find the first radical (by stroke) then go to index #
then by stroke count
find next part or character and this entry gives page #

著名语言学家、

中国科学院哲学社会科学部委员

吕叔湘先生和丁声树先生

分别于1956—1960年、1961—1978年

主持本词典的编写工作，

谨向为编纂我国第一部现代汉语词典

作出卓越贡献的两位先哲

致以崇高的敬意！

We wish to honour with greatest esteem the late Lü Shuxiang and Ding Shengshu, for their outstanding contributions to the compilation of the first contemporary Chinese dictionary in this country. These two great scholars – celebrated linguists and academicians of the Department of Philosophy and Social Sciences of the Chinese Academy of Sciences during their lifetime – presided over the compilation of this dictionary during the periods 1956 – 1960 and 1961 – 1978 respectively.

汉英双语

现代汉语词典

The Contemporary Chinese Dictionary

[Chinese-English Edition]

现代汉语词典（汉英双语）

The Contemporary Chinese Dictionary (Chinese-English Edition)

中国社会科学院语言研究所词典编辑室 编
外语教学与研究出版社语言学与辞书部双语词典编辑室 翻译编辑

Compiled by:

Dictionary Department, Institute of Linguistics, Chinese Academy of Social Sciences

Translated and Edited by:

Bilingual Dictionary Subdivision, Linguistics & Dictionary Division, FLTRP

. . . .

英文主审 English Editor:

凌　原 **Ling Yuan**

英文副审 Associate English Editors:

章思英 **Zhang Siying**　陈海燕 **Chen Haiyan**

英文顾问 English Consultants:

施晓菁 **Xiaojing Lynette Shi**

余薇芳 （加）**May Yee**　罗德帕梅拉 （英）**Pamela Lord**

新　月 （加）**Krisantha Sri Bhaggiyadatta**

英文翻译 English Translators:

（以姓氏笔画为序 in the order of number of strokes in surnames）

王寓帆 **Wang Yufan**　陈海燕 **Chen Haiyan**

何俊龙 **He Junlong**　张韶宁 **Zhang Shaoning**

赵艳玲 **Zhao Yanling**　顾文同 **Gu Wentong**

章挺权 **Zhang Tingquan**　章思英 **Zhang Siying**

程　宇 **Cheng Yu**　温晋根 **Wen Jingen**

董　黎 **Dong Li**　童孝华 **Tong Xiaohua**

责任编辑 Copy Editor:

陈　凯 **Chen Kai**

编校人员 Proof-readers:

申　葳 **Shen Wei**　唐晓萌 **Tang Xiaomeng**

杨镇明 **Yang Zhenming**　张红岩 **Zhang Hongyan**

许海峰 **Xu Haifeng**　周懿行 **Zhou Yixing**

董燕萍 **Dong Yanping**　沈中锋 **Shen Zhongfeng**

赵　红 **Zhao Hong**　游　媛 **You Yuan**

何　琳 **He Lin**　丁文娟 **Ding Wenjuan**

汉 英 双 语

（2002 年增补本）

现代汉語詞典

The Contemporary Chinese Dictionary

[Chinese-English Edition]

中国社会科学院语言研究所词典编辑室 编

外语教学与研究出版社

FOREIGN LANGUAGE TEACHING AND RESEARCH PRESS

(京) 新登字155号

图书在版编目(CIP)数据

现代汉语词典（汉英双语）/中国社会科学院语言研究所词典编辑室编.

-北京：外语教学与研究出版社，2002

ISBN 7-5600-3195-1

Ⅰ.现… Ⅱ.中… Ⅲ.① 汉语-现代-词典 ② 词典-汉、英 Ⅳ.H164

中国版本图书馆CIP数据核字（2002）第097395号

现代汉语词典（汉英双语）

中国社会科学院语言研究所词典编辑室 编

责任编辑　陈　凯
封面设计　朱　虹
出版发行　外语教学与研究出版社
社　　址　北京市西三环北路19号(100089)
网　　址　http://www.fltrp.com.cn
印　　刷　北京新华印刷厂
开　　本　880×1230　1/32
印　　张　87
版　　次　2002年11月第1版　2002年11月第1次印刷
书　　号　ISBN 7-5600-3195-1/H·1649
定　　价　99.90元

目　录
Contents

序 Preface　7

汉英双语版前言 Preface to the Chinese-English Edition　9

(中文版)前言 Introduction　16

(中文版)修订说明 Notes on the Revised Chinese Edition　18

(中文版)凡例 Guide to Using the Dictionary　21

音节表 Phonetic Guide　27

新旧字形对照表 Table of Comparison between Old and New Character Patterns　33

部首检字表 Radicals Guidc to Entries　34

词典正文(附新词新义、西文字母开头的词语) The Dictionary (including New Words and New Senses, and Acronyms and Words Beginning with Greek or Latin Letters)　1—2649

附录 Appendices　2651—2698

- 我国历代纪元表 Chronology of Chinese History　2653
- 计量单位表 Tables of Weights and Measures　2682
- 汉字偏旁名称表 Names of Radicals of Chinese Characters　2693
- 汉语拼音方案 Phonetic System of the Chinese Language　2696
- 元素周期表 Periodic Table of Chemical Elements　(封三)

序
Preface

根据一个母本翻译的双解词典首先要有一个好的母本,《现代汉语词典》是一部高质量的好词典,问世以来受到广大读者的欢迎,已经发行近4,000万册,产生了很大的社会影响。它的特点是宗旨明确、体例严密、收词精当、注释准确、举例简练。现在外研社组织人力将它译成英文,出版汉英双语版,这是我国汉英类词典出版业的一件大事。A good bilingual dictionary is based on translation from one language to another and thus calls for a good dictionary in the mother tongue. *The Contemporary Chinese Dictionary* is such a dictionary, having been well received by a wide range of readers since its publication. With an overall distribution exceeding 40 million copies, its social influence can hardly be overestimated. *The Contemporary Chinese Dictionary* is characterized by its well-designed goals, impeccable format, felicitous selection of entries, accurate definitions, and concise examples. By organizing the translation of this dictionary into English and publishing it in a bilingual format, Foreign Language Teaching and Research Press has made an originative contribution to the publication of Chinese-English dictionaries in China.

《现汉》是在国务院的指示下,遵照"推广普通话,促进汉语规范化"宗旨而编写的,它是一部现代汉语的规范词典。词语的规范化一般不能用行政命令的方式来实现,编纂高质量的词典是实现词语规范化的重要途径。高质量的词典编纂需要建立在科学研究的基础上,编纂者必须从现代汉语的语言事实出发,掌握第一手的资料,并且运用先进的语言学理论为指导。在前辈语言学大师吕叔湘先生、丁声树先生的主持下,一支一流的词典编纂队伍长期坚持工作,收集资料卡片上百万张,加上全面、认真的分析和综合,工作的繁杂和辛苦是难以想象的。辛勤的耕耘才换来丰硕的成果,这和当今许多词典粗制滥造、拼拼凑凑、甚至抄袭剽窃的做法形成何等鲜明的对照! *The Contemporary Chinese Dictionary* has been compiled at the request of the State Council to promote the popularization of standard Chinese. It serves as the standard dictionary of contemporary Chinese language usage. Standardization of a vocabulary cannot be achieved through administrative orders. Instead, the compilation of high-quality dictionaries on the basis of scientific research is an important means to reach this goal. In the instance of Chinese dictionaries, the lexicographers must obtain first-hand data on contemporary Chinese usage and organize it within the framework of advanced linguistic theories. The late linguists Lü Shuxiang and Ding Shengshu initiated the work on *The Contemporary Chinese Dictionary*, which has been carried on by a team of first-class lexicographers over many years. Their efforts are embodied in the more than one million index cards of data, and their intensive intellectual processing of the plethora of data eventually materialized in *The Contemporary Chinese Dictionary*, which was the first and still remains the best of its kind. Their diligence stands in sharp contrast with certain current practices that churn out dictionaries of poor quality or even plagiarize the work of others.

随着改革开放和现代化建设的进展,我国的社会生活正在发生着内容极为丰富的变化,这种变化必然要反映到语言中来,而且首先反映在词汇中,新词新义层出不穷。这次汉英双语版采用的是《现汉》最新的2002年增补本,这个版本在1996年修订本的基础上增收了近年来产生的新词新义1,200余条,基本上反映了现代汉语词汇的发展变化。词典的编纂和修订总是跟不上语言的发展变化，这是不足为奇的。As China continues to carry out reform and opening up to the outside world in its drive for modernization, social life in the country has been changing rapidly and becoming more enriched by the day. As such changes are reflected in language, countless new words and expressions keep entering daily usage. The 2002 Enlarged Edition of *The Contemporary Chinese Dictionary*, from which the English version has been translated, includes more than 1,200 new words and senses. While these additions basically represent the developments in contemporary Chinese language since 1996, the year the previous revised edition of the dictionary was published, it is not surprising that our work has already fallen behind the constant progress of the language.

语言工作者整理现代汉语的词汇，编纂和修订的工作任何时候不能一劳永逸。作为一本规范词典，不是所有的新词新义都要收录，因为有些新出现的词语时髦一时，不久就被淘汰，这样的情形并不少见。《现汉》在吸收新词新义方面采取的是既积极又慎重的方针，有利于现代汉语词汇的丰富和规范。As lexicographers of a contemporary language, we are fully aware of the need for continuous study of the language, its vocabulary in particular. There is no end to the compilation and revision of such dictionaries. On the other hand, as a standard reference book, *The Contemporary Chinese Dictionary* has not taken in new entries indiscriminately, as it is not uncommon for some words to become popular for a time but to disappear soon after. In order to enrich and at the same time standardize contemporary Chinese, the compilers have been both open and cautious in the choice of new words and senses.

我国和国外已经编纂出版的双语词典有不少是以《现汉》为蓝本的，例如享有盛誉的《汉英词典》就是其中之一。Quite a few Chinese-English dictionaries, published both in China and abroad, are based on *The Contemporary Chinese Dictionary*, such as the prestigious *A Chinese-English Dictionary* compiled by Beijing Foreign Studies University in the late 1970s.

现在十数位优秀的翻译家用英语将《现汉》原原本本地对译过来，这将进一步增强使用者对汉语词语的理解，提高汉语的使用水平。我相信，正在学习英语的中国人、翻译工作者、从事中英文信息处理和语言工程的人、以及从事对外汉语教学的老师和学习汉语的外国学生，都能从这个双语版中获得益处。作为《现汉》的第一个双语版本，其中难免会有不少错误和疏漏，这就要靠以后不断的修订来加以完善了。The English version of this dictionary has been rendered by more than a dozen highly qualified translators. The resulting bilingual edition of *The Contemporary Chinese Dictionary* should serve as a most useful reference book for English learners in China, translators working with Chinese and English, people involved in Chinese and English language information processing and technology, teachers teaching Chinese across the world, and non-native learners of Chinese. It should enable users to better understand the Chinese entries and to better use the Chinese language. As the first bilingual edition of *The Contemporary Chinese Dictionary*, this book has left something to be desired. Any errors and oversights will need to be corrected through the process of continuous revisions in the future.

沈家煊 Shen Jiaxuan
中国社会科学院语言研究所所长
Director of the Institute of Linguistics
Chinese Academy of Social Sciences

汉英双语版前言

Preface to the Chinese-English Edition

先后由吕叔湘、丁声树等著名语言学家主持，历经20年不惮繁复的增删修改而出版的《现代汉语词典》，是我国辞书史上一部里程碑式的中型详解语文词典。全书以收录规范的普通话词语为主，兼收部分有生命力的文言词语和方言，以及习见的百科词条，从而达到为推广普通话，确定词汇规范化服务的目的。因其收词精当，释义准确，举例典型而被视为现代汉语辞书的经典。*The Contemporary Chinese Dictionary*，first compiled under the direction of two renowned linguists — Lü Shuxiang and subsequently Ding Shengshu — published only after numerous revisions were made over a course of two decades，is a historic milestone in dictionary publishing in China. While the dictionary sets out to popularize standard Chinese and standardize its vocabulary，it also includes words from classical Chinese that have survived in contemporary usage as well as slang and words from Chinese dialects that have become widely used. The dictionary has been extolled as a classic of the contemporary Chinese language，thanks to its balanced compendium of words of everyday usage and encyclopedia of terms of standard reference，and to its accurate definitions and highly illustrative examples.

将这样一本影响巨大的汉语词典翻译成规范通畅的英语，无疑是出版界的一大盛事。《现汉》双语版的问世，将有助于规范的汉语拼音和标准的普通话在全世界范围进一步推广，在母语分别为汉语和英语的人们之间架设起又一座文化沟通的桥梁，给席卷国内的英语学习热潮增添活力，并为国外的汉语学习者提供一个不可或缺的工具。Translating such a hugely influential dictionary from Chinese into flawless English is undoubtedly an ambitious and tremendous undertaking. The publication of this bilingual edition of *The Contemporary Chinese Dictionary* will contribute to the further advancement of standard Chinese and its phonetic system of *pinyin* across the world，serve as a new bridge to facilitate cultural exchange between Chinese- and English-speaking peoples，add momentum to the surge in the study of English throughout China，and provide an essential tool for the study of Chinese as an international language.

《现汉》除了在收词、释义、举例方面举世公认的权威性和几近完美的编纂体系之外，其他优点也不胜枚举，并在双语版中得以完整、创新地体现。例如，《现汉》对成语、掌故，不仅释义，而且注明其在古典著作中的出处，提供不常见的文言原文，如今配上信达通畅的译文，使这个特点更加鲜明。如：*The Contemporary Chinese Dictionary* has a superb format and has been widely recognized for its authoritative selection of entries，definitions and examples. Apart from these distinctions，it has many other notable features that are fully and freshly apparent in this bilingual edition. For instance，the dictionary provides not only explanations for idioms and proverbs and allusions and metaphors but also their sources in original classical Chinese. For instance：

【高山流水】gāo shān liú shuǐ《列子·汤问》：'伯牙善鼓琴，钟子期善听。伯牙鼓琴，志在登高山，钟子期曰："善哉，峨峨兮若泰山！"志在流水，钟子期曰："善哉，洋洋兮若江河！"'后来用'高山流水'比喻知音或乐曲高妙。*Lie Zi·Yin Tang's Questions*：'Bo Ya was a good zither-player，and Zhong Ziqi had a good ear for music. When Bo strummed his zither，with his mind on mounting a lofty mountain，Zhong commented，"How delightful! It sounds as grand as Mount Taishan." When Bo meditated on flowing waters, Zhong said, "How delightful! It sounds as vast as the Yellow River and the Yangtze River."' This passage adds new meanings to the phrase "high mountains and flowing rivers", which is now a figurative expression for "bosom friends" or "musical virtuosity".

对那些对现代中国政治生活有重大影响的社科类名词,选其要者加以较为详细的介绍,如:Certain concepts from the social sciences have exerted a crucial influence on modern China's political and social life. These terms are treated with due commentary in this dictionary, such as:

【唯物辩证法】wéiwù biànzhèngfǎ 马克思、恩格斯所创立的建立在彻底的唯物主义基础上的辩证法。唯物辩证法认为物质世界本身有着自己的辩证运动规律,任何事物都是处在普遍联系和相互作用之中;任何事物都有它产生、发展和灭亡的过程;事物发展的根本原因在于事物内部的矛盾性,矛盾着的对立面又统一又斗争,由此推动事物的运动和变化。对立统一规律,是唯物辩证法的实质和核心。materialist dialectics; dialectics established by Marx and Engels on the basis of absolute materialism. According to materialist dialectics, the material world has its own dialectic law of motion; everything is in relation with and under the influence of everything else; everything has its own process of origin, development and end; the basic cause for the development of a thing is its internal contradiction. It is the opposing sides of a contradiction, both unified and opposite, that promote the motion and development of things. The law of unity and opposites is the essence and core of materialistic dialectics.

对典型的有关中国传统文化民俗民风的词条,给予足够的重视,如:Words and expressions concerning Chinese traditions and folklore have been given ample attention in this dictionary. The following is a typical example:

【本命年】běnmìngnián 我国习惯用十二生肖记人的出生年,每十二年轮回一次。如子年出生的人属鼠,再遇子年,就是这个人的本命年。year of (one's) birth; birth year; the year in which a person was born, recurring in a 12-year cycle associated with one of the 12 Earthly Branches, each marked by a symbolic animal. For example, a person born in the Year of *Zi* (The 1st Earthly Branch), which is customarily called, the Year of Rat, meets his year of birth when the Year of Rat occurs at a 12-year interval.

主要动植物品种,自然元素,常用工具,科学现象等百科词条,也有详略得当的解释,如:Encyclopedic terms, such as those involving flora and fauna, natural elements, common industrial tools or scientific phenomena, are written with appropriate details. For example:

【安全灯】ānquándēng ❶ 在矿井里用的可以防止引起混合气爆炸的灯。灯上有铜丝网罩,可以放散灯焰四周的热量。根据它的火焰变化,又可以估计矿井内气体的含毒量。safety lamp; miner's lighting device constructed to prevent immediate ignition of explosive gases. A copper-wire gauze cover is fixed on it to disperse the heat around the lamp. Changes in the lamp's oil-fuelled flame help one to determine the density of noxious gases in a mine. ❷ 泛指电压低于 36 伏或有安全设备的照明用具 general term for lighting equipment below 36 volts or fixed with a safety device

如此利用有限的空间对词语加以尽可能详细的注释,使《现汉》及其双语版成为意趣盎然、具有很高可读性的百科类词典。Definitions such as the above in *The Contemporary Chinese Dictionary* must be condensed to fit within the limited space yet detailed enough to provide sufficient information to the lay reader. With its faithful English rendering, the bilingual version of the dictionary makes for a highly readable encyclopedic work.

《现汉》在释疑解难方面亦堪称模范。某些词语特别是虚词,其性能,状态,存在的条件,以及词语间的相互搭配,是中小学语文教学的重点,对吴、粤、闽等方言地区的人们和学习汉语的外国人来说，则成为难点。《现汉》将这类语言现象以加框的“注意”两字标出，加以通俗的解释和精当的辨析。在双语版里，这些注疏被悉数译成英语，并用浅色网纹印刷，以提醒读者注意。*The Contemporary Chinese Dictionary* is exemplary in dealing with complex grammatical points in the language, such as function words and their varied combinations with other words under different conditions. Although these are emphasized when taught in middle and primary schools, they still pose difficulties for people in provinces such as Zhejiang, Jiangsu, Guangdong and Fujian, where people communicate mainly in local dialect. The compilers have gone out of their way to serve a diverse readership by appending special notes on the use of these words. The English equivalents of these notes are highlighted with a grey background screen.

全书插图、示意图和表格共48幅，在释义方面起到文字起不到的作用。有些疑难条目配以图解，图文并茂，一目了然，如【身体】、【骨骼】、【游标卡尺】、【仰角】、【斗拱】等。多幅几何图形，如【三角函数】、【波】、【多面体】之类，也有异曲同工之妙。而表格如‘海况表’、‘拉丁字母表’、‘地质年代表’等，将丰富的信息，浓缩在方寸之间。在双语版里，这些图表里的专用名称和资料均以双语列出，以备查考。The text of the dictionary offers 48 illustrations and tables, which illustrate relevant entries in ways that words cannot. Complicated entries, such as ‘body’, ‘skeleton’, ‘vernier calliper’, ‘angle of elevation’, and ‘corbel bracket’, are made clear at a glance with accompanying illustrations. The same is true of geometrical terms, such as ‘trigonometric function’, ‘wave’, ‘polyhedron’, etc. Tables like ‘Sea Conditions’, ‘Latin Alphabet’ and ‘Geological Time Scale’ condense rich detail into a small space. With English translation, these figures and tables provide quick reference for users seeking related information.

《现汉》2002年增补本的‘新词新义’和‘西文字母开头的词语’，是编纂者在推广、规范现代汉语方面锐意改革的成果。所收新词如【与时俱进】、【万维网】，新义如【下课】、【磨合】等都洋溢着时代的气息，双语版及时地将其译成英文以飨读者。其中江泽民同志的‘三个代表’的科学论说，首次被收入辞书，成为现代汉语的新词语：The additions of ‘New Words and New Senses’ and ‘Acronyms and Words Beginning with Greek or Latin Letters’ in the 2002 Enlarged Edition of *The Contemporary Chinese Dictionary* represent the lexicographers' timely observations and research into the most recent developments in the Chinese language. New words like *yushujujin* (keep pace with the times) and *wanweiwang* (World Wide Web), and new senses like *xiake* (resign) and *mohe* (break in), are fresh examples of current usage that have emerged over the recent years. Of particular significance is Comrade Jiang Zeming's scientific ‘Three Represents Theory’, included in a dictionary for the first time:

【三个代表】sān gè dàibiǎo 指中国共产党要始终代表中国先进生产力的发展要求，代表中国先进文化的前进方向，代表中国最广大人民的根本利益。这一重要思想是以江泽民为代表的中国共产党人，根据国际国内形势的新变化，总结党的历史经验作出的科学论断，是对马克思主义建党学说的新发展。Three Represents, i.e. the Communist Party of China is required to always represent the demand for the development of advanced productive forces in China, the direction for the advance of the advanced Chinese culture, and the fundamental interests of the broadest masses of the Chinese people. This major concept is a scientific conclusion the Chinese Communists represented by Jiang Zemin have reached in the light of new changes in the international and domestic situations and by summing up the historical experience of the Party; it is also a new development in the Marxist theory on Party building.

双语版的诸位译者力图以开阔的视野和全新的翻译理念，将所有条目，释义，举例原原本本地以英语演释了一遍，保留了母本的完整性和风采。通览全书，译者们刻意创新的努力在词里行间随处可见。例如：The English translators have striven to render the entries, including their definitions and examples, in a both faithful and innovative manner. While keeping intact the original Chinese text and format, they have sought out idiomatic and current English expressions in order to give readers a fresh sense of the target language. For example:

24/7 (连轴转。*Newsweek*: 'Conditions were brutal: the plant ran 24/7.'); have an instant connection (一见如故, e.g. We just started talking and had an instant connection.); open worlds to sb. (大开眼界); a hive of activity (繁忙景象); have a facial (美容); get into the swing of things (熟悉情况); fleet-fingered thief (三只手); bore one's eyes through by gazing anxiously (望眼欲穿); it ran me ragged (筋疲力尽); fallout (后果); be an eyeful (顺眼); whopper (弥天大谎); an inventor and a half (了不起的发明家); live it up (奢侈生活); two-timing (花心)。

本书收录的这些时常令英语学习者耳目一新的词汇,或许不一定是最好的,但它们至少为读者在学习、运用有关词语时提供了新的思路和更多的选择。Although these words and expressions may not always be the premium or most representative of English usage, they do provide more options for users in their study or work.

译者们还参考了众多的外版辞典,保证了专科词语尤其是那些源于西方的科技名词术语的译文正确性。母本里有些词条的释义不够完整,双语版则适当地加以补充,如【热】、【疟疾】、【人参】,【韧皮纤维】等。For the accuracy of specialist terms, especially those originally from the West, the translators have referred to a large number of native English dictionaries. Where the Chinese definitions fall short of a comprehensive explanation, the English version serves as a complement. Examples are 'heat', 'malaria', 'ginseng', and 'bast', etc.

另外,《现汉》中有些专科词语注释相当详细。以植物条目为例,注释将生态(一年生、二年生、多年生)、形态(根、茎、叶、花、果)、经济价值等逐一罗列。双语版则全文照译。所有动植物既给出英语俗名,又附之以拉丁文名称,以供专业人士参考。如雪莲 snow lotus (*Saussurea involucrata*)、鳕鱼 cod (*Gadus morrhua*)等。In *The Contemporary Chinese Dictionary*, some of the specialist entries are described almost in minute detail. Taking plant names for example, the definitions include not only their life cycle (annual, biennial, or perennial) and shape (of roots, stems, leaves, flowers, and fruits), but also their economic value. The English version has not only translated the names of plants and animals into English but added their Latin names as well, to serve as a more rigorous reference for the specialist reader, e.g. 'snow lotus (*Saussurea involucrata*)', 'cod (*Gadus morrhua*)', etc.

将详列各朝代列祖列宗的我国历史纪元表以汉英对照的形式出版,是《现汉》双语版的一个开先河之举。表中如'孛儿只斤铁木真','阿骨打','爱新觉罗努尔哈赤'这种读来诘屈聱牙的帝王姓名,常被译者视为畏途。双语版参考国际汉学约定俗成的拼法,将其全部译出,以为译者解难,为翻译界提供标准译文,也为杜绝乱译的现象作一份贡献。The 'Chronology of Chinese History', listing the names of kings and emperors in dynastic China, provides a brief yet useful reference for the general reader. The names of some emperors of minority ethnic origins, such as 'Borzigin Temuzin', 'Akutta', and 'Aisin-Gioro Nurhachi', are often challenges even for the experienced translator. The bilingual edition, with reference to conventions observed by international Sinologists and by Chinese scholars of the history of non-Han peoples in China, has rendered the names of kings and emperors into intelligible English. Such a table, perhaps the first of its kind to be found in any Chinese-English dictionary published so far, may serve as a reliable source of information for translators.

双语版对外来语的翻译颇费心血。这类词语大多通过音译的方式固定下来成为汉语的一部分,因而在将它们译成英语时,人们往往忽视其原来的形态而造成中国式英语。这种情况在翻译来自西方的借入语时不很严重，因为人们可以容易地把‘沙发’译成 sofa，将‘咖啡’译为 coffee 等等。问题常出现在处理源于稀有语种和少数民族的词语的时候。双语版注意到中译英工作中的这一难点，在翻译时决不用汉语拼音对付之，而注意还之以本来的民族面貌，或采用国际通用的译名。例如：月氏 Scyths、敕勒 Teleg、镶蓝旗 Hobot Hoh、畜仕 Suc Si、瓦剌 Qirat 等等。The translators have taken pains in the translation of words borrowed from foreign and national minority languages. Most of these loanwords have become standard Chinese in transliteration. When translating them into English, it is possible to overlook their true origin and transliterate them in *pinyin*, or Chinese phonetics. Such errors are not overly serious with words from the West. For example, 沙发 and 咖啡 can easily be recognized and translated back into English as 'sofa' and 'coffee'. More challenging are transliterations from national minority languages. The English version of such entries in this dictionary strictly follow their original-language pronunciation or international conventions. Thus 月氏 is rendered as 'Indo-Scythae', not its Chinese transliteration 'Yuezhi', 敕勒 as 'Teleg', 镶蓝旗 as 'Hobot Hoh', 畜仕 as 'Suc Si', 瓦剌 as 'Qirat', etc.

《现汉》作为一个特定时代的产物，也存在些许缺点。有些词条的释义已经落后于时代，如【本埠】(…平信～邮资一角外埠两角)；有些解释不够精确，如【接见】(跟来的人见面)、【挣扎】(用力支撑)。双语版对这些瑕疵采取了慎重的态度。有些疏漏，在征得社科院语言所的同意后，已在双语版里得到匡正。如有些标有‘旧时’而实际上仍在普遍使用的词语，在英译时不注 old。这些缺点瑕不掩瑜，而且已进入编纂者们的目光，会在将来出版的修订本中加以革除。As with any other dictionary of contemporary language, *The Contemporary Chinese Dictionary* has its temporal limitations. Some of its contents are outdated or not adequately precise, such as the example cited in the entry *benbu* (... A stamp for a local letter costs one *jiao*; and one for an out-of-town letter, two *jiao*), which we have translated as it is, and the explanation of *jiejian* (receive; give an interview to) and of *zhengzha* (struggle), which the translator has handled differently. The English editors have tried to be very careful in dealing with these types of minor flaws. The bilingual edition has corrected or modified some of the original interpretations, with the approval of the Institute of Linguistics of the Chinese Academy of Social Sciences. For instance, some expressions, though still in current use, were marked with 旧时 (old) in the Chinese version. In such cases, this word was deliberately not translated. The Chinese compilers have taken note of such shortcomings and are already making revisions for a future edition.

在此《现汉》双语版问世之际，不禁想起汉英类词典出版业数十年来的巨大变化。抚今追昔，不胜感慨。新中国最初的三十年里，国产的英汉词典如凤毛麟角，汉英词典出版一片空白。在我供职的那个国家对外传播部门，办公室里高据案头的几乎是清一色的英美词典。年长的同事们大多早年留洋，其中不乏超一流的译林高手，如黄品长、方矩成、段连城、林戊荪、任家桢等均荟萃其间，极一时之盛。摆在他们书案上的辞书，早已斑驳陈旧，纸张发黄，都是《牛津》、《韦伯斯特》之类。如我的老师黄品长先生，每天审定稿件时无数次翻动的那本《简明牛津词典》，久而久之在书上经常掀动的地方，竟留下触目的指痕。置身于老师们的翻译的情景中是一种美的享受。只见他们端坐在各自的打字机前，将键盘敲得‘滴答’直响，不用多时，文稿便如期译就。词典之于他们，是真正意义上的辅助工具。只有我等初出茅庐者，才会在面对一篇篇充满疑难生词的文稿时，感到工具书的缺乏。好在老师个个学贯中西，而且诲人不倦，有问必答，使我们在其卵翼下，好歹挨过了那没有汉英词典的尴尬时光。As I finish presiding over the translation work for this bilingual edition of *The Contemporary Chinese Dictionary*, I cannot help recalling the tremendous changes that have taken place in the publishing of Chinese-English dictionaries in this country over the past decades. In the first 30 years of the People's Republic, English-Chinese dictionaries compiled by Chinese lexicographers were a precious rarity and Chinese-English dictionaries were just not available. In the national publishing institute dedicated to international exchange where I worked as an English translator, almost all the English reference books were published in Britain or the United States. Most of my senior colleagues had studied abroad in their youth and many of them were the country's top translators, such as Huang Pinchang, Fang Jucheng, Duan Liancheng, Lin Wusun, and Ren Jiazhen. On their desks invariably sat Oxford and Webster dictionaries, with their covers worn out and pages turned yellow through long years of browsing. I can still visualize *The Concise Oxford Dictionary* my mentor Huang Pinchang used daily when he checked the final drafts of translated articles — with its conspicuous finger marks on frequently flipped pages. It was a joy to watch these senior translators at work, as they sat erect in front of their typewriters, with keys clicking away, issuing out one article in English after another. For them, dictionaries were of occasional reference value only. Novices like myself, on the other hand, were often baffled by unusual terms and at a loss as to where to look for their English equivalents, given there were almost no Chinese-English dictionaries available. Fortunately, we could always turn for help to our senior colleagues, who were well versed in both Chinese and Western scholarship, and never tired of answering our questions. Looking back now, I can never thank these trailblazers enough for their patient assistance over those years.

流年似水,当年驰骋在翻译领域的第一代元老们已几乎全部退出了舞台,他们那从不为词汇的匮乏和知识的贫瘠发愁的潇洒,已成为同业者的美谈。如今外语类辞书出版的空前繁荣,不仅使翻译工作变得十分便捷,也反映了我们国家整个外语环境的变化。As time flows on, New China's translators of the first generation are nearly all no longer on the scene. The ease with which they handled their work, without relying on bilingual dictionaries, and their wisdom that inspired younger colleagues have become legendary among translation circles. The recent flourishing in the publication of foreign-language dictionaries has made translation work so much easier today. With so many useful dictionaries now available, the landscape for China's vast contingent of English translators and learners is no longer the same.

如今,时代在呼唤更多的双语人才,前辈们的风采将长久地激励着我们,并在更多的后来者身上重现。倘若这本双语词典能够为此起一点作用,我们全体编者莫不将感到深深的欣慰。We are living in a time in China that calls for more and more bilingual specialists. To respond to this need, we should never cease to draw inspiration from our predecessors. We should also do our best to ensure that the legacy of their vast encyclopedic scholarship and professional ease be carried on by future generations. If this dictionary can contribute even a hair's breadth towards this goal, all the translators and editors would feel immensely gratified in our work.

《现汉》双语版得以顺利问世,首先应当归功于诸位同事的戮力同心,他们坦然面对了编写词典这种“吃力不讨好”的工作的繁琐、寂寞和艰辛。来自首都和外地的十数位翻译工作者分担了全书六万多个词条的翻译工作,将三百余万字的母本拓阔为八百余万字的大型辞书。The successful publication of the bilingual edition of *The Contemporary Chinese Dictionary* is owed first of all to the concerted efforts of all the translators and editors, who dedicatedly embraced the unglamorous drudgery involved in dictionary compilation. More than a dozen highly qualified translators rendered the original 3-million-character text into a new work of over 8 million words.

社会各界也对本书的翻译工作倾注了热诚的关注。加拿大籍专家余薇芳女士和新月先生、英籍专家罗德帕梅拉女士、以及美国蒙特里国际研究学院翻译研究院的施晓菁教授,联袂为本书润色,保证了译文质量。中国社科院语言研究所所长沈家煊和韩敬体、陆尊梧教授在本书翻译过程中始终和编者保持密切联系,提供咨询;前中国文学出版社资深编审吴善祥老师和社科院文学所党圣元副所长热情为有关古典文学的条目释疑解难;中国翻译工作者协会常务副会长林戊荪先生和翻译家汤博文先生为翻译问题提供了宝贵的指导；北京外国语大学的夏祖煃、周谟智、顾日国、陈国华、姚小平等教授拨冗审阅并亲手修改了部分样条。谨借此机会对以上各位先生表示由衷的谢意。During the process, we have received generous support from many people in various fields. The translations were refined by Canadian editors May Yee and Krisantha Sri Bhaggiyadatta, British editor Pamela Lord, and Professor Xiaojing Lynette Shi of the Graduate School of Translation and Interpretation, Monterey Institute of International Studies, USA.; Mr. Shen Jiaxuan, director of the Institute of Linguistics of the Chinese Academy of Social Sciences, and his colleagues, Han Jingti and Lu Zunwu maintained close consultation with the English editors. Mr. Wu Shanxiang, senior editor of the former Chinese Literature Press, and Mr. Dang Shengyuan, Deputy Director of the Institute of Literature, Chinese Academy of Social Sciences assisted our understanding of difficult terms from classical Chinese literature. Mr. Lin Wusun, permanent vice-chairman of the Chinese Translators' Association, and Mr. Tang Bowen, senior translator of the Foreign Language Press, provided invaluable advice on many issues involved in translation. Professors Xia Zukui, Zhou Mozhi, Gu Yueguo, Chen Guohua and Yao Xiaoping have taken time from their busy schedules to read and correct some of the translated entries. To all of the above people, along with many others that space does not permit me to name, I extend my most sincere thanks.

应当指出的是，本书作为翻译工作的产物，受能力、时间诸因素的影响，谬误和疏漏在所难免。恳切地希望广大的读者不吝指正，以便在再版时加以修订，使《现汉》双语版更臻完美地呈献给读者。I should point out that the bilingual edition of *The Contemporary Chinese Dictionary*, basically a work of translation, is of course not without its errors and oversights, due to limitations in our human capabilities and also a hectic schedule. We sincerely hope that our readers and users will kindly share any comments and suggestions, so that we may further improve the dictionary in future revisions.

凌 原 Ling Yuan

北京 Beijing, December 12, 2002

(中文版)前 言
Introduction

这部《现代汉语词典》是以记录普通话语汇为主的中型词典,供中等以上文化程度的读者使用。词典中所收条目,包括字、词、词组、熟语、成语等,共约五万六千余条。*The Contemporary Chinese Dictionary* is a medium-sized dictionary for readers with an average-level education and above. The more than 56,000 entries include characters, words, phrases, colloquialisms and idioms of standard Chinese.

这部词典是为推广普通话、促进汉语规范化服务的,在字形、词形、注音、释义等方面,都朝着这个方向努力。一般语汇之外,也收了一些常见的方言词语、方言意义,不久以前还使用的旧词语、旧意义,现在书面上还常见的文言词语,以及某些习见的专门术语。此外还收了一些用于地名、人名、姓氏等方面的字和少数现代不很常用的字。这些条目大都在注释中分别交代,或者附加标记,以便识别。With the objective of popularizing *putonghua* (standard Chinese pronunciation) and standardizing the Chinese language, we have taken great care in our choice of entries, the phonetic notation of pronunciations, and the definition of words and phrases. In addition to words of common usage, the dictionary includes words and meanings from Chinese dialects that have become widespread, along with old words and meanings that have faded out of use only recently, expressions in classical Chinese that are still used in writing, as well as specialist terms often found in everyday usage. Some entries are characters mainly used in place names, surnames and given names; and a small number of entries are characters of infrequent usage in modern Chinese. The specificities of such entries are either explained in definition or marked with symbols for the convenience of the reader.

1956年2月6日,国务院发布关于推广普通话的指示,责成中国科学院语言研究所*在1958年编好以确定词汇规范为目的的中型的现代汉语词典。我所词典编辑室1956年夏着手收集资料,1958年初开始编写,1959年底完成初稿,1960年印出'试印本'征求意见。经过修改,1965年又印出'试用本'送审稿。1973年,为了更广泛地征求意见,作进一步的修订,并为了适应广大读者的迫切需要,利用1965年'试用本'送审稿的原纸型印了若干部,内部发行。1973年开始对'试用本'进行修订,但由于'四人帮'的严重干扰和破坏,直至1977年底才全部完成修订工作,把书稿交到出版部门。On February 6, 1956, the State Council issued a directive for popularizing *putonghua*, and requested the Institute of Linguistics of the Chinese Academy of Sciences to finish compiling a medium-sized modern Chinese dictionary by 1958 to serve as the norm for a standard vocabulary of Chinese language. The Dictionary Department of the Institute of Linguistics began to collect data in the summer of 1956. The editors started to compile the dictionary in early 1958 and completed the first draft by the end of 1959. A 'trial-printed edition' was issued in 1960 for the purpose of soliciting comments . After numerous revisions were made , an ' edition for trial use' was printed in 1965 for official examination. In order to gather comments on a more exten-

---

*从1977年5月起改称中国社会科学院语言研究所。The Institute of Linguistics became part of the Chinese Academy of Social Sciences in May 1977.

sive scale for further improvements and to meet the urgent need of many users, a number of copies were printed in 1973 for internal circulation, using the original paper matrix of the 1965 'edition for trial use.' Revision of the 'edition for trial use' began in 1973, but the work was hampered by interference from the 'Gang of Four.' Thus the final manuscript was not ready for printing until 1977.

《现代汉语词典》在整个编写和修订过程中,得到了全国一些科研机构、大中学校、工矿企业、部队有关机关以及很多专家、群众的大力协助。我们在这里敬向有关单位和有关同志表示衷心的感谢。Throughout the process of compilation and revision of *The Contemporary Chinese Dictionary*, we have received strong support from research institutes, universities, middle schools, industrial enterprises and relevant army units from across the country, and from many experts as well as ordinary people. To all of them we would like to express our sincere thanks.

限于编写人员的水平,这部词典的缺点和错误一定还不少。我们恳切地希望广大读者多多提出宝贵意见,以便继续修订,不断提高质量,使这部词典在推广普通话、促进汉语规范化方面,在汉语教学方面,能起到应有的作用,更好地为社会主义革命和社会主义建设服务。We realize that the dictionary is not free of errors and shortcomings, due to the limits of our knowledge and expertise. Therefore, we look forward to comments and suggestions from our readers so that we may continue to improve the quality of our work. We hope the dictionary will play its due role in promoting the use of *putonghua* and standardizing the Chinese, in the teaching of Chinese, as well as in serving socialist revolution and construction.

中国社会科学院语言研究所
1978 年 8 月
Institute of Linguistics
Chinese Academy of Social Sciences
August 1978

这次重排仍照 1978 年 12 月第一版排印。1979 年底,因原版已损坏,须重新排版。1980 年初仅对某些条目稍作修改,即交出版单位,1980 年第二季度开始排版。The plates for this edition were set according to the first edition published in December 1978. Since the original plates had worn out by the end of 1979, new plates were prepared in the second quarter of 1980 after minor changes were made to some entries early that year.

1983 年 1 月
January 1983

（中文版）修订说明

Notes on the Revised Chinese Edition

《现代汉语词典》1978年出第一版。1980年曾对一些条目稍作修改，1983年出第二版。自本词典出版以来，随着社会的发展，语言也有演变，一些语词在运用上有了不少变化，并有不少的新词新语产生。为了适应读者的需要，词典编辑室在搜集的几十万条资料的基础上，进行了这次修订。修订工作主要是增、删、改。增，是增加一些新的词语；删，是删去一些过于陈旧的词语及一些过于专门的百科词条；改，是修改那些词语有变化、有发展，在词义和用法上需要改动或补充的词条。此外，对一些异体字和有异读的字，按照国家语言文字工作委员会的规定作了一些改动。增、删、改的原则仍依据《现代汉语词典》的编写宗旨，目的是使这部词典在推广普通话、促进汉语规范化方面，在汉语教学方面，继续起到它应有的作用。修订后的《现代汉语词典》共收字、词6万余条，其中语文条目增加较多。*The Contemporary Chinese Dictionary* was first published in 1978. With minor revisions to some entries in 1980, the second edition of the dictionary was published in 1983. Since then, alongside social developments in China, the Chinese language has seen continuous evolution, resulting in alterations in the use of words and phrases, and the emergence of new words and expressions. This current revision, based on several hundred thousand entries collected by the Dictionary Department, aims at providing an up-to-date dictionary for our readers. Specifically, we have added new words, deleted outdated items and encyclopedic terms that are overly technical for most users, and have rewritten entries that have undergone changes in meaning and/or usage. For characters that have variant written forms or pronunciations, we have checked them against the guidelines set by the State Language Commission and have made corrections where necessary. Overall, we have made alterations according to the principle of *The Contemporary Chinese Dictionary*, so as to continue to contribute to the promotion of *putonghua* and standardization of the Chinese language and the teaching of it. The current edition has more than 60,000 entries, with a considerable increase in the number of those concerning the Chinese language per se.

《现代汉语词典》始编于1958年，先后由吕叔湘先生和丁声树先生任主编，参加编写的人员有数十人，编写完和修订完后曾先后印出'试印本'和'试用本'送审稿，直至1978年正式出版。现在，借修订重排的机会，把曾参加过《现代汉语词典》编写工作的人员的名字按不同阶段分列如下：Compilation of *The Contemporary Chinese Dictionary* began in 1958, first with Mr. Lü Shuxiang and then with Mr. Ding Shengshu as its editor-in-chief. Several dozen editors participated in the project. A 'trial-printed edition' and an 'edition for trial use' were prepared after initial compilation and revision were finished. Not until 1978 was the first edition formally published. We have listed here the names of those who have contributed to the development of the dictionary at different stages, in recognition of our esteemed appreciation of their work.

'试印本'阶段 During the stage of the 'trial-printed edition':

主编 Editor-in-chief　　吕叔湘 Lü Shuxiang

参加编写的有 Editorial staff

孙德宣 Sun Dexuan　　孙崇义 Sun Chongyi　　何梅岑 He Meicen

李伯纯 Li Bochun　萧家霖 Xiao Jialin　孔凡均 Kong Fanjun
王述达 Wang Shuda　刘庆隆 Liu Qinglong　郭　地 Guo Di
李文生 Li Wensheng　刘洁修 Liu Jiexiu　莫　衡 Mo Heng
吴崇康 Wu Chongkang　李国炎 Li Guoyan　郑宣沐 Zheng Xuanmu
单耀海 Shan Yaohai　吕天琛 Lü Tianchen

'试用本'阶段 During the stage of the 'edition for trial use':

主编 Editors-in-chief　丁声树 Ding Shengshu　李　荣(协助) Li Rong (assistant)

参加修订的有 Editorial staff

孙德宣 Sun Dexuan　何梅岑 He Meicen　李伯纯 Li Bochun
刘庆隆 Liu Qinglong　莫　衡 Mo Heng　吴崇康 Wu Chongkang
李国炎 Li Guoyan　单耀海 Shan Yaohai　吕天琛 Lü Tianchen
吴昌恒 Wu Changheng　陆卓元 Lu Zhuoyuan　曲翰章 Qu Hanzhang
闵家骥 Min Jiaji　韩敬体 Han Jingti　刘洁修 Liu Jiexiu
舒宝璋 Shu Baozhang　李玉英 Li Yuying　张聿忠 Zhang Yuzhong
夏义民 Xia Yimin

先后参加资料工作的有 Those who participated in data collection in different periods of time

徐世禄 Xu Shilu　贺澹江 He Danjiang　高泽均 Gao Zejun
王焕贞 Wang Huanzhen　岳珺玲 Yue Junling　赵桂钧 Zhao Guijun
王蕴明 Wang Yunming　姚宝田 Yao Baotian　宋惠德 Song Huide
于庆芝 Yu Qingzhi

语言研究所其他研究室参加编写和修订的人员有 Editorial staff from other departments of the Institute of Linguistics:

徐萧斧 Xu Xiaofu　范继淹 Fan Jiyan　范方莲 Fan Fanglian
傅　婧 Fu Jing　金有景 Jin Youjing　姜　远 Jiang Yuan
王立达 Wang Lida

一些短时间参加的就不一一列名了。Those who worked only briefly for the project are not listed here.

《现代汉语词典》在 1993 年获中国社会科学院优秀科研成果奖,1994 年获中华人民共和国新闻出版署颁发的国家图书奖,这对编者来说,是鼓励,也是鞭策。*The Contemporary Chinese Dictionary* won an award for outstanding research achievement from the Chinese Academy of Social Sciences in 1993 and a National Book Award from the Administration of News and Press of the People's Republic of China in 1994. Both awards are tokens of recognition and encouragement for the work of the compilers.

当年参加编写的人中已有好几位离世了,他们对《现代汉语词典》的贡献将在书中永存。Several members of the editorial staff of previous editions have already passed away, but their contribution to *The Contemporary Chinese Dictionary* are forever inscribed between its pages.

这次修订工作从 1993 年开始。参加修订工作的人员有 The latest revision began in 1993. Participants include:

单耀海 Shan Yaohai　韩敬体(审订) Han Jingti (final check)
晁继周 Chao Jizhou　吴昌恒 Wu Changheng　吴崇康 Wu Chongkang
董　琨 Dong Kun　李志江 Li Zhijiang　刘庆隆 Liu Qinglong
李国炎 Li Guoyan　莫　衡 Mo Heng　吕天琛 Lü Tianchen
陆尊梧 Lu Zunwu　曹兰萍 Cao Lanping　贾采珠 Jia Caizhu
黄　华 Huang Hua

负责计算机处理和资料工作的人员有 Computer processing and data collection

王　伟 Wan Wei　　宋惠德 Song Huide　　郭小妹 Guo Xiaomei

张　彤 Zhang Tong　　张　林 Zhang Lin

在这次修订工作中，商务印书馆编辑部、出版部不少同志为我们做了许多工作，全国科学技术名词审定委员会的同志在本书科学技术术语的规范方面，也给予了帮助，在此谨向他们表示敬意。We would like to thank members of the Editorial Department and Production Department of the Commercial Press, and members of the China National Committee for Terms in Sciences and Technologies for their work and help in the revision process.

《现代汉语词典》出版后，承读者关心和爱护，不少读者来信指出不足，这里，谨表衷心感谢，并希望对修订本继续提出宝贵意见，以便不断修订。Since its first publication, *The Contemporary Chinese Dictionary* has drawn considerable attention from our readers. Some have written to us with valuable criticism. We would like to thank all our readers and hope you will continue to contribute your comments and suggestions and help us with future revisions of the dictionary.

中国社会科学院语言研究所词典编辑室

1994年10月

Dictionary Department, Institute of Linguistics

Chinese Academy of Social Sciences

October 1994

《现代汉语词典》修订本出版以来，受到广大读者的欢迎和关注，1998年重印时，参考专家和读者的意见，对个别条目稍作修改。Since its revised edition was published, *The Contemporary Chinese Dictionary* has been well received by users. When it was reprinted in 1998, we incorporated minor revisions to some entries at the suggestion of experts and readers.

1998年7月

July 1998

（中文版）凡　例

Guide to Using the Dictionary

Ⅰ　条目安排 Listing of Entries

1. 本词典所收条目分单字条目和多字条目。单字条目用比较大的字体。多字条目按第一个字分列于领头的单字条目之下。The entries are classified into single-character and multi-character categories. Single-character entries are of a larger type than the rest of the text. Immediately below most single-character entries are multi-character entries that begin with the head character, listed in alphabetical order according to the pronunciation of the second character.

2. 单字条目和多字条目都有同形而分条的，情况如下：Some words, both single-character and multi-character, may have more than one entry although they have the same written form.

(a)关于单字条目。形同而音、义不同的，分立条目，如'好'hǎo 和'好'hào，'长'cháng 和'长'zhǎng。形、义相同而音不相同，各有适用范围的，也分立条目，如'剥'bāo 和'剥'bō，'薄'báo 和'薄'bó。形同音同而在意义上需要分别处理的，也分立条目，在字的右肩上标注阿拉伯数字，如'按[1]'、'按[2]'，'白[1]'、'白[2]'、'白[3]'。Single-character words: those with the same written form but different pronunciations and senses, such as 好（pronounced hǎo and hào respectively）and 长（pronounced cháng and zhǎng respectively）and 薄（pronounced báo and bó respectively）; those with the same written form and meaning(s) but different pronunciations and uses, such as 剥（pronounced bāo and bō respectively）; those with the same written form and pronunciation but completely separate meanings, indicated by the small number to their upper right, such as 按[1] and 按[2]，白[1]，白[2] and 白[3].

(b)关于多字条目。形同而音、义不同的，分立条目，如【公差】gōngchā 和【公差】gōngchāi。形同音同，但在意义上需要分别处理的，也分立条目，在【　】外右上方标注阿拉伯数字，如：【大白】[1]、【大白】[2]，【燃点】[1]、【燃点】[2]；注音方式不同的，不标注阿拉伯数字，如：【借款】jiè//kuǎn 和【借款】jièkuǎn。Multi-character words: those with the same written form but different pronunciations and senses, such as【公差】（pronounced gōngchā and gōngchāi respectively）; those with the same written form and pronunciation but with completely separate meanings, indicated by the small number to their upper right, such as【大白】[1] and【大白】[2]，【燃点】[1] and【燃点】[2]; those with the same written form but separate meanings, indicated by slightly different phonetic transcriptions, such as【借款】（pronounced jiè//kuǎn and jièkuǎn）.

3. 本词典全部条目的排列法如下 Order of entry listings:

(a)单字条目按拼音字母次序排列。同音字按笔画排列，笔画少的在前，多的在后。笔画相同的，按起笔笔形横（一）、直（丨）、撇（丿）、点（丶）、折（乛）的顺序排列。Single-character words are listed in alphabetical order of their pronunciations. For characters with the same pronunciation, those with fewer strokes are listed before those with more strokes; words with the same number of strokes are listed in the order of their beginning stroke, i. e. horizontal line（一），vertical line（丨），left slash（丿），dot（丶），and straight stroke with a bending tip

(一).

(b)单字条目之下所列的多字条目不止一条的,依第二字的拼音字母次序排列。第二字相同的,依第三字排列,以下类推。Entries under the same head character are listed in alphabetical order of the pronunciation of the second character, or the third character if the second character is the same, and so on.

(c)轻声字一般紧接在同形的非轻声字后面,如'家'·jia 排在'家'jiā 的后面,【大方】dà·fang 排在【大方】dàfāng 的后面。但是'了'·le、'着'·zhe 等轻声字排在去声音节之后。For characters of the same written form and pronunciation, those spoken with a regular tone precede those with a neutral tone, such as 家, which may be pronounced with either a regular tone jiā or a neutral tone ·jia, and【大方】, which may be spoken with a regular tone dàfāng or a neutral tone dà·fang. Some characters with a neutral tone, such as 了·le and 着·zhe, are listed after the same character with a falling-tone pronunciation.

II 字形和词形 Written Forms of Characters and Words

4. 本词典单字条目所用汉字形体以现在通行的为标准。异体字(包括繁体)加括号附列在正体之后。括号内的异体字只适用于个别意义时,在异体字前头加上所适用的义项数码,如:彩(❷綵)。All single-character entries are written in the forms currently in use. Variant forms (including the original complex forms) are placed in parentheses next to the formal entry; those that are applicable to a restricted sense compared with the standard form are marked with a small number indicating the relevant sense, such as 彩(❷綵).

5. 不同写法的多字条目,注解后加'也作某',如:【缘故】…也作原故;【原原本本】…'原'也作源或元。Variant written forms of multi-character entries are put at the end of definitions, such as【缘故】... also 原故;【原原本本】... 原 also written as 源 or 元.

6. 书面上有时儿化有时不儿化,口语里必须儿化的词,自成条目,如:【今儿】、【小孩儿】。书面上一般不儿化,但口语里一般儿化的,在释义前加'(~儿)',如【米粒】条。释义不止一项的,如口语里一般都儿化,就把'(~儿)'放在注音之后,第一义项之前,如【模样】条。如只有个别义项儿化,就把'(~儿)'放在有关义项数码之后,如:牌❶(~儿)…❷(~儿)…。Words that may or may not be inflected with the character 儿 in written Chinese but must be spoken with the inflection are treated as independent entries, such as【今儿】and【小孩儿】. Those that are not inflected with 儿 in written Chinese but are usually spoken with the sound are indicated by adding the inflected form before the definition, such as【米粒】(~儿); if the entry has more than one definition, the indication is placed before the first definition, such as【模样】; if the character should be inflected in only certain of several definitions, (~儿) is placed before the specific definition, such 牌❶(~儿)... 牌❷(~儿).

7. 重叠式在口语中经常带'的'或'儿的',条目中一般不加'的'或'儿的',只在注解前面加'(~的)'或'(~儿的)',如:【白花花】…(~的),【乖乖】…(~儿的)。Entries consisting of repeated characters that are often spoken with the auxiliary word 的 or 儿的 are noted before the definitions, such as【白花花】... (~的) and【乖乖】... (~儿的).

III 注音 Phonetic Transcription

8. 每条都用汉语拼音字母注音。Every entry is noted with *pinyin*, i.e. Chinese phonetic transcription.

9. 有异读的词,已经普通话审音委员会审订过的,一般依照审音委员会的审订。Words with variant pronunciations are transcribed according to the rules set by the Examination Committee for Standard Chinese Pronunciation.

传统上有两读,都比较通行的,酌收两读,如:嘏(gǔ,又 jiǎ);酾(shī,又 shāi)。Words with two conventional pronunciations that are both in use are transcribed both ways, such as 嘏(gǔ, also jiǎ) and 酾(shī, also shāi).

10. 条目中的轻声字,注音不标调号,但在注音前加圆点,如:【便当】biàn·dang;【桌子】zhuō·zi。Characters pronounced with a neutral tone are transcribed not with a tone marker on top of the main vowel, as ordinary characters are, but with a dot before the initial consonant, such as【便当】biàn·dang and【桌子】zhuō·zi.

11. 一般轻读、间或重读的字,注音上标调号,注音前再加圆点,如【因为】注作 yīn·wèi,表示'因为'的'为'字一般轻读,有时也可以读去声。Characters usually pronounced with a neutral tone but occasionally with a stress are transcribed with both a tone marker and a dot before the initial consonant, such as【因为】yīn·wèi, where 为 is usually pronounced with a neutral tone but sometimes with a falling tone.

12. 插入其他成分时,语音上有轻重变化的词语,标上调号和圆点,再加斜的双斜线,如【看见】注作 kàn//·jiàn,【起来】注作 qǐ//·lái,表示在'看见'、'起来'中,'见'字'来'字轻读,在'看得见、看不见'、'起得来、起不来'中,'见'字'来'字重读。Characters that change tones in different combinations are transcribed with a tone marker, a dot before the initial consonant, and a pair of left slashes before the dot, such as【看见】kàn//·jiàn and【起来】qǐ//·lái, where 见 and 来 are normally pronounced with a neutral tone but with a stress in 看得见 or 看不见 and 起得来 or 起不来 respectively.

【起来】还有//·qǐ//·lái 的注法,表示用在动词、形容词后做补语时,如'拿起来'、'好起来'等,'起来'两字都有轻重的变化。例如在'拿起来'里,'起来'两字都轻读;插入'得、不'以后,如'拿得起来、拿不起来','起来'两字都重读。'起来'两字之间再加宾语,如'拿得起枪来','拿不起枪来','起'字重读,'来'字轻读。'上来'、'上去'、'下来'、'下去'、'出来'、'出去'等都可以有同样的变化,注音也用同样方式。【起来】is also transcribed as //·qǐ//·lái, where both characters are pronounced with a neutral tone when the word is used as a complement to a verb or adjective, such as 拿起来 and 好起来; when the auxiliary word 得 or adverb 不 is inserted between the verb and 起来 as the complement, both 起 and 来 are pronounced with their regular tones, as in 拿得起来 and 拿不起来; when an object is inserted between 起 and 来, as in 拿得起枪来 or 拿不起枪来, 起 is pronounced with a regular tone while 来 is neutral-toned. This pattern of tone changes applies to a number of other words, such as 上来,上去,下来,下去,出来,出去,etc.

13. 本词典一般不注变调。在普通话语音中两字相连的变调情形如下:As a norm, tone changes are not marked in this dictionary. In standard Chinese, adjacent characters change tones according to the following rules:

(a) 上声在阴平、阳平、去声、轻声前变半上。Falling-rising tone characters are pronounced with a semi-falling-rising tone when used immediately before characters of level, rising, falling, and neutral tones.

(b) 上声在上声前一般变阳平。For words consisting of two falling-rising-tone characters, the first character is changed into a rising tone.

但是一部分重叠式词语,如'沉甸甸、热腾腾',照实际读法注作 chéndiāndiān、rètēngtēng。Exceptions are made with some entries consisting of repeated characters, such as 沉甸甸

chéndiāndiān and 热腾腾 rèténgténg, in which 甸 and 腾 are marked with the tones with which they are actually pronounced in the combinations, not their regular tones.

14. 本词典对于儿化音的注法，只在基本形式后面加‘r’，如【今儿】jīnr，不标语音上的实际变化。普通话语音中儿化变音情形如下表：Transcription of 儿 inflection is represented by the consonant ‘r’, as in【今儿】(jīnr); actual pronunciations of inflections of different words are not transcribed in full. The following table provides a guideline for the pronunciations of different words when they are inflected with 儿：

ar	a 马	ai 盖	an 盘	*er*	e 歌	*or*	o 婆	*ər*	i 字	ei 辈	en 根		
iar	ia 匣		ian 点	*ier*	ie 碟			*iər*		i 皮	in 心		
uar	ua 花	uai 块	uan 玩			*uor*	uo 窝	*uər*		uei 味	uen 纹	*ur*	u 肚
üar			üan 远	*üer*	üe 月			*üər*		ü 鱼	ün 裙		
aor			ao 包	*our*	ou 头	*ãr*	ang 缸	*ə̃r*			eng 灯	*õr*	ong 工
iaor			iao 条	*iour*	iou 球	*iãr*	iang 秧	*iə̃r*			ing 影	*iõr*	iong 熊
						uãr	uang 黄	*uə̃r*			ueng 瓮		

附注 Notes：①表中儿化韵母之后列举相当的基本韵母，如 ar 后列举 a，ai，an，表示 a，ai，an 三个韵母儿化后都变 ar。每个基本韵母之下举一个字为例。For vowels with the same pronunciation when the characters they represent are inflected with 儿, only one of them is described in full transcription while the rest are listed after it, such as a, ai, and an, which are all pronounced as ar when the characters they represent are inflected with 儿. An example character is given below each vowel.

②普通话里，‘歌儿’和‘根儿’不同音，‘根儿’的韵母在本表里用 ər 表示。ər 是一种卷舌的中央元首。歌儿 and 根儿 are pronounced differently in standard Chinese. The inflected 根儿 is transcribed as ‘ər’ in the table, which represents a retroflex central vowel.

③zi，ci，si，zhi，chi，shi，ri 中的 i 是舌尖元音，儿化后变 ər，如：‘字儿’zər，‘事儿’shər。The i in zi, ci, si, zhi, chi, shi, and ri is an apical vowel. It is pronounced as ‘ər’ when the characters these transcriptions represent are inflected with 儿, such as 字儿(zər) and 事儿(shər).

④ã、ə̃、õ 表示鼻音化的 a、ə、o。ã, ə̃, and õ represent nasalized a, ə, and o respectively.

15. 多音词的注音，以连写为原则，结合较松的，在中间加短横‘-’；词组、成语按词分写。有些组合在中间加斜的双斜线‘//’，表示中间可以插入其他成分。在中间没有插入成分时连写；中间有插入成分时分写。Transcriptions of multi-character words are normally written as one; those that are loosely combined have a hyphen (-) in between; characters of phrases or idioms are transcribed separately; combinations into which other words can be inserted are indicated by a pair of left slashes (//) in between. In actual use, such combinations are transcribed as one when there is no insertion, and separately when other words are inserted.

16. 多音词的注音中,音节界限有混淆可能的,加隔音号('):Transcriptions for multi-character entries with ambiguous division of syllables are clarified with an apostrophe (') in between:

(a) 相连的两个元音,不属于同一个音节的,中间加隔音号,如【答案】dá'àn,【木偶】mù'ǒu。Two adjacent vowels belonging to different syllables are separated by an apostrophe, such as【答案】dá'àn and【木偶】mù'ǒu.

(b) 前一音节收-n尾或-ng尾,后一音节由元音开头的,中间加隔音号,如【恩爱】ēn'ài,【名额】míng'é。Transcriptions for entries consisting of characters ending with -n or -ng and characters beginning with vowels are separated by an apostrophe, such as【恩爱】ēn'ài and【名额】míng'é.

17. 专名和姓氏的注音,第一个字母大写。The first letter of transcriptions of special terms and names is capitalized.

IV 释义 Definitions

18. 分析意义以现代汉语为标准,不详列古义。Definitions are based on contemporary Chinese; archaic senses are not elaborated.

19. 一般条目中,标〈方〉的表示方言,标〈书〉的表示书面上的文言词语,标〈古〉的表示古代的用法,〈方〉、〈书〉等标记适用于整个条目各个义项的,标在第一义项之前;只适用于个别义项的,标在有关义项数码之后。Expressions from Chinese dialects are marked with〈方〉; expressions of written classical Chinese are marked with〈书〉; archaic senses are marked with symbols like〈方〉,〈书〉, etc. are placed before the first definition if all the definitions of the entry belong to the same category; otherwise it is placed immediately after the numeral indicator of the individual definition it refers to.

20. 有些单字条目,仅带一个多音词,这个多音词外面加上'[ ]',就附列在单字注中,不另立条目。如:艅 yú[艅艎](yúhuáng)古时一种木船。If a single-character word has only one multi-character entry under it, the latter is added to the former and enclosed in a pair of square brackets, such as 艅 yú [艅艎] (yúhuáng), a kind of wooden boat in ancient times.

21. 释义后举例中遇本条目,用'~'代替。不止一例的,例与例之间用竖线'|'隔开。例中用的是比喻义时,前面加'◇'。(释义中如已说明'比喻…',举例即不加'◇'。) Entries are represented by a '~' symbol when used in examples after the definitions. Examples illustrating the same definition are separated by a vertical bar (|); examples illustrating the figurative sense of the entry are preceded by a diamond sign (◇), which is omitted if the definition is about the figurative meaning.

22. '也说…'、'也叫…'、'也作…'、'注意…'等,前头有时加'‖'号,表示适用于以上几个义项,如:【数字】❶…❷…❸…‖也说数目字。表示❶❷❸三个义项都可以说成'数目字'。前头不加'‖'号的,只适用于本义项,如:【话筒】❶…❷…❸…也叫传声筒。表示只有第❸义项的物品也叫'传声筒'。A pair of vertical bars (‖) is placed before extra information about an

entry introduced by such words as 也说 ..., 也叫 ..., 也作 ..., or before 注意. The vertical bars indicate that the added information applies to all the definitions before it, such as 【数字】❶... ❷... ❸... ‖ also 数目字. The vertical bars are not used when the additional information is about the definition immediately before it, such as 【话筒】❶... ❷... ❸... also called 传声筒. In this example, only the object as described in the definition ❸ is called by the variant name 传声筒.

23. 一般音译的外来语附注外文,如:【沙发】…[英 sofa];【蒙太奇】…[法 montage]。'英、法'等字,表示语别。【鸸鹋】…[新拉 Rhea],'新拉'表示是新拉丁文。从我国少数民族来的词只附注民族名称,如【萨其马】条附注'[满]'。(释义中如已指明某民族,即不再附注民族名称。) Transliterations of foreign words are usually noted with their original languages, such as【沙发】[英 English: sofa],【蒙太奇】[法 French: montage], and【鸸鹋】[新拉 New Latin: Rhea]. Transliterations from the languages or dialects of ethnic minority peoples in China are noted with the name of their ethnic group, not the original written form of the entry, such as【萨其马】[满 Manchu]. (Such notation is omitted if the origin of the word is already stated in the definition.)

音 节 表
Phonetic Guide

（音节右边的号码指词典正文的页码。
The number that appears to the right of each syllable indicates the page number in this Dictionary.）

A

ā 1
á 2
ǎ 2
à 2
·a 2
āi 3
ái 4
ǎi 5
ài 5
ān 8
ǎn 12
àn 13
āng 17
áng 17
àng 17
āo 18
áo 18
ǎo 19
ào 19

B

bā 21
bá 26
bǎ 27
bà 29
·ba 31
bāi 31
bái 32
bǎi 39
bài 44
·bai 46
bān 46
bǎn 49
bàn 51
bāng 56
bǎng 57
bàng 58
bāo 59
báo 63
bǎo 63
bào 69
bēi 76
běi 79
bèi 81
·bei 87
bēn 88
běn 89
bèn 93
bēng 93
béng 94
běng 94
bèng 94
bī 95
bí 96
bǐ 97
bì 104
biān 112
biǎn 116
biàn 117
biāo 125
biǎo 128
biào 131
biē 131
bié 131
biě 133
biè 134
bīn 134
bìn 135
bīng 135
bǐng 139
bìng 141
bō 144
bó 147
bǒ 152
bò 152
·bo 152
bū 152
bú 153
bǔ 153
bù 155

C

cā 175
cǎ 175
cāi 175
cái 176
cǎi 179
cài 181
cān 182
cán 185
cǎn 187
càn 188
cāng 188
cáng 190
cāo 190
cáo 192
cǎo 192
cào 195
cè 195
cèi 197
cēn 198
cén 198
cēng 198
céng 198
cèng 199
chā 199
chá 202
chǎ 205
chà 205
chāi 207
chái 208
chǎi 209
chài 209
chān 209
chán 209
chǎn 212
chàn 213
chāng 214
cháng 215
chǎng 221
chàng 223
chāo 225
cháo 228
chǎo 230
chào 231
chē 231
chě 233
chè 234
chēn 235
chén 235
chěn 240
chèn 240
·chen 242
chēng 242
chéng 244
chěng 254
chèng 254
chī 255
chí 260
chǐ 262
chì 264
chōng 267
chóng 270
chǒng 273
chòng 273
chōu 274
chóu 276
chǒu 279
chòu 280
chū 280
chú 290
chǔ 292
chù 294
chuā 296
chuāi 296
chuái 296
chuǎi 296
chuài 297
chuān 297
chuán 298
chuǎn 302
chuàn 303
chuāng 304
chuáng 305
chuǎng 305
chuàng 306
chuī 307
chuí 308
chūn 310
chún 312
chǔn 313
chuō 314
chuò 314
cī 314
cí 315
cǐ 320
cì 321
cōng 323
cóng 324
còu 327
cū 327
cú 330
cù 330
cuān 331
cuán 331
cuàn 332
cuī 332
cuǐ 333
cuì 333
cūn 335
cún 335
cǔn 337
cùn 337
cuō 338
cuó 338
cuǒ 339
cuò 339

D

dā 342
dá 344
dǎ 345
dà 353
·da 367

dāi 367
dǎi 368
dài 368
dān 373
dǎn 378
dàn 379
dāng 383
dǎng 386
dàng 388
dāo 389
dáo 391
dǎo 391
dào 394
dē 401
dé 401
·de 404
dēi 405
děi 405
dèn 405
dēng 406
děng 408
dèng 410
dī 411
dí 414
dǐ 416
dì 419
diǎ 431
diān 432
diǎn 433
diàn 435
diāo 444
diǎo 446
diào 446
diē 450
dié 450
dīng 452
dǐng 454
dìng 457
diū 461
dōng 461
dǒng 465
dòng 465
dōu 470
dǒu 471
dòu 473
dū 475
dú 476
dǔ 480
dù 481
duān 483
duǎn 484
duàn 486
duī 489
duì 489
dūn 495
dǔn 496
dùn 496
duō 497
duó 500
duǒ 501
duò 501

E

ē 503
é 503
ě 505
è 505
·e 508
ê̄ 508
ế 508
ê̌ 508
ề 509
ēn 509
èn 509
ēng 509
ér 509
ěr 511
èr 514

F

fā 518
fá 524
fǎ 525
fà 528
·fa 529
fān 529
fán 532
fǎn 535
fàn 540
fāng 544
fáng 547
fǎng 550
fàng 551
fēi 555
féi 560
fěi 561
fèi 562
fēn 566
fén 573
fěn 573
fèn 575
fēng 577
féng 588
fěng 588
fèng 589
fiào 590
fó 590
fǒu 591
fū 592
fú 593
fǔ 601
fù 605

G

gā 618
gá 618
gǎ 619
gà 619
gāi 619
gǎi 620
gài 622
gān 624
gǎn 629
gàn 634
gāng 635
gǎng 638
gàng 639
gāo 639
gǎo 646
gào 647
gē 649
gé 652
gě 655
gè 655
gěi 657
gēn 658
gén 660
gěn 660
gèn 661
gēng 661
gěng 662
gèng 663
gōng 663
gǒng 676
gòng 677
gōu 680
gǒu 682
gòu 684
gū 686
gǔ 689
gù 697
guā 701
guǎ 703
guà 704
guāi 707
guǎi 707
guài 708
guān 709
guǎn 715
guàn 717
guāng 720
guǎng 724
guàng 726
guī 726
guǐ 732
guì 734
gǔn 736
gùn 737
guō 737
guó 738
guǒ 744
guò 746

H

hā 752
há 753
hǎ 753
hà 753
hāi 753
hái 753
hǎi 754
hài 759
hān 760
hán 761
hǎn 765
hàn 765
hāng 769
háng 769
hàng 772
hāo 772
háo 772
hǎo 774
hào 777
hē 780
hé 781
hè 791
hēi 792
hén 796
hěn 796
hèn 796
hēng 796
héng 797
hèng 800
hm 800
hng 800
hōng 800
hóng 801
hǒng 808
hòng 808
hōu 808
hóu 808
hǒu 809
hòu 809
hū 815
hú 817
hǔ 821
hù 822
huā 825
huá 831
huà 835
huái 841
huài 842
·huai 842
huān 842
huán 843
huǎn 845
huàn 846
huāng 849
huáng 850
huǎng 855
huàng 856
huī 856
huí 858
huǐ 864
huì 865
hūn 871
hún 872
hùn 873
huō 874
huó 875
huǒ 878
huò 884

J

jī 888
jí 900
jǐ 910
jì 912
jiā 923
jiá 931
jiǎ 931
jià 935
jiān 937
jiǎn 944
jiàn 950
jiāng 958
jiǎng 961
jiàng 963
jiāo 965
jiáo 973
jiǎo 973
jiào 979
jiē 984
jié 988
jiě 995
jiè 998
·jie 1002
jīn 1002
jǐn 1008
jìn 1010
jīng 1017
jǐng 1027
jìng 1030
jiōng 1034
jiǒng 1034
jiū 1035
jiǔ 1036
jiù 1038
·jiu 1043
jū 1043
jú 1046
jǔ 1047
jù 1049

juān	1054	kuān	1121	lī	1174	lǜ	1266	mēng	1324	nǎn	1392
juǎn	1055	kuǎn	1123	lí	1175	luán	1269	méng	1324	nàn	1392
juàn	1055	kuāng	1123	lǐ	1178	luǎn	1269	měng	1326	nāng	1392
juē	1057	kuáng	1124	lì	1183	luàn	1270	mèng	1327	náng	1392
jué	1057	kuǎng	1125	· li	1193	lüě	1271	mī	1328	nǎng	1393
juě	1063	kuàng	1125	liǎ	1193	lüè	1271	mí	1328	nàng	1393
juè	1063	kuī	1127	lián	1193	lūn	1272	mǐ	1331	nāo	1393
jūn	1063	kuí	1128	liǎn	1200	lún	1272	mì	1332	náo	1393
jùn	1067	kuǐ	1130	liàn	1201	lǔn	1275	mián	1335	nǎo	1394
		kuì	1130	liáng	1203	lùn	1275	miǎn	1336	nào	1396
K		kūn	1131	liǎng	1205	luō	1276	miàn	1338	né	1397
		kǔn	1132	liàng	1209	luó	1276	miāo	1341	nè	1397
kā	1068	kùn	1132	liāo	1211	luǒ	1279	miáo	1341	· ne	1397
kǎ	1068	kuò	1133	liáo	1211	luò	1280	miǎo	1342	něi	1398
kāi	1069			liǎo	1213	· luo	1284	miào	1343	nèi	1398
kǎi	1078	**L**		liào	1214			miē	1344	nèn	1401
kài	1079			liē	1216	**M**		miè	1344	néng	1402
kān	1079	lā	1136	liě	1216			mín	1345	ńg	1403
kǎn	1080	lá	1138	liè	1216	m̄	1285	mǐn	1349	ňg	1403
kàn	1081	lǎ	1139	· lie	1219	ḿ	1285	míng	1350	ǹg	1403
kāng	1083	là	1139	līn	1219	m̀	1285	mǐng	1359	nī	1403
káng	1083	· la	1141	lín	1220	mā	1285	mìng	1359	ní	1404
kàng	1084	lái	1141	lǐn	1225	má	1285	miù	1360	nǐ	1405
kāo	1085	lài	1144	lìn	1225	mǎ	1287	mō	1361	nì	1406
kǎo	1085	· lai	1145	líng	1226	mà	1292	mó	1361	niān	1408
kào	1087	lán	1145	lǐng	1232	· ma	1292	mǒ	1365	nián	1409
kē	1088	lǎn	1148	lìng	1235	mái	1293	mò	1365	niǎn	1412
ké	1091	làn	1149	liū	1236	mǎi	1293	mōu	1371	niàn	1413
kě	1092	lāng	1149	liú	1237	mài	1294	móu	1371	niáng	1413
kè	1095	láng	1150	liǔ	1245	mān	1297	mǒu	1372	niàng	1414
kēi	1099	lǎng	1151	liù	1246	mán	1297	mú	1372	niǎo	1414
kěn	1100	làng	1151	· lo	1248	mǎn	1298	mǔ	1372	niào	1415
kèn	1100	lāo	1152	lōng	1248	màn	1300	mù	1374	niē	1415
kēng	1101	láo	1153	lóng	1248	māng	1302			nié	1416
kōng	1101	lǎo	1156	lǒng	1251	máng	1302	**N**		niè	1416
kǒng	1105	lào	1163	lòng	1252	mǎng	1304			nín	1417
kòng	1106	lē	1164	lōu	1252	māo	1305	ń	1381	níng	1417
kōu	1107	lè	1164	lóu	1252	máo	1305	ň	1381	nǐng	1419
kǒu	1108	· le	1166	lǒu	1253	mǎo	1309	ǹ	1381	nìng	1419
kòu	1111	lēi	1166	lòu	1254	mào	1310	nā	1381	niū	1419
kū	1113	léi	1166	· lou	1256	· me	1312	ná	1381	niú	1419
kǔ	1114	lěi	1168	lū	1256	méi	1312	nǎ	1382	niǔ	1421
kù	1115	lèi	1169	lú	1256	měi	1317	nà	1383	niù	1422
kuā	1117	· lei	1171	lǔ	1258	mèi	1319	· na	1385	nóng	1422
kuǎ	1117	lēng	1171	lù	1259	mēn	1320	nǎi	1385	nòng	1425
kuà	1117	léng	1171	· lu	1264	mén	1320	nài	1386	nòu	1426
kuǎi	1118	lěng	1171	lǘ	1264	mèn	1323	nān	1387	nú	1426
kuài	1118	lèng	1174	lǚ	1265	· men	1324	nán	1387	nǔ	1426

nù 1427
nǚ 1427
nǜ 1428
nuǎn 1428
nüè 1429
nún 1430
nuó 1430
nuò 1430

O

ō 1431
ó 1431
ǒ 1431
ò 1431
ōu 1431
ǒu 1432
òu 1433

P

pā 1434
pá 1434
pà 1435
pāi 1435
pái 1436
pǎi 1440
pài 1440
pān 1441
pán 1441
pàn 1443
pāng 1445
páng 1445
pǎng 1447
pàng 1447
pāo 1447
páo 1448
pǎo 1449
pào 1450
pēi 1452
péi 1452
pèi 1454
pēn 1456
pén 1457
pèn 1458
pēng 1458
péng 1458
pěng 1460
pèng 1460
pī 1461
pí 1464
pǐ 1468
pì 1469
piān 1470
pián 1473
piǎn 1473
piàn 1473
piāo 1474
piáo 1476
piǎo 1476
piào 1477
piē 1477
piě 1478
piè 1478
pīn 1478
pín 1479
pǐn 1480
pìn 1482
pīng 1482
píng 1482
pō 1491
pó 1492
pǒ 1492
pò 1493
• po 1496
pōu 1496
póu 1496
pǒu 1497
pū 1497
pú 1499
pǔ 1500
pù 1502

Q

qī 1504
qí 1508
qǐ 1514
qì 1520
qiā 1526
qiá 1526
qiǎ 1526
qià 1527
qiān 1527
qián 1532
qiǎn 1539
qiàn 1540
qiāng 1541
qiáng 1543
qiǎng 1546
qiàng 1547
qiāo 1548
qiáo 1549
qiǎo 1550
qiào 1551
qiē 1553
qié 1553
qiě 1554
qiè 1554
qīn 1556
qín 1559
qǐn 1562
qìn 1562
qīng 1562
qíng 1574
qǐng 1577
qìng 1578
qióng 1579
qiū 1581
qiú 1582
qiǔ 1586
qū 1586
qú 1590
qǔ 1591
qù 1593
• qu 1594
quān 1594
quán 1595
quǎn 1600
quàn 1600
quē 1601
qué 1602
què 1602
qūn 1604
qún 1604

R

rán 1607
rǎn 1608
rāng 1608
ráng 1608
rǎng 1609
ràng 1609
ráo 1610
rǎo 1610
rào 1610
rě 1611
rè 1611
rén 1615
rěn 1622
rèn 1623
rēng 1625
réng 1625
rì 1626
róng 1628
rǒng 1632
róu 1632
ròu 1633
rú 1634
rǔ 1637
rù 1639
ruá 1642
ruán 1642
ruǎn 1642
ruí 1643
ruǐ 1644
ruì 1644
rún 1644
rùn 1644
ruó 1645
ruò 1645

S

sā 1647
sǎ 1647
sà 1648
sāi 1648
sài 1649
sān 1650
sǎn 1655
sàn 1656
sāng 1657
sǎng 1657
sàng 1658
sāo 1658
sǎo 1658
sào 1659
sè 1660
sēn 1661
sēng 1662
shā 1662
shá 1666
shǎ 1666
shà 1667
shāi 1667
shǎi 1668
shài 1668
shān 1668
shǎn 1672
shàn 1673
shāng 1676
shǎng 1678
shàng 1679
• shang 1687
shāo 1687
sháo 1689
shǎo 1689
shào 1690
shē 1691
shé 1692
shě 1693
shè 1694
shéi 1699
shēn 1699
shén 1704
shěn 1708
shèn 1709
shēng 1711
shéng 1721
shěng 1722
shèng 1722
shī 1726
shí 1733
shǐ 1748
shì 1750
• shi 1764
shōu 1764
shóu 1767
shǒu 1767
shòu 1773
shū 1777
shú 1783
shǔ 1784
shù 1787
shuā 1791
shuǎ 1792
shuà 1792
shuāi 1792
shuǎi 1793
shuài 1794
shuān 1794
shuàn 1795
shuāng 1795
shuǎng 1797
shuí 1798
shuǐ 1798
shuì 1805
shǔn 1806
shùn 1806
shuō 1808
shuò 1811
sī 1812
sǐ 1817
sì 1820
sōng 1824
sóng 1825
sǒng 1825
sòng 1826
sōu 1827
sǒu 1828
sòu 1828
sū 1828
sú 1829
sù 1830
suān 1834
suàn 1835
suī 1836
suí 1837
suǐ 1839
suì 1839
sūn 1840
sǔn 1841
suō 1841
suǒ 1843

T

tā 1847
tǎ 1848
tà 1849
tāi 1850
tái 1851
tǎi 1853
tài 1853

tān	1856	tuān	1945	wò	2014	xù	2166	yìng	2305	zè	2399
tán	1858	tuán	1945	wū	2015	· xu	2169	yō	2309	zéi	2399
tǎn	1860	tuǎn	1947	wú	2018	xuān	2169	· yo	2309	zěn	2400
tàn	1861	tuàn	1947	wǔ	2028	xuán	2171	yōng	2309	zèn	2400
tāng	1864	tuī	1947	wù	2036	xuǎn	2174	yóng	2311	zēng	2401
táng	1864	tuí	1950			xuàn	2175	yǒng	2311	zèng	2402
tǎng	1868	tuǐ	1950	**X**		xuē	2176	yòng	2313	zhā	2402
tàng	1868	tuì	1951			xué	2176	yōu	2314	zhá	2403
tāo	1869	tūn	1953	xī	2041	xuě	2179	yóu	2317	zhǎ	2404
táo	1870	tún	1954	xí	2051	xuè	2181	yǒu	2325	zhà	2405
tǎo	1872	tǔn	1954	xǐ	2053	xūn	2184	yòu	2332	· zha	2406
tào	1873	tùn	1954	xì	2055	xún	2185	yū	2335	zhāi	2406
tè	1875	tuō	1955	xiā	2060	xùn	2188	yú	2335	zhái	2407
· te	1877	tuó	1960	xiá	2061			yǔ	2342	zhǎi	2407
tēi	1877	tuǒ	1961	xià	2062	**Y**		yù	2346	zhài	2407
tēng	1877	tuò	1962	xiān	2069			yuān	2354	zhān	2408
téng	1877			xián	2074	yā	2191	yuán	2355	zhǎn	2410
tī	1878	**W**		xiǎn	2077	yá	2194	yuǎn	2365	zhàn	2411
tí	1880			xiàn	2079	yǎ	2196	yuàn	2367	zhāng	2415
tǐ	1883	wā	1964	xiāng	2085	yà	2197	yuē	2368	zhǎng	2417
tì	1886	wá	1964	xiáng	2092	· ya	2198	yuě	2369	zhàng	2418
tiān	1887	wǎ	1965	xiǎng	2093	yān	2198	yuè	2369	zhāo	2420
tián	1896	wà	1965	xiàng	2095	yán	2201	yūn	2374	zháo	2423
tiǎn	1899	· wa	1966	xiāo	2099	yǎn	2208	yún	2375	zhǎo	2424
tiàn	1899	wāi	1966	xiáo	2104	yàn	2214	yǔn	2377	zhào	2424
tiāo	1899	wǎi	1966	xiǎo	2104	yāng	2216	yùn	2378	zhē	2427
tiáo	1900	wài	1967	xiào	2114	yáng	2217			zhé	2428
tiǎo	1903	wān	1971	xiē	2117	yǎng	2222	**Z**		zhě	2430
tiào	1904	wán	1972	xié	2119	yàng	2225			zhè	2431
tiē	1906	wǎn	1975	xiě	2122	yāo	2225	zā	2383	· zhe	2432
tiě	1907	wàn	1977	xiè	2123	yáo	2228	zá	2383	zhèi	2433
tiè	1909	wāng	1979	xīn	2126	yǎo	2230	zǎ	2385	zhēn	2433
tīng	1909	wáng	1980	xín	2136	yào	2231	zāi	2385	zhěn	2437
tíng	1912	wǎng	1981	xǐn	2136	yē	2235	zǎi	2386	zhèn	2438
tǐng	1913	wàng	1983	xìn	2136	yé	2235	zài	2386	zhēng	2441
tìng	1914	wēi	1985	xīng	2139	yě	2236	zān	2390	zhěng	2444
tōng	1914	wéi	1989	xíng	2142	yè	2238	zán	2390	zhèng	2446
tóng	1919	wěi	1994	xǐng	2148	yī	2242	zǎn	2390	zhī	2453
tǒng	1925	wèi	1997	xìng	2149	yí	2260	zàn	2390	zhí	2459
tòng	1927	wēn	2003	xiōng	2152	yǐ	2266	· zan	2391	zhǐ	2465
tōu	1928	wén	2004	xióng	2154	yì	2270	zāng	2391	zhì	2470
tóu	1929	wěn	2009	xiòng	2155	yīn	2282	zǎng	2392	zhōng	2479
tǒu	1935	wèn	2010	xiū	2156	yín	2289	zàng	2392	zhǒng	2489
tòu	1935	wēng	2012	xiǔ	2159	yǐn	2291	zāo	2393	zhòng	2490
tū	1936	wěng	2012	xiù	2159	yìn	2295	záo	2394	zhōu	2494
tú	1938	wèng	2012	xū	2161	yīng	2297	zǎo	2394	zhóu	2497
tǔ	1942	wō	2012	xú	2165	yíng	2300	zào	2396	zhǒu	2497
tù	1944	wǒ	2014	xǔ	2165	yǐng	2304	zé	2398	zhòu	2497

zhū	2498	zhuài	2515	zhuì	2529	zōng	2553	zǔ	2564	zūn	2570
zhú	2501	zhuān	2515	zhūn	2530	zǒng	2555	zuān	2567	zǔn	2571
zhǔ	2503	zhuǎn	2518	zhǔn	2530	zòng	2558	zuǎn	2567	zùn	2571
zhù	2508	zhuàn	2521	zhuō	2532	zōu	2559	zuàn	2568	zuō	2571
zhuā	2513	zhuāng	2523	zhuó	2533	zǒu	2559	zuī	2568	zuó	2572
zhuǎ	2515	zhuǎng	2525	zī	2536	zòu	2562	zuǐ	2568	zuǒ	2572
zhuāi	2515	zhuàng	2525	zǐ	2539	zū	2562	zuì	2569	zuò	2574
zhuǎi	2515	zhuī	2527	zì	2543	zú	2563				

新旧字形对照表

Table of Comparison between Old and New Character Patterns

（字形后圆圈内的数字表示字形的笔画数。
The circled number on the right of each character pattern indicates the number of strokes contained in it.）

旧字形 Old Form	新字形 New Form	新字举例 Example of New Characters	旧字形 Old Form	新字形 New Form	新字举例 Example of New Characters
艹④	艹③	花草	直⑧	直⑧	值植
辶④	辶③	连速	黾⑧	黾⑧	绳鼋
幵⑥	开④	型形	咼⑨	咼⑧	過蝸
丰④	丰④	艳沣	垂⑨	垂⑧	睡郵
巨⑤	巨④	苣渠	飠⑨	飠⑧	飲飽
屯④	屯④	纯顿	郎⑨	郎⑧	廊螂
瓦⑤	瓦④	瓶瓷	彔⑧	录⑧	渌箓
反④	反④	板饭	昷⑩	昷⑨	温瘟
丑④	丑④	纽杻	骨⑩	骨⑨	滑骼
犮⑤	犮⑤	拔茇	鬼⑩	鬼⑨	槐嵬
印⑥	印⑤	茚	俞⑨	俞⑨	偷渝
耒⑥	耒⑥	耕耘	旣⑪	既⑨	溉厩
呂⑦	吕⑥	侣营	蚤⑩	蚤⑨	搔骚
攸⑦	攸⑥	修倏	敖⑪	敖⑩	傲遨
爭⑧	争⑥	净静	莽⑫	莽⑩	漭蟒
产⑥	产⑥	彦産	眞⑩	真⑩	慎填
羊⑦	羊⑥	差养	䍃⑩	䍃⑩	摇遥
幷⑧	并⑥	屏拼	殺⑪	殺⑩	摋鎩
吳⑦	吴⑦	蜈虞	黃⑫	黄⑪	廣横
角⑦	角⑦	解确	虛⑫	虚⑪	墟歔
奐⑨	奂⑦	换痪	異⑫	異⑪	冀戴
㡀⑧	㡀⑦	敝弊	象⑫	象⑪	像橡
耳⑧	耳⑦	敢嚴	奧⑬	奥⑫	澳襖
者⑨	者⑧	都著	普⑬	普⑫	谱氆

部首检字表
Radicals Guide to Entries

【说明】1. 本检字表采用的部首跟一般字典用的部首基本相同，略有改并。共有 189 部。部首次序按部首笔画数目多少排列，同画数的，按起笔（即书写时的第一笔）一（横）丨（直）丿（撇）丶（点）乛（折，包括亅ㄱ乚㇛等笔形）的顺序排列。同一部的字按除去部首笔画以外的画数排列，同画数的，按起笔 一丨丿丶乛的顺序排列。笔画新旧字形不同的，按新字形。The list of radicals as a guide to the entries in this dictionary is largely the same as those in other Chinese dictionaries, with only minor modifications. There are 189 radicals in all, listed from fewer to more strokes; those with the same number of strokes are listed in the order of their beginning stroke, i. e. horizontal line (一), vertical line (丨), left slash (丿), dot (丶), and straight stroke with a bending tip (乛) or with an extended bending stroke (such as 亅ㄱ乚㇛). Characters with the same radical are listed according to the number of strokes of their other parts; those with the same radical and the same number of strokes in their other parts are listed in the order of the beginning stroke of those parts, i. e. 一丨丿丶乛. New forms of radicals and characters are preferred when both old and new forms are currently in use.

2. 对于难检的字，解决的办法是：Characters with radicals that are difficult to classify are treated as follows:

(1) 有些字分收在几个部首内，如'古'字，分别收入十部、口部。Some are listed under different radicals, such as 古, which is listed under both the radicals of 十 and 口.

(2) 分不清部首的字，按起笔的笔形，收入一丨丿丶乙五个单笔部首内。Characters that do not have separable radicals are listed under the five single-stroke radicals of 一丨丿丶乙, depending on the beginning stroke of the characters concerned.

(3) 检字表后另有《难检字笔画索引》备查。An 'Index of Characters with Radicals Difficult to Classify' is provided for reference.

I 部首目录
Contents of Radicals

（部首右边的号码指检字表的页码。The number to the right of each radical indicates the page number in the 'Radical Guide'.）

一画

一 35
丨 36
丿 36
丶 36
乙（乛ㄱ乚） 36

二画

二 37
十 37
厂 37
匚 37
卜（⺊） 37
刂 37
冂 38
亻 38
八（丷） 39
人（入） 39
勹 39
⺈（见刀）
儿 40
几（⺇） 40
亠 40
冫 40
冖 40
讠（言） 40
卩（㔾） 41
阝（在左） 41
阝（在右） 41
凵 42
刀（⺈） 42
力 42
厶 42
又（㕛） 42
廴 42
㔾（见卩）

三画

工 42
土 43
士 44
艹 44
廾（在下） 46
大 46
尢 46
扌 46
寸 48
弋 48
小（⺌） 48
口 48
囗 50
巾 50
山 50
彳 51

彡 51
犭 51
夕 52
夂 52
饣(飠) 52
丬(爿) 52
广 52
门(門) 52
氵 53
忄(⺗) 55
宀 56
辶(辶) 56
彐(⺕彑) 56
尸 57
己(巳) 57
弓 57
屮 57
女 57
子(孑) 58
纟(糸) 58
马(馬) 59
幺 59
巛 59

四画

王 59
韦(韋) 60
木 60
犬 62
歹 62
车(車) 62
戈 62
比 62
瓦 62
止 63
攴 63
⺌(见忄)
日 63
曰(⺜) 63
水(氺) 63
贝(貝) 63
见(見) 64
牛(牜⺧) 64
手 64
毛 64
气 64
攵 64
片 65
斤 65
爪(⺤) 65
父 65
月(⺝) 65
欠 66
风(風) 66
殳 66
文 66
方 66
火 66
斗 67
灬 67
户 67
礻(示) 67
心 67
肀(⺻聿) 68
爿(见丬)
毋(母) 68

五画

示(⺬见礻) 68
石 68
龙(龍) 69
业 69
氺(见水)
目 69
田 69
罒 69
皿 69
钅(釒) 70
矢 71
禾 71
白 71
瓜 71
用 71
鸟(鳥) 71
疒 72
立 73
穴 73
衤 73
⺻(见聿)
艮(见艮)
疋(⺪) 73
皮 73
矛 73
母(见毋)

六画

耒 73
老 73
耳 73
臣 74
西(覀) 74
页(頁) 74
虍 74
虫 74
缶 75
舌 75
竹(⺮) 75
臼 76
自 76
血 76
舟 76
衣 76
羊(⺶⺷) 76
米 76
聿(见聿)
艮(⺙) 77
羽 77
糸(糹见纟) 77

七画

麦(麥) 77
走 77
赤 77
車(见车)
豆 77
酉 77
辰 78
豕 78
卤(鹵) 78
里 78
貝(见贝)
見(见见)
足(⻊) 78
身 78
采 78
谷 79
豸 79
角 79
言(訁见讠) 79
辛 79

八画

青 79
其 79
雨(⻗) 79
齿(齒) 79
黾(黽) 79
隹 79
金(釒见钅) 79
飠(见饣)
鱼(魚) 80
門(见门)

九画

革 80
頁(见页)
骨 80
鬼 80
食(飠见饣) 80
風(见风)
音 81
韋(见韦)

十画

鬥 81
髟 81
馬(见马)

十一画

麥(见麦)
鹵(见卤)
鳥(见鸟)
魚(见鱼)
麻 81
鹿 81

十二画以上

黑 81
黽(见黾)
鼠 81
鼻 81
齒(见齿)
龍(见龙)

II 检字表
Radicals Guide

(1. 字右边的号码指词典正文的页码。The number to the right of each character indicates the page number in the Dictionary. 2. 带圆括弧的字是繁体字或异体字。Characters in parentheses are the original complex forms or variant forms.)

一部

一 2242 2260 2270

一画

丁 452 2441
七 1504 1508

二画

三 1650
干 624 634
于 2335
上 1679
下 2062
丈 2418
兀 2015 2036
万 1365 1977
与 2336 2342 2346
才 176

三画

丰 577
开 1069
井 1027
夫 592 593
天 1887
元 2355
无 1361 2018
专 2515
丐 622
廿 1413
五 2028
(帀) 2383
丏 1336
卅 1648
不 153 155
不 496
冇 1309
丑 279
屯 1954 2530
互 822
牙 2194

四画

未 1999
末 1365
(末) 1312
击 888
正 2441 2446
甘 627
世 1752
卌 2055
且 1043 1554
可 1092 1095
(冊) 195
丙 139
丕 1461
册 195
平 1482
东 461
丝 1813

五画

(丢) 461
亚 2197
亘 661
再 2386
吏 1189
百 39
而 510
(亙) 661
夹 618 925

931
尧 2228
丞 248

六画

(𠀤) 1843
严 2202
巫 2017
求 1583
甫 601
更 661
663
束 1787
两 1205
丽 1175
1189
(夾) 618
931
来 1141

七画

奉 589
表 128
(長) 215
2417
(亞) 2197
(東) 461
事 1755
(兩) 1205
枣 2395
(面) 1338
(來) 1141
疌 990

八画

奏 2562
韭 1037
甚 1710
(甚) 1704
巷 772
2097
柬 944
歪 1966
面 1338
甩 2039
昼 2498

九画

艳 2214
蕈 685
哥 650
鬲 654
1192
孬 1393

十画以上

焉 2200
(暨) 380
(甦) 1828
(棗) 2395
棘 907
奡 19
皕 108
赝 1950
(壽) 1773
(爾) 511
奭 1764
赜 2399
(憂) 2315
鼒 2539
黇 1896
整 2444
噩 508
臻 2437
鬴 605
(豎) 2258
醶 870
橐 646
夔 1394
疊 2139
囊 1392

丨部

三画

丰 577
中 2479
2490
内 1398

四画

北 79
凸 1936
旧 1038
且 1043
1554
申 1699
甲 931
电 435
由 2318
冉 1608
史 1748
央 2216
目 2269
凹 18
1964
出 280

五至七画

师 1730
曳 2240
曲 1586
1591
肉 1633
串 303
非 558
畅 223

八画以上

临 1221
禺 2339
(暢) 223

丿部

一至二画

乂 2270
匕 97
九 1036
乃 1385
千 1527
乇 1955
川 297
久 1037
么 1312
(么) 1292
2225
及 900

三画

午 2032
壬 1622
升 1711
夭 2226
长 215
2417
币 104
反 535
爻 2228
乏 524
丹 373
氏 1751
2455
乌 2015
2036

四画

生 1712
生 619
失 1726
乍 2405
丘 1581
卮 2455
乎 815
甩 1793
氐 411
416
丱 717
乐 1164
2371

五画

年 1409
朱 2498
丢 461
乔 1549
乒 1482
乓 1445
向 2095
囟 2136
后 809
甪 1259
兆 2425

六画

我 2014
每 1317
兵 137
(兎) 1945
囱 323
(巵) 2455
龟 729
1066
1581
卵 1269
系 918
2056

七画

垂 308
乖 707
秉 139
卑 77
质 2473
周 2495

八画

拜 45
臿 199
重 271
2492
复 609
禹 2344
胤 2297

九画

甡 1702
乘 252
1724
(師) 1730
虒 1816

十画以上

(牾) 2033
(暨) 380
馗 1128
甥 1721
(喬) 1549
粤 2374
弑 1763
舞 2035
毓 2353
睾 646
甭 1387
疑 2265
孵 593
靠 1087
(舉) 1048
艚 573
(歸) 726
虋 1872
疊 2139
(譽) 1116
(釁) 808
(嚳) 2139
爨 332

丶部

二至三画

丫 2191
义 2270
丸 1972
之 2453
为 1989
1998

四画

主 2503
半 52
头 1929
永 2311

五画以上

州 2494
农 1422
良 1203
叛 1445
(為) 1989
1998
举 1048

乙(乛𠃌乚)部

乙 2266

一至三画

刁 444
了 1166
1213
乜 1344
1416
也 2236
乞 1514
飞 555
习 2051
孑 988
乡 2085
孓 1057
尹 2291
尺 233
262
夬 708
(弔) 446
丑 279
巴 23
以 2267
予 2336
2342
孔 1105
书 1777

四画

司 1812
民 1345
弗 593
疋 2196
(疋) 1468
电 435
(氹) 388
丱 717
发 518
528

五画

尕 475
尽 1008
1011
乩 892
买 1293

六至九画

乱 1270
肃 1831
乳 1637
承 249
亟 904
1525
昼 2498
咫 2470
(飛) 555
胤 2297

癸 734
(凾) 762

十画以上

(發) 518
(肅) 1831
(亂) 1270
豫 2354
嚮 2085

二部

二 514
干 624
634
亍 294
于 2335
2336
亏 1127
五 2028
亓 1508
井 1027
元 2355
2356
无 1361
2018
云 2375
些 2117
叆 7
叇 373

十部

十 1733

一至五画

支 2453
2454
卉 865
古 689
(卋) 1752
考 1085
毕 105
华 832
838
协 2119
芈 1332
克 1095
(皁) 2396
孛 81
147

六画

卓 2533
直 2460
卑 77
阜 609
卒 330
2564
丧 1657
1658
(協) 2119
卖 1295

七至十画

南 1381
1388
真 2435
隼 1841
(䘮) 1657
1658
索 1844
1845
乾 1537
(乾) 624
啬 1661
博 149
(喪) 1657
1658

十一画以上

(幹) 634
(嗇) 1661
(準) 2530
(榦) 634
斡 2015
兢 1024
嘏 697
934
疐 2479
(疐) 2479
翰 769
矗 296

厂部

厂 8
221

二至六画

厅 1909
仄 2399
历 1184
厄 505
厉 1186
压 2191
2198
厌 2214
厍 1694
励 1189
(厓) 2196
厔 2472
厕 195

七至八画

(厖) 1445
厘 1175
厚 813
(厛) 1909
厝 339
原 2358

九至十画

厢 2092
厣 2209
厩 1040
(厫) 18
厨 291
厦 1667
2069
(厤) 1184
雁 2215
厥 1062

十一画以上

(厪) 1010
(厭) 2214
(厨) 291
厮 1817
(厲) 1186
(厰) 221
靥 2242
魇 2213
餍 2216
(鴈) 2215
(歷) 654
1192
(歷) 1184
(曆) 1184
赝 2216
(橜) 1062
(壓) 2191
2198
黡 2213
(懕) 2199
(厴) 2209
(蹷) 1062
(贋) 2216
(靨) 2242
(魘) 2213
(饜) 2216
(黶) 2213

匚部

二至四画

区 1431
1586
匹 1468
巨 1049
叵 1492
匝 2383
匜 2260
匡 1123
匠 963

五画以上

匣 2061
医 2258
匦 732
匼 1088
匿 1408
匪 561
562
匮 1130
(區) 1431
1586
匾 117
(匯) 865
(匳) 1193
匵 2399
(匳) 1193
(匵) 480

卜(⺊)部

卜 152
153
上 1678
1679
1680
卝 1125
卡 1068
1526
占 2408
2411
外 1967
卢 1256
(朩) 1780
贞 2433
芈 1332
卣 2332
卦 704
卧 2014
卓 2533
卤 2124
桌 2532
(卨) 2124
(离) 2124

刂部

二至三画

刈 2272
刊 1079
刌 337

四画

刑 2142
刓 1972
列 1216
划 831
837
842
刚 635
则 2398
创 304
306
刖 2372
刎 2009
刘 1237

五画

刬 213
214
(刦) 990
(刓) 2275
(刪) 1671
别 131
132
134
钊 2420
利 1189
删 1671
刨 72
1448
判 1443
刜 595
刭 1028

六画

封 1128
刵 517
刺 314
321
刯 31
刲 1113
到 394
刿 734
剀 1078
制 2472
刮 702
刽 734
刹 206
1665
剁 502
(刴) 502
剂 919
刻 1096
刷 1791
1792

七画

荆 1022
剋 1099
(尅) 1095
剌 1139
(剌) 1139
剅 1252
(剄) 1028
削 2099
2176
剐 703
剑 954
剉 279
剒 339
前 1533
剃 1886

八画

剒 339
剚 2553
剞 894
(剗) 213
214
剕 566
剔 1878
(剛) 635
(剮) 703
(剠) 1576
剖 1496
剡 1674
2209
剜 1972
剥 63
146
剧 1051
剟 500

九至十一画

(剳) 874
副 613
(剴) 1078
剩 1725
(創) 304
306
割 651
蒯 1118
剽 1474
(劉) 1252
(剷) 213
剿 228
978

十二画以上

劂 1062
劄 2403
 2404
劁 1548
劚 2508
(劃) 838
 842
劐 703
(劌) 734
劋 874
(劇) 1051
(劍) 954
(劊) 734
(劉) 1237
劓 2281
(劑) 919
劗 950
劘 1365
(劚) 2508
劙 1178

冂部

(冄) 1608
冈 635
内 1398
冉 1608
(冊) 195
(囘) 858
同 1919
 1927
网 1981
肉 1633
冏 1034
周 2495
(岡) 635
罔 1982
(罣) 706

亻部

一画

亿 2270

二画

仁 1622
什 1704
 1735
仃 453
仆 1497
 1499
仉 2417
仇 276
 1582
化 825
 835
仍 1625
仂 1164
仅 1008
 1010

三画

仨 1647
仕 1753
仗 2419
代 368
付 605
仙 2069
仟 1529
仡 649
 2272
(仛) 1957
仪 2260
仫 1378
伋 901
们 1324
他 1847
伖 1426
仞 1624
仔 2536
 2541
(仔) 2386

四画

伕 592
伟 1994
传 298
 2521
休 2156
伍 2032
伎 915
伏 593
伛 2342
优 2314
伜 233
(佢) 1590
伐 525
仳 1468
伢 2195
佤 1965
仲 2491
仵 2033
件 952
任 1622
 1624
伤 1676
伥 214
价 935
 998
 1002
伦 1272
份 575
(伀) 2486
伧 189
 242
仰 2222
伉 1084
仿 550
伙 883
伪 1994
伫 2508
伈 2136
伊 2256
似 1755
 1822
伃 2336

五画

佞 1419
佉 1588
估 686
 697
体 1878
 1883
何 784
佐 2573
伾 1461
佑 2334
(佈) 171
𫢸 1251
伻 93
佧 1069
(佔) 2411
攸 2315
但 380
伸 1700
伷 2497
佃 441
 1897
佀 1823
佚 2275
作 2571
 2574
(作) 2579
伯 42
 148
 353
(佗) 1957
伶 1226
佣 2309
 2314
低 411
你 1406
佝 681
佟 1923
㑇 2497
住 2509
位 2000
伴 54
(佇) 2508
佗 1960
伺 321
 1823
伲 1406
佛 590
 595
伽 618
 926
 1553
佊 100

六画

侊 1123
佳 926
侍 1757
佶 904
佬 1162
佴 517
 1387
供 674
 679
使 1749
佰 42
侑 2334
侉 1117
㑷 1849
例 1191
侠 2061
侥 975
 2228
侄 2462
侦 2434
侣 1265
侗 469
 1923
 1925
侃 1080
侧 195
 2399
 2406
侏 2499
侁 1701
侹 1913
侨 1549
侜 2495
佺 1598
侩 1120
佻 1899
佾 2276
佩 1454
佹 732
佫 791
侈 264
侂 1957
侪 208
佼 975
佽 322
依 2258
佯 2221
(併) 141
侘 206
侬 1424
侔 1371

七画

俦 276
俨 2208
俅 1584
便 121
 1473
俩 1193
 1208
俪 1192
(俠) 2061
修 2157
俏 1552
俚 1180
俣 2344
保 65
俜 1482
促 330
俐 1192
俄 503
侮 2034
俭 944
俗 1829
俘 597
俛 602
 1337
 1349
(係) 2056
信 2136
(信) 2136
侻 1951
 1957
俤 428
俍 1203
侵 1556
侯 808
 814
侷 1047
俑 2312
俟 1511
 1823
俊 1067

八画

俸 590
倩 1541
债 2407
俵 131
(倀) 214
(倖) 2150
倻 2235
借 1000
偌 1646
值 2462
(傳) 2553
(倆) 1193
 1208
倷 1386
倴 93
倚 2269
俺 12
(倈) 1144
倢 993
倾 1568
倒 393
 395
俳 1436
俶 294
 1886
倬 2533
(條) 1900
倏 1780
脩 2158
(倐) 1780
倘 219
 1868
俱 1045
 1051
倮 1279
倡 214
 223
(個) 655
偭 1349
候 814
㑩 1278
倭 2013
倪 1405
俾 103
(倫) 1272
(保) 181
倜 1886
(俻) 81
倞 1031
 1210
俯 602
倅 333
(倣) 550
倍 85
倦 1056

倓 1858
倌 715
倥 1105
1106
健 955
倨 1051
倔 1061
1063

九画

(偰) 2124
偾 576
做 2579
偃 2212
(偪) 95
偭 1338
偕 2121
偿 221
偶 1432
偈 921
994
偎 1987
偲 175
1816
偢 279
1552
傀 731
1130
偊 2346
偷 1928
偛 243
偬 2558
(偺) 2385
2390
2391
停 1912
偁 241
偻 1253
1265
(偽) 1994
偏 1470
偓 2015
假 933
937
(偉) 1994

十画

傣 368
傲 19
傤 2389
(備) 81
傎 432
傅 615
傈 1193
傉 1427
(條) 1869
傛 2104
傥 1868
(傜) 2229
𫢸 7
傒 2048
(傖) 189
242
763
(傑) 990
(傽) 2497
(傚) 2116
傍 58
傢 930
傧 134
储 293
傕 1062
傩 1430

十一画

(僅) 1008
1010
(傳) 298
2521
(傴) 2342
僄 1477
(僂) 1253
1265
催 332
働 470
(傷) 1676
傻 1666
(傯) 2558
像 2098
傺 266
(傭) 2309
僇 1263

十二画

(僥) 975
2228
僖 2050
(僿) 1849
儆 1029
僡 870
(僊) 2069
僳 1834
僚 1212
僭 957
(僕) 1499
(僑) 1549
(僪) 1067
僬 973
(僞) 1994
僢 303
僦 1043
僮 1924
2527
(僮) 1924
僧 1662
(僱) 701
僝 211

十三画

僵 960
(價) 935
998
1002
(儋) 388
僶 1349
(儂) 1424
儇 2171
儃 2498
儌 978
(儉) 944
(儈) 1120
(僾) 7
(儍) 1666
儋 378
(億) 2270
(儀) 2260
僻 1469

十四画以上

儓 1852
(儔) 276
儒 1636
儗 1406
(儕) 208
(儐) 134
(儘) 1008
(優) 2314
(儏) 184
(儯) 1903
(償) 221
儡 1169
(儲) 293
(儭) 241
(儱) 1251
儵 1783
儴 1608
(儺) 1430
(儷) 1192
(儼) 2208
(儸) 1278
(儹) 2390
(儻) 1868
儽 1168

八(丷)部

八 21
26

一至二画

兮 2041
分 566
575
公 667

三至六画

兰 1145
半 52
只 2455
2465
并 137
141
关 709
共 677
兴 2139
2149
兑 494
兵 137
弟 428
卷 1055
(並) 141
具 1050
单 209
374
1674
典 433
(冟) 1979

七至八画

养 2223
(刱) 306
前 1533
酋 1584
首 1772
兹 317
2536
(奐) 847
(剏) 304
306
真 2435
益 2277
兼 942

九画以上

黄 850
兽 1776
普 1501
奠 443
尊 2570
孳 2538
曾 198
2401
巽 2190
(義) 2270
(與) 2336
2342
2346
(養) 1458
舆 2342
黇 1896
冀 923
(黺) 573
(興) 2139
2149
(灃) 1950
鼢 573
黉 808
馘 744
囅 213
夔 1129
蠲 1055
(黌) 808

人(入)部

人 1615
入 1639

一至三画

个 655
(亾) 1980
介 998
从 324
仑 1272
今 1003
以 2267
仓 188
仝 1919
丛 326
令 1226
1232
1235

四至六画

全 1596
会 865
1118
合 655
781
企 1514
氽 331
1954
众 2491
伞 1655
佘 1693
余 2336
巫 2017
(夾) 618
925
931
佥 1530
含 761
舍 1693
1696
(侖) 1272
命 1359
肏 195
臾 2337

七至十画

俞 2339
(俞) 1790
弇 2209
㑯 279
俎 2566
拿 1381
(倉) 188
衾 1559
龛 1080
盒 790
舒 1780
畲 1692
畬 1692
2340
翕 2048
(傘) 1655
禽 1560

十一画以上

(僉) 1530
(會) 865
1118
僰 151
(舖) 1502
(館) 715
(劍) 954
龠 2374
(龕) 1080

勹部

勺 1689
勿 2036
勼 1035
匀 2376
勾 680
684
句 681
1050
(句) 680
684
匆 323
匄 622
包 59
旬 2185
匈 2153

訇 1458
匍 442
匋 1870
(匊) 1045
匐 1499
匒 801
(匑) 290
匓 600
够 685
(夠) 685
匔 573

儿部

儿 509
兀 2015
2036
元 2355
允 2377
兄 2152
尧 2228
光 720
先 2070
(兇) 2152
充 269
克 1095
兕 1823
皃 1310
兑 494
兒 1404
(兒) 509
兖 2208
党 386
兜 470
兢 1024

几(⺇)部

几 888
910
(凡) 532
凡 532
凤 589
夙 1830
凫 594
壳 1091
1551
秃 1937
咒 2497
凯 1078
凭 1489
凰 854
(凱) 1078
(鳳) 589
(凴) 1489
凳 410

亠部

一至四画

亡 1980
卞 117
六 1246
1259
亢 769
1084
市 1754
玄 2171
交 965
亦 2273
产 212
亥 759
充 269

五至六画

亩 1373
亨 796
弃 1524
变 117
京 1017
享 2093
夜 2240
卒 330
2564
兖 2208
氓 1304
1324

七画

弯 1971
哀 3
亭 1912
亮 1209
(亱) 2240
弈 2277
奕 2277
彦 2214
帝 428
衰 1415
玅 1344

八画

衰 332
1792
(畝) 1373
衷 2488
高 640
亳 149
(棄) 2383
离 1175
衮 736
旁 1445

九画

毫 772
孰 1783
烹 1458
袅 2476
(袞) 736
(産) 212
商 1677
率 1267
1794
(率) 1794
袤 1311

十画

亵 2124
裔 1269
就 1041
(高) 1578
衰 1497
棄 253
1726
(棄) 1524

十一至十四画

(裏) 1179
禀 140
亶 379
382
(稟) 140
(亷) 1199
雍 2310
裹 746
(稟) 573
豪 773
膏 646
649
(齊) 915
1508
(稾) 2161
(稾) 2161
亵 2161
褒 63
(齍) 1324
羸 501
(褎) 63
嬴 2303
壅 2310

十五画以上

(褻) 2124
襄 2092
嬴 2303
(齋) 2406
羸 1280
羸 1168
(饔) 2012
(羸) 501
(齎) 898
(羸) 1280
亹 1323
1997
(齏) 899
(羸) 1279
饔 2311

冫部

一至七画

习 2051
冮 635
冯 588
1488
冱 823
冲 267
273
冰 135
沧 307
次 321
决 1057
冻 468
况 1125
冷 1171
泽 501
冶 2236
冽 1217
冼 2077
净 1030
(凃) 1941

八画以上

凊 1579
凌 1229
凇 1825
(凍) 468
凄 1505
准 2530
凋 444
凉 1203
1210
凑 327
减 945
(凔) 184
凓 1193
(凔) 307
凘 1817
(澤) 501
凛 1225
(凜) 1225
凝 1418
(凟) 480

冖部

冗 1632
写 2122
军 1063
(冐) 1100
罕 765
冠 715
718
冢 2490
冥 1358
冤 2354
幂 1334
(冪) 1334

讠(言)部

二画

计 912
订 457
讣 605
认 1623
讥 888

三画

讦 990
讨 2161
讧 808
讯 2188
讨 1872
让 1609
讪 1673
(託) 1955
讫 1524
训 2188
议 2272
记 914
(訑) 2261
讱 1624

四画

讲 961
讳 868
讴 1431
讵 1050
讶 2198
讷 1397
许 2165
讹 503
(訢) 2132
论 1273
1275
讼 1826
讽 588
设 1694
访 551
讵 2507
(訦) 240
诀 1058

五画

诋 953
证 2450
诂 692
诃 780
(訶) 780
评 1488
诅 2564
识 1741
2472
诇 2155
诎 1588
诈 2405
诉 785
诌 2261
诉 1830
诊 2437
诋 416
诏 2494
(註) 2510
(詝) 2507
(詑) 2261
(詠) 2311
词 315
诏 2425
诐 107
译 2276
诒 2261

六画

诓 1123
诔 1168
试 1758
诖 704
诗 1731
诘 904
990
(誇) 1117
诙 857
诚 249
诧 1393
诛 2499
诜 1701
话 840
诞 380
诟 685
诠 1599
诡 732
诣 2276
询 2187

(詾) 2153
诤 2451
该 619
详 2092
诧 206
诨 873
诩 2165

七画

诪 2496
诫 1000
(誌) 2471
(誖) 85
语 2344
2349
诬 2018
诮 1552
误 2039
诰 649
诱 2334
诲 868
诳 1125
说 1805
1808
2372
(認) 1623
诵 1827
(誒) 508
509

八画

请 1577
诸 2500
诹 2559
诺 1430
读 475
479
诼 2534
(諓) 953
诽 562
𫍲 295
课 1099
诿 1996
谀 2339
谁 1699
1798
(論) 1273
1275
谂 1709
调 447
1901
谄 213
谅 1210
谆 2530
谇 1840
谈 1858
谊 2278

九画

谋 1371
谌 240
谍 451
谎 855
谏 956
谐 2121
谑 2184
谒 2241
谓 2001
谔 507
𫍹 2114
谕 2352
(謚) 1763
谖 2170
谗 209
谘 2538
谙 12
谚 2215
谛 431
谜 1319
1330
(諠) 2170
谝 1473
(諱) 868
谞 2164

十画

(講) 961
(譁) 833
谟 1361
𬣙 651
谠 387
谡 1833
谢 2124
谣 2228
(謅) 2494
谤 59
谥 1763
谦 1531
谧 1334

十一画

谨 1010
(謳) 1431
谩 1298
1300
谪 2430
谫 949
𬤲 2295
谬 1360

十二画以上

(譊) 1393
谆 2050
(謿) 229
谭 1860
谮 2400
谯 1550
(譙) 1552
(譌) 503
(識) 1741
2472
谰 1147
谱 1502
𬣡 2522
(證) 2450
2453
谲 1062
(譏) 888
(護) 823
谳 2216
谴 1540
(譟) 2397
(譯) 2276
𬤊 2171
(譭) 864
谵 2409
(議) 2272
(譸) 2496
(讁) 2430
(讀) 475
479
𬤮 480
(譾) 949
(讅) 1708
(讌) 2216
(讔) 2295
讙 843
谶 242
(讒) 209
(讓) 1609
(讛) 2275
(讚) 2391
(讞) 2216
(讜) 387
(讟) 480

卩(㔾)部

卫 1997
卬 17
叩 1111
卮 2455
印 2295
卯 1310
仰 2222
危 1985
却 1602
即 903
卲 1691
(卹) 2167
卷 1055
卺 1008
卸 2124
(卻) 1602
卿 1569

阝(在左)部

二至四画

队 489
阢 2037
阡 1529
阱 1028
阮 1642
(阨) 505
阵 2439
(阯) 2466
阳 2219
(阪) 49
阶 984
阴 2283
阬 1101
防 547
阧 472

五画

际 918
陆 1247
1259
阿 1
503
(阿) 2
陇 1251
陈 238
阽 442
2205
阻 2564
阼 2578
陁 1960
附 608
陀 1960
陂 76
1466
1491
陉 2148

六至八画

陋 1254
陌 1367
陕 1673
𬮿 622
(陒) 733
降 963
2093
陔 619
限 2081
陡 472
(陝) 1673
陛 107
(陘) 2148
陟 2475
(陗) 1552
陧 1416
陨 2378
(陞) 1711
除 291
险 2078
院 2367
𬮱 2061
(陸) 1247
1259
陵 1230
陬 2559
(陳) 238
陲 309
陴 1467
(陰) 2283
陶 1871
2228
陷 2083
陪 1452

九画

(陿) 2061
隋 1837
堕 502
(墮) 858
随 1837
(階) 984
(隄) 412
(陽) 2219
隅 2340
隈 1987
𬯎 1950
(隉) 1416
隍 854
隗 1128
1997
(隂) 2283
隆 1248
1251
隐 2294
(隊) 489

十画以上

隞 18
隔 654
隙 2059
(隑) 622
(隖) 2037
隘 7
(隔) 654
(隙) 2059
(際) 918
(隲) 2310
障 2420
隟 2060
(隨) 1837
隩 20
2354
(隣) 1220
隧 1840
(險) 2078
隰 2052
(隱) 2294
隳 858
(隴) 1251

阝(在右)部

二至四画

邓 410
邗 761
邘 2336
邛 1579
邝 1125
邙 1302
邦 56
(邦) 56
邢 2143
(邨) 335
邪 2120
2235
(𨚗) 1384
邠 134
邬 2017
邡 547
祁 1508
那 1381
1383
1397
1401
(那) 1382
1386
1398

五画

邯 761
邴 139
邳 1461
邶 81
邺 2240

邮 2318
郇 1384
邱 1581
邻 1220
邸 416
邹 2559
邲 107
出阝 288
邵 1691
邰 1852

六画

邽 731
耶 2235
2236
郁 2348
郕 249
郏 931
郅 2472
邾 2499
郇 2052
郈 813
郐 1121
郃 787
郄 1555
2057
郇 845
2187
郊 969
郑 2451
郎 1150
1151
郓 2380
郛 2187

七画

郝 777
郚 2028
郦 1192
(郟) 931
郢 2304
郧 2377
郜 648
郗 258
2045
郤 2059
郛 597
郡 1067

八画

都 470
475
(郰) 2559
郪 1646
郴 235
郫 1505
(郵) 2318
(郳) 1404
郸 1466
郭 737
部 173
郸 378
郯 1858

九画

郾 2209
鄄 1056
鄂 507
鄅 2346
鄃 1780
鄋 1311
鄇 1315
(鄉) 2085

十至十一画

鄚 1311
鄗 1639
(鄔) 2017
(鄒) 2559
鄗 780
鄘 1866
鄢 2201
鄞 2290
鄠 825
鄙 103
鄜 2310
鄘 593
鄣 2416

十二画以上

(鄲) 378
鄱 1492
鄯 1675
(鄰) 1220
(鄭) 2451
(鄩) 2187
(鄧) 410
(鄴) 2240
(鄶) 1121
鄹 2559
(鄺) 1125
鄻 2317
鄼 339
2391
酃 1232
酆 588
酄 1595
(酈) 1192

凵部

凶 2152
击 888
凷 1118
凸 1936
出 280
凹 18
1964
函 388
画 838
函 762
幽 2316
鬯 223
凿 2394
豳 135

刀(⺈)部

刀 389
刃 1623
(刄) 1623
切 1553
1554
分 566
575
召 1691
2424
刍 290
危 1985
负 606
争 2441
色 1660
1668
(刧) 990
龟 729
1066
1581
奂 847
免 1336
初 288
(刼) 990
兔 1945
券 1601
2175
(奐) 847
(剏) 306
(剙) 306
象 2097
剪 946
棼 573
劈 1177
赖 1144
詹 2409
(麁) 327
夐 2156
劈 1463
1468
(錟) 2215
(劒) 954
(龜) 729
(釁) 2139

力部

力 1183

二至四画

办 51
劝 1600
功 672
夯 93
769
劢 1294
加 923
务 2036
幼 2333
动 465
劣 1217
(劤) 1015

五至六画

劫 990
励 1189
助 2508
男 1387
劬 1590
努 1426
劭 1691
劲 1015
1030
劻 1123
劼 990
势 1757
(効) 2116
劾 787

七至九画

勃 149
(勅) 266
(勁) 1015
1030
勋 2184
勉 1337
勇 2312
勍 920
(勑) 266
啓 655
勍 1574
勐 1326
勘 1079
勚 2278
勔 1338
勖 2167
(動) 465

十画以上

(勞) 1153
(勢) 1757
勤 1560
(勠) 1263
(勦) 228
978
(勱) 1294
(甥) 965
勰 2122
(勵) 1189
(勳) 2184
(勸) 1600
勷 1608

厶部

厶 1812
允 2377
2378
去 1593
1594
弁 117
台 1850
1851
牟 1371
1378
县 2080
矣 2269
叁 1655
参 183
198
1702
畚 92
能 1402
(參) 183
198
1702

又(ㄡ)部

又 2332

一至四画

叉 199
202
205
支 2453
友 2325
反 535
(収) 1764
邓 410
劝 1600
双 1795
圣 1722
对 489
发 518
528
戏 815
2055
叓 1748
观 711
718
欢 842

六至十画

取 1591
叔 1779
受 1774
变 117
艰 941
叟 1828
叙 2166
爱 2358
难 1390
1392
(隻) 2455
曼 1300
(叜) 1795

十一画以上

(叡) 2403
叠 451
(叡) 1644
燮 2126
(雙) 1795
(叢) 326
矍 1063

廴部

(廸) 209
(廵) 2186
廷 1912
延 2201
(廸) 414
(廹) 1440
1493
(廼) 1385
(廻) 858
建 953

工部

工 663
左 2572
巧 1550
邛 1579
功 672
巠 1017

式 1755
巩 676
(巠) 1017
贡 679
汞 676
攻 673
巫 2017
项 2096
差 199
206
208
209
315
巯 1586
(巰) 1586
曌 2427

土部

土 1942

二至三画

凷 1118
去 1593
圣 1722
圩 1990
2161
圬 2017
圭 728
在 2388
寺 1822
至 2470
尘 235
圪 649
圳 2438
圾 889
壮 2525
圹 1125
圮 1468
圯 2261
地 404
419
场 218
221

四画

坛 1858
坏 842
(坏) 1462
坜 1189
址 2466
坚 939
坝 29
圻 1508
2289
坂 49
坐 2576
(坐) 2579
坳 2553
坨 1275
坌 93
坋 93
575
坍 1856
坎 1080
均 1065
坞 2037
坟 573
坑 1101
坊 547
549
(壯) 2525
块 1119
坠 2529
(坳) 19

五画

坩 628
茔 2301
坷 1088
1095
坯 1462
坲 173
垄 1251
坪 1489
坫 442
垆 1256
坦 1860
坤 1131
(坤) 1856
坰 1034
(垧) 19
(坵) 1581
(坿) 608
坼 234
坻 261
416
垃 1136
幸 2150
坢 55
坨 1960
坭 1404
坡 1491
坶 1373
坳 19

六画

型 2148
垚 2228
垭 2193
垩 506
垣 2358
垮 1117
垯 367
城 251
垫 442
垤 450
垱 389
垌 469
1923
垲 1078
垡 525
埏 1672
垍 919
垧 1678
垢 685
垕 814
垛 501
502
(垜) 501
502
垝 733
垴 1394
垓 619
垟 2221
垞 202
(垵) 13
垠 2289
垦 1100
垒 1168

七画

埗 173
埁 1155
埔 173
1501
埂 662
埕 768
埕 251
埋 1293
1297
埘 1747
埙 2184
埚 737
袁 2358
(垔) 706
埙 2396
埒 1217
埇 1602
埣 2167
垩 2297
垸 2368
埌 1151
埇 2312
埃 4

八画

堵 481
埮 1174
(埡) 2193
(堊) 506
基 895
埴 2463
埴 2463
(埜) 2237
域 2351
(堅) 939
埼 1511
埯 13
堑 1541
堂 1865
埸 2278
堌 700
(堝) 737
埵 501
埦 1408
堆 489
埤 1467
1469
埠 174
(埨) 1275
(埰) 181
埝 1413
堋 1458
埦 1945
(埳) 1080
埻 2531
埪 1132
培 1453
埥 2351
(執) 2459
埠 1674
埮 1859
埭 373
埽 1660
堀 1114
堕 502
(堕) 858
埯 240
掇 500

九画

堾 312
(堯) 2228
堪 1080
堞 451
塔 367
1848
塃 849
堰 2215
堙 2288
堧 2227
堉 1961
(堿) 949
堧 1642
(堦) 984
堤 412
(場) 221
塄 1171
塅 488
堡 69
155
1503
(塊) 1119
堠 815
塆 1972
(報) 69
(塖) 254
堩 663
(堩) 663
塈 922
(壻) 2168
(塯) 1394

十画

塨 676
墓 1378
填 1898
塥 655
塬 2365
(塒) 1747
塌 1848
(塏) 1078
塍 638
塮 2125
(塢) 2037
塕 2012
塍 254
(塙) 1603
塘 1866
塝 59
塑 1833
(塋) 2301
(塗) 1941
塞 1649
1661
塱 1151
(塱) 1151
(塚) 2490

十一画

墕 2216
(墊) 442
墈 1082
墐 1017
墘 1537
墙 1545
(塼) 2518
墺 1798
墟 2164
(墟) 2161
墅 1791
墁 1300
(塲) 218
221
(墔) 2553
垫 2122
(墖) 1848
墊 1783
墉 2310
(塵) 235
境 1034
墒 1678
墚 1205
(墮) 502
(墜) 2529
墜 431
墕 1556
(墋) 240

十二至十四画

(墝) 1548
(墳) 573
(墶) 367
墼 2238
(墰) 1858
(墠) 1674
墨 1368
墦 533
墩 495
墡 1675
增 2401
(撈) 1155
墀 262
墼 899
(墻) 1545
壑 792
(壋) 389
(墾) 1100
壈 1148
(壇) 1858
(壈) 1148
壅 2310
壁 110
(壖) 1642
(壎) 2184
壕 774
(壙) 1125

十五画以上

(壘) 1168
(鼃) 1964
(壢) 1189
(壚) 1256
(壜) 1858

(壞) 842
(壠) 1251
(壟) 1251
疆 961
壤 1609
(巍) 1552
(壩) 29
(壪) 1972

士部

士 1750
吉 901
壮 2525
壳 1091
1551
志 2471
(壯) 2525
声 1719
毐 5
壶 819
壸 1132
(喆) 2430
喜 2054
壹 2260
(壼) 1132
鼓 695
(壺) 819
嘉 930
臺 1852
(臺) 1851
(槖) 1961
(壽) 1773
(賣) 1295
(隸) 1191
(嚭) 1469
(鼕) 464
(燾) 397
1869
嚭 1469
馨 2136
鼙 1468
懿 2281
鼟 1877

艹部

一至三画

艺 2272
艾 5
2272
艽 965
节 984
989
艿 1386
芳 1164
芋 2347
芏 481
芊 1529
芍 1689
芃 1458
芨 889
芒 1302
芝 2455
芑 1514
芎 2153
芗 2085

四画

芙 594
芫 2202
2357
芜 2027
苇 1994
芸 2377
芾 562
594
芰 917
苿 594
苈 1189
茈 1466
苊 505
苣 1050
1591
芽 2195
芷 2466
(茸) 1608
芮 1644
苋 2079
芼 1310
苌 218
花 825
826
芹 1559
苅 2275
芥 622
999
苁 323
芩 1560
芬 572
苍 189
芪 1509
芴 2037
芡 1540
芟 1671
(苆) 682
苄 117
芳 547
苇 1994
苎 2508
芦 1256
1258
芯 2132
2136
劳 1153
芭 25
苏 1828
苡 2269
苧 2508
2166
芤 1107

五画

茉 1367
苷 628
苦 1114
苯 92
苛 1088
苿 594
1478
若 1611
1645
茂 1310
茏 1250
茇 26
苹 1489
苫 1671
1673
苜 1378
苴 1043
苗 1341
苒 1608
英 2298
苜 2269
苘 1577
苲 2404
茌 261
苻 595
苽 686
茶 1416
苓 1228
茚 2297
苛 682
茆 1309
茑 1415
苑 2367
茔 291
苞 62
范 543
苧 1417
(苧) 2508
茓 2177
茔 2301
苾 107
茕 1580
苠 1349
茀 595
茁 2533
苕 1689
1901
茄 926
1553
茎 1017
苔 1850
1852
茅 1309
(苺) 1315

六画

茸 1628
荁 845
茜 1541
2045
茬 202
荐 954
荙 345
荚 931
荑 1880
2261
荛 1610
荜 107
茈 317
2541
草 192
茧 944
茼 1923
莒 1048
茵 2285
茴 863
荣 2499
莛 1912
苦 703
荞 1549
茯 597
荏 1623
荇 2151
荃 1599
荟 868
茶 202
(荅) 343
345
荀 2187
茻 302
茗 1358
荠 652
荠 919
1511
茭 969
茨 317
荒 849
荄 620
荛 270
茳 959
茫 1304
荡 389
荣 1629
荤 871
2184
荷 1212
荥 2148
2301
荦 1280
荧 2301
荨 1532
2187
莨 661
荩 1015
荫 1549
荫 2285
2297
茹 1636
荔 1192
荬 1294
荭 806
荮 2498
荪 1841
药 2231
(茲) 2536

七画

(華) 832
858
荻 1081
莲 209
(荅) 2151
莩 96
莆 1499
(荳) 473
(莢) 931
莽 1304
1305
莱 1144
莲 1197
(莖) 1017
莫 1367
莳 1747
1762
莴 2012
莉 1192
莠 2332
莪 504
莓 1315
荷 789
791
莜 2323
莅 1192
荼 1940
莶 2073
莝 339
莩 1837
莩 597
1476
获 885
莸 2323
荻 414
莘 447
莘 1702
2133
莎 1666
1841
莞 715
1975
莠 1580
莹 2302
莨 1151
1203
莺 2299
莙 1066
(莊) 2523
莼 312

八画

萚 94
菁 1022
萘 1897
(萇) 218
著 2432
2512
2534
菱 1230
萁 1511
菻 1225
菥 2046
菘 1825
堇 1009
菾 1387
(菴) 12
(萊) 1144
萋 1506
菝 27
(菴) 72
萚 1962
菲 560
562
菽 1780
菓 746
菖 214
萌 1324
萜 1907
萝 1278
菌 1066
1067
(萵) 2012
萎 1997

萸 2339
萑 845
萆 107
菂 429
菜 181
菍 1416
棻 573
菔 599
菟 1941
1945
萄 1871
萏 380
菊 1047
萃 334
菩 1499
（菸） 2199
菼 1861
菏 790
萍 1491
菹 2563
菠 147
菪 389
菅 943
菀 1975
2351
菮 1193
萤 2302
营 2302
莹 2299
萦 2303
萧 2102
菉 1260
1267
菡 768
萨 1648
菇 689
菰 689
菑 2537

九画

葜 1526
葑 587
590
葚 1625
1711
（葉） 2239
2240
葫 819
萷 2092
葳 1987
葴 213
葬 2392
蒈 1078
（韮） 1037
募 1378
葺 1525
（萬） 1977
葛 654
655
蒉 1130
葸 2055
萼 507
蓇 689
萩 1582
董 465
（蓚） 1903
葆 69
（蒐） 1827
（葠） 1702
葩 1434
葎 1268
（葅） 2563
葡 1499
葱 323
蒋 963
葶 1913
葹 1733
蒂 431
蒌 1253
（蔿） 1994
葓 807
蒎 1440
落 1527
落 1139
1163
1276
1281
（蓱） 1491
萱 2170
葵 1938
萹 113
117
葭 930
（葦） 1994
葇 1128
萩 1311

十画

蓁 2437
蒜 1835
蓍 1733
（蓋） 622
655
蓐 1641
蒱 1499
蓝 1147
（蒔） 1762
1747
（蓽） 107
墓 1378
幕 1379
蓦 1368
蒽 509
（夢） 1327
（蒨） 1541
（蓧） 447
蓨 1903
蓓 87
蓖 108
蓏 1280
蓤 7
（蒼） 189
蓊 2012
蒯 1118
蓟 922
蓬 1459
（蒻） 291
蓑 1842
蒿 772
（蓆） 2052
蒺 909
蓠 1177
薋 317
蔀 174
蒟 1049
蒡 59
1446
蓄 2168
蒹 943
蒴 1811
蒲 1499
（蒞） 1192
蒗 1152
（蓡） 1702
蓉 1630
蒙 1324
1326
蓂 1334
1359
蓥 2303
蒻 1646
（蔭） 2285
2297
蒸 2444
蓣 2353
（蓀） 1841

十一画

蔒 870
蔫 1408
蓺 2280
（蔕） 431
蔷 1546
（蓴） 312
蔌 1834
蓷 1950
（蔶） 1577
慕 1379
暮 1379
摹 1361
（蔞） 1253
蔓 1298
1300
1979
蔂 1168
蔑 1345
甍 1325
蘡 2299
蓰 2055
（蓯） 323
蔹 1201
（蔔） 152
蔀 471
蔡 182
蔗 2432
（蔴） 1286
蔟 330
蔺 1226
蔽 109
蔊 768
蕖 1590
蔻 1112
蓿 2169
蔼 5
蔚 2002
2353
（蔣） 963
蓼 1214
1263
（薌） 2085

十二画

（蕘） 1610
（蓮） 345
蕙 870
蕈 2190
蕨 1062
蕤 1644
（蕓） 2377
（蕋） 1644
蕞 2570
蕺 909
（蕢） 1294
瞢 1325
（蕪） 2027
蔾 1177
（蕎） 1549
蕉 973
1550
蕇 2354
蕃 529
533
（蔿） 1994
（蕕） 2323
蕲 1513
（蕩） 389
（蕅） 1433
蕰 2004
蕊 1644
（蕁） 1532
蔬 1783
蕿 1659
蕴 2382

十三画

蕻 807
808
（薔） 1546
（薑） 960
薤 2125
蕾 1169
𬞟 1480
（蘋） 1489
蕗 1263
薯 1787
薨 801
薙 1887
薐 1171
薛 2176
薇 1988
（薟） 2073
（薈） 868
（薆） 7
薢 2125
（薦） 954
薪 2136
薏 2281
蕹 2012
薮 1828
薄 63
151
152
（蕭） 2102
薜 109
（薩） 1648
薅 772

十四画

藉 910
1002
（藉） 1000
薹 1852
1853
藂 326
（藍） 1147
藏 190
2392
薷 1637
藊 117
薰 2185
（舊） 1038
藐 1343
藓 2079
藑 1581
薿 1406
臒 886
藁 647
（薺） 96
919
1511
藦 1476
（薴） 1417
（藎） 1015

十五画

藕 1433
爇 1646
（藝） 2272
藙 2281
（藪） 1828
藟 1169
（藠） 944
945
藜 1177
藠 983
藤 1878
（藷） 1787
藦 1364
藨 128
藩 529
（藭） 1580
2453
藥 2234
（藥） 2231

十六画

（蘂） 1532
（藶） 1189
藿 887
（蘀） 1962
蘧 1590
（蘆） 1256
1258
（蘄） 1513
蘖 1417
蘅 800
（蘇） 1828
（蘐） 2170
蘑 1364
（蘢） 1250
藻 2396
（蘂） 1644

十七画以上

蘸 780
蘩 535

蘗 1417
(蘒) 1201
蘘 1608
蘑 1331
(蘭) 1145
(蘖) 152
(蘺) 1177
(蘂) 1644
蘸 2414
(蘿) 1278
蘖 1417
蘼 1331
(虆) 1168

廾部

卉 865
弁 117
异 2273
弄 1252
1425
弃 1524
弆 1047
昇 121
畀 2339
弇 2209
弈 2277
羿 2277
葬 2392
弊 109
(彛) 2266
彝 2266

大部

大 353
368

一至四画

太 1853
央 2216
夯 93
769
夸 1117
夹 618
925
931
夺 500
尖 937
夼 1125
夷 2261
夽 509
奁 1193
(夾) 618
925
931
夿 25

五画

奉 589
奈 1386
奔 88
93
奇 894
1509
奄 2208
奋 575
奅 1450

六画

契 1525
2124
奎 1128
耷 342
耎 1643
奓 2403
2405
奖 962
奕 2277
美 1317
昚 1710
牵 1530

七至八画

套 1873
奚 2046
(昚) 1710
奘 2392
2525
匏 1449
奢 1691
爽 1797

九画以上

攲 1507
奤 753
(奤) 1853
奥 19
奠 443
(奩) 1193
(奪) 500
(奬) 962
樊 534
奭 1764
(奮) 575
奰 111
奲 501
(奲) 501

尢部

(尣) 2317
尤 2317
尥 1214
尪 1979
尬 619
尰 152
尴 629
(尷) 629
(尶) 629

扌部

一至二画

扎 2383
2402
2403
打 344
346
扑 1497
扒 24
1434
扔 1625

三画

扞 766
(扞) 633
扛 635
1083
扤 2037
扣 1112
扦 1529
托 1955
执 2459
扩 1133
扪 1323
扫 1658
扬 2217
扠 199

四画

扶 594
抏 1972
抚 601
抟 1947
技 917
抔 1496
抠 1107
扰 1610
扼 505
拒 1050
扽 405
找 2424
批 1461
扯 233
抄 225
㧏 636
折 1693
2427
2428
抓 2513
扳 46
1441
扨 304
抡 1272
1273
扮 54
抢 1541
1546
抈 2372
扺 2466
抑 2275
抛 1447
投 1932
抃 117
抆 2009
抗 1084
㧑 857
抖 472
护 823
抉 1058
扭 1421
把 27
28
29
报 69
拟 1405
㧐 1825
抒 1779
(抝) 19
1422

五画

抹 1285
1365
1367
(拑) 1537
(抴) 2240
拓 1849
1962
拢 1251
拔 26
(抛) 1447
抨 1458
拣 944
拤 1526
拈 1408
担 374
380
(担) 379
押 2193
抻 235
抽 274
拐 707
拙 2532
抶 266
拃 2404
拖 1956
拊 602
拍 1435
拆 175
207
拎 1219
拥 2309
抵 416
拘 1043
𢭃 276
抱 72
拄 2507
拉 1136
1139
拦 1146
拌 55
抂 1118
拧 1417
1419
拕 1957
抿 1349
拂 595
(抝) 1426
招 2420
(招) 2422
披 1462
拨 144
择 2399
2407
拚 1444
(拚) 1478
抬 1852
拇 1373
拗 19
1422

六画

拭 1760
挂 704
持 261
拮 991
拷 1086
𢭏 1162
拱 676
挜 2198
挎 1117
挞 1849
挟 2120
(挟) 925
挠 1393
挝 2012
2514
挡 386
389
拽 2515
(拽) 2240
挺 1913
括 703
1134
挢 975
拴 1794
挱 1648
1666
拾 1696
1744
挑 1899
1903
指 2467
挣 2443
2452
挤 911
拼 1478
挓 2403
挖 1964
按 13
挥 857
挦 2076
挪 1430
拯 2444
拶 2383
2390

七画

捞 1152
(捄) 1040
捕 155
捂 2028
2035
振 2439
(挾) 2120
捎 1687
1691
捍 768
捏 1415
捉 2532
捆 1132
捐 1054
损 1841
挹 2277
捌 25
捡 944
挫 339
捋 1265
1276
挼 1642
1645
换 847
挽 1975

捣 392
挩 1957
(挱) 1647
1666
1842
捃 1067
挶 1045
捅 1927
挨 4
捘 2571

八画

捧 1460
掭 1899
(掛) 704
(掗) 2198
掫 2236
(掫) 2496
措 339
描 1342
(捱) 4
捺 1385
掎 912
掩 2209
捷 993
捯 391
排 1436
1437
1438
1439
掯 1100
掉 449
掳 1258
掴 707
744
(捵) 235
(掆) 636
捶 309
推 1947
捭 42
掀 2073
(捨) 1693
捡 1560
(掄) 1272
1273
(採) 179
授 1776
捻 1412
捴 2558
搊 2496
掏 1869
(搯) 1872
掐 1526
掬 1045
掠 1271
掂 432
掖 2235
2241
捽 2572
掊 1496
1497
接 984
掷 2476
(捲) 1055
(掽) 1460
掸 379
1674
掞 1674
控 1107
捩 1218
掮 1537
探 1862
[illegible] 2103
(掃) 1658
1659
据 1045
1052
掘 1062
掺 188
209
1673
掇 500
掼 718

九画

揳 2117
揍 2562
揕 2440
揲 451
1693
搽 204
搭 342
揸 2403
揠 2198
揦 1139
(揀) 944
揻 1987
揰 1966
揩 1078
(揹) 77
(㨗) 993
揽 1148
(揝) 2149
提 413
1880
(揚) 2217
揖 2260
揾 2012
揭 987
揌 1648
揣 296
297
揟 819
揿 1562
插 200
揪 1036
(揑) 1415
搜 1827
(搥) 309
揄 2340
(揜) 2209
援 2364
搀 209
(搰) 800
揞 13
搁 650
654
搓 338
搂 1252
1253
揃 947
(撝) 857
搅 978
揎 2170
揢 1092
握 2015
揙 144
揆 1129
搔 1658
揉 1633
掾 2368

十画

搆 685
(搕) 1090
摄 1698
摸 1361
搢 1017
搏 150
摅 1782
(揘) 856
(搨) 1849
摁 509
摆 42
携 2122
(搗) 392
(摀) 2035
搋 296
搬 48
(搫) 1666
摇 2228
(搯) 1869
(搶) 1541
1546
(搇) 1562
(搩) 2404
(搊) 276
搞 646
摛 259
搪 1866
搒 59
1459
搐 295
搤 508
搛 943
搠 1812
搳 835
摈 135
(搾) 2406
(搧) 1672
(搉) 1604
搌 2411
搦 1430
(㨨) 1927
摊 1857
搡 1657

十一画

(摶) 1947
(摳) 1107
摽 128
131
(摲) 233
摴 290
(摣) 2403
(摟) 1252
1253
摝 1215
摞 1284
(摑) 707
744
摧 333
撄 2299
(搵) 2012
2514
(摠) 2558
(摐) 304
摭 2464
(擄) 1285
摘 2406
摔 1793
撇 1477
1478
撖 769
摺 2430
(摻) 188
209
1673

十二画

撵 1413
(撓) 1393
撷 2122
(撻) 1849
撕 1817
撒 1647
1648
撧 1068
(撢) 379
撅 1057
撩 1211
1212
(撂) 1215
(撲) 1497
(撐) 243
撑 243
撮 338
2573
(撣) 379
(撫) 601
撬 1552
(撟) 975
(撜) 405
(攜) 2122
播 147
擒 1561
(撝) 857
撸 1256
(撚) 1412
撴 495
撞 2527
撤 234
撙 2571
(撈) 1152
撺 331
(撏) 2076
撰 2522
(撥) 144
(撧) 1057

十三画

擀 633
撼 769
(擓) 1118
擂 1168
1170
(據) 1052
(擄) 1258
(擋) 386
389
操 190
195
(擇) 2399
2407
擐 849
(擉) 2515
撽 1553
(撿) 944
(擔) 374
380
擅 1675
(擁) 2309
擞 1828
(擨) 1648
(擩) 2103
擗 1469

十四画

(擡) 1852
(擣) 392
擩 1639
擤 2149
(擬) 1405
(擴) 1133
擿 1880
2479
(擠) 911
(擲) 2476
擆 2408
(擯) 135
擦 175
(擰) 1417
1419
擢 2535

十五至十七画

(擾) 1610
(攄) 1782
(擻) 1828
(擺) 42
攧 432
(擷) 2103
攉 875
攒 331
2390
(攏) 1251
(攙) 209
攘 1609
(攔) 1146

十八画以上

(攝) 1698
(攜) 2122
(攗) 1825
(攟) 1067
(攛) 331
(攤) 1857
(攈) 1067
(攩) 386
攫 1063
攥 2568
(攪) 978
(攬) 1148
攮 1393

寸部

寸 337

二至七画

刌 337
对 489
寺 1822
寻 2185
导 391
寿 1773
封 584
耐 1387
将 959
964
1543
(尅) 1095
1099
辱 1639
射 1696

八画以上

(專) 2515
尉 2001
2352
尊 2570
2571
(尋) 2185
(對) 489
(導) 391

弋部

弋 2270
(弌) 2260
弍 517
弎 1655
式 1755
忒 1875
1877
1947
甙 370
鸢 2354
贰 517
弑 1763

小(⺌)部

小 2104

一至三画

少 1689
1690
尔 511
尕 619
尘 235
尖 937
光 720
(尗) 1780
劣 1217
当 383
388

四至七画

肖 2099
2114
贞 1843
尚 1687
尜 618
省 1722
2148
尝 219
党 386

八画以上

雀 1548
1551
1602
堂 1865
常 219
辉 858
棠 1866
牚 243
255
掌 2418
(尠) 2079
2073
(當) 383
388
(嘗) 219
裳 221
1687
虩 2060
耀 2235
(黨) 386

口部

口 1108

二画

古 689
叶 2119
2239
右 2333
叮 453
可 1092
1095
号 772
777
778
占 2408
2411
卟 153
只 2455
2465
叭 25
史 1748
句 681
1050
兄 2152
叱 264
叽 888
司 1812
叼 444
叫 979
叩 1111
叨 390
391
1869
召 1691
2424
叻 1164
另 1235
加 923
台 1850
1851
叹 1861

三画

吁 2161
2335
2348
吉 901
吐 1944
吓 791
2069
(吘) 1381
吋 338
2297
吕 1265
吊 446
吃 255
吒 2403
(吒) 2405
向 2095
后 809
合 655
781
(吆) 2226
名 1350
各 655
657
吸 2044
吖 1
(启) 476
吗 1285
1291
1292
吆 2226

四画

呈 248
呋 592
吴 2027
吞 1953
呒 1285
呓 2275
呆 367
杏 2149
(呕) 1381
1403
吾 2027
吱 2456
2536
吥 173
否 591
1468
呔 368
1853
吠 562
呕 1432
呖 1189
(呆) 368
呟 805
呃 505
508
呠 233
吨 495
吡 100
1468
呀 2193
2198
吵 225
230
呗 44
87
员 2357
2377
2380
呙 737
呐 1384
1397
(呐) 1385
1397
吽 800
告 647
吪 503
听 1910
吟 2289
吩 572
呛 1541
1547
吻 2010
吹 307
呜 2017
吝 1225
吭 770
1101
(呌) 979
启 1515
吣 1562
(吢) 1562
(吚) 2259
君 1066
呎 263
2297
(吳) 2027
吲 2293
吧 25
31
邑 2275
吮 1806
吼 809

五画

味 2000
哎 3
咕 686
呵 780
1088
(呵) 2
咂 2383
呸 1452
咙 1250
咑 342
咔 1068
1069
咀 1047
2568
呷 618
2060
呻 1701
咒 2497
(呪) 2497
咄 500
(咼) 737
知 2456
咋 2385
2399
2403
和 785
786
791
817
875
884
咐 609
呱 686
702
703
呼 815
呤 1236
咎 1040
咚 465
鸣 1357
咆 1448
咛 1417
咜 506
咏 2311
呢 1397
1404
呶 1393
(呶) 1426
咖 618
1068
咍 753
呣 1285
呦 2316
亟 904
1525
咝 1815

六画

哐 1124
哪 57
哇 1964
1966
咭 894
者 683
哉 2385
咡 517
哄 801
808
哑 2194
2196
哂 1709
咸 2076
(咵) 1117
咳 857
哒 342
咧 1216
1219
咦 2261
哓 2100
哔 107
呲 315
(呲) 2538
呰 2541
咣 724
虽 1836
品 1480
咽 2198

2214
2241
唠 868
2369
咮 2498
咻 2157
哦 529
哗 831
833
咱 2385
2390
2391
咿 2259
响 2093
哌 1440
哙 1121
哈 752
753
咷 1870
哚 501
(哅) 2153
咯 649
1069
1248
1280
哆 264
500
哜 919
咬 2230
咨 2536
咳 753
1091
咩 1344
咲 2115
咪 1328
咤 2405
咹 11
12
哝 1424
哷 2187
2299
哪 1382
1385
1397
哏 660
哞 1371
哟 2309

七画

唝 1252
唛 1297
哇 470
哥 650
唢 680
808
哧 258
哮 2115
唠 1155
1163
哱 146
哺 155
哽 662
唔 2028
(唔) 1381
1403
哂 1209
2299
唇 312
唻 1145
唒 2403
哲 2430
(哔) 1344
哨 1691
唢 1845
哩 1174
1180
1193
2299
哭 1113
㖞 1966
唈 2277
哦 504
1431
(唣) 2396
唣 2396
唏 2045
唑 2579
唤 848
(啾) 415
唁 2214
哼 797
800
唐 1865
唻 1827
(唚) 1562
唧 894
啊 2
(唠) 1426
唉 4
6
唆 1842

八画

唪 589
啧 2399
唪 797
800
(啞) 2194
2196
喏 1430
1611
喵 1341
营 2302
啉 1223
(唡) 1209
2299
唵 12
13
唹 1432
啄 2534
啑 451
1667
啭 2522
啪 1434
啦 1138
1141
啡 560
啨 1100
啮 1416
唬 822
2069
(唻) 1145
唱 223
啰 1276
1278
1284
(啯) 1966
唾 1962
唯 1992
1997
售 1776
啤 1467
啥 1666
啥 1016
(唅) 2289
(唸) 1413
啁 2422
2496
啕 1871
(啗) 380
啯 817
啐 334
唼 1667
商 1677
啨 2309
啴 213
1857
兽 1776
啖 380
啵 152
啶 461
啷 1149
唳 1193
(启) 1515
啸 2117
(啢) 1791
啜 297
314

九画

(喫) 255
(喆) 2430
喷 1456
1458
喜 2054
喋 451
2404
嗒 343
1849
(喪) 1657
1658
喃 1392
喳 201
2403
喇 1138
1139
喓 2227
喊 765
喹 1966
喱 1177
喹 1129
喈 988
喈 2541
喁 2311
2340
喝 780
791
喂 2001
喟 1130
(單) 209
374
1674
(喦) 2205
喌 2496
喘 302
喎 1114
(唧) 2076
喏 46
(喭) 2385
啾 1036
(喬) 1549
嗖 1828
喤 854
喉 808
喻 2352
(喒) 2385
2390
2391
喨 1211
喑 2288
喭 2215
啼 1882
啻 266
善 1674
嗟 988
喽 1253
1256
嗞 2538
喾 1116
喧 2170
喀 1068
(嘅) 1078
喔 2013
喙 870

十画

嗪 1561
嗷 18
嗦 1833
嘟 476
嗜 1763
嗑 1090
1099
嗫 1416
(嘩) 831
833
嗬 780
嗔 235
嗦 1842
嗝 655
嗄 2
1667
(號) 772
778
(嗶) 107
嗣 1823
嗯 1381
1403
嗅 2161
嗥 773
(嗚) 2017
(嗁) 1882
嗲 431
嗳 5
7
(噯) 3
(嗆) 1541
1547
嗡 2012
嗽 2299
嗙 1447
嗌 7
2278
嗛 1540
嗍 1842
嗨 753
(嗨) 795
嗐 760
嗤 259
嗵 1919
嗓 1657
辔 1456
嗈 2310

十一画

嘒 870
嘉 930
(嘆) 1861
嘞 1164
1171
(槑) 1315
嘏 697
934
嘈 192
嗽 1828
(嘔) 1432
嘌 1477
嘁 1507
嘎 618
619
嘘 1733
2164
嘑 817
嘡 1864
(嘍) 1253
1256
嘣 94
嘤 2299
嘚 401
405
嫛 983
嗿 1272
嘝 820
嗻 2428
2432
嘛 1292
嗾 1828
嘀 413
415
嘐 382
嘧 1334
(嗽) 380

十二画

(嘵) 2100
嘻 2050
嘭 1458
(嗹) 342
噎 2235
(噁) 505
嘶 1817
噶 619
嘲 229
2423
噘 1057

嘹 1212
嚕 2390
噗 1498
嘬 297
2572
(嚚) 1525
(嘽) 213
1857
嘿 795
1368
(嘸) 1285
嶕 983
(嗥) 773
噢 1431
噏 2050
噙 1561
噜 1256
噇 305
噌 198
244
(嘮) 1155
1163
(嗕) 2187
噣 2508
噀 2190
噔 408
(噝) 1815
(嘰) 888

十三画

嚄 875
886
1431
嚆 772
噤 1017
噃 1171
噩 508
(噸) 495
(噦) 868
2369
噘 1480
嘴 2568
噱 1062
2179
(噹) 383
器 1525
(噥) 1424
噪 2397
噀 1848
噬 1764
嗷 983
(噲) 1121
(噯) 5
7
噷 800
噫 2260
(嚈) 2310
營
噻 1649
(嘯) 2117
噼 1464

十四画

(嚎) 1853
(嚇) 791
2069
嚏 1887
嚅 1637
(嚐) 219
嚎 774
(嚌) 919
嚙 765
嚓 175
202
(嚀) 1417
(嚮) 2095

十五至十七画

(嚥) 1432
嚚 2291
嚣 19
2104
嚜 1312
(嚙) 2214
(嚦) 1189
嚯 887
(嚴) 2202
(嚲) 213
(嚫) 241
(嚨) 1250
(嚾) 843
鼍 1961
(嚳) 1116
嚼 973
983
1063
嚷 1608
1609

十八画以上

(囁) 1416
(囈) 2275
(囀) 2522
曜 1590
(躡) 2104
(囌) 1828
(囅) 213
(囉) 1276
1278
1284
(囓) 1416
(囑) 2508
囔 1392
(鼉) 1961

囗部

一画

○

二至三画

囚 1582
四 1820
因 2282
团 1945
回 858
囟 2136
囡 1387
团 944
(囝) 1387

四画

(国) 738
园 2357
围 1990
困 1132
囤 496
1954
(囬) 858
囮 503
囱 323
囵 1273
囫 817
囥 1085

五至七画

国 738
固 697
囷 1604
囹 1228
图 1938
囿 2334
圃 1501
圄 2346
圂 873
圆 2362

八画以上

圊 1569
圉 2346
啬 1661
(國) 738
(圇) 1273
圈 1054
1056
1595
圌 309
(圌) 302
(圐) 1114
(圍) 1990
(園) 2357
(嗇) 1661
圙 1269
(團) 1945
(圖) 1938
(圙) 1272
圜 845
2365
圝 2325
(圞) 1269
(圞) 1269

巾部

巾 1002

一至四画

市 593
(帀) 2383
币 104
布 171
帅 1794
市 1754
师 1730
吊 446
帆 529
帏 815
帏 1991
帐 2419
希 2045
(帋) 2466
帊 1435

五画

帖 1906
1907
1909
帜 2472
帙 2472
帕 1435
帛 149
帑 2354
帘 1197
帚 2497
帑 1868
帔 1454

六至九画

帮 56
带 371
帧 2435
(帥) 1794
帝 428
帡 1490
卷 1055
1056
帱 276
395
帩 1552
(師) 1730
帨 1805
(帬) 1604
帻 2399
(帳) 2419
(帶) 371
常 219
帼 744
帷 1992
幄 1972
幅 600
帽 1311
(幏) 1549
(幃) 1132
幄 2015
幈 1491
(幃) 1991

十画以上

幕 1379
幌 856
幎 1334
幖 128
幔 1300
(幗) 744
幛 2420
(幣) 104
幮 292
幞 601
(幠) 815
(縣) 1335
幡 529
幢 305
2527
(幟) 2472
幪 1325
幧 1549
幨 209
(幫) 56
(幬) 276
395
(歸) 726
(幮) 292
幰 2079
(襴) 1148

山部

山 1668

三至四画

屼 2037
屿 2342
屾 1700
屹 649
2273
岁 1839
岌 902
岂 1514
岂 1514
岍 1529
岐 1509
岖 1588
岈 2196
岗 636
638
639
岘 2080
岙 19
岜 1273
岑 198
岔 205
岚 1146
岛 392
岜 25

五画

岵 824
岢 1095
岸 13
岩 2205
岽 465
岧 1128
岬 932
岫 2160
(岡) 635
岝 2578
岳 2372
岱 370
岭 1232
岣 683
岪 1310
岭 1923
峃 2177
岷 1349
岧 1901
(岹) 1901
峄 2276
峔 1373

六至七画

峙 1761
2475
耑 483
(耑) 2515

炭 1862
(炭) 1862
峡 2061
峣 2228
峒 469
1923
峤 980
1549
峇 25
峋 2187
峥 2443
峦 1269
峧 969
幽 2316
峷 1252
崁 1082
崂 1155
峬 153
(豈) 1514
峚 1691
(峽) 2061
崃 1144
峭 1552
峨 504
(峩) 504
(島) 392
崄 2079
[illegible] 2079
峪 2349
峰 587
(峯) 587
崀 1151
峻 1067

八画

崚 1171
(崧) 1825
(崠) 465
崖 2196
(崕) 2196
崎 1511
崦 2201
(崍) 1144
崭 2411
崑 1132
崮 701
(崗) 636
638
639
崔 332
崟 2289
(崯) 2289
(崙) 1273
崤 2104
崩 93
崞 738
崒 2564
(崪) 2564
崇 273
崆 1105
[illegible] 1260
崛 1062

九画

嵌 1082
1541
[illegible] 451
[illegible] 367
嵘 1630
嵖 204
(嵗) 1839
崴 1966
1987
嵎 2340
崽 2386
崿 508
(嵒) 2205
嵚 1559
嵬 1993
嵛 2340
嵯 338
嵝 1253
嵫 2538
嵋 1315

十画

嶅 18
(嵗) 1839
嵊 1726
嵲 1416
嵴 909
嵩 1825

十一至十二画

(嵽) 451
(嶇) 1588
(嶁) 1253
嶂 2420
嶍 2052
(嶍) 2052
(嶢) 2228
(嶠) 980
1549
嶲 2050
嶕 973
(嶴) 19
嶓 147
嶙 1224
嶒 199
(嶗) 1155
嶝 410

十三画以上

巘 2213
(嶩) 1393
(嶧) 2276
(嶼) 2342
(嶨) 2177
(嶮) 2079
(𡾊) 2079
嶰 2125
豳 135
(嶺) 1232
嶷 2266
(嶽) 2372
(嶸) 1630
巅 432
巇 2051
巍 1988
巉 212
(巋) 1128
巎 1394
(巖) 2205
(巒) 1269
(巘) 2213

彳部

彳 264

三至五画

行 769
772
797
2143
彻 234
役 2275
彷 551
1445
征 2442
徂 330
往 1982
彿 596
彼 100
径 1030

六至七画

衎 1082
待 368
372
徊 841
863
徇 2189
(徇) 2189
徉 2221
衍 2208
律 1266
很 796
(後) 809
衏 2368
徒 1940
徕 1144
(徑) 1030
徐 2165
[illegible] 771

八画

鸻 798
(術) 1787
徛 921
(徠) 1144
徘 1439
徙 2054
徜 221
得 401
402
405
衔 2076
(從) 324
(衒) 2175

九至十画

街 988
衖 2098
衕 1927
御 2352
(復) 609
610
徨 854
循 2187
(徧) 122
衙 2196
微 1987
徭 2229
徯 2049
(徬) 1445

十二画以上

衚 820
德 404
徵 2470
(徵) 2442
(衝) 267
273
(徹) 234
(衛) 1997
衠 2530
(徺) 2228
徼 978
983
衡 800
(衞) 1997
徽 858
(黴) 1316
衢 1591

彡部

形 2146
杉 1663
1671
尨 1303
1324
[illegible] 314
彤 1628
彣 1923
钐 1672
1674
衫 1672
参 182
198
1702
须 2161
彦 2214
彧 2349
彬 134
彪 128
彩 180
(彫) 444
445
參 182
彭 1458
彰 2416
影 2304
鬱 2348

犭部

二至四画

犰 1583
犯 540
犴 13
犷 726
犸 1291
狂 1124
犹 2319
狈 81
狄 414
狃 1422
(犯) 26
狁 2378
犼 809

五至六画

狉 1463
狙 1044
狎 2061
狌 1721
2140
狐 817
狝 2077
狗 683
狍 1448
狞 1417
狖 2334
狒 564
[illegible] 927
狓 1466
狭 2061
狮 1732
[illegible] 2277
独 477
狯 1121
(狥) 2189
狰 2443
狡 975
狩 1776
狱 2349
[illegible] 1267
狠 796
狲 1841

七画 1327

[illegible] 2079
(狹) 2061
狾 2476
狴 107
狸 1175
狷 1056
猁 1193
狳 2339
猃 2079
狺 2289
狼 1150
猂 760
[illegible] 1393
狻 1834

八画

猜 175
猪 2500
猎 1218
猫 1305
1309
猗 2260
猇 2103
猖 214
猡 1278
(猘) 2476
猊 1405
猞 1692
[illegible] 1857
[illegible] 817

猔 1022
猝 330
猕 1330
猛 1326

九画

猰 2198
猢 820
猹 204
猩 2142
猲 792
2124
猥 1997
猬 2002
猾 833
猴 809
㺄 2346
(猨) 2365
(猶) 2319
猸 1315
猱 1394

十至十三画

獉 2437
猿 2365
(獏) 1371
(獅) 1732
猺 2230
(猻) 1841
獕 333
(獄) 2349
獐 2416
獍 1034
獗 1062
獠 1213
(獲) 885
獴 1327
獭 1849
(獧) 1056
(獨) 477
(獫) 2079
(獪) 1121
獬 2125

十四画以上

(獮) 2077
獯 2185
(獷) 726
(獰) 1417
(獵) 1218
獾 887
玃 843
(獼) 1330
(玁) 2079
(玀) 1278

夕部

夕 2041
舛 302
名 1350
岁 1839
多 497
罗 1276
梦 1327
(夠) 685
飧 1841
(夢) 1327
夥 884
(夥) 883
夤 2291

夊部

处 292
294
(処) 292
294
冬 464
务 2036
各 655
657
条 1900
备 81
复 609
夏 2069
惫 87
(愛) 6
夐 2156
(憂) 2315
夔 1129

饣(食)部

二至四画

饤 457
饥 1822
饥 889
(飦) 2409
饦 1956
饧 1864
2146
饨 1954
饩 2056
饪 1625
饫 2348
饬 266
饫 2415
饭 541
饮 2293
2297

五至六画

饯 953
饳 502
饰 1758
饱 63
饲 1823
饴 2261
饵 514
饶 1610
饽 107
蚀 1747
(蚀) 1745
饸 1899
(飪) 1625
饷 2094
饹 789
饹 650
1166
饺 975
饻 2045
饼 140

七至八画

饽 146
铺 174
馃 1832
饾 475
饿 507
馀 2339
(餘) 2336
馁 1398
馂 1067
(餦) 2415
(餞) 953
馃 746
馄 873
馊 1278
(餧) 2001
(餚) 2228
馅 2084
(餣) 1055
馆 715

九至十一画

馇 820
馇 202
2406
(餳) 1864
2146
(餵) 2001
馈 1130
馉 695
馊 1828
馌 854
(餽) 1130
(餱) 809
馉 489
馋 210
馌 2242
馍 1361
馎 151
(餺) 107
(饁) 2056
馏 1244
1248
馐 1866
馑 2159
(餻) 646
馑 1010
馒 1298

十二画以上

(饒) 1610
馓 2280
馓 1656
(饍) 1675
馔 2523
(饑) 889
馇 2409
(饝) 1361
(饞) 210
(饠) 1278
馕 1393

丬(爿)部

爿 1441
壮 2525
(壯) 2525
妆 2523
(妝) 2523
(牀) 305
状 2526
(狀) 2526
戕 1543
斨 1543
牁 1090
将 959
964
1543
牂 2392
(將) 1543
(牆) 1545

广部

广 8
724

二至五画

庀 1468
邝 1125
庄 2523
庆 1578
庑 2033
床 305
庋 732
库 1115
庇 106
应 2297
2305
庐 1256
序 2166
庞 1445
店 442
庙 1344
府 602
底 405
417
庖 1448
庚 662
废 564

六至八画

庤 2475
度 482
501
庭 1912
庥 2158
庠 2093
席 2052
庯 153
(庪) 732
座 2579
唐 1865
庶 1789
庹 1961
庵 12
庼 1578
庾 2346
庳 107
廊 1151
康 1083
庸 2310

九至十一画

(廂) 2092
(廁) 195
(庽) 2352
廋 1828
廆 731
赓 662
(廐) 1040
(廄) 1040
廒 18
(廈) 1667
2069
廓 1135
廉 1199
(廕) 2297
廑 1010
1561
(廣) 724
725
廙 2280
腐 604
廖 1216

十二画

(廚) 291
(廝) 1817
(廟) 1344
(廠) 221
廛 211
(廡) 2033
(慶) 1578
(廢) 564

十三画以上

廨 2125
廪 1225
(廩) 1225
廱 2432
膺 2300
應 2297
2305
鹰 2300
(廬) 1256
(龐) 1445
譍 2300
2309
(廳) 1909

门(門)部

门 1320
(門) 1320

一至四画

闩 1794
闪 1672
(閆) 2207
闬 766
闭 105
问 2010
闯 305
闰 1644
(開) 1069
闱 1991
闲 2074
闳 805

间 940
952
(閒) 940
952
2074
闵 1349
闶 1083
1085
闷 1320
1323

五至六画

闸 2404
闹 1396
閟 107
闺 731
闻 2009
闼 1849
闽 1349
闾 1264
闿 1078
阀 525
阁 652
(閤) 791
阁 652
阎 2453
阂 789
(閧) 709

七至八画

阃 1132
阄 297
阉 1036
訚 2289
阅 2372
阆 1151
阇 476
1693
阈 2352
阉 2201
阊 214
阌 2059
阋 2009
阍 872
阎 2207
阏 507
2201
阐 213

九画

阛 2288
阑 1146
阒 1594
阓 870
(闆) 49
(闇) 15
阔 1134
(闈) 1991
阕 1603

十画以上

阖 791
阗 1898
阘 345
1849
(閭) 1078
阙 1602
1604
(闊) 1128
(闞) 1476
阚 1082
(闞) 765
(關) 709
(闥) 1849
(闡) 213
阛 845
(闢) 1463
1469

氵部

二画

汁 2455
汀 1910
汇 865
氿 732
氾 444
汉 765
氾 533
(氾) 542

三画

汗 761
766
(汙) 2017
污 2017
(汚) 2017
江 958
汛 2188
汏 367
沥 1979
汕 1673
汔 1524
汐 2045
(汎) 542
汍 1972
汲 902
汜 1823
池 260
汝 1637
汤 1676
1864
汊 205

四画

沣 584
汪 1979
1980
汧 1530
汫 1028
沅 2358
沄 2033
沛 1991
汽 1947
沄 2377
沐 1378
沛 1454
沔 1337
汰 1855
沤 1431
1433
沥 1191
沌 496
2521
沘 100
(沍) 823
沏 1505
沚 2466
沙 1663
1667
汩 692
汨 1332
(沖) 267
汭 1644
汽 1524
沃 2014
沂 2261
汶 608
沦 1273
汹 2153
汾 573
泛 542
(沿) 2206
沧 189
沨 584
沟 681
没 1312
1366
汴 117
汶 2012
沆 772
沩 1992
沪 824
沉 236
沈 1708
(沈) 236
沁 1562
(決) 1057
泐 1165

五画

沫 1319
沬 1367
浅 940
1539
法 525
526
泔 628
泄 2123
沽 687
沭 1788
河 787
泷 1250
1797
沾 2408
泸 1257
泪 1169
沮 1047
1051
油 2319
泱 2217
(況) 1125
泂 1035
泅 1584
泗 1823
泆 2276
泊 149
1491
(泝) 1833
沴 1191
泠 1228
泜 2458
泺 1332
泺 1280
(濼) 1491
泃 1044
沿 2206
泖 1310
泡 1448
1450
注 2510
泣 1525
泫 2175
泮 1444
泞 1419
沱 1960
泻 2123
泌 107
1332
泳 2312
泥 1404
1406
泯 1349
沸 565
泓 806
沼 2424
波 144
泼 1491
泽 2399
泾 1018
治 2474

六画

洭 1124
洼 1964
洁 991
洱 514
洪 806
洹 845
洒 1647
洧 1996
洏 511
洿 2018
洓 1849
洌 1217
浃 927
洟 1886
浇 969
泚 320
浈 2435
浉 1733
洸 724
(洩) 2123
浊 2533
洞 469
洇 2287
洄 864
测 196
洙 2499
洗 2053
2078
活 875
洑 597
613
涎 2076
浒 955
洎 919
洢 2259
洫 2167
派 1434
1440
浍 868
1121
洽 1527
洮 1870
洈 1992
洵 2187
(洶) 2153
浲 964
洛 1358
洺 1280
浏 1237
济 911
919
洨 2104
浐 213
洋 2221
洴 1490
洣 1332
洲 2496
浑 872
浒 822
2165
浓 1424
津 1006
浔 2187
浕 1015
洳 1641

七画

涛 1869
涝 1163
浡 149
浦 1501
浭 662
涑 1832
浯 2028
酒 1037
(浹) 927
涞 1144
涟 1197
浙 2432
(涇) 1018
涉 1697
消 2100
涅 1416
浬 754
1180
涠 1992
浞 2534
涓 1054
涡 737
2013
涢 2377
浥 2278
涔 198
浩 779
涐 504
海 754
浜 57
(涖) 1192
涂 1941
浠 2046
浴 2349
浮 597

洽 763
涣 848
浼 1319
涤 415
流 1239
润 1645
涧 955
涕 1886
浣 848
浪 1152
浸 1016
涨 2417
2420
涩 1661
涊 1412
涌 270
2312
涘 1823
浚 1067
2190

八画

清 1569
渍 2553
添 1896
渚 2507
(淩) 1229
鸿 807
淇 1511
淋 1223
1226
淅 2047
淞 1825
渎 480
涯 2196
淹 2201
(淶) 1144
涿 2533
(淒) 1505
渐 943
956
(淺) 940
1539
渠 1590
淑 1780
淖 1397
淌 1868
淏 780
混 873
涸 744
淠 1469
淟 1899
涠 790
渑 1338
1721
(渦) 737
2013
(淛) 2432
淮 841
淦 635
(淪) 1273
淆 2104
渊 2355
淫 2290
(淨) 1030
淝 561
渔 2339
淘 1872
(淊) 2201
淴 817
(涼) 1203
1210
淳 313
液 2241
淬 334
淤 2335
涪 600
淯 2352
湴 55
淡 380
淙 326
淀 443
涫 718
涴 2015
2355
(淚) 1169
深 1702
渌 1260
涮 1795
涵 763
渗 1710
淄 2538

九画

(湊) 327
溂 808
渍 573
湛 2414
港 638
渫 2124
渃 1848
湈 2303
湖 820
渣 2403
湘 2092
滞 2478
渤 150
湢 108
湮 2201
(湮) 2287
(減) 945
湎 1338
湝 988
湨 1047
湜 1747
渺 1343
(湯) 1676
湿 1733
温 2003
湦 1721
渴 1095
渭 2002
溃 1130
(潰) 870
1130
湍 1945
溅 957
(濺) 940
滑 833
湃 1441
湫 978
1582
(淵) 2355
溲 1828
湟 854
溆 2168
渝 2340
湲 2364
(滄) 184
溢 1458
湾 1972
渟 1913
渡 483
游 2323
溠 2406
渼 1319
溇 1253
湔 943
滋 2538
(溈) 1992
湉 1898
渲 2176
溉 623
渥 2015
湣 1350
(湋) 1991
湄 1315
湑 2164
2165
滁 292
湧 2312

十画

滟 2216
溱 1561
2437
(溝) 681
溘 1099
滠 1698
满 1298
漭 1305
漠 1368
溍 1017
滢 2303
滇 432
溥 1502
滆 655
溧 1193
溽 1641
(滅) 1344
(滙) 865
源 2365
(溼) 1733
滤 1268
滥 1149
滉 856
溻 1848
溷 874
滍 2479
溦 1988
滗 108
(滌) 415
滫 2159
溴 2161
(溮) 1733
溵 2288
滏 604
滔 1869
溪 2049
(滄) 189
滃 2012
溜 1236
1248
(溜) 1237
滦 1269
滈 780
滒 884
漓 1177
滚 736
溏 1866
滂 1445
滀 296
2169
溢 2280
溯 1833
滨 135
溶 1630
滓 2543
溟 1359
滘 983
溺 1408
1415
滩 1858
滪 2353
溰 2310

十一画

漖 983
(漢) 765
潢 855
(滿) 1298
(滯) 2478
潆 2303
漧 629
潇 2104
漤 1148
漆 1507
漹 1661
(漙) 1947
漕 192
漱 1791
(漚) 1431
1433
漂 1474
1476
1477
漘 313
(滷) 1258
漙 817
滮 128
(漊) 1253
漫 1300
潩 2280
漯 1284
1849
(漍) 744
漶 849
潅 333
漟 635
潋 1202
潴 2501
漪 2260
漈 923
(滾) 736
漉 1263
漩 2173
漳 2416
(滻) 213
滴 413
漾 2225
演 2213
(滬) 824
澉 633
漏 1254
(漲) 2417
2420
漻 1212
(滲) 1710
潍 1994

十二画

(潔) 991
滜 1435
潜 1537
(澆) 969
澍 1791
澎 1458
1459
(澾) 1849
澌 1817
澂 1648
(澫) 1979
潮 229
潸 1672
(潛) 1672
潓 870
潭 1860
潆 1062
潦 1163
1213
(澐) 2377
(潳) 1537
(澁) 1661
(澂) 254
(潿) 1992
(潕) 2033
潲 1691
(潷) 108
潟 2060
澔 780
澳 20
潘 1441
(潙) 1992
潼 1925
澈 235
澜 1147
澧 1499
潾 1224
(澇) 1163
(潯) 2187
潺 211
(潠) 2190
澄 254
410
(潑) 1491
潏 2354

十三画

濛 1325
(澣) 848
(濇) 1661
濑 1145
濒 135
濾 1054
濉 1837
(澠) 1338

1721
潞　1263
澧　1182
(濃)　1424
澡　2395
(澤)　2399
澴　845
(濁)　2533
澨　1764
激　899
(澮)　868
1121
澹　383
1860
澥　2125
2126
澶　211
濂　1199
(澱)　443
澼　1470

十四画

(濤)　1869
(濫)　1149
(濔)　1332
濡　1637
(濬)　1067
2190
(濕)　1733
(潕)　2033
濮　1500
濞　111
濠　774
(濟)　911
919
(濴)　2303
(濱)　135
(濘)　1419
(濜)　1015
(濶)　1134
(澀)　1661
濯　2536

十五画

(瀆)　480
瀫　697
(瀦)　2501
(濾)　1268
瀑　75
1503
(濺)　957
㶁　744
鸂　2051
(瀏)　857
瀍　211
瀌　128
(瀅)　2303
(瀉)　2123
(瀋)　1708
(濼)　1280

十六至十七画

瀚　769
(瀟)　2104
(瀝)　1191
瀣　2126
(瀘)　1257
瀵　2391
(瀧)　1250
1797
瀛　2303
(瀠)　2303
灌　719
瀹　2374
(瀲)　1202
瀼　1608
1610
瀵　576
瀽　950
瀰　1331

十八画以上

(灃)　584
(灄)　1698
灊　1539
灏　780
(灘)　1177
(灑)　1858
(灝)　1647
灞　528
(灠)　1148
灡　31
灢　1169
(灣)　1972
(灤)　1269
(灩)　2216
(灨)　635

忄(⺗)部

一至四画

忆　2272
忉　390
忏　628
忖　337
忓　213
忣　902
忙　1302
忝　1899
忨　1979
怃　2033
忮　2472
怀　841
怄　1433
忧　2315
忳　1954
忡　270
忤　2033
忾　1079
怅　223
忻　2132
(忷)　2153
忪　1824
2486
怆　307
忺　2073
忭　117
(忼)　1083
忱　238
快　1119
忸　1422

五画

怔　2443
2451
怯　1555
怗　824
怵　294
(怵)　294
怖　173
怦　1458
怗　1906
怛　345
怏　2225
怳　855
性　2150
怍　2578
怕　1435
怜　1196
怞　2498
怩　1405
怫　597
怊　225
怿　2276
怪　708
怡　2261

六画

恇　1124
恸　1927
恃　1762
恭　675
恒　797
恓　2045
恹　2199
(恠)　708
恢　857
(恆)　797
恍　855
恫　470
1914
恺　1078
恻　197
恬　1897
恤　2167
恰　1527
(恉)　2466
恂　2187
恟　2153
恪　1097
恼　1394
恔　759
恑　207
恽　2380
侬　1393
恨　796

七画

悖　277
悖　85
悚　1826
悟　2040
悂　1463
悭　1531
悄　1548
1551
悍　768
悝　1128
1180
悃　1132
(悞)　2039
悒　2278
悔　864
悕　2046
悯　1349
悦　2373
悌　1887
悢　1210
悛　1595

八画

情　1574
惬　1556
(悵)　223
悻　2151
惜　2047
(悽)　1505
惭　187
悱　562
悼　398
惝　222
1868
惧　1052
惕　1887
惧　1899
惘　1982
悸　921
惟　1992
惆　277
惛　872
惚　817
惊　1022
惇　495
惦　443
悴　334
惓　1599
惮　381
悰　326
悾　1105
惋　1976
惨　187
惙　314
惯　718

九画

(愜)　1556
愤　576
愫　451
慌　850
愊　108
惰　502
愐　1338
愠　2381
惺　2142
愒　792
1079
1525
愦　1131
愕　508
惴　2530
愣　1174
愀　1551
愎　108
惶　854
愧　1131
愉　2340
(愶)　1580
愔　2288
惼　117
慨　1078
(惛)　1350
(惱)　1394

十画

慠　20
愫　1833
慑　1698
慕　1379
慎　1711
(慄)　1192
(慖)　874
(愷)　1078
(愾)　1079
慥　2397
(愴)　307
(慆)　2498
慊　1541
1556

十一画

(慪)　1433
(慳)　1531
慓　1475
慢　1301
(慟)　1927
憏　266
慵　2310
慷　1083
(慴)　1698
(慘)　187

十二画

懂　465
憓　870
憭　1214
憯　188
憬　1029
(憚)　381
(憮)　2033
憔　1550
懊　20
憱　331
憧　270
(憐)　1196
憎　2402

十三画

(懜)　1327
憷　296
懒　1148
憾　769
(憹)　1393
懆　195
(懌)　2276
懁　2171
懈　2126
懔　1225
(懍)　1225
(憶)　2272
懔　858

十四画以上

(懤)　277
(懨)　2199

懦 1430
懵 1327
(懷) 841
(懽) 842
(懺) 213
(懾) 1698
(懼) 1052
(戁) 270

宀部

二至四画

宁 1417
1419
宂 732
(冗) 1632
它 1847
宇 2342
守 1770
宅 2407
安 8
字 2551
完 1972
宋 1826
宏 805
牢 1155
灾 2385

五至六画

宝 64
宗 2553
定 457
宕 388
宠 273
宜 2261
审 1708
宙 2498
官 713
宛 1975
实 1741
宓 1332
宣 2169
宦 847
宥 2334
宬 251
室 1762
宫 675
宪 2083
客 1097
(宩) 1828

七画

害 759
宽 1121
宧 2262
宸 240
家 927
1002
宵 2102
宴 2215
宾 134
宰 2386
宭 1604

八画

寇 1112
寁 2569
寅 2290
寄 921
寂 922
宿 1832
2159
2160
寀 181
182
(寃) 2354
密 1333

九至十一画

寒 763
富 615
寔 1747
寓 2352
(甯) 1417
1419
寐 1319
塞 1649
1661
骞 1532
寞 1368
寘 2479
寝 1562
(寖) 1016
寨 2408
赛 1649
搴 1532
(寬) 1121
(賓) 64
寡 703
察 205
(寧) 1417
1419
蜜 1335
寤 2040
(寢) 1562
(賔) 134
寥 1212
(實) 1741

十二画以上

骞 2074
寮 1213
(寫) 2122
2123
寯 1067
(審) 1708
(憲) 2083
褰 1532
寰 845
蹇 950
謇 950
寱 2281
(寶) 64
(寵) 273
(寳) 64

辶(辶)部

二至四画

辻 1736
边 112
辽 1211
迁 2335
达 344
迈 1294
过 737
746
讪 209
迁 1529
迄 1524
迅 2188
(迆) 2261
2269
巡 2186
进 1011
远 2365
违 1990
运 2378
还 753
843
连 1193
1194
迍 2530
迓 2198
迕 2033
近 1014
返 540
迎 2300
这 2431
2433
迒 770
迟 261

五画

述 1788
迪 414
迥 1034
迭 450
迮 2399
迤 2261
2269
迫 1440
1493
迩 514
(迯) 1870
迦 927
迢 1901
迨 370

六画

迺 1386
(迺) 1385
(迴) 858
选 2174
适 1134
1761
(适) 1134
追 2527
逅 814
逃 1870
逄 1445
迻 2261
迹 919
迸 95
送 1826
迷 1329
逆 1406
退 1951
逊 2189

七画

逑 1584
逋 152
速 1832
逗 475
逦 1180
逐 2502
逝 1762
(逕) 1030
逍 2100
逞 254
造 2396
透 1935
途 1940
逍 1134
逛 726
逖 1886
逢 588
(這) 2431
2433
递 428
通 1914
1927
逡 1604

八画

逵 1128
(迸) 93
逴 314
(逿) 1886
逻 1278
(過) 737
746
逶 1987
(進) 1011
(週) 2495
逸 2278
逭 848
逮 368
373
逯 1260

九画

(達) 344
逼 95
遇 2352
遏 507
遗 2001
2263
遌 508
遄 302
遑 854
遁 497
逾 2340
(遊) 2323
遆 1882
遒 1585
道 398
399
遂 1839
1840
(運) 2378
遍 122
遐 2061
(違) 1990

十画

遨 18
遘 685
(遠) 2365
遢 1848
遣 1539
遝 1849
(遞) 428
遥 2230
遛 1244
1247
(遡) 1833
(遜) 2189

十一画

遭 2393
(遯) 497
遮 2428
(適) 1761

十二画

(遶) 1610
(邁) 1294
(遷) 1529
(遼) 1211
暹 2074
遴 1224
遵 2571
(遲) 261
(選) 2174
遹 2354

十三画以上

遽 1054
(還) 753
843
邀 2227
邂 2125
邅 2409
避 110
(邇) 514
邈 1343
邃 1840
(邊) 112
邋 1138
(邐) 1180
(邏) 1278

彐(⺕彑)部

归 726
刍 290
寻 2185
当 383
388
灵 1226
录 1259
帚 2497
彖 1947
彗 869
(尋) 2185
彘 2478
(彙) 865
(彜) 2266
(歸) 726
彝 2266

蘐 2369
蠡 1178
1183
(蘐) 2369

尸部

尸 1726
彐

一至三画

尹 2291
尺 233
262
尻 1085
尼 1404
(启) 476
尽 1008
1011

四至六画

层 198
屁 1469
屃 108
2057
尿 1415
1836
尾 1994
2269
屄 1825
岜 29
局 1046
屉 1886
居 1044
届 999
屈 1588
鸤 1731
屄 95
(屄) 95
(屍) 1726
屋 2018
屌 446
昼 2498
咫 2470
屏 139
140
1490
屎 1750

七画以上

展 2410
屎 1584
屑 2124
屐 895
屙 503
屠 1941
㞘 476
(屜) 1886
屧 2125
屖 2049
属 1785
2507
𪨗 1057
屡 1265
孱 188
210
(屢) 1265
屣 2055
(屣) 1825
(屧) 2125
履 1266
屦 1054
(層) 198
(屨) 1054
(屩) 1057
(屬) 1785
2507
羼 214
(屭) 2057

己(巳)部

己 910
已 2266
巳 1820
(巳) 1820
巴 23
(回) 859
包 59
异 2273
导 391
岂 1514
忌 918
巷 772
2097

弓部

弓 667
(弔) 446
引 2291
弗 593
弘 801
弡 737
弛 260
弬 1108
张 2415
弝 29
弧 818
弥 1328
弦 2075
(弢) 1869
弩 1427
弨 225
弪 1031
弭 1332
弯 1971
弮 1594
弱 1646
(張) 2415
艴 600
(弳) 1031
弸 1458
弶 964
弹 381
1859
(強) 964
1543
1547
(弻) 108
弼 108
强 964
1543
1547
粥 2353
2496
(發) 518
528
(彉) 737
(彄) 1108
(彆) 134
(彈) 381
1859
(彊) 964
1543
1547
(彌) 1328
(彍) 737
疆 961
(彎) 1971

屮部

(艸) 192
蚩 259
(芻) 290

女部

女 1427

二至三画

奶 1386
奴 1426
奸 938
如 1634
(奼) 207
妁 1811
妆 2523
妄 1983
妇 607
妃 558
她 1847
好 774
778
妈 1285

四画

妍 2205
妩 2033
妘 2377
妓 918
妪 2348
妣 100
妙 1343
妊 1625
妖 2226
妥 1961
妗 1015
姊 2541
妨 549
妫 729
妒 482
妞 1419
(妝) 2523
姒 1823
妤 2337

五画

妹 1319
妺 1367
姑 687
妸 503
(妬) 482
妻 1505
1525
妲 345
姐 995
要 894
妯 2497
(姍) 1672
姓 2151
委 1986
1996
姁 2165
姗 1672
妾 1555
妮 1403
始 1750
姆 1285
1373

六画

㛃 990
娍 1825
娃 1964
姞 906
姥 1162
1373
娅 2198
姮 798
要 2226
2233
威 1986
耍 1792
姱 1117
姨 2261
娆 1610
(姪) 2462
姻 2288
姝 1779
娇 970
(姙) 1625
姤 685
姚 2228
姽 734
娈 1269
姣 970
姿 2536
姜 960
姘 1479
娄 1252
姹 207
娜 1385
1430
(姦) 938

七画

姬 895
娠 1702
孬 1393
娌 1180
娱 2339
娉 1482
娖 314
娟 1054
娲 1964
娥 504
娒 1315
娩 1338
1975
娴 2076
娣 429
娑 1842
娘 1413
娓 1996
娿 503
婀 503
娭 4
2046

八画

(娬) 2033
婧 1032
婊 130
婞 2151
(婭) 2198
娶 1593
婼 314
1646
媖 2299
婪 1146
婳 841
婕 994
婥 314
娼 214
(婁) 1252
婴 2299
(媧) 1964
婗 1405
婢 108
(婬) 2290
婚 872
婵 210
婆 1492
婶 1709
婉 1976
娵 1151
(婦) 607
㚢 1427

九画

媒 1315
媟 2125
媠 502
媢 1312
媪 19
(婣) 2288
嫂 1659
(媿) 1131
媭 2164
(媮) 1928
媕 12
媛 2364
2368
婷 1913
(媯) 729
媚 1320
婿 2168
婺 2040

十画

媾 685
嫫 1361
嫄 2365

媳 2052
媿 1469
媛 7
媵 2309
嫉 909
嫌 2077
嫁 937
嫔 1480
(嫋) 1415
嫱 260

十一画

嫠 1177
嫣 2201
嫛 2299
嫱 1546
嫩 1402
(嫗) 2348
嫖 1476
嫕 2280
嫛 2260
嫦 221
嫚 1297
1302
嫘 1168
嫛 983
嫜 2416
嫡 415
嫳 1478
嫪 1164

十二画以上

(嬈) 1610
嬉 2050
嫽 1213
(嬋) 210
(嫵) 2033
(嬌) 970
(嬀) 729
嬎 543
(嬙) 841
(嫺) 2076
(嬙) 1546
嬛 845
(嬝) 1415
(嬡) 7
嬗 1675
嬴 2303
孌 111
(孋) 1386
嬲 1415
嬷 1364
(嬪) 1480
(孀) 1709
嬿 2216
(嬾) 1148
孀 1797
(孃) 1413
(孌) 1269

子(子)部

子 2539
孑 988
孓 1057

一至五画

孔 1105
孕 2378
存 335
孙 1840
孖 1285
孝 2114
孛 81
147
孜 2214
孜 2536
孚 595
(李) 2177
孟 1327
孤 687
孢 62
享 2093
学 2177
孥 1426

六画以上

孪 1269
孩 754
(挽) 1338
(孫) 1840
孰 1783
孳 2538
孵 593
(學) 2177
孺 1637
(孽) 1417
(孿) 1269

纟(糸)部

二至三画

纠 1035
纡 2335
红 673
802
纣 2497
纤 1540
2072
纥 649
784
纠 2186
约 2226
2368
纨 1972
级 902
纩 1125
纪 911
915
纫 1625

四画

纬 1995
纭 2377
纮 806
纯 312
纰 1461
纱 1664
纲 636
纳 1384
纲 944
纴 1625
纵 2558
纶 713
1273
纷 1003
纷 572
纸 2466
纹 2008
(纹) 2012
纺 551
纻 2510
纽 2439
纽 1422
纾 1779

五画

线 2082
绀 634
绁 2124
绂 597
练 1201
绉 1257
组 2411
组 2565
绅 1702
细 2057
细 276
(细) 277
织 2458
绸 1035
绌 294
绂 2475
绳 1732
纱 2438
终 2487
绉 2498
(絃) 2075
绊 55
(紵) 2510
绋 597
绎 2277
绍 1691
经 1018
1031
给 370

六画

绑 57
绒 1629
绯 706
结 984
991
绔 1116
绌 367
(絙) 662
绕 1610
绖 451
绕 1126
(紲) 2124
绚 2288
幽 2316
(紝) 1625
绗 770
绘 869
给 657
911
绚 2175
绛 964
络 1163
1280
绝 1059
绞 975
统 1925
(絲) 1813

七画

绠 663
绠 1209
绡 1176
2054
(經) 1018
1031
绡 2102
(綑) 1132
绢 1056
娲 703
绣 2160
绨 259
绤 2059
绥 1837
绦 1869
继 920
绨 1880
1887

八画

绩 1541
绩 922
绪 2167
绫 1231
缀 2559
绑 235
1223
(緉) 1209
续 2167
绮 1519
(綫) 2082
绯 560
绰 225
314
绡 1687
绲 736
绳 1721
(綱) 636
(網) 1981
(緺) 703
绫 1643
维 1993
绵 1335
(綸) 713
1273
(綵) 180
绶 1776
绷 94
95
绸 277
(緍) 1349
绹 1872
绺 1246
绛 334
绻 1600
(緪) 662
综 2402
2554
绽 2414
绾 1977
缤 1193
绿 1260
1267
缀 2530
缁 2538

九画

缂 1099
(緤) 2124
缃 2092
(練) 1201
缄 943
缅 1338
缆 1148
缇 1882
缈 1343
缉 898
1507
缊 2375
2381
缋 870
缌 1817
缎 488
缏 123
1473
(緥) 69
缐 2084
缑 682
缒 2530
缓 845
缔 431
缕 1266
(緫) 2555
缅 662
编 113
缗 1349
(緯) 1995
缘 2364

十画

缙 1017
缜 2438
缚 616
缛 1641
(緻) 2476
缟 1848
(緜) 1869
(縚) 1869
缝 588
590
(縐) 2498
缞 333
缟 647
缠 210
缡 1177
缢 2280
缣 943
缤 135

十一画

缥 1475
1476
(縷) 1266
缦 1302
缧 1168
(繃) 94
95
缨 2299

(總) 2555
(縱) 2558
缭 182
(縫) 1540
缤 2213
缩 1834
1842
缪 1344
1361
1371
缫 1658

十二画

(繞) 1610
缬 2122
(縫) 367
(繖) 1655
(繐) 1840
缭 1213
缮 529
534
(織) 2458
缮 1675
缯 2402
(繩) 1547

十三画以上

缰 961
(繩) 1721
缱 1540
缲 1549
(繰) 1658
(繹) 2277
缳 845
缴 978
2535
(繪) 869
(繡) 2160
缥 2165
缥 2185
缮 2295
(纊) 1125
(繽) 135
(繼) 920
(續) 2167
缨 1371
(纏) 210
(纑) 1257
缵 2567
(纖) 2072
(纔) 176
(變) 117
(纕) 1609
(纚) 1176
2054
(纗) 1269
(纘) 1148

马(馬)部

马 1287
(馬) 1287

二至四画

驭 2347
驮 501
1960
驯 2189
闯 305
驰 260
驱 1588
驲 1628
驳 148
飒 529
驴 1264
驶 1059

五画

驵 2392
驶 1750
(罵) 1292
驷 1034
驷 1823
驼 1960
驸 609
驹 1045
驺 2559
驻 2511
驼 1960
驱 107
驽 1426
驾 935
驿 2276
骀 370
1852

六至十画

骃 514
骁 2100
骂 1292
骃 2288
骁 1702
骄 970
骅 833
骆 1280
(駮) 148
骇 759
骈 1473
骉 128
骊 1176
骋 254
骒 703
验 2215
骍 2142
骎 1559
骏 5
骏 1067
骐 1511
骑 1512
骓 560
骒 1099
(騧) 703
骓 2529
(騐) 2215
(騌) 2555
骕 1833
骎 1261
骖 184
骘 874
(驔) 192
骒 1882
骗 2340
骙 2555
骗 1474
(騗) 1474
骛 2478
骙 1129
骚 1658
骜 2040
骜 20
(驊) 833
腾 1877
骝 1245
(騶) 2559
骞 1532
骟 1675

十一画以上

(驅) 1588
骠 128
1477
骡 1797
骡 1279
骢 323
(驂) 184
(驍) 2100
(驚) 1022
(驕) 970
骣 495
骥 213
(驛) 2276
(驗) 2215
(驌) 1833
骤 2498
骥 923
(驢) 1264
骦 843
骦 1797
骧 2092
(驪) 1176

幺部

幺 2225
乡 2085
幻 846
幼 2333
(茲) 184
幽 2316
兹 317
2536
(幾) 888
910
畿 899

巛部

(災) 2385
甾 2385
邕 2310
巢 228

王部

王 1980
1983

一至四画

玉 2346
主 2503
玎 453
全 1596
玑 889
玏 1165
玕 628
弄 1252
1425
玙 2336
玓 427
玖 1037
玘 1515
玚 223
2220
玛 1291
玞 592
玩 1973
1974
玮 1995
环 844
玭 1479
玡 2196
现 2080
玫 1314
玠 999
玐 323
玢 134
572
玱 1542
玥 2372
玦 1059

五画

珏 1059
珓 2410
珐 529
珂 1088
珑 1250
玷 442
珅 1702
(珊) 1672
玳 370
珀 1493
皇 850
珍 2434
玲 1228
(珎) 2434
珠 1192
珊 1672
珌 107
珉 1349
珈 927
玻 146

六画

珪 731
珥 514
珙 677
莹 2302
项 2162
(琊) 2196
珖 724
珰 386
珠 2499
珽 1914
珩 798
珧 2228
(珮) 1454
玺 2054
珣 2187
珞 1281
琤 242
珓 980
班 47
珲 858
873
珝 2187

七画

琎 1016
球 1584
琏 1200
琐 1845
理 1180
琇 2160
琀 763
望 1984
琉 1244
琅 1151
珺 1067

八画

琫 94
琵 1467
琙 2035
琴 1560
琶 1435
琪 1512
瑛 2299
琳 1223
琦 1512
琢 2535
2572
(琖) 2410
琥 822
琨 1132
琌 1278
(琱) 445
琼 1580
斑 48
琰 2212
(琺) 529
琮 326
琯 716
琬 1977
(琊) 1151
琛 235
琭 1261
琚 1045

九画

瑟 1661
(瑇) 370
(聖) 1722
瑚 820
瑊 943
(瑒) 223
瑁 1312
瑞 1644
瑰 731
瑀 2346
瑜 2340
瑗 2368
瑄 2171
瑕 2061
(瑨) 1349

(瑋) 1995
瑑 2522
瑙 1396

十至十二画

璈 18
(瑴) 1059
璊 1323
瑨 1017
瑱 2440
(瑻) 107
瑶 2230
瑷 7
(瑲) 1542
(瑠) 1244
璃 1177
瑭 1866
瑢 1631
瑾 1010
璜 855
(璊) 1323
璀 333
瓔 2300
(璡) 1016
璁 323
(瑽) 323
璋 2416
璇 2173
(瑩) 2302
璆 1586
璅 1846
璞 1500
璟 1029
噩 508
璠 534
璘 1224
(璕) 2187
(璣) 889

十三画以上

瓛 845
璨 188
璩 1590
(璫) 386
璐 1263
璪 2396
(環) 844
(璵) 2336
(璦) 7
(璿) 2173
(瓊) 1580
璧 111
(璽) 2054
(瓈) 1177
(瓅) 1192
瓒 2391
璺 2012
瓌 731
(瓏) 1250
瓘 720
瓖 2092
(瓓) 1278
(瓛) 845

韦(韋)部

韦 1989
(韋) 1989
韧 1625
(韌) 1625
韨 223
韍 597
(韍) 597
韠 107
韡 1996
(韔) 223
韩 763
(韓) 763
韪 1997
(韙) 1997
韫 2381
(韞) 2381
(韡) 1996
韝 46
(韝) 46
韬 1869
(韜) 1869
(韠) 107
(韤) 1966

木部

木 1374

一画

本 89
未 1999
末 1365
(末) 1365
术 1787
2501
札 2403

二画

朽 2159
朴 1476
1491
1493
1500
朱 2498
朳 25
杀 1662
机 889
朵 501
杂 2383
(朶) 501
权 1595

三画

杆 628
629
(杇) 2017
杠 636
639
杜 481
杕 427
502
杖 2419
杌 2037
材 177
村 335
杙 2275
杏 2149
束 1787
杉 1663
1671
杓 125
(杓) 1689
条 1900
极 902
床 305
杗 1303
杞 1515
杝 1175
(杝) 502
2261
杨 2220
杈 199
205
李 1179
杩 1292

四画

枉 1982
林 1220
枝 2456
杯 76
枢 1779
枥 1191
柜 734
1047
枇 1466
枑 824
(枒) 2194
杪 1342
杳 2230
杲 646
果 744
(東) 461
枧 81
枘 1644
枫 636
枧 944
枣 2395
杵 293
枚 1314
枨 248
析 2045
板 49
枞 323
2553
采 179
181
松 1824
枪 1542
(枬) 1760
(杴) 2073
枫 584
枭 2099
枊 17
构 684
杭 770
枋 547
枓 472
杰 990
枕 2438
杻 279
(牀) 305
杷 1434
杼 2510

五画

标 125
柰 1387
栈 2411
柑 628
某 1372
柚 2277
荣 1629
枯 1113
栉 2475
柯 1088
柄 140
柘 2432
栊 1250
柩 1040
枰 1490
栋 469
栌 1257
查 203
2403
(查) 2403
相 2086
2097
柙 2061
枵 2099
柚 2322
2334
(柟) 1392
枳 2467
柷 294
(柺) 707
(柵) 1672
2405
柮 502
柬 944
柞 2405
2578
柂 502
1175
2261
柎 592
柏 42
149
152
柝 1962
栀 2458
柃 1228
柢 418
栎 1192
2372
枸 681
683
1048
栅 1672
2405
柳 1245
柊 2488
枹 62
(枹) 599
柱 2511
柿 1760
亲 1557
1579
栏 1146
柈 55
柒 1505
染 1608
柠 1417
柁 1961
(柁) 502
柲 107
枷 927
架 936
柽 242
树 1788
(柗) 1851
枲 2053
柔 1632

六画

框 1126
(栔) 1525
梆 57
栻 1762
(栞) 1079
桂 735
桔 993
1047
栲 1087
栳 1162
栽 2386
栱 677
桠 2194
桓 845
栖 1505
2045
栗 1192
(栢) 42
栭 511
桡 1610
桎 2475
桠 2514
柴 208
桌 2532
桢 2437
桄 724
726
档 389
(栧) 2277
(桒) 483
桐 1923
桤 1505
株 2400
梃 1914
栝 703
1134
桥 1549
栴 2409
栿 597
(栈) 525
梴 209
桦 840
柏 1040
臬 1416
桁 798
栓 1794
桧 735
869
桃 1870
(殺) 1662
桅 1992
栒 2187
桀 993
格 650
653

移 2262
栾 1269
桨 963
桩 2523
校 980
2115
(桒) 2383
栨 2260
核 789
819
样 2225
栟 88
139
桊 1056
桉 11
案 14
(桉) 13
根 658
栩 2165
桑 1657
(栘) 2390

七画

梼 1871
械 2124
梽 2476
棻 573
彬 134
梵 543
桲 1496
梗 663
梧 2028
梔 1193
梧 78
(梜) 930
梾 1144
梿 1197
梐 107
梢 1660
1688
(桿) 629
桯 1911
梩 1176
梈 240
梏 700
梨 1176
梅 1315
(梹) 135
139
(梟) 2099
(桗) 2458
检 944
桼 1506
桜 1644
桴 599
桷 1061
梓 2541
梳 1780
棁 2533
梯 1879
渠 1590
桫 1842
梁 1204
桹 1151
梷 1230
梫 1562
梮 1045
桶 1927
梭 1842

八画

棒 58
琹 1560
(棖) 248
棱 1171
1231
楮 293
(椏) 2194
棋 1512
(棊) 1512
椰 2235
楛 825
1115
植 2463
森 1661
(棶) 1144
棽 1704
棼 573
(棟) 469
棫 2352
棱 480
椅 2260
2270
椓 2535
(棲) 1505
椠 1541
(棧) 2411
棑 1439
棐 1439
椒 972
棹 2425
棠 1866
椇 1049
棵 1090
棍 737
棘 907
(棗) 2395
椤 1278
(棡) 636
椈 2459
棰 309
(棃) 1176
椎 309
2529
集 907
棉 1336
椑 78
1467
(椷) 2073
弑 1763
棚 1458
棔 872
椋 1204
椁 746
棄 253
1726
棓 58
87
(棄) 1524
棬 1595
椪 1460
棪 2212
棕 2555
(椗) 461
棺 715
(椀) 1977
椰 1151
棨 1519
楗 956
棣 431
椐 1045
椭 1961
(極) 902

九画

楔 2118
楧 517
椿 312
(楳) 1315
椹 1711
2437
楠 1392
楂 204
2403
楂 2403
楚 294
楝 1202
楷 988
1078
榄 1148
(業) 2238
(楊) 2220
楫 909
榅 2004
楬 994
椳 1987
楒 1817
楄 1482
楞 1171
楈 697
(榘) 1048
楸 1582
椴 488
楩 1473
槐 841
槌 309
楯 497
1806
榆 2341
(楥) 2176
(椶) 2555
楹 2303
椺 242
椸 2265
椆 1264
槎 204
楼 1253
榆 943
楢 2325
榉 1049
楦 2176
概 623
(槩) 623
楣 1315
椽 302

十画

榛 2437
(構) 684
榧 1408
榧 562
(槓) 639
榰 2459
(槀) 1961
榼 1090
(樺) 840
模 1361
1372
(榦) 634
1372
榑 601
榀 655
樌 935
榎 935
槛 957
1081
榥 856
榻 1849
(槑) 1315
(榿) 1505
榫 1841
槜 2570
榭 2125
槔 646
槃 1443
(槍) 1542
槊 995
榴 1245
榱 333
槁 647
(稾) 647
(槨) 746
榜 57
(牓) 59
1459
槊 1812
(榮) 1629
寨 2408
槟 135
139
榨 2406
榕 1631
槊 1151
槠 2501
榠 1359
榷 1604
榍 2125

十一画

槽 870
(椿) 2523
(槼) 729
槷 1416
槿 1010
横 798
800
樯 1546
槽 192
(樞) 1779
(標) 125
樵 2332
樾 1525
樗 290
(樝) 2403
樘 1866
(樓) 1253
(槾) 1302
樱 2300
(樢) 2514
(槐) 471
(樂) 1164
2371
(樅) 323
2553
橡 2099
橥 2501
槲 820
槺 1083
樟 2416
樀 414
(樣) 2225
(樑) 1204
橄 633
(橢) 1961
(槳) 963
槷 2295
樛 1036

十二画

(橈) 1610
樾 2374
(樹) 1788
檠 1576
(檄) 1576
(蕟) 326
橐 1961
橱 292
橛 1062
(橜) 1062
(樸) 1500
(橤) 483
橇 1549
(橋) 1549
(樵) 2570
樵 1550
(槔) 646
橋 1561
橹 1258
橦 1925
樽 2571
橤 1704
橤 1644
樨 2050
(橥) 2295
橙 254
橘 1047
橼 2365
(機) 889

十三画

(隸) 1191
(檉) 242
藁 647
檬 1325
(檣) 1546
檽 1168
(櫝) 1258
(檔) 389
(櫛) 2475
檑 1129
檄 2052
(檢) 944
(檜) 735
869
檐 2208

榭 998
檩 1225
檀 1860
（檁）1225
（檥）2269
檗 152

十四画

（檯）1851
（檮）1871
（櫃）734
（檻）957
1081
（橤）1577
（檳）135
139
檫 205
（檸）1417
（櫂）2425
（櫈）410
檵 923

十五画以上

（櫝）480
（櫫）2501
（櫟）1192
2372
（櫥）292
欂 152
（櫗）1962
（櫪）1191
（櫨）1257
（櫸）1049
（櫽）2295
（櫬）242
（櫳）1250
（龒）1250
（權）1595
（櫺）1230
櫼 944
（櫰）1794
（欄）1146
欋 1590
（欐）1193
（欏）1278
（欑）331
（欒）1269
（欖）1148
（欛）29
欙 1168
（欞）1230
（欝）2348

犬部

犬 1600
状 2526
戾 1191
（狀）2526
畎 1600
哭 1113
臭 280
2160
猋 128
献 2084
猷 2325
獒 18
（獃）367
獘 109
（獸）1776
（獻）2084

歹部

歹 368

二至四画

列 1216
夙 1830
死 1817
歼 939
（殀）2226
殁 1367

五至六画

残 185
殂 330
殃 2217
殇 1677
殄 1899
殆 372
毙 107
殊 1780
殉 2189

七画以上

殒 2378
殓 1202
殍 1476
殖 1764
2464
（殘）185
殚 378
殛 907
殢 1887
殨 870
（殗）1841
殠 280
殡 135
殣 1017
（殤）1677
殪 2281
（殫）378
（殭）960
（殮）1202
（斃）107
（殯）135
（殲）939

车(車)部

车 231
1043
（車）231
1043

一至四画

轧 618
2197
2404
轨 732
军 1063
轩 2169
轪 370
軏 2372
轫 1625
转 2515
2518
2521
轭 506
斩 2410
轮 1273
软 1642
轰 800

五画

轱 689
轲 1089
1095
轳 1257
轴 2497
2498
轵 2467
轶 2277
軱 689
轷 817
轸 2438
轹 1192
轺 2228
轻 1565

六画

轼 1762
载 2386
2389
輀 511
轾 2476
晕 2374
2380
轿 980
辀 2496
辁 1599
辂 1260
较 980

七至八画

辄 2430
辅 603
辆 1210
（輕）1565
（輓）1975
辇 1412
（輒）2430
（輛）1210
辈 87
辉 858
辊 736
辋 1982
輗 1405
（輪）1273
辌 1205
輨 716
辍 314
辎 2538

九至十画

辏 327
毂 689
697
辐 600
（輭）1642
辑 909
辒 2004
輴 312
输 1782
輶 2325
輮 1633
辕 2365
辖 2062
辗 2411
（辗）1412

十一画以上

（轉）2515
2518
2521
辘 1263
轇 973
轕 655
（轜）511
（轎）980
辙 2430
辚 1224
轗 1081
轘 845
849
（轟）800
（轢）1192
（轤）1257

戈部

戈 649

一至二画

戋 937
戊 2036
（戉）2372
戎 1628
划 831
837
842
戌 1594
2161
戍 1787
成 244
戏 815
2055

三至七画

戒 999
我 2014
（戔）937
或 884
戗 1543
1547
戕 1543
哉 2385
战 2412
咸 2076
威 1986
栽 2386
载 2386
2389
㦲 2386
盏 2410
彧 2349
戚 1506
戛 931

八至九画

戟 912
[illegible] 2553
裁 178
（戞）931
戢 907
（幾）888
910
戡 1080
（盞）2410
戥 410
戤 624
戣 1129

十画以上

戬 949
截 994
（戧）1543
1547
臧 2392
（戲）815
2055
戮 1263
畿 899
（戰）2412
戴 373
（戱）815
2055
戳 314

比部

比 97
毕 105
毗 1466
（毘）1466
皆 984
毖 107
毙 107

瓦部

瓦 1965
瓩 1529
瓯 1431
瓮 2012
瓴 1229
瓷 317
瓶 1490
瓸 259
（甌）638
瓻 197
瓿 174
甄 2437
甃 2498
（甆）317
[illegible] 1192
（甎）2518
（甌）1431
甏 95
[illegible] 1192
甑 2402
甔 378
（甕）2012

甓 1470
(甖) 2299
甗 2213

止部

止 2465
正 2441
2446
此 320
步 172
武 2033
歧 1510
肯 1100
歪 1966
耻 264
齿 2553
(歲) 1839
(歷) 1184
(歸) 726

攴部

(敁) 432
(敍) 2166
敔 1935
敩 2117
2179
(敠) 500
(敼) 481
敲 1548
(敺) 1588
(斅) 2117
2179

日部

日 1626

一至三画

旦 379
旧 1038
早 2394
旯 1138
旮 618
旭 2166
旬 2185
旰 634
旱 767
时 1738
旷 1125
旸 2221
昜 2093

四画

旺 1984
昊 779
昉 1996
昙 1858
昔 2045
杲 646
杳 2230
昃 2399
旾 310
昆 1131
昌 214
旹 1741
晛 2081
(昇) 1711
昕 2132
明 1353
昏 871
易 2276
昀 2377
昂 17
旻 1349
昉 551
炅 734
1034

五画

春 310
昧 1319
昰 1760
是 1760
昺 140
(昞) 140
昚 1710
昽 1250
显 2077
映 2307
星 2140
昳 450
2277
昨 2572
昫 2166
昴 1310
昝 2390
昱 2349
昡 2175
昶 222
昵 1406
昭 2422

六画

(時) 1738
耆 1511
晋 1015
晅 2175
晒 1668
晟 251
1724
晓 2114
(晉) 1015
晃 855
856
晔 2241
晌 1678
晁 228
晏 2214
晖 858
晕 2374
2380
(書) 1777

七画

匙 262
1764
晡 153
曹 192
晤 2040
晨 240
晢 2430
(晣) 2430
晦 869
晞 2046
晗 763
晚 1975
晛 1152
(晝) 2498

八画

晴 1576
替 1887
暑 1784
暎 2309
晰 2047
(晳) 2047
量 1205
1210
晻 15
2212
晳 2390
晶 1023
晹 2278
智 2477
晷 734
晾 1211
景 1028
晬 2569
普 1501
曾 198
2401

九画

韪 1997
(匙) 2079
暕 947
(暝) 1428
(暘) 2221
暍 2235
暑 848
暖 1428
暗 15
暅 663
(暆) 663
暄 2171
暇 2062
暋 1350
(暐) 1996
暌 1129

十至十二画

(曬) 1406
(曄) 2241
暮 1379
(嘗) 219
暧 7
暠 647
780
暝 1359
暴 2079
暴 74
(暴) 1503
(曏) 2093
(曉) 2114
曀 2281
暵 769
(曆) 1184
(曇) 1858
暵 2354
曌 2427
暾 1954
曈 1925

十三画以上

曚 1325
曙 1787
曟 2402
(曖) 7
(韙) 1997
(鼂) 228
曞 1508
曛 2185
(曠) 1125
曜 2234
曝 75
1503
(疊) 451
(曨) 1250
曦 2051
曩 1393
(曬) 1668

曰(⺜)部

曰 2368
旨 2466
曳 2240
者 2430
沓 344
1849
冒 1310
1367
曷 789
昇 121
(昜) 2167
曼 1300
冕 1338
最 2569

水(氺)部

水 1798
(氷) 135
永 2311
(氹) 388
求 1583
氽 331
氽 1954
凼 388
汞 676
录 1259
隶 1191
尿 1415
1836
沓 344
1849
泰 1856
荥 2148
2301
泵 94
泉 1599
桼 1506
浆 960
(漿) 965
淼 1343
颍 2304
黎 1177
滕 1878
(滎) 2148
2301
漦 2301
(漿) 960

贝(貝)部

贝 81
(貝) 81

二至四画

贞 2433
则 2398
负 606
贡 679
财 177
员 1843
员 2357
2377
2380
屃 2057
贮 2261
2275
责 2398
贤 2075
败 44
账 2419
货 884
质 2473
贩 543
贪 1856
贫 1479
贬 116
购 684
贮 2510
贯 718

五画

贰 517
贱 954
贲 88
107
贳 1760
贴 1906
(貼) 1906
贵 734
贶 1126
(買) 1293
贷 372
贸 1311
(貯) 2510
费 565
贺 791
贻 2261

六至七画

贼 2399
贾 695
932
贿 869
赀 2475
赀 2536
赁 1225
(賉) 2167
赂 1260
赃 2391

资 2536
赅 620
赆 1016
赇 1585
赈 2440
赉 1144
赊 1692
(賓) 134
(賔) 134
(實) 1741

八画

赋 614
䝼 1576
(賛) 2391
(賬) 2419
(賣) 1295
赌 481
(賫) 1144
赍 898
(賢) 2075
赎 1783
(賤) 954
赏 1678
赐 322
赑 108
(質) 2473
赒 2496
赓 662
赔 1453
赕 379
賨 326

九画以上

赖 1144
赗 590
(賮) 1016
赘 2530
(購) 684
赙 616
赚 2522
2568
赛 1649
(贄) 2475
赜 2399
賧 383
赞 2391
赟 2375
赠 2402
赡 1675
(贓) 2391
(贐) 1016
(贖) 1783
(贜) 2391
(贏) 2057
(贗) 2567

见(見)部

见 950
(见) 2080
(見) 950

二至七画

观 711
718
觃 2214
规 729
(覔) 1332
觅 1332
视 1759
觇 209
览 1148
𫌪 1278
觉 980
1059
𫌩 1823
觊 920
舰 956
觋 2052

八画以上

靓 1032
1210
(覩) 481
觌 415
觍 1899
䩄 1338
1899
觎 2342
(親) 1557
1579
觏 686
(覬) 920
觐 1017
觑 1590
1594
(覻) 1590
1594
(覸) 956
(覰) 1590
1594
(覺) 980
1059
觽 731
(覽) 1148
(覼) 1278
(覿) 415
(觀) 711
718

牛(牜⺧)部

牛 1419

二至四画

牝 1482
牟 1371
1378
牡 1373
告 647
牤 1302
(牠) 1847
牣 1625
牦 1309
牧 1378
物 2037

五至六画

荦 1280
牯 695
牵 1530
牲 1721
牮 954
牴 419
特 1875
牺 2045
牸 2553

七至八画

牾 2035
牻 1304
牿 701
犁 1177
(犕) 327
(牽) 1530
犊 480
犄 898
犋 1052
犇 89
(犂) 1177
犍 943
1537
犀 2049

九画以上

犏 1472
(犛) 1302
犒 1087
(犖) 1280
(犨) 2062
犛 1177
靠 1087
犤 1168
犟 965
(犢) 480
犨 276
(犧) 2045

手部

手 1767

四至八画

拜 45
(拏) 1381
挈 1556
挚 2475
拿 1381
挛 1269
拳 1599
挐 1382
挲 1647
1666
1842
掌 2418
掣 234
掱 1435
掰 31

九画

擘 2207

十画以上

摹 1361
搿 655
搴 1532
(摯) 2475
摩 1285
1362
擎 1576
(擏) 496
(擊) 888
(擧) 1048
擘 152
(擘) 31
攀 1441
(攣) 1269

毛部

毛 1305
尾 1994
2269
毡 2409
(毬) 1629
耄 1311
毨 2079
(毨) 2079
毪 1372
(毬) 1584
毫 772
毹 1632
毳 334
毰 1454
毯 1861
毽 956
毵 1655
毷 1312
毸 1648
毹 1783
(氂) 1309
麾 858
(毿) 1655
氅 222
氇 1264
氆 1502
(毹) 1632
(氄) 1632
(氍) 1591
毶 1660
(氊) 2409
(氈) 2409
氍 1591
氎 452

气部

气 1520
氕 1477
氘 390
氖 1386
氙 2073
氚 297
氛 572
氡 465
氟 597
氢 1567
氤 2198
氩 2288
氦 759
氧 2224
(氣) 1520
氨 11
氪 1099
(氫) 1567
氰 1576
(氳) 2198
氮 382
氯 1268
氲 2375

攵部

二至五画

(攷) 1085
收 1764
攻 673
攸 2315
改 620
孜 2536
败 44
攽 47
放 551
政 2451
故 698
畋 1897
(敂) 1111
(敃) 1350
敉 483
2277

六至七画

敖 18
致 2475
敌 414
效 2116
赦 1697
教 972
981
救 1040
(敎) 149
敕 266
敔 2346
敏 1349
(敍) 2166
敛 1200
敚 501
敝 108
(啓) 1515
敢 631

八画以上

散 1655
1656
敬 1032
敞 222
敦 495
(敭) 2217
敫 978
数 1786
1790
1812
敷 593
(數) 1786
1790
1812
(敵) 414
整 2444
徹 2430
(斁) 2277
憝 495
496
(斂) 1200
(斆) 2339

(黴)　1316
(變)　117

片部

片　1470
　1473
版　50
牍　480
(牋)　943
牌　1439
牒　451
(牐)　2404
(牕)　305
牓　58
牎　305
牖　2332
(牘)　480

斤部

斤　1002
斥　264
(劤)　1015
　1030
所　1843
斧　602
欣　2132
斨　1543
颀　1511
断　486
斯　1816
斮　2535
(斮)　339
新　2133
斲　2535
斶　296
(斷)　486
(斸)　2508

爪(爫)部

爪　2424
　2515
妥　1961
孚　595
采　179
　181
觅　1332
受　1774
爬　1434
乳　1637
爰　2358
舀　2231
爱　6
奚　2046
(爲)　1989
　1998
舜　1808
(愛)　6
(亂)　1270
叆　7
孵　593
虢　744
爵　1062
繇　2230
　2325
　2498
(靉)　7

父部

父　601
　605
爷　2235
斧　602
爸　29
釜　603
爹　450
(爺)　2235

月(⺝)部

月　2369

一至三画

(肊)　2281
有　2326
　2334
刖　2372
肌　892
肋　1164
　1169
肝　628
肟　2014
肛　636
肚　480
　482
肘　2497
肖　2099
　2114
(肐)　650
肜　1628
肓　849
肠　218

四画

(肨)　1447
肼　1028
肤　592
朊　1643
䏝　2517
肺　563
肢　2458
(肧)　1452
肽　1856
(肬)　2323
肱　674
肫　2530
肯　1100
肾　1709
肦　1343
肿　2489
肭　1385
胀　2419
肣　2045
肴　2228
朋　1458
肷　1539
股　692
肮　17
肪　549
育　2309
　2348
肩　940
肥　560
胁　2120
服　596
　609

五画

胠　1589
胡　818
胚　1452
胧　1250
胈　27
胨　469
胩　1069
背　77
　82
胪　1257
胆　378
胛　932
胂　1710
胃　2001
胄　2498
胜　1721
　1723
胙　2579
胍　703
胗　2435
胝　2458
朐　1590
胞　63
胖　1441
　1447
脉　1296
　1367
胥　2162
胐　561
胫　1031
胎　1850

六画

胹　511
胯　1118
(脈)　1315
胰　2262
胵　259
胱　724
胴　470
胭　2199
朒　1428
脡　1914
　1296
(脉)　1367
脍　1121
脎　1648
脁　1904
脊　911
脆　333
脂　2458
胸　2153
(胷)　2153
(胮)　1445
胳　618
　650
　654
(脃)　333
脏　2392
脐　1511
胶　971
脑　1394
胲　622
　754
胼　1473
朕　2440
脒　1332
朔　1811
胺　14
朗　1151
脓　1425
(脇)　2120
(脅)　2120
能　1402

七画

脚　976
　1062
脖　149
脯　604
　1499
脰　475
(脣)　312
豚　1954
脦　405
　1877
(脛)　1031
脶　1278
脢　1315
脸　1200
脞　339
脬　1448
(脗)　2010
脝　797
望　1984
脱　1957
脘　1976
脲　1415
朘　1054
　2568

八画

腈　1023
(脹)　2419
期　898
　1506
(朞)　898
腊　1139
　2048
朝　228
　2422
(腖)　469
(腎)　1709
腌　2
　2201
腓　561
腘　744
腆　1899
罥　1057
(腡)　1278
腴　2340
脾　1467
殽　2104
腋　2241
腑　604
(脺)　334
(勝)　1723
　1724
腙　2555
腚　461
腔　1543
腕　1979
胬　1520
腱　956
腒　1045

九画

腻　1408
腠　327
腩　1392
腷　108
腰　2227
腼　1338
腌　344
(腸)　218
腽　1966
腥　2142
腮　1648
腭　508
(腫)　2489
腹　616
腺　2085
膇　2530
腯　1941
腧　1790
(腳)　976
　1062
鹏　1459
腤　12
塍　254
媵　2309
腾　1877
腿　1950
(腦)　1394

十画

(膆)　1833
膜　1362
膑　235
膊　151
膈　655
　657
膔　1468
膏　646
　649
膀　58
　59
　1445
　1446
膂　1266
(膁)　1539
(膋)　1212
膑　135
膲　886

十一画

膵　334
膝　2050
(膞)　2517
膘　128
(膚)　592
膛　1866
(膕)　744
膗　296
滕　1878

膣 2479
(膠) 971

十二画

膨 1459
月(臈)
1139
膰 534
膧 1925
膪 297
膳 1675
臜 1878
(臢) 1877
縢 1878
膦 1226
膙 963

十三画

臌 697
朦 1325
(膿) 1425
臊 1658
1660
(臉) 1200
(膾) 1121
(膽) 378
膻 1672
膺 2300
臁 1199
臆 2281
臃 2311
(謄) 1725
(臢) 1878
臀 1954
臂 87
111

十四画以上

臑 1397
(臍) 1511
臜 1878
(臏) 135
(臕) 128
(臘) 1139
(臙) 2199
臛 887
(臚) 1257
臢 2383
(朧) 1250
(臟) 2392
臞 1591
臜 373

欠部

欠 1540

二至七画

次 321
欢 842
欤 2337
欧 1431
软 1642
欣 2132
炊 308
(欱) 780
欬 1079
欷 2046
欲 2351
(欵) 1123
欶 4
5
508
509

八画以上

款 1123
欺 1506
欹 1507
2260
歆 1081
欻 296
2164
歅 2288
歇 2118
歃 1667
歙 2342
歆 2136
歌 651
歉 1541
(歎) 1861
(歐) 1431
歔 2165
歈 2295
歙 1698
2050
(歘) 296
2164
歜 296
(歟) 2337
(歗) 2117
歠 314
(歡) 842

风(風)部

风 577
(風) 577
飏 2221
飐 2410
飑 127
飒 1648
(颱) 1851
(颳) 702
飓 1052
(颺) 2221
飔 1817
飕 1828
(颼) 1828
飖 2230
飗 1245
飘 1475
(飄) 1475
飙 128
(飆) 128
(飇) 128

殳部

殳 1777
殴 1431
殁 1367
段 486
殷 2199
2288
2294
般 47
146
1441
(般) 48
(殺) 1662
羖 695
(殼) 1091
1551
殽 475
毁 734
(殽) 475
殺 2104
(發) 518
毂 689
697
毂 685
骰 1935
毁 864
殿 444
(榖) 1059
榖 697
縠 697
(轂) 691
彀 1112
(毆) 1431
毅 2280
觳 821
斅 821

文部

文 2004
刘 1237
齐 915
1508
吝 1225
(李) 2177
忞 1349
斋 2406
虔 1536
紊 2010
斑 48
斌 135
斐 562
斒 49
斖 899
斓 1148

方部

方 544
邡 547
放 551
於 2017
2335
(於) 2335
房 549
旃 2339
(旆) 1456
施 1732
斿 2323
旆 1456
旄 1309
旂 1511
(旂) 1512
旅 1265
旃 2409
旁 1445
旌 1022
族 2564
旎 1406
旋 2173
2175
旒 2425
旒 1245
旗 1512
旖 2270
(旛) 529
(旟) 2339

火部

火 878
(⺣) 883

一至三画

灭 1344
灰 856
灯 406
灶 2396
灿 188
灸 1037
灼 2533
灾 2385
灵 1226
灺 2123
炀 2221
(災) 2385

四画

炜 1996
炬 1432
炬 1051
炖 496
炒 231
炅 734
1034
炘 2133
炝 1548
炊 308
炙 2474
炆 2009
炕 1085
炎 2205
炉 1257
炔 734
1601
炮 1434

五画

荧 2301
炳 140
炻 1747
炼 1201
炟 345
畑 1897
炽 266
炭 1862
(炭) 1862
炯 1035
炸 2404
2405
(炢) 1581
(炧) 2123
炣 817
烁 1811
炮 63
1448
1451
炷 2511
炫 2175
烂 1149
炤 2425
烃 1911
炱 1852

六画

烤 1087
烖 2386
耿 662
烘 801
烜 2175
烦 533
烧 1687
烛 2502
烔 1923
烟 2199
2288
烨 2241
烩 869
烙 1163
1281
烊 2222
2225
烫 1868
烬 1016

七至八画

(烲) 1646
焐 2040
(烴) 1911
焊 768
(焅) 1088
烯 2047
焓 763
焕 848
烽 587
焖 1323
烷 1975
烺 1151
焗 1047
焌 1067
1589
煐 2299
焚 573
焯 228
2533
焸 1035
焜 1132
焮 2139
焰 2215
焿 1035
(焠) 334
焙 87
焯 213
焱 296
2164
焱 2216

九画

煤 1315

(煠) 2404
煳 820
煏 108
(煙) 2199
(煉) 1201
(煗) 1428
(煬) 2221
煴 2375
2382
煜 2353
煨 1988
煅 488
煲 63
煌 854
(⿰火追) 1953
煖 2171
(煖) 1428
(煢) 1580
煊 2171
(煇) 858
煸 115
煺 1953
(煒) 1996
煣 1633

十至十一画

(燁) 2241
熄 2050
(熗) 1548
熘 1237
(榮) 1629
(滎) 2148
2301
(犖) 1280
(熒) 2301
熔 1631
煽 1672
熥 1877
熯 769
(熰) 1432
熛 128
(㷇) 1953
熳 1302
熜 324
熵 1678
⿰火闲 2216
熨 2354
2382
熠 2281

十二画

(燒) 1687
熺 2050
燂 1860
燎 1213
1214
熸 943
(燀) 213
燠 2354
燔 534
(燄) 2215
燃 1607
(燉) 496
(熾) 266
(燐) 1224
燧 1840
(歘) 296
2164
燚 2281
(螢) 2302
(營) 2302
(罃) 2299
(燙) 1868
(燈) 406
燏 2354

十三画

(燦) 188
燥 2397
(燭) 2502
(燬) 864
(燴) 869
(熝) 18

十四画以上

燹 2079
(爗) 2241
(燻) 2184
(爇) 1577
(燼) 1016
燿 2235
爆 75
爌 1088
爊 18
(爕) 2126
(爍) 1811
(爐) 1257
爔 2051
鶯 2299
爚 2374
爝 1063
(爛) 1149
爨 332

斗部

斗 471
473
戽 824
料 1215
(斚) 934
斜 2121
斛 819
斝 934
斟 2437
斠 983
斡 2015
斢 1904
斣 1046

灬部

四至八画

杰 990
炁 1525
点 433
(為) 1989
1998
烈 1217
热 1611
(烏) 2015
2036
羔 646
烝 2443
焘 397
1869
焉 2200
烹 1458
煮 2507
(無) 1361
2018
舄 2059
焦 972
(爲) 1989
1998
然 1607

九画以上

蒸 2444
煦 2169
照 2425
煞 1666
1667
煎 943
熬 18
熙 2049
罴 1468
熏 2184
2190
熊 2155
(熱) 1611
熟 1767
1783
熹 2050
燕 2201
2216
(燾) 397
(羆) 1869

户部

户 823
(戹) 505
启 1515
⿸户及 903
戾 1191
肩 940
所 1843
房 549
戽 824
扁 116
1470
扃 1034
扅 2262
扆 2270
扇 1672
1674
扈 825
扉 560
雇 701
扊 2212

礻(示)部

一至四画

礼 1178
⿰礻几 892
祁 1508
礽 1626
社 1694
祀 1823
祃 1292
祆 2073
祎 2259
祉 2467
视 1759
祈 1511
祇 1511
(衹) 2465
祊 93

五画

祛 1589
祜 825
祏 1747
(祐) 2334
祓 597
祖 2566
神 1705
祝 2511
祚 2579
祔 613
祗 2458
祢 1330
(祕) 107
1332
祠 317

六画以上

祯 2437
祫 2061
祧 1900
祥 2093
祷 394
祸 885
祲 1016
祾 1231
祺 1512
(禇) 2406
祼 719
(禍) 885
禅 210
1675
禄 1261
禊 2060
禖 1316
福 600
禋 2289
禘 431
(禕) 2259
禛 2437
禚 2535
禩 1823
禤 2171
禧 2055
禫 383
(禪) 210
1675
(禨) 892
(禮) 1178
(禱) 394
(禰) 1330
禳 1608

心部

心 2126

一至四画

必 104
志 2471
忑 1875
忒 1875
1877
1947
忐 1860
(⿱台心) 1562
忘 1983
忌 918
忍 1622
态 1856
㤅 6
忠 2486
怂 1825
念 1413
忿 576
忽 816
忞 1349

五画

毖 107
思 1648
1815
怎 2400
怹 1857
(怱) 323
怨 2367
急 904
总 2555
怒 1427
怼 495
怠 372

六画

恝 931
恚 869
恐 1106
(恥) 264
恶 505
506
2018
2039
恧 1428
虑 1267
恩 509
恁 1401
1417
息 2046
恋 1202
恣 2553
恙 2225
恳 1100
恕 1789

七至八画

悫 1602
悬 2171
2172
患 848
悠 2317
您 1417
(悤) 323
悉 2046
悳 2312

(惡) 505
506
2018
2039
惎 922
惹 1611
(悳) 404
惠 870
惑 886
悲 78
惄 1408
崽 2386
惩 253
惫 87

九至十画

(惷) 313
(㥦) 1556
想 2094
感 631
愚 2341
愁 277
愆 1532
愈 2353
(愛) 6
意 2278
慈 318
愙 1099
愍 1350
慝 1877
(愨) 1602
愿 2368
慁 874
罳 1817
慇 2289
愬 1834
(慂) 2312
(態) 1856

十一画

慧 870
憃 270
(慤) 1602
(慙) 187
(慼) 1506
(憂) 2315
慭 2297
(慮) 1267
(憇) 1526
慜 1350
(慫) 1825
(慾) 2351
(慶) 1578
憋 131
憨 761
慰 2002

十二至十三画

憙 2050
(憖) 2297
憩 1526
(憊) 87
憝 495
(憑) 1489
(憲) 2083
懃 1562
懋 1312
(懇) 1100
(應) 2297
2305
懑 1324

十四画以上

(懕) 2199
(懟) 495
(懣) 1324
(懲) 253
(懸) 2171
懿 2281
(戀) 1202
戇 639
2527

聿(肀⺻)部

聿 2348
(書) 1777
肃 1831
隶 1191
(晝) 2498
(畫) 838
肆 1823
肄 2278
(肅) 1831
(肇) 2427
(盡) 1011
肇 2427
盡 2060

毋(母)部

毋 2027
毌 717
母 1372
每 1317
毐 5
毑 995
毑 1382
毒 476
贯 718
(緐) 534
毓 2353

示部

示 1751
佘 1693
奈 1386
柰 1387
(祘) 1835
祟 1840
票 1477
祭 921
2408
禁 1007
1016
禀 140
禜 94
(禦) 2352

石部

石 379
1736

二至四画

(矴) 461
矶 892
矸 628
矼 636
岩 2205
矻 1113
矽 2045
矾 533
矿 1126
砀 388
码 1291
砉 2161
831
研 2206
2214
砆 592
砖 2518
砗 233
砘 496
砒 1463
砌 1525
1555
砑 2198
砂 1665
(碙) 1393
泵 94
砚 2214
斫 2533
砭 113
砜 586
砍 1081
砄 1059

五画

砝 528
砹 6
砵 146
砢 1090
砸 2385
砺 1192
砻 1250
砰 1458
砧 2437
砷 1702
砟 2404
砼 1923
砥 419
砾 1192
(硇) 1393
(砲) 1451
砫 2512
砬 1139
砣 1961
砩 597
础 293
砮 1427
破 1493
硁 1101

六至七画

硎 2148
硅 731
硭 1304
硒 2046
硕 1811
硖 2061
硗 1548
砦 2408
硐 470
硙 1992
(磑) 2002
(硃) 2498
硚 1550
硇 1393
硊 735
(硔) 769
硌 657
1281
硋 7
硬 2307
(硤) 2061
(硜) 1101
硝 2103
(硶) 240
硪 2015
硷 947
确 1603
硫 1244
硠 1151

八画

碔 2035
碛 1525
(碁) 1512
碏 1604
(碕) 1511
碍 7
碘 435
碓 495
碑 79
𬒈 2478
硼 1459
碉 445
碎 1840
碚 87
碰 1460
䃅 413
碇 461
碗 1977
碌 1247
1261
碜 240

九画

碶 1525
碧 109
碡 2497
(碪) 2437
碟 451
碴 202
204
碱 949
碹 2406
(碭) 388
碣 995
碨 2002
硆 508
碳 1863
碫 488
磈 1130
碲 431
磋 338
磁 318
碹 2176
碥 117
(磂) 1349

十画

磕 1090
磊 1169
(磑) 1992
磐 1443
磎 2050
磔 2430
(碻) 1603
磙 737
磅 59
1446
磏 1199
1532
(確) 1603
碾 1412
磉 1658

十一画

磬 1579
磡 1082
磺 855
(磚) 2518
磳 192
(䃘) 1101
磜 1525
磨 1363
1370
(磙) 737
(磸) 2176
磦 1590
(磂) 1139
磟 1248
(磣) 240

十二画以上

(磽) 1548
磹 1860
磼 2418
(磾) 413
(礄) 1550
礁 973
磻 1443
礅 496
磷 1224
磴 410
(磯) 892
礞 1325
(礎) 293
礓 961
礌 1168
(礆) 947
礤 175
(礪) 1192
(礙) 7
(礦) 1126
礸 175
(礬) 533
(礧) 1168
(礩) 2478
(礫) 1192
(礮) 1451
礴 152

礳 1371
(礱) 1250
礵 1797

龙(龍)部

龙 1248
(龍) 1248
垅 1303
1324
垄 1251
(壟) 1251
龚 2208
(龔) 2208
(龑) 1250
砻 1250
(礱) 1250
聋 1250
(聾) 1250
龚 676
(龔) 676
龛 1080
(龕) 1080
袭 2052
(襲) 2052
詟 2430
(讋) 2430

业部

业 2238
邺 2240
凿 2394
凿 2470
(業) 2238
黻 601
(叢) 326
黼 605

目部

目 1376

二至四画

盯 453
盱 2161
盲 1303
相 2086
2097
眍 1108
盹 1337
1341
盹 496
省 1722
2148
眇 1343
看 1079
1081
眊 1310
盾 496
盼 2059
盼 1444
眨 2404
眈 378
(眲) 279
眉 1314

五至七画

眛 1368
(眎) 1759
眡 695
(眘) 1710
眬 1250
眝 1257
眚 1722
(眡) 1759
智 2354
眩 2175
眠 1335
眙 266
2262
眶 1127
眭 1837
眦 2553
(眥) 2553
脈 1368
眺 1904
眵 259
睁 2443
睆 274
眷 1056
眯 1328
1330
眼 2209
眸 1371
睐 1673
睐 1144
睄 1691
睅 768
(睏) 1132
睊 1057
睋 504
睎 2047
睑 947
睏 1644
睊 956
睇 431
睆 848
鼎 456
睃 1842

八画

睛 1023
睹 481
睦 1379
睖 1174
瞄 1342
睚 2196
(睞) 1144
睫 994
晰 2411
督 476
睡 1806
睨 1408
睢 1837
睥 1469
睬 181
睟 1840
(睠) 1056
(睒) 1673
睩 1261

九至十画

睿 1644
瞅 279
瞍 1828
睺 809
(瞇) 1328
1330
瞜 1252
暌 1129
瞀 1312
瞌 1091
瞒 1298
瞢 1325
瞋 235
瞤 1237
瞎 2060
瞑 1359

十一画以上

(瞞) 1298
(縣) 2080
(瞘) 1108
瞟 1476
瞖 2281
瞠 244
(瞜) 1252
瞥 1478
瞰 1083
瞫 1709
瞭 1216
(瞭) 1213
瞧 1550
瞬 1808
瞳 1925
瞵 1224
瞩 2508
瞪 410
瞽 697
矇 1326
(矇) 1324
瞿 1054
1590
(瞼) 947
瞻 2409
(矑) 1257
(矓) 1250
(矙) 1083
(矚) 2508

田部

田 1896
甲 931
申 1699
由 2318
电 435

二至三画

町 453
1913
甿 1088
奋 1136
甸 442
亩 1373
男 1387
畀 107
(甽) 2438
备 81
(甿) 1324
畏 894
甾 2385

四画

畊 662
畎 1600
畏 2001
毗 1466
(毘) 1466
胃 2001
禺 2339
畋 1897
畈 543
界 999
畇 2377
畂 638
畑 1897
思 1648
1815

五至六画

(畢) 105
畠 1897
畖 1964
(畛) 1947
畛 2438
留 1237
(畝) 1373
畜 295
2167
畔 1445
畚 92
畦 1511
畤 2476
(異) 2273
略 1272
(畧) 1272
累 1166
1168
1170

七画以上

畴 277
(畱) 1237
畲 1692
2340
畬 1692
番 529
1441
富 615
(畫) 838
畯 1067
畨 1860
畸 898
(當) 383
388
畹 1977
畿 899
(奮) 575
(暘) 1678
疃 1947
疈 1415
(壘) 1168
(疇) 277
罍 1168
(纍) 1166
1168
1170
(疊) 451

罒部

四 1820

三至八画

罗 1276
罘 597
罚 525
罡 638
罢 30
(罷) 31
罟 695
罝 1045
罛 689
(罰) 1246
罣 706
(買) 1293
罥 1057
罦 600
詈 1193
署 1785
置 2478
罭 2353
罨 2212
罪 2569
罩 2427
蜀 1785

九画以上

罴 1468
罱 1148
罳 1817
(罵) 1292
罶 1246
(罸) 525
(罷) 30
罽 1834
麗 1263
罹 1177
罻 2002
羁 900
罿 923
罾 270
罽 2402
羃 111
(羆) 1468
(羅) 1276
羇 1055

皿部

皿 1349

三至五画

盂 2337
盂 1327
(盃) 76
(盇) 789
盅 2488
盆 1457
盈 2301
盏 2410
盐 2206
盍 789
盎 146

监	941
	955
盎	17
盉	790
(盌)	1977
益	2277

六至九画

盔	1128
盛	252
	1724
蛊	695
盄	1550
盘	1441
盒	790
盗	397
盖	622
	655
(盞)	2410
盟	1325
(監)	941
	955
盨	2165
(盡)	1011

十画以上

(盤)	1441
盬	697
(盧)	1256
盥	719
盦	12
盩	2497
(盞)	1550
(盪)	389
盬	697
盭	1193
(蠱)	2060
蠲	1055
(鹽)	2206
(豔)	

钅(金)部

一至二画

钇	2269
钆	618
针	2433
钉	453
	457
钋	1491
钊	2420
钌	1214
	1215

三画

(釬)	768
釭	636
钍	1944
(釦)	1112
钎	1530
钏	304
钐	1672
	1674
钓	447
钒	533
钔	1323
钕	1428
钖	2221
钗	207

四画

钘	2148
铁	592
钙	622
钚	173
钛	1856
鈜	806
钜	1051
(鉅)	1049
钝	496
鈚	1463
钞	225
(鈔)	225
钟	2488
钡	85
钠	1385
钢	636
	639
𫓨	222
鈲	1469
钣	51
𫓯	323
钤	1533
钥	2234
	2372
钦	1556
钧	1066
钨	2018
钩	681
钪	1085
钫	547
钬	884
钭	1935
钮	1422
钯	29
(鈀)	1435

五画

钰	2349
钱	1536
钲	2443
钳	1537
钴	695
钵	146
𫓶	1789
钷	1492
钹	149
钺	2372
钻	2567
	2568
钼	1378
𫓧	291
	1049
钽	1861
钾	933
钿	443
	1897
铀	2323
铁	1907
铂	149
铃	1229
铄	1811
𫓹	2054
(鉤)	681
铅	1531
	2207
铆	1310
(鉋)	72
铈	1763
铉	2175
铊	1847
(鉈)	1961
铋	107
铌	1405
铍	1463
	1466
鏺	1492
铎	501
鉧	1374

六画

铏	2148
铐	1087
铑	1162
铒	514
鉷	807
铓	1304
铕	2332
铖	253
铗	931
(銕)	1907
铙	1393
铚	2476
铘	2236
铛	243
	386
铝	1265
铜	1923
铞	450
铟	2288
铠	1078
铡	2404
铢	2500
铣	2054
	2079
铥	461
铤	461
	1914
铦	2073
鋋	209
铧	833
(鉆)	2098
(鈲)	1469
铨	1599
铩	1666
铪	752
铫	450
	2228
铭	1358
铬	657
铮	2443
	2453
铯	1661
铰	975
铱	2260
铲	213
铳	274
铴	1864
铵	13
银	2289
铷	1636

七画

铸	2512
铹	1155
銶	1585
铺	1498
	1502
铻	2028
	2346
(鋏)	931
铼	1144
铽	1877
链	1202
铿	1101
销	2103
锁	1845
(銲)	768
锃	2402
锂	1182
锄	291
(鋜)	2536
锅	738
锆	649
锈	2160
锇	504
锉	340
锊	1272
锋	587
锌	2133
锍	1246
锎	1078
锏	947
	956
锐	1644
锑	1879
锒	1151
锓	1562
锔	1045
	1047
锕	2

八画

锖	1543
(錶)	128
(鋹)	222
锗	2431
錤	898
错	340
锘	1430
锚	1309
锳	2299
锛	89
锜	1512
(錸)	1144
(錢)	1536
锝	404
锞	1099
锟	1132
锡	2049
锢	701
锣	1278
(鋼)	636
	639
(鍋)	738
锤	309
锥	2529
锦	1010
(錍)	1463
锧	2479
锨	2073
锪	874
錞	495
	313
锫	1454
锩	1055
锬	1860
(鍁)	2073
锭	461
(錧)	716
鎯	1151
键	957
(録)	1259
锯	1052
(鋸)	1045
錣	2530
锰	1327
锱	2538

九画

锲	1556
鎝	344
(鍊)	1201
	1202
(鍼)	2433
锴	1078
(鍚)	2221
锶	1817
锷	508
锸	202
锹	1548
(鍾)	2488
锻	488
锼	1828
锽	855
𫔍	2085
(鎚)	309
锾	845
锵	1543
锿	4
镀	483
镁	1319
镂	1254
镃	2539
镄	566
镅	1316

十画

镊	1416
(鏵)	833
镆	1370
镇	2440
镈	151
镉	655
(鎒)	1426
𬭎	1269
镋	1868
(鎧)	1078
镌	1055
镍	1416
(鎢)	2018
镎	96
	1463
(鎩)	1666
镏	1382

(鎗)　1542
镏　1245
1248
镐　647
780
镑　59
镒　2280
(鎌)　1199
(鎋)　2062
镓　931
镔　135
镕　1631
(鍽)　1674

十一画

镨　2533
镄　855
(鏗)　1101
镖　128
(鏚)　1506
镗　1864
1866
(鏤)　1254
镘　1302
镚　95
(鏦)　323
镛　2310
镞　2564
(鏇)　2175
镜　1034
(鏟)　213
镝　414
416
镦　1478
(鏘)　1543
镠　1245
镙　1846

十二画

镢　988
(鐃)　1393
(鐋)　1141
镡　211
1860
2136
(鐝)　1063
镣　1216
镤　1500
(鐫)　1055
镥　1259
镦　495
496
(鐘)　2488
镧　1148
(鐥)　1674
镨　1502
(鐒)　1155
(鐊)　1864
镩　331
镪　1543
1547
镫　408
410
(鐙)　1492
镭　1062

十三画

(鐵)　1907
镬　887
镭　1168
镰　1054
(鐺)　243
386
(鐸)　501
镯　2536
镰　1199
镱　2281
(鏽)　2160

十四画

(鑄)　2512
(鑑)　957
(鑛)　1126
(鑌)　135
镲　205

十五画

以上

(鑢)　1269
(鑤)　72
(鑕)　2479
镳　128
(鑠)　1811
镴　1141
(鑪)　1257
(鑰)　2234
2372
镵　212
镶　2092
(鑷)　1416
(鑹)　331
(鑼)　1278
(鑽)　2567
2568
(鑾)　1868
镬　1063

矢部

矢　1748
矣　2269
知　2456
矩　1048
矧　1709
矫　973
976
短　484
矬　338
矮　5
雉　2479
(矯)　973
976
矰　2402
矱　2369

禾部

禾　781

二至三画

利　1189
秃　1937
秀　2159
私　1813
秆　629
和　785
791
817
875
884
(秈)　2073
(秊)　1409
秉　139
委　1986
1996
季　918

四画

秬　1051
秕　101
秒　1343
香　2089
种　271
2489
2492
秭　2541
(秔)　1024
秋　1581
(秌)　1581
科　1089

五画

秦　1560
秫　1368
秣　1783
秤　254
乘　252
1724
租　2562
积　894
秧　2217
盉　790
秩　2476
称　241
242
(称)　254
秘　107
1332

六至七画

秸　987
秵　1265
秽　870
秾　1872
(秵)　502
移　2262
秾　1425
(秔)　1024
嵇　898
稍　1688
1691
(稈)　629
程　253
稀　2047
黍　1785
稃　593
稆　1582
税　1805
稂　1151

八画

(稜)　1171
1231
稙　2459
稞　1090
稚　2479
稗　46
稔　1623
稠　277
颓　1950
颖　2304
稣　1829
(稟)　140
稽　59
穇　188

九至十画

(稬)　1430
(稭)　987
馝　109
(種)　2489
2492
(稱)　241
242
稳　2010
稨　117
稧　923
(穀)　692
(稹)　2438
稽　898
1520
稷　923
稻　401
黎　1177
稿　647
(稾)　647
稼　937

十一画以上

(積)　894
穑　1661
馞　152
穆　1380
穨　1950
穄　923
(穅)　1083
(穇)　188
穗　1840
黏　1411
穜　2490
2494
穟　1840
(穉)　2479
(穫)　885
(穡)　1661
(穢)　870
馥　617
(穠)　1425
(穤)　1430
(穩)　2010
(穭)　1265
穮　128
(龢)　785
黏　1873
穰　1608
(穐)　1582

白部

白　32

一至八画

百　39
(阜)　2396
皂　2396
皃　1310
帛　149
的　404
414
428
皇　850
皆　984
泉　1599
皈　731
皋　639
皛　1897
皊　1229
皑　5
皎　976
皕　108
皓　780
皖　1977
皙　2049

九画以上

魄　151
1496
1963
皝　856
(皚)　5
(皤)　1335
皞　780
(皜)　780
皠　333
皤　1492
皦　978
皭　983

瓜部

瓜　701
瓞　149
瓝　1964
罛　689
瓞　451
瓠　825
瓟　63
瓢　1476
瓣　55
瓤　1609

用部

用　2313
甩　1793
甪　1259
甫　601
甬　2311
甭　94
甯　590

鸟(鳥)部

鸟　446
1414
(鳥)　446

1414

二至四画

(鳬) 594
鸠 1035
鸡 892
鸢 2354
鸣 1357
(鳳) 589
鸤 1731
䴓 1732
鸥 1432
鸦 2193
鸧 190
鸨 69
鸩 2439
䴗 1059
鴃 1059

五画

莺 2299
鸪 689
鸫 465
鸬 1257
鸭 2194
鸮 2100
鸯 2217
鸰 1229
鸱 259
鸲 1590
鸳 2354
䳑 291
鴥 2349
䴍 447
鸵 1961
鸶 1816

六至七画

䳕 676
鸸 511
䴕 1218
鸷 2476
鵄 259
鸹 703
鸺 2159
鸻 798
鸼 2496
鸽 650
鸾 1269
䴔 972
鸿 807
(鶂) 2216
鹀 2028
鹁 150
䴊 155
鹂 1177
鹍 1144
鹃 1054
䴋 240
鹄 695
819
鹅 504
(鵞) 504
(鵝) 504
鹆 2352
鵟 1125
鹇 2077
鹈 1882

八画

鹉 2035
鶄 1023
(鴉) 2193
鹊 1604
鹋 1342
(鶤) 1144
(鶇) 465
鹌 12
鹓 2355
鵢 1833
鹍 1132
鵹 1177
鶃 2278
(鶂) 2278
鹎 79
鹏 1459
鵩 600
(鵰) 445
鹐 1532
鹑 313
鹒 662
鹓 2355
鹔 1833

九画

鹕 820
鶒 266
鶪 1047
鶗 1882
鹖 791
鹗 508
鹘 697
820
鹙 1582
鸑 2374
鹚 320
(鷀) 320
(鵾) 1132
鹛 1316
鹜 2040

十画

鷇 1112
鹞 2280
鹢 2216
鶶 1880
䳺 2234
(鷄) 892
(鶬) 190
鹟 2012
鹠 1245
(鶵) 291
鹡 910
鹞 2280
鹣 943
(鶯) 2299
鶱 2074
鹤 792

十一画以上

(鷙) 2476
(鷗) 1432
鹥 2260
鷞 1797
鹦 2300
鹧 2432
鷟 2535
鹨 1248
(鷊) 2216
鹩 1213
鹪 973
鷔 19
鷭 535
鹫 1043
(鷴) 2077
鹬 2354
(鷥) 1816
鹱 825
鹲 1325
鹭 1263
鹮 845
鹯 2410
鹰 2300
(鷫) 1833
䴙 1470
(鸎) 2299
(鸑) 2374
(鸕) 1257
鹳 720
鹴 1797
鸜 1591
(鸝) 1177
(鸞) 1269

疒部

二至四画

疔 454
疖 984
疗 1211
疠 1191
疟 1429
2231
疝 1674
疙 649
疚 1040
疡 2221
疬 1192
疣 2323
疥 1000
疭 2559
疮 304
疷 1511
(疬) 2040
疯 586
疫 2277
疢 241
疤 25

五画

症 2443
2453
疳 629
疴 1090
病 142
痁 1672
疸 367
379
疽 1045
疾 906
痄 2406
疹 2438
痈 2310
疼 1877
疱 1452
疰 2512
痃 2171
(疿) 566
痂 927
疲 1466
痉 1031

六至七画

痔 2476
痖 2196
痏 1997
痍 2263
疵 315
(痌) 1914
痊 1599
痎 987
痒 2225
痕 796
痣 2477
痨 1156
痡 593
痦 2040
痘 475
痞 1468
(痙) 1031
痟 2355
痢 1193
痗 1319
痤 339
痪 848
痫 2077
痧 1666
痾 503
痛 1927
(痠) 1834

八画

瘏 1941
(瘂) 2196
瘄 330
痳 1287
瘃 2503
痱 566
痹 108
痼 701
痴 259
痿 1997
瘐 2346
(痺) 108
瘁 334
瘖 1452
(瘀) 2335
瘅 378
382
癌 5
痰 1860
痯 716
瘆 1711

九至十画

瘛 266
2479
瘩 345
瘌 1140
瘗 2280
(瘧) 2231
1429
(瘍) 2221
瘟 2004
瘦 1776
瘊 809
(瘉) 2353
(瘖) 2288
瘥 209
339
瘘 1254
瘕 935
瘙 1660
瘪 267
瘼 1370
(瘞) 2280
(瘯) 208
瘝 715
瘪 131
133
瘜 2050
瘢 49
(瘡) 304
瘤 1245
瘠 910
瘫 1858

十一至十三画

癀 855
瘭 128
(瘻) 1254
瘰 1280
瘿 2305
(瘲) 2559
瘵 2408
瘴 2420
(瘺) 1254
癃 1251
瘾 2295
瘸 1602
瘳 276
(瘮) 1711
瘢 49
(癘) 1191
(療) 1211
(癉) 378
382
癌 5
(癆) 1156
(癇) 2077
癞 1141
1145
癗 1169
(癤) 984
癙 1787
(癒) 2353
癔 2281
癜 444
癖 1469

十四画以上

(癟) 133
131
癣 2175

(癡) 259
(癢) 2225
癗 1169
(癥) 2443
癫 432
(癧) 1192
(癮) 2295
癯 1591
(癰) 2310
(癱) 1858

立部

立 1186

一画

产 212

三至六画

妾 1555
亲 1557
　1579
竑 806
竖 1789
彦 2214
飒 1648
站 2414
竞 1031
(竝) 141
(竚) 2508
章 2416
竟 1032
(産) 212
翊 2278
翌 2278

七画以上

竦 1826
童 1924
(竢) 1823
竣 1067
靖 1033
(竪) 1789
意 2278
竭 995
端 483
赣 635
(競) 1031
贛 635

穴部

穴 2176

一至六画

穵 1964
究 1035
穷 1579
空 1101
　1106
帘 1197
穸 2045
穹 1580
(穽) 1028
突 1937
窀 2530
窃 1555
穿 297
窆 116
窍 1552
窅 2231
窄 2407
窊 1964
容 1629
窌 981
窎 447
窈 2231
窒 2477
窑 2228
窕 1904
(窓) 304

七画以上

窦 475
窜 332
窝 2013
(窓) 304
窖 983
窗 304
窘 1035
窥 1128
窦 475
窠 1090
(窩) 2013
窣 1829
窟 1114
窬 2342
窨 2185
　2297
窭 1054
(窪) 1964
(藭) 1580
窳 2346
(窯) 2228
(窰) 2228
(窶) 304
(窻) 332
窸 2050
窿 1251
窾 1123
(竄) 332
(竅) 1552
(竇) 475
(竈) 2396
(竊) 1555

衤部

二至五画

补 153
初 288
衬 240
衫 1672
衩 205
　206
袆 858
衲 1385
衽 1625
袄 19
衿 1007
(衹) 2465
袂 1319
袜 1966
袪 1589
袒 1861
袖 2160
袗 2438
袍 1449
袢 1445
被 85
袯 149
袎 2234

六至八画

袺 994
袴 1116
裆 386
(裀) 2285
袱 613
(袵) 1625
袷 1526
(袷) 931
袼 650
裈 1132
裉 1100
(補) 153
裋 1790
裲 1209
(裌) 931
裢 1199
裎 254
(裡) 1179
裣 1201
裕 2353
裤 1116
裥 947
裙 1604
裱 898
裱 130
褂 706
褚 294
　2508
(裲) 1209
(裞) 1100
裸 1280
(裩) 1132
裼 1887
　2049
裨 108
　1467
裯 278
禅 378
裾 1046
裰 500

九至十画

褡 344
褙 87
褐 792
褃 1131
(複) 609
褓 69
褕 2342
褛 1266
褊 117
褪 1953
　1954
(褘) 858
褥 1641
褴 1147
褟 1848
褫 264
褯 1002
(褵) 1177
褦 1387

十一画以上

褾 130
(褸) 1266
褶 2431
襆 2122
襥 601
(襌) 378
(襍) 2383
(襖) 19
襕 1148
襁 1547
(襏) 149
襟 1007
(襠) 386
(襝) 1201
襜 209
(襪) 1966
(襤) 1147
襦 1637
襫 1764
襮 152
(襬) 42
(襯) 240
襳 373
襶 1609
(襵) 2431
襻 1445

疋(⺪)部

疋 2196
(疋) 1468
胥 2162
疍 380
蛋 382
(疎) 1781
疏 1781
楚 294
疐 2479
疑 2265

皮部

皮 1464
皯 152
皱 2498
(皰) 1452
颇 1492
皲 1066
(皶) 1392
皴 335
皵 109
(皺) 2498
(皻) 2403

矛部

矛 1308
柔 1632
矜 715
　1007
　1560
(務) 2036
矟 1811
矞 2353
(矡) 1560
蟊 1309

耒部

耒 1168
耔 2541
耕 662
耘 2377
耖 231
耗 779
耙 29
　1435
耜 1823
耠 874
耢 1164
(耡) 291
耥 1864
耦 1433
耧 1253
耩 963
耨 1426
耪 1447
(耬) 1253
(耮) 1164
耰 2317
(耲) 29
(耪) 128
耱 842
耱 1371

老部

老 1156
考 1085
耇 683
耆 1511
耄 1311
(耉) 683
耋 451

耳部

耳 512

二画

耵 454
耶 2235
　2236
取 1591

三画

耷 342
闻 2009

四画

耻 264
(聃) 378
耸 1825
耿 662
耽 378
(恥) 264
(聊) 2559

聂 1416

五至十画

聋 2167
聋 1250
聃 378
职 2463
聆 1230
聊 1212
聍 1418
聒 738
联 1197
(聖) 1722
聘 1482
(聝) 744
聚 1053
聩 1131
聪 323
聱 19

十一画以上

(聲) 1719
(聰) 323
(聳) 1825
(聯) 1197
(聶) 1416
(職) 2463
(聼) 1910
(聹) 1418
(聽) 1910
(聾) 1250

臣部

臣 235
卧 2014
(臥) 2014
臧 2392
(臨) 1221

西(覀)部

西 2041
覀要 2226
2232
栗 1192
贾 695
932
覂 589
票 1477
覃 1560
1860
粟 1833
覅 590
覆 617
(覇) 30
(覈) 789
(覊) 900

页(頁)部

页 2240
(頁) 2240

二至三画

顶 454
顷 1577
顸 760
项 2096
顺 1806
须 2161

四画

顼 2162
顽 1974
(顽) 1973
顾 700
顿 479
497
颀 1511
颁 48
颂 1827
颃 772
烦 533
预 2349

五至七画

硕 1811
颅 1258
颇 415
领 1233
颇 1492
颈 663
1028
颉 994
2122
颊 931
颉 2270
颋 1914
颌 654
790
颎 604
颀 1997
颕 2304
颊 1035
颏 1090
1092
颈 508
颐 2265
(頭) 1929
(頰) 931
(頸) 1028
663
频 1480
(頯) 240
颓 1950
颔 768
颖 2304

八至九画

颙 1507
颗 1090
颔 334
颇 1081
题 1882
颙 2311
(顋) 1648
颚 508
颛 2518
颜 2207
额 505

十至十二画

颞 1416
颟 1297
颠 432
(願) 2368
(顗) 2270
(類) 1170
颡 1658
(顢) 1297
颢 331
(顣) 2136
颢 780
嚣 19
(囂) 19
2104
颤 1550
颥 1171
(顧) 700

十三画以上

颤 214
2414
颦 1637
(顯) 2077
颦 1480
(顱) 1258
颧 1600
(顳) 1416

虍部

虎 821
824
(虎) 822
虏 1258
虐 1429
虒 1816
虓 2100
虔 1536
虑 1267
虚 2162
彪 128
(處) 292
294
(處) 292
294
虞 1052
虞 2341
(號) 772
777
(虜) 1258
(戲) 2055
815
觑 1590
1594
(膚) 592
(慮) 1267
虢 744
虤 75
(覷) 2403
(盧) 1256
(戲) 2055
815
(虧) 1127
虩 2060
(覷) 1590
1594
(覰) 1590
1594

虫部

虫 270

一至三画

虬 1584
虮 911
(虯) 1584
虱 1731
虹 806
964
虾 753
2060
虺 857
864
虿 209
虽 1836
虼 657
虻 1324
闽 1349
蚁 2269
(虵) 1693
蚤 2395
虷 2541
蚂 1285
1292

四画

蚌 58
95
蚨 597
蚕 186
(蚘) 864
蚍 1466
蚜 2196
(蚋) 1607
蚺 2494
蚋 1644
蚬 2079
蚝 772
蚧 1000
蚡 573
蚣 675
蚊 2009
蚄 547
蚪 473
蚓 2293
蚩 259

五画

蚶 760
萤 2302
蛄 689
695
蛱 994
蛎 1193
蛛 465
蛆 1589
蚰 2323
蚺 1607
蛊 695
蚱 2406
蚯 1582
蛉 1230
蛀 2512
蛇 2076
蛇 1693
2262
蛋 382
蛁 445
蛏 243
蚴 2334

六画

蛙 1964
蛄 1507
蛩 1580
蛰 677
(蛕) 864
蛱 931
蛰 2430
蛲 1393
蛭 2477
蛳 1817
蛸 386
蛐 1590
蛔 864
蛛 2501
蜓 1913
蛞 1134
蜒 2207
蛔 2094
蛤 654
753
蛸 614
蛮 1297
蛴 1512
蛟 972
蛘 2222
蛇 2406
蛑 1371

七画

蛐 994
(蜹) 1644
蜗 1209
蜃 1711
(蛺) 931
蜇 2427
2430
蛸 1688
2104
蜈 2028
蜎 2355
蜗 2014
蜀 1785
蜊 1177
蛾 504
2270
蜍 292
蜉 600
蜂 587
蛛 1543
蜕 1953
(蜋) 1151
蛹 2312

八画

蜯 59
蜻 1574
蜞 1512
蜡 1140
2406

蜥 2049
(蝀) 465
蜮 2353
(蜽) 1209
(蜨) 451
蜚 560
562
蜾 746
蝈 738
蜴 2280
蝇 2303
蝄 1983
(蝸) 2014
蜘 2459
蜺 1405
(蜺) 1405
蝂 51
蜱 1467
蜩 1903
蜷 1599
蝉 211
蜿 1972
蜜 1335
螂 1151
(蝃) 431
蜢 1327

九画

蝽 312
蝶 451
䗖 431
蝾 1631
蝴 820
蝻 1392
蝘 2213
蝲 1141
蝠 601
(蝡) 1637
蝰 1129
(蝨) 1731
蝎 2119
(蝟) 2002
蝌 1091
蝮 617
螋 1828
蟘 1877
蝗 855
蝓 2342
螹 961
(蝱) 1324
蝣 2325
蝼 1253
蝤 1586
2325
蝙 115
(蝦) 753
2060
蝥 1309

十画

螓 1561
螯 19
螚 1408
螨 1300
(蟇) 1287
蟒 1305
蟆 1287
(螙) 483
融 1631
螈 2365
(螘) 2269
螑 2159
螅 2050
(螄) 1817
螣 1878
(螣) 1877
螭 260
螗 1866
螃 1446
螠 2281
(螢) 2302
螟 1359

十一画

螫 1764
(蟄) 2430
蟥 855
(蟎) 1300
(螮) 431
蟏 2104
螬 192
螵 1476
蟚 1507
螳 1867
(螻) 1253
螺 1279
(蟈) 738
蟋 2050
螽 2489
蟅 2432
蟑 2417
蟀 1794
螾 2295
螲 2479
452
蟁 2009
(螹) 961
蟊 1309

十二画

(蟯) 1393
蟢 2055
蟛 1460
(蠆) 209
蟪 870
蟫 2291
(蟲) 270
(蟬) 211
蟠 1443
蟮 1676
(蟣) 911

十三画

(蟶) 243
蠖 887
蠓 1327
蟿 1526
(蟷) 386
(蠍) 2119
(蠅) 2303
蠋 2503
(蠘) 994
蟾 211
蟹 2126
(蠏) 2126
蠊 1200
蠃 1280
(蟻) 2269

十四画

蠚 780
蠛 1345
(蠣) 1193
蠕 1637
(蠔) 772
(蠐) 1512
(蠑) 1631
(蠙) 1479

十五画以上

蠢 313
蠡 1178
1183
(蠟) 1140
(蠠) 1408
(蠧) 483
(蠨) 2104
(蠭) 587
(蠱) 695
蠹 483
(蠶) 186
蠷 1591
蠵 2051
(蠻) 1297
蠼 1591

缶部

缶 591
缸 638
缺 1601
(缽) 146
䍃 2407
缿 2098
(缾) 1490
罂 2299
罄 1579
罅 2069
(罆) 720
(罈) 1858
(罇) 2571
(罋) 2012
罍 1168
(罏) 1256
(罎) 1858
罐 720

舌部

舌 1692
乱 1270
舍 1693
1696
舐 1763
甜 1897
鸹 703
舒 1780
辞 317
舔 1899
(舖) 1502
(舘) 715

竹(⺮)部

竹 2501

二至四画

竺 2502
竿 629
竽 2339
笈 904
(笆) 262
笃 480
笄 895
笕 944
笔 101
笑 2115
笊 2425
笫 2541
笏 825
笋 1841
笆 25

五画

笺 943
笻 1580
笨 93
笴 630
笸 1492
笼 1250
1252
笪 345
笛 415
笙 1721
笮 2399
2572
符 599
笭 1230
笯 1416
笱 683
笤 276
笠 1193
笥 1823
筤 1349
第 429
笤 1903
笳 930
笾 113
笞 259

六画

筐 1124
筀 735
等 408
筹 1087
筶 1163
筑 2513
策 197
筴 930
197
筘 1112
筚 108
筛 1667
筜 386
筒 1927
筥 1049
筅 2079
筈 1134
筏 525
筵 2207
筌 1599
答 343
345
筋 1007
(筍) 1841
筝 2444
筊 978
(筆) 101

七画

筹 278
筭 1835
筼 1252
筠 1066
2377
篣 1156
筮 1764
筻 639
(筴) 197
930
䈇 2430
筢 1435
筲 1688
(筯) 2513
筫 2377
筱 2114
(筰) 2572
签 1532
简 947
筷 1121
筦 716
(筞) 197
(節) 984
989
(筩) 1927

八画

箐 1579
箦 2399
箧 1556
箸 2513
箕 898
箬 1646
箴 2374
箣 197
箑 1667
(箝) 1537
箍 689
箨 1963
(箋) 943
(箎) 262
算 1835
箅 109
(箇) 655
箩 1279
箠 310
箄 79
1440
箙 601
箥 566
箪 378
箔 151
管 716
箜 1105
箢 2355

箫 2104
箓 1263
(箒) 2497
篨 1330
篸 188
2390

九画

(篋) 1556
(箑) 2240
葙 2092
(範) 543
箴 2437
箵 2142
篢 1131
箮 1817
篙 302
箯 115
篁 855
篌 809
(箷) 2265
篓 1254
箭 958
(篨) 2079
篇 1472
篠 292
篆 2522

十画

篝 682
篚 562
(築) 2513
篥 1193
篮 1147
篡 332
(篳) 108
篷 2397
(篠) 2114
(篩) 1667
篦 109
篪 262
篷 1459
(篛) 276
(篸) 1842
篙 646
篱 1177
篰 174
(篘) 1646

十一画

(簪) 869
簕 1166
簧 855
簌 1834
篹 2523
2567
(簍) 1254
篾 1345
(簻) 2514
簃 2266
篼 471
簏 1263
簇 331
簖 488
(簰) 1440
(簆) 1112
簋 734
(篸) 188
2390

十二至十三画

(簿) 149
簠 605
簟 444
簝 1213
簪 2390
(簞) 378
簰 1440
簡 1148
(簩) 1156
簨 1841
簦 408
簸 152
(簹) 2374
簵 1145
籀 2498
(簾) 1052
(簹) 386
(簽) 1532
(簷) 2208
(簾) 1197
簿 174
(簫) 2104

十四画以上

籍 910
(籌) 278
(籃) 1147
(籋) 1416
纂 2567
籑 2523
2567
(籐) 1878
(籔) 566
籓 111
(籜) 1963
籧 1591
(籙) 2304
(籠) 1250
1252
籯 2304
(籑) 2523
(籥) 2374
(籢) 1193
(籤) 1532
(籟) 1330
(籩) 113
(籬) 1177
(籪) 488
(籮) 1279
籰 2374
(籯) 2304
(籲) 2348

臼部

臼 1040
臾 2337
兒 1404
(兒) 509
舁 2339
臿 199
舀 2231
舂 270
舄 2059
(與) 2336
2342
2346
舅 1043
興 2342
(舉) 1048
(舊) 1038

自部

自 2543
臬 1416
臭 280
2160
息 2046
(皋) 639
(臯) 2569
臲 1416

血部

血 2123
2181
(卹) 2181
(衂) 1428
衃 1452
衄 1428
衅 2139
(衆) 2491
(衇) 1296
(衊) 1345
衋 2060

舟部

舟 2494
舡 302
舢 1672
舣 2269
舭 103
舰 956
舨 51
(舩) 302
舱 190
般 47
146
1441
(般) 48
航 771
舫 551
舸 655
舻 1251
舮 1258
舳 2503
盘 1441
舴 2399
舶 149
舲 1230
船 302
鸼 2496
舷 2077
舵 502
舨 1467
舾 2048
艇 345
艇 1914
艄 1688
艅 2341
艉 1997
(艎) 2425
艋 1327
艓 451
艘 1828
艎 855
(盤) 1441
艖 202
艏 1773
艑 123
艒 1850
(艙) 190
艕 59
艚 192
(艖) 345
(艗) 1850
艟 270
艨 1326
(艢) 1546
(艣) 1258
(艤) 2269
(艦) 956
(艪) 1258
(艫) 1258
(艭) 1251

衣部

衣 2257
2273

二至六画

表 128
哀 3
衰 332
1792
衷 2488
衾 1559
袅 1415
衰 2270
袭 2052
袤 2476
袋 373
袈 930
袤 1311
裁 178
裂 1216
1218
亵 2124
裒 1497
装 2524

七画以上

裘 1586
(裏) 1179
裔 2278
裟 1666
(裝) 2524
裴 1454
裳 221
1687
裹 746
(製) 2472
(褎) 2161
褒 2161
褒 63
(褧) 1035
褰 1532
(褻) 2124
襄 2092
(褒) 63
襞 111
(襲) 2052

羊(⺶⺷)部

羊 2218

一至六画

羌 1541
差 199
206
208
209
315
美 1317
养 2332
养 2223
姜 960
羖 695
羔 646
恙 2225
羞 2158
羘 2392
(羖) 695
着 2422
2423
2432
2534
盖 622
655
羚 1230
羝 412
羟 1547
(羢) 1629
羡 2084
善 1674
翔 2093

七画以上

(羥) 1547
(義) 2270
(羨) 2084
群 1604
(羣) 1604
羧 1842
羞 2404
(養) 2223
羯 995
羰 1864
羱 2365
羲 2050
羴 1672
(羶) 1672
羸 1168
羹 662

米部

米 1331

二至六画

籴 414
类 1170
籼 2073
(粈) 1704
屎 1750
娄 1252
籹 1428
籽 2541
粔 1051
(粃) 101
粯 2083
敉 1332
粉 573
料 1215
粑 25
粝 1193
粘 1411
2409
粗 327
粜 1904
粕 1496
粒 1193
粪 576
粞 2048
粟 1833
(粬) 1586
粤 2374
(粧) 2523
粢 315
2538
粥 2353
2496

七至十画

粳 1024
粲 188
粱 1205
粮 1205
精 1024
粼 1224
粹 334
粽 2559
糁 1656
1704
糊 817
820
825
糌 205
糇 809
(糉) 2559
糈 2390
糍 320
糈 2166
糅 1633
糒 87
糙 191
糗 1586
糖 1866
糕 646

十一画以上

糟 2393
(糞) 576
糜 1317
1330
糠 1083
(糡) 965
(糝) 1656
1704
(糲) 1193
(糧) 1205
糨 965
糵 1171
(糷) 1193
糯 1430
(糰) 1945
(糱) 1417
(糴) 414
鬻 2354
(糶) 1904

艮(艮)部

艮 660
661
良 1203
即 903
艰 941
垦 1100
既 920
恳 1100
暨 923
(艱) 941
鬙 923

羽部

羽 2343

三至八画

羿 2277
翅 266
(翄) 266
翃 807
(翝) 807
翀 270
翁 2012
扇 1672
1674
(習) 2051
翎 1230
翊 2278
翌 2278
翘 1550
1552
翙 870
翕 2048
翔 2093
翚 858
翛 2104
翥 2513
翡 562
翟 416
2407
翠 334

九画以上

(翫) 1974
翦 950
翩 1472
翰 769
翮 791
翱 19
翯 792
翳 2281
翼 2281
(翹) 1550
1552
(翶) 19
翻 530
(翽) 870
翾 2171

糸部

一画

系 918
2056

四至七画

素 1831
索 1844
(紮) 2383
2402
紧 1008
紊 2010
萦 2303
(紥) 2383
2402
累 1166
1168
1170
絫 373
絜 994
2122
綮 2464
紫 2541
絮 2168

八画以上

綦 1512
(緊) 1008
(緐) 534
縈 1520
1578
(緜) 1335
縠 821
(縣) 2080
(繄) 1443
縢 1878
(縈) 2303
(縶) 2464
繄 2260
繁 534
1492
繇 2230
2325
2498
縻 1330
纇 1171
(縈) 1644
(繫) 918
2056
纂 2567
(纍) 1166
1168
纛 401

麦(麥)部

麦 1294
(麥) 1294
麸 592
(麪) 1338
麹 231
(麯) 1586
麰 1371
(麩) 592
嬃 1590
(麵) 1338
(麴) 231

走部

走 2559

二至五画

赴 609
赵 2425
赳 1036
赶 629
赸 1674
起 1516
越 2373
趄 1045
1556
趁 241
(趂) 241
趋 1589
超 225

六画以上

趔 1219
趑 2538
(趙) 2425
(趕) 629
趣 1594
趟 1864
1869
(趦) 2538
(趨) 1589
趯 1887
趱 2390

赤部

赤 265
郝 777
赦 1697
赧 1392
(赧) 1392
赪 243
赩 2060
赫 792
(赬) 243
赭 2431
赯 1867

豆部

豆 473
剅 1252
豇 960
(豈) 1514
豉 264
壹 2260
短 484
登 407
踖 209
(豎) 1789
豌 1972
(頭) 1929
(豐) 577
(豔) 2214
(豓) 2214

酉部

酉 2332

二至五画

酊 454
456
酋 1584
酐 629
酎 2498
酌 2534
酒 1037
配 1454
酏 2269
酝 2381
酞 1856
酕 1309
酗 2167
酚 573
酡 1543
酘 475
(酖) 2439
酣 760
酤 689
酢 330
2580
酥 1829
酡 1961
酦 524
1492

六至七画

酮 1925
酰 2073
酯 2470
酩 1359
酪 1164
酱 964
酬 277
(酧) 277
酴 1425
酵 983
酽 2216
酺 1500
酾 1668
1733
酲 254
酷 1116
酶 1316
酴 1941
酹 1170
酿 1414
酸 1834

八至十画

醋 330
(醃) 2201

醌 1132
醄 1872
醇 313
醉 2570
醅 1452
醁 1263
醊 2530
醛 1600
醐 821
醍 1883
(醞) 2381
醒 2149
(醜) 279
醚 1330
醑 2166
醢 759
(䤚) 1543
醨 1177
(醣) 1866
醡 2406

十一画以上

(醫) 2258
(醬) 964
醪 1156
醰 1860
醭 153
醮 983
醯 2051
(醱) 524
1492
醵 1054
醴 1182
(醲) 1425
(醻) 277
醺 2185
(醼) 2216
醽 1232
(釀) 1414
醾 1331
(醿) 1331
(釃) 1668
(釅) 2216
(釁) 1733
(釄) 1331

辰部

辰 236
辱 1639
唇 312
晨 240
(脣) 312
蜃 1711
(農) 1422
(辳) 1422

豕部

豕 1748
豗 858
家 927
1002
(豘) 1954
象 2097
豝 26
(豛) 475
豢 848
豨 2049
豪 773
(豬) 2500
豵 2559
豫 2354
豮 573
豳 135
豯 2079

卤(鹵)部

卤 1258
(鹵) 1258
⿰卤亢 638
(⿰鹵亢) 638
(鹹) 2076
鹾 339
(鹺) 339
(鹻) 949
(鹼) 947

里部

里 1179
厘 1175
重 271
2492
野 2237
量 1205
1210
童 1924
(釐) 1175
2055

足(⻊)部

足 2563

二至四画

趴 1434
趸 496
趵 73
146
趿 1847
趼 945
趺 593
跂 1511
1525
距 1052
趾 2470
跃 2373
趻 240
跄 1543
1548
(跀) 2372

五画

践 956
跖 2464
跋 27
跕 450
(跕) 435
跌 450
跗 593
跅 1963
⿰𧾷氐 2459
跞 1193
1283
跔 1045
跚 1672
跑 1449
跎 1961
跏 930
跛 152

六画

跬 1130
跫 1580
(跴) 181
跨 1118
跶 367
跷 1548
跸 108
跐 315
320
跩 2515
跣 2079
跹 2073
⿰𧾷乔 1548
(⿰𧾷乔) 1057
跲 931
跳 1904
跺 502
(跥) 502
跪 735
路 1261
(跢) 502
跻 898
跤 973
(跡) 919
跰 1473
跟 659

七至八画

踌 278
踅 2179
踉 1205
1211
踊 1047
踞 923
踊 2313
踆 335
踖 910
踦 2270
踅 2391
(踐) 956
(踂) 566
踧 330
踔 314
(踹) 1864
踝 841
踢 1879
踏 1848
1849
踟 262
踒 2014
踬 2479
踩 181
踮 435
踣 151
踯 2464
(踡) 1599
(踫) 1460
踪 2555
踺 958
踞 1054

九至十画

踳 303
踸 240
蹀 451
蹅 205
(踁) 1966
踶 431
踹 297
⿰𧾷拜 32
踵 2490
踽 1049
(踰) 2340
2342
蹡 1543
1548
踱 501
蹄 1883
蹉 338
蹁 1473
(踴) 2313
蹂 1633
蹑 1416
蹒 1443
蹎 432
(蹕) 108
蹋 1850
(蹏) 1883
蹈 394
蹊 1507
2050
(蹌) 1543
1548
蹓 1237
1248
蹐 910
蹇 950
蹍 1413

十一画

(蹟) 919
躇 292
(蹣) 1443
蹙 331
蹚 1864
蹦 95
(蹤) 2555
蹠 2464
蹢 416
2465
(蹝) 1793
蹩 133
蹜 1834
(蹡) 1543
1548

十二画

(蹺) 1548
(躂) 367
(躉) 496
蹰 292
蹶 1062
1063
(蹷) 1062
蹽 1211
蹼 1502
(蹻) 1548
蹯 535
蹴 331
1043
(蹵) 331
蹾 496
蹲 337
496
蹭 199
蹿 331
蹬 408
411

十三画以上

躁 2397
躅 2503
躈 1553
躄 111
躃 111
(躊) 278
躏 1226
(躋) 898
(躑) 2464
(躍) 2373
(躚) 2073
(躒) 1193
1283
(躓) 2479
(躗) 2002
(躕) 292
躔 212
躐 1219
躜 2567
躞 2126
(躡) 1416
(躥) 331
(⿰𧾷屬) 2503

身部

身 1700
射 1696
躬 676
躯 1589
(躭) 378
(躰) 1883
(躳) 676
躲 501
(躱) 501
躺 1868
(躶) 1280
(⿰身叚) 752
(軀) 1589
(軃) 501

釆部

悉 2046
番 529
1441
釉 2334
释 1763

(釋) 1763
飜 532

谷部

谷 691
2348
(卻) 1602
郤 2059
欲 2351
鹆 2352
谿 2051
豀 2051
豁 835
875
886

豸部

豸 2472
豺 208
豹 73
貂 445
貆 845
貊 1368
貅 2159
貉 773
791
(貈) 1368
貌 1312
(貓) 1305
1309
(⿰豸契) 2198
(貐) 2346
貘 1371
貔 1468
(貛) 843

角部

角 973
1058
(觔) 1002
1007
斛 819
觖 1062
觞 1678
觚 689
(觝) 419
觜 2538
2568
觥 676
触 295
(觧) 995
1002
解 995
1002
2125
觫 1834
觭 899
觯 2479
觱 109
觳 821
(觴) 1678
(觶) 2479
(觸) 295
觿 2266
觱 109
觹 2051

言部

言 2203
訇 801
訄 1584
訚 2289
(這) 2431
詟 2430
詈 1193
訾 2538
2542
詹 2409
詧 204
誊 1878
誉 2353
誓 1764
霅 2406
諐 1532
謷 19
讆 2002
(謄) 1878
謇 950
謦 1578
警 1029
(譽) 2353
譻 2300
2309
譬 1470
(讏) 2002
(讐) 276
279
(讋) 2430

辛部

辛 2132
辜 689
辞 317
(辠) 2569
辟 108
1463
1469
辣 1140
(辤) 317
辨 123
辩 123
(辦) 51
辫 124
瓣 55
(辭) 317
(辮) 124
(辯) 123

青部

青 1562
靓 1032
1210
䴖 1023
靖 1033
静 1033
靛 444

其部

其 894
1509
甚 1710
(甚) 1704
基 895
(棊) 1512
(朞) 898
斯 1816
期 898
1506
欺 1506
(碁) 1512
(尠) 2079
⿰其页 1507
綦 1512

雨(⻗)部

雨 2344
2348

三至七画

雩 2339
雪 2179
(雲) 2375
雳 1193
雰 573
雯 2009
雱 1445
(電) 435
雷 1167
零 1231
雾 2040
雹 63
需 2164
霆 1913
霁 922
震 2440
霄 2104
霉 1316
霅 2406
霂 1380
霈 1456

八至十二画

霙 2300
霖 1224
霏 560
霓 1405
霍 886
霎 1667
(霑) 2408
霜 1797
霡 1297
霞 2062
(霛) 1226
(霢) 1297
(霤) 1248
(霶) 1445
(霧) 2040
霪 2291
霭 5
霨 2002
霫 2053
霰 2085

十三画以上

霸 30
露 1255
1263
(霶) 1445
霹 1464
霾 1293
(霽) 922
(靆) 373
(靂) 1193
(靈) 1226
(靉) 7

齿(齒)部

齿 263
(齒) 263
龀 241
啮 1416
龁 790
龂 2290
⿰齿介 2124
⿰齿巴 30
⿰齿可 1526
(⿰齒可) 1099
龃 1049
(齚) 2399
龄 1232
(齣) 281
龅 63
龆 1903
(齧) 1416
龇 2538
(齩) 2230
龈 2291
(齦) 1100
龉 2346
龊 314
齰 2399
齮 2270
齯 1405
齲 1593
龌 2015
(⿰齒堯) 2230
齼 294

黾(黽)部

黾 1337
1349
(黽) 1337
1349
鼋 2364
(黿) 2364
(鼂) 228
(鼃) 1964
(鼄) 2396
(鼇) 19
(鼈) 131
鼍 1961
(鼉) 1961

隹部

隹 2527

二至六画

隼 1841
隽 1056
(雋) 1067
难 1390
1392
(隻) 2455
雀 1548
1551
1602
售 1776
集 907
雁 2215
雄 2154
雅 2194
2197
(雋) 1056
焦 972
雇 701
睢 1046
雉 2479
雊 685
雏 292
雍 2310
雌 319
雒 1284
翟 416
2407

八画以上

雕 445
(雖) 1836
瞿 1054
1590
(雙) 1795
(雞) 892
(雛) 292
(雜) 2383
(離) 1175
雠 279
雝 2311
(難) 1390
1392
(讎) 276
279

金部

金 1003
崟 2289
蓥 2303
鉴 957
銎 1581
銮 1269
鋆 2377
鋬 1445
鋈 2040
錾 2391
(鍫) 1548
鍪 1372
鏊 20
(鎣) 2303
鎏 1245
鏖 19
鐾 87
(鑒) 957
鑫 2136
(鑾) 1269

(鑿) 2394

鱼(魚)部

鱼 2338
(魚) 2338

二至七画

鱽 391
魟 807
鲄 2167
魢 912
鱿 2323
鲀 1954
鲁 1258
鲂 550
鲃 26
鲅 30
鲆 1491
鲇 1411
鲈 1258
鲉 2325
鲊 2404
稣 1829
鲋 616
鲌 151
(鮁) 30
鮣 2297
鮈 1046
鲍 74
(鮌) 737
鲎 815
鮄 600
鲏 1467
鲅 147
鲐 1852
鲑 731
 2122
鲒 995
鲔 1997
鲕 511
鮆 321
鰤 1733
鲖 1925
鲛 735
鮰 864
鲗 2400
(鯈) 1903
鲘 815
鲙 1121
鮡 2427
鮠 1993
鮨 2280
鲚 923
鲛 973
鲜 2073
 2079
鲝 2404
鲞 2095
鮟 12
鲟 2188
鲠 663
鲡 1177
鲢 1199
鲹 184
鲣 943
鲤 1182
鲥 1747
鮸 1338
鲦 1903
鲧 737
(鯗) 2095
(鮷) 1883
鲨 1666
鲩 849
鲪 1066
鲫 923
鲬 2313

八至十画

鲭 1574
 2444
鲮 1232
鲯 1513
鲰 2559
鲱 886
鲱 560
鲲 1132
鲳 215
鲴 701
鲵 1405
(鯰) 1411
鲷 445
鲸 1027
鯥 1263
鲺 1733
鲹 1704
鲻 2539
䲠 312
鲼 576
鲽 452
鯻 1141
鲾 96
鰊 1203
鳀 1883
鳁 2004
鳂 1988
鳃 1649
鳄 508
鰗 835
鳅 1582
鳆 617
(鯿) 115
鳇 855
鳈 1600
鳉 961
(鰌) 1582
鳊 115
鱀 923
鰕 2061
鰇 1633
鳌 19
鳍 1513
(鰣) 1747
鳎 1849
鳏 715
(鰷) 1903
(鰤) 1733
鳐 2230
[illegible] 2012
鰧 1878
鳑 1446
鳒 943

十一画以上

鳓 1166
(鰹) 943
鳔 131
鳕 2181
鳗 1298
鳘 1350
鳙 2077
鰶 923
鳙 2311
鱇 1083
鳖 131
鳚 2002
(鱂) 961
鳛 2053
(鰺) 1704
鱚 2055
(鱘) 2188
鳜 735
(鱓) 1676
鳝 1676
鳞 1224
鳟 2571
(鱏) 2188
(鱍) 147
鳠 825
鳡 634
(鱥) 735
鳢 1182
(鱮) 2167
(鱟) 815
(鱠) 1121
鳣 2410
鳤 717
(鱭) 923
鱵 2437
鱲 1219
(鱷) 508
(鱸) 1258
(鱺) 1177

革部

革 652
 904

二至四画

靪 454
靰 897
勒 1165
 1166
靬 1537
靰 2040
靸 1648
(靭) 1625
靴 2176
靳 1016
靱 2295
靶 29

五画

靺 1368
靼 345
鞅 2217
 2225
靽 55
(鞀) 1872
鞁 87
靿 2234

六画

鞋 2122
(鞏) 676
鞑 345
鞒 1550
(鞉) 1872
鞍 12
鞌 12

七至八画

鞘 1553
 1689
鞓 1911
鞔 1298
鞛 94
鞡 1141
(鞝) 1687
鞞 141
鞠 1046
鞟 1135
䩬 94
鞚 1107
鞬 943

九画

鞯 943
鞨 791
鞦 1582
(鞦) 1582
鞭 115
鞥 509
鞫 1046
鞧 1582
鞣 1633

十画

鞲 682
(鞾) 2176
鞴 87
鞶 1443
鞵 2122
[illegible] 2012
(鞹) 1135

十二画以上

(韃) 345
(鞽) 1550
(鞿) 897
(韁) 961
韂 214
韆 1532
(韉) 943
(韊) 1148

骨部

骨 689
 693
骭 635
骫 1997
骱 1002
骰 1935
(骯) 17
骷 1114
骶 419
鹘 697
 820
骳 87
骴 315
骺 809
骼 655
骸 754
(骾) 663
髁 1091
髀 111
髃 2342
髅 1253
髂 1527
髆 152
髈 58
 1447
髋 1122
髌 135
(髏) 1253
髎 1213
(髒) 2392
髓 1839
(體) 1878
 1883
髑 480
(髖) 1122
(髕) 135

鬼部

鬼 733
魂 873
魁 1129
魅 1320
魃 27
魆 2165
魄 151
 1496
 1963
魇 2213
魉 1209
魈 2104
(魌) 1507
(魊) 2353
(魎) 1209
魍 1983
魏 2002
魑 260
魔 1364
(魘) 2213

食部

食 1745
 1823
 2277
(飡) 184
飧 1841
飨 2094
(飱) 1841
餍 2216
餈 320
餐 184
饕 1909

(饗) 2094
饕 1870
饔 2311
(饜) 2216

音部

音 2285
章 2416
竟 1032
歆 2136
韵 2381
韶 1689
(韻) 2381
(響) 2093

鬥部

(鬥) 1320
(鬦) 473
(鬧) 1396
(鬨) 808
(鬩) 2059
(鬭) 471
473
(鬮) 1036

髟部

(髠) 1132
髡 1132
髦 415
(髤) 2159
(髩) 135
(髥) 1607
髦 1309
髣 551
髴 382
(髮) 528
髯 1607
髷 1418
鬅 601
髫 1903
髲 109
髳 1309
髻 923
髭 2539
髹 2159
鬙 2444
鬎 1193
髽 2514
鬌 416
(鬆) 1824
鬘 2014
鬅 1460
鬈 1600
鬃 2555
(鬍) 818
鬁 1141
鬚 1962
鬏 1036
鬍 950
鬐 1513
鬒 2438
鬝 1887
鬑 1200
鬓 135
鬘 1298
(鬚) 2161
鬠 1662
鬟 845
(鬈) 1418
(鬢) 135
鬣 1219
(鬤) 2567

麻部

麻 1285
1286
麼 1362
(麽) 1312
摩 1285
1362
麾 858
磨 1363
1370
(糜) 1317
縻 1317
1330
縻 1330
靡 1331
1332
麿 1430
魔 1364
(黂) 1361
(靡) 1317

鹿部

鹿 1260
麂 912
麀 2317
(麄) 327
(麈) 235
麗 1263
麇 1066
1606
(麅) 1448
麈 2508
麃 931
麋 1330
(麐) 1225
麒 1513
麓 1263
(麗) 1175
1189
(麕) 1066
1606
麑 1405
麖 19
麝 1027
麛 1698
(麞) 2416
麟 1225
(麤) 327

黑部

黑 792
墨 1368
默 1370
黔 1538
黕 379
(點) 433
黜 296
黛 373
黝 2332
黠 2062
黡 2213
黟 2260
黢 1590
黣 480
(黨) 386
黧 1177
黥 1576
黦 2374
黪 188
黯 17
(黰) 2438
黱 373
(黴) 1316
(黲) 188
黵 2411
(黶) 2213
(黷) 480

鼠部

鼠 1786
鼢 573
鼫 1748
鼥 27
鼬 2335
鼪 1721
鼩 1590
鼧 1961
(鼦) 445
鼯 2028
鼱 1027
(鼴) 2213
鼹 2213
鼷 2051

鼻部

鼻 96
劓 2281
鼽 1586
鼾 761
(齀) 1428
齁 808
齆 2012
齇 2403
齉 1393

III 难检字笔画索引
Index of Characters with Radicals Difficult to Classify

(字右边的号码指字典正文的页码。The number to the right of each character indicates the page number in the Dictionary.)

一画

〇 1226
乙 2266

二画

丁 452
2441
七 1504
1508
乂 2270
九 1036
匕 97
乃 1385
刁 444
了 1166
1213
乜 1344
1416

三画

三 1650
干 624
634
亍 294
于 2335
亏 1127
下 2062
丈 2418
万 1365
1977
与 2336
2342
2346
才 176
上 1679
千 1527
乇 1955
乞 1514
川 297
义 2270
(亾) 1980
丸 1972
么 1312
(么) 1292
2225
久 1037
及 900
丫 2191
之 2453
卫 1997
也 2236
(刄) 1623
飞 555
习 2051
孑 988
乡 2085
孓 1057

四画

丰 577
亓 1508
开 1069
井 1027
天 1887
夫 592
593
元 2355
无 1361
2018
云 2375
专 2515
丐 622
廿 1413
不 496
五 2028
(帀) 2383
丏 1336
卅 1648
不 153
155
有 1309
屯 1954
2530
互 822
牙 2194
丬 1125
(爿) 1608
中 2479
2490
午 2032
壬 1622
升 1711
夭 2226
长 215
2417
反 535
爻 2228
乏 524
丹 373
氏 1751
2455
乌 2015
2036
卞 117
为 1989
1998
尹 2291
夬 708
尺 233
262
(弔) 446
丑 279
巴 23
以 2267
予 2336
2342
书 1777

五画

未 1999
末 1365
(朩) 1312
击 888
戋 937
正 2441
2446
甘 627
世 1752
卌 2055
本 89
术 1787
2501
丕 1461
可 1092
1095
丙 139
左 2572
右 2333
布 171
戊 2036
平 1482
东 461
(戉) 2372
卡 1068
1526
北 79
凸 1936
归 726
且 1043
1554
申 1699
甲 931
由 2318
电 435
冉 1608
史 1748
央 2216
目 2269
(冊) 195
凹 18
1964
出 280
生 619
生 1712
失 1726
乍 2405
丘 1581
斥 264
卮 2455
乎 815
丛 326
用 2313
甩 1793
氐 411
416
匆 323
乐 1164
2371
册 195
包 59
兰 1145
半 52
头 1929
必 104
司 1812
民 1345
弗 593
疋 2196
(疋) 1468
(癶) 388
丱 717
丝 1813

六画

(丢) 461
戎 1628
考 1085
亚 2197
亘 661
再 2386
吏 1189
戌 1594
2161
在 2388
百 39
而 510
戍 1787
死 1817
(亙) 661
成 244
夹 618
925
931
尧 2228
乩 892
师 1730
曳 2240
曲 1586
1591
肉 1633
年 1409
朱 2498
丢 461
乔 1549
乒 1482
乓 1445
向 2095
囟 2136
后 809
角 1259
兆 2425
产 212
关 709
州 2494
兴 2139
2149
农 1422
尽 1008
1011
丞 475
买 1293
丞 248

七画

戒 999
(甦) 1843
严 2202
巫 2017
甫 601
更 661
663
束 1787
两 1205
丽 1175
1189
求 1583
来 1141
(巠) 1017
芈 1332
串 303
我 2014
(兎) 1945
囱 323
(巵) 2455
希 2045
坐 2576
(坐) 2579
龟 729
1066
1581
卵 1269
岛 392
兑 494
弟 428
君 1066

八画

奉 589
武 2033
表 128

(長) 215
2417
者 2430
(亞) 2197
丧 1657
(東) 461
或 884
事 1755
(兩) 1205
枣 2395
卖 1295
(面) 1338
(來) 1141
疌 990
非 558
些 2117
果 744
畅 223
(咼) 737
垂 308
乖 707
秉 139
臾 2337
(乕) 1979
乳 1637
枭 2099
氓 1304
1324
卷 1055
单 209
374
1674
肃 1831
隶 1191
承 249
亟 904
1525
沓 1008

九画

奏 2562
哉 2385
甚 1710
(甚) 1704
巷 772
2097
柬 944
歪 1966
面 1338
虒 2039
韭 1037
卤 2124
临 1221
禺 2339
幽 2316
拜 45
臿 199
重 271
2492
禹 2344
㫗 1584
胤 2297
玅 1344
养 2223
(刱) 306
叛 1445
首 1772
举 1048
昼 2498
咫 2470
(飛) 555
癸 734

十画

艳 2214
冓 685
衰 2358
(喪) 1657
彧 2349
哥 650
鬲 654
1192
孬 1393
(卨) 2124
甡 1702
乘 252
1724
(島) 392
(師) 1730
虒 1816
鬯 223
虓 2100
(畝) 1373
离 1175
(刱) 306
弱 1646
哿 655
能 1402
(函) 762

十一画

焉 2200
(執) 2459
堇 1009
黄 850
乾 1537
(乾) 624
啬 1661
(專) 2515
戚 1506
匏 1449
爽 1797
(禼) 2124
匙 262
1764
(啎) 2033
(暨) 380
(梟) 2099
象 2097
够 685
馗 1128
(夠) 685
孰 1783
(産) 212
兽 1776
艴 600
胬 1427

十二画

(堯) 2228
(喆) 2430
戠 2553
(報) 69
(喪) 1657
(甦) 1828
棘 907
(棗) 2395
敧 1507
㝵 19
皕 108
赝 1950
黹 2553
辉 858
(單) 209
374
1674
甥 1721
(喬) 1549
(衆) 2491
粤 2374
舒 1780
就 1041
喾 1116
巯 1586
(發) 518
(幾) 888
910

十三画

鼓 695
(聖) 1722
(尠) 2079
(幹) 634
(嗇) 1661
勠 590
嗣 1823
(亂) 1270
(煢) 1580
(肅) 1831
叠 451

十四画

(壽) 1773
叆 7
嘉 930
臺 1852
(臺) 1851
截 994
赫 792
(壽) 1773
朅 1556
(榦) 634
斡 2015
兢 1024
嘏 697
934
(爾) 511
疐 2479
臧 2392
(巰) 1586
夥 884
(夥) 883
(暢) 223
舞 2035
毓 2353
睾 646
甯 1387
孵 593
脊 635
疑 2265
暨 923

十五画

犛 1177
(氂) 1309
奭 1764
逮 373
赜 2399
(疐) 2479
(憂) 2315
叕 2539
靠 1087
虢 856
(舖) 1502
虢 744
勰 2122
豫 2354

十六画

虤 75
(隸) 1191
黇 1896
翰 769
噩 508
整 2444
臻 2437
(舉) 1048
䠆 1416
(舘) 715
(贗) 1950
(餘) 2215
赠 573
辨 501
嬴 2303
(贈) 573

十七画

(嚭) 1469
戴 373
(韓) 763
(隸) 1191
黼 605
豳 135
(虧) 1127
(黨) 107
黏 1411
爵 1062
嬴 2303
馘 744
(嚮) 2095

十八画

(釐) 1175
2055
鬶 731
(鑒) 464
(豎) 2258
醺 870
虩 2060
(歸) 726
(龜) 729
1066
1581
颤 635
䩞 213

十九画

嚭 1469
(黿) 1964
夔 1394
橐 646
辫 501
(䩞) 213
鼗 1872
嬴 1280
羸 1168
蠖 2369
疆 961

二十画以上

馨 2136
耀 2235
疊 2139
(譽) 1116
鼙 1468
蠑 1480
赣 635
(嬴) 1280
懿 2281
囊 1392
(䩞) 213
韬 1873
(辮) 501
(鏈) 373
(龕) 899
(嬴) 1279
蠲 1055
纛 401
(競) 1552
(艷) 2214
矗 296
(釁) 808
鼕 1877
(靉) 7
(蠖) 2369
(疊) 2139
(豔) 2214
(鬱) 2348

A

ā（ㄚ）

吖 ā［吖嗪］（āqín）有机化合物的一类，呈环状结构，含有一个或几个氮原子，如吡啶、哒嗪、嘧啶等 azine; any of a group of heterocyclic compounds containing one or more nitrogen atoms in the ring, such as pyridine, pyridazine and pyrimidine

阿 ā〈方 *dial.*〉〈前缀 *prefix*〉❶ 用在排行、小名或姓的前面，有亲昵的意味［used before a pet name, monosyllabic surname, or number denoting order of seniority in a family, to make it sound more endearing］：～大 Ah Da（The Eldest）|～宝 Ah Bao|～唐 Ah Tang ❷ 用在某些亲属名称的前面［used before kinship terms］：～婆 grannie|～爹 dad; pa|～哥 elder brother

☞ 啊 ·a on p. 2 and ē on p. 503

【阿鼻地狱】ābí dìyù〈佛教 *Budd.*〉指犯了重罪的人死后灵魂受苦的地方 Avici Hell, the last and deepest of eight hot infernos where the condemned are put through round after round of misery, death and rebirth without letup［阿鼻，梵 Sanskrit：avīci］

【阿昌族】Āchāngzú 我国少数民族之一，分布在云南 Achang（Archangs）, one of China's ethnic minority groups, inhabiting Yunnan Province

【阿斗】Ā Dǒu 三国蜀汉后主刘禅的小名。阿斗为人庸碌，后来多比喻懦弱无能的人 jerk; fool; Ah Dou, pet name of Liu Shan（207-271）, last emperor of Shu Han（221-263）during the Three Kingdoms Period. Ah Dou was known for his weak and inept character, and so his name is oft. used figuratively for a weak-minded and ne'er-do-well person

【阿尔法粒子】ā'ěrfǎ lìzǐ alpha particle; ☞ 甲种粒子 jiǎzhǒng lìzǐ on p. 932; also α 粒子 ā'ěrfǎ lìzi［阿尔法，希腊字母的第一个字母 α, the first letter of the Greek alphabet］

【阿尔法射线】ā'ěrfǎ shèxiàn alpha ray; ☞ 甲种射线 jiǎzhǒng shèxiàn on p. 932; also α 射线 ā'ěrfǎ shèxiàn

【阿飞】āfēi 指身着奇装异服、举动轻狂的青少年流氓 young street ruffian;（teenager）hoodlum or hooligan

【阿公】āgōng〈方 *dial.*〉❶ 丈夫的父亲 father of one's husband ❷ 祖父 paternal grandfather ❸ 尊称老年男子 respectful term of address for an old man

【阿訇】āhōng 我国伊斯兰教称主持清真寺教务和讲授经典的人 ahung; imam; officiating priest of an Islamic mosque in China［波斯 Persian：ākhūnd］

【阿拉】ālā〈方 *dial.*〉❶ 我 I; me ❷ 我们 we; us

【阿拉伯人】Ālābórén 亚洲西南部和非洲北部的主要居民。原住阿拉伯半岛，多信伊斯兰教。Arab; Arabian（member of a Semitic people inhabiting Southwest Asia and Northern Africa）. The Arabs were native to the Arabian Peninsula, and most of them believe in Islamism.［阿拉伯 Arabia；阿拉伯语 Arabic］

【阿拉伯数字】Ālābó shùzì 国际通用的数字 Arabic numerals for universal use；就是 i. e. 0, 1, 2, 3, 4, 5, 6, 7, 8, 9

【阿兰若】ālánrě ☞ 兰若 lánrě on p. 1146［梵 Sanskrit：araṇya］

【阿罗汉】āluóhàn ☞ 罗汉 luóhàn on p. 1277［梵 Sanskrit：arhat］

【阿猫阿狗】āmāo āgǒu〈方 *dial.*〉泛指某些人或随便什么人（含轻蔑意 derog.）Tom, Dick, and Harry; everyman jack; general term for people of any description

【阿门】āmén 基督教祈祷的结束语，'但愿如此'的意思 amen; Christian incantation used after a prayer, creed or other formal statement to express solemn ratification or agreement［希伯来 Hebrew：āmēn］

【阿木林】āmùlín〈方 *dial.*〉容易上当受骗的人；傻瓜 fool; person who is easily taken in

【阿片】āpiàn 从尚未成熟的罂粟果里取出的乳状液体，干燥后变成淡黄色或棕色固体，味苦。医药上用做止泻、镇痛和止咳剂。常用成瘾，是一种毒品。用作毒品时，叫大烟、鸦片（雅片）或阿芙蓉。opium; inspissated juice abstracted from premature opium poppies that, when dried, becomes a light yellow or brown solid matter with a bitter taste; used clinically as an anti-diarrhoea and pain-killer and for the treatment of cough; addictive narcotic substance that, when used as such, is known as 大烟 dàyān, 鸦片 yāpiàn, or 阿芙蓉 āfúróng

【阿婆】āpó〈方 *dial.*〉❶ 丈夫的母亲 husband's mother; mother-in-law ❷ 祖母 grandma ❸ 尊称老年妇女 term of respect for an elderly woman

【阿Q】Ā Qiū，又 also Ā Kiū 鲁迅著名小说《阿Q正传》的主人公，是'精神胜利者'的典型，受了屈辱，不敢正视，反而用自我安慰的办法，说自己是'胜利者' Ah Q, also Akiu, protagonist in Lu Xun's novella *The True Story of Ah Q*. A typical 'champion of spiritual victory,' he espouses self-consolation by declaring himself a winner whenever he has been humiliated.

【阿嚏】ātì〈拟声词 *onom*.〉形容打喷嚏的声音 atishoo; ahchoo; sound of sneezing

【阿姨】āyí ❶〈方 *dial*.〉母亲的姐妹 aunt; mother's sister ❷ 称呼跟母亲辈分相同、年纪差不多的无亲属关系的妇女 auntie; form of address for a woman of one's parents' generation but not related to one's family：王～ Auntie Wang｜售票员～Auntie Conductress ❸ 对保育员或保姆的称呼 form of address for childcare worker or housemaid

啊(呵) ā〈叹词 *interj*.〉表示惊异或赞叹［expressing surprise or admiration］ah; oh：～，出虹了！Oh, there rises the rainbow！｜～，今年的庄稼长得真好哇！Wow, what a good crop this year!
☞ 呵 hē on p. 780 and kē on p. 1088

【啊呀】āyā〈叹词 *interj*.〉❶ 表示惊讶［expressing surprise］：～，他跑得真快呀！Man, see how fast he runs! ❷ 表示不满或为难［expressing resentment, dissatisfaction or embarrassment］：～，怎么弄了满地的水！Oh no, the floor is flooded! ｜～，这事不好办哪！Oh dear, a hard nut to crack!

【啊哟】āyō〈叹词 *interj*.〉表示惊讶、痛苦等［indicating surprise, pain, etc.］：～，好大的雪呀！Oh, my God, it's snowing so heavily! ｜～，头痛死啦！What a bad headache, it really hurts!

锕 ā 金属元素，符号 Ac (actinium)。有放射性。actinium (Ac), radioactive metalic element

腌 ā［腌臜］ā·zā〈方 *dial*.〉❶ 脏；不干净 filthy; dirty：房子里太～了，快打扫打扫吧。It's so dirty in this house; let's hurry to clean it up. ❷（心里）别扭；不痛快 ruffled; unhappy：晚到一步，事没办成，～极了。We were just one step away from getting it done. What a shame! ❸ 糟践；使难堪 insult; embarrass：算了，别～人了。Come on, stop treating him like dirt.
☞ yān on p. 2201

á (ㄚˊ)

啊(呵) á〈叹词 *interj*.〉表示追问［pressing for an answer or asking for a repetition of sth. just said］：～？你明天到底去不去呀？Well, are you going tomorrow or not? ｜～？你说什么？Eh? Pardon?
☞ 呵 hē on p. 780 and kē on p. 1088

嗄 á same as 啊 á
☞ shà on p. 1667

ǎ (ㄚˇ)

啊(呵) ǎ〈叹词 *interj*.〉表示惊疑［indicating surprise and doubt］：～？这是怎么回事啊？My, what is going on?
☞ 呵 hē on p. 780 and kē on p. 1088

à (ㄚˋ)

啊(呵) à〈叹词 *interj*.〉❶ 表示应诺（音较短）［expressing agreement or compliance (in a short syllable)］：～，好吧。Ah, all right. ❷ 表示明白过来（音较长）［expressing sudden realization (with a drawl)］：～，原来是你，怪不得看着面熟哇！Ah, so it's you! Small wonder you look so familiar. ❸ 表示惊异或赞叹（音较长）［expressing surprise or admiration (with a drawl)］：～，伟大的祖国！Oh, our great motherland!
☞ 呵 hē on p. 780 and kē on p. 1088

·a (·ㄚ)

啊(阿、呵) ·a〈助词 *aux*.〉❶ 用在句末表示赞叹的语气［attached to the end of a sentence to indicate admiration］：多好的天儿～！What a fine day! ❷ 用在句末表示肯定、辩解、催促、嘱咐等语气［attached to the end of a sentence to show approval or self-protectiveness or to urge or enjoin sb.］：这话说得是～！You've said a mouthful! ｜我没去是因为我有事情～。I didn't go because I was real busy. ｜快去～！Hurry up, will you? ｜你可要小心～！Do be careful! ❸ 用在句末表示疑问的语气［attached to the end of a sentence to indicate doubt］：你吃不吃～？Do you want to eat or not? ｜你这说的是真的～？Are you telling the truth? ❹ 用在句中稍作停顿，让人注意下面的话［sign of pause in the middle of a sentence to draw attention to what one is going to say next］：这些年～，咱们的日子越过越好啦。All the years, you see, our life is getting better. ❺ 用在列举的事项之后［attached to the end of each item enumerated］：书～，杂志～，摆满了一书架子。The bookshelf is stacked full of books, magazines, and whatnot. ‖ 注意 **NOTE**：'啊'用在句末或句中，常受到前一字韵母或韵尾的影响而发生不同的变音，也可以写成不同的字 When used at the end of a sentence or in the middle of it, the word 啊 ·a may be pronounced or written in a different way due to the influence of the head or tail vowels of the previous word.

前字的韵母或韵尾 Head or tail vowel of previous word	'啊'的发音和写法 Pronunciation and written form of 啊 ·a
a, e, i, o, ü	a → ia 呀 yā
u, ao, ou	a → ua 哇 wā
-n	a → na 哪 ·na
-ng	a →nga

☞ 阿 ā on p. 1 and ē on p. 503; 呵 hē on p. 780 and kē on p. 1088

āi (历)

哎(嗳) āi〈叹词 *interj*.〉❶ 表示惊讶或不满意 [showing surprise or disapproval]: ~! 真是想不到的事。Why, it's really unexpected! | ~! 你怎么能这么说呢! But how could you talk like that! ❷ 表示提醒 [remind sb. of sth.]: ~, 我倒有个办法, 你们大家看行不行? Listen, I have a way out; just let us see if it will work or not.

☞ 嗳 ǎi on p. 5 and ài on p. 7

【哎呀】āiyā〈叹词 *interj*.〉❶ 表示惊讶 [expressing surprise or amazement]: ~! 这瓜长得这么大呀! My goodness, what a large melon! ❷ 表示埋怨、不耐烦、惋惜等 [expressing complaint or showing impatience or pity]: ~, 你怎么来这么晚呢! Goodness, why did you come so late? | ~, 你就少说两句吧! O dear, can't you keep your mouth shut! | ~, 时间都白白浪费了。My, what a waste of time!

【哎哟】āiyō〈叹词 *interj*.〉表示惊讶、痛苦、惋惜等 [expressing astonishment, pain or pity]: ~! 都十二点了。Ouch, it's 12 now! | ~! 我肚子好疼! O dear, my stomach hurts! | ~, 咱们怎么没有想到他呀! How come we totally forgot about him?

哀 āi ❶ 悲伤; 悲痛 grieved; sorrowful: 悲~ grief; sorrow | ~鸣 plaintive whine; mournful cry; wail in sorrow ❷ 悼念 condolence: ~悼 express one's condolences | 默~ observe a (three-minute) silence ❸ 怜悯 pity: ~怜 feel compassion for | ~矜 sympathize with | ~其不幸 share sb.'s sorrow

【哀兵必胜】āi bīng bì shèng《老子》六十九章: '抗兵相若, 哀者胜矣。' 对抗的两军力量相当, 悲愤的一方获得胜利。指受压抑而奋起反抗的军队, 必然能打胜仗 an army being bullied is bound to win so long as it puts up a valiant resistance. *Laozi* · *Chapter 69*: 'When opposing troops equal in strength meet in combat, the sorrowful side will win.'

【哀愁】āichóu 悲哀忧愁 sad and distressed: 满腹~ be extremely distressed | ~的目光 anguished look in sb.'s eyes

【哀辞】āicí〈书 *fml*.〉哀悼死者的文章, 多用韵文 elegy; formal expression of sorrow or mourning, mostly in verse

【哀悼】āidào 悲痛地悼念(死者) lament for sb.'s death; feel and show grief for: ~死难烈士 mourn for those who died a martyr's death | 表示沉痛的~ extend one's heartfelt condolences (to the family of the deceased)

【哀的美敦书】āidìměidūnshū 最后通牒 (transliteration for) ultimatum

【哀告】āigào 苦苦央告 implore plaintively; entreat piteously: 四处~ supplicate high and low

【哀号】āiháo 悲哀地号哭 wail; cry piteously; also 哀嚎 āiháo

【哀嚎】āiháo ❶ 悲哀地嚎叫 wail mournfully: 饿狼~。Famished wolves were howling in the wilds. ❷ same as 哀号 āiháo

【哀鸿遍野】āi hóng biàn yě〈比喻 *fig*.〉到处都是呻吟呼号、流离失所的灾民 land swarmed with famished refugees; disaster victims moaning everywhere (哀鸿 *aihong*: 哀鸣的大雁 moaning wild goose)

【哀毁骨立】āi huǐ gǔ lì 形容遭父母之丧, 因非常悲痛而消瘦变样 be emaciated with grief at the loss of one's parent

【哀矜】āijīn〈书 *fml*.〉哀怜 feel compassion for; pity

【哀苦】āikǔ 悲哀痛苦 grieved and miserable: ~无依的孤儿 helpless child worn down by grief and misery

【哀怜】āilián 对别人的不幸遭遇表示同情 pity; feel compassion for sb.'s misfortune: 孤儿寡母, 令人~。No people are more piteous than orphans and widows.

【哀鸣】āimíng 悲哀地叫 whine plaintively: 寒鸦~ lament as plaintively as a jackdaw; lamentation of a dying crow

【哀戚】āiqī〈书 *fml*.〉悲伤 sad; woeful

【哀启】āiqǐ〈旧时 *old*〉死者亲属叙述死者生平事略的文章, 通常附在讣闻之后 brief biographical sketch of the deceased, usu. attached to an obituary written by kinsmen

【哀泣】āiqì 悲伤地哭泣 weep plaintively: 嘤嘤~ sob softly in sorrow

【哀切】āiqiè 凄切(多用来形容声音、眼神等 oft. used to describe sound, look, etc.) mournful; sad: 情辞~ plaintive in mood and word

【哀求】āiqiú 哀告请求 entreat; implore: ~饶命 plead for mercy | 苦苦~ implore piteously

【哀荣】āiróng〈书 *fml*.〉指死后的荣誉 posthumous honour

【哀伤】āishāng 悲伤 be grieved and heart-

A

broken：哭声凄切～ sad and melancholy weeps|请保重身体，切莫过于～。Take care and don't take it too much to heart.

【哀思】āisī 悲哀思念的感情 sad memories (of the deceased); grief：寄托～ give expression to one's grief over sb.'s death

【哀叹】āitàn 悲哀地叹息 sigh sorrowfully for; lament; bewail; bemoan：独自～ lament in solitude|～自己不幸的遭遇 bemoan one's misfortune

【哀恸】āitòng 极为悲痛 extreme sorrow or grief：伟人长眠，举世～。The death of this great man plunged the entire nation in deep sorrow.

【哀痛】āitòng 悲伤；悲痛 mourn sorrowfully; grieve deeply for：～欲绝 in extreme grief

【哀婉】āiwǎn 悲伤婉转 pathetic; sad in a moving way：歌声～动人。There is something sad and touching about the song.

【哀艳】āiyàn 〈书 *fml*.〉形容文辞凄切而华丽 (of diction) poignantly sad：～之词 words of sentimental appeal|诗句～缠绵。The lines of this poem are moving in a sentimental way.

【哀怨】āiyuàn 因委屈而悲伤怨恨 aggrieved; resentful：倾诉内心的～ vent one's resentment

【哀乐】āiyuè 悲哀的乐曲，专用于丧葬或追悼 funeral music; dirge

【哀子】āizǐ 〈旧时 *old*〉死了母亲的儿子称哀子 son bereaved of his mother; ☞ 孤哀子 gū'āizǐ on p. 687

埃[1] āi 灰尘；尘土 dust：尘～dust|黄～蔽天。The sky was obliterated by a dust storm.

埃[2] āi 长度单位，一埃等于一亿分之一厘米。主要用来计算光波等的波长。这个单位名称是为纪念瑞典物理学家埃斯特朗(Anders Jonas Ångström)而定的。angstrom; Angström; unit of linear measure. One angstrom equals one tenth of a millimicron or one ten-millionth of a millimetre, primarily used to express electromagnetic wavelengths. This unit of length is named after the Swedish physicist Anders Jonas Ångström (1814-74).

挨 āi ❶ 顺着(次序)；逐一 follow a regular order or sequence; do sth. in sequence or by turns：～个儿 one by one|～门～户地检查卫生 inspect sanitary house by house ❷ 靠近；紧接着 be or get close to; be next to：他家～着工厂。His house or apartment sits next to a factory.|学生一个～一个地走进教室。The students filed into the classroom one by one.

☞ ái on p. 4

【挨边】āi//biān (～儿 āi//biānr) ❶ 靠着边缘 keep close to the edge：上了大路，要挨着边儿走。Keep close to the side when walking on the road. ❷ 接近(某数，多指年龄) be near; be close to (a figure, usu. age)：我六十～儿了。I'm getting on sixty. ❸ 接近事实或事物应有的样子 be close to the truth of sth.; be relevant：你说的一点也不～儿! What you have said is totally irrelevant.

【挨次】āicì 顺次 take turns (doing sth.); do sth. one after another or in turn：～入场 file in|～检查机器上的零件 examine parts of a machine in due order

【挨个儿】āigèr 逐一；顺次 do sth. by turns or one by one：～检查 examine persons or things one at a time

【挨户】aihù 挨门 from door to door：挨家～ from house to house|～询问 make door-to-door enquiries

【挨家】āijiā (～儿 āijiār) 挨门 from door to door：～逐户 from one house to another

【挨肩儿】āijiānr 同胞兄弟姐妹排行相连，年岁相差很小 (of siblings) be close in age：这哥儿俩是～的，只差一岁。The two brothers are close in age, and one is only one year older than the other.

【挨近】āi//jìn 靠近 get close to; sneak up to：你～我一点儿。Move over and get closer to me.|两家挨得很近。The two families are close to each other.

【挨门】āimén (～儿 āiménr) 一家一家地 from house to house：～挨户 from door to door|～打听 make enquiries from one house to another

唉 āi ❶ 答应的声音 [sound indicating response]：～，我在这儿。Yes, I'm here.|～，我知道了。Yeah, I know. ❷ 叹息的声音 [sound of a deep breath] sighing loud：他双手抱着头，～～地直叹气。His head sunk between his hands, he let out one sigh after another.

☞ ài on p. 6

【唉声叹气】āi shēng tàn qì 因伤感、烦闷或痛苦而发出叹息的声音 moan and groan; heave deep sighs of grief, worry or anguish

娭 āi [娭毑] (āijiě) 〈方 *dial*.〉❶ 祖母 father's mother; grandma ❷ 尊称年老的妇女 [respectful form of address for elderly women]

☞ xī on p. 2046

欸 āi same as 唉 āi

☞ ǎi on p. 5 and ē on p. 509

锿 āi 金属元素，符号 Es (einsteinium)。有放射性，由人工核反应获得。einsteinium (Es), radioactive metal element obtained through man-made nuclear reaction

ái (劳)

挨(捱) ái ❶ 遭受；忍受 suffer; put up with：～打 be manhandled; get a beating; be spanked|～饿 go hungry ❷ 困难地度过(岁月) pull through (hard times);

drag out：～日子 eke out a living ❸ 拖延 delay；stall：～时间 stall for time；procrastinate
☞ āi on p.4

骇 ái〈书 *fml.*〉傻 foolish：痴～ stupid | 愚～ idiotic；silly

皑(皚) ái〈书 *fml.*〉洁白 pure white；snow white：～如山上雪，皎若云间月（of an old person's hair）as white as mountain snow，and as clear as the moon amidst the clouds

【皑皑】ái'ái 形容霜、雪洁白（of snow，frost，etc.）pure white：白雪～ vast expanse of white snow

癌 ái（旧读 formerly pronounced yán）上皮组织生长出来的恶性肿瘤，如胃癌、肝癌、食道癌、皮肤癌等。cancer or carcinoma；malignant and invasive growth of tumour，esp. one originating in epithelium，tending to recur after excision and metastasize to other sites. This includes stomach cancer，liver cancer，oesophagus cancer and skin cancer. also 癌瘤 áiliú or 癌肿 áizhǒng

【癌变】áibiàn 由良性病变转化为癌症病变（of a benign ailment）become malignant；develop into cancer；canceration

ǎi（ㄞˇ）

毐 ǎi 用于人名，嫪毐（Lào'ǎi），战国时秦国人 part of a given name；Lao'ai，man of Qin during the Warring States Period

欸 ǎi［欸乃］（ǎinǎi）〈书 *fml.*〉〈拟声词 *onom.*〉❶ 形容摇橹的声音 sound of sculling ❷ 划船时歌唱的声音 sound of singing when rowing
☞ āi on p.4 and ê on p.509

嗳(噯) ǎi〈叹词 *interj.*〉表示不同意或否定［expressing disagreement or negation］：～，不是这样的。No，it's not like that. | ～，话可不能那么说。Oh no，you cannot put it that way.
☞ 哎 āi on p.2 and ài on p.7

【嗳气】ǎiqì 胃里的气体从嘴里出来，并发出声音 eruct；belch；eject gas spasmodically and noisily from the stomach through the mouth；通称 general term for 打嗝儿 dǎ//gér

【嗳酸】ǎisuān 胃酸从胃里涌到嘴里 acid rising up into the mouth from the stomach（a symptom of hyperacidity of the gastric juice）

矮 ǎi ❶ 身材短 short of stature：～个儿 person of small build | 个头儿不～ not short of stature ❷ 高度小的 low：～墙 low wall | ～凳儿 low stool ❸（级别、地位）低 of low rank or grade：他在学校里比我～一级。He was a grade lower than I in school.

【矮墩墩】ǎidūndūn（～的 ǎidūndūn·de）形容矮而粗壮 pudgy；dumpy；stumpy

【矮小】ǎixiǎo 又矮又小 diminutive；petite；short and small：身材～ of short and small build | ～的草屋 low and small thatched cottage

【矮星】ǎixīng 光度小、体积小、密度大的恒星，如天狼星的伴星 dwarf star；star of relatively low luminosity and small volume but oft. very high in density，such as the companion stars of Sirius

【矮子】ǎi·zi 个子矮的人 low-built person；short person

蔼[1] ǎi 和气；态度好 friendly；amiable：和～ affable | ～然 genial

蔼[2] ǎi〈书 *fml.*〉繁茂 lush；luxuriant

【蔼蔼】ǎi'ǎi〈书 *fml.*〉❶ 形容树木茂盛（of trees）verdant；luxuriant ❷ 形容昏暗 dim；dark

【蔼然】ǎirán 和气；和善 affable；genial；kind：～可亲 amiable and endearing

霭 ǎi〈书 *fml.*〉云气 mist；haze：烟～ light blue mist | 暮～ dusky haze

ài（ㄞˋ）

艾[1] ài ❶ 多年生草本植物，叶子有香气，可入药，内服可做止血剂，又供灸法上用。也叫艾蒿或蕲艾。Chinese mugwort（*Artemisia argyi*），perennial plant with fragrant leaves that can be orally administered as a haemostatic drug or used for moxibustion ❷（Ài）姓 a surname

艾[2] ài〈书 *fml.*〉年老的，也指老年人 old；elderly；aged；elderly：耆～old age

艾[3] ài〈书 *fml.*〉停止 end；stop：方兴未～ be burgeoning；be in the ascendant

艾[4] ài〈书 *fml.*〉美好；漂亮 beautiful；handsome：少～（年轻漂亮的人）pretty teenager
☞ yì on p.2272

【艾虎】[1] àihǔ 哺乳动物，背部棕黄色或淡黄色。昼伏夜出，捕食小动物。毛皮可制衣物。fitch（*Mustela putorius*）；nocturnal mammal with a brown or light yellow back，living on small animals，its fur used for making coat；also 地狗 dìgǒu

【艾虎】[2] àihǔ 用艾做成的像老虎的东西，旧俗端午节给儿童戴在头上，认为可以驱邪 cloth tiger filled with moxa，worn by children during the Dragon Boat Festival to ward off evils

【艾绒】àiróng 把艾叶晒干捣碎而成的绒状物，中医用来治病 crushed dry leaves of Chinese mugworth for use in traditional Chinese medicine；☞灸 jiǔ on p.1037

【艾窝窝】àiwō·wo 用熟糯米做成的球形食品，有馅 steamed cone-shaped cake made of glutinous rice or millet with sweet filling；also

爱窝窝 àiwō·wo

懓 ài〈书 *fml.*〉same as 爱 ài

砹 ài 非金属元素，符号 At (astatium)。有放射性，自然界分布极少。astatine (At), radioactive nonmetal element, with scarce deposits on this globe

嗳 ài〈叹词 *interj.*〉表示伤感或懊悔[sigh of sadness or regret]：～，病了几天，把工作都耽误了。Whoops! My work was held up when I was ill the past few days. |～，好好的一套书弄丢了两本。What a pity! Two books are missing in this otherwise complete set. ☞ āi on p. 4

爱(愛) ài ❶ 对人或事物有很深的感情 love：～祖国 love one's motherland|～人民 love the people|～劳动 love manual labour|他～上了一个姑娘。He fell in love with a girl. ❷ 喜欢 like; be fond of; be keen on：～游泳 be fond of swimming|～看电影 enjoy watching films ❸ 爱惜；爱护 cherish; treasure; take good care of：～公物 take good care of public property|～集体荣誉 cherish the good name of the collective ❹ 常常发生某种行为；容易发生某种变化 be liable to; be apt to; in the habit of：～哭 be a tearbag|～开玩笑 be given to joking|铁～生锈。Iron rusts easily.

【爱不释手】ài bù shì shǒu 喜爱得舍不得放下 be so fond of sth. as not to let go of it

【爱财如命】ài cái rú mìng 形容非常吝啬或贪财 love money as one loves one's life; love money as much as life itself; be a money-grubber

【爱巢】àicháo 指新房，也指年轻夫妻的幸福家庭 love nest, referring to a bridal chamber or the happy family of a young couple

【爱称】àichēng 表示喜爱、亲昵的称呼 term of endearment; pet name

【爱答不理】ài dā bù lǐ（～的 ài dā bù lǐ ·de）像是理睬又不理睬，形容对人冷淡、怠慢 cold and indifferent; standoffish：别人同她说话，她～的。She's always standoffish whenever sb. wants to talk to her. also 爱理不理 ài lǐ bù lǐ

【爱戴】àidài 敬爱并且拥护 love and esteem：～领袖 adore one's leader

【爱抚】àifǔ 疼爱抚慰 be affectionate to; show affection for：～的眼神 with tenderness in one's eyes|母亲～地为女儿梳理头发。The mother caressed and combed her daughter's hair with love in her eyes.

【爱国】ài//guó 热爱自己的国家 love one's country：～心 be patriotic|～人士 patriot

【爱国主义】àiguó zhǔyì 指对祖国的忠诚和热爱的思想 patriotism

【爱好】ài//hǎo〈方 *dial.*〉(～儿 ài//hǎor) 顾惜体面，喜欢打扮 be particular about one's looks：她从小就～，总是穿得整整齐齐的。She had been particular about the way she looked since childhood, and was always neatly dressed. |我这么大岁数了，还爱什么好儿。At my age I'm past caring for how I look.

【爱好】àihào ❶ 对某种事物具有浓厚的兴趣 be fond of; have a weakness for：～体育 be keen on sports|他对打太极拳很～。He has a penchant for slow-motion boxing. ❷ 喜爱 like：供应人民～的日用品 supply the people with their favourite daily necessities

【爱河】àihé 指爱情（佛教认为爱情像河流一样，人沉溺其中，就不能自拔）river of love (According to Buddhism, love is like a river from which one cannot extricate oneself once one has fallen into it.)

【爱护】àihù 爱惜并保护 cherish; treasure; take good care of：～公物 take good care of public property|～年轻一代 care for the younger generation

【爱克斯射线】àikèsī shèxiàn 波长很短的电磁波，有很大穿透能力，能使照相胶片感光，使某些物质发荧光，并能使气体游离，对机体细胞有很强的破坏作用。广泛应用于科学技术和医疗方面。是德国物理学家伦琴发现的，所以又叫伦琴射线。也叫爱克斯光。通常写作 X 射线。X-ray; oft. X-rays, and also known as Roentgen ray because it was discovered by the German physicist Wilhelm Konrad Roentgen (1845-1923); a form of electromagnetic radiation similar to light but of shorter wavelength, capable of penetrating solids, exposing light-sensitive films and ionizing gases, and highly destructive to organic cells; widely used in science and technology and medical service

【爱怜】àilián 怜爱 show tender affection for：母亲～地抚摩着女儿的脸。The mother fondly caressed her daughter's face.

【爱恋】àiliàn 热爱而难以分离（多指男女之间 usu. between man and woman）be in love with; feel deeply attached to：信中流露出～之情。There were feelings of love between the lines of this letter.

【爱美的】àiměi·de 指业余爱好者 fan; person with a hobby [法 French: amateur]

【爱面子】ài miàn·zi 怕损害自己的体面，被人看不起 be concerned about face-saving; be sensitive about one's reputation：有错就承认，不要～。Own up to it whenever you have made a mistake — don't be afraid of losing face.

【爱莫能助】ài mò néng zhù 心里愿意帮助，但是力量做不到 be found lacking; willing but unable to help; The heart's willing, but the body's not.

【爱慕】àimù ❶ 喜欢羡慕 yearn for; envy：～虚荣 be vain; be given to vanity ❷ 喜爱倾慕 hold a torch for; admire; adore：～之情 feelings of admiration

【爱情】àiqíng 男女相爱的感情 amour; love between man and woman

【爱人】ài·ren ❶ 丈夫或妻子 husband or wife ❷ 指恋爱中男女的一方 sweetheart; lover

【爱斯基摩人】Àisījīmórén 居住在北美洲北冰洋沿岸的人，一小部分住在俄罗斯东北部楚克奇半岛一带，主要从事捕鱼和猎取海兽 Eskimo, member of a people of Mongoloid stock, inhabiting the shores of the Arctic Ocean in North America, with a small number living in and around Chukotsky Peninsula, whose main sources of living are fishing and sea-animal hunting

【爱窝窝】àiwō·wo same as 艾窝窝 àiwō·wo

【爱屋及乌】ài wū jí wū《尚书大传·大战篇》：'爱人者，兼其屋上之乌' *Grand Commentary on the Classic of Documents·Major Battles*: Love for a person extends even to the crows on his roof;〈比喻 *fig.*〉爱一个人而连带地关心到跟他有关系的人或物 Love me, love my dog.

【爱惜】àixī ❶ 因重视而不糟蹋 cherish; treasure: ～时间 make the most of one's time; use time efficiently | ～国家财物 cherish state property ❷ 疼爱；爱护 be fond of; love dearly: 全家对他都百般～。He is pampered by everybody in his family. *or* The entire family dotes on him.

【爱小】àixiǎo〈方 *dial.*〉好占小便宜 be greedy about petty gains; go after fringe advantages

【爱心】àixīn 指关怀、爱护人的思想感情 love; compassion; sympathy: 老妈妈对儿童充满～。The old lady is full of love for children.

【爱重】àizhòng 喜爱，尊重 love and respect: 他为人热情、正直，深受大家的～。He is loved and respected for his warm heart and integrity.

砹 ài〈书 *fml.*〉same as 碍 ài

僾(僾) ài〈书 *fml.*〉❶ 仿佛 seem: ～然 seem like (this or that) ❷ 气不顺畅 breathe with difficulty

【僾尼】àiní 部分哈尼族人的自称 Aini, name used by some of the Hanis (minority ethnic people in China) for themselves

隘 ài ❶ 狭窄 narrow: 狭～ narrow pass; defile | 林深路～。The forest is deep, and the road narrow. ❷ 险要的地方 place of strategic importance: 关～ pass; fortification | 要～ fort; major pass

【隘口】àikǒu 狭隘的山口 narrow mountain pass

【隘路】àilù 狭窄而险要的路 narrow and strategically important road

薆(薆) ài〈书 *fml.*〉❶ 隐蔽 cover; shelter ❷ 草木茂盛的样子 (of plant and tree) leafy; luxuriant

碍(礙) ài 妨碍；阻碍 hinder; obstruct; be in the way of: ～事 get in the way of | 有～观瞻 be an eyesore | 把地下的东西收拾一下，别让它～脚。Could you clear up the floor so that these things won't get in the way?

【碍口】ài//kǒu 怕难为情或碍于情面而不便说出 too embarrassed to bring sth. up: 求人的事，说出来真有点儿～。To ask for help — I don't know how to bring it up.

【碍面子】ài miàn·zi 怕伤情面 for fear of hurting sb.'s feelings: 有意见就提，别～不说。Speak your mind, and don't be afraid of offending people.

【碍难】àinán ❶ 难于（旧时公文套语 *fml. arch.*）find it difficult to do sth.: ～照办。I'm afraid I can't oblige. | ～从命。I find it hard to comply with your instruction. ❷〈方 *dial.*〉为难 do not know what to do

【碍事】ài//shì ❶ 妨碍做事；造成不方便；有妨碍 be in the way; be a hindrance to: 您站远一点儿，在这里有点儿～。Would you please stand a bit further away — I'm afraid you are somewhat in my way. | 家具多了，安置不好，倒～。Too much furniture, if not properly arranged, can get in the way. ❷ 严重；大有关系（多用于否定式 usu. in the negative）be of consequence; matter: 他的病不～。He has just a minor complaint. | 擦破点儿皮，不碍什么事。Nothing serious, just a slight scratch.

【碍手碍脚】ài shǒu ài jiǎo 妨碍别人做事 be in the way; be a hindrance: 咱们走吧，别在这儿～的。Let's get out of here and get out of the way.

【碍眼】ài//yǎn ❶ 不顺眼 offend the eye; be an eyesore: 东西乱堆在那里怪～的。The mess over there is something of an eyesore. ❷ 嫌有人在跟前不便 be out of place: 人家有事，咱们在这里～，快走吧！Since they are busy, we might be a hindrance here. Let's go!

嗳(嗳) ài〈叹词 *interj.*〉表示悔恨、懊恼 [expressing regret or annoyance]: ～，早知如此，我就不去了。Oh! I wouldn't have gone there if I'd known sooner.

☞ 哎 āi on p. 3 and ǎi on p. 5

嗌 ài 古书上指咽喉痛 sore throat (as used in ancient books)

☞ yì on p. 2278

嫒(嫒) ài ☞令嫒 lìng'ài on p. 1236

瑷(瑷) ài 瑷珲（Àihuī），地名，在黑龙江。今作爱辉。Aihui ('Aigun' in English), a county in Heilongjiang Province (now written as 爱辉 Àihuī)

叆(靉) ài [叆叇]（àidài）〈书 *fml.*〉形容浓云蔽日 overcast; enveloped in cloud: 暮云～。The dusky sky is enshrouded in clouds.

暧(暧) ài〈书 *fml.*〉日光昏暗 (of daylight) dim

【暧昧】àimèi ❶（态度、用意）含糊；不明白（of attitude, intention, etc.）noncommittal; ambiguous：态度～ take an equivocal attitude; be evasive ❷（行为）不光明；不可告人（of behaviour）shady; dubious：关系～dubious relationship

ān（ㄢ）

厂 ān same as 庵 ān（多用于人名 usu. in a given name）
☞ chǎng on p.221

广 ān same as 庵 ān（多用于人名 usu. in a given name）
☞ guǎng on p.725

安[1] ān ❶ 安定 calm; at ease：心神不～in a listless frame of mind | 坐不～，立不稳 be on tenterhooks ❷ 使安定（多指心情 oft. of one's mind, feelings, etc.）cause to calm down; set at ease：～民 bring peace to the people | ～神 soothe the nerves ❸ 对生活、工作等感到满足合适 be content; be satisfied：～于现状（满足于目前的状况，不求进步）be reconciled to the situation; take things as they are（rest on one's laurels）| ～之若素 bear（hardship, etc）with equanimity; regard（wrongdoing, etc.）with indifference ❹ 平安；安全（跟'危'相对 as opposed to 'danger'）safe; secure：公～public security | 治～public order | 转危为～pull through（a crisis, critical disease, etc.）❺ 使有合适的位置 place in a suitable position; find a place for：～插 place sb. in a certain position; assign sb. to a job | ～顿 find a place for; arrange for; settle in ❻ 安装；设立 install; fix：～门窗 fix doors and windows | ～电灯 install electric lights | 咱们村上～拖拉机站了。A tractor station has been set up in our village. ❼ 加上 level charge against; give a nickname to; impose：～罪名 bring a charge | ～个头衔 give an official title ❽ 存着；怀着（某种念头，多指不好的 oft. of not good idea）harbour; be up to：你～的什么心？What on earth are you up to? ❾（Ān）姓 a surname

安[2] ān〈书 *fml.*〉〈疑问代词 *interrog. pron.*〉❶ 问处所，跟'哪里'相同（same as 哪里 nǎ•li）where：而今～在？Where is it now? ❷ 表示反问，跟'怎么、哪里'相同（in rhetorical questions, same as 怎么 zěn•me or 哪里 nǎ•li）how：不入虎穴，～得虎子？Nothing venture, nothing have. *or* Unless you enter the tiger's lair, you can't catch the tiger's cub. | ～能若无其事？How can you behave as if nothing had happened?

安[3] ān 安培的简称 abbr. for 安培 ānpéi

【安邦定国】ān bāng dìng guó 使国家安定、巩固（of a ruler）bring peace and stability to the country

【安步当车】ān bù dàng chē 慢慢地步行，就当是坐车 stroll over instead of riding in a carriage; walk rather than ride：反正路也不远，我们还是～吧。Since it is a short walk, let's go there by foot.

【安瓿】ānbù 装注射剂用的密封的小玻璃瓶，用药时将瓶颈的上端弄破 ampoule（also ampul, ampule）; small glass vessel in which liquid for injection is hermetically sealed, to be opened by breaking its neck

【安插】ānchā（人员、故事情节、文章的词句等）放在一定的位置上 put in a certain position; insert（an episode, phrase, sentence, etc.）into（a story, play, article, etc.）：～亲信 plant one's confident in a key position

【安厝】āncuò 停放灵柩待葬或浅埋以待正式安葬 keep a coffin in a temporary shelter pending burial, or lay it in a temporary burial place to be reburied permanently later

【安定】[1] āndìng ❶（生活、形势等）平静正常；稳定（of livelihood, situation, etc.）stable; quiet; settled：生活～settled life | 情绪～in a calm frame of mind | 社会秩序～social stability ❷ 使安定 cause to stabilize：～人心 keep up the morale of the public; set people's mind at ease

【安定】[2] āndìng 药名，有机化合物，化学式 $C_{16}H_{13}ClN_2O$。黄白色结晶粉末。有镇静、抗惊厥、使横纹肌松弛等作用。valium; diazepam; tranquillizer, $C_{16}H_{13}ClN_2O$, that relieves anxiety, depression and muscular tension, in the form of a yellowish white crystal powder

【安堵】āndǔ〈书 *fml.*〉安定；安居 live in peace and security：～如常。Life goes on as usual in peace.

【安顿】āndùn ❶ 使人或事物有着落；安排妥当 help settle down（or in）; get sth. or everything arranged; find a place for：～老小 get everything settled for the entire family | 妈妈把家务事～得井井有条。Mum always manages to keep the house in order. ❷ 安稳 undisturbed; peaceful：睡不～ toss and turn（in bed）| 只有把事情做完心里才～。Only by getting things done can（I）feel at ease.

【安放】ānfàng 使物件处于一定的位置 put sth. where it belongs; lay：～铺盖 put the bedding where it belongs | 把仪器～好。Put the instruments in their proper places.

【安分】ānfèn 规矩老实，守本分 not go beyond one's bounds; be law-abiding; know one's place：～人 decent person | ～守己 know and keep one's place; abide by law and behave oneself | 这孩子不大～。The boy doesn't behave himself.

【安分守己】ān fèn shǒu jǐ 规矩老实，不做违法乱纪的事 abide by law and behave oneself; be content with one's lot and act one's part

【安抚】ānfǔ 安顿抚慰 pacify; aid and comfort (or console):～伤员 console the wounded|～人心 pacify the public

【安好】ānhǎo 平安 safe and sound; well:全家～,请勿挂念。You will be pleased to know that everyone in the family is well.

【安家】ān//jiā ❶ 安置家庭 settle down:～费 settling-in allowance|～落户 make one's home in a place; settle ❷ 组成家庭;结婚 set up a home; get married:他都快四十岁了,还没～。He's turning forty and hasn't got married yet.

【安家立业】ān jiā lì yè 安置家庭,建立事业 settle down and embark on a career

【安家落户】ān jiā luò hù 在他乡安置家庭并定居 resettle one's family in a new place:在山区～,当一辈子农民。Let's settle in the mountains and be a farmer the rest of our lives. ◇经过一年多的试养,武昌鱼已经在这里～了。After more than one year's trials and errors we have finally domesticated the Wuchang fish here.

【安静】ānjìng ❶ 没有声音;没有吵闹和喧哗 peace and quiet; peaceful:病人需要～。The patient needs peace and quiet. ❷ 安稳平静 calm; unperturbed:孩子睡得很～。The child is sound asleep.|过了几年～生活 live in peace and quiet for several years

【安居乐业】ān jū lè yè 安定地生活,愉快地劳动 live and work in peace and contentment

【安康】ānkāng 平安和健康 contented and in good health:祝全家～。Wishing your family happiness and the best of health!

【安澜】ānlán 〈书 *fml.*〉❶ 指河流平静,没有泛滥现象(of a river, etc.) limpid; unruffled ❷ 〈比喻 *fig.*〉太平 peaceful:天下～。The nation is at peace.

【安乐】ānlè 安宁和快乐 carefree:生活～live a carefree life

【安乐死】ānlèsǐ 指对无法救治的病人停止治疗或使用药物,让病人无痛苦地死去 euthanasia; mercy killing; act of putting to death painlessly a person suffering from a terminal and painful disease by medication or cancellation of medical treatment

【安乐窝】ānlèwō 指安逸舒适的生活处所 snug retreat; cosy nest

【安理会】Ānlǐhuì 安全理事会的简称 abbr. for 安全理事会 Ānquán Lǐshìhuì

【安谧】ānmì 安宁;安静 (of a place) tranquil; quiet; peaceful:～的山村 mountain village in sequestered repose; mountain hamlet that evinces a calm and settled security|月色是那么美丽而～。The moon looks so charming and serene.

【安眠】ānmián 安稳地熟睡 slumber; sleep well:～药 soporific; sleeping pill|喧嚣的车马声,让人终夜不得～。The din of traffic robbed everybody of a night's sound sleep.

【安民告示】ānmín gàoshì 原指官府发布的安定民心的告示,现多用来比喻政府或机关团体等在做某事之前,把有关内容、要求等先让人知道的通知 government notice to reassure the public; advance notice (of an event, agenda, etc.) issued by a government or an organization

【安宁】ānníng ❶ 秩序正常,没有骚扰 tranquil; imperturbable:地方～local peace and tranquillity|边境～peace on the border ❷ (心情)安定;宁静 (of mind) calm; composed; imperturbable:嘈杂的声音,使人不得～。The racket gave people no peace.

【安排】ānpái ❶ 有条理、分先后地处理(事物);安置(人员) arrange; handle things in an orderly fashion:～工作 make work arrangements|～生活 arrange one's daily life|～他当统计员。He was appointed as a statistician. ❷ 规划;改造 plan; remodel:重新～家乡的山河 transform the landscape of one's native place

【安培】ānpéi 电流强度的单位,导体横截面每秒通过的电量是1库仑时,电流强度就是1安培。这个单位名称是为纪念法国物理学家安培(André Ampère)而定的。ampere (A or amp.), named after the French physicist André Marie Ampère (1775-1836); metre-kilogramme-second unit of electric current, equal to the current that passes in a resistance of one ohm when a potential difference of one volt is applied; equivalent to one coulomb per second; 简称 abbr. 安 ān

【安培计】ānpéijì 测量电路中电流强度的仪器 ammeter; ampere-meter; instrument for measuring current in amperes; also 安培表 ānpéibiǎo and 电流表 diànliúbiǎo

【安贫乐道】ān pín lè dào 安于贫穷的境遇,乐于奉行自己信仰的道德准则 willing to suffer poverty while adhering to one's moral values

【安琪儿】ānqí'ér 天使 (transliteration for) angel

【安全】ānquán 没有危险;不受威胁;不出事故 safety; security; free from (danger, threat, accidents, etc.):～操作 ensure safety in operation|～地带 safety zone|注意交通～。Watch out for the traffic.

【安全岛】ānquándǎo 马路中间供行人穿过时躲避车辆的地方 safety island; pedestrian island; area in the middle of a roadway for the safety of pedestrians

【安全灯】ānquándēng ❶ 在矿井里用的可以防止引起混合气爆炸的灯。灯上有铜丝网罩,可以放散灯焰四周的热量。根据它的火焰变化,又可以估计矿井内气体的含毒量。safety lamp; miner's lighting device constructed to prevent immediate ignition of explosive gas-

A

es. A copper-wire gauze cover is fixed on it to disperse the heat around the lamp. Changes in the lamp's oil-fuelled flame help one to determine the density of noxious gases in a mine. ❷ 泛指电压低于 36 伏或有安全设备的照明用具 general term for lighting equipment below 36 volts or fixed with a safety device

【安全电压】ānquán diànyā 不致造成人身触电事故的电压，一般低于 36 伏 safe voltage, generally below 36 volts, that prevents a live wire from causing electric shock

【安全理事会】Ānquán Lǐshìhuì 联合国的重要机构之一。根据联合国宪章规定，它是联合国唯一有权采取行动来维持国际和平与安全的机构。由十五个理事国组成，中、法、苏（后由俄罗斯接替）、英、美为常任理事国，其余十国为非常任理事国，由联合国大会选出，任期两年。安全理事会的决议除程序性问题外必须得到常任理事国的一致同意。Security Council, major department of the United Nations. According to the Charter of the United Nations, the Security Council is the only department of the United Nations with the power to take actions to maintain world peace and security. It has 15 member states, with China, France, the Soviet Union (later replaced by Russia), the United Kingdom and the United States as permanent member states. The other 10 nations, which serve as non-permanent member states, are elected by the General Assembly of the United Nations for a term of two years. All the resolutions of the Security Council, with the exception of issues on procedures, shall be endorsed with the consensus of the five permanent member states. 简称 abbr. 安理会 Ānlǐhuì

【安全门】ānquánmén 太平门 emergency exit

【安全剃刀】ānquán tìdāo 保险刀 safety razor

【安全系数】ānquán xìshù 进行土木、机械等工程设计时，为了防止因材料的缺点、工作的偏差、外力的突增等因素所引起的后果，工程的受力部分实际上能够担负的力必须大于其容许担负的力，二者之比叫做安全系数。也指做某事的安全、可靠程度。safety coefficient or factor; ratio between the strength of a machine part, etc. and the force it is allowed to sustain. When a construction, machine-building or any other engineering project is being designed, it is imperative to ensure that the part of the project that is supposed to react to an external force should be able to sustain more such force than it is allowed to; also meaning degree of safety or reliability

【安然】ānrán ❶ 平安；安安稳稳地 safe and sound; (emerge) unscathed：～无事。Nothing has gone wrong.｜～返航（of a ship or plane) return home safe and sound from a voyage｜～脱险 escape unscathed ❷ 没有顾虑；很放心 be free from worry; feel at ease：～自若 be calm and composed｜只有把这件事告诉他，他心里才会～。Only by telling him the truth can he feel at ease.

【安如泰山】ān rú Tài Shān 形容像泰山一样稳固，不可动摇 rock firm; as solid as Mount Taishan; also 稳如泰山 wěn rú Tài Shān

【安设】ānshè 安装设置 install; set up：～空调器 install an airconditioner｜在山顶上～了一个气象观测站 set up a weather station on the mountaintop

【安身】ān//shēn 指在某地居住和生活（多用在困窘的环境下 oft. in an awkward situation) have a roof over one's head; take shelter：无处～have no roof over one's head; be homeless｜我有了～之地，母亲也就放心了。My mother finally set her mind at rest after I had settled down.

【安身立命】ān shēn lì mìng 生活有着落，精神有所寄托 settle down and get on with one's life：～之所 place for a settled life; a roof over one's head

【安神】ān//shén 使心神安定 calm or soothe the nerves; keep one's mind unruffled

【安生】ānshēng ❶ 生活安定 peaceful; restful：过～日子 live a restful life ❷ 安静；不生事（多指小孩子 usu. of children) quiet：睡个～觉 get a nice sleep｜这孩子一会儿也不～。The child simply will not keep quiet for a moment.

【安适】ānshì 安静而舒适 quiet and comfortable：～如常 as quiet and comfortable as usual｜心里～ in a comfortable frame of mind｜病员在疗养院里过着～的生活。The patients live in the sheltered quietude of the sanatorium.

【安睡】ānshuì 安静地睡觉；安歇 slumber; sleep soundly：夜深了，人们都已～。It's very late at night. Everybody is in a slumber.

【安泰】āntài 平安；安宁 domestic bliss; safe and sound：阖家～。Wish all the domestic bliss to your entire family.

【安恬】āntián 安逸恬适；安静 snug; quietude and seclusion (of a place)：～地睡了一觉 have a restful sleep

【安帖】āntiē 安定 feel at ease; set one's heart at rest; same as 塌实 tā•shi ②：事情都办妥，心里才算～。I have to see to it that everything is settled before I can set my heart at rest.

【安土重迁】ān tǔ zhòng qiān 在一个地方住惯了，不肯轻易迁移 be used to living in one's homeland and feel disinclined to move elsewhere; be attached to one's native land and reluctant to leave it

【安妥】āntuǒ 平安稳妥 be relieved; feel secure：把东西～地运到目的地。The goods have been shipped to their destination safe and sound.

【安慰】ānwèi ❶ 心情安适 be comforted; feel encouraged:有女儿在身边,她能得到一点~。She feels a little better with her daughter keeping her company. ❷ 使心情安适 comfort; console:~病人 comfort a patient|你要多~~他,叫他别太难过。Go out of your way to comfort him so that he won't feel too bad.

【安稳】ānwěn ❶ 稳当;平稳 smooth and steady:仪器要放~。Make sure to find a safe and steady place for the instruments.|这条船大,即使刮点风,也很~。The boat is so large, it's all smooth sailing even in the wind. ❷ 平静;安定 quiet; reposed:睡不~ have a restive sleep|过~日子 live a peaceful life ❸ (举止)沉静;稳重 (of behaviour, etc.) poised; composed

【安息】ānxī ❶ 安静地休息,多指入睡 rest; go to sleep:一路劳顿,请早点~。Please go to bed early after such a long journey. ❷ 对死者表示悼念的用语 rest in peace:~吧,亲爱的战友。May you rest in peace, comrade-in-arms!

【安息日】ānxīrì《圣经》记载,上帝在六日内创造天地万物,第七日完工休息。犹太教尊这天为圣日,名叫安息日(即星期五日落到星期六日落的一昼夜时间)。这一天礼拜上帝,不做工作。基督教以星期日为安息日,又称主日。Sabbath (day). According to the *Bible*, God blessed the seventh day (i.e., from sunset on Friday to sunset on Saturday) and made it holy, because on it he rested from all the work of creating that he had done. The Jews spend the Sabbath day worshipping God without working, whereas most Christians observe Sunday as their Sabbath day and they call it Lord's Day, but it is observed on Saturday in some Christian churches.

【安闲】ānxián 安静清闲 peaceful and carefree; relaxed:神态~in a relaxed mood|~自在 leisurely and carefree|他忙里忙外,一日不得~。Day in and day out, he bustles around without letup.

【安详】ānxiáng 从容不迫;稳重 serene; composed; imperturbable:面容~serene facial expression|举止~ carry oneself with composure; behave imperturbably|老人~地坐在靠椅里。The old man is a study of composure as he sits in his armchair.

【安歇】ānxiē ❶ 上床睡觉 go to bed; retire for the night:天已不早,大家该回房~了。It's getting late, time for everybody to go to bed in their rooms. ❷ 休息 take a rest:走得太累,先找个地方~一下。We are too tired to walk any further. Let's find a place for a break.

【安心】ān//xīn 存心;居心 harbour (an ulterior motive); be up to (sth. bad):~不善 mean harm; have a bad or evil intention|谁知他安的什么心? Who knows what he is up to?

【安心】ānxīn 心情安定 feel at ease; be relieved; set one's mind at rest:~工作 set one's mind to work; be devoted to one's work|家里事多,在外也难~。So much has happened back home to unsettle him, who is away making a living.

【安逸】ānyì 安闲舒适 leisurely; easy and comfortable:贪图~ be after comfort and ease; be bent on seeking comfort and ease

【安营】ān//yíng (队伍)架起帐篷住下 (of an army) pitch camp

【安营扎寨】ān yíng zhā zhài 原指军队架起帐篷、修起栅栏住下。现借指建立临时住地(多用于大规模的施工队伍)。(old, of an army) pitch tents and erect fences to stay for a period of time; (current, of a large construction crew) camp at the worksite

【安葬】ānzàng 埋葬(用于比较郑重的场合 a term used on solemn occasions) bury in state:~烈士遗骨 hold a solemn burial service for the remains of a martyr

【安枕】ānzhěn 放好枕头(睡觉),借指没有忧虑和牵挂 put the pillow in place for a nice sleep:~而卧 go to sleep free from anxiety

【安之若素】ān zhī ruò sù (遇到不顺利情况或反常现象)像平常一样对待,毫不在意 bear (adversity or hardship) with equanimity

【安置】ānzhì 使人或事物有着落;安放 allocate accommodation to sb.; put sb. or sth. in place:~人员 people to be re-allocated|~行李 put away the luggage|这批新来的同志都得到了适当的~。Each of the newcomers has been properly accommodated.

【安装】ānzhuāng 按照一定的方法、规格把机械或器材(多指成套的)固定在一定的地方 install; set up (a machine or complete set of equipment according to a prescribed method):~自来水管 install water pipes|~电话 mount a telephone set|~机器 install a machine

咹 ān same as 唵 ān
☞ ǎn on p.12

桉 ān 桉树,常绿乔木,树干高而直。原产澳大利亚,我国南部也种植。枝叶可提制桉油,树皮可制鞣料,木材供建筑用。eucalyptus (*Eucalyptus*); evergreen arbour with a straight and tall trunk, native to Australia but also planted in south China. Volatile oil can be extracted from its leaves and twigs, its bark is used as a tanning material, and its wood can be used for construction purposes. also 玉树 yùshù,黄金树 huángjīnshù and 有加利 yǒujiālì

氨 ān 氮和氢的化合物,化学式 NH_3。无色气体,有刺激性臭味,易溶于水。用做致冷剂,也用来做硝酸和氮肥。ammonia; pungent, colourless gaseous compound, NH_3, usu.

produced by direct combination of nitrogen and hydrogen gases; used as a refrigerant and in the manufacture of nitric acid and nitrogenous fertilizer; also 阿摩尼亚 āmóníyà; 通称 general term for 氨气 ānqì

【氨基】ānjī 氨分子失去 1 个氢原子而成的一价原子团($-NH_2$)amino or amino group; monovalent elementide ($-NH_2$) obtained by depriving the ammonia molecule of one hydrogen atom

【氨基酸】ānjīsuān 分子中同时含有氨基和羧基的有机化合物,是组成蛋白质的基本单位 amino acid; organic compound that contains at least one carboxyl group and one amino group and that serves as the basic unit for protein

唵 ān〈叹词 *interj.*〉❶ 表示答应[indicating response] yeah:'您开完会啦?''~,开完了。' 'So the meeting's over?' 'Yeah, it's over.' ❷ 表示提醒、商量(语气较委婉)[indicating the intention to remind or consult in a tactful manner]:你们责任重大,以后还得加油,~! This is real important work and you've got to work harder, right? |大家想的办法,~,我看很不错嘛! In my opinion your idea is a good one, right?

☞ ǎn on p.13

庵(菴) ān ❶〈书 *fml.*〉小草屋 tiny thatched hut:茅~ thatched cottage ❷ 佛寺(多指尼姑住的)Buddhist convent; nunnery:~堂 convent|尼姑~nunnery

【庵堂】āntáng 尼姑庵 nunnery; Buddhist convent

【庵子】ān•zi〈方 *dial.*〉❶ 小草屋 small thatched hut:稻草~ straw-thatched cottage ❷ 尼姑庵 nunnery

谙 ān〈书 *fml.*〉熟悉 be familiar with:不~水性 not good at swimming|素~针灸之术 be highly skilled in administering acupuncture and moxibustion

【谙达】āndá 熟悉(人情世故) be familiar with (ways of the world):~世情 be worldly-wise

【谙练】ānliàn〈书 *fml.*〉熟习;熟练;有经验 be well-versed in; be skilled at; be experienced in

【谙熟】ānshú 熟悉(某种事物) be proficient in (sth.):~地理 be knowledgeable about geography|培养~经济管理的人才 train people who are proficient in economic management

媕 ān [媕娿](ān'ē)〈书 *fml.*〉不能决定的样子 indecision; hesitation

鹌 ān [鹌鹑](ān•chún) 鸟,头小,尾巴短,羽毛赤褐色,不善飞 quail (*Coturnix*); bobwhite; small bird with tiny head and short tail and brownish feathers, not good at flying; also 鹑 chún

腤 ān〈书 *fml.*〉烹煮(鱼、肉) cook; stew (fish or meat)

鮟 ān [鮟鱇](ānkāng) 鱼,全身无鳞,头大而扁,常潜伏在海底捕食,能发出像老人咳嗽一样的声音。angler (*Pediculati*); scaleless pediculate fish having an immense mouth and a big, depressed head to which is attached a wormlike filament for luring prey, oft. ambushing its prey at the bottom of the sea, and emitting a sound evocative of an old man's cough; 通称 general term for 老头儿鱼 lǎotóuryú

鞍 ān 鞍子 saddle:马~horse saddle|~鞯 saddle and the cushion beneath it|马不歇~be combat ready

【鞍鼻】ānbí 鼻部畸形的一种,鼻梁中间凹陷,由鼻部外伤、梅毒、结核等引起 saddle nose; deformed nose with the bridge sunken in the middle, caused by injury, syphilis, tuberculosis, etc.

【鞍鞯】ānchàn 马鞍子和垫在马鞍子下面的东西 saddle and the cushion beneath it

【鞍鞯】ānjiān〈书 *fml.*〉same as 鞍鞯 ānchàn

【鞍马】ānmǎ ❶ 体操器械的一种,形状略像马,背部有两个半圆环,是木马的一种 pummelled horse; vaulting horse; sports apparatus in the rough shape of a horse with two semi-circular knobs on its back; a kind of wooden horse ❷ 男子竞技体操项目之一,运动员在鞍马上,手握半圆环或撑着马背做各种动作 gymnastic event for men, with the athlete doing stunts by propping himself up with hands on the knobs or the back of a vaulting horse ❸ 鞍子和马,借指骑马或战斗的生活 saddle and horse; horseback-riding or battle life:~劳顿 be fatigued by a long journey; travel-worn|~生活 life of a horseback-rider or soldier

【鞍马劳顿】ān mǎ láodùn 形容旅途或战斗的劳累 be fatigued by a long journey or a battle; travel-worn; foot-weary

【鞍前马后】ān qián mǎ hòu〈比喻 *fig.*〉跟随在别人身边,小心侍候 (of a faithful attendant) fuss around the master

【鞍子】ān•zi 放在牲口背上驮运东西或供人骑坐的器具,多用皮革或木头加棉垫制成 saddle; seat for a rider or goods on the back of a draught animal, mostly made of leather or wood with a cotton cushion underneath

韽 ān〈书 *fml.*〉same as 鞍 ān

盦[1] ān〈古时 *arch.*〉盛食物的器具 food container

盦[2] ān same as 庵 ān

ǎn (ㄢˇ)

咹 ǎn same as 唵[3] ǎn

☞ ān on p.11

俺 ǎn〈方 *dial.*〉〈代词 *pron.*〉❶ 我们(不包括听话的人) we or our (the person spoken to not included):你先去,~几个随后就到。You go first — we'll be there right away. ❷ 我 I or me:你们都走吧,就~一个人留下。Go, all of you, and I'll stay behind by myself.

堷(垵) ǎn ❶ 挖小坑点种瓜、豆等 dig a hole to dibble seeds:~豆子 dibble in the beans ❷ 点种时挖的小坑 hole to dibble ❸ (~儿 ǎnr)〈量词 *classifier*〉用于点种的瓜、豆等 melon, bean seeds or seedlings, etc., to be sown or planted by dibbling:一~儿花生 a cluster of peanut seedlings

【堷子】ǎn·zi 点种瓜、豆等挖的小坑:~田 dig holes to dibble seeds or seedlings|挖个~dig a hole for dibbling

唵[1] ǎn 把手里握着的粒状或粉末状的东西塞进嘴里 put granulated or powdered stuff into one's mouth:~了一口炒米。(He) put a mouthful of roasted rice into his mouth.|~了两口雪。(He) ate two mouthfuls of snow.

唵[2] ǎn same as 俺 ǎn

唵[3] ǎn 〈叹词 *interj.*〉表示疑问 [indicating doubt]:~,东西都收拾好了吗? You have put things together, haven't you?|怎么这两天没看到你呀,~? Haven't seen you the last couple of days — where have you been?

唵[4] ǎn 佛教咒语用字 Om; aum; word used in Buddhism as a mythic spell or as an object of meditation

☞ ān on p.12

铵 ǎn 从氨衍生所得的带正电荷的根,也就是铵离子 ammonium ion; ammonium; positive-carrying univalent ion which plays the part of a metal in the salt formed when ammonia reacts with an acid; also 铵根 ǎn'gen

揞 ǎn 用药面儿或其他粉末敷在伤口上 apply medicinal powder to a wound:伤口上抹点儿红药水,再~上点儿消炎粉。Daub mercurochrome on the wound, and then apply sulphadiazine powder to it.

àn (ㄢˋ)

犴 àn ☞ [狴犴](bì'àn) on p.107

岸[1] àn 江、河、湖、海等水边的陆地 bank; shore; coast:江~ river bank|上~go ashore|两~绿柳成阴。The rivers is flanked on both sides by green willows.

岸[2] àn 〈书 *fml.*〉❶ 高大 lofty; tall and big:伟~(of man) tall and broad shouldered; stalwart ❷ 高傲 proud:傲~haughty

【岸标】ànbiāo 设在岸上指示航行的标志,可以使船舶避开沙滩、暗礁等 navigational beacon; landmark set up on the shore of a river, sea, etc., to help ships steer clear of a beach, reefs, etc.

【岸然】ànrán 〈书 *fml.*〉严肃的样子 serious manner:道貌~assume the guise of a man of integrity; be a hypocrite

按[1] àn ❶ 用手或指头压 press; push down:~电铃 ring an electric bell|~图钉 nail a thumbtack in place ❷ 压住;搁下 leave aside; shelve; hold:~兵不动 hold one's troops where they are; abide by one's time|~下此事不说。Leave this aside for the moment. ❸ 抑制 restrain; check:~不住心头怒火 be unable to restrain, control or contain one's anger ❹ 用手压住不动 keep one's hand on; keep a tight grip on:~剑 keep one's hand on a sword ❺ 依照 in compliance with:~时上班 go to work on time|~质论价 fix the price according to quality|~制度办事 act in accordance with rules and regulations

按[2](案) àn ❶〈书 *fml.*〉考查;核对 check; refer to:有原文可~。There's the original to go by. ❷(编者、作者等)加按语 (of an editor or author) add a note or comment:编者~ editor's note

【按兵不动】àn bīng bù dòng 使军队暂不行动,等待时机。现也借指接受任务后不肯行动。hold one's troops where they are and bide one's time; take no action after receiving a task

【按部就班】àn bù jiù bān 按照一定的条理,遵循一定的程序 follow the prescribed order; keep to conventional ways of doing things:学习科学知识,应该~,循序渐进。In studying science it is imperative to follow a proper order and advance step by step.

【按键】ànjiàn 用手按的键 (as of a key board) key; push button; same as 键 jiàn ③

【按金】ànjīn 〈方 *dial.*〉押金;租金 deposit; rent

【按扣儿】ànkòur 子母扣儿 snap fastener

【按理】àn//lǐ 按照情理 normally; in the ordinary course of events:~我们应该先去看您的。Of course we should have come to see you first.|你这样做,不管按什么理都说不过去。You simply have no excuse for the way you behave.

【按例】ànlì 按照惯例 as a rule:生活困难,~可以申请补助。According to regulations those who are in financial difficulty may apply for government allowance.

【按脉】àn//mài 诊脉 feel (or take) the pulse

【按摩】ànmó 用手在人身上推、按、捏、揉等,以促进血液循环,增加皮肤抵抗力,调整神经功能 massage; act or technique of treating the body by pushing, pressing, kneading, rubbing, or the like, to stimulate blood circulation, increase the skin's resistance to diseases; and readjust the nerve's function; also 推拿 tuīná

【按捺】ànnà same as 抑制 yìzhì ②:~不住

A

激动的心情 cannot contain one's excitement; also 按纳 ànnà

【按钮】ànniǔ（～儿 ànniǔr）用手按的开关 push button

【按期】ànqī 依照规定的限期 on schedule; on time: ～交工 complete a project and hand it over on schedule | ～归还 return sth. on time

【按时】ànshí 依照规定的时间 on time; on schedule: ～完成 meet the deadline; finish in time | ～吃药 take medicine on time

【按说】ànshuō 依照事实或情理来说 normally; ordinarily: 这么大的孩子，～该懂事了。A child at his or her age should normally be well-behaved. | 五一节都过了，～该穿单衣了，可是一早一晚还离不了毛衣。It's past May Day. Normally we would be wearing summer clothing at this time of the year, yet we still can't do without woollen sweaters in the morning and at night.

【按图索骥】àn tú suǒ jì 按照图像寻找好马 look for a steed with the aid of a picture;〈比喻 *fig.*〉按照线索寻找，也比喻办事机械、死板 try to find sth. by following up a clue; deal with (or handle) sth. in a mechanical way

【按下葫芦浮起瓢】àn xià hú·lu fú qǐ piáo 〈比喻 *fig.*〉顾了这头就顾不了那头，无法使事情得到圆满解决 solve one problem only to find another cropping up

【按压】ànyā same as 抑制 yìzhì ②: ～不住的激情 cannot restrain one's excitement

【按验】ànyàn same as 案验 ànyàn

【按语】ànyǔ 作者、编者对有关文章、词句所做的说明、提示或考证 note or comment by an author or editor on a piece of writing or certain parts of it; also 案语 ànyǔ

【按照】ànzhào 根据；依照 according to; in (the) light of; in compliance with: ～事实说话 base one's opinions on facts | ～预定的计划执行 act on a plan

胺 àn 氨分子中的氢原子被烃基取代而成的有机化合物 amine; organic compounds derived from ammonia by replacement of one or more hydrogen atoms with hydrocarbon radical

案¹ àn ❶ same as '案子'¹ àn·zi: 条～narrow table or desk | 书～desk | 拍～而起 smite the table and rise to one's feet in indignation ❷〈古代 *arch.*〉进食用的木托盘 wooden saucer for serving meals: 举～齐眉 hold the tray level with the brows — husband and wife treating each other with courtesy; married couple loving and respecting each other

案² àn ❶ same as '案子'² àn·zi: 犯～commit a crime | 破～crack a case | 五卅惨～May 30th Massacre; slaughter of Chinese demonstrators by imperialist troops in foreign concessions in Shanghai on May 30, 1925 ❷ 案卷；记录 record; file: 备～register for the record | 有～可查 be documented; have records to be referred to | 声明在～。The statement is on the record. ❸ 提出计划、办法或其他建议的文件 plan, method or suggestion submitted for consideration: 方～work plan | 议～bill; motion | 提～proposal; motion ❹ same as 按² àn

【案板】ànbǎn 做面食、切菜用的木板，多为长方形 kneading or chopping board (usu. rectangular)

【案秤】ànchèng 一种小型的秤，商店中使用时常把它放在柜台上。有的地区叫台秤。counter scale; small scale put on a counter in a store; also known as 台秤 táichèng in some areas

【案底】àndǐ 治安机关指某人过去违法或犯罪行为的记录 file or record of previous offences

【案牍】àndú〈书 *fml.*〉公事文书 formal official documents or correspondence

【案犯】ànfàn 经司法机关批准逮捕的人或刑事法庭上被控告而尚未判定有罪的人；作案的人 suspect; criminal implicated in a case; person suspected of a crime and arrested with the approval of a judicial organ; person who has been prosecuted in court but not yet convicted of a crime

【案件】ànjiàn 有关诉讼和违法的事件 law suit; case: 刑事～criminal case | 重大贪污～major case of corruption

【案卷】ànjuàn 机关或企业等经过分类、整理的以备存查的文件材料 records; files; archives

【案例】ànlì 某种案件的例子 case in point: 经济～economic case in point | ～分析 case analysis; case study

【案目】ànmù〈旧时 *old*〉称剧场中为观众找座位的人 usher; someone who shows people to their seats in a theatre

【案情】ànqíng 案件的情节 details of a case: ～复杂 complicated case | 分析～analyse a case

【案头】àntóu ❶ 几案上或书桌上 on the table; on the desk: ～日历 desk calendar | ～放着一些参考书。There are some reference books on the desk. ❷ 指案头工作 same as 案头工作 àntóu gōngzuò

【案头工作】àntóu gōngzuò 指导演、演员在创作过程中所做的分析剧情、角色等的文字工作 notes written by a director or an actor in analysing a plot, a role, etc. in the course of creative writing or performance

【案验】ànyàn〈书 *fml.*〉调查罪证 investigate the evidence of a case; also 按验 ànyàn

【案由】ànyóu 案件的内容提要 brief; gist or brief of a case

【案语】ànyǔ same as 按语 ànyǔ

【案子】¹ àn·zi 一种旧式的狭长桌子或架起来代替桌子用的长木板 long, narrow table or long board propped up to serve as a table or counter：肉～meat counter｜裁缝～tailor's work bench

【案子】[2] àn·zi 案件 law suit；case：审～try or hear a case｜办了一件～finish handling a case

晻 àn same as 暗 àn
☞ yǎn on p. 2212

暗（❶❸闇）àn ❶ 光线不足；黑暗（跟'明'相对，下同 as opposed to 'bright'）dark；dim：～室 darkroom｜光线太～。The light is rather dim.｜太阳已经落山，天色渐渐～下来了。The sun has set，and it's getting dark. ❷ 隐藏不露的；秘密的 hidden；secret；clandestine：～号 secret signal or sign；cipher；countersign｜明人不做～事。An honest man does not do anything underhand.｜～自欢喜 feel a surge of innermost joy ❸〈书 *fml.*〉糊涂；不明白 muddled；confused：兼听则明，偏信则～。Listen to both sides，you'll be enlightened；listen to one side，and you'll be benighted.

【暗暗】àn'àn 在暗中或私下里，不显露出来 secretly；inwardly；to oneself：～吃了一惊 gasp inwardly｜他～下定决心。He made up his mind but did not show it.

【暗坝】ànbà 不露出水面的坝 underwater dam

【暗堡】ànbǎo 隐蔽的碉堡 bunker

【暗藏】àncáng 隐藏；隐蔽 hide；conceal：身上～凶器 have a weapon about one's person；illegally possess firearms｜消灭～的敌人 eliminate hidden enemy

【暗娼】ànchāng 暗地里卖淫的妓女 unlicensed (or unregistered) prostitute；call girl

【暗场】ànchǎng 不在舞台上表演，只在台词中交代，使观众意会的情节 plot in a drama not acted out on stage but to be understood through dialogue or monologue

【暗潮】àncháo〈比喻 *fig.*〉暗中发展，还没有表面化的事态（多指政治斗争、社会运动等 usu. in a political struggle，social movement，etc.）undercurrent；underlying tendency

【暗淡】àndàn（光、色）昏暗；不光明；不鲜艳（of light and colour）dim；faint；dismal；gloomy：光线～dim light｜色彩～dull colour ◇前景～bleak prospects

【暗道】àndào 隐蔽的道路；不露在外面的通道 secret path (passage，tunnel，etc.)

【暗地里】àndì·li 私下；背地里 secretly；inwardly；on the sly：～勾结 hand in glove (with sb.) on the sly｜～直掉眼泪 shed tears without being seen by others；also 暗地 àndì

【暗度陈仓】àn dù Chéncāng 公元前206年，刘邦攻下咸阳，被项羽封为汉王，带着人马到南郑去，途中烧毁了栈道。不久绕道北上，在陈仓（今陕西宝鸡市东）打败秦将章邯的军队，回到咸阳。小说家把这段历史演义为'明修栈道，暗度陈仓'。后来用'暗度陈仓'比喻暗中进行某种活动（多指男女私通）。make a feint in one direction while attacking in another；do one thing under cover of another. In 206 B.C. Liu Bang led his troops on a march to Nanzheng shortly after sacking Xianyang，for which Xiang Yu the Lord of Chu made him 'King of Han'. They burned down the plankway on the way，turned north by making a detour，and stormed back to Xianyang after routing General Zhang Han's army of Qin in a surprise attack at Chencang (east of present-day Baoji，Shaanxi Province). An ancient novelist summed up this episode in the famed idiom of 'pretending to prepare to advance along one path while secretly going along another.' The phrase is oft. used to imply clandestine activity (usu. adultery).

【暗房】ànfáng same as 暗室 ànshì ①

【暗沟】àngōu 地下的排水沟 sewer；underground drainage ditch

【暗害】ànhài 暗中杀害或陷害 murder；kill secretly；frame sb. up：险遭～narrowly escape a murder attempt

【暗含】ànhán 做事、说话包含某种意思而未明白说出 express or mean indirectly；imply；suggest：～不满情绪 imply one's resentment｜这几句话，～着对他的讥讽。These remarks imply much mockery of him.

【暗号】ànhào（～儿 ànhàor）彼此约定的秘密信号（利用声音、动作等）secret signal (or sign)；countersign；watchword：联络～contact signal

【暗合】ànhé 没有经过商讨而意思恰巧相合 coincide；agree without prior consultation：妈妈的话正与他的心意～。His mother said exactly what was on his mind.

【暗盒】ànhé 有遮光作用，专为放置没有曝光或冲洗的胶卷的小盒 cartridge；cassette；tiny lightproof metal or plastic container for a roll of film to be exposed or developed

【暗花儿】ànhuār 隐约的花纹，如瓷器上利用凹凸构成的花纹和纺织品上利用明暗构成的花纹 veiled design incised in porcelain or woven in fabric

【暗火】ànhuǒ 不冒火焰的火（区别于'明火'as compared with 'burning fire'）fire without flame；smouldering fire

【暗疾】ànjí 不好意思告诉别人的疾病，如性病之类 disease one is ashamed of，unmentionable disease，such as VD

【暗记儿】ànjìr 秘密的记号 secret mark

【暗间儿】ànjiānr 相连的几间屋子中不直接通向外面的房间，通常用做卧室或贮藏室 inner room (usu. used as a bedroom or storeroom)

【暗箭】ànjiàn〈比喻 *fig.*〉暗中伤人的行为或诡计 stab in the back；arrow shot from hiding — an attack by a hidden enemy：明枪易躲，～难防。It is easy to parry a spear thrust in the open，but hard to dodge an arrow shot in the dark.

【暗礁】ànjiāo ❶ 海洋、江河中不露出水面的礁

A

石，是航行的障碍 reef or rock under water ❷〈比喻 *fig.*〉事情在进行中遇到的潜伏的障碍 latent obstacle

【暗井】ànjǐng 地下采矿时，装有提升设备而无直通地面出口的垂直或倾斜的通道 winze; vertical or inclined shaft driven downward into a body of ore, equipped with a hoist for mining purposes but without a direct exit to the ground; also 盲井 mángjǐng

【暗里】àn·lǐ 暗中；背地里 in the dark; on the sly：～活动 manoeuvre on the sly; clandestine manoeuvring

【暗流】ànliú ❶ 流动的地下水 undercurrent ❷〈比喻 *fig.*〉潜伏的思想倾向或社会动态 latent ideological or social trend or tendency

【暗楼子】ànlóu·zi 屋内顶部可以藏东西的部分，在天花板上开一方口，临时用梯子上下 attic storeroom, accessible through an opening in the ceiling by a ladder

【暗码】ànmǎ（～儿 ànmǎr）〈旧时 *old*〉商店在商品标价上所用的代替数字的符号 mark on a price tag to replace a figure

【暗昧】ànmèi ❶ 暧昧 dim; obscure：～之事 carryings-on ❷ 愚昧 stupid; foolish：～懵懂 stupid and ignorant

【暗门子】ànmén·zi〈方 *dial.*〉暗娼 unlicensed whore

【暗盘】ànpán（～儿 ànpánr）指买卖双方在市场外秘密议定的价格 price secretly negotiated off the marketplace

【暗器】ànqì 暗中投射使人不及防备的兵器，如镖、袖箭等（多见于早期白话 usu. used in early vernacular）hidden weapon, such as darts hidden inside sleeves

【暗弱】ànruò ❶ 光线微弱，不明亮（of light）dim; faint：灯光～dim light｜星光渐渐～了。The stars are fading. ❷〈书 *fml.*〉愚昧软弱 stupid and weak：为人～be stupid and weak-willed; be a weakling｜昏庸～fatuous and incompetent

【暗杀】ànshā 乘人不备，进行杀害 murder premeditatedly and treacherously; assassinate：惨遭～be murdered in cold blood｜～事件 case of assassination

【暗沙】ànshā 海中由沙和珊瑚碎屑堆成的岛屿，略高于高潮线，或与高潮线相平 shoal; sandbar or coral islet that is exposed at or above the surface of the water when the sea is at high tide; also 暗砂 ànshā

【暗伤】ànshāng same as ❶ 内伤 nèishāng ② ❷ 物体上的不显露的损伤 indiscernible damage

【暗哨】ànshào 隐蔽的岗哨 secret sentry; on hidden sentry duty

【暗射】ànshè 影射 insinuate

【暗射地图】ànshè dìtú 有符号标记，不注文字的地图，教学时用来使学生辨认或填充 map with locations marked but not labelled, used as a teaching aid for identifying places on a map

【暗示】ànshì ❶ 不明白表示意思，而用含蓄的言语或示意的举动使人领会 drop a hint; hint; suggest：他用眼睛～我，让我走开。He hinted with his eyes that he wanted me to leave. ❷ 一种心理影响，用言语、手势、表情等使人不加考虑地接受某种意见或做某件事，如催眠就是暗示作用 hint; covert suggestion; intimation conveyed through language, gesture, facial expression, etc. that is meant to prompt sb. to accept an opinion or do sth. with no time for reflection, such as hypnotism

【暗事】ànshì 不光明正大的事 clandestine or illicit action：明人不做～。An honest man does nothing underhand.

【暗室】ànshì ❶ 有遮光设备的房间 darkroom; room from which the actinic rays of light are excluded ❷〈书 *fml.*〉指幽暗隐蔽的地方；无人之处 secret place：不欺～ be scrupulously honest even when there is no one around

【暗送秋波】àn sòng qiūbō 原指暗中眉目传情，泛指献媚取宠，暗中勾搭 ogle; make eyes at sb.; make secret overtures to sb.

【暗算】ànsuàn 暗中图谋伤害或陷害 plot against：险遭～ almost fall prey to a plot

【暗锁】ànsuǒ 嵌在门、箱子、抽屉上，只有锁孔露在外面的锁，一般要用钥匙才能锁上 built-in lock; mechanical device for securing a door or suitcase or drawer, etc., with only a hole exposed, to be locked only with a key

【暗滩】àntān 不露出水面的石滩或沙滩 hidden shoal

【暗探】àntàn ❶ 从事秘密侦察的人 secret agent; spy ❷ 暗中刺探 make out on the sly; pry; spy：～军机 spy on or fish for military secret

【暗无天日】àn wú tiān rì 形容社会极端黑暗 complete darkness — total absence of justice

【暗喜】ànxǐ 暗自高兴 feel pleased but not show it：心中～ cannot help feeling secretly delighted

【暗匣】ànxiá 暗箱 camera bellows; camera obscura

【暗下】ànxià 背地里；私下里 on the sly; surreptitiously：表面不露声色，～却加紧活动。Nothing seems unusual on the surface, but a conspiracy is brewing. also 暗下里 ànxià·li

【暗线】ànxiàn ❶ 文学作品中未直接描绘的人物活动或事件所间接呈现出来的线索（of literary work）hidden thread, lead or clue, etc. revealed through an activity or event that has left unsaid ❷ 暗中为己方进行侦察或做内应的人 mole; agent or spy planted inside an enemy

【暗箱】ànxiāng 照相机的一部分，关闭时不透光，前部装镜头、快门，后部装胶片 camera bellows; camera obscura; lightproof box-like device in a camera, with the lens and shutter fixed in the front and film loaded at its back

【暗笑】ànxiào ❶ 暗自高兴 glee secretly; laugh in or up one's sleeve:看到对方着急的样子,不禁心里~。At the sight of the other party's anxious look, (he) tried to suppress a grin in secret glee. ❷ 暗自讥笑 sneer secretly at:在场的人都~他无知妄说。Everyone on the scene was secretly laughing at his ignorant absurdity.

【暗影】ànyǐng 阴影 shadow

【暗语】ànyǔ 彼此约定的秘密话 code word; prescribed word used for secrecy of communication:说~communicate with code word|用~接头 contact sb. with code word in a rendezvous

【暗喻】ànyù 隐喻 metaphor

【暗中】ànzhōng ❶ 黑暗之中 in the dark:躲在~张望 hide in the dark and keep watch|~摸索 grope in the dark; explore by oneself ❷ 背地里;私下里;不公开的 in secret; on the sly:~打听 gather information in secret|~活动 carry on surreptitious activities

【暗转】ànzhuǎn 戏剧演至某一场或某一幕的中间,台上灯光暂时熄灭,表示剧情时间的推移,或者同时迅速换布景,表示地点的变动 (of the theatre) blackout in the middle of a scene or act (to indicate either a change in time, or, with a quick change of setting, a change in place)

【暗自】ànzì 私下里;暗地里 inwardly; to oneself; on the sly:~盘算 secretly calculate|~高兴 feel delighted but not show it

黯 àn 阴暗 dim:~淡 dim; faint

【黯淡】àndàn 暗淡 dim; faint:色彩~dim colour

【黯黑】ànhēi ❶ 乌黑 swarthy:脸色~swarthy complexion ❷ 昏黑 dim; gloomy:~的夜晚 dark night|天色已经~了。It is dark already.

【黯然】ànrán ❶ 阴暗的样子 dim, faint:~无光 dark and dim|工地上千万盏电灯光芒四射,连天上的星月也~失色。The worksite was ablaze with a myriad of lights so that even the moon and the stars appeared lustreless in comparison. ❷ 心里不舒服,情绪低落的样子 dejected; low-spirited; downcast:~泪下 cry despite oneself|~神伤 appear dejected or depressed

āng (尢)

肮(骯) āng [肮脏](āng·zāng) ❶ 脏;不干净 dirty; filthy:~衣服 dirty clothes|屋里又凌乱又~。It's messy and filthy in the room. ❷〈比喻 *fig.*〉卑鄙、丑恶 mean; foul; dirty:~交易 dirty deal|灵魂~dark soul

áng (尢)

卬 áng〈书 *fml.*〉❶ 我 I; me ❷ same as 昂 áng ❸ (Áng) 姓 a surname

昂 áng ❶ 仰着(头) hold (one's head) high:~首挺胸 be spirited; full of vigour; chin up and chest out ❷ 高涨 soaring:~贵 (of a commodity) very expensive|激~impassioned

【昂昂】áng'áng 形容精神振奋,很有气魄 in high spirits; looking brave:~然 high-spirited|气势~forceful; vigorous|雄赳赳,气~valiant and spirited

【昂藏】ángcáng〈书 *fml.*〉形容人的仪表雄伟 (of man) of tall and strong build:气宇~ tall and strong

【昂奋】ángfèn (精神)振奋;(情绪)高涨 in high spirits; buoyant; be full of zest

【昂贵】ángguì 价格很高 expensive; costly:物价~exorbitant price|~的代价 dear price

【昂然】ángrán 仰头挺胸无所畏惧的样子 chin up and chest out; upright and unafraid:~屹立 stand like a towering mountain|气概~daring spirit of character; full of valour

【昂首】ángshǒu 仰着头 hold one's head high:~望天 hold one's head high and gaze at the sky|战马~长鸣。The battle steed craned its neck and neighed.

【昂首阔步】áng shǒu kuò bù 仰起头,迈着大步向前。形容精神振奋,意气昂扬。stride along with one's chin up; stride proudly ahead

【昂扬】ángyáng ❶ (情绪)高涨 elated; spirited:斗志~with high morale ❷ (声音)高昂 (of voice, sound, etc.) high-pitched:歌声激越~inspiring and spirited singing

àng (尢)

枊 àng〈书 *fml.*〉拴马桩 post for hitching or tethering a horse

盎1 àng〈古代 *arch.*〉一种腹大口小的器皿 vessel with a big belly and a small mouth

盎2 àng〈书 *fml.*〉洋溢;盛(shèng) brimming; abundant:~然 overflowing; exuberant|~~ full of vigour

【盎格鲁撒克逊人】Àngélǔ-Sākèxùnrén 公元5世纪时,迁居英国不列颠的以盎格鲁和撒克逊为主的日耳曼人。这两个部落最早住在北欧日德兰半岛南部。Anglo-Saxon; member of the Germanic tribes of Angles and Saxons who lived in the south of the Julland Peninsula of northern Europe in the early days and settled in Britain in the 5th century

【盎然】àngrán 形容气氛、趣味等洋溢的样子 exuberant; rich:春意~。Spring is very much in the air.|趣味~appealing; full of interest

【盎司】àngsī 英美制重量单位,1盎司等于1/16

A

磅,约合28.35克 ounce; British and American unit of weight measurement, equal 1/16 pound or approximately 28.35 grammes; 旧称 formerly called 英两 yīngliǎng or 唡 yīngliǎng

āo(幺)

凹 āo 低于周围(跟'凸'相对 as opposed to 'convex') concave; sunken; dented; sag: ～地 depression | ～凸不平 bumpy

☞ wā on p. 1964

【凹版】āobǎn 雕刻的部分凹入版面的印刷版,如铜版、钢版、照相凹板。凹版印刷品,纸面上油墨稍微鼓起,如钞票、邮票等。intaglio; gravure (copper or steel plate for the intaglio process of photomechanical printing); banknote, stamp, etc. produced by gravure

【凹面镜】āomiànjìng 球面镜的一种,反射面为凹面,焦点在镜前,当光源在焦点上,所发出的光反射后形成平行光束 concave mirror; reflecting mirror with a concave spherical reflecting surface with its focus in front of it, and when the source of light is on the focus, the light reflected on the mirror's surface is converted into parallel rays; also 凹镜 āojìng or 会聚镜 huìjùjìng

【凹透镜】āotòujìng 透镜的一种,中央比四周薄,平行光线透过后向四外散射。近视眼镜的镜片就属于这个类型。concave lens, with its centre thinner than its edge, diverging in all directions the parallel rays that have penetrated its surface. The lenses of spectacles worn by a nearsighted person are of this type. also 发散透镜 fāsàn tòujìng

【凹陷】āoxiàn 向内或向下陷进去 cave in; sink: 两颊～sunken or hollow cheeks | 地形～。The ground caved in.

熬 āo 烹调方法,把蔬菜等放在水里煮 stew; boil vegetable, etc. in water: ～白菜 stewed cabbage | ～豆腐 stewed bean curd or tofu

☞ áo on p. 18

【熬心】āoxīn 〈方 *dial.*〉心里不舒畅;烦闷 vexed; upset; depressed

爊(爊) āo ❶〈书 *fml.*〉放在微火上煨熟 simmer sth. over a low fire ❷〈方 *dial.*〉烹调方法,用多种香料加工某种食品 cook with many spices: ～鸭 duck cooked with spices | ～鸡 spicy chicken ❸〈书 *fml.*〉same as 熬 āo

áo(幺)

敖 áo ❶ same as 遨 áo ❷ (Áo) 姓 a surname

【敖包】áobāo 蒙古族人做路标和界标的堆子,用石、土、草等堆成。旧时曾把敖包当神灵的住地来祭祀。也译作鄂博。aobao; pile of stones, earth and grass, used by Mongolians as a road or boundary sign, worshipped in the past as habitation of deities; also translated as 鄂博 èbó

隞 Áo 商朝的都城,在今河南郑州西北 Ao, capital of the Shang Dynasty (1600-1046 B.C.), to the northwest of present-day Zhengzhou, Henan Province; also 敖 Áo or 嚣 Áo

嶅 áo 嶅阳(Áoyáng),地名,在山东 Aoyang, name of a place in Shandong Province

遨 áo 〈书 *fml.*〉游玩 stroll; saunter

【遨游】áoyóu 漫游;游历 travel; roam: ～世界 go on a tour of the world | ～太空 travel through space

嗷 áo ☞ below

【嗷嗷】áo'áo 〈拟声词 *onom.*〉形容哀号或喊叫声 [sound of crying (of certain birds or animals, or of human beings in pain or suffering)]: ～叫 howl | ～待哺 (of an infant) cry out for the breast

【嗷嗷待哺】áo'áo dài bǔ 形容饥饿时急于求食的样子 (of starving children or young animals) cry piteously for food

廒(厫) áo 〈书 *fml.*〉贮藏粮食等的仓库 storehouse for grain, etc.: 仓～ granary; barn

璈 áo 古代的一种乐器 stringed musical instrument of ancient China

獒 áo 狗的一种,身体大,尾巴长,四肢较短,毛黄褐色。凶猛善斗,可做猎狗。mastiff; long-tailed and short-limbed large dog in a yellowish brown coat, trained as hunting dog for its ferocity and bravery

熬 áo ❶ 把粮食等放在水里,煮成糊状 cook (cereals, etc.) into porridge or thick soup: ～粥 make gruel; cook porridge ❷ 为了提取有效成分或去掉所含水分、杂质,把东西放在容器里久煮 extract sth.'s essence; dehydrate or purify sth. by long boiling: ～盐 make salt by boiling seawater | ～药 decoct medicine by boiling medicinal herbs ❸ 忍受(疼痛或艰苦的生活等) endure (pain, hard life, etc.); put up with: ～夜 stay up late at night | ～苦日子 drag out a miserable existence

☞ āo on p. 18

【熬煎】áojiān 〈比喻 *fig.*〉折磨 suffering; torment; torture: 受尽～have one's fill of suffering | 疾病时时～着他。He is bugged by illness from time to time.

【熬磨】áo·mó 〈方 *dial.*〉❶ 痛苦地度过(时间) endure; go through painfully ❷ 没完没了地纠缠 pester: 这孩子很听话,从不～人。The child is so well-behaved, he never causes me any trouble.

【熬头儿】áo·tour 经受艰难困苦后，可能获得美好生活的希望 hope for a better life after years of suffering; good days to look forward to

【熬刑】áo//xíng 犯人忍受酷刑，不肯承认被指控的罪行(of a suspect or convict) suffer torture rather than plead guilty：～不过，只得招供。The torture proved too much for the man, who had no alternative but to confess.

【熬夜】áo//yè 通夜或深夜不睡觉 stay up late or all night; burn the midnight oil

聱 áo ☞ 佶屈聱牙 jíqū áoyá on p. 904

螯 áo 螃蟹等节肢动物的变形的第一对脚，形状像钳子，能开合，用来取食或自卫 chela; pincers; (of crab or any other arthropod) pincer-like organ or claw that can open or close for feeding or self-defence

翱(翶) áo〈书 *fml.*〉展翅飞 take wing

【翱翔】áoxiáng 在空中回旋地飞 hover; soar in the sky：雄鹰在高空中～。Eagles hover high in the sky.

謷 áo〈书 *fml.*〉诋毁 slander; defamation; calumny

鳌(鼇) áo 传说中海里的大龟或大鳖 huge legendary turtle

【鳌山】áoshān〈旧时 *old*〉元宵节用灯彩堆叠成的山，像传说中的巨鳌形状 lanterns piled up in the shape of a huge turtle during the Lantern Festival (15th of the 1st lunar month)

【鳌头】áotóu 指皇宫大殿前石阶上刻的鳌的头，考上状元的人可以踏上。后来用'独占鳌头'比喻占首位或取得第一名。head of a legendary turtle carved on the stone steps leading to the main hall of the Imperial Palace to be ascended only by he who scored the top marks in the nation's highest imperial examination; (fig.) be the champion; win first prize

嚣 Áo〈书 *fml.*〉same as 隞 Áo
☞ xiāo on p. 2104

鏖 áo〈书 *fml.*〉鏖战 engage in a fierce battle：赤壁～兵 decisive Battle of Chibi between Cao Cao's army and the allied forces of Sun Quan and Liu Bei in 208 A.D. in present-day Hubei

【鏖战】áozhàn 激烈地战斗；苦战 fight with might and main; in the throes of a battle：与敌人～了三天三夜。(We) fought the enemy for three days and three nights.

ǎo（ㄠˇ）

拗(抝) ǎo〈方 *dial.*〉使弯曲；使断；折 bend or twist, break：把竹竿～断了 break a bamboo pole by bending it
☞ ào on p. 19 and niù on p. 1422

袄(襖) ǎo 有里子的上衣 lined Chinese-style coat or jacket：夹～lined jacket | 皮～leather coat; fur coat | 小棉～儿 short coat

媪 ǎo〈书 *fml.*〉年老的妇女 old woman

鹓 ☞ [鹓鹓](lái'ǎo) on p. 1144

ào（ㄠˋ）

岙(嶴) ào 浙江、福建等沿海一带称山间平地（多用于地名）level land in a mountain, usu. in place names in coastal Zhejiang and Fujian provinces：珠～Zhu'ao | 薛～Xue'ao

坳(垇、㘭) ào 山间平地 low-lying land between or amidst higher points in a mountain range：山～col

拗(抝) ào 不顺；不顺从 defy; disobey：～口(of sentence or word) tongue-twisting; hard to pronounce | 违～disobey; disobedience
☞ ǎo on p. 19 and niù on p. 1422

【拗口】àokǒu 说起来别扭，不顺口 be hard to pronounce; awkward to read：这两句话读着有点～，改一改吧。These two lines do not read smoothly. Let's change them.

【拗口令】àokǒulìng 绕口令 tongue twister

奡 ào〈书 *fml.*〉❶ 矫健 nimble-bodied：排～(of writing) vigorous and forceful ❷ same as 傲 ào

傲 ào 骄傲 proud; haughty：～慢 arrogant; cocky | 倨～haughty and standoffish

【傲岸】ào'àn〈书 *fml.*〉高傲；自高自大 proud; self-important

【傲骨】àogǔ〈比喻 *fig.*〉高傲不屈的性格 lofty and unyielding character

【傲慢】àomàn 轻视别人，对人没有礼貌 overbearing; cocky：态度～be contemptuous; put on airs | ～无礼 overbearing and insolent

【傲气】àoqì 自高自大的作风 haughtiness; arrogance：～十足 be condescending

【傲然】àorán 坚强不屈的样子 unyielding; dauntless：～挺立 tower or soar into the skies

【傲世】àoshì 傲视当世和世人 despise the world and the multitude

【傲视】àoshì 傲慢地看待 disdain; turn up one's nose at：～万物 regard all things on earth with contempt

【傲物】àowù〈书 *fml.*〉骄傲自大，瞧不起人 be arrogant and contemptuous; look down upon others：恃才～be proud of one's talent and contemptuous of one's peers

奥 ào ❶ 含义深，不容易理解 unfathomable; abstruse：深～profound | ～妙 subtle ❷〈古时 *arch.*〉指房屋的西南角，也泛指房屋的深处 southwestern corner or the innermost part of a house：堂～innermost recess of a hall ❸（Ào）姓 a surname

【奥博】àobó〈书 *fml.*〉❶ 含义深广 profound in meaning：文辞～abstruse in rhetoric ❷ 知识丰富（of a person）encyclopaedic；erudite；widely read

【奥林匹克运动会】Àolínpǐkè Yùndònghuì 世界性的综合运动会。因古代希腊人常在奥林匹亚（Olympia）举行体育竞技，1894 年的国际体育大会决定把世界性的综合运动会叫做奥林匹克运动会。第一届于 1896 年在希腊雅典举行，以后每四年一次，在会员国的某个城市举行。Olympic Games；Olympics；Olympiad；comprehensive international sports event. Representatives to an international conference on sports in Paris in 1894 decided to establish a worldwide comprehensive sports event and named it after Olympia，where the Greeks held sports competitions in ancient times. The First Olympic Games took place in 1896 in Athens，Greece，and since then it has been held once every four years by different cities of member countries. 简称 abbr. 奥运会 Àoyùnhuì

【奥秘】àomì 奥妙神秘 enigma；mystery：探索宇宙的～probe the mysteries of the universe

【奥妙】àomiào（道理、内容）深奥微妙（of reason，content）profound and subtle：～无穷 enigmatic；laden with subtleties and secrets｜难解其中的～hard to fathom the subtlety behind it

【奥义】àoyì 深奥的义理 profound or abstruse ideas：探求五经～probe into the profound implications of the Five Confucian Classics

【奥援】àoyuán〈书 *fml.*〉官场中暗中撑腰的力量；有力的靠山（多含贬义 oft. derog.）clout；power behind the scenes；powerful backing

【奥运会】Àoyùnhuì 奥林匹克运动会的简称 abbr. for 奥林匹克运动会 Àolínpǐkè Yùndònghuì

【奥旨】àozhǐ 深奥的含义 profound implication：深得其中～capable of appreciating the subtleties of something.

骜 ào〈书 *fml.*〉❶ 骏马 fine horse；steed ❷ same as 傲 ào

傲 ào〈书 *fml.*〉same as 傲 ào

隩 ào〈书 *fml.*〉same as 奥 ào ②
☞ yù on p. 2354

澳[1] ào ❶ 海边弯曲可以停船的地方（多用于地名 usu. as part of a place name）bay：三都～（在福建）Sandu Bay（Fujian）❷（Ào）指澳门 Macao：港～同胞 compatriots in or from Hong Kong and Macao

澳[2] Ào 指澳洲（现称大洋洲）Australia（present-day Oceania）：～毛（澳洲出产的羊毛）Australian wool

【澳抗】àokàng 人体血清中一种异常蛋白质，与流行性乙型肝炎的发病有密切关系 Australia antigen；abnormal protein in human serum closely associated with the incidence of hepatitis B

懊 ào 烦恼；悔恨 regret；remorse：～恨 regretful｜～恼 remorseful

【懊恨】àohèn 悔恨 feeling of self-reproach

【懊悔】àohuǐ 做错了事或说错了话，心里自恨不该这样 feel deep and painful regret for wrongdoing or slip of tongue：～不已 endless remorse

【懊侬】àonáo〈书 *fml.*〉烦恼；痛悔 heartfelt regret；remorse

【懊恼】àonǎo 心里别扭；烦恼 annoyed；vexed；upset；fret

【懊丧】àosàng 因事情不如意而情绪低落，精神不振 in low spirits；feel dejected or depressed because things do not turn out as one wishes：神情～ look downcast

【懊糟】ào·zao〈方 *dial.*〉懊丧，不痛快 in the doldrums；sullen

鏊 ào［鏊子］（ào·zi）烙饼的器具，用铁做成，平面圆形，中心稍凸 griddle，round iron pan with its bottom slightly protruding in the centre，for the baking of pancakes

B

bā（ㄅㄚ）

八 bā 数目，七加一后所得 eight; a numeral that is the result of seven plus one. 注意 **NOTE**: '八'字单用或在一词一句末尾或在阴平、阳平、上声字前念阴平(bā)，如'十八、一八得八、八十、八百'；在去声字前念阳平(bá)，如'八岁、八次'。When used alone, or at the end of a word or a sentence, or before a character pronounced with the first, second or third tone, 八 bā is pronounced with the first tone: 十八 shíbā, eighteen; 一八得八 yī bā dé bā, one times eight is eight; 八十 bāshí, eighty; 八百 bābǎi, eight hundred. When before a character pronounced with the fourth tone, 八 bā changes to the second tone: 八岁 básuì, eight years old, 八次 bácì, eight times. 本词典为简便起见，条目中的'八'字，都注阴平。For the sake of convenience, in all the following entries 八 bā is marked in the first tone. ☞数字 shùzì on p.1791

【八拜之交】 bā bài zhī jiāo 拜把子的关系 sworn brotherhood

【八宝菜】 bābǎocài 由核桃仁、莴笋、杏仁、黄瓜、花生米等混合在一起的酱菜 eight-treasure pickles; assorted walnut meats, asparagus lettuce, almonds, cucumber and peanuts, etc. pickled in soy sauce

【八宝饭】 bābǎofàn 糯米加果料儿、莲子、桂圆等多种食品蒸制的甜食 eight-treasure rice pudding; glutinous rice steamed with preserved fruits, sweetened bean paste, lotus seeds, longan, etc.

【八辈子】 bābèi·zi 好几辈子，形容程度深或时间长 eight lifetimes; long time; extremely: ～前的事儿。It happened long ago.｜倒了～霉。What interminable rotten luck!

【八成】 bāchéng ❶ 十分之八 eighty per cent: ～新 eighty per cent new; practically new｜事情有了～啦。Things are as good as settled. ❷（～儿 bāchéngr）多半；大概 most probably; most likely: 看样子～儿他不来了。He is probably not coming.

【八斗才】 bā dǒu cái〈比喻 *fig.*〉高才。唐李商隐《可叹》诗：'宓妃愁坐芝田馆，用尽陈王八斗才'（三国时，魏曹植，字子建，曾封为陈王）。宋无名氏《释常谈》：'谢灵运尝曰："天下才有一石，曹子建独占八斗，我得一斗，天下共分一斗。"' unusual literary talent; superb talent. From the poem *Regrettable* by Li Shangyin, a celebrated poet of the Tang Dynasty: 'Concubine Mi sat worriedly in Zhitian Hall, / Depleted of the superb talent of Prince Chen.' (During the Three Kingdoms Period, Cao Zhi, alias Zijian, was given the title Prince Chen.) From *On Dispelling Mediocrity* by an anonymous author of the Song Dynasty: 'Xie Lingyun once said, "Of the sum of talent under heaven, Cao Zijian possesses eight parts, I have one part, and the remaining one part is shared by the rest."'

【八方】 bāfāng 指东、西、南、北、东南、东北、西南、西北，泛指周围各地 eight points of the compass, i.e. east, west, south, north, southeast, northeast, southwest, northwest; all directions: 四面～all around｜一方有难，～支援。When trouble occurs in one place, help comes from all quarters.

【八分书】 bāfēnshū 汉字的一种字体，即汉隶 *lishu*; official script; a style of calligraphy dating back to the Han Dynasty (206 B.C.-A.D. 220)

【八竿子打不着】 bā gān·zi dǎ bù zháo 形容二者之间关系疏远或毫无关联 far-fetched; unrelated; 竿 also written as 杆 gān

【八哥】 bā·ge（～儿 bā·ger）鸟，羽毛黑色，头部有羽冠，吃昆虫和植物种子。能模仿人说话的某些声音。crested myna (*Acridotheres cristatellas*); crested bird with black feathers, lives off insects and seeds, can imitate certain sounds of human speech; also 鸲鹆 qúyù

【八股】 bāgǔ 明清科举制度的一种考试文体，段落有严格规定，每篇由破题、承题、起讲、入手、起股、中股、后股、束股等部分组成。从起股到束股的四个部分，其中都有两股相互排比的文字，共为八股。内容空泛，形式死板，束缚人的思想。现在多用来比喻空洞死板的文章、讲演等。Eight-Legged Essay; literary form prescribed for the imperial civil service examinations in the Ming and Qing dynasties, known for its rigidity of form and poverty of ideas. Each composition is composed of eight parts: setting the theme, exposition, explanation, proceeding to set hand, the starting leg, the middle leg, the rear leg and the ending leg. Each of the last four paragraphs consists of two pairs of parallel sentences, totalling eight pairs. Now a synonym for stereotyped writing or lecture.

B

【八卦】bāguà 我国古代的一套有象征意义的符号。用'—'代表阳,用'--'代表阴,用三个这样的符号组成八种形式,叫做八卦。每一卦形代表一定的事物。☰为乾,代表天;☷为坤,代表地;☵为坎,代表水;☲为离,代表火;☳为震,代表雷;☶为艮,代表山;☴为巽,代表风;☱为兑,代表沼泽。八卦互相搭配又得六十四卦,用来象征各种自然现象和人事现象。例如上面☷,下面☵,'地中有水'是师卦,上面☵,下面☷,'地上有水'是比卦。在《易经》里有详细的论述。八卦相传是伏羲所造,后来用来占卜。Eight Trigrams; a set of symbolic signs created in ancient China. A solid line represents '*yang* —', the masculine or positive principle in nature; a broken line represents '*yin* --', the feminine or negative principle in nature. Eight combinations of three lines — all solid, all broken, or a combination of solid and broken lines — form the Eight Trigrams, and each trigram represents a certain kind of matter. Qian (☰ 乾), represents heaven; Kūn (☷ 坤), represents earth; Kǎn (☵ 坎), represents water; Lí (☲ 离), represents fire; Zhèn (☳ 震), represents thunder; Gèn (☶ 艮), represents mountain; Xùn (☴ 巽), represents wind; Duì (☱ 兑), represents marsh. These are paired to form 64 hexagrams, representing various natural and social phenomena. For instance, the 师 Shī hexagram is formed by the 坤 Kūn trigram over the 坎 Kǎn trigram, meaning water under the ground; and the 比 Bǐ hexagram is formed by reversing these trigrams, meaning water above ground. The theory is expounded in detail in *The Book of Changes*. Said to be invented by Fuxi, the Eight Trigrams were used in divination.

【八卦教】Bāguàjiào 天理教的别称 another name for Tianli Sect. ☞ 天理教 Tiānlǐjiào on p. 1890

【八国联军】Bā Guó Liánjūn 1900 年英、美、德、法、俄、日、意、奥八国为了扑灭我国义和团反对帝国主义的运动而组成的侵略军队。八国联军攻占了天津、北京等地,于 1901 年强迫清政府签订《辛丑条约》。Eight-Power Allied Forces; invading troops sent by Britain, the United States, Germany, France, Russia, Japan, Italy and Austria in 1900, to suppress the popular Chinese anti-imperialist Yihetuan Movement, known in the West as the Boxer Rebellion. The Eight-Power Allied Forces attacked and occupied Tianjin and Beijing, and in 1901 forced the Qing government to sign the 'International Protocol'.

【八行书】bāhángshū 旧式信纸大多用红线直分为八行,因此称书信为八行书 letter; old-style letter paper divided by red vertical lines into eight columns 八行书; 简称 abbr. 八行 bāháng

【八角】bājiǎo ❶ 常绿小乔木,叶子长椭圆形,花红色,果实呈八角形 anise (*Pimpinella anisum*); star anise; evergreen shrub with prolate ellipsoid leaves, red flowers and octagonal fruits; also 八角茴香 bājiǎo huíxiāng or 大茴香 dàhuíxiāng ❷ 这种植物的果实,是常用的调味香料。内含挥发油,中医入药。是我国特产之一。在不同的地区有大料、茴香等名称。aniseed; seed of anise, often used in cooking, contains volatile oil, and used in traditional Chinese medicine, a special product of China; in some localities also called 大料 dàliào or 茴香 huíxiāng.

【八角枫】bājiǎofēng 落叶灌木或小乔木,叶子卵形或圆形,聚伞花序,花瓣白色。根、茎、叶可入药。木材可用来做家具等。alangium (*Alangium*); deciduous shrub or arboret, with oval or round leaves, white-coloured cyme, its roots, stems and leaves used in traditional Chinese medicine, its wood used in furniture; also 棿木 nìmù

【八节】bājié 指立春、春分、立夏、夏至、立秋、秋分、立冬、冬至八个节气 eight solar terms or periods — Beginning of Spring, Spring Equinox, Beginning of Summer, Summer Solstice, Beginning of Autumn, Autumn Equinox, Beginning of Winter and Winter Solstice: 四时～ four seasons and eight periods

【八进制】bājìnzhì 一种记数法,采用 0,1,2,3,4,5,6,7 八个数码,逢八进位。如十进制的 9,27 在八进制中分别记为 11,33。八进制的数较二进制的数书写方便,常应用在电子计算机的计算中。octal (number) system; number system with a base of eight, e.g. 9 and 27 in the decimal system are written 11 and 23 in the octal system. Octal numerals, more convenient to use than binary ones, are frequently used in computer computations.

【八九不离十】bā jiǔ bù lí shí 几乎接近(实际情况) about right; pretty close (to reality); very near: 我虽然没有亲眼看见,猜也能猜个～。Although I did not see it with my own eyes, I can make a pretty close guess.

【八路】Bālù 指八路军,也指八路军的干部、战士 abbr. for the Eighth Route Army; also cadres and soldiers of the Eighth Route Army

【八路军】Bā Lù Jūn 中国共产党领导的抗日革命武装,原是中国工农红军的主力部队,1937 年抗日战争开始后改编为国民革命军第八路军,是华北抗日的主力。第三次国内革命战争时期跟新四军和其他人民武装一起改编为中国人民解放军。Eighth Route Army — revolutionary anti-Japanese armed forces led by the Chinese Communist Party. Its predecessor was the main force of the Chinese Workers' and Peasants' Red Army, which was re-designated the Eighth Route Army of the National Revolutionary Army after the outbreak of the War of Resistance against Japan in 1937, and became the main army of resistance in North China. During the Third Revolutionary Civil War, the Eighth Route Army, the New Fourth Army and other popular military units were combined to form the Chinese People's Liberation Army.

【八面玲珑】bāmiàn línglóng 原指窗户宽敞明亮,后用来形容人处世圆滑,不得罪任何一方 (formerly) description of large, bright windows; someone smooth and tactful, who never offends

【八旗】bāqí 清代满族的军队组织和户口编制,以旗为号,分正黄、正白、正红、正蓝、镶黄、镶白、镶红、镶蓝八旗。后又增建蒙古八旗和汉军八旗。八旗官员平时管民政,战时任将领,旗民子孙永远当兵。Eight Banners; military organizations and household registration system of the Manchu ethnic people in the Qing Dynasty, distinguished by their banners of different colours — Xulun Xar (Yellow), Xulun Qagan (White), Xulun Ulaan (Red), Xulun Hoh (Blue), Hobot Xar (Bordered Yellow), Hobot Qagan (Bordered White), Hobot Ulaan (Bordered Red) and Hobot Hoh (Bordered Blue). Later, Eight Banners were also established among Mongols and Hans. Officials of the Eight Banners were civilians in peacetime and generals in wartime; descendants of Bannermen were hereditary soldiers.

【八下里】bāxià·li 〈方 *dial.*〉指方面太多(多表示照顾不过来) too many aspects (to be taken into account)

【八仙】bāxiān ❶ 古代神话中的八位神仙,就是汉钟离、张果老、吕洞宾、铁拐李、韩湘子、曹国舅、蓝采和、何仙姑。旧时常作为绘画的题材和美术装饰的主题。Eight Immortals, i. e. Han Zhongli, Zhang Guolao, Lü Dongbin, Li Tieguai, Han Xiangzi, Cao Guojiu, Lan Caihe, and He Xiangu, who in Taoist mythology frequently appeared in painting and other forms of art in old times ❷ 〈方 *dial.*〉 same as 八仙桌 bāxiānzhuō

【八仙过海】bāxiān guòhǎi 谚语'八仙过海,各显神通(或"各显其能")' from the saying 'The Eight Immortals cross the sea, each demonstrating their special skill'; 〈比喻 *fig.*〉各自有一套办法,或各自显示本领,互相竞赛 each displays his talent or skills to see who is best

【八仙桌】bāxiānzhuō (～儿 bāxiānzhuōr)大的方桌,每边可以坐两个人 Eight Immortals table; old-fashioned square table seating eight people

【八一建军节】Bā-Yī Jiànjūn Jié 中国人民解放军建军的节日。1927年8月1日,中国共产党领导了南昌起义,从此建立了中国人民的革命军队。Army Day (August 1, anniversary of the founding of the Chinese People's Liberation Army). On August 1, 1927, the Chinese Communist Party led the Nanchang Uprising, and founded the revolutionary army of the Chinese people.

【八一南昌起义】Bā-Yī Nánchāng Qǐyì 中国共产党为了挽救第一次国内革命战争的失败,于1927年8月1日在江西南昌举行的武装起义,领导人有周恩来、朱德、贺龙、叶挺等。起义部队于1928年4月到达井冈山,和毛泽东领导的秋收起义部队胜利会师,组成了中国工农红军第四军。August 1st Nanchang Uprising. To save the First Revolutionary Civil War from defeat, the Chinese Communist Party staged an armed uprising on August 1, 1927 in Nanchang, Jiangxi Province; the leaders were Zhou Enlai, Zhu De, He Long and Ye Ting. The troops then marched to Jinggang Mountains in April 1928, and joined the troops of the Autumn Harvest Uprising led by Mao Zedong, to form the Fourth Army of the Chinese Workers and Peasants Red Army.

【八音盒】bāyīnhé 一种器物,开动匣里的发条后,能奏出各种固定的乐曲 musical (music) box powered by a spiral power spring that plays a fixed tune; also 八音琴 bāyīnqín and 八音匣子 bāyīn xiá·zi

【八月节】Bāyuè Jié 中秋 Mid-Autumn Festival (15th day of the 8th lunar month)

【八字】bāzì (～儿 bāzìr)用天干地支表示人出生的年、月、日、时,合起来是八个字。迷信的人认为根据生辰八字可以推算出一个人的命运好坏。Eight Characters; characters in four pairs, indicating the year, month, day and hour of a person's birth, each pair consisting of one Heavenly Stem (天干) and one Earthly Branch (地支), used in fortune-telling

【八字没一撇】bā zì méi yī piě 〈比喻 *fig.*〉事情还没有眉目 not even the first stroke of the character 八 bā; (sth.) not even begun yet; no sign of success yet

【八字帖儿】bāzìtiěr 旧俗订婚时写明男方或女方生辰八字的帖子 (old custom) card written with the horoscope of a young man or woman sent as a proposal for betrothal; also 庚帖 gēngtiě

巴¹ bā ❶盼望 long for; await anxiously: ～不得 be only too anxious (to do sth.) | 朝～夜望 long for day and night ❷ 紧贴 cling to: 爬山虎～在墙上。The ivy clings to the wall. ❸ 粘住 stick to: 粥～了锅了。The porridge sticks to the pot. ❹ 粘在别的东西上的东西 that which adheres to sth. else: 锅～ rice crust ❺ 〈方 *dial.*〉挨着 be close to; be next to: 前不～村,后不～店 with no village ahead and no inn behind; be stranded in a place with no one to help ❻〈方 *dial.*〉张开 open; spread: ～着眼瞧 stare wide-eyed | 天气干燥，桌子都～缝儿啦。The tabletop is cracked because of the dry weather.

B

巴[2] Bā ❶ 周朝国名，在今四川东部和重庆市一带 Ba, state during the Zhou Dynasty, in the eastern part of what is now Sichuan Province and Chongqing Municipality ❷ 指四川东部和重庆市一带 eastern part of Sichuan Province and Chongqing Municipality ❸ 姓 a surname

巴[3] bā 压强单位，1平方厘米的面积上受到100万达因作用力，压强就是1巴，等于0.1兆帕斯卡。从前气象学上多用毫巴，声学上多用微巴。bar; unit of pressure equal to 1 million dynes per square centimetre, equal to 0.1 million pascals. The unit millibar is often used in meteorology, and microbar in acoustics.

巴[4] bā 巴士 bus: 大～ big bus; coach | 小～ mini-bus

【巴巴】bābā 用在形容词后，表示程度深 [used after an adjective] for emphasis: 干～dull and dry | 可怜～ very pitiful

【巴巴结结】bā·bajiējiē〈方 *dial.*〉❶ 凑合；勉强 perform with difficulty; manage with an effort: 一般书报他～能看懂。He can just about manage to read general publications. ❷ 勤奋；艰辛 diligent; hardships: ～地做着生活 work diligently | 他～从老远跑来为了啥? Why did he take all this trouble to come here from so far? ❸ 形容说话不流利 stammer; make involuntary stops and repetitions in one's speech

【巴巴儿地】bābār·de〈方 *dial.*〉❶ 迫切；急切 eagerly; anxiously: 他～等着他那老伙伴。He is waiting anxiously for his old pal. ❷ 特地 specially: ～从远道赶来 come specially from afar

【巴不得】bā·bu·de 迫切盼望 be very anxious (to do sth.); eagerly look forward to; earnestly wish: 他～立刻见到你。He is very anxious to meet you immediately.

【巴豆】bādòu ❶ 常绿小乔木，叶子卵圆形，花小，结蒴果 croton (*Croton tiglium*); evergreen arboret with oval leaves and small flowers that bear capsules ❷ 这种植物的种子，是剧烈的泻剂 croton seed, a strong purgative

【巴结】bā·jie ❶ 趋炎附势，极力奉承 fawn on; curry favour with; make up to: ～上司 fawn on one's superiors ❷〈方 *dial.*〉努力；勤奋 try hard; make great efforts to: 他工作很～。He works very hard.

【巴黎公社】Bālí Gōngshè 法国工人阶级在巴黎建立的世界上第一个无产阶级政权。1871年3月18日，巴黎工人武装起义，推翻了资产阶级政权，28日成立巴黎公社。由于当时没有马克思主义政党的领导，没有和农民取得紧密的联系，没有坚决镇压反革命，终于被国内外反动势力所扼杀。Paris Commune; world's first dictatorship of the proletariat, established by the French working class in Paris. On March 18, 1871, the workers of Paris rose up in arms and overthrew the bourgeois regime, establishing the Paris Commune on March 28. Lacking the leadership of a Marxist political party, and failing to foster close ties with the peasants and suppress the counter-revolutionaries the Paris Commune was defeated by domestic and foreign reactionary forces.

【巴里纱】bālǐshā 用较细的棉纱织成的薄而透气的平纹织物，可用来做窗帘或夏季服装 organdy; thin, transparent muslin with a stiff finish, used for window curtains or summer clothing; also 玻璃纱 bō·lishā

【巴儿狗】bārgǒu 哈巴狗 Pekingese (breed of dog); also 叭儿狗 bārgǒu

【巴山蜀水】Bā shān Shǔ shuǐ 巴蜀一带的山水，指四川 mountains and waters in the Ba-Shu region, referring to Sichuan

【巴士】bāshì〈方 *dial.*〉公共汽车 bus

【巴松】bāsōng 木管乐器，管身分短节、长节、底节和喇叭口四部分，双簧片由金属曲颈管连接，插在短节顶端 bassoon; tenor or bass double-reed woodwind instrument with a long, U-shaped conical tube connected to the mouthpiece by a thin metal tube; also 大管 dàguǎn

【巴头探脑儿】bā tóu tàn nǎor 伸着头(偷看) crane one's head and look about furtively

【巴望】bāwàng ❶ 盼望 look forward to; hope: ～儿子早日平安归来。I hope my son will come back safe and sound as soon as possible. ❷ 指望；盼头 good prospects: 今年收成有～。There is a good chance of a bumper harvest this year.

【巴乌】bāwū 哈尼族、彝族、苗族的管乐器。用竹子制成，形似笛子，有八个孔，上端有铜制簧片。横吹，振动簧片发音。bamboo musical instrument of the Hani, Yi and Miao ethnic minorities resembles a flute, with eight holes and a copper reed, played horizontally

【巴掌】bā·zhang 手掌 palm; hand: 拍～ clap one's hands

扒 bā ❶ 抓着可依附的东西 hold on to; cling to: ～墙头儿 hold on to the top of a wall | 孩子～着车窗看风景。Children clutch the window of the train as they admire the scenery. | 猴子～着树枝儿采果子吃。Monkeys cling to the branches as they pick fruits. ❷ 刨；挖；拆 dig up; rake; pull down: ～土 rake earth | ～堤 breach the dyke | ～了旧房盖新房 pull down the old house to build a new one in its place ❸ 拨动 push aside: ～开草棵 push aside the grass ❹ 脱掉；剥(bāo) strip off; take off：把鞋袜一～，光着脚蹚水 take off shoes and socks to wade in the water｜把兔子皮～下来 skin a rabbit

☞ pá on p.1434

【扒车】bā//chē 攀上低速行驶的火车、公共汽车等 hitch a ride on a slow-going train, bus, etc., without permission

【扒拉】bā·la ❶ 拨动 push lightly：～算盘子ル flick the beads of an abacus up and down｜把钟摆～一下 push the pendulum of a clock｜他把围着看热闹的人～开，自己挤了进去。He pushed aside the onlookers and elbowed his way through the crowd. ❷ 去掉；撤掉 get rid of; remove; take away：人太多了，要～下去几个。There are too many people; some must be dismissed.｜他的厂长职务叫上头给～了。He was dismissed from his post of factory director.

☞ pá·la on p.1434

【扒皮】bā//pí 〈比喻 *fig.*〉进行剥削 exploit; take advantage of

【扒头ル】bā·tour 往高处爬时可以抓住的东西 handhold for climbing up：峭壁连个～都没有，怎么往上爬呀？There are no handholds on the cliff face, how can I climb up?

叭 bā same as 吧 bā

【叭ル狗】bārgǒu same as 巴ル狗 bārgǒu

机 bā 〈书 *fml.*〉无齿的耙子 toothless rake

芭 bā 古书上说的一种香草 fragrant plant mentioned in ancient texts

【芭蕉】bājiāo ❶ 多年生草本植物。叶子很大，花白色，果实跟香蕉相似，可以吃。原产亚热带。Japanese banana (*Musa basjoo*); herbaceous perennial, with large leaves, white flowers, and edible fruits similar to bananas, originally from subtropical zones ❷ 这种植物的果实 fruits of this plant

【芭蕉扇】bājiāoshàn 用蒲葵叶子(不是芭蕉叶子)做的扇子 fans made of leaves from Chinese fan palm (not banana leaves)

【芭蕾舞】bālěiwǔ 一种起源于意大利的舞剧，用音乐、舞蹈和哑剧手法来表演戏剧情节。女演员舞蹈时常用脚趾尖点地。ballet; dance drama originally from Italy, combining music, dance and mime to tell a story. The ballerina often dances on her toes or points. also 芭蕾舞剧 bālěiwǔjù

夿 bā 夿夿屯(Hābātún)，地名，在北京 Habatun, place name in Beijing

吧 bā ❶〈拟声词 *onom.*〉：～的一声，把树枝折断了。The branch broke with a snap. ❷〈方 *dial.*〉抽(烟) draw on; pull at (cigarette or pipe, etc.)：他～了一口烟，才开始说话。He puffed on his pipe before speaking.

☞ ·ba on p.31

【吧哒】bādā 〈拟声词 *onom.*〉：～一声，闸门关上了。The sluice gate clanked shut.

【吧嗒】bā·da ❶ 嘴唇开合作声 smack one's lips (in surprise, alarm, etc.)：他～了两下嘴，一声也不言语。He smacked his lips but did not utter a word. ❷〈方 *dial.*〉抽(旱烟) puff at (a pipe, etc.)：他蹲在一边～着叶子烟。He squatted to one side and puffed at his pipe.

【吧唧】bājī 〈拟声词 *onom.*〉：他光着脚在雨地里～～地走。He squelched barefoot through the mud in the rain.

【吧唧】bā·ji ❶ 嘴唇开合作声 smack one's lips ❷〈方 *dial.*〉抽(旱烟) puff at (a pipe, etc.)：老汉不住地～着烟斗。The old man kept puffing at his pipe.

【吧女】bānǚ 酒吧间的女招待 waitress at a bar

岜 bā 石山 craggy mountain：～关岭(地名，在广西) Baguanling (place name in Guangxi)

峇 bā 峇厘(Bālí)，印度尼西亚岛名。现作巴厘。Bali, name of an island in Indonesia, now written as 巴厘 Bālí

疤 bā ❶ 疮口或伤口长好后留下的痕迹 mark left when injured tissue heals：疮～ scar left by a sore｜伤～scar left by a wound｜树干上有一个～。There is a scar on the tree trunk. ❷ 像疤的痕迹 sth. that resembles a scar：茶壶盖上有个～。There is a mark on the lid of the teapot.

【疤痕】bāhén 疤 scar：他左眼角下有一个很深的～。There is a deep scar under the corner of his left eye.｜这树有一个碗口大的～。There is a scar the size of a bowl on the tree trunk.

【疤瘌】bā·la 疤 scar; also 疤拉 bā·la

【疤瘌眼ル】bā·layǎnr ❶ 眼皮上有疤的眼睛 eye with a scar on the eyelid ❷ 眼皮上有疤的人 person with such scarring. ‖ also written 疤拉眼ル bā·layǎnr

捌 bā '八'的大写 full written form of numeral '八 eight' on cheques, etc. to avoid mistakes or alterations. ☞ 数字 shùzì on p. 1791

笆 bā 用竹片或树的枝条编成的片状器物 basketry; flat, thin woven trips of bamboo or tree twigs：竹篾～ bamboo basketry

【笆斗】bādǒu 柳条等编成的一种容器，底为半球形 round-bottomed basket woven of wicker, etc.

【笆篱】bālí 〈方 *dial.*〉篱笆 bamboo or branch fence

【笆篱子】bālí·zi 〈方 *dial.*〉监狱 prison; gaol

【笆篓】bālǒu 用树条或竹篾等编成的器物，多用来背东西 wicker or bamboo basket for carrying on the back

粑 bā 〈方 *dial.*〉饼类食物 cake：糍～glutinous rice cake｜糖～sweet cake

【粑粑】bābā 〈方 *dial.*〉饼类食物 griddle cake：玉米～corn cake

豝(豝) bā〈书 *fml*.〉母猪 sow

鲃 bā 鱼,体侧扁或略呈圆筒形,生活在淡水中,种类很多 barbel (*Barbus barbus*), freshwater fish of the large cyprinidae family, with flat or slightly cylindrical body

bá(ㄅㄚˊ)

八 bá ☞ 八 bā on p.21

茇 bá〈书 *fml*.〉❶ 草根 grass roots ❷ 在草间住宿 live among the grass

拔 bá ❶ 把固定或隐藏在其他物体里的东西往外拉;抽出 pull out; pull up:~草 pull up weeds; weed|~剑 draw one's sword|~刺 pick out a splinter◇~了祸根 eradicate the root of trouble ❷ 吸出(毒气等) suck out; draw out:~毒 remove toxic substances|~火 draw out body heat (traditional medical treatment) ❸ 挑选(多指人才) choose; select; pick (talent):选~ select talent ❹ 向高提 lift; raise:~嗓子 raise one's voice ❺ 超出;高出 stand out among; surpass:海~ altitude; height above sea level|出类~萃 surpass the ordinary ❻ 夺取;攻克(据点、城池等) capture; seize (stronghold, city, etc.):连~敌军三个据点 capture three enemy strongholds in succession ❼〈方 *dial*.〉把东西放在凉水里使变凉 cool sth. in water:把西瓜放在冰水里~一~ cool a watermelon in ice water

【拔白】bábái〈方 *dial*.〉(天)刚亮 dawn; daybreak

【拔除】báchú 拔掉;除去 eradicate; pull out; remove:~杂草 pull up weeds|~敌军据点 wipe out an enemy stronghold

【拔刀相助】bá dāo xiāng zhù 形容见义勇为,打抱不平 draw one's sword to help; help to set right a wrong; help sb. for the sake of justice

【拔份儿】bá//fènr〈方 *dial*.〉突出个人;出风头 push oneself forward; show off

【拔高】bá//gāo ❶ 提高 lift; raise:~嗓子唱 raise one's voice in singing ❷ 有意抬高某些人物或作品等的地位 deliberately boost the status of certain people or works:剧中对主人公过分~,反而失去了真实性。The role of the hero in the drama is exaggerated, resulting in a loss of authenticity.

【拔罐子】bá guàn·zi 一种治疗方法,在小罐内点火燃烧片刻,把罐口扣在皮肤上,造成局部郁血,达到治疗目的。对关节炎、肺炎、神经痛等症有疗效。有的地区说拔火罐儿(bá huǒguànr)。cupping; applying a cupping glass to the skin for therapeutic purposes so that vacuum is created in the glass by lighting a flame to it. The method is effective for treating arthritis, pneumonia and neuralgia. In some places it is also called 拔火罐儿 bá huǒguànr

【拔海】báhǎi same as 海拔 hǎibá

【拔河】bá//hé 一种体育运动,人数相等的两队队员,分别握住长绳两端,向相反方向用力拉绳,把绳上系着标志的一点拉过规定界线为胜 tug-of-war; sporting contest in which two teams equal in number tug on opposite ends of a rope and each try to pull the mark on the rope across a line on its side

【拔火罐儿】bá huǒguànr〈方 *dial*.〉same as 拔罐子 bá guàn·zi

【拔火罐儿】báhuǒguànr 一种上端较细的短烟筒,生炉子时把它放在炉口上,使火容易烧旺 detachable chimney; short tapered pipe over the flame when lighting a stove, to get the fire going; also 拔火筒 báhuǒtǒng

【拔尖】bá//jiān(~儿 bá//jiānr) ❶ 出众;超出一般 tiptop; top-notch:他们种的花生,产量高,质量好,在我们县里算是~的。The peanuts they grow are the best in our county for their high yield and fine quality. ❷ 突出个人;出风头 push oneself forward; be pushy; show off:他好逞强,遇事爱~。He is a show-off, and likes to be in the limelight whenever possible.

【拔脚】bá//jiǎo same as 拔腿 bá//tuǐ

【拔节】bá//jié 指水稻、小麦、高粱、玉米等农作物发育到一定阶段时,主茎的各节长得很快 jointing; at certain stages, the main stem joints of crops like rice, wheat, sorghum and corn grow very fast:小麦~孕穗时需要充分的养分。During the jointing and booting stages, wheat needs plenty of nutrients.

【拔锚】bá//máo 起锚 weigh anchor

【拔苗助长】bá miáo zhù zhǎng ☞ 揠苗助长 yà miáo zhù zhǎng on p.2198

【拔取】báqǔ 选择录用 select and recruit

【拔丝】básī ❶ 把金属材料制成条状或丝状物。通常在不加热的情况下进行。wire drawing; draw metal into wire, usu. without heating; also 拉丝 lāsī ❷ 烹调方法,把油炸过的山药、苹果之类的食物放在熬滚的糖锅里,吃时用筷子夹起来,糖遇冷就拉成丝状 cooking technique of tossing deep-fried yam or apple pieces in melted sugar which is pulled into fine threads when eaten:~山药 candied yam

【拔俗】bású〈书 *fml*.〉脱俗;超出凡俗 free from vulgarity; refined

【拔腿】bá//tuǐ ❶ 迈步 take a step (and begin to run, chase, etc.):他答应了一声,~就跑了。He answered and took to his heels. ❷ 抽身;脱身 leave (one's work); get away; free oneself:他事情太多,拔不开腿。He is too busy with his work to get away.

【拔营】bá//yíng 指军队从驻地出发转移 strike camp; march out of camp and move to another place

【拔擢】bázhuó〈书 *fml*.〉提拔 promote (person)

胈 bá〈书 *fml.*〉腿上的毛 hairs on the leg

菝 bá［菝葜］(báqiā)落叶藤木植物，叶子多为椭圆形，花黄绿色，浆果球形。根茎入中药。smilax (*Smilax*); deciduous vine with oval leaves, yellowish-green flowers and round juicy fruits; roots and stems used in traditional Chinese medicine

跋[1] bá 在山上行走 walk on a mountain：～山涉水 scale mountains and ford streams

跋[2] bá 一般写在书籍、文章、金石拓片等后面的短文，内容大多属于评介、鉴定、考释之类 postscript; short section at the end of a book, an article or rubbings from stone tablets or bronze vessels, oft. for commentary, appraisal or annotation：～语 postscript｜题～ preface and postscript

【跋扈】báhù 专横暴戾，欺上压下 domineering; overbearing：飞扬～ arrogant and domineering

【跋前疐后】bá qián zhì hòu〈比喻 *fig.*〉进退两难 encounter obstacles on all sides; beset with difficulties (疐 *zhì*：跌倒 fall; tumble)；疐 also written as 踬 zhì

【跋山涉水】bá shān shè shuǐ 翻越山岭，蹚水过河。形容旅途艰苦。scale mountains and ford streams; travel long distances under difficult conditions; difficult journey

【跋涉】báshè 爬山蹚水，形容旅途艰苦 trudge; trek：长途～ travel long distances under difficult conditions

【跋文】báwén same as 跋[2] bá

【跋语】báyǔ same as 跋[2] bá

魃 bá ☞ 旱魃 hànbá on p.767

鼥 bá ☞［鼧鼥］(tuóbá) on p.1961

bǎ (ㄅㄚˇ)

把[1] bǎ ❶ 用手握住 hold; grasp：～舵 hold the helm｜两手～着冲锋枪 hold the submachine gun with both hands ❷ 从后面用手托起小孩儿两腿，让他大小便 hold (a child up by its thighs for it to urinate or defecate)：～尿 hold a baby out for it to urinate ❸ 把持；把揽 control; monopolise; dominate：要信任群众，不要把一切工作都～着不放手。You must trust the people and not keep such a tight control on things. ❹ 看守；把守 guard; watch：～大门 guard a gate ❺ 紧靠 be close to; near：～墙角儿站着 stand at the corner of the wall｜～着胡同口儿有个小饭馆。There is a small restaurant at the entrance of the alley. ❻ 约束住使不裂开 bind together; attach closely：用铁叶子～住裂缝 use a binding iron to hold the crack ❼〈方 *dial.*〉same as 给 gěi ①② ❽ 车把 handle (of pushcart, etc.) ❾ (～儿 bǎr) 把东西扎在一起的捆子 bundle; bunch：草～ bundle of straw｜秫秸～ bundle of sorghum stalks ❿〈量词 *classifier*〉a) 用于有把手的器具［for object with a handle］：一～刀 a knife｜一～茶壶 a teapot｜一～扇子 a fan｜一～椅子 a chair b) (～儿 bǎr) 一手抓起的数量 handful of：一～米 a handful of rice｜一～花儿 a bunch of flowers｜抓了一～儿韭菜 hold a bunch of chives c) 用于某些抽象的事物［for certain abstract ideas］：一～年纪 getting on in years｜他可真有～力气。He is quite strong.｜为了提前完成任务，咱们还得加～劲。We need to make an extra effort to accomplish our task ahead of schedule.｜他在生产上真是一～好手。He is really a good hand at production. d) 用于手的动作［indicating the hand's action］：拉他一～ give him a tug; give (or lend) him a hand｜帮他一～ give him a helping hand; get him out of difficulty

把[2] bǎ〈介词 *prep.*〉❶ 宾语是后面动词的受事者，整个格式有处置的意思［used when the object is placed before the verb, and is the recipient of the action］：～头一扭 toss one's head｜～衣服洗洗 wash the clothes ❷ 后面的动词，是'忙、累、急、气'等加上表示结果的补语，整个格式有致使的意思［when used before a verb that is preceded by an object and followed by a complement indicating result, 把 and the verb function as a transitive verbal phrase, such as '(cause sb. to be) busy, tired, worried, angry, etc.'］：～他乐坏了。He is overwhelmed with joy.｜差点儿～他急疯了。He is worried almost to madness. ❸ 宾语是后面动词的施事者，整个格式表示不如意的事情［the object of 把 is the doer of the action, expressing an unsatisfactory state of affairs］：正在节骨眼上偏偏～老张病了。It was just when we needed Lao Zhang most that he fell ill. ‖ 注意 **NOTE**：a) ①②'把'的宾语都是确定的［In ①② the object of 把 is definite］ b) 用'把'的句子，动词后边有附加成分或补语，或前边有'一'等特种状语。但在诗歌戏曲里可以不带。［In a 把 construction, there is usu. a suffix or complement after the verb, or 一 yī before the verb; poetry or dramatic verse are exceptions］：领导人民～身翻。Leads the people to stand up.｜扭转身来～话讲。Turn around and speak. c) 用'把'的句子，动词后头一般不带宾语，但有时带［with a 把 construction, there is usu. no object after the verb, but there are exceptions］：～衣服撕了个口子 tear a hole in one's jacket｜～这两封信贴上邮票发出去。Stick stamps on these two letters and mail them. d) 用'把'的句子，有时候后面不说出具体的动作，这种句子多半用在骂人的场合［sometimes 把 is not followed by any action and expresses reproach］：我～你个糊涂虫啊！What a muddle head you are! e) 近代

B

汉语里'把'曾经有过'拿'的意思,现代方言里还有这种用法[in modern Chinese, 把 had the meaning of '拿 ná (use)', and this usage is still found in certain contemporary dialects]:那个人不住地~眼睛看我。That person keeps staring at me.

B

把3 bǎ 加在'百、千、万'和'里、丈、顷、斤、个'等量词后头,表示数量近于这个单位数(前头不能再加数词)[used after numerals and classifiers such as 百 bǎi,千 qiān,万 wàn,里 lǐ,丈 zhàng,顷 qǐng,斤 jīn,个 gè, etc. to show approximation (no other numerals can be used to modify the first)] about; or so:个~月 about a month; a month or so|百~块钱 some hundred dollars

把4 bǎ 指拜把子的关系 sworn brotherhood:~兄 sworn brother|~嫂 sworn sister-in-law

☞ bà on p.29

【把柄】bǎbǐng 器物上便于用手拿的部分 handle;〈比喻 *fig.*〉可以被人用来进行要挟或攻击的过失或错误等 mistake that can be used against oneself:他敢这样对待你,是不是你有什么~叫他抓住了? Does he have anything against you that he dare treat you like this?

【把场】bǎchǎng 戏曲演出时,在上场门对演员进行照料、提示,叫做把场 during a theatrical performance, the action of standing by the stage entrance to cater to and prompt the performers

【把持】bǎchí ❶〈贬义 *derog.*〉独占位置、权利等,不让别人参与 dominate; monopolise:~财权 monopolise financial power|~朝政 monopolise court administration ❷ 控制(感情等) control (feelings, etc.):~不住内心的激愤 unable to control one's indignation

【把舵】bǎ//duò 掌舵 hold the rudder; hold, take, be at the helm; steer

【把风】bǎ//fēng 望风 keep watch (in a clandestine activity); be on the lookout

【把关】bǎ//guān ❶ 把守关口 guard a pass ❷〈比喻 *fig.*〉根据已定的标准,严格检查,防止差错 check against criteria to prevent errors:集体编写的著作,应由主编负责~。A compilation of articles by many authors should be checked by the editor-in-chief.|把好产品质量关 guarantee the quality of products

【把家】bǎjiā〈方 *dial.*〉管理家务,特指善于管理家务 housekeeping, especially excellent housekeeping

【把角儿】bǎjiǎor 路口拐角的地方 street corner:胡同~有家早点铺。There is a breakfast shop at the street corner.

【把酒】bǎjiǔ〈书 *fml.*〉端起酒杯 raise one's wine cup:~临风 raise the cup and face into the wind|~问青天。Lifting my cup, I accost Heaven.

【把口儿】bǎ//kǒur 正当路口 road crossing; intersection:小街~有一家酒店。There is a tavern at the intersection.

【把揽】bǎ·lan 尽量占有;把持包揽 monopolise; take over completely

【把牢】bǎláo〈方 *dial.*〉坚实牢靠(多用于否定式 oft. used in the negative) steady; reliable:用碎砖砌的墙,不~。Walls built of broken bricks are not solid.|这个人做事不~。He is unreliable in everything he does.

【把脉】bǎ//mài〈方 *dial.*〉诊脉;按脉 feel the pulse

【把门】bǎ//mén (~儿 bǎ//ménr) ❶ 把守门户 guard a gate:这里门卫~很严,不能随便进去。The gate is closely guarded, no casual entrance is allowed. ◇这个人说话嘴上缺个~的。This person can't keep his mouth shut. ❷ 把守球门 be a goalkeeper (in sports)

【把势】bǎ·shi ❶ 武术 wushu; martial arts:练~的 wushu practitioner ❷ 会武术的人;精于某种技术的人 person skilled in wushu; skilled person:车~ skillful cart-driver|论庄稼活,他可真是个好~。He's a highly skilled farmer. ❸〈方 *dial.*〉技术 skill:他们学会了田间劳动的全套~。They have mastered all the skills of farm work. ‖ also 把式 bǎ·shi

【把手】bǎ·shou ❶ 拉手(lā·shou) handle ❷ 器物上手拿的地方;把儿(bàr) grip for the hand; place to hold by

【把守】bǎshǒu 守卫;看守(重要的地方) guard, watch over (important places):~关口 guard strategic pass|大桥有卫兵~。The bridge is guarded by soldiers.

【把头】bǎ·tóu 旧社会里把持某种行业从中剥削的人 persons who monopolised certain trades and reaped unearned profits in pre-1949 China:封建~ feudal gangmaster

【把玩】bǎwán〈书 *fml.*〉拿着赏玩 toy with; fondle (toys, valuables, etc.):~良久,不忍释手。He fondled it for a long time, reluctant to let it go.

【把稳】bǎwěn〈方 *dial.*〉稳当;可靠 trustworthy; dependable:他办事很~。He is dependable in whatever he does.

【把握】bǎwò ❶ 握;拿 hold; grasp:司机~着方向盘。The driver clasped the steering wheel. ❷ 抓住(抽象的东西) grasp (the abstract):~时机 seize the opportunity; seize the right time|透过现象,~本质 see past the appearance to grasp the essence ❸ 成功的可靠性(多用于'有'和'没'后 mostly after 有 yǒu or 没 méi) reliability of success; certainty of success:球赛获胜是有~的。Victory in the ball game is a certainty.

【把晤】bǎwù〈书 *fml.*〉会面握手;会晤(of friends) meet and shake hands; encounter

【把戏】bǎxì ❶ 杂技 acrobatics; juggling：耍～play tricks; juggle | 看～ watch acrobatics ❷ 花招；蒙蔽人的手法 trick; swindle; deceit：鬼～devilish trick | 收起你这套～，我不会上你的当。No tricks from you, I won't be deceived.

【把细】bǎxì 〈方 *dial.*〉小心谨慎；仔细 cautious; careful：做事很～act with caution | 凡事～一点儿好。It's better to be cautious whatever one does.

【把兄弟】bǎxiōngdì 指结拜的弟兄。年长的称把兄，年轻的称把弟。sworn brothers, an elder one is called 把兄 (bǎxiōng), a younger one 把弟 (bǎdì); also 盟兄弟 méngxiōngdì

【把斋】bǎ//zhāi 封斋 Islamic day of fasting

【把盏】bǎzhǎn 〈书 *fml.*〉端着酒杯(多用于斟酒敬客 oft. used in toast to a guest) raise wine cup

【把捉】bǎzhuō 抓住(多用于抽象事物 used for the abstract) grasp：～事物的本质 grasp the essence of the matter | ～文件的精神实质 grasp the gist of the document

【把子】[1] bǎ·zi 把东西扎在一起的捆子 bundle, number of articles fastened, tied or wrapped together：秫秸～sorghum stalk bundle ❷ 〈量词 *classifier*〉a)〈贬义 *derog.*〉人一群、一帮叫一把子(of people) group; band b)一手抓起的数量，多用于长条形东西 handful; fistful (of long, narrow pieces)：一～韭菜 a bundle of chives c)用于某些抽象的事物 [for certain abstract ideas]：加～劲儿 make an extra effort; give a bit extra

【把子】[2] bǎ·zi 戏曲中所使用的武器的总称，也指开打的动作 general name for weapons used in traditional opera; opening fighting moves：练～practice martial arts with weapons | 单刀～broadsword play

【把子】[3] bǎ·zi ☞ 拜把子 bài bǎ·zi on p.45

☞ bà·zi on p.29

屉

bǎ 〈方 *dial.*〉❶ 屎；粪便 excrement; faeces; dung：屙～ stool ❷ 拉屎 defecate; poop：想屎就屎，想～就～。Piss or poop as you please.

【屉屉】bǎ·ba 屎；粪便(多用于小儿语 oft. usd in baby talk) stool; faeces

钯

bǎ 金属元素，符号 Pd (palladium)。银白色，化学性质不活泼，能大量吸附氢气。用来制合金和牙科材料等。palladium (Pd), silver-white metallic element, inactive, highly hydrogen-absorbing, used in alloys and dental materials

☞ 钯 pá on p.1435

靶

bǎ 靶子 target：打～target practice | 环～round target | 胸～chest silhouette | 枪枪中～。Every shot hits the target.

【靶标】bǎbiāo 靶子 target：瞄准～aim at the target

【靶场】bǎchǎng 打靶的场地 shooting range; range

【靶台】bǎtái 打靶时射击者所在的位置 shooter's position at a shooting range

【靶心】bǎxīn 靶子的中心部位 centre of a target; bull's-eye

【靶子】bǎ·zi 练习射击或射箭的目标 target for shooting or archery practice

bà (ㄅㄚˋ)

坝(壩)

bà ❶ 拦水的建筑物 dam; barrier blocking the flow of water：拦河～ dam across a river ❷ 河工险要处巩固堤防的建筑物，如丁坝 dyke; embankment; reinforcing of a river dyke, e.g. spur dike ❸ 〈方 *dial.*〉沙滩；沙洲 sandbar ❹ same as 坝子 bà·zi ②(多用于地名 oft. in place names)：雁门～(在四川) Yanmenba (in Sichuan Province) | 留～(在陕西) Liuba (in Shaanxi Province)

【坝基】bàjī 堤坝的基础 foundation of a dyke

【坝埽】bàsào 从前黄河上用埽筑成的拦水护堤的建筑物 construction of tree branches, sorghum stalks or stones bound together on the Yellow River to protect the dikes; ☞ 埽 sào on p.1660

【坝塘】bàtáng 〈方 *dial.*〉山区或丘陵地区的一种小型蓄水工程 small reservoir in mountainous or hilly areas; also 塘坝 tángbà

【坝田】bàtián 山脚围绕的平坦农田 flat farmland at the foot of a mountain

【坝子】bà·zi ❶ same as 坝 bà ① ❷ 西南地区称平地或平原(in southwestern China) flatland, plain：川西～Western Sichuan Plain

把(欛)

bà (～儿 bàr) ❶ 器具上便于用手拿的部分 handle or grip for holding or grasping：缸子～儿 mug handle | 掸子～儿 duster handle ❷ 花、叶或果实的柄 stem; stalk (of leaf, flower or fruit)：花～儿 flower stem | 梨～儿 pear stalk

☞ bǎ on p.27

【把子】bà·zi same as 把 bà ①

☞ bǎ·zi on p.29

弝

bà ❶ 弓的中部，射箭时握弓的地方 grip of a bow where it is held in position ❷ 〈方 *dial.*〉same as 把子 bà·zi

爸

bà 父亲 dad; pa; father; also 爸爸 bà·ba

耙(耮)

bà ❶ 碎土、平地的农具。它的用处是把耕过的地里的大土块弄碎弄平。有钉齿耙和圆盘耙等。harrow, a farm implement set with spikes, or disks, used primarily for breaking up clods and levelling ploughed land ❷ 用耙弄碎土块 draw a harrow over (field); harrow：三犁三～plough thrice and harrow thrice | 那块地已经～过两

遍了。That piece of land has already been harrowed twice.

☞ pá on p. 1435

罢(罷) bà ❶ 停止 stop; cease: ～工 go on strike | 欲～不能 unable to stop even though one wants to ❷ 免去;解除 dismiss: ～职 remove from office | ～免 recall ❸ 完毕 end, finish: 吃～晚饭 finish dinner | 说～就走 finish talking and leave

〈古 *arch*.〉same as 疲 pí

☞ ·ba 吧 on p. 31

【罢笔】bà//bǐ 停止写作 stop writing

【罢黜】bàchù 〈书 *fml*.〉❶ 贬低并排斥 ban; exclude: ～百家,独尊儒术 proscribe all non-Confucian schools of thought and espouse Confucianism as the orthodox state ideology ❷ 免除(官职) dismiss (from office)

【罢工】bà//gōng 工人为实现某种要求或表示抗议而集体停止工作 workers' strike; work stoppage by a group of workers to protest or compel an employer to meet with their demands

【罢官】bà//guān 解除官职 dismiss from office

【罢教】bà//jiào 教师为实现某种要求或表示抗议而集体停止教学 teachers' strike; work stoppage by a group of teachers in order to protest or enforce compliance with their demands

【罢考】bà//kǎo 考生为实现某种要求或表示抗议而集体拒绝参加考试 examinees' strike; refusal by a group of examinees to take an examination, in order to protest or to enforce compliance with their demands

【罢课】bà//kè 学生为实现某种要求或表示抗议而集体停止上课 students' strike; refusal by a group of students to attend class, in order to protest or to enforce compliance with their demands

【罢了】bà·le 〈助词 *aux*.〉用在陈述句的末尾,有'仅此而已'的意思,常跟'不过、无非、只是'等词前后呼应[used at the end of a declarative sentence, to denote 'merely', 'nothing else', paired with 不过 bùguò, 无非 wúfēi and 只是 zhǐshì]: 这有什么,我不过做了我应该做的事～。It's nothing. I've merely done what I ought to.

【罢了】bàliǎo 表示容忍,有勉强放过暂不深究的意思;算了 let it pass; be done with it, denoting tolerance or unwilling acceptance: 他不愿来也就～。Let him stay away if he wishes.

【罢论】bàlùn 取消了的打算 abandoned idea: 此事已作～。The idea has already been dropped.

【罢免】bàmiǎn 选民或代表机关撤销他们所选出的人员的职务;免去(官职) dismiss (from office); removal of a popularly elected official by the electors or by their representative body: ～权 the right of recall | 我这个厂长如果当得不好,你们可以随时～我。You may dismiss me at any time if I fail to be a competent factory director.

【罢免权】bàmiǎnquán ❶ 选民或选民单位依法撤销他们所选出的人员职务的权利 legal right of dismissal of a popularly elected person by the electors or their representative body ❷ 政府机关或组织依法撤销其任命的人员职务的权利 legal right of dismissal of an appointed official by a government organ or organization

【罢赛】bà//sài 运动员为实现某种要求或表示抗议而拒绝参加比赛 athletes' strike; athletes refusal to take part in a competition as a protest or to enforce compliance with their demands

【罢市】bà//shì 商人为实现某种要求或表示抗议而联合起来停止营业 business strike; stoppage by a group of businesses and tradespeople to protest or to enforce compliance with their demands

【罢手】bàshǒu 停止进行;住手 give up; stop: 不试验成功,决不～。We will never give up until the experiment succeeds.

【罢讼】bà//sòng same as 罢诉 bà//sù

【罢诉】bà//sù 撤销诉讼,不再打官司 drop a lawsuit; withdraw a charge

【罢休】bàxiū 停止做某件事情(多用于否定句 oft. used in the negative) give up; let the matter drop: 不找到新油田,决不～。We'll never give up until we find a new oilfield.

【罢演】bà//yǎn 演员为实现某种要求或表示抗议而停止演出 actors' strike; actors' refusal to perform as a protest or to enforce compliance with their demands

【罢战】bàzhàn 结束战争;休战 truce; ceasefire; armistice

【罢职】bà//zhí 解除职务 remove from office; dismiss

䎬 bà 〈方 *dial*.〉牙齿外露 bucktooth; projecting front teeth

鲅(鲌) bà 鲅鱼,身体呈纺锤形,鳞细,背部黑蓝色,腹部两侧银灰色。生活在海洋中。Spanish mackerel (*Scomberomorus sinensis*); ocean fish tapered at both ends, with small fine scales, bluish-black back and silver belly; also 蓝点鲅 lándiǎnbà, 马鲛鱼 mǎjiāoyú or 燕鱼 yànyú

☞ 鲌 bó on p. 151

霸(覇) bà ❶ 古代诸侯联盟的首领 leader of an alliance of feudal lords: 春秋五～ Five Overlords of the Spring and Autumn Period (770-476 B.C.) ❷ 强横无理、依仗权势压迫人民的人 tyrant; despot; bully; one who abuses power to oppress the people: 恶～ local despot ❸ 指实行霸权主义的国家 hegemonist power; hegemonism; hegemony: 反帝反～ oppose imperialism and hegemonism

❹ 霸占 dominate; occupy and control: 军阀割据，各～一方。The country was torn apart by warlords, each dominating a certain region. ❺ (Bà)姓 a surname

【霸持】bàchí 强行占据；霸占 forcibly occupy; seize: ～文坛 dominate the literary circle | ～他人产业 seize other's properties

【霸道】bàdào ❶ 我国古代政治哲学中指凭借武力、刑法、权势等进行统治的政策 in ancient times, political philosophy of rule by military force, penal laws and raw power ❷ 强横不讲理；蛮横 domineering; overbearing; high-handed; unreasonable: 横行～ arrogant and domineering | 这人真～，一点理也不讲。This man is overbearing and impervious to all reason.

【霸道】bà·dao 猛烈；厉害(of liquor, medicine, etc.) strong; potent: 这酒真～，少喝点吧。This liquor is pretty strong, you'd better not drink too much.

【霸气】bàqì ❶ 蛮横，不讲道理 overbearing; high-handed; unreasonable: 这个人说话太～了。This person talks in a rude and belligerent manner. ❷ 专横的气势 aggressive manner

【霸权】bàquán 在国际关系上以实力操纵或控制别国的行为 hegemony; supremacy; (in international relations) dominant influence or authority of one nation over others

【霸王】bàwáng ❶ 秦汉之间楚王项羽的称号 Hegemon King (title assumed by Xiang Yu, 232-202 B.C.) in the late Qin Dynasty ❷〈比喻 *fig*.〉极端霸道的人 despot; one who abuses power

【霸王鞭】[1] bàwángbiān ❶ 表演民间舞蹈用的彩色短棍，两端安有铜片 rattle stick; coloured stick with copper clappers at both ends, used in folk dances ❷ 民间舞蹈，表演时一面舞动霸王鞭，一面歌唱 rattle stick dance; folk song and dance, performed with rattle sticks; also 花棍舞 huāgùnwǔ or 打连厢 dǎliánxiāng

【霸王鞭】[2] bàwángbiān 灌木状常绿植物，茎有五个棱，有成行的乳头状硬刺，开绿色小花。原产南洋群岛，在热带常栽培做绿篱。tropical evergreen shrub, with pentagonal-edged stalks, rows of papilla-shaped thorns, and small green flowers, native to the islands beyond South China Sea, oft. used for hedges

【霸业】bàyè 指称霸诸侯或维持霸权的事业 cause of leading feudal lords, or of maintaining hegemony

【霸占】bàzhàn 倚仗权势占为己有；强行占据 forcibly occupy; seize: ～民女 seize the women of ordinary people | ～土地 forcibly occupy the land

【霸主】bàzhǔ ❶ 春秋时代势力最大并取得首领地位的诸侯 powerful leader among feudal lords of the Spring and Autumn Period ❷ 在某一领域或地区最有声势的人或集团 overlord; hegemon, most influential person or group in a specific circle or region: 文坛～ towering figure of literary circles

灞 Bà 灞河，水名，在陕西 Bahe River, in Shaanxi Province

B

·ba (·ㄅㄚ)

吧(罢、罷) ·ba 〈助词 *aux*.〉❶ 在句末表示商量、提议、请求、命令 [used at the end of a sentence, implying soliciting sb.'s advice, suggestion, request or mild command]: 咱们走～！Let's go! | 帮帮他～！Lend him a hand! | 你好好儿想想～！Think it over! | 同志们前进～！Forward march, comrades! ❷ 在句末表示同意或认可 [used at the end of a sentence, indicating consent or approval]: 好～，我答应你了。Alright, I promise you. | 就这样～，明天继续干。Alright, let's continue tomorrow. ❸ 在句末表示疑问，带有揣测的意味 [used at the end of a sentence, to imply doubt or supposition]: 他大概不来了～？I don't suppose he will come. | 你不会不知道～？Surely you know. ❹ 在句末表示不敢肯定(不要求回答) [used at the end of a sentence, indicating doubt without seeking an answer]: 大概是前天～，他到我这儿来了。I think it was the day before yesterday that he came to me. | 是～，他好像是这么说的。It seems that's what he said. ❺ 在句中表示停顿，带假设的语气(常常对举，有两难的意味) [marking a pause in a presumable tune between positive and negative alternatives, implying a difficult choice]: 走～，不好；不走～，也不好。Going will not do, but neither will not going.

☞ bā on p.25 and 罢 bà on p.30

bāi (ㄅㄞ)

刯 bāi [刯划](bāi·huai)〈方 *dial*.〉❶ 处置；安排 deal with; arrange: 这件事你别管了，就交给他去～吧。Don't you bother, let him deal with it. ❷ 修理；整治 repair; renovate: 电子钟叫他给～坏了。He damaged the electronic clock with his tinkering.

掰(擘) bāi ❶ 用手把东西分开或折断 break off or divide with the hand: ～玉米 break off ears of corn | 把馒头～成两半儿 divide the steamed bun in two | 小弟弟～着手数数儿。Younger Brother counts on his fingers. ❷〈方 *dial*.〉(情谊)破裂 (of a relationship) breakoff: 他俩的交情早就～了。They were estranged long ago. ❸〈方 *dial*.〉分析；说 analyse; chat: 他胡～了半天，也没说

出个所以然。He talked a lot but made little sense.

☞ 擘 bò on p. 152

【掰腕子】bāi wàn·zi 比赛臂力、腕力。两人各伸出一只手互相握住，摆正后，各自用力，把对方的手压下去为胜。hand wrestling; contest of strength, with two people grasping opposite hands and trying to press the other's arm down, with the one who succeeds being the winner

B

蹳 bāi 〈方 *dial.*〉腿脚有毛病，行动不方便；瘸 lame; crippled：脚～手残 crippled in hands and feet

【蹳子】bāi·zi 〈方 *dial.*〉腿脚有毛病、行动不方便的人；瘸子 lame person; cripple

bái（ㄅㄞˊ）

白[1] bái ❶ 像霜或雪的颜色，是物体被日光或与日光相似的光线照射，各种波长的光都被反射时呈现的颜色（跟'黑'相对 as opposed to 'black'）white; colour, when a surface reflects sunlight without absorbing any of the visible rays; colour of fresh snow or frost ❷ 光亮；明亮 shiny; bright：东方发～ dawn is breaking｜大天～日 broad daylight ❸ 清楚；明白；弄明白 clear; plain; make clear：真相大～。The truth has come out.｜不～之冤 unredressed injustice ❹ 没有加上什么东西的；空白 pure; plain; blank：～卷 a blank examination paper｜～饭 plain cooked rice｜～开水 boiled water｜一穷二～ poor and empty ❺ 没有效果；徒然 in vain; to no purpose; for nothing：～跑一趟 make a fruitless trip｜～费力气。All efforts are in vain.｜一天的时光～～浪费了。A whole day was wasted. ❻ 无代价；无报偿 free of charge; gratis：～吃 eat free of charge｜～给 give away for free｜～看戏 go to a theatre free of charge ❼ 象征反动 White (symbol of reactionary political ideology)：～军 White Army｜～区 White Area ❽ 指丧事 funeral：红～事 weddings and funerals ❾ 用白眼珠看人，表示轻视或不满 give a scornful look; stare coldly：～了他一眼。I gave him a scornful look. ❿（Bái）姓 a surname

白[2] bái（字音或字形）错误（of a Chinese character）wrongly written or mispronounced：写～字 write the wrong character (one that sounds the same but is written differently)｜把字念～了。The character is mispronounced.

白[3] bái ❶ 说明；告诉；陈述 state; explain：表～ vindicate oneself｜辨～ plead innocence｜告～ explain oneself ❷ 戏曲或歌剧中在唱词之外用说话腔调说的语句 spoken lines in an opera, etc.：道～spoken lines of an opera｜独～monologue｜对～dialogue ❸ 指地方话 dialect ❹ 白话 vernacular：文～杂糅 mixed style of classical and vernacular｜半文半～ half-classical and half-vernacular

【白皑皑】bái'ái'ái（～的 bái'ái'ái·de）形容霜、雪等洁白（of snow, frost, etc.）pure white：～的雪铺满田野。The fields were covered with pure, white snow.

【白矮星】bái'ǎixīng 发白光而光度小的一类恒星，体积很小，密度很大。天狼星的伴星就属于白矮星。white dwarf; small fixed stars of great density that give off faint, white light, such as the companion star of Sirius.

【白案】bái'àn（～儿 bái'ànr）炊事人员分工上指做主食（如煮饭、烙饼、蒸馒头等）的工作（区别于'红案' as compared with 'red chopping board'）white (kneading) board; portion of a cook's work dealing with starchy foods, e.g. rice, pancakes and steamed buns

【白班】báibān（～儿 báibānr）白天工作的班次；日班 day shift

【白版】báibǎn 指书刊上没印出文字或图表，留下的成块空白 full blank page of book, etc.

【白报纸】báibàozhǐ 印报或印一般书刊用的纸 newsprint; cheap machine-finished paper used mostly for newspapers or ordinary publications

【白鼻子】báibí·zi 戏曲中丑角鼻梁上多抹有白色，借以指狡诈的人，也指汉奸或叛徒 white nose; cunning person, or traitor, from the clown characters in traditional dramas who have white-painted noses; also 白鼻头 báibí·tou

【白璧微瑕】bái bì wēi xiá 洁白的玉上面有些小斑点 slight flaw in white jade;〈比喻 *fig.*〉很好的人或事物有些小缺点 minor blemish in a thing of beauty; minor weaknesses in a person of integrity

【白璧无瑕】bái bì wú xiá 洁白的玉上面没有一点儿小斑点 flawless white jade;〈比喻 *fig.*〉人或事物完美无缺 impeccable moral integrity; perfection

【白醭】báibú（～儿 báibúr）醋、酱油等表面长的白色的霉 mould (on the surface of vinegar, soy sauce, etc.)

【白不呲咧】bái·bucīliē〈方 *dial.*〉（～的 bái·bucīliē·de）物件退色发白或汤、菜颜色滋味淡薄（of sth. with fading colour or a dish whose colour or taste is too light）colourless; tasteless：蓝衣服洗得有些～的，应该染一染了。The colour of this blue coat has faded from washing, and it needs dyeing.｜菜里酱油放少了，～的。This dish is tasteless from lack of soy sauce.

【白菜】báicài 二年生草本植物，叶子大，花淡黄色。品种很多，是普通蔬菜。Chinese cabbage (*Brassica penkinensis*), in many varieties, herbaceous biennial, common vegetable with large leaves and pale-yellow flowers; also 大白菜 dàbáicài or 菘菜 sōngcài

【白茬】báichá（～儿 báichár）❶ 农作物收割后没有再播种的（土地）unplanted（land）after crop harvest：～地 fallow land ❷（木制器物）未经油漆的 unpainted；bare（wooden implements）：～大门 unpainted gate|桌椅还是～，得请人油一油。The desks and chairs are still bare and need to be painted. also written 白槎 báichá or 白碴 báichá ❸（皮衣）未用布、绸等缝制面的（fur clothing）without cloth or silk outer covering：～老羊皮袄 old sheepskin coat without outer cloth covering. also written 白楂 báichá

【白茶】báichá 茶叶的一大类，是一种不发酵，也不经揉捻，制作技术特殊的茶。种类有银针白毫、贡眉、寿眉等。white tea；category of tea specially processed，without fermentation，pressing or kneading. Varieties include Yinzhen Baihao，Gongmei and Shoumei.

【白痴】báichī ❶ 病，患者智力低下，动作迟钝，轻者语言机能不健全，重者起居饮食不能自理 idiocy；disease of extreme mental deficiency，slow and clumsy movements. In light cases speech is impaired，in serious cases patients are unable to take care of themselves. ❷ 患白痴的人 idiot；person afflicted with idiocy

【白炽电灯】báichì diàndēng 最常用的一种电灯，灯泡是真空的或充有惰性气体的玻璃泡，里面有灯丝，电流通过时，灯丝白热，发出亮光 incandescent lamp；most commonly used electric light，made of glass bulb with a vacuum or inert gas inside，with filament which gives off light when heated to incandescence by an electric current

【白唇鹿】báichúnlù 鹿的一种，两腮和嘴边的毛纯白色，生活在高寒地区，是我国特产珍贵动物 white-lipped deer（*Cervus albirostris*）；rare animal unique to China，living in cold alpine areas，with white fur on both cheeks and around the mouth

【白醋】báicù 无色透明的食醋 white vinegar；colourless，transparent vinegar

【白搭】báidā 没有用处；不起作用；白费力气 no use；hopeless；waste of energy：这场球输定了，你上场也是～。The ball game is a sure lose. No use your joining in.

【白带】báidài 妇女的子宫和阴道分泌的乳白色或淡黄色的黏液 leucorrhoea；whites；milk white or pale yellow mucous discharge from female uterus and vagina

【白党】báidǎng 称俄国十月革命后外国武装干涉和国内战争时期由反革命分子结成的叛乱集团 White Party；counter-revolutionary rebel clique during the period of foreign armed intervention and civil war after the Russian October Revolution

【白道】báidào 月球绕地球运行的轨道 moon orbit around the earth

【白地】[1] báidì ❶ 没有种上庄稼的田地 unplanted land：留有一块～准备种白薯。Set aside a plot of unplanted land for growing sweet potatoes. ❷ 没有树木、房屋等的土地 land without trees or houses：村子被烧成一片～。The village was burnt to the ground.

【白地】[2] báidì（～儿 báidìr）白色的衬托面 white background：～红花儿 red flowers on a white background

【白癜风】báidiànfēng 皮肤病，多由皮肤不能形成黑色素引起。症状是皮肤上呈现一片片白斑，不痛不痒。vitiligo；skin disease caused by loss of melanin，appearing as white painless patches that do not itch；also 白斑病 báibānbìng

【白丁】báidīng 封建社会里指没有功名的人（in feudal times）person without academic titles or official ranks；commoner：谈笑有鸿儒，往来无～。Within，the laugh of cultured wit；where no gross soul intrudes（from a poem by Liu Yuxi 刘禹锡）.

【白垩】bái'è 石灰岩的一种，主要成分是碳酸钙，是由古生物的骨骼积聚形成的。白色，质软，分布很广，用做粉刷材料等。chalk；type of soft，white limestone，mainly calcium carbonate，formed by accumulation of remains of ancient organisms，widely distributed，used for whitewashing；also 白土子 báitǔ·zi or 大白 dàbái

【白矾】báifán 明矾的通称 general term for 明矾 míngfán

【白饭】báifàn ❶ 指不加菜、糖等做成并且不就菜吃的米饭 plain cooked rice，cooked rice without vegetables or sugar，and eaten alone ❷ 饭馆按份计价出售饭菜时，指另加的不搭配菜肴出售的米饭 portion of rice sold without accompanying dishes：给我们来七个份儿饭，另加一份～。Give us seven set meals，and a portion of rice.

【白费】báifèi 徒然耗费 waste：～力气 waste one's energy|～心思 bother one's head for nothing

【白费蜡】báifèilà〈比喻 *fig.*〉白白地耗费时间、精力 waste of time or energy：他不懂这种技术，你问他也是～。He knows nothing about this technology. Don't waste your breath.

【白粉】báifěn ❶ 白色的化妆粉 white face powder ❷〈方 *dial.*〉指粉刷墙壁用的白垩 lime for whitewashing walls ❸〈方 *dial.*〉same as 白面儿 báimiànr

【白干儿】báigānr 白酒，因无色、含水分少而得名 strong，colourless liquor

【白宫】Bái Gōng 美国总统的官邸，在华盛顿，是一座白色的建筑物。常用做美国官方的代称。White House；white-coloured official residence of the U.S. president，in Washington D.C.，often used to refer to the government of the United States

【白骨】báigǔ 指人的尸体腐烂后剩下的骨头 white bones（of the dead）；bleached bones

B

【白骨精】báigǔjīng 神话小说《西游记》中一个阴险狡诈善于伪装变化的女妖精。常用来比喻极为阴险毒辣的女人。White Bone Demon; wicked and treacherous female spirit in the novel *Journey to the West*;(fig.) dangerous and sinister woman

【白果】báiguǒ 银杏 ginkgo (*Ginkgo biloba*); gingko

【白果儿】báiguǒr〈方 *dial*.〉鸡蛋 chicken egg

【白鹤】báihè 鹤的一种,羽毛白色,翅膀大,末端黑色,能高飞,头顶红色,颈和腿很长,常涉水吃鱼、虾等。叫的声音高而响亮。white crane (*Grus leucogeranus*), species of crane with white feathers, large black-tipped wings, red crest, long neck and legs; wader which catches fish or shrimp, has loud, high-pitched cry and can fly at high altitudes; also 仙鹤 xiānhè or 丹顶鹤 dāndǐnghè

【白喉】báihóu 传染病,病原体是白喉杆菌。多在秋冬季流行,小儿最容易感染。患者有全身中毒症状,咽部有灰白色膜,不易剥离,有的声音嘶哑。常引起心肌发炎和瘫痪。diphtheria; acute infectious disease caused by Corynebacterium diphtheriae, mostly occurring in autumn and winter; symptoms include severe inflammation of the throat, with a persistent grayish-white membrane, and hoarse voice. Overall toxic reaction can lead to inflammation of the heart muscles and paralysis. Children are particularly susceptible.

【白虎星】báihǔxīng 迷信的人指给人带来灾祸的人 White Tiger Star; (superstitious belief) one who brings disaster to others

【白花】báihuā 皮辊花 lap waste; roller waste

【白花花】báihuāhuā (～的 báihuāhuā·de) 白得耀眼 dazzling white:～的银子 gleaming silver (coins) | 收棉季节,地里一片～的。During cotton-harvest time, the fields are a mass of dazzling white.

【白化】báihuà 生物体的病变部分由于缺乏色素或色素消退而变白 albation; albefaction; pathological whiteness due to deficiency or absence of pigment in an organism

【白化病】báihuàbìng 一种先天性疾病,患者体内缺乏色素,毛发都呈白色,皮肤呈粉白色,眼睛怕见光。患这种病的人俗称天老儿。albinism; congenital deficiency or absence of pigment in the skin, hair and eyes, resulting in white hair, pink skin and sensitivity to light. An albino is popularly called 天老儿 tiān·laor.

【白话】[1] báihuà ❶ 指不能实现或没有根据的话 exaggerated or unfeasible statement:空口说～ empty talk ❷〈方 *dial*.〉闲话;家常话 gossip, chitchat:她一边纳鞋底,一边和婆婆说～。She chatted about everyday matters with her mother-in-law as she stitched a sole of cloth shoe.

【白话】[2] báihuà 指现代汉语(普通话)的书面形式。它是唐宋以来在口语的基础上形成的,起初只用于通俗文学作品,到五四运动以后才在社会上普遍应用 vernacular; written form of modern Chinese (putonghua), which developed from the spoken language of the Tang and Song dynasties. First used only in popular literature, it later became the principal form of language after the May Fourth Movement in 1919:～文 writing in the vernacular | ～小说 story in the vernacular

【白话诗】báihuàshī 五四以后称打破旧诗格律用白话写成的诗 free-style verse in the vernacular, which eschews rules of rhyme and forms of classical poetic composition, popular after the May Fourth Movement of 1919

【白话文】báihuàwén 用白话写成的文章 writings in the vernacular; also 语体文 yǔtǐwén

【白桦】báihuà 落叶乔木,树皮白色,剥离呈纸状,叶子卵形。我国东北有出产。木材致密,可制木器。white birch (*Betula platyphylla*); deciduous tree growing in northeastern China, with paper-like white bark, oval leaves, and close-grained wood that can be used to make wooden articles

【白晃晃】báihuānghuāng (～的 báihuānghuāng·de) 白而亮 shining and bright; gleaming; glittering:～的照明弹 glittering flares

【白灰】báihuī 石灰的通称 common name for 石灰 shíhuī

【白芨】báijī 多年生草本植物,叶子长,开紫红色花。地下块茎白色,中医入药。hyacinth bletilla (*Bletilla striata*), herbaceous and perennial with long leaves and purplish-red flowers; its underground stem tuber, being white, is used in traditional Chinese medicine

【白鳖豚】báijìtún same as 白鳍豚 báiqítún

【白金】báijīn ❶ 铂的通称 common name for 铂 bó ❷〈古代 *arch*.〉指银子 historical name for silver

【白金汉宫】Báijīnhàn Gōng 英国王宫,位于伦敦。从1837年起,英国历代君主都住在这里。常用作英国王室的代称。Buckingham Palace; London home of British sovereigns since 1837, often used to denote the British royal family

【白净】bái·jing 白而洁净(of skin) fair and clear:皮肤～ fair skin

【白酒】báijiǔ 用高粱、玉米、甘薯等粮食或某些果品发酵、蒸馏制成的酒,没有颜色,含酒精量较高 white spirits; liquor distilled from fermented sorghum, maize, sweet potato or certain fruits, colourless and with high alcoholic content; also 烧酒 shāojiǔ or 白干儿 báigānr

【白驹过隙】bái jū guò xì 形容时间过得飞快,像小白马在细小的缝隙前一闪而过(见于《庄子·知北游》) fleeting passage of time, metaphor of 'a glimpse of a white colt flashing past a chink in a wall' (from *Zhuangzi · Knowledge Rambling in the North*)

【白卷】báijuàn（～儿 báijuànr）没有写出文章或答案的考卷 blank examination paper; examination paper left unanswered: 交～ hand in a blank examination paper

【白开水】báikāishuǐ 不加茶叶或其他东西的开水 plain boiled water without tea leaves or any other ingredient

【白口】[1] báikǒu 线装书书口的一种格式，版口中心上下都是空白的，叫做白口（区别于'黑口'as compared with 'black fore-edge'） white fore-edge; a form of fore-edge of thread-bound books, which is blank

【白口】[2] báikǒu（～儿 báikǒur）戏曲中的说白 spoken lines in traditional operas

【白蜡】báilà ❶ 白蜡虫分泌的蜡质，熔点较高，颜色洁白，是我国特产之一。可制蜡烛或药丸外壳，又可用来涂蜡纸，密封容器。white wax excreted by the wax insect, in white colour with a high melting point, a speciality product of China used in candles, wax pill coatings, and wax paper, and as a sealant ❷ 精制的蜂蜡，颜色洁白，可以制蜡烛 fine beeswax, used for candles

【白镴】báilà 焊锡 soldering tin

【白兰地】báilándì 用葡萄、苹果等发酵蒸馏制成的酒。含酒精量较高。brandy (transliteration); strong spirit distilled from fermented grapes or apples

【白痢】báilì ❶〈中医 Chin. med.〉指大便中含黏液或脓而不含血液的痢疾 dysentery characterised by white mucous stools (no blood) ❷ 某些幼畜的一种急性传染病，病原体是白痢杆菌，患病的动物粪便很稀 white diarrhea; acute contagious disease of certain young animals, caused by Bacillus dysenteriae, characterised by running stools

【白莲教】Báiliánjiào 一种秘密教派，因依托佛教的一个宗派白莲宗而得名。元、明、清三代在民间流行，农民军往往借白莲教的名义起事。White Lotus Religion; secret cult named after the White Lotus Sect of Buddhism, folk belief popular in the Yuan, Ming and Qing dynasties; peasant rebellions often fought in the name of the White Lotus Religion

【白蔹】báiliǎn 多年生蔓生草本植物，掌状复叶，浆果球形。根入药。Japan ampelopsis (*Ampelopsis japonica*); trailing, herbaceous, perennial plant, with palm-shaped compound leaves and round berries, its roots used in traditional Chinese medicine

【白亮】báiliàng 白而发亮 shiny and bright; gleaming; glistering: ～的刺刀 gleaming bayonet | 电灯照得屋里～～的。The electric lamp lights up the room brightly.

【白磷】báilín 磷的同素异形体，无色或淡黄色蜡状晶体，有大蒜的气味，毒性强，在空气中能自燃，在暗处发出磷光。用来制造普通火柴、焰火或烟幕弹等。white phosphorus; allotrope of phosphorus, in the form of colourless or pale yellow wax-like crystals that smells like garlic, is toxic, burns spontaneously when exposed to air, gives off phosphorescence in dark, and is used to make ordinary matches, fireworks or smoke shells; also 黄磷 huánglín

【白蛉】báilíng 昆虫，身体小，黄白色或浅灰色，表面有很多细长的毛。雄的吸食植物的汁。雌的吸人畜的血液，能传播黑热病和白蛉热。sandfly (*Phlebotomus*); small, yellow-white or pale gray insect with many fine, long hairs on its body, the male sucking plant sap, the female sucking blood from humans and animals, capable of spreading visceral leishmaniasis and sandfly fever; also 白蛉子 báilíng·zi

【白领】báilǐng 某些国家或地区指从事脑力劳动的职员，如管理人员、技术人员、政府公务人员等 white collar; (in some countries or regions) non-manual workers, e.g. managerial and technical personnel, and government functionaries: ～阶层 white-collar class

【白鹭】báilù 鹭的一种，羽毛白色，腿很长，能涉水捕食鱼、虾等 little egret (*Egretta garzetta*); genus of tall, long-legged white bird related to the heron, feeding on fish and shrimp; also 鹭鸶 lùsī

【白露】báilù 二十四节气之一，在 9 月 7、8 或 9 日 White Dew; one of the 24 solar terms that falls on September 7, 8, or 9; ☞ 节气 jié·qi on p. 989 and 二十四节气 èrshí sì jiéqì on p. 516

【白马王子】báimǎ wángzǐ 指少女倾慕的理想的青年男子 Prince Charming; ideal young man admired by young women

【白茫茫】báimángmáng（～的 báimángmáng·de）形容一望无边的白（用于云、雾、雪、大水等）(of cloud, mist, snow, floodwater, etc.) vast expanse of whiteness: 雾很大，四下里～的。The fog is very heavy, and all is white. | 辽阔的田野上铺满了积雪，～的一眼望不到尽头。The vast field is covered with snow, stretching white to the horizon.

【白毛风】báimáofēng〈方 dial.〉暴风雪 snowstorm; blizzard

【白茅】báimáo 多年生草本植物，春季先开花，后生叶子，花穗上密生白毛。根茎可以吃，也可入药，叶子可以编蓑衣。cogongrass (*Imperata cylindrica*); herbaceous perennial plant, blooming before sprouting leaves in spring, with white hairs on its flower spikes, edible roots and stems that are also used in traditional Chinese medicine, and leaves that can be woven into a rain cape; also 茅 máo

【白煤】báiméi ❶〈方 dial.〉无烟煤 anthracite ❷ 指用做动力的水流 waterpower; fall of water which can be harnessed to produce power

【白蒙蒙】báimēngmēng（～的 báimēngmēng·de）形容（烟、雾、蒸气等）白茫茫一片，模糊不清 (of smoke, fog, steam, etc.) hazy; misty: 海

面雾气腾腾，～的什么也看不见。A haze of mist veiled the sea, obliterating everything.

【白米】báimǐ 碾净了糠的大米(区别于'糙米')，有时泛指大米(as compared with 'unpolished rice') polished rice, sometimes the general term for rice

【白面】báimiàn 小麦磨成的粉 wheat flour：～馒头 steamed bread made of wheat flour

【白面儿】báimiànr 指作为毒品的海洛因 heroin

【白面书生】báimiàn shūshēng 指年轻的读书人，也指面孔白净的读书人 young scholar; pasty-faced bookworm

【白描】báimiáo ❶ 国画的一种画法，纯用线条勾画，不加彩色渲染 line drawing in traditional ink-and-brush painting, without any colour application ❷ 文字简练单纯，不加渲染烘托的写作手法 clean and straightforward style of writing; uncluttered writing

【白木耳】báimù'ěr 银耳 tremella (*Tremella fuciformis*)

【白内障】báinèizhàng 病，症状是眼球的晶状体混浊影响视力。最常见的是老年性白内障。cataract; an eye disease characterised by a loss of transparency of the crystalline lens, leading to blurred vision; most common form is senile cataract

【白嫩】báinèn (皮肤)白皙细嫩(of skin) fine and soft; delicate

【白皮书】báipíshū 政府、议会等公开发表的有关政治、外交、财政等重大问题的文件，封面为白色，所以叫白皮书。由于各国习惯和文件内容不同，也有用别种颜色的，如蓝皮书、黄皮书、红皮书。White Paper; White Book; official report on important political issues, foreign or financial affairs prepared by government or parliament and bound in a white cover. Different countries can use other colours for different contents, e.g. Blue Book, Yellow Book, or Red Book.

【白皮松】báipísōng 常绿乔木，树皮老时乳白色，叶子针状。种子可以吃。lacebark pine (*Pinus bungeana*); evergreen tree, whose bark turns white as it ages, with needle-like leaves and edible seeds; also 白果松 báiguǒsōng

【白票】báipiào 投票选举时，没有写上或圈出被选举人姓名的选票 unmarked ballot; in voting, ballot paper without either candidate's name or any mark against the name

【白旗】báiqí ❶ 战争中表示投降的旗子 white flag; signal of surrender in wartime ❷ 战争中敌对双方派人互相联络所用的旗子 white flag; flag used when opposing sides in wartime exchange intermediaries

【白鳍豚】báiqítún 哺乳动物，鲸的一种，生活在淡水中，比海里的鲸小，身体呈纺锤形，上部浅蓝灰色，下部白色。是我国特有的珍贵动物。flag dolphin (*Lipotes vexillifer*); mammal, rare species of freshwater whale, smaller than the marine whale, with sleek, spindle-shaped body, pale bluish-gray back and white belly, unique to China; also 白鱀豚 báijìtún

【白契】báiqì 指买卖田地房产未经官方登记盖印的契约（区别于'红契' as compared with 'red deed'）white deed; paper agreement of a real estate transaction without the official red seal

【白铅】báiqiān 锌的俗称 popular term for 锌 xīn

【白镪】báiqiǎng〈古代 *arch.*〉当做货币的银子 silver currency used in ancient times

【白区】báiqū 我国第二次国内革命战争时期称国民党统治的地区 White Area; Kuomintang-controlled area during the Second Revolutionary Civil War, 1927-1937

【白饶】báiráo ❶ 无代价地额外多给 give sth. extra free of charge：～碗高汤 an extra free bowl of soup ❷〈方 *dial.*〉白搭 no use; no good：过去的辛苦全算～，得打头儿重来。All past hard work was for nothing. We have to start all over again.

【白热】báirè 某些物质加高热（1，200—1,500℃）后发出白色的光亮，这种状态叫做白热。如果温度降低，就由白热转为红热。white heat; incandescence; white light produced when an object is heated to 1,200-1,500℃; as the temperature drops, white heat becomes red heat

【白热化】báirèhuà (事态、感情等)发展到最紧张的阶段(situation or emotion) reaches a climax; fever-pitch：斗争～。The struggle has reached fever pitch.

【白人】Báirén 指白种人 white man or woman; Caucasian

【白刃】báirèn 锋利的刀 sharp blade：～格斗 hand-to-hand combat

【白刃战】báirènzhàn 敌对双方接近时用枪刺、枪托等进行的格斗 bayonet charge; hand-to-hand combat when two opposing sides fight in close combat with bayonets and rifle butts, etc.; also 肉搏战 ròubózhàn

【白日】báirì ❶ 指太阳 the sun：～依山尽，黄河入海流。The sun sets behind the mountain, the Yellow River empties to the sea. ❷ 白天 daytime：～做梦 spin daydreams; indulge in wishful thinking

【白日见鬼】báirì jiàn guǐ〈比喻 *fig.*〉出现不可能出现的事 seeing a ghost in daytime; when the impossible occurs; also 白昼见鬼 báizhòu jiàn guǐ

【白日撞】báirìzhuàng〈方 *dial.*〉指白天趁人不备到人家里偷东西的小偷儿 thief that breaks in and steals in the daytime

【白日做梦】báirì zuò mèng〈比喻 *fig.*〉幻想根本不能实现 spin daydreams; indulge in wishful thinking; be in a fool's paradise

【白肉】báiròu 清水煮熟的猪肉 pork boiled in

plain water

【白润】báirùn （皮肤）白而润泽（of skin） fair and smooth; delicate

【白色】báisè ❶ 白的颜色 white colour ❷ 象征反动 White (symbol of political conservatism; reactionary):～政权 White Regime|～恐怖 White Terror

【白色恐怖】báisè kǒngbù 指在反动政权统治下，反革命暴力所造成的恐怖，如大规模的屠杀、逮捕等 White Terror; terror created by counter-revolutionary violence, such as massacre or arrests, under a reactionary regime

【白山黑水】báishān-hēishuǐ 长白山和黑龙江，指我国东北地区 White Mountains and Black River; Changbai Mountains and Heilong River, referring to Northeast China

【白鳝】báishàn 鳗鲡 eel(*Anguilla japonica*)

【白食】báishí 指不出代价而得到的饮食 free food:吃～ eat for free

【白事】báishì 指丧事 funeral:办～make funeral arrangements

【白手】báishǒu 空手；徒手 empty handed; barehanded:～起家 start from scratch|这一场～夺刀演得很精彩。This is an exciting performance of barehand vs. broadsword.

【白手起家】báishǒu qǐ jiā 形容原来没有基础或条件很差而创立起一番事业 build up from nothing; start from scratch; also 白手成家 báishǒu chéng jiā

【白首】báishǒu 〈书 *fml*.〉指年老；白头 hoary head; old age:～话当年。Recall the past when one is old.

【白薯】báishǔ 甘薯的通称 general term for 甘薯 gānshǔ

【白水】báishuǐ ❶ 白开水 plain boiled water ❷ 〈书 *fml*.〉明净的水 clear water

【白苏】báisū 一年生草本植物，茎方形，叶子卵圆形，花小，白花。嫩叶可以吃。种子通称苏子，可以榨油。common perilla (*Perilla frutescens*); herbaceous, annual plant with square stem, oval leaves, which are edible when new, small white flowers, oil-bearing seeds, generally called 苏子 sū·zi; also 荏 rěn

【白汤】báitāng 煮白肉的汤或不加酱油的菜汤 clear soup; meat or vegetable soup without soy sauce

【白糖】báitáng 甘蔗或甜菜的汁提纯后，分出糖蜜制成的糖，白色结晶，颗粒较小，味甜，供食用 (refined) white sugar; sweet-tasting and edible sucrose, in a white crystallised form, obtained by refining sugarcane or sugar beet juice

【白陶】báitáo 殷代用高岭土烧成的白色陶器 white pottery (of the Shang Dynasty, 1600-1046 B.C.) made from kaolin clay

【白体】[1] báitǐ 笔划较细的一种铅字字体，如老宋体等（区别于'黑体' as compared with 'bold face'） lean type, typeface characterised by thin strokes, e.g. Old Song typeface

【白体】[2] báitǐ 对照射在上面的白光能够完全反射的理想物体 white object; ideal object that can totally reflect white light beamed on to it; also 绝对白体 juéduì báitǐ

【白天】bái·tiān 从天亮到天黑的一段时间 daylight hours; day; time between dawn and dusk

【白田】báitián 没有种上庄稼的田地，有的地区专指没有种上庄稼的水田 farmland not planted with cereal crops; in certain places specifically rice paddy field that has not been planted with cereal crops

【白条】[1] báitiáo（～儿 báitiáor）财务上指非正式单据 unofficial receipt in accounting:打～ write a promissory note|～不能作报销凭证。A promissory note cannot be used as a receipt for reimbursement. also 白条子 báitiáo·zi

【白条】[2] báitiáo 商品上指家禽、牲畜宰杀后煺毛或去头、蹄、内脏的 slaughtered of domestic fowl or animal with feathers, head, hooves and internal organs removed:～鸡 dressed chicken|～猪 pig carcass

【白铁】báitiě 镀锌铁的通称 common term for 镀锌铁 dùxīntiě

【白厅】Bái Tīng 英国伦敦的一条大街。因过去有白厅宫而得名。现在是英国主要政府机关所在地。常用做英国官方的代称。Whitehall; street in London named after White hall, where many government offices are located; oft. used as synonym for the British government or policies

【白铜】báitóng 铜和镍的合金，颜色银白，用来制造日用器具等 copper nickel alloy, silvery white, used to make articles for daily uses

【白头】[1] báitóu 指年老 hoary head; old age:～偕老 live in conjugal bliss to a ripe old age

【白头】[2] báitóu 不署名或没有印章的 unsigned; anonymous:～帖子（不署名的字帖儿） unsigned note|～材料 unsigned material

【白头翁】[1] báitóuwēng 鸟，头部的毛黑白相间，老鸟头部的毛变成白色，生活在山林中，吃树木的果实，也吃害虫 Chinese bulbul (*Pycnonotus sinensis sineusis*); bird with black-and-white head feathers which turn completely white with age, inhabiting forests, feeding on fruits and insect pests

【白头翁】[2] báitóuwēng 多年生草本植物，花紫红色，果实有白毛，像老翁的白发。中医入药。root of Chinese pulsatilla (*Pulsatilla chinensis*); herbaceous, perennial plant with purplish-red flowers, white hairy fruits like a hoary head, and roots used in traditional Chinese medicine

【白头偕老】báitóu xié lǎo 夫妻共同生活到老 live in conjugal bliss to a ripe old age:百年好合，～（新婚颂词）。May you remain happily married to a ripe old age (congratulatory wish expressed at weddings).

【白玩儿】báiwánr ❶ 不付任何代价地玩儿 have fun free of charge ❷ 指做某种事轻而易举，不费力 a piece of cake; do sth. easily; effortless

B

【白文】báiwén ❶ 指有注解的书的正文 text of an annotated book：先读～，后看注解 read the text before consulting the annotations ❷ 指有注解的书不录注解只印正文的本子，如《十三经白文》unannotated edition of a book, e.g. *The Unannotated Edition of the Thirteen Classics* ❸ 印章上的阴文（跟'朱文'相对 in contrast to 'characters on a seal carved in relief'）intagliated characters on a seal

【白皙】báixī 〈书 *fml*.〉白净 (of skin) fair and clear

【白细胞】báixìbāo 血细胞的一种，比红细胞大，圆形或椭圆形，无色，有细胞核，产生在骨髓、脾脏和淋巴结中。作用是吞食病菌、中和病菌分泌的毒素等。white blood cell; leukocyte; colourless, round or oval cell formed in the myelopoietic, lymphoid, and reticular portions of the reticuloendothelial system of the body, larger than red blood cell, normally present in those sites and in the circulating blood. Formed in bone marrow, spleens and lymphs, white blood cells engulf pathogenic bacteria and neutralize the toxin excreted by pathogenic bacteria. also 白血球 báixuèqiú

【白鹇】báixián 鸟，雄的背部白色，有黑色的纹，腹部黑蓝色，雌的全身棕绿色。产于我国南部各省，是有名的观赏鸟。silver pheasant (*Lophura nycthemera nycthemera*); famous ornamental bird inhabiting various provinces in South China, having a dark blue belly, the male being white on the back with black stripes, and the female being brownish-green all over

【白鲞】báixiǎng 剖开晾干的黄鱼 cut open and dried yellow croaker

【白相】báixiàng 〈方 *dial*.〉玩；玩耍；玩弄 play; enjoy oneself

【白相人】báixiàngrén 〈方 *dial*.〉游手好闲，为非作歹的人；流氓 good-for-nothing; hooligan

【白血病】báixuèbìng 病，症状是白细胞异常增多，红细胞减少，脾脏肿大，眩晕等 leukaemia; disease of the blood with symptoms of progressive proliferation of abnormal leukocytes, reduction of red blood cells, enlargement of the spleen, and dizziness; 俗称 commonly called 血癌 xuè'ái

【白血球】báixuèqiú 白细胞 white blood cell; leukocyte

【白眼】báiyǎn 眼睛朝上或向旁边看，现出白眼珠，是看不起人的一种表情（跟'青眼'相对 opposite to 'good graces'）show the white of the eyes by looking upward or sideways; supercilious look：～看人 treat people superciliously; look with disdain｜遭人～be treated with disdain

【白眼儿狼】báiyǎnrláng 〈比喻 *fig*.〉忘恩负义的人 ungrateful person

【白眼珠】báiyǎnzhū (～儿 báiyǎnzhūr)眼球上白色的部分 the white of the eye

【白羊座】báiyángzuò 黄道十二星座之一 Aries; northern constellation; one of the 12 signs of the zodiac, represented as a ram; ☞ 黄道十二宫 huángdào shí'èrgōng on p. 851

【白药】báiyào 〈中药 *Chin. med*.〉成药，是一种白色粉末。能治出血疾患、跌打损伤等。云南出产的最著名。baiyao, white medicinal powder for treating haemorrhage, wounds, bruises, etc. The variety produced in Yunnan Province is the best known.

【白夜】báiyè 由于地轴偏斜和地球自转、公转的关系，在高纬度地区，有时黄昏还没有过去就呈现黎明，这种现象叫做白夜。出现白夜的地区从纬度49°起，纬度越高白夜出现的时期越长，天空也越亮。white night; phenomenon in high-latitude areas where dawn often breaks just as night falls, caused by the slant of the earth's axis, its auto rotation and revolution around the sun. White nights occur in areas above 49° latitude. The higher the latitude, the longer the white night becomes, and the brighter the sky.

【白衣苍狗】báiyī cānggǒu 杜甫《可叹》诗：'天上浮云似白衣，斯须改变如苍狗。'后来用白衣苍狗比喻变幻无常。white clouds change into gray dogs; changes in human affairs often take freakish forms, line from Du Fu's poem *Regrettable*: 'The floating clouds resemble white garments, in an instant changing to look like gray dogs.' also 白云苍狗 báiyún cānggǒu

【白衣天使】báiyī tiānshǐ 护士的美称 angel in white; laudatory term for nurses

【白衣战士】báiyī zhànshì 指医疗护理人员。因为他们身穿白色工作服，救死扶伤，跟疾病作斗争，所以称做白衣战士。warriors in white; medical workers, so named because they wear white overalls, heal the wounded, rescue the dying and combat disease

【白蚁】báiyǐ 昆虫，形状像蚂蚁，群居，吃木材。对森林、建筑物、桥梁、铁路等破坏性极大 termite (*Termitidae*); white ant; small, white, soft-bodied, social, wood-eating insects that resemble ants and do great damage to forests, buildings, bridges and railroads

【白翳】báiyì 〈中医 *Chin. med*.〉指眼球角膜病变后留下的疤痕，能影响视力 nebula; faint, opacity of the cornea that can affect eyesight

【白银】báiyín 银①的通称 common name for 银 yín ①

【白云苍狗】báiyún cānggǒu ☞ 白衣苍狗 báiyī

cānggǒu

【白斩鸡】báizhǎnjī 一种菜肴,用宰好的整只鸡放在水里煮熟后,捞出切成块,蘸作料吃 Tender Boiled Chicken, made by boiling a whole chicken in water and cutting into cubes, then dipping into seasonings

【白芷】báizhǐ 多年生草本植物,开白花,果实长椭圆形。根粗大,圆锥形,有香气,中医入药。dahurian angelica (*Angelica dahurica*); herbaceous perennial plant with white flowers, prolate elliptical fruits, and cony e-shaped bulky, fragrant roots that are used in traditional Chinese medicine

【白纸黑字】bái zhǐ hēi zì 白纸上写的黑字。指见于书面的确凿的证据 black ink characters written on white paper; written in black and white:这是~,赖是赖不掉的。This is evidence written in black and white and cannot be denied.

【白质】báizhì 脑和脊髓的白色部分,主要由神经细胞所发出的神经纤维组成 white matter; white substance; white-coloured part of the brain and spinal cord, consisting mainly of nerve fibres extending from nerve cells

【白种】Báizhǒng 欧罗巴人种 the white race; Caucasoid race

【白昼】báizhòu 白天 daytime; day:灯火通明,照得如同~一般。The brilliant lights make it all as bright as day.

【白术】báizhú 多年生草本植物,叶子椭圆形,花红色。根状茎中医入药。rhizome of large-headed atractylodes (*Atractylodes macrocephala*); herbaceous perennial plant with oval leaves, red flowers, and rhizome used in traditional Chinese medicine

【白字】báizì 写错或读错的字;别字 character misused or mispronounced through confusion with one that sounds or looks like it:写~ write a wrong character in mistake for one that resembles it|念~ pronounce a character wrongly because it resembles another one

【白族】Báizú 我国少数民族之一,主要分布在云南 Bai ethnic group or the Bais, one of China's ethnic minorities, mainly inhabiting Yunnan Province

【白族吹吹腔】báizú chuīchuīqiāng 白族戏曲剧种,历史悠久,流行于云南西部白族聚居的地区 *chuichuiqiang* of the Bais, an ancient traditional opera of the Bai ethnic group, popular in western Yunnan Province where the Bais live in compact communities

【白嘴儿】báizuǐr 〈方 *dial.*〉指光吃菜不就饭或光吃饭不就菜 eat rice, steamed bread, etc. without vegetables or other dishes, or vice versa:~吃菜 eat vegetable and meat dishes without any starch foods|~吃饭 eat starch foods without vegetables or meat

bǎi(ㄅㄞˇ)

百 bǎi ❶ 数目,十个十 hundred; numeral, product of 10 times 10 ❷〈比喻 *fig.*〉很多 numerous; variety; all kinds of:~草 numerous plants|~货 general merchandise|~科全书 encyclopaedia|~家争鸣 debate between a hundred schools of thought|~花齐放 hundreds of flowers in bloom|精神~倍 full of vigour|~闻不如一见。It is better to see once than to hear a hundred times.

【百般】bǎibān ❶ 形容采用多种方法 in every possible way; by every means:~阻挠 put up innumerable obstacles|~劝解 try by every means to persuade ❷ 各种各样 numerous; all kinds of:~花色 numerous designs and colours|~痛苦 all kinds of suffering

【百宝箱】bǎibǎoxiāng 储藏各种珍贵物品的箱子,多用于比喻(oft. fig.) treasure box; treasure chest

【百倍】bǎibèi 形容数量多或程度深(多用于抽象事物 for the abstract) hundred-fold; a hundred times:~努力 make greatest effort|精神~ full of vigour

【百步穿杨】bǎi bù chuān yáng 春秋时楚国养由基善于射箭,能在一百步以外射中杨柳的叶子(见于《战国策·西周策》)。后用'百步穿杨'形容箭法或枪法非常高明。shoot with great precision; during the Spring and Autumn Period, Yang Youji of the State of Chu was a fine archer able to shoot an arrow through a willow leaf at a hundred paces (from *Intrigues of the Warring States·Intrigues of the Western Zhou*); Hence the saying, 'shoot a willow leaf at a hundred paces', which describes fine marksmanship.

【百尺竿头,更进一步】bǎi chǐ gān tóu, gèng jìn yī bù 〈比喻 *fig.*〉学问、成绩等达到了很高的程度以后仍继续努力 make still further efforts; continue to improve after attaining high levels of learning or success

【百出】bǎichū 〈贬义 *derog.*〉形容出现次数很多 numerous; full of; plenty of:错误~ full of mistakes|矛盾~full of contradictions

【百川归海】bǎi chuān guī hǎi 条条江河流入大海。比喻大势所趋或众望所归。也比喻许多分散的事物汇集到一个地方。all rivers flow to the sea; (fig.)everything points in one direction; all hopes turn in one direction; concentration of dispersed things

【百儿八十】bǎi·erbāshí 一百或比一百略少 around a hundred; a hundred or so:~块钱 a hundred or so dollars|~人 about a hundred people

【百发百中】bǎi fā bǎi zhòng ❶ 每次都命中目标,形容射箭或射击非常准 a hundred bull's-eyes with a hundred shots; every shot hits the mark; shoot with unfailing accuracy; be a crack shot ❷〈比喻 *fig*.〉做事有充分把握,绝不落空 full of confidence; sure of success

【百废俱兴】bǎi fèi jù xīng 各种该办未办的事业都兴办起来 all neglected tasks are now being undertaken; all that was left undone is now being done; also 百废俱举 bǎi fèi jù jǔ; 俱 can be written as 具 jù

【百分比】bǎifēnbǐ 用百分率表示的两个数的比例关系,例如某班 50 个学生当中有 20 个是女生,这一班中女生所占的百分比就是 40% percentage; rate or proportion per hundred, e.g. 20 girls in a class of 50 students means 40 per cent are girls

【百分表】bǎifēnbiǎo 一种精度很高的量具,由表针、表盘等组成,利用杆杆原理进行工作,测量精度达 0.01 毫米。精度达到 0.001 毫米的叫千分表。clock gauge; precision measuring instrument consisting of a pointer and dial plate, works according to the lever principle, with a precision of 0.01 mm. A clock gauge with a precision of 0.001 mm is called 千分表 qiānfēnbiǎo.

【百分尺】bǎifēnchǐ 利用螺旋原理制成的精度很高的量具,测量精度达 0.01 毫米 micrometre; milscale; precision measuring instrument based on the spiral principle, with a precision of 0.01 mm; also 分厘卡 fēnlíkǎ and 千分尺 qiānfēnchǐ

【百分点】bǎifēndiǎn 统计学上称百分之一为一个百分点(in statistics) one percentage point: 同前一年相比,通货膨胀率减少三个～。Compared to the previous year, the inflation rate dropped three percentage points.

【百分号】bǎifēnhào 表示分数的分母是 100 的符号 percentage symbol (%)

【百分率】bǎifēnlǜ 两个数的比值写成百分数的形式,叫做百分率。如$\frac{2}{5}$用百分率表示是$\frac{40}{100}$。百分率指一个数占另一个数的百分之几或某一部分占整体的百分之几。percentage; per cent; ratio of two figures in the form of a percentage, e.g. 2/5 is 40%. Percentage indicates the ratio between two figures expressed in hundredths, or a part of a whole expressed in hundredths.

【百分数】bǎifēnshù 分母是 100 的分数,通常用百分号来表示,如$\frac{11}{100}$写作 11% fraction with 100 as the denominator, expressed with %, e.g. 11%

【百分之百】bǎi fēn zhī bǎi 全部;十足 one hundred per cent; out and out; absolutely: ～地完成了任务。The task is accomplished one hundred per cent. | 这件事我有～的把握,准能成功。I am absolutely sure this will succeed.

【百分制】bǎifēnzhì 学校评定学生成绩的一种记分方法。一百分为最高成绩,六十分为及格。hundred-mark system; grading system for registering students' marks, with 100 as the highest score, and 60 points the passing grade

【百感】bǎigǎn 各种各样的感触、感慨 many different feelings: ～交集 mixed feelings

【百合】bǎihé ❶ 多年生草本植物,鳞茎呈球形,白色或浅红色。花呈漏斗形,白色,供观赏。鳞茎供食用,中医入药。lily (*Lilium*); herbaceous perennial plant, with a round, white or pinkish bulb, its funnel-shaped, white flowers are ornamental. Fresh bulbs are edible, and used in traditional Chinese medicine. ❷ 这种植物的鳞茎 lily bulb

【百花齐放】bǎi huā qí fàng ❶〈比喻 *fig*.〉不同形式和风格的各种艺术作品自由发展 let a hundred flowers bloom; free development of different forms and styles in the arts ❷ 形容艺术界的繁荣景象 flourishing art circles

【百花齐放,百家争鸣】bǎi huā qí fàng, bǎi jiā zhēng míng 1956 年中国共产党提出的促进艺术发展、科学进步和社会主义文化繁荣的方针。提倡在党的领导下,艺术上不同的形式和风格可以自由发展,科学上不同的学派可以自由争论。let a hundred flowers blossom and a hundred schools of thought contend; policy set forth by the Communist Party of China in 1956 for promoting progress of the arts and sciences, and the development of a flourishing socialist culture, featuring unrestricted development of different forms and styles in the arts, and free debate of different schools of thought in sciences

【百货】bǎihuò 以衣着、器皿和日用品为主的商品的总称 general merchandise, mainly clothing, utensils and daily-use articles: 日用～ articles of daily use | ～公司 department store

【百家争鸣】bǎi jiā zhēng míng ❶ 春秋战国时代,社会处于大变革时期,产生了各种思想流派,如儒、法、道、墨等,他们著书讲学,互相论战,出现了学术上的繁荣景象,后世称为百家争鸣。a hundred schools of thought contend. The Spring and Autumn and the Warring States periods (770-221 B.C.) were a time of great social change, stimulating various schools of thought, such as Confucianism, Legalism, Taoism, and Mohism; and scholars wrote, lectured and debated vigorously, creating a lively academic environment later characterised as 'a hundred schools of thought contend'. ❷ ☞ 百花齐放,百家争鸣 bǎi huā qí fàng, bǎi jiā zhēng míng

【百科全书】bǎikē quánshū 比较全面系统地介绍文化科学知识的大型工具书,收录各种专门名词和术语,按词典形式分条编排,解说详细。也有专科的百科全书,如医学百科全书、农业百科全书等。encyclopaedia; reference work containing information on all branches of knowledge, using specialised terms, arranged alphabetically with detailed explanations; also specialised encyclopaedia, as medical encyclopaedia, agricultural encyclopaedia

【百孔千疮】bǎikǒng qiān chuāng〈比喻 *fig.*〉破坏得很严重或弊病很多 badly damaged; full of problems

【白口莫辩】bǎi kǒu mò biàn 即使有一百张嘴也辩解不清。形容事情无法说清楚(多用于受冤屈、被怀疑等情况 usu. when wronged or under suspicion) unable to argue one's innocence even with a hundred mouths; unable to make things clear

【百里挑一】bǎi lǐ tiāo yī 一百个里挑选出一个。形容十分出众。one in a hundred; cream of the crop

【百炼成钢】bǎi liàn chéng gāng〈比喻 *fig.*〉久经锻炼,变得非常坚强 (of iron) be tempered into steel—become strong through many trials

【百灵】bǎilíng 鸟,比麻雀大,羽毛茶褐色,有白色斑点。飞得很高,能发出多种叫声,吃害虫,对农业有益。lark (*Alaudidae*); song bird larger than a sparrow, with brown feathers spotted white, able to fly high, feeds on harmful insects, benefits agriculture

【百衲本】bǎinàběn 用许多不同的版本汇集而印成的书籍,如百衲本《二十四史》anthology; book containing selections from various editions or texts, e.g. *The Twenty-Four Histories*

【百衲衣】bǎinàyī ❶ 袈裟,因用许多长方形小块布片拼缀制成而得名 another name for 袈裟 jiāshā; *kasaya*, patchwork outer vestment worn by a Buddhist monk ❷ 泛指补丁很多的衣服(in a broad sense) heavily patched garment

【百年】bǎinián ❶ 指很多年或很长时期 hundred years; century; many years; long period of time:~大业 cause of vital and lasting importance|~不遇 once in a century ❷ 人的一生;终身 lifetime:~好合(新婚颂词) Wishing you life-long happiness and perfect harmony (at wedding)|~之后(婉辞,指死亡 euph. for death) after death

【百年不遇】bǎi nián bù yù 一百年也碰不到。形容很少见到或很少出现。not seen once in a hundred years; rarely seen; seldom appear

【百年大计】bǎinián dàjì 关系到长远利益的计划或措施 matter of fundamental importance for generations to come; project of vital and lasting importance:~,质量第一。A project of vital and lasting importance calls above all for good quality.

【百日咳】bǎirìké 传染病,由百日咳杆菌侵入呼吸道引起,患者多为十岁以下儿童。症状是阵发性的连续咳嗽,咳嗽后长吸气,发出特殊的哮喘声。whooping cough; pertussis; acute infectious disease of children under 10, caused by bordetella pertussis in the respiratory tract, and resulting in recurrent bouts of spasmodic coughing that continue until the breath is exhausted and the cycle ends in a noisy inspiratory stridor (whoop)

【百日维新】bǎi rì wéixīn 戊戌变法由颁布新法到变法失败,历时一百零三天,旧称百日维新 Hundred Days' Reform; former name of the Reform Movement of 1898, which lasted 103 days from the promulgation of new laws to its defeat; ☞ 戊戌变法 Wùxū Biànfǎ on p. 2036

【百十】bǎishí 指一百左右的大概数目 hundred or so:~个人 about a hundred people|~来年 a hundred or so years|~亩地 about a hundred *mu* of land

【百世】bǎishì 很多世代 many years; from generation to generation:流芳~ leave a good name for a hundred generations

【百事通】bǎishìtōng 万事通 knowledgeable person

【百思不解】bǎi sī bù jiě 反复思索,仍然不能理解 remain perplexed in spite of much thought; also 百思不得其解 bǎi sī bù dé qí jiě

【百万】bǎiwàn 一百万,泛指数目巨大 million; huge amount:~雄师 a million bold warriors|~富翁 millionaire

【百闻不如一见】bǎi wén bù rú yī jiàn 听到一百次也不如见到一次,表示亲眼看到的远比听人家说的更为确切可靠 seeing is believing; better to see once than to hear a hundred times; seeing for oneself is better than hearing from others

【百无禁忌】bǎi wú jìnjì 什么都不忌讳 nothing is taboo; everything is permitted

【百无聊赖】bǎi wú liáolài 精神无所依托,感到非常无聊 bored to death; feel things are meaningless

【百无一失】bǎi wú yī shī 形容绝对不会出差错 no danger of anything going wrong; no risk at all; perfectly safe

【百无一是】bǎi wú yī shì 没有一点对的地方 without a single redeeming feature; having no saving grace:孩子有错,应该批评教育,但不应把孩子说得~。When a child makes a mistake, we should point it out and correct him, instead of making him think he has no good qualities at all.

【百物】bǎiwù 各种物品 all kinds of articles:~昂贵。Everything is expensive.

【百响】bǎixiǎng〈方 *dial.*〉一百个爆竹编成的鞭炮,有时泛指鞭炮 string of 100 firecrackers; general term for firecrackers

【百姓】bǎixìng 人民(区别于'官吏' as compared with 'officials') common people:平民~the populace; ordinary folk

【百业】bǎiyè 各种行业 trades and professions:~萧条。Business is slack for all trades and professions.

【百叶】bǎiyè〈方 *dial.*〉❶ 千张 thin sheets of

dried beancurd ❷ (～儿 bǎiyèr)牛羊等反刍类动物的胃，做食品时叫百叶儿 stomach of ruminants such as oxen and sheep when prepared for cooking

【百叶窗】bǎiyèchuāng ❶ 窗扇的一种，用许多横板条制成，横板条之间有空隙，既可以遮光挡雨，又可以通风 shutter; blind; jalousie; cover or screen composed of horizontal laths for a window that limits the passage of light and rain, and yet allows ventilation ❷ 机械设备中像百叶窗的装置 mechanical device that looks like a shutter

【百叶箱】bǎiyèxiāng 放在室外、装有测量空气温度或湿度的仪器的白色木箱，四周有百叶窗，既可以使仪器不受辐射、降水和强风的影响，又可以让空气自由流通 thermometer screen; white wooden box placed outdoors, containing thermometers or psychrometers; its shutters on four sides provide good ventilation, yet protect the instruments from radiation, rainfall and strong wind

【百战不殆】bǎi zhàn bù dài 多次打仗都不失败 fight a hundred battles without a single defeat; emerge victorious from every battle; invincible (殆 *dai*:危险 danger)

【百折不挠】bǎi zhé bù náo 无论受多少挫折都不退缩，形容意志坚强 keep on fighting in spite of all setbacks; be undaunted by repeated setbacks; dauntless; indomitable; unrelenting; also 百折不回 bǎi zhé bù huí

【百足之虫，死而不僵】bǎi zú zhī chóng, sǐ ér bù jiāng 原指马陆这种虫子被切断致死后仍然蠕动的现象(《本草纲目·马陆》:弘景曰:'此虫甚多，寸寸断之，亦便寸行。故《鲁连子》云:"百足之虫，死而不僵"')。centipede continues to move even when cut into pieces (*Compendium of Materia Medica · Centipede*: Hongjing said, 'There are many such insects which when cut into inch-long sections still wriggle. Thus *Lulianzi* has this to say, 'A centipede still moves even when it is dead.''); 现用来比喻人或集团虽已失败，但其势力和影响依然存在(多含贬义 oft. derog.)(fig.) after a person or group has failed his or its influence still lingers; old institutions die hard

伯 bǎi ☞ 大伯子 dàbǎi·zi on p. 353
☞ bó on p. 148

佰 bǎi '百'的大写 used for the numeral 百 bǎi on cheques, etc. to avoid mistakes or alterations

柏(栢) bǎi ❶ 柏树，常绿乔木，叶鳞片状，果实为球果。可用来造防风林。木材质地坚硬，用来做建筑材料。cypress (*Cupressus funebris*); evergreen tree with overlapping leaves resembling scales and round fruits, planted in windbreak forests, its hard wood used as a building material ❷ (Bǎi) 姓 a surname
☞ bó on p. 149 and bò on p. 152

【柏油】bǎiyóu 沥青的通称 common name for 沥青 lìqīng

捭 bǎi 〈书 *fml*.〉分开 divide: ～阖 divide and unite

【捭阖】bǎihé 〈书 *fml*.〉开合，指运用手段使联合或分化 manoeuvre to divide or unite: 纵横～manoeuvre among various states or political groupings | ～之术 art of political manoeuvring

摆[1](擺) bǎi ❶ 安放；排列 put; place; arrange: 把东西～好 arrange things properly | 河边一字儿～开十几条渔船。Along the river a dozen of fishing boats were aligned in a line. | 书架上～着各种工具书。Various reference books are stacked on the bookshelf. ❷ 显示；炫耀 show off; display: ～阔 parade one's wealth | ～威风 give oneself airs; put on airs ❸ 摇动；摇摆 rock; wave: 他向我直～手。He waved frenetically at me. ❹ 悬挂在细线上的能做往复运动的重锤的装置。摆的长度不变且振幅不太大时，运动的周期恒等。pendulum; weight suspended on a string from a fixed point so as to swing freely to and fro under the action of gravity. When the length of the pendulum is fixed and the amplitude of the vibration is not too big, the period of motion is identically equal. ❺ 钟表或精密仪器上用来控制摆动频率的机械装置 device on a timepiece or precision instrument that controls the frequency of sways ❻ 说；谈；陈述 talk; say; spell out: ～事实，讲道理 present the facts and reason things out | 大家都把意见～出来。Let us lay out our arguments.

摆[2](擺、襬) bǎi 长袍、上衣、衬衫等的最下端部分 bottom part of a gown, jacket or shirt: 衣～lower part of a jacket | 下～lower hem | 前～ front hem | ～宽 width of the bottom hem

摆[3](擺) bǎi 傣族地区佛教仪式或庆丰收、物资交流、文艺会演等群众性活动的集会 gathering of the Dai people for Buddhist rituals, or for group activities to celebrate a bumper harvest, exchange goods, or for cultural festivals

【摆布】bǎi·bu ❶ 安排；布置 dispose; arrange: 这间屋子～得十分雅致。The room is tastefully furnished. ❷ 操纵；支配(别人行动) control; manipulate: 任人～let oneself be ordered about | 随意～人 boss people about

【摆荡】bǎidàng 摇晃动荡；摆动 swing; sway: 风起浪涌，船身～。As the winds rise and the waves heave, the boat rocks. | 柳枝随风～。The willow branches swayed in the breeze.

【摆动】bǎidòng 来回摇动；摇摆 swing; sway: 树枝儿迎风～。The tree branches swayed in the breeze. | 钟摆不停地～。The pendulum of the clock swings steadily.

【摆渡】bǎi//dù ❶ 用船运载过河 ferry across a river：先～物资，后～人。Ferry material first and people later. ❷ 乘船过河 take a boat across a river：会游泳的游泳过去，不会游泳的～过去。Those who could swim across the river, and those who could not took a boat.

【摆渡】bǎidù 摆渡的船；渡船 ferryboat; ferry

【摆份儿】bǎi//fènr〈方 dial.〉讲究排场，显示身份；摆架子 fond of ostentation and extravagance; show off social status; put on airs

【摆好】bǎi//hǎo 数说优点、长处 cite merits and strengths：评功～ speak of someone in glowing terms

【摆划】bǎi·hua〈方 dial.〉❶ 反复摆弄 fiddle：你别瞎～！Stop fiddling! ❷ 处理；安排 handle; deal with：这件事真不好～。This matter is really difficult to handle. ❸ 整治；修理 repair; renovate：～好了，就能把这些废渣变成宝贝。If things are properly done, the waste residue will become riches. | 这个收音机让他～好了。This radio works well after he repaired it.

【摆架子】bǎi jià·zi 指自高自大，为显示身份而装腔作势 put on airs; give oneself airs to show off one's social status

【摆件】bǎijiàn 用作摆设的工艺品 objets d'art displayed as ornaments：案头～ desk ornaments | 金银～ gold and silver ornaments

【摆款儿】bǎi//kuǎnr 摆架子 put on airs; give oneself airs

【摆阔】bǎi//kuò 讲究排场，显示阔气 parade one's wealth; be ostentatious and extravagant：就是经济宽裕，也不应～。Being well off is no reason to be ostentatious and extravagant.

【摆擂台】bǎi lèitái 搭起擂台招人来比武。现比喻欢迎人来应战或参加竞赛。set up a platform and invite people to a contest of martial arts; welcome those who take up a challenge; (fig.) welcome competitors to a competition; also 摆擂 bǎi//lèi

【摆列】bǎiliè 摆放；陈列 arrange; place; lay out：展品～有序。The exhibits are neatly arranged.

【摆龙门阵】bǎi lóngménzhèn〈方 dial.〉谈天或讲故事 chat; gossip; spin a yarn

【摆轮】bǎilún 钟表内等时运动系统中的主要元件。外为圆环，中有轮辐。balance wheel; main component of the isochronous movement system of a timepiece, consisting of a ring with spokes; also 摆盘 bǎipán

【摆门面】bǎi mén·miàn 讲究排场，粉饰外表 put up a front; maintain an outward show; keep up appearances

【摆弄】bǎinòng ❶ 反复拨动或移动 move about; tinker with; fiddle with：一个战士正在那里～枪栓。A soldier is tinkering with the rifle bolt. ❷ 摆布② same as 摆布 bǎi·bu ②；玩弄 order about; manipulate：受人～ let oneself be ordered about ❸〈方 dial.〉做某项工作 do sth.; perform：～牲口，他是行家。He is an expert in livestock dealings. | ～文字，我可不行。I am not good at writing.

【摆平】bǎi//píng ❶ 放平，比喻公平处理或使各方面平衡 be fair; be impartial：～关系 deal with people impartially | 两边要～ treat both sides fairly ❷〈方 dial.〉惩治；收拾 punish; deal with

【摆谱儿】bǎi//pǔr〈方 dial.〉❶ 摆门面 keep up appearances; be ostentatious：办事要节约，不要～。Practice strict economy and never be ostentatious. ❷ 摆架子 put on airs：他当了官好摆个谱儿。After becoming an official he likes to put on airs.

【摆设】bǎishè 把物品(多指艺术品 oft. of works of art)按照审美观点安放 furnish and decorate：屋子里～得很整齐。The room is neatly furnished and decorated.

【摆设】bǎi·she ❶ (～儿 bǎi·sher)摆设的东西(多指供欣赏的艺术品 oft. of works of art) objects on display：小～small ornaments | 会客室里的～十分雅致。The ornaments displayed in the reception room are in good taste. ❷ 指徒有其表而无实际用处的东西 objects or articles merely for show：书是供人读的，不是拿来当～的。Books are for reading, not for show.

【摆手】bǎi//shǒu ❶ 摇手 wave one's hand (in admonition or disapproval)：他连忙～，叫大家不要笑。He hastily waved his hand to stop people from laughing. ❷ 招手 beckon; wave：他俩在路上见了没有说话，只摆了下手。They did not speak when they met on the road, but merely waved at each other.

【摆摊子】bǎi tān·zi ❶ 在路旁或市场中陈列货物出售 set up a stall on roadside or in a market ❷ 把东西摆开(做开展工作的准备) lay things out (in preparation for work) ❸〈比喻 *fig.*〉铺张(含贬义 derog.) excessive：不要～，追求形式。Let us not be extravagant and overemphasise form only. ‖ also 摆摊儿 bǎi tānr

【摆脱】bǎituō 脱离(牵制、束缚、困难、不良的情况等) shake off; cast off; break away from; free (or extricate) oneself from (containment, constraint, difficulty, predicament, etc.)：～困境 extricate oneself from a predicament | ～苦恼 free oneself from worries | ～落后状态 be lifted out of backwardness | ～坏人的跟踪 shake off the pursuit of a scoundrel

【摆治】bǎi·zhì〈方 dial.〉❶ 整治；侍弄 attend to; look after：这块地他～得不错。He has prepared this piece of land well. | 小马驹病了，他～了一夜。The colt was sick, and he sat up with it the whole night. ❷ 折磨；整治

torment; punish：他把我～得好苦。He made me suffer a lot. ❸ 摆布；操纵 manipulate; control：他既然上了圈套，就不得不听人家～。Once he fell into the trap, he was at the mercy of others.

B

【摆钟】bǎizhōng 时钟的一种，用摆锤控制其他机件，使钟走得快慢均匀，一般能报点 pendulum clock; clock whose works are regulated by a pendulum, usu. strikes the hours

【摆轴】bǎizhóu 摆轮的主轴，是钟表的主要零件之一，用优质钢加工制成 balance staff of a balance wheel, major component of a timepiece, made of high-grade steel; also 天心 tiānxīn or 摆杆 bǎigān

【摆桌】bǎi//zhuō 指摆酒席；宴请 give a banquet; feast sb.

【摆子】bǎi·zi 〈方 *dial.*〉疟疾 malaria：打～ suffer from an attack of malaria

bài（ㄅㄞˋ）

呗 bài ☞ 梵呗 fànbài on p. 543
☞ ·bei on p. 87

败 bài ❶ 在战争或竞赛中失败（跟'胜'相对 as opposed to 'win'）be defeated; lose：战～国 vanquished nation｜立于不～之地 establish oneself in an unassailable position｜胜～乃兵家常事。To the soldier, victory and defeat are common place.｜甲队以二比三～于乙队。Team A lost to Team B 2 to 3. ❷ 使失败；打败（敌人或对手）defeat (enemy or opponent)：大～侵略军 inflict a crushing defeat on aggressor troops ❸（事情）失败（跟'成'相对 as opposed to 'success'）failure：功～垂成 fail when on the verge of success; suffer defeat when victory is within reach｜不计成～never give a thought to success or failure ❹ 毁坏；搞坏（事情）destroy; spoil：身～名裂 lose all standing and reputation｜伤风～俗 offend public decency; indecent; offensive｜成事不足，～事有余 unable to accomplish anything but liable to spoil everything ❺ 解除；消除 relieve; eliminate：～毒 alleviate internal heat｜～火 release a fever ❻ 破旧；败落；腐烂；凋谢 shabby; worn-out; dilapidated; decayed; withered：～絮 old cotton wadding｜～肉 rotten meat｜～叶 withered leaves｜开不～的花朵 flower that will not fade ❼ 使败落 dissipate; ruin：～家 dissipate a family fortune

【败北】bàiběi 打败仗（'北'本来是二人相背的意思，因此军队打败仗背向敌人逃跑叫败北）suffer defeat; lose a battle（北 běi formerly meant 'two people with their back to each other', thus 败北 describes a defeated army turning its back to flee from the enemy）：身经百战，未尝～。He has fought countless battles and never been defeated. ◇客队决赛中以二比三～。In the finals, the visitors lost to the home team 2 to 3.

【败笔】bàibǐ 写字写得不好的一笔；绘画中画得不好的部分；诗文中写得不好的词句 badly written character in calligraphy; poorly executed part of a painting; flawed writing in prose and verse

【败兵】bàibīng 打了败仗的兵；打败仗溃散的兵 defeated army; army in flight; defeated troops

【败草】bàicǎo 枯萎的草 withered grass：～残花 withered grass and faded flowers

【败坏】bàihuài ❶ 损害；破坏（名誉、风气等）ruin; corrupt; undermine (fame, mood, atmosphere, etc.)：～门风 corrupt family morals｜～声誉 damage sb.'s reputation｜～纪律 violate discipline ❷（道德、纪律等）极坏 rotten; extremely bad (morals, discipline, etc.)：道德～morally degenerate｜纪律～rotten discipline

【败火】bài//huǒ 〈中医 *Chin. med.*〉指清热、凉血、解毒等 relieve inflammation or internal heat：～药 medicine to lower fever｜绿豆汤能清心～。Mung bean soup can clear the heart and relieve internal heat.

【败绩】bàijì 〈书 *fml.*〉在战争中被打败 defeated in war; put to rout

【败家】bài//jiā 使家业败落 dissipate the family fortune：由投机起家的，也会因投机而～。Those who make a fortune through profiteering will also lose it that way.

【败家子】bàijiāzǐ（～儿 bàijiāzǐr）不务正业、挥霍家产的子弟。现常用来比喻挥霍浪费集体或国家财产的人。black sheep of the family; spendthrift; wastrel; (fig.) person who wastefully spends public or state monies

【败将】bàijiàng 打了败仗的将领，多用来指比试中比输的一方 defeated general; loser：手下～ opponent of a defeated army

【败局】bàijú 失败的局势 bad situation; losing battle：挽回～ save the day; recover

【败军】bàijūn ❶ 使军队打败仗 cause military defeat：～亡国 lead to military defeat and the annihilation of the nation ❷ 打了败仗的军队 defeated army：～之将 general of a defeated army

【败类】bàilèi 集体中的堕落或变节分子 riffraff; degenerate：无耻～ shameless degenerate｜民族～ scum of a nation

【败露】bàilù（隐蔽的事）被人发觉（of secret, hidden activity, etc.）uncover; expose：阴谋～。The conspiracy was brought to light.｜事情～，无法隐瞒了。The matter has been exposed and can no longer be concealed.

【败落】bàiluò 由盛而衰；破落；衰落 decline (in wealth and position); deteriorate：家道～ decline of a family｜半山坡有一座～的古庙。There is an ancient dilapidated temple halfway up the hill.

【败诉】bàisù 诉讼中当事人的一方受到不利的判决 lose a lawsuit

【败退】bàituì 战败而退却 retreat in defeat：节节～retreat in defeat again and again；keep on retreating

【败亡】bàiwáng 失败而灭亡 be defeated and wiped out

【败胃】bàiwèi 伤害胃使胃口变坏 spoil one's appetite；ruin the taste for：这东西吃多了～。Eating too much of this will spoil your appetite.

【败谢】bàixiè 凋谢 dim；wither ◇青春常在，永不～ keep the fervour of youth alive forever

【败兴】bài//xìng ❶ 因遇到不如意的事而情绪低落；扫兴 low spirits caused by disappointment；crestfallen：乘兴而来，～而归 set out in high spirits and return disappointed ❷〈方 *dial.*〉晦气；倒霉 unlucky；bad luck

【败絮】bàixù 破棉絮 poor quality cotton wool used as stuffing for quilts，etc.：金玉其外，～其中（比喻外表很好，实质很糟）gilded junk；（fig.）fair without but foul within

【败血症】bàixuèzhèng 病，由球菌、杆菌等侵入血液而引起。症状是寒战，发烧，皮肤和黏膜有出血点，脾脏肿大。septicaemia；systemic disease caused by multiplication of microorganisms such as coccus or bacillus in the circulating blood. Symptoms are shivering，fever，hemorrhagic spots on skin and mucosa，and enlargement of the spleen.

【败叶】bàiyè 干枯凋落的叶子 dry，withered leaf：枯枝～dry twigs and withered leaves

【败仗】bàizhàng 失利的战役或战斗 losing campaign or battle；defeat：打～ be defeated in battle；suffer a defeat｜吃了一个大～suffer a crushing blow

【败阵】bài//zhèn 在阵地上被打败 be defeated on the battlefield：～而逃 lose the field and take flight｜败下阵来 lose a battle；be beaten in a contest ◇甲队最后以二比三～。In the end，Team A lost 2 to 3.

【败子】bàizǐ 败家子 black sheep of the family：～回头（败家子觉悟悔改）return of the prodigal son；a prodigal son repents and mends his ways

拜 bài ❶ 一种表示敬意的礼节 respectful formality：回～pay a return courtesy visit｜叩～kowtow ❷ 见面行礼表示祝贺 congratulatory greeting：～年 pay a New Year's call｜～寿 present birthday greetings（to an elderly person）❸ 拜访 visit；pay a visit：新搬来的张同志～街坊来了。Comrade Zhang，who has moved here recently，visited the neighbours. ❹ 用一定的礼节授与某种名位或官职 confer title with ceremony；appoint to office：～相 appoint the Prime Minister｜～将 confer the rank of general ❺ 结成某种关系 enter into a relationship：～师 acknowledge as one's teacher｜～把子 become sworn brothers ❻〈敬辞 *pol.*〉用于人事往来[used before a verb to show respect]：～托 request a favour｜～领（收下赠品）have the honour of receiving（gift，etc.）｜～读大作 have the pleasure of reading your book ❼（Bài）姓 a surname

【拜把子】bài bǎ·zi 朋友结为兄弟 friends become sworn brothers

【拜拜】bài·bai ❶〈旧时 *old*〉指妇女行礼，就是万福 woman's bow；also 万福 wànfú ❷〈方 *dial.*〉指在节日或佛的诞辰日举行迎神赛会，宴请亲朋 religious festival or the Buddha's birthday，celebrated with parades and banquets

【拜忏】bài//chàn 僧道念经礼拜，代人忏悔消灾（of monks or Taoists）say prayers on behalf of the faithful for blessings and protection from calamities

【拜辞】bàicí〈敬辞 *pol.*〉告别 bid farewell：临行匆匆，未及～，请原谅。I left in a hurry and did not have time to take my leave. Please forgive me.

【拜倒】bàidǎo 跪下行礼 fall on one's knees；grovel；〈比喻 *fig.*〉崇拜或屈服（多含贬义 oft. derog.）worship；surrender

【拜读】bàidú〈敬辞 *pol.*〉阅读 read with respect；have the honour of reading：～大作，获益不浅。I had the pleasure of perusing your work，and have greatly benefited from it.

【拜访】bàifǎng〈敬辞 *pol.*〉访问 pay a visit；call on：～亲友 pay a visit to one's relatives and friends

【拜佛】bài//fó 向佛像行礼 kneel before the image of the Buddha；worship the Buddha：烧香～burn joss sticks and bow to the Buddha

【拜服】bàifú〈敬辞 *pol.*〉佩服 admire greatly；worship：他的博闻强识，令人～。His wide knowledge and deep understanding are truly admirable.

【拜贺】bàihè〈敬辞 *pol.*〉祝贺 express good wishes；congratulate：～新年 wish somebody a happy New Year

【拜会】bàihuì 拜访会见（今多用于外交上的正式访问 oft. for diplomacy）pay an official visit；call on

【拜火教】Bàihuǒjiào 起源于古波斯的宗教，认为世界有光明和黑暗（善和恶）两种神，把火当做光明的象征来崇拜。公元 6 世纪传入中国，称祆（xiān）教。Zoroastrianism；Mazdaism；religion of ancient Persia，based on the belief that good and evil，represented by the gods Ormazd and Ahriman respectively，are in constant warfare. Followers worship fire as the symbol of light and good. It spread into China in the 6th century，known as *xianjiao*.

B

【拜见】bàijiàn 拜会;会见(从客人方面说)(of a guest) pay a formal visit (to one's host); call to pay respects:～尊长 call on one's elders|～恩师 visit one's teacher

【拜节】bài//jié 向人祝贺节日 extend good wishes on a festive occasion

【拜金】bàijīn 崇拜金钱 money worship:～思想 mammonism

【拜客】bài//kè 拜访别人 pay a visit; make a call:出门～go out to visit friends

【拜盟】bài//méng 拜把子 become sworn brothers

【拜年】bài//nián 向人祝贺新年 pay a New Year's call; wish somebody a happy New Year

【拜认】bàirèn 举行一定仪式认别人为义父、义母、师父等 hold ceremony to acknowledge somebody as one's adoptive parents, master-teacher, etc.

【拜扫】bàisǎo 在墓前祭奠;扫墓 offer sacrifices at a grave; sweep tombs:～烈士墓 pay respects to a martyr at his tomb

【拜师】bài//shī 认老师;认师傅 formally request to become someone's pupil; take someone as one's master:～学艺 take a master to learn a craft|我愿拜他为师。I wish to acknowledge him as my teacher.

【拜识】bàishí〈敬辞 *pol.*〉结识 have the honour of making sb.'s acquaintance:～尊颜。It is an honour to meet you.|闻名已久,无缘～。Your reputation has preceded you and I am honoured to finally meet you.

【拜寿】bài//shòu 祝贺寿辰 present birthday greetings to an elderly person

【拜堂】bài//táng 旧式婚礼,新郎新娘一起举行参拜天地的仪式,也指参拜天地后拜见父母公婆 (of bride and groom) traditional ceremonial obeisance; perform the marriage ceremony; pay homage to parents and parents-in-law; also 拜天地 bài tiāndì

【拜天地】bài tiāndì same as 拜堂 bài//táng

【拜托】bàituō〈敬辞 *pol.*〉托人办事 request a favour:有一封信,～您带给他。Would you be kind enough to take a letter to him?

【拜望】bàiwàng〈敬辞 *pol.*〉探望 call to pay one's respects; call on:～师母 call to pay respects to the wife of one's teacher

【拜物教】bàiwùjiào ❶ 原始宗教的一种形式,把某些东西(如石头、树木、弓箭等)当做神灵崇拜,无一定的组织形式 fetishism; primitive belief that certain objects (e.g. stones, trees, bows, and arrows) are the embodiments of spirits. There is no formal organization. ❷〈比喻 *fig.*〉对某种事物的迷信 material object regarded with awe or reverence:商品～commodity fetishism

【拜谢】bàixiè 行礼表示感谢 action to show gratitude:登门～pay a thank-you call

【拜谒】bàiyè ❶ same as 拜见 bàijiàn:专诚～pay a special visit ❷ 瞻仰(陵墓、碑碣) pay homage (to a monument, mausoleum, etc.):～黄帝陵 pay homage to the Mausoleum of the Yellow Emperor

稗 bài ❶ 稗子 barnyard grass ❷〈书 *fml.*〉〈比喻 *fig.*〉微小、琐碎的 insignificant; unofficial:～史 unofficial history; historical anecdotes

【稗官野史】bàiguān yěshǐ 稗官,古代的小官,专给帝王述说街谈巷议、风俗故事,后来称小说为稗官,泛称记载逸闻琐事的文字为稗官野史 low-ranking officials whose duties were to report street gossip and news to the emperor. Later, novels were called 稗官, and books of tales and anecdotes are now called 稗官野史

【稗子】bài•zi ❶ 一年生草本植物,叶子像稻,果实像黍米。是稻田害草。但果实可以酿酒或做饲料,有时也当做一种作物来栽培 barnyard grass (*Echinochloa cursgalli*); annual herbaceous plant resembling rice plant with seeds like millet, and a common weed in paddy fields that can be fermented to make spirits, or used as feed, and sometimes grown as a crop ❷ 这种植物的果实 seeds of barnyard grass

韛(韛) bài〈方 *dial.*〉风箱 bellows:风～bellows|～拐子(风箱的拉手) bellows handle

•bai(•ㄅㄞ)

唄 •bai〈助词 *aux.*〉same as 呗•bei

bān(ㄅㄢ)

扳 bān ❶ 使位置固定的东西改变方向或转动 change the direction of a fixed object; turn:～闸 pull the switch|～枪栓 pull back the bolt of a rifle|～着指头算天数 count the days on one's fingers ❷ 把输掉的赢回来 turn defeat into victory:～本 win back one's losses|客队经过苦战,～回一球,踢成平局。The visiting team fought hard and equalised the score by making a goal.

☞ pān on p.1441

【扳本】bān//běn〈方 *dial.*〉(～儿 bān//běnr) 翻本 win back all one's losses

【扳不倒儿】bānbùdǎor 不倒翁 tumbler; roly-poly

【扳道】bān//dào 扳动道岔使列车由一组轨道转到另一组轨道上 pull railway switches so that a train can switch from one set of tracks to another:～工 pointsman; switchman

【扳机】bānjī 枪上的机件,射击时用手扳动它使枪弹射出 trigger; in firearms, a small lever pressed back by the finger to activate the firing mechanism

【扳手】bān·shou ❶ 拧紧或松开螺丝、螺母等的工具 spanner; wrench; any tools used for tightening or loosening nuts, bolts, etc.; also 扳子 bān·zi ❷ 器具上用手扳动的部分 lever, handle or other projection used to operate a machine

【扳指儿】bān·zhir 戴在拇指上的玉石指环,本来是射箭时戴,后来用做装饰品 thumb-ring; formerly archery ring made of jade and worn on the thumb as protection from taut bowstring, and later used as an ornament

【扳子】bān·zi same as 扳手 bān·shou ①

攽 bān〈书 *fml.*〉发给;分给 issue, promulgate; allocate

班 bān ❶ 为了工作或学习等目的而编成的组织 unit organized for the purposes of work or study: 大～top class in a kindergarten|作业～work team|进修～class for continued studies ❷ (～儿 bānr)指一天之内的一段工作时间 shift; duty: 上～ go to work|晚～儿 night shift|值～on duty|日夜三～ work three shifts a day ❸ 军队编制的基层单位 squad; smallest tactical unit, often subdivision of a platoon ❹ (～儿 bānr)戏班,旧时也用于剧团的名称 theatrical troupe; used in the name of a theatrical troupe in old times: ～规 theatrical troupe rules|搭～temporarily join a theatrical troupe|三庆～ Sanqing Theatrical Troupe ❺〈量词 *classifier*〉a)用于人群[used to denote a group of people]:这～姑娘真有干劲。These young women are full of energy. b)用于定时开行的交通运输工具[used for scheduled forms of transportation]:你搭下一～飞机走吧。Please take the next flight.|公共汽车每隔四分钟就有一～。The bus runs every four minutes. ❻ 按排定的时间开行的 mechanism which runs at regular intervals: ～车 shuttle bus|～机 shuttle flight ❼ 调回或调动(军队) move troops; withdraw troops: ～师 withdraw troops from the front ❽ (Bān) 姓 a surname

【班白】bānbái same as 斑白 bānbái

【班辈】bānbèi (～儿 bānbèir)行辈 order of seniority in family or clan: 古稀之年的人,～不会小的。A person in his seventies ought be high in seniority in a family.

【班驳】bānbó same as 斑驳 bānbó

【班车】bānchē 有固定的路线并按排定的时间开行的车辆,多指机关、团体专用的 shuttle bus; motor vehicle which runs along a set route and at set hours, mostly for government and other institutions

【班次】bāncì ❶ (学校)班级的次序 order of classes or grades at school ❷ 定时往来的交通运输工具开行的次数 number of times a scheduled form of transportation operates: 增加公共汽车～increase the frequency of bus runs

【班底】bāndǐ (～儿 bāndǐr) ❶〈旧时 *old*〉指戏班中主要演员以外的其他演员 supporting cast in an operatic troupe; also 底包 dǐbāo ❷ 泛指一个组织中的基本成员(in a broad sense) ordinary personnel of an organization

【班房】bānfáng ❶〈旧时 *old*〉衙门里衙役当班的地方。也指衙役。government, quarters for runners on duty; government runners ❷ 监狱或拘留所的俗称 commonly known as jail; house of detention; lockup

【班机】bānjī 有固定的航线并按排定的时间起飞的飞机 regular air service; shuttle flights

【班级】bānjí 学校里的年级和班的总称 general term for classes and grades in school

【班轮】bānlún 有固定的航线并按排定的时间起航的轮船 regular passenger or cargo ship; regular steamship service; scheduled voyage on set route

【班门弄斧】Bān mén nòng fǔ 在鲁班(古代有名的木匠)门前摆弄斧子,比喻在行家面前卖弄本领 show off one's skill with the axe in front of the master carpenter Lu Ban; (fig.) display one's imperfect skills before an expert

【班配】bānpèi same as 般配 bānpèi

【班期】bānqī ❶ 定期往返的轮船、飞机等开航的时间 schedule (for regular flights, boat trips, etc.): 客运～passenger service timetable ❷ 邮局投递信件等的固定日期(of a post office) timetable for mail delivery

【班师】bānshī〈书 *fml.*〉调回出去打仗的军队,也指出征的军队胜利归来 withdraw troops from the front; triumphal return of army

【班主】bānzhǔ〈旧时 *old*〉戏班的主持人 head of a theatrical troupe

【班主任】bānzhǔrèn 学校中负责一班学生的思想工作、集体活动等的教师或干部 teacher or administrator in charge of ideological matters and group activities of a class (in primary and middle school)

【班子】bān·zi ❶ 剧团的旧称 old term for 剧团 jùtuán ❷ 泛指为执行一定任务而成立的组织 (in a broad sense) group organized to accomplish a specific task: 领导～leading group|生产～production team

【班组】bānzǔ 企业中根据工作需要组成的较小的基层单位(in an enterprise) basic unit organized according to work needs: ～会 group meeting|优秀～ model work group

般[1] bān 种;样 kind, same as; just like: 这～ like this|百～安慰 comfort sb. in every possible way|十八～武艺 skill in wielding the 18 kinds of weapons; skills in various fields|暴风雨～的掌声 stormy (or thunderous) applause

般[2] bān same as 搬 bān

☞ bō on p.146 and pán on p.1441

【般配】bānpèi 结亲的双方相称(chèn)。也指人的身份跟衣着、住所等相称。well matched (in marriage, etc.); dress and home match one's position or status

颁 bān 发布;颁发 promulgate; issue: ～布 promulgation | ～行 announce and enforce | ～奖 bestow an award

【颁白】bānbái same as 斑白 bānbái

【颁布】bānbù 公布 promulgate; issue; publish: ～法令 promulgate (or issue) a decree | ～奖惩条例 announce regulations on rewards and penalties

【颁发】bānfā ❶ 发布(命令、指示、政策等) issue; promulgate (order, instruction, policy, etc.): 条例自～之日起执行。These regulations come into force upon promulgation. ❷ 授与(勋章、奖状、证书等) award (medal, certificate of merit, or credentials, etc.): ～奖章 award a medal

【颁奖】bān//jiǎng 颁发奖状、奖杯或奖品等 award medal, certificate of merit, or trophy, etc.: 向劳动模范～issue awards to model workers

斑 bān ❶ 斑点或斑纹 spot; speck; stripe: 红～red spots | 黑～black spots | 雀～freckles | ～痕 mark; trace ❷ 有斑点或斑纹的 spotted; striped: ～马 zebra | ～鸠 turtledove | ～竹 mottled bamboo

【斑白】bānbái 〈书 *fml*.〉(须发)花白(beard and hair) grey; grizzled: 两鬓～greying at the temples; also 班白 bānbái or 颁白 bānbái

【斑斑】bānbān 形容斑点很多 covered with stains or spots: 血迹～bloodstained

【斑驳】bānbó 一种颜色中杂有别种颜色,花花搭搭的 mottled; motley; mixed colours: 树影～dappled shadows of trees; also 班驳 bānbó

【斑驳陆离】bānbó lùlí 形容色彩繁杂 of many colours; many-hued

【斑点】bāndiǎn 在一种颜色的物体表面上显露出来的别种颜色的点子 distinctly coloured spot that contrasts with the background

【斑痕】bānhén 在一种颜色上显露出来的别种颜色的印子;痕迹 mark; trace of different colours: 白衬衣上有铁锈的～。There are rust stains on the white shirt.

【斑鸠】bānjiū 鸟,身体灰褐色,颈后有白色或黄褐色斑点,嘴短,脚淡红色。常成群在田野里吃谷粒,对农作物有害。turtledove (*Streptopelio orientalis orientalis*); greyish-brown bird with white or yellowish-brown spots on the back of its neck, short beak, and pale-red feet, often flocking to feed on grain in the fields, considered a pest

【斑斓】bānlán 〈书 *fml*.〉灿烂多彩 brilliant colours; bright-coloured: 五色～a riot of colours | ～的玛瑙 brilliant agates

【斑马】bānmǎ 哺乳动物,形状像马,全身的毛棕色和白色条纹相间,听觉灵敏。产在非洲,是一种珍贵的观赏动物。zebra (*Equus zebra*); African mammal resembling the horse, with distinctive white stripes on brown background, having acute hearing, and being a valuable and attractive animal

【斑马线】bānmǎxiàn 马路上标示人行横道的像斑马身上的白色条纹的横线,多用油漆涂成 zebra crossing; street crosswalk marked by painted white stripes to indicate where pedestrians may cross

【斑蝥】bānmáo 昆虫,触角呈鞭状,腿细长,鞘翅上有黄黑色斑纹,成虫危害大豆、棉花、茄子等农作物。可入药。cantharis (*Mylabris phalerata*); Chinese blister beetle; insect with whip-like feelers, long, thin legs, yellowish-black stripes on the wing case, destroying beans, cotton and eggplant when grown up, and used in traditional Chinese medicine

【斑秃】bāntū 皮肤病,局部头发突然脱落,经过一定时期,能自然痊愈 alopecia areata; skin disease characterised by circumscribed, non-inflamed areas of baldness on the scalp; spontaneous recovery occurs after some time; also 鬼剃头 guǐtìtóu

【斑纹】bānwén 在一种颜色的物体表面上显露出来的别种颜色的条纹 stripe; band of contrasting colour: 斑马身上有美丽的～。A zebra has beautiful stripes.

【斑竹】bānzhú 竹子的一种,茎上有紫褐色的斑点。茎可以制装饰品、手杖、笔杆等。mottled bamboo; variety of bamboo with purplish-brown spots on the stems, which can be used to make ornaments, walking sticks and the shaft of writing brushes; also 湘妃竹 xiāngfēizhú

搬(般) bān ❶ 移动物体的位置(多指笨重的或较大的) change the location of (large or heavy objects): ～砖 move bricks | ～运 transport | 把保险柜～走。Take the safe away. ◇把小说里的故事～到舞台上 adapt a story for performance on the stage; dramatise a novel ❷ 迁移 move from one place to another: ～家 move house | 他早就～走了。He moved out long ago.

【搬兵】bān//bīng 搬取救兵,多比喻请求援助或增加人力 call in reinforcements; (oft. fig.) ask for help or more manpower

【搬家】bān//jiā ❶ 把家迁到别处去 resettle; move (house) ❷ 泛指迁移地点或挪动位置 change the location of sth.: 这家工厂去年已经～了。This factory moved away last year.

【搬弄】bānnòng ❶ 用手拨动 move with hand; fiddle with: ～枪栓 fiddle with the rifle bolt ❷ 卖弄;有意显示 show off; display: 他总好～自己的那点儿知识。He likes to show off his bit of knowledge. ❸ 挑拨 instigate: ～是非 sow discord

【搬弄是非】bānnòng shìfēi 把别人背后说的话

传来传去，蓄意挑拨，或在别人背后乱加议论，引起纠纷 sow discord; tell tales; malicious gossip

【搬起石头打自己的脚】bān qǐ shí·tou dǎ zìjǐ·de jiǎo 〈比喻 *fig.*〉自作自受，自食恶果 pick up a stone only to drop it on one's own feet; lift a rock only to drop it on one's own toes; suffer from one's own actions

【搬迁】bānqiān 迁移 relocate; transfer; remove:～户 relocated household|～新居 move to a new house

【搬舌头】bān shé·tou 〈方 *dial.*〉搬弄是非 tell tales; sow discord

【搬演】bānyǎn 把往事或别处的事重演出来 replay past events or ones that occurred elsewhere:～故事 reproduce a past story

【搬移】bānyí ❶ 搬动；移动 move about; shift:～家具 move furniture ❷ 搬迁 relocate:这家商店已～到东街去了。This shop has moved to East Street.

【搬用】bānyòng 不顾实际情况，机械地采用(现成的规章、办法等) apply (existing regulations or methods) mechanically regardless of actual situation; use indiscriminately:这些做法可以参考，不能机械～。These methods may be consulted, but should not be copied mechanically.

【搬运】bānyùn 把物品从一个地方运到另一个地方 transport sth. from one place to another:～工 porter; docker|～行李 transport luggage|～货物 transport goods|～弹药 transport ammunition

煸 bān [煸斓](bānlán) same as 斑斓 bānlán

瘢 bān 疮口或伤口好了之后留下的痕迹 scar; mark left by the healing of injured tissue:刀～ scar from a knife wound|～痕 scar

【瘢痕】bānhén 瘢 scar:伤口已愈，却留下一道～。The wound has healed, but has left a scar.

癍 bān 皮肤上生斑点的病 abnormal pigmentary deposits on the skin; freckles

bǎn (ㄅㄢˇ)

坂(阪) bǎn 〈书 *fml.*〉山坡；斜坡 hillside; slope:如丸走～(比喻迅速) like a ball rolling down a hillside; (fig.) speedy, fast

板[1] bǎn ❶ (～儿 bǎnr)片状的较硬的物体 board; plank; sheet; flat, thin piece of hard material:木～ wooden plank|钢～ steel sheet|玻璃～plate glass ❷ (～儿 bǎnr)专指店铺的门板 shutter; blind (spec. for shops):铺子都上～儿了。The shops have all put up the shutters. ❸ 黑板 blackboard:～报 blackboard newspaper; blackboard bulletin|～书 blackboard writing ❹ 演奏民族音乐或戏曲时用来打拍子的乐器 clappers used to beat time in Chinese national music or traditional operas:檀～hardwood clappers ❺ (～儿 bǎnr)音乐和戏曲中的节拍 rhythm or tempo in music and traditional Chinese opera:快～儿 allegro|慢～ adagio|走～ be out of time; ☞ 板眼 bǎnyǎn ❻ 呆板 stiff; unnatural:他们都那样活泼，显得我太～了。They are all so lively, which makes me look too stiff. ❼ 硬得像板子似的 hard (as a plate):地～了，锄不下去。The ground is too hard to hoe. ❽ 表情严肃 stern expression; look serious:他～着脸不睬人。He did not smile or speak to anyone.

板[2](闆) bǎn ☞ 老板 lǎobǎn on p.1156

【板板六十四】bǎnbǎn liùshísì 〈方 *dial.*〉形容不知变通或不能通融 unaccommodating; inflexible

【板报】bǎnbào same as 黑板报 hēibǎnbào

【板壁】bǎnbì 分隔房间的木板墙 wooden partition between rooms

【板擦儿】bǎncār 擦黑板的用具，一般是在小块木板上加绒布或棕毛制成 blackboard eraser, made of flannel or palm fibre attached to small wooden block

【板锉】bǎncuò 横剖面呈长方形的锉 flat file; file whose transverse section is rectangular; also 扁锉 biǎncuò

【板荡】bǎndàng 〈书 *fml.*〉《诗经·大雅》有《板》、《荡》两篇，都是写当时政治黑暗、人民痛苦的。后来用'板荡'指政局混乱，社会动荡不安。*Censure* and *Warnings* are two poems in *The Book of Songs·Epics*, describing the oppressive politics and people's sufferings of the time; later the term *bandang* 板荡 is used to mean political chaos and social instability

【板凳】bǎndèng (～儿 bǎndèngr)用木头做成的一种凳子，多为长条形 wooden bench or stool, oft. long and narrow

【板斧】bǎnfǔ 刃平而宽的大斧子 broad axe; large axe with broad blade

【板鼓】bǎngǔ 打击乐器，一面蒙牛皮，鼓框内膛呈喇叭形，上口径约一寸，发音脆亮，是戏曲乐队中的指挥乐器 small percussion instrument shaped like a trumpet, the wide end one inch in diameter and covered with cowhide, producing a sharp, dry sound, and used to mark time in a traditional orchestra

【板胡】bǎnhú 胡琴的一种，琴筒呈半球形，口上蒙着薄板。发音高亢。bowed stringed instrument with semicircular soundbox covered with thin wooden soundboard; marked for its full sonorous tone

【板结】bǎnjié 土壤因缺乏有机质，结构不良，灌水或降雨后地面变硬，不利于农作物生长，叫做板结 harden; hardening of soil after irrigation or rainfalls caused by lack of organic substances and poor composition; unsuitable for crops

【板块】bǎnkuài 大地构造理论指由地质上的活动地带划分的岩石圈的构造单元。全球共分为六大板块,即欧亚板块、太平洋板块、美洲板块、非洲板块、印度洋板块和南极洲板块。大板块又可划分成小板块。plate; shifting segments of the earth's crust. According to geotectological theory, the earth is divided into six large plates, i.e. Eurasian Plate, Pacific Plate, American Plate, African Plate, Indian Plate and Antarctic Plate, which can be further divided into smaller plates

B

【板栗】bǎnlì 栗子 chestnut (*Castanea*)

【板上钉钉】bǎn shàng dìng dīng 〈比喻 *fig.*〉事情已定,不能变更 final; decided; no two ways about it

【板式】bǎnshì 戏曲唱腔的节拍形式,如京剧中的慢板、快板、二六、流水等 tempo in Chinese operatic music, such as slow, fast, *erliu*, *liushui*, etc.

【板实】bǎn·shi 〈方 *dial.*〉❶(土壤)硬而结实 (of soil) firm and hard:地~,不长庄稼。The soil is too hard for crops to grow. ❷(书皮、衣物等)平整挺括(of book cover, clothing, etc.) smooth and stiff:衣服叠得很~。The garments are folded neatly. ❸(身体)硬朗壮实(of physique) strong:老人身子骨还~。The old man is hale and hearty.

【板书】bǎnshū ❶在黑板上写字 write on the blackboard:需要~的地方,在备课时都作了记号。When preparing lessons, marks were made at the places where something had to be written on the blackboard. ❷也指在黑板上写的字 characters written on the blackboard; blackboard writing:工整的~ neat blackboard writing

【板刷】bǎnshuā 毛比较粗硬的刷子,板面较宽,没有柄,多用来刷洗布衣、鞋子等 scrubbing brush; wide-faced, handleless brush made with thick, stiff bristles, mostly used to scrub clothing, shoes, etc.

【板瓦】bǎnwǎ 瓦的一种,瓦面较宽,弯曲的程度较小 plain tile; wide tile with small curvature

【板鸭】bǎnyā 经盐渍并压成扁平状后风干了的鸭子 salted, pressed and dried duck

【板牙】bǎnyá ❶〈方 *dial.*〉门牙 front tooth; incisor ❷〈方 *dial.*〉臼齿 molar ❸切削外螺纹的刀具 screw-cutting die; threading die

【板烟】bǎnyān 压成块状或片状的烟丝 tobacco compressed into solid brick or sheet

【板眼】bǎnyǎn ❶民族音乐和戏曲中的节拍,每小节中最强的拍子叫板,其余的拍子叫眼。如一板三眼(四拍子)、一板一眼(二拍子)。strong and light beats in traditional Chinese music, e.g. one strong beat 板 bǎn and three light beats 眼 yǎn in a bar, similar to 4/4 time; and one strong beat (板) and one light beat (眼), similar to 2/4 time ❷〈比喻 *fig.*〉条理和层次 orderliness; system; method:他说话做事都很有~。He is very methodical in handling things. ❸〈方 *dial.*〉〈比喻 *fig.*〉办法、主意等 idea; notion:在我们班里,数他~多。He is the one who comes up with the most ideas in our class.

【板油】bǎnyóu 猪的体腔内壁上呈板状的脂肪 leaf fat on the walls of a hog's body cavity

【板障】bǎnzhàng ❶练习翻越障碍物用的设备,是用木板做成的,像板壁一样 plate barrier; wall-like barrier made of wooden planks used to practice surmounting obstacles ❷〈方 *dial.*〉same as 板壁 bǎnbì

【板正】bǎnzhèng ❶(形式)端正;整齐(of form) regular, neat:本子装订得板板正正的。The notebooks are neatly bound. ❷(态度、神情等)庄重认真(of attitude, manner) solemn; serious

【板滞】bǎnzhì (文章、图画、神情等)呆板(of writing, drawing, expression, etc.) stiff; dull:两眼~dull eyes

【板筑】bǎnzhù same as 版筑 bǎnzhù

【板子】bǎn·zi ❶片状的较硬的物体(多指木质的 oft. of wood) board; plank ❷〈旧时 *old*〉拷打或施行体罚用的长条形的木板或竹片 strip of bamboo or rod of birch used for corporal punishment

版 bǎn ❶上面有文字或图形的供印刷用的底子,从前用木板,现在用金属板 printing plate (or block); solid plate of type or graphics for printing, formerly made of wood and now of metal:锌~zinc plate | 铜~copper plate | 排~composing | 制~plate making ❷书籍排印一次为一版,一版可包括多次印刷 edition; one of a series of printings of the same book, the same edition can include several printings:第一~the first edition | 再~the second edition ❸报纸的一面叫一版 page of a newspaper:头~新闻 front-page news ❹筑土墙用的夹板 clamping boards for building wall of rammed earth:~筑 build with clamping boards

【版本】bǎnběn 同一部书因编辑、传抄、刻版、排版或装订形式的不同而产生的不同的本子 edition; same book issued at different times with alterations of text, typeface, layout or bindings, etc., or by different publishers

【版次】bǎncì 图书出版的先后次序。图书第一次出版的叫'第一版'或'初版',修订后重排出版的叫'第二版'或'再版',以下类推。order in which editions are printed, e.g. first edition, second edition, etc.

【版画】bǎnhuà 用刀子或化学药品等在铜版、锌版、木版、石版、麻胶版等版面上雕刻或蚀刻后印刷出来的图画 picture printed from an engraved or etched plate of copper, zinc, wood, stone or rubber

【版籍】bǎnjí 〈书 *fml.*〉❶ 登记户口、土地的簿册 books keeping registration of residents and property ❷ 泛指领土、疆域 territory; domain ❸ 书籍 books

【版刻】bǎnkè 文字或图画的木版雕刻 carving or engraving of text or graphics on woodblock

【版口】bǎnkǒu 木板书书框的中缝 fore-edge of a wood-block book; also 版心 bǎnxīn or 页心 yèxīn

【版面】bǎnmiàn ❶ 书报杂志上每一页的整面 (of book, newspaper or magazine) page ❷ 书报杂志的每一面上文字图画的编排形式(of book, newspaper or magazine) layout or makeup of a printed sheet: ～设计 layout design

【版纳】bǎnnà 云南西双版纳傣族自治州所属的旧行政区划单位,相当于县。1960 年版纳改为县,如版纳景洪改称景洪县。*banna*; formerly the term for an administrative division under the jurisdiction of Xishuangbanna Dai Autonomous Prefecture in Yunnan Province. The term was changed to 'county' in 1960, e.g. Banna Jinghong was changed to Jinghong County.

【版权】bǎnquán 即著作权。出版单位可以根据出版合同在合同有效期内获得作品的使用权。copyright; within the effective period of a publication contract, the publisher has the right of use of a work

【版权页】bǎnquányè 书刊上印着书刊名、著作者、出版者、发行者、版次、印刷年月、印数、定价等的一页 copyright page; page containing title, author, publisher, distributor, order of edition, date of printing, number of impression and price

【版式】bǎnshì 版面的格式 format; shape, size and general makeup of printed material

【版税】bǎnshuì 出版者按照出售出版物所得收入的约定百分数付给作者的报酬 royalty (on books); payment made to an author by the publisher for each copy of his work sold, calculated as a percentage of the retail price

【版图】bǎntú 原指户籍和地图,今泛指国家的领土、疆域 (formerly) books recording registration of residents and maps; national domain or territory: 我国～辽阔。Our country has a vast territory.

【版心】bǎnxīn ❶ 书刊等每面排印文字、图画的部分 type area; part of page printed with text or graphics ❷ 版口 fore-edge of a page

【版筑】bǎnzhù 〈书 *fml.*〉筑土墙用的夹板和杵(筑土墙时,夹板中填入泥土,用杵夯实)。泛指土木营造的事情。clamping boards and rammer used for building a wall of rammed earth (to build such a wall, clamping boards are erected and the space between is filled with earth, which is then rammed firm); civil engineering; also 板筑 bǎnzhù

钣 bǎn 金属板材 metal plate: 铝～aluminum plate | 钢～steel plate

舨 bǎn ☞ 舢舨 shānbǎn on p. 1672

蝂 bǎn ☞ 蝜蝂 fùbǎn on p. 614

bàn (ㄅㄢˋ)

办(辦) bàn ❶ 办理;处理; 料理 do; handle; manage; tackle; attend to: ～事 handle affairs | ～公 handle official business | ～交涉 carry on negotiations | ～入学手续 go through school entrance formalities ❷ 创设;经营 set up; operate: ～工厂 run a factory | 勤俭～一切事业。Practice the principle of thrift and hard work in all undertakings. ❸ 采购;置备 procure; purchase; prepare: 置～ purchase (durables) | ～货 procure (for an organization or enterprise) | ～酒席 prepare a feast | ～嫁妆 prepare a dowry ❹ 惩治 punish (by law); bring to justice: ～罪 punish (for a crime) | 严～punish with severity | 首恶必～。The principal perpetrator must be punished.

【办案】bàn//àn 办理案件 handle a legal case

【办差】bànchāi 〈旧指 *old*〉给官府办理征集夫役、征收财物等事 be in charge of government operations, such as collecting taxes and corvee labour

【办法】bànfǎ 处理事情或解决问题的方法 way to handle affairs; method: 想～find a way | 他不答应,你也拿他没～。If he does not agree, you can do nothing about it.

【办稿】bàn//gǎo 起草公文 draft an official document

【办公】bàn//gōng 办理公务;处理公事 handle official business; work (usu. in an office): ～会议 working meeting | 星期天照常～。Business is as usual on Sundays.

【办公会议】bàngōng huìyì 一个部门的有关负责人举行会议讨论并处理事务的工作方式 working meeting; regular meeting of department leaders to discuss and handle business

【办公室】bàngōngshì ❶ 办公的屋子 office; room for handling official matters ❷ 机关、学校、企业等单位内办理行政性事务的部门。规模大的称办公厅。department of institute, school or enterprise that handles administrative affairs. Larger ones are called General Office.

【办理】bànlǐ 处理(事务);承办 handle; conduct; transact: 这些事情你可以斟酌～。You may handle these matters as you see fit. | 本店～邮购业务。Our shop handles mail orders.

【办事】bàn//shì 做事 handle affairs; work:～机构 administrative body; working body|～认真 be conscientious in one's work|我们是给群众～的。We work for the masses.

【办事员】bànshìyuán 机关工作人员的一种职别,在科员之下 office worker; official rank of government hierarchy, lower than a section member

【办学】bànxué 兴办学校 run a school:集资～raise funds for a school

【办置】bànzhì 置办 buy (durables); purchase

半 bàn ❶ 二分之一;一半(没有整数时用在量词前,有整数时用在量词后)[used before classifier when there is no integral number, and after when there is] one half; half:～尺 half a *chi*|一斤～one and half *jin*|～价 half price|过～ more than half|一年～载 in a year or so; in about a year ❷ 在…中间 in the middle of; halfway:～夜 midnight|～路上 halfway|～山腰 halfway up a hill|～途而废 give up halfway ❸〈比喻 *fig*.〉很少 very little:一星～点 a tiny bit; a very small amount ❹ 不完全 partly; about half:～成品 semi-finished product|～新的楼房 half-new buildings|房门～开着。The door was left half open.

【半百】bànbǎi 五十(多指岁数 years of age) fifty:年过～over fifty years old

【半…半…】bàn…bàn… 分别用在意义相反的两个词或词素前面,表示相对的两种性质或状态同时存在[used before two words with opposite meanings indicating the simultaneous existence of two opposite states]:～文～白 semi-literary, semi-vernacular|～真～假 half-genuine, half-false|～信～疑 half-believing, half-doubting|～推～就 yield with a show of reluctance; give way after making a show of declining

【半半拉拉】bàn·banlālā 不完全;没有全部完成的 incomplete; unfinished:工作做了个～就扔下了。The work was left unfinished.

【半辈子】bànbèi·zi 指中年以前或中年以后的生活时间 half a lifetime (period of life before or after middle age):前(或上)～the first half of one's life|后(或下)～ the latter half of one's life

【半壁】bànbì〈书 *fml*.〉半边,特指半壁江山 half, esp. half of the country:江南～ the southern half of the country

【半壁江山】bànbì jiāngshān 指保存下来的或丧失掉的部分国土 (usu. referring to national territory retained or lost) half of the country

【半边】bànbiān ❶ (～儿 bànbiānr)指某一部分或某一方面 part or portion of sth.:～身子 part of the body|这块地的东～儿种玉米,西～儿种棉花。The eastern part of the field grows corn, and the western part cotton.|这个苹果～儿红,～儿绿。Half of the apple is red, and the other half green. ❷〈方 *dial*.〉旁边 side

【半边人】bànbiānrén〈方 *dial*.〉指寡妇 widow

【半边天】bànbiāntiān ❶ 天空的一部分 part of the sky:晚霞映红了～。The sunset glow tinted half of the sky a reddish hue. ❷〈比喻 *fig*.〉新社会妇女的巨大力量能顶半边天,也用来指新社会的妇女 women of the new society; womenfolk (from a saying, 'Women can hold up half of the sky.')

【半彪子】bànbiāo·zi〈方 *dial*.〉不通事理,行事鲁莽的人 brash, unreasonable person

【半…不…】bàn…bù… 略同'半…半…'(多含厌恶意 oft. derog.) similar to 半…半… bàn…bàn…:～明～暗 dimly lit|～新～旧 no longer new; show signs of wear|～生～熟 half-cooked; underdone|～死～活 neither dead nor alive

【半成品】bànchéngpǐn 加工制造过程未全部完成的产品 semi-manufactured goods; semi-finished articles; semi-finished products; also 半制品 bànzhìpǐn

【半大】bàndà 形体介乎大小之间的 medium-sized:～小子 adolescent boy|～桌子 medium-sized table

【半大不小】bàn dà bù xiǎo 指人未到成年但已不是儿童的年龄 age between adulthood and childhood

【半导体】bàndǎotǐ 导电能力介于导体和绝缘体之间的物质,如锗、硅、硒和很多氧化物、硫化物等。这种物质具有单向导电等特性。semiconductor; a class of solids (including germanium, silicon, selenium, and many oxides and sulphides) with electrical conductivity halfway between that of a conductor and an insulator. A semi-conductor has unidirectional conduction.

【半岛】bàndǎo 三面临水一面连接大陆的陆地,如我国的辽东半岛、雷州半岛等 peninsula; portion of land nearly surrounded by water and connected with a larger body by an isthmus, such as China's Liaodong Peninsula and Leizhou Peninsula

【半道儿】bàndàor 半路 halfway:～折回 turn back halfway

【半点】bàndiǎn (～儿 bàndiǎnr)表示极少 the least bit:一星～儿 a tiny bit|知识的问题是一个科学问题,来不得～的虚伪和骄傲。The question of knowledge is a matter of science, which permits no dishonesty and arrogance.

【半吊子】bàndiào·zi ❶ 不通事理,说话随便,举止不沉着的人 tactless and impulsive person ❷ 知识不丰富或技术不熟练的人 uninformed or unskilled person ❸ 做事不认真、有始无终的人 lackadaisical, irresolute person

【半封建】bànfēngjiàn 封建国家遭受帝国主义经济侵略后形成的一种社会形态,原来的封建经济遭到破坏,资本主义有了一定的发展,但仍然保持着封建剥削制度 semi-feudal; social structures and relationships in a feudal country after economic aggression by imperialism. The original feudal economy is damaged, and capitalism has developed to a certain degree, but the old feudal system of exploitation remains.

【半疯儿】bànfēngr ❶ 患有轻微精神病的人 half-mad; mildly deranged ❷ 指言语行动颠倒、轻狂的人 one who speaks and acts in a confused erratic way as if slightly insane ‖ also 半疯子 bànfēng·zi

【半规管】bànguīguǎn 内耳的一部分，由三个半圆形的管子构成，管内有淋巴液。有维持身体平衡状态的作用。semicircular canal in the inner ear; consisting of three semicircular membranous tubes that contain lymph and serve to maintain balance

【半价】bànjià 原价的一半 half price：～出售 sell at half price

【半截】bànjié (～儿 bànjiér)一件事物的一半；半段 half (a section)：～粉笔 half a piece of chalk|话说了～儿 unfinished speech; halfway through saying sth.

【半斤八两】bàn jīn bā liǎng 旧制一斤合十六两，半斤等于八两(in traditional Chinese weight system, one *jin* equals 16 *liang*, so half a *jin* equals eight *liang*) six of one and half a dozen of the other;〈比喻 *fig.*〉彼此一样，不相上下(多含贬义 oft. derog.) not much to choose between the two; two of a kind

【半径】bànjìng 连接圆心和圆周上任意一点的线段叫做圆的半径；连接球心和球面上任意一点的线段叫做球的半径 radius; line segment extending from the centre of a circle to the curve; line segment extending from the centre of a sphere to the surface

【半开门儿】bànkāiménr〈方 *dial.*〉指暗娼 unlicensed prostitute

【半空】[1] bànkōng ❶ 瘪；不充实 shrunken; half-empty：～着肚子 half-empty stomach ❷〈方 *dial.*〉(～儿 bànkōngr)指较小的不饱满的炒花生 small, dried-up roasted peanuts

【半空】[2] bànkōng 空中 in midair; in the air：柳絮在～飘荡。The willow catkins drift in midair. also 半空中 bànkōngzhōng

【半拉】bànlǎ〈方 *dial.*〉半个 half：～馒头 half a steamed bun|～苹果 half an apple|过了～月 after a fortnight

【半劳动力】bànláodònglì 指体力较弱只能从事一般轻体力劳动的人(多就农业劳动而言) one only able to do light manual labour (esp. farm work); also 半劳力 bànláolì

【半流体】bànliútǐ 介乎固体和流体之间的物质，如生鸡蛋的蛋白和蛋黄 semi-fluid; sth. between fluid and solid, e.g. raw egg albumen and yolk

【半路】bànlù (～儿 bànlùr) ❶ 路程的一半或中间 halfway; midway：走到～，天就黑了。We had gone halfway when it began to get dark. ❷〈比喻 *fig.*〉事情正处在进行的过程中 in progress：他听故事入了神，不愿意～走开。Enthralled by the story, he is reluctant to leave halfway through it. ‖ also 半道儿 bàndàor

【半路出家】bànlù chūjiā〈比喻 *fig.*〉原先并不是从事这一工作的，后来才改行从事这一工作 become a monk or nun late in life; switch to a completely new kind of work

【半票】bànpiào 半价的车票、门票等 half-price (train, bus, admission) ticket; half fare

【半瓶醋】bànpíngcù〈比喻 *fig.*〉对某种知识或某种技术只略知一二的人 half a bottle of vinegar; dabbler; smatterer; also 半瓶子醋 bànpíng·zicù

【半晌】bànshǎng〈方 *dial.*〉same as 半天 bàntiān：前～morning|后～afternoon|他想了～才想起来。It took him a long time to recall it.

【半身不遂】bàn shēn bù suí 偏瘫 hemiplegia; partial paralysis

【半生】bànshēng 半辈子 half a lifetime：前～ the first half of one's life|操劳～work hard for half a lifetime|～戎马 lead a soldier's life for many years

【半生不熟】bàn shēng bù shú ❶(食物等)没全熟 half-cooked; underdone：肉煮得～的，没法吃。The meat is underdone and inedible. ❷(～的 bàn shēng bù shú·de)不熟习；不熟练 unskilled, unfamiliar：他试着用～的英语跟外宾谈话。He tries to speak to foreigners in broken English.

【半世】bànshì 半辈子 half a lifetime

【半衰期】bànshuāiqī 放射性元素由于衰变而使原有量的一半成为其他元素所需的时间。放射性元素的半衰期长短差别很大，短的远小于一秒，长的可达许多万年。half-life; period during which the radioactivity of a radioactive substance, due to disintegration, is reduced to half of its original value. Radioactive elements vary enormously in their half life, the shortest lasting less than one second, the longest tens of thousands of years.

【半死】bànsǐ 形容受到的折磨、摧残极深 half-dead from suffering or torture：打个～be beaten within an inch of one's life|气得～furiously angry; faint with rage

【半死不活】bàn sǐ bù huó 形容没有精神，没有生气的样子 half-dead; more dead than alive

【半天】bàntiān ❶ 白天的一半 half the day：前～morning|后～afternoon ❷ 指相当长的一段时间；好久 long time; quite a while：等了～，他才来。He came after a long wait.

【半途】bàntú〈书 *fml.*〉半路 halfway; midway

【半途而废】bàntú ér fèi 做事情没有完成而终止 give up halfway; leave sth. unfinished

【半文盲】bànwénmáng 识字不多的成年人 sem-illiterate; adult who can read and write a little

【半无产阶级】bàn wúchǎn jiējí 只有极少的生产资料，需要出卖部分劳动力来维持生活的人。旧中国的绝大部分半自耕农、贫农、小手工业者、店员、小贩都是半无产阶级。semi-proletariat; people who possess very little means of production and need to live by selling part of their labour. In pre-1949 China, most of the semi-owner peasants, poor peasants, petty handicraftsmen, shop clerks and vendors belonged to this category.

【半休】bànxiū 指职工因病在一定时期内每日半天工作，半天休息 half-day rest; employee who works half time because of illness：～一周 work half-time for a week

【半夜】bànyè ❶ 一夜的一半 half the night：前～the first half of the night｜后～the latter half of the night｜上～before midnight｜下～after midnight ❷ 夜里十二点钟前后，也泛指深夜 around midnight; (in a broad sense) late at night：深更～deep in the night｜哥儿俩谈到～。The two brothers talked until midnight.

【半夜三更】bànyè sāngēng 深夜 late at night：～的，别再大声说话了。It's very late, don't talk so loudly.

【半音】bànyīn 把八度音划分为十二个音，两个相邻的音之间的音程叫半音 semitone; octave is divided into 12 intervals, and the tone at an interval of a half step from the next is called a semitone

【半元音】bànyuányīn 语音学上指擦音中气流较弱，摩擦较小，介于元音跟辅音之间的音，如普通话 yīn·wèi(因为)中的'y'和'w' (phonet.) semivowel; sound of fricative between a consonant and a vowel, characterised by weak air flow and light friction, e.g. 'y' and 'w' in 因为 yīn·wèi

【半圆】bànyuán ❶ 圆的直径的两个端点把圆周分成两条弧，每一条弧叫做半圆 semicircle; half circles formed by the diameter cutting the circumference in two ❷ 半圆(弧)和直径所围成的平面 surface between the boundary of a semicircle and the diameter

【半月刊】bànyuèkān 每半月出版一次的刊物 periodical published semimonthly; fortnightly

【半殖民地】bànzhímíndì 指形式上独立，但在政治、经济、文化各方面受帝国主义控制和压迫的国家 semi-colony; country independent in name only, in fact subject to imperialist control and political, economic and cultural oppression

【半制品】bànzhìpǐn 半成品 semi-manufactured goods

【半中腰】bànzhōngyāo 中间；半截 middle; halfway：他的话说到～就停住了。He broke off in the middle of a sentence.

【半子】bànzǐ〈书 *fml.*〉指女婿 son-in-law

【半自动】bànzìdòng 部分不靠人工而由机器装置操作的 semi-automatic; (of mechanical device) partly automatic and partly manually controlled

【半自耕农】bànzìgēngnóng 指耕种少量土地另需租种部分土地或出卖部分劳动力的农民 semi-tenant peasant; semi-owner peasant; peasant who owns a small plot of land and has to rent more land or sell his labour

扮 bàn ❶ 化装成(某种人物) dress up as; play the part of; disguise：女～男装 a woman disguised as a man｜《逼上梁山》里他～林冲。In the opera *Forced to Join the Liangshan Rebels* he plays the part of Lin Chong. ❷ 面部表情装成(某种样子) put on (an expression)：～鬼脸 grimace; make faces

【扮鬼脸】bàn guǐliǎn 指脸上装出怪样子 grimace; make faces

【扮戏】bàn//xì ❶ 戏曲演员化装 (of a traditional opera singer) put on makeup; make up ❷〈旧称 *old*〉演戏 put on a play; act in a play

【扮相】bànxiàng ❶ 演员化装成戏中人物后的外部形象 appearance of an actor or actress in costume and makeup：他的～和唱工都很好。He looks good and sings well. ❷ 泛指打扮成的模样 (in a broad sense) appearance：我这副～能见客人吗？Can I receive guests looking like this?

【扮演】bànyǎn 化装成某种人物出场表演 play the role of; act：她在《白毛女》里～喜儿。She played the part of Xi'er in *The White-Haired Girl*. ◇知识分子在民主革命中～了重要角色。Intellectuals played an important role in the democratic revolution.

【扮装】bànzhuāng (演员)化装 (of an actor, etc.) put on makeup; make up：～吧，下一场就该你上场了。Put on your makeup. It's your turn in the next act.

伴 bàn ❶ (～儿 bànr)同伴 companion; partner：搭个～儿 accompany each other｜结～同行 travel in a group｜让我来跟你做个～儿吧。Let us be partners. ❷ 陪伴；陪同 accompany：～唱 vocal accompaniment｜～送 see sb. off

【伴唱】bànchàng 从旁歌唱，配合表演 sing a supporting part in a performance; support singer

【伴当】bàndāng〈旧时 *old*〉指跟随着做伴的仆人或伙伴 follower or companion

【伴酒】bànjiǔ 陪伴人喝酒(多指在酒店或酒吧间里 oft. in a tavern or bar) one who drinks with customers

【伴郎】bànláng 男傧相 groomsman; best man

【伴侣】bànlǚ 同在一起生活、工作或旅行的人 companion; mate; partner in work, travel or life：终身～(指夫妻) lifelong companion (esp. husband or wife)｜长途跋涉中，有他做

～，就不寂寞了。With him as a companion, one will not feel lonesome on a long journey.

【伴娘】bànniáng 女傧相 bridesmaid

【伴生】bànshēng （次要的）伴随着主要的一起存在(secondary) coexists with the principal：～树 associated tree｜钛、铬、钴等常与铁矿～。Titanium, chromium and cobalt are often associated with iron mines.

【伴宿】bànsù 〈方 *dial.*〉出殡的前一天的夜里，亲属守灵不睡 all-night vigil by relatives beside the coffin before the day of burial; all-night wake

【伴随】bànsuí 随同；跟 accompany; follow：～左右，不离寸步 be always at sb.'s elbow; follow sb. closely｜～着生产的大发展，必将出现一个文化高潮。An upsurge in culture is bound to follow the rapid advance in production.

【伴同】bàntóng 陪同；一同 accompany; together：去年他曾～我到过这里。Last year he accompanied me here on my visit to this place.｜蒸发和溶解的过程常有温度下降的现象～发生。The process of evaporation and dissolving is often associated with a drop in temperature.

【伴舞】bànwǔ ❶ 陪伴人跳舞 partner sb. to dance：邀她去舞会上～。She is invited to the dance to partner others. ❷ 从旁跳舞，配合演唱 backup dancer; support dancer

【伴星】bànxīng 双星中较暗的一颗，围绕着主星旋转 companion (star); faint star seen in the same field with a bright one and revolving around it

【伴音】bànyīn 在电影和电视中配合图像的声音 sound track for film or television programme; also 伴声 bànshēng

【伴游】bànyóu ❶ 陪同游览或游玩 escort sb. on a travel ❷ 指陪同游览或游玩的人 travel companion; escort

【伴奏】bànzòu 歌唱、跳舞或独奏时用器乐配合 musical accompaniment for song, dance or instrumental solo

坢 bàn 〈方 *dial.*〉粪肥 muck, manure, dung：猪栏～pigpen manure｜牛栏～cattlepen dung

拌 bàn ❶ 搅和 mix：给牲口～草 mix fodder for draught animals｜把种子用药剂～了再种。Mix in agricultural chemicals with the seeds before sowing. ❷ 争吵 quarrel：～嘴 squabble

【拌和】bàn·huò 搅拌 mix and stir; blend：～饲料 mix fodder｜饺子馅要～匀了。The filling for dumplings should be well mixed.

【拌蒜】bàn//suàn 〈方 *dial.*〉指走路时两脚常常相碰，身体摇晃不稳 shuffle and stagger：酒喝多了，走起路来两脚直～。He staggered along because he was drunk.

【拌嘴】bàn//zuǐ 吵嘴 bicker; squabble; quarrel：两口子时常～。The couple quarrels very often.｜拌了几句嘴 have exchanged a few hot words

绊 bàn 挡住或缠住，使跌倒或使行走不方便 (cause to) stumble; trip; trip over：～手～脚 be in the way｜～了一跤 stumble and fall

B

【绊脚石】bànjiǎoshí 〈比喻 *fig.*〉阻碍前进的人或事物 stumbling block; obstacle; things that get in the way or hinder：骄傲是进步的～。Complacence (or Conceit) is an obstacle to progress.

【绊马索】bànmǎsuǒ 设在暗处用来绊倒对方人马的绳索 concealed trip; rope for trapping the opponents' troops

【绊儿】bànr same as 绊子 bàn·zi ①：他一使～就把我摔倒了。He tripped me up and I fell on the ground.

【绊手绊脚】bàn shǒu bàn jiǎo 妨碍别人做事；碍手碍脚 be in the way; be a hindrance

【绊子】bàn·zi ❶ 摔跤的一种着数，用一只腿别着对方的腿使跌倒 in wrestling, make the opponent stumble by blocking his leg with one's own：使～ trip sb. up (in wrestling) ❷ 系在牲畜腿上使不能快跑的短绳 hobble; short rope tied to the legs of draught animals so they cannot move fast

柈 bàn [柈子](bàn·zi)〈方 *dial.*〉大块的劈柴 large pieces of firewood

湴 bàn 〈方 *dial.*〉烂泥 mud; slush

靽 bàn 〈书 *fml.*〉驾车时套在牲口后部的皮带 breeching; leather strap that passes round the rump of a draught animal when it is hitched to a vehicle

瓣 bàn ❶ (～儿 bànr)花瓣 petal：梅花有五个～儿。A plum blossom has five petals. ❷ (～儿 bànr)植物的种子、果实或球茎可以分开的小块儿 segment or section (of a seed, fruit or corm)：豆～儿 bean segments｜橘子～儿 tangerine wedge｜蒜～儿 clove of garlic ❸ (～儿 bànr)物体自然地分成或破碎后分成的部分 fragment; natural or broken part of a whole; pieces：四角八～儿 four quarters and eight pieces｜碗摔成几～儿。The bowl is broken into several fragments. ❹ 瓣膜的简称 abbr. for 瓣膜 bànmó ❺ (～儿 bànr)〈量词 *classifier*〉用于花瓣、叶片或种子、果实、球茎分开的小块儿 [used for petals, leaves or segments of seeds, fruits and corms]：两～儿蒜 two cloves of garlic｜把西瓜切成四～儿 carve a watermelon into four pieces

【瓣膜】bànmó 人或某些动物的器官里面可以开闭的膜状结构 valve; membranous fold or structure in certain human or animal organs which opens and closes, allowing body fluids to flow in one direction only; 简称 abbr. 瓣 bàn

bāng（ㄅㄤ）

邦(邦) bāng 国 nation; state; country: ～交 diplomatic relations | 友～ friendly country | 邻～ neighbouring country

【邦交】bāngjiāo 国与国之间的正式外交关系 relations between two countries; diplomatic relations: 建立～establish diplomatic relations | 断绝～sever diplomatic relations | 恢复～resume diplomatic relations

【邦联】bānglián 两个或两个以上的国家为了达到某些共同的目的而组成的联合体。邦联的成员国仍保留完全的独立主权，只是在军事、外交等方面采取某些联合行动。confederation; league or alliance formed by two or more countries for some common purposes, with member countries maintaining total independence and sovereignty, but taking certain combined actions in defence and foreign affairs

帮[1](幫) bāng ❶ 帮助 help; assist; aid: 大孩子能～妈妈干活儿了。The older children can help their mother with chores. ❷ 指从事雇佣劳动 be hired: ～短工 serve as a seasonal labourer

帮[2](幫) bāng (～儿 bāngr) ❶ 物体两旁或周围的部分 side; edge: 桶～ edge of a pail | 鞋～儿 shoe upper | 船～side of a boat | 床～side of a bed ❷ ☞ 帮子[1] bāng·zi ①: 菜～ outer leaf of cabbage

帮[3](幫) bāng ❶ 群；伙；集团(多指为政治的或经济的目的而结成的) gang; band; clique (group of people who associate closely for political or economic purposes): 搭～join a gang | 马～horse caravan | 匪～bandit gang ❷〈量词 *classifier*〉用于人，是'群、伙'的意思 a group of (people): 一～小朋友 a group of children | 一～强盗 a pack of bandits ❸ 帮会 secret society; underworld gang: 青～ the Qing Gang | 洪～ the Hong Gang

【帮办】bāngbàn ❶〈旧时 *old*〉指帮助主管人员办公务 assist a leader in public duties: ～军务 assist in handling military affairs ❷〈旧时 *old*〉指主管人员的助手 deputy; one who acts as assistant to sb. with primary responsibilities

【帮补】bāngbǔ 在经济上帮助 aid economically: 我上大学时，哥哥经常寄钱～我。When I was studying at university, my elder brother often sent me money.

【帮衬】bāngchèn〈方 *dial.*〉❶ 帮助；帮忙 help, assist: 每逢集日，老头儿总～着儿子照料菜摊子。On market day, the old man would help his son at his vegetable stall. ❷ 帮补；资助 aid financially; subsidise ❸ 逢迎；凑趣(多见于早期白话 oft. in early vernacular) fawn; curry favour with

【帮厨】bāng//chú 非炊事人员下厨房帮助炊事员工作 help out in the kitchen

【帮凑】bāngcòu 凑集财物，帮助人解决困难 pool or contribute money to help sb. out: 大家给他～了点路费，送他回家。People pooled some money to pay for him to go home. | 你有困难，我们自会～你。We will help you out if you have any difficulties.

【帮倒忙】bāng dàománg 指因帮忙不得法，反而给人添麻烦 be more of a hindrance than a help; do sb. a disservice

【帮冬】bāng//dōng〈方 *dial.*〉在冬季帮工 winter hire

【帮工】bāng//gōng 帮助干活儿，多指受雇帮人干活 be hired to work for others: 他出外～去了。He hired himself out to work. | 大忙季节，请人帮了几天工。In the busy season, some extra labourers were hired for a few days.

【帮工】bānggōng 帮工的人 temporary hire; seasonal labourer; helper: 麦收时，他家雇了两个～。During the wheat harvest, his family hired two casual labourers.

【帮会】bānghuì〈旧社会 *pre-1949*〉民间秘密组织(如青帮、洪帮、哥老会等)的总称 secret society; underworld gang (e.g. the Qing Gang, the Hong Gang, and Gelao Society)

【帮教】bāngjiào 帮助和教育 help and educate: 对失足青少年要做好～工作。We should be effective in helping and educating juvenile delinquents.

【帮口】bāngkǒu〈旧社会 *pre-1949*〉地方上或行业中借同乡或其他关系结合起来的小集团 small group set up by people from the same hometown, province or for other reasons within a locality or a profession

【帮忙】bāng//máng (～儿 bāng//mángr) 帮助别人做事，泛指在别人有困难的时候给予帮助 offer help in a time of need; give (or lend) a hand; do a favour; do a good turn: 你搬家时我来～。When you move house I'll give you a hand. | 这件事我实在帮不上忙。There's nothing I can do in this matter.

【帮派】bāngpài 为共同的私利而结成的小集团 faction; small group formed to promote common private interests: ～思想 factionalism | ～活动 factionalist activities | 拉山头，搞～ form a faction to conduct factionalist activities

【帮浦】bāngpǔ 泵的旧称 old name for pump

【帮腔】bāngqiāng ❶ 某些戏曲中的一种演唱形式，台上一人主唱，多人在台后和着唱 backstage vocal accompaniment to the principal singer on stage in certain traditional Chinese operas ❷〈比喻 *fig.*〉支持别人，帮他说话 speak in support of sb.; back sb. up: ～助势 speak up in support | 他看见没有人～，也就不再坚持了。He did not insist when no one seconded him.

【帮手】bāng//shǒu 帮忙 help：帮不上手 can offer no assistance｜帮得上手 able to give a hand｜劳驾，请您过来帮把手。May I trouble you to come and give me a hand?

【帮手】bāng·shou 帮助工作的人 helper; assistant：找个～look for a helper

【帮套】bāngtào ❶ 在车辕外面的拉车的套 harness for a draught animal outside the shaft of a vehicle：加上一头牲口拉～add an animal to pull from the side ❷ 指在车辕外面拉车的牲口 extra draught animal that pulls from outside the shafts：一匹马拉不动，再加上个～。If one horse is not enough to pull the cart, add another to pull from the side.

【帮贴】bāngtiē 〈方 *dial.*〉从经济上帮助；贴补 aid financially; subsidise：过去，我拖家带口，他常～我。When I was burdened with a family, he often helped me out with money.

【帮同】bāngtóng 帮助别人一同（做事）work together with sb.：～母亲料理家务。I help my mother with household chores.

【帮闲】bāngxián ❶（文人）受有钱有势的人豢养，给他们装点门面，为他们效劳（of man of letters) serve the rich and powerful as a literary hack so they can keep up appearances：～凑趣 seek to please (the powerful) ❷ 帮闲的文人 literary hack

【帮凶】bāngxiōng ❶ 帮助行凶或作恶 abet in wicked or illegal activity ❷ 帮助行凶或作恶的人 accomplice; accessary; one who abets wicked or illegal activity

【帮佣】bāngyōng ❶ 为人做佣工 be hired as a labourer, servant, etc.：靠～度日 hire oneself out to make a living ❷ 做佣工的人 hired labourer; servant

【帮主】bāngzhǔ 帮会或帮派的首领 head of a secret society or faction

【帮助】bāngzhù 替人出力、出主意或给以物质上、精神上的支援 help; assist; aid; provide material, emotional support and offer advice or service：互相～help each other｜～灾民 help the victims of a natural calamity

【帮子】[1] bāng·zi ❶ 白菜等蔬菜外层叶子较厚的部分（of cabbage or other vegetable) outer thick leaf：白菜～ outer cabbage leaf ❷ 鞋帮 upper of a shoe

【帮子】[2] bāng·zi 〈量词 *classifier*〉群；伙 crowd, group：来了一～人。A group of people has come.｜这～年轻人劲头真足。These young people are full of energy.

啷 bāng 〈拟声词 *onom.*〉敲打木头的声音 rat-tat; rat-a-tat; sound of rapping or knocking on wood

【啷啷】bānglāng 〈拟声词 *onom.*〉撞击物体的声音 banging sound：～一声，大门被踹开了。With a sharp bang, the gate was kicked open.

梆 bāng ❶ 打更等用的梆子 clapper for sounding the watch ❷〈方 *dial.*〉用棍子等打；敲 strike with stick; knock：奶奶手握擀面杖要～他。Grandma wants to spank him with a rolling pin.｜～树上的红枣儿吃 beat the tree to knock the dates down ❸〈拟声词 *onom.*〉敲打木头的声音 rat-tat; rat-a-tat; sound of rapping or knocking on wood：～～～地使劲敲门 loud rapping on the door

【梆子】bāng·zi ❶ 打更用的器具，空心，用竹子或木头制成 clapper made of hollow bamboo or wood for sounding the watch ❷ 打击乐器，用两根长短不同的枣木制成，多用于梆子腔的伴奏 percussion instrument consisting of two wooden clappers of unequal length, mostly used for accompaniment of clapper operas ❸ same as 梆子腔 bāng·ziqiāng

【梆子腔】bāng·ziqiāng ❶ 戏曲声腔之一，因用木梆子加强节奏而得名 music of clapper operas, so named because clappers are used to pick out the rhythm ❷ 用梆子腔演唱的剧种的统称，如秦腔（陕西梆子）、山西梆子、河北梆子、山东梆子等 clapper opera; general term for local operas of Shaanxi, Shanxi, Hebei and Shandong provinces, performed to the accompaniment of 梆子 *bangzi* or clappers

浜 bāng 〈方 *dial.*〉小河 creek; streamlet：河～small river｜门前有条～。A creek runs by the door.

bǎng（ㄅㄤˇ）

绑 bǎng 用绳、带等缠绕或捆扎 bind or tie with strings, ropes, etc.：～担架 tie up a stretcher｜把行李～紧一点儿。Tie up the luggage more tightly.

【绑匪】bǎngfěi 指从事绑票的匪徒 kidnapper

【绑架】bǎng//jià 用强力把人劫走 kidnap; take a person by force

【绑票】bǎng//piào（～儿 bǎng//piàor）匪徒把人劫走，强迫被绑者的家属出钱去赎 kidnap (for ransom); seize and detain a person by force, and demand a ransom for his or her release

【绑腿】bǎngtuǐ 缠裹小腿的布带 leg wrappings; puttee

【绑扎】bǎngzā 捆扎；包扎 tie up; wrap up; bind up：～行李 tie up baggage｜～伤口 bind up (or dress) a wound

榜 bǎng ❶ 张贴的名单 list of names posted up：选民～ List of Eligible Voters｜光荣～ Honour Roll ❷〈古代 *arch.*〉指文告 proclamation; notice：～文 notice｜张～招贤 put up a notice to summon men of worth ❸ 匾额 horizontal board with an inscription written on it：题～inscribe on a board｜～额 a horizontal inscribed board

☞ 搒 bàng on p. 59 and 搒 péng on p. 1459

【榜额】bǎng'é same as 匾额 biǎn'é

【榜首】bǎngshǒu 榜上公布的名单中的首位，泛指第一名 first on a list of names; first place in a contest, etc.：名列～rank first; come first|该队异军突起，一跃而居大赛的～。This team has unexpectedly come to the fore, and now ranks first in the tournament.

【榜书】bǎngshū 原指写在宫阙门额上的大字。后来泛指招牌一类的大型字 (formerly) large characters inscribed on the board above the door of a palace; characters written on posters; also 擘窠书 bòkēshū

【榜尾】bǎngwěi 榜上公布的名单中的末位，泛指最后一名 last place on a list：在这次邀请赛上，该队只能名列～。This team ranks last in this invitational competition.

【榜文】bǎngwén〈古代 *arch.*〉指文告 proclamation; notice

【榜眼】bǎngyǎn 科举时代的一种称号。明清两代称殿试考取一甲（第一等）第二名的人。unofficial designation in the civil service examination; the second best examinee in the palace examination during the Ming and Qing dynasties

【榜样】bǎngyàng 作为仿效的人或事例（多指好的 oft. sth. good) example; model for others to follow：好～a good example|你先带个头，做个～让大家看看。You take the lead and set a good example.

膀 bǎng〈书 *fml.*〉same as 榜 bǎng

膀 bǎng ❶ 肩膀 shoulder：～阔腰圆 broad-shouldered and solidly built ❷（～儿 bǎngr）鸟类等的翅膀 wing (of bird)

☞ bàng on p. 59, pāng on p. 1445 and páng on p. 1446

【膀臂】bǎngbì ❶〈比喻 *fig.*〉得力的助手 capable assistant; reliable helper; right-hand man：你来得好，给我添了个～。You have come at the right moment to help me. ❷〈方 *dial.*〉same as 膀子 bǎng·zi ①

【膀大腰圆】bǎng dà yāo yuán 形容人的身体高大粗壮 broad-shouldered and solidly built; hefty; husky

【膀子】bǎng·zi ❶ 胳膊的上部靠肩的部分，也指整个胳膊 upper arm; whole arm：光着～be stripped to the waist ❷ 鸟类等的翅膀 wing (of bird)

髈 bǎng same as 膀 bǎng

☞ pǎng on p. 1447

bàng（ㄅㄤˋ）

蚌 bàng 软体动物，有两个椭圆形介壳，可以开闭。壳表面黑绿色，有环状纹，里面有珍珠层。生活在淡水中，有的种类产珍珠。clam (*Cyelina sinensis*); freshwater mussel; freshwater mollusk with two green-black elongated shells with a pearly lining that open and close. Some varieties produce pearls.

☞ bèng on p. 95

棒 bàng ❶ 棍子 stick; club; cudgel：木～wooden stick|炭精～carbon stick (or rod) ❷（体力或能力）强；（水平）高；（成绩）好 good; fine; excellent; strong：～小伙子 a strong young man|字写得真～write a good hand|功课～do well in school subjects

【棒冰】bàngbīng〈方 *dial.*〉冰棍儿 ice-lolly; popsicle

【棒疮】bàngchuāng 被棍棒打后皮肤或黏膜发生溃烂的疾病 sore on skin or mucous membrane caused by beating with club or stick

【棒槌】bàng·chui ❶ 捶打用的木棒（多用来洗衣服 oft. for washing clothes) wooden beater ❷ 指外行（多用于戏剧界 oft. in the theatre circles) amateur

【棒喝】bànghè〈比喻 *fig.*〉促人醒悟的警告 sharp warning to make people mindful of reality：一声～a loud warning shout; ☞ 当头棒喝 dāng tóu bànghè on p. 385

【棒球】bàngqiú ❶ 球类运动项目之一，规则和用具都像垒球而稍有不同，场地比垒球的大 baseball; ball game with rules and equipment similar to softball, played on a slightly larger field ❷ 棒球运动使用的球，较垒球小而硬 baseball, smaller and harder than the ball used in softball

【棒儿香】bàngrxiāng 用细的竹棍或木棍做芯子的香 stick of incense made from a thin piece of bamboo or wood

【棒针】bàngzhēn ❶ 一种编织毛线衣物的用具，较粗，多用竹子削制而成 knitting needle; thin pointed stick used for knitting by hand, mostly made of bamboo ❷ 用棒针编织的 knitted：～衫 a knitted sweater

【棒子】bàng·zi ❶ 棍子（多指粗而短的 esp. short and thick ones) stick; club; cudgel ❷〈方 *dial.*〉玉米 ear of maize (or corn); corncob：～面 corn flour

【棒子面】bàng·zimiàn〈方 *dial.*〉玉米面 cornmeal; corn flour

棓 bàng〈书 *fml.*〉same as 棒 bàng

☞ bèi on p. 87

傍 bàng ❶ 靠；靠近 be close to (in distance); draw near：船～了岸。The boat drew alongside the bank.|依山～水 at the foot of a hill and by a stream|你～我这边坐吧。Sit beside me. ❷ 临近（指时间）near (in time)：～晚 towards evening ❸〈方 *dial.*〉跟随 follow：～上他，别让他跑了。Follow him, don't let him escape.|他曾～梅兰芳拉二胡。He once accompanied Mei Lanfang on the *erhu*.

【傍边儿】bàng//biānr〈方 *dial.*〉靠近；接近 be

close to; draw near

【傍黑儿】bànghēir〈方 *dial.*〉傍晚 dusk:一早出的门,~才回家。He left early in the morning and did not get home until dusk.

【傍角儿】bàngjuér〈方 *dial.*〉❶ 为主角配戏或伴奏 play a supporting role or be accompanist to a leading role ❷ 指为主角配戏或伴奏的人 one who takes a supporting role, or is an accompanist

【傍亮儿】bàngliàngr〈方 *dial.*〉临近天明的时候 dawn; daybreak:天刚~他们就出发了。They set off at daybreak.

【傍明】bàngmíng〈方 *dial.*〉临近天明的时候 dawn; daybreak:~,雨停了。It stopped raining at dawn.

【傍人门户】bàng rén ménhù〈比喻 *fig.*〉依附别人,不能自主 live under another's roof; be dependent on

【傍晌】bàngshǎng〈方 *dial.*〉(~儿 bàngshǎngr)临近正午的时候 about noon

【傍晚】bàngwǎn (~儿 bàngwǎnr)临近晚上的时候 towards evening; at nightfall; at dusk

【傍午】bàngwǔ 临近正午的时候 about noon:~时分,突然下起了大雨。At noon, it suddenly began to pour.

【傍依】bàngyī 靠近;挨近 near (in distance); draw near:住宅小区~碧波荡漾的太平湖。The residential sub-district is near the rippling waters of the Taiping Lake.

谤 bàng〈书 *fml.*〉诽谤 slander; defame; vilify:毁~malign | ~议 calumny | ~书 libel

【谤毁】bànghuǐ〈书 *fml.*〉毁谤 slander; defame; vilify

【谤书】bàngshū〈书 *fml.*〉诽谤人的信件或书籍 libel; written or printed statement that damages a person's reputation with false information

【谤议】bàngyì〈书 *fml.*〉诽谤议论 oral slander; calumny; libel

塝 bàng〈方 *dial.*〉田边土坡;沟渠或土埂的边(多用于地名 oft. part of place name) slope at field's edge; side of canal or ridge in field:张家~(在湖北) Zhangjiabang, name of a place in Hubei Province

蒡 bàng ☞ 牛蒡 niúbàng on p. 1420
☞ páng on p. 1446

搒(榜) bàng〈书 *fml.*〉摇橹使船前进;划船 row a boat; paddle a boat
☞ péng on p. 1459 and 榜 bǎng on p. 57

棓 bàng [棓头](bàngtóu)〈方 *dial.*〉玉米 maize; corn

蚌 bàng〈书 *fml.*〉same as 蚌 bàng

膀 bàng ☞ 吊膀子 diàobàng·zi on p. 446
☞ bǎng on p. 58, pāng on p. 1445 and páng on p. 1446

磅[1] bàng ❶ 英美制重量单位。1 磅等于 16 盎司,合 453.59 克 pound; unit of weight of the British and US system, equal to 16 ounces or 453.59 grammes ❷ 磅秤 scales:过~ weigh | 搁在~上称一称。Put it on the scales and weigh. ❸ 用磅秤称轻重 weigh on the scales:~体重 weigh to determine body weight

磅[2] bàng 点[4]的旧称 old term for 点[4] diǎn
☞ páng on p. 1446

【磅秤】bàngchèng same as 台秤 táichèng ①

镑 bàng 英国、埃及等国的本位货币 pound; basic monetary unit of the currency of Britain, Egypt and some other countries

艕 bàng ❶ 船和船相靠 boats draw near to each other ❷ same as 搒 bàng

bāo(ㄅㄠ)

包 bāo ❶ 用纸、布或其他薄片把东西裹起来 wrap in paper, cloth or other thin material:~书 cover a book with paper; put a jacket (or cover) on a book | ~饺子 make *jiaozi* (dumplings) | 头上~着一条白毛巾 a white towel wrapped round one's head ❷ (~儿 bāor)包好了的东西 bundle; package; pack; packet; parcel:药~packet of medicine | 邮~ postal parcel | 打了个~wrap things up in a bundle ❸ 装东西的口袋 bag; sack:书~ schoolbag ◇病~儿 chronic invalid | 坏~儿 rascal; rogue | 淘气~儿 mischievous imp ❹〈量词 *classifier*〉用于成包的东西 package; bundle:两~大米 two sacks of rice | 一大~衣服 a big bundle of clothes ❺ 物体或身体上鼓起来的疙瘩 protuberance; swelling; lump:树干上有个大~。There is a big protuberance on the tree trunk. | 腿上起了个~ a swelling on the leg ❻ 毡制的圆顶帐篷 yurt; circular felt-covered tent over a collapsible frame:蒙古~Mongolian yurt ❼ 围绕;包围 surround; encircle; envelop:火苗~住了锅台。The flames envelop the pot. | 骑兵分两路~过去。The cavalry outflanks the enemy on both sides. ❽ 容纳在里头;总括在一起 include; contain:~含 include | ~罗 embody | 无所不~ all-embracing ❾ 把整个任务承担下来,负责完成 undertake the entire task:~医 contract for full medical coverage | ~教 contract for all instruction | ~片儿(负责完成一定地段或范围的工作) contract for work in a certain locality or field ❿ 担保 assure; guarantee:~你没错。No problem at all, I assure you. | ~你满意。Your satisfaction is guaranteed. ⓫ 约定专用 hire; charter:~车 hire (or charter) a car | ~场 book a whole theatre or cinema | ~了一只船 hire a boat ⓬ (Bāo)姓 a surname

【包办】bāobàn ❶ 一手办理,单独负责 take full

responsibility for everything：这件事你一个人～了吧。You'd better do the whole job yourself. ❷ 不和有关的人商量、合作，独自作主办理 decide and implement without consulting or cooperating with others; monopolise：把持～monopolise everything｜～婚姻 arranged marriage｜～代替 take over sb. else's work without consulting them

【包背装】bāobèizhuāng 图书装订法的一种，书页用线或纸捻装订成册，用厚纸或绫绢等包背粘连，纸捻和线不外露 wrapped-ridge binding; a form of book binding where the pages are bound with threads or spills of rolled paper, and the ridge covered with thick paper or silk, so the threads or spills are hidden

【包庇】bāobì 袒护或掩护（坏人、坏事）shield; harbour (evil doers); cover up (evil deeds)：互相～cover up for each other｜～贪污犯 harbour an embezzler

【包藏】bāocáng 包含；隐藏在里面 contain; harbour; conceal：～祸心 harbour evil intentions｜他的眼神～着抑郁之情。There is a despondent expression in his eyes.

【包藏祸心】bāocáng huòxīn 怀着害人的念头 harbour evil intentions; have bad intentions toward sb.

【包产】bāo//chǎn 根据土地、生产工具、技术、劳动力等条件订出产量指标，由个人或生产单位负责完成 contract with an individual or production unit with responsibility for output quotas based on land, tools of production, technology and labour：包工～draw up a production contract for labour and output quota｜～到户 fix farm output quotas for each household

【包场】bāo//chǎng 预先定下一场电影、戏剧等的全部或大部分座位 book a whole theatre or cinema; make a block booking

【包抄】bāochāo 绕到敌人侧面或背后进攻 outflank or envelop the enemy：分三路～过去 close in on the enemy in a three-pronged attack

【包车】bāo//chē 定期租用车辆 hire a vehicle for a set time：包一辆车 charter a vehicle

【包车】bāochē ❶ 个人或机关团体定期租用的人力车或机动车 motor vehicle or rickshaw hired for a set period of time by an individual or an organization：拉～pull a private rickshaw｜～夫 puller of a private rickshaw｜门前挤满了～。Private rickshaws crowded in front of the gate. ❷ 由若干乘务员负责一列列车或由司机、售票员共同负责一辆公共汽车、电车的使用、保管等任务，叫做包车 contract for a vehicle; crew (drivers and conductors) contracts to be responsible for use and maintenance of a train, bus or trolley bus：～组 contracting crew

【包乘制】bāochéngzhì 交通运输部门乘务员的一种工作负责制。如铁路部门由司机、副司机、司炉等组成若干包乘组，各组轮流驾驶一台机车，在指定区段值勤并负责保养。transportation contract system; responsibility system instituted by transport departments for train attendants or bus drivers and conductors. For instance, contracting train crews, each consisting of driver, assistant driver and stoker, are organized to take turns in running a train in designated sections, and are each responsible for its operation and maintenance.

【包打天下】bāo dǎ tiānxià 包揽打天下的重任 undertake to conquer the country single-handedly;〈比喻 *fig.*〉由个人或少数人包办代替，不放手让其他人干 monopolise a task; exclude others from a task

【包打听】bāodǎtīng〈方 *dial.*〉❶ same as 包探 bāotàn ❷ 指好打听消息或知道消息多的人 snooper; gossip monger; Nosy Parker

【包饭】bāo//fàn 双方约定，一方按月付饭钱，另一方供给饭食 supply meals at a fixed monthly rate; board：学校可为双职工子女～。The school provides paid meals for children with working parents.

【包饭】bāofàn 按月支付固定费用的饭食 meals supplied at a fixed monthly rate：孩子在街道食堂吃～。Children eat at the neighbourhood canteen for a monthly fee.

【包袱】bāo·fu ❶ 包衣服等东西的布 cloth-wrapper ❷ 用布包起来的包儿 bundle wrapped in a cloth ❸〈比喻 *fig.*〉某种负担 millstone round one's neck; load; weight; burden：思想～a load (or weight) on one's mind; inhibiting concerns｜不能把赡养父母看成是～。Supporting one's parents should not be considered a burden. ❹ 指相声、快书等曲艺中的笑料。把笑料说出来叫抖包袱。humorous content in comic dialogue or quick-patter. To say the funny pants is called 抖包袱 dǒu bāo·fu.

【包袱底儿】bāo·fudǐr〈方 *dial.*〉❶ 指家庭多年不动用的或最贵重的东西 family property, esp. valuables, accumulated over a long time; resources ❷〈比喻 *fig.*〉隐私 secrets; privacy; private matters：抖～disclose one's secrets ❸〈比喻 *fig.*〉最拿手的本领 unique skill; consummate skill：抖搂～（显示绝技）show off one's special skills

【包袱皮儿】bāo·fupír 包衣服等用的布 cloth-wrapper

【包干儿】bāogānr 承担一定范围的工作，保证全部完成 be responsible for a task until it is completed：分段～divide up the work and assign a part to each individual or group｜剩下的扫尾活儿由我们小组～。Our team will finish up the last of the job.

【包工】bāo//gōng 按照规定的要求和期限，完成某项生产或建设任务 undertake to complete

a task within a time limit and according to specifications:～包产 contract for a job|大楼由承建单位～。Construction of the high-rise is contracted to a construction unit.

【包工】bāogōng 承包工程的厂商或工头 contractor; person or firm that undertakes jobs (esp. construction) under contract

【包公】Bāogōng 包拯(zhěng),北宋时进士,曾任开封府知府,以执法严正著称。民间关于他断案的传说很多,尊称他为包公或包青天。小说戏曲中把他描写成刚正严明、不畏权势的清官的典型。Bao Zheng, of the Northern Song Dynasty, passed the highest level of the imperial examinations and served as prefect of Kaifeng, and was famous for his strict enforcement of the law. There are many popular tales about his rulings in lawsuits, for which he is also known as Lord Bao or Just-Minded Bao. In dramas and fictions he appears as the model of an upright official who is never intimidated by the rich and powerful.

【包谷】bāogǔ 〈方 *dial.*〉玉米 maize; corn; also 苞谷 bāogǔ

【包管】bāoguǎn 担保(表示说话的人的自信) assure; guarantee (expression of the speaker's confidence):～退换。Merchandise will be exchanged if found unsatisfactory.|他这种病～不用吃药就会好。He is sure to fully recover from this disease without taking any medicine.

【包裹】bāoguǒ ❶ 包;包扎 wrap up; bind up:用布把伤口～起来。Bandage up the wound. ❷ 包扎成件的包儿 bundle; package; parcel:他肩上背着一个小～。He carried a small bundle on his shoulder.|我到邮电局寄～去。I went to the post office to send a parcel.

【包含】bāohán 里边含有 contain; embody; include:这句话～好几层意思。This statement has quite a few implications.

【包涵】bāo·han 〈客套话 *pol.*〉请人原谅 excuse; forgive; bear with:唱得不好,大家多多～! Excuse me for my poor singing.

【包伙】bāo//huǒ same as 包饭 bāo//fàn

【包伙】bāohuǒ same as 包饭 bāofàn

【包机】bāojī ❶ 定期租用飞机 charter a plane:开展～业务 operate a charter plane business ❷ 包乘的飞机 chartered plane:一架旅游～a chartered tourist plane

【包剿】bāojiǎo 围剿 encircle and suppress

【包金】bāojīn ❶ 用薄金叶包在金属首饰外面 cover with gold leaf; gild; gold-plate:～项链 a gilded necklace ❷ same as 包银 bāoyín

【包举】bāojǔ 总括;全部占有 include; encompass:～无遗 all encompassing

【包括】bāokuò 包含(或列举各部分,或着重指出某一部分) include; consist of; comprise; incorporate:语文教学应该～听、说、读、写四项,不可偏轻偏重。The teaching of language should include four aspects — listening, speaking, reading and writing, and none should be stressed over the others.|我说'大家',自然～你在内。When I say 'everyone,' I naturally include you.

【包揽】bāolǎn 兜揽过来,全部承担 assume responsibility for the whole; take on everything:政府部门不可能把各种事务都～起来。It is impossible for government departments to manage everything.

【包罗】bāoluó 包括(指大范围) include; cover; embrace:民间艺术～甚广,不是三言两语所能说完的。Folk arts cover a wide range, and cannot be described in just a few words.

【包罗万象】bāoluó wànxiàng 内容丰富,应有尽有 rich in content and complete:这个博览会的展品真可说是～,美不胜收。The exhibits in this exposition cover all aspects and are a real feast for the eyes.

【包米】bāomǐ 〈方 *dial.*〉玉米 maize; corn; also 苞米 bāomǐ

【包赔】bāopéi 担保赔偿 guarantee to pay compensation:～损失。Compensation for losses is guaranteed.

【包皮】bāopí ❶ 包装的皮儿 wrapping; wrapper ❷ 阴茎前部覆盖龟头的外皮 prepuce; foreskin; free fold of skin covering the glans of a penis

【包票】bāopiào 保单。料事有绝对的把握时,说可以打包票。guarantee slip; warranty; expression of certainty:他一定能按时完成任务,我敢打～。He will accomplish the task on time, I guarantee. also 保票 bǎopiào

【包容】bāoróng ❶ 宽容 pardon; forgiveness:大度～be magnanimous and tolerant|一味～invariably forgive ❷ 容纳 contain; hold:小礼堂能～三百个听众。The small auditorium can seat 300 listeners.

【包身工】bāoshēngōng ❶〈旧社会 *pre-1949*〉一种变相的贩卖奴隶的形式。被贩卖的是青少年,由包工头骗到工厂、矿山做工,没有人身自由,工钱全归包工头所有,受资本家和包工头的双重剥削。indentured labour, a form of slavery. Young people were lured to work in factories or mines where they were deprived of personal freedom, and their pay were pocketed by the labour contractors. They were thus subjected to dual exploitation of both capitalists and contractors. ❷ 在包身工形式下做工的人 indentured labourer

【包探】bāotàn 〈旧时 *old*〉巡捕房中的侦缉人员 police detective

【包头】bāo·tóu ❶ 裹在头上的装束用品(多用于少数民族) head wrapper; head-dress worn by ethnic minorities:青～black kerchief ❷ (～儿 bāo·tóur)附在鞋头起保护作用的橡胶、皮革等 protective patch of rubber or leather on the shoe tip：打～儿 put a patch on the shoe tip

【包围】bāowéi ❶ 四面围住 surround; encircle：亭子被茂密的松林～着。The pavilion is surrounded by a thick pine forest. ❷ 正面进攻的同时，向敌人的翼侧和后方进攻 launch frontal attack and assault the enemy's flanks and rear at the same time ❸ 指包围圈 ring of encirclement：陷于～之中 find oneself surrounded

【包围圈】bāowéiquān 军事上指已形成的包围态势的圈子和已被包围的地区（mil.）encirclement; area under siege：冲出～ break through the enemy encirclement｜～越缩越小了。The area under siege is getting smaller.

【包席】bāo//xí 订整桌的酒席 order a complete menu：你们是点菜还是～？Do you wish to order a full menu or choose dishes a la carte?｜包三桌席 book three tables with full banquet menu

【包席】bāoxí 饭馆里指整桌供应的酒席 full banquet menu provided by a restaurant; also 包桌 bāozhuō

【包厢】bāoxiāng 某些剧场里特设的单间席位，一间有几个座位，多在楼上 box (at the theatre); small compartment for a group of spectators in a theatre or concert hall, oft. upstairs

【包销】bāoxiāo ❶ 指商人承揽货物，负责销售 have exclusive selling rights ❷ 指商业机构跟生产单位订立合同，把全部产品包下来销售 contract to be the sole sales agent for a production unit or a firm

【包心菜】bāoxīncài 〈方 *dial.*〉结球甘蓝 cabbage

【包银】bāoyín 〈旧时 *old*〉戏院按期付给剧团或主要演员的约定的报酬 agreed wages paid by a theatre to leading traditional opera singers

【包圆儿】bāoyuánr ❶ 把货物或剩余的货物全部买下 buy the whole lot：剩下的这点儿您～吧！Please buy up the remainder! ❷ 全部担当 assume in its entirety：剩下的零碎活儿我～了。I'll deal with all that's left of the work.

【包月】bāo//yuè 按月计价付款，如包饭按月付饭钱、包车按月付车钱等 make monthly payment, e. g. monthly payment for meals or a chartered vehicle

【包孕】bāoyùn 包含 contain; embody; include：她的信里～着无尽的思念之情。Her letter is full of nostalgia.

【包蕴】bāoyùn 包含 contain; embody; include：简短的几句话却～着很深的哲理。The few sentences, though short, contain some profound philosophy.

【包扎】bāozā 包裹捆扎 wrap up; bind up; pack：～伤口 bind up (or dress) a wound｜待运的仪器都～好了。The instruments awaiting shipment are already packed.

【包装】bāozhuāng ❶ 在商品外面用纸包裹或把商品装进纸盒、瓶子等 packaging; wrap in paper, paper box or bottle：定量～packaged in fixed quantities｜～商品要注意质量。Due attention should be paid to the quality of commodity packaging. ❷ 指包装商品的东西，如纸、盒子、瓶子等 packaging materials such as paper, boxes, bottles, etc.：～美观 attractive packaging｜运输不慎，～破损严重。The packaging has been badly damaged by careless transportation.

【包子】bāo·zi ❶ 食品，用菜、肉或糖等做馅儿，多用发面做皮，包成后，蒸熟 bun stuffed with minced vegetables, meat or sugar inside, wrapped in leavened dough and steamed ❷ 冶炼金属时盛金属溶液的器具 container for molten metal in metal smelting

【包租】bāozū ❶ 为了转租而租进房屋或田地等 rent land or house for subletting ❷ 不管年成丰歉，佃户都要按照规定数额交租，叫做包租 (old) mandatory fixed rent for farmland (to be paid no matter what the harvest) ❸ 在一段时期内专由某方租用 hire (a car, boat, etc.) for a period of time; charter：～汽车 charter a car

苞[1] bāo 花没开时包着花骨朵的小叶片 bud; small protuberance on the stem of a plant that may develop into a flower：花～ flower bud｜含～未放 in bud; budding

苞[2] bāo 〈书 *fml.*〉丛生而茂密 luxuriant; profuse; thick：竹～松茂 bamboo and pines growing in profusion

【苞谷】bāogǔ same as 包谷 bāogǔ

【苞米】bāomǐ same as 包米 bāomǐ

孢 bāo ☞ below

【孢子】bāozǐ 某些低等动物和植物产生的一种有繁殖作用或休眠作用的细胞，离开母体后就能形成新的个体 spore; unicellular hypnotic or reproductive cell produced by certain primitive plants and invertebrates, capable of developing into a new individual after leaving the parent plant; also 胞子 bāozǐ

【孢子植物】bāozǐ zhíwù 用孢子繁殖的植物，一般包括菌、藻、苔、藓、蕨类等植物，如海带、水绵等 cryptogam; plants reproduced by spores, including fungi, algae, bryophytes, mosses, and pteridophytes such as kelps and spirogyra

枹 bāo 枹树，落叶乔木，叶子互生，略呈倒卵形，边缘有粗锯齿，花单性，雌雄同株。种子可用来提取淀粉，树皮可以制栲胶。有的地区叫小橡树。glandbearing oak (*Quercus glandulifera*); Japanese silkworm oak; deciduous tree with alternate oval, serrated leaves, pistillate and staminate flowers growing on the same tree, seeds that can be used to make starch, and bark that can be made into glue;

known in some places as 小橡树 xiǎoxiàngshù ☞ 桴 fú on p.599

胞 bāo ❶ 胞衣 (human) afterbirth ❷ 同父母所生的;嫡亲的 born of the same parents:～兄 full or blood brothers | ～妹 full sisters | ～叔(父亲的胞弟) paternal uncle (father's full brother) ❸ 同一个国家或民族的人 fellow countrymen; compatriot:侨～ overseas compatriots | 藏～ Tibetan compatriots

【胞波】bāobō 缅语是同胞和亲戚的意思,缅甸人习惯用来称呼中国人,以表示亲切 meaning 'compatriot and relative' in the Myanmese language. The Myanmese people call Chinese people '胞波 bāobō' to show cordiality.

【胞衣】bāoyī 〈中医 *Chin. med.*〉把胎盘和胎膜统称为胞衣 (human) afterbirth (placenta and caul); also 衣胞 yībāo or 胎衣 tāiyī; 用做中药时叫紫河车 when used as medicinal ingredient, called 紫河车 zǐhéchē

【胞子】bāozǐ same as 孢子 bāozǐ

炮 bāo ❶ 烹调方法,用锅或铛在旺火上炒(牛羊肉片等),迅速搅拌 quick-fry (mutton or beef slices) in a wok over high heat; sauté:～羊肉 quick-fried mutton ❷ 烘焙 dry with heat:湿衣服搁在热炕上,一会儿就～干了。Spread damp clothes on the heated brick bed and they'll soon dry.

☞ páo on p.1448 and pào on p.1451

剥 bāo 去掉外面的皮或壳 shell; peel; skin:～花生 shell peanuts | ～皮 peel the skin off

☞ bō on p.146

龅 bāo [龅牙](bāoyá) 突出嘴唇外的牙齿 buckteeth; large projecting front teeth

煲 bāo 〈方 *dial.*〉❶ 壁较陡直的锅 deep pot:瓦～earthen pot | 沙～casserole | 铜～copper pot | 电饭～electric rice cooker ❷ 用煲煮或熬 cook in this kind of pot:～饭 simmer rice | ～粥 make gruel

褒(襃) bāo ❶ 赞扬;夸奖 praise; honour; commend (跟'贬'相对 as opposed to 'censure'):～奖 praise and honour | ～扬 commend ❷ 〈书 *fml.*〉(衣服)肥大 (of clothes) loose; large:～衣博带(宽袍大带) loose gown with wide girdle

【褒贬】bāobiǎn 评论好坏 assess; appraise:～人物 evaluate the merits and demerits of important figures | 一字～one word of appraisal | 不加～make no comment; express neither praise nor censure

【褒贬】bāo·bian 批评缺点;指责 speak ill of; cry down:有意见要当面提,别在背地里～人。If you have any criticisms, state them openly and refrain from speaking ill of people behind their back.

【褒词】bāocí 含有褒义的词,如'坚强'、'勇敢'等 commendatory term, such as 'staunchness' and 'bravery'; also 褒义词 bāoyìcí

【褒奖】bāojiǎng 表扬和奖励 praise and honour; commend and award:～有功人员 commend those who have rendered outstanding service | 在大桥落成庆典上,许多先进工作者受到了～。At the inauguration ceremony of the bridge, many outstanding workers were given commendations and awards.

【褒扬】bāoyáng 表扬 praise; commend:～先进 praise the advanced

【褒义】bāoyì 字句里含有的赞许或好的意思 commendatory (or complimentary) sense of word or sentence:～词 commendatory term

báo (ㄅㄠˊ)

瓝 báo 〈书 *fml.*〉❶ 小瓜 small melon ❷ ☞ 马瓝儿 mǎbáor on p.1287

雹 báo 冰雹 hail

【雹灾】báozāi 冰雹造成的灾害 disaster caused by hail

【雹子】báo·zi 冰雹的通称 general term for 冰雹 bīngbáo

薄 báo ❶ 扁平物上下两面之间的距离小(跟'厚'相对,下②③同 as opposed to 'thick', same as ②③ below) thin; have little extent from one surface to its opposite; flimsy:～板 thin plank | ～被 thin quilt | ～片 thin slice | 这种纸很～。This kind of paper is very thin. ◇家底～lack resources; not financially solid ❷ (感情)冷淡;不深 lacking in warmth; cold:待他的情分不～ treat him quite well ❸ 不浓;淡 weak; light:酒味很～。This is a light wine. ❹ 不肥沃 infertile; poor:变～地为肥田 transform infertile land into fertile land | 这儿土～,产量不高。The soil is infertile here, so the yield is low.

☞ bó on p.151 and bò on p.152

【薄饼】báobǐng 一种面食,用烫面做饼,很薄,两张相叠,烙熟后能揭开 thin pancake; cooked wheaten food, made of dough prepared with hot water; two thin pancakes lightly pressed together for bakery, and can then be separated when cooked

【薄脆】báocuì ❶ 一种糕点,形状多样,薄而脆 thin and crispy pastry made in many shapes ❷ 一种油炸面食,薄而脆 thin, crispy, dough fritter

bǎo (ㄅㄠˇ)

饱 bǎo ❶ 满足了食量(跟'饿'相对 as opposed to 'hungry') have eaten one's fill; be full:我～了,一点也吃不下了。I'm full and can't eat another bite. ❷ 饱满 full;

plump：谷粒儿很～。The grains are very plump. ❸ 足足地；充分 fully；to the full：～经风霜 endured countless hardships|～览大好河山 drink in the beauty of rivers and mountains ❹ 满足 satisfy：一～眼福 feast one's eyes on sth. ❺ 中饱 embezzle：克扣军饷，以～私囊 pocket a portion of the soldiers' pay and provisions

【饱餐】bǎocān 饱饱儿地吃 eat to one's heart's content：～了一顿 eat and drink one's fill

【饱尝】bǎocháng ❶ 充分地品尝 taste，savour；sample：～美味 sample the delicacies to please the palate ❷ 长期经受或体验 endure or experience over a long period of time：～艰苦 suffer untold hardships

【饱嗝儿】bǎogér 吃饱后打的嗝儿 belch；burp after eating one's fill

【饱含】bǎohán 充满 full of：眼里～着热泪 eyes brimming with tears|胸中～着对大好河山的热爱 heart full of love for the beautiful mountains and rivers of one's country

【饱汉不知饿汉饥】bǎo hàn bù zhī è hàn jī 〈比喻 *fig.*〉处境好的人，不能理解处于困境中的人的痛苦和难处 well-fed do not understand the suffering of the starving；those in comfortable circumstances do not understand the bitterness of misfortune

【饱和】bǎohé ❶ 在一定温度和压力下，溶液所含溶质的量达到最大限度，不能再溶解 saturation；stage at which no more of a substance can be absorbed into a solution ❷ 泛指事物在某个范围内达到最高限度 point at which no more can be absorbed or accepted：目前市场上洗衣机的销售已接近～。At present，the market for washing machines is approaching saturation point.

【饱经沧桑】bǎo jīng cāngsāng 形容经历过很多世事变迁 have experienced many vicissitudes

【饱经风霜】bǎo jīng fēngshuāng 形容经历过很多艰苦困难 worn；weather-beaten；have had one's fill of hardships

【饱满】bǎomǎn ❶ 丰满 full；plump：颗粒～full grains ❷ 充足 plenty：精神～full of vigour (or vitality)|～的热情 great fervour

【饱食终日】bǎo shí zhōngrì 一天到晚吃得饱饱的 do nothing but eat all day；〈比喻 *fig.*〉无所事事 lead an idle life

【饱学】bǎoxué 学识丰富 learned；erudite；scholarly：～之士 erudite person；learned scholar；man of learning

【饱以老拳】bǎo yǐ lǎo quán 用拳头狠狠地打 punch heavily with fists

【饱雨】bǎoyǔ 透雨 saturating (or soaking) rain；soaker

宝(寶、寳) bǎo ❶ 珍贵的东西 treasure：国～national treasure|献～present sth. valuable|粮食是～中之～。Grain is the treasure of all treasures. ❷ 珍贵的 precious；treasured：～刀 treasured knife|～剑 a double-edged sword|～石 precious stone；gem ❸ 旧时的一种赌具，方形，多用牛角制成，上有指示方向的记号(old) cubic gambling device，made of oxhorn，marked with directional signs；☞压宝 yā//bǎo on p.2193 ❹〈敬辞 *pol.*〉用于称对方的家眷、铺子等 [designating other party's wife，children，etc.]：～眷 your wife and children；your family|～号 your firm；your shop

【宝宝】bǎo·bǎo 对小孩儿的爱称(endearment for young child) darling；precious one

【宝贝】bǎobèi ❶ 珍奇的东西 treasured object；treasure ❷ (～儿 bǎobèir)对小孩儿的爱称 endearment for young child ❸〈方 *dial.*〉疼爱；喜爱 be fond of；dote on：老人可～这个孙子了。The grandparents dote on this grandson of theirs. ❹ 无能或奇怪荒唐的人(含讽刺意 used ironically) good-for-nothing or strange character：这个人真是个～！What a fellow!

【宝贝疙瘩】bǎobèi gē·da 〈方 *dial.*〉〈比喻 *fig.*〉非常受宠爱的孩子 parents' darling

【宝刹】bǎochà ❶ 指佛寺的塔 pagoda in a Buddhist temple ❷〈敬辞 *pol.*〉称僧尼所在的寺庙 designating temple or monastery where monks or nuns reside

【宝刀】bǎodāo 用做武器的稀有而珍贵的刀 precious or treasured sword；rare，fine sword

【宝刀不老】bǎodāo bù lǎo 〈比喻 *fig.*〉年纪虽老但功夫或技术并没减退 the man is old，but not his sword；elderly persons still at the height of their skills

【宝地】bǎodì ❶ 指地势优越或物资丰富的地方 place with favourable terrain or rich resources ❷〈敬辞 *pol.*〉对方所在的地方 designating the other party's place：借贵方一块～暂住几天。I would like to stay a few days in your honourable place.

【宝贵】bǎoguì ❶ 极有价值；非常难得；珍贵 valuable；rare；precious：～的生命 precious life|时间极为～。Time is extremely precious.|这是一些十分～的出土文物。These are rare archaeological finds. ❷ 当做珍宝看待；重视 value；treasure；set store by：这是极可～的经验。This is an extremely valuable experience.

【宝号】bǎohào ❶〈敬辞 *pol.*〉对方的店铺 your (honourable) shop ❷〈敬辞 *pol.*〉对方的名字 your (honourable) name

【宝货】bǎohuò ❶ 珍贵的物品 valuable article ❷ 活宝 humorous，lively person

【宝剑】bǎojiàn 原指稀有而珍贵的剑，后来泛指一般的剑 (formerly) rare，valuable double-edged sword；(in a broad sense) sword

【宝眷】bǎojuàn 〈敬辞 *pol.*〉对方的家眷 your (honourable) wife and children；your (respected) family

【宝库】bǎokù 储藏珍贵物品的地方,多用于比喻 treasure-house:知识～ treasure house of knowledge|艺术～ artistic treasure house|理论～ treasure house of theories

【宝蓝】bǎolán 鲜亮的蓝色 sapphire blue

【宝瓶座】bǎopíngzuò 黄道十二星座之一 Aquarius; Water Bearer; constellation, one of 12 signs of the zodiac; ☞ 黄道十二宫 huángdào shí'èrgōng on p. 851

【宝石】bǎoshí 颜色美丽、有光泽、透明度和硬度高的矿石,可制装饰品、仪表的轴承或研磨剂 precious stone; gem; bright coloured, transparent, lustrous, hard ore that can be cut and polished to make jewelry, instrument bearings or ground into abrasive powder

【宝塔】bǎotǎ 原为塔的美称,今泛指塔 (formerly) laudatory name for pagodas; (in a broad sense) pagodas

【宝玩】bǎowán 珍宝和古玩 treasures and antiques

【宝物】bǎowù 珍贵的东西 treasures; valuables

【宝藏】bǎozàng 储藏的珍宝或财富,多指矿产 stored treasures; spec. mineral deposits:发掘地下的～bring buried treasures to light ◇民间艺术的～真是无穷无尽。Folk arts are a truly inexhaustible treasure trove.

【宝重】bǎozhòng 珍惜重视 value greatly; treasure:他的书法作品深为世人～。His calligraphic works are greatly valued by ordinary people.

【宝座】bǎozuò 指帝王或神佛的座位,现多用于比喻 throne; ceremonial chair or seat of a king; pedestal of deity; (oft. used in a figurative sense) the highest place:登上冠军～ become the champion

保 bǎo ❶ 保护;保卫 protect; defend:～健 health care|～家卫国 protect our homes and defend our country ❷ 保持 keep; maintain; preserve:～温 heat preservation|～鲜 preserve freshness ❸ 保证;担保做到 guarantee; ensure:～质～量。Quality and quantity are both guaranteed.|这块地旱涝～收。This plot produces stable yields despite drought or excessive rain. ❹ 担保(不犯罪、不逃走等) stand guarantor (or surety) for; bail:～释 release on bail|取～候审(allow defendant) to obtain a guarantor and await trial out of custody ❺ 保人;保证人 guarantor:作～ be sb.'s guarantor|交～release on bail ❻〈旧时 *old*〉户籍的编制单位 *bao*; administrative system organized on the basis of households, with each 保 bǎo consisting of 10 甲 jiǎ; ☞ 保甲 bǎojiǎ ❼ (Bǎo) 姓 a surname

【保安】bǎo'ān ❶ 保卫治安 ensure public security:加强～工作 strengthen public security ❷ 保护工人安全,防止在生产过程中发生人身事故 ensure worker safety to prevent job-related accidents:～规程 safety standards|～制度 safety regulations

【保安队】bǎo'ānduì〈旧时 *old*〉一种具有警察性质的地方武装部队 Peace Preservation Corps; local armed forces similar to police

【保安族】Bǎo'ānzú 我国少数民族之一,分布在甘肃 Bonan (Pao'an) people, one of the ethnic minorities of China who inhabit Gansu Province

【保本】bǎo//běn (～儿 bǎo//běnr)保证本钱或资金不受损失 ensure value of principal or capital:～保值 (deposits) with principal and interest safeguarded against price increases

【保膘】bǎobiāo 保持牲畜肥壮 keep farm animals stout and strong

【保镖】bǎobiāo ❶ 会技击的人佩带武器,为别人护送财物或保护人身安全 (an armed person) charged with guarding another or escorting property ❷ 指做这种工作的人 bodyguard; armed escort

【保不定】bǎo·bu dìng same as 保不住 bǎo·buzhù ①

【保不齐】bǎo·bu qí〈方 *dial.*〉same as 保不住 bǎo·bu zhù ①

【保不住】bǎo·bu zhù ❶ 难免;可能 most likely; more likely than not; probably:这个天儿很难说,～会下雨。The weather is rather uncertain; most likely it's going to rain. ❷ 不能保持 unable to maintain:以前要是遇到这样的大旱,这块地的收成就～了。In the past, such a serious drought would have badly affected the yield of this plot of land.

【保藏】bǎocáng 把东西藏起来以免遗失或损坏 keep in store; preserve:～手稿 preserve the original manuscripts|把选好的种子好好～起来。Store the selected seeds carefully.

【保持】bǎochí 维持(原状),使不消失或减弱 keep; maintain; preserve:水土～ water and soil conservation|～冷静 remain calm|～物价稳定 maintain the stability of prices|跟群众～密切联系 maintain close ties with the masses

【保存】bǎocún 使事物、性质、意义、作风等继续存在,不受损失或不发生变化 preserve; conserve; keep; ensure no change or damage to object, quality, significance, attitude, etc.:～古迹 preserve historical sites|～实力 preserve one's strength; conserve one's forces|～自己,消灭敌人 preserve oneself and destroy the enemy

【保单】bǎodān ❶〈旧时 *old*〉为保证他人的行为或财力而写的字据 written guarantee for sb. else's behaviour or property ❷ 表示在一定期限和规定的范围内对所售或所修物品负责的单据,如修理钟表的保单 guarantee slip; warranty; written guarantee for the quality of a product, or for its repair, e.g. repair warranty for a clock or wristwatch

【保底】bǎo//dǐ ❶ same as 保本 bǎo//běn ❷ 指保证不少于最低限额 guarantee a minimum amount:上不封顶,下不～。There is neither a maximum nor a minimum.

【保固】bǎogù 承包工程的人保证工程在一定时期内不会损坏,损坏时由承包人负责修理 guarantee of durability of a construction project; guarantee of the quality of a construction project over a certain period of time and of the contractor's responsibility to repair any damage during that period

【保管】bǎoguǎn ❶ 保藏和管理 take care of; store and manage:图书～工作 storage of library books|这个仓库的粮食～得很好。The grain in this barn is well stored. ❷ 在仓库中做保藏和管理工作的人 warehouse keeper; custodian:老～veteran custodian|这个粮库有两个～。This grain depot has two warehousemen. ❸ 完全有把握;担保 for certain; assure:只要肯努力,～你能学会。I assure you that you will learn if you make the effort.

【保护】bǎohù 尽力照顾,使不受损害 care and protect from harm; safeguard:～眼睛 protect one's eyes|～妇女儿童的权益 safeguard the rights and interests of women and children

【保护关税】bǎohù guānshuì 为了保护本国工农业的发展,对进出口商品征收重税或实行减税、免税的政策 protective tariff; tariff on imported and exported commodities intended to protect the development of domestic industry and agriculture, including heavy taxes or tax reduction/exemption

【保护国】bǎohùguó 因被迫订立不平等条约将部分主权(如外交主权)交给别国而受其'保护'的国家。是殖民地的一种形式。protectorate; country under the 'protection' of another, forced to relinquish part of its sovereignty (e.g. over foreign affairs) to the 'protector' under the terms of an unequal treaty; form of colonization

【保护鸟】bǎohùniǎo 受人类保护,禁止随便捕杀的鸟。如许多益鸟和某些珍稀鸟类。protected birds; birds protected from capture and killing by humans, including many beneficial birds and certain rare species

【保护人】bǎohùrén 监护人 guardian

【保护伞】bǎohùsǎn 〈比喻 *fig.*〉可以起保护作用的有威慑性的力量或有权势的人(多含贬义 oft. derog.) power or status that protects owing to its capacity to deter; umbrella:核～nuclear umbrella|拉关系,找～seek protection by cultivating a network of connections|官僚主义往往是贪污分子的～。Bureaucracy often acts as a shield for the corrupt.

【保护色】bǎohùsè 某些动物身上的颜色跟周围环境的颜色类似,这种颜色叫做保护色。有保护色的动物不容易让别的动物发觉。protective colouration; camouflage body colour of certain animal species that blend into their surroundings. Animals with camouflage are nearly imperceptible to others.

【保皇】bǎohuáng 维护帝制或皇权 support the monarchy or imperial power;〈比喻 *fig.*〉效忠当权者 be loyal to those in power:～党 royalist party|～派 royalists

【保甲】bǎojiǎ 〈旧时 *old*〉统治者通过户籍编制来统治人民的制度,若干户编作一甲,若干甲编作一保,甲设甲长,保设保长,对人民实行层层管制 *bao-jia* system; administrative system organized on a households basis, with each *jia* made up of a set number of households, headed by the chief of *jia*, and a number of *jia* made up a *bao*, headed by the chief of *bao*, for governing the population at different levels

【保价】bǎojià 一种加收费用的邮递业务,用于寄递较贵重物品、有价证券、包裹等。如有遗失,邮电部门按保价金额负责赔偿。(value) insured; category of registered mail for sending valuables, securities, parcels, etc. If lost, the postal department is responsible for compensating the sender for the insured value:～信 insured letter|～包裹 insured parcel

【保驾】bǎo//jià 〈旧指 *old*〉保卫皇帝,现泛指保护某人(多用于开玩笑的场合 usu. humor.) protect the emperor;(in a broad sense) look after sb.:有老张给你～,你怕什么? With Old Zhang escorting you, what are you worried about?

【保荐】bǎojiàn 负责推荐(人) recommend sb. (for a job, etc.):～贤能 recommend worthy and capable persons

【保健】bǎojiàn 保护健康 health protection; health care:～室 infirmary|～站 health centre|～工作 health care undertaking

【保健操】bǎojiàncāo 综合运用我国医学中推拿、穴位按摩等方法而编制的一种健身运动,如眼睛保健操等 setting-up exercises; exercises worked out according to massage and pressure point techniques of traditional Chinese medicine, e.g., setting-up exercises for the eyes

【保健球】bǎojiànqiú 放在手里来回转动的小铁球。一般为两个。也有用玉、石等做成的。health preservation balls; small iron balls rolled in the palm. Generally they come in pairs; and are also made of jade or stone.

【保洁】bǎojié 保持清洁 keep clean; sanitation:～车 sanitation vehicle; street cleaner|加强公园的～工作 increase park clean-up

【保结】bǎojié 〈旧时 *old*〉写给官府保证他人身份或行为的文书 document certifying a person's identity or actions to government authorities

【保举】bǎojǔ 向上级荐举有才或有功的人,使得到提拔任用 recommend capable or meritorious person (for office) with personal guarantee

【保龄球】bǎolíngqiú ❶ 室内体育运动项目之一。球场是用硬质木料铺成的细长水平滑道。在滑道终端设10个大瓶柱，摆成三角形。比赛者在投掷线上投球撞击瓶柱。tenpin bowling; tenpins; bowling; indoor sports game in which a ball is rolled down an alley made of hardwood at a group of 10 bottles arranged in the shape of a triangle at the end of the alley ❷ 保龄球运动使用的球，用硬质胶木制成，空心 bowling ball; hollow ball used in bowling, made of hard bakelite ‖ also 地滚球 dìgǔnqiú

【保留】bǎoliú ❶ 保存不变 remain as before; retain：遵义会议会址还～着它当年的面貌。The site of the Zunyi Meeting looks the same as it did in the past. ❷ 暂时留着不处理 lay aside for future solution; put on hold：不同的意见暂时～，下次再讨论。Let's hold these different ideas for discussion next time. ❸ 表示不赞同或有异议 have reservations; disagree：他对这个决议持～态度。He has reservations about this resolution. ❹ 留下，不拿出来 retain：他的藏书大部分都赠给国家图书馆了，自己只～了一小部分。He has donated most of his book collection to the National Library, keeping only a small part for himself.｜有意见尽量谈出来，不要～。Please speak frankly without reservation.｜老师把宝贵的经验和知识毫无～地教给学生。The teacher has passed all of his valuable experience and knowledge on to his students without withholding anything.

【保留剧目】bǎoliú jùmù 指某个剧团或主要演员演出获得成功的并保留下来以备经常演出的戏剧 repertory; repertoire; drama, opera, or episode that is successfully performed by a company or a leading actor and retained for frequent performance

【保媒】bǎo//méi 说媒；做媒 be a matchmaker; arrange a match

【保密】bǎo//mì 保守机密，不泄漏出去 maintain secrecy; keep sth. secret; confidentiality：这事对外要绝对～。This is strictly confidential.｜大家都知道了，还保什么密！Everyone already knows; no point in trying to keep it secret!

【保苗】bǎomiáo 采取措施，使地里有足够株数的幼苗，并使苗壮生长 ensure a full stand of sturdy seedlings：灌溉～，战胜旱灾。Irrigate to maintain a full stand of seedlings and overcome the drought.

【保命】bǎo//mìng 维持生命；保住性命 save one's life; survive

【保姆】bǎomǔ ❶ 受雇为人照管儿童或为人从事家务劳动的妇女 housemaid; housekeeper; female servant employed to care for children or to do housework; also 保母 bǎomǔ ❷ 保育员的旧称 old term for 保育员 bǎoyùyuán

【保票】bǎopiào same as 包票 bāopiào

【保全】bǎoquán ❶ 保住使不受损失 save from damage; preserve：～性命 preserve life｜～名誉 preserve one's reputation ❷ 保护、维修机器设备，使正常使用 maintain; keep in good working order (machines, equipment)：～工 maintenance worker

【保人】bǎo·ren 保证人 guarantor

【保山】bǎoshān 〈旧称 *old*〉保人或媒人 guarantor or matchmaker

【保墒】bǎoshāng 使土壤中保存一定的水分，以适合于农作物出苗和生长。保墒的主要方法是耙地、镇压和中耕。preserve soil moisture for sprouting and growth of crops by such major measures as harrowing, rolling and intertilling

【保释】bǎoshì （犯人）取保获释 release on bail; bail：～出狱 release on bail

【保守】bǎoshǒu ❶ 保持使不失去 guard; keep：～秘密 keep secrets ❷ 维持原状，不求改进；跟不上形势的发展（多指思想）conservative; tending or disposed to maintain status quo; (of one's way of thinking) unable to keep up with a changing situation：思想～conservative ideas (or thinking)｜计划定得有些～，要重新制定。This plan is too conservative, and must be redone.

【保送】bǎosòng 由国家、机关、学校、团体等保荐去学习（of government departments, schools, organizations) recommend sb. for admission to school (without taking the entrance examination)：～留学生 student recommended for study abroad

【保外就医】bǎo wài jiù yī 犯人在服刑期间患有严重疾病经批准取保出狱医治（prisoner) be released on bail for medical treatment in cases of serious illness

【保外执行】bǎo wài zhíxíng 犯人在服刑期间取保监外执行 serve a sentence on bail outside prison; ☞ 监外执行 jiān wài zhíxíng on p. 942

【保卫】bǎowèi 保护使不受侵犯 defend; safeguard：～祖国 defend one's country｜～和平 safeguard peace｜加强治安～工作 strengthen public order and security

【保温】bǎowēn 保持温度，通常指使热不散出去 maintain temperature by preserving heat：～杯 thermos mug｜积雪可以～保墒。Snow preserves soil moisture and prevents freezing.

【保温杯】bǎowēnbēi 有保温作用的杯子。外壳用塑料、金属等做成，内装瓶胆，盖子可以扣紧 thermos mug, made from a plastic or metal outer case and a glass liner, with a tight lid

【保温瓶】bǎowēnpíng 日常用品，外面有竹蔑、铁皮、塑料等做成的壳，内装瓶胆。瓶胆由双层玻璃制成，夹层中的两面镀上银等金属，中间抽成真空，瓶口有塞子，可以在较长时间内保持瓶内的温度。盛热水的通常叫暖水瓶；盛冷食的通常叫冰瓶。vacuum flask (or bottle); thermos; article of daily use composed of an outer shell made of plaited bamboo, iron sheeting or plastic, with a cylindrical container inside made of double-layered glass with a vacuum in between and plated with silvery on both sides. The flask is closed with a stopper and can maintain a constant temperature inside for considerable periods of time. These for storing hot water are called 暖水瓶 nuǎnshuǐpíng, and those for cold food are called 冰瓶 bīngpíng.

【保鲜】bǎoxiān 保持蔬菜、水果、肉类等易腐食物的新鲜 keep vegetables, fruit, meat, etc. fresh; preserve freshness: ～纸 plastic cling-foil; handi-wrap | 食品～keep foodstuffs fresh | 改进水产品～技术 improve the technology for keeping aquatic products fresh

【保险】bǎoxiǎn ❶ 集中分散的社会资金,补偿因自然灾害、意外事故或人身伤亡而造成的损失的方法。参加保险的人或单位,向保险机构按期缴纳一定数量的费用,保险机构对在保险责任范围内所受的损失负赔偿责任。insurance; system for pooling scattered social resources to compensate people for losses caused by natural disasters, accidents, personal injuries or death; The insured individual or organization pays a regular premium, and the insurance company is responsible for indemnifying them for losses within the specified contingencies. ❷ 稳妥可靠 sure; safe: 这样做可不～。It's not safe to do this. ❸ 担保 assurance; for sure: 你依我的话,～不会出错。If you follow my advice, I can assure you nothing will go wrong.

【保险刀】bǎoxiǎndāo (～儿 bǎoxiǎndāor) 刮胡子的用具,刀片安在特制的刀架上,使用时不会刮伤皮肤 safety razor; razor provided with a guard for the blade to prevent cutting the skin; also 安全剃刀 ānquán tìdāo

【保险灯】bǎoxiǎndēng ❶ 一种带灯罩的大型手提煤油灯 safety lamp; large portable kerosene lamp with a lamp shade ❷〈方 *dial.*〉汽灯 gas lamp

【保险法】bǎoxiǎnfǎ 有关保险的机构、管理和保险关系当事人权利、义务等方面的法规 insurance law; laws governing the organization and management of insurance, and stipulating the rights and obligations of parties entering into insurance contracts

【保险柜】bǎoxiǎnguì 用中间夹有石棉的两层铁板做成的并装有特制的锁的柜子,可以防盗、防火 strongbox; safe; fire- and theft-proof chest made from two layers of iron plate with asbestos in between, and equipped with special locks

【保险丝】bǎoxiǎnsī 电路中保险装置用的导线,一般用铅、锡等熔点低的合金或细铜丝、铜银合金丝制成。当电路中的电流超过限度时,丝就烧断,电路也就断开了,可以防止发生火灾或烧毁电器。fuse; fuse-wire; electric circuit safety device consisting of a metal conductor of low melting point, such as lead or tin, thin wire of copper, or alloy of copper and silver, that melts and interrupts the circuit to prevent fires or burnout of electric appliances when the current exceeds a particular amperage

【保险箱】bǎoxiǎnxiāng 小型的保险柜,样子像箱子 strongbox; small safe that looks like a box

【保修】bǎoxiū ❶ 商店或工厂售出的某些商品,在规定限期内免费修理 sales warranty; guarantee by shop or factory to provide free repair service within a certain period of time: 本店所售钟表,～一年。Clocks and watches sold in this shop have a one year's guarantee. ❷ 保养修理;维修 maintenance, repair: 超额完成车辆～任务 over-fulfil the quota of vehicle maintenance

【保养】bǎoyǎng ❶ 保护调养 take good care of one's health: ～身体 health preservation ❷ 保护修理,使保持正常状态 maintain; keep in good repair: ～车辆 maintenance of vehicles | 机器～得好,可以延长使用年限。Keeping machinery in good repair can prolong its service life.

【保有】bǎoyǒu 拥有 possess; have: ～土地 possess land | 作者～修订的权利。The author reserves the right of revision.

【保佑】bǎoyòu 迷信的人称神力保护和帮助 blessing and protection of deity

【保育】bǎoyù 经心照管幼儿,使好好成长 child care; meticulous care of children so they grow up properly

【保育员】bǎoyùyuán 幼儿园和托儿所里负责照管儿童生活的工作人员 child-care worker; nurse in kindergarten or nursery

【保育院】bǎoyùyuàn 为保护、教育失去父母或父母无法照管的儿童而设的机构,内有托儿所、幼儿园、小学等 nursery school; organization set up for protection and education of orphans and children whose parents cannot do so, consisting of nursery, kindergarten, and primary school

【保障】bǎozhàng ❶ 保护(生命、财产、权利等),使不受侵犯和破坏 protect (life, property, rights, etc.) from damage or violation: ～人身安全 ensure personal safety | ～公民权利 guarantee citizen's rights ❷ 起保障作用的事物 guarantee: 安全是生产的～。Safety is the guarantee of production.

【保证】bǎozhèng ❶ 担保,担保做到 pledge; guarantee; assure; ensure: 我们～提前完成任务。We pledge to fulfil our tasks ahead of schedule. ❷ 确保既定的要求和标准,不打折扣 guarantee; promise to meet requirements and standards to the letter, without reservation: ～产品质量 guarantee the quality of products

|～科研时间 guarantee the time needed for scientific research ❸ 作为担保的事物 that which guarantees：安定团结是我们取得胜利的～。Stability and unity are the guarantees of our victory.

【保证金】bǎozhèngjīn ❶ 为了保证履行某种义务而缴纳的一定数量的钱 earnest money; cash deposit; payment to guarantee the performance of certain obligations ❷〈旧时 *old*〉被告人为了保证不逃避审讯而向法院或警察机关缴纳的一定数量的钱 bail; payment by the accused to court or police to guarantee due appearance in court

【保证人】bǎozhèngrén ❶ 保证别人的行为符合要求的人 guarantor; one who guarantees another's actions ❷ 担保被告人不逃避审讯并随传随到的第三人 guarantor; third party who guarantees the due appearance of the accused in court ❸ 法律上指担保债务人履行债务的第三人 guarantor; third party who guarantees the debtor will repay the debt

【保证书】bǎozhèngshū 为了保证做到某件事情而写成的书面材料 written pledge; guarantee; guaranty; letter of guarantee

【保值】bǎozhí 指保持货币购买力的原有价值 maintain the original value of the monetary purchasing power：～储蓄 deposits with principal and interest safeguarded against price increases

【保重】bǎozhòng (希望别人)注意身体健康 to express concern about another's health, take care of oneself：～身体。Take good care of yourself.｜只身在外，请多～。You are alone and away from home, so please look after yourself.

【保状】bǎozhuàng〈旧时 *old*〉法庭要保证人填写的有一定格式的保证书 pledge form filled out by a guarantor as required by the court

【保准】bǎozhǔn ❶ 可以信任；可靠 reliable; dependable; trustworthy：他说话不～。One cannot rely on his words.｜这片洼地要是改成稻田，收成就～了。Good yields are guaranteed if this low-lying land is transformed into rice paddies. ❷ 担保；担保做到 guarantee; assure; ensure：～办到 guarantee to get sth. done｜这是我的缺点，我～改。This is my weakness and I will correct it.

鸨 bǎo ❶ 鸟类的一属，头小，颈长，背部平，尾巴短，不善于飞，能涉水。大鸨就属于这一属。bustard (*Gruiformes*); any bird of the *Otididae* family featuring small head, long neck, flat back, and short tail, not good at flying but capable of wading across waters. Great bustard belongs to this family. ❷ 指鸨母 procuress：老～madam

【鸨母】bǎomǔ 开设妓院的女人 woman who runs a brothel; procuress; madam; also 鸨儿 bǎo'ér or 老鸨 lǎobǎo

葆[1] bǎo ❶〈书 *fml.*〉保持；保护 preserve; nurture：永～青春 keep alive the vigour of youth ❷ (Bǎo) 姓 a surname

葆[2] bǎo〈书 *fml.*〉草茂盛 luxuriant grass

堡 bǎo 堡垒 fort; fortress：碉～blockhouse｜地～bunker｜桥头～bridgehead; bridge tower

☞ bǔ on p. 155 and pù on p. 1503

【堡垒】bǎolěi ❶ 在冲要地点作防守用的坚固建筑物 fort; fortress; stronghold; blockhouse; solid building used for military defence at strategic location ❷〈比喻 *fig.*〉难于攻破的事物或不容易接受进步思想的人 diehard; hard nut to crack; person not willing to accept progressive ideas：封建～feudal diehard｜科学～scientific fortress｜顽固～(比喻十分顽固的人) (fig.) diehard

【堡寨】bǎozhài 四周有栅栏或围墙的村子 village fortified by paling or wall

褓(緥) bǎo 包婴儿的被子 swaddling clothes; ☞ 襁褓 qiǎngbǎo on p. 1547

bào (ㄅㄠˋ)

报(報) bào ❶ 告诉 report; announce; declare：～告 report｜～名 enter one's name; sign up｜～账 render an account; submit an expense account ❷ 回答 reply; respond; reciprocate：～友人书 a letter in reply to a friend ◇～以热烈的掌声 respond with warm applause ❸ 报答 recompense; requite：～效 render service to repay sb.'s kindness｜～酬 remuneration｜～恩 repay a debt of gratitude ❹ 报复 revenge：～仇 avenge｜～怨 complain ❺ 报应 retribution; judgement：现世～retribution in this life ❻ same as 报纸 bàozhǐ ①：日～daily newspaper｜机关～the official newspaper (of a political party, a government, etc.)｜登～publish in the newspaper｜看～read the newspaper ❼ 指某些刊物 periodical; journal：画～pictorial｜学～learned journal ❽ 指用文字报道消息或发表意见的某些东西 bulletin; report：喜～bulletin of good news｜海～playbill; poster｜黑板～blackboard newspaper ❾ 指电报 telegram; cable：发～send a telegraph

【报案】bào//àn 把违反法律、危害社会治安的事件报告给公安或司法机关 report illegal behaviour or incident jeopardizing public security to the public security authorities or the judicial department

【报表】bàobiǎo 向上级报告情况的表格 forms for reporting statistics, etc. to one's superior; report forms：生产进度～progress chart of production

B

【报偿】bàocháng 报答和补偿 repay; recompense:你能痛改前非,就是对老人最好的~。To thoroughly rectify your errors is the best way to repay your parents.

【报呈】bàochéng 用公文向上级报告 submit (a report) to one's superior:~上级备案 report the matter to a higher level for the record

【报仇】bào//chóu 采取行动,打击仇敌 revenge; avenge:~雪恨 avenge oneself; take revenge

【报酬】bào·chou 由于使用别人的劳动、物件等而付给别人的钱或实物 reward; remuneration; pay; pay for a service or use of an object:种花栽树,是我应尽的义务,不要~。Planting trees and flowers is my duty, and I don't want any payment.

【报答】bàodá 用实际行动来表示感谢 repay with action; requite:以优异的学习成绩~老师的辛勤培育。Repay the hard work and guidance of one's teacher with excellent academic results.

【报单】bàodān ❶ 运货报税的单据 declaration form for transported goods ❷〈旧时 *old*〉向得官、升官、考试得中的人家送去的喜报 notice sent to the home of a candidate announcing official appointment, promotion or success in an imperial examination; also 报条 bàotiáo

【报导】bàodǎo same as 报道 bàodào

【报到】bào//dào 向组织报告自己已经来到 report for duty; check in; register:新生今天开始~。The new students start registering today.

【报道】bàodào ❶ 通过报纸、杂志、广播、电视或其他形式把新闻告诉群众 report (news); cover in newspaper, magazine, on radio, television or in other ways:~消息 news dispatch ❷ 用书面或广播、电视形式发表的新闻稿 news report in the form of writing, or radio/television broadcast:他写了一篇关于小麦丰收的~。He wrote a report on the bumper wheat harvest.

【报德】bào//dé 对受到的恩德予以报答 repay a kindness:以德~ repay a kindness with kindness

【报端】bàoduān 报纸版面上的某部分 space in a newspaper:征稿启事已见~。The notice calling for contributions has appeared in the newspaper.

【报恩】bào//ēn 由于受到恩惠而予以报答 pay a debt of gratitude:知恩~know the kindness and repay it

【报废】bào//fèi 设备、器物等因不能继续使用或不合格而作废 discard as useless; reject; scrap:由于计算失误,这批零件全~了。Due to miscalculation, this whole batch of spare parts must be discarded.

【报复】bào·fù 打击批评自己或损害自己利益的人 make reprisals; retaliate against those who have criticised one or who have jeopardised one's interests:打击~attack vindictively|受到~suffer retaliation|~情绪 vengeful sentiments

【报告】bàogào ❶ 把事情或意见正式告诉上级或群众 report; report events or opinions to one's superior or to the public; make known:你应当把事情的经过向领导~。You should report what happened to the higher authorities.|大会主席~了开会宗旨。The chairman of the conference spoke about its purpose. ❷ 用口头或书面的形式向上级或群众所做的正式陈述 written or oral declaration made to a superior or to the public:总结~summary report|动员~mobilization speech

【报告文学】bàogào wénxué 文学体裁,散文中的一类,是通讯、速写、特写等的统称。以现实生活中具有典型意义的真人真事为题材,经过适当的艺术加工而成,具有新闻特点。reportage; form of literature, a category of prose, and a general term for news story, literary sketch and feature story, based on illustrative real events and people, but described with some artistic license

【报关】bào//guān 货物、行李或船舶等进出口时,向海关申报,办理进出口手续 declaration to customs of cargo, luggage or ships, and completion of import/export formalities; apply to customs:~单 declaration form|这批货已经报过关了。This batch of goods has been declared to customs.

【报馆】bàoguǎn 报社的俗称 popular term for 报社 bàoshè

【报国】bào//guó 为国家效力尽忠 dedicate oneself to the service of one's country:以身~ lay down one's life for one's country|精忠~ serve one's country with total loyalty

【报话】bàohuà ❶ 用无线电通讯工具传话 transmit message by a telecommunications device:~员 radio operator|~机 walkie-talkie ❷ 用无线电通讯工具传的话 radio message:他一上午收发了二十份~。During the morning he received and dispatched 20 radio messages.

【报话机】bàohuàjī 无线电通讯工具,可以用来收发电报或通话 walkie-talkie; apparatus for radio communication used to converse or send/receive telegrams

【报价】bào//jià ❶ 卖方提出商品的售价 quoted price offered by seller:~单 quotation sheet|外贸商品应统一~。Commodities for foreign trade should quote the same price. ❷ 提出所需的价款 offer; proposal:四家研制单位投标,中标单位的~比其他三家要低一百多万元。Of the four developers who submitted bids, the winning offer is over one million yuan lower than the other three.

【报捷】bào//jié 报告胜利的消息 report a success; announce a victory

【报警】bào//jǐng 向治安机关报告危急情况或向有关方面发出紧急信号 report an emergency to the police; send an urgent message to the appropriate department: 发生火灾要及时~。Whenever a fire takes place report it to the police immediately.

【报刊】bàokān 报纸和杂志的总称 general term for newspapers and periodicals

【报考】bàokǎo 报名投考 sign up for an examination: ~师范学院 register for the entrance examinations to the normal college | 有一千多名学生前来~。More than 1,000 students came to register for the examinations.

【报矿】bào//kuàng 向有关部门报告发现矿石或蕴藏矿产的地方 report to the concerned department about the discovery of ores or the location of mineral deposits

【报名】bào//míng 把自己的名字报告给主管的人或机关、团体等,表示愿意参加某种活动或组织 give one's name to the person, organization or institute in charge; sign up: ~投考 sign up for an examination | ~参赛 register for a competition | 你先替我报上名。Sign up for me.

【报幕】bào//mù 文艺演出时在每个节目演出之前向观众报告节目名称、作者和演员姓名,有时也简单地介绍节目内容 announce each item in a variety show, including the title, author, and performer, sometimes with a brief description: ~员 announcer

【报批】bàopī 报请上级批准 report (or submit) a request to the higher authorities for approval: 履行~手续 go through the report and approval procedures

【报屁股】bàopì·gu 指报纸版面上的最后的位置(含诙谐意 humor.) last page of a newspaper: ~文章 a last-page article

【报聘】bàopìn 〈旧时 *old*〉指代表本国政府到友邦回访 return visit to a friendly nation on behalf of one's government

【报请】bàoqǐng 用书面报告向上级请示或请求 (in official communications) submit a written report requesting instructions: ~上级批准 submit a written document to superior authorities requesting for approval

【报人】bàorén 指从事报刊工作的人 newspaper journalist: 老~ veteran newspaper journalist | 我以~的身份前去采访。I covered the event as a veteran journalist.

【报丧】bào//sāng 把去世的消息通知死者的亲友 inform relatives and friends of the death of a person

【报社】bàoshè 编辑和出版报纸的机构 press; general office of a newspaper

【报失】bàoshī 向治安机关或有关部门报告丢失了财物,请求查找 report the loss of sth. to police or the authorities concerned and request search

【报时】bào//shí 报告时间,特指广播电台向收听者或电话局向询问者报告准确的时间 give the correct time, esp. over radio or telephone to listeners or enquirers

【报数】bào//shù 报告数目,多指排队时每人依次报一个数目,以查点人数 number off; count off one by one in a line to check the number of people

【报条】bàotiáo same as 报单 bàodān ②

【报亭】bàotíng 出售报纸、期刊等的像亭子的小房子 kiosk selling newspapers and periodicals

【报童】bàotóng 在街头卖报的儿童 newsboy; children who sell newspaper in the streets

【报头】bàotóu 报纸第一版、壁报、黑板报等上头标报名、期数等的部分 masthead (of newspaper, etc.); part of a newspaper, wall bulletin, or blackboard newspaper that gives the title and issue number, etc.

【报务】bàowù 拍发和抄收电报的业务 send and receive telegraphs: ~员 telegraph operator; radio operator

【报喜】bào//xǐ 报告喜庆的消息 announce good news; report success

【报销】bàoxiāo ❶ 把领用款项或收支账目开列清单,报告上级核销 submit an expense account; apply for reimbursement: 车费可以凭票~。Bus fares can be reimbursed by handing in the tickets. ❷ 把用坏作废的物件报告销账 report damaged or rejected articles so they can be struck off the list ❸ 〈比喻 *fig.*〉从现有的人或物中除掉(多含诙谐意 oft. humor.) write off; wipe out: 桌上的菜他一个人全给~了。He devoured all the dishes on the table. | 我们两面夹攻,一个班的敌人很快就~了。We closed in from both sides, and quickly wiped out a squad of the enemy forces.

【报晓】bàoxiǎo 用声音使人知道天已经亮了(of cock, bell, etc.) herald the break of day; be a harbinger of dawn: 晨鸡~。The crowing of roosters at dawn heralded the break of day. | 远远传来~的钟声。From afar came the chimes of a bell announcing the break of day.

【报效】bàoxiào 为报答对方的恩情而为对方尽力 render service to repay sb.'s kindness: ~祖国 serve the country

【报信】bào//xìn 把消息通知人 notify; inform: 通风~ furnish secret information; tip sb. off | 你先给他报个信。You tip him off first.

【报修】bàoxiū 设备等损坏或发生故障,告知有关部门前来修理 report breakdown (of equipment) to relevant department for repair: 住房漏水,住户可向房管部门~。If there is a leakage, the resident may report to the housing administrative department for repair.

【报应】bào·yìng 〈佛教用语 *Budd.*〉原指种善因得善果，种恶因得恶果，后来专指种恶因得恶果 good is rewarded with good, evil with evil; retribution; due punishment

B

【报怨】bào//yuàn 对所怨恨的人做出反应 response made to resented person：以德～repay evil with good

【报站】bào//zhàn 乘务员向乘客报告车、船等所到站和即将到达的前方一站的站名 announce the name of a bus stop (railway station, harbour)：提前～，方便乘客。Announce the name of a bus stop in advance for the convenience of the passengers.

【报章】bàozhāng 报纸(总称) newspapers (collect.)：～杂志 newspapers and magazines

【报账】bào//zhàng 把领用或经手的款项的使用经过和结果报告主管人 render an account; submit an expense account; apply for reimbursement to the person in charge

【报纸】bàozhǐ ❶ 以国内外社会、政治、经济、文化等新闻为主要内容的散页的定期出版物，一般指日报 newspaper; printed loose leaf pages issued periodically containing domestic and international news of social, political, economic and cultural nature ❷ 纸张的一种，用来印报或一般书刊 newsprint; paper used for printing newspapers or ordinary books; also 白报纸 báibàozhǐ or 新闻纸 xīnwénzhǐ

【报子】bào·zi ❶ 报告消息的人；探子(多见于旧戏曲、小说 oft. in old drama and fiction) informer; detective ❷〈旧时 *old*〉给得官、升官、考试得中的人家报喜而讨赏钱的人 man who brought news of official appointment, promotion, or success in imperial examinations to the home of the candidate, in exchange for a tip ❸ same as 报单 bàodān ②：贴～put up a poster ❹ 指海报或广告 playbill, advertisement：新戏的～一贴，轰动了全城。Posters announcing the new play have caused a sensation in the city.

刨(鉋、鑤) bào ❶ 刨子或刨床 plane; planer; planing machine：～刃儿 plane iron|牛头～shaping machine|平～flat plane|槽～grooving plane ❷ 用刨子或刨床刮平木料或钢材等 make wood or steel smooth by use of a plane or planing machine：～木头 plane a wood|这张桌面没有～平。The surface of this table has not been planed smooth.

☞ páo on p.1448

【刨冰】bàobīng 一种冷食，把冰刨成碎片，加上果汁等，现做现吃 shave ice; cold snack of shaved ice flavoured with fruit juice：菠萝块儿～shave ice with pineapple cubes

【刨床】bàochuáng ❶ 金属切削机床，用来加工金属材料的平面和各种直线的成型面 planer; planing machine; metal cutting machine, used to process the surface of metal materials and flat shapes ❷ 刨子上的木制部分 the wooden part of a plane

【刨刀】bàodāo ❶ 刨床上用的刀具，结构跟车刀相似 planer tool, similar to a lathe tool in structure ❷ 木工用的机械刨的刀具，片状，扁长 flat, narrow and long cutting tool of carpenter's planing machine ❸ 刨子上刮削木料的部分 plane iron; also 刨铁 bàotiě or 刨刃儿 bàorènr

【刨工】bàogōng ❶ 用刨床切削金属材料的工种 planing; process of operating a planing machine to cut metal material ❷ 做上述工作的技术工人 planing machine operator; planer

【刨花】bàohuā 刨木料时刨下来的薄片，多呈卷状 wood shavings; thin layers planed off wood, usu. in rolls

【刨花板】bàohuābǎn 用刨花和经过加工的碎木料拌以胶合剂压制成的板材，可以制造家具、包装箱等 shaving board; board made by pressing wood shavings and pulverized wood mixed with adhesive, used as a material for making furniture, packaging crates, etc.

【刨子】bào·zi 刮平木料用的手工工具 plane; carpenter's tool for shaving a wood surface in order to make it smooth or level

抱[1] bào ❶ 用手臂围住 hold or carry in the arms; clasp in the arms; hug; embrace：母亲～着孩子。The mother is holding the child in her arms. ❷ 初次得到(儿子或孙子) have one's first child or grandchild：听说你～孙子了。I hear that you've had a grandson. ❸ 领养(孩子) adopt (a child)：这孩子是～的，不是她生的。This is her adopted child. ❹〈方 *dial.*〉结合在一起 hang together; band up：大家～成团，就会有力量。By banding together we will be powerful. ❺〈方 *dial.*〉(衣、鞋)大小合适 (of clothing, shoes) fit well：这件衣服～身儿。This jacket fits me perfectly.|这双鞋～脚儿。These shoes fit nicely. ❻ 心里存着(想法、意见) cherish; harbour：青年人都～着远大的理想。All young people cherish lofty ideals.|对他的这种决定，许多人～有看法。With regard to that decision of his, many people be to differ. ❼〈量词 *classifier*〉表示两臂合围的量 armful：一～草 an armful of straw

抱[2](菢) bào 孵(卵成雏) hatch (eggs); brood：～小鸡儿 hatch (out) chickens|～窝 brood; hatch; sit (on eggs)

【抱病】bào//bìng 有病在身 be ill; be in poor health：～工作 go on working despite poor health

【抱不平】bào bùpíng 看见别人受到不公平的待遇，产生强烈的愤慨情绪 be ready to intervene on behalf of an injured party：打～ champion the cause of a person who has suffered a wrong|他心里很替老王～。He felt indignant at the gross injustice done to Lao Wang.

【抱残守缺】bào cán shǒu quē 形容保守不知改进 be conservative; be a stick-in-the-mud; stick to old-fashioned ideas and refuse to change; cherish the old and preserve the outmoded

【抱粗腿】bào cūtuǐ 〈比喻 *fig.*〉攀附有权势的人 latch on to the rich and powerful; throw oneself under the protection of sb. of influence or power; attach oneself to bigwigs

【抱佛脚】bào fójiǎo 谚语:'平时不烧香,急来抱佛脚'。原来比喻平时没有联系,临时慌忙恳求,后来多指平时没有准备,临时慌忙应付。offering no incense to Buddha when things go well and beseech his help only when in need (a proverb); (formerly fig.) seek help from persons whom one does not ordinarily maintain contact; make a last-minute effort

【抱负】bàofù 远大的志向 aspiration; ambition; ideal: 有～ have aspirations; cherish ambitions|～不凡 have a great life ambition; cherish extraordinary ideals; entertain lofty aspirations

【抱憾】bàohàn 心中存有遗憾的事 repent; be filled with remorse: ～终生 be plagued by lifelong remorse

【抱恨】bàohèn 心中存有恨事 be overwhelmed with remorse: ～终天(含恨一辈子) be tormented by lifelong regret or resentment; be eaten up with eternal sorrow

【抱脚儿】bàojiǎor 〈方 *dial.*〉鞋的大小、肥瘦正合脚型 (of shoes) fit perfectly

【抱愧】bàokuì 心中有愧 feel ashamed: 在你困难的时候没能尽力,实在～。I feel ashamed of myself at being unable to help you out at this difficult time.

【抱歉】bàoqiàn 心中不安,觉着对不住别人 be sorry; regret: 因事负约,深感～。I deeply regret having to cancel our appointment.

【抱屈】bàoqū 因受委屈而心中不舒畅 feel wronged; feel aggrieved; also 抱委屈 bào wěi·qu

【抱拳】bào// quán 〈旧时 *old*〉一种礼节,一手握拳,另一手抱着拳头,合拢在胸前 (way of greeting between men) make an obeisance by cupping one hand in the other at chest level

【抱厦】bàoshà 房屋前面加出来的门廊,也指后面毗连着的小房子 Chinese-style portico; lean-to at the back of a house

【抱身儿】bàoshēnr 〈方 *dial.*〉衣服的大小、肥瘦正合体型 (of clothes) body-hugging; fit nicely

【抱头鼠窜】bào tóu shǔ cuàn 形容急忙逃走的狼狈相 put one's head into one's hands and scurry away; clasp one's head and scurry away in a panic; flee; turn tail and scuttle off like a frightened mouse

【抱团儿】bào// tuánr 抱成一团;结成一伙 hang together; stick together; gang up: 咱们只能～,不能散伙。We must stick together and never be divided. |几个人死死地抱成团儿。A few people stuck resolutely together.

【抱委屈】bào wěi·qu 抱屈 feel wronged; feel aggrieved

【抱窝】bào// wō 孵卵成雏 sit (on eggs); brood; hatch: 母鸡～。The hen is sitting on her eggs.

【抱薪救火】bàoxīn jiùhuǒ 〈比喻 *fig.*〉因为方法不对,虽然有心消灭祸害,结果反而使祸害扩大 take faggots to put out a fire — exacerbate a desperate situation by using a wrong method to remedy it; take counterproductive measures

【抱养】bàoyǎng 把别人家的孩子抱来当自己的孩子抚养 adopt (a child): 他们无儿无女,～了一个孩子。Being childless, they adopted a child.

【抱腰】bàoyāo 〈方 *dial.*〉〈比喻 *fig.*〉做他人的后援,撑腰 support sb.; back sb. up

【抱冤】bàoyuān 感到冤枉 feel wronged; bear a grudge

【抱怨】bào·yuàn 心中不满,数说别人不对;埋怨 complain; grumble; grouse: 做错事只能怪自己,不能～别人。You have only yourself to blame for this mistake and should not grumble about other people.

【抱柱对儿】bàozhùduìr 挂在柱子上的对联,用木板制成,稍曲,与柱体相合 a pair of slightly curved boards inscribed with antithetical couplets that are hung on pillars

趵 bào 〈方 *dial.*〉跳跃 spring forth; bounce: ～突泉(在济南) Baotu Spring (in Jinan, Shandong Province)

☞ bō on p.146

豹 bào ❶ 哺乳动物,像虎而较小,身上有很多斑点或花纹。性凶猛,能上树,捕食其他兽类,伤害人畜。常见的有金钱豹、云豹等。leopard (*Panthera pardus*); panther; ferocious mammal similar to, but smaller than a tiger, covered with spots or markings, capable of climbing trees, and preying on other animals and even humans. Common varieties include *Panthera pardus* and clouded leopard; also 豹子 bào·zi ❷ (Bào) 姓 a surname

【豹猫】bàomāo 哺乳动物,形状跟猫相似,头部有黑色条纹,躯干有黑褐色的斑点,尾部有横纹。性凶猛,吃鸟、鼠、蛇、蛙等小动物。毛皮可以做衣服。leopard cat (*Felis bengalensis Kerr*); ferocious catlike mammal with black stripes on its head, black-and-brown spots on its body, and horizontal stripes on its tail, feeding on small animals such as mice, snakes, frogs, and birds, its fur used to make clothes; also 山猫 shānmāo, 狸猫 límāo and 狸子 lí·zi

【豹头环眼】bào tóu huán yǎn 形容人的长相威

武勇猛 have a head like a leopard and big, round eyes; have a well-formed forehead and round eyes; (of a person) look courageous and powerful

【豹子】bào•zi 豹 leopard; panther

鲍 bào ❶ 鲍鱼 abalone ❷ (Bào) 姓 a surname

【鲍鱼】[1] bàoyú 〈书 *fml.*〉咸鱼 salted fish: 如入～之肆(肆:铺子),久而不闻其臭。If you stay long enough in a fish market, you will soon get used to the stench — long exposure to a bad environment accustoms one to evil ways.

【鲍鱼】[2] bàoyú 软体动物,贝壳椭圆形,生活在海中。肉可食。贝壳中医入药,称石决明。abalone (*Haliotis spp.*); sea mollusk whose oval shell is used in traditional Chinese medicine, and whose meat is edible; also 鳆鱼 fùyú

暴[1] bào ❶ 突然而且猛烈 sudden and fierce: ～雨 downpour; torrential rain; thunder storm | ～病 sudden attack of a disease | ～怒 fury; violent rage | ～饮～食 immoderate drinking and eating ❷ 凶狠;残酷 cruel; savage; violent; tyrannical: ～徒 rioter; ruffian; thug | ～行 atrocity; outrage; ferocity | 施～ use violence ❸ 残暴的人 cruel, ruthless person: 安良除～drive out the cruel and ruthless so that people may live in peace ❹ 急躁 hot-tempered; short-tempered: 他的脾气很～。He has a hot (or short) temper. ❺ (Bào) 姓 a surname

暴[2] bào ❶ 鼓起来;突出 protrude; stick out; stand out: 急得头上的青筋都～出来了 be so worried that the veins on one's forehead stand out ❷ 露出来;显现 expose; reveal: ～露 expose; reveal; lay bare; bring to light

暴[3] bào 〈书 *fml.*〉糟蹋 ruin; spoil: 自～自弃 give oneself up for lost

☞ 曝 pù on p. 1503

【暴病】bàobìng 突然发作来势很凶的病 sudden attack of disease

【暴跌】bàodiē (物价、声誉等)大幅度下降 (of price, reputation, etc.) fall steeply; drop; slump: 谷价～ sharp fall in grain prices | 声价～ one's reputation take a dive

【暴动】bàodòng 阶级或集团为了破坏当时的政治制度、社会秩序而采取的武装行动 rebellion; uprising; insurrection; class or group's armed resistance against the establishment

【暴发】bàofā ❶ 突然发财或得势(多含贬义 oft. derog.) suddenly become rich or rise to an important position: ～户 nouveau riche; upstart ❷ 突然发作 break out: 山洪～。Torrents of water rushed down the mountain.

【暴风】bàofēng ❶ 气象学上指 11 级风 (meteorol.) storm (force 11 wind); hurricane; ☞ 风级 fēngjí on p. 579 ❷ 泛指猛烈而急速的风 general term for wind storm; tempest: ～骤雨 violent storm; tempest; hurricane

【暴风雪】bàofēngxuě 大而急的风雪。有的地区叫白毛风。blizzard; in some places it is called 白毛风 báimáofēng

【暴风雨】bàofēngyǔ 大而急的风雨 rainstorm; storm; tempest ◇革命的～ a storm of revolution; a revolutionary tempest

【暴风骤雨】bào fēng zhòu yǔ 来势急遽而猛烈的风雨 violent storm; hurricane; tempest; 〈比喻 *fig.*〉声势浩大、发展迅猛的群众运动 gigantic and rapidly expanding mass movement

【暴光】bào//guāng same as 曝光 bào//guāng

【暴洪】bàohóng 来势猛而急的洪水 flash flood; sudden violent flood

【暴虎冯河】bào hǔ píng hé 〈比喻 *fig.*〉有勇无谋,冒险蛮干 act with reckless courage; be brave but not resourceful; bold but imprudent (暴虎 *bao hu*: 空手打虎 fight a tiger with bare hands; 冯河 *ping he*: 徒步渡河 wade across a river on foot)

【暴君】bàojūn 暴虐的君主 tyrant; despot

【暴库】bàokù 仓库里货物多到没有空地存放的程度 (of unsold goods) over-stocked warehouse; have a heavy surplus: 销路不畅,产品严重～。Impediments on the market have resulted in a glut of products.

【暴力】bàolì ❶ 强制的力量;武力 violence, force ❷ 特指国家的强制力量 force or violence as exercised by the state: 军队、警察、法庭对于敌对阶级是一种～。The armed forces, police, and courts are organs of force against hostile classes.

【暴利】bàolì 用不正当的手段在短时间内获得的巨额利润 exorbitant profits; sudden, huge profits; windfall; bonanza: 牟取～ seek to reap colossal profits; profiteer

【暴戾】bàolì 〈书 *fml.*〉粗暴乖张;残酷凶恶 savage; ruthless and tyrannical; cruel and fierce: 脾气～ have a fierce temper | ～成性 be violent-tempered; be ruthless and tyrannical

【暴戾恣睢】bàolì zìsuī 形容残暴凶狠,任意胡为 savage and despotic

【暴烈】bàoliè ❶ 暴躁刚烈 violent; fierce: 性情～ be hot-tempered; have a fiery temper ❷ 凶暴猛烈 fierce; violent; brutal: ～的行动 act of violence and brutality

【暴露】bàolù (隐蔽的事物、缺陷、矛盾、问题等)显露出来 expose; reveal; bring to light; lay bare (hidden matters, defects, contradictions, problems, etc.): ～目标 reveal one's objective | ～无遗 be thoroughly exposed; be completely unmasked

【暴露文学】bàolù wénxué 指只揭露社会黑暗面,而不能指出光明前景的文学作品,如清末的《官场现形记》等 literature of exposure; muckraking literature; literary work exposing the seamy side of society, but failing to point out the way out, such as the late-Qing novel *Revealing True Colours of Officialdom*

【暴乱】bàoluàn 破坏社会秩序的武装骚动 rebellion; riot; revolt; armed disturbance that undermines public order: 武装～ armed rebellion | 平定～ put down a riot; suppress (or quell or put down) a rebellion

【暴民】bàomín 参与暴动或暴乱的人 rioter; mob; person taking part in a riot or rebellion

【暴怒】bàonù 极端愤怒 violent rage; fury

【暴虐】bàonüè ❶ 凶恶残酷 brutal; tyrannical; despotic: ～无道 brutal and immoral ❷〈书 *fml.*〉凶恶残暴地对待 treat savagely; ride roughshod over: ～无辜 treat innocent people brutally | ～百姓 ride roughshod over the people

【暴晒】bàoshài 在强烈的阳光下久晒 be exposed to the sun (for a long time): 烈日～ exposed to the scorching sun | 洗好的丝绸衣服不宜～。Freshly washed silk clothes should not be exposed to the sun.

【暴尸】bàoshī 死在外面尸体没有收殓埋藏 leave a dead body unburied; exhibit a corpse: ～街头 leave one's dead body on the street

【暴殄天物】bào tiǎn tiān wù 任意糟蹋东西: recklessly waste what Mother Nature has provided; be recklessly wasteful of Nature's bounty (殄 *tian*: 灭绝 extinct; 天物 *tian wu*: 指自然界的鸟兽草木等 things that Mother Nature has provided, such as birds, animals and plants)

【暴跳】bàotiào 猛烈地跳脚,形容大怒的样子 stamp with fury: 稍不如意,就～起来 fly into a rage at the slightest provocation

【暴跳如雷】bào tiào rú léi 跳着脚喊叫,像打雷一样。形容大怒的样子。stamp with fury; be in a thundering (or towering) rage; fly into a violent temper

【暴突】bàotū 鼓起来;突出 protruding; bulging: 青筋～ bulging blue veins | 气得两眼～ eyes that bulge with rage

【暴徒】bàotú 用强暴手段迫害别人、扰乱社会秩序的坏人 rioter; ruffian; thug; undesirable person whose brutality persecutes others and upsets the social order

【暴行】bàoxíng 凶恶残酷的行为 outrage; atrocity; ferocity: 血腥～ bloody outrages | 书中写下了侵略者烧杀掳掠的～。This book records all the burning, killing, looting and other atrocities committed by the invaders.

【暴雨】bàoyǔ ❶ 我国指 24 小时内降雨量在 50－100 毫米之间的雨 rain 50－100 millimetres in precipitation in 24 hours ❷ 大而急的雨 downpour; rainstorm; torrential rain

【暴躁】bàozào 遇事好发急,不能控制感情 irritable; irascible, hot-tempered; short-tempered: 性情～ hot-tempered; irascible by nature

【暴涨】bàozhǎng ❶(水位)急剧上升 (of water level) rise suddenly and sharply: 河水～。The river suddenly rose. ❷(物价等)突然大幅度地上升 (of prices, etc.) rise suddenly and sharply: 米价～。The cost of rice soared (or skyrocketed).

【暴政】bàozhèng 指反动统治者残酷地剥削、镇压人民的政治措施 tyranny; despotic rule; political measures taken by reactionary rulers to exploit and brutally suppress the people

【暴卒】bàozú〈书 *fml.*〉得急病突然死亡 die of a sudden illness; die suddenly

虣 bào〈书 *fml.*〉same as 暴 bào (凶暴 xiōngbào)

瀑 Bào 瀑河,水名,在河北 Baohe River in Hebei Province

☞ pù on p. 1503

曝 bào (旧读 formerly pronounced pù) ☞ below

☞ pù on p. 1503

【曝光】bào//guāng ❶ 使照相底片或感光纸感光 exposure; sensitization of negatives or sensitive paper ❷〈比喻 *fig.*〉隐秘的事(多指不光彩的)显露出来,被众人知道 (of secret matters, usu. ignominious) lay bare (to the public): 事情在报上～后,引起了轰动 The affair caused a sensation after it hit the headline. ‖ also 暴光 bào//guāng

【曝光表】bàoguāngbiǎo 一种测量光线强度的仪表。常用于摄影,以便准确地确定摄影机的光圈和曝光速度等。exposure meter; instrument used in photography for measuring the intensity of light and indicating the appropriate aperture and shutter speed for correct exposure

爆 bào ❶ 猛然破裂或迸出 explode; burst: ～炸 explode; blast; dynamite; detonate | 豆荚～了。The pods burst open. | 子弹打在石头上,～起许多火星儿。Bullets glanced against the rock in a burst of sparks. ❷ 出人意料地出现;突然发生 appear or occur unexpectedly; crop up: ～冷门 surprise; unexpected turn of events | ～出特大新闻。A red-hot news item unexpectedly emerged. ❸ 烹调方法,用滚油稍微一炸或用滚水稍微一煮 quick-fry; quick boil: ～肚儿 quick-boiled tripe | ～鱿鱼卷 quick-fried squid rolls

【爆肚儿】bàodǔr 食品,把牛羊肚儿在开水里稍微一煮就取出来,吃时现蘸作料。另有用热油快煎再加作料芡粉的,叫油爆肚儿。quick-boiled tripe served with seasoning; quick-fried tripe

【爆发】bàofā ❶ 火山内部的岩浆突然冲破地壳,向四外迸出 (of a volcano) erupt; (of magmas in a volcano) suddenly burst out through the earth's crust, spewing out in all directions: 火山～。The volcano erupted. ❷ 通过外部冲突的形式而发生重大变化,例如用

革命的手段来推翻旧政权，建立新政权 break out; change greatly through external conflicts, e.g. use revolutionary measures to overthrow an old political power and establish a new one ❸（力量、情绪等）忽然发作；（事变）突然发生（of force, emotion, event, etc.）erupt; break out：～战争。War broke out.

【爆发变星】bàofā biànxīng 恒星的一种，由于星球内部原子反应所引起的爆炸，光度突然变化。新星和超新星都属于爆发变星。eruptive variable (star); a kind of fixed star whose luminosity changes suddenly due to explosion caused by internal automatic reactions, including novas and supernovas

【爆发力】bàofālì 体育运动中指在短暂间突然产生的力量，如起跑、起跳、投掷、抽球时使出的力量 explosive force in sports; sudden spurt of energy, such as the force exerted at the start of a race, jump, throw, or drive

【爆发音】bàofāyīn 塞音 explosive; plosive

【爆冷门】bào lěngmén（～儿 bào lěngménr）指在某方面突然出现意料不到的事情 unexpected turn of events; surprise：本届世界乒乓球锦标赛大～，一名新手淘汰了上届世界冠军。A bolt came from the blue during the current world pingpong championship, when the reigning world champion was eliminated by a newcomer in the final match.

【爆裂】bàoliè（物体）突然破裂 burst; crack; split：豆荚成熟了就会～。Pods burst open when ripe.

【爆满】bàomǎn 形容戏院、影院、竞赛场所等人多到没有空位的程度（of a theatre, cinema, stadium or gymnasium) be filled to capacity; sellout：剧院里观众～，盛况空前。It was a gala occasion, and the theatre was filled to capacity.

【爆棚】bàopéng〈方 *dial.*〉same as 爆满 bàomǎn

【爆破】bàopò 用炸药摧毁岩石、建筑物等 blow up; demolish; dynamite; blast (rocks, buildings, etc. with explosives)：定向～ guided demolition (or blast) | ～敌人的碉堡 blow up an enemy pillbox

【爆破筒】bàopòtǒng 一种爆破用的火器，在钢管内装上炸药和雷管。多用来破坏敌方的工事或铁丝网等障碍物。bangalore (torpedo); weapon consisting of a steel tube filled with explosives and detonators, usu. for destroying enemy fortifications, wire netting and other obstacles

【爆炸】bàozhà ❶ 物体体积急剧膨大，使周围气压发生强烈变化并产生巨大的声响，叫做爆炸。核反应、急剧的氧化作用和容器内部气体的压力突然增高等都能引起爆炸 explode; blast; detonate; dynamite; expand with violent force and in a huge boom, which may be caused by a nuclear reaction, rapid oxidization, or a sudden rise of air pressure in a container：炮弹～ blast a shell | 气球～ burst a balloon | ～了一颗氢弹 detonate a hydrogen bomb ❷ 形容数量急剧增加，突破极限 sharp increase (of sth.) that breaks through a limit：人口～ population explosion | 信息～ information explosion | 知识～ knowledge explosion

【爆炸性】bàozhàxìng〈比喻 *fig.*〉出人意外、使人震惊的 explosive; unexpected and sensational：～新闻 sensational news

【爆仗】bào·zhang same as 爆竹 bàozhú：放～ let off firecrackers

【爆竹】bàozhú 用纸把火药卷起来，两头堵死，点着引火线后能爆裂发声的东西，多用于喜庆事 firecracker; gunpowder rolled into paper blocked at both ends with a fuse that explodes with a loud noise when lit, usu. used on festive occasions; also 炮仗 pào·zhang or 爆仗 bào·zhang

bēi（ㄅㄟ）

陂 bēi〈书 *fml.*〉❶ 池塘 pond：～塘 pond | ～池 pond ❷ 水边；岸 waterside; bank ❸ 山坡 mountain slope

☞ pí on p. 1466 and pō on p. 1491

【陂塘】bēitáng〈书 *fml.*〉水塘 pond

杯（盃） bēi ❶ 杯子 cup：茶～ tea cup | ～盘狼藉。The dinner table was strewn with plates and dishes (after a banquet). | ～酒言欢 hobnob ❷ 杯状的锦标 (prize) cup; trophy：银～ silver cup | 奖～ prize cup | 捧～ (of sports competitions) win the cup | 夺～ win first prize (in a contest); win the championship

【杯葛】bēigé〈方 *dial.*〉抵制 boycott; break off relations with

【杯弓蛇影】bēi gōng shé yǐng 有人请客吃饭，挂在墙上的弓映在酒杯里，客人以为酒杯里有蛇，回去疑心中了蛇毒，就生病了（见于《风俗通义·怪神第九》）according to *Notes on Social Customs· Strange Gods* (*IX*), a man invited to a meal mistook the reflection of an archer's bow in his wine cup for a snake and became sick on returning home, suspecting he had imbibed its venom;〈比喻 *fig.*〉疑神疑鬼，妄自惊慌 be jittery and filled with fear for no valid reason; be extremely nervous and suspicious

【杯珓】bēijiào ☞ 珓 jiào on p. 980

【杯盘狼藉】bēi pán láng jí 杯盘等放得乱七八糟。形容宴饮后桌上凌乱的样子。(of a dinner table) strewn with plates and dishes (after a banquet)

【杯赛】bēisài 以某种奖杯命名的运动竞赛，如世界杯足球赛 sports competition of the same name as its prize cup, e.g. the World Cup soccer tournament

【杯水车薪】bēi shuǐ chē xīn 用一杯水去救一车着了火的柴 a cup of water to put out a burning cartload of faggots;〈比喻 *fig.*〉无济于事 using a cup — an utterly inadequate measure; action falling far short of the need; drop in the ocean

【杯中物】bēizhōngwù 指酒 wine; liquor: 酷好～ be addicted to alcohol; be very fond of drinking

【杯子】bēi·zi 盛饮料或其他液体的器具,多为圆柱状或下部略细,一般容积不大 cup; glass; vessel for alcoholic drinks or other liquids of a small volume, usu. cylindrical or slightly tapered

卑 bēi ❶〈书 *fml.*〉(位置)低 low; low-lying: 地势～湿 low-lying, damp terrain ❷(地位)低下 low; of low rank: ～贱 of low or humble origin or status | 自～ feel inferior; be diffident ❸(品质或质量)低劣 low character; inferior in quality: ～鄙 base; mean; despicable; contemptible | ～劣 base; mean; despicable | ～不足道 not worth mentioning; of little consequence; insignificant; negligible ❹〈书 *fml.*〉谦恭 humble; modest: ～辞 humble words; obsequious patter | ～恭 humble and respectable

【卑鄙】bēibǐ ❶(语言、行为)恶劣;不道德 (of language or behaviour) base; mean; contemptible; despicable: ～无耻 mean and shameless; base and brazen | ～龌龊(形容品质、行为恶劣) (of characters or behaviour) foul; sordid | ～行径 base (or mean) behaviour; sordid conduct ❷〈书 *fml.*〉卑微鄙陋 humble; modest

【卑不足道】bēi bù zú dào 极其卑下,不值一提 not worth mentioning; of little consequence; insignificant; negligible

【卑辞】bēicí 谦恭的话 humble words; obsequious patter; also 卑词 bēicí

【卑躬屈膝】bēi gōng qū xī 形容没有骨气,谄媚奉承 bow and scrape; cringe; act in a servile or obsequious manner; also 卑躬屈节 bēi gōng qū jié (屈节 *qu jie*: 丧失气节 humble oneself; forfeit one's honour)

【卑贱】bēijiàn ❶〈旧时 *old*〉指出身或地位低下 of lowly or humble origin or status: 出身～ be of lowly origin ❷卑鄙下贱 lowly; menial; mean and low: 行为～ mean and low behaviour

【卑劣】bēiliè 卑鄙恶劣 base; mean; despicable: 手段～ mean (or despicable) trick

【卑怯】bēiqiè 卑鄙怯懦 base and cowardly; abject: ～的心理 abject mentality

【卑微】bēiwēi 地位低下 petty and low: 门第～ come from a lowly family; be of low origin | 官职～ hold a low official post

【卑污】bēiwū 品质卑劣,心地肮脏 despicable in character; evil-minded: 人格～ despicable character | ～小人 vile knave; low cur

【卑下】bēixià ❶(品格、风格等)低下 (of character, etc.) base; lowly: 素质～ base quality ❷(地位)低微 low status (or station): 身份～ low status

【卑职】bēizhí ❶〈书 *fml.*〉低微的职位 humble position; lowly post ❷〈旧时 *old*〉下级官吏对上级的自称 [used by a subordinate official when addressing superior] your humble subordinate; I

背(揹) bēi ❶(人)用脊背驮 carry on the back: 把草捆好～回村去。Bundle up the straw, load it on to your back and return to the village. ❷负担 shoulder; bear: ～债 be saddled with debts | 这个责任我还～得起。I can bear this responsibility. ❸〈方 *dial.*〉〈量词 *classifier*〉一个人一次背的量 [used to indicate what can be borne by one person on his or her back]: 一～麦子 a bundle of wheat (to carry by back) | 一～柴火 a bundle of firewood

☞ bèi on p. 83

【背榜】bēi//bǎng 指在考试后发的榜上名列最末 be at the bottom of the list of successful candidates (issued after an examination)

【背包袱】bēi bāo·fu〈比喻 *fig.*〉有沉重的思想负担 have a weight or load on one's mind; take on a mental burden: 事情做错了,改了就好,不必～。It's good that you have corrected your mistake, and that it no longer weighs on your mind.

【背带】bēidài ❶搭在肩上系住裤子或裙子的带子 braces; suspenders; broad straps that stretch over one's shoulders and fasten on to a pair of trousers (to keep them from falling down) ❷背背包、枪等用的皮带或帆布带子 (of a knapsack) straps; (of a rifle) sling

【背负】bēifù ❶用脊背驮 carry on the back: ～着衣包 carry on the back a paper bag containing paper garments and paper money to be burned as offerings to the dead ❷担负 bear; have on one's shoulders: ～重任 hold a position of great responsibility | ～着人民的希望 carry in one's heart the expectations of the people; bear in mind the aspirations of the people

【背黑锅】bēi hēiguō〈比喻 *fig.*〉代人受过,泛指受冤枉 be made a scapegoat; be unjustly blamed; take the blame for others

【背饥荒】bēi jī·huang〈方 *dial.*〉指欠债 be in debt

【背头】bēitóu 男子头发由鬓角起都向后梳的发式 swept back hairstyle (from a man's temples); quiff: 留～ wear one's hair swept back

【背债】bēi//zhài 欠债;负债 be saddled with

debt

【背子】bēi·zi 用来背东西的细而长的筐子，山区多用来运送物品 back basket — long and narrow basket worn on the back for carrying things (common in mountainous areas)

B

棓 bēi〈书 *fml*.〉same as 杯 bēi

椑 bēi［椑柿］(bēishì) 古书上说的一种柿子，果实小，青黑色 a kind of small persimmon, of a green-and-black colour, mentioned in ancient literature

☞ pí on p. 1467

悲 bēi ❶ 悲伤 sad; sorrowful; melancholy: ～痛 grieved; painfully sad | ～喜交集 mixed feelings of grief and joy; grief mingled with joy ❷ 怜悯 compassion: 慈～ compassionate and merciful

【悲哀】bēi'āi 伤心 sad; sorrow; grief: 感到～ feel sadness (or grief) | 显出十分～的样子 look deeply sorrowful

【悲惨】bēicǎn 处境或遭遇极其痛苦，令人伤心 (of one's situation or experience) bitter; miserable; tragic: ～的生活 a bitter (or miserable) life | 身世～miserable life

【悲愁】bēichóu 悲伤忧愁 sad and worried: 她成天乐呵呵的，不知道什么叫孤独和～。She is always cheerful and merry and has no notion of sadness or worry.

【悲怆】bēichuàng〈书 *fml*.〉悲伤 sorrowful; melancholy: 曲调～凄凉。This is a mournful and distressing tune.

【悲悼】bēidào 伤心地悼念 mourn; grieve over sb.'s death: ～亡友 grieve over the death of a friend

【悲愤】bēifèn 悲痛愤怒 grief and indignation: ～填膺(悲愤充满胸中) be filled with sorrow and resentment

【悲歌】bēigē ❶ 悲壮地歌唱 mournful song sung with solemn fervour: 慷慨～ sing with solemn fervour | ～当哭 sing a song of lament instead of crying ❷ 指悲壮的或哀痛的歌 sad, stirring song; elegy; dirge: 一曲～ a sad, stirring song; an elegy; a dirge

【悲观】bēiguān 精神颓丧，对事物的发展缺乏信心(跟'乐观'相对 as opposed to 'optimistic') pessimistic; gloomy and doubtful about the development of sth.: ～失望 become pessimistic and lose heart; be disheartened | ～情绪 pessimism | 虽然试验失败了，但他并不～。Although the experiment was a failure, he did not lose heart.

【悲号】bēiháo 伤心地号哭 cry or howl with sorrow and pain; wail

【悲欢离合】bēi huān lí hé 泛指聚会、别离、欢乐、悲伤的种种遭遇 joys and sorrows, partings and reunions — vicissitudes of life

【悲剧】bēijù ❶ 戏剧的主要类别之一，以表现主人公与现实之间不可调和的冲突及其悲惨结局为基本特点 tragedy; major dramatic or literary form characterized by irreconcilable conflicts between the protagonist and reality, and a sad denouement ❷〈比喻 *fig*.〉不幸的遭遇 sad event: 决不能让这种～重演。This tragedy must never be repeated.

【悲苦】bēikǔ 悲哀痛苦 grief; sorrow: 脸上露出～的神情 one's face shows signs of sorrow

【悲凉】bēiliáng 悲哀凄凉 desolate; disconsolate; forlorn: ～激越的琴声 desolate, woeful music played on the lute

【悲鸣】bēimíng 悲哀地叫 utter a plaintive cry; lament: 号角～ lament played on a bugle | 绝望地～ lament despondently

【悲凄】bēiqī 悲伤凄切 mournful; melancholy; plaintive: 远处传来～的哭声。Piteous cries came from afar.

【悲戚】bēiqī 悲痛哀伤 sad; sorrowful: ～的面容 sad look; sorrowful demeanour

【悲泣】bēiqì 伤心地哭泣 sob sadly; wail: 暗自～ cry inwardly; sob secretly

【悲切】bēiqiè 悲哀；悲痛 sorrowful; mournful: 万分～ be overwhelmed by sorrow; be greatly sorrowful

【悲伤】bēishāng 伤心难过 sad; sorrowful; mournful: 他听到这消息，不禁～起来。On hearing the news, he could not suppress his sorrow.

【悲酸】bēisuān 悲痛心酸 sad and depressed; bitter; aggrieved: 阵阵～，涌上心头。Bitterness flooded my heart.

【悲叹】bēitàn 悲伤叹息 sign mournfully; lament: 老人～时光的流逝。The old man heaved a sad sigh over time gone by.

【悲天悯人】bēi tiān mǐn rén 对社会的腐败和人民的疾苦感到悲愤和不平 lament the state of heaven and pity the fate of man; bemoan the depraved state of society and the misery of the people

【悲恸】bēitòng 非常悲哀 be extremely grief; be grief-stricken: ～欲绝 be overcome with grief; abandon oneself to grief

【悲痛】bēitòng 伤心 sorrowful; grieved: ～万分 be in deep grief; be deeply grieved | 化～为力量 turn grief into strength

【悲喜交集】bēi xǐ jiāo jí 悲伤和喜悦的感情交织在一起 mixed feelings of grief and joy; grief mingled with joy: 劫后重逢，～! Their reunion after the disaster brought them mixed feelings of joy and sorrow.

【悲喜剧】bēixǐjù 戏剧类别之一，兼有悲剧和喜剧的因素。一般具有圆满的结局。tragicomedy; dramatic or literary form combining elements of both tragedy and comedy, usu. with a happy ending

【悲辛】bēixīn〈书 *fml*.〉悲痛辛酸 bitter; sad;

sorrowful

【悲咽】bēiyè 悲哀哽咽 sad and choking with sobs:说到伤心处,她不禁~起来。Speaking of her grief, she could not help but choke on her sobs.

【悲壮】bēizhuàng (声音、诗文等)悲哀而雄壮;(情节)悲哀而壮烈 (of sounds, poems, prose, etc.) solemn and stirring; (of plots) moving and tragic:~的曲调 a solemn and heroic tune|情节~,催人泪下 tragic, moving and lachrymose plot

碑 bēi 刻着文字或图画,竖立起来作为纪念物或标记的石头 stele; upright stone tablet engraved with characters or images, used as monuments or marks:界~ boundary tablet; boundary marker|里程~ milestone|人民英雄纪念~ Monument to the People's Heroes

【碑额】bēi'é 碑的上端 top section of a tablet; also 碑首 bēishǒu or 碑头 bēitóu

【碑记】bēijì 刻在碑上的记事文章 record of events inscribed on a tablet

【碑碣】bēijié〈书 *fml.*〉碑 upright stone tablet; stele:墓前立有~ stele placed in front of a tomb

【碑刻】bēikè 刻在碑上的文字或图画 engraving or inscription on a tablet:拓印~ rubbing of an engraving or inscription

【碑林】bēilín 石碑林立的地方,如陕西西安碑林 forest of steles; collection of ancient stone tablets, such as the Forest of Steles in Xi'an, Shaanxi Province

【碑铭】bēimíng 碑文 inscription on a tablet

【碑拓】bēità 碑刻的拓本 rubbings from ancient tablets

【碑帖】bēitiè 石刻、木刻法书的拓本或印本,多做习字时临摹的范本 rubbings from, or prints or woodcuts of, stone inscriptions compiled in a book (usu. used as a copybook for calligraphy)

【碑文】bēiwén 刻在碑上的文字;准备刻在碑上的或从碑上抄录、拓印的文字 inscription on a tablet; characters to be engraved, copied or rubbed from a tablet

【碑阴】bēiyīn 碑的背面 back or reverse side of a tablet

【碑志】bēizhì 碑记 record of events inscribed on a tablet

【碑座】bēizuò (~儿 bēizuòr)碑下边的底座 stand for a tablet

鹎 bēi 鸟类的一属,羽毛大部为黑褐色,腿短而细。吃果实和昆虫。bulbul (*Pycnonotidae*); bird with black-and-brown plumage and short spindle legs that feeds on fruits and insects

箄 bēi〈书 *fml.*〉捕鱼的小竹笼 small bamboo cage for fishing

☞ pái on p. 1440

běi (ㄅㄟˇ)

北[1] běi 四个主要方向之一,清晨面对太阳时左手的一边 north; one of the four main compass directions, to the left of a person facing the rising sun:~头儿 in the north|~面 north; northern side; face north|~风 north wind; boreas|~房 north house|城~ north of the city|往~去 go north|坐~朝南 (of a building) with a southern exposure; (of a posture) facing south

北[2] běi〈书 *fml.*〉打败仗 be defeated:败~ suffer defeat|连战皆~ lose several battles successively; suffer repeated defeats|追奔逐~(追击败逃的敌军) pursue and attack the defeated enemy

【北半球】běibànqiú 地球赤道以北的部分 Northern Hemisphere; half of the earth; north of the equator

【北边】běi·bian ❶(~儿 běi·bianr)北 north ❷ same as 北方 běifāng ②

【北朝】Běi Cháo 北魏(后分裂为东魏、西魏)、北齐、北周的合称 Northern Dynasties (386-581), namely, Northern Wei (北魏 Běi Wèi, 386-534, which was later split into Eastern Wei 东魏 Dōng Wèi, 534-550, and Western Wei 西魏 Xī Wèi, 535-556), Northern Qi (北齐 Běi Qí, 550-577) and Northern Zhou (北周 Běi Zhōu 557-581); ☞ 南北朝 Nán-Běi Cháo on p. 1388

【北辰】běichén 古书上指北极星(as recorded in ancient books) North Star; polar star:众星环~。The North Star is surrounded by a myriad of stars.

【北斗星】běidǒuxīng 大熊星座的七颗明亮的星,分布成勺形,用直线把勺形边上两颗星连接起来向勺口方向延长约五倍的距离,就遇到小熊座 α 星,即现在的北极星 Big Dipper; Plough; group of seven bright stars in Ursa Major, resembling a dipper in shape, which would meet the α star in Ursa Minor (the Little Dipper), i.e. Polaris, by extending approximately five times the distance between the two stars at the side of the 'dipper' at its mouth

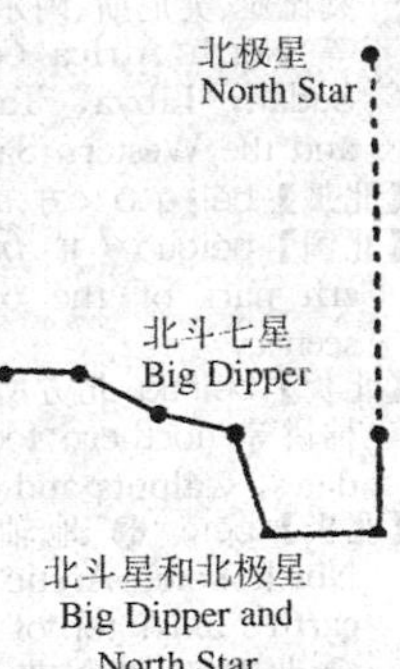

北斗星和北极星
Big Dipper and North Star

【北豆腐】běidòu·fu 食品,豆浆煮开后加入盐卤,使凝结成块,压去一部分水分而成,比南豆腐水分少而硬(区别于'南豆腐' as compared with 'southern-style beancurd') northern-style firm beancurd; firm tofu; foodstuff made by adding bittern to boiled soya-bean milk, condensed it into lumps, and with water squeezed out, less watery and more solid in texture than the southern-style beancurd

【北伐战争】Běifá Zhànzhēng 第一次国内革命战争时期,在中国共产党领导下,以国共合作的统一战线为基础进行的一次反对帝国主义和封建军阀统治的革命战争(1926—1927)。因这次战争从广东出师北伐,所以叫北伐战争。Northern Expedition (1926-1927); anti-imperialist and anti-feudal warlord revolutionary war during the period of the First Revolutionary Civil War (1924-1927) under the leadership of the Chinese Communist Party, based on the united front of the alliance between the KMT and CPC. The war, initiated in Guangdong, pushed northward, hence its name. ☞ 第一次国内革命战争 Dì Yī Cì Guónèi Gémìng Zhànzhēng on p.430

【北方】běifāng ❶ 北 north ❷ 北部地区,在我国一般指黄河流域及其以北的地区 northern part of the country, esp. the area north of the Yellow River

【北方话】běifānghuà 长江以北的汉语方言。广义的北方话还包括四川、云南、贵州和广西北部的方言。北方话是普通话的基础方言。northern dialect; Chinese dialect of the areas north of the Yangtze River, which, in a broad sense, also includes the dialects of Sichuan, Yunnan and Guizhou provinces, and north Guangxi Zhuang Autonomous Region, that serves as the basis for *putonghua*, (common speech of the modern Hans)

【北非】Běi Fēi 非洲北部,通常包括埃及、苏丹、利比亚、突尼斯、阿尔及利亚、摩洛哥、西撒哈拉等 North Africa (encompassing Egypt, the Sudan, Libya, Tunisia, Algeria, Morocco and the Western Sahara)

【北瓜】běi·guā 〈方 *dial.*〉南瓜 pumpkin

【北国】běiguó 〈书 *fml.*〉指我国的北部 northern part of the country: ～风光 northern scenery

【北货】běihuò 北方所产的食品,如红枣、核桃、柿饼等 northern food products (such as red dates, walnuts and dried persimmons)

【北极】běijí ❶ 地轴的北端,北半球的顶点 North Pole; Arctic Pole; north end of the earth's axis; top of the Northern Hemisphere ❷ 北磁极,用 N 来表示 north magnetic pole (indicated by N)

【北极星】běijíxīng 天空北部的一颗亮星,距天球北极很近,差不多正对着地轴,从地球上看,它的位置几乎不变,可以靠它来辨别方向。由于岁差,北极星并不是永远不变的某一颗星,现在是小熊座 α 星,到公元 14000 年将是织女星。Polaris; North Star; Polestar; bright star situated close to the North Celestial Pole, approximately opposite the earth's axis, used to take bearings because it hardly changes its position. Owing to the precession of the equinoxes, it is not a fixed star. At present, it is α Star in Ursa Minor, but in the year 14000, Vega (in the constellation Lyra) will serve as North Star. ☞ 北斗星 běidǒuxīng

【北京时间】Běijīng shíjiān 我国的标准时。以东经 120°子午线为标准的时刻,即北京所在时区的标准时刻。Beijing Time (standard time in China); standard time in the Beijing time zone as measured on the meridian 120° east longitude

【北京猿人】Běijīng yuánrén 中国猿人的一种,生活在距今约 70—20 多万年以前。1927 年在北京周口店龙骨山山洞发现了第一颗牙齿化石,1929 年发现了第一个完整的头骨化石。Peking Man (*Sinanthropus pekinensis*); a kind of Chinese ape-man living approximately 700,000-200,000 years ago; the first fossil of its tooth was discovered in 1927 in a cave at Longgu Mountain at Zhoukoudian of Beijing, followed in 1929 by discovery of the first fossil of its complete skull; also 北京人 Běijīng rén

【北欧】Běi Ōu 欧洲北部,包括丹麦、挪威、瑞典、芬兰和冰岛等国 North Europe (comprising Denmark, Norway, Sweden, Finland and Iceland)

【北齐】Běi Qí 北朝之一,公元 550—577,高洋所建 Northern Qi Dynasty (550-577), one of the Northern Dynasties established by Gao Yang; ☞ 南北朝 Nán-Běi Cháo on p.912

【北曲】běiqǔ ❶ 宋元以来北方诸宫调、散曲、戏曲所用的各种曲调的统称,调子豪壮朴实 powerful and simple melodies in the northern mode of ancient Chinese music, *sanqu* (type of opera popular in the Yuan, Ming and Qing dynasties with tonal patterns modelled on tunes drawn from folk music) and operas since the Song and Yuan dynasties ❷ 元代流行于北方的戏曲 northern operas of the Yuan Dynasty (and their derivatives); ☞ 杂剧 zájù on p.2384

【北山羊】běishānyáng 哺乳动物,形状似山羊而大,雄雌都有角,雄的角大,向后弯曲,生活在高山地带 ibex (*Capra ibex*); mammal that lives in mountainous regions, similar to but larger than a goat; both male and female have horns, those of the former bigger, curving up and backwards; also 羱羊 yuányáng

【北上】běishàng 我国古代以北为上,后来把去本地以北的某地叫北上 go up north; proceed northward; as north was regarded as the upper direction in ancient China, people later called going to a place north of the locality 'going up north':近日将动身～。We will set out up north in a few days.

【北宋】Běi Sòng 朝代,公元 960—1127,自太祖(赵匡胤)建隆元年起,到钦宗(赵桓)靖康二年止。建都汴京(今河南开封)。Northern Song Dynasty (960-1127), dating from the 1st year of the Longyuan reign of Emperor Taizu (Zhao Kuangyin) to the 2nd year of the Jingkang reign of Emperor Qinzong (Zhao Huan), which made Bianjing (present-day Kaifeng, Henan Province) its capital

【北魏】Běi Wèi 北朝之一,公元 386—534,鲜卑人拓跋珪所建,后来分裂为东魏和西魏 Northern Wei Dynasty (386-534), one of the Northern Dynasties established by Tuoba Gui of the ancint Xianbei nationality of Mongolian stock, which later split into the Eastern and Western Wei dynasties; ☞ 南北朝 Nán-Běi Cháo on p.1388

【北洋】Běiyáng 清末指奉天(辽宁)、直隶(河北)、山东沿海地区。特设北洋通商大臣,由直隶总督兼任。Beiyang, a region that covered the coastal provinces of Liaoning, Hebei and Shandong in the Qing Dynasty that were under the charge of the superintendent of the Northern ports, whose position was concurrently held by the governor-general of the metropolitan areas

【北洋军阀】Běiyáng Jūnfá 民国初年(1912-1927)代表北方封建势力的军阀集团,是清末北洋派势力的延续。最初的首领是袁世凯,袁死后分成几个派系,在帝国主义的支持下先后控制了当时的北京政府,镇压革命力量,出卖国家主权,连年进行内战。Northern warlords (1912-1927); warlord group that represented the northern feudal forces during the early period (1912-1927) of the Republic of China; continuation of the Northern forces at the end of the Qing Dynasty that split into several factions after the death of Yuan Shikai, its chieftan in the early days, controlling the then Beijing government, suppressing revolutionary forces, selling out national sovereignty, and waging a protracted civil war with imperialists' support

【北周】Běi Zhōu 北朝之一,公元 557—581,鲜卑人宇文觉所建 Northern Zhou Dynasty (557-581), one of the Northern Dynasties established by Yuwen Jue from the ancient Xianbei nationality; ☞ 南北朝 Nán-Běi Cháo on p.1388

bèi (ㄅㄟˋ)

贝(貝) bèi ❶ 软体动物的统称。水产上指有介壳的软体动物,如蛤蜊、蚌、鲍鱼等。mollusk; shellfish; scallop; a type of sea creature with a soft body covered by a hard shell, such as clam, freshwater mussel and abalone ❷ 〈古代 *arch.*〉用贝壳做的货币 cowry, cowrie used as money ❸ (Bèi) 姓 a surname

【贝雕】bèidiāo 把贝壳琢磨加工制成的工艺品 shell carving; handicraft carved out of shells

【贝多】bèiduō 贝叶树; talipot; also 桢多 bèiduō [梵 Sanskrit; pattra]

【贝壳】bèiké (～儿 bèikér) 贝类的硬壳 (hard) shell (of shellfish)

【贝勒】bèi·lè 清代贵族的世袭封爵,地位在亲王、郡王之下 *beile*; hereditary title of nobility below that of prince in the Qing Dynasty

【贝书】bèishū 指佛经,因古代印度用贝叶书写佛经而得名 Buddhist scripture (which was so named because it was originally written on pattra leaves); also 贝叶书 bèiyèshū

【贝塔粒子】bèitǎ lìzǐ 乙种粒子 beta particle; also β粒子 β lìzǐ

【贝塔射线】bèitǎ shèxiàn 乙种射线 beta ray; also β射线 β shèxiàn

【贝叶树】bèiyèshù 常绿乔木,高达 10 多米,茎上有环纹,叶子大,掌状羽形分裂,花淡绿而带白色。只开一次花,结果后即死亡。叶子叫贝叶,可以做扇子,又可以代替纸用来写字。talipot palm (*Corypha umbraculifera Linn.*); pattra; evergreen tree more than 10 metres in height, having a trunk with ring patterns and large hand-shaped pinnate leaves, blooming only once throughout its life, and dying right after it has borne fruit; also 贝多 bèiduō

【贝子】bèizǐ 清代贵族的世袭封爵,地位在贝勒之下 *beizi*; Qing-dynasty hereditary title of nobility below *beile*

孛 bèi 古书上指光芒四射的彗星 (as recorded in ancient books) comet shedding its rays in all directions
☞ bó on p.147

邶 Bèi 古国名,在今河南汤阴南 Bei, name of a state in ancient times south of present-day Tangyin, Henan Province

狈 bèi ☞ 狼狈 lángbèi on p.1150

棿 bèi [棿多](bèiduō) same as 贝多 bèiduō

备(備、俻) bèi ❶ 具备;具有 be equipped with; have; possess: 德才兼～ have (or possess) both ability and moral integrity ❷ 准备 prepare; get ready: ～用 reserve; alternative; spare; standby | ～料 get materials ready (for production) | ～而不用 have ready just in case; keep for possible future use ❸ 防备 provide (or prepare) for; take precautions against: 防旱～荒 make provision for drought and crop failure | 攻其不～ strike where or when the enemy is unprepared; catch sb. unawares ❹ 设备(包括人力物力) equipment (including manpower and material resources): 军～ military equipment; arms; armaments | 装～ equipment ❺ 表示完全 fully; in every possible way: 艰苦～尝 experience untold hardships | 关怀～至 show every consideration; take utmost care|～受欢迎 enjoy great popularity; be very popular

【备案】bèi//àn 向主管机关报告事由存案以备查考 put on record or on file; enter (a case) in the records:此事已报上级～。The case has been reported to the high-up authority and entered in the records.|本店开业一事,已向工商管理部门～。The shop's business application has been put on the file of the industrial and commercial administration department.

【备办】bèibàn 把需要的东西置办起来 get (what is necessary) ready; prepare:年货已经～齐了。All the goods needed for Spring Festival have been prepared.

【备不住】bèi·bu zhù〈方 *dial.*〉说不定;或许 perhaps; maybe; for all one knows:这件事他～是忘了。For all we know, he forgot about the matter. also 背不住 bèi·bu zhù

【备查】bèichá 供查考(多用于公文 oft. of official documents) keep for future reference:存档～ be kept on file for reference

【备份】bèifèn ❶ 备用的一份 spare (part):～伞(备用的降落伞) spare parachute|～节目 back-up programme ❷〈方 *dial.*〉充数;空设 fill a nominal post; serve as a figurehead

【备耕】bèigēng 为耕种做准备,包括修理农具、挖沟、积肥等 make preparations for plowing and sowing (including repairing farm tools, digging ditches and collecting manure):农民利用冬闲,加紧～工作。In this slack season of winter, the farmers are busy making preparations for plowing and sowing.

【备荒】bèi//huāng 防备灾荒 prepare against crop failure or famine:储粮～ store grains as a precaution against crop failure or famine

【备货】bèi//huò 准备供销售的商品 stock (a store or shop); (of a shop, etc.) get in a supply of goods:营业前要备好货。A shop should get its stock in before commencing business.|应节的商品应及早～。Seasonal goods should be stocked up as soon as possible.

【备件】bèijiàn 预备着供更换的机件 spare part

【备考】bèikǎo (书册、文件、表格)供参考的附录或附注 (appendix, note, etc. on a book, document or form) for reference

【备课】bèi//kè 教师在讲课前准备讲课内容 (of a teacher) prepare lessons (before a lecture or class):备完课,她又忙着改作业。Having prepared her lessons, she began to correct and grade the students' homework.

【备料】bèi//liào 准备供应生产所需材料 get the materials ready (for production):～车间 workshop for preparing matierials|上班前就备好了料 get the materials ready before commencing work

【备品】bèipǐn 储备待用的机件和工具等 machine parts, tools, etc. kept in reserve; spare parts or tools

【备取】bèiqǔ 招考时在正式录取名额以外再录取若干名以备正取不到时递补(区别于'正取' as compared with 'being officially enrolled') be on the waiting list for formal enrollment in a school:～生 be on the waiting list for enrollment

【备述】bèishù 详尽地叙述 narrate in detail:～其事 narrate the case in detail|其中细节,难以～。It is difficult to relate everything in detail.

【备忘录】bèiwànglù ❶ 一种外交文书,声明自己方面对某种问题的立场,或把某些事项的概况(包括必须注意的名称、数字等)通知对方 memorandum; aide-memoire; diplomatic document that states one's standpoint on an issue, or informs the other party of the general situation of certain matters (such as names or figures that require attention) ❷ 随时记载,帮助记忆的笔记本 memorandum book; Filofax; notebook in which to keep a record for quick reference

【备用】bèiyòng 准备着供随时使用 reserve; alternate; spare; standby (that can be used at any time):～件 spare unit; spare part|～物资 reserved goods and materials|随身携带以作～ take sth. with sb. as an alternative

【备战】bèi//zhàn 准备战争 prepare for war; be prepared against war:～物资 goods and materials in preparation for war|～备荒 be prepared for war and natural disasters

【备至】bèizhì 极其周到(多指对人的关怀等) to the utmost; take every possible measure to make provision (for sb.); in every possible way:关怀～ be very considerate; show meticulous care|爱护～ take utmost care (of sb.)

【备注】bèizhù ❶ 表格上为附加必要的注解说明而留的一栏 remarks column; column in a form for relevant notes or explanations ❷ 指在这一栏内所加的注解说明 remarks; relevant notes or explanations added in this column

背1 bèi ❶ 躯干的一部分,部位跟胸和腹相对 back; part of one's body opposite the chest and stomach (图见 ☞ figure for 身体 shēntǐ on p. 1701):后～ back|～影 view of sb.'s back; figure viewed from behind ❷ 某些物体的反面或后部 back of an object:手～ back of the hand|刀～儿 back of a knife|墨透纸～ (of brushwork in calligraphy or painting) so forceful that the ink soaks right through the paper

背2 bèi ❶ 背部对着(跟'向'相对 as opposed to 'facing') with one's back towards:～山面海 with hills to the rear and the sea in the front|～水作战 fight with one's back to the river or the wall — fight to win or die;

fight a last-ditch battle ◇人心向～ whether the people are for or against ❷ 离开 leave; go away:～井离乡 leave one's native place (esp. against one's will) ❸ 躲避;瞒 hide sth from; do sth. behind sb.'s back:光明正大,没什么～人的事。Being open and above-board, I have nothing to hide. ❹ 背诵 recite from memory; learn by heart or by rote:～台词 learn one's lines (by heart); recite (or speak) one's lines|书～熟了 have a lesson memorised ❺ 违背;违反 violate; break; act contrary to:～约 break an agreement; go back on one's word; fail to honour one's pledge or promise|～信弃义 faithless; perfidious ❻ 朝着相反的方向 turn away:他把脸～过去,装着没看见。He turned his face away, pretending he had not seen (us). ❼ 偏僻 out-of-the-way:～静 quiet and secluded|～街小巷 back (or side) street and small lanes|深山小路很～。The path to the deep mountains is very secluded. ❽ 不顺利;倒霉 unlucky:～时 unlucky|手气～have bad luck (at gambling) ❾ 听觉不灵 hard of hearing:耳朵有点～ be a little hard of hearing

☞ bēi on p. 77

【背包】bèibāo 行军或外出时背(bēi)在背上的衣被包裹 knapsack; rucksack; infantry pack; field pack blanket roll; wallet; clothes, quilt or bundle carried on one's back when marching or going away

【背不住】bèi·bu zhù same as 备不住 bèi·bu zhù

【背城借一】bèichéng jièyī 在自己的城下跟敌人决一死战,泛指跟敌人作最后一次的决战 wage a last-ditch fight with one's back against the city wall; fight to the last ditch; put up a stubborn resistance; also 背城一战 bèichéng yīzhàn

【背搭子】bèidā·zi 出门时用来装被褥、什物等的布袋 cloth bag for carrying one's bedding (when travelling); also 被褡子 bèidā·zi

【背道而驰】bèi dào ér chí 朝着相反的方向走 run in the opposite direction; run counter to; 〈比喻 *fig.*〉方向、目标完全相反 defeat the purpose; opposite in direction or objective

【背地】bèidì 私下;不当面 privately; behind sb.'s back; on the sly:不要～议论人。Don't talk about others behind their backs. also 背地里 bèidì·li

【背篼】bèidōu 〈方 *dial.*〉背(bēi)在背上运送东西的篼 basket carried on one's back

【背对背】bèiduìbèi 背靠背 back to back

【背风】bèifēng 风不能直接吹到 out of the wind; on the lee side; leeward:找个～的地方休息一下。Let's find a place on the lee side to take a rest.

【背旮旯儿】bèigālár 〈方 *dial.*〉偏僻的角落 remote corner; out-of-the-way place; hide-out

【背躬】bèigōng 戏曲的旁白 aside (in traditional operas):打～(说旁白) utter an aside

【背光】bèiguāng 光线不能直接照到 do sth. with one's back to the light; stand in one's own light:那儿～,请到亮的地方来。You're in a poor light there, please come over. It's a little brighter here.

【背后】bèihòu ❶ 后面 behind; at the back; in the rear:山～ behind a mountain ❷ 不当面 behind sb.'s back:有话当面说,不要～乱说。It's best to say sth. straight to a person's face rather than speak ill of them behind their back.

【背晦】bèi·hui same as 悖晦 bèi·hui

【背货】bèihuò 不合时宜而销路不畅的货物 unfashionable, unsaleable goods:处理～,使资金得以周转 sell outdated goods at reduced prices to turn over capital funds

【背集】bèijí 〈方 *dial.*〉没有集市的日子 non-marketing days; days on which no fair is held in a rural area:每逢～,他就挑起货担送货下乡。On the day when there was no market, he took goods on a shoulder pole to rural areas.

【背脊】bèijǐ 背部 back of the human body; spine

【背剪】bèijiǎn 反剪 with hands behind one's back:他～双手,来回走着。He paced back and forth, his hands clasped behind him.

【背角】bèijiǎo 不被人注意的角落 unnoticed corner; quiet place:两人在～处,不知嘀咕什么事。The two stood in a shady corner, whispering to each other.

【背井离乡】bèi jǐng lí xiāng 离开了故乡,在外地生活(多指不得已的 esp. against one's will) leave one's native place; also 离乡背井 lí xiāng bèi jǐng

【背景】bèijǐng ❶ 舞台上或电影、电视剧里的布景。放在后面,衬托前景。stage setting; backdrop; scenery; setting or scenery on a stage or for a film or TV series, placed at the rear to set off the foreground ❷ 图画、摄影里衬托主体事物的景物 background to a picture or photograph that sets off the main subject ❸ 对人物、事件起作用的历史情况或现实环境 background, historical situation or environment that has an effect on a person or an event:历史～ historical background|政治～ political background ❹ 指背后倚仗的力量 backstop; background support; behind-the-scenes backer; patron:听他说话的气势,恐怕是有～的。Judging by his tone of voice, it would appear he has a behind-the-scenes sponsor.

【背静】bèi·jing (地方)偏僻;清静 quiet and secluded:～的小巷 a secluded lane

【背靠背】bèikàobèi ❶ 背部靠着背部 back to

back：他俩～地坐着。They sat back to back. ❷ 指不当着有关人的面(批评、揭发检举等)(criticise, expose, report, etc.) through an intermediary or without facing the concerned person：为了避免矛盾激化，先～给他提些意见。In order to avoid sparking off antagonism, let's make back-to-back comments on his conduct. ‖ also 背对背 bèiduìbèi

【背筐】bèikuāng 背(bēi)在背上的筐 dosser; basket carried on the back

【背离】bèilí ❶ 离开 leave for another place：～故土，流浪在外 leave one's homeland and drift from place to place ❷ 违背 deviate from; depart from：不能～基本原则。One should not deviate from the basic principle.

【背理】bèi//lǐ 违背事理；不合理 unreasonable; irrational：这件事他做得有点儿～。It was unreasonable of him to act like that. also 悖理 bèilǐ

【背令】bèilìng 不合时令 out of season：～商品 out-of-season goods

【背篓】bèilǒu 〈方 *dial.*〉背(bēi)在背上运送东西的篓子 pack basket; basket carried on the back

【背面】bèimiàn ❶ (～儿 bèimiànr)物体上跟正面相反的一面 back; reserve side; wrong side (of an object)：在单据的～签字。Please sign on the back of the receipt. ❷ 指某些动物的脊背 back (of some animals)

【背谬】bèimiù same as 悖谬 bèimiù

【背年】bèinián 〈方 *dial.*〉指果树歇枝、竹子等生长得慢的年份 lean year (for fruit trees, bamboo, etc.)

【背叛】bèipàn 背离，叛变 betray; forsake：～祖国 betray one's country

【背鳍】bèiqí 鱼类背部的鳍 dorsal fin; fin on the back of fish; also 脊鳍 jǐqí；(图见 ☞ figure for 鳍 qí on p.1513)

【背气】bèi//qì 由于疾病或其他原因而突然暂时停止呼吸 apnoea; transient suspension of respiration owing to illness or other reasons：婴儿～了，要赶快做人工呼吸。This baby has stopped breathing and should be given artificial respiration immediately. | 气得他差点儿背过气去。He was almost breathless with anger.

【背弃】bèiqì 违背和抛弃 abandon; desert; renounce：～盟约 abandon the oath of alliance

【背人】bèi//rén ❶ 隐讳不愿使人知道 keep from public knowledge; cover up：他得过～的病。His illness was one he did not wish to make known. | 他干了不少～的事。He has done quite a few shady deals. ❷ 没有人或人看不到 out of the way; out of sight：找个～的地方谈话 find a secluded place to talk

【背时】bèishí ❶ 不合时宜 behind the times; out-of-date：～商品 out-of-date commodities ❷ 倒霉 unlucky：这些天真～，老遇上不顺心的事。My stars are really down these days, as I always seem to find myself in unsatisfactory situations. ‖ also 悖时 bèishí

【背书】bèi//shū 背诵念过的书 recite a lesson from memory; repeat a lesson：过去上私塾每天早晨要～，背不出书要挨罚。In the past, students attending private tutorial schools were required to recite a lesson from memory every morning, and those that failed would be punished.

【背书】bèishū 票据(多指支票)背面的签字或图章 endorsement; authorizing signature or seal on the back of a cheque

【背水一战】bèi shuǐ yī zhàn 在不利情况下和敌人作最后决战 fight with one's back to the river or the wall; 〈比喻 *fig.*〉面临绝境，为求得出路而作最后一次努力 fight to win or die; fight a last-ditch battle; conduct a desperate struggle to find a way out of a hopeless situation

【背水阵】bèishuǐzhèn 韩信攻赵，在井陉口背水列阵，大破赵兵。后来将领们问他这是什么道理，韩信回答说兵法里有'陷之死地而后生，置之亡地而后存'的话(见于《史记·淮阴侯列传》)。后来用'背水阵'比喻处于死里求生的境地。battle formation with a river to the rear. When attacking the State of Zhao, Han Xin arranged a battle formation at Jingjingkou with a river behind it, and completely defeated the enemy troops. When his generals asked him why he had done so, he told them that according to the art of war, 'A general should deploy troops in such a way as to leave them no route to retreat, consequently forcing them to fight for their lives and win the battle.' (*Records of the Historian · Biography of Marquis of Huaiyin*). (fig.) desperate situation where one must fight in order to survive

【背诵】bèisòng 凭记忆念出读过的文字 recite; repeat from memory：～课文 recite a text

【背心】bèixīn (～儿 bèixīnr)不带袖子和领子的上衣 sleeveless garment; waistcoat; vest

【背信弃义】bèi xìn qì yì 不守信用，不讲道义 faithless; perfidious

【背兴】bèixìng 〈方 *dial.*〉倒霉 unlucky; down on one's luck：真～，刚穿的新衣服拉了个口子。As luck would have it, I tore this new outfit just after putting it on.

【背眼】bèiyǎn (～儿 bèiyǎnr)人们不易看见的(地方) (of places) hidden; concealed

【背阴】bèiyīn (～儿 bèiyīnr)阳光照不到的(地方) shady; in the shade：楼后～的地方还有积雪。There is still some snow in the shady spots behind the building.

【背影】bèiyǐng (～儿 bèiyǐngr)人体的背面形象 view of sb.'s back; figure viewed from behind:父亲走远了,我看着他的～,不禁流下了眼泪。I could not help shedding tears at my father's receding figure.

【背约】bèi//yuē 违背以前的约定;失信 break an agreement; go back on one's word; fail to honour a promise:～毁誓 break one's promise

【背运】bèiyùn ❶ 不好的运气 unlucky fate:走～ be out of luck; have a run of bad luck ❷ 运气不好 unlucky; unfortunate:老不来好牌,真～。I haven't been dealt a good card for ages; my luck is really running low.

【背字儿】bèizìr 〈方 *dial.*〉same as 背运 bèiyùn ①:走～ be out of luck; have a run of bad luck

钡 bèi 金属元素,符号 Ba (baryum)。银白色,化学性质活泼,容易氧化,燃烧时发出绿色光,用来制合金、烟火和钡盐等。barium; Ba (barium), silver whitish metallic element with active chemical properties, which oxidises easily, burns with a green light, and is used to produce alloys, fire works, barium salts, etc.

【钡餐】bèicān 诊断某些食管、胃肠道疾患的一种检查方法。病人服硫酸钡后,用 X 射线透视或拍片检查有无病变。barium meal; method of examining throat, stomach problems and enteritis with X-rays after the patient has taken barium sulphate

倍 bèi ❶ 跟原数相等的数,某数的几倍就是用几乘某数 times; fold; number equal to the original; *n* times a number meaning to multiply it by *n*:二的五～是十。Five times two is ten. ❷ 加倍 double; redouble:事半功～ half the work with twice the results|勇气～增 redouble one's courage

【倍道】bèidào 〈书 *fml.*〉兼程 travel at double speed

【倍加】bèijiā 指程度比原来深得多 all the more:～爱惜 take extra care of|雨后的空气～清新。After a rainfall, the air is all the more fresh.

【倍率】bèilǜ 望远镜、显微镜的物镜焦距和目镜焦距的比值,比值越大,放大的倍数越大 magnifying power; ratio between the focuses of the object lens and the sight lens of a telescope or microscope, and the bigger the ratio, the bigger the magnifying power

【倍儿】bèir 〈方 *dial.*〉非常;十分 very; terribly:～新 awfully new|～亮 awfully bright|～精神 very energetic; full of vim and vigour

【倍式】bèishì 一个整式能够被另一整式整除,这个整式就是另一整式的倍式。如 a^2-b^2 是 $a+b$ 和 $a-b$ 的倍式。multiple formula; If one integral expression can be exactly divided by another, it is known as its multiple formula (e.g. a^2-b^2 is the multiple formula of $a+b$ and $a-b$).

【倍数】bèishù ❶ 一个数能够被另一数整除,这个数就是另一个数的倍数。如 15 能够被 3 或 5 整除,因此 15 是 3 的倍数,也是 5 的倍数。multiple; number that exactly contains another integral number of times (e.g. 15 can be exactly divided by 3 or 5, so 15 is a multiple of both 3 and 5) ❷ 一个数除以另一数所得的商。如 $a \div b = c$,就是说 a 是 b 的 c 倍,c 是倍数。quotient of one number divided by another; times (e.g. if $a \div b = c$, a is c times b, and c is the multiple)

【倍增】bèizēng 成倍地增长 double; redouble; multiply:信心～ double one's confidence|勇气～ redouble one's courage

悖(誖) bèi 〈书 *fml.*〉❶ 相反;违反 be contrary to; go against:并行不～ run parallel and non-conflicting; not mutually exclusive ❷ 违背道理;错误 erroneous; perverse:～谬 absurd; preposterous ❸ 迷惑;糊涂 puzzled; confused; muddle-headed:～晦 (oft. said of old people) confused; muddle-headed; senile

【悖晦】bèi·hui 〈方 *dial.*〉糊涂(多指老年人 oft. said of old people) confused; muddle-headed; senile; also 背晦 bèi·hui

【悖理】bèilǐ same as 背理 bèilǐ

【悖谬】bèimiù 〈书 *fml.*〉荒谬;不合道理 absurd; preposterous; also 背谬 bèimiù

【悖逆】bèinì 〈书 *fml.*〉指违反正道,犯上作乱 rebellious; insurrectional; subversive of the establishment:～之罪 crime of rebellion|～天道 offensive (or run counter) to the way of heaven

【悖入悖出】bèi rù bèi chū 用不正当的手段得来的财物,也会被别人用不正当的手段拿走;胡乱弄来的钱又胡乱花掉(语本《礼记·大学》:'货悖而入者,亦悖而出') ill-gotten, ill-spent; ill-gotten wealth never thrives; easy come, easy go (*The Book of Rites* · *Great Learning*: 'Ill-gotten wealth is also ill-spent.')

【悖时】bèishí same as 背时 bèishí

被[1] bèi 被子 quilt:棉～ cotton-padded quilt|夹～ lined quilt|毛巾～ towelling coverlet|做一床～ make a new quilt

被[2] bèi〈书 *fml.*〉❶ 遮盖 cover:～覆 cover ❷ 遭遇 meet with; encounter:～灾 suffer (or be hit by) disaster|～难 be killed in a disaster; suffer from a disaster

被[3] bèi ❶ 用在句子中表示主语是受事(施事放在被字后,但往往省略)[used in a passive sentence to indicate that the subject is the object of the action (the agent or doer usu. follows 被 bèi, and is oft. omitted)]:解放军到处～(人)尊敬。Men of the PLA are respected everywhere.|那棵树～(大风)刮倒了。The tree was uprooted (by the gale).|这部书～人借走了一本。One of the books in this series has been borrowed.|他～选为代表。He was elected a representative. ❷ 用在动词前构

B

成被动词组［used before a verb to form a passive phrase］：～压迫 oppressed | ～批评 criticised | ～剥削阶级 exploited class

【被褡子】bèidā·zi same as 背搭子 bèidā·zi

【被袋】bèidài 外出时装被褥、衣物等用的圆筒形的袋 bedding bag; cylindrical bag that contains bedding, clothes, etc. to be carried on the road

【被单】bèidān（～儿 bèidānr）❶ 铺在床上或盖在被子上的布（bed）sheet ❷ 单层布被 quilt cover ‖ also 被单子 bèidān·zi

【被动】bèidòng ❶ 待外力推动而行动（跟'主动'相对 as opposed to 'active'）passive; take action only when pushed by external forces：工作要主动，不要～。We should adopt an active rather than passive attitude. ❷ 不能造成有利局面使事情按照自己的意图进行（跟'主动'相对 as opposed to 'initiative'）land oneself in a passive position; be thrown into passivity; fail to create a favourable situation in which things develop according to one's will：由于事先考虑不周，事情搞得很～。Due to inadequate consideration before hand, we have been cast into passivity.

【被动式】bèidòngshì 说明主语所表示的人或事物是被动者的语法格式。汉语的被动式有时没有形式上的标志，如：他选上了|麦子收割了。有时在动词前边加助词'被'，如：反动统治被推翻了。有时在动词前边加介词'被'，引进主动者，如：敌人被我们歼灭了（口语里常常用'叫'或'让'in oral Chinese 叫 jiào or 让 ràng are oft. used）passive form; passive construction; grammatical form indicating that the person(s) or matter(s) indicated by the subject is the object of the action; in the passive form of the Chinese language, there is no formal sign（e.g. 他选上了。He was elected. |麦子收割了。The wheat has been harvested.）. Sometimes 被 bèi is placed before a verb as an auxiliary word, or a preposition to introduce the agent or doer（e.g. 敌人被我们歼灭了。The enemy was wiped out by us.）

【被服】bèifú 被褥、毯子和服装（多指军用的 esp. for army use）bedding and clothing：～厂 clothing factory

【被覆】bèifù ❶ 遮盖；蒙 cover; blanket; cocoon：山上～着苍翠的森林。The mountain is cocooned under a blanket of verdant forest. ❷ 遮盖地面的草木等 vegetation cover：滥伐森林，破坏了地面～。The wanton felling of trees has damaged the vegetation cover. ❸ 军事上指用竹、木、砖、石等建筑材料对建筑物的内壁和外表进行加固（mil.）coat; reinforce the inside walls and surfaces of a building with materials such as bamboo, wood, brick, stone, etc.

【被告】bèigào 在民事和刑事案件中被控告的人 defendant; the accused; also 被告人 bèigàorén

【被害人】bèihàirén 指刑事、民事案件中受犯罪行为侵害的人（leg.）injured party; victim

【被里】bèilǐ（～儿 bèilǐr）睡觉时被子贴身的一面 underside of a quilt

【被面】bèimiàn（～儿 bèimiànr）睡觉时被子不贴身的一面 facing or outside cover of a quilt

【被难】bèinàn ❶ 因灾祸或重大变故而丧失生命 be killed in a disaster or a major misfortune：飞机失事，乘客全部～。All passengers perished in the plane crash. ❷ 遭受灾难 suffer from a disaster：～的老百姓正在抢运东西。The disaster-stricken people rushed about salvaging their belongings.

【被褥】bèirù 被子和褥子；铺盖 bedding; bedclothes：那床～该拆洗了。The bedding must be unpicked and washed.

【被套】bèitào ❶ 外出时装被褥的长方形布袋，一面的中间开口 bedding bag; rectangle cloth bag to carry bedding, used by sb. on the road ❷ 为了拆洗的方便，把被里和被面缝成袋状，叫被套（bag-shaped）quilt case; quilt slip（to make unpicking and washing more convenient）❸ 棉被的胎 silk floss wadding for a quilt：丝绵～ silk floss wadding for a quilt

【被头】bèitóu ❶ 缝在被子盖上身那一头上的布，便于拆洗，保持被里清洁 piece of cloth sewn to the upper side of a quilt in order to keep it clean ❷〈方 *dial.*〉被子 quilt

【被窝儿】bèiwōr 为睡觉叠成的长筒形的被子 quilt folded round the body in the shape of a tube：他躺在～里不愿起来。Lying enfolded in his quilt, he was reluctant to get up.

【被卧】bèi·wo 被子 quilt：一床～ a quilt

【被选举权】bèixuǎnjǔquán ❶ 公民依法当选为国家权力机关代表或被选担任一定职务的权利 right to be elected; right of a citizen to be elected deputy to a state organ of power, or hold a certain post, according to the law ❷ 各种组织的成员当选为本组织的代表或领导人的权利 right to be elected; right of a member of an organiszation to be elected its representative or leader

【被罩】bèizhào 套在被子外面的罩子，可以随时取下换洗，多用宽幅的棉布或的确良做成 quilt slip; quilt case; cover of a quilt that can be removed in order to wash, usu. made from broad cotton cloth or dacron

【被子】bèi·zi 睡觉时盖在身上的东西，一般用布或绸缎做面，用布做里子，装上棉花或丝绵等 quilt; cover for one's body when sleeping, usu. made of cloth or silk, with a cotton underside, filled with cotton, silk floss, etc.

【被子植物】bèizǐ-zhíwù 种子植物的一大类，胚珠生在子房里，种子包在果实里。胚珠接受本花或异花雄蕊的花粉而受精。根据子叶数分为单子叶植物和双子叶植物（区别于'裸子植物'as opposed to 'gymnosperm'）angiosperm; a category of seed plant whose seeds grow in an ovary and are fertilized by pollen from the plant flower or from the stamens of another flower. Such plants are divided into subclasses monocotyledons and dicotyledons according to the number of cotyledons.

棓 bèi ☞ 五棓子 wǔbèizǐ on p. 2029
☞ bàng on p. 58

辈 bèi ❶ 行辈；辈分 rank or position in a (family or clan) generational hierarchy：长～ member of a higher (or elder or senior) generation of a family (or clan) hierarchy | 晚～ member of a younger (or junior) generation within the family (or clan) hierarchy | 同～ of the same generation | 老前～ elder generation; forebears; ancestors | 小一～ one generation younger than (or junior to) sb. ❷〈书 *fml.*〉等；类(指人) people of a certain kind; the like：我～ people of our group | 无能之～ incompetents; people without ability ❸ (～儿 bèir) 辈子 lifetime：后半～儿 latter part of one's life

【辈出】bèichū (人才)一批一批地连续出现 (of talented people) come forth in large numbers：英雄～ heroes come forth in large numbers | 新人～ people of a new type coming forth in large numbers

【辈分】bèi•fen 指家族、亲友之间的世系次第 seniority in generational hierarchy of a family or clan：论～，我是他叔叔。I am his uncle by virtue of seniority. | 他年纪比我小，～比我大。Though younger than I, he is my senior within the family generational hierarchy.

【辈行】bèiháng same as 辈分 bèi•fen

【辈数儿】bèishùr same as 辈分 bèi•fen：他虽然年纪轻，～小，但在村里很有威信。Although young in age and low within the family hierarchy, he enjoys high prestige in the village.

【辈子】bèi•zi 一世或一生 all one's life; lifetime：这～ all one's life; lifetime | 半～(半生) half a lifetime | 他当了一～教师。He worked as a teacher all his life.

惫(憊) bèi (旧读 formerly pronounced bài) 极端疲乏 exhausted; fatigued：疲～ tired out; exhausted

【惫倦】bèijuàn〈书 *fml.*〉疲惫困倦 be tired and drowsy：酒后～，昏昏欲睡 be overcome with fatigue and drowsiness under the influence of wine

焙 bèi 用微火烘(药材、食品、烟叶、茶叶等) (of medicine, food, tobacco, tea, etc.) bake over a slow fire：～干研碎 dry sth. over a fire and grind it into powder | ～一点花椒 cure a small amount of Chinese prickly ash seeds by drying them over a fire

【焙粉】bèifěn 发面用的白色粉末，是碳酸氢钠、酒石酸和淀粉的混合物。也叫发粉，有的地区叫起子。baking-powder; white powder used to leaven dough, integrated with sodium bicarbonate, tartaric acid and starch; also 发粉 fāfěn and (in some areas) 起子 qǐ•zi

【焙烧】bèishāo 把物料(如矿石)加热而又不使熔化，以改变其化学组成或物理性质 bake (raw materials such as ores, to such a degree that changes take place in their chemical composition or physical property without melting them); roast

B

蓓 bèi [蓓蕾](bèilěi) 没开的花；花骨朵儿 bud：桃树～满枝。The branches on the peach trees are strung with buds. ◇美术园地中的～ buds in the garden of fine arts

碚 bèi 地名用字 used in names of places：北～(在重庆) Beibei (in Chongqing Municipality) | 虾蟆～(在湖北宜昌西北) Hamabei (in the northwest of Yichang, Hubei Province)

鞁 bèi ❶〈书 *fml.*〉鞍辔的统称 general term for saddle and bridle ❷ same as 鞴[1] bèi

骳 bèi ☞ 骫骳 wěibèi on p. 1997

褙 bèi 把布或纸一层一层地粘在一起 paste or glue layers of cloth or paper together：裱～ mount | 袼～ pieces of old cloth or rags pasted together to make cloth shoes

【褙子】bèi•zi〈方 *dial.*〉袼褙 pieces of old cloth or rags pasted together to make cloth shoes：打～ glue pieces of cloth together, generally to make soles for cotton shoes

糒 bèi〈书 *fml.*〉干饭 cooked rice

鞴1 bèi 把鞍辔等套在马上 put saddle, etc. on a horse：～马 put saddle and a bridle on a horse

鞴2 bèi ☞ [韝鞴](gōubèi) on p. 682

鐾 bèi 把刀在布、皮、石头等物上面反复磨擦几下，使锋利 sharpen (a knife on a piece of cloth, leather or stone by repeated grinding); whet; strop：～刀 sharpen or whet a knife; strop a knife | ～刀布 piece of cloth on which a knife is sharpened

•bei (•ㄅㄟ)

呗 •bei〈助词 *aux.*〉❶ 表示事实或道理明显，很容易了解 [used to show that sth. is self-evident]：不懂，就好好学～。Didn't you know that? Well, you had better learn then. ❷ 表示勉强同意或勉强让步的语气 [used to express reluctant agreement or concession]：去就去～。Well, if I must go, go I must.
☞ bài on p. 44

臂 •bei ☞ 胳臂 gē•bei on p. 650
☞ bì on p. 111

bēn (ㄅㄣ)

奔 bēn ❶ 奔走;急跑 run quickly; dash; (of a horse) gallop:狂～ run like mad; dash (or tear) along|～驰 speed; run fast; dash ❷ 紧赶;赶忙或赶急事 hurry; hasten; rush:～命 run about on business; be kept on the run; be rushed off one's feet|～丧 hasten home for the funeral of one's parent or grandparent ❸ 逃跑 run away; flee:～逃 flee; run away|东～西窜 flee in all directions

☞ bèn on p.93

【奔波】bēnbō 忙忙碌碌地往来奔走 rush about; dash about; hurry back and forth:四处～ dash around; rush about|不辞劳苦,为集体～ rush about indefatigably for the collective

【奔驰】bēnchí (车、马等)很快地跑 dash; speed; run fast:骏马～sturdy steeds on the gallop|列车在广阔的原野上～。A train sped across the vast open country.

【奔窜】bēncuàn 走投无路地乱跑;狼狈逃跑 run away; flee; stampede:敌军被打得四处～。The enemy troops were defeated and fled in all directions.

【奔放】bēnfàng (思想、感情、文章气势等)尽情流露,不受拘束 (of thoughts, feelings, style of writing, etc.) bold and unrestrained; uninhibited:热情～ overflowing with enthusiasm; brimming with fervent emotion|笔意～ write in a vigorous and racy style

【奔赴】bēnfù 奔向(一定目的地) hurry; hasten; rush:～战场 rush to the battlefield|～前线 rush to the front

【奔劳】bēnláo 奔波劳碌 dash about; bustle about:日夜～ bustle about day and night

【奔流】bēnliú ❶ (水)急速地流;淌得很快 (of water) flow at a great speed; gush:大河～。The great river flows swiftly.|铁水～。Molten iron gushed out in a stream. ❷ 奔腾的流水;急流 flowing stream; racing current:～直下 hurtle downwards

【奔忙】bēnmáng 奔走操劳 bustle or dash about:他为料理这件事,～了好几天。He has been busy attending to this matter for days.

【奔命】bēnmìng 奉命奔走 be kept on the hop; be rushed off one's feet; ☞ 疲于奔命 pí yú bēn mìng on p.1467

☞ bèn//mìng on p.93

【奔跑】bēnpǎo 很快地跑;奔走 run; race:往来～ run about|～如飞 dash about; race off

【奔丧】bēn//sāng 从外地急忙赶回去料理长辈亲属的丧事 hasten home for the funeral of one's parent or grandparent

【奔驶】bēnshǐ (车辆等)很快地跑 move with great speed; speed

【奔逝】bēnshì (时间、水流等)飞快地过去 (time, water, etc.) pass rapidly:岁月～。Time passes quickly.|～的河水 a rapid stream

【奔逃】bēntáo 逃奔;逃跑 flee; run away:～他乡 flee one's hometown|四散～ run away (or scurry off) in all directions; flee helter-skelter|狼狈～ scurry off in disarray

【奔腾】bēnténg (许多马)跳跃着奔跑 gallop:一马当先,万马～。One horse galloped at the head of ten thousand. ◇思绪～ with one's mind racing|黄河～呼啸而来。The roaring waves of the Yellow River roll on and on.

【奔突】bēntū 横冲直撞;奔驰 dash about; run wildly:四下～ dash about in all directions|～向前 run forward wildly

【奔袭】bēnxí 向距离较远的敌人迅速进军,进行突然袭击 long-range raid:命令部队,轻装～ order the troops to pack light military equipment for a long-range raid

【奔泻】bēnxiè (水流)向低处急速地流 (of torrents) rush down; pour down:瀑布～而下。The waterfall thunders down.

【奔涌】bēnyǒng 急速地涌出;奔流 gush out; flow rapidly:大江～。The great river flows rapidly.|热泪～ hot tears gushing out (or streaming down)◇激情～ overflow with passion

【奔逐】bēnzhú 奔跑追逐 chase after:孩子们在田野里尽情地～嬉闹。The children are frolicking about in the fields, as happy as can be.

【奔走】bēnzǒu ❶ 急走;跑 run around; rush about; bustle about:～相告 run around passing on the message; rush about spreading the (exciting) news ❷ 为一定目的而到处活动 rush about; be busy running about (or around):～衣食 rush about in order to feed and clothe oneself|～了几天,事情仍然没有结果。After rushing about for days, still no result has been achieved.

【奔走呼号】bēnzǒu hūháo 一边奔跑,一边喊叫。形容为办成某事而到处宣传,以争取同情和支持。go campaigning (for a cause); canvass support; go hither and thither to call out for sth.; go around crying out for help and support

贲 bēn ❶ ☞ 虎贲 hǔbēn on p.821 ❷ (Bēn) 姓 a surname

☞ bì on p.107

【贲门】bēnmén 胃与食管相连的部分,是胃上端的口儿,食管中的食物通过贲门进入胃内 cardia; opening that connects the esophagus with the upper part of the stomach, through which food descending the esophagus enters the stomach; (图见 ☞ figure for 消化系统 xiāohuà xìtǒng on p.2100)

栟 bēn 栟茶(Bēnchá),地名,在江苏 Bencha, a place in Jiangsu Province

☞ bīng on p. 139

犇 bēn same as 奔 bēn

锛 bēn ❶ 锛子 adze ❷ 用锛子削平木料 cut with an adze：～木头 cut wood with an adze ❸〈方 *dial.*〉刃出现缺口 dent (edge of a knife, etc.)：刀使～了。The knife's edge was dented through use.｜这种刻刀不卷不～。This kind of graver is neither curling nor dented.

【锛子】bēn·zi 削平木料的工具，柄与刃具相垂直呈丁字形，刃具扁而宽，使用时向下向里用力 adze; tool with the flat and broad blade forming a T shape with the handle, used to shape pieces of wood by directing one's strength downward and inward

běn（ㄅㄣˇ）

本[1] běn ❶ 草木的茎或根 root or stem of a plant：草～ grass family｜木～ plants with stiff trunks; trunk of a tree｜水有源，木有～。A stream has its source, and a tree its roots. ❷〈书 *fml.*〉〈量词 *classifier*〉用于花木 used of flowering plants：牡丹十～ 10 peony bulbs (or plants) ❸ 事物的根本、根源（跟'末'相对 as opposed to 'tip' or 'end'）foundation; basis; origin：忘～ forget one's class origin; forget one's past suffering｜舍～逐末 attend to trifles and neglect essentials｜兵民是胜利之～。The militia is the foundation of our triumph. ❹（～儿 běnr）本钱；本金 capital; principal：下～儿 invest｜够～儿 gain enough to recoup the costs｜赔～儿 lose money｜还～付息 pay back the principal over and above the interest◇吃老～儿 live off one's past gains; sit on one's laurels ❺ 主要的；中心的 main; chief; central：～部 main or central part; headquarters｜～科 regular undergraduate course (as distinct from junior college or correspondence course) ❻ 本来；原来 original; initial：～意 original idea; original intention｜～色 inherent qualities; distinctive character｜～想不去 did not want to go (but actually went) ❼ 自己方面的 one's own; native：～厂 our factory｜～校 our school｜～国 our country ❽ 现今的 current; present; this：～年 this year; current｜～月 this month; current month ❾ 按照；根据 according to; based on; in line with：～着政策办事 handle affairs according to the principle｜这句话是有所～的。The statement is well founded.

本[2] běn ❶（～儿 běnr）本子 book：书～ book｜账～儿 account book; ledger ❷ 版本 version; edition：刻～ block-printed edition｜抄～ scribe's copy｜稿～ manuscript ❸（～儿 běnr）演出的底本 script：话～text of a story; script for story telling｜剧～ storyteller's script (in folk literature during the Song and Yuan dynasties); text of a story ❹ 封建时代指奏章 memorial presented to the emperor (in feudal times)：修～（拟奏章）write a memorial｜奏上一～ present a memorial to the throne ❺（～儿 běnr）〈量词 *classifier*〉a) 用于书籍薄册 [used for books of various kinds]：五～书 five books (or copies)｜两～儿账 two account books (one for actual, day-to-day use and the other for tax examiners) b) 用于戏 [used for traditional operas or their scripts]：头～《西游记》first part of the dramatised *Journey to the West* c) 用于一定长度的影片 [used for films of a certain length]：这部电影是十四～。This is a 14-reel film.

【本白布】běnbáibù 未经漂白、染色的布 unbleached cloth

【本本】běnběn 书本；本子 book：你看，～上写得很清楚嘛。Look, it is written in black and white in this book.

【本本主义】běn·běn zhǔyì 一种脱离实际的、盲目地凭书本条文或上级指示办事的作风 book worship (indicating a blind faith in dogma or punctilious adherence to written rules and directives); dogmatism

【本币】běnbì 本位货币的简称 abbr. for 本位货币 běnwèi huòbì

【本部】běnbù （机构、组织等）主要的、中心的部分 main or central part; headquarters：校～ major campus

【本埠】běnbù 本地（多用于较大的城镇 oft. a large town）this town or city：平信～邮资一角，外埠两角。A stamp for a local letter costs one *jiao*; and one for an out-of-town letter, two *jiao*.

【本初子午线】běnchū-zǐwǔxiàn 0°经线，是计算东西经度的起点。1884 年国际会议决定用通过英国格林尼治(Greenwich)天文台子午仪中心的经线为本初子午线。1957 年后，格林尼治天文台迁移台址。1968 年国际上以国际协议原点(CIO)作为地极原点，经度起点实际上不变。first meridian; prime meridian; 0° meridian, which is the starting point for calculating the east and west meridians. In 1884 it was decided at an international conference to use the meridian line passing through the Meridian Instrument Centre at the Greenwich Observatory in Britain as the first (or prime) meridian. In 1957 the Greenwich Observatory moved to another site. In 1968 the CIO became internationally regarded as the terrestrial pole origin, which actually made no change in the starting point of the meridians.

【本岛】běndǎo 几个岛屿中的主要岛屿，其名称和这几个岛屿总体的名称相同。例如我国的台湾包括台湾本岛和澎湖列岛、火烧岛、兰屿等许多岛屿。main island; island proper; major

B

island among several smaller ones, whose name refers both to itself and the others (e.g. Taiwan of China is a name that covers many islands, such as the Taiwan Main Island, Penghu Islands, Burning Fire Island and Orchid Island)

B

【本地】běndì 人、物所在的地区；叙事时特指的某个地区 local; this locality：～人 native; local inhabitant|～口音 local accent

【本分】běnfèn ❶ 本身应尽的责任和义务 one's job; one's duty：～的工作 one's job ❷ 安于所处的地位和环境 contented with the present status and environment; decent：～人 decent person|守～ keep one's place; never go beyond what is proper|这个人很～。He is a decent guy.

【本固枝荣】běn gù zhī róng（树木）主干强固，枝叶才能茂盛 when the roots are firm, the branches and leaves flourish;〈比喻 *fig.*〉事物的基础巩固了，其他部分才能发展 things only develop from sound foundations

【本行】běnháng ❶ 个人一贯从事的或长期已经熟习的行业 one's old profession; profession one has always engaged in or been trained for：他原来是医生，还是让他干老～吧。Let him take up his original profession as a doctor. ❷ 现在从事的工作 one's current profession or work：三句话不离～ unable to utter three sentences without talking shop; can hardly open one's mouth without talking shop|熟悉～业务 be well-versed in one's line of work

【本纪】běnjì 纪传体史书中帝王的传记，一般按年月编排重要史实，列在全书的前面，对全书起总纲的作用 primary chronicle (listing major events of a dynasty centred around the life of the reigning emperor); emperor's biography (page at the front of a biographical history book, in which important historical events are chronologically arranged, serving as a general outline)

【本家】běnjiā 同宗族的人 member of the same family; relative with the same surname：～兄弟 my brother

【本家儿】běnjiār〈方 *dial.*〉指当事人 person or party concerned：～不来，别人不好替他做主。If the party concerned is not present, others cannot take responsibility for a decision on his behalf.

【本金】běnjīn ❶ 存款者或放款者拿出的钱（区别于'利息' as compared with 'interest'）principal; sum of money drawn by a saver or money lender ❷ 经营工商业的本钱；营业的资本 capital; principal to manage industry and trade; money used in a business

【本科】běnkē 大学或学院的基本组成部分（区别于'预科、函授部'等 as compared with 'prior course', 'correspondence course', etc.）regular undergraduate course

【本来】běnlái ❶ 原有的 original：～面貌 true features; truth; objective reality|～的颜色 original hues ❷ 原先；先前 originally; at first：他～身体很瘦弱，现在很结实了。He used to be thin and weak, but is now very sturdy.|我～不知道，到了这里才听说有这么回事。I knew nothing about it until I came here. ❸ 表示理所当然 as a matter of course; naturally：～就该这样办。It should of course be handled that way.

【本利】běnlì 本金和利息 principal and interest

【本领】běnlǐng 技能；能力 skill; ability; capability：有～ be capable|～高强 excel in one's skill (or ability)

【本名】běnmíng ❶ 本来的名字；原来的名字（区别于'别号、官衔'等 as compared with 'alias' or 'official title'）original name ❷ 给本人起的名儿 (of foreigners) first name：有些外国人的全名分三部分，第一部分是～，第二部分是父名，第三部分是姓。The full names of some foreigners can be divided into three parts: the first part, the given name; the second part, the father's name; and the third part, the surname.

【本命年】běnmìngnián 我国习惯用十二生肖记人的出生年，每十二年轮回一次。如子年出生的人属鼠，再遇子年，就是这个人的本命年。year of (one's) birth; birth year; the year in which a person was born, recurring in a 12-year cycle associated with one of the 12 Earthly Branches, each marked by a symbolic animal. For example, a person born in the Year of *Zi* (The 1st Earthly Branch), which is customarily called, the Year of Rat, meets his year of birth when the Year of Rat occurs at a 12-year interval. ☞ 生肖 shēngxiào on p. 1718

【本末】běnmò ❶ 树的下部和上部，东西的底部和顶部 upper and lower parts of a tree; top and bottom of sth.;〈比喻 *fig.*〉事情从头到尾的经过 course of an event from beginning to end; ins and outs：详述～ tell the whole story from beginning to end ❷〈比喻 *fig.*〉主要的与次要的 the fundamental and the incidental：～颠倒 put the incidental before the fundamental; put non-essentials before fundamentals; put the cart before the horse

【本能】běnnéng ❶ 人类和动物不学就会的本领，如初生的婴儿会哭会吃奶，蜂酿蜜等都是本能的表现 instinct; inborn ability of humans and animals, such as a baby's ability to cry and suckle at its mother's breast, and a bee's ability to make honey, which are not based on learning ❷ 有机体对外界刺激不知不觉地、无意识地（作出反应）instinctive (behaviour); unconscious reaction of an organism towards external stimulation：他看见红光一闪，～地闭

上了眼睛。Dazzled by the red light, he instinctively closed his eyes.

【本钱】běn·qián ❶ 用来营利、生息、赌博等的钱财 capital; principal (used to gain or pursue profit, bear interest, gamble, etc.):做买卖得有～。Doing business requires capital. ❷〈比喻 *fig.*〉可以凭借的资历、能力、条件等 qualification, ability, condition, etc. that one can rely on; asset:强壮的身体是做好工作的～。A robust build is his basic asset for doing well at his job.

【本人】běnrén ❶ 说话人指自己 I; me; myself:这是～的亲身经历。This is my firsthand experience. ❷ 指当事人自己或前边所提到的人自己 oneself; in person:结婚要～同意,别人不能包办代替。A marriage should be agreed to by the person concerned, and not by others without consulting him or her.|他的那段坎坷经历,还是由他～来谈吧。It should be he himself that speaks of his experience of frustrations.

【本嗓】běnsǎng (～儿 běnsǎngr)说话或歌唱的时候自然发出的嗓音 natural voice (of speaking or singing)

【本色】běnsè 本来面貌 inherent qualities; distinctive character:英雄～ true qualities of a hero

【本色】běnshǎi (～儿 běnshǎir)物品原来的颜色(多指没有染过色的织物 of sth., usu. undyed fabrics) natural colour:～布 grey (or white) cloth

【本身】běnshēn 自身(多指集团、单位或事物 usu. of a group, unit or matter) oneself; in oneself:要挖掘企业～的潜力。It is imperative to tap the potentials of enterprises.|生活～就是复杂多样的。Life is itself complex and various.

【本生灯】běnshēngdēng 用煤气做燃料的一种产生高温的装置,由一个长管和一个套在外面的短管组成,旁边有孔,转动短管就可以调节管口火焰的大小。多用在化学实验室中。是德国化学家本生(Robert Wihelm Bunsen)发明的。通称煤气灯。Bunsen burner; type of gas burner invented by Robert Wihelm Bunsen, a German chemist, commonly used in chemical laboratories, which produces high temperature, comprising a long metal tube covered by a short one, both of which have adjustable holes at their base, through which to control the flame.

【本事】běnshì 文学作品主题所根据的故事情节 source material; original story (of the themes of literary works):～诗 original poem|这些诗词的～,年久失考。The original stories to these poems have been lost over the years.

【本事】běn·shi 本领 skill; ability; capability:有～ be capable (or talented)|学～ learn a skill|～大 be very capable (or talented)

【本题】běntí 谈话和文章的主题或主要论点(of a speech or an article) point at issue; subject under discussion:这一段文字跟～无关,应该删去。This paragraph has nothing to do with the topic, and should be deleted.

【本体】běntǐ ❶ 德国哲学家康德唯心主义哲学中的重要概念,指与现象对立的不可认识的'自在之物'。辩证唯物主义否认现象和本体之间有不可逾越的界限,认为只有尚未认识的东西,没有不可认识的东西。noumenon; thing-in-itself; object of purely intellectual perception, as compared with a phenomenon; important concept within the idealistic philosophy of Immanuel Kant, a German philosopher, while dialectical materialism denies the impassable limit between a phenomenon and the thing-in-itself, holding that there are only things that can be understood, and nothing is beyond understanding ❷ 机器、工程等的主要部分 main part or body (of a machine, project, etc.)

【本土】běntǔ ❶ 乡土;原来的生长地 one's native country or land:本乡～ native land; native soil; home village ❷ 指殖民国家本国的领土(对所掠夺的殖民地而言。也指一个国家固有的领土。as compared with the colonies plundered by it) metropolitan territory; native land of a colonialist power; inherent territory of a country ❸ 指本地的土壤 native soil:由于田里土层太薄,只有借客土加厚～,才能深耕。As the soil in this field is too shallow, deep culture can only be achieved by supplementing it with earth brought in from elsewhere.

【本位】běnwèi ❶ 货币制度的基础或货币价值的计算标准 standard; basis of monetary system or calculating criterion of monetary value:金～ gold standard|银～ silver standard|～货币 standard or basic unit of a national currency ❷ 自己所在的单位;自己工作的岗位 department or unit one works in:～工作 one's own job; work of one's own department|立足～,一专多能。Basing oneself at one's own job, one should strive to specialize in one aspect and be able at many.

【本位货币】běnwèi huòbì 一国货币制度中的基本货币,如我国票面为'圆'的人民币 standard or basic unit of a national currency (e. g. China's Renminbi bill in yuan denomination); 简称 abbr. 本币 běnbì

【本位主义】běnwèi zhǔyì 为自己所在的小单位打算而不顾整体利益的思想作风 working solely for the interests of one's own department or unit (at the expense of the wider considerations of overall interests); departmental egoism; (selfish) departmentalism

【本文】běnwén ❶ 所指的这篇文章 this article; this text: ～准备谈谈经济问题。This article deals with economic problems. ❷ 原文（区别于'译文'或'注解' as compared with 'translation' or 'footnote'）original text

B

【本息】běnxī 本金和利息 principal and interest: 偿还～ repay the principal and interest

【本戏】běnxì 成本演出的戏曲，内容包括一个完整的故事，有时不一定一次演完（区别于'折子戏' as compared with 'an aria'（of traditional Chinese opera）complete series; opera in episodes comprising a complete story, which is not always complete in one performance: 连台～ multi-part series（of traditional opera）

【本乡本土】běn xiāng běn tǔ（～的 běn xiāng běn tǔ·de）家乡；本地 native land; native soil; home village: 菜都是～的，请尝尝。These are all local dishes; please try them.｜都是～的，在外边彼此多照应点儿。As fellow townspeople, we should look after each other when away from our home.

【本相】běnxiàng 本来面目；原形 true features or colours: ～毕露 reveal one's true features completely

【本心】běnxīn 本来的心愿 original intention; motive: 出于～ of one's free will

【本性】běnxìng 原来的性质或个性 innate nature; inherent quality: 江山易改，～难移。Rivers and mountains may change, but it is hard to alter a man's character.

【本业】běnyè ❶ 本来的职业 original or primary occupation; original profession; previous line of business: 士农工商，各安～。Let soldiers, peasants, workers and merchants be settled in their respective occupations. ❷〈书 *fml.*〉指农业 agriculture

【本义】běnyì 词语的本来的意义，如'兵'的本义是武器，引申为战士（拿武器的人）original or primary meaning of a word; literal sense (e.g. the original meaning of 兵 bīng is weapons or arms; and its extended meaning, soldier — person with arms)

【本意】běnyì 原来的意思或意图 original intention; original idea: 他的～还是好的，只是话说得重了些。He meant well, but his words sounded a little sharp.

【本原】běnyuán 哲学上指一切事物的最初根源或构成世界的最根本实体 principle; first origin of all things or most fundamental substance that constitutes the world

【本源】běnyuán 事物产生的根源 origin; source

【本愿】běnyuàn 本心 original desire: 学医是我的～。It has always been my wish to study medicine.

【本职】běnzhí 指自己担任的职务 one's job; one's duty: 做好～工作 do one's own job well

【本质】běnzhì 指事物本身所固有的、决定事物性质、面貌和发展的根本属性。事物的本质是隐蔽的，是通过现象来表现的，不能用简单的直观去认识，必须透过现象掌握本质。essence; nature; innate character; intrinsic quality; innate essential property of a thing that decides its nature, features and development, which is both concealed and revealed by its superficial appearance; one must see beyond the surface to get to the essence, rather than perceiving directly through the senses

【本主儿】běnzhǔr ❶ 本人 oneself: ～一会儿就来，你问他得了。The man himself will be here in a moment, so you had better ask him about it. ❷ 失物的所有者 owner of lost property: 物归～ return sth. to its rightful owner｜这辆招领的自行车，～还没来取。The owner of this lost-and-found bike has not shown up to claim it yet.

【本字】běnzì 一个字通行的写法与原来的写法不同，原来的写法就称为本字，如'掰'的本字是'擘'，'搬'的本字是'般'，'喝'（喝酒）的本字是'欱' original form of a character, e.g. the original form of 掰 bāi is 擘 bò; 搬 bān, 般 bān; and 喝 hē（喝酒 hējiǔ），欱 hē

【本子】běn·zi ❶ 把成沓的纸装订在一起而成的东西；册子 book; notebook; sheets of paper fastened together: 笔记～ notebook｜改～（评改作业）correct students' homework; go over students' papers ❷ 版本 edition: 这两个～都是宋本。They are both Song editions. ❸ 指某些证件 licence; diploma; certificate: 考～（通过考试取得驾驶执照或其他合格证书）take a test to obtain a driver's licence (or other certificates)

苯 běn 有机化合物，化学式 C_6H_6。无色液体，有芳香气味，容易挥发和燃烧。可用做燃料、熔剂、香料等，也用来合成有机物质。benzene; organic chemical compound and colourless fragrant liquid (C_6H_6) that volatilises easily and burns quickly, used to make fuel, solvent, perfume, etc., and compound organisms

【苯甲基】běnjiǎjī 甲苯分子中甲基上失去一个氢原子而成的一价基团（$C_6H_5CH_2$-）benzyl; univalent atomic groups and radicals of toluene molecules formed by losing a hydrogen atom in methyl; also 苄基 biànjī

畚 běn ❶ same as 簸箕 bò·ji ① ❷〈方 *dial.*〉用簸箕撮 scoop up with a dustpan: ～土 scoop dirt with a dustpan｜～炉灰 scoop up stove ashes with a dustpan

【畚斗】běndǒu〈方 *dial.*〉簸箕（专用于撮、簸粮食）bamboo or wicker scoop; dustpan (esp. for scooping or winnowing grains)

【畚箕】běnjī〈方 *dial.*〉簸箕 dustpan; bamboo or wicker scoop

bèn(ㄅㄣˋ)

夯 bèn same as 笨 bèn(见于《西游记》、《红楼梦》等书 a word that can be seen in such books as *Journey to the West* and *A Dream of Red Mansions*)
☞ hāng on p.769

坋 bèn〈书 *fml.*〉尘埃 dust
☞ fèn on p.575

坌[1] bèn〈方 *dial.*〉翻(土);刨 dig; turn over:~地 dig the ground; turn over the soil

坌[2] bèn〈书 *fml.*〉❶ 尘埃 dust:尘~ dust|微~ fine dust ❷ 聚 gather; collect:~集 gather together; converge ❸ 粗劣 crude and inferior; shoddy ❹ 用细末撒在物体上面 spread with powder ❺ same as 笨 bèn

奔(逩) bèn ❶ 直向目的地走去 go straight to; head for; make straight for:投~ go to (a friend or a place) for shelter|直~工地 make straight for the construction site|他顺着小道直~那山头。Walking along the path, he headed for the hilltop. ❷〈介词 *prep.*〉朝;向 towards:~这边看 look this way|渔轮~渔场开去。The fishing vessel set sail towards the fishery. ❸ 年纪接近(四十岁、五十岁等)(of one's age) approach; get close to; be getting on for (40, 50, etc.):他是~六十的人了。He is getting on for 60. ❹ 为某事奔走 go about (some business):~球票 go and try to get a ticket to the ball game|你们生产上还缺什么材料,我去~。If you are still short of some of the material you need for production, I'll go and see if I can get it.
☞ bēn on p.88

【奔命】bèn//mìng 拼命赶路或做事 be in a desperate hurry:一路~,连续行军一百二十多里。The troops marched over 120 *li* rapidly without stopping.
☞ bēnmìng on p.88

【奔头儿】bèn·tour 经过努力奋斗,可指望的前途 sth. to strive for; sth. to gain; prospect:有~ have bright prospects; sth. worth striving for|没~ have nothing to look forward to

倴 bèn 倴城(Bènchéng),地名,在河北 Bencheng, a place in Hebei Province

笨 bèn ❶ 理解能力和记忆能力差;不聪明 stupid; dull; foolish; dense; of poor understanding and memory; not bright or clever:愚~ stupid|脑子~ stupid; slow-witted; dull-witted|他很~。He is very stupid. ❷ 不灵巧;不灵活 clumsy; awkward:嘴~ inarticulate|~手~脚 be clumsy; be gauche; be all fingers and thumbs ❸ 费力气的;笨重 cumbersome; awkward; unwieldy:~活儿 heavy unskilled work; heavy manual labour|搬大箱子、大柜子这些~家具得找年轻人。Young people should be asked to move cumbersome furniture such as large suitcases and cupboards.

【笨伯】bènbó〈书 *fml.*〉愚蠢的人 stupid person; dunce

【笨蛋】bèndàn 蠢人(骂人的话 curse) fool; idiot; dunce

【笨活儿】bènhuór 笨重的工作;粗活儿 heavy unskilled work; heavy manual labour

【笨口拙舌】bèn kǒu zhuō shé 嘴笨;没有口才 clumsy in speech; not particularly articulate; also 笨嘴拙舌 bèn zuǐ zhuō shé

【笨鸟先飞】bèn niǎo xiān fēi〈比喻 *fig.*〉能力差的人做事时,恐怕落后,比别人先行动(多用做谦辞 oft. hum.) clumsy birds must start flying before the rest; an inefficient person must start work earlier for fear of falling behind

【笨手笨脚】bèn shǒu bèn jiǎo 形容动作不灵活或手脚不灵巧 be clumsy; be gauche; be all fingers and thumbs

【笨头笨脑】bèn tóu bèn nǎo ❶ 形容人不聪明,反应迟钝 slow; slow-witted ❷ 形容式样蠢笨 clumsy; cumbersome:皮鞋做得~的,年轻人不爱穿。Young people do not like to wear cumbersome leather shoes.

【笨重】bènzhòng ❶ 庞大沉重;不灵巧 heavy; cumbersome; unwieldy:~家具 heavy cumbersome furniture|身体~ be clumsy ❷ 繁重而费力的 arduous and strenuous:用机器代替~的体力劳动 use machines rather than doing heavy manual work

【笨拙】bènzhuō 笨;不聪明;不灵巧 clumsy; awkward; stupid:动作~ clumsy (or awkward) in movement|笔法~ clumsy (or awkward) writing style

bēng(ㄅㄥ)

伻 bēng〈书 *fml.*〉使者 envoy

祊 bēng〈古代 *arch.*〉宗庙门内设祭的地方,也指在这个地方举行的祭祀 part of a temple where sacrifices were held; offering of sacrifices to gods or ancestors at such a place

崩 bēng ❶ 倒塌;崩裂 collapse:雪~ avalanche|山~地裂。Mountains collapse and the ground cracks. ❷ 破裂 burst; crack; split:把气球吹~了 burst a balloon◇两个人谈~了。Negotiations between the two of them broke down. ❸ 崩裂的东西击中 hit:炸起的石头差点儿把他~伤了。He was nearly hit by stone fragments from the explosion. ❹ 枪毙 shoot; execute by shooting ❺ 君主时代称帝

王死 (of emperor) pass away：驾～ (of emperor) die

【崩溃】bēngkuì 完全破坏；垮台(多指国家政治、经济、军事等 usu. of a nation's politics, economy, military, etc.) collapse; break down; crumble; fall apart

B

【崩裂】bēngliè (物体)猛然分裂成若干部分 burst or break apart; crack：炸药轰隆一声，山石～。The dynamite exploded with a boom, sending rocks flying.

【崩龙族】Bēnglóngzú 德昂族的旧称 Benglong, old name for De'ang, an ethnic minority people in Yunnan Province

【崩塌】bēngtā 崩裂而倒塌 collapse; crumble：江堤～。The embankment along the river collapsed.

【崩坍】bēngtān 悬崖、陡坡上的岩石、泥土崩裂散落下来；崩塌 (of a cliff or slope) crumble and fall; collapse：山崖～。The cliff collapsed.

绷[1] (繃) bēng ❶ 拉紧 stretch tight; strain：把绳子～直了。Straighten the rope. ❷ 衣服、布、绸等张紧 (of a dress, a piece of cloth or silk, etc.) tight; taut：小褂紧～在身上不舒服。This shirt is so tight that it is uncomfortable to wear. ❸ (物体)猛然弹起 spring; bounce：弹簧～飞了。The spring bounced away. ❹ 缝纫方法，稀疏地缝住或用针别上 baste; pin; tack; make rough stitches：红布上～着金字。Gold characters basted on a piece of red fabric. ❺〈方 *dial*.〉勉强支持；硬撑 be barely able to subsist; manage with difficulty：～场面 keep up appearances ❻ 用藤皮、棕绳等编织成的床屉子 framed matting (for a bed woven from rattan, coir rope, etc.)：棕～ framed matting made of palm fibre | 床～坏了，该修理了。The bed's framed matting is broken, and should be repaired. ❼ same as 绷子 bēng·zi ①：竹～ framed matting made of bamboo | ～架 embroidery frame

绷[2] (繃) bēng〈方 *dial*.〉骗(财物) swindle; cheat：坑～拐骗 use all possible means to swindle | 他～了人家几百块钱。He defrauded others out of several hundred yuan.

☞ běng on p. 94 and bèng on p. 95

【绷场面】bēng chǎngmiàn〈方 *dial*.〉撑场面 be barely able to keep the appearance of respectability; keep up appearances

【绷带】bēngdài 包扎伤口或患处用的纱布带 bandage; a piece of gauze for dressing a wound or an infected part (of a patient's body)

【绷弓子】bēnggōng·zi ❶ 装在门上用来自动关门的装置，用弹簧或竹片等制成 door-closing spring or bamboo bow ❷〈方 *dial*.〉弹弓 catapult

【绷簧】bēnghuáng〈方 *dial*.〉弹簧 spring

【绷子】bēng·zi ❶ 刺绣时用来绷紧布帛的用具，大件用长方形的木框子，小件用竹圈 embroidery frame; hoop; tambour; tool for keeping cloth or silk taut when embroidering; rectangle wooden frame is used for a large work of embroidery, while a bamboo hoop is used for a smaller work：花～ embroidery frame; hoop; tambour ❷ same as 绷 bēng ⑥：藤～ framed matting made from rattan | ～床 bed with framed matting

嘣 bēng〈拟声词 *onom*.〉形容跳动或爆裂的声音 sound of sth. bouncing, snapping, or bursting：心里～～直跳 relentless pounding (or thumping) of one's heart | ～的一声，气球爆了。The balloon burst with a bang.

甏 bēng same as 祊 bēng

béng (ㄅㄥˊ)

甭 béng〈方 *dial*.〉'不用'的合音，表示不需要 (composite tone of 不用 bùyòng) no need to：你既然都知道，我就～说了。As you already know all about it, there's no need for me to say anything. | 这些小事儿，你～管。No need to bother about these trifles.

běng (ㄅㄥˇ)

菶 běng [菶菶]〈书 *fml*.〉形容草木茂盛 lush or luxuriant (vegetation)

绷(繃) běng ❶ 板着 pull (a long face)：～脸 pull a long face ❷ 勉强支撑 strain oneself：咬住牙～住劲 clench one's teeth and strain one's muscles

☞ bēng on p. 94 and bèng on p. 95

【绷劲】běng//jìn (～儿 běng//jìnr) 屏住气息用力 pant from exertion; strain oneself：绷不住劲 be unable to push oneself any further | 他一～，就把大石头举过了头顶。Straining hard, he lifted the boulder above his head.

【绷脸】běng//liǎn 板着脸，表示不高兴 pull a long face; be sullen：他绷着脸，半天一句话也不说。Pulling a long face, he did not utter a word for a long time.

琫 běng〈古代 *arch*.〉刀鞘上端的饰物 pendent attached to the upper end of the sheath of a knife

鞛 běng same as 琫 běng

鞯 běng same as 琫 běng

bèng (ㄅㄥˋ)

泵 bèng ❶ 吸入和排出流体的机械，能把流体抽出或压入容器，也能把液体提送到高处。

平常按用途不同分为气泵、水泵、油泵。pump; machine for forcing liquids into or out of sth. or sending it upwards, usu. classified into gas, water, and petrol pumps according to usage; also 帮浦 bāngpǔ or 唧筒 jītǒng ❷ 用泵压入或抽出 pump-in and pump-out: ～入 pump-in | ～出 pump-out | ～油 pump oil

迸 bèng ❶ 向外溅出或喷射 spout; spurt; burst forth; blurt: 打铁时火星儿乱～ sparks of molten steel fly out in all directions | 潮水冲来，礁石边上～起乳白色的浪花。Foaming waves lashed the rocks, shooting up sprays of water as the tide rushed in. ◇沉默了半天，他才～出一句话来。It was quite a while before he was able to blurt out a few words and break the silence. ❷ 突然碎裂 suddenly burst into fragments: ～裂 split; burst (open) | ～碎 burst into fragments; break into pieces

【迸发】bèngfā 由内而外地突然发出 burst forth; burst out: 一锤子打到岩石上，～了好些火星儿。As the hammer pounded against the rock, showers of sparks burst out. ◇笑声从四面八方～出来。Laughter burst out from all directions.

【迸溅】bèngjiàn 向四外溅 splash (in all directions): 火花～ sparks flying out | 激流冲击着岩石，～起无数飞沫。The rapids dashed against the rocks, spraying out foam.

【迸裂】bèngliè 破裂；裂开而往外飞溅 split; burst (open): 山石～。The stones on the mountain burst. | 脑浆～ have one's brains dashed out

蚌 bèng 蚌埠(Bèngbù)，地名，在安徽 Bengbu, a city in Anhui Province
☞ bàng on p. 58

绷(繃) bèng ❶ 裂开 split open; crack: 西瓜～了一道缝儿。The watermelon has a crack in it. ❷ 用在'硬、直、亮'一类形容词的前面，表示程度深 [used before adjectives like 硬 yìng, 直 zhí, 亮 liàng, etc., as an intensifier]: ～硬 hard as rock | ～直 straight as a die | ～脆 crisp as starch | ～亮 star-bright
☞ bēng on p. 94 and běng on p. 94

【绷瓷】bèngcí (～儿 bèngcír)表面的釉层有不规则碎纹的瓷器。这种碎纹是由于坯和釉的膨胀系数不同而形成的。crackleware; porcelain with a cracked finish; porcelain with irregular cracked patterns on a glazed finish, formed through the various coefficients of expansion or dilation of its base and glaze

甏 bèng 〈方 *dial.*〉瓮；坛子 jar; vat: 酒～ vats of wine

镚 bèng ☞ below

【镚儿】bèngr same as 镚子 bèng·zi

【镚子】bèng·zi 原指清末不带孔的小铜币，十个当一个铜元，现在把小形的硬币叫钢镚子或钢镚儿 small coin; late Qing-dynasty small copper coin without a hole in it, ten of which were equivalent to a copper; small coin called 钢镚子 gāngbèng·zi or 钢镚儿 gāngbèngr; also 镚儿 bèngr

【镚子儿】bèngzǐr 〈方 *dial.*〉指极少量的钱 smallest denomination of money; penny: ～不值 not worth a penny | 一个～也不给 not give sb. even a penny

蹦 bèng 跳 leap; jump; spring: 欢～乱跳 alive and kicking | 皮球一拍～得老高。A mere tap is enough to send the ball bouncing high. | 他蹲下身子，用力一～，就～了六七尺远。Squatting on his heels, he sprang with all his might to a distance of six or seven feet. ◇他嘴里不时～出一些新词儿来。He would come up with a few new terms every now and then.

【蹦蹦儿戏】bèngbèngrxì 评剧的前身 predecessor for *pingju*; ☞ 评剧 píngjù on p. 1488

【蹦跶】bèng·da 蹦跳，现多比喻挣扎 bounce or jump about; (fig.) struggle; battle: 秋后的蚂蚱，～不了几天了。After autumn arrives, grasshoppers are on their last legs.

【蹦豆儿】bèngdòur 〈方 *dial.*〉❶ 铁蚕豆 roasted broad beans ❷ 小孩儿 small child

【蹦高】bènggāo (～儿 bènggāor) 跳跃 jump; leap: 乐得直～儿 jump for joy

【蹦跳】bèngtiào 跳跃 jump; prance: 他高兴得～起来。He jumped about in excitement. | 孩子们从院子里蹦蹦跳跳地跑进来。The children pranced and scampered from the courtyard into the room.

bī (ㄅㄧ)

屄(㞘) bī 阴门 vaginal orifice; vulva

逼(偪) bī ❶ 逼迫；给人以威胁 force; compel; press; drive: 威～ compel or threaten by force; coerce | 寒气～人。There is a nip in the air. | 形势～人。The situation is pressing. | 为生活所～ driven as a matter of life ❷ 强迫索取 press for; extort: ～租 press for rent payment | ～债 press for debt repayment; dun ❸ 靠近；接近 press on towards; advance on: ～视 look at from close-up; gaze fixedly at; stare intently at | ～真 lifelike; true to life | 大军已～城郊。The main troops advanced to the outskirts of the town. ❹ 〈书 *fml.*〉狭窄 narrow: ～仄 narrow; cramped

【逼宫】bī//gōng 指大臣强迫帝王退位。也泛指强迫政府首脑辞职或让出权力。(of officials) force a king or an emperor to abdicate; (in a broad sense) force the head of a government to resign or give up his power

【逼供】bīgòng 用酷刑或威胁等手段强迫受审人招供 extort a confession; force sb. to confess by use of torture, threats, etc.: 严刑～ extort a confession through torture

【逼婚】bīhūn 用暴力或威胁手段强迫对方(多为女方)跟自己或别人结婚 force sb. (usu. a female) to marry sb. by use of violence or coercion

【逼近】bījìn 靠近;接近 approach; close in on; press on towards: 小艇～了岸边。The small, light boat approached the bank. | 天色～黄昏。Dusk is falling. | 脚步声从远处渐渐～。The sound of approaching footsteps grew louder.

【逼良为娼】bī liáng wéi chāng 逼迫良家妇女当娼妓 force a young woman from a good family or a woman of virtue to engage in prostitution; 〈比喻 *fig.*〉迫使正直安分的人去做坏事 force an honest person to do sth. dishonest

【逼命】bīmìng ❶ 指用暴力威胁人 threaten sb. with violence ❷〈比喻 *fig.*〉催促得十分紧急,使人感到紧张,难以应付 press sb. to do sth. difficult to accomplish; put pressure on sb. to the extent they feel unequal to the demands of the situation: 真～! 这么大的任务,三天内怎能完成! It is unreasonable to expect such a difficult task to be accomplished in three days!

【逼迫】bīpò 紧紧地催促;用压力促使 force; compel; coerce: 在环境的～下,他开始变得勤奋了。Force of circumstances compelled him to be diligent.

【逼上梁山】bī shàng Liáng Shān《水浒传》中有林冲等人为官府所迫,上梁山造反的情节。后用来比喻被迫进行反抗或不得不做某种事。In the classic, *Outlaws of the Marsh*, Lin Chong and other heroes, forced by the intransigence of local authorities, join the Liangshan rebels. This is now used to mean sb. driven to rebel or compelled to act desperately.

【逼视】bīshì 向前靠近目标,紧紧盯着 look at from close up; gaze fixedly at; stare intently at: 光彩夺目,不可～ shining in dazzling splendour | 在众人的～下,他显得局促不安了。Under the stern gaze of everyone, he began to feel ill at ease.

【逼问】bīwèn 强迫被问者回答 press sb. to answer; interrogate: 无论怎么～,他就是不说。No matter how intensely you question him he will never let on.

【逼肖】bīxiào〈书 *fml.*〉很相似 bear a close resemblance to; be the very image of: 虽是绢花,却与真花～。Although these flowers are made of silk, they bear an uncanny resemblance to the real thing.

【逼仄】bīzè〈书 *fml.*〉(地方)狭窄 narrow; cramped: ～小径 narrow small path | 居室～ cramped living room

【逼真】bīzhēn ❶ 极像真的 lifelike; true to life: 情节～。This plot is true to life. | 这个老虎画得十分～。This painting of a tiger is incredibly lifelike. ❷ 真切 clearly; distinctly: 看得～ see distinctly | 听得～ hear clearly

锟 bī〈书 *fml.*〉❶ 钗 hairpin ❷ 篦子 fine comb

☞ pī on p. 1463

鲾 bī 鱼,身体小而侧扁,略呈卵圆形,青褐色,口小,鳞细。生活在近海。slipmouth (*Leiognathus*); small fish that has a greenish brown, laterally flat, and slightly egg-shaped body, a small mouth and fine scales, and lives in coastal waters

bí (ㄅㄧˊ)

荸 bí [荸荠](bí·qí) ❶ 多年生草本植物,通常栽培在水田里,地下茎扁圆形,皮赤褐色或黑褐色,肉白色,可以吃,又可以制淀粉 water chestnut (*Eleocharis tuberosa*); perennial herb normally cultivated in paddy fields, with an oval subterranean stem, reddish or darkish brown skin, and white edible pulp that can be used to produce starch ❷ 这种植物的地下茎 subterranean stem of such plant ‖ 有的地区叫地梨、地栗或马蹄 in some areas also called 地梨 dìlí, 地栗 dìlì or 马蹄 mǎtí

鼻 bí ❶ 鼻子 nose: ～梁 bridge of the nose | ～音 nasal sound ❷〈书 *fml.*〉开创 pioneer; originate: ～祖 earliest ancestor; originator (of a tradition, school of thought, etc.); founder; guru

【鼻翅儿】bíchìr 鼻翼的通称 general term for 鼻翼 bíyì

【鼻窦】bídòu 鼻旁窦的通称 general term for 鼻旁窦 bípángdòu

【鼻观】bíguàn〈书 *fml.*〉鼻孔 nostril: 花香沁人～。The fragrance of flowers assailed everyone's nostrils.

【鼻化元音】bíhuà yuányīn ☞ 元音 yuányīn on p. 2357

【鼻甲】bíjiǎ 把鼻腔分成窄缝的骨组织,左右鼻腔内各有三个,能使吸入的气流变得缓慢 turbinate; turbinated bones; bone tissue dividing the left and right nasal cavity into three narrow seams that regulate the inhaled air current

【鼻尖】bíjiān (～儿 bíjiānr)鼻子末端最突出的部分 tip of the nose; also 鼻子尖儿 bí·zijiānr

【鼻孔】bíkǒng 鼻腔跟外面相通的孔道 nostril; narrow passage that connects the nasal cavity to the exterior

【鼻梁】bíliáng (～儿 bíliángr)鼻子隆起的部分 bridge of the nose: 高～ steep bridge of the nose | 塌～儿 flat bridge of the nose; also 鼻梁子 bíliáng·zi

【鼻牛儿】bíniúr〈方 *dial.*〉鼻腔里干结的鼻涕 hardened mucus in nostrils; booger

【鼻旁窦】bípángdòu 头颅内部鼻腔周围的空腔 paranasal sinus; cavity that surrounds the nasal cavity in the head; 通称 general term for 鼻窦 bídòu

【鼻腔】bíqiāng 鼻子内部的空腔,分左右两个,壁上有细毛。上部黏膜中有嗅觉细胞,能分辨气味。nasal cavity; left and right cavity in the nose lined with fine, soft cilia, whose olfactory cells on the upper mucosa can distinguish smells

【鼻青脸肿】bí qīng liǎn zhǒng 鼻子青了,脸也肿了。形容面部被碰伤或打伤的样子。也比喻遭到严重打击、挫折的狼狈相。bloody nose and swollen face; (of one's face) be badly battered; be beaten black and blue; (fig.) sorry figure of sb. who has suffered a heavy blow or major setback

【鼻儿】bír ❶ 器物上面能够穿上其他东西的小孔 hole in an implement, utensil, etc. for sth. to be inserted into: 门～ bolt staple | 针～ eye of a needle ❷〈方 *dial.*〉像哨子的东西 whistle: 用苇子做了一个～ make a whistle from a reed

【鼻饲】bísì 病人不能用嘴饮食时,用特制的管子通过鼻腔插入胃内,把流质食物或药液从管子里灌进去 nasal feeding; liquid diet or medicine fed to a patient incapable of imbibing by mouth through a special tube inserted into the nasal cavity that extends directly to the stomach

【鼻酸】bísuān 鼻子发酸 feel a lump in one's throat;〈比喻 *fig.*〉悲伤心酸 feel sad; be sorrowful

【鼻涕】bítì 鼻腔黏膜所分泌的液体 nasal mucus; snivel; liquid secreted by the mucous membrane of nasal cavity

【鼻头】bí·tou〈方 *dial.*〉鼻子 nose

【鼻洼子】bíwā·zi 鼻翼旁边凹下去的部分 furrow beside the nose; also 鼻洼 bíwā

【鼻息】bíxī 从鼻腔出入的气息,特指熟睡时的鼾声 breath (that comes in and goes out of the nasal cavity), esp. sound of snoring of sb. who is fast asleep: ～如雷 snore like thunder

【鼻烟】bíyān (～儿 bíyānr) 由鼻孔吸入的粉末状的烟 snuff; tobacco made into powder for breathing into the nose: ～壶(装鼻烟的小瓶) snuff bottle

【鼻翼】bíyì 鼻尖两旁的部分 wing of nose; ala nasi; 通称 general term for 鼻翅儿 bíchìr

【鼻音】bíyīn 口腔气流通路阻塞,软腭下垂,鼻腔通气发出的音,例如普通话语音的 m, n, ng(ŋ) 等 nasal sound; sound made by obstructing the oral air passageway, drooping the soft palate, and aerating the nasal cavity, e. g. pronunciation of *putonghua* such as m, n, ng (ŋ)

【鼻韵母】bíyùnmǔ 鼻音收尾的韵母。普通话语音中有 an, ian, uan, üan, en, in, un, ün, ang, iang, uang, eng, ing, ong, iong 等。(in pronunciation of Chinese) vowel followed by a nasal consonant, such as the *putonghua* speech sounds an, ian, uan, uan, en, in, un, un, ang, iang, unag, eng, ing, ong and iong

【鼻中隔】bízhōnggé 把鼻腔分成左右两部分的组织,由骨、软骨和黏膜构成 nasal septum; tissue that separates nasal cavity into its left and right sections, made of bone, cartilage and mucosa

【鼻子】bí·zi 人和高等动物的嗅觉器官,又是呼吸器官的一部分,位于头部,有两个孔 nose; olfactory organ with two holes on the face of humans and higher animals; part of respiratory organs

【鼻子眼儿】bí·ziyǎnr same as 鼻孔 bíkǒng

【鼻祖】bízǔ〈书 *fml.*〉始祖 earliest ancestor; originator (of a tradition, school of thought, etc.);〈比喻 *fig.*〉创始人 founder

bǐ (ㄅㄧˇ)

匕 bǐ ❶ 古人取食的器具,后代的羹匙由它演变而来 a type of ancient spoon (that later developed into the current style of spoon) ❷〈书 *fml.*〉指匕首 dagger: 图穷～见 when the map is unrolled, the dagger is revealed — the true intention eventually comes to light

【匕鬯不惊】bǐ chàng bù jīng《周易·震》:'震惊百里,不丧匕鬯。'匕和鬯,都是古代祭祀用品,'匕鬯不惊'原指宗庙祭祀不受惊扰,后用来形容军纪严明,不惊扰百姓。*The Book of Changes· Thunder*, 'The army amazed all in the area of 100 *li* by not disturbing the sacrificial offerings to people's ancestors at ancestral shrines'; 匕 bǐ and 鬯 chàng, ancient sacrificial offerings; (original meaning) sacrificial offerings to ancestors at the ancestral shrines must not be disturbed; (of an army) maintain strict discipline so as not to cause the slightest violation of the people's interests

【匕首】bǐshǒu 短剑或狭长的短刀 dagger; short or pointed knife

比[1] bǐ ❶ 比较;较量 compare; contrast; compete; emulate: ～干劲 enthusiastically compete with each other | 学先进,～先进 learn from and compare oneself with advanced workers ❷ 能够相比 be like; be similar to; match: 近邻～亲 close neighbours are like relatives | 坚～金石 hard as rock or metal | 演讲不～自言自语。One should not adopt the manner of talking to oneself when giving a speech. ❸ 比画 gesture; gesticulate: 连说带～ gesticulate while speaking (or talking) ❹〈方 *dial.*〉对着;向着 aim at; direct towards: 别拿枪～着人,小心走火。Don't point guns at people, and take care they do not go off! ❺ 仿照 copy; do according to; model after: ～着葫芦画瓢(比喻模仿着做事) draw a gourd ladle on a calabash; (fig.) copy; do according to; model after ❻ 比方;比喻 compare to; liken to; draw an analogy: 打～ by way of analogy|人们常把聪明的人～做诸葛亮。People often compare a clever person to Zhuge Liang. ❼ 比较两个同类数量之间的倍数关系,叫做它们的比,其中一数是另一数的几倍或几分之几 ratio; proportion; comparison of the multiple relations between two similar quantities (*a and b*); *a* is *n* times *b*, while *b* is 1/n *a*:这里的小麦年产量和水稻年产量约为一与四之～。The local annual production of wheat and rice has a ratio of approximately one to four. ❽ 表示比赛双方得分的对比 (of a score) to: 甲队以二～一胜乙队。Team A beat Team B two to one. ❾〈介词 *prep.*〉用来比较性状和程度的差别[used to compare differences in properties and degrees] than; (superior or inferior) to: 今天的风～昨天更大了。The wind is stronger today than yesterday.|许多同志都～我强。Many comrades are superior to me. 注意 **NOTE**: a)'一'加量词在'比'的前后重复,可以表示程度的累进 adding 一 yī to a measure word and repeating it before and after 比 bǐ indicates progression: 人民的生活一年～一年富裕了。The lives of the people become more prosperous every year. b)比较高下的时候用'比',表示异同的时候用'跟'或'同' using 比 bǐ compares the differences of degree; and 跟 gēn or 同 tóng shows similarities and dissimilarities

比[2] bǐ (旧读 formerly pronounced bì)〈书 *fml.*〉❶ 紧靠;挨着 close together; next to: ～肩 shoulder to shoulder|鳞次栉～ row upon row of ❷ 依附;勾结 depend on; collude with; gang up with: 朋～为奸 gang up to do evil ❸ 近来 recently; of late: ～来 recently; of late ❹ 等到 by (then); by the time: ～及 when; at the time when; by the time

【比比】bǐbǐ〈书 *fml.*〉❶ 频频;屡屡 frequently; repeatedly ❷ 到处;处处 everywhere; all over: ～皆是(到处都是) can be seen everywhere; can be seen here, there and everywhere

【比方】bǐ·fang ❶ 用容易明白的甲事物来说明不容易明白的乙事物 compare to; liken to; draw an analogy between; use A, an easily understandable instance, to illustrate the meaning of B, which is easier to grasp: 他坚贞不屈的品德,可用四季常青的松柏来～。An analogy can be drawn between his faithful and unyielding character and evergreen pines and cypresses. ❷ 指用甲事物来说明乙事物的行为 act of illustrating A through comparing it with B: 打～ by way of analogy|这不过是个～。This is just an analogy. *or* This is only by way of analogy. ❸ 比如 take for instance or example: 郊游的事情都安排好了,～谁带队、谁开车,等等。All matters concerning the outing have been arranged, such as who will lead the group, and who will drive the bus. ❹ 表示'假如'的意思(用于有话要说而故意吞吐其词时) [used when sb. wants to say sth. but purposely pauses while speaking] if; suppose: 他的隶书真好,～我求他写一副对联儿,他不会拒绝吧? He is a calligrapher versed in official script. If I were to ask him to write a couplet for me, he wouldn't refuse, would he?

【比分】bǐfēn 比赛中双方用来比较成绩、决定胜负的得分 score; points scored by competitors in a match to compare who is the stronger: 最后一分钟,客队攻进一球,把～扳平。With a minute left to play, the visiting team levelled the score by scoring a goal.

【比附】bǐfù〈书 *fml.*〉拿不能相比的东西来勉强相比 draw a forced analogy; make a far-fetched comparison: 曲为～ make an unrealistic comparision

【比画】bǐ·hua ❶ 用手或拿着东西做出姿势来帮助说话或代替说话 gesture; gesticulate; use hands or objects to assist in or substitute for speech: 他在一张纸上～着,教大家怎样剪裁裤子。Through demonstrating with a piece of paper, he taught everyone how to cut out a pair of trousers. ❷ 指练武或比武 (as in martial arts) have a contest; practice: 我今天定要跟他～～,见个高低。I have arranged a contest with him for today to see who is the stronger of us. ‖ also 比划 bǐ·hua

【比基尼】bǐjīní 一种女子穿的游泳衣,由遮蔽面积很小的裤衩和乳罩组成 bikini; woman's bathing suit comprising panties and brassiere top; also 三点式游泳衣 sāndiǎnshì yóuyǒngyī

【比及】bǐjí〈书 *fml.*〉等到 when; at the time when; by the time: ～赶到,船已离岸。The ship had already sailed away by the time we arrived.

【比价】bǐ//jià 发包工程、器材或变卖产业、货物时,比较承包人或买主用书面形式提出的价格 price ratio or price comparison; comparing the prices put forward by the contractors or purchasers in written form when contracting for a project and equipment, or selling off one's properties or goods: ～单 price ratio or price comparison list

【比价】bǐjià 不同商品的价格比率或不同货币兑换的比率,如棉粮比价、外汇比价 parity; rate of exchange; price ratios of various products or rates of exchange of different currencies, e.g. price ratios between cotton and grains, and foreign exchange rate

【比肩】bǐjiān〈书 *fml*.〉❶ 并肩 shoulder to shoulder; side by side:～作战 fight side by side | ～而立 stand shoulder to shoulder; be very near ❷〈比喻 *fig*.〉相当;比美 be as good as; match:他虽然是票友,水平却可与专业演员～。Although he is an amateur, he performs as well as a professional.

【比肩继踵】bǐ jiān jì zhǒng 肩挨着肩,脚挨着脚,形容人多拥挤 stand shoulder to shoulder, and follow on the heels of another; be packed with people; (people) jostle each other in a crowd; also 比肩接踵 bǐ jiān jiē zhǒng

【比较】bǐjiào ❶ 就两种或两种以上同类的事物辨别异同或高下 compare; contrast; differentiate similarities from dissimilarities, or differences in degree:有～才能鉴别。Only by comparing can differences be distinguished. | 这两块料子～起来,颜色是这块好,质地是那块好。Comparing the two fabrics, this is of a better colour, while that is of a superior quality. ❷〈介词 *prep*.〉用来比较性状和程度的差别[used to compare differences in properties and degrees] than:这项政策贯彻以后,农民的生产积极性～前一时期又有所提高。Peasants have shown greater enthusiasm for production now than in the previous period since implementation of the policy. ❸〈副词 *adv*.〉表示具有一定程度 comparatively; relatively; fairly; rather:这篇文章写得～好。This article is comparatively well written.

【比较价格】bǐjiào jiàgé 不变价格 fixed price or cost; non-negotiable price

【比来】bǐlái〈书 *fml*.〉近来 recently; of late

【比例】bǐlì ❶ 表示两个比相等的式子,如 3 : 4 = 9 : 12 proportion; scale; formula that indicates two equal ratios, e.g. 3 : 4 = 9 : 12 ❷ same as 比[1] bǐ ⑦:教师和学生的～已经达到要求。The ratio of teachers to students meets the demand. ❸ same as 比重 bǐzhòng ②:在所销商品中,国货的～比较大。Home-made goods enjoy a high percentage in the commodities sales.

【比例尺】bǐlìchǐ ❶ 绘制地图或机械制图时,图上距离与它所表示的实际距离的比 scale; proportion between the distance as shown on a map or technical drawing and the actual distance ❷ 指线段比例尺,附在图边的表示比例的数字和线段 proportional scale; number and line segment shown in the legend on a map to indicate proportions ❸ 制图用的一种工具,上面有几种不同比例的刻度 architect's scale; engineer's scale; a map-drawing tool with several scale divisions of various proportions

【比例税制】bǐlì-shuìzhì 对同一课税对象不论数额多少,都按同一比例计征的税率制度 proportional taxation; system of collecting tax at the same rate, regardless of amount involved, for the same objective

【比量】bǐ·liang ❶ 不用尺而用手、绳、棍等大概地量一量 take rough measurements (with the hand, a stick, string, etc.):他用胳膊一～,那棵树有两围粗。He used his arm to take a rough measurement of the tree, which is two arm spans in girth. ❷ same as 比试 bǐ·shi ②:他拿起镰刀～了～,就要动手割麦子。After measuring up with the sickle, he set about reaping the wheat.

【比邻】bǐlín ❶〈书 *fml*.〉近邻;街坊 neighbour; next-door neighbour:海内存知己,天涯若～。A bosom friend afar brings a distant land nearer. ❷ 位置接近;邻近 be in the neighbourhood of; be located close to:～星(离太阳最近的一颗恒星) Proxima Centauri (the fixed star nearest to the sun)

【比率】bǐlǜ same as 比值 bǐzhí

【比美】bǐměi 水平不相上下,足以相比 compare favourably with; rival:乡镇企业的一些产品,已经可以跟大工厂的产品～。Some of the township enterprise products compare very favourably with those of large factories.

【比目鱼】bǐmùyú 鲽、鳎、鲆等鱼的统称。这几种鱼身体扁平,成长中两眼逐渐移到头部的一侧,平卧在海底。flatfish; flounder (*Pleuronectes flesus*); general term for right-eyed flounder, sole, left-eyed flounder, of type of fish with a thin flat body, whose eyes gradually grow to one side of the head, and that lays flat on the ocean bed; also 偏口鱼 piānkǒuyú

【比拟】bǐnǐ ❶ same as 比较 bǐjiào ①:无可～ beyond compare; matchless | 难以～ hardly comparable ❷ 修辞手法,把物拟做人或把人拟做物 analogy; metaphor; comparison; rhetoric comparing a thing to a person or vice versa

【比年】bǐnián〈书 *fml*.〉❶ 近年 in recent years:～以来,缠绵病榻 to have been bedridden with a lingering (or chronic) disease in recent years ❷ 每年;连年 each passing year:～不登 reap poor harvests for years running ‖ also 比岁 bǐsuì

【比配】bǐpèi 相称;相配 match; be compatible:这两件摆设放在一起很不～。These two decorations are incongruous when put together.

【比丘】bǐqiū〈佛教 *Budd*.〉指和尚 monk [梵 Sanskrit: bhiksu]

【比丘尼】bǐqiūní〈佛教 *Budd*.〉指尼姑 nun [梵 Sanskrit: bhiksuṇi]

【比热容】bǐrèróng 单位质量的物质,温度升高(或降低)1℃所吸收(或放出)的热量,叫做该物质的比热容 specific heat; heat absorbed (or released) by a unit quality substance when its temperature rises (or drops) 1℃; 简称abbr. 比热 bǐrè

【比如】bǐrú 举例时的发端语 for example; for instance; such as; phrase used when giving an example: 有些问题已经做出决定,～招多少学生,分多少班,等等。Decisions have been made on some questions, such as the number of students to be enrolled and how many classes there should be.

【比赛】bǐsài 在体育、生产等活动中,比较本领、技术的高低 match; contest; competition to see who has the greatest skill or strength in activities such as sports and production: 象棋～ chess match | ～篮球 have a basketball game

【比试】bǐ·shi ❶ 彼此较量高低 have a competition or contest: 咱们～一下,看谁做得又快又好。Let's have a competition to see who is swiftest and best. ❷ 做出某种动作的姿势 gesticulate: 他把大枪一～,不在乎地说,叫他们来吧。With a flourish of his rifle, he said carelessly, 'Let them come!'

【比索】bǐsuǒ ❶ 西班牙的旧本位货币 peso (former monetary unit of Spain) ❷ 菲律宾和一部分拉丁美洲国家的本位货币 [Spanish peso] monetary unit of the Philippines and some Latin American countries

【比武】bǐ//wǔ 比赛武艺 martial arts competition; competition in martial skills

【比翼】bǐyì 翅膀挨着翅膀(飞) fly wing to wing: ～齐飞 pair off wing to wing; fly side by side

【比翼鸟】bǐyìniǎo 传说中的一种鸟,雌雄老在一起飞,古典诗词里用做恩爱夫妻的比喻 mythological bird with only one wing that consequently can only fly in a pair; pair of love birds; (fig.) (in ancient poems) devoted couple

【比翼齐飞】bǐ yì qí fēi 〈比喻 *fig.*〉夫妻恩爱,朝夕相伴。也比喻互相帮助,共同前进。(of loving husband and wife) keep each other company; help each other to advance

【比喻】bǐyù 修辞手法,用某些有类似点的事物来比拟想要说的某一事物,以便表达得更加生动鲜明;打比方 metaphor; analogy; figure of speech; a method of comparing one thing to another with which it shares some similarities with the aim of achieving a more vivid form of expression; draw an analogy

【比照】bǐzhào ❶ 按照已有的(格式、标准、方法等);对比着 according to; in the light of: ～着实物绘图 draw a picture after a model ❷ 比较对照 contrast: 两种方案一～,就可看出明显的差异。Put the two plans side by side and you will see their obvious differences.

【比值】bǐzhí 两个数相比所得的值,即前项除以后项所得的商。如 8∶4 的比值是 2。specific value; ratio; rate; value of the proportion between two figures, i.e. quotient when the antecedent is divided by the consequent, e.g. the ratio between 8 and 4 is 2; also 比率 bǐlǜ

【比重】bǐzhòng ❶ 物质的重量和 4℃ 时同体积纯水的重量的比值,叫做该物质的比重 specific gravity; ratio between the weight of a substance and that of the same volume of pure water at 4℃ ❷ 一种事物在整体中所占的分量 proportion; amount of sth. in its entirety: 我国工业在整个国民经济中的～逐年增长。The proportion of industry as a whole within the national economy is growing year by year.

吡 bǐ ☞ below
☞ pǐ on p.1468

【吡啶】bǐdìng 有机化合物,化学式 C_5H_5N。无色液体,有臭味。用做溶剂和化学试剂。pyridine; organic chemical compound whose chemical formula is C_5H_5N; a colourless liquid with a strong odour used to make solvent and chemical reagent

【吡咯】bǐluò 有机化合物,化学式 C_4H_5N。无色液体,在空气中颜色变深,有刺激性气味。用来制药品。pyrrole; organic chemical compound whose chemical formula is C_4H_5N; a colourless liquid that turns dark when exposed to air, and used to make medicine and chemical reagents

佊 bǐ 〈书 *fml.*〉邪 evil

沘 Bǐ 沘江,水名,在云南 Bijiang River, in Yunnan Province

妣 bǐ 〈书 *fml.*〉已故的母亲 deceased mother: 先～ my deceased (or late) mother | 如丧考～(像死了父母一样) very sad or sorrowful (because of death of a parent)

彼 bǐ ❶ 那;那个(跟'此'相对 as compared with 'this') that; those; the other; another: ～时 at that time | 此起～伏 as one falls, another rises; rise one after another; rise here and subside there | 由此及～ from this to that; from one to another ❷ 对方;他 other party; one's opponent: 知己知～ know both one's opponent and oneself | ～退我进。As he retreats, I march forward.

【彼岸】bǐ'àn ❶〈书 *fml.*〉(江、河、湖、海的)那一边;对岸 (of a river, lake, sea, etc.) other bank; other side ❷〈佛教 *Budd.*〉认为有生有死的境界好比此岸,超脱生死的境界(涅槃)好比彼岸 other shore; Faramita. The realm of life and death is this shore; while the one freeing from life and death (nirvana) is the other. ❸〈比喻 *fig.*〉所向往的境界 realm to which one looks forward: 走向幸福的～ march towards the path of happiness

【彼此】bǐcǐ ❶ 那个和这个;双方 each other; one another: 不分～ share everything they have | ～互助 help each other ❷〈客套话 *pol.*〉表示大家一样(常叠用做答话) [used usu. in reduplication to indicate that all concerned are about the same]:'您辛苦啦!''～～!''You must have gone to a lot of trouble over this.''So must you!'

【彼一时,此一时】bǐ yī shí,cǐ yī shí 那是一个时候,现在又是一个时候,表示时间不同,情况有了改变 times have changed; the situation is better now; that was then, this is now:～,不要拿老眼光看新事物。Times have changed. You should not judge new things by old standards.

秕(粃) bǐ ❶ 秕子 blighted grain:～糠 chaff ❷ (子实)不饱满 (of grain) not plump; blighted:～粒 blighted seed|～谷子 blighted grains ❸ 〈书 *fml.*〉恶;坏 evil; bad:～政 bad government policy

【秕谷】bǐgǔ 不饱满的稻谷或谷子 blighted grains; also 秕谷子 bǐgǔ·zi

【秕糠】bǐkāng 秕子和糠 chaff;〈比喻 *fig.*〉没有价值的东西 worthless stuff

【秕子】bǐ·zi 空的或不饱满的子粒 blighted grain:谷～ blighted grains

笔(筆) bǐ ❶ 写字画图的用具 tool for writing and drawing:毛～ writing brush|铅～ pencil|钢～ pen|粉～ chalk|一枝～ a pen|一管～ a pen ❷ (写字、画画、作文的)笔法 calligraphy or drawing; technique of writing:伏～ foreshadowing|工～ traditional Chinese realistic painting characterized by fine brushwork and close attention to detail|败～ flaw in a good piece of writing; fly in the ointment|曲～ devious way of recording history adopted by the feudal historiographers in order to conceal the truth of an event from their contemporaries; devious way of writing; oblique reference ❸ 用笔写出 write; pen:代～ write down for sb.|直～ record faithfully; give a faithful account|亲～ in one's own handwriting; in one's own hand ❹ 手迹 handwriting:遗～ handwriting of a deceased person ❺ 笔画 stroke in Chinese painting or calligraphy:'大'字有三～。The character 大 (dà) has three strokes. ❻ 〈量词 *classifier*〉a)用于款项或跟款项有关的[used to indicate sums of money or the matters concerned]:一～钱 a sum of money|三～账 three accounts|五～生意 five deals b)用于书画艺术 [used to indicate painting and calligraphy]:写一～好字 write a good hand|他能画几～山水画。He is something of a hand at landscape painting.

【笔触】bǐchù 书画、文章等的笔法;格调 brushwork; brush stroke in Chinese painting and calligraphy; style of drawing or writing:他用简练而鲜明的～来表现祖国壮丽的河山。He depicted the magnificent mountains and rivers of the motherland in a succinct, distinct style.|他以锋利的～讽刺了旧社会的丑恶。He used an incisive pen to satirise the ugliness of the old society.

【笔答】bǐdá 书面回答 give a written answer; answer in writing:～试题 questions to be answered in writing

【笔底生花】bǐ dǐ shēng huā 〈比喻 *fig.*〉所写的文章非常优美 have elegant style of writing; write beautifully or brilliantly; also 笔下生花 bǐ xià shēng huā; ☞ 生花之笔 shēng huā zhī bǐ on p.1714

【笔底下】bǐdǐ·xia 指写文章的能力 ability to write:他～不错(会写文章)。He writes well.|他～来得快(写文章快)。He writes with facility. *or* He is a facile writer.

【笔调】bǐdiào 文章的格调 (of writing) tone; style:～清新 fresh, pure style|他用文艺～写了许多通俗科学读物。He has written numerous popular science books in a literary style.

【笔端】bǐduān 〈书 *fml.*〉指写作、写字、绘画时笔的运用以及所表现的意境 wielding of the pen or brush in an artistic conception of writing, calligraphy or painting:～奇趣横生。He writes in the most witty and pleasing manner.|愤激之情见于～。Indignation was apparent in the writing style.

【笔伐】bǐfá 用文字声讨 denounce or condemn in writing:口诛～ denounce in both speech and writing

【笔法】bǐfǎ 写字、画画、作文的技巧或特色 technique or characteristics of calligraphy, drawing or writing:他的字,～圆润秀美。He writes in a smooth, vital and elegant hand.|他以豪放的～,写出了大草原的风光。He depicted the vast grassland in a bold and unrestrained style.

【笔锋】bǐfēng ❶ 毛笔的尖端 tip of a writing brush ❷ 书画的笔势;文章的锋芒 touch; stroke; vigour of style in writing or painting; forcefulness of a piece of writing:～苍劲 write in bold and vigorous strokes|～犀利 wield a pointed pen; write in a poignant (or incisive) style

【笔杆儿】bǐgǎnr same as 笔杆子 bǐgǎn·zi ①②

【笔杆子】bǐgǎn·zi ❶ 笔的手拿的部分 shaft of a pen or writing brush (for holding) ❷ 指写文章的能力 ability to write:要～ wield the pen; write for one's living|他嘴皮子、～都比我强。He speaks more glibly and writes more effectively than I. *or* He is better than I in both verbal and writing abilities. ‖ also 笔杆儿 bǐgǎnr ❸ 指能写文章的人 effective writer; facile writer

【笔耕】bǐgēng 指写作 engage in writing:伏案～ bent over one's desk writing|～不辍 never give up writing

【笔供】bǐgòng 用笔写出来的供词 written confession

【笔管条直】bǐ guǎn tiáo zhí 笔直(多指直立着 usu. stand erect; stand upright) straight; bolt upright:这棵树长得~。This tree stands tall and erect.|大家~地站着等点名。Everyone was standing to attention, awaiting the roll call.

【笔画】bǐhuà ❶ 组成汉字的点、横、直、撇、捺等 strokes of a Chinese character, such as dot, horizontal, vertical, and left- and right-falling strokes ❷ 指笔画数 number of strokes:书前有汉字~索引。There is a stroke order index of Chinese characters at the front of the book. ‖ also 笔划 bǐhuà

【笔会】bǐhuì ❶ 以文章的方式对某个专题或专题的某个侧面进行探讨、报道等的活动 writers' forum; activities such as discussing or reporting on some special subject or topic or one of its aspects through writing articles or essays:文艺评论~ written forum on literary criticism ❷ 一种由作家联合成的组织 association or club of writers

【笔迹】bǐjì 每个人写的字所特有的形象;字迹 handwriting; writing; chirography; particular image of a character as written by sb.; style of personal writing:对~ identify sb.'s hand (or handwriting)|这可不像他的~。It does not look like his handwriting.

【笔记】bǐjì ❶ 用笔记录 take down (in writing):老人口述,请人~下来,整理成文。The old man asked the others to take notes of his oral account, and then write them up into article. ❷ 听课、听报告、读书时所做的记录 notes (of lectures, reports and readings); note-taking:读书~ reading notes|课堂~ class notes ❸ 一种以随笔记录为主的著作体裁,多由分条的短篇汇集而成 pen jottings; a type of literature consisting mainly of short sketches; sketch:~小说 literary sketches; sketchbook

【笔架】bǐjià (~儿 bǐjiàr)用陶瓷、竹、木、金属等制成的搁笔或插笔的架儿 pen rack; penholder; rack or stack made of ceramics, bamboo, wood, metal, etc., in which to keep pens

【笔尖】bǐjiān (~儿 bǐjiānr) ❶ 笔的写字的尖端部分 nib; tip of a pen for writing ❷ 特指钢笔的笔头儿 pen nib:换个~ change the nib of a pen

【笔力】bǐlì 写字、画画或做文章在笔法上所表现的力量 vigour of strokes in calligraphy or drawing; vigour of style in literary composition:~雄健 vigorous style in literary composition; powerful strokes|~遒劲 write with firm strokes; write with forceful and vigorous strokes

【笔立】bǐlì 直立 stand erect; tower:~的山峰 perpendicular mountain peak

【笔录】bǐlù ❶ 用笔记录 put down (in writing); take down:您口述,由我给您~。You tell the story, and I'll take it down in writing. ❷ 记录下来的文字 notes; records:口供~ transcript of testimony or confession; deposition

【笔路】bǐlù ❶ 笔法 technique of calligraphy, painting or writing ❷ 写作的思路 train of thought in writing; composition; organization

【笔帽】bǐmào (~儿 bǐmàor)套着笔头儿保护笔的套儿 protective cap of pen, pencil or writing brush

【笔名】bǐmíng 作者发表作品时用的别名,如鲁迅是周树人的笔名 pseudonym; pen name; another name of a writer used when publishing works, e.g. Lu Xun is the pen name (or pseudonym) of Zhou Shuren

【笔墨】bǐmò 指文字或诗文书画等 pen and ink; writing; words; articles:~流畅 easy and smooth writing|西湖美丽的景色,不是用~可以形容的。Words cannot describe the beautiful view of the West Lake. *or* The beauty of the scenery of the West Lake is beyond description.

【笔墨官司】bǐmò guān•si 指书面上的争辩 paper arguments; written polemics; battle of words:打~ fight a battle of words

【笔铅】bǐqiān 铅笔的芯子 pencil lead

【笔润】bǐrùn 润笔 brush moistener-remuneration or fee for writing, painting or calligraphic work

【笔试】bǐshì 要求把答案写出来的考试方法(区别于'口试' as compared with oral test) written examination; an examination method in which written answers are required

【笔势】bǐshì ❶ 写字、画画用笔的风格 style of writing or painting:~沉稳 in a steady style ❷ 诗文的气势 vigour of style in writing; vigour of literary style:这首七律,~犹如大江出峡,汹涌澎湃。This *qilü* poem (eight-line poem with seven characters to a line and a strict tonal pattern and rhyming scheme) is written in a bold and powerful style, like a turbulent great river gushing out of a gorge.

【笔受】bǐshòu〈书 *fml.*〉用笔记下别人口授的话 take (or write) down what is dictated

【笔顺】bǐshùn 汉字笔画的书写次序,如'文'的笔顺是 1)丶, 2)亠, 3)亣, 4)文 order of strokes observed in calligraphy (e.g. the order of strokes in writing 文 (wén): 1.丶, 2.亠, 3.亣, 4.文)

【笔算】bǐsuàn 用笔写出算式或算草来计算 do a sum in writing; written calculation

【笔谈】bǐtán ❶ 两人对面在纸上写字交换意见,代替谈话 written dialogue or conversation; (of two persons) written, rather than spoken, exchange of opinions ❷ 用书面发表意见代替谈话 written statement (instead of dialogue or conversation) ❸ same as 笔记 bǐjì ③ (oft. used in names of books):《梦溪～》*Dream Brook Sketchbook*

【笔套】bǐtào（～儿 bǐtàor）❶ 笔帽 cap of a pen, pencil or writing brush ❷ 用线、丝织成或用布做成的套笔的东西 sheath for a pen (made of thread, silk or cloth)

【笔体】bǐtǐ 各人写的字所特有的形象；笔迹 handwriting; a person's particular style of writing: 对～ check sb.'s handwriting (against an original, etc.)｜我认得出他的～。By comparison, I can identify his handwriting.

【笔挺】bǐtǐng ❶ 很直地（立着）(standing) very straight; straight as a ramrod; bolt upright: 卫兵～地站在一旁。The guards were standing bolt upright at the side. ❷（衣服）烫得很平而折叠的痕迹又很直 well-ironed; trim; stiff; (of clothes) well-ironed and neatly folded: 穿着一身～的西服 be dressed in an immaculate Western-style suit

【笔筒】bǐtǒng 用陶瓷、竹木等制成的插笔的筒儿 pen container; brush pot; pot made of ceramics, bamboo, wood, etc. for holding pens or brushes

【笔头儿】bǐtóur ❶ 毛笔、钢笔等用以写字的部分 nib; pen point; part of a writing brush or pen for writing ❷ 指写字的技巧或写文章的能力 ability to write; writing skill: 他～有两下子。He writes well.｜你～快，还是你写吧！You write quickly, so it would be better if you wrote it. also 笔头子 bǐtóu · zi

【笔误】bǐwù ❶ 因疏忽而写了错字 slip of the pen; clerical error: 这篇文章～的地方不少。Quite a few slips of the pen occurred in the writing of this article. ❷ 因疏忽而写错的字 mistakes in writing; words miswritten due to carelessness: 精神不集中，写东西常有～ often miswrite words owing to inattention

【笔洗】bǐxǐ 用陶瓷、石头、贝壳等制成的洗涮毛笔的用具 dish made from ceramic, stone or shells for rinsing writing brushes

【笔下】bǐxià ❶ 笔底下 ability to write ❷ 指写文章时作者的措辞和用意 wording and purport of what one writes: ～留情 be merciful when writing; forbear from making critical remarks (so as not to hurt sb.'s feelings); spare sb. from critical attack

【笔心】bǐxīn 铅笔或圆珠笔的芯子 pencil lead; refill (for a ball-point pen); also 笔芯 bǐxīn

【笔形】bǐxíng 指汉字的笔画和由笔画构成的形体，如'一'、'丿'、'亠'、'扌'等 (of Chinese characters) forms of strokes and their combinations (e. g., '一', '丿', '亠', '扌', etc.)

【笔削】bǐxuē 笔指记载，削指删改，古时在竹简、木简上写字，要删改得用刀刮去，后用做请人修改文章的敬辞 revise; polish (a piece of writing); edit. In ancient times an article was revised by scratching words off inscribed bamboo or wooden slips with a knife; now used as a polite way of asking sb. to revise or polish a piece of writing

【笔译】bǐyì 用文字翻译（区别于'口译' as compared with 'oral translation'）written translation; translate in writing

【笔意】bǐyì 书画或诗文所表现的意境 one's feeling or mood as conveyed in calligraphy, painting or literary work: ～超逸 write with rare grace and ease｜～清新 write in a fresh style

【笔札】bǐzhá 札是古代写字用的小木片，后来用笔札指纸笔，又转指书信、文章等 writing materials; writing; wooden slips used for writing in ancient times, later used to refer to writing materials, or letters, articles, etc.

【笔债】bǐzhài 指受别人约请而未交付的字、画或文章 commission as a writer, calligrapher or painter

【笔战】bǐzhàn 用文章来进行的争论 written polemics or controversy; paper battle

【笔者】bǐzhě 某一篇文章或某一本书的作者（多用于自称 usu. referring to oneself）the author; this writer; author or writer of an article or a book

【笔政】bǐzhèng 报刊编辑中指撰写重要评论的工作 (of journalism) writing of important commentaries

【笔直】bǐzhí 很直 very (or perfect) straight; straight as a ramrod; bolt upright: ～的马路 straight avenues｜站得～ stand bolt upright; stand straight as a ramrod; draw oneself up to one's full height

【笔致】bǐzhì 书画、文章等用笔的风格 style of painting, calligraphy or writing: ～高雅 elegant style

【笔资】bǐzī〈旧时 *old*〉称写字、画画、做文章所得的报酬 remuneration for calligraphy, painting or writing

【笔走龙蛇】bǐ zǒu lóng shé 形容书法笔势雄健活泼 make vigorous and graceful strokes in calligraphy

俾 bǐ〈书 *fml.*〉使（达到某种效果）in order to; so that; so as to: ～众周知 so as to make sth. known to all (or everyone); for the information of all｜～有所悟 in order to understand; so as to realize

舭 bǐ 船底和船侧间的弯曲部分 bilge; curved section between the bottom and sides of a ship

【舭舯】bǐdá 古代的一种船 a kind of ancient ship

鄙 bǐ ❶ 粗俗；低下 low; mean; vulgar; base: ～陋 shallow; ignorant｜卑～ base; mean; despicable ❷〈谦辞 *hum.*〉〈旧时 *old*〉用于自称 my: ～人 your humble servant; I｜～意 in my opinion; I beg to observe｜～见 my humble opinion ❸〈书 *fml.*〉轻视；看不起 despise; disdain; scorn; look down：～弃 disdain; loathe; spurn｜～薄 despise; scorn; look down on (or upon) ❹〈书 *fml.*〉边远的地方 out-of-the-way place; remote area：边～ remote area

B

【鄙薄】bǐbó ❶ 轻视；看不起 despise; scorn; look down on (or upon)：～势利小人 have great contempt for snobs｜脸上露出～的神情 face showing expression of contempt ❷〈书 *fml.*〉浅陋微薄（多用做谦辞 oft. hum.）shallow and meagre knowledge; ignorant and shallow：～之志（微小的志向）humble wish

【鄙称】bǐchēng ❶ 鄙视地称做 address in a derogatory manner; label contemptuously：不劳而食者被～为寄生虫。Those who live on other people's labour are contemptuously referred to as parasites. ❷ 鄙视的称呼 derogatory term; pejorative appellation：寄生虫是对不劳而食者的～。'Parasite' is a derogatory term for those who live off others' labour.

【鄙俚】bǐlǐ〈书 *fml.*〉粗俗；浅陋 vulgar; crude; philistine; uncouth：文辞～，不登大雅之堂 in coarse language, abhorrent to refined taste

【鄙吝】bǐlìn〈书 *fml.*〉❶ 鄙俗 vulgar ❷ 过分吝啬 mean; stingy; miserly

【鄙陋】bǐlòu 见识浅薄 shallow; ignorant：～无知 ignorant and shallow; superficial and poorly informed｜学识～ having shallow knowledge; little learning

【鄙弃】bǐqì 看不起；厌恶 disdain; loathe; spurn; despise：她～那种矫揉造作的演唱作风。She disdains affected singing styles.

【鄙人】bǐrén ❶〈书 *fml.*〉知识浅陋的人 mean and ignorant person ❷〈谦辞 *hum.*〉对人称自己 your humble servant; I

【鄙视】bǐshì 轻视；看不起 despise; disdain; contempt; belittle; look down upon：他向来～那些帮闲文人。He has always despised such hack scholars.

【鄙俗】bǐsú 粗俗；庸俗 vulgar; philistine：言词～ vulgar (or philistine) words

【鄙夷】bǐyí〈书 *fml.*〉轻视；看不起 disdain; despise; look down upon

【鄙意】bǐyì〈谦辞 *hum.*〉称自己的意见 in my opinion; I beg to observe

bì (ㄅㄧˋ)

币(幣) bì 货币 money; currency：硬～ coin｜银～ silver coin｜纸～ paper currency; note, bill｜人民～ RMB; renminbi

【币值】bìzhí 货币的价值，即货币购买商品的能力 currency value; purchasing power of currency

【币制】bìzhì 货币制度，包括拿什么做货币和货币的单位，以及硬币的铸造，纸币的发行、流通等制度 currency or monetary system (i.e. systems of determining currencies and monetary units, casting coins, and issuing and circulating paper currency)

必 bì ❶ 必定；必然 certainly; necessarily; surely：我明天三点钟～到。I will definitely be here at three o'clock tomorrow.｜不战则已，战则～胜。Fight no battle where victory is not certain. ❷ 必须；一定要 must; have to; ought to：事～躬亲 do everything oneself; attend to every detail in person｜事物的存在和发展，～有一定的条件。There must be certain conditions for the existence and development of a thing.

【必得】bìděi 必须；一定要 must; have to：捎信儿不行，～你亲自去一趟。Sending him a message will not do; you simply must go.

【必定】bìdìng〈副词 *adv.*〉❶ 表示判断或推论的确凿或必然 be bound to; be sure to; must：他得到信儿，～会来。He will surely come when he gets the message.｜有全组同志的共同努力，这项任务～能完成。This task is sure to be fulfilled through the common efforts of our whole group of comrades. ❷ 表示意志的坚决 be certain to; be resolved to：你放心，后天我～来接你。Don't worry. I will meet you the day after tomorrow.

【必恭必敬】bì gōng bì jìng 十分恭敬 reverent and respectful; extremely deferential; showing great respect; also 毕恭毕敬 bì gōng bì jìng

【必然】bìrán ❶ 事理上确定不移 inevitable; certain; necessary：～趋势 inexorable trend｜胜利～属于意志坚强的人。Strong-willed people are bound to succeed. ❷ 哲学上指不以人们意志为转移的客观发展规律 necessity; objective law of development independent of man's will：新事物代替旧事物是历史发展的～。The inevitable outcome of historical development is that the new replaces the old.

【必然王国】bìrán wángguó 哲学上指人在尚未认识和掌握客观世界规律之前，没有意志自由，行动受着必然性支配的境界 (philos.) realm of necessity; the mental state of humankind in which there is no freedom of will, and when actions are determined by necessity, prior to discovery of and learning the principles of the objective world; ☞ 自由王国 zìyóu wángguó on p. 2550

【必然性】bìránxìng 指事物发展、变化中的不可避免和一定不移的趋势。必然性是由事物的本质决定的，认识事物的必然性就是认识事物的本质（跟'偶然性'相对 as compared with 'contingency' or 'fortuity'）necessity; inevitability; certainty; inevitable and necessary course of development and change of a thing, which is determined by its nature; it is through the process of realising the necessity of a thing that its nature may be recognised

【必修】bìxiū 学生依照学校规定必须学习的(区别于'选修'as opposed to 'optional')(of a course, lesson, etc.) required; obligatory; compulsory; mandatory; (a course, lesson, etc.) that students must study according to the curriculum of a school: ～课 required course; obligatory course; compulsory course (or subject)

【必须】bìxū ❶ 表示事理上和情理上的必要;一定要 must; have to; necessary; be obliged to; reasonable and sensible necessity: 学习～刻苦钻研。Diligent and intensive study is a fundamental necessity. ❷ 加强命令语气 [used to add weight to an order]: 明天你～来。You must come here tomorrow. ‖ 注意 **NOTE**: '必须'的否定是'无须'、'不须'或'不必'。The negative of 'must; have to; necessary' is 'not have to; not be necessary; need not' or 'unnecessary'.

【必需】bìxū 一定要有的;不可少的 necessary; essential; indispensable: 日用～品 daily necessities; articles for daily consumption | 煤铁等是发展工业所～的原料。Coal, iron, etc. are the fundamental raw materials necessary for industrial development.

【必需品】bìxūpǐn 生活上不可缺少的物品,如粮食、衣服、被褥等 necessities; daily necessities; articles for daily consumption; indispensable daily life articles, such as grains, clothing, bedding

【必要】bìyào 不可缺少;非这样不行 necessary; essential; indispensable: 开展批评和自我批评是十分～的。It is essential to make criticisms and self-criticisms. | 为了集体的利益,～时可以牺牲个人的利益。Personal gains are to be given up in the interests of the collective when necessary.

【必要产品】bìyào chǎnpǐn 由劳动者的必要劳动生产出来的产品(跟'剩余产品'相对 as compared with 'surplus product') necessary product; commodity produced by the necessary labour of a worker

【必要劳动】bìyào láodòng 劳动者为了维持自己和家属的生活所必须付出的那一部分劳动(跟'剩余劳动'相对 as compared with 'surplus labour') necessary labour; labor that a worker must expend in order to support himself or herself and his or her family

毕(畢) bì ❶ 完结;完成 finish; complete; conclude: 礼～on conclusion of the ceremony; after the salute | ～其功于一役 accomplish the whole task at one stroke ❷〈书 *fml.*〉全;完全 fully; completely; altogether: ～力 do one's best; try one's utmost; exert oneself; use all one's strength | 群贤～至 all wise men arrive; all wise men gather at a place ❸ 二十八宿之一 one of the 28 constellations ❹ (Bì)姓 a surname

【毕恭毕敬】bì gōng bì jìng same as 必恭必敬 bì gōng bì jìng

【毕竟】bìjìng〈副词 *adv.*〉表示追根究底所得的结论;究竟;终归;到底 after all; all in all; in the final analysis; when all is said and done; in the long run; conclusion drawn by getting to the bottom of sth.: 这部书虽然有缺页,～是珍本。Despite having several pages missing, this book is, when all said and done, an extremely valuable edition.

【毕露】bìlù 完全暴露 reveal completely; be completely exposed: 原形～ utterly reveal one's true features; show one's true colours; expose one's true self; be shown for what one is | 凶相～ look thoroughly ferocious; be ferocity itself

【毕命】bìmìng〈书 *fml.*〉结束生命(多指横死 usu. a sudden or violent death) die

【毕生】bìshēng 一生;终生 lifetime; lifelong; all one's life; throughout one's life: ～的精力 energy throughout one's life

【毕肖】bìxiào 完全相像 be the very image of; resemble closely; be true to life: 神态～ lifelike

【毕业】bì//yè 在学校或训练班学习期满,达到规定的要求,结束学习 graduate; finish school; on completing one's term of study at a school or training course and meeting the requirements necessary to leave: 大学～ graduate from university | 他的学习成绩太差,毕不了业。His achievements in studies are insufficient for him to graduate.

闭 bì ❶ 关;合 shut; close: ～门 shut (or close) the door | ～口无言 remain silent; be left speechless; keep silent | ～目养神 refresh one's spirit by closing one's eyes; close one's eyes and rest one's mind; close eyes to take a rest ❷ 堵塞不通 obstruct; stop up; block up: ～气 hold one's breath | ～塞 stop up; block ❸ 结束;停止 stop; end: ～会 close (or end) a meeting; adjourn a meeting; adjournment | ～经 amenorrhoea ❹ (Bì) 姓 a surname

【闭关】bìguān ❶ 闭塞关口 block a pass; close a city gate;〈比喻 *fig.*〉不跟外界往来 have no contact with the outside world: ～政策 closed-door policy; closed-doorism ❷〈佛教 *Budd.*〉指僧人独居一处,静修佛法,不与任何人交往,满一定期限才外出 (of a monk) stay secluded meditating and studying scriptures for a period of time

【闭关锁国】bì guān suǒ guó 闭塞关口,封锁国境,不跟外国往来 block up the pass; close the border; have no contact with the outside world; close the country to the rest of the world; shut the door to the international community

【闭关自守】bì guān zì shǒu 闭塞关口，不跟别国往来 close the country to the outside world (by closing the pass); 〈比喻 *fig.*〉不跟外界交往 seclude oneself from the outside world

B

【闭合】bìhé ❶首尾相连的；封闭的 closed; with head and tail linked together: ～电路 closed-circuit | ～曲线 closed curve | 电冰箱各部分之间用管道相连，形成一个～循环系统。As the various parts of a refrigerator are connected by pipes, they form a closed circulatory system. ❷ 使首尾相连；封闭；合上 circularise; link head and tail: 电门一～，电流就通了。The electric current will be energized once it is switched on.

【闭合电路】bìhé diànlù 电荷沿电路绕一周后可回到原位置的电路 closed-circuit; circuit whose electric charge can return to its original position after completing a circuit

【闭会】bìhuì 会议结束 close (or end) a meeting; adjourn a meeting; adjournment

【闭架式】bìjiàshì 图书馆的一种借阅方式。由读者填写借书条交管理员到书架上取书，交给读者阅览。closed stacks (a system of library management which denies readers open access to bookshelves); method of borrowing books from a library, when the reader completes a slip and submits it to an assistant, who finds the book and lends it to the reader

【闭经】bìjīng 经闭 amenorrhoea

【闭卷】bìjuàn (～儿 bìjuànr)一种考试方法，参加考试的人答题时不能查阅有关资料(区别于'开卷' as compared with 'open-book' examination) closed-book; method of examination in which examinees are not allowed to consult any relevant materials

【闭口】bìkǒu 合上嘴不讲话 keep one's mouth shut; 〈比喻 *fig.*〉不发表意见 not speak out one's mind: ～不言 shut one's mouth; keep one's tongue still; remain mute

【闭口韵】bìkǒuyùn 拿双唇音 m 或 b 收尾的韵母 syllabic that ends in bilabials 'm' or 'b'

【闭路电视】bìlùdiànshì 图像信号只在有限的区域内通过电缆传送的电视系统。多应用于工业、教育、医学、科学研究等方面。closed-circuit television; television system whose image is transmitted through electric cable within a limited region only, usu. applied in industry, education, medical science and scientific studies

【闭门羹】bìméngēng ☞ 吃闭门羹 chī bìméngēng on p. 255

【闭门思过】bì mén sī guò 关上房门，独自反省过错。多指独自进行自我反省。shut oneself up and ponder over one's mistakes; mediate on one's own faults (or ponder over one's mistakes) in solitude (or behind closed doors); reflect on one's misdeeds in private

【闭门造车】bì mén zào chē 关上门造车 make a cart behind closed doors; 〈比喻 *fig.*〉只凭主观办事，不管客观实际 do whatever one likes without any reference to objective reality; shut oneself off from reality

【闭目塞听】bì mù sè tīng 闭着眼睛，堵住耳朵。形容对外界事物不闻不问或不了解。shut one's eyes and stop one's ears; take no notice or know nothing of external matters; cut oneself off from reality; be out of touch with reality

【闭幕】bì//mù ❶ 一场演出、一个节目或一幕戏结束时闭上舞台前的幕 curtain fall, or lowering of the curtain (when a show, performance or an act of a drama ends) ❷ (会议、展览会等)结束 (of a conference, an exhibition, etc.) close; conclude: ～词 closing address (or speech) | ～式 closing ceremony | 运动会胜利～。The sports meet has come to a successful close.

【闭气】bì//qì ❶ 呼吸微弱、失去知觉 be in a coma, breathe feebly: 跌了一跤，闭住气了 have a fall and lose consciousness ❷ 有意地暂时抑止呼吸 hold one's breath: ～凝神 hold one's breath while concentrating attention on doing sth. | 护士放轻脚步闭住气走到病人床前。Holding her breath, the nurse walked softly to the patient's bedside.

【闭塞】bìsè ❶ 堵塞 block; stop up; close up: 管道～ blocked pipe ❷ 交通不便；偏僻；风气不开 out-of-the-way; inaccessible; hard to get to; backward: 他住在偏远的山区，那里十分～。He lives in a remote and inaccessible mountainous region. ❸ 消息不灵通 unenlightened; out of touch: 老人久不出门，～得很。As the elderly man had not been out of his house for a long time, he was ill-informed.

【闭市】bì//shì 商店、市场等停止营业 (of a shop, market, etc.) close; suspend business

【闭锁】bìsuǒ ❶ 自然科学指某个系统与外界隔绝，不相联系 (of a system in natural sciences) close off; block; isolate from and lose contact with the external world ❷ 医学上旧指瓣膜等严密合拢 (med.) valvular sufficiency; tight closure of valve, etc.: 大动脉～不全。The major artery lacks valvular sufficiency.

庇 bì 遮蔽；掩护 shelter; cover; protect; shield; screen: 包～ shelter; harbour; cover up | ～护 shelter; protect; shield; put under one's protection; take under one's wing

【庇护】bìhù 袒护；保护 shelter; protect; shield; put under one's protection; take under one's wing: ～权 right of asylum | ～坏人 shelter (or shield) bad or wicked person

【庇护权】bìhùquán 国家对于因受政治迫害而来

避难的外国人给以居留的权利 right of asylum; right of residence granted by a nation to foreigners subjected to political persecution

【庇荫】bìyìn〈书 *fml.*〉❶（树木）遮住阳光（of a tree）give shade ❷〈比喻 *fig.*〉尊长的照顾或祖宗的保佑 shield; shelter; protect; harbour; care of one's elders and betters and the blessings of ancestors

【庇佑】bìyòu〈书 *fml.*〉保佑 bless; prosper; protect：神明～ God's blessings

邲 Bì 古地名，在今河南郑州东 place name in ancient China, in the east of the present Zhengzhou City, Henan Province

诐 bì〈书 *fml.*〉❶ 辩论 argue; debate; dispute ❷ 不正 evil; sinister：～辞（邪僻的言论）sinister (or evil) words

苾 bì〈书 *fml.*〉芳香 fragrant; aromatic

畀 bì〈书 *fml.*〉给；给以 give; confer：～以重任 entrust sb. with a heavy responsibility｜投～豺虎 throw (an evil doer) among beasts of prey — feel strong indignation (against)

闷 bì〈书 *fml.*〉❶ 闭门；闭 close; hide ❷ 谨慎 careful; cautious; secret

泌 bì 泌阳（Bìyáng），地名，在河南 Biyang, a place in Henan Province

☞ mì on p. 1332

骁 bì〈书 *fml.*〉马肥壮（of a horse）stout and strong

珌（琿） bì〈书 *fml.*〉刀鞘下端的饰物 ornament at the end of a sheath

贲 bì〈书 *fml.*〉装饰得很美 beautifully adorned (or decorated)

☞ bēn on p. 88

荜[1]（蓽） bì same as 筚 bì

荜[2]（蓽） bì same as 荜拨 bìbō

【荜拨】bìbō 多年生藤本植物，叶卵状心形，雌雄异株，浆果卵形。中医用果穗入药。long pepper (*Piper longum*), a perennial liana and dioecious plant with oval heart-shaped leaves and ovoid berries, whose grain is used in traditional Chinese medicine

【荜路蓝缕】bì lù lán lǚ same as 筚路蓝缕 bì lù lán lǚ

柲 bì〈书 *fml.*〉戈戟等兵器的柄 handle of a spear or halberd

毖 bì〈书 *fml.*〉谨慎小心 caution：惩前～后 punish wrongdoings so as to inhibit their future recurrence; learn from past errors to avoid future mistakes

哔（嗶） bì［哔叽］(bìjī) 密度比较小的斜纹的毛织品。另有一种斜纹的棉织品，叫充哔叽或线哔叽。serge; small-density twill wool fabric; 充哔叽 chōngbìjī or 线哔叽 xiànbìjī, another twill cotton fabric, 简称 abbr. 哔叽 bìjī［法 French: beige］

饽（饆） bì［饽馊］(bìluó) 一种食品 a kind of food

陛 bì〈书 *fml.*〉宫殿的台阶 flight of steps leading to a palace hall：石～ stone steps

【陛下】bìxià 对君主的尊称 Your Majesty; His or Her Majesty; honorific title for a sovereign

鞸（韠） bì〈古代 *arch.*〉朝服的蔽膝 knee cover in court dress

毙（斃） bì ❶ 死（用于人时多含贬义 derogative when used of people）die; get killed：～命 meet violent death; get killed; lose one's life｜击～ shoot dead; strike dead｜牲畜倒～。The animal fell dead. ❷ 枪毙 shoot; execute; shoot dead：昨天～了一个土匪头目。The bandit leader was executed by a firing squad yesterday. ❸〈书 *fml.*〉仆倒 fall; drop; collapse：多行不义必自～。An inveterate evil-doer is bound to meet his doom.

【毙命】bìmìng 丧命（含贬义 derog.）meet violent death; get killed; lose one's life

铋 bì 金属元素，符号 Bi (bismuthum)。白色或粉红色，质软，不纯时脆，凝固时有膨胀现象。用来制低熔合金，可做保险丝、安全阀等。bismuthum (Bi), white or pink soft metal element, which is fragile when impure and expands when it solidifies; used to produce low-thermo metal, and to make fuses, safety valves, etc.

秘（祕） bì ❶ 译音用字，如秘鲁（国名，在南美洲）word for translation, e.g. 秘鲁 (Bìlǔ) Peru (a country in the South America) ❷ (Bì) 姓 a surname

☞ mì on p. 1332

狴 bì［狴犴］(bì'àn)〈书 *fml.*〉❶ 传说中的一种走兽，古代常把它的形象画在牢狱的门上 mythological beast often painted on prison doors in ancient times ❷ 借指监狱 prison; gaol; jail

萆 bì ❶ same as 蓖 bì ❷ same as 萆薢 bìxiè

【萆薢】bìxiè 多年生藤本植物，叶互生，雌雄异株。根状茎横生，呈圆柱形，表面黄褐色，可入药。yam (*Dioscorea*), a perennial liana and dioecious plant with alternate leaves, overgrown with cylinder and root-shaped stems with yellowish brown surface, which may be used as medicine

梐 bì［梐枑］(bìhù)〈古代 *arch.*〉官署前拦住行人的东西，用木条交叉制成 railing, banister, balustrade in front of government office to keep out pedestrians, made of crisscross wooden slips

庳 bì〈书 *fml.*〉❶ 低洼 low-lying：陂塘污～ dirty and uneven pool ❷ 矮 low：宫室卑～（房屋低矮）low houses

敝 bì ❶〈书 *fml*.〉破旧;破烂 shabby; ragged; worn-out; tattered: ～衣 shabby clothes | 舌～唇焦 with a weary tongue and parched lips (as from talking too much); talk till one's tongue and lips are parched ❷〈谦辞 *hum*.〉〈旧时 *old*〉用于跟自己有关的事物 [used for matters concerned with oneself] my; our; this: ～姓 my surname | ～处 my place | ～校 our school ❸〈书 *fml*.〉衰败 decline; worsen: 凋～ destitute; depressed | 经久不～ prolonged; endured

【敝人】bìrén 对人谦称自己 your humble servant; I

【敝屣】bìxǐ〈书 *fml*.〉破旧的鞋 worn-out shoes;〈比喻 *fig*.〉没有价值的东西 worthless thing: 视功名若～ regard scholarly honour and official rank as a pair of old shoes

【敝帚自珍】bì zhǒu zì zhēn 破扫帚,自己当宝贝爱惜 value one's own old broom;〈比喻 *fig*.〉东西虽不好,可是自己珍视 cherish sth. of little value simply because it is one's own; also 敝帚千金 bì zhǒu qiān jīn

婢 bì 婢女 slave girl; servant girl: 奴～ maidservant; slave girl | 奴颜～膝 servile; subservient

【婢女】bìnǚ〈旧时 *old*〉有钱人家雇用的女孩子 slave girl; servant girl; girl employed by a rich family

皕 bì〈书 *fml*.〉二百 two hundred

赑 bì [赑屃](bìxì)〈书 *fml*.〉❶ 形容用力 strain one's muscles; exert one's strength ❷ 传说中的一种动物,像龟。旧时大石碑的石座多雕刻成赑屃形状。legendary animal like a tortoise; giant land turtle; bases of heavy stone tablets carved in the likeness of this animal in old times

筚(篳) bì〈书 *fml*.〉用荆条、竹子等编成的篱笆或其他遮拦物 bamboo or twig fence or other barrier: 蓬门～户 (house with) a wicker door | 蓬～生辉。Luster is lent to my humble abode (by your visit).

【筚篥】bìlì same as 觱篥 bìlì

【筚路蓝缕】bì lù lán lǚ《左传》宣公十二年:'筚路蓝缕,以启山林。'意思是说驾着柴车,穿着破旧的衣服去开辟山林 *The Zuo Commentary* · *Duke Xuan 12th Year*: 'Drive a cart full of faggots in threadbare clothes in order to reclaim mountain wilderness.' (筚路 *bi lu*: 柴车 faggot cart; 蓝缕 *lan lü*: 破衣服 threadbare clothes); 形容创业的艰苦 The phrase refers to hardships in pioneering work; also 荜路蓝缕 bì lù lán lǚ

湢 bì〈书 *fml*.〉浴室 bathroom

愊 bì [愊忆](bìyì)〈书 *fml*.〉烦闷 gloomy; depressed; also 腷臆 bìyì

愎 bì 乖戾;执拗 willful; self-willed: 刚～自用 headstrong; opinionated

弼(弻) bì〈书 *fml*.〉辅助 assistance: 辅～support

蓖 bì [蓖麻](bìmá)一年生或多年生草本植物,叶子大,掌状分裂。种子叫蓖麻子,榨的油叫蓖麻油,医药上做泻药,工业上做润滑油。castor-oil plant (*Ricinus communis*); annual or perennial herb with big palm-shaped leaves, whose seeds are called castor beans, and the oil extracted from them castor oil, which is used as a laxative in medicine and a lubricant in industry; also 大麻子 dàmázǐ

跸(蹕) bì〈书 *fml*.〉帝王出行时,开路清道,禁止通行。泛指跟帝王行止有关的事情。keep the road clear for the emperor, keep traffic away from the road; (in a broad serse) an emperor's tour: 驻～(帝王出行时沿途停留暂住) (of emperor on a tour) stay temporarily; stop over

腷 bì [腷臆](bìyì) same as 愊忆 bìyì

痹(痺) bì 痹症 disease of the limbs; trunk pain or numbness: 风～ wandering arthritis | 寒～arthralgia caused by cold | 湿～arthritis with fixed pain caused by damp

【痹症】bìzhèng〈中医 *Chin. med*.〉指由风、寒、湿等引起的肢体疼痛或麻木的病 disease of limbs, trunk pain or numbness caused by wind, cold, damp, etc.

煏 bì〈方 *dial*.〉用火烘干 dry by the fire

滗(潷) bì 挡住渣滓或泡着的东西,把液体倒出 decant; drain: ～汤药 strain decoction of medicinal ingredients | 把汤～出去 strain out the soup

裨 bì〈书 *fml*.〉益处 benefit; advantage: ～益 benefit | 无～于事(对事情没有益处)。It will not help. *or* It will not do any good.

☞ pí on p.1467

【裨益】bìyì〈书 *fml*.〉❶ 益处 benefit; advantage; profit: 学习先进经验,对于改进工作,大有～。Learning from advanced experience is of benefit to one's work. ❷ 使受益 bring benefit to; do good to: 植树造林是～当代、造福子孙的大事。Afforestation is a major endeavour beneficial to both present and future generations.

辟[1] bì〈书 *fml*.〉君主 monarch; sovereign: 复～ restore a dethroned monarch; restore the old order

辟[2] bì〈书 *fml*.〉❶ 排除 ward off; keep away: ～邪 ward off evil spirits (with talismans, incantations, etc.) ❷ same as 避 bì

辟[3] bì〈书 *fml*.〉帝王召见并授与官职 (of a sovereign) summon sb. and confer on him an official post: ～举(征召和荐举) ap-

point or recommend sb. to an office
☞ pī on p.1463 and pì on p.1469

【辟谷】bìgǔ 不吃五谷,方士道家当做修炼成仙的方法 refrain from eating grain or live without eating grain — ancient Taoist practice of asceticism for the purpose of achieving immortality

【辟邪】bì//xié 避免或驱除邪祟。一般用做迷信语,表示降伏妖魔鬼怪使不侵扰人的意思。ward off or exorcise evil spirits; a superstitious term meaning to dispel demons and ghosts so as to prevent them from casting spells on or bewitching people

【辟易】bìyì〈书 *fml.*〉退避(多指受惊吓后控制不住而离开原地 usu. in shock or panic) beat a retreat; back away in fear:～道侧 withdraw to the roadside|人马俱惊,～数里。The troops were badly shaken and beat a retreat of several miles.

碧 bì ❶〈书 *fml.*〉青绿色的玉石 green jade ❷ 青绿色 bluish green; blue:～草 green grass|澄～(of water or sky) blue and clear; azure

【碧波】bìbō 碧绿色的水波 blue wave:～荡漾 rippling|～万顷 boundless or vast expanse of blue water

【碧空】bìkōng 青蓝色的天空 pale blue sky; azure sky:～如洗 cloudless blue sky

【碧蓝】bìlán 青蓝色 bluish green; blue; turquoise:～的大海 blue sea|天空～～的。The sky is azure.

【碧绿】bìlǜ 青绿色 dark green:～的荷叶 dark green lotus leaf|田野一片～。The field is completely green.

【碧螺春】bìluóchūn 绿茶的一种,色泽青翠,蜷曲呈螺状,原产于太湖洞庭山 *biluochun*, green tea originally produced in the Dongting Mountains on the Taihu Lake, Jiangsu Province

【碧落】bìluò〈书 *fml.*〉天空 green void; the sky; heaven

【碧血】bìxuè《庄子·外物》:'苌弘死于蜀,藏其血,三年而化为碧。'后多用碧血指为正义事业而流的血。*Zhuangzi · External Things*: 'Three years after Chang Hong died in the state of Shu, his blood turned into jade.' usu. blood shed for a just cause:～丹心 loyal-hearted; deep patriotism; loyalty unto death

【碧油油】bìyōuyōu (～的 bìyōuyōu·de)绿油油 green and lush:～的麦苗 green and lush wheat seedlings

蔽 bì 遮盖;挡住 cover; shelter; hide:掩～ cover|遮～hide|衣不～体 dressed in rags|浮云～日。Clouds shut out the sun.

【蔽芾】bìfèi〈书 *fml.*〉形容树干树叶微小(of tree or plant) small of trunk and leaf

【蔽塞】bìsè 闭塞 ill-informed; out of the way

【蔽障】bìzhàng 遮蔽;障碍 shelter; obstacle

秘 bì [秘馞](bìbó)〈书 *fml.*〉形容香气很浓 strong scent or aroma

箅 bì [箅子](bì·zi)有空隙而能起间隔作用的器具,如蒸食物用的竹箅子,下水道口上挡住垃圾的铁箅子等 grate; frame with space between every two adjoining bars, such as a bamboo lattice for steaming food, or the iron grate over a sewer

弊 bì ❶ 欺诈蒙骗、图占便宜的行为 fraud; abuse; malpractice:作～cheat|营私舞～ engage in malpractice for selfish ends; practice graft ❷ 害处;毛病 disadvantage; harm:兴利除～ promote what is beneficial and abolish what is harmful|切中时～sharply criticize the ills of society; strike out hard at current social evils

【弊病】bìbìng ❶ 弊端 malady; evil; malpractice:管理混乱,恐有～。Confusion in management leads to malpractice. ❷ 事情上的毛病 drawback:制度不健全的～越来越突出了。The disadvantages of inadequate rules and regulations are becoming increasingly obvious.

【弊端】bìduān 由于工作上有漏洞而发生的损害公益的事情 flaws in work; practice resulting in harm to public interests; abuse:消除～ stem off abuses

【弊害】bìhài 弊病;害处 disadvantage; harm; drawback

【弊绝风清】bì jué fēng qīng 形容社会风气十分良好,没有贪污舞弊等坏事情 corruption swept away and social mores cleared; put an end to all corrupt practices to make way for a prevailingly wholesome atmosphere; also 风清弊绝 fēng qīng bì jué

【弊政】bìzhèng〈书 *fml.*〉有害的政治措施 harmful or pernicious policies or political measures:抨击～criticize harmful policies|革除～abolish corrupt politics

髲 bì〈书 *fml.*〉假发 wig

獘 bì〈书 *fml.*〉same as 毙 bì

薜 bì [薜荔](bìlì)木本植物,茎蔓生,叶子卵形。果实球形,可做凉粉。climbing fig (*Ficus pumila*), woody climbing fig with oval-shaped leaves and spherical fruit used to make bean jelly

觱 bì [觱篥](bìlì)〈古代 *arch.*〉管乐器,用竹做管,用芦苇做嘴,汉代从西域传入 Tartar pipe; bamboo pipe with a reed mouthpiece introduced from the Western Regions during the Han Dynasty; also 觱栗 bìlì,觱篥 bìlì and 筚篥 bìlì

篦 bì 用篦子梳 comb (for hair); double-edged fine-tooth comb:～头 comb one's hair with such a comb

【篦子】bì·zi 用竹子制成的梳头用具，中间有梁儿，两侧有密齿 double-edged fine-tooth bamboo comb

壁 bì ❶ 墙 wall：～报 wall newspaper｜～灯 wall lamp; bracket light｜家徒四～have nothing but bare walls in one's house — live in miserable penury ◇铜墙铁～bastion of iron (fig. impregnable fortress) ❷ 某些物体上作用像围墙的部分 part of sth. that serves as a wall：井～wall of a well｜锅炉～boiler wall｜细胞～cell wall ❸ 像墙那样直立的山石 wall-like stone：绝～precipice｜峭～steep; cliff ❹ 壁垒 barrier：坚～清野 fortify defence works, evacuate non-combatants and hide provisions and livestock; strengthen the defences and clear the fields ❺ 二十八宿之一 *Bi*, name of one of the 28 constellations

【壁报】bìbào 机关、团体、学校等办的报，把稿子张贴在墙壁上 newspaper published by a government office, organization, school, etc., that is pasted on the wall for all to read; also 墙报 qiángbào

【壁橱】bìchú 墙体上留出空间而成的橱 walk-in closet; built-in wardrobe or cupboard; also 壁柜 bìguì

【壁灯】bìdēng 装置在墙壁上的灯 wall lamp; bracket light

【壁挂】bìguà 挂在墙壁上的一种装饰性织物。包括毛织壁挂、印染壁挂、刺绣壁挂、棉织壁挂等。毛织壁挂也叫壁毯，挂毯。wall hangings; woollen, printed and dyed, embroidered, or cotton tapestry; woollen tapestry; also known as 壁毯 bìtǎn and 挂毯 guàtǎn

【壁虎】bìhǔ 爬行动物，身体扁平，四肢短，趾上有吸盘，能在壁上爬行。吃蚊、蝇、蛾等小昆虫，对人类有益。house gecko (*Hemidactylus*), a kind of reptile beneficial to humankind that has a flat body, short limbs and suction pads on its toes, that crawls up walls and preys on mosquitoes, flies and other insects; also 蝎虎 xiēhǔ; 旧称 formerly known as 守宫 shǒugōng

【壁画】bìhuà 绘在建筑物的墙壁或天花板上的图画 mural; fresco; wall or ceiling painting in a building：敦煌～Dunhuang murals

【壁垒】bìlěi ❶〈旧时 *old*〉军营的围墙，泛指防御工事 defensive wall; (in a broad sense) defence works; fortifications; defences ❷〈比喻 *fig.*〉对立的事物和界限 rival; demarcation line; bounds：～分明 be diametrically opposed; be sharply divided｜唯物主义和唯心主义是哲学中的两大～。Materialism and idealism are two rivaling and diametrically opposed philosophical theories in philosophy.

【壁垒森严】bìlěi sēnyán〈比喻 *fig.*〉防守很严密或界限划得很分明 closely guarded; strongly fortified or sharply divided

【壁立】bìlì （山崖等）像墙壁一样陡立 (of cliffs, etc.) stand like a wall：～千仞 sheer rise of eight thousand feet｜～的山峰 sheer cliff

【壁炉】bìlú 就着墙壁砌成的生火取暖的设备，有烟囱通到室外 fireplace, grate or hearth of a residence, set into a wall with a vertical passage, a chimney, to the exterior through which smoke escapes

【壁上观】bìshàngguān ☞ 作壁上观 zuò bì shàng guān on p. 2574

【壁虱】bìshī ❶ 蜱(pí) tick ❷〈书 *fml.*〉臭虫 bedbug

【壁毯】bìtǎn 毛织壁挂 tapestry (used as a wall hanging); also 挂毯 guàtǎn

【壁障】bìzhàng 像墙壁的障碍物（多用于比喻 usu. fig.）barrier or obstacle like a wall：消除双方之间的思想～remove the ideological misunderstanding between the two sides

【壁纸】bìzhǐ 贴在室内墙上做装饰用的纸 wallpaper; decorative paper for internal wall

【壁钟】bìzhōng 挂钟 wall clock; bracket clock

避 bì ❶ 躲开；回避 avoid：～雨 take shelter from the rain｜退～avoid｜～而不谈 evade the question; avoid the subject; keep silent about the matter ❷ 防止 prevent; keep away; repel：～孕 contraception｜～雷针 lightening rod

【避风】bì//fēng ❶ 躲避风 take shelter from the wind：找个～的地方休息休息 take a rest in the lee ❷〈比喻 *fig.*〉避开不利的势头 keep away from unfavourable situation; stay away from trouble; also 避风头 bì//fēng·tou

【避风港】bìfēnggǎng 供船只躲避大风浪的港湾 place of shelter for ships;〈比喻 *fig.*〉供躲避激烈斗争的地方 shelter from a fierce struggle

【避讳】bì//huì 封建时代为了维护等级制度的尊严，说话写文章时遇到君主或尊亲的名字都不直接说出或写出，叫做避讳 practice in feudal times of avoiding violating the taboo of uttering the personal names of the emperor or elders, in order to safeguard the dignity of the hierarchy

【避讳】bì·hui ❶ 不愿说出或听到某些会引起不愉快的字眼儿 word or phrase to be avoided as taboo：旧时迷信，行船的人～'翻'、'沉'等字眼儿。In former times there existed a superstition whereby people onboard a ship avoided uttering phrases such as 'capsize' and 'sink'. ❷ 回避 evade; dodge：都是自己人，用不着～。Since we are all friends, let us not avoid the issue.

【避忌】bìjì same as 避讳 bì·hui

【避坑落井】bì kēng luò jǐng 躲过了坑，掉进了井里 dodge a pit only to fall into a well;〈比喻 *fig.*〉避开一害，又遇另一害 out of the frying pan into the fire

【避雷器】bìléiqì 保护电气设备或无线电收音机等避免雷击的装置，原理和避雷针相同 lightning conductor; device designed on the same principle as the lightning rod, whose purpose is to protect electrical equipment, radio receivers, etc. from lightning damage

【避雷针】bìléizhēn 保护建筑物等避免雷击的装置。在高大建筑物顶端安装一个金属棒,用金属线与埋在地下的一块金属板连接起来,利用金属棒的尖端放电,使云层所带的电和地上的电逐渐中和。lightning rod; device that protects buildings, etc. from lightning damage; A metallic rod is placed at the apex of a high-rise building and connected to a metallic board at ground level by cables. The tip of the rod attracts the electricity in clouds and transmits it to the ground where it is neutralized.

【避免】bìmiǎn 设法不使某种情形发生;防止 prevent sth. from happening; avoid; refrain from; avert:～冲突 avoid conflicts|看问题要客观、全面,～主观、片面。One should take an objective and all-round, rather than subjective and one-sided, point of view on issues.

【避难】bì//nàn 躲避灾难或迫害 flee disaster or persecution; take refuge; seek asylum:～所 refuge; sanctuary; haven

【避让】bìràng 躲避;让开 avoid; dodge; get out of the way; step aside; make way:～道旁 dodge away to the roadside

【避世】bìshì 脱离现实生活,避免和外界接触 retire from the world; withdraw from society:～绝俗 withdraw from society and live in solitude

【避暑】bì//shǔ ❶ 天气炎热的时候到凉爽的地方去住 be away for summer holidays; spend a holiday at a summer resort:～胜地 summer resort|夏天到北戴河～spend a holiday at Beidaihe, a seaside summer resort ❷ 避免中暑 prevent sunstroke:天气太热,吃点～的药。It is very hot, so it would be advisable to take some medicine to prevent sunstroke.

【避嫌】bì//xián 避开嫌疑 avoid doing anything that may arouse suspicion; avoid arousing suspicion

【避邪】bìxié 迷信的人指用符咒等避免邪祟(of superstitious people) ward off evil spirits with talismans, incantations, etc.

【避孕】bì//yùn 用阴茎套、子宫环等用具或药物阻止精子和卵子相结合,使不受孕 use of a condom, intrauterine device (IUD), or birth pill in order to prevent sperm and ovum fusing, thus avoiding pregnancy; contraception

【避重就轻】bì zhòng jiù qīng 避开重要的而拣次要的来承担,也指回避主要的问题,只谈无关重要的方面 evade major responsibilities in favour of minor ones; avoid the important and dwell on the trivial

嬖 bì〈书 *fml.*〉❶ 宠爱 show favour to:～爱 dote on|～昵 be in favour (with sb.) ❷ 受宠爱 win sb.'s favour:～臣 favourite subject|～妾 favourite concubine ❸ 受宠爱的人 person enjoying favour

髀 bì〈书 *fml.*〉大腿,也指大腿骨 thigh; thighbone:抚～长叹 rest hands on thighs and heave a deep sigh

【髀肉复生】bì ròu fù shēng 因为长久不骑马,大腿上的肉又长起来了。形容长久安逸,无所作为。become flabby in one's thighs owing to lack of horseback-riding exercises — accomplish nothing in a life of comfort and ease; idle away one's life

潷 bì 漾潷(Yàngbì),地名,在云南 Yangbi, name of a place in Yunnan Province

臂 bì ❶ 胳膊 arm:左～left arm|～力 strength of the arm|振～高呼 raise one's arm and shout ❷ 人体解剖学上多指上臂 the upper arm in anthropometry

☞ · bei on p. 87

【臂膀】bìbǎng ❶ 胳膊 arm ❷〈比喻 *fig.*〉助手 aide; assistant

【臂膊】bìbó〈方 *dial.*〉胳膊 arm

【臂力】bìlì 臂部的力量 strength of the arm

【臂章】bìzhāng 佩带在衣袖(一般为左袖)上臂部分、表示身份或职务的标志 armband; band attached to the upper left sleeve to indicate one's rank or position

【臂助】bìzhù〈书 *fml.*〉❶ 帮助 help:屡承～,不胜感激。Thank you for your unfailing help. ❷ 助手 assistant:收为～accept sb. as one's assistant

奰 bì〈书 *fml.*〉❶ 怒 angry ❷ 壮大 big and tall

璧 bì 古代的一种玉器,扁平,圆形,中间有小孔 round flat piece of jade with a hole at its center used in ancient China:白～无瑕 flawless jade; impeccable (moral) integrity

【璧还】bìhuán〈书 *fml.*〉〈敬辞 *pol.*〉用于归还原物或辞谢赠品 return (a borrowed subject) with thanks; decline a gift:所借图书,不日～。I will return the books I borrowed in no time at all.

【璧谢】bìxiè〈书 *fml.*〉〈敬辞 *pol.*〉退还原物,并且表示感谢(多用于辞谢赠品) return a borrowed subject with thanks; decline a gift with thanks

襞 bì ❶〈书 *fml.*〉衣服上打的褶子,泛指衣服的皱纹 gathering or fold in clothes:皱～wrinkles (in crumpled clothes) ❷ 肠、胃等内部器官上的褶子 folds of an internal organ such as the stomach or intestines

躃 bì same as 躄 bì

躄 bì〈书 *fml.*〉❶ 仆倒 fall ❷ 腿瘸(qué) lame in the leg

箅 bì [箅篥](bìlì) same as 觱篥 bìlì

biān (ㄅ丨ㄢ)

边(邊) biān ❶ 几何图形上夹成角的射线或围成多边形的线段 side of a geometrical figure; lines that form angle or a multi-angle figure in geometry ❷ (～儿 biānr) same as 边缘 biānyuán ①: 海～seaside; seashore|村～ edge of a village|田～edge of fields|马路～儿 roadside; the side of a street ❸ (～儿 biānr)镶在或画在边缘上的条状装饰 striped decoration fixed or drawn on the edge of sth.: 花～儿 lace|金～儿 golden lace ❹ 边界;边境 border; frontier: ～疆 border area; borderland|～防 frontier (border) defence|戍～defend the border ❺ 界限 edge: ～际 limit; bound; boundary; margin|一望无～stretch as far as the eye can see; stretch to the horizon ❻ 靠近物体的地方 place next to a person or thing: 旁～side|身～at or by one's side; around ❼ 方面 side; party: 双～会谈 bilateral talks|这～那～都说好了。The two sides have reached an agreement. ❽ 用在时间词或数词后,表示接近某个时间或某个数目[used after a reference to time or to a numeral, meaning sth. close to the time or the numeral]: 冬至～上下了一场大雪。There was a heavy snow around the Winter Solstice.|活到六十～上还没有见过这种事。I have never seen anything like this, even though I am about 60. ❾ 两个或几个'边'字分别用在动词前面,表示动作同时进行[two or more 边 biān used before verbs to express the simultaneous progression or development of two actions]: ～干～学 learn while working|～收件,～打包,～托运 take goods, pack them and consign them for shipment ❿ (Biān) 姓 a surname

边(邊) ·bian (～儿·bianr) 方位词后缀[suffix of nouns of locality]: 前～in front of; before|里～inside|东～east side|左～left

【边岸】biān'àn 水边的陆地;边际 bank; shore; limit; boundary: 湖水茫茫,不见～。The lake is a vast expanse of waves, mighty and boundless.

【边鄙】biānbǐ 〈书 *fml.*〉边远的地方 remote border region; remote district

【边币】biānbì 抗日战争和解放战争时期,陕甘宁、晋察冀、冀热辽等边区政府银行所发行的纸币 border region currency consisting of currency notes issued by the governments of the Shaanxi-Gansu-Ningxia Border Region, the Shanxi-Chahar-Hebei Border Region, the Hebei-Rehe-Liaoning Border Region and other border regions during the War of Resistance against Japan (1937-1945) and the War of Liberation (1946-1949)

【边城】biānchéng 靠近国界的城市 border or frontier town

【边陲】biānchuí 边境 border area; frontier: ～重镇 important frontier town

【边地】biāndì 边远的地区 border district; borderland

【边防】biānfáng 国家边境地区布置的防务 frontier or border defence of the state: ～部队 frontier guards

【边锋】biānfēng 足球、冰球等球类比赛中担任边线进攻的队员 player on the wing, side section of the game area in football, ice hockey, etc.

【边幅】biānfú 布帛的边缘 edge of cloth and silk; 〈比喻 *fig.*〉人的仪表、衣着 one's attire or appearance: 不修～not care for one's appearance; be careless about one's dress

【边关】biānguān 边境上的关口 frontier pass: 镇守～ guard a frontier pass; hold a frontier command

【边患】biānhuàn 〈书 *fml.*〉边疆被侵扰而造成的祸害 external encroachment on the frontier: ～频仍。There were frequent foreign encroachments on the borders.

【边际】biānjì 边缘;界限(多指地区或空间 oft. an area or a space) limit; bound; boundary; margin: 一片绿油油的庄稼,望不到～。Shiny green crops stretch as far as the eye can see.|汪洋大海,漫无～boundless (limitless) ocean

【边疆】biānjiāng 靠近国界的领土 land near the line dividing two countries; border area; borderland; frontier; frontier region

【边角料】biānjiǎoliào 制作物品时,切割、裁剪下来的零碎材料 leftover bits and pieces of industrial material

【边界】biānjiè 地区和地区之间的界线(多指国界,有时也指省界、县界 mostly national boundary, sometimes provincial and county boundary or border) line dividing two regions: ～线 borderline; boundary line|越过～cross a boundary; cross the border

【边境】biānjìng 靠近边界的地方 border; area near the line dividing two countries; frontier, border area

【边款】biānkuǎn 刻于印章侧面或上端的文字、图案等 inscriptions or patterns carved on the sides or top of a seal

【边框】biānkuàng (～儿 biānkuàngr) 挂屏、镜子等扁平器物的框子 frame or edge of a scroll, mirror or other flat object

【边贸】biānmào 边境贸易 frontier trade; border trade: 近几年,这个地区的～发展很快。Border trade in the region has been burgeoning in recent years.

【边门】biānmén 旁门 side door; wicket door or gate

【边民】biānmín 边界一带的居民 people living on the frontiers; inhabitants of a border area

【边卡】biānqiǎ 边界上的哨所或关卡 border

checkpoint

【边区】biānqū 我国国内革命战争及抗日战争时期，共产党领导的革命政权在几个省连接的边缘地带建立的根据地，如陕甘宁边区、晋察冀边区等 border area or region established by the revolutionary government under the leadership of the Communist Party of China on the borders of several linked provinces during China's revolutionary civil wars (1924-1937), and the War of Resistance against Japan (1937-1945), including, for example, the Shaanxi-Gansu-Ningxia Border Region and the Shanxi-Chahar-Hebei Border Region

【边塞】biānsài 边疆地区的要塞 frontier fortress

【边式】biān·shi ❶〈方 *dial.*〉(装束、体态)漂亮俏皮(of one's dress or figure) smart; sexy ❷ 戏曲演员的表演动作潇洒利落(of acting) smart and graceful：他扮演的关羽，动作～，嗓音洪亮。His acting of the role of General Guan Yu is graceful and his voice is sonorous.

【边事】biānshì〈书 *fml.*〉与边境有关的事务，特指边防军情 border affairs, especially defence affairs：～紧急。The border situation is pressing.

【边务】biānwù 与边境有关的事务，特指国际事务 frontier affairs, especially international affairs

【边线】biānxiàn 足球、篮球、羽毛球等运动场地两边的界线 sideline, either of two lines that define the side boundaries of a football playing field, basketball or volleyball court, etc.

【边沿】biānyán same as 边缘 biānyuán ①：～地带 periphery

【边音】biānyīn 口腔中间通路阻塞，气流从舌头的边上通过而发出的辅音。如普通话语音的 l。consonant articulated so that breath passes along either or both sides of the tongue, e.g. l in *putonghua*; lateral (sound)

【边缘】biānyuán ❶ 沿边的部分 margin; edge; fringe; verge; brink; periphery：～区 verge; brink ◇处于破产的～on the verge of bankruptcy ❷ 靠近界线的；同两方面或多方面有关系的 pertaining to a margin; connected to two or more areas：～学科 marginal discipline

【边缘科学】biānyuán kēxué 以两种或多种学科为基础而发展起来的科学。如以地质学和化学为基础的地球化学、以物理学和生物学为基础的生物物理学等。science developed on the basis of two or more disciplines, e.g. geochemistry is based on geography and chemistry; biophysics is based on physics and biology; frontier science

【边远】biānyuǎn 靠近国界的；远离中心地区的 close to the national boundary; far from the centre; remote; outlying：～地区 outlying area|～县份 remote counties

【边寨】biānzhài 边境地区的寨子 village in a frontier region

砭 biān ❶ 砭石 stone acupuncture needle ❷〈古代 *arch.*〉用石针扎皮肉治病 method of curing illness by puncturing specified areas of the skin with stone needles：针～ ancient form of acupuncture; criticize; refute ◇寒风～骨。The cold wind cuts one to the marrow.|痛～时弊 castigate the abuses of the time

【砭骨】biāngǔ 刺入骨髓，形容使人感觉非常冷或疼痛非常剧烈 chill one to the bone; cut one to the marrow：朔风～。The icy wind cuts one to the marrow.

【砭石】biānshí〈古代 *arch.*〉治病用的石针或石片 stone acupuncture needle or piece used to cure illness

笾(籩) biān〈古代 *arch.*〉祭祀或宴会时盛果实、干肉等的竹器 bamboo container for fruit, dried meat or other delicacies for banquets or when offering sacrifices

萹 biān [萹蓄](biānxù)一年生草本植物，叶子互生，披针形，花被绿色，有白色边缘。全草入药。beggard-weed (*Polygonum aviculare*); annual herb with alternate, needle-shaped leaves whose flower perianths are green with white edges, and used entirely for medicine

☞ biǎn on p.117

编 biān ❶ 把细长条状的东西交叉组织起来 weave; plait; forming threads, twigs, etc. by drawing one out and putting another over it, repeating until a form of fabric has been completed：～筐 weave a basket|～辫子 plait one's hair|～草帽 weave a straw hat ❷ 把分散的事物按照一定的条理组织起来或按照一定的顺序排列起来 organize or arrange diverse matters according to a certain order：～组 organize or divide into groups|～队 organize into teams|～号 number; serial number ❸ 编辑 edit; editor：～报 edit a newspaper|～杂志 edit a magazine; work in the editorial department of a magazine ❹ 创作(歌词、剧本等) write (a play); compose (a song)：～歌 compose a song|～话剧 write a modern drama|～了个曲儿 compose a song ❺ 捏造 fabricate; concoct; trump up; make up; cook up：瞎～fabricate; invent; make up; cook up|～派 exaggerate (people's defects); fabricate; cook up ❻ 成本的书(常用做书名 oft. used as part of the titles of books) book：正～the first part; Book I|续～continuation or sequel (to a book or a story)|人手一～one copy for everybody; everybody has one copy|《故事新～》*Old Stories Retold* ❼ 书籍按内容划分的单位，大于'章' part; book; division of a book which comes before 'chapter'：上～the first part; Book I | 中～the second part; Book II | 下～the third part; Book III ❽ same as 编制 biānzhì ③:在～(of personnel) be on the permanent staff | 超～exceed the personnel quota; be overstaffed | ～外 not in the regular payroll; non-staff member; irregular or temporary staff; irregular

【编次】biāncì 按一定的次序编排 order of arrangement

【编导】biāndǎo ❶ 编剧和导演 write and direct (a play, film, etc.) ❷ 编剧和导演的人 writer and director (of a play, film, etc.)

【编订】biāndìng 编纂校订 compile and edit:～《唐宋传奇集》compile and edit *A Compilation of Classical-language Tales of Tang and Song*

【编队】biān//duì ❶ 把分散的人、运输工具等编成一定顺序或某种组织形式 put diverse people, means of transportation, etc. in order, or form them into an organization ❷ 军事上指飞机、军舰等按一定要求组成战斗单位 formation (of ships or aircrafts)

【编号】biān//hào 按顺序编号数 ascertain the number of:新买的图书～上架后才能出借。Newly acquired books will not be available for lending until they have been numbered.

【编号】biānhào 编定的号数 number:请把这本书的～填在借书单上。Please write the number of the book on the loan slip.

【编辑】biānjí ❶ 对资料或现成的作品进行整理、加工 edit; prepare data for publication or finalize pieces of writing by deciding what should remain or be left out, and correcting mistakes:～部 editorial department | ～工作 editing ❷ 做编辑工作的人 editor

【编校】biānjiào 编辑和校订 edit and revise; editor-reviser

【编结】biānjié same as 编 biān ①:～毛衣 weave or knit a sweater | ～鱼网 weave a fishing net

【编列】biānliè ❶ 编排 edit; compile:他把文章辑在一起,～成书。He edited and compiled a book of essays. ❷ 制定规程、计划等,安排有关项目 work out rules and regulations, plans, etc. make arrangements

【编录】biānlù 摘录并编辑 select excerpts and edit:该书～严谨。This books is well edited.

【编码】biān//mǎ 用预先规定的方法将文字、数字或其他对象编成数码,或将信息、数据转换成规定的电脉冲信号。编码在电子计算机、电视、遥控和通讯等方面广泛使用。use prescribed methods to convert a message, sequence of numbers or other objects into code, or covert information or data into specified electropulse signals; code; encode. Codes are extensively used in computer, TV, remote control, telecommunications, etc.

【编目】biān//mù 编制目录 make a catalogue; catalogue:新购图书尚未～。The newly acquired books have yet to be catalogued. | 本馆编了目的图书已有十万种。This library has 100,000 types of catalogued books.

【编目】biānmù 编制成的目录 catalogue:图书～catalogue of books

【编年】biānnián 按史实发生或文章写作的年、月、日顺序编排 arranged with earlier things or events preceding later ones; annalistic; chronological:～史 annals; annalistic history; chronicle | ～文集 chronologically collected works

【编年体】biānniántǐ 我国传统史书的一种体裁,按年、月、日编排史实。如《春秋》、《资治通鉴》等就是编年体史书。annalistic (historiographical or chronological) style of keeping records whereby earlier events come before later ones, as in *The Spring and Autumn Annals* and *Historical Events Retold as a Mirror for Government*

【编排】biānpái ❶ 按照一定的次序排列先后 arrange; lay out; place in desired order:课文的～应由浅入深。The texts should be arranged in the order of difficulty. ❷ 编写剧本并排演 write a play and rehearse:～戏剧小品 write and rehearse a skit

【编派】biān·pai 〈方 *dial.*〉夸大或捏造别人的缺点或过失;编造情节来取笑 exaggerate or fabricate (people's defects or failures); cook up; invent stories to mock sb.

【编遣】biānqiǎn 改编并遣散编余人员 reorganize (troops, etc.) and discharge surplus personnel

【编磬】biānqìng 〈古代 *arch.*〉打击乐器,在木架上悬挂一组音调高低不同的石制或玉制的磬,用小木槌敲打奏乐 stone and jade chimes; ancient Chinese percussion instrument composed of a set of high- and low-pitched stone or jade pieces hung on a wooden stand and struck with a small wooden stick for music

【编审】biānshěn ❶ 编辑和审定 read and edit, edit and finalise:～稿件 edit papers ❷ 做编审工作的人 editor

【编外】biānwài (军队、机关、企业等)编制以外的 not on the regular payroll; not on the permanent staff (in the military, government offices, enterprises, etc.):～人员 employee not on regular payroll; non-staff personnel; irregular

【编写】biānxiě ❶ 就现成的材料加以整理,写成书或文章 compile a book or academic paper using available materials:～教科书 compile a textbook ❷ 创作 write; compose:～剧本 write a play

【编选】biānxuǎn 从资料或文章中选取一部分加以编辑 select section of data or a paper to edit:～教材 compile teaching materials | ～摄影作品 select and compile photos

【编演】biānyǎn 创作和演出(戏曲、舞蹈等) write and produce (a play, dance, etc.);～文艺节目 create and put on a performance or show

【编译】biānyì ❶ 编辑和翻译 edit and translate ❷ 做编译工作的人 editor-translator

【编余】biānyú (军队、机关等)整编后多余的(of personnel) redundant after reorganization (of military or government offices, etc.):～人员 surplus personnel

【编造】biānzào ❶ 把资料组织排列起来(多指报表等 mostly statistical statements) compile materials:～名册 compile name rolls|～预算 draw up a budget ❷ 凭想像创造(故事) create (stories) from the imagination:《山海经》里有不少古人～的神话。*Book of Mountains and Seas* contains many myths invented by ancients. ❸ 捏造 fabricate; invent; make up:～谎言 fabricate or concoct lies

【编者】biānzhě 编写的人;做编辑工作的人 compiler; editor

【编者按】biānzhě'àn 编辑人员对一篇文章或一条消息所加的意见、评论等,常常放在文章或消息的前面 editor's note or editorial note expressing a specific opinion that generally precedes an article or a piece of news; also 编者案 biānzhě'àn

【编者案】biānzhě'àn same as 编者按 biānzhě'àn

【编织】biānzhī 把细长的东西互相交错或钩连而组织起来 weave; knit; plait; braid; interlace thread, yarn, strips, fibrous material, etc., so as to form a fabric:～毛衣 knit a sweater ◇根据民间传说～成一篇美丽的童话 compile popular legends into a beautiful fairy tale

【编制】biānzhì ❶ 把细长的东西交叉组织起来,制成器物 weave; knit; plait; braid; interlace thread, yarn, strips, fibrous material, etc., so as to form a fabric:用柳条～的筐子 baskets woven from willow twigs ❷ 根据资料做出(规程、方案、计划等)work out (regulations, programmes, plans, etc.) on the basis of materials available:～教学方案 draw up a teaching programme ❸ 组织机构的设置及其人员数量的定额和职务的分配 authorized organizational structure, size of staff, and distribution of posts of an organization or institution:扩大～augment the staff

【编钟】biānzhōng 〈古代 *arch.*〉打击乐器,在木架上悬挂一组音调高低不同的铜钟,用小木槌敲打奏乐 bell chimes; ancient Chinese percussion instrument comprising a set of high- and low-pitched copper bells hung from a wooden stand and struck with a small wooden stick

【编著】biānzhù 编写;著述 write; compile

【编撰】biānzhuàn 编纂;撰写 write; compile

【编缀】biānzhuì ❶ 把材料交叉组织成器物;编结 braid; plait; weave materials into an article:～花环 wreathe flowers into a garland ❷ 将有关的资料、文章等收集起来编成书;编集 edit relevant materials, articles, etc. into a book, edit:～成书 edit sth. into a book

【编组】biān//zǔ 把分散的人、交通工具等安排成一定形式的单位或单元 group; organize people, vehicles, etc. into groupings

【编纂】biānzuǎn 编辑(多指资料较多、篇幅较大的著作 mainly large books) edit:～词典 edit a dictionary|～百科全书 compile an encyclopaedia

煸 biān 烹饪方法,把菜、肉等放在热油里炒 stir-fry (vegetables or meat in hot oil):～锅 wok|～牛肉丝 stir-fried shredded beef

蝙 biān [蝙蝠](biānfú) 哺乳动物,头部和躯干像老鼠,四肢和尾部之间有皮质的膜,夜间在空中飞翔,吃蚊、蛾等昆虫。视力很弱,靠本身发出的超声波来引导飞行。bat (*Chiroptera*), flying nocturual mammal with a mouse-like body and modified forelimbs that serve as wings covered with a membranous skin that extends to the hind limbs, and feeding on insects such as mosquitoes and moths. Having poor sight (hence the expression, 'blind as a bat'), the bat transmits ultrasonic waves to navigate its flight path.

箯 biān [箯舆](biānyú) 古代的一种竹轿 a kind of bamboo bridge in ancient China

鳊(鯿) biān 鳊鱼,身体侧扁,头小而尖,鳞较细。生活在淡水中。bream (*Abramis*); a freshwater fish with a flat body, a small and pointed head, and fine scales

鞭 biān ❶ 鞭子 whip; lash ❷〈古代 *arch.*〉兵器,用铁做成,有节,没有锋刃 iron staff made up of several joints and no blade, used as a weapon:钢～iron staff|竹节～corrugated staff ❸ 形状细长类似鞭子的东西 sth. resembling a whip:教～teacher's pointer|竹～subterranean stem of bamboo ❹ 供食用或药用的某些雄兽的阴茎 penis of certain male animals used as medicine or cooked as food:鹿～deer's penis|牛～ox's penis ❺ 成串的小爆竹,放起来响声连续不断 string of small firecrackers which crackle continuously when set off until spent:一挂～a string of firecrackers|放～set off firecrackers ❻〈书 *fml.*〉鞭打 flog; whip; lash:～马 whip a horse|掘墓～尸 have the grave of sb. opened, take out the corpse and publicly flog it

【鞭策】biāncè 用鞭和策赶马 use a crop or whip to urge a horse on;〈比喻 *fig.*〉督促 spur on; urge on:要经常～自己,努力学习。We should constantly spur ourselves to study hard.

【鞭长莫及】biān cháng mò jí《左传》宣公十五年:'虽鞭之长,不及马腹。'原来是说虽然鞭子长，但是不应该打到马肚子上，后来借指力量达不到。*The Zuo Commentary · Duke Xuan 15th Year*：'The whip may be long, but it is not long enough to reach a horse's stomach.'（fig.）beyond the reach of one's power or authority; too far away to be helped

【鞭笞】biānchī〈书 *fml.*〉用鞭子或板子打 flog or lash with a whip; cane; castigate

【鞭打】biāndǎ 用鞭子打 whip; lash; flog; thrash

【鞭毛】biānmáo 原生质伸出细胞外形成鞭状物，一条或多条，有运动、摄食等作用。鞭毛虫以及各种动植物的精子等都有鞭毛。flagellum; lashlike appendage of a protoplasm for exercising and feeding. Flagellates and the sperms of all animals and plants have flagella

【鞭炮】biānpào ❶ 大小爆竹的统称 general term for firecrackers ❷ 专指成串的小爆竹 string of small firecrackers

【鞭辟入里】biān pì rù lǐ 形容能透彻说明问题，深中要害（of an argument, a theory, etc.）penetrating; trenchant; incisive（里 *li*：里头 inside）; also 鞭辟近里 biān bì jìn lǐ

【鞭挞】biāntà 鞭打 lash sb. or sth. with a whip;〈比喻 *fig.*〉抨击 lash; castigate：这部作品对旧社会的丑恶进行了无情的揭露和～。This piece of work is relentless in its exposure and condemnation of the evils of the old society.

【鞭子】biān·zi 赶牲畜的用具 instrument used to strike and urge on draft animals：马～ horsewhip

biǎn（ㄅㄧㄢˇ）

贬 biǎn ❶ 降低（封建时代多指官职，现代多指价值）（in imperial times）demote;（in modern times）depreciate：～黜 demote; dismiss｜～值 depreciate ❷ 指出缺点，给予不好的评价（跟'褒'相对 antonym of 'praise'）belittle; play down：他被～得一无是处。He was criticised as if he could never get anything right.

【贬斥】biǎnchì ❶〈书 *fml.*〉降低官职 demote ❷ 贬低并排斥或斥责 belittle and denounce

【贬黜】biǎnchù〈书 *fml.*〉same as 贬斥 biǎnchì ①；黜退 demote; dismiss

【贬词】biǎncí 含有贬义的词，如'阴谋'、'叫嚣'、'顽固'等 derogatory terms, such as conspiracy, clamour and die-hard; also 贬义词 biǎnyìcí

【贬低】biǎndī 故意降低对人或事物的评价 deliberately underestimate people or things：对这部电影任意～或拔高都是不客观的。It is not objective to arbitrarily putting down or overrating this film.

【贬官】biǎnguān ❶ 降低官职 demote：因失职而被～be demoted for dereliction of duty ❷ 被降职的官吏 demoted official

【贬损】biǎnsǔn 贬低 belittle; disparage; speak ill of：不能～别人，抬高自己。One should not underrate others and overrate oneself.

【贬义】biǎnyì 字句里含有的不赞成或坏的意思 derogatory sense; pejorative meaning：～词 derogatory term; expression of censure

【贬抑】biǎnyì 贬低并压制 belittle; depreciate

【贬责】biǎnzé 指出过失，加以批评；责备 blame; reproach; reprimand; point out mistakes and criticise：横加～blame｜不待～而深刻自省 examine oneself critically before being reprimanded

【贬谪】biǎnzhé 封建时代指官史降职，被派到远离京城的地方（in imperial times）banish from the court; relegate to an area far away from the capital

【贬值】biǎnzhí ❶ 货币购买力下降（of the purchasing value of a currency）decrease ❷ 降低本国单位货币的含金量或降低本国货币对外币的比价，叫做贬值 depreciate; devalue; devaluate; reduce the value of national currency or lower the exchange rate of national currency against other currencies ❸ 泛指价值降低 lessen the value or price of：商品～。Goods have diminished in value.

【贬职】biǎnzhí〈书 *fml.*〉降职 demote

窆 biǎn〈书 *fml.*〉埋葬 bury

扁 biǎn 图形或字体上下的距离比左右的距离小；物体的厚度比长度、宽度小 flat;（of a picture or handwriting）the height is shorter than the width. The thickness of an object is always smaller than its length and width：～圆 oval; oblate｜～体字 squat-shaped handwriting｜～盒子 flat case; shallow box｜馒头压～了。The loaf was pressed flat. ◇别把人看～了（不要小看人）。Never underestimate a person's ability. *or* Don't belittle people.

☞ piān on p. 1470

【扁柏】biǎnbǎi 常绿乔木，叶子像鳞片，果实呈球形。木材可做建筑材料和器物。false cypress（*Chamaecyparis*）; evergreen coniferous tree with scale-like leaves and timber used as a building material and in carpentry

【扁铲】biǎnchǎn 一种刃宽而较薄的凿子 flat chisel with a broad, thin blade

【扁锉】biǎncuò 板锉 flat file

【扁担】biǎn·dan 放在肩上挑东西或抬东西的工具，用竹子或木头制成，扁而长 carrying pole; shoulder pole; bamboo or wooden pole used to carry things on the shoulder

【扁担星】biǎn·danxīng 牛郎星和它附近两颗小星的俗称。民间相传小星是牛郎的两个孩子，牛郎挑着他们去见他们的母亲织女。popular name for Altair and the two adjacent stars.

According to an ancient Chinese fairy tale, the Cowherd (Altair) carries his two children (the two adjacent stars) on a shoulder pole on their way to visit their mother, the Weaving Maid (Vega).

【扁豆】biǎndòu ❶ 一年生草本植物,茎蔓生,小叶披针形,花白色或紫色,荚果长椭圆形,扁平,微弯。种子白色或紫黑色。嫩荚是普通蔬菜,种子可入药。hyacinth bean (*Dolichos lablab*); annual caulicolous and decumbent herb with small pointed leaves, white or purple flowers, and long, flat and slightly bent ellipsoid pods. Its seeds are white or purplish black, its tender pods are a common vegetable, and its seeds can be used for medicine. ❷ 这种植物的荚果或种子 pod or seed of this plant ❸〈方 *dial.*〉菜豆 kidney bean ‖ also written as 萹豆 biǎndòu, 稨豆 biǎndòu and 藊豆 biǎndòu

【扁骨】biǎngǔ 扁平的骨头,如髂骨、大多数颅骨等 flat bones such as ilium and most cranial bones

【扁平足】biǎnpíngzú 指足弓减低或塌陷,脚心逐渐变成扁平的脚,也指这样的脚病 condition in which the arch of the foot is flattened so that the entire sole rests upon the ground; flatfooted; pes planus; also 平足 píngzú

【扁食】biǎn·shi〈方 *dial.*〉饺子或馄饨 dumpling (with meat and vegetable stuffing); wonton

【扁桃】biǎntáo ❶ 落叶乔木,树皮灰色,叶披针形,花粉红色,果实卵圆形,光滑,易破裂。果仁供食用或药用。almond tree (*Prunus amygdalus*); deciduous tree with grey bark, pointed leaves, pink flowers, and smooth, oval, nut-like fruit, the kernel of which can be eaten or used to make medicine ❷ 这种植物的果实 almond, fruit of the plant ❸ 蟠(pán)桃(一种桃,果实扁圆形) flat peach

【扁桃体】biǎntáotǐ 分布在上呼吸道内的一些类似淋巴结的组织。通常指腭部的扁桃体,左右各一,形状像扁桃。tonsil, a prominent almond-shaped mass of lymphoid tissue on either side of the throat; also 扁桃腺 biǎntáoxiàn

【扁形动物】biǎnxíng dòngwù 无脊椎动物的一门,身体呈扁形,有的雌雄同体,如绦虫,有的雌雄异体,如血吸虫 flatworm; platyhelminth; worm of the phylum Plytyhelminthes, with a flat body, some (such as the tapeworm) being hermaphrodite, and others (such as blood flukes) gonochorisms

匾 biǎn ❶ 上面题着作为标记或表示赞扬文字的长方形木牌(也有用绸布做成的) horizontal inscribed board or a silk banner embroidered with words of praise: 横～ horizontal inscribed board | 绣金～ embroidered silk banner with words in gold | 门上挂着一块～。There is a horizontal inscribed board hanging over the door. ❷ 用竹篾编成的器具,圆形平底,边框很浅,用来养蚕或盛粮食 big round shallow basket made from bamboo strips for raising silkworms or holding grain

【匾额】biǎn'é same as 匾 biǎn ①

【匾文】biǎnwén 题在匾额上的文字 inscription on a horizontal board

萹 biǎn [萹豆] (biǎndòu) same as 扁豆 biǎndòu

☞ biān on p. 113

惼 biǎn〈书 *fml.*〉(心胸)狭窄 narrow (of mind): ～心 narrow-minded

碥 biǎn ❶ 在水旁斜着伸出来的山石 rock sticking out obliquely at the side of a river ❷ 山崖险峻地方的登山石级 stone steps along dangerous parts of a cliff

稨 biǎn [稨豆] (biǎndòu) same as 扁豆 biǎndòu

褊 biǎn〈书 *fml.*〉狭小; 狭隘 narrow; cramped

【褊急】biǎnjí〈书 *fml.*〉气量狭小,性情急躁 narrow-minded and short-tempered

【褊狭】biǎnxiá〈书 *fml.*〉狭小 narrow; cramped: 土地～ narrow strip of land | 气量～ small-minded

藊 biǎn [藊豆] (biǎndòu) same as 扁豆 biǎndòu

biàn (ㄅㄧㄢˋ)

卞 biàn ❶〈书 *fml.*〉急躁 irritable; irascible: ～急 irascible; testy ❷ (Biàn) 姓 a surname

弁 biàn ❶〈古代 *arch.*〉男子戴的帽子 man's cap ❷〈旧时 *old*〉称低级武职 low-ranking military officer: 武～ low-ranking military officer | 马～ bodyguard

【弁言】biànyán〈书 *fml.*〉序言; 序文 foreword; preface

苄 biàn [苄基] (biànjī) 苯甲基 benzyl

抃 biàn〈书 *fml.*〉鼓掌,表示欢喜 clap one's hands to express joy: ～舞 clap hands and dance for joy | ～踊(鼓掌跳跃,形容非常高兴) clap hands and dance for joy

汴 Biàn 河南开封的别称 another name for 开封 Kāifēng, major city in Henan Province

忭 biàn〈书 *fml.*〉欢喜; 快乐 glad; happy: 欢～ glad; happy | ～跃(欢欣跳跃) jump for joy

变(變) biàn ❶ 和原来不同; 变化; 改变 become different; change: 情况～了。The situation has changed. | ～了样儿 look different ❷ 改变(性质、状态); 变成 change in nature or state; change into: 沙漠～良田。The desert has been turned into cultivated land. | 后进～先进。The backward has now become the advanced. ❸ 使改变 change; turn; transform: ～废为宝 change waste material into things of value; recycle waste material|～农业国为工业国 turn an agricultural country into an industrial one ❹ 能变化的;已变化的 changeable; changed: ～数 variable|～态 metamorphosis; deformation ❺ 变卖 sell off: ～产 sell off one's property ❻ 变通 be flexible; make changes according to specific conditions; stretch a point: 通权达～ be flexible and untrammeled by convention; adapt oneself to circumstances; act as the occasion requires ❼ 有重大影响的突然变化 unexpected turn of major events: 事～incident|～乱 turmoil; social upheaval ❽ 指变文 popular form of narrative literature that flourished in the Tang Dynasty, with alternate lines of prose and poetry for recitation and singing (oft. on Buddhist themes): 目连～ *The Great Mahamaudgalyayana Rescues His Mother from Hell*

【变本加厉】biàn běn jiā lì 变得比原来更加严重 go from bad to worse; with ever-growing intensity

【变产】biàn//chǎn 变卖产业 sell off one's property

【变蛋】biàndàn same as 松花 sōnghuā

【变电站】biàndiànzhàn 改变电压的场所。为了把发电厂发出来的电能输送到较远的地方,必须把电压升高,变为高压电,到用户附近再按需要把电压降低。这种升降电压的工作靠变电站来完成。变电站的主要设备是开关和变压器。按规模大小不同,称为变电所、配电室等。transformer substation; place for changing the voltage of power grid. In order to transmit electricity to remote areas, the voltage must be increased to produce high-voltage electricity, but reduced to allow a particular piece of equipment to be used. All this is done at transformer substations. The major types of equipment in these substations are switches and transformers, referred to as transformer offices or distributing rooms according to their size.

【变调】biàndiào ❶ 字和字连起来说,有时发生字调和单说时不同的现象,叫做变调。例如普通话语音中两个上声字相连时,第一个字变成阳平。tonal modification; referring to a character's change of tone in a specific context, e.g. when two characters of the falling-rising (or third) tone are joined together, the first one is pronounced with a rising tone ❷ 转调 modulation; change to another tune

【变动】biàndòng ❶ 变化(多指社会现象 usu. of social phenomena) change: 人事～personnel change|国际局势发生了很大的～。The world situation has undergone great changes. ❷ 改变 change; alter; modify: 任务～了。Our assignment has changed.|根据市场需要,～蔬菜种植计划。Plans for growing vegetables will change in response to market demand.

【变法】biàn//fǎ 指历史上对国家的法令制度做重大的变革 political reform; institutional reform; major historical change in a country's laws and systems: ～维新 constitutional reform and modernization

【变法儿】biàn//fǎr 想另外的办法;用各种办法 try different ways; try in a thousand and one ways: 他变着法儿算计人。He tries every way possible to hatch plots against others.|食堂里总是～把伙食搞得好一些。The mess hall does everything it can to provide better food.

【变革】biàngé 改变事物的本质(多指社会制度而言 mostly of social systems) change the nature: ～社会 change society|伟大的历史～ great historical change

【变更】biàngēng 改变;变动 change; alter; modify: ～原定赛程 alter the original agenda for competitions|修订版的内容有些～。Some changes have been made to the content in this revised edition.

【变工】biàngōng 老解放区和五十年代初期曾经施行过的农业劳动互助的简单形式,是农民相互调剂劳动力的方法,有人工换人工、牛工换牛工、人工换牛工等 exchange work or labour; simple methods used by agricultural producers' mutual-aid organizations in the old liberated areas and in the early 1950s to regulate their work force by exchanging manpower for manpower, or the use of oxen for manpower or vice versa

【变故】biàngù 意外发生的事情;灾难 unforeseen event; accident; misfortune

【变卦】biàn//guà 已定的事,忽然改变(多含贬义 oft. derog.) go back on one's word; break an agreement: 昨天说得好好的,今天怎么～了? Yesterday you agreed. What made you change your mind? |别人一说,他就变了卦。Owing to the objections raised by others, he changed his mind.

【变化】biànhuà 事物在形态上或本质上产生新的状况 change in the state or nature of things: 化学～chemical change|～多端 vary a lot|情况发生了～。Changes have taken place in the situation.

【变幻】biànhuàn 不规则地改变 change irregularly; fluctuate: 风云～fast-changing or volatile situation|～莫测 changeable; unpredictable

【变换】biànhuàn 事物的一种形式或内容换成另一种(of things) vary; alternate; change in form or content: ～位置 shift one's position|～手法 vary one's tactics

【变价】biànjià 把实物按照时价折合(出卖) appraise at the current rate (and sell): ～出售

sell at the current price

【变节】biàn//jié 改变自己的节操，在敌人面前屈服 recant one's faith and yield to the enemy; make a political recantation; desert: ～分子 recanter; traitor; turncoat; apostate | ～自首 turn one's coat and go over to the enemy

【变局】biànjú 变动的局势；非常的局面 fluid situation; changing or volatile situation; sudden turn of events; emergency: 采取紧急措施以应付～ take emergency measures to cope with the changing situation or sudden turn of events

【变口】biànkǒu 北方曲艺表演中称运用各地方言为变口 (in northern folk art) variant tone; use of various dialects in a ballard-singing performance

【变脸】biàn//liǎn ❶ 翻脸 turn hostile: 他一～，六亲不认。Once he gets angry, he does not consider anybody's feelings. | 两个人为了一点儿小事变了脸。The two of them fell out over mere trifles. ❷ 戏曲表演特技，表演时以快速的动作改变角色的脸色或面容，多用来表示人物的极度恐惧、愤怒等 (dramatic technique in performance of a play) change facial expression rapidly to show extreme fear, anger, etc.

【变量】biànliàng 数值可以变化的量。如一天内的气温就是变量。variable quantity that changes, such as the temperature in a day

【变乱】biànluàn ❶ 战争或暴力行动所造成的混乱 turmoil; social upheaval caused by war or acts of violence ❷〈书 *fml.*〉变更并使紊乱 plunge into chaos; create disturbance: ～祖制 tamper with the system passed down by the emperor's ancestors | ～成法 alter established laws and decrees

【变卖】biànmài 出卖财产什物，换取现款 sell off one's property for cash: ～家产 sell off one's estate

【变迁】biànqiān 情况或阶段的变化转移 change of situation or shift of phases of development; vicissitudes: 陵谷～ mountains and valleys change | 人事～change of personnel | 时代～change of the times

【变色】biànsè ❶ 改变颜色 change colour; discolour: ～镜 sun-sensitive glasses; light-sensitive glasses | 这种墨水不易～。This ink will not easily change colour. ◇风云～(比喻时局变化) (fig.) volatile situation; change in a political situation ❷ 改变脸色(多指发怒) change countenance; show signs of displeasure or anger: 勃然～fly into a rage

【变色镜】biànsèjìng 镜片能随光线强弱而变色的眼镜 sun-sensitive glasses; light-sensitive glasses, glasses that change colour according to the light

【变色龙】biànsèlóng ❶ 脊椎动物，躯干稍扁，皮粗糙，四肢稍长，运动极慢。舌长，可舔食虫类。表皮下有多种色素块，能随时变成不同的保护色。chameleon dragon (*Chelosania brunnea Gray*); vertebrate with a slightly flat body, rough skin and short limbs, characterized by very slow locomotion, and a long projectile tongue with which it feeds on insects. The many chromatophores under its epidermis enable it to change its skin to different protective colours according to circumstances. ❷〈比喻 *fig.*〉在政治上善于变化和伪装的人 changeable or fickle person (esp. in politics)

【变生肘腋】biàn shēng zhǒu yè〈比喻 *fig.*〉事变发生在极近的地方 incident occurring close at hand

【变声】biànshēng 男女在青春期嗓音变粗变低。通常男子比女子显著。change of voice at puberty, with men usu. having more marked changes than women

【变数】biànshù ❶ 表示变量的数，如 $x^2+y^2=a^2$，$y=\sin x$ 中，x、y 都是变数 variable, for example, x and y in the formula $x^2+y^2=a^2$, $y=\sin x$ are variables ❷ 可变的因素 variable factors; variable: 事情在没有办成之前，还会有新的～。There will be new variable factors before the mission is accomplished.

【变速器】biànsùqì 改变机床、汽车、拖拉机等机器运转速度或牵引力的装置，由许多直径大小不同的齿轮组成。通常装在发动机的主动轴和从动轴之间。gear change; apparatus consisting of many gears of different diameters that change the speed or traction force of machine tools, automobiles such as tractors, and other machinery. The apparatus consists of many gears of different diameters and is usu. fixed between the main drive shaft and the driver of the engine.

【变速运动】biànsù yùndòng 物体在单位时间内通过的距离不等的运动 variable velocity; variable motion; motion of objects over different distances in a unit time

【变态】biàntài ❶ 某些动物在个体发育过程中的形态变化，例如某些昆虫(蚊、蝇等)经过卵、幼虫、蛹、成虫四个时期，称为完全变态；还有一些昆虫(蝉、蝗虫等)不经过蛹期直接变为成虫，称为不完全变态；还有一些昆虫(虱、衣鱼等)自卵孵化后的幼体，除体小、性未成熟外，其他形状、习性与成虫相似，称为无变态。此外，蛙类经过蝌蚪变为成熟的蛙也叫变态。metamorphosis; change of form in the development of some animals or insects, e.g., mosquitoes and flies undergo the four stages of eggs, larva, pupa and maturity known as complete metamorphosis. Other insects (such as cicadas and locusts) become adults without going through the stage of pupa, and their metamorphosis is incomplete. Still other insects (such as lice and silverfish) have forms and habits similar to those fully grown as soon as they hatch, although they are smaller and sexually immature; they are referred to as having undergone an ametabola; metamorphosis. ❷ 某些植物因长期受环境影响而在根、茎、叶的构造上、形态上和生理机能上发生特殊变化的现象。如马铃薯的块茎、仙人掌的针状叶等。deformation; anomaly; special changes in the structure, form or physiological function in the roots, stems or leaves of certaub plants as a result of long-term environmental impact, such as stem tubers on sweet potatoes and needles on cactuses ❸ 指人的生理、心理的不正常状态(跟'常态'相对 contrary to 'normalcy')(of people's physiology and psychology) deviating from normal; abnormal; aberrant; anomalous: ～心理 aberrant personality; abnormal psychology|～反应 allergy

【变天】biàn//tiān ❶ 天气发生变化,由晴变阴、下雨、下雪、刮风等 change of weather; changing from sunny to cloudy, rainy, snowy or windy ❷〈比喻 *fig.*〉政治上发生根本变化,多指反动势力复辟 fundamental political changes, mainly restoration of reactionary rule

【变通】biàn·tōng 依据不同情况,作非原则性的变动 make unprincipled changes in sth. to suit different circumstances; be flexible; accommodate or adapt sth. to circumstances:遇特殊情况,可以酌情～处理。Appropriate adaptations may be made in the light of specific conditions.

【变味】biàn//wèi (～儿 biàn//wèir)(食物等)味道发生变化(多指变坏)(of food) go bad:昨天做的菜,今天～了。The dish that was cooked yesterday has gone bad.|变了味儿的食品不能吃。Food that has gone bad cannot be eaten.

【变温动物】biànwēn dòngwù 没有固定体温的动物,体温随外界气温的高低而改变,如蛇、蛙、鱼等 poikilothermal animals such as snakes, frogs and fish that do not have a fixed temperature and whose temperature changes in line with the ambient temperature; 俗称 popularly called 冷血动物 lěngxuè dòngwù

【变文】biànwén 唐代兴起的一种说唱文学,多用韵文和散文交错组成,内容原为佛经故事,后来范围扩大,包括历史故事、民间传说等。如敦煌石窟里发现的《大目乾连冥间救母变文》、《伍子胥变文》等。popular form of narrative literature that flourished in the Tang Dynasty (618-907), with alternate prose and rhyming lines for recitation and singing (originally on Buddhistic themes and later extending to historical events, popular legends, etc.) such as *The Great Maudgalyayana Rescues His Mother from Hell* and *The Story of Wu Zixu*

【变戏法】biàn xìfǎ (～儿 biàn xìfǎr)表演魔术 perform conjuring tricks; conjure; juggle

【变相】biànxiàng 内容不变,形式和原来不同(多指坏事 oft. bad things) in disguised form; covert:～剥削 covert exploitation|～贪污 disguised form of corruption

【变心】biàn//xīn 改变原来对人或事业的爱或忠诚 change of heart; cease to be faithful (to sb. or sth.); change loyalties; break faith:海枯石烂,永不～。Though the seas may run dry and the rocks may crumble, our hearts will always remain true. *or* I will always be true to you even after the seas have dried up and the rocks have turned to dust.

【变星】biànxīng 光度有变化的恒星 variable star, a star whose luminosity changes

【变形】[1] biàn//xíng 形状、格式起变化(of shape or pattern) change; be out of shape; become deformed:这个零件已经～。The shape of this spare part has become distorted.|一场大病,瘦得人都～了。Following a serious illness, he had become so wasted that he lost his physique.

【变形】[2] biàn//xíng 童话或神话故事中指人变成某种动物的形状或动物变成人的形状 anamorphic; of people or certain animals in children's stories or fairy tales that turn into other form, e.g. the frog and the prince

【变型】biànxíng 改变类型 change category or type; change into a different type or category:转轨～change the management and category

【变性】biànxìng ❶ 物体的性质发生改变 denaturation; sth. deprived of its natural character and properties:～酒精 denatured alcohol ❷ 机体的细胞因新陈代谢障碍而在结构和性质上发生改变 degeneration; (of the cells of the body) deterioration in structure and quality due to obstructed metabolism

【变性酒精】biànxìng jiǔjīng 工业上用的含甲醇的酒精,有毒。通常加入颜料,使人容易辨认。denatured alcohol; toxic alcohol for industrial use, to which colour is usu. added to make it easily recognizable

【变压器】biànyāqì 利用电磁感应的原理来改变交流电压的装置,主要构件是初级线圈、次级线圈和铁心。在电路设备和无线电路中,常用作升降电压、匹配阻抗等。transformer; device by which electromagnetic induction changes alternating voltage, consisting mainly of primary coils, secondary coils and an iron core; usu. used to increase or reduce voltage or for matched impedance

【变样】biàn//yàng (～儿 biàn//yàngr)形状、样式发生变化 change in shape or appearance:几年没见,他还没～。He hasn't changed any since I saw him a few years ago.|这地方已经变了样了。This place has changed.

【变异】biànyì 同种生物世代之间或同代生物不同个体之间在形态特征、生理特征等方面所表现的差异 variation; formal and physiological differences between different generations of living things or between individual living things of the same generation

【变易】biànyì 改变;变化 change; alter; modify:～服饰 change dressings

【变质】biàn//zhì 人的思想或事物的本质变得与原来不同(多指向坏的方面转变 usu. becoming worse) people's thinking or the nature of things changing from what it was previously:蜕化～become morally degenerate|变了质的食品 food that has gone bad

【变种】biànzhǒng ❶ 早期生物分类学上指物种以下的分类单位,在特征方面与原种有一定区别,并有一定的地理分布。现在多指在单一互相交配而生育的种群中具有不连续变异的个体。variety; mutation; unit of classification in a species in early biological taxonomy, differing from its parent type in one or more physical characteristics, found only in certain geographical areas; now mainly referring to individuals that do not have the continuous variations in a species or group reproduced through unitary mating ❷〈比喻 *fig.*〉跟已有的形式有所变化而实质相同的错误或反动的思潮、流派等 erroneous or reactionary trend of thought, schools different from an existing form but the same in nature; variety; variant

【变子】biànzǐ 原子物理学中指数十种不稳定的基本粒子 varitron; one of dozens of elementary particles referred to in atomic physics

【变奏】biànzòu 乐曲结构原则,运用各种手法将主题等音乐素材加以变化重复 variation; music structural principle by which different means are used to vary and repeat the basic theme to make other melodies

【变奏曲】biànzòuqǔ 运用变奏手法谱写的乐曲,如贝多芬的《C小调三十二次变奏曲》music composed by using variations, such as Beethoven's 32 Variations in C Minor; variations in music

【变阻器】biànzǔqì 可以调节电阻大小的装置,接在电路中能调整电流的大小。一般的变阻器用电阻较大的导线(电阻线)和可以改变接触点以调节电阻线有效长度的装置构成。rheostat, adjustable resistor used for controlling the current in a circuit, generally consisting of a wire (resistive conductor) with considerable resistance, and a device with adjustable junction points for regulating the effective length of the resistive conductor

弁 biàn〈书 *fml.*〉❶ 光明 bright ❷ 欢乐 joy

便[1] biàn ❶ 方便;便利 convenient; handy:轻～light; portable|近～close and convenient|旅客称～。Travelers appreciate such convenience. ❷ 方便的时候或顺便的机会 when an opportunity arises; when it is convenient:～中 at one's convenience; when it is convenient|得～whenever it is convenient|搭～车 hitchhike one's way to somewhere; get a lift to somewhere ❸ 非正式的;简单平常的 informal; simple:～饭 homely meal; simple meal|～条儿 note ❹ 屎或尿 shit or piss; stool or urine:粪～excrement; night soil ❺ 排泄屎、尿 excrete; relieve oneself:大～shit; defecate; evacuate bowels|小～piss; urinate|～桶 commode; chamber pot|～血 hematochezia; have or pass blood in one's stool

便[2] biàn ❶〈副词 *adv.*〉就 then; in that case:没有各方面的通力合作,任务～无法顺利完成。Without the full cooperation of all quarters concerned, the task cannot be accomplished smoothly.|这几天不是刮风,～是下雨。These days the weather is either windy or wet. ❷〈连词 *conj.*〉表示假设的让步[indicating a hypothetical concession]even if:只要依靠群众,～是再大的困难,也能克服。As long as we rely on the people, we can overcome all difficulties, no matter how great.‖

注意 **NOTE:** '便'是保留在书面语中的近代汉语,它的意义和用法基本上跟'就'相同。便 is a formal modern Chinese character and means almost the same as 就 jiù.

☞ pián on p.1473

【便步】biànbù 队伍行进的一种步法,随意行走的姿势(区别于'正步' as compared with 'parade step' or 'goose step') a marching step, march at ease; route step

【便餐】biàncān same as 便饭 biànfàn

【便当】biàn·dang 方便;顺手;简单;容易 convenient; handy; easy:这里乘车很～。Transportation here is very convenient.|东西不多,收拾起来很～。There isn't too much stuff here, so it will be easy to tidy up.

【便道】biàndào ❶ 近便的小路;顺便的路 shortcut; shorter and quicker way:地里一条小道,是贪走～的人踩出来的。A path had been trodden through the field by people taking the shortcut. ❷ 马路两边供人行走的道路;人行道 pavement; sidewalk; walk-way on the two sides of a street or road:行人走～。Pedestrians walk on the pavement. ❸ 正式道路正在修建或修整时临时使用的道路 road made available when the official road is under construction or repair; makeshift road

【便饭】biànfàn ❶ 日常吃的饭食 everyday meal; ordinary meal; simple meal; potluck:家常～home-style food; homely meal ❷ 吃便饭 have a simple meal:明晚请来舍下～。Come to my home tomorrow evening and take potluck with us.

【便服】biànfú ❶ 日常穿的服装(区别于'礼服、制服'等 as compared with 'ceremonial robes', 'full dress', 'formal attire', or 'uniform') everyday clothes; informal dress ❷

专指中式服装 Chinese-style clothes

【便函】biànhán 形式比较简便的、非正式公文的信件(区别于'公函'as compared with 'official letter') short non-official letter

【便壶】biànhú 男人夜间或病中卧床小便的用具 bed urinal; chamber pot (used by men at night or when confined to bed due to illness)

【便笺】biànjiān ❶ 便条 informal note ❷ 供写便条、便函用的纸 notepaper; memo; memo pad

【便捷】biànjié ❶ 直捷而方便 direct and simple; convenient; easy: 比较起来,这种方法最为～。This method is the simplest of all. ❷ 动作轻快敏捷(of action) quick; nimble: 行动～。There is freedom of movement.

【便览】biànlǎn 总括说明;一览(内容多为交通、邮政或风景)(generally of transport, posts and telecommunications or scenery) brief guide; general survey; overview:《邮政～》*A Guide to Posts and Telecommunications*

【便利】biànlì ❶ 使用或行动起来不感觉困难;容易达到目的 not difficult to use or act upon; suitable for the purpose: 交通～have convenient communications; have good transport facilities; be conveniently located|附近就有百货公司,买东西很～。Shopping here is easy as there is a department store nearby. ❷ 使便利 facilitate: 扩大商业网,～群众。More shops should be built for the convenience of the people.

【便了】biànliǎo〈助词 *aux.*〉用在句末,表示决定、允诺或让步的语气,跟'就是了'相同(多见于早期白话 oft. in early vernacular) [used at the end of a sentence to indicate determination, promise or concession] same as the meaning of 就是了 jiùshì•le: 如有差池,由我担待～。I will be responsible for any mistake, you can be sure.

【便帽】biànmào 日常戴的帽子(区别于'礼帽'等 as compared with 'cap' or 'hat' that goes with formal dress) informal cap or hat

【便门】biànmén (～儿 biànwénr) 正门之外的小门 side door; wicket door

【便秘】biànmì 粪便干燥,大便困难而次数少的症状 constipation; condition of the bowels in which the faeces are dry and hardened and evacuation is difficult and infrequent

【便民】biànmín 便利群众 for the convenience of the people: ～措施 facilities for the convenience of the people|～商店 convenience shop

【便溺】biànniào ❶ 排泄大小便 urinate or defecate; relieve oneself: 不许随地～。Don't relieve yourself in the street. ❷ 屎和尿 excrement: 这种动物的～,有种特殊的气味。The excrement of this animal has a special odour.

【便盆】biànpén (～儿 biànpénr) 供大小便用的盆 bedpan

【便桥】biànqiáo 临时架设的简便的桥 temporary or makeshift bridge

【便人】biànrén 顺便受委托办事的人 sb. who happens to be on hand for an errand: 托～给他带去一本词典。I'll send a dictionary to you by someone going your way.

【便士】biànshì 英国等国的辅助货币 pence or penny; fractional currency in the United Kingdom, Ireland and other countries

【便所】biànsuǒ 厕所 lavatory; toilet; WC

【便条】biàntiáo (～儿 biàntiáor) 写上简单事项的纸条;非正式的书信或通知 brief written record; informal letter or notice

【便桶】biàntǒng 供大小便用的桶 commode; chamber pot

【便携式】biànxiéshì (形体)便于携带的 portable: ～计算机 laptop; portable computer|～罐装燃料 portable canned heat

【便鞋】biànxié 轻便的鞋,一般指布鞋 cloth shoe; slipper

【便血】biàn//xiě 粪便中带血或只排出血液而没有粪便 hematochezia; have or pass blood in one's stool

【便宴】biànyàn 比较简便的宴席(区别于正式宴会 as compared with formal banquet) informal dinner: 家庭～family dinner|设～招待 give a dinner for sb.

【便衣】biànyī ❶ 平常人的服装(区别于军警制服 as compared with military and police uniform) civilian clothes; plain clothes ❷ (～儿 biànyīr) 身着便衣执行任务的军人、警察等 plainclothes soldier or policeman on duty

【便宜】biànyí 方便合适;便利 convenient; advantageous

☞ pián•yi on p.1473

【便宜行事】biànyí xíng shì 经过特许,不必请示,根据实际情况或临时变化就斟酌处理(authorized to) act on one's discretion; act as one sees fit; also 便宜从事 biànyí cóng shì

【便于】biànyú 比较容易(做某事) easy to; convenient for: ～计算 be easy to calculate; be easily calculable|～携带 easy to carry

【便中】biànzhōng 方便的时候或有顺便的机会 at one's convenience; when it is convenient: 你家里托人带来棉鞋两双,请你～进城来取。Your family sent someone with two pairs of cloth shoes for you, so whenever it's convenient, come into the city and collect them.

【便装】biànzhuāng same as 便服 biànfú ①: 身着～dressed in everyday clothes

遍(徧) biàn ❶ 普遍;全面 all over; everywhere: ～身 all over the body|满山～野 over hill and dale; all over the mountains and plains ❷〈量词 *classifier*〉一个动作从开始到结束的整个过程为一遍(for action) once through; a time: 问了三～ask sb. for sth. three times|从头到尾看一～ read (a book) once from cover to cover

【遍布】biànbù 分布到所有的地方；散布到每个地方 be found everywhere; spread all over: 通信网～全国。Communication networks cover all over the country.

【遍地】biàndì 到处；处处 everywhere; all over the place: 黄花～。There are vast expanses of day lilies. | 牧场上～是牛羊。Cattle and sheep are all over the ranch.

【遍地开花】biàn dì kāi huā〈比喻 *fig.*〉好事情到处出现或普遍发展(of good things) blossom everywhere; spring up all over the place: 电力工业已经出现～的新局面。New projects in the power industry have sprung up like mushrooms after rain.

【遍及】biànjí 普遍地达到(extend or spread) all over: 影响～海外。The impact has extended abroad.

【遍体鳞伤】biàn tǐ lín shāng 满身都是伤痕，形容伤势重 seriously injured; be covered all over with cuts and bruises; be beaten black and blue; be a mass of bruises

【遍野】biànyě 遍布原野，形容很多 a lot of; large numbers of; all over the fields; everywhere; all around the field: ～碧绿的庄稼 green crops growing in fields all around

缏 biàn 缏子 plaited straw
☞ pián on p. 1473

【缏子】biàn·zi 草帽缏 plaited straw

艑 biàn〈书 *fml.*〉船 boat

辨 biàn 辨别；分辨 differentiate; distinguish; discriminate: ～明 differentiate; distinguish; discriminate | 明～是非 make a clear distinction between right and wrong

【辨白】biànbái same as 辩白 biànbái

【辨别】biànbié 根据不同事物的特点，在认识上加以区别 perceive the difference in or between; differentiate; distinguish; discriminate: ～真假 distinguish the true from the false | ～方向 take one's bearings

【辨明】biànmíng 辨别清楚 make a clear distinction; distinguish: ～方位 take one's bearings | ～是非 distinguish what is right from wrong

【辨认】biànrèn 根据特点辨别，做出判断，以便找出或认定某一对象 recognize or establish as being a particular person or thing; identify; recognize: ～笔迹 identify handwriting | 照片已模糊不清，无法～。The photo has faded beyond recognition.

【辨识】biànshí 辨认；识别 identify; recognize; distinguish: ～足迹 identify one's footprints | 烟雨蒙蒙，远处景物～不清。With that misty rain falling so steadily, the landscape is only a blur in the distance.

【辨析】biànxī 辨别分析 differentiate and analyse; discriminate: 词义～semantic discrimination and analysis | ～容易写错的字形 differentiate and analyse the Chinese characters that are most frequently miswritten

【辨正】biànzhèng 辨明是非，改正错误 differentiate between right and wrong and rectify the error; also 辩正 biànzhèng

【辨证】[1] biànzhèng same as 辩证 biànzhèng ①

【辨证】[2] biànzhèng 辨别症候 diagnose: ～求因 diagnose and find out the cause of the disease | ～论治 diagnosis and treatment based on an overall analysis of the illness and the patient's condition; also 辨症 biànzhèng

【辨证论治】biàn zhèng lùn zhì〈中医 *Chin. med.*〉指根据病人的发病原因、症状、脉象等，结合中医理论，全面分析、作出判断，进行治疗 diagnosis and treatment based on an overall analysis of the illness and the patient's condition; also 辨证施治 biàn zhèng shī zhì (证 zhèng same as 症 zhèng)

辩(辯) biàn 辩解；辩论 argue; dispute; debate: 分～ differentiate; distinguish; discriminate | 争～ argue; dispute; debate | 真理愈～愈明。The more truth is debated, the clearer it becomes.

【辩白】biànbái 说明事实真相，用来消除误会或受到的指责 offer an explanation of the situation so as to dispell misunderstanding or censure; try to justify oneself; plead innocence; defend oneself against a charge: 不必～了，大家没有责怪你的意思。You don't have to explain. We are not blaming you. also 辨白 biànbái

【辩驳】biànbó 提出理由或根据来否定对方的意见 dispute; refute; rebut; offer reason or grounds to prove the error in a person's opinion: 他说的话句句在理，我无法～。What he said seemed to me impossible to dispute.

【辩才】biàncái 辩论的才能 eloquence; oratory; power of fluent, forceful and appropriate speech: 在法庭上，年轻的女律师表现出出众的～。In court the young woman acting as defence counsel was outstandingly eloquent.

【辩辞】biàncí 辩解的话 explanation; argument; also 辩词 biàncí

【辩护】biànhù ❶ 为了保护别人或自己，提出理由、事实来说明某种见解或行为是正确合理的，或是错误的程度不如别人所说的严重 argue in favour of; defend; defend oneself or others by offering reasons and facts to prove that a particular point or action is correct and reasonable, or not as bad as it has been said to be; speak in defence of: 不要替错误行为～。Don't try to defend a wrongful act. | 我们要为真理～。We should defend truth. ❷ 法院审判案件时被告人为自己申辩或辩护人为被告人申辩 plead; defend; (of a defendant) defend himself; (of a defender) defend a defendant at a court hearing: ～人 defender; counsel | ～律师 defence counsel; counsel for the defence

【辩护权】biànhùquán 被告人对被控告的内容进行申述、辩解的权利 the right of the defendant to argue his case; right to defence

B

【辩护人】biànhùrén 受被告人委托或由法院许可或指定,在法庭上为被告人辩护的人 defender; counsel; person hired by the defendant or appointed by the court to defend the defendant at a court hearing

【辩解】biànjiě 对受人指责的某种见解或行为加以解释 make an explanation for one's opinion or action that has been censured; try to defend oneself:事实俱在,无论怎么~也是没有用的。The evidence is there; it is futile trying to explain it away.

【辩论】biànlùn 彼此用一定的理由来说明自己对事物或问题的见解,揭露对方的矛盾,以便最后得到正确的认识或共同的意见(of both sides) present reasons for and against an issue or problem, and prove the weaknesses of the other side in order to reach a correct or common understanding; argue; debate:~会 debate|他们为历史分期问题~不休。They argued time and again over the definition of historical periods.

【辩明】biànmíng 分辩清楚;辩论清楚 argue; justify:~事理 reason or argue things out

【辩难】biànnàn〈书 *fml.*〉辩驳或用难解答的问题质问对方 argue or retort with challenging questions; debate:互相~make taunting retorts to each other; challenge each other with disapproving remarks

【辩士】biànshì〈书 *fml.*〉能言善辩的人 eloquent person; orator; sophist

【辩诉】biànsù 法院审判案件时,被告人为自己申辩 defend oneself (rather than engage a lawyer) in a court case

【辩诬】biànwū 对错误的指责进行辩解 defend oneself against false accusations

【辩学】biànxué ❶ 关于研究辩论的学问 branch of learning concerned with debate ❷ 逻辑学的旧称 old term for logic

【辩正】biànzhèng same as 辨正 biànzhèng

【辩证】biànzhèng ❶ 辨析考证 textual research and discrimination; investigate; authenticate:反复~repeated authentication; also 辨证 biànzhèng ❷ 合乎辩证法的 dialectical:~关系 dialectical relationship|~的统一 dialectical unity

【辩证法】biànzhèngfǎ ❶ 关于事物矛盾的运动、发展、变化的一般规律的哲学学说。它是和形而上学相对立的世界观和方法论,认为事物处在不断运动、变化和发展之中,是由于事物内部的矛盾斗争所引起的。在历史上辩证法经历了自发、唯心、唯物三个阶段。辩证法只有发展到了马克思主义的唯物辩证法才成为一门真正的科学。dialectics; philosophic science about the general law of motion, development, and change in contradictions of things, representing the world outlook and methodology that are antagonistic to metaphysics and maintaining that things are in a constant state of motion, development and change owing to the contradictions in them; In history dialectics has gone through the three stages of spontaneous dialectics, idealistic dialectics, and materialistic dialectics. Dialectics did not become a science in the true sense of the term until it developed into Marxist materialistic dialectics. ❷ 特指唯物辩证法 materialistic dialectics

【辩证逻辑】biànzhèng luó•ji 马克思主义哲学的组成部分,是研究思维辩证法的科学。辩证逻辑要求人们必须把握、研究事物的总和,从事物本身矛盾的发展、运动、变化来观察它,把握它,只有这样,才能认识客观世界的本质。dialectical logic, part of Marxist philosophy and a science about the dialectics of thinking that calls on people to study the summation of things and observe the development, motion and change of contradictions in them, for only thus can they understand the nature of the objective world

【辩证唯物主义】biànzhèng wéiwù zhǔyì 马克思、恩格斯所创立的关于用辩证方法研究自然界、人类社会和思维发展的一般规律的科学,是无产阶级的世界观和方法论。辩证唯物主义认为世界从它的本质来讲是物质的,物质按照本身固有的对立统一规律运动、发展,存在决定意识,意识反作用于存在。辩证唯物主义和历史唯物主义是科学社会主义的理论基础,是无产阶级认识世界、改造世界的锐利武器。dialectical materialism, a science created by Marx and Engels whereby an dialectical approach is used to study the common laws governing the development of nature, human society and thinking. It is the world outlook and methodology of the proletariat. According to dialectical materialism, the world is material in nature, and matter undergoes motion and development in accordance with its intrinsic law of the unity of opposites. Man's social being determines his consciousness, and his consciousness reacts against his social being. Dialectical materialism and historical materialism constitute the theoretical foundation of scientific socialism and are effective tool through which the proletariat understands and transforms the world.

辫(辮) biàn ❶ (~儿 biànr) same as 辫子 biàn•zi ①:发~braid; plait|小~儿 pigtail ❷ (~儿 biànr) same as 辫子 biàn•zi ②:草帽~plait for a straw hat ❸〈方 *dial.*〉(~儿 biànr)〈量词 *classifier*〉用于编成的像辫子的东西 [for things like plait]:一~蒜 a braid of garlic ❹〈方 *dial.*〉编成(辫子)plait (into a braid):~辫子 plait one's hair|把蒜~

起来 braid the garlic

【辫子】biàn·zi ❶ 把头发分股交叉编成的条条儿 plaited braids of hair; plait; braid; pigtail: 梳～braid one's hair◇把问题梳梳～sort out the problems to be tackled ❷ 像辫子的东西 sth. resembling a braid: 蒜～braid of garlic ❸〈比喻 *fig.*〉把柄 mistake or shortcoming that may be exploited by an opponent; handle: 抓～seize on sb.'s mistake or shortcoming; capitalize on sb.'s vulnerable point | 揪住～不放 seize on sb.'s mistake or shortcoming; capitalize on sb.'s vulnerable point

biāo（ㄅㄧㄠ）

杓 biāo〈古代 *arch.*〉指北斗柄部的三颗星 three stars forming the handle of the Big Dipper

☞ 勺 sháo on p.1689

标(標) biāo ❶〈书 *fml.*〉树木的末梢 uppermost point of a tree ❷ 事物的枝节或表面 minor aspect; outward sign; symptom; superficiality: 治～不如治本 seek a permanent cure rather than a temporary solution ❸ 标志；记号 mark; sign: 路～road sign | 商～trademark | ～点 punctuation ❹ 标准；指标 standard; quota; target; norm: 达～reach the standard | 超～surpass the standard; exceed the quota ❺ 用文字或其他事物表明 label; mark sth. with words or other things; put a mark, tag or label on: ～上记号 make marks on sth. | 明码～价 with the price clearly marked ❻ 给竞赛优胜者的奖品 prize; sth. given as a reward to winners in a contest or competition: 锦～prize, trophy, title | 夺～win a championship ❼ 用比价的方式承包工程或买卖货物时各竞争厂商所标出的价格 tender; bid; bid to contract for a project at a given cost; or price offered by a rivalling firm in a bid for a contract or deal: 招～invite tenders; public bidding | 投～submit a tender; enter a bid ❽ 清末陆军编制之一，相当于后来的团 unit of ground forces in the late Qing Dynasty, equivalent to the present-day regiment ❾〈量词 *classifier*〉用于队伍，数词限用'一' [used on troops, only with the numeral '一' yī]: 斜刺里杀出一～人马。A detachment of troops charged out on a diagonal tack. also 彪 biāo

【标榜】biāobǎng ❶ 提出某种好听的名义，加以宣扬 flaunt sth. good; advertise; parade: ～自由 flaunt the banner of liberty ❷（互相）吹嘘；夸耀 boost (each other); excessively praise: 互相～heap praises on each other; exchange excessive praises

【标本】biāoběn ❶ 枝节和根本 root cause and symptoms of a disease: ～兼治 treat a disease by tackling both its root cause and symptoms; seek both a temporary solution and a permanent cure ❷ 保持实物原样或经过加工整理，供学习、研究时参考用的动物、植物、矿物 sample; specimen; animal, plant or ore kept in its original form as an example for research and study ❸ 指在同一类事物中可以作为代表的事物 example; model; one of a number of things taken to show the character of the whole: 我觉得苏州园林可以算作我国各地园林的～。I think the gardens of Suzhou are representative of Chinese-style gardening. ❹ 医学上指用来化验或研究的血液、痰液、粪便、组织切片等 sample; blood, phlegm, excrement, urine, tissue slice, etc., used for laboratory test or study

【标兵】biāobīng ❶ 阅兵场上用来标志界线的兵士。泛指群众集会中用来标志某种界线的人。parade guard spaced out along a parade route; person spaced out along a route in a mass rally ❷〈比喻 *fig.*〉可以作为榜样的人或单位 pace-setter; person or unit that sets an example: 树立～cite sb. as a pacemaker | 服务～model in a service trade

【标尺】biāochǐ ❶ 测量地面或建筑物高度或者标明水的深度用的有刻度的尺 scale for measuring the height of a building or the depth of water; surveyor's rod; staff; water conservancy staff gauge ❷ 表尺的通称 common name for 表尺 biǎochǐ

【标灯】biāodēng 作标志用的灯 light used as a sign; beacon light; beacon; sign lamp: 船尾有一盏讯号～。There is a signal light at the stern of the ship. | 邮电局门口安了玻璃～，上有'夜间电报'四个字。At the gate of the post office there is a glass lamp that says, 'Night Cable'.

【标底】biāodǐ 招标人预定的招标工程的价目 starting price of a bid

【标的】biāodì ❶ 靶子 target ❷ 目的 aim; purpose ❸ 指经济合同当事人双方权利和义务共同指向的对象，如货物、劳务、工程项目等 common objectives of both parties in a commercial contract with regard to their rights and duties in the execution of the project

【标点】biāodiǎn ❶ 标点符号 punctuation mark ❷ 给原来没有标点的著作（如古书）加上标点符号 add punctuation marks to writings (such as classical works) that have no punctuation: ～二十四史 punctuate the *Twenty-Four Histories*

【标点符号】biāodiǎn fúhào 用来表示停顿、语气以及词语性质和作用的书写符号，包括句号（。）、问号（？）、叹号（！）、逗号（，）、顿号（、）分号（；）、冒号（：）、引号（""、''）、括号（[]、()、〔〕、【】）、破折号（——）、省略号（……）、着重号（.）、连接号（—）、间隔号（·）、书名号（《》、〈〉）、专名号（___）等 marks used in writing to indicate a pause, tone or the nature or role of words, such as period (。), question mark (?), exclamation point (!), comma (,), slight-pause mark (、), semicolon (;), colon (:), quotation marks ("" and ''), brackets ([] and 【】), parentheses (() and 〔〕), dash (—), ellipsis (……), mark of emphasis (.), hyphen (-), separation dot (·), punctuation marks used in Chinese to enclose the title of a book, an article, etc. (《》、〈〉) and underline (____)

【标定】biāodìng ❶ 规定以某个数值或型号为标准 fix a certain number or type as standard ❷ 根据一定的标准测定 check according to set standards; standardize: 车间成立了技术小组,对装置进行全面～。A technical team was set up in the workshop to conduct standard test procedures on the device. | 勘探队跑遍了整个大山,～了十个采矿点。The prospecting team surveyed the entire mountain and demarcated 10 mining points. ❸ 符合规定标准的 standard; standardized: ～型自行车 standard (type) bicycle

【标杆】biāogān ❶ 测量的用具,用木杆制成,上面涂有红白相间的油漆,主要用来指示测量点 surveyor's pole; a wooden pole painted red and white and mainly used to indicate points of measurement ❷ same as 样板 yàngbǎn ③: ～钻井队 model drilling team

【标高】biāogāo 地面或建筑物上的一点和作为基准的水平面之间的垂直距离 vertical distance between a point on the ground or a building and the datum water level; surveying and drawing elevation; level

【标格】biāogé 〈书〉品格;风格 style; character

【标号】biāohào ❶ 某些产品用来表示性能(大多为物理性能)的数字。如水泥因抗压强度不同,而有200号、300号、400号、500号、600号等各种标号。numbers used to indicate the property (mostly physical) of some products, e.g. cement is divided into Grades 200, 300, 400, 500, or 600 according to its compression strength ❷ 泛指标志和符号 mark and symbol

【标记】biāojì 标志;记号 sign; mark; symbol

【标价】biāo//jià 标出货物价格 mark a price: 明码～at a marked price | 商品标了价摆上柜台 display priced goods on a counter

【标价】biāojià 所标出的价格 marked price: 所售商品均有～。All goods for sale are priced.

【标金】[1] biāojīn 投标时的押金 deposit or bond for a bid

【标金】[2] biāojīn 用硬印标明重量和成色的金条,成色为0.978上下 gold bar on which the weight and purity usu. 97.8 per cent are marked

【标量】biāoliàng 有大小而没有方向的物理量,如体积、温度等 scalar quantity; physical quantity having magnitude and no direction, such as volume, temperature, etc.

【标卖】biāomài ❶ 标明价目,公开出卖 put on sale at a marked price ❷ 用投标方式出卖 sell by auction

【标明】biāomíng 做出记号或写出文字使人知道 put a mark or marks on; write a note; mark; indicate: ～号码 number sth. | 车站的时刻表上～由上海来的快车在四点钟到达。According to the railway station timetable, the express train arrives at four.

【标牌】biāopái 作标志用的牌子,上面有文字、图案等 sign with words, a design, etc. on it; logo

【标签】biāoqiān (～儿 biāoqiānr)贴在或系在物品上,标明品名、用途、价格等的纸片 label; tag; a slip of paper bearing the name, use, price, etc. of the thing to which it is attached

【标枪】biāoqiāng ❶ 田径运动项目之一,运动员经过助跑后把标枪投掷出去 field event in which the competitor throws the javelin as far as possible after a run-up ❷ 田径运动使用的投掷器械之一,枪杆木制(或金属制),中间粗,两头细,前端安着尖的金属头 javelin, a throw shaft in a field event made of wood (or metal) and tipped with metal, thicker in the middle than at the tip ❸ 旧式武器,在长杆的一端安装枪头,可以投掷,用来杀敌或打猎 long metal-tipped shaft used in former times as a weapon, and thrown at an enemy or prey

【标石】biāoshí 标定某地点位置的标志,一般用岩石或混凝土制成,埋在地下或部分露出地面 markstone; marker usu. made of stone or concrete, buried entirely or partially in the ground to indicate the position of a place

【标示】biāoshì 标明;显示 mark; indicate: 他用笔在地图上划了一道红线,～队伍可从这里通过。He drew a red line on the map, indicating where troops could pass through.

【标书】biāoshū 写有招标或投标的标准、条件、价格等内容的文书 document specifying the standard, conditions, prices, etc. for public bidding; bidding document

【标题】biāotí 标明文章、作品等内容的简短语句 title; heading; headline; caption; brief sentence describing the content of an article and other works: 大～banner headline | 副～subheading; crosshead | 通栏～banner headline; banner

【标题音乐】biāotí yīnyuè 用题目标明中心内容的器乐曲 programme theme tune; music intended to convey the central theme through its title

【标图】biāotú 在军事地图、海图、天气图等上面作出标志 make marks on a military map, nautical chart or synoptic chart; plot

【标新立异】biāo xīn lì yì 提出新奇的主张,表示与一般不同 start sth. new just in order to be different; do sth. unconventional or unorthodox; create sth. new and original

【标语】biāoyǔ 用简短文字写出的有宣传鼓动作用的口号 slogan; poster; distinctive wording written for advertising or propaganda

【标志】biāozhì ❶ 表明特征的记号 sign; mark; symbol; mark showing the characteristics of sth.: 地图上有各种形式的～ marks (or signs) on a map ◇这篇作品是作者在创作上日趋成熟的～。This article signifies the extent to which its author has matured in creative writing. ❷ 表明某种特征 mark; symbolize; indicate a certain characteristic: 这条生产线的建成投产,～着这个工厂的生产能力提高到了一个新的水平。The completion and putting into operation of this production line signifies a new level in the productive capacity of the factory. ‖ also 标识 biāozhì

【标识】biāozhì same as 标志 biāozhì

【标致】biāo·zhi 相貌、姿态美丽(多用于女子 usu. of women) beautiful; handsome: 她穿上这身衣服,显得越发～了。She looks even prettier in that dress.

【标准】biāozhǔn ❶ 衡量事物的准则 standard; criterion; established rule for testing things: 技术～technical standard | 实践是检验真理的唯一～。Practice is the sole criterion for testing truth. ❷ 本身合于准则,可供同类事物比较核对的事物 serving as or conforming to a standard: ～音 standard pronunciation | ～时 standard time

【标准大气压】biāozhǔn dàqìyā 压强的一种单位,1 标准大气压等于 1,013.25 百帕 standard atmosphere, a unit of intensity of pressure. A standard atmosphere equals 1,013.25 hPa.

【标准粉】biāozhǔnfěn 指一百斤麦子磨出八十五斤白面的面粉 standard wheat flour (85 kg. out of every 100 kg. of wheat grain)

【标准化】biāozhǔnhuà 为适应科学发展和合理组织生产的需要,在产品质量、品种规格、零件部件通用等方面规定统一的技术标准,叫做标准化。我国现在通行的有国家标准和部标准(由部一级颁定的标准)两种。standardize; create and use an established standard for product quality, variety and specifications, and for standardization of spare parts, so as to meet the requirements of scientific development and rationally organize production. There are two levels of standards in universal use in China: national and ministerial.

【标准时】biāozhǔnshí ❶ 同一标准时区内各地共同使用的时刻,一般用这个时区的中间一条子午线的时刻做标准 standard time; civil time adopted for a region in a standard time zone, usu. that of the middle meridian running through the region ❷ 一个国家各地共同使用的时刻,一般以首都所在时区的标准时为准。我国的标准时(北京时间)就是东八时区的标准时,比以本初子午线为中线的零时区早八小时。civil time adopted for various localities in a country, usu. the standard time in the time zone where the country's capital is located. In China, Beijing time is the standard time of the east eight time zone, which is eight hours earlier than the zero time zone for which the 1st meridian is the middle meridian.

【标准时区】biāozhǔn shíqū 按经线把地球表面平分为二十四区,每一区跨十五度,叫做一个标准时区。以本初子午线为中线的那一区叫做零时区。以东经 15°,30°…165°为中线的时区分别叫做东一时区、东二时区…东十一时区。以西经 15°,30°…165°为中线的时区分别叫做西一时区、西二时区…西十一时区。以东经 180°(也就是西经 180°)为中线的时区叫做东十二时区,也就是西十二时区。相邻两个标准时区的标准时相差一小时。如东一时区比零时区早一小时,西一时区比零时区晚一小时。standard time zone, one of the surface of the 24 equal zones on earth divided by the meridians of longitude. Each zone takes up 15 degrees and is called a standard time zone. The zone for which the 1st meridian is the middle meridian is called the zero time zone. The time zones for which the 15°,30°…165° east longitudes are their respective middle meridians are known as east one time zone, east two time zone ... east 11 time zone. The time zones for which the 15°,30°…165° west longitudes are their respective middle meridians are known as west one time zone, west two time zone ... west 11 time zone. The time zone for which the 180° east longitude (i.e., the 180° west longitude) is the middle meridian is called the east 12 time zone (i.e., the west 12 time zone). The difference between two adjoining time zones is one hour. For example, the east one time zone is one hour earlier than the zero time zone, and the west one time zone is one hour later than the zero time zone. also 时区 shíqū

【标准音】biāozhǔnyīn 标准语的语音,一般都采用占优势的地点方言的语音系统,例如北京语音是汉语普通话的标准音 standard pronunciation; pronunciation of the standard speech, which is usu. the pronunciation system of the dialect of a dominant area. For example, the Beijing dialect is the standard pronunciation of *putonghua* (common speech) in the Chinese language.

【标准语】biāozhǔnyǔ 有一定规范的民族共同语,是全民族的交际工具,如汉语的普通话 standardised common speech of a nation, and the linguistic tool through which a whole nation communicates, e.g. *putonghua*; standard speech

飑 biāo 气象学上指风向突然改变,风速急剧增大的天气现象。飑出现时,气温下降,并可能有阵雨。squall; phenomenon of sudden change of wind direction or abrupt increase of the wind speed, accompanied by a drop in temperature and perhaps showers

骉 biāo 〈书 *fml.*〉许多马跑的样子 galloping horses

彪 biāo ❶〈书 *fml.*〉小老虎 young tiger; 〈比喻 *fig.*〉身材高大 hefty: ～形大汉 hefty fellow; burly chap ❷〈书 *fml.*〉虎身上的斑纹,借指文采 stripes of a tiger; (referring to) literary talent: ～炳 shining, splendid ❸〈量词 *classifier*〉same as 标 biāo⑨: 一～人马 a detachment of troops ❹ (Biāo) 姓 a surname

【彪炳】biāobǐng 〈书 *fml.*〉文采焕发;照耀 (of great literary talent) shining; splendid: ～青史 stand out in the annals of history | ～千古 shine through the ages

【彪炳千古】biāobǐng qiāngǔ 形容伟大的业绩流传千秋万代 (of great achievements) shine through the ages

猋 biāo 〈书 *fml.*〉❶ 迅速 rapid ❷ same as 飙 biāo

摽 biāo 〈书 *fml.*〉❶ 挥之使去 wave off ❷ 抛弃 abandon

☞ biào on p.131

【摽榜】biāobǎng 〈书 *fml.*〉标榜 brag about; boast

幖 biāo 〈书 *fml.*〉旗帜 flag 〈古 *arch.*〉same as 标 biāo

滮 biāo 〈书 *fml.*〉水流的样子 flow of water

骠 biāo ☞ 黄骠马 huángbiāomǎ on p.851 and piào on p.1477

膘(臕) biāo (～儿 biāor) 肥肉(多用于牲畜,用于人时带贬义或戏谑意 usu. of a domestic animal, derogative or playful when used for a person) fat: 长～get fat; put on flesh; flesh out | 蹲～(of livestock, etc.) fatten up in the shed | 跌～(变瘦) (of livestock, etc.) become thin | 这块肉～厚。This piece of meat has a lot of fat on it.

【膘情】biāoqíng 牲畜生长的肥壮情况 the condition of an animal, esp. with regard to its brawn or fat

熛 biāo 〈书 *fml.*〉火焰 flame

飙(飇、飈) biāo 〈书 *fml.*〉暴风 violent wind; whirlwind: 狂～ hurricane

【飙车】biāochē 〈方 *dial.*〉开快车 drive a car at top speed; speed: 酒后～,酿成惨祸。Reckless drunk driving leads to road accidents.

【飙风】biāofēng 〈书 *fml.*〉猛烈的风;疾风 strong wind; gale

镖 biāo 旧式武器,形状像长矛的头,投掷出去杀伤敌人 lance; old-fashioned weapon thrown to injure or kill: 飞～flying lance | 袖～ lance hidden up the sleeve and launched therefrom

【镖局】biāojú 保镖的营业机构 professional establishment which provides armed escorts; commercial firm for providing armed escort or bodyguards

【镖客】biāokè 〈旧时 *old*〉给行旅或运输中的货物保镖的人 armed escort (of travellers or merchants' caravans); also 镖师 biāoshī

瘭 biāo [瘭疽] (biāojū) 手指头或脚趾头肚儿发炎化脓的病,症状是局部红肿,剧烈疼痛,发烧 pyogenic infection of the pad of a finger or toe, with local redness, swelling, acute pain and fever as the symptoms

藨 biāo [藨草] (biāocǎo) 多年生草本植物,茎呈三棱形,叶子条形,花褐色,果实倒卵形。茎可织席、编草鞋,又可用来造纸。scirpus (*Scirpus triqueter*); meadowrush; bulrush; perennial herb with a three-sided stem from which grow linear leaves, brown flowers and obovate fruit, the stem can be used to make mats, shoes or paper

瀌 biāo [瀌瀌]〈书 *fml.*〉形容雨雪大 heavy (rain or snow)

镳[1] biāo 〈书 *fml.*〉马嚼子的两端露出嘴外的部分 bit (of a bridle); curb bit: 分道扬～ separate and go different ways

镳[2] biāo same as 镖 biāo

穮(穮) biāo 〈书 *fml.*〉除草 weeding

biǎo (ㄅㄧㄠˇ)

表(⑩錶) biǎo ❶ 外面;外表 surface; outside; external: ～面 appearance; surface | 地～earth's surface | 由～及里 proceed from the outside to the inside; penetrate the surface to get at the essence ❷ 中表(亲戚) relationship between the children or grandchildren of a brother and a sister or of sisters: ～哥 male cousin | ～叔 male cousin of one's mother | 姨～ female cousin of one's mother | 姑～relationship between the children of a brother and those of a sister (as viewed by the brother's family) ❸ 把思想感情显示出来;表示 express one's feeling; show; demonstrate: ～达 express | ～态 make known one's position; declare where one stands | 深～同情 show deep sympathy | 按下不～(说)。(in traditional story-telling) Let's suspend the narration for a while. ❹ 俗称用药物把感受的风寒发散出来 administer medicine to bring out the cold: 吃服(fù)药～一～,出身汗。Take medicine to draw out the cold and induce perspiration. ❺ 榜样;模范 model; example: ～率 model; example | 为人师～be an exemplary teacher; be worthy of the name of teacher; be a paragon of virtue and learning ❻〈古代 *arch.*〉文体奏章的一种,用于较重大

的事件 memorial to an emperor usu. on an important event or matter：诸葛亮《出师～》 Zhuge Liang's *Memorial on Dispatching the Army* ❼ 用表格形式排列事项的书籍或文件 book or document with events arranged in a table or form：《史记》十～ 10 tables of *Records of the Historian*｜统计～statistical table ❽〈古代 *arch.*〉测日影的标杆 pole used as a sundial；☞ 圭表 guībiǎo on p. 729 ❾ 测量某种量(liàng)的器具 metre；gauge：温度～thermometre｜电～kilowatt-hour metre；electric metre｜水～water metre｜煤气～gas metre ❿ 计时的器具，一般指比钟小而可以随身携带的 watch，a timepiece smaller than a clock and easy to carry：怀～pocket watch｜手～wrist watch｜秒～stopwatch｜电子～quartz watch；accutron

【表白】biǎobái 对人解释，说明自己的意思 explain；clarify；express or state clearly；explain oneself：再三～explain time and time again｜～心迹 lay bare one's true feelings

【表笔】biǎobǐ 测试仪表上用来接触被测物的笔状物 test pencil；pencil-like device on the testing metre (instrument) for touching what is to be tested；also 表棒 biǎobàng

【表册】biǎocè 装订成册的表格 collected statistical forms；collection of tables or forms

【表层】biǎocéng 物体表面的一层 surface layer

【表尺】biǎochǐ 枪炮上瞄准装置的一部分，按目标的距离，调节表尺可以提高命中率 rear sight，part of the gunsight；The percentage of on-target hits can be raised by adjusting the gun's rear sight to take into account the distance. also known as 标尺 biāochǐ

【表达】biǎodá 表示(思想、感情) express (one's ideas or feelings)；convey；voice：感激之情，难以～。I hardly know how to express my gratitude.｜提高学生的口头～能力 improve the students' ability in oral expression

【表格】biǎogé 按项目画成格子，分别填写文字或数字的书面材料 form；table；arrangement of words or numbers on squared paper

【表功】biǎo//gōng ❶ 表白自己的功劳(多含贬义 oft. derog.) brag about one's deeds：丑～brag unabashedly about one's own deeds ❷〈书 *fml.*〉表扬功绩 praise；commend；honour；cite

【表记】biǎojì 作为纪念品或信物而赠送给人的东西 sth. given as a token；souvenir；memento

【表决】biǎojué 会议上通过举手、投票等方式做出决定 vote；decide by voting through a show of hands or by casting ballots at a meeting：付～put to the vote；take a vote｜～通过 be voted through；adopt by a vote

【表决权】biǎojuéquán 在会议上参加表决的权利 right to vote at a meeting；vote

【表里如一】biǎo lǐ rú yī〈比喻 *fig.*〉思想和言行完全一致 think and act in one and the same way

【表链】biǎoliàn (～儿 biǎoliànr)系在怀表上的金属链 chain tied to a pocket watch

【表露】biǎolù 流露；显示 show；reveal：一个人的喜怒哀乐最容易在脸上～出来。A person's feelings are generally revealed by his or her facial expression.

【表蒙子】biǎoméng·zi 装在表盘上的透明薄片 watch glass；crystal

【表面】[1] biǎomiàn ❶ 物体跟外界接触的部分 surface；face；outside；appearance；outer part of a subject：地球～surface of the earth｜桌子～的油漆锃亮。The table has a gleaming，painted surface. ❷ 外在的现象或非本质的部分 appearance；superficiality：他～上很镇静，内心却十分紧张。He was outwardly calm，but inwardly very nervous.

【表面】[2] biǎomiàn〈方 *dial.*〉❶ 表盘 dial plate；dial ❷ 表蒙子 watch glass；crystal

【表面光】biǎomiànguāng 指事物只是外表好看 attractive on the surface；cheaply showy：对产品不能只求～，还要求高质量。A product requires more than good packaging — it must also be of high quality.

【表面化】biǎomiànhuà (矛盾等)由隐藏的变成明显的(of contradiction，etc.) come to the surface；become apparent：问题一经摆出来，分歧更加～了。When the issue was brought out into the open，the differences between the two sides became more apparent.

【表面积】biǎomiànjī 物体表面面积的总和 surface area

【表面张力】biǎomiàn zhānglì 液体表面各部分间相互吸引的力。在这个力的作用下，液体表面有收缩到最小的趋势。surface tension；elastic-like force that minimizes the surface of a liquid

【表明】biǎomíng 表示清楚 make known；make clear；state clearly；indicate：～态度 make known one's position；declare one's stand｜～决心 declare one's determination

【表盘】biǎopán 钟表、仪表上的刻度盘，上面有表示时间、度数等的刻度或数字。有的地区叫表面。dial plate；dial，a graduated plate，disk or face of a clock or sundial with graduations or figures for indicating time or measurement；in some areas also known as 表面 biǎomiàn

【表皮】biǎopí ❶ 皮肤的外层 epidermis；cuticle，outer layer of skin ❷ 植物体表面初生的一种保护组织，一般由单层、无色而扁平的活细胞构成 thin，colourless layer of living cells forming the outer integument of seed plants and ferns

【表亲】biǎoqīn 中表亲戚 cousin；cousinship；☞ 中表 zhōngbiǎo on p. 2480

【表情】biǎoqíng ❶ 从面部或姿态的变化上表达内心的思想感情 express one's feelings by facial expression or body posture：～传意 express one's feelings and ideas｜这个演员善于～。This actor knows how to perform. ❷ 表现在面部或姿态上的思想感情 feelings expressed by facial expression or posture；expression：～严肃 look serious｜脸上流露出兴奋的～look excited

【表示】biǎoshì ❶ 用言语行为显出某种思想、感情、态度等 show；express；indicate；express one's ideas，feelings，attitude，etc. with words or acts：～关怀 show concern｜～好感 express one's good opinion of sth. or sb.｜大家一起鼓掌～欢迎。We all applauded to extend a warm welcome. ❷ 事物本身显出某种意义或者凭借某种事物显出某种意义（of sth.）indicate meaning through itself or through sth. else：海上红色的灯光～那儿有浅滩或者礁石。The red light on the sea indicates a shoal or reef. ❸ 显出思想感情的言语、动作或神情 words，action or air expressing one's ideas and feelings；expression；indication：老师心里很喜欢他的直爽，但是脸上并没露出赞许的～。The teacher liked him for his frankness，but his face betrayed no sign of agreement.

【表述】biǎoshù 说明；述说 explain；state：～己见 state or air one's views

【表率】biǎoshuài 好榜样 good example；model：老师要做学生的～。A teacher must act as a model and set a good example to his students.

【表态】biǎo//tài 表示态度 make known one's position；declare one's stand；commit oneself：这件事，你得表个态，我才好去办。You must let me know your position on the matter before I deal with it.

【表土】biǎotǔ 地球表面的一层土壤。农业上指耕种的熟土层。topsoil；surface soil；layer of mellow soil for farming

【表现】biǎoxiàn ❶ 表示出来 show；display；manifest：他的优点，～在许多方面。His strengths are manifested in many respects. ❷ 行为或作风中表示出来的 behaviour；performance：他在工作中的～很好。He is doing very well in his work. ❸ 故意显示自己（含贬义 derog.）show off：此人一贯爱～，好出风头。This person always shows off and hogs the limelight.

【表象】biǎoxiàng 经过感知的客观事物在脑中再现的形象 idea；image；presentation；conception existing in the mind as a result of an understanding of objective things

【表演】biǎoyǎn ❶ 戏剧、舞蹈、杂技等演出；把情节或技艺表现出来 perform an opera，dance，acrobatics，etc.；act；play；perform a plot or display skills：化装～fancy dress show｜～体操 perform gymnastics ❷ 做示范性的动作 make demonstrations；demonstrate：～新操作法 demonstrate a new technique of operation

【表演唱】biǎoyǎnchàng 一种带有戏剧性质和舞蹈动作的演唱形式 a dramatic form of singing

【表演赛】biǎoyǎnsài 一种以宣传体育运动为目的，对技术、战术进行演示或示范的运动竞赛 exhibition match；match in which skills and tactics are displayed or demonstrated for the purpose of promoting sports

【表扬】biǎoyáng 对好人好事公开赞美 praise；commend；publicly extol good people and good deeds：～劳动模范 commend model workers｜他在厂里多次受到～。His factory commended him on several occasions.

【表意文字】biǎoyì wénzì 用符号来表示词或词素的文字，如古埃及文字、楔形文字等 ideography；ideogram；ideograph，written symbol that represents a word or morpheme，as in the Egyptian language

【表音文字】biǎoyīn wénzì 用字母来表示语音的文字 language in which letters are used to indicate pronunciation；phonography，phonetic spelling；☞ 拼音文字 pīnyīn wénzì on p.1479

【表语】biǎoyǔ 有的语法书用来指'是'字句'是'字后面的成分，也泛指名词性谓语和形容词性谓语[indicating what comes after 是 shì in a sentence containing this word]（referring to noun predicate and adjective predicate）predicative

【表彰】biǎozhāng 表扬（伟大功绩、壮烈事迹等）praise sb.（for his meritorious exploits，brave deeds，etc.）；cite（in dispatches）；commend：～先进 commend advanced individuals（organizations）

【表针】biǎozhēn 钟表或各种测试仪表上指示刻度的针（of timepiece，metres，etc.）hand；indicator；pointer

【表侄】biǎozhí 表弟兄的儿子 nephew；son of a male cousin on the distaff side

【表侄女】biǎozhínǚ 表弟兄的女儿 niece；daughter of a male cousin on the distaff side

【表字】biǎozì 人在本名外所取的与本名有意义关系的另一名字（多见于早期白话 oft. in early vernacular）[usu. related to one's official name in meaning] secondary name

婊 biǎo [婊子]（biǎo·zi）妓女（多用做骂人的话 oft. curse）prostitute；whore

裱 biǎo ❶ 用纸或丝织品做衬托，把字画书籍等装潢起来，或加以修补，使美观耐久 mount a calligraphic writing or a picture on paper，cloth or silk in order to embellish it：这幅画得拿去重～一～。I will have the painting mounted. ❷ 裱糊 paper

【裱褙】biǎobèi same as 裱 biǎo ①

【裱糊】biǎohú 用纸糊房间的顶棚或墙壁等 paper the walls or ceiling of a room

褾 biǎo 〈书 *fml.*〉❶ 袖子的前端 cuff of a sleeve ❷ 衣服上的绲边 trimming on clothing; braid; hemming

biào (ㄅㄧㄠˋ)

俵 biào 〈方 *dial.*〉 same as 俵分 biàofēn

【俵分】biàofēn 按份儿或按人分发 distribute according to the number of portions or persons

摽[1] biào ❶ 捆绑物体使相连接 tie; bind; fasten; draw things together with a cord, string, or the like, and knot: 桌子腿儿裂了,用铁丝～住吧! The table has a broken leg. Let's bind it with some steel wire. ❷ 用胳膊紧紧地钩住 arm in arm: 母女俩～着胳膊走。Mother and daughter walked arm in arm. ❸ 摽劲儿 (of competitors, etc.) strain every muscle; exert oneself to emulate or excel: 这两个小组一直在～着干。The two groups have been working hard with a silent resolve to excel. | 我跟你～上啦,你搬多少我就搬多少。I will strain every fibre to be your equal. ❹ 亲近;依附 (多含贬义 oft. derog.) be glued to; locked together; thick as thieves: 他们老～在一块儿。They are always locked together.

摽[2] biào 〈书 *fml.*〉 ❶ 落 fall ❷ 打;击 hit; strike

☞ biāo on p.128

【摽劲儿】biào//jìnr 双方因赌气或竞赛等憋着劲比着(干) compete with sb. and try to get the upperhand: 大伙儿摽着劲儿干。Everybody worked hard with a silent resolve to excel. | 贴光荣榜后没几天,好几个组就跟红旗小组摽上劲儿了。Only a few days after the red-banner group had been commended and placed on the honour roll, several other groups began to compete with, and try to outstrip it.

鳔 biào ❶ 某些鱼类体内可以胀缩的囊状物。里面充满氮、氧、二氧化碳等混合气体。收缩时鱼下沉,膨胀时鱼上浮。有的鱼类的鳔有辅助听觉或呼吸等作用。swimming bladder; air bladder in the body of a fish filled with a mixture of nitrogen, oxygen, carbon dioxide and other gases and, capable of expanding and contracting, swelling when the fish swims to the surface and shrinking when it swims deep into the water. The bladders of certain species of fish help it hear and respire. ❷ 鳔胶 isinglass; fish glue ❸ 〈方 *dial.*〉用鳔胶粘上 glue with isinglass

【鳔胶】biàojiāo 用鱼鳔或猪皮等熬制的胶,黏性大,多用来粘木器 isinglass; gelatine obtained from the air bladders of certain fish, e.g. sturgeon; very sticky and used mostly to glue wood

biē (ㄅㄧㄝ)

瘪(癟) biē [瘪三](biēsān)上海人称城市中无正当职业而以乞讨或偷窃为生的游民为瘪三 tramp; Shanghai appellation for a wretched-looking tramp who lives by begging or stealing

☞ biě on p.133

憋 biē ❶ 抑制或堵住不让出来 suppress; hold back: 劲头儿～足了 be bursting with energy | ～着一口气 hold one's breath | 他正～着一肚子话没处说。He is bursting with unspoken words. ❷ 闷 suffocate; feel oppressed: 心里～得慌 feel very much oppressed | 气压低,～得人透不过气来。It was so stuffy that one could hardly breathe.

【憋闷】biē·men 由于心里有疑团不能解除或其他原因而感到不舒畅 feel oppressed; be depressed; be dejected: 他挨了一通训,又没处诉说,心里特别～。He felt depressed after being reprimanded as he had no where to go to complain. | 在防空洞里时间长了,会觉得～。You feel depressed after staying too long in an air-raid shelter.

【憋气】biēqì ❶ 由于外界氧气不足或呼吸系统发生障碍等原因而引起呼吸困难 have difficulty in breathing owing to a lack of oxygen in the air, or a blockage in the respiratory system ❷ 有委屈或烦恼而不能发泄 choke with bottled up resentment; feel injured and resentful: 左也不是,右也不是,真叫人～。I find it depressing that I am believed to be wrong in all ways.

鳖(鱉) biē 爬行动物,生活在水中,形状像龟,背甲上有软皮 Chinese soft-shelled turtle (*Trionyx sinensis Wiegmann*), reptile similar to a tortoise that has a hard outer shell with a soft edge and that lives in water; soft-shelled turtle; also called 甲鱼 jiǎyú or 团鱼 tuányú; 有的地区叫鼋 in some places also known as 鼋 yuán; 俗称 popularly called 王八 wáng·ba

【鳖裙】biēqún 鳖的背甲四周的肉质软边,味道鲜美 calipash; the part of a soft-shelled turtle next to its upper shell which is considered a culinary delicacy; also 鳖边 biēbiān

bié (ㄅㄧㄝˊ)

别[1] bié ❶ 分离 leave; part: 告～say goodbye to sb.; leave, take leave of; part from | 临～纪念 parting souvenir; sth. to remember one by; memento | 久～重逢 meet again after a long separation ❷ 另外 other; another: ～人 someone else; other people; another person; others | ～称 another name; alternative name|～有用心 have ulterior motives; have an axe to grind ❸〈方 *dial*.〉转动;转变 turn; change:她把头～了过去。She turned her head.|这个人的脾气一时～不过来。His temper is difficult to change in a short time. ❹(Bié)姓 a surname

B

别² bié ❶ 区分;区别 differentiate; distinguish:辨～differentiate; distinguish|鉴～discern; discriminate; differentiate; distinguish|分门～类 classify; put into different category ❷ 差别 difference; distinction:天渊之～a world of difference; poles apart ❸ 类别 classification; category:性～sex distinction; sex|职～official rank|派～faction; group; school of thought|级～rank; level; grade; scale

别³ bié ❶ 用别针等把另一样东西附着或固定在纸、布等物体上 fasten sth. with a pin or clip to a piece of paper, cloth, etc.:把两张发票～在一起 pin or clip the two invoices together|胸前～着一朵红花 with a big red flower pinned to one's breast ❷ 插住;用东西卡住 stick in; insert in order to inhibit the movement of sth. or sb.:皮带上～着一支枪 with a gun stuck in one's belt|把门～上。Bolt the door. ❸ 摔跤时用腿使绊把对方摔倒 (in wrestling) cause sb. to stumble by a swinging movement of one's leg; trip up ❹ 两个人朝同一方向行车时,一方故意用车阻碍另一方车的前轮,使不能正常行进(when two bikes or cars are advancing in the same direction) deliberately hinder the advance of a bike or car with one's own:～车 stop an advancing bike or car with one's own

别⁴ bié ❶ 表示禁止或劝阻,跟不要的意思相同[used in giving commands or advice] don't; had better not (the meaning same as 不要 bùyào):～冒冒失失的。Don't act rashly.|你～走了,在这儿住两天吧。Don't leave. Stay here for a couple of days. ❷ 表示揣测,通常跟'是'字合用(所揣测的事情,往往是自己所不愿意的)[usu. followed by 是 shì, indicating conjecture of sth. against one's own wish]:约定的时间都过了,～是他不来了吧? He agreed to be here by now. I hope he hasn't changed his mind.

☞ biè on p.134

【别称】biéchēng 正式名称以外的名称,如湘是湖南的别称,鄂是湖北的别称 name other than formal one; another name; alternative name, e.g. Xiang is another name for Hunan, and È is another name for Hubei

【别出心裁】bié chū xīncái 独创一格,与众不同 adopt an original approach; try to be different

【别处】biéchù 另外的地方 other place; elsewhere:这里没有你要的那种鞋,你到～看看吧。We don't have the shoes you want. Try somewhere else.

【别动队】biédòngduì 指离开主力单独执行特殊任务的部队 special detachment; commando; fifth column; military unit designed to carry out special tasks independent of the main force

【别管】biéguǎn〈连词 *conj*.〉跟'无论'相同 no matter (who, what, etc.), having the same meaning as 无论 wúlùn:～是谁,一律按规章办事。No matter who it is, we shall act according to principle.

【别号】biéhào (～儿 biéhàor)名、字以外另起的称号 alias; another name (in addition to one's official and courtesy names):李白字太白,～青莲居士。Li Bai, whose courtesy name was Taibai, was also known as the Green Lotus Hermit.

【别集】biéjí 收录个人的作品而成的诗文集,如白居易《白氏长庆集》(区别于'总集' as compared with 'anthology') collected works of an individual, e.g. Bai Juyi's *Changqing Collected Works of Bai Juyi*

【别家】biéjiā 另外的人家或企业 other households, enterprises; etc.:我不是这里人,你到～打听一下看。I am new here; you had better ask somebody else.|～商店都关门了,只有这一家还在营业。All stores except this one are closed.

【别价】bié·jie〈方 *dial*.〉表示劝阻或禁止 indicating an attempt to prevent or forbid; please don't:您～,等等再说。Don't go. Please wait a bit longer.

【别具匠心】bié jù jiàngxīn 另有一种巧妙的心思(多指文学、艺术方面创造性的构思 mostly in creating literary and artistic works) show ingenuity; have originality

【别具一格】bié jù yī gé 另有一种风格 have a style of one's own; have a unique or distinctive style

【别具只眼】bié jù zhī yǎn 另有一种独到的见解 see what others fail to see; see what others cannot; have an original view; have a special or unique insight

【别开生面】bié kāi shēng miàn 另外开展新的局面或创造新的形式 be an eye-opener; break a new trail; break ground:在词的发展史上,苏轼和辛弃疾都是～的大家。Su Shi and Xin Qiji were both great masters that opened new vistas in the history of *ci* poetry.

【别离】biélí 离别 leave; take leave of:～了家乡,踏上征途 leave home and start out on a long journey

【别论】biélùn 另外的对待或评论 another or a different matter; different story:如果他确因有事,不能来,则当～。If he really is detained by urgent business, that makes it a different matter.

【别名】biémíng (～儿 biémíngr)正式名字以外

的名称 another name; alternative name; name other than the official one

【别情】biéqíng 离别的情怀 sorrow of separation; sentiment felt at parting:老友重逢,畅叙～。When the old friends met, they talked of their sad feelings after their previous parting.

【别人】biérén 另外的人 someone else:家里只有母亲和我,没有～。There are only my mother and I in our family — nobody else.

【别人】bié·ren 指自己或某人以外的人 other people; others:～都同意,就你一人反对。All others agree; only you do not. | 把方便让给～,把困难留给自己 leave the easy part of a job to others while taking the difficult part oneself; making things convenient for others at one's own expense

【别史】biéshǐ 编年体、纪传体以外,杂记历代或一代史实的史书 history books other than those written in a biographical or annalistic style; unofficial history; separate history (i.e. privately compiled history)

【别是】biéshì 莫非是 used in expressing anxiety about sth. untoward:他这时还没来,～不肯来吧! He hasn't come yet. I hope he is not unwilling to come.

【别树一帜】bié shù yī zhì 形容与众不同,另成一家 set up a new banner; found a new school of thought; have a style of one's own

【别墅】biéshù 在郊区或风景区建造的供休养用的园林住宅 villa; large and imposing garden residence built in suburbs or scenic spots

【别提】biétí 表示程度之深不必细说 no need to mention; needless to say; you can well imagine:他那个高兴劲儿啊,就～了。You can well imagine how happy he was.

【别无长物】bié wú chángwù 没有多余的东西。形容穷困或俭朴。be in possession of nothing other than (is absolutely necessary); be in reduced circumstances (长 cháng, formerly pronounced zhàng)

【别无二致】bié wú èr zhì 没有两样;没有区别 without the slightest difference; just the same; identical:这两个人的思想～。They are no different in their thinking.

【别绪】biéxù 离别时的情绪 surge of sentimental feeling at parting; sorrow of separation:离愁～parting sorrows

【别有洞天】bié yǒu dòng tiān 另有一种境界。形容景物等引人入胜。place of unique charm and beauty; scenery of exceptional charm; altogether different world

【别有风味】bié yǒu fēngwèi 另有一种趣味或特色 have a distinctive flavour or feature:围着篝火吃烤肉,～。It is really special to have a barbecue over a campfire.

【别有天地】bié yǒu tiān dì 另有一种境界。形容风景等引人入胜。place of unique charm and beauty; scenery of exceptional charm; altogether different world

【别有用心】bié yǒu yòngxīn 言论或行动中另有不可告人的企图 have ulterior motives; have an axe to grind

【别针】biézhēn (～儿 biézhēnr) ❶ 一种弯曲而有弹性的针,尖端可以打开,也可以扣住,用来把布片、纸片等固定在一起或固定在衣物上 safety pin; flexible bent pin with a pointed tip which can be opened and clicked shut, for holding pieces of cloth, paper, etc., or fastening them to clothing ❷ 别在胸前或领口的装饰品,多用金银、玉石等制成 brooch; ornament generally made of gold, silver or jade, pinned to the clothing for ornamentation

【别致】bié·zhì 新奇,跟寻常不同 original; novel; exquisite:这座楼房式样很～。The building is exquisite.

【别传】biézhuàn 记载某人逸事的传记 anecdotage; biography about one's anecdotes; informal biography; anecdotal biography

【别子】biézǐ 〈古代 *arch.*〉指天子、诸侯的嫡长子以外的儿子 younger son(s) of an emperor or lord

【别子】bié·zi ❶ 线装书的套子上或字画手卷上用来别住开口的东西,多用骨头制成 pin (usu. made of bone) for holding fast an old-fashioned hard-covered book, or a painting or calligraphy scroll ❷ 烟袋荷包的坠饰 pipe pouch pendant

【别字】biézì ❶ 写错或读错的字,比如把'包子'写成'饱子',是写别字;把'破绽'的'绽'(zhàn)读成'定',是读别字 incorrectly written or mispronounced character; malapropism, e.g. writing 包子 bāo·zi as 饱子 bǎo·zi and pronouncing 绽 zhàn in 破绽 pò·zhàn as 定 dìng; also 白字 báizì ❷ 别号 another name (in addition to one's official and courtesy names); alias

蹩 bié 〈方 *dial.*〉脚腕子或手腕子扭伤 sprain one's ankle or wrist:走路不小心,～痛了脚。By not looking where I was going, I sprained my foot.

【蹩脚】biéjiǎo 〈方 *dial.*〉质量不好;本领不强 inferior; shoddy:～货 inferior or shoddy goods; poor stuff; shoddy work

biě (ㄅㄧㄝˇ)

瘪(癟) biě ❶ 物体表面凹下去;不饱满 shrivelled; shrunken; deflated:干～dry and shrivelled; wizened | ～谷 blighted | 没牙～嘴儿 have a toothless, sunken mouth | 车带～了。The tyre is flat. | 乒乓球～了。The pingpong ball is squashed. ❷ 〈方 *dial.*〉为难;使为难 be in a spot; make things difficult for sb.：作～be in a spot；be in a dilemma|这话经不住问，一问就～。This is a preposterous statement.

☞ biē on p.131

【瘪子】biě·zi 〈方 *dial.*〉❶ 指处境窘迫；挫折 dilemma；setback：这次去，要是弄不好，那才作～呢。If you fail accomplish your mission, you will find yourself in a tricky predicament. ❷ 秕子 blighted grain：把种子放在水里，没长成的～就漂起来了。When you immerse seeds in water, any blighted grains float on the surface.

biè（ㄅㄧㄝˋ）

别（彆）biè 〈方 *dial.*〉改变别人坚持的意见或习性（多用于'别不过'usu. used in the phrase 别不过 biè·bu guò）persuade sb. to change his opinion or give up his idea：我想不依他，可是又～不过他。I don't want him to get his way, but I can't talk him round.

☞ bié on p.132

【别扭】biè·niu ❶ 不顺心；难对付 awkward；difficult；uncomfortable：这个天气真～，一会儿冷，一会儿热。The weather is unpredictable：cold one minute and hot the next.|他的脾气挺～，说话要注意。He is of uncertain temper；keep this in mind when you talk to him. ❷ 意见不相投 not see eye to eye；disagree：闹～be at odds；fall out|两个人有些别别扭扭的，说不到一块儿。The two of them are often at loggerheads；they simply don't see eye to eye with each other. ❸（说话、作文）不通顺；不流畅（of speech or writing）unnatural；awkward

【别嘴】bièzuǐ 〈方 *dial.*〉绕嘴 a bit of a mouthful；tongue-twister：这段文字半文不白，读起来～。This paragraph is a bit of a mouthful（or a tongue-twister）as it is part literary and partly in the vernacular.

bīn（ㄅㄧㄣ）

邠 Bīn ❶ 邠县，在陕西。今作彬县。county in Shaanxi Province；now written as 彬县 Bīnxiàn ❷ same as 豳 Bīn

玢 bīn 〈书 *fml.*〉玉名 a kind of jade

☞ fēn on p.572

宾（賓、賔）bīn ❶ 客人 guest（跟'主'相对 as compared with 'host' or 'hostess'）：外～foreign guest|～至如归（of a hotel, guesthouse, etc.）where guests feel as comfortable as if they were at home；home away from home ❷（Bīn）姓 a surname

【宾白】bīnbái 戏曲中的说白。中国戏曲艺术以唱为主，故称说白为宾白。spoken parts in a Chinese opera

【宾词】bīncí 一个命题的三部分之一，表示思考对象的属性等，如在'金属是导体'这个命题中，'导体'是宾词 predicate；one of three main constituents of a simple sentence indicating the state attributed to the subject, as 导体 dǎotǐ in 金属是导体 jīnshǔ shì dǎotǐ

【宾东】bīndōng 〈古代 *arch.*〉主人的坐位在东，客人的坐位在西，因此称宾与主为宾东（多用于幕僚和官长，家庭教师和家长，店员和店主）host and guest；ranking official and his staff；private tutor and his employer；shopkeeper and shop assistant

【宾服】bīnfú 〈书 *fml.*〉服从；归附 submit to；obey；be subordinated to

【宾服】bīn·fú 〈方 *dial.*〉佩服 admire；be convinced：你说的那个理，俺不～。I'm not convinced by what you said.

【宾馆】bīnguǎn 公家招待来宾住宿的地方。现指较大而设施好的旅馆。guesthouse；building used by an organization or enterprise to accommodate guests；now refers to a large and well-equipped hotel

【宾客】bīnkè 客人（总称）（collect.）guests；visitors

【宾朋】bīnpéng 宾客；朋友 friends and guests；guests：～满座。The house was filled with guests. *or* Visitors filled all the seats.

【宾语】bīnyǔ 动词的一种连带成分，一般在动词后边，用来回答'谁？'或'什么？'例如'我找厂长'的'厂长'，'他开拖拉机'的'拖拉机'，'接受批评'的'批评'，'他说他不知道'的'他不知道'。有时候一个动词可以带两个宾语，如'教我们化学'的'我们'和'化学'。object；part of a sentence generally following a verb, indicating 'who' or 'what', such as '厂长 chǎngzhǎng' in '我找厂长 wǒ zhǎo chǎngzhǎng'；'拖拉机 tuōlājī' in '他开拖拉机 tā kāi tuōlājī'；'批评 pīpíng' in '接受批评 jiēshòu pīpíng' and '他不知道 tā bùzhīdào' in '他说他不知道 tā shuō tā bùzhīdào'. Sometimes a verb has two objects after it, e.g. '我们 wǒmén' and '化学 huàxué' in '教我们化学 jiāo wǒmén huàxué'.

【宾至如归】bīn zhì rú guī 客人到了这里就像回到自己的家一样。形容旅馆、饭馆等招待周到。（of a hotel, guesthouse, etc.）where guests feel as comfortable as they would if they were at home；home away from home

【宾主】bīnzhǔ 客人和主人 host and guest

彬 bīn［彬彬］〈书 *fml.*〉形容文雅 refined；urbane：～有礼 refined and courteous；urbane|文质～ suave；urbane；quiet and scholarly

傧（儐）bīn［傧相］bīnxiàng ❶〈古代 *arch.*〉称接引宾客的人，也指赞礼的人 usher（for guests）；master of ceremonies ❷ 举行婚礼时陪伴新郎新娘的人 attendant to bride or bridegroom：男～best man｜女～bridesmaid

斌 bīn same as 彬 bīn

滨(濱) bīn ❶ 水边；近水的地方 water's edge; bank; brink; shore：海～seashore｜湖～lakeshore｜湘江之～on the banks of the Xiangjiang River ❷ 靠近(水边) be close to (the sea, a river, etc.); border on：～海 border on the sea｜～江 along the bank of a river

缤(繽) bīn［缤纷］(bīnfēn)〈书 *fml.*〉繁多而凌乱 in riotous profusion：五彩～riot of colours; multi-coloured｜落英(花)～profusion of falling petals

槟(檳、梹) bīn［槟子］(bīn·zi) ❶ 槟子树，苹果树的一种。果实比苹果小，红色，熟后转紫红，味酸甜带涩。big-fruit crabapple (*Malus platycarpa*), species of apple, redder and smaller than the more common variety, which, when ripe, turns purplish red, and has a slightly tart, piquant taste ❷ 这种植物的果实 binzi, fruit of the plant

☞ bīng on p. 139

镔(鑌) bīn［镔铁］(bīntiě) 精炼的铁 wrought iron

濒 bīn ❶ 紧靠(水边) be close to (the sea, river, etc.); border on：～湖 border the shores of a lake｜东～大海 face the sea to the east ❷ 临近；接近 on the brink of; on the point of：～危 be in imminent danger｜～行 about to leave; before setting out; on the eve of departure

【濒临】bīnlín 紧接；临近 be close to; border on; be on the verge of：我国～太平洋。China borders on the Pacific Ocean.｜精神～崩溃的边缘 on the verge of a nervous breakdown

【濒危】bīnwēi 接近危险的境地；病重将死 be in imminent danger; be critically ill：病人～。The patient is critically ill.

【濒于】bīnyú 临近；接近(用于坏的遭遇) be on the brink of (sth. bad)：～危险 be in imminent danger｜～绝望 be on the brink of desperation｜～破产 be on the brink of bankruptcy

豳 Bīn 古地名，在今陕西彬县、旬邑一带 ancient name of a place in today's Binxian and Xunyi counties in Shaanxi Province; also 邠 Bīn

bìn (ㄅㄧㄣˋ)

摈(擯) bìn〈书 *fml.*〉抛弃；排除 discard; get rid of：～诸门外 shut or lock sb. out｜～而不用 reject

【摈斥】bìnchì 排诉 reject; dismiss：～异己 dismiss those who hold different opinions

【摈除】bìnchú 排除；抛弃 discard; get rid of; dispense with：～陈规陋习 dispense with outdated conventions and practices

【摈弃】bìn qì 抛弃 abandon; discard; cast away：～旧观念 cast off antiquated values

殡(殯) bìn 停放灵柩；把灵柩送到埋葬或火化的地方去 lay a coffin in a memorial hall; carry a coffin to the burial place or the crematory：出～ carry a coffin to the cemetery; hold a funeral procession ｜～车 hearse

【殡车】bìnchē 出殡时运灵柩的车 hearse; vehicle for conveying a dead person to the place of burial or the crematory

【殡殓】bìnliàn 入殓和出殡 encoffin a corpse and carry it to the grave

【殡仪馆】bìnyíguǎn 供停放灵柩和办理丧事的机构 the undertaker's; funeral parlour or home; establishment where a bier is temporarily placed and a funeral is held

【殡葬】bìnzàng 出殡和埋葬 funeral and interment

膑(臏) bìn same as 髌 bìn

髌(髕) bìn ❶ 髌骨 kneecap; patella ❷ 古代削去髌骨的酷刑 chopping off the kneecaps (a punishment in ancient China)

【髌骨】bìngǔ 膝盖部的一块骨，略呈三角形，尖端向下 the triangular shaped bone at the front of the knee; kneecap; patella; also 膝盖骨 xīgàigǔ；(图见 ☞ figure for 骨骼 gǔgé on p. 693)

鬓(鬢、髩) bìn 鬓角 temples; hair over the temples：双～the temples｜两～斑白 greying at the temples

【鬓发】bìnfà 鬓角的头发 hair over the temples：～苍白 greying at the temples

【鬓角】bìnjiǎo (～儿 bìnjiǎor) 耳朵前边长头发的部位。也指长在这个部位的头发。part of the head in front of the ear where hair grows; temple; also 鬓脚 bìnjiǎo

【鬓脚】bìnjiǎo same as 鬓角 bìnjiǎo

bīng (ㄅㄧㄥ)

冰(氷) bīng ❶ 水在0℃或0℃以下凝结成的固体 ice; solid form of water at or below zero degree centigrade：湖里结～了。The water was frozen over. ❷ 因接触凉的东西而感到寒冷 feel cold from contact with cold things：刚到中秋，河水已经有些～腿了。It is only mid-autumn, yet the river is already a little iced over. ❸ 把东西和冰或凉水放在一起使凉 put sth. on the ice or in cold water to make it cool; ice：把汽水～上 put ice in soda water ❹ 像冰的东西 sth. resembling ice：～片 borneol｜～糖 crystal sugar; rock candy

【冰棒】bīngbàng 〈方 *dial.*〉冰棍儿 popsicle; ice lolly

【冰雹】bīngbáo 空中降下来的冰块，多在晚春和夏季的午后伴同雷阵雨出现，给农作物带来很大危害 hail; hailstone; precipitation in the form of pellets or balls of ice that usu. fall during afternoon thundershowers in spring and autumn; also 雹 báo; 通称 commonly known as 雹子 báo·zi; 有的地区叫冷子 in some places also called 冷子 lěng·zi

【冰碴儿】bīngchár 〈方 *dial.*〉冰的碎块或碎末；水面上结的一层薄冰 ice chip; thin coat of ice on water surface

【冰川】bīngchuān 在高山或两极地区，积雪由于自身的压力变成冰块(或积雪融化，下渗冻结成冰块)，又因重力作用而沿着地面倾斜方向移动，这种移动的大冰块叫做冰川 glacier; extended mass of ice formed from snow falling and accumulating over the years that moves very slowly; found on high mountains and at the north and south polar regions; also 冰河 bīnghé

【冰川期】bīngchuānqī 地质上的一个时期，在新生代的第四纪，当时气候非常寒冷，欧洲和美洲北部都被冰川所覆盖 ice age; glacial epoch; the geologically recent Pleistocene, when temperatures were sub-freezing; and when Europe and the northern part of America were covered by glaciers; also 冰河时代 bīnghé shídài

【冰床】bīngchuáng 冰上滑行的交通运输工具，形状像雪橇，可坐六七个人，用竿子撑，也可用人力或畜力推拉 sled; sledge; sleigh; vehicle like a sleigh that is drawn or pushed by men or draft animals and can be ridden by six or seven people when sliding over ice

【冰镩】bīngcuān 凿冰工具，头部尖，有倒钩 ice chisel; tool with a pointed tip and barb for cutting ice

【冰袋】bīngdài 装冰块的橡胶袋。装上冰块后，敷在病人身上某一部位，使局部的温度降低。ice bag; rubber bag for holding ice that is applied to the part of a patient's body that needs to be cooled

【冰刀】bīngdāo 装在冰鞋底下的钢制的刀状物。有球刀、跑刀和花样刀三种。ice skate blade; steel blades fitted to ice skates, of three broad types: for ice-hockey skates, racing skates and figure skating skates

【冰灯】bīngdēng 用冰做成的供人观赏的灯，灯体多为各种动植物、建筑物的造型，内装电灯或蜡烛，光彩四射 ice lantern; coloured ice of various shapes (usu. of animals, plants or buildings) enclosing a light

【冰点】bīngdiǎn 水凝固时的温度，也就是水和冰可以平衡共存的温度 freezing point; temperature at which water freezes and water and ice coexist

【冰雕】bīngdiāo 用冰雕刻形象的艺术。也指用冰雕刻成的作品。ice carving; carved ice; ice sculpture; skill of fashioning or cutting ice to produce work of art: ～展览 ice sculpture exhibition

【冰冻】bīngdòng ❶ 水结成冰 (of water) become hardened into ice; freeze ❷〈方 *dial.*〉冰 ice

【冰冻三尺，非一日之寒】bīng dòng sān chǐ, fēi yī rì zhī hán 〈比喻 *fig.*〉事物变化达到某种程度，是经过日积月累、逐渐形成的 it takes more than one cold day for the river to freeze three feet deep; Rome was not built in a day; the trouble is deep-rooted

【冰峰】bīngfēng 冰冻长年不化的山峰 mountain peak capped by ice all the year round; icy mountain peak

【冰糕】bīnggāo 〈方 *dial.*〉❶ 冰激凌 ice-cream ❷ 冰棍儿 ice-lolly; popsicle; ice-sucker; frozen sucker

【冰镐】bīnggǎo 凿冰用的工具，多用于攀登冰峰 ice axe; tool for cutting ice, used mostly when climbing an icy mountain peak

【冰挂】bīngguà 雨凇的通称 general term for 雨凇 yǔsōng

【冰柜】bīngguì 电冰柜的简称 abbr. for 电冰柜 diànbīngguì

【冰棍儿】bīnggùnr 一种冷食，把水、果汁、糖等混合搅拌冷冻而成，用一根小棍做把儿 popsicle; ice-sucker; frozen sucker; frozen food made of flavoured ice, a mixture of water, fruit juice, sugar, etc. on a stick; ice-lolly

【冰花】bīnghuā ❶ 指凝结呈花纹的薄薄冰层(多在玻璃窗上) ice-flake (as on a window pane in winter) ❷ 把花卉、水草、水果、活鱼等实物用水冻结，形成冰罩的艺术品 iced object of art (such as iced flowers, water plants, fruit, live fish, etc., as ornaments) ❸ 雾凇 frost flower; frost; rime: 路旁树上的～真是美。The frost flowers on the trees lining the road are very beautiful.

【冰激凌】bīng·jilíng 一种半固体的冷食，用水、牛奶、鸡蛋、糖、果汁等调和后，一面加冷一面搅拌，使凝结而成 ice cream; semisolid frozen food made by freezing and at the same time stirring the mixture of water, milk, eggs, sugar, fruit juice, etc.

【冰窖】bīngjiào 贮藏冰的地窖 icehouse; cellar for storing ice

【冰晶】bīngjīng 在0℃以下时空气中的水蒸气凝结成的结晶状的微小颗粒 ice crystal; precipitation consisting of small crystals of ice that occurs when the temperature drops below zero degrees centigrade

【冰冷】bīnglěng ❶ 很冷 ice-cold: 手脚冻得～。My hands and feet are freezing.｜不要躺在～的石板上。Don't lie on that ice-cold slab of stone. ❷ 非常冷淡 very cold; indifferent;

apathetic：表情～cold expression

【冰凉】bīngliáng （物体）很凉 ice-cold：浑身～。He was ice-cold all over.|～的酸梅汤 ice-cold sweet-sour plum juice

【冰凌】bīnglíng 冰 ice

【冰轮】bīnglún 〈书 *fml*.〉指月亮 the moon

【冰排】bīngpái 大块浮冰 ice raft；ice floe

【冰瓶】bīngpíng 大口的保温瓶，通常用来盛冰棍儿等冷食 vacuum bottle or flask for keeping popsicles and other frozen food；☞ 保温瓶 bǎowēnpíng on p.67

【冰期】bīngqī ❶ 冰川期 glacial epoch；ice age ❷ 指一次冰期中冰川活动剧烈的时期 active period of a glacial epoch

【冰淇淋】bīngqílín same as 冰激凌 bīng·jilíng

【冰橇】bīngqiāo 雪橇 sled；sledge；sleigh

【冰清玉洁】bīng qīng yù jié ☞ 玉洁冰清 yù jié bīng qīng on p.2347

【冰球】bīngqiú ❶ 一种冰上运动，用冰球杆把球打进对方球门得分，分多的为胜 ice hockey；game played on ice between two teams using hockey sticks to score goals by shooting the puck into the opposing team's net ❷ 冰球运动使用的球，饼状，用黑色的硬橡胶做成 puck；black disk of vulcanised rubber to be hit into the goal in ice hockey

【冰人】bīngrén 〈书 *fml*.〉称媒人 matchmaker；go-between

【冰山】bīngshān ❶ 冰冻长年不化的大山 glacier；mountain covered with ice all the year round；ice-covered mountain；icy mountain ❷ 浮在海洋中的巨大冰块，有时长到几里，高到一百米左右，是两极冰川末端断裂，滑落海洋中形成的 iceberg；large floating mass of ice, sometimes several km long and about 100 metres tall, that has become detached from glaciers in the polar regions and carried out to sea ❸〈比喻 *fig*.〉不能长久依赖的靠山 individual or group not to be relied upon for long

【冰释】bīngshì 像冰一样溶化 thaw or melt like ice；〈比喻 *fig*.〉嫌隙、怀疑、误会等完全消除 (of ill feeling；suspicions，misunderstandings，etc.) disappear；vanish；be dispelled：涣然～melt away like ice；vanish like air；clear up

【冰霜】bīngshuāng 〈书 *fml*.〉❶〈比喻 *fig*.〉有节操 moral integrity ❷〈比喻 *fig*.〉神情严肃 austere manner；stern countenance；austerity：凛若～be awe-inspiring；look frosty and stern

【冰炭】bīngtàn 〈比喻 *fig*.〉互相对立的两种事物 ice and burning coals；mutually exclusive：～不相容（比喻两种对立的事物不能并存）as incompatible or irreconcilable as ice and hot coals

【冰糖】bīngtáng 一种块状的食糖，用白糖或红糖加水使溶化成糖汁，经过蒸发，结晶而成。透明或半透明，多为白色或带黄色。crystal sugar；rock candy；white or yellowish transparent or semi-transparent edible lumps of sugar crystallized by evaporation；dissolved white or brown sugar

【冰糖葫芦】bīngtáng hú·lu （～儿 bīngtáng hú·lur）糖葫芦 candied haws or other fruits on a stick

【冰天雪地】bīng tiān xuě dì 形容冰雪漫天盖地，非常寒冷 world of ice and snow；wide tracts of ice-bound and snow-covered country

【冰坨】bīngtuó 水或含水的东西冻结成的硬块 lump of ice；block of ice

【冰箱】bīngxiāng ❶ 冷藏食物或药品用的器具，里面放冰块，保持低温 refrigerator；freezer；fridge；icebox；cabinet or chest with a partition for ice, used for keeping food, medicine, etc. cool ❷ 电冰箱的简称 abbr. for 电冰箱 diànbīngxiāng

【冰消瓦解】bīng xiāo wǎ jiě 〈比喻 *fig*.〉完全消释或崩溃 melt like ice and break like tiles — disintegrate；dissolve；be dispelled

【冰鞋】bīngxié 滑冰时穿的鞋，皮制，鞋底上装着冰刀 skating boots；ice-skates；leather shoe fitted with a metal blade for skating on ice

【冰镇】bīngzhèn 把食物或饮料和冰等放在一起使凉 ice；iced；cool food or beverages kept in ice, or with ice cubes added：～西瓜 iced watermelon|～汽水 iced soda water

【冰砖】bīngzhuān 一种冷食，把水、奶油、糖、果汁等物混合搅拌，在低温下冻成的砖形硬块 ice-cream brick；frozen food made by freezing a mixture of water, cream, sugar, fruit juice, etc.；ice-cream in the shape of a brick

【冰锥】bīngzhuī （～儿 bīngzhuīr）雪后檐头滴水凝成锥形的冰 icicle；pendant, tapering mass of ice formed from frozen dripping water；also 冰锥子 bīngzhuī·zi，冰柱 bīngzhù or 冰溜 bīngliū

并 Bīng 山西太原的别称 another name for Taiyuan in Shanxi Province

☞ bìng on p.141

兵 bīng ❶ 兵器 weapons；arms：短～相接 fight at close quarters|秣马厉～feed the horses and sharpen the weapons — prepare for battle ❷ 军人；军队 soldier；army；troops：当～join the army；be a soldier|～种 branch of one of the services|骑～cavalry；horse soldier；cavalryman ❸ 军队中的最基层成员 members of the army at the grassroots level；rank-and-file soldier；private：上等～private；first class ❹ 关于军事或战争的 military；related to war：～法 art of war；military strategy and tactics|～书 book or treatise on the art of war

【兵变】bīngbiàn 军队哗变 mutiny：发动～mutiny；commit mutiny

【兵不血刃】bīng bù xuè rèn 兵器上面没有沾

血，指未经交锋而取得胜利 with blades innocent of blood — win victory without shedding a drop of blood or firing a shot

【兵不厌诈】bīng bù yàn zhà 用兵打仗可以使用欺诈的办法迷惑敌人 Deception is justified in war; in war nothing is too deceitful; there can never be too much deception in war; all's fair in war; (不厌 *bu yan*: 不排斥；不以为非 it is justifiable to; it is not incorrect to)；语本《韩非子·难一》：'战阵之间，不厌诈伪' *Hanfeizi · Rebuttals* (*I*): 'There can never be too much deception in war.'

【兵差】bīngchāi 〈旧时 *old*〉军队强迫人民替他们做的劳役，主要是从事运输等 army corvée; conscript labour; corvée labour that civilians were forced into by the army in former times, mainly transport, etc.

【兵车】bīngchē ❶〈古代 *arch.*〉作战用的车辆 war chariot ❷ 指运载军队的列车 troop vehicle; troop train; military vehicle

【兵船】bīngchuán 指军舰 man-of-war; naval vessel; warship

【兵丁】bīng dīng 士兵的旧称 old name for rank-and-file soldier

【兵法】bīngfǎ 〈古代 *arch.*〉指用兵作战的策略和方法 art of war; military strategy and tactics: 熟谙～be well acquainted with the art of war

【兵符】bīngfú ❶〈古代 *arch.*〉调兵遣将的符节 military tally (used in former times as evidence of authority) ❷ 兵书 book or treatise on the art of war

【兵戈】bīnggē 〈书 *fml.*〉兵器，指战争 weapons; arms: 不动～without resorting to force | ～四起. There is war everywhere.

【兵革】bīnggé 〈书 *fml.*〉兵器和甲胄，借指战争 war; weapons and armour: ～未息 the war is still on; hostilities have not ceased

【兵工厂】bīnggōngchǎng 制造武器装备的工厂 arsenal; munitions or ordnance factory; factory for manufacturing military equipment or munitions

【兵贵神速】bīng guì shén sù 用兵以行动特别迅速最为重要(见于《三国志·魏书·郭嘉传》) *History of Three Kingdoms · Kingdom of Wei · Biography of Guo Jia*: speed is what counts in war; in war it is speed that counts

【兵荒马乱】bīng huāng mǎ luàn 形容战时社会动荡不安的景象 turmoil and chaos of war

【兵火】bīnghuǒ 战火，指战争 flames of war; war: ～连天 raging flames of war | 书稿毁于～。The manuscripts were destroyed in war and turmoil.

【兵家】bīngjiā ❶〈古代 *arch.*〉指军事家 military strategist ❷ 用兵的人 military commander; soldier: 胜败乃～常事。For a military commander, winning or losing a battle is common place. | 徐州历来为～必争之地。Xuzhou has long been a bone of contention among warring strategists.

【兵舰】bīngjiàn 军舰 warship

【兵谏】bīngjiàn 用武力胁迫君主或当权者接受规劝 coerce the monarch or ruler by force of arms into accepting one's exhortations; exhortations backed up by force of arms: 发动～coerce the monarch or ruler by force of arms into accepting one's exhortations

【兵来将挡，水来土掩】bīng lái jiàng dǎng, shuǐ lái tǔ yǎn 〈比喻 *fig.*〉不管对方使用什么计策、手段，都有对付办法。也比喻针对具体情况采取相应对策。counter measure for measure; confront soldiers with generals and stem flood water with earth — take such measures as the situation calls for; counter move for move

【兵力】bīnglì 军队的实力，包括人员和武器装备等 armed forces; troops; military strength including troops and weaponry: ～雄厚 formidable military strength | 集中～ concentrate one's forces or troops

【兵临城下】bīng lín chéng xià 指大军压境城被围困。形容形势危急。the enemy has reached the city gates; the city is under siege; enemy troops are at the city gate; the situation is dangerous

【兵乱】bīngluàn 由战争造成的骚扰和灾害；兵灾 turmoil caused by war: 屡遭～repeatedly ravaged by war

【兵马俑】bīngmǎyǒng 〈古代 *arch.*〉用来殉葬的兵马形象的陶俑 terracotta warrior; terracotta warriors and horses buried with the dead in ancient China

【兵痞】bīngpǐ 指在旧军队中长期当兵、品质恶劣、为非作歹的人 wicked seasoned soldier; army riffraff; army ruffian; soldier of fortune

【兵棋】bīngqí 特制的军队标号图型和人员、兵器、地物等模型，供各级指挥员在沙盘上研究作战和训练等情况时使用 war model; model of military symbols, troops, weapons, topographical features, etc., made for officers at various levels in order for them to study operations and carry out training

【兵器】bīngqì same as 武器 wǔqì ①

【兵强马壮】bīng qiáng mǎ zhuàng 形容军队实力强，富有战斗力 strong soldiers and sturdy horses — a well-trained and powerful army

【兵权】bīngquán 指挥和调动军队的权力 military leadership; military power: 掌握～ hold military power

【兵戎】bīngróng 指武器、军队 arms; weapons: ～相见(武装冲突的婉辞) resort to arms; open hostilities; cross swords with; meet on the battleground

【兵士】bīngshì 士兵 private; rank-and-file soldier

【兵书】bīngshū 讲兵法的书 book on the art of

war

【兵团】bīngtuán ❶ 军队的一级组织，下辖几个军或师 large military unit consisting of several armies or divisions; army group; formation; corps ❷ 泛指团以上的部队 army units above the regimental level; troop formation; armed force：主力～main force | 地方～local armed forces

【兵燹】bīngxiǎn 〈书 *fml.*〉战争造成的焚烧破坏等灾害 ravages of war：藏书毁于～。The books were destroyed in the war.

【兵饷】bīngxiǎng 军饷 soldier's pay and provisions

【兵役】bīngyì 指当兵的义务 military service：服～ serve in the army; do military service

【兵役法】bīngyìfǎ 国家根据宪法规定公民服兵役的法律制度 military service law; conscription law; law formulated by the government in accordance with the Constitution that defines national military service

【兵营】bīngyíng 军队居住的营房 military camp; barracks

【兵勇】bīngyǒng 〈旧指 *old*〉士兵 rank-and-file soldier; armyman

【兵油子】bīngyóu·zi 指久在行伍而油滑的兵 oily seasoned sergeant; army riffraff; army ruffian

【兵员】bīngyuán 兵；战士①（总称）（collect.）soldiers; troops：补充～replenish with more troops | 五十万～500,000 troops; 500,000 strong army

【兵源】bīngyuán 士兵的来源 manpower resources for military service; sources of troops：～充足 abundant sources of troops

【兵灾】bīngzāi 战乱带来的灾难 disaster of war; scourge of war

【兵站】bīngzhàn 军队在后方交通线上设置的供应、转运机构，主要负责补给物资、接收伤病员、接待过往部队等 supply and transfer station set up by the army along a line of communication, mainly in charge of supplies, caring for sick and wounded soldiers, and receiving passing troops; army service station; military depot

【兵种】bīngzhǒng 军种内部的分类，如步兵、炮兵、装甲兵、工程兵等是陆军的各兵种 branch of one of the services, e.g. the army is subdivided into infantry, artillery, armoured forces, and engineering troops

【兵卒】bīngzú 士兵的旧称 old name for soldier

屏 bīng [屏营]（bīngyíng）〈书 *fml.*〉形容惶恐的样子（多用于奏章、书札 oft. used in memorials to the throne, letters, etc.）in fear and trepidation; trembling with fear：不胜～待命之至 awaiting your Majesty's edict with fear and trepidation; anxiously awaiting your instructions

☞ bǐng on p. 140 and píng on p. 1490

栟 bīng [栟榈]（bīnglǘ）古书上指棕榈 name of palm in ancient books

☞ bēn on p. 88

槟（檳、梹） bīng [槟榔]（bīng·lang）❶ 常绿乔木，树干很高，羽状复叶。果实可以吃，也供药用。生长在热带地方。betel palm (*Piper betle*); areca; evergreen arbour with a tall trunk and double feather-like compound leaves, that grows in tropical zones; its fruits are edible and used in medicine ❷ 这种植物的果实 areca nut; betel nut

☞ bīn on p. 135

bǐng（ㄅㄧㄥˇ）

丙 bǐng ❶ 天干的第三位 3rd of the 10 Heavenly stems; ☞ 干支 gānzhī on p. 627 ❷ 〈书 *fml.*〉丙丁 fire：阅后付～set sth. on fire after reading it

【丙部】bǐngbù 子部 Category C (of books), under the ancient Chinese method of classification, which includes all works by various schools and scholars of thought

【丙丁】bǐngdīng 〈书 *fml.*〉火的代称 another name for fire：付～set on fire; burn

【丙纶】bǐnglún 合成纤维的一种，质轻，耐磨，吸水性小，制成的衣物不易走样。工业上用来制造绳索、滤布、渔网等。polypropylene fibre; a variety of synthetic fibres which is light, stands hard wear and is not very absorbent. Clothes made of polypropylene fibre do not easily lose their shape. Polypropylene fibre is used in industry to make rope, filter gauze, fishing nets, etc.

【丙种射线】bǐngzhǒng shèxiàn 镭和其他一些放射性元素的原子放出的射线，是波长极短的电磁波，穿透力比爱克斯射线更强，能穿透几十厘米厚的钢板。工业上用来探伤，医学上用来消毒、治疗肿瘤等。也叫伽马（gāmǎ）射线。也写作γ射线。gamma ray; γ ray; a ray emitted from radium and other radioactive elements; an electromagnetic wave with an extremely short wavelength that is stronger than an X ray and is capable of penetrating a steel plate dozens of centimetres thick; It is used in industry to detect defects, and in medicine to sterilize and treat tumours. also called 伽马射线 gāmǎ shèxiàn; written as γ射线 gāmǎ shèxiàn

邴 Bǐng 姓 a surname

秉 bǐng ❶ 〈书 *fml.*〉拿着；握着 grasp; hold：～笔 hold a pen | ～烛 hold a candle ❷ 〈书 *fml.*〉掌握；主持 control; preside over：～政 hold political power; be in power ❸ 〈古代 *arch.*〉容量单位，合16斛 capacity unit, equal to 16 *hu* ❹（Bǐng）姓 a surname

【秉承】bǐngchéng 承受；接受（旨意或指示）take (orders); receive (commands); also 禀

承 bǐngchéng

【秉持】bǐngchí 〈书 *fml.*〉主持；掌握 adhere to (principles, etc.); hold to

【秉公】bǐnggōng 依照公认的道理或公平的标准 justly; impartially; in accordance with a universally accepted principle or fair standard: ～办理 handle a matter impartially; act with justice

【秉性】bǐngxìng 性格 nature; temperament; disposition: ～纯朴 be simple and plain by nature | ～各异 all kinds of dispositions; diverse temperaments

【秉正】bǐngzhèng 〈书 *fml.*〉秉持公正 fair-minded; honest; upright: ～无私 be impartial and selfless

【秉烛】bǐngzhú 〈书 *fml.*〉拿着燃着的蜡烛 hold a candle: ～待旦 wait by candlelight until daybreak | ～夜游(指及时行乐) go out at night taking a lamp — make merry while one may

柄 bǐng ❶ 器物的把儿 handle of sth.: 刀～ handle of a knife | 勺～handle of a spoon ❷ 植物的花、叶或果实跟茎或枝连着的部分(of a flower, leaf or fruit) the part combined with the twig or stem: 花～stem of a flower | 叶～stem of a leaf ❸ 〈比喻 *fig.*〉在言行上被人抓住的材料 anything affording an advantage or pretext for an opponent: 话～subject for ridicule | 笑～laughing stock | 把～evidence against sb.; handle ❹ 〈书 *fml.*〉执掌 control: ～国 rule a country | ～政 hold political power ❺ 〈书 *fml.*〉权 power; authority: 国～national power ❻ 〈方 *dial.*〉〈量词 *classifier*〉用于某些带把儿的东西 [used of things with a handle]: 一～斧头 one axe | 两～锄头 two pickaxes

【柄子】bǐng·zi 〈方 *dial.*〉 same as 柄 bǐng ①

昺(昞) bǐng〈书 *fml.*〉明亮；光明 (多用于人名) mostly used in people's names) bright

饼 bǐng ❶ 泛称烤熟或蒸熟的面食，形状大多扁而圆 round flat cake made of flour by baking or steaming: 月～moon cake | 烧～sesame seed cake | 大～a kind of big flat pie ❷ (～儿 bǐngr)形体像饼的东西 sth. shaped like a cake: 铁～discus | 豆～bean cake | 柿～儿 dried persimmon

【饼铛】bǐngchēng 烙饼用的平底锅 baking pan

【饼饵】bǐng'ěr 〈书 *fml.*〉饼类食品的总称 cakes; pastry

【饼肥】bǐngféi 豆饼、花生饼等肥料的统称 general term for fertilizer cake

【饼干】bǐnggān 食品，用面粉加糖、鸡蛋、牛奶等烤成的小而薄的块儿 biscuit; cracker; a type of food made with sugar, eggs, milk and flour and baked

【饼子】bǐng·zi 用玉米面、小米面等贴在锅上烙成的饼 pancake baked with maize or millet

炳 bǐng 〈书 *fml.*〉光明；显著 bright; splendid; remarkable: 彪～shining; splendid | ～蔚 bright and beautiful

【炳蔚】bǐngwèi 〈书 *fml.*〉文采鲜明华美 remarkable literary talent

【炳耀】bǐngyào 〈书 *fml.*〉❶ (光彩)焕发 brilliant ❷ (光辉)照耀 illuminate; shine: ～千古 remain eternally glorious

屏 bǐng ❶ 抑止(呼吸) hold (one's breath): ～着呼吸 hold one's breath | ～着气 hold one's breath ❷ 除去；排除 reject; get rid of; abandon: ～除 get rid of; dismiss; brush aside | ～弃 discard; abandon; reject; throw away ☞ bīng on p. 139 and píng on p. 1490

【屏除】bǐngchú 摒除 (bìngchú) get rid of; dismiss; brush aside

【屏迹】bǐngjì 〈书 *fml.*〉❶ 敛迹；匿迹 lie low; go into hiding: 权贵～。The powerful families are all lying low. | 盗贼～。Robbers and thieves dare not go out. ❷ 隐居 live as a hermit; live in seclusion: ～山村 live in a mountain village as a recluse or hermit

【屏气】bǐng//qì 暂时抑止呼吸；有意地闭住气 hold one's breath: ～凝神 hold one's breath in concentration | 他放轻脚步屏住气向病房走去。Holding his breath, he walked softly towards the hospital ward.

【屏弃】bǐngqì 摒弃 (bìngqì) discard; reject; throw away; abandon

【屏退】bǐngtuì ❶ 使离开 order retainers, servants, etc. to retire: ～左右 order one's attendants to clear out | ～闲人 dismiss persons not concerned ❷ 〈书 *fml.*〉退隐 (of an official) retire from public life; go into retirement: 不乐仕进，常思～。Having no particular liking for an official career, he often toyed with the idea of retirement.

【屏息】bǐngxī 屏气 hold one's breath: 全场听众～静听。All the attendants listened with bated breath.

禀(稟) bǐng ❶ 禀报；禀告 report (to one's superior or senior); petition: 回～report back (to one's superior) | 待我～过家父，再来回话。I will give you an answer after I have reported this to my father. ❷ 〈旧时 *old*〉禀报的文件 official report; petition: ～帖 petition | 具～详报 report in great detail ❸ 承受 receive; be endowed with: ～承 take orders from; act in accordance with

【禀报】bǐngbào 指向上级或长辈报告 report (to one's superior or senior): 据实～give a full account; make a detailed report

【禀承】bǐngchéng same as 秉承 bǐngchéng

【禀赋】bǐngfù 人的体魄、智力等方面的素质 natural endowments (including physique and intelligence); gift: ～较弱 be born weak | ～聪明 be gifted with keen intelligence

【禀告】bǐnggào 指向上级或长辈告诉事情 report (to one's superior or senior):此事待我～家母后再定。The matter will be decided after I have reported it to my mother.

【禀帖】bǐngtiě 〈旧时 *old*〉百姓向官府有所报告或请求用的文书 report or petition to government authorities

【禀性】bǐngxìng 本性 natural disposition:～纯厚 be simple and honest by nature|江山易改,～难移。Rivers and mountains may change, but it is hard to alter a man's character.

鞞 bǐng 〈书 *fml.*〉刀鞘 sheath of a knife or sword

bìng (ㄅㄧㄥˋ)

并[1](**併**) bìng 合在一起 combine; merge; incorporate:归～incorporate into; merge into; amalgamate|合～combine; merge; incorporate|把三个组～成两个 merge three groups into two

并[2](**並、竝**) bìng ❶ 两种或两种以上的事物平排着(of two or more kinds of things) stand or place side by side:～肩前进 advance shoulder to shoulder|～蒂莲 twin lotus flowers on one stalk ❷〈副词 *adv.*〉表示不同的事物同时存在,不同的事情同时进行 side by side; equally; simultaneously:两说～存 two views coexist|相提～论 mention in the same breath; group together; place on a bar ❸〈副词 *adv.*〉用在否定词前面加强否定的语气,略带反驳的意味[used before a negative to reinforce it] actually; definitely:你以为他糊涂,其实他～不湖涂。You thought he was foolish, but he actually is not.|所谓团结～非一团和气。When we speak of unity, we do not mean unprincipled peace. ❹〈连词 *conj.*〉并且 and; besides:我完全同意～拥护领导的决定。I fully agree to and endorse the decision of the leader. ❺〈书 *fml.*〉用法跟'连'相同(常跟'而'、'亦'呼应 oft. accompanied by 而 ér or 亦 yì) [used in the same way as 连 lián]:～此而不知 do not know even that|～此浅近原理亦不能明 cannot even understand a principle as simple as that

☞ Bīng on p.137

【并存】bìngcún 同时存在 exist side by side; coexist:两种体制～。Two systems coexist or exist side by side.|不同的见解可以～。Different views can exist side by side.

【并蒂莲】bìngdìlián 并排地长在同一个茎上的两朵莲花,文学作品中常用来比喻恩爱的夫妻 twin lotus flowers on one stalk; (oft. fig.) devoted married couple in literary works

【并发】bìngfā 由正在患的某种病引起(另一种病)(of a disease) be complicated by another; (of two diseases) occur simultaneously:～症 complication|～肺炎 complications brought about by simultaneously falling ill with pneumonia

【并骨】bìnggǔ 〈书 *fml.*〉指夫妻合葬 burial of husband and wife in the same tomb

【并驾齐驱】bìng jià qí qū 〈比喻 *fig.*〉齐头并进,不分前后。也比喻地位或程度相等,不分高下。run neck and neck; keep abreast of sb.; keep pace with sb.; be on a par with sb.

【并肩】bìng//jiān ❶ 肩挨着肩 shoulder to shoulder; side by side; abreast:他们～在河边走着。They are walking side by side along the river. ❷〈比喻 *fig.*〉行动一致,共同努力 take unified action; make joint efforts:～作战 fight side by side

【并进】bìngjìn 不分先后,同时进行 progress abreast; run parallel:齐头～advance side by side

【并举】bìngjǔ 不分先后,同时举办 carry on (two or more things) at the same time; develop concurrently or simultaneously:工农业～simultaneous development of industry and agriculture

【并力】bìnglì 〈书 *fml.*〉一起出力 join forces; pool efforts:～坚守 join forces in defending (a position); jointly hold fast (to the position)

【并立】bìnglì 同时存在 exist side by side; exist simultaneously:群雄～。Separatist warlords existed side by side.

【并联】bìnglián ❶ 并排地相联接 parallel connection ❷ 把几个电器或元器件,一个个并排地联接,形成几个平行的分支电路,这种联接方法叫并联 join together electric devices or components in a parallel fashion to form parallel branch circuits

【并列】bìngliè 并排平列,不分主次 stand side by side; be juxtaposed:这是～的两个分句。These are two coordinate clauses.|比赛结果两人～第三名。The two of them tied for third place in the competition.

【并拢】bìnglǒng 合拢 close up; join together:两脚～put together one's feet|～翅膀(of a bird) fold its wings

【并茂】bìngmào 〈比喻 *fig.*〉两种事物都很优美 two things of equal excellence; of an equal match:图文～。The illustrations (in a book) match the quality of the text.|声情～sing in a good voice and with much expression

【并排】bìngpái 不分前后地排列在一条线上 side by side; abreast:三个人～地走过来。Three people walked over side by side.|这条马路可以～行驶四辆大卡车。This road can handle four trucks abreast.

【并且】bìngqiě 〈连词 *conj.*〉❶ 用在两个动词或动词性的词组之间,表示两个动作同时或先后进行[used between two verbs or verb phrases, indicating two actions that are carried out at the same time or successively] and; besides; moreover; furthermore:会上热烈讨论～一致通过了这个生产计划。Those attending the meeting had a heated discussion on the production plan, and, furthermore, unanimously adopted it. ❷ 用在复合句后一半里,表示更进一层的意思[used in the second half of a compound sentence, indicating increased degree]:她被评为先进生产者,～出席了先进生产者经验交流会。She was elected an advanced worker and went on to attend a meeting to swap experience with other advanced workers.

【并吞】bìngtūn 把别国的领土或别人的产业强行并入自己的范围内 swallow up; annex; absorb; forcibly attach the territory of another country or the property of another person to one's own

【并行】bìngxíng ❶ 并排行走 walk abreast; run side by side:携手～walk hand in hand ❷ 同时实行 carry on two or more things at the same time:～不悖 both can be accomplished without coming into conflict; not incompatible|治这种病要打针和吃药～。In order to be cured of this disease, you have to take both oral medicine and injections.

【并行不悖】bìngxíng bù bèi 同时实行,互不冲突 both can be accomplished without coming into conflict; not mutually exclusive; run parallel with one another

【并用】bìngyòng 同时使用 use two or more things simultaneously:手脚～ use both hands and feet

【并重】bìngzhòng 同等重视 lay equal stress on; pay equal attention to:预防和治疗～ lay equal stress on prevention and cure

病 bìng ❶ 生理上或心理上发生的不正常的状态 abnormal physiological or mental condition; disease; illness; sickness:疾～disease; illness; sickness|心脏～heart trouble; heart disease|他的～已经好了。He is well again. ❷ 生理上或心理上发生不正常状态 experience an abnormal physiological or mental condition; be ill; be sick:他着了凉,～了三天。He has been ill with a cold for three days. ❸ 心病;私弊 secret passion; syndrome; wrong; sore point; malady; evil:弊～malady; ill; malpractice ❹ 缺点;错误 fault; defect:语～ill-chosen word; faulty sentence; grammatically wrong sentence; illogical sentence; slip of the tongue|通～common problem ❺〈书 *fml.*〉祸害;损害 do harm to; injure:祸国～民 wreck the country and ruin the people ❻〈书 *fml.*〉责备;不满 be distressed about; disapprove of:诟～censure; denounce; condemn; castigate|为世所～draw public censure

【病案】bìng'àn 病历 medical record; case history

【病包儿】bìngbāor 多病的人(含诙谐意 humor.) person who is always falling ill; chronic invali:三天两头生病,真成了～了。He is always ill, and really seems to be becoming a chronic invalid.

【病变】bìngbiàn 由疾病引起的细胞或组织的变化,是病理变化的简称 pathology; change in the cell or tissue as a result of a disease; pathological change

【病病歪歪】bìng·bingwāiwāi (～的 bìng·bingwāiwāi·de)形容病体衰弱无力的样子(usu. followed by 的·de) sickly-looking

【病程】bìngchéng 指患某种病的整个过程 entire course of a disease

【病虫害】bìng chónghài 病害和虫害的合称 plant diseases and insect pests

【病床】bìngchuáng 病人的床铺,特指医院、疗养院里供住院病人用的床 sickbed; bed used by a sick person at a hospital or sanatorium; hospital bed

【病毒】bìngdú 比病菌更小、多用电子显微镜才能看见的病原体。一般能通过滤菌器,所以也叫滤过性病毒。天花、麻疹、脑炎、牛瘟等疾病就是由不同的病毒引起的。virus; pathogen which is smaller than a germ and visible only under an electronic microscope. Generally a virus can pass through a germ filter, so it is also called a filterable virus or filter passer. Smallpox, measles, cerebritis, rinderpest and other diseases are caused by viruses.

【病笃】bìngdǔ〈书 *fml.*〉病势沉重 be critically ill; be terminally ill

【病房】bìngfáng 医院、疗养院里病人住的房间 sickroom; ward of a hospital or sanatorium

【病夫】bìngfū 体弱多病的人(含讥讽意 ironic) weak and sick person; invalid

【病根】bìnggēn ❶(～子 bìnggēn·zi、～儿 bìnggēnr)没有完全治好的旧病 illness that has not been completely cured; old complaint:这是坐月子时留下的～儿。She contracted the disease during her confinement in childbirth. ❷〈比喻 *fig.*〉能引起失败或灾祸的原因 root cause of failure or trouble:我厂连年亏损的～要找出来。We must find out the root cause of the successive years of loss our factory has suffered.

【病故】bìnggù 因病去世 die of illness

【病害】bìnghài 由细菌、真菌、病毒、藻类、不适宜的气候或土壤等因素引起的植物体发育不良、枯萎或死亡 underdevelopment, withering or death of plants as a result of exposure to germs, eumycetes or viruses, or due to algae, or inappropriate climate or soil; (plant) disease

【病号】bìnghào (～儿 bìnghàor)部队、学校、机关等集体中的病人 patient; sick personnel in military units, schools, government offices or other collectives; person on the sick list:老～(经常生病的人) one who is always ill; chronic invalid|～饭(给病人特做的饭食) special food for patients; patient's diet

【病候】bìnghòu 泛指疾病反映出来的各种临床表现(in a broad sense) symptoms of illness

【病家】bìngjiā 病人和病人的家属(就医生、医院、药房方面说) patient and his family (as addressed by doctor, hospital or dispensary)

【病假】bìngjià 因病请的假 sick leave

【病句】bìngjù 在语法或逻辑上有毛病的句子 grammatically or logically faulty sentence:改正～ correct a faulty sentence

【病菌】bìngjūn 能使人或其他生物生病的细菌,如伤寒杆菌、炭疽杆菌等 pathogenic bacterium; germ that causes human beings or other living things to fall ill, such as typhoid bacillus and bacillus anthracis; also 致病菌 zhìbìngjūn or 病原菌 bìngyuánjūn

【病况】bìngkuàng 病情 state of an illness; patient's condition

【病理】bìnglǐ 疾病发生和发展的过程和原理 pathology; processes and principles of the occurrence and development of diseases

【病历】bìnglì 医疗部门记载病情、诊断和处理方法的记录,每个病人一份 medical record; case history; record kept by a medical institution for each patient about his condition, diagnosis, and treatment; also 病案 bìng'àn

【病例】bìnglì 某种疾病的例子。某个人或生物患过某种疾病,就是这种疾病的病例。case of illness; occurrence of any illness suffered by a human being or living thing

【病魔】bìngmó 〈比喻 *fig.*〉疾病(多指长期重病 oft. chronic disease) demon of disease — serious illness:～缠身 be possessed by the demon of disease — be afflicted with a lingering disease|战胜～recover from a troublesome disease; recover one's health

【病情】bìngqíng 疾病变化的情况 state of an illness; patient's condition:～好转。The patient's condition has taken a turn for the better. *or* The patient's condition is improving.|～恶化。The patient's condition is worsening or deteriorating.

【病人】bìngrén 生病的人;受治疗的人 sick person; invalid; person receiving medical treatment

【病容】bìngróng 有病的气色 sickly look:面带～ look ill; look unwell

【病入膏肓】bìng rù gāo huāng 病到了无法医治的地步 the disease has attacked the vitals — is beyond cure;〈比喻 *fig.*〉事情严重到了不可挽救的程度 situation is irrevocable or irretrievable;(膏肓 *gao huang*:我国古代医学上把心尖脂肪叫膏,心脏和膈膜之间叫肓,认为是药力达不到的地方 in classical Chinese medicine, the fat at the tip of the heart is called the 膏 gāo, the section between the heart and the diaphragm is called the 肓 huāng, and the place between the 膏 gāo and the 肓 huāng is considered untreatable)

【病史】bìngshǐ 患者历次所患疾病及诊疗情况 diseases contracted by patients and their treatment; medical history; case history

【病势】bìngshì 病的轻重程度 degree of seriousness of an illness; patient's condition:服药之后,～减轻。After he took some medicine the patient's condition improved slightly.

【病逝】bìngshì 因病去世 die of illness

【病榻】bìngtà 病人的床铺 sickbed:缠绵～be bedridden; be confined to a sickbed

【病态】bìngtài 心理或生理上不正常的状态 morbid or abnormal mental or physiological state; pathogenesis:～心理 morbid psychology or mentality|这不是正常的胖,而是一种～。His obesity is not normal; it indicates pathogeny. ◇社会～ social pathogenesis

【病体】bìngtǐ 患病的身体 sick body

【病痛】bìngtòng 指人所患的疾病(多指小病) minor illness; indisposition; ailment

【病退】bìngtuì 因病退职 retire for health reasons; resign from office on account of ill health:办～手续 complete the formalities required to retire on account of health reasons

【病危】bìngwēi 病势危险 be critically ill; be terminally ill:医院已经下了～通知。The hospital has issued a critical condition notice about this patient.

【病象】bìngxiàng 疾病表现出来的现象,如发烧、呕吐、咳嗽等 symptom of a disease such as fever, vomiting and coughing

【病休】bìngxiū 因病休息 be on sick leave:～一周 be on a week's sick leave

【病秧子】bìngyāng·zi 〈方 *dial.*〉多病的人 person who is chronically ill; chronic invalid; valetudinarian

【病疫】bìngyì 指流行性传染病;疫病 epidemic contagious disease

【病因】bìngyīn 发生疾病的原因 cause of disease; pathogeny:～尚未查明。The cause of the disease has yet to be determined.

【病友】bìngyǒu 称跟自己同时住在一个医院的病人 wardmate; patient who is in the same ward of a hospital at the same time as one

【病员】bìngyuán 部队、机关、团体中称生病的人员 sick personnel in military units, government offices or organizations; person on the sick list; patient

【病原】bìngyuán same as 病因 bìngyīn

【病原虫】bìngyuánchóng 寄生在人体内能引起疾病的原生动物,如疟原虫等 protozoon; animal of the phylum Protozoa that parasitizes a human body and causes disease, such as the malarial parasite; also 原虫 yuánchóng

【病原体】bìngyuántǐ 能引起疾病的细菌、霉菌、病原虫、病毒等的统称 pathogen; disease-producing organism such as germs, mould, protozoon and virus

【病源】bìngyuán 发生疾病的根源 cause of a disease

【病院】bìngyuàn 专治某种疾病的医院 hospital specializing in certain diseases; specialized hospital:精神～mental hospital|传染～infectious diseases hospital

【病灶】bìngzào 机体上发生病变的部分。如肺的某一部分被结核菌破坏,这部分就是肺结核病灶。focus (of infection) part of the body affected by disease; For example, if a part of the lungs is affected by the tubercle bacillus, there is a tuberculous focus in the lungs.

【病征】bìngzhēng 表现在身体外面的显示出是什么病的征象 symptom of a disease

【病症】bìngzhèng 病 disease; illness:专治疑难～specific treatment for difficult and complicated cases of illness

摒 bìng 排除 get rid of; brush aside; dismiss:～之于外 get rid of; brush aside; dismiss

【摒除】bìngchú 排除;除去 get rid of; renounce:～杂念 renounce selfish considerations

【摒挡】bìngdàng 〈书 *fml.*〉料理;收拾 arrange; put in order; get ready:～行李 get one's luggage ready|～婚事 arrange a wedding|～一切 put everything in order

【摒绝】bìngjué 排除 get rid of; dismiss; brush aside:～妄念 dismiss distracting thoughts; rid one's mind of all illusions|～一切应酬 stop or cut out all social engagements

【摒弃】bìng qì 舍弃 discard; reject; throw away; abandon:～杂务,专心学习 get rid of sundry duties to concentrate on one's studies

bō(ㄅㄛ)

拨(撥) bō ❶ 手脚或棍棒等横着用力,使东西移动 move or adjust with hand, foot, stick, etc.:～门 move the door bolt to open the door|～船 move the boat◇～开云雾 part the clouds and mist ❷ 分出一部分发给;调配 set aside; assign; allocate:～粮 allocate food|～款 allocate funds|～两个人到锻工车间工作 assign two people for work in the foundry ❸ 掉转 turn round:～头便往回走 turn round and go back ❹ (～儿 bōr)〈量词 *classifier*〉用于成批的人或物(for people) group; batch:工人们分成两～儿干活。The workers work in two groups.|大家轮～儿休息。We took it in turns to rest.

【拨发】bōfā 分出一部分发给 set aside for delivery:所需经费由上级统一～。The funds will come from higher authorities.

【拨付】bōfù 调拨并发给(款项) appropriate (a sum of money):～经费 appropriate funds

【拨号】bō//hào 按照要通话的电话号码,拨动拨号盘中的数字 dial; press the numbers on the dial of a telephone in order to call another number

【拨款】bō//kuǎn (政府或上级)拨给款项(of the government or higher authorities) allocate funds; appropriate money:拨了一笔款 appropriate a sum of money|～10 万元 allocate 100,000 yuan

【拨款】bōkuǎn 政府或上级拨给的款项 funds allocated by the government or higher authorities; appropriation:军事～military appropriation|预算的支出部分是国家的～。Budgetary expenditure is financed by government appropriations.

【拨拉】bō·la same as 拨 bō①:～算盘子儿 move the beads on an abacus

【拨浪鼓】bō·langgǔ (～儿 bō·langgǔr)玩具,带把儿的小鼓,来回转动时,两旁系在短绳上的鼓槌击鼓作声 drum-shaped rattle; rattle-drum; toy drum with a handle which when turned makes drumsticks affixed to the two sides of the drum beat it rapidly; also 波浪鼓 bō·langgǔ

【拨乱反正】bō luàn fǎn zhèng 治理混乱的局面,使恢复正常 bring order out of chaos; set to rights what has been thrown into disorder; restore things to order

【拨弄】bō·nong ❶ 用手脚或棍棒等来回地拨动 fiddle with; move to and fro with the hand, the foot, a stick, etc.:～琴弦 pluck the strings of a fiddle|他用小棍儿～火盆里的炭。He poked the charcoal in the brazier. ❷ 摆布 order about; manipulate:他想～人,办不到!If he thinks he can order other people about, he's wrong. ❸ 挑拨 stir up:～是非 stir things up

【拨冗】bōrǒng 〈客套话 *pol.*〉推开繁忙的事务,抽出时间 find time in the midst of pressing affairs:务希～出席。Your presence is cordially requested.

【拨云见日】bō yún jiàn rì 拨开乌云,看见太阳 dispel the clouds and see the sun;〈比喻 *fig.*〉冲破黑暗,见到光明 break away from darkness and see the light

【拨子】bō·zi ❶ 一种用金属、木头、象牙或塑料等制成的薄片,用以弹奏月琴、曼德琳等弦乐器 plectrum; pick; small piece of metal, wood, ivory, plastic, etc. for plucking the strings of a lyre, mandolin or other stringed instruments ❷ 高拨子的简称 abbr. for 高拨子 gāobō·zi ❸〈量词 *classifier*〉same as 拨 bō ④:刚才有一～队伍从这里过去了。A group of soldiers passed by just now.

波 bō ❶ 波浪 wave:～纹 ripple|随～逐流 drift with the tide or current ❷ 振动在介

质中的传播过程。波是振动形式的传播，介质质点本身并不随波前进。最常见的有机械波和电磁波。wave, the spread of vibration within medium. The wave is the spread of the vibration itself, whereas the medium particle does not move with the wave. The most common waves are mechanical and electromagnetic waves. also 波动 bōdòng ❸〈比喻 *fig.*〉事情的意外变化 unexpected turn of events：风～unexpected turn of events | 一～未平，一～又起。Hardly has one upheaval subsided when another occurs.

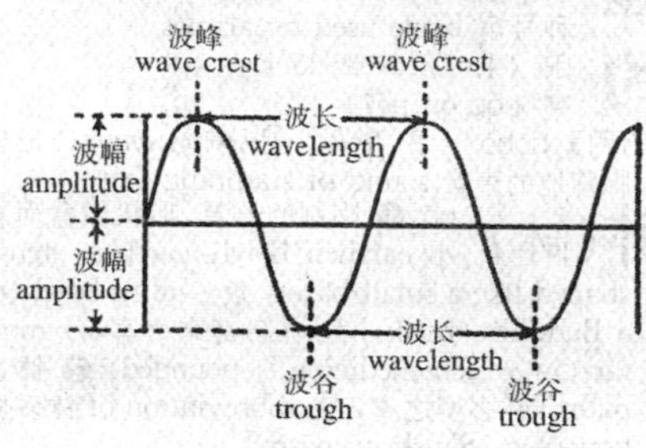

波 Wave

【波长】bōcháng 沿着波的传播方向，相邻的两个波峰或两个波谷之间的距离，即波在一个振动周期内传播的距离 wavelength; distance, measured in the direction of propagation of a wave, between two successive points in the wave that are characterised by the same phase of oscillation;（图见☞ figure for 波 bō）

【波荡】bōdàng 起落不定 rise and fall gently; drift; wave; flutter; heave; surge; same as 飘荡 piāodàng ①：海水～。The sea surges. | 悠扬的歌声在空中～。Melodious singing could be heard.

【波动】bōdòng ❶ 起伏不定；不稳定 undulate; fluctuate：情绪～in an anxious state of mind | 物价～price fluctuation ❷ same as 波 bō②

【波段】bōduàn 无线电广播中，把无线电波按波长不同而分成的段，有长波、中波、短波等 wave band; bands on a radio of different wave lengths, including long wave, medium wave and short wave

【波尔卡】bō'ěrkǎ 一种舞蹈，起源于捷克民族，是排成行列的双人舞，舞曲为 2/4 拍 polka（捷 Czech）; dance of Czech origin, a duet danced to music in two-quarter time

【波峰】bōfēng 在一周期内横波在横坐标轴以上的最高部分 wave crest; highest part of the axis of the transverse wave over the abscissa within a period;（图见☞ figure for 波 bō）

【波幅】bōfú 在横波中，从波峰或波谷到横坐标轴的距离 amplitude; distance between the wave crest or trough to the axis of the abscissa in a transverse wave;（图见☞ figure for 波 bō）

【波谷】bōgǔ 在一周期内横波在横坐标轴以下的最低部分 trough; highest part of the axis of the transverse wave over the abscissa within a period;（图见☞ figure for 波 bō）

【波及】bōjí 牵涉到；影响到 spread to; involve; affect：水灾～南方数省。The flood affected some southern provinces. | 事件～整个世界。The event affected the entire world. | 他怕此事～自身。He is afraid that the matter will affect him.

【波澜】bōlán 波涛，多用于比喻 great wave; billow (oft. used in a figurative sense)：～壮阔 surging forward with great momentum; unfolding on a magnificent scale | 激起感情的～stir up billows of emotion

【波澜壮阔】bōlán zhuàngkuò〈比喻 *fig.*〉声势雄壮浩大（多用于诗文、群众运动等 mostly of poems, mass movements, etc.）surging forward with great momentum; unfolding on a magnificent scale

【波浪】bōlàng 江湖海洋上起伏不平的水面 wave; disturbance on the surface of a river, lake or the sea：～起伏 waves rising and falling | ～翻滚 seething rolling waves

【波浪鼓】bō·langgǔ same as 拨浪鼓 bō·langgǔ

【波棱盖】bō·lenggài〈方 *dial.*〉（～儿 bō·lenggàir）膝盖 knee

【波罗密】[1] bōluómì〈佛教用语 *Budd.*〉指到彼岸。也译作波罗蜜多。arrival on the other shore; also transliterated as 波罗密多 bōluómìduō［梵 Sanckrit: pāramitā］

【波罗密】[2] bōluómì same as 菠萝蜜 bōluómì①

【波谱】bōpǔ 按照波长的长短依次排列而成的表 spectrum; table of waves ordered in accordance with their lengths

【波束】bōshù 指有很强的方向性的电磁波。用于雷达和微波通讯。beam; electromagnetic wave intensively focused in one direction, used in radar and microwave telecommunications

【波速】bōsù 波传播的速度，数值等于波长和频率的乘积 wave velocity, calculated by multiplying wave length by frequency

【波涛】bōtāo 大波浪 huge waves; billows：万顷～ a thousand huge waves | ～汹涌 waves surging turbulently; waves running high

【波纹】bōwén 小波浪形成的水纹 ripple, formed by little waves

【波源】bōyuán 能够维持振动的传播，并能发出波的物体或物体所在的位置 ripple source; object or an object's locations from which the spreading of vibrations can be maintained enough to generate waves

【波折】bōzhé 事情进行中所发生的曲折 twists and turns in the process of doing sth.：几经～，养殖场终于办起来了。After many twists and turns, the aquatic farm was finally set up.

【波磔】bōzhé 指汉字书法的撇捺 left-falling and right-falling strokes in Chinese calligraphy

B

玻 bō ☞ below

【玻璃】bō·li ❶ 一种质地硬而脆的透明物体。一般用石英砂、石灰石、纯碱等混合后,在高温下熔化、成型、冷却后制成。主要成分是二氧化硅、氧化钠和氧化钙。glass; hard and brittle transparent material, usu. made from quartzite, limestone and soda ash, the mixture of which is melted and shaped under high temperatures and then cooled down, its main elements being silica, sodium oxide and calcium oxide ❷ 指某些像玻璃的塑料 some glass-like plastics: ～丝 glass silk; glass fibre | 有机～ polymethyl methacrylate; plexiglass; perspex

【玻璃钢】bō·ligāng 用玻璃纤维及其织物增强的塑料,质轻而硬,不导电,机械强度高,耐腐蚀。可以代替钢材制造机器零件和汽车、船舶外壳等。glass-fibre-reinforced plastic; light and brittle plastics reinforced with glass fibre and its wool, which cannot conduct electricity, and possesses high mechanical strength and corrosion resistance; can be used as a substitute for iron and steel to manufacture machine components, hulls of vehicles and ships, etc.

【玻璃丝】bō·lisī 用玻璃、塑料或其他人工合成的物质制成的细丝,可用来制玻璃布、装饰品等 glass silk; thin thread made of glass, plastics or other synthetic materials, that can be used to make glass cloth, ornaments, etc.

【玻璃体】bō·litǐ 眼球内充满在晶状体和视网膜之间的无色透明的胶状物质,有支撑眼球内壁的作用 vitreous humour; vitreous body, of colourless, transparent jelly that fills the eyeball behind the lens, supporting the inner wall of the eyeball; (图见 ☞ figure for 眼 yǎn on p. 2209)

【玻璃纤维】bō·li xiānwéi 用熔融玻璃制成的极细的纤维,绝缘性、耐热性、抗腐蚀性好,机械强度高。用做绝缘材料和玻璃钢的原料等。glass fibre; fibreglass; extremely thin fibre made of melted glass, and possessing high insulating, heat- and corrosion-resistance and mechanical strength, used as raw material for making insulation, glass-fibre-reinforced plastics, etc.

【玻璃纸】bō·lizhǐ 透明的纸状薄膜,用纸浆经过化学处理或用塑料制成,可染成各种颜色,用于包装或装饰 cellophane; glassine, paper-like transparent film made of paper pulp through chemical treatment, or made of plastics, that can be dyed in various colours for packing or decorating

【玻璃砖】bō·lizhuān ❶ 指较厚的玻璃 thick glass ❷ 用玻璃制成的砖状建筑材料,多是空心的。坚固耐磨,能透光,隔音、隔热性能好。glass block; brick-like construction material made of glass, usu. hollow and possessing high durability, transmissibility, and sound and heat insulation capability

砵 bō ❶ 铜砵(Tóngbō),地名,在福建 Tongbo, a place name in Fujian Province ❷ same as 钵 bō

盋 bō〈书 *fml.*〉same as 钵 bō

哱 bō [哱罗](bōluó)〈古代 *arch.*〉军中的一种号角 bugle used by armies

趵 bō〈书 *fml.*〉踢 kick

☞ bào on p. 73

【趵趵】bōbō〈书 *fml.*〉〈拟声词 *onom.*〉形容脚踏地的声音 sound of stamping feet

钵(缽) bō ❶ 陶制的器具,形状像盆而较小 earthen bowl; earthen utensil shaped like a small basin: 饭～ alms bowl (of a Buddhist monk) | 乳～(研药末的器具) mortar (in which medicine is pounded) ❷ 钵盂 patra [钵多罗之省,梵 abbreviation of 钵多罗 bōduōluó, Sanskrit: pātra]

【钵头】bōtóu〈方 *dial.*〉same as 钵 bō ①

【钵盂】bōyú〈古代 *arch.*〉和尚用的饭碗,底平,口略小,形稍扁 alms bowl, used in ancient times by Buddhist monks, with a flat bottom, a small rim and a somewhat flat shape

【钵子】bō·zi〈方 *dial.*〉same as 钵 bō ①

般 bō [般若](bōrě) 智慧(佛经用语 used in Buddhist scriptures) wisdom [梵 Sanskrit: prajñā]

☞ bān on p. 47 and pán on p. 1441

饽 bō [饽饽](bō·bo)〈方 *dial.*〉❶ 糕点 pastry ❷ 馒头或其他面食,也指用杂粮面制成的块状食物 steamed bun (or bread); cake or other kinds of cooked bun-shaped wheaten foods: 棒子面儿～ maize cake | 贴～(贴饼子) baked wheat or corn pancakes

剥 bō 义同'剥'(bāo),专用于合成词或成语,如剥夺,生吞活剥 same as 剥 bāo, limited to use in compound words and idiomatic phrases, such as 剥夺 bōduó and 生吞活剥 shēng tūn huó bō

☞ bāo on p. 63

【剥夺】bōduó ❶ 用强制的方法夺去 rob sb. of sth.; take away by force: ～劳动成果 expropriate the fruits of sb.'s of labour ❷ 依照法律取消 deprive by law: ～政治权利 deprive sb. of political rights

【剥离】bōlí (组织、皮层、覆盖物等)脱落;分开 (of tissue, skin, coverings, etc.) come off; strip off; peel off: 岩石～ falling rocks | 胎盘早期～。The placenta came off prematurely.

【剥落】bōluò 一片片地脱落 come off in pieces; peel off: 门上的油漆～了。The paint on the door has peeled off.

【剥蚀】bōshí ❶ 物质表面因风化而逐渐损坏 erode; wear away; corrode; denude (of the surface of things) be gradually worn away because of weathering): 因受风雨的～，石刻的文字已经不易辨认。The inscriptions on the stone are barely legible because of erosion. ❷ 风、流水、冰川等破坏地球表面，使隆起的部分逐渐变平 (of the earth's surface) be levelled because of the erosion caused by wind, water, glacier, etc. ❸ 侵蚀 embezzle or seize bit by bit

【剥削】bōxuē 无偿地占有别人的劳动或产品，主要是凭借生产资料的私人所有权来进行的 exploit; seize or grab others' labour or products without paying compensation (usu. through private ownership of the means of production)

【剥削阶级】bōxuē jiējí 在阶级社会里占有生产资料剥削其他阶级的阶级，如奴隶主阶级、地主阶级和资产阶级 exploiting class; class of people in a class society that exploit other classes by possessing the means of production, such as the slave owner class, the landlord class, and the capitalist class or the bourgeoisie

【剥啄】bōzhuó 〈书 *fml.*〉〈拟声词 *onom.*〉形容轻轻敲门等的声音 sound of tapping gently on a door, or similar sounds

菠 bō ☞ below

【菠菜】bōcài 一年生或二年生草本植物，叶子略呈三角形，根略带红色，是普通蔬菜 spinach (*Spinacia oleracea*), annual or biennial herb with roughly triangular leaves and reddish roots, used as a common vegetable

【菠薐菜】bōléngcài 〈方 *dial.*〉菠菜 spinach

【菠萝】bōluó 凤梨 pineapple

【菠萝蜜】bōluómì ❶ 木菠萝 jack tree (*Artocarpus aeterophyllus*); jackfruit; also 波罗蜜 bōluómì ❷ 凤梨的俗称 popular name for 凤梨 fènglí

鲅(鱍) bō [鲅鲅]〈书 *fml.*〉鱼跳跃的样子 way that fish leap; splashing; flipping about

播 bō ❶ 传播；传扬 broadcast; spread: 广～ broadcast; on the air｜～音 broadcast; transmit; beam ❷ 播种 sow; seed: 条～ sow in drills｜点～ dibble seed; dibble｜夏～ summer sowing｜～了两亩地的麦子 sowed two *mu* of field with wheat ❸〈书 *fml.*〉迁移；流亡 move; remove; migrate; go into exile: ～迁 migrate; move to another place

【播发】bōfā 通过广播、电视发出 broadcast over the radio or on television: ～新闻 broadcast news

【播放】bōfàng ❶ 通过广播放送 broadcast over the radio: ～录音讲话 broadcast a taped speech ❷ 播映 show; screen; run; broadcast a TV programme: ～科教影片 screen a science and educational film｜电视台～比赛实况。The TV station is broadcasting a live telecast of the match.

【播幅】bōfú 垄沟中播种作物的宽度 width of a row of seeds sown

【播讲】bōjiǎng 通过广播、电视进行讲述或讲授 give a talk or lecture over radio or on television: ～评书 professional storytelling over the radio｜～英语 teach English on radio or television

【播弄】bō·nong ❶ 摆布 order sb. about: 人不再受命运～。People no longer take fate lying down. ❷ 挑拨 stir up; sow discord: ～是非 stir things up; stir up trouble with gossip or rumours; foment discord; pervert the truth; tell tales

【播撒】bōsǎ 撒播；撒 spread; scatter; sprinkle: ～树种 scatter seeds of trees｜～药粉 sprinkle medicinal powder

【播送】bōsòng 通过无线电或有线电向外传送 broadcast; transmit; beam; send out (broadcast) through wire or wireless communication systems: ～音乐 broadcast music｜～大风降温消息 broadcast news of a gale and drop in temperature

【播音】bō//yīn 广播电台播送节目 transmit; beam; broadcast over the radio: ～员 announcer｜今天～到此结束。That concludes today's broadcast.

【播映】bōyìng 电视台播放节目 broadcast a TV programme: ～权 authorization to broadcast; broadcast rights｜～国产故事影片 show a homemade feature film

【播种】bō//zhǒng 撒布种子 sow; seed; sow seeds: ～机 seeder; planter; sower; grain drill｜早～，早出苗。Early seeding, early sprouting.

【播种】bōzhòng 用播种(zhǒng)的方式种植 sow by seeding: ～冬小麦 plant winter wheat

皤 bō 皤冢(Bōzhǒng)，山名，在甘肃 Bozhong, name of a mountain in Gansu Province

bó (ㄅㄛˊ)

孛 bó 〈书 *fml.*〉same as 勃 bó
☞ bèi on p. 81

伯[1] bó ❶ 伯父 uncle; father's elder brother: 大～ uncle; father's eldest brother｜表～ uncle; father's male elder cousins from his father's sister's or mother's brother's or sister's families ❷ 在弟兄排行的次序里代表老大 the eldest among brothers: ～兄 eldest brother

B

伯[2] bó 封建五等爵位的第三等 earl; count; the third of the five ranks of nobility in feudal society: ～爵 earl; count

☞ bǎi on p.42

【伯伯】bó·bo 伯父 uncle; father's elder brother: 二～ second uncle | 张～ Uncle Zhang

【伯父】bófù ❶ 父亲的哥哥 uncle; father's elder brother ❷ 称呼跟父亲辈分相同而年纪较大的男子 uncle; term of address for a man of one's father's generation who is older than one's father

【伯公】bógōng 〈方 *dial.*〉❶ 伯祖 one's paternal grandfather's elder brother; great uncle ❷ 丈夫的伯父 elder brother of one's husband's father

【伯劳】bóláo 鸟,额部和头部的两旁黑色,颈部蓝灰色,背部棕红色,有黑色波状横纹。吃昆虫和小鸟。有的地区叫虎不拉(hù·bulǎ)。shrike (*Laniidae*); bird that has a black forehead, black cheeks, a bluish-grey neck and a reddish-brown back with black undulant bands, feeding on insects and small birds; also called 虎不拉 hù·bulǎ in some regions

【伯乐】Bólè 春秋时秦国人,善于相马 Bo Le, a legendary connoisseur of horses of the State of Qin, in the Spring and Autumn Period (770-476 B.C.);〈比喻 *fig.*〉善于发现和选用人才的人 good judge of talent: 各级领导要广开视野,当好～,发现和造就更多的人才。Leaders at all levels should broaden their vision and act like Bo Le to discover and foster more talents.

【伯母】bómǔ 伯父的妻子 aunt; wife of father's elder brother

【伯婆】bópó 〈方 *dial.*〉❶ 伯祖母 wife of (paternal) grandfather's elder brother; great aunt ❷ 丈夫的伯母 wife of the elder brother of one's husband's father

【伯仲】bózhòng 〈书 *fml.*〉指兄弟的次第 order of seniority among brothers;〈比喻 *fig.*〉事物不相上下 about the same: ～之间 be much the same

【伯仲叔季】bó zhòng shū jì 弟兄排行的次序,伯是老大,仲是第二,叔是第三,季是最小的 eldest, second, third and youngest of brothers; order of seniority among brothers

【伯祖】bózǔ 父亲的伯父 (paternal) grandfather's elder brother; grand-uncle (or great uncle)

【伯祖母】bózǔmǔ 父亲的伯母 wife of (paternal) grandfather's elder brother; grand-aunt (or great aunt)

驳[1](駁) bó 指出对方的意见不合事实或没有道理;说出自己的意见,否定别人的意见 refute; contradict; gainsay; point out sb.'s as contrary to facts or logic; present one's own opinion to refute another's: 批～ refute; criticize; rebut | 反～ refute; rebut; retort | ～价 counter-offer | 这种论点不值一～。This argument is not worth a response.

驳[2](駮) bó 〈书 *fml.*〉一种颜色夹杂着别种颜色;不纯净 parti-coloured; variegated; impure in colour: 斑～ parti-coloured; variegated

驳[3] bó ❶ 驳运 transport by lighter: 起～ start shipment by lighter | ～卸 unload by lighter ❷ 驳船 barge; lighter: 铁～ iron barge ❸〈方 *dial.*〉把岸或堤向外扩展 extend or widen (a bank or a dyke): 这条堤还不够宽,最好再～出去一米。This dyke is not wide enough and should be extended by one metre.

【驳岸】bó'àn 保护岸或堤使不坍塌的建筑物,多用石块筑成 low wall (usu. of stone) built along the water's edge to protect an embankment; revetment

【驳斥】bóchì 反驳错误的言论或意见 refute (a fallacy); rebut; contradict; denounce

【驳船】bóchuán 用来运货物或旅客的一种船,一般没有动力装置,由拖轮拉着或推着行驶 barge; lighter; a kind of boat, generally without a propulsion system but pulled or pushed by a towboat, for transporting passengers or goods

【驳倒】bó//dǎo 成功地否定了对方的意见 refute; outargue; demolish sb.'s argument; argue sb. down: 一句话就把他～了。He was refuted in one sentence. | 真理是驳不倒的。Truth stands up against any refutation.

【驳回】bóhuí 不允许(请求);不采纳(建议) reject (an appeal, request, proposal, etc.); turn down; overrule: ～上诉 reject an appeal | 对无理要求,一概～。Any unreasonable claim will be rejected.

【驳价】bó//jià (～儿 bó//jiàr) 驳回卖主提出的价格;还价 (of a buyer) haggle over prices; refuse to accept a seller's offer; counter-offer

【驳壳枪】bókéqiāng 手枪的一种,外有木盒,射击时可把木盒移装在枪后,作为托柄。能连续射击,射程比普通手枪远。有的地区叫盒子枪、盒子炮。Mauser pistol; a kind of pistol capable of continuous fire, with a longer range of fire than common pistols, packed in a wooden box which can be fixed at the back of the pistol as the buttstock when shooting; also called 盒子枪 hé·ziqiāng or 盒子炮 hé·zipào in some places

【驳面子】bó miàn·zi 不给情面 not spare sb.'s sensibilities; not show due respect for sb.'s feelings

【驳难】bónàn 〈书 *fml.*〉反驳责难 condemn as false or erroneous; refute and condemn: ～攻讦 rake up one's past and condemn; expose one's past misdeeds

【驳运】bóyùn 在岸与船、船与船之间用小船来往转运旅客或货物 transport passengers or

goods by barge between the shore and a ship, or between two ships

【驳杂】bózá 混杂不纯 multifarious; heterogeneous: 这篇文章又谈景物,又谈掌故,内容非常～。This article is a heterogeneous mass of scenic description and anecdotes.

帛 bó〈书 *fml.*〉丝织物的总称 general term for silk fabrics; silks: 布～ cloth and silks | 财～ wealth; riches | 玉～ jades and silks

【帛画】bóhuà 我国古代画在丝织品上的画 painting done on silk in ancient China

【帛书】bóshū 我国古代写在丝织品上的书 book copied on silk in ancient China

瓟 bó ❶〈书 *fml.*〉小瓜 small melon ❷ 古书上说的一种草 a kind of grass recorded in ancient books

泊 bó ❶ 船靠岸;停船 at anchor; moor; berth: 停～ lie at anchor | 船～港外。The ship was lying at anchor outside the harbour. ❷ 停留 stay for a time; stop over: 飘～ drift; wander aimlessly; lead a wandering life ❸〈方 *dial.*〉停放(车辆) park (vehicles): ～车 park a car

☞ pō on p.1491

【泊地】bódì 锚地 anchor ground; anchorage

【泊位】bówèi 航运上指港区内能停靠船舶的位置。能停泊一条船的位置称为一个泊位。berth (for a ship), a place in a harbour for a ship to lie at anchor

柏 bó 柏林(Bólín),德国城市名 transliteration of Berlin, capital of Germany

☞ bǎi on p. 42 and bò on p.152

勃(敦) bó〈书 *fml.*〉旺盛 vigorous; thriving; flourishing: 蓬～ vigorous; thriving; flourishing | ～发 vigorous

【勃勃】bóbó 精神旺盛或欲望强烈的样子 thriving; vigorous; exuberant; ambitious: 生气～ full of vitality | 朝气～ vigorous | 兴致～ full of zest | 野心～ overwhelmingly ambitious

【勃发】bófā〈书 *fml.*〉❶ 焕发;旺盛 thrive; prosper: 英姿～ dashing and spirited; bright and brave | 生机～ full of life ❷ 突然发生 break out: 战争～。War broke out. | ～事件 unexpected incident

【勃郎宁】bólángníng 手枪的一种,可以连续射击,因设计人美国的勃郎宁(John Moses Browning)而得名 Browning; a type of automatic pistol, named after its American designer, John Moses Browning

【勃然】bórán ❶ 兴起或旺盛的样子 vigorously; prosperously: ～而兴 spring up | ～而起 rise vigorously ❷ 因生气或惊慌等变脸色的样子 agitatedly; excitedly: ～不悦 become annoyed; irritated | ～大怒 fly into a rage; flare up

【勃豀】bóxī〈书 *fml.*〉家庭中争吵 family quarrel; tiff; squabble: 姑嫂～ tiff between the wife and her husband's sister

【勃谿】bóxī〈书 *fml.*〉same as 勃豀 bóxī

【勃兴】bóxīng〈书 *fml.*〉勃然兴起;蓬勃发展 burgeon; thrive

钹 bó 打击乐器,是两个圆铜片,中间突起成半球形,正中有孔,可以穿绸条或布片,两片合起来拍打发声 cymbals; percussion instrument consisting of two round pieces of copper with their centres swelling into half-spheres, and a hole right at the centre through which silk or cloth strips are fixed, that produces sounds by clapping

铂 bó 金属元素,符号 Pt (platinum)。银白色,质软,延展性强,化学性质稳定。用来制耐腐蚀的化学仪器等,也用做催化剂。platinum (Pt); soft silvery-white metal element that has great ductility and stable chemical properties, used to make things like corrosion-resistant chemical instruments, or as a catalytic agent; 通称 popularly known as 白金 báijīn

亳 Bó 亳州,地名,在安徽 Bozhou, name of a city in Anhui Province

浡 bó〈书 *fml.*〉振作;兴起 display vigour; cheer up

袯(襏) bó [袯襫](bóshì)〈古时 *arch.*〉指农夫穿的蓑衣之类 alpine rush, palm-bark rain cape or similar garments worn by peasants

舶 bó 航海大船 oceangoing ship: 船～ ship | 巨～ huge ship | 海～ seagoing ship

【舶来品】bóláipǐn〈旧时 *old*〉指进口的货物 imports

脖 bó (～儿 bór) ❶ 脖子 neck ❷ 器物上像脖子的部分 sth. neck-shaped: 这个瓶子～儿长。The bottle has a long neck.

【脖颈儿】bógěngr 脖子的后部 nape; back of the neck; also 脖颈子 bógěng·zi

【脖梗儿】bógěngr same as 脖颈儿 bógěngr

【脖领儿】bólǐngr〈方 *dial.*〉衣服领儿;领子 collar; also 脖领子 bólǐng·zi

【脖子】bó·zi 头和躯干相连接的部分 neck; the part of the body connecting the head and the trunk

博[1] bó ❶(量)多;丰富 rich; abundant; plentiful: 渊～ broad and profound | 地大物～ vast in territory and rich in natural resources | ～而不精 have wide but not expert knowledge; knowing a bit about everything ❷ 通晓 erudite; well-informed: ～古通今 possess a wide knowledge of things ancient and modern; erudite and informed ❸〈书 *fml.*〉大 loose; big: 宽衣～带 wearing loose garments

博[2](❷簙) bó ❶ 博取;取得 win; gain: 聊～一笑 just for your entertainment | 以～欢心 win sb.'s favour ❷ 古代的一种棋戏,后来泛指赌博 chess game in ancient times; (in a broad sense) gambling: ～徒 gambler | ～局 gambling party

【博爱】bó'ài 指对人类普遍的爱 universal fraternity (or brotherhood); universal love

【博大】bódà 宽广；丰富(多用于抽象事物 oft. of abstract things) broad; vast; extensive; erudite: ～的胸怀 broad-minded; liberal-minded | 学问～而精深 have extensive and profound knowledge

【博得】bódé 取得；得到(好感、同情等) win; gain (favour, sympathy, etc.): ～群众的信任 win the confidence of the masses | 这个电影～了观众的好评。This film was well received by the audience.

【博古】bógǔ ❶ 通晓古代的事情 conversant with things of the past: ～多识 have a sound knowledge of things of the past | ～通今 possess a wide knowledge of things ancient and modern; erudite and informed ❷ 指古器物，也指以古器物为题材的国画 ancient objects; paintings of ancient objects ❸ 仿照古器物或古代款式的 modelled after ancient objects; ancient-style: ～瓶 ancient-style bottle | ～架上摆放着古玩玉器。There are antiques and jade articles displayed on the ancient-style shelf.

【博古通今】bó gǔ tōng jīn 通晓古今的事情。形容知识渊博。possess a wide knowledge of things ancient and modern — erudite and informed

【博览】bólǎn 广泛阅览 read extensively (or widely): ～群书 be well-read

【博览会】bólǎnhuì 组织许多国家参加的大型产品展览会。有时也指一国的大型产品展览会。(international) fair; large-scale exhibition of products with the participation of many countries; (sometimes referring to) large-scale domestic product exhibition

【博洽】bóqià 〈书 *fml.*〉(学识)渊博 (of knowledge) erudite; well-informed: ～多闻 experienced and knowledgeable; erudite

【博取】bóqǔ 用言语、行动取得信任、重视等 gain; win; court (confidence, attention, etc.): ～欢心 curry favour | ～人们的同情 seek (or enlist) the people's sympathy

【博识】bóshí 学识丰富 learned; erudite: 多闻～ well-informed and learned

【博士】bóshì ❶ 学位的最高一级 doctor, the highest of the academic degrees: 文学～ Doctor of Letters; Doctor of Literature (Litt. D.) ❷〈古代 *arch.*〉指专精某种技艺的人 expert in some skill in ancient times: 茶～ doctor of tea | 酒～ doctor of wine ❸ 古代的一种传授经学的官员 court academician; official lecturing on Confucian classics in ancient times

【博闻强识】bó wén qiáng zhì 见闻广博，记忆力强 have encyclopaedic knowledge; possess wide learning and a powerful memory; also 博闻强记 bó wén qiáng jì

【博物】bówù 动物、植物、矿物、生理等学科的总称 natural science; general name for zoology, botany, mineralogy, physiology, etc.

【博物馆】bówùguǎn 搜集、保管、研究、陈列、展览有关革命、历史、文化、艺术、自然科学、技术等方面的文物或标本的机构 museum; institution dedicated to the collection, care, research, display and exhibition of cultural and historic relics or specimens concerning revolution, history, culture, art, natural science, technology, etc.

【博物院】bówùyuàn 博物馆 museum: 故宫～ Palace Museum (in Beijing)

【博学】bóxué 学问广博精深 learned; erudite: ～多才 learned and versatile

【博雅】bóyǎ 〈书 *fml.*〉渊博 learned; well-informed and refined: ～之士 scholar of profound knowledge | ～精深 learned and profound

【博引】bóyǐn 广泛地引证 quote (or cite) extensively; well documented: 旁征～ quote copiously to support one's thesis

葧 bó ☞ [荸葧] (pángbó) on p. 1446

鹁 bó ☞ below

【鹁鸽】bógē 鸽子的一种，身体上面灰黑色，颈部和胸部暗红色。可以饲养。pigeon (*Columba livia*); a kind of dove with a greyish-black body and dull red neck and chest, which can be bred domestically; also 家鸽 jiāgē

【鹁鸪】bógū 鸟，羽毛黑褐色，天要下雨或刚晴的时候，常在树上咕咕地叫 wood-pigeon (*Columba palumbus*), bird with dark brown features that often coos in the trees before rain or just after it clears; also 鹁鸪 gūgū

渤 Bó 渤海(Bóhǎi)，在山东半岛和辽东半岛之间 Bohai Sea, between the Shandong Peninsula and the Liaodong Peninsula

搏 bó ❶ 搏斗；对打 wrestle; fight; combat; struggle: 拼～ struggle hard; go all out | 肉～ fight hand to hand; hand-to-hand fight ❷ 扑上去抓 pounce on: 狮子～兔。The lion pounced on the hare. ❸ 跳动 beat; throb; pulsate: 脉～ pulse

【搏动】bódòng 有节奏地跳动(多指心脏或血脉 usu. of the heart, blood or pulse) beat rhythmically; throb; pulsate: 心脏起搏器能模拟心脏的自然～，改善病人的病情。A pacemaker can imitate the natural beating of the heart and improve a patient's condition.

【搏斗】bódòu ❶ 徒手或用刀、棒等激烈地对打 fight fiercely barehanded or with knife, club, etc.: 用刺刀跟敌人～ fight the enemy with bayonets ❷〈比喻 *fig.*〉激烈地斗争 struggle mentally: 与暴风雪～ battle with a snowstorm | 新旧思想的大～ tug-of-war between conservative and new ideas

【搏击】bójī 奋力斗争和冲击 fight vehemently; struggle: 奋力～ combat with all the strength one has; spare no effort in doing sth. | ～风浪 brave the winds and waves

【搏杀】bóshā 用武器格斗 fight with a weapon: 在同歹徒～中,受了重伤。(The man) got seriously injured in a fight with a ruffian. ◇两位棋手激烈～。The two chess players are locked in a hotly contested game.

鲌 bó 鱼类的一属,身体侧扁,嘴向上翘。生活在淡水中。Spanish mackerel (*Scomberomorus*); a kind of freshwater fish with a flat body and upward-bent mouth

☞ 鲅 bà on p. 30

馎 bó [馎饦](bótuō)〈古代 *arch.*〉一种面食 a kind of cooked wheaten food

僰 Bó 我国古代称居住在西南地区的某一少数民族 Bo people, one of ancient minority peoples who lived in southwest China

箔[1] bó ❶ 苇子或秫秸编成的帘子 screen (of reeds, sorghum stalks, etc.): 苇～ reed screen | 席～ sorghum stalk screen ❷ 蚕箔 bamboo tray for rearing silkworms; frame for silkworms

箔[2] bó ❶ 金属薄片 foil; tinsel: 金～儿 gold foil; gold-leaf | 镍～ nickel foil | 铜～ copper foil ❷ 涂上金属粉末或裱上金属薄片的纸(迷信的人在祭祀时当做纸钱焚化) paper powdered with metal or pasted with thin sheet metal; paper tinsel (burnt as offerings to the dead by the superstitious): 锡～ tin foil | 金银～ gold and silver foil

【箔材】bócái 铝箔、锡箔一类的材料,用做电工材料,也用于商品包装等 materials like aluminium foil and tin foil, used for electrical purposes, packaging for goods, etc.

魄 bó ☞ 落魄 luòbó on p. 1283

☞ pò on p. 1496 and tuò on p. 1963

膊 bó 胳膊 arm: 赤～ barebacked; bare to the waist

踣 bó〈书 *fml.*〉跌倒 fall; tumble

镈 bó ❶〈古代 *arch.*〉乐器,大钟 large bell used as a musical instrument in ancient times ❷〈古代 *arch.*〉锄一类的农具 hoe-like tool

薄[1] bó ❶ 轻微;少 slight; meagre; small: ～技 my slight skill | 广种～收 extensive cultivation | 这份礼太～。This present is too small. ❷ 不强健;不壮实 weak and unhealthy; frail: ～弱 weak; frail; vulnerable | 单～ thin and weak; frail ❸ 不厚道;不庄重 ungenerous; unkind; mean; harsh: ～待 treat sb. ungenerously | 刻～ unkind; harsh; mean | 轻～ frivolous; given to philandering ❹ 看不起;轻视;慢待 despise; belittle; look down on: 菲～ despise; belittle | 鄙～ despise; scorn | 厚今～古 stress the present rather than the past ❺ (Bó) 姓 a surname

薄[2] bó〈书 *fml.*〉迫近;靠近 approach; near: 日～西山。The sun is setting beyond the western hills. | ～海同欢。The whole world (or country) joins in the jubilation.

☞ báo on p. 63 and bò on p. 152

【薄产】bóchǎn〈书 *fml.*〉少量的产业 small property

【薄地】bódì 不肥沃的田地 infertile land; barren soil

【薄海】bóhǎi 指到达海边,泛指广大地区 up to the shores; vast areas: ～传诵 be widely read and admired; be eulogised everywhere | 普天同庆,～欢腾。The whole country joins in the jubilation.

【薄厚】bóhòu same as 厚薄 hòubó

【薄技】bójì 微小的技能,常用来谦称自己的技艺 (hum.) my limited skill: ～在身。I have very limited skill. | 愿献～。I'm ready to present my limited skill.

【薄酒】bójiǔ 味淡的酒,常用作待客时谦辞 (hum.) light wine (usu. used when treating guests): ～一杯,不成敬意。It's my pleasure to present this cup of light wine to you. | 略备～,为先生洗尘。I'm honoured to prepare this small dinner to welcome you.

【薄礼】bólǐ 不丰厚的礼物,多用来谦称自己送的礼物 (hum.) my small (or unworthy) gift: 些许～,敬请笑纳。Please accept my small present.

【薄利】bólì 微薄的利润 small profits: ～多销 small profits but quick turnover

【薄面】bómiàn 为人求情时谦称自己的情面 (hum.) for my sake: 看在我的～上,原谅他这一次。Forgive him this time for my sake.

【薄命】bómìng 指命运不好,福分不大(迷信,多用于妇女 superstitious term, usu. of women) born under an unlucky star; born unlucky: 红颜～ an ill-fated beauty

【薄暮】bómù 傍晚 dusk; twilight; nightfall: ～时分 at dusk; at nightfall

【薄情】bóqíng 不念情义;背弃情义(多用于男女爱情 oft. concerning love affairs) inconstant (unfaithful) in love; fickle; heartless

【薄弱】bóruò 容易挫折、破坏或动摇;不雄厚;不坚强 weak; frail; vulnerable to setbacks, damages; lacking in: 兵力～ lacking in military strength | 意志～ weak-willed | 能力～ lacking in ability | 加强工作中的～环节 work to improve weak points in one's work

【薄田】bótián same as 薄地 bódì

【薄物细故】bó wù xì gù〈书 *fml.*〉微小的事情 trifles; trivialities; trivia: ～,不足计较。Don't fuss over trifles.

【薄幸】bóxìng〈书 *fml.*〉薄情;负心 fickle;

heartless; inconstant in love

【薄葬】bózàng 从简办理丧葬 handle a funeral based on the principle of thrift: 提倡厚养～ advocate great care when one's parents are alive, and thrifty funerals after their death

馞 bó ☞［馝馞］(bìbó) on p.109

髆 bó〈书 *fml.*〉肩 shoulder

欂 bó［欂栌］bólú〈古代 *arch.*〉指斗拱(dǒugǒng) bracket on top of columns supporting the beams inside and the roof eaves outside

襮 bó〈书 *fml.*〉❶ 表露 expose: 表～(暴露) expose ❷ 外表 appearance

礴 bó ☞［磅礴］(pángbó) on p.1446

bǒ (ㄅㄛˇ)

尳 bǒ〈书 *fml.*〉same as 跛 bǒ

跛 bǒ 腿或脚有毛病,走起路来身体不平衡 lame; limp; walk unbalanced because of illness in one's leg or foot: ～脚 lame｜～行 walk with a limp; limp along

【跛鳖千里】bǒ biē qiān lǐ《荀子·修身》:'故跬步而不休,跛鳖千里'(跬步:半步)。意思是跛脚的鳖不停地走,也能走千里地,比喻只要努力不懈,即使条件很差,也能取得成就。*Xunzi·Self-Cultivation*: 'A lame tortoise can walk a thousand *li* as long as it keeps at it.'(fig.) success can be achieved against all odds through steady, continuous effort.

【跛脚】bǒjiǎo 因患病或受伤走路时身体不平衡的脚 foot that cannot walk steadily due to illness or injury

【跛子】bǒ·zi 跛脚的人;瘸子 lame person; cripple

簸 bǒ ❶ 把粮食等放在簸箕里上下颠动,扬去糠秕等杂物 winnow using a fan; fan: ～谷 winnow away the chaff; fan the chaff｜～扬 fan ❷ 泛指上下颠动 (in a broad sense) toss up and down: ～荡 roll; rock｜～动 roll; rock

☞ bò on p.152

【簸荡】bǒdàng 颠簸摇荡 roll; rock: 风大浪高,船身～得非常厉害。The ship was rolling heavily because of the huge waves and strong wind.

【簸动】bǒdòng 颠簸;上下摇动 roll; rock; jolt; bump; toss: 用簸(bò)箕～粮食,扬去糠秕 blow away particles of chaff by throwing grain into the air with a winnowing basket

【簸箩】bǒ·luo 笸箩 (pǒ·luo) wicker basket

【簸弄】bǒ·nong ❶ 摆弄 toy with; fiddle with ❷ 挑拨 instigate; incite; sow discord; foment discord: ～是非 foment discord

bò (ㄅㄛˋ)

柏 bò ☞ 黄柏 huángbò on p.851
☞ bǎi on p.42 and bó on p.149

薄 bò［薄荷］(bò·he) 多年生草本植物,茎有四棱,叶子对生,花淡紫色,茎和叶子有清凉的香味,可以入药,提炼出来的芳香化合物可加在糖果、饮料里 mint (*Mentha*); perennial herb with a four-edged stem, opposite leaves and small purplish flowers, both its refreshingly fragrant stems and leaves used as medicine, or processed to be used as essence in candy and beverages

☞ báo on p.63 and bó on p.151

檗(蘗) bò ☞ 黄檗 huángbò on p.851

擘 bò〈书 *fml.*〉大拇指 thumb: 巨～ giant among equals; authority in a certain field

☞ 掰 bāi on p.32

【擘画】bòhuà〈书 *fml.*〉筹划;布置 plan; arrange: ～经营 management plan｜机构新立,一切均待～。The institution has just been set up, and everything is yet to be arranged. also 擘划 bòhuà

簸 bò 义同'簸'(bǒ),只用于'簸箕' meaning the same as 簸 bǒ, only used in 簸箕 bò·ji

☞ bǒ on p.152

【簸箕】bò·ji ❶ 用竹篾或柳条编成的器具,三面有边沿,一面敞口,用来簸粮食等。也有用铁皮、塑料制成的,多用来清除垃圾。winnowing basket; a utensil made of bamboo strips or wicker and sometimes iron or plastic with three rimmed edges and one open edge, used to winnow grain, etc. ❷ 簸箕形的指纹 loop (of a fingerprint)

·bo (·ㄅㄛ)

卜(蔔) ·bo ☞ 萝卜 luó·bo on p.1278
☞ bǔ on p.153

啵 ·bo〈方 *dial.*〉〈助词 *aux.*〉表示商量、提议、请求、命令等语气 indicating consultation, suggestion, request, command, etc.: 你看要得～? Do you think it's necessary? ｜你的窍门多,想个办法,行～? You always have good ideas, so why not find a way to deal with it?

bū (ㄅㄨ)

逋 bū〈书 *fml.*〉❶ 逃亡 flee: ～逃 flee; abscond; flee from justice ❷ 拖欠;拖延 owe; delay; evade: ～欠 default; be behind in payments; be in arrears; fail to pay

【逋客】būkè〈书 *fml.*〉❶ 逃亡的人 fugitive

❷ 避世隐居的人 hermit; recluse; person who withdraws from society and lives in seclusion

【逋留】būliú 〈书 *fml.*〉逗留;稽留 stay; stop; detain: ～他乡数载 stay on in a distant land for years

【逋欠】būqiàn 〈书 *fml.*〉拖欠 default; be behind in payments; be in arrears: ～税粮 fail to pay tax and grain

【逋峭】būqiào 〈书 *fml.*〉same as 峬峭 būqiào

【逋逃】būtáo 〈书 *fml.*〉❶ 逃亡;逃窜 flee; abscond ❷ 逃亡的罪人;流亡的人 fugitive

【逋逃薮】būtáosǒu 〈书 *fml.*〉逃亡的人躲藏的地方 refuge for a fugitive

峬 bū [峬峭] (būqiào) 〈书 *fml.*〉(风姿、文笔)优美 (of bearing or writing) graceful; fine; also 庯峭 būqiào or 逋峭 būqiào

庯 bū [庯峭] (būqiào) 〈书 *fml.*〉same as 峬峭 būqiào

晡 bū 〈书 *fml.*〉申时,即下午三点钟到五点钟的时间 the period of the day from 3 p.m. to 5 p.m.

bú (ㄅㄨˊ)

不 bú ☞ 不 bù on p.155

醭 bú (旧读 formerly pronounced pú) (～儿 búr)醋、酱油等表面生出的白色的霉 white mould (found on the surface of soy sauce, vinegar, etc.)

bǔ (ㄅㄨˇ)

卜 bǔ ❶ 占卜 divine; tell fortunes: ～卦 divine by the Eight Trigrams | ～辞 oracle inscriptions | 求签问～ draw lots and consult oracles ❷ 〈书 *fml.*〉预料 foretell; predict: 预～ foretell | 存亡未～。Survival or death remains unknown. | 胜败可～。Victory or defeat can be foretold. ❸ 〈书 *fml.*〉选择(处所) choose (a place): ～宅 choose a house | ～邻 choose a neighbourhood | ～居 choose a dwelling place ❹ (Bǔ) 姓 a surname
☞ ·bo on p.152

【卜辞】bǔcí 殷代把占卜的时间、原因、应验等刻在龟甲或兽骨上的记录 oracle inscriptions concerning the time, reasons, results, etc. of divination on tortoise shells or animal bones in the Yin Dynasty (1300-1046 B.C.); ☞ 甲骨文 jiǎgǔwén on p.932

【卜居】bǔjū 〈书 *fml.*〉选择地方居住 choose a dwelling place

【卜课】bǔ//kè 起课 divination; fortune-telling; divine; practise divination

【卜筮】bǔshì 〈古代 *arch.*〉用龟甲占卜叫卜,用蓍草占卜叫筮,合称卜筮 divination; fortune-telling; divination using tortoiseshells is called 卜 bǔ, and using milfoil 筮 shì

叶 bǔ [叶吩] (bǔfēn)有机化合物,是叶绿素、血红蛋白等的重要组成部分 porphine; organic compound that is an important part of chlorophyll, haemoglobin, etc.

补(補) bǔ ❶ 添上材料,修理破损的东西;修补 mend; patch; repair: 缝～ mend by sewing | ～牙 fill a tooth | ～袜子 darn socks | 修桥～路 build bridges and repair roads ❷ 补充;补足;填补(缺额) fill (a vacancy); supply; make up for: 弥～ make up; remedy | 增～ augment; supplement | ～选 augment | 候～ be an alternate | 缺什么～什么 supply what is needed ❸ 补养 nourish; enrich; tonify: 滋～ nourish | ～品 tonic | ～脑 nourish the brain ❹ 〈书 *fml.*〉利益;用处 benefit; use; help: ～益 benefit; help | 不无小～ not be without some benefit; be of some help | 空言无～。A mere verbal statement is of no help.

【补白】bǔbái ❶ 报刊上填补空白的短文 filler; short articles to fill up the blank spaces in a newspaper or magazine ❷ 补充说明 additional remarks: 此事还有一点尚未谈及,想借贵报一角～几句。I've omitted something in discussing this matter, and I want to explain it on your newspaper.

【补办】bǔbàn 事后办理(本应事先办理的手续、证件等) go through (formalities, accreditation, etc.) after the event; make up for: ～住院手续 complete missing hospitalization procedures

【补报】bǔbào ❶ 事后报告;补充报告 make a report after the event; make a supplementary report: 调查结果将于近日～。Findings will be reported soon. ❷ 报答(恩德) repay (a kindness or a favour)

【补差】bǔchā 补足原工资和退休金之间的差额(用于退休人员继续工作时 when retired people continue to work) make up the balance between original salary and retirement pension

【补偿】bǔcháng 抵消(损失、消耗);补足(缺欠、差额) compensate; offset; make up: ～损失 compensate sb. for a loss

【补偿贸易】bǔcháng màoyì 国际贸易的一种方式,买方不以现汇支付,而以产品或加工劳务分期偿付进口设备、技术、专利等费用 compensation trade; form of international trade whereby the buyer pays in stages for the equipment, technology and patent he has imported with products or processing services, instead of cash

【补充】bǔchōng ❶ 原来不足或有损失时,增加一部分 replenish; supplement; complement; add: ～兵员 replenish (an army unit) to full strength; replace losses | ～枪支弹药 replenish firearms and ammunition | 对他的发言,我再做

两点～。I have two points to add to his speech. ❷ 在主要事物之外追加一些 additional; complementary; supplementary: ～任务 additional tasks | ～教材 supplementary teaching materials

B

【补丁】bǔ·ding 补在破损的衣服或其他物品上面的东西 patch; piece of material placed over a damaged or worn area on clothes or other things: 打～ put a patch on; patch up | ～摞～ covered with patches; also 补钉 bǔ·ding and 补靪 bǔ·ding

【补过】bǔ//guò 弥补过失 make amends for one's faults: 将功～ make amends for one's faults by good deeds

【补花】bǔhuā (～儿 bǔhuār)手工艺的一种，把彩色布片或丝绒缝在枕套、桌布、童装等上面，构成花鸟等图案 appliqué, a type of handicraft of sewing colourful pieces of cloth or velvet on pillowcases, tablecloths, children's wear, etc. to form patterns of flowers and birds, etc.

【补给】bǔjǐ 补充、供给弹药和粮草等 supply; replenish (ammunition, army provisions, etc.); provision; recharge: 前线急需及时～。The front is in urgent need of timely supplies.

【补给线】bǔjǐxiàn 军队作战时，输送物资器材的各种交通线的总称 supply line; general term for all transportation routes for moving goods, materials and equipment

【补假】bǔ//jià ❶ 职工应休假而未休假，事后补给假日 lieu time; days off for having worked overtime; take deferred holidays ❷ 补办请假手续 carry out procedures for leave retroactively

【补救】bǔjiù 采取行动矫正差错，扭转不利形势；设法使缺点不发生影响 remedy; take action to correct errors or mistakes, and to reverse unfavourable situations; manage to prevent defects from having an effect

【补苴】bǔjū 〈书 *fml.*〉❶ 缝补；补缀 sew; mend (by sewing) ❷ 弥补(缺陷) make up for (deficiencies): ～罅漏 make up for deficiencies

【补苴罅漏】bǔjū xiàlòu 指弥补文章、理论等的缺漏，也泛指弥补事物的缺陷 plug the loopholes in an article or theory; make up for deficiencies

【补考】bǔkǎo 因故未参加考试或考试不及格的人另行考试 make-up examination; remedial examination held for those who have missed an earlier examination for various reasons or those who had failed

【补课】bǔ//kè ❶ 补学或补教所缺的功课 make up a missed lesson: 老师放弃休息给同学～。The teacher gave up his time for a rest to help his pupils make up for the lessons they had missed. ❷〈比喻 *fig.*〉某种工作做得不完善而重做 do sth. badly done over again

【补漏】bǔlòu ❶ 修补物体上的漏洞 mend leaks or holes in objects: 船至江心～迟。It is too late to plug the leak when the boat is midstream. | 雨季临近，房屋～工作应该抓紧。The rainy season is coming, and the houses should be repaired soon. ❷ 弥补工作中的疏漏 make up the gaps, oversights and omissions in one's work: ～纠偏 make up for oversights and omissions, and rectify deviations

【补苗】bǔ//miáo 农作物幼苗出土后，发现有缺苗断垄现象时，用移苗或补种的方法把苗补全 fill in the gaps where seeds have failed to sprout

【补偏救弊】bǔ piān jiù bì 补救偏差疏漏，纠正缺点错误 remedy defects and rectify errors; rectify a deviation and correct an error

【补票】bǔ//piào 补买车票、船票等 buy one's ticket for the train or ship, etc. after the normal time

【补品】bǔpǐn 滋补身体的食品或药品 tonic; nourishing food or tonics

【补情】bǔqíng (～儿 bǔqíngr)报答情谊 repay a kindness

【补缺】bǔ//quē ❶ 填补缺额 fill a vacancy ❷ 弥补缺漏的部分 make up for a deficiency: ～堵漏 make up for deficiencies and gaps ❸〈旧时 *old*〉指候补的官吏得到实职 in ancient times, (of an alternate officer) get the actual post

【补色】bǔsè 两种色光以适当的比例混合而使人产生白色感觉时，这两种色光的颜色就互为补色 complementary colour; a term for the two colours that, when mixed in a proper proportion, give the impression of white; also 余色 yúsè

【补体】bǔtǐ 血清中能协助抗体杀灭病菌的化学物质 complement (in blood serum); chemical substance capable of helping antibodies kill bacteria or germs

【补贴】bǔtiē ❶ 贴补 subsidise; help (out) financially: ～家用 help out with the family expenses | ～粮价 subsidised grain price ❷ 贴补的费用 subsidy; allowance: 福利～ welfare subsidy | 副食～ non-staple food allowance

【补习】bǔxí 为了补足某种知识，在业余或课外学习 take lessons after school or work in order to catch up on certain kinds of knowledge; take a make-up course: ～学校 continuing-education school | ～外语 take foreign language lessons after school or work

【补血】bǔ//xuè 使红细胞或血色素增加 build or enrich the red blood cell or haemochrome: ～药 blood-building drug; antanemic; hematonic; hematicum; blood-tonifying drug

【补养】bǔyǎng 用饮食或药物来滋养身体 take

a tonic or nourishing food to build up one's health：大病刚好，还需要精心～。Nourishment, along with the best of care, is still needed after a critical illness.

【补药】bǔyào 滋补身体的药物 tonic; health-building drug

【补液】bǔyè ❶ 把生理盐水等输入患者静脉，以补充体液的不足（med.）fluid infusion; infusing saline, etc. into a patient's veins to meet the shortage of body fluids ❷ 有滋补作用的饮料 nourishing beverages or drinks：营养～ nourishing drinks

【补遗】bǔyí 书籍正文有遗漏，加以增补，附在后面，叫做补遗。前人的著作有遗漏，后人搜集材料加以补充，也叫补遗。addendum; supplement; parts attached to the end of a book that were omitted in the main body; new materials to supplement omissions in the works of predecessors

【补益】bǔyì〈书 *fml.*〉❶ 益处 benefit; help：大有～ be of great help (or benefit) ❷ 产生益处；使获得益处 bring about benefit; be of help (or benefit)：～国家 be of benefit to the country

【补语】bǔyǔ 动词或形容词后边的一种补充成分，用来回答'怎么样？'之类的问题，如'听懂了'的'懂'，'好得很'的'很'，'拿出来'的'出来'，'走一趟'的'一趟' complement; sentence element following a verb or adjective, as an additional remark to answer questions beginning with 'how', e. g. '懂 dǒng' in the phrase '听懂了 tīng dǒng·le', '很 hěn' in '好得很 hǎo·dehěn', '出来·chū//·lái' in '拿出来 ná·chū//·lái' and '一趟 yītàng' in '走一趟 zǒu yītàng'

【补正】bǔzhèng 补充和改正（文字的疏漏和错误）erratum (errata); supplements and corrections; supplement and correct omissions and errors in an article

【补助】bǔzhù 从经济上帮助（多指组织上对个人 oft. from an organization to an individual) help financially; subsidise; subsidy：～费 subsidy; allowance｜实物～ subsidy in kind

【补缀】bǔzhuì 修补（多指衣服 oft. clothes）mend; patch

【补足】bǔ//zú 补充使足数 bring up to full strength; make up a deficiency; fill (a vacancy, gap, etc.)：～缺额 fill all the vacancies

捕 bǔ 捉；逮 catch; seize; arrest：～鱼 catch fish｜～猎 hunt｜～捉 catch; seize｜追～ chase; pursue and capture

【捕风捉影】bǔ fēng zhuō yǐng〈比喻 *fig.*〉说话或做事时用似是而非的迹象做根据 speak or act on hearsay

【捕获】bǔhuò 捉到；逮住 catch; capture; seize：～猎物 capture｜罪犯已被～归案。The criminal has been arrested.

【捕捞】bǔlāo 捕捉和打捞（水生动植物）fish for (aquatic animals or plants); catch：近海～ inshore fishing｜～鱼虾 catch fish and prawns

【捕猎】bǔliè 捕捉（野生动物）；猎取 catch (wild animals); hunt：禁止～珍稀动物。Hunting endangered species is forbidden.

【捕杀】bǔshā 捕捉并杀死 catch and kill：～害虫 catch and kill pests

【捕食】bǔ//shí （动物）捕取食物 (of an animal) hunt for food; prey on; feed on

【捕食】bǔshí （动物）捉住别的动物并且把它吃掉 (of an animal) hunt and eat (another animal); prey on：青蛙～昆虫。Frogs feed on insects.

【捕捉】bǔzhuō same as 捉 zhuō ②：～野兽 hunt wild animals｜～逃犯 pursue a fugitive ◇～战机 seize the opportunity for battle; seize the right moment to strike

哺 bǔ ❶ 喂（不会取食的幼儿）feed (a baby)：～育 nurse; nurse｜～乳 breast-feed; suckle; nurse ❷〈书 *fml.*〉咀嚼着的食物 food being chewed in one's mouth：一饭三吐～。Each mouthful of food should be chewed three times.

【哺乳】bǔrǔ 用乳汁喂；喂奶 breast-feed; suckle; nurse：～期 lactation period

【哺乳动物】bǔrǔ dòngwù 最高等的脊椎动物，基本特点是靠母体的乳腺分泌乳汁哺育初生幼体。除最低等的单孔类是卵生的以外，其他哺乳动物全是胎生的。mammal; vertebrate of the highest class that feeds its young with milk from the female mammary glands, and brings forth living young rather than eggs, with the exception of the monotremes

【哺养】bǔyǎng 喂养 feed; rear

【哺育】bǔyù ❶ 喂养 feed：～婴儿 feed a baby ❷〈比喻 *fig.*〉培养 nurture; foster：学生在老师的～下茁壮成长。Under the care of their teachers, the students are growing up strong and healthy.

鸔 bǔ ☞ 地鸔 dìbǔ on p. 419

堡 bǔ 堡子（多用于地名 oft. used as part of a place name）town; village：吴～（在陕西）Wubu, in Shaanxi Provincc｜柴沟～（在河北）Chaigoubu, name of a place in Hebei Province

☞ bǎo on p. 69 and pù on p. 1503

【堡子】bǔ·zi ❶ 围有土墙的城镇或乡村 town or village surrounded with earthen walls ❷ 泛指村庄 (in a broad sense) village

bù（ㄅㄨˋ）

不 bù〈副词 *adv.*〉❶ 用在动词、形容词和其他副词前面表示否定［used before verbs,

adjectives, and other adverbs to indicate negation]：～去 not go | ～能 cannot | ～多 not many (much) | ～经济 uneconomic | ～很好 not very good (well) ❷ 加在名词或名词性词素前面，构成形容词 [used before certain nouns or nominal morphemes to form an adjective]：～法 lawless; illegal; unlawful | ～规则 irregular ❸ 单用，做否定性的回答(答话的意思跟问题相反) [used by itself as a negative answer]：他知道吗？——～，他不知道。Does he know? No, he doesn't. ❹〈方 *dial.*〉用在句末表示疑问，跟反复问句的作用相等 [attached to the end of a sentence to indicate doubt or question]：他现在身体好～？Is he in good health now? ❺ 用在动补结构中间，表示不可能达到某种结果 [used between a verb and its complement to indicate that sth. is impossible]：拿～动 find sth. too heavy to carry | 做～好 cannot do sth. well | 装～下 cannot hold sth. ❻ '不'字的前后叠用相同的词，表示不在乎或不相干(常在前边加'什么' usu. preceded by 什么 shén·me) [inserted between repeated words to show one's carelessness or indifference]：什么累～累的，有工作就得做。No matter how tired you are, you must do what comes to you. | 什么钱～钱的，你喜欢就拿去。Who cares how much it costs? Just get it if you like it. ❼ 跟'就'搭用，表示选择 [used correlatively with 就 jiù to indicate alteration]：晚上他～是看书，就是写文章。In the evening if he is not reading a book, then he is writing an article. ❽〈方 *dial.*〉不用；不要(限用于某些客套话 used in polite formulas only) don't; need not：～谢 don't mention it; not at all; you are welcome | ～送 don't bother to see me out | ～客气 don't mention it; not at all; you are welcome ‖ 注意 **NOTE**：a) 在去声字前面，'不'字读阳平声，如'～会'、'～是' said in rising tone when followed by words with falling tone, e.g. '～会' (cannot), or '～是' (not) b)动词'有'的否定式是'没有'，不是'不有' negative form of the verb '有' (have) is '没有' (have not) rather than '不有' (not have)

【不安】bù'ān ❶ 不安定；不安宁 untranquil; not peaceful; unstable; disturbed：忐忑～ restless | 坐立～ uneasy | 动荡～ in turmoil ❷〈客套话 *pol.*〉表示歉意和感激 expressing regret or thanks：总给您添麻烦，真是～。I'm sorry to trouble you so often.

【不白之冤】bù bái zhī yuān 指无法辩白或难以洗雪的冤枉 unrighted wrong; unredressed injustice; unexplainable or unrightable wrong：蒙受～ be grievously wronged

【不卑不亢】bù bēi bù kàng 既不自卑，也不高傲。形容言行自然、得体。neither haughty nor humble; neither supercilious nor obsequious; neither overbearing nor servile; (of speech or manner) natural and proper; also 不亢不卑 bù kàng bù bēi

【不比】bùbǐ 比不上；不同于 unlike; cannot compare with; no match for：虽然我们条件～他们，但我们一定能按时完成任务。Although things are not so favourable for us compared to them, we can still finish this task on time. | 海南～塞北，一年四季树木葱茏，花果飘香。Hainan Province, unlike areas north of the Great Wall, has lush trees and fragrant flowers and fruit throughout the year.

【不必】bùbì〈副词 *adv.*〉表示事理上或情理上不需要 need not; not have to：～去得太早 do not have to go there too early | 慢慢商议，～着急。Deliberate on it with patience and don't worry. | 为这点小事苦恼，我以为大可～。I don't think there is need to worry about such a trifling matter.

【不变价格】bùbiàn jiàgé 计算或比较各年工、农业产品总产值时，用某一时期的产品的平均价格作为固定的计算尺度，这种平均价格叫不变价格。如我国第一个五年计划时期，用1952年第三季度的产品平均价格为不变价格。fixed price; constant price; average price of products in a given period that serves as a fixed measure to calculate or compare gross annual industrial and agricultural output value, e.g. the average price of products in the third season of 1953 that served as the fixed price for the First Five-Year Plan period; also 比较价格 bǐjiào jiàgé，可比价格 kěbǐ-jiàgé or 固定价格 gùdìng jiàgé

【不便】bùbiàn ❶ 不方便；不适宜 inconvenient; inappropriate; unsuitable：行动～ have difficulty getting about | 边远山区，交通～。Remote mountainous areas have poor transport facilities. | 他有些不情愿，却又～马上回绝。He was somewhat unwilling to do it, but felt it inappropriate to flatly refuse. ❷ 指缺钱用 short of cash; be hard up：你如果一时手头～，我可以先垫上。If you have no money on hand now, I'll pay for you.

【不辨菽麦】bù biàn shū mài 分不清豆子和麦子；形容缺乏实际知识 unable to tell beans from wheat; have no practical knowledge

【不…不…】bù…bù… ❶ 用在意思相同或相近的词或词素的前面，表示否定(稍强调) [used before two words or expressions that are the same or similar in meaning to indicate negation (with slight stress)]：～干～净 unclean; filthy | ～明～白 obscure; dubious | ～清～楚 not clear | ～偏～倚 impartial; unbiased | ～慌～忙 unhurried; calm; leisurely | ～痛～痒 scratching the surface; superficial; perfunctory | ～知～觉 unconsciously; unwittingly | ～言～语 keep silent | ～声～响 quiet; silent |

～理～睬 ignore; take no notice of |～闻～问 not bother to ask or to listen; show no interest in sth. |～依～饶 not let (sb.) off easily |～屈～挠 unyielding; indomitable; dauntless |～折～扣 hundred per cent; to the letter; out-and-out ❷ 用在同类而意思相对的词或词素的前面,表示'既不…也不…' [used before two words or expressions of the same kind but opposite in meaning to indicate 'neither ... nor ...']: a)表示适中,恰到好处 moderate; just right: ～多～少 neither too much nor too little; just right |～大～小 neither too big nor too small; just right |～肥～瘦 neither fat nor thin b)表示尴尬的中间状态 awkward intermediate state: ～方～圆 neither square nor round |～明～暗 neither bright nor dark |～上～下 be suspended in midair; be in a fix |～死～活 neither dead nor alive; half dead; lifeless ❸ 用在同类而意思相对的词或词素的前面,表示'如果不…就不…' [used before words or expression of the same kind but opposite in meaning to indicate 'if not ... then not ...']: ～见～散 not leave without seeing each other |～破～立 no construction without destruction |～塞～流 no flowing without damming |～止～行 there is no motion without rest

【不才】bùcái 〈书 *fml.*〉没有才能;常用做'我'的谦称 without ability; I [usu. used as a humble address to call oneself]: 其中道理,～愿洗耳聆教。I'm ready to listen to your analysis of it.

【不测】bùcè 没有推测到的;意外 unexpected; unforeseen; accident; mishap; contingency: 天有～风云。A storm may arise from a clear sky — something unexpected may happen any time. |提高警惕,以防～。Sharpen vigilance, and be prepared for any contingency.

【不曾】bùcéng same as 没有[2] méi·yǒu ('曾经'的否定 negative form of 曾经 céngjīng) never (have done sth.): 我还～去过广州。I have never been to Guangzhou. |除此之外,～发现其他疑点。No questionable points were found except this.

【不差累黍】bù chā lěi shǔ 形容丝毫不差 not a whit (or an iota) of difference; accurate in every particular; without the slightest error (累黍 *lei shu*: 指微小的数量 very small amount)

【不差什么】bù chā shén·me ❶ 不缺什么 be short of nothing: 原材料已经～了,只是开工日期还没确定。Raw materials are all available, but the start date for construction is yet to be decided. ❷〈方 *dial.*〉差不多 almost; nearly: 这几个地方～我全都到过。I have been to almost all these places. ❸〈方 *dial.*〉平常;普通 ordinary; common; average: 这一袋粮食有二百斤,～的人还真扛不动。One bag of grain weighs as much as 200 *jin*, which is really hard for ordinary people to carry.

【不成】bùchéng ❶ same as 不行 bùxíng ①② ❷〈助词 *aux.*〉用在句末,表示推测或反问的语气,前面常常有'难道、莫非'等词相呼应 [attached to the end of a sentence to indicate inference or a rhetorical question, usu. preceded by 难道 nándào or 莫非 mòfēi]: 难道就这样算了～? How can we let it go like that? |他还不来,莫非家里出了什么事～? He hasn't come yet. Something wrong in his family?

【不成比例】bù chéng bǐlì 指数量或大小等方面差得很远,不能相比 (of amount, size, etc.) differing greatly and incomparable with sth. else

【不成材】bùchéngcái 不能做材料 unable to be used as material;〈比喻 *fig.*〉没出息 good-for-nothing; worthless; ne'er-do-well

【不成话】bùchénghuà ☞ 不像话 bù xiànghuà ①

【不成器】bùchéngqì 不成东西 unable to be made into anything; 〈比喻 *fig.*〉没出息 good-for-nothing; worthless; ne'er-do-well

【不成体统】bù chéng tǐtǒng 说话、做事不合体制,没有规矩 (of speech or behaviour) most improper; downright outrageous; very rude

【不成文】bùchéngwén 没有用文字固定下来的 unwritten; not fixed by unwritten language: ～的规矩 unwritten customs |多年的老传统～地沿袭了下来。Age-old traditions have been carried on.

【不成文法】bùchéngwénfǎ 不经立法程序而由国家承认其有效的法律,如判例、习惯法等(跟'成文法'相对 as opposed to 'written law') unwritten law; laws recognized as valid by a country without going through legislative procedures, e.g. case law, customary (common) law, etc.

【不逞】bùchěng 不得志 discontented; frustrated; disappointed: ～之徒(因失意而胡作非为的人) desperado; a bundle of resentment (one who behaves badly because of frustration)

【不齿】bùchǐ 〈书 *fml.*〉不愿意提到,表示鄙视 unwilling to mention; despise; hold in contempt: 人所～ held in contempt by the people

【不耻下问】bù chǐ xià wèn 不以向地位比自己低、知识比自己少的人请教为可耻 not feel ashamed to consult one's subordinates or people below

【不啻】bùchì 〈书〉❶ 不止;不只 not less than: 工程所需,～万金。The project requires a tremendous amount of money. ❷ 如同 as; like; as good as: 相去～天渊 difference tantamount to that between high heaven and deep sea; a world of difference

【不揣】bùchuǎi 〈谦辞 *hum.*〉不自量,用于向人提出自己的见解或有所请求时 overrate one's

abilities (used to put forward one's own opinion or ask for sth.); I venture to; may I take the liberty of: ～浅陋 I venture to | ～冒昧(不考虑自己的莽撞,言语、行动是否相宜) I venture to; may I take the liberty of (without considering whether one's speech or behaviour is appropriate)

B

【不辞】bùcí ❶ 不告别 without taking leave; without saying goodbye: ～而别 leave without saying goodbye ❷ 不推脱;不拒绝 not evade; not refuse: ～辛劳 spare no effort; take pains; take the trouble to; go to the trouble of doing sth.

【不错】bù cuò 对;正确 correct; right; yes: ～,情况正是如此。Yes, that's the case. | ～,当初他就是这么说的。Yes, that's what he said.

【不错】bùcuò 不坏;好 not bad; pretty good: 人家待你可真～。They treat you really well. | 虽然年纪大了,身体却还～。Old as he is, he is pretty healthy.

【不大离】bùdàlí 〈方 *dial.*〉(～儿 bùdàlír) ❶ 差不多;相近 pretty close; just about right: 两个孩子的身量～。The two children are almost of the same height. ❷ 还算不错 not bad: 这块地的麦子长得～。The wheat in this field is not bad.

【不带音】bù dàiyīn 发音时声带不振动 vocal cords having no vibration when pronouncing; ☞ 带音 dàiyīn on p.372

【不待】bùdài 用不着;不必 needless to; it goes without; unnecessary to: 自～言 needless to say; it goes without saying

【不逮】bùdài 〈方 *fml.*〉不及;不到 weakness; shortcomings: 匡其～(帮助他所做不到的) help sb. to do what he cannot do

【不单】bùdān ❶ same as 不止 bùzhǐ ②: 超额完成生产任务的,～是这几个厂。These are not the only factories that have surpassed the production target. ❷ 不但 not merely; not simply: 她～教孩子学习,还照顾他们的生活。She not only teaches her children to study, but takes care of them in daily life.

【不但】bùdàn 〈连词 *conj.*〉用在表示递进的复句的上半句里,下半句里通常有连词'而且、并且'或副词'也、还'等相呼应[used in the first half of a sentence with two or more clauses that are progressive in meaning, and usu. correlated with conjunctives like 而且 érqiě or 并且 bìngqiě, or with adverbs like 也 yě or 还 hái]: ～以身作则,而且乐于助人。He not only lives what he advocates, but also is ready to help others. | 这条生产线～在国内,即使在国际上也是一流的。This production line is advanced not only domestically but internationally. | 这样做～解决不了问题,反而会增加新的困难。This approach will only bring about new problems rather than solve the problem.

【不惮】bùdàn 不怕 not fear; not be afraid of: ～其烦(不怕麻烦) not mind taking the trouble; take great pains; be very patient

【不当】bùdàng 不合适;不恰当 unsuitable; improper; inappropriate: 处理～ not be handled properly | 用词～ inappropriate wording | ～之处,请予指正。Please point out my mistakes if there are any.

【不倒翁】bùdǎowēng 玩具,形状像老翁,上轻下重,扳倒后能自己起来 self-righting doll; tumbler; roly-poly, old-man-shaped toys that can self-right themselves because their centre of gravity is at the lower half of their body; also 扳不倒儿 bānbùdǎor

【不到黄河心不死】bù dào Huáng Hé xīn bù sǐ 〈比喻 *fig.*〉不到绝境不肯死心。也比喻不达到目的决不罢休。refuse to give up until all hope is gone; until it's all over, ambition survives; not stop until reaches one's goal

【不道德】bùdàodé 不符合道德标准的 immoral; unethical; not in line with moral standards: 随地吐痰是～的行为。It is immoral to spit everywhere.

【不得】·bu·de 用在动词后面,表示不可以或不能够[used after a verb to indicate disallowance or forbiddance] must not; may not; not be allowed: 去～ shouldn't go | 要～ be intolerable | 动弹～ cannot move | 老虎屁股摸～。No one dares to touch a tiger's backside. | 科学上来～半点虚假。No sophistry is tolerable in science.

【不得劲】bù déjìn (～儿 bù déjìnr) ❶ 不顺手;使不上劲 awkward; unhandy: 笔杆太细,我使着～。The pen is awkward because its shaft is too thin. ❷ 不舒适 indisposed; not feel well: 感冒了,浑身～。I'm not feeling too well because I've caught a cold. ❸ 〈方 *dial.*〉不好意思 feel embarrassed: 大伙儿都看着她,弄得她怪～儿的。She was embarrassed by so many guys staring at her.

【不得了】bù déliǎo ❶ 表示情况严重 (of situations) terrible; horrible; desperately serious: 哎呀,～,着火了! Oh, how awful! Fire! Fire! | 万一出了岔子,那可～。Should any accident happen, that would be terrible. ❷ 表示程度很深 (of degrees) extremely; exceedingly: 热得～ awfully hot | 她急得～,可又没办法。She is extremely anxious but of no help.

【不得已】bù déyǐ 无可奈何;不能不如此 act against one's will; have no alternative but to; have to; be forced to: 万～ out of absolute necessity | 实在～,只好亲自去一趟。I had no alternative but to go personally. | 他们这样做,是出于～。They did it that way because they had no choice.

【不等】bùděng 不一样；不齐 vary；differ：数目～ vary in quantity｜大小～ differ (or vary) in size｜水平高低～ vary in capability

【不等式】bùděngshì 表示两个数（或两个代数式）不相等的算式。两个数或两个代数式之间用不等号连接，如 5＞2，3a＜8，7m＋1≠9m＋2。(math.) inequality；mathematical formula indicating the relation between two quantities (or two algebraic expressions) that are not of equal value or magnitude，separated by a not-equal-to，less-than or greater-than sign，e.g. '5＞2'，'3a＜8' and '7m＋1≠9m＋2'

【不迭】bùdié ❶ 用在动词后面，表示急忙或来不及 [used after a verb to indicate being late or in a hurry to do sth.] cannot cope；find it too much：跑～ run quickly｜忙～ hasten (to do sth.)｜后悔～ too late for regrets ❷ 不停止 incessantly；profusely：称赞～ praise profusely｜叫苦～ complain incessantly

【不定】bùdìng 〈副词 *adv.*〉表示不肯定，后面常有表示疑问的词或肯定和否定相叠的词组 [indicating uncertainty，followed by question words or phrases consisting of both affirmative and negative forms of a word] hard to say；hard to predict；indefinite；indeterminate：孩子～又跑哪儿去了。Who knows where the children have gone.｜一天他～要问多少回。He asks I don't know how many times a day.｜我下星期还～走不走。It's not at all certain whether I'll go next week.｜这场球赛～谁输谁赢呢！It's hard to predict who will win the game.

【不定根】bùdìnggēn 不是从胚轴的下端生出来的根。有的不定根从茎的节上生出来，如禾本科植物的根；有的从叶片上生出来，如秋海棠的根。adventitious root；root that does not derive from the plumular axis，some deriving from the leaves，e.g. roots of the begonia

【不动产】bùdòngchǎn 不能移动的财产，指土地、房屋及附着于土地、房屋上不可分离的部分（如树木、水暖设备等）fixed assets；immovables；real estate；immovable property，e.g. land，house and the things that cannot be detached from them (e.g. trees，water supply，heating installations，etc.)；

【不动声色】bù dòng shēngsè 不说话，不流露感情。形容态度镇静。not change one's voice and expression because of emotion；maintain one's composure；stay calm and collected；not turn a hair；not bat an eyelid；also 不露声色 bù lù shēngsè

【不冻港】bùdònggǎng 较冷地区常年不结冰的海港，如旅顺、大连 ice-free ports that don't freeze throughout the year in rather cold regions，e.g. Lüshun Port and Dalian Port

【不独】bùdú 不但；不仅 not only：植树造林～有利于水土保持，而且还能提供木材。Afforestation not only helps to conserve water and prevent soil erosion，but can provide timber as well.

【不端】bùduān 不正派 improper；dishonourable：品行～ bad conduct；ill-behaved

【不断】bùduàn 连续不间断 unceasing；uninterrupted；continuous；constant：接连～ in succession｜～努力，～进步 make unceasing progress through continuous effort｜新生事物～涌现。New things are constantly emerging.

【不对】bù duì 不正确；错误 incorrect；wrong：数目～ wrong amount｜他没有什么～的地方。He's not in the wrong.

【不对】bùduì ❶ 不正常 amiss；abnormal；queer：那人神色有点儿～。That man doesn't quite look his usual self today.｜一听口气～，连忙退了出来。The moment he heard the abnormal tone，he beat a quick retreat. ❷ 不和睦；合不来 in disagreement；at odds：他们俩素来～。The two of them have always been at odds.

【不对茬儿】bù duìchár 不妥当；跟当时的情况不符合 not proper；not fit for the occasion：他刚说了一句，觉得～，就停住了。He had hardly uttered a sentence when he felt he was saying something improper for the occasion，so he stopped short.

【不对劲】bù duìjìn （～儿 bù duìjìnr）❶ 不称心合意；不合适 not satisfying：新换的工具，使起来～。The newly equipped tool feels awkward. ❷ 不情投意合；不和睦 in disagreement；at odds：俩人有点儿～，爱闹意见。The two of them are somewhat at odds and often quarrel with each other. ❸ 不正常 amiss；abnormal；queer：他越琢磨越觉得这事～，其中必有原因。The more he thought about it，the more he felt something was amiss，and figured there must be some reason.｜他觉得身上有点～就上床睡觉了。He didn't feel well and went to bed.

【不…而…】bù…ér… 表示虽不具有某条件或原因而产生某结果 gain results though without any condition or cause；do ... without doing ...：～寒～栗 shiver all over though not cold — tremble with fear；shudder｜～劳～获 reap without sowing；gain without pain｜～谋～合 agree without prior (or previous) consultation；(of two persons) happen to see eye to eye on sth.｜～期～遇 chance encounter；meet unexpectedly (or by chance)｜～言～喻 self-evident｜～约～同 do or think the same without prior consultation；happen to coincide｜～翼～飞 (of an object) disappear without trace；vanish into thin air｜～胫～走 get around fast；spread like wildfire

【不二法门】bù èr fǎmén 〈佛教用语 *Budd.*〉

'不二'指不是两极端。'法门'指修行入道的门径。意思是说，观察事物的道理，要离开相对的两个极端而用'处中'的看法，才能得其实在。Buddhist term that means only from the middle path and away from the extremes can one grasp the truth when seeking the law of things (不二 *bu er*: not the two extremes; 法门 *famen*: way to Buddhism); 〈比喻 *fig.*〉独一无二的门径 the one and only way; the only proper course to take

【不二价】bù èr jià 定价划一，卖给谁都是一样的价钱 fixed prices; uniform prices; one price: 童叟无欺，言～。One price for all customers, young or old.

【不贰过】bù èr guò 〈书 *fml.*〉犯过的错误不重犯 not repeat a previous mistake

【不乏】bùfá 不缺少，表示有相当数量 no lack of: ～其人 such people are not rare; there is no dearth of such people | ～先例。There are no lack of precedents.

【不法】bùfǎ 违反法律的 lawless; illegal; unlawful: ～行为 unlawful practice; illegal act | ～分子 lawbreaker; lawless person

【不凡】bùfán 不平凡；不平常 out of the ordinary; out of the common run; outstanding; uncommon: 出手～ make skillful opening moves | 自命～(自以为很了不起) consider oneself no ordinary being; have an unduly high opinion of oneself

【不犯】bùfàn 〈方 *dial.*〉犯不着；不值得 need not; not worthwhile: 这点小事～跟他计较。It's not worthwhile arguing with him over such a trivial matter.

【不妨】bùfáng 表示可以这样做，没有什么妨碍 there is no harm in; might as well: 这种办法没有用过，～试试。This method hasn't been used before. Why not give it a try? | 有什么意见，～当面提出来。You might as well make comments face to face if you've got any.

【不费吹灰之力】bù fèi chuī huī zhī lì 形容做事情非常容易，不费什么力气 as easy as blowing off dust; as easy as pie; very easy

【不忿】bùfèn (～儿 bùfènr)不服气；不平 not give in to; take offence; be resentful: 心中颇有～之意 remain very resentful

【不服】bùfú ❶ 不服从；不信服 refuse to obey (or comply); refuse to accept as final; remain unconvinced by; not give in to: ～管教 refuse to obey discipline | 说他错了，他还～。He refused to accept that he was wrong. ❷ 不习惯；不能适应 not accustomed to; not adapted to; not used to: ～水土 not accustomed to the climate of a new place; yet to be acclimatized | 这种烟我抽～。I'm not used to this type of cigarette.

【不服水土】bù fú shuǐtǔ 指不能适应某地的气候，饮食等 not accustomed to the climate, food and drink, etc. of a new place; not acclimatized

【不符】bùfú 不相合 not agree (or tally, square) with; not conform to; be inconsistent with: 名实～ have an undeserved reputation | 账面与库存～。The stock is inconsistent with what appears in the accounts book.

【不甘】bùgān 不甘心；不情愿 not reconciled to; not resigned to; unwilling: ～落后 not content to lag behind | ～示弱 unwilling to be outshone; not to be outdone

【不甘寂寞】bùgān jìmò 指不甘心冷落清闲、置身事外。指要表现自己或参加某一活动。hate to be neglected or overlooked; display oneself or take part in an activity

【不尴不尬】bù gān bù gà 左右为难，不好处理 in a dilemma; in an awkward predicament

【不敢当】bù gǎndāng 〈谦辞 *hum.*〉表示承当不起(对方的招待、夸奖等) I really don't deserve this; it's too great an honour; I'm overwhelmed; I'm much obliged; you flatter me (used in reply to a compliment or a complimentary gesture)

【不公】bùgōng 不公道；不公平 unjust; unfair: 办事～ unfair in handling matters | 分配～ unfair in distribution

【不共戴天】bù gòng dài tiān 不跟仇敌在一个天底下活着。形容仇恨极深。will not live under the same sky with one's enemy; absolutely irreconcilable

【不苟】bùgǒu 不随便；不马虎 not lax; not casual; careful; conscientious: ～言笑 reserved; reticent; taciturn; sober; sedate | 一丝～ not the least bit negligent; scrupulous about every detail; conscientious and meticulous

【不够】bùgòu 表示在数量上或程度上比所要求的差些 not enough; insufficient; inadequate (to what required): 材料～丰富。Materials are insufficient. | 分析得还～深入。The analysis lacks depth.

【不顾】bùgù ❶ 不照顾 have no consideration for; not concerned with: 只顾自己，～别人 just think of oneself and have no consideration for others ❷ 不考虑；不顾忌 in spite of; regardless of; have no regard for; ignore: 置危险于～ regardless of the danger | ～后果地一味蛮干 persist in acting blindly regardless of the consequences | 他～一切，跳到河里把孩子救了起来。Completely disregarding his own safety, he jumped into the river and saved the child.

【不管】bùguǎn 〈连词 *conj.*〉表示在任何条件或情况下结果都不会改变，后边常有'都、也'等副词与它呼应 [indicating that sth. will never change in any case, usu. correlated with adverbs like 都 dōu and 也 yě that follow it] regardless of; no matter (what, how, etc.): ～远不远他都不去。No matter how near or far, he refuses to go. | ～困难多大，我们也要克服。

We can overcome any difficulty, however great.

【不管不顾】bù guǎn bù gù ❶ 不照管 not look after; not mind: 他对家里的事全都～。He doesn't mind anything that happens in his family. ❷ 指人莽撞 rash; crude and impetuous: 他～地冲上去，挥起拳头就打。He rushed forward and struck with his fists.

【不管部长】bùguǎn bùzhǎng 某些国家的内阁阁员之一，不专管一个部，出席内阁会议，参与决策，并担任政府首脑交办的特殊重要事务 minister without portfolio; member of the cabinet in certain countries who is not designated to a single ministry, but attends cabinet meetings, participates in decision-making and handles important or special affairs assigned by the head of the government

【不管三七二十一】bùguǎn sān qī èrshí yī 不顾一切；不问是非情由 casting all caution to the wind; regardless of the consequences; recklessly; regardless of rights and wrong or how and why

【不光】bùguāng ❶ 表示超出某个数量或范围；不止 not the only one; beyond a certain number (amount) or range: 报名参加的～是他一个人。He was not the only one to sign up. ❷ 不但 not only: ～数量多，质量也不错 not only great in quantity, but fine in quality | 这里～出煤，而且出铁。This place produces not only coal but also iron.

【不轨】bùguǐ 指违反法纪或搞叛乱活动 against the law; breaking discipline; engaging in a rebellion: ～之徒 lawbreaker; lawless person | 行为～ dishonourable behaviour; bad conduct | 图谋～ plot sth. unlawful; engage in conspiratorial activities

【不过】bùguò ❶ 用在形容词性的词组或双音节形容词后面，表示程度最高 [attached to adjective phrases or disyllabic adjectives as an intensifier]: 再好～ couldn't be better | 最快～ couldn't be faster | 乖巧～的孩子 most lovely child ❷〈副词 *adv.*〉指明范围，含有往小里或轻里说的意味；仅仅 [indicating scope and implying relative smallness (of age) or lightness] only; merely; no more than: 当年她参军的时候～十七岁。She was only 17 when she joined the army. ❸〈连词 *conj.*〉用在后半句的开头儿，表示转折，对上半句话加以限制或修正 [used at the beginning of the latter half of a compound sentence to indicate a change in meaning, and to limit or amend the former half] but; however; same as 只是 zhǐshì: 病人精神还不错，～胃口不大好。The patient feels not bad, but his appetite is not good.

【不过意】bù guòyì 过意不去 be sorry; feel apologetic: 总来打扰您，心里实在～。I'm terribly sorry to always trouble you.

【不含糊】bù hán·hu ❶ 认真；不马虎 careful; not negligent; prudent; cautious: 她办起事来丁是丁，卯是卯，一点儿～。She is cautious and conscientious in her work. ❷ 不错；不一般 not ordinary; really good: 他那两笔字还真～。His handwriting is really good. | 质量是没说的，可是价钱也～。The quality is undisputed, but the price is really amazing. ❸ 不示弱；不畏惧 not be afraid of: 在高手面前，他也～。He's not afraid of master-hands.

【不寒而栗】bù hán ér lì 不寒冷而发抖。形容非常恐惧。shudder; shiver all over though not cold — tremble with fear

【不好意思】bù hǎoyì·si ❶ 害羞 shy; embarrassed; bashful; feel ill at ease: 他被大伙儿笑得～了。He felt embarrassed by their laughter. ❷ 碍于情面而不便或不肯 find it inappropriate or embarrassing to do sth. due to one's feelings: 虽然不大情愿，又～回绝 find it difficult to refuse though unwilling to do sth.

【不合】bùhé ❶ 不符合 not conform to; be unsuited to; be not in keeping with: ～手续 not conform to the formalities | ～时宜 out of touch with the times; incompatible with present needs; inopportune or inappropriate ❷〈书 *fml.*〉不应该 should not; ought not: 早知如此，当初～叫他去。Had we foreseen that, we would not have asked him to go. ❸ 合不来；不和 not get along well; on bad terms: 性格～ incompatible with each other in disposition

【不和】bùhé 不和睦 not get along well; on bad terms; at odds: 姑嫂～ wife and sister-in-law being on bad terms with each other | 感情～ not get along well

【不哼不哈】bù hēng bù hā 不言语，多指该说而不说 keep silent, usu. when one should say sth.: 有事情问到他，他总～的，真急人。When asked for his advice in an emergency, he always keeps silent. He can be really trying!

【不遑】bùhuáng 〈书 *fml.*〉来不及；没有闲暇（做某事）have no time; be too busy: ～顾及 have no time to attend to sth.

【不讳】bùhuì 〈书 *fml.*〉❶ 不忌讳；无所避讳 without concealing anything: 直言～ speak without any reservation; not mince words; call a spade a spade; talk straight ❷〈婉辞 *euph.*〉指死亡 die

【不惑】bùhuò 〈书 *fml.*〉《论语·为政》：'四十而不惑。'指人到了四十岁，能明辨是非而不受迷惑。后来用'不惑'指人四十岁。'At 40 I became free from doubts' (Confucius' *Analects·Governance*); later referring to the age of 40: 年届～ turn 40; be 40 years old | ～之年 the age of 40

【不羁】bùjī 〈书 *fml.*〉不受束缚 unruly; uninhibited: 放荡～ unconventional and unrestrained

【不及】bùjí ❶ 不如；比不上 not as good as; inferior to: 这个远～那个好。This one is far inferior to that one. | 在刻苦学习方面我～他。I don't study anywhere as hard as he does. ❷ 来不及 find it too late: 后悔～ too late for regrets | 躲闪～ too late to dodge

【不即不离】bù jí bù lí 既不亲近也不疏远 be neither familiar nor distant; keep sb. at arm's length

【不计】bùjì 不计较；不考虑 have no consideration for; disregard: ～成本 not consider costs | ～个人得失 disregard personal gain

【不计其数】bù jì qí shù 无法计算数目。形容极多。countless; innumerable

【不济】bùjì 不好；不顶用 poor; no good; of no use; not of any help: 精力～ short of energy | 眼神儿～。(His) eyesight is failing.

【不济事】bù jìshì 不顶事；不中用 not good; of no use: 这办法也～。This method isn't of any help either.

【不假思索】bù jiǎ sīsuǒ 用不着想。形容说话做事迅速。(act, respond, etc.) readily; offhand; without need of thinking; without hesitation

【不见】bùjiàn ❶ 不见面 not see; not meet: ～不散 (let's) not leave without seeing each other | 这孩子一年～，竟长得这么高了。It's only a year since I last saw the child, and he's grown so tall. ❷ (东西)不在了；找不着 (后头必须带'了' must be followed by 了·le) (of things) lost; out of sight; hard to find: 我的笔刚才还在，怎么转眼就～了？My pen was here just now. Where could it have gone in such a flash?

【不见得】bù jiàn·dé 不一定 not necessarily; not likely: 这雨～下得起来。It is unlikely to rain. | 看样子，他～能来。It seems that he's not likely to come.

【不见棺材不落泪】bù jiàn guān·cai bù luò lèi 〈比喻 *fig.*〉不到彻底失败的时候不知痛悔 refuse to repent until failing completely

【不见经传】bù jiàn jīng zhuàn 经传中没有记载。指人或事物没有什么名气，也指某种理论缺乏文献上的依据。not to be found in the classics; (of people or things) not authoritative; unknown; (of a theory) lacking support from previous documents

【不解之缘】bù jiě zhī yuán 不能分开的缘分。指亲密的关系或深厚的感情。indissoluble bond; irrevocable commitment; intimate relationship or deep affection

【不禁】bùjīn 抑制不住；禁不住 cannot help (doing sth.); cannot refrain from: 忍俊～ cannot help laughing | 读到精彩之处，他～大声叫好。He couldn't help shouting 'bravo' at the splendid parts of the book.

【不禁不由】bùjīn bùyóu (～儿的 bùjīn bùyóur·de)不由自主地 cannot help (doing sth.); involuntarily: 看着孩子们跳舞，他～地打起拍子来。He couldn't help keeping the beat when watching the children dancing.

【不仅】bùjǐn ❶ 表示超出某个数量或范围；不止 beyond a quantity or scope; not the only one: 这～是我个人的意见。I'm not the only one who holds this view. ❷ 不但 not only: ～方法对头，而且措施得力。Not only is the method correct, but the measures are effective. | 他们～提前完成了生产任务，而且还支援了兄弟单位。They not only completed their production target ahead of time, but gave support to fellow units.

【不尽然】bùjìnrán 不一定是这样；不完全如此 not necessarily like this; not completely like this: 要说做生意能赚钱，也～，有时也会亏本。Business doesn't necessarily mean gains; sometimes it means loss.

【不近人情】bù jìn rénqíng 不合乎人之常情。多指性情、言行怪僻。not amenable to reason; unreasonable; (usu. of disposition, speech and behaviour) eccentric; ☞ 人情 rénqíng on p. 1619

【不经一事，不长一智】bù jīng yī shì, bù zhǎng yī zhì 不经历一件事情，就不能增长对于那件事情的知识 one cannot gain knowledge without practice; wisdom comes from experience

【不经意】bùjīngyì 不注意；不留神 carelessly; by accident: 稍～，就会出错。You'll make mistakes if you don't give all your attention to it.

【不经之谈】bù jīng zhī tán 荒诞的、没有根据的话 absurd and groundless statement; cock-and-bull story(经 *jīng*:正常 regular)

【不景气】bù jǐngqì ❶ 经济不繁荣 depression; recession; slump ❷ 泛指不兴旺 in a depressed state

【不胫而走】bù jìng ér zǒu 没有腿却能跑。形容传布迅速。able to run without legs; get round fast; spread like wildfire (胫 *jìng*:小腿 lower leg)

【不久】bùjiǔ 指距离某个时期或某件事情时间不远 soon; before long; not long ago: 前～他曾在电台发表谈话。He made a speech on the radio not long ago. | 工厂建成，～即正式投产。The factory has been set up, and it will go into production soon.

【不咎既往】bù jiù jì wǎng ☞ 既往不咎 jì wǎng bù jiù on p. 920

【不拘】bùjū ❶ 不拘泥；不计较；不限制 not stick to; not confine oneself to: ～一格 not stick to one pattern; not limited to one type (or style) | ～小节 not bother about trifles; not niggling | 字数～。No limit is set on the number of words. | 长短～。No limit is set on the length. ❷ 不论 no matter (what, who, etc.); whatever: ～什么事，我都愿意把它做

好。Whatever it may be, I'm ready to do it well.

【不拘小节】bùjū xiǎojié 不为无关原则的琐事所约束，现多指不注意生活小事 not bother about trifles unrelated to principles; (usu.) not care about minor matters in daily life; not niggling

【不拘一格】bùjū yī gé 不局限于一种规格或方式 not stick to one pattern; not limited to one type (or style)：文艺创作要～，体裁可以多样化。Literary and artistic creation should not be limited to any one pattern; it can be diverse in form.

【不绝如缕】bù jué rú lǚ 像细线一样连着，差点儿就要断了。多用来形容局势危急或声音细微悠长。hanging by a thread; (of situations) critical; precarious; almost fatal; (of sound) linger on faintly

【不刊之论】bù kān zhī lùn 〈比喻 *fig*.〉不能改动或不可磨灭的言论 unalterable or irrefutable argument; unalterable truth; truth for all times (刊 *kan*：古代指削除刻错了的字，不刊是说不可更改 erasing wrong characters; 不刊 *bu kan* meaning unalterable)

【不堪】bùkān ❶ 承受不了 cannot bear; cannot stand：～其苦 cannot bear the hardships | ～一击 cannot withstand a single blow; collapse at the first blow ❷ 不可；不能(多用于不好的方面 usu. referring to sth. undesirable) cannot：～入耳 intolerable to the ear; revolting; disgusting | ～设想 too ghastly (or dreadful) to contemplate | ～造就 cannot be made (or trained) ❸ 用在消极意义的词后面，表示程度深 [used after words of negative meaning, as an intensifier of degree] utterly; extremely：疲惫～ extremely tired; dog-tired | 破烂～ in rags (or tatters) | 狼狈～ in an extremely awkward position; in a sorry plight; in dire straits ❹ 坏到极深的程度 extremely bad (or undesirable)：他这个人太～了。He is impossible.

【不堪回首】bùkān huíshǒu 不忍再去回忆过去的经历或情景 cannot bear to look back on; find it unbearable to recall

【不堪设想】bùkān shèxiǎng 事情的结果不能想像。指会发展到很坏或很危险的地步。(of consequences) too ghastly to contemplate; cannot be imagined; will be extremely bad or dangerous

【不可】bùkě ❶ 不可以；不能够 cannot; should not; must not：～偏废 cannot do one thing and neglect the other | ～动摇 unshakable; inflexible | 二者缺一～。Neither one shall be neglected. ❷ '非…不可'，表示必须或一定 [used in 非…不可 fēi…bùkě to indicate the necessity to do sth.]：今天这个会很重要，我非去～。Today's meeting is very important, so I simply must go.

【不可告人】bù kě gào rén 不能告诉别人，多指不正当的打算或计谋不敢公开说出来 not to be divulged; hidden; cannot bear the light of day; ulterior; sinister

【不可救药】bù kě jiù yào 病重到已无法救治 (of disease) incurable; beyond cure; 〈比喻 *fig*.〉人或事物坏到无法挽救的地步 incorrigible; hopeless; beyond remedy

【不可开交】bù kě kāi jiāo 无法摆脱或结束(只做'得'后面的补语 used only as a complement after 得·de) cannot avoid or finish：忙得～up to one's ears in work; awfully (or terribly) busy | 打得～ locked in a fierce struggle

【不可抗力】bùkěkànglì 法律上指在当时的条件下人力所不能抵抗的破坏力，如洪水、地震等。因不可抗力而发生的损害，不追究法律责任。(leg.) force majeure; destructive power beyond human control in terms of the consequences brought on by a disaster, e.g. flood, earthquake, etc.; thus ensuing damages are exempted from any investigation into responsibility under the law

【不可理喻】bù kě lǐ yù 不能够用道理使他明白。形容愚昧或态度蛮横，不讲道理。cannot make sb. understand by reasoning; foolish or rude, and unreasonable; impervious to reason; won't listen to reason

【不可名状】bù kě míng zhuàng 不能够用语言形容：begs description; indescribable; beyond description (名 *ming*：说出 describe)

【不可收拾】bù kě shōu·shi 原指事物无法归类整顿。后借指事情坏到无法挽回的地步。(of things) unclassifiable and hard to be sorted out; (later meaning) irremediable; unmanageable; out of hand; hopeless

【不可思议】bù kě sīyì 不可想像，不可能理解(原来是佛教用语，含有神秘奥妙的意思 originally a Buddhist term meaning mysterious and profound) inconceivable; unimaginable; unthinkable

【不可同日而语】bù kě tóng rì ér yǔ 不能放在同一时间谈论。形容不能相比，不能相提并论。cannot be mentioned in the same breath; there's no comparison between them; cannot be put on a par with

【不可向迩】bù kě xiàng ěr 不能接近 cannot approach：烈火燎原，～ cannot approach because of the raging fire

【不可一世】bù kě yī shì 自以为在当代没有一个人能比得上。形容极其狂妄自大。consider oneself unsurpassed in the world; overweening (or insufferable) arrogance

【不可知论】bùkězhīlùn 一种唯心主义的认识论，认为除了感觉或现象之外，世界本身是无法认识的。它否认社会发展的客观规律，否认社会实践的作用。agnosticism; a type of idealist epistemology that believes we cannot understand the world itself but only the sensations or appearance of things, denying the objective laws of social development and the function of social practice

【不可终日】bù kě zhōng rì 一天都过不下去。形容局势危急或心中惶恐。unable to carry on even for a single day; in a desperate situation: 惶惶～ in a constant state of anxiety; on tenterhooks

【不克】bùkè 〈书 *fml.*〉不能(多指能力薄弱,不能做到 usu. because of poor capability) unable to; cannot: ～自拔 unable to get away from |～分身 unable to attend to; not able to get around to (doing sth.)

【不快】bùkuài ❶(心情)不愉快 unhappy; displeased; in low spirits: 怏怏～ unhappy; displeased; depressed; in low spirits ❷(身体)不舒服 indisposed; feel under the weather; be out of sorts: 几天来身子～。I'm not feeling well these days.

【不愧】bùkuì 当之无愧;当得起(多跟'为'或'是'连用 usu. followed by 为 wéi or 是 shì) worthy of; deserve to be called; prove oneself to be: 郑成功～为一位民族英雄。Zheng Chenggong proved to be a national hero.

【不赖】bùlài 〈方 *dial.*〉不坏;好 not bad; good; fine: 字写得～。The handwriting is not bad. |今年的庄稼可真～。This year's crops are doing really fine.

【不郎不秀】bù láng bù xiù 〈比喻 *fig.*〉不成材或没出息(元明时代官僚、贵族的子弟称'秀',平民的子弟称'郎') useless; worthless; good-for-nothing (the sons of bureaucrats or nobles were called 秀 xiù, and those of the ordinary people were called 郎 láng in the Yuan and Ming dynasties)

【不劳而获】bù láo ér huò 自己不劳动而取得别人劳动的成果 reap without sowing; profit by or reap the fruits of other people's toil

【不离儿】bùlír 〈方 *dial.*〉不坏;差不多 not bad; pretty good: 你看他画得还真～呢。Look, he is really drawing well.

【不力】bùlì 不尽力;不得力 not do one's best; not exert oneself; ineffective: 办事～ not do one's best in one's work; be slack in one's work |打击～ fail to make effective attacks

【不利】bùlì 没有好处;不顺利 unfavourable; disadvantageous; harmful; detrimental: 扭转～的局面 put an end to an unfavourable situation |地形有利于我而～于敌。The terrain is to our advantage rather than to the enemy's.

【不良】bù liáng 不好 bad; harmful; unhealthy: ～现象 unhealthy tendencies |消化～ indigestion |存心～ harbour evil intentions; have ulterior motives

【不了】bùliǎo 没完(多用于动词加'个'之后 usu. attached to the structure 'verb + 个 gè') without end; endless: 忙个～ always busy |大雨下个～。The rain kept pouring down.

【不了了之】bù liǎo liǎo zhī 该办的事情没有办完,放在一边不去管它,就算完事 conclude a matter by leaving it unsettled; end up with nothing definite; fizzle out

【不料】bùliào 没想到;没有预先料到 unexpectedly; to one's surprise: 今天本想出门,～竟下起雨来。I had planned to go out today, but who would have thought it would rain!

【不吝】bùlìn 〈客套话 *pol.*〉不吝惜(用于征求意见 used in asking advice) not stint; not grudge; be generous with: 是否有当,尚希～赐教。We hope that you will not spare your comments on it.

【不伦不类】bù lún bù lèi 不像这一类,也不像那一类。形容不成样子或不规范。be like neither this kind nor that; neither fish nor fowl; nondescript: 翻译如果不顾本国语言的特点,死抠原文字句,就会弄出一些～的句子来,叫人看不懂。If one remains confined to the original language in translating regardless of the characteristics of one's own national language, the result will be some strange sentences that are hard to understand.

【不论】bùlùn ❶〈连词 *conj.*〉表示条件或情况不同而结果不变,后面往往有并列的词语或表示任指的疑问代词,下文多用'都、总'等副词跟它呼应 [indicating same result in spite of changeable conditions or circumstances, usu. followed by coordinate phrases or wh- pronouns with indefinite reference, and often correlated with 都 dōu or 总 zǒng] no matter (what, who, how, etc.); whether ... or ...; regardless of: ～困难有多大,他都不气馁。However great the difficulties, he never loses heart. |他～考虑什么问题,总是把集体利益放在第一位。He always puts the collective interests first no matter what is on his mind. ❷〈书 *fml.*〉不讨论;不辩论 not discuss; not argue: 存而～ leave the question open

【不落窠臼】bù luò kējiù 〈比喻 *fig.*〉文章或艺术等有独创风格,不落俗套 (of articles, arts, etc.) not follow the beaten track; have an original style; show originality; be unconventional

【不满】bùmǎn 不满意 resentful; discontented; dissatisfied: ～情绪 discontent |人们对不关心群众疾苦的做法极为～。The people are very resentful about the neglect over their weals and woes.

【不蔓不枝】bù màn bù zhī 原指莲茎不分枝杈 (of lotus stems) neither spreading about nor branching out;〈比喻 *fig.*〉文章简洁 (of articles) concise; succinct

【不毛之地】bù máo zhī dì 不长庄稼的地方,泛指贫瘠、荒凉的土地或地带 barren and bleak land; desert

【不免】bùmiǎn 免不了 cannot avoid; cannot

help but; inevitably; invariably; bound to; unavoidable: 旧地重游,～想起往事。Revisiting a once familiar place is bound to bring old memories to mind.

【不妙】bù miào 不好(多指情况的变化 of a turn of events) not too encouraging; far from good; anything but reassuring

【不敏】bùmǐn 〈书 *fml.*〉不聪明。常用来表示自谦。not intelligent (used in self-deprecation): 敬谢～。Thanks.

【不名数】bùmíngshù 不带有单位名称的数。如 -9,106。abstract number, e.g. -9,106

【不名一文】bù míng yī wén 一个钱也没有(名 míng:占有 have) without a penny to one's name; penniless; also 不名一钱 bù míng yī qián

【不名誉】bùmíngyù 对名誉有损害;不体面 disreputable; disgraceful: 一时糊涂,做下～的蠢事。What a fool to have committed such a disgrace.

【不摸头】bù mōtóu 摸不着头绪;不了解情况 not get the feel of sth. or the situation; not acquainted with the situation; not up on things: 我刚来,这些事全～。I'm a newcomer and therefore not familiar with local affairs.

【不谋而合】bù móu ér hé 没有事先商量而彼此见解或行动完全一致 agree without prior (or previous) consultation; happen to hold the same view

【不能自已】bù néng zì yǐ 不能控制自己的感情 cannot control oneself; lose self-control; can't help; be beside oneself

【不宁唯是】bù nìng wéi shì 〈书 *fml.*〉不仅如此 moreover; and what is more

【不佞】bùnìng 〈书 *fml.*〉没有才能。旧时用来谦称自己。(used in self-deprecation in old times) not capable

【不怕】bùpà 〈方 *dial.*〉〈连词 *conj.*〉用法跟'哪怕'相同[same as 哪怕 nǎpà in usage]: ～天气再冷,他也要用冷水洗脸。No matter how cold it is, he still washes his face with cold water.

【不配】bùpèi ❶ 不相配;不般配 ill matched; not match; incompatible: 上衣和裤子的颜色～。The coat and the trousers do not match in colour. | 这一男一女在一起有点儿～。This man and this woman are not right for each other. ❷ (资格、品级等)够不上;不符合 not qualified: 我做得不好,～当先进工作者。My performance is not good enough to qualify me as a model worker.

【不偏不倚】bù piān bù yǐ 指不偏袒任何一方,表示公正或中立。也形容不偏不歪,正中目标。even-handed; impartial; unbiased; also used to describe being perfectly on target

【不平】bùpíng ❶ 不公平 injustice; unfairness; wrong; grievance: 看见了～的事,他都想管。He will not tolerate any injustice that he comes across. ❷ 不公平的事 injustice; unfairness; wrong; grievance: 路见～,拔刀相助 stand out boldly to redress an injustice; come to the rescue of a wronged party ❸ 因不公平的事而愤怒或不满 resentful; indignant about sth. unjust: 愤愤～ boil with resentment or indignation ❹ 由不公平的事引起的愤怒和不满 indignation or resentment caused by unfairness: 消除心中的～ allay one's resentment

【不平等条约】bùpíngděng tiáoyuē 订约双方(或几方)在权利义务上不平等的条约。特指侵略国强迫别国订立的破坏别国主权、损害别国利益的这类条约。unequal treaty, especially those forced upon weaker nations by imperialist countries

【不平则鸣】bù píng zé míng 指对不公平的事情表示愤慨 injustice provokes outcry; Where there is injustice, there will be protest.

【不期而遇】bù qī ér yù 没有约定而意外地相遇 meet unexpectedly (or by chance); have a chance encounter; bump into sb.

【不期然而然】bù qī rán ér rán 没有料想到如此而竟然如此 happen unexpectedly; contrary to one's expectations; also 不期而然 bù qī ér rán

【不起眼儿】bù qǐyǎnr 不值得重视;不引人注目: ～的小人物 not attract attention; not be noticeable; not be attractive

【不情之请】bù qíng zhī qǐng 〈客套话 *pol.*〉不合情理的请求(向人求助时称自己的请求) my presumptuous request

【不求甚解】bù qiú shèn jiě 原指读书要领会精神实质,不必咬文嚼字。现多指只求懂得个大概,不求深刻了解。(formerly) get to the bottom of things without paying too much attention to the wording; not seek deep understanding; be content with a superficial understanding; not seek to understand things thoroughly

【不屈】bùqū 不屈服 unyielding; unbending: 坚贞～ faithful and unbending | 宁死～ rather die than surrender; unbending

【不然】bùrán ❶ 不是这样 not so: 抄抄写写看起来很容易,其实～。Copying a text may seem an easy job, but actually it is not the case. ❷ 用在对话开头,表示否定对方的话 [used at the beginning of a sentence to express disagreement] no: ～,事情不像你说的那么简单。No, it is not as simple as what you said. ❸〈连词 *conj.*〉表示如果不是上文所说的情况,就发生或可能发生下文所说的情况 or else; otherwise; if not: 快走吧,～,就要迟到了。Hurry up, otherwise, we'll be late. | 明天我还有点事儿,～倒可以陪你去一趟。I've got things to do tomorrow, or I can accompany you there. | 他晚上不是读书,就是写点儿什么,再～就是听听音乐。At night, he either reads or writes, or listens to music.

【不人道】bùréndào 不合乎人道 inhuman; ☞ 人道 réndào on p. 1616

【不仁】bùrén ❶ 不仁慈 not benevolent; heartless: 为富～ rich but heartless ❷(肢体)失去知觉 numb: 麻木～ apathy | 手足～。The limbs feel numb.

【不忍】bùrěn 心里忍受不了 cannot bear to: 于心～ cannot stand; not have the heart to | ～释手 cannot bear to put sth. down; cannot bear to tear oneself away from sth. | ～卒读(不忍心读完,多形容文章悲惨动人) cannot bear to read to the end (oft. of a tragic and touching text)

【不日】bùrì 要不了几天;几天之内(限用于未来 future tense only) within the next few days: ～启程 will set off soon | 代表团～抵京。The delegation will arrive in Beijing within days.

【不容】bùróng 不许;不让 not tolerate; not allow; not brook: ～置疑 beyond doubt; undoubtedly | ～置喙 allow no interference by any one; brook no interference | 任务紧迫,～拖延。This is an urgent task that allows no delay.

【不容置喙】bù róng zhì huì 指不容许别人插嘴说话 not allow others to interfere; tolerate no intervention

【不容置疑】bù róng zhì yí 不容许有什么怀疑,指真实可信 allow for (or admit) no doubt; not be open to doubt; be beyond doubt

【不如】bùrú 表示前面提到的人或事物比不上后面所说的 not equal to; not as good as; inferior to: 走路～骑车快。Walking is not as fast a riding. | 论手巧,大家都～他。Few can equal (or compare with) him in manual dexterity.

【不入虎穴,焉得虎子】bù rù hǔ xué, yān dé hǔ zǐ 不进老虎洞,怎能捉到小老虎 how can you catch tiger cubs without entering the tiger's lair; 〈比喻 *fig*.〉不历艰险,就不能获得成功 nothing ventured, nothing gained

【不三不四】bù sān bù sì ❶ 不正派 dubious; shady: 不要跟那些～的人来往。Don't hang around with those dubious characters. ❷ 不像样子 neither one thing nor the other; neither fish nor fowl; nondescript: 这篇文章改来改去,反而改得～的。Instead of inproving it, the repeated changes turned the article into a mess.

【不善】bùshàn ❶ 不好 bad; ill: 处理～ not handle properly; mishandle: 来意～ come with ill intent ❷ 不长于 not good at (also 不善于 bùshànyú): ～管理 not good at managing things ❸〈方 *dial*.〉很可观;非同小可 impressive; considerable (also 不善乎 bùshàn·hu): 别看他身体不强,干起农活来可～。He may not look strong, but he is quite impressive in farm work.

【不甚了了】bù shèn liǎo liǎo 不太了解;不怎么清楚 not know much (about sth.)

【不胜】bùshèng ❶ 承担不了;不能忍受 cannot bear (or stand): 体力～ be physically unequal to (a task); be physically incapable of coping with (a job) | ～其烦 be bored beyond endurance ❷ 表示不能做或做不完(前后重复同一动词) [used between two identical verbs to indicate difficulty or impossibility of fulfilment]: 防～防(防不住) cannot find a foolproof solution; cannot avoid (danger, mistake. etc.) in all cases | 数～数(数不完) countless; numerable ❸ 非常;十分(用于感情方面 used in expressing feelings) very; extremely: ～感激 be much obliged; be deeply grateful | ～遗憾 be very sorry; much to one's regret ❹〈方 *dial*.〉不如 less than; worse than: 身子一年～一年。His health is getting worse with each passing year.

【不失为】bùshīwéi 还可以算得上 can yet be regarded as; may after all be accepted as: 这样处理,还～一个办法。This, after all, is one way of doing it.

【不识抬举】bù shí tái·ju 不接受或不珍视别人对自己的好意(用于指责人) fail to appreciate sb.'s kindness; not know how to appreciate a favour

【不识闲儿】bùshíxiánr 〈方 *dial*.〉闲不住: 他手脚～,从早忙到晚。He keeps himself busy all day long.

【不识之无】bù shí zhī wú 指不识字('之'和'无'是常用的字) illiterate

【不时】bùshí ❶ 时时;经常不断地 from time to time; frequently; often: 一边走着,一边～地四处张望 look around from time to time while walking | 在丛林深处,～听到布谷鸟的叫声。The chirps of cuckoos could be constantly heard from the depth of the forests. ❷ 随时;不是预定的时间 at any time; at an unexpected moment: 以备～之需 prepare for emergency needs

【不是】bù·shi 错处;过失 fault; blame: 好意劝他,反倒落个～。Out of good intentions, (I) tried to persuade him, but got blamed for it in the end. | 你先出口伤人,这就是你的～了。It's your fault, because you were the first to speak bitingly.

【不是话】bù shì huà (话)没道理;不对头 unreasonable, wrong; absurd; amiss

【不是玩儿的】bù shì wánr·de 不是儿戏 it's no joke: 多穿上点儿,受了寒可～! It's no joke catching a cold. Better put on more clothes.

【不是味儿】bù shì wèir ❶ 味道不正 not the right flavour; not quite right; a bit off: 这个菜炒得～。This dish doesn't taste quite right. ◇他的民歌唱得～。The way he sings folk songs is a bit off. ❷ 不对头;不正常 fishy; queer; amiss: 一听这话～,就反过来追问。

Hearing the words and feeling something amiss, he retorted instead of giving an answer. ❸(心里感到)不好受 feel bad; be upset: 看到孩子们上不了学,心里很～。(I) was upset when (I) saw many children couldn't go to school. ‖ also 不是滋味儿 bù shì zīwèir

【不适】bùshì (身体)不舒服 unwell; indisposed: 偶感～ feel a bit unwell

【不爽】[1] bùshuǎng (身体、心情)不爽快 not well; be out of sorts; be in a bad mood

【不爽】[2] bùshuǎng 没有差错 without discrepancy; accurate: 毫厘～ not deviate a hair's breadth; be perfectly accurate; be right in every detail | 屡试～ prove to be successful time and again

【不送气】bù sòngqì 〈语音学 *phonet*.〉指发辅音时没有显著的气流出来 unaspirated; also 不吐气 bù tǔqì

【不速之客】bù sù zhī kè 指没有邀请而自己来的客人 uninvited (or unexpected) guest; gatecrasher (速 *su*:邀请 invite)

【不随意肌】bùsuíyìjī 平滑肌 involuntary muscle

【不遂】bùsuì 不如愿 fail; fail to materialize: 谋事～ fail to carry out one's plan | 稍有～,即大发脾气 fly into a rage at the slightest setback

【不特】bùtè 〈书 *fml*.〉不但 not only

【不祧之祖】bù tiāo zhī zǔ 〈旧时 *old*〉〈比喻 *fig*.〉创立某种事业受到尊崇的人 revered earliest ancestor; patriarch; founder; forefather; (祧 *tiao*:古代指远祖的祠堂。家庙中祖先的神主,辈分远的要依次迁入祧庙合祭,只有创业的始祖或影响较大的祖宗不迁,叫做不祧 ancestral temple or clan hall for remote ancestors. Of the ancestors being honoured in the family temple in the form of wooden tablets bearing their names, those of the oldest generations are moved according to the order of seniority to the *tiao* or ancestral temple, where they can be collectively worshipped. But the tablets for the founding ancestors of a clan or those of influence are not moved into the *tiao*. That is called 不祧 bùtiāo.)

【不同凡响】bù tóng fánxiǎng 〈比喻 *fig*.〉事物(多指文艺作品)不平凡 (usu. of literary and artistic works) outstanding; out of the ordinary; above the common run (凡响 *fanxiang*:平凡的音乐 ordinary music)

【不图】bùtú ❶不追求 not seek; not strive for: ～名利 not seek fame or gain ❷〈书 *fml*.〉不料 unexpectedly; contrary to expectation

【不吐气】bù tǔqì ☞ 不送气 bù sòngqì

【不外】bùwài 不超出某种范围以外 not beyond the scope of; nothing more than: 大家所谈论的～工作问题。What we talked about was no more than our work. also 不外乎 bùwài·hu

【不为已甚】bù wéi yǐ shèn 指对人的责备或处罚适可而止 not go too far; refrain from going to extremes; never go beyond reasonable limits (已甚 *yi shen*:过分 undue)

【不惟】bùwéi 〈书 *fml*.〉不但;不仅 not only: 此举～无益,反而有害。The practice will not only be of no good, but will bring harm.

【不韪】bùwěi 〈书 *fml*.〉过失;不对 fault, wrongdoing: 冒天下之大～ dare do what the whole world considers to be wrong

【不谓】bùwèi 〈书 *fml*.〉❶不能说(用于表示否定的语词前面 used before a negative phrase) cannot be said: 任务～不重。The task cannot be said to be unimportant. | 时间～不长。It cannot be said that the time is not long. ❷不料;没想到 unexpectedly; to one's surprise: 离别以来,以为相见无日,～今又重逢。I thought that we wouldn't see each other for good after our departure, but unexpectedly we met each other today.

【不闻不问】bù wén bù wèn 既不听也不问。形容漠不关心。not bother to ask or to listen; show no interest in sth.; be indifferent to sth.

【不稳平衡】bùwěn-pínghéng 受到微小的外力干扰就要失去平衡的平衡状态,如鸡蛋直立时的状态 unstable equilibrium; becoming unbalanced under the tiniest effects of outside force, e.g. an egg set on end

【不无】bùwú 不是没有;多少有些 more or less: ～小补 be of some help | ～裨益 be more or less helpful | ～关系 be more or less related | ～遗憾 feel somewhat regretful

【不惜】bùxī 不顾惜;舍得 not stint; not spare: ～工本 regardless of cost | ～牺牲一切(do sth.) at all cost | 倾家荡产,在所～ disregard any cost, even the loss of all one's property

【不暇】bùxiá 没有时间;忙不过来 have no time (for sth.): 应接～ have too much work to cope with | 自顾～ be too busy to attend to sth.

【不下】bùxià ❶ same as 不下于 bùxiàyú ② ❷用在动词后,表示动作没有结果或没有完成 [used after a verb to indicate an action is not completed or has not achieved the desired result]: 屡攻～。The repeated attacks have all failed. | 相持～ be at a stalemate | 放心～ cannot stop worrying | 委决～ hesitate to make a decision

【不下于】bùxiàyú ❶不低于;不比别的低 not lower than; not inferior to: 这种自来水笔虽是新产品,质量却～各种名牌。Although this type of pen is a new product, its quality is as good as the brand-names. ❷不少于;不比某个数目少 as many as; no less than: 新产品～二百种。There are as many as 200 new products on show. also 不下 bùxià

【不相上下】bù xiāng shàng xià 分不出高低，形容程度相等 equally matched; about the same; almost on a par：本领～ of equal ability | 年岁～ of similer age

【不详】bùxiáng ❶ 不详细；不清楚 not detailed; not quite clear：言之～ be stated too briefly; not be given in detail | 地址～。The address is not quite clear. | 历史情况～。The historical background is not quite clear. ❷ 不细说（书信中用语 used in letters) no need to go into details

【不祥】bùxiáng 不吉利 inauspicious：～之兆 an ill (or evil) omen

【不想】bùxiǎng 不料；没想到 unexpectedly; who would have expected：～事情结局竟会如此。Who would have expected that the ending turned out this way?

【不像话】bù xiànghuà ❶（言语行动）不合乎道理或情理 unreasonable：整天撒泼耍赖，实在～。Constant unreasonable quarrels are really intolerable. ❷ 坏得没法形容 shocking; outrageous：屋子乱得～。The room is in a shocking mess.

【不消】bùxiāo 不需要；不用 not necessary; needless：～说 needless to say; it goes without saying | ～一会儿工夫，这个消息就传开了。The news got out in no time.

【不孝】bùxiào ❶ 不孝顺 show no filial duty ❷〈旧时 *old*〉父母丧事中用于自称 I, the unfilial son or daughter

【不肖】bùxiào 品行不好（多用于子弟 of children) unworthy：～子孙 unworthy posterity

【不屑】bùxiè ❶ 认为不值得（做） disdain to do sth.; not worth doing; feel it beneath one's dignity to do sth.：～一顾 not worth a glance | ～置辩 not worth arguing about; also 不屑于 bùxièyú ❷ 形容轻视 belittle; look down on：脸上现出～的神情。Disdain was written on his face.

【不懈】bùxiè 不松懈 untiring; unremitting; indefatigable：坚持～ persistent | ～地努力 unremitting efforts | 进行～的斗争 wage an unremitting struggle

【不兴】bùxīng ❶ 不流行；不合时尚 out of fashion; outmoded：绣花鞋这里早就～了。Embroidered shoes are no longer fashionable in this part of the country. ❷ 不许 impermissible; not allowed：～欺负人。You are not allowed to bully others. ❸ 不能（限用于反问句 only used in rhetorical questions) can't：你干吗嚷嚷，～小点儿声吗？Why are you shouting, can't you speak a little more softly?

【不行】bùxíng ❶ 不可以；不被允许 not be allowed; will not do; be impossible：开玩笑可以，欺负人可～。To joke around is all right, but to bully people just won't do. ❷ 不中用 be no good; will not work：你知道，我在工程技术方面是～的。You know, I'm not good at engineering. ❸ 接近于死亡 dying：老太太病重，眼看～了。The old lady is so ill that it looks like she is dying. ❹ 不好 be not good; be poor：这件衣服的手工～。This coat was poorly made. ❺ 表示程度极深；不得了（用在'得'字后做补语 used as a complement after 得·de) awfully; extremely：累得～ awfully tired; be spent | 大街上热闹得～。The streets are extremely busy.

【不省人事】bù xǐng rénshì ❶ 指人昏迷，失去知觉 lose consciousness; be unconscious; be in a coma ❷ 指不懂人情世故 not know the ways of the world

【不幸】bùxìng ❶ 不幸运；使人失望、伤心、痛苦的 unfortunate; despairing and painful：～的消息 tragic news ❷ 表示不希望发生而竟然发生 (referring to) unwished-for or unexpected (events)：～身亡。To our great sorrow he died. | ～而言中。Unfortunately the prediction has come true. ❸ 指灾祸 disaster：惨遭～ encounter disaster

【不休】bùxiū 不停止（用做补语 used as a complement) endlessly; ceaselessly：争论～ argue endlessly; keep on arguing | 喋喋～ talk endlessly

【不修边幅】bù xiū biānfú 形容不注意衣着、容貌的整洁 not care about one's appearance; be slovenly (边幅 *bianfu*：布帛的边缘，比喻仪容、衣着 edge of a piece of cloth; further meaning appearance and clothes one wears)

【不朽】bùxiǔ 永不磨灭（多用于抽象事物 oft. for abstract things) immortal：～的业绩 immortal deeds | 人民英雄永垂～。Eternal glory to the people's heroes.

【不锈钢】bùxiùgāng 含铬13%以上的合金钢，有的还含有镍钛等其他元素。具有耐蚀和不锈的特性。多用来制造化工机件、耐热的机械零件、餐具等。stainless steel; iron alloy containing over 13% of chromium and, in some varieties, nickel, titanium or other elements, and resistant to erosion and rust, mostly used as a material for the making of chemical machine parts, heat-resistant components, food containers, etc.

【不许】bùxǔ ❶ 不允许 be not allowed; must not：～说谎。You must not tell lies. ❷ 不能（用于反问句 used in rhetorical questions) can't：何必非等我，你就～自己去吗？Why do you need to wait for me? Can't you go by yourself?

【不恤】bùxù 不顾及；不忧虑；不顾惜 disregard; could not care less; not be concerned with：～人言（不管别人的议论） disregard other people's comments

【不学无术】bù xué wú shù 没有学问，没有能力 have neither learning nor skill; be ignorant and incompetent

【不逊】bùxùn 没有礼貌；骄傲；蛮横 rude；impertinent：出言～ make impertinent remarks

【不言而喻】bù yán ér yù 不用说就可以明白 it goes without saying；it is self-evident

【不厌】bùyàn ❶ 不厌烦 not mind (doing sth.)；not tire of；not object to：～其详 go into details；dwell at length upon ❷ 不排斥；不以为非 not repel：兵～诈。There can never be too much deception in war.

【不扬】bùyáng （相貌）不好看 not good-looking：其貌～ not good-looking

【不要】bùyào 表示禁止和劝阻 don't：～大声喧哗。Don't talk loudly.｜～麻痹大意。Don't slacken your vigilance.

【不要紧】bù yàojǐn ❶ 没有妨碍；不成问题 it's not serious；it doesn't matter；never mind：这病～，吃点儿药就好。Your illness is not serious，and you will feel better after you take some medicine.｜路远也～，我们派车送你回去。Never mind how far it is，we will arrange for your drive back. ❷ 表面上似乎没有妨碍（下文有转折）it may appear all right，but ...：你这么一叫～，把大伙儿都惊醒了。You may think it's all right for you to shout，but you've woken everybody up.

【不一】bùyī ❶ 不相同（只做谓语，不做定语 only as a predicate，not as an attribute）different；not the same：质量～ differ in quality｜长短～ differ in length ❷ 书信用语，表示不一一详说 used in letters to indicate the deliberate omission of details：匆此～ without going into details

【不一而足】bù yī ér zú 不止一种或一次，而是很多 not an isolated case；numerous

【不依】bùyī ❶ 不听从；不依顺 not comply；not go along with：孩子要什么，她没有～的。She always lets her child have his way. ❷ 不允许；不宽容 not let off easily；not let sb. get away with sth.：～不饶 unwilling to let go or give in｜你要不按时来，我可～你。If you don't come on time，I won't let you off so easily.

【不宜】bùyí 不适宜 not suitable；inadvisable：这块地～种植水稻。This land is not suitable for growing rice.｜解决思想问题要耐心细致，～操之过急。You must be patient with ideological problems；haste is not advisable.

【不遗余力】bù yí yú lì 用出全部力量，一点也不保留 spare no pains (or effort)；do one's utmost

【不已】bùyǐ 继续不停 endlessly；incessantly：鸡鸣～。The cock is crowing incessantly.｜赞叹～ praise again and again

【不以为然】bù yǐ wéi rán 不认为是对的，表示不同意（多含轻视意 oft. derog.）not consider sth. to be right；disagree：～地一笑 a smile of denial｜他嘴上虽然没有说不对，心里却～。Although he did not state his objections，he felt it was not right.

【不以为意】bù yǐ wéi yì 不把它放在心上，表示不重视，不认真对待 pay no attention to；take no notice of；not mind

【不义之财】bù yì zhī cái 不应该得到的或以不正当的手段获得的钱财 ill-gotten wealth (or gains)

【不亦乐乎】bù yì lè hū 原意是'不也是很快乐的吗？'（见于《论语·学而》）现常用来表示达到极点的意思。*Analects · Learning*：'Isn't it a pleasure to learn and then carry into practice what has been learned?'；(used as a complement after 得·de) extremely；awfully：他每天东奔西跑，忙得～。Always on the go every day，he is awfully busy.

【不易之论】bù yì zhī lùn 内容正确、不可更改的言论 perfectly sound proposition；undeniable truth；irrefutable argument

【不意】bùyì 不料；没想到 unexpectedly：出其～ do the unexpected｜～大雨如注，不能起程。This downpour came so suddenly，it was impossible for us to set off right away.

【不翼而飞】bù yì ér fēi ❶ 没有翅膀却能飞。比喻东西突然不见了。(of an object) disappear without trace；vanish into thin air ❷ 形容消息、言论等传布迅速（of news，word，etc.）spread quickly as if on wings；spread like wildfire

【不用】bùyòng 表示事实上没有必要 need not：～介绍了，我们认识。There was no need for introductions because we knew each other.｜大家都是自己人，～客气。We are all among friends，so make yourself at home. ☞ 甭 béng on p. 94

【不由得】bùyóu·de ❶ 不容 cannot help；cannot but：他说得这么透彻，～你不信服。He spoke so cogently that you couldn't help being convinced. ❷ 不禁 cannot help：想起过去的苦难，～掉下眼泪来。I cannot help bursting into tears when thinking about my past hardships.

【不由自主】bù yóu zì zhǔ 由不得自己；控制不了自己 cannot help；involuntarily

【不虞】bùyú 〈书 *fml.*〉❶ 意料不到 unexpected：～之誉 unexpected praise｜～之患 unexpected disease ❷ 出乎意料的事 eventuality；contingency：以备～。Prepare for contingencies. ❸ 不忧虑 not worry about：～匮乏 fear no shortage of material resources；not worry about running out of supplies

【不约而同】bù yuē ér tóng 没有事先商量而彼此见解或行动一致 without prior consultation，(two persons) do or think the same；happen to coincide

【不在】bùzài ❶ 指不在家或不在某处 not be in；be out：您找我哥哥呀，他～。If you're looking for my brother，he is out.｜他～办公室，可能是联系工作去了。He's not in the office, but has probably gone out on some work. ❷〈婉辞 *euph*.〉指死亡(常带'了' oft. with 了·le) died: 我奶奶去年就~了。My grandmother died last year.

B

【不在乎】bùzài·hu 不放在心上 not mind; not care: 自有主张,~别人怎么说。Make up your mind and don't worry about what others might say.|青年人身强力壮,多干点活儿~。It's no problem for young people to work a little more, since they are strong and healthy.

【不在话下】bù zài huà xià 指事物轻微,不值得说,或事属当然,用不着说 be nothing difficult; be a cinch; it goes without saying

【不赞一词】bù zàn yī cí《史记·孔子世家》:'至于为《春秋》,笔则笔,削则削,子夏之徒不能赞一词。'原指文章写得很好,别人不能再添一句话。现在说'不赞一词'也指一言不发。*Records of the Historian · Hereditary House of Confucius*: 'In writing *The Spring and Autumn Annals* the author knew where to be elaborate and where to be succinct, so that the disciples of Zi Xia could not insert a single word in it; referring to sth. written so well that others could say nothing more; (later used to mean) not say a word; keep silent; make no comment

【不则声】bù zéshēng 〈方 *dial*.〉不做声 keep silent

【不择手段】bù zé shǒuduàn 为了达到目的,什么手段都使得出来(含贬义 derog.) by fair means or foul; by hook or by crook; unscrupulously

【不怎么样】bù zěn·meyàng 平平常常;不很好 just so-so; not particularly good: 这个人~。This person is pretty mediocre.|这幅画儿的构思还不错,就是着色~。The theme of the painting is quite good, but its colours are not very good.

【不振】bùzhèn 不振作;不旺盛 listless: 精神~ listless|一蹶~ cannot recover from defeat|国势~。The nation's influence is at low ebb.

【不支】bùzhī 支持不住;不能支撑下去 cannot support; cannot hold up: 精力~ exhausted|身体~。The body is too weak to support any further effort.

【不知凡几】bù zhī fán jǐ 不知道一共有多少。指同类的人或事物很多。can't tell how many there are (there being countless similar cases)

【不知进退】bù zhī jìn tuì 形容言语行动冒失,没有分寸 have no sense of propriety; not know when to stop

【不知死活】bù zhī sǐ huó 形容不知厉害,冒昧从事 act recklessly without considering the risks

【不知所措】bù zhī suǒ cuò 不知道怎么办才好。形容受窘或发急。be at a loss; be at one's wits' end

【不知所云】bù zhī suǒ yún 不知道说的是什么。指语言紊乱或空洞。scarcely know what one is saying (referring to confused or empty talk)

【不知所终】bù zhī suǒ zhōng 不知道结局或下落 not know the outcome or whereabouts of sth. or sb.

【不知天高地厚】bù zhī tiān gāo dì hòu 形容见识短浅,狂妄自大 not know the height of the heavens or the depth of the earth — have an exaggerated opinion of one's abilities

【不织布】bùzhībù 无纺织布 adhesive-bonded fabric; non-woven fabric.

【不止】bùzhǐ ❶ 继续不停 incessant; without end: 大笑~ roar with laughter|血流~。The bleeding is incessant. ❷ 表示超出某个数目或范围 more than; not limited to: 他恐怕~六十岁了。He is probably over 60.|类似情况~一次发生。It happened more than once.

【不只】bùzhǐ 不但;不仅 not only; not merely: ~生产发展了,生活也改善了。Not only has production developed but life has also improved.|河水~可供灌溉,且可用来发电。River water can be used not only for irrigation but also for the generation of electricity.

【不至于】bùzhìyú 表示不会达到某种程度 cannot go so far; be unlikely: 他~连这一点道理也不明白。He must have more sense than that.|两人有矛盾,但还~吵架。There are conflicts between them, but they cannot go so far as to quarrel.

【不治之症】bù zhì zhī zhèng 医治不好的病 incurable disease;〈比喻 *fig*.〉去除不掉的祸患或弊端 chronic malady; inveterate bane

【不致】bùzhì 不会引起某种后果 not in such a way as to; not likely to: 事前做好准备,就~临时手忙脚乱了。If you had arranged everything in advance you wouldn't be in such a rush at the moment.

【不置】bùzhì 〈书 *fml*.〉不停止 incessant; continuous: 赞叹~ admire again and again|懊丧~ cannot stop regretting

【不置可否】bù zhì kě fǒu 不说对,也不说不对 decline to comment; not express an opinion; be noncommittal; hedge

【不中】bùzhōng 〈方 *dial*.〉不中用;不可以;不好 no good; useless: 这个法子~,还得另打主意。This will not work and we must find another way.

【不周】bùzhōu 不周到;不完备 not attentive and satisfactory; thoughtless; inconsiderate: 考虑~ thoughtless|招待~ not be attentive enough to guests

【不周延】bù zhōuyán 一个判断的主词(或宾词)所包括的不是其全部外延,如在'有的工人是共青团员'这个判断中主词(工人)是不周延的,因为它说的不是所有的工人 non-distributional. What is entailed in the subject or predicate of a judgement does not cover the entirety of its denotation. For example, in the judgemental sentence, 'Some workers are Youth League members', the subject 'workers' is non-distributional because it does not refer to all the workers.

【不着边际】bù zhuó biānjì 形容言论空泛,不切实际;离题太远 not to the point; wide of the mark; neither here nor there; irrelevant

【不赀】bùzī 〈书 *fml.*〉没有限量,表示多或贵重(多用于财物 oft. property) immeasurable; incalculable: 价值～ immeasurable value | 工程浩大,所费～。The project is on such a gigantic scale that the cost is hard to calculate.

【不自量】bù zìliàng 过高地估计自己 not take a proper measure of oneself; overrate one's own abilities: 如此狂妄,太～。He is wildly arrogant and overrates his abilities.

【不自量力】bù zì liànglì 不能正确估计自己的力量(多指做力不能及的事情 oft. things beyond one's capability) not take a proper measure of oneself; overrate one's own abilities; also 自不量力 zì bù liànglì

【不足】bùzú ❶ 不充足;不满(某个数目) not enough; insufficient; inadequate: 先天～ congenital deficiency | 估计～ underestimate | ～三千人 less than 3,000 people ❷ 不值得 not worth: ～道 not worth mentioning | ～为奇 not enough to attract attention | ～挂齿 nothing to speak of ❸ 不可以;不能 cannot; should not: ～为训 not to be taken as an example | 非团结～图存。(We) cannot survive unless we unite.

【不足道】bùzúdào 不值得说 not worth mentioning; inconsiderable; of no consequence: 微～ too trivial or insignificant to mention | 个人的得失是～的。An individual's gain and loss is not worth mentioning.

【不足挂齿】bù zú guàchǐ 不值得一提 not worth mentioning; nothing to speak of: 区区小事,～。My paltry efforts are not worth mentioning.

【不足为奇】bù zú wéi qí 不值得奇怪。指事物、现象等很平常。not at all surprising; nothing to be surprised at

【不足为训】bù zú wéi xùn 不能当做典范或法则 not fit to serve as a model; not to be taken as an example; not an example to be followed; not to be taken as authoritative

【不做声】bù zuòshēng 不出声;不说话 keep silent; say not a word

布[1] bù ❶ 用棉、麻等织成的,可以做衣服或其他物件的材料 cotton cloth; cloth: 棉～ cotton cloth | 麻～ gunny cloth | 花～ cotton print | 粗～ coarse cloth | ～鞋 cloth shoes ❷ 古代的一种钱币 an ancient coin ❸ (Bù) 姓 a surname

布[2](佈) bù ❶ 宣告;宣布 declare; announce; publish; proclaim: 发～ issue; release | 公～ publish; issue | ～告 public notice | 开诚～公 frank and sincere ❷ 散布;分布 spread; disseminate: 阴云密～。The sky is overcast. | 铁路公路遍～全国。There are railways and highways all over the country. ❸ 布置 fix up; arrange; decorate: ～局 layout; overall arrangement | ～防 place troops on garrison duty | ～下天罗地网。Arrange a dragnet from which there will be no escape.

【布帛】bùbó 棉织品和丝织品的总称 general term for cotton and silk textiles

【布菜】bù//cài 把菜肴分给座上的客人 serve food (to guests at a meal)

【布道】bù//dào 指基督教宣讲教义 preach the gospel; sermonise

【布丁】bùdīng 用面粉、牛奶、鸡蛋、水果等制成的西餐点心 pudding; a Western dessert made with flour, milk, eggs, fruit, etc.

【布尔乔亚】bù'ěrqiáoyà 资产阶级的音译 translit eration: bourgeoisie [法 French: bourgeoisie]

【布尔什维克】bù'ěrshíwéikè 列宁建立的苏联共产党用过的称号,意思是多数派。1903年俄国社会民主工党召开第二次代表大会,在讨论党纲及组织原则问题上分成两派,拥护列宁主张的一派在选举党的领导机构时获得多数选票,所以有这称号。后来这一派成为独立的马克思列宁主义政党,改称苏联共产党(布尔什维克),简称联共(布)。Bolshevik, meaning 'majority party', old name for the Communist Party of the Soviet Union founded by Lenin. The name was coined at the Second Congress of the Russian Social Democratic Party in 1903, when the party split into two factions on issues concerning the Party programme and organizational principles, and the faction that supported Lenin's ideas won the majority position when voting for the Party's leading organ. The Bolsheviks later became an independent Marxist-Leninist party and renamed it as the Communist Party of the Soviet Union. abbr. 联共(布)[俄 Russian: большевик]

【布防】bù//fáng 布置防守的兵力 place troops on garrison duty; organize a defence: 沿江～ station troops along a river

【布告】bùgào ❶ (机关、团体)张贴出来告知群众的文件 notice; bulletin; proclamation: 出～ issue a public notice | 张贴～ paste up a notice ❷ 用张贴布告的方式告知(事项) announce by posting notice; notice: 特此～ hereby announce | ～天下 notice to the public

【布谷】bùgǔ 杜鹃(鸟名) cuckoo

【布景】bùjǐng ❶ 舞台或摄影场上所布置的景物 (theatre) setting; scenery setting ❷ 国画

用语，指按照画幅大小安排画中景物 composition (of a painting)

【布局】bùjú ❶ 全面安排(多指作文、绘画等 of writing, painting, etc.) overall arrangement; structure; composition：画面～匀称。The composition of the painting is well-proportioned. | 工业～不尽合理。The geographical distribution of industry is not reasonable. ❷ 围棋、象棋竞赛中指一局棋的开始阶段 the beginning of a chess match

【布控】bùkòng (对罪犯等的行踪)布置人员予以监控 (of activities and whereabouts of criminals) keep under surveillance

【布拉吉】bùlā·ji 连衣裙 dress; transliteration of Russian platye [俄 Russian: платье]

【布朗族】Bùlǎngzú 我国少数民族之一，分布在云南 Blang (Pulang) ethnic group, one of China's minority groups living in Yunnan Province

【布雷】bù//léi 布设地雷或水雷 lay mines; mine：～舰 mine-laying fleet | ～区 mined areas

【布雷舰】bùléijiàn 专门布设水雷的军舰，设有水雷储放舱，并装备有自卫火炮 minelayer; mine-laying warship with installations for the storage and release of mines, as well as guns for protection

【布匹】bùpǐ 布(总称)(collect.)cloth

【布设】bùshè 分散设置；布置 distribute; lay：～地雷 lay landmines | ～声呐 lay sonar mines | ～圈套 set a trap

【布施】bùshī 〈书 *fml.*〉把财物等施舍给人 almsgiving; charitable deed

【布头】bùtóu (～儿 bùtóur) ❶ 成匹的布上剪剩下来的不成整料的部分(多在五六尺以内 oft. less than five or six *chi*) remnants of a bolt of cloth ❷ 剪裁后剩下的零碎布块儿 remnants; odd bits of cloth

【布纹纸】bùwénzhǐ 一种印照片、放大照片用的纸，上面有像布的纹理 wove paper; light-sensitive paper showing a pattern of cloth-like fine mesh, used for printing or enlarging pictures

【布衣】bùyī ❶ 布衣服 cotton clothes：～蔬食 coarse clothes and simple fare — a thrifty and simple life ❷〈古时 *arch.*〉指平民(平民穿布衣) commoner：～出身 come from a commoner's family | ～之交 friends between commoners

【布依族】Bùyīzú 我国少数民族之一，分布在贵州 Bouyei (Buyei) ethnic group, one of China's minority groups living in Guizhou Province

【布置】bùzhì ❶ 在一个地方安排和陈列各种物件使这个地方适合某种需要 fix up; arrange; decorate：～会场 arrange a place for a meeting | ～新房。Decorate the bridal chamber. ❷ 对一些活动做出安排 assign; make arrangement for; give instructions about：～学习 make study arrangements | ～工作 assign work

步[1] bù ❶ 行走时两脚之间的距离；脚步 step; pace：正～ parade step | 跑～ run; jog | 寸～难移 be unable to move even a single step ◇ 走了一～棋 make a move (in chess, etc.) ❷ 阶段 stage; step：初～ primary stage | 事情一～比一～顺利。Things get smoother step by step. ❸ 地步；境地 condition; situation; state：不幸落到这一～。Unfortunately, things got to such a state. ❹ 旧制长度单位，1步等于5尺 old measure of length, equivalent to five *chi* ❺ 用脚走 walk; go on foot：～入会场 walk into an assembly hall | 亦～亦趋 imitate sb.'s every move ❻〈书 *fml.*〉踩；踏 tread：～人后尘 follow in sb.'s footsteps ❼〈方 *dial.*〉用脚步等量地 measure by paces; pace out：～一～这块地够不够三亩。Pace out this piece of land, and see if it's three *mu* in area. ❽ (Bù) 姓 a surname

步[2] bù 同'埠'。多用于地名，如盐步，禄步，炭步(都在广东)。same as 埠 bù; used as part of a place name, such as Yanbu, Lubu and Tanbu, all in Guangdong Province

【步兵】bùbīng 徒步作战的兵种，是陆军的主要兵种 infantry; foot soldier

【步步为营】bù bù wéi yíng 军队前进一步就设下一道营垒 advance gradually and dig in at every step;〈比喻 *fig.*〉行动谨慎，防备严密 consolidate at every step; act cautiously

【步调】bùdiào 行走时脚步的大小快慢，多比喻进行某种活动的方式、步骤和速度 (of certain activity) pace; step：统一～ concerted action | ～一致 march in step; keep in step; act in unison

【步伐】bùfá ❶ 指队伍操练时脚步的大小快慢 step; pace：～整齐 (march) in step ❷ 行走的步子 step：矫健的～ vigorous strides

【步弓】bùgōng same as 弓 gōng ③

【步履】bùlǚ 〈书 *fml.*〉行走 walk：～轻盈 walk with springy steps | ～维艰(行走艰难) have difficulty walking; walk with difficulty

【步枪】bùqiāng 步兵用的一种枪，枪管比较长，有效射程约400米 rifle; gun with a long rifled barrel with an effective range of 400 metres

【步人后尘】bù rén hòu chén 踩着人家脚印走 follow in sb.'s footsteps;〈比喻 *fig.*〉追随、模仿别人 imitate sb.; emulate

【步哨】bùshào 军队驻扎时担任警戒的士兵 sentry; sentinel

【步谈机】bùtánjī 体积很小、便于携带的无线电话收发机，通话距离不大。作战时，营、连、排、班之间用它来联络。walkie-talkie; handy two-way radio carried on the person for short-range communication, used as a liason tool during a war between battalions, companies, platoons and squads; also 步话机 bùhuàjī;通称 popularly known as 步行机 bùxíngjī

【步武】bùwǔ 〈书 *fml.*〉❶〈古时 *arch.*〉以六尺为步,半步为武。指不远的距离。a pace and a half — a very short distance:相去～ not far away; near ❷ 跟着别人的脚步走 follow upon sb.'s heels; follow in sb.'s footsteps;〈比喻 *fig.*〉效法 emulate; imitate:～前贤 emulate past sages as opposed to 'take a ride in a vehicle,' 'ride a horse', etc.

【步行】bùxíng 行走(区别于坐车、骑马等 as opposed to 'take the bus' or 'ride a horse') go on foot; walk:下马～ dismount from horseback and go on foot | 与其挤车,不如～。It is better to walk than to take a crowded bus.

【步行街】bùxíngjiē 不准车辆通行的街,大都是商业繁华地段 pedestrians' street; street (usu. in the busy shopping areas) where motor traffic is prohibited

【步韵】bù//yùn 依照别人做诗所用韵脚的次第来和(hè)诗 use the rhyme sequence of a poem (when replying to it)

【步骤】bùzhòu 事情进行的程序 step; measure:有计划、有～地开展工作。Carry on the work step by step in a planned way.

【步子】bù·zi 脚步 step; pace:放慢～ slow down one's steps | 队伍的～走得很整齐。The soldiers marched in step.

吥 bù 哏吥(Gòngbù),柬埔寨地名 Kampot, name of a place in Cambodia

埗 bù 茶埗(Chábù),地名,在福建 Chabu, name of a place in Fujian Province

怖 bù 害怕 fear; be afraid of:恐～ frightening | 阴森可～ ghastly and bloodcurdling

钚 bù 金属元素,符号 Pu(plutonium)。银白色,有放射性,用作核燃料等。plutonium (Pu), silver radioactive metal element used as nuclear fuel

埔 bù 大埔(Dàbù),地名,在广东 Dabu, name of a place in Guangdong Province ☞pǔ on p. 1501

埗 bù 同'埠' same as 埠 bù; 多用于地名 oft. used in place names:深水～(在香港) Sham Shui Po in Hong Kong

部 bù ❶ 部分;部位 part; section:内～ inner part or side | 上～ upper part | 胸～ chest | 局～ portion ❷ 某些机关的名称或机关企业中按业务而分的单位 unit; ministry; department; board:外交～ foreign ministry | 编辑～ editorial department | 门市～ department ❸〈军队 *mil.*〉(连以上)等的领导机构或其所在地 headquarters of an army unit above the company level:连～ seat of a company | 司令～ commander's headquarters ❹ 指部队 army; troop:率～突围 lead the army to make a breakthrough of an encirclement ❺〈书 *fml.*〉统辖;统率 lead; head; preside; govern:所～ control; command | ～领 commander ❻〈量词 *classifier*〉a)用于书籍、影片等(for books, films, etc.):两～字典 two dictionaries | 一～记录片 a documentary film | 三～电视剧 three TV plays; b) 用于机器或车辆(for machines and vehicles):一～机器 a machine | 两～汽车 two cars ❼ (Bù) 姓 a surname

B

【部队】bùduì 军队的通称 army; armed forces:野战～ a field army unit | 驻京～ armies stationed in Beijing | 武警～armed police corps | 从～转业到地方 (of an army man) transferred from the army to civilian work

【部分】bù·fen 整体中的局部;整体里的一些个体 part; section; share; individual part in sth. as an integral whole:检验机器各～的性能。Check the performance of each part of the machine. | 我校～师生参加了夏令营活动。Some of our teachers and students went to summer camp.

【部件】bùjiàn 机器的一个组成部分,由若干零件装配而成 (of a machine) components, consisting of a number of parts

【部类】bùlèi 概括性较大的类 category; division:这个百货商场的货物～齐全。The department store has a complete range of products.

【部落】bùluò 由若干血缘相近的氏族结合而成的集体 clan; tribe; collective formed on the basis of blood relations

【部门】bùmén 组成某一整体的部分或单位 department; branch:工业～ industrial sector | 文教～ cultural and educational sector | ～经济学(如工业经济学、农业经济学) departmental economics (such as industrial economics and agricultural economics) | 一本书要经过编辑、出版、印刷、发行等～,然后才能跟读者见面。Before a book is presented to its readers it must go through the departments of editing, publication, printing and distribution.

【部首】bùshǒu 字典、词典根据汉字形体偏旁所分的门类,如山、口、火、石等 radicals by which characters are arranged in traditional Chinese dictionaries

【部属】bùshǔ 部下 subordinate

【部署】bùshǔ 安排;布置(人力、任务) organize; delegate (human resources, tasks); deploy:～工作 delegate work | 战略～ strategic planning | ～了一个团的兵力。The troops of a regiment have been deployed.

【部头】bùtóu (～儿 bùtóur)书的厚薄和大小(主要指篇幅多的书) size (of a voluminous work):大～著作 large book

【部委】bùwěi 我国国务院所属的部和委员会的合称 ministries and commissions under the State Council

B

【部位】bùwèi 位置(多用于人的身体 usu. of parts of the human body) position; location: 发音～ the position of the tongue in pronunciation | 消化道～ the location of parts of the digestive tract

【部下】bùxià 军队中被统率的人,泛指下级 troops under one's command; (in a broad sense) one's subordinates

铺 bù same as 餔子 bù·zi

【餔子】bù·zi 婴儿吃的糊状食物 paste-like food for a baby

埠 bù ❶ 码头,多指有码头的城镇 port; wharf; pier: 船～ wharf | 本～ this town | 外～ out of town; city or town other than where one is ❷ 商埠 commercial port: 开～ open a commercial port

【埠头】bùtóu 〈方 *dial.*〉码头 wharf

瓿 bù 〈书 *fml.*〉小瓮 small jar

蔀 bù 〈书 *fml.*〉 ❶ 遮蔽 shade; obscure; close over; shield ❷ 〈古代 *arch.*〉历法称七十六年为一蔀 seventy-six years in ancient calendar

篰 bù 〈方 *dial.*〉竹子编的篓子 bamboo basket

簿 bù 簿子 notebook; book for writing in: 账～ account book | 练习～ notebook | 收文～ register of incoming dispatches | 记录～ minute book

【簿册】bùcè 记事记账的簿子 books for taking notes or keeping accounts

【簿籍】bùjí 账簿、名册等 account books; registers; records, etc.

【簿记】bùjì ❶ 会计工作中有关记账的技术 bookkeeping techniques ❷ 符合会计规程的账簿 account book in accordance with accounting rules

【簿子】bù·zi 记载某种事项的本子 notebook; book for writing in

C

cā（ㄘㄚ）

拆 cā〈方 *dial.*〉排泄（大小便）discharge (faeces or urine); shit or piss; poop
☞ chāi on p. 207

【拆烂污】cā lànwū〈方 *dial.*〉〈比喻 *fig.*〉不负责任，把事情弄得难以收拾 do sloppy work; skimp on a job; leave things in a mess; be irresponsible（烂污 *lanwu*：稀屎 semi-liquid stool）

擦 cā ❶ 摩擦 rub：～火柴 strike a match｜摩拳～掌 rub one's fists and palms — be eager for action or fight; champ at the bit｜手～破了皮。(My) hands were bruised raw. ❷ 用布、手巾等摩擦使干净 wipe clean with a rag or towel：～汗 wipe the sweat｜～桌子 wipe a table｜～玻璃 clean a windowpane ◇～亮眼睛 keep one's eyes peeled ❸ 涂抹 apply, spread on：～油 coat with oil｜～粉 powder; put on powder｜～红药水 apply mercurochrome ❹ 贴近；挨着 touch lightly or come close to in passing; shave; brush：～黑儿 evening; dusk; sunset; sundown｜～肩而过 brush past sb.｜球～桌边了。It's a line ball.｜燕子～着水面飞。The swallow skims over the water. ❺ 把瓜果等放在礤床儿上来回摩擦，使成细丝儿 grate a vegetable or fruit into shreds：把萝卜～成丝儿 shred turnips

【擦背】cā//bèi〈方 *dial.*〉搓澡 rub one's back with a towel while taking a bath

【擦黑儿】cāhēir〈方 *dial.*〉天快要黑的时候；傍晚 dusk; sunset; evening：赶到家时，天已经～了。It was dusk when I got home.

【擦屁股】cā pì·gu〈比喻 *fig.*〉替人做未了的事或处理遗留的问题（多指不好办的 usu. sth. difficult）clear up the mess left by sb.

【擦拭】cāshì same as 擦 cā ②：～武器 clean weapons

【擦洗】cāxǐ 用湿布块儿或酒精等擦拭使干净 clean (with wet rag or alcohol)：～餐桌 clean the dining table｜这个手表该～～了。This watch needs cleaning.

【擦音】cāyīn 口腔通路缩小，气流从中挤出而发的辅音，如普通话语音中的 f、s、sh 等 fricative, consonant sound characterised by the audible friction of moving air forced between vocal organs, such as f, s, sh in standard Chinese

【擦澡】cā//zǎo 用湿毛巾等擦洗全身，不用水冲 rub oneself down with a wet towel instead of taking a shower or bath

嚓 cā〈拟声词 *onom.*〉：摩托车～的一声停住了。The motorcycle screeched to a halt.
☞ chā on p. 202

礤 cā ☞［礓礤儿］(jiāngcār) on p. 961

cǎ（ㄘㄚˇ）

礤 cǎ〈书 *fml.*〉粗石 coarse stone

【礤床儿】cǎchuángr 把瓜、萝卜等擦成丝儿的器具，在木板、竹板等中间钉一块金属片，片上凿开许多小窟窿，使翘起的鳞状部分成为薄刃片 grater; utensil made of wood or bamboo board set with a piece of metal that has a punched, sharp-scaled surface for grating cucumber, turnips and other vegetables

cāi（ㄘㄞ）

偲 cāi〈书 *fml.*〉多才 talented
☞ sī on p. 1816

猜 cāi ❶ 根据不明显的线索或凭想像来寻找正确的解答；猜测 seek the correct answer by clue or by imagination; guess; conjecture; reckon; speculate; surmise：～谜语 solve a riddle｜你～谁来了？Guess who's here?｜他的心思我～不透。I can't figure out what's on his mind. ❷ 起疑心 suspect; have doubts about：～忌 distrust; suspicion｜两小无～（of a little boy and a girl）be intimate childhood playmates; innocent intimacy between a boy and a girl in childhood

【猜测】cāicè 推测；凭想像估计 judge or reach an opinion (about sth.) by reasoning; estimation based on imagination：这件事非常复杂，而且一点儿线索也没有，叫人很难～。The matter is so complex that it is hard to even hazard a guess without a clue.

【猜度】cāiduó 猜测；揣度 surmise; conjecture：心里暗自～，来人会是谁呢？(He) wondered, who can it be?

【猜忌】cāijì 猜疑别人对自己不利而心怀不满 be suspicious and hostile：互相～ be suspicious of one another

【猜料】cāiliào 猜测；估计 speculate; estimate:

事情的结果，现在还很难～。It is still hard to speculate on the result.

【猜枚】cāiméi 一种游戏(多用为酒令)，把瓜子、莲子或黑白棋子等握在手心里，让别人猜单双、个数或颜色，猜中的算胜(usu. drinkers') wager game, in which the players guess the number (odd or even) or colour of melon seeds, lotus seeds, or *weiqi* pieces held in a closed hand

C

【猜谜儿】cāi//mèir ❶ 猜谜底；捉摸谜语的答案 guess a riddle; try to find the answer to a riddle ❷〈比喻 *fig.*〉猜测说话的真实意思或事情的真相 guess the speaker's real intention or the truth of the matter：你有什么话就说出来，别让人家～。Say what you want to say, don't keep us guessing.

【猜谜】cāi//mí〈书 *fml.*〉same as 猜谜儿 cāi//mèir

【猜摸】cāi·mo 猜测；估摸 try to figure out; guess：他的心思叫人～不透。You can't tell what's on his mind.

【猜拳】cāi//quán 划(huá)拳 (play) a finger-guessing game

【猜嫌】cāixián same as 猜忌 cāijì

【猜想】cāixiǎng same as 猜测 cāicè：我～他同这件事有关。I suspect that he is involved in this matter.

【猜疑】cāiyí 无中生有地起疑心；对人对事不放心 groundless suspicion or doubt; mistrust; to have no trust or confidence in (sb. or sth.); to have misgivings：这件事过几天就要向大家说明，请不要胡乱～。No more guessing please. This will be explained in a few days.

cái (ㄘㄞˊ)

才[1] cái ❶ 才能 talent; ability：德～兼备 have both ability and integrity | 多～多艺 versatile; all-round; myriad-minded ❷ 有才能的人 capable person：干～person of experience and ability | 奇～prodigy; unusual talent ❸(Cái)姓 a surname

才[2]**(纔)** cái〈副词 *adv.*〉❶ 表示以前不久 a very short time ago：你怎么～来就要走？Why leave so soon? You've just arrived. ❷ 表示事情发生得晚或结束得晚 [indicating that something has taken place later than the usual, proper or expected lapse of time]：他说星期三动身，到星期五～走。He said he'd be leaving on Wednesday, but he didn't start out until Friday. | 大风到晚上～住了。The wind kept blowing until evening fell. ❸ 表示只有在某种场合条件下然后怎样(前面常常用'只有、必须'或含有这类意思)[oft. preceded by 只有 zhǐyǒu, 必须 bìxū or a sentence of similar meaning] not unless under certain conditions：只有依靠群众，～能把工作做好。Only by relying on the masses can we do a good job. ❹ 表示发生新情况，本来并不如此 not until：经他解释之后，我～明白是怎么回事。I didn't know what was going on until he explained it to me. ❺ 对比起来表示数量小，次数少，能力差，程度低等等 [indicating that sth. is less in quantity or frequency, worse in ability, or lower in level, etc., in comparison] only, merely：这个工厂开办时～五百工人，现在已有几千工人了。Now the factory has several thousand workers, up from a mere 500 at the beginning. ❻ 表示强调所说的事(句尾常用'呢'字)[indicating an emphatic tone, usu. followed by 呢·ne]：麦子长得～好呢！The wheat is coming along just fine.

【才分】cáifèn 才能；才智 talent; gift; innate ability; inherent capability

【才干】cáigàn 办事的能力 ability; competence; capability：增长～ improve one's ability | 他既年轻，又有～。He is both young and able.

【才刚】cáigāng〈方 *dial.*〉刚才 a short time ago; just now：他～还在这里，这会儿出去了。He was here just a short time ago, but now he's gone out.

【才华】cáihuá 表现于外的才能(多指文艺方面 esp. in arts) obvious talent：～横溢 be endowed with talent; of considerable talent; of great endowment; be richly endowed | ～出众 with unusual talent; be singularly endowed

【才具】cáijù〈书 *fml.*〉same as 才能 cáinéng：～有限 of or with limited ability

【才力】cáilì 才能；能力 ability; capability; talent：～超群 of or with superior ability

【才略】cáilüè 政治或军事上的才能和智谋 talent and resourcefulness in politics or military affairs：～过人 highly resourceful

【才能】cáinéng 知识和能力 learning and ability; power：施展～ make use of one's ability; give full play to one's ability; exert one's powers

【才气】cáiqì same as 才华 cáihuá

【才情】cáiqíng 才华；才思 literary or artistic endowment; imaginative power; brilliance：卖弄～ show off one's brilliance

【才识】cáishí 才能和见识 ability and insight：～卓异 with outstanding ability and insight

【才疏学浅】cái shū xué qiǎn 见识不广，学问不深(多用于自谦 oft. self-depreciatory) have little talent and less learning

【才思】cáisī 写作诗文的能力 imagination and creativeness in writing：～敏捷 have quick-witted imagination

【才学】cáixué 才能和学问 talent and learning; scholarship

【才艺】cáiyì 才能和技艺 gift and skill：～超绝

extraordinary talent and skill

【才智】cáizhì 才能和智慧 ability and wisdom; intelligence:充分发挥每个人的聪明～ give full play to each person's ability and wisdom

【才子】cáizǐ 指有才华的人 talented scholar; gifted person; wit

材 cái ❶ 木料,泛指材料① wood; timber; materials; (in a broad sense) 材料 cáiliào ①:木～timber; lumber|钢～steel; rolled steel|药～medicinal materials; crude drugs|就地取～draw on local resources; engage local people for office ❷ 棺材 coffin:寿～a coffin prepared before one's death|一口～a coffin ❸ 资料 material:教～teaching material|题～subject matter; theme|素～material; source material (for literature and art) ❹ 有才能的人 capable person:人～ person of ability; talented person; talent; competent person; qualified personnel

【材积】cáijī 单根树木或许多树木出产木材的体积 volume of processed timber obtainable from a single tree or many trees

【材料】cáiliào ❶ 可以直接造成成品的东西,如建筑用的砖瓦、纺织用的棉纱等 substance or things from which something else is made, e. g. bricks, tiles for construction, and cotton yarn for textiles:建筑～building materials|做一套衣服,这点～不够。The material isn't enough to make a suit. ❷ 提供著作内容的事物 facts, information, etc., to be used in writing:他打算写一部小说,正在搜集～。Intending to write a novel, he is collecting material. ❸ 可供参考的事实 facts for reference:人事～personnel information or date ❹〈比喻 *fig.*〉适于做某种事情的人才 talent for doing certain things; makings; stuff:我五音不全,不是唱歌的～。Without an accurate ear for the scales, I don't have the makings of a singer.

【材质】cáizhì ❶ 木材的质地 quality or texture of timber:楠木～细密。*Nanmu* is fine in texture. ❷ 材料的质地;质料 quality of material:各种～的浴缸 bathtubs made of various kinds of materials|大理石～的家具 marble furniture

财 cái 钱和物资的总称 general term for money and property:～产 property; assets; fortune|～物 property; belongings|理～management of money; finance; governing wealth

【财宝】cáibǎo 钱财和珍贵的物品 money and valuables

【财帛】cáibó 钱财(古时拿布帛作货币)wealth; money so called because in ancient times cloth and spunsilt were used as currency

【财产】cáichǎn 指拥有的金钱、物资、房屋、土地等物质财富 wealth owned, such as money, goods, real estate, land, etc.; possessions; assets:国家～state property|私人～private property

【财产权】cáichǎnquán 以物质财富为对象,直接与经济利益相联系的民事权利,如所有权、继承权等 property rights; civil right to material wealth, which is directly related to economic interests, e. g. ownership, right of inheritance; abbr. 产权 chǎnquán

【财大气粗】cái dà qì cū 形容人仗着钱财多而气势凌人 money talks; he who has wealth speaks louder than others; be a bully or braggart because of one's wealth

【财东】cáidōng ❶〈旧时 *old*〉商店或企业的所有者 owner of a store or enterprise; shop owner; store owner ❷ same as 财主 cái·zhu

【财阀】cáifá 指垄断资本家。一般指金融寡头。monopoly capitalist; financial oligarch; financial magnate; plutocrat; tycoon; *zaibatsu*

【财富】cáifù 具有价值的东西 weath; property; riches; thing or things of value:自然～natural riches|物质～material wealth|精神～spiritual wealth|创造～produce wealth

【财经】cáijīng 财政、经济的合称 finance and economics:～学院 College of Finance and Economics

【财会】cáikuài 财务、会计的合称 finance and accounting:～科 accounting department|～人员 accountants

【财礼】cáilǐ same as 彩礼 cǎilǐ

【财力】cáilì 经济力量(多指资金 usu. referring to funds) financial resources or capacity

【财贸】cáimào 财政、贸易的合称 finance and trade (or commerce):～系统 finance and trade circles

【财迷】cáimí 爱钱入迷、专想发财的人 moneygrubber; miser:他是个老～。He is an old miser.

【财气】cái·qì (～儿 cái·qìr)指获得钱财的运气;财运 luck in money matter:～不佳 have bad or ill luck in money matter

【财权】cáiquán ❶ 财产的所有权 property ownership; right of property ❷ 经济大权 control over financial affairs:掌握～have control over financial matters

【财神】cáishén 迷信的人指可以使人发财致富的神,原为道教所崇奉的神仙,据传姓赵名公明,亦称赵公元帅 God of Wealth; God of Fortune. Some superstitious people believe that there is a god who makes people rich. The God of Wealth originally worshipped by Taoists is Zhao Gongming, or Marshel Zhao. also 财神爷 cáishényé

【财势】cáishì 钱财和权势 wealth and influence:依仗～,横行乡里 use one's wealth and influence to rule as a despot or lord it over one's home village

【财税】cáishuì 财政、税务的合称 finance and tax:～部门 financial and tax departments

【财团】cáituán 指资本主义社会里控制许多公

司、银行和企业的垄断资本家或其集团 consortium; temporary alliance of two or more business firms and banks in a common venture, or the monopoly capitalist in control

【财务】cáiwù 机关、企业、团体等单位中,有关财产的管理或经营以及现金的出纳、保管、计算等事务 finance; financial affairs; affairs concerning the management or operation of financial assets, and receipt and payment, safekeeping and counting of cash in a governmental department, enterprise or any other organization, financial affairs:~处 financial department|~管理 financial management

【财物】cáiwù 钱财和物资 money and goods; property (real estate not included); belongings:爱护公共~ take good care of public property

【财源】cáiyuán 钱财的来源 financial resources; source of revenue:~茂盛 rich in financial resources|~枯竭。The financial resources are exhausted or drained.|发展经济,开辟~ develop the economy and open up more sources of revenue

【财运】cáiyùn 发财的运气 luck in matters concerning money:~亨通 have good luck in making money

【财政】cáizhèng 国家对资财的收入与支出的管理活动 finance; fiscal administration; the managing of money matters of a nation; government finance; public economy:~收入 revenue|~赤字 financial deficits; budgetary deficit

【财主】cái·zhu 占有大量财产的人 very wealthy person; rich (moneyed) person; moneybags:土~ local moneybags|大~ person of great wealth;tycoon

裁 cái ❶ 用刀、剪等把片状物分成若干部分 cut (paper, cloth, etc.) into parts with a knife or scissors:~纸 cut a sheet of paper|~衣服 cut out garments ❷ 整张纸分成的相等的若干份;division of standard-size printing paper; same as 开[1] kāi ⑲:对~(整张的二分之一) folio|八~报纸 octavo newspaper ❸ 把不用的或多余的去掉;削减 reduce by paring off a useless or unnecessary part or parts; cut down; reduce; lessen; curtail:~军 disarmament|~员 reduce staff;streamline ❹ 安排取舍(多用于文学艺术 oft. for literary or art works) mental plan; idea:别出心~adopt an innovative approach|《唐诗别~》*Innovative Poetry of the Tang Dynasty* ❺ 文章的体制、格式 style, form of writing:体~style ❻ 衡量;判断 judge; adjudicate; arbitrate:~判 judge; umpire; referee; judgement|~决 judge; decide; rule; adjudicate; verdict; arbitration; ruling; adjudication ❼ 控制;抑止 check; sanction:~制 sanction|制~sanction; ban|独~dictatorship; autocratic rule; exercise dictatorship

【裁兵】cái//bīng 〈旧指 *old*〉裁减军队 disarmament; reduce troops

【裁并】cáibìng 裁减合并(机构) cut down and merge (organizations)

【裁撤】cáichè 撤消;取消(机构等)(of organization, etc.) close; dissolve:~关卡 reduce customs passes|~重叠的科室 remove overlapping departments and offices

【裁处】cáichǔ 考虑决定并加以处置 consider and solve; make a decision and take action:酌情~handle sth. with due consideration to circumstances

【裁答】cáidá 〈书 *fml.*〉用书信、诗歌等答复 reply with a formal letter or a poem

【裁定】cáidìng 法院在案件审理过程中就某个问题做出决定 (of a court) make a legal decision; pass judgement on; judge; rule; ruling; adjudication

【裁断】cáiduàn 裁决判断;考虑决定 consider and decide; decision:丛书所收书目由主编~。The editor-in-chief decides what titles are to be included in the series.

【裁夺】cáiduó 考虑决定 consider and decide:此事如何处置,恳请~。Please decide how this matter should be dealt with.

【裁度】cáiduó 〈书 *fml.*〉推测断定 weigh; consider and decide; deduce; infer

【裁缝】cái·féng 裁剪缝制(衣服) tailor:虽是布衫布裤,但~得体。The jacket and trousers are of cotton, but well tailored.

【裁缝】cái·feng 做衣服的工人 tailor; seamstress

【裁减】cáijiǎn 削减(机构、人员、装备等) cut down; reduce (the size of organization, staff, equipment, etc.):~军备 reduce military preparations; reduction of armaments

【裁剪】cáijiǎn 缝制衣服时把衣料按一定的尺寸裁开 tailor; cut material according to a certain size and shape while making a garment:~技术 tailoring skills|这套衣服~得很合身。This suit is well tailored.

【裁决】cáijué 经过考虑,做出决定 make a ruling; judge; decide after consideration; adjudicate:如双方发生争执,由当地主管部门~。Any dispute that occurs between the two parties shall be adjudicated by local authorities.

【裁军】cáijūn 裁减武装人员和军事装备 disarmament; reduction of armed personnel and military equipment

【裁判】cáipàn ❶ 法院依照法律,对案件做出的决定,分为判决和裁定两种 adjudication; decision made by the court on a case according to the law, including the verdict and ruling ❷ 根据体育运动的竞赛规则,对运动员竞赛的成

绩和竞赛中发生的问题做出评判 referee; judge the outcome of sports contests and render a decision when a dispute occurs, in accordance with the rules of the game ❸ 在体育竞赛中执行评判工作的人 judge (in sports meets); referee (in basketball, football and boxing matches); umpire (in volleyball, table tennis, badminton, tennis and baseball matches); official who administers the rules in sports contests:足球～ referee | 国际～ international judge (referee, umpire); also 裁判员 cáipànyuán

【裁汰】 cáitài 〈书 *fml.*〉裁减(多余的或不合用的人员) dismiss; disemploy, discharge (unnecessary or unsuitable personnel)

【裁员】 cáiyuán 机关、企业裁减人员 reduction in the number of persons employed; reduction of staff in governmental organizations or enterprises

【裁酌】 cáizhuó 斟酌决定 consider and decide: 处理是否妥当,敬请～。Please decide whether the matter was settled properly.

cǎi (ㄘㄞˇ)

采[1] (採) cǎi ❶ 摘(花儿、叶子、果子)pick; pluck; gather; cull (flowers, leaves or fruits):～莲 pluck lotus seedpods|～茶 pick tea-leaves ◇到海底～珠子 dive for pearloysters at the bottom of the sea ❷ 开采 mine; quarry:～煤 mine coal|～矿 tap mineral ore; mine ❸ 搜集 gather; collect:～风 collect folk songs|～矿样 collect mineral samples ❹ 选取;取 choose; select; adopt:～购 purchase; select and purchase; procure|～取 adopt; take on; take up

采[2] cǎi 精神;神色 spirit; esprit; vitality; air; mien; complexion; expression:神～ look; expression; demeanour; air; mien; appearance|兴高～烈 in high spirits

采[3] cǎi same as 彩 cǎi
☞ cài on p. 181

【采办】 cǎibàn same as 采购 cǎigòu:～年货 do Spring Festival shopping

【采编】 cǎibiān 采访和编辑 gather and edit (news):新闻～ news gathering and editing|电视台的～人员 reporters and editors at a TV station; TV crew and editors

【采茶戏】 cǎicháxì 流行于江西、湖北、广西、安徽等地的地方戏,由民间歌舞发展而成,跟花鼓戏相近 *caicha* opera; local opera popular in Jiangxi, Hubei, Guangxi and Anhui provinces, which developed from folk songs and dancing, similar to the flower-drum opera

【采伐】 cǎifá 在森林中砍伐树木,采集木材 fell (trees in the forest for lumber); lumber; cut down; cut over:～林木 fell trees; woodcutting

【采访】 cǎifǎng 搜集寻访 have an interview with; cover (news-making event, people etc.); make enquiries; be on assignment (for a newspaper); gather material:～新闻 cover a news item; gather news|加强图书～工作 step up acquisition of book titles

【采风】 cǎi//fēng 搜集民歌 collect folk songs

【采购】 cǎigòu ❶ 选择购买(多指为机关或企业 for an organization or enterprise) make purchases; purchase; procure:～员 purchaser; purchasing agent; buyer|～建筑材料 purchase building materials ❷ 担任采购工作的人 people whose work is purchasing materials; purchaser; purchasing agent; buyer:他在食堂当～。He works as a buyer at the canteen.

【采光】 cǎiguāng 设计门窗的大小和建筑物的结构,使建筑物内部得到适宜的光线 lighting; ushering proper daylight into a building through designing the sizes of its doors and windows and its structure lighting; daylighting

【采集】 cǎijí 收集;搜罗 collect; gather:～标本 collect specimens|～民间歌谣 collect folk songs

【采掘】 cǎijué 挖取;开采(矿物)dig; excavate; mine (minerals):～金矿 mine gold|加快～进度 speed up excavation

【采矿】 cǎi//kuàng 把地壳中的矿石开采出来。有露天采矿和地下采矿两类。mining; process of removing ores, coal, and precious metals from the earth, which includes open-cut and underground mining

【采莲船】 cǎiliánchuán 跑旱船 folk dance depicting girls picking lotus seedpods from a boat

【采录】 cǎilù ❶ 采集并记录:collect and record:～民歌 collect folk songs ❷ 采访并录制 conduct an interview and record it on audio or visual tape:电视台～了新年晚会节目。The TV station has produced a programme on the New Year's Eve variety show. ❸〈书 *fml.*〉选取录用(人员) interview and select job applicants

【采买】 cǎimǎi 选择购买(物品)select and purchase; buy for an organization

【采纳】 cǎinà 接受(意见、建议、要求) accept (opinions, suggestions, requests, etc.); adopt; take (sb.'s advice)

【采暖】 cǎinuǎn 设计建筑物的防寒取暖装置,使建筑物内部得到适宜的温度 heating; design the heating facilities so that the interior of a building will have a suitable temperature

【采取】 cǎiqǔ ❶ 选择施行(某种方针、政策、措施、手段、形式、态度等) adopt (a certain policy, measure, means, way, etc.); assume (an attitude):～守势 take the defensive|～紧急措施 adopt emergency measures ❷ 取 take:～指纹 take or register sb.'s fingerprints

【采撷】cǎixié〈书 *fml.*〉❶ same as 采摘 cǎizhāi：～野果 pick wild fruit ❷ same as 采集 cǎijí

【采写】cǎixiě 采访并写出 cover; interview and write about：好人好事，要及时～，及时报道。Good people and good deeds should be covered and reported promptly.

【采血】cǎi//xiě 为检验等目的从人的静脉采取血液 draw blood from the vein for a test

【采样】cǎiyàng 采集样品；取样 take a sample; collect samples; sampling：食品～检查 food sampling for inspection

【采用】cǎiyòng 认为合适而使用 adopt sth. as suitable; use; employ：～新工艺 adopt new technology｜～举手表决方式 adopt voting by raising hands｜那篇稿子已被编辑部～。The editorial department has decided to publish the article.

【采油】cǎi//yóu 开采地下的石油 extract oil; oil drilling; petroleum production

【采择】cǎizé 选取；选择 select and adopt; pick; choose：提出几种方案，以供～。There are a few plans to choose from.

【采摘】cǎizhāi 摘取（花儿、叶子、果子）pluck; pick (flowers, leaves, fruits)：～葡萄 pluck grapes｜～棉花 pick cotton

【采制】cǎizhì ❶ 采集加工 gather and process：～春茶 pick and process spring tea ❷ 采访并录制 interview and record news items：～电视新闻 put together a TV news program

【采种】cǎi//zhǒng 采集植物的种子 gather seeds

彩（❷綵）cǎi ❶ 颜色 colour：五～ of different colours; multicoloured｜～云 rosy clouds ❷ 彩色的丝绸 coloured or variegated silk; colour festoons：剪～ cut the ribbon at an opening ceremony｜张灯结～ decorate with lanterns and colourful ribbons ❸ 称赞夸奖的欢呼声 applause; cheer：喝～ acclaim; cheer; applaud; root for｜博得满堂～ win, command, draw forth or receive general applause ❹ 花样；精彩的成分 variety; splendour; brilliance; artistry; gracefulness：丰富多～ rich and colourful ❺ 赌博或某种游戏中给得胜者的东西 lottery prize; winnings from certain games：得～ win a lottery｜中～ win a prize in a lottery｜～票 lottery ticket; raffle ticket ❻ 戏曲里表示特殊情景时所用的技术；魔术里用的手法 special effects in Chinese theatre; magic tricks：火～ special effects symbolizing fire｜带～ with tricks｜～活 (magicians') tricks ❼ 指负伤流血 be wounded and bleeding：挂～ be wounded｜～号 wounded soldier; the wounded

【彩绸】cǎichóu 彩色的丝绸 coloured silk

【彩带】cǎidài 彩色的丝绸带子 coloured ribbon or streamer

【彩旦】cǎidàn 戏曲中扮演女性的丑角。年龄比较老的也叫丑婆子。clown who plays a female role, the older ones also called 丑婆子 chǒupó·zi

【彩电】cǎidiàn ❶ 彩色电视的简称 abbr. for 彩色电视 cǎi sè diànshì：～中心 colour TV broadcasting centre ❷ 指彩色电视机 colour TV set：一台～ a colour TV set

【彩号】cǎihào（～儿 cǎihàor）指作战负伤的人员 wounded soldier：慰劳～ bring gifts to comfort wounded soldiers｜重～需要特别护理。Seriously wounded soldiers need special care.

【彩虹】cǎihóng 虹 rainbow

【彩绘】cǎihuì ❶ 器物、建筑物等上的彩色图画 coloured drawing or pattern on utensil, building, etc.：这次出土的陶器都有朴素的～。The pottery ware unearthed this time all bear simple coloured patterns. ❷ 用彩色绘画 paint with colours：古老建筑已～一新。The old buildings have been painted anew.

【彩轿】cǎijiào 花轿 bridal sedan chair

【彩卷】cǎijuǎn（～儿 cǎijuǎnr）彩色胶卷 colour film

【彩扩】cǎikuò 彩色照片扩印 enlarge and print colour film：电脑～ computerized enlargement and printing｜本店代理～业务。Our store enlarges and prints colour film.

【彩礼】cǎilǐ 旧俗订婚时男家送给女家的财物 (old custom) betrothal gifts from the bridegroom to the bride's family

【彩练】cǎiliàn same as 彩带 cǎidài

【彩排】cǎipái ❶ 戏剧、舞蹈等正式演出前的化装排演 dress rehearsal (before a play, dance, etc. is to take place) ❷ 节日游行、游园等大型群众活动正式开始前的化装排练 dress rehearsal (before a large-scale event such as a festival parade or a gala party)

【彩牌楼】cǎipái·lou 表示喜庆、纪念等活动中用竹、木等搭成并用花、彩绸、松柏树枝做装饰的牌楼 bamboo or wooden archway decorated with flowers, coloured streamers and pine and cypress twigs for events of celebration or commemoration

【彩棚】cǎipéng 用彩纸、彩绸、松柏树枝等装饰的棚子，用于喜庆活动 tent or marquee decorated with coloured paper and silk, and pine and cypress twigs for celebrations

【彩票】cǎipiào 奖券的通称 general term for 奖券 jiǎngquàn

【彩旗】cǎiqí 各种颜色的旗子 buntings; colourful flags：迎宾大道上，～飘扬。There are colourful flags waving along the street to welcome the guests.

【彩色】cǎisè 多种颜色 multicolour; colour：～照片 colour picture or photo

【彩色电视】cǎisè diànshì 荧光屏上显示彩色画面的电视 colour television; 简称 abbr. 彩电 cǎidiàn

【彩色片儿】 cǎisèpiānr same as 彩色片 cǎisèpiàn

【彩色片】 cǎisèpiàn 带有彩色的影片(区别于'黑白片' as compared with 'black-and-white' film) colour film

【彩声】 cǎishēng 喝彩的声音 applause; cheer: 一阵～ a burst of applause; a round of cheers | ～四起。There was a storm of applause.

【彩饰】 cǎishì 彩色的装饰 colourful decoration; polychrome: 因年久失修,梁柱上的～已经剥落。The colourful decorations on the beams have peeled as a result of long years of neglect.

【彩塑】 cǎisù 民间工艺,用黏土捏成各种人物形象,并涂上彩色颜料 colour modelling; coloured sculpture; painted sculpture; folk handicraft art of various clay figures that are hand-sculpted and colourfully painted

【彩陶】 cǎitáo 新石器时代的一种陶器,上面绘有彩色花纹 painted pottery; coloured pottery (a kind of pottery painted with colourful patterns dating back to the Neolithic Age)

【彩陶文化】 cǎitáo wénhuà ☞ 仰韶文化 Yǎngsháo wénhuà on p. 2223

【彩头】 cǎitóu ❶ 获利或得胜的预兆(迷信) (superstition) good sign; sign of future prosperity or triumph: 得了个好～。I got a good sign. ❷ 指中奖、赌博或赏赐得来的财物 money or prizes received from lotteries, gambling, or as a reward

【彩霞】 cǎixiá 彩色的云霞 rosy clouds; roseate clouds

【彩印】 cǎiyìn ❶ 彩色印刷 colour printing ❷ 洗印彩色照片 developing and printing colour photos

【彩云】 cǎiyún 由于折射日光而呈现彩色的云,以红色为主,多在晴天的清晨或傍晚出现在天边 rosy or roseate clouds; clouds that take on rosy hues as a result of refraction of sunlight, often appearing over the horizon in the morning or early evening in fine weather

【彩照】 cǎizhào 彩色照片 colour picture or photo

【彩纸】 cǎizhǐ ❶ 彩色的纸张 colour paper ❷ 彩色印相纸 printing paper for colour photos

寀 cǎi 〈古代 *arch.*〉指官 official
☞ cài on p. 182

睬(倸) cǎi 答理;理会 pay attention to; take notice of: 理～ pay attention to; show interest in | 不要～他。Ignore him. *or* Take no notice of him. | 人家对你说话,你怎么能～也不～? How come you pay no attention when someone is talking to you?

踩(跴) cǎi ❶ 脚底接触地面或物体 step on; stamp; tread; trample (to touch the ground or some object with the sole of a foot): 当心～坏了庄稼。Be careful not to tread on the crops. | 妹妹～在凳子上贴窗花。My little sister is standing on a stool, pasting paper-cuts on the windowpanes. ❷ 〈比喻 *fig.*〉贬低、糟蹋 belittle; disparage; degrade; debase; discredit; cry down: 这种人既会捧人,又会～人。This sort of person is capable of both flattering and belittling people. ❸ 〈旧时 *old*〉指追踪(盗匪)或追查(案件) track down (criminals) or investigate (cases): ～捕 investigate; pursue and capture | ～案 investigate a case

【踩道】 cǎidào (～儿 cǎidàor) 盗贼作案前察看地形 (of a thief) case the site before committing a crime

【踩点】 cǎidiǎn same as 踩道 cǎidào

【踩墒】 cǎishāng 在播种的地方踩实土壤,达到保墒目的 tramp down the earth over sown seeds to keep soil moist

【踩水】 cǎishuǐ 一种游泳方法,人直立深水中,两腿交替上抬下踩,身体保持不沉,并能前进 tread water (to advance or keep body almost upright in the water and the head above water with a treading motion of the feet)

cài (ㄘㄞˋ)

采(埰) cài [采地] (càidì) 〈古代 *arch.*〉诸侯分封给卿大夫的田地(包括耕种土地的奴隶) feudal estate; fief; feoff; benefice (an estate in land that a feudal prince invested his high officials with, usu. including the slaves working on it); also 采邑 càiyì
☞ cǎi on p. 179

菜 cài ❶ 能做副食品的植物;蔬菜 vegetable; greens; herbaceous plant grown for an edible part which is usu. eaten with the main meal: 种～ grow vegetables | 野～ edible wild herbs ❷ 专指油菜 rape: ～油 rapeseed oil; colza oil ❸ 经过烹调供下饭下酒的蔬菜、蛋品、鱼、肉等 dish; item or course on a menu such as vegetable, eggs, fish, meat and other food prepared to go with rice or wine: 荤～ meat dish | 川～ Sichuan dishes; Sichuan cuisine | 四～一汤 four dishes and a soup

【菜案】 cài'àn 厨房分工上指做菜的工作;红案 cooking that deals with dishes, both meat and vegetable

【菜场】 càichǎng same as 菜市 càishì

【菜单】 càidān (～儿 càidānr) 开列各种菜肴名称的单子 menu; menu card; bill of fare; list of dishes served at a meal; also 菜单子 càidān·zi

【菜刀】 càidāo 切菜切肉用的刀 kitchen knife; chopper; knife for cutting vegetable and meat

【菜点】 càidiǎn 菜肴和点心 dishes and desserts: 风味～ local dishes and desserts | 宫廷～ court dishes and desserts | 西式～ Western dishes and desserts

【菜豆】càidòu ❶ 一年生草本植物，茎蔓生，小叶阔卵形，花白色、黄色或带紫色，荚果较长，种子球形，白色、褐色、蓝黑色或绛红色，有花斑。嫩荚是普通蔬菜。种子可作粮食，也可入药。kidney bean (*Phaseolus vulgaris*); common bean; French bean; haricot bean; annual herbaceous climbing plant, with small, broad oval-shaped leaves, white or yellow blossoms or with a purple hue, elongated pods, spherical seeds, in colours ranging from white, brown purple, bluish black or deep red, and with contrasting patterns. The immature pods are a common vegetable, and the mature seeds can be a staple food or used as medicine. ❷ 这种植物的荚果或种子 pod or seed of the plant ‖ 通称 commonly known as 芸豆 yúndòu or 四季豆 sìjìdòu；有的地区叫扁豆 also 扁豆 biǎndòu in some areas

【菜瓜】càiguā ❶ 一年生草本植物，茎蔓生，叶子心脏形，花黄色。果实长形或椭圆形，皮白绿色，是一种蔬菜。snake melon (*Cucumis melo* var. *flexuosus*); serpent melon; annual herbaceous climbing plant, with heart-shaped leaves, yellow flowers, and elongated or oval-shaped fruit with a greenish-white skin, used as a vegetable ❷ 这种植物的果实 the fruit of the plant ‖ also 越瓜 yuèguā；有的地区叫老腌瓜 in some areas also called 老腌瓜 lǎoyānguā

【菜馆】càiguǎn 〈方 *dial.*〉(～儿 càiguǎnr) 饭馆 restaurant; also 菜馆子 càiguǎn·zi

【菜花】càihuā (～儿 càihuār) ❶ 油菜的花 rape flower ❷ 花椰菜的通称 popular name for 花椰菜 huāyēcài ❸ 花椰菜的花，是普通蔬菜 inflorescence of cauliflower, used as a vegetable

【菜金】càijīn 用作买副食的钱（多指机关、团体的 usu. of government departments or organizations) food expenses

【菜枯】càikū 油菜子经榨油后压成饼状的渣滓，是一种肥料 cake-shaped rapeseed dregs, used as fertilizer

【菜篮子】càilán·zi 盛菜的篮子，借指城镇的蔬菜、副食品的供应 vegetable basket, also refers to supply of vegetables and non-staple foods in cities and towns：经过几年的努力，本市居民的～问题已基本解决。After years of hard work, the shortage of non-staple food for residents of the city has been basically resolved.

【菜码儿】càimǎr 〈方 *dial.*〉面码儿 shredded or sliced vegetables to go with noodles

【菜牛】càiniú 专供宰杀食用的牛 cattle raised for beef; beef cattle; steer

【菜农】càinóng 以种植蔬菜为主的农民 vegetable grower; peasant who mainly lives on growing vegetables

【菜圃】càipǔ same as 菜园 càiyuán

【菜谱】càipǔ ❶ same as 菜单 càidān ❷ 介绍菜肴制作方法的书（多用做书名 usu. used as part of a cookbook's title) cookery book; cookbook; book containing recipes and instructions for cooking：《大众～》*A Cook Book of Popular Dishes*

【菜畦】càiqí 有土埂围着的一块块排列整齐的种蔬菜的田 small sections of a vegetable plot, divided by ridges; vegetable bed

【菜青】càiqīng 绿中略带灰黑的颜色 dark greyish green

【菜色】càisè 指人因靠吃菜充饥而营养不良的脸色 famished (or emaciated) look; sickly pallor of one living on wild herbs and suffering from malnutrition

【菜市】càishì 集中出售蔬菜和肉类等副食品的场所 food market; place used for selling food

【菜蔬】càishū ❶ 蔬菜 vegetables; greens ❷ 家常饭食或宴会所备的各种菜 dishes prepared for a meal or a banquet

【菜薹】càitái 某些十字花科蔬菜植物的花茎，如油菜薹、芥菜薹 tender flower stalk of some cruciferous plants, such as rape and mustard

【菜系】càixì 不同地区菜肴烹调在理论、方式、风味等方面具有独特风格的体系 cuisine; style of cooking of a particular area with distinctive characteristics of theory, method and taste

【菜羊】càiyáng 专供宰杀食用的羊 sheep raised for mutton

【菜肴】càiyáo 经过烹调供下饭下酒的鱼、肉、蛋品、蔬菜等 cooked dishes, such as of fish, meat, eggs and vegetable, etc.

【菜油】càiyóu 用油菜子榨的油，有的地区叫清油 rapeseed oil; also called 菜子油 càizǐyóu and 清油 qīngyóu in some areas

【菜园】càiyuán 种蔬菜的园子 vegetable garden; vegetable farm; also 菜园子 càiyuán·zi

【菜子】càizǐ ❶ (～儿 càizǐr) 蔬菜的种子 vegetable seeds ❷ 专指油菜子 especially rapeseed

【菜子油】càizǐyóu ☞ 菜油 càiyóu

寀 cài 〈书 *fml.*〉same as 采 cài ☞ cǎi on p. 181

蔡[1] Cài ❶ 周朝国名，在今河南上蔡西南，后来迁到新蔡一带 Cai, the name of a state during the Zhou Dynasty, located southwest of today's Shangcai, Henan Province, later moved to today's Xincai ❷ 姓 a surname

蔡[2] cài 〈书 *fml.*〉大龟 large turtle; tortoise：蓍～（占卜）augury

縩 cài ☞ 綷縩 (cuìcài) on p. 334

cān (ㄘㄢ)

参[1] (參) cān ❶ 加入；参加 join; enter; take part in; participate in：～军 join the army | ～赛 enter a competition ❷ 参考 consult; refer to：～看 see (also); cf. | ～阅 consult; refer to

参[2]（參） cān ❶ 进见；谒见 call to pay one's respects to：～谒 pay one's respects to｜～拜 pay a courtesy call；formally call on；pay homage to ❷ 封建时代指弹劾 impeach an official before the emperor in feudal times：～劾 impeach｜～他一本（'本'指奏章）submit a memorial to the emperor to impeach an official

参[3]（參） cān〈书 *fml.*〉探究并领会（道理、意义等）penetrate（truth）；reach into the realm of understanding：～破 penetrate；understand（mysteries，profundities，etc.）｜～透 perceive；understand；see through（mysteries，profundities，etc.）
☞ cēn on p.198 and shēn on p.1702

【参拜】cānbài 以一定的礼节进见敬重的人或瞻仰敬重的人的遗像、陵墓等 pay a formal call to a respected person；pay homage to the image or tomb of a respected person：大礼～ present oneself to sb. ceremoniously｜～孔庙 pay homage to Confucius' Temple

【参半】cānbàn 各占一半 half；half-and-half：疑信～half believing，half doubting

【参禅】cānchán 佛教徒静坐冥想领会佛理叫参禅（of Buddhists）sit in deep meditation to attain Buddhist truths：～悟道 meditation on and understanding of the truth

【参订】cāndìng 参校订正 proofread and correct：这部书由张先生编次，王先生～。Mr. Zhang compiled the book，and Mr. Wang proofread it.

【参观】cānguān 实地观察（工作成绩、事业、设施、名胜古迹等）visit；observe（work achievements，utilities，facilities，places of interest，etc.）：～团 visiting group｜～游览 visit places of interest；go sightseeing｜～工厂 visit a factory｜谢绝～visitors not admitted

【参合】cānhé〈书 *fml.*〉参考并综合 consult and sum up：～其要 draw on the essence of sth.｜本书～了有关资料写成。This book was written after consulting and summing up some relevant documents.

【参加】cānjiā ❶ 加入某种组织或某种活动 join a group or an organization；attend；engage in；take part in；participate in；go in for（activities）：～工会 join the trade union｜～会议 attend a meeting｜～选举 participate in an election｜～绿化劳动 take part in tree planting ❷ 提出（意见）offer；give；tender（advice，suggestions，etc.）：这件事儿，请你也～点儿意见。Please come and give us your view on this matter.

【参见】[1] cānjiàn same as 参看 cānkàn②（多用于书或文章的注解 usu. used in references）

【参见】[2] cānjiàn 以一定礼节进见；谒见 pay one's respects to（a superior，etc.）：～师父 pay respects to one's master

【参校】cānjiào ❶ 为别人所著的书做校订的工作 proofread；proof（a book written by another person）❷ 一部书有两种或几种本子，拿一种做底本，参考其他本子，加以校订 check versions of a book against a master copy

【参军】cān//jūn 参加军队 join the army；join up；enlist；enroll；sign up

【参看】cānkàn ❶ 读一篇文章时参考另一篇 refer to；read sth. for reference：那篇报告写得很好，可以～。The report is well written，and can be used as a reference. ❷ 文章注释用语，指示读者看了此处后再看其他有关部分 see（used in notes of articles），referring the reader to other relevant parts of an article

【参考】cānkǎo ❶ 为了学习或研究而查阅有关资料 consult（relevant material for the purpose of study or research）；read sth. for reference；refer to：～书 reference book｜作者写这本书，～了几十种书刊。To write this book，the author consulted scores of books and periodicals. ❷ 利用有关材料帮助了解情况 refer to；look at sth. for information：仅供～for reference only ❸ same as 参看 cānkàn②

【参考系】cānkǎoxì 为确定物体的位置和描述其运动而被选作标准的另一物体或物体系 reference system；reference frame；rigid framework relative to which positions and movements may be measured；also 参照系 cānzhàoxì or 参照物 cānzhàowù

【参量】cānliàng 数值可以在一定范围内变化的量。当这个量取不同数值时，反映出不同的状态或性能。parametre；quantity as a variable within certain limits，whose value determines the state or characteristics of sth.

【参谋】cānmóu ❶ 军队中参与指挥部队行动、制定作战计划的干部 staff officer；commissioned officer appointed to assist a commanding officer，concerned with administrative matters，planning，etc.，rather than with participation in combat ❷ 泛指代人出主意 give advice；advise；suggest；offer an opinion：这事该怎么办，你给～一下。Could you advise me on this matter? ❸ 指代出主意的人 adviser；counsellor；consultant；one who gives advice：他给你当～。He'll give you some advice.

【参赛】cānsài 参加比赛 participate in a match or contest：～作品 work of a contestant｜～选手 contestant｜取消～资格 debar；disqualify；expel

【参数】cānshù ❶ 方程中可以在某一范围内变化的数，当此数取得一定值时，就可以得到该方程所代表的图形。如在方程 $x^2+y^2=r^2$ 中，当 r 取得一定值时，就可以画出该方程所代表的圆，r 就是圆周的参数。parametre；a variable in an equation，whose values determine the figure the equation expresses. For example，in the equation $x^2+y^2=r^2$，when r， the parametre, takes on a certain value, the circle this equation expresses can be drawn; also 参变数 cānbiànshù ❷ 表明任何现象、机构、装置的某一种性质的量，如导电率、导热率、膨胀系数等 quantity whose value characterizes any phenomenon, organization or apparatus, e. g., electric conductivity, thermal conductivity, coefficient of expansion, etc.

【参天】cāntiān （树木等）高耸在天空中（of trees, etc.）reach to the sky; tower：古柏～ old cypress reaching high up to the sky|～大树 towering tree

【参透】cān//tòu 看透；透彻领会（道理、奥秘等）see through; perceive; make out; penetrate (truth, mystery, etc.)：参不透 cannot make out|～禅理 understand the truth of Zen|～机关（看穿阴谋或秘密）see through tricks (a scheme or secret)

【参详】cānxiáng 详细地观察、研究 study; ponder over; think over; contemplate：～了半天，忽有所悟 suddenly understand after much contemplation|我先把拟订的计划摆出来，请同志们～。Please study this plan I've drawn up.

【参验】cānyàn 考察检验；比较验证 investigate and check; compare and verify

【参谒】cānyè 进见尊敬的人；瞻仰尊敬的人的遗像、陵墓等 pay one's respects to; pay homage to sb. (before his or her tomb or image)：～黄帝陵 pay homage to the Yellow Emperor before his tomb

【参议】cānyì ❶〈书 *fml.*〉参与谋议 participate in consultation; counsel; advise：～国事 participate in consultation on state affairs ❷ 官名。明代在布政使、通政使司下设参议一职，清代通政使司下也设参议。民国时期参议多为闲职。official position, which was under the Provincial Administration Commissioner and Office of Transmission during the Ming Dynasty, under the Office of Transmission during the Qing Dynasty, was established and became mostly a nominal position during the period of Republic of China (1912-1949)

【参议院】cānyìyuàn 某些国家两院制议会的上议院 senate; upper house of the legislature of certain countries

【参与】cānyù 参加（事务的计划、讨论、处理）partake; participate in; take part in; be a part of; play a part in; have a say in：～其事 have a hand in the matter |他曾～这个规划的制订工作。He once participated in formulating this plan. also 参预 cānyù

【参预】cānyù same as 参与 cānyù

【参阅】cānyuè same as 参看 cānkàn：写这篇论文，～了大量的图书资料。To write this paper, (I) consulted a lot of books and materials.

【参赞】cānzàn ❶ 使馆的组成人员之一，是外交代表的主要助理人。外交代表不在时，一般都由参赞以临时代办名义暂时代理使馆事务。counsellor; chargé d'affaires; official of an embassy, the major assistant to a diplomatic representative, who does the latter's job temporarily in his or her absence ❷〈书 *fml.*〉参与协助 assist; aid：～军务 assist in military affairs|～朝政 assist in affairs of state

【参展】cānzhǎn 参加展览 attend an exhibition (or show)：～单位 participant in an exhibition|～的商品有一千余种。There are over a thousand kinds of merchandise on display.

【参战】cānzhàn 参加战争或战斗 enter a war; take part in a battle：～国 belligerent state|～部队 combat troops

【参照】cānzhào 参考并仿照（方法、经验等）consult (a method, experience, etc.) and follow suit：～执行 carry out by following the example of sth.

【参政】cān//zhèng 指参与政治活动或参加政治机构 participate in political activities or join a political organization

【参酌】cānzhuó 参考实际情况，加以斟酌 consider (a matter) in light of actual conditions; deliberate：～处理 handle (a matter) in light of the reality|～具体情况，制订工作计划 formulate a work plan in light of the specific conditions

骖（驂） cān〈古代 *arch.*〉指驾在车两旁的马 outer pair of a team of horses that draws a carriage

鳘 cān［鳘鲦］(cāntiáo) 鱼，身体小，呈条状，侧扁，白色。生活在淡水中。hemiculter (*Hemiculter leucisculus*); freshwater fish with a small, elongated and thin body, white in colour; also called 鳘鱼 cānyú or 鲦鱼 tiáoyú

餐（飡、湌） cān ❶ 吃（饭）eat; dine; take a meal; fare：聚～dine together; have a dining party|野～picnic; go on a picnic ❷ 饭食 food; meal：午～ lunch|中～ Chinese food|西～ Western food ❸〈量词 *classifier*〉一顿饭叫一餐［of meals］：一日三～three meals a day

【餐车】cānchē 列车上专为旅客供应饭食的车厢 restaurant car; dining car; diner; railroad car equipped as a restaurant for passengers

【餐风宿露】cān fēng sù lù 形容旅途或野外生活的艰苦 eat in the wind and sleep in the dew — hardships of a wayfarer; also 风餐露宿 fēng cān lù sù

【餐馆】cānguǎn 饭馆 restaurant; eating house

【餐巾】cānjīn 用餐时为防止弄脏衣服放在膝上或胸前的方巾 napkin; rectangular piece of material (cloth or paper) used to wipe the lips or fingers, and protect the clothes while eating

【餐巾纸】cānjīnzhǐ 专供进餐时擦拭用的纸 napkin; paper napkin; a piece of paper used at the table to wipe the lips or fingers; also 餐纸 cānzhǐ

【餐具】cānjù 吃饭的用具,如碗、筷、羹、匙等 table ware; dinner service; dinner set; bowls, chopsticks, spoons, etc., used at the table

【餐厅】cāntīng 供吃饭用的大房间,一般是宾馆、火车站、飞机场等附设的营业性食堂,也有的用做饭馆的名称 dining room; dining hall; large room in which meals are eaten, as in a hotel, railway station, airport, etc., sometimes used as part of a restaurant's name

【餐桌】cānzhuō (～儿 cānzhuōr) 饭桌 dining table

cán (ㄘㄢˊ)

残(殘) cán ❶ 不完整;残缺 incomplete; deficient:～品 defective goods; substandard product; damaged article|～废 maimed; crippled; disabled|身～志不～broken in health but not in spirit|这部书很好,可惜～了。It is a very good book, but unfortunately something's missing in it. ❷ 剩余的;将尽的 remnant; remaining:～冬 the last days of winter|～敌 remnants of enemy forces|风卷～云 strong wind scattering the last clouds ❸ 伤害;毁坏 injure; damage; abuse; break:摧～ wreck; destroy; damage; devastate|～害 molest ❹ 凶恶 cruel; savage; barbarous; ferocious:～忍 cruel; vicious; brutal; inhuman|～酷 cruel; ruthless; relentless; harsh; unrelenting

【残败】cánbài 残缺衰败 dilapidated; ruined; in ruins; broken-down; deteriorated; decadent; decayed:～不堪 in ruins; gone to wrack and ruin|一片～的景象 a dilapidated scene

【残暴】cánbào 残忍凶恶 cruel; ferocious; brutal; savage:～不仁 cruel and heartless; relentless; tyrannical|～成性 be cruel by nature|～的侵略者 brutal invaders

【残杯冷炙】cán bēi lěng zhì 指吃剩下的酒食 (of food) leftovers; orts; leavings; remnants of a meal

【残本】cánběn 残缺不全的本子(多指古籍 oft. refers to ancient books) book with part of it or some pages missing

【残编断简】cán biān duàn jiǎn ☞ 断编残简 duàn biān cán jiǎn on p.486

【残兵】cánbīng 残存下来的兵士 remnants of army troops:～败将 remnants of a routed army

【残部】cánbù 残存下来的部分人马 remnants of sb.'s defeated troops

【残喘】cánchuǎn 临死时仅存的喘息 lingering breath of life:苟延～linger on the last breath of life; be on one's last legs; linger on in a steadily worsening condition

【残存】cáncún 未被消除尽而保存下来或剩下来 remnant; remaining; surviving:～的封建思想 remnants of feudal thought|初冬,树上还～几片枯叶。It's early winter, and there are a few withered leaves left on the trees.

【残敌】cándí 残存的敌人 remnants of enemy troops

【残毒】cándú ❶ 凶残狠毒 brutal; ruthless; vicious:～的掠夺 brutal pillage ❷ 果实、蔬菜、谷物、牧草等里面残存的有毒农药或其他污染物质;动物吃了含毒植物后残存在肉、乳、蛋里面的有毒农药或其他污染物质 residue of poisonous pesticide or other pollutants found in fruit, vegetables, grains, forage grass, meat, milk or eggs

【残匪】cánfěi 残存的土匪 remnants of a group of bandits

【残废】cánfèi ❶ 四肢或双目等丧失一部分或者全部的机能 handicapped; disabled; crippled; loss of proper function of limbs, eyes, etc.:他的腿是在一次车祸中～的。His legs were crippled in a traffic accident. ❷ 残废的人 disabled person; handicapped person; lame person; handicapped; lame; crippled; cripple

【残羹剩饭】cán gēng shèng fàn 指吃剩下的菜汤和饭食 leftovers; orts; leavings; remains of a meal; crumbs from the table

【残骸】cánhái 人或动物的尸骨,借指残破的建筑物、机械、车辆等 remains of a human being or animal; wreckage; remains or fragments of sth. that has been wrecked, such as a building, machine, vehicle, etc.:寻找失事飞机的～ looking for the wreckage of a crashed airplane

【残害】cánhài 伤害或杀害 slaughter; cruelly injure or kill; maltreat; murder:～肢体 cause bodily injury|～生命 slaughter people|～儿童 abuse children

【残货】cánhuò 残缺或不合规格的货物 damaged or substandard goods; shopworn goods

【残积】cánjī 基岩经风化作用后残留在原地的岩石风化产物 saprolite; soft, disintegrated, usu. more or less decomposed bedrock remaining in the original place as a result of weathering; also 残积物 cánjīwù

【残疾】cán·jí 肢体、器官或其功能方面的缺陷 deformity; disability; handicap; defect in a limb or organ, or in their functions:～儿童 handicapped child|他的左腿没有治好,落下～。His left leg was crippled after failing to respond to medical treatment.

【残迹】cánjì 事物残留下的痕迹 remains; trace; relic; vestige; mark, trace, or visible evidence of sth. that is no longer present or in existence:当日巍峨的宫殿,如今只剩下一点儿～了。The grand palace of old has been reduced to a mere pile of ruins.

【残局】cánjú ❶ 棋下到快要结束时的局面(多指象棋 oft. game of chess) end-game; ending; final phase of a game of chess; last stage ❷ 事情失败后或社会变乱后的局面 situation after the failure of an undertaking or after social unrest:收拾～clear up the mess; pick up the pieces|维持～cope with a wretched situation

C

【残酷】cánkù 凶狠冷酷 cruel; brutal; ruthless; bloodthirsty:～无情 ruthless; relentless|～的压迫 ruthless oppression|手段十分～ with great cruelty

【残留】cánliú 部分地遗留下来 partly remain; be left over:面颊上还～着泪痕 traces of tears remaining on the face|他头脑中～着旧观念。He still holds on to the old mentality.

【残年】cánnián ❶ 指人的晚年(of a person) twilight years of life; declining years:风烛～ the decline of life; when life burns low like a candle in the wind; old and ailing like a candle flickering in the wind|～暮景 declining years ❷ 一年将尽的时候 the last days of the year:～将尽。The year is drawing to an end.|倏忽过了～。The last days of the year have passed in the blink of an eye.

【残虐】cánnüè ❶ 凶残暴虐 cruel; brutal; tyrannical:～的手段 brutal means ❷ 残酷虐待 maltreat; ill-treat; cruelly abuse:～囚犯 submit a prisoner to cruel abuse

【残篇断简】cán piān duàn jiǎn ☞ 断编残简 duàn biān cán jiǎn on p. 486

【残品】cánpǐn 有毛病的成品 defective goods; damaged article; substandard goods

【残破】cánpò 残缺破损 dilapidated; broken:～的古庙 dilapidated temple

【残棋】cánqí 没有下完的棋 end game of chess:一盘～ an end game

【残缺】cánquē 缺少一部分;不完整 incomplete; with parts missing; fragmentary:～不全 incomplete; fragmentary

【残忍】cánrěn 狠毒 cruel; ruthless; merciless; brutal:手段凶狠～ means of sheer brutality

【残杀】cánshā 杀害 kill savagely; murder; massacre; slaughter; butcher:自相～ slaughter each other|～无辜 massacre the innocent

【残生】cánshēng ❶ same as 残年 cánnián①:了此～ end one's remaining years ❷ 侥幸保存住的生命 life that survives on chance

【残损】cánsǔn (物品)残缺破损(of goods) broken; damaged; spoiled:这部线装书有一函～了。One part of the binding of the thread-bound book is torn.|由于商品包装不好,在运输途中～较多。Many of the goods were broken because of bad packing.

【残效】cánxiào 农药使用后,在一定时期内残留在植株上的药效 residue effect (of a pesticide sprayed on plants for a certain period):～期 period of residue effect

【残雪】cánxuě 没有融化尽的积雪 incompletely thawed snow

【残阳】cányáng 快要落山的太阳 setting sun

【残余】cányú ❶ 剩余;残留 remnants; remains; survivors; vestiges:～势力 remaining (or surviving) forces ❷ 在消灭或淘汰的过程中残留下来的人、事物、思想意识等 people, things or ideology remaining after an elimination process:封建～remnants of feudalism; feudal remnants

【残垣断壁】cán yuán duàn bì 残缺不全的墙壁。形容房屋遭受破坏后的凄凉景象。broken wall; scene of delapidation of a damaged building; also 颓垣断壁 tuí yuán duàn bì or 断壁残(颓)垣 duàn bì cán (tuí) yuán

【残月】cányuè ❶ 农历月末形状像钩的月亮 waning moon; crescent moon near the end of the month according to the Chinese Lunar Calendar ❷ 快落的月亮 setting moon

【残渣余孽】cán zhā yú niè 〈比喻 *fig.*〉残存的坏人 dregs and leftover evils; dross and remnant evils

【残照】cánzhào 落日的光辉 sunset glow; evening glow; rays of the setting sun

蚕(蠶) cán 家蚕、柞蚕等的统称,通常专指家蚕 silkworm (*Bombyx mori*); generic name for the domestic silkworm, tussah, etc., usu. referring to the domestic silkworm;☞家蚕 jiācán on p. 928 and 柞蚕 zuòcán on p. 2578

【蚕宝宝】cánbǎobǎo 〈方 *dial.*〉蚕(爱称) pet name for silkworm

【蚕箔】cánbó 养蚕的器具,用竹篾等编成,圆形或长方形,平底 round or rectangular bamboo tray with a flat bottom for breeding silkworms

【蚕蔟】cáncù 供蚕丝作茧的设备,有圆锥形、蛛网形等式样。有的地区叫蚕山。bundle of straw, etc., in the shape of a cone or web, for silkworms to spin cocoons on; also called 蚕山 cánshān in some areas

【蚕豆】cándòu ❶ 一年生或二年生草本植物,茎方形,中心空,花白色有紫斑,结荚果。种子供食用。broad bean (*Vicia faba*); annual or biannual herbaceous pod-bearing plant with a hollow, square stalk and purple-dotted white flowers ❷ 这种植物的荚果或种子 pod or seed of the plant ‖ also 胡豆 húdòu

【蚕蛾】cán'é 蚕的成虫,白色,触角羽毛状,两对翅膀,但不善飞,口器退化,不取食 silk moth; silkworm moth; white imago of the silkworm, with feather-shaped antennas, two pairs of wings and vestigial mouth parts, which does not fly or eat

【蚕茧】cánjiǎn 蚕吐丝结成的壳,椭圆形,蚕在里面变成蛹。是缫丝的原料。silkworm cocoon;

silky, oval envelope spun by the larvae of silkworms that serves as a covering in the pupal stage; used to reel silk

【蚕眠】cánmián 蚕每次蜕皮前不食不动的现象，蚕在生长过程中要蜕皮四次 inactive state of the silkworm before it sheds its skin, which occurs four times in its growth

【蚕农】cánnóng 以养蚕为主的农民 silkworm breeder; sericulturist

【蚕沙】cánshā 家蚕的屎，黑色的颗粒。中医入药。silkworm excrement, made up of black particles, used as an ingredient in traditional Chinese medicine

【蚕山】cánshān 〈方 *dial.*〉 same as 蚕蔟 cáncù

【蚕食】cánshí 蚕吃桑叶 (silkworm) nibble (mulberry leaves); 〈比喻 *fig.*〉逐步侵占 encroach on: ～政策 policy of 'nibbling' at another country's territory | ～邻国 encroach on a neighbouring country

【蚕丝】cánsī 蚕吐的丝，主要用来纺织绸缎，是我国的特产之一 natural silk; silk; filament obtained from silkworm cocoon, mainly used to reel silks and satins, one of the special products of China; also 丝 sī

【蚕蚁】cányǐ 刚孵化出来的幼蚕，身体小，颜色黑，像蚂蚁，所以叫蚕蚁 newly hatched silkworm, with a black, small body like that of an ant; also 蚁蚕 yǐcán

【蚕纸】cánzhǐ 养蚕的人通常使蚕蛾在纸上产卵，带有蚕卵的纸叫蚕纸 silkworm-egg sheet; a sheet of paper on which silk moths lay eggs

【蚕子】cánzǐ (～儿 cánzǐr) 蚕蛾的卵 silkworm egg

惭(慚) cán 惭愧 feel ashamed: 羞～ be ashamed | 大言不～ be shamelessly boastful; boast; brazenly brag | 自～形秽 feel ashamed of one's own unworthiness; have a sense of inferiority or inadequacy

【惭愧】cánkuì 因为自己有缺点，做错了事或未能尽到责任而感到不安 ashamed; abashed; feeling shame; distressed or embarrassed by one's own shortcomings, feelings of guilt, or failure to perform one's responsibility: 深感～ feel deeply ashamed | ～万分 be very much ashamed; be heartily ashamed

【惭色】cánsè 〈书 *fml.*〉惭愧的神色 shamedface expression: 面有～look ashamed

【惭颜】cányán 〈书 *fml.*〉羞愧的表情 shamedface expression

【惭怍】cánzuò 〈书 *fml.*〉惭愧 be ashamed: 自增～feel more ashamed

cǎn (ㄘㄢˇ)

惨(慘) cǎn ❶ 悲惨；凄惨 miserable; tragic: ～不忍睹 too horrible to look at; so horrible (miserable) that one cannot bear looking at it | ～绝人寰 tragic beyond human compare; rare tragedy on earth; so miserable and rare in human life; extremely tragic; extremely brutal | 死得好～ die a tragic death ❷ 程度严重；厉害 to a serious degree; disastrous: ～重 heavy; grievous; disastrous; calamitous | 冻～了 freeze to death | 敌人又一次～败。The enemy was severely defeated again. ❸ 凶恶；狠毒 cruel; savage; inhuman; merciless: ～无人道 inhuman; brutal

【惨案】cǎn'àn ❶ 指反动统治者或外国侵略者制造的屠杀人民的事件 massacre done by reactionaries or foreign invaders: 五卅～the May 30th Massacre of 1925 ❷ 指造成人员大量死伤的事件 tragedy; disastrous incident; disaster; event resulting in heavy casualty: 那里曾发生一起列车相撞的～。A tragic train collision happened there.

【惨白】cǎnbái ❶ (景色)暗淡 (of a scene) dim; gloomy ❷ (面容)苍白 (of face) pale; ghostly (deathly) pale: 脸色～ look deathly pale

【惨败】cǎnbài 惨重失败 crushingly or disastrously defeated; debacle; rout: 敌军～。The enemy was utterly defeated. ◇客队以〇比九～。The visiting team was crushed zero to nine.

【惨变】cǎnbiàn ❶ 悲惨的变故 tragic turn of fortune; disastrous turn of events: 家庭的～令人心碎。The tragedy of the family is heartbreaking. ❷ (脸色)改变得很厉害(多指变白 usu. pale) (of facial expression) change drastically: 吓得脸色～ turn pale from fear; change colour from fear

【惨不忍睹】cǎn bù rěn dǔ 悲惨得不忍心看。形容极其悲惨。too horrible (tragic) to look at; extremely tragic

【惨怛】cǎndá 〈书 *fml.*〉忧伤悲痛 grieved; heartbroken; sad: ～于心 feel grieved

【惨淡】cǎndàn ❶ 暗淡无色 gloomy; bleak; dim; sombre; dusky; dull: 天色～ gloomy weather | ～的灯光 dim lamplight ❷ 凄凉；萧条；不景气 dismal; dreary; dull; depressing; miserable: 秋风～wretched autumn wind | 神情～miserable expression | 生意～dull business ❸ 形容苦费心力 taking great pains: ～经营 take great pains to complete one's work under difficult circumstances; run a business by years of persistence ‖ also 惨澹 cǎndàn

【惨毒】cǎndú 残忍狠毒 brutal and vicious; ruthless and venomous: 手段～ with brutal and vicious methods

【惨祸】cǎnhuò 惨重的灾祸 horrible disaster; frightful calamity

【惨景】cǎnjǐng 凄惨的景象 tragic sight; miserable scene

【惨境】cǎnjìng 悲惨的境地 extremely miserable condition; dire straits; tragic circumstances;

陷入～ be trapped in dire straits

【惨剧】cǎnjù 指惨痛的事情 tragic event; dreadful event; calamity; disaster; tragedy

【惨绝人寰】cǎn jué rén huán 人世上还没有过的悲惨。形容悲惨到了极点。tragic beyond compare in the human world; rare tragedy on earth; extremely tragic; extremely brutal

【惨苦】cǎnkǔ 凄惨痛苦 miserable; forlorn; woebegone

【惨厉】cǎnlì 凄凉;凄惨 miserable; desolate; sad and shrill:风声～with the wind moaning|～的叫喊声 sad and shrill cries

【惨烈】cǎnliè ❶ 十分凄惨 miserable; desolate: ～的景象 a sad scene ❷ 极其壮烈 extremely heroic:～牺牲 die a heroic death; die heroically ❸ 猛烈;厉害 fierce; violent; vehement; severe:报复～violent retaliation|为害～cause severe harm|～的斗争 fierce fight

【惨然】cǎnrán 形容悲惨的样子(of facial expression, appearance, etc.) saddened; grieved

【惨杀】cǎnshā 残杀 massacre; murder; kill by cruel or violent means; slaughter:～无辜 massacre the innocent|遭受～be barbarously murdered

【惨死】cǎnsǐ 悲惨地死去 die a tragic death

【惨痛】cǎntòng 悲惨痛苦 bitter; agonizing; grievous; painful; deeply grieved:～的教训 a bitter lesson

【惨无人道】cǎn wú rén dào 残酷到了没有一点人性的地步。形容凶恶残暴到了极点。inhuman; brutal; cold-blooded; extremely cruel; savage

【惨笑】cǎnxiào 内心痛苦、烦恼而勉强作出笑容 sad smile; smile sadly; wry smile; bitter smile; force a smile (when feeling sad or frustrated)

【惨重】cǎnzhòng (损失)极其严重 (of loss or damage) heavy; grievous; disastrous:损失～ suffer heavy (grievous) losses|伤亡～suffer heavy casualties|～的失败 a disastrous defeat

【惨状】cǎnzhuàng 悲惨的情景、状况 miserable condition; pitiful sight; horrible sight

䅟(穇) cǎn [䅟子](cǎn·zi) ❶ 一年生草本植物,茎有很多分枝,叶子狭长。子实椭圆形,可以吃。billion-dollar grass (*Eleusine coracana*); annual herbaceous plant with a forked stalk, long, narrow leaves, and edible oval fruit ❷ 这种植物的子实 fruit of this plant

篸(篸) cǎn 〈方 *dial*.〉一种簸箕 winnowing pan

☞ zān on p. 2390

憯 cǎn 〈书 *fml*.〉same as 惨 cǎn

黲(黲) cǎn 〈书 *fml*.〉❶ 浅青黑色 dark: ～发 dark hair ❷ 昏暗 bleak; dismal; dim

càn (ㄘㄢˋ)

灿(燦) càn 光彩耀眼 bright; brilliant; dazzling; illuminating; glorious: ～然 brilliant; bright; cheerful|～若云锦 as shiny like brocade|黄～～的菜花 golden rape flowers

【灿烂】cànlàn 光彩鲜明耀眼 brilliant; resplendent; splendid; glorious:星光～stars shining brightly|～辉煌 glorious and resplendent; magnificent; splendid

【灿然】cànrán 形容明亮 bright; brilliant:阳光～brilliant sunshine|～炫目 dazzling; glaring; splendent; lustrous|～一新 look brand-new

掺(摻) càn 〈古代 *arch*.〉一种鼓曲 a kind of drum music:渔阳～(就是渔阳三挝) Three Stanzas of Yuyang (or 渔阳三挝 yúyáng sānzhuā)

☞ chān on p. 209 and shǎn on p. 1673

孱 càn 义同'孱'(chán),用于'孱头' same as 孱 chán in meaning; used in 孱头 càn·tou

☞ chán on p. 210

【孱头】càn·tou 〈方 *dial*.〉软弱无能的人(骂人的话 curse) weakling; coward; softy; chicken

粲 càn 〈书 *fml*.〉鲜明;美好 bright; brilliant; beaming:～然 beautiful and bright|云轻星～fleecy clouds and brilliant stars

【粲然】cànrán 〈书 *fml*.〉❶ 形容鲜明发光 shining; bright; beaming; brilliant:星光～bright star; shining star ❷ 形容显著明白 obvious; apparent; evident; manifest:～可见 obvious ❸ 笑时露出牙齿的样子 smiling broadly; cheerful; beaming:～一笑 give a beaming smile; grin with delight

璨 càn ❶ 美玉 jade ❷ same as 粲 càn

cāng (ㄘㄤ)

仓(倉) cāng ❶ 仓房;仓库 storehouse; warehouse:粮食满～。The granary is brimming with grain. ❷ (Cāng) 姓 a surname

【仓储】cāngchǔ 用仓库储存 keep grain, goods, etc., in a storehouse

【仓促】cāngcù 匆忙 hurried; hasty; hastily; hurriedly; in a hurry:～应战 go into battle in haste; accept a challenge in haste (in a hurry); take (pick) up the glove (gauntlet; gauge) without much forethought|时间～,来不及细说了。We have no time to talk about it at length. also 仓猝 cāngcù

【仓猝】cāngcù same as 仓促 cāngcù

【仓房】cāngfáng 储藏粮食或其他物资的房屋

warehouse; storehouse; building in which grains or other things are stored

【仓庚】cānggēng same as 鸧鹒 cānggēng

【仓皇】cānghuáng 匆忙而慌张 in a hurry; in a flurry; in a panic: ～失措 be disconcerted; be scared out of one's wits; be panic-stricken|～逃命 flee (run; fly) for one's life in confusion; flee in panic; flee helter-skelter; also 仓黄 cānghuáng and 仓惶 cānghuáng and 苍黄 cānghuáng

【仓库】cāngkù 储藏大批粮食或其他物资的建筑物 warehouse; storehouse; depository; building in which grains or other things are stored: 粮食～granary|军火～arsenal

【仓廪】cānglǐn〈书 *fml.*〉储藏粮食的仓库 granary

【仓容】cāngróng 仓库的容量 capacity of a storehouse: ～有限。The storehouse has a limited capacity.

伧(傖) cāng〈书 *fml.*〉粗野 rough; impolite; uncivil; unpolished; rude: ～父(粗野的人)a rough person; low or vulgar fellow; vulgarian

☞ ·chen on p. 242

【伧俗】cāngsú 粗俗鄙陋 vulgar; inelegant; distasteful; tasteless; in bad or poor taste: 言语～ use vulgar language

苍(蒼) cāng ❶ 青色(包括蓝和绿) dark green or blue: ～松翠柏 green pines and cypresses ❷ 灰白色 grey; ashen: ～髯 grey beard ❸〈书 *fml.*〉指天或天空 blue sky; sky above: 上～Heaven; God|～穹 the vault of heaven; firmament ❹ (Cāng) 姓 a surname

【苍白】cāngbái ❶ 白而略微发青;灰白 pale; pallid; wan: 脸色～look pale|～的须发 white beard and hair ❷ 形容没有旺盛的生命力 lifeless; flat; dull; colourless: 作品中的人物形象～无力。The characters in the work are lifeless.

【苍苍】cāngcāng ❶ (头发)灰白 (of hair) grey: 白发～ white-haired|两鬓～be greying at the temples ❷ 深绿色 dark green: 松柏～ verdant pine and cypress ❸ same as 苍茫 cāngmáng: 海山～ wide sea and hazy mountains|夜幕初落,四野～ vast expanse of land at dusk

【苍翠】cāngcuì (草木等)深绿 (of trees, grass, etc.) green; verdant: 林木～ green trees|～的山峦 verdant hills

【苍黄】[1] cānghuáng ❶ 黄而发青;灰暗的黄色 greenish yellow: 病人面色～。The patient has a sallow complexion.|时近深秋,竹林变得～了。It's almost late autumn, and the bamboo forest has turned yellow. ❷〈书 *fml.*〉青色和黄色。素丝染色,可以染成青的,也可以染成黄的(见于《墨子·所染》)。比喻事物的变化。black or yellow; (fig.) changeable (from the Mohist saying that white silk can be dyed either black or yellow in *Mozi·Dyeing*)

【苍黄】[2] cānghuáng same as 仓皇 cānghuáng

【苍劲】cāngjìng (树木、书画等)苍老挺拔(of trees) old and strong; (of calligraphy, painting, etc.) vigorous; bold: ～的古松 hardy, old pines|他的字写得～有力。He writes with a bold, vigorous hand.

【苍老】cānglǎo ❶ (面貌、声音等)显出老态(of appearance) old; (of voice, etc.) hoary; hoarse: 病了一场,人比以前显得～多了。He looks much older after his illness. ❷ 形容书画笔力雄健(of calligraphy or painting) vigorous; bold

【苍凉】cāngliáng 凄凉 desolate; bleak: 月色～ bleak moonlight

【苍龙】cānglóng ❶ 二十八宿中东方七宿的合称 collective name for the seven constellations of the eastern group of the 28 constellations; also 青龙 qīnglóng ❷ 古代传说中的一种凶神恶煞。现在有时用来比喻极其凶恶的人。evil spirit in ancient lore; (fig.) vicious person

【苍茫】cāngmáng 空阔辽远;没有边际 vast; boundless: ～大地 boundless land|暮色～ gathering dusk|云水～ vast expanse of sea and cloudy sky

【苍莽】cāngmǎng〈书 *fml.*〉same as 苍茫 cāngmáng

【苍穹】cāngqióng〈书 *fml.*〉天空 vault of heaven; firmament; also 穹苍 qióngcāng

【苍生】cāngshēng〈书 *fml.*〉指老百姓 common people

【苍天】cāngtiān 天(古代人常以苍天为主宰人生的神)Heavens (the God or celestial powers that determine human fate); also 上苍 shàngcāng

【苍蝇】cāng·ying 昆虫,种类很多,通常指家蝇,头部有一对复眼。幼虫叫蛆。成虫能传染霍乱、伤寒等多种疾病。fly; housefly; any of the numerous insects of the order *Diptera*, esp. of the family *Muscidae*, known as the common housefly, with a pair of compound eyes. The larva of the fly is called maggot. The mature fly transmits various diseases such as cholera and typhoid, etc .

【苍郁】cāngyù〈书 *fml.*〉(草木)苍翠茂盛 (of grass and trees) verdant and luxuriant

【苍术】cāngzhú 多年生草本植物,开白色或淡红色的花。根可入药。Chinese atractylodes (*Atractylodes chinensis*); perennial herbaceous plant with white or pale red flowers and roots that can be used as Chinese medicine.

沧(滄) cāng (水)青绿色 (of water) greenish-blue; sea-green: ～海 sea; deep blue sea

【沧海】cānghǎi 大海(因水深而呈青绿色)deep blue sea; sea

【沧海桑田】cāng hǎi sāng tián 大海变成农田，农田变成大海 vicissitudes; seas change into fields and fields change into seas;〈比喻 *fig*.〉世事变化很大 Time brings great changes to the world. also 桑田沧海 sāng tián cāng hǎi

【沧海一粟】cāng hǎi yī sù 大海里的一颗谷粒 a drop in the ocean;〈比喻 *fig*.〉非常渺小 tiny; paltry; insignificant:群众智慧无穷无尽,个人的才能只不过是～。Compared with the infinite intelligence of the collective, an individual's talent is but a drop in the ocean.

C

【沧桑】cāngsāng 沧海桑田的略语 abbr. for 沧海桑田 cāng hǎi sāng tián:饱经～(比喻经历了许多世事变化) be time-weathered; have experienced many vicissitudes of life

鸧(鶬) cāng [鸧鹒](cānggēng)黄鹂 oriole; also 仓庚 cānggēng

舱(艙) cāng 船或飞机中分隔开来载人或装东西的部分 cabin; hold; enclosed space for temporary occupancy by people or cargo, as in a vessel or aeroplane: 货～cargo cabin | 客～passenger cabin | 前～front cabin | 头等～first-class cabin

【舱室】cāngshì 舱(总称) cabin (collect.)

【舱位】cāngwèi 船、飞机等舱内的铺位或座位 seat or berth in a cabin

cáng (ㄘㄤˊ)

藏 cáng ❶ 躲藏;隐藏 hide; conceal; ensconce; hide away; stow away; store away:包～conceal; harbour; withhold; hold in; dissemble | 暗～hide; conceal | ～龙卧虎 hidden dragons and crouching tigers — people of talent remain in oblivion | 他～起来了。He has hidden himself. ❷ 收存;储藏 collect; store:收～collect | 珍～treasure; cherish | 冷～refrigerate; refrigeration; cold storage | ～书 collection of books

☞ zàng p. 2392

【藏躲】cángduǒ same as 躲藏 duǒcáng:无处～have no place to hide oneself

【藏锋】cángfēng ❶〈书 *fml*.〉使锋芒不外露 refrain from outspoken attack; sheathe one's talent:～守拙 sheathe one's talent ❷ 书法中指笔锋不显露 (of calligraphy) not show the tips of strokes

【藏富】cángfù 富有而不表露出来(of a rich man) conceal one's wealth

【藏垢纳污】cáng gòu nà wū〈比喻 *fig*.〉包容坏人坏事 shelter evil people and countenance evil practices; also 藏污纳垢 cáng wū nà gòu

【藏奸】cángjiān ❶ 心怀恶意 harbour evil intentions; harbour malice: 笑里～hide one's evil intentions behind smiles ❷〈方 *dial*.〉不肯拿出全副精力或不肯尽自己的力量帮助别人 be unwilling to exert one's full strength or do one's best to help others:～耍滑 hide one's treachery and act in a slick way

【藏龙卧虎】cáng lóng wò hǔ〈比喻 *fig*.〉潜藏着人才 talented people remain to be found

【藏猫儿】cángmāor 捉迷藏 play hide-and-seek

【藏闷儿】cángmēnr〈方 *dial*.〉捉迷藏 play hide-and-seek

【藏匿】cángnì 藏起来不让人发现 conceal; hide; go into hiding:在山洞里～了多天 remain hiding in a cave for several days

【藏品】cángpǐn 收藏的物品 collected article; collected object:私人～personal collection

【藏身】cángshēn 躲藏;安身 hide oneself; go into hiding:～之所 hiding place; hideaway; hideout; shelter; refuge; haven

【藏书】cáng//shū 收藏书籍 collect books:～家 book collector | 这个图书馆～百万册。This library boasts a collection of millions of books.

【藏书】cángshū 收藏的图书 collection of books:把～捐给学校 donate one's book collection to a school

【藏书票】cángshūpiào 贴在书籍封面封底或书内的纸片,记有藏书日期和人名等,一般印制精美 book collector's stamp; a piece of paper pasted on the front or back cover of a book or inside a book, bearing the date of collection, name of collector, etc., usu. in fine printing

【藏头露尾】cáng tóu lù wěi 形容说话办事故意露一点留一点,不完全表露出来 show the tail but conceal the head; hide one part of sth. on purpose; give a partial account; tell part of the truth but not all of it

【藏掖】cángyē ❶ 怕人知道或看见而竭力掩藏 try to cover up (for fear of being discovered):～躲闪 dodge and hide ❷ 遮掩住的弊端 covert malpractice:他为大家办事完全公开,从来没有～。He serves everyone openly, without concealing anything.

【藏拙】cángzhuō 怕丢丑,不愿让别人知道自己的见解或技能 hide one's inadequacy or incompetence by keeping quiet; be unwilling to show one's opinion or skill for fear of being mocked

【藏踪】cángzōng 隐藏踪迹;躲藏 conceal one's tracks; hide oneself

cāo (ㄘㄠ)

操 cāo ❶ 抓在手里;拿 grasp; hold:～刀 grab a knife | ～起扁担就往外走 grab a shoulder pole and head out ❷ 掌握;驾驶 control; operate:～舟 sail a boat | ～纵 manoeuvre; control; steer | 稳～胜券 have full assurance of success; be sure to win | ～生杀大权 have people completely at one's mercy; wield power of life and death over people ❸ 做

(事);从事 do; act; be engaged in:～作 operate; manipulate; handle|～劳 work hard|重～旧业 take up one's old trade again; resume one's old profession ❹ 用某种语言、方言说话 speak (a language or dialect):～英语 speak English|～吴语 speak the Wu dialect ❺ 操练 drill; exercise:～演 demonstration; drill; exercise|出～hold a drill; perform a drill ❻ 由一系列动作编排起来的体育活动 exercise composed of a series of movements:体～gymnastics|早～morning exercise|工间～work-break exercise|健美～aerobics dancing (exercises) ❼ 品行;行为 conduct; behaviour:～守 discretion in conduct; moral fortitude; integrity; virtue|～行 behaviour or conduct (of a student) ❽ (Cāo)姓 a surname

☞cào p.195

【操办】cāobàn 操持办理 manage affairs; make preparations or arrangements for:～婚事 make preparations for a wedding

【操场】cāochǎng 供体育锻炼或军事操练用的场地 playground; sports ground; drill ground; outdoor area used specifically for exercises or military drills

【操持】cāochí ❶ 料理;处理 manage; handle:～家务 manage household affairs|这件事由你～。I'll leave the matter in your hands. ❷ 筹划;筹办 make plans; make arrangements

【操典】cāodiǎn 记载军事操练要领等的书,如步兵操典、骑兵操典等 drill regulations; drill manual; drill book; book containing principles of military drills, such as a drill manual for infantry, a drill manual for cavalry

【操劳】cāoláo 辛辛苦苦地劳动;费心料理(事务)work hard; take care of or look after (affairs):日夜～work day and night|～过度 be overworked

【操练】cāoliàn ❶ 以队列形式学习和练习军事或体育等方面的技能 drill; train; instruct and practise military formations or athletic skills:～人马 drill the troops ❷ 泛指训练或锻炼 exercise:～身体 do exercises; perform physical exercises

【操切】cāoqiè 指办事过于急躁 rash; hasty:～从事 act with undue haste|这件事他办得太～了。He was too hurried in handling the matter.

【操琴】cāo//qín 演奏胡琴(多指京胡 esp. Beijing *huqin*) play the *huqin*

【操神】cāo//shén 劳神 take trouble:～受累 put sb. to trouble; bother sb.|他为这事可操了不少神了。He has taken much trouble over this matter.

【操守】cāoshǒu 指人平时的行为、品德 conduct; behaviour; personal integrity:～清廉 be honest and upright; be free from corruption

【操心】cāo//xīn 费心考虑和料理 worry; take trouble; take pains; be concerned over (with):为国事～put one's heart and soul into state affairs|为儿女的事操碎了心 go to a lot of trouble for one's children

【操行】cāoxíng 品行(多指学生在学校里的表现 usu. of a student at school) behaviour or conduct

【操演】cāoyǎn 操练;演习(多用于军事、体育 usu. for military or sports)drill; train:学生在操场里～。Students are doing drills on the training ground.|～一个动作,先要明了要领。One should understand the essentials of a movement before practising it.

【操之过急】cāo zhī guò jí 办事情过于急躁 act with undue haste:这事得分步骤进行,不可～。This matter should be handled step by step instead of in haste.

【操纵】cāozòng ❶ 控制或开动机械、仪器等 control; operate (machinery, equipment, etc.):～自如 operate with skill; operate with facility|远距离～remote control|一个人～两台机床。Each person operates two machine tools. ❷ 用不正当的手段支配、控制 manipulate; rig:～市场 rig the market|幕后～manipulate from behind the scenes; pull strings|那个组织曾一度被坏人所～。That organization once fell under the control of evil persons.

【操纵台】cāozòngtái 装有仪表、开关线路或其他机件,控制机器或电气设备运转的工作台 control panel; switchboard or control panel containing instruments, switches, cords, etc., that controls the operation of machines or electric equipment

【操作】cāozuò ❶ 按照一定的程序和技术要求进行活动 operate; manipulate; act according to a certain process and technical requirements:～方法 operating method|～规程 operating rules and regulations ❷ 泛指劳动;干活 work:在家帮助母亲～help one's mother with household chores

【操作规程】cāozuò guīchéng 操作时必须遵守的规定,是根据工作的条件和性质而制定的 operating rules and regulations; rules and regulations to be followed during operation, which are formulated according to the conditions and nature of the work:技术～rules and regulations for technical operation|安全～rules and regulations for safe operation

糙 cāo 粗糙;不细致 rough; coarse; crude; unrefined:～粮 coarse food grain|～纸 rough paper|这活儿做得很～。This is slipshod work.

【糙粮】cāoliáng 〈方 *dial.*〉粗粮 coarse food grain

【糙米】cāomǐ 碾得不精的大米 brown rice; unpolished rice; half-polished rice; coarse rice

cáo(ㄘㄠˊ)

曹[1] cáo ❶〈书 *fml.*〉辈 people of the same kind：吾～all of us；we|尔～all of you；you ❷〈古代 *arch.*〉分科办事的官署 government department

曹[2] Cáo ❶ 周朝国名，在今山东西部 name of a state in the Zhou Dynasty，located in the west of present-day Shandong Province ❷ 姓 a surname

嘈 cáo（声音）杂乱 noisy；booming（noise）；clamorous：～～ clamorous；clamouring；vociferous；noisy|～杂 noisy

【嘈杂】cáozá（声音）杂乱；喧闹 noisy；clamorous；vociferous；clamouring：人声～ hubbub of voices|声音～刺耳 make a harsh，deafening noise

漕 cáo 漕运 water transport：～粮 grain transported to the capital by water|～渠 canal|～船（运漕粮的船）boat for carrying grain to the capital in former times

【漕渡】cáodù 军事上指用船、筏子渡河（mil.）cross a river by boat or raft

【漕河】cáohé 运漕粮的河道 river for transporting grain to the capital in former times

【漕粮】cáoliáng 漕运的粮食 grain transported to the capital by water

【漕运】cáoyùn〈旧时 *old*〉指国家从水道运输粮食，供应京城或接济军需 water transport of grain by the government to supply the capital city or meet military needs

槽 cáo ❶ 盛牲畜饲料的长条形器具 trough；manger；feed box；long，narrow，open receptacle，used chiefly to hold water or food for animals：猪～ pig's trough|马～ manger ❷ 盛饮料或其他液体的器具 container used to hold drinks or other liquid：酒～ cask|水～ water trough；sink ❸（～儿 cáor）两边高起，中间凹下的物体，凹下的部分叫槽 groove；slot；furrow；tunnel；notch；slit；long，narrow cut or indentation in an object or surface：河～ tunnel|在木板上挖个～ cut a notch in the board ❹〈方 *dial.*〉〈量词 *classifier*〉门窗或屋内隔断的单位 unit of door，window or any other thing that partitions a room：两～隔扇 two partition windows|一～窗户 a window ❺〈方 *dial.*〉〈量词 *classifier*〉喂猪从买进小猪到喂壮卖出叫一槽 period to raise a piglet until it is big enough for sale：今年他家喂了两～猪。They have raised two litters of piglets this year.

【槽床】cáochuáng 安放槽的架子或台子 trough bed；groove bed；slot bed；trough stand；groove stand；slot stand；stand or table to put a trough on

【槽坊】cáo·fang 酿酒的作坊 traditional brewery or distillery

【槽糕】cáogāo〈方 *dial.*〉用模子制成的各种形状的蛋糕 cake made with moulds；also 槽子糕 cáo·zigāo

【槽头】cáotóu 给牲畜喂饲料的地方 trough（in a livestock shed）

【槽牙】cáoyá 臼齿的通称 general term for 臼齿 jiùchǐ

【槽子】cáo·zi same as 槽 cáo ①②③

【槽子糕】cáo·zigāo same as 槽糕 cáogāo

碏 cáo 斫碏(Zhuócáo)，地名，在湖南 Zhucao，name of a place in Hunan Province

螬 cáo ☞［蛴螬］(qícáo) on p. 1512

艚 cáo〈书 *fml.*〉一种木船 wooden boat

【艚子】cáo·zi 载货的木船，有货舱，舵前有住人的木房 wooden cargo boat（with living quarters in the stern）

cǎo(ㄘㄠˇ)

草[1]（艸、❹騲）cǎo ❶ 高等植物中栽培植物以外的草本植物的统称 grass；herbage in general，except cultivated plants：野～ weeds|青～ green grass|水～ water weeds；water plants；aquatic plants；aquatic weeds ❷ 指用做燃料、饲料等的稻、麦之类的茎和叶 stalks and leaves of rice，wheat，etc.，used as fuel，fodder，etc.：稻～ paddy straw|～绳 straw rope；grass rope|～鞋 straw sandals ❸〈旧指 *old*〉山野、民间 the wild；the country：～贼 outlaw in the woods；bandit；brigand|落～为寇 take to the woods and become a bandit|～泽医生 folk doctor ❹ 雌性的（多指家畜或家禽 usu. of domestic animals or fowls）female：～驴 female donkey；jenny ass|～鸡 hen

草[2]（艸）cǎo ❶ 草率；不细致 careless；hasty；sloppy：潦～sloppy|字写得很～。The handwriting is very sloppy. ❷ 文字书写形式的名称（of calligraphy）cursive hand；running style；handwritten forms a)汉字形体的一种 a style of Chinese characters：～书 cursive hand；running hand|～写 cursive hand；running hand|真～隶篆 regular，cursive，official and seal scripts b)拼音字母的手写体 handwritten form（of Romanized letters）：大～ large handwritten form|小～ small handwritten form ❸ 初步的；非正式的（文稿）（of documents）draft；not final：～案 draft；ground plan|～稿 draft；rough draft；manuscript ❹〈书 *fml.*〉起草 draft：～拟 draw up；draft；rough in

【草案】cǎo'àn 拟成而未经有关机关通过、公布的，或虽经公布而尚在试行的法令、规章、条例等 draft（of a decree，regulation，rule，etc.）that has not been passed and promulgated by relevant authorities, or promulgated but is on trial implementation:土地管理法～ draft law for land administration | 交通管理条例～ draft of the regulations for communications management

【草包】cǎobāo ❶ 用稻草等编成的袋子 straw bag; straw sack; bag woven with rice straw, etc. ❷ 装着草的袋子 bag (sack) containing straw;〈比喻 *fig.*〉无能的人。有的地区也比喻做事毛手毛脚、常出差错的人。idiot; blockhead; good-for-nothing; incapable person; (also in a figurative sense in some areas) careless person; person who always makes mistakes:这点儿事都办不了,真是～一个! He's a real good-for-nothing to have failed such a simple task!

【草本】[1] cǎoběn 有草质茎的(植物)(of plant) herbaceous; herbal; having a stem that does not become woody

【草本】[2] cǎoběn 文稿的底本 master copy (of a manuscript); original

【草本植物】cǎoběn zhíwù 有草质茎的植物。茎的地上部分在生长期终了时就枯死。herb; herbage; non-woody vegetation with a stem that withers at the end of the growing period

【草编】cǎobiān 一种民间手工艺,用玉米苞叶、小麦茎、龙须草、金丝草等编成提篮、果盒、杯套、帽子、拖鞋、枕席等 straw weaving; straw plaiting; folk handicraft, weaving baskets, fruit boxes, glass holders, hats, slippers, mats to cover pillows, etc., with corn husks, wheat stalks, Chinese alpine rush, *Hypericum patulum*, etc.

【草标儿】cǎobiāor 用草茎或草做的标志,集市中插在比较大的物品(多半是旧货)上表示出卖 wisp of straw marking larger-sized goods (usu. used goods) for sale on the market

【草草】cǎocǎo 草率;急急忙忙 carelessly; hastily; hurriedly:～了事 rush through the work; get the work done any old way|～收场 hastily wind up; come to a hasty conclusion|～地看过一遍 give a (cursory) glance; take a glance at; leaf through

【草测】cǎocè 工程开始之前,对地形、地质的初步测量,精确度要求不很高 preliminary survey of topography and location, made before a project starts, which does not require a high accuracy:新的铁路线已开始～。A preliminary survey of the new railway line has started.

【草场】cǎochǎng 长有牧草的大片土地,有天然的和人工的两种 grazing land; grassland; pastureland; pasture; vast stretch of natural or cultivated land covered with grass or herbage, used for the grazing of livestock

【草虫】cǎochóng ❶ 栖息在草丛中的虫子,如蛐蛐儿等 insect living in grass, such as the cricket ❷ 以花草和昆虫为题材的中国画 grass-and-insect painting; traditional Chinese painting that focuses on the subject matter of flowers, grass and insects

【草创】cǎochuàng 开始创办或创立 start; establish or found:～时期 initial (or pioneering) stage

【草刺儿】cǎocìr〈比喻 *fig.*〉很细小的东西 very tiny thing

【草苁蓉】cǎocōngróng same as 列当 lièdāng

【草丛】cǎocóng 聚生在一起的很多的草 thick growth of grass

【草底儿】cǎodǐr same as 草稿 cǎogǎo:作文先要打个～。You need to formulate a rough draft before writing a composition.

【草地】cǎodì ❶ 长野草或铺草皮的地方 lawn; stretch of grass-covered land ❷ 草原或种植牧草的大片土地 grassland; meadow; pasture; vast stretch of land covered with grass or herbage, used for the grazing of livestock

【草甸子】cǎodiàn·zi〈方 *dial.*〉长满野草的低湿地 grassy marshland:前面是一大片～。A vast grassy marshland stretches before us.

【草垫子】cǎodiàn·zi 用稻草、蒲草等编的垫子 straw mattress; pallet; rush cushion; rush mat

【草稿】cǎogǎo (～儿 cǎogǎor)初步写出的文稿或画出的画稿等 rough draft; preliminary draft:打～make a rough draft

【草荒】cǎohuāng 农田因缺乏管理,杂草丛生,妨碍了农作物的生长,叫草荒 farmland with more weeds than crops as a result of neglect

【草灰】cǎohuī ❶ 草木植物燃烧后的灰,可做肥料 plant ash (can be used as fertilizer) ❷ 灰黄的颜色 greyish yellow:～的大衣 greyish yellow overcoat

【草鸡】cǎojī〈方 *dial.*〉❶ 母鸡 hen ❷〈比喻 *fig.*〉软弱或胆小畏缩 cowardly; timid; chicken-hearted

【草菅人命】cǎo jiān rénmìng 把人命看得和野草一样,指任意残杀人民 treat human life as if it were not worth a straw; act with utter disregard for human life; wantonly slaughter people

【草荐】cǎojiàn 铺床用的草垫子 straw mattress; pallet

【草芥】cǎojiè〈比喻 *fig.*〉最微小的、无价值的东西 trifle; mere nothing; trash; tiniest, worthless thing; straw:视富贵如～ regard wealth and rank as worthless

【草寇】cǎokòu〈旧指 *old*〉出没山林的强盗 robbers in the woods; brigands

【草料】cǎoliào 喂牲口的饲料 fodder; feed

【草绿】cǎolǜ 绿而略黄的颜色 grass green colour

【草码】cǎomǎ ☞ 苏州码子 Sūzhōu mǎ·zi p.1829

【草莽】cǎomǎng ❶ same as 草丛 cǎocóng ❷〈旧指 *old*〉民间 common people; ordinary people

【草帽】cǎomào（～儿 cǎomàor）用麦秆等编成的帽子，夏天用来遮阳光 straw hat，used to block sunlight in summer

【草帽缏】cǎomàobiàn（～儿 cǎomàobiànr）用麦秆一类东西编成的扁平的带子，是做草帽、提篮、扇子等的材料 sennit；braided straw；plaited straw（used in making hats，baskets，fans，etc.）；also 草帽辫 cǎomàobiàn

【草莓】cǎoméi ❶ 多年生草本植物，匍匐茎，叶子有长柄，花白色。花托红色，肉质，多汁，味道酸甜，供食用。strawberry（*Fragaria*）；perennial herbaceous plant having stolons，long leaf stalks，white blossoms，red，edible fruit that is fleshy and juicy and tastes sour-sweet ❷ 这种植物的花托和种子 receptacle and seeds of the plant ‖ 有的地区叫草果或杨梅 in some areas also called 草果 cǎoguǒ or 杨梅 yángméi

【草昧】cǎomèi〈书 *fml.*〉未开化；蒙昧 uncivilized；primitive

【草棉】cǎomián 一年生草本植物，花一般淡黄色，果实的形状像桃儿，内有白色的纤维和黑褐色的种子。纤维就是棉絮，是纺织工业中最主要的原料。种子可以榨油。cotton plant（*Gossypium*）；annual herbaceous plant，usu. having light yellow flowers，peach-shaped fruit that contains white fibre and dark brown seeds，fibre that is a major raw material in the textile industry，and seeds that can be used to extract oil. 通称 commonly called 棉花 miánhuā

【草民】cǎomín 平民 common people

【草木灰】cǎomùhuī 草、木、树叶等燃烧后的灰，含钾很多，是一种常用的肥料 plant ash（ash of grass，wood，leaves，etc.，which contains much potassium and is a commonly used fertilizer）

【草木皆兵】cǎo mù jiē bīng 前秦苻坚领兵进攻东晋，进抵淝水流域，登寿春城瞭望，见晋军阵容严整，又远望八公山，把山上的草木都当成晋军，感到惊惧。后来用'草木皆兵'形容惊慌时疑神疑鬼。every bush and tree looking like an enemy soldier；a state of extreme suspicion and fear（According to history，Fu Jian，King of the Former Qin Dynasty，led his army to attack the Eastern Jin Dynasty. As he approached the Feishui River valley，Fu Jian mounted the city wall of Shouchun and saw the orderly battle formation of the Eastern Jin army. When he turned to look at the Bagongshan Mountain in the distance he panicked，for he mistook the grass and trees on the slopes for Eastern Jin troops.）

【草拟】cǎonǐ 起草；初步设计 draw up；draft；prepare：～文件 draw up a document｜～本地区发展的远景规划 draft a long-term plan for local development

【草皮】cǎopí 连带薄薄的一层泥土铲下来的草，用来铺成草坪，美化环境，或铺在堤岸表面，防止冲刷 turf；short grass and the surface layer of soil used for making lawns，to beautify environment，or for protecting dams against scouring

【草坪】cǎopíng 平坦的草地 flat area of closely cut grass；lawn

【草签】[1] cǎoqiān same as 草标儿 cǎobiāor

【草签】[2] cǎoqiān 缔约国代表在条约草案上临时签署自己姓名（多用简写或者第一个字母）。草签后还有待正式签字。也泛指一般协议、合同在正式签字前临时签署姓名。initial；representatives of signatory parties sign their names，usually in simplified form or initials，on a draft treaty before it is officially signed；the provisional signature of agreements and contracts in general

【草食】cǎoshí 以草类、蔬菜等为食物（of animals）feeding on herbs and vegetables：～动物 herbivorous animal；herbivore

【草市】cǎoshì 指农村的定期集市 village fair held at regular intervals

【草书】cǎoshū 汉字字体，特点是笔画相连，写起来快 cursive script；form of Chinese calligraphy，with characters executed swiftly and strokes flowing together

【草率】cǎoshuài（做事）不认真，敷衍了事 careless；sloppy；perfunctory；（do one's work）in a careless manner；attend to a matter negligently：～从事 act rashly；take hasty action｜～收兵 withdraw troops in a careless way；call off a battle perfunctorily｜没经过认真讨论，就做了决定，太～了。It's rash to make a decision without thorough discussion.

【草台班子】cǎotái bān·zi 演员较少，行头、道具等较简陋的戏班子，常在乡村或小城市中流动演出 small，lightly-equipped travelling theatrical troupe that performs in villages and small towns

【草滩】cǎotān 靠近水边的大片草地 meadow by the waterside

【草炭】cǎotàn 主要由古代的水草和藻类形成的泥炭，浅褐色，比重小，能浮于水面。主要用于干馏。weed coal；light-brown peat composed of waterweeds and mosses of ancient times，light in weight and able to float on water，mainly used for dry distillation；also 草煤 cǎoméi；☞ 泥炭 nítàn on p. 1405

【草体】cǎotǐ ❶ same as 草书 cǎoshū ❷ 拼音字母的手写体 hand written form of Romanized letters

【草头王】cǎotóuwáng〈旧指 *old*〉占有一块地盘的强盗头子 king of the bushes — bandit chief

【草图】cǎotú 初步画出的机械图或工程设计图，不要求十分精确 sketch；simple，rough machinery drawing or engineering design，done rapidly and without much detail

【草屋】cǎowū 屋顶用稻草、麦秸等盖的房子，大多简陋矮小 thatched hut；plain little hut with a straw roof; also 茅草屋 máocǎowū

【草鞋】cǎoxié 用稻草等编制的鞋 straw sandals

【草写】cǎoxiě 草体 cursive hand: '天'字的～是什么样儿? What does the cursive of 'sky' look like? | *a* 是 a 的～。'*a*' is the cursive of a.

【草药】cǎoyào〈中医 *Chin. med.*〉指用植物做的药材 herbal medicine

【草野】cǎoyě ❶〈旧时 *old*〉指民间 common people: ～小民 common people ❷〈书 *fml.*〉粗野;鄙陋 rough, shallow

【草鱼】cǎoyú 身体圆筒形,生活在淡水中,吃水草。是我国重要的养殖鱼之一。grass carp (*Ctenopharyngoden idellus*); barrel-shaped freshwater fish feeding on water weeds, widely cultivated in China; also 鲩 huàn

【草原】cǎoyuán 半干旱地区杂草丛生的大片土地,间或杂有耐旱的树木 grasslands; prairie; large semi-arid area covered with grass, sometimes with scattered drought-hardy trees

【草约】cǎoyuē 未正式签字的契约或条约 draft treaty; draft agreement; protocol

【草泽】cǎozé ❶ 低洼积水野草丛生的地方 tract of low wetlands covered with water and weeds: 深山～ remote mountains and swamps ❷〈旧指 *old*〉民间 common people: ～医生 doctor of the common people | 匿迹～ seclude oneself in the wilderness

【草纸】cǎozhǐ 用稻草等做原料制成的纸,一般呈黄色,质地粗糙,多用来做包装纸或卫生用纸 rough straw paper; toilet paper; a kind of rough yellow paper made from straw, often used as packing or toilet paper

【草质茎】cǎozhìjīng 木质部不发达,比较柔软的茎,例如水稻和小麦的茎 stalk; culm; soft stem of plants, like that of rice or wheat

【草字】cǎozì ❶ 草书汉字 Chinese character written in cursive hand ❷〈旧时 *old*〉谦称自己的别名(字) my humble style (name)

慅 cǎo [慅慅]〈书 *fml.*〉忧愁不安的样子 anxious; sad; worried

cào (ㄘㄠˋ)

肏 cào 骂人用的下流话,指男子的性交动作 (curse) fuck

操 cào same as 肏 cào

☞ cāo on p.190

【操蛋】càodàn 捣乱;无理取闹(多用作骂人的话 oft. curse) make trouble; make trouble out of nothing

cè (ㄘㄜˋ)

册(冊) cè ❶ 册子 volume; book: 名～ register; roll | 画～ an album of paintings | 纪念～ commemorative album ❷〈量词 *classifier*〉: 这套书一共六～。This book is in six volumes. ❷〈书 *fml.*〉皇帝封爵的命令 imperial order to confer a title: ～封 confer a title upon sb.

【册封】cèfēng 帝王通过一定仪式把爵位、封号赐给臣子、亲属、藩属等 emperor confers title or rank to officials, royal family members or nobility through certain ceremonies

【册立】cèlì 帝王确定皇后、太子等的身份 emperor crowns sb. as empress or prince

【册页】cèyè 分页装裱的字画 album of paintings or calligraphy; also 册叶 cèyè

【册子】cè·zi 装订好的本子 a set of blank or printed sheets bound in a tablet; book; volume: 相片～ photo album | 户口～ residence booklet | 写了几个小～(书) wrote a few booklets

厕[1](廁) cè 厕所 lavatory; toilet; washroom; W.C.: 男～ men's (room or toilet) | 女～ women's (room or toilet) | 公～ public lavatory | 茅～(方言中读 máo·si) latrine; latrine pit (pronounced máo·si in local dialect)

厕[2](廁) cè〈书 *fml.*〉夹杂在里面;参与 mingle with; participate in: ～身 occupy a humble place among others | 杂～(混杂) place among others

【厕身】cèshēn〈书 *fml.*〉参与;置身(多用作谦辞 oft. used as a self-depreciatory expression) occupy an unimportant place in; be an unqualified member of: ～士林 occupy an unimportant place among scholars | ～教育界 happen to move in educational circles also 侧身 cèshēn

【厕所】cèsuǒ 专供人大小便的地方 lavatory; toilet; W.C.; rest room

【厕足】cèzú〈书 *fml.*〉插足;涉足 set foot in; participate in: ～其间 set foot there; get involved; also 侧足 cèzú

侧 cè ❶ 旁边(跟'正'相对 as opposed to 'front')(a position or space beside one) side: 左～ left side | ～面 side | 公路两～种着杨树。Poplars are planted on both sides of the highway. ❷ 向旁边歪斜 incline to one side: ～耳 incline one's ears | ～着身子进去 enter by walking sideways

☞ zè on p.2399 and zhāi on p.2406

【侧扁】cèbiǎn 从背部到腹部的距离大于左右两侧之间的距离,如鲫鱼的身体 laterally flat; distance between the back and belly exceeds that between the two sides, like the body of a crucian

【侧耳】cè'ěr 侧转头,使一边的耳朵向前边歪斜。形容认真倾听。turn the head and incline the ear; strain one's ears; listen attentively: 他探身窗外,～细听。He leaned out of the window and listened attentively.

【侧根】cègēn 从主根向周围长出来的根 lateral root;root growing around the main root

【侧击】cèjī 从侧面攻击 attack the side of; make a flank attack

【侧记】cèjì 关于某些活动的侧面的记述(多用于报道文章的标题 oft. used in news headlines) incidental information on a subject:《全市中学生运动会~》'Sidelights of the Municipal Games for Middle School Students'

C

【侧近】cèjìn 附近 nearby:找~的人打听一下 consult somebody nearby

【侧门】cèmén 旁门 side door; side entrance

【侧面】cèmiàn 旁边的一面(区别于'正面' other than 'front') side; flank; aspect side of an object:从~打击敌人 made a flank attack on the enemy|小门在房子的~。The small door is at the side of the house. ◇从~了解 learn from indirect sources|注意正面的材料,也要注意~和反面的材料。In studying the materials we shall take note of both positive and negative examples.

【侧目】cèmù 不敢从正面看,斜着眼睛看。形容畏惧而又愤恨 cast sidelong glances (with fear or indignation):~而视 look askance at sb.|世人为之~ be resented by the common people

【侧身】cèshēn ❶ 歪斜身子 turn or move sideways:他一~躲到树后。He turned and hid himself behind the tree. ❷ same as 厕身 cèshēn

【侧视图】cèshìtú 由物体的一侧向另一侧做正投影得到的视图 lateral view; side view, profile

【侧室】cèshì ❶ 房屋两侧的房间 side room ❷〈旧时 *old*〉指偏房;妾 concubine

【侧线】cèxiàn 鱼类身体两侧各有一条由许多小点组成的线,叫做侧线。每一小点内有一个小管,管内有感觉细胞,能感觉水流的方向和压力。lateral line; on fish, a row of sensory organs along both sides of the head and body for detecting the direction and pressure of currents

【侧芽】cèyá 在叶子和茎相连的部分生长出来的芽 auxiliary bud; buds growing on the joint between a branch and the stem of a leaf; also 腋芽 yèyá

【侧翼】cèyì 作战时部队的两翼 flank; right or left side of an army

【侧影】cèyǐng 侧面的影像 profile; silhouette; side view of the face:在这里我们可以仰望宝塔的~。We can view the profile of the pagoda here. ◇通过这部小说,可以看到当时学生运动的一个~。The novel reflected one aspect of the student movement at that time.

【侧泳】cèyǒng 游泳的一种姿势,身体侧卧水面,两腿夹水,两手交替划水 sidestroke; do the sidestroke; swimming stroke performed, while lying sideways in the water, by working the arms alternately backward and forward while executing a scissor-kick with the legs

【侧枝】cèzhī 由主枝周围长出的小枝 small branches around the trunk; lateral branch; side shoot

【侧重】cèzhòng 着重某一方面;偏重 lay special emphasis on one aspect;emphasize; lay particular stress on:~农业 lay special emphasis on agriculture|这几项工作应有所~。Special emphasis shall be laid on these tasks.

【侧足】cèzú〈书 *fml.*〉❶ 两脚斜着站,不敢移动。形容非常恐惧 standing at an angle; horrified;panic-stricken:~而立 stand at an angle ❷ same as 厕足 cèzú

测 cè ❶ 测量 survey; fathom; measure:~绘 mapping|目~eye measurement|深不可~ fathomless; abysmal ❷ 推测;推想 infer; guess; imagine; reckon:变化莫~ change unpredictably; changeable

【测报】cèbào 测量并报告 measure and notify:~虫情 pest assessment and identification|气象~ weather prediction and report

【测定】cèdìng 经测量后确定 ascertain by measuring or surveying; determine:~方向 determine the direction|~气温 air temperature measurement

【测度】cèduó 推测;揣度 estimate; infer:她的想法难以~。It's difficult to figure out her opinion.|根据风向~,今天不会下雨。Judging by the direction of the wind, it won't rain today.

【测候】cèhòu 观测(天文、气象) astronomical or meteorological observation

【测绘】cèhuì 测量和绘图的统称 general designation for survey and drawing; mapping; cartography

【测控】cèkòng 观测并控制 observation and control:卫星~中心 satellite observation and control centre

【测量】cèliáng ❶ 用仪器确定空间、时间、温度、速度、功能等的有关数值 survey; measure; gauge; to ascertain the space, time, temperature, speed or capacity of something using instruments:~水温 measure the water temperature|~空气的清洁度 gauge the purity of the air ❷ 有关地形、地物等的测定工作 operation of surveying the form, extent and surface features, etc. of an area of land:地质~ geological survey|筑路前要做好~工作。We must make a careful survey before building the road.

【测试】cèshì ❶ 考查人的知识、技能 test; prove the knowledge and skills of a person:专业~ professional test|经~合格方可录用 must be tested before hiring ❷ 对机械、仪器和电器等的性能和精度进行测量 measure the performance and precision of machinery, instrument or electrical appliance：每台电视机出厂前都要进行严格～。Every TV set must be strictly tested before leaving the factory.

【测算】cèsuàn 测量计算；推算 measure and calculate：用地震仪～地震震级 measure and calculate the magnitude of earthquake with seismic instruments｜经过反复～，这项工程年内可以完成。After repeated calculations, it is estimated that the project will be completed by the end of this year.

【测探】cètàn ❶ 推测，探寻 estimate；detect：～她心里的想法 figure out her inner thoughts ❷ 测量勘探 probe；explore：～海底的矿藏 explore the mineral resources of the seabed

【测验】cèyàn ❶ 用仪器或其他办法检验 prove by means of instruments or other methods ❷ 考查学习成绩等 examination；test：算术～ arithmetic test (or quiz)｜时事～current events examination｜智力～intelligence test

【测字】cè∥zì 把汉字的偏旁笔画拆开或合并，作出解说来占吉凶（迷信） fortune-telling by analysing the component parts of a Chinese character；divine by means of characters；glyphomancy；also 拆字 chāi∥zì

恻 cè ❶ 悲伤 sorrowful；sad：凄～ grieved｜～然 grieved；sorrowful ❷〈书 *fml.*〉诚恳 sincere；earnest

【恻然】cèrán〈书 *fml.*〉悲伤的样子 grieved；sorrowful

【恻隐】cèyǐn 对受苦难的人表示同情；不忍 feel compassion for sb. suffering：～之心 latent compassion of one's heart；sympathy；sense of pity；compassion

策[1]（筞） cè ❶〈古代 *arch.*〉写字用的竹片或木片 bamboo or wooden slips used for writing on：简～ inscribed wooden or bamboo slips ❷〈古代 *arch.*〉考试的一种文体，多就政治和经济问题发问，应试者对答 questions on political or economic affairs set for imperial examinations：对～countermeasure｜～问 personal interview ❸ 我国数学上曾经用过的一种计算工具，形状跟'筹'相似。清代初期把乘法的九九口诀写在上面以计算乘除和开平方。a kind of counting instrument used for multiplication, division or extraction of square roots in ancient China；☞ 筹 chóu on p.278 ❹ 计谋；办法 plan；scheme：上～good plan｜献～submit a scheme｜束手无～fold one's hands helplessly；at one's wits' end ❺〈书 *fml.*〉谋划；筹划 plan；scheme：～反 incite mutiny｜～应 support by coordinated action ❻（Cè）姓 a surname

策[2]（筞） cè ❶〈古代 *arch.*〉赶马用的棍子，一端有尖刺，能刺马的身体，使它向前跑 spur；pointed stick used by horsemen to poke a horse's body to urge the animal forward ❷ 用策赶马 spur a horse：鞭～ spur｜～马前进 spur a horse on ❸〈书 *fml.*〉拐杖 cane；walking stick：扶～而行 walk with a cane

【策动】cèdòng 策划鼓动 instigate；engineer；stir up：～政变 plot to stage a coup d'état

【策反】cèfǎn 深入敌对一方的内部，秘密进行鼓动，使敌对一方的人倒戈 instigate rebellion within the enemy camp；incite defection or mutiny

【策划】cèhuà 筹划；谋划 plan；plot；scheme：幕后～plot behind the scenes｜这部影片怎么个拍法，请你来～一下。Please offer ideas on how to make the movie.

【策励】cèlì 督促勉励 encourage；spur on：时刻～自己 constantly spur oneself ahead

【策略】cèlüè ❶ 根据形势发展而制定的行动方针和斗争方式 action guidelines or struggle methods in accordance with the developing situation；tactics：斗争～ tactics of struggle ❷ 讲究斗争艺术，注意方式方法 showing or having tact；tactful：谈话要～一点 speak in a tactful way｜这样做不够～。It's not tactful to do so.

【策论】cèlùn 封建时代指议论当前政治问题、向朝廷献策的文章 essay on current affairs presented to the emperor as advice on government policy

【策士】cèshì 封建时代投靠君主或公卿为其划策的人，后来泛指有谋略的人 one who plotted for an emperor or duke in feudal society, later referring to a schemer, plotter or contriver in a generic sense

【策应】cèyìng 与友军相呼应，配合作战 support by coordinated action；make supporting movements to cut off enemy

【策源地】cèyuándì 战争、社会运动等策动、起源的地方 place of origin；source of a war or a social movement：北京是五四运动的～。Beijing was where the May 4th Movement started.

筴（筴） cè〈书 *fml.*〉same as 策 cè ☞ jiā on p.930

箣 cè［箣竹］(cèzhú) 竹的一种，茎高达 20 米，质坚韧，可做扁担、家具等 common bamboo (*Bambusa stenostachya*), a genus of bamboo reaching heights of about 20 metres, with stalk durable enough to make shoulder poles or furniture

cèi（ㄘㄟˋ）

瓻 cèi（瓷器、玻璃等）打碎；摔碎 break (china or glass) into pieces；smash：～了一个碗 smash a bowl｜不小心把杯子～了 break a teacup due to carelessness

cēn (ㄘㄣ)

参(參) cēn ☞ below
☞ cān on p. 183 and shēn on p. 1702

【参差】cēncī ❶ 长短、高低、大小不齐；不一致 long and short; different in length, height or size; uneven not uniform: 水平～不齐 at different levels ❷〈书 *fml.*〉大约；几乎 nearly; almost: ～是 almost true; almost so ❷〈书 *fml.*〉差错；蹉跎 go wrong; be delayed; waste time; idle away: 佳期～。The wedding was delayed.

【参错】cēncuò〈书 *fml.*〉❶ 参差交错 interlock; crisscross: 阡陌纵横～ labyrinth of footpaths between fields ❷ 错误脱漏 errors and omissions: 传(zhuàn)注～ errors and omissions in the commentaries on classics

cén (ㄘㄣˊ)

岑 cén ❶〈书 *fml.*〉小而高的山 high hill ❷〈书 *fml.*〉崖岸 scarp ❸ (Cén) 姓 a surname

【岑寂】cénjì〈书 *fml.*〉寂静；寂寞 quiet and still; lonely

涔 cén〈书 *fml.*〉❶ 积水 rainwater in puddles ❷ 雨水多 a lot of rainwater

【涔涔】céncén〈书 *fml.*〉❶ 形容汗、泪、水等不断地流下(of sweat, tears, water, etc.) dripping; streaming: 汗～下 sweat streaming down; dripping with sweat ❷ 形容天色阴沉 murky; cloudy; gloomy ❸ 形容胀痛或烦闷 agonized

cēng (ㄘㄥ)

噌[1] cēng〈拟声词 *onom.*〉: 麻雀～的一声飞上房。The sparrow whizzed up onto the roof.

噌[2] cēng〈方 *dial.*〉叱责 scold; shout at; upbraid; rebuke: 挨～ get a scolding
☞ chēng on p. 244

céng (ㄘㄥˊ)

层(層) céng ❶ 重叠；重复 one on top of another; overlapping: ～峦叠嶂 topographic turmoil of mountains | ～出不穷 emerge in an endless stream ❷ 重叠事物的一个部分 layer; level; component part in a sequence: 外～outer layer | 云～ clouds ❸〈量词 *classifier*〉a) 用于重叠、积累的东西 storey; tier; stratum; anything that can be arranged one above another: 五～大楼 a five-storey building | 两～玻璃窗 double-tier window b) 用于可以分项分步的东西 component part of a sequence: 去了一～顾虑 allay misgivings | 还得进一～想 give it further consideration c) 用于可以从物体表面揭开或抹去的东西 sth. spread over sth. else that can be taken or wiped off: 一～薄膜 a thin layer of plastic film | 擦掉一～灰 wipe away dust from

【层报】céngbào 一级一级地向上报告 report a matter to the higher authorities level by level

【层出不穷】céng chū bù qióng 接连不断地出现，没有穷尽 emerge in an endless stream; appear one after another; come out thick and fast

【层次】céngcì ❶ (说话、作文)内容的次序 arrangement of ideas (in writing or speech): ～清楚 well arranged; coherent ❷ 相属的各级机构 relevant administrative levels: 减少～，精简人员 simplify the administrative structure and reduce the staff ❸ 同一事物由于大小、高低等不同而形成的区别 arrange something in different grades according to size or level; gradation: 多～服务 multi-level service | 举行高～领导人会谈 hold high-level discussions | 年龄～不同，爱好也不同 hobbies vary at different ages | 房子面积还可以，就是朝向和～不理想。The suite is large enough but has an unfavourable exposure, and it's not on an ideal floor.

【层叠】céngdié 重叠 one on top of another: 冈峦～ ranges of hills | 层层叠叠的雪峰 range upon range of snowcapped mountains

【层见叠出】céng jiàn dié chū 屡次出现 occur frequently; appear repeatedly; also 层出叠见 céng chū dié jiàn

【层林】cénglín 一层层的树林 row upon row of trees: 深秋季节，～尽染，景色宜人。The deep hues of the woods make the scenery of late autumn pleasing.

【层峦】céngluán 重重叠叠的山岭 range upon range of hills: ～叠翠 range upon range of green hills

【层面】céngmiàn ❶ 某一层次的范围 scope; range: 设法增加服务～try to enlarge the scope of service | 这次事件影响的～极大。The event's repercussion is wide spread. ❷ 方面 aspect; field: 经济～ economic aspect | 谈话涉及的～很广。The discussion covers many fields.

曾 céng 曾经 [indicating that an action once happened in the past or a state once existed]: 几年前我～见过她。I met her once several years ago.
☞ zēng on p. 2401

【曾几何时】céng jǐ hé shí 时间过去没有多久 before long; not long after; it was not long before . . . ; in a not too long time: ～，这里竟

发生了那么大的变化。It was not long before so many changes took place.

【曾经】céngjīng 〈副词 *adv.*〉表示从前有过某种行为或情况 once; used to; indicating that an action once happened in the past or a state once existed: 他～说过这件事。He had mentioned that matter once. | 这里～闹过水灾。A flood once hit here.

【曾经沧海】céng jīng cāng hǎi 元稹诗《离思》:'曾经沧海难为水,除却巫山不是云。'后来用'曾经沧海'比喻曾经经历过很大的场面,眼界开阔,对比较平常的事物不放在眼里。one who has seen the ocean thinks nothing of rivers — to a sophisticated person there is nothing new under the sun; have seen much of the world; having seen and experienced much (from Yuan Zhen's poem *The Sorrow of Departure*: 'Speak not of lakes and streams to him who has once seen the sea. / The clouds that circle Wushan are the only clouds for me.')

嶒 céng [崚嶒](léngcéng)〈书 *fml.*〉形容山高 (of a mountain) high

cèng (ㄘㄥˋ)

蹭 cèng ❶ 摩擦 rub; scrape; scratch: 手～破一点儿皮 graze one's hand ❷ 因擦过去而沾上 rub against sth. and get stained: 留神～油! Take care not to stain your clothes with oil. | 墨还没干,当心别～了。The ink is still wet; be careful that you don't stain your clothes. ❸〈方 *dial.*〉就着某种机会不出代价而跟着得到好处;揩油 obtain for free by begging or sponging; cadge; scrounge; bum: 坐～车 go on a bus or train without buying a ticket; steal a ride; bum a lift | 看～戏 watch a play without buying a ticket | ～吃～喝 scounge meals and drinks | ～了一顿饭 have bummed a meal ❹ 慢吞吞地行动 move slowly: 磨～dawdle; loiter | 他的脚受伤了,只能一步一步地往前～。His fcct were injured, so he could only drag himself along inch by inch.

【蹭蹬】cèngdèng〈书 *fml.*〉遭遇挫折;不得意 meet with setbacks; be down on one's luck; run into mishaps: 仕途～ frustrated in officialdom

chā (ㄔㄚ)

叉 chā ❶ 一端有两个以上的长齿而另一端有柄的器具 instrument with a handle at one end and two or more pointed prongs on the other; fork: 钢～steel fork | 鱼～ harpoon | 吃西餐用刀～。Knives and forks are used to eat a Western-style meal. ❷ 用叉取东西 work with a fork; fork: ～鱼 spear fish; harpoon fish ❸ (～儿 chār)叉形符号'×',一般用来标志错误的或作废的事物 ×—mark to show something is wrong or deleted; cross out

☞ chá on p. 202, chǎ on p. 205 and chà on p. 205

【叉车】chāchē 铲运车 forklift

【叉烧】chāshāo 烤肉的一种方法,把腌渍后的瘦猪肉挂在特制的叉子上,放入炉内烧烤。也有把腌渍过的肉过油后再烧烤的 grilled or barbecued (marinated pork): ～肉 grilled pork

【叉腰】chā//yāo 大拇指和其余四指分开,紧按在腰旁 with hands on hips and thumbs apart from other fingers: 两手～站在那里 stand with arms akimbo

【叉子】chā·zi 小叉 fork

扠 chā same as 叉 chā ②

杈 chā 一种农具,一端有两个以上的略弯的长齿,一端有长柄,用来挑(tiǎo)柴草等 hayfork; pitchfork; a kind of farm tool with a long handle at one end and two or more crooked pointed prongs at the other, used for lifting or tossing hay, straw, etc.

☞ chà on p. 205

臿 chā ❶〈书 *fml.*〉same as 锸 chā ❷〈方 *dial.*〉舂 pound; pestle: ～米 husk rice with mortar and pestle

差 chā ❶ same as 差 chà ①: ～别 difference; disparity | ～异 difference; discrepancy ❷ 减法运算中,一个数减去另一个数所得的数。如 6－4＝2 中,2 是差。amount by which one quantity differs from another; remainder of subtraction, e. g. in the equation 6－4＝2, 2 is the difference; also 差数 chāshù ❸〈书 *fml.*〉稍微;较;尚 slightly; barely: 天气～暖。It's slightly warm. | ～可告慰 barely consolable

☞ chà on p. 206, chāi on p. 208, chài on p. 209 and cī on p. 315

【差别】chābié 形式或内容上的不同 difference in form or content; difference; disparity: 毫无～。There is no difference at all. | 缩小～ reduce the difference | 两者之间～很大。There is a world of difference between the two.

【差池】chāchí same as 差错 chācuò; also 差迟 chāchí

【差错】chācuò ❶ 错误 mistake; error; slip: 精神不集中,就会出～。You will make mistakes if you don't concentrate. ❷ 意外的变化(多指灾祸 usu. a disaster) unexpected event; mishap; accident: 万一有什么～,那可不得了。It would be terrible if anything went wrong.

【差额】chā'é 跟作为标准或用来比较的数额相差的数 amount by which one quantity differs from another; difference; differential; balance; margin: 补足～ make up the balance (or difference)|贸易～ trade deficit

【差额选举】chā'é xuǎnjǔ 候选人名额多于当选人名额的一种选举办法(区别于'等额选举' as compared with 'single-candidate election') election with more candidates than posts; competitive election; multi-candidate election; selective election

【差价】chājià 同一商品因各种条件不同而产生的价格差别,如批发和零售的差价、地区差价、季节差价 difference in the price of a commodity caused by different conditions such as purchase price, region or season

【差距】chājù 事物之间的差别程度,也指距离某种标准的差别程度 difference; gap; difference between different objects or disparity from a certain standard: 学先进,找～。Learn from others' strengths, and find where one falls short.|他俩在看法上有很大～。There is a great difference between their opinions.

【差可】chākě 勉强可以 barely acceptable: 成绩～ barely acceptable score|～告慰 barely consolable

【差强人意】chā qiáng rényì 大体上还能使人满意 just passable; barely satisfactory: 那几幅画都不怎么样,只有这一幅梅花还～。Those paintings are no good, with the exception of this one of plum blossoms which is barely satisfactory.

【差失】chāshī 差错;失误 error; mistake

【差误】chāwù 错误 error; mistake; slip: 工作出了～ make a mistake in one's work

【差异】chāyì 差别;不相同 difference; divergence; discrepancy; diversity: 南北气候～很大。There is a great difference between the climate in the south and in the north.|赛场上几个评委的打分有～。The marking of the panel members differs.

【差之毫厘,谬以千里】chā zhī háo lí, miù yǐ qiān lǐ 开始相差得很小,结果会造成很大的错误。强调不能有一点儿差错。也说差以毫厘,失之千里。An error the breadth of a single hair can lead you a thousand *li* astray. A slight discrepancy leads to a gigantic error.

插 chā ❶ 长形或片状的东西放进、挤入、刺进或穿入别的东西里 stick in; insert; to put or pierce something thin into something else: ～秧 transplant rice seedlings|双峰～云 double peaks penetrating the clouds|～翅难飞 unable to escape even if given wings|把插销～上 slide the bolt in place ❷ 中间加进去或加进中间去 interpose; insert: ～手 take part in; have a hand in|安～plant|～花地 alternatively|～一句话 get a word in

【插班】chābān 学校根据转学来的学生的学历和程度编入适当班级(of a new or transferred student) join a class in the middle of a semester according to academic record and level; be placed in the appropriate class: ～生 student who joins a class in the middle of a semester

【插播】chābō 临时插进已经编排好的节目中间播放 interrupt a scene or programme: 电视台准备随时～奥运会比赛新闻。The TV program will be interrupted anytime with news of the Olympic Games.

【插翅难飞】chā chì nán fēi 形容被围或受困而难以逃脱 besieged and can't escape; unable to escape even if given wings; also 插翅难逃 chā chì nán táo

【插床】chāchuáng 金属切削机床,用来加工键槽。加工时工作台上的工件做纵向、横向或旋转运动,插刀做上下往复运动,切削工件。slotting machine; a kind of machine for making slots (the machine moves vertically, horizontally or in a circle, while the slotting tool moves up and down repeatedly to cut sth.)

【插戴】chādài 女子戴在头上的装饰品,即首饰,特指旧俗定婚时男方送给女方的首饰 women's head ornament, especially jewellery presented by a man to a woman at the time of engagement in old times

【插袋】chādài also 插兜 chādōu

【插定】chādìng 〈旧时 *old*〉定婚由男方送给女方的礼品 gifts presented by a man's family to a woman's family at their engagement; betrothal gifts: 下～ send betrothal gifts

【插兜】chādōu ❶ 用布或纸做成的口袋形的东西,一般由许多个连成一排或许多排,用来插放信件、报纸等 a row or several rows of pockets made of cloth or paper to hold letters or newspapers ❷ 〈方 *dial.*〉衣兜 pocket: 裤子两边有～。The trousers have pockets on both sides. ‖ also 插袋 chādài

【插队】chā//duì ❶ 插进队伍中去 jump a queue: 请排队顺序购票,不要～。Please line up for tickets and don't jump the queue. ❷ 指城市知识青年、干部下到农村生产队 (of school graduates and government officials in cities) be sent to live and work in the countryside as member of a production team: ～落户 settle in the countryside as a member of a production team|他过去到农村插过队。He was sent to the countryside to live and work with the production teams.

【插杠子】chā gàng·zi 〈比喻 *fig.*〉中途参与谈话或做事(多含贬义 oft. derog.) butt in; poke one's nose into: 这事与你无关,你不要再插一杠子。It's none of your business, don't poke your nose into it.

【插关儿】chā·guanr 〈方 *dial.*〉小门闩(shuān) small bar or bolt

【插花】chā//huā ❶ 把各种供观赏的花适当地搭配着插进花瓶、花篮里 arrange flowers in a vase or basket: ～艺术 the art of flower arrangement ❷〈方 *dial.*〉绣花 embroidery

【插花】chāhuā 夹杂;交错 be mixed up with:～地 be mingled with|玉米地里还～着种豆子。Soya beans have been sown between the rows of maize.|农业副业～着搞 go into sideline production while farming

【插话】chā//huà 在别人谈话中间插进去说几句 interpose a remark, etc.; chip in:我们在谈正事,你别～。Don't interrupt while we are talking business.|插不上一句话 can't get a word in

【插话】chāhuà ❶ 在别人的谈话中间插进去说的话 interposed remark ❷ 插在大事件中的小故事 small event occurring as part of a big event; episode; digression; same as 插曲 chāqǔ②

【插画】chāhuà 艺术性的插图 illustration (in a book); plate

【插架】chājià ❶ 把书刊放在架上 place a book on a shelf:～万轴(形容藏书极多) have a big collection of books; collection of tens of thousands of books|～的地方志有五百部。There are 500 local chronicles on the shelf. ❷〈旧时 *old*〉悬在墙壁上的架子,类似后来的书架 shelves hung on walls, similar to present bookshelves

【插脚】chā//jiǎo ❶ 站到里面去(多用于否定式 usu. in the negative) put one's foot in:屋里坐得满满的,后来的人没处～。The room was so crowded that people coming late could hardly find a place to stand. ❷〈比喻 *fig.*〉参与某种活动 participate in (some activity):这样的事你何必去插一脚? There is no need for you to participate in such a matter.

【插犋】chājù 指农民两家或几家的牲口、犁耙合用,共同耕作 livestock and farming tools shared by several farmer families

【插科打诨】chā kē dǎ hùn 指戏曲演员在演出中穿插些滑稽的谈话和动作来引人发笑 make gags; (of actors) make impromptu comic gestures and remarks

【插空】chā//kòng 利用空隙时间 take advantage of intervals:参加会演的演员还～去工厂演出。Actors participating in the joint performance took advantage of the intervals to put on shows in factories.

【插口】chā//kǒu same as 插嘴 chā//zuǐ

【插口】chākǒu 可以插入东西的孔 hollow piece or part into which something fits; socket; jack:扩音器上有两个～,一个插麦克风,一个插电唱头。There are two sockets in the amplifier, one for a microphone, and the other for an acoustic pickup.

【插屏】chāpíng (～儿 chāpíngr)摆在桌子上的陈设品,下面有座,上面插着有图画的镜框、大理石或雕刻品 table plaque or table screen with a stand, on which either a framed picture, a piece of marble or a piece of sculpture is displayed

【插瓶】chāpíng 花瓶;胆瓶 vase

【插曲】chāqǔ ❶ 配置在电影、电视剧或话剧中比较有独立性的乐曲 interlude; independent music played during a film, TV programme or stage play ❷〈比喻 *fig.*〉连续进行的事情中插入的特殊片段 special event occurring as a part of a bigger one; episode; interlude

【插身】chāshēn ❶ 把身子挤进去 squeeze in; edge in ❷〈比喻 *fig.*〉参与 participate; take part in; involve:他不想～在这场纠纷中间。He doesn't want to get involved in this dispute.

【插手】chā//shǒu ❶ 帮着做事 take part in; lend a hand:想干又插不上手 want to help but don't know how ❷〈比喻 *fig.*〉参与某种活动 take part in; get involved in:那件事你千万不能～。You must not get involved in that.

【插穗】chāsuì 用于扦插的枝条 cutting wood; seed piece; also 插条 chātiáo

【插头】chātóu 装在导线一端的接头,插到插座上,电路就能接通 plug; electrical device connected by wire and fitted into an outlet, thus making contact or closing the circuit; also 插销 chāxiāo

【插图】chātú 插在文字中间帮助说明内容的图画,包括科学性的和艺术性的 illustration; plate; diagram; drawings (artistic or scientific in nature) used to help explain or make something clear

【插销】chāxiāo ❶ 门窗上装的金属闩 bolt (for a door, window, etc.) ❷ same as 插头 chātóu

【插叙】chāxù 一种叙述方式,在叙述时不依时间次序插入其他情节 narration interspersed with flashbacks

【插秧】chā//yāng 把水稻的秧从秧田里移栽到稻田里 transplant rice seedlings from the seedling bed to the field

【插页】chāyè 插在书刊中印有图表照片等的单页 insert; inset; extra page of photos or tables inserted in a publication

【插足】chāzú〈比喻 *fig.*〉参与某种活动 participate; take part in (some activity)

【插嘴】chā//zuǐ 在别人说话中间插进去说话 interrupt; chip in:你别～,先听我说完。Don't interrupt me until I finish speaking.|两位老人家正谈得高兴,我想说又插不上嘴。The two seniors were talking in such high spirits, I wanted to say something but couldn't get a word in.

【插座】chāzuò 连接电路的电器元件,通常接在电源上,跟电器的插头连接时电流就通入电器 socket; outlet; electrical element in a wiring system where the current is obtained by inserting a plug

喳

chā ☞ below
☞ zhā on p. 2403

【喳喳】chāchā 小声说话的声音 whispering sound：喊喊～ jabbering

【喳喳】chā•cha 小声说话 whisper：打～whisper|他在老伴儿的耳边～了两句。He whispered a few words in the ear of his wife.

馇 chā ❶ 边拌边煮（猪、狗的饲料）cook and stir (feed for pigs or dogs)：～猪食 cook and stir feed for pigs ❷〈方 *dial.*〉熬（粥）cook：～粥 cook gruel

☞ •zha p. 2406

碴 chā ☞胡子拉碴 hú•zilāchā on p. 819

☞ chá on p. 204

锸 chā 挖土的工具；铁锹 tool used for digging; spade

艖 chā〈书 *fml.*〉小船 small boat

嚓 chā〈拟声词 *onom.*〉：喀～ crack|啪～ crash

☞ cā on p. 175

chá（ㄔㄚˊ）

叉 chá〈方 *dial.*〉挡住；卡住 block (up); jam：车辆～住了路口，过不去了。Traffic was blocked at the crossroads and we couldn't get through.

☞ chā on p. 199, chǎ on p. 205 and chà on p. 205

垞 chá 小土山。多用于地名，如胜垞（在山东）。small mound (oft. used in place names, e.g. Shengcha of Shandong Province)

茬 chá (～儿 chár) ❶ 农作物收割后留在地里的茎和根 stubble; short stumps of grain left standing after harvesting：麦～儿 wheat stubble|豆～儿 bean stubble ❷ 指在同一块地上，作物种植或生长的次数，一次叫一茬 crop; times of yield of any farm product in one place：换～change crops|二～韭菜（割了一次以后又生长的韭菜）the second crop of Chinese chives (Chinese chives that grow after the first crop is reaped)|这块菜地一年能种四五～。This vegetable plot can produce 4-5 crops a year. ❸ same as 碴儿 chár

【茬口】chá•kǒu ❶ 指轮作作物的种类和轮作的次序 crops for rotation：选好～，实行合理轮作 select the right crops and rotate them rationally ❷ 指某种作物收割以后的土壤 soil on which a crop has been planted and harvested：西红柿～壮，种白菜很合适。A crop of tomatoes enriches the soil and makes it suitable for growing cabbage. ❸〈方 *dial.*〉(～儿 chá•kǒur)时机；机会 chance; opportunity：这事抓紧办，现在正是个～。We shall seize this opportunity to deal with the matter.

【茬子】chá•zi same as 茬 chá ①：刨～dig up the stubble|～地 land with stubble

茶 chá ❶ 常绿灌木，叶子长椭圆形，花白色，种子有硬壳。嫩叶加工后就是茶叶。是我国南方最重要的经济作物之一。tea; white-flowered evergreen plant with oval leaves and hard-shell seeds, the tender leaves of which can be processed to make a beverage, being one of the most important cash crops in southern China ❷ 用茶叶做成的饮料 beverage made from tea leaves：喝～drink tea; take tea|品～ sip tea ❸〈旧时 *old*〉指聘礼（古时聘礼多用茶）betrothal gifts (tea was oft. used as betrothal gifts in ancient China)：下～send betrothal gifts|代～ betrothal gifts ❹ 茶色 dark brown; tawny：～镜 tawny glasses|～晶 brown crystal ❺ 某些饮料的名称 certain kinds of drinks or liquid foods：奶～ milky tea|果～ fruit tea ❻ 指油茶树 oil-tea camellia (*Camellia oleifera*)：～油 tea oil ❼ 指山茶 camellia：～花 camellia

【茶场】cháchǎng ❶ 从事培育、管理茶树和采摘茶叶的单位 tea plantation; organization engaged in breeding, managing tea plantations and picking tea leaves ❷ 培育茶树和采摘茶叶的地方 tea plantation; place for breeding tea trees and picking tea leaves

【茶匙】cháchí (～儿 cháchír)调饮料用的小匙子，比汤匙小 teaspoon; small spoon used in stirring beverages

【茶炊】cháchuī 用铜铁等制的烧水的器具，有两层壁，在中间烧火，四围装水，供沏茶用。也叫茶汤壶，有的地区叫茶炊子、浇心壶。tea-urn; samovar; double-walled metal urn used for boiling water for tea, heated by passing a tube filled with hot charcoal through the hollow centre; also called 茶汤壶 chátānghú; in some places known as 茶炊子 cháchuī•zi, or 浇心壶 jiāoxīnhú

【茶点】chádiǎn 茶水和点心 tea and pastries; refreshments

【茶饭】cháfàn 茶和饭，泛指饮食 tea and rice — food and drink; food

【茶房】chá•fáng〈旧时 *old*〉称在旅馆、茶馆、轮船、火车、剧场等处从事供应茶水等杂务的人 waiter (who serves tea and does odd jobs in a hotel, teahouse, ship, train or theatre, etc.)

【茶缸子】chágāng•zi 比较深的带把儿的茶杯，口和底一样大或差不多大 mug; drinking cup, usually cylindrical and with a handle

【茶馆】cháguǎn (～儿 cháguǎnr)卖茶水的铺子，设有座位，供顾客喝茶 teahouse; place where tea and other refreshments are served

【茶褐色】cháhèsè 赤黄而略带黑的颜色 dark brown; also 茶色 chásè

【茶花】cháhuā (～儿 cháhuār)山茶、茶树、油茶树的花。特指山茶的花。flowers of camellia, tea plant or oil-tea camellia; camellia flowers

【茶话会】cháhuàhuì 备有茶点的集会 tea party at which the participants chat or give talks

【茶会】cháhuì 用茶点招待宾客的社交性集会 tea party; party at which tea, among other things, is served

【茶几】chájī (～儿 chájīr)放茶具用的家具,比桌子小 tea table; teapoy; side table; small table on which a tea set is placed

【茶鸡蛋】chájīdàn 用茶叶、五香、酱油等加水煮熟的鸡蛋 tea egg; egg boiled in water with tea, spices, soy, etc.; also 茶叶蛋 cháyèdàn

【茶晶】chájīng 颜色像浓茶汁的水晶,多用来做眼镜的镜片 dark-brown crystal, used to make lenses

【茶镜】chájìng 用茶晶或茶色玻璃做镜片的眼镜 glasses with citrine or brown-coloured lenses; sunglasses

【茶具】chájù 喝茶用具,如茶壶、茶杯等 tea-things; tea service; tea set; teapot and other accessories used at tea

【茶枯】chákū 油茶树的种子榨油后压成饼状的渣滓,可以做肥料 dregs of the tea-oil seeds after extraction, often used as fertilizer; also 茶子饼 chá·zibǐng

【茶楼】chálóu 有楼的茶馆(多用做茶馆的名称 oft. used in the name of a teahouse) teahouse with two or more storeys

【茶炉】chálú 烧开水的小火炉或锅炉,有的地区也指供应或出售热水、开水的地方 water boiler; places serving boiled water: 烧～ tend the water boiler

【茶卤儿】chálǔr 很浓的茶叶 strong tea

【茶农】chánóng 以种植茶树为业的农民 tea grower; tea planter

【茶盘】chápán (～儿 chápánr)放茶壶茶杯的盘子 tea tray; teaboard; tray for carrying teapots and teacups to serve tea; also 茶盘子 chápán·zi

【茶钱】chá·qián ❶ 喝茶用的钱 payment for tea (in a teahouse or restaurant) ❷ 小费的别称 another name for tip

【茶青】cháqīng 深绿而微黄的颜色 dark brownish green

【茶色】chásè 茶褐色 dark brown: ～玻璃 brown-coloured glass

【茶社】cháshè 茶馆儿或茶座儿 ①(多用做茶馆儿或茶座儿的名称 oft. used in the name of a teahouse) teahouse; tearoom; same as 茶座儿 cházuòr ①

【茶食】chá·shi 糕饼、果脯等食品的总称(collect.) cakes and sweetmeats

【茶水】cháshuǐ 泛称茶或开水(多指供给行人或旅客用的) tea or plain boiled water (supplied to travellers): ～站 tea-stall | ～自备 bring one's own drinks

【茶汤】chátāng ❶ 糜子面或高粱面用开水冲成糊状的食品 a kind of paste made by mixing millet or sorghum powder with boiled water ❷〈书 *fml.*〉same as 茶水 cháshuǐ

【茶汤壶】chátānghú〈方 *dial.*〉same as 茶炊 cháchuī

【茶托】chátuō (～儿 chátuōr)垫在茶碗或茶杯底下的器皿 saucer (for holding a teacup)

【茶锈】cháxiù 茶水附着在茶具上的黄褐色沉淀物 tea residue; brown matter of tea remaining at the bottom of a teapot or a teacup

【茶叶】cháyè 经过加工的茶树嫩叶,可以做成饮料 tea; cured tea leaves which make a beverage

【茶艺】cháyì 有关烹茶、饮茶及以茶款待客人的艺术 art of brewing, drinking or serving tea

【茶余饭后】chá yú fàn hòu 指茶饭后的一段空闲休息时间 over a cup of tea or after a meal; also 茶余酒后 chá yú jiǔ hòu

【茶园】cháyuán ❶ 种植茶树的园子 tea plantation ❷〈旧时 *old*〉称戏院 theatre

【茶砖】cházhuān 砖茶 brick of tea

【茶资】cházī same as 茶钱 chá·qián

【茶座】cházuò (～儿 cházuòr) ❶ 卖茶的地方(多指室外的 oft. referring to outdoors) tea-stall with seats: 树阴下面有～儿。There's a tea-stall with seats under the shady trees. ❷ 卖茶的地方所设的座位 seats in a teahouse or tea garden: 茶馆有五十多个～儿。There are more than 50 seats in this teahouse.

查 chá ❶ 检查 check; examine: 盘～ interrogate and examine; question | ～收 check and accept | ～户口 check on household occupants | ～卫生 make a public health and sanitation check | ～出病来了没有? Have you had your illness checked? ❷ 调查 look into; investigate: ～访 investigate | ～勘 survey; explore ❸ 翻检着看 look up; consult: ～词典 look up a word in a dictionary | ～地图 consult a map | ～资料 consult reference materials ☞ zhā on p. 2403

【查办】chábàn 查明犯罪事实或错误情节,加以处理 investigate and deal with accordingly: 撤职～ dismiss (or discharge) sb. from his post and prosecute | 严加～ make strict investigation and deal with accordingly

【查抄】cháchāo 清查并没收犯罪者的财产 make an inventory of and confiscate a criminal's possession: ～逆产 confiscate a traitor's property

【查处】cháchǔ 查明情况,进行处理 investigate and treat: 严肃～ investigate and treat in a strict manner | 对违章车辆,管理部门已予～。The competent authorities have dealt with drivers who have broken the rules accordingly.

【查点】chádiǎn 检查数目 check the number or amount of; make an inventory of: ～人数 check the number of people

【查对】cháduì 检查核对 check and verify: ～材料 check the data | ～账目 check the account | ～原文 check against the original text

【查访】cháfǎng 调查打听(案情等) go around and make enquiries; investigate: 暗中～ investigate quietly

【查封】cháfēng 检查以后,贴上封条,禁止动用 seal up; close down; secure the contents of by closing with a seal:～赃物 seal up the stolen goods

【查岗】chá//gǎng same as 查哨 cháshào

【查核】cháhé 检查核对(账目等) check (accounts, etc.):反复～,结算无误 check repeatedly to make sure the account is correctly settled

【查获】cháhuò 侦查或搜查后获得(罪犯、赃物、违禁品等) ferret out; track down; hunt down and seize (criminals, stolen goods, contraband, etc.):～毒品 track down and seize drugs

【查缉】chájī ❶ 检查(走私、偷税等活动);搜查 investigate and track down on (smuggling, tax evasion, etc.); search :～走私物品 seize smuggled goods ❷ 搜查捉拿(犯人) search and arrest (criminals):～凶手 track down a murderer|～逃犯 track down a fugitive

【查检】chájiǎn ❶ 翻检查阅(书刊、文件等) search; retrieve; consult:这部书立类得法,～方便。The book is easy to retrieve since its content is properly classified. ❷ 检查 inspect; examine:行李须经～,方可托运。The luggage has to be inspected before consignment.

【查禁】chájìn 检查禁止 ban; prohibit; suppress:～赌博 ban gambling|～黄色书刊 ban pornographic publications

【查究】chájiū 调查追究 investigate; try to ascertain (cause, responsibility, etc.); look into and find out:～责任 find out who should be held responsible|对事故必须认真～,严肃处理。The accident must be investigated thoroughly and dealt with seriously.

【查勘】chákān 调查探测 survey; prospect:～矿产资源 prospect for mineral deposits

【查看】chákàn 检查、观察事物的情况 look over; examine (the state of affairs):～灾情 look into a disaster|亲自到现场～ examine the field situation oneself

【查考】chákǎo 调查研究,弄清事实 investigate; try to ascertain; do research on:作者的生卒年月已无从～。There is no way to ascertain the author's date of birth and death.

【查铺】chá//pù (干部)到集体宿舍检查睡眠情况 (officers) go on bed rounds (in barracks) at night; bed check

【查哨】chá//shào 检查哨兵执行任务的情况 go on rounds of guard posts; inspect the sentries; also 查岗 chá//gǎng

【查实】cháshí 查证核实 check and verify:反复～ check time and again|案情已经～。The case has been verified after a thorough investigation.

【查收】cháshōu 检查后收下(多用于书信 usu. refers to letters, notes, etc.) check and accept (what is sent herewith):寄去词典一部,请～。Please find a dictionary enclosed herewith.

【查问】cháwèn ❶ 调查询问 enquire about:～电话号码 ask for somebody's phone number ❷ 检查盘问 question; interrogate:～过往行人 question the passenger

【查寻】cháxún same as 查找 cházhǎo:邮局办理挂号邮件的～业务。Registered mail can be sought at the post office.|～失散多年的亲人 search for relatives who have lost touch for years

【查巡】cháxún 巡查 patrol; make one's rounds

【查询】cháxún same as 查问 cháwèn ①

【查验】cháyàn 检查验看 check; examine:～证件 examine a certificate

【查夜】chá//yè 夜间巡查 night patrol; go on rounds at night

【查阅】cháyuè (把书刊、文件等)找出来阅读有关的部分 consult (books, magazines, papers, etc.); look up:～档案材料 consult files

【查账】chá//zhàng 检查账目 check (or audit) accounts:年终～ the year-end audit

【查找】cházhǎo 查;寻找 look for:～资料 gather data|～失主 try to find the owner of lost property|～原因 try to find the cause

【查照】cházhào 〈旧时公文用语 *fml. arch.*〉叫对方注意文件内容,或按照文件内容(办事) please note (and act accordingly):即希～。Please consider and act accordingly.|希～办理。Please note and take appropriate action.

【查证】cházhèng 调查证明 investigate and verify; check:～属实 be checked and found to be true; be verified|犯罪事实已～清楚。The facts of the crime have been verified.

搽 chá 用粉末、油类等涂(在脸上或手上等) put powder, ointment, etc., on (face or hands, etc.); apply:～粉 powder|～碘酒 apply tincture of iodine|～雪花膏 put on vanishing cream

嵖 chá 嵖岈(Cháyá),山名,在河南 Chaya Mountain (in Henan Province)

猹 chá 野兽,像獾,喜欢吃瓜(见于鲁迅小说《故乡》) badger-like wild animal fond of melons (described in *Hometown* by Lu Xun)

楂 chá (～儿 chár) ❶ 短而硬的头发或胡子(多指剪落的、剪而未尽的或刚长出来的) short, bristly hair or beard; stubble ❷ same as 茬 chá

☞ zhā on p. 2403

槎[1] chá 〈书 *fml.*〉木筏 raft:乘～take a raft|浮～ floating raft

槎[2] chá same as 茬 chá

詧 chá 〈书 *fml.*〉same as 察 chá

碴 chá 〈方 *dial.*〉碎片碰破(皮肉) cut (flesh) on broken glass, china, etc.:手让

玻璃～破了 cut one's hand on broken glass
☞ chā on p. 202

【碴口】chákǒu 东西断或破的地方 broken surface; fracture: 电线断了,看～像是刀割的。The wire is broken, and the fracture shows that it was cut by a knife.

【碴儿】chár ❶ 小碎块 broken pieces; fragments: 冰～ small pieces of ice | 玻璃～ fragments of glass ❷ 器物上的破口 sharp edge of broken glass, china, etc.: 碰到碗～上,拉(lá)破了手。(I) happened to touch the sharp edge of the broken bowl and cut my finger. ❸ 嫌隙;引起双方争执的事由 feeling of animosity; grudge; cause of a quarrel: 找～ pick a quarrel | 过去他们俩有～,现在好了。They held a grudge against each other in the past, but now they have patched it up. ❹ 指提到的事情或人家刚说完的话 [sth. said or mentioned]: 答～ take the cue | 话～ cue; hint | 接～ take the hint ❺ 〈方 *dial.*〉势头 situation: 那个～来得不善。That situation is not favourable.

察 chá 仔细看;调查 examine; look into; scrutinize: 观～ observe | 考～ survey | ～其言,观其行 examine his words and watch his deeds; check what he says against what he does

【察察为明】chá chá wéi míng 形容专在细枝末节上显示精明 be astute in trivial matters

【察访】cháfǎng 通过观察和访问进行调查 make firsthand observations and enquiries; make an investigation trip; go on a fact-finding mission: ～民情 investigate the condition of the people | 暗中～ go on a secret fact-finding mission

【察觉】chájué 发觉;看出来 be conscious of; become aware of; perceive: 我～他的举动有点儿异样。I am aware that his behaviour is a bit odd. | 心事被人～read sb.'s mind

【察看】chákàn 为了解情况而细看 inspect; watch; look carefully at; observe: ～风向 watch which way the wind is blowing | ～动静 look around to see if anything is afoot

【察言观色】chá yán guān sè 观察言语脸色来揣摩对方的心意 weigh a person's words and watch his expression; watch a person's every mood

【察验】cháyàn 察看,检验 inspect; examine: ～物品的成色 examine the quality of the goods

楂 chá [楂子](chá·zi)〈方 *dial.*〉玉米等磨成的碎粒儿 coarsely ground maize (or corn)

檫 chá 檫树,落叶乔木,叶子大如手掌,总状花序,果实球形。木材坚韧,供建筑、造船、制家具等用。sassafras (*Sassafras albidum*); a kind of deciduous tree with palm-sized leaves, raceme, and ball-like fruits, often used for construction, shipbuilding and furniture

chǎ (ㄔㄚˇ)

叉 chǎ 分开成叉(chā)形 part so as to form a fork; fork: ～着腿 stand with one's legs apart
☞ chā on p. 199, chá on p. 202 and chà on p. 205

衩 chǎ ☞ 裤衩 kùchǎ on p. 1116
☞ chà on p. 206

蹅 chǎ 踏;踩 trudge (in mud, snow, etc.): ～了一脚泥。The shoes were covered with mud.

镲 chǎ 钹(bó),一种打击乐器 small cymbals; a kind of percussion instrument

chà (ㄔㄚˋ)

叉 chà ☞ 排叉儿 páichàr on p. 1437 and 劈叉 pǐchà on p. 1468
☞ chā on p. 199, chá on p. 202 and chǎ on p. 205

汊 chà 分支的小河;汊港 branched river; branch of a river: 河～ river branch; river arm | 湖～ arm of a lake

【汊港】chàgǎng 水流的分支 branch of a river

【汊流】chàliú same as 岔流 chàliú

【汊子】chà·zi same as 汊 chà

杈 chà 杈子 branch (of a tree): 树～ tree branch | 打棉花～ trim cotton plants
☞ chā on p. 199

【杈子】chà·zi 植物的分枝 branch of a plant or tree: 树～ tree branch | 打～(除去分枝) prune; trim (remove certain branches)

岔 chà ❶ 分歧的;由主干分出来的(道路) branch off; road branching from a main road: ～路 sideroad | 三～路口 fork in the road; junction of three roads ❷ 离开原来的方向而偏到一边儿 turn off from the original direction: 车子～上了小道。The car turned into a side path. ❸ 转移话题: 打～ diverge; change the topic or subject of a conversation; interrupt; butt in | 他用别的话～开了。He changed the topic. ❹ 错开时间,避免冲突 stagger time to avoid conflict: 要把这两个会的时间～开。The time of the two meetings should be staggered. ❺ (～儿 chàr) same as 岔子 chà·zi ②: 出～儿。Something has gone wrong. ❻〈方 *dial.*〉(嗓音)失常 lose one's voice; become hoarse: 她越说越伤心,嗓音都～了。As she told her story, her grief grew until she lost her voice.

【岔道儿】chàdàor same as 岔路 chàlù

【岔换】chàhuàn 〈方 *dial.*〉❶ 掉换 exchange; swap ❷ 调剂(心情、口味等) change (one's mood, taste in food, etc.)

【岔口】chàkǒu 道路分岔地方 fork (in a road); place where a road branches off: 往前走,碰到~向右拐。Go straight ahead, and when you get to a fork in the road, turn right.

【岔流】chàliú 从河流干流的下游分出的流入海洋的支流 (of a river) tributary branching off at the lower section of a river and emptying into the sea; also 汊流 chàliú

【岔路】chàlù 分岔的道路 branch road; by-road; byway; ~口 fork in the road; junction of three roads|过了石桥,有一条到刘庄的~。On the other side of the stone bridge, there is a sideroad leading to the Liu Village. also 岔道儿 chàdàor

【岔气】chà//qì 指呼吸时两肋觉得不舒服或疼痛 feel pain or discomfort in the chest when breathing

【岔曲儿】chàqǔr 在单弦开始前演唱的小段曲儿。内容多为抒情、写景。lyrical prelude to a single-stringed-fiddle recital, either conveying the performer's feelings or scenic description

【岔眼】chà//yǎn (马、骡等)因视觉错乱而惊恐 (of draught animals like horses, mules, etc.) visually misjudge and get alarmed: 这匹马一~,猛地一尥蹶子,飞也似地跑起来。The horse, startled by a false vision, suddenly kicked backward and started to gallop like mad.

【岔子】chà·zi ❶ same as 岔路 chàlù ❷ 事故;错误 accident; mistake: 你放心吧,出不了~。Don't worry, nothing will go wrong.

侘 chà [侘傺](chàchì)〈书 *fml*.〉失意的样子 frustrated or disappointed look

刹 chà 佛教的寺庙 Buddhist monastery or temple: 古~ Buddhist temple or monastery; ancient Buddhist temple [刹多罗之省,梵 abbreviation of 刹多罗 chàduōluō, Sanskrit: kṣetra]

☞ shā on p.1665

【刹那】chànà 极短的时间;瞬间 instant; a split second: 一~ in an instant; in a flash; in a blink of an eye [梵 Sanskrit: kṣaṇa]

衩 chà 衣服旁边开口的地方 vent or slit in the side of a garment

☞ chǎ on p.205

诧 chà 惊讶 surprised; amazed; astonished; astounded: ~异 be surprised; be astonished; be astounded|~然 be astonished|~为奇事 surprised by sth. strange

【诧愕】chà'è〈书 *fml*.〉吃惊而发愣 so surprised as to be in a daze; be astonished; be astounded

【诧然】chàrán 诧异的样子 surprised look

【诧异】chàyì 觉得十分奇怪 be astounded by sth. sudden and unexpected: 听了这突如其来的消息,我们都十分~。We were all astonished at the unexpected news.

差 chà ❶ 不相同;不相合 differ from; fall short off: ~得远 fall far short of ❷ 错误 wrong; mistaken: 说~了。What you said was wrong. *or* You're wrong there. ❸ 缺欠: ~点儿 be wanting; short a little; fall short of |还~一个人。We are short of one person. ❹ 不好;不够标准 inferior; subpar; under standard: 质量~ be poor in quality; of low or inferior quality

☞ chā on p.199, chāi on p.208, chài on p.209 and cī on p.315

【差不多】chà·bu duō ❶ (在程度、时间、距离等方面)相差有限;相近 (of degree, time or distance) be about the same; That's about it; almost; be similar: 这两种颜色~。The two colours look very much the same.|两人~同时到达终点。The two persons reached the destination at almost the same time. ❷ '差不多的',指一般的、普通的人 average person; ordinary people: 这包大米二百斤重,~的扛不起来。This sack of rice weighs 100 kg.; an ordinary person cannot lift and carry it.

【差不离】chà·bu lí (~儿 chà·bu lír) same as 差不多 chà·bu duō

【差点儿】chà//diǎnr ❶ (质量)稍次 (of quality) be a little bit inferior; not quite up to the mark; not quite good enough: 这种笔比那种笔~。This pen is not quite as good as that one. ❷〈副词 *adv*.〉表示某种事情接近实现或勉强实现。如果是说话的人不希望实现的事情,说'差点儿'或'差点儿没'都是指事情接近实现而没有实现。如'差点儿摔倒了'和'差点儿没摔倒'都是指几乎摔倒但是没有摔倒。如果是说话的人希望实现的事情,'差点儿'是惋惜它未能实现,'差点儿没'是庆幸它终于勉强实现了。如'差点儿赶上了'是指没赶上;'差点儿没赶上'是指赶上了。almost; nearly; on the verge of [indicating that sth. comes near to happening but has not happened. If the speaker does not wish it to happen, then '差点儿' or '差点儿没 chà// diǎnr méi' refers to the event that comes close to becoming a reality but actually doesn't. e.g. '差点儿摔倒了 chà // diǎnr shuāidǎo · le' and '差点儿没摔倒 chá// diǎnr méi shuāidǎo' both mean that someone almost fell but actually did not. If the speaker wishes it to happen, then '差点儿' indicates the speaker's regret, while '差点儿没' indicates the speaker's rejoicing that it has happened at last. ‖ also 差一点儿 chàyīdiǎnr

【差劲】chàjìn (质量、品质、能力)差;不好 (of quality, ability, etc.) bad; no good; disappointing: 这酒~,味儿不正。This wine is no good; it doesn't taste right.|答应了的事,又不兑现,真~。You made a promise but didn't honour it. How disappointing!

【差生】chàshēng 学业不良的学生 slow student; student who is poor at studying: 帮助

一些～补习功课 help a slow or poor student with his lessons

【差事】chàshì 不中用；不合标准 no good; of poor or inferior quality：这东西可太～了，怎么一碰就破了！This thing was indeed of poor quality — it broke at the slightest touch!

☞ chāi·shi on p. 208

侘 chà［侘傺］(chàchì)〈书 *fml*.〉same as 侘傺 chàchì

姹(奼) chà〈书 *fml*.〉美丽 beautiful

【姹紫嫣红】chà zǐ yān hóng 形容各种好看的花 brilliant purples and bright reds — beautiful flowers(嫣 *yan*：娇艳 bright and gorgeous)：花园里，～，十分绚丽。With lovely flowers everywhere, the park is a blaze of colour.

chāi (ㄔㄞ)

拆 chāi ❶ 把合在一起的东西打开 tear open or take apart sth.：～信 open a letter|～洗 unstitch (garments or bedding) for washing ❷ 拆毁 pull down; dismantle; demolish：～墙 pull down a wall|把旧房子～了。The old house was demolished.

☞ cā on p. 175

【拆白党】chāibáidǎng〈方 *dial*.〉骗取财物的流氓集团或坏人 gang of swindlers who cheat people out of their money or possessions

【拆除】chāichú 拆掉(建筑物等) pull down (as of buildings, etc.); dismantle; demolish：～脚手架 tear down the scaffolding|～防御工事 demolish the defence works

【拆穿】chāichuān 揭露；揭穿 tear open in order to expose; unmask; debunk：～阴谋 expose a scheme|～骗局 expose a fraud|～西洋镜 expose a trick; give away the show

【拆东墙，补西墙】chāi dōngqiáng, bǔ xīqiáng〈比喻 *fig*.〉顾此失彼，处境困难 take apart the east wall to repair the west wall — resort to a makeshift solution in a difficult situation; rob Peter to pay Paul

【拆兑】chāiduì〈方 *dial*.〉为应急而临时借用(钱、物) borrow (money or sth.) for a short while to tide over immediate needs：跟您～一点儿钱以应急需。I want to borrow some money from you to tide me over for some urgent needs.

【拆毁】chāihuǐ same as 拆除 chāichú

【拆伙】chāi//huǒ 散伙 break up or dissolve a partnership; part company

【拆借】chāijiè 短期借贷(按日计息的) make a short-term loan (usu. at a daily interest)：向银行～两千万元。Make a short-term loan of 20 million yuan from the bank.

【拆零】chāilíng 拆散零售 retail; sell piece by piece (instead of the whole lot)：以～、批发、送货上门等服务吸引顾客。Attract customers with such services as selling piecemeal (retailing), wholesaling and home deliveries.

【拆卖】chāi//mài 拆开零卖 sell by the piece (for things usu. sold by the set)：这套家具不～。This set of furniture cannot be sold by the piece.

【拆迁】chāiqiān 拆除原有的建筑物，居民迁移到别处 tear down old houses and resettle the inhabitants elsewhere：～户 household to be resettled|限期～ tear down old houses and resettle the inhabitants before a deadline

【拆墙脚】chāi qiángjiǎo〈比喻 *fig*.〉拆台 undermine; pull the rug (out) from under sb.'s feet; pull away a prop

【拆散】chāi//sǎn 使成套的物件分散 break apart (things of a set)：这套瓷器千万不要～了。These pieces of china form one set. On no account should they be separated.

【拆散】chāi//sàn 使家庭、集体等分散 break up (a family, a group, a collection, etc.)：～婚姻 break up a marriage|～联盟 break up a coalition

【拆台】chāi//tái 用破坏手段使人或集体倒台或使事情不能顺利进行。有的地区叫拆台脚。use ulterior means to cause sb. or a collective to fall from power or to hinder the smooth progress of sth.; also 拆台脚 chāi táijiǎo in some regions

【拆息】chāixī 存款放款按日计算的利率 daily interest (as in banking); (of deposits or loans) interest rate calculated on a daily basis

【拆洗】chāixǐ (棉衣、棉被等)拆开来洗干净后又缝上 unpick, wash, and remake; (of padded coats, quilts, etc.) remove the padding or lining, wash and sew them back together

【拆卸】chāixiè 把机器等拆开并卸下部件 disassemble; dismantle; take apart (a machine, equipment, etc.) and remove the parts

【拆账】chāi//zhàng〈旧时 *old*〉某些行业(如戏班、饮食、理发等行业)的工作人员无固定工资，根据收入和劳动量，按比例分钱。也泛指按比例分配某种利益。workers of service trades, such as opera troupes, catering, and hairdressing, had no fixed wages but rather got paid in proportion to the total business earning and the amount of work they have done. Now, this generally means the portioning of profits or interests among a group of people or parties.

【拆字】chāi//zì 测字 fortune-telling by taking apart a chosen or given Chinese character

钗 chāi〈旧时 *old*〉妇女别在发髻上的一种首饰，由两股簪子合成 hairpin (formerly worn by women for adornment, usu. joined together with two hair clasps)：金～ a gold hairpin|荆～布裙(形容妇女装束朴素) thornwood hairpins and hemp skirt — simple low ly dress of a poor woman

差 chāi ❶ 派遣(去做事) send on an errand; dispatch:～遣 dispatch|鬼使神～ unexpected happening; curious coincidence, almost like it has been caused by a ghost's or a fairy's doing|立即～人去取。Send someone over for it immediately. ❷ 被派遣去做的事;公务;职务 job sb. is dispatched to do; official post; job:兼～ moonlight; hold more than one job concurrently|出～ on a business trip ❸〈旧时 *old*〉指被派遣的人;差役 one sent on an errand; hireling; runner or bailiff in a yamen:听～ errand-boy; servant|解(jiè)～ (in old times) one who escorted criminals or captives

☞ chā on p. 199, chà on p. 206, chài on p. 209 and cī on p. 315

【差旅费】chāilǚfèi 因公外出时的交通、食宿等费用 allowances for a business trip; travel expenses, such as for board and lodging when one is on an official business trip

【差遣】chāiqiǎn 分派人到外面去工作;派遣:dispatch; assign; send sb. on an errand or mission (usu. outside of the present work unit):听候～await assignment; be at sb.'s disposal; be at sb.'s beck and call

【差使】chāishǐ 差遣;派遣 send; dispatch; assign

【差使】chāi·shi〈旧时 *old*〉指官场中临时委任的职务,后来也泛指职务或官职 official post one is temporarily assigned to; later popularly used to refer to official post

【差事】chāi·shi ❶ 被派遣去做的事情 errand; assignment; sth. one is dispatched to do ❷ same as 差使 chāi·shi

☞ chàshì on p. 207

【差役】chāiyì ❶ 封建统治者强迫人民从事的无偿劳动 corvée; unpaid work that feudal rulers forced the people to do in old times ❷〈旧时 *old*〉称在衙门中当差的人 runner or bailiff in a yamen

chái (ㄔㄞˊ)

侪(儕) chái〈书 *fml.*〉同辈;同类的人 people of the same generation; fellows; associates:吾～ we as a group; people like us|～辈 people of the same generation|同～contemporaries

【侪辈】cháibèi〈书 *fml.*〉同辈 people of the same generation

柴(❷㾴) chái ❶ 柴火 firewood:木～ firewood|～草 faggot|上山打～ collect firewood in the hills ❷〈方 *dial.*〉干瘦;不松软;纤维多,不易嚼烂 (of food) tough; hard and dry; not soft; with too much tissues, not easy to chew:这芹菜显得～。The celery seems rather dry and woody.|酱肘子肥而不腻,瘦而不～。These pork joints simmered in brown sauce taste rich but not greasy, lean but not dry. ❸〈方 *dial.*〉质量低或品质、能力差 of poor quality, character or abilities; inferior; lousy:这支笔刚用就坏,太～了。This pen is so shoddy that it broke down after one use.|他棋下得特～。He is a lousy chess player. ❹ (Chái)姓 a surname

【柴草】cháicǎo 做柴用的草、木;柴火 grass and wood used as firewood; firewood:小山土薄,只长些～。The hill is arid. Only firewood can grow on it.

【柴扉】cháifēi〈书 *fml.*〉same as 柴门 cháimén

【柴火】chái·huo 做燃料用的树枝、秫秸、稻秆、杂草等 faggot; grass, plant stalks, tree branches etc., used as fuel

【柴鸡】cháijī 指身体较小,产的蛋也小,腿下部一般没有毛的鸡 chicken with a small body, usu. no feathers on the lower part of their legs, and lay small eggs

【柴门】cháimén 用散碎木材、树枝等做成的简陋的门。旧时用来比喻贫苦人家。simple door made of small sticks and broken pieces of wood, usu. referring to a poor family

【柴米】cháimǐ 做饭用的柴和米,泛指必需的生活资料 firewood and rice for making a meal, (in a broad sense) daily necessities

【柴米油盐】chái mǐ yóu yán 泛指人们的日常生活必需品 fuel, rice, oil and salt — chief daily necessities

【柴油】cháiyóu 轻质石油产品的一类,从石油中经分馏、裂化等而得。挥发性比润滑油高,比煤油低,用做燃料。diesel oil; light oil used as fuel, produced from petroleum through fractionation and cracking, whose volatility is higher than that of lubricant oils but lower than that of kerosene

【柴油机】cháiyóujī 用柴油做燃料的内燃机,比汽油机功率大而燃料费用低,广泛应用在载重汽车、机车、拖拉机、轮船、舰艇和其他机器设备上 diesel engine; internal combustion engine using diesel oil as fuel, stronger than the gasoline engine but lower in fuel cost, widely used for trucks, locomotives, tractors, ships, and warships; also 狄塞尔机 dísài'ěrjī

豺 chái 哺乳动物,形状像狼而小,耳朵比狼的短而圆。贪食,残暴,常成群围攻牛、羊等家畜。jackal (*Canis Linnaeus*), mammal resembling a wolf in appearance but with a smaller body. Its ears are shorter and rounder than a wolf's. Greedy and cruel, it usu. attacks domesticated animals such as cows, oxen and sheep, in packs. also 豺狗 cháigǒu

【豺狼】cháiláng 豺和狼 jackals and wolves;〈比喻 *fig.*〉凶恶残忍的人 cruel and evil people:～当道 jackals and wolves hold sway|～成性 as cruel and evil as jackals and wolves

【豺狼当道】cháiláng dāngdào〈比喻 *fig*.〉坏人当权 jackals and wolves hold sway — the cruel and the wicked are in power

chǎi (ㄔㄞˇ)

茝 chǎi 古书上说的一种香草 a kind of fragrant plant recorded in ancient books

蹅 chǎi (～儿 chǎir) 碾碎了的豆子或玉米 ground beans or maize or corns: 豆～儿 ground beans | 把玉米磨成～儿。Grind the maize into powder.

chài (ㄔㄞˋ)

虿(蠆) chài 蝎子一类的有毒的虫 insects and arachnoid as poisonous the insect-like scorpion: 蜂～ wasps and scorpions

差 chài〈书 *fml*.〉same as 瘥 chài
☞ chā on p. 199, chà on p. 206, chāi on p. 208 and cī on p. 315

瘥 chài〈书 *fml*.〉病愈 recover from an illness: 久病初～ have just recovered from a long illness
☞ cuó on p. 339

chān (ㄔㄢ)

辿(䢟) chān 地名用字,如龙王辿,在山西 *chan*; character used in the name of a place, e. g. Longwangchan, in Shanxi Province

觇 chān〈书 *fml*.〉窥视; 观测 peep; observe; survey: ～视 peep | ～望 observe | ～标 surveyor's beacon

【觇标】chānbiāo 一种测量标志,标架用几米到几十米高的木料或金属等制成,架设在被观测点上作为观测、瞄准的目标 surveyor's beacon; mark held up on a timber or metal structure several metres to dozens of metres in height. Erected on the spot to be surveyed, it is used as a target for aiming or observing.

梴 chān〈书 *fml*.〉形容木长 long log

掺(摻) chān same as 搀[2] chān: ～兑 adulterate; dilute | ～杂 mix
☞ càn on p. 188 and shǎn on p. 1673

搀[1](攙) chān 搀扶 help by the arm; support with one's hand: ～着奶奶慢慢走。Give grandma some support and walk slowly.

搀[2](攙) chān 把一种东西混合到另一种东西里去 mix one thing into another: ～和 mix together | 饲料里再～点水 mix the feed with a bit more water | 初期白话文,～用文言成分的比较多。Most early vernacular writings had mixed in more classical Chinese.

【搀兑】chānduì 把成分不同的东西混合在一起 mix different substances (esp. liquids) together: 把酒精跟水～起来。Mix alcohol with water.

【搀扶】chānfú 用手轻轻架住对方的手或胳膊 support gently by the hand or arm: 同学们轮流～老师爬山。The students take turn rendering a supporting arm to their teacher as they climb up the hill.

【搀和】chān·huo ❶ 搀杂混合在一起 mix; mingle: 把黄土、石灰、砂土～起来铺在小路上。Mix earth, cement and sand together and pave the road with it. ❷ 参加进去(多指搅乱、添麻烦 usu. causing trouble) meddle; interfere; tamper: 这事你少～。Stop butting in on this matter. | 人家正忙着呢,别在这里瞎～。We are very busy. Please stop messing things up.

【搀假】chān//jiǎ 把假的搀在真的里面或把质量差的搀在质量好的里面 mix what is sham into what is genuine; mix things of poor quality into those of good quality

【搀杂】chānzá 混杂; 使混杂 mix up; jumble up: 别把不同的种子～在一起 don't mix up different kinds of seeds | 喝骂声和哭叫声～在一起 noises of cursing mixed with crying | 依法办事不能～私人感情。One should do one's work according to the rule, and ought not allow one's personal feelings to interfere (with one's work).

幨 chān〈书 *fml*.〉车帷子 carriage curtain

襜 chān〈书 *fml*.〉❶ 短衣 short jacket ❷ 车帷子 carriage curtain

【襜褕】chānyú〈书 *fml*.〉一种短的便衣 a kind of short, casual jacket

chán (ㄔㄢˊ)

单(單) chán [单于](chányú) 匈奴君主的称号 *chanyu*; title of the chief of the Xiongnu people in ancient China
☞ dān on p. 374 and Shàn on p. 1674

铤 chán〈古代 *arch*.〉一种铁把的短矛 short spear with an iron handle

谗(讒) chán 在别人面前说某人的坏话 accuse or slander or backbite (sb. behind his back): ～言 malicious, false accusation | ～害 calumniate; frame a person for blame

【谗害】chánhài 用谗言陷害 slander a person in order to harm him: ～忠良 vilify and harm loyal and good (courtiers)

【谗佞】chánnìng〈书 *fml*.〉说人坏话和用花言巧语巴结人的人 slanderer; those who say bad words about others behind their backs or fawn on sb.

【谗言】chányán 毁谤的话；挑拨离间的话 false accusation; words that sow discord between people：进～(of a subordinate) falsely accuse someone (to his superior)|听信～(of a superior) believe false accusation against sb.

婵(嬋) chán ☞ below

【婵娟】chánjuān〈书 *fml*.〉❶(姿态)美好，多用来形容女子 (oft. of women) lovely; graceful; beautiful ❷ 指月亮 the moon：千里共～。May we share the beauty of the moonlight, though we are thousands of miles apart.

【婵媛】[1] chányuán〈书 *fml*.〉same as 婵娟 chánjuān ①

【婵媛】[2] chányuán〈书 *fml*.〉牵连；相连 be linked together; be related：垂条～。The drooping twigs are all intertwined.

馋(饞) chán ❶ 看见好的食物就想吃；专爱吃好的 greedy; gluttonous; want to eat whatever delicious food one sets eyes upon; interested in eating delicious foods：嘴～greedy; gluttonous; like to eat; enjoy eating a lot ❷ 羡慕；看到喜爱的事物希望得到 envy; wish to take as one's own when seeing things one likes：眼～envy|看见下棋他就～得慌。His hands itch when he sees others play chess. *or* His hands itch at the sight of a game of chess.

【馋鬼】chánguǐ 指嘴馋贪吃的人 greedy pig; glutton, greedy-guts, someone who wants to eat all the time

【馋猫】chánmāo 指嘴馋贪吃的人(含讥讽意 sarcastic) greedy pig; glutton, greedy-guts

【馋涎欲滴】chánxián yù dī 馋得口水要流下来。形容十分贪吃，有时也用于比喻。one's mouth is almost drooling, used to describe one is very greedy for food, sometimes also used as figurative speech

【馋嘴】chánzuǐ ❶ 指贪吃 greedy for food; gluttonous ❷ 指贪吃的人 greedy eater

禅(禪) chán ❶〈佛教用语 *Budd*.〉指排除杂念，静坐 refer to sitting in meditation cleansing one's mind：坐～ sit in meditation (with crossed legs)|参～ Buddhist practice of using meditation to gain truth ❷ 泛指佛教的事物 (in a broad sense) related to Buddhism：～林 Buddhist monasteries or temples|～杖 Buddhist monk's stick [梵 Sanskrit: dhyāna]

☞ shàn on p. 1675

【禅房】chánfáng 僧徒居住的房屋，泛指寺院 Buddhist monks' abode, generally refers to Buddhist temples

【禅机】chánjī 禅宗和尚说法时，用言行或事物来暗示教义的诀窍 allegorical words or gestures used by monks of the Chan (Zen) Sect in expounding Buddhist teachings

【禅理】chánlǐ 指佛教的教义 Buddhist tenets or doctrine

【禅林】chánlín 指寺院 Buddhist monasteries or temples

【禅门】chánmén 佛门 Buddhism; gate to Buddhism; belonging to Buddhism

【禅师】chánshī 对和尚的尊称 master (complimentary term of address for Buddhist monk)

【禅堂】chántáng 僧尼参禅礼佛的处所；佛堂 Buddhist meditation hall; (Buddhist) hall of the shrine

【禅悟】chánwù〈佛教 *Budd*.〉指对教义的领悟 awakening to truth; realization of truth

【禅学】chánxué 指佛教禅宗的教义 doctrine of Chan or Zen Buddhism

【禅院】chányuàn 佛寺；寺院 Buddhist monastery or temple

【禅杖】chánzhàng 佛教徒坐禅欲睡时，用来使惊醒的竹杖。泛指僧人用的手杖。bamboo stick used to awaken a monk when he is about to fall asleep during meditation; anything used by monks serving that function

【禅宗】chánzōng 我国佛教宗派之一，以静坐默念为修行方法。相传南朝宋末(五世纪)由印度和尚菩提达摩传入我国，唐宋时极盛。Chan Sect; one of the Buddhist sects in China that advocates achieving enlightenment through meditation and silent reciting of Buddhist scriptures. According to Buddhist literature, it was introduced to China by the Indian monk Budhidharma towards the end of the Song Dynasty (420-479) of the Southern Dynasties (420-589), and reached its heyday during the Tang (618-907) and Song (960-1279) dynasties.

孱 chán〈书 *fml*.〉瘦弱；软弱 frail; thin and feeble; weak and feeble：～羸 weak and feeble|～弱 frail

☞ càn on p. 188

【孱弱】chánruò〈书 *fml*.〉❶(身体)瘦弱 (of physique or health) frail; weak; feeble ❷ 软弱无能 weak; powerless; impotent ❸ 薄弱；不充实 insubstantial; thin

缠(纏) chán ❶ 缠绕 twine; wind：～线 wind a thread|用铁丝～了几道。It is twined with a few rounds of wire. ❷ 纠缠 pester; trouble; tie up; tangle：琐事～身 be tied down with trivial matters|胡搅蛮～ pester sb. endlessly; harass sb. with endless demands ❸〈方 *dial*.〉应付 deal with：这人真难～，好说歹说都不行。This fellow is really hard to deal with! *or* This fellow is such a nuisance! I simply can't shake him off, whatever I say.

【缠绑】chánbǎng 缠绕绑扎 bind; tie up; bandage：受伤的左腿～着纱布。The wounded left leg is bandaged.

【缠绵】chánmián ❶ 纠缠不已，不能解脱(多指病或感情 of illness or emotion) lingering;

abiding：～病榻 be bedridden with a lingering or chronic disease｜情意～ abiding affection ❷ 宛转动人 touching; moving; sentimental：歌声柔和～。The singing was soft and sweet and had a lingering effect on one.

【缠绵悱恻】chánmián fěicè 形容内心悲苦难以排遣 inextricable and commiserative; having lingering sad and sentimental feelings that cannot be dispelled or relieved

【缠磨】chán·mo 纠缠；搅扰 bother; pester：孩子老～人，不肯睡觉。The child is really a pest. He simply wouldn't fall asleep.｜许多事情～着他，使他忙乱不堪。He's got so many things pestering him and he is always very busy and in a state of chaos.

【缠扰】chánrǎo 纠缠，困扰 bother; pester; harass：被杂事～着 tied up with trivial matters

【缠绕】chánrào ❶ 条状物回旋地束缚在别的物体上（of wires, strips, or cord-like things）turn, twist, wind, or twine repeatedly, esp. round an object：枯藤～ twined by a dead vine｜电磁铁的上面～着导线。The electromagnetic iron was wound with wires. ❷ 纠缠；搅扰 pester; bother; harass：烦恼～心头 haunted by troubles｜这孩子～得我什么也干不成。The child is so pestering that I can't do anything.

【缠绕茎】chánràojīng 不能直立，必须缠在别的东西上才能向上生长的茎，如紫藤、牵牛等的茎 vine; stem of any creeping or climbing plant that cannot stand on its own and must climb around sth. else to grow, e.g. the vines of wisteria or morning glory

【缠身】chánshēn 缠扰身心 bog one down; tied down：杂事～tied down with trivial affairs｜长年重病～ long pestered by a serious illness

【缠手】chán//shǒu ❶ 脱不开手 tie down：孩子小，太～。The child is small and my hands are full just looking after it.｜喂牲口这种事很～。Feeding draught animals can really tie you down. ❷（事情）难办（of things）troublesome; hard to deal with：大家的想法不一致，事情看来有些～。Everyone has his or her own opinions. It looks like it is going to be troublesome.

【缠足】chán//zú 裹脚 foot-binding

蝉（蟬） chán 昆虫，种类很多，雄的腹部有发音器，能连续不断发出尖锐的声音。幼虫生活在土里，吸食植物的根。成虫刺吸植物的汁。cicada (*Cicada*); a kind of insect with many varieties, the male having a sound-producing organ in its abdomen that continually produces a shrill singing noise, and the larva living in the earth and sucking liquid from roots of plants while the adult sucks sap from plants with a needle-like organ

【蝉联】chánlián 连续（多指连任某个职务或继续保持某种称号）continue to hold a post or title：～世界冠军 retain a world championship; win a world championship for yet another time

【蝉蜕】chántuì ❶ 蝉的幼虫变为成虫时蜕下的壳，中医入药 cicada slough shed by the larva when it becomes an adult, used in traditional Chinese medicine ❷〈书 *fml.*〉〈比喻 *fig.*〉解脱 free or extricate oneself from

【蝉衣】chányī 中药上指蝉蜕 cicada slough (in Chinese medicine)

僝 chán［僝僽］(chánzhòu)〈书 *fml.*〉❶ 憔悴；烦恼 haggard; careworn; fretful; troubled ❷ 折磨 torment; harass ❸ 埋怨；嗔怪 complain; blame ❹ 排遣 divert oneself (from loneliness and boredom)

廛 chán〈古代 *arch.*〉指一户平民所住的房屋 house of a commoner's family：市～ marketplace (usu. among commoners' houses)

潺 chán 水流动的声音 soft sound of water flowing

【潺潺】chánchán〈拟声词 *onom.*〉形容溪水、泉水等流动的声音 murmur; babble; gurgle; sound of a stream or brook flowing：～流水 murmuring stream

【潺湲】chányuán〈书 *fml.*〉形容河水慢慢流的样子（of water）flow slowly：溪水～。The stream flows gently and slowly.

澶 chán 澶渊（Chányuān），古地名，在今河南濮阳西南 Chanyuan, name of a place in ancient times, in the southwest of present-day Puyang, Henan Province

镡 Chán 姓 a surname

☞ Tán on p. 1860 and xín on p. 2136

瀍 Chán 瀍河，水名，在河南 Chanhe River in Henan Province

蟾 chán 指蟾蜍 toad：～酥 dried venom of toads; toad-cake

【蟾蜍】chánchú ❶ 两栖动物，身体表面有许多疙瘩，内有毒腺，能分泌黏液，吃昆虫、蜗牛等小动物，对农业有益 toad (*Bufonidae*); frog-like amphibian whose skin is studded with small swellings with venomous glands that can produce a white, sticky mucus, and which feeds on insects and snails and is good for agriculture; 通称 popularly called 癞蛤蟆 làihá·ma or 疥蛤蟆 jièhá·ma ❷ 传说月亮里面有三条腿的蟾蜍，因此，古代诗文里常用来指月亮 Legend has it there is a three-legged toad in the moon, so the toad was oft. used in ancient poetry and prose to refer to the moon.

【蟾宫】chángōng〈书 *fml.*〉指月亮 moon

【蟾宫折桂】chángōng zhé guì 科举时代比喻考取进士 win laurels in the moon palace — be successful in the highest imperial examination

【蟾光】chánguāng〈书 *fml.*〉指月光 moonlight

【蟾酥】chánsū 蟾蜍表皮腺体的分泌物，白色乳状液体，有毒。中医入药。dry toad venom;

white, sticky secretion from the venomous glands on a toad's skin, which is poisonous and used as a traditional Chinese medicine

巉 chán 〈书 *fml.*〉山势高险的样子 dangerously steep; precipitous

【巉峻】chánjùn 〈书 *fml.*〉形容山势高而险(of mountains or cliffs, etc.) precipitous: ~的悬崖 steep cliff; sheer overhanging cliff

【巉岩】chányán 〈书 *fml.*〉高而险的山岩 precipitous crag: 峭壁~ perpendicular cliff|~林立 jungle of precipitous crags

躔 chán 〈书 *fml.*〉❶ 兽的足迹 trails or traces left by wild beasts or animals ❷ 天体的运行 orbiting of celestial bodies

镵 chán ❶〈古代 *arch.*〉一种铁制的刨土工具 trowel; shovel; digging tool made of iron ❷〈书 *fml.*〉same as 刺 cì ①

chǎn (ㄔㄢˇ)

产(產) chǎn ❶ 人或动物的幼体从母体中分离出来 give birth to (cubs or babies); deliver; breed; bear: ~妇 woman in labour; woman who has just given birth|~科 obstetrics; maternity department|~卵 lay eggs ❷ 创造物质财富或精神财富;生产 create wealth for material or cultural progress; produce: ~销 production and marketing|增~ increase production|转~ shift production ❸ 出产 produce; manufacture: ~粮 produce grain|~煤 produce coal ❹ 物产;产品 produce; products: 土~ native produce|特~ special local product|水~ aquatic products ❺ 产业 property; estate: 家~ family property; family possession|财~ property|破~ bankrupt

【产程】chǎnchéng 分娩的过程 childbirth; parturition; process of giving birth to a child

【产道】chǎndào 胎儿脱离母体时所经过的通道,包括骨产道(骨盆)和软产道(子宫颈和阴道)两部分 birth canal; canal the foetus goes through during deliverance, including two parts — bone canal (pelvis) and soft canal (cervix of womb and vagina)

【产地】chǎndì 物品出产的地方 place of origin; place where sth. is made

【产儿】chǎn'ér 刚出世的婴儿 newborn baby ◇ 这种工具正是技术革新运动的~。This implement is a product of the technical innovation drive.

【产房】chǎnfáng 供产妇分娩用的房间 delivery room

【产妇】chǎnfù 在分娩期或产褥期中的妇女 woman who is in labour or has just given birth; woman in puerperium

【产科】chǎnkē 医院中专门负责孕妇的孕期保健,辅助产妇分娩等的一科 obstetrics and department of obstetrics; maternity department; department in a hospital that specializes in providing medical care for pregnant women, childbirth, and other related services

【产量】chǎnliàng 产品的总量 output; yield

【产品】chǎnpǐn 生产出来的物品 product; produce: 农~ farm produce|畜~ livestock products|~出厂都要经过检验。All the products shall be examined before they leave the factory.

【产婆】chǎnpó 〈旧时 *old*〉以接生为业的妇女 midwife; woman who makes a living by helping pregnant women give birth

【产钳】chǎnqián 助产用的一种器械,在某些分娩过程中(如难产)用来牵引胎儿 obstetric forceps; medical instrument used to help deliver the baby in case of a difficult labour

【产权】chǎnquán 指财产的所有权 property right; title; ownership of property

【产褥期】chǎnrùqī 产妇产出胎儿后到生殖器官恢复一般状态的一段时期 puerperium; period of time after a woman gives birth and before her reproductive organs completely recover

【产生】chǎnshēng 由已有事物中生出新的事物;出现 give rise to; bring about; evolve; come into being; emerge: ~矛盾 conflicts emerge|在中华民族悠久的历史中,~了许许多多可歌可泣的英雄人物。A great multitude of laudable heroes emerged in the long Chinese history.

【产物】chǎnwù 在一定条件下产生的事物;结果 things produced under certain conditions; outcome; result: 迷信是愚昧落后的~。Superstition results from ignorance and backwardness.

【产销】chǎnxiāo 生产和销售 production and marketing: ~结合 coordination between production and marketing|~合同 contract of production and marketing

【产业】chǎnyè ❶ 土地、房屋、工厂等财产(多指私有的 oft. of private ownership) land, houses, factories, and other properties ❷ 关于工业生产的(用于定语 oft. used as attributive) industrial: ~工人 industrial worker|~部门 industrial department|~革命 industrial revolution

【产业工人】chǎnyè gōngrén 在现代工业生产部门中劳动的工人,如矿工、钢铁工人、纺织工人、铁路工人等 industrial worker; employees working in the production departments of modern industries, such as miners, steel workers, textile workers, railway workers, etc.

【产院】chǎnyuàn 为产妇进行产前检查以及供产妇度过分娩期和产后期的医疗机构 maternity hospital; medical institution that provides medical care for pregnant women before, during, and after delivery

【产值】chǎnzhí 在一个时期内全部产品或某一产品以货币计算的价值量 value of output; output value; value of one product or all products calculated in currency within a specified period

刬(剗) chǎn same as 铲 chǎn ②:～除 eradicate; eliminate

☞ chàn on p. 214

浐(滻) Chǎn 浐河,水名,在陕西 Chanhe River, in Shaanxi Province

谄 chǎn 谄媚 flatter; fawn on; toady to; curry favour with:～笑 smile obsequiously; ingratiating smile|～上欺下 be servile to one's superiors and tyrannical to one's subordinates; fawn on those above and bully those below

【谄媚】chǎnmèi 用卑贱的态度向人讨好 flatter (obsequiously); fawn on; toady to (sb. in a servile manner):～上司 toady to one's superior|羞于～ refrain from flattery; feel ashamed to flatter; consider it beneath one to flatter

【谄笑】chǎnxiào 为了讨好,故意做出笑容 smile ingratiatingly; force a smile in order to curry favour with sb.:胁肩～ cringe and smile obsequiously

【谄谀】chǎnyú 为了讨好,卑贱地奉承人;谄媚阿谀 flatter sb. servilely so as to fawn on him; curry favour with; lick sb.'s boots:～之态,令人齿冷。Such ingratiating manners are utterly contemptible.

啴(嘽) chǎn 〈书 *fml.*〉宽缓 lenient; relaxed:～缓 mild and lenient

☞ tān on p. 1857

铲(鏟、剷) chǎn ❶ (～儿 chǎnr)一种用具,像簸箕或像平板,带长把(bà),多用铁制 shovel; tool either flat or resembling a duster in shape, with a long handle and usu. made of iron:煤～ coal shovel|锅～ slice ❷ 用锹或铲撮取或清除 lift or remove with a shovel or spade:～煤 shovel coal|～草 weed; remove weeds|把地～平了 scrape the ground even; level the ground with a shovel or spade

【铲除】chǎnchú 连根除去;消灭干净 root out; uproot; eradicate; eliminate:～杂草 weed; root out the weeds|～祸根 root out the cause for more disaster|～旧习俗,树立新风尚 eradicate old customs while fostering new practices

【铲趟】chǎntāng 在作物的行间锄草、松土和培土 weeding, loosening soil and hilling (between lines of crops)

【铲土机】chǎntǔjī 铲土、运土用的机器,刮刀刮下的土可以自动装入斗中运走 carry-scraper; scraper; machine for spading or removing earth, capable of automatically filling the tip body with removed earth and carrying it away; also 铲运机 chǎnyùnjī

【铲运车】chǎnyùnchē 一种搬运机械,车前部装有钢叉,可以升降,用来搬运、装卸货物 forklift truck; machine with a moveable steel fork on its front used for lifting, lowering, and carrying heavy goods; also 叉车 chāchē and 铲车 chǎnchē

【铲子】chǎn·zi same as 铲 chǎn ①

阐(闡) chǎn 讲明白 make clear; explain clearly:～明 expound; clarify|～述 elaborate

【阐发】chǎnfā 阐述并发挥 elucidate; explain and develop (an idea, theory):～无遗 elucidate in great detail|文章详细～了技术革命的历史意义。The article elucidates the historical significance of technological revolution in great detail.

【阐明】chǎnmíng 讲明白(道理) clarify; make clear; expound (a truth):历史唯物主义是～社会发展规律的科学。Historical materialism is a science that expounds the laws of social development.

【阐释】chǎnshì 阐述并解释 explain; interpret:～精微 explain the fine details

【阐述】chǎnshù 论述 elaborate; expound:～自己的见解 elaborate one's views|报告对宪法草案作了详细的～。The report elaborates on the draft of the Constitution in great detail.

【阐扬】chǎnyáng 说明并宣传 expound and propagate or promote:～真理 expound and propagate a truth

蒇 chǎn 〈书 *fml.*〉完成 finish; complete:～事 finish the work; be through with the job

燀(燀) chǎn 〈书 *fml.*〉❶ 燃烧;烧 burn; be on fire ❷ 火花飞迸的样子 sparkle; send out sparks in all directions ❸ 炽热 intense heat; sizzling

骣 chǎn 骑马不加鞍辔 riding an unsaddled horse:～骑 ride a horse without a saddle

冁(囅、辴) chǎn 〈书 *fml.*〉笑的样子 the way one smiles:～然而笑 break into a smile

chàn (ㄔㄢˋ)

忏(懺) chàn ❶ 忏悔 repent; be penitent ❷ 僧尼道士代人忏悔时念的经文 scripture monks, nuns and Taoists read to atone for sb.'s sins:拜～ (of a monk or a nun) read a scripture to atone for sb.'s sins [梵 Sanskrit: ksama]

【忏悔】chànhuǐ ❶ 认识了过去的错误或罪过而感觉痛心 feel repentant on realizing one's past mistakes or sins ❷ 向神佛表示悔过,请求宽恕 confess (one's sins) to God, the Buddha or a priest to ask for forgiveness

刬(剗) chàn ☞ 一刬 yīchàn on p. 2244
☞ chǎn on p. 213

颤 chàn 颤动;发抖 quiver; vibrate; tremble; shiver: ～抖 tremble|声音发～ voice quivers|两腿直～ shiver in one's shoes
☞ zhàn on p. 2414

【颤动】chàndòng 短促而频繁地振动 tremble; vibrate in a short and repeated manner: 汽车驶过,能感到桥身的～。When a car shoots past, one can feel the shaking of the bridge.|他激动得说不出话来,嘴唇在微微～。He was too excited to say anything — his lips trembled slightly.

【颤抖】chàndǒu 哆嗦;发抖 tremble; shake; shiver; give a start: 冻得全身～ shiver all over with cold ◇树枝在寒风中～。The branches quivered in the cold wind.

【颤巍巍】chànwēiwēi (～的 chànwēiwēi·de)抖动摇晃(多用来形容老年人或病人的某些动作 usu. used to describe certain actions of sick or very old people) tottering; faltering

【颤音】chànyīn 舌尖或小舌等颤动时发出的辅音,例如俄语中的 P 就是舌尖颤音 consonant produced by trembling of the tongue tip or the uvula (or tonguelet), e. g. 'P' in the Russian language

【颤悠】chàn·you 颤动摇晃 shake; quiver; flicker; sway: 他的脚步正合着那扁担～的节拍。The carrying-pole on his shoulder swayed exactly to the rhythm of his footsteps.

羼 chàn 搀杂 mix; mingle: ～入 mix in|～杂 adulterate

【羼杂】chànzá 搀杂 adulterate

韂 chàn ☞ 鞍韂 ānchàn on p. 12

chāng (ㄔㄤ)

伥(倀) chāng 伥鬼 ghost of a man devoured by a tiger: 为虎作～ ghost of a man devoured by a tiger helps the tiger devour others

【伥鬼】chāngguǐ 传说中被老虎咬死的人变成的鬼,这个鬼不敢离开老虎,反而给老虎做帮凶 Legend has it that a man devoured by a tiger would become a ghost which, daring not leave the tiger, helps to find others for the tiger to devour. ☞ 为虎作伥 wèi hǔ zuò chāng on p. 1998

昌 chāng ❶ 兴旺;兴盛 prosperous; flourishing: ～盛 prosperous; flourishing|～明 thriving ❷〈书 *fml.*〉正当(dàng);美好 proper; fair; fair and proper: ～言 appropriate remarks; worthy words ❸ (Chāng)姓 a surname

【昌化石】chānghuàshí 一种以叶蜡石为主要成分的石料,一般是淡粉色,或带红色斑点,也有全红色的,产于浙江昌化,是制印章的名贵材料 Changhua stone; stone with pyrophyllite as its main component, usu. pale pink in colour, some with red spots are completely red, produced in quantity in Changhua County, Zhejiang Province, and is a valuable stone for making seals

【昌隆】chānglóng 兴旺发达 thriving and prosperous: 国运～。The country is flourishing.

【昌明】chāngmíng ❶ (政治、文化)兴盛发达 (of politics and culture) flourishing; well-developed: 科学～。Science is thriving. ❷ 使昌明 make flourish; prosper; promote: ～文化 make culture flourish|～大义 promote what is righteous

【昌盛】chāngshèng 兴旺;兴盛 prosperous; flourishing: 文化～ flourishing culture|把祖国建设成为一个繁荣～的国家。Build our fatherland into a prosperous country.

【昌言】chāngyán〈书 *fml.*〉❶ 正当的言论;有价值的话 appropriate remarks; proper words or comments; worthy advice ❷ 直言无隐 speak frankly; make a straightforward statement; not mince words

倡 chāng〈书 *fml.*〉❶ 指以演奏、歌舞为业的人 singer, dancer or musician ❷ same as 娼 chāng
☞ chàng on p. 223

【倡优】chāngyōu ❶〈古代 *arch.*〉指擅长乐舞、谐戏的艺人 entertainers specialized in singing, dancing, and comedies ❷〈书 *fml.*〉娼妓和优伶 prostitutes; actors or actresses

菖 chāng [菖蒲](chāngpú)多年生草本植物,生在水边,地下有淡红色根茎,叶子形状像剑,肉穗花序。根茎可做香料,也可入药。calamus; sweet flag (*Acorus calamus*); perennial herb growing in marshy places and having sword-like leaves, flowers borne on a spadix, and pink rhizomes used in perfumery and medicine

猖 chāng〈书 *fml.*〉凶猛;狂妄 ferocious; fierce; savage; outrageous

【猖獗】chāngjué ❶ 凶猛而放肆 ferocious and rampant; wild and unrestrained; raging: ～的敌人 savage enemy ❷〈书 *fml.*〉倾覆;跌倒 collapse; decline

【猖狂】chāngkuáng 狂妄而放肆 fierce and unruly; outrageous; savage: 打退敌人的～进攻 beat back the enemy's furious attack

阊 chāng [阊阖](chānghé)神话传说中的天门;宫门 (in mythical stories) gate of the palace in heaven; heavenly gate; palatial entrance

娼 chāng 妓女 prostitute; streetwalker: 暗～ unlicensed prostitute; unregistered prostitute|沦落为～ reduced to prostitution; become a prostitute|逼良为～ drive or force a woman to prostitution

【娼妇】chāngfù 妓女（多用于骂人 oft. curse）whore
【娼妓】chāngjì 妓女 prostitute; streetwalker
【娼门】chāngmén 妓院 brothel; whorehouse; house of ill repute

鲳 chāng 鲳鱼，身体短而侧扁，没有腹鳍。生活海洋中。butterfish (*Stromateidae*); silvery pomfret; marine fish with a short, laterally flat body without abdominal fin; also 银鲳 yínchāng, 镜鱼 jìngyú and 平鱼 píngyú

cháng（ㄔㄤˊ）

长(長) cháng ❶ 两点之间的距离大（跟'短'相对 as opposed to 'short'）long a) 指空间 refers to space: 这条路很～。This road is very long. | ～～的柳条垂到地面。Long willow twigs hang, all the way to the ground. b) 指时间 refers to time: 夏季昼～夜短。In summer days are long and nights short. | ～寿 long life; longevity ❷ 长度 length: 南京长江大桥气势雄伟，铁路桥全～6,772米。The imposing Yangtze River Bridge of Nanjing is 6,772 metres long. *or* The imposing Yangtze River Bridge of Nanjing is 6,772 metres in length. ❸ 长处 strong points; forte: 特～ specialty; strong points | 取～补短 make up for each other's deficiencies | 一技之～ proficiency in one particular field; professional skill; useful trade ❹ 对某事做得特别好 be strong in; be good at: 他～于写作。He is good at writing. *or* He is a good writer. ❺（旧读 formerly pronounced zhàng）多余；剩余 extra; spare; surplus: ～物 anything that can be spared

☞ zhǎng on p. 2417

【长安】Cháng'ān 西汉隋唐等朝的都城，在今陕西西安一带。也泛指都城。Chang'an; China's capital during the Han, Sui, and Tang dynasties, situated roughly where Xi'an, capital of Shaanxi Province, now stands; (in a broad sense) capital
【长臂猿】chángbìyuán 类人猿的一种，身体比猩猩小，前肢特别长，没有尾巴，能直立行走。生活在亚洲热带森林中。gibbon (*Hylobates Illiger*); anthropoid ape whose body is smaller than a chimpanzee, has very long arms but no tail, and can walk upright, living in tropical forests of Asia
【长编】chángbiān 在写定著作之前，搜集有关材料并整理编排而成的初步稿本 preliminary draft of a book compiled and sorted out of materials collected before the writing begins
【长别】chángbié ❶ 长久离别 long separation; long absence: 倾诉～的心情 unbosom oneself of one's feelings (to sb.) after a long separation ❷ 永别 part forever; parted by death
【长波】chángbō 波长30,000米—3,000米（频率10—100千赫）的无线电波。以地波方式传播，用于超远程无线电通讯和导航等方面 long wave; radio waves with wavelengths between 30,000 and 3,000 metres (frequency 10-100 kilohertz), transmitted in the form of surface wave and used in super-distance communication and navigation
【长策】chángcè 能起长远作用的策略 good policy; sound plan; long-term strategy (capable of producing long-term effects): 治国～ sound plan for running a state | 权宜之计，决非～。An expedient is by no means a sound long-term plan.
【长城】Chángchéng 指万里长城，也用来比喻坚强雄厚的力量、不可逾越的障碍等 Ten-thousand-*li* Great Wall; (fig.) strong and powerful bulwark; insurmountable barrier: 中国人民解放军是保卫祖国的钢铁～。The People's Liberation Army is a great wall of steel in safeguarding our fatherland.
【长程】chángchéng 路程远的；长距离的 long trip; long distance: ～车票 long-distance ticket ◇～计划 long-term plan | ～目标 long-term goal
【长虫】cháng·chong 蛇 snake
【长处】cháng·chu 特长；优点 strong point; merit; virtue; forte
【长川】chángchuān same as 常川 chángchuān
【长辞】chángcí 和人世永别，指去世 leave this world forever — die; pass away: ～人间 leave this world | 与世～ depart from this world
【长此以往】cháng cǐ yǐ wǎng 老是这样下去（多就不好的情况说 mostly said of bad things or situations) if things go on like this; if things continue this way; if things remain what they are
【长笛】chángdí 管乐器，多用金属制成，上面有孔，孔上有键 flute; orchestral musical instrument in the form of a long tube mostly made of metal with holes on it and keys over the holes
【长度】chángdù 两点之间的距离 length; distance between two points
【长短】chángduǎn ❶（～儿 chángduǎnr）长度 length: 这件衣裳～儿正合适。This coat is just the right length. ❷ 意外的灾祸、事故（多指生命的危险 mostly said of danger to one's life) accident; mishap: 他独自出海，家人提心吊胆，唯恐有个～。He went out to sea by himself, so his family was left in a constant state of fear, worrying about accidents. ❸ 是非；好坏 right and wrong; merits and demerits; good and bad: 背地里说人～是不应该的。It is not right to gossip about a person behind his back. ❹〈方 *dial.*〉表示无论如何 anyway; whatsoever; no matter what: 明天的欢迎大会你～要来。You must come to

tomorrow's welcome party, no matter what.

【长短句】chángduǎnjù 词②的别称 another name for *ci* poem

【长法】chángfǎ (～儿 chángfǎr)为长远利益打算的办法 long-term solution; overall solution: 头疼医头,脚疼医脚,不是个～儿。Treating the symptoms but not the disease is no long-term solution.

【长方体】chángfāngtǐ 六个长方形(有时相对的两个面是正方形)所围成的立体 cuboid; rectangular parallelepiped; three-dimensional object formed by six rectangles, sometimes two opposite sides being squares

【长方形】chángfāngxíng 矩形 rectangle; oblong

【长歌当哭】cháng gē dàng kū 以放声歌咏代替哭泣,多指用诗文抒发胸中的悲愤 roar out a somber song instead of weeping, singing in a loud voice to vent one's grief in place of crying and weeping; compose or recite poetry to express one's sorrow and indignation

【长庚】chánggēng 我国古代指傍晚出现在西方天空的金星 ancient Chinese name for Venus (appearing in the western sky at dusk)

【长工】chánggōng 旧社会长年出卖劳力,受地主、富农剥削的贫苦农民 long-term hired hand; farm labourer hired by the year; poor peasant reduced to selling his labour to land owners or rich peasants by the year and were often exploited in old times

【长骨】chánggǔ 长管状的骨,如股骨、肱骨等 long bone, e.g. thighbone and humerus, etc.

【长鼓】chánggǔ ❶ 朝鲜族打击乐器,圆筒形,中间细而实,两端粗而中空,用绳绷皮做鼓面 long drum; Korean cylindrical percussion instrument, thin and solid in the middle while thick and empty at both ends, with both sides covered with hide tightened with ropes ❷ 瑶族打击乐器,长筒形,腰细而实 long drum; cylindrical percussion instrument of the Yao people, with a thin and solid mid section.

【长号】chánghào 管乐器,发音管可自由伸缩 trombone; large brass musical instrument with a long sliding tube that is made longer or shorter to vary the note; commonly called 拉管 lāguǎn

【长河】chánghé 长的河流 long river; 〈比喻 *fig.*〉长的过程 long process: 历史的～ the long process of history

【长话短说】cháng huà duǎn shuō 把要用很多话才能说完的事用简短的话说完 make a long story short

【长活】chánghuó ❶ 长工的活儿 long-term job (of a hired farmhand): 扛～ be hired as a long-term farmhand ❷〈方 *dial.*〉same as 长工 chánggōng

【长假】chángjià 〈旧时 *old*〉机关或军队中称辞职为请长假 resignation from a government or military post

【长江后浪推前浪】Cháng Jiāng hòulàn tuī qiánlàng 〈比喻 *fig.*〉人或事物不断发展更迭,新陈代谢 in the Yangtze River the waves behind drive on those before; (of persons or things) the new would always push on the old

【长颈鹿】chángjǐnglù 哺乳动物,颈很长,不会发声,雌雄都有角,身上有花斑。跑得很快,吃植物的叶子,产于非洲森林中,是陆地上身体最高的动物。giraffe (*Giraffa camelopardalis*); extremely tall and fast-running mammal living in African forests with a very long neck and dark spots on its body, feeding on leaves from branches of trees, both the male and female having antlers on their heads, unrefutably the tallest animal on land

【长久】chángjiǔ 时间很长;长远 long time; lasting; prolonged: ～打算 long-term plan | 这种混乱状况不会～的。Such a chaotic situation won't last long.

【长局】chángjú 可以长远维持的局面(多用在'不是'后 often used in the negative) permanent situation; lasting solution: 这样拖下去终久不是～。Such delaying is no permanent solution after all.

【长卷】chángjuàn 长幅的字画 long scroll (of painting or calligraphy): 山水～ long scroll of landscape painting

【长空】chángkōng 辽阔的天空 vast sky: 万里～ vast expanse of the sky

【长款】cháng//kuǎn 指结账时现金的数额多于账面的数额 more cash than can be accounted for

【长龙】chánglóng 〈比喻 *fig.*〉排成的长队 long queue or line

【长毛绒】chángmáoróng 用毛纱做经,棉纱做纬织成的起绒织物,正面有挺立平整的长绒毛。适宜于做冬季服装。plush; fabric woven with wool yarn as warp and cotton yarn as weft. On the right side, it has a fur-like standing, and even down, suitable for making winter clothes.

【长眠】chángmián 〈婉辞 *euph.*〉指死亡 eternal sleep; death

【长明灯】chángmíngdēng 昼夜不灭的大油灯,大多挂在佛像或神像前面 altar lamp which burns day and night, usu. hung before statutes of Buddhas or other deities

【长命锁】chángmìngsuǒ 旧俗挂在小孩儿脖子上的锁状饰物,象征长寿,多用金属制成 (old custom) 'long-life lock'; ornament resembling a lock in shape, worn by a child around the neck as a mascot for longevity, usu. made of metal

【长年】chángnián ❶ 一年到头;整年 all the year round; from year to year; for a long time：～在野外工作 do fieldwork year in, year out ❷〈方 *dial.*〉same as 长工 chánggōng ❸〈书 *fml.*〉same as 长寿 chángshòu

☞ zhǎngnián on p.2417

【长年累月】cháng nián lěi yuè 形容经历很多年月；很长时期 year in year out; over the years; for a very long time

【长袍儿】chángpáor 男子穿的中式长衣 man's traditional Chinese long gown

【长跑】chángpǎo 长距离赛跑 long-distance running; distance race

【长篇】chángpiān ❶篇幅长的 of length; long：～小说 novel｜～演讲 long speech ❷篇幅长的作品(多指小说 oft. novel) full-length literary work：这部小说是他创作的第一部～。This is his first novel.

【长篇大论】cháng piān dà lùn 滔滔不绝的言论或篇幅冗长的文章 lengthy speech or article

【长篇小说】chángpiān xiǎoshuō 篇幅长的小说，情节复杂，人物较多 novel; work of full-length fiction with complex plots and many characters

【长期】chángqī 长时期 long-term; long-lasting：～计划 long-term plan｜～贷款 long-term loan

【长枪】chángqiāng ❶长杆上安铁枪头的旧式兵器 spear; long pole with a sharp iron point at one end, used as a weapon ❷枪筒长的火器的统称，包括步枪、马枪、卡宾枪等 general term for long-barrelled gun, such as rifle, carbine etc.

【长驱】chángqū 迅速地向很远的目的地走 push deep; (of an army) make a long drive or march (towards a faraway destination)：～南下 push deep south｜～直入 drive or ride straight in

【长驱直入】cháng qū zhí rù (军队)长距离地、毫无阻挡地向前挺进(of an army) drive straight in; march straight forward over a long distance without meeting any barrier

【长日照植物】chángrìzhào zhíwù 需要比较长的光照才能开花的植物，一般每天需要光照12小时以上。如大麦、豌豆、油菜等。long-day plant; plant that needs a comparatively long sunshine time to bloom, usu. over 12 hours per day, such as barley, pea, rape, etc.

【长衫】chángshān 男子穿的大褂儿 unlined (traditional Chinese) long gown (worn by men)

【长舌】chángshé〈比喻 *fig.*〉爱扯闲话，搬弄是非 long tongued — fond of gossip; gossipy：～妇 gossipy woman

【长生】chángshēng 永远活着 long life; longevity：～不老(多作颂词) perpetually youthful; perpetually young; immortality (complementary address or message)

【长生果】chángshēngguǒ〈方 *dial.*〉落花生 peanut

【长逝】chángshì 一去不回来，指死亡 be gone forever; pass away：溘然～ pass away quite unexpectedly

【长寿】chángshòu 寿命长 long life; longevity：～老人 person who lives to a ripe old age

【长叹】chángtàn 深深地叹息 heave a deep sigh：仰天～ heave a deep sigh with one's head looking towards the sky

【长天】chángtiān 辽阔的天空 vast sky：仰望～ look up into the vast sky

【长亭】chángtíng〈古时 *arch.*〉设在城外路旁的亭子，多作行人歇脚用，也是送行话别的地方 wayside pavilion outside a city or town for wayfarers to rest in or for people to stop over and say goodbye to friends：～送别 bid a friend farewell at a wayside pavilion

【长途】chángtú ❶路程遥远的；长距离的 long trip; long distance：～旅行 long trip｜～汽车 long-distance bus｜～电话 long-distance call ❷指长途电话或长途汽车 long-distance call or bus

【长物】chángwù (旧读 formerly pronounced zhàngwù)原指多余的东西，后来也指像样儿的东西 formerly refers to anything that can be spared — surplus, later it also refers to anything presentable — valuables：身无～(形容穷困或俭朴) possess nothing of value — live a very poor or spartan life

【长线】chángxiàn〈比喻 *fig.*〉(产品、专业等)供应量超过需求量(跟'短线'相对 as opposed to 'in short supply') (of products, specialities, etc.) overproduction; oversupply：～产品 products in excessive supply｜缩短～，发展短线，把国民经济的比例关系协调好。Coordinate the national economy by reducing overproduced goods and increasing production of those in short supply.

【长线产品】chángxiàn chǎnpǐn 企业生产的大于社会需要的产品 products in oversupply; products whose supply exceeds demand

【长行】chángxíng〈书 *fml.*〉远行 go on a long journey

【长性】chángxing same as 常性 chángxìng ①：这孩子没有～，才写几个字又去玩球了。The child has little power of concentration — no sooner has he written a few characters than he starts playing the ball again.

【长袖善舞】cháng xiù shàn wǔ《韩非子·五蠹》：'鄙谚曰："长袖善舞，多钱善贾。"此言多资之易为工也。' *Hanfeizi · Five Vermin*：'Biyan said, "With long sleeves one is good at dancing and with plentiful money one is good at business." This means success hinges on one's advantageous points.'〈比喻 *fig.*〉做事有所凭借，就容易成功。后多用来形容有财势、有手腕的人善于钻营取巧。powerful backing ensures success; (of the wealthy and the clever) know how to manoeuvre in business dealings

【长吁短叹】cháng xū duǎn tàn 因伤感、烦闷、痛苦等不住地唉声叹气(because of sadness, boredom, grief etc.) moan and groan; heaving long and short sighs

【长夜】chángyè ❶ 漫长的黑夜 long night; eternal night;〈比喻 *fig.*〉黑暗的日子 period of dark days:～难明。There seemed to be no ending to the dark days.|～漫漫 long night; endless night ❷ 通宵;整夜 all night; through the night:～不眠 sleepless all night long|～之饮 spend the whole night carousing

【长缨】chángyīng〈书 *fml.*〉长带子;长绳子 long rope

【长于】chángyú (对某事)做得特别好;擅长 skilful at a certain task or sth.; having a specialized skill; be good at:他～音乐。He is good at music.

【长圆】chángyuán 像鸡蛋之类的东西的形状 oval; egg-shaped

【长远】chángyuǎn ❶ 时间很长(指未来的时间) long-term; long-range (referring to the future):～打算 long-term plan|眼前利益应该服从～利益。Immediate interests shall be subordinate to long-term ones. ❷〈方 *dial.*〉时间很长(指过去的时间) long time (referring to the past):～未见 haven't seen for a long time|他好～没有来了。It's been a long time since he was last here.

【长斋】chángzhāi ☞ 吃长斋 chī chángzhāi on p.256

【长征】chángzhēng ❶ 长途旅行;长途出征 expedition; long march ❷ 特指中国工农红军1934—1935年由江西转移到陕北的二万五千里长征 Long March of the Chinese Workers' and Peasants' Red Army, which set off from Jiangxi in 1934 and finally succeeded in reaching northern Shaanxi in 1935 after traversing 25,000 *li*

【长支】chángzhī〈旧时 *old*〉店员向店主借支款项,到年终结算,叫做长支(of a shop assistant paid by the year) advance pay requested by an employee, to be deducted from the employee's yearly pay at the end of the year

【长治久安】cháng zhì jiǔ ān 指社会秩序长期安定太平 long period of peace and stability; prolonged political stability

【长足】chángzú 形容进展迅速 by leaps and bounds — progress rapidly:～的进步 rapid progress

场(場、塲) cháng ❶ 平坦的空地,多用来翻晒粮食,碾轧谷物 level open space (oft. used as a threshing ground, etc.):打～ threshing|起～ store up aired crops ❷〈方 *dial.*〉集;市集 country fair; rural market:赶～ go to the country fair ❸〈量词 *classifier*〉用于事情的经过[indefinite article used to indicate a process]:一～透雨 a heavy rain|一～大战 a fierce battle
☞ chǎng on p.221

【场屋】chángwū 盖在打谷场上或场院里供人休息或存放农具的小屋子 threshing-ground lodge (for the watchman to rest in, as well as for storing farm tools)
☞ chǎngwū on p.222

【场院】chángyuàn 有墙或篱笆环绕的平坦的空地,多用来打谷物和晒粮食 threshing ground; sunning ground; level open space oft. surrounded with walls or fences and used for threshing or sunning crops

苌(萇) cháng ❶ ☞ 苌楚 chǎngchǔ ❷ (Cháng) 姓 a surname

【苌楚】chángchǔ 古书上说的一种类似猕猴桃的植物 a kind of plant resembling the kiwi fruit, recorded in ancient books

肠(腸) cháng ❶ 消化器官的一部分,形状像管子,上端连胃,下端通肛门。分为小肠、大肠两部分,起消化和吸收作用。intestine; part of the digestive organ resembling a tube connecting the stomach with the anus, divided into small intestine and large intestine, whose function is to digest food and absorb nourishment; 通称 commonly called 肠子 cháng·zi; also 肠管 chángguǎn ❷ (～儿 chángr)在肠衣里塞进肉、淀粉等制成的食品 food made by stuffing a casing with meat, starch, etc.:香～ sausage|鱼～fish sausage|腊～ Chinese sausage

【肠断】chángduàn〈书 *fml.*〉形容极度悲痛 heart-broken; broken-hearted; grief-stricken; gut-wrenching (describing sb. is extremely sad and sorrow)

【肠骨】chánggǔ 髂(qià)骨 ilium

【肠管】chángguǎn same as 肠 cháng①

【肠绒毛】chángróngmáo 小肠内壁黏膜上像绒毛的组织,内含小血管,有吸收养料的作用 intestinal villi which contain veins and have a function of absorbing nutrients; downy tissue on the mucous membrane of the small intestines

【肠胃】chángwèi 肠和胃,指人的消化系统 intestines and stomach; stomach (refers to the digestive organs of the human body):我～不大好,不能吃生冷的东西。I'm having problems with my digestive system, and I cannot eat raw or cold food.

【肠系膜】chángxìmó 腹膜的一部分,包在小肠和大肠的外面,把肠连接在腹腔的后壁上 mesentery; part of the peritoneum, which wraps the small and large intestines and connects the intestines with the back of the abdominal cavity

【肠炎】chángyán 肠黏膜的炎症,通常多指小肠黏膜的炎症。症状是腹痛、发烧、腹泻等。enteritis; inflammation of the mucous membrane of intestines, usu. referring to the inflammation of the mucous membrane of small intestines, with symptoms like stomachache, high fever, diarrhoea, etc.

【肠液】chángyè 由小肠黏膜腺分泌的消化液，含有很多种酶，能进一步消化食物中的糖类、脂肪等 intestinal juice; digesting juice excreted by the glands of the mucous membrane of small intestines, containing multiple enzymes which further digest the carbohydrate and fat in food

【肠衣】chángyī 用火碱脱去脂肪晾干的肠子，一般用羊肠或猪的小肠等制成，可用来灌香肠，做羽毛球拍的弦、缝合伤口的线等 casing for sausages; sheep's intestines or pig's small intestines degreased (with caustic soda) and dried, used for stuffing to make sausages, as strings of a racket, or threads for stitching a wound, etc.

【肠子】cháng·zi 肠①的通称 general term for 肠 cháng ①

尝[1]（嘗、嚐）cháng ❶ 吃一点儿试试；辨别滋味 try some food; taste; have a taste of: ～～咸淡 try a bit to see if a dish or food tastes just right ❷ 经历；体验 experience; be aware of: 艰苦备～ experience all the hardships|～到了体育锻炼的甜头 come to know the good of physical exercise; become aware of the benefits of physical exercise

尝[2]（嘗）cháng 曾经 ever; once: 未～ not; never|何～ never (used in rhetorical questions to emphasize negation)

【尝鼎一脔】cháng dǐng yī luán 尝尝鼎里的一片肉，可以知道整个鼎里的肉味 taste a piece of the meat in the pot and you know the whole lot; 〈比喻 *fig.*〉根据部分推知全体 know the whole by sampling a part; straw shows which way the wind blows

【尝试】chángshì 试；试验 attempt; try; have a go at; venture: 他们为了解决这个问题，～过各种方法。They have tried a variety of ways to solve the problem.

【尝鲜】cháng//xiān 吃鲜美的食品；尝新 taste what is just in season; have delicious food

【尝新】cháng//xīn 吃应时的新鲜食品 have a taste of what is just in season: 这是刚摘下的荔枝，尝尝新吧。These litchis are just plucked from the tree. Have a taste.

倘 cháng [倘佯](chángyáng) same as 徜徉 chángyáng

☞ tǎng on p. 1868

常 cháng ❶ 一般；普通；平常 ordinary; common; normal: ～人 ordinary person|～识 common sense|～态 normal state ❷ 不变的；经常 invariable; constant: ～数 constant|冬夏～青 remain green throughout the year; evergreen ❸ 时常；常常 often; frequently; usually: ～来～往 pay frequent calls on each other; exchange frequent visits|我们～见面。We see each other quite often. ❹〈书 *fml.*〉指伦常 morality; mores: 三纲五～ the three cardinal guides and the five virtues (in Confucian ethics) ❺(Cháng)姓 a surname

【常备】chángbèi 经常准备或防备 be always on hand or available; constantly stand by: ～车辆 vehicles that are constantly in service|～药物 medicines that are always available|～不懈 be ever prepared and available

【常备军】chángbèijūn 国家平时经常保持的正规军队 standing army; regular army that a state usu. keeps in peaceful times

【常常】chángcháng (事情的发生)不止一次，而且时间相隔不久 (occurrence of things) more than once; at short intervals; often; frequently; usually; generally: 他工作积极，～受到表扬。He is hard-working in his work, so he receives praises quite often.

【常川】chángchuān 经常地；连续不断地 frequently; constantly: ～往来 keep in constant touch|～供给 keep sb. constantly supplied

【常服】chángfú 日常穿的服装(区别于'礼服' as compared with 'formal attire') daily wear; ordinary, everyday clothes: 居家～ daily clothes

【常规】chángguī ❶ 沿袭下来经常实行的规矩；通常的做法 convention; rule; routine; common practice: 打破～ break with conventions ❷ 医学上称经常使用的处理方法，如'血常规'是指红细胞计数、白细胞计数、白细胞分类计数等的检验 regular practice followed in medical examination, e.g. 'routine blood test', referring to red blood cell count, white blood cell count, and white blood cell classification count etc.

【常规武器】chángguī wǔqì 通常使用的武器，如枪、炮、飞机、坦克等，也包括冷兵器(区别于'核武器' as compared with 'nuclear arms') conventional weaponry, such as guns, cannons, planes, tanks etc., also including cold steel

【常规战争】chángguī zhànzhēng 用常规武器进行的战争(区别于'核战争' as compared with 'nuclear warfare') conventional warfare (fought with conventional weapons)

【常轨】chángguǐ 正常的、经常的方法或途径 normal or usual practice (or course): 改变了生活～ change the usual course of life|这类事件，可以遵循～解决。These matters can be resolved in conformity with normal practice.

【常衡】chánghéng 英美重量制度，用于金银、药物以外的一般物品(区别于'金衡、药衡' as compared with 'troy weight' and 'apothecaries weight') avoirdupois; weight of the United Kingdom and the United States, used to measure ordinary goods other than gold and medicine

【常会】chánghuì 规定在一定期间举行的会议；

例会 regular session or meeting (held at fixed times or fixed intervals)

【常客】chángkè 经常来的客人 denizen; frequent guest or customer; frequenter

【常理】chánglǐ (～儿 chánglǐr)通常的道理 common sense; customary practice:按～我应该去看望他。I should pay him a visit by social convention.

【常例】chánglì same as 常规 chángguī ①;惯例 common practice; normal procedure:沿用～ follow common practice|不能按～行事。This time we cannot (or should not) follow normal procedure.

【常量】chángliàng 在某一过程中,数值固定不变的量。如等速运动中的速度就是常量。constant quantity; sth., esp. a number or quantity, that never varies during a certain process, e.g. the speed in uniform motion; also 恒量 héngliàng

【常年】chángnián ❶ 终年;长期 all the year round; year in and year out; over a long period of time:山顶上～积雪。The mountaintop is clad in snow all the year round.|战士们～守卫在祖国的边防。The soldiers defend the frontiers of our country year in and year out. ❷ 平常的年份 average year:这儿小麦～亩产五百斤。In this area, the per *mu* yield of wheat for an average year is 500 *jin*.

【常情】chángqíng 通常的心情或情理 reason; common sense; human nature:按照～,要他回来,他会回来的。Common sense would have it that he will come back if asked to.

【常人】chángrén 普通的人;一般的人 ordinary person; man in the street; woman next door:他的性格与～不同。His personality is rather unique. *or* His personality is different from the man in the street.|这种痛苦,非～所能忍受。No ordinary person can bear such pain.

【常任】chángrèn 长期担任的 permanent; standing:～理事 standing member of a council

【常设】chángshè 不是临时设立的(组织、机构等)(of an organization) not temporarily established; standing; permanent:全国人民代表大会常务委员会是全国人民代表大会的～机关。The Standing Committee of the National People's Congress is the permanent organ of the National People's Congress.

【常识】chángshí 普通知识 general knowledge; elementary knowledge:政治～general knowledge of politics|科学～ the ABC of science|生活～ common sense in everyday life

【常事】chángshì 平常的事情;经常的事情 everyday experience; routine; common occurrence:看书看到深夜,这对他来说是～。Reading far into the night is almost a matter of everyday practice with him.

【常数】chángshù 表示常量的数,如圆周率 π 的值 3.1415926…就是常数 constant; number whose value never varies, e.g. the value of π is always 3.1415926...

【常态】chángtài 正常的状态(跟'变态'相对 as opposed to 'abnormal') normality; normalcy; normal behaviour; normal state of affairs:一反～ contrary to one's normal behaviour|恢复～ return or come back to normal

【常套】chángtào 常用的陈陈相因的办法或格式 convention; usual pattern; routine; formula:摆脱才子佳人小说的～ break away from the old convention of portraying gifted scholars and beautiful ladies in fiction

【常委】chángwěi ❶ 某些机构由常务委员组成的领导集体;常务委员会 leading collective formed with standing members of certain organizations; standing committee:人大～ Standing Committee of the National People's Congress ❷ 常务委员会的成员 member of a standing committee

【常温】chángwēn 一般指 15—25℃ 的温度 normal atmospheric temperature (between 15-25℃)

【常务】chángwù 主持日常工作的 in charge of day-to-day business; run routine work:～委员 member of the standing committee|～副市长 executive vice mayor

【常行军】chángxíngjūn 部队按正常的每日行程和时速进行的行军 (of an army) march at normal speed and schedule

【常性】chángxìng ❶ 能坚持做某事的性子 perseverance; tenacity:他无论学什么都没～,学个三五天就不干了。He cannot persevere in anything. He would just stop after three or five days. ❷〈书 *fml.*〉一定的习性 habit; custom; nature

【常言】chángyán 习惯上常说的像谚语、格言之类的话,如'不经一事,不长一智'、'人勤地不懒' well-known wise statement; saying; proverb, e.g. 'wisdom stems from experience' and 'where the tiller is diligent, the land is productive'

【常用对数】chángyòng-duìshù 以 10 为底的对数,用符号 lg 表示 Brigg's logarithm; common logarithm; number of times a fixed number (usu. 10) must be multiplied by itself to equal a stated number, symbolized by 'lg'; also 十进对数 shíjìn-duìshù; ☞ 对数 duìshù on p.493

【常住】chángzhù ❶ 经常居住 reside permanently; stay (at a place) frequently:～之地 permanent residence|～人口 permanent residents ❷〈佛教 *Budd.*〉指佛法无生灭变迁 permanency; immutability ❸ 佛教、道教指寺观及其田产什物等 Buddhist or Taoist temple and its assets

偿(償) cháng ❶ 归还;抵补 repay; redeem; compensate:～还 repay | 得不～失 the loss overweighs the gain; win a pyrrhic victory ❷ 满足 fulfil; satisfy; meet the need of:如愿以～。One's call is answered.

【偿付】chángfù same as 偿还 chánghuán:如期～ pay back as scheduled | ～债务 repay a debt

【偿还】chánghuán 归还(所欠的债) repay; pay back; redeem:～贷款 pay back a loan | 无力～ insolvent, unable to pay back

【偿命】cháng//mìng (杀人者)用生命抵偿 pay with one's life (for a murder); a life for a life

徜 cháng [徜徉](chángyáng)闲游;安闲自在地步行 stroll; saunter; amble; also 倘佯 chángyáng

裳 cháng 〈古代 *arch.*〉指裙子 skirt
☞ ·shang on p.1687

嫦 cháng [嫦娥](Cháng'é)神话中由人间飞到月亮上去的仙女 Goddess of the Moon (the lady in Chinese mythology who stole an elixir from her husband, swallowed it, and flew to the moon); also 姮娥 Héng'é

chǎng (ㄔㄤˇ)

厂(廠、厰) chǎng ❶ 工厂 factory; mill; plant; works:钢铁～ iron and steel mill | 纺织～ textile mill ❷same as 厂子② chǎng·zi:煤～ coal yard | 木材～ timber yard
☞ ān on p.8

【厂房】chǎngfáng 工厂的房屋,通常专指车间 factory building; manufactory; (in most cases) workshop of a factory

【厂规】chǎngguī 一个工厂所定的本厂成员必须遵守的规章 factory regulations; regulations a factory has made that all staff members and workers must observe

【厂家】chǎngjiā 指工厂 factory:这次展销会有几百个～参加。Several hundred manufacturers attended the exposition fair.

【厂矿】chǎngkuàng 工厂和矿山的合称 factories and mines

【厂礼拜】chǎnglǐbài 工厂里选定的代替星期日休假的日子 day off for a factory (usu. on a workday) specified by the factory management

【厂区】chǎngqū 工厂中进行生产的区域。通常包括车间、仓库、动力设施(如锅炉房)及运输道路等 production area of a factory, usu. including workshops, storage houses, power facilities (a boiler room), roads for transportation etc.

【厂商】chǎngshāng 工厂和商店(多指私营的 usu. of private ownership) factories and shops:营造～ manufacturer | 承包～ contractor

【厂丝】chǎngsī 缫丝厂用机械缫制的生丝 filature silk; raw silk reeled with a reeling machine in a reeling mill

【厂休】chǎngxiū 工厂规定的本厂职工的休息日 day of rest for staff as specified by the factory management; also 厂礼拜 chánglǐbài

【厂子】chǎng·zi ❶ 工厂 factory; mill; workshop:我们～里新建一个车间。Our factory has built a new workshop. ❷ 指有宽敞地面可以存放货物并进行加工的商店 yard; depot; facility having a wide area for storing and processing goods

场(場、塲) chǎng ❶ (～儿 chǎngr)适应某种需要的比较大的地方:large place where people gather for a specific purpose:会～meeting place | 操～ playground | 市～ market place | 剧～ theatre | 广～ square ❷ 舞台 stage:上～ enter stage (used in a script, scenario, libretto, etc.) | 下～ exit stage ❸ 指某种活动范围 scope of a certain activity; 官～ officialdom | 名利～ vanity fair | 逢～作戏 join in the fun on occasion ❹ 事情发生的地点 scene of an accident:现～ spot; scene | 当～ on the spot | 事故发生时我正好在～。I happened to be present when the accident occurred. ❺ 指表演或比赛的全场 whole process of a game or performance:开～ beginning (of a game or performance) | 终～ ending (of a game or performance) ❻ 戏剧中较小的段落,每场表演故事的一个片段 scene; small section in one act, portraying a small part of the story ❼ 〈量词 *classifier*〉用于文娱体育活动 [used as an indefinite article or together with a quantity in entertainment and sports activities]:三～球赛 three ball games | 跳一～舞 have a dance ❽ 电视接收机中,电子束对一幅画面的奇数行或偶数行完成一次隔行扫描,叫做一场。奇数场和偶数场合为一帧完整画面。round; one round during which an electronic beam finishes scanning the even-numbered or odd-numbered lines of a picture a television receives. When both the odd-numbered and even-numbered lines are scanned, a complete picture forms. ❾ 物质存在的一种基本形态,具有能量、动量和质量。实物之间的相互作用依靠有关的场来实现。如电场、磁场、引力场等。field; basic form of existence of matter characterized by energy, motion and quantity. The interaction between material objects is realized through certain fields, such as electric field, magnetic field, gravitational field, etc.
☞ cháng on p.218

【场次】chǎngcì 电影、戏剧等演出的场数 number of showings of a film, play, etc. 增加～,满足更多观众的需要。The number of performances shall be increased to meet the demand of the audience.

【场地】chǎngdì 空地，多指供文娱体育活动或施工、试验等用的地方 space; place; site (used for recreational and sports activities or for construction or doing experiments)

【场馆】chǎngguǎn 体育场和体育馆的合称 sports grounds or gymnasiums (stadiums)：比赛～ gymnasiums and stadiums for holding competitions｜新建五处体育～。Five stadiums and gymnasiums were built recently.

C

【场合】chǎnghé 一定的时间、地点、情况 occasion; situation：在公共～，要遵守秩序。One should abide by rules on public occasions.

【场记】chǎngjì 指摄制影视片或排演话剧时，详细记录摄影情况或排演情况的工作。也指做这项工作的人。log; work of keeping a detailed record of progress when shooting a film or TV drama or rehearsing a play; log keeper; script holder

【场景】chǎngjǐng ❶ 指戏剧、电影、电视剧中的场面 scene in theatre, film and TV ❷ 泛指情景 sight; scene; picture：热火朝天的劳动～ scene of people working with overflowing enthusiasm

【场面】chǎngmiàn ❶ 戏剧、电影、电视剧中由布景、音乐和登场人物组合成的景况 scene, composed of setting, music and characters on the stage in a play, film or drama ❷ 叙事性文学作品中，由人物在一定场合相互发生关系而构成的生活情景 scene in narrative literature brought about by the interaction between characters on a certain occasion ❸ 指戏曲演出时伴奏的人员和乐器，分文武两种，管乐和弦乐是文场面，锣鼓是武场面 musical accompaniment (musicians and musical instruments) for a theatrical performance, including orchestral accompaniment and percussional accompaniment; also 文场 wénchǎng or 武场 wǔchǎng ❹ 泛指一定场合下的情景 spectacle; occasion; scene：～壮观 grand spectacle or occasion｜热烈的～ manifestation of enthusiasm and excitement ❺ 表面的排场 ostentation; appearance; front; facade：摆～(讲排场) be ostentatious; go in for ostentation and extravagance; put on a show｜撑～ keep up appearances

【场面话】chǎngmiànhuà 指敷衍应酬的话 polite platitude for the occasion; civil banalities; unctuous words

【场面人】chǎngmiànrén ❶ 指善于在交际场合应酬的人 man about town; very sociable person ❷ 在社会上有一定地位的人 person of prestige; celebrity

【场面上】chǎngmiàn·shang 指社交场合 on social occasions; in social life：他在～混得很熟。He is very adept at these social occasions.｜～都称他为'三爷'。On social occasions, everyone addressed him as Third Master.｜大家都是～的人物，不必为这点儿小事伤了和气。Since we are all persons about town, we shall not allow such a trivial thing to hurt our friendship.

【场所】chǎngsuǒ 活动的处所 place (for an activity); venue：公共～ public place｜娱乐～ place of entertainment or recreation

【场屋】chǎngwū 科举考试的场所 hall for the imperial civil service examination
☞ chángwū on p. 218

【场子】chǎng·zi 适应某种需要的比较大的地方 large place (for a certain activity)：大～ big place (or ring, or hall)｜空～ empty place (or ring)

锃(鋹) chǎng 〈书 *fml.*〉锐利 sharp; keen-edged

昶 chǎng ❶〈书 *fml.*〉白天时间长 long day light ❷〈书 *fml.*〉舒畅；畅通 relaxed and easy; unimpeded; unblocked ❸ (Chǎng)姓 a surname

惝 chǎng，又 also tǎng［惝恍］(chǎnghuǎng，又 also tǎnghuǎng)〈书 *fml.*〉❶ 失意；不高兴 depressed; upset; unhappy ❷ 迷迷糊糊；不清楚 vague; hazy ‖ also 惝怳 chǎnghuǎng

敞 chǎng ❶ (房屋、庭院等)宽绰；没有遮拦 (of houses, yards, etc.) spacious; roomy：宽～ spacious｜这屋子太～。The room is too spacious indeed. ❷ 张开；打开 uncovered; open：～胸露怀 bare one's chest｜～着门 leave the door open｜～着口儿 leave the mouth (of a jar, bottle, etc.) open

【敞车】chǎngchē ❶ 没有车篷的车 open wagon; open car ❷ 铁路上指没有车顶的货车 flatcar (of a train)

【敞开】chǎngkāi ❶ 大开；打开 open wide; open：～衣襟 unbutton one's shirt｜大门～着。The door is wide open. ◇～思想 speak up; get things off one's chest ❷ 放开，不加限制；尽量 deregulate; decontrol; open up; put no limit on：～价格，随行就市 deregulate the prices and let them fluctuate in the market｜你有什么话就～说吧。Say whatever is on your mind.

【敞快】chǎng·kuài 爽快 frank; straightforward; forthright：他是个～人，说做就做。He is a forthright man who gets down to business the moment his mind is made up.

【敞亮】chǎngliàng 宽敞明亮 bright and spacious; clear-minded：三间～的平房 three bright and spacious one-storey houses ◇听了一番开导，心里～多了。My mind is clear up after hearing your enlightenment.

【敞篷车】chǎngpéngchē 没有篷子的车(多指机动车 mostly of motor vehicles) open car

氅 chǎng 外套 cloak：大～(大衣) overcoat

chàng(ㄔㄤˋ)

玚(瑒) chàng 古代祭祀用的一种圭 article of elongated, pointed jade used for worship in ancient China; also 玚圭 chàngguī

☞ yáng on p.2220

怅(悵) chàng 不如意 disappointed; sorry:～惘 listless|惆～ melancholy; disconsolate

【怅怅】chàngchàng〈书 *fml.*〉形容因不如意而感到不痛快 disappointed; upset; cheerless; frustrated and disconsolate:～不乐 disappointed and unhappy|～离去 depart with regret; in a disconsolate state

【怅恨】chànghèn 惆怅恼恨 regretful and depressed:无限～ chew the bitter cud of regret

【怅然】chàngrán same as 怅怅 chàngchàng:～而返 return disappointed and downcast|～若失 feel depressed and lost

【怅惋】chàngwǎn 惆怅惋惜 downcast with regret; deeply regret

【怅惘】chàngwǎng 惆怅迷惘;心里有事,没精打采 listless; downcast; anxious and in low spirits:神情～ look anxious and sad

韔(韔) chàng〈书 *fml.*〉❶ 装弓的袋子 bow case ❷ 把弓装入弓袋 put a bow in its case

畅(暢) chàng ❶ 无阻碍;不停滞 unimpeded; smooth:～达 smooth; easily accessible|～行无阻 pass unimpeded; go unhindered ❷ 痛快;尽情 free; uninhibited:～谈 talk freely|～所欲言 speak one's mind freely ❸ (Chàng) 姓 a surname

【畅达】chàngdá (语言、文章、交通)通畅;顺畅 (of language, article, traffic) smooth; fluent:译文～ smooth and fluent translation|车辆往来～。The traffic is very smooth.

【畅怀】chànghuái 尽情;开怀 to one's heart's content; as much as one likes:～痛饮 drink one's fill|～大笑 laugh open heartedly

【畅快】chàngkuài 舒畅快乐 carefree; happy; free from inhibitions:心情～ have ease of mind and be in a happy mood

【畅所欲言】chàng suǒ yù yán 尽情地说出想说的话 speak one's mind freely; speak out freely; speak without reservation

【畅谈】chàngtán 尽情地谈 chat or talk freely and happily:开怀～ talk freely

【畅通】chàngtōng 无阻碍地通行或通过(of passage) unimpeded; unblocked:铁路～ normal railway traffic|血脉～。Blood circulation is smooth.|～无阻。Road traffic is going smoothly.

【畅想】chàngxiǎng 敞开思路,毫无拘束地想像 give free rein to one's imagination; imagine freely; have no boundaries for one's imagination:～曲 fantasia; reverie|～未来 call up in one's mind a delightful picture of the future

【畅销】chàngxiāo (货物)销路广,卖得快 (of goods) sell well; have a ready market; be in great demand:～货 goods in great demand|～各地 sell well everywhere

【畅行】chàngxíng 顺利地通行 pass unimpeded:车辆～。The traffic proceeds without hindrance.

【畅叙】chàngxù 尽情地叙谈 chat cheerfully (usu. about old times):～别情 talk freely of the time after the last departure

【畅饮】chàngyǐn 尽情地喝(酒) drink one's fill (usu. alcoholic drink):开怀～ drink to one's heart's content|～几杯 drink a few glasses freely

【畅游】chàngyóu ❶ 尽情地游览 enjoy a sightseeing tour:～黄山 make a delightful trip to Mount Huangshan ❷ 畅快地游泳 have a good swim:～长江 have a good swim in the Yangtze River

倡 chàng ❶ 带头发动;提倡 initiate; advocate:～导 initiate and lead|～议 propose ❷〈书 *fml.*〉same as 唱 chàng

☞ chāng on p.214

【倡办】chàngbàn 带头开办;创办 initiate (an activity etc.); start or initiate the organization of (an undertaking etc.):联合～文化活动中心 jointly initiate to set up a culture centre|～单位多达十几家。More than a dozen units joined in the proposition.

【倡导】chàngdǎo 带头提倡 initiate; propose; promote:～新风尚 initiate new trend or practices

【倡首】chàngshǒu 带头做某事或提出某种主张;首倡 initiate; lead the way; take the lead in:此事由他～,我们附议。This matter was initiated by him and we seconded it.

【倡言】chàngyán 公开地提出来 propose; initiate; advocate:～革命 advocate a revolution

【倡议】chàngyì ❶ 首先建议;发起 propose; launch (an activity):～书 (written) proposal|我们～开展劳动竞赛。We propose launching a labour emulation drive. ❷ 首先提出的主张 first proposal:这个～得到了热烈的响应。The proposal is greeted with warm welcome.

鬯[1] chàng 古代祭祀用的一种酒 sacrificial wine used in ancient China

鬯[2] chàng〈书 *fml.*〉same as 畅 chàng

唱 chàng ❶ 口中发出(乐音);依照乐律发出声音 sing; utter a series of words or sounds in musical tones:～歌 sing a song|～戏 sing in an opera|独～ solo|合～ chorus|演～sing in a performance ❷ 大声叫 call; cry:

～名 roll call | 鸡～三遍。The rooster has crowed three times. ❸ (～儿 chàngr)歌曲；唱词 song; singing part of a Chinese opera:《穆柯寨》这出戏里，杨宗保的～儿不多。In the opera *Muke Stockaded Village*, the character of Yang Zongbao does not have much singing. ❹ (Chàng) 姓 a surname

【唱本】chàngběn (～儿 chàngběnr)曲艺或戏曲唱词的小册子 libretto or script of a ballad-singer

C

【唱酬】chàngchóu〈书 *fml*.〉same as 唱和 chànghè ①

【唱词】chàngcí 戏曲、曲艺中唱的词句 libretto; words of a ballad

【唱碟】chàngdié〈方 *dial*.〉same as 唱片 chàngpiàn

【唱独角戏】chàng dújiǎoxì〈比喻 *fig*.〉一个人独自做某件事 put on a one-man show; go it alone; play a monodrama; work alone

【唱段】chàngduàn 戏曲中一段完整的唱腔 aria; solo vocal piece with instrumental accompaniment; melody in an opera

【唱对台戏】chàng duìtáixì〈比喻 *fig*.〉采取与对方相对的行动，来反对或搞垮对方 put on a rival show against; enter into rivalry with (to oppose or ruin the opposite side)

【唱反调】chàng fǎndiào 提出相反的主张，采取相反的行动 sing a different tune; speak or act contrary to; sound or strike a discordant note

【唱付】chàngfù 营业员找给顾客钱时大声说出所找的钱数 (of a salesperson) shout the amount of money when giving the change to a customer

【唱高调】chàng gāodiào (～儿 chàng gāodiàor)说不切实际的漂亮话；光说得好听而不去做 make high-sounding statements; indulge in high-flown rhetoric:反对光～不干实事的作风。Such practice of indulging only in high-sounding words should be opposed.

【唱工】chànggōng (～儿 chànggōngr)戏曲中的歌唱艺术 singing; art of singing in theatrical performance:～戏 Chinese opera featuring singing (rather than acting or acrobatics); also 唱功 chànggōng

【唱功】chànggōng same as 唱工 chànggōng

【唱和】chànghè ❶ 一个人做了诗或词，别的人相应作答(大多按照原韵) when one writes a poem, the other comes up with another in reply, usu. using the same rhyme sequence:他们经常以诗词～。They often write and respond with poems to each other. ❷ 指唱歌时此唱彼和，互相呼应 one sings a song and the others join in the chorus

【唱机】chàngjī 留声机和电唱机的统称 general term for phonograph and gramophone

【唱空城计】chàng kōngchéngjì ❶〈比喻 *fig*.〉用掩饰自己力量空虚的办法，骗过对方 play the empty-city stratagem (bluffing the enemy by opening the gates of a weakly defended city); present a bold front to conceal a weak defence; ☞空城计 kōngchéngjì on p. 1102 ❷〈比喻 *fig*.〉某单位的人员全部或大部不在 have all or most of the staff vacated

【唱名】chàng//míng 高声点名 roll call:～表决 vote by roll call

【唱名】chàngmíng 指唱歌时所用的 do, re, mi, fa, sol, la, si (或 ti)七个固定音节 singing system of associating each note of a scale with a syllable, i. e., doh, ray, me, fah, soh, lah and te

【唱盘】chàngpán same as 唱片 chàngpiàn

【唱片儿】chàngpiānr same as 唱片 chàngpiàn

【唱片】chàngpiàn 用虫胶、塑料等制成的圆盘，表面有记录声音变化的螺旋槽纹，可以用唱机把所录的声音重放出来 phonograph (or gramophone) record; circular piece of plastic or shellac disc on which sound is stored so that it can be played back at any time (on a record player)

【唱票】chàng//piào 投票选举后，开票时大声念出选票上写的或圈定的名字 (after a voting is finished) call out the names of candidates on a ballot while counting ballots:～人 the person who calls out the name on the ballot while counting ballots

【唱腔】chàngqiāng 戏曲音乐中的声乐部分，即唱出来的曲调 melodies for the singing part in a Chinese opera

【唱喏】chàng//rě〈方 *dial*.〉作揖(在早期白话中，'唱喏'是一面作揖，一面出声致敬) bow; (in early vernacular) exchange pleasantries while bowing with folded hands held out before one

【唱诗】chàngshī ❶ 基督教指唱赞美诗 sing hymns:～班(做礼拜时唱赞美诗的合唱队) choir (for singing hymns in a church) ❷〈书 *fml*.〉吟诗 recite poetry

【唱收】chàngshōu 营业员收到顾客钱时大声说出所收的钱数 (of a salesperson) shout the amount of money when receiving money from a customer

【唱头】chàngtóu 唱机上用来发声的器件 pick-up head (of a phonograph, etc.)

【唱戏】chàng//xì 演唱戏曲 sing in an opera; put on a theatrical performance

【唱针】chàngzhēn 唱机的唱头上装的针，一般是钢制的或人造宝石的 gramophone needle; stylus; needle installed on the pick-up of a gramophone, usu. made of steel or synthetic gemstone

【唱主角】chàng zhǔjué〈比喻 *fig*.〉担负主要任务或在某方面起主导作用 play the leading role; shoulder most of the responsibilities:这项任务由老张～。Old Zhang will play the leading role in this task.

chāo（彳幺）

抄[1]（❶钞）chāo ❶ 誊写 copy; transcribe:～文件 copy the document|～稿子 make a copy of the manuscript ❷ 照着别人的作品、作业等写下来当做自己的 copy; plagiarize; lift (things from the works of others as one's own)

抄[2] chāo ❶ 搜查并没收 search and confiscate; make a raid upon: ～家 confiscate a family's property|查～ search and confiscate ❷ 从侧面或较近的小路过去 take a shortcut; outflank:～近道走。Take a shortcut. ❸ 两手在胸前相互地插在袖筒里 fold (one's hands) in the sleeves:～着手 with arms folded in the sleeves for warmth

抄[3] chāo 抓取;拿 grab;take: ～起一把铁锹就走。Grab a spade and walk away at once.

【抄靶子】chāo bǎ·zi〈方 *dial.*〉〈旧时 *old*〉巡警等拦住行人进行抄身叫抄靶子(of a patrolling policeman) search a pedestrian; frisk sb.

【抄本】chāoběn 抄写的本子 hand-copied book; transcript

【抄查】chāochá 搜查违禁的东西并没收;查抄 search for and confiscate (contraband goods); confiscate:～毒品 search for and confiscate illegal or narcotic drugs

【抄道】chāo//dào (～儿 chāo//dàor)走较近便的路 take a shortcut: ～进山 take a shortcut into the mountains

【抄道】chāodào (～儿 chāodàor)近便的路 shortcut:走～去赶集要近五里路。If you take the shortcut to the market fair, it would be five *li* closer.

【抄肥】chāoféi〈方 *dial.*〉指捞外快 wrangle extra money other than one's salary; earn grey income

【抄后路】chāo hòulù 绕到背后袭击 outflank and attack (the enemy) in the rear; turn the enemy's rear

【抄获】chāohuò 搜查并获得 search and seize; search and confiscate:～赃物 search for and confiscate illicit possessions

【抄家】chāo//jiā 查抄家产(in ancient China) search the home of a condemned court official and confiscate his property; ransack sb.'s home

【抄件】chāojiàn 送交有关单位参考的文件(多指复制的上级所发的文件) papers sent to relevant departments for reference — copy; duplicate (of a report, document, etc.)

【抄近儿】chāo//jìnr 走较近的路 take a shortcut

【抄录】chāolù same as 抄写 chāoxiě:～名人名言 quote wise sayings of a celebrity

【抄没】chāomò 搜查并没收 search and confiscate:～家产 search sb.'s house and confiscate his property; ransack sb.'s house

【抄身】chāo//shēn 搜检身上有无私带的东西 search sb.; frisk sb.

【抄收】chāoshōu 收听并抄录(电报等) receive and record (radio signals):～电讯 receive and record (telegram) dispatches

【抄手】chāo//shǒu 两手在胸前相互插在袖筒里或两臂交叉放在胸前 fold one's arms (in the sleeves or across one's chest):抄着手在一旁看热闹。Look on with folded arms.

【抄手】chāoshǒu〈方 *dial.*〉馄饨 wonton; dumpling soup

【抄袭】[1] chāoxí ❶ 把别人的作品或语句抄来当做自己的 plagiarize; lift or copy (sb.'s works or sayings as one's own) ❷ 指不顾客观情况，沿用别人的经验方法等 copy; borrow indiscriminately (from other's experience)

【抄袭】[2] chāoxí (军队)绕道到敌人侧面或后面袭击 (of an army) launch a surprise attack (on the enemy) by making a detour

【抄写】chāoxiě 照着原文写下来 copy (by hand); transcribe:～员 copyist

【抄用】chāoyòng 抄袭沿用 copy; imitate; apply mechanically:好经验应该学，但不能简单～。One should learn from valuable experiences of others but not try to copy it.

【抄造】chāozào 把纸浆造成纸 make (pulp into) paper

吵 chāo ☞ below
☞ chǎo on p. 230

【吵吵】chāo·chao〈方 *dial.*〉许多人乱说话 making lots of noisy (as in a lot of people speaking); make a row:别嚷～了，听他把话说完。Stop making such a row. Let's hear him out.

怊 chāo〈书 *fml.*〉悲愤 grieved and indignant

弨 chāo〈书 *fml.*〉❶ 弓松弛的样子 like a loosened bow ❷ 弓 bow

钞[1] chāo 指钞票 banknote; paper money:现～ cash

钞[2] chāo same as 抄[1] chāo ①

【钞票】chāopiào 纸币 banknote; paper money; bill

绰[1] chāo 抓取 grab:～起一根棍子 grab a stick|～起活儿就干 plunge right into a job

绰[2] chāo same as 焯 chāo
☞ chuò on p. 314

超 chāo ❶ 超过 exceed; surpass; overtake:～额 exceed the quota|～龄 overage|～音速 supersonic speed ❷ 超出寻常的 ultra-; super-; extra-:～级 super|～高温 super-high temperature ❸ 在某个范围以外的;不受限制的 transcend; go beyond (a certain limit):～自然 supernatural|～现实 go beyond reality|

～阶级 transcending class ❹〈书 *fml.*〉跳跃；跨过 leap over；stride over：挟泰山以～北海 carry Mount Taishan over the North Sea — attempt to do the impossible

【超拔】chāobá ❶ 高出一般；出众 outstanding；transcendent；superb：才情～ of outstanding talent ❷ 提升 be promoted：～擢用 promote to a higher rank，usu. more than expected ❸ 脱离（不良环境）；摆脱（坏习惯）free from（an undesirable environment）；break away from（a bad habit）：恶习一旦养成，则不易～。Once a bad habit is established，it is not easy to get rid of.

【超编】chāobiān 超出组织、机构人员编制的定额 overstaff；exceed the personnel quota

【超标】chāobiāo 超过规定的标准 surpass the set standard；exceed the quota：这个工厂因～排污被罚了款。This factory was fined for excessive discharge of waste material.

【超产】chāochǎn 超过原定生产数量 exceeds a production target（or quota）：～百分之二十 20 per cent in excess of a production target；exceed the production quota by 20 per cent

【超常】chāocháng 超过寻常；超出一般 extraordinary；hypernormal；supernormal；be above average：～儿童（智商特别高的儿童）supernormal child（whose intelligence quotient is extraordinarily high）|竞技水平～发挥 give an extraordinary performance；surpass（or outperform）oneself

【超车】chāo//chē （车辆）从旁边越过前面同方向行驶的车辆 overtake（other vehicles going in the same direction on the road）：切莫强行～。Don't try to overtake by forcing it.

【超尘拔俗】chāo chén bá sú 形容人品超过一般，不同凡俗 be outstanding in moral character；transcend the petty and vulgar；stand head and shoulders above the common crowd；also 超尘出俗 chāo chén chū sú

【超出】chāochū 越出（一定的数量或范围）exceed；go beyond（a certain quantity or limit）；overstep：～定额 exceed the quota|～规定 overstep the regulations

【超导电性】chāodǎodiànxìng 某些金属、合金或化合物，在温度降到接近绝对零度（-273.15℃）时，电阻突然减小为零，这种性质叫超导电性 superconductivity；ability of certain metals，alloys and chemical compounds to allow electricity to pass without resistance when the temperature is near absolute zero（-273.15℃）

【超导体】chāodǎotǐ 显示出超导电性的物体 superconductor；substance that possesses the quality of superconductivity

【超低温】chāodīwēn 比低温更低的温度，物理学上指低于-263℃的液态空气的温度 ultra-low temperature；temperature below -263℃（at which air turns to a liquid）

【超度】chāodù 佛教和道教用语，指念经或做法事使鬼魂脱离苦难（Buddhist or Taoist term）expiate the sins of the dead through making offerings and saying prayers：～亡魂 expiate the sins of the dead

【超短波】chāoduǎnbō 波长10米—1米（频率30—300兆赫）的无线电波。近似直线传播，用于电视广播、通信、雷达等方面。ultrashort wave；radio wave whose length is between 1-10 metres（frequency 30-300 megahertz），and whose transmission approximates linear transmission，widely used in television，telecommunications，radar，etc.；also 米波 mǐbō

【超短裙】chāoduǎnqún 一种裙身极短，不及膝盖的裙子 miniskirt；skirt with length above the knee

【超额】chāo'é 超过定额 overfulfil or exceed the quota：～完成任务 exceed the target set by the task|～百分之十 exceed the target by 10 per cent

【超凡】chāofán ❶ 超越凡人 overcome the worldly desire and attain sainthood：～入圣 transcend worldliness and attain holiness ❷ 超出平常 out of the common run；unusual；outstanding：技艺～ unusually skilful

【超凡入圣】chāo fán rù shèng 超出凡人，达到圣人的境界。多形容造诣精深。transcend worldliness and attain holiness；（in most cases）reach the pinnacle of literary fame；become a person of unrivalled wisdom

【超固态】chāogùtài 物质存在的一种形态，这种形态下的固体物质，由于压力和温度增加到一定程度，原子核和电子紧紧挤在一起，原子内部不再有空隙。白矮星内部和地球中心区域都有超固态物质。state of ultra-solidity；one of the existing forms of substance，a state in which，as pressure and temperature increase to a certain degree，an atomic nucleus and electrons squeeze tightly together so that no interspace exists inside an atom. There is ultra-solid substance inside the white dwarf star and in the centre of the earth.

【超过】chāoguò ❶ 由某物的后面赶到它的前面 overtake；outstrip；surpass；exceed；pass after catching up with；outweigh：他的车从左边～了前面的卡车。His car overtook the truck from the left side. ❷ 高出…之上 above；more than；exceeding：队员平均年龄～23岁。The average age of the team members is above 23 years old.|各车间产量都～原定计划。The output of every workshop exceeded what had been stated in the plan.

【超级】chāojí 超出一般等级的 super；beyond ordinary：～显微镜 super microscope|～豪华卧车 super-luxury car

【超级大国】chāojí dàguó 指凭借比其他国家强大的军事和经济实力谋求世界霸权的国家 superpower；country that seeks hegemony in the world by relying on its more powerful military and economic strength than other countries

【超级市场】chāojí shìchǎng 一种新型的综合商店,一般不设或少设售货员,让顾客自行选取所需的商品,到出口处结算付款 supermarket; large self-service retail market that employs none or a few salespeople and requires customers to pay at the exit; also 自选商场 zìxuǎn shāngchǎng

【超巨星】chāojùxīng 光度、体积比巨星大而密度较小的恒星 supergiant star; star that is brighter and larger than a giant star but of lesser density

【超绝】chāojué 超出寻常 unique; superb; extraordinary:技艺~ superb skill|~的智慧 extraordinary wisdom

【超龄】chāolíng 超过规定的年龄 overage:~团员 overage members of the Communist Youth League

【超期】chāoqī 超过规定的期限 overdue; past due; exceeding or beyond the fixed term of service:~服役 extended service in the army

【超迁】chāoqiān〈书 *fml.*〉(官吏)越级提升(of an official) be promoted by more than one grade at a time

【超前】chāoqián ❶ 超越当前的 exceed; outdo; surmount; surpass; transcend:~消费 unduly high level of consumption; overconsumption|~意识 foresight; farsightedness|~教育 future-oriented education ❷ 指超过前人 outdo or surpass one's predecessors:~绝后 unrivalled in the past and not likely to be matched in the future

【超群】chāoqún 超过一般 head and shoulders above all others; surpassing everyone else; the best in the group; preeminent; superior; outstanding:武艺~ with superior skills in martial arts

【超然】chāorán 不站在对立各方的任何一方面 aloof; detached; taking neither side (in a rivalry):~物外 be above worldly considerations; keep oneself aloof from earthly concerns|~不群 stand above and aloof from others; be stand-offish|~自得 be contented and free from worldly concerns

【超然物外】chāorán wù wài ❶ 超出于社会斗争之外 be above worldly considerations; stay away from scenes of contention ❷〈比喻 *fig.*〉置身事外 be above worldly concerns; stay away from scenes of contention; stand aloof

【超人】chāorén ❶(能力等)超过一般人(of ability) be out of the common run:~的记忆力 an exceptionally good memory ❷ 德国哲学家尼采(Friedrich Wilhelm Nietzsche)提出的所谓最强、最优、行为超出善恶,可以为所欲为的人。尼采认为超人是历史的创造者,平常人只是超人的工具。superman; person who, according to German philosopher Friedrich Wilhelm Nietzsche, is a man of exceptional strength and ability, lives at a level of experience beyond standards of good and evil, and can do whatever he wants to do; Nietzsche believed that supermen are the creators of history and ordinary people are but their tools

【超升】chāoshēng ❶〈佛教用语 *Budd.*〉指人死后灵魂升入极乐世界 (of a dead person's soul) rise to paradise ❷〈书 *fml.*〉越级提升 be promoted by more than one grade:破格~ be promoted as an exceptional case

【超生】chāoshēng ❶〈佛教用语 *Budd.*〉指人死后灵魂投生为人 reincarnation; rebirth of the soul of a dead person in another body ❷〈比喻 *fig.*〉宽容或开脱 be lenient; tolerate; exculpate:笔下~ spare sb. when one gives the verdict; show tolerance in passing a judgement; be lenient in one's critique or comments

【超声波】chāoshēngbō 超过人能听到的最高频(20,000 赫兹)的声波。超声波沿直线传播,有方向性,并能反射回来,对物体有破坏性。广泛应用在各技术部门。ultrasonic wave; supersonic wave; sound wave of acoustic frequencies above the range audible to the human ear, or above approximately 20,000 hertz; ultrasonic waves spread in a straight line in one direction, can be reflected and can cause damage to things; widely used in various technical fields

【超声速】chāoshēngsù 超过声速(340 米/秒)的速度 ultrasonic speed; speed that exceeds the speed of sound at 340 metres a second; also 超音速 chāoyīnsù

【超收】chāoshōu ❶ 收入超过计划或规定 above-norm earning; earn more than planned for or stipulated ❷ 收进的款项或实物(经过折价)超过应收金额的部分 receive cash or things (after being converted into money) in excess of what is stipulated

【超俗】chāosú 超脱世俗;不落俗套 be free from banality or vulgarity; not be inhibited by convention; be unconventional:~绝世 incomparably free from all convention|舞姿洒脱~。(She) danced uninhibitedly.

【超速】chāosù 超过规定的速度 exceed the speed limit:严禁~行车。Speeding is strictly prohibited.

【超脱】chāotuō ❶ 不拘泥成规、传统、形式等 unconventional; original; free from conventions, traditions, forms, etc.:性格~ unconventional character|他的字不专门学一家,信笔写来,十分~。Untrammelled by the established rules of any one calligraphic school, his calligraphy work is original, flows easily, and exhibits a graceful sense of freedom. ❷ 超出；脱离 overstep; go beyond; break away; be divorced from：～现实 detach oneself from reality｜～尘世 stand aloof from worldly affairs ❸ 解脱；开脱 be relieved; extricate from; disentangle

【超新星】chāoxīnxīng 超过原来光度一千万倍的新星 supernova; new star that is 10 million times brighter than its former self

【超一流】chāoyīliú 超出一流水平，指达到极高的境界 first rate; superior; superlative; super：～棋手 super chess player

【超逸】chāoyì（神态、意趣）超脱而不俗（of expression and interests）unconventional and graceful; free and natural：风度～ gracious demeanour｜笔意～ handwriting with rare grace and ease

【超员】chāo//yuán 超过规定的人数 exceed seating capacity; be overloaded：列车～百分之十。The train was overloaded by 10 per cent.

【超越】chāoyuè 超出；越过 go beyond; overstep; transcend; surpass; outdo：～前人 surpass one's predecessor｜～时空 transcend time and space｜我们能够～障碍，战胜困难。We can surmount obstacles and overcome difficulties.

【超载】chāozài 超过运输工具规定的载重量 be overloaded; be weighed down; load with more than the carrying capacity of a vehicle

【超支】chāozhī ❶ 支出超过规定或计划 overspend; spend more than planned or stipulated ❷ 领取的款项或实物（经过折价）超过应得金额的部分 money and things (after being converted into money) that one draws in excess of what one deserves

【超重】chāo//zhòng ❶ 物体超过原有的重量。是由于物体沿远离地球中心的方向作加速运动而引起的。如升降机向上起动时就有超重现象。(of an object) become heavier; phenomenon caused by the object making an accelerated motion to move away from the centre of the earth, e.g. when an elevator starts to move upward ❷ 超过了车辆的载重限度 overload; exceed the carrying capacity of a vehicle ❸ 超过规定的重量 overweigh; exceed the stipulated weight

【超卓】chāozhuó〈书 *fml.*〉超绝；卓越 unique; extraordinary; superb; excellent

【超擢】chāozhuó〈书 *fml.*〉越级提升 be promoted by more than one grade at a time

【超子】chāozǐ 质量超过中子的基本粒子，能量极高，很不稳定 hyperon; elementary particle that is unstable with mass greater than the neutron and high energy

【超自然】chāozìrán 属于自然界以外的，即宗教迷信和唯心主义哲学中所谓神灵、鬼魂等 supernatural; of or relating to existence outside the natural world, such as the so-called spirits and ghosts in religions, superstitions and idealism

焯 chāo 把蔬菜放在开水里略微一煮就拿出来 scald; cook vegetables by putting in boiling water for a few seconds：～菠菜 scald spinach

☞ zhuō on p. 2533

剿（勦） chāo〈书 *fml.*〉抄取；抄袭 plagiarize; copy

☞ jiǎo on p. 978

【剿说】chāoshuō〈书 *fml.*〉因袭别人的言论作为自己的说法 plagiarize; use and pass off the ideas or writings of others as one's own

【剿袭】chāoxí〈书 *fml.*〉same as 抄袭[1] chāoxí

cháo（ㄔㄠˊ）

晁（鼂） Cháo 姓 a surname

巢 cháo ❶ 鸟的窝，也称蜂、蚁等的窝 nest of a bird; beehive; anthill：鸟～ bird's nest｜蜂～ beehive ❷〈比喻 *fig.*〉盗匪等盘踞的地方 lair; den; nest; hideout：匪～ bandits' lair｜倾～出动 turn out in full force ❸（Cháo）姓 a surname

【巢窟】cháokū same as 巢穴 cháoxué

【巢穴】cháoxué ❶ 鸟兽藏身的地方 nest of a bird; den of an animal; lair; hideout ❷〈比喻 *fig.*〉盗匪等盘踞的地方 lair; den; nest; place that bandits occupy：直捣敌人的～ launch a direct attack on the lair of the enemy

朝 cháo ❶ 朝廷（跟'野'相对 as opposed to 'opposition party'）court; government; governing party：上～ go to court ◇在～党（执政党）party in power; ruling party ❷ 朝代 dynasty：唐～Tang Dynasty｜改～换代 dynasty changes ❸ 指一个君主的统治时期 ruling period of a monarch; emperor's reign：康熙～ the reign of Emperor Kangxi ❹ 朝见；朝拜 have an audience with an emperor; make a pilgrimage to：～觐 have an audience with; be received by an emperor｜～顶 make a pilgrimage to a monastery in the mountains to pay homage to the Buddha ❺ 面对着；向 face：脸～里 face inwards｜坐东～西 sit facing the west ❻〈介词 *prep.*〉表示动作的方向 indicating the direction of a movement (towards; in the direction of)：～南开门。The door opens towards the south.｜～学校走去 walk towards the school ❼（Cháo）姓 a surname

☞ zhāo on p. 2422

【朝拜】cháobài 君主时代官员上朝向君主跪拜；宗教徒到庙宇或圣地向神、佛礼拜 pay homage to; pay respects to; make obeisance (to a sovereign); (of officials) kneel down and kowtow to a monarch; (of religious believers) make a pilgrimage to a temple to worship the gods and Buddhas

【朝代】cháodài 建立国号的君主(一代或若干代相传)统治的整个时期 dynasty; ruling period of the founder of a country and the succession of rulers from the same family line

【朝顶】cháodǐng 佛教徒登山拜佛 (of Buddhist believers) climb up a mountain to worship the Buddha in a monastery

【朝奉】cháofèng 宋朝官阶有'朝奉郎'、'朝奉大夫',后来徽州方言中称富人为朝奉,苏、浙、皖一带也用来称呼当铺的管事人 term first used in the middle-ranking official titles of 朝奉郎 (gentleman for court service) and 朝奉大夫 (grand master for court service) in the Song Dynasty; later this term refers to a rich man in the Huizhou dialect, also a pawnshop manager in Jiangsu, Zhejiang and Anhui provinces

【朝服】cháofú 封建时代君臣上朝时所穿的礼服 court dress worn by emperors and government officials in feudal times

【朝纲】cháogāng 朝廷的法纪 court laws and discipline: ～不振 laxness and ineffectiveness of court laws and discipline

【朝贡】cháogòng 君主时代藩属国或外国的使臣朝见君主,敬献礼物 (for envoy from a vassal state or a foreign country) pay tribute to an emperor

【朝见】cháojiàn 臣子上朝见君主 (of subjects) meet with the emperor; have an audience with the monarch

【朝觐】cháojìn ❶〈书 *fml.*〉朝见 have an audience with the monarch ❷ 指宗教徒拜谒圣像、圣地等 (of religious believers) make a pilgrimage to worship a holy statue, place, etc.

【朝山】cháoshān 佛教徒到名山寺庙烧香参拜 (of Buddhist believers) make a pilgrimage to a temple on a famous mountain

【朝圣】cháoshèng ❶ 宗教徒朝拜宗教圣地,如伊斯兰教徒朝拜麦加 (of religious believers) make a pilgrimage to a sacred place, e.g. Islamic believers paying a pilgrimage to Mecca ❷ 到孔子诞生地(山东曲阜)去拜谒孔府、孔庙、孔林 make a trip to Qufu in Shandong Province, the birthplace of Confucius, to pay a formal visit to Confucius' Residence, the Confucian Temple, and the Confucian graveyard

【朝廷】cháotíng 君主时代君主听政的地方。也指以君主为首的中央统治机构。royal or imperial court, where the king or emperor meets with his subjects to discuss state affairs; royal or imperial government

【朝鲜族】Cháoxiǎnzú ❶ 我国少数民族之一,主要分布在吉林、黑龙江和辽宁 Korean ethnic group of China, mainly distributed in Jilin, Heilongjiang and Liaoning provinces ❷ 朝鲜和韩国的人数最多的民族 Koreans, the ethnic people who make up the majority of the population of North and South Korea

【朝向】cháoxiàng (建筑物的正门或房间的窗户)正对着的方向 (of the main gate of a building or window of a room) exposure: 这套房子设备不错,只是～不理想。The house is well-furnished but has an unfavourable exposure.

【朝阳】cháoyáng 向着太阳,一般指朝南 face the sun (usu. the south); have a sunny or southern exposure: 这间房子是～的。The room faces the south. *or* The room has a southern exposure.

☞ zhāoyáng on p. 2423

【朝阳花】cháoyánghuā 向日葵 sunflower (*Helianthus annus*)

【朝野】cháoyě〈旧时 *old*〉指朝廷和民间。现在用来指政府方面和非政府方面 the court and the commonalty; now meaning government and populace or whole nation: 权倾～ (of an official) be the most powerful in the court and among the people | ～一致赞成此项方案。Both the government and the people are in favour of this project.

【朝政】cháozhèng 朝廷的政事或政权 court administration; affairs of state: 议论～ discuss state affairs | 把持～ control the court; monopolize state power

【朝珠】cháozhū 清代高级官员等套在脖子上的串珠,下垂至胸前,多用珊瑚、玛瑙等制成 long string of coral or agate beads worn around the neck by senior officials of the Qing Dynasty

嘲(謿) cháo (旧读 formerly pronounced zhāo)嘲笑 ridicule; deride; sneer; jeer at: ～弄 mock; make fun of sb. | 冷～热讽 scathing sarcasm and caustic satire; biting sarcasm

☞ zhāo on p. 2423

【嘲讽】cháofěng 嘲笑讽刺 sneer at; taunt

【嘲弄】cháonòng 嘲笑戏弄 mock; poke fun at; deride; be a travesty on sb.

【嘲笑】cháoxiào 用言辞笑话对方 make fun of sb.; jest; jeer at; laugh at a person or thing with caustic remarks

【嘲谑】cháoxuè 嘲笑戏谑 tease; deride; ridicule

潮[1] cháo ❶ 潮汐,也指潮水 tide; tidewater: 早～ morning tide | 海～ sea tide ◇心～澎湃 be overcome by a wave of feelings and thoughts ❷〈比喻 *fig.*〉大规模的社会变动或运动发展的起伏形势 large-scale social upheaval; rise and fall of a campaign; current; tide: 革命高～ revolutionary upsurge ❸ 潮湿 humid; wet; damp: 衣服受～了。The clothes got damp. | 阴天东西容易返～。Things get damp easily on a cloudy day.

潮[2] cháo〈方 *dial.*〉❶ 成色低劣 of low or inferior quality:～银 inferior silver ingot |～金 impure gold ingot ❷ 技术不高 not skilled; not skilful:手艺～。The craftsmanship is quite poor.

潮[3] Cháo 指潮州 short for Chaozhou in Guangdong Province

C

【潮白】cháobái 蔗糖的一种,颜色微黄,颗粒小,产于广东潮安(今属潮州)一带 a kind of sugar in tiny yellowish grains, made from sugarcane and produced in Chao'an (present-day Chaozhou), Guangdong Province

【潮红】cháohóng 两颊泛起的红色 blush (on the cheeks)

【潮呼呼】cháohūhū (～的 cháohūhū·de)微湿的样子 damp; dank; clammy:连接下了几天雨,屋子里什么都是～的。After several days of rain, everything in the house became damp and clammy. also 潮乎乎 cháohūhū

【潮解】cháojiě 某些晶体因吸收空气中的水蒸气而在晶体表面逐渐形成饱和溶液 deliquesce; (of some crystalloids) gradually form saturated solutions on the surface by absorbing moisture from the air

【潮剧】cháojù 流行于广东潮州、汕头等地的地方戏曲剧种。在腔调上还保留着唐宋以来的古乐曲和明代弋阳腔的传统。Chao Opera; local opera popular in Chaozhou and Shantou in Guangdong Province, which still retains the traditions of ancient music from the Tang and Song dynasties and the *Yiyang* melodies from the Ming Dynasty

【潮流】cháoliú ❶ 由潮汐而引起的水流运动 tide; tidal current ❷〈比喻 *fig.*〉社会变动或发展的趋势 trend of social change or development:革命～ revolutionary trend | 历史～ historical trend

【潮气】cháoqì 指空气里所含水分 moisture in the air; humidity:仓库里～太大,粮食就容易发霉。If humidity goes too high the grain will easily go mouldy.

【潮润】cháorùn ❶(土壤、空气等)潮湿 (of soil, air, etc.) damp; humid; wet:海风轻轻吹来,使人觉得～而有凉意。The breeze from the sea blows gently, moist and cool. ❷(眼睛)含有泪水 (of eyes) teary; blurred with tears:说到这儿,她两眼～了,转脸向窗外望去。As she said this, she turned to look out of the window, her eyes moist with tears.

【潮湿】cháoshī 含有比正常状态下较多的水分 humid; damp; moist; containing more moisture than in a normal state:雨后新晴的原野,～而滋润。The fields, bathed in the sun after the rain, look moist and refreshing.

【潮水】cháoshuǐ 海洋中以及沿海地区的江河中受潮汐影响而定期涨落的水 tidewater; tide; regular rising water in the sea and rivers in coastal areas caused by the tides:人像～一样涌进来。People swarmed in like tides.

【潮位】cháowèi 受潮汐影响而涨落的水位 tidemark; level of the tidal current at its rise and ebb

【潮汐】cháoxī ❶ 由于月亮和太阳的引力而产生的水位定时涨落的现象 tidal wave; morning and evening tide; regular rising and ebbing of water level caused by the gravitational pull of the moon and the sun ❷ 特指海潮 sea tide

【潮信】cháoxìn ❶ 指潮水,因其涨落有一定的时间 spring tide; tidewater; water rising and ebbing regularly ❷〈书 *fml.*〉〈婉辞 *euph.*〉指月经 menstrual period; menstruation

【潮绣】cháoxiù 广东潮州出产的刺绣,色彩斑斓,富于民间特色 embroidery produced in Chaozhou, with beautiful colours and folk flavour

【潮汛】cháoxùn 一年中定期的大潮 spring tide; big tide at fixed times in a year

【潮涌】cháoyǒng 像潮水那样涌来 swarm in like the tide:人们从四面八方～而来。People streamed in from all directions.

chǎo(ㄔㄠˇ)

吵 chǎo ❶ 声音杂乱扰人 disturb others by making noise:～得慌 terribly noisy | 把孩子～醒了。You are so noisy, you've woken the child. ❷ 争吵 quarrel; squabble; have words with; argue:两人说着说着～了起来。As they talked on, the two started quarrelling. | 不要～,有话好好说。Don't quarrel. Let's talk it over.

☞ chāo on p. 225

【吵架】chǎo//jià 剧烈争吵 quarrel vehemently; argue vehemently:拌嘴～ have a quarrel | 他俩吵了一架。The two had a quarrel.

【吵闹】chǎonào ❶ 大声争吵 wrangle; kick up a row; quarrel in a loud voice:～不休 quarrel on and on ❷ 扰乱,使不安静 disturb; harass; break up or destroy the peace and quiet:他在休息,不要去～。He's resting, so don't disturb him. ❸(声音)杂乱 (of sound) din; hubbub:人声～。A hubbub was heard.

【吵嚷】chǎorǎng 乱喊叫;乱哄哄地争吵 make a racket; clamour:一片～声。The place seemed to be drowned in a big clamour.

【吵扰】chǎorǎo ❶ 吵闹使人不得安静;打扰 disturb; break up or destroy the tranquillity:～你半天,很过意不去。I'm really sorry to have troubled you for such a long time. ❷〈方 *dial.*〉争吵 quarrel; kick up a row; wrangle

【吵人】chǎo//rén 声音大而扰人 (of sound) loud and disturbing; noisy:机器噪声太～。The noises of the machine are really disturbing me.

【吵子】chǎo·zi〈方 *dial.*〉引起争吵的事；纠纷 cause of trouble; bone of contention：有什么～回家再说。If there's anything that you're displeased with, leave it till we get home.

【吵嘴】chǎo//zuǐ 争吵 quarrel; wrangle; bicker：俩人～。The two had a quarrel.｜吵了几句嘴 have a petty bickering with sb.

炒 chǎo ❶ 烹调方法，把食物放在锅里加热并随时翻动使熟，炒菜时要先放些油 stir-fry; sauté; way of cooking by putting oil in a hot wok or pan, adding ingredients and stirring quickly：～辣椒 stir-fried hot peppers｜～鸡蛋 scrambled eggs｜糖～栗子 roasted sweet chestnuts｜～花生 roasted peanuts ❷ 指倒买倒卖 speculate illegally：～地皮 speculate illegally in real estate｜～外汇 speculate illegally in foreign currency ❸〈方 *dial.*〉指解雇 sack; fire

【炒肝】chǎogān（～儿 chǎogānr）一种食品，用猪肝、肥肠加大蒜、黄酱等作料勾芡烩成 stew of pork liver and intestine with onion and fermented bean paste, thickened with starch

【炒更】chǎogēng〈方 *dial.*〉指业余时间（多为晚上）再从事别的工作挣钱 moonlight (for extra money); work at another job in one's spare time, oft. at night, in addition to one's full-time job

【炒汇】chǎohuì 指倒买倒卖外汇 trade illegally in a foreign currency; speculate illegally in foreign currencies

【炒货】chǎohuò 商店里出售的干炒食品（如瓜子、蚕豆、花生等）的总称 general term for roasted seeds and nuts (e.g. sunflower seeds, broad beans, peanuts, etc.) in a store

【炒家】chǎojiā 指专门进行倒买倒卖的人 speculator; broker; person who is adept at speculation

【炒冷饭】chǎo lěngfàn〈比喻 *fig.*〉重复已经说过的话或做过的事，没有新的内容 heat leftover rice — repeat what's been said or done without adding anything original; dish up the same old stuff; say or do the same old thing

【炒买炒卖】chǎomǎi-chǎomài 指转手买进和卖出，从中牟利 buy quick and sell quick so as to make profits; speculate

【炒米】chǎomǐ ❶ 干炒过的或煮熟晾干后再炒的米 parched rice; rice that is stir-fried or rice that is cooked, dried and then stir-fried：～花 puffed rice｜～团 puffed rice ball ❷ 蒙古族人民的日常食物，用煮熟后再炒的糜子米拌牛奶或黄油做成 staple food of the Mongolian people, prepared with stir-fried millet and milk or butter

【炒面】chǎomiàn ❶ 煮熟后再加油和作料炒过的面条 chow mein; noodles prepared in two steps: first cooking in boiling water and then stir-frying with shredded meat and vegetables ❷ 炒熟的面粉，做干粮，通常用开水冲了吃 parched flour as solid food, usu. prepared with boiling water

【炒勺】chǎosháo 炒菜用的带柄的铁锅，形状像勺子 wok; ladle-shaped iron pan with a handle

【炒鱿鱼】chǎo yóuyú 鱿鱼一炒就卷起来，像是卷铺盖 (of squid) roll up when being cooked, like rolling up one's quilt to prepare for departure;〈比喻 *fig.*〉解雇 be fired; be sacked

麸（麨） chǎo〈书 *fml.*〉炒熟的米粉或面粉 stir-fried rice or wheat flour

chào（ㄔㄠˋ）

耖 chào ❶ 一种像耙的农具，能把耙过的土块弄碎 harrow-like implement for pulverizing soil ❷ 用耖整地 level land with such an implement：～田 level land with a harrow

chē（ㄔㄜ）

车（車） chē ❶ 陆地上有轮子的运输工具 vehicle; conveyance with wheels：火～ train｜汽～ automobile; auto｜马～ cab; chariot; horse-drawn carriage ❷ 利用轮轴旋转的工具 tool with wheel and axle：纺～ spinning wheel｜滑～ pulley｜水～ waterwheel ❸ 机器 machine：开～ start a machine; set a machine going｜～间 workshop ❹ 车削 metal-turning with a lathe：～圆 make sth. round with a lathe｜～螺丝钉 lathe a screw ❺ 用水车取水 lift water by a waterwheel：～水 lift water by a waterwheel ❻〈方 *dial.*〉用车运东西 transport things with a vehicle：～垃圾 cart away the garbage ❼〈方 *dial.*〉用缝纫机缝制衣服 sew clothes with a sewing machine：～衣 make clothes on a sewing machine ❽〈方 *dial.*〉转动（多指身体 usu. the body) turn：～过头来 turn around ❾（Chē）姓 a surname

☞ jū on p. 1043

【车把】chēbǎ 骑车、推车、拉车时用手把住的部分 shaft (of a wheelbarrow, handcart, etc.); handlebar (of a bicycle, motorcycle, etc.)

【车把势】chēbǎ·shi 赶大车的人 cart driver; also 车把式 chēbǎ·shi

【车帮】chēbāng 卡车、大车等车体两侧的挡板 side or sideboard of a cart or truck

【车厂】chēchǎng ❶〈旧时 *old*〉租赁人力车或三轮车的处所 place where one can hire a rickshaw or pedicab; rickshaw or pedicab rental centre; also 车厂子 chēchǎng·zi ❷ 制造人力车或三轮车的工厂 factory where rickshaws or pedicabs are manufactured

【车场】chēchǎng ❶ 集中停放、保养和修理车辆的场所 place where vehicles are parked, maintained and repaired; garage ❷ 铁路车站内按用途划分的线路群 marshalling yard; railway routes grouped according to their use in a railway station ❸ 公路运输和城市公共交通企业的一级管理机构 road transport or public transit pool; administrative unit in charge of road transport and urban public transit

C

【车床】chēchuáng 金属切削机床，主要用来加工内圆、外圆和螺纹等成型面。加工时工件旋转，车刀移动着切削。lathe; machine for shaping a piece of metal into round and screw shapes, by rotating it while pressing it against a fixed, moving cutting or abrading tool; also 旋床 xuànchuáng

【车次】chēcì 列车的编号或长途汽车行车的次第 train number or coach number to indicate the order of departure

【车到山前必有路】 chē dào shān qián bì yǒu lù 〈比喻 *fig.*〉事到临头，总会有解决的办法 in the end things will mend

【车道】chēdào 专供车辆行走的道路(区别于'人行道' as compared with 'pedestrian lane') traffic lane：拓宽后的马路由原来的四～变为六～。The four-lane road has been widened into a six-lane affair.

【车队】chēduì ❶ 成队的车辆 motorcade ❷ 交通运输部门的一级组织 unit of a motor transport department

【车份儿】chēfènr 〈方 *dial.*〉租人力车、三轮车等拉客的人付给车主的租金 rent or money paid to the owner of a vehicle by the renter

【车夫】chēfū 〈旧时 *old*〉指以推车、拉车、赶兽力车或驾驶汽车为职业的人 chauffeur; rickshaw puller; cart driver; driver; one who drives a vehicle for a living

【车工】chēgōng ❶ 使用车床进行切削的工种 type of work using a lathe ❷ 使用车床的技术工人 turner; lathe operator

【车公里】chēgōnglǐ 〈复合量词 *compound classifier*〉计算车辆运行工作量的单位，一辆车运行一公里为一车公里 vehicle kilometre; unit used to measure the workload of vehicles, meaning one vehicle driving one km.

【车钩】chēgōu 火车车皮或机车两端的挂钩，有连接、牵引及缓冲的作用 railway coupling; hook at both ends of a train wagon or a locomotive, used to connect and tow wagons, and as a buffer between wagons

【车轱辘话】chēgū·luhuà 指重复、絮叨的话 repetitious talk

【车祸】chēhuò 行车(多指汽车)时发生的伤亡事故 traffic accident; road accident

【车技】chējì 杂技的一种，演员用特制的车表演各种动作 trick cycling by acrobatic performers who execute stunts on a specially made bicycle

【车驾】chējià 帝王的马车 imperial carriage

【车间】chējiān 企业内部在生产过程中完成某些工序或单独生产某些产品的单位 workshop; unit in an enterprise that produces certain parts in a production process or manufactures some products by itself

【车筐】chēkuāng 装在自行车车把前面或后架侧面，用来盛物品的筐子 bike basket; basket that is fixed either in the front or on the side of the back rack of a bicycle

【车况】chēkuàng 交通运输部门指车辆的性能、运行、保养等情况 performance, operation and maintenance conditions of a vehicle

【车老板】chēlǎobǎn 〈方 *dial.*〉(～儿 chēlǎobǎnr)赶大车的人 cart driver; also 车老板子 chēlǎobǎn·zi

【车辆】chēliàng 各种车的总称 vehicle; automobile; general term for different kinds of vehicles

【车裂】chēliè 〈古代 *arch.*〉一种残酷的刑法，用五辆车把人分拉撕裂致死 severe form of capital punishment, in which a person is torn apart with five chariots running in different directions

【车流】chēliú 道路上像河流似的连续不断行驶的车辆 traffic; incessant stream of vehicles on the road; traffic flow

【车轮战】chēlúnzhàn 几个人轮流跟一个人打，或几群人轮流跟一群人打，使对方因疲乏而战败 several persons taking turns in fighting an opponent to tire him out; or several groups of people taking turns in fighting one group to tire them out so as to defeat them

【车马费】chēmǎfèi 因公外出时的交通费 travel allowance for a business trip

【车门】chēmén ❶ 车上的门 door of a vehicle ❷ 大门旁专供车马出入的门 door specially opened near the main gate for the convenience of chariots and horses

【车棚】chēpéng 存放自行车等的棚子 bicycle shed; shed for parking bicycles

【车篷】chēpéng 车上遮蔽日光、风雨等的装置，用铁、木等做架，上盖布、皮等 awning for protecting a vehicle from sunlight, wind and rain; iron or wood canopy covered with cloth, leather, etc.

【车皮】chēpí 铁路运输上指机车以外的每一节车厢(多指货车) railway wagon or carriage; freight truck; railway car of a train (usu. a freight train)

【车钱】chēqián 乘车所付的费用 fare (for riding in a vehicle)

【车圈】chēquān 瓦圈 rim of a bicycle wheel, cart wheel, etc.

【车身】chē//shēn 〈方 *dial.*〉转身 turn round：没等我说完，他～就走了。He turned round and left before I finished speaking. | 她又车过

身来看了看熟睡的孩子。She turned round and took another look at her child in sound sleep.

【车身】chēshēn 车辆用来载人装货的部分,也指车辆整体 body of a vehicle or area in a vehicle to seat people or load freight:～宽,胡同窄,进不去。The vehicle is too wide to enter the narrow lane.|～过长,车库的门关不上。The vehicle is so long that the door of the garage cannot be closed.

【车手】chēshǒu 参加赛车比赛的选手 drivers in a car race

【车水马龙】chē shuǐ mǎ lóng 车像流水,马像游龙。形容车马或车辆很多,来往不绝。incessant stream of horses and carriages; heavy traffic

【车速】chēsù ❶ 车辆运行的速度 speed of a vehicle ❷ 车床等运转的速度 speed of a lathe in operation

【车胎】chētāi 轮胎的通称 general term for 轮胎 lúntāi

【车条】chētiáo 辐条 spokes (of a wheel)

【车头】chētóu 火车、汽车等车辆的头部,特指机车 front of a train, car, etc., esp. referring to the engine of a train or locomotive

【车瓦】chēwǎ 指安在木制车轮辋外的铁箍 iron rim of a wooden wheel

【车位】chēwèi 供汽车停放的位置 parking spot; parking space

【车厢】chēxiāng 火车、汽车等用来载人或装东西的部分 railway carriage; space to hold passengers or store freight in a train or car; also 车箱 chēxiāng

【车箱】chēxiāng same as 车厢 chēxiāng

【车削】chēxiāo 用车床进行金属切削 cut a piece of metal with a lathe

【车辕】chēyuán 大车前部驾牲口的两根直木 shaft (of a cart); two straight pieces of wood that control a draught animal in the front of a cart

【车载斗量】chē zài dǒu liáng 形容数量很多,多用来表示不足为奇 enough to fill carts and be measured by the bushel — usu. meaning common and numerous

【车闸】chēzhá 机动车、自行车等用来减低速度或停止前进的装置 brake; device that makes a vehicle or a bicycle go slowly or bring it to a stop

【车站】chēzhàn 陆路交通运输线上设置的停车地点,是上下乘客或装卸货物的场所 station; depot; stop; designated places along transport routes, where public vehicles regularly stop so that passengers can get on and off, and goods can be loaded and unloaded

【车照】chēzhào 行车的执照;检查车辆合格,准许行驶的凭证 driving license; document to permit the eligible operation of a vehicle on the road

【车辙】chēzhé 车辆经过后车轮压在道路上凹下去的痕迹 rut; trace left in the ground by a wheel

【车轴】chēzhóu 穿入车轱辘承受车身重量的圆柱形零件 axle; cylindrical part that connects two wheels and bears the weight of a vehicle

【车主】chēzhǔ ❶ 车辆的所有者 owner of a vehicle ❷〈旧时 *old*〉称经营车厂的人 person who runs a rickshaw rental business

【车资】chēzī same as 车钱 chēqián

【车子】chē·zi ❶ 车(多指小型的 usu. small) vehicle ❷ 自行车 bicycle

【车组】chēzǔ 公共电、汽车或火车上负责一辆车或特定运行任务的全体成员 crew; all the people working on a trolley bus, public bus or train; group of people working together for a particular purpose

伡 chē ☞ 大车[2] dàchē on p. 354

咔 chē [咔嗻](chēzhē)厉害;很(多见于早期白话 oft. in early vernacular) terrific; much

砗 chē [砗磲](chēqú) 软体动物,介壳略呈三角形,大的长达1米左右。生活在热带海底。肉可以吃。giant clam(*Tridacna gigas L.*); tridacna; mollusc with a triangle-shaped shell, at largest one metre long, living in the bottom of tropical seas; its flesh is edible

chě(ㄔㄜˇ)

尺 chě 我国民族音乐音阶上的一级,乐谱上用做记音符号,相当于简谱的'2' note of the scale in traditional Chinese musical notation, corresponding to 2 (re) in numbered musical notation; ☞ 工尺 gōngchǐ on p. 664

☞ chǐ on p. 262

扯(撦) chě ❶ 拉 drag; pull: 拉～ drag; tug|没等他说完～着他就走 pull him away without waiting for him to finish speaking ◇～开嗓子喊 shout at the top of one's lungs; shout at the top of one's voice ❷ 撕;撕下 tear; tear off:～五尺布 buy five *chi* of cloth|把墙上的旧广告～下来。Tear the old poster down from the wall. ❸ 漫无边际地闲谈 chat; gossip; engage in a chitchat: 闲～ gossip; chat; chew the fat|东拉西～ drag in all sorts of irrelevant matters; talk at random; ramble

【扯白】chě//bái〈方 *dial.*〉说假话 lie; tell a lie

【扯淡】chě//dàn〈方 *dial.*〉闲扯;胡扯 talk nonsense

【扯后腿】chěhòutuǐ〈比喻 *fig.*〉利用亲密的关系或感情牵制别人的行动(含贬义 derog.) take advantage of intimate relations or personal feelings to hold sb. back from action; be a drag on sb.; be a hindrance to sb.

【扯谎】chě//huǎng 说谎 lie; tell a lie

【扯皮】chě//pí 无原则地争论;争吵 dispute over trivial matters at the sacrifice of principles; argue back and forth; bicker:扯了几句皮 have an argument over trifles|好了,我们不要～了,还是谈正题吧。OK, let's stop arguing over nothing and come back to the main point.

【扯臊】chě//sào〈方 *dial.*〉胡扯;瞎扯(骂人的话 curse) talk sheer nonsense; tell shameless lies; spout bare-faced lies; shoot off one's mouth

【扯手】chě·shou〈方 *dial.*〉缰绳 rein; halter

【扯谈】chětán 闲谈;攀谈 engage in small talk; chitchat:他们一边吃,一边～赶集的事。While they were eating, they chatted about the fair.

【扯腿】chě//tuǐ same as 扯后腿 chě//hòutuǐ

【扯闲篇】chě xiánpiān (～儿 chě xiánpiānr)谈与正事无关的话;闲谈 chat; chit-chat; also 扯闲天儿 chě xiántiānr

chè(ㄔㄜˋ)

彻(徹) chè 通;透 thorough; penetrating; complete:～夜 whole night; all through the night|～骨 to the bone|响～云霄 resounding across the sky

【彻底】chèdǐ 一直到底;深而透 thorough; thoroughgoing; downright; from A to Z:～改正错误 thoroughly correct one's mistakes|～改变旧作风 make a radical change to one's working style; also 澈底 chèdǐ

【彻骨】chègǔ 透到骨头里 to the bone; to the marrow;〈比喻 *fig.*〉程度极深 indicating degree:～痛恨 hate sb. to the marrow|严寒～。The icy cold chills one to the bone.

【彻头彻尾】chè tóu chè wěi 从头到尾,完完全全 out and out; through and through; downright; dyed-in-the-wools:～的谎言 sheer lie

【彻悟】chèwù 彻底觉悟;完全明白 be fully aware of; fully recognize; come to understand thoroughly

【彻夜】chèyè 通宵;整夜 all night; through the night; from dusk to dawn:～不眠 lie awake all night

坼 chè〈书 *fml.*〉裂开 split open; crack:天寒地～。The ground cracked in the severe cold.

【坼裂】chèliè〈书 *fml.*〉裂开 split open; crack

掣 chè ❶ 拽(zhuài);拉 pull; tug:～肘 hold sb. back by pulling their elbow; impede sb. from doing sth. ❷ 抽 draw:～签 draw lots|他赶紧～回手去。He quickly drew back his hand. ❸ 一闪而过 flash past:电～雷鸣。Lightning flashed and thunder rolled.

【掣电】chèdiàn〈书 *fml.*〉闪电;打闪 bolt; (of lightning) flash

【掣肘】chèzhǒu 拉住胳膊 hold sb. back by their elbow;〈比喻 *fig.*〉阻挠别人做事 prevent sb. from doing sth.:相互～,谁也做不成事。We'll get nowhere if we deliberately make things difficult for each other.

撤 chè ❶ 除去 remove; take away:～职 dismiss sb. from a position|把障碍物～了。The obstacle has been removed. ❷ 退 withdraw; evacuate:～退 evacuate; retreat|～兵 withdraw troops ❸〈方 *dial.*〉减轻(气味、分量等)(of smell, weight, etc.) reduce; lose:～味儿 lessen the smell|～分量 take some weight off

【撤编】chèbiān 撤销编制 disestablish; deactivate; inactivate:部队奉命～,他转业到地方工作。He was demobilized and transferred to civilian work as the troops were deactivated.

【撤兵】chè//bīng 撤退或撤回军队 withdraw troops

【撤差】chè//chāi〈旧时 *old*〉称撤销官职 dismiss sb. from his official post; remove sb. from office

【撤除】chèchú 除去;取消 dismantle; get rid of; annul; abolish; abrogate; call off:～工事 dismantle the defence works|～代表 call back the representatives

【撤佃】chè//diàn 地主强制收回租给农民耕种的田地 (of a landlord) take back the land rented to a peasant

【撤防】chè//fáng 撤除防御的军队和工事 withdraw a garrison; withdraw from a defended position

【撤换】chèhuàn 撤去原有的,换上另外的(人或物) dismiss and replace; recall; replace:～人选 recall and replace candidates|木料糟了的都得～。The weather-beaten wood should be replaced.

【撤回】chèhuí ❶ 使驻在外面的人员回来 recall; withdraw:～军队 recall troops|～代表 recall representatives ❷ 收回(发出去的文件等) revoke; retract; withdraw (issued documents, etc.):～提案 retract a proposal

【撤军】chè//jūn 撤出军队 withdraw troops

【撤离】chèlí 撤退;离开 withdraw from; leave; evacuate:～现场 quit the scene|～防地 abandon a position

【撤诉】chèsù (原告)撤回诉讼 (of an accuser) withdraw one's charges; revoke a court action; (of the plaintiff) withdraw an accusation; drop a lawsuit

【撤退】chètuì (军队)放弃阵地或占领的地区 (of troops) evacuate; retreat; withdraw; abandon a position or occupied area

【撤消】chèxiāo same as 撤销 chèxiāo

【撤销】chèxiāo 取消 cancel; rescind; revoke:

~处分 rescind or annul a punishment|~职务 dismiss sb. from a post; also 撤消 chèxiāo

【撤职】chè//zhí 撤销职务 dismiss from a post; remove from office: ~查办 discharge sb. from his post and prosecute him|科长因违纪被撤了职。The section chief was removed from office for breaching the rules.

澈 chè 水清 (of water) clear; limpid: 清~ clear; limpid|澄~ crystal clear

【澈底】chèdǐ same as 彻底 chèdǐ

chēn (ㄔㄣ)

抻(**捵**) chēn 拉;扯 pull out; draw out; stretch: ~面 hand-pulled noodles|~着脖子看 crane one's neck to see|皮筋儿越~越长。The more a rubber band is stretched, the longer it becomes.

【抻面】chēn//miàn 用手把和(huó)好的面团抻成面条儿 make noodles by stretching the dough by hand

【抻面】chēnmiàn 用手抻成的面条儿 hand-pulled noodles

郴 Chēn 郴州,地名,在湖南 Chenzhou, a place in Hunan Province

綝 chēn〈书 *fml.*〉❶ 止 stop; cease ❷ 善 kind; good

☞ lín on p. 1223

琛 chēn〈书 *fml.*〉珍宝 treasure

嗔 chēn ❶ 怒;生气 angry; displeased: 似~非~ look as if angry|转~为喜 go from being angry or annoyed to being pleased ❷ 对人不满;生人家的气;怪罪 be dissatisfied with; be annoyed with; blame (sb.): ~怪 blame; rebuke|~责 reproach; upbraid

【嗔怪】chēnguài 对别人的言语或行动表示不满 complain; blame; rebuke; be displeased with others' talk or behaviour: 他~家人事先没同他商量。He was displeased with his family for not discussing it with him beforehand.

【嗔怒】chēnnù 恼怒;生气 get angry; become angry

膜 chēn〈书 *fml.*〉肿胀 swollen; tumefied

瞋 chēn〈书 *fml.*〉发怒时睁大眼睛 stare angrily; glare; become wide-eyed with anger: ~目而视 stare at sb. angrily

chén (ㄔㄣˊ)

臣 chén ❶ 君主时代的官吏,有时也包括百姓 subject; minister; officials and common people under a feudal ruler: 忠~ loyal official|君~ monarch and his courtiers ❷ 官吏对皇帝上书或说话时的自称 [how a court official referred himself when addressing the emperor] I, your vassal

【臣服】chénfú〈书 *fml.*〉❶ 屈服称臣,接受统治 submit oneself to the rule of; acknowledge allegiance to ❷ 以臣子的礼节侍奉(君主) serve a ruler as his subject

【臣僚】chénliáo 君主时代的文武官员 civil and military officials in feudal times

【臣民】chénmín 君主国家的臣子和百姓 subjects; officials and populace of a feudal ruler

【臣子】chénzǐ 臣 official in feudal times

尘(**塵**) chén ❶ 飞扬的或附在物体上的细小灰土 dust; dirt; cloud of fine, dry particles: 粉~ dust; fine, dry particles of matter|吸~器 vaccum cleaner; dust remover|一~不染 not a particle of dust; spotless ❷ 尘世 this world: 红~ this mortal world; the earthly vanity of the world|~俗 human world; mortal life ❸〈书 *fml.*〉踪迹 trace: 步人后~ follow in sb.'s footsteps; trail behind sb.; follow suit

【尘埃】chén'āi same as 尘土 chéntǔ: 桌面上满是~。The desk was covered with a layer of dust.

【尘暴】chénbào 挟带大量尘沙的风暴,发生在沙漠或半干旱地区 dust storm; severe windstorm that sweeps clouds of dust across an extensive area, esp. in an arid region; also 沙暴 shābào

【尘毒】chéndú 含有有毒物质的粉尘 toxic industrial dust

【尘肺】chénfèi 职业病,由长期吸入一定量工业生产中的粉尘引起。症状是肺结疤,弹性减弱,劳动力也逐渐减退,并容易感染肺结核、肺炎等。可分为硅肺、煤肺等。pneumoconiosis; occupational disease of the lungs, e. g. anthracosis or silicosis, caused by prolonged inhalation of industrial dusts, with such symptoms as scarred lungs with decreased flexibility, gradual loss of work ability, and susceptibility to tuberculosis and pneumonia

【尘封】chénfēng 搁置已久,被尘土盖满 be covered with dust; be dust-laden

【尘垢】chéngòu 灰尘和污垢 dust and filth; dirt

【尘寰】chénhuán 尘世;人世间 mundane world; human world; this earthly world; this mortal life: 脱离~ break away from this mortal life; live in seclusion

【尘芥】chénjiè 尘土和小草 dirt and weeds〈比喻 *fig.*〉轻微的事物 trifles; trivial matters

【尘虑】chénlǜ 指对人世间的人和事的思虑 earthly concerns; worldly cares: 置身此境,~全消。Staying in this environment lifts one above all earthly concerns.

【尘世】chénshì 佛教徒或道教徒指现实世界,跟他们所幻想的理想世界相对 this world; this mortal life; earthly or practical world in the eyes of a Buddhist or Taoist believer, as opposed to their imagined world

【尘事】chénshì 世俗的事 worldly affairs：不问～ be above worldly affairs; stay aloft of society

【尘俗】chénsú ❶ 世俗 earthly; worldly; mundane：这儿仿佛是另一世界，没有一点儿～气息。This place seems another world, without any of the mundane cares of the earthly world. ❷〈书 *fml.*〉人间 human world; mortal life

【尘土】chéntǔ 附在器物上或飞扬着的细土 dust; fine particles that get stuck to an object or float in the air

C

【尘雾】chénwù ❶ 像雾一样弥漫着的尘土 cloud of dust; foggy dust：狂风怒吼，～弥漫。The gale howled, kicking up clouds of choking dust. ❷ 尘土和烟雾 dust and smoke

【尘嚣】chénxiāo 人世间的纷扰喧嚣 hubbub; uproar：远离～ stay away from the hubbub of the human world

【尘烟】chényān ❶ 像烟一样飞扬着的尘土 dust floating about like smoke; cloud of dust：汽车飞驰，卷起滚滚～。A car sped by, raising clouds of dust in its trail. ❷ 烟和尘土 smoke and dust：炮声响过，～四起。A cloud of dust and smoke arose with the rumble of artillery fire.

【尘缘】chényuán 佛教称尘世间的色、声、香、味、触、法为'六尘'，人心与'六尘'有缘分，受其拖累，叫做尘缘。泛指世俗的缘分。predestined bonds (to earthly or mortal life); human bondage; Buddhist doctrines say that there are 'six dusts' in the human world — carnal desire, sound, fragrance, taste, touch, and dharma; (in a broad sense) human mind is predestined to be bonded with, and hence weighed down by：～未断 have not broken free from the bonds of this world; have not yet severed one's links with mortal life

辰[1] chén 地支的第五位 fifth of the twelve Earthly Branches; ☞ 干支 gānzhī on p. 627

辰[2] chén ❶ 日、月、星的统称 general term for the sun, the moon and the stars; celestial bodies：星～ stars ❷〈古代 *arch.*〉把一昼夜分作十二辰 any of the traditional twelve two-hour periods of the day：时～ period of two hours ❸ 时光；日子 time; day：良～美景 good time of fine weather and beautiful scenery | 诞～ birthday

辰[3] Chén 指辰州（旧府名，府治在今湖南沅陵）Chenzhou (name of a prefecture, whose seat is in present-day Yuanling, Hunan Province)：～砂 cinnabar; cinnabarite; vermillion

【辰光】chénguāng〈方 *dial.*〉时候 time; time of the day

【辰砂】chénshā 朱砂。旧时以湖南辰州府出的最著名，因而得名。cinnabar; vermillion; named after Chenzhou Prefecture, Hunan Province, where the best cinnabar was produced in old times

【辰时】chénshí〈旧式 *old*〉计时法指上午七点钟到九点钟的时间 period of the day from 7 a.m. to 9 a.m.

沉(沈) chén ❶（在水里）往下落（跟'浮'相对 as opposed to 'float'）(in water) sink：石～大海 (disappear) like a stone dropped into the sea ◇星～月落，旭日东升。The moon is down, the stars have set, and the sun has risen in the eastern sky. ❷ 物体往下陷 subside; sink; keep down：地基下～ settling of the foundation ❸ 使降落；向下放（多指抽象事物 usu. of abstract matter) keep down; lower; sink：～下心来 settle down to one's work; concentrate on one's work, studies, etc. | ～得住气 able to hold back one's excitement or anger ◇把脸一～ put on a stern expression; pull a long face ❹（程度）深 (of degree) deep; profound：～醉 deadly drunk; heavily drunk | ～痛 deep feeling of grief or remorse | 睡得很～ be in sound sleep ❺ 分量重 heavy：箱子里装满了书，很～。Packed full with books, the trunk is very heavy. ❻ 感觉沉重（不舒服）feel heavy or uncomfortable; fell not well：胳膊～ have sore arms | 头～ feel dizzy
☞ 沈 shěn on p. 1708

【沉沉】chénchén ❶ 形容沉重 heavy：谷穗儿～地垂下来。The ears hang heavy on the stalks. ❷ 形容深沉 deep; heavy; to a great extent：暮气～ lifeless; apathetic; lethargic

【沉甸甸】chéndiāndiān（～的 chéndiāndiān·de）形容沉重 heavy：装了～的一口袋麦种 loaded with a heavy sack of wheat seeds ◇任务还没有完成，心里老是～的。The unaccomplished mission weighed heavily on my mind.

【沉淀】chéndiàn ❶ 溶液中难溶解的物质沉到溶液底层 precipitate; (of insoluble substances in solution) form a sediment at the bottom of a solution ❷ 沉到溶液底层的难溶解的物质 sediment; insoluble substances at the bottom of solutions ❸〈比喻 *fig.*〉凝聚，积累 accumulate; accrete：情感需要～，才能写出好诗。Accumulation of emotions is the premise of creating a good poem. | 过多的资金～对于流通是不利的。Excessive accretion of funds is harmful to the circulation of money.

【沉浮】chénfú〈比喻 *fig.*〉起落或盛衰消长 ups and downs; vicissitudes：与世～ swim with the tide; drift along | 宦海～ rise and fall of an official career

【沉痼】chéngù〈书 *fml.*〉长久而难治的病 chronic disease; serious illness;〈比喻 *fig.*〉难以改掉的坏习惯 incurable bad habit

【沉酣】chénhān〈书 *fml.*〉指深深地沉浸在某种境界或思想活动中 indulge; be lost in a certain ambience or thought：睡梦～ be fast asleep|歌舞～ indulge in song and dance |～经史 be immersed in the study of classics

【沉积】chénjī ❶ 水流、风等流体在流速减慢时，所挟带的砂石、尘土等沉淀堆积起来（of sand, dust, etc. carried by water or wind）deposit when current or wind slow down ❷ 指物质在溶液中沉淀积聚起来（of material）settle to the bottom of a liquid ❸ 某些生物在生命活动中产生的物质堆积起来，如海洋生物的遗体堆积等 pile up; accumulate; (of substances produced by some life forms, e.g. remains of some sea creatures) ❹〈比喻 *fig.*〉沉淀，积聚（多用于抽象事物 oft. used for abstract matters）accumulate; accrete：文化～ cultural sediment|历史～ accumulation of history

【沉积岩】chēnjīyán 地球表面分布较广的岩层，是地壳岩石结过机械、化学或生物的破坏后沉积而成，大部分是在水中形成的，如砂岩、页岩、石灰岩等。其中常夹有生物化石，含有煤、石油等矿产。sedimentary rock; widely distributed terrane or terrain on the surface of the earth, formed by rock from the earth's crust that is deposited when eroded through mechanical, chemical or biological power; most sedimentary rock, e.g. gritstone, shale, limestone, etc., is formed in water and carries biological fossils and minerals like coal, oil, etc. also 水成岩 shuǐchéngyán

【沉寂】chénjì ❶ 十分寂静 quiet; still：～的深夜 in the still of night ❷ 消息全无 no news：音信～。There's no news whatsoever.

【沉降】chénjiàng（地层、浮在气体或液体中的物体）向下沉（of stratum, objects floating in air or liquid）sink：地面～。The ground has sunk.

【沉浸】chénjìn 浸入水中。多比喻处于某种境界或思想活动中 be soaked in water; be immersed in water; be steeped in; (fig.) be lost in thought：～在幸福的回忆中 be immersed in happy memories

【沉静】chénjìng ❶ 寂静 quiet; calm：夜深了，四周～下来。It was late at night and silence reigned. ❷（性格、心情、神色）安静；平静（of temperament, mood and facial expression）calm; serene; placid：他性情～，不爱多说话。He is quiet and taciturn by temperament.

【沉疴】chénkē〈书 *fml.*〉长久而严重的病 serious chronic disease; serious and lingering illness：妙手回春，～顿愈。With the doctor's wonderful skill, he completely recovered from a severe illness.

【沉雷】chénléi 声音大而低沉的雷 muffled thunder

【沉沦】chénlún 陷入罪恶的、痛苦的境界 hit bottom; sink into (sin, grief, sorrow, etc.)：不甘～ refuse to sink into depravity|～于浩劫 sink into a great calamity

【沉闷】chénmèn ❶（天气、气氛等）使人感到沉重而烦闷（of weather, atmosphere, etc.）dreary; oppressive; depressing; suffocating ❷（心情）不舒畅；（性格）不爽朗（of mood）depressed; in low spirits; (of temperament) not outgoing; withdrawn; introverted

【沉迷】chénmí（对某种事物）深深地迷恋 be infatuated with; be addicted to; indulge in; wallow in：～于跳舞 indulge in dancing

【沉绵】chénmián〈书 *fml.*〉疾病缠绵，经久不愈 be afflicted with a lingering illness; be tormented by severe illness：～不起 be bedridden because of severe illness|～枕席 be bedridden

【沉湎】chénmiǎn〈书 *fml.*〉沉溺 indulge in; wallow in; be given to; abandon oneself to sth.; allow oneself to be controlled by (a feeling, desire, etc.)：～酒色 be addicted to wine and women

【沉没】chénmò 没入水中 sink; founder：战舰触礁～。The warship collided into a reef and foundered. ◇落日～在远山后面。The setting sun sank behind the distant mountains.

【沉默】chénmò ❶ 不爱说笑 quiet; reticent：～寡言 taciturn ❷ 不说话 silent：他～了一会儿又继续说下去。He continued (speaking) after a pause.

【沉溺】chénnì 陷入不良的境地（多指生活习惯方面），不能自拔 be consumed with; wallow in (usu. referring to bad habits); be given to ill desires and whims：～于酒色 be addicted to wine and women

【沉潜】chénqián ❶ 在水里潜伏；沉没 lie hidden underwater; go to the bottom：这种鱼常～于水底。This species of fish often stays at the bottom of the water. ❷〈书 *fml.*〉思想感情深沉，不外露 reserved; unruffled; composed：～坚忍，处逆境而不馁。Composed and determined, he never feels disheartened in adversity. ❸ 集中精神；潜心 concentrate on; be devoted to：他～在研究工作中，废寝忘食。He's so devoted to the research work that he often sacrifices sleep and forgets to eat.

【沉睡】chénshuì 睡得很熟 be fast asleep; be in a sound sleep

【沉思】chénsī 深思 contemplate; ponder; meditate; muse：～良久 be lost in thought for a long time|敲门声打断了他的～。The knock on the door interrupted his contemplation.

【沉痛】chéntòng ❶ 深深的悲痛 deep grief; deep remorse：十分～的心情 be deeply grieved ❷ 深刻；严重 profound; severe; grave; bitter：应该接受这个～的教训。It is necessary to learn a lesson from this bitter and painful experience.

【沉稳】chénwěn ❶ 稳重 steady; staid; sedate; calm：举止～carry oneself in a steadfast way|这个人很～，考虑问题细密周到。Calm and steady, he is meticulous and thorough in handling all problems. ❷ 安稳 sound; untroubled: 睡得～ be fast asleep; be sound asleep

【沉陷】chénxiàn ❶ 地面或建筑物的基础陷下去 (of the ground or a foundation of a building) sink; cave in ❷ 深深地陷入 be lost in; be stranded: 车子～在泥泞中。The car was stuck in the mud. ◇老人～于往事的回忆中。The old man was lost in memories of the past.

C

【沉香】chénxiāng ❶ 常绿乔木,茎很高,叶子卵形或披针形,花白色。产于亚热带。木材质地坚硬而重,黄色,有香味,可入药。agalloch eaglewood (*Aquilaria agallocha*); tall evergreen tree, growing in subtropical zones, having oval or acicula leaves, white flowers, and yellow, fragrant and heavy, hard wood that can be used in medicine ❷ 这种植物的木材 wood of this tree; also 伽南香 qiénánxiāng or 奇南香 qí'nánxiāng

【沉箱】chénxiāng 一种在水底作业的设备,用金属或混凝土制成,形状像箱子,下面没有底。用时沉入水底,同时通入压缩空气将水排出,人在里面工作。caisson; bottomless trunk of metal or concrete for underwater operation; when sunk to the bottom of the water, compressed air is injected to squeeze water out so that a worker can stay in it and carry on work underwater

【沉雄】chénxióng (气势、风格)深沉而雄伟 (of bearing and style) serene and magnificent; calm and majestic: 字体～浑厚。The handwriting is unadorned and powerful. | 歌声～悲壮。The singing is solemn and moving.

【沉抑】chényì 低沉抑郁;沉郁 depressed; gloomy; in low spirits: 心情～ in low spirits | ～的曲调在深夜里显得分外凄凉。The depressing melody in the still of the night sounded all the more sorrowful.

【沉毅】chényì 沉着坚毅 steady and strong: 行动～ act steadily and resolutely

【沉吟】chényín ❶ 低声吟咏(文辞、诗句等) intone; recite (articles and poems) in a singing tone: ～章句 recite paragraphs and phrases in a low voice ❷ (遇到复杂或疑难的事)迟疑不决,低声自语 hesitate and mutter to oneself; be unable to make up one's mind (in the face of complications or difficulties): 他～半天,还是拿不定主意。He hesitated for a long time but still could not make up his mind.

【沉勇】chényǒng 沉着勇敢 composed and brave; calm and bold: 机智～ resourceful and brave

【沉鱼落雁】chén yú luò yàn《庄子·齐物论》:'毛嫱、丽姬,人之所美也;鱼见之深入,鸟见之高飞,麋鹿见之决骤,四者孰知天下之正色哉?'后来用'沉鱼落雁'形容女子容貌极美。*Zhuangzi·The Sorting Which Evens Things Out* said: 'Mao Qiang and Li Ji are beauties. At the sight of them, fish sink to the bottom of the sea, birds soar into the sky and elks and deer immediately flee. How do these four species of animals know the beauty in this human world?' Fish sinking and birds alighting, a description of the stunning beauty of a woman

【沉郁】chényù 低沉郁闷 depressed; downcast; gloomy: 心绪～ feel depressed; be in a gloomy mood

【沉冤】chényuān 难以辩白或久未昭雪的冤屈 gross injustice of long standing; unrighted wrong: ～莫白 suffer a grievous wrong that one does not know how to right

【沉渣】chénzhā 沉下去的渣滓 sediment; scum; dregs; 〈比喻 *fig.*〉残存下来的腐朽无用的事物 decayed, useless remains: ～泛起。The dregs rose to the surface.

【沉滞】chénzhì 〈书 *fml.*〉凝带 stagnant; heavy; low: 目光～ with a stagnant and heavy look in one's eyes

【沉重】chénzhòng 分量大;程度深 heavy; to a great extent: ～的脚步 heavy steps | 这担子很～。This burden is heavy. | 给敌人以～的打击 deal a heavy blow to the enemy | 他这两天的心情特别～。His mood has been especially gloomy and heavy in the past couple of days.

【沉住气】chén zhù qì 在情况紧急或感情激动时保持镇静 keep calm at a critical moment or at a moment of excitement; keep cool; be composed: 沉得住气 be able to hold oneself under control and keep cool | 沉不住气 be unsteady; easily flare up | 别慌,千万要～。Keep calm; don't lose your head.

【沉着】[1] chénzhuó 镇静;不慌不忙 cool-headed; composed; steady; calm: ～应战 meet an attack calmly; accept a challenge with calm and composure | 勇敢～ brave and steady

【沉着】[2] chénzhuó 非细胞性的物质(色素、钙质等)沉积在有机体的组织中 non-cell substances (pigment, calcium, etc.) accumulating in organic tissues

【沉醉】chénzuì 大醉,多用于比喻 (oft. fig.) be drunk; become intoxicated: ～在节日的欢乐里 be intoxicated with the joy of a festival

忱 chén 〈书 *fml.*〉情意 sincere feeling; true sentiment: 热～ zeal; warmth; enthusiasm | 谢～ gratitude; thanks | 略表微～。This is just to show my gratitude to you.

陈[1]**(陳)** chén ❶ 安放;摆设 lay out; put on display: ～列 display; exhibit | ～设 exhibit; display; set out ❷ 叙说 narrate; tell: ～述 explain; state | 另函详～。The matter will be explained in detail in a separate letter.

〈古 *arch.*〉 same as 阵 zhèn

陈[2]（陳） chén 时间久的；旧的 old；stale：～酒 old wine；mellow wine｜新～代谢 metabolism｜推～出新 weed through the old to bring forth the new

陈[3]（陳） Chén ❶ 周朝国名，在今河南淮阳一带 Chen，name of a kingdom in the Zhou Dynasty，situated around Huaiyang，Henan Province ❷ 南朝之一，公元557—589，陈霸先所建 Chen Dynasty（557-589），one of the Southern Dynasties founded by Chen Baxian；☞ 南北朝 Nán-Běi Cháo on p.1388 ❸ 姓 a surname

【陈兵】chénbīng 部署兵力 deploy troops；mass troops：～百万 deploy troops of a million soldiers

【陈陈相因】chén chén xiāng yīn《史记·平准书》：'太仓之粟，陈陈相因。'国都粮仓里的米谷，一年接一年地堆积起来。*Records of the Historian·Records on Price and Circulation Regulation* said：'Rice and grains in the state granaries keep piling up year after year.'〈比喻 *fig.*〉沿袭老一套，没有改进 follow a set routine；stay in the same old groove

【陈词滥调】chén cí làn diào 陈旧而不切合实际的话 obsolete expressions；hackneyed words；stereotyped expressions；clichés；platitude

【陈醋】chéncù 存放较久的醋，醋味醇厚 mature，well-aged vinegar；strong-flavoured，long-stored vinegar

【陈放】chénfàng 陈设；安放 set out；lay out；display；exhibit；place：样品～在展柜里。The samples are displayed in the showcase.

【陈腐】chénfǔ 陈旧腐朽 old and decayed；stale；worn-out；decadent：内容～ stale in content｜打破～的传统观念 smash decadent traditional values

【陈谷子烂芝麻】chén gǔ·zi làn zhī·ma〈比喻 *fig.*〉陈旧的无关紧要的话或事物 old and inessential words or things；stale topics of conversation：老太太爱唠叨，说的尽是些～。The old lady prattled on but there was no point in what she said.

【陈规】chénguī 已经不适用的规章制度；陈旧的规矩 outmoded conventions and practices：～陋习 outmoded regulations and irrational practices；bad customs and habits

【陈货】chénhuò 存放时间久的货物；过时的货物 old stock；shopworn goods

【陈迹】chénjì 过去的事情 thing of the past：历史～ historical record；historical site

【陈酒】chénjiǔ ❶ 存放多年的酒，酒味醇 liquor stored and aged for a long time；mellow wine ❷〈方 *dial.*〉黄酒 rice wine

【陈旧】chénjiù 旧的；过时的 old；outdated；obsolete；outmoded；unfashionable：设备虽然有点儿～，但还能使用。Although the equipment is a bit outdated，it still works.｜～的观念，应该抛弃。Outmoded notions should be abandoned.

【陈粮】chénliáng 上年余存的或存放多年的粮食 surplus grain from the previous year；grain in storage for years

【陈列】chénliè 把物品摆出来供人看 display；set out；exhibit：～品 exhibit｜商店～着许多新到的货物。Many new goods are on display in the store.

【陈年】chénnián 积存多年的 of long standing；preserved for a long time：～老酒 old vintage wine｜～老账 long-standing debt；old score

【陈酿】chénniàng same as 陈酒 chénjiǔ

【陈皮】chénpí 晒干了的橘子皮或橙子皮，可入药 dried tangerine or orange peel，used in medicine

【陈情】chénqíng 述说理由、意见等；陈诉衷情 give a full account；make a plea；explain：恳切～ make an earnest plea

【陈请】chénqǐng 向上级或有关部门陈述情况，提出请求 plead；petition；submit a report to one's superiors or relevant departments for consideration：～领导审定 report to one's superiors for approval

【陈绍】chénshào 存放多年的绍兴酒 Shaoxing rice wine preserved for years

【陈设】chénshè ❶ 摆设 display；set out：屋里～着新式家具。The room is furnished in the latest fashion. ❷ 摆设的东西 furnishing：房间里的一切～都很简单朴素。The furnishings in the room are all simple and basic.

【陈胜吴广起义】Chén Shèng Wú Guǎng Qǐyì 我国历史上第一次大规模农民起义。公元前209年，贫苦农民陈胜、吴广率戍卒九百人在蕲县大泽乡（今安徽宿县东南）起义，迅速得到全国的响应。起义军建立了自己的政权，国号张楚。这次起义导致秦王朝的灭亡。Chen Sheng-Wu Guang Uprising，the first large-scale peasant uprising in China's history. In 209 B.C.，two poor peasants，Chen Sheng and Wu Guang，led 900 border soldiers in a revolt in Dazexiang（southeast of present-day Suxian County，Anhui Province）. They were quickly echoed by people across the country，and founded their own regime under the title of Zhangchu. The uprising led to the fall of Qin Dynasty. also 大泽乡起义 Dàzéxiāng Qǐyì

【陈世美】Chén Shìměi 戏曲《铡美案》中的人物，考中状元后喜新厌旧，被招为驸马而抛弃结发妻子，后被包公处死。用来指地位提高而变心的丈夫，也泛指在情爱上见异思迁的男子。Chen Shimei，a notorious character in the traditional Chinese opera *The Beheading of an Ungrateful Husband*. Chen，after coming first in the imperial examination，abandons his wife and marries a princess，for which he is later beheaded by Lord Bao. The name Chen Shimei thus becomes a derisive title for a man who abandons his wife after successfully climbing the social ladder, and generally also for men who desert their old loves in favour of new romances.

【陈述】chénshù 有条有理地说出 enunciate; declare in a systematic way:～理由 give (one's) reasons; reason things out|～意见 state one's opinions

【陈述句】chénshùjù 述说一件事情的句子(区别于'疑问句、祈使句、感叹句'),如:'这是一部词典。''今年年成很好。'在书面上,陈述句后面用句号。declarative sentence; sentence declaring a fact (as compared with an interrogative sentence, imperative sentence or explanatory sentence). For example, 'This is a dictionary.' 'There has been a good harvest this year.' In written form, a declarative sentence ends with a period.

【陈说】chénshuō same as 陈述 chénshù:～利害 state the advantages and disadvantages|～事件的经过 recount the whole course of an incident

【陈诉】chénsù 诉说(痛苦或委屈) pour out (pain or grievances):～冤情 pour out one's grievances

【陈套】chéntào 陈旧的格式或办法 out-of-date form, style or method:这幅画构思新颖,不落～。This painting has a novel conception that conforms to no conventional pattern.

【陈言】[1] chényán 陈述理由、意见等 speak out; give reasons, opinions, etc.:率直～ state one's opinions in an unreserved, candid fashion

【陈言】[2] chényán〈书 *fml.*〉陈旧的话 hackneyed words and expressions:～务去。Hackneyed words and expressions should be avoided.

【陈账】chénzhàng 老账 old debts; longstanding debts:这些事都是多年～,不必提了。All this happened years ago, there's no need to bring it up now.

宸 chén ❶〈书 *fml.*〉屋宇;深邃的房屋 house or mansion; tall, palatial residence ❷ 封建时代指帝王住的地方,引申为王位、帝王的代称 emperor's residence during the feudal era; later extended to become a synonym of throne or emperor:～章(帝王写的文章) article written by an emperor|～衷(帝王的心意) the emperor's wishes

【宸垣】chényuán〈书 *fml.*〉京师 capital city of a country

梣 chén 小叶白蜡树 bunge ash (*Fraxinus bungeana*)

晨 chén 早晨,有时也泛指半夜以后到中午以前的一段时间 morning, sometimes also referring to the period between midnight and noon:清～ early morning|凌～五时 five o'clock in the morning

【晨炊】chénchuī 早晨烧火做饭 light a fire to cook breakfast

【晨光】chénguāng 清晨的太阳光 morning sunlight:～熹微 the first (faint) rays of dawn

【晨昏】chénhūn〈书 *fml.*〉早晨和晚上 morning and evening:～定省(早晨和晚上服侍问候双亲) respectful greeting to parents in the morning and in the evening

【晨练】chénliàn 在早晨进行的练习或锻炼 do morning exercises:参加～的老人,有的做气功,有的打太极拳。Among the seniors that do morning exercises, some practice *qigong* (breathing exercises), and others *taijiquan* (shadow boxing).

【晨曦】chénxī same as 晨光 chénguāng

【晨星】chénxīng ❶ 清晨稀疏的星 early morning stars that are few and far between:寥若～as scarce as morning stars ❷ 天文学上指日出以前出现在东方的金星或水星 Venus or Mercury appearing over the eastern horizon before dawn

【晨钟暮鼓】chén zhōng mù gǔ ☞ 暮鼓晨钟 mù gǔ chén zhōng on p. 1380

谌(❶訦) chén ❶〈书 *fml.*〉相信 believe ❷〈书 *fml.*〉的确;诚然 indeed, honestly ❸ (Chén,也有读 also pronounced Shèn)姓 a surname

鸩 chén〈方 *dial.*〉(～儿 chénr)小鸟 little bird

chěn (ㄔㄣˇ)

墋(墋) chěn ❶ same as 碜 chěn ❷〈书 *fml.*〉混浊 muddy; turbid:～黩(混浊不清) muddy; turbid; unclean

趻 chěn [趻踔](chěnchuō)〈书 *fml.*〉跳跃 bound; jump; leap

碜[1](磣、硶) chěn 食物中杂有沙子 gritty food; ☞ 牙碜 yá·chen on p. 2194

碜[2](磣、頳) chěn 丑;难看 ugly; unpleasant to the eye; unpleasant to look at

踸 chěn [踸踔](chěnchuō) same as 趻踔 chěnchuō

chèn (ㄔㄣˋ)

衬(襯) chèn ❶ 在里面托上一层 put a lining inside sth.:～上一层纸 mount sth. on a piece of paper ❷ 衬在里面的 material put inside sth.:～布 lining cloth|～衫 shirt; blouse|～裤 underpants; pants ❸ (～儿 chènr)附在衣裳、鞋、帽等某一部分的里面的布制品 lining; cotton cloth attached to the inside of certain parts of clothes, shoes, hats, etc.:帽～儿 cap lining|袖～儿 cuff lining ❹ 陪衬;衬托 serve as a contrast to; set off; serve as a foil to：绿叶把红花～得更好看了。The red flowers look even more beautiful against green leaves.

【衬布】chènbù 缝制服装时衬在衣领、两肩或裤腰等部分的布 cloth lining; cloth sewed to the inside of collars, shoulders of coats, or waists of trousers

【衬裤】chènkù 穿在里面的单裤 underpants; pants

【衬里】chènlǐ 服装的里子或衬料 lining

【衬料】chènliào 衬在服装面子和里子中间的用料 lining mass; cloth sewn between the outer and the inner fabric of a costume

【衬领】chènlǐng 扣在外衣领子里面的领子，可随时摘下来洗涤 removable collar affixed to the inside of the collar of a coat for ease of washing; also 护领 hùlǐng

【衬裙】chènqún 穿在裙子或旗袍里面的裙子 underskirt; petticoat; skirt worn beneath another skirt or Chinese cheongsam

【衬衫】chènshān 穿在里面的西式单上衣 shirt; blouse; Western-style, unlined inner clothes

【衬托】chèntuō 为了使事物的特色突出，用另一些事物放在一起来陪衬或对照 set off; make sth. stand out by putting it with sth. else for contrast

【衬衣】chènyī 通常穿在里面的单衣 shirt; blouse; unlined inner clothes

【衬字】chènzì 曲子在曲律规定字以外，为了行文或歌唱的需要而增加的字。例如《白毛女》：'北风(那个)吹，雪花(那个)飘'。括弧内的'那个'就是衬字。extra word; word inserted in a line of verse for the purpose of balance and euphony, such as the lines from the Chinese opera *The White-Haired Girl*: 'The wind is (that) blowing. *or* The snow is (that) flying.' 'That' in brackets is an extra word.

疢 chèn〈书 *fml.*〉病 sick; ill：～疾 disease; sickness; illness

龀 chèn〈书 *fml.*〉小孩子换牙(乳牙脱落，长出恒牙) (of a child) grow permanent teeth (milk teeth fall out and permanent teeth grow)

称(稱) chèn 适合；相当 fit; match; suit：～体 fit sb. or sth. well｜～心 be satisfied; be gratified｜对～ symmetry｜匀～ proportional; well-proportioned

☞ chēng on p. 242 and 秤 chèng on p. 254

【称钱】chèn//qián same as 趁钱 chèn//qián

【称身】chèn//shēn (衣服)合身 (of a garment) fit; body-hugging

【称体裁衣】chèn tǐ cái yī 量体裁衣 cut a garment according to the wearer's figure; act in light of actual circumstances

【称心】chèn//xīn 符合心愿；心满意足 (of things) turning out the way one wants; to one's heart's content; be content with：～如意 after one's own heart; to one's heart's content

【称愿】chèn//yuàn 满足愿望(多指对所恨的人遭遇不幸而感觉快意 usu. at a time when misfortune befalls a rival) feel gratified

【称职】chènzhí 思想水平和工作能力都能胜任所担任的职务 be well qualified for a post; able; prove to be competent at one's job, as regards mentality and capability

傢(儭、䞋) chèn〈旧时 *old*〉布施僧道 give alms to monks or Taoists：～钱 give money as alms

趁(趂) chèn ❶ 利用(时间、机会) take advantage of (time, opportunity, etc.)：～热打铁 strike while the iron is hot｜～风起帆 set sail while the wind is fair ❷〈方 *dial.*〉富有；拥有 rich; possess：～钱 have pots of money; be very rich｜～几头牲口 own a few head of cattle ❸〈书 *fml.*〉追逐；赶 pursue; track down; run after; catch up with; overtake

【趁便】chèn//biàn 顺便 by the way; at one's convenience; when it is convenient：你回家的时候，～给我带个口信。Would you please deliver a message for me when you arrive home?

【趁火打劫】chèn huǒ dǎ jié 趁人家失火的时候去抢人家的东西 rob the owner while his house is on fire; loot a burning house;〈比喻 *fig.*〉趁紧张危急的时候侵犯别人的权益 profit by sb. else's misfortune

【趁机】chènjī 利用机会 seize the chance; take advantage of the opportunity：～溜走 seize the chance and sneak away

【趁钱】chèn//qián〈方 *dial.*〉有钱 have lots of money：很趁几个钱儿 have a fortune; also 称钱 chèn//qián

【趁热打铁】chèn rè dǎ tiě〈比喻 *fig.*〉做事抓紧时机，加速进行 strike while the iron is hot; seize the chance and lose no time to get things done

【趁墒】chènshāng 趁着土壤里有足够水分的时候播种 sow while there is sufficient moisture in the soil

【趁势】chènshì 利用有利的形势；就势 ride the tide of; take advantage of a favourable situation; take the chance; seize the moment：他越过对方后卫，～把球踢入球门。He dribbled past the fullback, and seizing his chance, scored a goal.

【趁手】chènshǒu〈方 *dial.*〉随手 at hand; at one's convenience：走进屋～把门关上。Please close the door on your way in.

【趁早】chènzǎo (～儿 chènzǎor) 抓紧时机或提前时间(采取行动) as soon as possible; before it is too late; seize a chance or take action ahead of time：～动身 start off as early as possible｜～罢手 stop doing sth. before it is too late

榇(櫬) chèn 〈书 *fml.*〉棺材 coffin

谶 chèn 迷信的人指将来要应验的预言、预兆 portent; premonitory sign; prediction or omen a superstitious person believes will come true in the future:～语 prophecy

【谶纬】chènwěi 谶和纬。谶是秦汉间巫师、方士编造的预示吉凶的隐语,纬是汉代神学迷信附会儒家经义的一类书。谶 chèn, mystical words fabricated by sorcerers and alchemists to predict good or bad luck in Qin and Han dynasties; 纬 wěi, books on Han-dynasty theology and superstitions said to be derived from Confucian doctrines:～之学 divination combined with mystical Confucian belief

【谶语】chènyǔ 迷信的人指事后应验的话 prophecy that a superstitious person believes will come true

·chen (·ㄔㄣ)

伧(傖) ·chen ☞ 寒伧 hán·chen on p. 763
☞ cāng on p. 189

chēng (ㄔㄥ)

柽(檉) chēng [柽柳](chēngliǔ)落叶小乔木,老枝红色,叶子像鳞片,夏秋两季开花,花淡红色,结蒴果。能耐碱抗旱,适于造防沙林。Chinese tamarisk (*Tamarix chinensis*); deciduous tree with red sprigs and scale-like leaves that blossom twice a year, in summer and autumn, whose pink blossoms turn into capsules; alkali-and drought-resistant and therefore suitable for afforestation against encroachment of a desert. Also called 三春柳 sānchūnliǔ 或 or 红柳 hóngliǔ

琤 chēng ☞ below

【琤琤】chēngchēng 〈书 *fml.*〉〈拟声词 *onom.*〉形容玉器相击声、琴声或水流声 jangling of jade, twangling of string instrument, or gurgling of flowing water

【琤𪸩】chēngcōng 〈书 *fml.*〉〈拟声词 *onom.*〉形容玉器相击声或水流声 jangling of jade or gurgling of flowing water:玉佩～jangling of jade ornaments | ～的溪流 a creek flowing with a rich susurrus

称¹(稱) chēng ❶ 叫;叫做 call, name as:自～call oneself; self-styled as | 他足智多谋,人～智多星。Intelligent and resourceful, he is known as a wizard. | 队员都亲切地～他为老队长。He is affectionately called 'Old Team Leader' by fellow team members. ❷ 名称 name; title:简～abbreviation | 俗～ popular name ❸ 说 say; speak:～快 express one's joy, gratification or jubilation | ～便 find sth. a great convenience; convenient | 连声～好 repeatedly hail sth. ❹〈书 *fml.*〉赞扬 commend; praise:～叹 sigh with admiration | ～赏 praise; speak highly of | ～许 praise; commendation

称²(稱) chēng 测定重量 weigh:把这袋米～一～。Please weigh this bag of rice.

称³(稱) chēng 〈书 *fml.*〉举 raise:～觞祝寿 raise a wine cup in a toast to celebrate one's birthday
☞ chèn on p. 241 and 秤 chèng on p. 254

【称霸】chēngbà 倚仗权势,欺压别人 lord it over; control others by power and force; dominate by force:～一方 ride roughshod over an area

【称便】chēngbiàn 认为方便 find sth. a great convenience:公园增设了快餐部,游客无不～。All visitors to the park consider the newly established fast food restaurant to be a great convenience.

【称兵】chēngbīng 〈书 *fml.*〉采取军事行动 launch a military attack; take military action

【称病】chēngbìng 以生病为借口 call in sick; use illness as an excuse; plead illness:～不出 claim to be ill and stay at home; stay at home on the pretext of illness | ～辞职 resign on the ground of poor health

【称臣】chēngchén 自称臣子,向对方屈服,接受统治 declare oneself a vassal or subject; pledge allegiance to a ruler:俯首～bow one's head in submission and declare oneself a subject

【称大】chēng//dà 显示自己的尊长地位;摆架子 show off one's status or rank; put on airs:他从不在晚辈面前～。He never pulls rank on those of the younger generation.

【称贷】chēngdài 向别人借钱 borrow money from others; incur a debt; ask for a loan

【称道】chēngdào 称述;称赞 speak approvingly of; praise; acclaim:人人～ be widely acclaimed | 这是我应尽的责任,不值得～。This is my responsibility and not a matter for praise.

【称孤道寡】chēng gū dào guǎ 〈比喻 *fig.*〉妄以首脑自居(古代君主自称'孤'或'寡人') address oneself as king; act like a monarch (Chinese monarchs of yore called themselves 'gū' or 'guǎrén')

【称号】chēnghào 赋予某人、某单位或某事物的名称(多用于光荣的 mostly as an honour) honorary title; title conferred on a person, work unit or event:荣获先进工作者～ be awarded the title of advanced worker

【称贺】chēnghè 道贺 congratulate:登门～ go to sb.'s house to offer one's congratulations

【称呼】chēng·hu ❶ 叫 call; address: 你说我该怎么～她? ～大婶行吗? How should I address her? Is it all right to call her aunt? ❸ 当面招呼用的表示彼此关系的名称,如同志、哥哥等 term of address, such as comrade, brother, etc.

【称快】chēngkuài 表示快意 express one's gratification, joy or jubilation: 拍手～ clap hands in glee; clap and cheer; clap one's hands for joy

【称奇】chēngqí 称赞奇妙 express wonder: 啧啧～ exclaim in surprise

【称赏】chēngshǎng 称赞赏识 extol; speak highly of: 老师对他的作文很是～。The teacher spoke highly of his composition.

【称述】chēngshù 述说 relate; narrate; state: 晚会节目很多,无法一一～。The evening party included many events, so I will mention just a few.

【称说】chēngshuō 说话的时候叫出事物的名字 mention names of things during course of conversation: 他～着这些产品,如数家珍。He names these products as if he were enumerating his family valuables.

【称颂】chēngsòng 称赞颂扬 extol; praise; eulogize: ～民族英雄 eulogize national heroes | 丰功伟绩,万民～。All the people extol his great achievements and contributions.

【称叹】chēngtàn 赞叹 praise: 连声～ express adimiration repeatedly

【称谓】chēngwèi 人们由于亲属和别的方面的相互关系,以及身份、职业等而得来的名称,如父亲、师傅、厂长等 term of address; title that indicates relationship, status, or occupation, such as father, master, director, etc.

【称羡】chēngxiàn 称赞羡慕 praise with admiration; envy: 他们夫妻和睦,令人～。The couple lives an enviably harmonious life.

【称谢】chēngxiè 道谢 express one's gratitude; thank

【称兄道弟】chēng xiōng dào dì 朋友间以兄弟相称,表示关系亲密 friends that call each other brother to indicate intimacy; brother sb.

【称雄】chēngxióng 凭借武力或特殊势力统治一方 dominate; rule a region with military forces or special clout: 割据～ practise warlordism; establish a separatist regime and tear the country apart

【称许】chēngxǔ 赞许 praise; commend: 他做生意童叟无欺,深受群众～。He was highly commended for his honesty and fairness in business dealings.

【称扬】chēngyáng 称赞;赞扬 praise; commend: 交口～ praise unanimously; be held in public esteem; be praised by one and all

【称引】chēngyǐn 〈书 *fml*.〉引证;援引(言语、事例) quote or cite as proof or evidence; reference; quotation; cite (words, examples, etc.); quote

【称誉】chēngyù same as 称赞 chēngzàn: 这部影片高超的拍摄技巧,为人们所～。The film was highly acclaimed for its superb cinematography.

【称赞】chēngzàn 用言语表达对人或事物的优点的喜爱 praise; use language to express one's fondness for sb. or sth.: 他做了好事,受到老师的～。His good deed earned him the teacher's praise.

蛏(蟶) chēng 蛏子 razor clam: ～田 field for raising razor clams | ～干 dried razor clam meat

【蛏干】chēnggān 干的蛏子肉 dried razor clam meat

【蛏田】chēngtián 福建、广东一带海滨养蛏类的田 razor clam raising farms along the Fujian and Guangdong coasts

【蛏子】chēng·zi 软体动物,有两扇形状狭长的介壳。生活在近岸的海水里。肉可以吃。razor clam(*Solenidae*); a kind of seawater mollusc that lives near the coast, with a long rectangular shell in two parts enclosing edible flesh

铛(鐺) chēng 烙饼用的平底锅 pan; pot with a level bottom used to bake unleavened pancake: 饼～ baking pan

☞ dāng on p. 386

偁 chēng 〈书 *fml*.〉same as 称[1] chēng

橕 chēng 〈书 *fml*.〉same as 撑 chēng

☞ chèng on p. 255

赪(赬) chēng 〈书 *fml*.〉红色 red

撑(撐) chēng ❶ 抵住 prop up; support: 两手～着下巴沉思 be lost in a reverie with one's chin on both hands ❷ 用篙抵住河底使船行进 punt; move a boat forward by setting bamboo pole against the bottom of a river and pushing: ～船 punt a boat; move a boat with a pole ❸ 支持 maintain; support: 说得他自己也～不住,笑了。He couldn't help laughing in the middle of a remark he was making. ❹ 张开 open, unfurl: ～伞 open an umbrella | 把麻袋的口儿～开 hold open a sack ❺ 充满到容不下的程度 fill to the point of overflowing: 少吃点,别～着。Don't eat so much, otherwise you'll be bursting at the seams. | 装得连口袋都～破了。The sack was stuffed so full that it burst open.

【撑场面】chēng chǎngmiàn 维持表面的排场 maintain an appearance; keep up appearances; also 撑门面 chēng mén·mian

【撑持】chēngchí 勉强支持 barely able to prop up, support or sustain: ～危局 shore up a shaky situation

【撑杆跳高】chēnggān tiàogāo 田径运动项目之一。运动员双手握住一根杆子,经过快速的助跑后，借助杆子反弹的力量，使身体腾起，跃过横杆。pole vault; pole jump, a field sporting event in which a competitor carries a pole in both hands, sprints a short distance, sets the pole down and propels himself over a high bar through the pole's recoil force

【撑门面】chēng mén·mian also 撑场面 chēng chǎng·mian

【撑死】chēngsǐ 〈方 *dial.*〉表示最大的限度；至多 maximum; at the most; no more than：这手表～值十块钱。This watch is worth ten dollars at the most. | 他的文化水平～也就小学毕业。Primary school was as far his education advanced.

【撑腰】chēng//yāo 〈比喻 *fig.*〉给予有力的支持 give strong support to; back up; bolster up：～打气 give support to and encourage sb. | 有群众～，你大胆干吧！Having the backing of the masses, go ahead and do it!

噌 chēng [噌吰](chēnghóng)〈书 *fml.*〉形容钟鼓的声音 sound of a bell or a drum ☞ cēng on p. 198

瞠 chēng 〈书 *fml.*〉瞪着眼看 stare

【瞠乎其后】chēng hū qí hòu 在后面干瞪眼，赶不上 gaze at helplessly from behind, being unable to catch up to

【瞠目】chēngmù 〈书 *fml.*〉眼直直地瞪着，形容受窘、惊恐的样子 eyes fixed on sth. in embarrassment, panic, etc.：～以对 stare at each other | ～相视 look at each other goggle-eyed

【瞠目结舌】chēng mù jié shé 瞪着眼睛说不出话来，形容受窘或惊呆的样子 stupefaction; stare with eyes wide open but unable to utter a word; stare tongue-tied; be dumbfounded (usu. in embarrassment, panic, etc.)

chéng (ㄔㄥˊ)

成[1] chéng ❶ 完成；成功（跟'败'相对 as opposed to 'defeat, failure'）finish; succeed; accomplish：大功告～。The great mission has been accomplished. | 事情～了。It's done. ❷ 成全 help sb. achieve sth.：～人之美 kindly help sb. achieve sth. | 玉～其事 kindly help sb. attain a worthy goal; assist sb. in accomplishing a task ❸ 成为；变为 become; turn into：百炼～钢。Constant smelting turns iron into steel. | 雪化～水。The snow thawed and became water. ❹ 成果；成就 result; yield; achievement：坐享其～ reap where one has not sown; do nothing and enjoy the results achieved by others | 一事无～ be a complete failure; accomplish nothing ❺ 生物生长到定形、成熟的阶段 maturing phase of a creature：～虫 mature worm | ～人 adult; grownup ❻ 已定的；定形的；现成的 established; finalized; existing：～规 established practice; set rules | ～见 prejudice; bias | ～例 common practice | ～药 ready-to-take, patent medicine ❼ 表示达到一个单位（强调数量多或时间长）reaching certain degree (in considerable numbers or amounts)：～批生产 batched production; mass production | ～千～万 tens of thousands | ～年累月 for months and years; year in and year out ❽ 表示答应、许可 agree; approve：～！就这么办吧。Good! Let's do it this way! ❾ 表示有能力 able; capable：他可真～！什么都难不住他。He's so capable! Nothing can stop him. ❿ (Chéng) 姓 a surname

成[2] chéng (～儿 chéngr) 十分之一叫一成 one tenth; one out of ten：九～金 gold with a rate of purity of 90 per cent | 村里今年收的庄稼比去年增加两～。This year's village harvest was 20 per cent higher than last.

【成败】chéngbài 成功或失败 make or break; success or failure：～利钝 success or failure, going smoothly or not | ～在此一举。Success or failure hinges on this one action.

【成本】chéngběn 生产一种产品所需的全部费用 total cost to manufacture a product：～核算 cost accounting

【成本会计】chéngběn kuàijì 为了求得产品的总成本和单位成本而核算全部生产费用的会计 accountant who calculates net production costs in order to assess total and unit costs

【成才】chéngcái 成为有才能的人 emerge as a talent：自学～ amount to sth. by self-education | ～之路 the road to accomplishment

【成材】chéngcái 可以做材料 grow into useful timber;〈比喻 *fig.*〉成为有才能的人 grow up to be a talented person：树要修剪才能长得直，孩子不教育怎能～呢？A tree needs pruning in order to grow straight, so how can a child grow up to be a competent person without guidance?

【成材林】chéngcáilín 已经长成，能够供应木料的树林 full-grown trees ready for felling; standing timber; mature timber

【成虫】chéngchóng 发育成熟能繁殖后代的昆虫，例如蚕蛾是蚕的成虫，蚊子是孑孓的成虫 imago; insect at a sexually mature stage after metamorphosis, such as a silkworm that has matured into a silk moth, and a wiggler that has become a mosquito

【成法】chéngfǎ ❶ 已经制定的法规 established laws：恪守祖宗～ abide by the rules established by one's ancestors ❷ 现成的方法 existing methods：经济改革没有～可循，要因时因地制宜。Since there are no established methods, it is imperative to reform the economy according to the actual situation.

【成方】chéngfāng (～儿 chéngfāngr) 现成的药方（区别于医生诊病后所开的药方 as compared with prescription written by a doctor after clinical examination) set prescription

【成分】chéng·fèn ❶ 指构成事物的各种不同的物质或因素 composition; element; ingredients or elements that constitute an object or a thing: 化学～chemical composition | 营养～nutritious ingredients | 减轻了心里不安的～alleviate one's restlessness ❷ 指个人早先的主要经历或职业 identity; status; main experiences or occupation of a person in the past: 工人～identified as a worker | 他的个人～是学生。His identity is student. also 成份 chéng·fèn

【成份】chéng·fèn same as 成分 chéng·fèn

【成风】chéngfēng 形成风气 become common practice; become the order of the day; come into vogue: 蔚然～become the latest fashion

【成服】chéngfú ❶ 旧俗丧礼中死者的亲属穿上丧服叫做成服 bereaved relatives putting on mourning clothes for a funeral service: 遵礼～put on mourning clothes according to rites ❷ 制成后出售的服装 ready-made clothes: 该厂年生产～12 万件。The factory produces 120,000 pieces of ready-to-wear clothing annually.

【成个儿】chénggèr ❶ 生物长到跟成熟时大小相近的程度 (of things) more or less full-grown; grow to a good size: 果子已经～了。The fruit has grown to a good size. ❷〈比喻 *fig.*〉具备一定的形状 be well shaped; be in the proper form: 字写得不～。His handwriting lacks proper form.

【成功】chénggōng 获得预期的结果(跟'失败'相对 as opposed to 'fail') succeed; boffo; achieve the desired or hoped-for results: 试验～了。The experiment was successful. | 大会开得很～。The conference was a great success. | 大家都希望这项革新得到～。Everyone wishes this innovation great success.

【成规】chéngguī 现成的或久已通行的规则、方法 set rules; groove; rut; regulations or methods already established or in force for a long time: 打破～eschew the beaten tracks

【成果】chéngguǒ 工作或事业的收获 achievement in one's career; positive result: 丰硕～great success; substantial achievements | 劳动～the fruits of labour

【成化】Chénghuà 明宪宗(朱见深)年号(公元1465—1487) title of the reign (1465-1487) of Emperor Xianzong or Zhu Jianshen of Ming Dynasty

【成婚】chénghūn 结婚 get married; marry

【成活】chénghuó 培养的动植物没有在初生或种植后的短时期内死去 survive; young animals and plants that survive after birth or after being planted: ～率 survival rate | 树苗～的关键是吸收到充足的水分。The key to the saplings' survival is adequate moisture absorption.

【成绩】chéngjì 工作或学习的收获 fruits of work or study: 学习～study grade; mark | ～优秀 excellent marks | 我们各方面的工作都有很大的～。We have made great achievements in all aspects of our work.

【成家】[1] chéng//jiā (男子)结婚 (of a man) get married: ～立业 get married and embark on a career | 几个姐姐都出嫁了,哥哥也成了家。My elder sisters got married, and so did my elder brother.

【成家】[2] chéng//jiā 成为专家 become a specialist or expert: 成名～establish one's reputation as an authority in one's field

【成家立业】chéng jiā lì yè 指结了婚,有了一定的职业或建立某项事业 get married and have a successful career

【成见】chéngjiàn ❶ 对人或事物所抱的固定不变的看法(多指不好的 usu. unfavourable) fix; obsessive preoccupation; unchanged opinions about certain people or things: 消除～dispel prejudices | 不要存～。Don't harbour a prejudice ❷ 形成的个人见解;定见 personal opinions; preconceived idea: 对每个人的优点、缺点,她心里都有个～。She has a personal opinion on everyone's strength and weakness.

【成交】chéng//jiāo 交易成功;买卖做成 strike a bargain; conclude a transaction; clinch a deal: 拍板～strike a bargain | 展销会上～了上万宗生意。Nearly 10,000 deals were made at the fair.

【成就】chéngjiù ❶ 事业上的成绩 achievements in one's career; accomplishment; attainment: ～辉煌 glorious achievement | 巨大的～great achievement ❷ 完成(多指事业 of an undertaking) accomplish: ～革命大业 accomplish a great revolutionary task

【成句】chéngjù 前人用过的现成文句 sentence or aphorism created by predecessors: '东风压倒西风'不过是古人的～罢了。'The east wind prevails over the west' is an aphorism handed down from ancients.

【成立】chénglì ❶ (组织、机构等)筹备成功,开始存在 (of an organization, institution, etc.) start to exist as a result of good preparation: 1949 年 10 月 1 日,中华人民共和国～。The People's Republic of China was founded on October 1, 1949. ❷ (理论、意见)有根据,站得住 (of a theory or view) hold water; be tenable; hold ground; be well grounded: 这个论点理由很充分,能～。The ample arguments contained in this thesis make it tenable.

【成例】chénglì 现成的例子、办法等 ready example, method, etc.: 援引～cite a precedent; explain by way of examples | 他不愿意模仿已有的～。He was not prepared to follow stereotypes.

【成殓】chéngliàn 入殓 put the remains of a dead person in a coffin

【成龙配套】chéng lóng pèi tào 配搭起来，成为完整的系统 link up the parts to form a whole：该产品的生产、销售、维修已经～。A complete manufacturing, sales and maintenance chain for the product has taken shape. also 配套成龙 pèi tào chéng lóng

【成寐】chéngmèi〈书 *fml.*〉入睡；成眠 fall asleep; go to sleep：难以～ have difficulty falling asleep|夜不～ lie awake all night

【成眠】chéngmián 入睡；睡着（zháo）fall asleep; go to sleep

【成名】chéng//míng 因某种成就而有了名声 come to fame; make a name for oneself; become famous through a certain achievement; earn fame by virtue of achievements：一举～ make a name for oneself overnight; become famous overnight

【成命】chéngmìng 指已发布的命令、决定等 order, decision, etc. already issued：收回～ counter or retract an order; revoke a command

【成年】[1] chéngnián 指人发育到已经成熟的年龄，也指高等动物或树木发育到已经长成的时期 (of a person) come of age ; (of a higher animal or a tree) reach maturity：～人 grown-up; adult|～树 full-grown tree

【成年】[2] chéngnián 整年 whole year; all year round：～累月 all year round; year in, year out|～在外奔忙 work away from home all year around

【成年累月】chéng nián lěi yuè 形容历时长久 months and years; long period of time：他～在田里劳作，非常辛苦。He toiled in the field for years on end.

【成品】chéngpǐn 加工完毕，可以向外供应的产品 finished product; end product

【成气候】chéng qìhòu〈比喻 *fig.*〉有成就或有发展前途(多用于否定式 usu. in a negative) be hopeful of prospective developments：不～ fail to amount to anything|成不了什么气候 get nowhere

【成器】chéngqì〈比喻 *fig.*〉成为有用的人 amount to sth.; grow up to be a useful person; be successful：孩子～是父母的最大安慰。A successful child is the greatest comfort to the parents.

【成千成万】chéng qiān chéng wàn 形容数量非常多 tens of thousands; thousands upon thousands; large quantity; also 成千累万 chéng qiān lěi wàn and 成千上万 chéng qiān shàng wàn

【成亲】chéng//qīn 结婚的俗称 common term for getting married

【成趣】chéngqù 使人感到兴趣；有意味 intriguing; interesting; fascinating：湖光塔影，相映～。The splendour of the lake and the reflection of the pagoda in it make an interesting contrast. |信手拈来，涉笔～。Whatever issues from his pen becomes an interesting piece of writing.

【成全】chéngquán 帮助人，使达到目的 help sb. attain his or her goal：～好事 help sb. fulfil his wish; aid sb. in doing a good deed

【成人】chéng//rén 人发育成熟 (of human beings) grown up; mature：长大～ grow up

【成人】chéngrén 成年的人 grown-up; adult：～教育 adult education|孩子怎能同～比？How can a child compare with an adult?

【成人教育】chéngrén jiàoyù 通过职工学校、夜大学、广播电视学校、函授学校等对成年人进行的教育 adult education; adults attending a vocational college or night school, or take radio, television or correspondence courses

【成人之美】chéng rén zhī měi 成全人家的好事 help sb. attain a goal; help sb. fulfil a wish; aid sb. in doing a good deed

【成仁】chéngrén ☞ 杀身成仁 shā shēn chéng rén on p. 1663

【成日】chéngrì 整天 whole day; all day long：～无所事事 be idle all day long

【成色】chéngsè ❶ 金币、银币或器物中所含纯金、纯银的量 percentage of pure gold and silver in a gold and silver coin or gold and silver object; relative purity of gold or silver：这对镯子的～好。This pair of bracelets contains a high percentage of gold. ❷ 泛指质量 (in a broad sense) quality：茶的～好，味也清香。The quality of the tea is good, so it has a fine flavour.

【成事】chéng//shì 办成事情；成功 accomplish sth.; succeed：～之后，定当重谢。When you have got it done I'll show my appreciation by giving you a big award. |一味蛮干，成不了事。We're bound to fail if we persist in acting foolishly.

【成事】chéngshì〈书 *fml.*〉已经过去的事情 bygone events; thing that is past or finished：～不说。Don't mention the past.

【成事不足，败事有余】chéng shì bù zú, bài shì yǒu yú 指人办事极其无能 unable to accomplish anything but likely to spoil everything; never able to achieve anything but always capable of ruin; never make, but always break

【成书】chéngshū ❶ 写成书 be published in book form：《本草纲目》～于明代。*Compendium of Materia Medica* was first published in Ming Dynasty. ❷ 已流传的书 book in circulation

【成熟】chéngshú ❶ 植物的果实等完全长成，泛指生物体发育到完备的阶段 (of fruit) be ripe; (in a broad sense) (of creatures) mature; grow to maturity ❷ 发展到完善的程度 develop to perfection：我的意见还不～。My opinions are not yet well considered. |条件～了。Conditions were ripe.

【成数】[1] chéngshù 不带零头的整数，如五十、二百、三千等 round numbers, such as 50, 200, 3,000, etc.

【成数】[2] chéngshù 一数为另一数的几成，泛指比率 rate; percentage; ratio; figure showing the number of times one quantity contains another：应在生产组内找标准劳动力，互相比较，评～。We should find the standard labour force within the production group and obtain a ratio through comparison.

【成说】chéngshuō ❶ 现成的通行的说法 accepted theory or formulation：研究学问，不能囿于～。In scientific research, one should not be fettered by accepted theories. ❷〈书 *fml.*〉已有的约定；成议 agreement already set; accord：业有～。We have already reached an agreement.

【成算】chéngsuàn 早已做好的打算 premeditation; preconceived idea or plan：心有～，遇事从容 be at ease no matter what happens because one has worked out a plan

【成套】chéng//tào 配合起来成为一整套 complement each other to form a complete set：～设备 a complete set of equipment

【成天】chéngtiān 整天 all day long; all the time：～忙碌 be kept busy all day long

【成为】chéngwéi 变成 become; turn into：～先进工作者 become a model worker

【成文】chéngwén ❶ 现成的文章 ready-made article;〈比喻 *fig.*〉老一套 old-fashioned method：抄袭～ copy from a book or article; plagiarize ❷ 用文字固定下来的；成为书面的 regularize sth. in a written form：～法 written law; statute law; statutory law

【成文法】chéngwénfǎ 由国家依立法程序制定，并用文字公布施行的法律（跟'不成文法'相对 as opposed to 'unwritten law'）statute law; statutory law; written law laid down and promulgated by the state according to a legislative process

【成想】chéngxiǎng same as 承想 chéngxiǎng

【成效】chéngxiào 功效 effect; result; same as 效果 xiàoguǒ ①：～显著 achieve remarkable success; produce an obvious effect | 这种药防治棉蚜虫，很有～。This medicine is very effective in prevention and control of the cotton aphid.

【成心】chéngxīn 故意 intentionally; on purpose; deliberately：～捣乱 intentionally make a mess of sth. | ～跟他过不去 make trouble for him on purpose | 那是巧合，不是～的。This was pure coincidence, and not intentional.

【成行】chéngxíng 旅行、访问等得到实现 go on a trip as planned：去南方考察月内可～。We will go south on an investigative tour this month as planned.

【成形】chéngxíng ❶ 自然生长或加工后而具有某种形状 take shape as a result of natural growth or processing：浇铸～ pour molten steel into a mold ❷ 医学上指修复受到损伤的组织或器官（med.）repair damaged tissue or organ：～外科 plastic surgery | 骨～术 osteoplasty ❸ 医学上指具有正常的形状（med.）have a normal form：大便～。The stool is normal in shape.

【成型】chéngxíng 工件、产品经过加工，成为所需要的形状（of work or products）take the required shape through processing

【成性】chéngxìng 形成某种习性（多指不好的 usu. negative）become second nature; by nature：懒惰～ be lazy by nature | 流氓～ villain by nature

【成宿】chéngxiǔ 整夜 whole night; all night long：～侍候病人 attend to a sick person through the whole night

【成药】chéngyào 药店或药房里已经配制好了的各种剂型的药品 medicine ready-made by a pharmacy; patent medicine

【成也萧何，败也萧何】chéng yě Xiāo Hé, bài yě Xiāo Hé 宋代洪迈《容斋续笔·萧何给韩信》：'信之为大将军，实萧何所荐；今其死也，又出其谋，故俚语有"成也萧何，败也萧何"之语。'比喻事情的成败或好坏都是由同一个人造成的。Hong Mai of the Song Dynasty wrote in his *A Sequel to the Notes of the Tolerance Studio·Xiao He Cheating Han Xin*: 'It was none other than Xiao He who recommended Han Xin as the command-in-chief, and it was also Xiao He who plotted to have him killed.' Hence the saying, '成也萧何，败也萧何', meaning that either success or failure boils down to the same person.

【成夜】chéngyè 整夜 whole night; all night long：成日～ day and night | ～不睡 stay up the whole night

【成衣】chéngyī ❶〈旧时 *old*〉指做衣服的（工人或铺子）tailor's shop; dressmaking shop：～匠 tailor; dressmaker | ～铺 tailor's shop ❷ 制成后出售的衣服 ready-made clothes for sale：出售的～开架让顾客挑选。The ready-made garments are kept on open shelves so as to help customers make their selections.

【成议】chéngyì 达成的协议 agreement reached：已有～。An agreement has been reached.

【成因】chéngyīn（事物）形成的原因 reasons why an event happens; cause of formation; origin：海洋的～ cause of the formation of the ocean | 探讨这一事变的～ investigate the causes behind what has happened

【成阴】chéngyīn 指树木枝叶繁茂，形成树阴 patch of shade left by big, lush trees：绿树～。Verdant trees cast a large patch of shade.

【成语】chéngyǔ 人们长期以来习用的、简洁精辟的定型词组或短句。汉语的成语大多由四个字组成，一般都有出处。有些成语从字面上不难理解，如‘小题大做’、‘后来居上’等。有些成语必须知道来源或典故才能懂得意思，如‘朝三暮四’、‘杯弓蛇影’等。idiom; concise and meaningful phrases or short sentences that have been in long public usage. Most Chinese idioms have an historical origin and consist of four Chinese characters. The meanings of some are obvious, e.g. ‘trivial topic, long article’ and ‘latecomers become the first,’ but some can be understood only by knowing their sources, or the stories behind them, e.g. ‘three in the morning, four in the evening’ and ‘the shadow of a bow in a cup mistaken for a snake’.

【成员】chéngyuán 集体或家庭的组成人员 members of a group or a family: 家庭～ members of a family | 协会～ members of an association | 联合国～国 member states of the United Nations

【成约】chéngyuē 已订的条约；已有的约定 signed treaty; existing agreement: 违背～ breach an agreement | 有～在先，谁也不能后悔。We have reached an agreement, so there can be no regrets.

【成章】chéngzhāng ❶ 成文章 take the shape of an article: 下笔～。Whatever flows from his pen becomes an excellent article. | 出口～ beautiful words flowing from one's mouth as if from the pen of a master; improvise a polished speech ❷ 成条理 systematic; logical: 顺理～ in a reasonable and systematic way; in a natural and logical way

【成长】chéngzhǎng ❶ 生长而成熟；长成 grow to maturity; grow up: 前年栽的果树还没有～。The fruit trees planted the year before last are not yet fully grown. ❷ 向成熟的阶段发展；生长 develop into maturity; grow: 年轻的一代在茁壮～。The young generation is growing up sturdy and strong. ❸〈方 *dial.*〉发展；增长 develop; increase; grow: 经济～率 economic growth rate | 经济～减缓。Economic development has slowed down.

【成竹在胸】chéng zhú zài xiōng ☞ 胸有成竹 xiōng yǒu chéng zhú on p. 2154

【成总儿】chéngzǒngr ❶ 一总 altogether; in a lump sum: 这笔钱我还是～付吧！I'll pay in full. ❷ 整批地 in quantities; in bulk: 用得多就～买，用得少就零碎买。Buy goods used a lot in bulk, and those not on a piecemeal basis.

丞 chéng 古代辅助的官吏 assistant to an official in ancient China: ～相 prime minister | 县～ county magistrate's assistant

【丞相】chéngxiàng 古代辅佐君主的职位最高的大臣 prime minister; minister of the highest rank in ancient China

呈 chéng ❶ 具有（某种形式）；呈现（某种颜色、状态）take (certain form or shape); display or appear (in certain colour or state): 果实～长圆形。The fruit is oval in shape | 毛皮～暗褐色。The fur is dark brown in colour. ❷ 恭敬地送上去 submit or present sth. with respect: 谨～ respectfully present | ～上名片 present one's name card ❸（～儿 chéngr）呈文 petition; memorial: 签～ sign on a petition

【呈报】chéngbào 用公文报告上级 submit a report to one's superior: ～中央批准 submit a report to the central authorities for approval

【呈递】chéngdì 恭敬地递上 present or submit with great respect: ～国书 present a letter of credence | ～公文 present a government report; submit a business report

【呈览】chénglǎn〈书 *fml.*〉送上审阅 submit sth. to a higher authority for deliberation

【呈露】chénglù 呈现 appear; expose: 海水退潮，～出一片礁石。The seawater ebbed, exposing a cluster of rocks.

【呈请】chéngqǐng 用公文向上级请示 apply to the higher authorities for consideration and approval: ～立案 apply to register sth. for the record; place a case on file for investigation and prosecution | ～院部核示 submit a report or application to the headquarters of an institute for examination and approval

【呈送】chéngsòng 恭敬地赠送或呈递 present sth. as a gift or pass sth. on to sb. with respect; deliver: ～礼品 present a gift to sb. | ～公函 deliver a document to sb.

【呈文】chéngwén〈旧时 *old*〉公文的一种，下对上用 memorial; petition; document submitted to the higher authority by the subordinate

【呈现】chéngxiàn 显出；露出 appear; display; present; emerge: 到处～欣欣向荣的景象。Everywhere there is a scene of prosperity. | 暴风雨过去，大海又～出碧蓝的颜色。The storm subsided, and the ocean was again an expanse of deep blue.

【呈献】chéngxiàn 把实物或意见等恭敬地送给集体或敬爱的人 present sth. in due formality; respectfully present an object or pass on an opinion to one's work unit or respected people

【呈阅】chéngyuè 送上级审阅 present sth. to one's superior for examination and approval

【呈正】chéngzhèng〈书 *fml.*〉〈敬辞 *pol.*〉把自己的作品送请别人批评改正 term of respect when sending a piece of writing to sb. for criticism and correction; also 呈政 chéngzhèng

【呈子】chéng·zi 呈文（多指老百姓给官府的 usu. submitted by the rank-and-file to the authorities）petition

枨（棖） chéng〈书 *fml.*〉触动 touch: ～触 touch; be moved

【枨触】chéngchù〈书 *fml.*〉❶ 触动 touch ❷ 感动 be moved

郕 Chéng 周朝国名，在今山东汶上北 Cheng, name of a kingdom in the Zhou Dynasty in north Wenshang in today's Shandong Province

诚 chéng ❶ 真实的（心意）sincere; honest; real: ～心～意 wholeheartedly; in all seriousness; honestly | 开～布公 speak frankly and sincerely; in all sincerity and frankness; lay all the cards on the table; wear one's heart on one's sleeve ❷〈书 *fml.*〉实在；的确 honestly; indeed; actually: ～然。It's true. ❸〈书 *fml.*〉如果；果真 if; given that: ～能如是，则相见之日可期。If this is the case, then we can expect to see each other soon.

【诚笃】chéngdǔ 诚实真挚 honest and sincere: ～君子 honest and sincere gentleman

【诚惶诚恐】chéng huáng chéng kǒng 惶恐不安。原是君主时代臣下给君主奏章中的套语。be on tenterhooks; upset; live in panic and uncertainty; polite words used in a memorial submitted to the monarch

【诚恳】chéngkěn 真诚而恳切 honest and sincere: 态度～ sincere attitude | 言出肺腑，～感人。What he said was from the bottom of his heart, sincere and touching.

【诚朴】chéngpǔ 诚恳朴实 honest; sincere and simple: 为人～ be honest and sincere to others

【诚然】chéngrán ❶ 实在 truly; really: 他很爱那几只小鸭，小鸭也～可爱。He loves those ducklings, as they really are adorable. ❷ 固然（引起下文转折 used correlatively with 'but'）no doubt; to be sure; certainly: 文章流畅～很好，但主要的还在于内容。It's certainly good to have an article that reads fluently, but it is content that counts.

【诚实】chéng•shí 言行跟内心思想一致（指好的思想行为）；不虚假 unaffected; honest; what one says and does is in accordance with what one thinks (good thought and behaviour): 这孩子很～，不会撒谎。The child is honest and does not tell lies.

【诚心】chéngxīn ❶ 诚恳的心意 sincerity; honesty: 一片～ in all sincerity; in all seriousness ❷ same as 诚恳 chéngkěn: 很～ be sincere | 我们～向您求教。We earnestly ask your advice.

【诚信】chéngxìn 诚实，守信用 honest; keep or live up to one's promise; credit: 生意人应当以～为本。A businessman must take honesty as his cardinal principle.

【诚意】chéngyì 真心 sincerity; good faith; bona fide: 用实际行动来表示～ express one's sincerity through one's actions

【诚挚】chéngzhì 诚恳真挚 sincere; cordial: 会谈是在～友好的气氛中进行的。The talks proceeded in a cordial and friendly atmosphere.

承 chéng ❶ 托着；接着 support; hold; bear: ～尘 ceiling; canopy over a seat | ～重 load-bearing ❷ 承担 bear; undertake; assume: ～印 undertake the printing of sth. | ～制中西服装 undertake the work of making clothes in both Chinese and Western styles ❸〈客套话 *pol.*〉承蒙 term of politeness; be indebted to sb.: 昨～热情招待，不胜感激。I am very much indebted to you for your hospitality yesterday. ❹ 继续；接续 continue; go on; carry on: 继～ inherit; succeed (to); carry on; carry forward | ～上启下 link the preceding with the following; form a link between the foregoing and the following | ～先启后 form a link between the past and the future; inherit the legacy of the past while opening up a new field ❺ 接受（命令或吩咐）take (orders or instructions): 秉～ honestly carry out; act in line with; be obedient to | 敢不～命。I dare not go against you. *or* I cannot but do as you say. ❻ (Chéng) 姓 a surname

【承办】chéngbàn 接受办理 undertake; sponsor; initiate; host: ～土木工程 undertake civil engineering projects | 比赛由市体协和电视台联合～。The contest was co-sponsored by the municipal sports association and the television station.

【承包】chéngbāo 接受工程、订货或其他生产经营活动并且负责完成 make a contract to do sth.; conduct business on a contracted basis; take full responsibility for an engineering project, ordering materials, or other production and management activities from the very beginning to the end

【承尘】chéngchén ❶〈古代 *arch.*〉在座位顶上设置的帐子 canopy over a seat ❷〈方 *dial.*〉天花板 ceiling

【承担】chéngdān 担负；担当 bear; undertake; assume: ～义务 be obliged to do sth. | ～责任 assume (bear or take) responsibility; answer for sth. one has done

【承当】chéngdāng ❶ 担当 bear; take on; take up: ～罪责 claim responsibility for a crime | 这事我可～不起。This is too much for me to bear. ❷〈方 *dial.*〉答应；应承 agree; promise; consent to: 借车的事，我已～了人家。I've promised to lend my bicycle to him.

【承乏】chéngfá〈书 *fml.*〉〈谦辞 *hum.*〉表示所在职位因一时没有适当人选，只好暂由自己充任 polite expression to say the speaker himself will take up a certain position for the time being as there is currently no other appropriate person

【承欢】chénghuān〈书 *fml.*〉迎合人意，博取欢心。特指侍奉父母使感到欢喜 cater to; pander to; play up to; especially, wait on one's parents and make them happy:～膝下 take good care of one's parents and make them happy

【承继】chéngjì ❶ 给没有儿子的伯父叔父等做儿子 be adopted as heir to one's uncle who has no son ❷ 把兄弟等的儿子收做自己的儿子 adopt one's brother's son ❸ 继承 inherit; carry on:～遗产 inherit property

C

【承建】chéngjiàn 承担建筑任务;承包并修建(工程) undertake the construction of; contract to take full responsibility for constructing (an engineering project)

【承接】chéngjiē ❶ 用容器接受流下来的液体 hold out a container as receptacle for liquid being poured into it ❷ 承担;接受 undertake; accept:本刊～广告。This magazine welcomes advertisements.|～来料加工 accept customers' materials for processing; undertake the processing of supplied materials ❸ 接续 continue; carry on:～上文 continued from the preceding paragraph

【承揽】chénglǎn 接受(对方所委托的业务);承担 accept (the business entrusted by the other party); undertake:～车辆装修 undertake the repair of vehicles

【承溜】chéngliù 〈书 *fml*.〉檐沟 eaves gutter; gutter

【承蒙】chéngméng 〈客套话 *pol*.〉受到 be accorded (a kindness); be granted (a favor); be indebted to:～指点。Thank you for your advice.|～热情招待,十分感激。I am most grateful to you for your hospitality.

【承诺】chéngnuò 对某项事务答应照办 agree to do sth.; promise; pledge:慨然～ make a generous commitment

【承平】chéngpíng 〈书 *fml*.〉太平 peaceful:～盛世 time of peace and prosperity

【承前启后】chéng qián qǐ hòu same as 承先启后 chéng xiān qǐ hòu

【承情】chéng//qíng 〈客套话 *pol*.〉领受情谊 term of politeness, used when one receives care and friendship:～关照 be much obliged for sb.'s care; be grateful for sb.'s concern|别说得那么好听,没人承你的情。Don't be so effusive; no one will appreciate it.

【承认】chéngrèn ❶ 表示肯定,同意,认可 agree; consent; admit; acknowledge; recognize; allow:～错误 admit one's mistake; acknowledge one's fault ❷ 国际上指肯定新国家、新政权的法律地位 recognize the legal status of a newly established country or government

【承上启下】chéng shàng qǐ xià 接续上面的并引起下面的(多用于写作等) link the preceding and the following; form a link between the foregoing and the following (in a piece of writing, etc.); 启 also put as 起 qǐ

【承受】chéngshòu ❶ 接受;禁(jīn)受 receive; bear; endure:～考验 stand a test; put up with an ordeal|这块小薄板～不住一百斤的重量。This thin board won't bear the weight of 50 kg. ❷ 继承(财产、权利等) inherit (property; right, etc.):～遗产 inherit a legacy

【承题】chéngtí 八股文的第二股,用三句或四句,承接破题,对题目作进一步说明 second part of an eight-legged essay (a literary composition prescribed for the imperial civil service examinations, noted for its rigidity of form and poverty of ideas), which expounds the subject further in three or four sentences; ☞ 八股 bāgǔ on p.21

【承望】chéngwàng 料到(多用于否定式,表示出乎意外 usu. used in the negative) expect; anticipate:不～你这时候来,太好了。I never expected you to come at such a moment, and it's wonderful that you have.

【承袭】chéngxí ❶ 沿袭 adopt; carry on; follow:～旧制 carry on the old system ❷ 继承(封爵等) inherit (a title etc.):～衣钵 inherit the *kasaya* and alms bowl; inherit a legacy|～先人基业 inherit the business or property of one's ancestor

【承先启后】chéng xiān qǐ hòu 继承前代的并启发后代的(多用于学问、事业等 usu. in knowledge or an undertaking) inherit the past and give enlightenment to the following generation; also 承前启后 chéng qián qǐ hòu

【承想】chéngxiǎng 料想;想到(多用于否定 oft. in the negative) expect; think of:不～ contrary to one's expectation|没～会得到这样的结果 never expected such a result|谁～今天又刮大风呢!Who ever would have expected it to be windy again today! also 成想 chéngxiǎng

【承印】chéngyìn 承担印刷 undertake the printing of:～商标 undertake the printing of a trademark|～中外文名片 undertake the printing of name cards in Chinese and foreign languages

【承应】chéngyìng 应承 agree; consent; promise

【承运】chéngyùn (运输部门)承担运输业务 (of transportation department) provide transport services:～日用百货 transport general merchandise|行李～处 baggage check-in counter; baggage-handling counter

【承载】chéngzài 托着物体,承受它的重量 bear the weight of an object ◇～人口压力 stand the pressure of a population

【承重】chéngzhòng 承受重量(用于建筑物和其他构件 used in architecture and other components) load-bearing; bearing

【承重孙】chéngzhòngsūn 按宗法制度,如长子比父母先死,长孙在他祖父母死后举办丧礼时替长子做丧主,叫承重孙 eldest grandson; under the patriarchal system, if the eldest son has died earlier than his parents, it is the eldest grandson that presides over his grandparents' funeral

【承转】chéngzhuǎn 收到上级公文转交下级，或收到下级公文转送上级 forward a document to one's subordinate or superior

【承租】chéngzū 接受出租；租用 lease; rent：～人 renter; lessee｜～公房 rent a state-owned apartment

【承做】chéngzuò 承担制做 undertake; take the responsibility for doing sth.：～各式男女服装 accept orders for men's and women's clothes in different styles

城 chéng ❶ 城墙 city wall：～外 outside the city; out of the city｜万里长～ the Great Wall ❷ 城墙以内的地方 within the city wall：～区 urban area｜东～ eastern part of a city ❸ 城市(跟'乡'相对 as opposed to 'the countryside or rural areas') town; city; urban area; metropolis：山～ city in an mountainous area｜满～风雨 town hit by gusts of wind and heavy rain; become the talk of the town; cause a sensation｜连下数～ conquer a number of cities in a sweep｜～乡物资交流 exchange of goods between urban and rural areas

【城堡】chéngbǎo 堡垒式的小城 castle; citadel

【城池】chéngchí 城墙和护城河，指城市 city wall and moat; city：～失守 lose the control of a city｜攻克几座～ overrun several cities

【城垛】chéngduǒ ❶ 城墙向外突出的部分 outreaching section of a city wall; battlements ❷ 城墙上面呈凹凸形的矮墙 parapet; rampart; also 城垛口 chéngduǒkǒu; 城垛子 chéngduǒ•zi

【城防】chéngfáng 城市的防卫或防务 city defence：～巩固 closely guarded city｜～工事 city defence works

【城府】chéngfǔ〈书 *fml*.〉〈比喻 *fig*.〉待人处事的心机 be sophisticated in dealing with others：～很深 astute; (of a person) hard to fathom｜胸无～(为人坦率) (of a person) unsophisticated

【城根】chénggēn (～儿 chénggēnr)指靠近城墙的地方 area close to the city wall

【城关】chéngguān 指城外靠近城门的一带地方 area just outside a city gate

【城郭】chéngguō 城墙(城指内城的墙，郭指外城的墙)，泛指城市 city wall (literally, 城 chéng means the wall of the inner city and 郭 guō means the wall of the outer city); (gen.) city

【城壕】chéngháo 护城河 moat; river that surrounds and protects a city

【城隍】chénghuáng ❶〈书 *fml*.〉护城河 moat ❷ 迷信传说中指主管某个城的神 (in superstition and legend) town god

【城建】chéngjiàn 城市建设(规划、工程) urban construction (plans and projects)

【城郊】chéngjiāo 城市周围附近的地区 outskirts of a city; suburbs

【城楼】chénglóu 建筑在城门洞上的楼 tower atop a city gate; gate tower

【城门失火，殃及池鱼】chéng mén shī huǒ, yāng jí chí yú 城门着了火，大家都用护城河的水救火，水用尽了，鱼也干死了 When the city gate catches fire, water from the moat is used to put it out, and as the water is used up, the fish die;〈比喻 *fig*.〉因牵连而受祸害或损失 suffer from disaster or damage because of connection or implication; innocent people often fall victim to the actions of others; be a scapegoat for sb. else's wrongdoing

【城墙】chéngqiáng〈古代 *arch*.〉为防守而建筑在城市四周的又高又厚的墙 thick, high walls built around a city for protective proposes

【城区】chéngqū 城里和靠城的地区(区别于'郊区' as compared with 'suburbs') city and districts close to the city; city proper

【城阙】chéngquè〈书 *fml*.〉❶ 城门两边的望楼 watchtower on either side of a city gate ❷ 宫阙 palace

【城市】chéngshì 人口集中、工商业发达、居民以非农业人口为主的地区，通常是周围地区的政治、经济、文化中心 city; metropolis; area densely inhabited by a non-agricultural population and with developed industry and commerce, usu. the political, economic and cultural centre of the surrounding areas

【城市贫民】chéngshì pínmín〈旧时 *old*〉称城市中无固定职业，依靠自己劳动而生活贫苦的人 urban poor; city dweller without a regular job and trying to make ends meet by doing physical labour

【城下之盟】chéng xià zhī méng 敌军到了城下，抵抗不了，跟敌人订的盟约，泛指被迫签订的条约 treaty reached with the enemy at the city gate; treaty signed under pressure; terms accepted under duress

【城厢】chéngxiāng 城内和城门外附近的地方 city proper; areas in and just outside the city gates

【城垣】chéngyuán〈书 *fml*.〉same as 城墙 chéngqiáng

【城镇】chéngzhèn 城市和集镇 cities and towns：～居民 urban dwellers

宬 chéng〈古代 *arch*.〉藏书的屋子 room for keeping books; library：皇史～(明清皇家档案库) imperial library (where archives were kept in the Ming and Qing dynasties)

埕[1] chéng 指蛏(chēng)田 fields for raising razor clams

埕[2] chéng〈方 *dial*.〉酒瓮 wine jar

晟 Chéng 姓 a surname
☞ shèng on p. 1724

乘[1] chéng ❶ 用交通工具或牲畜代替步行；坐 take a journey by means of vehicles or animals; ride：～船 travel by boat｜～马 ride on horseback｜～火车 travel by train ❷ 利用（机会等）make use of (an opportunity); avail oneself of a chance：～势 take advantage of; take the chance to｜～胜直追 exploit victories through hot pursuit; continue one's triumphant pursuit 注意 NOTE：口语里多说'趁'chèn。趁 chèn is often used to replace 乘 chéng in spoken Chinese. ❸ 佛教的教义 Buddhist teachings：大～ Mahayana｜小～ Hinayana ❹（Chéng）姓 a surname

乘[2] chéng 进行乘法运算 multiply ☞ shèng on p. 1724

【乘便】chéngbiàn 顺便（不是特地）when it is convenient; at one's convenience (do sth. but not specifically or specially)：请你～把那本书带给我。Please bring me the book at you convenience.

【乘除】chéngchú ❶ 乘法和除法，泛指计算 multiply and divide; count ❷〈书 *fml.*〉指世事的消长盛衰 growth and decline or rise and fall of things in the world

【乘法】chéngfǎ 数学中的一种运算方法。最简单的是数的乘法，即几个相同数连加的简便算法。如 2+2+2+2+2，5 个 2 相加，就是 2 乘以 5。multiplication, an arithmetic operation, such as 2 × 5, which means 2+2+2+2+2

【乘方】chéngfāng ❶ 求一个数自乘若干次的积的运算，如数 a 自乘 3 次（$a \times a \times a$），就是 a 的 3 次乘方，写作 a^3 involution; power; an arithmetic operation which solves the problem of a number times itself several times, such as number 'a' times itself three times (a × a × a), written as a^3 ❷ 一个数自乘若干次所得的积 product of a number times itself several times; also 乘幂 chéngmì

【乘风破浪】chéng fēng pò làng《宋书·宗悫(què)传》：'愿乘长风破万里浪。'现比喻不畏艰险勇往直前。也形容事业迅猛地向前发展。*History of Song·Biography of Zong Que*：'I would like to take a ride on the wind and brave the waves for thousands of miles.' (fig.) going forward despite difficulties and hardships; prosperous and fast-developing undertaking

【乘机】chéngjī 利用机会 seize the chance; seize the opportunity：～逃脱 take the chance and flee｜～反扑 seize the chance to counterattack

【乘积】chéngjī 乘法运算中，两个或两个以上的数相乘所得的数。如 2×5=10 中，10 是乘积。product of two or more numbers multiplied, such as 2×5=10; 简称 abbr. 积 jī

【乘警】chéngjǐng 列车上负责治安保卫工作的警察 police responsible for the safety of passengers on a train

【乘客】chéngkè 搭乘车、船、飞机的人 passenger; person travelling by automobile, boat or plane

【乘凉】chéng//liáng 热天在凉快透风的地方休息 rest in a cool place on a hot day; relax in a cool place：在树下乘了一会儿凉。(They) have enjoyed the cool shade under a tree for a while.

【乘人之危】chéng rén zhī wēi 趁着人家危急的时候去侵害人家 take advantage of sb.'s precarious position (difficulties or trouble); make use of the precarious situation sb. is in

【乘时】chéngshí 利用时机 seize the chance; take the opportunity：～而起 take the chance to rise; rise to the occasion

【乘势】chéngshì ❶ 利用有利的形势；就势 make use of a favourable situation; avail oneself of an opportune moment：～进击 make use of a favourable situation to continue an attack ❷〈书 *fml.*〉凭借权势 rely on one's power and influence：～欺人 use one's power and influence to hoodwink others

【乘务】chéngwù 指火车、飞机、轮船等交通工具上为乘客服务的各种事务（of a train, plane, ship, etc.）passenger service：～员 attendant on a train; air steward or stewardess｜～组 service crew

【乘务员】chéngwùyuán 在火车、轮船、飞机上为乘客服务的工作人员。电车、公共汽车上的工作人员，也叫乘务员。attendant on a train; air steward or stewardess; conductor or conductress on a public bus or passenger ship

【乘隙】chéngxì 利用空子；趁机会 take advantage of a loophole; turn another's mistake to one's own account; take the chance：～逃脱 take the chance to escape｜～休整 take the opportunity to have a rest

【乘兴】chéngxìng 趁着一时高兴 while one is in high spirits：～而来，兴尽而返 arrive in high spirits and depart after enjoying oneself to one's heart's content

【乘虚】chéngxū 趁着空虚 take advantage of a weak point in an opponent's defence; act when sb. is off guard：～而入 find a way in by taking advantage of an opponent's weak defences; infiltrate by taking advantage of the enemy's unpreparedness; break through at a weak point

【乘员】chéngyuán 乘车、船、飞机等交通工具的人员的统称 passenger; general term for people who travel by train, ship, plane, etc.

【乘坐】chéngzuò 坐（车、船等）take a ride (in a car, ship, etc.)：～火车 ride in a train; travel by train｜～飞机 take a plane; travel by air

盛 chéng ❶ 把东西放在器具里 put sth. into a container or vessel; fill; ladle：～饭 fill a bowl with rice|缸里～满了水。The crock is full of water. ❷ 容纳 hold; contain:这间屋子小,～不了这么多东西。The room is too small for all this stuff.

☞ shèng on p. 1724

【盛器】chéngqì 盛东西的器具 vessel; receptacle

铖 chéng 用于人名 used in a name

程 chéng ❶ 规矩;法则 regulation; rule:章～rules; constitution|～式 form; pattern; formula; modality ❷ 程序 order; procedure; course; sequence; schedule:议～ agenda|课～ course; curriculum ❸ (旅行的)道路;一段路 (of travelling) road; journey; leg of a journey:启～ set out on a journey; embark on a journey|送你一～。I will accompany you on the first leg of the journey. ❹ 路程;距离 journey; distance:里～碑 milestone|射～ range of fire|行～ distance travelled; course; journey ❺〈书 *fml.*〉衡量;估量 weigh; measure; estimate; calculate:计日～功 estimate exactly how much time is needed to complete a project; be sure of success as planned|～其器能 make an evaluation of one's qualifications and ability ❻ (Chéng) 姓 a surname

【程度】chéngdù ❶ 文化、教育、知识、能力等方面的水平 (of literacy, education, knowledge, capability, etc.) extent; level; standard; degree:文化～ level of education; level of literacy|自动化～ level of automation ❷ 事物变化达到的状况 extent or degree to which sth. undergoing change reaches:天气虽冷,还没有到上冻的～。Although the weather is cold, it is not yet freezing.|他有肝病已恶化到十分严重的～。His liver disease has advanced to an extremely serious degree.

【程控】chéngkòng 程序控制 programme control:～设备 programme-controlled equipment|～电话 programme-controlled telephone

【程门立雪】Chéng mén lì xuě 宋代杨时在下雪天拜谒著名学者程颐,程颐瞑目而坐,杨时不敢惊动,在旁站立等待。程颐醒来,门前积雪已经一尺深了(见于《宋史·杨时传》)。后来用'程门立雪'形容尊师重道,恭敬受教。Yang Shi of the Song Dynasty paid a visit to the celebrated scholar Cheng Yi one snowy day. According to *History of Song·Biography of Yang Shi*, when Yang arrived, he saw the scholar sitting there with his eyes closed. As Yang Shi did not want to disturb the scholar, he stood aside, waiting. When Cheng Yi woke up, the snow had accumulated a foot deep on the ground before his door. This anecdote was later used as an example of reverence for a teacher.

【程式】chéngshì 一定的格式 formula; pattern; form:公文～ forms and formulas of official documents|表演的～ stylized movement in a performance

【程限】chéngxiàn〈书 *fml.*〉❶ 程式和限制 patterns and restrictions:创作是没有一定的～的。Creative writing knows no rules or formulas. ❷ 规定的进度 fixed rate of progress:宽其～ make allowances for patterns and restrictions|读书日有～ make daily progress in one's studies

【程序】chéngxù 事情进行的先后次序(of things) order; procedure; course; sequence:工作～ working procedure|会议～ agenda of a meeting

【程序控制】chéngxù kòngzhì 通过事先编制的固定程序实现的自动控制。广泛应用于控制各种生产和工艺加工过程。automatic control through pre-fixed program; gen. used to control manufacturing and processing procedures

【程子】chéng·zi〈方 *dial.*〉一段时间 period of time:这～他很忙。He's very busy lately.|到农村住了～ live in the country for a period of time

惩(懲) chéng ❶ 处罚 punish; penalize:～一警百 punish one in order to warn a hundred|～恶扬善 punish the wicked in order to elevate the virtuous|严～不贷 mete out severe punishment with no hint of leniency ❷〈书 *fml.*〉警戒 warn; exhort:～前毖后 learn from past mistakes to avoid future errors

【惩办】chéngbàn 处罚 punish; chastise:严加～ punish severely

【惩处】chéngchǔ 处罚 punish; penalize; administer justice:依法～ give a penalty according to law; punish sb. in accordance with the law

【惩罚】chéngfá 严厉地处罚 punish severely; chastise:从重～ mete out severe or rigorous punishment|无论是谁,犯了罪都要受到～。Whoever has committed a crime will be punished.

【惩戒】chéngjiè 通过处罚来警戒 punish sb. to teach them a lesson; discipline sb. as a warning

【惩前毖后】chéng qián bì hòu 吸取过去失败的教训,以后小心,不致重犯错误 learn from past failures to avoid future mistakes (毖 *bì*:谨慎;小心 prudently; carefully)

【惩一警百】chéng yī jǐng bǎi 惩罚少数人以警戒多数人 punish a few to warn a great number of people; 警 jǐng also 儆 jǐng; also 惩一戒百 chéng yī jiè bǎi

【惩治】chéngzhì same as 惩办 chéngbàn:依法～ punish according to the law|～罪犯 punish criminals

椉 chéng〈书 *fml.*〉same as 乘 chéng

☞ shèng on p. 1726

裎 chéng 〈书 *fml.*〉光着身子 with no clothes on：裸～ naked
☞ chěng on p. 254

塍(堘) chéng 〈方 *dial.*〉田间的土埂子 path between fields：田～ path between fields

酲 chéng 〈书 *fml.*〉喝醉了神志不清 drunken; addled; intoxicated under the influence of alcohol

澄(澂) chéng ❶（水）很清（of water）clean; limpid：江～如练。The limpid water looks like a veil of white gauze. ❷ 澄清；使清明 clarify; clear up
☞ dèng on p. 410

【澄碧】chéngbì 清而明净 clear, clean and bright：湖水～。The lake water is crystal clear.

【澄彻】chéngchè same as 澄澈 chéngchè

【澄澈】chéngchè 清澈透明 transparently clear; crystal clear; limpid：清溪～见底。The creek is so clear that you can see the bottom. also 澄彻 chéngchè

【澄清】chéngqīng ❶ 清亮 limpid; clear and bright：湖水碧绿～。The lake water is blue and crystal clear. ❷ 使混浊变为清明 make sth. clear; clear up; clarify;〈比喻 *fig.*〉肃清混乱局面 clarity：～天下 clarify sth. before the public ❸ 弄清楚（认识、问题等）be clear about (a subject, problem, etc.)：～事实 clarify the facts
☞ dèngqīng on p. 410

【澄莹】chéngyíng 清亮 fresh and clear：雨后，月亮更显得～皎洁。The moon looked clearer and brighter after a rainfall.

橙 chéng ❶ 常绿乔木或灌木，叶子椭圆形，果实圆形，多汁，果皮红黄色，味道酸甜 orange (*Citrus*); evergreen tree or bush having oval leaves and round, juicy, sweet and sour fruit with thick reddish yellow skin ❷ 这种植物的果实 fruit of the orange tree ❸ 红和黄合成的颜色 combined red and yellow colours; orange

【橙红】chénghóng 像橙子那样红里带黄的颜色 red tinted with yellow; orange red

【橙黄】chénghuáng 像橙子一样黄里带红的颜色 yellow tinted with red; orange yellow

【橙子】chéng·zi（旧读 formerly pronounced chén·zi）橙树的果实 fruit of the orange tree; orange

chěng（ㄔㄥˇ）

逞 chěng ❶ 显示（自己的才能、威风等）；夸耀 display (one's talents, strength or power, etc.); show off：～能 show off one's skill or capability; parade one's ability | ～强 show off one's power | ～威风 show off one's strength or power; swagger about ❷ 实现意愿；达到目的（多指坏事 mostly negative）succeed in doing sth.：得～ have one's way (in a plot or scheme) | 以求一～ in a bid for success ❸ 纵容；放任 spoil; indulge; give free rein to：～性 act wilfully; do sth. on impulse; act waywardly

【逞能】chěng//néng 显示自己能干 flaunt one's abilities; parade oneself; show off one's talent：不是我～，一天走个百把里路不算什么。I don't mean to show off, but it's really nothing for me to travel 50 km. in one day.

【逞强】chěng//qiáng 显示自己能力强 show off one's abilities：～好胜 be fond of showing off and upstaging others | 你一个人是搬不动的，别～了！You cannot move it by yourself, stop trying to show off.

【逞性】chěngxìng 任性 wilful; wayward; headstrong：～妄为 be wayward and reckless | 孩子爱在父母面前～。Children are likely to act wilfully before their parents. also 逞性子 chěngxìng·zi

【逞凶】chěngxiōng 做凶暴的事情；行凶 act violently; go berserk; commit a crime：暴徒～。The rioters committed crimes of violence.

骋 chěng 〈书 *fml.*〉❶（马）跑（of horse）gallop：驰～ gallop about a place ❷ 放开 give free rein to：～怀 give free rein to one's thoughts and feelings | ～目 look as far as one's eyes can see; look into the distance

【骋怀】chěnghuái 〈书 *fml.*〉开怀 give free rein to one's thoughts and feelings; enjoy oneself to one's heart's content：～痛饮 drink to one's heart's content

【骋目】chěngmù 〈书 *fml.*〉放眼往远处看 look as far as one's eyes can reach; look into the distance：凭栏～ lean on a railing for a panorama of the scenery

裎 chěng 古代的一种对襟单衣 unlined, front-buttoned jacket in ancient China
☞ chéng on p. 254

chèng（ㄔㄥˋ）

秤(称) chèng 测定物体重量的器具，有杆秤、地秤、台秤、弹簧秤等多种。特指杆秤。steelyard or lever scales, platform scales, spring scales, etc.; esp. steelyard; ☞ 杆秤 gǎnchèng on p. 629
☞ 称 chèn on p. 241 and chēng on p. 242

【秤锤】chèngchuí 称物品时用来使秤平衡的金属锤 sliding weight of a steelyard; also 秤砣 chèngtuó

【秤杆】chènggǎn（～儿 chènggǎnr）杆秤的组成部分，用木棍制成，上面镶着计量的秤星 arm or beam of a steelyard, usu. made of wood inscribed with gradations

【秤钩】chènggōu 杆秤上的金属钩子，用来挂所

称的物体 steelyard hook on which object to be weighed is hung

【秤毫】chènghάo 杆秤上手提的部分,条状物,多用绳子或皮条制成 lifting cord of a steelyard, usu. made of a rope or leather strap

【秤花】chènghuā〈方 *dial.*〉same as 秤星 chèngxīng

【秤纽】chèngniǔ same as 秤毫 chènghάo

【秤盘子】chèngpán·zi 盘秤一端系的金属盘子。用来盛(chéng)所称的物品。scale pan; metal pan tied to one end of a steelyard and in which objects to be weighed are placed; ☞ 盘秤 pánchèng on p.1442

【秤砣】chèngtuó same as 秤锤 chèngchuí

【秤星】chèngxīng (~儿 chèngxīngr)镶在秤杆上的金属的小圆点,是计量的标志 gradations; little metal dots on the arm of a steelyard to show the measurement; ☞ 杆秤 gǎnchèng on p.629

牚 chèng ❶ 斜柱 tilting pillar ❷ (~儿 chèngr)桌椅等腿中间的横木 horizontal bar connecting the legs of a chair or a desk ☞ chēng on p.243

chī (彳)

吃[1] **(喫)** chī ❶ 把食物等放到嘴里经过咀嚼咽下去(包括吸、喝)(including suck and drink) put food into one's mouth, chew and swallow; eat: ~饭 have dinner (breakfast, lunch, etc.)|~奶 (of a baby) take milk from its mother; breastfeed|~药 take medicine ❷ 在某一出售食物的地方吃;按某种标准吃 eat at a place that sells food; eat by certain standard: ~食堂 have meals at a dining hall; dine in a canteen|~馆子 eat in a restaurant; eat out; dine out|~大灶 eat from a big pot|~小灶 eat from a special pot; have dishes prepared for a special group of people ❸ 依靠某种事物来生活 live off; live on; scrounge off: ~老本 live off past achievements; live on one's old skills|靠山~山,靠水~水。Those living in a mountain live on the mountain and those living by a river get a living from the water — to subsist on what resources are available ❹ 吸收(液体) absorb (liquid); soak up: 道林纸不~墨。Dowling paper does not absorb ink well. ❺ 某物体进入另一物体 one object entering into another: ~刀 penetration of a cutting tool|这条船~水浅。The boat has a low draught. ❻ 消灭(多用于军事、棋戏 mostly in war or a chess game) annihilate; wipe out: ~掉敌人一个团 wipe out an enemy regiment|拿车~他的炮 wipe out his horse with my chariot ❼ 领会;把握 understand; grasp: ~透文件精神 grasp the gist of the document|他的心思我还~不准。I'm not sure what's in his mind. ❽ 承受;禁受 endure; withstand; take: ~得消 can endure or handle (hardship, arduous work, etc.)|这根绳子~不住这么重的分量。This rope cannot support such a heavy weight. ❾ 受;挨 suffer; incur; bear: ~亏 suffer losses|~惊 be startled; be taken aback; be surprised; be shocked|~批评 be criticized ❿ 耗费 consume; exhaust: ~力 laborious; strenuous|~劲 energy-consuming ⓫ 被(多见于早期白话 oft. in the passive voice in the early vernacular) by: ~他耻笑 be laughed at and insulted by sb.

吃[2] chī ☞ 口吃 kǒuchī on p.1108

【吃白饭】chī báifàn ❶ 吃饭时光吃主食不就菜 eat rice or a steamed bun with no dishes to go with it ❷ 吃饭不付钱 have free meals; have a meal at sb. else's expense ❸ 只吃饭而不干活(多指没有工作),也指寄居别人家里,靠别人生活 eat but do not work, referring to people who have no job and live off others

【吃白食】chī báishí〈方 *dial.*〉白吃别人的饭食等 have meals at others' expense; have free meals; live off others; sponge on sb.

【吃闭门羹】chī bìméngēng 被主人拒之门外或主人不在,门锁着,对于上门的人叫吃闭门羹 be denied entry; (of a visitor) find the host not at home and the door locked

【吃瘪】chībiě〈方 *dial.*〉❶ 受窘;受挫 be humiliated; eat humble pie: 当众~ be humiliated in public ❷ 被迫屈服;服输 be forced to give in; be forced to admit or concede defeat

【吃不服】chī ·bu fú 不习惯于吃某种饮食 not used or accustomed to certain food or drink: 生冷的东西我总~。Cold and raw things don't agree with me.

【吃不开】chī ·bu kāi 行不通;不受欢迎 do not work; be unpopular: 你这老一套现在可~了。Your old methods no longer work. *or* The old practices you use are no longer popular.

【吃不来】chī ·bu lái 不喜欢吃;吃不惯 not fond of (certain food); not used to (certain food): 辣的可以,酸的我~。I can eat hot food but do not care for pickled dishes.

【吃不了,兜着走】chī ·bu liǎo, dōu·zhe zǒu〈方 *dial.*〉指出了问题,要承担一切后果 take full responsibility for consequences; get more than one has bargained for; land oneself in serious trouble; be left holding the baby: 主意是你出的,出了事儿你可~! It's your idea, so if anything goes wrong you'll be in serious trouble!

【吃不上】chī ·bu shàng 吃不到 have nothing to eat; be unable to get sth. to eat: 快走吧,再晚了就~饭了。Hurry up, or we'll be too late to get anything to eat.

【吃不消】chī ·bu xiāo 不能支持;支持不住;受

不了 be unable to stand or bear：爬这么高的山，上年纪的人身体怕～。This mountain is too high for the aged to climb. | 这文章写得又长又难懂，真让看的人～。No reader can tolerate such a long and obscure article.

【吃不住】chī·bu zhù 承受不起；不能支持 be unable to bear or stand：机器太沉，这个架子恐怕～。The stand is not strong enough for this heavy machine.

C

【吃不准】chī·bu zhǔn 把握不定；确定不了 be unsure：这句话什么意思，我还～。I'm not quite sure of the meaning of this sentence.

【吃长斋】chī chángzhāi 信佛的人长年吃素，叫吃长斋 (of a believer in Buddhism) be a vegetarian

【吃吃喝喝】chī·chīhēhē 吃饭喝酒，多指以酒食拉拢关系 eat and drink; indulge in merry-making, usu. for the purpose of weaving a network of connections

【吃醋】chīcù 产生嫉妒情绪（多指在男女关系上 usu. of a rival in affairs of the heart) be jealous

【吃大锅饭】chī dàguōfàn〈比喻 *fig.*〉不论工作好坏，贡献大小，待遇、报酬都一样 eat from the same big pot; get the same reward or pay regardless of work performance or contribution

【吃大户】chī dàhù ❶〈旧时 *old*〉遇着荒年，饥民团结在一起到地主富豪家去吃饭或夺取粮食 (of starving people) seize meals or grain by force in a landlord's houses during a famine ❷ 指借故到经济较富裕的单位或个人那里吃喝或索取财物 dine off the wealthy; get the rich to pay up; eat and drink or ask for things in a financially rich unit or at a person's house under a pretext

【吃刀】chīdāo 切削金属时刀具切入工件 penetrate; (of a cutting tool) cut into a metal piece：～深浅要适宜。It is imperative to have an appropriate penetration.

【吃得开】chī·de kāi 行得通；受欢迎 workable; practical; be popular：他手艺好，又热心，在村里很～。He is skilful and warm-hearted, and quite popular in the village.

【吃得来】chī·de lái 吃得惯（不一定喜欢吃）be able to eat (not necessarily fond of)：牛肉我还～，羊肉就吃不来了。Beef is all right, but mutton doesn't agree with me.

【吃得消】chī·de xiāo 能支持；支持得住；受得了 be able to stand; endure or stand：一连几天不睡觉，人怎么能～！You haven't had any sleep in the last few days! How can you bear it!

【吃得住】chī·de zhù 承受得住；能支持 be able to bear or support：这座木桥过大卡车也能～。This wooden bridge can bear the weight of a lorry.

【吃豆腐】chī dòu·fu〈方 *dial.*〉❶ 调戏（妇女）harass (a woman); flirt with (a woman) ❷ 指开玩笑 crack a joke; make fun of sb.; tease ❸ 旧俗丧家准备的饭菜中有豆腐，所以去丧家吊唁吃饭叫吃豆腐 attend a funeral; by old Chinese custom, the meals a bereaved family prepares for well-wishers usu. contain bean-curd dishes, so the Chinese refer to attending a funeral as 'eating bean curd'; also 吃豆腐饭 chī dòu·fufàn

【吃独食】chī dúshí（～儿 chī dúshír）❶ 有东西自己一个人吃，不给别人 have all the food to oneself; refuse to share food with others ❷〈比喻 *fig.*〉独占利益，不让别人分享 keep benefits all to oneself; refuse to share with others

【吃饭】chī//fàn 泛指生活或生存 eat a meal; live on or make a living：靠打猎～（以打猎为生）making a living by hunting

【吃粉笔灰】chī fěnbǐhuī 指教书工作（含诙谐意 humor.）live off chalk dust — live by teaching

【吃干醋】chī gāncù 在与自己不相干的事情上产生嫉妒情绪；没来由地嫉妒 be jealous about sth. unrelated to one; be jealous without reason

【吃功夫】chī gōng·fu 耗费精力；用功力 time-consuming; energy-consuming; with pains-taking efforts：在《挑滑车》里演高宠可不容易，那是个～的角色。Playing the role of Gao Chong in *Breaking Through the Chariot Formation* is not easy as it requires painstaking effort.

【吃官司】chī guān·si 指被控告受处罚或关在监狱里 be brought to court; be sentenced to jail

【吃馆子】chī guǎn·zi 到饭馆里吃饭 eat out; dine out

【吃喝儿】chīhēr 指饮食 food and drink：这里物价高，～不便宜。Prices are high here, and food and drinks are quite expensive too.

【吃后悔药】chī hòuhuǐyào 指事后懊悔 feel remorse or regret after an event

【吃皇粮】chī huángliáng〈比喻 *fig.*〉在政府部门或靠国家开支经费的事业单位任职 live on imperial grains; work with government pay; receive government subsidies or other financial support

【吃回扣】chī huíkòu 接受回扣 accept a kick-back

【吃货】chīhuò 光会吃不会做事的人（骂人的话 curse）good-for-nothing; person who only knows how to eat but nothing about working

【吃讲茶】chī jiǎngchá〈方 *dial.*〉旧指有争执的双方及调解人到茶馆里边喝茶边评理，解决纠纷 have mediation tea; (of two arguing parties and a mediator) come to a tea house and settle a dispute over tea

【吃教】chījiào〈旧时 *old*〉称信天主教或基督教为吃教，含讥讽的意味，因为那时有些信教的人凭借教会的势力来谋生或图利 be converted to and live off Catholicism or Christianity; usu. in an ironic sense because a convert may take advantage of the church to make a living or even a fortune

【吃紧】chījǐn ❶（情势）紧张 (of a situation) tense; critical:形势～ tense situation|银根～。The money market is tight.|眼下正是农活儿～的时候。It is busy farming season right now. ❷ 重要;紧要 important; essential:这事我去不去不～,你不去可就办不成了。Whether or not I go is not important, but if you don't go it won't succeed.|先把那些～的地方整修一下,其他的以后再说吧。Please fix the parts that require immediate attention first; the rest can wait for a while.

【吃劲】chī//jìn (～儿 chī//jìnr) 承受力量 sustain weight:他那条受过伤的腿走路还不～。The leg he injured before still does not bear his weight when he walks.|肩上东西太重,我可吃不住劲儿了。The load on my shoulders is too heavy to bear.

【吃劲】chījìn ❶ (～儿 chījìnr) 费劲;吃力 painstaking; strenuous:他挑百儿八十斤也并不～。He can carry 50 kg. without feeling the strain. ❷〈方 *dial.*〉感觉重要或有关系(多用于否定 usu. in the negative) regard as important:这出戏不怎么样,看不看不～。The play is only so-so; it doesn't matter if you don't go and see it.

【吃惊】chī//jīng 受惊 be surprised; be shocked:令人～get a surpise|～受怕 be apprehensive; be surprised and frightened|大吃一惊 get a big surprise

【吃开口饭】chī kāikǒufàn〈旧时 *old*〉以表演戏曲、曲艺等谋生叫做吃开口饭 make a living by theatrical performing, ballad-singing or storytelling

【吃空额】chī kòng'é 主管人员向上级虚报人数,非法占有虚报名额的薪饷等 embezzle by doctoring the payroll; put non-existent names on the payroll and illegally draw pay under them; also 吃空饷 chī kòngxiǎng

【吃口】chīkǒu ❶ 家庭吃饭的人 mouths to feed; members of a family to be fed:他家里～多,生活比较困难。He is hard up because he has many mouths to feed in the family. ❷ 吃到嘴里的感觉 taste of food in the mouth:面包～松软。This kind of bread has a soft, spongy texture.|这种梨水分少,～略差。This kind of pear is not very juicy, so it doesn't taste as good as expected. ❸ 牲畜吃食物的能力(of livestock) intake of feed:这头牛～好,膘力足。This ox has a good appetite and is strong and sturdy.

【吃苦】chī//kǔ 经受艰苦 bear hardships; suffer:～耐劳 bear hardship and hard work; be used or inured to hardship and toil|～在前,享乐在后 be the first to bear hardships and the last to enjoy comforts

【吃苦头】chī kǔ·tou 遭受痛苦或磨难 suffer; experience an ordeal; get into trouble:他流浪异乡,吃过很多苦头。He led a vagrant's life and suffered a great deal.

【吃亏】chī//kuī ❶ 受损失 suffer losses; come to grief; get the worst of it:决不能让群众～。We should never let the masses suffer a loss.|他吃了不老实的亏。He has come to grief owing to his dishonesty. ❷ 在某方面条件不利 be at a disadvantage; be in an unfavourable situation:这场球赛,他们吃了经验不足的亏,否则不会输。Their lack of experience put them at a disadvantage in the match, otherwise they would not have lost the game.

【吃劳保】chī láobǎo 指职工因长期生病、因公致残等享受劳保待遇 live off labour insurance because of prolonged illness or industrial injury

【吃老本】chī lǎoběn (～儿 chī lǎoběnr) 原指消耗本金,现多指只凭已有的资历、功劳、本领过日子,不求进取和提高 live on the principal; rest on one's laurels; live off one's past experience, contributions and skills without making more progress and improvement

【吃里爬外】chī lǐ pá wài 受着这一方的好处,暗地里却为那一方尽力 eat sb.'s food and cater to his enemy; live on one person while secretly serving another; 爬 also put as 扒 pá

【吃力】chīlì ❶ 费力 strenuous; painstaking:爬山很～。Mountain climbing is a backbreaking experience.|～不讨好 work hard but get little thanks; spare no pains but get no gains ❷〈方 *dial.*〉疲劳 tired; exhausted:跑了一天路,感到很～。I feel exhausted after a long day on the road.

【吃粮】chīliáng〈旧时 *old*〉指当兵 join the army

【吃零嘴】chī língzuǐ 吃零食 have snacks between meals; eat between meals

【吃派饭】chī pàifàn 临时下乡的工作人员到当地安排的农户家吃饭 (of officials who go to inspect work in the countryside) board with local peasant families in rotation

【吃偏饭】chī piānfàn 在共同生活中吃好于别人的饭食 eat better-than-average meals in a collective life;〈比喻 *fig.*〉得到特别的照顾 enjoy special treatment; enjoy privileges; also 吃偏食 chī piānshí

【吃枪子】chī qiāngzǐ (～儿 chī qiāngzǐr) 指被枪打死(骂人的话 offens.) be hit by a bullet; be shot dead

【吃青】chīqīng 庄稼还没有完全成熟就收下来吃(多在青黄不接食物缺乏时 mostly at times of food shortage between two harvests) get in crops before they are ripe

【吃请】chīqǐng 接受邀请(多指对自己有所求的人的邀请)去吃饭(usu. given by someone asking a favour) accept a dinner invitation：～受贿 accept a dinner invitation intended as a bribe

【吃儿】chīr 吃的东西 eatables; food：家里没～了。There's no food in the house.

【吃食】chī//shí (～儿 chī//shír)(鸟、兽等)吃食物(of birds; animals, etc.) feed：母鸡生病，不～了。The hen is sick and refuses food.

C

【吃水】[1] chīshuǐ 吸取水分 absorb moisture：这块地不～。This field absorbs little moisture. | 和面时玉米面比白面～。Corn flour needs more water than wheat flour when mixed.

【吃水】[2] chīshuǐ ❶ 取用生活用水 fetch water：高山地区～困难。It's difficult to get water in mountainous areas. ❷〈方 *dial.*〉供食用的水(区别于洗东西用的水 as compared with water used for washing) drinking water

【吃水】[3] chīshuǐ 船身入水的深度 draught or draft of a boat

【吃素】chīsù ❶ 不吃鱼、肉等食物。佛教徒的吃素戒律还包括不吃葱蒜等。abstain from eating fish or meat; (of a Buddhist believer) also abstain from onion and garlic; be a vegetarian ❷〈比喻 *fig.*〉不事杀伤(多用于否定式 usu. in the negative) benign; not effective：你敢捣乱？告诉你，我的拳头可不是～的。Do you dare to throw your weight around here? Let me tell you. My fists are not merely for decoration.

【吃透】chī//tòu 理解透彻 have a thorough understanding of sth.：～会议精神 thoroughly understand the spirit of the meeting | 这话是什么意思，我还吃不透。I haven't yet grasped the meaning of these words.

【吃瓦片儿】chī wǎpiànr 指依靠出租房子生活 make a living by renting out rooms; live on rent

【吃闲饭】chī xiánfàn 指只吃饭而不做事，没有经济收入 unemployed and without income; be a loafer：两个孩子都工作了，家里没有～的了。His two children have work and no one in the family stays idle at home.

【吃现成饭】chī xiànchéngfàn〈比喻 *fig.*〉不劳而获，坐享其成 reap without sowing; feed on the fruits of others' labour

【吃香】chīxiāng 受欢迎；受重视 popular; in great demand; much sought after：这种产品在市场上很～。This kind of product sells like hot cake on the market. | 手艺高超的人在哪里都～。People of expertise are much sought after.

【吃相】chīxiàng 吃东西时的姿态神情 table manners：～不雅 unpleasant table manners | ～难看 rough table manners

【吃小灶】chī xiǎozào〈比喻 *fig.*〉享受特殊照顾 eat specially-made dishes; receive special care; enjoy privileges：学校准备在考试前给学习成绩差的学生～。The school decided to give remedial lectures to students with low grades before the examinations.

【吃心】chī//xīn〈方 *dial.*〉疑心；多心 be suspicious; be oversensitive：我是说他呢，你吃什么心？I'm speaking about him, why are you so suspicious?

【吃鸭蛋】chī yādàn〈比喻 *fig.*〉在考试或竞赛中得零分 eat a duck egg; get no score in an exam or competition; fail an exam

【吃哑巴亏】chī yǎ·bakuī 吃了亏无处申诉或不敢声张，叫吃哑巴亏 suffer losses but have no recourse to justice or do not dare to speak out; swallow a bitter pill in silence; have no alternative but to keep one's grievances to oneself

【吃一堑，长一智】chī yī qiàn, zhǎng yī zhì 受一次挫折，长一分见识 a fall into the pit, a gain in your wit; experience through suffering is instructive; experience teaches

【吃斋】chī//zhāi ❶ same as 吃素 chīsù ①：～念佛 abstain from meat and fish and chant Buddhist scriptures | 吃长斋 practise a lifelong abstinence from meat and fish ❷(和尚)吃饭(of monks) have a meal ❸(非出家人)在寺院吃饭(of lay people) have a vegetarian meal at a Buddhist temple

【吃重】chīzhòng ❶(所担负的责任)艰巨(of responsibility) onerous; arduous; hard; formidable：他在这件事上很～。It is an onerous task for him. ❷ 费力 energy consuming; strenuous; laborious：搞翻译，对我来讲，是很～的事。I find translation arduous work. ❸ 载重 loading capacity：这辆车～多少？What's the loading capacity of that lorry?

【吃准】chī//zhǔn 认定；确认 be certain; be sure：吃不准 be unsure | 吃得准 be absolutely sure | 他～老张过几天就会回来。He's sure that Old Zhang will be back in a couple of days.

【吃嘴】chī//zuǐ〈方 *dial.*〉❶ 吃零食 have snacks between meals ❷ 贪吃；嘴馋 fond of eating; gluttonous; greedy

【吃罪】chīzuì 承受罪责 take the blame：～不起 cannot afford to take the blame | ～不轻 bear much of the blame

郗 Chī 姓 a surname
☞ Xī on p. 2045

哧 chī〈拟声词 *onom.*〉：～的一声撕下一块布来 rip off a piece of cloth with a sharp tearing sound | ～～地笑 titter; laugh up or in one's sleeve; laugh under one's breath or to oneself

【哧溜】chīliū〈拟声词 *onom.*〉形容迅速滑动的声音 sound of slipping or sliding at speed：～一下，滑了一跤。Swish! Someone slipped and fell.

蚩 chī〈书 *fml.*〉❶ 无知;傻 ignorant; stupid ❷ same as 嗤 chī ❸ same as 媸 chī

眵 chī ☞ 膍眵 píchī on p. 1468

鸱 chī 古书上指鹞鹰 owl (recorded in ancient books)

【鸱尾】chīwěi 中式房屋屋脊两端的陶制装饰物,形状略像鸱的尾巴 ceramic ornament shaped somewhat like an owl's tail, fixed at either end of a Chinese-style house's roof ridge

【鸱吻】chīwěn 中式房屋屋脊两端陶制的装饰物 ceramic ornament at either end of the roof ridge of a Chinese-style house

【鸱枭】chīxiāo same as 鸱鸮 chīxiāo

【鸱鸮】chīxiāo 鸟类的一科,头大,嘴短而弯曲。吃鼠、兔、昆虫等小动物,对农业有益。鸺鹠、猫头鹰等都属于鸱鸮科。typical owl (*Strigidae*), with a big head and short, hooked beak that feed on rats, rabbits, insects and other small animals; good for agriculture. The owl and the barred owlet belong to this family; also 鸱枭 chīxiāo

【鸱鸺】chīxiū 猫头鹰 owl(*Strigiformes*)

絺 chī 细葛布 fine ko-hemp cloth

鸰 chī same as 鸱 chī

眵 chī 眼睑分泌出的黄色液体 eye secretion; gum of the eyes; yellow liquid secreted by eyelids; also 眼眵 yǎnchī;有的地区叫眼屎或眵目糊 in some areas also known as 眼屎 yǎnshǐ or 眵目糊 chīmù·hu

笞 chī〈书 *fml.*〉用鞭、杖或竹板子打 beat sb. with a whip, a cane, or a bamboo strip:鞭～ whip; lash; flog

瓻 chī 陶制的酒壶 pottery wine jar

摛 chī〈书 *fml.*〉舒展;散布 smooth out; spread:～藻(铺张辞藻)(of writing) turgid

嗤 chī〈书 *fml.*〉嗤笑 sneer:～之以鼻 hold sth. in contempt; scorn

【嗤笑】chīxiào 讥笑 sneer at; jeer at; laugh at:为人～ be the laughing stock|～他不懂道理。He was laughed at for his lack of common sense.

【嗤之以鼻】chī zhī yǐ bí 用鼻子吭气,表示看不起 turn up one's nose at sb. or sth.; pooh-pooh; give a snort of contempt; despise; turn one's nose up at

痴(癡) chī ❶ 傻;愚笨 silly; foolish; stupid:～呆 mentally retarded; idiotic|～人说梦 tale told by an idiot; idiotic nonsense ❷ 极度迷恋某人或某种事物 be infatuated with; be head over heels in love with:～情 passionate love|书～ a lover of books ❸〈方 *dial.*〉由于某种事物影响变傻了的;精神失常 become silly because of certain things; deranged; crazy; insane:～子 idiot; mad person

【痴騃】chī'ái 痴呆;不灵敏 stupid; slow in action

【痴呆】chīdāi ❶ 举止呆滞,不活泼 slow in action; inactive:两眼～地望着前面 eyes staring blankly ahead ❷ 傻 stupid; silly; idiotic; foolish; mentally retarded:经过那次变故,他有点～了。He has looked a bit vacant since that incident.

【痴肥】chīféi 肥胖得难看 abnormally fat; obese:～臃肿 corpulent and ugly

【痴话】chīhuà 傻话;不合常理的话 silly words; nonsense

【痴狂】chīkuáng 形容着迷程度极深 be infatuated; be obsessed:她是个演员,～地爱着自己的事业。As an actress, she is head over heels in love with her career.

【痴梦】chīmèng 迷梦 daydream; hallucination; illusion

【痴迷】chīmí ❶ 沉迷 be infatuated with; be obsessed with; be crazy about:～不悟 too infatuated to shake free ❷ 深深地迷恋 be head over heels in love with; be crazy about:他读大学时,对电影艺术曾～过一段时间。He was crazy about film during his university years.

【痴男怨女】chī nán yuàn nǚ 指沉湎于情爱中的男女 men and women in love

【痴情】chīqíng ❶ 痴心的爱情 passionate love:一片～ of passionate devotion ❷ 多情达到痴心的程度 be obsessed:～女子 a foolishly sentimental girl|她对音乐很～。She is obsessed by music.

【痴人说梦】chī rén shuō mèng〈比喻 *fig.*〉说根本办不到的荒唐话 tale told by an idiot; idiotic nonsense or lunatic ravings that cannot be realized

【痴想】chīxiǎng ❶ 发呆地想 be lost in thought or reverie:他一面眺望,一面～,身上给雨打湿了也不觉得。Looking into the distance and lost in thought, he did not even feel the rain as it drenched him. ❷ 不能实现的痴心的想法 wishful thinking

【痴笑】chīxiào 傻笑 laugh foolishly; giggle

【痴心】chīxīn ❶ 沉迷于某人或某种事物的心思 obsession over sb. or sth.; infatuation:一片～ case of pure infatuation; adoring love ❷ 形容沉迷于某人或某种事物 be dead gone on sb.; infatuated or obsessed with sb. or sth.:～情郎 man in love

【痴心妄想】chī xīn wàng xiǎng 指一心想着不可能实现的事 wishful thinking; daydreaming; hallucination; illusion

【痴长】chīzhǎng〈谦辞 *pol.*〉年纪比较大的人,说自己白白地比对方大若干岁 be older; be

sb.'s senior：我～你几岁，没多学到什么东西。Although I'm several years your senior, I have no more knowledge than you.

【痴子】chī·zi〈方 *dial.*〉❶ 傻子 fool; idiot ❷ 疯子 mad person; lunatic

【痴醉】chīzuì 对某种事物着迷并为之陶醉；迷醉 be infatuated with sth.; be fascinated; be spellbound：精湛的表演令人～。The audience was mesmerized by the excellent performance.

媸 chī〈书 *fml.*〉相貌丑（跟'妍'相对 as opposed to 'beautiful'）ugly：不辨妍～ fail to distinguish between beauty and ugliness; fail to tell the beautiful from the ugly

螭 chī ❶ 古代传说中没有角的龙。古代建筑中或工艺品上常用它的形状做装饰。*chi*, hornless dragon in Chinese mythology, oft. a decorative motif in traditional architecture, arts and crafts ❷ same as 魑 chī

魑 chī ☞ below

【魑魅】chīmèi〈书 *fml.*〉传说中指山林里能害人的妖怪 man-eating monsters dwelling in high mountains and deep forests in legendary stories：～魍魉 evil spirits; demons; monsters

【魑魅魍魉】chīmèi wǎngliǎng〈比喻 *fig.*〉各种各样的坏人 evil spirits; demons; monsters; evil people of all descriptions

chí（彳）

池 chí ❶ 池塘 pond; pool：游泳～ swimming pool｜养鱼～ fish pond｜盐～ salt lake ❷ 旁边高中间洼的地方 depression; low-lying land：花～ flower bed｜乐（yuè）～ orchestra pit ❸〈旧时 *old*〉指剧场正厅的前部 front part of a theatre; stalls in a theatre：～座 front seats in a theatre; front stalls ❹〈书 *fml.*〉护城河 moat：城～ city ❺（Chí）姓 a surname

【池汤】chítāng 澡堂中的浴池（区别于'盆汤' as compared with a 'bathtub' or a 'cubicle'）bathing pool in a bathhouse; also 池塘 chítáng and 池堂 chítáng

【池塘】chítáng ❶ 蓄水的坑，一般不太大，比较浅 pond; pool; body of shallow water smaller than a lake：～养鱼 raise fish in a pond ❷ same as 池汤 chítāng

【池盐】chíyán 从咸水湖采取的盐，成分和海盐相同 lake salt; salt obtained from a salt lake, with the same composition as sea salt

【池鱼之殃】chí yú zhī yāng〈比喻 *fig.*〉因牵连而受到的灾祸 disaster that befalls sb. because of implication; also 池鱼之祸 chí yú zhī huò; ☞ 城门失火，殃及池鱼 chéng mén shī huǒ, yāng jí chí yú on p. 251

【池浴】chíyù 在池汤里洗澡（区别于'盆浴' as compared with 'bathing in a bathtub'）bathe at a public bath

【池沼】chízhǎo 比较大的水坑 large water pit

【池子】chí·zi ❶ 蓄水的坑 pond; pool ❷ 指浴池 bathing pool ❸ 指舞池 dance floor of a ballroom ❹〈旧时 *old*〉指剧场正厅的前部 stalls in a theatre

【池座】chízuò 剧场正厅前部的座位 stalls in a theatre

弛 chí〈书 *fml.*〉松开；松懈 relax; slacken; loosen：～禁 lift a ban; annul a prohibition｜一张一～ alternate tension with relaxation

【弛缓】chíhuǎn ❶（局势、气氛、心情等）变和缓（of situation, ambience, mood, etc.）become relaxed; calm down; feel relieved：他听了这一番话，紧张的心情渐渐～下来。On hearing these words, he gradually calmed down. ❷ 松弛舒缓 loose; slow; at leisure：纪律～ lax discipline

【弛禁】chíjìn〈书 *fml.*〉开放禁令 annul a prohibition; lift a ban

【弛懈】chíxiè〈书 *fml.*〉松弛；松懈 loose; slack; lax：刻苦自励，不可一日～ work hard without slackening one's effort for even a single day

驰 chí ❶（车马等，使车马等）跑得很快（of vehicles, horses, etc.）gallop; drive at a high speed：～行 run fast｜～逐 pursue at high speed｜飞～而过 drive past as if flying; flee past ◇风～电掣 swift as the wind and quick as lightning ❷ 传播 disseminate; popularize; promote：～名 become known; become famous ❸〈书 *fml.*〉（心神）向往（of heart）long for; be eager to (or for)：神～ long for｜～想 be carried away; be lost in a reverie

【驰骋】chíchěng（骑马）奔驰（on horseback）gallop：无边的牧场，任人策马～。The pastureland is so vast, a rider can gallop as fast as his horse will go. ◇～文坛 play an outstanding role in the literary world

【驰电】chídiàn 迅速发出电报 send an emergency telegraph：～告急 send an emergency telegraph for help

【驰名】chímíng 声名传播很远 become known far and wide; become famous; become renowned：～中外 renowned at home and abroad

【驰目】chímù〈书 *fml.*〉放眼（往远处看）stretch one's eye over (many a mile of terra incognita); look (into the distance)：～远眺 look into the distance

【驰驱】chíqū ❶（骑马）快跑（on horseback）run quickly; gallop; trot：～疆场 fight valiantly in the battlefield ❷〈书 *fml.*〉指为人奔走效力 bustle about for sb. else's sake

【驰书】chíshū〈书 *fml.*〉迅速传信 dispatch a message express：～告急 send an emergency message for help

【驰突】chítū〈书 *fml.*〉快跑猛冲 run quickly about; charge:往来～,如入无人之境 charge this way and that as if in a no-man's land

【驰骛】chíwù〈书 *fml.*〉奔驰;奔走 gallop; run quickly

【驰誉】chíyù 声誉传播得很远 become known far and wide:～学界 become well-known in academic circles|～全国 become known across the country

【驰援】chíyuán 奔赴援救 dash to the rescue of sb.:星夜～ rush to the rescue on a starry night

【驰骤】chízhòu〈书 *fml.*〉驰骋 gallop:纵横～ gallop freely

迟(遲) chí ❶ 慢 slow; tardy:～～不决 still undecided after hesitating for some time; unable to make up one's mind; hesitate to make a decision|事不宜～ lose no time in doing sth.; need immediate attention ❷ 比规定的时间或合适的时间靠后 fall behind schedule; late:～到 be late|昨儿睡得太～了。I went to sleep very late last night. ❸ (Chí) 姓 a surname

【迟到】chídào 到得比规定的时间晚 arrive later than the arranged time; be late (for work, class, etc.)

【迟钝】chídùn (感官、思想、行动等)反应慢,不灵敏 (of senses, thinking, movement, etc.) dull; slow in response:感觉～ be insensitive to sth.|反应～ be slow in reacting; react slowly

【迟缓】chíhuǎn 不迅速;缓慢 slow; sluggish:动作～ doddering

【迟暮】chímù ❶ 天快黑的时候;傍晚 dusk; twilight:到达目的地已是～时分。It was dusk when we arrived at our destination. ❷〈书 *fml.*〉〈比喻 *fig.*〉晚年 evening years; past one's prime:～之感 feel old

【迟误】chíwù 迟延耽误 delay; postpone:事关重要,不得～。So much is at stake, it tolerates no delay.|他每天准时上班,从来没有～过。He came to work on time every day, and was never once late.

【迟延】chíyán 耽搁;拖延 delay; put off:情况紧急,不能再～了。We have no time to lose at this critical point.

【迟疑】chíyí 拿不定主意;犹豫 be unable to decide; hesitate:～不决 hesitate when making a decision|他～片刻,才接着说下去。He hesitated for a moment and then resumed talking.

【迟早】chízǎo 或早或晚;早晚 sooner or later; someday in the future:他～会来的。He will come sooner or later.|问题～要解决。The problem will be resolved sooner or later.

【迟滞】chízhì ❶ 缓慢;不通畅 slow; sluggish; not smooth:河道淤塞,流水～。The river is silted up and its water flows sluggishly. ❷ 呆滞 dull; inert; lifeless:目光～ with a dull look in one's eyes ❸ 阻碍,使延迟或停滞 stall; delay:节节阻击,～敌人的行动。Our successive victories have impeded the enemy's deployment.

坻 chí〈书 *fml.*〉水中的小块陆地 small patch of land in the water

☞ dǐ on p.416

茌 chí 茌平(Chípíng),地名,在山东 Chiping, a place in Shandong Province

持 chí ❶ 拿着;握着 hold; grasp:～枪 hold a gun ◇～法 enforce the law ❷ 支持;保持 support; keep; maintain:坚～ insist on; persevere in; stick to; adhere to|～久 protracted; long-term ❸ 主管;料理 administrate; manage; run:操～ manage; be in charge of|主～ be in charge of; preside ❹ 控制;挟制 control; take advantage of sb.'s weakness and control them; force sb. to do one's bidding:劫～ kidnap; hijack|挟～ hold sb. under duress ❺ 对抗 resist; oppose:僵～ refuse to budge; be in a stalemate|相～不下 be locked in a stalemate

【持法】chífǎ 执行法律 enforce the law:～严明 be strict and impartial in enforcing the law

【持家】chíjiā 料理家务 do household chores; run a household:勤俭～ be industrious and thrifty in running a household

【持久】chíjiǔ 保持长久 abiding; lasting; enduring; protracted:肥效～ lasting effect of fertilizer|争取～和平 fight for lasting peace

【持久战】chíjiǔzhàn 持续时间较长的战争。是在一方较强大并企图速战速决的条件下,另一方采取逐步削弱敌人、最后战胜敌人的战略方针而形成的。protracted war in which the weak side adopts the strategy of gradually wearing the strong side down and finally defeating it, as the latter seeks to win the war quickly

【持论】chílùn 提出主张;立论 submit a proposal; put forward a proposal; present an argument:～公平 state a case fairly; hold impartial views|～有据 argue on the basis of actual facts; put forward a well-grounded argument

【持平】chípíng ❶ 公正;公平 unbiased; fair:～之论 unbiased view ❷ (与相对比的数量)保持相等 equal to (the amount compared to):鲜鱼上市三百万斤,与去年～。Three million *jin* of fresh fish were sold this year, as much as last year.|钢窗和木制门窗的价格基本～。The prices of steel and wooden window frames are basically the same.

【持身】chíshēn 对待自己;要求自己 make demands on oneself:～严正 set strict demands on oneself; be strict with oneself

【持续】chíxù 延续不断 last; sustain; continue: ～的干旱造成粮食大幅度减产。Sustained drought has substantially reduced grain output.|两国经济和文化的交流已经～了一千多年。Economic and cultural exchange between the two countries has lasted for more than a thousand years.

【持斋】chízhāi 信某种宗教的人遵守不吃荤或限制吃某种东西的戒律 hold a fast (of religious believers) eat no meat, fish or other foods that are taboo in a religion or custom

C

【持正】chízhèng〈书 *fml.*〉❶ 主持正义 uphold justice: ～不阿 upright and above flattery ❷ 不偏不倚 unbiased; fair; same as 持平 chípíng ①: 平心～ be fair and free from bias

【持之以恒】chí zhī yǐ héng 长久地坚持下去 make unremitting effort; pursue with determination; persevere in doing sth.; persist in: 努力学习,～ study assiduously and perseveringly|锻炼身体要～。Perseverance is essential in physical exercise.

【持之有故】chí zhī yǒu gù 见解或主张有一定的根据 be well-grounded in one's views; argue with well-supported facts

【持重】chízhòng 谨慎;稳重;不浮躁 prudent; cautious; discreet; circumspect: 老成～ mature and prudent

匙 chí 匙子 spoon: 汤～ soup spoon|茶～ tea spoon|羹～ broth spoon

☞ ·shi on p. 1764

【匙子】chí·zi 舀液体或粉末状物体的小勺 ladle, used to scoop up liquid or powder

漦 chí〈书 *fml.*〉口水;涎沫 spit; saliva

墀 chí〈书 *fml.*〉台阶上面的空地;台阶 level ground that a staircase leads to; landing: 丹～ red painted stone terrace in front of the imperial palace

踟 chí ☞ below

【踟蹰】chíchú 心里迟疑,要走不走的样子 demur; hesitate; be uncertain about whether to move or not: ～不前 hesitate to move forward; also 踟躇 chíchú

【踟躇】chíchú same as 踟蹰 chíchú

篪(竾、箎) chí 古代的竹管乐器,像笛子,有八孔 *chi*, an ancient bamboo flute with eight holes, similar to *dizi*, another kind of Chinese bamboo flute

chǐ (彳)

尺 chǐ ❶ 长度单位。10 寸等于 1 尺,10 尺等于 1 丈。1 市尺合 1/3 米。traditional Chinese unit of length; one *chi* comprises 10 *cun* and one *zhang* comprises 10 *chi*; one *chi* is about one third of a metre ❷ 量长度的器具 tool for measuring length; ruler: 皮～ tape measure; tape|卷～ tape measure; band tape ❸ 画图的器具 tool for drawing: 丁字～ T-square|放大～ pantograph ❹ 像尺的东西 sth. shaped like a ruler: 镇～ horizontal bronze paperweight|计算～ slide rule ❺ 尺中的简称 abbr. for 尺中 chǐzhōng, one of the three points where the pulse is felt in traditional Chinese medicine; ☞ 寸口 cùnkǒu on p. 337

☞ chě on p. 233

【尺寸】chǐ·cun ❶ 长度(多指一件东西的长度 oft. length of an article) length; size: 这件衣服～不合适。This garment is the wrong size. ❷ 分寸 propriety; suitability: 他办事很有～。He has a sense of propriety when handling matters.|说话要掌握好～。The way one speaks should accord with the situation at hand.

【尺牍】chǐdú 书信(古代书简约长一尺) letter; correspondence; epistolary writing (the bamboo strip, about one *chi* long, on which characters were written):《～大全》(教人如何写信的书) *A General Guide to Letter Writing* (a guide to writing letters)

【尺度】chǐdù 标准 standard; yardstick; criterion; measure: 放宽～ lower the standard|实践是检验真理的～。Practice is the sole criterion for judging truth.

【尺短寸长】chǐ duǎn cùn cháng《楚辞·卜居》:'尺有所短,寸有所长。'由于应用的地方不同,一尺也有显着短的时候,一寸也有显着长的时候。*The Elegies of Chu · Divination*: In different places, a *chi* may prove too short while a *cun* may prove too long;〈比喻 *fig.*〉人或事物各有各的长处和短处(of things and people) have both strength and weakness

【尺幅千里】chǐ fú qiān lǐ 一尺长的图画,把千里的景象都画进去 a one-*chi*-long scroll encompasses a thousand *li* of landscape;〈比喻 *fig.*〉事物的外形虽小,但包含的内容非常丰富 a tiny object may be rich in content

【尺骨】chǐgǔ 上端是三棱形的长骨,在桡骨的内侧。上端较粗大,与肱骨相接,下端与腕骨相接。ulna; long bone of the forearm on the inner side of the radius that has a relatively thick triangle-shaped upper end that connects to the humerus, and a lower end that connects to the carpal bone; (图见☞ figure for 骨骼 gǔgé on p. 693)

【尺蠖】chǐhuò 尺蠖蛾的幼虫,行动时身体向上弯成弧状,像用大拇指和中指量距离一样,所以叫尺蠖 looper; inchworm; geometer; geometrid moth worm, which moves with its body arching upward, like a person using thumb and middle finger to measure length

【尺蠖蛾】chǐhuò'é 昆虫的一种,身体和脚都很细，翅膀阔，只有复眼。幼虫叫尺蠖。种类很多，是果树和森林的主要害虫之一。geometrid moth (*Geometridae*); insect with a thin body and limbs, wide wings and compound eyes; known as looper or inchworm at its larval stage; geometrid moth and all its variants are a major pest of fruit trees and forests

【尺码】chǐmǎ（～儿 chǐmǎr）❶ 尺寸（多指鞋帽）(of hats and shoes) size：各种～的帽子都齐全。There's a supply of hats of all sizes. ❷ 尺寸的大小；标准 yardstick; standard：两件事性质不一样，不能用一个～衡量。These two matters are completely different and cannot be measured by the same yardstick.

【尺头儿】chǐtóur〈方 *dial.*〉❶ 尺寸的大小；尺码 measurement; size ❷ 零碎料子；零头 odd bits of cloth; a small piece of cloth

【尺头】chǐ·tou〈方 *dial.*〉布帛 cloth; silk; textile：一匹～ a bolt of cloth

【尺页】chǐyè 一尺见方的书画单页或书画册 work of calligraphy, painting, book or album the size of one square *chi*：一帧～ a 33.3 cm. by 33.3 cm. painting | 一部～ a 33.3 cm. by 33.3 cm. album

【尺中】chǐzhōng ☞ 寸口 cùnkǒu on p.337

【尺子】chǐ·zi 量长度的器具 instrument to measure length; ruler

呎 chǐ 又 also yīngchǐ 英尺旧也作呎 foot (英尺) formerly known as 呎 yīngchǐ

齿(齒) chǐ ❶ 人类和高等动物咀嚼食物的器官，由坚固的骨组织和釉质构成，每个齿分三部分。下部细长成锥形，叫齿根，上部叫齿冠，齿根和齿冠之间叫齿颈。按部位和形状的不同，分为门齿、犬齿、前臼齿和臼齿。通称牙或牙齿。tooth, organ of humans and advanced animals used to masticate food, commonly known as 牙 yá or 牙齿 yáchǐ and composed of solid bone tissue and enamel. Each tooth comprises three parts: the thin, conical root, the upper crown, and the middle neck. A set of teeth consists of incisors, canines, premolars and molars, according to their location and shape. ❷（～儿 chǐr）物体上齿形的部分 tooth-like part of an object; dentate：锯～儿 saw teeth; dent of a saw | 梳～儿 teeth of a comb ❸ 带齿儿的 dentate：～轮 dentate wheel; gear ❹〈书 *fml.*〉并列；引为同类 stand side by side; stand shoulder to shoulder; of the same kind：～列 stand side by side | 不～于人类 not regarded as human; be unworthy of humanity ❺〈书 *fml.*〉年龄 age：序～ arranged in order of seniority | ～德俱尊 win respect because of one's age and moral integrity ❻〈书 *fml.*〉说到；提起 speak of; mention：～及 speak of | 不足～数 not worth mentioning

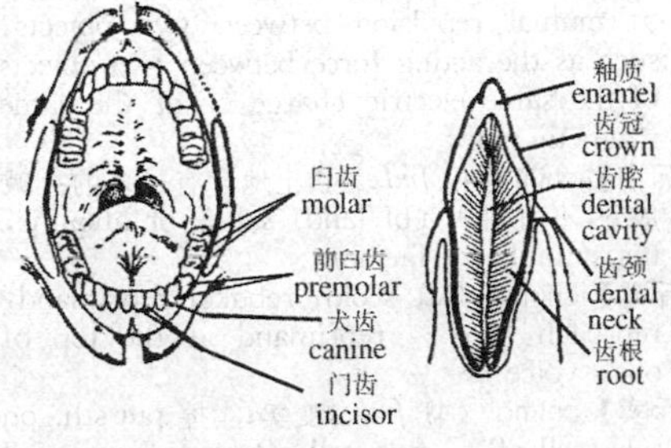

人的齿
Human Teeth

【齿唇音】chǐchúnyīn 上齿和下唇接触而发出的辅音，例如普通话语音中的 f labio-dental sound produced by the upper teeth touching the lower lip, such as 'f' in Mandarin Chinese phonetics; also called 唇齿音 chúnchǐyīn

【齿及】chǐjí〈书 *fml.*〉说到；提及 speak of; mention：区区小事，何足～。Such a trivial matter is hardly worth mentioning.

【齿冷】chǐlěng〈书 *fml.*〉耻笑（笑则张口，时间长了，牙齿就会感觉到冷）laugh at; sneer at (when sb. laughs at length, therefore opening his mouth, the teeth begin to feel cold)：令人～ arouse one's infinite scorn

【齿录】chǐlù〈书 *fml.*〉❶ 录用 hire; employ：未蒙～ fail to be hired or employed ❷ 科举时代同登一榜的人，各具姓名、年龄、籍贯、三代，汇刻成册，叫做齿录 book listing the name, age, hometown, and ancestors of people who passed the imperial civil exams in China's feudal society

【齿轮】chǐlún 机器上有齿的轮状机件。通常是成对啮合，其中一个转动，另一个被带动。作用是改变传动方向、转动方向、转动速度、力矩等。gear wheel or gear; usu. in pairs, where one moves and the other is moved by it. Its function is to change the drive direction, turning direction, turning speed and moment of force. 通称 popularly known as 牙轮 yálún

【齿腔】chǐqiāng 牙齿当中的空腔，充满齿髓 inside of a tooth, filled with tooth pulp;（图见 ☞ figure for 齿 chǐ）

【齿数】chǐshǔ〈书 *fml.*〉说起；提起 speak of; mention; refer to：不足～（不值得提起）not worth mentioning

【齿髓】chǐsuǐ 齿腔中的髓质，质地疏松、柔软，含有很多小血管和神经 tooth pulp; puffy and soft substance with numerous small blood vessels and nerves

【齿龈】chǐyín 包住齿颈的黏膜组织，粉红色，内有很多血管和神经 gum; soft epithelial tissues surrounding the tooth neck, inside which are numerous blood vessels and nerves; also 牙龈 yáyín; 通称 commonly known as 牙床 yáchuáng; 有的地区叫牙花 in some places known as 牙花 yáhuā

侈 chǐ 〈书 *fml*.〉❶ 浪费 waste：奢～extravagant｜豪～ extremely luxurious；extravagant ❷ 夸大 exaggerate：～谈 talk glibly about；prate about；prattle about；brag about

【侈靡】chǐmí 〈书 *fml*.〉奢侈浪费 extravagant and wasteful；excessively extravagant；also 侈靡 chǐmí

【侈谈】chǐtán 〈书 *fml*.〉❶ 夸大而不切实际地谈论 talk glibly about；prate about；prattle about ❷ 夸大而不切实际的话 empty talk

哆 chǐ 〈书 *fml*.〉张开（嘴）open（one's mouth）：～口 open one's mouth
☞ duō on p. 500

耻（恥） chǐ ❶ 羞愧 shame：可～ disgraceful｜知～ have a sense of shame ❷ 耻辱 disgrace；humiliation；insult：雪～ avenge an insult；exonerate from disgrace or humiliation｜奇～大辱 dreadful humiliation；deep disgrace｜不以为～，反以为荣 glory in sth. utterly disgraceful

【耻骨】chǐgǔ 骨盆下部靠近外生殖器的骨头，形状不规则，左右两块结合在一起 pubis；part of either innominate bone that，together with its corresponding section，forms the front of the pelvis；（图见☞ figure for 骨骼 gǔgé on p. 693）

【耻辱】chǐrǔ 声誉上所受的损害；可耻的事情 shame；disgrace；humiliation：蒙受～ suffer humiliation｜莫大的～ gross insult

【耻笑】chǐxiào 鄙视和嘲笑 sneer at；mock

豉 chǐ ☞ 豆豉 dòuchǐ on p. 473

褫 chǐ 〈书 *fml*.〉❶ 脱去；解下 take off；strip off；doff：解佩而～绅 take off one's jade ornaments as well as one's broad belt ❷ 剥夺 deprive；dismiss；divest：～革 remove sb. from office｜～职 be dismissed from office

【褫夺】chǐduó 剥夺 deprive；divest；disown；dispossess：～继承权 deprive sb. of their inheritance；disinherit sb.

【褫革】chǐgé 〈书 *fml*.〉开除；撤职 fire sb.；dismiss sb. from office

chì（彳）

彳 chì［彳亍］（chìchù）〈书 *fml*.〉慢步走，走走停停 walk slowly；saunter；stroll：独自在河边～ take a walk alone by a river

叱 chì 〈书 *fml*.〉大声责骂 denounce or rebuke loudly：怒～ curse angrily｜～问 interrogate angrily；question loudly

【叱呵】chìhē 大声怒斥；怒喝（hè）rebuke angrily and loudly；shout angrily at；bawl at：～部下 bawl at one's subordinates｜～牲口 shout angrily at the draught animal

【叱喝】chìhè same as 叱呵 chìhē：厉声～ yell at sb. in a stern tone of voice

【叱令】chìlìng 呵斥责令；喝令 order；demand loudly：～退出 order sb. to retreat or withdraw from｜～匪徒放下武器 order the bandits to put down their arms

【叱骂】chìmà 责骂 rebuke；curse；scold

【叱问】chìwèn 责问；大声问 interrogate angrily；question loudly

【叱责】chìzé 斥责 scold；upbraid；rebuke：他从不当着客人的面～孩子。He never scolds his children in front of guests.

【叱咤】chìzhà 〈书 *fml*.〉发怒吆喝 flare up and shout

【叱咤风云】chì zhà fēng yún 形容声势威力很大 command the wind and clouds；thundering；extremely powerful

斥[1] chì ❶ 责备 upbraid；blame；scold；reprimand；denounce：申～ rebuke；reprimand｜驳～ refute；rebut；contradict｜痛～ denounce vehemently｜怒～ rebuke angrily；denounce indignantly ❷ 使离开 expel；oust；drive away：排～ repel；exclude；dismiss｜～逐 expel；drive away；oust ❸〈书 *fml*.〉拿出（钱）；支付 take out（money）；pay：～资 allocate funds；invest ❹〈书 *fml*.〉扩展 enlarge；expand；open up：～地 expand land

斥[2] chì 〈书 *fml*.〉侦察 reconnoiter；scout：～候 scout；reconnoiter｜～骑（担任侦察的骑兵）scouts on horseback

斥[3] chì 〈书 *fml*.〉same as 斥卤 chìlǔ

【斥地】chìdì 〈书 *fml*.〉开拓疆土 expand territory：～千里 expand territory by a thousand *li*

【斥革】chìgé 开除；取消 be fired；be dismissed：～功名 be dismissed from one's titles and positions

【斥候】chìhòu 〈旧时 *old*〉军队称侦察（敌情）。也指进行侦察的士兵。gather intelligence about（the enemy）；also referring to scouts on a reconnaissance mission

【斥力】chìlì 物体之间相互排斥的力。带同性电荷的物体之间、同性磁极之间的作用力就是斥力 mutual repulsion between two objects，such as the acting force between two objects of the same electric charge or of the same magnetic pole

【斥卤】chìlǔ 〈书 *fml*.〉指土地含有过多的盐碱成分，不宜耕种（of land）saline or alkaline，not suitable for farming

【斥骂】chìmà 责骂 scold；rebuke；reprimand；reproach：高声～ reprimand at the top of one's voice

【斥卖】chìmài 〈书 *fml*.〉变卖；卖掉 put sth. on sale；sell off：～房产 sell off one's house and other property

【斥退】chìtuì ❶〈旧时 *old*〉指免去官吏的职位

或开除学生的学籍 remove a civil servant from his office or expel sb. from school ❷ 喝令旁边的人退出去 yell at sb. to leave the scene：～左右 order one's men to evacuate with a yell

【斥责】chìzé ❶ 用严厉的言语指出别人的错误或罪行 reprimand；rebuke；denounce：受到～ be severely reprimanded|～这种不讲公德的行为 denounce this kind of immoral behaviour

【斥逐】chìzhú〈书 *fml*.〉驱逐 drive away；expel；oust：～入侵之敌 drive away the invading enemy

【斥资】chìzī〈书 *fml*.〉支付费用 pay expenses：～百万 invest one million dollars|～创建学校 allocate funds for the construction of a school

赤 chì ❶ 比朱红稍浅的颜色 vermillion；shade of colour slightly lighter than red ❷ 泛指红色 red in a general sense：～小豆 red beans|面红耳～ blushed ❸ 象征革命，表示用鲜血争取自由 red，symbol of revolution meaning that freedom is achieved through bloodshed：～卫队 Red Guards ❹ 忠诚 loyal；sincere：～胆 be absolutely loyal to；be completely dedicated to；be committed to|～诚 absolutely sincere ❺ 光着；露着（身体）（of body）naked：～脚 bare-footed|～膊 be stripped to the waist ❻ 空 bare；empty：～手空拳 bare-handed；unarmed ❼ 指赤金 pure gold：金无足～。No piece of gold is pure.

【赤背】chì//bèi 光着上身 be stripped to the waist；bare-backed

【赤膊】chì//bó 光着上身 be stripped to the waist；bare-backed：～上阵 go into battle bare-backed|男人们赤着膊在地里锄草。Stripped to the waist，the men were busy weeding in the fields.

【赤膊】chìbó 光着的上身 naked torso

【赤膊上阵】chì bó shàng zhèn〈比喻 *fig*.〉不讲策略或毫无掩饰地做某事 go into battle stripped to the waist；expedite matters using neither disguise nor strategy

【赤忱】chìchén〈书 *fml*.〉❶ same as 赤诚 chìchéng：～相见 be absolutely frank ❷ 极真诚的心意 sincere wish；ardent expectations：一片～ ardent expectations

【赤诚】chìchéng 非常真诚 absolutely honest and sincere：～待人 treat sb. with genuine sincerity

【赤胆忠心】chì dǎn zhōng xīn 形容十分忠诚 utter devotion；complete dedication；absolute loyalty or commitment

【赤道】chìdào ❶ 环绕地球表面距离南北两极相等的圆周线。它把地球分为南北两半球，是划分纬度的基线，赤道的纬度是0° equator，imaginary line around the surface of the earth equidistant from its poles. Dividing the earth into the southern and northern hemispheres，the equator is the basic line from which to calculate latitude. The latitude of the equator is zero. ❷ 指天球赤道，就是地球赤道面和天球相交形成的大圆圈 celestial equator；great circle of the celestial sphere，lying on the same plane as the earth's equator

【赤地】chìdì〈书 *fml*.〉旱灾或虫灾严重时，寸草不生的土地 barren land devoid of green at times of draught or locust plague：～千里 a thousand *li* of barren land；scene of utter desolation

【赤红】chìhóng 红色 crimson；red：～脸儿 crimson complexion

【赤脚】chì//jiǎo 光着脚（一般指不穿鞋袜，有时只指不穿袜子）bare-footed（not wearing socks and shoes or without socks）：～穿草鞋 wear a pair of straw sandals without socks|农民赤着脚在田里插秧。Bare-footed farmers are transplanting rice seedlings in the fields.

【赤脚】chìjiǎo 光着的脚 bare foot：一双～ a pair of bare feet

【赤脚医生】chìjiǎo yīshēng 指农村里亦农亦医的医务工作人员 bare-footed doctors；part-time paramedic workers in rural areas who also take part in farming work

【赤金】chìjīn 纯金 pure gold；solid gold

【赤佬】chìlǎo〈方 *dial*.〉鬼；鬼子（骂人的话 curse）devil；rascal

【赤露】chìlù（身体）裸露（of body）naked：～着胸口 bare chest

【赤裸】chìluǒ ❶（身体）裸露（of body）naked；nude：全身～ stark naked；without a stitch of clothing on|～着上身 be stripped to the waist|他～着脚走路。He walks bare-footed. ❷〈比喻 *fig*.〉毫无遮盖掩饰 with nothing to cover up：～的原野 barren plains

【赤裸裸】chìluǒluǒ ❶ 形容光着身子，不穿衣服 naked without a stitch of clothing on；stark naked ❷ 形容毫无遮盖掩饰 with nothing to cover up；undisguised；naked：～的侵略行径 downright act of invasion

【赤贫】chìpín 穷得什么也没有 extremely poor without a penny to one's name；impoverished；destitute；in dire poverty：～如洗 utterly destitute；as poor as a church mouse；poverty-stricken

【赤身】chìshēn ❶ 光着身子 naked：～裸体 naked without a stitch of clothing on ❷〈比喻 *fig*.〉人一无所有 without a penny to one's name：他上无老，下无小，是个无牵无挂的～汉。He has neither parents nor children to support；he is a single man with nothing to worry about.

【赤手空拳】chì shǒu kōng quán 形容两手空空，没有任何可以凭借的东西 bare-handed；without anything to rely on

【赤条条】chìtiáotiáo 形容光着身体，一丝不挂，

毫无遮掩 stark naked; not wearing a stitch of clothing

【赤县】Chìxiàn 指中国 poetic name for China; ☞ 神州 Shénzhōu on p. 1708

【赤小豆】chìxiǎodòu ❶ 一年生草本植物,叶子互生,花黄色。种子暗红色,供食用。red bean (*Phaseolus angularis*); annual herb with yellow flowers and dark red edible seeds ❷ 这种植物的种子 seeds of red bean; also called 小豆 xiǎodòu or 红小豆 hóngxiǎodòu

【赤心】chìxīn 真诚的心 honest; sincere:～相待 treat sb. with genuine sincerity|～报国 devote oneself to one's motherland

【赤子】chìzǐ ❶ 初生的婴儿 new-born baby:～之心(比喻纯洁的心) the heart of a new-born; (*fig.*) pure and innocent ❷ 对故土怀有纯真感情的人 person who cherishes deep feelings for his or her hometown:海外～ person who lives abroad but cherishes deep feelings for his or her motherland

【赤字】chìzì 指经济活动中支出多于收入的差额数字。簿记上登记这种数目时,用红笔书写。deficit; in red; excess of liabilities over assets in financial dealings, usu. written in red

【赤足】chìzú same as 赤脚 chì//jiǎo

饬 chì 〈书 *fml.*〉❶ 整顿;整治 put in order; readjust; rectify:整～ put in order; strengthen ❷ 饬令 order; instruct:～其遵办 order sb. to do as told ❸ 谨慎 careful; prudent:谨～ prudent; careful; circumspect; cautious

【饬令】chìlìng 上级命令下级(多用于旧时公文 mostly used in formerly official documents) order from one's superior:～查办 investigate at the order of one's superior

抶 chì 〈书 *fml.*〉鞭打;笞 whip; lash; flog; thrash

炽(熾) chì ❶〈书 *fml.*〉(火)旺 (of fire) ablaze ❷ 热烈旺盛 enthusiastic and energetic:～热 white-hot; blazing; fervent|～烈 fervent; flaming

【炽烈】chìliè (火)旺盛猛烈 (of fire) burning fiercely:篝火在～地燃烧。The camp fire is ablaze.◇～的感情 passion

【炽情】chìqíng 热烈的感情 compassion; passion; zeal; ardour:满腔～ full of enthusiasm

【炽热】chìrè 极热 extremely hot; scorching; blazing:～的阳光 scorching sun ◇～的情感 compassion

【炽盛】chìshèng 〈书 *fml.*〉很旺盛 vigorous; exuberant

翅(翄) chì ❶ 昆虫的飞行器官,一般是两对,呈膜状,上面有翅脉,有的前翅变成角质或革质。通常又指鸟类等动物的飞行器官。wing; one of the pair of thin, lateral extensions on the body of an insect which enable it to fly; the fore wings of some insects have turned into cutin; also the wings of birds;通称 generally put as 翅膀 chìbǎng ❷ 翅果向外伸出呈翅状的果皮 outstretched wing-like peel of a samara ❸ 鱼翅 shark's fin:～席 banquet that serves shark's-fin dishes ❹ (～儿 chìr)物体上形状像翅膀的部分 wing-like part of an object:纱帽有两个～儿。The gauze hat has two wings.

〈古 *arch.*〉same as 啻 chì

【翅膀】chìbǎng ❶ 翅①的通称 general name for 翅 chì ① ❷ 物体上形状或作用像翅膀的部分 part of an object that looks or functions like a wing:飞机～ wings of a plane

【翅果】chìguǒ 果实的一种,一部分果皮向外伸出,像翅膀,借着风力把种子散布到远处,如榆钱 samara; one kind fruit, part of whose peel stretches outward like its wing so that its seeds can be spread to faraway places by wind, such as elm

【翅脉】chìmài 昆虫翅上分布成脉状的构造,有支撑的作用 veins that form the framework of an insect's wing

【翅席】chìxí 指菜肴中有鱼翅的宴席 banquet whose dishes include shark's fin

【翅子】chì·zi ❶ 鱼翅 shark's fin ❷〈方 *dial.*〉same as 翅膀 chìbǎng

眙 chì 〈书 *fml.*〉❶ 直视;注视 stare; gaze; eyes fixed on sth. ❷ 惊视 stare in surprise; gaze in shock

☞ yí on p. 2262

敕(勅、勑) chì 皇帝的诏令 imperial order; edict:宣～ announce an imperial decree|～命 imperial order|～封 (of a monarch) appoint sb. to a post; confer a reward or title on sb.|～撰 write on the imperial order

【敕封】chìfēng 指朝廷以敕令封赏(官爵、称号) confer a reward (official rank or title) on sb. at an imperial order

【敕建】chìjiàn 奉帝王命令修建 build sth. at the decree of the emperor

【敕令】chìlìng ❶ 皇帝下达命令 (of an emperor) issue an edict ❷ 皇帝下达的命令 order from the emperor; imperial edict

【敕书】chìshū 皇帝颁给朝臣的诏书 imperial edict issued to a minister by the emperor

【敕造】chìzào 奉帝王命令建造 build at the decree of the emperor

啻 chì 〈书 *fml.*〉但;只;仅 but; only; just:不～ not only|何～ can it be any less than ...|奚～ can it be any less than ...

傺 chì ☞ [侘傺](chàchì) on p. 206

鶒 chì ☞ [鸂鶒](xīchì) on p. 2051

瘈 chì [瘈疭](chìzòng) same as 瘛疭 chìzòng ☞ zhì on p. 2479

憏 chì ☞ [侘憏](chàchì) on p. 207

瘛 chì［瘛疭］(chìzòng)中医指痉挛的症状 symptoms of a convulsion in traditional Chinese medicine

chōng (ㄔㄨㄥ)

冲[1]（沖、衝）chōng ❶ 通行的大道；重要的地方 thoroughfare；important place：要～ place of strategic importance｜首当其～ bear the brunt；be the first to be affected (by a disaster, etc.) ❷ 很快地朝某一方向直闯，突破障碍 storm；make a rapid charge in one direction and break through a barrier：横～直撞 push or shove one's way through；jostle and elbow one's way；dash around madly；barge about｜～出重围 break through a tight encirclement｜直～云霄 soar into the sky ◇～口而出 blurt out ❸ 猛烈地撞击(多用于对对方思想感情的抵触方面 mostly used to describe conflicting feelings and thoughts) clash；collide：～突 conflict；collision｜～犯 offend ❹ 指冲喜 arrange a wedding for a young man who is dangerously ill, in the hope that the joyous occasion will ward off imminent death ❺ 太阳系中，除水星和金星外，其余的某一个行星(如火星、木星或土星)运行到跟地球、太阳成一条直线而地球正处在这个行星与太阳之间的位置时，叫做冲。这时，太阳从地平线升起，这个行星从西边落下；太阳下山时，这个行星从东方升起。opposition；situation of two heavenly bodies when their longitudes or right ascensions differ by 180 degrees. In the solar system, all planets (such as Mars, Jupiter and Saturn) other than Mercury and Venus arrive on the same line as the earth and the sun, at which time the earth is directly between them and the sun. When the sun rises from the horizon, the planets set in the west, and when it sets, the planets rise in the east.

冲[2]（沖、衝）chōng ❶ 用开水等浇 pour boiling water on：～茶 make tea｜～鸡蛋 pour boiling water into a bowl of raw egg ❷ same as 冲洗 chōngxǐ①；冲击 rinse；flush：用水把碗～干净 rinse the bowls｜大水～坏了河堤。The floods washed away the dam. ❸ 互相抵消 offset；cancel out；counteract：～账 strike a balance；reverse an entry；balance an account

冲[3]（沖）chōng〈方 *dial.*〉山区的平地 level land in mountainous areas：～田 cultivated level land in hilly areas｜韶山～ Shaoshan Terrace｜翻过山就有一个很大的～。There's an expanse of level land on the other side of the mountain.

☞ chòng on p. 273

【冲程】chōngchéng 内燃机工作时活塞在汽缸中往复运动，从汽缸的一端到另一端叫做一个冲程 stroke；(of operation of an internal combustion engine) one of a series of alternating continuous movements of pistons back and forth through the same line within a cylinder；also 行程 xíngchéng

【冲冲】chōngchōng 感情激动的样子 excited；emotional：兴～ in a state of excitement；in high spirits｜怒气～ in a rage；furiously

【冲刺】chōngcì 跑步、滑冰、游泳等体育竞赛中临近终点时全力向前冲(of sports competition, such as running, ice-skating or swimming, etc.) make a final dash for the finishing line；sprint

【冲淡】chōngdàn ❶ 加进别的液体，使原来的液体在同一个单位内所含成分相对减少 dilute；reduce the strength of a fluid by adding water or other solvents：把 80 度酒精～为 50 度 dilute the alcohol from 80 degrees to 50 degrees ❷ 使某种气氛、效果、感情等减弱 weaken the atmosphere, effect and feelings；water down；play down；downgrade：加了这一场，反而把整个剧本的效果～了。This extra scene has weakened the effect of the whole play.

【冲抵】chōngdǐ same as 冲销 chōngxiāo

【冲动】chōngdòng ❶ 能引起某种动作的神经兴奋 impulse；impetus；a wave of excitement that will bring about certain action：创作～ impulse to write ❷ 情感特别强烈，理性控制很薄弱的心理现象 strong emotional impulse difficult to rationalize：不要～，应当冷静考虑问题。Don't act on impulse；calm down and think it over.

【冲犯】chōngfàn 言语或行为与对方抵触，冒犯了对方 offend；affront；cause offence or resentment by one's words and behaviour：他一时不能够控制自己，说了几句话，～了叔父。He lost control of himself and spoke in a manner that offended his uncle.

【冲锋】chōngfēng 进攻的部队向敌人迅猛前进，用冲锋枪、手榴弹、刺刀等和敌人进行战斗(of troops) charge at the enemy in a sweeping manoeuvre and fight with tommy guns, grenades and bayonets, etc.

【冲锋枪】chōngfēngqiāng 单人使用的自动武器。枪身较短，用于近战和冲锋，有效射程约 300—400 米。submachine gun；tommy gun；small in size and used by a single person in face-to-face combat and assault, with a shooting range of 300-400 metres.

【冲锋陷阵】chōng fēng xiàn zhèn ❶ 向敌人冲锋，深入敌人阵地。形容作战英勇。charge toward the enemy and into the enemy's domain；fight bravely in a battle ❷ 泛指为正义事业英勇斗争(in a broad sense) fight heroically for a just cause

【冲服】chōngfú 服药的一种方式，用水或酒等调药吃下去 take medicine after mixing with water or wine

【冲击】chōngjī ❶（水流等）撞击物体（of water）break against an object; collide with; pound; lash: 海浪～着石崖。Waves pounded against the rocks. ❷ same as 冲锋 chōngfēng: 向敌人阵地发起～ launch an attack on the enemy position ❸〈比喻 *fig.*〉干扰或打击使受到影响 interfere or attack so as to exert an influence on sth.; come under fire: 在外国商品～下，当地一些工厂停止生产。Some local factories stopped operation in the face of an influx of foreign commodities.

C

【冲击波】chōngjībō ❶ 通常指核爆炸时，爆炸中心压力急剧升高，使周围空气猛烈震荡而形成的波动。冲击波以超音速的速度从爆炸中心向周围冲击，具有很大的破坏力，是核爆炸重要的杀伤破坏因素之一。shock wave; blast; sudden increase in pressure caused by an explosion which makes the surrounding air vibrate and which causes destruction, as it radiates in all directions at a speed faster than sound; one of the fatal elements of a nuclear explosion; also 爆炸波 bàozhàbō ❷ 指由超音速运动产生的强烈压缩气流 strong compressed air flow caused by a body moving faster than sound ❸〈比喻 *fig.*〉使某种事物受到影响的强大力量 powerful strength that exerts great influence on certain things

【冲积】chōngjī 高地的砂砾、泥土被水流带到河谷低洼地区沉积下来 alluvium; sand and soil from high areas washed down to river valleys or low-lying areas

【冲剂】chōngjì 中药剂型的一种，把药材煎汁、浓缩加糖等制成，颗粒状，用开水冲服 sweetened Chinese herb concoction condensed into grains, taken after being mixed with boiling water

【冲决】chōngjué ❶ 水流冲破堤岸（of water）burst through: ～河堤 breach a dyke ❷ 突破某种束缚、限制 cast off shackles; break through limitations: ～罗网 smash the trammels

【冲扩】chōngkuò 冲洗并扩印（照片）develop and print（photographs）: ～机 developing machine | ～彩照 develop colour photographs

【冲浪】chōnglàng 水上体育运动之一。运动员脚踏特制的冲浪板随海浪快速滑行，用全身的协调动作保持身体的平衡。surfing; surf-riding, a sports event where the competitor stands on a surfboard and is carried rapidly along the crest of surging waves, while attempting to maintain balance through body movements

【冲力】chōnglì 运动物体由于惯性作用，在动力停止后还继续运动的力量 thrust; momentum; inertial force compelling an object to move continuously forward after driving force ceases

【冲凉】chōng//liáng〈方 *dial.*〉洗澡 take a cold shower

【冲量】chōngliàng 作用在物体上的力和力的作用时间的乘积叫做冲量 impulse, momentum; the product of average force acting upon an object and the time it takes

【冲龄】chōnglíng〈书 *fml.*〉幼年（多用于帝王 mostly applied to an emperor）tender age, very young: ～登基 ascend the throne at a tender age

【冲破】chōngpò 突破某种状态、限制等 break through（a certain situation, limitation, etc.）; breach: ～封锁 breach a blockade | ～禁区 break into a forbidden zone | ～障碍物 surmount obstacles | 火光～漆黑的夜空。Flames penetrated the pitch-dark firmament.

【冲杀】chōngshā 在战场上迅速前进，杀伤敌人 rush ahead; charge and fight the enemy on the battlefield: 奋勇～ fight heroically in a battle; fight desperately

【冲刷】chōngshuā ❶ 一面用水冲，一面刷去附着的东西 wash off dirt; wash down: 把汽车～得干干净净 give the car a thorough wash-down ❷ 水流冲击，使土石流失或剥蚀（of soil and stone）eroded or scoured through water flow: 岩石上有被洪水～过的痕迹。The rocks still bear the marks left by scouring floods.

【冲腾】chōngténg（气体等）向上冲；升腾（of air, vapour, steam, etc.）rush out; leap up; rise up: 热气～而出。Hot steam shot upwards.

【冲天】chōngtiān 冲向天空 soar into the sky;〈比喻 *fig.*〉情绪高涨而猛烈（of mood）high-flying; violent; soaring: 怒气～ flare up; explode; lose control; fly into a rage | ～的干劲 boundless enthusiasm

【冲田】chōngtián 丘陵地区的谷地水稻田，地势较平缓 paddy fields or other cultivated lands in hilly areas, with a relatively level topography

【冲突】chōngtū ❶ 矛盾表面化，发生激烈争斗 conflict; clash; intense fight caused by contradiction: 武装～ armed conflict | 言语～ conflict of words ❷ 互相矛盾；不协调 contradiction; be out of harmony with; inconsistent: 文章的论点前后～。The arguments in this article are inconsistent. | 因时间～，会开不成了。Owing to a time clash, this meeting is cancelled.

【冲洗】chōngxǐ ❶ 用水冲，使附着的东西去掉 rinse off; scour; wash: 路面经大雨～后，显得格外干净了。The road looked much cleaner after the rain. ❷ 把已经曝光的胶片，进行显影、定影等的总称 develop; treat photographic film so as to make the latent image visible: ～放大 develop and enlarge（a film）

【冲喜】chōng//xǐ〈旧时 *old*〉迷信风俗，家中有人病重时，用办理喜事（如迎娶未婚妻过门）等举动来驱除邪祟，希望转危为安 benevolent or happy event (such as a wedding) arranged in the hope that this joyous occasion might ward off evil and bring a seriously ill person in the family back to health

【冲销】chōngxiāo 会计上指将有关账户内原记的数额部分或全部减除 write off; abate; partly or fully reverse an entry in an account

【冲要】chōngyào ❶ 处于全国的或某一个地区的重要道路的会合点,因而形势重要 place of strategic importance, usu. the hub of transportation in a region or a country:徐州地处津浦铁路和陇海铁路的交叉点,是个十分～的地方。Located at the intersection of the Tianjin-Nanjing and Lanzhou-Lianyungang railways, Xuzhou is a place of strategic importance. ❷〈书 *fml.*〉指重要的职位 important position:久居～ hold an important post for a long time; be in a key position for a long time

【冲账】chōng//zhàng 收支账目互相抵消,或两户应支付的款项互相抵消 balance income and expense accounts; balance accounts

【冲撞】chōngzhuàng ❶ 撞击 collide; bump; jostle:海浪～着山崖。Ocean waves beat against the cliffs. ❷ same as 冲犯 chōngfàn:我很后悔不该失言～她。I regret very much offending her by speaking out of turn.

充 chōng ❶ 满;足 full; sufficient:～满 be full of|～分 full; ample; sufficient|～其量 at the most ❷ 装满;塞住 fill; fill up; pack up:～电 charge a battery|～塞 stuff; fill up|～耳不闻 turn a deaf ear to ❸ 担任;当 assume office; act as; serve as:～当 play the role of; act as; pose as|～任 assume the office of ❹ 冒充 disguise as; pretend to be; pass off as:～行家 pretend to be an expert; pose as an expert|以次～好 pass shoddy goods off as certified goods|打肿脸～胖子 slap one's face until swollen in an effort to look impressive; puff oneself up at one's own cost; an impudent attempt to pass off one's failure as triumph ❺(Chōng) 姓 a surname

【充畅】chōngchàng (商品的来源、文章的气势)充沛畅达 (of supply of commodities) plentiful and constant; (of style of writing) vigorous and fluent:货源～ plentiful and constant supply of goods

【充斥】chōngchì 充满;塞满(含厌恶意 derog.) fill; fill up; be full of; be flooded with:不能让质量低劣的商品～市场。Shoddy commodities should not be allowed to inundate the market.

【充磁】chōng//cí 使磁性物质磁化或使磁性不足的磁体增加磁性。一般是把要充磁的物体放在有直流电通过的线圈所形成的磁场里。magnetize an object or increase the properties of a magnet, usu. by putting it into a magnetic field of coils through which a direct current passes

【充当】chōngdāng 取得某种身份;担任某种职务 serve as; act as; play the part of; assume the office of:～调解人 act as a mediator|～大会主席 act as chairman of a conference

【充电】chōng//diàn 把直流电源接到蓄电池的两极上使蓄电池获得放电能力 charge a battery; store energy in a battery by linking a direct current to its two poles

【充耳不闻】chōng ěr bù wén 塞住耳朵不听。形容不愿听取别人的意见。stuff one's ears and refuse to listen; turn a deaf ear to

【充分】chōngfèn ❶ 足够(多用于抽象事物 oft. used to describe the abstract) enough; sufficient; ample:你的理由不～。Your reasons are insufficient.|准备工作做得很～。Sufficient preparations have been made. ❷ 尽量 to the best of sb.'s abilities or knowledge; try one's best; try one's utmost:～利用有利条件 make full use of favourable conditions|必须～发挥群众的智慧和力量。It is necessary to make full use of the wisdom and strength of the masses.

【充公】chōng//gōng 把违法者或犯罪者与案情有关的财物没收归公 confiscate crime-related property of a law-breaker or criminal

【充饥】chōng//jī 解饿 stave off hunger; allay or appease one's hunger:他带了几个烧饼,预备在路上～。He brought a few pancakes with him in case he became hungry on the trip.

【充军】chōngjūn 封建时代的一种流刑,把罪犯解到边远地方去当兵或服劳役 banish; punishment administered in feudal society where a law-breaker was sent to the frontier to serve in the army or work in a labour camp

【充满】chōngmǎn ❶ 填满;布满 cram; be full of; be filled with; bristle with:眼里～了泪水 eyes filled with tears|欢呼声～了会场。The assembly hall resounded with loud cheers. ❷ 充分具有:be brimming with; be permeated or imbued with; be saturated with; be full of:～激情 overflow with passion|歌声里～着信心和力量 songs brimming with confidence and strength; songs imbued with confidence and strength

【充沛】chōngpèi 充足而旺盛 plentiful; abundant; energetic:精力～ energetic|雨水～ abundant rainfall|～的感情 passionate feelings

【充其量】chōngqíliàng 表示做最大限度的估计;至多 at most; at best:这箱苹果～不过六十斤。This box of apples at the most weighs 30 kg.|～十天就可以完成这个任务。It should take no more than ten days to finish the task.

【充任】chōngrèn 担任 hold the position of; act as; serve as:挑选懂得管理并精通技术的人～车间主任 choose a person who knows management and is a technological expert to be the workshop director

【充塞】chōngsè 塞满;填满 be stuffed with; be filled with; cram:库房里～着杂乱物品。The depot is crammed with miscellaneous goods.

【充实】chōngshí ❶ 丰富;充足(多指内容或人员物力的配备)rich; abundant; (of content or supply of labour force and materials) substantial:库存～ abundant stocks | 文字流畅,内容～ fluent language and substantial content ❷ 使充足;加强 substantiate; enrich; replenish:选拔优秀干部～基层 select excellent civil servants to strengthen grass-roots organizations

【充数】chōng//shù 用不胜任的人或不合格的物品来凑足数额 make up numbers by including incompetent or unqualified people or things:滥竽～ pass oneself off as a player in an ensemble; serve as a stopgap | 要是人手实在不够,就由我去充个数吧。If you're really short of hands, I'll serve as a stopgap.

【充血】chōngxuè 局部组织或器官,因小动脉、小静脉以及毛细血管扩张而充满血液。如消化时的胃肠、运动时的肌肉都有充血现象。congestion; hyperaemia, an abnormally large amount of blood in any part of the body, caused by the dilatation of arteriole, vein or blood capillary. This symptom is also found in the stomach and intestines as food is digested, and in muscles while being exercised.

【充溢】chōngyì 充满;流露 be filled to overflowing; brim with; be permeated with; be imbued with; overflow with:诗里～着江南的田园情趣。The poem is imbued with a pastoral aura evocative of the region south of the Yangtze River. | 孩子们的脸上～着幸福的笑容。The faces of the children were wreathed in happy smiles.

【充盈】chōngyíng ❶ same as 充满 chōngmǎn:泪水～ be filled with tears | 山谷里～着清越的歌声。The valley echoes with a clear and melodious song. ❷ (肌肉)丰满 (of muscle) full and round:肌肤～ (of muscle) well-developed

【充裕】chōngyù 充足有余;宽裕 abundant; ample; plentiful:经济～ be well-off | 时间～ have plenty of time

【充足】chōngzú 多到能满足需要 ample; abundant; enough to satisfy the demand:光线～ abundant light | 经费～ have sufficient funds | 理由～ sufficient reasons

忡(忡) chōng〈书 *fml*.〉忧虑不安 anxious; worried; upset

【忡忡】chōngchōng 忧愁的样子 in an anxious mood; deeply worried:忧心～ laden with anxiety; careworn; heavy-hearted

茺 chōng [茺蔚](chōngwèi) 益母草 motherwort (*Leonurus heterophyllus*)

涌 chōng〈方 *dial*.〉河汊,多用于地名 tributary; mostly used in place names:河～ tributary | 虾～(在广东)Xiachong (in Guangdong Province)

☞ yǒng on p. 2312

翀 chōng〈书 *fml*.〉鸟直着向上飞 (of bird) soar; fly upward

舂 chōng 把东西放在石臼或乳钵里捣去皮壳或捣碎 husk or pound with mortar and pestle:～米 husk rice with mortar and pestle | ～药 pound herbs in a mortar

憃 chōng〈书 *fml*.〉愚笨 stupid; ignorant; foolish

憧 chōng ☞ below

【憧憧】chōngchōng 往来不定;摇曳不定 flickering; moving to and fro:人影～ shadows of people moving about | 灯影～ flickering lamplight

【憧憬】chōngjǐng 向往 yearn for; long for; look forward to:～着幸福的明天 yearn for a brighter future | 心里充满着对未来的～ cherish a hope for a brighter future

罿 chōng〈书 *fml*.〉捕鸟的网 bird-catching net

艟 chōng ☞ [艨艟](méngchōng) on p. 1326

chóng (ㄔㄨㄥˊ)

虫(蟲) chóng (～儿 chóngr) 虫子 insect; worm

【虫草】chóngcǎo 冬虫夏草的简称 abbr. for 冬虫夏草 dōngchóng-xiàcǎo

【虫吃牙】chóngchīyá 龋齿(qǔchǐ)的俗称 common or lay term for carious or decayed tooth

【虫害】chónghài 某些昆虫或蜘蛛纲动物引起的植物体的破坏或死亡 insect pest; damage or death of plants caused by certain insects or spiders

【虫口】chóngkǒu 指一定范围内某些昆虫个体的数量 number of insects or worms in a given district:～密度 insect density

【虫情】chóngqíng 农业害虫潜伏、发生和活动的情况 reports about the latency, out-breaks and activities of pests:做好～预报、预测工作 do a good job at pest forecasting

【虫牙】chóngyá 龋齿(qǔchǐ)的俗称 common or lay term for carious or decayed tooth

【虫眼】chóngyǎn (～儿 chóngyǎnr)果肉、种子、树木、木器等上面虫蛀的小孔 small holes left by insect bites in fruit, seeds, trees and timber

【虫瘿】chóngyǐng 植物体受到害虫或真菌的刺激,一部分组织畸形发育而形成的瘤状物 lumps or plant tissue deformation caused by pests or bacteria; also 瘿 yǐng

【虫灾】chóngzāi 因虫害较大而造成的灾害 plague caused by a major insect pest
【虫豸】chóngzhì 〈书 *fml*.〉same as 虫子 chóng·zi
【虫子】chóng·zi 昆虫和类似昆虫的小动物 insect or insect-like small creature; hexapod; worm

种 Chóng 姓 a surname
☞ zhǒng on p.2489 and zhòng on p.2492

重 chóng ❶ 重复 repeat:～出 republish|书买～了。(I) bought another copy of the same book by mistake. ❷ 重新;再 again; once more:～逢 meet again|～见天日 see the light of the dam once more; lost freedom regained|旧地～游 revisit a place ❸ 层 layer; stratum; tier:云山万～ thick clouds|突破一～又一～的困难 overcome one difficulty after another ❹〈方 *dial*.〉使重叠在一起;摞 overlap; pile up:把两领席～在一起。Put the two mats one on top of the other.
☞ zhòng on p.2492

【重版】chóngbǎn (书刊)重新出版 (of books, periodicals, etc.) be republished
【重瓣胃】chóngbànwèi 反刍动物的胃的第三部分,容积比蜂巢胃略大,内壁有书页状的褶。反刍后的食物进入重瓣胃继续加以磨细。manyplies; omasum; psalterium; the third stomach of a ruminant, a little larger than the reticulum and with page-like creases on the inside. Food ingested by a ruminant goes into the manyplies where the digestion process continues; also 瓣胃 bànwèi
【重播】chóngbō ❶ 已播过种子的地方重新播上种子 re-sow fields ❷ (广播电台、电视台)重新播放已播放过的节目 (of radio and television stations) rerun; rebroadcast programme; repeat
【重茬】chóngchá 连作 continuous cropping
【重唱】chóngchàng 两个或两个以上的歌唱者,各按所担任的声部演唱同一歌曲。按人数多少,可分为二重唱、三重唱、四重唱等。ensemble of two or more singers, each singing one part of a song, such as duo, trio, quartet, etc.
【重重】chóngchóng 一层又一层,形容很多 layer upon layer; ring upon ring; many; a large number; a great amount:～包围 be encircled ring upon ring|困难～ be bristled with difficulties; with multiple difficulties|顾虑～ full of apprehension; full of misgivings
【重出】chóngchū 重复出现(多指文字、文句 mostly referring to words and sentences) show up repeatedly; redundent
【重蹈覆辙】chóng dǎo fù zhé 再走翻过车的老路 follow the track of an overturned cart;〈比喻 *fig*.〉不吸取失败的教训,重犯过去的错误 follow the same disastrous road to ruin; learn nothing from past failures and make the same mistake
【重叠】chóngdié (相同的东西)一层层堆叠 (of the same things) overlap; pile up:山峦～ blue smudge of mountains in the distance; topographical turmoil of mountains|精简～的机构 streamline overlapping administrative organs
【重读】chóngdú 学生因成绩不合格而留在原来的年级重新学习 (of pupils) fail in studies and repeat the same grade:～生 repeater
☞ zhòngdú on p.2493
【重逢】chóngféng 再次遇到(多指长时间不见的 after a long departure) meet again:故友～ old friends' reunion|久别～ meet again after a long separation
【重复】chóngfù ❶ (相同的东西)又一次出现 (of the same content) appear again; reappear:内容～ repeated content|这一段的意思跟第二段～了。This paragraph repeats the meaning of the second paragraph. ❷ 又一次做(相同的事情) do once again (the same thing):他把说过的话又～了一遍。He repeated what he had just said.
【重光】chóngguāng ❶ 重新见到光明 see light once more:大地～。Light shone on the earth once more. ❷ 光复 recover; retrieve:驱逐外寇,～河山 drive away invaders and recover lost territory
【重合】chónghé 两个或两个以上的几何图形占有同一个空间叫做重合 two or more geometrical graphs occupying the same space; coincide
【重婚】chónghūn 法律上指已有配偶而又同别的人结婚 (leg.) bigamy; crime of marrying while already having a legal spouse; commit bigamy
【重茧】[1] chóngjiǎn 〈书 *fml*.〉厚的丝绵衣 thick silk-floss padded clothes
【重茧】[2] chóngjiǎn same as 重趼 chóngjiǎn
【重趼】chóngjiǎn 手上或脚上磨的厚趼子 thick callus on hand or foot; same as 重茧 chóngjiǎn
【重见天日】chóng jiàn tiān rì 〈比喻 *fig*.〉脱离黑暗环境,重新见到光明 emerge from darkness and see light once more; be delivered from oppression or persecution
【重九】Chóngjiǔ same as 重阳 Chóngyáng
【重峦叠嶂】chóng luán dié zhàng 重重叠叠的山峰 range upon range of mountains; undulating mountains
【重落】chóng·luo 〈方 *dial*.〉病有转机后又变严重 have relapse after initial recovery from illness:他的病前几天刚好了点儿,现在又～了。He was getting better over the past few days, but then had a relapse.
【重名】chóngmíng (～儿 chóngmíngr)同名 of the same name
【重申】chóngshēn 再一次申述 reaffirm; reiter-

ate; restate: ～我国的对外政策 reiterate our country's foreign policies

【重审】chóngshěn 原审法院的判决在第二审程序中被上级法院撤消而重新审理 re-examine a case after the original verdict has been nullified at a second trial by a higher level court

【重生】chóngshēng ❶ 死而复生 be reborn; be revived or resurrected; be resuscitated ❷ 机体的组织或器官的某一部分丧失或受到损伤后,重新生长 regrowth after injury or loss of body tissue or organ

【重生父母】chóngshēng fùmǔ ☞ 再生父母 zàishēng fùmǔ on p. 2387

【重孙】chóngsūn 孙子的儿子 grandson's son; great-grandson; also 重孙子 chóngsūn·zi

【重孙女】chóngsūn·nǚ (～儿 chóngsūn·nǚr) 孙子的女儿 grandson's daughter; great-granddaughter

【重沓】chóngtà 〈书 *fml.*〉重复繁冗 repetitive and redundant; wordy

【重围】chóngwéi 层层的包围 tight encirclement: 杀出～ break through a tight encirclement

【重温旧梦】chóng wēn jiù mèng 〈比喻 *fig.*〉把过去的事重新经历或回忆一次 recall an old dream; relive or recall past experience

【重文】chóngwén 〈书 *fml.*〉异体字 variant of a character

【重五】Chóngwǔ same as 重午 Chóngwǔ

【重午】Chóngwǔ 旧时称端午 old-fashioned term for 端午 Duānwǔ; also 重五 Chóngwǔ

【重霄】chóngxiāo 〈书 *fml.*〉指极高的天空。古代传说天有九重。empyrean, the highest of the heavens which, according to Chinese legend, had nine layers or spheres; also 九重霄 jiǔchóngxiāo

【重新】chóngxīn 〈副词 *adv.*〉❶ 再一次 once again; once more: ～抄写一遍 make another copy | 他～来到战斗过的地方。He returned to the battlefield once again. ❷ 表示从头另行开始(变更方式或内容) start from the very beginning; start afresh (in terms of method or content): ～部署 rearrange; redeploy | ～做人 start one's life afresh; turn over a new leaf

【重行】chóngxíng 重新另行开始(做某种动作或事情) start afresh; take sth. up again; begin again: ～颁布 reissue; re-stipulate | ～起草 re-draft; make another draft

【重修】chóngxiū ❶ 重新翻修(建筑物等) renovate; rebuild; reconstruct: ～古寺 renovate an ancient temple | ～马路 repair highway ❷ 重新修订或编写 revise or re-compile: ～县志 revise the county annals

【重修旧好】chóng xiū jiù hǎo 恢复已往的交谊 renew past cordial relations; become reconciled; bury the hatchet

【重言】chóngyán 修辞方式,重叠单字,以加强描写效果,如'桃之夭夭,灼灼其华'(《诗经·周南·桃夭》),'天苍苍,野茫茫,风吹草低见牛羊'(北朝乐府诗《敕勒歌》) duplicated word; used to strengthen descriptive effect, such as 桃之夭夭,灼灼其华 in *The Book of Songs · Folksongs of South of Zhou · Like the Slender Peach* and 天苍苍,野茫茫,风吹草低见牛羊 in *The Song of Teleg*, a *yuefu* folksong of the Northern Dynasties

【重演】chóngyǎn 重新演出 recur; restage; 〈比喻 *fig.*〉相同的事再次出现 reenact; repeat: 历史的悲剧不许～。History's tragedies should not be repeated.

【重阳】Chóngyáng 我国传统节日,农历九月初九日。在这一天有登高的风俗。Double Ninth Festival, a traditional Chinese festival which falls on the ninth day of the ninth lunar month, when it is the custom for Chinese people to go hiking and mountain climbing

【重洋】chóngyáng 一重重的海洋 boundless seas and oceans: 远涉～ travel across the vast ocean; (of the departure of an ocean-going vessel) bound to distant climes

【重样】chóngyàng (～儿 chóngyàngr) 样式相同 of the same pattern or style: 买了五张邮票,没有～的。I bought five stamps, each with a different design.

【重译】chóngyì ❶ 经过好几次翻译 translate several times ❷ 从译文翻译 retranslate from a translation ❸ 重新翻译 retranslate

【重印】chóngyìn (书刊)重新印刷 (of books and periodicals) reprint

【重圆】chóngyuán 亲人长久分离、失散后重又团聚 family reunion after a long separation: 多年离散,今日～,悲喜交集。At their reunion after so many years of departure joy and sorrow flowed copiously from the hearts of all family members.

【重张】chóngzhāng 指商店重新开业 reopen a shop; restart a business

【重整旗鼓】chóng zhěng qí gǔ 指失败之后,重新集合力量再干(摇旗和击鼓是古代进军的号令) draw together forces to start afresh after a defeat; re-rally (waving a flag and beating a drum was the signal to charge the enemy in ancient China); also 重振旗鼓 chóng zhèn qí gǔ

【重奏】chóngzòu 两个或两个以上的人各按所担任的声部,同时用不同乐器或同一种乐器演奏同一乐曲。按人数的多少,可分为二重奏、三重奏、四重奏等。ensemble of two or more musicians playing either the same or different instruments, each assigned to play a part in a particular piece of music, such as duet, trio, quartet, etc. (according to the number of musical players in an ensemble)

【重足而立】chóng zú ér lì 后脚紧挨着前脚,不敢迈步。形容非常恐惧。one foot close to another; dare not move; stand transfixed in panic

崇 chóng ❶ 高 high; lofty; sublime: ～山峻岭 undulating high mountains ❷ 重视;尊敬 attach importance to; respect; esteem: 尊～ respect; adore; worship | 推～ hold sb. in high esteem ❸ (Chóng) 姓 a surname

【崇拜】chóngbài 尊敬钦佩 respect; admire; worship: ～英雄人物 worship heroes

【崇奉】chóngfèng 信仰;崇拜 believe in; worship: ～礼教 abide by rites and proprieties | ～圣人 worship saints

【崇高】chónggāo 最高的;最高尚的 lofty; sublime; high; noble: 品格～ of noble character | ～的理想 a lofty ideal | 致以～的敬礼! I take this opportunity of extending to you my highest salutations!

【崇敬】chóngjìng 推崇尊敬 respect; revere; hold sb. in high esteem: ～的心情 a feeling of great reverence for | 英雄的高尚品质为人～。The people hold this hero's noble attributes in high esteem.

【崇论闳议】chóng lùn hóng yì 指高出一般人的议论或见解 comments or arguments superior to all other's; brilliant discourses; 闳 also put as 宏 hóng

【崇山峻岭】chóng shān jùn lǐng 高而险峻的山岭 towering and precipitous mountains

【崇尚】chóngshàng 尊重;推崇 uphold; advocate: ～正义 uphold justice | ～俭朴 advocate thrift

【崇洋】chóngyáng 崇拜外国 make a fetish of foreign countries: 盲目～ have a blind faith in things foreign | ～媚外 worship things foreign and toady to foreigners or foreign powers | ～思想 idea of adulation of things foreign

【崇仰】chóngyǎng 崇拜信仰;崇敬仰慕 worship and believe in; revere and admire; hold in high esteem: ～真理 believe in truth

【崇祯】Chóngzhēn 明思宗(朱由检)年号(公元1628—1644) title of the reign (1628-1644) of Emperor Sizong or Zhu Youjian of the Ming Dynasty

chǒng (ㄔㄨㄥˇ)

宠(寵) chǒng 宠爱;偏爱 bestow favour on; dote on; pamper: 得～ win the favour of sb. | 别把孩子～坏了。Don't spoil the child.

【宠爱】chǒng'ài (上对下)喜爱;娇纵偏爱 (of the superior to the subordinate or the old to the young) dote on; pamper; indulge: 她是母亲最～的女儿。She is her mother's most beloved daughter.

【宠儿】chǒng'ér 〈比喻 *fig.*〉受到宠爱的人 beloved; favourite: 时代的～ darling of the times

【宠辱不惊】chǒng rǔ bù jīng 受宠或受辱都不为所动,形容把得失置之度外 be unaffected by favour or humiliation, success or defeat; be neither carried away by success nor upset by failure; keep one's cool over either gains or losses

【宠物】chǒngwù 指家庭豢养的受人喜爱的小动物,如猫、狗等 pet; small animals kept and raised by families, such as cats, dogs, etc.

【宠信】chǒngxìn 宠爱信任(多含贬义 oft. derog.) cherish; excessive fondness for and place undue trust in: ～奸佞 place undue trust in crafty sycophants | 深得上司～ win the confidence of one's superior

【宠幸】chǒngxìng (地位高的人对地位低的人)宠爱 (of a superior towards a subordinate) love; patronize; bestow favour on

【宠用】chǒngyòng 宠爱任用 assign sb. to a post out of favouritism: 倍受～ receive double favouritism

chòng (ㄔㄨㄥˋ)

冲[1](衝) chòng ❶ 劲头儿足;力量大 vigorously; with plenty of dash: 这小伙子干活儿真～。This young man works with vim and vigour. | 水流得很～。The water is torrential. ❷ 气味浓烈刺鼻 (of smell) strong and pungent: 酒味儿很～。This liquor smells pungent. ❸ 〈方 *dial.*〉斥责 scold; reprimand; chide; revile: 他一说话就～人。Whenever speaks he tends to offend people.

冲[2](衝) chòng ❶ 向着或对着 towards; facing: 他扭过头来～我笑了笑。He turned around and smiled at me. ❷ 凭;根据 because of; on the basis of; according to: 就～着这几句话,我也不能不答应。On hearing this statement, I had no recourse but to comply. | ～他们这股子干劲儿,一定可以提前完成任务。Working with such vigour, they are bound to finish the task ahead of time.

冲[3](衝) chòng 冲压 punch; press: ～床 punching machine | ～模 punching mould

☞ chōng on p. 267

【冲床】chòngchuáng 冲压使金属板成型或在金属板上冲孔的机器。汽车外壳等就是用冲床加工制成的。punching machine; machine for punching holes in a metal board, embossing a design, or stamping a die on a metal board, such as required for the exterior frame of a car; also 冲压机 chòngyājī and 压力机 yālìjī

【冲盹儿】chòng//dǔnr 〈方 *dial.*〉打盹儿 doze off; have a nap

【冲劲儿】chòngjìnr ❶ 敢做、敢向前冲(chōng)的

劲头儿 drive; bold spirit; drive and vigour:这姑娘挺有～,一个人干了两个人的活儿。The girl worked with such drive that she single-handedly finished the work of two people. ❷ 强烈的刺激性 strong smell; strongly stimulating:这酒有～,少喝点儿。This liquor is pretty strong, so don't drink too much. *or* This liquor has a kick; don't drink too much.

【冲模】chòngmú 装在冲床上用来使被加工的材料成型的模型,一般都是凹凸成对的 die or mould; incorporated into a punching machine with which to work on materials, usu. in a pair, one concave and the other convex

【冲压】chòngyā 用冲床进行金属加工 punching press; process metal with a punching machine

【冲子】chòng·zi punching pin; puncher; 用金属做成的一种打眼器具 metal tool used to punch holes; also 铳子 chòng·zi

眈 chòng〈方 *dial.*〉困极小睡 nap:瞌～ doze off|～一～ take a nap

铳 chòng 一种旧式火器 old-style blunderbuss; shotgun:火～ shotgun|鸟～ shotgun

【铳子】chòng·zi same as 冲子 chòng·zi

chōu(ㄔㄡ)

抽[1] chōu ❶ 把夹在中间的东西取出 take sth. from within sth. else:从信封里～出信纸 take a letter out of its envelope ◇～不出身来 too busy to extricate oneself ❷ 从中取出一部分 take a part of the whole:～查 spot check; make a random sampling of sth.|～肥补瘦 take from the fat to replenish the lean; take from those with too much and give to those with too little ❸(某些植物体)长出 (of certain plants) grow; put forth:～芽 put forth buds|谷子～穗。The millet is earing. *or* The millet is in the ear. ❹ 吸 absorb; inhale:～烟 draw on a pipe; smoke a cigarette|～水 pump water

抽[2] chōu ❶ 收缩 shrink:这件衣服刚洗一水就～了不少。The garment shrank after its first wash. ❷ 打(多指用条状物 with certain strip-like objects) whip or flog:～陀螺 whip a top|鞭子一～,马就跑了起来。The horse started galloping at a crack of the whip.

【抽测】chōucè 抽取一部分进行测量或测验 sample survey:～学习成绩 spot-check the students' study|～车速 spot-check the speed of cars

【抽查】chōuchá 抽取一部分进行检查 take samples and examine; make a random sampling:最近～了一些伙食单位,卫生工作都做得很好。Recent random spot checks carried out in some restaurants prove that they have done a good job of improving their standards of hygiene.

【抽抽儿】chōu·chour ❶ 收缩 shrink:这块布一洗就～了。The garment shrank after the first wash. ❷ 干瘪;萎缩 dry and shrivel; shrink; wither:枣儿一晒就～了。The dates shrivelled in the sun.|这牛怎么越养越～? Why is this cow growing thinner?

【抽搐】chōuchù 肌肉不随意地收缩的症状,多见于四肢和颜面 twitch; tic; uncontrollable twitching of muscle, usu. in limbs or face muscles; also 抽搦 chōunuò

【抽打】chōudǎ (用条状物)打 lash; whip; flog (with sth. strip-like):赶车人挥着鞭子,不时地～着牲口。The cart driver lashed his oxen from time to time.

【抽打】chōu·da 用掸子、毛巾等在衣物上打,以除掉灰尘 beat clothes etc. with a duster or a towel so as to get rid of dust:大衣上满是土,得～～。That dusty coat needs a good beating.

【抽搭】chōu·da 一吸一顿地哭泣 sob:那孩子捂着脸不停地～。The child covered his face with his hands and sobbed inconsolably.|抽抽搭搭地哭 sob

【抽调】chōudiào 从中调出一部分(人员、物资) transfer part of (personnel or material):机关～了一批干部加强农业生产第一线。A batch of cadres was transferred from the office to strengthen the agricultural front.

【抽丁】chōu//dīng〈旧时 *old*〉统治者强迫青壮年去当兵(of rulers) force young men to join the army; press-gang sb. into the army; also 抽壮丁 chōu zhuàngdīng

【抽斗】chōudǒu〈方 *dial.*〉same as 抽屉 chōu·ti

【抽肥补瘦】chōu féi bǔ shòu〈比喻 *fig.*〉抽取有余的补给不足的,使相互平均或平衡 take from those who have more to give to those who have less so as to make a balance

【抽风】[1] chōu//fēng ❶ 手脚痉挛、口眼歪斜的症状 convulsion; symptoms such as spasms of the hands and feet, or an askew mouth and rolling eyes ❷〈比喻 *fig.*〉做事违背常情 do sth. abnormal or perverse; be out of one's mind:你抽什么风,半夜三更了还唱歌? Are you crazy, singing at midnight?

【抽风】[2] chōu//fēng 利用一定装置把空气吸进来 pump air with specific equipment:～灶(利用自然抽风代替电力吹风的灶) air pumping stove (using natural air rather than an electric fan)

【抽工夫】chōu gōng·fu (～儿 chōu gōng·fur) 抽空儿 manage to find time:他们正等你呢,你先～去一趟吧。They are waiting for you; you had better find the time to go there now.|本来我也想去,可是抽不出工夫来。I would like to go but I'm too busy.

【抽检】chōujiǎn same as 抽查 chōuchá:～的产品中,符合标准的占大多数。Most of the products from which samples have been taken measure up to standard.

【抽奖】chōu//jiǎng 用抽签的方式确定获奖者 draw lots to determine the prize-winners; draw a winning number (in lottery or raffle):～活动 event where prizes are won by drawing tickets|～仪式 prize-winning ticket drawing ceremony

【抽筋】chōu//jīn ❶ 抽掉筋 pull a tendon:剥皮～ skin and pull out tendons ❷ (～儿 chōu//jīnr)筋肉痉挛 muscle convulsion; cramp:腿受了寒,直～儿。The cold has given me leg cramp.

【抽考】chōukǎo 抽出部分人或某科目进行考试 examination on certain selected subject, given to a randomly selected group of people:在几个中学的初二学生中举行～,我校成绩优良。Among the second-grade junior students of schools that were given selective exams, our students achieved particularly good scores.|这次代数～,得满分的超过一半。More than half of the students selected to take part in the algebra test got full marks.

【抽空】chōu//kòng (～儿 chōu//kòngr)挤出时间(做别的事情) manage to find time (to do other things):工作再忙,也要～学习。Time should be taken to study, no matter how busy the work schedule.

【抽冷子】chōu lěng·zi 〈方 *dial.*〉突然;乘人不备 suddenly; do sth. without warning:～一瞧,把人吓一跳。A sudden glance was enough to scare one away.|他抽个冷子跑了出来。He slipped away when he saw the chance.

【抽搦】chōunuò same as 抽搐 chōuchù

【抽气机】chōuqìjī 真空泵 vacuum pump; air extractor; air pump

【抽泣】chōuqì 一吸一顿地哭泣 sob:暗自～ sob to oneself|低声～ weep in silence

【抽签】chōu//qiān (～儿 chōu//qiānr)从许多做了标志的签儿中抽出一根或若干根,用来决定先后次序或输赢等 draw or cast lots; draw one or more marked lots to decide the order of winners and losers

【抽青】chōu//qīng (草、木)发芽变绿 (of grass and trees) sprout and turn green; put forth buds:老树抽了青。The old tree is putting forth buds.|草木～。The grass and trees are sprouting.

【抽取】chōuqǔ 从中收取或取出 collect or draw from:～版税 receive a royalty|～部分资金 draw part of the funds|～地下水 draw underground water

【抽纱】chōushā ❶ 刺绣的一种。在亚麻布或棉布等材料上,根据图案设计,抽去花纹部分的经线或纬线,形成透空的花纹 drawn work; a kind of embroidery on linen or cotton cloth, which draws longitudinal or latitudinal threads from the fabric so as to form hollowed-out patterns:～工艺 drawnwork ❷ 用抽纱方法制成的窗帘、台布、手帕等工艺品 drawnwork artifacts such as curtain, tablecloth and handkerchief, etc.

【抽身】chōu//shēn 脱身离开 leave one's work; get away; extricate oneself from:工作很忙,他一直抽不出身来。He's very busy working and has no time to spare.

【抽水】[1] chōu//shuǐ 用水泵吸水 pump water

【抽水】[2] chōu//shuǐ 缩水 shrink:这种布～厉害,得多买点儿。This kind of cloth has heavy shrinkage, so we had better buy more.

【抽水机】chōushuǐjī 水泵 pump

【抽水马桶】chōushuǐ mǎtǒng 上接水箱,下通下水道的瓷质马桶 flush toilet; porcelain toilet that has a pipe connected to a water closet above and a sewer system below

【抽税】chōu//shuì 按税率收取税款 tax; levy or impose a tax according to a tax rate

【抽穗】chōu//suì 指小麦、高粱、谷子、玉米等农作物由叶鞘中长出穗 (of wheat, sorghum, cereal, corn, etc.) put forth ears; ear up; head

【抽缩】chōusuō 机体因受刺激而收缩 (of a body) shrink or contract under stimulus:四肢～ limbs contracted

【抽薹】chōu//tái 油菜、韭菜等蔬菜长出薹来 (of rape, chives, etc.) pullulate; sprout

【抽屉】chōu·ti 桌子、柜子等家具中可以抽拉的盛放东西用的部分,常作匣形 drawer; movable box-shaped container within a desk, wardrobe or other piece of furniture

【抽头】chōu//tóu (～儿 chōu//tóur) ❶ 赌博时从赢得的钱里抽一小部分归赌博场所的主人或供役使的人 percentage of gambling gains given to casino owner and attendants ❷ 泛指经手人从中获取好处 commission; benefits taken by person in charge of business:这些产品在销售中几经转手,环环～,损害了消费者的利益。These products have been sold and resold several times, which has (as each transaction earns money for certain people) jeopardized consumers' interests.

【抽闲】chōuxián same as 抽空 chōu//kòng

【抽象】chōuxiàng ❶ 从许多事物中,舍弃个别的、非本质的属性,抽出共同的、本质的属性,叫抽象,是形成概念的必要手段 draw on common nature or essence of a number of things and abandon their individual and non-essential property in order to formulate a concept ❷ 不能具体经验到的,笼统的;空洞的 not applicable or practical; general; empty:看问题要根据具体的事实,不能从～的定义出发。We should look at matters from a factual perspective rather than one of abstract definition.

【抽象劳动】chōuxiàng láodòng 撇开各种具体形式的人类一般劳动。即劳动者的脑力、体力在生产中的消耗。在商品生产条件下，抽象劳动形成商品的价值(跟'具体劳动'相对 as opposed to 'concrete labour')。abstract labour, such as the consumption of a labourer's mental and physical strength, of an intangible form. In commodity production, it is abstract labour that decides the value of commodities.

C

【抽象思维】chōuxiàng sīwéi 逻辑思维 logical thinking; abstract thought; abstraction

【抽雄】chōuxióng 指某些作物(如玉米)的雄穗露出顶端 (of crops such as corn) grow stamens; also 出雄 chūxióng

【抽芽】chōu//yá 植物长出芽来 (of plants) bud; sprout

【抽验】chōuyàn 抽取一部分进行检验 take a part out of the whole and check; spot-check: ～产品性能 spot-check the function of products

【抽样】chōuyàng 取样 sample: ～检查 spot-check | ～化验 sampling test

【抽噎】chōuyē same as 抽搭 chōu•da

【抽咽】chōuyè same as 抽搭 chōu•da

【抽绎】chōuyì same as 紬绎 chōuyì

【抽印】chōuyìn 从整本书或刊物的印刷版中抽取一部分来单独印制 offprint part of a book or a journal: ～本 offprint | ～三百份 offprint 300 copies

【抽壮丁】chōu zhuàngdīng same as 抽丁 chōu//dīng

搊[1](**搊**) chōu 〈方 *dial.*〉弹奏(乐器) play (musical instrument); pluck stringed instrument

搊[2](**搊**) chōu 〈方 *dial.*〉❶ 搀扶 help sb. walk or stand properly; support: ～着老人走上讲台。Help the elderly man onto the stage. ❷ 从器具的一端或一侧用力使它翻倒 turn sth. over by pushing from one end or side: 把箱子～过来 turn the trunk over on its side

紬 chōu 〈书 *fml.*〉引出;缀辑 expound; clarify; clear up; sort out
☞ 绸 chóu on p. 277

【紬绎】chōuyì 〈书 *fml.*〉引出头绪 sort out; clear up; also 抽绎 chōuyì

篘(**篘**) chōu 〈书 *fml.*〉❶ 滤酒的器具 filter; porous device for removing impurities or solid particles from alcohol ❷ 过滤(酒) filter (wine)

瘳 chōu 〈书 *fml.*〉❶ 病愈 recover from an illness ❷ 损害 harm; damage

犨 chōu 〈书 *fml.*〉❶ 牛喘息的声音 snort; sound of breathing of an ox ❷ 突出 outstanding

chóu (ㄔㄡˊ)

仇(**讎**、**讐**) chóu ❶ 仇敌 enemy; foe: 疾恶如～ hate evil like an enemy; abhor evil | 同～敌忾 share a bitter hatred of the enemy; burning with a common hatred (for the enemy) ❷ 仇恨 hatred; enmity; grudge: 结～ fall out with each other and become enemies; incur hatred; start a feud | 血泪～ hatred filled with blood and tears | ～深似海 hatred as deep as the ocean
☞ Qiú on p. 1582

【仇敌】chóudí 仇人;敌人 foe; enemy: 视为～ regard sb. as an enemy

【仇恨】chóuhèn ❶ 因利害冲突而强烈地憎恨 hate bitterly or intensely because of a conflict of interests: 热爱人民，～敌人 love the people and hate the enemy ❷ 因利害冲突而产生的强烈憎恨 hostility; bitter or intense hatred caused by conflicts of interest: 民族的～ national hatred

【仇家】chóujiā same as 仇人 chóurén

【仇人】chóurén 因有仇恨而敌视的人 enemy or foe; person hated or opposed by sb.: ～相见，分外眼红。When the enemies come face to face, their eyes blaze with hatred.

【仇杀】chóushā 因有仇恨而杀害 murder committed out of hatred: ～案 murder case committed out of revenge

【仇视】chóushì 以仇敌相看待 look upon sb. with hostility; be hostile to; look at sb. as an enemy: 互相～ look at each other with hatred | ～侵略者 harbour hatred for the invaders

【仇外】chóuwài 仇视外国 be hostile to foreign countries: ～心理 hostile feelings towards foreign countries

【仇隙】chóuxì 〈书 *fml.*〉same as 仇恨 chóuhèn: 素无～ bear no grudge at all

【仇冤】chóuyuān 冤仇 enmity; rancour; hatred: 结～ fall out with each other and become enemies; earn sb.'s hatred | 报～ revenge oneself; avenge a wrong

【仇怨】chóuyuàn 仇恨;怨恨 hatred; grievance; resentment: ～极深 inveterate hatred

俦(**儔**) chóu 〈书 *fml.*〉❶ 伴侣 companion: ～侣 companion | ～伴 comrade; mate; companion ❷ 等;辈 class; generation: ～类 the same generation; peers; same kind

【俦类】chóulèi 〈书 *fml.*〉同辈的人;同类 peers; of same class or generation; also 畴类 chóulèi

【俦侣】chóulǚ 〈书 *fml.*〉伴侣 companion

帱(**幬**) chóu 〈书 *fml.*〉❶ 帐子 bed curtains; mosquito net ❷ 车帷 carriage curtains
☞ dào on p. 395

俦(儔) chóu [俦俦]〈书 *fml.*〉忧愁的样子 worried; sad; depressed; gloomy; melancholy

惆 chóu〈书 *fml.*〉失意;悲痛 disappointed; depressed; sad; grief-stricken

【惆怅】chóuchàng 伤感;失意 sentimental; melancholy; gloomy: ～的心绪 sentimental mood | 别离之后,她心里感到一阵～。She felt a spasm of sadness on leaving.

绸(紬) chóu 绸子 silk fabric; silk: 纺～ soft plain-weave silk fabric | ～缎 silk and satin

☞ 紬 chōu on p. 276

【绸缎】chóuduàn 绸子和缎子,泛指丝织品 silks and satins; (in a broad sense) all kinds of silk fabric

【绸缪】chóumóu〈书 *fml.*〉❶ 缠绵 sentimentally attached: 情意～ be deeply in love; be head over heels in love ❷ ☞ 未雨绸缪 wèi yǔ chóumóu on p. 2000

【绸纹纸】chóuwénzhǐ 一种洗印、放大照片用的纸,上面有像绸子的纹理(纹理比布纹纸细) matte paper; a kind of standard paper for photography, which has silk-like veins finer than those on woven paper

【绸子】chóu·zi 薄而软的丝织品 fine, soft silk fabric

畴(疇) chóu〈书 *fml.*〉❶ 田地 field; farmland: 田～ farmland | 平～千里 vast expanse of cultivated land ❷ 种类;类别 kind; type; division: 范～ range; category | 物各有～。All things fall under certain categories.

【畴日】chóurì〈书 *fml.*〉same as 畴昔 chóuxī

【畴昔】chóuxī〈书 *fml.*〉从前 in former times; formerly

酬(酧、醻) chóu ❶〈书 *fml.*〉主人向客人敬酒 (of a host) propose a toast to a guest; toast: ～酢 exchange of toasts ❷ 报答 repay a kindness; reward: ～谢 reward sb. for kindness ❸ 报酬 payment; remuneration: 按劳取～ work paid according to the amount done | 同工同～ equal pay for equal work ❹ 交际往来 social intercourse; exchange: 应～ socialize; entertain; treat with courtesy | ～答 thank sb. with a gift; reward sb. for his kindness ❺ 实现 realize; materialize; fulfil: 壮志未～ lofty aspirations left unfulfilled

【酬报】chóubào ❶ 用财物或行动来报答 reward one's kindness with money, gift or action; remunerate: ～救命之恩 reward sb. for saving one's life ❷ 报酬 payment: ～较高 relatively high payment

【酬宾】chóubīn 商业上指以优惠价格出售商品给顾客 sell commodities to customers at discount: ～展销 bargain sales | 开业头三天,以九五折～。All goods will be sold at a five per cent discount for the first three days after the shop starts doing business.

【酬唱】chóuchàng 用诗词互相赠答 respond to a poem written to one by writing one's own poem

【酬答】chóudá ❶ same as 酬谢 chóuxiè: 太感谢他了,真不知怎么～才好。I am so grateful to him I really don't know how to express my gratitude. ❷ 用言语或诗文应答 respond with a poem or speech: 这是一首～友人的小诗。This is a short poem to reciprocate my friend.

【酬对】chóuduì 应对;应答 respond; reply: 善于～ be quick to give answers

【酬和】chóuhè 用诗词应答 respond with a poem: 即席～ improvise a poem

【酬金】chóujīn 酬劳的钱 payment; remuneration; recompense: ～丰厚 generous remuneration; handsome pay

【酬劳】chóuláo ❶ 酬谢(出力的人) thank sb. for his service: 他备了一桌酒席,～帮助搬家的朋友。He offered wine and dishes to his friends as a token of appreciation for their help in his move to a new house. ❷ 给出力的人的报酬 pay sb. for his service; recompense: 这点钱请收下,这是您应得的～。Please accept the money you deserve.

【酬谢】chóuxiè 用金钱、礼物等表示谢意 express gratitude with money, gifts, etc.

【酬应】chóuyìng ❶ same as 应酬 yìng·chou① : 他不善于～。He is not a good socializer. *or* He's not good at dealing with people. ❷〈书 *fml.*〉应答;应对 answer; reply; respond: ～如流 be at ease with social activities

【酬酢】chóuzuò〈书 *fml.*〉宾主互相敬酒,泛指应酬 (of a host and a guest) exchange toasts; (in a broad sense) socialize

稠 chóu ❶ 液体中含某种固体成分很多(跟'稀'相对 as opposed to 'thin') (of a liquid) thick: 粥很～ thick porridge | 墨要研得～些。Ink should be thickly ground. ❷ 稠密 dense: 地窄人～ (of an area) small but densely inhabited | ～人广众 big crowd; large audience; big gathering

【稠糊】chóu·hu〈方 *dial.*〉same as 稠 chóu ①

【稠密】chóumì 多而密 of a great, densely concentrated number: 人烟～ densely populated | 枝叶～ thick foliage | 人口～ dense population

【稠人广众】chóu rén guǎng zhòng 指人多的场合 large audience; big gathering; big crowd; also 稠人广坐 chóu rén guǎng zuò

愁 chóu ❶ 忧虑 worry; be anxious: 发～ be worried | 不～吃,不～穿 not have to worry about food or clothing ❷ 忧伤的心情 melancholy; sadness; sorrow: 乡～ homesickness | 离～ sorrow at parting

【愁肠】chóucháng 指郁结愁闷的心绪 pent-up feelings of anxiety or sadness：～百结 with anxiety gnawing at one's heart; be weighed down with anxiety|～寸断 be eaten up with deep sorrow

【愁城】chóuchéng〈书 *fml.*〉指愁苦的境地 in a state of misery, distress or anxiety：陷入～ be overcome with grief; plunge into a state of misery; be eaten up with anxiety

【愁楚】chóuchǔ 忧愁痛苦 anxiety and sorrow; depression and agony：满腹～ be deeply worried and grieved; be deeply depressed and agonized

【愁怀】chóuhuái 愁苦的情怀 trauma; blues; depression：一腔～ full of anxiety and sorrow; be extremely depressed

【愁苦】chóukǔ 忧愁苦恼 melancholy; anxiety; gloom：～的面容 melancholy expression

【愁眉】chóuméi 发愁时皱着的眉头 brows knit at times of anxiety and sorrow：～不展 knit one's brows in worry|～紧锁 tightly knitted brows

【愁眉苦脸】chóu méi kǔ liǎn 形容愁苦的神情 worried look; wear a distressed expression; pull a long face; look miserable

【愁眉锁眼】chóu méi suǒ yǎn 形容忧愁、苦恼的样子 knit one's brows in melancholy; look melancholy and distressed; look downcast (锁 *suo*：紧皱 knit brows tightly)

【愁闷】chóumèn 忧愁烦闷 feel the blues; be in low spirits; be depressed：一席话，说得他心中～全消。In speaking he dispelled the pent-up gloom in his heart.

【愁容】chóuróng 发愁的面容 melancholy look; gloomy look：面带～ look gloomy

【愁思】chóusī 忧愁的思绪 feelings of anxiety; melancholy：～百结 fall into a state of profound melancholy; harbour melancholy feelings

【愁绪】chóuxù 忧愁的情绪 mood of melancholy; anxious feelings：～萦怀 be in a melancholy mood; feel extremely distressed

【愁云】chóuyún〈比喻 *fig.*〉忧郁的神色或凄惨的景象 melancholy look or a dreadful scene：～惨雾 a wretched scene|满脸～ a melancholy look

【愁云惨雾】chóu yún cǎn wù 形容使人感到愁闷凄惨的景象或气氛 scenario or atmosphere that evokes gloom and depression

筹(籌) chóu ❶ 竹、木或象牙等制成的小棍儿或小片儿，主要用来计数或作为领取物品的凭证 chip, usu. made of bamboo, wood, or ivory and mainly used to count, or as a collection token：竹～ bamboo chip|酒～(行酒令时所用的筹) chips used to keep count in a drinking game ❷ 筹划；筹措 prepare; plan; raise：统～ in an overall way|自～资金 raise funds on one's own|～饷(筹措军饷) raise money (for troops' pay and provisions) ❸ 计策；办法 resource; way; means：一～莫展 at the end of one's resources; at one's wit's end|运～帷幄 devise strategies in a tent; map out a well-conceived plan

【筹办】chóubàn 筹划办理 make preparations; make arrangements：～婚事 make preparations for a wedding

【筹备】chóubèi 为进行工作、举办事业或成立机构等事先筹划准备 make preparations for work to get under way; prepare for an undertaking, the establishment an institution, etc.：～粮饷 collect grains and raise funds|～展览 make preparations for an exhibition|～工作已经完成。The preliminary work has completed.

【筹措】chóucuò 设法弄到(款子、粮食等) raise (money, grains, etc.)：～旅费 scrape up money for travelling expenses|～军粮 raise troops' provisions

【筹划】chóuhuà ❶ 想办法；定计划 look for a way; make a plan：这里正在～建设一座水力发电站。Plans are being drawn up to build an hydroelectric station here. ❷ same as 筹措 chóucuò：～资金 raise funds|～建筑材料 prepare building materials

【筹集】chóují 筹措聚集 try to collect; raise：～资金 raise funds

【筹建】chóujiàn 筹划建立 make preparations for setting sth. up：～化肥厂 make preparations for the construction of a chemical fertilizer plant

【筹借】chóujiè 设法借(财物) borrow (money or things)：～款项 try to get a loan

【筹码】chóumǎ ❶ 计数和进行计算的用具，旧时常用于赌博 chip or counter used to keep count of sth., oft. used for gambling in the past ❷ 旧时称货币和能够代替货币的票据 (of old times) money and vouchers that function as money; also 筹马 chóumǎ

【筹谋】chóumóu 筹划谋虑；想办法 make plans; consider strategy：～解决问题的途径 rack one's brains to find a solution to the problem

【筹商】chóushāng 筹划商议 discuss; consult：～对策 discuss countermeasures

【筹算】chóusuàn ❶ 用筹来计算；计算 count by way of chips or counters; calculate ❷ 谋划 make plans; devise strategies

【筹资】chóuzī 筹集资金 raise funds：～办厂 raise money for setting up a factory

裯 chóu〈书 *fml.*〉❶ 单层的被子 quilt ❷ 床上的帐子 mosquito net

踌(躊) chóu ☞ blow

【踌躇】chóuchú ❶ 犹豫 hesitate; shilly-shally：颇费～ consider and reconsider before making a decision|～不决 hesitate in decision-making; be irresolute | ～了半天，我终于直说了。I finally spoke out after hesitating for a long time. ❷〈书 *fml.*〉停留 sojourn ❸〈书 *fml.*〉得意的样子 complacent; self-satisfied: ～满志 be extremely proud of one's success ‖ also 踌躇 chóuchú

【踌躇满志】chóu chú mǎn zhì 对自己的现状或取得的成就非常得意 be enormously proud of one's situation or success

【踌伫】chóuzhù〈书 *fml.*〉踌躇不前 hesitate to move forward; be indecisive

雠[1]（讎、讐）chóu 校对文字 collate; proofread: 校～ proofread〈古 *arch.*〉same as 售 shòu

雠[2]（讎、讐）chóu same as 仇 chóu

chǒu（ㄔㄡˇ）

丑[1] chǒu ❶ 地支的第二位 second of the twelve Earthly Branches; ☞ 干支 gānzhī on p. 627 ❷（Chǒu）姓 a surname

丑[2]（醜）chǒu ❶ 丑陋；不好看（跟'美'相对 as opposed to 'beautiful'）ugly; unpleasant to look at: ～媳妇 ugly wife | 长相太～ bad-looking; (of looks) unpleasant to look at ❷ 叫人厌恶或瞧不起的 detestable; shameful: ～态 grotesque or ludicrous performance; buffoonery | 出～ make a fool of oneself; cut a poor or sorry figure; bring shame on oneself ❸〈方 *dial.*〉坏；不好 bad; not good: 脾气～ bad temper

丑[3] chǒu 戏曲角色行当，扮演滑稽人物，鼻梁上抹白粉，有文丑、武丑之分 comedian; clown; comic role in traditional Chinese opera, recognized by the patch of white paint around the eyes and nose, subdivided into civil and martial clown; also 小花脸 xiǎohuāliǎn or 三花脸 sānhuāliǎn

【丑八怪】chǒubāguài 指长得很丑的人 very ugly person; hideous-looking person

【丑表功】chǒubiǎogōng 不知羞耻地吹嘘自己的功劳 brag shamelessly about one's deeds; claim undeserved merit

【丑旦】chǒudàn 彩旦 female clown in traditional Chinese opera

【丑诋】chǒudǐ 用很难听的话骂人 slander; vilify; defame; curse in coarse language

【丑恶】chǒu'è 丑陋恶劣 ugly; repulsive; hideous: ～嘴脸 ugly face; repulsive features

【丑化】chǒuhuà 把本来不丑的事物弄成丑的或形容成丑的 vilify; defame; paint a distorted picture of sth.: ～现实生活 paint a distorted picture of everyday life | 人物形象受到～。The image of the character has been vilified.

【丑话】chǒuhuà ❶ 粗俗难听的话 vulgar or coarse language: 这种～不堪入耳。This sort of vulgar language is repulsive to the ear. ❷ 指不中听的话（多带有提醒、警告的意思）blunt words (to warn or remind sb.): 咱们把～说在前头，以后要出了问题，你可别来找我。Let's not mince words; should anything go wrong in the future, don't come to me for help.

【丑剧】chǒujù 指有戏剧性的丑恶事情 absurd drama; farce

【丑角】chǒujué（～儿 chǒujuér）❶ 戏曲角色行当中的丑 the role of clown in traditional Chinese opera ❷ 指在某一事件中充当的不光彩角色 ignoble role in an event

【丑类】chǒulèi 指恶人，坏人 wicked people; rascals; scoundrels

【丑陋】chǒulòu（相貌或样子）难看（of appearance or looks）ugly; hideous: 相貌～ ugly looks

【丑婆子】chǒupó·zi 戏曲中扮演中老年妇女的丑角 female clown playing the role of a middle-aged or old woman in traditional Chinese opera

【丑时】chǒushí 旧式计时法指夜里一点钟到三点钟的时间 period of the day from 1 a. m. to 3 a. m. in old times

【丑史】chǒushǐ 丑恶的历史；不光彩的经历（多指个人的 of an individual）scandalous past; ignoble experience

【丑事】chǒushì 丑恶的事情；不光彩的事情 disgraceful affair; scandal

【丑态】chǒutài 指令人厌恶的样子和举动 abominable appearance and behaviour; ugly or ludicrous performance; buffoonery: ～百出 cut a despicable figure; put on an abominable show | ～毕露 reveal one's most hideous features; be utterly nauseating

【丑闻】chǒuwén 指有关人的阴私、丑事的传言或消息 scandal; rumours or revelations about one's privacy: 官场～ scandals in officialdom

【丑行】chǒuxíng 丑恶的行为 disgraceful conduct; shameful or scandalous behaviour; misconduct; misdemeanour: ～败露。Their scandalous conduct was exposed.

杻 chǒu〈古代 *arch.*〉刑具，手铐之类 instruments of torture or punishment, such as handcuffs

☞ niǔ on p. 1422

刍（㑇）Chǒu 姓 a surname

俅 chǒu same as 瞅 chǒu

☞ qiào on p. 1552

瞅（田）chǒu〈方 *dial.*〉看 look at: 我往屋里～了一眼，没～见他。I took a look inside the room but saw no sign of him.

【瞅见】chǒu//jiàn〈方 *dial.*〉看见 see; catch a glimpse of sth.: 瞅得见 able to see | 瞅不见 cannot see | 她～我来了，打了个招呼。She greeted me when she saw me.

chòu (ㄔㄡˋ)

臭 chòu ❶(气味)难闻(跟'香'相对 as opposed to 'fragrant')(of smell) stinky; smelly; foul: ～气 stench; offensive odour; stink|～味儿 bad smell ❷惹人厌恶的 disgusting; disgraceful: ～架子 disgusting manner|～名远扬 notorious ❸拙劣;不高明 inferior; poor; bad: ～棋 bad move|这一着真～。That was a cheap trick. ❹狠狠地 severely; harshly; relentlessly: ～骂 give sb. a good dressing-down|～揍一顿 give sb. a good beating ❺〈方 *dial.*〉(子弹)坏;失效 (of a bullet) ineffective; no longer of use: 这颗子弹～了。This bullet is a dud.

☞ xiù on p.2160

【臭虫】chòuchóng 昆虫,身体扁平,赤褐色,腹大,体内有臭腺。吸人畜的血液。bedbug (*Cimex lectularius*); brown, flat, wingless, bloodsucking hemipterous insect, brown with a big belly and a foetid gland; also 床虱 chuángshī; 有的地区叫壁虱 in some areas known as 壁虱 bìshī

【臭椿】chòuchūn 落叶乔木,羽状复叶,有臭味,花白色带绿,果实是翅果。根和皮可入药。tree of heaven (*Ailanthus altissima*); deciduous tree with smelly pinnate leaves, greenish white flowers, samara fruit, and roots and bark that can be used as herbs; also 樗 chū

【臭豆腐】chòudòu·fu 发酵后有特殊气味的小块豆腐,可作菜 odd-odour bean curd; preserved beancurd with a strong, distinctive flavour

【臭烘烘】chòuhōnghōng (～的 chòuhōnghōng·de)形容很臭 stinking; foul; smelly

【臭乎乎】chòuhūhū (～的 chòuhūhū·de)形容有些臭 somewhat foul-smelling: 这块肉怎么～的,是不是坏了? How come that meat smells a bit off? Is it rotten?

【臭骂】chòumà 狠狠地骂 curse roundly; scold angrily: ～一顿 give sb. a dressing-down

【臭美】chòuměi 讥讽人显示自己漂亮或能干 showing off unabashedly (about one's beautiful looks or talent); feel immensely pleased with oneself: 穿件新衣裳,有什么值得～的? Is there anything worth showing off about your new dress? |别～,谁不知道你那两下子。Don't show off, everyone knows what you are worth.

【臭名】chòumíng 坏名声 bad reputation; notoriety: ～昭著 infamous; of ill repute

【臭皮囊】chòupínáng 〈佛教用语 *Budd.*〉指人的躯体 human body

【臭棋】chòuqí 下棋时拙劣的着数;拙劣的棋术 ill-calculated move in chess; inferior skills in playing chess; bad move

【臭味相投】chòu wèi xiāng tóu 思想作风、兴趣等相同,很合得来(专指坏的 esp. derog.) be close to each other in notoriety; be birds of a feather; be two of a kind; get along well due to being of the same mentality, style and interests

【臭腺】chòuxiàn 某些动物体内分泌臭液或放出臭气的腺,如臭虫和黄鼠狼体内都有臭腺 foetid gland, as in the bedbug and the weasel, which produces an offensive liquid or odour

【臭氧】chòuyǎng 氧的同素异形体,化学式 O_3。无色,有特殊臭味,溶于水。放电时或在太阳紫外线的作用下,空气中的氧变为臭氧。用做氧化剂、杀菌剂等。ozone; a form of oxygen, chemical formula O_3, that is colourless, of a peculiar odour and that dissolves in water. When electricity is discharged through the air, as in lightning, or when it is exposed to the sun's ultraviolet rays, it changes into ozone; may be used to make an oxidizing agent, germicide, etc.

【臭氧层】chòuyǎngcéng 平流层中臭氧集中的一层,距地面20—30公里。太阳射向地球的紫外线大部分被臭氧层吸收。ozonosphere; ozone layer; layer of air in the stratosphere 20-30 km. above the earth surface, containing large amounts of ozone that absorbs most of the harmful ultraviolet rays from the sun before it reaches the earth; ☞ 大气层 dàqìcéng on p.361

殠 chòu〈书 *fml.*〉same as 臭 chòu

chū (ㄔㄨ)

出[1] chū ❶从里面到外面(跟'进'、'入'相对 as opposed to 'enter') proceed from inside to outside: ～来 come out|～去 go out|～门 go out of the house; leave home|～国 go abroad|～院 be discharged from hospital ❷来到 be at (an event): ～席 be present|～场 go on stage ❸超出 exceed: ～轨 derail|～界 go beyond the boundary|不～三年 within three years ❹往外拿 give: ～钱 pay money|～布告 put up a bulletin|～题目 prepare (exam) questions|～主意 put forth ideas ❺出产;产生;发生 produce; give rise to; happen: ～煤 produce coal|～活儿 get work done|我们厂里～了不少劳动模范。Many model workers have come forth in our factory.|～问题 get into trouble|这事儿～在1962年。This happened in 1962. ❻出版 publish: 这家出版社～了不少好书。This press has published many good books. ❼发出;发泄 emit; release: ～芽儿 sprout|～汗 sweat|～天花 suffer from smallpox|～气 vent one's anger ❽引文、典故等见于某处(of a quotation or allusion) quoted from: 语～《老子》quoted from *Laozi* ❾显露 become conspicuous: ～名 become famous|～面 appear personally; take it upon oneself (to do sth.) | ～头 act as the leader; act on behalf of | ～丑 make a fool of sb. or oneself ❿ 显得量多 appear in big quantity: 机米做饭～饭。Long-grained non-glutinous rice rises well when cooked. | 这面蒸馒头～数儿。Buns made of this flour swell big when steamed. ⓫ 支出 spend: ～纳 expenditure and income | 量入为～ spend within the limit of one's income; live within one's means ⓬〈方 *dial.*〉跟'往'连用,表示向外 [used after 往 wǎng to mean 'outward']: 散会了,大家往～走。When the meeting was over, everyone walked out.

出[2]（齣） chū 一本传奇中的一个大段落叫一出。戏曲的一个独立剧目也叫一出 classifier for a chapter of a classical novel; opera or play: 三～戏 three plays

出[3] //·chū 用在动词后表示向外、显露或完成 [used after a verb to indicate an outward movement, a conspicuous state or sth. accomplished]: 看得～clear to see | 看不～ cannot see clearly; cannot tell | 拿～一张纸 take out a sheet of paper | 跑～大门 run out of the gate | 看～问题 discern a problem | 做～成绩 accomplish

【出版】chūbǎn 把书刊、图画等编印出来;把唱片、音像磁带等制作出来 edit and publish books, periodicals, pictures, etc.; produce records, audio and visual tapes, etc.: ～社 press; publishing house | ～物 publication | 那部书已经～了。That book has been published. | 录音录像制品由音像出版单位～。Audio and visual products are published by specialized publishers.

【出榜】chū//bǎng ❶ 贴出被录取或被选取人的名单 publish the names of successful examinees or candidates: 考试后三日～。The names of successful examinees will be published three days after the test. ❷ 旧时指贴出大张的文告 (in old times) put up a big-character public notice: ～安民 put up a notice to reassure the public

【出奔】chūbēn same as 出走 chūzǒu: 仓促～run away in great haste | ～他乡 leave one's homeland for somewhere else

【出殡】chū//bìn 把灵柩运到安葬或安厝的地点 carry a coffin to the cemetery or a temporary burial site

【出兵】chū//bīng 出动军队(作战) dispatch troops (for a battle)

【出彩】chū//cǎi ❶ 旧时戏曲表演杀伤时,涂抹红色表示流血,叫出彩 apply red colour to indicate injury in traditional Chinese opera ❷ 指出丑(含诙谐意 humor.) make a fool of sb. or oneself: 我揭了老底,让他当场出了彩。I embarrassed him on the spot by pulling the skeleton out of his closet.

【出操】chū//cāo 出去操练 go out for drill: 他脚崴了,今天出不了操。He's sprained his ankle and so cannot drill today.

【出岔子】chū chà·zi 发生差错或事故 (of sth.) go wrong; have an accident: 手术中千万不能～。We cannot afford anything to go wrong in a surgical operation.

【出差】chū//chāi ❶ (机关、部队或企业单位的工作人员)暂时到外地办理公事 (of employees from a government department, enterprise or organization, or of servicemen) go on a business trip: 去北京～go on a business trip to Beijing | 出了一个月的差 be on a business trip for a month ❷ 出去担负运输、修建等临时任务 be assigned a temporary transportation or building task away from one's normal work place

【出产】chūchǎn ❶ 天然生长或人工生产 naturally available or artificially produce: 云南～大理石。Yunnan produces marble. | 景德镇～的瓷器是世界闻名的。Chinaware manufactured in Jingdezhen is world-famous. ❷ 出产的物品 things that are produced: ～丰富 rich produce or products

【出厂】chū//chǎng 产品运出工厂 ship products out of the factory: 产品注明～日期。Products are stamped with the date of manufacture.

【出场】chū//chǎng ❶ 演员登台(表演) (of actors) come on stage to perform; walkabout ❷ 运动员进入场地(参加表演或竞赛) (of athletes) enter the arena to perform or compete

【出超】chūchāo 在一定时期(一般为一年)内,对外贸易中出口货物的总值超过进口货物的总值(跟'入超'相对 as opposed to 'import surplus') export surplus; situation in which the total value of export surpasses that of import within a certain period (usu. a year)

【出车】chū//chē 开出车辆(载人或运货) drive a vehicle (to transport passengers or cargo): 你出趟车送他们去机场。Please drive them to the airport.

【出乘】chū//chéng (乘务员)随车、船等出发工作 serve as an attendant on a vehicle, ship, etc.

【出丑】chū//chǒu 露出丑相;丢人 be disgraced; lose face: 当众～lose one's face in public

【出处】chūchǔ〈书 *fml.*〉出仕和退隐 take up and retire from an official post

【出处】chūchù (引文或典故的)来源 source (of a quotation or allusion): 文章中的引文应注明～。The sources of quotations in an article should be noted.

【出倒】chūdǎo 私营工商业主因亏损或其他原因,将企业的设备、商品和房屋、地基等全部出售,由别人继续经营 sale of a private industrial or commercial company, including its equipment, products, and property, to someone else to operate, due to financial failure or other reasons

【出道】chū//dào 学徒学艺期满，开始从事某项工作或事业 begin a job or launch a career after completing the term of one's apprenticeship

【出典】[1] chūdiǎn 典故的来源；出处 source of an inference; source：'守株待兔'这个成语的～见《韩非子·五蠹》。The idiom 'expect gains without pains' comes from *Hanfeizi · Five Vermin*.

【出典】[2] chūdiǎn 指一方把土地、房屋等押给另一方使用，换取一笔钱，不付利息，议定年限，到期还款，收回原物 mortgage, transfer the use of land or a house by one party to another in return for the use of a sum of money without paying interest for an agreed period of time, at the end of which each shall get back what has been contributed

【出店】chūdiàn〈方 *dial.*〉〈旧时 *old*〉商店中担任接送货物等外勤工作的人员 shop assistant responsible for receiving and delivering goods and for running errands

【出顶】chūdǐng〈方 *dial.*〉指把自己租到的房屋转租给别人 sublease a house or room

【出动】chūdòng ❶（队伍）外出活动 (of troops) set out：队部命令一分队做好准备，待令～。The headquarters ordered the first squad to be prepared for action. ❷ 派出（军队）dispatch (troops)：～伞兵，协同作战 send paratroopers to coordinate in a battle ❸（许多人为某些事）行动起来 (of many people) get into action：昨天大扫除，全校师生都～了。All the teachers and students of the school joined yesterday's cleaning-up.

【出尔反尔】chū ěr fǎn ěr《孟子·梁惠王》：'出乎尔者，反乎尔者也。'原意是你怎么做，就会得到怎样的后果。今指说了又翻悔或说了不照着做，表示言行前后自相矛盾，反复无常。*Mencius · Duke Hui of Liang*：'You will reap what you have sowed.' It originally meant that one must take the consequences of what one has done. The present-day sense of this idiom is to go back on one's word, fail to do what one has promised, contradict one's word with one's deed, or be inconsistent.

【出发】chūfā ❶ 离开原来所在的地方到别的地方去 leave the original location for another place：～日期还没有确定。The date of departure has not been set.｜收拾行装，准备～。Pack your bags and get ready to leave. ❷ 考虑或处理问题时以某一方面为着眼点 focus of attention when considering or handling an issue：从生产～ as regards production｜从长远利益～ keep long-term interest in mind

【出发点】chūfādiǎn ❶ 旅程的起点 starting point of a journey ❷ 最根本的着眼的地方；动机 most essential point of emphasis; motive：全心全意地为人民服务，一切为了人民的利益，这就是我们的～。Our point of departure is to serve the people whole-heartedly and to proceed in all cases from the interest of the people.｜双方的～不同，而要达到的目的则是一致的。Despite different intentions, the two sides seek for the same goal.

【出饭】chūfàn 做出来的饭多 (of rice) rise well when cooked：这种米比别的米～。This rice swells larger than other kinds.

【出访】chūfǎng 到外国访问 go on a visit abroad：～欧美 go on a tour of Europe and America

【出份子】chū fèn·zi ❶ 各人拿出若干钱合起来送礼 club together to buy a gift ❷ 指到办红白事的人家去送礼并参加庆贺或吊唁 bring a present to a wedding or funeral to express congratulations or condolences

【出风头】chū fēng·tou 出头露面显示自己 show off：他就是爱～。He likes to seek the limelight.｜出够了风头 attract more than enough attention

【出伏】chū//fú 出了伏天；伏天结束 over with or end of the hot season：一～，天就凉快了。The weather turns cool as soon as the hot season is over.

【出阁】chū//gé same as 出嫁 chū//jià

【出格】chū//gé ❶ 言语行动与众不同；出众 extraordinary in word and deed; outstanding：在这一带，他的才学是～的。He is prominent for his learning in the area. ❷ 越出常规；出圈儿 over-the-top; go beyond what is proper; be bad：这孩子淘得出了格。The child is exceedingly naughty.

【出工】chū//gōng 出发上工；出勤 go to work; show up for work：时间快到，就要～了。It'll soon be time for work.｜他每天～，从不请假。He goes to work everyday, never asking for a leave.

【出恭】chū//gōng 排泄大便 go to the lavatory (for a bowel movement)

【出轨】chū//guǐ ❶（火车、有轨电车等）行驶时脱离轨道 (of a train, tramcar, etc.) derail; also 脱轨 tuō//guǐ ❷〈比喻 *fig.*〉言语行动出乎常规之外 (of speech and behaviour) improper：这话说得～了。What you say goes too far.

【出国】chū//guó 离开本国到别国去 go abroad：～留学 study abroad｜～考察 go on a fact-finding tour abroad

【出海】chū//hǎi（船只）离开停泊地点到海上去；（海员或渔民）驾驶船只到海上去 (of a ship) leave the port for the sea; (of sailors or fishermen) put to sea：～打鱼 go fishing on the sea

【出航】chū//háng（船或飞机）离开港口或机场去航行 (of a ship or plane) set out from a port or airport

【出号】chū//hào〈旧时 *old*〉指商店里的伙计离

开商店（of a shop assistant) leave the place of employment

【出号】chūhào（～儿 chūhàor)比头号的还大；特大号的 bigger than the large size; (of size) extra large：小伙子挑着两个～的大水桶。The young man carries a pair of extra-large wooden pails.

【出活】chū//huó（～儿 chū//huór) ❶ 干出活儿 get work done：有了新式机器，干活又轻巧，～又快。With the new machine, we can do our work with much ease and efficiency. ❷ 单位时间内干出较多的活 have a large amount of work done per unit time：下午虽然只干了两个钟头，可是很～。We worked only two hours in the afternoon, but we accomplished a lot.

【出击】chūjī ❶ 部队出动，向敌人进攻（of troops) launch an attack on the enemy ❷ 泛指在斗争或竞赛中发动攻势 attack first in a fight or competition：发现罪犯踪迹，主动～。Start the offensive as soon as we discover the criminal's traces.

【出继】chūjì 过继给别人做儿子 be adopted as a son

【出家】chū//jiā 离开家庭到庙宇里去做僧尼或道士 renounce the family to become a monk, nun, or Taoist：～修行 live and cultivate oneself as a monk or Taoist｜～为尼 be tonsured to become a nun

【出家人】chūjiārén 指僧尼或道士 monk, Taoist, or nun

【出价】chū//jià 在商品交易中买方提出愿付的价格 price offered by a buyer in a deal：这幅山水画他～三千元。He offered three thousand yuan for this landscape painting.｜您要真想买，就出个价吧。If you really want it, please give a price.

【出嫁】chū//jià 女子结婚（of a woman) get married

【出尖】chū//jiān（～儿 chū//jiānr) ❶ 超出一般；拔尖儿 better than usual; be the top or best：～露众 distinguish oneself ❷〈方 *dial*.〉装满而且稍高出容器 be full to the brim：碗里的米饭已经～了。The bowl is filled to the brim with rice.

【出将入相】chu jiàng rù xiàng 出战可为将，入朝可为相。旧时指人文武兼备。也指官居高位。be a general in the field or a minister at court; (in old times) applause of a man with both military and administrative competence; hold high office

【出界】chū//jiè 越出界线；越过边界 exceed the boundary; cross the border

【出借】chūjiè 借出去（多指物品 oft. things) lend：新到的期刊暂不～。We do not loan out new periodicals.

【出境】chū//jìng ❶ 离开国境 leave the country：驱逐～deport｜办理～手续 go through exit formalities ❷ 离开某个地区 leave an area：这条河是县界，过了河就～了。The river is the border; you are in a different county once you cross it.

【出九】chū//jiǔ 出了数九的日子 be over with the cold season：虽说还没有～，天气却暖和多了。Although the cold season has yet to end, the weather is turning much warmer.

☞ 九 jiǔ ② on p.1037

【出局】chū//jú 指棒球、垒球比赛击球员或跑垒员在进攻中因犯规等被判退离球场，失去继续进攻机会 be out of the game; In baseball or softball, a batter or fielder is ousted and loses his chance to attack when he fouls.

【出具】chūjù 开出；写出（证明、证件等）issue; write (certificate, papers, etc.)：～介绍信 provide a letter of introduction｜～健康证明 issue a health certificate

【出圈】chū//juàn same as 起圈 qǐ//juàn

【出科】chū//kē 指在科班学戏期满 complete the term of learning or training at a professional theatrical school

【出口】chū//kǒu ❶ 说出话来 speak out：～伤人 speak bitingly｜～成章 talk eloquently; make a polished impromptu speech ❷（船只)驶出港口（of a ship) depart from the port ❸ 本国或本地区的货物运出去（of goods) transport out of a country or locality：～货 export goods｜～税 export tax

【出口】chūkǒu 从建筑物或场地出去的门或口儿 door or opening through which one leaves a building or place：车站～ exit of a railway or bus station｜会场的～ exit of a meeting place

【出口成章】chū kǒu chéng zhāng 话说出来就是一篇文章。形容文思敏捷或言语精炼，擅长辞令。What one speaks is like a written article. (fig.) quick in writing or succinct in speech; have the gift of gab

【出口伤人】chū kǒu shāng rén 一张口说话就污辱人、伤害人 talk harshly; offend in word the moment one begins to talk; insult or offend sb. with rude remarks

【出来】chū//·lái ❶ 从里面到外面来 move from inside to outside：出得来 be able to come out｜出不来 be unable to come out｜你～，我跟你说句话。Come out please. I have a word with you. ❷ same as 出现 chūxiàn：经过讨论，～两种相反的意见。The discussion led to two opposite views.

【出来】//·chū//·lái ❶ 用在动词后，表示动作由里向外朝着说话的人[used after a verb to indicate an act directed from inside a place towards the speaker]：拿～ take out｜拿得～ be able to take out｜拿不～ be unable to take out｜从屋里走出一个人来。Someone comes out of the room. ❷ 用在动词后，表示动作完成或实现 [used after a verb to indicate completion or realization of an action]：开出很多荒地来。Much wasteland has been reclaimed.

|创造出新产品来。A new product has been developed. ❸ 用在动词后,表示由隐蔽到显露[used after a verb to indicate sth. coming to light or being driven home]:我认出他来了。I recognized him.|听着听着渐渐听出点意思来了。I gradually made out the meaning as I listened.|天黑了,字都看不~了。It's so dark, the characters are hardly discernible.

【出栏】chū//lán ❶ 猪羊等长成,提供屠宰叫出栏 (of livestock) grow big enough for slaughtering:今年养猪十万多头,卖给国家六万多头,~率达百分之六十。We raised more than 100,000 pigs this year and sold 60,000, or 60%, to the state. ❷〈方 *dial*.〉起圈 clean up a domestic animal's place:~垫土 remove manure and dirt from a pen and cover it with new earth

【出类拔萃】chū lèi bá cuì《孟子·公孙丑》:'出于其类,拔乎其萃。'后来用'出类拔萃'形容超出同类之上。*Mencius · Gongsun Chou*: 'Be of but above the same kind.' (fig.) excel one's fellow beings; also 出类拔群 chū lèi bá qún or 出群拔萃 chū qún bá cuì

【出力】chū//lì 拿出力量;尽力 exert oneself; do one's best:~不讨好 receive no credit for one's effort|他为人耿直,干工作又肯~。He is honest and straightforward, and hardworking, too.

【出列】chūliè 从队列中向前走出并立定 step out of the ranks and stand still

【出猎】chūliè 出去打猎 go hunting

【出溜】chū·liu〈方 *dial*.〉滑;滑行 slip; slide:脚底下一~,摔了一跤 slip and fall|他从沙堆上~下来。He dropped from the sand dune. ◇这孩子的学习近两个月有点往下~。The child's been doing less well in his study the past two months.

【出笼】chū//lóng ❶ 馒头等蒸熟后从笼屉取出 remove buns, etc., from the steamer when they are done ❷〈比喻 *fig*.〉囤积居奇的货物大量出售,通货膨胀时钞票大量发行。也比喻坏的作品发表或伪劣商品上市等。hoard up goods and subsequently sell them in large quantities; issue huge amount of banknotes during an inflation; publish a bad work; market shoddy goods

【出炉】chū//lú 取出炉内烘烤、冶炼的东西 remove sth. from an oven or furnace:刚~的烧饼 freshly baked cakes|一号高炉准时~。No. 1 Blast Furnace began the tapping on time.

【出路】chūlù ❶ 通向外面的道路 way out:在森林里迷失方向,找不到~ lose one's way in a forest ❷〈比喻 *fig*.〉生存或向前发展的途径;前途 ways and means for survival or making progress; future:另谋~ find a different way out|农业的根本~在于机械化。Mechanization is the fundamental way out for agriculture. ❸〈比喻 *fig*.〉销售货物的去处 sales outlet for commodities:品质优良的产品,不愁没有~。We can always find a market for quality products.

【出乱子】chū luàn·zi 出差错;出毛病 go wrong; in trouble:你放心,出不了乱子。Don't worry; nothing will go wrong.

【出落】chū·luo 青年人(多指女性)的体态、容貌向美好的方面变化 (of young people, esp. females) grow prettier in body shape and looks:半年没见,小妞儿~得更漂亮了。The little girl has turned even more beautiful since I saw her half a year ago.

【出马】chū//mǎ ❶ 原指将士上阵作战,今多指出头做事 (orig. of officers and men) take to the field; take the lead in doing sth.:老将~,一个顶俩。A veteran is better than two novices.|那件事很重要,非你亲自~不行。That is a very important matter and you have to attend to it personally. ❷〈方 *dial*.〉same as 出诊 chū//zhěn

【出卖】chūmài ❶ 卖;出售 sell; offer for sale:~房屋 sell a house|~劳动力 offer one's labour ❷ 为了个人利益,做出有利于敌人的事,使国家、民族、亲友等利益受到损害 do sth. for personal interest, or in the service of the enemy, at the expense of the state, nation, family or friends:~灵魂 sell one's soul|~情报 sell information |~民族利益 betray national interests

【出毛病】chū máo·bìng 出差错;出故障;出事故 go wrong; be out of order; have an accident:机器要保养好,免得~。The machine needs to be well maintained to avoid malfunction.

【出梅】chū//méi 出了黄梅季;黄梅季结束 over with or end of the rainy season; also 断梅 duàn//méi; ☞ 黄梅季 huángméijì on p. 853

【出门】chū//mén ❶ (~儿 chū//ménr)外出 go out:他刚~,你等一会儿吧。He's just gone out. Please wait a little while. ❷ (~儿 chū//ménr)离家远行 leave home for a long journey:~在外 be away from home|~后时常接到家里来信 receive frequent correspondence from one's family while away from home ❸〈方 *dial*.〉same as 出嫁 chū//jià

【出门子】chū mén·zi〈方 *dial*.〉same as 出嫁 chū//jià

【出面】chū//miàn 以个人或集体的名义(做某件事)(do sth.) in the name of a person or collective:这事你~交涉吧。You can be the negotiator for this matter.|由工会~,组织这次体育比赛。The sports meet was organized under the auspices of the trade union.

【出苗】chū//miáo ☞ 露苗 lòu//miáo on p. 1255

【出名】chū//míng ❶ 有名声;名字为大家所熟知 be famous; (of one's name) be well known:他是我们厂里~的先进生产者。He is a renowned advanced worker in our factory. ❷ (~儿 chú//míngr) same as 出面 chū//miàn

【出没】chūmò 出现和隐藏 appear and disappear:～无常 come and go unpredictably|森林里常有野兽～。The forest is the haunt of wild animals.

【出谋划策】chū móu huà cè 出主意,定计策 offer advice; work out a strategy

【出纳】chūnà ❶ 机关、团体、企业等单位中现金、票据的付出和收进 (of an organization or enterprise) payment and receipt of cash or bills:～科 cashier's section ❷ 担任出纳工作的人 cashier ❸ 泛指发出和收进的管理工作,如图书馆有出纳台 (in a broad sense) management of loaning and returning, such as the circulation desk in a library

【出盘】chūpán〈方 dial.〉same as 出倒 chūdǎo

【出品】chūpǐn ❶ 制造出来产品 manufacture a product:这个牌子的彩电是本厂～的。This brand of colour TV is made in my factory. ❷ 生产出来的物品;产品 things produced; product:这是本厂的新～。This is a new product of my factory.|这些～经过检验,完全合格。These products have passed quality tests and proved fully up to standard.

【出聘】chūpìn ❶ same as 出嫁 chū//jià:她的闺女去年～了。Her daughter got married last year. ❷〈书 fml.〉same as 出使 chūshǐ

【出圃】chūpǔ 指苗木长到一定阶段从苗圃移植别处 remove saplings from a nursery for transplanting:苗圃施了大量肥料,树苗长得旺,～早。Saplings of the nursery have grown very well due to rich fertilization; they can be transplanted elsewhere at an early date.

【出其不意】chū qí bù yì 趁对方没有料到(就采取行动) take the opponent by surprise:～,攻其无备 take action out of (an opponent's) expectation and attack where (the opponent) is not prepared

【出奇】chūqí 特别;不平常 particular; unusual:今年早春真暖得～。The weather was rather warm for early spring this year.|山村的夜,～的安静。Such a serene night is unique in a mountain village.

【出奇制胜】chū qí zhì shèng 用奇兵或奇计战胜敌人 defeat the enemy by a surprise move or strategy;〈比喻 fig.〉用对方意想不到的方法来取胜 gain the upper hand by taking an opponent unawares

【出气】chū//qì 把心里的怨愤发泄出来 give vent to one's anger:在外面受了委屈,不该拿家人～。You should not take it out on your family when you have been wronged elsewhere.

【出气筒】chūqìtǒng〈比喻 fig.〉被人用来发泄怨气的人 punching bag

【出勤】chū//qín ❶ 按规定的时间到工作场所工作 show up for work on time:～率 ratio of attendance ❷ 外出办理公务 go out for business

【出去】chū//·qù 从里面到外面去 go from inside to outside:出得去 be able to go out|出不去 be unable to go out|～走走,呼吸点新鲜空气。Let's get out to breathe some fresh air.

【出去】//·chū//·qù 用在动词后,表示动作由里向外离开说话的人[used after a verb to indicate an act directed away from the speaker]:走得～ be able to leave|走不～ be unable to go away|送出大门去 see sb. off outside the gate

【出圈儿】chūquānr〈比喻 fig.〉越出常规、范围 go beyond common rules or limits:这样做就～了。This goes too far.|话说得出了圈儿了 speak improperly

【出缺】chūquē 因原任人员(多指职位较高的)离职或死亡而职位空出来 (oft. of a high post) fall vacant due to resignation or death of the person concerned

【出让】chūràng 不以谋利为目的而卖出(个人自用的东西 of things for one's own use) sell, but not for profit:～家具 sell one's furniture|廉价～ sell one's stuff at low prices

【出人头地】chū rén tóu dì 超出一般人;高人一等 rise head and shoulders above others; make one's mark

【出人意料】chū rén yì liào (事物的好坏、情况的变化、数量的大小等)出于人们的意料之外 (of the good or bad side of sth., the change of a situation, or the size of a quantity) be beyond people's expectations; also 出人意表 chū rén yì biǎo

【出任】chūrèn 出来担任(某种官职) take up (an official post):～要职 assume an important position|～驻外使节 take up the mission as an envoy abroad

【出入】chūrù ❶ 出去和进来 go out and come in:～随手关门。Close the door behind you.|东西堆在过道,～不方便。Things stacked in corridor are getting in the way. ❷ (数目、内容等)不一致;不相符 (of numbers, contents, etc.) inconsistent; discrepant:现款跟账上的数目没有～。Cash on hand tallies with the figure in the accounts.|你俩说的话有～。The two of you have a different story of the same event.

【出丧】chū//sāng same as 出殡 chūbìn

【出色】chūsè 特别好;超出一般的 excellent; top-notch; extremely good:表演～。The performance was superb.|他们～地完成了任务。They have done an extraordinary job.

【出山】chū//shān〈比喻 fig〉出来做官,也泛指出来担任某种职务,从事某项工作 take up an official post (a career, or a job):他这次任篮球教练,已是二度～。This is his second term as a basketball coach.

【出身】chūshēn ❶ 指个人早期的经历或由家庭经济情况所决定的身份 one's identity as related to one's early experience or family background, especially financial status: 店员～ be from a shop assistant's family | 工人家庭～ come of a worker's stock ❷〈旧时 *old*〉指做官的最初资历 initial status of an official: 翰林～ begin one's official career as a member of the Hanlin Academy | 赐进士～ confer the status of metropolitan graduate on sb.

【出神】chū//shén 因精神过度集中而发呆 be spellbound because of high concentration: 孩子们听故事,听得出了神。The children were totally absorbed in the story. | 上课的铃声响了,他还对着窗口～。He was still staring out of the window in a trance, oblivious to the bell for class.

【出神入化】chū shén rù huà 形容技艺达到了绝妙的境界 (of skills) reach the acme: 这一支曲子演奏得～,听众被深深地吸引住了。The audience was mesmerized by the enchanting performance of the number.

【出生】chūshēng 胎儿从母体中分离出来 (of a baby) come out of its mother's body: ～地 birthplace | 爷爷 1900 年～于北京。Grandpa was born in Beijing in 1900.

【出生率】chūshēnglǜ 每年出生婴儿数在总人口中所占的比率,通常用千分率来表示 birth rate; ratio of the number of newborn babies in a year to the total population, usu. on a per thousand basis

【出生入死】chū shēng rù sǐ 形容冒着生命危险 brave the risk of one's life; go through thick and thin

【出师】[1] chū//shī (徒弟)期满学成 (of an apprentice) complete the term of learning with the master: 学徒三年～。The apprenticeship is three years.

【出师】[2] chūshī〈书 *fml.*〉出兵打仗 dispatch troops into battle: ～讨伐 send troops on a punitive expedition | ～不利 be thwarted in the first battle

【出使】chūshǐ 接受外交使命到外国去 take on a diplomatic mission abroad: ～北欧诸国 visit North European countries in the capacity of an envoy

【出示】chūshì ❶ 拿出来给人看 take (sth.) out to show others: ～手稿 display one's manuscripts | ～乘车月票 show one's metro pass | ～黄牌警告 show a yellow card ❷〈书 *fml.*〉贴出布告 post a bulletin: ～安民 put up a notice to reassure the people

【出世】chūshì ❶ same as 出生 chūshēng: 那年他还没有～。He was not yet born that year. ❷ 产生 come into being: 旧制度灭亡,新制度～。At the demise of the old system, a new one took shape. ❸ 超脱人世,摆脱世事的束缚 be detached from the world; extricate oneself from the bondage of worldly affairs: ～思想 thoughts to renounce the world ❹ 指高出人世 way above the human world: 横空～ span the sky (横亘太空 héng gèn tài kōng and 高出人世 gāo chū rén shì, 形容山极高 describe the great height of a mountain)

【出世作】chūshìzuò〈旧时 *old*〉指一生中最早问世的作品 first work known to the public in one's life; maiden work

【出仕】chūshì〈书 *fml.*〉出任官职 take up an official post

【出事】chū//shì 发生事故 meet with an accident or mishap: ～地点 site of an accident | 那里围了很多人,好像出了什么事。People have crowded over there. Something seems to have happened.

【出手】chū//shǒu ❶ 卖出货物(多用于倒把、变卖等); same as 脱手 tuō//shǒu② sell goods (for profiteering, etc.); dispose of: 那批货急于～。The stock needs to be cleared away as soon as possible. | 货物很快就出了手。The goods were snatched up pretty soon. ❷ 拿出来 give: 一～就给他两千块钱。(Someone) gave him two thousand yuan offhand.

【出手】chūshǒu ❶ 指袖子的长短 length of a sleeve ❷ 开始做某件事情时表现出来的本领 skill displayed in setting sth. in motion: 我跟他下了几着,就觉得他～的确不凡。I found him an excellent player after only a few moves. ❸ ☞ 打出手 dǎ chūshǒu on p. 347

【出首】chūshǒu ❶ 检举、告发别人的犯罪行为 report a crime to the authorities ❷ 自首(多见于早期白话 mostly in early vernacular) turn oneself in

【出售】chūshòu 卖 sell: ～商品 sell commodities | 降低～ sell (sth.) at a reduced price

【出数儿】chū//shùr 产生的数量大 become larger in number or size: 机米做饭～。Long-grained non-glutinous rice rises well when cooked.

【出台】chū//tái ❶ 演员上场 (of an actor or actress) appear onstage: ～演出 perform onstage ❷〈比喻 *fig.*〉公开出面活动 do sth. in public: ～干涉 openly intervene ❸ (政策、措施等)公布或予以实施 publish or implement (a policy, measure, etc.): 管理体制的改革方案正式～。The reform plan for the management system has been formally promulgated.

【出摊】chū//tān (～儿 chū//tānr) 在路旁、广场或集市上摆出货摊(售货) put up a stall by the road, on a public square, or in a market place (to sell goods): 这家饭馆一直坚持～卖早点,方便过路群众。The restaurant serves simple breakfast by the road, to the convenience of passersby.

【出逃】chūtáo 逃出去(脱离家庭或国家) flee (one's home or country): 仓皇～ run away in panic; flee helter-skelter | 离家～ escape from home

【出挑】chū·tiāo（青年人的体格、相貌、智能向美好的方面）发育、变化、成长（of young people）grow better or mature（in physique, appearance, intelligence）：这姑娘～得越发标致了。The young girl has turned even more beautiful.｜不满一年，他就～成师傅的得力助手。He became a competent assistant to his master within a year.

【出粜】chūtiào 卖出（粮食）sell（grain）：把粮食运到外地～ transport grain to other places to sell

【出庭】chū//tíng 诉讼案件的关系人（如原告人、被告人、辩护人、代理人、律师等）到法庭上接受审讯或讯问（of people related to a case, such as the plaintive, defendant, defender, agent, lawyer, etc.）appear in court for questioning

【出头】chū//tóu ❶ 从困苦的环境中解脱出来 be freed from a miserable condition：盼到了～之日 see the end of bitter days ❷（物体）露出顶端（of things）show the top：～的椽子先烂（比喻冒尖的人最容易受到打击）。Rafter that protrudes rots first. *or*（fig.）Those in the fore are most vulnerable to attack.｜堆放杉篙，不能～太多。When you pile up fir logs, make sure that not many of them stick out. ❸ 出面；带头 do sth. in person; take the lead：～露面 be active in public｜我们厂的体育活动，是他～搞起来的。It was he who initiated sports activities in our factory. ❹（～儿 chū//tóur）用在整数之后表示有零数［used after an integer to indicate a reminder after that］：小麦亩产八百斤～。The output of wheat per *mu* was more than 400 kg.｜你已是三十～的人了，该成家了。It's time for you to get married now that you are over 30 years old.

【出头露面】chūtóu lòumiàn ❶ 在公众的场合出现 appear in public：他不爱～。He doesn't like to be in the limelight. ❷ 出面（做事）take the lead in doing sth.：大家推他～去商谈这件事。We all recommended him to negotiate the matter.

【出徒】chū//tú（徒工）期满学成；出师 complete one's apprenticeship; finish learning with one's master：我刚进厂两年，还没～呢！I've been in the factory for only two years and am still an apprentice.

【出土】chū//tǔ（古器物等）被发掘出来（of antiques）be unearthed; be exhumed：～文物 cultural relics excavated from underground｜这一批铜器是在寿县～的。These bronze wares were dug up in Shouxian County.

【出脱】chūtuō ❶ 货物卖出（of merchandise）sell out; get rid of; same as 脱手 tuō//shǒu② ❷ same as 出落 chū·luo：这孩子的模样～得更好看了。The child has become even prettier. ❸ 开脱（罪名）find excuse（for a criminal charge）：他的诡辩不过是自我～。He resorted to sophistry in the hope of exonerating himself.

【出外】chūwài 到外地去 leave one's hometown for another place：～谋生 make a living away from home

【出亡】chūwáng 出走；逃亡 run away（from one's home）; flee for life：～他乡 flee home and live in exile

【出席】chū//xí 有发言权和表决权的成员（有时也泛指一般人）参加会议 be present at a meeting, with or without the right to present a speech or to vote：～代表大会 take part in a congress｜报告～人数 report the number of participants

【出息】chū·xi ❶ 指发展前途或志气 prospect or aspiration：不管做什么工作，只要对人民有贡献，就有～。Whatever we do is meaningful as long as it contributes to the welfare of the people.｜懦夫懒汉是没～的。There's no future for cowards and lazybones. ❷〈方 *dial.*〉长进；出落 make progress; same as 出落 chū·luo：这孩子比去年～多了。The child is doing much better than last year.｜那姑娘～得更漂亮了。The young woman has turned even more beautiful. ❸〈方 *dial.*〉培养使有出息 train（a person）to become more able：这个学校就是～人。This school is indeed an incubator of talents. ❹〈方 *dial.*〉收益 income：咱这儿种稻子比种高粱～大。We make more money planting paddy rice than sorghum in this area.

【出险】chū//xiǎn ❶（人）脱离险境（of a person）escape from a dangerous situation：他一定有办法保护你～。He's definitely able to come to your rescue. ❷（堤坝等工程）发生危险（of a dam or other engineering projects）be in perils：加固堤坝，防止～。Let's reinforce the dam to ensure safety.

【出现】chūxiàn 显露出来；产生出来 materialize; come into sight：比赛前半小时运动员已经～在运动场上了。The athletes appeared on the sports ground half an hour before the competition.｜近年来～了许多优秀作品。Many fine works have come to the fore in recent years.

【出线】chū//xiàn 在分阶段进行的比赛里，参赛的人员或团体取得参加下一阶段比赛的资格，叫做出线（of an individual or team）qualify for the next round of competition

【出项】chūxiàng 支出的款项 expenses：这几年家里人多了，～也增加了不少。With the increase of members in recent years, the family expenditures are also on the rise.

【出血】chū//xiě〈方 *dial.*〉〈比喻 *fig.*〉拿出钱或拿出东西 give out money or things

【出行】chūxíng 外出；到外地去 take to the

road; go to another place:这次～,跑了不少地方。We've been to quite a few places on this trip.

【出虚恭】chū xūgōng〈婉辞 *euph.*〉指放屁 break wind

【出巡】chūxún 出外巡视 make an inspection tour:～江南 go to areas south of the Yangtze River on an inspection tour

【出芽】chū//yá ❶ 抽芽 sprout ❷ 某些低等动物或植物生出芽体(of certain invertebrates or lower plants) gemmate

【出言】chūyán 说出话来 say; speak:～有章(说话有条理) talk with logic|～不逊(说话不客气) speak impolitely

【出演】chūyǎn 演出;扮演 perform; act; be cast as:在这出戏里他～包公。He plays the role of Lord Bao in the play.

【出洋】chū//yáng 指到外国去 go abroad:～考察 make a study tour abroad

【出洋相】chū yángxiàng 闹笑话;出丑 make a laughing stock of oneself; be held up for mockery (in front of a crowd); same as 出丑 chū//chǒu.

【出游】chūyóu 出去游历 go on a sightseeing tour:～未归(of a person) has yet to return from a sightseeing trip

【出语】chūyǔ 说出话语 say; speak:～惊人 make electrifying remarks

【出院】chū//yuàn(住院病人办理手续后)离开医院(of an inpatient) be discharged from hospital after going through necessary procedures

【出月】chū//yuè 过了本月 after the end of the month:这个月没时间,～才能把稿子写完。I have no time this month. I won't be able to finish writing the paper untill next month.

【出月子】chūyuè·zi 指妇女生育满一个月(of a woman who has given birth) complete a full month of maternity confinement

【出展】chūzhǎn ❶ 到外地展览 put on an exhibition away from home:新产品～欧洲获得好评。The new product drew raves while on display in Europe. ❷ 展出 exhibit; display:优秀美术作品即将在京～。Fine works of art will be put on show in Beijing soon.

【出战】chūzhàn 出兵打仗;跟进攻的敌人作战 send troops into battle; fight against an offensive enemy:～失利 lose a battle ◇中国足球队～世界杯外围赛。The Chinese Football Team took part in the preliminary heat of the World Cup.

【出账】chū//zhàng 把支出的款项登上账簿 enter an item of expenditure in the accounts:这笔开支违反规定,不能～。We can't enter this payment into the accounts, as it is against the rules.

【出账】chūzhàng〈方 *dial.*〉支出的款项;开支 item of expenditure; expense:这个月～太多。We've spent too much this month.

【出蛰】chūzhé 动物结束冬眠,出来活动(of certain animals) wake up from hibernation and become active

【出诊】chū//zhěn 医生离开医院或诊所到病人家里去给病人治病(of a doctor) leave the hospital or clinic to see a patient at home; go or make one's rounds

【出阵】chū//zhèn ❶ 上战场打仗 go into battle ❷〈比喻 *fig.*〉参加某种活动 take part in an activity:这场拔河比赛,连退休老人都～了。Even retirees joined in the tug-of-war competition.

【出征】chū//zhēng 出去打仗 be out to fight:率兵～ lead troops on an expedition

【出众】chūzhòng 超出众人 stand out among the ordinary:成绩～ accomplish outstanding achievement

【出资】chūzī 拿出钱财 provide funding:这次比赛是由几家企业～赞助的。The competition was sponsored by several enterprises.

【出走】chūzǒu 被环境逼迫不声张地离开家庭或当地 be forced by circumstances to leave one's home or place of living in secret:仓促～ leave in haste|离家～ run away from home

【出租】chūzū 收取一定的代价,让别人暂时使用 let; rent out; hire out; give sth. to sb. for temporary use in return for rent:～图书 rent out books

【出租汽车】chūzū qìchē 供人临时雇用的汽车,多按时间或里程收费 taxi, vehicle for hire, mostly for payment charged by the hour or mileage; also 出租车 chūzūchē

郘 chū 郘江(Chūjiāng),地名,在四川 place name, in Sichuan Province

初 chū ❶ 开始的;开始的部分 beginning; initial part:～夏 early summer|年～ commencement of a year ❷ 第一个 first one:～伏 first ten days of the hot season|～旬 first ten days of a month|～一(农历每月的第一天,等于'第一个一',区别于'十一、二十一') first day of a month on the Chinese lunar calendar, or the 'very first day'(as compared with the '11th day' and the '21st day')|～十(农历每月的第十天,等于'第一个十',区别于'二十、三十') tenth day of a month on the Chinese lunar calendar, or the 'first 10th day'(as compared with the '20th day' and the '30th day') ❸ 第一次;刚开始 first time; very beginning:～试 initial test|～次见面 meet for the first time|～学乍练 begin to learn or do sth. ❹ 最低的(等级) primary (grade):～级 rudimentary level|～等 primordial grade ❺ 原来的;原来的情况 original; earliest condition:～心 initial feelings|～志 aspiration to begin with|和好如～(of a relationship) become as good as before ❻

(Chū) 姓 a surname

【初版】chūbǎn ❶（书籍）出第一版（of a book）be published for the first time：本书 1956 年～。The book was first published in 1956. ❷（书籍的）第一版（of a book）first edition：这部书～印了两万册。The first edition of the book had a print run of 20,000 copies.

【初步】chūbù 开始阶段的；不是最后的或完备的 of the initial stage; not final or complete：提出～意见 make a tentative comment | 这些问题已经得到～解决。These problems have been initially solved.

【初潮】chūcháo 指女子第一次来月经 first menses

【初出茅庐】chū chū máolú〈比喻 *fig.*〉刚进入社会或刚到工作岗位上来，缺乏经验 just enter society or take up a new job; without experience

【初创】chūchàng 刚刚创立 newly established：～阶段 beginning stage (of an enterprise); in infancy

【初春】chūchūn 春季的一段时间，即农历正月；早春 early spring; part of the spring season, i.e. the first month of the Chinese lunar calendar

【初等】chūděng ❶ 比较浅近的 of a simple level：～数学 elementary mathematics ❷ 初级 elementary：～小学（旧称）(old name for) primary school | ～教育 elementary education

【初等教育】chūděng jiàoyù 小学程度的教育。是对少年儿童实施的全面基础教育和对成人实施的相当于小学程度的教育。elementary education; education at the primary level; education that provides overall basic school training for children or adults

【初冬】chūdōng 冬季的一段时间，即农历十月 early winter; part of the winter season, i.e. the 10th lunar month

【初度】chūdù〈书 *fml.*〉原指初生的时候，后称生日为初度 (orig.) time when one was born; birthday：四十～ fortieth birthday

【初犯】chūfàn 第一次犯罪或犯错误、过失等 commit a crime or make a mistake for the first time：因是～，还能原谅。A pardon may be possible for first offenders.

【初伏】chūfú ❶ 夏至后的第三个庚日，是三伏头一伏的第一天 the third *geng* day after the Summer Solstice, or the first day of the first of the three ten-day periods of the hot season ❷ 通常也指从夏至后第三个庚日起到第四个庚日前一天的一段时间 usu. the period from the third *geng* day to the day before the fourth *geng* day after the Summer Solstice ‖ also 头伏 tóufú; ☞ 三伏 sānfú on p. 1651

【初稿】chūgǎo 第一次的稿子，也泛指未定稿 first draft; draft in general

【初花】chūhuā ❶ 植株在一年中第一次开花（of a plant）blossom for the first time in the year：刺槐在云南 3 月 15 日～，北京 4 月 29 日～。Locust begins to bloom on March 15 in Yunnan Province and on April 29 in Beijing. ❷ 植物最早开出的花 earliest flowers of a plant

【初会】chūhuì 第一次见面 meet for the first time：我们是～，彼此都有点儿拘束。We were both a little ill at ease at our first meeting.

【初婚】chūhūn ❶ 第一次结婚 first marriage ❷ 刚结婚不久 newly married

【初级】chūjí 最低的阶段 beginner's stage：～读本 primer | ～形式 initial form

【初级小学】chūjí xiǎoxué 我国实施过的前一阶段的初等教育的学校 junior primary school once in practice in China; 简称 abbr. 初小 chūxiǎo

【初级中学】chūjí zhōngxué 我国实施的前一阶段的中等教育的学校。junior middle school; 简称 abbr. 初中 chūzhōng

【初交】chūjiāo 认识不久或交往不久的人 person of new acquaintance：我们是～，对他不太了解。We've just got acquainted, so I don't know much about him.

【初亏】chūkuī 日食或月食过程中，月亮和太阳圆面或地球阴影和月亮圆面第一次外切时的位置关系，也指发生这种位置关系的时刻。初亏是日食或月食过程的开始。beginning of a solar or lunar eclipse; during a solar or lunar eclipse, the positional relation between the moon and the sun or between the shadow of the earth and the moon when they first become externally tangent; moment when this occurs

【初来乍到】chū lái zhà dào 初次来到某个地方 be a newcomer to a place：～，不周之处请多包涵。Please bear with me if I make a slip or two, since I'm new here.

【初恋】chūliàn ❶ 第一次恋爱 first love ❷ 刚恋爱不久 just fall in love

【初露锋芒】chū lù fēng máng〈比喻 *fig.*〉刚显露出某种力量或才能 display certain ability or talent for the first time

【初露头角】chū lù tóu jiǎo〈比喻 *fig.*〉刚显露出某种才华 begin to show certain talent; cut a striking figure：这次展出的作品，作者大多是～的青年画家。The works on show are mostly by fledgling young painters.

【初民】chūmín 指远古时代的人 primitive people in remote antiquity

【初年】chūnián 指某一历史时期的最初一段 first few years of a historical period：民国～ early years of the Republic

【初评】chūpíng 初次或初步评比或评选 first or initial evaluation or screening

【初期】chūqī 开始的一段时期 beginning period：抗战～ early phase of the War of Resistance against Japan | 这病的～症状是厌食。The initial symptom of the disease is loss of appetite.

【初秋】chūqiū 秋季的一段时间,即农历七月 period of the autumn season, i.e. the seventh month of the Chinese lunar calendar

【初赛】chūsài 多轮次的体育、文艺等竞赛的第一轮比赛(of multi-round sports and artistic contests) preliminary

【初丧】chūsāng 家中刚发生丧事的一段时期 early in the mourning period of a family that has just lost a member

C

【初审】chūshěn ❶ 初次审查 first examination: ～合格 pass the first quality or qualification check ❷ 初步审问 initial interrogation: 经过～,案犯供认了犯罪事实。The suspect pleaded guilty at the first trial.

【初生之犊】chū shēng zhī dú 刚生出来的小牛。俗语说:'初生之犊不畏虎' newborn calf, as in the idiom 'A newborn calf is not afraid of the tiger'; 〈比喻 *fig.*〉青年人勇敢大胆,敢作敢为 dauntless young people; young daredevil

【初时】chūshí 起先,起初 at the beginning: ～我只当他说说而已,岂知他当真去了。I thought he didn't mean it, but who would have expected him to go for real.

【初试】chūshì ❶ 初次试验 first test ❷ 分两次举行的考试的第一次 primary of a two-phase examination; ☞ 复试 fùshì on p.611

【初速】chūsù ❶ 运动物体在一个特定运动过程开始时的速度 initial speed of an object in a given process of motion ❷ 特指弹头脱离枪、炮口瞬间的运动速度 speed of a bullet or cannonball just fired

【初岁】chūsuì 〈书 *fml.*〉指一年刚开始的时候 beginning of a year

【初探】chūtàn 初步探索或探讨(多用做书名或论文标题 oft. used for a book or thesis title) initial exploration or discussion of a topic: 《大陆架成因～》*An Initial Discussion on Formation of the Continental Shelf*

【初头】chūtóu 〈方 *dial.*〉一年或一月开始不久的日子 beginning days of a year or month: 1947 年～ early 1947|8 月～ early August

【初夏】chūxià 夏季的一段时间,即农历四月 period of the summer season, i.e. the fourth month of the Chinese lunar calendar

【初小】chūxiǎo 初级小学的简称 abbr. for 初级小学 chūjí xiǎoxué

【初心】chūxīn 最初的心愿 original ishes: 不改～。The aspiration remains unchanged.

【初学】chūxué 刚开始学或学习不久 just begin to learn or be in the early stage of learning: ～乍练 begin to learn or practise sth.|这本书对～的人很合适。This book is appropriate for beginners.

【初雪】chūxuě 入冬后第一次下的雪 first snowfall in winter

【初旬】chūxún 每月的第一个十天 first ten days of a month

【初叶】chūyè 指某一历史时期的最初一段 first phase of a historical period: 20 世纪～ early 20th century|明朝～ beginning of the Ming Dynasty

【初夜】chūyè ❶ 指进入夜晚不久的时候 not long after nightfall ❷ 指新婚第一夜 wedding night

【初愿】chūyuàn 起初的志愿或愿望 original aspiration or wishes: 他的～是当个中学教师,没想到后来成了大学教授。At first he wanted to become a middle school teacher, but ended up a university professor.

【初月】chūyuè 农历月初形状如钩的月亮 waxing moon at the beginning of a month of the Chinese lunar calendar

【初战】chūzhàn 战争或战役开始的第一仗 first battle in a war or campaign: ～告捷 win the first battle; also 序战 xùzhàn

【初诊】chūzhěn 医院或诊疗所指某个病人初次来看病 patient's first visit to the doctor at a hospital or clinic

【初志】chūzhì 〈书 *fml.*〉最初的志向 earliest aspiration: ～既定,终生不变。I will never change my ambition set early in my life.

【初中】chūzhōng 初级中学的简称 abbr. for 初级中学 chūjí zhōngxué

【初衷】chūzhōng 最初的心愿 original intention: 有违～ be against the initial intent|虽然经过百般挫折,也不改～ stick to one's goal despite many setbacks

摴 chū [摴蒱](chūpú)same as 樗蒲 chūpú

樗 chū 臭椿 heaven tree (*Ailanthus altissima*)

【樗蒲】chūpú 古代一种游戏,像后代的掷色子 ancient game, similar to dice-throwing; also 摴蒱 chūpú

chú(ㄔㄨˊ)

刍(芻) chú 〈书 *fml.*〉❶ 喂牲口用的草 hay: ～秣 fodder|反～ ruminate ❷ 割草 cut grass: ～荛 cut grass and firewood ❸ 〈谦辞 *hum.*〉称自己的(见解等) my own opinion: ～言 (my) humble remark|～见 (my) humble comment

【刍秣】chúmò 〈书 *fml.*〉草料 fodder

【刍荛】chúráo 〈书 *fml.*〉❶ 割草打柴 gather grass and firewood: ～有禁。Cutting grass and firewood is restricted. ❷ 指割草打柴的人 person who gathers grass and firewood: 询于～ enquire with a woodcutter ❸ 〈谦辞 *hum.*〉在向别人提供意见时把自己比作草野鄙陋的人 [refer to oneself as a rustic person when offering comments]: ～之言(浅陋的话) (my) shallow remark

【刍议】chúyì 〈书 *fml.*〉〈谦辞 *hum.*〉指自己的议论 one's own remark

刍(蒭) chú same as 刍 chú

除[1] chú ❶ 去掉 get rid of：根～root out | 铲～eradicate | 为民～害 wipe out evils for the people ❷ 不计算在内 not including：～外 except or besides | ～此而外 apart from this ❸ 用一个数对另一个数进行除法运算叫除，例如用 2 除 6 得 3 divide, e. g. 6 divided by 2 is 3 ❹〈书 *fml*.〉授；拜（官职）confer; appoint (sb. to an official post)

除[2] chú〈书 *fml*.〉台阶 step：庭～ courtyard | 阶～ flight of steps

【除暴安良】chú bào ān liáng 铲除暴徒，安抚人民 root out thugs to reassure the people

【除弊】chúbì 除去弊端 abolish malpractice：兴利～ engage in beneficial causes and eliminate malpractice

【除尘】chúchén 清除悬浮在气体中的粉尘，以免污染大气 remove suspended particles from the air or a gas to prevent atmospheric pollution

【除恶务尽】chú è wù jìn 清除坏人坏事或邪恶势力必须彻底 One must do a thorough job when wiping out wicked people, bad things, or evil forces. also 除恶务本 chú è wù běn

【除法】chúfǎ 数学中的一种运算方法。最简单的是数的除法，即从一个数连减相同数的简便算法。如从 10 中减去相同数 2，总共可以减去 5 个，就是 10 除以 2，或者说是 2 除 10。Division, a method of calculation in mathematics. The simplest form is the division of a number, or the successive subtraction of the same number from a number. For example, one can subtract 2 from 10 by five times. In other words, 10 divided by 2 is 5, or divide 10 by 2 you get 5.

【除非】chúfēi ❶〈连词 *conj*.〉表示唯一的条件，相当于'只有'，常跟'才、否则、不然'等合用 [usu. used correlatively with 才 cái, 否则 fǒuzé and 不然 bùrán, etc.] only if：若要人不知，～己莫为。Whatever one does is sure to leave a trace. | ～修个水库，才能更好地解决灌溉问题。Only by building a reservoir can we resolve the issue of irrigation. ❷ 表示不计算在内相当于'除了' including, not included, equivalent to 除了 chú·le：上山那条道，～他没人认识。No one but him knows the path to the top of the mountain.

【除服】chúfú〈书 *fml*.〉指守孝期满，脱去丧服 take off mourning clothes at the end of the mourning period

【除根】chú//gēn（～儿 chú//gēnr）从根本上消除 wipe out entirely; uproot：斩草～ cut the weeds and dig up the roots; annihilate | 治这种病就怕除不了根儿。The disease is unlikely to be cured completely.

【除旧布新】chú jiù bù xīn 破除旧的，建立新的 abolish the old to establish the new

【除开】chúkāi same as 除了 chú·le

【除了】chú·le〈介词 *prep*.〉❶ 表示所说的不计算在内 with the exception：那条山路，～他，谁也不熟悉。Nobody knows the mountain road except him. ❷ 跟'还、也、只'连用，表示在什么之外，还有别的 [used correlatively with 还 hái, 也 yě and 只 zhǐ to mean 'besides']：他～教课，还负责学校里工会的工作。He is in charge of the trade union besides teaching. | 他～写小说，有时候也写写诗。He occasionally writes poems in addition to stories. ❸ 跟'就是'连用，表示不这样就那样 [used correlatively with 就是 jiùshì to mean 'either of two alternatives']：刚生下来的孩子，～吃就是睡。All a newborn baby does is to eat or sleep.

【除名】chú//míng 使退出集体，从名册中除掉姓名 expel from a collective; expunge from the rolls

【除却】chúquè 除去；去掉 get rid of; do away with

【除日】chúrì〈书 *fml*.〉农历十二月的最后一天 last day of the 12th month of the Chinese lunar calendar

【除丧】chúsāng same as 除服 chúfú

【除外】chúwài 不计算在内 not including or included：图书馆天天开放，星期一～。The library is open everyday except Monday.

【除夕】chúxī 一年最后一天的夜晚，也泛指一年最后的一天 New Year's Eve; last day of the year：～之夜 New Year's eve | ～联欢会 New Year's Eve party

【除夜】chúyè 除夕晚上 New Year's Eve

钼 chú〈书 *fml*.〉same as 锄 chú ☞ jǔ on p. 1049

鸰(鶵) chú ❶ ☞ [鹓鸰]（yuānchú）on p. 2355 ❷〈书 *fml*.〉same as 雏 chú

厨(廚、厨) chú ❶ 厨房 kitchen：下～ cook ❷ 厨师 cook：名～ famous chef

【厨房】chúfáng ❶ 做饭菜的屋子 kitchen ❷〈旧时 *old*〉指厨师 cook

【厨具】chújù 做饭菜的用具，如锅、炒勺、菜刀等 cooking utensils, like wok, frying pan, kitchen knife, etc.

【厨师】chúshī 长于烹调并以此为业的人 cook; chef

【厨司】chúsī〈方 *dial*.〉same as 厨师 chúshī

【厨子】chú·zi 指厨师 cook

锄(耡) chú ❶ 松土和除草用的农具 farm tool used to dig soil and to weed：大～ big hoe | 小～ small hoe ❷ 用锄松土除草 dig soil and weed with a hoe：～草 hoe up weeds | 这块地～过三遍了。This field has been weeded three times. ❸ 铲除 annihilate：～奸 ferret out traitors

【锄奸】chú//jiān 铲除通敌的坏人 eliminate

traitors

【锄强扶弱】chú qiáng fú ruò 铲除强暴，扶助弱者 wipe out a tyrant and aid the weak

【锄头】chú·tou ❶ 南方用的形状像镐的农具 pickaxe, farm tool used in southern China ❷ 〈方 *dial*.〉same as 锄 chú ①

【锄头雨】chútóuyǔ 〈方 *dial*.〉锄地前庄稼正需要雨水时下的雨 rain that falls right before weeding, when the crop needs it most

滁 Chú 滁州，地名，在安徽 Chuzhou, place name in Anhui Province

蜍 chú ☞ 蟾蜍 chánchú on p. 211

雏(雛) chú 幼小的(多指鸟类) young (bird)：～鸡 chick｜～燕 baby swallow ◇～形 initial shape

【雏鸡】chújī 孵出不久的小鸡 newly hatched chick

【雏妓】chújì 未成年的妓女 child prostitute

【雏儿】chúr ❶ 幼小的鸟 nestling：燕～ young swallow｜鸭～duckling ❷〈比喻 *fig*.〉年纪轻、阅历少的人 young, inexperienced person

【雏形】chúxíng ❶ 未定型前的形式 embryonic form：蛹显示出成虫的触角、腿、翅膀的～ undeveloped antennae, legs, and wings of an adult insect as in the pupa ❷ 依照原物缩小的模型 scaled-down model：看了这座建筑物的～也可想见它的规模之大了。Just look at the model, and you can imagine the sheer size of the building.

㡡(幮) chú 〈古代 *arch*.〉一种形状像橱的帐子 wardrobe-like gaze net

篨 chú ☞ [籧篨](qúchú) on p. 1590

橱(櫥) chú (～儿 chúr) 放置衣服、物件的家具 furniture for keeping clothes or other stuff：衣～ wardrobe｜书～ bookcase｜碗～ cupboard

【橱窗】chúchuāng ❶ 商店临街的玻璃窗，用来展览样品 shop window facing the street, used to display samples ❷ 用来展览图片等的设备，形状像橱而较浅 glass fronted billboard, used to display photographs, etc.

【橱柜】chúguì ❶ (～儿 chúguìr) 放置餐具的柜子 cupboard ❷ 可以做桌子用的矮立柜 low cupboard that can serve as a table

躇 chú ☞ 踌躇 chóuchú on p. 278

蹰(躕) chú ☞ 踟蹰 chíchú on p. 262

chǔ (ㄔㄨˇ)

处(處、處、処) chǔ ❶〈书 *fml*.〉居住 reside：穴居野～ live in caves and the wild ❷ 跟别人一起生活；交往 live with sb.; get along (with sb.)：～得来 get along well｜～不来 difficult to get along｜他的脾气好，容易～。He is good-tempered and easy to get along with. ❸ 存；居 harbour; be situated at：～心积虑 scheme for a long time｜设身～地 put oneself in another's shoes｜我们工厂正～在发展、完善的阶段。Our factory is in a period of development and improvement. ❹ 处置；办理 handle; deal with：论～ punish (according to law, etc.)｜～理 deal with ❺ 处罚 discipline：惩～ punish｜～以徒刑 mete out a prison sentence
☞ chù on p. 294

【处变不惊】chǔ biàn bù jīng 面对变乱，能镇定自若，不惊慌 keep calm in the face of a crisis

【处罚】chǔfá 对犯错误或犯罪的人加以惩治 punish sb. for a wrongdoing or crime; penalize

【处方】chǔfāng ❶ 医生给病人开药方 prescribe：不是医生，没有～权。Only a doctor has the right to prescribe to a patient. ❷ 开的药方 prescription：按～抓药 fill a prescription

【处分】chǔfèn ❶ 对犯罪或犯错误的人按情节轻重做出处罚决定，也指这种处罚的决定 decision of punishment; mete out punishment on a criminal or wrongdoer according to the seriousness of the case：～违反校规的学生 discipline students who have breached school rules｜给予记大过的～ record a serious demerit ❷〈书 *fml*.〉处理安排 handle; deal with

【处境】chǔjìng 所处的境地(多指不利的情况下 oft. unfavourable) circumstances：～困难 be in a difficult situation｜～危险 be in danger

【处决】chǔjué ❶ 执行死刑 carry out a death penalty：～犯人 execute the criminal｜立即～ execute immediately ❷ 处理决定 deal with and decide：大会休会期间，一切事项由常委会～。The standing committee takes care of all issues during the recess.

【处理】chǔlǐ ❶ 安排(事物)；解决(问题) arrange (things); solve (a problem)：～日常事务 handle routine work ❷ 处治；惩办 discipline; punish：依法～ punish in accordance with law｜～了几个带头闹事的人。Those who first stirred up trouble were punished. ❸ 指减价或变价出售 sell (a commodity) at reduced price：～品 goods on sale ❹ 用特定的方法对工件或产品进行加工，使工件或产品获得所需要的性能 treat a workpiece or product by a special process to add a required property to it：热～ heat treatment

【处理品】chǔlǐpǐn 减价或变价出售的物品 goods sold at reduced prices

【处女】chǔnǚ ❶ 没有发生过性行为的女子 virgin; maiden ❷〈比喻 *fig*.〉第一次 first time：～航 maiden voyage or flight｜～作 maiden work

【处女地】chǔnǚdì 未开垦的土地 virgin land

【处女峰】chǔnǚfēng 没有人攀登过峰顶的山峰 mountain peak that has not been surmounted

【处女航】chǔnǚháng ❶ 轮船或飞机在某航线上第一次航行 (of a ship or plane) the first voyage or flight on a route ❷ 新制成的轮船或飞机第一次航行 (of a new ship or plane) the first voyage or flight

【处女膜】chǔnǚmó 阴道口周围的一层薄膜,有一个不规则的小孔 hymen; thin membranous fold partially closing the lower end of the virginal vagina

【处女作】chǔnǚzuò 作者的第一个作品 author's first work

【处身】chǔshēn 置身;安身 (of a person) be in (a situation); make a living in a place:～涉世(立身处世) make a living and conduct oneself in society|～在艰险的环境中 live under dangerous and difficult circumstances

【处士】chǔshì 原来指有德才而隐居不愿做官的人,后来泛指没有做过官的读书人(orig.) man of virtue and talent who prefers to live in seclusion to keep away from officialdom; (in a broad sense) learned man who has never been an official

【处世】chǔshì 在社会上活动,跟人往来相处 conduct oneself in society:立身～ live and conduct oneself in society|～为人 conduct oneself and get along with others

【处事】chǔshì 处理事务 handle affairs; deal with matters:他～严肃,态度却十分和蔼。He is serious and yet friendly in handling business.

【处暑】chǔshǔ 二十四节气之一,在8月22,23或24日 one of the 24 seasonal dates on the Chinese lunar calendar, marking climate changes and farming times, which falls on August 22, 23 or 24; ☞ 节气 jié·qi on p. 989 and 二十四节气 èrshísì jiéqì on p. 516

【处死】chǔsǐ 处以死刑 put to death; execute

【处心积虑】chǔ xīn jī lǜ 千方百计地盘算(多含贬义 oft. derog.) rack one's brains to scheme

【处刑】chǔxíng 法院依照法律对罪犯判处刑罚 (of a court) sentence a criminal according to law

【处于】chǔyú 在某种地位或状态 be in a certain position or state:～优势 be at an advantage|伤员～昏迷状态。The injured person is in a coma.

【处之泰然】chǔ zhī tài rán 对待发生的紧急情况或困难,安然自得,毫不在乎 remain calm and collected in the face of an urgent or difficult situation

【处治】chǔzhì 处分;惩治 discipline; punish:严加～ mete out severe punishment

【处置】chǔzhì ❶ same as 处理 chǔlǐ:～失当 mismanage|～得宜 handle (a situation, etc.) appropriately ❷ 发落;惩治 punish; deal with:依法～ punish by the law

【处子】chǔzǐ 〈书 *fml.*〉 same as 处女 chǔnǚ

杵 chǔ ❶ 一头粗一头细的圆木棒,用来在臼里捣粮食等或洗衣服时捶衣服 pestle; wooden club with one end thick and the other thin, used to pound food in a mortar or beat laundry:～臼 mortar and pestle|砧～ hammering block and pestle ❷ 用杵捣 beat with a pestle:～药 pound medicinal herbs with a pestle ❸ 用细长的东西戳或捅 poke or prick with a long, thin instrument:用手指头～了他一下。(Someone) gave him a nudge with the finger.|得拿棍子往里～一～。We need a stick to poke inside.

【杵乐】chǔyuè 台湾省高山族的一种歌舞。三五成群的妇女站在石臼周围,手执长杵,一边捣臼,一边歌唱。pestle dance; song and dance form of the Gaoshan ethnic group in Taiwan Province. In groups of three or five, the women stand around a mortar and pound with a long pestle while singing. also 杵舞 chǔwǔ

础(礎) chǔ same as 础石 chǔshí ①:基～ plinth; foundation|月晕而风,～润而雨。A halo around the moon foretells wind and a damp plinth heralds rain — one can predict occurrence of an event through certain signs.

【础石】chǔshí ❶ 垫在房屋柱子底下的石头 stone base on which the column of a house stands ❷ 基础 base:勤劳善良的人民,是社会的中坚与～。The hard-working and honest people are the backbone and cornerstone of the society.

楮 chǔ ❶ 楮树,落叶乔木,叶子卵形,叶子和茎上有硬毛,花淡绿色,雌雄异株。树皮是制造桑皮纸和宣纸的原料。paper mulberry (*Broussonetia papyrifera*); deciduous, dioecious tree that has egg-shaped leaves, bristly hair on the leaves and trunk, and pale-green blossoms. The bark can be used to produce mulberry paper and *Xuan* paper. also 构² gòu or 榖 gǔ ❷ 〈书 *fml.*〉指纸 paper:～墨 paper and ink

【楮墨】chǔmò 〈书 *fml.*〉 ❶ 纸和墨 paper and ink:珍藏～ cherished paper and ink ◇堪付～(可交付印刷) ready for publication ❷ 借指诗文或书画 literary writing, painting, or calligraphy:寄心～ set one's heart on literary writing, painting, and calligraphy

储(儲) chǔ ❶ 储藏;存放 store; stockpile:～蓄 savings|～金 deposit|～粮备荒 store up grain against crop failure ❷ 已经确定为继承皇位等最高统治权的人 person designated as the successor to the throne or monarch:立～ designate an heir to the throne|王～ crown prince|～君 appoint sb. monarch ❸(Chǔ) 姓 a surname

【储备】chǔbèi ❶ (物资)储存起来准备必要时应用 store up (materials) for use in times of need:～粮食 lay up grain ❷ 储存备用的东西 reserve:动用～ use reserved goods | ～年年增长。The stock is increasing year by year.

【储藏】chǔcáng ❶ 保藏 keep in store:～室 warehouse | 把器具～起来。Keep the instruments in a proper place. ❷ 蕴藏 contain (a natural resource):～量 reserves | 铁矿～丰富 rich in iron ore deposits

【储存】chǔcún (物或钱)存放起来,暂时不用 put away (materials or money) for later use:～大白菜 store up Chinese cabbage | ～资料 accumulate data

【储户】chǔhù 银行等称存款的个人或团体为储户 depositor, either individual or institutional

【储积】chǔjī ❶ 储存积聚;积蓄 stockpile; amass:～余粮,以备急需。Store up surplus grain for use in times of need. ❷ 积蓄的财物 accumulated property

【储集】chǔjí 储存聚集 save and collect

【储君】chǔjūn 帝王的亲属中已经确定继承皇位等最高统治权的人 crown prince; member of the royal family who has been designated to succeed the throne or monarch

【储量】chǔliàng (自然资源)储藏量 (of natural resources) reserves:探明油田的～ verify the reserves of an oil field | 矿产～极为丰富 abundance of mineral resources

【储青】chǔqīng 储存青饲料 reserve green fodder:打草～ cut grass as green-fodder reserves

【储蓄】chǔxù ❶ 把节约下来或暂时不用的钱或物积存起来,多指把钱存到银行里 save money or materials for later use; oft. deposit money in the bank:～所 savings bank | 踊跃～,支援国家建设。Let us put our savings in the bank to support national construction. ❷ 指积存的钱或物 (of money or materials) reserves:家家有～。Every family has savings deposits.

楚[1] chǔ ❶〈书 *fml.*〉痛苦 pain:苦～ misery | 凄～ sad ❷ 清晰;整齐 clear; neat:清～ transpicuous | 齐～ tidy

楚[2] Chǔ ❶ 周朝国名,原来在今湖北和湖南北部,后来扩展到今河南、安徽、江苏、浙江、江西和四川 kingdom during the Zhou Dynasty (1046-221B. C.), which first covered present-day Hubei and the northern part of Hunan, and which later expanded to present-day Henan, Anhui, Jiangsu, Zhejiang, Jiangxi, and Sichuan provinces ❷ 指湖北和湖南,特指湖北 Hubei and Hunan provinces, esp. Hubei ❸ 姓 a surname

【楚楚】chǔchǔ ❶ 鲜明;整洁 fresh; tidy:衣冠～ neatly dressed ❷ (姿态)娇柔;纤弱;秀美 (of body posture) charming; delicate; pretty:～可怜 lovely | ～动人 attractive | 门前垂柳,～可人。The willows in front of the house are delicate and lovely.

【楚剧】chǔjù 湖北地方戏曲剧种之一,由湖北黄冈、孝感一带的花鼓戏发展而成,流行湖北全省和江西部分地区 *chuju* opera; one of the local operas of Hubei Province, originated from the flower-drum drama in the Huanggang and Xiaogan areas, popular in Hubei and parts of Jiangxi Province

褚 Chǔ 姓 a surname
☞ zhǔ on p. 2508

齼 chǔ〈书 *fml.*〉牙齿酸痛 toothache

chù (ㄔㄨˋ)

亍 chù ☞ [彳亍](chìchù) on p. 264

处(處、處、処) chù ❶ 地方 place:住～ living quarters | 心灵深～ deep of the heart; inner world | 大～着眼,小～着手 take into consideration important issues but start by solving problems at hand ❷ 机关组织系统中按业务划分的单位(一般比局小,比科大),也指某些机关 department; business division in an organization (smaller than a bureau and bigger than a section); organization:科研～ research department | 总务～ general affairs department | 办事～ office | 联络～ liaison office
☞ chǔ on p. 292

【处处】chùchù 各个地方;各个方面 everywhere; all aspects:祖国～有亲人。One can find friends as close as family everywhere in one's country. | 教师～关心学生。The teachers' care for their students knows no bounds.

【处所】chùsuǒ same as 地方 dì·fang①:找个～避雨 find a shelter from the rain

怵(怵) chù 害怕;恐惧 be afraid; fear:～头 be afraid to do sth. | 心里直犯～ feel diffident

【怵场】chùchǎng same as 憷场 chùchǎng

【怵目惊心】chù mù jīng xīn 看到某种严重的情况使人十分紧张、害怕或震惊 horrid; ghastly; be nervous, horrified, or shocked at the sight of sth. terribly wrong

【怵惕】chùtì〈书 *fml.*〉恐惧警惕 fearful and alert:～不宁 fearful and agitated; palpitation caused by fright

【怵头】chùtóu same as 憷头 chùtóu

绌 chù〈书 *fml.*〉❶ 不够;不足 inadequate; insufficient:左支右～ be in financial straits or unable to cope with a situation | 相形见～ stand no comparison ❷ same as 黜 chù

柷 chù 古代乐器,木制,形状像方形的斗 ancient musical instrument fashioned out of wood, in the shape of a square *dou* (a measurer for grain)

俶 chù〈书 *fml.*〉❶ 开始 begin ❷ 整理 sort out:～装(整理行装) pack (things for travel)

☞ tì on p. 1886

【俶尔】chù'ěr 〈书 *fml.*〉忽然 sudden(ly)：鱼游水中，～远逝。The fish was swimming in the water, but disappeared all of a sudden.

畜 chù 禽兽，多指家畜 (mostly domestic) animals：六～ pig, cattle, sheep, horse, chicken, and dog; domestic animals | 牲～ livestock | 耕～ farming animals | 种～ breeding animals

☞ xù on p. 2167

【畜肥】chùféi 用做肥料的牲畜粪尿 animal excrement used as manure

【畜类】chù·lei same as 畜生 chù·sheng

【畜力】chùlì 能够使用在运输或牵引农具等方面的牲畜的力量 draught animal used in transportation or farming：山区还得用～运输。Mountainous areas still depend on animal power for transportation.

【畜生】chù·sheng 泛指禽兽(常用做骂人的话 oft. used as an insult) (in a broad sense) animals; also 畜牲 chù·sheng

【畜疫】chùyì 家畜的传染病，如马鼻疽、猪瘟、牛瘟等 epidemic disease of domestic animals, such as glanders, hog cholera, and cattle plague

诎 chù [诎诡](chùguǐ) 〈书 *fml.*〉❶ 奇异 strange ❷ 滑稽 funny

搐 chù 牵动；肌肉抽缩 cause to move; (of a muscle) twitch：抽～ (of a part of the body) tic

【搐动】chùdòng (肌肉等)不随意地收缩抖动 involuntary contraction or quiver (of a muscle, etc.)：全身～了一下。The whole body gave a jerk.

【搐搦】chùnuò 抽搐 (of a part of the body) tic

【搐缩】chùsuō 抽缩 shrink; contract

触(觸) chù ❶ 接触；碰；撞 come into contact; bump; collide：抵～ contravene | ～电 get an electric shock | 一～即发 (of a tense situation) be on the verge of eruption ❷ 触动；感动 touch; move：～起前情 be reminded of one's old love | 忽有所～ be moved all of a sudden

【触电】chù//diàn 人或动物接触较强的电流。机体触电会受到破坏，甚至死亡。(of a person or animal) get into contact with a strong electric current, which may cause injury, even death

【触动】chùdòng ❶ 碰；撞 bump; collide：他在暗中摸索了半天，忽然～了什么，响了一下。He fumbled in the darkness. Suddenly he bumped into something, producing a noise. ❷ 冲撞；触犯 go against; infringe upon：～现行体制 violate rules of an established system | ～了当权者的利益。The interests of those in power were affected. ❸ 因某种刺激而引起(感情变化、回忆等) stir up (emotions, memories, etc.) by a stimulus：这些话～了老人的心事。These words reminded the old man of the things that worry him.

【触发】chùfā 受到触动而引起某种反应 cause a reaction by contact：雷管爆炸，～了近旁的炸药。Explosion of the detonator touched off the explosive nearby. | 电台播放的家乡民歌～了他心底的思乡之情。He became homesick upon hearing a folk song of his hometown on the radio.

【触犯】chùfàn 冒犯；冲撞；侵犯 offend; affront; infringe：～众怒 incur public anger | 不能～人民的利益。We cannot encroach upon the interests of the people.

【触机】chùjī 触动灵机 be inspired：不假思索，～即发。With inspiration, one hits upon an idea without so much as thinking it over.

【触及】chùjí 触动到 touch：～痛处 strike a nerve; touch the sore spot | 他不敢～问题的要害。He dares not to get to the essence of the problem.

【触礁】chù//jiāo ❶ 船只在航行中碰上暗礁 (of a ship) run upon a submerged rock or reef ❷〈比喻 *fig.*〉事情进行中遇到障碍 (of sth.) meet with an obstacle：婚姻～。The marriage is in trouble. | 谈判～。The negotiation stalled.

【触角】chùjiǎo 昆虫、软体动物或甲壳类动物的感觉器官之一，生在头上，一般呈丝状 antenna; one of the sense organs on the head of an insect, mollusc, or crustacean, usu. hair-like; also 触须 chùxū

【触景生情】chù jǐng shēng qíng 受到当前情景的触动而产生某种感情 (of feelings, emotions, etc.) be evoked by the sight of sth.：旧地重游，～，当年的人和事浮上脑际。Memories of the people and events of the past came to mind when I visited where I had lived before.

【触觉】chùjué 皮肤、毛发等与物体接触时所产生的感觉 (of skin, hair, etc.) sense upon touch of an object; tactile or tactual sensation

【触类旁通】chù lèi páng tōng 掌握了关于某一事物的知识，而推知同类中其他事物 comprehend by analogy; knowledge of a single example leads to understanding of the entire category

【触霉头】chù méitóu 〈方 *dial.*〉碰到不愉快的事；倒霉 encounter sth. unpleasant; stroke of bad luck; also 触楣头 chù méitóu

【触摸】chùmō 用手接触后轻轻移动 touch and caress gently with the hand：受伤处稍一～即疼痛难忍。The wound hurts badly to the touch.

【触目】chùmù ❶ 视线接触到；目光所及 set eyes on; come in sight：～皆是 be everywhere in sight or evidence ❷ 显眼；引人注目 conspicuous; eye-catching：门上的金字招牌非常～。

The golden signboard on the door is very striking.

【触目惊心】chù mù jīng xīn 看到某种严重的情况引起内心的震动 be appalled at a serious situation

【触怒】chùnù 惹人发怒 infuriate：他的无理取闹～了众人。He enraged everybody by stirring up trouble for no reason.

【触杀】chùshā 因接触而杀死 kill upon touch：这种农药对蚜虫等有较高的～效果。This pesticide is quite effective in killing aphids upon touch.

【触手】chùshǒu 水螅等低等动物的感觉器官，多生在口旁，形状像丝或手指，又可以用来捕食 tentacle; one of the hair or finger-like tactile organs by the mouth of a low animal, like leech, also used for catching food

【触须】chùxū same as 触角 chùjiǎo

滀 chù〈书 *fml*.〉(水)聚积 (of water) gather
☞ xù on p.2169

憷 chù 害怕；畏缩 be afraid; shy：发～ feel diffident|～头 shrink from difficuties; be somewhat reluctant |～场 be timid on an public occasion |这孩子～见生人。The child holds back from meeting strangers.

【憷场】chùchǎng 害怕在公众场合讲话、表演等 be afraid to speak or perform in public; be stage shy; also 怵场 chùchǎng

【憷头】chùtóu 遇事胆怯，不敢出头，觉着难办 be timid, afraid, or diffident when doing sth; shrink from difficuties also 怵头 chùtóu

歜 chù〈书 *fml*.〉盛怒；气盛 in a fury; wild with anger; in a rage

黜 chù〈书 *fml*.〉罢免；革除 dismiss; discharge：罢～ remove sb. from office|～退 sack; fire; relieve sb. of a post

【黜免】chùmiǎn〈书 *fml*.〉罢免(官职) depose; dismiss

【黜退】chùtuì 免除(职务) remove or dismiss sb. from office

斶 chù 用于人名，颜斶，战国时齐国人 name of a person, as in 颜斶(Yan Chu) of the State of Qi during the Warring States period (475-221 B.C.)

矗 chù〈书 *fml*.〉直立；高耸 stand upright; tower：～立 stand high|～入云霄 soar into the clouds

【矗立】chùlì 高耸地立着 tower：大街两旁～着高楼大厦。The street is lined with tall buildings. |电视发射塔像擎天柱一般～在山顶上。The TV tower stands tall on the hilltop like a heavenly pillar.

chuā (ㄔㄨㄚ)

欻(歘) chuā〈拟声词 *onom*.〉[sound of steady steps]：仪仗队走起来～～的，非常整齐。The guard of honour tramped away in perfect unison. |～的一下把信撕开了 rip open a letter with a brittle sound
☞ xū on p.2164

【欻拉】chuālā〈拟声词 *onom*.〉sizzle：～一声，把菜倒进了油锅 drop vegetables into the boiling oil with a sizzle

chuāi (ㄔㄨㄞ)

揣 chuāi ❶ 藏在衣服里 put sth. in one's clothes：这张照片儿～在我口袋里很久了。I've kept the photograph in my pocket for a long time. ❷〈方 *dial*.〉牲畜怀孕 (of a domestic animal) conceive：母猪～崽儿。The sow is pregnant. |骒马～上驹了。The jenny is pregnant.
☞ chuǎi on p.296 and chuài on p.297

【揣手儿】chuāi//shǒur 两手交错放在袖子里 tuck each hand in the opposite sleeve

搋 chuāi ❶ 以手用力压和揉 press and knead forcibly with hand：～面 knead dough|把衣服洗了又～。(Someone) washed and rubbed the clothes again and again. ❷ 用搋子疏通下水道 dredge a drain with a suction pump：大便池堵住了，你去～～。The toilet is blocked. You go and dredge it.

【搋子】chuāi·zi 疏通下水道的工具，由长柄和橡胶碗制成 suction pump, consisted of a long handle and a rubber bowl, used to dredge a sewer

chuái (ㄔㄨㄞˊ)

膗 chuái〈方 *dial*.〉肥胖而肌肉松 fat and flabby：看他那～样。See how fat and floppy he is.

chuǎi (ㄔㄨㄞˇ)

揣 chuǎi ❶ 估计；忖度 estimate; speculate：～测 guess|～度 surmise|不～冒昧。Excuse me for taking the liberty. ❷ (Chuǎi) 姓 a surname
☞ chuāi on p.296 and chuài on p.297

【揣测】chuǎicè 推测；猜测 infer; guess：我～他已经离开北京了。I guess he's already left Beijing. |他善于～别人的心思。He's good at reading other people's mind.

【揣度】chuǎiduó〈书 *fml*.〉估量；推测 assess; deduce

【揣摩】chuǎimó 反复思考推求 ponder; try to figure out; think over：这篇文章的内容，要仔细～才能透彻了解。This article requires careful thinking to figure out what it is driving at. |我始终～不透他的意思。I was never able to figure out what he meant.

【揣摸】chuǎi·mo same as 揣摩 chuǎimó

【揣想】chuǎixiǎng 推测；猜想 infer; guess：他心里～着究竟什么原因使她生气。He was trying to make out why she was upset.

chuài（ㄔㄨㄞˋ）

闼 chuài ☞［阐闼］(zhèngchài) on p. 2453

啜 Chuài 姓 a surname

☞ chuò on p. 314

揣 chuài ☞ 囊揣 nāngchuài on p. 1392 and 挣揣 zhèngchuài on p. 2452

☞ chuāi on p. 296 and chuǎi on p. 296

嘬 chuài〈书 *fml.*〉咬；吃 bite; eat

☞ zuō on p. 2572

踹 chuài ❶ 脚底向外踢 kick (outward with the sole of one's foot)：一脚就把门～开了 kicked the door open with one go｜小马蹄子只顾乱～。The colt kept kicking aimlessly. ❷ 踩 tread; stamp：没留神一脚～在水沟里 stepped in a ditch inadvertently

膪 chuài ☞ 囊膪 nāngchuài on p. 1392

chuān（ㄔㄨㄢ）

川 chuān ❶ 河流 river：河～ river｜高山大～ high mountains and big rivers｜百～归海。All rivers flow into the sea. ❷ 平地；平野 flat land; plain：米粮～land of rice and grain｜一马平～ vast level land｜八百里秦～ the vast Central Shaanxi Plain ❸(Chuān) 指四川 Sichuan Province：～马 Sichuan horse｜～菜 Sichuan cuisine

【川菜】chuāncài 四川风味的菜肴 Sichuan cuisine; dishes of Sichuan flavour：～馆 Sichuan cuisine restaurant｜正宗～ genuine Sichuan cuisine

【川地】chuāndì 山间或河流两边的平坦低洼的土地 flat low-lying land between mountains or along river banks

【川费】chuānfèi 路费；川资 travel expenses

【川红】chuānhóng 茶叶品种之一，主要产于四川筠连 a variety of tea, mainly produced in Junlian of Sichuan Province

【川剧】chuānjù 四川地方戏曲剧种之一，流行于四川全省和贵州、云南两省的部分地区 Sichuan Opera; folk opera of Sichuan Province, popular in parts of Guizhou and Yunnan provinces as well

【川军】chuānjūn 大黄(dàihuáng)，旧称'将军'，四川出产的最好，所以叫川军 rhubarb (*Rheum rhaponticum*), called 'general' in old times, also known as Sichuan rhubarb, because what is produced in Sichuan is the best

【川流不息】chuān liú bù xī（行人、车马等）像水流一样连续不断 (of people, vehicles, etc.) come and go like an endless stream

【川马】chuānmǎ 四川产的马，身体比较矮小，但能负重爬山 breed of horse from Sichuan, short and small in stature, but good at travelling mountainous areas even under a heavy load

【川芎】chuānxiōng 多年生草本植物，羽状复叶，花白色，果实椭圆形。产于四川及云南等地。根茎入药。rhizome of *chuanxiong* (*Ligusticum wallichii*), a perennial plant with feather-like compound leaves, white flowers, elliptic seeds, produced in Sichuan, Yunnan and some other places; its rhizome used as a traditional Chinese medicine; also 芎䓖 xiōngqióng

【川资】chuānzī 旅费；路费 travel expenses

氚 chuān 氢的同位素之一，符号 T (tritium) 或 $^3_1$H。原子核中有一个质子和两个中子。有放射性，用于热核反应。Tritium (T or $^3_1$H), radioactive isotope of hydrogen, with one proton and two neutrons in the nucleus. It is used as a fuel in thermonuclear reaction. also 超重氢 chāozhòngqīng

穿 chuān ❶ 破；透 pierce through; penetrate：把纸～了个洞 poke a hole in the paper｜水滴石～。Dripping water wears through a rock. ❷ 用在某些动词后，表示破、透或彻底显露 used after certain verbs to mean thoroughness of damage, penetration or exposure：射～ shoot through｜磨～ wear out｜看～了他的心思 read his mind｜戳～阴谋诡计 uncover a conspiracy ❸ 通过(孔洞、缝隙、空地等) find one's way through; pass through (a hole, a crack, or an open land)：～针 thread a needle｜～过森林 pass a forest｜从这个胡同～过去。Go through the alley. ❹ 用绳线等通过物体把物品连贯起来 string together：～糖葫芦 string sugar coated haws on a stick｜用珠子～成珠帘 string beads into a curtain ❺ 把衣服鞋袜等物套在身体上 wear clothes, shoes, socks, etc.：～鞋 put on shoes｜～衣服 put on clothes

【穿插】chuānchā ❶ 交叉 alternate：突击任务和日常工作～进行，互相推动。Urgent tasks and routine work are juggled to the benefit of both.｜人流、车辆相互～，使交通格外拥挤。Pedestrians and vehicles got tangled, jamming the traffic. ❷ 小说戏曲中，为了衬托主题而安排一些次要的情节 weave in minor plots in a novel or drama to set off the subject：一些农村生活细节的～，使这个剧的主题更加鲜明。Details of country life make the theme of the play stand out.

【穿刺】chuāncì 为了诊断或治疗，用特制的针刺入体腔或器官而抽出液体或组织。如肝穿刺、关节穿刺等。puncture; pierce into the body or an organ with a special needle to draw out fluid or tissue as a means of diagnosis or treatment, such as liver puncture, joint puncture

【穿戴】chuāndài ❶ 穿和戴,泛指打扮 wear clothes; (in a broad sense) dress: 她～得很时髦。She's fashionably dressed. ❷ 指穿的和戴的衣帽、首饰等 clothes, hats, accessories, etc: 一身好～ well dressed and adorned

C

【穿甲弹】chuānjiǎdàn 能穿透坦克、装甲车等外部钢板的炮弹和枪弹 armour piercer; shell or bullet designed to tear the steel exterior of a tank or armoured vehicle

【穿孔】chuānkǒng ❶ 胃、肠等的壁遭到破坏,形成孔洞 (of stomach, intestines, etc.) perforate due to damage ❷ 打孔 bore or pierce a hole: ～机 puncher

【穿廊】chuānláng 二门两旁的走廊 covered corridor on either side of the second gate in a traditional Chinese courtyard

【穿连裆裤】chuān liándāngkù 〈方 *dial.*〉〈比喻 *fig.*〉互相勾结、包庇 in league with; collude with and cover up for one another

【穿山甲】chuānshānjiǎ 哺乳动物,全身有角质鳞甲,没有牙齿,爪锐利,善于掘土。生活在丘陵地区,吃蚂蚁等昆虫。鳞片可入药。pangolin (*Manis*), toothless mammal living off ants and other insects, in hilly areas, with a body covered with horny scales and sharp claws for digging earth, its scales used as a traditional Chinese medicine; also 鲮鲤 línglǐ

【穿梭】chuānsuō 像织布的梭子来回活动,形容来往频繁 shuttle back and forth; frequent coming and going: ～外交 shuttle diplomacy | 人流如～ people streaming back and forth

【穿堂风】chuāntángfēng 过堂风 draught

【穿堂门】chuāntángmén (～儿 chuāntángménr) 两巷之间有供穿行的小巷,在小巷口所造的像门一样的建筑物 gate-like structure leading to a small alley that connects two small streets

【穿堂儿】chuāntángr 指前后有门能穿行的厅堂 hallway

【穿线】chuānxiàn 〈比喻 *fig.*〉从中撮合、联系 serve as a go-between or liaison: 从中～搭桥 bridge a relationship

【穿小鞋】chuān xiǎoxié (～儿 chuān xiǎoxiér) 〈比喻 *fig.*〉受人(多为有职权者)暗中刁难、约束或限制 make it hot for sb.; secretly make things difficult for or set restrictions on sb. by abusing one's power: 不容许给发表不同意见的群众～。We must not make things difficult for those who have expressed different views.

【穿孝】chuān//xiào 旧俗,人死后亲属和亲戚中的晚辈或平辈穿孝服,表示哀悼 (old custom) wear mourning clothes for a deceased family member who was one's elder or peer

【穿行】chuānxíng (从孔洞、缝隙、空地等)通过 pass through (a hole, a crack, or an open land): 火车在隧道中～。The train was passing through the tunnel. | 施工重地,过路行人不得～。Passersby: Keep away from the construction site.

【穿靴戴帽】chuān xuē dài mào 〈比喻 *fig.*〉写文章或讲话中套用一些空洞说教,因多在开头和结尾部分,所以说穿靴戴帽 cliché, usu. used to begin and end an article, evocative of the hat and shoes one's wearing; also 穿鞋戴帽 chuān xié dài mào

【穿衣镜】chuānyījìng 可以照见全身的大镜子 full-length mirror

【穿窬】chuānyú 〈书 *fml.*〉钻洞和爬墙(多指偷窃) (of a burglar) cut through or climb over a wall: ～之辈 thieves and burglars

【穿越】chuānyuè 通过;穿过 pass through; braid across; cross: ～沙漠 go through the desert | ～边境 cross the border

【穿云裂石】chuān yún liè shí (声音)穿过云层,震裂石头。形容乐器声或歌声高亢嘹亮。(of sound) so high-pitched as to pierce through the clouds and split a rock; used figuratively to describe spirited singing or music

【穿凿】chuānzáo (也有读 also pronounced chuānzuò)非常牵强地解释,把没有这种意思的说成有这种意思 explain sth. in a far-fetched way; read too much into sth.: ～附会 make a forced analogy

【穿针引线】chuān zhēn yǐn xiàn 〈比喻 *fig.*〉从中撮合联系,使双方接通关系 act as a go-between or liaison

【穿着】chuānzhuó 衣着;装束 dress; attire: ～朴素 simply clothed | ～入时 fashionably dressed | 讲究～ be particular about one's clothing

chuán (ㄔㄨㄢˊ)

传(傳) chuán ❶ 由一方交给另一方;由上代交给下代 pass from one to another; hand down from one generation to the next: 流～ pass down | 由前向后～ pass from front to back | 古代～下来的文化遗产 cultural legacy bequeathed from ancient times ❷ 传授 teach: 师～ trained by a master | 把自己的手艺～给人 pass one's skills on to someone else ❸ 传播 promulgate: 宣～ publicize | 胜利的消息～遍全国。News of victory spread all over the country. ❹ 传导 transmit: ～电 transmit electricity | ～热 transmit heat ❺ 表达 express: ～神 graphic, lifelike | ～情 express one's feelings ❻ 发出命令叫人来 demand the presence of sb.: ～讯 summon sb. for interrogation; subpoena | 把他～来。Bring him over. ❼ 传染 infect: 这种病～人。This disease is contagious.

☞ zhuàn on p. 2521

【传本】chuánběn 书册流传的版本（of a book）edition in circulation

【传播】chuánbō 广泛散布 spread far and wide：～花粉 pollinate|～消息 propagate news|～先进经验 publicize advanced experience

【传布】chuánbù same as 传播 chuánbō：～病菌 diffuse germs|～消息 spread news|～新思想 disseminate new ideas

【传唱】chuánchàng （歌曲等）流传歌唱（of a song, etc.）go from lip to lip：～千古 be sung throughout the ages|这首歌已在群众中广为～。This song has been going the rounds among the people.

【传抄】chuánchāo 辗转抄写 copy and circulate (a manuscript, etc.)：～本 a hand-copied book

【传承】chuánchéng 传授和继承 impart and inherit：木雕艺术经历代～，至今已有千年的历史。The art of woodcarving has been handed down from generation to generation over a thousand years.

【传出神经】chuánchū-shénjīng 把中枢神经系统的兴奋传到各个器官或外围部分的神经 efferent nerve or motion nerve; nerve that conducts excitation from the central nerve system to the organs or peripheral parts; also 运动神经 yùndòng shénjīng

【传达】chuándá ❶ 把一方的意思告诉给另一方 pass on the meaning of one party to another：～命令 pass on an order|～上级的指示 relay instructions from a higher authority ❷ 在机关、学校、工厂的门口管理登记和引导来宾的工作 reception and registration of visitors at an organization, school, or factory：～室 reception room ❸ 在机关、学校、工厂的门口担任传达工作的人 receptionist

【传代】chuán//dài 一代接一代地继续生存或保留下去 survive or pass on from generation to generation

【传单】chuándān 印成单张向外散发的宣传品 leaflet; handbill：印～ print leaflets|撒～ leaflet (passersby or place)

【传导】chuándǎo ❶ 热或电从物体的一部分传到另一部分 transmit or conduct heat or electricity from one part to another ❷ 神经纤维把外界刺激传向大脑皮层，或把大脑皮层的活动传向外围神经（of nerve fibres）transmit external stimuli to the cerebral cortex or the activities of the cerebral cortex to peripheral nerves

【传道】chuándào ❶ 布道 preach ❷〈旧时 *old*〉指传授古代圣贤的学说 teach the doctrines of ancient sages

【传灯】chuándēng〈佛教 *Budd.*〉称佛法能像明灯一样照亮世界，指引迷途，因以传灯比喻传授佛法 teach Buddhism, which is believed to light up the world like a lamp and lead the road for those who are astray：～弟子 indoctrinate a disciple with Buddhism

【传递】chuándì 由一方交给另一方；辗转递送 deliver sth. from or by one party to another; relay：～消息 transmit news|～信件 deliver|～火炬 relay a torch

【传动】chuándòng 利用构件或机构把动力从机器的一部分传递到另一部分 transmit power from one part to another of a machine through certain components or mechanism：机械～ mechanical transmission|液压～ hydraulic transmission

【传动带】chuándòngdài 机器上传动的环形带，套在皮带轮上 transmission belt; loop-shaped belt fitted on a belt pulley

【传粉】chuánfěn 雄蕊花药里的花粉借风或昆虫做媒介，传到雌蕊的柱头上或直接传到胚珠上，是子房形成果实的必要条件 pollinate; pollination; the transfer of pollen grains in the anther of the stamen, by wind or insects, to the stigma of the pistil or directly to the ovule, a prerequisite for the ovary to develop into fruit

【传告】chuángào 把消息、话语等转告给别人 pass on news or word to others：互相～ relay (sth.) to each other|奔走～ go around passing on (some news)|～喜讯 disseminate a piece of good news

【传观】chuánguān 传递着看 pass (sth.) round for a look：他拿出纪念册来让我们～。He took out an autograph album for us to look at.

【传呼】chuánhū 电信局通知受话人去接长途电话；管理公用电话的人通知受话人去接电话（of a telecommunication office）send for sb. to answer a long distance call;（of a public telephone custodian）ask sb. to answer the phone：夜间～answering service at night|公用～电话 phone booth; public telephone with a custodian providing answering service

【传呼电话】chuánhū diànhuà 指有人管传呼的公用电话 public telephone with a custodian providing answering service

【传话】chuán//huà 把一方的话转告给另一方 pass on a message：他让我给你传个话，他实在帮不了你的忙。He asked me to tell you that he was really unable to help you.

【传唤】chuánhuàn ❶ 传话呼唤；招呼 call (on)：有事～一声。Let me know if there's anything I can do. ❷ 法院、检察机关用传票或通知叫与案件有关的人前来（of a court or a procuratorial organ）subpoena or summon those related to a case

【传家】chuánjiā 家庭里世代相传 hand down from generation to generation in a family：～宝 family heirloom|忠厚～ honesty as a family trait

【传家宝】chuánjiābǎo 家庭里世代相传的宝贵物品 sth. precious handed down from generation to generation in a family ◇艰苦朴素的

作风是劳动人民的～。Hard work and plain living is a cherished tradition of the working people.

【传见】chuánjiàn 通知人来见面(用于上级对下级)(of a superior) summon (a subordinate) for an interview:～学生代表 call the student representative|听候～ wait to be interviewed

【传教】chuán//jiào ❶〈书 *fml*.〉传播教化 disseminate knowledge; cultivate; educate ❷ 指宣传宗教教义,劝人信教 do missionary work; propagate religious doctrines in an effort to convert the listener

C

【传教士】chuánjiàoshì 基督教会(包括旧教和新教)派出去传教的人 missionary of Christianity (both Catholicism and Protestantism)

【传戒】chuánjiè〈佛教用语 *Budd*.〉指寺院里召集初出家的人受戒,使成为正式的和尚或尼姑 (of a Buddhist monastery or nunnery) initiate novices into monkhood or nunhood at a ceremony

【传经】chuán//jīng ❶ 传授儒家经典 teach Confucian doctrines ❷ 传授经验 pass on experience:～送宝 share one's valuable experience

【传令】chuán//lìng 传达命令 transmit an order:～兵 messenger|司令部～嘉奖。The headquarters dispatched a citation.

【传流】chuánliú same as 流传 liúchuán

【传媒】chuánméi ❶ 传播媒介,特指报纸、广播、电视等各种新闻工具 media, particularly the news media of newspaper, radio, and TV:国内外数十家新闻～对这一有趣的民俗作了介绍。Dozens of domestic news media have reported on the interesting folk custom. ❷ 疾病传染的媒介或途径 agent or channel for the transmission of a disease:游泳池会成为红眼病的～。The swimming pool may become a vehicle of conjunctivitis.

【传票】chuánpiào ❶ 法院或检察机关签发的传唤与案件有关的人到案的凭证 summon; subpoena ❷ 会计工作中据以登记账目的凭单 voucher for accounting record

【传奇】chuánqí ❶ 唐代兴起的短篇小说,如《李娃传》、《会真记》等 classical-language tale; a genre of short stories originated in the Tang Dynasty, e.g. '*The Story of Li Wa*' and '*A Tale of an Encounter with an Immortal*' (another name for 'The Story of Yingying') ❷ 明清两代盛行的长篇戏曲,一般每本由二十余出至五十余出组成。如明代汤显祖的《牡丹亭》、清代孔尚任的《桃花扇》等。full-length operas popular during the Ming and Qing dynasties, each consisting of 20 to 50 or more acts, like *The Peony Pavilion* by Tang Xianzu of the Ming and *The Peach Blossom Fan* by Kong Shangren of the Qing ❸ 指情节离奇或人物行为超越寻常的故事 legend; tale of strange plots or of characters with odd behaviours:～式的人物 legendary figure|他一生的经历充满了～色彩。He's led a fabulous life.

【传情】chuán//qíng 传达情意(多指男女之间 mostly between a man and a woman) express amorous feelings:眉目～ show one's feelings through the eye

【传染】chuánrǎn ❶ 病原体侵入生物体,使生物体产生病理反应,叫做传染。有明显症状的叫显性传染,无明显症状的叫隐性传染。infect; contagion; pathological reaction of an organic body to the invasion by pathogen; known as dominant contagion when obvious symptoms occur, and as recessive contagion when no obvious symptoms occur ❷〈比喻 *fig*.〉因接触而使情绪、感情、风气等受影响,发生类似变化 be influenced in mood, feelings, or way of doing things because of certain contact:他的不安情绪迅速～给了在座的人。His restlessness soon affected everyone present.

【传染病】chuánrǎnbìng 由病原体传染引起的疾病。如肺结核、麻风、天花、伤寒等。infectious or contagious disease; disease infected by pathogen, such as TB, leprosy, smallpox, typhoid, etc.

【传人】chuán//rén ❶ 传授给别人(多指特殊的技艺) pass on (mostly special skills) to others:祖传秘方向来不轻易～。By tradition an age-old family recipe is never passed on to outsiders. ❷(疾病)传染给别人 (of disease) infect others:感冒容易～。Colds are highly contagious. ❸ 发话叫人来 call sb. over:～问话 summon sb. for questioning

【传人】chuánrén 能够继承某种学术、技艺而使它流传的人 person who is able to inherit and pass on certain scholarship or craft:京剧梅(兰芳)派～ exponent of the Mei (Lanfang) school of Peking Opera|濒于失传的绝技如今有了～。A unique skill on the brink of extinction has found a worthy successor.

【传入神经】chuánrù-shénjīng 把各个器官或外围部分的兴奋传到中枢神经系统的神经 afferent nerve; nerve that transmits excitement from the organs or periphery nerves to the central nervous system; also 感觉神经 gǎnjué shénjīng

【传神】chuánshén (优美的文学、艺术作品)描绘人或物,给人生动逼真的印象 (of fine literary or artistic work) give the reader or viewer a true-to-life impression of people or things:他画的马非常～。The horses he paints are extremely lifelike.|这段对话把一个吝啬鬼刻画得如见其人,可谓～之笔。This passage represents a miser so vividly that we seem to see him in person.

【传声器】chuánshēngqì 微音器 microphone

【传声筒】chuánshēngtǒng ❶ same as 话筒 huàtǒng ③ megaphone ❷〈比喻 *fig*.〉照着人

家的话说，自己毫无主见的人 person who can only echo others without one's own idea

【传世】chuánshì 珍宝、书画、著作等（多指古代的）流传到后世（of treasures, calligraphic works, paintings, literary works, etc.）be handed down from ancient times：～珍品 treasure from ancient times

【传授】chuánshòu 把学问、技艺教给别人 pass on knowledge, skill, etc., to others：～技术 pass on a skill or technique｜～经验 share one's experience｜这门手艺是他祖父～下来的。The handicraft was handed down from his grandfather.

【传输】chuánshū 输送（能量、信息等）transmit（energy, information, etc.）：直线～ rectilinear transmission｜～装置 transmission device

【传输线】chuánshūxiàn 传送电能的导线。如传送电力的输电线、有线通讯的电缆和无线电发射机与天线的连线。wire for transmitting electric power, such as transmission line, communication wire, and the line connecting a radio transmitter and an antenna

【传述】chuánshù same as 传说 chuánshuō①：～故事 retold story

【传说】chuánshuō ❶ 辗转述说 relay：～他家有人立功了，不知道是他弟兄俩的哪一位。One of the two brothers of the family is said to have won a merit citation, but we do not know which one. ❷ 群众口头上流传的关于某人某事的叙述或某种说法 narration or description of sb. or sth. by word of mouth：鲁班的～ the legend of Lu Ban, the Sage Carpenter｜这种～并没什么根据。This story proved unfounded.

【传送】chuánsòng 把物品、信件、消息、声音等从一处传递另一处 deliver or transmit goods, mail, news, sound, etc., from one location to another：～电报 transmit a telegraph｜～消息 dispatch news

【传送带】chuánsòngdài ❶ 生产流水线中传送材料、机件、成品等的装置 conveyer belt; assemble used for transporting materials, parts, finished products, etc. in a production line ❷ 特指装置上的传送皮带 belt itself on a conveyer assemble

【传诵】chuánsòng 辗转传布诵读；辗转传布称道（of a story, poem, song, etc.）go the rounds：～一时 be widely read for a time｜他的名字在民间广为～。His name is widely applauded among the people.

【传颂】chuánsòng 辗转传布颂扬（of a good deed, act of heroism, etc.）go the rounds：全村人～着他英勇救人的事迹。All the villagers are applauding his heroic deed of saving a life.

【传统】chuántǒng 世代相传、具有特点的社会因素，如文化、道德、思想、制度等 tradition; social factors or elements carried forward from generation to generation and with unique characteristics, such as culture, ethics, ideology, system, etc.：发扬艰苦朴素的优良～ develop the fine tradition of hard work and plain living｜～剧目 traditional drama or opera

【传闻】chuánwén ❶ 辗转听到 hear indirectly：～不如亲见。Seeing believing.｜～他已出国。It is said that he has gone abroad. ❷ 辗转流传的事情 hearsay：～失实。The rumour is groundless.

【传习】chuánxí 传授和学习知识、技艺等 teach and learn knowledge, skills, etc.：～气功疗法 learn and pass on *qigong* therapy, a deep breathing exercise

【传檄】chuánxí〈书 *fml.*〉传布檄文 promulgate a call to arms or a letter of denunciation：～声讨 circulate a letter of condemnation

【传写】chuánxiě 传抄 circulate and copy（a manuscript, document, etc.）by hand：竞相～ vie to copy and disseminate｜几经～，讹误颇多。Copies upon copies have led to many errors.

【传讯】chuánxùn（司法机关、公安机关等）传唤与案件有关的人到案受讯问 subpoena;（of a judicial or public security organization）summon those related to a case for interrogation

【传言】chuányán ❶ 辗转流传的话 hearsay; rumour：不要轻信～。Give no credence to rumours。｜关于此事，外界～很多。Rumours run rampant about the incident. ❷ 传话 pass on a message：～送语 pass on word

【传扬】chuányáng（事情、名声等）传播（of an event, one's name, etc.）spread：这事要是～出去，他可就被动了。If this is made public, he'll be in an awkward situation.｜他的英雄事迹很快地～开了。His heroic deed soon became widely known and applauded.

【传艺】chuányì 传授技艺 impart skills：收徒～ train an apprentice

【传译】chuányì 从一种语言、文字翻译成另一种语言、文字 interpret or translate one language into another：学术报告厅有六种语言同声～系统。The academic auditorium has a system for simultaneous interpretation in six languages.

【传语】chuányǔ same as 传话 chuán//huà

【传阅】chuányuè 传递着看 pass around（or circulate）for perusal：～文件 pass around a document｜这篇稿子请大家～并提意见。Please pass the draft around and make your comments.

【传真】chuánzhēn ❶ 指画家描绘人物的形状 draw the portrait of a person; same as 写真 xiězhēn① ❷ 利用光电效应，通过有线电或无线电装置把照片、图表、书信、文件等的真迹传送到远方的通讯方式 facsimile transmission; telecommunication system, wired or wireless, of transmitting a photograph, a chart, a letter, or a document by scanning it photoelectrically and reproducing it xerographically at another location

【传种】chuán//zhǒng 动植物繁殖后代 (of animals and plants) propagate; reproduce: 养马要选择优良的品种来～。To raise horses, one should select fine breeds.

【传宗接代】chuán zōng jiē dài 子孙一代接一代地延续下去(of a family line) continue generation upon generation; keep the family line alive

舡 chuán 〈书 *fml.*〉 same as 船 chuán

船(舩) chuán 水上的主要运输工具 boat; ship: ～体 body of a ship | ～身 hull | 拖～tugboat; towboat | 帆～sailboat | 一只小～ one small boat | 两艘轮～ two steamers

【船帮】[1] chuánbāng 船身的侧面 side of a boat; shipboard

【船帮】[2] chuánbāng 成群结队的船 merchant fleet

【船舶】chuánbó 船(总称) (collect.) boats and ships

【船埠】chuánbù 停船的码头 harbour; port

【船舱】chuáncāng 船内载乘客、装货物的地方 cabin, either for passengers or cargo

【船夫】chuánfū 在木船上工作的人 man working on a wooden boat

【船户】chuánhù ❶ same as 船家 chuánjiā ❷ 指以船为家的水上住户 people who make their home on a boat

【船家】chuánjiā 〈旧时 *old*〉靠驾驶自己的木船为生的人 boatman; one who owns a boat and makes a living as a boatman

【船老大】chuánlǎodà 〈方 *dial.*〉木船上的主要的船夫,也泛指船夫 chief crewman of a wooden boat; (in a broad sense) boatmen

【船民】chuánmín 以船为家从事水上运输的人 person who lives on a boat and makes a living as a boatman

【船篷】chuánpéng ❶ 小木船上的覆盖物,用来遮蔽日光和风雨 awning ❷ 船上的帆 sail

【船钱】chuán•qián 雇船或搭船的人所付的费用 boat rent; boat fare

【船艄】chuánshāo 船尾 stern

【船台】chuántái 制造轮船、舰艇等用的工作台,有坚固的基础。船只在船台上拼装、制成后沿轨道下水。shipway; working platform with a solid base, on which a steamer or ship is built and assembled before taking to the water by the slip

【船位】chuánwèi 某一时刻轮船在海洋上的位置 position of a ship on the sea in a given time

【船坞】chuánwù 停泊、修理或制造船只的地方 dock; shipyard; place or facility where a ship is repaired or built

【船舷】chuánxián 船两侧的边ㄦ side of a ship or boat

【船员】chuányuán 在轮船上工作的人员 crew of a ship

【船闸】chuánzhá 使船只能在河道上水位差较大的地段通行的水工建筑物,由闸室和两端的闸门构成。船只驶入闸室后,关闭后闸门,调节水位,使与前面航道的水位相平或接近,然后开启前闸门,船只就驶出闸室而前进。lock; facility built on a river section with different water levels, consisting of gates and sluices; When a ship or boat enters the section confined by the facility, the back gate is closed and the water level within is adjusted to the water level in the front. Then the front gate is opened to allow the ship or boat to sail out.

【船长】chuánzhǎng 轮船上的总负责人 captain; skipper

【船只】chuánzhī 船(总称) (collect.) ships and boats: 捕捞队有大小～二十艘。The fishing fleet has 20 boats of different sizes.

遄 chuán 〈书 *fml.*〉 ❶ 迅速地 quickly: ～往 go in haste | ～返 return rapidly ❷ 往来频繁 frequent coming and going; busy traffic

椽 chuán same as 椽子 chuán•zi

【椽笔】chuánbǐ 〈书 *fml.*〉如椽的大笔,用来称颂别人的文章或写作才能 writing brush as big as a rafter, used figuratively to praise someone's written work or writing ability

【椽子】chuán•zi 放在檩上架着屋面板和瓦的木条 wooden pieces placed on the purlins to support the covering or tiles of a roof; (图见 ☞ figure for 房子 fáng•zi on p. 550)

篅(圌) chuán 〈方 *dial.*〉一种盛粮食等的器物,类似囤 container for grain, similar to a grain bin

☞圌 Chuí on p. 309

chuǎn (ㄔㄨㄢˇ)

舛 chuǎn 〈书 *fml.*〉 ❶ 差错 error: 乖～ mishap; uneven ❷ 违背 go against: ～驰(相背而驰) flee in the opposite direction ❸ 不顺遂;不幸 hard; unfortunate: 命途多～ life full of twists and turns

【舛错】chuǎncuò 〈书 *fml.*〉 ❶ 错误 mistake: 引文～ misquotation ❷ 意外的事;意外的变化(多指灾祸 oft. a disaster) accident; unexpected change ❸ 参差不齐;交错 uneven; interlace

【舛讹】chuǎn'é 〈书 *fml.*〉谬误;错乱 falsehood; disorder

【舛误】chuǎnwù 错误;差错 blunder; lapse

荈 chuǎn 〈书 *fml.*〉晚采的茶 late-season tea

喘 chuǎn ❶ 急促呼吸 breathe rapidly; pant: ～口气 take a breath | 累得直～ pant from exertions ❷ 气喘的简称 abbr. for 气喘 qìchuǎn：哮～ asthma

【喘气】chuǎn//qì ❶ 呼吸；深呼吸 breathe; breathe deeply：累得大口～ gasp for air from fatigue｜跑得喘不过气来 ran out of breath ❷ 指紧张活动中的短时休息 short rest in between intensive activities：忙了半天，也该喘喘气儿了。We've been working quite awhile. Let's take a break.

【喘息】chuǎnxī ❶ 急促呼吸 pant：～未定 pant nonstop ❷ 指紧张活动中的短时休息 short rest in between intensive activities：忙得连～的机会都没有。We are so busy as to have no time for a break.

【喘吁吁】chuǎnxūxū（～的 chuǎnxūxū·de）形容喘气的样子 gasp and wheeze; puff and blow：累得～的 puff and blow from exertions; also 喘嘘嘘 chuǎnxūxū

僢 chuǎn〈书 *fml.*〉same as 舛 chuǎn

踳 chuǎn〈书 *fml.*〉same as 舛 chuǎn

chuàn（ㄔㄨㄢˋ）

串 chuàn ❶ 连贯 string together：贯～ run through｜～讲 explain a text sentence by sentence; summarize an article or a book ❷（～儿 chuànr）〈量词 *classifier*〉用于连贯起来的东西 string：一～珍珠 a string of pearls｜两～儿糖葫芦 two strings of sugar-coated haws ❸ 勾结（做坏事）conspire：～供 collude so as to cover each other when under interrogation｜～骗 plot to cheat ❹ 错误地连接 connect wrongly：电话～线（of telephone lines）get crossed｜字印得太密，容易看～行。The print is so tight it's easy to skip lines. ❺ 由这里到那里走动 go from one place to another：～亲戚 go visiting relatives｜到处乱～ run about｜～街游乡 rove from village to village ❻ 担任戏曲角色 play a role in a theatric performance：客～perform as an amateur or guest actor｜反～ play a role that is not one's specialty｜～演 act

【串供】chuàn//gòng 互相串通，捏造口供（of suspects）collude to make consistent confessions：犯人～。The criminals colluded to make their confessions tally.

【串花】chuànhuā 不同品种的作物进行有性杂交，一般指天然杂交（of different species of plants）sexual or natural hybridization

【串换】chuànhuàn（互相）掉换 exchange：～优良品种 exchange for a fine breed or strain

【串讲】chuànjiǎng ❶ 语文教学中逐字逐句解释课文的意思（in teaching the Chinese language）explain a text sentence by sentence ❷ 一篇文章或一本书分段学习后，再把整个内容连贯起来做概括的讲述 sum up an article or book after studying it by the paragraph or section

【串联】chuànlián ❶ 一个一个地联系；为了共同行动，进行联系 link one by one; establish ties for concerted action：～几户乡亲合办了一个养鸡场。Several villagers pooled their efforts and money to set up a chicken farm. ❷ 把几个电器或元器件一个接一个相继联接起来，电路中的电流顺次通过，这种联接方法叫串联 series connection; connecting several electric appliances or parts together so as to allow electric current to run through them one by one ‖ also 串连 chuànlián

【串铃】chuànlíng ❶ 中空的金属环，装金属球，可以套在手上，摇动发声，走江湖给人算命、看病的人多用来招揽顾客（in old times）a hollow metal ring containing metal balls, worn on the wrist by a fortune-teller or an itinerant doctor, to attract customers ❷ 连成串的铃铛，多挂在骡马等的脖子上 string of bells hung around the neck of a horse, mule, etc.

【串门】chuàn//mén（～儿 chuàn//ménr）到别人家去闲坐聊天儿 stop by other people's home to chat：老太太好到四邻串个门儿。The old lady likes to visit her neighbours. also 串门子 chuànmén·zi

【串皮】chuànpí 指药物或酒类等进入人体后，作用散布到周身皮肤，使皮肤发痒或变红（of medicine or alcoholic drink）cause the skin to itch or redden

【串骗】chuànpiàn 互相串通，进行诈骗 conspire in a fraud; collude to cheat

【串气】chuànqì 互通声气；串通 keep one another informed; collude：暗中～ connive in secret

【串亲戚】chuànqīn·qi 到亲戚家看望 call on a relative; also 串亲 chuànqīn

【串通】chuàntōng ❶ 暗中勾结，使彼此言语行动互相配合 conspire：～一气 work hand in glove ❷ 串联；联系 establish a tie; connect：两家结亲的事，已由老村长～妥当。The old village head has arranged for a marriage between the two families.

【串通一气】chuàntōng yīqì 暗中勾结，互相配合 hand in glove：他们俩～来算计我。The two of them plotted against me.

【串味】chuàn//wèi（～儿 chuàn//wèir）食品、饮料等同其他有特殊气味的物品放在一起，染上特殊气味（of foods, drinks, etc.）absorb the smell of sth. with a special flavour because of close contact：茶叶切勿与化妆品放在一起，以免～。Don't store tea together with cosmetics so it won't get tainted in flavour.

【串戏】chuàn//xì 演戏，特指非专业演员参加专业剧团演戏 act, especially of an amateur actor playing a part in a professional performance

【串线】chuàn//xiàn 不同的线路相互连通（of different lines）linked together：电话～了。

The telephone lines got crossed.

【串烟】chuàn//yān 用柴灶做饭时，饭菜因受烟熏而有烟味 (of food) tainted with the smell of smoke from burning firewood in a traditional Chinese cooking stove

【串演】chuànyǎn 扮演 act：早年间，她在《天河配》里～过织女。In her early years she played the role of the Weaving Girl in *The Cowherd and the Weaving Girl*.

C

【串秧儿】chuànyāngr 不同品种的动物或植物杂交，改变原来的品种 (of animals or plants of different species) cross-breed; hybridize

【串游】chuàn·you 闲逛；散步 stroll; take a walk：四处～ idle about

【串珠】chuànzhū 成串的珠子 stringed beads

【串子】chuàn·zi 连贯起来的东西 stringed things：钱～ a string of coppers (money used in old times each with a hole in the centre)

钏 chuàn 镯子 bracelet：玉～jade bracelet|金～gold bracelet

chuāng (ㄔㄨㄤ)

创(創) chuāng 创伤 wound：～口 open wound|予以重～ deal a heavy blow|～巨痛深 deep wound causing great pain

☞ chuàng on p. 306

【创痕】chuānghén 伤痕 scar

【创口】chuāngkǒu 伤口 open wound; cut

【创面】chuāngmiàn 创伤的表面 surface of a wound

【创伤】chuāngshāng ❶ 身体受伤的地方；外伤 trauma; part of the body that is injured：腿上的～已经治愈。The wound on the leg has healed. ❷〈比喻 *fig.*〉物质或精神遭受的破坏或伤害 suffer material or spiritual injury：战争的～the trauma of war|精神上的～ mental scar; traumatic experience

【创痛】chuāngtòng 因受创伤而感到的疼痛；痛苦 feel painful from a wound; hurt：忍受着腿部中弹的剧烈～ bear the severe pain from the bullet wound in the leg|她用歌声安慰母亲心灵上的～。She sang to comfort mother's traumatized mind.

【创痍】chuāngyí same as 疮痍 chuāngyí

扨(摐) chuāng〈书 *fml.*〉用手或器具撞击物体 strike sth. with hand or an instrument：～钟鼓 ring the bell and beat the drum

疮(瘡) chuāng ❶ 通常称皮肤上或黏膜上发生溃烂的疾病 (usu. of skin or mucous membrane) ulcerate：口～aphtha|褥～ bedsore|冻～ chilblain|毒～malignant fester ❷ 外伤 open wound：刀～ cut|金～迸裂 cut by a metal weapon

【疮疤】chuāngbā ❶ 疮好了以后留下的疤 scar left on the body after an ulcer has healed：背上有一块～。There is a scar on the back. ❷〈比喻 *fig.*〉痛处、短处或隐私 sore spot; weak point; personal secret：别老揭人的～。Stop rubbing it in.

【疮痂】chuāngjiā 疮口表面所结的痂 scab; dry, rough crust that forms over a cut or wound during healing

【疮口】chuāngkǒu 疮的破口 infection of an ulcer：～化脓 (of an ulcer) fester

【疮痍】chuāngyí〈书 *fml.*〉创伤 trauma;〈比喻 *fig.*〉遭受破坏或灾害后的景象 scene of massive damage or disaster：满目～view of devastation everywhere|～凄景 sight of devastation and misery; also 创痍 chuāngyí

【疮痍满目】chuāngyí mǎn mù 眼睛看到的都是创伤。形容遭受战乱、灾祸严重破坏后的景象。view of devastation everywhere, used figuratively to describe the aftermath of war or disaster; also 满目疮痍 mǎn mù chuāngyí

窗(窓、牎、牕) chuāng (～儿 chuāngr) 窗户 window：纱～ gauze screen of a window|玻璃～glass window|～明几净 (of a room) with bright windows and clean tables; neat and tidy

【窗洞】chuāngdòng (～儿 chuāngdòngr) 墙上开的通气透光的洞 opening in a wall to let in light and air

【窗格子】chuānggé·zi 窗户上用木条或铁条交错制成的格子 window lattice, made of wooden or iron pieces; (图见☞ figure for 房子 fáng·zi on p. 550)

【窗户】chuāng·hu 墙壁上通气透光的装置 window, a structure in the wall to let in light and air; (图见☞ figure for 房子 fáng·zi on p. 550)

【窗花】chuānghuā (～儿 chuānghuār) 剪纸的一种，多作窗户上的装饰 paper-cut used for window decoration

【窗口】chuāngkǒu ❶ same as 窗户 chuāng·hu ❷ (～儿 chuāngkǒur) 窗户跟前 in front of a window：站在～远望 look afar in front of the window ❸ (售票处、挂号室等)墙上开的窗形的口，有活扇可以开关 window-like opening, with a movable door, in the wall of ticket or registration room ❹ 指直接为群众生活服务的 (of a trade) service-rendering：～单位 service unit|～行业 service industry ❺〈比喻 *fig.*〉渠道；途径 channel; means：工厂开设门市部，可以成为了解市场信息的～。The sales department of a factory can serve as its channel for collecting market information. ❻〈比喻 *fig.*〉反映或展示精神上、物质上各种现象或状况的地方 sth. that reflects a general mental or physical situation：眼睛是心灵的～。The eyes are the windows of the mind.|王府井是北京商业的～。Wangfujing is a window on Beijing's commercial landscape.

【窗帘】chuānglián (～儿 chuāngliánr)挡窗户的东西,用布、绸子、呢绒等制成,或用线编织而成 window curtain, made of cloth, silk, flannel, or knitted with thread

【窗棂】chuānglíng 〈方 *dial.*〉same as 窗格子 chuānggé·zi; also 窗棂子 chuānglíng·zi

【窗幔】chuāngmàn 窗帘(多指大幅的 mostly large in size) window curtain

【窗明几净】chuāng míng jī jìng 窗子明亮,几案洁净。形容室内十分整洁。(of a room) with bright windows and clean tables; spick-and-span

【窗纱】chuāngshā 安在窗户上的冷布、铁纱等 gauze or iron screen on a window

【窗扇】chuāngshàn (～儿 chuāngshànr)窗户上像门扇一样可以开合的部分 casement

【窗台】chuāngtái (～儿 chuāngtáir)托着窗框的平面部分 window sill; ledge or sill supporting the window frame; (图见☞ figure for 房子 fáng·zi on p.550)

【窗屉子】chuāngti·zi 〈方 *dial.*〉窗户上糊冷布或钉铁纱用的木框子 casement for fabric or metal gauze on a window

【窗帷】chuāngwéi same as 窗幔 chāngmàn

【窗沿】chuāngyán (～儿 chuāngyánr)窗台 windowsill

【窗友】chuāngyǒu 指同学 classmate; schoolmate

【窗纸】chuāngzhǐ 糊窗格子的纸 paper used to paste on a window

【窗子】chuāng·zi same as 窗户 chuāng·hu

牕(牎) chuāng same as 窗 chuāng

chuáng (ㄔㄨㄤˊ)

床(牀) chuáng ❶ 供人躺在上面睡觉的家具 bed:铁～iron bed|单人～single bed|一张～one bed ❷ 像床的器具 tool or instrument shaped like a bed:冰～ sledge|机～ machine tool ❸ 某些像床的地面 a piece of land similar to a bed:苗～seedbed|河～ riverbed ❹ 〈量词 *classifier*〉用于被褥等 for quilts, cotton-padded mattress, etc:两～被 two quilts|一～铺盖 one set of bedding

【床板】chuángbǎn 搭床用的木板 wooden boards of a bed

【床单】chuángdān (～儿 chuángdānr)铺在床上的长方形布 bed sheet; a piece of rectangular cloth spread on the bed; also 床单子 chuángdān·zi

【床铺】chuángpù 床和铺的总称 general term for bed and bedding

【床榻】chuángtà 床 bed:卧病～ bedridden

【床头柜】chuángtóuguì 放在床头边的小柜子 bedside cupboard

【床帏】chuángwéi 床上的帐子,借指男女私情 drapes over a bed, metaphorically referring to love between a man and a woman:～秘事 secret romance

【床位】chuángwèi 医院、轮船、集体宿舍等为病人、旅客、住宿者设置的床 bed for an inpatient, a dormitory resident, or a ship passenger (bunk)

【床沿】chuángyán (～儿 chuángyánr)床的边缘 edge of a bed; bedside

【床罩】chuángzhào (～儿 chuángzhàor)罩在床上的长方形单子,边上多有装饰性的穗子或荷叶边 bedspread; rectangular sheet with decorative edges used to cover the entire bed

【床子】chuáng·zi ❶ 机床 machine tool ❷〈方 *dial.*〉像床的货架 shelf shaped like a bed:菜～vegetable shelf|羊肉～ mutton shelf

噇 chuáng 〈方 *dial.*〉无节制地狂吃狂喝 gluttonize:～得烂醉 drink till drunk

幢 chuáng ❶〈古代 *arch.*〉旗子一类的东西 pennant; streamer ❷ 刻着佛号(佛的名字)或经咒的石柱子 stone pillar inscribed with the name of the Buddha or incantations:经～ scripture pillar|石～ stone pillar ☞ zhuàng on p.2527

【幢幢】chuángchuáng 〈书 *fml.*〉形容影子摇晃 (of a shadow) flickering; dancing:人影～ flittering shadows of people|灯影～ fluttering shadows of lamps

chuǎng (ㄔㄨㄤˇ)

闯 chuǎng ❶ 猛冲;勇猛向前 charge; bolt:～劲 pioneering spirit|～进去 force one's way in|横冲直～rampage ❷ 闯练 temper:他这几年～出来了。He's been seasoned the past few years. ❸ 为一定目的而到处活动;奔走 manoeuvre; go from place to place:～关东 take a risky journey to the Northeast to eke out a living|～江湖 live a vagrant's life; make a living in the wide world|走南～北 roam the world; tramp north and south or from place to place ❹ 惹起 incur:～祸 get into trouble|～乱子 cause trouble

【闯荡】chuǎngdàng 指离家在外谋生或经受锻炼 leave home to make a living or gain experience:～江湖(闯江湖) roam about the world in search of a foothold

【闯关】chuǎng//guān 冲过关口,多用于比喻 [used figuratively in most cases] bolt a pass:～夺隘 bolt one fortification and conquer another|我国男女单打选手都连闯几关,获得出线权。The Chinese players have stormed all the way to the finals in both singles and doubles.

【闯关东】chuǎng Guāndōng 〈旧时 *old*〉山东、河北一带的人到山海关以东的地方谋生,叫闯关东 people from Shandong and Hebei provinces left home for areas east of the Shanhai Pass in order to make a living

【闯红灯】chuǎng hóngdēng 车辆遇红灯信号不停下来，继续行驶，叫闯红灯 (of a vehicle) run the red traffic light

【闯祸】chuǎng//huò 因疏忽大意，行动鲁莽而引起事端或造成损失 cause trouble or damage due to carelessness or rash behaviour：孩子淘气，三天两头儿地～。The naughty child is always making trouble.

【闯江湖】chuǎng jiāng·hú 〈旧时 *old*〉指奔走四方，流浪谋生，从事算卦、卖艺、卖药治病等职业 roam from place to place to make a living as a fortune-teller, an acrobatic performer, or a practitioner

【闯将】chuǎngjiàng 勇于冲锋陷阵的将领，多用于比喻 brave general who always fights in the van, used figuratively in most cases：做技术革新中的～ take the lead in technical renovations

【闯劲】chuǎngjìn（～儿 chuǎngjìnr）猛冲猛干的劲头 pioneering spirit：我很喜欢他这股勇于开拓的～。I like his trailblazing spirit.

【闯练】chuǎngliàn 走出家庭，到实际生活中锻炼 leave one's home to experience real life：年轻人应到外边～～。Young people should temper themselves in the outside world.

【闯牌子】chuǎng pái·zi 创(chuàng)牌子 make a brand name (of merchandise) known

【闯世界】chuǎng shìjiè 指奔走四方，流浪谋生 lead a vagrant life：他年轻时就跟着叔叔外出～。He wandered from place to place with his uncle for a living when he was young.

chuàng（ㄔㄨㄤˋ）

创(創、刱、剏) chuàng 开始(做)；(初次)做 begin (to do sth.); do sth. for the first time：～办 set up|首～ launch|～新记录 set a new record

☞ chuāng on p. 304

【创办】chuàngbàn 开始办 begin to do sth.：～学校 set up a school|～杂志 start a magazine|许多乡镇都～了农机修造厂。Many townships have set up farm machine repair shops.

【创编】chuàngbiān 创作(剧本、体操、舞蹈等) write (a script); choreograph gymnastic movements or a dance：～历史剧 write a historical play

【创汇】chuànghuì 使成品出口的外汇净收入多于外汇支出，叫做创汇 earn net foreign exchange profit through exports

【创获】chuànghuò 过去没有过的成果或心得；第一次发现 new achievement or idea; new discovery：在技术革新中，许多技术人员、工人有不少的～。Many technicians and workers have made new contributions to technical renovation.

【创见】chuàngjiàn 独到的见解 original idea：他对明清文学的研究很有～。His study of the Ming and Qing literature is very innovative.

【创建】chuàngjiàn same as 创立 chuànglì：～学校 establish a school

【创举】chuàngjǔ 从来没有过的举动或事业 unprecedented undertaking or cause

【创刊】chuàngkān 开始刊行(报刊) start publishing (a newspaper or a journal)：～号 first issue|《人民日报》于 1948 年 6 月 15 日～。The *People's Daily* was first published on 15 June, 1948.

【创刊号】chuàngkānhào 报刊开始刊行的一期 first issue of a newspaper or a journal

【创立】chuànglì 初次建立 found; initiate; establish：～信用合作社 set up a credit cooperative|～新的学术体系 initiate a new academic system

【创利】chuànglì 通过经营工商业等活动，创造利润 make a profit through industrial or commercial operation：增收～ increase income and make profit|该厂人均～超万元。The average profit per capita of the factory is over 10,000 yuan.

【创牌子】chuàng pái·zi 以产品质量或服务质量赢得顾客信任，从而提高产品或企业的知名度 win customer trust and make the brand name of a product better known by providing quality product or service

【创设】chuàngshè ❶same as 创办 chuàngbàn：～研究所 establish a research institute ❷ 创造(条件) create (conditions)：为技术攻关～有利的条件 provide favourable conditions for tackling technical problems

【创始】chuàngshǐ 开始建立 initiate：～人 founder|中国是联合国的～国之一。China is a founding member of the United Nations.

【创收】chuàngshōu 学校、科研机关等非营业单位利用自身条件投入社会创造收入 (of non-profit organizations, such as schools and scientific research institutes) make money by investing their resources in society

【创税】chuàngshuì 纳税单位向国家财政部门交纳税款叫创税 (of organizations) pay tax to a state financial department：这家公司一年为国家～上百万元。This company pays up to a million yuan in taxes to the state every year.

【创新】chuàngxīn ❶ 抛开旧的，创造新的 blaze a new trail：要有～精神。We should have a pioneering spirit. ❷ 指创造性；新意 creativity; new idea：那是一座很有～的建筑物。The architecture of that building is quite original.

【创业】chuàngyè 创办事业 start an undertaking：～史 history of pioneering work|～守成 establish a cause and maintain it|艰苦～ pioneer an enterprise with arduous efforts

【创议】chuàngyì ❶ 倡议 propose：～开展劳动竞赛 propose a labour emulation campaign ❷ 首先提出的建议 initial proposal：这一～得到

了全厂工人的热烈响应。The proposal met with warm response from the workers of the factory.

【创造】chuàngzào 想出新方法、建立新理论、做出新的成绩或东西 create a new method, theory, achievement, or thing:～性 creativity|～新记录 chalk up a new record|劳动人民是历史的～者。The working people are the creators of history.

【创造性】chuàngzàoxìng ❶ 努力创新的思想和表现 creativity:充分调动广大群众在劳动中的积极性和～。We should bring into full play the initiatives and creativity of the people in their work. ❷ 属于创新的性质 of innovative quality:～的劳动 inventive work

【创制】chuàngzhì 初次制定(多指法律、文字等) institute (a law); formulate (a written language, etc.):帮助没有文字的少数民族～文字 help minority ethnic groups to invent a written form for their spoken language

【创作】chuàngzuò ❶ 创造文艺作品 create literary and art works:～经验 creative experience ❷ 指文艺作品 works of literature and art:划时代的～ epoch-making work

沧(滄) chuàng 〈书 *fml.*〉寒冷 cold

怆(愴) chuàng 〈书 *fml.*〉悲伤 sad:凄～ miserable|悲～ heartbroken

【怆然】chuàngrán 〈书 *fml.*〉悲伤的样子 sad:～泪下 burst into tears

【怆痛】chuàngtòng 悲痛 grieved:万分～in deep sorrow

chuī(ㄔㄨㄟ)

吹 chuī ❶ 合拢嘴唇用力出气 blow or puff with the mouth:～灯 blow out a lamp|～一口气 give a puff ❷ 吹气演奏 play (a wind instrument):～笛子 play the flute ❸ (风、气流等)流动;冲击 (of wind, air current, etc.) blow; strike:风～雨打 weather beaten|～风机 blower; bellows ❹ 说大话;夸口 exaggerate; boast:先别～,做出成绩来再说。Don't brag before you have anything done.|他胡～一通,你还真信。He's a big mouth and you take him for real. ❺ 吹捧 flatter:又～又拍 flatter and soft-soap ❻ (事情、交情)破裂;不成功 (of sth. or a relationship) break up; fail:婚事告～。The marriage was cancelled.|这个月的计划又～了。This month's plan has fallen through again.

【吹吹打打】chuī•chuīdǎdǎ 原指乐器合奏,借指对事渲染、夸耀,以张大声势,引人注意 put up an ensemble; ballyhoo; make a big fanfare

【吹打】chuīdǎ ❶ 用管乐器和打击乐器演奏 play wind and percussion instruments ❷ (风、雨)袭击 (of wind and rain) attack:经不住～ unable to stand wind and rain

【吹大气】chuī dàqì 〈方 *dial.*〉夸口 brag

【吹灯】chuī//dēng ❶ 把灯火吹灭 blow out a lamp ❷ 〈方 *dial.*〉〈比喻 *fig.*〉人死亡 (of a person) die; go west; kick the bucket:去年一场病,差点儿～。(He) almost died of a serious disease last year. ❸ 〈方 *dial.*〉〈比喻 *fig.*〉失败;垮台;散伙 fail; fall from power; collapse:前几回都没有搞成,这回又～啦。We've failed again, like the previous times.|两人不知为了什么就～了。The two have broken up for no apparent reason.

【吹灯拔蜡】chuī dēng bá là 〈方 *dial.*〉〈比喻 *fig.*〉人死亡或垮台 (of a person) kick the bucket or fall from power

【吹法螺】chuī fǎluó 佛教管讲经说法叫吹法螺 expound Buddhist doctrines;〈比喻 *fig.*〉说大话 talk big; also 大吹法螺 dà chuī fǎluó

【吹风】chuī//fēng ❶ 被风吹,身体受风寒 catch a chill because of exposure to wind:吃了药别～。Keep away from wind after you've taken the medicine. ❷ 洗发后,用吹风机把热空气吹到头发上,使干而伏贴 dry hair and have it done into a desired shape with a hairdryer after a wash ❸ (～儿 chuī//fēngr)有意透露意向或信息使人知道 fill sb. in on sth.; leak one's intention or information on purpose:他～儿要咱们邀请他参加晚会。He's hinted us to invite him to the party.|我先给你们吹吹风,大家好有个思想准备。I'll fill you in on it so you can stay prepared.

【吹风机】chuīfēngjī 鼓风机,多指型号较小的,如理发店或炊事上所用的 hairdryer; blower (for kitchen use)

【吹拂】chuīfú (微风)掠过;拂拭 (of a breeze) brush past; skim over:春风～大地。Spring breeze wafts caressingly across the land.

【吹鼓手】chuīgǔshǒu ❶ 旧式婚礼或丧礼中吹奏乐器的人 players of wind music at an old-fashioned wedding or funeral ❷ 〈比喻 *fig.*〉为某人或某事进行吹嘘捧场的人(贬义 derog.) eulogist of sb. or sth.

【吹管】chuīguǎn 以压缩氧气和其他可燃气体为燃料喷出高温火焰的管状装置。可以用来焊接金属或切割金属板。blowpipe; tube-like facility used to intensify the heat of a flame by blowing oxygen and other combustible gas through it at high pressure, for welding or cutting metal plates

【吹胡子瞪眼】chuī hú•zi dèng yǎn 形容发脾气或发怒的样子 foam and glare in rage

【吹灰之力】chuī huī zhī lì 〈比喻 *fig.*〉很小的力量(多用于否定式 mostly in negative form) little effort:不费～with no effort at all

【吹火筒】chuī huǒtǒng 吹火用的器具,多用打通竹节的竹子做成 stove pipe, mostly made of bamboo with the joints broken through

【吹喇叭】chuī lǎ•ba 〈比喻 *fig.*〉为人吹嘘捧场

flatter and beef up：～，抬轿子 blow the trumpet and carry sb. in a sedan chair — make a big show

【吹擂】chuīléi 夸口，吹嘘 boast；brag

【吹冷风】chuī lěngfēng 〈比喻 *fig.*〉散布冷言冷语 throw cold water on；make sarcastic remarks

【吹毛求疵】chuī máo qiú cī 故意挑剔毛病，寻找差错 find fault (with)；be hypercritical

C

【吹牛】chuī//niú 说大话；夸口 talk big；brag；also 吹牛皮 chuī niúpí

【吹拍】chuīpāi 吹捧奉承 flatter；fawn on

【吹捧】chuīpěng 吹嘘捧场 flatter；lavish praise on：无耻～ shameless fawning

【吹腔】chuīqiāng 徽剧主要腔调之一，用笛子伴奏。京剧、婺剧等剧种也吸收运用这种腔调。one of the major tunes of Anhui opera, accompanied by the flute, also used in Peking Opera and *wuju*, one of the local operas of Zhejiang Province

【吹求】chuīqiú 挑剔（毛病）find fault (with)

【吹台】chuītái （事情、交情）破裂；不成功 (of sth. or a relationship) fizzle out；fail：这事看来又得～。This is likely to fall through again.｜两人谈恋爱时间不长就～了。The two parted shortly after they began to date.

【吹嘘】chuīxū 夸大地或无中生有地说自己或别人的优点；夸张地宣扬 crow about；exaggerate or make up merits of oneself or another person；overstate：自我～ self-boast｜这点事不值得那么～。We should not overpaint such a small thing.

【吹奏】chuīzòu 吹某种乐器，泛指演奏各种乐器 play wind instruments in particular, or musical instruments in general

【吹奏乐】chuīzòuyuè 用管乐器演奏的音乐 band music；wind music

炊 chuī 烧火做饭 cook a meal：～具 cooking utensil｜～烟 cooking smoke

【炊具】chuījù 做饭菜用的器具 cooking utensil

【炊事】chuīshì 做饭、做菜及厨房里的其他工作 cooking and other kitchen work：～员（担任炊事工作的人）cook；kitchen staff

【炊烟】chuīyān 烧火做饭时冒出的烟 smoke from a cooking stove：～袅袅 cooking smoke in curling and uncurling ascent

【炊帚】chuī·zhou 刷洗锅碗等的用具 kitchen brush, used to clean pots and bowls

chuí（ㄔㄨㄟˊ）

垂 chuí ❶东西的一头向下 hang：下～ hang down｜～柳 drooping willows ❷〈书 *fml.*〉〈敬辞 *pol.*〉用于别人（多是长辈或上级）对自己的行动 [used before a verb to describe an act of a senior person directed towards the recipient]：～念 keep in mind｜～问 ask about ❸〈书 *fml.*〉流传 hand down：永～不朽 live for ever｜名～千古 (of one's name) go down in history ❹〈书 *fml.*〉将近 approach：～暮 gathering dusk｜～危 imminent danger｜功败～成 fall short of success at the last moment

【垂爱】chuí'ài 〈书 *fml.*〉〈敬辞 *pol.*〉称对方（多指长辈或上级）对自己的爱护（多用于书信 oft. used in letters） Your Concern, used as a modest term to a correspondent who is one's senior or superior

【垂钓】chuídiào 垂竿钓鱼 angle：湖边～ angle by the lake

【垂范】chuífàn 〈书 *fml.*〉给下级或晚辈示范；做榜样 set an example for one's subordinates or juniors：～后世 set an example for posterity

【垂拱】chuígǒng 〈书 *fml.*〉垂衣拱手，古时多指统治者以无所作为，顺其自然的方式统治天下 dress casually and fold one's arms, used to describe a laissez-faire government by ancient rulers：～而治 rule by laissez-faire

【垂挂】chuíguà 物体上端固定于某点而下垂 (of an object) hang down with the upper part fixed on a point：卧室～着深绿色的窗帘。The bedroom window is hung with deep-green curtains.

【垂花门】chuí·huāmén 旧式住宅在二门的上头修建像屋顶样的盖，四角有下垂的短柱，柱端雕花彩绘，这种门叫垂花门 gate with a floral-pendant portico, the second gate of an old-fashioned courtyard house with a short column with an elaborately carved and painted lower end hanging on each of the four corners of the roof of the portico；also 垂花二门 chuí·huāèrmén

【垂帘】chuílián 唐高宗在朝堂上跟大臣们讨论政事的时候，在宝座后挂着帘子，皇后武则天在里面参与决定政事，后来把皇后或皇太后掌握朝政叫垂帘 When Emperor Gaozong of the Tang Dynasty (618-907) held court, Empress Wu Zetian would sit behind a screen behind the throne to take part in decision-making. The phrase has since come to mean court rule by an empress or empress dowager：～听政 (of an empress or empress dowager) hold court from behind a screen

【垂柳】chuíliǔ 落叶乔木，树枝细长下垂，叶子呈条状披针形，春季开花，黄绿色，雌雄异株 weeping willow (*Salix*)；deciduous, dioecious tree that has slender, drooping branches, narrow leaves, and blooms in spring in yellowish green flowers；通称 generally known as 垂杨柳 chuíyángliǔ

【垂落】chuíluò 挂着的东西一头向下落；物体因失去支持而掉下来 (of an object) hang down with something suspended on the lower end；fall：两行眼泪簌簌地～下来。Two strings of tears streamed down. ◇日沉西山，夜幕～。The sun has gone down in the western hills, giving reign to the night.

【垂暮】chuímù〈书 *fml.*〉天将晚的时候 dusk：～之时，炊烟四起。Cooking smoke rose everywhere at dusk. ◇～之年（老年）evening years (old age)

【垂青】chuíqīng〈书 *fml.*〉古时黑眼珠叫青眼，对人正视表示看得起叫青眼相看。'垂青'表示重视。In ancient China, the pupil of the eye was called 青眼 qīngyǎn (black eye). 'To fix one's black eyes on sb.' meant 'to look upon sb. with appreciation.' Thus 垂青 means 'to lavish one's attention on sb.'：多蒙～。Thank you for your attention (or appreciation).

【垂手】chuíshǒu ❶ 下垂双手，表示容易 (of both hands) hang by one's side; easy：～而得 obtain sth. without lifting a finger ❷ 双手下垂，表示恭敬 stand with one's hands down, a gesture to show respect：～侍立 stand respectfully in attendance

【垂手可得】chuí shǒu kě dé 形容不费力气即可得到 be extremely easy to obtain; obtain sth. without lifting a finger; also 垂手而得 chuí shǒu ér dé

【垂首帖耳】chuí shǒu tiē ěr 形容非常驯服恭顺 extremely obedient（含贬义 derog.）；帖 also put as 贴 tiē

【垂死】chuísǐ 接近死亡 approach death：～挣扎 put up a last-ditch (or desperate) struggle; be in one's death throes

【垂体】chuítǐ 内分泌腺之一，在脑的底部，体积很小，能产生多种激素调节动物体的生长、发育和其他内分泌腺的活动 hypophysis; pituitary body or gland; one of the endocrine glands, a tiny body attached to the base of the brain, secretes various hormones to adjust the growth, development, and other endocrine activities of the body; also 脑下垂体 nǎoxià chuítǐ；(图见☞ figure for 脑 nǎo on p. 1394)

【垂髫】chuítiáo〈书 *fml.*〉小孩子头发扎起来下垂着，指幼年 early childhood; (of a child's hair) tied and hanging down

【垂头丧气】chuí tóu sàng qì 形容情绪低落、失望懊丧的神情 be in low spirits; be crestfallen

【垂危】chuíwēi ❶ 病重将死 (of a patient) dying：生命～ dying｜～病人 dying patient ❷（国家、民族）临近危亡 (existence of country, nation, etc.) at stake

【垂问】chuíwèn〈书 *fml.*〉〈敬辞 *pol.*〉表示别人（多是长辈或上级）对自己的询问 (of one's senior or superior) enquire with oneself

【垂涎】chuíxián 因想吃而流口水 slaver over food;〈比喻 *fig.*〉看见别人的好东西想得到 desire for sth. good that belongs to sb. else：～欲滴 crave for｜～三尺 drool with envy

【垂涎欲滴】chuíxián yù dī ❶ 形容非常贪馋想吃的样子 salivate over sth.; drool over (food) ❷〈比喻 *fig.*〉看到好的东西，十分羡慕，极想得到（含贬义 derog.）slaver after or over sth. good

【垂直】chuízhí 两条直线相交成直角，这两条直线就互相垂直。这个概念可推广到一条直线与一个平面或两个平面的垂直。(of two straight lines, a straight line and a plane, or two planes) be perpendicular to each other to form a right angle

陲 chuí〈书 *fml.*〉边地 border：边～ frontiers

捶（搥）chuí 用拳头或棒槌敲打 punch with the fist or a club：～背 pound the back (as in massage)｜～衣裳 beat laundry with a wooden club

【捶打】chuídǎ 用拳头或器具撞击物体 strike with the fist or an instrument：用榔头～铁板 hit the iron plate with a hammer

【捶胸顿足】chuí xiōng dùn zú 用拳头打胸部，用脚跺地。形容非常焦急、懊丧或极度悲痛的样子。beat one's chest and stamp one's feet in great anxiety, deep depression, or extreme sorrow

棰 chuí〈书 *fml.*〉❶ 短木棍 short wooden club ❷ 用棍子打 beat with a club ❸ same as 箠 chuí ❹ same as 槌 chuí

椎 chuí ❶ same as 槌 chuí ❷ same as 捶 chuí ☞ zhuī on p. 2529

【椎心泣血】chuí xīn qì xuè 捶打胸膛，哭得眼中出血。形容极度悲痛的样子。beat one's chest and shed tears of blood — be heartbroken

圌 Chuí 圌山，山名，在江苏镇江东 name of a hill in the east of Zhenjiang, Jiangsu Province

☞ 篅 chuán on p. 302

槌 chuí（～儿 chuír）敲打用的棒，大多一头较大或呈球形 club with one end larger than the other or in the shape of a ball：棒～ wooden bludgeon｜鼓～儿 drumstick

锤（鎚）chuí ❶ 古代兵器，柄的上头有一个金属圆球 mace; ancient weapon consisting of a handle and a round, metal head ❷ 像锤的东西 object in the shape of a mace：秤～ weight of a steelyard ❸（～儿 chuír）锤子 hammer：铁～ iron hammer｜钉～ nail hammer ❹ 用锤子敲打 hammer (as a verb)：千～百炼 be steeled over and over again; go through many trials

【锤骨】chuígǔ 内耳听骨之一，形状像锤子，跟鼓膜相连，能把声音的振动传给砧骨和镫骨 malleus; hammer; one of the inner ear bones, shaped like a hammer, that transmits sound vibrations from the eardrum to the incus and stirrup bone；(图见☞ figure for 耳朵 ěr·duo on p. 512)

【锤炼】chuíliàn ❶ 磨炼 go through trials and tribulations：在艰苦的环境里～自己 temper oneself in hard conditions ❷ 刻苦钻研，反复琢磨使艺术等精炼、纯熟 hone one's artistic skills to excellence：～艺术表现手法 work on and improve one's artistic techniques

【锤子】chuí·zi 敲打东西的工具。前有金属等材料做的头，有一个与头垂直的柄。hammer; pounding tool consisting of a metal head and a handle that is perpendicular to the head

箠 chuí〈书 *fml*.〉❶ 鞭子 whip ❷ 鞭打 flog; whip

chūn（ㄔㄨㄣ）

旾 chūn〈书 *fml*.〉same as 春 chūn

春 chūn ❶ 春季 spring：～景 scene of spring | 温暖如～ as warm as spring ❷ 指一年的时间 a year：一卧东山三十～。(He) lived in the eastern hills for a span of 30 years. ❸ 指男女情欲 love between a man and a woman：怀～ be lovesick | ～心 desire for love ❹〈比喻 *fig*.〉生机 life; vitality：妙手回～ (of a doctor) cure a patient of a serious disease ❺ (Chūn) 姓 a surname

【春饼】chūnbǐng 一种薄饼，立春日应节的食品 spring pancake, served on the day marking the Beginning of Spring, which falls on February 4th or 5th

【春播】chūnbō 春季播种 sow in spring; spring sowing

【春不老】chūnbùlǎo〈方 *dial*.〉雪里红 potherb mustard (*Brassica cernua*)

【春绸】chūnchóu ☞ 线春 xiànchūn on p. 2083

【春大麦】chūndàmài 春季播种的大麦 barley wheat sowed in spring

【春凳】chūndèng 宽而长的凳子，工料比较讲究，是一种旧式家具 old-fashioned bench of fine workmanship

【春分】chūnfēn 二十四节气之一，在 3 月 20 或 21 日。这一天，南北半球昼夜都一样长。Spring Equinox, the 4th of the 24 farming-related seasonal divisions of a year according to the Chinese lunar calendar, which falls on March 20 or 21, when the day and night on both the northern and southern hemispheres are of the same length; ☞ 节气 jié·qi on p. 989 and 二十四节气 èrshísì jiéqì on p. 516

【春分点】chūnfēndiǎn 赤道平面和黄道的两个相交点的一个，冬至后，太阳从南向北移动，在春分那天通过这一点 Spring Equinox point, one of the two points where the ecliptic and equatorial planes intersect; after the Winter Solstice, the sun moves from south to north and passes the point on Spring Equinox.

【春风】chūnfēng ❶ 春天的风 spring breeze：～送暖 warmth brought by spring breeze ❷〈书 *fml*.〉〈比喻 *fig*.〉恩惠 favour; grace ❸〈比喻 *fig*.〉和悦的神色 (of facial expression) kindly and pleasant：～满面 look pleased and contented

【春风得意】chūnfēng déyì 唐代孟郊《登科后》诗：'春风得意马蹄疾，一日看尽长安花。'形容考上进士后得意的心情。后来用'春风得意'称进士及第，也用来形容人官场腾达或事业顺心时扬扬得意的样子。flushed with success. *Success in the Imperial Examinations* by Meng Jiao of the Tang Dynasty: 'I have succeeded in the imperial examinations and even my horse scampered with pleasure; / Thus I have enjoyed all the flowers in Chang'an within one day.' The lines describe the poet's great happiness after he passed the highest level of imperial exams for recruiting civil servants.

【春风化雨】chūnfēng huàyǔ 适宜于草木生长的风雨 breeze and rain conducive to the growth of grass and plants;〈比喻 *fig*.〉良好的教育 fine education

【春风满面】chūnfēng mǎn miàn 形容愉快和蔼的面容 (of a person) look pleasant and kindly

【春耕】chūngēng 春季播种之前，翻松土地 plough before sowing in spring

【春宫】chūngōng ❶ 封建时代太子居住的宫室 living quarters of the crown prince in feudal times ❷ 指淫秽的图画 erotic picture; also 春画 chūnhuà

【春灌】chūnguàn 春季对农作物灌水 irrigate crops in spring

【春光】chūnguāng 春天的景致 spring scenery：～明媚 sunny and pretty spring scene | 大好～ beautiful spring sights

【春寒】chūnhán 指春季出现的寒冷天气 spring chill; chilly weather in spring：～料峭 (of weather) chill in the air in early spring

【春华秋实】chūn huá qiū shí 春天开花，秋天结果(多用于比喻 oft. fig.) bloom in spring and fruit in autumn

【春画】chūnhuà (～儿 chūnhuàr) same as 春宫 chūngōng ②

【春荒】chūnhuāng 指春天青黄不接时的饥荒 grain shortage in spring, when the granary is near empty but the crop is still in the blade：度～ tide over the spring food shortage | ～时期 spring time when grain is in shortage

【春晖】chūnhuī〈书 *fml*.〉春天的太阳 spring sunshine;〈比喻 *fig*.〉父母的恩惠 parental love

【春季】chūnjì 一年的第一季，我国习惯指立春到立夏的三个月时间，也指农历'正、二、三'三个月 spring; spring season, three months from the Beginning of Spring to the Beginning of Summer in China, or the 1st, 2nd, and 3rd months of the Chinese lunar calendar ☞ 四季 sìjì on p. 1821

【春假】chūnjià 学校春季放的假，多在四月初 (of schools) spring break, usu. in early April

【春节】Chūn Jié 农历正月初一，是我国传统节日，也指正月初一以后的几天 Spring Festival, the 1st day of the 1st month of the Chinese lunar calendar; the first few days in the 1st lunar month

【春酒】chūnjiǔ ❶ 春天酿制成的酒 wine brewed in spring ❷ 指春节期间的宴席 feast during the Spring Festival：吃～ attend a Spring Festival dinner｜请～ offer a Spring Festival dinner

【春卷】chūnjuǎn (～儿 chūnjuǎnr) 食品，用薄面皮裹馅，卷成长条形，放在油里炸熟 spring roll，made of a thin sheet of dough with stuffing rolled in，deep fried before serving

【春困】chūnkùn 指春季精神困倦 spring fatigue：～秋乏(指春秋两季人易困倦) prone to fatigue in spring and autumn

【春兰】chūnlán same as 兰花 lánhuā ①

【春兰秋菊】chūn lán qiū jú 春天的兰草，秋天的菊花，在不同的季节里，各有独特的优美风姿 orchid in spring and chrysanthemum in autumn，each with its unique charm；〈比喻 *fig*.〉各有专长 (of people) each having his or her own abilities

【春雷】chūnléi 春天的雷声(多用于比喻 mostly in a figurative sense) spring thunder：平地一声～ spring thunder out of the blue

【春联】chūnlián (～儿 chūnliánr) 春节时贴的对联 Spring Festival couplets；couplets posted on gateposts or door panels during the Spring Festival，expressing good wishes for the year

【春令】chūnlìng ❶same as 春季 chūnjì ❷ 春季的气候 spring weather：冬行～(冬天的气候像春天) spring-like winter；mild winter

【春麦】chūnmài same as 春小麦 chūnxiǎomài

【春梦】chūnmèng 〈比喻 *fig*.〉转瞬即逝的好景或空幻的不能实现的愿望 transient joy；wishful thinking

【春牛】chūnniú 用泥土做成的牛。旧时立春日用红绿鞭抽打春牛以迎春。earthen ox，(beaten with a red and green whip in old times as a gesture to usher in spring) on the Beginning of Spring day；☞ 打春 dǎchūn ① on p. 347

【春情】chūnqíng same as 春心 chūnxīn

【春秋】chūnqiū ❶ 春季和秋季，常用来表示整个一年，也泛指岁月 spring and autumn；a year；years：苦度～ lead a hard life ❷ 指人的年岁 age：～正富(年纪不大，将来的日子很长) of a young age｜～已高 advanced in years｜～鼎盛 heyday

【春秋】Chūnqiū ❶ 我国古代编年体的史书，相传鲁国的《春秋》经过孔子修订。后来常用为历史著作的名称。history book in ancient China，and legend has it that *The Spring and Autumn Annals* of the state of Lu was revised by Confucius；historical books in general ❷ 我国历史上的一个时代(公元前 722—公元前 481)，因鲁国编年史《春秋》包括这一段时期而得名。现在一般把公元前 770 年到公元前 476 年，划为春秋时代。Spring and Autumn Period (722-481 B.C.)，covered in *The Spring and Autumn Annals* of the state of Lu；Spring and Autumn Period，770-476 B.C.，according to modern division of historical periods

【春秋笔法】chūnqiū bǐfǎ 相传孔子修《春秋》，一字含褒贬。后来称文章用笔曲折而意含褒贬的写作手法为春秋笔法。Autumn and Spring style；use of subtle language in writing，as Confucius did in revising *The Spring and Autumn Annals*

【春色】chūnsè ❶ 春天的景色 spring scenery：满城～ city bathed in spring｜～宜人(of a place) look its seasonal best in spring ❷ 指脸上呈现的喜色或酒后脸上泛起的红色(of a person) look pleased；flush after drinking wine：满面～(of a person) look joyful

【春上】chūn·shang same as 春季 chūnjì：今年～雨水多。There was much rain this spring.

【春试】chūnshì 明清两代科举制度，会试在春季举行，叫做春试 general examinations for recruiting civil servants during the Ming and Qing dynasties，held in spring for successful candidates in the provincial examinations

【春笋】chūnsǔn 春季长成或挖出的竹笋 bamboo shoot，dug up in spring for food

【春天】chūntiān same as 春季 chūnjì ◇迎来科学技术发展的～ usher in the spring for science and technology

【春条】chūntiáo 〈方 *dial*.〉(～儿 chūntiáor) 春节时贴的用红纸写着吉利话的字条儿 narrow sheet of red paper written with wishes for the New Year，pasted on doors or walls during Spring Festival

【春头】chūntóu 〈方 *dial*.〉初春 beginning of spring：正当～，家家都在忙着农活儿。Every family is busy with farm work in early spring.

【春闱】chūnwéi 〈书 *fml*.〉same as 春试 chūnshì

【春宵】chūnxiāo 春天的夜晚 spring night：～苦短。Spring nights are too short. *or* Night of tryst goes by all too soon.

【春小麦】chūnxiǎomài 春季播种的小麦 also called 春麦 chūnmài

【春心】chūnxīn 指爱慕异性的心情 love for the opposite sex

【春汛】chūnxùn ☞ 桃花汛 táohuāxùn on p. 1871

【春药】chūnyào 刺激性欲的药 aphrodisiac

【春意】chūnyì ❶ 春天的迹象或情景 sign or sight of spring：～盎然。Spring is very much in the air.｜树梢发青，已经现出了几分～。The tips of tree branches are turning green，showing signs of spring ❷ same as 春心 chūnxīn

【春蚓秋蛇】chūn yǐn qiū shé 形容书法拙劣，字写得像蚯蚓和蛇爬行一样弯曲难看 awkward calligraphy，with the strokes crawling like an earthworm or snake

【春游】chūnyóu 春天到郊外游玩(多指集体组织的 usu. organized) spring outing:明天去香山~。Let's go to the Fragrant Hills for an outing tomorrow.

【春运】chūnyùn 运输部门指春节前后一段时间的运输业务 transportation services during the Spring Festival

【春装】chūnzhuāng 春季穿的服装 spring clothing

堾 chūn〈方 *dial.*〉地边上用石块垒起来的挡土的墙 low stone wall by the fields for stopping soil from eroding

椿 chūn ❶ 椿树,就是香椿,有时也指臭椿 Chinese mahogany (*Cedrela sinensis*); tree of heaven ❷(Chūn) 姓 a surname

【椿象】chūnxiàng 昆虫的一科,种类很多,身体圆形或椭圆形,头部有单眼。有的椿象能放出恶臭。吸植物茎和果实的汁。多数是害虫。stink bug; shield bug, family of insects, with a round or oval body and a single eye on the head; Some emit a foul smell as a defence. They live on plant sap or fruit juice. Many are pests. also 蝽 chūn

【椿萱】chūnxuān〈书 *fml.*〉〈比喻 *fig.*〉父母 one's parents:~并茂(比喻父母都健在)。(fig.)Both parents are in good health.

辎 chūn ❶〈书 *fml.*〉灵车 hearse ❷ 古代用于泥泞路上的交通工具 ancient vehicle for moving on muddy road

䲠 chūn 䲠鱼,形状跟鲅鱼相似而稍大,尾部两侧有棱状突起。生活在海中。Spanish mackerel(*Cybiidae*), living in the sea and related to mackerel but larger, with edges on either side of the tail

蝽 chūn same as 椿象 chūnxiàng

chún (ㄔㄨㄣˊ)

纯 chún ❶ 纯净;不含杂质 pure; unmixed:~金 pure gold; fine gold |~水 pure or purified water ❷ 纯粹;单纯 of one kind only:~白 pure white|~黑 all black ❸ 纯熟 skilful:工夫不~,还得练 (of a person) not very skilful yet and need to practise more

【纯粹】chúncuì ❶ 不掺杂别的成分的 unadulterated:陶器是用比较~的黏土制成的。Pottery is made of relatively pure clay. ❷〈副词 *adv.*〉表示判断、结论的不容置疑(多跟'是'连用 used correlatively with 是 shì) purely; only:他说的~是骗人的鬼话。What he said are downright lies. | 这种想法~是为目前打算。The idea is good for the moment only.

【纯度】chúndù 物质含杂质多少的程度。杂质愈少,纯度愈高。degree of purity, depending on the content of impurities in a material

【纯洁】chúnjié ❶ 纯粹清白,没有污点;没有私心 pure; unselfish:心地~(of a person) above any ultra intentions ❷ 使纯洁 purify:~组织 clean up an organization

【纯净】chúnjìng ❶ 不含杂质;单纯洁净 pure; simple and clean:~的水,看起来是透明的。Pure water is transparent. ❷ 使纯净 purify:优美的音乐也能~人们的灵魂。Beautiful music can cleanse people's soul.

【纯利】chúnlì 企业总收入中除去一切消耗费用后所剩下的利润 net profit; profit after all production costs are deducted

【纯良】chúnliáng 纯洁善良 pure and kind:心地~ kind-hearted and honest

【纯美】chúnměi 纯正美好;纯洁美丽 honest and good; pure and beautiful:风俗~ fine traditions and customs|心灵~ pure and beautiful heart

【纯朴】chúnpǔ same as 淳朴 chúnpǔ

【纯情】chúnqíng ❶(女子)纯洁的感情或爱情 (of a woman) unaffected feeling or love:一片~ heart filled with true love|少女的~ artless love of a young girl ❷ 感情或爱情纯洁真挚 (of feelings or love) natural and sincere:~少女 innocent young girl

【纯然】chúnrán ❶ 形容纯净而不混杂 clean; untainted:~一色 of a single colour ❷ 单纯地;单单 purely; only:这段描写~是为了主题的需要而臆造出来的。This passage was fabricated merely to accentuate the theme.

【纯熟】chúnshú 很熟练 very skilful:技术~ highly skilled

【纯一】chúnyī 单一 single; simple:想法~simple thinking

【纯音】chúnyīn 一般的声音是由几种振动频率的波组成的,只有一种振动频率的声音叫做纯音,如音叉所发出的声音 ordinary sound consists of the waves of several vibration frequencies; pure or simple tone has only one vibration frequency, like that produced by a tuning fork

【纯贞】chúnzhēn 纯洁忠贞 chaste; pure and faithful:~的爱情 pure and steadfast love

【纯真】chúnzhēn 纯洁真诚 pure and sincere:~无邪 innocent and genuine

【纯正】chúnzhèng ❶ same as 纯粹 chúncuì ①:他说的是~的普通话。He speaks standard *putonghua*. ❷ 纯洁正当 untainted and proper:动机~ motive free of ulterior intentions

莼(蓴) chún [莼菜](chúncài) 多年生水草,叶子椭圆形,浮在水面,茎上和叶的背面有黏液,花暗红色。嫩叶可以吃。water shield (*Brasenia schreberi*); perennial water plant, with oval leaves that float on the water. There is a sticky sap on the stem and the back of leaves. It blooms in dark red flowers and its tender leaves are edible.

唇(脣) chún 人或某些动物口的周围的肌肉组织 lip; either of the fleshy parts that form the edge of the mouth of humans and certain animals；通称 known as 嘴唇 zuǐchún in general

【唇齿】chúnchǐ〈比喻 *fig*.〉互相接近而且有共同利害的两方面 lips and teeth — two aspects of sth. that are closely related and share common interests：互为～ be lips and teeth to each other｜～相依 mutually dependent；as interdependent as lips and teeth

【唇齿相依】chún chǐ xiāng yī〈比喻 *fig*.〉关系密切，互相依存 be closely related and mutually dependent；as interdependent as lips and teeth

【唇齿音】chúnchǐyīn ☞ 齿唇音 chǐchúnyīn on p. 263

【唇膏】chúngāo 口红 lipstick

【唇红齿白】chún hóng chǐ bái 形容人容貌秀美（多用于儿童、青少年 of a child or young person）pretty or handsome with rosy lips and white teeth

【唇焦舌敝】chún jiāo shé bì 嘴唇说干了，舌头说破了。形容话说得太多。talk till one's lips become parched and one's tongue worn out；also 舌敝唇焦 shé bì chún jiāo

【唇裂】chúnliè 先天性畸形，上唇直着裂开，饮食不方便，说话不清楚 cleft lip；congenital split in the upper lip，affecting both eating and speaking；also 兔唇 tùchún；通称 commonly known as 豁嘴 huōzuǐ

【唇枪舌剑】chún qiāng shé jiàn 形容争辩激烈，言辞锋利 cross verbal swords；intense debate；also 舌剑唇枪 shé jiàn chún qiāng

【唇舌】chúnshé〈比喻 *fig*.〉言辞 words；speech：这件事儿恐怕还得大费～。I'm afraid it will take some hard argument on this matter.

【唇亡齿寒】chún wáng chǐ hán 嘴唇没有了，牙齿就会觉得冷 The teeth will be exposed to the cold once the lips are gone.〈比喻 *fig*.〉关系密切，利害相关 as closely related as the lips and the teeth

【唇吻】chúnwěn〈书 *fml*.〉嘴唇 lips；〈比喻 *fig*.〉口才、言辞 speech talent；eloquence

【唇音】chúnyīn 双唇音、齿唇音的统称（general term for）labial and labio-dental sounds

淳 chún〈书 *fml*.〉淳朴 honest：～厚 simple and honest

【淳厚】chúnhòu same as 淳朴 chúnpǔ：风俗～ unsophisticated folk customs；also 醇厚 chúnhòu

【淳美】chúnměi 纯美 pure and beautiful：音色～ pure and sweet voice

【淳朴】chúnpǔ 诚实朴素 honest and simple：外貌～ honest and plain in appearance｜民情～ artless folk customs；also 纯朴 chúnpǔ

【淳于】Chúnyú 姓 a surname

錞 chún［錞于］（chúnyú）古代一种铜制乐器 ancient bronze musical instrument
☞ duì on p. 495

鹑 chún 鹌鹑（ān·chún）quail

【鹑衣】chúnyī〈书 *fml*.〉指破烂不堪、补丁很多的衣服 ragged clothes：～百结 ragged and patched clothes

漘 chún〈书 *fml*.〉水边 waterside

醇 chún ❶〈书 *fml*.〉含酒精多的酒 spirit ❷〈书 *fml*.〉纯粹 pure ❸ 有机化合物的一大类，是烃分子中的氢原子被羟基取代而成的化合物（不包括苯环上的氢原子被羟基取代而成的化合物）。如乙醇（酒精）、胆固醇。category of organic chemical compounds，such as ethanol（alcohol）and cholesterol，acquired when the hydrogen atom of a hydrocarbon molecule is replaced by a hydroxyl group（excluding chemical compounds when the hydrogen atom of a benzene ring is replaced by a hydrocarbon radical）

【醇和】chúnhé（性质、味道）纯正平和（of quality，flavour）unmixed and mild：酒味～ wine of a mellow taste

【醇厚】chúnhòu ❶（气味、滋味等）纯正浓厚（of smell，taste，etc.）pure and rich：香味～ rich aroma ❷ same as 淳厚 chúnhòu

【醇化】chúnhuà 使更纯粹，达到完美的境界 purify；enhance：经过文艺工作者的努力，这种艺术更加～，更加丰富多彩。This art form has been further improved and enriched with the effort of artists and writers.

【醇酒】chúnjiǔ 味道纯正的酒 wine of good taste

【醇美】chúnměi 纯正甜美 pure and sweet：～的嗓音 beautiful voice｜酒味～ wine of mellow taste

【醇香】chúnxiāng（气味、滋味）纯正芳香（of smell，taste）balmy；savoury

【醇正】chúnzhèng（滋味、气味）浓厚纯正（of taste，smell）rich and undiluted

chǔn（ㄔㄨㄣˇ）

蠢[1] chǔn〈书 *fml*.〉蠢动 wriggle

蠢[2]（惷）chǔn ❶ 愚蠢 stupid ～材 fool ❷ 笨拙 clumsy：～笨 awkward

【蠢笨】chǔnbèn ❶ 笨拙 clumsy：～的狗熊 gawky bear ❷ 不灵便 maladroit：～的牛车 maladroit ox-drawn cart

【蠢材】chǔncái 笨家伙（骂人的话 abuse）idiot

【蠢蠢】chǔnchǔn〈书 *fml*.〉❶ 蠢动的样子 wriggling：～而动 restless and ready to stir up trouble ❷ 动荡不安 turbulent：王室～。The royal family is in turmoil.

【蠢蠢欲动】chǔnchǔn yù dòng 指敌人准备进行攻击或坏分子策划破坏活动（of an enemy）prepare to strike；（of evil persons）plot sabotage; itch for a go; be up to sth.

【蠢动】chǔndòng ❶ 虫子爬动 (of an insect) crawl ❷ (敌人或坏分子)进行活动 (of an enemy or evil persons) in action

【蠢话】chǔnhuà 愚蠢的话;不合常情的话 stupid uttering; nonsense

【蠢货】chǔnhuò 蠢材;笨家伙(骂人的话 abuse) donkey; dunce

【蠢人】chǔnrén 愚笨的人 stupid person

【蠢事】chǔnshì 愚蠢的事 stupidity: 不能干那种亲者痛、仇者快的～。Don't do dumb things that offend your friends but please your enemy.

【蠢头蠢脑】chǔn tóu chǔn nǎo 形容蠢笨痴呆的样子 dumb looking

chuō (ㄔㄨㄛ)

逴 chuō 〈书 *fml*.〉 ❶ 远 far ❷ 超越 surpass

踔 chuō 〈书 *fml*.〉 ❶ 跳跃 jump: 踸～ hop ❷ 超越 outdo

【踔厉】chuōlì 〈书 *fml*.〉精神振奋 be in high spirits: ～风发 spirited and energetic | 发扬～ (指意气昂扬,精神奋发) high-spirited and full of vigour

戳 chuō ❶用力使长条形物体的顶端向前触动或穿过另一物体 poke or pierce with a stick-like object: 一～就破 break at a slight jab ❷ 〈方 *dial*.〉(长条形物体)因猛戳另一物体而本身受伤或损坏 get hurt or damaged for striking into sth.: 打球～了手 sprain one's hand while playing a ball game | 钢笔尖儿～了。The nib was blunted. ❸ 〈方 *dial*.〉竖立;站 stand sth. on end; stand: 把棍子～起来。Set the cane erect. | 大伙儿都走了,他一个人还～在那儿。He was still standing there after everybody had left. ❹ (～儿 chuōr)图章 seal: ～记 seal mark | 邮～ postmark | 盖～ stamp on

【戳穿】chuōchuān ❶ 刺穿 pierce: 刺刀～了胸膛。The bayonet stabbed through the chest. ❷ 说破;揭穿 reveal; lay bare: 假话当场被～。The lies were disproved on the spot.

【戳脊梁骨】chuō jǐ·lianggǔ 指在背后指责 criticize behind sb.'s back: 办事要公正,别让人家～。Do things in a fair way so nobody can talk behind your back.

【戳记】chuōjì 图章(多指机关、团体的 of a government department or an organization) seal

chuò (ㄔㄨㄛˋ)

辵 chuò 〈书 *fml*.〉忽走忽停 hesitate in walking

娖 chuò 〈书 *fml*.〉 ❶ 谨慎 cautious ❷ 整顿(队伍) straighten up (troops)

啜 chuò 〈书 *fml*.〉 ❶ 喝 drink: ～茗(喝茶) sip tea ❷ 抽噎的样子 sob: ～泣 sob
☞ Chuài on p. 297

【啜泣】chuòqì 抽噎;抽抽搭搭地哭 sob: ～不止 blubber without stop | 低声～ sob quietly | 嘤嘤～ sob softly

惙 chuò 〈书 *fml*.〉 ❶ 忧愁 worry ❷ 疲乏 fatigue ❸ (气)短;弱 short of breath; weak: 气息～然 breathe feebly

【惙惙】chuòchuò 〈书 *fml*.〉忧愁的样子 looking worried: 忧心～ deeply concerned

婼 chuò 〈书 *fml*.〉不顺 uneven
☞ ruò on p. 1646

婥 chuò [婥约] (chuòyuē) 〈书 *fml*.〉same as 绰约 chuòyuē

绰 chuò 〈书 *fml*.〉 ❶ 宽绰 spacious; ample: ～有余裕 have more than enough ❷ (体态)柔美 (of body shape) delicate and pretty: ～丽 delicate and beautiful | 柔情～态 tender and pretty in a faminine way
☞ chāo on p. 225

【绰绰有余】chuòchuò yǒu yú 形容很宽裕,用不完 more than enough

【绰号】chuòhào 外号 nickname: 小张的～叫小老虎。Xiao Zhang is nicknamed Little Tiger.

【绰约】chuòyuē 〈书 *fml*.〉形容女子姿态柔美的样子 (of a woman's appearance) pretty and graceful: ～多姿 statuesque | 丰姿～ beautiful

辍 chuò 中止;停止 stop; cease: ～学 drop out of school | 时作时～ on and off | 日夜不～ nonstop in day and night

【辍笔】chuòbǐ 写作或画画儿没有完成而停止 stop midway in writing or painting: 中途～ give up writing or painting half way through | 他到晚年也不曾～。He kept writing (or painting) way into his old age.

【辍学】chuòxué 中途停止上学 drop out of school: 因病～ drop out of school due to illness

【辍演】chuòyǎn (戏剧等)停止演出 stop staging (a play, show, etc.)

龊 chuò ☞ [龌龊] (wòchuò) on p. 2015

歠 chuò 〈书 *fml*.〉 ❶ 吸;喝 suck; drink ❷ 指可以喝的,如粥、羹汤等 liquid food, like porridge, soup, etc.

cī (ㄘ)

刺 cī 〈拟声词 *onom*.〉 sound of slipping: ～的一声,滑了一个跟头 slipped and fell with a swish | 花炮点着了,～～地直冒火星。The firecracker wheezed and sparkled after it was ignited.
☞ cì on p. 321

【刺啦】cīlā 〈拟声词 *onom*.〉形容撕裂声、迅速划动声等 sound of tearing or scratching：～一声，衣服撕了个口子。The garment was ripped open with a crisp sound.｜～一声划着了火柴。Scratch! A match was struck.

【刺棱】cīlēng〈拟声词 *onom.*〉动作迅速的声音 sound of quick movement：猫～一下跑了。The cat scampered away in no time.

【刺溜】cīliū〈拟声词 *onom.*〉脚底下滑动的声音；东西迅速滑过的声音 sound of slipping or rapid sliding：不留神，～一下滑倒了。(He) carelessly slipped and fell.｜子弹～～地从耳边擦过去。A bullet whistled past the ear.

呲 cī（～儿 cīr）申斥；斥责 reprimand; rebuke：挨～儿 get a dressing down or tongue lashing｜我～了她两句她就哭了。I just chided her a little bit and she began to cry.
☞ 龇 zī on p. 2538

差 cī ❶〈书 *fml.*〉等级；等次 grade; level ❷ ☞ 参差 cēncī on p. 198
☞ chā on p. 199, chà on p. 206, chāi on p. 208 and chài on p. 209

疵 cī 缺点；毛病 defect; flaw：吹毛求～ find fault with

【疵点】cīdiǎn 缺点；毛病 defect; flaw：这匹布洁白光滑，没有什么～。This bolt of cloth is so white and smooth; it is flawless.

【疵品】cīpǐn 有缺点的产品 substandard product

【疵瑕】cīxiá same as 瑕疵 xiácī

粢 cī［粢饭］(cīfàn)〈方 *dial.*〉一种食品，将糯米掺和粳米，用冷水浸泡，沥干后蒸熟，吃时中间裹油条等捏成饭团 mixture of sticky and non-glutinous rice, steamed after soaking in cold water, served with a deep-fried dough twist wrapped inside
☞ zī on p. 2538

跐 cī 脚下滑动 sound of slipping of the foot：脚一～，摔倒了。(He) slipped and fell with a thud.｜登～了，摔下来了。(Someone) slipped when climbing up and fell down.
☞ cǐ on p. 320

【跐溜】cīliū 脚下滑动 slip of the foot：他脚一～，摔了个脸朝天。He slipped and fell flat on his back.

骴 cī〈书 *fml.*〉肉未烂尽的骸骨 skeleton with bits of flesh attached

cí（ㄘˊ）

词 cí ❶（～儿 cír）说话或诗歌、文章、戏剧中的语句 words in speech, poem, article, or play：戏～ actor's lines｜义正～严 in categorical terms｜～不达意 (of words) fail to get the message across｜他问得我没～儿回答。His question rendered me speechless. ❷ 一种韵文形式，由五言诗、七言诗和民间歌谣发展而成，起于唐代，盛于宋代。原是配乐歌唱的一种诗体，句的长短随着歌调而改变，因此又叫做长短句。有小令和慢词两种，一般分上下两阕。*ci*; rhymed verse based on five- or seven-character lines and folk rhymes, originating in the Tang Dynasty (618-907) and fully developed in the Song Dynasty (960-1279), with variation in line lengths according to the tunes to which a specific verse was first composed, thus also called long and short verse. A *ci* poem can be short (小令 xiǎolìng) or long (慢词 màncí), usu. with two stanzas in each composition. ❸（～儿 cír）语言里最小的、可以自由运用的单位 smallest unit of a language that can be used freely

【词典】cídiǎn 收集词汇加以解释供人检查参考的工具书 dictionary; reference book that lists words and provides explanations for their meanings; also 辞典 cídiǎn

【词调】cídiào 词的调子 tonal patterns and rhyme schemes of *ci* poem

【词法】cífǎ 语言学上的形态学，有时也包括构词法 morphology, sometimes including word-formation

【词锋】cífēng 犀利的文笔，好像刀剑的锋芒 pungent style of writing：～锐利 trenchant writing style

【词赋】cífù same as 辞赋 cífù

【词根】cígēn 词的主要组成部分。是词义的基础。如'老虎'里的'虎'，'桌子'里的'桌'，'工业化'里的'工业'，'观察'里的'观'和'察'。root; word on which a phrase is based, such as 虎 in 老虎 lǎohǔ, 桌 in 桌子 zhuō·zi, 工业 in 工业化 gōngyèhuà, 观 and 察 in 观察 guānchá

【词根语】cígēnyǔ 没有专门表示语法意义的附加成分、缺少形态变化的语言。这种语言句子里词与词的语法关系依靠词序和虚词来表示。radical language; language that depends on word order and function words, instead of accessory elements or morphological changes, to express grammatical relations; also 孤立语 gūlìyǔ

【词话】cíhuà ❶ 评论词的内容、形式，或记载词的作者事迹的书，如《碧鸡漫志》、《人间词话》commentary book on the contents and forms of *ci* poems, or biographies of *ci* poets, such as *Random Notes of Biji Studio* and *Worldly Notes on Ci Poems* ❷ 散文里间杂韵文的说唱文艺形式，是章回小说的前身，起于宋元，流行到明代，如《大唐秦王词话》。明代也把夹有词曲的章回小说叫做词话，如《金瓶梅词话》。*cihua*, prose interspersed with verse as a form of storytelling accompanied by singing, the predecessor of traditional Chinese novels with chapter headings, originating in the Song Dynasty (960-1279) and popular in the Ming Dynasty (1368-1644), such as *The Story of King Qin of the Great Tang*; novels with chapter headings and including prose interspersed with verse as a form of storytell-

C

ing accompanied by singing, such as *The Plum in a Golden Vase*

【词汇】cíhuì 一种语言里所使用的词的总称,如汉语词汇、英语词汇。也指一个人或一部作品所使用的词,如鲁迅的词汇。vocabulary; all the words of a language, such as Chinese vocabulary, English vocabulary; also the vocabulary of a writer or a literary work, such as Lu Xun's vocabulary

【词汇学】cíhuìxué 语言学的一个部门,研究语言或一种语言的词汇的组成和历史发展 lexicology, a branch of linguistics for the study of word formation and its historical development

【词句】cíjù 词和句子;字句 words and sentences:～不通 ungrammatical or unidiomatic expression|净说好听的～ sweet talk

【词类】cílèi 词在语法上的分类。各种语言的词类数目不同,现代汉语的词一般分十二类:名词、动词、形容词、数词、量词、代词(以上实词),副词、介词、连词、助词、叹词、拟声词(以上虚词) parts of speech, which vary in number from language to language. Modern Chinese has 12 parts of speech: noun, verb, adjective, numeral, classifier, and pronoun (the above being notional words); adverb, preposition, conjunction, auxiliary word, interjection, and onomatopoeia (the above being function words).

【词令】cílìng same as 辞令 cílìng

【词牌】cípái 词的调子的名称,如'西江月'、'蝶恋花' tune; name of the tune to which a *ci* poem is composed, such as *Xi Jiang Yue* (*Moon on the Western River*) and *Die Lian Hua* (*Butterfly Loves Flowers*)

【词谱】cípǔ 辑录各种词调的格式供填词的人应用的书,如《白香词谱》collection of various tunes of *ci* poems for poets to choose from; *Baixiang's Tunes for Ci Poems* is one such example.

【词曲】cíqǔ 词和曲的总称 general term for *ci* poems and *qu* verses

【词人】círén ❶ 擅长填词的人 *ci* poet ❷ 擅长文辞的人 person of literary talent

【词讼】císòng 诉讼 legal case; also 辞讼 císòng

【词素】císù 语言中最小的有意义的单位,词根、前缀、后缀、词尾都是词素。有的词只包含一个词素,如'人、蜈蚣'等。有的词包含两个或更多的词素,如'老虎'包含'老'和'虎'两个词素,'蜈蚣草'包含'蜈蚣'和'草'两个词素,'图书馆'包含'图'、'书'和'馆'三个词素。morpheme; the smallest language unit with a meaning, such as root, prefix, suffix, and ending. Some words consist of a single morpheme, such as 人 rén and 蜈蚣 wúgōng; others consist of two or more morphemes, such as 老虎 lǎohǔ, 蜈蚣草 wú·gōngcǎo, and 图书馆 túshūguǎn

【词头】cítóu ☞ 前缀 qiánzhuì on p. 1536

【词尾】cíwěi 加在词的最后,表示词形变化的词素,如'站着'的'着','孩子们'的'们'。汉语语法著作中常用'词尾'兼指后缀和词尾。end morpheme; morpheme added to the end of a word to indicate morphological change, such as 着·zhe in '站着 zhàn·zhe' and 们 mén in '孩子们 háizi·mén'; In Chinese grammar books, end morpheme includes both suffix and inflectional endings. ☞ 后缀 hòuzhuì on p. 813

【词性】cíxìng 作为划分词类的根据的词的特点,如'一把锯'的'锯'可以跟数量词结合,是名词,'锯木头'的'锯'可以带宾语,是动词 features that classify parts of speech; for example, 锯 (saw) as a noun in '一把锯 (a saw)', but a verb in '锯木头 (saw wood)'

【词序】cíxù 词在词组或句子里的先后次序。在汉语里,词序是一种主要语法手段。词序的变动能使词组或句子具有不同的意义,如'不完全懂'和'完全不懂','我看他'和'他看我'。word order in a phrase or a sentence. In Chinese, word order has important grammatical significance. Change in word order will change the meaning of a phrase or a sentence, such as '不完全懂 (partially understand)' as against '完全不懂 (understand nothing)', and '我看他 (I look at him.)' as against '他看我 (He looks at me.)'.

【词义】cíyì 词的语音形式所表达的意义,包括词的词汇意义和语法意义 meaning of a word in speech, including lexical and grammatical significance

【词余】cíyú 曲①的别称,意思是说曲是由词发展而来的 different term for 曲 qǔ ①, meaning that *qu* developed on the basis of *ci* poems

【词语】cíyǔ 词和短语;字眼 word and phrase; wording:写文章要尽量避免方言～。One should avoid the use of slang in writing.|对课文中的生僻～都做了简单的注释。Unusual words in the text are noted with simple explanations.

【词韵】cíyùn 填词所押的韵或所依据的韵书 rhymes of *ci* poems, or a rhyme book of *ci* poems

【词藻】cízǎo same as 辞藻 cízǎo

【词章】cízhāng same as 辞章 cízhāng

【词缀】cízhuì 词中附加在词根上的构词成分。常见的有前缀和后缀两种。affix; bound elememt, usu. prefix and suffix, added to a base or stem to form a new word ☞ 前缀 qiánzhuì on p. 1536 and 后缀 hòuzhuì on p. 813

【词组】cízǔ 两个或更多的词的组合(区别于'单词'),如'新社会,打扫干净,破除迷信' phrase, such as '新社会 (new society)', '打扫干净 (clean up)', and '破除迷信 (do away with superstition)', as compared with individual words

茈 cí ☞ 凫茈 fúcí on p. 594
☞ zǐ on p. 2541

茨 cí ❶ 用茅或苇盖屋子 thatch a roof with cogongrass or reed ❷ 蒺藜 puncture vine

【茨冈人】Cígāngrén ☞ 吉卜赛人 Jíbǔsàirén on p. 901 [茨冈,俄 цыган: Russian name for Gypsy]

【茨菰】cí·gu same as 慈姑 cí·gu

兹 cí 龟兹(Qiūcí),古代西域国名,在今新疆库车县一带 Kuqa, an ancient kingdom in the Western Regions, in present-day Kuqa County of Xinjiang Uygur Autonomous Region
☞ zī on p. 2536

祠 cí 祠堂 ancestral temple; memorial temple:宗～ clan hall

【祠堂】cítáng ❶ 在封建宗法制度下,同族的人共同祭祀祖先的房屋 memorial hall for the ancestors of the same clan under the patriarchal clan system of feudal society ❷ 在封建制度下,社会公众或某个阶层为共同祭祀某个人物而修建的房屋 under the feudal system, a memorial hall built for someone appreciated by the public or a certain class of people

瓷(甆) cí 用高岭土等烧制成的材料,质硬而脆,白色或发黄,比陶质细致 porcelain or china, made of kaolin clay, hard and brittle, white or yellowish in colour, and finer than pottery in texture

【瓷公鸡】cígōngjī 〈比喻 *fig*.〉非常吝啬的人 porcelain rooster, from which you cannot pluck a single feather; miser:这人是个～,一毛不拔。He's so tight-fisted, he won't give a penny.

【瓷瓶】cípíng ❶ 瓷质的瓶子 porcelain vase ❷ 绝缘子的俗称 popular name for 绝缘子 juéyuánzǐ

【瓷漆】cíqī same as 磁漆 cíqī

【瓷器】cíqì 瓷质的器皿 chinaware

【瓷实】cí·shi 〈方 *dial*.〉结实;扎实 solid; firm:打夯以后,地基就～了。The foundation became solid after ramming.|他用心钻研,学习得很～。He studies hard and masters everything he's learned.

【瓷土】cítǔ 烧制瓷器用的黏土,主要指高岭土。有的地区叫坩子土。clay for making porcelain, mainly kaolin clay; also called 坩子土 gān·zitǔ in some places

【瓷窑】cíyáo 烧瓷器的窑 porcelain kiln; china kiln

【瓷砖】cízhuān 用瓷土烧制的建筑材料,一般是方形,表面有釉质。主要用来装饰墙面、地面。ceramic or glazed tile, usu. square, for wall or floor decoration

赍 cí 〈书 *fml*.〉堆积杂草 pile up weeds

辞[1](辭、辤) cí ❶ 优美的语言;文辞;言辞 refined language; diction; wording:～藻 ornate diction|修～ rhetoric ❷ 古典文学的一种体裁 genre of classical literature:楚～ *The Elegies of Chu*|～赋 special form of rhapsodic poem; descriptive poetic poem ❸ 古体诗的一种 a type of classical poetry:《木兰～》*The Ballad of Mulan* ‖ 注意 **NOTE**:在很多合成词里'辞'也作词。In many compounds 辞 cí also put as 词 cí.

辞[2](辭、辤) cí ❶ 告别 take leave:～行 say goodbye before leaving|告～ take leave|不～而别 leave without saying goodbye ❷ 辞职 resign:～呈 letter of resignation|～去主任职务 resign one's post as director ❸ 辞退;解雇 dismiss; lay off:他被经理～了。He was dismissed by the manager. ❹ 躲避;推托 elude; shirk:推～ decline|不～辛苦 brave difficulties

【辞别】cíbié 临行前告别 bid farewell to:～母校,走上工作岗位 graduate from one's alma mater to start work

【辞呈】cíchéng 请求辞职的呈文 written request for resignation

【辞典】cídiǎn same as 词典 cídiǎn

【辞费】cífèi 话多而无用(多用于批评写作 oft. in critiques) superfluous

【辞赋】cífù 汉朝人集屈原等所作的赋称为楚辞,因此后人泛称赋体文学为辞赋 *cifu* is a genre of writing originally called 赋 *fu*, a combination of prose and poetry. The works of *fu* by Qu Yuan (c. 340-278 B.C.) and his contemporaries were called *chuci* in the Han Dynasty (206 B.C.-A.D. 220). Thus *fu* is also known as *cifu*. also 词赋 cífù

【辞工】cí//gōng 雇主辞退佣工,也指佣工主动要求解雇 dismiss an employee; quit one's job:东家辞了他的工。The boss dismissed him.|他要回老家,～不干了。He's quit his job to go home.

【辞活】cí//huó (～儿 cí//huór) same as 辞工 cí//gōng

【辞灵】cí//líng 出殡前亲友向灵柩行礼告别 bow to a coffin before it is carried to the grave

【辞令】cílìng 交际场合应对得宜的话语 words or speech appropriate to the occasion:外交～ diplomatic language|他应对敏捷,善于～。He has an agile mind and is eloquent in speech. also 词令 cílìng

【辞年】cí//nián same as 辞岁 cí//suì

【辞让】círàng 客气地推让 decline as a gesture of being polite:他～了一番,才坐在前排。He took a seat in the front row after politely declining the offer first.

【辞色】císè 〈书 *fml*.〉说的话和说话时的态度 speech and manner in speaking:不假～ without the use of words|欣喜之情,形于～ express one's happiness both in words and in the way one speaks

【辞书】císhū 字典、词典等工具书的统称 general term for dictionaries and similar reference books

【辞讼】císòng same as 词讼 císòng

【辞岁】cí//suì 农历除夕晚上家人相聚宴饮,互祝平安 (of family members) gather together for dinner on the traditional Chinese New Year's Eve and share good wishes for the New Year

【辞退】cítuì ❶ 解雇 dismiss:~保姆 dismiss a nanny ❷ 辞谢,不接受 politely decline:~礼物 refuse to accept a gift|导演请他饰演该片的主要角色,他~了。He declined the director's offer for him to play the leading role in the film.

【辞谢】cíxiè 很客气地推辞不受 politely decline:对方送给酬劳,他~了。He courteously declined the payment offered to him.

【辞行】cí//xíng 远行前向亲友告别 say goodbye to family, friends, etc. before going on a journey:我们明天启程南下,特来向老师~。We've come to say goodbye to our teacher before leaving for the south tomorrow.

【辞藻】cízǎo 诗文中工巧的词语,常指运用的典故和古人诗文中现成词语 ornate diction, usu. the use of expressions in allusions and classics:~华丽 flowery language|堆砌~ laden with florid vocabulary; also 词藻 cízǎo

【辞灶】cí//zào 旧俗腊月二十三日或二十四日送灶神上天(old custom) send the god of stove up to Heaven on the 23rd or 24th of the 12th lunar month

【辞章】cízhāng ❶ 韵文和散文的总称 general term for prose and verse ❷ 文章的写作技巧;修辞 art of writing; rhetoric ‖ also 词章 cízhāng

【辞职】cí//zhí 请求解除自己的职务 request to resign:~书 letter of resignation|要求~ ask for resignation

慈 cí ❶ 和善 kind:~母 loving mother|心~手软 soft-hearted and lenient ❷ 〈书 *fml.*〉(上对下)慈爱(of a senior person) love (a junior person):敬老~幼 respect for the old and care for the young ❸ 指母亲 mother:家~ mother ❹ (Cí) 姓 a surname

【慈爱】cí'ài (年长者对年幼者)仁慈怜爱 (of a senior person) affectionately love (a junior person):~的目光 kind eye|~的母亲 doting mother

【慈悲】cíbēi 慈善和怜悯(原来是佛教用语 originally a Buddhist term) benevolence and mercy:~为怀 with a heart of mercy|大发~ show great mercy

【慈姑】cí·gu ❶ 多年生草本植物,生在水田里,叶子像箭头,开白花。地下有球茎,黄白色或青白色,可以吃。arrowhead (*Sagittaria sagittaria*); perennial plant with arrowhead-shaped leaves above water surface, white flowers, and an edible corm in yellowish or greenish white colour ❷ 这种植物的地下茎 corm of arrowhead ‖ also 茨菰 cí·gu

【慈和】cíhé 慈祥和蔼 kindly and amicable:面容~ look kind and agreeable

【慈眉善目】cí méi shàn mù 形容仁慈善良的样子 (of a person's countenance) benign looking

【慈善】císhàn 对人关怀,富有同情心 considerate; compassionate:~心肠 kind-hearted

【慈祥】cíxiáng (老年人的态度、神色)和蔼安详 (of an old person's bearing and expression) kind and serene:祖母的脸上露出了~的笑容。Grandmother smiled kindly.

【慈颜】cíyán 尊亲的容颜(多指父母的) appearance (of one's parents)

磁[1] cí 物质能吸引铁、镍等金属的性能 magnetism; attractive quality of a material to iron, nickel and other metals

磁[2] cí same as '瓷'cí

【磁暴】cíbào 地球磁场的方向和强度发生急剧而不规则变化的现象,是太阳表面上耀斑异常活跃时发出的大量带电粒子经过地球附近引起的。发生时,磁针剧烈颤动,电讯受到严重干扰。magnetic storm; disturbance of the magnetic field of the earth, caused by large amounts of charged particles passing through the space close to the earth when the solar flare is unusually active, demonstrated by violent tremble of magnetic needles and causing serious jamming to telecommunications

【磁场】cíchǎng 传递物体间磁力作用的场。磁体和有电流通过的导体的周围空间都有磁场存在,指南针指南就是地球磁场的作用。magnetic field; region around a magnet or a charged conductor around which the force of magnetism acts. The compass works on the magnetic field of the earth. ☞ 场 chǎng ⑨ on p. 221

【磁场强度】cíchǎng qiángdù 在任何磁介质中,磁场中某点的磁感应强度和同一点上的磁导率的比值 magnetic field intensity; ratio between the magnetic induction intensity of a point in the magnetic field of any magnetic medium and the magnetic conductivity of the same point

【磁带】cídài 涂着氧化铁粉等磁性物质的塑料带子,用来记录声音、影像等 tape; strip of plastic coated with magnetic materials such as ferric oxide powder, used to record sound or image; ☞ 录像机 lùxiàngjī on p. 1260 and 录音机 lùyīnjī on p. 1260

【磁感应】cígǎnyìng 物体在磁场中受磁力作用的现象,如铁在磁场中被磁化,磁针在磁场中偏转等 magnetic induction; phenomenon of an object being magnetized in a magnetic field, such as magnetization of iron and the deflection of a magnetic needle

【磁化】cíhuà 使某些物体具有磁性。如把铁放在较强的磁场里，铁就会被磁化。cause sth. to become magnetic, such as magnetization of iron in a strong magnetic field

【磁极】cíjí 磁体上磁性最强的部分。任何磁体总有成对出现的两个磁极。条形、针形磁体的磁极在两端，磁针指北的一端叫北极，指南的一端叫南极。magnetic pole; each of the two points of any magnet where its magnetic force is the strongest, such as either end of a strip or needle-shaped magnet, known as the northern and southern poles as indicated by a magnetic needle

【磁力】cílì 磁体之间相互作用的力 magnetic force; attractive or repulsive force between two magnets

【磁力线】cílìxiàn 表明磁场强度和磁力方向的线。磁力线上的各点的切线方向跟磁场上相应点的磁场方向一致。在磁场中放一块玻璃板，板上撒一些铁屑，轻轻一敲，铁屑排列的形状就显示出磁力线来。line of magnetic flux; line that indicates the intensity of a magnetic field and the direction of its flux; The tangent on each point of the line gives the direction of magnetic flux at that point. If we scatter bits of iron on a plate glass, place it in a magnetic field, tap it gently and the shape of the iron bits shows the line of the magnetic flux.

【磁能】cínéng 磁体场所具有的能，如磁体吸引铁、镍等物质就是磁能的表现 magnetic energy; as manifested by the attraction of a magnet to iron, nickel, and other metals

【磁漆】cíqī 漆的一种，用清漆、颜料等制成。用来涂饰机器、家具等。lacquer made of varnish, pigments, etc., used to paint machines, furniture, etc.; also 瓷漆 cíqī

【磁石】císhí ❶ same as 磁铁 cítiě ❷ 磁铁矿的矿石 magnetite

【磁体】cítǐ 具有磁性的物体。磁铁矿、磁化的钢、有电流通过的导体以及地球、太阳和许多天体都是磁体。通常指永磁体。magnet, usu. permanent, such as magnetite, magnetized steel, conductor carrying electric current, the earth, the sun, and many other celestial bodies

【磁铁】cítiě 用钢或合金钢经过磁化制成的磁体，有的用磁铁矿加工制成 magnet; magnetized steel, alloy, or processed magnetite; also 磁石 císhí or 吸铁石 xītiěshí

【磁通量】cítōngliàng 通过一个截面的磁力线的总数，数值上等于所在处磁感应强度和截面面积的乘积。单位是韦伯。magnetic flux; total number of lines of induction through a given cross section of a surface. It is measured by the intensity of magnetic induction of the cross section times the proportions of the cross section, and usu. expressed in webers. 简称 abbr. 磁通 cítōng

【磁头】cítóu 录音机和录像机中重要的换能元件。不同的磁头能记录、重放、消去声音或图像。magnetic head; important transverter of an audio or video recorder, used to record, reproduce, or erase sound or image

【磁效应】cíxiàoyìng 电流通过导体产生跟磁铁相同作用的现象，如使磁针偏转 magnetic effect; phenomenon of magnetization when an electric current runs through a conductor, such as causing deflection of a magnetic needle

【磁性】cíxìng 磁体能吸引铁、镍等金属的性质 property of a magnet to attract iron, nickel, or other metals

【磁针】cízhēn 针形磁铁，通常是狭长菱形。中间支起，可在水平方向自由转动，受地磁作用，静止时两个尖端分别指着南和北。指南针和罗盘是磁针的应用。magnetic needle, usu. in the shape of a long, narrow rhombus, supported in the middle so that it can move freely horizontally, with each end pointing to the north and south respectively at the force of the earth's magnetic field. The needle on a compass is an example of the application of a magnetic needle.

雌 cí 生物中能产生卵细胞的（跟'雄'相对 as opposed to 'male'）female sex of living things that produces eggs: ～性 female | ～花 female flower | ～蕊 pistil | ～兔 doe

【雌蜂】cífēng 雌性的蜂类，特指雌性的蜜蜂，包括蜂王和工蜂 female bee; queen and workers among honeybees

【雌伏】cífú〈书 *fml.*〉❶ 屈居人下 be in a lower status than one should: 丈夫当雄飞，安能～！A man should cherish high ambitions. How can he remain obscure! ❷〈比喻 *fig.*〉隐藏起来，无所作为 lie low and do nothing: ～以待 lie low and bide one's time

【雌花】cíhuā 只有雌蕊的单性花 female flower; unisexual flower with only one pistil

【雌黄】cíhuáng ❶ 矿物，成分是三硫化二砷，晶体多呈柱状，柠檬黄色，略透明，燃烧时放出大蒜气味。可用来制颜料或做退色剂。orpiment; citrine, semi-transparent mineral consisting of arsenic trisulphide, in columnar crystal, emitting a garlic smell when burning, an ingredient of pigments and decolourants ❷ 古人抄书、校书常用雌黄涂改文字，因此称乱改文字、乱发议论为'妄下雌黄'，称不顾事实，随口乱说为'信口雌黄' practice in ancient times of using orpiment as a correction material in copying and proof-reading has given rise to a number of phrases to mean 'making irresponsible changes to a written work 妄下雌黄 wàng xià cíhuáng' or 'telling tales 信口雌黄 xìn kǒu cíhuáng'

【雌蕊】círuǐ 花的重要部分之一，一般生在花的中央，下部膨大部分是子房，发育成果实；子房中有胚珠,受精后发育成种子;中部细长的叫花柱,花柱上端叫柱头。pistil; important part of a flower, usu. in the centre of it, comprising the style (the long, narrow organ in the middle), the stigma (top of the style), and the ovary (the bulky base) that grows into fruit. The ovary contains one or more ovules that develop into seed(s) after being fertilized. (图见☞ figure for 花 huā on p.826)

C

【雌性】cíxìng 生物两性之一,能产生卵子 female sex of living things that produces eggs: ～动物 female animal

【雌雄】cíxióng ❶ 雌性和雄性 female and male: ～同株 monoecism ❷〈比喻 *fig.*〉胜负、高下 success and failure; relative superiority and inferiority: 决一～ fight it out

【雌雄同体】cí xióng tóng tǐ 精巢和卵巢生在同一动物体内,如蚯蚓 monoecia; (of animals) with the testis and ovary growing in the same body, such as the earthworm

【雌雄同株】cí xióng tóng zhū 雄花和雌花生在同一植株上,如玉米 monoecia; male and female flowers growing on the same plant, such as corn

【雌雄异体】cí xióng yì tǐ 精巢和卵巢分别生在雄性动物和雌性动物体内,高等动物都是雌雄异体的 dioecism; (of animals) with the testis and the ovary growing in the male and the female respectively, such as all higher animals

【雌雄异株】cí xióng yì zhū 雄花和雌花分别生在两个植株上,如大麻、银杏等 dioecism; (of plants) with the male and female flowers growing on different plants respectively, such as hemp and gingko

鹚(鷀) cí ☞ [鸬鹚](lúcí) on p.1257

瓷 cí〈书 *fml.*〉same as 糍 cí

糍 cí [糍粑](cíbā) 把糯米蒸熟捣碎后做成的食品 glutinous rice cake, made of steamed glutinous rice pounded into paste

cǐ (ㄘˇ)

此 cǐ ❶ 表示近指的代词(跟'彼'相对 a pronoun as opposed to 'that');这;这个 this: ～人 this person | ～时 this time | 由～及彼 from this to that | ～呼彼应 a call here, a reply there ❷ 表示此时或此地 here and now: 就～告别。Let's say goodbye here and now. | 谈话就～结束。Let's put an end to our talk now. | 从～病有起色。The disease will turn for the better from now on. | 由～往西 from here to the west ❸ 这样 like this: 长～以往 go on like this | 当时听劝,何至于～。If you had taken my advice then, how could you become like this.

【此岸】cǐ'àn〈佛教 *Budd.*〉指有生有死的境界 state where there are life and death; ☞ 彼岸 bǐ'àn ② on p.100

【此地】cǐdì 当地;这个地方 this place: 此时～ here and now | 居住～多年 lived here for many years

【此地无银三百两】cǐ dì wú yín sān bǎi liǎng 民间故事说,有人把银子埋在地里,上面写了个'此地无银三百两'的字牌;邻居李四看到字牌,挖出银子,在字牌的另一面写上'对门李四未曾偷'。比喻打出的幌子正好暴露了所要掩饰的内容。folk tale has it that once a man had buried an amount of silver underground, he placed a plaque on the site bearing the words: 'No 300 taels of silver here.' His neighbour Li Si saw the plaque, dug out the silver, and wrote on the other side of the plaque: 'Your neighbour Li Si did not steal it.' The phrase is figuratively used to mean the backfiring of a cover-up trick.

【此后】cǐhòu 从这以后 hence forth: 三年前和他车站握别,～就没见过面。I've never seen him again after bidding farewell to him with a handshake at the station three years ago.

【此间】cǐjiān 指自己所在的地方;此地 place where one is at; here: ～天气渐暖,油菜花已经盛开。With the weather here turning warm, the rape flowers are in full bloom.

【此刻】cǐkè 这时候 this moment: ～台风已过,轮船即将起航。The typhoon being over, the steamer will set sail immediately.

【此起彼伏】cǐ qǐ bǐ fú 这里起来,那里落下,表示连续不断 rise and fall continuously; also 此伏彼起 cǐ fú bǐ qǐ and 此起彼落 cǐ qǐ bǐ luò

【此前】cǐqián 在某时或某事以前 prior to a given time or event: 写小说是近几年的事,～他曾用笔名发表过一些诗作。Before he began to write novels a few years ago, he used to publish poems under a penname.

【此生】cǐshēng 这一辈子 this life: 不虚～ not to live one's life in vain

【此外】cǐwài 指除了上面所说的事物或情况之外的 besides; in addition (to what has been mentioned): 院子里种着两棵玉兰和两棵海棠,～还有几丛月季。There are a few clusters of Chinese rose in the yard, besides two magnolia and two crabapple trees.

【此一时,彼一时】cǐ yī shí, bǐ yī shí 现在是一种情况,那时又是一种情况。指情况已与过去不相同。the present situation is different from what it was before; times have changed

泚 cǐ〈书 *fml.*〉❶ 鲜明;清澈 fresh; clear ❷ 流汗 perspire ❸ 用笔蘸墨 dip a writing brush in ink: ～笔作书 dip the writing brush in ink to begin a work of calligraphy

跐 cǐ ❶ 为了支持身体用脚踩;踏 step on sth. to steady the body; stamp: ～着门槛儿 stand on the threshold ❷ (脚尖着地)抬起

脚后跟 stand on tiptoe：～着脚往前头看 stand on tiptoe in order to see farther

☞ cī on p.315

鲨 cí 鱼类的一属，体侧扁，上颌骨向后延长，有的可达臀鳍。生活在近海。ratmouth barbel (*Ptychidio jordani Myers*) sea fish living in coastal waters, with a laterally flat body and an upper jaw extending to the anal fin

cì（ㄘˋ）

次 cì ❶ 次序；等第 order; ranking：名～ ranking; place in a sequence｜座～seating arrangement｜车～ train number｜依～前进 march forward in sequence ❷ 次序在第二的；副的 second; next：～子 second son｜～日 next day ❸ 质量差；品质差 sub-standard; inferior quality：～品 sub-standard products｜这个人太～，一点也不讲究社会公德。This guy is really bad. He has practically no sense of social morality. ❹ 酸根或化合物中少含两个氧原子的 hypo-;（of acid radicals or compounds）with two fewer oxygen atoms than standard：～氯酸 hypochlorous acid ❺〈量词 *classifier*〉用于反复出现或可能反复出现的事情［used for repeated occurrences or likely to be repeated events］occurrence; time：第一～国内革命战争 First Revolutionary Civil War｜我是初～来北京。This is my first visit to Beijing.｜试验了十八～才成功。Success came only after 18 tests. ❻〈书 *fml.*〉出外远行时停留的处所 resting place on a journey：途～ traveller's lodging｜旅～lodging (on a trip); hotel｜舟～ berth on a boat ❼〈书 *fml.*〉中间 in the midst of：胸～in one's heart; mind｜言～ in one's own words or remarks ❽（Cì）姓 a surname

【次大陆】cìdàlù 面积比洲小，在地理上或政治上有某种程度独立性的陆地。如喜马拉雅山把印度、巴基斯坦、孟加拉地区和亚洲其他部分分割开，在地理上形成一个独立的单元，称为'南亚次大陆'。subcontinent; land mass smaller than a continent, with a certain degree of independence geographically or politically. For example, the South Asian subcontinent, consisting of India, Pakistan and Bangladesh, is separated from the rest of Asia by the Himalayas to become a self-contained independent geographical unit

【次等】cìděng 第二等 second-class; second-rate; inferior：～货 inferior goods

【次第】cìdì ❶ same as 次序 cìxù ❷ 一个挨一个地 one after another：～入座 take seats one after another

【次货】cìhuò 质量较低的货 inferior goods; sub-standard commodities

【次贫】cìpín 贫穷的程度比赤贫较低的 poor but not destitute

【次品】cìpǐn 不符合质量标准的产品 sub-standard products; defective goods; shoddy products; seconds

【次日】cìrì 第二天 next day：～起程 leave the next day

【次生】cìshēng 第二次生成的；间接造成的；派生的 secondary; derivative; sub-：～林 second growth｜～矿物 secondary mineral｜～灾害 second-level disaster

【次生林】cìshēnglín 原有森林经采伐或破坏后又自然恢复起来的森林 second growth; secondary forest; naturally recovered forest after being cut down or destroyed

【次声波】cìshēngbō 低于人能听到的最低频(20赫兹)的声波。次声波在传播过程中衰减很小，可用来预测风暴、地震和探矿等。infrasonic sound; infrasonic wave, sound waves with frequencies below the minimum (20Hz) people can hear. As it decreases little in the course of transmission, it can be used to forecast storms and earthquakes and locate mineral deposits.

【次数】cìshù 动作或事件重复出现的回数 number of times or occurrences; frequency：练习的～越多，熟练的程度越高。The more you practise, the more skilful you'll become.

【次序】cìxù 事物在空间或时间上排列的先后 order; sequence：按照～入场 enter in proper order｜这些文件已经整理过，不要把～弄乱了。These papers have been put into order. Please keep them in place.

【次要】cìyào 重要性较差的 less important; secondary; subordinate; minor：～地位 position of less importance｜内容是主要的，形式是～的，形式要服从内容。Form is subordinate to and must comply with content.

【次韵】cìyùn 按原诗的韵及韵脚次序和(hè)诗 use the rhyme sequence of a poem when responding to it; also 步韵 bù//yùn

伺 cì［伺候］(cì·hou) 在人身边供使唤，照料饮食起居 wait upon sb.; serve：～病人 take care of a patient

☞ sì on p.1823

刺 cì ❶ 尖的东西进入或穿过物体 stab; prick; pierce; thrust：～伤 stab and wound｜～绣 embroider ❷ 刺激 irritate; stimulate：～耳 harsh; grating on the ear ❸ 暗杀 assassinate：遇～be assassinated｜被～be assassinated ❹ 侦探；打听 detect; pry; spy：～探 make secret enquiries ❺ 讽刺 criticize：讥～ ridicule; satirize ❻（～儿 cìr）尖锐像针的东西 thorn; splinter：鱼～fish bone｜手上扎了个～ get a thorn (splinter) in one's hand ◇话里别带～儿。Take the sting out of your words. ❼〈书 *fml.*〉名片 visiting card：名～ visiting card

☞ cī on p.314

【刺柏】cìbǎi ☞ 桧 guì on p. 735

【刺刺不休】cì cì bù xiū 说话没完没了；唠叨 talk incessantly; chatter on and on; chatter like a magpie; gabble on and on; repeat endlessly; keep on clamouring; run off at the mouth; talk one's head off; talk a leg off a donkey

【刺刀】cìdāo 枪刺 bayonet

【刺耳】cì'ěr 声音尖锐、杂乱或言语尖酸刻薄，使人听着不舒服 jangling; grating on the ear; irritating (unpleasant) to the ear; jarring; ear-piercing; harsh: ～的刹车声 screeching of a car braking | 他这话听着有点儿～。What he said sounds a bit too sarcastic.

【刺骨】cìgǔ 寒气侵人入骨，形容极冷 piercing to the bone; cut to the bone; piercing; biting: 寒风～。The cold wind chills one to the bone.

【刺槐】cìhuái 落叶乔木，枝上有刺，羽状复叶，花白色，有香气，结荚果 locust (tree) (*Robinia pseudoacacia*); tall deciduous tree with thorny branches, pinnately compound leaves, drooping racemes of white fragrant flowers, and pods; also 洋槐 yánghuái

【刺激】cìjī ❶ 现实的物体和现象作用于感觉器官的过程；声、光、热等引起生物体活动或变化的作用 stimulation; stimulus; incitation; incitement; fillip; stimulation of sensory end organs by material things and phenomena through which activity is evoked; sound, light, heat, etc., that produces a temporary increase of physiological activity in an organism or in any of its parts ❷ 推动事物，使起积极的变化 give fillip to; stimulate; goad; excite; animate; whet; encourage; urge on: ～食欲 whet one's appetite | ～生产力的发展 stimulate the development of productivity ❸ 使人激动；使人精神上受到挫折或打击 excite; provoke; irritate; upset: 多年的收藏毁于一旦，对他～很大。He was terribly upset after his collection of many years was destroyed overnight.

【刺客】cìkè 用武器进行暗杀的人 assassin; murderer (who kills with a weapon)

【刺目】cìmù same as 刺眼 cìyǎn

【刺挠】cì·nao〈方 *dial.*〉很痒 itchy: 有好些天没洗澡了，身上～得很。I haven't had a shower for days and am itching all over.

【刺配】cìpèi〈古代 *arch.*〉在犯人脸上刺字，并发配到边远地方，叫做刺配 tattoo the face of a criminal and send him into exile

【刺儿话】cìrhuà 讥讽人的话 scathing or sarcastic remarks; biting words; vinegary remarks: 说～speak sarcastically; carry a sting in one's words

【刺儿头】cìrtóu〈方 *dial.*〉遇事刁难，不好对付的人 fastidious person; fault-finder; person who is hard to deal with; hard nut to crack

【刺杀】cìshā ❶ 用武器暗杀 assassinate; kill sb. (esp. an important politician, ruler) treacherously and violently: 被人～be assassinated ❷ 用上了枪刺的步枪同敌人拼杀的技术 bayonet charge: 练～practise bayonetting

【刺丝】cìsī 腔肠动物刺细胞内丝状的管子，捕食或自卫时立刻射出来，刺入对方体内并分泌毒液 ecthoraeum; stinging thread; thread-like tube in the nematocysts of coelenterates which, in times of preying and self-defence, projects from the cells, penetrates into the body of the prey or offender, and secretes venom

【刺探】cìtàn 暗中打听 make indirect or secret enquiries; detect; pry; spy: ～军情 spy out military secrets; gather military intelligence

【刺猬】cì·wei 哺乳动物，头小，四肢短，身上有硬刺。昼伏夜出，吃昆虫、鼠、蛇等，对农业有益。hedgehog (*Erinaceus europaeus*); nocturnal mammal with a small head, short limbs and sharp spines standing out from its back, being beneficial to agriculture as it feeds on insects, rats and snakes; also 猬 wèi

【刺细胞】cìxìbāo 腔肠动物身体表面的一种特殊细胞，内有刺丝，外有刺针，是捕食和自卫的器官 cnidoblast; nematocyst; trichocyst; nettle cell; stinging cell; sting cell; special type of cell for preying and self-defence on the surface of coelenterates with trichites inside and aculeus outside

【刺绣】cìxiù ❶ 手工艺的一种，用彩色丝线在纺织品上绣出花鸟、景物等 type of hand-embroidered ornamental cloth with needlework of colourful flowers, birds and scenes ❷ 刺绣工艺的产品，如苏绣、湘绣等 embroidery; embroidered needlework, such as Suzhou embroidery and Hunan embroidery

【刺眼】cìyǎn ❶ 光线过强，使眼睛不舒服 dazzling; (of light) too bright to see clearly ❷ 惹人注意并且使人感觉不顺眼 offensive to the eye; hard to look at: 他这身大红大绿的穿戴，显得特别～。He is loudly dressed in bright red and green.

【刺痒】cì·yang 痒 itchy: 蚊子咬了一下，很～。This mosquito bite is very itchy.

【刺针】cìzhēn 腔肠动物刺细胞外面的针状物，是感觉器官 aculeus; acicular sense organ on the surface of the nematocysts of coelenterates

【刺字】cì//zì 在皮肤上刺文字，古代特指在罪犯脸上刺文字 tattoo the skin with characters; (in ancient times) brand a criminal by tattooing

佽 cì〈书 *fml.*〉帮助 help; aid: ～助 help

赐 cì ❶〈旧指 *old*〉地位高的人或长辈把财物送给地位低的人或晚辈 (sb. of higher status or of an older generation) grant (confer, bestow) properties to (sb. of lower status or of a younger generation)：～予 grant ❷ 敬称别人对自己的指示、光顾、答复等 favour; grant; reply：～教 grant instruction | ～顾 favour me with a visit | 请即～复。Please favour me with an early reply. ❸ 〈敬辞 *pol.*〉指所受的礼物 gift; present：厚～受之有愧。I feel unworthy of the precious gift you have bestowed on me.

【赐教】cìjiào 〈敬辞 *pol.*〉给予指教 condescend to teach; grant instruction：不吝～please favour (or enlighten) me with your instruction; be so kind as to give me a reply

【赐予】cìyǔ 赏给 grant; bestow; confer：～爵位 confer a title of nobility; also 赐与 cìyǔ

cōng (ㄘㄨㄥ)

匆(悤、怱) cōng 急；忙 hastily; hurriedly：～忙 hurriedly | ～促 in a hurry

【匆匆】cōngcōng 急急忙忙的样子 hurriedly; in a rush; in haste：来去～come and go in a hurry | 行色～be in a rush getting ready for a journey

【匆卒】cōngcù same as 匆猝 cōngcù

【匆促】cōngcù 匆忙；仓促 hastily; in a hurry：因为动身的时候太～了，把稿子忘在家里没带来。Since we set out too hastily, I forgot to take my draft with me.

【匆猝】cōngcù same as 匆促 cōngcù; also 匆卒 cōngcù

【匆遽】cōngjù 〈书 *fml.*〉急忙；匆促 hastily, hurriedly：神色～ wearing a hurried look

【匆忙】cōngmáng 急急忙忙 in haste; in a hurry：临行～，没能来看你。I left in such a hurry that I didn't have time to visit you. | 他刚放下饭碗，又匆匆忙忙地回到车间去了。Immediately after he finished eating, he hurried back to the workshop.

苁(蓯) cōng [苁蓉] (cōngróng) 草苁蓉和肉苁蓉的统称。desert cistanche (*Cistanche deserticola*), general name for broomrage (*Boschniakia rossica*), and cistanche salsa (*Saline cistanche*)

囱 cōng ☞ 烟囱 yāncōng on p. 2199

玐(瑽) cōng [玐琮] (cōngróng) 〈书 *fml.*〉〈拟声词 *onom.*〉形容佩玉相碰的声音 tinkling of jade

枞(樅) cōng 冷杉 fir
☞ zōng on p. 2553

鏦(鏦) cōng 古兵器，短矛 short spear (a weapon used in ancient times)

【鏦鏦】cōngcōng 〈书 *fml.*〉〈拟声词 *onom.*〉形容金属相击的声音 tinkling of metal

葱 cōng ❶ 多年生草本植物，叶子圆筒形，中间空，鳞茎圆柱形，开小白花，种子黑色。是普通蔬菜或调味品。shallot (*Allium ascalonicum*); Chinese green onion; fistulous onion; perennial herbal plant with hollow tubular leaves, an edible rounded bulb, small white flowers and black seeds, commonly used as a vegetable or seasoning ❷ 青色 green：～翠 fresh green | ～绿 light green

【葱白】cōngbái 最浅的蓝色 very light blue

【葱白儿】cōngbáir 葱的茎 scallion stalk

【葱葱】cōngcōng 草木苍翠茂盛的样子 (of grass and trees) verdant：郁郁～ lush and green | 松柏～ verdant pines and cypresses

【葱翠】cōngcuì (草木)青翠 (of plants) fresh green; luxuriantly green：群山～fresh green mountains | ～的竹林 green bamboo grove

【葱花】cōnghuā (～儿 cōnghuār)切碎的葱，用来调味 chopped green onion (to add flavour)

【葱茏】cōnglóng (草木)青翠茂盛 (of plants) verdant; luxuriantly green：林木～luxuriant vegetation | 春天来了，大地一片～。When spring comes, the earth is covered in verdure.

【葱绿】cōnglǜ ❶ 浅绿而微黄的颜色 pale yellowish green; light green; verdant; leek-green; also 葱心儿绿 cōngxīnrlǜ ❷ (草木)青翠 (of plants) verdant：～的田野 verdant fields | 雨后的竹林更加～可爱。The bamboo grove after the rain looks all the more verdant and lovely.

【葱头】cōngtóu 洋葱 onion

【葱郁】cōngyù same as 葱茏 cōnglóng：～的松树林 verdant pine forest

骢 cōng 〈书 *fml.*〉毛色青白相间的马 piebald; type of horse with black and white spots

璁 cōng 〈书 *fml*〉像玉的石头 jade-like stone; jadeite

聪(聰) cōng ❶〈书 *fml.*〉听觉 faculty of hearing：左耳失～become deaf in the left ear ❷ 听觉灵敏 acute hearing：耳～目明 able to see and hear clearly ❸ 聪明；心思敏捷 intelligent; quick-witted：～慧 smart | ～颖 clever

【聪慧】cōnghuì 聪明；有智慧 smart; wise; intelligent：～过人 far surpass others in intelligence; be exceptionally bright

【聪敏】cōngmǐn 聪明敏捷 intelligent and quick-witted; smart：天资～ born intelligent and smart

【聪明】cōng·míng 智力发达，记忆和理解能力强 clever; intelligent; quick in learning and comprehension：这个孩子既～又用功，学习上进步很快。The child is smart and hardworking, and has made rapid progress in his studies.

【聪悟】cōngwù 〈书 *fml.*〉聪明；颖悟 clever and quick on the uptake

【聪颖】cōngyǐng 〈书 *fml.*〉聪明 bright; clever

熜 cōng〈书 *fml.*〉❶ 微火 slow fire ❷ 热气 steam; heat

cóng(ㄘㄨㄥˊ)

从[1](從) cóng(⑤⑥⑦旧读 formerly pronounced zòng)❶ 跟随 follow:～征 go on a military expedition ❷ 顺从;听从 comply with; obey:胁～ intimidate sb. into obedience|力不～心 have the will but not the strength ❸ 从事;参加 join; be engaged in:～艺 take up art (as a profession)|～军 join the army; enlist ❹ 采取某种方针或态度 in a certain manner; according to a certain principle:～缓办理 postpone working on sth.|一切～简 dispense with all unnecessary formalities|坦白～宽,抗拒～严。Leniency towards those who confess their crimes and severe punishment to those who refuse to do so. *or* Those who own up are leniently treated, and those who don't are severely punished|其余～略。The rest are omitted here. ❺ 跟随的人 follower; retainer:随～ attendant; retinue|侍～ servant ❻ 从属的;次要的 secondary; accessory:主～ principal and subordinate|～犯 accessory to a crime ❼ 堂房(亲属) relationship between cousins, etc., of the same paternal grandfather, great-grandfather or an earlier common ancestor; of the same clan:～兄 elder male cousin (on the paternal side)|～叔 uncle (father's younger male cousin) ❽(Cóng) 姓 a surname
〈古 *arch.*〉also same as 纵 zòng in 纵横 zònghéng

从[2](從) cóng ❶〈介词 *prep.*〉起于,'从…'表示'拿…做起点' from (a time, a place, or a point of view):～上海到北京 from Shanghai to Beijing|～这儿往西 go west from here|～现在起 from now on|～不懂到懂 from ignorance to enlightment|～无到有 grow out of nothing|～少到多 from few to abundance ❷〈介词 *prep.*〉表示经过,用在表示处所的词语前面 via, through, or past (a place):～窗缝里往外望 peep outside through a crevice in the window|你～桥上过,我～桥下走。You go over the bridge, and I'll go under it.|～他们前面经过 pass in front of them ❸〈副词 *adv.*〉从来,用在否定词前面 [followed by a negative] ever:～没有听说过 never heard of it|～未看见中国人民像现在这样意气风发,斗志昂扬。The Chinese people have never before been seen to exude such vigour and high spirits.

【从长计议】cóng cháng jì yì 慢慢儿地多加商量。指不急于做出决定。give the matter further thought and discussion; take one's time in reaching a decision

【从此】cóngcǐ 从这个时候起 from this time onwards; from now on; from then on; henceforth; thereupon:这条铁路全线通车,～交通就更方便了。Ever since the whole railway line was opened to traffic, travel has been much more convenient.

【从打】cóngdǎ〈方 *dial.*〉自从 since; ever since:～小张来后,我们的文体活动活跃多了。Cultural and sports activities have increased greatly since Xiao Zhang came.

【从动】cóngdòng 由其他零件带动的 driven (by other parts); slave:～轮 driven pulley; driven wheel; engaged wheel

【从而】cóng'ér〈连词 *conj.*〉上文是原因、方法等,下文是结果、目的等;因此就 (connecting reasons, methods, etc., with results, purposes, etc.) thus; thereby; hence:由于交通事业的迅速发展,～为城乡物资交流提供了更为有利的条件。The transportation system has developed rapidly, thus providing better conditions for the exchange of produce between the city and the countryside.

【从犯】cóngfàn 在共同犯罪中,帮助主犯实行犯罪的起次要作用的罪犯(区别于'主犯' as compared with 'principal') accessory; accessory criminal; accessory offender; person joining in or contributing to a crime, but not as the main perpetrator

【从简】cóngjiǎn 采取简单的办法或方式(办理) conform to the principle of simplicity; be simple; forgo the formalities:手续～simplify procedures|仪式～dispense with unnecessary formalities

【从教】cóngjiào 从事教育工作 teach; engage in teaching:他～近半个世纪,如今是桃李满天下。He has been teaching for nearly half a century and has students throughout the country.

【从井救人】cóng jǐng jiù rén 跳到井里去救人。原来比喻徒然危害自己而对别人并没有好处的行为,现多用来比喻冒极大的危险去拯救别人。jump into a well to save a drowning person — risk one's own life or compromise one's own interests without doing others any good; (now oft. fig.) take great risk to save others

【从军】cóngjūn 参加军队 join the army; enlist; enter the services:少小～ join the army at a young age

【从来】cónglái 从过去到现在 from the past till the present; always; at all times; all along:他～不失信。He never breaks his promises.|这种事我～没听说过。I've never heard of such a thing before.

【从良】cóng//liáng 指妓女脱离卖身的生活而嫁人(of a prostitute) get married and start a new life

【从轮】cónglún 机车或其他机械上,由动轮带动的轮子 trailing wheel; driven wheel, wheel driven by a driving wheel on locomotives or other machines

【从略】cónglüè 省去某些部分不说；省略 omit; be omitted：具体办法～。Detailed procedures are omitted here.

【从命】cóngmìng 听从吩咐 do sb.'s bidding; comply with sb.'s wish; obey an order：欣然～gladly comply with sb.'s wish｜恭敬不如～。It's better to accept deferentially than to decline courteously (in accepting gifts, etc.). *or* It's better to do as sb. asks instead of standing on ceremony. *or* Obedience is a better way of showing respect than outward reverence.

【从前】cóngqián 过去的时候；以前 before; formerly; in the past：想想～悲惨遭遇，更加感到今天生活的幸福美满。Recalling our miserable life in the past, we more keenly feel the happiness we enjoy now.｜～的事儿，不必再提了。Let bygones be bygones.

【从权】cóngquán 采用权宜的手段 as a matter of expediency：～处理 do what is expedient

【从戎】cóngróng〈书 *fml.*〉参加军队 join the army; enlist; enter the services：投笔～ throw aside the writing brush and join the army; renounce the pen for the sword

【从容】cóngróng（旧读 formerly pronounced cōngróng）❶ 不慌不忙；镇静；沉着 calm; unhurried; leisurely：举止～ deport oneself in a calm, unhurried manner｜～不迫 calm and unhurried｜～就义（毫不畏缩地为正义而牺牲）go to one's death unflinchingly; meet one's death like a hero; fearlessly die a martyr; meet death with great composure; tread the path of virtue calmly ❷（时间或经济）宽裕 (of time or financial status) plentiful; sufficient; enough：时间很～，可以仔仔细细地做。There's plenty of time for you to work on it very carefully.｜手头～ be quite well off; be not short of money; have enough money to spare

【从容不迫】cóng róng bù pò 非常镇静、不慌不忙的样子 take it leisurely; take one's time; go easy; in easy stages; calm and unhurried; self-possessed; in a leisurely manner; calmly; confidently and without haste：他满脸挂笑，～地走上了讲台。(He) took the rostrum composed and steady with a smiling face.

【从善如流】cóng shàn rú liú 形容能很快地接受别人的好意见，像水从高处流到低处一样自然 follow what is right as a stream follows its course; readily accept good advice; follow correct opinions or well-intentioned advice as naturally as water flows swiftly and smoothly downward

【从师】cóngshī 跟师傅（学习）follow a teacher or a master：～习艺 follow a master to learn a craft

【从实】cóngshí 按真实情况；如实 in the light of the fact (that ...); based on the fact：～回答 answer honestly (frankly)

【从事】cóngshì ❶ 投身到（事业中去）pursue; go in for; devote oneself to; throw oneself into; work on; occupy oneself with; take part in; go about; take up; be engaged in; be bound up in：～革命 devote oneself to revolutionary work｜～文艺创作 engage in literary and artistic creation ❷（按某种办法）处理 (in certain way) deal with：军法～ deal with according to military law; court-martial sb.

【从属】cóngshǔ 依从；附属 subordinate; dependent：～关系 relationship of subordination; affiliation

【从俗】cóngsú ❶ 按照风俗习惯；遵循通常做法 follow local custom; follow tradition; conform to convention：～办理 proceed according to local customs｜～就简 conform to conventions while adhering to the principle of simplicity ❷ 指顺从时俗 follow what the majority are doing：～浮沉experience ups and downs like most people do; live an ordinary life without much of a struggle to better one's situation

【从速】cóngsù 赶快；赶紧 as soon as possible; without delay：～处理 deal with the matter as soon as possible; settle the matter quickly｜存货不多，欲购～。Buy now, while they last.

【从头】cóngtóu（～儿 cóngtóur）❶ 从最初（做）from the beginning; from scratch：～儿做起 start from the very beginning ❷ 重新（做）afresh; anew; once again：～儿再来 start afresh; start all over again

【从先】cóngxiān〈方 *dial.*〉same as 从前 cóngqián：他身体比～结实多了。He's much stronger than before.

【从小】cóngxiǎo（～儿 cóngxiǎor）从年纪小的时候 from childhood; as a child：他～就爱运动。He has been a sports fan from childhood.

【从心所欲】cóng xīn suǒ yù same as 随心所欲 suí xīn suǒ yù

【从新】cóngxīn same as 重新 chóngxīn

【从刑】cóngxíng 随附主刑的刑罚，包括罚金、剥夺政治权利和没收财产三种（这几种刑罚也可单独施用）accessory penalty; accessory punishment, penalties including fines, deprivation of political rights and confiscation of property (which can also be imposed separately) that are imposed together with a principal punishment; also 附加刑 fùjiāxíng

【从业】cóngyè 从事某种职业或行业；就业 obtain employment; take up an occupation; get a job：～机会 job opening (offer)｜～人员 the employed

【从业员】cóngyèyuán 商业工作人员和服务性行业工作人员的统称 general term for employees of commercial and service industries

【从艺】cóngyì 从事艺术事业(多指表演艺术 mostly performing arts) take up art (as a profession); engage in artistic work

【从影】cóngyǐng 从事电影事业(多指当演员 mostly as actor or actress) take part in the motion picture industry

【从优】cóngyōu 给予优待 preferential treatment:价格~ at special or bargain prices

【从征】cóngzhēng 随军出征 go on a military expedition

【从政】cóngzhèng 参政;进入政界(多指做官) go into politics; take up a government post

【从中】cóngzhōng 在其间;在其中 out of; from among; therefrom:~取利 reap profits from; profit from; cash in on; seek one's own gain out of|~作梗 place obstacles in the way; come between; create difficulties; hinder sb. from carrying out a plan; make things difficult for sb.; put a spoke in sb.'s wheel

【从众】cóngzhòng 指按多数人的意见或流行的做法(行事) follow the crowd; follow majority opinion or prevalent practices

丛(叢、樷) cóng ❶ 聚集 crowd together:~生 grow thickly|~集 crowd together ❷ 生长在一起的草木 clump; thicket; grove:草~a patch of grass|树~a clump of trees; grove ❸ 泛指聚集在一起的人或东西 crowd; collection:人~a crowd of people|论~a collection of essays; collected essays|刀~剑树 forest of bayonets and swords — very dangerous situation ❹(Cóng) 姓 a surname

【丛残】cóngcán〈书 *fml.*〉指琐碎的逸闻、遗事 trivial anecdotes and incidents of ages past:掇拾~ collect trivial and historical anecdotes

【丛脞】cóngcuǒ〈书 *fml.*〉细碎;烦琐 trivial; trifling

【丛集】cóngjí ❶(许多事物)聚集在一起 crowd together; pile up; converge:百感~all sorts of feelings welling up|诸事~。Things are piling up. ❷ 选取若干种书或其中的一些篇章汇集编成的一套书 collected writings; selected books or articles on a common topic that are published as a series

【丛刊】cóngkān 丛书(多用做丛书的名称 oft. used in series titles) series of books; collection:《四部~》*Collected Writings of Four Basic Branches of Literature*

【丛刻】cóngkè 刻板印刷的丛书(多用做丛书名称 oft. used in series titles) block-printing series

【丛林】cónglín ❶ 茂密的树林 jungle; forest:热带~tropical forest ❷ 和尚聚集修行的处所,泛指大寺院。后道教也沿用此名 place where Buddhist monks gather and practise their rituals — Buddhist monastery; later adopted by Taoism to refer to a Taoist temple as well

【丛莽】cóngmǎng 大片茂盛的草 large thick growth of grass:密林~dense forest and thick grass; jungle

【丛山】cóngshān 连绵的群山 rolling mountains (hills):~峻岭 undulating high mountains

【丛生】cóngshēng ❶(草木)聚集在一处生长 (of plants) grow thickly; overgrow:杂草~growth of weeds|荆棘~ be infested with brambles ❷(疾病等)同时发生 (of diseases, etc.) break out:百病~ all kinds of diseases and ailments break out|百弊~ all manner of corruption creep in

【丛书】cóngshū 由许多书汇集编成的一套书,如《知不足斋丛书》、《历史小丛书》series of books; collection; series, such as *Collected Books of the Zhibuzu Studio*, *Mini-series of History*

【丛谈】cóngtán 性质相同或相近的若干部分合成的文章或书(多用做篇名或书名 oft. used in book titles) collected writings; essay or book composed of a number of parts that are same or similar in nature:《掌故~》*A Collection of Anecdotes*

【丛杂】cóngzá 多而杂乱 motley:事务~have too many things to attend to

【丛葬】cóngzàng 许多尸体合葬在一起的埋葬方式,也指这样的坟墓 multiple burial; multiple grave

【丛冢】cóngzhǒng〈书 *fml.*〉乱葬在一片地方的许多坟墓 mass of unkept grave mounds

淙 cóng [淙淙]〈拟声词 *onom.*〉流水的声音 gurgling:泉水~ gurgling stream

悰 cóng〈书 *fml.*〉心情;情绪 mood; emotion; feeling:离~grief at parting; feeling of separation; parting sorrows|欢~feeling of joy; happiness; delightfulness

琮 cóng〈古代 *arch.*〉一种玉器,方柱形,中有圆孔 long hollow piece of jade with rectangular sides

【琮琤】cóngchēng 形容玉石撞击的声音,也形容水石相击的声音 jingling sound of jade objects; gurgling sound of a stream:溪水~。The brook gurgles along.

赍 cóng 秦汉间今四川、湖南一带少数民族交纳的赋税名称,交的钱币叫赍钱,交的布匹叫赍布。这一部分民族也因此叫赍人 tax paid by minority groups during the Qin (221 B.C.-A.D. 207) and Han (206B.C.-A.D. 220) dynasties in present-day Sichuan and Hunan provinces; the currency they paid in was called '赍钱'(*cong* money) and the cloth they paid as tax in kind was called '赍布' (*cong* cloth), therefore the people were called '赍人'(*Cong* people)

藂 cóng〈书 *fml.*〉聚集 crowd; gather together

còu (ㄘㄡˋ)

凑(湊) còu ❶ 拼凑;聚集 gather; pool; collect:～钱 pool money; start a fund|～足了人数 gather together enough people; get quorum|大家～到这里来听他讲故事。The folks gathered here to listen to his storytelling. ❷ 碰;赶;趁 happen by chance; take advantage of:～巧 luckily|～热闹 join in the fun ❸ 接近 move close to; press near:往前～～move closer to the front|～到跟前 press near sb. or a place|她拿起一束鲜花～着鼻子闻。She picked a bouquet of fresh flowers and pressed it to her nose to smell it.

【凑搭】còu·da 〈方 *dial.*〉拼凑 rake together; pool

【凑胆子】còu dǎn·zi 〈方 *dial.*〉聚合许多人以壮声势 build up strength by gathering a lot of people

【凑份子】còu fèn·zi ❶ 各人拿出若干钱合起来送礼或办事 pool money to give to sb. as a gift or to achieve sth. ❷〈方 *dial.*〉指添麻烦 add to the trouble

【凑合】còu·he ❶ 聚集 gather together; collect; assemble:下班以后大伙儿都～在一起练习唱歌。We gathered together after work to practise singing. ❷ 拼凑 improvise:预先把发言提纲准备好,不要临时～。Please prepare your speech before coming to the meeting, rather than speak offhand. ❸ 将就 make do; not too bad:没有什么好菜,～着吃点吧。Sorry that the dishes are nothing special. Just make do with them.|这两年日子过得还～。Life wasn't too bad the past two years.

【凑集】còují 凑在一起;聚集 gather together:人烟～be densely populated|～技术力量 pool a technical force

【凑近】còujìn 朝某个目标靠近 get closer; get nearer:他～小王的耳朵,叽里咕噜说了一阵。He whispered something in Xiao Wang's ear.

【凑拢】còulǒng 朝一个地点靠近 get closer:大伙～一点,商量一下明天的工作。Come closer, everybody, to discuss what to do tomorrow.

【凑钱】còu//qián 凑集钱(办某事);筹集款项 pool money; start a fund:大家～买了些图书资料。Everyone chipped in to buy some books and materials.

【凑巧】còuqiǎo 表示正是时候或正遇着所希望的或所不希望的事情 luckily; fortunately; as luck would have it:我正想去找他,～他来了。I was just about to look for him when he showed up.|真不～,我还没有赶到车站,车就开了。What bad luck! The train left just before I got to the station.

【凑趣儿】còu//qùr ❶ 迎合别人的兴趣,使高兴 join in (a game, etc.) just to please others ❷ 逗笑取乐 make a joke about; poke fun at:他跟我很熟,所以故意拿我～。As a close acquaintance, he often pokes fun at me.|没事时姐妹们在一起～。The girls joke around when they have free time together.

【凑热闹】còu rè·nào (～儿 còu rè·nàor) ❶ 到热闹的地方跟大家一起玩儿 join in the fun; take part in the merry-making:孩子们玩得很起劲,我也去凑个热闹。The children are playing with such spirit that I'm going to join in the fun. ❷ 指添麻烦 add trouble to:这里够忙的,别再来～了! We're already busy enough, don't make more trouble for us.

【凑手】còu//shǒu 使用起来方便;顺手(常指手边的钱、物、人等) at hand; within easy reach:这把钳子～。This pair of pliers is easy to use.|钱不～,下次再买吧。I don't have that much money on me; let's buy it next time.

【凑数】còu//shù (～儿 còu//shùr) ❶ 凑足数额 make up the number or amount ❷ 充数 serve as a stopgap:人员要精干,不能随便找几个人～。The employees must be capable and efficient, and not just anyone to fill the vacancies.

【凑整儿】còu//zhěngr 凑成整数 make a round number:这里有九十八元,你再出两元,凑个整儿吧。I've got 98 yuan with me. Please give me two yuan to make a round hundred.

辏 còu 〈书 *fml.*〉车轮的辐集中到毂上 concentrate around one point, as spokes on an axis:～集 crowd together|辐～converge

腠 còu [腠理](còulǐ)〈中医 *Chin. med.*〉指皮肤的纹理和皮下肌肉之间的空隙 space between the texture of skin and the subcutaneous flesh

cū (ㄘㄨ)

粗(觕、麤、麁) cū ❶(条状物)横剖面较大 wide (in diameter); thick (跟'细'相对,②至⑥同 as opposed to 'slender'; applies to ② through ⑥):～纱 low-count yarn|这棵树很～。This tree has a thick trunk. ❷(长条形)两长边的距离不十分近 wide (in breadth); thick:～线条 thick lines|～眉大眼 bushy eyebrows and big eyes ❸ 颗粒大 coarse; crude; rough:～沙 coarse sand; grit ❹ 声音大而低 gruff; husky:嗓门儿～ husky voice|～声～气 deep, gruff voice; coarse, heavy voice ❺ 粗糙 (跟'精'相对 as opposed to 'refined') coarse; rough:去～取精 discard the dross, and select the essential or keep the finer part|这个手工活太～了。This is too sloppy a piece of handicraft. ❻ 疏忽;不周密 careless; negligent:～疏 inattentive|～心大意 careless ❼ 鲁莽;粗野 rude;

unrefined; vulgar: ～暴 rude and violent; rough and hot-tempered | ～话 vulgar language | ～人 roughneck; rough fellow (person) ❽ 略微 roughly; slightly; a little: ～知一二 have a rough idea; know a little about sth. | ～具规模 put roughly into shape

【粗暴】cūbào 鲁莽;暴躁 crude and hot-tempered; rude and violent; rough; savage: 性情～be rude and brutal in temperament

【粗笨】cūbèn ❶ (身材、举止)笨拙;不灵巧(of stature, behaviour) clumsy; unwieldy: 手脚～clumsy in doing things | 那人身高体大,但动作并不～。Tall and strong as the guy is, he is not clumsy in action. ❷ (物体)笨重;不精细 (of objects) unwieldy; heavy; bulky; cumbersome: 这些～家具搬起来挺费劲。It is hard work moving such heavy furniture.

【粗鄙】cūbǐ same as 粗俗 cūsú: 言语～vulgar in speech | 举止～vulgar in behaviour

【粗布】cūbù ❶ 一种平纹棉布,质地比较粗糙 coarse cloth ❷ 土布 hand-woven (hand-loomed) cloth; homespun

【粗糙】cūcāo ❶ (质料)不精细;不光滑 (of texture) coarse; rough; not smooth: 皮肤～rough skin | 这种瓷器比较～,赶不上江西瓷。This type of chinaware is too rough to match that produced in Jiangxi Province. ❷ (工作等)草率;不细致 (of work) careless; inattentive: 这套衣服的手工很～。This suit was badly made.

【粗茶淡饭】cū chá dàn fàn 指简单的、不精的饮食。有时用来形容生活简朴。plain tea and simple food; homely fare; lowly fare; sometimes used figuratively to refer to a simple life

【粗大】cūdà ❶ (人体、物体)粗 (of human body, object) thick and big; bulky: 长年的劳动使他的胳膊～有力。Long years of toil have made his arms thick and strong. | 他跟伙伴抬木头,总是自己抬～的一头。He always takes the heavier side when carrying wood with a partner. ❷ (声音)大 loud: 嗓音～loud voice | 睡在周围的人发出～的鼾声。Those sleeping in the same room with him snored thunderously.

【粗纺】cūfǎng 纺织过程中把棉条纺成粗纱的工序 slub; turn slivers of cotton, wool, etc. into rove (slightly twisted strands in preparation for spinning)

【粗放】cūfàng ❶ 农业上指在同一土地面积上投入较少的生产资料和劳动进行浅耕粗作,用扩大耕地面积的方法来提高产品总量(跟'集约'相对)。这种经营方式叫做粗放经营。extensive farming on large areas of land with minimum outlay and labour, aimed at raising total output by expanding farming acreage (as opposed to 'intensive'). This approach to farming is called extensive operation. ❷ 粗疏;不细致 careless; slipshod: 管理～careless management ❸ 粗犷豪放 coarse and unrestrained; straightforward and uninhibited: ～的笔触 free and unrestrained style of writing or painting | 这部影片在艺术处理上～简练。This film has a straightforward and succinct artistic style.

【粗浮】cūfú 粗暴浮躁 gruff and impetuous; rugged and impulsive: 气质～rugged and impulsive in nature

【粗工】cūgōng ❶ 指技术要求较低、劳动强度较大的工种;粗活 crude work; work with low skill but extensive labour requirements ❷ 壮工 unskilled worker; roustabout

【粗估】cūgū 粗略地估计;毛估 rough estimation: ～这幅画价值千元。This painting is roughly estimated at 1,000 yuan in value.

【粗犷】cūguǎng ❶ 粗野;粗鲁 rough; rude; boorish: ～无理 boorish and unreasonable ❷ 粗豪;豪放 straightforward and uninhibited; bold and unrestrained; rugged: 歌声～sing in a bold and unrestrained manner | ～的笔触 straightforward and uninhibited style of writing

【粗豪】cūháo ❶ 豪爽 forthright; straightforward; generous but paying no attention to niceties: 性情～be straightforward in nature; have an unsophisticated temperament | ～坦率 forthright and candid ❷ 豪壮 raucous; gruff; strident: 汽笛发出～的声音。The siren emits a strident sound.

【粗话】cūhuà 粗俗的话 vulgar language; coarse language, esp. obscene language

【粗活】cūhuó (～儿 cūhuór)指技术性较低、劳动强度较大的工作 heavy manual labour; unskilled work; work that demands little brain but lots of brawn

【粗狂】cūkuáng 粗豪狂放 bold and unruly; forthright and unrestrained: 风格～bold and unrestrained in style

【粗拉】cū·la same as 粗糙 cūcāo: 活儿做得太～。It is a slipshod piece of work.

【粗粝】cūlì ❶ 〈书 *fml.*〉糙米 unpolished rice ❷ same as 粗糙 cūcāo: ～的饭食 simple and coarse food

【粗粮】cūliáng 一般指大米、白面以外的食粮,如玉米、高粱、豆类等(区别于'细粮' as compared with 'refined grain') coarse food grain, e.g. maize, sorghum, millet, etc.

【粗劣】cūliè 粗糙低劣 of poor quality; cheap; shoddy: ～的饭食 shoddily made food | 这套书的插图太～。The illustrations in the book are of very poor quality.

【粗陋】cūlòu ❶ 粗糙,不精美 coarse and crude; simple (living quarters); rash: 陈设～plainly furnished ❷ 粗俗丑陋 ill-mannered and ugly: 面貌～vulgar and ugly in appearance ❸ 粗略

浅陋 sketchy and superficial：那篇评介文章较为～。The review was quite sketchy and superficial.

【粗鲁】cū·lǔ 粗暴鲁莽 rough；rude；impolite；boorish；rash：性格～boorish in disposition｜他是个火性人，说话～，你别介意。He is hot-tempered by nature and has a coarse mouth. Please do not take offence. also 粗卤 cū·lǔ

【粗略】cūlüè 粗粗地；大略；不精确 rough；sketchy；not accurate，not detailed：事先只能做～的估计。We can only make a rough estimate beforehand.｜～地看了看产品的制作过程 take a cursory look at the product's manufacturing process

【粗莽】cūmǎng same as 粗鲁 cū·lǔ：～汉子 boorish man｜性格～have a rough disposition；be rude in temper

【粗浅】cūqiǎn 浅显；不深奥 superficial；shallow；basic；simple；elementary：像这样～的道理是很容易懂的。Such simple truth is easy to understand.

【粗人】cūrén ❶ 鲁莽、不细心的人 boor；rough character ❷ 指没有文化的人(多用作谦辞 oft. used to refer to oneself in courtesy) unrefined person；uneducated person；person of little refinement；person good only at heavy labour

【粗纱】cūshā 纺纱过程中的半成品，供细纺用 roving；ends；textile roving；low-count yarn；material in an intermediate stage between sliver and yarn

【粗实】cū·shi 粗大结实 (of furniture，boxes，etc.) solid；strong：～的腰身 plump and solid waist｜树干长得很～。The tree trunks grow solid and sturdy.

【粗手笨脚】cū shǒu bèn jiǎo 形容手脚粗笨 ham-fisted；all thumbs；clumsy：别看他～的，心眼儿可多呢。Clumsy as he is，he is full of unnecessary misgivings.

【粗疏】cūshū ❶ 不细心；马虎 overlooking details；careless；inattentive：此书校对～，错误很多。This book was carelessly proof-read with many mistakes overlooked. ❷ (毛发、线条等)粗而稀疏(of hair，lines，etc.) sparse：鬃毛～sparse hair (of horses，pigs，etc.)｜线条～few and sparsely drawn lines

【粗率】cūshuài 粗略草率；不精确，不周到 rough and careless；not accurate；rash；ill-considered：文字～thoughtless writing｜言谈～rash talk｜～表态 ill-considered statement

【粗饲料】cū sìliào 营养价值较低的饲料，如秸秆、干草、荚壳等 coarse fodder；roughage；coarse，rough foodstuff with low nutrition，such as straw，dry weeds，pods，etc.

【粗俗】cūsú (谈吐、举止等)粗野庸俗 (of speech，behaviour，etc.) vulgar；coarse

【粗通】cūtōng 略微懂得一些 have a rough idea；know a little：～文墨 possess rudimentary literacy

【粗细】cūxì ❶ 粗细的程度 (degree of) thickness：碗口～的钢管 steel tubes as big as the mouth of a bowl｜这样～的沙子最合适。This coarseness of sand is most suitable. ❷ 粗糙和细致的程度 degree of finish；quality of work：桌面平不平，就看活儿的～。Whether the surface of the table is smooth or not depends on the quality of the work.

【粗线条】cūxiàntiáo ❶ 指笔道画得粗的线条，也指用粗线条勾出的轮廓 thick lines；rough outline ❷〈比喻 *fig.*〉粗率的性格、作风或方法 (of manners，approaches，etc.) rough-and-ready；slapdash；straightforward；having little regard for niceties；frank but without tact ❸〈比喻 *fig.*〉文章等粗略的构思或叙述 (of writing，etc.) sketchy conception or narration

【粗心】cūxīn 疏忽；不细心 careless；thoughtless：～大意 negligent；careless；inadvertent；scatterbrain｜一时～，铸成大错。A moment's carelessness can become a lifelong mistake.

【粗哑】cūyǎ 声音低而沙哑 gruff；hoarse：嗓音～ hoarse voice

【粗野】cūyě 粗鲁；没礼貌 rough；boorish；uncouth；rustic and coarse；unpolished；unrefined：举止～behave boorishly

【粗枝大叶】cū zhī dà yè〈比喻 *fig.*〉做事不细致，不认真 'thick branches and big leaves'—crude and careless (in doing things)；done in broad strokes or rough outline；in a cursory fashion；in a slipshod manner；negligent in one's work；roughly finished；sketchy；sloppy；slapdash

【粗制滥造】cū zhì làn zào 指产品制作粗劣，不讲究质量。也指工作不负责任，草率从事。manufacture in a rough and slipshod way；turn out in quantity without any regard for quality；crudely made；poorly and hastily manufactured

【粗制品】cūzhìpǐn 初步制成的毛坯产品 semi-finished product；blank，metal piece ready to be machined into a finished product

【粗重】cūzhòng ❶ 声音低沉有力 (of voice，etc.) loud and jarring；rough；harsh；gruff：～的嗓音 gruff voice；heavy voice｜～的喘息声 loud gasps ❷ (手或脚)粗大有力 (of limbs) big and strong：～的手 big strong hands ❸ (物体)笨重 big and heavy；bulky：～的东西都留下，只带走细软。Leave behind the heavy things and bring only the valuables. ❹ (条状物)宽而颜色浓 (of long or stick-like objects) thick and heavy：～的笔道儿 powerful strokes｜他的眉毛显得浓黑～。He has bushy black eyebrows. ❺ (工作)繁重费力 strenuous；heavy (work)：～的活儿，他总是

抢先去做。He is always the first to take on heavy work.

【粗壮】cūzhuàng ❶（人体）粗实而健壮（of the human body）thick and sturdy；brawny：身材～ have a brawny（sturdy）figure ❷（物体）粗大而结实（of objects）thick and strong：～的绳子 thick strong cord or rope ❸（声音）大而有力（of voice）deep and resonant

cú（ㄘㄨˊ）

徂 cú〈书 *fml.*〉❶ 往；到 go：自西～东 go from west to east ❷ 过去；逝（of time）pass：岁月其～。Time flies by. *or* The years flowed on. ❸ 开始 begin：六月～暑。June is the beginning of summer. ❹ same as 殂 cú

殂 cú〈书 *fml.*〉死亡 pass away；die

【殂谢】cúxiè〈书 *fml.*〉死亡 pass away；die

cù（ㄘㄨˋ）

卒 cù same as 猝 cù
☞ zú on p.2564

【卒中】cùzhòng 中风 apoplexy

促 cù ❶ 时间短（of time）short；hurried；urgent：短～of very short duration｜急～ hurried；pressing；brief ❷ 催；推动 urge；promote：催～urge；press；hasten｜督～supervise and urge｜～进 promote ❸〈书 *fml.*〉靠近 close to；near：～膝谈心 sit knee to knee for an intimate talk

【促成】cùchéng 推动使成功 help to bring about；facilitate；help to materialize；favour：这件事是他大力～的。It was he whose great efforts brought about this deal.

【促进】cùjìn 促使前进；推动使发展 promote；advance；accelerate；boost；facilitate；encourage；further；gear up：～派 progressive；promoter of progress｜～工作 advance work｜～两国的友好合作 promote friendship and cooperation between the two countries

【促请】cùqǐng 催促并请求 urge and petition：～上级早作决定 urge and petition the higher authorities to make a decision at their earliest convenience

【促声】cùshēng 指入声（跟'舒声'相对 as opposed to 'level tone'）entering tone

【促使】cùshǐ 推动使达到一定目的 precipitate；impel；urge；spur：～发生变化 make changes happen｜～生产迅速发展 promote the rapid development of production

【促膝】cùxī 膝盖对着膝盖，指两人面对面靠近坐着 sit knee to knee；sit close，face-to-face：～谈心 sit side by side and talk intimately；have a heart-to-heart talk；have an intimate chat together；draw close together and chat

【促狭】cùxiá〈方 *dial.*〉刁钻，爱捉弄人 mischievous：～鬼（促狭的人）mischievous person；mischief；practical joker；person who likes to play jokes on others

【促销】cùxiāo 推动商品销售 promote sales：利用广告～promote sales by advertising｜～手段不力 ineffective marketing campaign

【促织】cùzhī 蟋蟀 cricket

猝 cù〈书 *fml.*〉猝然 sudden；abrupt；unexpected：～不及防 be taken by surprise

【猝不及防】cù bù jí fáng 事情突然发生，来不及防备 be caught off guard；be caught unprepared；be taken by surprise；be put off one's guard

【猝尔】cù'ěr〈书 *fml.*〉突然 suddenly；unexpectedly

【猝发】cùfā 突然发作 burst：因过于兴奋，导致心脏病～。He had a heart attack due to overexcitement.

【猝然】cùrán 突然；出乎意外 suddenly；abruptly；unexpectedly：～而至 arrive unexpectedly｜～发问 raise a question abruptly

【猝死】cùsǐ 医学上指不是由于暴力而是由于体内潜在的进行性疾病引起的突然死亡（med.）sudden death because of a progressive disease latent in the body，rather than from violence

酢 cù〈书 *fml.*〉same as 醋 cù
☞ zuò on p.2580

瘄 cù［瘄子］（cù·zi）〈方 *dial.*〉麻疹 measles

蔟 cù 蚕蔟 small bundle of straw，etc.，for silkworms to spin cocoons on：上～spread bundles of straw for silkworms to spin cocoons on；prepare silkworms to spin cocoons

醋 cù ❶ 调味用的有酸味的液体 vinegar；acidic-tasting liquid used as seasoning：米～vinegar｜陈～mature vinegar ❷〈比喻 *fig.*〉嫉妒（多指在男女关系上 usu. in a love affair）jealousy：～意（feeling of）jealousy｜吃～feel jealous

【醋大】cùdà same as 措大 cuòdà

【醋罐子】cùguàn·zi same as 醋坛子 cùtán·zi

【醋劲儿】cùjìnr 嫉妒的情绪（feeling of）jealousy

【醋坛子】cùtán·zi〈比喻 *fig.*〉在男女关系上嫉妒心很强的人 bottle of vinegar；extremely jealous wife or husband；also 醋罐子 cùguàn·zi

【醋心】cù·xīn 胃里发酸 upset stomach；have heartburn

【醋意】cùyì 嫉妒心（多指在男女关系上 usu. of man-woman relationship）jealousy

踧[1] cù〈书 *fml.*〉惊惧不安的样子 timid and unease

踧[2] cù〈书 *fml.*〉same as 蹙 cù

【踧踖】cùjí〈书 *fml.*〉恭敬而不安的样子 in mincing steps or manner as a show of respect

憱 cù〈书 *fml*.〉心里不安的样子 uneasiness of mind

颇 cù〈书 *fml*.〉皱(眉头) knit one's eyebrows; frown

簇 cù ❶ 聚集 form a cluster; pile up:～拥 gather round (sb.) ❷ 聚集成的团或堆 cluster; bouquet; pile:花团锦～bouquets of flowers and piles of brocades; rich multicoloured decorations ❸〈量词 *classifier*〉用于聚集成团成堆的东西 cluster; bunch:一～鲜花 a bunch of flowers

【簇居】cùjū 聚居 live in a community:这里的少数民族多～山区。Minority nationalities here mostly live in compact communities in mountainous areas.

【簇生】cùshēng 植物体或其一部分聚集成团或成堆地生长(of plants, flowers, etc.) grow in clusters

【簇新】cùxīn 极新;全新 brand new:～的大衣 brand new overcoat

【簇拥】cùyōng (许多人)紧紧围着 (of many people) cluster round:孩子们～着老师走进教室。The children walked into the classroom, clustering round their teacher.

蹙 cù〈书 *fml*.〉❶ 紧迫 pressed; cramped:穷～in dire straits ❷ 皱(眉头);收缩 knit (one's brows):～额 frown

【蹙额】cù'é〈书 *fml*.〉皱着眉头,形容愁苦的样子 knit one's brows; frown; miserable looking:疾首～ shake one's head and knit one's brows (in disapproval, etc.)

蹴(蹵) cù〈书 *fml*.〉❶ 踢 kick:～鞠(踢球) play football ❷ 踏 strike the ground with foot; stamp; tread:一～而就 reach a goal in one step; accomplish one's aim in one move

☞ ·jiu on p. 1043

cuān (ㄘㄨㄢ)

氽 cuān ❶ 烹调方法,把食物放到沸水里稍微一煮 quick-boil:～汤 quick-boiled soup|～丸子 quick-boiled meatballs in soup|～黄瓜片 quick-boiled sliced cucumbers ❷〈方 *dial*.〉用氽子放到旺火中很快地把水烧开 boil water quickly by placing a small metal pot on a big fire

【氽子】cuān·zi 烧水用的薄铁筒,细长形,可以插入炉子火口里,使水开得快 small cylindrical metal pot that can be thrust into a fire to boil water quickly

撺(攛) cuān〈方 *dial*.〉❶ 抛掷 throw; fling ❷ 跳入 jump:～入水中 dive into the water ❸ 匆忙地做 do sth. in a hurry:临时现～improvise; do hurriedly at the last moment ❹ 发怒 fly into a rage:他～儿了。He flared up.

【撺掇】cuān·duo 从旁鼓动人(做某事);怂勇 urge; egg on (sb. to do sth.):他一再～我学滑冰。He kept urging me to learn skating.|他说他本来不想做,都是你～他做的。He said he didn't want to do it in the first place, and it was you who egged him on.

【撺弄】cuān·nong same as 撺掇 cuān·duo

镩(鑹) cuān ❶ 一种凿冰工具,头部尖,有倒钩 ice pick; pointed tool with a barb for chipping ice:冰～ice pick ❷ 用冰镩凿(冰) cut or break (ice) with an ice pick:～冰 chip ice with an ice pick

【镩子】cuān·zi 冰镩 ice pick

蹿(躥) cuān ❶ 向上或向前跳 leap up; leap forward:身子往上一～把球接住 leap up and catch the ball|猫～到树上去了。The cat leapt into the tree.|他一下子～得很远。He leaps far in one go. ❷〈方 *dial*.〉喷射 spray; spurt:鼻子～血。Blood spurted from the nose.

【蹿房越脊】cuān fáng yuè jǐ 跳上房顶在上面飞快地走(多见于旧小说 of swordsmen, robbers, etc. in old Chinese novels) leap from roof to roof; jump up onto the roof and run quickly

【蹿个儿】cuān//gèr 身材在较短时间里明显长高 grow notably taller in a short span of time:孩子～了,去年的衣服穿着短了一大截。The kid has shot up, and last year's clothes are much too short for him now.

【蹿火】cuān//huǒ〈方 *dial*.〉冒火 flare up; burn with anger

【蹿腾】cuān·teng〈方 *dial*.〉乱蹦乱跳 jump randomly:大青马一声长嘶,便～开了。The grey horse neighed loudly before jumping away restlessly.

【蹿稀】cuān//xī〈方 *dial*.〉指泻肚 have loose bowels

cuán (ㄘㄨㄢˊ)

攒(欑) cuán 聚拢;拼凑 collect together; assemble:～钱 save up; save money (to do sth.)|他买了各种零件～了一辆自行车。He bought the parts and assembled a bicycle himself.

☞ zǎn on p. 2390

【攒动】cuándòng 拥挤在一起晃动(of a crowd) move to and fro endlessly:街上人头～。The street is a mass of bobbing heads.

【攒盒】cuánhé 一种分层或分格可装多种食品的盒子 a kind of stackable food container to hold many dishes

【攒集】cuánjí same as 攒聚 cuánjù

【攒聚】cuánjù 紧紧地聚集在一起 congregate; gather closely together; huddle together; crowd together:教室前～了许多学生。Many students gathered in front of the classroom.

【攒眉】cuánméi 紧皱双眉 knit the brows：～苦思 knit one's brows and rack one's brains; think hard

【攒三聚五】cuán sān jù wǔ 三三五五，聚在一起 (of people) gather in knots; gather in threes and fours

【攒射】cuánshè (用箭或枪炮)集中射击 fire a volley (of gunshots, arrows, etc.)

C

cuàn (ㄘㄨㄢˋ)

窜(竄) cuàn ❶ 乱跑；乱逃(用于匪徒、敌军、兽类 of gangs, enemy troops, beasts, etc.) flee; scurry：流～flee hither and thither｜抱头鼠～cover the head and scurry away like a rat ❷〈书 *fml.*〉放逐；驱逐 exile; expel ❸ 改动(文字) change (the wording in a text, manuscript, etc.); alter：～改 alter｜点～make some alterations (in wording)

【窜犯】cuànfàn (股匪或小股的敌军)进犯(gang of bandits or a small number of enemies) raid; make an inroad into; invade; intrude into：～边境 invade the border area

【窜改】cuàngǎi 改动(成语、文件、古书等) alter (proverbs, documents, ancient books, etc.); change：～原文 alter the original text

【窜扰】cuànrǎo 窜犯骚扰 invade and harass

【窜逃】cuàntáo 逃窜 flee in disorder; scurry off

篡 cuàn 夺取，多指篡位 usurp; seize (oft. the throne)：～权 usurp power｜王莽～汉 The Usurpation of Power by Wang Mang. Wang Mang was the nephew of the wife of Emperor Yuandi 元帝 and mother of Emperor Chengdi 成帝 of the Western Han Dynasty (206 B.C.-A.D. 24) who rose in power and seized the throne in 8 A.D., establishing a new dynasty which lasted for only 15 years.

【篡夺】cuànduó 用不正当的手段夺取(地位或权力) usurp; seize and hold (a position or power) without legal rights：～领导权 usurp leadership

【篡改】cuàngǎi 用作伪的手段改动或曲解(经典、理论、政策等) distort (classical works, theories, policies, etc.); misrepresent; tamper with; falsify; manipulate

【篡国】cuàn//guó 篡夺国家政权 usurp state power

【篡权】cuàn//quán 篡夺权力(多指政权 usu. political power) usurp power：窃国～usurp state power

【篡位】cuàn//wèi 臣子夺取君主的地位 usurp the throne

爨 cuàn ❶〈书 *fml.*〉烧火煮饭 light the fire and cook：分～have separate kitchens｜分居异～(旧时指弟兄分家过日子) (in former times) divide the household among brothers ❷〈书 *fml.*〉灶 earthen cooking stove：执～cook; prepare meals ❸ (Cuàn) 姓 a surname

cuī (ㄘㄨㄟ)

衰 cuī ❶ ☞ 等衰 děngcuī on p.409 ❷ same as 缞 cuī

☞ shuāi on p.1792

崔 cuī ❶ ☞ 崔巍 cuīwēi and 崔嵬 cuīwéi ❷ (Cuī) 姓 a surname

【崔巍】cuīwēi〈书 *fml.*〉(山、建筑物)高大雄伟 (of mountains, buildings) lofty; towering

【崔嵬】cuīwéi〈书 *fml.*〉❶ 有石头的土山 rocky mound ❷ 高大 high; towering

催 cuī ❶ 叫人赶快行动或做某事 urge sb. to do sth.; hurry; press：图书馆来信，～他还书。The library sent him a letter, urging him to return the books he had borrowed. ❷ 使事物的产生和变化加快 hasten; expedite; speed up：～生 expedite child delivery｜～眠 lull (to sleep)｜～肥 fatten

【催巴儿】cuī·bar〈方 *dial.*〉听人使唤当下手干杂事的人 person who is ordered about to do trivial work or run errands; servant; underling; gofer

【催办】cuībàn 催促办理(某事) urge; press sb. to do sth.：此事已去信～，很快会有答复的。We sent a letter urging them to work on it, and should receive a reply soon.

【催逼】cuībī 催促逼迫 press (for payment of debt, etc.); hasten：～还债 press sb. to pay a debt

【催产】cuī//chǎn 用药物或其他方法使孕妇的子宫收缩，促使胎儿产出 induce labour (using drugs or other means to bring on labour in a pregnant woman); expedite child delivery; hasten parturition; also 催生 cuīshēng

【催促】cuīcù 催 urge; hasten; press; prompt：一再～，他才动身。We had to press him time and again before he set out on his journey.

【催肥】cuīféi 肥育 (animal husbandry) fatten

【催化】cuīhuà 某些物质在化学反应中改变反应速度，而本身的量和化学性质并不改变 catalyse; alter the rate of a chemical reaction through the use of certain substances that remain quantitatively and chemically unchanged

【催化剂】cuīhuàjì 能改变化学反应速度，而本身的量和化学性质并不改变的物质。通常把加速化学反应的物质叫正催化剂，延缓化学反应的物质叫负催化剂。catalyst; catalytic agent; catalyser; catalyte; substance that brings about changes in rates of chemical reaction while itself remaining unchanged quantitatively and chemically; 旧称 formerly called 触媒 chùméi

【催泪弹】cuīlèidàn 装填有催泪性毒剂的弹种。爆炸后强烈刺激眼睛流泪。tear gas; tear-gas grenade; tear-gas cannister; lachrymatory bomb; explosive charged with a solid, liquid or gaseous substance that on dispersion in the atmosphere blinds the eyes with tears but does not damage them

【催眠】cuīmián 对人或动物用刺激视觉、听觉或触觉来引起睡眠状态,对人还可以用言语的暗示引起 lull (to sleep) through hypnotic suggestion; hypnotize; induce (a person or an animal) into a state that resembles normal sleep by stimulating their sense of vision, hearing and touch, and by also verbal suggestion for human subjects

【催眠曲】cuīmiánqǔ 催婴儿入睡时唱的歌 lullaby; cradle song; song to lull babies to sleep

【催眠术】cuīmiánshù 催眠的方法,一般用言语暗示 hypnotism; mesmerism; act or practice of inducing hypnosis

【催命】cuī//mìng 催人死亡 pressure sb. to death;〈比喻 *fig.*〉紧紧地催促 persistently urge or pressure sb.

【催奶】cuī//nǎi 用药品或食物使产妇分泌出乳汁 promote lactation; stimulate the secretion of milk in a new mother through medicine or food

【催迫】cuīpò same as 催逼 cuībī

【催情】cuīqíng 用人工方法促使雌性动物发情 induce oestrus; (animal husbandry) artificially promote the sexual maturity of female animals

【催生】cuī//shēng same as 催产 cuī//chǎn

【催收】cuīshōu same as 催讨 cuītǎo:～货款 press for repayment of a loan

【催讨】cuītǎo 催人归还(债款、实物等) press sb. for repayment of a debt or return of sth. borrowed; dun sb. for repayment of debt; persistently demand repayment or return

缞 cuī 用粗麻布制成的丧服 mourning apparel; funeral garment made of coarse linen cloth

榱 cuī〈书 *fml.*〉same as 椽子 chuán·zi

摧 cuī 折断;破坏 break; destroy:～折 break|～毁 smash|无坚不～ nothing is indestructible; capable of destroying any stronghold

【摧残】cuīcán 使(政治、经济、文化、身体、精神等)蒙受严重损失 wreck; destroy; devastate; ruin; damage; trample; humiliate; wreak severe damage to (politics, economy, culture, body, mind, etc.)

【摧毁】cuīhuǐ 用强大的力量破坏 smash; wreck; knock out; destroy with great force:猛烈的炮火～了敌人的阵地。Intense fire destroyed the enemy ramparts.

【摧枯拉朽】cuī kū lā xiǔ 枯指枯草,朽指烂了的木头 (as easy as) crushing dry weeds and smashing rotten wood; break a dead branch from a tree;〈比喻 *fig.*〉腐朽势力很容易打垮 easily destroy and pull apart sth. already in a state of ruin or decay; crumple sth. like sweeping up dead leaves; tear away a withered stump; make a clean sweep; need no great strength to; easily overcome

【摧眉折腰】cuī méi zhé yāo 形容低头弯腰阿谀逢迎的媚态 bow and scrape; bow unctuously; lower one's eyebrows and bend down — act servilely

【摧陷廓清】cuī xiàn kuò qīng 攻入敌阵,彻底肃清。多比喻清除陈腐言论。defeat and completely wipe out (an enemy); uproot (enemy ramparts, etc.) and clear the ground; (fig.) eradicate outdated opinions

【摧心剖肝】cuī xīn pōu gān 心肝破裂 break one's heart and liver;〈比喻 *fig.*〉极大的悲痛 great sorrow; deep grief; anguish

【摧折】cuīzhé ❶ 折断 break; snap:狂风～幼株。Wild winds broke the saplings. ❷ 挫折 setback; reverse:历尽～,终于回到祖国。After many setbacks, he finally returned to his motherland.

獕 cuī ☞ 猥獕 wěicuī on p. 1997

cuǐ(ㄘㄨㄟˇ)

漼 cuǐ〈书 *fml.*〉❶ 水深的样子 (of water) deep ❷ 涕泪流下的样子 weep appearance

璀 cuǐ [璀璨](cuǐcàn)形容珠玉等光彩鲜明 (of jade, pearl etc.) bright; resplendent:～夺目 dazzling|这座古塔是我国古代建筑史上一颗～的明珠。This pagoda is a resplendent pearl in the history of ancient Chinese architecture.

皠 cuǐ〈书 *fml.*〉洁白 pure white

cuì(ㄘㄨㄟˋ)

倅 cuì〈书 *fml.*〉副;副职 deputy; assistant

脆(脃) cuì ❶ 容易折断破碎(跟'韧'相对 as opposed to 'pliable but strong') fragile; brittle; vulnerable:这种纸不算薄,就是太～。This type of paper is not thin but too fragile. ❷ (较硬的食物)容易弄碎弄裂 (of food) crisp:～枣 crisp date|这瓜又甜又～。The melon is sweet and crisp. ❸ (声音)清脆 (of voice) clear; crisp:她的嗓音挺～。She has a very clear voice. ❹〈方 *dial.*〉说话做事爽利痛快;干脆 neat, clear-cut:这件事办得很～。That was a job neatly done.

【脆骨】cuìgǔ 动物的软骨作为食品时叫脆骨 gristle (as food)

【脆快】cuìkuài〈方 *dial.*〉(说话、做事)干脆爽快;简捷痛快,不拖拉 straightforward; direct; clear-cut:～了当 clear-cut and straightforward|他答应得～。He readily and directly agreed.|他办起事来总是那么～。He always gets things done quickly and neatly.

【脆亮】cuìliàng (声音)清脆响亮 (of sound or voice) clear and sharp

【脆弱】cuìruò 禁不起挫折;不坚强 brittle; fragile; frail; weak; tender:感情～be easily upset|～的心灵 fragile heart

【脆生】cuì·sheng〈方 *dial.*〉❶(食物)脆 (of food) crisp:凉拌黄瓜,又～又爽口。Cold cucumbers in sauce are crisp and refreshing. ❷(声音)清脆 (of sound or voice) clear and sharp:这炮仗的声音可真～。The noise of the firecrackers is quite sharp.

【脆性】cuìxìng 物体受拉力或冲击时,容易破碎的性质。玻璃、生铁、砖、石都是脆性物质。brittleness; fragility; tendency to break or snap easily with pulling or impact. Glass, unrefined iron, brick and stone are all brittle materials.

【脆枣】cuìzǎo〈方 *dial.*〉(～儿 cuìzǎor)焦枣 crisp dates

萃 cuì〈书 *fml.*〉❶聚集 come together; assemble:荟～ assemble ❷聚在一起的人或物 gathering of people or a collection of objects; regiment:出类拔～be far above the average; outstanding ❸(Cuì)姓 a surname

【萃聚】cuìjù〈书 *fml.*〉聚集 gather; assemble:群英～ congregation of heroes of our times

【萃取】cuìqǔ 在混合物中加入某种溶剂,利用混合物的各种成分在该溶剂中溶解度不同而将它们分离。如在含有硝酸铀酰的水溶液中加入乙醚,硝酸铀酰就从水中转入乙醚中而杂质仍留在水中。extract; exhaust; dissolve a mixture in a solvent so as to separate its ingredients through their varying degrees of solubility. For example, add diethyl ether in the solution with uranyl nitrate, and uranyl nitrate will dissolve into diethyl ether, while foreign substances remain in the water.

啐 cuì ❶用力从嘴里吐出来 spit; expectorate:～了一口唾沫 expectorate some spittle ❷〈叹词 *interj.*〉表示唾弃、斥责或辱骂 [expressing scorn, reproach or disgust] bah; pah; phooey:呀～!休要胡说!(多见于早期白话 oft. in early vernacular) Hey! Stop that nonsense!

淬(焠) cuì same as 淬火 cuì//huǒ

【淬火】cuì//huǒ 把金属工件加热到一定温度,然后浸入冷却剂(油、水等)急速冷却,以增加硬度 quench; temper (a metal workpiece) by dipping in water, oil, etc., to harden it; 通称 generally called 蘸火 zhàn//huǒ

悴 cuì〈书 *fml.*〉❶忧伤 depressed in appearance; sorrowful:愁～ laden with grief; weighed down with sorrow ❷衰弱不振 weary, thin and drawn

綷 cuì〈书 *fml.*〉五色相杂;合 multicoloured; motley

【綷縩】cuìcài〈书 *fml.*〉〈拟声词 *onom.*〉行动时衣服磨擦的声音 rustling sound:华妆～ dressed nobly with rich ornamentation

毳 cuì〈书 *fml.*〉鸟兽的细毛 down; lanugo; fine soft hair on birds or animals

【毳毛】cuìmáo 医学上指除头发、阴毛、腋毛以外,其他部位所生的细毛 (med.) lanugo; fine soft hair other than that grown on one's head, pubes and armpits

瘁 cuì 过度劳累 overworked; exhausted:鞠躬尽～bend one's body and exhaust one's energy — spare no effort in the performance of one's duty; devote oneself entirely to sth.; tire oneself out in official duties; work with utter devotion; give oneself entirely to public duties; use the last (remnant) of one's strength|心力交～be mentally and physically exhausted; be utterly fatigued both mentally and physically; be utterly fatigued in mind and body; both the mind and strength were worn out

顇 cuì ☞[颠顇](qiáocuì) on p.1550

粹 cuì〈书 *fml.*〉❶纯粹 pure:～白 pure white|～而不杂 pure and unadulterated ❷精华 essence; best:精～essence; quintessence

【粹白】cuìbái〈书 *fml.*〉❶纯粹 pure ❷纯白 pure white:～之裘 pure-white fur coat

翠 cuì ❶翠绿色 emerald green; green:～竹 green bamboo|～玉 blue jade|～鸟 kingfisher (*Alcedo atthis*) ❷指翡翠① kingfisher:点～(用翡翠鸟的羽毛来做装饰的手工工艺) handicraft using kingfisher feathers for ornamentation ❸指翡翠② jadeite:珠～pearls and jade jewellery|～花 jadeite flower; flower made with kingfisher feathers

【翠绿】cuìlǜ 像翡翠那样的绿色 emerald green; jade green; viridity; bluish green:满山～ mountain covered with jade green trees and grass|～的松林 viridian pine forest

【翠生生】cuìshēngshēng (～的 cuìshēngshēng·de)形容植物青翠鲜嫩 (of plants) fresh and green:～的秧苗 fresh green rice seedlings

【翠微】cuìwēi 青绿的山色,也泛指青山 (of mountains) verdant; lush and green; (in a broad sense) green mountains; green hills

膵(脺) cuì [膵脏](cuìzàng)胰的旧称 old name for pancreas

cūn（ㄘㄨㄣ）

村（❶邨）cūn ❶（～儿 cūnr）村庄；泛指人口聚居的地方 village; hamlet：工人新～New Workers' Village ❷ 粗俗 rustic; boorish：～野 boorish｜撒～act wildly; behave atrociously

【村夫俗子】cūnfū súzǐ 指粗野鄙俗的人 uneducated person; boorish person

【村话】cūnhuà 粗俗的话（多指骂人的话 esp. curses）vulgar language

【村落】cūnluò same as 村庄 cūnzhuāng

【村民】cūnmín 乡村居民 villager; village people：～大会 villagers' meeting

【村塾】cūnshú〈旧时 *old*〉农村中的私塾 village school; also 村学 cūnxué

【村野】cūnyě ❶ 乡村和田野 villages and fields; countryside：过～生活 lead a rustic existence ❷ 粗鲁；粗俗 rustic; countrified; rough：性情～rustic in disposition｜～难听的话语 coarse and offensive remarks

【村寨】cūnzhài 村庄；寨子 fortified village; village：～相望 villages within sight of each other

【村镇】cūnzhèn 村庄和小市镇 villages and small townships

【村庄】cūnzhuāng 农民聚居的地方 village; hamlet

【村子】cūn•zi same as 村庄 cunzhuang

皴 cūn ❶（皮肤）因受冻而裂开（of skin）chapped（from the cold）; cracked：手～了。（My）hands are chapped from the cold. ❷〈方 *dial.*〉皮肤上积存的泥垢 dirt accumulated on skin：一脖子～ neck full of dirt ❸ 国画画山石时，勾出轮廓后，为了显示山石的纹理和阴阳面，再用淡干墨侧笔而画，叫做皴 method of depicting the shades and texture of rocks and mountains by light ink strokes in traditional Chinese landscape painting

【皴法】cūnfǎ 皴③的各种方法 texturing methods, or types of texture strokes（e.g. for trees, rocks, mountains, etc.）; wrinkle method

【皴裂】cūnliè same as 皴 cūn ①

踆 cūn〈书 *fml.*〉❶ 踢 kick ❷ 退；止 move back; retreat; stop

【踆乌】cūnwū〈古代 *arch.*〉传说太阳中的三足乌，后来借指太阳 legendary bird with three feet, later used to refer to the sun

cún（ㄘㄨㄣ）

存 cún ❶ 存在；生存 exist; live; survive：残～ remnant; surviving｜父母俱～。Both parents are still living. ❷ 储存；保存 store; keep：封～seal up for safekeeping｜～粮 store grain ❸ 蓄积；聚集 accumulate; collect：～食 suffer from indigestion｜新建的水库已经～满了水。A large quantity of water is stored in the new reservoir. ❹ 储蓄 save; deposit：～款 savings｜～折 deposit book; bank book｜零～整取 monthly small deposits for lump sum withdrawal at a specified time｜把暂时不用的现款～在银行里 deposit spare cash in the bank ❺ 寄存 leave with; check：～车处 parking lot（for bicycles）; bicycle park（shed）｜行李先～在这儿，回头再来取。Let's check our luggage in here and come back for it later. ❻ 保留 reserve; retain：～疑 leave a question unanswered｜～而不论 leave a question open｜去伪～真 get rid of the false and retain the true ❼ 结存；余留 remain on balance; be in stock：库～ stock; reserve｜收支相抵，净～二百元。The accounts show a surplus of 200 yuan. ❽ 心里怀着（某种想法）cherish; harbour：～心 intentionally; on purpose｜心～侥幸 leave things to chance; take a chance｜不～任何顾虑 have no misgivings whatsoever; without the slightest hesitancy

【存案】cún//àn 在有关机构登记备案 register with the proper authorities; keep on file; register officially for the record

【存查】cúnchá 保存起来以备查考（多在批阅公文时用 oft. for official documents）file for reference; keep on file for future reference：交会计科～send sth. to the accounting section to file for future reference

【存储】cúnchǔ 储存 store; memorize：～量 memory capacity

【存储器】cúnchǔqì 电子计算机中用来存贮程序、数据等信息的装置 memory device; memory unit; storage unit; device in a computer used to store programmes, data, etc. also called 存贮器 cúnchǔqì

【存单】cúndān 银行、信用合作社等给存款者作为凭证的单据 certificate of deposit; deposit receipt（from a bank, credit cooperative, etc.）

【存档】cún//dàng 把处理完毕的公文、资料、稿件等归入档案，留供以后查考 place on file; file for later reference; store（processed documents, materials, manuscripts, etc.）in archives

【存底】cúndǐ 商店指储存待售的货物 existing stock（of a shop）; goods available for sale：清出～take inventory of goods; take stock｜～不多了，要赶快进货。There are not many left, so we should replenish stocks quickly.

【存而不论】cún ér bù lùn 保留起来不加讨论 leave a question open; exclude a problem from consideration though aware of its existence; put the problem aside; table the question and not discuss it for the time being：这

个问题可以暂时～,先讨论其他问题。Let's leave this question aside for the time being and discuss other problems first.

【存放】cúnfàng 寄存;储存 leave with; leave in sb.'s care:～行李 check one's luggage｜临动身前,把几箱子书～在朋友家里。I left a few boxes of books with a friend of mine before departure.｜把节余的钱～在银行里 put surplus money in the bank; deposit the balance in the bank

C

【存根】cúngēn 开出票据或证明后留下来的底子,上面记载着与票据或证明同样的内容,以备查考 counterfoil; stub; office copy; portion of a cheque, receipt, etc., kept by the sender as a record for future reference

【存户】cúnhù 在银行、信用合作社等存款的户头 (bank) depositor

【存活】cúnhuó 生存,多指生命受到威胁后生存下来 survive, usually after a life threatening event:～率 survival rate; liveability; chance of survival

【存货】cún//huò 储存货物 stock up (goods)

【存货】cúnhuò 商店中储存待售的货物 goods in stock; existing stock; inventory; remainder; stock:～有限,欲购从速。There are not many in stock, so buy them while they last.

【存款】cún//kuǎn 把钱存在银行里 deposit money (in a bank):～手续简便。It's simple and convenient to deposit money.｜到银行去～ go to the bank to deposit some money

【存款】cúnkuǎn 存在银行里的钱 deposit; money on deposit; savings deposits:一笔～ a sum of money on deposit｜到银行去取～ go to the bank to withdraw one's savings deposits

【存栏】cúnlán 指牲畜在饲养中(多用于统计 usu. statistical) livestock on hand:全乡生猪～头数达两万余。The total livestock of pigs of the whole township is over 20,000.

【存粮】cún//liáng 储存粮食 stock up food grain:～备荒 stock up grain to protect against famine

【存粮】cúnliáng 储存的粮食 grain in store; grain in reserve:这里家家都有～。Every family here has surplus grain in store.

【存留】cúnliú 留存 keep, be kept, remain:他的著作～下来的不多。Only a few of his works remain to this day.

【存念】cúnniàn 保存下来作为纪念 for keepsake; as a memento

【存身】cún//shēn 安身 take shelter; make one's home; settle down:～之所 place to shelter sb.

【存食】cúnshí 吃了东西不消化,停留在胃里 suffer from indigestion:孩子老不想吃饭,想是～了吧? The child has been reluctant to eat anything for a long time. Is it indigestion?

【存世】cúnshì 留存在世间 be extant; remain in existence:他身后还有一部诗作～。There is still one of his works of poetry extant.｜据考证,这尊佛像是～极少的国家一级文物。Textual research shows that this statue of Buddha is an A-level national historical relic rarely found extant now.

【存亡】cúnwáng 生存和死亡;存在和灭亡 live or die; survive or perish:～未卜 the destiny (of a nation, etc.) cannot be foretold; there is no telling whether sb. is dead or alive｜1937年到1945年的抗日战争是关系中华民族生死～的战争。The War of Resistance against Japan from 1937 to 1945 was a life-and-death struggle for the Chinese nation.

【存息】cúnxī 存款的利息 interest (of deposit)

【存项】cúnxiàng 储存或余存的款项 credit balance; balance:手里留点儿～,有事就不着急了。Keep some nest eggs, so you won't have to worry in an emergency.

【存心】cún//xīn 怀着某种念头 cherish certain intentions:～不良 harbour evil designs (or intentions); mean ill｜他说这番话,不知存着什么心。It's hard to say what his intentions were in saying that.

【存心】cúnxīn 有意;故意 intentionally; deliberately; on purpose:你这不是～叫我为难吗? You mean to put me in a fix, don't you?

【存蓄】cúnxù ❶ 储存 save; reserve:～饮用水 reserve potable water ❷ 指积存的钱或物 money or goods saved; savings:这些年多少有了些～。I've saved a bit of money after all these years.

【存疑】cúnyí ❶ 对疑难问题暂时不做决定 leave a question open; leave a matter for future consideration:这件事只好暂时～,留待将来解决。We have to table this matter for the time being, and hope for a resolution in the future. ❷ 存在心中的疑问 remaining doubt; unanswered question; unsettled point:他终于把心中多年的～说了出来。At last, he spoke the doubt that had lain buried in his heart for years.

【存在】cúnzài ❶ 事物持续地占据着时间和空间;实际上有,还没有消失 be; exist; remain; having been in space and time and continuing to be:东西还～,经检点,完好无损。A careful check shows that everything is intact.｜事情已解决,不～任何问题。The matter has been settled and no problem remains. ❷ 哲学上指不依赖人的意识并不以人的意识为转移的客观世界,即物质(philos.) being; existence; physical world as considered independent of human consciousness and in contrast to nonexistence:～决定意识,不是意识决定～。Social being determines consciousness, not vice versa.

【存照】cúnzhào ❶ 把契约文件等保存起来以备查考核对 file a document; keep a document for future reference ❷ 指保存起来以备查考核对的契约文件等 document on file kept for future reference

【存折】cúnzhé 银行、信用合作社等给存款者作为凭证的小本子 deposit book; bankbook; small passbook issued by a bank or credit cooperative, etc., containing a record of a customer's account

【存正】cúnzhèng〈客套话 *pol.*〉送人作品时请人批评或提意见 request valuable comment or advice (when sending sb. one's work)

【存执】cúnzhí same as 存根 cúngēn

蹲 cún〈方 *dial.*〉腿猛然落地,因震动而受伤 sprain; injure one's foot by bringing it down too heavily: ～了腿 sprained one's leg by a sudden and heavy landing on the feet ☞ dūn on p.496

cǔn (ㄘㄨㄣˇ)

刌 cǔn〈书 *fml.*〉割;截断 cut; sever

忖 cǔn 细想;揣度 turn over in one's mind; ponder; speculate: 自～ponder by oneself; turn over in one's mind

【忖度】cǔnduó 推测;揣度 speculate; conjecture; surmise; presume; suppose: 我～他今天不会来了。I presume he won't come today.

【忖量】cǔnliàng ❶ 揣度 conjecture; guess: 一边走,一边～着刚才他说的那番话的意思。As I walked along, I kept wondering about the meaning of what he'd said. ❷ 思量 think over; turn over in one's mind; ponder: 她～了半天,还没有想好怎么说。She turned the matter over in her mind for a long while but still did not know what to say.

【忖摸】cǔn·mo 估摸;揣度 reckon; estimate; conjecture

cùn (ㄘㄨㄣˋ)

寸 cùn ❶ 长度单位。10 分等于一寸,10 寸等于一尺。*cun*, a unit of length (1/3 decimetre) that equals 10 *fen* and 1/10 *chi* ❷ 形容极短或极小 very little; very short; small: ～功 small contribution; meagre achievement |～进 a little progress|～土必争 fight for every inch of land|～步不离 follow sb. closely|鼠目～光 as short-sighted as a mouse; very short-sighted ❸〈方 *dial.*〉凑巧 as luck would have it: 你来得可真～。You came just at the right time. ❹ same as 寸口 cùnkǒu ② ❺ (Cùn) 姓 a surname

【寸步】cùnbù 指极短的距离 tiny step; single step — very short distance: ～难行 difficult to move even one step | ～不离 follow sb. closely; keep close to sb.; be always at sb.'s elbow | ～不让 refuse to yield an inch; not budge an inch

【寸步难行】cùn bù nán xíng 形容走路、行动困难 move even a single step;〈比喻 *fig.*〉开展某项工作困难重重 be unable to; be unable to do anything; cannot take a step; cannot move a single step; be forced into a corner; find it extremely hard to make a single move in doing sth; be impossible to do anything; also 寸步难移 cùn bù nán yí

【寸草不留】cùn cǎo bù liú 连小草都不留下。形容遭到天灾人祸后破坏得非常严重的景象。be devastated; be left in total devastation; leave not even a blade of grass — complete devastation (of land)

【寸草春晖】cùn cǎo chūn huī 唐代孟郊《游子吟》:'谁言寸草心,报得三春晖。'后来用'寸草春晖'比喻父母恩情子女难以报答。young grass and spring sunshine — children owe parents what young grass owes to spring sunshine. (*Song of the Wanderer* by Meng Jiao of the Tang Dynasty, 'Who says that the heart of an inch-long plant can requite the radiance of full spring?')

【寸断】cùnduàn 断成许多小段 break into tiny pieces ◇肝肠～(形容极其悲伤) broken heart — extreme grief

【寸功】cùngōng 极小的功劳 small achievement (or contribution): 身无～ achieve nothing at all; have not the slightest merit

【寸进】cùnjìn〈书 *fml.*〉微小的进步 a little progress; small advance: 略有～ made just a little progress

【寸劲儿】cùnjìnr〈方 *dial.*〉❶ 巧妙的用力方法 appropriate strength (in doing things): 折断麻经儿得靠～,不能硬拽。To break flaxen thread, you have to apply just the right force instead of tugging it. ❷ 凑巧的机会 coincidence: 这种东西早已不兴了,赶上～,还能买到旧的。Such things went out of fashion long ago. If you are lucky, you might be able to buy a used one.

【寸楷】cùnkǎi 一寸大小的楷体字 regular script in one-*cun*-size characters: ～羊毫 small-sized writing brush made of goat's hair

【寸刻】cùnkè 极短的时间 very short time: ～不离 follow sb. closely; keep close to sb.; not leave sb. even for a second — be very intimate with one another

【寸口】cùnkǒu ❶〈中医 *Chin. med.*〉指手腕上边用手按时可以觉到脉搏的部分,是切脉常取的部位 area of the wrist where the pulse is usually taken for diagnosis ❷ 特指寸口脉中距手腕最近的部分。中医把上述广义的寸口脉由下而上地分为寸口、关上、尺中三个部分。狭义的寸口简称寸,关上简称关,尺中简称尺。one of the three pulse-taking spots on the wrist (*cunkou* pulse) closest to the palm. In

C

traditional Chinese medicine, the *cunkou* pulse is broadly divided into three parts: *cunkou*, *guanshang* and *chizhong* from the bottom up respectively. In a narrow sense, *cunkou* is called *cun*, *guanshang guan*, and *chizhong chi* for short

【寸头】cùntóu 男子发式,顶上头发留约一寸,两鬓及后边缘的头发比头顶上头发短 crewcut; men's closely cropped style of haircut

【寸土】cùntǔ 指极小的一片土地 inch of land—a very small piece of land:～必争 contest every inch of land|～不让 never to yield an inch of ground; not to surrender a single inch of one's land

【寸心】cùnxīn ❶ 指中心;内心 heart; mind:～如割(形容痛苦不堪)(as painful as) a knife cutting one's heart|得失～知。Only he himself knows whether he gains or loses. ❷ 微小的心意;小意思 this humble heart; feelings:聊表～ as a small token of my feelings; just to show my appreciation in a small way

【寸阴】cùnyīn〈书 *fml*.〉日影移动一寸的时间,指极短的时间 time indicated by a shadow moving a *cun* —a very short time

吋 cùn 又 also yīngcùn 英寸旧也作吋 inch (英寸) formerly known as 吋 yīngcùn

cuō (ㄘㄨㄛ)

搓 cuō 两个手掌反复摩擦,或把手掌放在别的东西上来回揉 rub with the hands; twist:急得他直～手。He wrung his hands in anxiety.|～一条麻绳儿 make cord by twisting hemp fibres between the palms

【搓板】cuōbǎn (～儿 cuōbǎnr)搓洗衣服的木板,上面有窄而密的横槽 washboard; board with ridges to wash clothes

【搓弄】cuō·nòng 揉搓 rub, knead, or twist idly:她两手～着手绢,一句话也不说。She sat twisting her handkerchief, saying not a word.

【搓手顿脚】cuō shǒu dùn jiǎo 形容焦急不耐烦 wring one's hands and stamp one's feet —become anxious and impatient:遇到困难要设法克服,光～也不解决问题。We should try to overcome difficulties instead of uselessly growing anxious and impatient.

【搓洗】cuōxǐ 把衣物等浸泡在水里,用两手反复揉搓,去掉衣物上的污垢 hand-wash (clothes); scrub; soak clothes in water and rub them against one's hands again and again to get rid of dirt

磋 cuō ❶ 把象牙加工成器物 grind; polish (ivory into instruments):切～ cut and grind ❷ 商量讨论 consult; discuss:～商 exchange views; consult

【磋磨】cuōmó〈书 *fml*.〉切磋琢磨 exchange views; consult; discuss:相互～ exchange views with each other

【磋商】cuōshāng 反复商量;仔细讨论 consult; hold a discussion; exchange views; deliberate:经过多次～,双方总算达成协议。After repeated consultations, the two sides finally reached an agreement.

撮 cuō ❶〈书 *fml*.〉聚合;聚拢 gather; bring together ❷ 用簸箕等把东西聚在一起 scoop up (with a dustpan or shovel):～了一簸箕土 scoop up a dustpan of dirt ❸〈方 *dial*.〉用手指捏住细碎的东西拿起来 pick up or hold (dust, powder, etc.) between the thumb and first finger:～药 fill a prescription of Chinese herbal medicine|～了点儿盐 take a pinch of salt ❹ 摘取(要点)extract; summarize:～要 make extracts ❺〈方 *dial*.〉吃 eat; have dinner:我请你上馆子～一顿。Let me take you to dinner at a restaurant. ❻ 容量单位。10撮等于1勺。现用市撮,1市撮合1毫升。traditional unit of capacity (1 millilitre) ❼〈量词 *classifier*〉a)〈方 *dial*.〉用于手所撮取的东西 pinch:一～盐 a pinch of salt|一～芝麻 a pinch of sesame b)借用于极少的坏人或事物 handful (of bad people or events):一小～坏人 a handful of evil people

☞ zuǒ on p.2573

【撮合】cuō·he 从中介绍促成(多指婚姻) make a match; act as go-between

【撮箕】cuōjī〈方 *dial*.〉撮垃圾的簸箕 dustpan

【撮口呼】cuōkǒuhū ☞ 四呼 sìhū on p.1821

【撮弄】cuōnòng ❶ 戏弄;捉弄 make fun of; play a trick on; tease:～人 make fun of sb. ❷ 教唆;煽动 abet; instigate; incite:他本不想做买卖,是别人～入股的。He didn't want to go into business at the beginning; he was provoked to claim his share.

【撮要】cuōyào ❶ 摘取要点 make an abstract; outline essential points; distil:把工作内容～报告 submit an outline report on one's work ❷ 摘取出来的要点 abstract; synopsis; extracts:论文～ abstract of a thesis

蹉 cuō〈书 *fml*.〉❶ 差误 err ❷ (经某地)通过 pass by (a place); via

【蹉跌】cuōdiē〈书 *fml*.〉失足跌倒 trip and fall〈比喻 *fig*.〉失误 make a slip; make an error

【蹉跎】cuōtuó 光阴白白地过去 waste time; idle away:岁月～。The years drift by.|一再～ let one opportunity after another slip away

cuó (ㄘㄨㄛˊ)

嵯 cuó [嵯峨](cuó'é)〈书 *fml*.〉山势高峻 (of mountains) lofty and rugged

矬 cuó〈方 *dial*.〉❶ (身体)短小;短 (of build) short:～个儿 short person; dwarf ❷ 把身子往下缩 bend down (the body):这孩

子不让人领着，直往下～。The kid hates to be led and kept crouching down. ❸ 削减 reduce：～了他一块钱工钱。One yuan was deducted from his pay.

【矬子】cuó·zi〈方 *dial.*〉身材短小的人 short person；dwarf

痤 cuó［痤疮］(cuóchuāng)皮肤病，多生在青年人的面部，有时也生在胸、背、肩等部位。通常是圆锥形的小红疙瘩，有的有黑头。多由皮脂腺分泌过多、消化不良、便秘等引起。acne；skin disease common among adolescents；pimples and blackheads on the face，and sometimes on the chest，back and shoulders as well；mostly caused by the overactive secretion of sebaceous glands，indigestion，constipation，etc.；通称 generally known as 粉刺 fěncì

瘥 cuó〈书 *fml.*〉病 disease
☞ chài on p. 209

鹾(鹺) cuó〈书 *fml.*〉❶ 盐 salt ❷ 咸味 salty

鄌 Cuó 鄌城，地名，在河南永城西 Cuocheng，name of a place，west of Yongcheng County in Henan Province
☞ Zàn on p. 2391

cuǒ(ㄘㄨㄛˇ)

脞 cuǒ〈书 *fml.*〉细小而繁多；琐细 trivial and numerous；trivial；trifling：～语 petty talk or comment｜～谈 gossip；tittle-tattle｜丛～trivial

cuò(ㄘㄨㄛˋ)

剉 cuò ❶〈书 *fml.*〉折伤 break and hurt ❷ same as 锉 cuò

剒(斮) cuò〈书 *fml.*〉斩；割 chop；scrape off

莝 cuò〈书 *fml.*〉❶ 铡(草) cut up with a hay cutter ❷ 铡碎的草 chopped fodder

【莝草】cuòcǎo〈方 *dial.*〉铡碎的草 chopped fodder

厝 cuò ❶〈书 *fml.*〉放置 lay；place：～火积薪 put or place a fire under a pile of fire wood；hidden danger ❷〈书 *fml.*〉把棺材停放待葬，或浅埋以待改葬 place a coffin in a temporary shelter pending burial，or bury a coffin in a shallow pit before moving it to a permanent grave：暂～put the coffin some where pending formal burial｜浮～lay the coffin temporarily somewhere ❸〈方 *dial.*〉房屋 house：～后边跑出一条大黄狗。A big yellow dog runs out from behind the house.

【厝火积薪】cuò huǒ jī xīn 把火放在柴堆下面 set a fire beneath a pile of wood；〈比喻 *fig.*〉潜伏着很大的危险 hidden danger；in imminent danger；latent troubles；also 积薪厝火 jī xīn cuò huǒ

挫 cuò ❶ 挫折 defeat；frustrate ❷ 压下去；降低 subdue；lower：抑扬顿～rising and falling in cadence；rhythmical｜～敌人的锐气，长自己的威风。Deflate the enemy's arrogance and boost one's own morale.

【挫败】cuòbài ❶ 挫折与失败 setback and defeat：这个企业多次从～中奋起。This enterprise has fought its way out of setbacks many times. ❷ 击败 defeat；foil；frustrate；thwart：～敌军的几次进攻 thwart several enemy attacks

【挫伤】cuòshāng ❶ 身体因碰撞或突然压挤而形成的伤，皮肤下面呈青紫色，疼痛，但不流血 contusion；bruise；contused wound；injury by a knock or sudden pressure to the body so that the skin is discoloured and aches but does not bleed ❷ 损伤(积极性、上进心等) deflate；dampen；discourage；blunt (one's enthusiasm，eagerness for progress，etc.)

【挫损】cuòsǔn 因挫折而受损 be blunted by setbacks：～锐气 deflate sb.；cut sb. down to size；take the keen edge off the spirit of；blunt the edge of one's advance

【挫折】cuòzhé ❶ 压制，阻碍，使削弱或停顿 subdue；frustrate；hinder (sth. in order to weaken or stop it)：不要～群众的积极性。Don't throw cold water on people's enthusiasm. ❷ 失败；失利 defeat；setback；reverse；frustration：经过多次～，终于取得了胜利。They won the battle at last after several setbacks.

措 cuò ❶ 安排；处置 arrange；manage；handle：～置 arrange；handle｜惊惶失～be seized with panic；be frightened out of one's wits｜不知所～be at a loss about what to do；be at one's wits end ❷ 筹划 make plans：筹～款项 raise funds

【措办】cuòbàn 筹划办理 plan and administer：～善后事宜 deal with problems arising from sth.｜如款项数目不大，还可～。If the amount required is not too high，it's still possible to raise the fund.

【措辞】cuò//cí 说话或作文时选用词句 wording；diction：～不当 inappropriate wording｜全文条理清楚，～严谨。The article is logical in structure and careful in wording. also 措词 cuò//cí

【措大】cuòdà〈旧时 *old*〉指贫寒的读书人(含轻蔑意 derog.) poor miserable scholar：～习气(寒酸气) habitual practices of a poor scholar；miserable and shabby appearance；also 醋大 cùdà

【措举】cuòjǔ 举措 move；step：这样决定，也是不得已之～。This decision was a forced move.

【措施】cuòshī 针对某种情况而采取的处理办法

(用于较大的事情) measure or step taken to deal with a certain situation (for large projects or plans): 计划已经订出,～应该跟上。The plan is in place and specific measures should be taken immediately.

【措手】cuòshǒu 着手处理;应付 deal with; manage: 无从～ do not know what to do

【措手不及】cuò shǒu bù jí 临时来不及应付 be caught unprepared; be taken by surprise; be caught unawares; be too surprised to defend oneself; be too late to do anything about sth.: 必须做好防洪准备工作,以免雨季到来时～。We must be well-prepared for floods, or we will be thrown off guard when the rainy season comes.

【措意】cuòyì 〈书 *fml.*〉留意;用心 pay attention to; be careful; look out: 读书虽多,然于诗词不甚～。Wide-read though he is, he does not pay much attention to poetry.

【措置】cuòzhì 安排;料理 handle; manage; arrange: 只要～得当,不会有什么问题。If it's properly handled, there should be no problems.

锉 cuò ❶ 手工工具,条形,多刃,主要用来对金属、木料、皮革等表层做微量加工。按横截面的不同分为扁锉、圆锉、方锉、三角锉等。file; grater; linear, multiple-edged hand tool mainly used to lightly polish the surface of metal, wood and leather, including flat file, round file, square file and triangular file based on their different cross-sections; also 锉刀 cuòdāo ❷ 用锉进行切削 file; make smooth with a file: 圆孔用圆锉～一～ file a circular hole smooth with a round file

【锉刀】cuòdāo same as 锉 cuò ①

错¹ cuò ❶ 参差;错杂 interlocked and jagged; intricate; complex: 交～ crisscross | ～落 well-proportioned ❷ 两个物体相对磨擦 grind; rub: 上下牙～得很响 grind the teeth noisily ❸ 相对行动时避开而不碰上 make way; move out of the way: ～车 (of a vehicle) make way for another vehicle ◇～过了机会 missed an opportunity ❹ 安排办事的时间使不冲突 schedule events so as to avoid conflicts in timing; alternate; stagger: 这两个会不能同时开,得～一下。The two meetings cannot be held at the same time and must be staggered. ❺ 不正确 wrong; mistaken; erroneous: ～字 wrongly written character | 这道题算～了。This exercise is calculated incorrectly. ❻ (～儿 cuòr) 过错;错处 fault; demerit: 没～儿 no problem | 出～儿 do sth. wrong ❼ 坏;差 (用于否定式 used in the negative) bad; poor: 这幅画儿画得不～。This picture is not bad. | 今年的收成～不了。This year's harvest is sure to be good. ❽〈方 *dial.*〉错非 except: ～了你,换个人我也不说这话。I won't talk about it with any other person except you.

错² cuò 在凹下去的文字、花纹中镶上或涂上金、银等 inlay or plate (an etched character or decorative pattern) with gold, silver, etc.: ～金 inlay with gold

错³ cuò 〈书 *fml.*〉❶ 打磨玉石的石头 grindstone for polishing jade ❷ 打磨玉石 polish jade: 攻～ polish jade; hone

【错爱】cuò'ài〈谦辞 *hum.*〉表示感谢对方爱护 undeserved kindness (to show one's appreciation)

【错案】cuò'àn 错判的案件 misjudged case

【错别字】cuòbiézì 错字和别字 wrongly written or mispronounced character

【错车】cuò//chē 火车、电车、汽车等在单轨上或窄路上相向行驶,或后车超越前车时,在铺设双轨的地方或路边让开,使双方顺利通行 one vehicle gives another the right of way; (of trains, trolleys and buses that run in opposite directions on a single-track railway or narrow path, or that intend to overtake other vehicles ahead) drive on different sides of a double-track so as to make way for each other

【错处】cuò·chu 错误的地方;过错 fault; demerit

【错待】cuòdài 亏待 treat unfairly; treat badly: 他不会～你,你放心好了。You can rest assured that you'll be treated well.

【错讹】cuò'é (文字、记载)错误 error (in writing or recording): 校对不严,～甚多。There are a lot of errors due to poor proof-reading.

【错愕】cuò'è 仓促惊讶;惊愕 stunned; dumbfounded: ～良久 struck dumb for a long time | 他的突然到来使她大为～。She was greatly shocked by his unexpected arrival.

【错非】cuòfēi〈方 *dial.*〉除非;除了 except: ～这种药,没法儿治他的病。His illness can't be cured except with this medicine.

【错怪】cuòguài 因误会而错误地责备或抱怨人 blame sb. wrongly due to misunderstanding; make complaints against sb. unjustly: 是我不了解情况,～了你。It was I who blamed you unjustly without knowing what had happened.

【错过】cuòguò 失去(时机、对象) let slip; miss (an opportunity, object): 不要～农时。Don't miss the right farming time. | ～这个村就没有那个店了。If you bypass this village, you won't find such a shop again — take this chance, or you'll miss it forever.

【错会】cuòhuì 错误地理解 understand wrongly; misinterpret: 你～了我的意思。You misunderstood me.

【错金】cuòjīn 特种工艺的一种,在器物上用金属丝镶嵌成花纹或文字 inlay with gold; process or art of inlaying the surface of utensils with metal wire in the form of flowers or characters

【错觉】cuòjué 由于某种原因引起的对客观事物的不正确的知觉。如筷子放在有水的碗内，由于光线折射，看起来筷子是弯的，就是一种错觉。illusion; wrong or false impression; wrong or incorrect perception of objective reality because of certain factors. For example, put a chopstick in a bowl of water and one will get the wrong impression that it is bent because of the refraction of light.

【错开】cuò//kāi （时间、位置）互相让开，避免冲突 stagger (time, position)：为了避免公共车辆的拥挤，工厂、机关上下班的时间最好～。To avoid overcrowding in buses, factories and government departments should better stagger their office hours.

【错漏】cuòlòu 错误和遗漏 mistakes and omissions：文稿誊清后请再核对一遍，以免～。Please proof-read the drafts again after copying to avoid mistakes and omissions.

【错乱】cuòluàn 无次序；失常态 in disorder; in confusion; deranged：颠倒～topsy-turvy; upside down｜精神～mentally deranged; insane

【错落】cuòluò 交错纷杂 in disorderly profusion; strewn at random; scattered and interlocked; irregular：～有致 in picturesque disorder; well-proportioned; (the branches and leaves) are well-spaced; well-arranged｜～不齐 disorderedly and uneven; all at sixes and sevens; higgledy-piggledy; topsy-turvy; scattered here and there｜苍松翠柏，～其间 dotted with green pines and cypresses; with pines and cypresses interspersed

【错谬】cuòmiù 错误；差错 error; mistake：～之处，请多指正。Please kindly correct the mistakes and offer your advice.

【错时】cuòshí 错开时间 stagger the times：要求各单位～上下班，缓解市区交通拥挤状况。Government departments and institutions are required to stagger their office hours to alleviate traffic jams in the downtown area.

【错位】cuò//wèi 离开原来的或应有的位置 dislocation; malposition; misplacement：骨关节～dislocated elbow ◇名和利使他心中的荣辱观、羞耻感发生了～。Fame and gain gave him a misplaced sense of honour and shame.

【错误】cuòwù ❶ 不正确；与客观实际不符合 wrong; mistaken; incorrect; erroneous：～思想 wrong thinking; mistaken idea｜～的结论 wrong conclusion ❷ 不正确的事物、行为等 mistake, error, blunder; fault; falsehood：犯～ make a mistake; commit an error｜改正～ correct a mistake

【错银】cuòyín 特种工艺的一种，在器物上用银丝镶嵌成花纹或文字 inlay with silver; process or art of inlaying the surface of a utensil with silver wire in the form of patterns or characters

【错杂】cuòzá 两种以上的东西夹杂在一起 mixed; heterogeneous; jumbled; of mixed content

【错字】cuòzì 写得不正确的字或刻错、排错的字 wrongly written character; misprint

【错综】cuòzōng 纵横交叉 criss-crossed; intricate：～复杂 complex and intricate｜公路～ criss-crossed highways｜枝叶～，繁花似锦 with criss-crossed branches and leaves and abundant flowers

【错综复杂】cuòzōng fùzá 形容头绪繁多，情况复杂 perplexing; complicated and confused; complex and mixed; intricate and complex; wheels within wheels; very complicated

D

dā(ㄉㄚ)

咑 dā (发音短促)吆喝牲口前进的声音[sound (pronounced quickly) to urge draught animals forward] Da!

耷 dā 〈书 *fml*.〉耳朵大 big ear

【耷拉】dā·la 下垂 droop; hang down:～着脑袋 hang one's head|黄狗～着尾巴跑。The yellow dog is running with its tail drooping. also 搭拉 dā·la

哒(噠) dā ❶〈似声词 *onom*.〉same as 嗒 dā ❷ 赶牲口的声音[sound made to urge draught animals on] Da!

【哒嗪】dāqín 有机化合物,化学式 $C_4H_4N_2$。是嘧啶的同分异构体。diazine, any of three isomeric compounds having the formula $C_4H_4N_2$; isomer of metadiazine

搭 dā ❶ 支;架 put up; build:～桥 put up a bridge|～棚 set up a shed|喜鹊在树上～了个窝。The magpie built a nest in the tree. ❷ 把柔软的东西放在可以支架的东西上 hang soft things over sth. that can be propped up:把衣服～在竹竿上 hang the clothes on a bamboo pole|肩膀上～着一条毛巾 drape a towel over one's shoulder ❸ 连接在一起 connect; join:两根电线～上了。The two wires are touching.|前言不～后语 speak incoherently ◇～伙 join as partner|～街坊 being neighbours ❹ 凑上;加上 throw in more (people, money, etc.); add:把这些钱～上就够了。It should be enough with this money thrown in.|这个工作不轻,还得～上个人帮他才成。It's not an easy job — we better send someone to help him. ◇差点儿连命也给～上 nearly cost one's life ❺ 搭配;配合 arrange in pairs or groups:粗粮和细粮～着吃 eat coarse grain and fine grain together|大的小的～着卖 sell the large and the small together ❻ 共同抬起 lift sth. together:把桌子～起来在下面垫上几块砖 rig up a table by putting bricks under its legs|书柜已经～走了。The bookcase has been carried away. ❼ 乘;坐(车、船、飞机等)take (a bus, ship, plane, etc.); travel (or go) by:～轮船到上海 go to Shanghai by boat|～下一班汽车 take the next bus|～国际航班 catch an international flight

【搭班】dā//bān (～儿 dā//bānr) ❶〈旧时 *old*〉指艺人临时参加某个戏班 temporarily join a theatrical troupe to put on performances:～唱戏 put a theatrical troupe together to stage an opera ❷ 临时参加作业班或临时合伙 temporarily join in a group's work:出车时,老张总是找老工人～,装卸车时助他们一臂之力。Lao Zhang always teams up with elder workers when he is out driving a truck, so that he can help them load and unload.

【搭伴】dā//bàn (～儿 dā//bànr)趁便做伴 join sb. on a trip; travel together:半路上遇见几个老朋友,正好～一起去。I met several old friends on the way, and we got to travel together.|他也到新疆去,你们搭个伴儿吧。He's going to Xinjiang too, so you may as well travel together.

【搭帮】dā//bāng〈方 *dial*.〉(许多人)结伴 (many people) travel together:～结伙 form a group and travel together|搭个帮一块儿去 join sb. and travel together

【搭帮】dābāng〈方 *dial*.〉托福;依靠;多亏 thanks to; depend on; owing to

【搭帮】dā·bang〈方 *dial*.〉帮忙;照顾 help; take care of:大家～着点儿,困难就解决了。With everyone's rendering a hand, the difficulty was tackled.

【搭背】dābèi〈方 *dial*.〉搭腰 stand on sb's back

【搭便】dābiàn 顺便 do sth. in addition to what one is already doing:他是出差路过这里的,～看看大家。He's coming to see us while travelling on business.

【搭补】dābǔ 补贴;帮补 subsidize; financially assist:～家用 help out with the family expenses

【搭碴儿】dā//chár same as 答碴儿 dā//chár

【搭档】dādàng ❶ 协作 cooperate; work together:我们两个人～吧。Let's work together. ❷ 协作的人 partner; workmate:老～ old partner ‖ also 搭当 dādàng

【搭话】dā//huà ❶ 搭腔 strike up a conversation; get a word in:问他几遍,他就是不～。We have asked him several times, but he kept out of the conversation. ❷〈方 *dial*.〉捎带口信 send word; take a message

【搭伙】[1] dā//huǒ 合为一伙 join as a partner:成群～ join as partners in a group|他们搭了

伙，一起做买卖。They became partners and went into business together.

【搭伙】[2] dā//huǒ 加入伙食组织 eat regularly (in a cafeteria, etc.)：在食堂～ take meals regularly at a canteen

【搭架子】dā jià·zi ❶ 搭起间架 build a framework；〈比喻 *fig*.〉事业开创或文章布局略具规模 launch (an undertaking, etc.)；draft an outline for a piece of writing：先搭好架子，然后再充实内容。First make an outline, then fill in the content. ❷〈方 *dial*.〉摆架子 put on airs

【搭脚儿】dā//jiǎor〈方 *dial*.〉因便免费搭乘车船 free travel by bus or boat；thumb a lift

【搭街坊】dā jiē·fang〈方 *dial*.〉做邻居 be neighbours

【搭界】dājiè ❶ 交界 have a common boundary：这里是两省～的地方。This is where the two provinces meet. ❷〈方 *dial*.〉发生联系（多用于否定 oft. in the negative）have some contact with；have sth. to do with：这件事跟他不～。This has nothing to do with him.｜少跟这种人～。Better not have anything to do with these people.

【搭救】dājiù 帮助人脱离危险或灾难 rescue；go to the rescue of

【搭客】dā//kè〈方 *dial*.〉（车船）顺便载客（of an auto driver or a boatman）take on passengers at one's convenience

【搭配】dāpèi ❶ 按一定要求安排分配 arrange in pairs or groups according to need：车、犁、耙、套、鞭等农具，随牲口合理～。These farm tools — cart, plough, rake, harness and whip, etc. — should be matched with different draught animals.｜这两个词～得不适当。These two words don't correlate. ❷ 配合；配搭 cooperate：师徒两人～得十分合拍。The master and apprentice cooperate harmoniously. ❸ 相称 match：两人一高一矮，站在一起不～。The two of them, one tall and one short, do not match when standing together.

【搭腔】dā//qiāng ❶ 接着别人的话来说 answer；respond：我问了半天，没人～。I kept asking questions, but nobody answered. ❷〈方 *dial*.〉交谈 talk to each other：从前他俩合不来，彼此不～。In the past the two of them did not get along, and weren't even on speaking terms.‖also 答腔 dā//qiāng

【搭桥】dā//qiáo ❶ 架桥 put up (or build) a bridge：逢山开路，遇水～ cut paths through mountains and build bridges across rivers ❷〈比喻 *fig*.〉撮合；介绍 act as a matchmaker；introduce：牵线～ act as go-between ❸ 用病人自身的一段血管接在阻塞部位的两端，使血流畅通 bypass surgery；surgical procedure in which the two ends of an obstructed hollow organ are connected by a section of blood vessel from the patient so as to unblock the blood flow：心脏～手术 heart bypass surgery

【搭讪】dā·shàn 为了想跟人接近或把尴尬的局面敷衍过去而找话说 strike up a conversation with sb.；say sth. to smooth over an embarrassing situation；also 搭赸 dā·shàn and 答讪 dā·shàn

【搭赸】dā·shàn same as 搭讪 dā·shàn

【搭手】dā//shǒu 替别人出力；帮忙 give a hand；help others：搭把手 give help｜搭不上手 too many helping hands｜见我忙，他赶紧跑过来～。When he saw I was busy, he hurried over to give me a hand.

【搭头】dā·tou（～儿 dā·tour）配搭的、非主要的东西 minor and unimportant thing attached to a major thing：买了个大瓜，这个小瓜是～儿。I bought a big watermelon, with this small one as a supplement.

【搭腰】dā·yao 牲口拉车时搭在背上使车辕、套绳不致掉下的用具，多用皮条或绳索做成。有的地区叫搭背。harness pad on animals' backs used for pulling a cart, that prevents shaft and rope from dropping, mostly made of leather or rope. In some areas, it is also called 搭背 dābèi

嗒 dā〈拟声词 *onom*.〉：～～的马蹄声 clatter of horse hoofs｜机枪～～地响着。The machine guns rattled away.

☞ tà on p. 1849

答（荅） dā 义同'答'(dá)，专用于'答应、答理'等词［same as 答 dá, esp. used in such words as 答应 dā·ying and 答理 dā·li］

☞ dá on p. 345

【答碴儿】dā//chár〈方 *dial*.〉接着别人的话说话 pick up the thread of a conversation and join in：他的话没头没脑，叫人没法～。His talk is pointless, nobody can make conversation with him.｜他问了半天，没一个答他的碴儿。He kept on asking, but nobody answered. also 搭碴儿 dā//chár, 搭茬儿 dā//chár and 答茬儿 dā//chár

【答理】dā·li 对别人的言语行动表示态度（多用于否定句 usu. in the negative）acknowledge (sb.'s greeting, etc.)；respond；answer：不爱～人 be standoffish｜路上碰见了，谁也没有～谁。They didn't greet each other when they met on the road.｜我叫了他两声，他没～我。I called him twice, but he didn't respond. also 搭理 dā·li

【答腔】dā//qiāng same as 搭腔 dā//qiāng

【答讪】dā·shàn same as 搭讪 dā·shàn

【答言】dā//yán 接着别人的话说；搭腔 pick up the thread of a conversation and join in；answer；respond：一连问了几遍，没有人～。I asked several times, but nobody gave an answer.｜又没问你，你答什么言！I didn't ask you, why did you butt in?

【答应】dā·ying ❶ 应声回答 answer; respond: 喊了好几声,也没有人～。I shouted several times, but nobody responded. ❷ 应允;同意 agree; comply with: 他起初不肯,后来～了。He refused at first, but later agreed.

膛 dā ☞ 肥膛膛 féidādā on p. 560

锘 dā ☞ 铁锘 tiědā on p. 1909

褡 dā ☞ below

【褡包】dā·bāo 长而宽的腰带,用布或绸做成,系(jì)在衣服外面 long, broad girdle made of cotton or silk attached to the clothes

【褡裢】dā·lián ❶ (～儿 dā·liánr)长方形的口袋,中央开口,两端各成一个袋子,装钱物用,一般分大小两种,大的可以搭在肩上,小的可以挂在腰带上 long, rectangular bag sewn up at both ends with an opening in the middle for holding money and other things; in big and small sizes, the small one usu. worn round the waist, while the big one is slung across the shoulder ❷ 摔跤运动员所穿的一种用多层布制成的上衣 jacket made of several layers of cloth, worn by wrestlers

D

dá (ㄉㄚˊ)

打 dá 〈量词 *classifier*〉十二个为一打 twelve makes a dozen: 一～铅笔 a dozen pencils|两～毛巾 two dozen towels

☞ dǎ on p. 346

达(達) dá ❶ 通 extend: 铁路四通八～。Railways radiate in all directions. |在上海坐火车可以直～北京。One can take the train in Shanghai and reach Beijing directly. ❷ 达到 reach; attain; amount to: 抵～ reach|目的已～ achieve one's aim ❸ 懂得透彻;通达(事理) understand thoroughly; understanding and reasonable: 知书～理 educated and reasonable|通权～变 not bound by old rules ❹ 表达 express; communicate: 转～ convey; pass on|传～报告 transmit a report|词不～意。The words fail to convey the idea. ❺ 显达 eminent; distinguished: ～官贵人 ranking officials and noble lords ❻ (Dá) 姓 a surname

【达标】dábiāo 达到规定的标准 reach the standard: 质量～。The quality is up to standard. |英语考试～ pass a qualifying English test

【达成】dáchéng 达到;得到(多指商谈后得到结果) reach (agreement); conclude (usu. a business negotiation): ～协议 reach agreement

【达旦】dádàn 直到第二天早晨 until dawn: 通宵～ all night long|～不寐 no sleep through the night till past dawn

【达到】dá//dào 到(多指抽象事物或程度 usu. abstract objective or degree) achieve; attain; reach: 达得到 reachable (objective)|达不到 fail to live up to|～目的 achieve the goal|～国际水平 measure up to international standards

【达尔文主义】Dá'ěrwén zhǔyì 英国生物学家达尔文(Charles Robert Darwin)所创关于生物界历史发展一般规律的学说,主要内容包括生物的变异性和遗传性、物种的起源、生存斗争等 Darwinism, a theory developed by British biologist Charles Robert Darwin on the general rules governing the process of evolution of living things, which, among other things, covers the origin of species and the interplay of three principles — variation in all forms of life, heredity that transmits similar organic forms from one generation to another, and the struggle for survival in a given environment. also called 进化论 jìnhuàlùn

【达观】dáguān 对不如意的事情看得开 optimistic; philosophical: 生性～ optimistic in nature; be a born optimist|遇事要～些,不要愁坏了身体。You'd better take things philosophically and not worry too much.

【达官】dáguān 〈旧时 *old*〉指职位高的官吏 high officials: ～贵人 high officials and noble lords|～显宦(职位高而声势显赫的官吏) high officials with power and influence

【达姆弹】dámǔdàn 枪弹的一种,弹头射入身体后炸裂,造成重创。国际公约禁止使用。因首先是英国人在印度达姆达姆(Dumdum)的兵工厂制造而得名。dumdum; hollow-nosed or soft-nosed bullet that expands on impact, inflicting a severe wound, banned by international regulations, named after Dum-Dum, a town in India where the bullets were made by the British

【达斡尔族】Dáwò'ěrzú 我国少数民族之一,主要分布在黑龙江、内蒙古和新疆 Daur (Tahur) ethnic group, or the Daurs (Tahurs), distributed over Heilongjiang Province, the Inner Mongolia Autonomous Region, and the Xinjiang Uygur Autonomous Region.

【达奚】Dáxī 姓 a surname

【达意】dáyì (用语言文字)表达思想 get the message across; express (or convey) ideas by language: 抒情～ express one's thoughts and feelings

【达因】dáyīn 力的单位,使1克质量的物体产生1厘米/秒^{2}的加速度所需的力,叫做1达因。1达因 = 10^{-5}牛顿。dyne; centimetre-gram/second unit of force, equal to the force that produces an acceleration of one centimetre per second on a mass of one gram. One dyne is equal to 10^{-5} newton.

沓 dá (～儿 dár) 〈量词 *classifier*〉用于重叠起来的纸张和其他薄的东西(一般不很厚)

pile (of paper or other thin things); pad: 一～信纸 a pad of letter paper|我把报纸一～一～地整理好了。I have arranged the newspapers in piles.

☞ tà on p. 1849

【沓子】dá·zi 沓(dá) pile (of paper, etc.): 一～钞票 a wad of money or bills

怛 dá〈书 *fml.*〉❶ 忧伤;悲苦 worried; troubled; saddened: 惨～ misery|～伤 worried ❷ 畏惧;惧怕 fear; dread

妲 dá 用于人名,妲己,商纣王的妃子 Da, surname; Daji, the concubine of King Zhou of the Shang Dynasty

迖(薘) dá ☞ [莙迖菜] (jūndácài) on p. 1066

炟 dá 用于人名,刘炟,东汉章帝 used as a given name; Liu Da, or Emperor Zhang of the Eastern Han Dynasty

笪 dá ❶〈方 *dial.*〉一种用粗竹篾编成的形状像席的东西,通常铺在地上晾晒粮食 rough bamboo mat (usu. placed on the ground for airing grain) ❷〈书 *fml.*〉拉船的绳索 hemp rope for pulling boats ❸ (Dá)姓 a surname

答(荅) dá ❶ 回答 answer; respond: 对～ answer|一问一～ one asks and the other answers|～非所问 give an irrelevant answer ❷ 受了别人的好处,还报别人 return (help, etc.): ～谢 express appreciation (for sb.'s kindness or hospitality)|报～ return; pay back

☞ dā on p. 343

【答案】dá'àn 对问题所做的解答 answer; solution; key: 寻求～ seek a solution

【答拜】dábài 回访 pay a return visit

【答辩】dábiàn 答复别人的指责、控告、问难,为自己的行为或论点辩护 reply (to a charge, query or argument); defend one's own behaviour or points of view: 法庭上允许被告～ the accused is permitted to defend himself in court|进行论文～ defend one's thesis

【答词】dácí 表示谢意或回答时所说的话 thank-you speech; answering speech; reply: 致～ make a speech in reply

【答对】dáduì 回答别人的问话 answer sb.'s question; reply: ～得体 answer in the proper way|我叫他问得没法～。I am baffled by his questions.

【答非所问】dá fēi suǒ wèn 回答的不是所问的内容 give an irrelevant answer to a question; also 所答非所问 suǒ dá fēi suǒ wèn

【答复】dá·fù 对问题或要求给以回答 formal reply: ～读者提出的问题 reply to readers' questions|等研究后再～你。I'll give you a reply after further study.|会给你一个满意的～的。We can give you a satisfactory reply.

【答话】dáhuà 回答(多用于否定式 usu. in the negative) answer; reply: 人家问你,你怎么不～? I asked you a question. Why don't you answer?

【答卷】dá//juàn 解答试卷 answer questions in a test paper: 认真地～ carefully answer the questions in a test paper

【答卷】dájuàn 对试题做了解答的卷子 completed test paper: 标准～ standard answers in a test paper ◇人生的意义究竟是什么? 他用自己的行动交了一份很好的～。What's the meaning of life? He gave a good answer with his own actions.

【答礼】dá//lǐ 回礼 return a salute

【答数】dáshù 算术运算求得的数 answer to an arithmetic problem; also 得数 déshù

【答谢】dáxiè 受了别人的好处或招待,表示谢意 express appreciation (for sb.'s kindness or hospitality): ～宴会 return banquet|我们简直不知道怎样～你们的热情招待。We simply don't know how to repay your kind hospitality.

【答疑】dáyí 解答疑问 (of a teacher, speaker, etc.) answer questions: 课堂～ answer questions in class

躂(韃) dá ☞ 舭躂 bǐdá on p. 103

闒 dá〈方 *dial.*〉楼上的窗户 window on a upper floor

☞ tà on p. 1849

靼 dá ☞ [鞑靼] (Dádá) on p. 345

瘩 dá [瘩背] (dábèi)〈中医 *Chin. med.*〉指生在背部的痈 carbuncle on the back

鞑(韃) dá [鞑靼] (Dádá) 古时汉族对北方各游牧民族的统称。明代指东蒙古人,住在今内蒙古和蒙古国的东部。Tartar, as the Han people called all nomadic peoples in northern China in ancient times. In the Ming Dynasty, this referred to eastern Mongolians living in today's Inner Mongolia Autonomous Region and east of the Republic of Mongolia.

dǎ (ㄉㄚˇ)

打[1] dǎ ❶ 用手或器具撞击物体 knock or hit by hand or using a tool: ～门 knock at the door|～鼓 beat a drum ❷ 器皿、蛋类等因撞击而破碎 break; smash (container, egg, etc.): 碗～了。The bowl is broken.|鸡飞蛋～。The hen has flown away and the eggs are broken. ❸ 殴打;攻打 beat; fight; attack: ～架 fight|～援 attack enemy reinforcements ❹ 发生与人交涉的行为 deal with sb. or sth.: ～官司 go to court|～交道 come into contact with ❺ 建造;修筑 construct; build: ～坝 construct a dam|～墙 build a wall ❻ 制造(器物、食品) make (articles of daily use or food): ～刀 forge a knife|～家具 make furniture|～烧饼 make sesame seed cakes ❼ 搅拌 mix; stir; beat:～馅儿 stir filling|～糨子 mix paste ❽ 捆 tie up; pack:～包裹 pack one's luggage|～铺盖卷儿 set up a bed|～裹腿 wind a puttee ❾ 编织 knit; weave:～草鞋 weave straw sandals|～毛衣 knit a sweater ❿ 涂抹;画;印 draw; paint; make a mark on:～蜡 wax|～个问号 put a question mark|～墨线 draw an ink line|～格子 draw squares|～戳子 put a stamp|～图样儿 paint a picture ⓫ 揭;凿开 open; dig:～开盖子 take off the lid|～冰 dig ice|～井 dig a well|～眼儿 drill a hole ⓬ 举;提 hoist; raise:～旗子 unfurl a banner|～灯笼 carry a lantern|～伞 hold an umbrella|～帘子 raise the curtain ◇～起精神来 cheer up ⓭ 放射;发出 send; dispatch; project:～雷 thunder|～炮 fire a cannon|～信号 give a signal|～电话 make a phone call ⓮ 付给或领取(证件) issue or receive (a certificate, etc.):～介绍信 write out a letter of introduction for sb. ⓯ 除去 remove; get rid of:～旁杈 prune the side branches ⓰ 舀取 ladle; draw:～水 draw water|～粥 ladle gruel ⓱ 买 buy:～油 buy oil|～酒 buy a drink|～车票 buy a bus ticket ⓲ 捉(禽兽等) catch; hunt:～鸟 shoot birds|～鱼 catch fish ⓳ 用割、砍等动作来收集 gather in; reap; collect:～柴 gather firewood|～草 collect grass ⓴ 定出;计算 calculate; reckon; estimate; work out:～草稿 work out a draft|～主意 think of a plan|成本～二百块钱 estimate (or reckon) the cost at 200 yuan ㉑ 做;从事 do; engage in:～杂儿 do odds and ends|～游击 fight a guerrilla warfare; work (eat, sleep) in no fixed place|～埋伏 lie in ambush or keep sth. in reserve|～前站 act as an advance party ㉒ 做某种游戏 play:～球 play ball|～扑克 play cards|～秋千 go on the swing ㉓ 表示身体上的某些动作 go through (some physical action):～手势 make a gesture|～哈欠 yawn|～嗝儿 hiccup|～踉跄 stagger|～前失 stumble|～滚儿 roll about|～晃儿(huàngr) sway before falling down ㉔ 采取某种方式 adopt; use:～官腔 talk like a bureaucrat|～比喻 draw an analogy|～马虎眼 act dumb ㉕ 定(某种罪名) convict sb. of a crime:他曾被～成右派。He was convicted as a Rightist.

打² dǎ〈介词 *prep.*〉从 from; since:～这儿往西,再走三里地就到了。Head west from here, and you'll reach the place after walking three *li*.|他～门缝里往外看。He looked out through a crack in the door.|～今儿起,每天晚上学习一小时。From now onwards, you should study one hour at night every day.

☞ dá on p. 344

【打把势】dǎ bǎ·shi ❶ 练武术 practise Wushu ❷ 泛指手舞足蹈 gesticulating with hands and feet ‖ also 打把式 dǎ bǎ·shi

【打靶】dǎ//bǎ 按一定规则对设置的目标进行射击 target shooting based on certain rules:练习～ practise shooting

【打白条】dǎ báitiáo (～儿 dǎ báitiáor) ❶ 开具非正式的收据等 give an informal receipt ❷ 收购时用单据代替应付的现款,日后再予以兑付,叫做打白条 write out a marked note when purchasing sth., to be paid in cash later accordingly

【打摆子】dǎ bǎi·zi〈方 *dial.*〉患疟疾 suffer from malaria

【打败】dǎ//bài ❶ 战胜(敌人) defeat; beat (the enemy):～侵略者 beat the invaders ❷ 在战争或竞赛中失败;打败仗 suffer a defeat in war or a match; defeated:这场比赛如果你们～了,就失去决赛资格。If you are defeated in this game, you will not make it into the playoff.

【打扮】dǎ·ban ❶ 使容貌和衣着好看;装饰 do up; dress up; make up; deck out:参加国庆游园,得～得漂亮点儿。One should dress up to attend National Day celebrations in the parks.|节日的天安门～得格外壮观。Tiananmen Square is magnificently decked out for festive occasions. ❷ 打扮出来的样子;衣着穿戴 way or style of dressing:学生～ be dressed like a student|看他的～,像是一个教员。Judging from his dress he appears to be a teacher.

【打包】dǎ//bāo ❶ 用纸、布、麻袋、稻草等包装物品 pack with paper, cloth, gunny-bag, straw, etc.:～机 baler|～装箱 packing and binding ❷ 打开包着的东西 unpack:～检查 unpack and examine

【打苞】dǎbāo (～儿 dǎbāor) 小麦、高粱等谷类作物孕穗 (of wheat, sorghum, etc.) form ears

【打抱不平】dǎ bàobùpíng 帮助受欺压的人说话或采取某种行动 take up the cudgels for the injured party; defend sb. against an injustice; be the champion of the oppressed

【打奔儿】dǎ//bēnr〈方 *dial.*〉❶ 说话或背诵接不下去,中途间歇 stumble (in speech) ❷ 走路时腿脚发软或被绊了一下,几乎跌倒 stumble (in walking), almost fall down

【打比】dǎbǐ ❶ 用一件事物来说明另一件事物;比喻 draw an analogy; use a metaphor or simile:讲抽象的事情,拿具体的东西～,就容易使人明白。People understand you better if you draw concrete analogies when talking about abstractions. ❷〈方 *dial.*〉比较;相比 compare; contrast:他六十多岁了,怎能跟小伙子～呢? He's over sixty, so how can you compare him with a young man?

【打边鼓】dǎ biāngǔ 敲边鼓 speak up for sb. from the sidelines

【打草惊蛇】dǎ cǎo jīng shé〈比喻 *fig.*〉采取机

密行动时，由于透露了风声，惊动了对方 beat the grass and startle the snake — act rashly and alert the enemy

【打喳喳】dǎchā·cha〈方 *dial.*〉小声说话；耳语 whisper

【打岔】dǎ//chà 打断别人的说话或工作 interrupt; cut in：你别～，听我说下去。Listen to me and do not butt in. | 他在那儿做功课，你别跟他～。Do not interrupt him while he is studying.

【打场】dǎ//cháng 麦子、高粱、豆子等农作物收割后在场上脱粒 thresh grain (wheat, sorghum, beans, etc.) on the threshing ground

【打场子】dǎ chǎng·zi 跑江湖的曲艺、杂技演员用敲锣鼓、吆喝等方式把观众招引来围成圆形的表演场地，叫做打场子 [of itinerant artists, such as performers of *quyi* (Chinese storytelling and ballad-singing) and acrobatics] attract audiences by beating gongs or drums or yelling：～卖艺 make a living as a street performer

【打成一片】dǎ chéng yī piàn 合为一个整体(多指思想感情融洽 usu. refers to harmony in thought and feeling) become one with; identify oneself with; merge with：干部跟群众～。The cadres become one with the masses.

【打冲锋】dǎ chōngfēng ❶（进攻部队）率先前进，担负起冲锋的战斗行动 charge (in a battle)：这次战斗由一连～。Company One will charge in this battle. ❷〈比喻 *fig*.〉行动抢在别人前面 be in the vanguard：青年人在各项工作中都应该～。Young people should always bear the brunt of all fields of endeavour.

【打抽丰】dǎ chōufēng same as 打秋风 dǎ qiūfēng

【打出手】dǎ chūshǒu ❶（～儿 dǎ chūshǒur）戏曲演武打时，以一个角色为中心，互相投掷和传递武器 (in traditional opera) throw weapons back and forth; also 过家伙 guò jiā·huo ❷〈方 *dial*.〉指动手打架 start a fight; come to blows：大～ strike violently

【打春】dǎ//chūn ❶ 立春(〈旧时 *old*〉府县官在立春前一天迎接用泥土做的春牛，放在衙门前，立春日用红绿鞭抽打，因此俗称立春为打春) celebrate the beginning of spring. County magistrates made it a point to erect a clay cow at the front gate of the *yamen* the day before spring began, so that the advent of spring could be marked by beating the cow with red and green whips, which is why the Beginning of Spring was also called 'beating spring'. ❷〈旧时 *old*〉湖南一带无业游民，在春节前后，敲打小锣、竹板等，唱着歌词，挨户索取钱财，叫做打春 In what is now Hunan Province, wandering beggars used to ask for money going from house to house beating small drums and bamboo clappers and singing songs before or after the Spring Festival, which was also called 'beating spring'.

【打从】dǎcóng〈介词 *prep*.〉❶ 自从(某时以后) since：～春上起，就没有下过透雨。Since the beginning of spring, there has been no heavy rain. ❷ 表示经过，用在表示处所的词语前面 (used before words indicating places) past; by：～公园门口经过 go past the park entrance

【打倒】dǎ//dǎo ❶ 击倒在地 knock down to the ground：一拳把他～ knock him down with one punch ❷ 攻击使垮台；推翻 overthrow; down with：～帝国主义！Down with imperialism!

【打道】dǎdào 封建时代官员外出或返回时，先使差役在前面开路，叫人回避 clear the way (for officials in imperial times)：～回府 head homeward

【打的】dǎ//dí〈方 *dial*.〉租用出租汽车；乘坐出租汽车 hail a taxi; take a taxi

【打底子】dǎ dǐ·zi ❶ 画底样或起草稿 sketch a plan, picture, etc.：画工笔画必须先学会～。Learners of meticulous Chinese painting should be given a good grounding in sketching. | 这篇文章你先打个底子，咱们再商量着修改。You should make a draft of the essay, and then we will discuss revisions. ❷ 垫底儿 put sth. under sth. else：地面用三合土～ put lime-sand-clay mixture under the floor ❸ 奠定基础 lay a foundation：这次普查给今后制订规划打下了底子。This general survey will lay the groundwork for making plans in the future.

【打点】dǎ·dian ❶ 收拾；料理；准备(礼物、行装等) arrange; get (gifts, luggage, etc.) ready：～行李 pack the luggage | ～家务 do family chores ❷ 送人钱财，请求照顾 bribe sb. to request a favour

【打点滴】dǎ diǎndī 利用输液装置把葡萄糖溶液、生理盐水等通过静脉输入病人体内，叫做打点滴 I. V.; intravenous glucose and normal saline drip into a patient's body using infusion equipment

【打叠】dǎdié 收拾；安排；准备 pack; arrange; prepare：～行李 pack one's luggage | ～停当。Everything is arranged. ◇～精神(打起精神) cheer up

【打动】dǎdòng 使人感动 move; touch：这一番话～了他的心。He was moved by these words.

【打斗】dǎdòu 打架争斗；厮打搏斗 fight; struggle; fight and quarrel：影片中有警匪～的场面。There is a fight scene between the police and gangsters in the film.

【打嘟噜】dǎ dū·lu (舌或小舌)发生颤动的声音；嘴发颤，发音含混不清 (tongue or uvula) pronounce with a trill; unclear pronunciation：听不清他在说什么，光听到他嘴里打着嘟

噜。I can't catch what he is saying, he is speaking with a trill.

【打赌】dǎ//dǔ 拿一件事情的真相如何或能否实现赌输赢 bet; wager: 打个赌 take up a bet | 他明天一定会来,你要不信,咱们可以~。He will definitely come tomorrow, you can bet on it.

【打盹儿】dǎ//dǔnr 小睡;断续地入睡(多指坐着或靠着 usu. sitting or leaning) doze off; take (or have) a nap: 打个盹儿 take a nap | 晚上没睡好,白天老是~。When I sleep badly at night, I always doze off in the daytime.

【打趸儿】dǎdǔnr ❶ 成批地(买或卖) buy or sell in batches: 这车西瓜是~买来的。This truck-load of watermelons was bought in batches. ❷ 归总;打总儿 take altogether: 你们把这几个月的钱~领去。Take your money for those months all at once.

【打发】dǎ·fa ❶ 派(出去) send; dispatch: 我已经~人去找他了。I have sent for him. ❷ 使离去 dismiss; send away: 他连说带哄才把孩子~走了。He sent the children away through persuasion and coaxing. ❸ 消磨(时间、日子) while away (one's time): ~余年 while away one's remaining years | 他躺在病床上,觉得一天的时间真难~。He found it difficult to while away the time just lying in the bed. ❹ 安排;照料(多见于早期白话 usu. seen in early vernacular) arrange; take care of: ~众人住下 put everybody up for the night

【打榧子】dǎ fěi·zi 把拇指贴紧中指面,再使劲闪开,使中指打在掌上发声 make noise by snapping the fingers

【打嗝儿】dǎ//gér ❶ 呃逆的通称 general term for 呃逆 ènì ❷ 嗳气的通称 general term for 嗳气 ǎiqì

【打工】dǎ//gōng 做工(多指临时的 usu. temporarily) do manual work: ~仔 working man | 暑假里打了一个月工 work one month during the summer vacation

【打躬作揖】dǎ gōng zuò yī 弯身作揖,多用来形容恭顺恳求 bow and clasp one's hands in salute; fold the hands and make deep bows modestly and imploringly

【打钩】dǎgōu 在公文、试题等上画一个'√',表示认可或肯定 tick; indicating approval or answers by checkmarks on documents or test questions

【打鼓】dǎ//gǔ 〈比喻 *fig.*〉没有把握,心神不定 feel uncertain (or nervous): 能不能完成任务,我心里直~。I feel extremely uncertain whether I can finish the task or not.

【打瓜】dǎguā ❶ 西瓜的一个品种,果实较小,种子多而大。栽培这种瓜,主要是为收瓜子。a kind of small watermelon with many big seeds, planted chiefly for harvesting the seeds ❷ 这种植物的果实。吃时多用手打开,所以叫打瓜。'smacking watermelon', a popular name for this watermelon, since it is opened by striking with the hand

【打卦】dǎ//guà 把卦扔到地上,根据卦象推算吉凶 divine by casting lots, and fortune-telling according to the symbols: 求神~pray to gods and divinities

【打官腔】dǎ guānqiāng 指说一些原则、规章等冠冕堂皇的话对人进行应付、推托、责备 speak in a bureaucratic tone; talk like a bureaucrat; stall with official jargon when making excuses or blaming: 动不动就~训斥人 always criticizing others in a bureaucratic tone

【打官司】dǎ guān·si 进行诉讼 go to court; engage in a lawsuit

【打光棍儿】dǎ guānggùnr 指成年人过单身生活(多用于男子 usu. of men) remain a bachelor

【打鬼】dǎ//guǐ ☞ 跳布扎 tiào bùzhá on p. 1904

【打滚】dǎ//gǔn (~儿 dǎ//gǔnr) ❶ 躺着滚来滚去 roll about: 疼得直~ writhe with pain | 毛驴在地上~。The little donkey rolled on the ground. ❷ 〈比喻 *fig.*〉长期在某种环境中生活 live in a certain environment for a long time: 他从小在农村~长大的。He grew up in the countryside.

【打哈哈】dǎ hā·ha 开玩笑 make fun; crack a joke: 别拿我~! Don't make fun of me! | 这是正经事,咱们可别~! This is a serious matter; let's not joke about it!

【打哈欠】dǎ hā·qian 困倦时嘴张开,深深吸气,然后呼出。有的地区也说打呵(hē)欠。yawn; also called 打呵欠 dǎ hē·qiàn in some areas

【打鼾】dǎ//hān 睡着时由于呼吸受阻而发出粗重的声音 snore

【打夯】dǎ//hāng 用夯把地基砸实 ram; tamp

【打横】dǎhéng (~儿 dǎhéngr)围着方桌坐时,坐在末座叫打横 take the least important seat at a square table

【打呼噜】dǎhū·lu same as 打鼾 dǎ//hān

【打滑】dǎhuá ❶ 指车轮或皮带轮转动时产生的摩擦力达不到要求而空转 skid around when the friction caused by wheels or a conveyor belt is not enough: 雪天行车要防止~。While driving on snowy days make sure to prevent cars from skidding. ❷ 〈方 *dial.*〉地滑站不住,走不稳 slip (on slippery ground): 走在冰上两脚直~ walking on the ice with feet slipping

【打谎】dǎ//huǎng 〈方 *dial.*〉撒谎 lie

【打晃儿】dǎ//huàngr (身体)左右摇摆站立不稳 (of one's body) sway before falling down: 病刚好,走路还有点儿~。I just recovered, and still stagger a bit when walking.

【打诨】dǎhùn 戏曲演出时,演员(多是丑角)即兴说些可笑的话逗乐,叫做打诨 (of clowns in Chinese opera) make impromptu comic gestures and remarks

【打火机】dǎhuǒjī 一种小巧的取火器。按其燃料不同分为液体打火机和气体打火机;按其发火方式不同分为火石打火机和电子打火机。lighter, fuelled with liquid or gas, and fixed with a flint or an electric device

【打伙儿】dǎ//huǒr 结伴；合伙 join together; form a group：成帮～ team up|几个人～上山采药。They went together to gather herbs in the mountains.

【打击】dǎjī ❶ 敲打；撞击 hit; strike：～乐器 percussion instrument ❷ 攻击；使受挫折 attack; frustrate：不应该～群众的积极性。We shouldn't do anything to dampen the masses' enthusiasm.|给敌军以歼灭性的～ deal a fatal blow at the enemy

【打击乐器】dǎjī yuèqì 指由于敲打乐器本身而发音的乐器，如锣、鼓、木鱼等 percussion instrument, such as gong, drum and wooden clappers, etc.

【打饥荒】dǎ jī•huang〈比喻 *fig.*〉经济困难或借债 be in straitened circumstances; be in debt

【打家劫舍】dǎ jiā jié shè 指成群结伙到人家里抢夺财物 loot; plunder

【打价】dǎ//jià（～儿 dǎ//jiàr）还价（多用于否定 usu. in the negative）bargain：不～儿。No bargaining.

【打架】dǎ//jià 互相争执殴打 come to blows; fight; scuffle：有话好说，不能～。Calm down and talk, do not fight.

【打尖】[1] dǎ//jiān 旅途中休息下来吃点东西 stop for refreshment when travelling; have a snack (at a rest stop)：打过尖后再赶路。Have a snack before hitting the road again.

【打尖】[2] dǎ//jiān 掐去棉花等作物的顶尖儿 pinching the top of crops like cotton; also 打顶 dǎ//dǐng

【打浆】dǎjiāng 搅拌纸浆，使纤维分散开，均匀地悬浮在水里，是造纸的重要工序 beating, an important procedure in paper-making; stir paper pulp until fibres are evenly suspended in the water

【打交道】dǎ jiāo•dao 交际；来往；联系 come into (or make) contact with; have dealings with：我没跟他打过交道。I've never had any dealings with him.◇他成年累月和牲口～，养牲口的经验很丰富。He has rich experience in raising animals since he has dealt with them year in, year out.

【打脚】dǎ//jiǎo〈方 *dial.*〉因鞋不合适，走路时脚发疼甚至磨破 (of tight shoes) pinching

【打搅】dǎjiǎo ❶ 扰乱 disturb; trouble：人家正在看书，别去～。He is reading, don't disturb him. ❷〈婉辞 *euph.*〉指受招待 receive hospitality：～您了，明儿见吧！Sorry to have troubled you. See you tomorrow.

【打醮】dǎ//jiào 道士设坛念经做法事 perform Taoist rituals

【打劫】dǎ//jié 抢夺（财物）rob; plunder; loot：趁火～ fish in troubled waters

【打紧】dǎ//jǐn〈方 *dial.*〉要紧（多用于否定 usu. in the negative）urgent; serious：缺你一个也不～。Nothing matters without you.

【打开】dǎ//kāi ❶ 揭开；拉开；解开 open; unfold：～箱子 open the box|～抽屉 pull out the drawer|～书本 open the book|～包袱 untie a bundle ❷ 使停滞的局面开展，狭小的范围扩大 make a breakthrough; broaden the scope：～局面 open up new prospects

【打开天窗说亮话】dǎ kāi tiānchuāng shuō liàng huà〈比喻 *fig.*〉毫无隐瞒地公开说出来 frankly speaking; let's not mince matters; let's be frank and put our cards on the table; also 打开窗子说亮话 dǎ kāi chuāng•zi shuō liàng huà

【打垮】dǎ//kuǎ 打击使崩溃；摧毁 defeat completely; rout：～封建势力 defeat feudal forces|～了敌人的精锐师团 put the enemy's crack troops to rout

【打捞】dǎlāo 把沉在水里的东西（如死尸、船只等）取上来 get (corpses and shipwrecks) out of the water; salvage：～队 salvage team|～沉船 salvage a sunken ship

【打雷】dǎ//léi 指云层放电时发出巨大响声 thunder

【打擂台】dǎ lèitái ☞ 擂台 lèitái on p.1170

【打冷枪】dǎ lěngqiāng 藏在暗处向没有防备的人突然开枪 shoot from a hiding-place; snipe

【打冷战】dǎ lěng•zhan 因寒冷或害怕身体突然颤动一两下 shudder because of cold or fear; also 打冷颤 dǎ lěng•zhan

【打冷颤】dǎ lěng•zhan same as 打冷战 dǎ lěng•zhan

【打愣】dǎ//lèng〈方 *dial.*〉（～儿 dǎ//lèngr）发呆；发愣 stare blankly; be in a daze

【打连厢】dǎ liánxiāng ☞ 霸王鞭[1] bàwángbiān on p.31

【打量】dǎ•liang ❶ 观察（人的衣着、外貌）measure with the eye; look sb. up and down; size up：对来人上下～了一番。I looked the visitor up and down. ❷ 以为；估计 think; suppose：你还想瞒着我，～我不知道？You think I don't know?

【打猎】dǎ//liè 在野外捕捉鸟兽 go hunting in the wild

【打零】dǎlíng〈方 *dial.*〉❶ 做零工 do odd jobs ❷ 指孤单一个；孤独无伴 single; lonely

【打落水狗】dǎ luòshuǐgǒu〈比喻 *fig.*〉彻底打垮已经失败了的坏人 beat a drowning dog — completely crush a defeated enemy

【打马虎眼】dǎ mǎ•huyǎn 故意装糊涂蒙混骗人 pretend to be ignorant of sth.; act dumb

【打埋伏】dǎ mái•fu ❶ 预先隐藏起来，待时行动 lie in ambush to wait for a chance; ambush：留下一排人在这里～。Leave a platoon here to ambush them. ❷〈比喻 *fig.*〉隐藏物资、人力或隐瞒问题 hold sth. (material, manpower or a problem) back for one's own use; keep sth. in reserve：这个预算是打了埋伏的，要认

真核查一下。You should carefully check this budget, which keeps enough in reserve.

【打鸣儿】dǎ//míngr (公鸡)叫 (roosters) crows

【打磨】dǎ·mó 在器物的表面磨擦,使光滑精致 (of surfaces) polish; burnish; shine: 手工~ polish by hand

【打蔫儿】dǎ//niānr ❶ 植物枝叶萎缩下垂 (of leaves) shrivel; fade; wither; droop: 高粱都旱得~了。The sorghum drooped in the drought. ❷〈方 *dial.*〉形容无精打采;精神不振 spiritless; droopy

【打泡】dǎ//pào 手脚等部分由于磨擦而起泡 get blisters on the hands and feet: 才割了半天麦子,手就~了。I got blisters on my hands only after half a day of cutting wheat. | 在行军中,他脚上打了泡。He got blisters on his feet during the march.

【打炮】dǎpào ❶ 发射炮弹 fire a gun ❷〈旧时 *old*〉名角儿新到某个地点登台的头几天演出拿手好戏 famous actor or actress shines in his or her opening performances: ~戏 one's specialty | ~三天 perform three days

【打屁股】dǎ pì·gu〈比喻 *fig.*〉严厉批评(多含诙谐意 oft. humor.) take sb. to task; get punished: 任务完不成就要~。You'll be spanked if you can't finish the task.

【打平手】dǎ píngshǒu 比赛结果不分高下 come to a draw; tie: 甲乙两队打了个平手。Team A and Team B tied.

【打破】dǎ//pò 突破原有的限制、拘束等 break; smash (old rules and restrictions, etc.): ~常规 break free from conventions | ~记录 chalk up a record | ~情面 lose esteem for sb. | ~沉默 break the silence

【打破沙锅问到底】 dǎpò shāguō wèn dào dǐ〈比喻 *fig.*〉对事情的原委追问到底。'问'跟'璺'谐音。insist on getting to the bottom of matters, with a pun on 问 wèn (ask) and 璺 wèn (crack)

【打谱】dǎ//pǔ ❶ 按照棋谱把棋子顺次摆出来,学习下棋的技术 place the pieces on the chessboard according to a chess manual ❷ (~儿 dǎ//pǔr) 订出大概的计划 draw a general plan: 你得先打个谱儿,才能跟人家商订合同。You should have a general plan before discussing the contract with others. ❸ 合计;打算 think; intend

【打气】dǎ//qì ❶ 加压力使气进入(球或轮胎等) inflate; pump up (ball or tire, etc.) ❷〈比喻 *fig.*〉鼓动 bolster; encourage; cheer up: 撑腰~ brace and bolster

【打千】dǎ//qiān (~儿 dǎ//qiānr) 旧时的敬礼,右手下垂,左腿向前屈膝,右腿略弯曲: way of salute in old days by lowering the right hand and going down on the left knee: ~请安 pay respect to sb. by going down on one's left knee

【打钎】dǎqiān 采矿、开隧道等爆破工程中,用钎子在岩石上凿孔 drill a blasting hole in rock with a hammer and a drill rod, when mining or tunnelling

【打前失】dǎ qián·shi (驴、马等)前蹄没站稳而跌倒或几乎跌倒 (of horses or mules) stumble

【打前站】dǎ qiánzhàn 行军或集体出行的时候,先有人到将要停留或到达的地点去办理食宿等事务,叫打前站 act as an advance party; set out in advance to make arrangements for board and lodging

【打钱】dǎ//qián 卖艺的人向观众收钱 (of a street-performer) collect money from the audience

【打枪】dǎqiāng ❶ 发射枪弹 fire a gun ❷ ☞ 枪替 qiāngtì on p.1542

【打秋风】dǎ qiūfēng 指假借某种名义向人索取财物 try to sponge off people; also 打抽丰 dǎ chōufēng

【打趣】dǎ//qù 拿人开玩笑;嘲弄 tease; make fun of: 几个调皮的人围上来,七嘴八舌~他。Some naughty people surrounded him and made fun of him.

【打圈子】dǎ quān·zi 转圈子 circle: 飞机在天空嗡嗡地~。The plane hummed while circling in the sky. ◇应该全面地考虑问题,不要只在一些细节上~。We should think the question over as a whole, instead of getting bogged down in minor issues. also 打圈圈 dǎ quānquān

【打拳】dǎ//quán 练拳术 go shadow boxing

【打群架】dǎ qúnjià 双方聚集许多人打架 engage in a gang fight

【打扰】dǎrǎo ❶ 扰乱;搅扰 disturb; trouble: 工作时间,请勿~。Please don't disturb during office hours. ❷〈婉辞 *euph.*〉指受招待 be received: 在府上~多日,非常感谢! Thank you very much for letting me stay at your home for so long!

【打扫】dǎsǎo 扫除;清理 sweep; clean: ~院子 sweep the courtyard | ~战场 clean up the battlefield

【打闪】dǎ//shǎn 云层发生放电现象 (of lightning) flash: 天上又打雷又~,眼看雨就来了。There is thunder and lightning — it's going to rain.

【打扇】dǎ//shàn (给别人)扇 (shān) 扇子 fan sb.

【打食】[1] dǎ//shí (~儿 dǎ//shír) (鸟兽)到窝外寻找食物 (of birds and beasts) seek food

【打食】[2] dǎ//shí 用药物帮助消化或使肠胃里停滞的东西排出体外 use medicine to aid digestion or ease constipation

【打手】dǎ·shou 受主子豢养,替主子欺压、殴打人的恶棍 hired roughneck (or thug); hatchet man

【打算】dǎ·suan ❶ 考虑;计划 plan; intend: 通盘~ comprehensive plan | 你~几时走? When do you intend to leave? ❷ 关于行动的方向、

方法等的想法；念头 plan; consideration; calculation：毕业生有一个共同的～，就是到祖国最需要的地方去。The common plan of all graduates is to go where the country needs them most.

【打算盘】dǎ suàn·pan ❶ 用算盘计算 calculate on an abacus ❷ 合计；盘算 calculate; scheme：别总在一些小事上～。Cut all the scheming on minor things.

【打胎】dǎ// tāi 人工流产的通称 common reference to 人工流产 réngōng liúchǎn

【打探】dǎtàn 打听；探听 enquire about; ask about：～消息 ask for information

【打铁】dǎ// tiě 锻造钢铁工件 forge iron; work as a blacksmith

【打听】dǎ·ting 探问 ask about; enquire about：～消息 ask for information|～同伴的下落 ask about the whereabouts of one's companion

【打挺儿】dǎ tǐngr 头颈用力向后仰，胸部和腹部挺起 bend one's head and neck backwards and stretch one's chest and stomach：这孩子不肯吃药，在妈妈的怀里直～。The child bent backwards in his mother's arms, refusing to take the medicine.

【打通】dǎ// tōng 除去阻隔使相贯通 get through; open up：把这两个房间～。Make an opening between these two rooms. ◇～思想 straighten out sb.'s thinking; talk sb. round

【打通关】dǎ tōngguān 筵席上一个人跟在座的人顺次划拳喝酒(at banquets) play a finger-guessing game with each other in sequence

【打头】[1] dǎ// tóu (～儿 dǎ// tóur) same as 抽头 chōu// tóu

【打头】[2] dǎ// tóu (～儿 dǎ// tóur) 带头；领先 take the lead：谁先打个头？Who will take the lead? |～的都是小伙子。Those who took the lead were all young men.

【打头】dǎtóu 〈方 *dial.*〉(～儿 dǎtóur) 从头 from the beginning：失败了再～儿来。Let's do it all over again if it fails.

【打头风】dǎtóufēng 逆风 against the wind

【打头阵】dǎ tóu zhèn 〈比喻 *fig.*〉冲在前边带头干 fight in the van; spearhead the attack; take the lead：每次抗洪救灾，当地驻军总是～。The army of the local garrison always fight in the van whenever flood or any other disaster occurs.

【打退堂鼓】dǎ tuìtánggǔ 封建官吏退堂时打鼓，现在比喻做事中途退缩 (of an official in feudal days) dismiss a court session by beating a drum; beat a retreat; back up; give sth. up midway：有困难大家来克服，你可不能～。Let's stick together and overcome the difficulties. Don't give up.

【打围】dǎ// wéi 许多打猎的人从四面围捕野兽，也泛指打猎 encircle and hunt down (animals); go hunting

【打问】[1] dǎwèn 〈方 *dial.*〉打听 ask about：把事情的底细～清楚。Ask about what really happened.

【打问】[2] dǎwèn 〈书 *fml.*〉拷问 torture sb. during interrogation

【打问号】dǎ wènhào 表示产生怀疑 doubt：出现这种情况，我对他不得不打个问号。When such things happen, I have to doubt him.

【打问讯】dǎ wènxùn same as 问讯 wènxùn ③

【打下】dǎ// xià ❶ 攻克(某地点) sack; capture (a place) ❷ 奠定(基础) lay a foundation

【打下手】dǎ xiàshǒu (～儿 dǎ xiàshǒur)担任助手 act as assistant

【打先锋】dǎ xiānfēng ❶ 作战或行军时充当先头部队 fight in the vanguard; be a pioneer ❷〈比喻 *fig.*〉带头奋进 lead the way：要为经济建设～。We should strive in the van of economic development.

【打响】dǎxiǎng ❶ 指开火；接火 start shooting; open fire：先头部队～了。The advance detachment opened fire. ❷〈比喻 *fig.*〉事情初步成功 win initial success：这一炮～了，下一步就好办了。Success at this stage will make the next step easier.

【打消】dǎxiāo 消除(用于抽象的事物) give up (an idea, etc.); dispel (a doubt, etc.)：～顾虑 dispel misgivings|这个念头趁早～。You'd better give up the idea as soon as possible.

【打斜】dǎxié 坐立时斜对着尊长或客人 sit or stand with one's body inclined towards an elderly person or guest in a gesture of respect：～坐在一边儿 sit inclined to one side

【打雪仗】dǎ xuězhàng 把雪团成球，互相投掷闹着玩 have a snowball fight; throw snowballs at each other for fun

【打鸭子上架】dǎ yā·zi shàng jià ☞ 赶鸭子上架 gǎn yā·zi shàng jià on p. 630

【打牙祭】dǎ yájì 〈方 *dial.*〉原指每逢月初、月中吃一顿有荤菜的饭，后来泛指偶尔吃一顿丰盛的饭 originally referring to a meal with meat or fish eaten at the beginning and middle of every month; now a reference to splurging on a sumptuous meal occasionally

【打哑谜】dǎ yǎmí 没有明确地把意思说出来或表示出来，让对方猜 not speak out but let others guess：有话直说，用不着～。Say what you have to say, and don't let me guess.

【打掩护】dǎ yǎnhù ❶ 在主力部队的侧面或后面跟敌人作战，保护主力部队完成任务 provide cover for the main force ❷〈比喻 *fig.*〉遮盖或包庇(坏事、坏人) shield; give refuge to (bad person or thing, etc.)：事情已经调查清楚，你用不着再替他～了。We have found out, you needn't shield him any more.

【打眼】[1] dǎ//yǎn (～儿 dǎ// yǎnr) 钻孔 punch (or bore) a hole; drill：往墙上打个眼 drill a hole in the wall|～放炮 drill and blast

【打眼】[2] dǎ// yǎn 〈方 *dial.*〉买东西没看出毛病，上了当 be double-crossed when buying goods

【打眼】[3] dǎ//yǎn〈方 *dial.*〉惹人注意 catch the eye; attract attention: 这件红衣服真～。This red dress is really eye-catching.

【打佯儿】dǎ//yángr〈方 *dial*〉装做不知道的样子 pretend ignorance or innocence: 我问他,他跟我～。I asked him and he pretended he did not know anything.

【打样】dǎ//yàng ❶ 在建筑房屋、制造器具等之前,画出设计图样 draw a design before the construction of a house or the production of goods, etc. ❷ 排版完了,印刷之前,印出样张来供校对用 produce a proof before printing

【打烊】dǎ//yàng〈方 *dial.*〉(商店)晚上关门停止营业 (of shops) put up the shutters; close for the night

D

【打药】dǎyào ❶ 泻药 laxative; cathartic; purgative ❷〈方 *dial.*〉〈旧时 *old*〉走江湖的医生卖的药(多为外敷的) ointment sold by quacks (mostly for external application) to treat wounds

【打野外】dǎ yěwài (军队)到野外演习 (of army) do exercises in the wild

【打夜作】dǎ yèzuò 夜间工作 work late into the night: 接连打了两个夜作 work overtime for two consecutive nights

【打印】dǎ//yìn 盖图章 affix a seal on; stamp

【打印】dǎyìn 打字油印 cut a stencil and mimeograph; mimeograph: ～文件 print documents

【打印机】dǎyìnjī 由微型电子计算机控制的打字机,没有键盘,把字符的代码转换成字符并印出来 printer, controlled by a microcomputer, without a keyboard, transferring character codes into characters, and printing them

【打印台】dǎyìntái same as 印台 yìntái

【打油】dǎ//yóu ❶ 用油提子舀油,借指零星地买油 scoop up oil — buy oil (in a small quantity with one's own container ❷〈方 *dial.*〉榨油 extract oil (from a plant, etc.) ❸ 上油 add oil: 给皮鞋打点儿油 polish leather shoes with oil

【打油诗】dǎyóushī 内容和词句通俗诙谐、不拘于平仄韵律的旧体诗。相传为唐代张打油所创,因而得名。doggerel; classical Chinese poetry with easily understandable sentences not strict in tonal patterns, named after Zhang Dayou, of the Tang Dynasty, who was said to have initiated the style

【打游击】dǎ yóujī ❶ 从事游击活动 fight as a guerrilla ❷〈比喻 *fig.*〉从事没有固定地点的工作或活动(诙谐的说法 humor.) operate like a guerrilla — work, eat, sleep, etc., at no fixed place

【打圆场】dǎ yuánchǎng 调解纠纷,缓和僵局 mediate a dispute; smooth things over: 他俩正在争吵,你去打个圆场吧。Those two are quarrelling, you'd better smooth things over. also 打圆盘 dǎ yuánpán

【打援】dǎ//yuán 攻打增援的敌军 attack (or ambush) enemy reinforcements: 围城～ besiege a city and attack enemy reinforcements

【打杂儿】dǎ//zár 做杂事 do odds and ends: 他没技术,只能在车间～。He has no special skills, and has to do odd jobs in the workshop.

【打造】dǎzào 制造(多指金属器物) make (metal work); forge: ～农具 make farm tools | ～船只 build ships

【打战】dǎzhàn 发抖 shiver; tremble: 冻得直～ so cold as to shiver; also 打颤 dǎzhàn

【打颤】dǎzhàn same as 打战 dǎzhàn

【打仗】dǎ//zhàng 进行战争;进行战斗 fight; go to war; make war ◇我们在生产战线上打了个漂亮仗。We made remarkable achievements in production.

【打招呼】dǎ zhāo·hu ❶ 用语言或动作表示问候 (by words or gestures) greet sb.; say hello: 路上碰见熟人,打了个招呼。I met an acquaintance on the way and greeted him. ❷(事前或事后)就某项事情或某种问题予以通知、关照 notify; let sb. in on sth. (beforehand or afterwards): 已经给你们打过招呼,怎么还要这样干? I already informed you, now why did you still do it in this way?

【打照面儿】dǎ zhàomiànr ❶ 面对面地相遇 meet unexpectedly (or by chance); have a chance encounter: 他俩在街上打个照面儿,一时都愣住了。They met on the street and both were struck speechless. ❷ 露面 make a brief appearance: 他刚才在会上打了个照面儿就走了。He just showed his face at the meeting and left.

【打折扣】dǎ zhékòu ❶ 降低商品的定价(出售) sell at a discount; give a discount; ☞ 折扣 zhékòu on p. 2429 ❷〈比喻 *fig.*〉不完全按规定的、已承认的或已答应的来做 fall short of a requirement or promise: 要保质保量地按时交活儿,不能～。We should carry out our pledge to meet quality and quantity requirements and get the job done on time.

【打针】dǎ//zhēn 把液体药物用注射器注射到有机体内 give or get an injection

【打整】dǎ·zheng〈方 *dial.*〉收拾;准备 get things ready

【打皱】dǎzhòu〈方 *dial.*〉(～儿 dǎzhòur)起皱纹 crumple; wrinkle: 脸上～ wrinkles on the face | 衣服～了,熨平了再穿。The clothes have became crumpled, iron them before wearing.

【打主意】dǎ zhǔ·yi 想办法;设法谋取 think out a plan; try to obtain: 这事还得另～。This has to be done some other way. | 做事不能只在钱上～。Making money should not be your only goal.

【打住】dǎ//zhù ❶ 停止 come to a halt; (in speech or writing) stop: 他说到这里突然～了。

He suddenly stopped talking at that point.｜在小院门口～了脚步 stop at the gate of the yard ❷〈方 *dial*.〉在别人家里或外地暂住 temporarily live in sb. else's home or other place

【打转】dǎzhuàn（～儿 dǎzhuànr）绕圈子；旋转 spin；rotate；revolve；turn around and around：急得张着两手乱～。He was so worried that he kept twisting his hands.｜眼睛滴溜溜地直～ eyeballs spinning around and around ◇他讲的话老是在我脑子里～。His words kept ringing in my mind. also 打转转 dǎzhuànzhuàn

【打桩】dǎ//zhuāng 把木桩、石桩等砸进地里，使建筑物基础坚固 pile driving；piling；drive wooden or stone piles into the earth to lay a solid foundation

【打字】dǎ//zì 用打字机把文字打在纸上 typewrite；type

【打字机】dǎzìjī 按键或把手把字和符号打印在纸上的机械，有手打和电打两种 typewriter (manual or electric)

【打总儿】dǎzǒngr 把分为几次做的事情合并为一次做 at one go；in a batch；altogether：～算账 settle the account once and for all｜～买 buy the whole lot

【打嘴】dǎ//zuǐ ❶ 打嘴巴 slap sb.'s face ❷〈方 *dial*.〉才夸口就出丑 slap one's own face — fail to make good one's boast：～现眼 fail to make good one's boast and lose face

【打嘴仗】dǎ zuǐzhàng 指吵架 quarrel

【打坐】dǎ//zuò 我国古代一种养生健身法，也是僧道修行的方法。闭目盘膝而坐，调整气息出入，手放在一定位置上，不想任何事情。(of a Buddhist or Taoist monk) sit in meditation, adjusting breathing, putting the hands in certain positions and thinking of nothing, a way of cultivating and maintaining good health

dà（ㄉㄚˋ）

大¹ dà ❶ 在体积、面积、数量、力量、强度等方面超过一般或超过所比较的对象（跟'小'相对 as opposed to 'small'）big；large；great (in volume, area, quantity, force, strength, etc.)：房子～ big house｜地方～ big place｜年纪～ old age｜声音太～ too loud｜外面风～。The wind is blowing hard.｜团结起来力量～。Unity is strength.｜❷ 大小的程度 size；age：那间房子有这间两个～。That room is twice the size of this one.｜你的孩子现在多～了？How old is your child? ❸ 程度深 high degree：～红 bright red｜真相～白。The truth has been revealed.｜～吃一惊 be greatly surprised｜天已经～亮了。It's already broad daylight.｜病已经～好了 almost recovered ❹ 用于'不'后，表示程度浅或次数少（in the negative) not very；not often：不～爱说话 not like to talk｜还不～会走路 cannot walk steadily｜不～出门 not often go out ❺ 排行第一的 eldest：老～ the eldest (son, daughter, etc.)｜～哥 eldest brother ❻ 年纪大的人 adult；grown-up：一家～小 whole family ❼〈敬辞 *pol*.〉称与对方有关的事物 your：尊姓～名 your honourable name｜～作 your article｜～札 your letter ❽ 用在时令或节日前，表示强调 [used before time or festival for emphasis]：～清早 early in the morning｜～热天 hot day｜～年初一 first day of the lunar year ❾ (Dà) 姓 a surname

大² dà〈方 *dial*.〉❶ 父亲 father：俺～叫我来看看你。My father asked me to visit you. ❷ 伯父或叔父：father's brother；uncle：三～是一个劳动英雄。Third Uncle is a model worker.

〈古 *arch*.〉又同'太''泰'(tài)，如'大子''大山' same as 太 tài and 泰 tài, such as 大子 'crown prince' and 大山 'huge mountain'

☞ dài on p. 368

【大白】¹ dàbái〈方 *dial*.〉粉刷墙壁用的白垩 whitewash；chalk

【大白】² dàbái（事情的原委）完全清楚 come out；become known：真相～。The truth has come out.｜～于天下。It has become known to all.

【大白菜】dàbáicài same as 白菜 báicài

【大伯子】dàbǎi·zi 丈夫的哥哥 husband's elder brother

【大班】¹ dàbān〈方 *dial*.〉❶〈旧时 *old*〉称洋行的经理 taipan；big boss (a term for the manager of a foreign firm) ❷〈旧时 *old*〉称轿夫 carriage driver

【大班】² dàbān 幼儿园里由五周岁至六周岁儿童所编成的班级 top class in a kindergarten, consisting of children five to six years old

【大半】dàbàn ❶ 过半数；大部分 more than half；greater part；most：这个车间～是年轻人。Most of the members of this workshop are young. ❷〈副词 *adv*.〉表示较大的可能性 most probably；most likely：他这时候还不来，～是不来了。He most probably isn't coming as he still hasn't come yet.

【大鸨】dàbǎo 鸟，高约3—4尺，背部有黄褐色和黑色的斑纹，腹部灰白色，不善于飞而善于走。吃谷类和昆虫。great bustard (*Otis tarda dybowskii*)；bird with a height of 3-4 *chi*, yellow and black stripes on the back, grey-white belly, chiefly terrestrial and ground-running, eating grains and insects；also 地鹔 dìbǔ

【大暴雨】dàbàoyǔ 指24小时内，雨量达100—200毫米的雨 downpour, with a precipitation of 100-200mm. within 24 hours

【大本营】dàběnyíng ❶ 指战时军队的最高统帅部 supreme headquarters ❷ 泛指某种活动的

策源地 base camp for certain activity

【大便】dàbiàn ❶ 屎 faece; stool ❷ 拉屎 defecate; poop

【大兵】dàbīng ❶ 指士兵(含贬义 derog.)common soldier ❷ 兵力强大的军队 powerful army:～压境 the main force is approaching

【大伯】dàbó ❶ 伯父 father's elder brother; uncle ❷ 尊称年长的男人(a polite form of address for an elderly man) uncle

【大脖子病】dàbó·zibìng〈方 *dial.*〉甲状腺肿 goitre, an enlargement of the thyroid gland on the front and sides of the neck, usu. symptomatic of abnormal thyroid secretion, esp. hypothyroidism due to a lack of iodine in the diet

D

【大不了】dà·buliǎo ❶ 至多也不过 at the worst:赶不上车,～走回去就是了。The worst that can happen if we miss the bus is we will have to walk back. ❷ 了不得(多用于否定式 usu. in the negative) alarming; serious:这个病没有什么～,吃点药就会好的。It's nothing serious, you will be fine after taking some medicine.

【大步流星】dà bù liú xīng 形容脚步迈得大,走得快 with vigorous strides; at a stride

【大材小用】dà cái xiǎo yòng 大的材料用在小处。多指人事安排上不恰当,屈才。large resource put to small use — one's talent wasted on a petty job; not do justice to sb.'s talent

【大菜】dàcài ❶ 酒席中后上的大碗的菜,如全鸡、全鸭、肘子等 big dish served late at a banquet, such as whole chicken, whole duck, pork joint, etc. ❷ 指西餐 Western meal

【大肠】dàcháng 肠的一部分,上连小肠,下通肛门,比小肠粗而短。分为盲肠、结肠和直肠三部分。主要作用是吸收水分和形成粪便。large intestine, the broad, shorter part of the intestines, comprising the cecum, colon and rectum, that absorbs water from and eliminates the residues of digestion

【大氅】dàchǎng 大衣 overcoat; cloak; cape:羊皮～ sheepskin coat

【大钞】dàchāo 大面额的钞票 bill of a big denomination:百元～ one-hundred-yuan bill

【大潮】dàcháo ❶ 一个朔望月中最高的潮水。朔日和望日,月亮和太阳对地球的引力最大(是二者引力之和),按理大潮应该出现在这两天,由于一些复杂因素的影响,大潮往往延迟两三天出现。spring tide, the heaviest flooding tide of the month; On the 1st and 15th days of the lunar month, the earth feels the strongest gravitational pull from the sun and the moon (the sum of the two); in theory the spring tide should appear on these two days, but it always appears two or three days later due to some complicating factors. ❷〈比喻 *fig.*〉声势大的社会潮流 influential social trend:改革的～ tide of reform

【大车】[1] dàchē 牲口拉的两轮或四轮载重车 cart with two or four wheels driven by draught animals

【大车】[2] dàchē 对火车司机和轮船上负责管理机器的人的尊称 respectful term for an engine driver or the chief engineer of a ship; also 大伡 dàchē

【大臣】dàchén 君主国家的高级官员 minister (of a monarchy)

【大乘】dàchéng 公元1,2世纪流行的佛教派别,自以为可以普度众生,所以自命为大乘 Mahayana, a school of Buddhism popular in the 1st and 2nd centuries, characterized by belief in salvation; ☞ 小乘 xiǎochéng on p. 2106

【大吃一惊】dà chī yī jīng 形容对发生的意外事情非常吃惊 be aghast; be quite taken aback

【大冲】dàchōng 火星离地球最近的时期,隔15—17年重复一次。因为距地球近,这时火星显得最亮。favourable opposition, when Mars is nearest to and looks clearest from earth every 15 to 17 years; ☞ 冲[1] chōng⑤ on p. 267

【大虫】dàchóng〈方 *dial.*〉老虎 tiger

【大出血】dàchūxuè 由动脉破裂或内脏损伤等引起的大量出血的现象 massive haemorrhage caused by damage to artery or injury of internal organs

【大处落墨】dà chù luò mò 绘画或写文章在主要的地方下工夫(of painting or writing) devote to major parts;〈比喻 *fig.*〉做事从主要的地方着眼,不把力量分散在枝节上 concentrate on the key points, and not get diverted by trifles

【大疮】dàchuāng 梅毒、软性下疳等性病在身体表面上形成的溃疡 mycotic ulcer caused by venereal diseases such as syphilis and haemophilus

【大吹大擂】dà chuī dà léi〈比喻 *fig.*〉大肆宣扬 make a great fanfare; make a big noise; beat the drum

【大吹法螺】dà chuī fǎluó 佛家把讲经说法叫吹法螺。现比喻说大话。expound the doctrines of Buddhism; (fig.) blow one's own trumpet; talk big; brag

【大春】dàchūn〈方 *dial.*〉❶ 指春季 spring ❷ 指春天播种的作物,如稻子、玉米 crops sown in spring (rice, corn, etc.); also 大春作物 dàchūn zuòwù

【大醇小疵】dà chún xiǎo cī 大体上完美,只是个别小地方有些毛病 fine on the whole despite a few defects

【大词】dàcí 三段论中结论的宾词(major logic term) predicate of the conclusion in a syllogism; ☞ 三段论 sānduànlùn on p. 1650

【大葱】dàcōng 葱的一种,叶子和茎较粗大 Chinese green onion with thick leaves and stem; ☞ 葱 cōng on p. 323

【大…大…】dà…dà… 分别用在名词、动词或形容词的前面，表示规模大，程度深［used before nouns, verbs or adjectives to show a large scale or high degree］：～手～脚 wasteful｜～鱼～肉 plenty of meat and fish; rich food｜～摇～摆 swaggering｜～吵～闹 kick up a row; make a scene｜～吃～喝 make a pig of oneself｜～红～绿 loud colours

【大大】dàdà 强调数量很大或程度很深 greatly; enormously：费用～超过了预算。Expenses exceeded the budget by a huge margin.｜室内有了通风装置，温度～降低了。The temperature in the room has been greatly decreased after the ventilation equipment was installed.

【大大咧咧】dà·daliēliē（～的 dà·daliēliē·de）形容随随便便，满不在意 careless; casual

【大大落落】dà·daluōluō〈方 *dial.*〉形容态度大方 natural and poised

【大胆】dàdǎn 有勇气；不畏缩 bold; daring; be the opposite of discreet; audacious：～革新 bold innovation｜～探索 daring exploration

【大刀阔斧】dà dāo kuò fǔ〈比喻 *fig.*〉办事果断而有魄力 make snap and bold decisions

【大抵】dàdǐ 大概；大都 generally speaking; in the main; on the whole：情况～如此。That's roughly the whole situation.｜他们几个人是同一年毕业的，后来的经历也～相同。They graduated in the same year and then had similar experiences.

【大地】dàdì ❶ 广大的地面 earth; ground：～回春。Spring is here again.｜阳光普照～。The sun shines all over the world. ❷ 指有关地球的 concerning the earth：～测量 earth measurement

【大典】dàdiǎn 隆重的典礼（指国家举行的）grand ceremony (held by a state)：开国～ceremonies to proclaim the founding of a state

【大殿】dàdiàn ❶ 封建王朝举行庆典、接见大臣或使臣等的殿 audience hall in feudal society for holding ceremonies and meeting officials or foreign envoys ❷ 寺庙中供奉主要神佛的殿 main hall of a Buddhist temple

【大动干戈】dà dòng gāngē 原指发动战争，现多比喻兴师动众或大张声势地做事 go to war; get into a fight; (fig.) do sth. in a big way：这部机器没有多大毛病，你却要大拆大卸，何必如此～呢？There is nothing seriously wrong with this machine, why did you make such a big fuss and tear it down?

【大动脉】dàdòngmài ❶ 主动脉 main artery ❷〈比喻 *fig.*〉主要的交通干线 trunk line of transportation：京广铁路是我国南北交通的～。The Beijing-Guangzhou Railway is a main artery between the north and south of our country.

【大豆】dàdòu ❶ 一年生草本植物，花白色或紫色，有根瘤，豆荚有毛。种子一般黄色，供食用，也可以榨油。soya bean (*Glycine max*); annual plant of the legume family, with white or purple flowers, root nodules, hairy pods, yellow seeds, chiefly for food and oil extraction ❷ 这种植物的种子 seed of the plant

【大都】dàdū 大多 mostly; for the most part：杜甫的杰出诗篇～写于安史之乱前后。Most of Du Fu's masterpieces were written around the Turmoil of the An Lushan-Shi Siming Insurrection.

【大肚子】dàdù·zi ❶ 指怀孕 pregnant ❷ 指饭量大的人（用于不严肃的口气 humor.）big eater

【大肚子痞】dàdù·zipǐ〈中医 *Chin. med.*〉指肝脏和脾脏肿大，腹部膨大，并有腹水的症状，常见于黑热病、晚期血吸虫病等 distension of liver, spleen and abdomen, accompanied by ascites, oft. seen in kala-azar and terminal snail fever

【大度】dàdù〈书 *fml.*〉气量宽宏能容人 magnanimous：豁达～be generous and open-minded｜～包容 be magnanimous and tolerant

【大端】dàduān〈书 *fml.*〉（事情的）主要方面 main aspects or features; salient points：举其～ point out the main features

【大队】dàduì ❶ 队伍编制，由若干中队组成 military unit corresponding to a battalion or regiment; group ❷ 军队中相当于营或团的一级组织 organization equivalent to the battalion or regiment level

【大多】dàduō 大部分；大多数 for the most part; mostly：大会的代表～是先进工作者。The representatives at the meeting are mostly advanced workers.｜树上的柿子～已经成熟。Most of the persimmons on the tree have ripened.

【大多数】dàduōshù 超过半数很多的数量 great majority; vast majority; bulk：～人赞成这个方案。The great majority agreed with this plan.

【大而无当】dà ér wú dàng 虽然大，但是不合用 large but impractical; unwieldy

【大发】dà·fa〈方 *dial.*〉超过了适当的限度；过度（后面常跟'了'字 oft. followed by the character 了·le) beyond the proper limits; excessive：病～了 cruelly ill｜这件事闹～了。The whole thing has got out of control.

【大发雷霆】dà fā léitíng〈比喻 *fig.*〉大发脾气，高声训斥 be furious; fly into a rage; scream at sb. angrily

【大法】dàfǎ ❶ 指国家的根本法，即宪法 fundamental laws and principles (of a state); constitution ❷〈书 *fml.*〉重要的法令、法则 important law

【大凡】dàfán〈副词 *adv.*〉用在句首，表示总括一般的情形，常跟'总、都'等呼应［used at the beginning of a sentence and oft. correlative with 总 zǒng, 都 dōu, etc.］generally; in most cases：～搞基本建设的单位，流动性都比较大。Generally speaking, units engaged in capital construction have noticeable fluidity.

【大方】[1] dàfāng〈书 *fml*.〉指专家学者；内行人 expert; scholar：～之家 learned man; scholar | 贻笑～ incur the ridicule of experts

【大方】[2] dàfāng 绿茶的一种，产于安徽歙县、浙江淳安等地 *dafang*; a kind of green tea produced in Shexian County in Anhui Province, and Chun'an in Zhejiang Province

【大方】dà·fang ❶ 对于财物不计较；不吝啬 generous; liberal：出手～ be open-handed | 他很～，不会计较这几个钱。A generous man, he would not begrudge this small sum of money. ❷（言谈、举止）自然；不拘束 natural and poised; easy; unaffected：举止～ have an easy manner | 可以大大方方的，用不着拘束。You may relax and make yourself comfortable. ❸（样式、颜色等）不俗气（pattern, colour, etc.）in good taste：陈设～ tastefully furnished | 这种布的颜色和花样看着很～。The pattern and colour of this fabric are in good taste.

【大放厥词】dà fàng jué cí 大发议论（今多含贬义 oft. derog.）talk a lot of nonsense; let loose a torrent of empty rhetoric

【大粪】dàfèn 人的粪便 human excrement

【大风】dàfēng ❶ 气象学上指 8 级风 fresh gale; ☞ 风级 fēngjí on p. 579 ❷ 泛指风力很大的风 gale; strong wind：～警报 gale warning

【大风大浪】dà fēng dà làng〈比喻 *fig*.〉社会的大动荡，大变化 great social turbulence; vast changes

【大夫】dàfū 古代官职，位于卿之下，士之上 grand master; official title in feudal China, below a minister and higher than a councillor;
☞ dài·fu on p. 368

【大副】dàfù 轮船上船长的主要助手，驾驶工作的负责人。大副之下有时还有二副和三副。first (or chief) mate to the captain in charge of navigating a ship, with second and third mates under him

【大腹贾】dàfùgǔ 指富商（含讥讽意 sarcastic）potbellied merchant; rich merchant

【大腹便便】dà fù piánpián 肚子肥大的样子（含贬义 derog.）potbellied; big-bellied

【大盖帽】dàgàimào 军人、警察或其他机关人员戴的一种顶大而平的制式帽子 peaked cap; uniform cap worn by the military, police or other staff; also 大檐帽 dàyánmào

【大概】dàgài ❶ 大致的内容或情况 general idea; broad outline：他嘴上不说，心里却捉摸了个～。Although he did not say anything, he got a general idea about the situation. ❷ 不十分精确或不十分详尽 general; rough：他把情况做了个～的分析。He made a general analysis of the situation. | 这件事我记不太清，只有个～的印象。I don't remember it clearly, I only have a rough impression. ❸〈副词 *adv*.〉表示有很大的可能性 probably; most likely：雪并没有多厚，～在半夜就不下了。It did not snow heavily, probably stopping at midnight. | 从这里到西山，～有四五十里地。It is approximately 40 to 50 *li* from here to the Western Hills.

【大概其】dàgàiqí〈方 *dial*.〉大概 general; rough：这本书我没细看，只～翻了翻。I didn't read the book carefully, but only skimmed through it. | 他说了半天，我只听了个～。He talked at length, but I only caught the general idea. '其'有时也作齐。其 qí can sometimes be replaced by 齐 qí

【大纲】dàgāng（著作、讲稿、计划等）系统排列的内容要点 outline; compendium of (work, text of a speech, plan, etc.)：教学～ teaching programme

【大哥】dàgē ❶ 排行最大的哥哥 eldest brother ❷ 尊称年纪跟自己相仿的男子 elder brother (a polite form of address for a man about one's own age)

【大革命】dàgémìng ❶ 大规模的革命 great revolution：法国～ French Revolution ❷ 特指我国第一次国内革命战争 First Civil Revolutionary War of China (1924-27)

【大公国】dàgōngguó 以大公（在公爵之上的爵位）为国家元首的国家，如卢森堡大公国（在西欧）grand duchy, the territory ruled by a duke or duchess, such as Luxembourg (in Western Europe)

【大公无私】dà gōng wú sī ❶ 完全为人民群众利益着想，毫无自私自利之心 selfless; give no thought to self ❷ 处理公正，不偏袒任何一方 be perfectly impartial

【大功告成】dà gōng gào chéng 指大的工程、事业或重要任务宣告完成（of a project, work, etc.）be accomplished; be crowned with success

【大姑子】dà·gū·zi 丈夫的姐姐 husband's elder sister; sister-in-law

【大鼓】dàgǔ 曲艺的一种，用韵文演唱故事，夹有少量说白，用鼓、板、三弦等伴奏。流行地区很广，因地区和方言、曲调的不同而有不同的名称，如京韵大鼓、乐亭大鼓、山东大鼓、湖北大鼓等。*dagu*; folk tale sung in verse accompanied by a small drum, clappers, *sanxian* (a three-stringed plucked instrument), etc., popular in many places, named after different dialects and tunes, such as *Jingyun dagu*, *Leting dagu*, *Shandong dagu*, and *Hubei dagu*

【大故】dàgù〈书 *fml*.〉❶ 重大的事故，如战争、灾祸等 dreadful accident, such as war and disaster：国有～。The country suffered a disaster. ❷ 指父亲或母亲死亡 (of one's parent)

die

【大褂】dàguà（～儿 dàguàr）身长过膝的中式单衣 unlined long Chinese gown

【大观】dàguān 形容事物美好繁多 grand sight; magnificent spectacle：蔚为～ afford magnificent view｜洋洋～ grandiose; spectacular

【大管】dàguǎn ☞ 巴松 bāsōng on p. 24

【大锅饭】dàguōfàn 供多数人吃的普通伙食 food prepared in a large canteen cauldron：吃～ everyone eating from the same big pot (a typical Chinese term for egalitarianism); have one's meals in a canteen

【大海捞针】dà hǎi lāo zhēn 海底捞针 fish for a needle in the ocean; look for a needle in a haystack

【大寒】dàhán 二十四节气之一，在1月20日或21日，一般是我国气候最冷的时候 Greater Cold — the last of the 24 solar terms, the day marking the beginning of the last solar term (Jan. 20 or 21), after which the weather grows slowly warmer. ☞ 节气 jiéqì on p. 989 and 二十四节气 èrshísì jiéqì on p. 516

【大汉】dàhàn 身材高大的男子 big (or hefty, burly) fellow：彪形～ husky fellow

【大旱望云霓】dàhàn wàng yúnní〈比喻 *fig.*〉渴望解除困境，好像大旱的时候盼望雨水一样 long for a rain cloud during a drought — look forward to relief from distress

【大好】dàhǎo ❶ 很好；美好 very good; excellent：～形势 very good situation｜～时光 golden years ❷（病）完全好 (of illness) completely cured

【大号】[1] dàhào ❶〈尊称 *honor.*〉他人的名字 given name ❷（～儿 dàhàor）较大的型号 large size：～皮鞋 large-size leather shoes

【大号】[2] dàhào 铜管乐器，装有四个或五个活塞。吹奏时声音低沉雄浑。tuba; bass horn or brass wind, having four or five plungers, and producing low and resonant sound

【大合唱】dàhéchàng 包括独唱、对唱、重唱、齐唱、合唱等形式的集体演唱，有时还穿插朗诵和表演，常用管弦乐队伴奏，如《黄河大合唱》cantata; chorus, including solo, antiphonal singing, an ensemble of two or more singers, unison, chorus, sometimes with recital and performance accompanied by an orchestra, such as *The Yellow River Cantata*

【大亨】dàhēng 称某一地方或某一行业的有势力的人 big shot; bigwig; magnate：金融～ financial magnate

【大轰大嗡】dà hōng dà wēng 形容不注重实际，只在形式上轰轰烈烈 make a terrific din; rousing but impractical situation

【大红】dàhóng 很红的颜色 bright red; scarlet

【大后方】dàhòufāng 指抗日战争时期国民党统治下的西南、西北地区 area of southwestern and northwestern China under KMT rule during the War of Resistance against Japan

【大后年】dàhòunián 紧接在后年之后的那一年 three years from now

【大后天】dàhòutiān 紧接在后天之后的那一天 three days from now; also 大后儿 dàhòur

【大户】dàhù ❶〈旧时 *old*〉指有钱有势的人家 rich and influential family ❷ 人口多、分支繁的家族 big family：王姓是该村的～。The Wangs are a big family in the village. ❸ 指在某一方面数量比较大的单位或个人 unit or individual possessing certain characteristics in large measure：冰箱生产～ large producer of refrigerators｜用电～ unit or individual consuming an unusual amount of electricity

【大花脸】dàhuāliǎn 戏曲中花脸的一种，注重唱工，如铜锤、黑头等 'big flowery face', a type of the flowery-face role in Chinese opera, which requires more skill in singing than in acting, including roles like 'bronze hammer' and 'black face'

【大话】dàhuà 虚夸的话 big talk; boast; bragging：说～ talk big; brag

【大黄鱼】dàhuángyú 黄鱼的一种，鳞小，背部灰黄色，鳍黄色，是我国重要海产鱼类之一 large yellow croaker (*Pseudosciaena crocea*); important sea fish in China having tiny scales, a grey yellow back, and yellow fins

【大会】dàhuì ❶ 国家机关、团体等召开的全体会议 (of a government department or people's organization) plenary session; congress ❷ 人数众多的群众集会 mass meeting; mass rally：动员～ mobilization meeting｜庆祝～ celebratory meeting or gathering

【大伙儿】dàhuǒr '大家'[2] we all; you all; everybody：～要是没意见，就这么定了。If all of you have no objection, it is thus settled. also 大家伙儿 dàjiāhuǒr

【大吉】dàjí ❶ 非常吉利 very lucky; highly auspicious：～大利 good luck and great prosperity (an expression of good wishes)｜万事～ everything is great｜开市～ open or reopen a business with success ❷ 用在动词或动词结构后表示诙谐的说法 [used after a verb or verb structure]：溜之～ slope off｜关门～ put up the shutters; close down for good

【大几】dàjǐ 用在二十、三十等整数后面，表示超过这个整数(多指年龄) [used after a whole number, oft. indicating sb.'s age, such as 'twenty something' and 'thirty something']：二十～的人了，怎么还跟小孩子一样。You are in your twenties. How come you are still behaving like a kid?

【大计】dàjì 重要的计划；重大的事情 major programme of lasting importance; matter of fundamental importance：百年～ project having a major impact on future generations｜方针～ important policy｜共商～ discuss matters of vital importance

【大蓟】dàjì 多年生草本植物，茎有刺，叶子羽状，花紫红色，瘦果椭圆形。可入药。setose thistle (*Circium japonicum*); herbaceous perennial plant having a stem with thorns, pinnate leaves, purplish red flowers, and oval akenes, and used for medicine; also 蓟 jì

【大家】[1] dàjiā ❶ 著名的专家 great master; authority: 书法～ great master of calligraphy | ～手笔 work of a master ❷ 世家望族 old and eminent family; distinguished family: ～闺秀 young lady of a noble family

【大家】[2] dàjiā 〈代词 *pron.*〉指一定范围内所有的人 all, everybody: ～的事～办。Everybody's business should be everybody's responsibility. | ～坐好，现在开会了。Take your seats, please, let's start the meeting. 注意 **NOTE**: a) 某人或某些人跟'大家'对举的时候，这人或这些人不在'大家'的范围之内 When sb. or some people are talking to others, they are not included in 'everyone'. Example: 我报告～一个好消息。I have some good news for you all. | 你讲个笑话给～听听。Please tell us a joke. | 他们一进来，～都鼓掌表示欢迎。As soon as they came in, all the people applauded. b) '大家'常常放在'你们、我们、咱们'后面做复指成分 It oft. comes after 'you and we as a whole'. Example: 明天咱们～开个会谈谈。We'll have a meeting to discuss it tomorrow.

【大家庭】dàjiātíng 人口众多的家庭，多比喻成员多、内部和谐的集体 big family; community; harmonious group with many people: 民族～ great family of people of different ethnic backgrounds

【大驾】dàjià ❶ 〈敬辞 *pol.*〉称对方 your good self — you: 恭候～。We request the pleasure of your company. | 这件事只好有劳～了。I'm sorry but I have to bother you with this matter. ❷ 〈古代 *arch.*〉帝王乘坐的一种车子。也用作帝王的代称。The carriage for a sovereign or emperor; also referring to an emperor

【大建】dàjiàn 农历有30天的月份 lunar month of 30 days; also 大尽 dàjìn

【大奖】dàjiǎng 奖金数额大的或荣誉高的奖励 award at the highest level or with large prize: ～赛 grand prix | 这部故事片荣获～。The feature film won the highest award.

【大将】dàjiàng ❶ 军衔，某些国家将官的最高一级 (mil.) senior general, the top-ranking officer in some countries ❷ 泛指高级将领。比喻得力的部属或集体中的重要人物 high-ranking officer; (fig.) capable subordinate; key person of a group: 她是篮球队里的一员～。She is the key player on the basketball team.

【大街】dàjiē 城镇中路面较宽、比较繁华的街道 main street

【大节】dàjié ❶ 指有关国家、民族存亡安危的大事 political integrity ❷ 指临难不苟的节操 loyalty in the face of adversity: ～凛然 awe-inspiring loyalty | ～不辱 retain loyalty ❸ 〈书 *fml.*〉大纲；大体 outline

【大捷】dàjié 战争中取得的大胜利 great victory

【大姐】dàjiě ❶ 排行最大的姐姐 eldest sister ❷ 对女性朋友或熟人的尊称 elder sister (a polite form of address for a woman about one's own age): 刘～ Sister Liu | 王～ Sister Wang

【大解】dàjiě 排泄大便 go to the lavatory; defecate

【大襟】dàjīn 纽扣在一侧的中装的前面部分，通常从左侧到右侧，盖住底襟 front of a Chinese garment that buttons on the right

【大尽】dàjìn same as 大建 dàjiàn

【大惊小怪】dà jīng xiǎo guài 形容对于不足为奇的事情过分惊讶 be surprised or alarmed at sth. quite normal; make a fuss about nothing

【大静脉】dàjìngmài 体内的静脉汇集成的一条上腔静脉和一条下腔静脉，直接与右心房相连，统称为大静脉 vena cava, consisting of precava and postcava, directly connected with the right atrium of the heart

【大舅子】dàjiù·zi 妻子的哥哥 wife's elder brother; brother-in-law

【大局】dàjú 整个的局面；整个的形势 overall (or general, whole) situation: 顾全～ consider the situation as a whole | ～已定。The outcome is a foregone conclusion. | 无关～ have no bearing on the general situation

【大举】dàjǔ ❶ 大规模地进行(多用于军事行动) carry out (a military operation) on a large scale: ～进攻 mount a large-scale offensive ❷ 〈书 *fml.*〉重大的举动 important action: 共商～ discuss an important action

【大军】dàjūn ❶ 人数众多，声势浩大的武装部队 main forces; army: 百万～ army a million strong | ～压境。The main forces are approaching the border. ❷ 指从事某种工作的大批人 large contingent: 产业～ a large contingent of industrial workers | 地质～ a large contingent of geologists

【大卡】dàkǎ 热量的实用单位，是1卡路里的1,000倍 kilocalorie; large (or great) calories; also 千卡 qiānkǎ

【大楷】dàkǎi ❶ 手写的大的楷体汉字 regular script in big characters, as in Chinese calligraphy exercises ❷ 拼音字母的大写印刷体 block letters; block-writing of Pinyin letters

【大考】dàkǎo 学校中学期终了的考试 end-of-term examination; final exam

【大课】dàkè 课堂教学的一种形式，集合不同班级的许多学生或学员在一起上课听讲 lecture given to a large number of students from different classes and grades; enlarged class

【大快人心】dà kuài rén xīn 指坏人受到惩罚或打击，使大家非常痛快 (usu. of the punishment of an evil-doer) affording general satisfaction; most gratifying to the people; to the immense satisfaction of the people

【大块头】dàkuàitóu 胖子;身材高大的人 fat person; person of big build; fatty

【大款】dàkuǎn 指很有钱的人 moneybags; moneyed man

【大牢】dàláo same as 监狱 jiānyù

【大老婆】dàlǎo·po 有妾的人的妻子。有的地区叫大婆儿。wife of a man with a concubine; in some places also called 大婆儿 dàpór

【大礼拜】dàlǐbài ❶ 每两个星期或十天休息一天,休息的那天叫大礼拜 fortnightly holiday; day off every ten days ❷ 每两个星期休息三天,休息两天的那个星期或那个星期的休息日叫大礼拜 big week (in which one takes both Saturday and Sunday off and which alternates with a week when one takes only Sunday off); big weekend (with both Saturday and Sunday off)

【大理石】dàlǐshí 大理岩的通称。一种变质岩,由粒状方解石和白云石等组成,一般是白色或带有黑、灰、褐等色的花纹,有光泽,多用做装饰品及雕刻、建筑材料。我国云南大理产的最有名,所以叫大理石。marble, metamorphosed limestone consisting chiefly of recrystallized calcite or dolomite, occurring in a wide range of colours such as white, black, grey and brown as well as variegations, and oft. used in sculpture and as a building material. It is named after Dali in China's Yunnan Province, famous for its high-quality marble.

【大力】dàlì ❶ 很大的力量 major effort: 出~ work with might and main | 下~ devote major efforts to ❷ 用很大的力量 go all out: ~支持 give energetic support | ~协作 devote great effort to cooperation

【大丽花】dàlìhuā 多年生草本植物,有块根,叶子对生,分裂成羽状,花有多种颜色,供观赏 dahlia (*Dahlia pinnata*); perennial plant of the grass family, having root tubers and opposite leaves breaking into a pinniform, cultivated for its showy, vary-coloured flower tops; also called 西番莲 xīfānlián

【大殓】dàliàn 丧礼中把尸体装进棺材,钉上棺盖叫大殓 encoffining ceremony; put the corpse into a coffin and nail the cover in pomp and ceremony

【大梁】dàliáng ☞ 脊檩 jǐlǐn on p. 911

【大量】dàliàng ❶ 数量多 large number; mega-amount; great quantity: ~节日用品源源不断运来。A large number of holiday goods are brought in continuously. | ~生产化肥,支援农业生产 mass-produced fertilizer for agricultural production ❷ 气量大,能容忍 generous; magnanimous: 宽宏~ magnanimous and large-minded

【大料】dàliào same as 八角 bājiǎo②

【大龄】dàlíng 年龄较大的 above-average age: ~学童 school child older than a school-ager | ~青年(指超过法定婚龄较多的未婚青年人) single man or woman above the average age for marriage

【大溜】dàliù 河心速度大的水流 rapidly flowing water in the middle of a river ◇随~ follow the majority

【大陆】dàlù ❶ 广大的陆地 continent; mainland: 亚洲~(不包括属于亚洲的岛屿) Asian continent (islands excluded) ❷ 特指我国领土的广大陆地部分(对我国沿海岛屿而言) mainland of China (when contrasting with the country's islands): 台胞回~探亲。Taiwan compatriots return to the mainland of China to visit relatives.

【大陆岛】dàlùdǎo 原来和大陆相连的岛屿,多在靠近大陆的地方,地质构造上和邻近的大陆有联系。如我国的台湾岛、海南岛。island originally connected with the mainland, near the continent and related in geological structure to the land by it, such as Taiwan Island and Hainan Island in China

【大陆架】dàlùjià 大陆从海岸向外延伸,开头坡度较缓,相隔一段距离后,坡度突然加大,直达深海底。坡度较缓的部分叫大陆架,坡度较大的部分叫大陆坡或陆坡。continental shelf, the part of a continent that is submerged in relatively shallow sea, with a gentle slope near the shore and a steep slope extending to the bottom of the sea. The part with a gentle slope is called the continental shelf, while the steep slope is called the continental slope; also 大陆棚 dàlùpéng, 陆棚 lùpéng or 陆架 lùjià

【大陆性气候】dàlùxìng qìhòu 大陆内地受海洋影响不明显的气候,全年和一天内的气温变化较大,空气干燥,降水量少,多集中在夏季 continental climate; climate of the hinterland where the influence from the ocean is little felt, the temperature changes conspicuously through the day and through the year, the air is dry, and precipitation is scarce and concentrated in summer

【大路】dàlù ❶ 宽阔的道路 main road; highway: 顺着~往前走 walk along the main road ❷ 指商品质量一般而销路广的 popular goods of reliable quality: ~菜 popular dish | ~产品 popular products of reliable quality

【大路活】dàlùhuó (~儿 dàlùhuór) 原料较次,加工较粗的成品 run-of-the-mill goods; products made with poor materials and rough processing

【大路货】dàlùhuò 质量一般而销路广的货物 popular goods of reliable quality

【大略】dàlüè ❶ 大致的情况或内容 general idea; broad outline: 这个厂的问题我只知道个~。I have only a rough idea about this factory. ❷ 大概;大致 roughly; generally: 时间不多了,

你～说说吧。There isn't much time left, could you just speak briefly? ❸ 远大的谋略 bold vision：雄才～（person of）great talent and bold vision

【大妈】dàmā ❶ 伯母 father's elder brother's wife ❷ 尊称年长的妇人 aunt (an affectionate or respectful form of address for an elderly woman)

【大麻】dàmá 一年生草本植物，雌雄异株，雌株叫苴麻（jūmá），雄株叫枲麻（xǐmá）。掌状复叶，小叶披针形，花淡绿色。纤维可以制绳。种子叫麻仁，可以榨油，又可入药。marijuana (*Cannabis sativa*); hemp, annual herbal, heterogony, the female called 'juma', the male called 'xima', having palm-like compound leaves, lanceolate leaflets, light green flowers, its fibres used for making rope, seeds called 'maren', and used for oil or as medicine; also 线麻 xiànmá

【大麻风】dàmáfēng 麻风 leprosy

【大麻哈鱼】dàmáhǎyú 鱼，身体长约 2—3 尺，嘴大，鳞细，生活在太平洋北部海洋中，夏初或秋末成群入黑龙江等河流产卵。刺少，肉味鲜美。chum salmon (*Oncorhynchus keta*), northern Pacific salmon, occurring in rivers such as the Heilongjiang in the early summer or late fall, having a body 2-3 *chi* long, a large mouth, thin scales and few bones, and delicious in taste; also 大马哈鱼 dàmǎhǎyú

【大麻子】dàmázǐ ❶ 大麻的种子 seeds of marijuana ❷ 蓖麻 castor-oil plant ❸ 蓖麻的种子 castor bean

【大马趴】dàmǎpā 身体向前跌倒的姿势 fall on one's face：摔了个～ fell on one's face

【大麦】dàmài ❶ 一年生草本植物，叶子宽条形，子实的外壳有长芒。是一种粮食作物。麦芽可以制啤酒和饴糖。barley (*Hordeum vulgare*); annual herb having leaves with broad stripes and long beards that grow out of the fruit; the grain of this plant is used as food and in making beer and ale ❷ 这种植物的子实 seeds of this plant

【大忙】dàmáng 工作集中，繁忙而紧张 very busy：三夏～季节 rush (or busy) season

【大猫熊】dàmāoxióng same as 猫熊 māoxióng

【大毛】dàmáo 长毛的皮料，如狐肷、滩羊皮等 long-haired pelt, such as fox fur and *tanyang* (a kind of sheep raised in Ningxia and Gansu) wool

【大门】dàmén 大的门，特指整个建筑物（如房屋、院子、公园）临街的一道主要的门（区别于二门和各房各屋的门 as compared with the doors of other yards or rooms) gate; (house, yard or park) entrance; front door of a building, mainly facing the street

【大米】dàmǐ 稻的子实脱壳后叫大米。现在一般指好大米。(husked) rice; rice of high quality

【大面儿】dàmiànr 〈方 *dial.*〉❶ 表面 surface：～上搞得很干净，柜子底下还有尘土。It's clean on the surface, but there is dust under the cabinet. ❷ 面子 reputation; face：顾全～ save face

【大民族主义】dà mínzú zhǔyì 大民族中的剥削阶级思想在民族关系上的一种表现，认为本民族在政治、经济、文化上比别的民族优越，应居支配地位，享有各种特权，其他民族理应受到歧视和压迫 ethnocentrism; big-nation chauvinism, believing in the prestige and dominant role of one's own nationality in politics, economy and culture over all other nationalities; biased devotion to any group

【大名】dàmíng ❶ 人的正式名字 formal personal name：他小名叫老虎，～叫李金彪。His formal name is Li Jinbiao, and his pet name is Laohu (Tiger). ❷ 盛名 well-known name：～鼎鼎（名气很大）be very famous | 久闻～。I have long heard of your great name.

【大谬不然】dà miù bù rán 大错特错，完全不是这样 downright wrong; grossly mistaken

【大漠】dàmò 大沙漠 vast desert

【大模大样】dà mú dà yàng 形容傲慢、满不在乎的样子 in an ostentatious manner

【大拇哥】dà·mǔgē 〈方 *dial.*〉拇指 thumb

【大拇指】dà·mǔzhǐ 拇指 thumb

【大拿】dàná 〈方 *dial.*〉❶ 掌大权的人 person with power：他现在是我们县的～。He is the man with the final say in our county. ❷ 在某方面有权威的人 authority; expert：技术～ technical expert

【大男大女】dà nán dà nǚ 指超过法定婚龄较多的未婚男女 single men or women above the average age for marriage

【大脑】dànǎo 中枢神经系统中最重要的部分，正中有一道纵沟，分左右两个半球，表面有很多皱襞。大脑表层稍带灰色，内部白色。人的大脑最发达，是人类在漫长的进化历史中劳动实践的结果。cerebrum, the most important part of the central nervous system, consisting of two halves divided by a vertical furrow and covered by wrinkles, having a grey surface and white interior, the most developed part of a human being, the result of labour over long years of evolution

【大脑脚】dànǎojiǎo 中脑的一部分，前部由神经纤维构成，后部由网状组织构成，内有神经核。有直接传递中枢兴奋和使有机体运动协调的作用。cerebral peduncle, part of midbrain, the front consisting of nerve fibre, the rear of a net structure with a nerve core inside, having the function of directly transferring central excitement and harmonizing organism movement (图见 ☞ figure for 脑 nǎo on p. 1394)

【大脑皮层】dànǎo-pícéng 大脑两半球表面的一层，稍带灰色，由神经细胞组成。记忆、分析、判断等思维活动都得通过它，是高级神经系统的中枢，也是保证有机体内部统一并与周围环境统一的主要机构。cerebral cortex, the furrowed outer layer of grey matter in the cerebrum of the brain, consisting of a subnucleus associated with the higher brain functions, such as voluntary movement, coordination of sensory information, learning and memory and the expression of individuality; the main centre of the nervous system and an organ that guarantees harmony within an organism as well as the surrounded environment; also 大脑皮质 dànǎo-pízhì; abbr. 皮层 pícéng or 皮质 pízhì; (图见 ☞ figure for 脑 nǎo on p.1394)

【大脑炎】dànǎoyán 流行性乙型脑炎的通称 (general term for) encephalitis B

【大内】dànèi 〈旧时 *old*〉指皇宫 imperial palace

【大鲵】dàní 两栖动物,身体长而扁,眼小,口大,四肢短,生活在山谷的溪水中,在我国多产在广西。叫的声音像婴儿,所以俗称娃娃鱼。giant salamander (*Megalobatrachus daridianus*); amphibian with a long and flat body, small eyes, large mouth and short arms, that lives in valley streams; in China, mainly found in Guangxi; also called 'baby fish' for its baby-like cries.

【大逆不道】dà nì bù dào 封建统治者对反抗封建统治、背叛封建礼教的人所加的重大的罪名 treason and heresy; greatest outrage; serious charge that feudal rulers filed against those opposed to their rule and feudal ethics code

【大年】dànián ❶ 丰收年 good year; bumper year; (of fruit trees) bearing-year:今年是个~,一亩地比往年多收百十来斤粮食。This is a good year, with the yield per *mu* over one hundred *jin* more than previous years. |今年的梨是~,树枝都快压折了。It is an fertile year for pears, with the branches of the trees almost breaking from too much fruit. ❷ 农历十二月有 30 天的年份 lunar year in which the last month has 30 days ❸ 指春节 Spring Festival

【大年夜】dàniányè 〈方 *dial.*〉农历除夕 lunar New Year's Eve

【大娘】dàniáng ❶ 伯母 wife of father's elder brother; aunt:三~Aunt Third ❷ 尊称年长的妇人 (affectionate or respectful form of address for an elderly woman) aunt ❸ 〈方 *dial.*〉大老婆 wife of a man with a concubine

【大排行】dàpáiháng 叔伯兄弟姐妹依长幼排列次序 order of seniority among cousins in an extended family or descendants of the same paternal grandfather:他~是老三。He is the third child in his extended family.

【大炮】dàpào ❶ 通常指口径大的炮 artillery; big gun; cannon ❷〈比喻 *fig.*〉好说大话或好发表激烈意见的人 one who speaks boastfully or forcefully; one who loudly overstates things

【大篷车】dàpéngchē 指商业部门送货下乡的货车,多为临时加篷的卡车 delivery truck

【大批】dàpī same as 大量 dàliàng①:火车运来了~货物。The train brought large quantities of goods.

【大辟】dàpì 〈古代 *arch.*〉指死刑 capital punishment

【大票】dàpiào (~儿 dàpiàor)面额较大的钞票 bill of large denomination

【大谱儿】dàpǔr ❶ 设想的大致轮廓 general idea:究竟怎么做,心里应该先有个~。Before you start anything, you ought to have a general idea of what you are going to do. ❷ 大略;大致 roughly; generally:我~算了一下,盖三间房得花近万元。It will cost nearly 10,000 yuan to build a house with three rooms, based on my rough calculations.

【大漆】dàqī 生漆 raw lacquer

【大起大落】dà qǐ dà luò 形容起伏变化极快极大 change radically; major fluctuations:市场价格~。The market price is changing radically. |这部小说没有~的故事情节。The novel has no dramatic plots.

【大气】dàqì ❶ 包围地球的气体,是干燥空气、水汽、微尘等的混合物 atmosphere; air; mixture of dry air, vapour and dust ❷ (~儿 dàqìr)粗重的气息 heavy breathing:吓得他~也不敢出。He held his breath in fear.

【大气层】dàqìcéng 地球的外面包围的气体层。按物理性质的不同,通常分为对流层、平流层、中层、热层和外层等层次。atmospheric layer, the outer atmosphere of the earth. The layers are divided according to different physical characteristics into the troposphere, stratosphere, mesosphere, thermosphere, outer atmosphere, etc. also 大气圈 dàqìquān

【大气候】dàqìhòu ❶ 一个广大区域的气候,如大洲的气候、全球的气候 macroclimate, such as continental climate and global climate ❷〈比喻 *fig.*〉出现在较大范围内的某种政治、经济形势或思潮 (of politics, economics or thought) general tendency; general political climate

【大气磅礴】dà qì pángbó 形容气势盛大 of great momentum; powerful; grand and magnificent:这张画尺幅千里,~。This painting, capturing a thousand-*li* landscape, is monumental.

【大气压】dàqìyā ❶ 大气的压强,随着距离海面的高度增加而减小,如高空的大气压比地面上的大气压小 atmosphere; atmospheric pressure, decreases as sea level increases, with the atmospheric pressure in the upper air lower than that on the ground ❷ 指标准大气压 standard atmospheric pressure

【大器晚成】dà qì wǎn chéng 指能担当大事的人物要经过长期的锻炼,所以成就比较晚 Great vessels take years to produce. *or* Great minds mature slowly.

【大千世界】dàqiān-shìjiè 原为佛教用语，世界的千倍叫小千世界，小千世界的千倍叫中千世界，中千世界的千倍叫大千世界。指广阔无边的世界。Great Chiliocosm, originally a Buddhist term of space which is 1,000 times the Medium Chiliocosm, which in its turn is 1,000 times the Small Chiliocosm, and the Small Chiliocosm is 1,000 times as large as the world. The term also refers to the boundless universe.

【大前年】dàqiánnián 前年以前的一年 three years ago

【大前提】dàqiántí 三段论的一个组成部分，含有结论中的宾词，是作为结论依据的命题 one part of a syllogism, major premise; ☞ 三段论 sānduànlùn on p.1650

D

【大前天】dàqiántiān 前天以前的一天 three days ago; also 大前儿 dàqiánr

【大钱】dàqián ❶ 旧时的一种铜钱，较普通铜钱大，作为货币的价值也较高。泛指钱。large copper coin; money; old Chinese coin of a higher denomination than common coins：不值一个～ worthless ❷ 指大量的钱 large sum of money：赚～ make a fortune

【大庆】dàqìng ❶ 大规模庆祝的事（多指国家大事 usu. referring to state affairs）grand celebration of an important event; great occasion：十年～ festive occasion of the 10th anniversary ❷〈敬辞 *pol.*〉称老年人的寿辰 birthday of an old person who commands respect：七十～ seventieth birthday

【大秋】dàqiū ❶ 指九、十月收割玉米、高粱等作物的季节 harvest season in September and October：～一过，天气就冷起来了。It becomes cold after the harvest season. ❷ 指大秋作物或大秋时的收成 crops harvested in autumn; autumn harvest：今年～真不错。We have a good autumn harvest this year.

【大秋作物】dàqiū zuòwù 秋季收获的大田作物，如高粱、玉米、谷子等 autumn-harvested crops; crops sown in spring and reaped in autumn, such as Chinese sorghum, corn and millet

【大全】dàquán 指内容丰富，完备无缺。多用做书名，如《农村日用大全》、《中国戏曲大全》。[usu. in the title of a book with complete and rich contents] complete collection, such as *A Complete Rural Collection for Everyday Use*, and *A Complete Collection of Chinese Traditional Operas*

【大权】dàquán 处理重大事情的权力，多指政权 power over major issues：独揽～ keep a tight grip of power in one's hands | ～旁落 lose one's power to sb. else

【大人】dà·rén〈敬辞 *pol.*〉称长辈（多用于书信 usu. used in letters）address for parents or people of an older generation：父亲～ Dear Father

【大人】dà·ren ❶ 成人（区别于'小孩儿' as opposed to children）adult; grownup：～说话，小孩儿别插嘴。Kids should not interrupt when adults are talking. ❷〈旧时 *old*〉称地位高的官长 [address for a high official] Your Excellency; His Excellency：巡抚～ His Excellency the Imperial Inspector (in the Ming Dynasty); His Excellency the Governor (in the Qing Dynasty)

【大人物】dàrénwù 指有地位有名望的人 bigwig; important person; great personage; big shot; VIP

【大肉】dàròu 指猪肉 pork

【大儒】dàrú〈旧指 *old*〉学问渊博而有名的学者 well-known learned scholar; pundit

【大赛】dàsài 大型的、级别较高的比赛 match on a large scale and high level：世界杯排球～ World Cup Volleyball Games | 国际芭蕾舞～ International Ballet Competition

【大扫除】dàsǎochú 室内室外全面打扫 general cleaning; thorough cleanup：春节前，要进行一次～。A thorough cleanup is needed before the Spring Festival.

【大嫂】dàsǎo ❶ 大哥的妻子 elder brother's wife; sister-in-law ❷ 尊称年纪跟自己相仿的妇人 [polite form of address for a woman about one's own age] elder sister

【大厦】dàshà 高大的房屋，今多用做高楼名，如'友谊大厦' large building, mansion (used in names of large buildings), such as Friendship Mansion

【大少爷】dàshào·ye 指好逸恶劳、挥霍浪费的青年男子 spoilt son of a rich family; spendthrift：～作风 behaviour typical of the spoilt son of a rich family; extravagant ways

【大舌头】dàshé·tou 舌头不灵活，说话不清楚。也指有这种毛病的人 thick-tongued person; one who lisps：他说话有点儿～。He speaks with a lisp. | 他是个～。He is a thick-tongued person.

【大赦】dàshè 国家依法对全国犯人（除某些例外）一律实行赦免（减轻或免除刑罚）amnesty; general pardon; government mandate to reduce or write off punishment of criminals all over the country

【大婶儿】dàshěnr 尊称跟母亲同辈而年纪较小的妇人 aunt; affectionate or respectful form of address for a woman about one's mother's age

【大声疾呼】dà shēng jí hū 大声呼喊，提醒人们注意 raise a cry of warning; loudly appeal to the public

【大失所望】dà shī suǒ wàng 非常失望 greatly disappointed; to one's great disappointment

【大师】dàshī ❶ 在学问或艺术上有很深的造诣，为大家所尊崇的人 great master; virtuoso; master (of knowledge or art)：艺术～ great master of art ❷ 某些棋类运动的等级称号 (of some board games) Great Master：国际象棋特

级～ Great Master of special class of chess ❸ 对和尚的尊称 honourific term to address a Buddhist monk

【大师傅】dàshī·fu 对和尚的尊称 honourific term to address a Buddhist monk

【大师傅】dà·shi·fu same as 厨师 chúshī

【大使】dàshǐ 由一国派驻在他国的最高一级的外交代表,全称特命全权大使 ambassador, the highest-ranking diplomatic representative sent by a country (full name: ambassador extraordinary and plenipotentiary)

【大事】dàshì ❶ 重大的或重要的事情 great (or major) event; important matter: 国家～ state affairs|终身～ event of life-long impact (referring to marriage) ❷ 大力从事 in a big way: ～渲染 enormously exaggerate; play up

【大事记】dàshìjì 把重大事件按年月日顺序记载,以便查考的材料 chronicle of events

【大势】dàshì 事情发展的趋势(多指政治局势)(of political situation) general trend of events: ～所趋 trend of the times; general trend

【大是大非】dà shì dà fēi 指原则性的是非问题 major matters of principle; cardinal questions of right and wrong

【大手笔】dàshǒubǐ ❶ 名作家的著作 work of a well-known writer ❷ 名作家 well-known writer

【大手大脚】dà shǒu dà jiǎo 形容花钱、用东西没有节制 wasteful; extravagant

【大叔】dàshū 尊称跟父亲同辈而年纪较小的男子 uncle; polite form of address for a man about one's father's age

【大暑】dàshǔ 二十四节气之一,在7月22,23或24日。一般是我国气候最热的时候。Greater Heat — the 12th of the 24 solar terms, the day marking the beginning of the 12th solar term (July 22, 23, or 24, in the midst of the three *fu*, or ten-day periods, when the heat is greatest). ☞ 节气 jiéqì on p. 989 and 二十四节气 èrshísì jiéqì on p. 516

【大率】dàshuài 〈书 *fml.*〉大概;大致 general; roughly: ～如此。That's the general idea.

【大肆】dàsì 无顾忌地(多指做坏事 oft. of evil-doing) with impunity; without restraint; wantonly: ～吹嘘 loudly advocate|～挥霍 wantonly squander|～活动 stop at nothing in doing sth.

【大蒜】dàsuàn 蒜 garlic

【大踏步】dàtàbù 迈着大步(多虚用 oft. abstract in usage) in big strides: ～前进 stride along

【大堂】dàtáng ❶ 指衙门中审理案件的厅堂 courtroom in a *yamen* ❷ 指宾馆、饭店的大厅 lobby of a hotel: ～经理 lobby manager

【大…特…】dà…tè… 分别用在同一个动词前面,表示规模大,程度深 repeat a verb for emphasis: ～书～书 write volumes about|～吃～吃 eat extravagantly|老一套的工作方法非～改～改不可。The old working methods need to be drastically reformed.

【大提琴】dàtíqín 提琴的一种,体积比小提琴大四五倍,音比中提琴低八度 violoncello; cello; musical instrument four or five-times the size of a violin, with notes an octave lower than that of a viola

【大体】dàtǐ ❶ 重要的道理 cardinal principle: 识～,顾大局 bear cardinal principles in mind, and take the overall situation into account ❷ 就多数情形或主要方面说 roughly; more or less; on the whole; by and large; approximately: 我们的看法～相同。On the whole we have the same opinion.

【大天白日】dà tiān bái rì 白天(强调)(with emphasis) broad daylight: ～的,你怎么走迷了路! How could you have got lost in broad daylight!

【大田】dàtián 指大面积种植作物的田地 land for growing large-scale crops

【大田作物】dàtián zuòwù 在大田上种植的作物,如小麦、高粱、玉米、棉花等 field crops, such as wheat, Chinese sorghum, corn, cotton, etc.

【大厅】dàtīng 较大的建筑物中宽敞的房间,多用于集会或招待宾客等 lobby; hall; spacious room in a large building, mainly for gatherings or receptions

【大庭广众】dà tíng guǎng zhòng 人很多的公开场合 (before) a big crowd; (on) a public occasion: 在～之中发言应该用普通话。When making a public speech we should speak standard Chinese.

【大同】dàtóng ❶ 指人人平等、自由的社会景象。这是我国历史上某些思想家的一种理想。Great Harmony (an ideal or perfect society), the ideal of some thinkers in Chinese history ❷ 主要的方面一致 have common ground on major issues: 求～,存小异 seek common ground on major issues while reserving differences on minor issues

【大同乡】dàtóngxiāng 指籍贯跟自己是同一个省份的人(对'小同乡'而言 as compared with 'fellow villager' or 'fellow townsman') person from the same province; fellow provincial

【大同小异】dà tóng xiǎo yì 大部分相同,只有小部分不同 much the same with only minor differences

【大头】dàtóu ❶ 套在头上的一种假面具 mask ❷ 指民国初年发行的铸有袁世凯头像的银元 silver coin minted in the early years of the Republic (1912-1916) with the head of Yuan Shikai on the obverse side ❸ (～儿 dàtóur)大的那一端;主要的部分 bigger end; major part: 抓～儿 aim at the major part; focus on the major problem ❹ 冤大头 squanderer;

dupe：拿～（拿人当做冤大头）sponge off a spendthrift；dupe sb.

【大头菜】dàtóucài ❶ 二年生草本植物，芥（jiè）菜的变种，根部肥大，有辣味，花黄色。块根和嫩叶供食用。rutabaga（*Brassica juncea* var. *megarrhiza*）；biennial plant，mutation of leaf mustard（*Brassica juncea*），with yellow flowers and a thick bulbous root having a peppery flavour，both root and leaves（when tender）being edible ❷ 这种植物的块根 root of this plant ❸〈方 *dial.*〉结球甘蓝 cabbage（*Brassica oleracea* var. *capitat*）

【大头针】dàtóuzhēn 用来别纸等的一种针，一头尖，一头有个小疙瘩 pin used for fastening paper or in dressmaking，with a point at one end and a blunt head at the other

D

【大团结】dàtuánjié ❶ 指印有表现全国各族人民大团结图案的拾元面额的人民币 ten-yuan banknote in Renminbi；picture depicting the unity of all the ethnic groups of China as seen on a 10 yuan Renminbi banknote ❷ 泛指人民币（in a broad sense）Renminbi，the Chinese currency

【大团圆】dàtuányuán ❶ 指全家人团聚在一起 family reunion ❷ 小说、戏剧、电影中主要人物经过悲欢离合终于团聚的结局 happy ending；（of a novel，play or movie）reunion after a long sad separation

【大腿】dàtuǐ 下肢从臀部到膝盖的一段 thigh；upper human leg from hip to knee；also 股 gǔ

【大腕】dàwàn（～儿 dàwànr）指有名气、有实力的人（多指文艺界的）big name；star；celebrated and talented person，esp. within the sphere of literature and art

【大王】dàwáng ❶ 指垄断某种经济事业的财阀 magnate or tycoon of a monopoly：石油～ oil magnate｜钢铁～ steel baron ❷ 指长于某种事情的人 person highly skilled in sth.；master：足球～ football ace｜爆破～ demolition expert ☞ dài·wang on p. 368

【大为】dàwéi〈副词 *adv.*〉表示程度深、范围大 to a large extent；greatly；considerably：～提高 greatly improved｜～改观 changed considerably｜～高兴 overjoyed｜～失望 extremely disappointed

【大尉】dàwèi 军衔，某些国家尉官的最高一级 senior captain；military rank，the highest rank of lieutenancy in certain countries

【大我】dàwǒ 指集体（跟'小我'相对 as compared with 'individual self'）collective self：牺牲小我的利益，服从～的利益 sacrifice one's individual benefit for the sake of the collective

【大无畏】dàwúwèi 什么都不怕（指对于困难、艰险等）unafraid of difficulty or danger：～的精神 dauntlessness；fearlessness

【大五金】dàwǔjīn 比较粗大的金属材料的统称，如铁锭、钢管、铁板等 general term for large pieces of metal，such as iron ingot，steel pipe，iron plate，etc.

【大喜】dàxǐ 大喜事 bliss：您～啦！Congratulations！｜哪天是你们～的日子（指结婚日期）？When is your wedding？

【大喜过望】dà xǐ guò wàng 结果比原来希望的更好，因而感到特别高兴 overjoyed；delighted that things are even better than expected

【大戏】dàxì ❶ 大型的戏曲，情节较为复杂，各种角色齐全，伴奏乐器较多 full-length traditional opera with an intricate plot，a full cast，and the accompaniment of a wide assemblage of musical instruments ❷〈方 *dial.*〉京戏 Peking Opera

【大显身手】dà xiǎn shēnshǒu 充分显露自己的本领 display one's skills to the full；give full scope to one's ability：运动员在赛场上～。Competing athletes bring their very best into full play.

【大限】dàxiàn 指寿数已尽、注定死亡的期限（迷信）（superstition）the day on which one is destined to die；one's predestined hour of death

【大相径庭】dà xiāng jìngtíng《庄子·逍遥游》：'大有径庭，不近人情焉。'后来用'大相径庭'表示彼此相差很远或矛盾很大。*Zhuangzi·Transcendent Bliss*：'Things so worlds apart as to defy reason，' meaning totally different. widely divergent：他们的意见～，无法折中。Their opinions are poles apart and could never reach a compromise.

【大小】dàxiǎo ❶（～儿 dàxiǎor）指大小的程度 size：这双鞋我穿上～正合适。This pair of shoes fits me perfectly. ❷ 辈分的高低 degree of seniority：不分～ regardless of seniority｜没～ age is no longer a consideration；speak without proper respect for elderly people ❸ 大人小孩儿 adults and children：全家～五口。There are altogether 5 family members.｜大大小小六个人。There are 6 people old and young. ❹ 或大或小，表示还能算得上 at the very least：～是个干部。His status is at least that of cadre. ～是笔生意。In any event，this is a deal. ❺ 大的和小的 big and small：这条街～商店有几十家。There are dozens of shops on this street，large and small.｜～要搭配起来。The big should team up with the small.

【大校】dàxiào 军衔，某些国家校官的最高一级 senior colonel；military rank，the highest of colonelcy in certain countries

【大写】dàxiě ❶ 汉字数目字的一种笔画较繁的写法，如'壹、贰、叁、肆、拾、佰、仟'等，多用于账目和文件等中（跟'小写'相对 as opposed to 'low case'）capital form of a Chinese numeral，such as 'one，two，three，four，ten，one hundred, one, etc.,' most frequently used in accounts and on documents; ☞ 数字 shùzì on p.1791 ❷ 拼音字母的一种写法,如拉丁字母的A、B、C,多用于句首或专名的第一个字母(跟'小写'相对 as opposed to 'low case') capitalize; write in capital form; (of phonetic letters) written in capital form, e.g. A, B, C, and used as the first letter of the first word of a sentence, and the first letter of a proper name

【大兴土木】dà xīng tǔmù 大规模兴建土木工程,多指盖房子 go in for large-scale construction, oft. referring to housing development

【大猩猩】dàxīng·xing 类人猿中最大的一种,身体高4—5尺,毛黑褐色,前肢比后肢长,能直立行走。产在非洲,生活在密林中,吃野果、竹笋等。gorilla (*Gorilla gorilla*); the largest anthropoid ape indigenous to African jungles, which feeds on wild fruit and bamboo shoots, and is of a height of around 4 to 5 *chi*, with dark brown hair, longer front than hind limbs, and the ability to stand erect

【大行星】dàxíngxīng 指太阳系的九大行星 nine planets of the solar system

【大型】dàxíng 形状或规模大的 large; large-scale; full-length: ～钢材 large steel products | ～歌剧 grand opera; full-length opera | ～比赛 championship; tournament; games | ～展销会 large fair

【大姓】dàxìng ❶ 指世家大族 clan ❷ 人多的姓,如张、王、李、刘等 common surname such as Zhang, Wang, Li, or Liu

【大熊猫】dàxióngmāo same as 猫熊 māoxióng

【大熊座】dàxióngzuò 星座,位置离北极星不远,北斗七星是大熊星座中最亮的七颗星 Ursa Major; Great Bear, constellation in the region near Polaris containing the seven brightest stars that form the Big Dipper

【大修】dàxiū 指对房屋、机器、车船等进行全面彻底的检修 overhaul; dismantle or cxamine in order to make necessary or thorough repairs to a house, machinery, vehicle or ship

【大选】dàxuǎn 指某些国家对国会议员或总统的选举 general election; elective system of certain countries employed to elect candidates for congress or presidency

【大学】dàxué 实施高等教育的学校的一种,在我国一般指综合大学 university; institution of higher learning, in the PRC generally referring to a university that offers bachelor degrees in both humanities and sciences; ☞ 综合大学 zōnghé dàxué on p.2554

【大学生】dàxuéshēng 在高等学校读书的学生 college or university student; student enrolled in a college or university

【大学生】dàxué·sheng ❶ 年岁较大的学生 senior high school student ❷〈方 *dial.*〉年岁较大的男孩子 big boy

【大雪】dàxuě ❶ 二十四节气之一,在12月6,7或8日 Great Snow; one of the 24 seasonal divisions, falling on Dec. 6, 7 or 8; ☞ 节气 jiéqì on p.989 and 二十四节气 èrshísì jiéqì on p.516 ❷ 指24小时内降雪量达5毫米以上的雪 heavy snow with a 24-hour precipitation of 5 mm or more

【大循环】dàxúnhuán 体循环 systemic circulation

【大牙】dàyá ❶ 槽牙 molar; molar tooth ❷ 门牙 front tooth: 笑掉～ laugh one's head off; split one's sides

【大雅】dàyǎ〈书 *fml.*〉风雅 elegance; refinement; good taste: 无伤～ offend no one's sensibilities; not to matter much | 不登～之堂 unpresentable; unrefined; indecorous

【大烟】dàyān 鸦片的通称 common term for 鸦片 yāpiàn

【大言不惭】dà yán bù cán 说大话而毫不感到难为情 unashamedly brag; talk big; rodomontade; braggart

【大盐】dàyán 用海水熬制或晒制的盐 salt extracted from sea water

【大雁】dàyàn 鸿雁(鸟名) wild goose

【大洋】dàyáng ❶ same as 洋 yáng ②: 四～ Four Oceans ❷ 银元 silver dollar: 五块～ five silver dollars

【大样】dàyàng ❶ 报纸的整版的清样(区别于'小样' as compared with 'galley proof') final proof (of a newspaper); full-page proof ❷ 工程上的细部图 detailed drawing; detail: 足尺～ drawing to the last detail; detailed drawing

【大摇大摆】dà yáo dà bǎi 形容走路挺神气、满不在乎的样子 walk with pompous bearing; strut; swagger: ～地闯了进去 make an imposing entrance; wager through the door

【大要】dàyào 主要的;概要 gist; keynote: 举其～ list the main points

【大爷】dàyé 指不好劳动、傲慢任性的男子 arrogant and wilful male lazybones: ～作风 arrogant manners; indolent egomania | ～脾气 rude and willful temperament

【大爷】dà·ye ❶ 伯父 father's elder brother; uncle ❷ 尊称年长的男子 respectful term of address for an elderly man

【大业】dàyè 伟大的事业 great undertaking: 雄图～ blueprint

【大衣】dàyī 较长的西式外衣 overcoat; topcoat; great coat

【大姨】dàyí (～儿 dàyír)最大的姨母 mother's eldest sister; aunt

【大姨子】dàyí·zi 妻子的姐姐 wife's elder sister; sister-in-law

【大义】dàyì 大道理 general principle; great truth: 深明～ be deeply conscious of the righteousness of a cause | 微言～ sublime words with profound implications

【大义凛然】dà yì lǐnrán 严峻不可侵犯的样子。形容为了正义事业坚强不屈。stern and uncompromising; unyielding in defence of justice

【大义灭亲】dà yì miè qīn 为了维护正义，对违反国家人民利益的亲人不徇私情，使受国法制裁 impartially subject a law-breaking family member or relative to due punishment under state law in order to defend justice

【大意】dàyì 主要的意思 main idea; general idea; main points; gist; tenor: 段落～ gist of a paragraph | 把他讲话的～记下来就行了。Just jot down the main points of what he says.

D

【大意】dà·yi 疏忽；不注意 unobservant; inattentive: 粗心～ careless | 他太～了，连这样的错误都没检查出来。It was negligent of him to overlook such an error.

【大油】dàyóu 猪油 lard

【大有可为】dà yǒu kě wéi 事情很值得做，很有发展前途 worth doing; having good prospects

【大有作为】dà yǒu zuòwéi 能充分发挥作用；能做出重大贡献 be able to employ one's talents fully and make great contributions

【大鱼吃小鱼】dàyú chī xiǎoyú 〈比喻 *fig.*〉势力大的欺压、并吞势力小的 the big tyrannizing or swallowing up the small

【大雨】dàyǔ ❶ 指 24 小时内雨量达 25—50 毫米的雨 rainfall reaching a level of 25-50 mm. within 24 hours ❷ 指下得很大的雨 heavy rain

【大员】dàyuán 〈旧时 *old*〉指职位高的人员（多用于委派时）high-ranking official (esp. one appointed as an inspector): 考察～ government inspector | 接收～ commissioner assigned to take over the property of a bogus government or national traitor

【大圆】dàyuán 球面被通过球心的平面所截而成的圆，是球面能够截取的最大的圆 great circle; circle described by the intersection of the surface of a sphere by a plane passing through its centre; the largest possible circle created by intersecting a sphere with a plane

【大约】dàyuē 〈副词 *adv.*〉❶ 表示估计的数目不十分精确（句子里有数字）probably; approximately; indicating an estimated, rather than exact, number (with a certain number following within the same sentence): 他～有六十开外了。He is probably on the wrong side of 60. ❷ 表示有很大的可能性 most probably: 他～是开会去了。He has probably gone to a meeting.

【大约摸】dàyuē·mo 〈方 *dial.*〉大约 about: ～有七八百人。There are approximately seven hundred people. | 他～还不知道这件事。He is probably still unaware of this.

【大月】dàyuè 阳历有 31 天或农历有 30 天的月份 long month; solar month of 31 days or lunar month of 30 days

【大杂烩】dàzáhuì 用多种菜合在一起烩成的菜。比喻把各种不同的事物胡乱拼凑在一起的混合体（含贬义）。hotchpotch; hodgepodge; medley; potpourri; mishmash; miscellany; dish with a wide range of ingredients, or mixture of dishes; (fig.)(derog.) mixture of dissimilar ingredients without appropriate order or arrangement

【大杂院儿】dàzáyuànr 有许多户人家居住的院子 compound occupied by a number of households

【大灶】dàzào ❶ 用砖土砌成的固定的炉灶 fixed stove or kitchen range made of bricks and earth ❷ 集体伙食标准中最低的一级（区别于'中灶'、'小灶' as compared with 中灶 zhōngzhào or 小灶 xiǎozhào) fare cooked for a mess

【大泽乡起义】Dàzéxiāng Qǐyì ☞ 陈胜吴广起义 Chén Shèng Wú Guǎng Qǐyì on p. 239

【大战】dàzhàn ❶ 大规模的战争，也用于比喻 war; great battle; three-dimensional armed fighting; also used figuratively: 世界～ world war | 足球～ critical football match ❷ 进行大规模的战争或激烈的战斗 wage a large-scale, mortal battle or heavy-arms attack: ～中原 fierce showdown in Central China

【大站】dàzhàn ❶ 铁路、公路沿线规模较大、快车和慢车都停靠的车站 main junction along a railroad or highway where buses and trains converge ❷ 公共汽车快车、慢车都停靠的上下乘客较多的车站 large bus station with heavy flow of passengers

【大张旗鼓】dà zhāng qí gǔ 〈比喻 *fig.*〉声势和规模很大 on a grand scale; with a great fanfare

【大丈夫】dàzhàng·fu 指有志气或有作为的男子 real man; strong man; true man; man: ～敢做敢当 true man has the courage to act and be responsible whatever the outcome; man unhesitatingly accepts responsibility for his doings; real man is not afraid to face the consequences

【大政】dàzhèng 重大的政务或政策 important or decisive political matter or policy: 总揽～ assume full responsibility for major government affairs; have overall authority | ～方针 fundamental policy; guiding principles

【大旨】dàzhǐ 〈书 *fml.*〉主要的意思 gist; keynote: 究其～ explore the central idea; also 大指 dàzhǐ

【大指】dàzhǐ ❶ 拇指 thumb ❷ same as 大旨 dàzhǐ

【大治】dàzhì 指国家政治安定，经济繁荣 (of a state) be able to maintain political stability and achieve economic prosperity: 天下～ world of peace and abundance

【大致】dàzhì ❶ 大体上 in general; substantially：两家的情况～相同。The circumstances of the two families are generally the same. ❷ 大概；大约 approximately；roughly：看看太阳，～是十一点钟的光景。Judging by the sun，it's about 11 a. m.

【大智若愚】dà zhì ruò yú 指有智慧有才能的人，不炫耀自己，外表好像很愚笨（of an intelligent or talented person）never show off，and may appear slow witted；wise look dull；man of great wisdom oft. appears unprepossessing or lacking in talent

【大众】dàzhòng 群众；民众 masses；populace；commonalty；common people；general public：～化 popularize | 劳苦～ toiling masses

【大众化】dàzhònghuà 变得跟广大群众一致；适合广大群众需要 identifying with the masses，and conforming to their needs

【大轴子】dàzhòu•zi 一次演出的若干戏曲节目中排在最末的一出戏 last performance of a programme of traditional opera；also 大轴 dàzhóu

【大主教】dàzhǔjiào 基督教某些派别的神职人员的一种头衔。在天主教和英国圣公会（新教的一派）等是管理一个大教区的主教，领导区内各个主教（原名各不相同，都译成'大主教'）。archbishop；clerical title within some Christian Churches，esp. the Catholic church，and Anglican（a branch of Protestantism）Church of England administering an archdiocese or province，and having authority over the bishops there

【大专】dàzhuān ❶ 指大学和专科学院 four-year and three-year college ❷ 大学程度的专科学校的简称 short for a junior college：～学历 associate college degree

【大篆】dàzhuàn 指笔画较繁复的篆书，是周朝的字体，秦朝创制小篆以后把它叫做大篆 ancient style of calligraphy，with complicated strokes，current in the Zhou Dynasty，called 'da zhuan' subsequent to the creation of the 'xiao zhuan' style during the Qin Dynasty

【大庄稼】dàzhuāng•jia〈方 *dial.*〉大秋作物 autumn harvest；autumn crops

【大自然】dàzìrán 自然界 nature：征服～ conquer nature

【大宗】dàzōng ❶ 大批（货物、款项等）large quantity，amount（of goods，money，etc.）：～货物 goods in bulk；bulk freight ❷ 数量最大的产品、商品 staple：本地出产以棉花为～。Cotton is the local staple. *or* Cotton is the staple produce here.

【大族】dàzú 指人口多、分支繁的家族 clan with lots of kindred members and branches

【大作】[1] dàzuò〈敬辞 *pol.*〉称对方的著作 referring to sb. else's work；your celebrated work，book，article，etc.

【大作】[2] dàzuò 猛烈发作；大起 sudden and violent break-out of sth.；eruption：狂风～。A strong gale suddenly blew up. | 枪声～。Heavy gunfire broke out.

汏 dà〈方 *dial.*〉洗；涮 wash：～头 wash one's hair | ～衣裳 wash the clothes；do the laundry

•da（•ㄉㄚ）

垯（墶）•da ☞ 圪垯 gē•da on p. 649

繨（縺）•da ☞［纥繨］（gē•da）on p. 649

疸 •da ☞ 疙疸 gē•da on p. 649 ☞ dǎn on p. 379

塔 •da ☞ 圪塔 gē•da on p. 649 ☞ tǎ on p. 1848

嶅 •da ☞［圪塔］（gē•da）on p. 649

跶（躂）•da ☞ 蹦跶 bèng•da on p. 95 and ☞ 蹓跶 liū•da on p. 1237

dāi（ㄉㄞ）

呆（獃）dāi ❶（头脑）迟钝；不灵敏（of brain）blunt；dull：～头～脑 idiotic；thick-witted；moronic ❷ 脸上表情死板；发愣 wear a blank face；look vacant；dumbstruck：发～ sit or stare in a trance | 吓～了 be aghast at sth.；be scared stiff；be dumbfounded ❸ same as 待 dāi

【呆板】dāibǎn（旧读 formerly pronounced áibǎn）死板，不灵活 rigid；inflexible：这篇文章写得太～。This article is written in too hackneyed a style. | 别看他样子～，心倒很灵活。He is actually very smart despite his mediocre appearance.

【呆若木鸡】dāi ruò mù jī 呆得像木头鸡一样，形容因恐惧或惊讶而发愣的样子 dumbstruck；look like a wooden chicken，frightened or shocked to the extent of being unable to speak or move

【呆傻】dāishǎ 头脑迟钝糊涂 mentally sluggish；mentally retarded：他一点儿也不～，内心明白得很。He is by no means dull-witted，being innately intelligent.

【呆头呆脑】dāi tóu dāi nǎo 形容迟钝的样子 dull and vacant-looking

【呆小症】dāixiǎozhèng 胎儿期或婴儿期中，先天性甲状腺机能低下或发生障碍引起的疾病。患儿头大，身材矮小，四肢短，皮肤干黄，脸部臃肿，舌头大，智力低下。congenital condition caused by a thyroid hormone deficiency during prenatal development or infancy，characterized in childhood by a large head，short stature and limbs，yellowish skin，tumid face，swollen tongue and mental retardation；also 克汀病 kètīngbìng

【呆账】dāizhàng 会计上指收不回来的账 non-collectible accounts; dead loan; bad debt: 清理～ recover bad debts

【呆滞】dāizhì ❶ 迟钝;不活动 slow; stolid; lagging; inactivity: 脸色苍白,两眼～无神 pale faced and dull eyed ❷ 不流通;不周转 lack of circulation or flow: ～商品 idle commodities|避免资金～avoid letting capital lay idle

【呆子】dāi·zi 傻子 blockhead; idiot; nitwit

呔(呀) dāi〈叹词 *interj*.〉突然大喝一声,使人注意(多见于早期白话 oft. used in early vernacular)[make a sudden outburst to call attention] Ta!; Yo-ho!

☞ tǎi on p.1853

D

待 dāi 停留 stay: ～一会儿再走。Why not stay for a short while? also 呆 dāi

☞ dài on p.372

dǎi(ㄉㄞˇ)

歹 dǎi 坏(人、事 of sb. or sth.) evil: ～人 gangster|～徒 attacker; robber, mugger, burglar or murderer|为非作～ do evil; perpetrate outrages

【歹毒】dǎidú 阴险狠毒 malevolent; sinister and treacherous: 心肠～ evil-minded

【歹人】dǎirén 坏人,多指强盗 evil person; criminal

【歹徒】dǎitú 歹人;坏人 law-breaker; evildoer; attacker

逮 dǎi 捉 catch: 猫～老鼠。Cats catch mice.

☞ dài on p.373

傣 Dǎi 指傣族 the Dais, a minority ethnic people in China

【傣剧】dǎijù 傣族戏曲剧种之一,流行于云南傣族聚居的地区 Dai opera, popular among the Dai communities of Yunnan

【傣族】Dǎizú 我国少数民族之一,分布在云南 the Dai people, one of the ethnic minorities in China that inhabit Yunnan Province

dài(ㄉㄞˋ)

大 dài 义同'大'(dà),用于'大城、大夫、大黄、大王' same meaning as 大 dà, used in 大城 Dàichéng, 大夫 dài·fū, 大黄 dàihuáng, 大王 dài·wang

☞ dà on p.353

【大城】Dàichéng 地名,在河北 name of a place in Hebei

【大夫】dài·fu same as 医生 yīshēng

☞ dàfū on p.356

【大黄】dàihuáng 多年生草本植物,叶子大,花小,黄白色,瘦果褐色。地下块根有苦味,可入药。rhubarb (*Rheum rhaponticum*); pie plant; perennial plant with large leaves, small yellowish-white flowers, brown fruit and bitter-tasting roots which can be used as medicine; also 川军 chuānjūn

【大王】dài·wang 戏曲、旧小说中对国王或强盗首领的称呼 [term of address for a king or a bandit chief, used in traditional opera and old-time novels] chief; king

☞ dàwáng on p.364

代[1] dài ❶ 代替 take the place of: ～课 take over a class for sb.|～笔 write for sb.; ghost-write|～销 be commissioned to sell sth.; sell sth. on a consignment basis; consignment sale ❷ 代理 acting: ～局长 acting director ❸(Dài) 姓 a surname

代[2] dài ❶ 历史的分期;时代 historical period; times: 古～ ancient times; antiquity|近～ modern times|现～ present days; modern times|当～英雄 contemporary hero ❷ 朝代 dynasty: 汉～ Han Dynasty|改朝换～ dynastic changes ❸ 世系的辈分 generation: 第二～ second generation|老一～ older generation|我们这一～ our generation|爱护下一～ show caring for the younger generation ❹ 地质年代分期的第一级,根据动植物进化的顺序分地质年代为太古代、元古代、古生代、中生代和新生代,代以下为纪。跟代相应的年代地层单位叫做界。era; first division of geologic time, subdivided into the Archean Era, the Proterozoic Era, the Palaeozoic Era, the Mesozoic Era and the Cenozoic Era. The division subsequent to 'era' is 'period', the corresponding stratigraphic system to which is called erathem

【代办】dàibàn ❶ 代行办理 be an agent; act for another: ～托运 consign; undertake commissions for shipment|邮政～所 postal agency ❷ 一国以外交部长名义派驻另一国的外交代表 diplomatic representative accredited by the government of one state to the minister of foreign affairs of another ❸ 大使或公使不在职时,在使馆的高级人员中委派的临时负责人员,叫临时代办 chargé d'affaires; official temporarily in charge of a diplomatic mission in the absence of the ambassador or minister; also called chargé d'affaires ad interim

【代笔】dàibǐ 替别人写文章、书信或其他文件 write an article, letter or official document for sb.; act as ghost-writer: 他不便亲自写信,只好由我～。He has no time to write letters personally, so I write them on his behalf.

【代表】dàibiǎo ❶ 由行政区、团体、机关等选举出来替选举人办事或表达意见的人 deputy; delegate; representative; representative elected by an administrative area, organization or government office to act or speak on behalf of the voters: 人大～ deputy to the National People's Congress ❷ 受委托或指派代替个人、

团体、政府办事或表达意见的人 representative authorized or appointed to act or speak for an individual, organization or government office：全权～ plenipotentiary ❸ 显示同一类的共同特征的人或事物 person or thing bearing the common character of all others of the same classification：～作 representative work; trademark work ❹ 代替个人或集体办事或表达意见 act as representative for an individual or collective; represent：副部长～部长主持开幕典礼。The vice minister hosted the opening ceremony on behalf of the minister. ❺ 人或事物表示某种意义或象征某种概念 person or thing that stands for or symbolizes sth.：这三个人物～三种不同的性格。These three characters represent three distinctive personalities.

【代表作】dàibiǎozuò 指具有时代意义的或最能体现作者的水平、风格的著作或艺术作品 masterpiece; masterwork; book or artistic work truly reflecting the times, or the distinctive skill and talent of the writer, in supremely characteristic style

【代步】dàibù〈书 *fml.*〉❶ 替代步行，指乘车、骑马等 ride instead of walk ❷ 指代步的车、马等 vehicle or horse for travelling

【代称】dàichēng 代替正式名称的另一名称 informal name：我国木刻书版向来用梨木和枣木，所以梨枣成了木刻书版的～。In China engraving boards for wood block printing are generally made from pear and jujube, so 'pear and jujube' is the alternative term for such engraving board wood.

【代词】dàicí 代替名词、动词、形容词、数量词、副词的词，包括［any word that functions in place of a noun, verb, adjective, numerical-classifier, adverb, including］：a)人称代词，如'我、你、他、我们、咱们、自己、人家'：personal pronoun, such as 'I (me), you, he (him) or she (her), we (us), myself (himself; herself; yourself; themselves; ourselves; yourselves), the other, another or others'; b)疑问代词，如'谁、什么、哪儿、多会儿、怎么、怎样、几、多少、多么'：interrogative pronoun, such as 'who (whom), what, where, how long, how, how much'; c)指示代词，如'这、这里、这么、这样、这么些、那、那里、那么、那样、那么些'：demonstrative pronoun, such as 'this, these, that, those, here, there'

【代代花】dàidàihuā 常绿灌木，小枝细长，有短刺。叶椭圆形。花白色，有香气，可熏茶和制香精。sour orange (*Citrus aurantinum* var. *amara*); evergreen shrub, having long thin prickly twigs, elliptic leaves and white fragrant flowers which can be used to scent tea or make flavouring essence; also 玳玳花 dàidàihuā

【代电】dàidiàn〈旧时 *old*〉一种公文形式，文字简单，像电报，但作快信邮寄，名为快邮代电，简称代电 written message, esp. an official communication, in the concise writing style of a telegram, but sent by express mail, therefore called 快邮代电 kuàiyóu dàidiàn; 简称 abbr. 代电 dàidiàn

【代沟】dàigōu 指两代人之间在价值观念、心理状态、生活习惯等方面的差异 generation gap; differences in value, mentality, life style, etc., between the older and the younger generations：目前青年一代与老一代的～问题是一个热门话题。The generation gap between the young and the old is currently a hot topic.

【代号】dàihào 为简便或保密用来代替正式名称(如部队、机关、工厂、产品、度量衡单位等的名称)的别名、编号或字母 code name; alias, number(s) or letter(s) assumed instead of an official name of a troop, office, factory, product, measure unit, etc., for the purposes of convenience or secrecy

【代价】dàijià ❶ 获得某种东西所付出的钱 money required in payment for a purchase ❷ 泛指为达到某种目的所耗费的物质或精力 price; cost; (in a broader sense) at the expense of sth., such as the materials or effort necessary for the attainment of a goal：胜利是用血的～换来的。The price of victory is blood.｜用最小的～办更多的事情 accomplish a great deal at minimum cost

【代金】dàijīn 按照实物价格折合的现金，用来代替应该发给或交纳的实物 cash equivalent; money paid in cash at the equivalent value of goods

【代课】dài//kè 代替别人讲课 teach a class in the absence of the regular teacher：～教师 substitute teacher｜王老师病了，由李老师～。Teacher Li took over the class when Teacher Wang fell ill.

【代劳】dàiláo ❶ (请人)代替自己办事 ask sb. to do sth. for one：我明天不能去，这件事就请你～了。I am not available tomorrow, so must ask you, please, to deal with the matter. ❷代替别人办事 do sth. for sb.：这事由我～，您甭管了。Leave it to me. *or* I will take care of it for you.

【代理】dàilǐ ❶ 暂时代人担任某单位的负责职务 temporarily act for sb. in a responsible position：～厂长 acting director of the factory ❷ 受当事人委托，代表他进行某种活动，如贸易、诉讼、纳税、签订合同等 be entrusted and authorized by sb. to conduct, on his or her behalf, activities related to trade, law suits, taxes, contracts, etc.

【代理人】dàilǐrén ❶ 受当事人委托，代表他进行某种活动(如贸易、诉讼、纳税、签订合同等)的人 agent; procurator; surrogate; vicegerent; person who is entrusted or authorized by sb. to carry out such activities as trade, litigation, payment of tax, signing of contracts, etc. ❷ 指实际上为某人或集团的利益(多指非法利益)服务的人 proxy; person serving an individual or group, often for illicit gains

【代码】dàimǎ 为简便或保密用来代替某个单位、某个项目等名称的一组数码 code name for a unit, program etc., used for convenience or secrecy

【代名词】dàimíngcí ❶ 替代某种名称、词语或说法的词语 word or phrase used in substitution of a name, another word or phrase or expression: 他所说的'研究研究'不过是敷衍、推托的～。His talk of further consideration is just a way of evading the issue. ❷ 有些语法书中称代词 (in some grammar books) pronoun

D

【代庖】dàipáo 〈书 *fml.*〉替别人做事 take responsibility for sb.'s job; act in the place of sb.; ☞ 越俎代庖 yuè zǔ dài páo on p. 2374

【代乳粉】dàirǔfěn 用大豆和其他有营养的原料制成的粉,可以代替鲜奶 dairy milk powder substitute composed of soya bean and other nourishing ingredients

【代数】dàishù same as 代数学 dàishùxué

【代数方程】dàishù fāngchéng 用代数式表示的方程,如 $ax^m+bx^{m-1}+\cdots+kx+l=0$, $\sqrt{x^2-2}+7x=14$ 等 equation in algebraic expressions; algebraic equation, such as $ax^m+bx^{m-1}+\cdots+kx+l=0$, $\sqrt{x^2-2}+7x=14$, etc.

【代数式】dàishùshì 用代数运算法(加、减、乘、除、乘方、开方)把数和表示数的字母联结起来的式子。如 $a-b$, $8x+5y$。statement expressing a relationship using numbers and letters symbolizing certain amounts within algebraic calculations (addition, subtraction, multiplication, division, involution, evolution, etc.); such as $a-b$, $8x+5y$, etc.

【代数学】dàishùxué 数学的一个分支,用字母代表数来研究数的运算性质和规律,从而把许多实际问题归结为代数方程或方程组。在近代数学中,代数学的研究由数扩大到多种其他对象,研究更为一般的代数运算的性质和规律。branch of mathematics in which symbols, usu. letters of the alphabet, represent numbers to treat the relations and properties of quantity, therefore reducing many practical problems to algebraic equations. In modern mathematics, algebra shifts focus from numbers to other subjects in exploration of more general properties and relationships in algebraic calculations.

【代替】dàitì 以甲换乙,起乙的作用 substitute A for B and take the place of B: 用国产品～进口货 substitute homemade products for imported goods | 他不能去,你～他去一趟吧! He is unable to go. Could you make the trip in his stead?

【代为】dàiwéi 代替 on behalf of; for sb.: ～执行 implement a mission on behalf of sb. | ～保管 be entrusted with sth.; entrust sth. to sb.

【代谢】dàixiè 交替;更替 supersession; alternation: 四时～ changes of the four seasons | 新陈～ metabolism

【代序】dàixù 代替序言的文章(多自有标题) article used instead of a preface (oft. with a subtitle)

【代言人】dàiyánrén 代表某方面(阶级、集团等)发表言论的人 spokesperson; mouthpiece; person who speaks for a group or class

【代议制】dàiyìzhì 一种政治制度。采取这种制度的国家,在宪法中规定议会有立法和监督政府的权力,政府由议会产生并对议会负责。representative system; political system whereby the state stipulates in its constitution that parliament has legislative power and supervises the government, and that the government is elected within parliament and answers to parliament; also 议会制 yìhuìzhì

【代用】dàiyòng 用性能相近或相同的东西代替原用的东西 substitute; replace the original with material or thing of the same or similar property: ～品 substitute; succedaneum | ～材料 ersatz materials; substitute

轪 dài 〈古代 *arch.*〉指车毂上包的铁帽。也指车轮。iron cap on the axis of a wheel; also referring to a wheel

甙 dài 有机化合物的一类,由糖类和非糖类的各种有机化合物缩合而成,多为白色晶体,广泛存在于植物体中 organic compound, condensed from various sugar or non-sugar compounds, mostly occurring in white crystalline substance and widely distributed in plants; also 配糖物 pèitángwù, 葡糖苷 pútánggān or 糖苷 tánggān

岱 Dài 泰山的别称 another name for Mount Taishan; also 岱宗 Dàizōng or 岱岳 Dàiyuè

迨 dài 〈书 *fml.*〉❶ 等到 wait until ❷ 趁着 when

绐 dài 〈书 *fml.*〉欺哄 coax; cajole; wheedle

骀 dài [骀荡] (dàidàng) 〈书 *fml.*〉❶ 使人舒畅(多用来形容春天的景物 oft. used to describe spring-time scenery) refreshing: 春风～。The spring breeze has a soothing effect on the soul. ❷ 放荡 be corrupt in virtue; immoral; licentious

☞ tái on p. 1852

玳(瑇) dài ☞ below

【玳玳花】dàidàihuā same as 代代花 dàidàihuā

【玳瑁】dàimào 爬行动物,形状像龟,甲壳黄褐色,有黑斑,很光润。产在热带和亚热带海中。hawksbill (*Eretmochelys imbricata*); tropical sea turtle, with a yellowish-brown, black spotted, smooth, shiny shell that is known as tortoiseshell or mother-of-pearl and used to make ornaments and jewellery

带[1]（帶） dài ❶（～儿 dàir）带子或像带子的长条物 band; long thin strip: 皮～ leather belt｜鞋～儿 shoe lace｜传送～ conveyer belt ❷ 轮胎 tire: 车～ tire｜汽车外～ tire ❸ 地带；区域 belt; zone; area: 温～ temperate zone｜黄河一～ Yellow River valley ❹ 白带 leucorrhoea; whites: ～下 morbid leucorrhoea

带[2]（帶） dài ❶ 随身拿着；携带 carry with oneself; take; bring: ～行李 bring along one's luggage｜～干粮 take some food with oneself ❷ 捎带着做某事 do sth. incidentally or in passing: 上街～包茶叶来(捎带着买) Get me some tea while you are out.｜你出去请把门～上(随手关上)。Please shut the door after you. ❸ 呈现；显出 show; have; bear: ～笑容 wear a smile ❹ 含有 have sth. hidden inside: 这瓜～点儿苦味。This melon has a slightly bitter taste.｜说话～刺儿。These remarks smack of sarcasm. ❺ 连着；附带 have sth. attached; while: ～叶的橘子 tangerines fresh with leaves｜连说～笑 talking and laughing｜放牛～割草 cut grass while herding cattle ❻ 引导；领 lead; head: ～队 head a group or team｜～徒弟 train (or take on) an apprentice ❼ 带动 drive; promote; give impetus to: 以点～面 use the experience of pilot units to promote progress in an entire area｜他这样一来～得大家都勤快了。In this way he encouraged all to be diligent.

【带班】dài//bān 带领人值班(巡逻、劳动等) head a working party or patrol: 今夜排长亲自～。Tonight our platoon leader will head the patrol.｜老主任出马，～操作。The senior director will take personal charge of the operation.

【带刺儿】dài//cìr 指说的话里暗含讽刺意味(of sth. said) notable by the use of satire; be sarcastic: 有意见就提，不要话里～。Speak open and frankly. Do not try to be ironic. *or* Say what you mean, don't be sarcastic.

【带电】dài//diàn 物体上带有正电荷或负电荷 charged; electrified; (of a particle or body) having a net amount of positive or negative electric charge

【带动】dàidòng ❶ 通过动力使有关部分相应地动起来 cause connected parts to function by supplying the motivating force or power: 机车～货车 a locomotive engine powers a freight train ❷ 引导着前进；带头做并使别人跟着做 guide or direct sb. to achieve an objective; lead the way for others to follow: 抓好典型，～全局。Set a good example to give impetus to the work as a whole.｜在校长的～下，参加义务植树的人越来越多。With our president taking the lead, more and more people join in volunteer tree planting.

【带好儿】dài//hǎor 转达问候 pass sb.'s best regards to: 你回校时给王老师～。Give my best regards to Mr. Wang when you go back to school.｜你见到他时，替我带个好儿。Say hello to him for me when you see him.

【带话】dài//huà（～儿 dà//huàr）捎话 take or bring a message; deliver a message; give a message

【带劲】dàijìn ❶（～儿 dàijìnr）有力量；有劲头儿 energetic; forceful: 他干起活来可真～。He works like a horse.｜他的发言挺～。His speech is uplifting indeed. ❷ 能引起兴致；来劲 interesting; full of fun: 下象棋不～，还是打球吧。Chess is too sedentary, let's play tennis instead.｜什么时候我也会开飞机，那才～呢！When I am eventually able to pilot an airplane, that will be truly terrific.

【带菌】dài//jūn（人或其他物体）带有病菌 (of a human body or object) carry disease germs: ～者 virus carrier｜吃了～食物引起腹泻。He ate something contaminated, and it caused diarrhoea.

【带累】dàilěi 使(别人)连带受损害；连累 get sb. into trouble through one's own problem: 是我～了你，真对不起。Sorry to have unloaded my troubles on you.

【带领】dàilǐng ❶ 在前带头使后面的人跟随着 guide; lead: 老同学～新同学去见老师。Seniors take freshmen to meet their teachers. ❷ 领导或指挥(一群人进行集体活动) lead or direct an activity to be carried out by a group of people: 老师～同学们去支援麦收。The teacher took his students to help harvest wheat.

【带路】dài//lù 引导不认得路的人行进 show by leading the way: ～人 guide｜你在前面～。You lead the way and we will follow.

【带挈】dàiqiè same as 挈带 qièdài

【带声】dàishēng same as 带音 dàiyīn

【带手儿】dàishǒur〈方 *dial.*〉顺便 in passing: 你去吧，你的事我～就做了。You go on, I can handle this matter for you on my way.

【带头】dài//tóu 首先行动起来带动别人；领头儿 be the first; take the lead: ～人 leader; forerunner｜～作用 play a leading role ◇～学科 leading subject

【带下】dàixià〈中医 *Chin. med.*〉指白带不正常的病 abnormal discharge of leucorrhoea; morbid leucorrhoea

【带孝】dài//xiào 死者的亲属和亲戚，在一定时期内穿着孝服，或在袖子上缠黑纱、辫子上扎白绳等，表示哀悼 mourning dress; a band of black cloth (or crape) worn on the arm, or a piece of white string tied to plaited hair, by bereaved relatives, for a certain period of time in order to show grief for a deceased parent or relative; wear mourning (for sb.);

be in mourning; also 戴孝 dài//xiào

【带音】dàiyīn 发音时声带振动叫做带音,声带不振动叫不带音。普通话语音中元音都是带音的,辅音中的 l、m、n、ng、r 等也是带音的。别的辅音如 p、f 等都不带音。带音的是浊音,不带音的是清音。speech sound pronounced with vibration of the vocal cords, as compared with the sound pronounced without vibrating vocal cords that is voiceless. In *putonghua* (common Chinese speech with standard pronunciation), all vowels, and some consonants such as l, m, n, ng, r, are voiced, while other consonants such as p and f are voiceless. Voiced consonants are called *zhuoyin*, and voiceless consonants are *qingyin*.

D

【带鱼】dàiyú 鱼,体长侧扁,形状像带子,银白色,全身光滑无鳞。是我国重要海产鱼类之一。有的地区叫刀鱼。hairtail (*Trichiuridae*); silver white, scale-less fish, with a long, thin, sleek body resembling a belt; one of the main fish species found in the seas of China; also known as bladefish or cutlassfish in some areas

【带子】dài·zi ❶ 用皮、布等做成的窄而长的条状物,用来绑扎衣物 belt; long narrow strip of leather or cloth used for bundling clothes ❷ 录音带、录像带的俗称 informal name for a audio tape or videotape

殆 dài 〈书 *fml*.〉❶ 危险 dangerous: 知彼知己,百战不~ know yourself and your enemy, and you will survive a hundred battles ❷ 几乎;差不多 nearly; almost: 敌人伤亡~尽。The enemy were practically wiped out.

贷 dài ❶ 贷款 loan; credit: 信~ credit | 农~ farming loans ❷ 借入或借出 borrowing or lending money: 向银行~款 raise (or obtain) a loan from a bank | 银行~给工厂一笔款。The bank granted a loan to the factory. ❸ 推卸(责任) shirk (a duty or responsibility); shrug off the blame; clear oneself of the blame: 责无旁~ indisputable responsibility; be duty bound ❹ 饶恕 forgive; pardon; mercy: 严惩不~ inflict severe punishment; punish without leniency or mercy

【贷方】dàifāng 付方 charging side; credit side; creditor

【贷款】dài//kuǎn 甲国借钱给乙国;银行、信用合作社等机构借钱给用钱的部门或个人。一般规定利息、偿还日期 (of a country) lend money to another country; (of a bank, credit bank, etc.) lend money to an organization or individual, with fixed interest and date of repayment: 向银行~五十万元 get a bank loan of 500,000 yuan

【贷款】dàikuǎn 甲国贷给乙国的款项;银行、信用合作社等机构贷给用钱的部门或个人的款项 loan; money lent by one country to another; money granted as a loan to an organization or individual: 还清~ pay off one's loan

待[1] dài ❶ 对待 treat; approach; deal with; serve: 优~ give preferential (or special) treatment | 以礼相~ be polite to sb.; treat sb. with courtesy | ~人和气 treat sb. nicely ❷ 招待 entertain; receive: ~客 entertain a guest

待[2] dài ❶ 等待 wait; expect: ~业 awaiting a job | 严阵以~ stand ready in battle formation; lay in wait for | 有~改进 leave something to be desired; have yet to be improved ❷ 需要 need: 自不~言 it goes without saying ❸ 要;打算 be about to; want to do sth.: ~说不说 hesitate to say sth. (or speak out) | ~要上前招呼,又怕认错了人 be about to go forward and say hello but hesitating for fear of greeting the wrong person

☞ dāi on p. 368

【待承】dài·cheng 招待;看待 treat; entertain: 老汉拿出最好的东西~客人。The old man did his utmost to entertain the guests.

【待机】dàijī 等待时机 wait for one's time (or chance or opportunity); bide one's time: ~而动 wait for an opportune moment to act | ~行事 wait for the right time to do sth.

【待考】dàikǎo 暂时存疑,留待查考 needing to be verified due to some trace of doubt; need checking; awaiting verification

【待理不理】dài lǐ bù lǐ 像要答理又不答理,形容对人态度冷淡 coldly ignore sb.; snub sb.; give cold shoulder to sb.

【待命】dàimìng 等待命令 await orders: 集结~ assemble and await orders

【待人接物】dài rén jiē wù 跟人相处 manner of dealing with people

【待业】dàiyè (非农业户口的人)等待就业 (of non-rural residents) wait for employment: ~青年 youth awaiting employment | ~人员 future employees; the unemployed | 在家~ be home waiting for a job

【待遇】dàiyù ❶ 对待(人) deal with a person ❷ 对待人的情形、态度、方式 way or manner of dealing with people: 周到的~ consideration when dealing with people | 冷淡的~ cold shoulder ❸ 指权利、社会地位等 enjoy certain power and social status: 政治~ political treatment | 平等~ equality ❹ 物质报酬;工资福利 material return; salary or wages and benefits: 生活~ materiat benefits | ~优厚 high pay; treat sb. well

【待字】dàizì 〈书 *fml*.〉指女子尚未定亲 (of a woman) be as yet unattached or unengaged (字 *zi*: 许嫁 betrothal): ~闺中 not yet betrothed; still a maiden (in her boudoir); not yet affianced

怠 dài ❶ 懒惰;松懈 slothful; slack: ~惰 slothful | 懈~ lax ❷ 轻慢;不恭敬 rude;

showing no respect：～慢 treat a guest rudely；be rude to sb.

【怠惰】dàiduò same as 懒惰 lǎnduò

【怠工】dài//gōng 有意地不积极工作，降低工作效率 deliberately slow down，work with less efficiency：消极～ slacken work pace

【怠慢】dàimàn ❶ 冷淡 slight；give cold shoulder to sb.：不要～了客人。See that none of the guests is neglected. ❷〈客套话 *pol.*〉表示招待不周 polite expression，showing modesty before a guest：～之处，请多包涵。Please forgive me for being so negligent or inconsiderate.

埭 dài〈方 *dial.*〉坝，多用于地名 dam，oft. used in a place name：石～（在安徽）Shidai（in Anhui）| 钟～（在浙江）Zhongdai（in Zhejiang）

袋 dài ❶（～儿 dàir）口袋 bag：布～ cloth bag | 衣～ pocket | 米～ rice bag ❷（～儿 dàir）〈量词 *classifier*〉用于装口袋的东西 amount of sth. a bag can hold：两～儿面 two sacks of flour | 一～儿洗衣粉 a packet of washing powder ❸〈量词 *classifier*〉用于水烟或旱烟 used for pipe smoking（water pipe or long Chinese pipe）：一～烟（smoke）a pipe

【袋鼠】dàishǔ 哺乳动物的一科，前肢短小，后肢粗大，善于跳跃，尾巴粗大，能支持身体。雌的腹部有皮质的育儿袋。吃青草、野菜等。产在大洋洲。kangaroo（*Macropodidae*），having short forelimbs and large hind limbs adapted for leaping，and a long，tapered tail strong enough to support the body，the female carriying her young in an external abdominal pocket of skin. Kangaroos are herbivores and inhabit Oceania.

【袋子】dài·zi 口袋 bag；sack：面～ flour bag

紿 dài 旦[3]（纤度单位）的旧称 former name for dan 旦[3]（unit of measurement for fibre）

逮[1] dài〈书 *fml.*〉到；及 reach：力有未～ beyond one's power

逮[2] dài 义同'逮'（dǎi），只用于'逮捕' same as 逮 dǎi，only used in the word 逮捕 dàibǔ ☞ dǎi on p. 368

【逮捕】dàibǔ 捉拿（罪犯）arrest；capture；nab：～归案 arrest and bring to justice

叇（靆） dài ☞［叆叇］（àidài）on p. 7

戴 dài ❶ 把东西放在头、面、颈、胸、臂等处 adorn；wear sth. on the head，face，neck，chest，arm，etc.：～帽子 wear a hat | ～花 wear a flower for ornamentation | ～眼镜 wear glasses | ～红领巾 wear a red scarf ◇ 披星～月 toil day and night | 不共～天之仇 deadly feud；inveterate hatred ❷ 拥护尊敬 support；respect：爱～ love | 感～ feel gratitude and respect for sb. ❸（Dài）姓 a surname

【戴高帽子】dài gāomào·zi〈比喻 *fig.*〉对人说恭维的话 flatter；lay it on thick；praise to the skies；over praise；also 戴高帽儿 dài gāomàor

【戴绿帽】dài lǜmào（～儿 dài lǜmàor）〈比喻 *fig.*〉妻子有外遇（of a man）having an unfaithful wife；be made a cuckold

【戴胜】dàishèng 鸟，羽毛大部为棕色，有羽冠，嘴细长而稍弯。吃昆虫，对农业有益。hoopoe（*Upupa epops*）；bird，oft. having brown plumage，a crest and a slender，downward-curving bill，insect-eating and therefore beneficial to agriculture；通称 generally known as 呼哱哱 hūbō·bo or 山和尚 shānhé·shang

【戴孝】dài//xiào same as 带孝 dài//xiào

【戴罪立功】dài zuì lì gōng 在承当某种罪名的情况下建立功劳 atone for a sin，a mistake or failure by meritorious service

黛 dài 青黑色的颜料，古代女子用来画眉 black pigment，used by women in ancient times to paint their eyebrows：粉～（指妇女）dame

【黛绿】dàilǜ 墨绿 dark green：深秋的树林，一片～，一片金黄。The trees in late autumn are a smudge of green and gold.

黱 dài〈书 *fml.*〉same as 黛 dài

襶 dài ☞［褦襶］（nàidài）on p. 1387

dān（ㄉㄢ）

丹 dān ❶ 红色：～砂 cinnabar | ～枫 fiery maple trees ❷ 依成方制成的颗粒状或粉末状的中药（从前道家炼药多用朱砂，所以称为'丹'）pellet；powder；Chinese medicine prepared according to a prescription（in former times oft. used by Taoist alchemists，hence called 'dan'）：丸散膏～ pills，powder，extract and pellets | 灵～妙药 wonder drug；panacea ❸ 指丹砂 cinnabar ❹（Dān）姓 a surname

【丹顶鹤】dāndǐnghè 白鹤 red-crested white crane

【丹毒】dāndú 病，由丹毒链球菌侵入皮肤的小淋巴管引起。最常发病的部位是面部和小腿。症状是突发高热，病变部分呈片状红斑，疼痛，发热，与正常组织之间界限很清晰。erysipelas，a disease caused by the penetration of erysipelatous streptococcus into the minute lymphatic skin vessels，oft. apparent on the face and calf，characterized by a sudden high fever，localized red inflammation，a burning sensation and an appearance distinct from that of uninfected skin

【丹方】dānfāng ❶ same as 单方 dānfāng ❷〈书 *fml.*〉炼丹的方术 alchemy，art or skill of making magical pellets；home remedy；folk prescription

【丹凤眼】dānfèngyǎn 眼角向上微翘的眼睛 almond-shaped eyes; slanting eyes

【丹青】dānqīng〈书 *fml*.〉❶ 红色和青色的颜料，借指绘画 red and green pigments, a borrowed term for painting: ～手(画师)painter | ～妙笔 magic touch of an artist | 擅长～ excel in painting ❷ 指史册；史籍 history scrolls or books; historical records; annals

【丹砂】dānshā 朱砂 cinnabar

【丹田】dāntián 指人体脐下一寸半或三寸的地方(of a human body) region one and half to three inches below the navel; pubic region: 气沉～ hold a deep breath down in the abdomen; inhale deeply

【丹心】dānxīn 赤诚的心 loyal heart; bottom of one's heart; loyalty: 一片～sheer loyalty

D

担(擔) dān ❶ 用肩膀挑 carry sth. on a shoulder pole: ～水 carry water with pails hanging from a carrying pole | 人家两个人抬一筐，他一个人～两筐。While others carry one basket to a pair, he manages two by himself. ❷ 担负；承当 undertake; take on; be burdened with: 承～ take on | 分～ share | 把任务～起来 commit oneself to a task; take the responsibility for an assignment | 你叫我师傅，我可～不起(不敢当)。I do not measure up to the title of master you have given me. *or* I do not think I deserve the title, master.
☞ 掸 dǎn on p.379 and dàn on p.380

【担保】dānbǎo 表示负责，保证不出问题或一定办到 be responsible for; see that nothing goes wrong or that sth. happens; guarantee; assure: 出不了事，我敢～。Nothing can go wrong, I guarantee it. | 交给他办，～错不了。Leave it to him, and rest assured there will be no mistakes.

【担不是】dān bù·shi 承当过错 take the blame: 万一出了问题，也不能让他一个人～。If anything should go wrong, he is not solely to blame. *or* In case something goes wrong, we should not pin all the blame on him.

【担待】dāndài ❶ 原谅；谅解 forgive; let pass; be tolerant: 孩子小，不懂事，您多～。He is a callow, unversed boy, please forgive him. ❷ 担当(责任)take on (the responsibility): ～不起。This is too much to ask for me. | 你放心吧！一切有我～。Don't worry, I will be responsible for everything.

【担当】dāndāng 接受并负起责任 ready to accept and bear the responsibility: ～重任 take on a heavy burden | 再艰巨的工作，他也勇于～。He is ready to take on any job, however tough.

【担负】dānfù 承当(责任、工作、费用)sustain; bear; be answerable for (a blame, responsibility or expense): ～重任 shoulder an important task

【担搁】dān·ge same as 耽搁 dān·ge

【担架】dānjià 医院或军队中抬送病人、伤员的用具，用木棍、竹竿等做架子，中间绷着帆布或绳子(used by hospital or army in battle) a piece of canvas (or framework of ropes) stretched over long wooden or bamboo poles, used to transport the sick or wounded: 一副～ a litter or stretcher

【担惊受怕】dān jīng shòu pà 提心吊胆，害怕遭受祸害 remain in a state of apprehension; have misgivings about sth.; live in fear of possible misfortune

【担名】dān//míng (～儿 dān//míngr) 承当某种名分 bear a certain name: 他只是担个名儿，并没做什么工作。He bears a meaningless or undeserved title.

【担任】dānrèn 担当某种职务或工作 assume the office of; hold the post of: ～小组长 be a group leader | ～运输工作 be responsible for transportation

【担心】dān//xīn 放心不下 be anxious about; take sth. to heart; worry oneself about: ～情况有变 fear an unexpected change | 一切都顺利，请不要～。Everything is going smoothly, rest assured.

【担忧】dānyōu 发愁；忧虑 worried; anxious; apprehensive: 儿行千里母～。A mother always worries about a son who is far away. *or* A mother's thoughts are never far from her son. | 不必～，他不会遇到危险的。Don't worry, he will be safe.

单(單) dān ❶ 一个(跟'双'相对 as opposed to 'pair' or 'double') one; single: ～扇门 a single-leaf door | ～人床 single bed ❷ 奇数的(一、三、五、七等，跟'双'相对) odd number (1, 3, 5, 7, etc., as opposed to 'even'): ～数 odd number; singular (grammar) | ～号 odd numbers | ～日 odd days ❸ 单独 single; alone; by oneself; on one's own: ～身 living alone; unmarried; bachelor | ～干 self-employed; work on one's own; do sth. by oneself | ～打一 concentrate on one thing at a time | ～枪匹马 single-handed | 形～影只 solitary ❹ 只；仅 only; alone: 干工作不能～凭经验。Experience alone is not sufficient for competence at a job. | 别的不说，～说这件事。Let's talk about this matter alone. ❺ 项目或种类少；不复杂(of items or types) small in number; lacking in variety: 简～ simple | ～纯 alone; purely; simply | ～调 dull; monotonous ❻ 薄弱 thin; weak; insubstantial: ～薄 lack strength or magnitude | ～弱 weak; frail; delicate | 势孤力～ be in a helpless, isolated plight, running out of strength or supplies ❼ 只有一层的(衣服等) unlined clothing: ～衣 unlined garment; (wearing) a single shirt, jacket, coat, etc. | ～裤 unlined trousers ❽ (～儿 dānr) same as 单子 dān·zi

①：被～儿 sheet | 床～子 bedspread; sheet ❾ (～儿 dānr) same as 单子 dān·zi ②：名～ name list | 传～ handbill; leaflet | 清～ detailed list; inventory | 账～ bill | 货～ indenture; waybill; manifest; list of goods; invoice

☞ chán on p. 209 and Shàn on p. 1674

【单帮】dānbāng 〈旧时 *old*〉指从甲地贩商品到乙地出卖的单人商贩 trader, travelling by oneself from one place to another to sell goods：跑～ travel around carrying a small quantity of goods; travel as a lone merchant | ～客人 customer who patronizes a travelling trader

【单薄】dānbó ❶ 指天凉或天冷的时候穿的衣服薄而且少 thinly clad in cold weather; underdressed：冰天雪地的，穿这么～，行吗？ It's freezing, how can you stand the cold wearing so little? ❷（身体）瘦弱 (of a human body) thin and weak; feeble; frail; emaciated：她从小多病，身子～。She was sickly as a child, small and thin. ❸（力量、论据等）薄弱；不充实(of strength or proof) weak; insubstantial：人手～ be short of hands | 兵力～ be in need of military strength | 内容～。The content is insubstantial.

【单产】dānchǎn 在一年或一季中单位土地面积上的产量 annual or quarterly yield per unit area

【单车】dānchē ❶指单独运行的一辆车（多指汽车、拖拉机 oft. a truck or tractor) operation of a single vehicle：～收入日报表 daily report for per-vehicle income | 这个汽车服务公司的～效益较好。This transportation company enjoys good returns from single vehicle service. ❷〈方 *dial.*〉自行车 bicycle

【单程】dānchéng 一来或一去的行程（区别于'来回' as compared with 'round trip') single trip to or from：～车票 one-way ticket

【单传】dānchuán ❶ 几代相传都只有一个儿子 patrilineal line of descent with just one son in each generation：三世～ three successive paternal generations, each having a descendant son only ❷〈旧时 *old*〉指一个师傅所传授，不杂有别的流派 pass on a skill from a single master to apprentices without influence from other schools

【单纯】dānchún ❶ 简单纯一；不复杂 pure; uniform; uncomplicated; simple：思想～ unsophisticated | 情节～ simple plot ❷ 单一；只顾 pure; merely：～技术观点 from a purely technical point of view | ～追求数量 put a premium on quantity alone; simply seek quantity

【单纯词】dānchúncí 只包含一个词素的词（区别于'合成词' as compared with 'compound word') single-morpheme word；就汉语说，有时只用一个字来表示，如'马、跑、快'。有时用两个字来表示。必须合起来才有意义，如'葡萄、徘徊、朦胧'。In Chinese may be found examples of one-character words like 马(mǎ), 跑(pǎo) and 快(kuài), and sometimes two inseparable characters that combine to form a complete meaning, such as 葡萄(pútáo), 徘徊(páihuái) and 朦胧(ménglóng).

【单词】dāncí ❶ 单纯词 single-morpheme word ❷ 词（区别于'词组' as compared with 'phrase') word

【单打】dāndǎ 某些球类比赛的一种方式，由两人对打，如乒乓球、羽毛球、网球等都可以单打 (of some ball games) singles; form of competition between two players, such as pingpong, badminton, and tennis

【单打一】dāndǎyī 集中力量做一件事或只接触某一方面的事物，而不管其他方面 concentrate on one thing at a time

【单单】dāndān 〈副词 *adv.*〉表示从一般的人或事物中指出个别的 [introducing a particular item or exception among a group of people or things] only; alone：别人都来了，～他没来。Everyone else is here except him. | 其他环节都没问题，～这里出了毛病。There are no problems anywhere else but here.

【单刀】dāndāo ❶ 短柄长刀，武术用具 martial arts weapon, broadsword with a short handle; short-hilted broadsword ❷ 武术运动项目之一，表演或练习时只用一把单刀 single-broadsword event; martial arts event solely using broadsword when giving a show or practising

【单刀直入】dān dāo zhí rù 〈比喻 *fig.*〉说话直截了当，不绕弯子 speak out without beating about the bush; confront a subject directly; come straight to the point

【单调】dāndiào 简单、重复而没有变化 tediously repetitious; lacking in variety; monotonous：色彩～ bland colour | 样式～ unvarying style | 只做一种游戏，未免～。Playing just one game is tedious.

【单独】dāndú 不跟别的合在一起；独自 without the presence of another or others; by oneself; independently; on one's own：～行动 take independent action | 请你抽空到我这里来一下，我要～跟你谈谈。Please take some time to come over, I want to talk with you alone. | 他已经能够离开师傅，～操作了。He is capable of working without his master and operating alone.

【单方】dānfāng 民间流传的药方 folk prescription; also 丹方 dānfāng

【单放机】dānfàngjī ❶ 只能放录音磁带而不能收音或录音的机器 cassette player without radio or recording function ❷ 指放像机 video player

【单干】dāngàn 不跟人合作，单独干活 go it alone; working without help; do sth. by oneself; self-employed: ～户 peasant family farming on its own without any cooperation with other farmers; independent farming family | 一个人～ self-employed; do sth. single-handedly

【单杠】dāngàng ❶ 体操器械的一种,用两根支柱架起一根铁杠做成 horizontal bar, gymnastic apparatus consisting of a single bar mounted on two posts ❷ 竞技体操项目之一,运动员在单杠上做各种动作 gymnastics event on the horizontal bar where the gymnast performs various swinging manoeuvres

【单个儿】dāngèr ❶独自一个 alone; individually: 说好了大家一齐去,他偏要～去。It was agreed that we all go together, but he insisted on going alone. ❷ 成套或成对中的一个 one of a pair or set: 这套家具不～卖。This set of furniture is not sold by the piece.

【单轨】dānguǐ 单线的铁道 single track; monorail

【单果】dānguǒ 果实的一类,由一朵花的一个成熟子房发育而成。如桃、李、杏、棉、向日葵等的果实。fruit that grows from a single mature ovary in a flower, such as the peach, plum, apricot, cotton, and sunflower; also known as 单花果 dānhuāguǒ

【单过】dānguò (分开)单独过日子 live separately or independently from one's parents; live on one's own; live alone: 儿子结了婚,和老人分居～了,只在节假日回来。After getting married, the son moved away from his parents, and only came back at holidays.

【单寒】dānhán ❶ 衣服穿得少,不能御寒 too underdressed to stand the cold ❷〈旧指 *old*〉家世寒微,没有地位 be from a humble family and low in social status

【单簧管】dānhuángguǎn 管乐器,由嘴子、小筒、管身和喇叭口四部分构成,嘴上装有单簧片 clarinet, wind instrument, consisting of mouthpiece, cylindrical tube, keyed body, flaring bell, with a single reed fixed to the mouthpiece; also 黑管 hēiguǎn

【单季稻】dānjìdào 在同一块稻田里,一年之内只插一次秧,收割一次的,叫单季稻 single-crop rice; rice annually transplanted and cropped

【单价】dānjià 商品的单位价格 unit price of a commodity

【单间】dānjiān (～儿 dānjiānr)❶只有一间的屋子 house with just one room: ～铺面 a single room shop ❷ 饭馆、旅馆内供单人或一起来的几个人用的小房间 (in a restaurant or hotel) separate room for one or a few guests to share; single room (as in a hotel); separate room (as in a restaurant)

【单晶体】dānjīngtǐ 原子按照统一的规则排列的晶体。具有一定的外形,其物理性质在各个方向各不相同。monocrystal, crystal with atomic structure in a uniform arrangement, featuring a distinctive appearance, and different physical properties from different angles

【单句】dānjù 不能分析成两个或两个以上的分句的句子 simple sentence; (of a sentence) having no coordinate or subordinate clauses

【单据】dānjù 收付款项或货物的凭据,如收据、发票、发货单、收支传票等 documented proof of incoming and outgoing sums of money or goods, such as receipt, bill, invoice, and slip

【单口】dānkǒu 曲艺的一种表演形式,只有一个演员进行表演,如京韵大鼓、山东快书、单口快板等 solo, form of folk art with only one performer, such as ballad singing in the Beijing dialect, Shandong clapper ballads, clapper monologues

【单口相声】dānkǒu xiàng·sheng 只有一个人表演的相声 one-man comic talk; comic monologue; ☞ 相声 xiàng·sheng on p. 2097

【单利】dānlì 计算利息的一种方法,只按照本金计算利息 simple interest; interest paid on the principal only and not on the interest accrued

【单列】dānliè (项目等)单独开列 (of items or programmes) be drawn on separately from others: 计划～市 municipality with independent budgetary status | 这笔款项收支～。Put the funds on separate statements showing receipt and payment.

【单名】dānmíng 只有一个字的名字 single-character given name

【单名数】dānmíngshù 只带有一个单位名称的数。如 3 尺、4.5 丈。number used with only one measurement unit, such as 3 *chi*, 4.5 *zhang*

【单皮】dānpí 类似小鼓的一种打击乐器,戏曲演出时用来指挥其他乐器 *danpi*, percussion instrument similar to a bongo drum, and a leading instrument in traditional opera orchestras

【单枪匹马】dān qiāng pǐ mǎ〈比喻 *fig.*〉单独行动,没有别人帮助 act on one's own; do sth. without help; single-handed; also 匹马单枪 pǐ mǎ dān qiāng

【单亲】dānqīn 只有父亲或母亲的 (of a family) with either a father or mother only: ～家庭(指孩子只随父亲或母亲一方生活的家庭) single-parent family (family with a child or children living with just one parent)

【单弱】dānruò ❶ (身体)瘦弱;不结实 (of a human body) thin and weak; of delicate constitution ❷ (力量)单薄 (of strength) insubstantial: 兵力～be weak in military strength

【单身】dānshēn 没有家属或没有跟家属在一起生活 not yet having a spouse or living away from one's spouse; live singly or alone: ～汉 bachelor | ～宿舍 living quarters for the unmarried; single dorm; bachelor's quarters | ～在外 live away from home as a single person

【单身汉】dānshēnhàn 没有妻子或没有跟妻子一起生活的人 bachelor; unmarried man or man who is not living with his wife

【单数】dānshù ❶ 正的奇数,如1,3,5,7等 odd number, such as 1, 3, 5, 7, etc. ❷ 某些语言中由词本身形式表示的单一的数量。例如英语里 pen 表示一支钢笔,是单数。singular; (word in certain languages) denoting a single person or thing, e.g. the English word 'pen' denotes a pen, so it has a singular number

【单瘫】dāntān 一个上肢或一个下肢发生瘫痪。多由局部神经受外伤以及脑、脊髓等疾患引起。monoplegia, complete paralysis of a single limb, oft. caused by partial nerve injury, brain or spinal problems

【单条】dāntiáo (~儿 dāntiáor)立轴(区别于'屏条'as compared with 'a set of wall scrolls') wall scroll painting or calligraphy hung vertically

【单位】dānwèi ❶ 计量事物的标准量的名称。如厘米为计算长度的单位,克为计算质量的单位,秒为计算时间的单位等。amount or quantity taken as a standard of measurement, such as 'centimetre' as a unit of length, 'gramme' as a unit of weight, 'second' as a unit of time ❷ 指机关、团体或属于一个机关、团体的各个部门 unit; government office, organization regarded as a whole or an elementary structure of a whole: 直属~ unit under the direct jurisdiction of a higher authority | 下属~subordinate unit | 事业~ institution | 参加竞赛的有很多~。Many units participated in the competition.

【单弦儿】dānxiánr 曲艺的一种,用弦子和八角鼓伴奏,八角鼓由唱者自己摇或弹。流行于华北、东北等地。form of folk art; performance by a single singer accompanied by a 3-stringed instrument and a small octagonal drum, popular in north and northeast China

【单线】dānxiàn ❶ 单独的一条线 single line ❷ 只有一组轨道的铁道或电车道,不能供相对方向的车辆同时通行(区别于'复线' as compared with 'dual track' or 'double track') single-rail track for a train or tram, not having the capability of serving trains or trams moving in opposite directions

【单相思】dānxiāngsī 指男女间仅一方对另一方爱慕 unrequited love; be lovesick for sb. without his or her knowledge or with no return of feelings

【单项】dānxiàng 单一的项目 individual event: 体操~比赛 individual gymnastic competition

【单行】dānxíng ❶ 就单一事项而实行的(条例等);仅在某个地方颁行和适用的(法规等) (of rules or regulations) be implemented for a particular situation; (of laws or regulations) made for or applied to a particular case ❷ 单独降临 come singly: 祸不~ misfortune never comes singly ❸ 单独印行 print singly: ~本 separate edition; offprint ❹ 向单一的方向行驶 move in one direction: ~线 one-way road

【单行本】dānxíngběn ❶ 从报刊上或从成套成部的书里抽出来单独印行的著作 separately printed book of a collection of newspaper articles or a particular volume from a set of books ❷ 在报刊上分期发表后经整理、汇集而印行的著作 separate edition; offprint; book published after sorting and collecting serialized newspaper articles

【单行线】dānxíngxiàn 只供车辆向一个方向行驶的路 one-way road or street; road permitting movement of vehicles in one direction only; also 单行道 dānxíngdào

D

【单姓】dānxìng 只有一个字的姓,如张、王、刘、李等 surname consisting of just one character, such as Zhang, Wang, Liu, Li, etc.

【单眼】dānyǎn 节肢动物的一种眼,只有一个水晶体。单眼的数目,各种节肢动物不同,如蜜蜂有三只,蜘蛛类有两只到八只。单眼只能分辨光的强弱,不能分辨颜色。stemma, eye of arthropod having a single lens. Various arthropods have different numbers of simple eyes, e.g. a bee has three simple eyes; a spider has two to eight. A simple eye can detect the degree of brightness, but not colour.

【单眼皮】dānyǎnpí (~儿 dānyǎnpír)上眼皮下缘没有褶儿的叫单眼皮 single-edged eyelid; single-layer eyelid; eyelid without a fold at its lower section

【单一】dānyī 只有一种 single; unitary; monotonous: ~经济 single-product economy | 品种~single variety; single breed | ~的全民所有制 unitary system of ownership by the whole people

【单衣】dānyī 只有一层的衣服 unlined garment

【单音词】dānyīncí 只有一个音节的词,如'笔、水、花儿(huār)、吃、走、大、高'等 monosyllable; monosyllabic word; word with a single syllable, such as '笔 bǐ, 水 shuǐ, 花儿 huār, 吃 chī, 走 zǒu, 大 dà, 高 gāo', etc.

【单元】dānyuán 整体中自成段落、系统,自为一组的单位(多用于教材、房屋等 oft. used in referring to a textbook or house) unit, separate part, system or group of a whole: ~练习 unit exercises | ~房 an apartment | 三号楼二~六室 Room No. 6, Entrance 2, Building 3

【单质】dānzhì 由同种元素组成的纯净物,如氢、氧、溴、汞、铁、铜等。有些元素可以形成不同的单质,如元素磷有白磷、红磷等单质。simple substance; pure substance composed of one element, e.g. hydrogen, oxygen, bromine, mercury, iron, or copper that may form a different simple substance. The element phosphorus may include red and white phosphorus.

【单子】dān·zi ❶ 盖在床上的大幅布 large cloth cover on a bed：布～ cloth；sheet | 床～ bed sheet ❷ 分项记载事物的纸片 piece of paper on which to list things separately：菜～ menu | 要买些什么，请开个～。Please make a shopping list.

【单字】dānzì ❶ 单个的汉字 individual Chinese character ❷ 指外国语中一个个的词 single word of a foreign language：学外语记～很重要。Word memorization is important when learning a foreign language.

【单作】dānzuò 在一块耕地上，一茬只种植一种作物 single-crop farming；grow a single crop on a piece of land

D

眈 dān [眈眈]形容眼睛注视 fix one's eyes on；gaze at；stare at：～相向 with eyes fixed on each other | 虎视～(凶猛地注视) gloat over sb. or sth.；cast a menacing look at

耽[1] (躭) dān 延误；迟延 delay；hold up；procrastinate；suspend：～搁 hold up；delay | ～误 hold up；delay；make or become worse because of delay

耽[2] dān〈书 *fml.*〉沉溺；入迷 abandon oneself to；indulge in；wallow in：～玩 indulge in pleasure seeking；spend lots of time playing around | ～于幻想 indulge in illusion

【耽搁】dān·ge ❶ 停留 stay：因为有些事情没办完，在上海多～了三天。As he still had unfinished business to attend to，he stayed in Shanghai for three more days. ❷ 拖延 delay；procrastinate：～时间 delay；waste time | 事情再忙也不要～治病。However busy you are，you must not put off treatment of illness. ❸ 耽误 make worse because of delay：庸医误诊，把病给～了。The patient's illness became worse because of a wrong diagnosis given by a charlatan. ‖ also 担搁 dān·ge

【耽误】dān·wu 因拖延或错过时机而误事 be late for sth. or fail to achieve a desired task or perform a job because of delay：快走吧，别～了看电影。Hurry up，let's not be late for the film. | 手续烦琐，实在～时间。Too much red tape wastes time.

郸(鄲) dān 郸城(Dānchéng)，地名，在河南 name of a place in Henan Province

聃(耼) dān 用于人名，老聃，古代哲学家 used as a given name，Lao Dan，ancient Chinese philosopher

殚(殫) dān〈书 *fml.*〉尽；竭尽 devote；use up；exhaust：～心 devote oneself heart and soul to | ～力 spare no efforts；strain every nerve；go to all lengths；do one's utmost | ～思极虑(用尽心思) rack one's brains；think of everything one can；devote one's entire thoughts to

【殚精竭虑】dān jīng jié lǜ 用尽精力，费尽心思 devote one's entire energy and thought to

瘅(癉) dān [瘅疟](dānnüè)〈中医 *Chin. med.*〉指疟疾的一种，症状是发高烧，不打寒战，烦躁，口渴，呕吐等 a kind of malaria distinguished by a high fever but no shivering，fretfulness，thirst，or vomiting

☞ dàn on p. 382

禅(襌) dān〈书 *fml.*〉单衣 unlined garment

箪(簞) dān〈古代 *arch.*〉盛饭用的圆形竹器 round food container made of bamboo

【箪食壶浆】dān sì hú jiāng〈古时 *arch.*〉老百姓用箪盛饭，用壶盛汤来欢迎他们爱戴的军队，后用来形容军队受欢迎的情况 greet the arrival of an army with food and drink

儋 Dān 儋县，地名，在海南 Danxian，name of a place in Hainan Province

甔 dān〈书 *fml.*〉瓶 bottle

dǎn (ㄉㄢˇ)

胆(膽) dǎn ❶ 胆囊的通称 general term for 胆囊 dǎnnáng ❷ (～儿 dǎnr)胆量 courage；guts；pluck：壮～儿 embolden；infuse courage；pluck up one's courage；nerve oneself；take heart | ～怯 quail；be timid；be faint-hearted | 斗～ venture (to do sth.)；make bold | ～大心细 brave but not reckless | ～小如鼠 as timid as a mouse；as scared as a mouse；chicken-hearted ❸ 装在器物内部，可以容纳水、空气等物的东西 vacuum flask or bladder fixed inside a container to hold water，air，etc.：球～ rubber bladder of a ball | 瓶～ glass liner inside a vacuum flask，thermos bottle，etc.

【胆大包天】dǎn dà bāo tiān 形容胆量极大(多用于贬义 oft. derog.) downright audacious

【胆大妄为】dǎn dà wàng wéi 毫无顾忌地胡作非为 act in foolhardy manner；daredevil；desperate；devil-may-care

【胆敢】dǎngǎn 竟有胆量敢于(做某事) dare；have the gall (to do sth.)：敌人～来侵犯，坚决把它彻底消灭。If the enemy dare to invade，we will resolutely wipe them out.

【胆固醇】dǎngùchún 醇的一种，白色的结晶，质地软。人的胆汁、神经组织、血液中含胆固醇较多。是合成胆酸和类固醇激素的重要原料。胆固醇代谢失调会引起动脉硬化和胆石病。cholesterol；sterol of a white soapy crystalline substance，mostly contained in bile，nerve tissues and blood，and an important constituent of cholic acid and steroid hormones. Unbalanced metabolism of cholesterol tends to cause arteriosclerosis and cholelithiasis.

【胆管】dǎnguǎn 肝脏的输出管，与十二指肠相连接。肝内生成的胆汁通过它流入十二指肠。

bile duct; excretory passage in the liver opening into the duodenum through which bile secreted in the liver passes and discharges into the duodenum; also 胆道 dǎndào

【胆寒】dǎnhán 害怕 be terrified; be alarmed; lose one's nerve; feel one's blood run cold; shiver in one's shoes

【胆力】dǎnlì 胆量和魄力 courage and dash: ～过人 of great courage

【胆量】dǎnliàng 不怕危险的精神;勇气 pluck; courage; defiance of danger; dauntlessness: ～小 not brave enough | 有～ have plenty of guts or spunk; be full of pluck

【胆略】dǎnlüè 勇气和智谋 courage and resourcefulness: ～超群 have unusual courage and resourcefulness; bold vision

【胆囊】dǎnnáng 储存胆汁的囊状器官,在肝脏右叶的下前方,与胆管相连接。通称胆或苦胆。muscular sac for storing bile, located under the right lobe of the liver, joined with bile duct, and generally known as 胆 dǎn or 苦胆 kǔdǎn;(图见 ☞ figure for 消化系统 xiāohuà xìtǒng on p. 2100)

【胆瓶】dǎnpíng 颈部细长而腹部大的花瓶,形状有点像胆 vase with a slender neck and a bulging belly, in the shape of a gallbladder

【胆气】dǎnqì 胆量和勇气 daring and courage

【胆怯】dǎnqiè 胆小;畏缩 timid; timorous; cower; quail: 初上讲台,还真有几分～。She felt a little self-conscious when standing on the rostrum for the first time.

【胆识】dǎnshí 胆量和见识 courage and vision; courage and insight: ～非凡 (man) of great enterprise; enterprising

【胆小鬼】dǎnxiǎoguǐ 胆量小的人(含讥讽意 derog.) coward; mouse; craven; poltroon; scaramouch

【胆战心惊】dǎn zhàn xīn jīng 形容非常害怕 tremble with fear; shake like an aspen leaf; be scared out of one's wits

【胆汁】dǎnzhī 肝脏产生的消化液,有苦味,黄褐色或绿色,储存在胆囊中。能促进脂肪的分解、皂化和吸收。bile; gall, bitter, brownish-yellow or greenish digestive fluid secreted from the liver and stored in the gallbladder; aids in the decomposition, digestion and absorption of fats

【胆壮】dǎnzhuàng 胆子大 audacious; fearless: 他见到有人支持他,就更～了。On seeing he had support, he became all the more daring.

【胆子】dǎn·zi 胆量 courage; guts; nerve; hardiness: ～不小 be bold; have the guts

疸 dǎn ☞ 黄疸 huángdǎn on p. 851
☞ ·da on p. 367

掸(撢、撣、担) dǎn 用掸子或别的东西轻轻地抽或扫,去掉灰尘等 brush with light sweeping movement to remove dust, using a feather duster or other cleaning implement: 墙壁和天花板都～得很干净。The walls and the ceiling were all dusted clean. | ～掉衣服上的雪 brush the snow off one's coat

☞ Shàn on p. 1674, 担 dān on p. 374 and dàn on p. 380

【掸子】dǎn·zi 用鸡毛或布绑成的除去灰尘的用具 feather duster; duster made of chicken feathers or strips of cloth

赕 dǎn 奉献 donate; offer: ～佛 donate money, etc., to a Buddhist temple [傣 term popular among the Dais]

【赕佛】dǎnfó 我国信奉佛教的某些少数民族向庙宇捐献财物,求佛消灾赐福(of Buddhists from certain minority peoples in China) donate money or tribute to a temple for the blessing of the Buddha

亶 dǎn 〈书 *fml.*〉实在;诚然 indeed; truly
☞ dàn on p. 382

黕 dǎn 〈书 *fml.*〉❶ 污垢 filth ❷ 乌黑 pitch-black; sootiness

dàn (ㄉㄢˋ)

石 dàn 容量单位,10 斗等于 1 石 unit of dry measure, 1 *dan* = 10 *dou*;(在古书中读 shí,如'二千石、万石'等 pronounced shí in ancient books, such as two thousand *shi*, ten thousand *shi*, etc.)

☞ shí on p. 1736

旦[1] dàn ❶〈书 *fml.*〉天亮;早晨 dawn; daybreak; morning: ～暮 dawn and dusk; | ～夕 this morning and evening | 通宵达～ all through the night; all night | 枕戈待～ pillow a sword in wait for the day to come; keep battle-alert ❷ (某一)天 (a) day: 一～ a day | 元～ New Year's Day

旦[2] dàn 戏曲角色,扮演妇女,有青衣、花旦、老旦、武旦等区别 *dan*, female role in traditional opera; There are four female roles, i. e. *qingyi*, *huadan*, *laodan* and *wudan*

旦[3] dàn 纤度单位,9,000 米长的天然丝或化学纤维重量为多少克,它的纤度就是多少旦。旦数愈小,纤维愈细。denier; unit of fineness for fibres, based on a standard mass per 9,000 metres of silk yarn or chemical fibres, the bigger the dan measurement, the thicker the yarn; 旧称 formerly called 紽(dài) [法 French: denier]

【旦角】dànjué (～儿 dànjuér) 旦[2],有时特指青衣、花旦 *dan*, sometimes referring in particular to such Peking Opera roles as *qingyi* and *huadan*

【旦夕】dànxī 〈书 *fml.*〉早晨和晚上 this morning or evening;〈比喻 *fig.*〉短时间 in a short while: 危在～ hang by a thread or hair; be in imminent danger; peril or destruction is close at hand or impending|人有～祸福。Sudden changes of fortune are just part of life. *or* Life is unpredictable. *or* Fortune is fickle. *or* Men are subject to sudden changes of fortune.

但 dàn ❶ 只 merely; only; just: ～愿如此。If only it were so or true. *or* May this be true. *or* I hope so.|不求有功，～求无过 aspire after no merit, praying only to commit no error; aim only at playing safe|辽阔的原野上，～见麦浪随风起伏。In the vast fields you see nothing but wheat undulating in the wind. ❷ 但是 but; yet; still; in spite of: 屋子小，～挺干净。The room is small but clean.|工作虽然忙，～一点也没放松学习。Although he is tied up with work, he nevertheless maintains the rigor of his studies. ❸ (Dàn) 姓 a surname

【但凡】dànfán 凡是；只要是 in every case; as long as; without exception: ～有一线希望，也要努力争取。Try your best to grasp even the slimmest hope.|～过路的人，没有一个不在这儿打尖的。Whoever passes here always stops for a snack.

【但是】dànshì 〈连词 *conj.*〉用在后半句话里表示转折，往往与‘虽然、尽管’等呼应 [used to introduce the next part of a sentence and indicate unexpectedness or exception]: 他想睡一会儿，～睡不着。He wanted to have a nap, but could not sleep.|他虽然已经七十多了，～精力仍然很健旺。Although he is already in his 70s, he is still full of energy.

【但书】dànshū 法律条文中‘但’字以下的部分，指出本条文的例外 proviso; qualifying clause; article or clause in any legal document, usu. beginning with the word ‘Provided’, indicating a condition, qualification or restriction

担(擔) dàn ❶ 担子 carrying pole and the loads thereon; load; burden: 货郎～ pedlar's goods carried on a shoulder pole|勇挑重～ take up a heavy load or task with courage and determination ❷ 重量单位，100 斤等于 1 担 *dan*, unit of weight, 1 *dan* = 100 *jin* ❸ 〈量词 *classifier*〉用于成担的东西 [as much as a shoulder pole can carry] pole: 一～水 a pole of water (with water carried in a bucket hung from either end of the pole)|两～柴 two poles of firewood (with firewood carried in two bundles hung from both ends of the pole)

☞ dān on p. 374 and 掸 dǎn on p. 379

【担子】dàn·zi ❶ 扁担和挂在两头的东西 carrying pole and the loads on both ends thereon: 一副～ a carrying pole and the loads thereon ❷ 〈比喻 *fig.*〉担负的责任 burden to bear; responsibility to shoulder: 我们不怕～重，一定要把事情办好。We are not afraid of this heavy task and are determined to do a good job.

诞[1] dàn ❶ 诞生 birth: ～辰 birthday ❷ 生日 birthday; one's natal day: 华～ your birthday|寿～ birthday (usu. of an elderly person)

诞[2] dàn 荒唐的；不实在的；不合情理的 absurd; fantastic; preposterous; without rhyme or reason: 虚～ fictitious and senseless|荒～ nonsensical|怪～ bizarre; weird

【诞辰】dànchén 生日(多用于所尊敬的人 for the old and venerable) birthday

【诞生】dànshēng (人)出生 (of a person) be born ◇ 1949 年 10 月 1 日，中华人民共和国～了。The People's Republic of China was founded on Oct. 1, 1949.

疍(蜑) dàn [疍民](dànmín) ☞ 水上居民 shuǐshàng jūmín on p. 1802

萏 dàn ☞ [菡萏](hàndàn) on p. 768

啖[1] **(啗、噉)** dàn 〈书 *fml.*〉❶ 吃或给别人吃 eat or feed: ～饭 eat one's meal|以枣～之 feed sb. with dates ❷ 拿利益引诱人 entice or lure with the promise of reward: ～以重利 allure or lure sb. with handsome rewards

啖[2] Dàn 姓 a surname

淡 dàn ❶ 液体或气体中所含的某种成分少；稀薄(跟‘浓’相对 as opposed to ‘thick or dense’) (of a liquid or gas) low content of certain ingredients; light thin; low in density: ～墨 light ink|天高云～。The sky is clear with scattered clouds. ❷ (味道)不浓；不咸 (of wine or other alcoholic drinks) lacking the proper strength; weak; (of food) tasteless; lacking salt; mild: 一杯～酒 a glass of weak wine|～而无味 light and tasteless|菜太～，再放点盐。This dish is bland, it needs a little more salt. ❸ (颜色)浅 (of colour) light; tinge: ～青 light greenish blue|～绿 light green|轻描～写 understate; mention casually; describe with a delicate touch; play down ❹ 冷淡；不热心 indifferent; cold; lacking interest; with little enthusiasm: ～然处之 be indifferent to; not care a straw, fig or whit about; act in a devil-may-care manner|～～地答应了一声 reply coolly ❺ 营业不旺盛 (of business) lacking in activity; slack; sluggish: ～季 slack season; off-season|～月 slack month ❻ 没有意味的；无关紧要的 meaningless; unimportant; trivial: ～话 mere words|～事 trifling matter|扯～ bullshit; gibberish

【淡泊】dànbó 〈书 *fml.*〉不追求名利 not woo fame and fortune; be above fame and fortune: ～名利 be indifferent to fame and fortune|～寡欲 lead a tranquil life without worldly desires|～明志 show one's purpose of life by simple living; also 澹泊 dànbó

【淡薄】dànbó ❶(云雾等)密度小(of cloud or fog) not dense; thin: 浓雾渐渐地～了。The thick fog slowly dispersed ❷(味道)不浓 weak: 酒味～。This wine tastes weak. ❸(感情、兴趣等)不浓厚(of emotion, interest, etc.) cool down; lessen; abate: 人情～ benumbing of people's feelings toward each other|他对象棋的兴趣逐渐～。His interest in Chinese chess has worn off. ❹(印象)因淡忘而模糊(of memory or impression) become blurred; dim; faint: 时间隔得太久,印象非常～了。It's been so long that my memory is fading.

【淡而无味】dàn ér wú wèi 指食物淡,没有滋味(of food) void of taste; insipid; flat; flavourless;〈比喻 *fig.*〉事物平淡,不能引起人的兴趣(of things) lacking liveliness, animation or interest; vapid

【淡化】[1] dànhuà ❶(问题、情感等)逐渐冷淡下来,变得不被重视或无关紧要(of problem, emotion, etc.) be gradually forgotten; become less thought of; fade: 家族观念～了 weakening of clannish concepts ❷使淡化 put less emphasis on; give less prominence to: ～情节 simplify the plot

【淡化】[2] dànhuà 使含盐分较多的水变成可供人类生活或工农业生产用的淡水 make saline water fresh by removing its salts so that it is suitable for daily life or industrial and agricultural purposes: ～海水 desalination of sea water|咸水～ desalination of saline water

【淡季】dànjì 营业不旺盛的季节或某种东西出产少的季节(跟'旺季'相对 as opposed to 'busy season or high season') slack season; off-season; dull season; inactive season for business or season with no bountiful supply of a certain farm produce: 蔬菜～ off-season for vegetables|旅游～ slack season for tourism

【淡漠】dànmò ❶没有热情;冷淡 lack enthusiasm; indifferent; apathetic; impassive: 反应～ be indifferent to sth. |～的神情 unconcerned look ❷记忆不真切;印象淡薄 not clear in the memory; dim in the mind: 十几年过去了,这件事在人们的记忆里已经～了。More than a decade has passed, and the matter has now become a faint memory.

【淡青】dànqīng 浅蓝而微绿的颜色 light greenish blue

【淡然】dànrán〈书 *fml.*〉形容不经心;不在意 unconcerned; casual; indifferent: ～置之 be indifferent to; take it easy|～一笑 smile drily; also 澹然 dànrán

【淡水】dànshuǐ 含盐分极少的水 fresh water: ～湖 fresh water lake|～养鱼 freshwater fish-farming

【淡忘】dànwàng 印象逐渐淡漠以至于忘记 become unclear in memory or be forgotten: 许多年过去,这件事被人～了。It has been many years, the matter has already faded from memory.

【淡雅】dànyǎ 素净雅致;素淡典雅 simple but elegant; quietly elegant; of seemingly effortless refinement: 服饰～be tastefully dressed in a simple style|色彩～ simple and graceful colours

【淡月】dànyuè 营业不旺盛的月份(跟'旺月'相对 as opposed to 'busy month') slack month

【淡妆】dànzhuāng 淡雅的妆饰 wearing less make-up; lightly made-up; dressed in understated, good taste

惮(憚) dàn〈书 *fml.*〉怕 fear; dread: ～烦 fear trouble|肆无忌～ reckless and without inhibition; unscrupulous; unbridled|过则勿～改。Do not be afraid to correct a fault when it emerges.

弹(彈) dàn ❶(～儿 dànr)弹子 ball; pellet: ～丸 ball; pellet|泥～儿 mud ball ❷枪弹;炮弹;炸弹 cartridge; slug; bullet; shot; shell; cannon ball; shot bomb; bombshell; crump: 中～ be hit; be stricken; be shot|投～bomb; drop a bomb; throw a grenade|手榴～ grenade; hand grenade|燃烧～ incendiary; incendiary bomb; flaming projectile|信号～ signal flare|原子～ atomic bomb; A-bomb; atom bomb|氢～ hydrogen bomb; H-bomb|导～missile ❸ same as 蛋 dàn

☞ tán on p. 1859

【弹道】dàndào 弹头射出后所经的路线。因受空气的阻力和地心引力的影响,形成不对称的弧线形。trajectory; ballistic path; path of a projectile, which forms a dissymmetric curve due to air resistance and gravity

【弹弓】dàngōng 用弹(tán)力发射弹丸的弓,古代用做武器,现在有时用来打鸟 catapult; slingshot, apparatus made from a Y-shaped stick with an elastic strap attached to its prongs, used as a weapon for flinging small stones or pellets (in ancient times) or to shoot birds

【弹痕】dànhén 弹着点的痕迹 shot mark; mark made by a fired bomb or bullet on a surface or the ground; bullet or shell hole: ～遍地。The ground is honeycombed with bullets. |～累累 be riddled with bullets

【弹壳】dànké ❶药筒的通称 general term for 药筒 yàotǒng ❷炸弹的外壳 shell case; jacket; outer metal shell of a bomb or bullet; cartridge case

【弹坑】dànkēng 炮弹、地雷、炸弹等爆炸后,在地面或其他东西上形成的坑 surface; crater; pit left by the explosion of an artillery shell, mine, bomb, etc. on the ground

【弹片】dànpiàn 炮弹、炸弹等爆炸后的碎片 shrapnel; (bomb) splinter; fragment from an exploded artillery shell or bomb

【弹头】dàntóu 枪弹、炮弹、导弹等的前部，射出后能起杀伤和破坏作用 bullet; projectile nose; warhead; forward part of a projectile, such as a cartridge, artillery shell, missile, etc., capable of death and destruction when fired

【弹丸】dànwán ❶ 弹弓所用的铁丸或泥丸 pellet; metal ball or clay ball used as a catapult projectile ❷ 枪弹的弹头 bullet; shot ❸〈书 *fml.*〉〈比喻 *fig.*〉地方狭小(of a place) very small; tiny: ～之地 a pellet of land; a tiny place

【弹药】dànyào 枪弹、炮弹、手榴弹、炸弹、地雷等具有杀伤能力或其他特殊作用的爆炸物的统称 ammunition, general term for fired or detonated material capable of killing or other purposes, such as bullets, shells, grenades, bombs, and mines

【弹着点】dànzhuódiǎn 枪弹或炮弹着落的地点 point of impact; hitting point; point of impact by a bullet or a shell

【弹子】dàn·zǐ ❶ 用弹弓弹(tán)射的弹丸 pellet shot from a catapult ❷〈方 *dial.*〉台球① billiards: ～房 billiard room

【弹子锁】dàn·zisuǒ〈方 *dial.*〉same as 撞锁 zhuàngsuǒ

蛋 dàn ❶ 鸟、龟、蛇等所产的卵 ovum produce by a bird, turtle, snake, etc. ❷ (～儿 dànr) 球形的东西 sth. having the ovoid-shape of an egg or the round shape of a ball: 泥～儿 mud ball | 山药～ potato

【蛋白】dànbái ❶ 鸟卵中透明的胶状物质，包在卵黄周围，由蛋白质组成 albumen; glair; egg white; (in the egg of a bird) gelatinous substance surrounding the yolk consisting of protein ❷ 指蛋白质 protein: 动物～ animal protein | 植物～ vegetable protein

【蛋白胨】dànbáidòng 有机化合物，由蛋白质经酸、碱或蛋白酶分解后而成。医学上用做细菌的培养基，也用来治疗消化道疾病。peptone, organic compound obtained by partial hydrolysis of a protein by an acid, alkali or enzyme during digestion and used in culture media in bacteriology; 简称 abbr. 胨 dòng

【蛋白酶】dànbáiméi 有机化合物，主要存在于动物体内，作用是把蛋白质分解成便于吸收的氨基酸。种类很多，如胃蛋白酶、胰蛋白酶等。protease; proteinase; proteolytic enzyme, organic compound, found in animals, that catalyzes the hydrolytic breakdown of proteins into amino acids. There are various enzymes, such as pepsin and trypsin.

【蛋白质】dànbáizhì 天然的高分子有机化合物，由多种氨基酸组成。是构成生物体活质的最重要部分，是生命的基础，种类很多。旧称朊。protein, group of complex organic macromolecules, composed of chains of amino acids. Proteins are fundamental components of all living cells — the bases of life, and are various; formerly known as 朊 ruǎn

【蛋糕】dàngāo 鸡蛋和面粉加糖和油制成的松软的糕 cake, soft baked food made of eggs and flour with sugar and oil

【蛋羹】dàngēng 鲜蛋去壳打匀后，加适量的水和作料蒸成的食物 egg custard, egg shelled, mixed with water and flavouring ingredients, and steamed

【蛋黄】dànhuáng (～儿 dánhuángr) 鸟卵中黄色胶状的物体，球形，周围有蛋白 yolk; yellow, usu. spherical gelatinous portion of the egg of a bird, surrounded by the albumen; also 卵黄 luǎnhuáng

【蛋品】dànpǐn 各种蛋类(如鸡蛋、鸭蛋、鹅蛋、鹌鹑蛋等)和各种蛋类制品(如松花蛋、冰蛋、糟蛋等)的统称 general term for eggs, i. e. chicken, duck, goose, quail eggs, as well as various egg products, such as preserved eggs, frozen eggs, pickled eggs, etc.

【蛋青】dànqīng 像青鸭蛋壳的颜色 pale blue

【蛋清】dànqīng (～儿 dànqīngr) same as 蛋白① dànbái

【蛋子】dàn·zi same as 蛋 dàn②

氮 dàn 气体元素，符号 N (nitrogen)。无色，无臭，不能燃烧，也不能助燃，化学性质很不活泼。氮在空气中约占 4/5，是植物营养的重要成分之一。用来制造氨、硝酸和氮肥，也用来填充灯泡。nitrogen, gaseous element, abbreviated as N, colourless and odourless, noncombustible, non-combustion-supporting, chemically inert, comprising four fifths of the atmosphere by volume, forming an important vegetable nutrient, used to manufacture ammonia, nitric acid and fertilizers. It can also be used to charge an electric bulb; 通称 generally called 氮气 dànqì

【氮肥】dànféi 含氮为主的肥料，能促进作物的茎叶生长，如硫酸铵、硝酸铵、厩肥、绿肥、人粪尿等 nitrogenous fertilizer; chemical fertilizer composed mostly of nitrogen, such as ammonium sulphate, ammonium nitrate, barnyard manure, green manure, human waste, etc., which promotes growth of stems and leaves in a crop

【氮气】dànqì 氮的通称 general term for 氮 dàn

亶 dàn〈书 *fml.*〉same as 但 dàn①②
☞ dǎn on p. 379

瘅(癉) dàn〈书 *fml.*〉❶ 由于劳累而得的病 illness resulting from strain or overwork ❷ 憎恨 hate; detest; condemn; denounce: 彰善～恶 praise good and denounce evil; uphold virtue and condemn vice
☞ dān on p. 378

髧 dàn〈书 *fml.*〉头发下垂的样子 hair falling or cascading

啗 dàn〈书 *fml.*〉same as 啖[1] dàn

赕 dàn〈书 *fml*.〉❶ 买东西预先付钱 money advanced for a purchase ❷ 书册或书画卷轴卷头上贴绫的地方 top of a scroll or back of a thread-bound book, usu. bound with silk

澹 dàn〈书 *fml*.〉安静 hush; quietude; tranquillity

☞ tán on p.1860

【澹泊】dànbó same as 淡泊 dànbó

【澹然】dànrán same as 淡然 dànrán

禫 dàn〈古时 *arch*.〉丧家除服的祭祀 ritual held to mark the end of a mourning period

dāng(ㄉㄤ)

当[1](當) dāng ❶ 相称 equal; match: 相～ fit; match; be worthy of | 门～户对 be from equal or similiar family background | 罚不～罪 unwarranted punishment for a crime; be unduly punished ❷ 应当 ought to; should; must: 该～ ought to; should | 理～如此 as it should be | 能省的就省，～用的还是得用。Save what you can, but use what you must. ❸ 面对着；向着 facing; confronting; to sb.'s face: ～面 in sb.'s presence | ～众宣布 declare publicly | 首～其冲 be the first to suffer impact; bear the brunt ❹ 正在（那时候、那地方）just at (a time or place): ～今 nowadays; now; today; at present | ～初 at the beginning; in the first place; originally | ～地 local; in the locality | ～场 on the spot; then and there; extempore

当[2](當) dāng ❶ 担任；充当 act as; work as; be: ～干部 be a cadre, official, public servant or government employee | 选他～代表 elect him deputy ❷ 承当；承受 bear; accept; deserve: 敢做敢～ have the courage to accept the consequences of what one has done | ～之无愧 deserve (one's title, honour, award, or praise) | 我可～不起这样的夸奖。I do not deserve such praise. ❸ 掌管；主持 administer; be in charge of; control; manage: ～家 run a household; housekeeping | ～权 be in power; be in control; wield power; wield authority | ～政 be in office; be in power | 独～一面 take full charge of sth.; be soly responsible for sth. ❹〈书 *fml*.〉阻挡；抵挡 stop; prevent; obstruct: 螳臂～车 brave but rash attempt to do what is far beyond one's ability | 锐不可～ be invincible; (of an army's combatant power) too overwhelming to check

当[3](當) dāng〈书 *fml*.〉顶端 tip; top; end: 瓦～ tile end; eaves tile

当[4](當、噹) dāng〈拟声词 *onom*.〉撞击金属器物的声音 tinkle; clank; clang; sound made by striking metals

☞ dàng on p.388

【当班】dāngbān 在规定的时间内担任工作或参加劳动；值班 work on a regular schedule; be on duty; be on a shift: 轮流～ work on a rotating shift | ～工人正在紧张地劳动。The workers are busy at their posts.

【当差】dāng//chāi〈旧时 *old*〉指做小官吏或当仆人 work as a petty official or servant

【当差】dāngchāi〈旧指 *old*〉男仆 male servant

【当场】dāngchǎng 就在那个地方和那个时候 then and there; on the spot; extempore: ～出丑 make a spectacle of oneself; make a gaffe | ～捕获 be caught red-handed (or in the act) | 他～就把这种新的技术表演了一次。He demonstrated the innovation on the spot.

【当场出彩】dāngchǎng chūcǎi 戏剧表演杀伤的时候，用红色水涂抹，装做流血的样子，叫做出彩。现在多比喻当场败露秘密或显出丑态。(seen in a theatrical performance or drama) scene of bloodshed accomplished using red ink; (fig.) make a spectacle of oneself; give the whole show away there and then

【当初】dāngchū 泛指从前或特指过去发生某件事情的时候 in the beginning; at first; originally; at that time: ～这里是一片汪洋。In the early days this region was covered with water. | 早知今日，何必～？If I had known things would be like this, would I have done it in the first place?

【当代】dāngdài 当前这个时代 present age; contemporary time; of the day: ～文学 contemporary literature | ～英雄 hero of the day or time; hero of our time

【当道】dāngdào ❶（～儿 dāngdàor）路中间 in the middle of the road: 别在～站着。Don't stand in the way. ❷ 掌握政权（含贬义 derog.）be in power; hold sway; take the reins: 奸佞～。The wicked toadeaters wield the scepter. ❸〈旧时 *old*〉指掌握政权的大官 influential officials; powers that be: 取悦于～curry favour with the powers that be

【当地】dāngdì 人、物所在的或事情发生的那个地方；本地 origin of a person or thing; place where sth. happens; in the locality; local: ～百姓 local people | ～风俗 local customs

【当归】dāngguī 多年生草本植物，羽状复叶，花白色，伞形花序。有许多细根，果实长椭圆形，整个植物有特殊香气。根可入药。Chinese angelica (*Angelica archangelica*); angelica, perennial herb, having pinnately compound leaves and white flowers in compound umbels, multiple thin roots and long oval fruit, with a distinctive fragrance, and its roots used as medicine

【当行出色】dānghǎng-chūsè 做本行的事，成绩特别显著 distinguish oneself in one's own profession or trade; be outstanding in one's field

【当机立断】dāng jī lì duàn 抓住时机，立刻决断 make a prompt decision; decide on the spot

【当即】dāngjí 立即；马上就 at once; right away; immediately; at short notice：接到命令，～出发。We are ready to start the moment we receive the order.

【当家】dāng//jiā 主持家务 manage household affairs; run a house; keep house：不～不知柴米贵。One has to keep house to know the price of rice and firewood.｜她是个会～的好主妇，家里的事情处理得井井有条。She is a good housewife and keeps the house in good order. ◇人民～作主。The people are now masters of their own country.

【当家的】dāngjiā·de ❶ 主持家务的人；家主 housekeeper; householder; head of a household ❷ 主持寺院的和尚 Buddhist abbot; head monk of a Buddhist temple ❸〈方 *dial.*〉丈夫(zhàng·fu) husband

【当间儿】dāngjiànr〈方 *dial.*〉中间 in the middle：堂屋～放着一张大方桌。There is a big square table in the middle of the hall.

【当街】dāngjiē ❶ 靠近街道；临街 near the street; facing the street：这里的酒店，都是～一个曲尺形的大柜台。Each restaurant here has a large L-shaped counter facing the street. ❷〈方 *dial.*〉街上 in the street：出了院门，直奔～(walking or running) out of the yard and into the street

【当今】dāngjīn ❶ 如今；现时；目前 now; at present; nowadays; today：～世界 world today｜～最新技术 the most advanced technology of the time ❷ 封建时代称在位的皇帝 reigning emperor; emperor on the throne in feudal China

【当紧】dāngjǐn〈方 *dial.*〉要紧 urgent; important

【当局】dāngjú 指政府、党派、学校中的领导者 government, party or school authorities：政府～ the authorities; the government｜学校～ school authorities

【当局者迷】dāng jú zhě mí '当局者迷，旁观者清'，当局者指下棋的人，旁观者指看棋的人 what bewilders the player, the onlooker sees clearly; spectator sees the whole game; the player sees less clearly than the bystander. 'The player' refers to a chess player while 'the bystander' is the spectator.〈比喻 *fig.*〉当事人往往因为对利害得失的考虑太多，认识不全面，反而不及旁观的人看得清楚 Those deeply involved in a matter tend to have their vision obscured by the prospect of possible defeat, while outsiders have a sounder, more objective judgement.

【当空】dāngkōng 在上空；在天空 high above in the sky：烈日～。The sun is high in the sky and scorching hot.｜皓月～。The moon shines bright above.

【当口儿】dāng·kour 事情发生或进行的时候 at the very moment when sth. happens：正是抗旱紧张的～，他们送来了一台抽水机。Just at the most critical juncture of the drought, they sent a pump.

【当啷】dānglāng〈拟声词 *onom.*〉金属器物磕碰的声音 clank; clang; hitting sound of metals

【当量】dāngliàng 科学技术上指与某标准数量相对应的某个数量，如化学当量、热功当量、核装置的梯恩梯当量 equivalent (weight); corresponding element under an equivalence relation, such as chemical equivalent; mechanical equivalent of heat; TNT equivalent of a nuclear device

【当令】dānglìng 合时令 in season：现在是伏天，西瓜正～。During these dog days, watermelons are in season.

【当面】dāng//miàn (～儿 dāng//miànr) 在面前；面对面(做某件事) to sb.'s face; in sb.'s presence; right in sb.'s face; face to face：～对质 confront sb. (with a question, fact, etc.)｜～说清楚 make clear face to face

【当面锣对面鼓】dāng miàn luó duì miàn gǔ〈比喻 *fig.*〉面对面地商谈或争论 openly; negotiate or argue face to face

【当年】dāngnián ❶ 指过去某一时间 in those years or days; that year：～旧事 bygone happenings｜～我离开家的时候，这里还没有火车。The year when I left home, trains were still unavailable here. ❷ 指身强力壮的时期 in the prime of life：他正～，干活一点儿也不觉得累。He is at his best, and never feels the slightest bit tired at work.

☞ dàngnián on p. 388

【当前】dāngqián ❶ 在面前 facing one; before one：大敌～ confronted by an arch enemy｜国难～ at this time of national crisis ❷ 目前；现阶段 present; current：～的任务 current job or task

【当权】dāng//quán 掌握权力 hold power or authority; wield power or authority; be in power; take the reins of government：～者 potentate; person in power; authority｜这件事谁～就由谁作主。The matter is the responsibility of whoever is in power.

【当儿】dāngr ❶ 当口儿 in the nick of time; at the very moment; just as; when：正在犯愁的～，他来帮忙了。He came to my aid just as I was starting to get anxious. ❷ 空儿；空隙 gap; break; space：两张床中间留一尺宽的～。Leave a one-foot space between the beds.

【当然】dāngrán ❶ 应当这样 naturally; it goes without saying：理所～ as it should (be) ❷ 合于事理或情理，没有疑问 in accordance with reason or sense; without doubt：群众有困难

～应该帮助解决。It goes without saying that we should help people in need.

【当仁不让】dāng rén bù ràng《论语·卫灵公》：'当仁不让于师。'后泛指遇到应该做的事，积极主动去做，不退让。do not leave to others what one should do oneself. *Analects · Duke Ling of Wei*: 'You should take it upon yourselves to be the source of benevolence, and should not lag behind even your teacher in this regard.' In a broad sense, this phrase means one should not pass on to others what one is called upon to do.

【当日】dāngrì 当(dāng)时；当初 at that time; back then
☞ dàngrì on p. 388

【当时】dāngshí 指过去发生某件事情的时候 then; at that time：～不清楚，事后才知道。I knew nothing about it until after it had happened.｜他这篇文章是1936年写成的，～并没有发表。He wrote this article in 1936, but it was not printed at that time.
☞ dàngshí on p. 388

【当事人】dāngshìrén ❶ 指参加诉讼的一方，如民事诉讼中的原告、被告，刑事诉讼中的自诉人、被告 litigant; party engaged in a lawsuit, such as a prosecutor or defendant in a civil lawsuit; a private prosecutor or defendant in a criminal lawsuit ❷ 跟事物有直接关系的人 person or party concerned

【当头】dāngtóu ❶ 正对着头；迎头 head-on：～一棒 telling blow; great shock; stunning blow; stern alarm ❷（事情）到了眼前；临头 facing or confronting; imminent：那时国难～，全国人民同仇敌忾，奋起抗战。When the country was imperilled by foreign aggression, the people all rose to resist and fought with a common hatred of the enemy. ❸ 放在首位 put in the first place; give priority to; come first：敢字～ bravery overcomes｜不能遇事钱～。Whatever you do, don't take money as the first consideration.
☞ dàng·tou on p. 388

【当头棒喝】dāng tóu bàng hè 佛教禅宗和尚接待来学的人的时候，常常用棒一击或大声一喝，促其领悟 when a monk of the Chan sect of Chinese Buddhism received a disciple, he oft. struck him on the head with a cudgel or shouted at him at the top of his voice in order to get his message arose;〈比喻 *fig*.〉促人醒悟的警告 give sb. a wake-up warning

【当头一棒】dāng tóu yī bàng ❶〈比喻 *fig*.〉促人醒悟的警告 severe warning to wake sb. up from error ☞ 当头棒喝 dāng tóu bàng hè ❷〈比喻 *fig*.〉给人以突然打击 sudden shock or blow

【当务之急】dāng wù zhī jí 当前急切应办的事 business or task of the greatest urgency; most pressing matter of the moment; top priority

【当下】dāngxià 就在那个时刻；立刻 at once; immediately：我一听这话，～就愣住了。I was instantly dumbfounded at the remark. *or* I was speechless on hearing this.

【当先】dāngxiān ❶ 赶在最前面 up front; at the head; in the vanguard：奋勇～ take the lead with courage; fight bravely in the vanguard｜一马～，万马奔腾。When one horse leads, ten thousand horses follow at full gallop.（oft. used figuratively to show the importance of a leading role）❷〈方 *dial*.〉当初 originally; in the beginning

【当心】[1] dāngxīn 小心；留神 be careful; watch out; be on guard：慢点儿走，～地上滑。Watch your step, the road is slippery.｜跟这种人打交道，你可千万～。You must be careful in your dealings with such a person.

【当心】[2] dāngxīn〈方 *dial*.〉胸部的正中，泛指正中间 centre of the chest;（in a broad sense）in the middle; at the centre：～一拳 punch sb. on the chest｜拖拉机停在场院～。The tractor was parked in the middle of the threshing ground.

【当选】dāngxuǎn 选举时被选上 be elected; win an election：他再次～为工会主席。He was once more elected chairman of the trade union.

【当央】dāngyāng〈方 *dial*.〉当中；正中 in the middle; at the centre：堂屋～摆着八仙桌。At the centre of the hall is a Chinese square table.

【当腰】dāngyāo 中间（多指长条形物体）middle section（of an object of some length）：两头细，～粗 thin at both ends and thick at the waist

【当院】dāngyuàn〈方 *dial*.〉（～儿 dāngyuànr）院子里 in the courtyard：吃完晚饭，大家都在～乘凉。After supper everyone goes out to the courtyard to keep cool.

【当政】dāngzhèng 掌握政权 be in power; be in office

【当中】dāngzhōng ❶ 正中 in the centre：烈士纪念碑坐落在广场～。The monument to the martyrs stands in the centre of the square. ❷ 中间；之内 in the midst of; among：谈话～流露出不满情绪 reveal one's dissatisfaction when in conversation｜在这些英雄人物～，他的事迹最感人。Among these heroes, what he did was the most touching.

【当中间儿】dāngzhōngjiànr 正中 right in the middle：照片的右边是哥哥、嫂子，左边是我和弟弟，～是爸爸、妈妈。On the right are my elder brother and sister-in-law, on the left are my younger brother and me, and my father and mother are right in the middle.

【当众】dāngzhòng 当着大家 in the presence of all; in public; before a crowd：～表态 make one's position known to all | ～宣布结果 declare the result in public

【当子】dāng·zi 〈方 *dial.*〉same as 当儿 dāngr ②：不要留那么大的～，靠近一点。Come closer, don't stand at such a distance from us.

珰(璫) dāng〈书 *fml.*〉❶ 妇女戴在耳垂上的一种装饰品 eardrop; earring, item of jewellery worn by women, on or pendant from the ear, esp. the earlobe ❷ 指宦官。汉代宦官侍中、中常侍等的帽子上有黄金珰的装饰品。a reference to eunuch, originating in the fact that during the Han Dynasty, a eunuch who was a palace attendant or palace attendant-in-ordinary wore gold jewellery on their caps.

铛(鐺) dāng〈拟声词 *onom.*〉撞击金属器物的声音 clank; clang; metallic sound

☞ chēng on p. 243

裆(襠) dāng ❶ 两条裤腿相连的部分 fly; section of a pair of pants, underpants, or shorts where the two leg panels join：裤～ fly; crotch | 横～hip (hip width of a pair of trousers) | 直～rise (length from crotch to waist of a pair of trousers) | 开～裤 open-seat pants (for a baby or small child) ❷ 两条腿的中间 place between the tops of the legs of the human body; crotch：腿～ crotch | 胯～crotch; groin

蚂(蟷) dāng ☞ [螳蚂] (diédāng) on p. 452

筜(簹) dāng ☞ [筼筜] (yúndāng) on p. 2377

dǎng (ㄉㄤˇ)

挡(擋、攩) dǎng ❶ 拦住；抵挡 keep off; ward off; withstand：拦～ blockade; block; hold back | ～住去路 stand in one's way | 兵来将～，水来土掩 stop an army with a troop, stop a breach with earth | 一件单衣可～不了夜里的寒气。A single coat cannot keep out the chill of night. ❷ 遮蔽 shelter from; block：～风 keep out the wind | ～雨 shelter from the rain | 山高～不住太阳。Even the highest mountain cannot shut out the sun. *or* No high mountain can obliterate the sun. ❸ (～儿 dǎngr) 挡子 fender：火～ fire screen | 炉～儿 fender; fire screen ❹ 排挡的简称 abbr. for 排挡 páidǎn：二～ second gear | 空～ neutral gear | 挂～ put into gear ❺某些仪器和测量装置用来表明光、电、热等量的等级 gauge; grading; scale of measurement on certain instruments or apparatus used to measure light, electricity, heat, etc.

☞ dàng on p. 389

【挡车】dǎng//chē 纺织工业指看管一定数量纺织机器，并负责所看管机器上的产品的产量和质量的工作 (of a textile worker) oversee or operate a certain number of looms while checking the quality and quantity of the cloth produced：～工 loom tender; spinner

【挡横儿】dǎng//hèngr 从中干涉、拦阻 intervene; interfere; meddle in; get in the way：没你的事儿，你挡什么横儿？This does not concern you, why meddle?

【挡驾】dǎng//jià 〈婉辞 *euph.*〉谢绝来客访问 turn away a visitor with some excuse; decline to see a guest：凡上门来求情的他一概～。He forestalled all those who came to plead for leniency.

【挡箭牌】dǎngjiànpái 盾牌 shield; 〈比喻 *fig.*〉推托或掩饰的借口 excuse to shirk or evade sth.; pretext：你不想去就对他直说，别拿我做～。If you don't want to go, tell him frankly — don't use me as an excuse.

【挡子】dǎng·zi 遮挡用的东西 blind; shade; screen; fender：窗～ window blind or shade

党(黨) dǎng ❶ 政党，在我国特指中国共产党 party; political party; (in China) the Communist Party; the Party：～章 Party Constitution | ～校 Party school | 入～ join the Party; become a Party member ❷ 由私人利害关系结成的集团 clique; faction; clan; junto; ring; crew; gang; horde; circle or group of people whose association stems from a common interest：死～ sworn followers | 结～营私 clique; band together for clandestine and illegal activities ❸ 〈书 *fml.*〉偏袒 be partial to; favour; take sides with：～同伐异 support one's colleagues and attack those who are not; be narrowly partisan ❹ 〈书 *fml.*〉指亲族 kinsfolk; relatives：父～ father's kinsfolk | 母～ mother's kinsfolk | 妻～ wife's kinsfolk ❺ (Dǎng) 姓 a surname

【党报】dǎngbào 政党的机关报，是政党的纲领、路线和政策的宣传工具 party organ; newspaper serving as the mouthpiece of a political party and its programme, line and policy

【党阀】dǎngfá 指政党内把持大权、专横跋扈、进行宗派活动的头目 party bigwig; party tyrant, despotic political party leader who wields power clannishly

【党费】dǎngfèi ❶ 政党的活动经费 fund needed for the operation of a political party ❷ 党员按期向所在的党的基层组织交纳的钱 membership dues; money paid periodically by a member to a party's grass-roots organization

【党纲】dǎnggāng 党章的总纲，是一个政党的最基本的政治纲领和组织纲领 party programme; platform, general programme of a party's constitution; fundamental political and organizational programme of a political party

【党锢】dǎnggù 〈古代 *arch.*〉指禁止某一集团、派别及其有关的人担任官职并限制其活动

party sanction; prevention of a certain clique or clan from assuming office or pursuing more activities than allowed

【党棍】dǎnggùn 政党中依仗权势作恶多端的人 corrupt and tyrannical party boss; person from a political party who abuses power for personal gain

【党国】dǎngguó 国民党统治时期指国民党及其所掌握的国家政权(used by the KMT during its regime) reference to the Kuomintang (KMT) and its government

【党籍】dǎngjí 申请入党的人被批准后取得的党员资格 party membership; party affiliation; party membership granted to an applicant after he or she is recruited

【党纪】dǎngjì 一个政党所规定的该党党员必须遵守的纪律 party discipline; rules of conduct or discipline stipulated by a political party

【党课】dǎngkè 中国共产党的组织为了对党员进行党章教育而开的课,有时也吸收申请入党的人听课 party lesson; party lecture; lecture arranged by the Party to educate its members and aspiring members on the Party Constitution

【党魁】dǎngkuí 政党的首领(多含贬义 oft. derog.) party boss; chieftain; chief

【党龄】dǎnglíng 党员入党后经过的年数 party membership seniority, length of time as a party member

【党派】dǎngpài 各政党或政党中各派别的统称 clans; factions; cliques; party groupings; general term for various political parties or different groups within a party

【党旗】dǎngqí 代表一个政党的旗帜。中国共产党的党旗是左上角有金黄色的镰刀和铁锤的红旗。party flag; flag that represents a political party. The CPC party flag is a red flag emblazoned with a golden hammer and sickle in its upper left-hand corner.

【党同伐异】dǎng tóng fá yì 跟自己意见相同的就袒护,跟自己意见不同的就加以攻击。原指学术上派别之间的斗争,后用来指一切学术上、政治上或社会上的集团之间的斗争。shield those who agree and attack those who differ; originally referring to conflicts between various academic schools; later referring generally to conflicts among academic schools or political and social groups

【党徒】dǎngtú 参加某一集团或派别的人(含贬义 derog.) henchman; partisan; follower; adherent; person who joins a clique or clan

【党团】dǎngtuán ❶ 党派和团体的简称,在我国特指共产党和共青团 political party and its affiliated organizations for short; (in China) the Chinese Communist Party and the Chinese Communist Youth League; the Party and the League ❷ 某些国家议会中,属于同一政党的代表的集体 (in some parliaments) caucus, parliamentary group that belongs to or stands for the same party

【党委】dǎngwěi 某些政党的各级委员会的简称,在我国特指中国共产党的各级委员会 committees of a political party at different levels for short; (in China) committees of the CPC at different levels; Party committee

【党务】dǎngwù 政党内部有关组织建设等的事务 party work; party affairs; work, affairs, etc., associated with the organizational construction of a political party

【党项】Dǎngxiàng〈古代 *arch.*〉羌族的一支,北宋时建立西夏政权,地区包括今甘肃、陕西、内蒙古的各一部分和宁夏 Tanguts; branch of the Qiang tribe that, during the Northern Song Dynasty, set up the Western Xia regime that encompassed present-day Ningxia and parts of Gansu, Shaanxi and Inner Mongolia

【党校】dǎngxiào 共产党培养、训练党的干部的学校 Party school; school set up by the CPC to prepare members for leading posts or to train cadres

【党性】dǎngxìng ❶ 阶级性最高最集中的表现。不同的阶级或政党有不同的党性。highest epitome of class character or spirit; different classes or political parties each have a different party character ❷ 特指共产党员的党性,就是无产阶级的阶级性最高最集中的表现,是衡量党员阶级觉悟的高低和立场是否坚定的准绳 Party spirit; Party character; referring specifically to the Party spirit of a CPC member that epitomizes the character of the proletarian class, and the criterion that indicates the class awareness and stand of a Party member

【党羽】dǎngyǔ 指某个派别或集团首领下面的追随者(含贬义 derog.) adherent; henchman; partisan; protégé; follower of a party or clan chief

【党员】dǎngyuán 政党的成员,在我国特指中国共产党的成员 member of a political party; member of the Chinese Communist Party

【党章】dǎngzhāng 一个政党的章程,一般规定该党的总纲、组织机构、组织制度及党员的条件、权利、义务和纪律等项 constitution of a political party, which generally prescribes its programme, organizational structure, organizational system as well as qualifications, rights, obligations, and discipline for members

【党证】dǎngzhèng 政党发给党员的证明其党籍的证件 party membership card; certificate that verifies party membership issued by a political party

谠(讜) dǎng〈书 *fml.*〉正直的(话)(of advice or comment) honest; outspoken; straightforward: ~言 candid remarks | ~辞 sincere words | ~论 unbiased comment; candid statement

dàng（ㄉㄤˋ）

当[1]（當） dàng ❶ 合宜；合适 proper；right；appropriate：恰～ suitable｜妥～ appropriate｜得～ proper｜用例不～ use improper examples｜举措失～ make an ill-advised move ❷ 抵得上 be equal to；match：割麦子他一个人能～两个人。He can do the work of two people in harvesting wheat. ❸ 作为；当做 treat as；regard as；take for：安步～车 walk over leisurely instead of riding in a carriage；go on foot rather than by car｜不要把我～客人看待。Don't treat me as a guest. ❹ 以为；认为 think：～真 really｜我～你回来了，原来还在这儿。I thought you had left，but you're still here. ❺ 指事情发生的(时间) that very (day，year，etc.)：～时 the same moment；at the moment｜～天 the same day；that very day｜～年 that same year；in that year

当[2]（當、儅） dàng ❶ 用实物作抵押向当铺借钱 pawn：～当 pawn things｜典～ pawn ❷ 押在当铺的实物 sth. pawned；pawn；pledge：当～ sth. in pawn｜赎～ redeem sth. pawned
☞ dāng on p. 383

【当成】dàngchéng 当做 regard as；treat as；take for：看错了眼，我把他弟弟～是他了。My eyes failed me，for I mistook his younger brother for him.

【当当】dàngdàng 到当铺当东西 pawn things；put things in pawn

【当家子】dàngjiā·zi〈方 *dial.*〉同宗族的人；本家 members of the same clan；distant relatives with the same family name

【当年】dàngnián 就在本年；同一年 the same year；that very year：这个工厂～兴建，～投产。The factory started production the year it was constructed.
☞ dāngnián on p. 384

【当票】dàngpiào 当铺所开的单据，上面写明抵押品和抵押的钱数，到期凭此赎取抵押品 pawn receipt；document given by a pawnshop to attest to the things pawned and the amount of money with which the pawned things can be redeemed before an expiry date

【当铺】dàng·pù 专门收取抵押品而借款给人的店铺。借款多少，按抵押品的估价而定。到期不赎，抵押品就归当铺所有。pawnshop；shop specializing in lending money on interest against pawned objects as security，where the amount lent is determined by the value of the pawned objects，which will belong to the pawnshop if not redeemed in due time

【当日】dàngrì 当(dàng)天 the same day；that very day：～事，～做完 finish the day's work on the same day
☞ dāngrì on p. 385

【当时】dàngshí 就在那个时刻；马上；立刻 right away；at once；immediately：他一听到这个消息，～就跑来了。He came over right away after he heard the news.
☞ dāngshí on p. 385

【当天】dàngtiān 就在本天；同一天 the same day；that very day：路不远，早晨动身，～就能赶回来。It is not far away；if you go in the morning，you can come back on the same day.

【当头】dàng·tou 向当铺借钱时所用的抵押品 sth. pawned；pawn；pledge
☞ dāngtóu on p. 385

【当晚】dàngwǎn 本天的晚上；同一天的晚上 that evening；on the evening of the same day：早晨进城，～就赶回来了。He went to town in the morning and made his way back in the evening.

【当夜】dàngyè 本天的夜里；同一天的夜里 the same night；that very night：傍晚接到命令，～就出发了。He got the order in the evening and started off the same night.

【当月】dàngyuè 就在本月；同一月 the same month；that very month：月票～有效。The monthly metro pass is good only for the prescribed month.

【当真】dàngzhēn ❶ 信以为真 take seriously：这是跟你闹着玩儿的，你别～。Don't take it seriously；I was only joking. ❷ 确实；果然 really；true；sure enough：这话～？Is it true?｜那天他答应给我画幅画儿，没过几天，～送来了一幅。He promised to do a painting for me that day，and，sure enough，he sent me one in a few days' time.

【当做】dàngzuò 认为；作为；看成 treat as；regard as；look on as：不要把群众的批评～耳旁风。Don't turn a deaf ear to the masses' criticisms.｜参军后我就把部队～自己的家。After joining the army，I regarded the army as my own home.

凼（氹） dàng〈方 *dial.*〉水坑；田地里沤肥的小坑 water hole；compost pit in the fields：水～ pond｜粪～ cesspool

【凼肥】dàngféi 我国南方把垃圾、树叶、杂草、粪尿等放在坑里沤制成的肥料 wet compost or water-logged compost. In South China，wet compost is made by putting organic waste，leaves，weeds，night soil，etc. into a pool.

砀（碭） dàng 砀山 (Dàngshān)，地名，在安徽 name of a place in Anhui Province

宕 dàng〈书 *fml.*〉❶ 拖延 delay：延～ procrastinate；keep putting off｜推～ put off；postpone ❷ 放荡；不受拘束 with abandonment；freedom from restraint；indulgent：跌～ unrestrained；unbridled；varied

垱(壋) dàng〈方 *dial*.〉为便于灌溉而筑的小土堤 embankment built for irrigation：筑～挖塘 build embankments and dig ponds for irrigation

荡¹(蕩、盪) dàng ❶ 摇动；摆动 swing；sway；wave：动～ undulate；turmoil｜飘～ flutter；wander about｜～桨 pull on the oars｜～秋千 play on a swing ❷ 无事走来走去；闲逛 loaf about：游～ loaf about｜闲～ idle about ❸ 洗 rinse：冲～ rinse out；wash away｜涤～ rinse；wash ❹ 全部搞光；清除 clear away；sweep off：扫～ mopping up；mopping-up operation｜倾家～产 lose the entire family fortune；be broke ❺ 广阔；平坦 vast；broad and level：浩～ vast and mighty｜坦～ broad and level；magnanimous

荡²(蕩) dàng 放纵，行为不检点 loose in morals；debauched；licentious：放～ dissolute；dissipated｜浪～ loiter about；loaf about｜淫～ loose in morals；lascivious；licentious；lewd

荡³(蕩) dàng ❶ 浅水湖 shallow lake；marsh：黄天～Huangtian Marsh｜芦花～ reed marsh ❷ same as 凼 dàng

【荡除】dàngchú 清除 clear away；get rid of：～积习 do away with old habits and customs

【荡涤】dàngdí〈书 *fml*.〉洗涤 cleanse；clean up；wash away ◇山光水色足以～胸襟。The beautiful mountains and rivers are enough to cleanse all worries from the mind.

【荡平】dàngpíng 扫荡平定 wipe out；quell；stamp out：～天下 conquer all the land under the sky

【荡气回肠】dàng qì huí cháng ☞ 回肠荡气 huí cháng dàng qì on p. 859

【荡然】dàngrán〈书 *fml*.〉形容原有的东西完全失去 all gone；nothing left：～无存。Everything is gone.｜资财～。No money and property is left.

【荡漾】dàngyàng (水波)一起一伏地动 ripple；undulate：湖水～。There are ripples on the lake.｜◇歌声～。The singing rose and fell in waves.｜春风～ like ripples in the spring breeze

【荡子】dàng·zi〈方 *dial*.〉浅水湖 shallow lake

挡(擋) dàng ☞ 摒挡 bìngdàng on p. 144 ☞ dǎng on p. 386

档(檔) dàng ❶ 带格子的架子或橱，多用来存放案卷 shelves (for files)；pigeonholes：归～ file a document；place a document on file ❷ 档案 files；records；archives：查～ look into the records or files｜调～ transfer files ❸ (～儿 dàngr)(器物上)起支撑固定作用的木条或细棍儿 crosspiece (of a table, etc.)：床～ crosspiece of a bed｜桌子的横～儿 crosspiece of a table ❹ (商品、产品的)等级 (of commodities or products) grade：～次 grades；levels｜低～货 low-grade goods｜高～产品 high-grade product ❺〈方 *dial*.〉货摊；摊档 open-air booth or stall：鱼～ fish stall｜大排～ pavement stall；food stand；roadside eatery

【档案】dàng'àn 分类保存以备查考的文件和材料 files；archives；records；dossier；documents and materials kept in a catalogued fashion for reference：人事～ personnel dossier｜科技～ scientific and technological files

【档次】dàngcì 按一定标准分成的不同等级 grading；grade：商品种类多，～全 commodities in all grades and full specifications｜奖勤罚懒，拉开分配的不同～。In order to reward those who are hardworking and punish those who are lazy, the gaps between different grades of distribution must be widened.

【档子】dàng·zi〈方 *dial*.〉〈量词 *classifier*〉❶ 用于事件 [used as a definite article before an event or issue]：这～事我来管吧。Leave the matter to me. same as 档儿 dàngr ❷ 用于成组的曲艺杂技等 integrated group of performances：刚过去两～龙灯，又来了一～旱船。Two teams of dragon dancers had just passed when a team of land-boat dancers arrived.

宕 dàng ☞ [莨宕] (làngdàng) on p. 1151

dāo (ㄉㄠ)

刀 dāo ❶ 古代兵器，泛指切、割、削、砍、铡的工具，一般用钢铁制成 ancient weapon；generally referring to steel tools for cutting, mowing, hacking or chopping：菜～ kitchen knife；butcher knife｜军～ soldier's sword；sabre｜铡～ folder chopper；hand hay cutter｜铣～ milling cutter ❷ 形状像刀的东西 sth. shaped like a knife：冰～ ice skates｜双～电闸 twin-knife main switch；twin-knife master switch ❸〈量词 *classifier*〉计算纸张的单位，通常一百张为一刀 [unit for counting sheets of paper that entails 100 sheets of paper] ❹ (Dāo) 姓 a surname

【刀把儿】dāobàr ❶〈比喻 *fig*.〉权柄 military power；power ❷〈方 *dial*.〉〈比喻 *fig*.〉把柄 evidence against sb. ‖ also 刀把子 dāobà·zi

【刀背】dāobèi (～儿 dāobèir) 刀上与刀口相反、不用来切削的一边 opposite side of a knife blade, the side not for cutting；back of a knife

【刀笔】dāobǐ〈古代 *arch*.〉在竹简上记事，用刀子刮去错字，因此把有关公文案卷的事叫做刀笔，后世多指写状子的事(多含贬义 oft. derog.) In ancient times people wrote on bamboo slips and scraped out wrong words with a knife, so documents and files were called 'knife and brush' — the writing of indictments and appeals：～吏 petty official who draws up indictments, etc.; official pettifogger|～老手 old hand in drawing up indictments; seasoned pettifogger|长于～ good at drawing up indictments and appeals

【刀兵】dāobīng 泛指武器，转指战事 generally refers to weapons or arms; in a roundabout way also refers to fighting or war：动～ resort to arms; resort to force|～相见 meet in battle; declare war on sb.; fight each other|～之灾 calamities of war

【刀锋】dāofēng 刀尖；刀刃 point of a knife; knife edge

【刀耕火种】dāo gēng huǒ zhòng 一种原始的耕种方法，把地上的草木烧成灰做肥料，就地挖坑下种 slash-and-burn cultivation; primitive farming method of burning the grass and plants on the land to use the ashes as fertilizer, digging holes in the ground, and sowing the seeds

【刀光剑影】dāo guāng jiàn yǐng 形容激烈的厮杀、搏斗或杀气腾腾的气势 glint and flash of steel; fierce fighting; under the flashes of knives and the shadows of swords

【刀具】dāojù 切削工具的统称，包括车刀、铣刀、刨刀、钻头、铰刀等 general term for all cutting tools, including lathe tool, milling cutter, planer, drill bit, reamer, etc.; also 刃具 rènjù

【刀锯】dāojù 刀和锯，古代的刑具，用于割刑和刖刑。旧时泛指刑罚。knife and saw; ancient instruments of torture; corporal punishment in ancient times; formerly referring to punishment

【刀口】dāokǒu ❶刀上用来切削的一边 blade; side of a knife used to cut; knife edge：～锋利 the sharp edge of a knife ❷〈比喻 *fig.*〉最能发挥作用的地方 where sth. can be put to best use; crucial point; right spot：钱要花在～上。Use your money where it is most needed.|把力量用在～上。Focus your efforts on the crucial point. ❸动手术或受刀伤时拉开的口子 cut; incision：～尚未愈合。The cut hasn't healed yet.

【刀螂】dāo·lang〈方 *dial.*〉螳螂 mantis

【刀马旦】dāomǎdàn 戏曲中旦角的一种，扮演熟习武艺的妇女，着重唱、念和做工 *daomadan*; actress skilled in acrobatic fighting, with emphasis on singing, reciting and acting

【刀片】dāopiàn ❶装在机械、工具上，用来切削的片状零件 cutter blade; fly bar; sharp flat spare parts set in machines for cutting or paring ❷（～儿 dāopiànr）夹在刮脸刀架中刮胡须用的薄钢片 razor blade

【刀枪】dāoqiāng 刀和枪，泛指武器 sword and spear; weapons：～剑戟 swords, spears, sabres and halberds|～入库，马放南山（形容战争结束，天下太平）the weapons have been put back in the arsenal and the battle horses let out to graze on the hillside (referring to war being over and there being peace throughout the land); enjoy peace and worry no more about war

【刀儿】dāor 小的刀 small knife; pocket knife：小～ small knife|剃～ razor|铅笔～ pencil sharpener; pen-knife

【刀刃】dāorèn （～儿 dāorènr）same as 刀口 dāokǒu ①②：好钢用在～上 use the best steel to make the best blade; use resources where they are needed most

【刀山火海】dāo shān huǒ hǎi〈比喻 *fig.*〉非常艰险和困难的地方 mountain of swords and sea of flames — most dangerous places; most severe trials; also 火海刀山 huǒ hǎi dāo shān

【刀削面】dāoxiāomiàn 一种面食，先用面加水和成较硬的面团，再用刀削成窄而长的面片儿，煮着吃 shaved noodles; after a fairly hard dough is made with wheat flour and water, a knife is used to whittle off strips of it into a pot of boiling water; also 削面 xiāomiàn

【刀子】dāo·zi 小刀儿 small knife; pocket knife

【刀子嘴】dāo·zizuǐ 形容说话尖刻，也指说话尖刻的人 sharp tongue; bitter tongue; person with a sharp or bitter tongue

【刀俎】dāozǔ〈书 *fml.*〉刀和砧板 butcher's knife and chopping block;〈比喻 *fig.*〉宰割者或迫害者 oppressor; persecutor：人为～，我为鱼肉。I am at other people's mercy (like fish or meat on a chopping board).

叨 dāo ☞ below

☞ dáo on p. 391 and tāo on p. 1869

【叨叨】dāo·dao 没完没了地说；唠叨：talk on and on; chatter away：别一个人～了，听听大家的意见吧。Don't be the only person talking away, but listen to what other people have to say.

【叨登】dāo·deng〈方 *dial.*〉❶翻腾 turn things over; move things around：把衣服～出来晒晒。Turn your clothes out to air them. ❷重提旧事 harp on things past：事情已经过去了，还～什么！Why harp on things already over and done with?

【叨唠】dāo·lao 叨叨 talk on and on; chatter away：为了一点小事就～个没完没了 talk about a small thing on and on

【叨念】dāoniàn same as 念叨 niàndāo

忉 dāo [忉忉]〈书 *fml.*〉形容忧愁 worried; sad; depressed

氘 dāo 氢的同位素之一，符号 D (deuterium) 或 $^2_1$H。原子核中有一个质子和一个中子，普通的氢中含有 0.02%的氘。用于热核反应。deuterium (D or $^2_1$H), one of the isotopes of hydrogen whose atomic nucleus consists of one proton and one neutron. Naturally occurring hydrogen contains 0.02% deuterium, which is used for thermonuclear reaction. also called 重氢 zhòngqīng

鱽 dāo 古书上指身体形状像刀的鱼，如带鱼、鲚(jì)鱼 in ancient books, referring to knife-shaped fish, e.g. hairtail and anchovy

dáo (ㄉㄠˊ)

叨 dāo [叨咕] (dáo·gu) 〈方 *dial.*〉 小声絮叨 grumble in a low voice: 他一肚子不满意，一边收拾一边～。He is full of complaints, grumbling the whole time he is tidying up. ☞ dāo on p.390 and tāo on p.1869

捯 dáo 〈方 *dial.*〉 ❶ 两手替换着把线或绳子拉回或绕好 pull in thread or string and wind it using two hands: 把风筝～下来。Pull in the kite. | 我撑着线，请你帮我～～。While I hold up the thread, would you please wind it for me. ❷ 两脚交替着迈出 stride along with alternating feet: 爸爸走得快，孩子小腿儿紧～都跟不上。His father was walking so quickly, the child could not keep up despite his best attempts to stride with his short legs. ❸ 追究 look into; find out; investigate: ～老账 rake up (or look into) an old score | 这件事儿已经～出头儿来了。We have found a clue to the mystery.

【捯饬】 dáo·chi 〈方 *dial.*〉 修饰；打扮 dress up; make up; decorate

【捯根儿】 dáo//gēnr 〈方 *dial.*〉 追究事情的根源 get to the root of a matter

【捯气儿】 dáo//qìr 〈方 *dial.*〉 ❶ 指临死前急促、断续地呼吸 gasp for breath on one's death-bed ❷ 形容上气不接下气 short of breath; out of breath; panting: 他说得那么快，都捯不过气儿来了。He talked so fast that he could hardly catch his breath.

dǎo (ㄉㄠˇ)

导(導) dǎo ❶ 引导；疏导 lead; guide; channel: ～航 pilot; navigation | ～游 guide a sightseeing tour; tour guide | 先～ lead the way; be in the vanguard | 倡～ initiate | ～淮入海 channel the Huai River into the sea | 因势利～ make the best use of a situation by guiding sth. with the flow; adroitly guide action according to circumstances ❷ 传导 transmit; conduct: ～热 transmit heat | ～电 conduct electricity | 半～体 semiconductor ❸ 开导 instruct; give guidance: 教～ teach; instruct | 指～ guide; instruct | 训～ admonish; advise; guide; counsel; teach ❹ 导演 direct: ～戏 direct a play or a film | 执～ director of a film or a play

【导板】 dǎobǎn same as 倒板 dǎobǎn

【导标】 dǎobiāo 航标的一种，多设在港口附近的岸上或航道狭窄的地方。一般由前低后高的两标志组成。当见到两标志形成上下一直线时，对着它航行，就是安全航行的方向。navigation marker, generally set on shores by a port or a narrow part of a channel, usu. consisting of two markers with the one in front lower than the one behind, so that when the two markers meet in one straight line, ships can sail towards it as the safe direction for navigation

【导出单位】 dǎochū-dānwèi ☞ 国际单位制 guójì dānwèizhì on p.740

【导弹】 dǎodàn 装有弹头和动力装置并能制导的高速飞行武器。依靠控制系统制导，能使弹头击中预定目标。种类很多，可以从地面上、舰艇上或飞机上发射出去，轰击地面、海上或空中的目标。guided missile; weapon that has a warhead and a propulsion system, can fly at high speed, relying on a guidance system to hit the chosen target, and can be launched from the ground, ships or planes to attack targets on the ground, in the sea or in the air

【导电】 dǎodiàn 让电流通过。一般金属都能导电。transmit electric current; conduct electricity. Generally metals are all electrically conductive.

【导读】 dǎodú 对读书给予引导；指导阅读(书籍) give guidance to readers; guide to reading: 世界名著～ guide to world classics

【导发】 dǎofā 引发 lead to; induce; cause: 由于疏忽～了事故。The accident was caused by carelessness.

【导购】 dǎogòu 对购买货物给予引导；指导购买(商品) provide guidance for purchases: ～小姐 saleslady

【导管】 dǎoguǎn ❶ 用来输送液体的管子 conduit; duct; pipe ❷ 动物体内输送液体的管子 (in animals) vessel; tube ❸ 植物体木质部内输送水分和无机盐的管子 sieve tubes in the phloem of plants

【导航】 dǎoháng 利用航行标志、雷达、无线电装置等引导飞机或轮船等航行 pilot; navigate; use navigation markers, radar and radio signals to guide navigation of planes, ships, etc.

【导火线】 dǎohuǒxiàn ❶ 使爆炸物爆炸的引线 blasting fuse; also 导火索 dǎohuǒsuǒ ❷ 〈比喻 *fig.*〉直接引起事变爆发的事件 apparently insignificant incident leading to a major conflict: 1914 年奥国皇太子被刺事件，是第一次世界大战的～。In 1914 the assassination of the Austrian crown prince touched off the First World War.

【导坑】 dǎokēng 开凿隧洞时，先开一个较小的洞，逐步扩大到设计需要的大小。所开的小洞叫做导坑。guide pit; guide hole; small pit dug first when tunnelling, and gradually enlarged to the intended size

【导轮】 dǎolún 装在机车或某些机械前部、不能自动而只有支撑作用的轮子 nose wheel;

D

wheel installed in front of a locomotive or certain machines, that cannot turn but has a supportive function

【导纳】dǎonà 具有电阻、电感和电容的电路对交流电所起的引导和容纳作用。导纳的数值等于阻抗的倒数。admittance; conducting and holding role played in an alternating current by the circuit that has resistance, inductance and capacitance. The numerical value of admittance is the reciprocal of impedance.

【导热】dǎorè same as 热传导 rèchuándǎo

【导师】dǎoshī ❶ 高等学校或研究机关中指导人学习、进修、写作论文的人员 tutor; adviser; supervisor; people who give tuition, supervision and guidance to students in universities and research institutes on how to do research and write papers: 博士生～ adviser to Ph.D. candidates ❷ 在大事业、大运动中指示方向、掌握政策的人 teacher; mentor; guide in a great cause: 革命～ revolutionary teacher

【导体】dǎotǐ 具有大量能够自由移动的带电粒子,容易传导电流的物体。这种物体也容易导热。一般金属都是导体。conductor; substance that has a large amount of freely moving charged particles, is good for transmitting electric current, and can also be heat conductive. Generally, metals are conductors.

【导线】dǎoxiàn 输送电流的金属线,多用铜或铝制成 electric lead; conducting wire; metal wire used to transmit electric current, mostly made of bronze or aluminium

【导向】dǎoxiàng ❶ 使向某个方面发展 head toward; make for; lead to: 会谈～两国关系的正常化。The talks led to normalization of relations between the two countries. ❷引导方向 lead; guide: 这种火箭的～性能良好。This type of rocket has an excellent guidance system. | 气垫火车也是靠路轨来～的。Air-cushion trains are also guided by rails. ❸ 指导行动或发展的方向 direction; orientation: 宣传工作对社会潮流的～极为重要。Publicity work is extremely important for the orientation of social trends. | 产品结构调整应以市场为～。The adjustment of product mix must be market-oriented.

【导言】dǎoyán 绪论 preamble; foreword; introduction; introductory remarks

【导演】dǎoyǎn ❶ 排演戏剧或拍摄影视片的时候,组织和指导演出工作 direct a play, film, etc.: 他～过五部电影。He directed five films. ❷ 担任导演工作的人 director

【导扬】dǎoyáng 〈书 *fml*.〉鼓吹宣扬 advocate; propagate: ～风化 advocate morals and manners

【导游】dǎoyóu ❶ 带领游览;指导游览 conduct a sightseeing tour; guide a tour: ～者 a guide | 《西湖～》*Guide to the West Lake* ❷ 担任导游工作的人 tour guide

【导语】dǎoyǔ 长篇新闻报道的开头,概括消息内容、背景等的简短文字 synopsis of a long article

【导源】dǎoyuán ❶ 发源(后面常带'于' oft. followed by 于 yú) (of a river) originate: 黄河～于青海。The Yellow River rises in Qinghai Province. ❷ 由某物发展而来(后面常带'于' oft. followed by 于 yú) originate; derive: 认识～于实践。Knowledge is derived from practice.

【导致】dǎozhì 引起 lead to; bring about; result in; cause: 由矛盾～决裂。The contradictions between them led to a breakup.

岛(島) dǎo 海洋里被水环绕、面积比大陆小的陆地。也指湖里、江河里被水环绕的陆地。island; piece of land surrounded by water in a sea, lake or river

【岛国】dǎoguó 全部领土由岛屿组成的国家 island country; country consisting of one or more islands

【岛弧】dǎohú 排列成弧形的群岛。如千岛群岛、琉球群岛。island archipelago, e.g. Kuril Islands and Ryukyu-gunto

【岛屿】dǎoyǔ 岛(总称) islands and islets

捣(搗、擣) dǎo ❶ 用棍子等的一端撞击 pound with a pestle, etc.; beat; smash: ～蒜 pound garlic into pulp | ～米 husk rice with a mortar and pestle | 用胳膊肘～了他一下 (sb.) gave him a nudge | ◇直～敌营 storm straight into the enemy camp ❷ 捶打 beat; strike: ～衣 beat clothes (while washing) ❸ 搅乱 make trouble; create a disturbance: ～乱 harass; disturb | ～麻烦 create a disturbance

【捣蛋】dǎo//dàn 借端生事,无理取闹 make trouble; find an excuse to stir up trouble; kick up a row for no reason at all: 调皮～ be mischievous

【捣鼓】dǎo·gu 〈方 *dial*.〉❶ 反复摆弄 fiddle with; meddle with: 他下了班就爱～那些无线电元件。He loves to fiddle with radio gadgets after work. ❷ 倒(dǎo)腾;经营 rummage; move; shift; buy in and sell out; deal in; trade in: ～点儿小买卖 trade in small deals

【捣鬼】dǎo//guǐ 使用诡计 play tricks; do mischief: ～有术 good at playing tricks | 暗中～ play dirty tricks behind sb.'s back

【捣毁】dǎohuǐ 砸坏;击垮 smash (up); demolish; destroy: ～敌巢 destroy the lair of the enemy

【捣乱】dǎo//luàn ❶ 进行破坏;扰乱 make or cause trouble; create a disturbance ❷ (存心)跟人找麻烦 make trouble for; disturb

【捣麻烦】dǎo má·fan 有意寻事,使人感到麻烦 create trouble; make things hard for sb.; be troublesome

【捣腾】dǎo·teng same as 倒腾 dǎo·teng

倒[1] dǎo ❶（人或竖立的东西）横躺下来 fall; topple; tumble down: 摔～ slip and fall down|卧～ lie down|风把树刮～了。The gale uprooted the tree. ❷（事业）失败;垮台 collapse; fail; go bankrupt; go out of business: ～闭 go bankrupt|～台 fall|打～ defeat (sb. or sth.); put down; down with ❸ 进行反对活动,使政府、首脑人物等垮台 wage a movement to overthrow a government or a political leader: ～阁 overturn a cabinet|～袁（世凯）campaign against Yuan Shikai ❹（戏曲演员的嗓子）变低或变哑（of a singer) become hoarse; lose one's voice: 他的嗓子～了,不再登台。He has lost his voice and will not perform again. ❺（食欲）变得不好 spoil (appetite): ～胃口 have no appetite; lose one's appetite

倒[2] dǎo ❶ 转移;转换 transfer; shift: ～车 change bus or train|～班 change shifts|～手 do sth. through a third party ❷ 腾挪; make room for; move around: 地方太小,～不开身儿。This place is so small, there is no room to move around. ❸ 出倒 sell out: 铺子～出去了。The shop has been sold. ❹ 倒买倒卖 profiteer; speculate: ～汇 profiteer through foreign exchange|～粮食 profiteer from trades in food grains ❺ 指倒爷 scalper; speculator; profiteer

☞ dào on p. 395

【倒把】dǎobǎ 利用物价涨落,买进卖出取利 buy low and sell high to make profit by using the rises and falls in price: 投机～ engage in speculation and profiteering

【倒班】dǎo//bān 分班轮换 work in shifts: ～生产 work by turns|昼夜～ work in shifts round the clock

【倒板】dǎobǎn 戏曲唱腔的一种特定板式,一般作为成套唱腔的先导部分 *daoban*; stylized tune in traditional Chinese opera, usu. preceding an integrated singing part. also 导板 dǎobǎn

【倒闭】dǎobì 工厂、商店等因亏本而停业 close down; go bankrupt; go into liquidation, such as a factory being closed down or an enterprises going bankrupt due to losses

【倒毙】dǎobì 倒在地上死去 drop dead (on the ground): ～街头 drop dead in the street

【倒仓】[1] dǎo//cāng ❶ 把仓里的粮食全取出来,晾晒之后,再装进去 take grain out of a granary to sun, and then put it back ❷ 把一个仓里的粮食转到另一个仓里去 transfer grain from one granary to another

【倒仓】[2] dǎo//cāng 指戏曲演员在青春期发育时嗓音变低或变哑（of a young opera singer) change of voice (in puberty)

【倒茬】dǎochá 轮作 rotation of crops

【倒车】dǎo//chē 中途换车 transfer: 现在这里可以直达北京,不用到省城再～了。We can now take a direct train from here to Beijing, instead of making a transfer in the provincial capital.

☞ dào//chē on p. 396

【倒伏】dǎofú 农作物因根茎无力,支持不住叶子和穗的重量而倒在地上 (of a farm crop) lay flat; lodge; collapse because stems and roots are too weak to hold up leaves and ears

【倒戈】dǎogē 在战争中投降敌人,反过来打自己人 change sides in a war; turncoat; transfer one's allegiance; surrender to the enemy during a war, and then turn back to fight against one's own people

【倒海翻江】dǎo hǎi fān jiāng ☞ 翻江倒海 fān jiāng dǎo hǎi on p. 531

【倒换】dǎohuàn ❶ 轮流替换 rotate; take turns: 几种作物～着种 rotate several crops ❷ 掉换;交换 rearrange (sequence, order, etc.); replace; exchange: ～次序 rearrange the order|～麦种 exchange wheat seeds

【倒汇】dǎo//huì 倒买倒卖外汇 deal illegally in foreign currencies; speculate in foreign currencies

【倒嚼】dǎojiào same as 倒嚼 dǎojiào

【倒嚼】dǎojiào 反刍的通称 general term for 反刍 fǎnchú; also 倒嚼 dǎo//jiào

【倒买倒卖】dǎo mǎi dǎo mài 低价买进,高价卖出以取利的投机活动 buy low and sell high to make profit by using the rise and fall in prices

【倒卖】dǎomài 低价买进,高价卖出。多指投机倒把 speculative buying and selling; buy at low price and sell at high price; engage in speculation and profiteering: 转手～ resell at a profit; speculate|～粮食 secretly hoard and sell food grain; scalp food grain

【倒霉】dǎo//méi 遇事不利;遭遇不好 have bad luck; be out of luck; be down on one's luck: 真～,赶到车站车刚开走。What lousy luck! When I reached the station, the train had just left. also 倒楣 dǎo//méi

【倒牌子】dǎo pái·zi 指产品或服务质量下降,失去信誉 ruin one's established trade name; lose or spoil one's good reputation

【倒儿爷】dǎoryé 倒爷 speculator; profiteer

【倒嗓】dǎo//sǎng 指戏曲演员嗓音变低或变哑 (of opera singers) lose one's voice; have one's voice become hoarse

【倒手】dǎo//shǒu ❶ 把东西从一只手转到另一只手 shift or move from one hand to the other: 他没～,一口气把箱子提到六楼。He carried the suitcase all the way to the sixth floor without so much as to shift hands. ❷ 把东西从一个人的手上转到另一个人的手上(多指货物买卖) change hands (of merchandise, etc.): ～转卖 resell from one hand to another

【倒塌】dǎotā（建筑物）倒下来 (of buildings)

collapse；topple over；cave in：房屋～。The house collapsed.

【倒台】dǎo//tái 垮台 fall from power；fall down；collapse

【倒腾】dǎo·teng ❶ 翻腾；移动 rummage；move；shift：把粪～到地里去 carry manure to the fields ❷ 掉换；调配 replace；exchange；rearrange：人手少，事情多，～不开。It is hard to cope，with so few hands and so much to do. ❸ 买进卖出；贩卖 buy low and sell high；deal in；trade in：～牲口 trade in cattle | ～小买卖 deal in a small business ‖ also 捣腾 dǎo·teng

【倒替】dǎotì 轮流替换 take turns；work in turn：两个人～着看护病人。The two took turns looking after the patient.

【倒头】dǎo//tóu ❶ 躺下 lie down；touch the pillow：～就睡 fall asleep the moment one touches the pillow ❷〈方 *dial.*〉指人死（常用做咒骂的话 oft. used as a curse）die

【倒胃口】dǎo wèi·kou ❶ 因为腻味而不想再吃 spoil one's appetite；upset one's stomach：再好吃的吃多了也～。Too much food，no matter how good it is，will spoil one's appetite. ❷〈比喻 *fig.*〉对某事物厌烦而不愿接受（of things）be so disgusting as to kill one's interest or dampen one's spirits：啰啰唆唆，词不达意，让人听得～。His talk，repetitive and full of platitudes，is so distasteful.

【倒休】dǎoxiū（职工）掉换工作日和休息日（of workers and staff）exchange working days and holidays；stagger holidays

【倒牙】dǎoyá〈方 *dial.*〉吃了较多的酸性食物，牙神经受过分刺激，咀嚼时感觉不舒服（of sour food）set or put one's teeth on edge

【倒爷】dǎoyé 指从事倒买倒卖活动的人（含贬义 derog.）scalper；speculator；profiteer；also 倒儿爷 dǎoryé

【倒运】dǎo//yùn〈方 *dial.*〉倒霉 have a run of bad luck；be unlucky；be out of luck；be down on one's luck

【倒运】dǎoyùn ❶ 把甲地货物运到乙地出卖，再把乙地货物运到甲地出卖（多指非法活动）buy sth. at a low price in one place and sell it at a high price in another place；profiteer ❷ 把货物从一地运到另一地；转运 ship from one place to another；tranship

【倒灶】dǎo//zào〈方 *dial.*〉❶ 垮台；败落 decline；collapse ❷ 倒霉 be down on one's luck；be out of luck：背时～ be behind the times；at the wrong time and unlucky

【倒账】dǎozhàng ❶ 欠账不还；赖账 evade or repudiate a debt：～卷逃 evade debts by disappearing and taking all the money and valuables ❷ 收不回来的账 debt that cannot be recovered；bad debt

祷(禱) dǎo ❶ 祷告 pray：祈～ pray for | ～祝 pray and wish ❷ 盼望（旧时书信用语）（used in old-style letters）ask earnestly；beg：盼～ earnestly hope that | 是所至～。That is what I am most eagerly hoping for.

【祷告】dǎogào 向神祈求保佑 pray；say one's prayers

【祷念】dǎoniàn 祷告 pray

【祷祝】dǎozhù 祷告祝愿 pray and make a wish

蹈 dǎo ❶〈书 *fml.*〉践踏；踩 tread；step：赴汤～火 go through fire and water — defy all difficulties and dangers | 重～覆辙 follow the same old way to ruin；repeat the same mistake ◇循规～距 not step out of bounds；tow the line；observe rules and conventions ❷ 跳动 move up and down；skip；trip：舞～ dance | 手舞足～ dance for joy；move one's limbs up and down

【蹈海】dǎohǎi〈书 *fml.*〉跳到海里（自杀）throw oneself into the sea（to commit suicide）：～自尽 drown oneself in the sea | ～而死 commit suicide by throwing oneself into the sea

【蹈袭】dǎoxí 走别人走过的老路；因袭 follow other's way slavishly；copy：～前人 mechanically follow one's predecessors | ～覆辙 get into a rut

dào（ㄉㄠ）

到 dào ❶ 达于某一点；到达；达到 get to a place；arrive；reach：～期 become due；mature；expire | 迟～ be late | 火车～站了。The train has arrived at the station. | 从星期三～星期五 from Wednesday to Friday ❷ 往 go to；leave for：～郊外去 go to the suburbs | ～群众中去 go to the masses（people）❸ 用做动词的补语，表示动作有结果［as the complement of a verb indicating the result of an action］：看～ have seen sth. | 办得～ can do sth. | 说～一定要做～。One must do what he says；be as good as one's word | 想不～你来了。I didn't expect that you would come. ❹ 周到 considerate；thoughtful；thorough：想得很～。You have thought of everything. | 有不～的地方请原谅。Hope you will forgive me if I have not been thoughtful enough. ❺（Dào）姓 a surname

【到案】dào'àn 审理案件时，与案件有关的人出庭（of those involved in a case）appear in court

【到场】dào//chǎng 亲自到某种集会或活动的场所 turn up；show up；be present：展览会开幕的时候，许多专家学者都～表示祝贺。When the exhibition opens，many experts are present to express their congratulations.

【到处】dàochù 各处；处处 all about；at all places；everywhere：祖国～是欣欣向荣的景

象。Signs of prosperity are everywhere in our motherland. | ～找也没有找到。I looked all around for it but still could not find it.

【到达】dàodá 到了(某一地点、某一阶段) arrive; get to; reach (a place or a period): 火车于下午3时～北京。The train arrived in Beijing at 3:00 in the afternoon.

【到底】dào//dǐ 到尽头;到终点 to the end; to the finish: 一竿子～ get to the bottom of the matter | 将革命进行～ carry the revolution through to the end

【到底】dàodǐ 〈副词 *adv*.〉❶ 表示经过种种变化或曲折最后实现的情况 at last; eventually; finally: 新方法～试验成功了。The new method has finally proved to be a success. | 我想了好久,～明白了。After thinking for a long while, I finally saw the point. ❷ 用在问句里,表示深究 [used in a question for emphasis] after all: 火星上～有没有生命? Is there any life on Mars after all? | 你跟他们～有什么关系? What relations do you have with them after all? ❸ 毕竟 after all; when all is said and done: ～还是年轻人干劲大。It is the young people who have the greatest vigour after all. | 南方～是南方,四月就插秧了。After all, the south is the south, so though it is still April, rice seedlings have already been transplanted.

【到点】dào//diǎn 达到规定的时间 fixed time (is up): 商店到了点就开门。The shop is open at a fixed time. | 快～了,咱们赶紧进场吧。It is almost time. Let's hurry up and get in.

【到顶】dào//dǐng 到顶点;到了尽头 reach to the limit; for all there is in it; go as far as possible: 要破除增产～的思想。We must get rid of the idea that production has reached its limit.

【到家】dào//jiā 达到相当高的水平或标准 consummate; reach a rather high level or standard: 把工作做～ do the work perfectly | 他的表演还不～。His performance is still far from perfect.

【到来】dàolái 来临(多用于事物) arrival; advent: 在雨季～之前做好防汛准备。All preparations for flood prevention must be completed before the arrival of the monsoon season. | 生产建设的新高潮已经～。A new upsurge in production and construction has been reached.

【到了儿】dàoliǎor 〈方 *dial*.〉到终了;到底 at last; in the end; finally: 我这样为你卖命,～还落个不是。I worked myself to the bone for you, and in the end I was still in the wrong. | 今天盼,明天盼,～还没盼到他回来。(She) longed for him day after day, and in the end still did not get to see his return.

【到手】dào//shǒu 拿到手;获得 in one's hands; in one's possession: 眼看就要～的粮食,决不能让洪水冲走。The grain is nearly in our hands. We mustn't allow the flood to carry it away.

【到头】dào//tóu (～儿 dào//tóur) 到了尽头 to the end; at an end

【到头来】dàotóulái 〈副词 *adv*.〉到末了儿;结果(多用于坏的方面 mostly used in the negative) in the end; only to; finally: 倒行逆施,～只能搬起石头砸自己的脚。You are trying to put the clock back and go against the tide. In the end it amounts to lifting a rock only to drop it on your own foot.

【到位】dào//wèi 到达适当的位置或预定的地点 be in place or position; reach the designated place: 传球～。The ball is passed where it is needed. | 资金～。The capital is in place. | 发电机组已安装～。The generating set has been entirely installed.

【到职】dào//zhí 接受任命或委派,来到工作岗位 assume office; take up one's post

帱(幬) dào 〈书 *fml*.〉覆盖 cover; ☞ chóu on p. 276

倒[1] dào ❶ 上下颠倒或前后颠倒 inverted; upside down; inverse: ～影 inverted image; inverted reflection in water | ～悬 hang by the feet | ～数第一行 first line from the bottom | 这几本书次序放～了。These books have been placed in the reverse order. ❷ 反面的;相反的 reverse; converse: ～彩 booing; hooting; catcalls | ～算 counterattack to settle old scores | ～找钱 pay instead of receiving money ❸ 使向相反的方向移动或颠倒 move backward; turn upside down; reverse; invert: ～车 reverse a car | ～退 go backwards; fall back; regress; retrogress ❹反转或倾斜容器使里面的东西出来;倾倒 tip; pour; dump: ～茶 pour tea | ～垃圾 dump rubbish; empty out the garbage ◇他恨不能把心里的话都～出来。He wanted to pour out everything that was on his mind.

倒[2] dào 〈副词 *adv*.〉❶ 表示跟意料相反 [contrary to what is expected or thought]: a)相反的意思较明显 [the opposite meaning is obvious]: 本想省事,没想～费事了。He thought it would be easy, but it was more difficult than he had expected. | 你太客气,～显得见外了。You are so polite that you make me feel like a stranger. b)相反的意思较轻微 [mildly contrary meaning]: 屋子不宽绰,收拾得～还干净(没想到)。The room isn't large but it is kept (unexpectedly) clean and tidy. | 你有什么理由,我～要听听(我还以为你没有什么可说了呢)。What are your reasons? I have to hear them. (I thought you would have nothing to say.) | 说起他来,我～想起一件事来了(你不说我不会想起来)。Speaking of him, I am reminded of something. 注意 **NOTE**: a 类可以改用'反倒', b 类不能 In the case of (a) 倒 dào can be replaced with 反倒 fǎndào, but in the case of (b) it cannot be replaced. ❷ 表示事情不是那样,有反说的语气 [used to indicate the contrary]: 你说得～容易,可做起来并不容易。It's easier said than done. ❸ 表示让步 [used to indicate concession]: 我跟他认识～认识,就是不太熟。I know him all right, but not very well. ❹ 表示催促或追问,有不耐烦的语气 [used to urge sb. to respond quickly, indicating impatience]: 你～说呀! Out with it! *or* Well, say it then! | 你～去不去呀? So are you going or not?

☞ dǎo on p.393

【倒背如流】dào bèi rú liú 倒着背诵像流水那样顺畅,形容诗文等读得很熟 can recite sth. backwards; know sth. (e.g. a poem or article) by heart

【倒彩】dàocǎi 倒好儿 booing; hooting; catcalls: 喝～ make catcalls; boo and hoot

【倒插门】dàochāmén (～儿 dàochāménr) 俗称男子到女方家里结婚并落户 (of a man) marry into and reside with the wife's family

【倒产】dàochǎn same as 逆产[2] nìchǎn

【倒车】dào//chē 使车向后退 back; drive a vehicle backwards

☞ dǎo//chē on p.393

【倒春寒】dàochūnhán 春天的一种反常现象,早春回暖后,由于寒潮侵入,气温下降到正常年份同期平均值以下 unusual cold spell in an otherwise warm early spring

【倒打一耙】dào dǎ yī pá 〈比喻 *fig.*〉不仅拒绝对方的指摘,反而指摘对方 make unfounded countercharges; blame one's victim; recriminate

【倒读数】dàodúshù 人造卫星、宇宙飞船等在发射前几十秒钟时倒着读出数字,如5、4、3、2、1,读完最后一个数发射 countdown before the launching of a satellite, spaceship, etc., e.g. 5, 4, 3, 2, 1

【倒风】dàofēng 风从烟筒出口灌入,烟气排不出去,叫做倒风 wind blowing in through a chimney choked with smoke

【倒挂】dàoguà ❶ 上下颠倒地挂着 hang upside down: 崖壁上古松～。Old pine trees hang downwards from the precipice. ❷ 〈比喻 *fig.*〉应该高的反而低,应该低的反而高 be contrary to the natural order of things; be in an inverted order: 购销价格～(指商品收购价格高于销售价格) inverted purchasing and selling prices (purchasing price is higher than selling price)

【倒灌】dàoguàn 河水、海水等因潮汐、台风等原因由低处流向高处 (of river or sea water, etc.) flow from a lower to higher place due to the morning and evening tides, typhoon, etc.: 海水～。The sea water is flowing up towards the highlands. | 江水～市区。The river water is flooding the urban areas.

【倒过儿】dào//guòr 颠倒;使颠倒 transpose; switch the order: 这两个字写倒了过儿了。The order of the two numbers is wrong. | 把号码倒个过儿就对了。These two numbers should be transposed.

【倒好儿】dàohǎor 对艺人、运动员等在表演或比赛中出现差错,故意喊'好'取笑,叫'喊倒好儿' catcall; boo; hoot; (what audiences mockingly shout when stage artists or athletes make mistakes during performance) 'Bravo!'

【倒剪】dàojiǎn 反剪 with one's hands clasped or tied behind one's back: ～双手 with hands clasped at the back

【倒立】dàolì ❶ 顶端朝下地竖立 stand upside down: 水中映现出～的塔影。The pagoda is reflected upside down in the water. ❷ 武术用语,指用手支撑全身,头朝下,两腿向上。有的地区叫拿大顶。(in martial arts) handstand; also 拿大顶 ná//dàdǐng in some regions

【倒流】dàoliú ❶ 向上游流 flow backwards: 水不能～。Rivers don't flow backwards. ❷ 〈比喻 *fig.*〉向跟正常流动相反的方向流动 flow in the opposite direction: 商品～ flow of goods back to their places of origin | 人口～ backward flow of population; reverse migration | 时光不会～。Time can't go backwards.

【倒卵形】dàoluǎnxíng 叶子的一种形状,跟鸡蛋相似,较窄的一端靠近叶柄 (of leaves) obovate; shaped like an upside-down egg

【倒轮闸】dàolúnzhá 自行车上的一种刹(shā)车装置,脚向后登时,车就停住 back-pedalling brake (of a bicycle); coaster brake

【倒赔】dàopéi 指不但不赚,反而赔本 lose instead of making money: 经营不善,～了两万元。He lost 20,000 yuan due to his poor management.

【倒是】dàoshì 〈副词 *adv.*〉❶ 表示跟一般情理相反;反倒 [used to indicate contrast to what is usu. true] but instead: 该说的不说,不该说的～说个没完没了 harp on what one shouldn't instead of speaking what one should ❷ 表示事情不是那样(含责怪意) [used to indicate what is contrary to facts, with a touch of criticism]: 说的～容易,你做起来试试! Though it's easy to say, would you try to do it yourself? ❸ 表示出乎意料 [used for sth. unexpected]: 还有什么理由,我～想听一听。If you have any other reasons, I would certainly like to hear them. ❹ 表示让步 [used to indicate concession]: 东西～好东西,就是价钱太贵。This thing may be good, only it is too expensive. ❺ 表示转折 [used to indicate a turn in meaning]: 屋子不大,布置得～挺讲

究。Though the room may not be very big, it is beautifully decorated. ❻ 用来缓和语气 [used to modify or tone down a preceding statement]：如果人手不够，我～愿意帮忙。If there really are not enough people, then I would like to go and help. ❼ 表示催促或追问 [used to press or question sb.]：你～快说呀！Out with it then! | 你～去过没去过，别吞吞吐吐的。So did you go there or not? Don't mince your words.

【倒数】dàoshǔ 逆着次序数（shǔ）；从后向前数（shǔ）count backwards; count from bottom to top, or from rear to front：～计时 countdown | ～第一名（最后一名）first from the bottom (last one)

【倒数】dàoshù 如果两个数的积是 1，其中一个数就叫做另一数的倒数。如 2 的倒数是 1/2，1/5的倒数是 5。reciprocal. If the product of two numbers is 1, each number is the reciprocal of the other, e.g. the reciprocal of 2 is 1/2, and the reciprocal of 1/5 is 5.

【倒算】dàosuàn 指地主向农民夺回由革命政权分给的土地、财产等，这种活动大多依靠反革命武装进行 settle old scores; retaliate; referring to the activity of landlords who, usu. by relying on counter-revolutionary armed forces, seize back from the peasants the land and properties distributed by a revolutionary political power

【倒贴】dàotiē 泛指该收的一方反向该付的一方提供财物 lose money instead of making a profit; pay instead of getting paid：这东西别说卖钱，就是～些钱送人都没人要。Nobody would want this even with an accompanying gift of money, to say nothing of buying it.

【倒退】dàotuì 往后退；退回（后面的地方、过去的年代、以往的发展阶段）go backwards; regress; fall back (into an old place, old times, or past development period)：迎面一阵狂风把我刮得～了好几步。A gust of strong wind pushed me a few steps backwards. | ～三十年，我也是个壮小伙子。Thirty years back, I was a strapping young fellow too.

【倒行逆施】dào xíng nì shī 原指做事违反常理，现多指所作所为违背社会正义和时代进步方向 behave counter to normal practices; go against the trends of the times; try to put the clock back; push a reactionary policy

【倒序】dàoxù same as 逆序 nìxù

【倒叙】dàoxù 文章、电影等的一种艺术手法。先交代故事结局或某些情节，然后回过来交代故事的开端和经过。flashback; artistic method in writing, film-making, etc., where usu. a story's ending or some later episodes come before earlier scenes in due course

【倒悬】dàoxuán〈书 *fml.*〉头向下脚向上地悬挂着 hang by the feet;〈比喻 *fig.*〉处境异常困苦、危急 be in dire straits：解民于～ retrieve ordinary people from their dire predicament

【倒烟】dàoyān 指烟不从烟筒正常排出，而从炉灶口冒出 smoke going down a chimney (not coming up out of the chimney as usual but coming out from the mouth of the stove)

【倒仰】dàoyǎng〈方 *dial.*〉（～儿 dàoyǎngr）仰面跌倒 fall backwards

【倒影】dàoyǐng（～儿 dàoyǐngr）倒立的影子 inverted image; inverted reflection in water：湖面映着峰峦的～ inverted reflection of the mountain peaks on the lake | 石拱桥的桥洞和水中的～正好合成一个圆圈。The opening of the stone arched bridge and its reflection in the water form a perfect circle.

【倒映】dàoying 物体的形象倒着映射到另一物体上 reflection; inverted image of one object reflected on another：垂柳～在湖面上。Swaying willows are reflected in the lake.

【倒栽葱】dàozāicōng 摔倒时头先着地 fall head over heels; fall headlong; nose-dive：一个～，从马鞍上跌下来 fall headlong from horseback | 风筝断了线，来了个～。The kite fell headlong after the thread broke.

【倒找】dàozhǎo 本应对方付给钱物，反倒付给对方钱物 reversal of payment; instead of getting paid by sb. as expected, one has to pay them

【倒置】dàozhì 倒过来放，指颠倒事物应有的顺序 place upside down; invert — mess up the order of things：本末～ placing the superficial above the essential | 轻重～ putting the trivial before the important

【倒转】dàozhuǎn ❶ 倒过来；反过来 turn the other way round; reverse：～来说，道理也是一样。The same reasoning is true the other way round. ❷〈方 *dial.*〉反倒 (contrary to reason or one's expectations)：你把字写坏了，～来怪我。You messed up your writing badly, but now you put the blame on me.

【倒转】dàozhuàn 倒着转动 turn backwards; go backwards：历史的车轮不能～。You can never turn back the clock of history.

【倒座儿】dàozuòr ❶ 四合房中跟正房相对的房屋 rooms opposite the principal rooms in a quadrangle courtyard：一进大门，左手三间～是客厅。Just inside the main gate, the three rooms on the left and opposite the main rooms are the reception rooms. ❷ 车船上背向行驶方向的座位 seats in a bus or ship facing the direction opposite to the direction of navigation

焘（燾） dào 又 also tāo〈书 *fml.*〉same as 帱 dào

盗 dào ❶ 偷 steal; rob; burgle; commit burglary：～窃 steal; burgle | 偷～ steal; pilfer; filch | 欺世～名 gain fame by deceiving the public; win an undeserved name by cheating | 监守自～ steal what is entrusted to one's care ❷ 强盗 robber; burglar: ～贼 thief; robber; burglar | 海～ pirate; sea-rover | 窃国大～ arch usurper of state power | 开门揖～ open one's door to invite robbers in

【盗版】dào//bǎn 未经版权所有者同意而翻印或翻录 illegally copy; pirate; reprint publications without getting the permission of the copyright holder: ～书 illegally copied books; pirate copies of a book

【盗版】dàobǎn 未经版权所有者同意而偷印或偷录的版本:这本书在海外有三种～。This book has three pirated versions abroad.

D

【盗匪】dàofěi 用暴力劫夺财物,扰乱社会治安的人(总称) those who rob and disturb social order using violence

【盗汗】dào//hàn 因病或身体虚弱睡眠时出汗 profuse sweating when one is sleeping due to illness or poor health

【盗劫】dàojié 盗窃掠夺 rob; loot: ～文物 rob cultural relics

【盗寇】dàokòu 强盗 bandit; robber

【盗卖】dàomài 盗窃并出卖(公物、公产) steal and sell (public property)

【盗墓】dào//mù 挖掘坟墓,盗取随葬的东西 grave looting; tomb raiding; dig out a tomb and loot the buried contents

【盗骗】dàopiàn 盗窃和骗取 steal and cheat: ～国家财产是犯罪行为。Appropriation of state property is a crime.

【盗窃】dàoqiè 用不合法的手段秘密地取得 steal; burglarize; obtain sth. secretly through illegal means: ～犯 thief; burglar | ～文物 steal cultural relics

【盗用】dàoyòng 非法使用公家的或别人的名义、财物等 embezzle; illegally use public or sb. else's names, goods, etc.: ～公款 embezzle public funds | ～他人名义 usurp sb.'s name

【盗贼】dàozéi 强盗和小偷(总称) thieves and robbers; bandits

悼 dào 悼念 mourn for: 追～ express condolences for the deceased | 哀～ lament for the deceased | ～亡 mourn for the deceased | ～词 memorial speech

【悼词】dàocí 对死者表示哀悼的话或文章 obituary; remarks or articles to mourn the dead; also 悼辞 dàocí

【悼辞】dàocí same as 悼词 dàocí

【悼念】dàoniàn 怀念死者,表示哀痛 grieve over the dead: 沉痛～ mourn with deep grief | ～亡友 mourn for a deceased friend

【悼亡】dàowáng 〈书 *fml.*〉悼念死去的妻子,也指死了妻子 mourn for one's deceased wife; lose one's wife

【悼唁】dàoyàn 悼念死者并慰问死者亲属 mourn for the dead and express condolences to the bereaved: 致电～ send a message of condolence to the bereaved by telegraph or cable

道[1] dào ❶ (～儿 dàor) 道路 way; road; path: 铁～ railway | 人行～ pedestrian road | 康庄大～ broad road | 羊肠小～ small and winding path ❷ 水流通行的途径 course; channel: 河～ course of a river | 下水～ sewer | 黄河故～ old course of the Yellow River ❸ 方向;方法;道理 orientation; way; method; justice: 志同～合 cherish the same ideals and follow the same path | 头头是～ clear and logical; tightly reasoned and well argued | 即以其人之～,还治其人之身 deal with a man as he deals with you; pay sb. back in his own coin | 得～多助,失～寡助。Whoever has justice on his side will enjoy abundant support, and those who have not will find little. ❹ 道德 morality; virtue: ～义 morality and justice; moral obligations ❺ 技艺;技术 technique; skill; art: 医～ medical skill | 茶～ tea ceremony | 花～ art of flower arrangement | 书～ method of reading books ❻ 学术或宗教的思想体系 (academic, religious or ideological) doctrine; principle: 尊师重～ respect teachers and revere established ways | 传～ spread doctrines | 卫～士 apologist or defender of outdated morality ❼ 属于道教的,也指道教徒 Taoism; Taoist: ～院 Taoist temple | ～士 Taoist priest | ～姑 Taoist nun | 老～ Taoist priest | 一僧一～ monk and priest ❽ 指某些封建迷信组织 superstitious sect: 一贯～ *Yiguandao* (a secret society) ❾ (～儿 dàor) 线条;细长的痕迹 line; thin and long mark: 画了两条横～儿,一条斜～儿 drew two horizontal lines and one slanting line ❿ 〈量词 *classifier*〉 a) 用于江、河和某些长条形的东西;条 [of rivers and certain long and narrow things]: 一～河 a river | 一～擦痕 a scratch mark | 万～霞光 myriad of sun rays; b) 用于门、墙等 [of doors, walls, etc.]: 两～门 two entrances | 三～防线 three lines of defence | 一～围墙 one surrounding wall; c) 用于命令、题目等 [of orders, questions, etc.]: 一～命令 an order | 十五～题 15 questions; d) 次 [indicating number of times or layers]: 上了三～漆 painted three coats | 省一～手续 save one step in the process ⓫ (～儿 dàor) 计量单位,忽米的通称 measuring unit; popular term for 忽米 hūmǐ

道[2] dào ❶ 我国历史上行政区域的名称。在唐代相当于现在的省,清代和民国初年在省的下面设道 circuit; administrative area in Chinese history, equivalent to a present-day province, in the Tang Dynasty, and below the provincial level in the Qing Dynasty and the early Republican years ❷ 某些国家行政区域的名称 circuit, administrative regional division in some countries

道[3] dào ❶ 说 say; talk; speak: ～白 spoken parts in an opera | 能说会～ have the gift of gab; have a glib tongue; able to talk very well and convincingly | 一语～破 lay bare the truth with one penetrating remark ❷ 用语言表示(情意) (of feeling) express; extend: ～喜 congratulate | ～歉 apologize ; make an apology | ～谢 express thanks; thank; extend gratitude ❸ 说(跟文言'曰'相当,多见于早期白话 equivalent to 曰 yuē in classical Chinese, oft. found in early vernacular) say ❹ 以为;认为 suppose; think: 我～是谁呢,原来是你。So it's you! I thought it was somebody else.

【道白】dàobái 戏曲中的说白 spoken parts in an opera; also 念白 niànbái

【道班】dàobān 养路工人的基层组织,每个班负责若干公里铁路或公路的养路工程 basic squad of railway or highway maintenance workers, with each squad responsible for the maintenance of a certain length of railway or highway: ～工人 road or rail maintenance workers | ～房(道班工人集体居住的房屋) maintenance workers' dormitory

【道别】dào//bié ❶ 离别;分手(一般要打个招呼或说句话) say goodbye; bid farewell: 握手～ shake hands and say goodbye | 过了十字路口,两人才～。Only after they had passed the crossroads did they bid each other farewell. ❷ 辞行 take leave: 起程前他到邻居家一一～。Before starting out on his journey, he bid farewell to all the neighbours.

【道…不…】dào…bù…〈方 *dial.*〉嵌入意义相反的两个单音的形容词,表示'既不…也不…'的意思 usu. followed by two monosyllabic adjectives opposite in meaning, indicating 'neither ... nor ...': ～长～短(说长不算长,说短不算短) neither long nor short | ～高～矮 neither tall nor short | ～大～小 neither big nor small | ～多～少 neither too many nor too few

【道不拾遗】dào bù shí yí ☞ 路不拾遗 lù bù shí yí on p. 1261

【道岔】dàochà (～儿 dàochàr) ❶ 从道路干路分出的岔路 feeder road; side road branching out from the main road; also 道岔子 dàochà·zi ❷ 使列车由一组轨道转到另一组轨道上去的装置 switching device; mechanism which switches a train from one track onto another

【道场】dàochǎng 和尚或道士做法事的场所,也指所做的法事 Buddhist or Taoist rites (performed to redeem the souls of the dead); where such rites are performed

【道床】dàochuáng 指铺在铁路路基和枕木之间的一层碎石和炉渣等,能缓和列车对铁轨的冲击,巩固轨道的位置 roadbed; track bed — the layer of crushed stones, slag, etc., between the railway bed and sleepers, which can alleviate the impact of the train on the tracks

【道道儿】dào·daor ❶ 办法;主意 way; method; idea: 只要大家肯动脑筋,完成任务的～就多了。So long as everyone uses their brain, there are many ways to accomplish the new task. ❷ 门道 way; knack: 听了半天也没听出个～来。We listened for a long time but still did not understand what it was about. | 你不懂这里面的～,千万要留神。You don't understand the ways here, so you must pay attention.

【道德】dàodé 社会意识形态之一,是人们共同生活及其行为的准则和规范。道德通过社会的或一定阶级的舆论对社会生活起约束作用。morals; morality; ethics, social ideology which serves as the norms for people's life and behaviour. Morals keep social life within bounds through public opinion of the society or a certain class

【道地】dàodì ❶ 真正是有名产地出产的 authentic; (of a product) produced in its place of origin: ～药材 authentic medicinal herbs ❷ 真正的;纯粹 genuine; real; pure: 一口～的北京话 standard Beijing speech

【道钉】dàodīng ❶ 把铁轨固定在枕木上的钉子 railway spikes that fasten the track and sleepers ❷ 能够反射夜间汽车灯光的装置,用工业塑料等制成,装在马路的隔离带上或盘山公路的转弯处,以提示司机注意安全。道钉的内部构造酷似猫眼,俗称猫眼道钉。highway reflector; device that can reflect the lights of automobiles at night, made of industrial plastics and set up on divider fencing along the road, or at the turns on winding mountain roads, to warn drivers. As these highway reflectors are shaped like an eye of a cat, they are also popularly called 'cat's eyes'.

【道乏】dào//fá 因为别人为自己出力而向人慰问,表示感谢 extend thanks for taking trouble: 你帮了他大忙了,他要亲自来给你～呢。He is coming to call in person to thank you for all the trouble you have taken on his behalf.

【道高一尺,魔高一丈】dào gāo yī chǐ, mó gāo yī zhàng 原为佛家告诫修行的人警惕外界诱惑的话,意思是修行到一定阶段,就会有魔障干扰破坏而可能前功尽弃。后用来比喻取得一定成就后遇到的障碍会更大,也比喻正义终将战胜邪恶。as virtue grows by one foot, vice rises by ten; the greater the illumination, the more the temptation. Originally, this was a saying from Buddhism to warn all adherents to be on guard against worldly temptations, meaning when they reached a certain stage on their way to enlightenment, the power of vice would interfere and create trouble, and all their previous efforts could be wasted. Later this term is oft. used to indicate that greater difficulties oft. come after achievements are attained, yet justice can ultimately triumph over evil.

【道姑】dàogū 女道士 Taoist nun

【道观】dàoguàn 道教的庙 Taoist temple

【道光】Dàoguāng 清宣宗(爱新觉罗旻宁)年号(公元 1821—1850) Daoguang, title of the reign (1821-1850) of Aisin Gioro Minning, 6th emperor of the Qing Dynasty, called Emperor Xuanzong after his death

【道贺】dàohè same as 道喜 dàoxǐ

【道行】dào•héng 僧道修行的功夫 supernatural skill possessed by a Buddhist or Taoist priest; 〈比喻 *fig*.〉技能本领 skill or workmanship: ～深 great skill

【道家】Dàojiā 先秦时期的一个思想派别,以老子、庄子为主要代表。道家的思想崇尚自然,有辩证法的因素和无神论的倾向,但是主张清静无为,反对斗争。Taoist school; school of thought originating in the pre-Qin period, with the main representatives being Lao Zi and Zhuang Zi, advocating nature and the natural course of things. Taoists had tendencies towards dialectics and atheism, but stood for quietude and a theory of letting things take their own course and opposing the waging of any struggles.

【道教】Dàojiào 我国宗教之一,由东汉张道陵创立,到南北朝时盛行起来。创立时,入道者须出五斗米,所以又叫'五斗米道'。道教徒尊称张道陵为天师,因而又叫'天师道'。道教奉老子为教祖,尊称他为'太上老君'。Taoism; indigenous Chinese religion that was founded by Zhang Daoling of the Eastern Han Dynasty, and flourished in the Northern and Southern Dynasties. In the beginning, those who became followers had to pay five *dou* of rice, so it was also called the 'Religion of Five *Dou* of Rice', and since the believers called Zhang Daoling 'Tianshi' ('Teacher or Prophet from Heaven'), the religion was also called 'Tianshi Religion'. Taoists revered Lao Zi as the originator of Taoism and called him 'Taishang Laojun', or Grand Alchemist and Supreme Patriarch.

【道具】dàojù 演剧或摄制电影电视片时表演用的器物,如桌子、椅子等叫大道具,纸烟、茶杯等叫小道具 stage property; props; objects used for performance when a drama is being staged or a film made; big things such as tables and chairs are called large props; and small things like cigarettes and teacups are small props

【道口】dàokǒu (～儿 dàokǒur) 路口。特指铁路与公路交叉的路口。road junction; crossing where a railway and a highway intersect

【道劳】dào//láo same as 道乏 dào//fá

【道理】dào•li ❶ 事物的规律 truth; principle; hows and whys: 他在跟孩子们讲热胀冷缩的～。He told the children why objects expand when heated and contract when cooled. ❷ 事情或论点的是非得失的根据;理由;情理 reason; argument; sense; grounds for why matters can exist and why arguments can stand: 摆事实,讲～ present the facts and reason things out|你的话很有～,我完全同意。What you said is very reasonable, and I completely agree with you. ❸ 办法;打算 way to do sth.; plan; intention: 怎么办我自有～。I know how to deal with it.|把情况了解清楚再作～。It is essential to find out everything about it before making any decision.

【道林纸】dàolínzhǐ 一种比较高级的纸,用木材为原料制成,按纸面的有无光泽分为毛道林纸和光道林纸两种。因最初为美国道林(Dowling)公司制造而得名。Dowling paper; high-quality paper made from wood, classified into two different types — crude and glossy — according to the degree of lustre on its surface, and named after the Dowling Company, where it was first produced in the United States of America

【道路】dàolù ❶ 地面上供人或车马通行的部分 road; part of land meant for people to walk or for horses and vehicles to run on: ～宽阔 broad road; wide road|～平坦 level road ◇ 人生～ way of life|走上富裕的～ get on the road to a prosperous life ❷ 两地之间的通道,包括陆地的和水上的 passage between two places, including land and water

【道貌岸然】dàomào ànrán 形容神态庄严(现多含讥讽意 now mostly in satire) be sanctimonious; appear as if one were a person of high morals

【道门】dàomén ❶ 指道家、道教 Taoists, Taoism ❷ (～儿 dàoménr)〈旧时 *old*〉某些封建迷信的组织,如一贯道、先天道等 superstitious sects and secret societies, e. g. *Yiguandao*, and *Xiantiandao*

【道木】dàomù same as 枕木 zhěnmù

【道袍】dàopáo 道士穿的袍子。也指过于肥大的袍子。robe worn by a Taoist priest; loose robe

【道破】dàopò 说穿 point out frankly; lay bare; reveal: 一语～天机 reveal the secret with one remark

【道歉】dào//qiàn 表示歉意,特指认错 be apologetic; offer an apology after realizing one is in the wrong: 赔礼～ apologize; make an apology

【道情】dàoqíng 以唱为主的一种曲艺,用渔鼓和简板伴奏,原为道士演唱的道教故事的曲子,后来用一般民间故事做题材 chanting folk tales to the accompaniment of simple percussion instruments; originally the chanting of Taoist tales by Taoist priests, but later it came to refer to any chanting of folk tales, also 渔鼓(鱼鼓) yúgǔ or 渔鼓道情(鱼鼓道情) yúgǔ dàoqíng

【道人】dào·ren ❶〈旧时 *old*〉对道士的尊称 respectful form of address for a Taoist priest ❷〈古代 *arch.*〉也称佛教徒为道人 Buddhist disciple ❸〈方 *dial.*〉佛寺中打杂的人 person who does the cleaning and other odd jobs in a Buddhist temple

【道士】dào·shi 道教徒 Taoist priest

【道听途说】dào tīng tú shuō 从道路上听到,在道路上传说。泛指传闻的、没有根据的话。hearsay; rumour; gossip; what one has heard on the way

【道统】dàotǒng 宋、明理学家称儒家学术思想授受的系统。他们自认为是继承周公、孔子的道统的。Confucian orthodoxy adhered to by the Confucian school of idealist philosophy of the Song and Ming dynasties, whose champions called themselves adherents to the orthodoxy of the Duke of Zhou and Confucius

【道喜】dào//xǐ 对人有喜庆事表示祝贺 congratulate sb. on a happy occasion: 登门~ call at sb.'s place to give congratulations

【道谢】dào//xiè 用言语表示感谢 express thanks; extend gratitude; thank: 当面向他~。They expressed their thanks to him in person.

【道学】dàoxué ❶理学 Confucian school of idealist philosophy of the Song Dynasty; Neo-Confucianism ❷形容古板迂腐 of pedantic learning: ~气 pedantic | ~先生 pedant; scholar rigidly adhering to principles, esp. Confucian principles

【道牙】dàoyá 马路牙子,用一块一块的凸形水泥构件连接而成 curb; curbstone made with cement blocks; also 道牙子 dàoyá·zi

【道义】dàoyì 道德和正义 morality and justice: 给以~上的支持 moral support

【道院】dàoyuàn ❶道士居住的地方;道观 Taoist residence; Taoist hermitage or temple ❷指修道院 monastery or convent

【道藏】dàozàng 道教书籍的总汇,包括周秦以下道家子书及六朝以来道教经典 Taoist Canon (collected Taoist scriptures), including the Taoist books after the Zhou and Qin dynasties and the Taoist scriptures after the Six Dynasties

【道砟】dàozhǎ 铺在铁路路基上面的石子 railway ballast

【道子】dào·zi same as 线条 xiàntiáo

稻 dào ❶一年生草本植物,叶子狭长,花白色或绿色。子实叫稻谷,去壳后叫大米。是我国重要的粮食作物。主要分水稻和陆稻两大类。通常指水稻。rice (*Oryza sativa*); annual plant with long leaves and white or green flowers, whose seed is called rice or paddy. An important grain crop in China, rice is roughly classified into paddy rice and dry rice, but the term generally refers to paddy rice. ❷这种植物的子实 seeds of rice

【稻草】dàocǎo 脱粒后的稻秆。可打草绳或草帘子,又可造纸,也可做饲料、燃料等。rice straw; stalks of rice after the grain is threshed, which can be used to make straw ropes and mats and paper, or as fodder and fuel

【稻草人】dàocǎorén 稻草扎成的人 scarecrow; human figure tied with rice straw; 〈比喻 *fig.*〉没有实际本领和力量的人 people who have no real skill and strength

【稻谷】dàogǔ 没有去壳的稻的子实 seeds of rice with husk on

【稻糠】dàokāng 稻谷经过加工脱出的外壳;砻糠 husk left from the processing of rice; rice chaff

【稻子】dào·zi 稻 rice; paddy

纛 dào〈古代 *arch.*〉军队里的大旗 big army banner

dē(ㄉㄜ)

嘚 dē〈拟声词 *onom.*〉形容马蹄踏地的声音 clatter of a horse's hoofs

☞ dēi on p.405

【嘚啵】dē·bo〈方 *dial.*〉絮叨;唠叨 garrulous; long-winded: 没功夫听他瞎~。I've no time for his long-winded chitchat.

【嘚嘚】dē·de〈方 *dial.*〉叨叨 talk on and on; chatter away: 一点小事,别再~了。Don't keep chattering on about such a trifle.

dé(ㄉㄜˊ)

得[1] dé ❶得到(跟'失'相对 as opposed to 'lose') get; obtain; gain; win: 取~ obtain; gain | ~益 benefit from; profit from | 不入虎穴,焉~虎子。How can you catch tiger cubs without entering the tiger's lair? *or* Nothing ventured, nothing gained. ❷演算产生结果 (of a calculation) equal; make; result in: 二三~六。Two times three equals six. *or* Two multiplied by three is six. | 五减一~四。Five minus one is four. ❸适合 fit; proper: ~用 handy; fit for use | ~体 appropriate to the occasion; befitting one's position or dignity ❹〈书 *fml.*〉得意 satisfied; complacent: 扬扬自~ be self-satisfied; show smug complacency ❺完成 be finished; be done; be ready: 饭~了。Dinner is ready. | 衣服还没有做~。The clothes are not finished. ❻用于结束谈话的时候,表示同意或禁止[used in ending a statement to indicate agreement or prohibition]: ~,就这么办。All right! We'll do it that way. | ~了,别说了。That's enough talking. Let it go at that. ❼ 用于情况不如人意的时候，表示无可奈何[used in a bad situation indicating helplessness]：～，这一张又画坏了！Look! This picture is messed up again.

得[2] dé ❶ 用在别的动词前，表示许多（多见于法令和公文）[used before other verbs to express permission, usu. in documents and stipulations]：这笔钱非经批准不～擅自动用。No one would use this money without permission. ❷〈方 *dial.*〉用在别的动词前，表示可能这样（多用于否定式）[used before other verbs indicating probability, usu. in the negative]：水渠昨天刚动手挖，没有三天不～完。The digging of the ditch just began yesterday, and will not be finished for at least three days.

☞ ·de on p. 405 and děi on p. 405

【得便】débiàn 遇到方便的机会 when it's convenient：这几样东西，请您～捎给他。Please take these things to him at your convenience.

【得病】dé//bìng 生病 fall ill; contract a disease：不讲卫生容易～。It's easy to fall ill if you don't pay attention to hygiene.

【得不偿失】dé bù cháng shī 得到的抵不上失去的 the loss outweighs the gain; not worth powder and shot

【得逞】déchěng （坏主意）实现；达到目的（of bad ideas）succeed; have one's way as intended; prevail as planned：～于一时 have one's way for the time being | 阴谋未能～。The plot fell through.

【得宠】dé//chǒng 受宠爱(含贬义 derog.) find favour with sb.; be in sb.'s good graces：君主昏庸，奸臣～。The monarch was muddle-headed, so the treacherous officials found favour with him.

【得寸进尺】dé cùn jìn chǐ〈比喻 *fig.*〉贪得无厌 try for a yard after getting an inch; give him an inch and he'll take a yard; be insatiably avaricious; be insatiable

【得当】dédàng （说话或做事）恰当；合适（of speech or action）apt; appropriate; proper; suitable：措词～ aptly worded; appropriate wording | 处理～ deal with a problem properly

【得到】dé//dào 事物为自己所有；获得 get; obtain; gain; receive：～鼓励 receive encouragement | ～一张奖状 be awarded a certificate of merit | ～一次学习的机会 get an opportunity to study; a learning opportunity | 得不到一点儿消息。Not a word of news was received.

【得道多助】dé dào duō zhù 坚持正义就能得到多方面的支持（语本《孟子·公孙丑下》：'得道者多助，失道者寡助'）A just cause wins supports from all sides. *Mencius · Gongsun Qiu II*：'A just cause enjoys abundant support, while an unjust cause finds little.'

【得法】défǎ （做事）采用正确的方法；找到窍门（in doing things）work in a proper way; have the knack：管理～，庄稼就长得好。With proper management, the crops will grow well.

【得分】dé//fēn 游戏或比赛时得到分数 score; make the score（in a game, competition, etc.）

【得分】défēn 游戏或比赛时得到的分数 score of a game or a competition

【得过且过】dé guò qiě guò 只要勉强过得去就这样过下去；敷衍地过日子。也指对工作不负责任，敷衍了事。get by however one can; muddle along or on; drift along; work perfunctorily and muddle along

【得计】déjì 计谋得以实现（多含贬义 oft. derog.）succeed in one's scheme：自以为～ believing one is in the right whether or not that's the case

【得济】dé//jì 得到好处，特指得到亲属晚辈的好处 reap a reward for one's efforts (esp. from one's children or relatives)

【得劲】déjìn （～儿 déjìnr）❶ 舒服合适 feel well：这两天感冒了，浑身不～。He caught the flu and hasn't been feeling well for the last few days. ❷ 称心合意；顺手 fit for use; handy：改进后的工具用起来很～。The improved tools fit the job very well.

【得救】déjiù 得到救助，脱离险境 be rescued; be saved：落水儿童～了。The child who had fallen into the water was finally rescued. | 大火被扑灭，这批珍贵的文物～了。With the fire put out, the invaluable relics were saved.

【得空】dé//kòng （～儿 dé//kòngr）有空闲时间 be free (with time); have leisure：白天上班，晚上要照顾病人，很少～。He had no time since he worked during the day and looked after a patient at night.

【得了】dé·le ❶ 表示禁止或同意；算了；行了 (usu. indicating prohibition, dismissal, or agreement) well, well; that's enough; come off it：～，别再说了。That's enough! Can we stop talking about it! | ～，就这么办吧。Well then, let's do it that way! ❷〈助词 *aux.*〉用于陈述句，表示肯定[used in a declarative sentence to indicate affirmation]：你走～，不用挂念家里的事。You should just go, and don't worry about us at home.

☞ déliǎo

【得力】dé//lì ❶ 得益；见效 benefit from; be effective：～于平时的勤学苦练 benefiting from diligent study and practice | 我吃这个药很～。The medicine is very effective for me. ❷ 得到帮助 get help from; be assisted by：我得他的力很不小。I benefited a lot from his assistance.

【得力】délì ❶ 做事能干；有干才 capable; competent：～助手 capable assistant; right-hand man | ～干部 competent cadre ❷ 坚强有力

strong; efficient: 领导～ exercise strong leadership

【得了】déliǎo 表示情况很严重(用于反问或否定式 oft. used in the negative, or in a rhetorical question to express astonishment or shock) really serious; awful: 这还～吗? How can that be? That's awful! | 不～啦,出了事故啦! Good Heavens! An accident has happened!

☞ dé·le

【得陇望蜀】dé Lǒng wàng Shǔ 后汉光武帝刘秀下命令给岑彭:'人苦不知足,既平陇,复望蜀。'教他平定陇右(今甘肃一带)以后领兵南下,攻取西蜀(见于《后汉书·岑彭传》)。后来用'得陇望蜀'比喻贪得无厌。According to *History of Later Han · The Life of Cen Peng*, Liu Xiu, or Emperor Guangwudi, issued the order to Cen Peng: 'It is human nature to be unable to be content with what we have; having captured Long we now have our eye on Shu.' The message here is that the general, after he took Longyou (around present-day Gansu), should lead his troops southward to attack Xishu. Later, people use the expression to refer to 'insatiable desires'.

【得其所哉】dé qí suǒ zāi 指得到适宜的处所。也用来指安排得当,称心满意。find one's proper place; feel at home after proper arrangements are made

【得人】dérén〈书 *fml*.〉用人得当 use people properly

【得人儿】dérénr〈方 *dial*.〉得人心 enjoy public support

【得人心】dé rénxīn 得到多数人的好感和拥护 be popular; have the support of the people

【得胜】dé//shèng 取得胜利 win a victory; triumph: ～回朝 return to the imperial court with news of victory | 旗开～,马到成功 win a speedy victory in the first battle

【得失】déshī ❶ 所得和所失;成功和失败 gain and loss; success and failure: 不计较个人的～ never give a thought to personal gain or loss ❷ 利弊;好处和坏处 advantages and disadvantages; pluses and minuses; merits and demerits: 两种办法各有～。Each of the two methods has its advantages and disadvantages.

【得时】dé//shí 遇到好时机;走运 be in luck; ride the crest of fortune

【得势】dé//shì 得到权柄或势力(多用于贬义 oft. derog.) be in power; get the upper hand; be in the ascendant: 小人～ villains holding sway

【得手】dé//shǒu 做事顺利;达到目的 go smoothly; succeed; come or bring off: 屡屡～ succeed in a row | 侥幸～ bring sth. off by sheer luck

【得手】déshǒu 指得心应手;顺手 come in handy; be convenient and easy to use: 刀太笨,用起来不～。The knife is too heavy, and not convenient to use. | 怎么～就怎么干吧。Do whatever is convenient for you.

【得数】déshù 答数 solution (of a mathematical problem)

【得体】détǐ (言语、行动等)得当;恰当;恰如其分 (of language or behaviour) appropriate to the occasion; befitting one's position or dignity: 应对～ give the right answers | 话说得很不～ speak in a most improper manner

【得天独厚】dé tiān dú hòu 独具特殊优越的条件,也指所处的环境特别好 be richly endowed by nature; abound in gifts of nature; enjoy exceptional advantages

【得闲】déxián 得空儿 have leisure; be free

【得心应手】dé xīn yìng shǒu 心里怎么想,手就能怎么做。形容运用自如。able to do with one's hands whatever is on one's mind; do with facility or with high proficiency

【得样儿】déyàngr〈方 *dial*.〉(服装、打扮)好看;有样子 (of clothes or appearance) look smart; fine; nice

【得宜】déyí 适当 proper; appropriate; suitable: 措置～ handle properly | 剪裁～ properly cut

【得以】déyǐ (借此)可以;能够 so that; so as to; as a result: 必须放手发动群众,让群众的意见～充分发表出来 boldly mobilize the masses so that they can fully express their opinions

【得意】dé//yì 称心如意;感到非常满意 pleased with oneself; proud of oneself; complacent; conceited: ～之作 favourite work | ～门生 favourite pupil | ～扬扬 be immensely proud | 自鸣～ preen oneself

【得意忘形】dé yì wàng xíng 形容浅薄的人稍稍得志,就高兴得控制不住自己 grow dizzy with success; have one's head turned by success

【得用】déyòng 适用;得力 handy; fit for use: 这把剪子不～。This pair of scissors is not handy. | 这几个都是很～的干部。They are very able cadres.

【得鱼忘筌】dé yú wàng quán《庄子·外物》:'筌者所以在鱼,得鱼而忘筌。'筌是用来捕鱼的,得到了鱼,就忘掉筌。forget the means by which an end is attained. *Zhuangzi · External Things*: 'The trap used to catch fish is forgotten as soon as the fish is caught.'〈比喻 *fig*.〉达到目的以后就忘了原来的凭借 forget things or conditions that helped bring success once a goal is reached

【得志】dé//zhì 志愿实现(多指满足名利的欲望)(oft. indicating the desire for personal fame and gain) achieve one's ambition; have a successful career: 少年～ enjoy success when young | 郁郁不～ be depressed over one's lack of success

【得主】dézhǔ 在比赛或评选中获得奖杯、奖牌等的人 winner of a cup or a medal in a game or competition：奥运会金牌～ winner of a gold medal in the Olympic Games；Olympic gold-medalist

【得罪】dé·zuì 招人不快或怀恨；冒犯 displease；offend；give offence to (sb.)：出言不逊，多有～。I spoke insolently，and my words might have offended you.｜他做了很多～人的事儿。He did many displeasing things.

锝 dé 金属元素，符号 Tc(technetium)，有放射性，由人工核反应获得。是第一种人工合成的元素。technetium (Tc)，radioactive metallic element that is obtained from nuclear reaction，and the first synthetic element

D

德(悳) dé ❶ 道德；品行；政治品质 virtue；morality；moral character；political character：品～ moral character；moral integrity｜公～ social morality；civic virtue；social responsibility｜～才兼备 combine high ability with moral integrity；have both moral integrity and professional competence ❷ 心意 mind；heart：一心一～ one mind and one heart｜离心离～ dissension and discord ❸ 恩惠 kindness；favour：感恩戴～ be deeply grateful；feel deeply indebted｜以怨报～ return evil for good；repay kindness with ingratitude ❹ (Dé) 姓 a surname

【德昂族】Dé'ángzú 我国少数民族之一，分布在云南 De'ang people，or the De'angs，one of China's minority ethnic peoples living in Yunnan Province

【德高望重】dé gāo wàng zhòng 品德高尚，名望很大 (of old people) possessing high moral character and enjoying high esteem；be of good moral standing and undisputed reputation

【德行】déxíng 道德和品行 moral integrity；moral conduct

【德行】dé·xing 讥讽人的话，表示看不起他的仪容、举止、行为、作风等 [expression to ridicule sb.'s appearance，behaviour，conduct，manner，etc.] disgusting；shameful；same as 德性 dé·xing

【德育】déyù 政治思想和道德品质的教育 political，ideological and moral education

【德政】dézhèng 有益于人民的政治措施 good government；political measures or policies beneficial to the well-being of the people

·de (·ㄉㄜ)

地 ·de 〈助词 *aux.*〉表示它前边的词或词组是状语 [used after an adjective or phrase to form an adverbial adjunct before the verb]：天渐渐～冷了。It is gradually getting cold.｜合理～安排和使用劳动力。Labour forces are rationally arranged and utilized.｜实事求是～处理问题。Problems must be handled practically and realistically.

☞ dì on p.419

的[1] ·de ❶ 〈助词 *aux.*〉(②—⑤同)，用在定语的后面 [used after an attribute from ② through ⑤]：a)定语和中心词之间是一般的修饰关系 [when the attribute modifies the noun in the usual way]：铁～纪律 iron discipline｜幸福～生活 happy life b)定语和中心词之间是领属关系 [when the attribute indicates possession]：我～母亲 my mother｜无产阶级～党 the proletarian party c)定语是人名或人称代词，中心词是表示职务或身份的名词，意思是这个人担任这个职务或取得这个身份 [when the attribute is a personal pronoun or name，and the modified noun indicates role or position]：今天开会是你～主席。At today's meeting，you are the chairman.｜谁～介绍人？Who played matchmaker for you? d)定语是指人的名词或人称代词，中心词和前边的动词合起来表示一种动作，意思是这个人是所说的动作的受事 [when the attribute is a personal pronoun or noun standing for a person，and the modified noun indicates the action received by the former]：开他～玩笑 play a joke on him｜找我～麻烦。(He is out to) make trouble for me. ❷ 用来构成没有中心词的'的'字结构 [used at the end of a nominal structure，equivalent to a noun phrase]：a)代替上文所说的人或物 substitute for sb. or sth. already mentioned：这是我～，那才是你～。This is mine and that is yours.｜菊花开了，有红～，有黄～。Chrysanthemums are blooming，some red and others yellow. b)指某一种人或物 [indicate a class category of people or things]：男～ male｜送报～ postman；messenger｜我爱吃辣～。I love spicy hot food. c)表示某种情况 [emphasize what precedes it]：大星期天～，你怎么不出去玩儿玩儿？Today is Sunday，so why don't you go out and enjoy yourself?｜无缘无故～，你着什么急？It has nothing to do with you，so why worry about it? d)用跟主语相同的人称代词加'的'字做宾语，表示别的事跟这个人无关或这事儿跟别人无关 [indicate that there is no connection between a person and a matter or between the matter and other people]：这里用不着你，你只管睡你～去。You have no business here. Just go to sleep. e)'的'字前后用相同的动词、形容词等，连用这样的结构，表示有这样的，有那样的 [used between identical verbs，adjectives，etc.，to constitute a sequence of contrasts]：推～推，拉～拉。Some push while others pull.｜说～说，笑～笑。Some talk while others laugh.｜大～大，小～小。The big ones are too big，while the small ones are too small. ❸ 用在谓语动词后面，强调这动作的施事者或时间、地点、方式等 [used between a verb and its object for emphasis of the subject, time, venue, way, etc. of an action]：谁买～书？Who bought the book? | 他是昨天进～城。He went to town yesterday. | 我是在车站打～票。I bought the ticket at the station. 注意 NOTE：这个用法限于过去的事情 This usage is restricted only to things that happened in the past. ❹ 用在陈述句的末尾，表示肯定的语气 [used at the end of a statement to indicate certainty]：这件事儿我知道～。True, I know about this matter. ❺ 用在两个同类的词或词组之后，表示'等等、之类'的意思 [used after words or phrases belonging to the same part of speech to imply further enumeration]：破铜烂铁～，他捡来一大筐。He picked up a basketful of scrap iron and stuff. | 老乡们沏茶倒水～，待我们很亲热。The folks made tea and served hot drinks, treating us warmly. ❻ 用在两个数量词中间 [used between numerals]：a) 表示相乘 [used to indicate multiplication]：这间屋子是五米～三米，合十五平方米。This room is five metres by three metres, which makes fifteen square metres. b)〈方 *dial.*〉表示相加 [used to indicate addition]：两个～三个，一共五个。Two plus three is five.

的[2] ·de same as 得 ·de ②③
☞ dí on p. 414 and dì on p. 428

【的话】·dehuà〈助词 *aux.*〉用在表示假设的分句后面，引起下文 [used at the end of a conditional clause]：如果你有事～，就不要来了。Don't come if you are busy.

底 ·de same as 的[1] ·de ①b
☞ dǐ on p. 417

得 ·de〈助词 *aux.*〉❶ 用在动词后面，表示可能 [used after certain verbs to indicate possibility]：她去～，我也去～。She can go, and so can I. | 对于无理要求我们一步也退让不～。We never make concessions on any unreasonable demands. 注意 NOTE：否定式是不得。The negative form is 不得 ·bu·de：哭不～，笑不～。(He) was at a loss whether to cry or laugh. ❷ 用在动词和补语中间，表示可能 [used between a verb and its complement to indicate possibility]：拿～动 can carry sth. | 办～到 can do sth. | 回～来 can come back | 过～去 can pass 注意 NOTE：否定式是把'得'换成'不'。The negative form changes 得 ·de to 不 bù：拿不动 can't take sth. | 办不到 can't do sth. ❸ 用在动词或形容词后面，连接表示结果或程度的补语 [used after a verb or an adjective to introduce a complement of result or degree]：写～非常好 write extremely well | 天气热～很。It is too hot. 注意 NOTE：a)'写得好'的否定式是'写得不好。' The negative form of 'write well' is 'write badly'. b) 动宾结构带这类补语时，要重复动词，如。'写字写得很好'不说'写字得很好' When such a complement appears in a verb-object structure, the verb is repeated, as in 写字写得很好 (write with good penmanship), with the verb 写 xiě repeated. ❹ 用在动词后面，表示动作已经完成（多见于早期白话 oft. found in early vernacular）[used after a verb to indicate the completion of an action]：出～门来 having come out of the house
☞ dé on p. 402 and děi on p. 405

肋 ·de 又 also ·te ☞「肋脦」(lē·de) on p. 1164

dēi (ㄉㄟ)

嘚 dēi (～儿 dēir) 赶驴、骡前进的吆喝声 sound to urge on a donkey or mule
☞ dē on p. 402

děi (ㄉㄟˇ)

得 děi ❶ 需要 need; require; take：这个工程～三个月才能完。This project will take three months to complete. | 修这座水库～多少人力？How much labour do you need to build this reservoir? ❷ 表示意志上或事实上的必要 must; have to; needs of will or reality：咱们绝不能落后，～把工作赶上去。We mustn't lag behind, but must work hard to catch up. | 要取得好成绩，就～努力学习。You must study hard if you want to have good grades. 注意 NOTE：'得'的否定是'无须'或'不用'，不说'不得'。The negative form of 得 děi is 无须 wúxū, or 不用 bùyòng, not 不得 bùděi. ❸ 表示揣测的必然 will; be sure to：快下大雨了，要不快走，就～挨淋。It will rain soon. We must hurry, or we will get wet. ❹〈方 *dial.*〉舒服；满意 comfortable; cozy; contented：这个沙发坐着真～。The sofa is comfortable.
☞ dé on p. 402 and ·de on p. 405

【得亏】děikuī〈方 *dial.*〉幸亏；多亏 fortunately; luckily：～我来得早，不然又赶不上了。Fortunately, I came early, or I would have lagged behind.

dèn (ㄉㄣˋ)

扽(撜) dèn ❶ 两头同时用力，或一头固定而另一头用力，把线、绳子、布匹、衣服等猛一拉 tug; pull at both ends, or at one end with the other fixed; pull hard on things such as thread, rope, cloth, clothes, etc.：～～袖口 tug at the sleeve | 轻一点儿，别把丝线

～折(shé)了。Don't pull too hard, or you will break the thread. ❷〈方 *dial.*〉拉紧 grasp tightly; pull hard; tug hard: 你～住了,不要松手。Pull it hard and don't let go.

dēng(ㄉㄥ)

灯(燈) dēng ❶ 照明或做其他用途的发光的器具 lamp; light; lantern; device that emits light for illumination and other purposes: 一盏～ a lamp | 电～ electric lamp or light | 红绿～ traffic light | 探照～ searchlight | 太阳～ sunlamp ❷ 燃烧液体或气体用来对别的东西加热的器具 burner; apparatus used to give heat by burning liquid or gas: 酒精～ alcohol burner; spirit lamp | 本生～ Bunsen burner ❸ 俗称收音机、电视机等的电子管 valve; tube part in a radio, television set etc.: 五～收音机 five-valve or tube radio set

【灯标】dēngbiāo ❶ 航标的一种,装有灯光设备,供夜间航行使用 beacon light; a kind of marker with a lamp inside it for navigation at night ❷ 用灯装饰的或做成的标志或标语 electrically lit decorations or signs: 夜市～ decorative lights for a night fair

【灯彩】dēngcǎi ❶ 指民间制造花灯的工艺 decorative lantern-making; lantern-making as a folk art ❷〈旧时 *old*〉演戏时用做舞台装饰或表演道具的花灯 coloured lanterns formerly used as decorations or props on stage: 满台～。The stage is decorated with many coloured lanterns. ❸ 泛指做装饰用的彩色花灯 decorative coloured lanterns and lights: 室内～交辉。The room is illuminated by decorative coloured lanterns and lights. | 国庆节用的～全部安装就绪。The decorative coloured lanterns and lights are all set up for the National Day.

【灯草】dēngcǎo 灯心草的茎的中心部分,白色,用做油灯的灯心 central part of the stem of rushes, white in colour, and used as lamp wicks

【灯光】dēngguāng ❶ 灯的光亮 light of a lamp; lamplight: 夜深了,屋里还有～。There is still light from the lamp in the room in the middle of the night. ❷ 指舞台上或摄影棚内的照明设备 lighting on a stage or in a film studio: ～布景 lighting and scenery

【灯红酒绿】dēng hóng jiǔ lǜ 形容寻欢作乐的腐化生活。也形容都市或娱乐场所夜晚的繁华景象。red lanterns and green wine — scene of feasting and revelry; scene of debauchery; colourful and bustling night scene

【灯虎】dēnghǔ (～儿 dēnghǔr)灯谜 riddles written on lanterns; lantern riddles: 打～儿 pose and guess lantern riddles

【灯花】dēnghuā (～儿 dēnghuār)灯心燃烧时结成的花状物 snuff (of a candlewick); candlewick forming a flower shape when burned

【灯会】dēnghuì 元宵节举行的群众观灯集会,集会上悬挂着各式各样的彩灯。有的灯会还有高跷、狮子、旱船、杂技表演等娱乐活动。Chinese Lantern Festival; on the 15th day of the 1st lunar month, people gather together to hang up various coloured lanterns and give all kinds of performances, e.g. stilt-walking, lion dance, land-boat dance, acrobatics, etc.

【灯火】dēnghuǒ 泛指亮着的灯 lights: ～辉煌 brilliantly illuminated; ablaze with lights | 万家～ myriad of twinkling lights

【灯节】Dēng Jié 元宵节 Lantern Festival (15th of the 1st lunar month)

【灯具】dēngjù 各种照明用具的统称 lamps and lanterns

【灯亮儿】dēngliàngr 灯的光亮;灯火 lights; illumination of lights: 屋里还有～,他还没有睡。There is still a light on in the room, so he has not gone to bed yet.

【灯笼】dēng·long 悬挂起来的或手提的照明用具,多用细竹篾或铁丝做骨架,糊上纱或纸,里边点蜡烛。现在多用电灯做光源,用来做装饰品。lantern; illumination apparatus hung up or held by the hand. Lanterns are made using thin bamboo strips or iron wire for the frame, with gauze or paper pasted over, and a lit candle inside. Nowadays lanterns use electric bulbs as their light source and are used for decoration.

【灯笼裤】dēng·longkù 裤子的一种,裤腿肥大,下端缩口紧箍在脚腕上 sweat pants; loose, knee-length or ankle-length sports pants

【灯谜】dēngmí 贴在灯上的谜语(有时也贴在墙上或挂在绳子上) riddles written on sheets of paper and pasted on lanterns (sometimes pasted on walls or hung on a string): 猜～是一种传统的娱乐活动。Guessing riddles is a traditional recreational activity.

【灯苗】dēngmiáo (～儿 dēngmiáor)油灯的火焰 tongue of a flame of a lamp

【灯捻】dēngniǎn (～儿 dēngniǎnr)用棉花等搓成的条状物或用线织成的带状物,放在油灯里,露出头儿,点燃照明 wick; lamp wick; narrow strip made of cotton or string, which is put in the lamp oil, with one end sticking out to be lit for illumination; also 灯捻子 dēngniǎn·zi

【灯泡】dēngpào (～儿 dēngpàor)电灯泡 light bulb; electric bulb; also 灯泡子 dēngpào·zi

【灯伞】dēngsǎn 灯上伞状的罩子 umbrella lampshade

【灯丝】dēngsī 灯泡或电子管内的金属丝,多为细钨丝,通电时能发光、发热、放射电子或产生射线 filament (in a light bulb or tube); thin metal filament in a light bulb or tube, mostly of thin tungsten, which gives out light and heat, and emits electrons or produces rays

【灯塔】dēngtǎ 装有强光源的高塔，晚间指引船只航行，多设在海岸或岛上 lighthouse; beacon; high tower with strong light source in it for guiding navigation at night, mostly located on the seashore or islands

【灯台】dēngtái 灯盏的底座 lampstand

【灯头】dēngtóu ❶ 接在电灯线末端、供安装灯泡用的装置 lamp holder; electric light socket; device at the end of an electric wire for installing an electric bulb: 螺丝口的～ screw socket ❷ 指电灯盏数 number of lamps: 这间屋里有五个～。There are five lamps in the room. ❸ 煤油灯上装灯心、安灯罩的部分 holder for the wick and chimney of a kerosene lamp

【灯心】dēngxīn 油灯上用来点火的灯草、纱、线等 lamp wick; wick; rush, gauze, string, etc., used to light a lamp in oil; also 灯芯 dēngxīn

【灯心草】dēngxīncǎo 多年生草本植物，茎细长，叶子狭长。花黄绿色。茎的中心部分用做油灯的灯心，可入药。rush (*Juncaceae*); perennial plant with long thin stems, long narrow leaves, and yellow and blue flowers. The central part of its stem can be used as wicks for oil lamps, and the whole plant can be used for medicinal purposes.

【灯心绒】dēngxīnróng 面上有像灯心的绒条的棉织品 corduroy; cotton fabrics with surface velvety ribs that look like lamp wicks; also 条绒 tiáoróng

【灯芯】dēngxīn same as 灯心 dēngxīn

【灯油】dēngyóu 点灯用的油，通常指煤油 lamp oil; kerosene; paraffin oil

【灯语】dēngyǔ 通讯方法之一，用灯光一明一暗的间歇做出长短不同的信号 lamp signal; communication method, which, by switching on and off a lamp, gives long or short signals

【灯盏】dēngzhǎn 没有灯罩的油灯（总称）oil lamp (minus its chimney)

【灯罩】dēngzhào (～儿 dēngzhàor) 灯上集中灯光或防风的东西，如电灯上的灯伞，煤油灯上的玻璃罩儿 lampshade; lamp chimney (for an oil lamp); device fixed above a lamp, which serves to focus the rays of the lamp or protect it from the wind; for an electric light it looks like an umbrella, and for an oil lamp it looks like a chimney and is made of glass; also 灯罩子 dēngzhào·zi

登1 dēng ❶ (人)由低处到高处(多指步行) (of people) climb; ascend; mount; scale; ascend from a low place to a high place (mostly on foot): ～山 climb a mountain|～陆 land; disembark|～车 get on a bus ◇一步～天 ascend to the heavens in a single step — attain the zenith of power in one leap ❷ 刊登或记载 publish; record; enter: ～报 publish an article in a newspaper|～记 get registered|他的名字～上了光荣榜。His name is entered in the honour roll. ❸ (谷物)成熟 (of grain) ripen: 五谷丰～ bumper harvest of all cereal grains

登2 dēng ❶ 踩；踏 tread; step: ～在窗台儿上擦玻璃 step onto the sill to clean the window ❷ 穿(鞋、裤等) put on; wear (shoes or trousers): ～上鞋 put one's shoes on|脚～长筒靴 wear a pair of high boots ❸ same as 蹬(dēng) ①

【登场】dēng//cháng (谷物)收割后运到场(cháng)上 (of grain) be gathered and taken to the threshing ground: 大豆～之后，要马上晒。After the soya bean crops are harvested, they must be immediately dried on the threshing ground.

【登场】dēng//chǎng (剧中人)出现在舞台上 (of characters in a drama) appear on stage; go on stage; enter: ～人物 character on stage|粉墨～ make oneself up and go on stage; appear on the stage in full make-up

【登程】dēngchéng 上路；起程 set off; set out; start off on a journey: 已收拾好行装，明日破晓～。I have finished packing up and will start off on the journey tomorrow morning.

【登第】dēngdì 登科，特指考取进士 pass the imperial examinations, esp. the palace examination

【登峰造极】dēng fēng zào jí 〈比喻 *fig.*〉达到顶峰 reach the peak and attain perfection; achieve a very high level (of scholastic attainment or technical skill); reach great heights

【登高】dēnggāo ❶ 上到高处 ascend a height; climb up: ～望远 ascend a height to enjoy a distant view ◇祝步步～。May every step you take bring you new progress. ❷ 古时风俗，重阳节登山叫登高 (old custom) climb up a mountain on the Double Ninth Festival: 重九～ mountain climbing on the 9th day of the 9th lunar month

【登基】dēng//jī 帝王即位 ascend the throne; be enthroned

【登极】dēng//jí same as 登基 dēngjī

【登记】dēngjì 把有关事项写在特备的表册上以备查考 register; enter one's name; check in; write down events or matters on a form for reference: 户口～ residence registration|～图书 keep a record of the books in a library

【登记吨】dēngjìdūn 计算船只容积的单位，1 登记吨 等于 2.83 立方米（合 100 立方英尺）registered tonnage; unit for the capacity of a ship, where 1 registered ton equals 2.83 cubic metres (or 100 cubic feet); 简称 abbr. 吨 dūn

【登科】dēngkē 科举时代应考人被录取 (in imperial times) pass the civil-service examinations

【登临】dēnglín 登山临水，泛指浏览山水名胜 climb a hill or a tall building that commands

D

a broad view; visit famous mountains, places of interest, etc.: ～名山大川,饱览壮丽景色 tour famous mountains and rivers to enjoy the magnificent scenery

【登陆】dēng//lù 渡过海洋或江河登上陆地,特指作战的军队登上敌方的陆地 land; disembark; cross seas or rivers to reach land, esp. referring to operative troops landing in enemy territory: ～演习 landing manoeuvre ◇台风～ typhoon hitting land

【登陆场】dēnglùchǎng 军队在强渡江河或渡海作战的时候,在敌方的岸上所夺取的一部分地区,用来保障后续部队渡河和上岸 beachhead; area that troops first capture on enemy shores across a river or sea, in order to let the rest of the troops cross over and get ashore to fight the enemy

【登陆艇】dēnglùtǐng 运送登陆士兵和武器装备靠岸登陆的舰艇。有各种类型,艇底平,船舷高,船头有可以打开的门,便于人员、坦克、车辆迅速登上陆地。landing craft; naval ships and boats to transport troops and weapons to the shore for landing; in different types, e.g. flat bottomed, with high sides and gate in the front for troops, tanks and vehicles to pass through for quick landing

【登录】dēnglù 登记 register: ～在案 be recorded; be put on record

【登门】dēng//mén 到对方住处 call at sb.'s house: ～拜访 pay sb. a visit | 我从来没有登过他的门。I have never called at his house.

【登攀】dēngpān 攀登 climb; clamber; scale

【登山】dēng//shān ❶ 上山 mountain climbing; mountaineering: ～临水 climb a hill to enjoy the scenery | ～越岭 cross over mountain after mountain ❷ 特指登山运动 mountain climbing; mountaineering: ～服 mountaineering apparel | ～协会 mountaineers' association

【登山服】dēngshānfú ❶ 登山运动员登山时穿的一种特制防寒服装 high-altitude wear; specially-made clothes for mountaineers to ward off the cold when they climb high mountains ❷ 一种防寒冬装,多用尼龙绸和羽绒等制作,一般有风帽 anorak; parka; winter coat for warding off the cold, generally made of nylon, down, etc., and having a hood

【登山运动】dēngshān yùndòng 一种体育运动,攀登高山。登山运动能锻炼人的毅力和勇敢精神,对于科学研究和资源开发等有重要意义。mountaineering; mountain-climbing sport which helps people cultivate willpower and courage, and is of major significance for scientific research, exploration of natural resources, etc.

【登时】dēngshí 立刻(多用于叙述过去的事情 used in narration of past events) at once; immediately; then and there: 说干就干,大家～动起手来了。Once agreed, everyone set to work straight away.

【登市】dēngshì (季节性的货物)开始在市场出售;上市 (of seasonal commodities) be in season: 下月初,鲜桃即可～。Peaches will be in season by early next month.

【登台】dēng//tái ❶ 走上讲台或舞台 mount the rostrum; go onstage: ～演讲 mount the rostrum to address the audience | ～表演 take the stage and perform ❷ 〈比喻 *fig.*〉走上政治舞台 enter the political arena: ～执政 enter the arena and take power

【登堂入室】dēng táng rù shì ☞ 升堂入室 shēng táng rù shì on p. 1712

【登载】dēngzǎi (新闻、文章等)在报刊上印出 (of news, articles, etc.) publish in newspapers or magazines

噔 dēng 〈拟声词 *onom.*〉沉重的东西落地或撞击物体的声音 thump; thud; sound produced by the falling or crashing of heavy things: ～～～地走上楼来 come thumping up the stairs

镫 dēng ❶ 古代盛肉食的器皿 ancient vessel for holding meat and food ❷ 〈书 *fml.*〉同'灯',指油灯 same as 灯 dēng, esp. oil lamp

☞ dèng on p. 410

簦 dēng ❶ 古代有柄的笠 ancient bamboo or straw hat with a conical crown, broad rim and handle ❷ 〈方 *dial.*〉笠 bamboo or straw hat with a conical crown and broad rim

蹬 dēng ❶ 腿和脚向脚底的方向用力 press down with the foot; pedal; treadle: ～水车 pedal the waterwheel | ～三轮儿 pedal a tricycle ❷ same as 登[2] dēng ①②

☞ dèng on p. 411

【蹬腿】dēng//tuǐ ❶ 伸出腿 stretch one's legs: 他一～坐起身。Stretching his legs, he sat up. ❷ (～儿 dēng//tuǐr)指人死亡(含诙谐意 humor.) kick the bucket; die

děng (ㄉㄥˇ)

等[1] děng ❶ 等级 class; grade; rank: 同～ same class | 优～ of an excellent (or superior) grade | 共分三～ classified into three grades ❷ 种;类 kind; sort: 这～事 things like this | 此～人 this kind of people ❸ 程度或数量上相同 equal; same in degree or in quantity: 相～ equal | ～于 equal | 大小不～ different in size; of different size ❹ same as 戥 (děng)

等[2] děng ❶ 等候;等待 wait; await: ～车 wait for a train, bus, etc. | 请稍～一会儿。Would you mind waiting a minute, please. | ～他来了一块儿去。Wait for him and go together with him. ❷ 等到 by the time;

when; till: ～我写完这封信再走也不晚。It wouldn't be late for you to leave if you wait till I finish writing this letter.

等[3] dĕng〈助词 *aux.*〉❶〈书 *fml.*〉用在人称代词或指人的名词后面,表示复数[used after a personal pronoun or a noun referring to people to indicate a plural number]: 我～ we|彼～ they ❷ 表示列举未尽(可以叠用 may be used in reiterative locution) and so on; and so forth; etc.: 北京、天津～地 Beijing, Tianjin and other cities|纸张文具～～ stationery and other things ❸ 列举后煞尾[used to end a list]: 长江、黄河、黑龙江、珠江～四大河流 four large rivers — Yangtze, Yellow, Heilongjiang and Pearl rivers

【等差】dĕngchā〈书 *fml.*〉same as 等次 dĕngcì

【等次】dĕngcì 等级高低 grade; rank; place in a series: 产品按质量划分～。The products are graded according to quality.

【等衰】dĕngcuī〈书 *fml.*〉等次 place in a series; grade; rank

【等待】dĕngdài 不采取行动,直到所期望的人、事物或情况出现 wait; await; expect; stay on without doing anything till the expected people, event or situation emerges: ～时机 bide one's time; wait for a favourable opportunity|耐心～ wait patiently

【等到】dĕngdào〈连词 *conj.*〉表示时间条件[used to indicate time condition] by the time; when; till: ～我们去送行,他们已经走了。By the time we went to see them off, they had already left.

【等第】dĕngdì〈书 *fml.*〉名次等级(指人) rank; grade (of people)

【等额选举】dĕng'é xuănjŭ 候选人名额相等于当选人名额的一种选举办法(区别于'差额选举'as compared with 'competitive election') nominating one candidate for election to each post; single-candidate election

【等而下之】dĕng ér xià zhī 由这一等再往下 from that grade down; lower down: 名牌货质量还不稳定,～的杂牌货就可想而知了。Even the quality of the famous brands is unstable, to say nothing of those lower down.

【等份】dĕngfèn (～儿 dĕngfènr)分成的数量相等的份儿 equal divisions; equal portions: 把这筐桃分成十～。Divide the basket of peaches into ten equal portions.

【等号】dĕnghào 表示两个数(或两个代数式)的相等关系的符号(＝) equal sign; equality sign; sign indicating the equal relation of two numerals or two algebraic expressions

【等候】dĕnghòu 等待(多用于具体的对象 usu. concrete things) wait; await; expect: ～命令 await orders; wait for instructions|～远方归来的亲人 wait for dear ones' return from afar

【等级】dĕngjí ❶ 按质量、程度、地位等的差异而作出的区别 grade; rank; distinctions made according to the differences in quality, degree, social status, etc.: 按商品～规定价格。Prices of goods are set according to their grades. ❷ 达到某种等级标准的;区分等级的 order and degree; graded standards; differences in grades: ～厨师 certified cooks|～工资制 graded wage scale ❸ 奴隶占有制度和封建制度下,在社会地位上和法律地位上不平等的社会集团。等级成分是世代相传的。例如封建时代的法国有三个等级:1)僧侣,2)贵族,3)农民、商人和手工业者。caste; stratum; social groups unequal in social strata and legal status under the slave-owning and feudal systems; this stratification of society was handed down from generation to generation, e.g. in feudal France, there were three social strata: (1) monks and priests, (2) aristocracy, (3) peasants, merchants and tradesmen

D

【等价】dĕngjià 不同商品的价值相等 of equal value; equal in value; equal value of different commodities: ～交换 exchange of equal value

【等价物】dĕngjiàwù 能体现另一种商品价值的商品。货币是体现各种商品价值的一般等价物。equivalent; commodity that embodies the value of another commodity, currency being the general equivalent for all commodities

【等离子态】dĕnglízĭtài 物质存在的一种形态,是物质的等离子体状态。高温、强大的紫外线、X射线和丙种射线等都能使气态物质变成等离子态。plasma state; a type of state of substance existence. High temperatures, strong ultraviolet radiation, X-rays, gamma rays, etc., all can turn substances in a gaseous state into a plasma state

【等离子体】dĕnglízĭtĭ 由正离子、自由电子组成的物体,是物质的高温电离状态,不带电,导电性很强。太阳等大多数星体都存在等离子体。plasma; body of substance consisting of positive ions and free electrons, that is an ionized state for certain substances at an extremely high temperature, not electrified and has a very high electric conductivity; most celestial bodies like the sun exist in a plasma state

【等量齐观】dĕng liàng qí guān 不管事物间的差异,同等看待 equate; put on a par; treat matters all the same regardless of the differences between them

【等日】dĕngrì〈方 *dial.*〉过些时候;过几天 some time later; in a few days: 这两天没空,～再去看你。I am busy these days, and will come see you in a few days.

【等身】dĕngshēn 跟某人身高相等(多用来形容数量多 of a great number or amount) be equal to oneself in height: ～雕像 life-size statue|著作～ have published the equivalent of one's height in books; have published a great number of books; have many works to one's credit

【等式】děngshì 表示两个数(或两个代数式)相等的算式,两个数(或两个代数式)之间用等号连接,如 3+2=4+1,$a=4$。equality; equation using an equal sign to indicate two equal numerals or two equal algebraic expressions, e.g. 3+2=4+1, a=4

【等同】děngtóng 当做同样的事物看待 be equal; equate; put on a par (with); mention one thing or person in the same breath as another: 不能把这两件事~起来。You mustn't equate the two matters.

D

【等外】děngwài 质量在等级标准以外的 substandard: ~品 substandard product

【等闲】děngxián 〈书 *fml*.〉❶ 平常 ordinary; unimportant: ~之辈 quite ordinary | ~视之 treat lightly; regard as unimportant | 红军不怕远征难,万水千山只~。The Red Army fears not the trials of the Long March,/ Holding light ten thousand crags and torrents. ❷ 随随便便;轻易 easily; casually; lightly: 莫~白了少年头,空悲切。Should youthful heads easily turn grey,/ For what would we rue the day? ❸ 无端;平白地 for no reason at all; for nothing: ~平地起波澜。A storm broke out over the calm sea — an undesirable event occurred unexpectedly.

【等因奉此】děngyīn fèngcǐ '等因'和'奉此'都是旧时公文用语,'等因'用来结束所引来文,'奉此'用来引起下文(used in official documents in old times) in view of the above, we therefore ...; whereas ... therefore ...; '等因奉此'泛指文牍 general reference to government documents; 〈比喻 *fig*.〉例行公事,官样文章 officialese

【等于】děngyú ❶ 某数量跟另一数量相等 equal to; equivalent to: 三加二~五。Three plus two equals five. ❷ 差不多就是,跟…没有区别 amount to; be tantamount to; be the same as: 不识字就~睁眼瞎子。Not being able to read or write is like not being able to see with two good eyes. | 说了不听,~白说。If no one is listening to you, it's talking in vain.

【等于零】děngyúlíng 跟零相等,指没有效果或不起作用 amount to nothing; be of no use: 说了不办,还不是~。Words not backed up by deeds amount to nothing.

戥 děng 用戥子称东西 weigh with a small scale: 拿戥子~一~这点儿麝香有多重。Please weigh this package of musk. also 等 děng

【戥子】děng·zi 测定贵重物品或药品重量的小秤,构造和原理跟杆秤相同,盛物体的部分是一个小盘子,最大单位是两,小到分或厘 small scale for weighing precious metal, medicine, etc.; also 等子 děng·zi

dèng (ㄉㄥˋ)

邓(鄧) Dèng 姓 a surname

凳(櫈) dèng (~儿 dèngr) 凳子 stool; bench: 方~ square stool | 板~ bench | 竹~儿 bamboo stool

【凳子】dèng·zi 有腿没有靠背的、供人坐的家具 stool; bench; furniture with legs but without a back, for people to sit on

嶝 dèng 〈书 *fml*.〉山上可以攀登的小道 path up a hill

澄 dèng ❶ 使液体里的杂质沉下去 (of liquid) become clear; settle: ~清 become clear; clarify ❷ 〈方 *dial*.〉挡着渣滓或泡着的东西,把液体倒出;滗 strain; decant: 把汤~出来。Strain the soup till it becomes clear.

☞ chéng on p. 254

【澄浆泥】dèngjiāngní 过滤后除去了杂质的极细腻的泥,特指制细陶瓷等用的泥 filtered fine clay, esp. for making delicate porcelain

【澄清】dèng//qīng 使杂质沉淀,液体变清 (of liquid) become clear; settle; clarify: 这水太浑,~之后才能用。This water is too muddy. Wait till it has settled before you use it.

☞ chéngqīng on p. 254

【澄沙】dèngshā 过滤后较细的豆沙 refine (by filtering) sweet bean paste: ~馅儿月饼 refine sweet bean paste for mooncakes

磴 dèng ❶ 〈书 *fml*.〉石头台阶 stone steps ❷ (~儿 dèngr)〈量词 *classifier*〉用于台阶、楼梯等 [used to refer to the number of steps, stairs, etc.]: 五~台阶 five steps on a flight of stairs | 这楼梯有三十来~。This flight of stairs has thirty steps.

瞪 dèng ❶ 用力睁大(眼) open one's eyes wide: 他把眼睛都~圆了。He gazed with round eyes. ❷ 睁大眼睛注视,表示不满意 glare with displeasure: 老秦~了她一眼,嫌她多嘴。Old Qin glared at her, displeased that she was so long-winded.

【瞪眼】dèng//yǎn ❶ 睁大眼睛;眼看着 open one's eyes wide; stare; glare: 干~ look on helplessly ❷ 指跟人生气或耍态度 get angry with sb.; glare or glower at sb.: 他就爱跟别人~。He is always glaring at others. | 有话好说,你瞪什么眼? You can talk to me. Why are you glowering?

镫 dèng 挂在鞍子两旁供脚登的东西,多用铁制成 stirrup; iron piece on either side of a saddle for riders to set their feet: 马~ stirrups

☞ dēng on p. 408

【镫骨】dènggǔ 听骨之一,形状像马镫,外面跟砧骨相连,里面的一端跟内耳相连 stapes; bone of the middle ear that is shaped like a stirrup, with its outside end connected to the incus and the other with the inner ear;(图见 ☞ figure for 耳朵 ěr·duo on p. 512)

【镫子】dèng·zi 镫 stirrup

蹬 dèng ☞蹭蹬 cèngdèng on p. 199
☞ dēng on p. 408

dī(ㄉㄧ)

氐 dī ❶ 二十八宿之一 one of the 28 constellations ❷(Dī)我国古代民族,居住在今西北一带,东晋时建立过前秦(在今黄河流域)、后凉(在今西北) the Di people, an ancient ethnic people of Tibetan stock who lived in northwestern China, and established the states of Former Qin (along the Yellow River) and Later Liang (in present-day northwestern China) during the Eastern Jin Dynasty
☞ dǐ on p. 416

低 dī ❶ 从下向上距离小;离地面近(跟'高'相对,②③同 as opposed to 'tall'; the same is true for ② and ③) at a short distance from the ground; low: ～空 low sky | 飞机～飞绕场一周。The airplane flew round the airfield at low altitude. | 水位降～了。The water level dropped. ❷ 在一般标准或平均程度之下 below average; low: ～地 low-lying land | 声音太～。The voice is too low. | 眼高手～ have high ambitions but low ability ❸ 等级在下的 low in grade or rank: ～年级学生 junior-year students | 我比哥哥～一班。I am one grade below my brother. ❹(头)向下垂 hang down; droop: ～着头 hang one's head

【低倍】dībèi 倍数小的 low power: ～放大镜 low-power magnifying glass

【低层】dīcéng ❶ 低的层次 of or on a lower level, floor, layer, etc.: 他住在高层,我住在～。I live on a lower floor than he does. ❷ 低的等级 low-ranking; lowly; low: ～职员 junior clerk; petty functionary

【低产】dīchǎn 产量低 low yield: ～田 low-yield land | ～作物 low-yielding crop

【低潮】dīcháo ❶ 在潮的一个涨落周期内,水面下降的最低潮位(in a cycle of ebb and flow, the sea's level on a coast gradually reaches its lowest) low tide; low ebb ❷〈比喻 *fig.*〉事物发展过程中低落、停滞的阶段 lowest point; nadir; at the low, stagnant period of sth. in its development: 那时革命正处于～。The revolution was at a low tide at that time.

【低沉】dīchén ❶ 天色阴暗,云层厚而低 overcast; gloomy ❷(声音)低 (of voice) low and deep ❸(情绪)低落 (of mood) low-spirited; downcast

【低档】dīdàng 质量差,价格较低的(商品) low gear; low-grade; inferior in quality; cheap (goods): ～服装 low-grade clothes | ～食品 inferior-quality food

【低等动物】dīděng dòngwù 在动物学中,一般指身体结构简单、组织及器官分化不显著的无脊椎动物 lower animal form; invertebrate; animals referred to in zoology as having bodies of simple structure, and tissues and organs of indistinct differentiation

【低等植物】dīděng zhíwù 一般指构造简单,无茎叶分化,生殖细胞多为单细胞结构的植物。旧时的低等植物范围较大,包括苔藓类和蕨类植物。现在以胚的有无作为区分高等植物与低等植物的标准。lower plant; plant with simple structure, no differentiation of stems and leaves, and germinating from a single cell; in the past lower plant forms had a wider range, including bryophytes and pteridophytes, but now the standard to differentiate higher and lower plants is based on whether or not they have embryos

【低调】dīdiào(～儿 dīdiàor)低的调门儿 low-key; low-pitched tune;〈比喻 *fig.*〉缓和的或比较消沉的论调 mild or low-spirited view

【低估】dīgū 过低估计 underestimate; underrate: 不要～群众的力量。Don't underestimate the strength of the masses.

【低缓】dīhuǎn ❶(声音)低而缓慢 (of sound and voice) low and slow: 他语调～,但口气很坚决。He spoke in a low but firm voice. ❷(地势)低而坡度小 (of topography) low-lying and flat: 这里地势～,气候温和。This place is low-lying with gentle slopes and temperate climate.

【低回】dīhuí〈书 *fml.*〉❶ 徘徊(huái) pace up and down ❷ 留恋 be reluctant to leave; linger; yearn: 使人～不忍离去 cause sb. to be reluctant to leave ❸ 回旋起伏 full of twists and turns; tangled; sentimental: 思绪～ lost in a tangle of thoughts | ～婉转的乐曲 sentimental music ‖ also 低徊 dīhuí

【低徊】dīhuí same as 低回 dīhuí

【低级】dījí ❶ 初步的;形式简单的 elementary; rudimentary; low; junior ❷ 庸俗的 vulgar; coarse; low: ～趣味 bad taste; vulgar interests

【低级神经活动】dījí shénjīng huódòng 大脑皮层之下各部位的神经活动,包括以无条件反射为基础的本能活动,是人类和动物所共有的神经活动 activities of the nerves under the cerebral cortex, including instinctive activities based on unconditioned reflexes that are common activities of the nerves in human beings and other animals

【低贱】dījiàn ❶(地位)低下 (of status) low and degrading; lowly; humble; mean: 出身～ of humble birth and unworthy of notice ❷(价钱)低 cheap; low in price: 谷价～ low grain prices; cheap grain

【低空】dīkōng 距离地面较近的空间 low altitude; low level; space near the ground: ～飞行 low-altitude (or low-level) flight | 在～是暖而湿润的西南气流。At low altitudes is found the warm, humid southwest airflow.

【低栏】dīlán 女子径赛项目之一,规定距离为 80 米,栏架高 76.2 厘米;规定距离为 100 米,栏架高 84 厘米 low hurdles; women's track event with a distance of 80 metres and a hurdle height of 76.2 centimetres, or a distance of 100 metres and a hurdle height of 84 centimetres

【低廉】dīlián (价钱)便宜(pián·yi) (of price) cheap; low-priced; low in price: 价格～。Prices are low. | 收费～。Fees are low.

D

【低劣】dīliè (质量)很不好 (of quality) inferior; substandard; low-grade: ～产品 substandard products | 品质～ bad character; bad quality

【低落】dīluò 下降 low; downcast; depressed: 价格～。Prices have been reduced. | 士气～。The army's morale is low. | 情绪～ downcast; depressed

【低能】dīnéng 能力低下 of low ability; mental deficiency; feeble-mindedness

【低能儿】dīnéng'ér 智力不发达、近于痴呆的儿童。也泛指智能低下的人。mentally disabled child; child with mental disabilities; mentally retarded child; imbecile; simpleton

【低频】dīpín ❶ 一般指低于射频或中频的频率,频率范围与声频相近 low frequency; frequency range that is lower than radio or intermediate frequencies and close to acoustic frequencies ❷ 指 30—300 千赫范围内的频率 frequencies within 30-300 kilohertz

【低热】dīrè same as 低烧 dīshāo

【低人一等】dī rén yī děng 比别人低一个等级 of inferior status; inferior to others: 职业不同是社会分工不同,不存在哪个行业～的问题。Different jobs are the different divisions of labour in society, in which no job is inferior to others.

【低三下四】dī sān xià sì 形容卑贱没有骨气 abject; subservient; servile; obsequious

【低烧】dīshāo 人的体温在 37.5—38℃ 叫低烧 low fever, with body temperature at 37.5-38℃; also 低热 dīrè

【低声下气】dī shēng xià qì 形容恭顺小心的样子 humble and submissive; humble and meek; servile

【低首下心】dī shǒu xià xīn 形容屈服顺从的样子 bow and scrape; obsequiously submissive

【低俗】dīsú 低级庸俗 vulgar; low; coarse: 言语～ vulgar language | ～的格调 low and vulgar style

【低糖】dītáng (食品的)含糖量低 (of food) low sugar: ～糕点 low-sugar pastry

【低头】dī//tóu ❶ 垂下头 hang or lower one's head: ～不语 hang one's head silently ❷〈比喻 *fig.*〉屈服 yield; submit: 他在任何困难面前都不～。He never bows to difficulties.

【低洼】dīwā 比四周低的(地方) low-lying: 地势～ low-lying land | ～地区必须及时采取防涝、排涝的措施。Timely measures must be taken to prevent waterlogging, and drain flooded fields.

【低微】dīwēi ❶ (声音)细小 (of voice or sound) low; faint: ～的呻吟 faint groans ❷ 少;微薄 low; little; meagre: 收入～ low income | 待遇～ low pay ❸〈旧时 *old*〉指身份或地位低 lowly; humble: 门第～ low family status

【低温】dīwēn 较低的温度。物理学上指 -192 到 -263℃ 的液态空气的温度 low temperature, the temperature of liquid-air at -192 to -263℃ in physics

【低下】dīxià ❶ (生产水平、经济地位等)在一般标准之下的 (of living standards, economic status, etc.) sub-par; below average; low; inferior: 能力～ low ability | 技术水平～ low technical level ❷ (品质、格调等)低俗 (of quality, taste, etc.) lowly; vulgar; cheap: 情趣～ in vulgar taste

【低压】dīyā ❶ 较低的压强 low pressure ❷ 较低的电压 low voltage ❸ 心脏舒张时血液对血管的压力 blood pressure on blood vessels when the heart is diastolic

【低压槽】dīyācáo 在同高度上低气压中心向外伸展的槽形部分。一般向南或西南方向延伸。(in meteorology) trough; extended trough-shaped sector of central low pressure at the same altitude, usu. extending southward or southwestward

【低音提琴】dīyīn tíqín 提琴的一种,体积最大、发音最低 double bass; contrabass

【低语】dīyǔ 低声说话 speak softly; speak in a low voice; whisper: ～密谈 talk in whispers in a secretive manner | 悄声～ whisper | 他在老王耳边～了几句。He whispered a few words in Old Wang's ear.

【低云】dīyún 距离地面约 2 公里以下的云 low clouds less than 2 km. above ground

羝 dī〈书 *fml.*〉公羊 ram; buck

堤(隄) dī 沿河或沿海的防水建筑物,多用土石等筑成 dyke; embankment; structures set up along a river or sea to prevent floods: 河～ embankment along a river | 海～ dyke along a seashore | 修～筑坝 build dams and dykes

【堤岸】dī'àn 堤 embankment

【堤坝】dībà 堤和坝的总称,也泛指防水、拦水的建筑物 dykes and dams; structures for preventing and holding back flood waters: 要加紧修筑～,以防水患 speed up the building of dykes and dams to prevent floods

【堤防】dīfáng 堤 weir; dyke; embankment: 汛

期以前,要加固～ strengthen the dykes before the floods arrive

【堤围】dīwéi 堤 weir; dyke; embankment

【堤堰】dīyàn 堤坝;堤 dyke; embankment; levee: 整修～ mend and reinforce an embankment

提 dī 义同'提'(tí)①,用于下列各条[same as 提 tí ①; used in the following entries] ☞ tí on p.1880

【提防】dī·fang 小心防备 take precautions against; be on guard against; beware of: 对他你要～着点儿。You must be on guard against him.

【提溜】dī·liu 〈方 *dial.*〉提 carry in hand; bring along: 手里～着一条鱼 carry a fish in his hand ◇～着心(不放心) have one's heart in one's mouth; with an unsettled mind

䃅(磾) dī 用于人名,金日䃅,汉代人 used in personal names, such as Jin Ridi of the Han Dynasty

嘀 dī ☞ below ☞ dí on p.415

【嘀嗒】dīdā same as 滴答 dīdā

【嘀嗒】dī·da same as 滴答 dī·da

【嘀里嘟噜】dī·lidūlū 形容说话很快,使人听不清 speak quickly and indistinctly; slur one's words; 嘀 same as 滴 dī

滴 dī ❶ 液体一点一点地向下落 drip; (of liquid) fall drop by drop: ～水穿石。Dripping water makes holes in stone. | 汗往下直～。Sweat kept dripping from his face. ❷ 使液体一点一点地向下落 let liquid fall drop by drop: ～眼药 put drops of medicine in one's eyes | ～上几滴油 put in a few drops of oil ❸ 一点一点地向下落的液体 drops; beads: 汗～ bead of sweat | 水～ drop of water ❹ 〈量词 *classifier*〉用于滴下的液体的数量[used with dripping liquid]: 一～汗 a bead of sweat | 两～墨水 two drops of ink

【滴答】dīdā 〈拟声词 *onom.*〉形容水滴落下或钟表摆动的声音 ticktack; drip; tick-tock; sound of dripping water or a clock: 屋里异常寂静,只有钟摆～～地响着。The room was very quiet except for the ticking of the clock. | 窗外滴滴答答,雨还没有停。The rain kept pattering outside the window. also 嘀嗒 dīdā

【滴答】dī·da 成滴地落下 drip: 汗直往下～。Sweat dripped down from (his) face. | 屋顶上的雪化了,～着水。The snow on the roof melted and dripped down. also 嘀嗒 dīdā

【滴滴涕】dīdītì 杀虫剂,成分是二氯二苯三氯乙烷,白色晶体。杀虫效力大,效用持久。通常用的有粉剂、乳剂和油溶剂。DDT; insecticide dichloro-diphenyl-trichlo-roethane, a white crystal that is very potent and has a long-lasting effect, usu. used in powder or emulsion form, or as an oil-soluble preparation

【滴定】dīdìng 化学容量分析中,将标准溶液(已知浓度的溶液)滴入被测物质的溶液里,反应终了时,根据所用标准溶液的体积,计量被测物质的含量 titration; (in chemical analysis) the controlled dripping of a standard solution (of known concentration) into a test solution to produce an observable chemical reaction; when the reaction ends, the concentration of the test solution is calculated according to the volume of the standard solution used in the titration

【滴定管】dīdìngguǎn 化学容量分析用的细长玻璃管,有刻度,下端有活栓 buret; burette; long thin glass tube for chemical tests, with calibrations and a removable cork

【滴灌】dīguàn 灌溉的一种方法,使水流通过设置的管道系统,不断滴到植物体的根部和土壤中 drip irrigation; trickle irrigation; a kind of irrigation where water drips into the soil around the roots of plants through a pipe system

【滴里嘟噜】dī·lidūlū ❶ 形容大大小小的一串东西显得很累赘,不利落 (of a whole series of things put loosely together) appear cumbersome or clumsy: 他腰带上～地挂着好多钥匙。A big bunch of keys hung clumsily from his waist. ❷ same as 嘀里嘟噜 dī·lidūlū

【滴沥】dīlì 〈拟声词 *onom.*〉水下滴的声音 sound of water dripping or pattering: 雨水～ dripping of rain | 泉水～ dripping spring

【滴溜溜】dīliūliū (～的 dīliūliū·de)形容旋转或流动 motion of rolling or flowing: 孩子不停地抽打着陀螺,只见陀螺在地上～地转动。The child kept whipping the top, which turned round and round on the ground.

【滴溜儿】dīliūr ❶ 形容极圆 perfectly round: ～滚圆 perfectly round ❷ 形容很快地旋转或流动 turn or flow around quickly; roll: 眼珠～乱转 with one's eyes rolling round and round

【滴水】dī·shui ❶ 滴水瓦的瓦头,略呈三角形 top of a drip-tile in the shape of triangle ❷ 一座房屋和毗邻的建筑物之间为了房檐上宣泄雨水而留下的隙地 throating; drip channel; space left on the eaves for the draining of rainwater between a house and its neighbouring house

【滴水不漏】dī shuǐ bù lòu 形容说话、做事十分周密,没有漏洞 speak in a watertight or leakproof manner, leaving nothing for people to pick on; make one's argument flawless: 她能言善辩,说出的话～。She has the gift of the gab, and leaves nothing for people to criticize when she speaks.

【滴水成冰】dī shuǐ chéng bīng 水一滴下来就冻成冰,形容天气十分寒冷 water freezes as it drips; freezing cold

【滴水穿石】dī shuǐ chuān shí ☞ 水滴石穿 shuǐ dī shí chuān on p.1798

【滴水瓦】dī·shuiwǎ 一种传统式样的瓦,一端带着下垂的边儿,边儿正面有的有花纹,盖房顶时放在檐口 drip-tile; traditional tile with one end hanging down and a decorative pattern on its front face, placed at the end of an eaves

楠 dī［楠楠］〈书 *fml*.〉叩门声 sound of knocking on the door

镝 dī 金属元素，符号 Dy（dysprosium）。是一种稀土金属。用于原子能工业和激光材料等。dysprosium（Dy），a rare-earth metal used in the atomic energy industry and for the making of laser materials

☞ dí on p. 416

dí（ㄉㄧˊ）

狄 dí ❶ 我国古代称北方的民族 ancient name for the tribes in the north ❷（Dí）姓 a surname

迪（廸） dí〈书 *fml*.〉开导；引导 enlighten; guide: 启～ enlightenment; inspiration

【迪斯科】dí·sikē ❶ 摇摆舞音乐的一种，起源于黑人歌舞，节奏快而强烈（transliteration）disco; a type of rock-and-roll music originating from a form of dance music of black people, with a quick, lively rhythm ❷ 最早流行在美洲黑人间的一种节奏快而强烈的舞蹈，后广泛流传世界各地 disco dancing; lively dancing originating from African-Americans and then spreading worldwide: 跳～ dance at a discothèque; disco｜老年～senior citizens' disco

的 dí〈书 *fml*.〉真实；实在 true; really: ～当 proper; appropriate; suitable｜～是高手 truly a master

☞ ·de on p. 405 and dì on p. 428

【的当】dídàng 恰当；非常合适 apt; appropriate; proper; suitable: 这个评语十分～。This comment is quite appropriate.

【的款】díkuǎn 确实可靠的款项 definitely available sum of money

【的确】díquè 完全确实；实在 indeed; really: 他～是这样说的。He really did say that.｜这的的确确是宋刻本。This is really a Song-dynasty copy.

【的确良】díquèliáng 涤纶的纺织物，有纯纺的，也有与棉、毛混纺的。的确良做的衣物耐磨，不走样，容易洗，干得快。dacron; terylene; polyester fibre, of pure polyester as well as cotton and wool polyester blends. Clothes made of dacron are durable and easy to wash, do not lose their shape easily, and dry quickly.

【的士】díshì〈方 *dial*.〉出租小汽车（transliteration）taxi

【的证】dízhèng 确凿的证据 reliable evidence; irrefutable proof

籴（糴） dí 买进（粮食）（跟'粜'相对 as opposed to 'sell out'）buy in (grain): ～麦子 buy in wheat

荻 dí 多年生草本植物，形状像芦苇，地下茎蔓延，叶子长形，紫色花穗，生长在水边。茎可以编席箔。Amur silvergrass（*Miscanthus saccbariflorus*）; reed-like perennial herb with thriving subterranean stems, long leaves and purple flowers, growing in marshland, its stem suitable for making mats

敌（敵） dí ❶ 有利害冲突不能相容的 of diametrically opposed interests: ～人 enemy｜～军 enemy troops ❷ 敌人 enemy; foe: 仇～ sworn enemy｜残～ remnant enemy troops｜分清～我 make a distinction between the enemy and ourselves ❸ 对抗；抵挡 oppose; resist; stand up to: 所向无～ invincible; ever victorious｜寡不～众 having too few men to resist a large enemy army; be hopelessly outnumbered ❹（力量）相等的 equal in strength; match; rival: 匹～ be one's match｜势均力～ evenly matched in strength

【敌敌畏】dídíwèi 一种有机磷杀虫剂，无色油状液体，有挥发性，用来防治棉蚜等农业害虫，也用来杀死蚊蝇等 DDVP（dimethyl-dichlorovinyl-phosphate）; organic phosphate insecticide in the form of a colourless volatile liquid in oil form, which is used for the prevention and control of plant diseases, and elimination of pests such as cotton aphids as well as mosquitoes and flies

【敌对】díduì 利害冲突不能相容；仇视而相对抗 hostile; antagonistic; belligerent: ～态度 hostile（antagonistic）attitude｜～势力 hostile forces｜～行动 hostile acts

【敌国】díguó 敌对的国家 enemy state

【敌后】díhòu 作战时的敌人的后方 behind enemy lines: 深入～ penetrate deep behind enemy lines｜建立～根据地 establish base areas behind enemy lines｜～武工队（during the War of Resistance against Japan）armed work teams operating behind enemy lines

【敌忾】díkài〈书 *fml*.〉对敌人的愤恨 hatred towards the enemy: 同仇～ nuture a common hatred for the enemy

【敌寇】díkòu 侵略者；敌人 aggressors; enemy: 抗击～ resist the aggressors｜歼灭～ wipe out the aggressors

【敌情】díqíng 敌人的情况，特指敌人对我方采取行动的情况 enemy situation; enemy activities; esp. enemy action towards our side: 了解～ get to know the enemy; gather information about the enemy｜侦察～ reconnoitre the enemy situation｜发现～ uncover the enemy｜～观念（对敌人警惕的观念）alertness to the presence of the enemy; vigilance against the enemy

【敌酋】díqiú 敌人的头子 enemy chieftain; enemy commander: 活捉～ capture the enemy chieftain alive

【敌人】dírén 敌对的人;敌对的方面 enemy; foe

【敌视】díshì 当做敌人看待;仇视 be hostile or antagonistic to: 互相～ be hostile to each other|～的态度 adopt a hostile attitude towards (sb. or sth.)

【敌手】díshǒu 力量能相抗衡的对手 match; opponent; adversary: 棋逢～,将遇良才。As an ace chess player meets his match, so a general will find his own match in military talent. |比技术,咱们几个都不是他的～。So far as skills are concerned, we are no match for him.

【敌台】dítái 敌方的电台 enemy radio station

【敌探】dítàn 敌方派遣的刺探我方机密的间谍 enemy spy

【敌特】dítè 敌方派来的特务(tè·wu) enemy spy; enemy agent

【敌伪】díwěi 指我国抗日战争时期日本侵略者、汉奸及其政权 enemy and their puppet regime during the War of Resistance against Japan: ～时期 period of Japanese occupation; during the Japanese occupation|没收～财产 confiscate the property of the enemy and the puppet regime

【敌我矛盾】dí-wǒ máodùn 敌对阶级之间由于根本利害冲突而产生的矛盾 conflicts between two opposing groups (ourselves and the enemy)

【敌焰】díyàn 敌人的气焰 enemy's arrogance: ～嚣张。The enemy's arrogance is rampant.

【敌意】díyì 仇视的心理;敌对的情感 hostility; enmity; animosity; antagonism: 心怀～ harbour hostility|露出～的目光 reveal hostility in one's eyes; show hostile looks

【敌阵】dízhèn 敌人的阵地 enemy position: 冲入～ charge into the enemy position

涤(滌) dí 洗 wash; cleanse: 洗～ wash; wash up|～荡 wash away; clean up

【涤除】díchú 清除;去掉 wash away; do away with; eliminate: ～污垢 clean up the filth|～旧习 do away with old customs

【涤荡】dídàng 洗涤;清除 wash away; clean up; cleanse: ～邪祟 exorcize evil spirits|～污泥浊水 wash away the sludge and filth

【涤卡】díkǎ 用涤纶纤维和棉纱织成的咔叽布,一般用来做制服 dacron drill; dacron khaki; cloth woven with polyester fibres and cotton, usu. used to make uniforms

【涤纶】dílún 合成纤维的一种,用乙二醇、对苯二甲酸二甲酯等原料合成。强度高、弹性大。用来织的确良或制造绝缘材料、绳索等。terylene; synthetic polyester fibre with a high degree of strength and elasticity used to make dacron, insulating materials, rope, etc.

【涤棉布】dímiánbù 涤纶与棉的混纺织物的统称 polycotton; fabric made from a polyester and cotton blend; 俗称 popularly known as 棉的确良 miándíquèliáng

頔 dí〈书 *fml.*〉美好,多用于人名 beautiful and good (oft. used in people's names)

笛 dí ❶ 管乐器,用竹子制成,上面有一排供吹气、蒙笛膜和调节发音的孔,横着吹奏 bamboo flute; flute; wind instrument made of bamboo, with a row of holes, bamboo membrane and a sound-adjusting hole, played by being held horizontally; also 横笛 héngdí ❷ 响声尖锐的发音器 whistle: 汽～ steam whistle|警～ police whistle; siren

【笛膜】dímó (～儿 dímór)从竹子或芦苇的茎中取出的薄膜,用来贴在笛子左端第二个孔上,吹笛时振动发声 membrane obtained from inside bamboo or reed stalks, pasted on the second hole on the left end of a flute, producing a tremulous sound when blown

【笛子】dí·zi same as 笛 dí ①

觌(覿) dí〈书 *fml.*〉见;相见 see; meet

【觌面】dímiàn〈书 *fml.*〉见面;当面 meet each other

髢 dí (旧读 formerly pronounced dì) [髢髢] (dí·dí)〈方 *dial.*〉假头发 wig

嘀(啲) dí [嘀咕] (dí·gu) ❶ 小声说;私下里说 whisper; talk in whispers; gossip (in a low voice): 俩人一见面就～上了。The two of them began to talk in whispers the minute they met. ❷ 猜疑;犹疑 be apprehensive; have qualms; be unsettled: 他看到这种异常的情形,心里直犯～。The sight of the unusual situation unsettled him profoundly.

☞ dī on p. 413

嫡 dí ❶ 宗法制度下指家庭的正支(跟'庶'相对 as opposed to a concubine, under the feudal-patriarchal system) of or by the wife: ～出 born of the wife|～长子(妻子所生的长子) eldest son by the wife ❷ 家族中血统近的 of lineal descent; closely related: ～亲 closest by blood; of the same father; of the same paternal grandfather|～堂 once removed from the direct paternal line ❸ 正宗;正统 orthodox; authentic: ～派 direct line of descent; disciples personally instructed by a master|～传 handed down in a direct line from the master; authentic

【嫡出】díchū〈旧指 *old*〉妻子所生(区别于'庶出' as compared with one born of a concubine, under the feudal-patriarchal system) born of the wife

【嫡传】díchuán 嫡派相传(表示正统) handed down in a direct line from the master (of orthodoxy): ～弟子 disciples personally instructed by the master

【嫡母】dímǔ 宗法制度下妾所生的子女称父亲的妻子 mother of the direct line (as used by children of a concubine, in reference to their

D

father's official wife in feudal times)

【嫡派】dípài ❶ 嫡系 direct line of descent：～子孙 children of the direct line of descent ❷ 得到传授人亲自传授的一派(多指技术、武艺)(usu. of technique, martial arts) disciples personally instructed by a master：～真传 personal instruction by the master

【嫡亲】díqīn 血统最接近的(亲属) closest by blood; by the same father; of the same paternal grandfather：～姐姐 elder sister by the same father｜～侄子 son of one's own brother

【嫡堂】dítáng 血统关系较近的(亲属) relationship between cousins of the same paternal grandfather：～兄弟 (male) cousins of the same paternal grandfather｜～叔伯 first cousins of one's father; uncles

【嫡系】díxì ❶ 宗法制度下指家族的正支 direct line of descent：～后裔 progeny of the direct line of descent (from sb.) ❷ 一线相传的派系，亲信派系 under the direct control of a faction：～部队 troops under one's direct control; one's own (or personal) troops

【嫡子】dízǐ 〈旧指 *old*〉妻子所生的儿子，特指嫡长子(区别于'庶子' as compared with 'son born of a concubine') son, esp. oldest son born of the wife

翟 dí ❶ 古书上指长尾的野鸡 long-tailed pheasant, referred to in ancient books ❷ 〈古代 *arch.*〉用做舞具的野鸡的羽毛 pheasant feather used as a prop in dancing ❸ (Dí) 姓 a surname

☞ Zhái on p. 2407

镝 dí 〈书 *fml.*〉箭头，也指箭 arrowhead; arrow：锋～ blade and arrowhead; weaponry; war｜鸣～ twanging arrow

☞ dī on p. 414

髢 dí [髢髻] díjì 〈书 *fml.*〉假发盘成的髻 hairpiece; bun (of false hair worn at the back or on top of the head)

蹢 dí 〈书 *fml.*〉蹄子 trotter; hoof

☞ zhí on p. 2465

dǐ (ㄉㄧˇ)

氐 dǐ 〈书 *fml.*〉根本 foundation; base

☞ dī on p. 411

邸 dǐ ❶ 高级官员的住所 residence of a high official：官～ residence of an official｜私～ private house ❷ (Dǐ) 姓 a surname

【邸宅】dǐzhái 第宅；府第 mansion

诋 dǐ 〈书 *fml.*〉说坏话；骂 speak ill of; slander; defame：～毁 slander; vilify; calumniate; defame｜丑～(辱骂) slander; insult; vilify; calumniate

【诋毁】dǐhuǐ 毁谤；污蔑 slander; vilify; calumniate; defame; do sb. down：～别人，抬高自己 vilify others so as to build up oneself

坻 dǐ 宝坻(Bǎodǐ)，地名，在天津 name of a place near Tianjin

☞ chí on p. 261

抵[1] dǐ ❶ 支撑 support; prop; hold; sustain：～住门别让风刮开。Prop sth. against the door so that it won't get blown open by the wind.｜他用手～着下巴颏儿。He propped his chin in his hands. ❷ 抵挡；抵抗 resist; withstand ❸ 抵偿 compensate for; make good; make up for：～命 pay with one's own life ❹ 抵押 mortgage：用房屋做～ mortgage a house ❺ 抵消 balance; set off：收支相～。Income and expenditure are exactly equal. ❻ 相当；能代替 be equal to; match：一个～两个。One can do the work of two.

抵[2] dǐ 〈书 *fml.*〉抵达；到 reach; arrive at：平安～京 arrive in Beijing safe and sound

【抵补】dǐbǔ 补足所缺的部分 make up for; compensate：～损失 compensate for (or make good) a loss

【抵偿】dǐcháng 用价值相等的事物作为赔偿或补偿 compensate for; make good; give sth. by way of payment for：～消耗 make up for the depreciation (or loss)｜拿实物作～ compensation in kind

【抵触】dǐchù 跟另一方有矛盾 conflict; contravene; clash; oppose：～情绪 resentment｜相互～ at odds with each other; resent each other｜在个人利益和集体利益有～的时候，应该服从集体利益。When individual and collective interests conflict, those of the collective should prevail. also 牴触 dǐchù

【抵达】dǐdá 到达 arrive; reach：～目的地 reach one's destination

【抵挡】dǐdǎng 挡住压力；抵抗 keep out; ward off; check; withstand：～严寒 keep out the wind and the cold｜攻势太猛，～不住。The attack was too fierce to check.

【抵还】dǐhuán 以价值相当的物品偿还 compensate with goods of equal value：把房产作价～ compensate sb., or pay back a debt, with (the sale of) a house

【抵换】dǐhuàn 以另一物代替原物 substitute for; take the place of

【抵抗】dǐkàng 用力量制止对方的进攻 resist; stand up to：奋力～ rise in resistance｜～敌人入侵 resist the invasion of the enemy

【抵赖】dǐlài 用谎言和狡辩否认所犯过失或罪行 deny; disavow; disclaim; use lies and cunning tricks to deny one's mistakes or crimes：铁证如山，不容～。The evidence is conclusive and cannot be denied.

【抵命】dǐ//mìng 偿命 a life for a life; pay with one's life：杀人～ pay with one's life (for a murder, etc.)

【抵事】dǐ//shì 顶事；中用(多用于否定式 oft.

used in the negative) be effective; serve the purpose: 谁说人少了不～! Who says we can't do the job just because we are small in number! 究竟抵不抵事,还要试一试看。We'll have to try it to find out if it works.

【抵死】dǐsǐ 拼死(表示态度坚决 indicating determination) risk one's life; fight desperately: ～也不承认 refuse to admit (a crime, etc.) until death

【抵牾】dǐwǔ 矛盾 contradiction; conflict; also 牴牾 dǐwǔ

【抵消】dǐxiāo 两种事物的作用因相反而互相消除 offset; cancel out; counteract: 这两种药可别同时吃,否则药力就～了。Don't take the two medicines at the same time because they will counteract each other.

【抵押】dǐyā 债务人把自己的财产押给债权人,作为清偿债务的保证 mortgage; pledge: ～品 security; pledge | 用房产做～ raise a mortgage on one's house

【抵御】dǐyù 抵挡;抵抗 resist; withstand; ward off: ～外侮 resist foreign aggression | ～风沙侵袭 withstand the onslaught of sandstorms

【抵债】dǐ//zhài 抵偿债款 repay a debt in kind or through labour

【抵账】dǐ//zhàng 用实物或劳力等来还账 pay a debt in kind or through labour

【抵制】dǐzhì 阻止某些事物,使不能侵入或发生作用 boycott; resist; combat; reject: ～不正之风 combat evil social trends | ～会议的召开 boycott a meeting

【抵罪】dǐzuì 因犯罪而受到适当的惩罚 be punished for a crime; be punished by law

底¹ dǐ ❶ (～儿 dǐr)物体的最下部分 bottom; base: 锅～儿 bottom of a pot | 井～ bottom of a well | 海～ bottom of the sea ❷ (～儿 dǐr)事情的根源或内情 origin or bottom of sth.; heart of the matter; ins and outs: 交～ give sb. the bottom line; put all one's cards on the table | 摸～儿 try to sound sb. out | 刨根问～ get to the bottom of sth. ❸ (～儿 dǐr)底子④ rough draft; draft text: ～本 copy kept as a record | ～稿儿 draft | 留个～儿 keep a copy on file; duplicate and file (a letter, etc.) ❹ (年和月的)末尾 end of a year or month: 年～ end of the year | 月～ end of the month ❺ 花纹图案的衬托面 background; foundation: 白～红花 red flowers on a white background ❻ 底数①的简称 abbr. for 底数 dǐshù① ❼〈书 *fml.*〉达到 end up with; end in; come to: 终～于成 end in victory; succeed in the end | 伊于胡～? (到什么地步为止?) Where will all this end? ❽ (Dǐ) 姓 a surname

底² dǐ〈书 *fml.*〉何;什么 what: ～处 what place; where | ～事 what matter; what

底³ dǐ〈书 *fml.*〉❶ 此;这 here; this: 竹篱茅舍,～是藏春处。A cottage with a bamboo fence, here is where spring can be found. ❷ 如此;这样 so; such: 长歌～有情。The song is so sentimental.

☞ ·de on p. 405

【底版】dǐbǎn 底片 photographic plate; negative (of a photograph)

【底本】dǐběn ❶ 留做底子的稿本 copy for the record, or for reproduction; master copy ❷ 抄写、刊印、校勘等所依据的本子 text against which other copies are checked; original text

【底册】dǐcè 登记事项留存备查考的册子 bound copy of documents kept on file; file copy: 清抄两份,一份上报,一份留做～。Make two copies, one copy to send to the leadership and the other to keep on file.

【底层】dǐcéng ❶ 建筑物地面上最底下的一层。泛指事物最下面的部分 ground floor; also a general term for the lowest part of sth.: 大楼的～是商店。The ground floor of the building is a department store. | 白鱼晚上就游回水的底层。Silver carp swim to the bottom of the river (or lake) in the evening. ❷ 社会、组织等的最低阶层: the lowest stratum of a society or organization: 生活在社会～ live at the bottom rung of the social ladder

【底肥】dǐféi 基肥 base fertilizer: ～不足,麦苗长得不好。The wheat seedlings did not grow well for lack of base fertilizer.

【底稿】dǐgǎo (～儿 dǐgǎor)公文、信件、文章等的原稿,多保存起来备查 draft of an official document, a letter, an article, etc., usu. kept on record

【底工】dǐgōng 基本工夫(多指戏曲表演技艺等) basic skills (of a theatrical performer): ～扎实 solid basic skills; also 底功 dǐgōng

【底火】dǐhuǒ ❶ 指增添燃料以前炉灶中原有的火 fire in a stove before new fuel is added ❷ 枪弹或炮弹底部的发火装置,是装着雷汞的铜帽或钢帽,受撞针撞击时,就引起发射药的燃烧 primer; ignition apparatus on the base of a bullet or cannon ball, a copper or steel cap containing mercury fulminate that ignites propellant powder when struck by a firing pin

【底价】dǐjià 招标、拍卖前预定的价钱 base price; price set before bidding or auction: 这套邮票拍卖～130 元,成交价 160 元。This set of stamps was priced at 130 yuan before the auction, but was actually sold for 160 yuan.

【底襟】dǐjīn (～儿 dǐjīnr)纽扣在一侧的中装,掩在大襟底下的狭长部分 narrow piece of cloth under the front of a traditional Chinese jacket buttoned on the right side

【底里】dǐlǐ〈书 *fml.*〉内部的实情 inside story: 不知～ do not know the ins and outs of sth. | 探听～ pry into the bottom of things

【底码】dǐmǎ ❶ 商业中指商品的最低售价 floor price, the lowest possible price for merchandise ❷ 银钱业中指规定的最低限度的放款利息额 base interest; minimum interest of a loan in banking

【底牌】dǐpái ❶ 扑克牌游戏中最后亮出来的牌 last card in one's hand in a card game ❷〈比喻 *fig*.〉内情 inside story: 摸清对方～,再考虑如何行动。Let's find out what the other side is up to before considering our action. ❸〈比喻 *fig*.〉留着最后动用的力量 sth. kept as the last resort: 不到万不得已,别打这张～。Don't play this card unless absolutely necessary.

【底盘】dǐpán ❶ 汽车、拖拉机等的一个组成部分,包括传动机构、行驶机构和控制机构 chassis; base frame of a motor vehicle like a car or tractor, consisting of transmission, driving, and control gears ❷ 电子仪器内安装大部分零件的板 framework of an electronic instrument on which most parts are installed ❸〈方 *dial*.〉器物的底座 base of a utensil

【底片】dǐpiàn ❶ 拍摄过的胶片,物像的明暗和实物相反。这种胶片用来印制相片。negative, characterized by the absence rather than presence of distinguishing features, used for developing prints ❷ 没有拍摄过的胶片(of photography) film ‖ also 底版 dǐbǎn

【底气】dǐqì ❶ 指人体的呼吸量 lung power: ～不足,爬到第三层就气喘了。(I) don't have very strong lungs and begin to pant after climbing to the third floor. | 他～足,唱起歌来嗓音洪亮。He has strong lungs and sings with a resounding voice. ❷ 泛指气力或劲头 (in general) strength or energy: 看到新一代的成长,教师们干工作的～更足了。Seeing the growth of the new generation, the teachers work even more energetically.

【底情】dǐqíng 内情;实情 bottom of things; real situation: 了解～ get to know the real situation

【底墒】dǐshāng 种庄稼以前土壤中已有的水分 soil moisture before sowing or planting: 今春雨水多,～好。There was much rain this spring so that the soil contains enough moisture.

【底数】dǐshù ❶ 求一个数的若干次乘方时,这个数就是底数,如求 a^n, a 就是底数 base number; a number in which other numbers are expressed as logarithms. For example, a is the base number in a^n; 简称 abbr. 底 dǐ ❷ 事情的原委;预定的计划、数字等 ins and outs of sth.; prepared plan or figure: 心里有了～ know what's going on | 告诉你个～。Give you a tip.

【底土】dǐtǔ 心土下面的一层土壤 layer of soil beneath subsoil

【底细】dǐ·xì (人或事物的)根源;内情 origin (of sb. or sth.); inside story: 摸清～ get to the bottom of sth. | 不了解这件事的～ do not know the ins and outs of the matter

【底下】dǐ·xia ❶ 下面 under; below; beneath: 树～ under a tree | 窗户～ below a window ◇ 手～工作多 have much work on hand | 笔～不错(会写文章) good at the pen; write well ❷ 以后 afterwards; later; next: 他们～说的话我就听不清了。I couldn't hear clearly what they were talking about afterwards.

【底下人】dǐ·xiarén ❶ 下人 servant ❷ 手下的人;下属 subordinate: 上边没说话,～不好做主。A subordinate cannot make a decision without word from his superior.

【底线】[1] dǐxiàn 足球、篮球、羽毛球等运动场地两端的界线 baseline of a football field, or a basketball or tennis court

【底线】[2] dǐxiàn 暗藏在对方内部刺探情况或进行其他活动的人 planted agent; spy in an opponent's camp for collecting information or conducting other activities

【底薪】dǐxīn ❶ 过去物价不稳定时的计算工资的基数。有的在这基数之外另加津贴,成为实际的工资。有的根据当时若干种主要生活必需品的物价指数,对基数加以调整,折算实际的工资。base salary; basic amount of salary during a time of erratic price fluctuations in the past. The actual salary included the base and various subsidies; in some cases the base salary was adjusted according to the prices indexes of several major daily necessities. ❷ 基本工资 basic salary

【底蕴】dǐyùn〈书 *fml*.〉详细的内容;内情 detailed content; inside story: 不知其中～ do not know what really happened

【底止】dǐzhǐ〈书 *fml*.〉止境 limit; boundary: 永无～ go on endlessly

【底子】dǐ·zi ❶ same as 底[1] dǐ ①: 鞋～ sole ❷ 底细;内情 details; inside story: 把～摸清了 get to the bottom (of sth.) ❸ 基础 base: ～薄 with a weak base or foundation | 他的～不大好,可是学习很努力。Although he has little pre-knowledge, he studies very hard. ❹ 可做根据的(多指草稿) sth. (usu. a manuscript) used for the record: 发出的文件要留个～。Keep a copy of each document issued. | 画画儿要打个～。Draw a sketch before painting or drawing. ❺ 东西剩下的最后一部分 remainder; leftover: 货～ remainder of stock | 粮食～ remnants of grain ❻ 花纹图案的衬托面 background of a design or pattern: 她穿件白～小紫花的短衫。She's wearing a blouse with purple patterns on white.

【底座】dǐzuò (～儿 dǐzuòr) 座子(多指在上面安装各种零件或构件的) base (on which sth. else is installed); pedestal; foundation: 磅秤的～ base of a platform scale | 台灯的～ pedestal of a table lamp | 柱子的～是大理石的。The foundation of the pillar is marble.

柢 dǐ 树根 root of a tree: 根深～固 same as 根深蒂固 gēn shēn dì gù

牴(觝) dǐ ☞ below

【牴触】dǐchù same as 抵触 dǐchù

【牴牾】dǐwù same as 抵牾 dǐwù

砥 dǐ(旧又读 formerly also pronounced zhǐ)〈书 *fml.*〉细的磨刀石 fine-grained whetstone:～石 whetstone

【砥砺】dǐlì〈书 *fml.*〉❶ 磨刀石 whetstone ❷ 磨炼 temper:～风节 temper one's character and sense of justice|～革命意志 temper one's revolutionary will ❸ 勉励 encourage:互相～ encourage each other

【砥柱中流】Dǐzhù zhōngliú ☞ 中流砥柱 zhōngliú Dǐzhù on p.2482

骶 dǐ 腰部下面尾骨上面的部分 sacrum; part (of the spine) below the waist and above the tailbone

【骶骨】dǐgǔ 腰椎下部五块椎骨合成的一块骨,呈三角形,上宽下窄,上部与第五腰椎相连,下部与尾骨相接 sacrum; inverted triangular bone formed from the five vertebrae below the 5th lumber vertebra and above the tailbone; also 骶椎 dǐzhuī,荐骨 jiàngǔ or 荐椎 jiànzhuī;(图见 ☞ figure for 骨骼 gǔgé on p.693)

dì(ㄉㄧˋ)

地 dì ❶ 地球;地壳 earth; earth's crust:天～ heaven and earth|～层 stratum|～质 geology ❷ 陆地 land:～面 earth's surface|～势 terrain|高～ highland|低～ lowland|山～ mountainous area|～下水 underground water ❸ 土地;田地 land; field:荒～ wasteland|下～干活ㄦ go to work in the field ❹ same as 地面 dìmiàn ②:水泥～ cement surface ❺ same as 地区 dìqū ①:各～various localities|内～inland area|外～places other than one's hometown ❻ same as 地区 dìqū ②:省～领导 provincial and prefectural leader|～县两级干部 cadres at prefectural and county levels ❼ same as 地方(dìfāng)①:军～两用人才 personnel qualified for both military and civil services ❽ same as 地方(dì·fang)①:无～自容 extremely embarrassed or ashamed ❾ 地点 location:目的～ destination|所在～ location ❿ 地位 position:易～以处 put oneself in another's shoes ⓫ 地步 situation:置之死～ back (sb.) to a dead corner|预为之～ condition to achieve sth. ⓬(～ㄦ dìr)花纹或文字的衬托面 base of a pattern or characters:白～红花ㄦ的大碗 big white bowl with red patterns|白～黑字的木牌 white wooden plaque written with characters in black ⓭ 路程(用于里数、站数后)[used after a mileage or station number] distance:二十里～distance of 20 *li*|两站～ distance of two stops

☞ ·de on p.404

【地板】dìbǎn ❶ 室内铺在地面上的木板,有时也指木质楼板 flooring; wooden board laid on the floor; wooden floor ❷ same as 地面 dìmiàn②:～革 plastic flooring|水磨石～ terrazzo floor ❸〈方 *dial.*〉田地 field

【地磅】dìbàng same as 地秤 dìchèng

【地保】dìbǎo 清朝和民国初年在地方上为官府办差的人(during the Qing Dynasty and early years of the Republic) person running errands for a local government

【地堡】dìbǎo 供步枪、机枪射击用的低矮工事,有顶,通常为圆形 blockhouse; dome-shaped low structure protecting riflers and machine gunners

【地表】dìbiǎo 地球的表面,也就是地壳的最外层 earth's surface; outermost layer of the earth's crust:～温度 surface temperature on the earth

【地鳖】dìbiē 昆虫,身体扁,棕黑色,雄的有翅,雌的无翅。常在住宅墙根的土内活动。可入药。ground beetle (*Eupolyphaga sinensis*); flat-bodied, brownish-dark insect, the male having wings while the female is wingless, living underground near the walls of a house, and used as a medicine; also called 䗪虫 zhèchóng;通称 generally known as 土鳖 tǔbiē

【地波】dìbō 指沿着地球表面传播的无线电波 surface wave; radio wave transmitting along the earth's surface; also 地面波 dìmiànbō

【地鵏】dìbǔ ☞大鸨 dàbǎo on p.353

【地步】dìbù ❶ 处境;景况(多指不好的 usu. undesirable) condition; plight:真没想到他会落到这个～。Who'd have expected him to come to this? ❷ 达到的程度 extent; degree:他兴奋得到了不能入睡的～。He's so excited that he could not fall asleep. ❸ 言语行动可以回旋的地方 leeway; elbowroom:留～ leave room for manoeuvre

【地财】dìcái〈方 *dial.*〉指私人埋藏在地下的财物 private valuables buried underground

【地层】dìcéng 地壳是由一层一层的岩石构成的,这种岩石层次的系统叫做地层 stratum; layers of rock that form the earth's crust

【地产】dìchǎn 属于个人、团体或国家所有的土地 real estate; land belonging to an individual, a group, or a state

【地潮】dìcháo ☞ 固体潮 gùtǐcháo on p.698

【地秤】dìchèng 秤的一种,安装在地上,放物体的部分跟地面一般平,一次可以称数吨至数十吨,多用于仓库和车站 weighbridge; weighing scale installed on the ground, with the platform at the same level of the ground, capable of scaling a weight up to several dozen tons, usu. installed in a warehouse or railway station; also 地磅 dìbàng

【地磁】dìcí 地球磁场,地球所具有的磁性,在其周围形成磁场。罗盘指南和磁力探矿都是地磁的利用。terrestrial magnetism; geomagnetism; magnetic properties of the earth and its magnetic fields, as manifested by the compass and the magnetic detector for mineral deposits

【地磁极】dìcíjí 地球的磁南极和磁北极，与地球的南北两极不重合，而且位置经常缓慢移动。1970年磁北极在北纬76°、西经101°，磁南极在南纬66°、东经140°。geomagnetic pole; either of the north and south geomagnetic poles of the earth, which do not match with the north and south poles of the earth and which are constantly moving at a slow pace. In 1970, the north magnetic pole was at 76° north altitude and 101° west longitude; the south magnetic pole was at 66°south altitude and 140° east longitude.

D

【地大物博】dì dà wù bó 土地广大，物产丰富 large territory that abounds in natural resources：我国～，人口众多。Our country has a big territory, rich natural resources and a large population.

【地带】dìdài 具有某种性质或范围的一片地方 tract of land with a certain feature or boundary：丘陵～ hilly area|草原～ grassland|危险～ danger zone

【地道】dìdào 在地面下掘成的交通坑道（多用于军事 usu. for military purposes）underground tunnel for transportation

【地道】dì·dao ❶ 真正是有名产地出产的 from the place well-known for a certain product：～药材 genuine medicine ❷ 真正的；纯粹 real; pure：她的普通话说得真～。She speaks standard *putonghua*. ❸（工作或材料的质量）实在；够标准（quality of work or material）good; up to standard：他干的活儿真～。His work is really well done.

【地点】dìdiǎn 所在的地方 locale：开会～在大礼堂。The big auditorium is the place for meetings.|在这里设个商场，～倒还适中。This should be an appropriate site for a department store.

【地动】dìdòng 地震的俗称 popular term for 地震 dìzhèn

【地动仪】dìdòngyí 候风地动仪的简称 abbr. for 候风地动仪 hòufēng dìdòngyí

【地洞】dìdòng 在地面下挖成的洞 hole dug in the ground; underground cave

【地段】dìduàn 指地面上的一段或一定区域 section or district (of a town)：繁华～busy district|这里是属东城区管辖的～。This area is under the administration of the East District.

【地方】dìfāng ❶ 各级行政区划的统称（跟'中央'相对 as opposed to 'central'）local administration：中央工业和～工业同时并举 attach equal importance to centrally and locally administrated industries alike ❷ 本地；当地 native or local place：他在农村的时候，常给～上的群众治病。He used to provide medical treatment to the local people while in the countryside.

【地方】dì·fang ❶（～儿 dì·fangr）某一区域；空间的一部分；部位 a certain region; space; place：你是什么～的人？Where are you from?|你听，飞机在什么～飞？Can you hear where the plane is flying?|会场里人都坐满了，没有～了。The meeting place is so crowded that there is no room left.|我这个～有点疼。I feel painful here. ❷ 部分 part：这话有对的～，也有不对的～。Part of what you say is right, part of it wrong.

【地方病】dìfāngbìng 经常发生在某一地区的疾病，例如我国东北的克山病 endemic disease; disease that frequently occurs in a certain region, such as the Keshan disease in China's northeast

【地方民族主义】dìfāng mínzú zhǔyì 在民族关系上表现出来的一种反动思想。它打着维护本民族利益的幌子，实际上是破坏民族团结和国家统一。local nationalism; reactionary ideology concerning relations between different ethnic groups that does harm to ethnic and national unity in the name of safeguarding the interests of one's own ethnic group; also 狭隘民族主义 xiá'ài mínzú zhǔyì

【地方时】dìfāngshí 各地因经度不同，太阳经过各地子午线的时间也不相同，把太阳正对某地子午线的时间定为该地中午十二点，这样定出的时间叫做地方时 local time. Due to difference in longitude of the earth, the sun shines at the meridian of different zones at different times. Local time is the common standard time of a zone established with 12 a. m. set at the point of time when the sun shines directly at the meridian of that zone.

【地方税】dìfāngshuì 根据财政制度规定，划归地方管理并由地方征收留用的税款 local tax; tax collected and used by local governments in accordance with state finance policies

【地方戏】dìfāngxì 产生在某一地区，用当地方言演唱，具有乡土色彩的剧种，如汉剧、湘剧、川剧、越剧等 local opera; opera that originated in a certain region and is performed in local dialect with local features, such as Hubei, Hunan, Sichuan, and Zhejiang operas

【地方性植物】dìfāngxìng zhíwù 多分布在一个区域或一个地方的植物 endemic plant; plant that grows in a certain region or locality; also 风土性植物 fēngtǔxìng zhíwù

【地方志】dìfāngzhì same as 方志 fāngzhì

【地方主义】dìfāng zhǔyì 只强调本地方的利益、不顾全局利益的错误思想 regionalism; localism; idea or thought that emphasizes regional or local interests to the neglect of overall interests

【地府】dìfǔ 迷信的人指人死后灵魂所在的地方 underworld; place where ghosts stay, as believed by the superstitious：阴曹～ Hades; nether world

【地覆天翻】dì fù tiān fān ☞ 天翻地覆 tiān fān

dì fù on p. 1889

【地根儿】dìgēnr〈方 *dial.*〉根本；从来（多用于否定 usu. in a negative sense) essential; ever: ～就不行 absolutely impossible | 我～不认识他。I don't know him at all.

【地埂】dìgěng（～儿 dìgěngr）田地间的埂子 narrow ridge between fields; also 地埂子 dìgěng·zi

【地宫】dìgōng ❶ 帝王陵墓地面下安放棺椁的建筑物 underground palace; structure underneath the tumulus of an emperor's tomb, where the coffin is placed: 定陵～ Dingling Underground Palace ❷ 佛寺保藏舍利、器物等的地下建筑物 underground structure of a Buddhist temple where sarīras and other Buddhist relics are concealed

【地沟】dìgōu 地下的沟渠，多用来灌溉或排除雨水、污水等 underground drainage or canal for irrigation, or rain or sewage drainage

【地瓜】dìguā〈方 *dial.*〉❶ 甘薯 sweet potato (*Ipomoea batatas*) ❷ 豆薯 yam bean (*Pachyrrhizus erosus*)

【地核】dìhé 地球的中心部分，半径约 3,470 公里 earth's core, with a radius of about 3,470 km.

【地黄牛】dìhuángniú 玩具，用竹筒做成的陀螺，旋转时发出嗡嗡的声音 spinning top fashioned out of bamboo tube, producing a wheezing sound when turning

【地积】dìjī 土地的面积，过去通常用顷、亩、分等单位来计算，现在用平方米来计算 measure of land, usu. in terms of hectare, *mu*, and *fen* in the past, now mostly in terms of square metre

【地基】dìjī ❶ 承受建筑物重量的土层或岩层，土层一般经过夯实。有的地区叫地脚（dì·jiǎo）foundation; layer of usu. rammed earth or rock to sustain the weight of a building; also called 地脚 dì·jiǎo in some places ❷ same as 地皮 dìpí ②：挖沟占了他家的～。The (newly dug) ditch infringed upon his family estate.

【地极】dìjí 地球的南极和北极 either of the north and south poles of the earth

【地脚】dìjiǎo 书页下边的空白处 lower margin of a book page: 天头～ upper and lower margins

【地脚】dì·jiǎo〈方 *dial.*〉same as 地基 dìjī①：挖～ dig up earth to lay a foundation | 打～ lay a foundation

【地脚螺丝】dìjiǎo luósī 把机器等紧紧固定在基础上用的螺丝 anchor bolt, used to fix a machine to a base; also 地脚螺栓 dàjiǎo luóshuān

【地窖】dìjiào 保藏薯类、蔬菜等的地洞或地下室 cellar; underground cave or room used to keep potatoes and vegetables

【地界】dìjiè ❶ 两块土地之间的界线 boundary between two pieces of land: 去掉田塍～，增加耕地面积。Level the ridges between fields to increase the arable acreage. ❷ 地区；管界 district; administrative area: 出了北京市就是河北～。Once out of Beijing, you are in the area of Hebei Province.

【地牢】dìláo 地面下的牢狱 dungeon: 打入～ throw sb. into a dungeon

【地老天荒】dì lǎo tiān huāng ☞天荒地老 tiānhuāng dì lǎo on p. 1890

【地雷】dìléi 一种爆炸性武器，多埋入地下，装有特种引火装置 (land) mine; explosive weapon, usu. buried underground, with a special igniting device

【地梨】dìlí ❶ 多年生草本植物，野生在湿地里，地下茎像荸荠而较小，可以吃 wild water chestnut, perennial herb found in wet land, with an edible tuber growing underground that is smaller than water chestnut ❷ 这种植物的地下球茎 underground tuber of this herb ❸〈方 *dial.*〉荸荠 water chestnut (*Eleocharis tuberosa*)

【地理】dìlǐ ❶ 全世界或一个地区的山川、气候等自然环境及特产、交通、居民点等社会经济因素的总的情况 natural features of the world or a region, such as mountains and rivers, and climate, and the comprehensive conditions of products, transportation, settlements and other socio-economic factors: 自然～ physical geography | 经济～ economic geography ❷ 地理学 geography ❸〈方 *dial.*〉风水 *fengshui*: ～先生（看风水的人）geomancer (person good at telling *fengshui*)

【地理学】dìlǐxué 以地理为研究对象的学科。通常分为自然地理学和经济地理学。自然地理学研究人类社会的自然环境，经济地理学研究生产的地理布局以及各国和各地区生产发展的条件和特点，两者之间有不可分割的联系。geography; study of geographical features, usu. in two branches: physical geography, which deals with the natural environment of human society and the geographical arrangement of production, and economic geography, which studies the conditions and features of individual countries and regions

【地力】dìlì 土地肥沃的程度 soil fertility: 多施底肥，增加～ supply more base fertilizer to increase soil fertility

【地利】dìlì ❶ 地理的优势 advantage in geographical position: 天时～ opportune time and position ❷ 土地有利于种植作物的条件 land conditions favourable for growing crops: 充分发挥～，适合种什么就种什么。In order to make the best of a piece of land, one should plant what is appropriate with its conditions.

【地栗】dìlì〈方 *dial.*〉荸荠 water chestnut

【地邻】dìlín 甲乙两方的耕地邻接，彼此互为地邻 bordering of two fields

【地垄】dìlǒng 在耕地上培成的一行一行的土埂 lines of earthen ridges on tilled land

【地漏】dìlòu（～儿 dìlòur）试验室、厨房、浴室、厕所等地面上设置的排水孔，和下水道相通 floor drain; drainage hole on the floor of a lab, kitchen, bathroom, or toilet, connected with the sewage

【地脉】dìmài 迷信的人讲风水所说的地形好坏 favourable or unfavourable conditions of a terrain, or *fengshui*, as believed by the superstitious

【地幔】dìmàn 地球内介于地壳和地核之间的部分，厚度约2,900公里 earth's mantle, between its crust and core, about 2,900 km. thick

【地貌】dìmào 地球表面的形态 landform; general configuration of the earth's surface

【地面】dìmiàn ❶ 地的表面 land surface：高出～五尺 five *chi* above ground｜两边空出三尺宽五尺长的～ leave a space of three *chi* wide and five *chi* long on either side ❷ 房屋等建筑物内部以及周围的地上铺筑的一层东西，材料多为木头、砖石、混凝土等 floor or pavement of an area around a house or building, mostly built of wood, brick, stone, or concrete：瓷砖～ floor laid with ceramic tiles｜水磨石～ terrazzo floor or pavement ❸ 地区(多指行政区域)(administrative) area：这里已经进入山东～。We are already in Shandong (Province) here. ❹（～儿 dìmiànr）当地 local place：他在～儿上很有威信。He has a high prestige in this area.

【地膜】dìmó 覆盖作物的塑料薄膜，主要用来保护幼株，抵挡风寒 mulch film; plastic sheet used to cover seedlings, protecting them against wind and cold：～覆盖育苗 grow seedlings under a plastic-film cover｜推广～植棉 popularize mulching for growing cotton seedlings

【地亩】dìmǔ 田地（总称）(collect.) farmland：丈量～ measure farmland

【地菍】dìniè 多年生草本植物，叶子倒卵形或椭圆形，花紫红色，浆果球形。全草入药。*Melastoma dodecandrum Lour.*; perennial herb with egg-shaped or oval leaves, purplish red flowers, and ball-like berries, the entire herb used as a medicine; also 铺地锦 pūdìjǐn or 地石榴 dìshí·liu

【地盘】dìpán（～儿 dìpánr）❶ 占用或控制的地方；势力范围 domain; territory under one's occupation or control：争夺～ fight for control of an area ❷〈方 *dial.*〉建筑物的地基 foundation of a building：～下沉。The foundation is sinking.

【地皮】dìpí ❶（～儿 dìpír）地的表面 ground：下雨以后，～还没有干。The rain has left the ground wet. ❷ 供建筑等用的土地 land for construction purposes：城市里～很紧张。There isn't much land left for construction in the city.

【地痞】dìpǐ 地方上的坏分子 local thugs：～流氓 thugs and rascals

【地平线】dìpíngxiàn 向水平方向望去，天跟地交界的线 horizon; line at which the sky and the earth seem to meet when observed horizontally at a distance：一轮红日，正从～上升起。The red sun is rising from the horizon.

【地铺】dìpù 把铺盖铺在地上做成的铺位 makeshift bed on the floor：打～ prepare a makeshift bed on the floor｜睡～ sleep in a makeshift bed

【地契】dìqì 买卖土地时所立的契约 title deed for land transfer

【地壳】dìqiào 由岩石构成的地球外壳，主要成分是氧、硅、铝、镁、铁等。平均厚度大陆地壳约35公里，海底地壳约6公里。earth's crust of rocks, consisting mainly of oxygen, silicon, aluminium, magnesium, iron, etc., about 35 km. thick on land and six km. on seabed

【地勤】dìqín 航空部门指在地面上执行的各种工作，如维修飞机等(区别于'空勤'as compared with 'air service') ground service; work related to aviation that is performed on the ground, such as repair of aircraft, etc.：～人员 ground crew or personnel

【地球】dìqiú 太阳系九大行星之一，按离太阳由近而远的次序计为第三颗，形状像球而略扁，赤道半径约6,378.2公里，极半径约6,356.8公里，自转一周的时间是一昼夜，绕太阳一周的时间是一年。周围有大气层包围，表面是陆地和海洋，有人类和动植物等生存。有一个卫星(月球)。earth; the third, in terms of distance from the sun, of the nine planets of the solar system, shaped like a ball with a small degree of fatness. The earth's equatorial radius is about 6,378.2 km., its polar radius about 6,356.8 km. The earth's one rotation is a day and a night, and one revolution around the sun is a year. Surrounded by atmosphere and covered by land and oceans, the earth is inhabited by human beings, animals and plants. It has one natural satellite, the moon. (图见 ☞ figure for 太阳系 tàiyángxì on p. 1855)

【地球仪】dìqiúyí 地球的模型，装在支架上，可以转动，上面画着海洋、陆地、河流、山脉、经纬线等。供教学和军事上用。terrestrial globe; model of the earth which is installed on a stand and can be rotated to indicate oceans, land, rivers, mountains, meridian, parallel lines, etc., for teaching and military purposes

【地区】dìqū ❶ 较大范围的地方 large area：湖北西部～ western region of Hubei (Province)｜多山～ mountainous area｜这个～最适宜种小麦。This region is most appropriate for growing wheat. ❷ 我国省、自治区设立的行政区域，一般包括若干县、市 prefecture; administrative region with several counties and cities under its jurisdiction;〈旧称 *old*〉专区

zhuānqū ❸ 指未获得独立的殖民地、托管地等 colonial territory; trust territory

【地权】dìquán 土地所有权 land ownership

【地儿】dìr 坐或立的地方;容纳的地方 place for sitting or standing; place for containing sth.:在那间房里腾个～放书柜。Find a space in that room to place a bookcase.|里边有～,请里边坐。There's room inside; pleased come in and sit down.

【地热】dìrè 指存在于地球内部的热 terrestrial heat; heat inside the earth:开发利用～资源 develop and use terrestrial heat; also 地下热 dìxiàrè

【地煞】dìshà ❶ 星相家指主管凶杀的星 star in charge of killings on earth, according to astrologers ❷ 指凶神恶鬼 ominous spirit or ghost;〈比喻 *fig*.〉恶势力 evil force

【地上茎】dìshàngjīng 植物的茎生长在地面以上的部分 aerial stem; part of the stem of a plant growing above ground

【地势】dìshì 地面高低起伏的形势 terrain; features of a piece of land being high or low:～险要 strategically located terrain with difficult access|～平坦 flat terrain

【地摊】dìtān (～儿 dìtānr)就地陈列货物出卖的摊子 street stall, where a vendor displays his goods on the ground:摆～儿 set up a street stall

【地毯】dìtǎn 铺在地上的毯子 carpet; rug

【地铁】dìtiě ❶ 地下铁道的简称 abbr. for 地下铁道 dìxià tiědào:～车站 subway station ❷ 指地铁列车 tube train:坐～比坐公共汽车快。It's faster to take the tube than the bus.

【地头】[1] dìtóu ❶ (～儿 dìtóur)田地的两端 either edge of a field:～地脑 edges of a field|请大家在～休息一会儿。Please take a break by the edges of the field, everybody. ❷〈方 *dial*.〉目的地 destination:快到～了,你准备下车吧。We'll soon arrive at your station. You can prepare to get off. ❸〈方 *dial*.〉(～儿 dìtóur)本地方;当地 local place:你～儿熟,联系起来方便。As you know the place well, it's easy for you to make contacts there.

【地头】[2] dìtóu 书页下端的空白处 lower margin of a page; ☞天地头 tiāndìtóu on p.1888

【地头蛇】dìtóushé 指当地的强横无赖、欺压人民的坏人 snake in its old haunt; local thug or bully who suppresses the people

【地图】dìtú 说明地球表面的事物和现象分布情况的图,上面标着符号和文字,有时也着上颜色 map; picture that shows the distribution of things and phenomena on the earth, marked with symbols and words, and coloured in some cases:军用～ military map|中华人民共和国～ Map of the People's Republic of China|一张大～ a large map|世界～ map of the world

【地位】dìwèi ❶ 人或团体在社会关系中所处的位置 (of a person or group) position or status in social relations:学术～ academic position|国际～ international standing|～平等 equal status|提高～ improve one's status ❷ (人或物)所占的地方 place or space (occupied by sb. or sth.)

【地温】dìwēn 地表面和土层不同深度的温度 ground or earth temperature; temperature on the surface or at different depths of the earth

【地物】dìwù 分布在地面上的固定性物体,如居民点、道路、水利工程建筑等 surface features; fixed structures on the ground, such as residential quarters, roads, and irrigation projects, etc.:利用地形～做掩护 take terrain and surface features for cover

【地峡】dìxiá 海洋中连接两块陆地的狭窄陆地 isthmus; narrow strip of land in the sea, connecting two larger pieces of land

【地下】dìxià ❶ 地面之下;地层内部 underground; subterranean:～水 groundwater|～铁道 tube; subway|～商场 underground store ❷ 秘密活动的;不公开的 (of activity) secret; underground:～党 underground party|～工作 underground work|转入～ go underground

【地下】dì·xia 地面上 on the ground:钢笔掉在～。The pen fell on the ground.|～一点灰尘都没有,像洗过的一样。There is not a speck of dust on the ground, as if it has just been washed.

【地下茎】dìxiàjīng 植物的茎生长在地面以下的部分,如根茎、块茎、鳞茎等 subterranean stem; part of the stem of a plant that grows underground, such as rhizome, tuber, bulb, etc.

【地下室】dìxiàshì 全部或一部分建筑在地下的房间(多为多层建筑的最下一层)(oft. the lowest floor of a multi-floored building) basement; room completely or partially underground

【地下水】dìxiàshuǐ 地面下的水,主要是雨水和其他地表水渗入地下,聚积在土壤或岩层的空隙中形成的 groundwater, mainly rain and other surface water that has seeped underground and gathered in soil or gaps between rocks

【地下铁道】dìxià tiědào 修建在地下隧道中的铁道 tube; subway; railway built in an underground tunnel

【地线】dìxiàn 电器与地相接的导线。无线电技术上,常将地线作为高频电路的一个回路。其他电器的金属外壳常接上地线,以防电器内部绝缘破坏时使外壳带电而发生触电事故。ground wire; earth wire; wire used to connect an electrical appliance with the ground. In radio technology, ground wire is oft. formed into a loop of a high-frequency circuit. The metal case of an electrical appliance is oft. linked with a ground wire to prevent accidents of electric shock when the case becomes electrified due to damage of insulation inside the appliance.

【地心说】dìxīnshuō〈古时 *arch.*〉天文学上一种学说，认为地球居于宇宙中心静止不动，太阳、月球和其他星球都围绕地球运行 geocentricism; theory in ancient astronomy contending that the earth remains still in the centre of the universe, while the sun, the moon, and other planets rotate around it

【地心引力】dìxīn yǐnlì 地球吸引其他物体的力，力的方向指向地心。物体落到地上就是这种力作用的结果。terrestrial gravity; gravity; force of the earth that attracts other objects towards its core, an instance of which is seen in the fall of things onto the ground; also 重力 zhònglì

【地形】dìxíng ❶ 地理学上指地貌（geog.）topography; terrain ❷ 测绘学上地貌和地物的总称 general term for terrain and surface features in cartography

【地形图】dìxíngtú 表示地面上地貌、水系、植被、工程建筑、居民点等的地图 topographic map; map that shows the terrain, water systems, vegetation, engineering projects, residential areas, etc., on the ground

【地学】dìxué 地质学、地球物理学、地球化学、古生物学、海洋学、大气物理学、自然资源考察等的统称 earth science; general term for geology, geophysics, geochemistry, palaeontology, oceanology, atmospheric physics, the survey of natural resources, etc.

【地衣】dìyī 低等生物的一类，是藻类与某些低等光合生物的共生联合体，种类很多，生长在地面、树皮或岩石上 lichen; a class of low plant that is a composite of algae and some low photosynthetic organisms, of a large variety, growing on the ground, on tree barks or rocks

【地窨子】dìyìn·zi ❶ 地下室 basement ❷ 地窖 cellar

【地狱】dìyù ❶ 某些宗教指人死后灵魂受苦的地方（跟‘天堂’相对 as opposed to ‘heaven’）hell; place where souls of the dead suffer, as believed in some religions ❷〈比喻 *fig.*〉黑暗而悲惨的生活环境 dark and miserable living conditions

【地域】dìyù ❶ 面积相当大的一块地方 large area：～辽阔 vast in territory ❷ 地方（指本乡本土）local place：～观念 regionalism

【地震】dìzhèn 由地球内部的变动引起的地壳的震动，分为陷落地震、火山地震和构造地震三种。俗称地动。earthquake; seism; shaking of the earth's crust, caused by movements within the earth, known in general terms as 地动 dìdòng. There are three types of earthquake: depression, volcanic and structural.

【地震波】dìzhènbō 由于地震而产生的向四外传播的震动。主要由横波、纵波组成。seismic wave; radiating vibration caused by an earthquake, mainly in horizontal and vertical directions; also 震波 zhènbō

【地震烈度】dìzhèn lièdù 地震发生后在地面上造成的影响或破坏的程度，与地震震级并不成比例。地震烈度分为十二度。earthquake intensity; degree of influence or damage on the ground caused by an earthquake, which is divided into 12 scales and not necessarily in proportion with its magnitude; 简称 abbr. 烈度 lièdù

【地震震级】dìzhèn zhènjí 划分震源放出的能量大小的等级。释放能量越大，地震震级也越大。地震震级分为九级。一般小于 2.5 级的地震人无感觉；2.5 级以上人有感觉；5 级以上的地震就会造成破坏。earthquake magnitude; energy released from a seismic focus. The greater the energy, the bigger the magnitude, which is divided into nine (Richter) scales. Earthquake below 2.5 magnitude on the Richter scale cannot be felt by human beings; that above 2.5 can be felt; that above 5 will cause damage. 简称 abbr. 震级 zhènjí

【地政】dìzhèng 有关土地的管理、利用、征用等行政事务 land administration; administrative affairs concerning management, use, requisition of land, etc.

【地支】dìzhī 子、丑、寅、卯、辰、巳、午、未、申、酉、戌、亥的总称，传统用做表示次序的符号 Earthly Branches; *zi*, *chou*, *yin*, *mao*, *chen*, *si*, *wu*, *wei*, *shen*, *you*, *xu*, *hai* — traditional terms indicating order; also 十二支 shí'èrzhī; ☞干支 gānzhī on p. 627

【地址】dìzhǐ（人、团体）居住或通信的地点（of a person or group）place of residence; mailing address; address

【地质】dìzhì 地壳的成分和结构 composition and structure of the earth's crust

【地质年代】dìzhì niándài 地壳中不同年代的岩石形成的时间和先后顺序。相对地质年代主要依据岩石的层位和岩石中的化石，指明岩石生成时间的顺序，如古生代、中生代、新生代等；绝对地质年代依据岩石中放射性同位素蜕变产物的含量，指明岩石生成至今的年数。geochronology; dating of rock formation of the earth's crust. Relative age, such as Palaeozoic, Mesozoic and Cenozoic, refers to the time order in which rocks have formed by studying their position and the fossils contained in them. Absolute age refers to the number of years between the formation of rocks and the present, established by studying radioactive decay of isotopes in the rocks. ☞地质年代表 dìzhì niándàibiǎo

【地质学】dìzhìxué 研究构成地球的物质和地壳构造，以探讨地球的形成和发展的学科 geology; science that studies the substance, formation and development of the earth, and the structure of the earth's crust

地质年代表 Geological Time Scale*

宙 Eon	代 Era	纪 Period	符号 Sign	同位素年龄 Isotopic age (单位百万年 million years) 开始时间 Start	持续时间 Duration	生物发展的阶段 Development of organisms
显生宙 Phanerozoic (PH)	新生代 (KZ) Cenozoic	第四纪 Quaternary	Q	2.6	20.7	本纪初期人科出现 appearance of early man in the Early Quaternary
		新近纪 Neogene	N	23.3	41.7	植物和动物逐渐接近现代。出现三趾马(*Hipparion*)。有孔虫为 N_4—N_{23} 带。fauna and flora gradually approaching modern forms; appearance of *Hipparion*; foraminifers of the N_4—N_{23} zones
		古近纪 Paleogen	E	65	72	植物和动物发育。有孔虫为 P_1—P_{22} 带。development of fauna and flora; foraminifers of the P_1—P_{22} zones
	中生代 (MZ) Mesozoic	白垩纪 Cretaceous	K	135	68	本纪后期,被子植物大量发现。有孔虫兴盛。菊石和箭石渐趋绝迹。爬行类至后期急剧减少。appearance of abundant angiosperms in the Late Cretaceous; flourishing foraminifers; ammonites and belemnites approaching extinction; rapid decrease of reptiles in the Late Mesozoic
		侏罗纪 Jurassic	J	203	47	真蕨、苏铁、银杏和松柏类等繁荣。箭石和菊石兴盛。巨大的爬行类(恐龙)发展。鸟类出现。flourishing pteridophytes, gymnosperms, ginkgo, pine, and cypress; abundant belemnites and ammonites; rise of giant reptiles (dinosaurs); appearance of birds
		三叠纪 Triassic	T	250	45	裸子植物进一步发展。腕足类减少。菊石和瓣鳃类发育。迷齿类绝迹。爬行类发展。哺乳类出现。further development of gymnosperms; decrease of brachiopods; development of ammonites and lamellibranches; extinction of labyrinthodonts; emergence of reptiles; appearance of mammals
	古生代 (PZ) Palaeozoic	二叠纪 Permian	P	295	60	至晚期,木本石松、芦木、种子蕨、科达树等趋于衰落,裸子植物如松柏类等开始发展。菊石、腕足类等继续发展。本纪末,四射珊瑚、床板珊瑚、三叶虫、蜓类绝灭。decline of woody lycopods, calamites, pteridosperms and *Cordaioxylon*, and rise of gymnosperms like pine and cypress, in the Late Permian; continued development of ammonites and brachiopods; extinction of tetradactyl corals, tabulatas, trilobites and fusulinids by the end of the Paleozoic
		石炭纪 Carboniferous	C	355	65	真蕨、木本石松、芦木、种子蕨、科达树等大量繁荣。笔石衰亡。珊瑚、蜓类、腕足类很多。两栖类进一步发展。爬行类出现。great abundance of woody lycopods, calamites, pteridosperms and *Cordaioxylon*; decline and disappearance of graptolites; abundant

						corals, fusulinids and brachiopods; further development of amphibians; appearance of reptiles
显生宙 Phanerozoic (PH)	古生代 (PZ) Palaeozoic	泥盆纪 Devonian	D	410	25	在早期裸蕨类繁荣，中期后，蕨类植物和原始裸子植物出现。腕足类和珊瑚发育。原始菊石出现。昆虫和原始两栖类（迷齿类）最初发现。鱼类发展。至晚期，无颌类趋于绝灭。abundance of psilophytes in the Early Devonian; appearance of pteridophytes and primordial gymnosperms after the Middle Devonian; development of brachiopods and corals; appearance of earliest ammonites; first insects and primordial amphibians (labyrinthodonts); development of fishes; Agnatha approaching extinction in the late Devonian
		志留纪 Silurian	S	435	65	在末期，裸蕨类开始出现。腕足类和珊瑚繁荣。三叶虫和笔石仍繁盛。无颌类发育。至晚期，原始鱼类出现。appearance of psilophytes in the Late Silurian; flourishing brachiopods and corals; continued abundance of trilobites and graptolites; development of Agnatha; appearance of primitive fishes in the Late Silurian
		奥陶纪 Ordovician	O	500	60	藻类广泛发育。海生无脊椎动物和三叶虫、笔石、头足类、腕足类、棘皮动物（海林檎）等非常繁盛，板足鲎类出现。发现可靠的四射珊瑚。钙藻发育。extensive development of algae; extraordinary abundance of marine invertebrates, trilobites, graptolites, cephalopods, brachiopods, echinoderms (cystoideas); appearance of eurypterids; discovery of anthentic tetradactyl corals; development of calcareous algae
		寒武纪 Cambrian	Є	540	40	红藻、绿藻等开始繁盛。与元古代化石记录相比，若干门类无脊椎动物，尤其是三叶虫等开始繁荣。低等腕足类、古杯动物等发育。rise of red and green algae; growing abundance of sevearal phyla and classes of invertebrates, esp. trilobites compared to fossil records of the Proterozoic; development of low forms of brachiopods and Archaeocyatha

元古宙 Protorozoic (PR)	新元古代 Neoproterozoic	新元古纪 III Neoproterozoic III	NP_3	650	110	出现全球后生动物,具刺疑源类再度繁盛,并出现早期胚胎化石 appearance of metazoa; re-prosperity of acathomorphita acritarchs; appearance of early fossilization of embryos
		成冰纪 Cryogenian	NP_2	850	200	全球雪球事件,为生物低潮 'snow ball' in many countinents; lower evolution of fauna and flora
		拉伸纪 Tonian	NP_1	1000	150	首次出现大型具刺凝源类 first appearance of acathomorphite acritarchs
	中元古代 Mesoproterozoic	狭带纪 Stenian	MP_3	1200	200	蓝藻、褐藻发育,出现大型宏观藻类 development of blue green algae and brown algae; appearance of macro-paleoalgae
		延展纪 Ectasian	MP_2	1400	200	
		盖层纪 Calymmian	MP_1	1600	200	
	古元古代 Paleoproterozoic	固结纪 Statherian	PP_4	1800	200	蓝藻、细菌繁盛 prosperity of blue green algae and bacteria
		造山纪 Orosirian	PP_3	2050	250	
		层侵纪 Rhyacian	PP_2	2300	250	
		成铁纪 Siderian	PP_1	2500	200	
太古宙 (AR) Archeozoic		没有国际性的划分方案 no internationally acknowledged time boundary		4500	2100	晚期有菌类和低等蓝藻存在,但可靠的化石记录不多 existence of bacteria and low forms of blue green algae, with few reliable fossil records available

* 译者注:征得中国社会科学院语言研究所同意,双语版根据国际地层委员会和中国地层委员会各自公布的最新地层年表,更新了本表部分内容,以浅色网纹标出。Translator's Note: The latest International Stratigraphic Charts published respectively by the International Commission on Stratigraphy and the Chinese Commission on Stratigraphy have rendered some of the information provided in the table in the 2002 Enlarged Edition of *The Contemporary Chinese Dictionary* obsolete. With permission from the Chinese Academy of Social Sciences Institute of Linguistics, we have made some alterations accordingly, which are highlighted with a grey screen.

【地轴】dìzhóu 地球自转的轴线,和赤道平面相垂直 earth's axis; axis of the earth's rotation, which is perpendicular to its equatorial plane

【地主】dìzhǔ ❶ 占有土地,自己不劳动,依靠出租土地剥削农民为主要生活来源的人 landlord; landowner who does not till the land but collects rents from peasants working on rented land ❷ 指住在本地的人(跟外地来的客人相对 as opposed to guest) host:略尽~之谊 offer a host's friendship

【地租】dìzū 依靠土地所有权获得的收入。在封建制度下,地租是地主从农民直接剥削来的。在资本主义经营的形式下,土地所有者出租土地给农业资本家,农业资本家把超过平均利润的那部分剩余价值作为地租交给土地所有者。land rent; income from ownership of land. Under the feudal system, land rent came from direct exploitation of peasants by landlords. Under capitalist management, landowners leased land to farming capitalists, who paid as rent to the former surplus value above the average profit.

玓 dì [玓珠](dìlì)〈书 *fml.*〉珠光 lustre of pearl

杕 dì〈书 *fml.*〉形容树木孤立 (of a tree) stand alone

☞ duò on p. 502

弟 dì ❶ 弟弟 younger brother：二～ second younger brother | 小～ youngest brother | 胞～ full younger brother | 堂～ younger (male) cousin whose father is one's paternal uncle ❷ 亲戚中同辈而年纪比自己小的男子 younger male cousins or in-laws：表～younger (male) cousin related to one's paternal aunt, or maternal uncle or aunt | 妻～ wife's younger brother；brother-in-law ❸ 朋友相互间的谦称（多用于书信 oft. in written correspondence）modest reference to oneself among (male) friends ❹ (Dì) 姓 a surname
〈古 *arch*.〉same as 第 dì in 第[1] and 第[3]；also same as 悌 tì

D

【弟弟】dì·di ❶ 同父母（或只同父、只同母）而年纪比自己小的男子 younger brother of the same parents (or one of the parents) ❷ 同辈而年纪比自己小的男子 younger male cousin：叔伯～ younger cousin who is the son of one's paternal uncle

【弟妇】dìfù 弟弟的妻子 wife of one's younger brother；sister-in-law

【弟妹】dìmèi ❶ 弟弟和妹妹 younger brother and sister ❷ same as 弟妇 dìfù

【弟兄】dì·xiong 弟弟和哥哥 younger brother and elder brother a) 不包括本人［excluding oneself］：他没有～，只有一个姐姐。He does not have any brothers, only an elder sister. b) 包括本人［including oneself］：他们是亲～。They are blood brothers. | 他（们）～两个 the two brothers | 他就～一个（没有哥哥或弟弟）。He does not have any brothers. ◇支援农民～ provide aid to our peasant brothers

【弟子】dìzǐ〈旧称 *old*〉学生；徒弟 disciple；pupil or student；apprentice

的 dì 箭靶的中心 bull's eye：目～ purpose；goal | 无～放矢 shoot an arrow without aiming at a target | 众矢之～ target of public criticism
☞ ·de on p. 405 and dí on p. 414

佛 dì 用于人名 used as a given name；same as 弟 dì

帝 dì ❶ 宗教徒或神话中称宇宙的创造者和主宰者 God；Supreme Being；creator and governor of the universe as described in religion or mythology：上～ God | 天～ Heavenly King | 玉皇大～ Jade Emperor of Heaven ❷ 君主；皇帝 king；emperor：称～ ascend the throne | 三皇五～ three emperors (Fuxi, Suiren, and Shennong; or Heavenly, Earthly, and Human Emperors) and five kings (Huangdi, Zhuanxu, Di Ku, Tang Yao, and Yu Shun)；legendary rules of ancient China ❸ 帝国主义的简称 abbr. for 帝国主义 dìguó zhǔyì：反～斗争 struggle against imperialism

【帝俄】Dì'é 指沙皇统治下的俄国 Russia under the czar；also 沙俄 Shā'é

【帝国】dìguó ❶ 一般指版图很大或有殖民地的君主国家，如罗马帝国、英帝国。没有帝王而向外扩张的国家，有时也称为帝国，如希特勒统治下的德国叫第三帝国。empire；monarchical state with a large territory or colonies, such as the Roman Empire and the British Empire；country without a monarchy but that extends its power and influence abroad, such as the Third Reich (Germany under Hitler's rule) ❷〈比喻 *fig*.〉经济实力强大的企业集团 business empire；enterprise group：石油～ oil empire

【帝国主义】dìguó zhǔyì ❶ 资本主义发展的最高阶段。它的基本特征是垄断代替了自由竞争，形成金融寡头的统治。imperialism；the highest level of capitalism, characterized by monopoly instead of free competition and the rule of financial oligarchs ❷ 指帝国主义国家 imperialist state

【帝君】dìjūn 迷信的人对地位较高的神的称呼，如文昌帝君 respectful reference to gods with a high status, such as the god of literature

【帝王】dìwáng 指君主国的最高统治者 emperor；king；monarch；the highest ruler of a monarchical state

【帝制】dìzhì 君主专制政体 autocratic monarchy：推翻～ overthrow autocratic monarchy

递（遞） dì ❶ 传送；传递 hand over；pass：投～ deliver | 把报～给我。Please pass me the newspaper. | 呈～国书 present state credentials | 给她～了个眼色。(I) gave her a wink. ❷ 顺次 progressively：～增 increase step by step | ～减 decrease steadily | ～升 rise higher and higher | ～降 drop constantly

【递补】dìbǔ 顺次补充 supplement in order：委员出缺，由候补委员～。Vacancies in the committee will be filled by alternate members in a proper order.

【递加】dìjiā same as 递增 dìzēng

【递减】dìjiǎn 一次比一次减少 decrease successively：劳动生产率逐步提高，产品的成本也随着～。With gradual rise of productivity, the cost of products has dropped step by step.

【递降】dìjiàng 一次比一次降低 become lower and lower：改进工艺，使原材料消耗逐月～。Improved techniques have led to a monthly reduction of consumption of raw materials.

【递交】dìjiāo 当面送交 present in person：～本人 deliver (sth.) to sb. in person | ～国书 present state credentials

【递解】dìjiè〈旧时 *old*〉指把犯人解往外地，由沿途官府派人递相押送 escort a criminal to another place, relayed by men designated by local governments along the way：～还乡 escort (a criminal) to his hometown in such manner

【递升】dìshēng 一次比一次升高 rise higher and higher

【递送】dìsòng 送(公文、信件等);投递 send (document, letter, etc.); deliver:～邮件 deliver mail|～情报 send out information

【递增】dìzēng 一次比一次增加 increase progressively:收入逐年～ income on the rise year by year|产销两旺,税利～。Thriving production and brisk sales lead to steady increase of tax payments and profits.

娣 dì ❶〈古时 *arch.*〉妇人称丈夫的弟妇为娣,丈夫的嫂子为姒(sì) wife of husband's younger brother, while *si* refers to wife of husband's elder brother:～姒(妯娌) wives of husband's younger and elder brothers ❷〈古时 *arch.*〉姐姐称妹妹为娣 form of address for a woman to call her younger sister

菂 dì〈书 *fml.*〉莲子 lotus seed

第1 dì ❶用在整数的数词的前边,表示次序,如第一、第十 [used before integers to indicate order, such as first, tenth] ❷〈书 *fml.*〉科第 grading of successful candidates in imperial examination:及～ candidates who passed palace-level imperial examination |落～fell in township-level imperial examination |不～fail in imperial examination

第2 dì 封建社会官僚的住宅 residence of a high official in feudal times:府～ official mansion|宅～ grand mansion|门～ social status of a fmily|进士～ residence of a successful candidate in imperial examination at the palace level

第3 dì〈书 *fml.*〉❶但是 but; however ❷仅;只 only

【第二产业】dì èr chǎnyè 指工业(包括采掘业、制造业、自来水、电力、蒸汽、热水、煤气)和建筑业 secondary industry (including mining, manufacturing, water works, power, steam energy, hot water supply, and coal gas) and construction

【第二次国内革命战争】Dì Èr Cì Guónèi Gémìng Zhànzhēng 1927—1937年中国人民在中国共产党领导下反对国民党反动统治的战争。这期间,党领导人民在许多省份开辟了农村根据地,实行了土地改革,成立了工农民主政府,建立了中国工农红军,多次粉碎了国民党反动派的'围剿',胜利地进行了二万五千里长征。Second Revolutionary Civil War (1927-1937), against the reactionary rule of the Kuomintang, during which the Communist Party of China opened up bases in the rural areas of many provinces, carried out land reform, established democratic political power of workers and peasants, founded the Chinese Workers and Peasants Red Army, defeated several campaigns of encirclement and suppression staged by the Kuomintang, and successfully completed the 25,000-*li* Long March; also 土地革命战争 Tǔdì Gémìng Zhànzhēng

【第二次世界大战】Dì Èr Cì Shìjiè Dàzhàn 1939—1945年法西斯国家德国、意大利、日本发动的世界规模的战争。这次战争从1931年日本侵占我国东北起开始酝酿,到1939年德国进攻波兰,英、法对德宣战而正式爆发。全世界人民的反法西斯斗争和中、苏、美、英、法等国结成的反法西斯联盟,最后取得胜利。Second World War (1939-1945); World War II; worldwide war staged by fascist Germany, Italy and Japan. The war began to brew up when Japan invaded China's northeast in 1931 and broke out on full scale when Germany launched attacks on Poland in 1939, leading to Britain and France's declaration of war against Germany. Anti-fascist struggles across the world and the anti-fascist alliance formed by China, the Soviet Union, the United States, Britain and France won final victory in the war.

【第二次鸦片战争】Dì Èr Cì Yāpiàn Zhànzhēng 1856—1860年英法等国对我国发动的侵略战争。第二次鸦片战争使我国继鸦片战争之后又一次大量丧失领土主权。Second Opium War (1856-1860); war of aggression against China started by Britain and France, which led to China's another massive loss of sovereign rights over its territory following the Opium War (1840-1842)

【第二审】dì'èrshěn 指上级法院按照上诉程序对第一审案件进行审理 second instance; (of a higher-level court) hear a first-instance case, in accordance with the procedure for appeal; 简称 abbr. 二审 èrshěn

【第二世界】dì èr shìjiè 指处在超级大国和发展中国家之间的发达国家(总称 general term) second world, referring to countries between superpower(s) and developing countries

【第二信号系统】dì èr xìnhào xìtǒng 语言或文字的刺激通过人的大脑皮层中相应的区域,就形成条件联系,大脑皮层的这种机能系统叫做第二信号系统。第二信号系统是人类特有的。因此,人类才能进行抽象的思维。第二信号系统以第一信号系统为基础,二者又紧密联系。例如吃过酸杏的人看见酸杏会分泌唾液,酸杏就是酸味的信号,这是第一信号。听到说'酸杏',也会分泌唾液,听到的'酸杏'是信号的信号,所以叫做第二信号。second signal system, referring to the physiological system of the cerebral cortex that forms conditional links when relevant areas of the cerebral cortex are stimulated by spoken or written language. The second signal system enables human beings to think in abstract terms. It is based on and closely related to the first signal system. For instance, those who have tasted sour apricots before will salivate at the sight of the fruit (first signal), and do the same when they hear the fruit mentioned (second signal).

【第二宇宙速度】dì èr yǔzhòu sùdù 宇宙速度的一级，物体具有11.2公里/秒的速度时，就可以克服地心引力，脱离地球，在太阳系中运行，这个速度叫做第二宇宙速度 second cosmic speed or velocity, 1.2km./second, at or above which an object can break away from the earth's gravity to move in the solar system; also 脱离速度 tuōlí sùdù

【第二职业】dì èr zhíyè 指职工在本职工作以外所从事的收取报酬的工作 second job; moonlighting

【第三产业】dì sān chǎnyè 通常指为生活、生产服务的行业，如商业、饮食业、修理业、旅游业、市内客运、货运、金融、保险、通信、信息、咨询、法律事务、文化教育、科学研究事业等 tertiary industry; service sector, including commerce, catering trade, repair trade, tourism, municipal transportation, cargo transportation, finance, insurance, telecommunications, information, consulting, legal services, culture and education, science and research, etc.

【第三次国内革命战争】Dì Sān Cì Guónèi Gémìng Zhànzhēng 1946—1949年中国人民在中国共产党领导下反对国民党反动派的战争。这次战争消灭了八百万国民党军队，推翻了国民党在大陆的反动统治，解放了全国绝大部分土地，完成了新民主主义革命，成立了中华人民共和国，并把帝国主义势力赶出中国大陆。Third Revolutionary Civil War or the War of Liberation (1946-1949), in which the Chinese people, under the leadership of the Communist Party of China, fought against the reactionary Kuomintang. The war wiped out 8 million Kuomintang troops, overthrew its rule in the mainland of China, liberated most part of the country, brought the New Democratic Revolution to completion, led to the founding of the People's Republic of China and drove the imperialist forces out of the country. also 解放战争 jiěfàng zhànzhēng

【第三人】dìsānrén 法律上指相对于原告和被告的第三位对案件具有利害关系的人 third party, as distinct from the plaintiff and the defendant, who is an interested person in a legal case

【第三世界】dì sān shìjiè 指亚洲、非洲、拉丁美洲以及其他地区的发展中国家(总称 general term) third world; general reference to developing countries in Asia, Africa, Latin America and other regions

【第三宇宙速度】dì sān yǔzhòu sùdù 宇宙速度的一级，物体具有16.7公里/秒的速度时，就可以脱离太阳系而进入其他星系，这个速度叫做第三宇宙速度 third cosmic speed or velocity, 16.7km./second, at which an object can break away from the solar system to enter into other galaxies

【第三者】dìsānzhě ❶ 当事双方以外的人或团体 third party; person or group as distinct from the two parties directly concerned with a legal case ❷ 特指插足于他人家庭，跟夫妇中的一方有不正当的男女关系的人 third party; person who has illicit sexual relations with either one of a married couple: ～插足 (of a third party) wedge in between a married couple

【第五纵队】dì wǔ zòngduì 1936年10月西班牙内战时，叛军用四个纵队进攻首都马德里，把潜伏在马德里城内进行破坏活动的反革命组织叫做第五纵队。后来泛指内部潜藏的敌方组织。fifth column. During the Spanish Civil War, the rebellious army applied four columns to attack the capital Madrid and called the reactionary organization engaged in sabotage within the city, the 'fifth column'. The term is later used as a general term for enemy organization planted in one's camp.

【第一】dìyī ❶ 排列在最前面的 first; foremost: 他考了～名。He came out number one in the exam. ❷ 最重要 most important: 百年大计，质量～。It is a project to last for a hundred years; quality comes first.

【第一把手】dì yī bǎ shǒu 领导班子中居于首位的负责人 first in command; chief; person holding primary responsibility in a leading group

【第一产业】dì yī chǎnyè 指农业(包括林业、牧业、渔业等) agriculture (including forestry, animal husbandry, fishery, etc.)

【第一次国内革命战争】Dì Yī Cì Guónèi Gémìng Zhànzhēng 1924—1927年中国人民在中国共产党领导下进行的反对帝国主义、北洋军阀的战争。这次战争以国共合作的统一战线为基础，1926年从广东出师北伐，很快发展到长江流域。由于国民党右派发动了反革命政变和党内右倾机会主义的错误领导，致使革命中途失败。First Revolutionary Civil War (1924-1927), waged by the Chinese people under the leadership of the Communist Party against the imperialists and the Northern Warlords. It laid the foundation for the first cooperation between the Communist Party of China and the Kuomintang. The revolution soon spread to the Yangtze River valley after the Northern Expedition started from Guangdong in 1926, but ended in failure due to a reactionary coup staged by the right wing of the Kuomintang and erroneous leadership of Rightist opportunists within the Communist Party.

【第一次世界大战】Dì Yī Cì Shìjiè Dàzhàn 1914—1918年帝国主义国家为了重新瓜分殖民地和争夺世界霸权而进行的第一次世界规模的战争。

参战的一方是德国、奥匈帝国等,称为同盟国;另一方是英、法、俄、美等,称为协约国。中国后来也加入了协约国。最后同盟国失败。First World War (1914-1918); World War I; first worldwide war between imperialist countries to re-divide up colonies and contend for world supremacy. On one side were the Central Powers of Germany and Austro-Hungarian Empire; on the other were the Entente countries of Britain, France, Russia and the United States. China became one of the Entente countries later. The war ended with the defeat of the Central Powers.

【第一次鸦片战争】 Dì Yī Cì Yāpiàn Zhànzhēng ☞鸦片战争 Yāpiàn Zhànzhēng on p. 2194

【第一审】 dìyīshěn 指法院对诉讼案件的初次审判 first instance; (of a court) first trial of a case; 简称 abbr. 一审 yīshěn

【第一世界】 dì yī shìjiè 指超级大国(总称 general term) first world, generally referring to superpowers

【第一手】 dìyīshǒu 亲自实践、调查得来的;直接得来的 firsthand; (of sth.) obtained from practice and investigation in person: ~材料 firsthand material | ~知识 firsthand knowledge

【第一信号系统】 dì yī xìnhào xìtǒng 直接的刺激作用于感受器,就在大脑皮层中相应的区域形成条件联系,大脑皮层的这种机能系统叫做第一信号系统。第一信号系统是人类和一般高等动物所共有的。first signal system, common to human beings and other higher animals; physiological system of the cerebral cortex to form conditional links in corresponding areas when the senses receive direct stimulus; ☞第二信号系统 dì èr xìnhào xìtǒng

【第一宇宙速度】 dì yī yǔzhòu sùdù 宇宙速度的一级,物体具有 7.9 公里/秒的速度时,就和地心引力平衡,环绕地球运行,不再落回地面,这个速度叫做第一宇宙速度 first cosmic speed or velocity, 7.9 km./second, at which an object obtains a force parallel to the earth's gravity and can move around the earth without falling onto the ground; also 环绕速度 huánrào sùdù

谛 dì 〈书 *fml.*〉 ❶ 仔细(看或听 look or listen) carefully: ~视 examine closely | ~观 observe carefully | ~听 listen attentively ❷ 〈佛教 *Budd.*〉指真实而正确的道理,泛指道理 *satya*; truth; axiom; reason: 真~ true meaning | 妙~profound knowledge

【谛视】 dìshì 〈书 *fml.*〉 仔细地看 examine closely: 凝神~ examine with high concentration

【谛听】 dìtīng 〈书 *fml.*〉仔细地听 listen attentively: 屏息~ listen with bated breath

蒂(蔕) dì 瓜、果等跟茎、枝相连的部分;把儿(bàr) base of a fruit, connecting the fruit and the stem or branch: 并~莲 twin lotus flowers on the same root | 瓜熟~落 fall of the base when a melon is ripe | 根深~固 engrained; deeply rooted; well established

棣[1] dì ❶ ☞棣棠 dìtáng ❷ ☞ 棠棣 tángdì on p. 1866

棣[2] dì 〈书 *fml.*〉 弟 younger brother: 贤~ wise younger brother

【棣棠】 dìtáng 落叶灌木,叶子略呈卵形,花黄色,果实黑褐色。可供观赏。kerria (*Kerria japonica*); deciduous shrub with oval leaf, yellow flower and darkish brown fruit, appreciated for its beauty

睇 dì ❶ 〈书 *fml.*〉斜着眼看 look askance ❷ 〈方 *dial.*〉看;望 look; look afar

缔 dì 结合;订立 form; establish: ~交 establish diplomatic relations | ~约 conclude a treaty | ~盟 form an alliance

【缔交】 dìjiāo ❶ 〈书 *fml.*〉(朋友)订交 form (a friendship); become friends ❷ 缔结邦交 establish diplomatic ties: 两国~以后,关系一直正常。Relations between the two countries have been normal since they established diplomatic ties.

【缔结】 dìjié 订立(条约等) conclude (treaty, etc.): ~同盟 establish an alliance | ~贸易协定 sign a trade agreement

【缔盟】 dìméng 结成同盟 form an alliance

【缔约】 dìyuē 订立条约 conclude or sign a treaty: ~国 signatory country to a treaty

【缔约国】 dìyuēguó 共同订立某项条约的国家 signatory countries to a certain treaty

【缔造】 dìzào 创立;建立(多指伟大的事业) found; establish (oft. a great cause)

禘 dì 古代一种祭祀 ancient sacrificial rite

碲 dì 非金属元素,符号 Te (tellurium)。银白色结晶或棕色粉末。是半导体材料,也用来加入金属或合金中,以改变它们的性能。tellurium (Te); nonmetallic element, in the form of white crystal or brown powder, used as a semiconductor or added to metal or alloy to change their property

墬 dì 〈书 *fml.*〉 same as 地 dì

蝃(蝃、蝃) dì [蝃蝀] (dìdōng) 〈书 *fml.*〉 虹 rainbow

踶 dì 〈书 *fml.*〉 踢;踏 kick; stamp

diǎ (ㄉㄧㄚˇ)

嗲 diǎ ❶ 形容撒娇的声音或姿态 (of voice or posture) coquettish: ~声~气 speak in the manner of a pampered child ❷ 好;优异 good; excellent: 味道~! Yummy! Delicious!

diān (ㄉㄧㄢ)

掂(敁) diān 用手托着东西上下晃动来估量轻重 weigh sth. in the hand:你~一~这块铁有多重。Weigh how heavy this piece of iron is in your hand.

【掂对】diān·dui〈方 *dial.*〉❶ 斟酌 consider:大家~~,看怎么办好。You decide to do what you see fit. ❷ 掉换;对调 exchange; swap:我这儿有玉米,想和你~点儿麦子。I have some corn, which I'd like to swap for some wheat with you.

【掂掇】diān·duo ❶ 斟酌 consider:你~着办吧。Do it as you see fit. ❷ 估计 estimate:我~着这么办能行。I guess this will do.

【掂斤播两】diān jīn bō liǎng〈比喻 *fig.*〉过分计较小事 be fussy about trivial things; also 掂斤簸两 diān jīn bǒ liǎng

【掂量】diān·liáng ❶ 掂 weigh in the hand:他~了一下西瓜,说有八斤来重。He weighed the watermelon in his hand and said it was about four km.◇你好好~~老师这句话的分量。Think carefully about what the teacher has said. ❷ 斟酌 consider:事情就是这些,各组回去~着办得了。These are the things to be done; each group should go back and do what you see fit.

傎 diān〈书 *fml.*〉颠倒错乱 upside down; disorderly

滇 Diān 云南的别称 Dian, another name for Yunnan Province:~红 Yunnan black tea|川~公路 Sichuan-Yunnan highway

【滇红】diānhóng 云南出产的红茶 Yunnan black tea

【滇剧】diānjù 云南主要戏曲剧种之一,腔调以皮黄为主,流行于云南全省和贵州、四川的部分地区 Yunnan opera; one of the local operas in Yunnan, characterized by *xipi* and *erhuang* tunes, popular in Yunnan, and parts of Guizhou and Sichuan provinces

颠[1] diān ❶ 头顶 crown (of the head):华~(头顶上黑发白发相间) silver-haired ❷ 高而直立的东西的顶 top of sth. tall and erect:山~ hilltop|塔~ top of a pagoda

颠[2] diān ❶ 颠簸 bump:路不平,车~得厉害。The car jolted badly on the bumpy road. ❷ 跌落;倒下来 fall; fall down:~覆 overthrow|~扑不破 indisputable ❸〈方 *dial.*〉(~儿 diānr)跳起来跑;跑 jump and run:连跑带~ skip along|跑跑~~be on the go

颠[3] diān same as 癫 diān

【颠簸】diānbǒ 上下震荡 bump:风大了,船身更加~起来。As the wind rose higher, the ship jolted more violently.

【颠倒】diāndǎo ❶ 上下、前后跟原有的或应有的位置相反 turn upside down; transpose; reverse:把这两个字~过来就顺了。Change the order of these two words and the sentence will read fine.|这一面朝上,别放~了。This side up; don't place it on the wrong side. ❷ 错乱 confused:神魂~ be totally confused

【颠倒黑白】diāndǎo hēibái 把黑的说成白的,把白的说成黑的。形容歪曲事实,混淆是非。confound black and white; confuse right and wrong; stand facts on their heads

【颠倒是非】diāndǎo shìfēi 把对的说成不对,不对的说成对 confuse right and wrong; confuse truth and falsehood

【颠覆】diānfù ❶ 翻倒 topple:防止列车~prevent a train from overturning ❷ 采取阴谋手段从内部推翻合法的政府 subversion; bring down a legitimate government with conspiracy from within:~活动 subversive activity

【颠来倒去】diān lái dǎo qù 翻过来倒过去,来回重复 over and over again

【颠连】[1] diānlián〈书 *fml.*〉困苦 hardship:~无告 have no one to tell one's suffering

【颠连】[2] diānlián〈书 *fml.*〉形容连绵不断 endless:群山~起伏。The mountains undulate far into the distance.

【颠末】diānmò〈书 *fml.*〉自始至终的经过情形 details of sth. from beginning to end:细述~ tell sth. from beginning to end in minute detail

【颠沛】diānpèi 穷困;受挫折 poverty and hardship; frustration:~流离(生活艰难,四处流浪) drift from place to place (be hard up; wander about)

【颠仆】diānpū 跌倒 fall down

【颠扑不破】diān pū bù pò 无论怎样摔打都不破 remain intact despite repeated tattering;〈比喻 *fig.*〉永远不会被推翻(多指理论 oft. of theory) irrefutable:~的真理 indisputable truth

【颠三倒四】diān sān dǎo sì (说话、做事)错乱,没有次序 (of speech or manner of doing things) confused; disorderly

蹎 diān〈书 *fml.*〉跌倒 fall down

攧 diān 跌(多见于早期白话 oft. in early vernacular) fall:~下来 fall down

巅 diān 山顶 peak; summit:珠峰之~ summit of Mount Qomolangma

癫 diān 精神错乱 mentally deranged; insane:疯~ mad; crazy

【癫狂】diānkuáng ❶ 由精神病引起的言语或行动异常 deranged; abnormal speech or behaviour caused by mental illness ❷ (言谈举止)轻佻;不庄重 (of speech and behaviour) frivolous

【癫痫】diānxián 病,由脑部疾患或脑外伤等引起。发作时突然昏倒,全身痉挛,意识丧失,有的口吐泡沫。epilepsy; neurological disorders characterized by sudden loss of consciousness, convulsive seizures and sometimes foaming in the mouth; 通称 in generally known as 羊痫风 yángxiánfēng or 羊角风 yángjiǎofēng

【癫子】diān·zi 〈方 *dial.*〉疯子 madman

diǎn (ㄉㄧㄢˇ)

典[1] diǎn ❶ 标准;法则 standard; canon:~范 example|~章 laws and rules ❷ 典范性书籍 standard work of scholarship:词~dictionary|引经据~ quote from classics ❸ 典故 allusion:用~use of allusion|出~source of an allusion ❹ 典礼 ceremony:盛~ grand ceremony|开国大~ founding ceremony of a sovereign state ❺ 〈书 *fml.*〉主持;主管 be in charge of:~试 examiner|~狱 warden ❻ (Diǎn) 姓 a surname

典[2] diǎn 一方把土地或房屋等押给另一方使用,换取一笔钱,不付利息,议定年限,到期还款,收回原物 pawn; give land or real estate as security for the payment of money borrowed free of interest, with the two parties retrieving their money and property respectively by the end of the agreed period

【典当】diǎndàng ❶ 典和当(dàng) pawn; also 典押 diǎnyā ❷ 〈方 *dial.*〉当铺 pawn shop

【典范】diǎnfàn 可以作为学习、仿效标准的人或事物 model; example:树立~ set up an example|~作品 model work

【典故】diǎngù 诗文里引用的古书中的故事或词句 allusion or quotation from classical works

【典籍】diǎnjí 记载古代法制的图书,也泛指古代图书 ancient records of laws and rules; ancient books:文献~ documents and historical records

【典借】diǎnjiè ☞典[2] diǎn

【典礼】diǎnlǐ 郑重举行的仪式,如开幕典礼、结婚典礼、毕业典礼等 ceremony, such as opening, wedding or graduation ceremony

【典型】diǎnxíng ❶ 具有代表性的人物或事件 model; typical person or event:用~示范的方法推广先进经验 popularize advanced experience by demonstration ❷ 具有代表性的 typical; representative:这件事很~,可以用来教育群众。This is a typical case, which is educational for the people. ❸ 文学艺术作品中用艺术概括的手法,表现出人的某种社会特征的艺术形象,它既表现了人的一定的阶级特征,同时又具有鲜明的个性特征 representation; technique of literary writing, featuring certain social characteristics of a person who is not only representative of his social class but also has his own personality

【典押】diǎnyā same as 典当 diǎndàng ①

【典雅】diǎnyǎ 优美不粗俗 refined; elegant:词句~polished wording|风格~ graceful style

【典章】diǎnzhāng 法令制度 laws and rules:文物~ cultural relics and ancient documents|《元~》(书名,元朝的法令汇编) *The Code of Yuan* (collection of decrees of the Yuan Dynasty)

点[1](點) diǎn ❶ (~儿 diǎnr)液体的小滴 drop of liquid:雨~儿 raindrop ❷ (~儿 diǎnr)小的痕迹 dot; speck:墨~儿 ink spot|斑~ speckle ❸ (~儿 diǎnr)汉字的笔画,形状是'、'dot; stroke of the Chinese character, shaped like '、' ❹ 几何学上指没有大小(即没有长、宽、高)而只有位置,不可分割的图形。如两直线的相交处、线段的两端都是点。(geom.) point; dimensionless geometric object having no properties except location, such as the point where two lines cross and either end of a line ❺ (~儿 diǎnr)小数点,如 432.5 读作四三二点儿五或四百三十二点儿五 decimal point; point, such as 432.5, read as four hundred and thirty-two point five ❻ (~儿 diǎnr)〈量词 *classifier*〉表示少量 a little:一~儿小事 small matter|吃~儿东西再走。Have something to eat before you leave. ❼ 〈量词 *classifier*〉用于事项 [for items]:两~意见 two suggestions|他的错误主要有三~。His mistake boils down to three points. ❽ 一定的地点或程度的标志 point to mark a location or degree:起~ starting point|终~ terminal point|冰~ freezing point|沸~ boiling point|据~ stronghold|先突破一~make a breakthrough at one point first ❾ 事物的方面或部分 aspect or part of sth.:优~ strong point|重~ important aspect|特~ speciality ❿ 用笔加上点子 write a point with a pen:~一个点儿 write a point|评~ comment|画龙~睛 add eyes to a (painted) dragon; add finishing touch to a piece of writing or art to brighten it up ⓫ 触到物体立刻离开 touch:蜻蜓~水(of a dragonfly) skip on water surface|他用篙一~就把船撑开了。He punted the boat away with a touch at the shore. ⓬ same as 踮 diǎn ⓭ (头或手)向下稍微动一动立刻恢复原位 nod; wave one's hand slightly downward:他~了~头。He nodded. ⓮ 使液体一滴滴地向下落 cause liquid to drip:~卤 add drops of bittern|~眼药 apply eye drops ⓯ 点播[1] sow seeds in holes:~花生 dibble peanuts|~豆子 dibble beans ⓰ 一个个地查对 check one by one:~名 call the roll|~数 count the number|清~货品 make an inventory of goods ⓱ 在许多人或事物中指定 select from many persons or things:~菜 order a dish|~播节目 request a programme to be aired ⓲ 指点;启发 advise; enlighten:他是聪明人,一~就明白了。A clever man, he is able to pick up the slightest cue. ⓳ 引着火 light a fire:~灯 light a lamp|~火 start a fire ◇老李是火暴性子,一~就着。Lao Li is

D

so hot-tempered that he flares up at the slightest provocation. ⑳ 点缀 embellish：装～ decorate｜～染 polish｜～景儿（点缀景物，应景儿）add decorative

点²（點）diǎn ❶ 铁制的响器，挂起来敲，用来报告时间或召集群众 iron bell, used to report time or call an assembly ❷〈旧时 *old*〉夜间计时用更点，一更分五点 watch; one of the five points of time of each of the two-hour periods into which the night was divided：五更三～third point of the fifth watch ❸ 时间单位，一昼夜的二十四分之一 hour ❹ 规定的钟点 appointed time：误～ miss the time｜到～了。It's time.

D

点³（點）diǎn 点心 pastry; dim sum：茶～ tea pastry｜早～ breakfast｜糕～ pastry

点⁴（點）diǎn 印刷上计算活字及字模的大小的单位，约等于 0.35 毫米（of printing）point; unit of measurement for type, about 0.35mm.

【点播】[1] diǎnbō 播种的一种方法，每隔一定距离挖一小坑，放入种子 dibble; method of sowing seeds in holes at even intervals; also 点种 diǎnzhòng

【点播】[2] diǎnbō 指定节目请广播电台、电视台播送 request a radio or TV station to broadcast a programme：听众～的音乐节目 music programme requested by a listener

【点拨】diǎn·bo same as 指点 zhǐdiǎn ①

【点补】diǎn·bu 吃少量的食物解饿 have a snack：这里有饼干，饿了可以先～～。Here are some biscuits; you can have some if you are hungry.

【点穿】diǎnchuān same as 点破 diǎnpò

【点窜】diǎncuàn 改换（字句）reword：经他一～，这篇文章就好多了。The article looks much better after his rewording.

【点滴】diǎndī ❶ 形容零星微小 bits and pieces：重视别人的～经验 pay attention to all the experiences of others｜这批资料是点点滴滴积累起来的。These data have been accumulated bit by bit. ❷ 指零星的事物 sporadic things：足球大赛～ bits of news of the grand football match ❸ ☞打点滴 dǎ diǎndī on p. 347

【点厾】diǎndū 画家随意点染（of a painter）add random touches to a painting

【点发】diǎnfā same as 点射 diǎnshè

【点化】diǎnhuà 道教传说，神仙运用法术使物变化。借指僧道用言语启发人悟道。也泛指启发指导。（of Taoist immortals）transform things by magic;（of a Buddhist or Taoist monk）enlighten people with words; enlighten or advise

【点火】diǎn//huǒ ❶ 引着火；使燃料开始燃烧 light a fire; cause fuel to burn：上午七点整，火箭发动机～。The rocket engine was ignited at 7 o'clock sharp. ❷〈比喻 *fig.*〉挑起是非，制造事端 stir up trouble：煽风～instigate

【点饥】diǎn//jī 稍微吃点东西解饿 eat a little snack to mitigate hunger

【点将】diǎn//jiàng〈旧时 *old*〉主帅对将官点名分派任务。现比喻指名要某人做某项工作（of a commander）summon generals and officers for assignment;（fig.）name a person for a particular job

【点卯】diǎn//mǎo〈旧时 *old*〉官厅在卯时（上午五点到七点）查点到班人员，叫点卯。现指到时上班应付差事。roll call; call the roll in the *yamen* from 5 a.m. to 7 a.m.; perform one's duty in the workplace in a perfunctory manner

【点名】diǎn//míng ❶ 按名册查点人员时一个个地叫名字 roll call; call the roll ❷ 指名 name a person（to do sth.）：他要求派人支援，～要你去。He needs someone to help and has asked for you.

【点明】diǎnmíng 指出来使人知道 point out：～主题 make clear the theme｜～学习的要点 point out the gist of learning

【点破】diǎnpò 用一两句话揭露真相或隐情 lay bare a truth or secret with a few words：事情不必～，大家心照不宣算了。It's a matter understood by all; let's just not talk about it.

【点燃】diǎnrán 使燃烧；点着 cause to burn; ignite：～火把 light a torch

【点染】diǎnrǎn 绘画时点缀景物和着色，也比喻修饰文字 add touches and colours to a painting;（fig.）polish a piece of writing：一经～，形象更加生动。The image is even more lively after a few more touches.

【点射】diǎnshè 用机关枪、冲锋枪、自动步枪等自动武器进行断续的射击 fire machine gun, submachine gun, automatic rifle, etc., in bursts

【点收】diǎnshōu 接收货物或财产时一件件地查点 check goods or other forms of property upon reception：按清单～ check goods against a list

【点题】diǎn//tí 用扼要的话把谈话或文章的中心意思提示出来 highlight the central theme of a conversation or piece of writing in a few words

【点铁成金】diǎn tiě chéng jīn 神仙故事中说仙人用手指一点使铁变成金子 golden touch;（of a celestial being）transform iron into gold with a touch;〈比喻 *fig.*〉把不好的作品改好 turn a piece of bad writing into one of good readability

【点头】diǎn//tóu（～儿 diǎn//tóur）头微微向下一动，表示允许、赞成、领会或打招呼 nod（with agreement, appreciation, understanding, or as a form of greeting）：他见我进来，点了下头。He nodded to me as I came in.｜这种做法需经局领导～批准。We need approval from the bureau leader for doing this. | 他听他说得有理，不由得连连～。He kept nodding his agreement to what he had heard.

【点头哈腰】diǎntóu-hāyāo 形容恭顺或过分客气 bow and scrape — be unduly compliant or cordial

【点心】diǎn//xīn 〈方 *dial.*〉same as 点饥 diǎn//jī

【点心】diǎn•xin 糕饼之类的食品 pastry; dim sum

【点穴】diǎn//xué 相传是拳术家的一种武功，把全身的力量运在手指上，在人身某几处穴道上点一下，就可以使人受伤，不能动弹 acupoint touch; (of Chinese boxing) injure or disable by touching certain acupoints of an opponent

【点验】diǎnyàn 一件件地查对检验 check item by item：按清单～物资 check goods against a list

【点种】diǎn//zhǒng 点播种子 dibble in seeds

【点种】diǎnzhòng ☞点播[1] diǎnbō

【点缀】diǎn•zhuì ❶ 加以衬托或装饰，使原有事物更加美好 embellish to set off sth. or make sth. look better：蔚蓝的天空～着朵朵白云 blue sky dotted with white clouds | 青松翠柏把烈士陵园～得格外肃穆。The cemetery of martyrs looks extraordinarily solemn under green pines and cypresses. ❷ 装点门面；应景儿；凑数儿 decorative; ornament; accessory

【点子】[1] diǎn•zi ❶ 液体的小滴 drop of liquid：雨～ raindrop ❷ 小的痕迹 speck：油～ grease spot ❸ 指打击乐器演奏时的节拍 beat of a percussion instrument：鼓～ drumbeat ❹〈方 *dial.*〉〈量词 *classifier*〉表示少量 a little：这个病抓～药吃就好了。The disease can be cured with a little Chinese herbal medicine.

【点子】[2] diǎn•zi ❶ 关键的地方 key point：这句话说到～上了。You've put your finger on it. | 劲儿没使在～上。We missed the goal in our effort. ❷ 主意；办法 idea; way (of doing things)：出～ make a suggestion | 想～ think of a way out

【点字】diǎnzì ☞盲字 mángzì on p. 1304

碘 diǎn 非金属元素，符号 I (iodine)。紫黑色晶体，有金属光泽，容易升华，蒸气紫色，有毒。用来制药品、染料等。iodine; lustrous, purplish-black, poisonous nonmetal element, easy to sublimate into purple vapour, used to make medicine and dye, etc.

【碘酊】diǎndīng 药名，碘和碘化钾的稀酒精溶液，棕红色，用做消毒剂 tincture of iodine; alcoholic solution of iodine and potassium iodide, brownish red, used as a disinfectant; 通称 generally known as 碘酒 diǎnjiǔ

【碘钨灯】diǎnwūdēng 白炽灯的一种。在石英玻璃等制成的外壳中装有钨丝，并充入一定量的碘，通电后钨丝灼热发光。iodine tungsten lamp, with tungsten filament inside quartz glass bulb filled with a certain amount of iodine

踮(跕) diǎn 抬起脚后跟用脚尖站着 stand on tiptoe：他人矮，得～着脚才能看见。Being short, he has to stand on tiptoe to see things clearly. also 点 diǎn

☞ 跕 diē on p. 450

【踮脚】diǎnjiǎo 〈方 *dial.*〉(～儿 diǎnjiǎor) 一只脚有病，走路做点地的样子 limp

diàn (ㄉㄧㄢˋ)

电(電) diàn ❶ 有电荷存在和电荷变化的现象。电是一种很重要的能源，广泛用在生产和生活各方面，如发光、发热、产生动力等。electricity; physical phenomena arising from the existence and change of electric charge, an important energy used extensively in production and daily life to provide light, heat, power, etc. ❷ 触电 get an electric shock：电门可能有毛病了，我一开灯，～了我一下。Something is wrong with the switch; I got an electric shock when turning on the lamp. ❸ 电报 telegraph：急～ express telegraph | 唁～ telegraph of condolences | 通～致贺 send a telegraph of congratulations ❹ 打电报 send a telegram：～贺 send a congratulatory telegram | 即～上级请示。Send a telegram to the higher authorities at once for instructions.

【电棒】diànbàng 〈方 *dial.*〉(～儿 diànbàngr) 手电筒 torch; flashlight

【电报】diànbào ❶ 用电信号传递文字、照片、图表的通信方式。有无线电报和有线电报两种。发电报的方面把文字、照片、图表变成信号，用电流或无线电波发出去，收电报的方面把收到的符号还原。telegraph; communications system, either wired or wireless, that transmits and receives text, photograph, chart, etc. The sender turns text, photograph, or chart into signals and transmit them through electric current or radio wave, while the receiver converts the signals back into their original forms. ❷ 用电报装置传递的文字、图表等 use telegraph facilitics to transmit text, picture, chart, etc：打～ send a telegram

【电报挂号】diànbào guàhào 向当地电报局申请后编定的号码，用来代替申请单位的地址和名称 cable address; telegraphic address, obtained from local telegraph office to replace address and name of an organization

【电笔】diànbǐ 试电笔 test pencil

【电表】diànbiǎo ❶ 测量电压、电流、电阻、电功率等的各种电气仪表的统称 any meter for measuring electricity, such as ammeter or voltmeter ❷ 瓦特小时计的通称 general term for 瓦特小时计 wǎtèxiǎoshíjì

【电冰柜】diànbīngguì 一种冷藏装置，工作原理跟电冰箱相同，冷藏温度在 0℃ 以下 freezer;

same as refrigerator in working principle, used to store things at temperatures below 0℃；简称 abbr. 冰柜 bīngguì

【电冰箱】diànbīngxiāng 一种冷藏装置，在隔热的柜子中装有盘曲的管道，电动机带动压缩机，使冷凝剂在管道中循环产生低温。电冰箱中低温在0℃以下的部分叫做冷冻室，在0℃以上的部分叫做冷藏室。refrigerator; appliance in the form of a cabinet or room for storing food or other substances at a low temperature. The adiabatic appliance is equipped with a wound-up pipe. A compressor, powered by an electromotor, presses condensate to circulate in the pipe to keep temperatures low. 简称 abbr. 冰箱 bīngxiāng

【电波】diànbō ☞电磁波 diàncíbō

【电铲】diànchǎn 掘土机 power shovel

【电场】diànchǎng 传递电荷与电荷间相互作用的场。电荷周围总有电场存在。electric field; region around a charged particle within which a force would be exerted on other charged particles; ☞ 场 chǎng ⑨ on p. 221

【电唱机】diànchàngjī 用电动机做动力，并使用电唱头和扩音器的留声机。有的地区叫电转儿 electric gramophone; turntable; known as 电转儿 diànzhuànr in some places

【电唱头】diànchàngtóu 拾音器 pickup (of a gramophone)

【电车】diànchē 用电做动力的公共交通工具，电能从架空的电源线供给，分无轨和有轨两种 tram; trackless trolley; public transport vehicle powered by electricity supplied from overhead wire

【电陈】diànchén 用电报陈述(事由) state via telegraph：谈判一有结果，迅即～。Report the result of the negotiation via telegraph as soon as it's out.

【电池】diànchí 把化学能或光能等变成电能的装置。如手电筒用的干电池，汽车用的电瓶，人造卫星上用的太阳能电池等。(electric) cell; battery; device that converts chemical or light energy into electricity, such as torch battery, storage battery in an automobile and solar cell for a man-made satellite

【电船】diànchuán 〈方 *dial.*〉汽艇 motorboat

【电瓷】diàncí 瓷质的电绝缘材料，具有良好的绝缘性和机械强度，如绝缘子 ceramic insulating material, with fine insulating quality and strong mechanical strength, such as ceramic insulator

【电磁】diàncí 物质所表现的电性和磁性的统称，如电磁感应、电磁波 electromagnetism; general term for the electric and magnetic properties of matter, such as electromagnetic induction and electromagnetic wave

【电磁波】diàncíbō 在空间传播的周期性变化的电磁场。无线电波和光线、X射线、γ射线等都是波长不同的电磁波。electromagnetic wave; electromagnetic field transmitted in the air with periodical changes, such as radio wave, light, X-ray and γ-ray; also 电波 diànbō

【电磁场】diàncíchǎng 电场和磁场的统称。变化着的电场和磁场往往同时并存，并且互相转化。electromagnetic field; general term for electric field and magnetic field, which usu. exist simultaneously and transform into each other

【电磁感应】diàncí-gǎnyìng 当导体回路中的磁通量发生变化时，导体两端产生电动势，并在闭合电路中产生电流的现象 electromagnetic induction; occurrence of electric current when magnetic flux in the return circuit of a conductor changes to produce electro-motive force at either end of the conductor

【电磁炉】diàncílú 利用电磁感应引起涡流加热的灶具 electromagnetic stove, with heat produced by the vertex flow of electromagnetic induction

【电大】diàndà 电视大学的简称 abbr. for 电视大学 diànshì dàxué

【电导】diàndǎo 表述导体导电性能的物理量。导体的电阻愈小，电导就愈大，数值上等于电阻的倒数。单位是西门子。conductance; physical measure for conductivity; the small the resistance, the greater the conductance, with the latter equal to the reciprocal of the former; unit: siemens

【电灯】diàndēng 利用电能发光的灯，通常指白炽电灯 electric lamp; electric light

【电灯泡】diàndēngpào (～儿 diàndēngpàor) 白炽电灯上用的发光器件，一般呈梨形 electric (light) bulb, usu. shaped like a pear; also 电灯泡子 diàndēngpào·zi；通称 generally known as 灯泡 dēngpào ☞ 白炽电灯 báichì diàndēng on p. 33

【电动】diàndòng 用电力使机械运转的(of machinery) power-driven：～机 motor | ～玩具 electric toy

【电动机】diàndòngjī 把电能变为机械能的机器，是近代工业的重要动力装备 (electric) motor; machine that converts electricity into mechanical energy; important equipment in modern industry; 通称 generally known as 马达 mǎdá

【电动势】diàndòngshì 单位正电荷沿回路移动一周所作的功，叫做电源的电动势。电源不输出电流时，电源的电动势等于两极间的电势差。单位是伏特。electro-motive force (EMF); work done by unit positive charge moving one circle along a return circuit; equal to potential difference of the mains when not supplying electricity; unit: volt

【电镀】diàndù 利用电解作用，在金属表面上均匀地附上薄薄一层别的金属或合金。电镀可以防止金属器物表面生锈，使外形美观，或增加耐磨、导电、光反射等性能。electroplate; apply to the surface of a piece of metal an even, thin layer of another metal or alloy to prevent rusting, make it look pretty, or strengthen its wearability, conductivity, reflectability

【电风扇】diànfēngshàn same as 电扇 diànshàn

【电镐】diàngǎo 用电能做动力开凿岩层和矿石的工具 electric pick; power-driven tool to cut rock and mine

【电告】diàngào 用电报通知或报告 notify or report by telegraph:请速将详情～中央。Please report the details by telegraph to the Central Committee immediately.

【电工】diàngōng ❶ 电工学 electrical engineering ❷ 制造、安装各种电气设备的技术工人 electrician

【电工学】diàngōngxué 研究电能应用的基础理论学科。电机、电器以及电在产业部门和生活上的应用原理都是电工学研究的对象。electrical engineering; electrotechnics; basic science concerned with the application of electricity, as in electric motors and appliances, in industry and daily life

【电功率】diàngōnglǜ 电流在单位时间所做的功,单位是瓦特,实用单位是千瓦 electric power; work done by electric current within unit time; unit: watt; unit in use: kilowatt

【电灌】diànguàn 用电力扬水灌溉 power-driven irrigation:～站 electric pumping station

【电光】diànguāng 电能所发的光,多指雷电的光 light produced by electricity (oft. lightning)

【电滚子】diàngǔn·zi 〈方 *dial.*〉❶ 发电机 generator; dynamo ❷ 电动机(electric) motor

【电焊】diànhàn 电弧焊接的通称 general term for 电弧焊接 diànhú hànjiē

【电贺】diànhè 发电报祝贺 convey one's congratulations via telegraph:～中国队荣获冠军。Send a congratulatory telegram to the Chinese team for winning the championship.

【电荷】diànhè 物体或构成物体的质点所带的正电或负电。异种电荷相吸引,同种电荷相排斥。单位是库仑。electric charge; charge, with attraction between different charges (positive v. negative) and repulsion between the same charges; unit: coulomb

【电弧】diànhú 正负两电极接近到一定距离时所产生的持续的火花放电。电弧能产生高温、强光和某些射线,用于照明、焊接、炼钢等。electric arc; continuous sparkling discharge when anode and cathode come within a close distance. The intense heat, light and certain rays produced by electric arc are used for lighting, welding and smelting steel

【电弧焊接】diànhú hànjiē 把要焊接的金属作为一极,焊条作为另一极,两极接近时产生电弧,使金属和焊条熔化的焊接方法叫做电弧焊接 (electric) arc welding; method of welding by placing the metal to be welded and the welding rod close enough to produce electric arc to melt both; 通称 general term for 电焊 diànhàn

【电化教育】diànhuà jiàoyù 利用录音、广播、电视、幻灯、电影等使用电的设备进行的教育 education with electrical aids, such as recording, radio, TV, slide and film; 简称 abbr. 电教 diànjiào

【电话】diànhuà ❶ 利用电流使两地的人互相交谈的装置,主要由发话器、受话器和线路三部分组成 telephone; device consisting mainly of a speaker, a receiver and wires, for people in different places to speak to each other through electric current ❷ 用电话装置传递的话 message conveyed via telephone:打～ make a telephone call|我没有接到他的～。I did not receive his call.

【电话会议】diànhuà huìyì (不在一个地方的人)利用电话装置举行的会议 telephone conference, participated by people in different places via telephone

【电话亭】diànhuàtíng 设在路旁或邮电局内形状像小亭子的供公众打电话的设施 telephone kiosk, by the roadside or in a post office for public use

【电汇】diànhuì ❶ 通过电报办理汇兑 remittance by telegram:急需用款,盼速～五千元。Money badly needed. Please remit 5,000 yuan by telegram. ❷ 通过电报办理的汇款 telegraphic money order:昨日收到一笔～。I received a telegraphic money order yesterday.

【电机】diànjī 产生和应用电能的机器,特指发电机或电动机 machinery for generating and using electricity, esp. generator and motor

【电极】diànjí 电源或电器上用来接通电流的地方 electrode (of a power source or electric appliance)

【电键】diànjiàn 使电路开合或改变线路的装置。种类很多,特指发电报用的按键。key; button; device to switch on and off, or change, a circuit; esp. telegraph key

【电教】diànjiào 电化教育的简称 abbr. for 电化教育 diànhuà jiàoyù:～馆 hall for teaching with electrical aids|～中心 centre of education with electrical aids

【电解】diànjiě 电流通过电解质溶液或熔融状态的电解质,使阴阳两极发生氧化还原反应。可用来冶炼或精炼金属,也用来电镀。electrolysis; deoxidization of an electrolyte by an electric current, applied in smelting or purifying of metals and electroplating

【电解质】diànjiězhì 在水溶液中或在熔融状态下能形成离子,因而能导电的化合物。如食盐、硫酸、氢氧化钠等。electrolyte; chemical compound that ionizes when dissolved or molten to produce an electrically conductive medium, such as salt, vitriol and sodium hydroxide

【电介质】diànjièzhì 不导电的物质,如空气、玻璃、云母片、胶木等 dielectric; nonconductive material, such as air, glass, isinglass and bakelite

【电抗】diànkàng 电感或电容在电路中对交流电的阻碍作用。单位是欧姆。reactance; opposition to the flow of alternating current caused by the inductance and capacitance in a circuit; unit: ohm

【电缆】diànlǎn 装有绝缘层和保护外皮的导线,通常是比较粗的,由多股彼此绝缘的导线构成。多架在空中或装在地下、水底,用于电讯或电力输送。electric cable; cable; thick wire wrapped in insulating and protective layers, consisting of several wires insulative to one another, oft. for overhead, underground or underwater telecommunications or power transmission

D

【电离】diànlí ❶ 液体、气体的原子或分子受到粒子撞击、射线照射等作用而变成离子 ionization; formation of or separation into ions of liquid or gas atom or molecule by the impact of particle or radiation ❷ 电解质在溶液中或在熔融状态下形成自由移动的离子 free-moving ions formed of electrolyte when dissolved or molten

【电力】diànlì 电所产生的作功能力,通常指做动力用的电 electric power; energy produced by electricity; generally referring to electricity used to operate a device

【电力网】diànlìwǎng 由发电厂、变电站和各种不同电压的输电线路组成的电力系统 power grid, consisting of power plant, substation and transmission wires with different voltages

【电力线】diànlìxiàn ❶描述电场分布情况的假想曲线。曲线上各点的切线方向与该点的电场方向一致,曲线的疏密程度与该处的电场强度成正比。electric line of force; imaginary curve describing the distribution of an electric field, with tangent lines of the points of the curve in the same direction of the field and the density of the curve in proportion to the density of the field ❷ 称输送动力用电的导线 power line

【电量】diànliàng 物体所带电荷的多少 electric quantity, referring to the quantity of electric charges

【电疗】diànliáo 物理疗法的一种,利用电器装置发热或电流刺激来治疗疾病 electrotherapy; physiotherapy using electric heat or current to treat certain diseases

【电料】diànliào 电气器材的统称,如电线、开关、灯泡、插头等 electrical materials and appliances, such as wire, switch, bulb, plug, etc.

【电铃】diànlíng 利用电磁铁特性通电后使铃发出音响信号的装置 electric bell; doorbell; facility using special properties of electromagnet to produce sound

【电流】diànliú ❶ 定向流动的电荷。电流通过导体会产生热效应、磁效应、化学效应、发光效应等。electric current; electric charge moving along one direction, producing thermal, magnetic, chemical and luminescent effects when passing through a conductor ❷ 指电流强度 current intensity

【电流表】diànliúbiǎo same as 安培计 ānpéijì

【电流强度】diànliú qiángdù 单位时间内通过导体横截面的电量。电流强度的单位是安培。current intensity; electric quantity passing through the cross section of a conductor within unit time; unit: ampere

【电炉】diànlú 利用电能产生热量的设备,有电弧电炉、电阻电炉、感应电炉等几种。用于取暖、炊事以及工业上加热、烘干、冶炼等。electric stove; hot plate; facility using electric power to produce heat, such as electric arc stove, resistance stove, induced stove, for heating, cooking, drying, smelting, etc.

【电路】diànlù 由电源、用电器、导线、电器元件等连接而成的电流通路 (electric) circuit, consisting of power source, appliance, wire and other components connected into a current passage

【电路图】diànlùtú 用规定的符号代表各种元件、器件装置,表示所组成的电路的图 circuit diagram; schematic diagram using conventional symbols to indicate connections between components in an electronic device

【电驴子】diànlǘ·zi 〈方 *dial.*〉摩托车 motorbike

【电码】diànmǎ ❶ 指打电报的时候所用的符号,通常有两种。一种是用时间长短不同的电流脉冲(点和画)来组成各种符号代替字母和数字,叫做不均匀电码。一种是用时间长短相同而电流方向不同或有电、无电的电流脉冲来组成各种符号,叫做均匀电码。telegraphic code; system of signals used to represent letters or numbers in transmitting messages, usu. of two types, one using electric current pulses of different lengths (dot and graph) to make up different symbols to stand for letters and numbers, known as uniform code, the other using electric current of the same time length but of different directions, or power-on and power-off current pulses to make up various symbols, known as asymmetry code ❷ 我国用汉字打电报时,用四个数字代表一个汉字,也叫电码 telegraphic code, consisting of four numbers standing for one Chinese character

【电门】diànmén 开关①的通称 general term for 开关 kāiguān ①

【电脑】diànnǎo same as 电子计算机 diànzǐ jìsuànjī

【电脑病毒】diànnǎo bìngdú 计算机病毒 computer virus

【电能】diànnéng 电所具有的能。可以用导线输送到远处,并易于转换成其他形式的能。通常也指电量。electric power; electricity, which can be transmitted to far-away places through wire and which can easily be converted into other forms of energy; also referring to electric quantity

【电钮】diànniǔ 电器开关或调节等设备中通常用手操作的部分。有按下、扳动和转动等几种，多用胶木、塑料等绝缘材料制成。push button; button; part of the switch or regulator of an electric appliance, which can be pushed, pulled or rotated with hand, oft. made of bakelite, plastic and other insulating materials

【电瓶】diànpíng 蓄电池的通称 general term for 蓄电池 xùdiànchí

【电瓶车】diànpíngchē 用自身携带的电瓶做动力来源的车 storage battery car; electromobile

【电气】diànqì same as 电 diàn ①

【电气化】diànqìhuà 为了提高劳动生产率，减轻体力劳动，把电力广泛应用到国民经济的各个领域，特别是用做机器的动力 electrify; apply electric power extensively in all areas of the national economy, esp. using machines, to improve production efficiency and reduce labour intensity

【电器】diànqì ❶ 电路上的负载以及用来控制、调节或保护电路、电机等的设备，如扬声器、开关、变阻器、熔断器等 electric device; load on an electric circuit and other facilities for controlling, regulating or protecting the circuit or appliance, such as loudspeaker, switch, rheostat ❷ 指家用电器，如电视机、录音机、电冰箱、洗衣机等 electric home appliance, such as TV, cassette tape recorder, refrigerator and washing machine

【电热】diànrè 利用电能加热 heat with electric power: ～杯 electric heating mug | ～毯 electric blanket

【电容】diànróng ❶ 导体储藏电荷的能力。单位是法拉。electric capacity; capacitance unit: farad ❷ 指电容器 condenser; capacitor

【电容器】diànróngqì 电路中用来储存电量的器件，由两个接近并相互绝缘的导体构成。capacitor; electric circuit element used to store charge, consisting of two conductors separated and insulated from each other; also 容电器 róngdiànqì

【电扇】diànshàn 利用电动机带动叶片旋转，使空气流动的装置。天气炎热时用来使空气流动，让人有凉爽的感觉。常见的有吊扇、台扇、落地扇等。electric fan; device using electric power to drive the vanes and move the air, such as ceiling fan, desk fan and standard fan

【电石】diànshí 把生石灰和焦炭放在电炉里加热制成的灰色石块状物质，化学成分是碳化钙，工业上用来制造乙炔 calcium carbide; made from lime and coke heated in electric stove; used to produce acetylene in industry

【电视】diànshì ❶ 利用无线电波传送物体影像的装置。由发射台把实物的影像变成电能信号传播出去，电视机把收到的信号再变成影像映在荧光屏上。电视除了用在文化娱乐和教育方面外，也广泛地用在其他技术和军事方面。television; TV; facility for transmitting visual images via radio wave. The launch pad transmits images in electric signals, which are converted back into images on the screen of a television set. Television is used extensively in military and other technologies, as well as for cultural, entertainment and educational purposes. ❷ 用上述装置传送的影像 television images: 黑白～ black and white TV | 彩色～ colour TV | 看～ watch TV | 放～ turn on TV

【电视大学】diànshì dàxué 通过电视实施高等教育的一种教学机构 TV university; 简称 abbr. 电大 diàndà

【电视电话】diànshì diànhuà 带有电视装置的电话，通话时彼此可以看见 video telephone; telephone with visual facilities so that the speakers can see each other

【电视发射塔】diànshì fāshètǎ 发射电视广播的天线，支架结构的形状像塔 TV tower; television transmission antenna (or aerial), with a tower-like mast; 通称 commonly called 电视塔 diànshìtǎ

【电视接收机】diànshì jiēshōujī 接收电视广播的装置，由接收图像和接收声音的两个部分合成 television receiver; television set; set for receiving television broadcasts, consisting of an image receiver and a sound receiver; 通称 commonly called 电视机 diànshìjī

【电视剧】diànshìjù 为电视台播映而编写、录制的戏剧 TV drama; TV play; teledrama; drama written and produced for television broadcast

【电视片】diànshìpiàn 供电视台播送的片子，内容多为介绍人物、地区风貌等 TV documentary; TV film or programme portraying lives of real people, features of an area, etc.

【电视台】diànshìtái 播送电视节目的场所和机构 TV station; television station; building or organization for the production and broadcasting of TV programmes

【电势】diànshì 单位正电荷从某一点移到无穷远时，电场所作的功就是电场中该点的电势。正电荷越多，电势也越高。(electric) potential; work required to bring a unit of positive electric charge from a certain point in an electric field to infinity; the more positive electric charges there are, the higher the electric potential becomes; also 电位 diànwèi

【电势差】diànshìchā 带电体或导体在电路中两点之间电势的差。电势差的单位是伏特。potential difference; difference of potential between two points in the circuit of a charged body or conductor, measured in volts; also 电位差 diànwèichā and 电压 diànyā

【电台】diàntái ❶ 无线电台的通称 general

term for 无线电台 wúxiàn-diàntái ❷ 指广播电台 radio broadcasting station

【电烫】diàntàng 用电热烫发，使鬈曲 perm; permanent wave or hair-styling; application of electric heat to set a wave in the hair

【电梯】diàntī 多层建筑物中作垂直方向运动的电动机械 lift; elevator; electric mechanism to move people and things up and down a multistory building; ☞ 升降机 shēngjiàngjī on p. 1711

【电筒】diàntǒng 手电筒 electric torch; flashlight

【电头】diàntóu 电讯开头的几个字，包括通讯社名称，发报的地点、日期等，如'新华社北京5月1日电' dateline; giving the name of the news agency, place of origin and date of a news dispatch, etc., e.g. 'from Xinhua News Agency, Beijing, May 1'

【电网】diànwǎng ❶ 用金属线架设的可以通电的障碍物，多用来防敌或防盗 electrified wire fence; barrier built with electrified wires, oft. used to guard against intruders ❷ 指由发电、输电系统形成的网络 power grid; network of power-generating and power-transmitting systems

【电文】diànwén 电报的文字、内容 text of a telegram: 起草～ draft a telegram

【电匣子】diànxiá·zi 〈方 *dial.*〉收音机 radio; radio set; wireless (set)

【电线】diànxiàn 传送电力的导线，多用铜或铝制成。有各种规格，如单股的或多股的，裸露的或用绝缘体套起来的。(electric) wire; length of wire, usu. copper or aluminium, consisting either of a single filament or several filaments woven or twisted together, exposed or insulated with a dielectric material, used as a conductor of electricity

【电信】diànxìn 利用电话、电报或无线电设备传递消息的通讯方式 telecommunications; transmission of information by telephone, telegraph, or radio

【电刑】diànxíng ❶ 使电流通过人的身体，用来逼供的刑罚 torture by electricity; passing electricity through a person's body as a form of torture to extort a confession ❷用电椅处死犯人的刑罚 electrocution; execution (of a criminal) in an electric chair

【电讯】diànxùn ❶ 用电话、电报或无线电设备传播的消息 (telegraphic) dispatch; information transmitted by telephone, telegraph, or radio ❷ 无线电信号 radio signals

【电压】diànyā 电势差 voltage; (electric) potential difference

【电压表】diànyābiǎo ☞ 伏特计 fútèjì on p. 594

【电压计】diànyājì ☞ 伏特计 fútèjì on p. 594

【电眼】diànyǎn ❶ 在某些自动控制设备中指光电管 electronic eye; light sensor tube; photoelectric cell; photocell; phototube; component in certain types of automatic control equipment ❷ 无线电装置中指示调谐程度的电子管 tuning eye; tuning indicator tube (in a radio)

【电唁】diànyàn 发电报吊唁 send a telegram containing a message of condolence

【电椅】diànyǐ 装有电极的椅子式的刑具 electric chair; electrified chair used to execute criminals

【电影】diànyǐng (～儿 diànyǐngr) 一种综合艺术，用强灯光把拍摄的形象连续放映在银幕上，看起来像实在活动的形象 film; movie; motion picture; comprehensive art form where a sequence of images of filmed objects are thrown onto a screen by a projector through a bright beam of light in succession to give the illusion of natural movement

【电影剧本】diànyǐng jùběn 专门为拍摄电影写的剧本，分两种，一种是跟一般剧本只稍有不同，不分场幕，叫做电影文学剧本，另一种是电影分镜头剧本 written form of a story prepared for motion-picture production, which comes in two categories: film novels and screenplays (or shooting script), the former having no division of scenes

【电影摄影机】diànyǐng shèyǐngjī 拍摄电影用的机械，有自动连续曝光及输片的机构 motion-picture camera; film camera; machine used to shoot movies, which has automatic continuous exposing and film transporting devices; 简称 abbr. 摄影机 shèyǐngjī

【电影院】diànyǐngyuàn 专供放映电影的场所 cinema; movie theatre

【电源】diànyuán 把电能供给电器的装置，如电池、发电机等 power supply; power source; (electrical) main; source of electrical power, e.g. batteries, electric generators, etc., for operating electric or electronic devices

【电灶】diànzào 利用电能发热的炉灶 electric cooking stove (or range)

【电闸】diànzhá 指较大型的电源开关 main switch; master switch; also 闸 zhá

【电钟】diànzhōng 利用电力运转的时钟。现在用的电钟多采用有旋转轴的电磁感应装置。electric clock, nowadays usu. having an electromagnetic induction device with a rotation axis

【电珠】diànzhū 小的电灯泡，如手电筒里所用的 tiny light bulb (e.g. in a flashlight)

【电转儿】diànzhuànr 〈方 *dial.*〉电唱机 electronic gramophone; phonograph; record player

【电子】diànzǐ 构成原子的基本粒子之一，质量极小，带负电，在原子中围绕原子核旋转 electron; elementary particle that is a constituent of atom, with a negative charge and a minimal mass, and that spins around the nucleus in a atom

【电子管】diànzǐguǎn 无线电技术上的重要器件。在玻璃或金属的容器内装特制的电极，通过阴极放射的电子与其他电极相作用进行各种工作，最重要的作用是整流、检波、放大和振荡。简单的电子管有两个极，叫二极管。按电极数可分为三极管、四极管、五极管等。一般常用的都是高度真空的，所以也叫真空管。electron tube; valve; important device in radio engineering, in which two or more electrodes are enclosed in an envelope of glass or metal, and the electrons provided by the emission of one negative electrode interact with the other electrodes, the most important reactions being rectification, detection, amplification, and oscillation. A simple electron tube with two electrodes is called a diode or two-electrode valve. There are also triode, tetrode, pentode, and so on, according to the number of electrodes. An electron tube is usu. evacuated, so it is also called a vacuum tube.

【电子计算机】diànzǐ jìsuànjī 用电子管、晶体管或集成电路等构成的复杂机器，能对输入的数据或信息非常迅速、准确地进行运算和处理。电子计算机根据工作原理，一般分为数字式和模拟式两种，广泛应用在工程技术、科学研究等方面。computer; any complex machine consisting of electron tubes, transistors, integrated circuits, etc., that calculates and processes received data or information rapidly and accurately. A computer can be digital or analogue according to its principle of operation. It is widely used in engineering, scientific research, etc.

【电子流】diànzǐliú 自由电子在空间做定向运动所形成的电流 electron current; current resulting from free electrons moving in a certain direction in a space

【电子枪】diànzǐqiāng 示波管、摄像管、电子束加工装置等器件中产生和聚焦电子束的电极系统，电子束的方向和强度可以控制，通常由热阴极、控制电极和若干加速阳极等组成 electron gun; electron system in an oscillotron, camera tube, electron beam process equipment, etc., that consists of a thermic cathode, a control electrode and several accelerating anodes, and produces and focuses an electron beam. The direction and intensity of the beam are controlled by electrodes in the gun

【电子琴】diànzǐqín 键盘乐器，采用半导体集成电路，对乐音信号进行放大，通过扬声器产生音响。有多种类型。electronic organ; electronic keyboard; keyboard instrument that uses a semiconductor integrated circuit to amplify musical signals and produce sounds through a loudspeaker; there are various types of electronic organs

【电子手表】diànzǐ shǒubiǎo 含有电子线路的手表。根据所用振动系统或振荡器的不同，可分为摆轮电子手表、音叉手表和石英手表等。electronic watch; any watch that contains an electronic circuit; according to the vibration systems or oscillators used, there are pendulum watches, tuning-fork electronic watches, and electronic quartz watches; also 电子表 diànzǐbiǎo

【电子束】dinzǐshù 由阴极射线产生的束状电子流。电子显微镜和电视机就是利用电子束形成影像的。electron beam; beam of electron current generated by a cathode ray; used for image-forming in electron microscopes and television sets

【电子显微镜】diànzǐ xiǎnwēijìng 一种新型的显微镜，使高速电子流通过物体，经过电磁的放大装置，使物体的影像显现在荧光屏上。放大倍数比光学显微镜大得多，一般可达几十万倍。electron microscope; new type of microscope which passes a beam of energetic electrons through the sample and a magnetic magnifying device, and then focus it onto a fluorescent screen, thus producing a visible image. The magnification of the electron microscope can be several hundred thousand times.

【电子音乐】diànzǐ yīnyuè 指用电子计算机的技术手段编制创作出来的音乐。也指用电子乐器演奏的音乐。electronic music; music composed by using computer techniques; the term also refers to music played with electronic or synthesized musical instruments

【电阻】diànzǔ ❶ 导体对电流通过的阻碍作用。导体的电阻随长度、截面大小、温度和导体成分的不同而改变。电阻的单位是欧姆。electric resistance; resistance; property of a conductor by virtue of which the passage of current is opposed; resistance of a conductor varies with its length, the area of its cross section, its temperature and composition; unit of electric resistance is the ohm ❷ 利用这种阻碍作用做成的元件 resistor; device possessing such resistance

【电钻】diànzuàn 利用电做动力的钻孔机 electrodrill; electric drill; electrical drill; drill operated by electricity

【电嘴】diànzuǐ〈方 *dial.*〉火花塞 spark plug; ignition plug; igniter

佃 diàn 租种土地 rented land：～了五亩地 have rented five *mu* of land

☞ tián on p. 1897

【佃东】diàndōng〈旧时 *old*〉佃户称租给他土地的地主 landlord or landlady; name used by tenant farmers to refer to their landlord or landlady

【佃户】diànhù 租种某地主土地的农民称为某地主的佃户 tenant farmer (of a certain landlord or landlady)

【佃农】diànnóng 自己不占有土地，以租种土地为生的农民 tenant-peasant; tenant farmer;

person who owns no farmland but lives on tilling land rented from another person

【佃权】diànquán 佃户继续租种土地的权利 tenant right; tenant farmer's right to maintain the renting of a farmland

【佃租】diànzū 佃户交纳给地主的地租 land rent; cash or produce paid by tenant farmers to their landlord or landlady

甸 diàn ❶〈古代 *arch.*〉指郊外的地方 suburb; outskirts ❷ 甸子(多用于地名 usu. used as a part of a place name) area; region: 桦～(在吉林) Huadian (in Jilin Province) | 宽～(在辽宁) Kuandian (in Liaoning Province)

【甸子】diàn·zi〈方 *dial.*〉放牧的草地 pasture

阽 diàn 又 also yán〈书 *fml.*〉临近(危险)(danger) close to; be on the edge of: ～危 on the edge of danger; in an hour of danger; in a state of danger | ～于死亡 at one's last gasp; close to death; near one's end; approaching death

坫 diàn ❶〈古时 *arch.*〉室内放置食物、酒器等的土台子 earthen table where food and wine wares were set ❷〈书 *fml.*〉屏障 protective screen; defence

店 diàn ❶ 客店 inn: 小～儿 small inn | 住～ stop at an inn ❷ 商店 shop; store: 布～ cloth shop | 百货～ department store | 零售～ retail shop; retail store

【店东】diàndōng〈旧时 *old*〉称商店或旅店的主人 shopkeeper; innkeeper

【店家】diànjiā ❶〈旧时 *old*〉指旅店、酒馆、饭铺的主人或管事的人 hotel, restaurant or shop owner or manager ❷〈方 *dial.*〉店铺 shop; store

【店面】diànmiàn 商店的门面;铺面 storefront; shop front: ～房 shop building; house with a shop front | 两间～ two-storefront property | 装潢～ decorate the storefront

【店铺】diànpù 泛指商店 shop; store

【店堂】diàntáng 商店、饭馆等进行营业的屋子 building or house that houses a business, a shop or restaurant; commercial section: ～宽敞明亮。The dining hall (shop, etc.) is spacious and bright.

【店小二】diànxiǎo'èr 饭馆、酒馆、客店中接待顾客的人(多见于早期白话 usu. in early vernacular) waiter; attendant; person who waits on tables, e.g. in a restaurant, hotel, etc.

【店员】diànyuán 商店的职工,有时兼指服务性行业的职工 shop assistant; salesclerk; clerk; salesman or saleswoman; term sometimes refers to a waiter or an attendant

玷 diàn ❶ 白玉上面的斑点 flaw in a piece of white jade: 白圭之～ flaw in a jade tablet; spot on white jade ❷ 使有污点 blemish; stain; mar; taint; sully; smudge; spot; disgrace: ～污 blemish; stain; sully; smear; tarnish | ～辱 bring humiliation; bring disgrace on; dishonour

【玷辱】diànrǔ 使蒙受耻辱 bring disgrace on; be a disgrace to; dishonour; bring humiliation: ～祖先 bring shame upon one's ancestors | ～门户 disgrace one's family

【玷污】diànwū ❶ 弄脏 stain; blemish; smear; tarnish;〈比喻 *fig.*〉辱没 bring disgrace to; be unworthy of: ～名声 foul one's name; stain (bring disgrace on) one's reputation | ～光荣称号 be unworthy of a title of honour; sully the honour ❷ 奸污 rape; violate; assault

垫(墊) diàn ❶ 用东西支、铺或衬,使加高、加厚或平正,或起隔离作用 support; prop; fill up; pad; bolster; cushion; wad; put sth. under sth. else to raise it or make it thicker or level, or to separate it from another thing: ～猪圈 bed down the pigs; spread earth in a pigsty | 把桌子～高些 pad the table higher | 熨衣服最好在上面～一块布。It's better to put a piece of cloth on top of the clothes when you iron them. ❷ 填补空缺 fill a vacancy: 正戏还没开演,先～一出小戏。(We)'ll give a preview performance before the play opens. ❸ 暂时替人付钱 pay for sb. and expect to be repaid later: 我先给你～上,等你取了款再还我。I'll pay for you. You can pay me back after you've got money from the bank. ❹ (～儿 diànr) 垫子 bolster; cushion; pad; hassock; upholstery: 靠～ cushion; back cushion; pillow | 鞋～儿 inner sole; insole

【垫背】diàn//bèi〈方 *dial.*〉〈比喻 *fig.*〉代人受过 be sb.'s scapegoat; suffer for the faults of others

【垫补】diàn·bu〈方 *dial.*〉❶ 钱不够用时暂时挪用别的款项或借用别人的钱 use money budgeted for other purposes; borrow money ❷ 吃点心;点补; eat refreshments, pastry or sth. light (usu. before meal time)

【垫底儿】diàn//dǐr ❶ 在底部放上别的东西 put sth. at the bottom: 鱼缸里是用细沙～的。The bottom of the fishbowl is covered with a layer of fine sand. ❷ 先少吃点东西以暂时解饿 have a bite to stave off hunger: 你先吃点东西垫垫底儿,等客人来齐了再吃。Have a bite of something to stave off your hunger and wait till the guests are all here to have dinner. ❸〈比喻 *fig.*〉做基础 lay a foundation; establish a base: 有了你以前的工作～,今后我的工作就好开展了。With what you've done previously as a base, I can do my end of the job well in the future.

【垫付】diànfù 暂时替人付钱 pay for sb. and expect to be repaid later: 由银行～货款。The bank will advance money for the loan.

【垫话】diànhuà 相声演员表演正式节目前所说的开场白，用以引起观众注意或点出下面正式节目的内容 opening remarks made by comic dialogue performers before a show begins to draw the attention of the audience or give a clue to the subject of the show

【垫肩】diànjiān ❶ 挑或扛东西的时候放在肩膀上的垫子，用来减少摩擦，保护衣服和皮肤 shoulder pad; pad put on the shoulder when carrying a heavy weight on the shoulder to reduce friction and protect the clothes and skin ❷ 衬在上衣肩部的三角形衬垫物，使衣服穿起来美观 shoulder pad; triangular pad sewn into the shoulder of a jacket to give a better and tailored look

【垫脚】diàn·jiao 铺垫牲畜棚、圈的干土、碎草等 litter; dry earth and straw used as bedding for animals in a stable, cowshed, barn, etc.

【垫脚石】diànjiǎoshí 〈比喻 *fig.*〉借以向上爬的人或事物 stepping-stone; person or thing one uses to climb up the social ladder

【垫圈】diàn//juàn 给牲畜的圈铺垫干土、碎草等 litter; use dry earth, straw, hay, etc., for litter

【垫圈】diànquān (～儿 diànquānr) 垫在被连接件与螺母之间的零件。一般为扁平形的金属环，用来保护被连接件的表面不受螺母擦伤、分散螺母对被连接件的压力。nut collar; insertion ring; joint-packing; packing collar; washer; flat metal ring put between the connected part and the nut to protect the surface of the connected part from being worn from friction with the nut, and to distribute pressure from the nut

【垫上运动】diànshàng-yùndòng 指在垫子上做的各种运动 mat work; movements and exercises done on a mat; mat tumbling; ground tumbling

【垫支】diànzhī 暂时代替支付；垫付 advance expenditure

【垫子】diàn·zi 垫在床、椅子、凳子上或别的地方的东西 mat; pad; cushion; bolster; mattress; hassock: 椅～ chair cushion | 褥～ cotton-padded mattress | 草～ straw mattress | 弹簧～ spring mattress | 垫上个～。Use a cushion.

钿 diàn 用金片做成的花朵形的装饰品，或木器上和漆器上用螺壳镶嵌的花纹 flower-patterned ornament made of gold foil; shell-inlaid flower pattern on wooden or lacquer ware: 金～ woman's hair ornament of gold flowers | 螺～ shell-inlaid flower pattern; mother-of-pearl inlay | 宝～ woman's hair ornament | 翠～ woman's hair decoration studded with kingfisher feathers

☞ tián on p. 1897

淀¹(澱) diàn 沉淀 form sediment; settle; precipitate: ～粉 starch; amylum

淀² diàn 浅的湖泊，多用于地名，如茶淀(在天津)、白洋淀(在河北) shallow lake, usu. used as part of a place name, e.g. Chadian Lake in Tianjin and Baiyangdian Lake in Hebei Province

【淀粉】diànfěn 有机化合物，化学式 $(C_6H_{10}O_5)_n$，是二氧化碳和水在绿色植物细胞中经光合作用形成的白色无定形的物质。多存在于植物的子粒、块根和块茎中，是主要的碳水化合物食物。工业上应用广泛。starch; organic compound $(C_6H_{10}O_5)_n$, in the form of a white substance with various and variable molecular shape and/or configuration produced in the cells of green plants through photosynthesis, mostly existing in the seeds, root tubers and stem tubers of plants as a major carbohydrate food that is also widely used in industry

惦 diàn 挂念 remember with concern; be concerned about; keep thinking about: ～记 keep thinking about; be concerned about | 老师傅虽然退休了，但心里总～着厂里的工作。Although he has retired, the old worker often finds himself thinking about work in the factory.

【惦记】diàn·jì (对人或事物)心里老想着，放不下心 remember with concern; keep thinking of; be concerned about; worry (oneself) about: 老人孩子有我照顾，你什么也不要～。Don't worry about your parents and kids. I'm taking care of them.

【惦念】diànniàn same as 惦记 diàn·jì: 母亲十分～在外地工作的女儿。The mother worries herself very much over her daughter who works far away.

奠¹ diàn 奠定；建立 establish; found; set up: ～都 establish a capital; found a capital | ～基 lay a foundation

奠² diàn 用祭品向死者致祭 make offerings to the spirits of the dead: 祭～ hold a memorial ceremony for | ～仪 gift of money made on the occasion of a funeral

【奠定】diàndìng 使稳固；使安定 establish; settle: ～基础 build up a foundation; lay a foundation

【奠都】diàndū 确定首都的地址 establish a capital; found a capital: ～北京 make Beijing the capital

【奠基】diànjī 奠定建筑物的基础 lay a foundation: ～石 foundation stone; cornerstone | 举行～典礼 hold a foundation-stone laying ceremony | 人民英雄纪念碑是 1949 年 9 月 30 日～的。The foundation of the Monument to the People's Heroes was laid on Sept. 30, 1949. ◇鲁迅是中国新文学的～人。Lu Xun was a founder of the New Literature of China.

【奠基石】diànjīshí 建筑物奠基用的刻石，上面刻有奠基的年月日等 foundation stone; cornerstone; stone, carved with the date and other information for the laying of a foundation, which represents the starting place in the construction of a building

【奠酒】diànjiǔ 祭祀时的一种仪式，把酒洒在地下 libation; pouring out of wine in an offering ritual

【奠仪】diànyí 指送给丧家用于祭奠的财物 gift of money given to the bereaved on the occasion of a funeral

殿1 diàn 高大的房屋，特指供奉神佛或帝王受朝理事的房屋 hall; palace; temple; large and stately building, esp. where a deity is enshrined, or a monarch handles state affairs: 佛～ Hall of the Buddha | 大雄宝～ Mahavira Hall | 太和～ Hall of Supreme Harmony | 金銮～ emperor's audience hall; throne room

殿2 diàn 在最后 bring up (follow in or close) the rear: ～后 bring up the rear follow in the rear; close the rear | ～军 rear guard; rear

【殿后】diànhòu 行军时走在部队的最后 bring up the rear (in a march): 大部队开始转移，由三连～。The main troops are starting to leave, and the Third Company brings up the rear.

【殿军】diànjūn ❶ 行军时走在最后的部队 rear guard; rear; that part of the army or fleet that brings up the rear ❷ 体育、游艺竞赛中的最末一名，也指竞赛后入选的最末一名 person who finishes last in a contest or among the winners; last of the successful candidates

【殿试】diànshì 科举制度中最高一级的考试，在皇宫内大殿上举行，由皇帝亲自主持 palace examination, the final imperial examination that takes place in the imperial palace and is presided over by the emperor; ☞ 科举 kējǔ on p. 1089

【殿堂】diàntáng 指宫殿、庙宇等高大建筑物 palace; palace hall; temple hall; sanctuary; large stately building

【殿下】diànxià 对太子或亲王的尊称。现用于外交场合。Your (His or Her) Highness, or Excellency; respectful form of address to a prince or princess; now the term is used on diplomatic occasions

靛 diàn ❶ 靛蓝 indigo ❷ 深蓝色，由蓝和紫混合而成 indigo-blue, a colour resulting from blue and purple mixed together

【靛颏儿】diànkér 红点颏和蓝点颏的统称 general name for the Siberian rubythroat (*Luscinia calliope*) and bluethroat (*Luscinia svecica svecica*)

【靛蓝】diànlán 有机染料，深蓝色，用蓼蓝的叶子发酵制成，也有人工合成的。用来染布，颜色经久不退。通称蓝靛，有的地区叫靛青。indigo; dark blue organic dye obtained from the leaves of plants of the genus *Indigofera* by fermentation, or made synthetically; used for dyeing cloth, producing a durable colour, commonly known as 蓝靛 lándiàn; also called 靛青 diànqīng in some areas

【靛青】diànqīng ❶ 深蓝色 indigo-blue; dark blue ❷〈方 *dial.*〉靛蓝 indigo

簟 diàn〈方 *dial.*〉竹席 bamboo mat: 晒～(摊晒粮食等的席子) sun-drying mat (mat used to dry grain in the sun)

癜 diàn 皮肤上长紫斑或白斑的病 any skin disease characterized by purplish or white patches on the skin: 紫～ purpura | 白～风 vitiligo; leukoderma; leucoderma; piebald skin

diāo (ㄉㄧㄠ)

刁 diāo ❶ 狡猾 tricky; artful; sly: 放～ make difficulties for sb.; act in a rascally manner | 逞～ act cunningly ❷〈方 *dial.*〉挑食过分 be picky over food: 嘴～ be picky (or particular) about food ❸ (Diāo)姓 a surname

【刁悍】diāohàn 狡猾凶狠 cunning and fierce; crafty and fierce; wicked and ferocious: 性情～ be of cunning and fierce disposition

【刁滑】diāohuá 狡猾 cunning; guileful; crafty; crooked; insidious

【刁难】diāonàn 故意使人为难 make things difficult for sb.; deliberately cause trouble for sb.: 百般～ create all kinds of difficulties; make it hard for sb.; put up innumerable obstacles

【刁顽】diāowán 狡猾顽固 cunning and unyielding

【刁钻】diāozuān 狡猾；奸诈 tricky; cunning; artful; wily; crafty; deceitful; guileful: ～古怪 sly and capricious; cranky

叼 diāo 用嘴夹住(物体一部分) hold (a part of sth.) in the mouth: 嘴里～着烟卷 with a cigarette dangling from one's lips; hold a cigarette between one's lips | 黄鼠狼～走了小鸡。A weasel ran off with a chick in its mouth.

汈 diāo 汈汊 (Diāochà)，湖名，在湖北 Diaocha, name of a lake in Hubei Province

凋(彫) diāo 凋谢 wither; fade (away); wilt: ～零 withered; wilted; faded away (or out); fallen off; wasted away | 松柏后～。The pine and the cypress do not wither.

【凋败】diāobài 凋谢衰败 wither; wilt: 草木～。All the trees and plants have withered.

【凋敝】diāobì (生活)困苦；(事业)衰败 (of life) hard; destitute; (of business) depressed: 民生～。The people live in destitution. | 百业～。All business languished.

【凋零】diāolíng ❶（草木）凋谢零落（of plants）wither；wilt：万木～。All the trees have withered. ❷ 衰落 decline；fall；go downhill；be on the wane；be on the downward track：家道～。The fortune of the family is waning.

【凋落】diāoluò same as 凋谢 diāoxiè

【凋谢】diāoxiè ❶（草木花叶）脱落（of flowers and leaves of plants）fall off：百花～。All the flowers have withered and fallen. ❷ 指老年人死（of old people）die；pass away：老成～ passing away of a worthy old person

蛁 diāo 古书上指蝉 cicada，referred to in ancient books

貂（鼦）diāo 哺乳动物的一属，身体细长，四肢短，耳朵三角形，听觉敏锐，种类很多，毛皮珍贵，如我国出产的紫貂 marten（*Martes*）；any of several mammal species with a slender body，sharp，triangular ears，and a valuable coat，e. g. the sable of China

碉 diāo ☞ below

【碉堡】diāobǎo 军事上防守用的坚固建筑物，多用砖、石、钢筋混凝土等建成 pillbox；blockhouse；fortified structure for defence，usu. built of bricks，stone，and steel-reinforced concrete

【碉楼】diāolóu 防守和瞭望用的较高建筑物 watchtower；tower on which soldiers defend against enemies and keep watch

雕[1]（彫、琱）diāo ❶ 在竹木、玉石、金属等上面刻画 carve；cut pictures or patterns out of bamboo，wood，jade，metal，etc.：～版 cut blocks for printing｜～漆 carved lacquerware｜～花 carve patterns on woodwork｜～塑 carve and mould；sculpture ❷ 指雕刻艺术或雕刻作品 carving；sculpture：石～ stone carving｜玉～ jade carving｜浮～ relief（sculpture）❸ 有彩画装饰的 decorated with colour drawings：～梁画栋 carved beams and lacquered columns；richly ornamented building

雕[2]（鵰）diāo 鸟类的一属，猛禽，嘴呈钩状，视力很强，腿部有羽毛 vulture（*Accipitridae*）；bird of prey with a hooked beak，sharp eyesight，and feathered legs；also 鹫 jiù

【雕版】diāobǎn same as 刻板 kèbǎn ①

【雕虫小技】diāo chóng xiǎo jì〈比喻 *fig.*〉微不足道的技能（多指文字技巧 usu. referring to writing skill）petty craft；trifling skill

【雕红漆】diāohóngqī ☞ 剔红 tīhóng on p. 1879

【雕花】diāohuā ❶ 一种工艺，在木器上或房屋的隔扇、窗户等上头雕刻图案、花纹 carving；art of cutting out designs or patterns in wood ware，partition boards in a house，windows，etc.：～匠 carver engaged in this kind of craft ❷ 雕刻成的图案、花纹 carved patterns or designs on woodwork

【雕镌】diāojuān〈书 *fml.*〉雕刻 carve；engrave

【雕刻】diāokè ❶ 在金属、象牙、骨头或其他材料上刻出形象 carve；engrave；sculpt：精心～ carve elaborately（or painstakingly）❷ 雕刻成的艺术作品 work of carving：这套～已散失不全。Part of this set of carving is missing.

【雕梁画栋】diāo liáng huà dòng 指房屋的华丽的彩绘装饰。也指有这样装饰的房屋。carved beams and lacquered pillars；gorgeous ornamentation of a building；richly ornamented building

【雕漆】diāoqī 特种工艺的一种，在铜胎或木胎上涂上好些层漆，阴干后浮雕各种花纹。也指这种雕漆的器物。北京和扬州出产的最著名。lacquerware carving；special art form which involves coating a copper or wooden base with layers of lacquer and drying it in the shade before carving various relief patterns in it；carved lacquerware. Lacquerware from Beijing and Yangzhou is the most famous. also 漆雕 qīdiāo

【雕砌】diāoqì 雕琢堆砌（文字）（of writing）overwrought；overelaborate；florid；flowery；excessively flowery in style；marked by rhetorical elegance；in a laboured and ornate style：写文章切忌～。Floridity should be avoided in writing.

【雕饰】diāoshì ❶ 雕刻并装饰 carve and decorate：精心～ carve and decorate elaborately｜柱子上的盘龙～得很生动。The dragon coiling around the column is vividly carved. ❷ 雕刻的花纹、图形装饰 carving；carved ornamental pattern or design：门扇上的～已经残破了。The carvings in the doors and windows have become worn down and broken. ❸ 指过分地刻画修饰）（overwrought；overworked；overdone；overacted：她表演适度，不加～，显得很自然。Her performance struck the right balance，being unaffectedly easy and natural.

【雕塑】diāosù 造型艺术的一种，用竹木、玉石、金属、石膏、泥土等材料雕刻或塑造各种艺术形象 sculpture；art that involves forming（e. g. by carving，modelling，or welding）materials such as bamboo，wood，jade，metals，plastic and earth into works of art

【雕琢】diāozhuó ❶ 雕刻（玉石）carve and polish（jade）；carve：这是用翡翠～成的西瓜。This watermelon is a piece of jade carving. ❷ 过分地修饰（文字）（of writing）overwrought；florid；flowery

鲷 diāo 鱼类的一属，身体侧扁，背部稍微凸起，头大，口小，侧线发达。生活在海里。最常见的是真鲷。porgy（*Calamus*）；sea fish that is characterized by a flat body，slightly bulging back，big head，small mouth，and well-developed lateral lines；the most common kind is the red porgy

diǎo (ㄉㄧㄠˇ)

鸟(鳥) diǎo same as 屌 diǎo;旧小说中用做骂人的话 used in old-style novels as a term of abuse

☞ niǎo on p. 1414

屌 diǎo 男性生殖器的俗称 vulgar name for the male genital organ

diào (ㄉㄧㄠˋ)

D

吊[1](弔) diào ❶ 悬挂 hang; suspend:门前～着两盏红灯。Two red lamps are hanging in front of the gate. ❷ 用绳子等系着向上提或向下放 hoist or lower sth. fastened at one end of a rope:把和好的水泥～上去。Hoist up the mixed cement. ❸ 把球从网上轻轻打到对方难以接到的地方 make a drop shot; hit the ball so softly over the net that it falls to a place the opponent(s) find hard to reach:近网轻～ make a drop shot near the net|打～结合 alternate spikes with drop shots ❹ 把皮桶子加面子或里子缝成衣服 line, as to put in a fur lining (in a jacket):～皮袄 line a coat with fur|～里儿 line a coat ❺ 收回(发出去的证件) revoke; withdraw; annul; cancel (an issued certificate):～销 withdraw; cancel

吊[2](弔) diào 〈旧时 *old*〉钱币单位,一般是一千个制钱叫一吊[monetary unit, equal to a string of 1,000 smallest coins] string

吊[3](弔) diào 祭奠死者或对遭到丧事的人家、团体给予慰问 mourn; condole; grieve or lament for the dead, or express sympathy with a bereaved family or organization:～丧 offer condolences to the bereaved|～唁 express one's grief

【吊膀子】diàobàng·zi 〈方 *dial.*〉调情 flirt

【吊车】diàochē 起重机的通称 general term for 起重机 qǐzhòngjī

【吊窗】diàochuāng 可以向上吊起来的旧式窗子 old-style window hinged at the top

【吊床】diàochuáng 两端挂起来可以睡人的用具,多用网状织物、帆布等临时拴在固定物体上 hammock; hanging bed made of netted cord, canvas, etc.

【吊带】diàodài ❶ 围绕在腰部从两侧垂下来吊住长筒袜子的带子 suspender belt; garter belt; undergarment with garters, worn by women to hold up stockings ❷ 围绕在腿上吊着袜子的带子 garter; sock suspender; suspender; elastic band worn around the leg for holding up a stocking or sock ‖ also 吊袜带 diàowàdài

【吊灯】diàodēng 悬空垂挂的灯 hanging lamp; ceiling lamp; drop light

【吊儿郎当】diào·erlángdāng 形容仪容不整、作风散漫、态度不严肃等 careless and casual; slovenly; frivolous

【吊环】diàohuán ❶ 体操器械的一种,在架上挂两根绳,下面各有一个环 rings; hand rings; gymnastic apparatus that consists of two ropes hanging from a frame and a ring at the lower end of each rope ❷ 男子竞技体操项目之一,运动员用手握住吊环做各种动作 rings; athletic gymnastic event, where a gymnast holds on the rings and does various movements

【吊祭】diàojì 祭奠 hold a mourning ceremony; attend a funeral

【吊脚楼】diàojiǎolóu same as 吊楼 diàolóu ①

【吊卷】diào//juàn same as 调卷 diào//juàn

【吊扣】diàokòu 收回并扣留(发出的证件) withdraw; suspend (an issued certificate):～驾驶执照 suspend sb's driver's licence

【吊楼】diàolóu ❶ 后部用支柱架在水面上的房屋 house on stilts; house supported over the water by stilts under its rear part; also 吊脚楼 diàojiǎolóu ❷ 山区的一种木板房或竹房子,下面用木桩做支柱,用梯子上下 wooden or bamboo house in some mountainous areas that is supported by wooden stakes, and access to it is by a ladder

【吊毛】diàomáo 戏曲中表演突然跌跤的动作。演员身体向前,头向下,然后腾空一翻,以背着地 (of an actor performing traditional Chinese opera) make a forward somersault in the air and land on one's back

【吊民伐罪】diào mín fá zuì 慰问受苦的民众,讨伐有罪的统治者 console the suffering people and launch a punitive expedition against their oppressive rulers

【吊盘】diàopán 建造竖井时,悬吊在井筒中可以升降的工作台 hanging scaffold; work platform which moves up and down in a vertical shaft

【吊铺】diàopù 吊起来的简易的铺位 hanging bed

【吊钱儿】diào·qiánr 〈方 *dial.*〉贴在门楣上镂有图案和文字的刻纸 papercut of patterns and characters pasted on the lintel of a doorframe

【吊桥】diàoqiáo ❶ 全部或一部分桥面可以吊起、放下的桥。多用在护城河及军事据点上。现代在通航的河道上,为了便利船只通过,也有架吊桥的。drawbridge; bridge that may be entirely or partly drawn up or let down, mostly built over a moat or at a military stronghold. In modern times, a drawbridge is built over a navigable waterway so as to leave an open passage for boats. ❷ 在河上、山谷等处架起两根钢索,然后用很多铁条把桥面吊在钢索上,用这种方式造成的桥梁叫吊桥 suspension bridge; bridge built by drawing two steel cables over a river, a valley, etc., and suspending a platform with many iron bars from the cables; also 悬索桥 xuánsuǒqiáo

【吊丧】diào//sāng 到丧家祭奠死者 pay a condolence call; visit the bereaved to offer one's condolences

【吊嗓子】diào sǎng ·zi 戏曲或歌唱演员在乐器伴奏下锻炼嗓子 vocalizing exercise; (of traditional Chinese opera actors or actresses, or singers) train (or exercise) one's voice to the accompaniment of a musical instrument

【吊扇】diàoshàn 安装在顶棚上的电扇 ceiling fan; electric fan hanging from the ceiling

【吊桶】diàotǒng 桶梁上拴着绳子或竹竿的桶,用来从井中打水,或从高处向河中、坑中打水 well-bucket; bucket; pail; bucket with a rope or bamboo pole tied to its handle, used to draw water from a well, a river, or a pond

【吊袜带】diàowàdài same as 吊带 diàodài

【吊胃口】diào wèikǒu 用好吃的东西引起人的食欲,也比喻让人产生欲望或兴趣 stimulate sb.'s appetite with delicious food; (fig.) tantalize; arouse one's desire or interest

【吊线】diào//xiàn 瓦工、木工工作时,用线吊重物形成垂线,借以取直 plumb-line; cord with a weight attached to one end, used by bricklayers and carpenters to determine perpendicularity

【吊销】diàoxiāo 收回并注销(发出去的证件) revoke; withdraw (an issued certificate):~护照 revoke a passport|~营业执照 revoke a business licence

【吊孝】diào//xiào same as 吊丧 diào//sāng

【吊唁】diàoyàn 祭奠死者并慰问家属 mourn the dead and condole the bereaved; express one's grief for the dead and offer one's condolences to the bereaved

【吊装】diàozhuāng 用人工或机械把预制构件吊起来安装在预定的位置 hoist; lift a prefabricated structure to a predetermined place manually or mechanically

【吊子】diào·zi same as 铫子 diào·zi

钓 diào ❶ 用钓竿捉鱼或其他水生动物 angle; fish with a fishing pole:~鱼 fishing; ❷〈比喻 *fig.*〉用手段猎取(名利) angle for; fish for; attempt to get (fame or wealth) by artful means:沽名~誉 fish for fame and compliments ❸ 指钓钩 fishhook; hook:操竿下~ take up the fishing pole and cast the hook

【钓饵】diào'ěr 钓鱼时用来引鱼上钩的食物,也比喻用来引诱人的事物 bait; food used as a lure in fishing; (fig.) anything used to entice or lure

【钓竿】diàogān (~儿 diàogānr) 钓鱼或水中其他动物用的竿子,一端系线,线端有钩 fishing rod; fishing pole; angling rod; casting rod; rod with a line and hook at one end, for use in fishing

【钓钩】diàogōu 钓鱼的钩儿 fishhook; hook;〈比喻 *fig.*〉引诱人的圈套 hook; snare; trap

【钓具】diàoju 钓鱼用具,如钓竿、钓钩等 fishing tackle; equipment, e.g. rods, lines, hooks, etc., used in fishing

茶(蓧) diào〈古代 *arch.*〉除草用的农具 weeding tool

寫 diào 深远 deep; distant; far

【寫远】diàoyuǎn (距离)遥远 (of distance) far-away; far off

调[1] diào ❶ 调动;分派 transfer; shift; move:对~ exchange; swap|~职 be transferred to another post|~兵遣将 deploy forces; commission generals and dispatch troops; mobilize troops|他是新~来的干部。He is a cadre newly transferred here. ❷ 调查 investigate; enquire into:函~ enquire by mail|内查外~ make investigations both inside and outside an organization

调[2] diào ❶ (~儿 diàor)腔调 accent:南腔北~ speak a language heavily corrupted by one's accent; mixture of accents|这人说话的~儿有点特别。This person speaks with a peculiar accent. ❷ (~儿 diàor)论调 view; opinion; argument:两个人的意见是一个~。The two of them have the same view. ❸ 乐曲以什么音做 do,就叫做什么调。例如以 C 做 do 就叫做 C 调,以'上'做 do 就叫做'上'字调 key; principal tonality of a composition of music, classified by the tone used as the keynote, e.g. the key of C means C is the keynote, and the key of '上 *shang*' in Chinese music means '*shang*' is the keynote ❹ (~儿 diàor)音乐上高低长短配合的成组的音 tune; air; melody; a succession of musical sounds, which can be high, low, long and short, to make a tune:这个~很好听。This is a very pleasant tune. ❺ 指语音上的声调 tone; tune:~类 tone category|~号 classification and symbols of tunes

☞ tiáo on p. 1901

【调包】diào//bāo same as 掉包 diào//bāo

【调拨】diàobō ❶ 调动拨付(多指物资) allocate and transfer (usu. goods or supplies); allot:~款项 allocate funds|~小麦种子 allocate wheat seeds ❷ 调遣 assign; dispatch:人员都听从他的指挥和~。Everyone is to obey his commands and dispatches.

☞ tiáobō on p. 1901

【调查】diàochá 为了了解情况进行考察(多指到现场) investigate; enquire into; look into; survey; (usu. on the spot) to search so as to learn the facts:~事实真相 probe into the truth of sth.|没有~,就没有发言权。No investigation, no right to speak. | 事情还没有～清楚，不能忙着处理。We should not handle this matter hastily without a thorough investigation.

【调调】diào·diao (～儿 diào·diaor) ❶ same as 调 diào² ③ ④ ❷ 论调 view; argument

【调动】diàodòng ❶ 更动（位置、用途）shift; transfer; move (from one place to another); change the use of sth.: ～队伍 move troops | ～工作 transfer sb. to a new post ❷ 调集动员 assemble and put into action; mobilize; actuate; muster: ～群众的生产积极性 fire the masses with enthusiasm for production

【调度】diàodù ❶ 管理并安排（工作、人力、车辆等）organize and dispatch (people, trains, buses, etc.); manage or control (work, human resources, etc.) ❷ 指做调度工作的人 dispatcher

【调防】diào//fáng 换防 relieve a garrison

【调函】diàohán 调动工作人员工作的公函，一般由上级机关或用人单位发出 official letter for personnel transfer (usu. issued by higher authorities or an employing unit)

【调号】diàohào (～儿 diàohàor) ❶ 表示字调的符号。《汉语拼音方案》的调号，阴平是'ˉ'(ā)，阳平是'ˊ'(á)，上声是'ˇ'(ǎ)，去声是'ˋ'(à)，轻声无号(a)。tone mark; according to 'The Plan for Chinese Phonetic Alphabet', the symbols of the four tones are respectively ā, á, ǎ, à, with the neutral tone having no symbol ❷ 音乐上指用以确定乐曲主音高度的符号 key signature; symbol that indicates the pitch of the key

【调虎离山】diào hǔ lí shān 〈比喻 *fig.*〉为了便于乘机行事，想法子引诱有关的人离开原来的地方 lure the tiger from the mountain; try to lure sb. away from his original location so as to take advantage of him

【调换】diàohuàn same as 掉换 diàohuàn

【调集】diàojí 调动使集中 muster; assemble; gather: ～军队 muster the troops; assemble the troops | ～防汛器材 assemble flood-prevention equipment

【调卷】diào//juàn 提取案卷、考卷 ask for files or examination papers: ～复审 ask for files for re-examination or for a retrial; also 吊卷 diào//juàn

【调侃儿】diào//kǎnr 〈方 *dial.*〉同行业的人说行话 (of people of the same profession) talk in professional jargon; also 调坎儿 diào//kǎnr

【调类】diàolèi 有声调的语言中声调的类别。古汉语的调类有四个，就是平声、上声、去声、入声。普通话的调类有五个，就是阴平、阳平、上声、去声、轻声。tone category of a tonal language. Ancient Chinese has four tones — level, rising, falling, brief (which can be level, rising, falling-rising or falling). Modern Chinese has five tones — level, rising, falling-rising, falling, neutral.

【调令】diàolìng 调动工作人员工作的命令 transfer order; order for transferring sb. to a new post

【调门儿】diàoménr ❶ 歌唱或说话时音调的高低 pitch of tone when one sings or speaks: 我今天嗓子不好，～定低点儿。My voice is not good today, so please set the pitch at a lower key. | 你说话老是那么大声大气，～放低点儿行不行？You are always talking so loudly. Can you lower your voice? ❷ 指论调 view; point of view; argument: 这几个人的发言都是一个～。In their speeches these people talked very much in the same vein.

【调派】diàopài 调动分派（指人事的安排）assign; send; transfer (personnel): 上级决定～大批干部支援农业。The higher authorities decided to assign large numbers of government and Party functionaries to aid agriculture.

【调配】diàopèi 调动分配 allocate; deploy: 劳动力和工具～得合理，工作进行就顺利。Rational allocation of human resources and tools will help the work go on smoothly.
☞ tiáopèi on p. 1902

【调遣】diàoqiǎn 调派；差遣 dispatch; assign; transfer; send: ～部队 dispatch troops; send troops | 听从～ (be ready to) accept an assignment

【调任】diàorèn 调动职位，担任另一工作 be transferred to another post: ～新职 be transferred to a new post

【调式】diàoshì 乐曲中的几个音根据它们彼此之间的关系而联结成体系，并且有一个主音，这些音的总和叫做调式 mode; scale; (in a piece of music) sum total of a keynote and the tones arranged around it according to their relations

【调头】diào//tóu same as 掉头 diào//tóu ②

【调头】diàotóu 论调 point of view; argument; remark: 空洞抽象的～必须少唱。We should refrain from using empty and abstract arguments.

【调头】diào·tou 〈方 *dial.*〉❶ 调子 tune; melody ❷ 语气 tone; manner of speaking

【调研】diàoyán 调查研究 investigation; research; survey; study: 开展市场～ make investigation into the market | 深入实际，进行～ dig deeply into reality to conduct the investigation

【调演】diàoyǎn 从某些地方或文艺团体抽调演员选定节目集中在一起演出 gather performers from different localities or troupes for a joint performance or a theatrical festival: 全省戏剧～ provincial joint theatrical performance

【调用】diàoyòng 调配使用 allocate; transfer: ～物资 allocate materials | ～干部 allocate and transfer cadres

【调运】diàoyùn 调拨和运输 allocate and transport:～工业品下乡 allocate and deliver industrial products to rural areas

【调值】diàozhí 有声调的语言中各调类的实际读法,即字音的高低升降。两个不同的方言,字调的分类法(调类)可以相同,每一调类的实际读法(调值)却可以不同。如北京语音(普通话标准音)的阴平读高平调,天津话的阴平读低平调。tone pitch; actual pronunciation of tones in a tonal language, or the rising and falling pitches of the pronunciation of words; different dialects may have the same classification of tones, but the actual pronunciation of the tones can be different, e.g. in the Beijing dialect (standard Chinese or *putonghua*), the first tone is pronounced with a higher pitch than in the Tianjin dialect

【调职】diào//zhí 从某个单位调到另一个单位去工作 be transferred to a new post

【调转】diàozhuǎn ❶调动转换(工作等) transfer to a new post:他的～手续已经办好了。He has gone through the procedure for a transfer. ❷ same as 掉转 diàozhuǎn

【调子】diào·zi ❶ 一组音的排列次第和相互关系 mode; sequencing and relation of a group of notes ❷ 音乐上高低长短配合成组的音 tune; melody; air; a succession of musical sounds different in pitch and duration ❸ 说话时带的某种情绪 tone; mood in a speech:他说话的～很忧郁。He speaks in a gloomy tone. ❹ 指论调;精神(jīngshén)② view; spirit:文章只作了文字上的改动,基本～没有变。In the article some changes have been made in wording, but its basic spirit remains the same.

掉[1] diào ❶ 落① fall; drop; shed:～眼泪 shed tears|被击中的敌机～在海里了。The stricken enemy fighter plane dropped into the sea. ❷ 落在后面 fall behind; lag behind:～队 lag behind; fall behind ❸ 遗失;遗漏 lose; be missing:钢笔～了。The pen was lost.|这篇文章里～了几个字。There are a few characters missing in the article. ❹ 减少;降低 reduce; drop:～价儿 lose face; lose one's dignity; lower one's dignity|别让牲口～膘。Don't let the cattle lose weight.

掉[2] diào ❶ 摇动;摆动 wag; swing:尾大不～ big tail does not wag; the tail wags the dog; (of an organization) too cumbersome to be efficient|～臂而去(甩胳膊就走) leave with a swing of the arm; walk out on sb. ❷ 回;转 turn; spin; swing:把车头～过来 turn the car around|他～过脸来向送行的人一一招呼。He turned around to say goodbye to everyone seeing him off. ❸ 互换 change; exchange; shift; swap; switch; trade; barter:～换 swap; exchange|～过儿 shift positions ❹ 卖弄 show off:～文 write in a showy style|～书袋 make literary quotations

掉[3] diào 用在某些动词后,表示动作的结果[used after certain verbs to indicate the consequence of an act]:扔～ throw away|除～ get rid of|抹～ erase; wipe off|改～坏习气 correct and get rid of bad habits

【掉包】diào//bāo (～儿 diàobāor)暗中用假的换真的或用坏的换好的 stealthily substitute the fake for the real or the bad for the good:～计 scheme of substitution|他的东西叫人掉了包。His belongings were stealthily substituted. also 调包 diào//bāo

【掉秤】diào//chèng〈方 *dial*.〉折(shé)秤 lose weight when reweighed

【掉点儿】diào//diǎnr 落下稀疏的雨点(of rain) spatter:～了,快去收衣服吧!It's spattering. Hurry over to collect the clothes!

【掉队】diào//duì ❶ 结队行走时落在队伍的后面 drop behind; fall behind; lag; fail to keep pace with the group:在接连三天的急行军中,没有一个人～。No one dropped behind in the three-day forced march. ❷〈比喻 *fig*.〉落在客观形势的后边 lag behind; become outdated or old-fashioned:只有加紧学习才不致～。One can only keep pace with the times by studying hard.

【掉过儿】diào//guòr 互相掉换位置 swap or exchange places with sb.; switch positions:这两件家具～放才合适。It would be better to switch these two pieces of furniture around.|你跟他掉个过儿,你就看得见台上的人了。You can see the people on the stage if you change seats with him.

【掉换】diàohuàn ❶ 彼此互换 exchange; swap; switch:～位置 swap positions|咱们俩～一下,你上午值班,我下午值班。Let's swap shifts. You work on the morning shift, and let me do the afternoon shift. ❷ 更换 change; replace:～领导班子 change the leading group|这根木料太细,～一根粗的。This log is too thin. Please change it for a thicker one. ‖ also 调换 diàohuàn

【掉价】diào//jià (～儿 diào//jiàr) ❶ 价格降低 fall (or drop) in price; go down in price:菠菜～了。The price of spinach has dropped. ❷〈比喻 *fig*.〉身份、排场降低 lower (or lose) one's dignity; lose one's social position

【掉枪花】diào qiānghuā〈方 *dial*.〉耍花招 get up to tricks; play tricks

【掉色】diào//shǎi 颜色脱落(多指纺织品经日晒或水洗后)(usu. of textiles after washing or exposure to sun) lose colour; fade

【掉书袋】diàoshūdài 讥讽人爱引用古书词句,卖弄才学(usu. satirical) fling or drop one's bag of books — padding one's speech or writing with quotations and allusions

【掉头】diào//tóu ❶ (人)转回头(of people)

turn around：他掉过头去，装作没看见。He turned away, pretending not to see it. ❷（车、船等）转成相反的方向（of vehicles, boats, etc.）turn about; turn around; veer about：～车 returned bus｜胡同太窄，车子掉不了头。The lane is too narrow for the car to turn around. also 调头 diào//tóu

【掉以轻心】diào yǐ qīng xīn 表示对某种问题漫不经心，不当回事 treat (take) sth. lightly; let down one's guard; relax one's vigilance

【掉转】diàozhuǎn 改变成相反的方向 turn round; make a U-turn：～船头 turn the boat around; also 调转 diàozhuǎn

铞 diào ☞［钌铞儿］（liàodiàor）on p. 1215

铫 diào（～儿 diàor）same as 铫子 diào·zi：药～儿 medicine pot｜沙～儿 earth pot
☞ yáo on p. 2228

【铫子】diào·zi 煎药或烧水用的器具，形状像比较高的壶，口大有盖，旁边有柄，用沙土或金属制成 pot-shaped earthen or metal utensil for concocting herbal medicine or boiling water, with large mouth, lid and handle; also 吊子 diào·zi

diē（ㄉㄧㄝ）

爹 diē 父亲 father; dad; daddy; pa：～娘 father and mother; mum and dad; ma and pa; parents｜～妈 father and mother; mum and dad; ma and pa; parents

【爹爹】diē·die〈方 *dial.*〉❶ 父亲 father; dad; daddy; pa ❷ 祖父 grandfather; grandpa

跕 diē〈书 *fml.*〉跌倒；降落 fall; tumble; topple; descend
☞ 跕 diǎn on p. 435

跌 diē ❶ 摔 ① tumble; topple; fall：～跤 have a fall｜～倒了又爬起来了 fall down and get up ❷（物体）落下（of objects）drop; fall; descend：～水 drop into the water; fall into the water ❸（物价）下降（of prices）drop; fall; go down; plummet：金价～了百分之二。The price of gold dropped by 2%.

【跌宕】diēdàng〈书 *fml.*〉❶ 性格洒脱，不拘束；放荡不羁（of character）free and easy; bold and unconstrained; uninhibited ❷ 音调抑扬顿挫或文章富于变化（of tone）rhythmical; in measured tones; (of writing) richly varied：乐曲起伏～。The music is rhythmical.｜文笔～有致 write in a style free and rich with variation; also 跌荡 diēdàng

【跌荡】diēdàng same as 跌宕 diēdàng

【跌跌撞撞】diē·diezhuàngzhuàng（～的 diē·diezhuàngzhuàng·de）形容走路不稳 tumble along; stagger; lurch

【跌份】diē//fèn〈方 *dial.*〉（～儿 diē//fènr）降低身份；丢面子 lower (or lose) one's dignity; lose face

【跌价】diē//jià 商品价格下降 fall (or drop) in price; go down in price

【跌跤】diē//jiāo ❶ 摔跟头 fall; tumble：小孩儿学走路免不了要～。A baby learning to walk falls a lot.｜跌了一跤 have a fall; have a tumble; ❷〈比喻 *fig.*〉犯错误或受挫折 make a mistake; suffer a setback; be frustrated ‖ also 跌跤子 diē//jiāo·zi

【跌落】diēluò ❶（物体）往下掉（of objects）fall; drop ❷（价格、产量等）下降（of prices, yields, etc.）drop; fall; go down; plummet

【跌水】diēshuǐ ❶ 突然下降的水流 drop; sudden drop in water flowing ❷ 水利工程中使水流突然下降的台阶（of a water conservancy project）a series of steps to make water plunge

【跌眼镜】diē yǎnjìng〈方 *dial.*〉指事情的发展出乎意料，令人感到吃惊（多跟'大'连用 usu. used with 大 dà）to one's surprise; surprise; amaze; astonish; dumbfound; flabbergast：出现这样的结果，令不少行家大～。Such a result astonished many experts.

【跌足】diēzú〈方 *dial.*〉跺脚 stamp one's foot：～长叹 stamp one's foot and sigh｜～捶胸 stamp one's foot and thump one's chest

dié（ㄉㄧㄝˊ）

迭 dié ❶ 轮流；替换 alternate; substitute：更～ change; rotate; alternation; rotation ❷ 屡次 repeatedly; again and again; time and again; over and over：～挫强敌 defeat powerful enemies time and again｜～有新发现 make new discoveries one after another ❸ same as 及[1] jí ②：忙不～ hasten to do sth.

【迭出】diéchū 一次又一次地出现 appear time and again：花样～ play trick after trick｜名家～ famous experts appear one after another

【迭次】diécì 屡次；不止一次 repeatedly; more than once; over and over; again and again：～会商 repeatedly consult each other｜影片中惊险场面～出现。Thrilling scenes occurred again and again in the movie.

【迭起】diéqǐ 一次又一次地兴起、出现 occur repeatedly; happen frequently：比赛高潮～。One climax after another occurred in the match.

垤 dié〈书 *fml.*〉小土堆 mound; hill：丘～ mound; hill｜蚁～（蚂蚁做窝时堆在穴口的小土堆）anthill, mound thrown up by ants (when digging their nest)

昳 dié〈书 *fml.*〉太阳偏西 sun going down in the west：日～。The sun sets in the west.
☞ yì on p. 2277

绖 dié〈古时 *arch.*〉丧服上的麻布带子 hemp band on a mourning garment

瓞 dié〈书 *fml.*〉小瓜 small melon: 绵绵瓜～(比喻子孙昌盛) may the family grow and prosper like spreading melon-vines

咥 dié same as 喋 dié
☞ shà on p. 1667

【咥血】diéxuè same as 喋血 diéxuè

谍 dié ❶ 谍报活动 espionage; spying ❷ 从事谍报活动的人 spy; agent; undercover agent: 间～ spy; agent; intelligence agent; undercover agent | 防～ prevent spying

【谍报】diébào 刺探到的关于敌方军事、政治、经济等的情报 information on an enemy's military affairs, politics, economy, etc., obtained through espionage; intelligence report; intelligence: ～员(从事谍报工作的人) spy; intelligence agent; undercover agent

堞 dié 堞墙 battlements: 雉～ battlements | 城～ battlements

【堞墙】diéqiáng 城墙上呈凹凸形的矮墙 battlements; crenelation; parapet or city wall with regularly alternating merlons and crenels

耋 dié〈书 *fml.*〉七八十岁的年纪,泛指老年 septuagenarian; sb. over seventy or eighty years in age; old age; advanced in years: 耄(mào)～之年 advanced age; senile age; venerable age

揲 dié〈书 *fml.*〉折叠 fold
☞ shé on p. 1693

喋 dié ☞ below
☞ zhá on p. 2404

【喋喋】diédié 没完没了地说话 talk endlessly; talkative: ～不休 chatter away; rattle on; talk endlessly

【喋血】diéxuè〈书 *fml.*〉血流遍地(杀人很多) bloodshed; bloodbath; massacre; also 咥血 diéxuè and 蹀血 diéxuè

嵽(嵽) dié [嵽嵲](diéniè)〈书 *fml.*〉形容山高 (of a mountain) high; lofty; towering; to wery; soaring; skyscraping

惵 dié〈书 *fml.*〉恐惧;害怕 fearful; afraid; frightened; scared; terrified

牒 dié ❶ 文书或证件 official document or note; credentials; certificate: 通～ diplomatic note | 度～ monk's or nun's certificate issued by the government ❷ 簿册;书籍 book; volume; tome: 谱～ family tree; genealogy | 史～ history; historical records

叠(疊、曡) dié ❶ 一层加上一层;重复 lap; overlap; pile up; repeat: 重～overlapping | ～石为山 pile up rocks into hills | 层见～出 occur frequently; appear repeatedly ❷ 折叠(衣被、纸张等) fold (a quilt, paper, etc.): ～衣服 fold clothes | 把信～好装在信封里 fold a letter and put it into an envelope

【叠床架屋】dié chuáng jià wū〈比喻 *fig.*〉重复累赘 needless duplication (or repetition); repetitiousness

【叠翠】diécuì 林木青翠重叠 (of forest, woods) heaping up rich piles of foliage; verdant; green; emerald: 峰峦～ mountains clad in verdure | 层林～ verdant forests

【叠罗汉】diéluóhàn 人上架人,重叠成各种形式,是体操、杂技表演项目之一 pyramid; gymnastic event or acrobatic performance where a group of people pile one on top of another in various forms

【叠印】diéyìn 电影、电视片中把两个或两个以上的内容不同的画面重叠印在一起,用于表现剧中人的回忆、幻想,或构成并列形象 (in films or TV) dissolve; overlapping dissolve; dissolving view in which two or more different scenes are overlapped to reveal the memories and fantasies of a character or different images in juxtaposition

【叠韵】diéyùn 两个字或几个字的韵母相同叫叠韵,例如'阑干'、'千年' rhyming compound; compound consisting of two or more syllables that rhyme with one another, e. g. 阑干 lángān and 千年 qiānnián

【叠嶂】diézhàng 重叠的山峰 jumble of mountains; great cluster of mountains; turmoil of rocky eminencies: 重峦～ peaks upon peaks; topographic turmoil of mountains

碟 dié (～儿 diér)碟子 small plate; saucer; dish

【碟子】dié·zi 盛菜蔬或调味品的器皿,比盘子小,底平而浅 small plate; saucer; dish; any container, shallow and concave and smaller than a plate, for serving or holding vegetables, seasonings or condiments

蝶(蜨) dié 蝴蝶 butterfly

【蝶骨】diégǔ 头骨之一,形状像蝴蝶,在脑颅的底部,枕骨之前 sphenoid bone; butterfly-shaped compound bone at the bottom of the cranium and in front of the occipital bone

【蝶泳】diéyǒng ❶ 游泳的一种姿势,也是游泳项目之一,跟蛙泳相似,但两臂划水后须提出水面再向前摆去,因形似蝶飞而得名 butterfly stroke; swimming stroke similar to the breaststroke, where both arms are brought out of the water after moving through the water and then swung forward, thus named because it looks like a flying butterfly ❷ 指海豚泳 dolphin (swimming); dolphin butterfly; dolphin fishtail

艓 dié〈书 *fml.*〉小船 small boat

蹀 dié〈书 *fml.*〉蹈;顿足 step; tread; stamp one's foot

【蹀躞】diéxiè〈书 *fml.*〉❶ 小步走路 mince

(walk in a prim manner); walk with a mincing gait; walk with short steps ❷ 往来徘徊 pace up and down

【蹀血】diéxuè same as 喋血 diéxuè

蛭 dié [蛭蛸](diédāng)一种生活在地下洞穴中的蜘蛛 *Latouchia davidi*; ctenizid; a species of spider living in underground caves

☞ zhì on p. 2479

鰈 dié 鱼类的一科,身体侧扁像薄片,长椭圆形,有细鳞,两眼都在右侧,左侧向下卧在沙底。生活在浅海中。flatfish (*Heterosomata*); right-eyed flounder; sole; fish with a flat, elongate oval body covered with fine scales, having both eyes on the right side, usu. lying on its left side on the seabed, and living in shallow seawater

D

氎 dié〈书 *fml.*〉棉布 cotton cloth

dīng(ㄉㄧㄥ)

丁[1] dīng ❶ 成年男子 grown man: 成~ reach manhood; come of age; reach the age of adulthood | 壮~ able-bodied man ❷ 指人口 member of a family; population: 添~ have a baby born into the family | ~口 population | 人~ population; family member ❸ 称从事某些职业的人 person engaged in a certain occupation: 园~ gardener ❹(Dīng) 姓 a surname

丁[2] dīng 天干的第四位 the 4th of the 10 Heavenly Stems; ☞ 干支 gānzhī on p. 627

丁[3] dīng (~儿 dīngr)蔬菜、肉类等切成的小块 cube; small cubes of meat or vegetable: 黄瓜~儿 diced cucumber | 辣子炒鸡~ diced chicken with hot pepper

丁[4] dīng〈书 *fml.*〉遭逢;碰到 meet with; run into; encounter; confront; face: ~忧 encounter a parent's death; in mourning for one's parent | ~兹盛世 born into this prosperous age

☞ zhēng on p. 2441

【丁坝】dīngbà 一端跟堤岸连接成丁字形的坝,能改变水流,使河岸不受冲刷 spur dike; dike built at a right angle to the bank of a river to reduce erosion of the bank by changing the direction of the water current

【丁部】dīngbù 集部 collection of literary works

【丁册】dīngcè〈旧时 *old*〉指户口簿 residence registration booklet

【丁村人】Dīngcūnrén 古代人类的一种,生活在旧石器时代中期,化石在 1954 年发现于山西襄汾县丁村 Dingcun Man, primitive man dating back to the mid-Palaolithic Age, whose fossil remains were found in Dingcun Village in Xiangfen County, Shanxi Province, in 1954

【丁当】dīngdāng〈拟声词 *onom.*〉形容金属、瓷器、玉饰等撞击的声音 jingle; clatter; dingdong; clink; tinkle; sound made by metal pieces, porcelain ware, jade ornaments, etc., striking against each other: 环佩~ tinkling of jade ornaments | 铁马~ tinkling of metal chimes hanging from the eaves of pagodas and temples | 碟子碗碰得丁丁当当的。Dishes and bowls clinked against each other. also 叮当 dīngdāng or 玎珰 dīngdāng

【丁点儿】dīngdiǎnr〈方 *dial.*〉〈量词 *classifier*〉表示极少或极小(程度比'点儿'深 to a larger degree than '点儿' diǎnr) a tiny bit; a little bit; the tiniest; the slightest: 一~毛病也没有。There isn't the slightest flaw. | 这~事何必放在心上。Don't worry yourself over such trifles.

【丁东】dīngdōng〈拟声词 *onom.*〉形容玉石、金属等撞击的声音 tinkle; clink; dingdong; jingle; sound produced by two pieces of jade, metal, etc., striking against each other: 玉佩~ tinkling of jade ornaments; also 丁冬 dīngdōng

【丁冬】dīngdōng same as 丁东 dīngdōng

【丁艰】dīngjiān〈书 *fml.*〉丁忧 encounter a parent's death

【丁零】dīnglíng〈拟声词 *onom.*〉形容铃声或小的金属物体的撞击声 tinkle; jingle; ding-a-ling; dingling; ring; sound of a bell or of small objects striking against each other: 铜铃~~地响。The copper bell is ringing.

【丁零当啷】dīng·lingdānglāng〈拟声词 *onom.*〉形容金属、瓷器等连续撞击声 jingle-jangle; cling-clang; ding-dong; sound produced by pieces of metal, porcelain, etc., continuously striking against each other

【丁宁】dīngníng same as 叮咛 dīngníng

【丁是丁,卯是卯】dīng shì dīng, mǎo shì mǎo 形容对事情认真,一点儿不含糊、不马虎 keep *ding* (a Heavenly Stem) distinct from *mao* (an Earthly Branch) — be strict, precise or unaccommodating; also 钉是钉,铆是铆 dīng shì dìng, mǎo shì mǎo

【丁香】[1] dīng xiāng ❶ 落叶灌木或小乔木,叶子卵圆形或肾脏形,花紫色或白色,有香味,花冠长筒状。供观赏。lilac (*Syringa vulgaris*); deciduous shrub or tree with oval or kidney-shaped leaves and fragrant tubular white or purple flowers ❷ 这种植物的花 flower of this plant ‖ also 丁香花 dīngxiānghuā or 紫丁香 zǐdīngxiāng

【丁香】[2] dīng xiāng 常绿乔木,叶子长椭圆形,花淡红色,果实长球形。生在热带地方。花可入药,种子可以榨丁香油,用做芳香剂。clove (*Eugenia aromatica*); evergreen tree with elongated oval leaves, pale-red flowers, and oblong bulb-shaped fruits, growing in tropical areas, the flowers of which are used as medicine, and the seeds for making clove oil, an aromatic

【丁忧】dīngyōu〈书 *fml*.〉遭到父母的丧事 in mourning for a deceased parent

【丁字尺】dīngzìchǐ 绘图的用具,多用木料或塑料制成,形状像丁字 T-square; T-shaped ruler used in drawing, oft. made of wood or plastic

【丁字钢】dīngzìgāng 断面呈 T 形的条状钢材 steel bar with T-shaped fracture; T-steel; commonly known as 丁字铁 dīngzìtiě

【丁字街】dīngzìjiē 呈 T 形的街道 T-shaped road junction; T-junction

仃 dīng ☞ 伶仃 língdīng on p. 1226

叮 dīng ❶(蚊子等)用针形口器插入人或牛马等的皮肤吸取血液 sting; bite; (of insects like mosquitoes) to prick with a sting into the skin of human beings or livestock to suck blood: 腿上叫蚊子~了一下 got a mosquito bite on the leg ❷ 叮嘱 admonish; exhort; say or ask again to make sure: 千~万嘱 admonish repeatedly ❸ 追问 enquire: 跟着我又~了他一句,他说明天准去,我才放心。I asked him again and was relieved when he said he would be there tomorrow.

【叮当】dīngdāng same as 丁当 dīngdāng

【叮咛】dīngníng 反复地嘱咐 urge; exhort: 他娘千~万嘱咐,叫他一路上多加小心。His mother exhorted him again and again to be careful along the way. also 丁宁 dīngníng

【叮问】dīngwèn〈方 *dial*.〉追问 question persistently; make a detailed enquiry

【叮咬】dīngyǎo same as 叮 dīng ①: 蚊虫~ bitten by insects

【叮嘱】dīngzhǔ 再三嘱咐 urge again and again; warn; exhort: 老师~他,在新的环境里仍要继续努力。His teacher urged him to continue with his efforts in the new place.

玎 dīng ☞ below

【玎珰】dīngdāng same as 丁当 dīngdāng

【玎玲】dīnglíng〈拟声词 *onom*.〉多形容玉石等撞击的声音 (of precious stones, etc.) clink; jingle; ting; sound made by pieces of precious stones, such as jade, striking against each other

盯 dīng 把视线集中在一点上;注视 fix one's eyes on; gaze at; stare at: 轮到她射击,大家的眼睛都~住了靶心。When it was her turn to shoot, everybody fixed their eyes on the bull's eye. also 钉 dīng

【盯梢】dīng//shāo same as 钉梢 dīng//shāo

町 dīng 畹町(Wǎndīng),地名,在云南 used in place names: Wanding (in Yunnan Province)

☞ tǐng on p. 1913

钉[1] dīng(~儿 dīngr) same as 钉子 dīng·zi ①: 螺丝~儿 screw

钉[2] dīng ❶ 紧跟着不放松 follow closely; tail behind: 小李~住对方的前锋,使他没有得球机会。Xiao Li tailed the forward of the other team to prevent him from getting the ball. ❷ 督促;催问 urge; press: 你要经常~着他一点儿,免得他忘了。You must remind him every now and then of the matter, in case he forgets. ❸ same as 盯 dīng

☞ dìng on p. 457

【钉齿耙】dīngchǐbà 用大铁钉做齿的耙,用来弄碎土块,平整地面。使用时平放在地面上,用牲畜或机器牵引。spike-tooth harrow; farm implement with spikes, which is laid flat on the ground and drawn by a draught animal or tractor, used for breaking up the soil and levelling the ground

【钉锤】dīngchuí 钉钉子用的小锤,锤头一端是方柱形,另一端扁平,有的中间有起钉子用的狭缝 hammer; claw hammer; tool for pounding, with one end of its head in the shape of a square column, and the other end being flat or having a pronged claw for pulling nails

【钉螺】dīngluó 螺的一种,卵生,壳圆锥形。生活在温带和亚热带的淡水里和陆地上。是传染血吸虫病的媒介。snail (*Helicidae*); oncomelania; freshwater or terrestrial snail in temperate and subtropical zones, with a cone-shaped shell, which is the intermediate host of the blood fluke

【钉帽】dīngmào 钉的顶端,是承受锤打或旋转的部分 head of a nail, the part to be pounded or screwed

【钉耙】dīngpá 用铁钉做齿的耙子,是碎土、平土的农具 iron-toothed rake; farm tool with iron teeth for breaking and levelling the ground

【钉梢】dīng//shāo 暗中跟在后面(监视人的行动 so as to observe the movements of sb.) shadow; tail; follow in secret; also 盯梢 dīngshāo

【钉是钉,铆是铆】 dīng shì dīng, mǎo shì mǎo same as 丁是丁,卯是卯 dīng shì dīng, mǎo shì mǎo

【钉鞋】dīngxié ❶ 旧式雨鞋,用布做帮,用桐油油过,鞋底钉上大帽子钉 old-style rain shoes with tung-oil-cloth uppers and spiked soles ❷ 体育运动上跑鞋和跳鞋的统称 general term for spiked shoes; soccer shoes

【钉子】dīng·zi ❶ 金属制成的细棍形的物件,一端有扁平的头,另一端尖锐,主要起固定或连接作用,也可以用来悬挂物品或做别的用处 nail; tapered piece of metal with a pointed end and a flattened head, mainly used to fix things, hold pieces or parts together, hang things on, etc. ❷〈比喻 *fig*.〉难以处置或解决的事物 matter that is difficult to handle: ~户 tartar; sb. who refuses to move but bargains for high compensation when his land is requisitioned for a construction project ❸〈比喻 *fig.*〉埋伏的人 saboteur：安插～ plant a saboteur

【钉子户】dīng·zihù 指在城市建设征用土地时，讨价还价，不肯迁走的住户 (in cities) sb. who refuses to move but bargains for high compensation when his land is requisitioned for a construction project

疔 dīng〈中医 *Chin. med.*〉指病理变化急骤并有全身症状的小疮，坚硬而根深，形状像钉 malignant boil (or furuncle); deep-rooted boil; hard, nail-shaped, deep-rooted sore that worsens quickly and is accompanied by pervasive general symptoms; also 疔疮 dīngchuāng

【疔毒】dīngdú〈中医 *Chin. med.*〉指症状严重的疔疮 malignant boil (or furuncle) with serious symptoms

耵 dīng [耵聍](dīngníng) 耳垢 earwax; cerumen

酊 dīng 酊剂的简称 abbr. for 酊剂 dīngjì [拉 Latin: tinctura]

☞ dǐng on p.456

【酊剂】dīngjì 把生药浸在酒精里或把化学药物溶解在酒精里而成的药剂，如颠茄酊、橙皮酊、碘酊等 tincture; medication made of an alcohol preparation containing dried medicinal herbs or chemical drugs, e.g. belladonna tincture, flavedo tincture, iodine tincture, etc.; 简称 abbr. 酊 dīng

靪 dīng 补鞋底 resole：～前掌 resole a shoe

dǐng (ㄉㄧㄥˇ)

顶 dǐng ❶ (～儿 dǐngr) 人体或物体上最高的部分 top; summit; tip-top; peak; pinnacle; crest; crown; uppermost part of a human body or an object：头～ top of the head | 屋～ roof | 山～ top of the mountain; crest of the hill | 塔～儿 crest of the pagoda ❷ 用头支承 carry on the head：～碗（杂技）pagoda of bowls (in acrobatics) ◇～天立地 of gigantic stature; upright and high-minded | 他～着雨就走了。He left in the rain. ❸ 从下面拱起 push from below or behind; push up; prop up; jack up：种子的嫩芽把土～起来了。The sprouts have pushed up the earth. ❹ 用头或角撞击 gore; butt; head：～球 head a ball | 这头牛时常～人。This bull often gores people. ❺ 支撑；抵住 prop; sustain; support; hold up：拿杠子～上门 prop up the door with a bar | 列车在前，机车在后面～着走。The engine is pushing the train from behind. ❻ 对面迎着 go against; head against：～风 against the wind | ～头 coming directly towards sb. ❼ 顶撞 retort; talk back; rebut：他听了姑母的话很不满意，就～了她几句。Displeased at his aunt's words, he talked back. ❽ 担当；支持 handle; cope with; stand up to：活儿重，两个人～不下来。The work is too heavy for two people to cope with. ❾ 相当；抵 equal; equal to; be equivalent to：他一个人～两个人。He can do the work of two. ❿ 顶替 substitute; replace; displace; change; change for; substitute for; take the place of; double for：～名儿 assume sb. else's name or title | 不能拿次货～好货。You can't pass inferior goods for superior ones. ⓫ 指转让或取得企业经营权、房屋租赁权 take over the operating right of a business or the lease of a house：～盘 take over a business | ～出去 turn (sth.) over (to sb.) | ～进来 take over from ⓬〈方 *dial.*〉到（某个时间）by (a certain time); till; until：～下午两点他才吃饭。He didn't eat lunch until 2 p.m. ⓭〈量词 *classifier*〉用于某些有顶的东西 [as an indefinite article for sth. with a top]：一～帽子 a cap; a hat | 一～帐子 a mosquito net ⓮〈副词 *adv.*〉表示程度最高 very much; greatly; extremely; highly：～大 very large | ～好 excellent; superb | ～讨厌 very annoying | ～喜欢唱歌 like singing very much | ～有劲儿 very strong

【顶班】dǐng//bān (～儿 dǐng//bānr) 替班 work as a substitute for sb. who is absent：车间有人病了，他就去～。He works as a substitute in the workshop whenever someone calls in sick.

【顶班】dǐngbān 在规定时间内做顶一个劳动力的工作：～劳动 do the work of a labour hand within specified time; do the work assigned for sb. else

【顶板】dǐngbǎn ❶ 矿井内巷道顶上的岩石层 roof; rock stratum that forms the ceiling of a mine tunnel ❷ 天花板 ceiling

【顶承】dǐngchéng ❶ 承担 bear; undertake; take on：出了什么问题，由我～。I'll take the responsibility if anything goes wrong. ❷ 承受 bear; stand; endure; take

【顶灯】dǐngdēng ❶ 汽车车顶上安装的灯，灯罩上用文字或用颜色表示车辆的用途 (of vehicles) dome light; overhead light, which is set on the roof of a vehicle, and whose cover bears words or colours showing the use of the vehicle ❷ 安装在天花板上的灯 ceiling lamp; ceiling light

【顶点】dǐngdiǎn ❶ 角的两条边的交点；锥体的尖顶 point; angular point; point of intersection of two lines; apex or vertex (of a cone or pyramid) ❷ 最高点；极点 apex; zenith; acme; pinnacle：比赛的激烈程度达到了～。The game reached its climax.

【顶端】dǐngduān ❶ 最高最上的部分 top; peak; apex：登上电视塔的～ reach the top of the television tower ❷ 末尾 end：我们走到大

桥的～。We walked to the end of the bridge.

【顶风】dǐng//fēng 迎着风 against the wind:～冒雪 brave (or defy) the wind and snow|～逆水,船走得更慢了。The boat progresses slowly going against the wind and current.

【顶风】dǐngfēng 跟(人、车、船等)前进的方向相反的风 headwind; wind blowing in the direction opposite the course (of sb., vehicle, ship, etc.)

【顶峰】dǐngfēng ❶ 山的最高处 peak; summit; crest; pinnacle; top of a mountain:登上泰山～ climb to the top of Mount Tai ❷〈比喻 *fig.*〉事物发展过程中的最高点 peak of a trend or a development; apex; acme; pinnacle; summit; zenith; culmination:攀登科学的～ scale the heights of science

【顶缸】dǐng//gāng〈比喻 *fig.*〉代人承担责任 take blame or responsibility for someone else

【顶岗】dǐnggǎng〈方 *dial.*〉顶班 work as a substitute in sb.'s absence:～劳动 work as someone's substitute|～任教 teach as someone's substitute

【顶杠】dǐng//gàng 争辩 argue; debate; contend; quarrel; squabble:他脾气坏,爱跟人～。He has a bad temper, and argues a lot. also 顶杠子 dǐng//gàng·zi

【顶格】dǐnggé (～儿 dǐnggér)书写或排版时,把字写在或排在横行最左边的一格或直行最上边的一格 (in writing or typesetting) flush; characters or type that is written or set from the left edge of a horizontal margin or the top edge of a perpendicular margin, with no indentation:这行要～书写。Write this line flush.

【顶骨】dǐnggǔ 头骨之一,略呈扁方形,在头的顶部,左右各一块 parietal bone; either of a pair of squarish bones forming the central part of the sides and top of the skull

【顶呱呱】dǐngguāguā (～的 dǐngguāguā·de)形容顶好 super-duper; tip-top; first-rate; superb; excellent; also 顶刮刮 dǐngguāguā

【顶尖】dǐngjiān (～儿 dǐngjiānr) ❶ 顶心 tip:打掉棉花～ knock off the cotton tips ❷ 泛指最高最上的部分 tip; top; apex; cusp:镀金塔的～在阳光下十分耀眼。The tip of the gilded pagoda shines brilliantly in the sun. ❸ 达到最高水平的 top; first-rate; first-class; top-notch; supreme:～大学 elite university|～人物 top-notch figure

【顶礼】dǐnglǐ 跪下,两手伏在地上,用头顶着所尊敬的人的脚。是佛教徒最高的敬礼。prostrate oneself before sb. and press one's head against his feet (Buddhist salute of the highest respect):～膜拜 prostrate oneself in worship; idolize; (〈比喻 *fig.*〉对人特别崇敬 admire sb. to the extreme;现多用于贬义 oft. derog.)

【顶梁柱】dǐngliángzhù〈比喻 *fig.*〉起主要作用的骨干力量 pillar; backbone; mainstay; main support

【顶楼】dǐnglóu 楼房的最上面的一层 top floor; top storey

【顶门儿】dǐngménr 头顶前面的部分 front of the top of the head:～上的头发已经脱光了。The front of his scalp has gone bald.

【顶命】dǐng//mìng 抵命 a life for a life; pay with one's life

【顶牛儿】[1] dǐng//niúr〈比喻 *fig.*〉争持不下或互相冲突 lock horns like bulls; clash; conflict:他们两人一谈就顶起牛儿来了。The two of them began to wrangle the moment they started talking.|这两节课排得～了。The schedules of the two classes are in conflict.

D

【顶牛儿】[2] dǐng//niúr 骨牌的一种玩法,两家或几家轮流出牌,点数相同的一头互相衔接,接不上的人从手里选一张牌扣下,以终局不扣牌或所扣点数最小者为胜 domino-type game, where two or more parties play the pieces in turn, joining those with the same number of points; party who fails to join their piece with the others chooses a piece from their own hand and puts it aside; winner is the one who has put aside none or the least number of pieces. also 接龙 jiē//lóng

【顶盘】dǐngpán (～儿 dǐngpánr)指买下出倒的工厂或商店,继续营业 take over a business (e.g. factory or shop)

【顶棚】dǐngpéng same as 天棚 ① tiānpéng

【顶事】dǐng//shì (～儿 dǐng//shìr)能解决问题;有用 be able to do the job; be helpful; be useful; serve the purpose:别看他个子小,干起活来可～呢。He may be a small man, but he's an efficient worker.|多穿件夹衣也还～。An additional lined jacket will help.|吃这药不～。This medication doesn't work.

【顶视图】dǐngshìtú ☞ 俯视图 fǔshìtú on p. 603

【顶数】dǐng//shù (～儿 dǐng//shùr) ❶ 充数 serve as a fill-in (or stopgap); make up the number:别拿不合格的产品～。Don't make up the number with inferior products. ❷ 有效力;有用(多用于否定式 usu. in the negative) useful; adequate; valid:你说的不～。What you say doesn't carry enough weight.

【顶替】dǐngtì 顶名代替;由别的人、物接替或代替 take sb.'s place; replace; substitute sb. or sth. with sb. or sth. else; substitute for sb. or sth.:冒名～ assume the identity of another person; imposture|他没来,我临时～一下。He didn't come, so I'm taking his place.

【顶天立地】dǐng tiān lì dì 形容形象高大,气概雄伟豪迈 of gigantic stature and indomitable spirit; dauntless; brave

【顶头】dǐngtóu 迎面 coming directly towards one:～风 headwind|一出胡同,～碰上了李大妈。I ran into Aunt Li the moment I stepped out of the lane.

【顶头上司】dǐngtóu shàng·si 指直接领导自己的人或机构 one's immediate (or direct) superior or authority

【顶箱】dǐngxiāng 立柜上面的小柜 top case; small case on the top of a wardrobe

【顶心】dǐngxīn 棉花等作物主茎的顶端 tip; top of the main stem of a plant, such as cotton; also 顶尖 dǐngjiān

【顶用】dǐng//yòng 有用;顶事 be of use or help; serve the purpose; be useful; be helpful; be able to do the job:小牛再养上一年就～了。The calf will be of use in a year.|这件事需要你去,我去不顶什么用。You are needed to settle this matter; I'd be of little help.

D

【顶账】dǐng//zhàng 抵账 repay a debt (in another form)

【顶针】dǐngzhēn same as 顶真[2] dǐngzhēn

【顶针】dǐng·zhen (～儿 dǐng·zhenr)做针线活时戴在手指上的工具,用金属或其他材料制成,上面有许多小窝儿,用来抵住针鼻儿,使针容易穿过活计而手指不至于受伤 thimble; small ring of metal or other materials, covered with small holes, worn on the finger for protection against the needle while sewing

【顶真】[1] dǐngzhēn 〈方 *dial.*〉认真 be serious; be earnest:大事小事他都很～。He takes everything seriously whether it is important or trivial.

【顶真】[2] dǐngzhēn 一种修辞方法,用前面结尾的词语或句子作下文的起头。例如李白《白云歌送刘十六归山》:'楚山秦山皆白云。白云处处长随君。长随君;君入楚山里,云亦随君渡湘水。湘水上,女罗衣,白云堪卧君早归。' rhetorical device calling for a sentence to begin with the last word or phrase of the previous one, e.g. the poem *A Song of White Clouds — Farewell to Liu Shiliu Who Is Returning to the Mountains* by Li Bai: 'Mountains in Hubei and Shaanxi are mantled in white clouds. /White clouds go with you everywhere. / Everywhere they go with you; /You enter into mountains in Hubei, /And with you the clouds cross the Xiang River. Over the River of Xiang, /Where the hermit lives, /The white cloud is waiting for you.' also 顶针 dǐngzhēn

【顶珠】dǐngzhū (～儿 dǐngzhūr)清朝官吏装在帽顶正中的饰物,下有金属小座,座上面安一个核桃大小的圆珠,珠的质料和颜色表示一定品级 rank button; walnut-sized ball set on a small metal stand in the centre of the top of a Qing-dynasty official's headgear, the texture and colour of which are symbols of rank; also 顶儿 dǐngr and 顶子 dǐng·zi

【顶撞】dǐngzhuàng 用强硬的话反驳别人(多指对长辈或上级)(usu. to one's elder or superior) contradict; talk back:他后悔不该～父亲。He regretted contradicting his father.

【顶子】dǐng·zi ❶ 亭子、塔、轿子等顶上的装饰部分 ornamentation on the top of a pavilion, pagoda, sedanchair, etc. ❷ same as 顶珠 dǐngzhū ❸ 房顶 roof:挑(tiǎo)～(拆修房顶) overhaul the roof

【顶嘴】dǐng//zuǐ 争辩(多指对尊长)(usu. to one's elder) reply defiantly; answer back; talk back:小孩子不要跟大人～。Children should not talk back to their elders.

【顶罪】dǐng//zuì ❶ 代替别人承担罪责 bear the blame for sb. else ❷ 抵罪 be punished for a crime; bear the punishment; expiate one's crime; atone for a crime:罚不～ punishment not in keeping with the crime; be unduly punished

酊 dǐng ☞ [酩酊] mǐngdǐng on p. 1359
☞ dīng on p. 454

鼎[1] dǐng ❶〈古代 *arch.*〉煮东西用的器物,三足两耳 tripod cauldron for cooking, with three legs and two ears ❷〈书 *fml.*〉〈比喻 *fig.*〉王位、帝业 throne:定～ found a kingdom or state|问～ attempt to usurp the throne; try to be a winner or champion ❸〈书 *fml.*〉大 great; enormous; remarkable:～力 great effort|～言 weighty advice ❹〈方 *dial.*〉锅 pot

鼎[2] dǐng〈书 *fml.*〉正当;正在 enter upon a period of; when:～盛 in a period of great prosperity

【鼎鼎】dǐngdǐng 盛大 great; magnificent; grand; imposing:～大名 very famous; of great celebrity; great reputation; well-known

【鼎沸】dǐngfèi〈书 *fml.*〉形容喧闹、混乱,像水在锅里沸腾一样 noisy and chaotic, like water boiling in a cauldron; uproarious; tumultuous:人声～ hubbub of voices|舆论～ uproar of public opinion

【鼎革】dǐnggé〈书 *fml.*〉除旧布新,指改朝换代 discarding the old traditions in favour of the new, referring to change of dynasty or regime; dynastic change; ☞ 革故鼎新 gé gù dǐng xīn on p. 652

【鼎力】dǐnglì〈书 *fml.*〉〈敬辞 *pol.*〉大力(表示请托或感谢时用) your kind efforts (used to request sb.'s help or express thankfulness): 多蒙～协助,无任感谢!(We) are extremely grateful to you for your kind efforts on our behalf.

【鼎立】dǐnglì 三方面的势力对立(像鼎的三条腿) confrontation of three forces (like the three legs of a tripod); tripartite confrontation; tripartite balance of forces:赤壁之战决定了魏、蜀、吴三国～的局面。The Battle of the Red Cliffs determined the tripartite balance of power of the three states of Wei, Shu and Wu.

【鼎盛】dǐngshèng 正当兴盛或强壮 in a period of great prosperity; at the height of power and splendour:～时期 period of full bloom; prime; heyday|春秋～(正当壮年) prime of one's life

【鼎新】dǐngxīn 〈书 *fml.*〉革新 innovate; make innovations; introduce new blood: 革故～ drop old ways and build anew

【鼎言】dǐngyán 〈书 *fml.*〉有分量的言论 weighty remarks

【鼎峙】dǐngzhì 〈书 *fml.*〉三方面对立。鼎有三足,所以叫鼎峙。tripartite confrontation; confrontation of three rival powers like the three legs of a tripod cauldron

【鼎足】dǐngzú 鼎的腿 three legs of a tripod; 〈比喻 *fig.*〉三方面对立的局势 situation of tripartite confrontation:～而三(of three rival powers) stand like the legs of a tripod cauldron|势成～ form a situation of tripartite confrontation

dìng(ㄉㄧㄥˋ)

订 dìng ❶ 经过研究商讨而立下(条约、契约、计划、章程等) make a plan or commitment; make or form a treaty, contract, plan, regulations, etc., after study and discussion:～婚 be engaged to; be betrothed to; engage|～合同 conclude (or enter into, make, set) a contract ❷ 预先约定 subscribe to; book; order:～报 subscribe to a newspaper|预～ order; book ❸ 改正(文字中的错误) amend; revise; correct (mistakes in a text):～正 make corrections; correct|修～ revise|校～ check against the authoritative text; blue-pencil ❹ 装订 staple together; bind:～书机 stapler|用纸～成一个本子 staple sheets of paper together into a notebook

【订单】dìngdān 订购货物的合同、单据 order for goods; order form; contract or document for purchasing goods; also 定单 dìngdān

【订购】dìnggòu 约定购买(货物等) order; place an order for (goods, etc.); book:～机票 book an air ticket; also 定购 dìnggòu

【订户】dìnghù 由于预先约定而得到定期供应的个人或单位,如报刊的订阅者,牛奶的用户等 subscriber (to newspaper or magazine); person, household or unit receiving service regularly on order e. g. periodical publications, milk delivery, etc.; also 定户 dìnghù

【订婚】dìng//hūn 男女订立婚约 engage (to be married); be engaged to; be betrothed to; enter into betrothal; also 定婚 dìng//hūn

【订货】dìng//huò 订购产品或货物 order goods or products; place an order for goods:～会 meeting for the placement of orders|～合同 contract to order goods|订了一批货 ordered a batch of goods; also 定货 dìng//huò

【订货】dìnghuò 预订的产品或货物 ordered goods or products:～已如期发运。The ordered goods have been sent as scheduled. also 定货 dìnghuò

【订交】dìngjiāo 彼此结为朋友 pledge friendship; form a friendship; establish friendly relations

【订金】dìngjīn 定钱 deposit; down payment; advance; also 定金 dìngjīn

【订立】dìnglì 双方或几方把商定的事项用书面形式(如条约、合同等)肯定下来 conclude or make an agreement; (two or more parties) confirm their decision (e. g. for a treaty or contract) made through discussion in a written form:～卫生公约 conclude a health treaty|两国在平等互利的基础上～了贸易协定。The two countries entered into a trade agreement on the basis of equality and mutual benefit.

【订阅】dìngyuè 预先付款订购(报纸、期刊) subscribe to reading material (newspaper, periodical, etc.); also 定阅 dìngyuè

【订正】dìngzhèng 改正(文字中的错误) make corrections; correct (mistakes in a text)

饤 dìng ☞ 饾饤 dòudìng on p. 475

钉 dìng ❶ 把钉子捶打进别的东西;用钉子、螺丝钉等把东西固定在一定的位置或把分散的东西组合起来 hammer a nail into sth.; nail; fix sth. to a position with a nail or screw; fasten things together:～钉(dīng)子 drive in a nail|～马掌 nail on horseshoes|门上～上两个合叶 nail two hinges onto the door|他用几块木板～了个箱子。He made a case with a few wooden boards. ❷ 用针线把带子、纽扣等缝住 sew on (a ribbon, button, etc.):～扣子 sew a button on

☞ dīng on p. 453

定 dìng ❶ 平静;稳定 calm; stable; placid:立～ stand still|坐～ sit down|心神不～ agitated; with an unsettled mind; be on tenterhooks; feel ill at ease ❷ 固定;使固定 fix; set; fasten; secure:～影 photographic fixing; fixation|～睛观看 gaze at ❸ 决定;使确定 decide; set; fix:商～ agree on; decide through consultation|～计划 make a plan|开会时间～在明天上午。The meeting is scheduled for tomorrow morning. ❹ 已经确定的;不改变的 fixed; settled; set; established; decided; determined:～理 theorem|～论 final conclusion|～局 foregone conclusion; inevitable outcome ❺ 规定的 arranged; fixed; set; prescribed; stipulated:～量 ration|～时 at regular times|～期 at regular dates; periodic ❻ 约定 subscribe to; book; order:～报 subscribe to a newspaper|～单 order for goods|～了一批货 ordered a batch of goods ❼ 〈书 *fml.*〉

必定;一定 surely; certainly; definitely:~可取得胜利 sure to win ❽ (Dìng) 姓 a surname

【定案】dìng//àn 对案件、方案等做最后的决定 decide on a case or plan; make a decision; reach a conclusion:拍板~ give the final verdict

【定案】dìng'àn 对案件、方案等所做的最后决定 final conclusion (or decision) on (a case, plan, etc.); verdict:这个问题已有~,不要再讨论了。This issue has come to a conclusion and needs no further discussion.

【定本】dìngběn 校正后改定的本子 definitive edition

【定编】dìngbiān 确定编制 finalize an organizational structure

【定常流】dìngchángliú 稳定流 stable current

【定场白】dìngchǎngbái 戏曲中角色第一次出场说的自我介绍的独白 (of traditional Chinese opera) monologue in which characters introduce themselves at their first appearance onstage

【定场诗】dìngchǎngshī 戏曲中角色第一次出场开头所念的诗,通常是四句 (in traditional Chinese opera) poem (usu. of four lines) recited by a character first appearing in a scene

【定单】dìngdān same as 订单 dìngdān

【定当】 dìngdàng 〈方 *dial*.〉停当;妥当 settled; set; ready; finished:商量~ talk over sth. and reach an agreement|安排~ have finished all preparations; be ready

【定点】dìngdiǎn ❶ 选定或指定在某一处 fixed point:~供应 rationed supply (of sth.) at fixed locations|~跳伞 parachute to an accurate landing ❷ 选定或指定专门从事某项工作的 designated (for a special task):涉外~饭店 hotel or restaurant designated for foreign visitors|该厂是生产冰箱的~厂。This is a designated manufacturer of refrigerators. ❸ 规定时间的 at a fixed time:~航船 regular, scheduled sailing|~作业 work or operate at a fixed time

【定鼎】dìngdǐng 〈书 *fml*.〉相传禹铸九鼎,为古代传国之宝,保存在王朝建都的地方。后来称定都或建立王朝为定鼎。cast a tripod cauldron — found a state; establish a capital. It was said that King Yu had nine tripod cauldrons cast to be state heirlooms and kept in the city designated as the capital of the kingdom; therefore 'cast a tripod cauldron' refers to founding a state or establishing a capital.

【定都】dìng//dū 把首都设在(某地) establish a capital; make (a place) the capital of a state

【定夺】dìngduó 对事情做可否或取舍的决定 make a final decision; decide; come to a choice; determine:等讨论后再行~。We'll make a decision after discussion.

【定额】dìng'é ❶ 规定数额 stipulate an amount or number; set a quota; ration:~管理 quota management|~供应 rationed supply ❷ 规定的数额 quota; set quantity:提前完成生产~ meet the production quota ahead of schedule

【定稿】dìnggǎo ❶ 修改并确定稿子 finalize a text:全书由主编~。The editor-in-chief finalized the whole book. ❷ 修改后确定下来的稿子 final text (or version):年内可把~交出版社。The final text will be handed to the publisher by the end of this year.

【定格】dìnggé ❶ 电影、电视片的活动画面突然停止在某一个画面上,叫做定格 freeze frame; freeze; (in a movie or TV film) all action stops ❷ 固定不变的格式;一定的规格 fixed (or set) form:写小说并无~。There's no set form for novel writing.

【定更】dìnggēng 〈旧时 *old*〉晚上八点钟左右,打鼓报告初更开始 beat the drum to report the start of the first watch at about 8 p.m.

【定购】dìnggòu same as 订购 dìnggòu

【定规】dìngguī ❶ 一定的规矩;成规 established rule or practice; set pattern:月底盘点,已成~。It is an established practice to draw up an inventory at the end of each month. ❷ 〈方 *dial*.〉一定(专指主观意志 esp. of one's mind) be bent on; be determined; insist on; insist:叫他不要去,他~要去。He was told not to go, but he insisted on going.

【定户】dìnghù same as 订户 dìnghù

【定滑轮】dìnghuálún 位置固定的滑轮,使用时轮子转动而整个滑轮不发生位移。使用这种滑轮能够改变力的方向,但不能省力,也不能缩短路程。fixed pulley; pulley at a fixed position that turns without changing its position; such a pulley can change the direction of a force, but cannot save energy or reduce the distance

【定婚】dìng//hūn same as 订婚 dìng//hūn

【定货】dìnghuò same as 订货 dìnghuò

【定价】dìng//jià 规定价钱 fix a price; set a price; price sth.:合理~ set reasonable prices|你先定个价吧。Please set a price first.

【定价】dìngjià 规定的价钱 price; fixed price:~便宜 of a cheap price|降低~ lower the price

【定见】dìngjiàn 确定的见解或主张 get a fix on sth. or sb.; fixation

【定金】dìngjīn same as 订金 dìngjīn

【定睛】dìngjīng 集中视线 fix one's eyes on; gaze at; stare at:~细看 scrutinize

【定居】dìng//jū 在某个地方固定地居住下来 settle down (in a certain place):回国~ return to settle in one's home country|~北京 settle down in Beijing

【定居点】dìngjūdiǎn 指牧民、渔民等定居的地点 settlement (of herdsmen, fishermen, etc.)

【定局】dìngjú ❶ 做最后决定 settle finally; make a final decision:事情还没~,明天还可以再研究。The matter isn't settled yet. We can take it up again tomorrow. ❷ 确定不移的形势 foregone conclusion; inevitable outcome:今年丰收已成～。It's a foregone conclusion that we'll have a bumper harvest this year.

【定礼】dìnglǐ 彩礼 betrothal gifts

【定理】dìnglǐ 已经证明具有正确性、可以作为原则或规律的命题或公式,如几何定理 theorem; statement or formula that has been proved correct and can be regarded as a principle or law, e.g. geometry theorem

【定例】dìnglì 沿袭下来经常实行的规矩 usual (or regular) practice; set pattern; routine:每到星期六我们厂总要放场电影,这差不多成了～了。It's the usual practice in our factory to have a film shown on Saturday.

【定量】dìngliàng ❶ 测定物质所含各种成分的数量 determine the quantities of different components in a substance:～分析 quantitative analysis ❷ 规定数量 fix the quantity:～供应 ration; fixed supply|定质～ with set quality and quantity ❸ 规定的数量 fixed quantity:超出～ exceed the fixed quantity

【定量分析】dìngliàng fēnxī 分析化学上测定某种物质所含各种成分数量多少的方法 quantitative analysis; analysis of a substance to determine the amounts of its constituents

【定律】dìnglǜ 科学上对某种客观规律的概括,反映事物在一定条件下发生一定变化过程的必然关系 law; general statement of a certain objective law, reflecting the actions and relations of things in nature, observed to be always the same under given conditions

【定论】dìnglùn 确定的论断 final conclusion:此事已有～。This matter has been decided already.

【定苗】dìng//miáo 按一定株距留下长得好的幼苗,把多余的苗去掉 single seedlings; final singling of seedlings; remove extra seedlings, leaving good ones with uniform spacing between them

【定名】dìng//míng 确定名称;命名(不用于人 not used for human beings) name; denominate; title:这个连队被～为爱民模范连。This company was named Model Company on Friendly Terms with Civilians.

【定盘星】dìngpánxīng ❶ 戥子或杆秤上标志起算点(重量为零)的星儿 zero point on a steelyard or scale ❷〈比喻 *fig.*〉一定的主张(多用于否定句问句);准主意 (usu. in the negative) fixed idea; definite thought:他做事没有～。He acts in a haphazard way.

【定评】dìngpíng 确定的评论 final judgement; accepted opinion:这部作品早有～。There is already an accepted opinion on this work.

【定期】dìngqī ❶ 定下日期 fix (or set) a date:～召开代表大会 set a date for an assembly of representatives ❷ 有一定期限的 regular schedule; at regular intervals; periodical:～刊物 periodical; periodical publication|～检查 regular examination|～存款 fixed deposit; periodic deposits

【定钱】dìng·qián 购买或租赁时预先付给的一部分钱,作为成交的保证 deposit; down payment; a part of the total amount of money paid in advance as a pledge of purchase or rent

【定亲】dìng//qīn 订婚(多指由父母做主的 oft. arranged by one's parents) engage; betroth

【定然】dìngrán 必定 certainly; definitely; surely

【定神】dìng//shén ❶ 集中注意力 concentrate one's attention:听见有人叫我,～一看原来是小李。I heard someone calling me and, after paying attention, I saw that it was Xiao Li. ❷ 使心神安定 collect oneself; compose oneself; pull oneself together; calm sb. down

【定时】dìngshí ❶ 按规定的时间;准时 at regular intervals; at fixed times:～吃药 take medication at regular intervals|～起床 get up at a fixed time ❷ 一定的时间 fixed time:吃饭要有～。There should be fixed times for taking meals.

【定时炸弹】dìngshí zhàdàn ❶ 雷管由计时器控制的炸弹,能按预定的时间爆炸 time bomb; bomb in which the detonator is controlled by a timer to explode at a set time ❷〈比喻 *fig.*〉潜在的危险 potential danger; hidden danger

【定式】dìngshì 长期形成的固定的方式或格式 set; fixed way or pattern formed after a long time:心理～ mind-set|思维～ set mode of thinking; also 定势 dìngshì

【定说】dìngshuō 确定的说法 final conclusion:这种病的起因尚无～。No final conclusion has yet been reached on the cause of this disease.

【定位】dìngwèi ❶ 用仪器对物体所在的位置进行测量 orientate; position; locate; fix the position of an object with an instrument ❷ 经测量后确定的位置 position (fixed by measuring); location ❸ 把事物放在适当的地位并做出某种评价 evaluate sth. after putting it in proper perspective:循名～ evaluate according to the name|抓好产品价值～ do a good job in evaluating the products

【定息】dìngxī 我国私营工商业实行全行业公私合营后,国家对工商业者的资产进行核定,在一定时期内按固定利率每年付给的利息 fixed interest rate (an annual rate of interest paid by the state on the money value of assets for a given period of time, for the conversion of private industry and commerce into joint state-private enterprises)

【定弦】dìng//xián (～儿 dìng//xiánr) ❶ 调整乐器弦的松紧以校正音高 tune (a stringed instrument); adjust the tightness of the strings of a musical instrument to correct the pitch ❷〈方 *dial.*〉〈比喻 *fig.*〉打定主意 make up one's mind:你先别追问我,我还没~呢。Don't ask me yet, since I still haven't made up my mind.

【定向】dìngxiàng ❶ 测定方向 find the direction:~台(装有特种接收设备,能测定被测电台电波发射方向的无线电台) directive station (radio station installed with special receiving equipment that is able to find the direction of waves of another radio station) ❷ 指有一定方向 directional:~爆破 directional blasting|~招生 directed enrollment

【定向培育】dìngxiàng péiyù 利用一定的生活环境促使动植物的遗传性向人们所要求的方向变化,如提高耐寒性、抗病能力等 directive breeding; using certain environments to genetically modify the heredity of animals or plants accordingly, e.g. to improve cold resistance and disease resistance

【定向天线】dìngxiàng tiānxiàn 有方向性的天线,在接收机上常作环形,在雷达通讯设备上常作凹面镜形 directional antenna; circular antenna of a receiver, or one in the shape of a concave mirror on radar communication equipment

【定心丸】dìngxīnwán (~儿 dìngxīnwánr)〈比喻 *fig.*〉能使思想、情绪安定下来的言论或行动 remark or action capable of settling sb.'s mind or putting sb.'s mind at ease

【定刑】dìngxíng 审判机关认定犯人应判处某种刑罚 (for a judicial organ to) determine the penalty (that a convict deserves):~过重。The penalty is too harsh.

【定型】dìng//xíng 事物的特点逐渐形成并固定下来 fall into a pattern; become set; settle into a shape (or form); (character of an event) take shape and gradually become set

【定性】dìng//xìng 对犯有错误或罪行的人,确定其问题的性质 determine the nature of an error or offence:这个案子~准确,量刑恰当。The nature of the case was determined correctly, and the penalty imposed properly.

【定性】dìngxìng 测定物质包含哪些成分及性质 determine the chemical composition and properties of a substance:~分析 qualitative analysis

【定性分析】dìngxìng fēnxī 分析化学上测定某种物质含有哪些成分的方法 qualitative analysis; analysis of a substance to determine its constituents

【定洋】dìngyáng same as 定钱 dìng•qián

【定义】dìngyì 对于一种事物的本质特征或一个概念的内涵和外延的确切而简要的说明 definition; exact, concise statement of the nature of sth. or the connotation and denotation of a concept

【定音鼓】dìngyīngǔ 打击乐器,形状像锅,用铜制成,在开口的一面蒙皮,装有螺旋,能松紧鼓面来调整音高。主要用于交响乐队。kettledrum; timpano; pot-shaped percussion instrument, made of copper and a piece of vellum covering its open end, with a screw that can be turned to adjust the pitch by changing the tightness of the vellum, mainly used in orchestras

【定影】dìngyǐng 把经过显影的感光材料放入配好的药液里,溶去全部卤化银,只留下银质的影像,并把影像固定下来,不再变化。通常在暗室里进行。(in photography) fixing; fix; to put developed light-sensitive material into a preparation to render the silver image permanent by removing all silver halides, usu. in a darkroom

【定语】dìngyǔ 名词前边的表示领属、性质、数量等等的修饰成分。名词、代词、形容词、数量词等都可以做定语。例如'国家机关'的'国家'(领属),'新气象'的'新'(性质),'三架飞机'的'三架'(数量)。attribute; modifier used before a noun to indicate pertinence, character, quantity, etc. of the modified; attribute can be a noun, pronoun, adjective, classifier, etc., e.g. 'state' in 'state organs' (indicating relevance), 'new' in 'new atmosphere' (indicating character), and 'three' in 'three aeroplanes' (indicating quantity)

【定员】dìngyuán ❶ 规定人数 fix the number of persons:~定编 fix the number of people employed ❷ 规定的人数,指机关、部队等人员编制的名额,或车船等规定容纳乘客的数目 fixed number of persons, referring to the number of staff members of an organization or a military unit, or the seating capacity of a passenger vehicle, ship, etc.

【定阅】dìngyuè same as 订阅 dìngyuè

【定植】dìngzhí 树苗在苗圃里生长1—2年后移植到固定的地方,也指蔬菜秧苗生长到一定时间或程度后移植到田地里 field planting (or setting); moving a sapling to a permanent place after growing it for one or two years in a nursery garden, or moving a vegetable shoot into the field after it has grown for some time

【定址】dìngzhǐ ❶ 把建筑工程的位置设在(某地) situate; locate; set; place; establish sth. in a place:轿车总装厂~武汉。The general car-assembling plant was situated in Wuhan. ❷ 固定的住址 fixed address:他成年东跑西颠,没有个~。He travels all over throughout the year, and has no fixed address.

【定准】dìngzhǔn ❶ (~儿 dìngzhǔnr) 确定的标准 set standard:工作要有个~,不能各行其是。We should have a set standard for the work instead of each acting in his or her own way. ❷ 一定;肯定 certainly; surely; sure; certain:你看见了~满意。You'll surely be satisfied when you see it.|究竟派谁去,现在还没~。

It's not certain yet who will be sent.

【定子】dìngzǐ 电动机和发电机中,跟转子相应而固定在外壳上的部分 stator; portion of an electric motor or generator that remains fixed on the case with respect to rotating parts

【定罪】dìng//zuì 审判机关认定某违法行为符合刑事法律规定的某个罪名 convict sb. (of a crime); (a judicial organ) decide that a certain illegal action is a certain crime according to provisions of criminal law

啶 dìng ☞ 吡啶 bǐdìng on p.100

铤 dìng 〈书 *fml*.〉未经冶铸的铜铁 copper or iron ore

☞ tǐng on p.1914

腚 dìng 〈方 *dial*.〉屁股 buttocks

碇(矴、椗) dìng 系船的石墩 killock; killick; heavy stone used as an anchor: 船已下～。The boat has been anchored.

锭 dìng ❶ 锭子 spindle; ❷ 做成块状的金属或药物等 ingot-shaped metal or medicine: 金～ gold ingot | 钢～ steel ingot | 万应～ cure-all; panacea ❸〈量词 *classifier*〉用于成锭的东西 used for ingot-shaped objects: 一～墨 a cake of Chinese ink; an ink stick

【锭剂】dìngjì 药物粉末制成的硬块,供患者吞服、研汁内服或外用,如万应锭、紫金锭、蟾酥锭等 lozenge; pastille; troche; small tablet made of medicinal powder to be taken orally or used externally, e.g., panacea pastille, toad cake, etc.

【锭子】dìng·zi 纱锭 spindle

【锭子油】dìng·ziyóu 黏度中等的精制润滑油,适用于纺纱机的锭子和各种负荷小、速度高的轴承和摩擦部分 spindle oil; bobbin oil; spindle lubricant; refined lubricant with medium viscosity, suitable for spindles in a spinning machine and various light-loading, high-speed bearings and rubbing parts

diū (ㄉㄧㄡ)

丢(丟) diū ❶ 遗失;失去 lose; forfeit; drop; be missing: 钱包～了 lose a wallet ◇～了工作 lose a job ❷ 扔 throw; cast; toss: 不要随地～果皮。Please don't litter the place with fruit peel. ❸ 搁置;放 toss aside; lay aside; pigeonhole; put on the shelf: 技术～久了就生疏了。A skill that hasn't been used for a long time will become rusty. | 只有这件事～不开。That's the one thing that keeps worrying me.

【丢丑】diū//chǒu 丢脸 lose face; be disgraced: 他不愿在众人面前～。He doesn't want to be disgraced in public.

【丢掉】diūdiào ❶ 遗失 lose: 不小心把钥匙～了 accidentally lose one's key ◇～饭碗(失业) be unemployed; lose one's job ❷ 抛弃 give up; abandon; discard; throw away; cast away; scrap; shed: ～幻想 cast away illusions

【丢份】diū//fènr〈方 *dial*.〉(～儿 diū//fènr)有失身份;丢人 suffer a loss of face; lose one's dignity; be disgraced; also 丢份子 diū//fèn·zi

【丢脸】diū//liǎn 丧失体面 lose face; be disgraced

【丢面子】diūmiàn·zi same as 丢脸 diū//liǎn

【丢弃】diūqì 扔掉;抛弃 abandon; discard; scrap; give up: 虽是旧衣服,他也舍不得～。Although the clothes are old, he hates to throw them out.

【丢却】diūquè ❶ 丢弃 abandon; give up; discard: 那件心事总～不下 can't take a load off one's mind ❷ 遗失 lose: 书不慎～,心里好不懊恼。I lost the book accidentally and am very vexed.

【丢人】diū//rén 丢脸 lose face; be disgraced: ～现眼 make a fool of oneself; make a spectacle of oneself

【丢三落四】diū sān là sì 形容马虎或记忆力不好而好忘事 forgetful; scatterbrained; be always forgetting things because of carelessness or bad memory

【丢失】diūshī 遗失 lose: ～行李 lose one's luggage | ～文件 lose a document

【丢手】diū//shǒu 放开不管 wash one's hands of; give up: ～不干 wash one's hands (of sth.) | 这种事趁早丢开手。It's better to wash your hands of such a matter.

【丢眼色】diū yǎnsè 用眼光暗示;使眼色 wink at sb.; give sb. the eye

铥 diū 金属元素,符号 Tm (thulium)。是一种稀土金属。银白色,质软。用作 X 射线源等。thulium (Tm); soft, silvery metallic element of a rare earth group, used as a source of X-rays, etc.

dōng (ㄉㄨㄥ)

东(東) dōng ❶ 四个主要方向之一,太阳出来的一边 east; one of the four directions, where the sun rises from: ～边儿 east side | ～方 the east | ～风 east wind | ～城 eastern part of a city | 城～ east of a city | 大江～去。The great river runs eastward. ❷ 主人(古时主位在东,宾位在西) host (in ancient times, the host sat on the east side, while the guest sat on the west side); master; owner: 房～ landlord or landlady | 股～ shareholder | ～家 master ❸ (～儿 dōngr)东道 host: 我做～,请你们吃饭。I'd like to play host and treat you to dinner. ❹ Dōng 姓 a surname

【东半球】dōngbànqiú 地球的东半部,从西经 20°

起向东到东经 160°止。陆地包括欧洲、非洲的全部，亚洲和大洋洲的绝大部分以及南极洲的大部分。Eastern Hemisphere; eastern half of the globe, from longitude 20° W to 160° E; territorial areas include the entire continents of Europe and Africa, most parts of Asia and Oceania, and the major part of Antarctica

【东北】dōngběi ❶ 东和北之间的方向 northeast：风向～。The wind comes from the northeast. ❷ (Dōngběi)指我国东北地区，包括辽宁、吉林、黑龙江三省以及内蒙古自治区的东部 Northeast China, which includes the provinces of Liaoning, Jilin and Heilongjiang and the eastern part of the Inner Mongolia Autonomous Region

D

【东边】dōng·bian (～儿 dōng·bianr) same as 东 dōng ①

【东不拉】dōngbùlā same as 冬不拉 dòngbùlā

【东昌纸】dōngchāngzhǐ 毛头纸 a kind of coarse soft white paper, used for papering windows or wrapping things

【东窗事发】dōng chuāng shì fā 传说宋朝秦桧在他家东窗下定计杀害了岳飞，地藏王(神名)化为一个行者到人间作证说东窗事犯了，秦桧不久就死了(见于元孔文卿《地藏王证东窗事犯杂剧》)。明田汝成《西湖游览志余》卷四里说，秦桧死后他老婆请方士做法事，方士看见秦桧在阴间身带铁枷受苦，秦桧对他说：'可烦传语夫人，东窗事发矣。'后来'东窗事发'指罪行、阴谋败露。disclosure of a crime or plot; plot has come to light; secret is out. It is said that in the Song Dynasty, Qin Hui plotted and murdered Yue Fei by the east window in his home, and Ksitigarbha (Overlord of Hell) disguised himself as a monk to bear witness to the east-window plot in the human world, and before long Qin Hui died (*Supreme Ruler of Hell Testifying on the East-Window Plot* by Kong Wenqing of the Yuan Dynasty). According to Volume 4 of *Notes on Touring the West Lake* by Tian Rucheng of the Ming Dynasty, after Qin Hui's death, his wife asked a necromancer to hold a religious ceremony for Qin Hui. The necromancer saw Qin bearing an iron cangue and being tortured, and heard Qin Hui tell him: 'Please tell my wife that the east-window plot has been exposed.' Hence the term, referring to exposure of a crime or plot; also 东窗事犯 dōng chuāng shì fàn

【东床】dōngchuáng 晋代太尉郗鉴派一位门客到王导家去选女婿。门客回来说：'王家的年轻人都很好，但是听到有人去选女婿，都拘谨起来，只有一位在东边床上敞开衣襟吃饭的，好像没听到似的。'郗鉴说：'这正是一位好女婿。'这个人就是王羲之。于是把女儿嫁给他(见于《晋书·王羲之传》)。因此，后来也称女婿为东床。son-in-law. In the Jin Dynasty, Xi Jian, a military officer, sent one of his hangers-on to select a son-in-law for him from Wang Dao's family. The hanger-on returned and reported, 'The young men at the Wang's are all very good, but they all acted in a reserved manner when they heard that someone had come to select a son-in-law from among them, except one, who sat bare-chested on the eastern bed, eating his meal as nothing had happened.' Xi Jian said, 'This one will make a good son-in-law.' This young man was none other than Wang Xizhi, who Xi married his daughter to (*History of Jin · Biography of Wang Xizhi*). Hence the term, referring to son-in-law.

【东倒西歪】dōng dǎo xī wāi ❶ 形容行走、坐立时身体歪斜或摇晃不稳的样子 unsteady; tottering; staggering ❷ 形容物体杂乱地歪斜或倒下的样子 jumbled; in a mess; rickety; tumbled down

【东道】dōngdào ❶ 请客的主人 host：做～ play the host; treat | 略尽～之谊 perform the duties of a host ❷ 指请客的事儿或义务 duty of a host; entertaining guests：做～ play host; stand treat | 打个～ play host; stand treat

【东道国】dōngdàoguó 负责组织、安排国际会议、比赛等在本国举行的国家 host country; country responsible for organizing and arranging an international meeting, competition, etc.

【东道主】dōngdàozhǔ 请客的主人 host

【东佃】dōngdiàn 地主和佃户的合称 landlord or landlady and his or her tenant peasant

【东方】Dōngfāng 姓 a surname

【东方】dōngfāng ❶ same as 东 dōng ①：～红，太阳升。As the east turns red, the sun rises. ❷ (Dōngfāng) 指亚洲(习惯上也包括埃及) the East; the Orient, referring to Asia (usu. including Egypt)

【东非】Dōng Fēi 非洲东部，包括索马里、吉布提、埃塞俄比亚、肯尼亚、乌干达、卢旺达、布隆迪、坦桑尼亚和塞舌尔等 East Africa, including Somalia, Djibouti, Ethiopia, Kenya, Uganda, Rwanda Burundi, Tanzania, Seychelles, etc.

【东风】dōngfēng ❶ 指春风 east wind, spring wind ❷〈比喻 *fig.*〉革命的力量或气势 driving force of revolution; revolutionary force：～压倒西风。The East Wind prevails over the West Wind.

【东风吹马耳】dōngfēng chuī mǎ'ěr 〈比喻 *fig.*〉对别人的话无动于衷 turn a deaf ear to what sb. else says; (of words) go in one ear and out the other

【东宫】dōnggōng 封建时代太子住的地方，借指太子 Eastern Palace (the residence of the crown prince), referring to the crown prince

【东郭】Dōngguō 姓 a surname

【东郭先生】Dōngguō xiān·sheng 明马中锡《中

山狼传》中的人物。因救助被人追逐的中山狼；差点儿被狼吃掉，是对坏人讲仁慈的典型。Master Dongguo, a character in *The Story of a Wolf in Zhongshan* by Ma Zhongxi of the Ming Dynasty, who nearly got eaten by a wolf after he had helped it to hide from a hunter, and hence an example of people who show mercy to evil people

【东汉】Dōng Hàn 朝代，公元 25—220，自光武帝（刘秀）建武元年起到献帝（刘协）延康元年止。建都洛阳。Eastern Han Dynasty (A. D. 25-220), starting from the 1st year of the Jianwu reign of Emperor Guangwu (Liu Xiu), and ending in the 1st year of the Yankang reign of Emperor Xian, its capital being Luoyang; also 后汉 Hòu Hàn

【东胡】Dōng Hú 我国古代民族，居住在今内蒙古东南一带 Donghu, a people in ancient China, living in the southeast of today's Inner Mongolia

【东家】dōng•jia 受人雇用或聘请的人称他的主人；佃户称租给他土地的地主 master; boss; term used by an employee to refer to or address his employer, or by a tenant-peasant to his landlord

【东晋】Dōng Jìn 朝代，公元 317—420，自元帝（司马睿）建武元年起到恭帝（司马德文）元熙二年止。建都建康（今南京）。Eastern Jin Dynasty (317-420 A. D.), starting from the 1st year of the Jianwu reign of Emperor Yuandi (Sima Rui), and ending in the second year of the Yuanxi reign of Emperor Gongdi (Sima Dewen), its capital being Jiankang (today's Nanjing)

【东经】dōngjīng 本初子午线以东的经度或经线 east longitude; longitude or longitude line to the east of the prime meridian; ☞ 经度 jīngdù on p. 1019 and 经线 jīngxiàn on p. 1021

【东鳞西爪】dōng lín xī zhǎo ☞ 一鳞半爪 yī lín bàn zhǎo on p. 2248

【东南】dōngnán ❶ 东和南之间的方向 southeast ❷ (Dōngnán) 指我国东南沿海地区，包括上海、江苏、浙江、福建、台湾等省市 southeast China; southeastern coastal areas in China, including Shanghai, Jiangsu, Zhejiang, Fujian, Taiwan, etc.

【东南亚】Dōngnán Yà 亚洲的东南部，包括越南、柬埔寨、老挝、泰国、缅甸、马来西亚、新加坡、菲律宾、印度尼西亚和文莱等国 Southeast Asia, including Vietnam, Cambodia, Laos, Thailand, Myanmar, Malaysia, Singapore, Philippines, Indonesia, Brunei, etc.

【东欧】Dōng Ōu 欧洲东部，包括罗马尼亚、波兰、捷克、斯洛伐克、匈牙利等国和前苏联的欧洲部分 Eastern Europe, including Romania, Poland, Czech, Slovakia, Hungary, and the European part of the former Soviet Union

【东三省】Dōng Sān Shěng 东北辽宁、吉林、黑龙江三省的总称 Three Northeastern Provinces, i. e. Liaoning, Jilin and Heilongjiang in northeast China

【东山再起】Dōng Shān zài qǐ 东晋谢安退职后在东山做隐士，后来又出任要职 Xie An, an official of the Eastern Jin Dynasty, resigned from office and lived in the Dongshan Mountains as a hermit, and later took an important post again; 〈比喻 *fig.*〉失势之后，重新恢复地位 (of one who once lost his power) resume one's former position; stage a comeback; return to power

【东施效颦】Dōngshī xiào pín 美女西施病了，皱着眉头，按着心口。同村的丑女人看见了，觉得姿态很美，也学她的样子，却丑得可怕（见于《庄子•天运》）。后人把这个丑女人称做东施。'东施效颦'比喻胡乱模仿，效果很坏。imitate awkwardly; crude imitation with ludicrous effect. When Xi Shi, a famous beauty, fell ill, she knitted her brows and pressed her chest with her hand. An ugly woman in the same village saw her and found the pose beautiful. So she copied her gestures only to look more ugly (*Zhuangzi • The Revolution of Heaven*). Later an ugly woman was thus called Dong Shi. The idiom is used to describe one who blindly copies others and makes himself look foolish.

【东魏】Dōng Wèi 北朝之一，公元 534—550，元善见所建 Eastern Wei Dynasty (534-550), one of the Northern Dynasties; ☞ 北魏 Běi Wèi on p. 81

【东西】dōngxī ❶ 东边和西边 east and west ❷ 从东到西（距离）from east to west: 这座城～三里，南北五里。The city is three *li* across from east to west and five *li* from north to south.

【东…西…】dōng…xī… 表示'这里…那里…'的意思 ... here ... there: ～奔～跑 rush about busily; run to and fro | ～张～望 look this way and that; peer around; look all around | ～拼～凑 put all sorts of things together; scrape together | ～倒～歪 reel right and left; dilapidated; rickety; staggering; tumbling; walk unsteadily | ～涂～抹 paint casually; paint at random | ～一句，～一句 talk incoherently

【东西】dōng•xi ❶ 泛指各种具体的或抽象的事物 thing; stuff; matter: 他买～去了。He's gone shopping. | 雾很大，十几步以外的～就看不见了。The fog is so heavy that one can't see beyond a dozen steps. | 语言这～，不是随便可以学好的，非下苦功不可。One can't learn a language well without making painstaking efforts. | 咱们写～要用普通话。We should write in standard Chinese. ❷ 特指人或动物（多含厌恶或喜爱的感情 used to refer to a person or animal with either negative or affectionate feelings) thing; creature: 老～ old creature | 笨～ idiot | 这小～真可爱。What a cute little thing!

【东乡族】Dōngxiāngzú 我国少数民族之一，主要分布在甘肃 Dongxiang people, one of China's ethnic minority groups, inhabiting parts of Gansu Province

【东亚】Dōng Yà 亚洲东部，包括中国、朝鲜、韩国、蒙古和日本等国 East Asia, including China, North Korea, South Korea, Mongolia, Japan, etc.

【东洋】Dōngyáng 指日本 Japan：～人 Japanese (people) | ～货 Japanese goods

【东野】Dōngyě 姓 a surname

【东瀛】dōngyíng 〈书 *fml*.〉❶ 东海 East China Sea ❷ 指日本 Japan：留学～ go to study in Japan

D

【东正教】Dōngzhèngjiào ☞ 正教 Zhèngjiào on p. 2448

【东周】Dōng Zhōu 朝代，公元前 770—公元前 256，自周平王（姬宜臼）迁都洛邑（在今河南洛阳市西）起，到被秦灭亡止 Eastern Zhou Dynasty (770-256 B. C.), which was established when King Ping of Zhou (Ji Yijiu) moved the capital to Luoyi (west of present-day Luoyang, Henan Province), and ended when it was overthrown by the State of Qin

冬[1] dōng ❶ 冬季 winter：隆～ mid-winter | ～耕 winter ploughing | ～眠 hibernation | 在北京住了两～ have passed two winters in Beijing ❷ (Dōng) 姓 a surname

冬[2]（鼕）dōng 〈拟声词 *onom*.〉形容敲鼓或敲门等声音 rub-a-dub; rat-tat; rat-a-tat; sound of beating a drum, knocking at a door, etc.

【冬不拉】dōngbùlā 哈萨克族的弦乐器，形状略像半个梨加上长柄，一般有两根弦或四根弦 *tamboura*; musical instrument with a body shaped like half a pear and two or four strings, used by the Kazak people; also 东不拉 dōngbùlā

【冬菜】dōngcài ❶ 用白菜或芥菜叶腌制成的干菜 preserved, dried cabbage or mustard greens ❷ 冬季贮存、食用的蔬菜，如大白菜、胡萝卜等 vegetables stored as food in winter, e. g. Chinese cabbage, carrot, etc.

【冬虫夏草】dōngchóng-xiàcǎo 真菌的一种，寄生在鳞翅目昆虫的幼体中，被害的幼虫冬季钻入土内，逐渐形成菌核，夏季从菌核或死虫的身体上长出菌体的繁殖器官来，形状像草，所以叫冬虫夏草。可入药。Chinese caterpillar fungus (*Cordyceps sinensis*); a kind of fungus parasite in the larvae of lepidopteran insects that get into the earth to winter; the insects die and in summer the cycocore in the dead insects grow into fungi resembling a weed, hence the name, meaning 'winter insect and summer grass; 简称 abbr. 虫草 chóngcǎo

【冬耕】dōnggēng 为保墒、除虫、培养地力，在冬季翻松土地 winter ploughing; ploughing the field in winter to protect the moisture of the soil, get rid of insects, and keep the soil fertile

【冬菇】dōnggū 冬季采集的香菇 dried mushrooms (picked in winter)

【冬瓜】dōngguā ❶ 一年生草本植物，茎上有卷须，能爬蔓，叶子大，开黄花。果实球形或长圆柱形，表面有毛和白粉，是普通蔬菜。皮和种子可入药。wax gourd (*Benincasa hispida*); white gourd; annual climbing plant with tassels, big leaves, yellow flowers and ball- or cylinder-shaped edible fruits, skin and seeds, which are used as medicine ❷ 这种植物的果实 fruit of this plant

【冬灌】dōngguàn 冬季往田里灌水，使土壤储水，防止春旱 winter irrigation; irrigate fields in winter to increase the water content of the soil and avoid spring drought

【冬烘】dōnghōng（思想）迂腐，（知识）浅陋（含讽刺意 sarcastic）(of sb.'s thinking and knowledge) shallow but pedantic：～先生 pedant | 头脑～ with a pedantic mind

【冬候鸟】dōnghòuniǎo 冬季在某个地区生活，春季飞到较远而且较冷的地区繁殖，秋季又飞回原地区的鸟。如野鸭、大雁就是我国的冬候鸟。winter bird; bird living in a certain area in winter, flying to a remote and cold region in spring and returning in autumn, like the wild duck and wild goose

【冬季】dōngjì 一年的第四季，我国习惯指立冬到立春的三个月时间，也指农历'十、十一、十二'三个月 winter; the last season of the year from the 19th solar term to the 1st solar term, or the 10th, 11th and 12th lunar months in China; ☞ 四季 sìjì on p. 1821

【冬节】dōngjié same as 冬至 dōngzhì

【冬令】dōnglìng ❶ 冬季 winter ❷ 冬季的气候 winter weather：春行～（春天的气候像冬天）wintry weather in spring; harsh spring

【冬眠】dōngmián 某些动物对不利生活条件的一种适应。如蛙、龟、蛇、蝙蝠、刺猬等，冬季僵卧在洞里，血液循环和呼吸非常缓慢，神经活动几乎完全停止 hibernation; hibernate; winter sleep; way some animals, e. g. frogs, snakes, turtles, bats and hedgehogs, etc., adjust themselves to adverse conditions by lying motionless in caves in a state of suspended animation, their blood circulation and respiration very slow, and nervous activity almost stopped

【冬青】dōngqīng 常绿乔木，叶子长椭圆形，前端尖，花白色，雌雄异株，果实球形，红色，种子和树皮可入药 holly (*Ilex aquifolium*); Chinese ilex; evergreen tree with oblong-ecliptic sharp-pointed leaves, white flowers and clusters of bright-red berries, the seed and bark of which used as herbal medicine

【冬笋】dōngsǔn 冬季挖的毛竹的笋。生长在向阳而温暖的地方，肉浅黄色，质嫩可食。winter

bamboo shoots; pale-yellow tender edible shoots of moso bamboo, which grows in warm, sunny places, dug up in winter for consumption

【冬天】dōngtiān same as 冬季 dōngjì

【冬瘟】dōngwēn 〈中医 *Chin. med.*〉称冬季流行的瘟病 epidemic febrile diseases in the winter

【冬闲】dōngxián 指冬季农事较少(时节) slack winter season (in farming):利用～做好室内选种工作 make use of the slack winter season to do a good job in selecting seeds

【冬小麦】dōngxiǎomài 指秋天播种第二年夏天收割的小麦 wheat (*Triticum*), sowed in autumn and harvested the next summer; also 冬麦 dōngmài

【冬学】dōngxué 农民在冬季农闲时学习文化的组织 organization where farmers learn to read and write in the slack winter season

【冬训】dōngxùn 冬季训练 winter training:篮球队即将投入～。The basketball team is going to start its winter training.

【冬衣】dōngyī 冬季穿的御寒的衣服 winter clothes

【冬泳】dōngyǒng 冬季在江河湖海里游泳 winter outdoor swimming (in a river, lake or sea):～比赛 winter swimming contest|不畏严寒,坚持～ defy severe cold and keep on swimming in winter

【冬月】dōngyuè 指农历十一月 eleventh month of the lunar calendar

【冬运】dōngyùn 运输部门指冬季的运输业务 winter transportation

【冬蛰】dōngzhé same as 冬眠 dōngmián

【冬至】dōngzhì 二十四节气之一,在12月21、22或23日。这一天太阳经过冬至点,北半球白天最短,夜间最长。Winter Solstice; one of the 24 solar terms, when the sun is the farthest south of the celestial equator on about Dec. 21, 22 or 23, which is thus the day of the year having the shortest period of sunlight in the Northern Hemisphere; ☞ 节气 jiéqì on p.989 and 二十四节气 èrshísì jiéqì on p.516

【冬至点】dōngzhìdiǎn 黄道上最南的一点,冬至这天太阳经过这个位置 winter solstice point; the farthest south point of the celestial equator which the sun passes at winter solstice

【冬至线】dōngzhìxiàn 南回归线 Tropic of Capricorn; ☞ 回归线 huíguīxiàn on p.860

【冬装】dōngzhuāng 冬季穿的御寒的服装 winter dress (or clothes)

咚 dōng same as 冬² dōng

岽(崬) dōng 岽罗(Dōngluó),地名,在广西 name of a place in Guangxi

氡 dōng 气体元素,符号 Rn (radon)。无色,在大气中含量极少,有放射性,用来治疗恶性肿瘤 radon (Rn); radioactive, colourless gaseous chemical element, minute quantities of which are found in the atmosphere; used to treat malicious tumours

鸫(鶇) dōng 鸟的一科,嘴细长而侧扁,翅膀长而平,叫的声音好听 thrush (*Muscicapidae*); veery (*Hylocichla fuscescens*); songbird with a long and thin beak and long flat wings and pleasant singing

蛛(蝀) dōng ☞ [䗖蛛](dìdōng) on p.431

dǒng (ㄉㄨㄥˇ)

董 dǒng ❶〈书 *fml.*〉监督管理 direct; superintend; supervise:～理 supervise|～其成 supervise the project until its completion ❷ 董事 director; trustee:校～ board of trustees of a college, school, etc.|商～ board of directors of the chamber of commerce ❸ (Dǒng) 姓 a surname

【董酒】dǒngjiǔ 贵州遵义出产的一种白酒 liquor produced in Zunyi, Guizhou Province

【董事】dǒngshì 董事会的成员 director; trustee; member of the board of directors

【董事会】dǒngshìhuì 某些企业或学校、团体等的领导机构 board of directors (in an enterprise); board of trustees (in an educational institution); leading body in some enterprises, schools or organizations

懂 dǒng 知道;了解 understand; know:～事 sensible; intelligent|～行 know the business|～英语 understand English|他的话我听～了。I understood what he said.

【懂得】dǒng·de 知道(意义、做法等) understand; know; grasp (meaning, method, etc.):～规矩 know the rules|你～这句话的意思吗? Do you understand the meaning of this sentence?

【懂行】dǒngháng 熟悉某一种业务 know the business; know the ropes; know one's job:向～的人请教 consult those who know the business

【懂事】dǒng//shì 了解别人的意图或一般事理 capable of understanding other people and events; sensible; intelligent:～明理 sensible; intelligent|这孩子很～。He is a sensible child.

dòng (ㄉㄨㄥˋ)

动(動) dòng ❶ (事物)改变原来位置或脱离静止状态(跟'静'相对 as opposed to 'still') change the place or position of sth.; move; stir:流～ flow|风吹草～。The grass sways as the wind rises.|你坐着别～。Sit there and don't move.|这东西一个人拿不

～。No one can move that singlehandedly. ❷ 动作;行动 act; get moving:轻举妄～ act rashly｜一举一～ every act and every move｜只要大家～起来,什么事都能办。Anything can be achieved with our joint efforts. ❸ 改变(事物)原来的位置或样子 cause to become different; change; alter; shift:搬～ move｜挪～ shift｜改～ change｜～用 employ｜兴师～众 arouse the masses (to do sth.) ❹ 使用;使起作用 use; make use of:～笔 take up the pen｜～手 start work｜～脑筋 use one's head ❺ 触动(思想感情) touch (one's heart); arouse; provoke:～心 be touched; moved｜～怒 lose one's temper｜～了公愤 incur public indignation ❻ 感动 move; touch:这出戏演得很～人。This play is touching. ❼〈方 *dial*.〉吃;喝(多用于否定式 usu. in the negative) eat or drink:这病不宜～荤腥。Consumption of meat and fish is not advisable for those with this illness.｜他向来不～酒。He doesn't drink. ❽ 动不动;常常 easily; frequently; usu.; tend to:～辄得咎 be liable to accusation no matter what one does｜影片一经上演,观众～以万计。Immediately after its release, the film drew audiences of tens of thousands.

【动笔】dòng//bǐ 用笔写或画(多指开始写或画);落笔 take up the pen; start writing or drawing:好久没～了 have not written anything for a long time｜～之前,先要想一想。Think it all out before you start writing.

【动兵】dòng//bīng 出动军队打仗 send out troops to fight

【动不动】dòng•budòng 表示很容易产生某种行动或情况(多指不希望发生的),常跟'就'连用[usu. followed by 就 jiù] (of an act or situation, usu. unwished for) appearing frequently, easily; frequently; at every turn; at every move; at the drop of a hat; at the slightest provocation:～就感冒 easily catch cold｜～就发脾气 be apt to lose one's temper; often get into a temper

【动产】dòngchǎn 可以移动的财产,指金钱、器物等 movables; personal property; movable assets like cash, household goods, etc.

【动词】dòngcí 表示人或事物的动作、存在、变化的词,如'走、笑、有、在、看、写、飞、落、保护、开始、起来、上去' verb; any of a class of words expressing an action, state of being, or occurrence, e.g. walk, laugh, have, be, look, write, fly, drop, protect, start, rise, climb, etc.

【动荡】dòngdàng ❶ 波浪起伏 heaving and subsiding:湖水～。The water in the lake rises and ebbs. ❷〈比喻 *fig*.〉局势、情况不稳定;不平静 turbulence; upheaval; unrest; turmoil:社会～ social upheaval｜～不安 turbulent; in turmoil｜～的年代 turbulent age

【动肝火】dòng gānhuǒ 指发脾气;发怒 get angry; flare up:有话慢慢说,不要～。Take time to explain yourself and do not get angry.

【动感】dònggǎn 指绘画、雕刻、文艺作品中的形象等给人以栩栩如生的感觉 (of images in paintings, sculpture, literature, etc.) dynamic; vibrant with life; lively; vivid:塑像极富～。The sculpture is full of life.

【动工】dòng//gōng ❶ 开工(指土木工程) begin construction; come under construction:～不到三个月,就完成了全部工程的一半。Half of the project was completed only three months after construction began. ❷ 施工 construct; build:这里正在～,车辆不能通过。This area is under construction and there is no thoroughfare.

【动滑轮】dònghuálún 位置不固定的滑轮,使用时整个滑轮发生位移。使用这种滑轮可以省力。fall block; movable pulley; pulley block with unfixed position, providing mechanical advantage and saving emergy for pulling or hoisting large, heavy objects

【动画片儿】dònghuàpiānr same as 动画片 dònghuàpiàn

【动画片】dònghuàpiàn 美术片的一种,把人、物的表情、动作、变化等分段画成许多画幅,再用摄影机连续拍摄而成 animated cartoon; cartoon; motion picture made by filming a series of drawings each showing a stage of movement of a person or an object slightly changed from the one before, so that the figures in them seem to move when the drawings are projected in rapid succession

【动换】dòng•huan 动弹;活动 move; stir:车内太挤,人都没法～了。One cannot move in this bus crammed with so many people.

【动火】dòng//huǒ (～儿 dòng//huǒr)发怒 get angry; flare up:什么事值得这么～? What made you flare up like that?｜他一听这话就动起火来。He got angry upon hearing what was said.

【动机】dòngjī 推动人从事某种行为的念头 motive; intention; inner drive that causes a person to do sth.:～好,方法不对头,也会把事办坏。Good intentions can also mess things up if the method is not appropriate.

【动劲儿】dòngjìnr〈方 *dial*.〉使力气 exert strength; work hard

【动静】dòng•jing ❶ 动作或说话的声音 sound; voice:屋子里静悄悄的,一点～也没有。It was quiet in the room; nothing was stirring. ❷ (打听或侦察的)情况 movements (apprehended or learned of); happenings; events; conditions; activities:察看对方的～ study the activities of the other side｜一有～,要马上报告。Report as soon as anything happens.

【动力】dònglì ❶ 使机械作功的各种作用力,如水力、风力、电力、畜力等 power; motive power; force or energy that puts machinery to work, e.g. hydropower, wind power, electric power, livestock power, etc.; ❷〈比喻 *fig.*〉推动工作、事业等前进和发展的力量 impetus; drive; driving force; force stimulating the development of work or a cause: 人民是创造世界历史的～。People are the driving force of world history.

【动力机】dònglìjī 发动机 motor; engine

【动量】dòngliàng 表示运动物体运动特性的一种物理量。动量是一个矢量,它的方向和物体运动的方向相同,它的大小等于运动物体的质量和速度的乘积。momentum; physical quantity representing the moving character of an object, in the direction of the movement of the object and equal to the product of its mass and velocity

【动乱】dòngluàn (社会)骚动变乱 (social) turmoil; disturbance; upheaval; turbulence

【动轮】dònglún 机车或其他机械上跟动力直接相连的轮子 driving wheel; wheel of a locomotive or other kinds of machinery, that receives power from the engine

【动脉】dòngmài ❶ 把心脏中压出来的血液输送到全身各部分的血管 artery; blood vessels that carry blood away from the heart to every part of the body ❷〈比喻 *fig.*〉重要的交通干线 artery; main road or channel

【动脉弓】dòngmàigōng 主动脉弓 arch of the aorta

【动脉硬化】dòngmài yìnghuà 病,动脉管壁增厚,弹性减弱,管腔狭窄,甚至完全堵塞。多由高血压、血液中胆固醇含量增多等引起。arteriosclerosis; disease characterized by the abnormal thickening, narrowing, loss of elasticity and even blockage of the arteries, usu. caused by hypertension and an increase of cholesterol in the blood

【动脉粥样硬化】dòngmài zhōuyàng yìnghuà 动脉硬化的一种,大、中动脉内膜出现含胆固醇、类脂肪等的黄色物质,多由脂肪代谢紊乱、神经血管功能失调引起。常导致血栓形成、供血障碍等。arteriosclerosis; a kind of arteriosclerosis, with yellow substances containing cholesterol and quasi-fat in arteries and veins, usu. caused by a disorder of the fat metabolism, oft. leads to thrombophlebitis and blockage of blood vessels; also 粥样硬化 zhōuyàng yìnghuà

【动摩擦】dòngmócā 接触物体之间保持相对运动的摩擦 dynamic friction; kinetic friction; running friction; friction between two contacting objects in relative motion

【动能】dòngnéng 物体由于机械运动而具有的能,它的大小是运动物体的质量和速度平方乘积的 1/2 kinetic energy; energy of motion; energy of an object that results from its motion, equal to half of the product of the mass of the object and the square of its velocity

【动怒】dòng//nù 发怒 lose one's temper; flare up; be enraged; be vexed

【动气】dòng//qì 生气 take offence; get angry: 病中不宜～。Better not get angry while you are ill. | 我从来没有看见他动过气。I have never seen him get angry.

【动情】dòng//qíng ❶ 情绪激动 get worked up; become excited: 她越说越～,泪水哗哗直流。She got so worked up talking about it that her tears flowed freely. ❷ 产生爱慕的感情 become enamoured; have one's passions aroused

【动人】dòngrén 感动人 moving; touching: 美丽～ beautiful and touching | ～的歌声 enchanting sound of singing

【动人心弦】dòng rén xīnxián 激动人心;非常动人 tug at one's heartstrings; be deeply moving; be exciting: 这是个多么～的场面! What a moving scene! also 动人心魄 dòng rén xīnpò

【动容】dòngróng 脸上出现受感动的表情 change countenance; be visibly moved: 观者无不为之～。The entire audience was moved.

【动身】dòng//shēn 启程;出发 go (or set out) on a journey; leave (for a distant place); set off: 行李都打好了,明天早上就～。We've already packed and will leave tomorrow morning.

【动手】dòng//shǒu ❶ 开始做;做 start work; get to work; get moving: 早点儿～早点儿完。The sooner we start, the sooner we'll finish. | 大家一齐～。Everyone got to work. ❷ 用手接触 touch; handle: 展览品只许看,不许～。Please just look and don't touch the exhibits. ❸ 指打人 raise a hand to strike sb.; hit out at: 两人说着说着就动起手来了。The two came to blows in the middle of a conversation.

【动态】dòngtài ❶ (事情)变化发展的情况 the general tendency or course (of events); trends; developments: 科技～ developments in science and technology | 从这些图片里可以看出我国建设的～。These pictures embody the trends of reconstruction of our country. ❷ 艺术形象表现出的活动神态 dynamism of an artistic image: 画中人物,～各异,栩栩如生。The figures in the painting, with their different bearings, are as vivid as live figures. ❸ 运动变化状态的或从运动变化状态考察的 kinestate; dynamic state; dynamic condition; dynamic; motional; relating to an object in motion: ～工作点 dynamic operation point | ～电流 dynamic current | ～分析 dynamic analysis

【动弹】dòng·tan (人、动物或能转动的东西)活动 (human being, animal or animated object) move; stir: 两脚发木,～不得。Both feet went numb and could not move. | 风车不～了。The windmill has stopped.

【动听】dòngtīng 听起来使人感动或者感觉有兴

趣 interesting or pleasant to the ear; moving; persuasive:娓娓～ be pleasant to the ear|极平常的事儿,让他说起来就很～。He can make ordinary things sound interesting.

【动土】dòng//tǔ 刨地(多用于建筑、安葬等 usu. of civil engineering projects and burials) break ground; start building

【动问】dòngwèn 〈客套话 *pol.*〉请问 may I ask:不敢～,您是从北京来的吗? Excuse me for asking, but are you from Beijing?

【动武】dòng//wǔ 使用武力(包括殴打、发动战争) use force; start a fight; come to blows

【动物】dòngwù 生物的一大类,这一类生物多以有机物为食料,有神经,有感觉,能运动 animal; a category of living beings that can move about independently, have specialized sense organs, and usu. take other organisms as food

【动物纤维】dòngwù xiānwéi 来源于动物的纤维,如蚕丝、羊毛等 animal fibre; fibres from animals, e.g. silk, wool, etc.

【动物学】dòngwùxué 研究动物的形态、生理、生态、分类、分布和怎样控制动物的学科 zoology; science that deals with animals, their structure, physiology, habits, classification, distribution and control

【动物油】dòngwùyóu 从动物取得的油脂,如牛油、猪油、鲸油等。供食用,也可以做润滑剂和化工原料。animal oil; edible oils obtained from animals, e.g. butter (from cows), lard (from pigs), blubber (from whales), etc., and also oils obtained from animals to be used as lubricants and chemical materials

【动物园】dòngwùyuán 饲养许多种动物(特别是科学上有价值或当地罕见的动物),供人观赏的公园 zoo; zoological park; place where wild animals (esp. rare species and those valuable in science) are kept for public showing

【动向】dòngxiàng 活动或发展的方向 trend; tendency:思想～ trends of thought |市场～ market trends |侦察敌人的～ reconnoitre enemy movements

【动心】dòng//xīn 思想、感情发生波动 one's mind is disturbed; one's desire, enthusiasm or interest is aroused:见财不～ not moved by money|经人一说,他也就动了心了。People tried to persuade him, and his interest was aroused.

【动刑】dòng//xíng 施用刑具 subject sb. to torture; torture

【动眼神经】dòngyǎn-shénjīng 第三对脑神经,从大脑脚发出,分布在眼球的肌肉上,主管眼球的运动 oculomotor nerves; third pair of cranial nerves, arise from the midbrain, and supply most muscles of the eye, controlling movements of the eyeball

【动摇】dòngyáo ❶ 不稳固;不坚定 vacillate; waver:～分子 wavering (or vacillating) element |意志坚定,绝不～ never waver in one's determination ❷ 使动摇 shake:～军心 shake the morale of the army |环境再艰苦也～不了这批青年征服自然的决心。No matter how difficult the situation, nothing can shake these young people's resolve to conquer nature.

【动议】dòngyì 会议中的建议(一般指临时的) motion; (usu. provisional) proposal to be discussed at a meeting:紧急～ urgent motion

【动用】dòngyòng 使用 put to use; employ; draw on; resort to:～公款 draw upon public funds|～武力 resort to arms|不得随意～库存粮食。Random drawing upon grain reserves is not allowed.

【动员】dòngyuán ❶ 把国家的武装力量由和平状态转入战时状态,以及把所有的经济部门(工业、农业、运输业等)转入供应战争需要的工作 mobilize; cause the armed forces to become ready for service and turn all of economic departments (industry, agriculture, transportation, etc.) to the needs of war ❷ 发动人参加某项活动 call upon people to participate in a certain activity:～报告 mobilization speech |全体～,大搞卫生 mobilize everyone to improve on general sanitation

【动辄】dòngzhé 〈书 *fml.*〉动不动就 easily; frequently; at every turn:～得咎 be blamed for everything whatever one does |～恶语相加 swear at sb. on the least pretext

【动辄得咎】dòng zhé dé jiù 动不动就受到责备或处分 be constantly taken to task; be liable to blame for whatever one does

【动嘴】dòngzuǐ 指说话 talk; speak:别光～,快干活! Don't just talk. Get down to business.

【动作】dòngzuò ❶ 全身或身体的一部分的活动 movement of the body or a part of the body; motion; action:这一节操有四个～。This segment of the exercise is composed of four movements. |～敏捷 quick-limbed; quick in one's movements ❷ 活动;行动起来 act; start moving:弹钢琴要十个指头都～。It takes the action of all ten fingers to play the piano.

冻(凍) dòng ❶ (液体或含水分的东西)遇冷凝固 (of liquid or things containing water) freeze; change from liquid to solid due to extreme cold:不～港 ice-free port; open port|缸里的水～了。The water in the urn froze. |白菜要抢收入窖,不能让它～坏。(We) have to do an emergency harvest of Chinese cabbage and store them in cellars, since we can't let them be damaged by frost. ❷ (～儿 dòngr)汤汁等凝结成的半固体 jelly; savoury food made from juice or gelatine, which jiggles when moved:肉～儿 meat jelly |鱼～儿 fish jelly ❸ 受冷或感到冷 feel very cold; freeze; be frostbitten:我的脚～了。My feet were frostbitten. |今天衣服穿少了,真～

得慌。I did not put on enough clothes and really froze today.

【冻疮】dòngchuāng 局部皮肤因受低温损害而成的疮 chilblains; frostbite; painful swelling on the skin caused by overexposure to cold

【冻豆腐】dòngdòu·fu 经过冰冻的豆腐 frozen bean curd

【冻害】dònghài 农业上指由于气温下降使植物体的组织受到破坏(agriculture) frost damage; tissue damage to plants caused by a sharp decline in temperature

【冻结】dòngjié ❶ 液体遇冷凝结;使物体受冻凝结 congeal; change or be changed from liquid to solid by cold; freeze ❷〈比喻 *fig.*〉阻止流动或变动(指人员、资金等) not allow (money or personnel) to be used or changed freeze:～存款 freeze a deposit ❸〈比喻 *fig.*〉暂不执行或发展 freeze; withhold:协议～ freeze the agreement | ～双方关系 freeze the bilateral relations

【冻馁】dòngněi〈书 *fml.*〉寒冷饥饿;受冻挨饿 cold and hunger

【冻伤】dòngshāng 机体的组织由于低温而引起的损伤。轻的皮肤红肿,灼痛或发痒,重的皮肤起水泡,最重的引起皮肤、肌肉甚至骨骼坏死。frostbite; injury to tissue caused by extreme cold, ranging from red and swollen skin, causalgia, itching, to blisters, and even necrosis of the skin, muscle and bone

【冻雨】dòngyǔ 一种特殊的降水现象,这种雨从天空落下时是0℃以下的过冷却水滴,一落地就结为固态的冰 sleet; freezing rain; rain that freezes as it falls

【冻瘃】dòngzhú〈方 *dial.*〉冻疮 chilblains

侗 Dòng 侗族 the Dongs, an ethnic minority people

☞ tóng on p. 1923 and tǒng on p. 1925

【侗剧】dòngjù 侗族戏曲剧种,流行于贵州、广西等地侗族聚居的地区 Dong opera; a kind of drama of the Dong people, prevailing in Guizhou and Guangxi

【侗族】Dòngzú 我国少数民族之一,分布在贵州、湖南和广西 Dong people, a minority people inhabiting in Guizhou and Hunan provinces, and the Guangxi Zhuang Autonomous Region

垌 dòng〈方 *dial.*〉田地(多用于地名)(usu. used in place names) field:合伞～(在贵州) Hesandong (in Guizhou Province) | 儒～(在广东) Rudong (in Guangdong Province)

☞ tóng on p. 1923

栋(棟) dòng ❶〈书 *fml.*〉脊檩;正梁 ridgepole ❷〈量词 *classifier*〉房屋一座叫一栋 building

【栋梁】dòngliáng 房屋的大梁,比喻担负国家重任的人 ridgepole; (fig.) sb. who is a pillar of the state:～之才 person of tremendous ability and strength; sb. with the makings of a statesperson | 社会～ pillars of society

峒 dòng 山洞(多用于地名)(usu. in a place name) cave; cavern:吉～坪(在湖南) Jidongping (in Hunan Province) | ～中(在广东) Dongzhong (in Guangdong Province)

☞ tóng on p. 1923

胨(腖) dòng 蛋白胨的简称 abbr. for 蛋白胨 dànbáidòng

洞 dòng ❶(～儿 dòngr)物体中间的穿通的或凹入较深的部分 hole; cavity; hollow or hollowed-out place in an object:～穴 cave; cavern | 山～ cave | 衣服破了一个～。There is a hole in the garment. ◇漏～ flaw; loophole ❷〈书 *fml.*〉穿透 penetrate; pierce through:弹～其腹。His belly was pierced by a bullet. ❸ 说数字时用来代表'0' used in place of '0' when speaking of figures ❹ 深远;透彻 profound; thorough; clear:～晓 have a clear knowledge of | ～察一切 have a keen insight into matters; see right through | ～若观火 see sth. as clearly as a blazing fire; as clear as day

【洞察】dòngchá 观察得很清楚 see clearly; see through; have insight into:～下情 (for sb. in a high position) know the feelings of the people clearly | ～其奸 see through a trick

【洞彻】dòngchè 透彻地了解 understand thoroughly; see clearly; see through:～事理 be perfectly aware and sensible

【洞达】dòngdá 很明白;很了解 understand thoroughly:～人情世故 in possession of worldly wisdom; understand human nature and the workings of the world

【洞房】dòngfáng 新婚夫妇的房间 bridal (or nuptial) chamber:闹～ charivari in the bridal chamber; celebrate a wedding in the bridal chamber | ～花烛(旧时结婚的景象,新婚之夜,洞房里点花烛) nuptial chamber with painted candles (in old tradition); wedding night

【洞府】dòngfǔ 神话传说深山中神仙所住的地方 cave dwelling; abode, usu. in the mountains, of fairies and immortals in fairy tales

【洞见】dòngjiàn 很清楚地见到 see very clearly:～肺腑(形容诚恳坦白) see clearly through to the depths of the heart

【洞开】dòngkāi (门窗等)大开 (of doors, windows, etc.) be wide open:门户～。The door was wide open.

【洞若观火】dòng ruò guān huǒ 形容看得清楚明白 see sth. as clearly as a blazing fire; very clear-sighted; as clear as day

【洞天】dòngtiān〈道教 *Taoism*〉指神仙居住的地方,现在多用来指引人入胜的境地 paradise of Taoism, referring to an attractive place:别有～ hidden but beautiful spot; world all its own

【洞天福地】dòngtiān fúdì〈道教 *Taoism*〉指神

仙居住的地方，现泛指名山胜境 cave paradise and blessed land — fairyland; heavenly abode; scenic beauty of a famous mountain

【洞悉】dòngxī 很清楚地知道 know clearly; understand thoroughly：～内情 know clearly the inside story

【洞箫】dòngxiāo 箫，因不封底而得名 vertical bamboo flute

【洞晓】dòngxiǎo 透彻地知道；精通 have a clear knowledge of：～音律 thoroughly understand tonality, the principle and rules of sound and music｜～其中利弊 have a clear understanding of the advantages and disadvantages

D

【洞穴】dòngxué 地洞或山洞（多指能藏人或东西的）（indicating to hide people or things) cave; cavern

【洞烛其奸】dòng zhú qí jiān 形容看透对方的阴谋诡计 see through sb.'s tricks

【洞子】dòng·zi ❶〈方 *dial.*〉冬天培植花草、蔬菜等的暖房 greenhouse for flowers, plants and vegetables in the winter：花儿～ greenhouse｜～货 plants from a greenhouse ❷ same as 洞穴 dòngxué

【洞子货】dòng·zihuò〈方 *dial.*〉指冬天在暖房培植的花草或蔬菜 plants or vegetables cultivated in greenhouses in winter

恫 dòng〈书 *fml.*〉恐惧；恐吓 fear; fright：～恐 fear｜～吓 threaten; intimidate

☞ tōng on p. 1914

【恫吓】dònghè 威吓；吓（xià）唬 threaten; intimidate：不怕武力～ defy any intimidation of arms

胴 dòng ❶ 躯干（gàn） trunk; torso ❷〈书 *fml.*〉大肠 large intestine

【胴体】dòngtǐ ❶ 躯干，特指牲畜屠宰后，除去头、尾、四肢、内脏等剩下的部分 trunk (esp. of a slaughtered animal with the head, tail, limbs, bowels, etc., removed) ❷ 指人的躯体 human body

硐 dòng 山洞、窑洞或矿坑 cave; cave dwelling; pit

働 dòng 用于'劳働' used in 劳働 láodòng, same as '劳动' láodòng

dōu（ㄉㄡ）

都 dōu〈副词 *adv.*〉❶ 表示总括，所总括的成分一般在前 whole extent or quantity of; all：全家～搞财贸工作。All the members of the family are engaged in finance and trade.｜他无论干什么～很带劲儿。Whatever he did, he did with vigour. ❷ 跟'是'字合用，说明理由［used with 是 shì to show the cause］：～是你磨蹭，要不我也不会迟到。It was all because of your dawdling that I got late.｜～是昨天这场雨，害得我们耽误了一天工。It was all because of the rain yesterday that our work was delayed for a day. ❸ 表示'甚至' even：你待我比亲姐姐～好。You treat me even better than my own sister does.｜今天一点儿～不冷。It is not cold at all today.｜一动～不动 without even a single movement ❹ 表示'已经' already：饭～凉了，快吃吧。The food is already cold. Hurry and eat.

☞ dū on p. 475

哣 dōu 怒斥声（多见于早期白话 usu. seen in early vernacular) exclamation of angry dismissal

兜[1] dōu ❶（～儿 dōur）口袋一类的东西 bag; pocket; sack; pouch：网～儿 net bag｜裤～儿 trouser pocket｜中山服有四个～儿。A Sun Yat-sen uniform has four pockets. ❷ 做成兜形把东西拢住 wrap; envelop; enfold：小女孩儿的衣襟里～着几个海棠果儿。The little girl is carrying some plum-leaf crab apples wrapped in the turned-up front of her jacket.｜老大娘用手巾～着几个鸡蛋。The old woman carries a few eggs wrapped up in a towel. ❸ 绕 move around; circle; revolve：～抄 round up; envelop｜～圈子 circle ◇许多感想～上心头。All sorts of feelings welled up in my mind. ❹ 招揽 solicit; canvass：～销 drum up trade｜～生意 canvass business orders seek business orders ❺ 承担或包下来 take upon oneself; take care of; take the responsibility for：没关系，有问题我～着。Don't worry, I'll take care of things if there's any problem. ❻ 兜底 expose; disclose; reveal：把他的老底全给～出来 bring up everything about his past ❼ 正对着；冲着 towards; against; on：～头盖脸 straight on the head; right in the face ❽ same as 篼 dōu

兜[2] dōu same as 蔸 dōu

【兜抄】dōuchāo 从后面和两旁包围攻击 round up; envelop; close in on sb. or sth. from the rear and both flanks

【兜底】dōu//dǐ（～儿 dōu//dǐr）把底细全部揭露出来（多指隐讳的事 usu. of sth. disreputable) reveal all the details：他的事儿全让人兜了底。His hanky-panky was all exposed.

【兜兜】dōu·dou 兜肚 undergarment covering the chest and abdomen

【兜兜裤儿】dōu·doukùr 小孩儿夏天穿的带兜肚的小短裤儿 sun suit (for a child)

【兜肚】dōu·du 贴身护在胸部和腹部的像菱形的布，用带子套在脖子上，左右两角钉带子束在背后 diamond-shaped undergarment covering the chest and abdomen, with bands going around the neck and waist

【兜翻】dōu·fan〈方 *dial.*〉❶ 翻弄（旧存的东西）rummage through (old things)：老太太又在开箱子～她那点儿绣花的活计。The old lady is rummaging through the chest for her embroidery work again. ❷ 重新提起(旧事旧话) dig up (old stories); bring up again; mention again:过去的那些事别~了。Don't dig up the past. ❸ 揭穿(隐讳的事情) expose; disclose; reveal (disreputable things): 把他的老底都给~出来了。His past has been revealed.

【兜风】dōu//fēng ❶ (船帆、车篷等)挡住风 (of sails, hoods, etc.) catch the wind:破帆不~。Torn sails don't catch the wind. ❷ 坐车、骑马或乘游艇兜圈子乘凉或游逛 go for a drive, ride or sail; go for a spin:他开着车~去了。He's gone for a spin in his car.

【兜揽】dōulǎn ❶ 招引(顾客) canvass; solicit: ~生意 solicit customers; drum up trade ❷ 把事情往身上拉 take upon oneself:他就爱~个事儿。He likes taking things on himself.

【兜鍪】dōumóu 〈古代 *arch.*〉作战时戴的盔 helmet

【兜圈子】dōu quān·zi 绕圈儿 go around in circles; circle:飞机在树林子上空兜了两个圈子就飞走了。The airplane circled over the forest a couple of times and left. ◇别跟我~,有话直截了当地说吧。Stop talking in circles with me, and just get straight to the point.

【兜售】dōushòu same as 兜销 dōuxiāo

【兜头盖脸】dōu tóu gài liǎn 正对着头和脸 direct to one's head and face; right in the face: 一盆水~全泼在他身上。A basin of water was poured right on him. also 兜头盖脑 dōu tóu gài nǎo

【兜销】dōuxiāo 到处找人购买(自己手上的货物) peddle; hawk:~存货 hawk the goods in stock

【兜子】dōu·zi ❶ 口袋一类的东西 pocket; bag; sack; pouch:车~ bicycle pouch | 裤~ trouser pocket ❷ same as 篼子 dōu·zi

【兜嘴】dōuzuǐ 〈方 *dial.*〉❶ 围嘴儿 bib ❷ 笼嘴 muzzle (for a draft animal)

蔸(橷) dōu 〈方 *dial.*〉❶ 指某些植物的根和靠近根的茎: root and stem of certain plants 禾~ stem of a plant ❷ 〈量词 *classifier*〉same as 棵 kē or 丛 cōng (of plants): 一~树 a tree | 两~白菜 two heads of Chinese cabbage | 三~禾 three seedlings

篼 dōu 竹、藤、柳条等做成的盛东西的器具 basket; container made of bamboo, wicker, rattan, etc.; 背~ basket carried on the back

【篼子】dōu·zi 〈方 *dial.*〉用竹椅子捆在两根竹竿上做成的交通工具,作用跟轿子相同 bamboo sedan chair; litter; bamboo chair for carrying one person on two poles by two people; also 兜子 dōu·zi

dǒu (ㄉㄡˇ)

斗 dǒu ❶ 容量单位。10 升等于 1 斗,10 斗等于 1 石 *dou*, unit of dry measure for grain (now about a decalitre, equal to 10 *sheng* or 1/10 *dan*) ❷ 量(liáng)粮食的器具,容量是一斗,方形,也有鼓形的,多用木头或竹子制成 *dou* measure, square or drum-like, made of wood or bamboo ❸ (~儿 dǒur)形状略像斗的东西 object shaped like a cup or dipper: 漏~ funnel | 风~儿 vent | 烟~ pipe ❹ 圆形的指纹 whorl (of a fingerprint) ❺ 古代盛酒的器具 ancient wine vessel ❻ 二十八宿之一,通称南斗 (usu. called 南斗 nándǒu) 8th of the 28 constellations into which celestial space was divided in ancient Chinese astronomy (consisting of six stars in the shape of a ladle in Sagittarius) ❼ 北斗星的简称(abbr. for 北斗星 běidǒuxīng) Big Dipper; Dipper: ~柄 handle of the Dipper ❽ same as 陡 dǒu ☞ dòu on p.473

【斗笔】dǒubǐ 一种大型毛笔,笔头儿安装在一个斗形部件里,上安笔杆儿 large writing brush, the tip of which is fixed in a *dou*-like socket

【斗车】dǒuchē 工地、矿区常用的一种运输工具,车身有点像斗,下面有轮,放在轨道上移动 trolley (*dou*-like vehicle used in a mine or on a construction site); tram

【斗胆】dǒudǎn 形容大胆(多用做谦辞 usu. hum.) make bold; venture: 我~说一句,这件事情您做错了。May I make so bold as to suggest that you did it wrong.

【斗方】dǒufāng (~儿 dǒufāngr)书画所用的方形纸张,也指一二尺见方的字画 square sheet of paper used for painting or calligraphy; painting or calligraphy done on a (one- or two-*chi* square sheet of paper

【斗方名士】dǒufāng míngshì 指以风雅自命的无聊文人 pretender to culture and refinement; poseur; literary hack

【斗拱】dǒugǒng, 又 also dòugǒng 我国建筑特有的一种结构。在立柱和横梁交接处,从柱顶上加的一层层探出成弓形的承重结构叫拱,拱

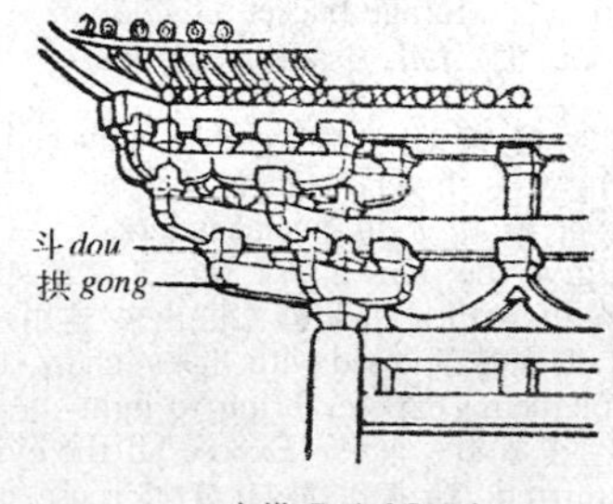

斗拱 Corbel Bracket

与拱之间垫的方形木块叫斗。合称斗拱。corbel bracket; unique Chinese architectural structure, comprising a system of tiers of brackets inserted between the top of a pillar and a crossbeam (each bracket being in the form of a bow-shaped arc, called *gong*, cushioned with trapezoidal blocks called *dou*); also 枓拱 dǒugǒng and 枓栱 dǒugǒng

【斗箕】dǒu·ji 指印,因指纹有斗有箕,所以把指印叫做斗箕 whorl and loop; fingerprint

【斗笠】dǒulì 遮阳光和雨的帽子,有很宽的边,用竹篾夹油纸或竹叶等制成 bamboo hat (broad brimmed hat made of bamboo slips and leaves, or oiled paper, that gives shelter from sun or rain)

【斗门】dǒumén 指农田灌溉系统中斗渠的水闸 (of agricultural irrigation system) sluice valve; sluice gate

【斗篷】dǒu·peng ❶ 披在肩上的没有袖子的外衣 cape; cloak; wrap-like outer garment fastened at the throat and falling straight from the shoulder ❷〈方 *dial.*〉斗笠 bamboo hat

【斗渠】dǒuqú 由支渠引水到毛渠或灌区的渠道 (of a water conservancy and irrigation system) lateral canal

【斗筲】dǒushāo〈书 *fml.*〉斗和筲都是容量不大的容器,比喻气量狭小或才识短浅: literally, *dou* and *shao*, both mean small containers; (fig.) narrow-mindedness; shallow understanding; poor ability :～之器 man of shallow understanding | ～之辈 petty-minded people; minnows

【斗室】dǒushì〈书 *fml.*〉指极小的屋子 tiny room: 身居～ dwell in a small room; live in a tiny room

【斗烟丝】dǒuyānsī 烟斗丝 pipe tobacco

【斗转星移】dǒu zhuǎn xīng yí 北斗转向,众星移位。表示时序变迁,岁月流逝。turning of the handle of the Big Dipper and changing position of the stars — change of season; passage of time

【斗子】dǒu·zi ❶ 煤矿里盛煤的器具,也指家庭中盛煤的铁桶 coal bucket (used in a coal mine or in the home) ❷ 用树条、木板等制成的盛东西的器具 container made of twigs or wood: 料～ forage bucket

阧 dǒu〈书 *fml.*〉same as 陡 dǒu

抖 dǒu ❶ 颤动;哆嗦 tremble; shiver; quiver: 发～ shiver; tremble 浑身直～ tremble all over ❷ 振动;甩动 shake; jerk: ～一～马缰绳 give the reins a jerk | ～开被窝 spread the quilt with a flick ❸ (跟'出来'连用)全部倒出;彻底揭穿 [used with 出来//chū//·lái as complement] expose; bring to light: 把他干的那些丑事都～出来。Expose all the evil he committed. ❹ 振作;鼓起(精神) rouse; muster up; stir up: ～起精神往前直赶 pull oneself together and pursue ❺ 称人因为有钱有地位等而得意(多含讥讽意 usu. ironic) self-satisfied at having achieved a measure of wealth and position: 他如今当了官,～起来了。Now that he has a position of authority he has begun throwing his weight about.

【抖颤】dǒuchàn 发抖;颤抖 shiver; quiver; tremble

【抖动】dǒudòng ❶ 颤动: tremble: 她气得咬紧嘴唇,身子剧烈～。She was so angry that she bit her lips and her whole body trembled. ❷ 用手振动物体: shake; vibrate 他～了一下缰绳,马便向草原飞奔而去。He gave the reins a jerk and the horse began to gallop towards the grassland.

【抖搂】dǒu·lou〈方 *dial.*〉❶ 振动衣、被、包袱等,使附着的东西落下来 shake off (clothing, bedding, wraps, etc.); shake out of sth.: 把衣服上的雪～干净 shake the snow off the jacket ❷ 全部倒出或说出;揭露 shake out (a container, etc.); make a clean breast of (a secret); expose; bring to light: ～箱子底儿 tip things out of a case or trunk | 把以前的事全给～出来 bring everything sb. did to light ❸ 浪费;胡乱用(财物) waste; squander: 别把钱～光了,留着办点儿正事。Don't waste all of the money, leave some for important business.

【抖擞】dǒusǒu 振作 enliven; rouse; invigorate: 精神～ full of energy; full of beans; in high spirits | ～精神 brace up; pull oneself together

枓 dǒu [枓拱][枓栱](dǒugǒng) same as 斗拱 dǒugǒng

陡 dǒu ❶ 坡度很大,近于垂直 steep; precipitous: ～坡 steep slop | 山很～,爬上去很困难。The mountain is very steep and difficult to climb. ❷ 陡然 suddenly; unexpectedly; abruptly: ～变 change suddenly

【陡壁】dǒubì 像墙壁那样直立的岸或山崖: wall-like perpendicular bank or mountain; cliff; precipice ～悬崖 precipices and cliffs

【陡变】dǒubiàn 突然改变或变化 change suddenly: 面色～ sb.'s countenance changed abruptly | 天气～。The weather changed suddenly.

【陡峻】dǒujùn (地势)高而陡 high and precipitous: 山崖～。The cliff stands high and steep.

【陡立】dǒulì (山峰、建筑物等)直立 (of a mountain, a building etc.) rise steeply

【陡坡】dǒupō 和水平面所成角度大的地面;坡度大的坡 steep slope

【陡峭】dǒuqiào (山势等)坡度很大,直上直下的 (of mountain etc.) precipitous: 这个～的山峰连山羊也上不去。The peak is so steep that even goats cannot climb it.

【陡然】dǒurán 突然 suddenly; unexpectedly; abruptly: ～醒悟 suddenly come to realize; realize in a flash

蚪 dǒu ☞ 蝌蚪 kēdǒu on p. 1091

dòu (ㄉㄡˋ)

斗(鬥、鬦、鬭) dòu ❶ 对打 fight; tussle: 械～ fight with weapons (between groups of people) | 拳～ fist fight; fisticuffs ❷ same as 斗争 dòuzhēng ②: ～恶霸 denounce a local despot ❸ 使动物斗 make animals fight (as a sport or amusement): ～鸡 cockfight | ～蛐蛐儿 cricket fight; ❹ 比赛争胜 contest with; contend with: ～智 fight a battle of wits ～嘴 quarrel; banter ❺ 往一块儿凑;凑在一块儿 come together; put together; fit together: ～眼 cross-eyed | ～榫儿 fit a tenon into the mortise; dovetail | 这件小袄儿是用各色花布～起来的。This little jacket is made by stitching together pieces of cloth in different colours.
☞ dǒu on p. 471

【斗法】dòu//fǎ 用法术相斗(旧小说中的虚构) (as described in old novels) exercise magic powers against each other; 〈比喻 *fig*.〉使用计谋,暗中争斗 use stratagems; outwit sb.

【斗拱】dòugǒng '斗拱'(dǒugǒng)的又音 variant pronunciation of 斗拱 dǒugǒng

【斗鸡】dòu//jī ❶ 使公鸡相斗的一种游戏 cockfight; cockfighting (a sport) ❷ 一种游戏,一只脚站立,另一条腿弯曲着,两手捧住脚,彼此用弯着的腿的膝盖互相冲撞 game in which a person grasps one leg with both hands and while hopping on the other leg, manoeuvres his knee to kick an opponent

【斗鸡走狗】dòu jī zǒu gǒu 使鸡相斗,嗾使着狗跑。多用来指纨袴子弟游手好闲,不务正业。let cocks fight and dogs race; used to describe the way some young people loiter about frittering away their time rather than engaging in decent work; also 斗鸡走马 dòu jī zǒu mǎ

【斗口齿】dòu kǒuchǐ 〈方 *dial*.〉 same as 斗嘴 dòu//zuǐ

【斗殴】dòu'ōu 争斗殴打 fight; scuffle: 相互～ two people fighting

【斗牌】dòu//pái 玩纸牌、骨牌等比输赢 play cards or dominoes

【斗气】dòu//qì 为意气相争: take things personally and nurse a personal grudge (against sb); act perversely out of resentment or anger :有话好好说,用不着～。You must try to talk reasonably, being angry with each other is of no use.

【斗士】dòushì 勇于斗争的人 courageous fighter (for a cause)

【斗心眼儿】dòu xīnyǎnr 用心思相斗(含贬义 derog.) try to outwit; contend in petty scheming

【斗眼】dòuyǎn (～儿 dòuyǎnr) 内斜视的通称 general term for 内斜视 nèixiéshì

【斗争】dòuzhēng ❶ 矛盾的双方互相冲突,一方力求战胜另一方 fight; combat; struggle; exert strength, energy, and force; work or strive: 阶级～ class struggle | 思想～ ideological struggle | 跟歪风邪气作坚决的～。Resolutely combat insidious trends and harmful practices. ❷ 群众用说理、揭发、控诉等方式打击敌对分子或坏分子 censure; condemn (of a mass of people); combat hostile or bad elements by reasoning, exposing their crimes or levelling charges against them: 开～会 hold a gathering to denounce (hostile elements) ❸ 努力奋斗 strive for: 为建设美好的未来而～ strive for a bright future

【斗志】dòuzhì 战斗的意志 fighting will: 激励～ inspire one's fighting will | ～昂扬 have high morale; be militant

【斗智】dòu//zhì 用智谋争胜 fight a battle of wits

【斗嘴】dòu//zuǐ (～儿 dòu//zuǐr) ❶ 争吵 quarrel; bicker; squabble; have an angry exchange: ～怄气 fall out with sb. and sulk ❷ 耍嘴皮子;互相开玩笑 exchange banter; make fun of each other: 取笑～ play jokes and banter with each other

豆¹ dòu ❶ 古代盛食物用的器具,有点像带高座的盘 ancient stemmed cup or bowl ❷ (Dòu) 姓 a surname

豆²(❶荳) dòu (～儿 dòur) ❶ same as 豆子 dòu·zi ①②: 黄～ soya bean | 绿～ mung bean ❷ same as 豆子 dòu·zi ③: 花生～儿 peanut kernel

【豆瓣儿酱】dòubànrjiàng 大豆或蚕豆发酵后制成的酱,里面有豆瓣儿 thick soya bean or broad-bean sauce (containing broad bean segments)

【豆包】dòubāo (～儿 dòubāor)用豆沙做馅儿的包子 steamed bun with sweetened bean paste filling

【豆饼】dòubǐng 大豆榨油后剩下的渣子压成饼形,叫豆饼。可以用来制造大豆胶,也用做肥料或饲料。soya bean cake; bean cake (dregs of beans after oil is extracted, and pressed into cakes, to be used as raw material for glue, fertilizer or fodder)

【豆䜺儿】dòuchǎir 〈方 *dial*.〉碾碎的豆子,用来做糕点或熬粥等 crushed beans, used to cook porridge; also 豆䜺子 dòuchǎi·zi

【豆豉】dòuchǐ 食品,把黄豆或黑豆泡透蒸熟或煮熟,经过发酵而成。有咸淡两种,都可放在菜里调味,淡豆豉也入药。fermented soya beans, salted or otherwise, used as flavouring for food or medicine

【豆腐】dòu·fu 食品,豆浆煮开后加入石膏或盐卤使凝结成块,压去一部分水分而成 bean curd; foodstuff made from soya bean milk curdled with gypsum or brine, and with part of the water squeezed out of it

【豆腐饭】dòu·fufàn〈方 *dial.*〉指丧家招待前来吊唁的亲友吃的饭食(多为素食) dinner (usu. vegetarian) for friends and relatives attending a funeral

【豆腐干】dòu·fugān (～儿 dòu·fugānr)食品,用布包豆腐加香料蒸制而成 dried bean curd; bean curd wrapped up in cloth, steamed with spice, and dried as preserved food

【豆腐脑儿】dòu·funǎor 食品,豆浆煮开后,加入石膏而凝结成的半固体 jellied bean curd

D

【豆腐皮】dòu·fupí ❶ (～儿 dòu·fupír)煮熟的豆浆表面上结的薄皮,揭下晾干后供食用 film-like skin of soya bean milk dried in sun ❷〈方 *dial.*〉千张 thin sheets of dried bean curd

【豆腐乳】dòu·furǔ 食品,用小块的豆腐做坯,经过发酵、腌制而成 fermented bean curd; also 腐乳 fǔrǔ or 酱豆腐 jiàngdòu·fu

【豆腐渣】dòu·fuzhā 豆渣 bean residue after making soya bean milk; bean dregs

【豆花儿】dòuhuār〈方 *dial.*〉食品,豆浆煮开后,加入盐卤而凝结成的半固体,比豆腐脑儿稍老 condensed bean curd jelly (made by adding brine to boiled bean milk)

【豆荚】dòujiá 豆类的果实 pod; fruit of any leguminous plant, consisting of a long case that contains several seeds and splits along both sides when ripe

【豆浆】dòujiāng 食品,黄豆泡透磨成的浆,加水去渣煮开而成 soya bean milk (produced by grinding soaked soya beans, boiling the mash and removing the dregs); also 豆腐浆 dòu·fujiāng or 豆乳 dòurǔ

【豆角儿】dòujiǎor 豆荚(多指鲜嫩可做菜的) pod, usu. fresh kidney beans used as vegetable

【豆秸】dòujiē 豆类植物脱粒后剩下的茎 beanstalk (left after threshing)

【豆蔻】dòukòu ❶ 多年生草本植物,外形似芭蕉,花淡黄色,果实扁球形,种子像石榴子,有香味。果实和种子可入药。round cardamom (*Amomum cardamomum*); perennial herbaceous plant looking like *bajiao* banana (*Musa basjoo*), having light yellow flowers, flat round fruit, and fragrant seeds that look like those of a pomegranate, with both fruit and seeds being of medical value ❷ 这种植物的果实或种子 fruit or seed of round cardamom ‖ also known as 草果 cǎoguǒ or 草豆蔻 cǎodòukòu

【豆蔻年华】dòukòu niánhuá 唐代杜牧《赠别》诗:'娉娉袅袅十三余,豆蔻梢头二月初。'后来称女子十三四岁的年纪为豆蔻年华。adolescence; (of a girl) in early teens like a blooming cardamon, an idiom derived from the Tang-dynasty poet Du Mu's poem *On Our Departure*: 'A supple and elegant thirteen-year old girl,/Like blooming cardamom in the early spring.'

【豆绿】dòulǜ 像青豆一样的绿色 pea green

【豆萁】dòuqí〈方 *dial.*〉same as 豆秸 dòujiē

【豆青】dòuqīng same as 豆绿 dòulǜ

【豆蓉】dòuróng 木豆、大豆、豌豆或绿豆煮熟晒干后磨成的粉,用来做糕点的馅儿 fine bean mash, used as stuffing for cakes: ～月饼 moon cake with bean mash stuffing

【豆乳】dòurǔ ❶ 豆浆 soya bean milk ❷〈方 *dial.*〉same as 豆腐乳 dòu·furǔ

【豆沙】dòushā 食品,红小豆、红豇豆或云豆煮烂捣成泥或干磨成粉,加糖制成,用做点心的馅儿 sweetened bean paste, used for stuffing: ～包 bun with bean paste stuffing | ～月饼 moon cake with bean paste stuffing

【豆薯】dòushǔ ❶ 藤本植物,叶子略呈圆形,花浅蓝色或淡红色,块根像甘薯,可以生吃 yam bean (*Pachyrrhizus erosus*); jicama; liana plant with roughly round leaves, light blue or pink flowers and edible tuberous root ❷ 这种植物的块根 tuberous root of this plant ‖ 有的地区叫凉薯或地瓜 in some areas known as 凉薯 liángshǔ or 地瓜 dìguā

【豆芽儿】dòuyár 蔬菜,用黄豆、黑豆或绿豆过水发芽而成,芽长二三寸 bean sprouts (obtained by first soaking soya beans, mung beans or black soya beans, then pouring away the water and letting sprouts grow from the beans); also 豆芽菜 dòuyácài

【豆油】dòuyóu 大豆榨的油,供食用,加氢硬化后是制肥皂的原料,又供制假漆和涂料 soya bean oil (used as food, or, when hardened with hydrogen, as material for soap; also as material for varnish and paint)

【豆渣】dòuzhā 制豆浆剩下的渣滓,可做饲料 residue from beans after making soya bean milk; bean dregs; also known as 豆腐渣 dòu·fuzhā

【豆汁】dòuzhī ❶ (～儿 dòuzhīr)制绿豆粉时剩下来的汁,味酸,可做饮料 fermented drink made from ground mung beans ❷〈方 *dial.*〉豆浆 soya bean milk

【豆猪】dòuzhū 体内有囊虫寄生的猪。因囊虫为黄豆大小的囊泡,所以叫豆猪。pig with parasitic cysticercosis; pig suffering from cysticercosis (cysticerci manifesting themselves as soya bean-sized sacs with a scolex, hence the name, 'pig with soya bean-like sacs)

【豆子】dòu·zi ❶ 豆类作物 pod-bearing plant; legume; pulse; pea; bean ❷ 豆类作物的种子 seeds of pod-bearing plant: 剥～ shell beans ❸ 样子像豆的东西 bean-shaped thing: 金～ gold bean | 狗～ tick on dog's body

【豆嘴儿】dòuzuǐr 泡开的大豆或刚刚露芽的大豆,做菜用 soya beans soaked or with tiny sprouts, used as foodstuff

逗[1]（鬥、鬦、鬬）dòu ❶ 引逗 tease; tantalize; play with: 他正拿着一枝红花～孩子玩。He is teasing that child with a bunch of flowers. ❷ 招引 entice; attract: 这孩子两只灵活的大眼睛很～人喜欢。The child has bewitchingly large eyes. ❸〈方 *dial.*〉逗笑儿 amusing; funny: 这话真～! What a funny remark! | 她是一个爱说爱～的姑娘。She's a girl fond of chatting and joking.

逗[2] dòu ❶ 停留 stay; stop ❷ same as 读 dòu

【逗点】dòudiǎn same as 逗号 dòuhào

【逗哏】dòu//gén 用滑稽有趣的话引人发笑（多指相声演员 esp. in comic dialogue performances) crack jokes; provoke laughter with funny remarks

【逗号】dòuhào 标点符号(,),表示句子中较小的停顿 comma (,); punctuation mark indicating a slight pause in a spoken sentence, and used to list items, or to separate a nonrestrictive clause or phrase from a main clause; also 逗点 dòudiǎn

【逗乐儿】dòu//lèr 引人发笑 amuse; try to make people laugh; clown around: 人都快急疯了,你还有心思～。Here we are worried to death, yet you're cracking jokes!

【逗留】dòuliú 暂时停留 stay; stop: 今年春节在家乡～了一个星期。I stayed at my hometown for a week over the Spring Festival. also 逗遛 dòuliú

【逗遛】dòuliú same as 逗留 dòuliú

【逗闷子】dòu mèn•zi〈方 *dial.*〉开玩笑 crack a joke; joke; make fun of

【逗弄】dòu•nong ❶ 引逗 tease; kid; make fun of: 老人在～孙子玩。The old man is teasing his grandson. ❷ 作弄;要笑 make a fool of sb.; play pranks on: ～人可不该。One should not play pranks on others.

【逗趣儿】dòu//qùr 逗乐打趣 make people laugh (by funny remarks, etc.); amuse; also 斗趣儿 dòu//qùr

【逗笑儿】dòuxiàor 引人发笑 amusing

【逗引】dòuyǐn 用言语、行动逗弄对方借以取乐 tease; play with: ～小孩儿玩 play with a child

饾 dòu ☞ below

【饾版】dòubǎn 木刻水印的旧称。因为是由若干块版拼凑而成,有如饾饤,故名饾版。old name for watercolour block printing (a plate made from several woodblocks, that looks like 饾饤 dòudìng, hence the term)

【饾饤】dòudìng〈书 *fml.*〉❶ 供陈设的食品 food for display ❷〈比喻 *fig.*〉堆砌词藻 writing of a wordy, ornate style

读（讀）dòu 语句中的停顿。古代诵读文章,分句和读,极短的停顿叫读,稍长的停顿叫句,后来把'读'写成'逗'。现代所用逗号就是取这个意义,但分别句逗的标准不同。slight pause when reading aloud (when reading unpunctuated ancient writing, the longer pause is called *ju* and the shorter one *dou*, later also written as 逗 dòu); ☞ 句读 jùdòu on p. 1050

☞ dú on p. 479

酘 dòu〈书 *fml.*〉再酿的酒 double fermented wine or liquor

脰 dòu〈书 *fml.*〉脖子;颈 neck

痘 dòu ❶ 天花 smallpox ❷ 痘苗 (bovine) vaccine; inoculate (a person) with vaccine so as to produce immunity against a specific disease: 种～ vaccinate ❸ 出天花时或接种痘苗后,皮肤上出的豆状疱疹 smallpox pustule; small inflamed elevated area of skin containing pus appearing on the body of a smallpox patient

【痘疮】dòuchuāng ☞天花[1] tiānhuā

【痘苗】dòumiáo 从患牛痘病的牛身上取出痘疱中的浆液,接种到牛犊身上,使发病,再从牛犊身上的痘疱中取出痘浆,把所含病毒的毒力减弱,用甘油保存起来,叫做痘苗。痘苗接种到人体上,可以预防天花。(bovine) vaccine; preparation containing the cowpox virus, used for vaccination; also 牛痘苗 niúdòumiáo

窦 dòu 西窦(Xīdòu)地名,在广西 Xidou, name of place in Guangxi

窦（竇）dòu ❶ 孔;洞 hole: 狗～ dog kennel, doghouse | 疑～(可疑的地方) cause for suspicion; doubtful point ❷ 人体某些器官或组织的内部凹人的部分 cavity in human body: 鼻～ paranasal | 鼻旁～ paranasal sinus ❸ (Dòu)姓 a surname

dū (ㄉㄨ)

厾（豛）dū 用指头、棍棒等轻击轻点 lightly touch with a finger, writing brush, stick, etc.: ～一个点儿 make a dot by tapping lightly (with one's finger or brush, etc.) | 点～(国画指用笔随意点染) adding dots or short touches (in traditional Chinese painting)

都 dū ❶ 首都 capital (of a country): 建～ establish a capital ❷ 大城市,也指以盛产某种东西而闻名的城市 big city; metropolis (also a city famous for a certain produce): ～市 city | 通～大邑 metropolis | 瓷～ porcelain city | 煤～coal city ❸〈旧时 *old*〉某些地区县与乡之间的政权机关 administrative unit between county and township levels ❹ (Dū)姓 a surname

☞ dōu on p. 470

【都城】dūchéng 首都 capital (of a country)
【都督】dū·du〈古时 *arch.*〉军事长官。民国初年各省也设有都督,兼管民政。commander-in-chief; provincial military governor in the early years of the Republic of China (1911-1949) who was also in charge of civil administration
【都会】dūhuì same as 都市 dūshì
【都市】dūshì 大城市 big city; metropolis

阇 dū〈书 *fml.*〉城门上的台 platform above a city gate

☞ shé on p. 1693

屌(启) dū [屌子](dū·zi)〈方 *dial.*〉❶ 屁股 buttocks; bottom; bum ❷ 蜂或蝎子等的尾部 tail end of a scorpion or wasp

督 dū 监督指挥 superintend and direct: ~战 supervise (military) operations | ~办 superintend; oversee | ~师 supervise a military operation | ~率 command; lead
【督办】dūbàn ❶ 督促办理;督察办理 supervise and manage; superintend; oversee: ~粮秣 superintend the supply of army provisions ❷ 指担任督办工作的人 superintendent; overseer; supervisor
【督察】dūchá ❶ 监督察看: superintend; supervise :派人前往~ send person or people to supervise sth. ❷ 指担任督察工作的人 superintendent; supervisor
【督促】dūcù 监督催促 supervise and exhort: 已经布置了的工作,应当认真~检查。(We) must supervise and accelerate fulfilment of the assignments.
【督导】dūdǎo〈书 *fml.*〉监督指导 supervise and direct; superintend: ~员 supervisor; superintendent | 莅临~ come to give directions
【督抚】dūfǔ 总督和巡抚,明清两代最高的地方行政长官 governor general and inspector general, highest local officials during the Ming and Qing dynasties
【督军】dūjūn 民国初年一省的最高军事长官 provincial military governor in the early years of the Republic of China (1911-1949)
【督学】dūxué 教育行政机关中负责视察、监督学校工作的人员 educational inspector; inspector of schools
【督战】dūzhàn 监督作战 supervise military operations: 亲临前线~ personally supervise military operations on frontline positions

嘟[1] dū〈拟声词 *onom.*〉honk; toot: 汽车喇叭~地响了一声。The car tooted its horn.

嘟[2] dū〈方 *dial.*〉(嘴)向前突出;撅着 thrust out (the lips); pout: 弟弟听说不让他去,气得~起了嘴。The brother pouted sulkily on hearing that he was not allowed to go.
【嘟噜】dū·lu ❶〈量词 *classifier*〉用于连成一簇的东西 bunch; cluster: 一~葡萄 a cluster of grapes | 一~钥匙 a bunch of keys ❷ 向下垂着;耷拉 hang down in a bunch; sag; dangle: ~着脸 have a long face ❸ (~儿 dū·lur) 连续颤动舌或小舌发音 trill: 打~儿 pronounce with a trill; utter a tremulous sound by vibrating the tongue tip or the uvula
【嘟囔】dū·nang 连续不断地自言自语 mutter to oneself; mumble: 你在~什么呀? What are you mumbling about?
【嘟哝】dū· nong same as 嘟囔 dū·nang

dú (ㄉㄨˊ)

毒 dú ❶ 进入有机体后能跟有机体起化学变化,破坏体内组织和生理机能的物质 poison; toxin; substance that kills, injures, or impairs an organism by its chemical action: 病~ virus | 中~ poisoning, toxicosis | 蝎子有~。The scorpion is a poisonous insect. ❷ 指对思想意识有害的事物 anything pernicious to the mind: 肃清流~eradicate pernicious influences ❸ 毒品 narcotics; (narcotic) drugs: 吸~take drugs | 贩~ traffic in drugs ❹ 有毒的 poisonous; noxious; poisoned: ~蛇 venomous snake | ~药 poison ❺ 用毒物害死 kill with poison; poison: 买药~老鼠 buy poison to kill rats ❻ 毒辣;猛烈 malicious; cruel; fierce: ~打 beat relentlessly | ~计 vicious scheme | 他的心肠真~! How cruel he is! | 七月的天气,太阳正~。In July the sun is at its fiercest.
【毒草】dúcǎo 有毒的草 poisonous weeds;〈比喻 *fig.*〉对人民、对社会进步有害的言论和作品 harmful speech, writing, etc. (from an ideological point of view)
【毒打】dúdǎ 残酷地打;狠狠地打 beat relentlessly; beat up: 挨了一顿~ be beaten black and blue | 遭到~ get a vicious beating
【毒饵】dú'ěr 在麦麸或其他食物中混入砒霜或有毒农药制成的毒物,撒在地面上,用来毒杀蝼蛄、蛴螬等害虫,也可用来毒杀老鼠、害鸟等 poisoned bait (bran or food mixed with arsenic or pesticide to kill pests, rats and harmful birds)
【毒害】dúhài ❶ 用有毒的东西使人受害 defile; poison (sb.'s mind); harm (sb.'s health) with narcotics: 黄色录像~人们的心灵。Pornographic video tapes defile people's minds. ❷ 能毒害人的事物 vermin; destructive or harmful thing; poisonous stuff: 清除~ get rid of pernicious things
【毒化】dúhuà ❶ 指用毒品(如鸦片等)残害人民 harm sb.'s health with drugs (e.g. opium) ❷ 利用教育、文艺等向人民灌输落后、反动思想 spread backward or reactionary ideas among the people through education, art and literature ❸ 使气氛、关系、风尚等变得恶劣 poison (relationship, atmosphere, etc.);

spoil：～社会风气 debase social morality

【毒计】dújì 毒辣的计策 venomous scheme；deadly trap：设下～ set a deadly trap

【毒剂】dújì 军事上指专门用来毒害人、畜的化学物质，大多是毒气 toxic；toxicant；(in war) chemical substances，usu. poisonous gas，used specifically to kill humans or animals)

【毒辣】dúlà (心肠或手段)狠毒残酷 sinister；diabolic；malignant：阴险～ sinister and ruthless | 手段～ ruthless means

【毒瘤】dúliú 恶性肿瘤的通称 (general term) malignant tumour；cancer

【毒谋】dúmóu 阴险毒辣的计谋 sinister and treacherous scheme；deadly trap

【毒品】dúpǐn 指作为嗜好品用的鸦片、吗啡、海洛因等 substance whose effect is addictive e.g. opium，morphine，heroin，etc.；narcotics；(narcotic) drugs

【毒气】dúqì ❶ 气体的毒剂。旧称毒瓦斯。poisonous (or poison) gas；gaseous poison (as used in war)；formerly known as 毒瓦斯 dúwǎsī ❷ 泛指有毒的气体 (in a broad sense) harmful or poisonous gas

【毒蛇】dúshé 有毒的蛇，头部多为三角形，有毒腺，能分泌毒液。毒蛇咬人或动物时，毒液从毒牙流出使被咬的人或动物中毒。蝮蛇、白花蛇等就是毒蛇。毒液可供医药用。poisonous or venomous snake；viper (whose head is usu. triangular with a poisonous gland that poisons the humans or animals bitten，and that is also used in medicine)

【毒手】dúshǒu 杀人或伤害人的狠毒手段 violent treachery；murder plot：下～ lay murderous hands on sb. | 险遭～ nearly fall victim to a murder plot

【毒素】dúsù ❶ 某些有机体产生的有毒的物质，例如蓖麻种子中含的毒素，毒蛇的毒腺中所含的毒素等。有些毒素毒性很猛烈，能造成死亡，但把适量的毒素注射到动物体内，能产生抗毒素，含有抗毒素的动物血清有治疗作用。toxin；poison；poisonous substance secreted by certain organisms capable of causing toxicosis when introduced into the body tissues，but also capable of inducing a counteragent or an antitoxin ❷〈比喻 *fig.*〉言论、著作中对思想意识有腐蚀作用的成分 harmful elements in speech or works；poison：封建～ feudalist poison

【毒瓦斯】dúwǎsī 毒气①的旧称 (formerly known as) poisonous (or poison) gas

【毒物】dúwù 有毒的物质 poisonous substance；poison

【毒腺】dúxiàn 动物体内分泌毒素的腺体 poison gland；gland in an animal's body that secretes poisonous substances

【毒刑】dúxíng 残酷的肉刑 brutal corporal punishment；horrible torture：～拷打 subject sb. to torture

【毒药】dúyào 能危害生物体生理机能并引起死亡的药物 poison；toxicant；substance that causes injury，illness or death

独(獨) dú ❶ 一个 only；single：～子 only son | ～木桥 single-plank (or single-log) bridge | 无～有偶 not come singly but in pairs (generally in reference to evil-doers or evil deeds)；curious coincidence ❷ 独自 alone；by oneself；in solitude：～揽 arrogate to oneself | ～断～行 make arbitrary decisions and take peremptory action；act arbitrarily ❸ 年老没有儿子的人 old people without offspring；childless：鳏寡孤～ widows，widowers，orphans and old and childless people ❹ 唯独 solely；only：大伙儿都齐了，～有他还没来。He's the only one yet to arrive. ❺ 自私；容不得人 egoistic；standoffish；selfish；not tolerant：他这个人真～，他的东西谁也碰不得。He's very standoffish and does not allow anybody to touch his things.

【独霸】dúbà 独自称霸；独占 dominate exclusively；monopolize：～一方 lord it over a district；be a local despot | ～市场 corner the market

【独白】dúbái 戏剧、电影中角色独自抒发个人情感和愿望的话 soliloquy；monologue

【独步】dúbù 指超出同类之上，没有可以相比的 be unrivalled：～文坛 be the unrivalled literary colossus of the age；be unsurpassed in the literary world；be a titan in the world of letters

【独裁】dúcái 独自裁断。多指独揽政权，实行专制统治 make arbitrary decisions；dictatorship；autocratic rule：～者 dictator | 个人～ autocracy | ～统治 autocratic rule；autocracy

【独唱】dúchàng 一个人演唱歌曲，常用乐器伴奏 (vocal) solo (oft. accompanied with musical instruments)

【独出心裁】dú chū xīn cái 原指诗文的构思有独到的地方，后来泛指想出来的办法与众不同 show originality；be original

【独处】dúchǔ 一个人单独生活 live alone；live on one's own

【独创】dúchuàng 独特的创造 original creation：～精神 creative spirit | ～一格 create a style of one's own

【独当一面】dú dāng yī miàn 单独担当一个方面的任务 single-handedly take charge of a department or locality with facility；assume responsibility for a certain sector alone

【独到】dúdào 与众不同(多指好的) original，unique：～之处 distinctive qualities；specific characteristics | ～的见解 original view

【独断】dúduàn 独自决断；专断 arbitrary；dictatorial

【独断专行】dú duàn zhuān xíng 行事专断，不考虑别人的意见 make arbitrary decisions and take peremptory action; act arbitrarily; act willfully on one's own; also 独断独行 dú duàn dú xíng

【独夫】dúfū 残暴无道为人民所憎恨的统治者 ruthless ruler forsaken by all; tyrant; autocrat: ～民贼 tyrant and the enemy of the people

【独孤】Dúgū 姓 a surname

【独家】dújiā 单独一家 sole; only one; exclusive: ～新闻 exclusive report | ～经营 be the sole agent (of a product, etc.)

【独角戏】dújiǎoxì ❶ 只有一个角色的戏,比喻一个人做一般不是一个人做的工作 play with only one role; mono-drama; one-man show; (fig.) job undertaken by one person that is normally done by several persons ❷ 滑稽② one man's comic talk ‖ also 独脚戏 dújiǎoxì

【独具匠心】dú jù jiàng xīn 指具有与众不同的巧妙的构思 show ingenuity; have originality

【独具只眼】dú jù zhī yǎn 能看到别人看不到的东西,形容眼光敏锐,见解高超 be able to see what others cannot; show unusual insight and sense of judgement

【独揽】dúlǎn 独自把持 arrogate to oneself; monopolize: ～大权 arrogate all powers to oneself

【独力】dúlì 单独依靠自己的力量(做) by one's own efforts; on one's own: ～经营 manage affairs by oneself; go into business on one's own

【独立】dúlì ❶ 单独地站立 stand alone: ～山巅的苍松 pine tree standing alone on a mountain peak ❷ 一个国家或一个政权不受别的国家或别的政权的统治而自主地存在 (of a nation or government) independence: 宣布～ proclaim independence ❸ 军队在编制上不隶属于高一级的单位而直接隶属于更高级的单位的,如不隶属于团而直接隶属于师的营叫独立营 independent; (of a military unit) under direct command of a higher authority than its direct leadership, e. g. an independent battalion that is subordinate to a division instead of a regiment ❹ 脱离原来所属单位,成为另一单位 become independent of or separate from an organization: 民俗研究室已经～出去了,现在叫民俗研究所。The former Folklore Research Office has become an independent entity known as the Folklore Institute. ❺ 不依靠他人 independently; on one's own: ability to analyse and solve problems on one's own: ～思考 think for oneself | ～工作 work independently

【独立国】dúlìguó 有完整主权的国家 sovereign state; independent country

【独立王国】dúlì wángguó 〈比喻 *fig*.〉不服从上级的指挥和领导,自搞一套的地区、部门或单位 independent kingdom; realm, department or area under one's own control and free from any higher authority or outside scrutiny

【独立自主】dúlì zìzhǔ (国家、民族或政党等)不受外来力量控制、支配,自己行使主权 independence and self-reliance; (of country, nation, party, etc.) free from foreign control, possessing the autonomy to maintain independence and keep initiative; act independently and on one's own initiative

【独龙族】Dúlóngzú 我国少数民族之一,分布在云南 Derung (Tulung) people, an ethnic minority that lives in Yunnan Province

【独轮车】dúlúnchē 只有一个车轮的小车,多用手推着走 wheelbarrow; simple vehicle for carrying small loads, typically an open container supported by a wheel at the front and two legs at the rear

【独门】dúmén (～儿 dúménr) ❶ 只供一户人家进出的门 (of a family etc.) having one's own entrance or gate: ～独院 compound with houses around a courtyard occupied by a single family | ～进出,互不干扰。(The households) each have their own courtyard and entrance, so that none of them interferes with the others. ❷ 一人或一家独有的某种技能或秘诀 (of a skill, recipe, etc.) possessed by one individual or family only: ～儿绝活 special skill possessed solely by one individual or family

【独苗】dúmiáo (～儿 dúmiáor) 一家或一个家族唯一的后代 only son or heir of a family; only offspring of a clan; also 独苗苗 dúmiáo·miao

【独木不成林】dú mù bù chéng lín 一棵树不能成为树林 one tree doesn't make a forest; 〈比喻 *fig*.〉一个人力量有限,做不成大事 one person without support can't accomplish much; also 独树不成林 dú shù bù chéng lín

【独木难支】dú mù nán zhī 一根木头支持不住高大的房子 one log cannot prop up a tall building; 〈比喻 *fig*.〉一个人的力量难以支撑全局 one person alone cannot accomplish a major undertaking

【独木桥】dúmùqiáo 用一根木头搭成的桥 single-plank (or single-log) bridge; 〈比喻 *fig*.〉艰难的途径 difficult path: 你走你的阳关道,我走我的～。Take what you see as your open road and leave me to travel along my rugged path. *or* You go your way, and I'll go mine.

【独幕剧】dúmùjù 不分幕的小型戏剧,一般情节比较简单紧凑 one-act play

【独辟蹊径】dú pì xī jìng 独自开辟一条路 blaze a new trail by oneself; 〈比喻 *fig*.〉独创一种新风格或者新方法 create a new style or a method of one's own; become a school in one's own right

【独善其身】dú shàn qí shēn《孟子·尽心》:'穷则独善其身。'意思是做不上官,就搞好自身的修养。现在也指只顾自己,缺乏集体精神。maintain one's own integrity (*Mencius*·*Ex-*

haustion of Mental Constitution: When out of office, one will try to maintain one's own personal integrity.) The term is interpreted today as 'self-centred' or 'lacking the collective spirit'.

【独擅胜场】dú shàn shèng chǎng 独揽竞技场上的胜利。形容技艺高超。sweep a game; win every game, round, etc., of a series of contests; be exceptionally good at doing sth.

【独身】dúshēn ❶ 单身 live away from one's home and family; live alone: ～一人 live by oneself | 十几年～在外 be away from home and family for over 10 years ❷ 不结婚的 remain unmarried or single (as a lifestyle); unmarried; single: ～主义 celibacy

【独生女】dúshēngnǚ 唯一的女儿 only daughter

【独生子】dúshēngzǐ 独子 only son

【独树一帜】dú shù yī zhì 单独树立起一面旗帜 fly one's own colours; blaze one's own path; 〈比喻 *fig.*〉自成一家 develop a school of one's own

【独特】dútè 独有的;特别的 unique; distinctive: 风格～ unique style | ～的见解 original point of view

【独吞】dútūn 独自占有 keep all to oneself; take exclusive possession of sth.; hog: ～家产 appropriate the family property | ～胜利果实 hog the fruits of victory

【独舞】dúwǔ 单人表演的舞蹈。可以单独表演,也可以是舞剧或集体舞中的一个部分。solo dance; dance performed by one person, as an independent show, or part of a company dance drama; also 单人舞 dānrénwǔ

【独行】dúxíng ❶ 独自走路 walk alone: 踽踽～ walk in solitude and silence ❷ 按自己的主张去做 go one's own way; stick to one's own way of doing things: 独断～ make one's own decisions and go one's own way | ～其是 go it alone; take a different course from others; paddle one's own canoe ❸ 〈书 *fml.*〉独特的行为、操守 unique character; distinctive behaviour: 特立～ noteworthy conduct and independent character

【独眼龙】dúyǎnlóng 瞎了一只眼的人(含诙谐意 humor.) person blind in one eye; one-eyed person

【独一无二】dú yī wú èr 没有相同的;没有可以相比的 unique; unparalleled; unmatched; unrivalled: 他的棋下得很高明,在全校是～的。He is an unrivalled chess player in this school.

【独院】dúyuàn (～儿 dúyuànr) 只有一户人家住的院子 one-family courtyard; one-household compound: 独门～compound with houses around a courtyard and occupied by a single family

【独占】dúzhàn 独自占有或占据 have sth. all to oneself; monopolize: ～市场 corner the market | ～资本 monopolize capital

【独占鳌头】dú zhàn áo tóu 科举时代称中状元。据说皇宫石阶前刻有鳌(大鳖)的头,状元及第时才可以踏上。后来比喻占首位或第一名。be the only one to take the turtle head (in front of the imperial palace); privilege awarded the candidate with the highest marks in a civil examination in feudal times; (fig.) come first; head the list of successful candidates; emerge as the winner

【独资】dúzī 指由一个人或一方单独拿出资金(办企业) (of an enterprise) wholly-owned; exclusive investment: ～经营 exclusive ownership and management | ～企业 enterprise of exclusive ownership; wholly-owned (foreign) enterprise

【独子】dúzǐ 唯一的儿子 only son; also 独生子 dúshēngzǐ

【独自】dúzì 自己一个人 alone; by oneself: ～玩耍 play by oneself | 就他一人～在家。He is home alone.

【独奏】dúzòu 由一个人用一种乐器演奏,如小提琴独奏、钢琴独奏等,有时也用其他乐器伴奏 (instrumental) solo, e.g. violin solo, piano solo, etc., sometimes to the accompaniment of other instruments

顿 dú ☞ 冒顿 Mòdú on p.1367
☞ dùn on p.497

读(讀) dú ❶ 看着文字念出声音 read aloud: 朗～ read aloud | 宣～ read out in public; announce | ～报 read a newspaper aloud | 老师～一句,同学们跟着～一句。Students read after the teacher, sentence by sentence. ❷ 阅读;看(文章) read (silently): ～者 reader | 默～ read silently | 这本小说很值得一～。This novel is worth reading. ❸ 指上学 attend school: 他～完高中,就参加了工作。He found a job after finishing high school. ❹ 字的念法;读音 pronounce: 破～ variant pronunciation (of a Chinese character) | ～破 variant pronunciation (of a Chinese character)
☞ dòu on p.475

【读本】dúběn 课本(多指语文或文学课本 usu. literary reader) reader; textbook

【读后感】dúhòugǎn 读过一本书或一篇文章以后的感想(多指书面的 usu. written) thoughts or reflections on reading sth.; notes on a book or essay; comments after reading a book or essay

【读经】dújīng 讽诵、阅读儒家经典《五经》或《十三经》reading Confucian classics such as the *The Five Classics* or *The Thirteen Classics*

【读破】dúpò 同一个字形因意义不同而有两个或几个读音的时候,不照习惯上最通常的读音来读,叫做读破,如'长幼'的'长'不读 cháng 而读 zhǎng,'喜好'的'好'不读 hǎo 而读 hào。zhǎng、hào 的音叫做破读。读破了的字叫破读字。pronounce a Chinese character in one or more variant ways different from the most generally known articulation and with different meaning(s). For example, the character 长 in 长幼 zhǎngyòu is pronounced zhǎng, not its most common pronunciation cháng; 好 in 喜好 xǐhào is pronounced hào, not hǎo. Characters with such pronunciations are called 破读字 pòdúzì. ☞ 破读 pòdú on p. 1494

【读破句】dú pòjù 断句错误,把上一句末了的字连到下一句读,或者把下一句头上的字连到上一句读 pause at the wrong places when reading aloud (esp. traditional unpunctuated writing); make incorrect stops when reading

【读书】dú//shū ❶ 看着书本,出声地或不出声地读 read aloud or silently: ～声 sound of reading aloud | ～笔记 reading notes | ～得间(读书时能发现问题) be able to solve problems by reading books ❷ 指学习功课 study one's lessons: 他～很用功。He is a diligent (or hardworking) student. ❸ 指上学 attend a school or university: 当时,我还在～。I was still a student then. | 他在那个中学读过一年书。He studied for a year at that middle school.

【读书人】dúshūrén ❶ 指知识分子;士人 scholar; intellectual ❷〈方 dial.〉学生 student

【读数】dúshù 仪表、机器上,由指针或水银柱等指出的刻度的数目 reading (on meters or instruments, indicated by hands or a mercury column)

【读物】dúwù 供阅读的东西,包括书籍、杂志、报纸等 reading matter (or material); books, magazines, newspapers, etc.: 儿童～ reading matter for children | 通俗～ popular literature | 农村～ books for rural readers

【读音】dúyīn (字的)念法 pronunciation: 这个字是多音字,有两个～。This word has two pronunciations.

【读者】dúzhě 阅读书刊文章的人 reader (of a book, newspaper, article, etc.)

渎[1](瀆、瀆) dú〈书 *fml.*〉轻慢;不敬 show disrespect or contempt: ～犯 offend; affront | 亵～blaspheme; profane | 烦～ put sb. to trouble | 有～清神(书信套语 used as a formula of courtesy in correspondence) have subjected you to so much inconvenience; have caused you tremendous bother

渎[2](瀆) dú〈书 *fml.*〉沟渠;水道 ditch; drain: 沟～ ditch

【渎职】dúzhí 不尽职,在执行任务时犯严重过失 malfeasance; dereliction of duty: ～罪 crime of misconduct in office; offence of dereliction of duty | ～行为 malfeasance; malpractice; dereliction of duty

椟(櫝、匵) dú〈书 *fml.*〉匣子 casket; case; box: 买～还珠 buy the nice-looking box but return the pearl contained in it to the seller — show poor sense of judgement

犊(犢) dú 犊子 calf: 初生之～不畏虎。Newborn calves do not fear tigers. *or* The young are courageous.

【犊子】dú·zi 小牛 calf: 牛～ calf

牍(牘) dú ❶ 古代写字用的木简 wooden tablets or slips for writing (in ancient times) ❷ 文件;书信 documents; archives; correspondence: 文～ official documents and correspondence | 案～official documents and correspondence | 尺～ correspondence; models of epistolary writing

讟(讟) dú〈书 *fml.*〉怨言 complaint

黩(黷) dú〈书 *fml.*〉❶ 玷污 blacken; defile ❷ 轻率;轻举妄动: act wantonly: ～武 militaristic; warlike

【黩武】dúwǔ〈书 *fml.*〉滥用武力 militaristic; warlike; bellicose: 穷兵～ indulge in incessant wars of conquest | ～主义 militarism

髑 dú [髑髅] (dúlóu)〈书 *fml.*〉死人的头骨; 骷髅 skull (of a dead person)

dǔ (ㄉㄨˇ)

肚 dǔ (～儿 dǔr) 肚子 (dǔ·zi) tripe: 羊～儿 mutton tripe | 拌～丝儿 sliced pork tripe mixed with cucumber or other vegetables in soy sauce
☞ dù on p. 482

【肚子】dǔ·zi 用做食品的动物的胃 food made from animal's stomach: 猪～ pork tripe | 羊～ mutton tripe
☞ dù·zi on p. 482

笃 dǔ ❶ 忠实;一心一意 faithful; sincere; earnest: ～志 devote oneself to; be dedicated to | ～行而不倦 go in for sth. tirelessly and in all sincerity | 情爱甚～ be deeply in love with each other ❷ (病势)沉重 (of an illness) serious; critical: 危～ be mortally ill | 病～ be in a critical condition

【笃爱】dǔ'ài 深切地爱 love deeply; be devoted to: ～自己的事业 be devoted to one's career

【笃诚】dǔchéng 诚笃 sincere and faithful: ～之士 sincere and faithful man

【笃定】dǔdìng〈方 *dial.*〉❶ 有把握;一定 be sure of; be certain of: 三天完成任务,～没问题。I am certain the task will be finished in three days. ❷ 从容不迫,不慌不忙 calm and unhurried; be composed: 神情～ be composed

【笃厚】dǔhòu 忠实厚道 honest and kind-hearted

【笃实】dǔshí ❶ 忠诚老实 honest and loyal: ～敦厚 loyal and sincere ❷ 实在 solid; sound: 学问～ sound scholarship

【笃守】dǔshǒu 忠实地遵守 abide by faithfully; faithfully follow the teachings of: ～遗教 faithfully abide by the instructions of the deceased|～诺言 keep one's word to the letter

【笃信】dǔxìn 忠实地信仰 sincerely believe in; be a devout believer in: ～佛教 be a devout follower of Buddhism

【笃学】dǔxué 专心好学 diligent in study; devoted to study; studious: ～不倦 diligently and tirelessly study Confucian classics

【笃志】dǔzhì〈书 *fml.*〉专心一意 be steadfast in one's purpose; devote oneself to: ～经学 devote oneself to study

堵 dǔ ❶ 堵塞 stop up; block up: 把窟窿～上 stop up the hole|你～着门,叫别人怎么走哇? How is anyone supposed to go out with you blocking the doorway? ❷ 闷;憋气 stifled; suffocated; oppressed: 我要不跟他说说,心里～得慌。This will continue to weigh heavily on my mind if I don't talk to him. ❸〈书 *fml.*〉墙 wall: 观者如～。The crowd was like a barricade. ❹〈量词 *classifier*〉用于墙 used of walls: 一～围墙 a wall ❺ (Dǔ) 姓 a surname

【堵车】dǔchē 因道路狭窄或车辆太多,车辆无法顺利通行 traffic jam; traffic congestion: 上下班时间,这个路口经常～。Traffic congestion is commonplace at this crossing during rush hour.

【堵截】dǔjié 迎面拦截 intercept: 围追～ encircle, pursue and intercept|～增援的敌军 intercept enemy reinforcements

【堵塞】dǔsè 阻塞(洞穴、通道)使不通 stop up; block: 公路被塌下来的山石～了。The highway is blocked by fallen mountain rocks. ◇～工作中的漏洞 stop up all loopholes at work

【堵心】dǔxīn 心里憋闷 depressing; frustrating: 想起这件事儿就觉得怪～的。I feel depressed whenever I think of this.

【堵嘴】dǔ//zuǐ〈比喻 *fig.*〉不让人说话或使人没法开口 gag sb.; silence sb.; 自己做错了,还想堵人嘴,不让人说。He made a mistake, yet he didn't want anyone to speak out about it.

赌 dǔ ❶ 赌博 gamble: ～钱 gambling|～场 casino|聚～ set up a gambling party ❷ 泛指争输赢 (in a broad sense) bet: 打～ make a bet|～东道 bet where the loser stands a treat

【赌本】dǔběn 赌博的本钱 money to gamble with;〈比喻 *fig.*〉从事冒险活动时所凭借的力量 resources for a risky venture

【赌博】dǔbó 用斗牌、掷色子等形式,拿财物作注比输赢 gamble; play games of chance for money ◇政治～ political gamble

【赌场】dǔchǎng 专供赌博的场所 gambling house; casino

【赌东道】dǔ dōngdào 用做东道请客来打赌 bet where the loser stands a treat; also 赌东儿 dǔ dōngr

【赌棍】dǔgùn 指精于赌博并以此为生的人 hardened or professional gambler

【赌局】dǔjú 赌博的集会或场所 gambling party; gambling joint: 设～ set up a gambling party

【赌具】dǔjù 赌博的用具,如牌、色子(shǎi·zi)等 gambling paraphernalia, e.g. cards, dice, etc.

【赌气】dǔ//qì 因为不满意或受指责而任性(行动) feel wronged and act rashly; be discontented and act rashly; act willfully or in a fit of pique: 他一～就走了。He went off in a fit of pique.

【赌钱】dǔ//qián 赌博 gamble

【赌咒】dǔ//zhòu 发誓 take an oath; swear

【赌注】dǔzhù 赌博时所押的财物 stake

【赌资】dǔzī 用来赌博的钱 money to gamble with; gambling money

睹(覩) dǔ 看见 see: 耳闻目～ what one hears with one's ears and sees with one's eyes|有目共～ anyone with eyes can see|熟视无～ turn a blind eye to; ignore|～物思人 seeing a thing makes one think of the person associated with it; sth. that reminds one of its owner; memento is reminiscent of the person who gave it

dù (ㄉㄨˋ)

芏 dù ☞ [茳芏] (jiāngdù) on p. 959

杜[1] dù ❶ 棠梨。通称杜树。birchleaf pear ❷ (Dù) 姓 a surname

杜[2] **(殬)** dù 阻塞 shut out; stop; prevent: ～门谢客 close one's door to visitors|以～流弊 so as to put an end to abuse

【杜衡】dùhéng 多年生草本植物,野生在山地里,开紫色小花。根茎可入药。wild ginger (*Asarum canadense*); perennial herbaceous plant having a solitary brownish flower and an aromatic root that is used as medicine; also 杜蘅 dùhéng

【杜蘅】dùhéng same as 杜衡 dùhéng

【杜鹃】[1] dùjuān 鸟,身体黑灰色,尾巴有白色斑点,腹部有黑色横纹。初夏时常昼夜不停地叫。吃毛虫,是益鸟。多数把卵产在别的鸟巢中。cuckoo (*Cuculidae*); bird with greyish plumage, a tail with white spots and a characteristic two-note call, that eats caterpillars and usu. lays its eggs in other birds' nests; also 杜宇 dùyǔ, 布谷 bùgǔ, or 子规 zǐguī

【杜鹃】[2] dùjuān ❶ 常绿或落叶灌木,叶子椭圆形,花多为红色。供观赏。azalea (*Azalea*);

evergreen or deciduous bush with oval leaves and ornamental red flowers ❷ 这种植物的花 flower of this plant ‖ also 映山红 yìngshānhóng

【杜绝】dùjué ❶ 制止;消灭(坏事) stop; put an end to: ～贪污和浪费 put an end to corruption and waste|～一切漏洞 plug up all loopholes ❷〈旧时 *old*〉出卖田地房产,在契约上写明不得回赎叫杜绝 used in title deed, etc. waive all rights to buy back the real estate one sells

【杜康】dùkāng 相传最早发明酿酒的人,文学作品中用来指酒 Du Kang, China's legendary inventor of wine; (liter.) wine

【杜门】dùmén〈书 *fml.*〉闭门 shut the door; shut oneself up: ～谢客 close one's door to visitors; shut oneself up and refuse to see visitors

【杜撰】dùzhuàn 没有根据地编造;虚构 fabricate; make up; coin: 这个故事写的是真人真事,不是～的。This is a true story and not a fabrication.

肚 dù (～儿 dùr) 肚子(dù·zi) belly; abdomen; stomach

☞ dǔ on p. 480

【肚带】dùdài 围绕着骡马等的肚子,把鞍子等紧系在背上的皮带 belly band; girth; band that goes around a horse's belly to keep the saddle in position

【肚量】dùliàng ❶ same as 度量 dùliàng ❷ 饭量 appetite; capacity or need for food: 小伙子～大。Young men have good appetites. *or* Young men eat a great deal.

【肚皮】dùpí〈方 *dial.*〉腹部;肚子(dù·zi) belly

【肚脐】dùqí (～儿 dùqír)肚子中间脐带脱落的地方 navel; belly button; also 肚脐眼儿 dùqíyǎnr

【肚子】dù·zi ❶ 腹①的通称 belly; abdomen ❷ 物体圆而凸起像肚子的部分 prominent and round-shaped thing; belly-shaped thing: 腿～ calf (of leg)

☞ dǔ·zi on p. 480

妒(妬) dù 忌妒: be jealous (or envious) of; envy: 嫉贤～能(对品德、才能比自己强的人心怀怨恨) be jealous of capable and virtuous people

【妒火】dùhuǒ 指极强烈的忌妒心 agony of jealousy: ～中烧 be burning with jealousy

【妒忌】dùjì 忌妒 be jealous (or envious) of; envy

度 dù ❶ 计量长短 linear measure: ～量衡 length, capacity and weight; weights and measures ❷ 表明物质的有关性质所达到的程度,如硬度、热度、浓度、湿度等 degree of intensity, hardness, heat, concentration, density or humidity ❸ 计量单位名称 unit of measurement a)弧或角,把圆周分为360等份所成的弧叫1度弧。1度弧所对的圆心角叫1度角。1度等于60分。degree for arcs and angles, a degree has 60 minutes b)经度或纬度,如北纬38度 longitude or latitude, e.g. 38 degrees north latitude c)电量,1度即1千瓦小时 kilowatt-hour (kwh) ❹ 程度 extent; degree: 极～ extraordinary|知名～ fame; reputation|透明～ transparency; openness|高～的责任感 strong sense of duty; strong sense of responsibility ❺ 限度 limit; bounds; ceiling: 劳累过～ be tired from overwork|以能熔化为～ to the point that it melts ❻ 章程;行为准则 constitution; regulations; rules; guideline; principles: 法～ law|制～ system; institution ❼ 哲学上指一定事物保持自己质的数量界限。在这个界限内,量的增减不改变事物的质,超过这个界限,就要引起质变。(philos.) cross-over point (between quantitative and qualitative change) ❽ 对人对事宽容的程度 tolerance; magnanimity: ～量 tolerance; magnanimity|气～ tolerance ❾ 人的气质或姿态 temperament; mien; bearing; attitude: 风～ bearing|态～ attitude ❿ 一定范围内的时间或空间 space or time of a certain extent: 年～ year|国～ country ⓫ 所打算或计较的 consideration; calculation: 生死早已置之～外 give no thought to personal safety ⓬〈量词 *classifier*〉次 occasion; time: 再～声明 proclaim once again|一年一～ once a year|这个剧曾两～公演。The play has been staged twice. ⓭ 过(指时间) spend; pass: 欢～春节 joyously celebrate the Spring Festival|光阴没有虚～ have not frittered away one's time ⓮ 僧尼道士劝人出家 (of Buddhist monks or nuns, or Daoist priests) (try to) convert ⓯ (Dù)姓 a surname

☞ duó on p. 501

【度牒】dùdié〈旧时 *old*〉官府发给和尚、尼姑的证明身份的文书 certificate of ordination; letter of credence issued by the government to a Buddhist monk or nun; also 戒牒 jièdié

【度假】dùjià 过假日 spend one's holidays; go vacationing: ～村 holiday village|去海边～ spend holiday by sea

【度量】dùliàng 指能宽容人的限度 tolerance; magnanimity: 他脾气好,～大,能容人。He has a gentle disposition and is tolerant. also 肚量 dùliàng

【度量衡】dùliànghéng 计量长短、容积、轻重的统称。度是计量长短,量是计量容积,衡是计量轻重 length, capacity and weight; weights and measures

【度命】dùmìng 维持生命(多指在困境中) live from hand to mouth; live at subsistence level; make a meager living

【度曲】dùqǔ〈书 *fml.*〉❶ 作曲 set to music; compose (music): 工于～ be a skilled composer ❷ 照现成的曲调唱 sing to a tune

【度日】dùrì 过日子(多指在困境中) eke out a living or an existence: ～如年(形容日子难熬)

one day seems like a year; days drag on like years; time hangs heavily

【度数】dù·shu 按度计算的数目 number of degrees; reading: 用电～逐月增加。Power consumption increases month by month.

斁 dù 〈书 *fml*.〉败坏 ruin; corrupt; undermine
☞ yì on p.2277

渡 dù ❶ 由这一岸到那一岸;通过(江河等) cross (a river, the sea, etc.): 横～ cross (a river, etc.)|远～重洋 fly (sail, etc.) across the ocean|飞～太平洋 fly (across) the Pacific|红军强～大渡河。The Red Army forced its way across the Dadu River. ◇～过难关 tide over a difficulty ❷ 载运过河 ferry (people, goods, etc.) across: ～船 ferry boat|请您把我们～过河去。Please ferry us across the river. ❸ 渡口(多用于地名 usu. used as part of a place name) ferry crossing: 茅津～(黄河渡口,在山西河南之间) Maojin Ferry Crossing (on the Yellow River on the Shanxi-Henan boader)|深～(新安江渡口,在安徽) Shendu Crossing (on the Xin'an River, Anhui Province)

【渡槽】dùcáo 跨越山谷、道路、水道的桥梁式水槽,两端与渠道相接 aqueduct; conduit designed to transport water over a valley, road or canal

【渡船】dùchuán 载运行人、货物、车辆等横渡江河、湖泊、海峡的船 ferryboat; ferry; vessel for transporting passengers and usu. vehicle across a body of water, esp. as a regular service

【渡口】dùkǒu 有船或筏子摆渡的地方 ferry crossing

【渡轮】dùlún 载运行人、货物、车辆等横渡江河、湖泊、海峡的轮船 ferry steamer; ferryboat

【渡头】dùtóu 渡口 ferry crossing

镀 dù 用电解或其他化学方法使一种金属附着到别的金属或物体表面上,形成薄层 plating; covering of a metal with a layer, or plating it, with another metal, by chemical, clectrolytic or other means: ～金 gold-plating; gilding|～银 silver-plating; silvering

【镀层】dùcéng 镀在其他金属或物体表面上的金属薄层 coating; layer or film spread over a surface for protection or decoration

【镀金】dù//jīn ❶ 在器物的表面上镀上一薄层金子 gold-plating; gilding ❷ 讥讽人到某种环境去深造或锻炼,只是为了取得虚名 (ironical) become gilded (said of sb. attending school or studying abroad with the express purpose of raising his reputation or social status); acquire a gilded reputation: 出国留学不是为了～。Studying abroad is not merely to gain a gilded reputation.

【镀锡铁】dùxītiě 表面镀锡的铁皮,不易生锈,多用于罐头工业上 tinplate; thin steel sheet coated with a layer of tin that protects it from corrosion; also 马口铁 mǎkǒutiě

【镀锌铁】dùxīntiě 表面镀锌的铁皮,不易生锈 galvanized iron; generally known as 铅铁 qiāntiě or 白铁 báitiě

蠹(螙、蠧、蠹) dù ❶ 蠹虫① moth; a kind of insect whose larvae eats into books, clothing, etc.: 木～ wood moth; carpenter moth|书～ bookworm ❷ 蛀蚀 moth-eaten; worm-eaten: 流水不腐,户枢不～。Running water is never stale and a door-hinge never gets moth-eaten.

【蠹弊】dùbì 〈书 *fml*.〉弊病① malady; malpractice; abuse; corrupt practice

【蠹虫】dùchóng ❶ 咬器物的虫子 moth; a kind of insect whose larvae eats into books, clothing, etc. ❷〈比喻 *fig*.〉危害集体利益的坏人 harmful person; vermin; person who undermines collective interests: 清除社会～ get rid of social vermin

【蠹鱼】dùyú ☞ 衣鱼 yīyú on p.2257

duān (ㄉㄨㄢ)

耑 duān 〈书 *fml*.〉same as 端 duān
☞ 专 zhuān on p.2515

端1 duān ❶ (东西的)头 end; limit; extremity: 笔～ tip of a pen|两～ both ends|尖～ pointed end; peak; top-of-the-line; sophisticated ❷ (事情的)开头 beginning; start: 发～ make a start|开～ onset; beginning ❸ 原因;起因 reason; cause: 无～ groundless; unprovoked|借～生事 use sth. as a pretext to make trouble ❹ 方面;项目 aspect; point; item: 举其一～ for instance; just to mention one example|变化多～ varied; unpredictably changeable

端2 duān ❶ 端正 upright; proper: ～坐 sit up straight|品行不～ of loose morals; of improper behaviour ❷ 平举着拿 hold sth. level with both hands; carry: ～饭上菜 serve a meal|～出两碗茶来 bring in two cups of tea ◇把问题都～出来讨论 bring up issues for discussion ❹ (Duān) 姓 a surname

【端的】duāndì ❶ 果然;的确 really; indeed; sure enough: 武松读了印信榜文,方知～有虎。On reading the notice, Wu Song realized that tigers were indeed there. ❷ 究竟 after all; in the end; actually; exactly: 这人～是谁? Who exactly is this man? ❸ 事情的经过;底细 what actually happened; whole story; ins and outs: 我一问起,方知～。It was only when I asked that I got to know the whole story. ‖ 注意 **NOTE:** '端的'多见于早期白话。端的 is usu. used in early vernacular.

【端方】duānfāng 〈书 *fml*.〉端正;正派 proper;

upright; correct: 品行～ proper and upright; of integrity

【端架子】duān jià·zi 〈方 *dial.*〉拿架子 put on airs

【端节】Duān Jié ☞ 端午 Duānwǔ

【端丽】duānlì 端正秀丽 neat and graceful; beautiful; comely; graceful: 字体～ write with a graceful hand | 姿容～ have comely features

【端量】duān·liang 仔细地看;打量 look sb. up and down; size up; weigh up: 他把来人仔细～了一番。He carefully weighed up the newcomer.

【端面】duānmiàn (～儿 duānmiànr)圆柱形工件两端的平面 (of either end of a cylinder) face; surface

D

【端木】Duānmù 姓 a surname

【端倪】duānní ❶ 事情的眉目;头绪;边际 clue; indication; inkling: 略有～ have a vague notion about a matter | 莫测～ impossible to predict; have not the faintest clue | ～渐显 begin to get some inkling ❷ 指推测事物的始末 predict; conjecture: 千变万化,不可～。The situation is so changeable that it is impossible to make any predictions.

【端五】Duānwǔ same as 端午 Duānwǔ

【端午】Duānwǔ 我国传统节日,农历五月初五日。相传古代诗人屈原在这天投江自杀,后人为了纪念他,把这天当做节日,有吃粽子、赛龙舟等风俗。Dragon Boat Festival (the fifth day of the fifth lunar month); traditional Chinese festival which falls on the anniversary of the day the ancient poet Qu Yuan committed suicide by jumping into a river, when dragon boat races are held and *zongzi* (pyramid shaped dumplings made of glutinous rice wrapped in bamboo or reed leaves) are eaten; also 端五 Duānwǔ

【端线】duānxiàn 底线[1] (sports) finishing line

【端详】duānxiáng ❶ 详情 details: 听～ hear the details | 说～ give a full and detailed account; give full particulars ❷ 端庄安详 dignified and serene: 举止～ dignified and serene in manner

【端详】duān·xiang 仔细地看 look sb. up and down: ～了半天,也没认出是谁。(I) looked him up and down for while but (I) did not recognize him.

【端绪】duānxù 头绪 thread of thought; inkling; clue: 谈了半天,仍然毫无～。(We) talked the matter over for quite some time but got nowhere.

【端砚】duānyàn 用广东高要端溪地方出产的石头制成的砚台,是砚台中的上品 a kind of quality ink-slab made in Duanxi of Gaoyao, Guangdong Province

【端阳】Duānyáng ☞ 端午 Duānwǔ

【端由】duānyóu 原因 cause; reason: 他把事情的～说了一遍。He related the cause of the incident.

【端正】duānzhèng ❶ 物体不歪斜;物体各部分保持应有的平衡状态 balanced and symmetrical; upright; regular: 五官～ have regular features | 字写得端端正正 write a neat hand ❷ 正派;正确 proper; upright; correct: 品行～ having good conduct; well-behaved; behave with moral rectitude ❸ 使端正 rectify; correct: ～学习态度 adopt a correct attitude towards study

【端庄】duānzhuāng 端正庄重 stately; dignified; sedate: 神情～ look calm and sedate; look dignified | 举止～ have a graceful and dignified manner

duǎn (ㄉㄨㄢˇ)

短 duǎn ❶ 两端之间的距离小(跟'长'相对 as opposed to 'long') short; brief a) 指空间 [of space]: ～刀 short knife | ～裤 shorts; pants b) 指时间[of time]: ～期 short period | 夏季昼长夜～。In summer the days are long and the nights short. ❷ 缺少;欠 lack; owe: 理～ be in the wrong; have no justification | 缺斤～两 give short measure or weight | 别人都来了,就～他一个人了。All the others are here; he is the only one missing. | ～你三块钱。(I) owe you three yuan. ❸ (～儿 duǎnr) 缺点 shortcoming; deficiency; weak point; fault: 取长补～ learn from other's strong points in order to offset one's own weaknesses | 说长道～ comment on other people's merits and demerits | 揭～儿 rake up sb.'s faults; touch a raw nerve | 不应该护～。One should not defend a shortcoming or fault.

【短兵相接】duǎn bīng xiāng jiē 双方用刀剑等短兵器进行搏斗 fight at close quarters; engage in hand-to-hand fighting (or close combat); 〈比喻 *fig.*〉面对面地进行针锋相对的斗争 face-to-face struggle; give sb. tit for tat

【短波】duǎnbō 波长 50—10 米(频率 6—30 兆赫)的无线电波。以天波的方式传播,用于无线电广播和电报通讯等方面。shortwave (wavelength between 50-10 metres and frequency between 6-30 MHz), with radio signals transmitted by way of sky waves for broadcasting and telegraph telecommunication purposes

【短不了】duǎn ·bu liǎo ❶ 不能缺少 cannot do without; find indispensable: 人～水。Man cannot live without water. ❷ 免不了 cannot avoid; have to: 我跟他住在一个院子里,每天出来进去,～要点个头,说句话。Living in the same courtyard, it's natural that he and I should nod to each other or exchange greetings as we come and go on a daily basis.

【短程】duǎnchéng 路程短的;距离小的 short distance; short range: ～运输 short-distance haul|～导弹 short-range missile

【短秤】duǎn//chèng 亏秤 give short weight

【短处】duǎn·chu 缺点;弱点 shortcoming; failing; fault; weakness: 大家各有长处,各有～,应该取长补短,互相学习。Each of us having both strengths and weaknesses, we should learn from each other's strong points.

【短促】duǎncù (时间)极短;急促 of very short duration; very brief: 生命～。Life is short.|声音～ short burst of sound|～的访问 short visit; hasty visit

【短打】duǎndǎ ❶ 戏曲中武戏表演作战时,演员穿短衣开打(theat.) hand-to-hand fight wearing tights: ～戏 hand-to-hand fight scene|～武生 actor who plays hand-to-hand fight scenes ❷ 短装 be dressed in a Chinese-style jacket and trousers (rather than long gowns): 一身～ dressed in jacket and trousers

【短笛】duǎndí 管乐器,构造与长笛相同,比长笛短 piccolo

【短工】duǎngōng 临时的雇工 casual labourer; seasonal labourer: 打～ work as a casual labourer|农忙时要雇几个～。A few short-term farmhands are employed during busy farming seasons.

【短骨】duǎngǔ 近似立方体的骨,如腕骨、跗骨等 short bone, e.g. carpus bone, tarsal bone

【短号】duǎnhào 管乐器,和小号的结构相似而号管较短 cornet; three-valved brass instrument of the trumpet family

【短见】duǎnjiàn ❶ 短浅的见解 shortsighted view ❷ 指自杀 suicide: 自寻～ attempt suicide; commit suicide

【短路】duǎnlù ❶ 电路中电势不同的两点直接碰接或被阻抗(或电阻)非常小的导体接通时的情况。发生短路时电流强度很大,往往损坏电气设备或引起火灾。short circuit; accidentally established low-resistance connection between two points in an electric circuit which oft. damages electric apparatuses or causes a fire ❷〈方 *dial.*〉拦路抢劫 waylay; mug

【短跑】duǎnpǎo 短距离赛跑。包括男、女 100 米、200 米、400 米,少年 60 米等。dash; sprint; short-distance run, including men's and women's 100m., 200m. and 400m. races, and children's 60m. race

【短篇小说】duǎnpiān xiǎoshuō 比较简短的小说,人物不多,结构紧凑 short story; short piece of fiction, usu. with one or two central characters, in a compact structure

【短平快】duǎn píng kuài ❶ 排球比赛的一种快攻打法,二传手传出弧度很小的球后,扣球手迅速跃起扣出高速、平射的球 short, quick smash (as in volley-ball) ❷〈比喻 *fig.*〉企业、工程等投资少,历时短,收效快 (enterprise or project) of low investment, short construction period, and quick returns: ～项目 project yielding quick returns with a relatively low investment|～产品 product that requires a relatively low level of investment but brings quick returns

【短评】duǎnpíng (报刊上)简短的评论 short commentary in a newspaper or journal; brief comment: 时事～ short commentary on current affairs

【短期】duǎnqī 短时期 short-term: ～贷款 short-term loan|～训练班 short training course

【短气】duǎnqì 缺乏自信心;灰心丧气 lose heart; get discouraged; be disheartened: 振作起来,不要说～的话。Let's pull ourselves together, cheer up, and stop talking about this depressing subject.

【短浅】duǎnqiǎn (对事物的认识和分析)狭窄而肤浅 narrow (in vision) and shallow (in understanding): 目光～ be short-sighted|见识～ be superficial in one's view|～之见 narrow vision

【短欠】duǎnqiàn 欠;欠缺 owe; be in arrears; be short of; lack: 款项～二十万元。The sum is short by 200,000 yuan.

【短枪】duǎnqiāng 枪筒短的火器的统称,如各种手枪 side arm; handgun; pistol

【短缺】duǎnquē 缺乏;不足 shortage: 物资～ shortage of material|经费～ shortage of funds|人手～ under-staffed; shortage of manpower

【短日照植物】duǎnrìzhào-zhíwù 在较短的日照条件下才能发育开花的植物,每天需要 14 小时以上的连续黑暗才能生长良好。如大豆、玉米等 short-day plant, i.e. plant that flowers and yields fruit in a short photoperiod (less than 14 hours a day) only, such as soya bean, corn, etc.

【短少】duǎnshǎo 缺少(多指少于定额) deficient; short; missing: 保存的东西,一件也不～。Nothing is missing from the stores.

【短视】duǎnshì ❶ 近视 nearsightedness; myopia ❷ 眼光短浅 lack foresight; be shortsighted: 要纠正那种不从长远看问题的～观点。Shortsighted views must be rectified.

【短途】duǎntú 路程近的;短距离的 short distance: ～运输 short-distance transport; short haul|～贩运 short-distance transport of goods for sale

【短线】duǎnxiàn 短的线 short line;〈比喻 *fig.*〉(产品、专业等)需求量超过供应量(跟'长线'相对 as opposed to 'excessive supply') (of products) be in short supply; be in pressing demand: 增加～材料的生产 increase the output of materials that are in short supply|扩大～专业的招生名额 enroll more students on the specialities that are short in supply

【短线产品】duǎnxiàn chǎnpǐn 企业生产的少于

社会需要的产品 products in short supply

【短小】duǎnxiǎo ❶ 短而小 short and small; short; small: 篇幅～ limited in length ❷ (身躯)矮小 short in stature: ～精干 short but strong and tough | 身材～ of small stature

【短小精悍】duǎnxiǎo jīnghàn ❶ 形容人身材矮小而精明强干 not of imposing stature but strong and capable ❷ 形容文章、戏剧等篇幅不长而有力 (of a piece of writing) short and pithy; terse and forceful

【短语】duǎnyǔ 词组 phrase

【短暂】duǎnzàn (时间)短 of short duration; transient; brief: 经过～的休息,队伍又开拔了。After a short rest, the troops set out again. | 我跟他只有过～的接触。He and I were together for only a short time.

【短装】duǎnzhuāng 只穿中装上衣和裤子而不穿长衣叫短装 be dressed in a Chinese style jacket and trousers (rather than a long gown): ～打扮儿 dressed in jacket and trousers; also 穿短装 chuān duǎnzhuāng

duàn (ㄉㄨㄢˋ)

段 duàn ❶〈量词 *classifier*〉a)用于长条东西分成的若干部分 (of long object) section; segment; part: 两～木头 two logs | 一～铁路 a section of railway b)表示一定距离 duration (of time), distance: 一～时间 a period of time | 一～路 a road section c)事物的一部分 part (of anything); paragraph; passage: 一～话 a passage of speech | 一～文章 a paragraph of an article ❷ 段位 rank (in *weiqi*): 九～国手 level nine *weiqi* master (the highest) ❸ 工矿企业中的一级行政单位 section (as an administrative level in a mine or factory): 工～ work section; (work) shop ❹ (Duàn) 姓 a surname

【段落】duànluò (文章、事情)根据内容划分成的部分 division (of an article, project, etc.); paragraph; phase; stage: 这篇文章～清楚,文字流畅。This article is well paragraphed and reads smoothly. | 我们的工作到此告一～。Our work has come to an end at this stage.

【段位】duànwèi 根据围棋棋手技能划分的等级,共分九段,棋艺水平越高,段位越高 level; *duan* (in *weiqi*, level nine being the highest)

【段子】duàn·zi 大鼓、相声、评书等曲艺中可以一次表演完的节目 (of comic talk, ballad singing, etc.) aria; number

断[1](斷) duàn ❶ (长形的东西)分成两段或几段 cut (sth. long) into two or more sections; break; snap: 砍～ chop off | 割～ sever by cutting | ～砖 break a brick | 绳子～了。The rope snapped. ❷ 断绝;隔绝 break off; cut off; stop: ～水 cut off the water supply | ～电 power failure; power cut; blackout | ～了关系 lose contact with sb. | 音讯～了 have one's correspondence with sb. cut off ❸ 拦截 intercept: 把对方的球～了下来 intercept the opponent's ball ❹ 戒除(烟酒) give up (smoking, drinking, etc.); abstain from: ～烟 give up (or quit) smoking | ～酒 keep off alcohol

断[2](斷) duàn ❶ 判断;决定 judge; decide: ～语 conclusion; judgement | 诊～ diagnose | 独～独行 make arbitrary decisions and take peremptory actions; act willfully on one's own ❷〈书 *fml.*〉〈副词 *adv.*〉绝对;一定(多用于否定式 usu. in the negative) absolutely; decidedly: ～无此理 absolutely untenable (or unreasonable); height of absurdity | ～不能信 absolutely incredible

【断垵】duàn//ǎn 条播的粟、黍等农作物在间苗时,用小手锄把垄断开,使苗成为一丛一丛的 cut up a ridge planted with millet, corn, etc., to thin out the plants and form clusters of earth round the remaining plants

【断案】duàn//àn 审判诉讼案件 settle a lawsuit: 秉公～ settle a lawsuit with impartiality

【断案】duàn'àn 结论① conclusion (of a syllogism)

【断编残简】duàn biān cán jiǎn 残缺不全的书本或文章 stray fragments of text; also 断简残编 duàn jiǎn cán biān, 断简残篇 duàn jiǎn cán piān or 残篇断简 cán piān duàn jiǎn

【断层】duàncéng ❶ 由于地壳的变动,地层发生断裂并沿断裂面发生垂直、水平或倾斜方向的相对位移的现象 fault; break in the continuity of a rock formation, caused by a shifting or dislodging of the earth's crust ❷ 连续性的事业或人员的层次中断,不相衔接 break (in lineage); gap: 人才～ break in intellectual lineage

【断肠】duàncháng 形容悲伤到极点 heartbroken

【断炊】duàn//chuī 穷得没米柴做饭 run out of rice and fuel; fail to keep the pot boiling; go hungry

【断代】duàn//dài ❶ 没有后代;断后(duàn//hòu) have no offspring ❷〈比喻 *fig.*〉事业中断或后继无人 (of a profession or undertaking) have no successor to carry on

【断代】duàndài 按时代分成段落 division of history into periods: ～史 periodic history; dynastic history | 对历史进行～研究 study of the history by period

【断代史】duàndàishǐ 记述某一个朝代或某一个历史阶段的史实的史书,如《汉书》、《宋史》等 dynastic history; periodic history, e.g. *History of Han*, *History of Song*, etc.

【断档】duàn//dàng 指某种商品脱销 be out of stock; be sold out: 顾客需要的日用小百货不能～。(We) must be sure to keep a large stock of small daily use articles that our customers need.

【断定】duàndìng 下结论 conclude; form a judgement; decide; determine: 我敢～这事是他干的。I am certain that this was his work. | 这场比赛的结果,还难以～。It's too early yet to predict the result of the match.

【断断】duànduàn 绝对(多用于否定式 usu. in the negative) absolutely: ～使不得。That will never do. *or* That simply won't do.

【断断续续】duànduànxùxù 时而中断,时而继续 off and on; intermittently: 沿路可以听到～的歌声。Sporadic singing can be heard along the way. | 这本书～写了五年才完成。This book was finished after five years of spasmodic writing.

【断顿】duàn//dùn (～儿 duàn//dùnr) 断了饭食,形容穷得没有饭吃 cannot afford the next meal; go hungry

【断根】duàn//gēn (～儿 duàn//gēnr) ❶ 断后(duàn//hòu) have no heir; have no progeny: ～绝种 have no heir to a lineage ❷〈比喻 *fig.*〉彻底除去 be completely cured; effect a permanent cure: 顽疾难以～。A stubborn illness is difficult to cure completely.

【断喝】duànhè 急促地大声叫喊 give a loud shout; bawl suddenly: 他一声～,把所有的人都镇住了。He gave a loud shout that shocked everyone into stopping what they were doing.

【断后】duàn//hòu 没有子孙延续 have no progeny

【断后】duànhòu 军队撤退时,派一部分人在后面掩护,叫断后 bring up the rear; cover a retreat

【断乎】duànhū 绝对(多用于否定式 usu. used in the negative) absolutely: ～不可 absolutely impermissible

【断简残编】duàn jiǎn cán biān ☞ 断编残简 duàn biān cán jiǎn

【断交】duàn//jiāo 绝交 break off a friendship; sever diplomatic relations with

【断井颓垣】duàn jǐng tuí yuán 形容建筑等残破的景象 dilapidated wells and crumbling walls — a scene of devastation

【断句】duàn//jù 古书无标点符号,诵读时根据文义作停顿,或同时在书上按停顿加圈点,叫做断句。这种'句'往往比现在语法所讲的'句'短。pauses made when reading an unpunctuated piece of ancient writing; punctuate unpunctuated writings

【断绝】duànjué 原来有联系的失去联系;原来连贯的不再连贯 break off; cut off; sever: ～关系 sever (or break off) diplomatic relations | ～来往 break contact | ～交通 stop all traffic

【断口】duànkǒu 矿物受外力后不依一定结晶方向破裂的断开面。不同的矿物断口的形状不同,可以利用来鉴定矿物的种类。fracture (characteristic appearance of a fresh mineral surface broken by a hammer, etc.)

【断粮】duàn//liáng 粮食断绝 run out of grain or food: ～绝草 run out of food and forage (草 *cao*: 特指喂马的草料 referring esp. to fodder for horses)

【断垄】duàn//lǒng 条播作物的垄中有些地段缺苗,这种现象叫做断垄 patches of a drill-sown ridge devoid of plants

【断路】duànlù ❶ 拦路抢劫 waylay; hold up: ～劫财 | hold up travellers and seize all their money ❷ 电路断开,电流不能通过 open circuit; broken circuit

【断奶】duàn//nǎi 婴儿或幼小的哺乳动物不继续吃母奶,改吃别的食物 wean; process (with child or young mammal) of feeding on a surrogate mother's milk for solid nourishment

D

【断片】duànpiàn 片段 part; passage; extract; fragment: 这些回忆是他这一时期的生活～。These memoirs are about his life during that period of time.

【断七】duàn//qī 迷信风俗,人死后每七天叫一个'七',满七个'七'即四十九天时叫'断七',常请和尚道士来念经超度亡魂 service held on the 49th day after sb.'s death, during which a Buddhist or Daoist priest is usu. invited to pray for redemption of the deceased's soul

【断气】duàn//qì 停止呼吸;死亡 breathe one's last; die

【断然】duànrán ❶ 坚决;果断 resolute; drastic: ～拒绝 flatly refuse | ～措施 drastic measures ❷ 断乎 absolutely; flatly; categorically: ～不可 absolutely cannot do (sth.) | 思路不通,～写不出好文章。It is impossible to write a good article without a clear train of thought.

【断送】duànsòng 丧失;毁灭(生命、前途等) forfeit (one's life, future, etc.); ruin: ～了性命 lose one's life

【断头台】duàntóutái 执行斩刑的台,台上竖立木架,装着可以升降的铡刀,18 世纪末法国资产阶级革命时期用过。现多用于比喻。guillotine; block on which one's head is placed to receive the axe, used during the late 18th-century French Revolution; now figuratively used as a reference to death penalty

【断弦】duàn//xián 指死了妻子(古时以琴瑟比喻夫妇) snap the lute string — lose one's wife (in ancient times the husband-wife relationship is compared to that between lute and zither): ～再续 second marriage after the death of one's first wife

【断线风筝】duànxiàn fēng·zheng〈比喻 *fig.*〉一去不返或不知去向的人或东西 kite with a broken string; person or thing that is irretrievable

【断想】duànxiǎng 片段的感想 brief comments; notes: 学诗～ notes on learning poems | 忽生～ hit upon an idea | 看完电影写了篇～的小文。After seeing the film, I wrote a brief commentary on it.

【断行】duànxíng 断然施行 resolutely execute or carry out: ～有效办法 resolutely take effective measures

【断言】duànyán ❶ 十分肯定地说 say (or state) with certainty; assert categorically; affirm: 可以～,这种办法行不通。It may be said with certainty that this method does not work. ❷ 断定的话;结论 judgement; conclusion: 作出这样的～未免过早。It's early yet to come to this kind of conclusion.

【断语】duànyǔ 断定的话;结论 conclusion; judgement: 妄下～ come to an unwarranted conclusion

【断狱】duànyù 〈书 *fml.*〉审理案件 try a case in court; try a case and pass a verdict: ～如神 pass judgement with miraculous accuracy | 老吏～(比喻熟练) as experienced and skilful as a veteran magistrate

【断垣残壁】duàn yuán cán bì 形容建筑物倒塌残破的景象 crumbling walls — a desolate scene

【断章取义】duàn zhāng qǔ yì 不顾全篇文章或谈话的内容,而只根据自己的需要孤立地取其中一段或一句的意思 quote out of context; garble a statement, etc.

【断种】duàn//zhǒng 断了后代;绝种 die without issue; have no progeny

【断子绝孙】duàn zǐ jué sūn 绝了后代(常用做咒骂的话 usu. offens.) may you die sonless (or without sons); may you be the last of your line

塅 duàn 〈方 *dial.*〉指面积较大的平坦的地区(多用于地名 used mostly in place names) vast plain area: 中～(在福建) Zhongduan (in Fujian) | 田心～(在湖南) Tianxinduan (in Hunan) | 他们在～上种稻子。They are planting rice seedlings in the fields on the plain.

缎 duàn 缎子 satin: 绸～ silks and satins | 锦～ brocade | 素～(没有花纹的) plain satin

【缎子】duàn·zi 质地较厚、一面平滑有光彩的丝织品,是我国的特产之一 satin; thick silk fabric, glossy on one side and matte on the other, produced in China

椴 duàn 椴树,落叶乔木,花黄色或白色,果实球形或卵圆形。木材用途很广。树皮中纤维很多,可制造绳索。(Chinese) linden (*Tilia*); tree with yellow or white blossom and round or oval fruit, the timber of which is used widely and from whose fibrous bark rope is made

煅 duàn ❶ 放在火里烧(中药制法) calcine (a method of treating certain Chinese medical minerals or herbs): ～石膏 calcined gypsum ❷ same as 锻 duàn

【煅烧】duànshāo 把物料加热到低于熔点的一定温度,使其除去所含结晶水、二氧化碳或三氧化硫等挥发性物质。如加热石灰石,除去二氧化碳而成生石灰。calcine; incineration; heat a material to a temperature below its melting point to remove crystal water, carbon dioxide, sulphide trioxide and other impurities, such as heating limestone to get rid of carbon dioxide and obtain quick lime

碫 duàn 〈书 *fml.*〉砺石 whetstone; grindstone

锻 duàn 锻造 forge: ～铁 forge iron | ～工 forger | ～接 forge welding

【锻锤】duànchuí 金属压力加工用的机器,由动力带动锤头锤打而产生压力。常见的有空气锤、蒸气锤等。forging hammer

【锻工】duàngōng ❶ 把金属材料加热到一定温度,锻造工件或毛坯的工种 forging; shape by heating in a forge and hammering ❷ 做这种工作的工人 blacksmith; forger

【锻件】duànjiàn 经锻造制成的毛坯或工件 forging(s)

【锻炼】duànliàn ❶ 指锻造或冶炼 forge; smelt; temper ❷ 通过体育运动使身体强壮,培养勇敢、机警和维护集体利益等品德 work out; do keep-fit exercise; take physical training (so as to build up physique, and boost courage, alertness and awareness in defending collective interests): 体育～ physical exercise | ～身体,保卫祖国 build up a good physique and defend the country ❸ 通过生产劳动、社会斗争和工作实践,使觉悟、工作能力等提高 temper; steel; enhance one's political awareness and work ability through productive labour, social practice, etc.

【锻铁】duàntiě 含碳量在 0.15%以下的铁,用生铁精炼而成,有韧性、延性,强度较低,容易锻造和焊接,不能淬火。用来制造铆钉、链条、镰刀等。wrought iron (form of iron containing less than 0.15 per cent carbon, refined from pig iron, readily forged and welded but incapable of being quenched, used to make nails, chains, sickles, etc.); also 熟铁 shútiě

【锻压】duànyā 锻造和冲压的统称 forging and pressing

【锻造】duànzào 用锤击等方法,使在可塑状态下的金属材料成为具有一定形状和尺寸的工件,并改变它的物理性质 forge; form (metal) by heating in a forge and beating or hammering into shape

簖(籪) duàn 拦河插在水里的竹栅栏,用来阻挡鱼、虾、螃蟹,以便捕捉 bamboo weir (for catching fish, shrimps, crabs etc.): 鱼～ bamboo fish weir

duī(ㄉㄨㄟ)

堆 duī ❶ 堆积 pile up; heap up; stack: 粮食～满仓,果子～成山。The granaries are full, and fruit is piled high on the ground. ❷ 用手或工具把东西堆积起来 pile up; heap up; stack: 场上的人在～麦秸。People are piling up wheat stalks on the threshing ground. | 把书～在桌子上 stack the books on the table ❸ (～儿 duīr) 堆积成的东西 heap; pile; stack: 柴火～ a pile (or stack) of firewood | 土～ mound ❹ 小山(多用于地名 oft. used as part of a place name) hillock; mound: 滟滪～(在四川长江中,1958年整治航道时已炸平) Yanyu Mound (in the Yangtse River, blown up in 1958 when the water passage was dredged) | 双～集(在安徽) Shuangduiji (in Anhui Province) ❺ 〈量词 *classifier*〉用于成堆的物或成群的人 heap; pack; pile; crowd: 一～黄土 a pile of earth | 一～人 a crowd of people

【堆叠】duīdié 一层一层地堆起来 place one on top of another; pile up; stack: 案上～着大批新书。There are lots of new books stacked on the table.

【堆房】duī·fang 贮藏杂物或货物的房间 storeroom

【堆放】duīfàng 成堆地放置 pile up; stack: 不要在人行道上～建筑材料。Do not stack building materials on the sidewalk.

【堆肥】duīféi 把杂草、落叶、秸秆、骨屑、泥土、粪尿等堆积起来发酵腐烂后制成的有机肥料。肥力持久,多用作底肥。compost; mixture consisting largely of decayed organic matter, such as straw, crop stalks, fallen leaves, mud, and dung, used as manure

【堆积】duījī (事物)成堆地聚集 pile up; heap up: 货物～如山。Goods heaped up into a mound. | 工地上～着大批木材和水泥。Logs and cement are piled high on the construction site.

【堆集】duījí 成堆地聚在一起;堆积 pile up; heap up: 案头～着画轴。There are painting scrolls piled up on the desk.

【堆砌】duīqì ❶ 垒积砖石并用泥灰黏合 pile up (hewn rocks, etc. to build sth.): ～台阶 build a flight of steps | ～假山 pile up a rockery ❷ 〈比喻 *fig*.〉写文章时使用大量华丽而无用的词语 (of a piece of writing) be bristled with fancy phrases: ～辞藻 load with ornate phrases

【堆栈】duīzhàn 供临时寄存货物的地方 storehouse; warehouse

馅 duī 古时的一种蒸饼 a kind of steamed cake in ancient times

duì(ㄉㄨㄟˋ)

队(隊) duì ❶ 行列 row of people; line: 站～ stand in line; queue up | 排～上车 get on a bus (or train, etc.) one by one in a line ❷ 具有某种性质的集体 team; group: 球～ ball team | 舰～ fleet | 生产～ production team | 消防～ fire brigade | 游击～ guerrilla forces; guerrilla detachment ❸ 特指少年先锋队 esp. referring to the Chinese Young Pioneers: ～礼 Young Pioneer's salute | ～旗 Young Pioneer's flag | ～日 Young Pioneer's Day ❹ 〈量词 *classifier*〉 file; column; rank; line: 一～人马 a file of soldiers and horses

〈古 *arch*.〉 same as 坠 zhuì

【队礼】duìlǐ 中国少年先锋队队员行的礼,右手五指并紧,手掌向前,高举头上,表示人民利益高于一切 Young Pioneer's salute (right hand raised above the head with palm facing forward, signifying that the people's interests are above everything else)

【队列】duìliè 队伍的行列 formation: ～训练 formation drill | ～整齐 in neat formation

【队日】duìrì 少年先锋队举行集体活动的日子 Young Pioneer's Day (a day of collective activity for Young Pioneers): 过～ have a Young Pioneer's Day

【队伍】duì·wu ❶ 军队 armed forces; troops: 从～上转业回来 be demobilized from the army ❷ 有组织的集体 contingent; force: 干部～ contingent of public functionaries | 知识分子～ contingent of intellectuals ❸ 有组织的群众行列 ranks; formations: 游行～ contingents of marchers; procession; parade | 排好～ (of a group of people) form neat lines

对(對) duì ❶ 回答 answer; reply: ～答 answer; reply | 无言以～ have nothing to say in reply ❷ 对待,对付 treat; cope with; counter: ～事不～人 be concerned with the facts rather than individuals | ～症下药 suit the medicine to the illness | 刀～刀,枪～枪 sword against sword and spear against spear ❸ 朝着;向着(常跟'着' oft. followed by 着·zhe) be trained on; be directed at: ～着镜子理理头发 smooth one's hair while looking in the mirror | 枪口～着敌人 train a gun on an enemy ❹ 二者相对;彼此相向 facing each other; face to face; vis-a-vis: ～调 exchange | ～流 convection | ～立 contradict | ～抗 antagonism; oppose ❺ 对面的;敌对的 opposite; opposing: ～岸 opposite bank; other side of the river | ～方 other side; opposite side; other party | ～手 opponent; adversary; rival | 作～ set one against; be antagonistic to; oppose ❻ 使两个东西配合或接触 bring (two things) into contact; fit one into the other: ～对子 make a couplet; provide the second of a pair of antithetical sentences | 把门～上 fit the doorflaps | ～个火儿 ask sb. for a light to light a cigarette ❼ 投合;适合 suit; agree; get along: ～劲儿 be to one's liking; suit one | ～心眼儿 find each other's company congenial | 两个人越说越投缘,越说越～脾气。The more the two talked, the more they found each other's company congenial. ❽ 把两个东西放在一起互相比较,看是否符合;对证 compare; check; identify: ～质 confrontation in a law court between two parties | 校～ proofread | ～表 set one's watch; synchronize watch | ～笔迹 identify handwriting | ～号码 check numbers ❾ 调整使合于一定标准 adjust; tune up: ～好照相机的焦距 adjust the focus of a camera | 拿胡琴来～～弦 tune the *erhu* fiddle ❿ 相合;正确;正常 right; correct; true; normal: 你的话很～。What you say is quite true. | ～,就这么办。All right, just go ahead. | 数目不～,还差得多。This number is wrong; it is short by a large amount. | 神气不～ don't give yourself airs ⓫ 搀和(多指液体)(usu. of liquid) mix; add; adulterate: 茶壶里～点儿开水。add some boiling water to the tea pot | 朱砂里～上一点儿藤黄 mix some gamboge yellow in the cinnabar ⓬ 平均分成两份 divide into halves: ～半儿 half-and-half; fifty-fifty | ～开纸 folio ⓭ (～儿 duìr)对子 antithetical couplet; couplet: 喜～ wedding couplet | 五言～儿 five-syllable couplets ⓮ (～儿 duìr)〈量词 *classifier*〉双 pair; couplet: 一～鹦鹉 a pair of parrots | 一～儿椅子 a pair of chairs | 一～模范夫妻 a model couple (of husband and wife) ⓯〈介词 *prep.*〉用法基本上跟'对于'相同 with regard to; concerning; to: ～他表示谢意 extend thanks to him | 决不～困难屈服 never submit to difficulties | 你的话～我有启发。Your remarks are inspiring to me. | 大家～他这件事很不满意。Nobody feels satisfied with what he has done. 注意 **NOTE**: '对'和'对于'的用法差不多,但是'对'所保留的动词性较强,因此有些用'对'的句子不能改用'对于',如上面头两个例子 Though used roughly in the same way, 对 duì and 对于 duìyú are not always interchangeable, as 对 is used in a more verbal sense, as is shown in the above two examples.

【对岸】duì'àn 一定水域互相对着的两岸互称对岸 opposite bank; other side of the river, lake, etc.

【对白】duìbái 戏剧、电影中角色之间的对话 dialogue (between roles in a drama, film, etc.)

【对半】duìbàn (～儿 duìbànr) ❶ 各半 half-and-half; fifty-fifty: ～儿分 divide half-and-half; go halves ❷ 一倍 double: ～儿利 double profit

【对本】duìběn 利润或利息跟本钱相等 profit, or interest equivalent to capital

【对比】duìbǐ ❶ (两种事物)相对比较 contrast; balance: 古今～ contrast the present with the past | 新旧～ comparison of new and old ❷ 比例 ratio: 双方人数～是一对四。The ratio between the two sides is one to four.

【对比度】duìbǐdù 指荧光屏上图像各部分之间的明暗对比程度 contrast (of brightness on a screen, etc.)

【对比色】duìbǐsè 色相性质相反,光度明暗差别大的颜色。如红与绿、黄与紫、橙与青等。contrasting colours (e.g. red and green, yellow and violet, orange and blue)

【对簿】duìbù〈书 *fml.*〉受审问 be interrogated; face a charge: ～公堂 go to court

【对不起】duì·bu qǐ 对人有愧,常用为表示抱歉的套语 I'm sorry; sorry; excuse me; pardon me; I beg your pardon: ～,让您久等了。I'm sorry to have kept you waiting for so long. also 对不住 duì·bu zhù

【对策】duìcè ❶ 古代应考的人回答皇帝所问关于治国的策略 policies to be employed in running a state (as a candidate's answer to the emperor in the imperial examinations in ancient China) ❷ 对付的策略或办法 way to deal with a situation; countermeasure; countermove: 商量～ discuss countermeasures

【对茬儿】duì//chár〈方 *dial.*〉吻合;相符 tally; agree: 这事情很不～,应该对证一下。This matter does not seem right; we had better look into it. | 他们两人说的话根本对不上茬儿。The two stories they told do not tally.

【对唱】duìchàng 两人或两组歌唱者的对答式演唱 musical dialogue in antiphonal style; antiphonal singing (between two singers or two groups of singers)

【对称】duìchèn 指图形或物体对某个点、直线或平面而言,在大小、形状和排列上具有一一对应关系。如人体、船、飞机的左右两边,在外观上都是对称的。symmetry; exact correspondence in position or form to a given point, line, or plane

【对词】duì//cí (～儿 duì//cír)演员在排练中互相对台词 (of actors) practise lines together: 她俩正在～走场子。They are practising their lines together.

【对答】duìdá 回答(问话) answer; reply: ～如流 respond fluently | 问他的话他～不上来。He failed to answer the question.

【对答如流】duì dá rú liú 回答问话像流水一样流畅,形容反应快,口才好 field sb.'s questions; be ready at repartee; deliver one's dissertation as easily as the flow of water

【对待】duìdài ❶ 处于相对的情况 be relative

to：高山与平地～，不见高山，哪见平地？Plains are relative to mountains, as without them there would be no plains.｜工作和休息是互相～的，保证充分的休息，正是为了更好地工作。Work and rest are complementary; taking a good rest makes for better work. ❷ 以某种态度或行为加之于人或事物 treat; approach; handle：～朋友要真诚。One should treat one's friends with sincerity.｜要正确～群众的批评。One must adopt a correct attitude towards criticism from the masses.

【对得起】duì·de qǐ 对人无愧；不辜负 not let sb. down; treat sb. fairly; be worthy of：只有学好功课，才～老师。It is only by doing one's lessons well that one can be worthy of one's teacher. also 对得住 duì·de zhù

【对等】duìděng （等级、地位等）相等 reciprocity; equity：双方应派～人员进行会谈。The two parties should send persons of equal status to the negotiation table.

【对调】duìdiào 互相掉换 exchange; swap：～工作 exchange jobs｜把你们两个的座位～一下。You two exchange (or swap) your seats.

【对方】duìfāng 跟行为的主体处于相对地位的一方 other (or opposite) side; other party：老王结婚了，～是幼儿园的保育员。Old Wang got married; his wife is a kindergarten nurse.｜打球要善于抓住～的弱点来进攻。A ball player should know how to attack the opponents' vulnerable spot.

【对付】duì·fu ❶ 应付① deal with; cope with; counter; tackle：学了几个月的文化，看信也能～了。After a few months of schooling, it is possible to manage reading a letter.｜这匹烈马很难～。This temperamental horse is hard to control. ❷ 将就 make do：旧衣服扔了可惜，～着穿。It would be a pity to throw away these old clothes, so make do with them.｜这支笔虽然不太好，～～也能用。This pen is not good enough, but we can make do with it. ❸ 〈方 *dial*.〉感情相投合 get along with; be on agreeable terms：两口儿最近好像有些不～。The couple does not seem to be getting along recently.

【对歌】duìgē 双方一问一答地唱歌。是一种民间的歌唱形式，多流行于我国某些少数民族地区。singing in antiphonal style (popular in regions of Chinese ethnic minorities)

【对工】duìgōng ❶ 戏曲表演上指适合演员的行当 part or role appropriate for an actor ❷ 〈方 *dial*.〉（～儿 duìgōngr）合适；恰当 appropriate; suitable：你说得～。What you say is quite right.

【对光】duì//guāng ❶ 照相时，调整焦点距离、光圈大小和曝光时间 set (or focus) a camera ❷ 使用显微镜、望远镜等光学仪器时，调节光线 focus a microscope, telescope, etc.

【对过】duìguò （～儿 duìguòr）在街道、空地、河流等的一边称另一边 opposite; across the way：我家～就是邮局。The post office is just opposite my house.｜剧院的斜～有家书店。There is a bookshop across from the theatre.

【对号】duì//hào （～儿 duì//hàor）❶ 查对相合的号数 check the number：～入座 take one's seat according to the number on the ticket; sit in the correct seat ❷ 与有关事物、情况对照，相互符合 fit; tally; match：理论要与现实～ link theory with practice｜他说的与实际对不上号。What he has said does not tally with the facts.

【对号】duìhào （～儿 duìhàor）表示正确的符号，用于批改学生作业或试卷。如'○'、'✓'等。check mark (○ or ✓); tick (used when correcting students' homework or papers, etc.)

【对号入座】duì hào rù zuò 〈比喻 *fig*.〉把有关的人或事物跟自己对比联系起来，也比喻把某人所做的事跟规章制度相比，联系起来。see where one fits into sth.; how sth. one does relates to rules and regulations

【对话】duìhuà ❶ 两个或更多的人之间的谈话（多指小说或戏剧里的人物之间的 between characters in fiction or drama）dialogue; conversation：精彩的～ brilliant dialogue｜～要符合人物的性格。A dialogue should accord with the characters' personalities. ❷ 两方或几方之间的接触或谈判 dialogue (talk or contact between two or more sides)：两国开始就边界问题进行～。The two countries have begun talks on the border issue.｜领导和群众经常～可以加深彼此的了解。Dialogues between leaders and the rank-and-file may increase their mutual understanding.

【对换】duìhuàn 相互交换；对调 exchange; swap：～座位 exchange seats｜我跟你～一下，你用我这支笔。Let's swap pens; you use mine.

【对火】duì//huǒ （～儿 duì//huǒr）吸烟时借别人燃着的烟点燃自己的烟 use sb.'s lighted cigarette to light one's own

【对家】duìjiā ❶ 四人玩牌时坐在自己对面的一方 party sitting opposite one (in a mah-jong game, etc.) ❷ 指说亲时的对方 other party in a proposed marriage; intended husband or wife：本家叔父给他提亲，～能力强，人品也好。His uncle proposed a girl in marriage to him who is both capable and of high moral fibre.

【对接】duìjiē 指两个或两个以上航行中的航天器（航天飞机、宇宙飞船等）靠拢后接合成为一体 dock; link up; (of two or more spacecraft) connect (in space navigation)

【对襟】duìjīn （～儿 duìjīnr）中装上衣的一种式样，两襟相对，纽扣在胸前正中 a kind of Chinese-style jacket with buttons down the front

【对劲】duìjìn （～儿 duìjìnr）❶ 称心合意；合适 be to one's liking; suit one：这支笔太秃，写起字来不～。This pen is blunt; it doesn't write well. ❷ 合得来；相投 get along (well); be on good terms with: 他们俩一向很～。The two of them have always got along very well.

【对局】duìjú 下棋。也指球类比赛。play a game of chess, etc.; ball game

【对开】duìkāi ❶（车船等）由两个地点相向开行 (of trains, buses or ships) run from opposite directions ❷ 印刷上指相当于整张纸的二分之一 (print.) folio ❸ 对半分配，即双方各占一半 divide into two halves; go fifty-fifty

【对抗】duìkàng ❶ 对立起来相持不下 antagonism; confrontation; eyeball to eyeball: 阶级～ class antagonism | 不能对同志的批评抱～情绪。Don't take a defiant attitude towards your comrades' criticism. ❷ 抵抗 resist; oppose: 武装～ armed resistance

【对抗赛】duìkàngsài 两个或几个技术水平相近单位之间组织的单项体育运动比赛 dual; sports meet between two, or among several, teams of equal strength

【对抗性矛盾】duìkàngxìng máodùn 必须采取外部冲突形式才能解决的矛盾 antagonistic contradiction; contradiction that can be solved only through external conflict

【对空台】duìkōngtái 地面指挥部门对空中飞机进行指挥引导的电台 ground radar navigation station

【对口】[1] duìkǒu 〈中医 *Chin. med.*〉指生在脑后、部位跟口相对的疽。deep-rooted ulcer at the back of the head (above the nape); also 脑疽 nǎojū

【对口】[2] duìkǒu ❶ 相声、山歌等的一种表演方式，两个人交替着说或唱 (of two performers) speak or sing alternately: ～相声 comic dialogue | ～山歌 mountain song sung by two singers in turns ❷（～儿 duìkǒur）互相联系的两方在工作内容和性质上相一致 (of two parties) compatible in career; fit in with one's vocational training or speciality: 工作～ the kind of work one is trained for | 专业～ job suited to one's special training | ～协作 cooperation between similar departments of different institutions ❸（味道）合口 to one's taste; palatable: 这几个菜都不～。These dishes are unpalatable.

【对口词】duìkǒucí 曲艺的一种，由两个人对口朗诵唱词，结合动作表演，一般不用乐器伴奏 rhymed dialogue between two actors with actions, but without musical accompaniment

【对口快板儿】duìkǒu kuàibǎnr 由两个人对口表演的快板儿 rhymed clapper dialogue; ☞ 快板儿 kuàibǎnr on p. 1119

【对口相声】duìkǒu xiàng·sheng 由两个人表演的相声 cross talk; comic dialogue; ☞ 相声 xiàng·sheng on p. 2097

【对垒】duìlěi 指两军相持，也用于下棋、赛球等 stand facing each other, ready for battle or contest; be pitted against each other: 两军～。Two armies pitted against each other. | 中国队将于明天与日本队～。The Chinese team is to meet the Japanese team tomorrow.

【对立】duìlì ❶ 两种事物或一种事物中的两个方面之间的相互排斥、相互矛盾、相互斗争 contradiction; antagonism: ～面 opposite; antithesis | ～事物 opposite; antithesis | ～的统一 unity of opposites | 不能把工作和学习～起来看。It is not possible to think of work and study as mutually exclusive. ❷ 互相抵触；敌对 antagonism; conflict; clash: ～情绪 be resentful; antagonistic

【对立面】duìlìmiàn 处于矛盾统一体中的相互依存、相互斗争的两个方面 opposite; antithesis; two mutually dependent yet conflicting aspects in a unity of opposites

【对立统一规律】duìlì tǒngyī guīlǜ 唯物辩证法的根本规律。它揭示出一切事物都是对立的统一，都包含着矛盾。矛盾的对立面又统一，又斗争，并在一定条件下互相转化，推动着事物的变化和发展。对于任何一个具体的事物来说，对立的统一是有条件的、暂时的、过渡的，因而是相对的，对立的斗争则是无条件的、绝对的。law of the unity of opposites, the fundamental law of materialist dialectics that indicates everything in the universe contains contradictions. Between the opposites in a contradiction there is at once unity and struggle, and they convert to each other under certain circumstances, thereby impelling things to move and change. In any given phenomenon or thing, the unity of opposites is conditional, temporary and transitory, and hence relative, whereas the struggle of opposites is unconditional and absolute.

【对联】duìlián（～儿 duìliánr）写在纸上、布上或刻在竹子上、木头上、柱子上的对偶语句 antithetical couplet (written on paper or cloth, or inscribed in bamboo, wood or pillars)

【对流】duìliú 液体或气体中较热的部分和较冷的部分通过循环流动使温度趋于均匀，是流体传热的主要方式 convection; major method for the transference of heat in a flowing substance, whereby heat is transferred by the cylic movement of the warm and cold sections of a gas or liquid medium to achieve a balance in temperature

【对流层】duìliúcéng 大气层的一个层次，接近地面，经常有对流现象发生，层内气温随高度而下降。雨、雪、雹等天气现象发生在这一层。它的厚度在中纬度约 10—12 公里，在赤道约 17—18 公里，在两极约 8—9 公里。troposhere; inner layer of the atmosphere that is close to earth's surface, within which convection is a common occurrence, the temperature drops with increase in height, and all weather conditions — rain, snow, hail, etc. — manifest themselves. The troposhere varies in height between 10 and 12 km. above the middle latitudes, 17 and 18 km. above the equator, and 8 and 9 km. above the North and South Poles.

【对路】duìlù ❶ 合于需要；合于要求 satisfy the need：～产品 products needed in the market | 这种货运到山区可不～。These are not the goods needed in mountainous regions. ❷ 对劲① be to one's liking; suit one：他觉得干这个工作挺～。He feels that this job suits him very well.

【对门】duìmén（～儿 duìménr）❶ 大门相对（of two houses）face each other：～对户 live across the street ❷ 大门相对的房子 opposite building or room：别看他俩住～，平常可很少见面。Living in opposite rooms, they seldom see each other. | 我们家～新搬来一家广东人。A family from Guangdong recently moved to the house opposite ours.

【对面】duìmiàn ❶（～儿 duìmiànr）对过 opposite：他家就在我家～。His house is opposite mine. ❷ 正前方 right in front：～来了一个人。A man came towards us. ❸（～儿 duìmiànr）面对面 face to face：这事儿得他们本人～儿谈。They should talk about this face to face.

【对牛弹琴】duì niú tán qín〈比喻 *fig.*〉对不懂道理的人讲道理，对外行人说内行话。现在也用来讥笑说话的人不看对象。play the lute to a cow — address the wrong listener; talk over sb.'s head; cast pearls before a swine

【对偶】duì'ǒu 修辞方式，用对称的字句加强语言的效果。如：下笔千言，离题万里。沉舟侧畔千帆过，病树前头万木春。(rhetoric) antithesis; use of phrases or sentences that are matched in sound and sense for reiteration purposes, e. g. 'Having written one thousand words, the theme is still ten thousand miles distant.' 'Thousands of boats sail past a sunken ship; ten thousand trees blossom before a withered tree.' ☞律诗 lǜshī on p. 1267 and 骈文 piánwén on p. 1473

【对生】duìshēng 叶序的一种，茎的每个节上长两个叶子，彼此相对，如槭树、紫丁香等的叶子都是对生的（of leaf arrangements）opposite (as are the leaves on the oak, and on clover, etc.)

【对手】duìshǒu ❶ 竞赛的对方 opponent; adversary：我们的～是个素负盛名的球队。Our opponent is a ball team of high reputation. ❷ 特指本领、水平不相上下的竞赛的对方 matchup; match; equal：棋逢～ equals in chess | 讲拳术，他不是你的～。He's no match for you at boxing.

【对数】duìshù 如果 $a^k = b(a>0, a\neq1)$，k 就叫做以 a 为底的 b 的对数，记作$\log_a{}^b = k$。其中 a 叫做底数，简称底；b 叫做真数。If $a^k = b(a>0,\ a\neq1)$, k is the logarithm of b with a as its base number, and it is put as $\log_a{}^b = k$. Of this, a is known as 'base number', or 'base' for short, and b 'antilogarithm', or 'antilog' for short.

【对台戏】duìtáixì 两个戏班为了互相竞争，同时演出的同样的戏 rival show；〈比喻 *fig.*〉双方竞争的同类工作或事情 job of the same nature done by competitors：唱～ stage a competitory choral concert | 演～ put on a rival show

【对头】duì//tóu ❶ 正确；合适 correct; on the right track：方法～，效率就高。When the method is correct, efficiency is high. *or* Good methods make for high efficiency. ❷ 正常（多用于否定 usu. in the negative）normal; right：他的脸色不～，恐怕是病了。He does not look well; I'm afraid he is ill. ❸ 合得来（多用于否定 usu. in the negative）get on well; hit it off：两个人脾气不～，处不好。The two of them do not get along.

【对头】duì·tou ❶ 仇敌；敌对的方面 enemy：死～ sworn enemy | 冤家～ opponent and foe ❷ 对手 opponent; adversary

【对外贸易】duìwài-màoyì 本国（或本地区）跟外国（或外地区）进行的贸易 foreign trade

【对味儿】duì//wèir ❶ 合口味 to one's taste; tasty：这道菜很～。This dish is very nice. ❷〈比喻 *fig.*〉适合自己的思想感情（多用于否定式 usu. in the negative）seem to be all right：我觉得他的话不大～。I don't think what he said is quite right.

【对虾】duìxiā 节肢动物，身体长 15—20 厘米，甲壳薄而透明。第二对触角上的须很长。肉味鲜美，是我国的特产之一。主要产在黄海和渤海湾中。过去市场上常成对出售，所以叫对虾。prawn (*Palaemon*); 15-20 cm. long edible decapod crustaceans that resemble shrimps, with large compressed abdomens, chiefly found in China's Yellow Sea and Bohai Sea gulf; also 明虾 míngxiā

【对象】duìxiàng ❶ 行动或思考时作为目标的人或事物 target; object：革命的～ targets of the revolution | 研究～ object of study ❷ 特指恋爱的对方 boy or girl friend：找～ look for a boy or girl friend or partner in marriage | 他有～了。He is going steady with a woman.

【对消】duìxiāo 互相抵消 offset; cancel each other out：力量～ forces applied cancel out one another | 功过～ good deeds cancel out faults

【对眼】duìyǎn ❶ 合乎自己的眼光；满意 to one's liking：几块花布看着都不～。None of the pieces of cloth suits me. ❷（～儿 duìyǎnr）内斜视的通称（general term for）cross-eyed

【对弈】duìyì〈书 *fml.*〉下棋（of two people）play chess

【对应】duìyìng ❶ 一个系统中某一项在性质、作用、位置或数量上跟另一系统中某一项相当（two systems of quality, function, position, and quantity, etc.）corresponding; homologous ❷ 针对某一情况的；与某一情况相应的 relevant; suitable; corresponding: ～措施 corresponding measure; countermeasure|～行动 corresponding action

【对于】duìyú 〈介词 *prep.*〉引进对象或事物的关系者 with regard to; concerning; to: 我们～公共财产，无论大小，都应该爱惜。We must take good care of all public property, be it large or small.|大家～这个问题的意见是一致的。Everyone is of the same opinion regarding this problem.

【对仗】duìzhàng（律诗、骈文等）按照字音的平仄和字义的虚实做成对偶的语句 antithesis; (in poetry, etc.) matching of both tone and sense in two lines, sentences, etc., the corresponding words usu. being the same part of speech

【对照】duìzhào ❶ 互相对比参照 compare; place side by side; check: 俄汉～(of a dictionary, reading, etc.) in Russian and Chinese|把译文～原文加以修改 check a text of translation against the original and make corrections ❷（人或事物）相比；对比 contrast; compare: 你拿这个标准～一下自己，看看差距有多大。Measure yourself by this standard and see what you must do to reach it.

【对折】duìzhé 一半的折扣 50% discount: 打～ sell at half price|～处理 half-price sale

【对着干】duì·zhegàn ❶ 采取与对方相对的行动，来反对或搞垮对方 adopt a confrontational approach; set oneself against ❷ 跟对方做同样的工作，比赛着干 compete with sb. at work

【对阵】duìzhèn 双方摆开交战的阵势，比喻在竞赛、竞争中交锋（of two rivalling armies, teams, etc.）be poised for a battle or a contest: 两军～。The two armies are poised to give battle.|两国排球队五次～，主队三胜二负。The volleyball teams representing the two countries played five games, of which the host team won three.

【对证】duìzhèng 为了证明是否真实而加以核对 verify; check; give testimony in court; establish evidence through personal confrontation or signed statements, etc.: ～笔迹 identify handwriting|和事实～一下，看看是不是有不符合的地方。Verify the facts and see if there are any discrepancies (in a testimony, statement, etc.).

【对症】duì//zhèng 针对具体病情: be the right cure; give a correct diagnosis: ～下药 suit the medicine to the illness

【对症下药】duì zhèng xià yào 〈比喻 *fig.*〉针对具体情况决定解决问题的办法 suit the medicine to the illness; suit the remedy to the case; prescribe the right remedy for an illness; take proper steps

【对质】duìzhì 诉讼关系人在法庭上面对面互相质问，也泛指和问题有关联的各方当面对证 confrontation (in a law court between two parties); compare the statements or evidence of the relevant parties

【对峙】duìzhì 相对而立 stand facing each other; confront each other: 两山～。Two mountains stand facing each other. ◇两军～（相持不下）。The two armies are locked in a face-off.

【对酌】duìzhuó 相对饮酒 (of two people) drink together

【对子】duì·zi ❶ 对偶的词句 a pair of antithetical phrases, etc.: 对～ supply the antithesis to a given phrase, etc. ❷ 对联 antithetical couplet (written on scrolls, etc., and hung on pillars, etc.): 写～ write hanging couplets ❸ 成对的或相对的人或物 pair of persons or things: 结成互帮互学的～ form pairs to help and learn from each other.

兑[1] duì ❶ 用旧的金银首饰、器皿向银楼换取新的 exchange (old jewellery, gold or silverware for new); convert ❷ 凭票据支付或领取现款 honour (a bill, etc.); cash (a money order, cheque, etc.): ～付 cash (a cheque)|汇～ remittance

兑[2] duì 八卦之一，卦形是☱，代表沼泽 one of the Eight Trigrams in the shape of ☱, standing for marsh; ☞ 八卦 bāguà on p. 22

【兑付】duìfù 凭票据支付现款 cash (a cheque, etc.)

【兑换】duìhuàn 用证券换取现金或用一种货币换取另一种货币 exchange; convert (currencies): ～现金 convert (a bill, money order, gold or silver, etc.) into cash|用美圆～人民币 convert US dollars into Renminbi

【兑换券】duìhuànquàn 旧时地方政府或没有纸币发行权的银行，以及银号、钱庄、商号为了资金周转或补助市面货币不足而发行的周转券或流通券，可以向发行处兑换现金 bank certificates convertible into cash at their bank of issue, used in former times by a local government or by banks unauthorized to issue paper money

【兑奖】duìjiǎng 凭中奖的彩票或奖券兑换奖品 claim a prize; cash in a lottery ticket (that has won a prize)

【兑现】duìxiàn ❶ 凭票据向银行换取现款，泛指结算时支付现款 cash (a check, etc.); pay a dividend, bonus or balance in cash (when the accounts have been finalized): 这张支票不能～。This cheque cannot be cashed.|年终～时，共收入近三千元。When the accounts were settled at the year-end, the income totalled three thousands yuan. ❷ 〈比喻 *fig.*〉诺言的实现 honour (a promise, etc.); fulfil; make good: 答应孩子的事，一定要～。One must honour a promise made to a child.

怼(懟) duì〈书 *fml.*〉怨恨 rancour; resentment: 怨～ bitterly resentful

敦 duì 古代盛黍稷的器具 ancient grain container

☞ dūn on p.495

碓 duì 舂米用具,用柱子架起一根木杠,杠的一端装一块圆形的石头,用脚连续踏另一端,石头就连续起落,去掉下面石臼中的糙米的皮。简单的碓只是一个石臼,用杵捣米。treadle-operated tilt hammer for hulling rice, a more simple type consisting of a stone mortar

【碓房】duìfáng 舂米的作坊 hulling house; also 碓屋 duìwū

镦 duì〈书 *fml.*〉矛戟柄末的平底金属套 flat-bottom metal hood at the end of a spear or halberd

☞ chún on p.313

憝 duì〈书 *fml.*〉❶ 怨恨 resentment; grudge ❷ 坏;恶 wicked; evil: 大～ arch criminal; man of iniquity

镦 duì same as 镦 duì

☞ dūn on p.496

dūn(ㄉㄨㄣ)

吨(噸) dūn ❶ 公制重量单位,1 吨等于1,000公斤,合2,000市斤 ton (t.) (equal to 1,000 kg or 2,000 *jin*); also 公吨 gōngdūn ❷ 英美制重量单位。英国为英吨,美国为美吨 British and US weight unit; (short for) long ton or short ton [法 French: tonne] ❸ 登记吨的简称 abbr. for 登记吨 dēngjìdūn ❹ 船舶运输时按货物的体积计算运费用的单位,根据不同的货物定出体积换算成吨数的不同标准 (in shipping) tonnage; unit for calculating transportation expenses according to the volume of freight, there being different standards for converting cargo volume into tonnage

【吨公里】dūngōnglǐ 货物运输的计量单位,1 吨货物运输 1 公里为 1 吨公里,如 3 吨货物运输 100 公里,就是 300 吨公里 ton-kilometre (unit of freight carriage equal to the transportation of one metric ton of freight one km.; e.g. 300 ton-kilometres indicate transportation of 3 tons of freight for 100 km.)

【吨海里】dūnhǎilǐ 海运货物的运输量计算单位,1 吨货物运输 1 海里为 1 吨海里 ton-sea (or nautical) mile (unit of freight carriage equal to the transportation of one metric ton of freight for one mile)

【吨位】dūnwèi ❶ 车、船等规定的最大载重量。船舶的吨位为满载排水量减去空船排水量。(capacity of a ship) tonnage; maximum cargo-carrying capacity of a vessel, defined by the volume of water displaced by the vessel in question in a fully loaded condition minus the volume of water displaced by it when empty ❷ 计算船舶载重量时按船的容积计算,以登记吨为一吨位 registered ton; unit of internal capacity of a ship equal to 100 cubic feet

惇 dūn〈书 *fml.*〉敦厚;笃厚 sincere and honest

敦 dūn ❶ 诚恳 honest; sincere: ～厚 honest and sincere | ～促 urge | ～聘 cordially invite | ～请 invite in earnest ❷ (Dūn) 姓 a surname

☞ duì on p.495

【敦促】dūncù 催促 urge; press: ～赴会 urge sb. to attend a meeting

【敦厚】dūnhòu 忠厚 honest and sincere: 温柔～ gentle and honest | 质朴～ simple and honest; unsophisticated

【敦睦】dūnmù〈书 *fml.*〉使亲善和睦 promote friendly relations: ～邦交 promote friendly diplomatic relations between two countries

【敦聘】dūnpìn〈书 *fml.*〉诚恳地聘请 offer to engage or employ; cordially invite sb. (to serve in some capacity)

【敦请】dūnqǐng 诚恳地邀请 cordially invite; earnestly request: ～先生与会共商大事。(We) cordially invite you to a meeting to discuss important (state) affairs.

【敦实】dūn·shi 粗短而结实 stocky: 这人长得很～。He has a stocky build. | 这个坛子真～。This jar is rather squat and looks durable.

墩 dūn ❶ 土堆 mound: 土～ mound | 挖塘取水,垒土为～ dig for water and heap the earth into a mound ❷ (～儿 dūnr) 墩子 block of stone or wood: 树～ stump | 门～儿 wood or stone block supporting the pivot of a door; gate pier ❸ 像墩子的坐具 squat stool or cushion: 锦～ silk-covered cushion | 坐～儿 stool ❹ 用拖把擦(地) mop (the floor, etc.): 把地扫干净了再～。Sweep the floor clean before mopping it. ❺〈量词 *classifier*〉用于丛生的或几棵合在一起的植物 [used for densely growing plants] cluster: 一～荆条 a cluster of chaste tree twigs | 这块地方栽稻秧三万～。In this field 30,000 clusters of rice seedlings have been planted.

【墩布】dūnbù 拖把 mop; swab (for use on a ship)

【墩子】dūn·zi 厚而粗大的一整块石头或木头 block of wood or stone: 菜～(切菜用具) chopping block | 坐在石～上 sit on a stone block

撴 dūn〈方 *dial.*〉揪住;拽(zhuài) catch hold of; seize: 死死～住他的手 grab his hand and hold it firmly | 一伸手把他～住 seize him

驐 dūn〈方 *dial.*〉去掉雄性家畜家禽的生殖器 castrate: ～牛 castrate a bull | ～鸡 castrate a rooster

礅 dūn 厚而粗大的一整块石头 large stone：石～ stone block

镦 dūn ❶ 冲压金属板，使其变形。不加热叫冷镦，加热叫热镦。stamping；punching；cold punching；hot punching ❷ same as 礅 dūn

☞ duì on p.495

蹾(撴) dūn〈方 *dial*.〉重重地往下放 lay down heavily；put down with force；dump：箱子里有仪器，不要往地下～。Please lay the box down gently, as there are instruments inside it.

蹲 dūn ❶ 两腿尽量弯曲，像坐的样子，但臀部不着地 squat on the heels：两人在地头～着谈话。They are squatting at the side of a field, chatting. ❷〈比喻 *fig*.〉呆着或闲居 be idle；stay：他整天～在家里不出门。He stays at home all day long.

☞ cún on p.337

【蹲班】dūn//bān 留级（of pupils，etc.）fail to advance to the next grade or year；stay down；repeat the year's work：全班学生没有一个～的。None of the students in the class failed to advance to the next grade.｜他去年蹲了一班，没有毕业。He stayed down（or failed to pass）last year and did not graduate.

【蹲膘】dūn//biāo（～儿 dūn//biāor）多吃好的食物而少活动，以致肥胖（多指牲畜，用于人时带贬义）（of cattle，etc.，and also pejoratively applied to a person getting fat）fatten in the shed：催肥～ fatten in the shed

【蹲点】dūn//diǎn 到某个基层单位，参加实际工作，进行调查研究（of leaders，etc.）stay at a selected grass-roots unit，take part in the practical work，and carry out surveys and research so as to improve the overall level of work there：下乡～ go and stay in a village to gain first-hand experience｜他在西村蹲过点，对那里情况很熟悉。He knows Xicun Village very well because he once worked there for a time to gain first-hand experience.

【蹲苗】dūnmiáo 在一定时期内控制施肥和灌水，进行中耕和镇压，使幼苗根部下扎，生长健壮，防止茎叶徒长 restrict the growth of seedlings by controlling application of fertilizer and irrigation and by intertilling and tamping down the earth，so as to develop the roots，ensure healthy growth of the crop and prevent stalks and leaves from spindling

dǔn（ㄉㄨㄣˇ）

不 dǔn［不子］（dǔn·zi）〈方 *dial*.〉❶ 墩子 block of wood or stone ❷ 特指砖状的瓷土块，是制造瓷器的原料 brick of clay used to make porcelain

盹 dǔn（～儿 dǔnr）很短时间的睡眠 doze；take a nap：打～儿 doze off；have a nap｜醒～儿 wake up from a nap

趸(躉) dǔn ❶ 整批 wholesale：～批 wholesale｜～买～卖 buy and sell wholesale ❷ 整批买进（准备出卖）buy wholesale（for retail trading）：～货 buy goods wholesale｜现～现卖 sell goods immediately after buying them

【趸船】dǔnchuán 无动力装置的矩形平底船，固定在岸边、码头，以供船舶停靠，上下旅客，装卸货物 landing stage；pontoon

【趸批】dǔnpī 整批（多用于买卖货物 of goods）wholesale：～买进 buy wholesale｜～出卖 sell wholesale

dùn（ㄉㄨㄣˋ）

囤 dùn 用竹篾、荆条、稻草编成的或用席箔等围成的盛粮食的器具 grain bin：粮食～ grain bin｜大～满，小～流。All bins，big or small，were filled to overflowing（from a bumper harvest）.

☞ tún on p.1954

沌 dùn ☞ 混沌 hùndùn on p.873

☞ Zhuàn on p.2521

炖(燉) dùn ❶ 烹调方法，加水烧开后用文火久煮使烂熟（多用于肉类）stew；cook（meat，etc.）by long，slow simmering：清～排骨 stew spareribs ❷ 把东西盛在碗里，再把碗放在水里加热 warm sth. by putting the container in boiling water：～酒 warm up wine｜～药 warm（herbal）medicine in a container

砘 dùn 播种后，用石砘子把松土压实：这块地已经～过一遍 ram loose soil with a stone-roller after sowing

【砘子】dùn·zi 播种覆土以后用来镇压的农具 roller（to ram loose soil）

钝 dùn ❶ 不锋利（跟‘快、利、锐’相对 as opposed to ‘sharp’）blunt；dull：刀～了，要磨一磨。This knife is blunt；it should be sharpened. ◇成败利～ success or failure，plain sailing or rough going ❷ 笨拙；不灵活 stupid；dull-witted：迟～ slow；dull-witted｜鲁～ obtuse；stupid

【钝角】dùnjiǎo 大于直角（90°）而小于平角（180°）的角 obtuse angle（greater than 90° but less than 180°）

盾[1] dùn ❶ 盾牌 shield；buckler ❷ 盾形的东西 shield-shaped object：金～ gold shield｜银～ silver shield

盾[2] dùn ❶荷兰的旧本位货币 guilder；former basic monetary unit of the Netherlands ❷越南、印度尼西亚等国的本位货币 dong，monetary unit of Vietnam；rupiah，monetary unit of Indonesia，etc.

【盾牌】dùnpái ❶ 古代用来防护身体、遮挡刀箭的武器 shield; buckler ❷〈比喻 *fig.*〉推托的借口 pretext; excuse

顿[1] dùn ❶ 稍停 pause: 他～了一下,又接着往下说。After a short pause, he carried on. ❷ 书法上指用力使笔着纸而暂不移动 (in Chinese calligraphy) pause in writing in order to reinforce the beginning or ending of a stroke: 一横的两头都要～一～。(of calligraphy) Reinforce both the beginning and the end of a horizontal stroke. ❸ (头)叩地;(脚)跺地 kowtow; stamp: ～首 kowtow | ～足 stamp one's feet ❹ 处理;安置 arrange; settle: 整～ consolidate; straighten out | 安～ settle in ❺ 立刻;忽然 suddenly; immediately; at once: ～然 suddenly | ～悟 suddenly realize the truth, etc.; attain enlightenment | ～生邪念 wicked thought (or idea) suddenly occurs to one ❻〈量词 *classifier*〉用于吃饭、斥责、劝说、打骂等行为的次数 [used to indicate frequency of food, reproach, admonishment, beating, etc.]: 一天三～饭 three meals a day | 被他说了一～ be reproached by him ❼ (Dùn) 姓 a surname

顿[2] dùn 疲乏 tired: 困～ dog-tired; fatigued | 劳～ fatigued; exhausted
☞ dú on p. 479

【顿挫】dùncuò (语调、音律等)停顿转折 pause or transition (in rhythm or tone): 抑扬～ lowering, raising, pausing and transition — all variations of one's tone; modulation in tone

【顿号】dùnhào 标点符号(、),表示句子内部并列词语之间的停顿。主要用在并列的词或并列的较短的词组中间。slight-pause mark (、), usu. used to set off items in a series

【顿开茅塞】dùn kāi máo sè ☞ 茅塞顿开 máosè dùn kāi on p. 1309

【顿然】dùnrán 忽然;突然 suddenly; immediately: ～醒悟 come to realize sth. immediately | 登上顶峰,～觉得周围山头矮了一截。After having climbed to the peak one sees the surrounding mountains as lower.

【顿时】dùnshí 立刻(只用于叙述过去的事情 used only when recounting a past event) suddenly; immediately; at once: 喜讯传来,人们～欢呼起来。People broke into cheers as soon as they heard the good news.

【顿首】dùnshǒu 磕头(多用于书信 usu. used after the signature in old-style letters) kowtow

【顿悟】dùnwù 佛教指顿然破除妄念,觉悟真理。也泛指忽然领悟。suddenly come to realize (the truth in Buddhism); be suddenly enlightened; realize in a flash

【顿足捶胸】dùn zú chuí xiōng ☞ 捶胸顿足 chuí xiōng dùn zú on p. 309

遁(**遯**) dùn ❶ 逃走 escape; flee; run away: ～走 run away | 逃～ escape | 远～ flee far away ❷ 隐藏;消失 hide; lie low; disappear: ～迹 lie low; go into hiding | ～形 lie low; hide one's identity | 隐～ go into hiding

【遁词】dùncí 因为理屈词穷而故意避开正题的话 subterfuge; pretext

【遁迹】dùnjì〈书 *fml.*〉逃避人世;隐居 live in seclusion; withdraw from society and live in solitude: ～潜形 live in seclusion and hide one's identity | ～空门(出家) withdraw from temporal life and become a Buddhist monk or nun

【遁世】dùnshì〈书 *fml.*〉避世;避开现实社会而隐居 withdraw from the world; live in seclusion: ～绝俗 withdraw from the world and renounce temporal life

楯 dùn〈书 *fml.*〉same as 盾 dùn
☞ shǔn on p. 1806

duō (ㄉㄨㄛ)

多[1] duō ❶ 数量大(跟'少'或'寡'相对 as opposed to 'few') many; much; more; a lot of: ～年 many years | ～种～样 in various kinds; varied; diversified | ～才～艺 versatile | ～快好省 achieve greater, faster, better and more economical results ❷ 超出原有或应有的数目;比原来的数目有所增加(跟'少'相对 as opposed to 'few') exceed the original, correct or required number or amount; be in excess, or have too many or too much: 这句话～了一个字。There is one word too many in this sentence. | 你的钱给～了,还你吧。You have overpaid, let me give you the balance. ❸ 过分的;不必要的 excessive; overly: ～心 oversensitive; suspicious | ～嘴 shoot off one's mouth | ～疑 oversensitive; oversuspicious ❹ (用在数量词后)表示有零头 [used after a number] more; over; odd: 五十～岁 over fifty years old | 两丈～高 more than two *zhang* high | 三年～ more than three years ❺ 表示相差的程度大 much more; much less; far more; far less: 他比我强～了。He has done far better than I have. *or* He is far more capable than I am. | 这样摆好看得～。It looks far more beautiful arranged this way. ❻ (Duō) 姓 a surname

多[2] duō〈副词 *adv.*〉❶ 用在疑问句里,问程度 [used in questions] to what extent: 他～大年纪? How old is he? | 你知道天安门～高? Do you know how high Tian'anmen is?
注意 **NOTE**: 大都用于积极性的形容词,如'大、高、长、远、粗、宽、厚'等等。多 is used largely to modify adjectives in positive senses such as 大 dà, 高 gāo, 长 cháng, 远 yuǎn, 粗 cū, 宽 kuān and 厚 hòu, etc. ❷ 用在感叹句

里，表示程度很高［used in exclamations to express a specific extent］：你看他老人家～有精神！Look how spirited the old man is！| 这问题～不简单哪！This question is so difficult！❸ 指某种程度［to an unspecified extent］：无论山有～高，路有～陡，他总是走在前面。No matter how high the mountain, or how steep the road, he is always ahead. | 有～大劲使～大劲。Exert your every ounce of strength.

【多半】duōbàn（～儿 duōbànr）❶ 超过半数；大半 greater part; most; more often than not: 同学～到操场上去了，只有少数还在教室里。Most of the students were in the playground, only a few stayed in the classroom. ❷ 大概 most probably; very likely: 他这会儿还不来，～不来了。As he still hasn't arrived, he most probably won't come. ‖ also 多一半 duōyībàn

D

【多宝槅】duōbǎogé 分成许多格子的架子，用来放置古玩、工艺品等 lattice framework for curios or bric-à-brac; curio shelves; also 多宝架 duōbǎojià

【多边】duōbiān 由三个或更多方面参加的，特指由三个或更多国家参加的 multilateral; involving three or more countries: ～会谈 multilateral talks | ～条约 multilateral treaty | ～贸易 multilateral trade

【多边形】duōbiānxíng 由三条或三条以上的边构成的图形 polygon; closed plane figure bounded by three or more straight sides

【多才多艺】duō cái duō yì 具有多方面的才能、技艺 versatile; gifted in many ways

【多愁善感】duō chóu shàn gǎn 形容人感情脆弱，容易发愁或感伤 mawkish; excessively sentimental

【多此一举】duō cǐ yī jǔ 做不必要的、多余的事情 be superfluous; make an unnecessary move: 何必～。Why take the trouble to do that?

【多端】duōduān 多种多样 varied; in various ways: 变化～ most changeable; highly volatile | 诡计～ have a whole bag of tricks; be very crafty

【多多益善】duō duō yì shàn 越多越好 the more, the better

【多发】duōfā 发生率较高的 occur frequently: ～病 frequently occurring disease | 事故～地段 accident-prone area or section (of a road, etc.)

【多方】duōfāng 多方面 in many ways; in every way: ～设法 try all possible means; make every effort

【多分】duōfèn〈方 *dial.*〉多半 most likely: ～是这样。That is probably the case. | 我看这事～没希望了。I'm afraid the matter is hopeless.

【多寡】duōguǎ 指数量的大小 number; amount: ～不等 vary in amount or number

【多会儿】duō·huìr 什么时候；几时 when; what time: a) 用在疑问句里，问时间［used in questions］when: 你是～来的？When did you come? b) 指某一时间或任何时间 ever; at any time: 在工作中他～也没叫过苦。He never complains of hardship at work. | 现在还不敢说定了，～有空～去。I can't yet say exactly when, but I'll go whenever I'm free.

【多晶体】duōjīngtǐ 由许多小晶体组成的晶体。原子在整个晶体中不是按统一的规则排列的，无一定的外形，其物理性质在各个方向都相同。polycrystal; rock or metal composed of aggregates of individual crystals, in which atoms are arrayed irregularly and have no fixed external form, but their physical property is the same in all directions

【多口相声】duōkǒu-xiàng·sheng 由几个人表演的相声 cross talk (or comic dialogue) performed by more than two persons; ☞ 相声 xiàng·sheng on p. 2097

【多亏】duōkuī 表示由于别人的帮助或某种有利因素，避免了不幸或得到了好处 thanks to; luckily: ～你来了，否则我们要迷路的。We are lucky to have you as our guide, otherwise we would have lost our way.

【多棱镜】duōléngjìng 棱镜，多指三棱镜 (optical) prism; triangular prism

【多么】duō·me〈副词 *adv.*〉❶ 用在疑问句里，问程度［used in questions, oft. replaced by 多 in spoken language］to what extent; how: 洛阳离这里有～远？How far is Luoyang from here? ❷ 用在感叹句里，表示程度很高［used in exclamations to indicate high degree］what; how: 他的品德～高尚！How noble-minded he is. | 国家培养一个人才是～不容易呀！The state has gone to such great lengths to cultivate a person's talent. ❸ 指较深的程度 to a great extent: 不管风里雨里，～冷，～热，战士们总是不停地在苦练杀敌本领。Rain or shine, no matter how hot or cold, soldiers train rigorously in combat skills. 注意 **NOTE**: '多么'的用法基本上跟'多²'相同，'多么'用于感叹句为主，其他用法不如'多'普通。Usage of 多么 is akin to 多² duō. 多么 is usu. used in exclamations, otherwise it is less commonly used than 多².

【多面手】duōmiànshǒu 指擅长多种技能的人 many-sided person; versatile person; all-rounder; person of many parts

【多面体】duōmiàntǐ 四个或四个以上多边形所

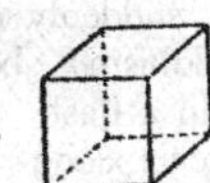
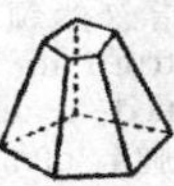

多面体 Polyhedrons

围成的立体 polyhedron; solid figure consisting of four or more closed plane figures (all polygons)

【多谋善断】duō móu shàn duàn 很有智谋,又善于决断 resourceful and decisive; sagacious and resolute

【多幕剧】duōmùjù 分做若干幕演出的大型戏剧,一般比独幕剧人物多,情节复杂。依照分幕数目的多少,可以分为三幕剧、四幕剧、五幕剧等。play of several acts; full-length drama

【多难兴邦】duō nàn xīng bāng 国家多灾多难,可以激发人民发愤图强,战胜困难,使国家兴盛起来 distress can regenerate a nation; deep distress resurrects a nation

【多年生】duōniánshēng 能连续生活多年的,如乔木、灌木等木本植物和蒲公英、车前等草本植物 (of plant) perennial, e.g. woody plants and herbs like the dandelion and Asiatic plantain

【多情】duōqíng 重感情(多指重爱情) tender and affectionate (to a person of the opposite sex): 自作~ imagine oneself the favourite of one (of the opposite sex)

【多如牛毛】duō rú niú máo 形容极多 as numerous as the hairs on an ox; countless; innumerable

【多少】duōshǎo ❶ 指数量的大小 number; amount: ~不等,长短不齐 vary in amount or number and in length ❷ 或多或少 somewhat; more or less; to some extent: 这句话~有点道理。There is something in this statement. ❸ 稍微 a little; slightly: 一立秋,天气~有点凉意了。One begins to feel a slight chill when autumn comes.

【多少】duō·shao 〈疑问代词 *interrog. pron.*〉 ❶ 问数量 how many; how much: 这个村子有~人家? How many households are there in this village? | 今年收了~粮食? How much grain has been reaped this year? ❷ 表示不定的数量 [expressing an unspecified amount or number]: 我知道~说~。I'll tell you all I know. | 有~人,准备~工具。Prepare as many tools as there are people.

【多神教】duōshénjiào 不止信奉一个神的宗教,如佛教、道教等(区别于'一神教' as compared with 'monotheism') polytheism (e.g. Buddhism, Daoism, etc.); worship of or belief in more than one god

【多时】duōshí 很长时间 long time: 等候~ have waited a long time | ~未见面 have not seen each other for a long time (or for ages)

【多事】duō//shì ❶ 做多余的事 do what is unnecessary or superfluous: 不找他他也会来的,你不必多那个事了。He will come whether or not you ask for him, so don't bother. ❷ 做没必要做的事 be meddlesome: 他总爱~,惹是非。He is meddlesome and often causes trouble.

【多事之秋】duō shì zhī qiū 事故或事变多的时期,多用来形容动荡不安的政局 eventful period or year; troubled times

【多数】duōshù 较大的数量 majority; most: 绝大~ overwhelming majority | 少数服从~。The minority should submit to the majority. | ~人赞成这个方案。The majority agrees with this proposal.

【多头】duōtóu ❶ 从事股票交易、期货交易的人,预料货价将涨而买进期货,伺机卖出,这种人叫多头(因为买进的货等待卖出,所以叫'多头';跟'空头'相对 as opposed to 'bear') (on the stock exchange) bull; person who, confident that prices will go up in time, buys futures in order to sell when the prices rise; ☞ 买空卖空 mǎi kōng mài kōng on p. 1294 ❷ 不只一个方面的 more than one channel; too many bosses: ~领导 with too many bosses; overlapping leadership | ~政治 polyarchy

【多嫌】duō·xian 〈方 *dial.*〉认为多余而嫌弃(多指人) regard (sb.) as superfluous; cold-shoulder: 你别胡思乱想,哪会~你一个? Don't let your imagination run away with you, nobody thinks of you as superfluous.

【多谢】duōxiè 〈客套话 *pol.*〉表示感谢 many thanks; thanks a lot

【多心】duō//xīn 乱起疑心;用不必要的心思 oversensitive; suspicious: 你别~,他不是冲你说的。Don't get him wrong. His remarks are not directed at you.

【多样】duōyàng 多种样式 diverse; varied: ~化 diversification | 多种~ diversified

【多一半】duōyībàn 多半 more than half; a good half

【多疑】duōyí 疑虑过多;过分疑心 oversensitive; oversuspicious; given to suspicion; prone to suspicion: 不必~。Don't be suspicious without cause. | 生性~ be oversuspicious by nature

【多义词】duōyìcí 具有两个或更多意义的词,如'接'有'连接'(接电线)、'接受'(接到一封信)、'迎接'(接客人)等义。多义词的意义之间往往有共同点或某些联系,如'接'的三个意义都表示'使分散的人或事物合在一起'。polysemous word; polysemant; word having two or more meanings. For example the Chinese character 接 jiē means 'connect' (as in 'connecting two wires'), 'receive' (as in 'have received a letter'), and 'greet' (as in 'greeting a guest'). The different meanings of a polysemant often hold sth. in common or are related. For example, the three meanings of 接 jiē all indicate 'putting together things originally scattered'.

【多余】duōyú ❶ 超过需要数量的 surplus: 把~的粮食卖给国家 sell surplus grain to the state ❷ 不必要的 unnecessary; surplus; superfluous; uncalled-for: 把文章中~的字句删掉 cut out superfluous words and phrases from an article or essay | 你这种担心完全是～的。Your worries are needless.

【多元论】duōyuánlùn 一种唯心主义的哲学观点，认为世界是由多种独立的、不互相依存的实体构成(跟'一元论'相对 as opposed to 'monism') pluralism (an idealist theory that the world is composed of many entities that are independent of each other)

【多云】duōyún 我国气象上，中、低云云量占天空面积 4/10—7/10 或高云云量占天空面积 6/10—10/10 叫做多云。cloudy; overcast (in Chinese meteorology, cloudy weather indicates that 4/10-7/10 of the sky is covered by medium or low cloud, or that 6/10-10/10 of the sky is covered by high cloud)

D

【多咱】duō·zan〈方 *dial.*〉什么时候；几时(用法跟'多会儿'相同 of the same usage as '多会儿' duō·huir) what time; when: 咱们～走? When are we leaving? | 这是～的事? When did that happen? *or* When was that?

【多早晚】duō·zaowǎn 多咱('多咱'就是由'多早晚'变来的) same as 多咱 duō·zan (being a corrupted form of 多早晚)

【多嘴】duō//zuǐ 不该说而说 speak out of turn; shoot one's mouth off; have a big mouth: ～多舌 gossipy and meddlesome; long-tongued| 你不了解情况，别～! You don't know the facts, so keep your mouth shut!

咄 duō〈书 *fml.*〉表示呵斥或惊异 (used to show amazement or to berate) tut-tut

【咄咄】duōduō〈叹词 *interj.*〉表示惊诧或感叹 tut! tut!: ～怪事 monstrous absurdity|～称奇 cannot help wondering out loud

【咄咄逼人】duōduō bī rén 形容气势汹汹，盛气凌人 overbearing; aggressive: 他说话的口气～，令人十分难堪。He spoke with an overbearing air, making the listener feel most awkward.

【咄嗟】duōjiē〈书 *fml.*〉吆喝 shout

【咄嗟立办】duōjiē lì bàn 原指主人一吩咐，仆人立刻就办好，现在指马上就办到(of a servant in former times) get things done promptly at a boss' bidding; carry out (an order) immediately

哆 duō [哆嗦] (duō·suō) 因受外界刺激而身体不由自主地颤动 tremble; shiver: 冻得直～ shiver with cold | 气得浑身～ tremble with rage

☞ chǐ on p. 264

剟 duō〈书 *fml.*〉❶ 刺；击 stab; attack ❷ 削；删除 cut; delete ❸ 割取 cut down and take

堶 duō 塘堶(Tángduō)，地名，在广东 Tangduo, name of a place in Guangdong Province

掇(敠) duō ❶ 拾取；采取 pick up; pluck ❷〈方 *dial.*〉用双手拿；搬(椅子、凳子等) hold with both hands; carry (a chair, stool, etc.)

【掇弄】duōnòng〈方 *dial.*〉❶ 收拾；修理 fix up: 机器坏了，经他一～就好啦。The machine was out of order, but worked again after he had fixed it. ❷ 播弄；怂恿 stir up (trouble, etc.); manipulate; incite: 受人～ manipulated by others

【掇拾】duōshí〈书 *fml.*〉❶ 拾掇 tidy up; put in order ❷ 搜集 collect; gather: ～旧闻 collect old-time anecdotes

裰 duō ❶ 缝补(破衣) mend (clothing): 补～ mend (or patch) (clothes) ❷ ☞ 直裰 zhíduō on p. 2460

duó (ㄉㄨㄛˊ)

夺[1](奪) duó ❶ 强取；抢 take by force; seize; wrest: 掠～ plunder; pillage | 巧取豪～ get by cheating or by force ◇强词～理 use lame arguments; resort to sophistry ❷ 争先取到 contend for; compete for; strive for: ～高产 strive for high yields| ～红旗 contend for the red banner (in an emulation campaign); strive to be the pacesetter ❸ 胜过；压倒 overwhelm; defeat; surpass: 巧～天工 ingenuity surpassing nature| 先声～人 overawe others by displaying one's prowess ❹ 使失去 deprive: 剥～ deprive sb. of sth. | 褫～ deprive; dispossess ❺〈书 *fml.*〉失去 lose: 勿～农时。Do not miss the farming season.

夺[2](奪) duó〈书 *fml.*〉做决定 decide: 定～ make a final decision | 裁～ come to a verdict

夺[3](奪) duó〈书 *fml.*〉(文字)脱漏 omission (in a text): 讹～ errors and omissions

【夺杯】duó//bēi 夺取奖杯，特指夺取冠军 win the (first) prize (in a contest); win the championship: 我国排球队在这次邀请赛中～。China's volleyball team carried off the first prize in this invitational tournament.

【夺标】duó//biāo ❶ 夺取锦标，特指夺取冠军 win the trophy; win the championship: 这场大赛中数她～呼声最高。She is the most likely champion of this competition. ❷ 承包人或买主所投的标在投标竞争中中(zhòng)标 have one's tender accepted: 这家公司在同其他八家厂商的竞争中～。This company won the tender in competition with eight other companies.

【夺冠】duó//guàn 夺取冠军 carry off the first prize; win first place; win the championship

【夺魁】duó//kuí 争夺第一；夺取冠军 pocket the first prize; win first place; win the championship: 这个厂的电视机在全国评比中～。

TV sets produced by this factory won first place in a nationwide evaluation.

【夺目】duómù（光彩）耀眼 dazzle the eyes：鲜艳～ brilliant; dazzling

【夺取】duóqǔ ❶ 用武力强取 capture; seize; wrest：～敌人的阵地 capture an enemy position ❷ 努力争取 strive for：～新的胜利 strive for new victories｜～农业丰收 strive for a good harvest

【夺权】duó//quán 夺取权力（多指夺取政权）seize power; take over (usu. political) power

泽（澤）duó ☞ 凌泽 língduó on p. 1229

度 duó〈书 *fml.*〉推测；估计 surmise; estimate：揣～ make a rough estimate of｜测～ estimate｜～德量力 make an appraisal of one's own position

☞ dù on p. 482

【度德量力】duó dé liàng lì 衡量自己的品德能否服人，估计自己的能力能否胜任 estimate one's own moral and material strength; make an appraisal of one's own position

铎（鐸）duó 古代宣布政教法令时或有战事时用的大铃 big bell used in ancient China when issuing proclamations or at times of war：木～ wooden bell｜铃～ bell｜振～ strike a bell; issue a clarion call

敓 duó〈书 *fml.*〉same as 夺 duó

踱 duó 慢步行走 pace; stroll：～来～去 pace to and fro; pace up and down｜～方步 walk with measured steps

duǒ（ㄉㄨㄛˇ）

朵（朶）duǒ ❶〈量词 *classifier*〉用于花朵和云彩或像花和云彩的东西［used of flowers, clouds and things that look as such］：两～牡丹 two peonies｜一～白云 a whitish cloud｜激起～～浪花 dash up two waves ❷（Duǒ）姓 a surname

【朵儿】duǒr ❶ 花朵 flower：牡丹花开的～多大呀！How large the peony flowers are! ❷〈量词 *classifier*〉same as 朵 duǒ

【朵颐】duǒyí〈书 *fml.*〉指鼓动腮颊嚼东西的样子 munch; chew：大快～（形容食物鲜美，吃得很满意）eat with great relish

垛（垜）duǒ 垛（duǒ）子 crenel; battlements：城墙～口 crenel; battlement

☞ duò on p. 502

【垛堞】duǒdié same as 垛口 duǒkǒu

【垛口】duǒkǒu 城墙上呈凹凸形的短墙 battlement; crenel

☞duòkǒu on p. 502

【垛子】duǒ·zi 墙上向外或向上突出的部分 buttress; battlements：门～ gate buttress｜城～ battlements on a city wall

☞ duò·zi on p. 502

哚 duǒ ☞［吲哚］（yǐnduǒ）on p. 2293

埵 duǒ〈书 *fml.*〉坚硬的土 hard soil

躲（躱）duǒ 躲避；躲藏 hide (oneself); avoid; dodge：～雨 take shelter from the rain｜～车 give way to a car (truck, bicycle, train, etc.)｜～债 hide from a creditor｜明枪易～，暗箭难防。It's easy to dodge an open spear thrust but difficult to guard against an arrow from behind.

【躲避】duǒbì ❶ 故意离开或隐蔽起来，使人看不见 hide (oneself)：这几天他好像有意～我。He seems to have been hiding from me these past days. ❷ 离开对自己不利的事物 avoid; elude; dodge：～风雨 take shelter from wind and rain｜不应该～困难。One should not avoid difficulties.

【躲藏】duǒcáng 把身体隐蔽起来，不让人看见 hide (or conceal) oneself; go into hiding; entrench

【躲躲闪闪】duǒ·duoshǎnshǎn 指有意掩饰或避开事实真相 be evasive; hedge; equivocate：你谈问题要和盘托出，不要～。Say everything that is on your mind; don't be evasive.

【躲懒】duǒ//lǎn（～儿 duǒ//lǎnr）逃避工作或劳动；偷懒 shy away from work; shirk

【躲让】duǒràng 躲闪；让开 dodge; get out of the way：一辆救护车急驰而来，人们纷纷往两边～。As an ambulance came charging down the road, people stepped quickly out of its path.

【躲闪】duǒshǎn 迅速使身体避开 dodge; evade：小王～不及，和他撞了个满怀。It was too late for Xiao Wang to dodge out of the way and he bumped into him.

【躲债】duǒ//zhài 欠债人因无钱还债，避开跟债主见面 shun a creditor

亸（嚲、軃）duǒ〈书 *fml.*〉下垂 hang down; droop

軃（𩠄）duǒ〈书 *fml.*〉same as 亸 duǒ

【軃都】Duǒdū 宋时西夏毅宗年号（公元 1057—1062）Duodu, title of the reign of Emperor Yizong of the Western Xia Dynasty (1057-1062) during the Song Dynasty

duò（ㄉㄨㄛˋ）

驮 duò［驮子］（duò·zi）❶ 牲口驮（tuó）着的货物 pack; load carried by a pack-animal：把～卸下来，让牲口休息一会儿。Unload the animal and let it rest for a while. ❷〈量词 *classifier*〉用于牲口驮（tuó）着的货物［used of caravan goods］：来了三～货。Three loads of goods have arrived.

☞ tuó on p.1960

杕 duò 〈书 *fml.*〉 same as 舵 duò

☞ dì on p.427

剁(剁) duò 用刀向下砍 chop; cut: ～排骨 cut spareribs | 饺子馅儿～得很细 chop the stuffing for dumplings real fine | 他把柳条～成了三段。He chopped a willow branch into three pieces.

【剁斧石】duòfǔshí 一种人造石料,制作过程是用石屑、石粉、水泥等加水拌和,抹在建筑物的表面,半凝固后,用斧子剁出像经过细凿的石头那样的纹理 artificial stone made of stone powder and chips mixed with cement, with stone-like grains hacked out with an axe as it solidifies after being plastered on the walls of a building; also 剁假石 duòjiǎshí or 斩假石 zhǎnjiǎshí

饳 duò ☞ [馉饳] (gǔduò) on p.695

垛(垜、稑) duò ❶ 整齐地堆 pile up neatly; stack: 把晒干的稻草捆好～起来。Bale the hay and pile it up. ❷ 整齐地堆成的堆 pile; stack: 麦～stack of wheat | 砖～ pile of bricks | 柴火～ pile of firewood

☞ duǒ on p.501

【垛口】duòkǒu 指曲艺演员将好几句押韵的唱词一句紧接一句地唱出来 sing rhymed lines in regular succession

☞ duǒkǒu on p.501

【垛子】duò·zi 整齐地堆成的堆 stack; pile: 麦秸～ pile of wheat (stems)

☞ duǒ·zi on p.501

柮 duò ☞ [榾柮] (gǔduò) on p.697

柂(杝) duò 〈书 *fml.*〉 ❶ same as 舵 duò ❷ 沟通;引 communicate; connect; link

☞ yí on p.2261 and 杝 lí on p.1175

舵(柁) duò 船、飞机等控制方向的装置 rudder; helm: 掌～ be at the helm | 升降～ elevator | 方向～ rudder

☞ 柁 tuó on p.1961

【舵轮】duòlún 轮船、汽车等的方向盘 steering wheel; helm

【舵盘】duòpán same as 舵轮 duòlún

【舵手】duòshǒu ❶ 掌舵的人 steersman; helmsman ❷ 〈比喻 *fig.*〉把握方向的领导者 leader; helmsman

堕(墮) duò 落;掉 fall; sink: ～落 degenerate | ～地 fall on the ground | ～入海中 sink in the sea

☞ 隳 huī on p.858

【堕落】duòluò ❶ (思想、行为)往坏里变 (of morality or behaviour) degenerate; sink low: 腐化～ corruption and degeneration ❷ 沦落;流落(多见于早期白话 usu. in early vernacular) fall low; come down in the world: ～风尘 stoop to street-walking; be driven to prostitution

【堕马】duòmǎ 〈书 *fml.*〉从马上摔下来 fall from horseback

【堕胎】duò//tāi 人工流产 have an abortion

惰 duò 懒 (跟'勤'相对 as opposed to 'diligent') lazy; indolent: 懒～ lazy; slothful

【惰性】duòxìng ❶ 某些物质化学性质不活泼,不易跟其他物质发生化学反应的性质 inertia; inertness; (of chemical elements) quality of having little or no ability to react ❷ 不想改变生活和工作习惯的倾向(多指消极落后的) passivity; passive attitude (towards life and work)

【惰性气体】duòxìng qìtǐ 指氦、氖、氩、氪、氙、氡六个元素。它们化学性质极不活泼,一般不易跟其他元素化合。inert gas; any of the unreactive gaseous elements, such as helium, neon, argon, krypton, xenon, and radon; also 稀有气体 xīyǒu qìtǐ

媠 duò 〈书 *fml.*〉 same as 惰 duò

跺(跥、跢) duò 用力踏地 stamp (one's foot): ～脚 stamp one's foot

【跺脚】duò//jiǎo 脚用力踏地,表示着急、生气、悔恨等情绪 stamp one's foot (in anxiety, fury, resentment, etc.)

E

ē (ㄜ)

阿[1] ē ❶ 迎合；偏袒 play up to; pander to; cater to：～附 fawn on and echo; toady to and chime in with|～谀 fawn on; flatter; ingratiate oneself with sb.|刚直不～ upright and above flattery|～其所好 play up to sb.'s likes and tastes ❷〈书 *fml.*〉大的丘陵 big hill; large mound：崇～ lofty hill ❸〈书 *fml.*〉弯曲的地方（topography) twist; turn; bend：山～ mountain nook; col

阿[2] Ē 指山东东阿 Dong'e County in Shandong Province：～胶 E-gelatin; donkey-hide gelatin

☞ ā on p.1 and 啊 ·a on p.2

【阿附】ēfù〈书 *fml.*〉逢迎附和 curry favour with; ingratiate oneself with：～权贵 curry favour with the powerful and influential

【阿胶】ējiāo 中药上指用驴皮加水熬成的胶，原产山东东阿，有滋补养血的作用 E-gelatin; donkey-hide gelatin; traditional Chinese tonic for nourishing the blood, made by stewing donkey hide with water, orig. produced in Dong'e County in Shandong Province; also 驴皮胶 lǘpíjiāo

【阿弥陀佛】Ēmítuófó〈佛教 *Budd.*〉指西方极乐世界中最大的佛，也译作无量寿佛或无量光佛。信佛的人用做口头诵念的佛号，表示祈祷或感谢神灵等意思。Amitabha in Sanskrit; Buddha's attainment of Nirvana; It is also translated as Buddha of Eternal Life (Amitayus) or Buddha of Eternal Light. Buddhist pilgrims oft. chant this name to seek blessings from or express their gratitude to the Buddha.

【阿谀】ēyú 迎合别人的意思，说好听的话（含贬义 derog.）speak good things in order to cater to others：～奉承 flatter sb. so as to curry favour|～曲从 go against one's conscience to flatter sb.

婀 ē [婀娜]（ēnuó）〈书 *fml.*〉same as 婀娜 ēnuó

屙 ē〈方 *dial.*〉排泄（大小便）loosen the bowels and bladder; excrement or urine：～屎 take poop; poop|～尿 urinate; piss|～痢 suffer from dysentery

婴 ē ☞ [媕婴]（ān'ē）on p.12

婀 ē [婀娜]（ēnuó，旧读 formerly pronounced ěnuǒ)（姿态）柔软而美好（of posture) lithe and graceful; supple and elegant：～多姿 pretty and charming; graceful|体态～（of a woman's body) curvaceous; statuesque

痾 ē〈书 *fml.*〉病 disease; illness

é (ㄜ́)

讹（❶譌）é ❶ 错误 incorrect; mistake; error：～字 incorrect words|以～传～ circulate erroneous reports; spread a wrong message ❷ 讹诈 blackmail; extort; bluff：～钱 extort money by blackmail

【讹传】échuán 错误的传说 false or unfounded rumour：纯系～，切勿轻信。It's pure rumour; don't believe it.

【讹舛】échuǎn〈书 *fml.*〉（文字）错误；舛误（of words in a text) mistake; error：校订粗疏，～甚多。The book is full of mistakes because of the proofreader's carelessness.

【讹夺】éduó〈书 *fml.*〉same as 讹脱 étuō

【讹赖】élài〈方 *dial.*〉same as 讹诈 ézhà

【讹谬】émiù 错误；差错 mistake; error

【讹脱】étuō（文字上的）错误和脱漏（of words in a text) error and omission

【讹误】éwù（文字、记载）错误（of words or records) error：该文记述与史实不符，～颇多。There are many references that do not tally with historical facts in the article.

【讹诈】ézhà ❶ 假借某种理由向人强行索取财物 extort or blackmail on certain grounds; blackmail under false pretences：～钱财 extort money under false pretences ❷ 威胁恫吓 threaten; intimidate; imperil：核～ nuclear blackmail|政治～ political blackmail

吪 é〈书 *fml.*〉❶ 动；行动 move; act ❷ 化；教化 cultivate; educate; train

囮 é [囮子]（é·zi）捕鸟时用来引诱同类鸟的鸟 decoy bird; bird used to lure other birds of the same variety; also 圝子 yóu·zi

俄[1] é〈书 *fml.*〉时间很短；突然间 in a short time; suddenly; all of a sudden：～顷 soon; presently; shortly|～而阴云密布。The sky was soon covered with dark clouds.

俄[2] É ❶ 指俄罗斯帝国 Russian Empire (1721-1917) ❷ 指俄罗斯联邦 Russian

Federation ❸〈旧时 *old*〉指苏联 another name for the Union of the Soviet Socialist Republics

【俄而】é'ér〈书 *fml.*〉不久;一会儿 soon afterwards; then; presently: ～日出,光照海上。Presently the sun rose and shone over the sea.

【俄尔】é'ěr same as 俄而 é'ér

【俄罗斯族】Éluósīzú ❶ 我国少数民族之一,主要分布在新疆 Russian people, a minority ethnic group in China, mainly inhabiting the Xinjiang Uygur Autonomous Region ❷ 俄罗斯联邦的人数最多的民族 Russians, who comprise the overwhelming majority of the population of the Russian Federation

【俄顷】éqǐng〈书 *fml.*〉很短的时间 all of a sudden; presently; suddenly

【俄延】éyán〈书 *fml.*〉拖延;迟延 delay; put off

莪 é ☞ below

【莪蒿】éhāo 多年生草本植物,叶子像针,花黄绿色,头状花序。生在水边。sagebrush (*Artemisia*); herbaceous perennial shrub which grows by the water, and has wedge-shaped leaves, yellowish-green flowers and head-shaped inflorescence

【莪术】ézhú 多年生草本植物,叶子长椭圆形,根状茎圆柱形或卵形,花黄色。根状茎可入药,叫郁金。aromatic turmeric (*Curcuma aromatica*); herbaceous perennial plant with oval leaves, yellow flowers, and cylindrical or egg-shaped tuberous rhizomes that are used as a medicine called *yujin*

哦 é〈书 *fml.*〉吟咏 chant: 吟～ chant ☞ ó on p. 1431 and ò on p. 1431

峨(峩) é〈书 *fml.*〉高 high; lofty; towering: 巍～lofty; towering|～冠博带 tall hat and broad waistband (worn by the literati in ancient China)

【峨冠博带】éguān bódài 高高的帽子和宽大的衣带,古时士大夫的装束 high hat and broad waistband worn by the literati in ancient China

涐 É 古水名,就是现在的大渡河 old name for today's Dadu River

娥 é 美女 pretty woman; beauty: 宫～ palace maid|娇～ beautiful woman

【娥眉】éméi ❶ 形容美人细长而弯的眉毛 beautiful eyebrows of a pretty woman: 皓齿～(形容女子美貌) bright white teeth and beautiful eyebrows (of a pretty woman) ❷ 指美人 pretty person; beauty ‖ also 蛾眉 éméi

睋 é〈书 *fml.*〉❶ 望;看 look; watch ❷ 突然;不久 suddenly; soon

锇 é 金属元素,符号 Os (osmium)。灰蓝色,质硬而脆,比重是金属中最大的。用于制催化剂等,锇铱合金可作钟表、仪器的轴承。osmium (Os); metallic element, greyish-blue in colour, and hard and brittle of texture, having the densest gravity among all metals, used in making catalysts. The alloy of osmium and iridium is used for gears in timepieces and other instruments.

鹅(鵞、䳘) é 家禽,羽毛白色或灰色,额部有橙黄色或黑褐色肉质突起,雄的突起较大。颈长,嘴扁而阔,脚有蹼,能游泳,耐寒,吃青草、谷物、蔬菜、鱼虾等。goose (*Anser domestica*); domesticated bird with white or grey feathers, a long neck, a flat and wide beak, webbed feet, and an orange or brown fleshy crown on its forehead, the male having a bigger crown than the female, good at swimming, cold-resistant, and feeding on grass, grain, vegetables, fish, shrimp, etc.

【鹅蛋脸】édànliǎn 指微长而丰满,上部略圆,下部略尖的脸庞 goose-egg face; oval face with a round upper part and a relatively pointed jaw

【鹅黄】éhuáng 像小鹅绒毛那样的颜色;嫩黄 soft yellow; colour of the down of a young goose

【鹅卵石】éluǎnshí 卵石的一种,直径 40—150 毫米左右,是一种天然的建筑材料 a type of cobblestone, usu. with a diameter of 40-150 mm., used as a natural building material; ☞ 卵石 luǎnshí on p. 1270

【鹅毛】émáo 鹅的羽毛 goose feather;〈比喻 *fig.*〉极轻微的东西 sth. as light as a goose feather: 千里送～,礼轻情意重。The gift itself may be as light as goose feather, but coming from a faraway place, it conveys deep feelings.

【鹅绒】éróng 鹅的绒毛,细软,能保温,可以絮被褥等 goose down; fine, soft and warm and used to make quilts

【鹅行鸭步】é xíng yā bù 像鹅和鸭子那样走路,形容行动迟缓 move slowly; waddle along like a duck or a goose; also 鸭步鹅行 yā bù é xíng

【鹅掌风】ézhǎngfēng〈中医 *Chin. med.*〉指手癣 fungal infection on the hand; tinea manuum

【鹅掌楸】ézhǎngqiū 落叶乔木,茎高 17—20 米,叶子大,形状像鹅掌,花黄绿色,果穗长纺锤形。是世界上珍贵的树种之一。产于我国江西、湖北等地。Chinese tulip tree (*Liriodendron chinense*); yellow poplar; one of the most precious timber trees in the world, usu. 17-20 metres high, with large, goose-feet-like leaves, yellowish-green blossoms and cone-like clusters of terminally winged fruit, growing in Jiangxi and Hubei provinces in China

蛾 é 蛾子 moth ☞ yǐ on p. 2270

【蛾眉】éméi same as 娥眉 éméi

【蛾子】é·zi 昆虫,腹部短而粗,有四个带鳞片的翅膀。多在夜间活动,常飞向灯光。其中很多种是农业害虫。moth (*Lepidoptera*); winged insect with a round belly and four scaly wings, which is active at night and attracted to light. There are a variety of moths, most of which are harmful to agriculture.

额[1] é ❶ 人的眉毛以上头发以下的部分,也指某些动物头部大致与此相当的部位 forehead; flat part of a human face above the eyes and below the hair; similar part of animal's head; 通称 generally callad 额头 é·tóu ❷ 牌匾 board; tablet: 匾～ board with inscriptions | 横～ horizontal board inscribed with words

额[2] é 规定的数目 specified number or amount; quota: 名～ specified number of people to be enrolled; vacancies | 定～ quota; norm | 总～ total amount; gross amount | 余～ balance; remaining sum | 空～ vacancy yet to be filled; opening | 超～ overfulfil | ～外 extra; additional; added

【额定】édìng 规定数目的 specified or set number; quota: ～人数 quota of people | ～工资 salary cap

【额角】éjiǎo 额的两旁 frontal eminence

【额鲁特】Élǔtè 瓦剌(Wǎlà)在清代的称呼 Oirad Mongols; name of a Mongolian tribe during the Qing Dynasty

【额手称庆】é shǒu chēng qìng 以手加额,表示庆幸 raise one's hand to one's forehead as a sign of joy or solace

【额数】éshù 规定的数目;定额 prescribed number or amount; quota

【额头】é·tóu 额[1] ① 的通称 general term for forehead

【额外】éwài 超出规定的数量或范围 extra; additional; above-norm; beyond specified amount or range: ～负担 added burden | ～开支 extra expenses

ě (ㄜˇ)

恶(惡、噁) ě [恶心] (ě·xin) ❶ 有要呕吐的感觉 feel nauseated; feel like vomitting; feel queasy; feel sick: 胃里不舒服,一阵一阵地～。I feel like throwing up time and again. ❷ 令人感到厌恶 disgusting; repugnant: 这种丑事,让人～。This scandal is disgusting. ❸ 〈方 *dial.*〉揭人短处,使难堪 expose sb.'s weaknesses to make him embarrassed; humiliate: 他太抠门儿,得找个机会～～他。He's just too stingy; let's find an opportunity to show him up.

☞ è on p. 506, wū on p. 2018 and wù on p. 2039

è (ㄜˋ)

厄(戹、❶阨) è 〈书 *fml.*〉❶ 险要的地方 place of strategic importance: 险～ dangerous but strategically important place; strategic pass ❷ 灾难;困苦 disaster; catastrophe; hardship: 困～ dire straits; difficult situation | ～运 adversity; misfortune ❸ 受困 be stranded; be in distress: 海轮～于风浪。The liner was caught in a storm.

【厄境】èjìng 苦难的境遇 miserable plight; adverse situation; predicament: 身处～ be in an adverse situation

【厄难】ènàn 灾难;苦难 disaster; distress; misery: 屡遭～ suffer from repeated misfortune

【厄运】èyùn 困苦的遭遇;不幸的命运 adversity; misfortune

苊 è 碳氢化合物的一类,化学式 $C_{12}H_{10}$。无色针状结晶,可做媒染剂。acenaphthene; a kind of needle-shaped, crystallized hydrocarbon with the chemical formula $C_{12}H_{10}$, colourless and used as a mordant

扼 è ❶ 用力掐住 clutch; grip with force: ～杀 kill by strangulation; strangle; smother; throttle ❷ 把守;控制 guard; control: ～守 hold (a strategic place); guard | ～制 restrain; control

【扼杀】èshā ❶ 掐住脖子弄死 kill by strangulation; strangle sb. to death ❷ 〈比喻 *fig.*〉压制、摧残使不能存在或发展 put high pressure on or torment sth. so as to kill or prevent its development: ～新生事物 nip new things in the bud

【扼守】èshǒu 把守(险要的地方) guard (a place of strategic importance)

【扼死】èsǐ 掐住脖子弄死 kill by gripping tightly at sb.'s neck; strangle sb. to death

【扼腕】èwàn 〈书 *fml.*〉用一只手握住自己另一只手的手腕,表示振奋、惋惜等情绪 hold one's own wrist as a sign of one's excitement, regret, etc.: ～叹息 sigh while wringing one's hands

【扼要】èyào 抓住要点(多指发言或写文章 of speech or article) to the point: 简明～ brief and to the point

【扼制】èzhì 抑制;控制 bring under control; control; restrain; check: ～心里的怒火 check one's anger; bring one's anger under control | ～通往内河的航道 hold the access to a water way leading to inland rivers

呃 è 〈叹词 *interj.*〉表示感叹、提醒等 [expressing an exclamation, or as a reminder, etc.]: ～,你还在这里啊! Why, you're still here! | ～,别忘了带钥匙。Oh, don't forget to bring your key.

☞ ·e on p.508

【呃逆】ènì 由于膈肌痉挛，急促吸气后，声门突然关闭，发出声音。hiccup; loud sound caused by a sudden tightening of a muscle just below the chest, shortness of breath and the closing of the glottis; 通称 popularly known as 打嗝儿 dǎ//gér

轭 è 牛马等拉东西时架在脖子上的器具 yoke; wooden bar fastened over the neck of a draft ox or horse

呝 è〈书 *fml.*〉❶ same as 呃 è ❷ 形容鸟鸣声 chirping of a bird

垩(堊) è ❶ 白垩 chalk, soft white earthen limestone ❷〈书 *fml.*〉用白垩涂饰 whiten with chalk ❸〈方 *dial.*〉施(肥) spread manure; apply fertilizer to the fields

恶(惡) è ❶ 很坏的行为；犯罪的事情(跟'善'相对 as opposed to 'benevolence') evil conduct; vice; wickedness, vicious; crime: 作～ do evil | 罪大～极 commit atrocious crimes | 惩～劝善 punish evildoers and encourage people to do good | 疾～如仇 hate evil like an enemy; detest evil ❷ 凶恶；凶狠；凶猛 fierce; ferocious: ～霸 local tyrant or despot | ～骂 shout vicious abuse | ～战 fierce battle ❸ 恶劣；坏 bad; evil; wicked: ～习 bad habit | ～意 wicked intention

☞ ě on p. 505, wū on p. 2018 and wù on p. 2039

【恶霸】èbà 独霸一方，欺压人民的坏人 local tyrant who controls an area and bullies its people

【恶变】èbiàn 医学上指肿瘤由良性转变成恶性 (med.) (of a tumour) grow from benign to malignant

【恶病质】èbìngzhì 医学上指人体显著消瘦、贫血、精神衰颓等全身机能衰竭的现象，多由癌症和其他严重慢性病引起 (med.) cachexia; physical symptoms of sudden emaciation, anaemia and depression and deterioration of other functions, usu. caused by cancer and other serious chronic diseases

【恶臭】èchòu ❶ 难闻的臭气 foul smell; stench: 一股～让人喘不过气来。A foul smell struck the nostrils, choking everyone at the scene. ❷ 很臭 stinking; foul: 名声～ foul reputation; notoriety

【恶斗】èdòu 凶猛激烈的争斗 fierce fight; ferocious fight: 一场～ a fierce fight

【恶毒】èdú (心术、手段、语言)阴险狠毒 (of intention, means and language) vicious; malicious; venomous: 用心～harbour evil | ～攻击 vicious attack

【恶感】ègǎn 不满或仇恨的情绪 dissatisfaction or hatred; malicious mood

【恶贯满盈】è guàn mǎn yíng 作恶极多，已到末日 be guilty of too many crimes and deserve judgement; face retribution for all of one's iniquity

【恶棍】ègùn 凶恶无赖，欺压群众的坏人 ruffian; scoundrel; uncontrollable, unpleasant person who bullies others

【恶果】èguǒ 坏结果；坏的下场 deplorable result; bad consequence: 自食～ suffer the consequences of one's own evildoings; sow the wind and reap the whirlwind | 任其发展，会引起严重～。If left unchecked, it will cause serious consequences.

【恶狠狠】èhěnhěn (～的 èhěnhěn·de)形容非常凶狠 fierce; ferocious; venomous: ～地瞪了他一眼 give him a malicious stare

【恶化】èhuà ❶ 向坏的方面变 deteriorate; go downhill; take a turn for the worse: 防止病情～ prevent the deterioration of a disease | 两国关系日趋～。Bilateral relations are going downhill with each passing day. ❷ 使变坏 worsen: 军备竞赛，～了国际局势。Military competition aggravated the world situation.

【恶疾】èjí 令人厌恶的、不容易治好的疾病 nasty, hard-to-cure disease

【恶浪】èlàng ❶ 来势凶猛的浪头 surging waves; crashing waves; torrential waves: 狂风～ howling wind and surging waves | ～掀天 huge cresting waves rising high into the sky ❷〈比喻 *fig.*〉邪恶的势力 evil forces

【恶劣】èliè 很坏 bad, vile; odious: 品行～ be morally corrupt | 手段～ mean or dirty tricks | 环境～ adverse circumstances | ～的作风 abominable work style | ～的天气 bad weather; foul weather

【恶露】èlù 产妇分娩后由子宫排出的余血和浊液。正常情况下，产后 2 至 3 周完全排尽。lochia; blood and liquid expelled out of the fetus after a woman gives birth; In normal cases, lochia is completely expelled within two to three weeks after delivery.

【恶名】èmíng 坏名声 bad reputation; infamy: 蒙受～ (unfairly) get a bad reputation; be wronged with a bad reputation

【恶魔】èmó ❶〈佛教 *Budd.*〉称阻碍佛法及一切善事的恶神、恶鬼 evil spirit; term in Buddhism for all that prevents the spread of Buddhist doctrines or a good deed ❷〈比喻 *fig.*〉十分凶恶的人 vicious person; ferocious person

【恶念】èniàn 邪恶的想法；犯罪的念头 vicious idea; wicked intention; evil idea: 心生～。An evil idea arose in his mind.

【恶气】èqì ❶ 难闻的气味；臭气 foul smell; bad odour: ～熏人 be unexpectedly assailed by a foul smell ❷ 指受到的欺压、侮辱等 insult; humiliation: 他闷闷不乐，是受谁的～了？He's in low spirits. Who has humiliated him? ❸ 指心中的怨恨、不满等 grievance; resentment; dissatisfaction: 出了一口～ vent one's grievances; redress one's grievances

【恶人】èrén 品质恶劣的人;心肠恶毒的人 morally corrupt person; vicious person; wicked person

【恶煞】èshà 迷信的人指凶神 ogre; ferocious god;〈比喻 *fig.*〉凶恶的人 wicked and ferocious person:凶神～ fiends; fierce demons

【恶少】èshào 品行恶劣、胡作非为的年轻人 young ruffian; rogue; morally corrupted and dissipated young man from a wealthy or influential family:洋场～ rich urban young rogue

【恶声】èshēng ❶ 谩骂的话;坏话 abusive language; angry curses:～对骂 curse each other angrily; call each other names angrily ❷〈书 *fml.*〉坏名声 bad reputation; infamy

【恶声恶气】è shēng è qì 形容语调、态度凶狠 angry tone and ferocious attitude; angry voices and rude remarks

【恶俗】èsú ❶ 不好的风俗;陋俗 bad practices or customs ❷ 粗俗;庸俗 vulgar:语言～ vulgar language|趣味～ vulgar tastes

【恶习】èxí 坏习惯,多指赌博、吸食毒品等 bad habit, usu. referring to gambling, drug abuse, etc.:沾染～ pick up a bad habit; fall into evil ways|痛改～ resolutely reform a bad habit; make a clear break from one's evil ways

【恶性】èxìng 能产生严重后果的 of serious consequences; malignant; pernicious; vicious:～循环 vicious circle|～肿瘤 malignant tumour|～事故 fatal accident

【恶性循环】èxìng xúnhuán 若干事物互为因果,循环不已,越来越坏 go from bad to worse; vicious circle

【恶性肿瘤】èxìng zhǒngliú 肿瘤的一种,周围没有包膜,细胞异常增生,形状、大小很不规则,与正常组织之间的界限不明显。能在体内转移,破坏性很大。癌和肉瘤都属于恶性肿瘤。malignant tumour; tumour that has no membrane covering it, whose cells grow abnormally and quickly in irregular shapes and sizes, with no clear demarcation between the tumour and the normal tissues; possessing destructive abilities, it is able to move to other parts of the body. Cancer and sarcoma are malignant tumours; 通称 generally called 毒瘤 dúliú

【恶意】èyì 不良的居心;坏的用意 evil or ill intention; malice:一句玩笑,并无～。It's only a joke. No hard feelings.|不要把人家的一片好心当成～。Don't treat people's good intentions as wicked.

【恶语】èyǔ 粗野的言语;恶毒的话 rude remarks; vicious slander:秽言～ foul language; obscene language|～伤人。Vicious remarks hurt people.

【恶战】èzhàn 非常激烈的战斗 fierce battle; savage fight

【恶仗】èzhàng 恶战 fierce battle; savage fight

【恶浊】èzhuó 污秽;不干净 foul; filthy; dirty:空气～ foul air

【恶作剧】èzuòjù 捉弄耍笑,使人难堪 embarrass sb. by making practical jokes or acting mischievously:不要搞～。No more of your practical jokes!

饿 è ❶ 肚子空,想吃东西(跟'饱'相对 as opposed to 'full') be hungry; have an empty stomach; feel hungry:饥～ go hungry; starve|～虎扑食 like a starved tiger pouncing on its prey ❷ 使挨饿 starve:牲口多拉几趟不要紧,可别～着它。It doesn't matter if you want to use the draught animals on a few more hauls — just please don't starve them!

【饿饭】è//fàn 挨饿 go hungry; starve

【饿虎扑食】è hǔ pū shí〈比喻 *fig.*〉动作迅速而猛烈 like a hungry tiger pouncing on its prey; swift and powerful action; also 饿虎扑羊 è hǔ pū yáng

【饿殍】èpiǎo〈书 *fml.*〉饿死的人 people who were starved to death; people who died of famine; victim of starvation

鄂 È ❶ 湖北的别称 another name for Hubei Province ❷ 姓 a surname

【鄂博】èbó 敖包 Mongolian cairn or obo; heap of sand, stones or earth set up as a road marker

【鄂伦春族】Èlúnchūnzú 我国少数民族之一,分布在内蒙古和黑龙江 Oroqen (Olunchun) people; one of China's ethnic groups inhabiting Inner Mongolia and Heilongjiang

【鄂温克族】Èwēnkèzú 我国少数民族之一,分布在内蒙古和黑龙江 Ewenki (Owenk) people; one of China's ethnic groups living in Inner Mongolia and Heilongjiang

阏 è〈书 *fml.*〉❶ 堵塞 block; stop; close up ❷ 闸板 sluice-gate

☞ yān on p. 2201

谔 è [谔谔]〈书 *fml.*〉形容直话直说 speak frankly; call a spade a spade:千人之诺诺,不如一士之～(有许多人说顺从奉承的话,不如有一个人直言不讳)。It is better to have one man speaking out the truth than a thousand nodding obediently.

萼 è 花萼 calyx

【萼片】èpiàn 环列在花的最外面一轮的叶状薄片,一般呈绿色。花萼是由若干萼片组成的。sepal; thin, oft. green, leaf-like parts surrounding the outmost petals of a flower; part of the calyx of a flower; (图见 ☞ figure for 花 huā on p. 826)

遏 è 阻止;禁止 check; hold back; prohibit:～止 check; hold back; restrain|响～行云 (of singing) be so resonant as to stop the passing clouds; pierce the clouds|怒不可～

cannot restrain one's anger; be livid at sb./sth.; boil with indignation

【遏抑】èyì 压制;抑止 suppress; contain; keep down:~不住胸中的怒火 cannot restrain one's anger; boil with indignation|百感交集,难以~ hardly able to contain chaotic feelings welling up in one's heart

【遏止】èzhǐ 用力阻止 hold back with force; check; restrain:洪流滚滚,不可~。There is no holding back the torrential tide.

【遏制】èzhì 制止;控制 restrain; control; keep within limits:~对方的攻势 restrain the rival's momentum of attack|~不住的激情 uncontrollable passion

遌 è〈书 *fml.*〉遇到 meet; come across

崿 è〈书 *fml.*〉山崖 cliff:危岩峭~ grotesque monoliths and precipitous cliffs

愕 è 惊讶;发愣 stunned; astounded; dazed:~然 stunned; astounded|惊~ shocked;

【愕然】èrán 形容吃惊 stunned; astounded:意外的消息传来,大家都为之~。Everyone was shocked by the unexpected news.

頞 è〈书 *fml.*〉鼻梁 bridge of a nose

搤 è〈书 *fml.*〉same as 扼 è

腭 è 口腔的上壁。前部由骨和肌肉构成,叫硬腭,后部由结缔组织和肌肉构成,叫软腭 palate; roof of the mouth, consisting of an anterior bony portion called the hard palate and a posterior muscular portion called the soft palate; 通称 generally called 上膛 shàngtáng

【腭裂】èliè 先天性畸形,常与唇裂同时出现。患者的腭部部分或全部裂开,饮食不方便,说话不清楚。cleft palate; congenital defect in which a longitudinal fissure partly or completely cleaves the roof of the mouth and the lip, making it difficult for the sufferer to eat, drink and speak clearly

碍 è [碍嘉](Èjiā)地名,在云南 name of a place in Yunnan Province

鹗 è 鸟,背部褐色,头、颈和腹部白色。性凶猛。在树上或岩石上筑巢,常在水面上飞翔,吃鱼类。osprey (*Pandion haliceetus*); fish hawk; sea eagle (*Haliaeetus*); bird having a brown back, white head, neck and belly and a ferocious nature, it builds nests on trees and rocks, oft. flying over water, and feeding on fish; 通称 also known as 鱼鹰 yúyīng

锷 è〈书 *fml.*〉刀剑的刃 blade of a sword

颚 è ❶ 某些节肢动物摄取食物的器官 mandible; organ of some arthropods, used to take food:上~ upper mandible|下~ lower mandible ❷ same as 腭 è

噩 è 凶恶惊人的 evil and terrifying:~梦 nightmare|~耗 terrible news of the death of a loved one

【噩耗】èhào 指亲近的人死亡的消息 terrible news of the death of sb. beloved

【噩梦】èmèng 可怕的梦 terrifying dream; nightmare

【噩运】èyùn 坏的运气 bad luck

【噩兆】èzhào 坏的兆头 ill or bad omen

鳄(鱷) è 爬行动物的一属,大的身体长达3—6米,四肢短,尾巴长,全身有灰褐色的硬皮。善于游泳,性凶恶,捕食鱼、蛙和鸟类,有的也吃人、畜。多产在热带和亚热带,其中扬子鳄是我国的特产。crocodile (*Crocodylidae*); alligator; a kind of reptile, the largest of which is 3-6 meters long, with short limbs, a long tail and grey and brown hard skin; of a ferocious nature, the crocodile is a good swimmer and feeds on fish, frogs, birds, and even domesticated animals and sometimes human beings. Crocodiles mostly live in tropical and subtropical regions, among which the Chinese alligator is a rare species; 俗称 popularly known as 鳄鱼 èyú

【鳄鱼眼泪】èyú yǎnlèi 西方古代传说,鳄鱼吞食人畜,一边吃,一边掉眼泪 crocodile tears, Western legend has it that the crocodile sheds tears while swallowing humans and livestock; 〈比喻 *fig.*〉坏人的假慈悲 An evil person puts on a false show of compassion.

·e (·ㄜ)

呃 ·e〈助词 *aux.*〉用在句末,表示赞叹或惊异的语气[used at the end of a sentence to express admiration or surprise]:红霞映山崖~! Oh, look at the red glow over the cliffs!

☞ è on p. 505

ē (ㄝ)

欸(誒) ē 又 also ēi〈叹词 *interj.*〉表示招呼[calling attention]:~,你快来! Hey! Come over here.

é (ㄝˊ)

欸(誒) é 又 also éi〈叹词 *interj.*〉表示诧异[used to expressing surprise]:~,他怎么走了! Why, he's gone!

ě (ㄝˇ)

欸(誒) ě 又 also ěi〈叹词 *interj.*〉表示不以为然[expressing disapproval]:~,你这话可不对呀! Huh, you're wrong to say so!

ê（ㄝ̀）

欸（誒）ê 又 also èi〈叹词 *interj*.〉表示答应或同意[used to express approval or consent]：～，我这就来！Yeah, I'm coming!｜～，就这么办！All right! Let's do it this way!

☞ āi on p.4 and ǎi on p.5

ēn（ㄣ）

奀 ēn〈方 *dial*.〉瘦小（多用于人名 mostly used in names）thin and small

恩 ēn ❶ 恩惠 favour; kindness; grace：～德 favour｜～深似海 infinite kindness; numerous favours｜忘～负义 be ungrateful; bite the hand that feeds one; ingratitude ❷（Ēn）姓 a surname

【恩爱】ēn'ài（夫妻）亲热（of a married couple）be deeply in love with each other; conjugal love：～夫妻 affectionate couple; couple deeply in love｜小两口儿十分～。The young couple love each other affectionately.

【恩赐】ēncì 原指帝王给予赏赐，现泛指因怜悯而施舍（orig. of an emperor）grant favours and rewards to sb.;（in a broad sense）give out of compassion

【恩德】ēndé 恩惠 benevolence; favour; kindness; grace

【恩典】endiǎn ❶ 恩惠 favour; kindness; grace ❷ 给予恩惠 be clement to; bestow a favour or kindness on sb.：恳请大人～。I beg for Your Excellency's clemency.

【恩断义绝】ēn duàn yì jué 感情破裂，情义断绝。多指夫妻离异。（of feelings）be estranged（mostly used to refer to a divorce）

【恩惠】ēnhuì 给予的或受到的好处 favour; grace; kindness; bounty

【恩将仇报】ēn jiāng chóu bào 用仇恨报答恩惠 requite kindness with enmity; return hate for love; bite the hand that feeds one

【恩情】ēnqíng 深厚的情义；恩惠 loving kindness; favour：报答～ repay sb.'s kindness｜～似海深 kindness as deep as the ocean

【恩人】ēnrén 对自己有大恩的人 benefactor; person who confers benefit; kindly helper：救命～ lifesaver

【恩师】ēnshī 称对自己有恩情的师傅或老师 esteemed teacher; honourable master, form of address for a master or teacher to whom one owes a debt of deep gratitude

【恩同再造】ēn tóng zài zào 形容恩惠极大，如同重新给予生命 extraordinary kindness tantamount to giving sb. a new lease on life

【恩怨】ēnyuàn 恩惠和仇恨（多偏指仇恨 meaning resentment in most cases）gratitude and resentment：～分明 know clearly whom one should love or hate｜不计个人～ not allow oneself to be swayed by personal feelings

【恩泽】ēnzé 称帝王或官吏给予臣民的恩惠 bounties bestowed by a monarch or an official

蒽 ēn 有机化合物，化学式 $C_{14}H_{10}$。无色晶体，有荧光，是菲的同分异构体。用来制染料等。anthracene; chemical formula $C_{14}H_{10}$; organic chemical compound, crystal-shaped and colourless with a slight blue fluorescence; the isomer of phenanthrene, and used as a colouring agent

èn（ㄣ̀）

摁 èn（用手）按（with the hand）press：～电铃 ring a bell; press or push the button of an electric bell｜～动快门 press or click the shutter｜一把将他～倒在地 pin him down on the ground

【摁钉儿】èndīngr 图钉 thumbtack; push-pin

【摁扣儿】ènkòur 子母扣儿 snap fastener; snap buttons

ēng（ㄥ）

鞥 ēng〈书 *fml*.〉马缰绳 reins for a horse; halter

ér（ㄦ́）

儿[1]（兒）ér ❶ 小孩子 child; kid; tot 婴～ infant; baby; toddler｜幼～ kid｜～童 child ❷ 年轻的人（多指青年男子 mostly referring to young men）youngster; youth：男～ young man｜健～ healthy young man｜～女英雄 heroic young men and women ❸ 儿子 son：～孙 son and grandson｜～媳 daughter-in-law｜生～育女 raise children｜妻～老小 wife, parents and children; family ❹ 雄性的 male：～马 male horse; stallion

儿[2]（兒）ér〈后缀 *suffix*〉（注音作 r transcribed as 'r' in *Pinyin*）❶ 名词后缀，主要有下面几种作用[used as a noun suffix, which functions as follows]：a）表示微小，如：盆儿、棍儿、窟窿儿、小车儿[added after a noun to indicate smallness, such as 'little basin', 'small stick', 'tiny hole' and 'small vehicle'] b）表示词性变化，如：吃儿、盖儿、卷（juǎn）儿（动词名词化）；亮儿、热闹儿、零碎儿（形容词名词化）[added after a verb or an adjective to turn it into a noun, such as 'food', 'cover', 'roll'（the verb turned into a noun）; 'light', 'bustling scene' and 'odds and ends' (the adjective turned into a noun)] c)表示具体事物抽象化,如:门儿、根儿、油水儿[added after a concrete noun to turn it into an abstract noun, e.g. 'a way to do sth.', 'origin' and 'benefit'] d)区别不同事物,如:白面—白面儿(海洛因),老家—老家儿(父母和家中其他长辈)[added to a noun to change its original meaning, e.g. 白面 (wheat flour) becomes 白面儿(heroin), 老家 (hometown) becomes 老家儿 (one's parents and other members of the older generation)] ❷ 少数动词的后缀 [used as a suffix for a limited number of verbs]:玩～ play | 火～ flare up; ☞ 儿化 érhuà

☞ 兒 Ní on p.1404

【儿歌】 érgē 为儿童创作的、适合儿童唱的歌谣 children's song; nursery rhymes

【儿化】 érhuà 汉语普通话和某些方言中的一种语音现象,就是后缀'儿'字不自成音节,而和前头的音节合在一起,使前一音节的韵母成为卷舌韵母。例如'花儿'的发音是 huār,不是 huā'ér。phonetic phenomenon in standard Chinese and some dialects, where the suffix '儿 ér' is itself not a syllable but when used together with a syllable, and the vowel in the preceding syllable becomes a retroflex one, e.g. the pronunciation of 花儿 is 'huār', not 'huā'ér'.

【儿皇帝】 érhuángdì 五代时,石敬瑭勾结契丹,建立后晋,对契丹主自称儿皇帝。后来泛指投靠外国,取得统治地位的卖国贼。puppet emperor; during the Five Dynasties, Shi Jingtang set up the Later Jin Dynasty with the help of the Khitan Kingdom and called himself an 'Erhuangdi' before the King of Khitan. The term was later widely used to refer to a traitor who comes to power with the support of a foreign force.

【儿科】 érkē 医院中专门为儿童治病的一科 department of paediatrics, that treats children in a hospital; also 小儿科 xiǎo'érkē

【儿郎】 érláng ❶ 男儿;男子 young man; man ❷ 儿子 son ❸ 称士兵或喽啰 soldiers; men:三千～ three thousand troops

【儿马】 érmǎ 公马 male horse; stallion

【儿男】 érnán ❶ 男子汉 man:见义勇为的好～ upright young man ready to help others ❷ 男孩儿 boy:只有一女,别无～ only have a daughter but no son

【儿女】 érnǚ ❶ 子女 sons and daughters; children:把～抚养成人 bring up children ◇英雄的中华～ heroic sons and daughters of the Chinese nation ❷ 男女 man and woman:～情长(指过分看重情爱或与家人之间的感情) abiding love between a man and woman, or affection for one's family

【儿孙】 érsūn 儿子和孙子,泛指后代 sons and grandsons; posterity; (in a broad sense) descendants

【儿童】 értóng 较幼小的未成年人(年纪比'少年'小 younger than 'juveniles') children; kids:～读物 readings for children

【儿童节】 Értóng Jié 六一儿童节 International Children's Day, which falls on June 1

【儿童团】 Értóngtuán 民主革命时期中国共产党在革命根据地领导建立的少年儿童组织 Children's Corps; children's organization set up in revolutionary bases by the Chinese Communist Party during the National Democratic Revolution

【儿童文学】 értóng wénxué 为少年儿童创作的文学作品。具有适应少年儿童的年龄、智力和兴趣等特点。children's literature; literary works catered to the age, intelligence and interests of children

【儿媳妇儿】 érxí·fur 儿子的妻子 daughter-in-law

【儿戏】 érxì 像小孩子游戏那样闹着玩儿 have fun by playing games like children; 〈比喻 *fig.*〉对工作或事情不负责、不认真 take an irresponsible and careless attitude towards one's work or sth.:视同～ regard sth. as a trifling matter | 不能拿工作任务当～。Don't treat your work as inconsequential.

【儿子】 ér·zi 男孩子(对父母而言) (in relation to parents) son:二～ second son ◇ 人民的好～ good son of the people

而 ér ❶〈连词 *conj.*〉(不连接名词 not used to connect nouns) and a)连接语意相承的成分 [used to connect two parts that are consistent in meaning]:伟大～艰巨的任务 great and arduous task | 战～胜之 fight and defeat sb. | 取～代之 replace sth. or sb. | 我们正从事一个伟大的事业,～伟大的事业必须有最广泛的群众的参加和支持。We're undertaking a great cause, and we must have the widest participation and support of the masses. b)连接肯定和否定互相补充的成分[used to connect an affirmative element and a negative element that complement each other]:栀子花的香,浓～不烈,清～不淡。The fragrance of the gardenia is strong but not pungent, light but not bland. | 马克思主义叫我们看问题不要从抽象的定义出发,～要从客观存在的事实出发。Marxism teaches us to look at things from the perspective of objective, existing facts rather than abstract definitions. c)连接语意相反的成分,表示转折 [used to connect two elements opposite in meaning that show a contrast]:如果能集中生产～不集中,就会影响改进技术、提高生产。If we could not centralize production where we could, this will affect the improvement of our technology and output of products. d)连接事理上前后相因的成分 [used to connect cause and effect]:因困难～畏惧～退却～消极的人,不会有任何成就。

A person who flinches and takes a passive attitude in the face of difficulty will achieve nothing. ❷〈连词 *conj.*〉有'到'的意思［used to indicate change from one state to another］：一～再，再～三 again and again; time and again｜由秋～冬 from autumn to winter｜由南～北 from south to north ❸ 把表示时间或方式的成分连接到动词上面［used to connect an adverbial phrase of time or manner with a verb］：匆匆～来 come in a hurry｜挺身～出 step forward bravely; rise courageously; enter the scene boldly｜盘旋～上 spiral upwards｜相辅～行 go forward by helping each other ❹ 插在主语谓语中间，有'如果'的意思［inserted between subject and predicate to indicate a condition］：民族战争～不依靠人民大众，毫无疑义将不能取得胜利。A national war that does not rely on the support of the people is doubtlessly doomed.

【而后】érhòu 以后；然后 after that; then：确有把握～动手 start to work after one is certain of sth. 注意 **NOTE**：'以后'可以单用，表示从现在以后，'而后'不能单用。The phrase 以后 yǐhòu can be used independently to express the future, while the phrase 而后 érhòu can not be used independently.

【而今】érjīn same as 如今 rújīn

【而况】érkuàng〈连词 *conj.*〉何况 much less; let alone：这么多的事情一个人一天做完是困难的，～他又是新手。It is difficult for a person to finish so many things within a day, let alone a new hand like him. 注意 **NOTE**：'何况'前可以加'更、又'，'而况'前不能加。The characters 更 gèng and 又 yòu can be added before 何况 hékuàng but not before 而况 érkuàng.

【而立】érlì〈书 *fml.*〉《论语·为政》：'三十而立。'指年至三十，学有成就。后来用'而立'指人三十岁。'I took my stand at thirty', a sentence in *Analects·Governance* that means one has made some achievements at the age of thirty; later 而立 érlì came to refer to thirty years of age：年届～ thirty years old｜～之年 thirty years of age

【而且】érqiě〈连词 *conj.*〉表示进一步，前面往往有'不但、不仅'等跟它呼应［often preceded by 不但 bùdàn or 不仅 bùjǐn］and; but also：他不仅会开汽车，～还会修理。He cannot only drive a car but also repair it.｜不但战胜了各种灾害，～获得了丰收。(We) not only came through the natural disaster, but also had a bumper harvest.

【而已】éryǐ〈助词 *aux.*〉罢了 nothing more; nothing but; only：如此～，岂有他哉。That's all there is to it!｜我只不过是随便说说～，不必过于认真。That was only a casual remark on my part; don't take it too seriously.

洏 ér ☞ 涟洏 lián'ér on p.1197

栭 ér〈书 *fml.*〉❶ 斗拱 set of brackets on top of a column supporting the beam within and roof eaves without ❷ 朽木上生的蕈类 fungus that grows on rotten wood

輀（轜） ér〈书 *fml.*〉丧车 hearse：灵～ hearse

胹 ér〈书 *fml.*〉煮；煮烂 boil; boil sth. until it becomes soft

鸸 ér［鸸鹋］(érmiáo) 鸟，形状像鸵鸟，嘴短而扁，羽毛灰色或褐色。翅膀退化，腿长，有三趾，善于走，产在澳洲森林中，吃树叶和野果。emu (*Dromaius novaehollandiae*); large, flightless, ratite bird, resembling the ostrich but smaller, with a short, flat beak, grey or brown feathers, degenerating wings, long legs, and three-toed feet, inhabiting the forests of Australia, good at walking, and feeding on tree leaves and wild fruit

鲕 ér〈书 *fml.*〉鱼卵 fish roe

ěr（儿）

尔（爾） ěr〈书 *fml.*〉❶ 你 you：～曹 you people; you and your kind｜非～之过 not your fault ❷ 如此；这样 so; like that：果～ if so｜不过～～ just so-so｜何其相似乃～。What a striking similarity! ❸ 那；这 that; this：～日 that day｜～时 at that time ❹〈助词 *aux.*〉而已；罢了 only; just：无他，但手熟～。He's gone, I'm used to that. ❺ 形容词后缀（这类形容词多用做状语）［suffix to an adjective which is oft. used as an adverb］：率～ hastily; rashly｜卓～不群 be preeminent; be outstanding; rise above the common herd｜莞～而笑 give a winsome smile

【尔曹】ěrcáo〈书 *fml.*〉你们这些人 you people; you and your kind

【尔代节】Ěrdài Jié 开斋节(of Islamism) Lesser Bairam; Fast-Breaking Festival; *'Id al-Fitr*

【尔耳】ěr'ěr〈书 *fml.*〉如此罢了；如此而已 just so-so; nothing out of the ordinary：不过～。It's nothing out of the ordinary.｜聊复～。This is just a brief note in reply.

【尔格】ěrgé 功的单位，是 1 达因的力使物体在力的方向上移动 1 厘米所作的功 erg; centimetre-gramme-second unit of work or energy, equal to the work done by a force of one dyne to directly move a mass a distance of one centimetre

【尔后】ěrhòu 从此以后 thereafter; subsequently：前年在上海见过一面，～就不知他的去向了。I met him in Shanghai two years ago but have since had no idea of his whereabouts.

【尔虞我诈】ěr yú wǒ zhà 彼此猜疑,互相欺骗 mutual deception; each trying to outwit the other; also 尔诈我虞 ěr zhà wǒ yú

耳[1] ěr ❶ 耳朵 ear:～聋眼花 deaf ears and dim eyes|～闻目睹 hear with one's own ears and see with one's own eyes ❷ 形状像耳朵的东西 sth. in the shape of an ear:木～ edible black fungus|银～ tremella ❸ 位置在两旁的 on both sides; flank; side:～房 anteroom; smaller room on either side of the main room (usu. in a courtyard)|～门 smaller door on either side of a gate, or beside the main entrance

耳[2] ěr 〈书 *fml.*〉〈助词 *aux.*〉而已;罢了 only; just:想当然～。It is mere conjecture.|技止此～。The skill is just so-so.

【耳报神】ěrbàoshén 〈方 *dial.*〉〈比喻 *fig.*〉暗中通风报信的人(多含贬义 derog.) informer

【耳背】ěrbèi 听觉不灵 be hard of hearing; deaf:老人身体还硬朗,就是有点～。The old man is physically strong, but he is a bit hard of hearing.

【耳边风】ěrbiānfēng 耳边吹过的风 a puff of wind that passes through the ear; sth. that goes in one ear and out the other;〈比喻 *fig.*〉听过后不放在心上的话(多指劝告、嘱咐) unheeded advice; turn a deaf ear to; also 耳旁风 ěrpángfēng

【耳鬓厮磨】ěr bìn sī mó 指两人的耳朵和鬓发相接触,形容亲密相处(多指小儿女 oft. of a boy and a girl) play together ear to ear and temple to temple; be very intimate during childhood:青梅竹马,～ be childhood playmates and share the joys of innocent intimacy

【耳沉】ěrchén 〈方 *dial.*〉耳背 be hard of hearing; deaf; hearing impaired

【耳垂】ěrchuí (～儿 ěrchuír)耳郭的一部分,在耳轮的下面 earlobe; lower part of the helix; (图见 ☞ figure for 耳朵 ěr·duo)

【耳聪目明】ěr cōng mù míng 听得清楚,看得分明。形容头脑清楚,眼光敏锐。hear and see clearly; have good eyesight and hearing; be clear-headed and clear-sighted; keep updated about a situation

【耳朵】ěr·duo 听觉器官。人和哺乳动物的耳朵分为外耳、中耳、内耳三部分。内耳除管听觉外,还管身体的平衡。ear (hearing organ); The ear of a human or a mammal comprises three parts: the outer ear, middle ear and inner ear. The inner ear controls one's hearing and the balance of the body as well.

【耳朵底子】ěr·duo dǐ·zi 〈方 *dial.*〉中耳炎 inflammation of the middle ear; otitis media

【耳朵软】ěr·duo ruǎn 形容没有主见,容易轻信别人的话 credulous; easily influenced; susceptible to flattery:她～,听人家一说就信以为真了。She believes what everyone tells her.

【耳朵眼儿】ěr·duoyǎnr ❶ 外耳门的通称 general term for 外耳门 wài'ěrmén ❷ 为了戴耳环等装饰品,在耳垂上扎的孔 holes pierced in the earlobes for wearing earrings

【耳房】ěrfáng 跟正房相连的两侧的小屋,也指厢房两旁的小屋 small room on either side of the main room; wing room

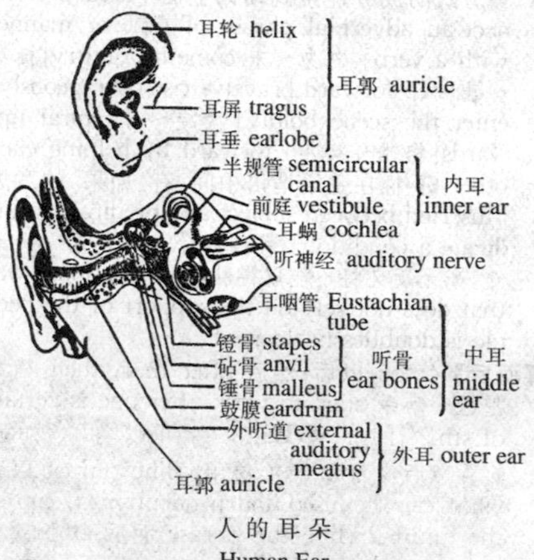

人的耳朵
Human Ear

【耳风】ěr·feng 〈方 *dial.*〉指听来的不一定可靠的消息 hearsay; rumour; unreliable news that one hears

【耳福】ěrfú 听到美好的音乐、戏曲、曲艺等的福分 have the luck to listen to part of a piece of beautiful music, opera, etc:大饱～ have the good fortune to enjoy wonderful music; fully satisfy one's acoustic sense

【耳根】ěrgēn ❶ 耳朵的根部 root of the ear ❷ 耳朵 ear:～清净 have peace for one's ears; have a quiet and peaceful environment; be free from worldly discord ‖ also 耳根子 ěrgēn·zi

【耳垢】ěrgòu 外耳道内皮脂腺分泌的蜡状物质,黄色,有湿润耳内细毛和防止昆虫进入耳内的作用 earwax; cerumen; yellow waxy secretion produced by the sebaceous gland in the outer ear, which moistens the fine hair in the ear and prevents small insects from entering; also 耵聍 dīngníng;俗称 popularly known as 耳屎 ěrshǐ

【耳鼓】ěrgǔ same as 鼓膜 gǔmó

【耳刮子】ěrguā·zi 耳光 slap on the face; boxing the ears

【耳掴子】ěrguāi·zi 〈方 *dial.*〉same as 耳刮子 ěrguā·zi

【耳管】ěrguǎn 外听道 external auditory canal

【耳光】ěrguāng 用手打在耳朵附近的部位叫打耳光 slap on the face; boxing the ear ◇事实给了造谣的人一记响亮～。The truth is a resounding slap to the face for the rumour-mongers. also 耳光子 ěrguāng·zi

【耳郭】ěrguō 外耳的一部分,主要由软骨构成,有收集声波的作用 auricle; pinna; part of the external ear, mainly comprising cartilage, and able to receive sound waves; also 耳廓 ěrkuò; (图见 ☞ figure for 耳朵 ěr·duo)

【耳环】ěrhuán 戴在耳垂上的装饰品,多用金、银、玉石等制成 earring; ornament pinned to the earlobe, mainly made of gold, silver and jade

【耳机】ěrjī ❶ 受话器 earphone; ear cup; receiver; device applied to the ear to aid hearing, listen to music, or receive radio, telephone communications, etc. ❷ 通常指受话器和发话器连在一起的电讯器件 general term for a set of headphones, oft. with a microphone attached ‖ also 听筒 tīngtǒng and 耳机子 ěrjī·zi

【耳尖】ěrjiān 形容听觉锐敏 sharp-eared

【耳孔】ěrkǒng 外耳门 external auditory meatus

【耳力】ěrlì 听力 sense of hearing; hearing: ~不济 have poor hearing; be hard of hearing

【耳轮】ěrlún 耳郭的边缘,大部分向前卷曲,下连耳垂 helix; rim of the outer ear, which connects with the earlobe and curves forward; (图见 ☞ figure for 耳朵 ěr·duo)

【耳门】ěrmén 大门两侧的小门;正门旁边的小门 smaller door on either side of a gate, or beside the main entrance

【耳鸣】ěrmíng 外界并无声音而患者自己觉得耳朵里有鸣叫的声音。多由中耳、内耳或神经系统的疾病引起。tinnitus; ringing in the ear; illness in which one hears noises, esp. ringing in one's ears although there's no noise around, usu. caused by an illness in the middle ear, inner ear or nerve system

【耳膜】ěrmó same as 鼓膜 gǔmó

【耳目】ěrmù ❶ 耳朵和眼睛 ears and eyes: 掩人~(比喻以假象欺骗蒙蔽别人) cover sb.'s eyes and ears; (fig.) deceive sb. with false appearances; prevent sb. from seeing or hearing sth. ❷ 指见闻 what one sees and hears; knowledge; information: ~所及 from what one sees and hears; from what one knows | ~一新 find everything fresh and new; find a completely new world | ~不广 ill-informed ❸ 指替人刺探消息的人 informer; one who spies for sb. else: ~众多 have many informers around; have many spies

【耳目一新】ěr mù yī xīn 听到的看到的都换了样子,感到很新鲜 find everything fresh and new; find a completely new world

【耳旁风】ěrpángfēng 耳边风 breeze flitting by one's ears; unheeded advice; sth. that goes in one ear and out the other

【耳屏】ěrpíng 外耳门前面的突起,由软骨和皮肤构成,能遮住外耳门 tragus; prominence in front of the external auditory meatus, composed of cartilage and skin and able to cover the external auditory meatus; (图见 ☞ figure for 耳朵 ěr·duo)

【耳热】ěrrè 指极端兴奋或害臊 burning ears; blushing due to extreme excitement or shyness: 酒酣~ burning ears because of drinking too much | 说到婚事,姑娘顿觉脸红~。The girl blushed at the mere mention of marriage.

【耳濡目染】ěr rú mù rǎn 形容见得多听得多了之后,无形之中受到影响 be imperceptibly influenced by what one sees and hears

【耳软心活】ěr ruǎn xīn huó 耳朵软,心眼活。指没有主见,容易轻信别人的话。credulous and pliable; gullible; easily influenced by gossip, and lacking a sense of judgement

【耳塞】ěrsāi ❶ 小型受话器,可塞在耳中,常用在收音机和助听器上 small earphone put inside the ear to aid hearing or receive radio or telephone communications ❷ 可以塞在耳中的塞子,游泳时用来防止水进入耳内,也可以用来减低噪声干扰 earplug; small piece of wax placed in the ear to protect against water and noise

【耳塞】ěr·sai same as 耳垢 ěrgòu

【耳生】ěrshēng 听着生疏(跟'耳熟'相对 as opposed to 'familiar to the ear') unfamiliar to the ear; strange-sounding: 不知谁在说话,听着~。Who is speaking outside? The voice sounds unfamiliar.

【耳食】ěrshí 〈书 *fml*.〉指听到传闻不加审察就信以为真 be credulous; readily believe what one is told without examination

【耳屎】ěrshǐ 耳垢的俗称 popular term for 耳垢 ěrgòu

【耳熟】ěrshú 听着熟悉(跟'耳生'相对 as opposed to 'strange-sounding') sound familiar: 人我不认识,可名字听着怪~的。I don't know the man but his name sounds quite familiar to me.

【耳熟能详】ěr shú néng xiáng 听的次数多了,熟悉得能详尽地说出来 be so familiar with what one hears repeatedly that one can repeat it in detail; sound familiar

【耳顺】ěrshùn ❶〈书 *fml*.〉《论语·为政》:'六十而耳顺。'指年至六十,听到别人的话,就能深刻理解其中的意思。后来用'耳顺'指人六十岁。According to *Analects·Governance*, 'A person at sixty years of age will thoroughly understand the meaning of others' words.' The phrase '耳顺 ěrshùn' later came to mean 60 years old: 年逾~ over 60 years old | ~之年 at the age of 60 ❷ 顺耳 pleasant to the ear: 这个唱腔我听着倒还~。This kind of singing sounds pleasant to me.

【耳提面命】ěr tí miàn mìng 《诗经·大雅·抑》:'匪面命之,言提其耳。'意思是不但当面告诉他,而且揪着他的耳朵叮嘱。后来用'耳提面命'形容恳切地教导。hold sb. by the ear and teach him face to face; give earnest exhortations. The song 'Yi' in *The Book of Songs•Epics•Admonition* has a line which means to give earnest exhortations not only in front of sb. but into his ears. Later, people used the line to describe earnest teaching.

【耳挖子】ěrwā•zi 掏耳垢用的小勺儿 earpick, used to take out earwax

【耳闻】ěrwén 听说 hear of: ～不如目见。Seeing is believing. | 这事略有～，详细情况不很清楚。I've heard something about it, but don't know the details.

【耳蜗】ěrwō 内耳的一部分，在内耳的最前部，形状像蜗牛壳，内部有淋巴和听神经，是听觉的感受器 cochlea; acoustic labyrinth; spiral-shaped, tube-like part at the front of the inner ear where there are lymph and nerves for hearing（图见 ☞ figure for 耳朵 ěr•duo)

【耳下腺】ěrxiàxiàn same as 腮腺 sāixiàn

【耳性】ěr•xìng 受了告诫之后，没有记在心上，依然犯同样的毛病，叫做没有耳性（多指小孩子 oft. used in the negative with a child) remember commands; be unable to remember commands and repeat the same mistakes

【耳穴】ěrxué 人体某一部分有病时，就会反应在耳郭的一定部位上，这些部位就是耳针治疗的刺激点，统称为耳穴 acupuncture points on the ears, each of which reflects certain diseases and must be pierced by a needle in order to cure the disease

【耳咽管】ěryānguǎn 从中耳向下通咽部的管子，由骨和软骨构成，有调节鼓膜内外压力的作用 Eustachian tube; auditory tube; either of the pair of tubes that join the ears to the throat, composed of bone and cartilage, and able to balance the outer and inner pressure of the eardrum; also 咽鼓管 yāngǔguǎn;（图见 ☞ figure for 耳朵 ěr•duo)

【耳音】ěryīn 听力 sense of hearing; hearing ability: 瞧你这～，连我的声音也听不出来了。How poor your hearing is! You even cannot recognize my voice.

【耳语】ěryǔ 凑近别人耳朵小声说话；咬耳朵 whisper into sb.'s ear

【耳坠】ěrzhuì (～儿 ěrzhuìr) 耳环（多指带着坠儿的 oft. with eardrops) earring; also 耳坠子 ěrzhuì•zi

【耳子】ěr•zi 器物两旁供人提的部分 ears or handles of a utensil or pot

迩(邇) ěr〈书 *fml.*〉近 near; close: 遐～驰名（远近闻名）be known far and wide; enjoy great renown

【迩来】ěrlái〈书 *fml.*〉近来 recently; lately

洱 ěr 洱海(Ěrhǎi)，湖名，在云南 Erhai Lake in Yunnan Province

饵 ěr ❶ 糕饼 cake; pastry: 果～ candies and cakes; confectionery ❷ 钓鱼时引鱼上钩的食物 bait; food used to entice fish: 鱼～ bait | 钓～ fishing bait ❸〈书 *fml.*〉用东西引诱 entice; allure; tempt: ～以重利 entice sb. with the prospect of wealth; tempt sb. by offering piles of money

【饵料】ěrliào ❶ 养鱼业上指鱼的食物；鱼饵 bait; food for fish ❷ 拌上毒药，诱杀蝼蛄等害虫的食物 insect killer; insecticide; poisonous food to lure and kill insects such as mole crickets, etc.

【饵子】ěr•zi 鱼饵 fishing bait

駬 ěr ☞［騄駬］(lù'ěr) on p. 1261

珥 ěr〈书 *fml.*〉用珠子或玉石做的耳环 earrings made of pearl or jade

铒 ěr 金属元素，符号 Er (erbium)。是一种稀土金属。暗灰色，质软，用来制有色玻璃、搪瓷等。erbium (Er); soft silvery metallic element of the lanthanide series, used to make coloured glass, porcelain, etc.

èr (儿)

二 èr ❶ 数目，一加一后所得 two; sum of one plus one; ☞ 数字 shùzì on p. 1791

注意 **NOTE**: '二'和'两'用法上的分别，☞ 两 liǎng on p. 1205 difference in usage of the two characters, 二 èr and 两 liǎng ❷ 两样 different: 不～价 fixed price; no bargaining | 不～法门 same old trick | 心无～用 cannot keep one's mind on two things at the same time

【二八】èrbā〈书 *fml.*〉指十六岁 sixteen years old: 年方～ be only sixteen years old

【二把刀】èrbǎdāo〈方 *dial.*〉❶ 对某项工作知识不足，技术不高 have a smattering idea of a subject; have half-baked knowledge or skill ❷ 称某项工作知识不足，技术不高的人 dabbler; smatterer

【二百二】èrbǎi'èr 汞溴红的通称 general term for mercurochrome; also 二百二十 èrbǎi èrshí

【二百五】èrbǎiwǔ ❶ 讥称有些傻气，做事莽撞的人 (ironic) person who is a bit stupid and acts rashly ❷〈方 *dial.*〉半瓶醋 half a bottle of vinegar; dabbler; smatterer; dilettante

【二部制】èrbùzhì 中小学把学生分成两部轮流在校上课的教学组织形式 teaching arrangement where primary school students and middle school students take turns to come to classes

【二重性】èrchóngxìng 指事物本身所固有的互相矛盾的两种属性，即一种事物同时具有两种互相对立的性质。如商品，一方面它有使用价值，另一方面它有价值。dual character; dual nature; duality; two intrinsic contradictory aspects, in one thing. In other words, a thing has two opposite natures existing within it at the same time, e.g. merchandise has its value and use value as well. also 两重性 liǎngchóngxìng

【二次能源】èr cì néngyuán 指依靠一次能源来产生或制取的能源，如水力发电产生的电能，分馏石油制取的汽油、柴油等 secondary energy, produced from a primary energy, such as electricity generated from waterpower, gas and diesel produced from distilling oil, etc.

【二道贩子】èr dào fàn·zi 指从商店或别人手中买进货物，转手倒卖，从中牟利的人（多含贬义 usu. derog.）merchant who makes profits by buying cheap and selling dear

【二地主】èrdìzhǔ 向地主租入大量土地，自己不耕种，转租给别人，以收取地租为主要生活来源的人 sub-landlord; person who rents land from a landlord and sub-leases it out to others instead of tilling it himself so as to live off collecting rent

【二房】èrfáng ❶〈旧时 *old*〉家族中排行第二的一支 second male branch of an extended family; branch headed by the second son; cadet branch ❷ 小老婆；妾 concubine

【二房东】èrfángdōng 指把租来的房屋转租给别人而从中取利的人 sub-landlord; person who rents a room from a landlord and sublets it to make a profit

【二伏】èrfú 中伏 second of the three hottest ten-day periods of summer

【二副】èrfù 轮船上船员的职务名称，职位次于大副 second mate; second officer on a ship, with a rank lower than the chief officer; ☞ 大副 dàfù on p. 356

【二锅头】èrguōtóu 一种较纯的白酒，在蒸馏时，除去最先出的和最后出的酒，留下来的就是二锅头 *erguotou*; strong, colourless liquor of high purity, produced from the second distillation in the course of brewing

【二胡】èrhú 胡琴的一种，比京胡大，琴筒用木头做成，前端稍大，蒙蟒皮，有两根弦，声音低沉圆润 *erhu*; two-stringed bowed instrument having a low but mellow sound, slightly larger than the two-stringed fiddle used in Peking Opera, its resonator being made of wood and covered with boa skin; also 南胡 nánhú

【二乎】èr·hu〈方 *dial.*〉❶ 畏缩 shrink back in fear; flinch: 他在困难面前向来不～。He never flinches from hardship. ❷ 心里犹疑，不能确定 be perplexed; feel uncertain: 你越说越把我弄～了。The more you talk about it, the more puzzled I am. ❸ 指望不大 unpromising; of little hope: 我看这件事～了，你说呢？There's hardly any hope in this matter, don't you think so? ‖ also 二忽 èr·hu

【二花脸】èrhuāliǎn 架子花 painted face in Peking Opera; male role with a painted face, laying more emphasis on postures and acting rather than on singing

【二话】èrhuà 别的话；不同的意见（指后悔、抱怨、讲条件等，多用于否定句 referring to regret, complaint and argument; oft. used in the negative）other words; different opinions: ～不提 without much ado; without demur | 尽管吩咐就是了，我决无～。If you have any instructions, please let me know. I'll do as told.

【二黄】èrhuáng 戏曲声腔之一，用胡琴伴奏。跟西皮合称皮黄。*erhuang*; one of the types of music in traditional Chinese opera, usu. accompanied by the *huqin*; called 皮黄 píhuáng together with another kind of traditional Chinese music 西皮 xīpí; also 二簧 èrhuáng

【二婚】èrhūn 再婚（多指妇女再嫁 usu. of a woman）remarry

【二婚头】èrhūntóu 指再嫁的妇女（含轻视意 derog.）remarried woman; also 二婚儿 èrhūnr

【二极管】èrjíguǎn 有两个电极的电子管或晶体管 diode; two-element electron tube; semiconductor; ☞ 晶体管 jīngtǐguǎn on p. 1023 and 电子管 diànzǐguǎn on p. 441

【二进制】èrjìnzhì 一种记数法，采用 0 和 1 两个数码，逢二进位。如十进制的 2,5 在二进制中分别记为 10,101。二进制广泛应用在电子计算机的计算中。binary system; system of numerical notation to the base 2, which uses only two numerals 0 and 1, e.g. 2 and 5 in the decimal notation are expressed as 10 and 101 respectively in the binary system; binary system is widely adopted in a computer

【二郎腿】èrlángtuǐ 坐着的时候把一条腿搁在另一条腿上的姿势 cross-legged; sitting posture with one leg placed on the other

【二老】èrlǎo 指父母 parents: ～双亲 father and mother; parents

【二愣子】èrlèng·zi 指鲁莽的人 rash fellow

【二流子】èrliú·zi 游手好闲、不务正业的人 loafer; idler; bum

【二毛】èrmáo〈书 *fml.*〉❶ 花白的头发 grey or grizzled hair ❷ 指头发花白的老人 old people with grey hair or greying temples

【二门】èrmén（较大的院落等）大门里面的一道总的门 (of a big courtyard) second gate leading to the main living quarters; inner gate

【二拇指】èr·muzhǐ 第二个手指头；食指 forefinger; index finger

【二年生】èrniánshēng 种子萌发的当年只长出根和叶子，次年才开花结实，然后死亡的，如萝卜、白菜、洋葱等植物都是二年生的 biennial; (of a plant) grow roots and leaves in the first year, and flower and bear fruit and die in the second, e.g. radish, cabbage, onion, etc.

【二七大罢工】Èr-Qī Dà Bàgōng 1923 年京汉铁路工人在中国共产党领导下举行的反帝、反军阀的政治罢工。2 月 7 日，军阀吴佩孚在汉口、长辛店等地镇压罢工工人，造成流血惨案，所以这次罢工叫二七大罢工。Great Strike of February 7, 1923; anti-imperialist, anti-warlord strike by the Beijing-Hankou railway workers led by the Chinese Communist Party in 1923. On February 7, 1923, the warlord Wu Peifu masterminded a massacre of the workers on strike in Hankou and Changxindian. Hence the term.

【二人台】èrréntái ❶ 流行于内蒙古自治区的一种曲艺，用笛子、四胡、扬琴等乐器伴奏，由二人对唱对舞 popular Inner-Mongolian song-and-dance duet, accompanied by musical instruments such as the flute, *sihu*, dulcimer, etc. ❷ 由曲艺二人台发展而成的地方戏曲剧种 local opera based on such song-and-dance duets

【二人转】èrrénzhuàn ❶ 流行于黑龙江、吉林、辽宁一带的曲艺，用板胡、唢呐等乐器伴奏，一般由二人舞蹈说唱 song-and-dance duet, popular in Heilongjiang, Jilin and Liaoning provinces, accompanied by musical instruments like the *banhu*, *suona*, etc. ❷ 由曲艺二人转发展而成的地方戏曲剧种 local opera based on such song-and-dance duets

【二审】èrshěn ☞ 第二审 dì'èrshěn on p. 429

【二十八宿】èrshíbā xiù 我国古代天文学家把天空中可见的星分成二十八组，叫做二十八宿，东西南北四方各七宿。东方苍龙七宿是角、亢、氐(dī)、房、心、尾、箕；北方玄武七宿是斗、牛、女、虚、危、室、壁；西方白虎七宿是奎、娄、胃、昴(mǎo)、毕、觜(zī)、参(shēn)；南方朱雀七宿是井、鬼、柳、星、张、翼、轸(zhěn)。印度、波斯、阿拉伯古代也有类似我国二十八宿的说法。lunar mansions; 28 constellations; Ancient Chinese astronomers divided the stars that they could see into 28 constellations, which were further divided into four major groups, each group taking up one of the four quadrants of the sky. The eastern quadrant is Dragon (苍龙), which comprises seven constellations of jiǎo (角), kàng (亢), dī (氐), fāng (房), xīn (心), wěi (尾) and jī (箕); the northern quadrant is Black Warrior (玄武), which comprises dǒu (斗), níu (牛), nǚ (女), xū (虚), wēi (危), shì (室) and bì (壁); the western quadrant is White Tiger (白虎), which comprises kuí (奎), lóu (娄), wèi (胃), mǎo (昴), bì (毕), zī (觜) and shēn (参); and the southern quadrant is Scarlet Bird (朱雀), which comprises jǐng (井), guǐ (鬼), liǔ (柳), xīng (星), zhāng (张), yì (翼) and zhěn (轸). Ancient India, Persia and Arab had similar theories on constellations.

【二十四节气】èrshísì jiéqì 指立春、雨水、惊蛰、春分、清明、谷雨、立夏、小满、芒种、夏至、小暑、大暑、立秋、处暑、白露、秋分、寒露、霜降、立冬、小雪、大雪、冬至、小寒、大寒等二十四个节气。二十四节气表明气候变化和农事季节，在农业生产上有重要的意义。twenty-four seasonal division points by which the solar year is divided according to the Chinese lunar calendar, including: Beginning of Spring (立春), Rain Water (雨水), Waking of Insects (惊蛰), Vernal Equinox (春分), Pure Brightness (清明), Grain Rain (谷雨), Beginning of Summer (立夏), Grain Budding (小满), Grain Forming (芒种), Summer Solstice (夏至), Small Heat (小暑), Great Heat (大暑), Beginning of Autumn (立秋), Limit of Heat (处暑), White Dew (白露), Autumnal Equinox (秋分), Cold Dew (寒露), Frost's Descent (霜降), Beginning of Winter (立冬), Small Snow (小雪), Great Snow (大雪), Winter Solstice (冬至), Small Cold (小寒) and Great Cold (大寒). The 24 solar terms, which indicate the change of climate and timing for agricultural activities, are of great significance to agriculture.

【二十四史】èrshísì shǐ 指旧时称为正史的二十四部纪传体史书，即：《史记》、《汉书》、《后汉书》、《三国志》、《晋书》、《宋书》、《南齐书》、《梁书》、《陈书》、《魏书》、《北齐书》、《周书》、《隋书》、《南史》、《北史》、《唐书》(旧唐书)、《新唐书》、《五代史》(旧五代史)、《新五代史》、《宋史》、《辽史》、《金史》、《元史》、《明史》 Twenty-four Histories, which are official history books written in the form of a series of biographies, including *Records of the Historian*, *History of Han*, *History of Later Han*, *Records of Three Kingdoms*, *History of Jin*, *History of Song*, *History of Southern Qi*, *History of Liang*, *History of Chen*, *History of Wei*, *History of Northern Qi*, *History of Zhou*, *History of Sui*, *History of Southern Dynasties*, *History of Northern Dynasties*, *Old History of Tang*, *New History of Tang*, *Old History of the Five Dynasties*, *New History of the Five Dynasties*, *History of Song*, *History of Liao*, *History of Jin*, *History of Yuan*, and *History of Ming*

【二十五史】èrshíwǔ shǐ 二十四史与《新元史》的合称 Twenty-five Histories; Twenty-four Histories plus the *New History of Yuan*

【二手】èrshǒu (～儿 èrshǒur) 指间接的；辗转得来的(事物) second-hand; attained indirectly: ～资料 second-hand materials | 从国外购进的～设备 second-hand equipment bought from abroad

【二踢脚】èrtījiǎo 双响(一种爆竹) double-bang firecracker

【二天】èrtiān 〈方 *dial*.〉过一两天；改天 within a day or two; another day; some other time: ～有空我再来看你。I'll come to see you some other day.

【二五眼】èr·wuyǎn 〈方 *dial*.〉❶ (人)能力差；(物品)质量差 (of a person) incompetent; mediocre; (of things) of low quality; of inferior quality ❷ 能力差的人 incompetent person

【二线】èrxiàn ❶ 战争中的第二道防线 second line of defence in a war ❷〈比喻 *fig.*〉不负有直接领导责任的地位 position of less responsibility: 退居～ step down from an important position and take a secondary position

【二心】èrxīn ❶ 不忠实;异心 two-time; be a two-timer; be fealty with two hearts: 怀有～ be disloyal; be unfaithful ❷ 不专心;三心二意 absent-minded; half-hearted ‖ also 贰心 èrxīn

【二性子】èrxìng·zi 两性人的通称 general term for bisexual person; hermaphrodite; androgynous person

【二氧化碳】èryǎnghuàtàn 无机化合物,化学式 CO_2。无色无臭的气体,比空气重,空气中含量约为 0.04%。动物呼吸时吸入氧气,呼出二氧化碳;绿色植物进行光合作用时放出氧气,吸入二氧化碳。用来制纯碱、清凉性饮料等,也用来灭火。carbon dioxide; carbonic-acid gas; carbonic anhydride; colourless, odourless gas, chemical formula CO_2, heavier than the air and occupying 0.04% of the atmosphere, produced during respiration by animals and humans who inhale oxygen and exhale carbon dioxide, and consumed during the photosynthesis of green plants that inhale carbon dioxide and exhale oxygen, used extensively in manufacturing soda ash and soft drinks, and in fire extinguishers as well; also 碳酐 tàngān or 碳酸气 tànsuānqì

【二一添作五】èr yī tiān zuò wǔ 本是珠算除法的一句口诀,是 1/2 = 0.5 的意思,借指双方平分 one of the abacus rhymes, meaning 1/2 equalling 0.5; go halves; share sth. on a fifty-fifty basis; go Dutch

【二意】èryì same as 二心 èrxīn: 决无～ with utter devotion; be loyal for ever | 三心～ waver and hesitate; be of two minds; be half-hearted

【二元论】èryuánlùn 一种企图调和唯物主义和唯心主义的哲学观点,认为世界的本原是精神和物质两个实体。二元论实质上坚持精神离开物质而独立存在,归根结底还是唯心的。dualism; philosophy that tries to compromise materialism with idealism, believing that the origin of the world comprises the two basic entities of spirit and matter; In essence, dualism insists on the existence of spirit independent of matter, so it boils down to nothing more than idealism.

【二战】Èrzhàn 第二次世界大战的简称 abbr. for 第二次世界大战 Dì Èr Cì Shìjiè Dàzhàn

弎 èr same as 二 èr

刵 èr〈古代 *arch.*〉割耳朵的酷刑 savage torture by cutting off one's ears

佴 èr〈书 *fml.*〉停留;置 stay for a time; sojourn; place; set

☞ Nài on p. 1387

贰 èr ❶ '二'的大写 upper case of the Chinese character for the numeral two; ☞ 数字 shùzì on p. 1791 ❷ 变节;背叛 betray; become a turncoat: ～臣 court official who transfers his allegiance to a new ruler; turncoat official

【贰臣】èrchén 指在前一朝代做了官,投降后一朝代又做官的人 court official who surrenders to and becomes an official in the new dynasty after the fall of the old one; turncoat official

【贰心】èrxīn same as 二心 èrxīn

咡 èr〈书 *fml.*〉口旁;两颊 cheek

樲 èr 古书上指酸枣树 wild jujube tree in ancient books

F

fā (ㄈㄚ)

发(發) fā ❶ 送出;交付 deliver; dispatch; send out; hand over; turn over:～货 deliver; dispatch goods|～稿 distribute news dispatch; (of manuscripts, etc.) go to the press|分～ distribute; issue; dispense; hand out|印～ circulate; print and distribute ❷ 发射 launch; project; discharge; fire:～炮 fire shells; open fire|百～百中 every shot hitting the bull's-eye; shoot with unfailing precision ❸ 产生;发生 produce; engender; cause; happen; occur; arise; take place:～芽 germinate; sprout|～电 generate (electricity or power)|～水 flood|～病(of a disease) burst; occur; (of a person) fall ill; be taken ill; come down with (a disease) ❹ 表达 express; convey; voice:～表 state; announce; issue; deliver; publish; (of newspapers, journals, etc.) carry|～布 issue; promulgate; release|～誓 vow; pledge; swear; take an oath|～言 speak; address; make a statement; deliver a speech; take the floor ❺ 扩大;开展 enlarge; expand; extend; broaden; develop; launch; promote; carry out:～展 develop; expand; grow; promote|～扬 promote; foster; carry on or forward|～育 growth; development ❻ 因得到大量财物而兴旺 flourish through obtaining a great deal of wealth:～家 build up a family fortune|暴～户 upstart; nouveau riche|他这两年跑买卖可～了。His travelling around doing business over the past two years has made him quite a fortune. ❼ 食物因发酵或水浸而膨胀(of foodstuffs) rise or expand when leavened or soaked:面～了。The dough has risen.|～海参 ferment sea cucumbers ❽ 放散;散开(of smoke, scent, etc.) diffuse; disperse:～散 (of rays, etc.) diverge; diffuse|挥～ volatilize|蒸～ evaporation ❾ 揭露;打开 expose; unmask; unveil; open; unfold; bring to light; lay bare:～现 find; discover|揭～ expose; unmask; disclose; lay bare; bring light to|～掘 excavate; unearth; dig ❿ 因变化而显现、散发 appear, or emit a smell due to certain changes:～黄 turn yellow|～潮 become damp; feel damp|～臭 stench; stink|～酸 turn sour; taste sour ⓫ 流露(感情) reveal (one's feelings):～怒 get angry; flare up; fly into a rage|～笑 laugh; burst out laughing|～愁 worry; be anxious; become sad ⓬ 感到(多指不愉快的情况 oft. an unpleasant condition) feel; sense; perceive:～麻 tingle; feel numb|～痒 itch; feel itchy|嘴里～苦 have a bitter taste in the mouth ⓭ 起程 set out; start a journey:出～ leave; set off; set out; start (off)|整装待～ packed up and ready to go; ready to start|朝～夕至 start at dawn and arrive at dusk — a short journey ⓮ 开始行动 start doing sth.:～起 initiate; sponsor|奋～ rouse oneself; exert oneself; brace oneself|先～制人 preempt; take the wind out of sb.'s sails; gain the initiative by striking first; forestall (an opponent) enemy, etc. ⓯ 引起;启发 generate; arouse; stimulate; inspire; enlighten; set off; touch off; bring about:～人深省 provide much food for thought; call for deep thought; prompt sb. to think deeply ⓰〈量词 *classifier*〉颗,用于枪弹、炮弹 [of bullets and shells]:一～子弹 one bullet|上百～炮弹 more than a hundred rounds of shells

☞ fà on p.528

【发榜】fā//bǎng 考试后公布考试成绩的名次或被录取者的名单 announce the results of an exam in the form of a list of names in descending order; issue a list of successful candidates:本市高考首批录取新生今起～。A list of the first group of students in this city who have passed the entrance exams and enrolled in colleges will be published today.

【发包】fābāo 把建筑、加工、订货等任务交给承担单位或个人承包 contract a construction or processing project out to, or place an order with, a unit or individual

【发报】fā//bào 用无线电或有线电装置把消息、情报等发给收报人 transmit news or information by radio or wired equipment to an individual receiver

【发标】fā//biāo 〈方 *dial.*〉发威风;发脾气 flare up; throw one's weight about

【发表】fābiǎo ❶ 向集体或社会表达(意见);宣布 announce; declare; express one's opinions; air one's views (to a collective or society):～谈话 address the public|～声明 issue or make a statement|代表团成员已经确定,名单尚未正

式～。The delegate members have been determined, but the name list has not yet been officially announced. ❷ 在刊物上登载(文章、绘画、歌曲等) publish (articles, paintings, songs, etc.) in a periodical: ～论文 publish an academic paper

【发兵】fā//bīng 派出军队(作战) send out troops; dispatch troops (to fight)

【发病】fā//bìng 某种疾病在有机体内开始发生 outbreak or onset of a disease in an organism: ～率 incidence (of a disease) | 秋冬之交容易～。(People) are prone to illness during the time of the year when autumn gives way to winter.

【发布】fābù 宣布(命令、指示、新闻等) issue or release (orders, instructions, news, etc.): ～战报 issue a war communique | 新闻～会 news conference; press conference

【发财】fā//cái ❶ 获得大量钱财 obtain a great deal of money or wealth; hit the jackpot: ～致富 become rich; make a fortune | 升官～ get a promotion and become rich ❷〈客套话 *pol*.〉问人在哪里工作称在哪里发财 ask sb. where he or she works by way of asking where he or she makes a fortune

【发车】fā//chē (从车站或停放地点)开出车辆 (from a station or parking lot) dispatch or send off a vehicle: 每隔五分钟～一次 dispatch a bus every five minutes | 首班车早晨五点半～。The first bus departs at 5:30 a.m.

【发痴】fā//chī〈方 *dial*.〉❶ 发呆 stupefied; look blank; in a trance; in a daze ❷ 发疯 go (or become) mad; go crazy; become insane

【发愁】fā//chóu 因为没有主意或办法而感到愁闷 be worried about; feeling of being gloomy about a problem one is not sure how to deal with: 你先别～,资金问题我来想办法解决。Please don't worry about the investment problem, I will try to find a solution.

【发出】fāchū ❶ 发生(声音、疑问等) produce (sound, etc.); ask (a question): ～笑声 laugh ❷ 发表;发布(命令、指示) issue; deliver; distribute; circulate; publish; give out; send out; give an order; promulgate a decree: ～号召 call for; call on | ～通告 issue a public notice ❸ 送出(货物、信件等);开出(车辆等) deliver; forward (goods, letters, etc.); dispatch (vehicles, etc.)

【发憷】fāchù〈方 *dial*.〉胆怯;畏缩 timid; cowardly; recoil; cringe; shrink: 初次登台,心里有点～。Feel a little nervous at one's first stage appearance.

【发达】fādá ❶ (事物)已有充分发展;(事业)兴盛 (of sth.) fully developed; (of a cause) flourish: 肌肉～ muscular; brawny | 四肢～ full-limbed; sound in body; physically sound | 工业～ well-developed industry; flourishing or thriving industry | 交通～ convenient communication; well-developed transportation system ❷ 使充分发展 enable sth. to develop fully: ～经济 develop or promote the economy | ～贸易 develop or promote trade

【发呆】fā//dāi 因着急、害怕或心思有所专注,而对外界事物完全不注意 dazed; nonplussed; flabbergasted; completely ignore what is happening around one due to anxiety, fear, or preoccupation with sth.: 他话也不说,眼直直地瞪着,坐在那儿～。He sat there, staring blankly, not saying a word.

【发单】fādān same as 发票 fāpiào

【发嗲】fādiǎ〈方 *dial*.〉撒娇 behave like a spoiled child; play the pampered child

【发电】fādiàn ❶ 发出电力 generate electricity or power: 水力～ hydro-power; water power | 原子能～ atomic power; nuclear power ❷ 打电报 send a telegram

【发动】fādòng ❶ 使开始 start; initiate; launch: ～战争 launch (or start or unleash) a war | ～新攻势 unleash a new attack ❷ 使行动起来 mobilize; arouse; call into action: ～群众 arouse (or mobilize) the masses ❸ 使机器运转 rev up; start a machine; get a machine started; set a machine going: 天气太冷,柴油机不容易～。It is too cold to start a diesel engine.

【发动机】fādòngjī 把热能、电能等变为机械能的机器,用来带动其他机械工作。如电动机、蒸汽机、涡轮机、内燃机、风车。motor or engine, a piece of machinery, such as a motor, steam engine, turbine, internal combustion engine, or windmill, that transposes power contained in steam, electricity, etc., to achieve movement in other machines; also 动力机 dònglìjī

【发抖】fādǒu 由于害怕、生气或受到寒冷等原因而身体颤动 tremble; shake; shiver because of fear, anger or cold etc.: 吓得～ tremble with fear; shake in one's shoes | 冻得浑身～ shiver all over with cold; shake from head to foot

【发端】fāduān 开始;开端 start; beginning

【发端词】fāduāncí 发语词 function word

【发凡】fāfán 陈述全书或某一学科的要旨 introduction to (or explanation of) the main idea or points of a book or a subject: ～起例(说明全书要旨,拟定编撰体例) (of a book) introduction and guide (to the main idea or points, and style of compilation)

【发放】fāfàng ❶ (政府、机构)把钱或物资等发给需要的人 (of a government or an organization) grant, issue and distribute money, or goods and materials to people in need: ～贷款 grant (or extend) a loan | ～救济粮 distribute (or dole out) relief grains | ～经营许可证 issue a business license ❷ 发出;放出 release; send up; send out: ～信号弹 send up a signal flare

❸ 处理；处置（多见于早期白话 mostly in early vernacular）deal with；treat

【发粉】fāfěn ☞ 焙粉 bèifěn on p. 87

【发奋】fāfèn ❶ 振作起来；奋发 activate oneself；bestir oneself；exert oneself；rouse oneself：～努力 work hard；exert oneself｜～有为 energetic and promising；with firm resolve to succeed ❷ same as 发愤 fāfèn

【发愤】fāfèn 决心努力 make a firm resolution；make a determined effort：～忘食 be so absorbed in one's work or study as to forget one's meals；work or study so hard as to forget to eat｜～图强 make determined efforts to better oneself；resolve to make one's country strong；also 发奋 fāfèn

【发疯】fā//fēng ❶ 精神受到刺激而发生精神病的症状 go mad；suffer from a disease of the brain or disorder of the mind because of traumatic experience ❷〈比喻 *fig.*〉做事出于常情之外 state contrary to reason or against common sense：你～啦，这么大热天，还穿棉袄！You're crazy to wear a cotton-padded jacket on such a hot day.

【发福】fā//fú〈客套话 *pol.*〉称人发胖（多用于中年以上的人 usu. of older people）grow stout；put on weight

【发付】fāfù 打发（多见于早期白话 oft. in early vernacular）dispatch；arrange；send on an errand

【发绀】fāgàn 皮肤或黏膜呈现青紫色。由呼吸或循环系统发生障碍，血液中缺氧引起。cyanosis；skin or mucosa turning purple and green owing to the circulation of imperfectly oxygenated blood caused by an obstruction within the respiratory or circulatory system；also 青紫 qīngzǐ

【发糕】fāgāo 用米粉、面粉等发酵做成的糕，有的还加糖、枣儿、青丝等 steamed sponge cake，made of leavened ground rice or flour，sometimes with added sugar，dates and finely cut green plums，etc.

【发稿】fā//gǎo 发出稿件。如通讯社发送电讯稿给报社，编辑部门把书刊、图片等稿件交给出版部门或印刷厂。（of a news agency）dispatch news releases to newspapers；（of an editorial department）submit the manuscripts of books or journals or pictures to a publishing department or the press

【发汗】fā//hàn（用药物等）使身体出汗 induce perspiration（through medication）

【发行】fāháng 批发 sell wholesale
☞ fāxíng on p. 523

【发号施令】fā hào shī lìng 发布命令；指挥 issue orders；give orders；command；boss around

【发狠】fā//hěn ❶ 下决心，不顾一切 make a determined effort；resolve to do sth.；do sth. at any cost：～读书 make a determined effort to study｜他一～，三天的任务，两天就完成了。Through determined effort，he completed a three-day assignment in two days. ❷ 恼怒；动气 angry；irritated；furious

【发横】fā//hèng 发脾气；要横 explode；flare up；lose control；act in an unreasonable or headstrong way：有理讲理，发什么横？Please try to be rational，why are you acting in such an unreasonable fashion?

【发花】fā//huā 眼睛看东西模糊不清 experience blurred vision：饿得两眼～。I was so hungry I couldn't see straight.

【发话】fā//huà ❶ 给予口头指示；口头上提出警告或要求 give（verbal）orders or instructions；give（verbal）warnings；voice requirements：到底该怎么办，你～吧。What shall we do? Please tell us your requirements.｜人家早～啦，不许咱再到这里来。They have already given orders to disallow us from coming here again. ❷ 气冲冲地说出话 speak angrily

【发还】fāhuán 把收来的东西还回去（多用于上对下 usu. to one's subordinate）give（or send）back；return sth.：～原主 return sth. to its rightful owner；send sth. back to its original owner

【发慌】fā//huāng 因害怕、着急或虚弱而心神不定 feel disturbed and upset because of fright，anxiety or debility：沉住气，别～。Keep calm! Don't be nervous.

【发挥】fāhuī ❶ 把内在的性质或能力表现出来 demonstrate the inner property or ability of sth.：～积极性 give full play to one's initiative；bring one's initiative into full play；give free reign to one's initiative｜～模范作用 play an exemplary role｜～技术水平 give play to one's technical knowledge or skill｜～炮兵的威力 bring the artillery into play ❷ 把意思或道理充分表达出来 fully express（idea or argument）：～题意 elaborate（meaning or theme）｜借题～ seize upon a pretext through which to give vent to one's own views or feelings；make use of the topic under discussion to put across one's own ideas（which are unrelated to it）

【发昏】fā//hūn 神志不清 feel giddy（dizzy；confused）：头脑～ feel giddy；lose control of oneself

【发火】fā//huǒ ❶ 开始燃烧 fire；ignite：～点 firing point；ignition point ❷ 子弹、炮弹的底火经撞击后火药爆发 cause the gunpowder inside a bullet or shell to explode after its primer has been struck ❸〈方 *dial.*〉发生火警；失火 catch fire；be on fire ❹（炉灶）生火容易旺（of a stove）draw well ❺（～儿 fā//huǒr）发脾气 get angry；flare up；lose one's temper；lose control：有话好好说，不必～。Don't get angry，let's talk it over calmly.

【发急】fā//jí 着急 become impatient or anxious; lose patience: 他还不来,让人等得~。He still hasn't arrived, and the waiting makes everybody impatient.

【发迹】fā//jì 指人变得有钱有势(of a poor man) gain fame and fortune; go from rags to riches: ~变泰 rise to position of power and influence

【发家】fā//jiā 使家庭变得富裕 help one's family to go wealthy: ~致富 become rich; build up a family fortune

【发贱】fā//jiàn 因不自重而表现出让人看不起的举动 act cheap; cheapen oneself due to a lack of self-respect

【发酵】fā//jiào 复杂的有机化合物在微生物的作用下分解成比较简单的物质。发面、酿酒等都是发酵的应用。ferment; process whereby complex organic chemical compounds are broken down into comparatively simple substances under the influence of a micro-organism, such as leavening dough and brewing wine; also 酦酵 fājiào

【发酵酒】fājiàojiǔ 酿造后不经过蒸馏而可以直接饮用的酒,酒精含量较低,如黄酒、葡萄酒等 fermented wine, such as rice wine and grape wine, of low alcohol content, that can be imbibed without having gone through a distillation process; also 酿造酒 niàngzàojiǔ

【发窘】fājiǒng 感到为难;表现出窘态 be abashed; become embarrassed; be ill at ease

【发酒疯】fājiǔfēng 撒酒疯 be drunk and act foolishly; be roaring drunk; be in a drunken fit or brawl

【发觉】fājué 开始知道(隐藏的或以前没注意到的事) sense; realize; become aware of a concealed matter or sth. previously unnoticed: 火扑灭了以后,他才~自己受了伤。He did not realize he was injured until after the fire had been extinguished.

【发掘】fājué 挖掘埋藏在地下的东西 excavate; unearth; explore sth. buried underground: ~古物 excavate antiquities | ~宝藏 explore a treasurehouse; excavate a precious mineral deposit ◇~潜力 tap potential | ~人才 seek out gifted (or talented) people

【发刊词】fākāncí 刊物创刊号上说明本刊的宗旨、性质等的文章 foreword or introduction in the first issue of a periodical explaining its aims and character

【发棵】fākē 〈方 *dial.*〉(~儿 fākēr) ❶ 分蘖 tiller ❷ 植株逐渐长大 (of plant) grow

【发狂】fā//kuáng 发疯 go mad; crazy; become lunatic (or insane); go berserk; lose control

【发困】fākùn 感到困倦,想睡觉 feel sleepy; feel drowsy: 今天起得过早,午饭后有点儿~。Having got up early this morning, I felt sleepy after lunch.

【发懒】fālǎn 因身体或心情不好,懒得动 feel sluggish due to poor health or ill humour

【发愣】fā//lèng 发呆 be stunned; be in a trance; be in a daze

【发利市】fālìshì 〈方 *dial.*〉❶ 商店把开门后做成第一笔买卖叫做发利市 make the first transaction of the day after opening shop ❷ 泛指获得利润 (in a broad sense) profit

【发令】fālìng 发出命令或口令 give or issue an order or a word of command: ~枪 starting gun or pistol | ~开火 give the order to fire

【发令枪】fālìngqiāng 径赛、游泳比赛等开始时,用来发出声音信号的器械,形状像手枪 gun or pistol, used to give the signal to begin a track or field event, a swimming competition, etc.

【发聋振聩】fā lóng zhèn kuì 发出很大的响声,使耳聋的人也能听见 make a noise loud enough to rouse the deaf and awaken the unhearing;〈比喻 *fig.*〉用语言文字唤醒糊涂的人 enlighten the ignorant or the benighted through spoken or written words

【发落】fāluò 处理;处置 handle; deal with (an offender): 听候~ wait for one's decision

【发毛】fā//máo ❶ 害怕;惊慌 be scared; be frightened; get gooseflesh: 他从没见过这阵势,心里直~。Never having seen such a scenario, he was scared. ❷〈方 *dial.*〉发脾气 lose one's temper; lose control

【发霉】fā//méi 有机质滋生霉菌而变质 go mouldy; become mildewed◇思想~ ossified way of thinking

【发蒙】fāmēng 糊涂;弄不清楚 confused; bewildered; in a muddle; at a loss: 一人一个说法,听得我~。Each of you has a different story, making me confused.

【发蒙】fāméng 〈旧时 *old*〉教少年、儿童开始识字读书 teach a child to read and write; teach a child his ABC: ~读物 primer; beginner's book

【发面】fā//miàn 使面发酵 leaven dough

【发面】fāmiàn 经过发酵的面 leavened dough: ~饼 leavened pancake

【发明】fāmíng ❶ 创造(新的事物或方法) invent (new things or methods): ~指南针 invent the compass | 火药是中国最早~的。Gunpowder was first invented by the Chinese. ❷ 创造出的新事物或新方法 newly invented things or methods: 新~ new invention | 四大~ four major inventions (the compass, gunpowder, papermaking and printing) ❸〈书 *fml.*〉创造性地阐发 expound; set forth a theme; develop (an idea, theme, etc.); same as 发挥 fāhuī ②: ~文义 expound the theme of an article | 本书对《老子》的哲理颇多~。This book expounds in detail the philosophy of *Laozi*.

【发墨】fā//mò 指砚台磨墨易浓 (of inkstones) good for grinding an inkstick: 这种砚石细腻如玉,~也快。This inkstone is as smooth as jade and effective for grinding inksticks.

【发难】fā//nàn ❶ 发动反抗或叛乱 rise in revolt; start a rebellion; launch an attack:辛亥革命在武昌首先～。The first attack of the Revolution of 1911 was launched in Wuchang. ❷〈书 *fml.*〉问难 raise a difficult question; start discussion on a doubtful or difficult point:提问～ raise questions about one's view

【发蔫】fāniān ❶ 花木、水果等显现出萎缩(of flowers, plants, fruits, etc.) fade; wither; droop; shrivel up:几天没浇水,海棠花有些～了。Not having been watered over the past few days, the Chinese flowering crab apple withered. ❷ 表现出精神不振 spiritless; listless; downcast:他这两天有点～,不像往日爱说爱笑。He looks a bit listless recently, and has not been talking animatedly and laughing merrily as he usually does.

【发苶】fānié 委靡不振; dispirited; in low spirits; same as 发蔫 fāniān ②

【发怒】fā//nù 因愤怒而表现出粗暴的声色举动 be enraged; behave crudely due to anger

F 【发排】fāpái 把稿子交给排印部门排版 send a manuscript to the typesetting and printing departments

【发胖】fāpàng (身体)变胖 (of body) get fat; put on (or gain) weight

【发配】fāpèi 充军(多见于早期白话 oft. in early vernacular) send sb. into exile; be escorted to a remote place for penal servitude

【发脾气】fā pí·qi 因事情不如意而吵闹或骂人 quarrel or swear due to dissatisfaction; vent one's spleen on sb. or sth.

【发飘】fāpiāo 感觉轻飘飘的 feel light:这把木锨使着～。This wooden winnowing shovel feels too light.|头沉得厉害,脚下有点儿～feel dizzy and a bit shaky

【发票】fāpiào 商店或其他收款部门开出的收款单据 receipt; invoice

【发起】fāqǐ ❶ 倡议(做某件事情) advocate; initiate:～人 sponsor; initiator|他们～组织一个读书会。They organized a reading association under their sponsorship. ❷ 发动(战役、进攻等) start or launch (a war, an attack, etc.):～冲锋 launch an assault|～反攻 launch a counter-attack

【发情】fāqíng 雌性的高等动物卵子成熟前后,生理上要求交配 in heat; physiological characteristic of a female mammal, whereby it to mates at ovulation:～期 heat (period); oestrus

【发球】fā//qiú 球类比赛时,一方把球发出,使比赛开始或继续(of a ball game) serve

【发热】fā//rè ❶ 温度增高;产生热量 give out heat; generate heat:恒星本身发光～。Fixed stars emit light and heat by themselves. ❷ 发烧 run a fever; have a temperature ❸〈比喻 *fig.*〉不冷静,不清醒 temperamental:头脑～ be hotheaded; be impetuous

【发人深省】fā rén shēn xǐng 启发人深刻醒悟 set people thinking; provide much food for thought; 省 also put as 醒 xǐng

【发轫】fārèn〈书 *fml.*〉拿掉支住车轮的木头,使车前进 remove the wooden wedge from underneath a wheel to set a vehicle in motion;〈比喻 *fig.*〉新事物或某种局面开始出现 new thing or situation starts to emerge:～之作 maiden work; work that signals the beginning of one's writing career|新文学运动～于五四运动。The May Fourth Movement precipitated the New Culture Movement.

【发散】fāsàn ❶(光线等)由某一点向四周散开(of rays, etc.) diverge; diffuse:～透镜 divergent lens ❷〈中医 *Chin. med.*〉用发汗的药物把体内的热散出去,以治疗疾病 disperse internal heat with sudorifics to cure disease

【发丧】fā//sāng ❶ 丧家向亲友宣告某人死去 announce a death to relatives and friends ❷ 办理丧事 hold a funeral (procession); arrange a funeral

【发痧】fā//shā〈方 *dial.*〉中暑(zhòng//shǔ) have a heatstroke or sunstroke

【发傻】fā//shǎ ❶ 因为某种意外情况出现而目瞪口呆 dumbstruck; dumbfounded ❷ 说傻话或做傻事;犯傻 speak or act foolishly

【发烧】fā//shāo 体温增高。人的正常体温是37℃左右,如超过37.5℃,就是发烧,是疾病的一种症状。have or run a temperature or fever; symptom of a disease when one's body temperature exceeds 37.5℃, when the normal temperature is around 37℃; also 发热 fā//rè

【发烧友】fāshāoyǒu〈方 *dial.*〉对某项事业或活动非常迷恋专注的人;狂热的爱好者 devotee; aficionado; buff; fanatic; zealot

【发射】fāshè 射出(枪弹、炮弹、火箭、电波、人造卫星等) discharge; shoot; fire (a bullet); transmit (electric waves); launch (a man-made satellite, rocket, etc.)

【发身】fāshēn 男女到青春期,生殖器官发育成熟,身体其他各部分也发生变化,逐渐长成成年人的样子,这种生理变化叫做发身 pubescence, stage of physical development during puberty in both males and females when their reproductive organs become mature, and when other parts of their bodies gradually develop, giving them an adult appearance

【发神经】fā shénjīng same as 发疯 fā//fēng ②

【发生】fāshēng ❶ 原来没有的事出现了;产生 happen; occur; new things appear; take place:～变化 changes take place|～事故 accident occurs or happens|～关系 establish a relationship; have an affair; have sexual intercourse ❷ 卵子受精后逐渐生长的过程 gradual development of an embryo (from a fertilized egg)

【发市】fā//shì 指商店等一天里第一次成交(of a shop, etc.) make the first transaction in a day's business

【发誓】fā//shì 庄严地说出表示决心的话或对某事提出保证 vow, swear and make a pledge:指天～ swear by the sun|～要为烈士报仇 vow to avenge the martyrs

【发事】fā//shì 出事 have an accident; meet with a mishap:～地点 site or scene of an accident

【发售】fāshòu 出售 sell; put on sale:公开～ public sale|～纪念邮票 put commemorative stamps on sale

【发抒】fāshū 表达(意见、感情) express; voice (one's opinions or feelings):～己见 express one's own view; speak one's mind

【发水】fā//shuǐ 闹水灾(of a river) overflow; in flood

【发送】fāsòng ❶ 无线电发射机把无线电信号发射出去 transmit radio-signals by a transmitter ❷ 发出;送出 send out; dispatch (letters, etc.):～文件 dispatch documents|这个火车站每天～旅客在五万人以上。This railway station dispatches over fifty thousand passengers every day.

【发送】fā·song 办丧事,特指殡葬 hold a funeral procession, esp. for a burial

【发酸】fāsuān ❶ 食物变酸(of food) turn sour; taste sour:碱放少了,馒头～。Steamed buns taste a little sour if insufficient soda is used in mixing the dough. ❷ 要流泪时眼睛、鼻子感到不舒适 tingle experienced in one's eyes and nose before breaking down and weeping:看到感人之处,鼻子一阵～ feel a tingle in one's nose when reading a particularly moving passage|两眼～,泪水止不住流了下来 one's eyes tingle as tears begin to roll down one's cheeks ❸ 因疾病或疲劳而感到肢体酸痛无力(of limbs and body) feel weak and sore because of illness or fatigue:站了一天了,两腿～。(I) feel weak and sore in the legs after standing the whole day.

【发文】fā//wén 发出公文 issue or dispatch a document, etc.:中央三个单位联合～。Three central government departments issued a jointly document.

【发文】fāwén 本单位发出的公文 outgoing document:～簿(登记发文的本子) registration book on outgoing documents, letters, etc.

【发问】fāwèn 口头提出问题 ask, pose and raise a question

【发物】fā·wù 指富于营养或有刺激性,容易使疮疖或某些病状发生变化的食物,如羊肉、鱼虾等 stimulating food; nutritious foods such as mutton, fish and shrimp, that stimulate or aggravate sores, boils or certain clinical symptoms

【发现】fāxiàn ❶ 经过研究、探索等,看到或找到前人没有看到的事物或规律 find out; discover (esp. after studies and explorations of sth. unknown to predecessors):～新的基本粒子 discover a new elementary particle|有所发明,有所～,有所创造。Make new inventions and discoveries and create new things. ❷ 发觉 detect; notice; find out; become aware of:这两天,我～他好像有什么心事。In the last couple of days I have noticed that he seems to have something on his mind.

【发祥】fāxiáng 〈书 *fml.*〉❶ 指发生吉祥的事 occurrence of an auspicious event ❷ 兴起;发生 originate; begin; start; initiate:～地 place of origin; birthplace

【发祥地】fāxiángdì 原指帝王祖先兴起的地方,现用来指民族、革命、文化等起源的地方 cradle; place of origin of an emperor or one's ancestor; birthplace (of a nation, a revolution, a culture, etc.):黄河流域物产丰富,山河壮丽,是我国古代文化的～。The Yellow River Valley, with its rich resources and magnificent landscape, was the cradle of ancient Chinese culture.

【发笑】fāxiào 笑起来 laugh; burst into laughter:引人～ make one laugh; provoke laughter; be ridiculous

【发泄】fāxiè 尽量发出(情欲或不满情绪) give vent to; take (one's lust, grievances or discontent) out on sb.:～兽欲 give rein to one's bestial lust|～私愤 vent personal grudges

【发行】fāxíng 发出新印制的货币、债券或新出版的书刊、新制作的电影等(of new currency, bonds, books, periodicals, films, etc.) issue; publish; distribute; release

☞ fāháng on p.520

【发虚】fāxū ❶ 因胆怯或没有把握而感到心虚 feel diffident or lack self-confidence owing to timidity, or uncertainty ❷ (身体)显得虚弱(of body) feel feeble and weak:他病刚好,身子还有些～。He has just recovered, and still feels weak.

【发噱】fāxué 〈方 *dial.*〉能引人发笑;可笑 amusing; funny; comical

【发芽】fā//yá 种了的胚发育长大,突破种皮而出(embryo of a seed) breaks through its shell after germinating

【发言】fā//yán 发表意见(多指在会议上 usu. at a meeting) state one's view:积极～ take the floor actively|～权 right to speak|他已经发过言了。He has already made his speech.

【发言】fāyán 发表的意见(多指在会议上 made mostly at a meeting) statement:他在大会上的～很中肯。He made a sincere and pertinent speech at the meeting.

【发言人】fāyánrén 代表某一政权机关或组织发表意见的人 spokesman; spokesperson; person who speaks on behalf of a government or organization：外交部～ Foreign Ministry spokesperson

【发扬】fāyáng ❶ 发展和提倡（优良作风、传统等）develop and promote（fine practice，tradition，etc.）：～光大 carry forward；develop；enhance|～民主 promote democracy|～勤俭节约、艰苦奋斗的精神 keep up the spirit of diligence，thrift，plain living and hard work ❷ 发挥 make the most of；make full use of；give full play to：～火力，消灭敌人 make full use of firepower to annihilate the enemy

【发扬踔厉】fāyáng chuōlì 指精神奋发，意气昂扬 vigorous and full of spirit；energetic；also 发扬蹈厉 fāyáng dǎolì

【发扬光大】fāyáng guāngdà 发展提倡，使日益盛大 enhance；develop，carry forward

【发洋财】fā yángcái 原指在与外国人有关的活动中发财，后泛指获得意外的财物（orig.）make a great fortune or profit from activities related to foreigners；（in a broad sense）acquisition of unexpected wealth

【发疟子】fā yào·zi 患疟疾 have an attack of malaria；suffer from malarial fever

【发音】fā//yīn 发出语音或乐音，也泛指发出声音 pronounce；make sounds；enunciate（in a broad sense）：练习～ practise pronunciation|～方法 manner of articulation

【发引】fāyǐn〈古代 *arch.*〉出殡时送丧的人用绋牵引灵柩作前导，叫作发引。后来也指出殡时抬出灵柩。（of a funeral procession）draw the bier with a cord；（later referring to）carry coffin to a burial

【发语词】fāyǔcí 文言虚词，用于一篇或一段文章的开头，如'夫、盖、维' function words such as '夫 fú，盖 gài，维 wéi' at the beginning of a piece of classical Chinese writing，or a paragraph；also 发端词 fāduāncí

【发育】fāyù 生物体成熟之前，机能和构造发生变化，如植物开花结果，动物的性腺逐渐成熟 growth；development，the change of function and structure of an organism shortly before becoming mature，such as plants blossoming and bearing fruit，and the gonads of animals gradually becoming mature

【发源】fāyuán（河流）开始流出；起源（of a river）headwater；originate：～地 birthplace；place of origin；source|淮河～于桐柏山。The Huai River rises in the Tongbai Mountain.

【发愿】fāyuàn 表明心愿或愿望 express one's wish or desire：起誓～ make a pledge or promise；take an oath

【发运】fāyùn（货物）运出去 send（goods）by freight：装船～ ship；load a ship with cargo to be shipped|订货已经～，不日即可收到。The goods ordered have been sent by freight，and will soon reach you.

【发展】fāzhǎn ❶ 事物由小到大、由简单到复杂、由低级到高级的变化 develop；change into a larger，more complex or advanced state：事态还在～。Events are still developing.|社会～规律 social development law ❷ 扩大（组织、规模等）expand（an organization，scale，etc.）：～新会员 recruit（or admit）new members|～轻纺工业 develop or promote the light textile industry

【发怔】fāzhèng 发呆 be stupefied；be in a daze or trance；be stunned；stare blankly

【发纵指示】fā zòng zhǐ shì 放出猎狗，指示方向，要它追捕野兽 unleash hunting dogs after a quarry；〈比喻 *fig*〉指挥、调度 command and dispatch；pull strings；also 发踪指示 fā zōng zhǐ shì

【发作】fāzuò ❶（隐伏的事物）突然暴发或起作用（of latent things）act up；suddenly break out or show effect：胃病～ have a sudden bout of stomach-ache|酒力～ begin to feel the effect of wine；The liquor began to act up.|药性～。The medicine began to take effect. ❷ 发脾气 have a fit of anger；flare up；lose one's temper（or control）：心怀不满，借机～ take the opportunity to give vent to one's spleens|他有些生气，但当着大家的面不好～。He was angry，but as everybody was present，he kept his temper in check.

酦（醱） fā［酦酵］（fā//jiào）same as 发酵 fā//jiào

☞ pō on p. 1492

fá（ㄈㄚˊ）

乏 fá ❶ 缺乏 lack；deficient；insufficient；be short of：～味 uninteresting；dull；tasteless|贫～ impoverished；poor；destitute|不～其人。There is no shortage of such people. ❷ 疲倦 tired；weary：疲～ weary；tired|解～ recover from fatigue；refresh oneself|走～了 be tired after a long walk|人困马～。Both men and horses are exhausted. *or* Everyone is worn out. ❸〈方 *dial.*〉没力量；不起作用 exhausted；worn-out；useless：～话 useless words；ineffective talk|～煤 partially burned coal|贴～了的膏药 worn-out plaster

【乏货】fáhuò〈方 *dial.*〉不中用的人（骂人的话 curse）good-for-nothing；jerk；fathead

【乏力】fálì ❶ 身体疲倦，没有力气 weary；worn-out：浑身～ feel dog-tired；completely exhausted ❷ 没有能力；能力不足 incapable（of doing sth.）；lack of ability：回天～ not able to turn the tide；powerless to salvage a desperate situation

【乏煤】fáméi 燃烧过而没有烧透的煤 partially burned coal

【乏汽】fáqì 从蒸汽机、汽轮机等排出的已经做过功的蒸汽 dead steam；steam exhaust（from a steam engine or steam turbine, etc.)

【乏术】fáshù 没有办法;缺少办法 lack means; have no effective means: 进攻～ have no means of launching an attack | 回春～。There is no way to bring this patient back to life.

【乏味】fáwèi 没有趣味;缺少情趣 uninteresting; dull; tasteless; boring: 语言～ dull (or tedious) language | 这种单调的生活实在～得很。This monotonous way of life is really boring.

伐[1] fá ❶ 砍(树) fell; chop; cut down (trees): ～木 lumbering; felling | ～了几棵树 cut down several trees ❷ 攻打 strike; attack; send an expedition against: 征～go on a punitive expedition | 讨～ send armed forces to suppress | 北～ Northern Expedition (1926-1927)

伐[2] fá 〈书 *fml.*〉自夸 sing one's own praises; blow one's own trumpet; boast about oneself: ～善 boast about one's own advantages; sing one's own praises | 不矜不～(不自大自夸) unpretentious; neither conceited nor boastful; modest and unassuming

【伐木】fámù 采伐林木 lumbering; felling; cutting: 上山～ go up the mountain to cut trees | ～工人 logger; lumberman; lumberjack; timber cutter

【伐善】fáshàn 〈书 *fml.*〉夸耀自己的长处 brag; sing one's own praises

罚(罸) fá 处罚 punish; penalize; discipline: 惩～ punish; penalize | 责～ punish | 赏～分明 be fair in meting out rewards and punishments; be discriminating in one's rewards and punishments; keep strictly to the rules of reward and punishment | ～他喝一杯 (make sb.) drink a cup of wine as a forfeit

【罚不当罪】fá bù dāng zuì 处罚和所犯的罪行不相当。多指处罚过重。undeserved punishment; unduly (oft. too severely) punish; suffer inappropriate punishment

【罚金】fájīn ❶ 司法机关强制罪犯缴纳一定数额的钱,是一种刑事处罚,常作为附加刑使用 fine; criminal sanction oft. used as an accessory punishment imposed by judicial organs requiring submission of an amount of money ❷ 被判罚金时缴纳的钱 money submitted as a fine (or forfeit)

【罚款】fá//kuǎn ❶ 行政机关强制违法者缴纳一定数量的钱,是一种行政处罚 administrative penalty imposed by administrative organs forcing a lawbreaker to submit an amount of money ❷ 订合同的一方处罚违反合同的另一方以一定数量的钱 fine (or forfeit) imposed by one party of a contract on the other for violating its terms

【罚款】fákuǎn 被罚款时缴纳的钱 money submitted as a fine (forfeit, or penalty)

【罚没】fámò 行政机关强制违法者缴纳罚金和没收其非法所得的财物 confiscate; (of administrative organs) compel a lawbreaker to pay a fine, and confiscate their illegal gains

【罚球】fá//qiú 足球、篮球等球类比赛中,一方队员犯规时,由对方队员执行射门、投篮等处罚 penalty; (in football, basketball and other ball games) when a player in one team commits a foul, the opposing team is awarded a free kick or shot

垡[1] fá 〈方 *dial.*〉❶ 耕地翻土 dig and turn over soil: 耕～ turn up soil; plough a field ❷ 翻耕过的土块 tilled soil; ploughed land: 打～ plough a field | 深耕晒～ plough deep to expose the upturned soil to the sun

垡[2] fá 地名用字 used in place names only: 榆～(在北京) Yufa (in Beijing) | 落～(在河北) Luofa (in Hebei)

【垡子】fá·zi 〈方 *dial.*〉❶ 翻耕出来或掘出的土块 upturned soil; also 垡头 fá·tóu ❷ 指相当长的一段时间 fairly long period of time; quite a long time: 这一～ these days | 那一～ those days

阀[1] fá 指在某一方面有支配势力的人物、家族或集团 person, family or group dominant in a certain field: 军～ warlord | 财～ financial magnate; plutocrat

阀[2] fá 管道或机器中调节和控制流体的流量、压力和流动方向的装置,种类很多,如气阀、水阀、油阀等 valve; device on a pipe or machine that adjusts and controls the flow, pressure and direction of fluid, and having diverse applications, e.g. steam, water and oil valves; also 阀门 fámén and 凡尔 fán·ěr; 通称 generally called 活门 huómén

【阀阅】fáyuè 〈书 *fml.*〉❶ 功勋 meritorious service or deed ('阀' *fa*: 指功劳 contribution; credit; meritorious service; also 伐 fá; 阅 *yue*: 指经历 experience) ❷ 指有功勋的世家 family of distinction

筏(栰) fá 筏子 raft: 竹～ bamboo raft | 木～ wooden raft | 皮～ sheepskin or oxskin raft

【筏子】fá·zi 水上行驶的竹排或木排,也有用牛羊皮、橡胶等制造的 bamboo or wooden rafts; cattle-hide, sheepskin and rubber dinghy

fǎ (ㄈㄚˇ)

法[1] fǎ ❶ 体现统治阶级的意志,由国家制定或认可,受国家强制力保证执行的行为规则的总称,包括法律、法令、条例、命令、决定等 lex; law; act; code; general term for rules and regulations established or recognized by the state, and enforced under the guarantee of national mandatory power, such as laws, ordinances, regulations, orders, decisions, etc.: 合～ legal; lawful; legitimate | 犯～

break (or violate) the law; go against the law|变～ political reform; institutional reform|军～ military law|婚姻～ marriage law|绳之以～ punish sb. according to law; bring sb. to justice; enforce law upon sb. ❷ 方法；方式 method; way; mode:办～ way; means; measure; approach|用～ usage; use; application|土～ indigenous method; local method; traditional method|加～ addition ❸ 标准；模范；可以仿效的 standard; model; sth. imitable:～帖 model calligraphy|～书 model calligraphy|效～ take as a model; follow (suit)|取～乎上 aim high; set a high standard (or criterion) ❹ 仿效；效法 follow; emulate:师～ model oneself after (a great master); take as a model; imitate|～其遗志 fulfil sb.'s unfulfilled wish ❺〈佛教 *Budd.*〉道理 Law; Way; dharma: 佛～ Buddhist doctrine; Buddha's teachings|现身说～ draw a moral from one's own experience; advise sb. by using one's own experience as an example ❻ 法术 magic; trick; magic arts:作～ exercise magic|斗(dòu)～ contend by artifice or trickery; contend; (in mythology) contest in magic arts ❼ (Fǎ)姓 a surname

F

法[2] fǎ 法拉的简称 abbr. for 法拉 fǎlā

【法案】fǎ'àn 提交国家立法机关审查讨论的关于法律、法令问题的议案 motion; bill; draft act or law; legislative bill of law or decree submitted to a national legislative body for examination and discussion

【法办】fǎbàn 依法惩办 deal with sb. according to law; punish by law:逮捕～ arrest sb. and bring him or her to justice

【法宝】fǎbǎo ❶〈佛教 *Budd.*〉指佛说的法，也指和尚用的衣钵、锡杖等 Buddha's doctrine; monk's mantle, alms bowl and stick headed with a tin ring ❷ 神话中说的能制伏或杀伤妖魔的宝物 magic weapon; (in mythology) object with the magic power to subdue or kill monsters and demons ❸〈比喻 *fig.*〉用起来特别有效的工具、方法或经验 effective tool, formula or experience:群众路线是我们工作的～。The mass line is the talisman for our work.

【法币】fǎbì 1935 年以后国民党政府发行的纸币 paper currency issued by the KMT government from 1935 to 1948

【法场】fǎchǎng ❶ 僧道做法事的场所；道场 domain; bodhimanda, where Buddhist rites are performed ❷〈旧时 *old*〉执行死刑的地方；刑场 executioner's ground

【法典】fǎdiǎn 经过整理的比较完备、系统的某一类法律的总称，如民法典、刑法典 code; statute book; corpus juris; collection of certain organized, comprehensive and systematic laws, such as civil (law) code and penal (law) code

【法定】fǎdìng 由法律、法令所规定 statutory; legal; lawful; provided by law or decree:～人数(legal) quorum|～婚龄 legal age of marriage|～计量单位 official measuring unit|按照～的手续办理 go through the legal formalities

【法定人数】fǎdìng rénshù 正式规定的为召开会议或通过有效决议所必要的人数 quorum, formally prescribed minimum number of participants needed for a meeting or to be convened an effective decision to be made

【法度】fǎdù ❶ 法令制度；法律 legal system; laws and decrees ❷ 行为的准则；规矩 moral standard; established norm; rule:不合～ not up to the standard; not conforming to the norm

【法古】fǎgǔ 效法古代、古人 follow the example of ancient practices or sages:他的书法～而不泥古，别具神韵。His calligraphy draws on the styles of ancient masters without sticking to the rules, and has a charm uniquely his own.

【法官】fǎguān 法院中审判人员的通称 (general term for) justice; judge; judicial official

【法规】fǎguī 法律、法令、条例、规则、章程等的总称 statute; general term for laws, decrees, rules, regulations, etc.

【法纪】fǎjì 法律和纪律 law and discipline:遵守～ observe law and discipline; be law-abiding|目无～ act in total disregard of law and discipline; flout (or defy) law and discipline

【法家】Fǎjiā 先秦时期的一个思想流派，以申不害、商鞅、韩非为代表，主张法治，反对礼治，代表了当时新兴地主阶级的利益 Legalist School; pre-Qin school of thought represented by Shen Buhai, Shang Yang and Han Fei, advocating the rule of law instead of the rule of rites, and representing the interests of the then rising landlord class

【法警】fǎjǐng 司法警察。法院、检察院中执行逮捕或押送犯人，传唤当事人、证人和维持法庭秩序等任务的警察。bailiff; marshal; policeman employed by a court or procuratorate to make an arrest, escort a prisoner or captive to a designated place, summon the litigant and witness, and keep order in the court

【法拉】fǎlā 电容单位，1 个电容器，充以 1 库仑电量时，电势升高 1 伏特，电容就是 1 法拉。这个单位名称是为纪念英国物理学家法拉第(Michael Faraday)而定的。farad; unit of capacitance named after the English physicist Michael Faraday (1791-1867). When a capacitor is charged with 1 coulomb of electricity, its potential will rise by one volt, and thus the electric capacity is 1 farad. 简称

abbr. 法 fǎ

【法郎】fǎláng ❶法国等国的旧本位货币 Franc; old basic monetary unit of France and a few other countries ❷ 瑞士等国的本位货币 Franc; the basic monetary unit of Switzerland and a few other countries [法 French: Franc]

【法老】fǎlǎo 〈古代 *arch*.〉埃及国王的称号 pharaoh, title of the king of Egypt [希腊 Greek: pharao]

【法理】fǎlǐ ❶ 法律的理论根据 *ratio juris*; theoretical basis of law ❷〈书 *fml*.〉法则 rules; law ❸ 佛法的义理 Buddhist doctrine

【法力】fǎlì 佛法的力量。也泛指神奇的力量。power of the Buddhist doctrine; dharma power; (in a broad sense) magic power: ～无边。The dharma is all-powerful.

【法令】fǎlìng 政权机关所颁布的命令、指示、决定等的总称 laws and decrees; collection of orders, instructions and decisions, etc., promulgated by a state organ

【法律】fǎlǜ 由立法机关制定,国家政权保证执行的行为规则。法律体现统治阶级的意志,是阶级专政的工具之一。lex; juristic method; law; code of conduct formulated by a legislative body, whose enforcement is guaranteed by state power, which embodies the will of the ruling class, and serves as one of the ruling tools

【法螺】fǎluó 软体动物的一属,多生活在海洋中,壳圆锥形,壁厚,长约 1 尺,表面有很多瘤状突起。磨去尖顶的壳吹起来很响,古代做佛事时用来做乐器,所以叫法螺。渔船、航船等也用来做号角。conch (*Strombus*); marine gastropod mollusk, with a large, thick, spiralled shell. When the top of the shell of a conch is rubbed off and blown, it emits a loud, distinctive sound; used as a musical instrument in Buddhist rites in ancient times, hence its name 'conch of the law'; also used on board fishing boats and ships as a foghorn

【法盲】fǎmáng 缺乏法律知识的人 person lacking legal knowledge; person ignorant of the law

【法门】fǎmén ❶〈佛教 *Budd*.〉指修行者入道的门径 dharmaparaya; dharma dar; gateway to the Law; way to be initiated in Buddhism; also 佛门 fómén ❷ 泛指门径;方法(in a broad sense) access; approach; methodology

【法名】fǎmíng 指出家当僧尼或道士后由师父另起的名字 monastic name; clerical name; Taoist name

【法器】fǎqì 和尚、道士等举行宗教仪式时所用的器物,如钟、鼓、铙、钹、木鱼和瓶、钵、杖等 ritual utensil; ritual implement used by monks or Taoist priests, such as drum, cymbal, wooden fish, bottle, alms bowl, staff, etc.

【法权】fǎquán 权利;特权 right; privilege; power

【法人】fǎrén 法律上指根据法律参加民事活动的组织,如公司、社团等。法人享有与其业务有关的民事权利,承担相应的民事义务(区别于'自然人' as compared with 'natural person') corporation; legal or juristic person; organization participating in civil activities on a legal basis, such as companies and mass organizations, that enjoy the civil power related to their business, and that bear corresponding civil duties

【法师】fǎshī 对和尚或道士的尊称 Master of the Law; respectful title for a Buddhist or Taoist priest

【法式】fǎshì 标准的格式 rule; method; model: 《营造～》*Rules of Architecture*

【法事】fǎshì 指僧道拜忏、打醮等事 religious service or ceremony, such as the Buddhist ritual for redemption and the performance of Taoist rites

【法书】fǎshū ❶ 有高度艺术性的可以作为书法典范的字 model calligraphy of high artistic value ❷〈敬辞 *pol*.〉称对方写的字 your calligraphy; your writing

【法术】fǎshù ❶ 指法家的学术(in the Legalist school of thought) law and methods of governance ❷ 道士、巫婆等所用的画符念咒等骗人手法 witchcraft; deceitful tricks used by a Taoist priest or witch, such as drawing magic figures and reciting incantations

【法堂】fǎtáng ❶〈旧时 *old*〉官吏审理案件的地方;公堂 law court; hall where a magistrate hears cases ❷ 讲说佛法的场所 hall for preaching Buddhist doctrines

【法帖】fǎtiè 供人临摹或欣赏的名家书法的拓本或印本 calligraphic copybook, consisting of rubbings or reprints of works by accomplished calligraphers

【法庭】fǎtíng ❶ 法院所设立的审理诉讼案件的机构 court; law court; court of justice ❷ 法院审理诉讼案件的地方 courtroom; tribunal

【法统】fǎtǒng 宪法和法律的传统,是统治权力的法律根据 constitutional and legal tradition, the legal basis of a ruling power

【法王】fǎwáng ❶〈佛教 *Budd*.〉对释迦牟尼的尊称 Dharmaraja; King of the Law, respectful term of address for Sakyamuni ❷ 元明两代授予喇嘛教首领的封号 King of the Law, title conferred on the head of Lamaism in the Yuan and Ming dynasties

【法网】fǎwǎng〈比喻 *fig*.〉严密的法律制度 meshes of the law; arm of the law: 难逃～ cannot escape the net of justice; will eventually be brought to justice | 落入～ be caught in the net of justice; be brought to justice

【法西斯】fǎxīsī ❶ '权标'(拉丁 fasces)的译音,权标是意大利法西斯党的标志 fascism, transliteration of the Latin term of fasces, symbol of Italian fascists ❷ 指法西斯主义的(倾向、运动、体制等) fascist (tendencies, movement, systems, etc.)

【法西斯蒂】fǎxīsīdì 指法西斯主义的组织或成员 fascist organization or its member [意 Italian: fascisti (fascista 的复数 pl. of fascista)

【法西斯主义】fǎxīsī zhǔyì 一种最反动最野蛮的独裁制度和思想体系。对内实行恐怖统治,对外实行武力侵略和民族压迫。起源于意大利独裁者墨索里尼的法西斯党。fascism; most reactionary and brutal dictatorship and ideological system that originated in the fascist party led by the Italian dictator Benito Mussolini, exercising terrorist rule at home while pursuing armed invasion and national oppression abroad

【法学】fǎxué 研究国家和法的学科 jurisprudence; science of law; *juris doctrina*

【法眼】fǎyǎn 〈佛教 *Budd.*〉指能认识到事物真相的眼力,泛指敏锐深邃的眼力 dharma eye, eye of wisdom which discerns the truth; (in a broad sense) keen and profound eye

【法衣】fǎyī 和尚、道士等在举行宗教仪式时穿的衣服 monastic habit; garment worn by a Buddhist or Taoist priest at a religious ceremony

【法医】fǎyī 法院中专门负责用法医学来协助审理案件的医生 forensic doctor (or physician); person employed by a court to help trying cases by forensic medicine

【法医学】fǎyīxué 医学的一个分科,研究并解决法律案件中有关医学的问题,如创伤或死亡的原因等 forensic medicine; medical jurisprudence; branch of medical science pertaining to the study and solving of medical aspects of legal cases, such as finding out the reasons for an injury or a death, etc.

【法院】fǎyuàn 独立行使审判权的国家机关 court; tribunal; *judicatus*; court of law

【法则】fǎzé ❶ 规律 rule; law: 自然～law of nature ❷ 〈书 *fml.*〉法规 *norma*; norms; formal laws and regulations ❸ 〈书 *fml.*〉模范;榜样 model; good example

【法政】fǎzhèng 〈旧时 *old*〉对法律和政治的合称 law and politics

【法旨】fǎzhǐ 神的意旨(迷信) (superstition) god's wish; Buddha's will

【法制】fǎzhì 统治阶级按照自己的意志,通过政权机关建立起来的法律制度,包括法律的制定、执行和遵守,是统治阶级实行专政的方法和工具 legality; legal institutions; legal system established by the ruling class according to its will through state apparatuses, including the formulation, enforcement and observation of law, serving as the means to exercise dictatorship: 健全～ improve the legal system; tighten up the legal institutions | 增强～观念 enhance awareness of law; enhance the sense of legality

【法治】fǎzhì ❶ 先秦时期法家的政治思想,主张以法为准则,统治人民,处理国事 Legalist school of thought prior to the Qin Dynasty, advocating the rule of the people and the handling of state affairs by law ❷ 指根据法律治理国家 rule of law

【法子】fǎ·zi 方法 way; method; solution: 想～ think of (or find out) a way | 没～ can do nothing about it; cannot help it

砝 fǎ [砝码](fǎmǎ)天平上作为重量标准的物体,通常为金属块或金属片,可以表明较精确的重量 weight; objects used on a balance as a standard weight, usu. metal lumps or pieces, which indicate accurate weight

灋 fǎ 〈书 *fml.*〉 same as 法 fǎ

fà (ㄈㄚˋ)

发(髮) fà 头发 hair: 毛～ hair | 须～ beard and hair | 白～ white hair | 假～ wig; hairpiece | 理～ have a haircut; have one's hair cut

☞ fā on p. 518

【发胶】fàjiāo 理发或烫发后用来固定发型的化妆品 hairspray; hair lacquer; cosmetic used to fix a hairstyle after having a haircut or perm

【发蜡】fàlà 用凡士林加香料制成的化妆品,抹在头发上,使有光泽而不蓬松 pomade, hair cosmetic made of vaseline and perfume, rubbed on hair to make it glossy but not fluffy

【发廊】fàláng 美容理发店,多指小型的个体美容理发店 barber's; hairdresser's; beauty salon

【发妻】fàqī 指第一次娶的妻子(古诗'结发为夫妻',结发指初成年) first wife; woman who was married to a man when both had just come of age and, usu. who remains as his wife into old age. The term is derived from the line in a poem by the Western-Han poet Su Wu (?-60 B.C.): 'United in wedlock when we were both young, we remain husband and wife to this day.'

【发卡】fàqiǎ 妇女用来别头发的卡子 hair clip

【发式】fàshì 头发梳理成的式样 hairstyle; hairdo; coiffure

【发网】fàwǎng 妇女罩头发用的网子 hairnet used by a woman

【发型】fàxíng 发式 hairstyle; hairdo; coiffure; hair fashion

【发指】fàzhǐ 头发竖起来。形容非常愤怒。with one's hair standing on end; filled with indignation; bristle or boil with anger: 令人～ make sb. boil with anger | 为之～ get one's hackles up

珐(琺) fà ☞ below

【珐琅】fàláng 用石英、长石、硝石和碳酸钠等加上铅和锡的氧化物烧制成的像釉子的物质。涂在铜质或银质器物上,经过烧制,能形成不同颜色的釉质表面,用来制造景泰蓝、证章、纪念章等。enamel, substance resembling glaze and prepared by melting quartz, feldspar, niter and soda with lead and tin oxides, applied on bronze or silver utensils to form a coloured surface after baking; a material that may be used to produce cloisonne, badges, and souvenir pins

【珐琅质】fàlángzhì ☞ 釉质 yòuzhì on p. 2334

•fa (•ㄈㄚ)

哦 •fa 〈方 *dial.*〉〈语助词 *aux.*〉相当于'吗' [used at the end of a sentence to form a question, equivalent to 吗 •ma]:番茄要～? Do you want a tomato? |夜饭吃过～? Have you had supper?

fān (ㄈㄢ)

帆 fān ❶ 挂在桅杆上的布篷,利用风力使船前进 sail; large sheet of strong cloth fixed to the mast of a ship which, when the wind fills, propels the vessel:～樯 mast|一～风顺 smooth sailing; bon voyage|扬～远航 set sail for a long voyage ❷〈书 *fml.*〉指帆船 sailboat; sailing boat:征～ boat or ship on a long voyage|千～竞发。Thousands of sails shoot ahead.

【帆布】fānbù 用棉纱或亚麻等织成的一种粗厚的布,用来做帐篷、行军床、衣服、鞋等 canvas, strong cloth woven with cotton yarn or flax to make tents, camp beds, clothes, shoes, etc.

【帆布床】fānbùchuáng 行军床 camp bed; cot

【帆船】fānchuán 利用风力张帆行驶的船 boat or ship with sails that travels by the force of wind

【帆樯】fānqiáng〈书 *fml.*〉船上挂帆的杆子,借指船只 pole from which hangs the sail of a boat; (reference to) vessels:～林立 forest of masts

飒 fān〈书 *fml.*〉same as 帆 fān

番[1] fān 指外国或外族 foreign country or nation:～邦 foreign country; barbarian land; alien people or nation|～茄 tomato |～薯 sweet potato (*Ipomoea batatas*)

番[2] fān〈量词 *classifier*〉❶ 种;样[used with the numeral 一 (only)] kind; sort:别有一～天地 place of unique beauty; scenery of exceptional charm ❷ 回;次;遍 time:思考一～ give careful consideration (to sth.); think it over|几～周折 after repeated (several) setbacks|三～五次 time and again|翻了一～(数量加了一倍) double; increase twofold
☞ pān on p. 1441

【番邦】fānbāng〈旧时 *old*〉外国或外族 foreign country or nation

【番菜】fāncài 西餐的旧称 old name for Western-style food:～馆 Western-style restaurant; restaurant serving Western food

【番瓜】fānguā〈方 *dial.*〉南瓜 pumpkin

【番号】fānhào 部队的编号 designation of a military unit

【番椒】fānjiāo 中药上指辣椒 (Chin. med.) chilli (*Capsicum anuum*); (hot) pepper

【番茄】fānqié ❶ 一年生或二年生草本植物,全株有软毛,花黄色。结浆果,球形或扁圆形,红或黄色,是普通蔬菜。tomato (*Lycopersicon esculentum*); annual or biennial downy solanaceous plant with blooming yellow flowers, and bearing red or yellow spherical or oval berries, which serve as a common vegetable ❷ 这种植物的果实 tomato; fruit of the plant‖ also 西红柿 xīhóngshì

【番薯】fānshǔ〈方 *dial.*〉甘薯 sweet potato (*Ipomoea batatas*)

蕃 fān same as 番[1] fān
☞ fán on p. 533

幡(旛) fān 一种窄长的旗子,垂直悬挂 streamer, long, narrow flag hung vertically

【幡儿】fānr 旧俗出殡时举的窄长像幡的东西,多用白纸剪成 long narrow flag, oft. fashioned out of white paper, carried in a funeral procession; also 引魂幡 yǐnhúnfān

【幡然】fānrán same as 翻然 fānrán

【幡子】fān•zi〈方 *dial.*〉same as 幡儿 fānr

缗 fān same as 翻 fān ⑥
☞ fán on p. 534

藩 fān ❶ 篱笆 hedge; fence:～篱 fence; hedge ❷〈书 *fml.*〉屏障 (protective) screen; barrier:屏～ border defence facility; protectorate ❸ 封建王朝的属国或属地 feudatory; dependent state; vassal state:～国 vassal state|外～ outlying vassal state

【藩国】fānguó 封建时代作为宗主国藩属的国家 vassal states of a metropolitan state during the period of feudalism

【藩篱】fānlí 篱笆 fence; hedge;〈比喻 *fig.*〉门户或屏障 gateway or protective screen

【藩属】fānshǔ 封建王朝的属地或属国 colony, vassal, or dependent state of a feudal dynasty

【藩镇】fānzhèn 唐代中期在边境和重要地区设节度使,掌管当地的军政,后来权力逐渐扩大,兼管民政、财政,形成军人割据,常与朝廷对抗,历史上叫做藩镇(of the mid-Tang Dynasty) military governorship established at the prefectural level in border regions and important areas, which later gradually extended its power to local civil and financial affairs until it gave rise to a separatist warlords that were oft. at loggerheads with the imperial court

翻 fān ❶ 上下或内外交换位置；歪倒；反转 turn (over, up, upside down, inside out, etc.); reverse：推～ overthrow; overturn｜～身 turn over; stand up｜车～了 (of a vehicle) overturn｜人仰马～ both men and horses thrown off their feet; shocking mess of things; men and horses toppled ❷ 为了寻找而移动上下物体的位置 rummage; search; look through：～箱倒柜 rummage through chests and cupboards (in a thorough house-search); ransack boxes and chests｜从箱子底下～出来一条旧围巾 search out an old scarf from under a case ❸ 推翻原来的 reverse; overturn：～供 withdraw a confession; retract a testimony｜～案 reverse a verdict ❹ 爬过；越过 cross; get over; climb over：～墙而过 climb over a wall｜～山越岭 tramp over mountains and through ravines; cross one mountain after another; tramp over hill and dale ❺（数量）成倍地增加 multiply; double：～番 double; twice as much (or many) as｜～了几倍 double and redouble ❻ 翻译 translate; interpret：把德文～成中文 translate sth. from German into Chinese ❼（～儿 fānr）翻脸 break up; fall out：闹～了 fall out; quarrel and split up｜把他惹～了 make him angry; get his back up

【翻案】fān//àn ❶ 推翻原定的判决 reverse or overturn a verdict：为蒙冤者～ overturn or reverse the wrong verdict passed on an innocent person ❷ 泛指推翻原来的处分、结论、评价等 (in a broad sense) overturn the original punishment, conclusion or comment, etc.：～文章 article or work representing a radically different view on a historical incident or figure

【翻把】fān//bǎ〈方 *dial.*〉❶ 敌对的一方被打败以后重占上风 (of one's rival) come back from a defeat to gain the upper hand once more; also 反把 fǎnbǎ ❷ 不承认说过的话；不认账 deny what one has said or done

【翻白眼】fān báiyǎn（～儿 fān báiyǎnr）黑眼珠偏斜，露出较多的眼白，是为难、失望、愤恨或不满时眼睛的表情，有时是病势危险时的生理现象 glare; show the whites of one's eyes (from embarrassment, despair, resentment or dissatisfaction, or as a physiological symptom of someone dangerously ill)

【翻版】fānbǎn ❶ 翻印的版本 reprint; reproduction; copy ❷〈比喻 *fig.*〉照搬、照抄或生硬模仿的行为 mechanically copy or rigidly imitate

【翻本】fānběn（～儿 fānběnr）赌博时赢回已经输掉的钱 win back (money lost in gambling, etc.)

【翻茬】fān//chá 农作物收割后进行浅耕，将留下的茎和根翻入土中 plough under the stubble after a harvest

【翻场】fān//cháng 翻动摊晒在场上的农作物，使干得快，容易脱粒 turn over the grain on the threshing ground so as to dry it quickly, making it easy to thresh

【翻车】fān//chē ❶ 车辆翻覆 (of a vehicle) overturn：发生一起～事故。A traffic accident occurred in which a car overturned. ❷〈比喻 *fig.*〉事情中途受挫或失败 suffer a setback or failure midway through one's work

【翻车】fānchē〈方 *dial.*〉水车 waterwheel

【翻船】fān//chuán ❶ 船只翻覆 (of a boat or ship) capsize ❷〈比喻 *fig.*〉事情中途受挫或失败 suffer a setback or upset midway; be defeated：夺魁呼声最高的北京队在半决赛中～。The Beijing Team, which was most favoured for the championship, lost in the semi-finals.

【翻动】fāndòng 改变原来的位置或样子 shift sth. from its original place or change its appearance：～身子 turn over｜要勤～，免得受热不均。Stir frequently so as to avoid heating unevenly.

【翻斗】fāndǒu 指可以翻转的、形状略像斗的车厢 reversible sidecar shaped like a dipper：～车 tipcart; skip car

【翻番】fān//fān 数量加倍 double; be twice as much (or many) as：钻井速度～。The drilling speed has doubled.｜这个县工农业总产值十年翻了两番。The total agricultural and industrial output value of the county quadrupled in ten years.

【翻覆】fānfù ❶ same as 翻 fān ①：车辆～。A vehicle toppled over. ❷ 巨大彻底的变化 great and thorough change：天地～ earth-shaking change; world-shaking change ❸ 来回翻动身体 toss and turn; toss from side to side：夜间～不成眠 toss and turn sleeplessly at night ❹〈书 *fml.*〉same as 反复 fǎnfù ②

【翻改】fāngǎi 把旧的衣服拆开另行改做 turn (old clothes); remake：～大衣 have an overcoat turned or remade

【翻盖】fāngài 把旧的房屋拆除后重新建造 rebuild or renovate (a house)

【翻跟头】fān gēn·tou ❶ 身体向下翻转而后恢复原状 (of one's body) roll downward and then return to its original upright position; turn a somersault ❷〈比喻 *fig.*〉受挫 suffer a setback

【翻个儿】fān//gèr 翻过来；颠倒过来 turn over; turn upside down or inside out：场上晒的麦子该～了。It is time to turn over the wheat on the threshing ground.

【翻工】fān//gōng〈方 *dial.*〉返工 do (poorly-done work) over again; redo one's job

【翻供】fān//gòng 推翻自己以前所供认的话 withdraw or revoke a confession; retract one's testimony

【翻滚】fāngǔn ❶ 上下滚动;翻腾 seethe; roll upward or downward:白浪~。The waves rolled and foamed.|乌云~。Dark clouds were rolling. ◇桩桩往事在脑子里~。Past events rolled through the mind. ❷ 来回翻身打滚儿;翻转滚动 toss and turn; tumble about:两个人扭打起来,满地~。The two came to blows, heaving and turning on the ground.

【翻黄】fānhuáng 竹黄 bamboo chips stripped of its outer green layer for the making of basketry; also 翻簧 fānhuáng

【翻悔】fānhuǐ 对以前允诺的事后悔而不承认 back out (of a commitment, promise, etc.):这件事原是他亲口答应的,如今却~不认账了。He made a personal promise to do this, but is now backing out.

【翻检】fānjiǎn 翻动查看(书籍、文件等) consult; look through (books, papers, etc.):~词典 look through a dictionary|~资料 consult reference materials

【翻建】fānjiàn 翻盖 rebuild:~危房 rebuild dilapidated housing

【翻江倒海】fān jiāng dǎo hǎi 形容水势浩大,多用来比喻力量或声势非常壮大 vast flow of water; (of a river) deluge with the momentum of an avalanche; (fig.) overwhelming force or momentum; also 倒海翻江 dǎo hǎi fān jiāng

【翻浆】fān//jiāng 春暖解冻的时候,地面或道路表面发生裂纹并渗出水分和泥浆 (of road surface) become sodden and muddy (usu. when spring thaw sets in)

【翻卷】fānjuǎn 上下翻动 twirl; spin; whirl round; wheel about:红旗~。The red flag unfurled and flapped.|雪花在空中~。Snowflakes swirled in the air.|船尾~着层层浪花。Layer upon layer of spray whirled around the stern.

【翻刻】fānkè 按照原版重新雕版(印刷) (in block-printing) cut blocks based on a printed book or article:~本 block-printed edition|~重印 reprint a book by block-printing

【翻来覆去】fān lái fù qù ❶ 来回翻身 toss and turn; toss from side to side:躺在床上~,怎么也睡不着 toss and turn in bed, unable to sleep ❷ 一次又一次;多次重复 repeatedly; again and again:这话已经~说过不知多少遍。This is what I have been saying over and over again.

【翻脸】fān//liǎn 对人的态度突然变得不好 wax hostile; fall out:~无情 turn against a friend without mercy; be treacherous and ruthless|~不认人 turn against a friend, turn one's back on an old associate|两口子从来没翻过脸。The couple has never fallen out.

【翻领】fānlǐng (~儿 fānlǐngr)衣领的一种样式,领子上部翻转向外,或全部翻转向外,领口敞开 lapel; turndown collar; collar, whose upper section turns down, or that completely turns down, and whose collar band folds down on each side:~衬衫 shirt with a turndown collar

【翻录】fānlù 照原样重录磁带(多指不是原出版者重录 usu. by one other than the original publisher) duplicate a tape

【翻毛】fānmáo (~儿 fānmáor) ❶ 毛皮的毛朝外的 fur (on exterior):~大衣 fur coat ❷ 皮革的反面朝外的 reverse side of leather turned out:~皮鞋 suede shoes

【翻弄】fānnòng 来回翻动 turn (back and forth):他心不在焉地~着报纸。He absent-mindedly turned the pages of a newspaper.

【翻拍】fānpāi 以图片、文稿等为对象拍摄复制 reproduce (a photo or manuscript):~照片 reproduce a photo|~文件 reproduce a document

【翻皮】fānpí same as 翻毛 fānmáo ②

【翻然】fānrán 很快而彻底地(改变) (change) quickly and completely:~改进 make quick, marked improvement|~悔悟 quickly wake up to one's error; make a clean break with one's past; also 幡然 fānrán

【翻砂】fānshā ❶ 铸工①的通称 popular term for 铸工 zhùgōng ① ❷ 制造砂型 founding; moulding; casting

【翻晒】fānshài 在阳光下翻动物体使吸收光和热 turn over sth. in the sun to absorb light and heat:~粮食 turn over grain on the threshing ground|~被褥 turn over quilts and bedding in the sun

【翻身】fān//shēn ❶ 躺着转动身体 turn over (in bed) ❷〈比喻 *fig.*〉从受压迫、受剥削的情况下解放出来 emancipate oneself from oppression and exploitation; stand up:~户 emancipated household|~作主 stand up and be master(s) of one's own ❸〈比喻 *fig.*〉改变落后面貌或不利处境 deliver oneself from backwardness or a predicament:只有进行改革,我厂的生产才能~。Only by carrying out reform can production in our plant effect a turn for the better. ❹〈方 *dial.*〉转身;回身 turn round

【翻腾】fān·téng ❶ 上下滚动 roll up and down:波浪~ churning (or seething) wave ◇许多问题在他脑子里像滚了锅一样~着。His mind seethed with problems like boiling water in a pot. ❷ 翻动 rummage; turn sth. over and over:几个柜子都~到了,也没找到那件衣服。I rummaged through all the cupboards but still could not find the coat. ◇那些事儿,不去~也好。It would be better not to bring that up.

【翻天】fān//tiān ❶ 形容吵闹得很凶 make a racket:吵~ have a violent quarrel; kick up a terrific row|闹翻了天 rough-house; make (or raise) a rumpus ❷〈比喻 *fig.*〉造反 rebel

【翻天覆地】fān tiān fù dì ❶ 形容变化巨大而彻底 earthshaking and thorough change：农村面貌有了～的变化。Earthshaking changes have taken place in rural areas. ❷ 形容闹得很凶 quarrel (or fight) furiously：这一闹，把家闹得个～。They kicked up a terrific row in the family.

【翻胃】fān//wèi ☞ 反胃 fǎnwèi on p.538

【翻箱倒柜】fān xiāng dǎo guì 形容彻底地翻检、搜查 thorough search by rummaging through everything; also 翻箱倒箧 fān xiāng dǎo qiè

【翻新】fānxīn ❶ 把旧的东西拆了重做(多指衣服 usu. of clothes) refurbish or remake ❷ 从旧的变化出新的 (of the new) emerges out of the old：手法～ innovations in style | 花样～ put old wine in a new bottle

【翻修】fānxiū 把旧的房屋、道路等拆除后就原有规模重建 rebuild a house, a road, etc., according to its original scale after tearing it down

【翻译】fānyì ❶ 把一种语言文字的意义用另一种语言文字表达出来(也指方言与民族共同语、方言与方言、古代语与现代语之间一种用另一种表达)；把代表语言文字的符号或数码用语言文字表达出来 translate; convert a piece of writing or speech from one language to another (also the conversion of a dialect to the standard national language, of one dialect into another in the same language or of an archaic language into a modern one); decode symbols or numerals in the form of a written language：～外国小说 translate a foreign novel | 把密码～出来 decode a secret cipher ❷ 做翻译工作的人 translator：他当过三年～。He worked as a translator for three years.

【翻印】fānyìn 照原样重印书刊、图画等(多指不是原出版者重印 usu. sb. other than the original publisher) reprint (books, periodicals or pictures, etc.)：版权所有，～必究。All rights reserved; those responsible for unauthorized reproduction will be prosecuted.

【翻涌】fānyǒng (云、水等)上下滚动；翻腾 seethe; surge; (of cloud and water, etc.) roll up and down：波涛～ billowing waves ◇热血～ seethe with righteous indignation; one's blood seethes | 思绪～ one's mind seethes with thoughts

【翻阅】fānyuè 翻着看(书籍、文件等) look over or leaf (glance) through (a book, document, etc.)：～杂志 look over a magazine

【翻越】fānyuè 越过；跨过 surmount; get over：～山岭 climb over mountains and hills | ～障碍物 get over (or surmount) an obstacle

【翻云覆雨】fān yún fù yǔ 唐杜甫诗《贫交行》：'翻手作云覆手雨，纷纷轻薄何须数。'后来用'翻云覆雨'比喻反复无常或玩弄手段。like a weathercock in the wind; produce clouds with one turn of the hand and rain with another. The phrase originated from the poem *Friends from Days of Poverty* by the Tang poet Du Fu, 'Today there are those as changeable as clouds or rain, their numbers too great to be counted.'

【翻造】fānzào 拆除旧的重新建造；翻盖 rebuild; renovate

䌓 fān same as 翻 fān

fán (ㄈㄢˊ)

凡[1](亢) fán ❶ 平凡 ordinary; commonplace：～庸 mediocre | 自命不～ think oneself a prodigy; think a great deal of oneself ❷ 宗教迷信和神话故事中称人世间 (in religious or superstitious stories and mythology) mundane world; earth：思～ (of an immortal) long for this mortal world | 天仙下～。A fairy descended on the mundane world.

凡[2](亢) fán ❶ 凡是 all; every; any：～年满十八岁公民都有选举权与被选举权。Every citizen who has reached the age of 18 has the right to vote and stand for election. ❷〈书 *fml.*〉总共 altogether; in all：不知～几 innumerable; countless | 全书～二十卷。The book comprises 20 volumes. ❸〈书 *fml.*〉大概；要略 outline; gist：大～ generally; in most cases | 发～起例 introduction and guide (to a book or a subject)

凡[3](亢) fán 我国民族音乐音阶上的一级，乐谱上用做记音符号，相当于简谱的'4' *fan*, a note of tradition Chinese music scale, used on a music score as a symbol, equivalent to '4' in numbered musical notation; ☞ 工尺 gōngchǐ on p.664

【凡尘】fánchén 佛教、道教或神话故事中指人世间；尘世 (in Buddhism, Taoism or Chinese mythology) this mortal world; mundane world

【凡尔丁】fán'ěrdīng 一种平纹单色毛织品，常用线做经、纱做纬织成，质地薄而挺括，适宜于做夏季服装 valetin; plain monochromatic wool fabric, often woven with threads as warps, and yarns as wefts, with a thin and strong texture, suitable for making summer clothes

【凡夫】fánfū 凡人 mortal man; ordinary person; common folk：～俗子 ordinary people; common run

【凡例】fánlì 书前关于本书体例的说明 notes on or guide to the style of a book

【凡人】fánrén ❶ 平常的人 ordinary (or common) people：～琐事 ordinary people and trifling matters ❷ 指尘世的人(区别于'神仙' as compared with 'immortals') mortals

【凡士林】fánshìlín 石蜡和重油的混合物，半透明，半固态，淡黄色，精炼后成纯白色。医药上用来制油膏，工业上用做防锈剂和润滑剂。vaseline, soft yellow semitranslucent and semisolid mixture of paraffin wax and heavy oil, which turns pure white after refinement, used to make ointment and other medical products, and industrial products such as antirusting agents and lubricants; also 矿脂 kuàngzhī

【凡事】fánshì 不论什么事情 everything：～多跟群众商量总有好处。It is always beneficial to consult the masses before doing something.

【凡是】fánshì 总括某个范围内的一切 every; any; without exception：～新生的事物总是在同旧事物的斗争中成长起来的。All new things achieve development during the course of fighting against the old.

【凡俗】fánsú 平凡庸俗；平常 ordinary; common：不同～ out of the ordinary; out of the common run｜流于～ end up in mediocrity

【凡响】fánxiǎng 平凡的音乐 common or ordinary music：不同～ outstanding; out of the ordinary｜非同～ quite extraordinary

【凡心】fánxīn 僧道指对尘世的思念、留恋之心 (of Buddhists and Taoists) reluctance to renounce the temporal world

【凡庸】fányōng 平平常常；普普通通（多形容人）(of a person) ordinary; commonplace：才能～ ordinary talent｜～之辈 common herd; person of mediocre abilities

氾 Fán 姓 a surname

☞ 泛 fàn on p.542

矾（礬） fán 泛称某些金属硫酸盐的含水复盐，如明矾、胆矾、绿矾 general term for water-bearing salt of certain metal sulphates, such as alum, and blue and green vitriol

钒 fán 金属元素，符号 V (vanadium)。银白色，质硬，耐腐蚀，用来制造合金钢等。vanadium (V), a silvery white corrosion-resistant metal element of a hard quality, used to make alloy steel and certain other materials

烦 fán ❶ 烦闷 annoyed; vexed; upset：～恼 worried; upset; vexed｜心～意乱 be terribly upset; be vexed and lost ❷ 厌烦 be tired of; fed up：耐～ be patient｜这些话都听～了。I have heard enough. ❸ 又多又乱 superfluous and confusing：～杂 tediously miscellaneous｜要言不～ terse and to the point; spell out the essentials in a few words ❹ 烦劳 trouble：有事相～。I have a favour to ask of you.｜～您给带个信儿。May I trouble you to pass on a message?

【烦劳】fánláo〈敬辞 *pol.*〉表示请托 trouble：～您顺便给我们捎个信儿去。Would you mind taking along a message from us?

【烦乱】fánluàn ❶（心情）烦躁不安 depressed and perturbed：心里～极了，不知干什么好 feel extremely upset, not knowing what to do ❷ same as 繁乱 fánluàn

【烦闷】fánmèn 心情不畅快 unhappy, depressed; moody

【烦难】fánnán same as 繁难 fánnán

【烦恼】fánnǎo 烦闷苦恼 upset; worried; vexed：自寻～ work oneself up for no reason at all｜不必为区区小事而～。Don't be upset over such trifles.

【烦请】fánqǐng〈敬辞 *pol.*〉表示请求 request：～光临。May I request the honour of your presence?

【烦扰】fánrǎo ❶ 搅扰 disturb; bug; bother：他太累了，我实在不忍心再～他。He is so tired. I don't have the heart to disturb him. ❷ 因受搅扰而心烦 disturbed; annoyed

【烦人】fánrén 使人心烦或厌烦 annoying; vexing：～的毛毛雨下起来没完没了。This irritating drizzle carried on endlessly.

【烦冗】fánrǒng ❶（事务）繁杂 (of a workload) diverse and complex ❷（文章）烦琐冗长 (of articles) long and tedious; wordy and insipid; also 繁冗 fánrǒng

【烦琐】fánsuǒ 繁杂琐碎 over-elaborate; loaded down with trivial details; petty and tedious：手续～ over-elaborate formalities｜～的考据 pedantic textual research; also 繁琐 fánsuǒ

【烦嚣】fánxiāo（声音）嘈杂扰人 noisy and irritating：～的集市 din and traffic of a market｜这里～的声音一点也听不到了，只有树叶在微风中沙沙作响。There is no troublesome noise to be heard here. What one can hear is only the rustling of leaves in the breeze.

【烦心】fánxīn ❶ 使心烦 annoying; vexing; wearying：别谈这些～的事情了。Don't talk about such annoying matters. ❷〈方 *dial.*〉费心；操心 go to all lengths：孩子太淘气，真让人～。The child is so naughty, he is really a pain in the neck.

【烦言】fányán〈书 *fml.*〉❶ 气愤或不满的话 complaint; grievance：啧有～ grumble time and again; be full of complaints｜心无结怨，口无～ bear no grudge and never complain ❷ 烦琐的话 tedious words or remarks：～碎辞 gossip; also 繁言 fányán

【烦忧】fányōu 烦恼忧愁 worried and depressed

【烦杂】fánzá same as 繁杂 fánzá

【烦躁】fánzào 烦闷急躁 agitated; fretful; irritable and restless：～不安 have (get) the fidgets; set one's nerves on edge

墦 fán〈书 *fml.*〉坟墓 tomb; grave

蕃 fán〈书 *fml.*〉❶（草木）茂盛 (of grass, trees, etc.) luxuriant; lush; grow in abundance：～茂 luxuriant; lush｜～昌 thrive ❷ 繁殖 multiply; reproduce：～息 multiply (or reproduce) rapidly; proliferate｜～孳 multiply

☞ fān on p. 529

【蕃息】fánxī 〈书 *fml*.〉滋生众多;繁殖增多 multiply quickly; proliferate: 万物~。All living creatures proliferate.

【蕃衍】fányǎn same as 繁衍 fányǎn

樊 fán ❶〈书 *fml*.〉篱笆 fence: ~篱 fence; hedge ❷(Fán)姓 a surname

【樊篱】fánlí 篱笆 fence; hedge;〈比喻 *fig*.〉对事物的限制 obstacle or restriction to sth.: 冲破旧礼教的~ shake off the shackles of old-fashioned morals

【樊笼】fánlóng 关鸟兽的笼子 bird cage;〈比喻 *fig*.〉受束缚而不自由的境地 shackles

缗 fán [缗帑](fányuān)〈书 *fml*.〉❶ 风吹摆动的样子 fluttering ❷ 乱取 grab

☞ fān on p. 529

璠 fán 〈书 *fml*.〉美玉 beautiful jade

膰 fán 〈古代 *arch*.〉祭祀所用的熟肉 sacrificial meat

燔 fán 〈书 *fml*.〉❶ 焚烧 burn: ~烧 burn; set on fire ❷ 烤 roast; bake: ~之炙之 roast and broil

繁(緐) fán ❶ 繁多;复杂(跟'简'相对 as opposed to 'simple') complicated: 纷~ numerous and complicated|~杂 miscellaneous; many and diverse|~星 galaxy of stars|删~就简 cut out the superfluous to bring out the essential; simplify by weeding out superfluities ❷ 繁殖(牲畜)(of livestock) multiply; procreate; propagate: 自~自养 livestock propagated and raised by oneself

☞ Pó on p. 1492

【繁本】fánběn 有多种版本的著作中内容、文字较多的版本;改写成简本或缩写本所根据的原本 unexpurgated edition; original manuscript of a work before being adapted into an abridged or concise edition

【繁博】fánbó (引证)多而广泛(of citation and quotation) prolific and wide-ranging

【繁多】fánduō (种类)多;丰富 numerous; various: 花色~ of all patterns and colours|品种~ various in kind; of great variety|名目~ multifarious items

【繁复】fánfù 多而复杂 heavy and complicated: 手续~ complicated procedures|~的组织工作 complex organizational work

【繁花】fánhuā 繁茂的花;各种各样的花 flowers in full bloom; variety of flowers: ~似锦 flowers blooming like a length of brocade; a multitude of blooming flowers|万紫千红,~怒放。Flowers of all kinds are blooming in a riot of colour.

【繁华】fánhuá (城镇、街市)繁荣热闹(of cities and towns and downtown streets) thriving; prosperous; bustling; busy: 王府井是北京~的商业街。Wangfujing is a busy downtown street in Beijing.

【繁丽】fánlì (辞藻)丰富华丽(of diction) rich and flowery

【繁乱】fánluàn (事情)多而杂乱(of affairs) miscellaneous; many and diverse: 头绪~ too many loose ends; also 烦乱 fánluàn

【繁忙】fánmáng 事情多,不得空 busy; bustling: 工作~ busy with work; busily engaged

【繁茂】fánmào (草木)繁密茂盛(of grass and trees, etc.) lush; luxuriant: 花木~ lush growth of flowers and trees|枝叶~,苍翠欲滴 lush emerald-green foliage

【繁密】fánmì 多而密 thick; dense: 人口~ densely populated|~的树林 dense forest|~的鞭炮声 cacophony of firecrackers

【繁难】fánnán 复杂困难 troublesome; hard nut to crack: 工作~ arduous work|遇到了~的事 come across a knotty problem; also 烦难 fánnán

【繁闹】fánnào 繁荣热闹 bustling with activity: 昔日偏僻的渔村,如今已是~的市镇。The formerly sleepy fishing village has become a prosperous and bustling town.

【繁荣】fánróng ❶(经济或事业)蓬勃发展;昌盛(of an economy or a cause) prosperous; flourishing; booming: 经济~ thriving economy; prosperous economy|把祖国建设得~富强。Build our motherland into a rich, strong and prosperous country. ❷ 使繁荣 make prosper; promote: ~经济 promote economic prosperity; bring about a prosperous economy|~文化艺术事业 promote cultural and artistic undertakings

【繁冗】fánrǒng same as 烦冗 fánrǒng

【繁缛】fánrù 〈书 *fml*.〉多而琐碎 over-elaborate: 礼仪~ tedious rituals

【繁盛】fánshèng ❶ 繁荣兴盛 prosperous; flourishing; thriving: 这个城市越来越~了。The city becomes more prosperous on a daily basis. ❷ 繁密茂盛 exuberant; luxuriant: 花草~ exuberant growth of flowers and grass

【繁琐】fánsuǒ same as 烦琐 fánsuǒ

【繁体】fántǐ ❶ 笔画未经简化的(of Chinese characters) original complex form: ~字 original complex form of the simplified Chinese characters ❷ 指繁体字 characters in such a form: '车'的~是'車'。'車' is the original form of '车'.

【繁体字】fántǐzì 已有简化字代替的汉字,例如'禮'是'礼'的繁体字 Chinese character that has been replaced by a simplified one, for example, '禮' is the original complex form of '礼'; ☞ 简化汉字 jiǎnhuà Hànzì on p. 948

【繁文缛节】fán wén rù jié 烦琐而不必要的礼节,也比喻其他烦琐多余的事项 nagging formalities; red tape; (fig.) other miscellaneous and unnecessary items; also 繁文缛礼 fán wén rù lǐ

【繁芜】fánwú（文字等）繁多芜杂（of writing, etc.）wordy; weighed down with unnecessary words; rambling; verbose

【繁星】fánxīng 多而密的星星 myriad stars：～点点 star-spangled｜～满天。The sky was studded with stars.

【繁言】fányán same as 烦言 fányán ②

【繁衍】fányǎn 逐渐增多或增广 multiply; procreate; increase gradually in number or quantity：子孙～ procreate descendants｜～生息 live and procreate; also 蕃衍 fányǎn

【繁育】fányù 繁殖培育 raise; breed：～虾苗 breed young shrimps｜～优良品种 breed fine strains or breeds

【繁杂】fánzá（事情）多而杂乱（of affairs）miscellaneous; many and varied：内容～ complex and diverse content｜～的家务劳动 miscellaneous household chores; also 烦杂 fánzá

【繁征博引】fán zhēng bó yǐn 形容论证时大量引用材料 quote from many sources; quote extensively

【繁殖】fánzhí 生物产生新的个体，以传代（of living things）reproduce new individuals from generation to generation

【繁重】fánzhòng（工作、任务）多而重（of work or task）heavy; strenuous; onerous：机械化取代了～的体力劳动。Strenuous manual labour has given way to mechanization.

鷭 fán 鸟，外形略像鸡，身体黑灰色或黑褐色，前额有红色块状物。生活在沼泽或河、湖岸边，捕食昆虫、小鱼等。coot（*Fulica atra*）; dark-grey or dark-brown bird resembling chicken in appearance, with red protuberances on its forehead, that inhabits marshes, or the banks of rivers or lakes, and feeds on insects and small fish

蹯 fán〈书 *fml.*〉兽足 paw：熊～（熊掌）bear's paw

蘩 fán〈书 *fml.*〉白蒿 wormwood（*Artemisia absinthium*）; artemisia

fǎn（ㄈㄢˇ）

反 fǎn ❶ 颠倒的；方向相背的（跟'正'相对 as opposed to 'obverse'）in a reverse; inside out：适得其～。The result is quite the reverse.｜绒衣穿～了 wear one's sweat shirt inside out（or the wrong side out）❷（对立面）转换；翻过来 reverse;（of the opposite side）turn over：易如～掌 as easy as turning over one's palm｜～败为胜 turn defeat into victory; turn the tide｜物极必～。Things turn into their opposite when they reach the extreme. ❸ 回；还 return; counter：～光 reflection of light｜～攻 counter-offensive; counter-attack｜～问 retort; ask（a question）in reply ❹ 反抗；反对 oppose; combat; be against：～霸 oppose hegemonism｜～封建 oppose feudalism; be anti-feudal｜～法西斯 fight against fascism; anti-fascist struggle ❺ 背叛 rebel; revolt：～叛 revolt; rebel; defect｜官逼民～。Oppressive governments drive the people to revolt. ❻ 指反革命、反动派 counter-revolutionaries; reactionaries：镇～ suppress counter-revolutionaries｜有～必肃。Every counter-revolutionary must be eliminated. ❼ 类推 analogize; reason by analogy：举一～三 draw inferences from one example ❽ 反而；相反地 instead; on the contrary：他遇到困难，不但没有气馁，～更坚强起来。Instead of being discouraged in the face of difficulties, he became stronger. ❾ 用在反切后头，表示前两字是注音用的反切。如'塑，桑故反'。used behind a *fanqie* in which the two preceding words are used to indicate pronunciation（e.g. the pronunciation of 塑 sù is indicated as 桑故反 sāng gù fǎn, meaning the combination of the consonant s in 桑 sang and the vowel u from 故 gù）; ☞ 反切 fǎnqiè

【反把】fǎn//bǎ〈方 *dial.*〉☞ 翻把 fān//bǎ ①

【反霸】fǎnbà ❶ 指反对霸权主义 oppose hegemonism ❷ 指反对地方上或行业中的恶霸，特指土地改革运动中清算恶霸地主的罪行 struggle against despots in a locality or trade; reference to the liquidation of the crimes of despotic landlords during the Land Reform（1950-1953）

【反绑】fǎnbǎng 两手绑在背后 bind sb.'s arms behind him or her

【反比】fǎnbǐ ❶ 两个事物或一事物的两个方面，一方发生变化，其另一方随之起相反的变化，如老年人随着年龄的增长，体力反而逐渐衰弱，就是反比 inverse proportion; Of two things or two aspects of one thing, as one changes, the other changes inversely. For example, as a person's age increases, his（or her）physical strength declines. ❷ 把一个比的前项作为后项，后项作为前项，所构成的比和原来的比互为反比。如9∶3和3∶9互为反比。When exchanging the positions of the antecedent and consequent of a proportion, each of the new and original ratio is the inverse proportion of the other, e.g., 9∶3 and 3∶9.

【反比例】fǎnbǐlì 两个量（a 和 b），如果其中的一个量（a）扩大到若干倍，另一个量（b）反而缩小到原来的若干分之一，或一个量（a）缩小到原来的若干分之一，另一个量（b）反而扩大到若干倍，这两个量的变化关系叫做反比例，记作 $a \propto \frac{1}{b}$ inverse proportion（or ratio）. Given two quantities,（a）and（b）, as（a）increases in proportion,（b）decreases, or vice versa. The change in their relation is called inverse proportion（or ratio）, marked as $a \propto \frac{1}{b}$

【反驳】fǎnbó 说出自己的理由,来否定别人跟自己不同的理论或意见 rebut; refute; give one's own reasons for refuting a theory or opinion different from one's own

【反哺】fǎnbǔ 传说雏乌长大后,衔食喂母乌 According to legend, a nestling crow will feed its mother when it has grown up. 〈比喻 *fig.*〉子女长大奉养父母 Children support and look after their parents when they grow up: ～之情 filial piety

【反侧】fǎncè〈书 *fml.*〉❶(身体)翻来覆去,形容睡卧不安(of one's body) toss and turn; toss from side to side; sleep uneasily: 辗转～ toss about in bed; toss and turn ❷ 不顺从;不安定 defiant; disobedient; insubordinate: ～之民 rebellious people ❸ 反复无常 changeable; capricious; unpredictable: 天命～。The will of God is unpredictable.

【反差】fǎnchā ❶ 照片、底片或景物等黑白对比的差异 contrast between black and white in a photo, negative or scene ❷ 指人或事物优劣、美丑等方面对比的差异 contrast between good and bad, and the beautiful and the ugly in people or things: 今昔对比,～强烈。There is a striking contrast when the present is compared with the past.

【反常】fǎncháng 跟正常的情况不同 abnormal; unusual; strange: 天气～ unusual weather | 态度～ strange attitude | ～现象 abnormal phenomenon | ～心理 abnormal psychology

【反衬】fǎnchèn 从反面来衬托 set off by contrast; serve as a foil for: 对英雄的赞美就～着对懦夫的嘲讽。Praise for a hero serves as a foil for ridicule of a coward.

【反冲力】fǎnchōnglì 与冲力方向相反的作用力 recoil; reactive force in the opposite direction of an applied force

【反刍】fǎnchú ❶ 偶蹄类的某些动物把粗粗咀嚼后咽下去的食物再反回到嘴里细细咀嚼,然后再咽下 ruminate; (of some artiodactyls) regurgitate coarsely masticated food and chew it again more finely before swallowing; 通称 generally called 倒嚼 dǎojiào ❷〈比喻 *fig.*〉对过去的事物反复地追忆、回味 mull over past events

【反串】fǎnchuàn 戏曲演员临时扮演自己行当以外的角色(of an opera actor) take on a role other than one's customary one; act a role other than one's own; play a reverse role

【反唇相讥】fǎn chún xiāng jī 受到指责不服气而反过来讥讽对方(《汉书·贾谊传》原作'反唇而相稽',稽:计较) answer back sarcastically when unconvinced by a criticism, a phrase that originated from 反唇而相稽 fǎn chún ér xiāng jī in *History of Han·Biography of Jia Yi*; 稽 jī meaning fuss about

【反倒】fǎndào 反而 instead; on the contrary: 让他走慢点ル,他～加快了脚步。Instead of walking more slowly as told to, he sped up. | 好心帮助他,～落下许多埋怨。To the contrary of our good wishes, our help to him incurred much of his hard feelings.

【反调】fǎndiào 指相反的观点、言论 different views or opinions: 唱～ sing a different tune; express opposite views

【反动】fǎndòng ❶ 指思想上或行动上维护旧制度,反对进步,反对革命(of one's mind or action) safeguarding the old system and opposing progress and revolution: ～阶级 reactionary class | 思想～ reactionary mind ❷ 相反的作用 reaction: 从历史来看,党八股是对于五四运动的一个～。From an historical perspective, stereotyped Party writing was a reaction to the May 4th Movement.

【反动派】fǎndòngpài 反对进步、反对革命事业的集团或分子 reactionaries; group or elements opposing progress and the revolutionary cause

【反对】fǎnduì 不赞成;不同意 oppose; be against; object: ～侵略 anti-aggression; oppose invasion | ～平均主义 combat egalitarianism | 有～的意见没有? Are there any objections?

【反对党】fǎnduìdǎng 某些国家中的在野党 opposition party

【反而】fǎn'ér〈连词 *conj.*〉表示跟上文意思相反或出乎预料和常情 on the contrary; instead: 风不但没停,～越来越大了。Instead of subsiding, the wind is blowing even harder. | 你太拘礼了,～弄得大家不方便。You are too punctilious, which, contrary to your wishes, is inconvenient to us.

【反方】fǎnfāng 指辩论中对某一论断持相反意见的一方(跟'正方'相对 as opposed to 'pro') (in a debate) con; side that holds a negative view on a topic

【反复】fǎnfù ❶ 一遍又一遍;多次重复 repeatedly; again and again; over and over: ～思考 ponder on; turn sth. over in one's mind again and again | ～实践 practise repeatedly ❷ 颠过来倒过去;翻悔 back out; go back on one's word; chop and change: ～无常 unpredicable; capricious; change like a weathercock | 说一是一,说二是二,决不～。I mean what I say and will not change my mind. ❸ 重复的情况 reversal; relapse; setback: 斗争往往会有～。There are often setbacks in a struggle.

【反感】fǎngǎn 反对或不满的情绪 dislike; be disgusted with; be averse to: 你这样说话容易引起他们的～。Speaking to them in that way is likely to antagonize them.

【反戈】fǎngē 掉转兵器的锋芒(进行反击),多用于比喻 turn one's weapon around (to counter-attack), oft. used in figurative way: ～一击 turn one's weapon around to strike those who misled; cross over

【反革命】fǎngémìng ❶ 与革命政权对立,进行

破坏活动,企图推翻革命政权的 counter-revolutionary; engage in disruptive activities in an attempt to overthrow a revolutionary power:～活动 counter-revolutionary activities |～言论 counter-revolutionary opinions ❷ 反革命分子 counter-revolutionaries:镇压～ suppress counter-revolutionaries; crack down on counter-revolutionaries

【反攻】fǎngōng 防御的一方对进攻的一方实行进攻 counter-attack; counter-offensive; (of a defensive party) launch an offensive against an attacking party

【反攻倒算】fǎngōng dàosuàn 指被打倒的地主阶级借反革命势力反过来打击农民,夺取经革命政权分配给农民的土地、财产等。也指被打倒的阶级敌人对群众实行打击报复。counter-attack to settle old scores; retaliate; (as of the overthrown landlord class with the support of a counter-revolutionary power) launch a vindictive counter-attack against peasants to seize back land and property distributed among them by a revolutionary power; (as of members of an overthrown class) retaliate against the masses

【反躬自问】fǎn gōng zì wèn 反过来问问自己 ask oneself; examine oneself; also 抚躬自问 fǔ gōng zì wèn

【反光】fǎnguāng ❶ 使光线反射 reflect light:～镜 reflector|白墙～,屋里显得很敞亮。The reflection from its white walls makes the room look bright and spacious. ❷ 反射的光线 reflection of light:雪地上的～让人睁不开眼。Reflection from the snow on the ground dazzled me.

【反光灯】fǎnguāngdēng 利用反光镜把强烈的光线集中照射的灯,主要用在舞台或高大建筑物上 reflector lamp, one which emit bright light usu. on a platforms or high building

【反话】fǎnhuà 故意说的跟自己真正意思相反的话 irony; sarcasm; words that are the opposite of what is actually meant

【反悔】fǎnhuǐ 翻悔 go back on one's word (or promise):一言为定,决不～。Once (I) give my word, I will never renege.

【反击】fǎnjī 回击 counter-attack; strike back; beat back:～战 counterblow|奋起～ rise in counter-attack

【反剪】fǎnjiǎn 两手交叉地放在背后或绑在背后 have one's hands placed or tied behind one's back

【反间】fǎnjiàn 原指利用敌人的间谍使敌人获得虚假的情报,后专指用计使敌人内部不团结 (orig.) give false information to one's enemy through their spies; sow distrust or dissent among one's enemies:～计 stratagem of sowing discord among one's enemies

【反诘】fǎnjié 反问 ask in retort; counter with a question

【反抗】fǎnkàng 用行动反对;抵抗 revolt or resist with action:～精神 rebellious spirit; spirit of revolt|～侵略 resist invasion or aggression|哪里有压迫,哪里就有～。Where there is oppression, there is resistance.

【反客为主】fǎn kè wéi zhǔ 客人反过来成为主人,多用来比喻变被动为主动 turn from guest to host; (fig.) turn from passivity into positivity

【反口】fǎnkǒu 推翻原来说的话 go back on one's word (or promise); back out:话已说出,不能～。Since (you) have already said it, you cannot go back on it.

【反馈】fǎnkuì ❶ 把放大器的输出电路中的一部分能量送回输入电路中,以增强或减弱输入讯号的效应。增强输入讯号效应的叫正反馈;减弱输入讯号效应的叫负反馈。正反馈常用来产生振荡;负反馈能稳定放大,减少失真,因而广泛应用于放大器中。feedback; process of returning part of the energy of the output circuit of a loudspeaker to the input circuit to aid the effect of input signals (positive feedback) or to enfeeble them (negative feedback). Positive feedback is oft. used to produce vibration, while negative feedback is widely applied in loudspeakers due to its property of stabilizing amplification and reducing distortion. ❷ 医学上指某些生理的或病理的效应反过来影响引起这种效应的原因。起增强作用的叫正反馈;起减弱作用的叫负反馈。feedback; physiological or pathological effects that conversely affect their causes, either adding to the effects (positive feedback) or opposing them (negative feedback) ❸ (信息、反映等)返回 feedback (of information, reactions etc.):市场销售情况的信息不断～到工厂。The factory constantly received feedbacks on market sales.

【反面】fǎnmiàn ❶ (～儿 fǎnmiànr)物体上跟正面相反的一面 back; reverse side; wrong side:这块缎子正面儿是蓝地儿黄花儿,～儿全是蓝的。The right side of the satin is dotted with yellow flower patterns against a blue background, while the wrong side is pure blue. ❷ 坏的、消极的一面(跟'正面'相对 as opposed to 'positive') opposite, negative side:～教员 teacher by negative example|～角色 negative role ❸ 事情、问题等的另一面 other or reverse side of a state of affairs, a problem, etc.:不但要看问题的正面,还要看问题的～。We must see the reverse as well as the obverse side of matters.

【反面人物】fǎnmiàn rénwù 指文学艺术作品中反动的、被否定的人物(of literary and artistic works) villain; negative character; negative role

【反目】fǎnmù 不和睦(多指夫妻 esp. between husband and wife) fall out:～成仇 quarrel with each other and become enemies

【反派】fǎnpài 戏剧、电影、电视、小说中的坏人；反面人物 villain (in drama, films, television programmes and novels, etc.); negative character

【反叛】fǎnpàn 叛变；背叛 rebel; revolt; betray：～封建礼教 rebel against the feudal ethical codes

【反叛】fǎn·pàn 叛变的人；背叛者 traitor; renegade; rebel

【反批评】fǎnpīpíng 针对别人的批评做出的解释，以表达自己不同的观点（多指学术论争） counter-criticism (to express one's different views, usu. academic arguments)

【反扑】fǎnpū （猛兽、敌人等）被打退后又扑过来 (of a beast of prey or an enemy) pounce on sb. again after being beaten off once

【反其道而行之】fǎn qí dào ér xíng zhī 采取跟对方相反的办法行事（见于《史记·淮阴侯列传》） act in a diametrically opposite way; do exactly the opposite. The phrase originated in the *Records of the Historian • Biography of Marquis of Huaiyin*.

【反潜】fǎnqián 对潜入一定海域的敌潜艇进行搜索、封锁、限制或消灭等战斗行动 anti-submarine (action); searching out, enforcing blockades, restricting or wiping out enemy submarines lurking in certain waters

【反潜机】fǎnqiánjī 海军用来搜索和攻击敌潜艇的飞机 naval plane used to search out and attack enemy submarines

【反切】fǎnqiè 我国传统的一种注音方法，用两个字来注另一个字的音，例如'塑，桑故切（或桑故反）'。被切字的声母跟反切上字相同（'塑'字声母跟'桑'字声母相同，都是 s），被切字的韵母和字调跟反切下字相同（'塑'字的韵母和字调跟'故'相同，都是 u 韵母，都是去声）。*fanqie*; traditional method of indicating the correct pronunciation of a Chinese character by using two other characters, the first having the same consonant as the given character and the second having the same vowel and tone. For example, the pronunciation of 塑 sù is indicated as 桑故反 sāng gù fǎn, meaning a combination of the consonant s in 桑 sāng and the vowel u in 故 gù, which are both in falling tone

【反求诸己】fǎn qiú zhū jǐ 指从自己方面寻找原因或对自己提出要求 seek the cause in oneself; or impose a demand on oneself

【反射】fǎnshè ❶ 光线、声波从一种媒质进入另一种媒质时返回原媒质的现象 reflect; (of light or sound wave) revert to its original medium when entering into another ❷ 有机体通过神经系统，对于刺激所发生的反应，如瞳孔随光刺激的强弱而改变大小，吃东西时分泌唾液 reflective; reaction of an organism to stimulation through the nervous system. For example, the pupil of the eye changes its size according to the degree of intensity of light stimulation, and a mouth secretes saliva when eating. ☞条件反射 tiáojiàn fǎnshè on p.1900 and 非条件反射 fēitiáojiàn fǎnshè on p.559

【反身】fǎnshēn 转过身子；转身 (of a person) turn round; face about：见她～要走，我急忙拦住。She turned round and was about to leave when I made haste and stopped her.

【反噬】fǎnshì 〈书 *fml.*〉反咬 trump up a countercharge against one's accuser; make a false countercharge

【反手】fǎn//shǒu ❶ 反过手来；手放到背后 turn one's hand over; have one's hand(s) behind one's back：进了屋～把门拉上。Shut the door behind you when you enter the room. ❷ 形容事情容易办到 get sth. done easily：～可得 ready for the picking

【反水】fǎn//shuǐ 〈方 *dial.*〉❶ 叛变 defect; turn traitor or renegade ❷ 反悔；变卦 break a promise; go back on one's words

【反思】fǎnsī 思考过去的事情，从中总结经验教训 mull over past events to sum up one's experience and lessons：～过去，是为了以后。To reflect upon one's past is to live a better life in the future.

【反诉】fǎnsù 在同一诉讼中，被告向法院对原告提出的诉讼 counterclaim; recriminate; countercharge in lawsuit brought by a defendant against the plaintiff

【反锁】fǎnsuǒ 人在屋里，门由外面锁上；人在屋外，门由里面锁上 be locked in or locked out

【反弹】fǎntán ❶ 压紧的弹簧弹回；运动的物体遇到障碍物后向相反的方向弹回 (of tightly compressed spring) bounce off; (of a moving object) rebound in the opposite direction after meeting an obstacle ❷ 〈比喻 *fig.*〉价格、行情回升 (of price or market conditions) rebound (after a fall)：股市～。The stock market surged once again.

【反坦克炮】fǎntǎnkèpào 弹道低，直射距离大，发射速度快，配有高速穿甲弹的火炮，主要用来射击坦克和装甲车辆 anti-tank gun; gun with a low ballistic path, long battle range and fast shooting speed, equipped with armour piercers, mainly used to shoot tanks and armoured cars or vehicles; 旧称 formerly known as 防坦克炮 fángtǎnkèpào and 战防炮 zhànfángpào

【反胃】fǎnwèi 指食物咽下后，胃里不舒服，恶心甚至呕吐 feel discomfort in the stomach or nausea after ingesting food; also 翻胃 fān//wèi

【反问】fǎnwèn ❶ 反过来对提问的人发问 ask (a question) in reply; ask a question by way of retorting：我等他把所有的问题都提完了，～他一句，'你说这些问题该怎么解决呢？' After he had raised all the questions, I responded by asking, 'How would you suggest solving all these problems?' ❷ 用疑问语气表达与字面相反的意义,例如'难道我不想搞好工作?' retort; make one's point by reversing the meaning of a sentence by the interrogative mood, e.g., 'I really want to do a good job, don't I?'

【反诬】fǎnwū 不承认对方的揭发指摘,反过来诬告对方 countercharge; deny the charge and make a countercharge

【反响】fǎnxiǎng 回响;反应 echo; repercussion; reverberation:她曾经登台演出,~不一。She was once a stage performer, and evoked conflicting reviews.|此事在报上披露后,在社会上引起强烈~。The incident has raised strong public repercussions after the press brought it to light.

【反省】fǎnxǐng 回想自己的思想行动,检查其中的错误 self-examine; reflect on one's thoughts and actions and examine one's mistakes:停职~ be suspended from one's duties for self-examination

【反咬】fǎnyǎo (被控告的人)诬赖控诉人、检举人、见证人(of the accused) falsely incriminate the accuser, informant or witness:~一口 make a false countercharge; retort with a countercharge

【反义词】fǎnyìcí 意义相反的词,如'高'和'低'、'好'和'坏'、'成功'和'失败' antonym; word opposite in meaning to another word, e.g. 'tall' and 'short','good' and 'bad', and 'success' and 'failure'

【反应】fǎnyìng ❶ 有机体受到体内或体外的刺激而引起的相应的活动 reaction; corresponding activities of an organism resulting from interior or exterior stimulation ❷ 化学反应 chemical reaction ❸ 打针或服药所引起的呕吐、发烧、头痛、腹痛等症状 symptom such as vomiting, fever, headache and stomachache in reaction to injection or medication ❹ 原子核受到外力作用而发生变化 nuclear reaction; transformation of nuclei under external force:热核~ thermo-nuclear reaction ❺事情所引起的意见、态度或行动 response; repercussion; reaction:他的演说引起了不同的~。His speech elicited varying reactions.

【反应堆】fǎnyìngduī 原子反应堆的简称 abbr. for yuánzǐ fǎnyìngduī

【反映】fǎnyìng ❶ 反照 reflect; mirror;〈比喻 *fig.*〉把客观事物的实质表现出来 display the essence of sth. objective:这部小说~了现实的生活和斗争。This novel reflects real life and struggle. ❷ 把情况、意见等告诉上级或有关部门 report; make known; inform authorities or department concerned of a situation, opinions, etc.:把情况~到县里 report the situation to county leaders|他~的意见值得重视。His opinions merit attention. ❸ 指有机体接受和回答客观事物影响的活动过程 reflect; (of an organism) active process of receiving and responding to the influence of objective matters

【反映论】fǎnyìnglùn 唯物主义的认识论。辩证唯物主义的反映论认为人的感性、理性的全部认识过程都是客观世界在人脑中的反映。并认为社会实践是认识的基础和检验真理的标准,反映过程是积极的,能动的,辩证发展着的。materialist theory of knowledge. According to the materialist theory of reflection, the whole process of man's cognition of both perceptual and rational knowledge is the reflection of the objective world in the human brain. Social practice serves as the foundation for knowledge and the criterion for testing truth. The process of reflection is actively, dynamically and dialectically developed.

【反语】fǎnyǔ same as 反话 fǎnhuà

【反照】fǎnzhào 光线反射 reflection of light; also 返照 fǎnzhào

【反正】fǎnzhèng ❶ 指复归于正道 restore things to order; put things on the right track:拨乱~ bring order out of chaos ❷ 敌方的军队或人员投到己方(of troops or personnel) come over from the enemy's side

【反正】fǎn·zhèng〈副词 *adv.*〉❶ 表示情况虽然不同而结果并无区别[used to indicate the same result despite different circumstances]:~去不去都是一样。It makes no difference whether (you) go or not.|不管你怎么说,~他不答应。Whatever you say, he will not budge an inch. ❷ 表示坚决肯定的语气 indicating certainty or resolution:你别着急,~不是什么要紧的大事。Don't worry, in any event it's nothing important.

【反证】fǎnzhèng ❶ 可以驳倒原论证的证据 disproof; counter evidence ❷ 由证明与论题相矛盾的判断是不真实的来证明论题的真实性,是一种间接论证 counterevidence; prove to the contrary; demonstration of the truthfulness of a proposition by proving the untruthfulness of its contradictory judgement

【反证法】fǎnzhèngfǎ 证明定理的一种方法,先提出和定理中的结论相反的假定,然后从这个假定中得出和已知条件相矛盾的结果来,这样就否定了原来的假定而肯定了定理 method of disproof; rebuttal of evidence; proof by contradiction; reduction to absurdity; a method of proving a theorem by obtaining a result contradictory to the known conditions from the contrary assumption of its conclusion, thus denying the original assumption, while affirming the theorem; also 归谬法 guīmiùfǎ

【反之】fǎnzhī 与此相反,反过来说或反过来做 otherwise; whereas; on the contrary

【反坐】fǎnzuò 指把被诬告的罪名所应得的刑罚加在诬告人身上 retaliation; retribution; sentence false accuser to the punishment originally facing the person falsely accused

【反作用】fǎnzuòyòng ❶ 承受作用力的物体对于施力的物体的作用。反作用力和作用力的大小相等,方向相反,并在同一条直线上。reaction; effect of the object subjected to force on the object applying it; reacting and acting forces are equal in magnitude but opposite in direction, and remain on the same straight line ❷ 相反的作用 reaction effect; counterreaction; retroaction:填鸭式的教学方法只能起～。A cramming (or force-feeding) method of teaching is counter-productive.

返 fǎn 回 return; come or go back:往～ round trip; to and fro|遣～ repatriate|流连忘～ indulge in sth. so much as to forget to go home; linger on with no thought of leaving|一去不复～ gone forever

【返场】fǎn//chǎng 指演员演完下场后,应观众要求,再次上场表演(of a performer) give an encore at the request of the audience after a performance

【返潮】fǎn//cháo 由于空气湿度很大或地下水分上升,地面、墙根、粮食、衣物等变得潮湿 get damp; (of ground, foot of a wall, grain, clothing and other articles of daily use) become damp or moist because of the high humidity or rising groundwater

【返程】fǎnchéng 归程;归途 return journey; on one's way back

【返防】fǎn//fáng (军队)回到驻防的地方(of troops) return to station

【返工】fǎn//gōng 因为质量不合要求而重新加工或制作 redo; remake; redo poorly done work because its quality does not meet specified requirements

【返归】fǎnguī 回返;回归 return; go back:～自然 return to nature; back to nature

【返航】fǎn//háng (船、飞机等)驶回或飞回出发的地方(of a boat, plane, etc.) return to the point of departure

【返还】fǎnhuán 归还;退还 return; restore; give or send back:～定金 give back down payment

【返回】fǎnhuí 回;回到(原来的地方) return; (come or go) back to the original place

【返老还童】fǎn lǎo huán tóng 由衰老恢复青春 regain one's youth; feel rejuvenated in one's old age

【返聘】fǎnpìn 聘请离休、退休人员回原单位继续工作 be employed or re-posted after retirement

【返璞归真】fǎn pú guī zhēn ☞ 归真返璞 guī zhēn fǎn pú on p.728

【返青】fǎn//qīng 指某些植物的幼苗移栽或越冬后,由黄色转为绿色并恢复生长(of winter crop or transplanted seedling) turn back to green from yellow and recover growth

【返俗】fǎn//sú 还俗 (of Buddhist monks and nuns or Taoist priests) return to secular life

【返销】fǎnxiāo ❶ 把从农村征购来的粮食再销售到农村 resells esp. grains to a rural area where it was purchased:～粮 resold grain (state-purchased grain sold back to a grain-producing area in the case of natural disaster, etc.) ❷ 从某个国家或地区进口原料或元器件等,制成产品后再销售到那个国家或地区 resell products to the country or region from where the raw materials, elements or parts are imported

【返修】fǎnxiū 退给原修理者重新修理;退给出品单位修理 refix or repair again at the same repair shop; return to the producer to repair:～率 repair rate|这台彩电,先后～了两次。This colour TV set has been repaired twice.

【返照】fǎnzhào same as 反照 fǎnzhào

fàn (ㄈㄢˋ)

犯 fàn ❶ 抵触;违犯 offend; violate; go against; encroach on:～法 violate or break the law|～规 break the rules or regulations|～忌讳 violate a taboo|众怒难～。One cannot afford to incur public wrath. ❷ 侵犯 attack; invade; assail:进～ invade; intrude|秋毫无～ (of troops) there has not been the slightest violation of discipline; no encroachment on people's interests in the least|人不～我,我不～人;人若～我,我必～人。We will not attack unless we are attacked; if we are attacked, we will certainly counterattack.|井水不～河水。Well water does not impinge on river water. ❸ 罪犯 offender; criminal; culprit:主～ principal offender or culprit|盗窃～ thief; robber ❹ 发作;发生(多指错误的或不好的事情) recurrence of (wrong or bad things):～愁 worry; feel anxious|～错误 make (or commit) a mistake (or an error)|～脾气 flare up; be in a bad mood|他的胃病又～了。He had another bout of stomachache.

【犯案】fàn//àn 指作案后被发觉(of an offender) be found out (and brought to justice)

【犯病】fàn//bìng 病重新发作 have an attack of one's old illness; have a relapse:出院后他很注意调养,没犯过病。After taking good care of himself since leaving hospital, he has not suffered any relapse.

【犯不上】fàn·bu shàng same as 犯不着 fàn·bu zháo:他不懂事,跟他计较～。It is not worthwhile arguing with an unreasonable fellow like him.

【犯不着】fàn·bu zháo 不值得 unworthy; not worthwhile; not worth doing:～为这点小事情着急。It is no use getting worried about such trifles.

【犯愁】fàn//chóu 发愁 worry; be anxious; feel

uneasy：现在吃穿不用～了。There are no worries over food and clothing now. | 孩子上学问题，真叫我犯了愁。I am troubled about my child's schooling opportunity.

【犯憷】fàn//chù 〈方 *dial.*〉胆怯；畏缩 be nervous; feel timid; grow apprehensive：初上讲台，她有点儿～。She felt nervous as it was the first time she had given a lecture. | 不管在什么场合，他从没犯过憷。He has never, on any occasions, felt nervous.

【犯得上】fàn·de shàng 犯得着 worth doing：一点小事，跟孩子发脾气～吗？Is it worthwhile losing your temper with a child over such a trifle?

【犯得着】fàn·de zháo 值得(多用于反问 oft. in rhetorical questions) worthwhile：为这么点小事～再去麻烦人吗？Is it worthwhile bothering others again over such trifles?

【犯法】fàn//fǎ 违反法律、法令 violate (or break) the law：知法～ know the law but break it; deliberately flout the law | 谁犯了法都要受到法律的制裁。Anyone who breaks the law will be punished by it.

【犯规】fàn//guī 违犯规则、规定 break the rules or regulations：比赛中他有意～。He deliberately fouled during the competition. | 六号队员犯了规，被罚下场。No. 6 player was sent off for committing a foul.

【犯讳】fàn//huì ❶〈旧时 *old*〉指不避尊亲或上级的名讳 mention oft. inadvertently, the name of an elder or leader — a practice regarded as irreverent ❷ 说出忌讳的事或会引起不愉快的字眼儿 verbally break a taboo or enunciate an unpleasant word：这个地方，早晨起来谁要是说'蛇'、'虎'、'鬼'什么的，就被认为是～，不吉利。In this area, anyone mentioning 'snake', 'tiger' or 'ghost' in the early morning is regarded as inauspicious, as they have broken a local taboo.

【犯浑】fàn//hún 说话做事不知轻重，不合情理 be perversely tactless in one's behaviour or speech; act unreasonably：我一时～，说话冲撞了您，请您多原谅。I'm sorry to have offended you by the improper remarks I made. | 他犯起浑来，谁的话都不听。When he is on a roll, he listens to nobody's admonitions.

【犯忌】fàn//jì 违犯禁忌 violate a taboo：你说的话犯了他的忌。Your words have violated his taboo. | 过去在船上话里带'翻'字是～。In the past, anyone who mentioned 'turn (over)' onboard a boat would be regarded as violating a taboo.

【犯贱】fàn//jiàn 行动不自重，显得轻贱 conduct oneself in a manner below one's dignity; behave badly

【犯节气】fàn jié·qi 指某些慢性病在季节转换、天气有较大变化时发作 suffer attack of a chronic disease as a result of change of season or weather：我这病～，立冬以后就喘得厉害。Having been through an attack of this disease, I am almost asthmatic at the Beginning of Winter.

【犯戒】fàn//jiè 违犯戒律 break or violate religious discipline or commandment

【犯禁】fàn//jìn 违犯禁令 violate a ban or prohibition

【犯困】fàn//kùn 困倦想睡 feel sleepy or drowsy

【犯难】fàn//nán 感到为难 feel embarrassed or awkward; feel uneasy; be perplexed：这件事叫我犯了难。I was at a loss as to how to handle this problem. | 你有什么～的事，可以给大家说说。You may tell us what is troubling you.

【犯人】fànrén 犯罪的人，特指在押的 criminal (esp. convict)

【犯傻】fàn//shǎ 〈方 *dial.*〉❶ 装糊涂；装傻 pretend not to know; feign ignorance; pretend to be naive or stupid：这事情很清楚，你别～啦。You know this perfect well, don't pretend you don't. ❷ 做傻事 act foolishly：你怎么又～了，忘了上次的教训了？Why are you so stupid? Have you forgotten the previous lesson? ❸ 发呆 be in a daze (or trance); stare blankly：别人都走了，他还坐在那儿～呢。All people had left, but he still sat there staring blankly.

【犯上】fàn//shàng 触犯长辈或上级 offend one's elders or superiors：～作乱 go against one's superiors and make trouble; rebel against authority

【犯事】fàn//shì 做犯罪或违纪的事 commit a crime or an offence

【犯颜】fànyán 〈书 *fml.*〉冒犯君主或尊长的威严 offend the dignity of a monarch or one's elders：～直谏 voice one's outspoken criticisms before the monarch without considering the consequences

【犯疑】fàn//yí 起疑心 be suspicious; also 犯疑心 fàn yíxīn

【犯嘴】fàn//zuǐ 〈方 *dial.*〉争辩；吵架 quarrel; argue; dispute; have a row

【犯罪】fàn//zuì 做出犯法的、应受处罚的事(of a person) commit a crime or an offence for which punishment is imposed

饭 fàn ❶ 煮熟的谷类食品 cooked rice or other cereals：稀～ porridge; congee | 干～ cooked rice ❷ 特指大米饭 (particular reference) cooked rice：吃～吃面都行。Either rice or noodles will do. ❸ 每天定时吃的食物 regular meal：早～ breakfast | 中～ lunch | 晚～ supper; dinner

【饭菜】fàncài ❶ 饭和菜 meal; repast; food ❷ 下饭的菜(区别于'酒菜' as compared with 'food to go with wine or liquor') dishes to go with staple food like rice, steamed buns, etc.

【饭店】fàndiàn ❶ 较大而设备好的旅馆 (large) hotel (equipped with good facilities):北京~ Beijing Hotel ❷〈方 *dial*.〉饭馆 restaurant; eatery

【饭馆】fànguǎn (~儿 fǎnguǎnr)出售饭菜供人食用的店铺 restaurant; eatery; luncheonette

【饭盒】fànhé (~儿 fànhér)用来装饭菜的盒子,用铝、不锈钢等制成 lunch box; food container made of aluminium or stainless steel

【饭局】fànjú 宴会;聚餐 feast; banquet; dinner party

【饭口】fànkǒu (~儿 fànkǒur)吃饭的当口儿 meal time; dinner time; time to eat:一到~时间,饭馆里顾客络绎不绝。At meal times, this restaurant is kept busy with a stream of customers.

【饭粒】fànlì (~儿 fànlìr)饭的颗粒 grain of cooked rice:嘴边粘着~ a grain of rice stuck in the corner of one's mouth|锅里还剩几个~儿。There are only a few grains of rice left in the pot.

【饭量】fàn·liàng 一个人一顿饭能吃的食物的量 appetite; quantity of food one can eat at a meal:~小 be a small eater; have a poor appetite (or stomach)|~增加 enlarge one's appetite

【饭囊】fànnáng 装饭的口袋 rice bag;〈比喻 *fig*.〉没有用的人 fathead; good-for-nothing:~衣架(比喻庸碌无能的人)clothes-horse and food-bag; (fig.) worthless person; good-for-nothing

【饭铺】fànpù (~儿 fànpùr)规模较小的饭馆 (small) restaurant; eating house

【饭时】fànshí〈方 *dial*.〉指吃早饭、午饭或晚饭的时候 meal time; time for breakfast, lunch or supper

【饭食】fàn·shi (~儿 fàn·shir)饭和菜(多就质量说 esp. with regard to its quality)fare; food:这里~不错,花样多。The food here is pretty good, and of a great variety.

【饭厅】fàntīng 专供吃饭用的比较宽敞的房子 dining hall

【饭桶】fàntǒng 装饭的桶 rice bucket;〈比喻 *fig*.〉只会吃饭而不会做事的人 fathead; good-for-nothing; worthless person

【饭碗】fànwǎn ❶ 盛饭的碗 rice bowl ❷ (~儿 fànwǎnr)〈比喻 *fig*.〉职业 job; means of livelihood:找~ look for a job|铁~ iron rice bowl — a secure lifelong job

【饭辙】fànzhé〈方 *dial*.〉吃饭的门路;维持生活的门路 job; means of livelihood

【饭庄】fànzhuāng 规模较大的饭馆 big restaurant

【饭桌】fànzhuō (~儿 fànzhuōr)供吃饭用的桌子 dining table

泛(汎、❺氾) fàn ❶〈书 *fml*.〉漂浮 float:~舟 go boating; float about on a boat|~萍浮梗 floating duckweed and plant stems|沉渣~起。The dregs rise to the surface — long-suppressed vices stage a comeback. ❷ 透出;冒出 be suffused with; send forth:脸上~红 with one's cheeks suffused with blushes|~出香味儿 smell sweet; emit fragrance ❸ 广泛;一般地 broad; extensive; general; nonspecific:~论 general discussion (on sth.)|~指 in a general sense; general reference ❹ 肤浅;不深入 superficial; shallow:浮~ unspecified; superficial and full of generalities|空~ containing nothing but generalities; vague and devoid of content ❺ 泛滥 flood; inundate; overflow:黄~区(黄河泛滥过的地方) areas formerly flooded by the Yellow River

☞ 氾 Fán on p.533

【泛称】fànchēng 总称;统称 general term

【泛泛】fànfàn ❶ 不深入 general; not thoroughgoing:~之交 nodding acquaintance; casual acquaintance|~而谈 talk in generalities; speak in vague terms|~地一说 talk about sth. in general terms ❷ 普通;平平常常 ordinary; common

【泛滥】fànlàn ❶ 江河湖泊的水溢出 swallen (river or lake); be flooded; overflow; inundate:洪水~ deluge of floods|~成灾 run rampant; run wild; disaster caused by flooding water ❷〈比喻 *fig*.〉坏的事物不受限制地流行 (of evil things) run unchecked:不能让错误思想和言行自由~。We must not allow erroneous ideas, speeches and actions to spread unchecked.

【泛神论】fànshénlùn 一种哲学理论,主张神不存在于自然之外,自然便是神的体现。在有些哲学家那里,曾用泛神论的形式表达唯物主义的自然观。后来变成企图调和科学和宗教的唯心主义哲学,认为世界存在于神之中。pantheism; philosophical theory which holds that God does not exist beyond nature, while nature is the manifestation of God. Some philosophers used to express the materialist conception of nature in the form of pantheism. Later it became an idealistic philosophy attempting to compromise science and religion, which held that the world existed within God.

【泛酸】fàn//suān〈方 *dial*.〉指胃酸过多而上涌 pantothenic acid; hyperchlorhydria surge

【泛音】fànyīn 一般的乐音都是复音,一个复音中,除去基音(频率最低的纯音)外,所有其余的纯音叫做泛音 overtone; harmonic; general musical sounds of complex tones. Except for the fundamental tone (pure tone in the lowest frequency), all other pure tones within a complex tone are called overtones or harmonics. also 陪音 péiyīn

【泛舟】fànzhōu〈书 *fml.*〉坐船游玩 go boating; float on a boat:～西湖 go boating upon the West Lake

范[1]**(範)** fàn ❶〈书 *fml.*〉模子 mould; pattern; matrix:钱～ coin mould|铁～ rion matrix ❷ 模范;好榜样 model; good example:典～ example; model to be followed|规～ standard; criterion; norm|示～ demonstrate; set an example|～例 example; model ❸ 范围 limits; range; scope:～畴 domain; range; scope|就～ submit; give in ❹〈书 *fml.*〉限制 restriction:防～ be on guard; remain vigilant

范[2] Fàn 姓 a surname

【范本】fànběn 可做模范的样本(多指书画 usu. for calligraphy and painting) model copy:习字～ calligraphy copybook

【范畴】fànchóu ❶ 人的思维对客观事物的普遍本质的概括和反映。各门科学都有自己的一些基本范畴,如化合、分解等,是化学的范畴;商品价值、抽象劳动、具体劳动等,是政治经济学的范畴;本质和现象、形式和内容、必然性和偶然性,是唯物辩证法的基本范畴。category; summarization and reflection of human thoughts on the general nature of objective matters. Each science has its own basic category. For example, chemical combination and decomposition fall under the category of chemistry; commodity value, abstract labour and concrete labour under political economy; and nature and phenomenon, form and content, and necessity and contingency under materialist dialectics. ❷ 类型;范围 domain; scope; realm; range:汉字属于表意文字的～。Chinese characters are a kind of ideograph.

【范例】fànlì 可以当做典范的事例 model; example; case in point:我们一个团打垮了敌人三个团,创造了以少胜多的战斗～。Our regiment defeated three enemy regiments, thus setting an outstanding example of victors over an enemy with a superior force.

【范围】fànwéi ❶ 周围界限 limits; scope; extent; range:地区～ regional scope|工作～ scope of work; business scope|活动～ range (or scope) of activities|他们谈话的～很广,涉及政治、科学、文学等各方面。The topics on which they talk are broad in scope, involving various fields, such as politics, science, literature, etc. ❷〈书 *fml.*〉限制;概括 set limits to; limit the scope of:纵横四溢,不可～ overrun all limits

【范文】fànwén 语文教学中作为学习榜样的文章 model essay (in Chinese teaching):熟读～ read a model essay carefully over and over again|讲解～ explain a model essay

【范性】fànxìng ☞塑性 sùxìng on p. 1833

贩 fàn ❶(商人)买货 (of businessmen) buy to resell:～货 buy and resell products|～牲口 buy and sell draught animals|～药材 traffic in medicinal herbs ❷ 贩卖东西的人 trader; vendor; peddler:小～ vendor; hawker|摊～ vendor; street peddler|商～ peddler; small retailer; small-time merchant

【贩毒】fàndú 贩卖毒品 traffic in narcotics; drug trafficking

【贩夫】fànfū〈旧时 *old*〉指小贩 peddler; vendor; hawker:～走卒(旧时泛指社会地位低下的人) small tradesmen and porters (people of a low social status in the old days)

【贩卖】fànmài 商人买进货物再卖出以获取利润 (of businessmen) buy and resell products for a profit:～干鲜果品 peddle fresh and dried fruits ◇打着辩证法的旗号～不可知论的哲学观点 peddle the philosophical views of agnosticism under the banner of dialectics

【贩私】fànsī 贩卖私货 illegal vending; traffic in smuggled goods; sale of illegal goods:严厉打击～活动 crack down severely on the vending of illegal goods

【贩运】fànyùn (商人)从甲地买货运到乙地(出卖) (of businessmen) transport goods bought in one place to another in order to sell; traffic:～货物 shipping (goods)|短途～ short haul of goods for sale

【贩子】fàn·zi 往来各地贩卖东西的人(多含贬义 oft. derog.) person who comes and goes to various places to sell products:牲口～ cattle trader ◇战争～ warmonger

畈 fàn〈方 *dial.*〉❶ 田地(多用于地名 oft. used in place names) field; land:～田 big tract of farmland|周党～(在河南) Zhoudangfan (in Henan Province)|白水～(在湖北) Baishuifan (in Hubei Province)|葛～(在浙江) Gefan (in Zhejiang Province) ❷〈量词 *classifier*〉用于大片田地 fan, a unit for measuring large tracts of land:一～田 a big tract of farmland

梵 fàn ❶ 关于古代印度的 of ancient India:～语 Sanskrit|～文 Sanscrit ❷ 关于佛教的 Buddhist:～刹 Buddhist temple [梵 Sanskrit: brahmā (清静 quiet)]

【梵呗】fànbài 佛教作法事时念诵经文的声音 sound of chanting scriptures in a Buddhist service or ceremony:空山～ chant a eulogy on an open and silent mountain

【梵刹】fànchà 佛寺 Buddhist temple

【梵宫】fàngōng 佛寺 Buddhist temple

【梵文】fànwén 印度古代的一种语言文字 Sanskrit, an ancient Indian language

【梵哑铃】fànyǎlíng 小提琴 violin

嬎 fàn〈方 *dial.*〉鸟类下蛋 (of fowls) lay an egg:鸡～蛋。Hens lay eggs.

F

fāng(ㄈㄤ)

方[1] fāng ❶ 四个角都是90°的四边形或六个面都是方形的六面体 square; quadrilateral with 90° angles at its four corners, or hexahedron with six square-shaped surfaces: 正～ square|长～ rectangle|～块字 square-shaped characters|这块木头是～的。This piece of wood is square. ❷ 乘方 involution; power: 平～ square|立～ cube|2 的 3 次～是 8。The cube of 2 is 8. ❸〈量词 *classifier*〉a)用于方形的东西[for square things]: 一～手帕 a handkerchief|两～腊肉 two slices of bacon|三～图章 three seals|几～石碑 several stone tablets b)平方或立方的简称,一般指平方米或立方米 abbr. for 平方 píngfāng or 立方 lìfāng, usu. referring to square metre or cubic metre: 铺地板十五～ tile a 15-square-metre floor|土石～ cubic metres of earth and stone ❹ 正直 upright; honest; morally square: 品行～正 have an upright character ❺ (Fāng)姓 a surname

方[2] fāng ❶ 方向 direction: 东～ east|那一～ that direction|四面八～ in all directions ❷ 方面 party; side: 我～ our side (or party)|甲～ Party A|对～ the other party; the opposite side|双～ both sides (or parties); two sides (or parties) ❸ 地方 place; region; locality: 远～ remote (or faraway) place|～言 dialect; patois; local dialect|天各一～ (of family members or friends) be far apart from each other

方[3] fāng ❶ 方法 method; way: ～略 general plan|千～百计 make every attempt; leave no stone unturned; by hook or crook|教导有～ know how to teach and guide ❷ (～儿 fāngr)药方 prescription: 验～ proven formula|偏～儿 folk prescription

方[4] fāng〈书 *fml.*〉〈副词 *adv.*〉❶ 正在;正当 just; at the time when: ～兴未艾 burgeoning; be just unfolding|来日～长。There will be a time for this.|～今盛世 at the present time of prosperity ❷ same as 方才 fāngcái ②: 如梦～醒 as if just awakening from a dream|年～二十 be just 20 years old; have just turned 20

【方案】fāng'àn ❶ 工作的计划 scheme; plan; programme: 教学～ teaching plan|建厂～ plan for the construction of a factory ❷ 制定的法式 rule: 汉语拼音～ rule of the Chinese phonetic alphabet

【方便】fāngbiàn ❶ 便利 convenient: 大开～之门 do everything for sb.'s convenience|北京市的交通很～。Getting around is rather convenient in Beijing.|把～让给别人,把困难留给自己 take the difficulties on oneself and make things easy for others ❷ 使便利;给予便利 make things convenient for sb.: ～群众 make things convenient for the people ❸ 适宜 suitable: 这儿说话不～。It's not convenient to talk here. *or* This is not the right place for talking. ❹〈婉辞 *euph.*〉指有富裕的钱 have money to spare or lend: 手头儿不～ have little money to spare ❺〈婉辞 *euph.*〉指大小便 go to the lavatory: 车停一会儿,大家可以～～。The car will wait here for a while and you can use the lavatory (or wash your hands).

【方便面】fāngbiànmiàn 烘干的熟面条,用开水冲泡,加上调料就可以吃 instant noodles; baked noodles made ready for eating by pouring boiling water over them

【方步】fāngbù 斯斯文文的大而慢的步子 measured steps: 踱～ stroll|迈～ walk in measured steps

【方才】fāngcái ❶ 不久以前;刚才 just now: ～的情形,他都知道了。He found out what had just happened. ❷〈副词 *adv*.〉表示时间或条件关系,跟'才'相同而语气稍重[same as 才 cái, but more emphatic]: 等到天黑,他～回来。He came back only after it had gotten dark.

【方材】fāngcái 截面呈方形或长方形的木材 square-edged timber; lumber; timber; square cut; also 方子 fāng·zi

【方程】fāngchéng 含有未知数的等式,如 $x+1=3$, $x+1=y+2$ equation with unknown value, e.g. $x+1=3$, $x+1=y+2$; equation; also 方程式 fāngchéngshì

【方尺】fāngchǐ ❶ 一尺见方 one *chi* square ❷ 平方尺 square *chi*

【方寸】fāngcùn ❶ 一寸见方 one *cun* square: ～之木 a square *cun* of wood ❷ 平方寸 square *cun* ❸〈书 *fml.*〉指人的内心;心绪 heart: ～已乱 with one's heart troubled and in turmoil; with one's mind in turmoil; greatly agitated and disturbed

【方队】fāngduì 方形的队列 square formation

【方法】fāngfǎ 关于解决思想、说话、行动等问题的门路、程序等 method; means; technique; process; procedure; way; tool; ways or procedures of thoughts, speeches or actions: 工作～ working method|学习～ study method|思想～ method of thinking; way of thinking; mentality

【方法论】fāngfǎlùn ❶ 关于认识世界、改造世界的根本方法的学说 science of methods of cognition and transformation of the world; a branch of philosophy dealing with the science of method and change methodology ❷ 在某一门具体学科上所采用的研究方式、方法的综合 methodology; a set of methods or ways of doing research in a particular subject

【方方面面】fāng fāng miàn miàn 各个方面 every aspect; every side: 要办好一件事,须要考虑到～的问题。You have to take all aspects into consideration to do a good job.

【方根】fānggēn 一个数的 n 次幂(n 为大于 1 的整数)等于 a,这个数就是 a 的 n 次方根。如 16 的 4 次方根是 +2 和 −2。root; quantity that, when multiplied by itself a certain number of times, produces a given quantity, e.g. +2 and −2 are the fourth roots of 16; 简称 abbr. for 根 gēn

【方技】fāngjì〈旧时 *old*〉总称医、卜、星、相之类的技术 general term for Chinese folk medicine, necromancy, astrology, physiognomy, etc.

【方剂】fāngjì same as 药方 yàofāng ①

【方家】fāngjiā '大方之家'的简称,本义是深明大道的人,后多指精通某种学问、艺术的人 abbr. for 大方之家 dàfāng zhī jiā; expert; scholar; orig. referring to those who deeply understood the principles of Nature, and later to those proficient in learning or in a certain school of art

【方将】fāngjiāng〈书 *fml.*〉正要 just about to

【方巾气】fāngjīnqì 指思想、言行迂腐的作风习气 (of thoughts, ideas or behaviour) conservative; pedantic (方巾 *fangjin*: 明代书生日常戴的帽子 a kind of kerchief used as a hat by scholars in the Ming Dynasty)

【方今】fāngjīn 如今;现时 now; nowadays: ~盛世 in this age of prosperity

【方块字】fāngkuàizì 指汉字,因为每个汉字一般占一个方形面积 square-shaped characters; Chinese characters

【方框图】fāngkuàngtú 表示电路、程序、工艺流程等内在联系的图形。方框内表示各独立部分的性能、作用等,方框之间用线连接起来,表示各部分之间的相互关系。square diagram; a kind of diagram showing the internal relations of circuits, procedures and the technological process, by connecting the squares describing the performance and functions of independent parts with lines; 简称 abbr. 框图 kuàngtú; also 方块图 fāngkuàitú

【方腊起义】Fāng Là Qǐyì 北宋末年(公元 1120 年)方腊领导的江东(今安徽南部和江西东北部)、两浙(今浙江全省和江苏南部)农民起义 Fang La Uprising; peasant uprising in the south of Anhui, northeast of Jiangxi, Zhejiang, and south of Jiangsu provinces, led by Fang La in A.D. 1120 during the late Northern Song Dynasty

【方里】fānglǐ ❶ 一里见方 one *li* in circumference ❷ 平方里 square *li*

【方略】fānglüè 全盘的计划和策略 general plan: 作战~ general plan of operation

【方面】fāngmiàn 就相对的或并列的几个人或几个事物之一说,叫方面 side; in the area of ...; one of the parties or objects in opposite or parallel positions: 优势是在我们~,不是在敌人~。Our side, not the enemy, holds the advantage. | 必须不断提高农业生产~的机械化水平。We shall continuously improve the mechanization of agricultural production.

【方面军】fāngmiànjūn 担负一个方面作战任务的军队的最高一级编组,辖若干集团军(兵团)或军 front army; highest grouping in an operational army that commands several corps

【方枘圆凿】fāng ruì yuán záo ('凿'也有读 zuò 的)《楚辞·九辩》:'圆凿而方枘兮,吾固知其钼铻而难入。'意思是说,方榫头和圆卯眼,两下合不起来。形容格格不入。out of tune; as incompatible as a round peg and a square hole; misfitting. *The Elegies of Chu · Nine Changes*: 'The peg is round and the hole square; / That's why I know it's hard to put the peg into the hole.' (凿 also pronounced zuò); also 圆凿方枘 yuán záo fāng ruì

【方胜】fāngshèng〈古代 *arch.*〉一种首饰,形状是由两个斜方形一部分重叠相连而成,后也泛指这种形状 jewellery in the shape of two overlapping slanting squares; also referring to the shape similar to this

【方始】fāngshǐ same as 方才 fāngcái ②: 斟酌再三,~下笔 think over and over before putting pen to paper | 现在种的树,要过几年~见效益。The benefit of the trees just planted will not show until several years later.

【方士】fāngshì〈古代 *arch.*〉称从事求仙、炼丹等活动的人 necromancer; alchemist; persons engaged in necromancy, alchemy, etc.

【方式】fāngshì 说话做事所采取的方法和形式 way; fashion; pattern; ways and manners of behaviour: 工作~ working method | 批评人要注意~。We must pay attention to method and style when criticizing others.

【方术】fāngshù〈旧时 *old*〉指医、卜、星、相、炼丹等技术;方技 profession such as medicine, divination, alchemy, and similar arts

【方外】fāngwài〈书 *fml.*〉❶ 中国以外的地方;异域 places beyond China; foreign land: ~之国 foreign country ❷ 尘世之外 beyond this world: ~之人 person outside the boundaries of this earthly world, i.e. Buddhist monks or Taoist priests

【方位】fāngwèi ❶ 方向。东、南、西、北为基本方位;东北、东南、西北、西南为中间方位。points of the compass, with east, west, north and south as the cardinal points, and northeast, southeast, northwest and southwest as mid-points ❷ 方向和位置 bearings; direction and position: 下着大雨,辨不清~ be unable to find the way in heavy rain

【方位词】fāngwèicí 名词的一种,是表示方向或位置的词,分单纯的和合成的两类。单纯的方位词是'上、下、前、后、左、右、东、西、南、北、里、外、中、内、间、旁'。合成的方位词由单纯的方位词用下面的方式构成。noun of locality, including both single-morpheme and compound words. Single-morpheme nouns of location

F

are up（上），down（下），front（前），back（后），left（左），right（右），east（东），west（西），south（南），north（北），inside（里），outside（外），centre（中），inside（内），in between（间），beside（旁）. Compound nouns of location take the following forms：a)前边加'以'或'之'，如'以上、之下'single-morpheme noun of location preceded by 以 yǐ or 之 zhī，such as 以上'above' and 之下 'below' b)后边加'边、面、头'，如'前边、左面、里头'single-morpheme noun of location followed by 边 biān，面 miàn，or 头·tou，such as 前面'in front of'，左面'to the left'，and 里面'inside' c)对举，如'上下、前后、里外'combination of two opposite single-morpheme nouns of location，such as 上下 'above and below'，前后 'front and rear'，and 里外 'inside and out' d)其他，如'底下、头里、当中'other forms，including 底下'underneath'，里头 'interior' and 当中 'in the middle'

【方向】fāngxiàng ❶ 指东、南、西、北等 directions. e.g. east，south，west，north，etc.：在山里迷失了～ lost one's way in the mountain ❷ 正对的位置；前进的目标 direction；orientation：军队朝渡口的～行进。The troops marched in the direction of the ferry.

【方向】fāng·xiang〈方 *dial.*〉情势 way things stand；trend of events：看～做事 act according to the circumstances

【方向舵】fāngxiàngduò 用来控制飞机向左或向右飞行的片状装置，装在飞机的尾部，和水平面垂直 rudder；vertical rudder；piece of metal hinged vertically at the tail of an aircraft，used for steering

【方向盘】fāngxiàngpán 轮船、汽车等的操纵行驶方向的轮状装置 steering wheel；wheel-like equipment or mechanism for steering a car，boat，etc.

【方兴未艾】fāng xīng wèi ài 事物正在发展，一时不会终止 be fast unfolding；be ascendant；be still growing with no sign of stopping；be still making progress；be in full swing with no signs of slowing down

【方言】fāngyán 一种语言中跟标准语有区别的、只在一个地区使用的话，如汉语的粤方言、吴方言等 dialect；localism；a form of language different from the standard，used only in a part of the country，such as the Guangdong dialect and Wu dialect of Chinese

【方药】fāngyào〈中医 *Chin. med.*〉药方中用的药 medicinal ingredients，as in prescriptions for Chinese medicine；also 方剂 fāngjì

【方音】fāngyīn 方言的语音，包括 phonetic aspect of a dialect；dialectal accent，which consists of：a)方言所特有的元音、辅音、声调，例如作为声母的舌根鼻音 ng（上海话'牙、我'的声母）vowels，consonants and tones，e.g. vela rhinolalia ng as an initial consonant（as in Shanghai dialect）b)方言与标准语同有而使用上有分歧的元音、辅音、声调，例如昆明话把'雨'读如'椅'，西安话把'税'读如'费'等 vowels，consonants and tones same as those in standard Chinese but used differently，e.g. 雨 yǔ pronounced as 椅 yǐ in Kunming dialect，and 税 shuì pronounced as 费 fèi in Xi'an dialect

【方圆】fāngyuán ❶ 指周围 neighbourhood；vicinity：～左近的人，他都认识。He knows everyone in the neighbourhood. ❷ 指周围的长度 surrounding area；circumference：～几十里见不到一个人影。Not a single human being could be found in this area of several dozen *li*. ❸ 方形和圆形 square and circle；〈比喻 *fig.*〉一定的规则或标准 rules；established practice or standards：不依规矩，不能成～。Without ruler and compass，you cannot draw a proper square or circle. *or* One can accomplish nothing without complying with norms and rules.

【方丈】fāngzhàng ❶ 一丈见方 area of a square *zhang* ❷ 平方丈 square *zhang*

【方丈】fāng·zhang ❶ 佛寺或道观中住持住的房间 room of the abbot in a Buddhist or Taoist temple ❷ 寺院的住持 abbot of a Buddhist or Taoist temple

【方针】fāngzhēn 引导事业前进的方向和目标 policy；direction or target of a task；orientation；guiding principle：～政策 general and specific policies｜教育～ guiding principles for education

【方正】fāngzhèng ❶ 成正方形，不偏不歪 upright and four-square：字写得很～。When writing，make the characters square and upright. ❷ 正直 straightforward；upright；righteous：为人～ be an upright man｜～不阿 upright；righteous

【方志】fāngzhì 记载某一地方的地理、历史、风俗、教育、物产、人物等情况的书，如县志、府志等 gazetteer；records of the geography，history，customs，education，products，personages，etc.，of an area，such as 'county gazetteer' and 'prefecture gazetteer'；also 地方志 dìfāngzhì

【方舟】[1] fāngzhōu〈书 *fml.*〉两船相并 two boats sailing abreast

【方舟】[2] fāngzhōu《圣经》故事中义士诺亚（Noah）为躲避洪水造的长方木柜形大船 Noah's ark；from a Biblical story，the huge coffer-shaped ark built by the righteous man Noah to survive the great flood

【方桌】fāngzhuō 桌面是方形的桌子 square table

【方子】[1] fāng·zi same as 方材 fāngcái；also 枋子 fāng·zi

【方子】[2] fāng·zi ❶ 药方 prescription ❷ 配方的

通称 general term for 配方 pèifāng

邡 fāng 什邡(Shífāng),地名,在四川 *fang*, as in 'Shifang', name of a place in Sichuan Province

坊 fāng ❶ 里巷(多用于街巷名 usu. used in street names) lane: 白纸～(在北京) Baizhifang (White Paper Lane) (in Beijing) ❷ 牌坊 memorial archway: 节义～ virtuous arch of chastity and righteousness ☞ fáng on p.549

【坊本】fāngběn 〈旧时 *old*〉书坊刻印的书籍的版本 block-printed edition prepared by a bookshop

【坊间】fāngjiān 街市上(旧时多指书坊 usu. referring to bookshops in old times) in the streets

芳 fāng ❶ 香 fragrant; sweet-smelling: 芬～ fragrant|～草 fragrant grass|～香 fragrant; aromatic; sweet fragrance ❷ 花卉 flowers and grass: 群～ beautiful and fragrant flowers; beautiful women; women of the same profession|众～ all kinds of flowers ❸ 美好的(德行、名声) good (conduct or reputation); virtuous: ～名 (polite way of referring to) one's name|流～百世 leave a good name for posterity ❹ 〈书 *fml.*〉〈敬辞 *pol.*〉用于对方或跟对方有关的事物 [used in referring to things relevant to a person]: ～邻 one's neighbour ❺ (Fāng)姓 a surname

【芳菲】fāngfēi 〈书 *fml.*〉 ❶ 花草的芳香 fragrance of flowers and plants: 春草～fragrance of grasses of spring ❷ 花草 grass and flowers: ～满园,蝶飞燕舞。The garden is full of flowers and plants with butterflies and swallows flying around.

【芳邻】fānglín 〈书 *fml.*〉 ❶ 好邻居 good neighbours ❷ 〈敬辞 *pol.*〉称别人的邻居 sb. else's neighbour

【芳龄】fānglíng 指女子的年龄,一般用于年轻女子 age of a young woman

【芳名】fāngmíng ❶ 指女子的名字,一般用于年轻女子 referring to the name of a young woman ❷ 美好的名声 good reputation: ～永垂 leave a good name for posterity

【芳香】fāngxiāng 香味(多指花草) (of flowers or grass) fragrant: 梅花的～沁人心脾。The fragrance of plum blossoms refreshes one's mind (or goes right to one's heart.)

【芳心】fāngxīn 〈书 *fml.*〉指年轻女子的心 heart of a young woman

【芳泽】fāngzé ❶ 〈古代 *arch.*〉妇女润发用的有香气的油,泛指香气 scented hair oil used by women; (in a broad sense) fragrance ❷ 〈书 *fml.*〉借指妇女的风范、容貌 looks and manners of a woman

枋[1] fāng 古书上说的一种树,木材可以做车 tree mentioned in ancient texts as timber used for making carriages or vehicles

枋[2] fāng ❶ 方柱形的木材 piece of timber shaped like a square pillar ❷ 〈书 *fml.*〉两根柱子间起连接作用的方形横木 square timber connecting two pillars

【枋子】fāng·zi ❶ same as 方子[1] fāng·zi ❷ 〈方 *dial.*〉棺材 coffin

钫[1] fāng 金属元素,符号 Fr (francium)。有放射性。francium (Fr), a radioactive metal

钫[2] fāng ❶ 〈古代 *arch.*〉盛酒器皿,青铜制成,方口大腹 *fang*, square-mouthed, round-bellied bronze wine vessel ❷ 〈书 *fml.*〉锅一类的器皿 pot; pan

蚄 fāng ☞ [虸蚄] zǐfāng on p.2541

fáng (ㄈㄤˊ)

防 fáng ❶ 防备 guard against; provide against: 预～ prevent; take precautions against|～涝 prevent waterlogging|以～万一。Be prepared for all contingencies. *or* Take precautions against the unexpected.|谨～假冒。Beware of counterfeits. ❷ 防守;防御 defence: 国～ national defence|边～ border security|海～ coastal defence|布～ organize a defence; take preventive measures ❸ 堤;挡水的建筑物 dam; dyke; embankment; structure to block water: 堤～ dyke ❹ (Fáng)姓 a surname

【防暴】fángbào 防止暴力或暴动 antiriot: ～术 antiriot skills|～警察 riot police|～武器 antiriot weapons

【防备】fángbèi 做好准备以应付攻击或避免受害 take precautions against possible danger or harm; guard against: ～敌人突然袭击 be prepared for surprise attacks by the enemy|路上很滑,走路要小心,～跌倒。The road is slippery. Mind your step and guard against falling.

【防不胜防】fáng bù shèng fáng 要防备的太多,防备不过来 have too many things to guard against; hard to guard against; cannot reckon with all eventualities

【防潮】fángcháo ❶ 防止潮湿 damp-proof; moisture-proof: ～纸 moisture-proof paper; tarred paper|储存粮食要注意～。Take measures to keep the grain away from moisture. ❷ 防备潮水 protection against the tide: ～闸门 tidal gate

【防除】fángchú 预防和消除(害虫等) prevent and kill off (e.g. pests): ～白蚁 prevent and exterminate termites

【防弹】fángdàn 防止子弹射进 bullet cannot pierce; bulletproof; shellproof: ～服 bulletproof clothes|～玻璃 bulletproof glass

【防盗】fángdào 防止坏人进行盗窃 guard against theft; take precautions against burglars:～门 burglar-proof door|节日期间要注意防火～ beware of fire and burglars during holidays

【防地】fángdì (军队)防守的地区或地段 defence sector or area (of a unit)

【防冻】fángdòng ❶ 防止遭受冻害 prevent frostbite:冬贮大白菜要注意～。Take measures to prevent frostbite when storing Chinese cabbage in winter. ❷ 防止结冰 freeze-proofing; antifreezing:～剂 freeze-proofing agent; antifreezing agent

【防毒】fángdú 防止毒物对人畜等的危害 antitoxin; gas defence; protect (people or animals) against poisonous substances:～面具 gas mask

【防毒面具】fángdú miànjù 戴在头上,保护呼吸器官、眼睛和面部,免受毒剂、细菌武器和放射性物质伤害的器具 gas mask; respirator; device worn over the head to protect the respiratory organs, eyes and face from the harm of poisonous gases, bacteriological or biological weapons and radioactive substances

F

【防范】fángfàn 防备;戒备 be on guard; keep a lookout:对走私活动必须严加～ take strict precautions against smuggling

【防风林】fángfēnglín 在干旱多风的地区,为了降低风速、阻挡风沙而种植的防护林 a row of trees planted in a dry and windy area to slow down the wind and block sand; windbreak (forest)

【防腐】fángfǔ 用药品等抑制微生物的生长、繁殖,以防止有机体腐烂 use medicine to prevent infection, decay, etc., by inhibiting the action of microorganisms:～剂 antiseptic; preservative

【防寒】fánghán 防御寒冷;防备寒冷的侵害 cold-proof; winter protection:穿件棉衣,可以～ put on cotton-patted clothes to protect from the cold|采取～措施,确保苗木安全越冬 take protective measures for the nursery stock to survive through winter

【防洪】fánghóng 防备洪水成灾 prevent flood; flood protection:修筑堤堰,疏浚河道,～防涝 build up dams and dredge rivers to prevent flood and waterlogging

【防护】fánghù 防备和保护 protect; shelter:这些精密仪器在运输途中要严加～。The precision machinery must be kept under close protection during transportation.

【防护林】fánghùlín 为了调节气候,减免水、旱、风、沙等自然灾害所营造的林带或大片森林 shelter-forest; shelterbelt; forest or forest belt established to moderate the climate and reduce disasters like flood, draught, wind and sand storms

【防患未然】fáng huàn wèi rán 在事故或灾害尚未发生之前采取预防措施 take preventive measures before an accident or disaster; prevent against possible trouble; prevent the worst from happening

【防火墙】fánghuǒqiáng 两所房子之间或者一所房屋的两个部分之间的厚而高的墙,可以防止火灾蔓延 fire wall; high, thick wall between two houses or two parts of a house to prevent the spread of fire

【防空】fángkōng 为防备敌人空袭而采取各种措施 air defence; measures against air attacks by an enemy

【防空洞】fángkōngdòng ❶ 为了防备敌人空袭减少损害而挖掘的洞 air-raid shelter; bomb shelter; shelter for reducing the damage of air attacks by the enemy ❷〈比喻 *fig.*〉可以掩护坏人、坏思想的事物 hideout for evildoers; cover for wrong thinking

【防空壕】fángkōngháo 为了防备敌人空袭减少损害而挖掘的壕沟 air-raid dugout; trench dug for reducing the casualties and damage of air attacks by the enemy

【防老】fánglǎo 防备年老时供养无着 support oneself in later years:～钱 money to support oneself in later years|养儿～。Bring up children to prevent destitution in old age. *or* Children are reared to provide support for one's old age.

【防凌】fánglíng 防止解冻的时候冰块阻塞水道 reduce the menace of ice runs

【防区】fángqū 防守的区域 defence area; garrison area

【防身】fángshēn 保护自身不受侵害 defend oneself against violence and harm:～术 self-defence techniques or martial arts

【防守】fángshǒu ❶ 警戒守卫 defend; guard:～军事重镇 defend a key position (in military operation) ❷ 在斗争或比赛中防备对方进攻 defence; guard against the offence of the other side in a struggle or a game:这个队不仅～严密,而且能抓住机会快速反击。The team is tight in defence and quick to take opportunities to strike back.

【防暑】fángshǔ 防止受到暑热的侵害;预防中暑 prevent heatstroke (or sunstroke):～茶 heatstroke-prevention tea|～降温 cooling down to prevent heatstroke

【防特】fángtè 防止特务活动 guard against enemy agents

【防微杜渐】fáng wēi dù jiàn 在错误或坏事萌芽的时候及时制止,不让它发展 take precautions; nip a vice in the bud; check for erroneous ideas or faults at the outset so as to stop their development; be cautious before sth. wrong happens

【防卫】fángwèi 防御和保卫 defend:正当～ justifiable defence; legitimate defence|加强～力量 strengthen defence capabilities

【防务】fángwù 有关国家安全防御方面的事务 defence; matters pertaining to national security and defence

【防线】fángxiàn 防御工事连成的线 defence; line of defence: 钢铁～ iron line of defence | 突破敌军～ break through the enemy's line of defence

【防汛】fángxùn 在江河涨水的时期采取措施，防止泛滥成灾 take measures to prevent flood; flood prevention; flood control

【防疫】fángyì 预防传染病 epidemic prevention: ～针 (prophylactic) inoculation | ～站 epidemic prevention station | ～措施 epidemic prevention measures

【防雨布】fángyǔbù 雨水浸不透的纺织品。用致密的帆布、亚麻布或亚麻和棉的混纺织品浸在防水液体中制成。粗而厚的做遮盖货物的苫布，细而薄的用来做雨衣。waterproof cloth; tarpaulin; waterproof textile produced by immersing fine canvas, linen or blended fabrics of flax and cotton in waterproof liquid, the rough and thick kind used to cover goods, and the fine and light kind used to make raincoats

【防御】fángyù 抗击敌人的进攻 defend; guard; guard against attacks by the enemy: ～战 war of defence | 不能消极～，要主动进攻 take active offence instead of passive defence

【防震】fángzhèn ❶ 采取一定的措施或安装某种装置，使建筑物、机器、仪表等免受震动 keep buildings, machinery or instruments free from shocks by taking certain measures or installing certain devices: ～手表 shockproof watch ❷ 防备地震 take precautions against earthquakes: ～棚 earthquake shelter

【防止】fángzhǐ 预先设法制止(坏事发生) forestall; avoid; prevent (bad things) from happening; guard against: ～煤气中毒 guard against gas poisoning | ～交通事故 try to forestall traffic accidents

【防治】fángzhì 预防和治疗(疾病、病虫害等) prevention and treatment (of diseases, pests, etc.); administer prophylaxis and treatment: ～结核病 prevention and treatment of tuberculosis | ～蚜虫 control and eliminate aphis

坊 fáng 小手工业者的工作场所 workshop of small handicraft business: 作～workshop | 油～oil mill (for processing vegetable oil) | 染～dyeing mill | 磨～mill | 粉～flour mill ☞ fāng on p. 547

妨 fáng 妨碍 hinder; hamper; impede; obstruct; interfere with: ～害 impair | 不～事 no harm

【妨碍】fáng'ài 使事情不能顺利进行；阻碍 hinder; hamper; impede; obstruct; make difficult: 大声说话～别人学习。Talking loudly disturbs those who are studying. | 这个大柜子放在过道里，～走路。The big cupboard in the hallway stands in the way.

【妨害】fánghài 有害于 impair; jeopardize; be harmful to: 吸烟～健康。Smoking harms one's health. | 雨水过多，会～大豆生长。Too much rain will impair the growth of the soya beans.

肪 fáng ☞ 脂肪 zhīfáng on p. 2458

房[1] fáng ❶ 房子 house: 一所～ a house | 瓦～ tile-roofed house | 楼～ building | 平～ single-storey house ❷ 房间 room: 卧～ bedroom | 客～ guestroom | 书～ study | 厨～ kitchen ❸ 结构和作用像房子的东西 house-like structure: 蜂～ beehive; honeycomb | 莲～(莲蓬) lotus pod ❹ 指家族的分支 branch of an extended family: 长～ branch headed by the eldest son | 堂～ branch of the same clan | 远～ distant relatives ❺〈量词 *classifier*〉: 两～儿媳妇 two daughters-in-law ❻ 二十八宿之一 *fang*, one of the 28 constellations ❼ (Fáng) 姓 a surname

房[2] fáng same as 坊 fáng

【房舱】fángcāng 轮船上乘客住的小房间 passenger cabins in a ship

【房产】fángchǎn 个人或团体保有所有权的房屋 real estate or property owned by an individual or an organization

【房产主】fángchǎnzhǔ 出租房屋的人 landlord; owner of a house for rent

【房东】fángdōng 出租或出借房屋的人(对'房客'而言 as opposed to lodger) landlord or landlady; owner or lessor of a house or room

【房改】fánggǎi 住房制度改革 reform of the housing system: ～方案 scheme of housing reform

【房管】fángguǎn 房地产管理 housing management: ～局 bereau of housing management | ～人员 housing management staff

【房基】fángjī 房屋的地基 foundations of a building: ～下沉。The foundations have sunken.

【房间】fángjiān 房子内隔成的各个部分 room; space within a building enclosed by walls or partitions: 这套房子有五个～。This house has five rooms.

【房客】fángkè 租房或借房居住的人(对'房东'而言 as opposed to 'landlord') lodger; tenant of a house

【房契】fángqì 买卖房屋时所立的契约 title deed (for a house); contract signed in the purchase of a house

【房钱】fáng·qián same as 房租 fángzū

【房山】fángshān ❶ 山墙 gable wall ❷〈方 *dial.*〉泛指房屋四周的墙 walls surrounding the house: 前～front wall | 后～back wall

【房事】fángshì 指人性交的事 sexual intercourse

【房帖】fángtiě (～儿 fángtiěr) 贴在门口或街头

的房屋招租启事 notice posted on doorways or the street of a house for rent

【房屋】fángwū 房子(总称)(collect.) houses; buildings

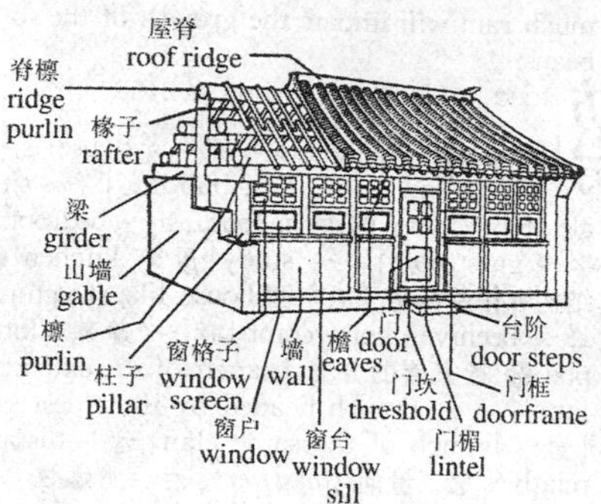

房 子
House

【房檐】fángyán (～儿 fángyánr)房顶伸出墙外的部分 eaves; edges of a roof projecting beyond the sides of a building

【房子】fáng·zi 有墙、顶、门、窗,供人居住或做其他用途的建筑物 house; building; building with a roof, walls, doors and windows for people to live in

【房租】fángzū 租房屋的钱 rent; money for renting a house

鲂 fáng 鱼,形状跟鳊鱼相似而较宽,银灰色,胸部略平,腹部中央隆起。生活在淡水中。triangular bream (*Megalobrama terminalis*); grey freshwater fish resembling bream, with a flat breast and bulging belly

【鲂鮄】fángfú 鱼类的一科,身体略呈圆筒状,后部稍侧扁,头部有骨质板。生活在海中。triglidae (*Megalobrama terminalis*); sea robin; a sea fish, with a cylinder-shaped body slightly flat at the end and a broad head covered with bone plates

fǎng (ㄈㄤˇ)

仿(倣) fǎng ❶ 仿效;效法 imitate; copy: ～造 copy; be modelled on|～着原样做了一个 make sth. from a model ❷ 类似;像 resemble; be like:他长得跟他舅舅相～。He resembles his uncle in features. ❸ 依照范本写的字 characters written after a calligraphy model: 判～ mark letters|写了一张～ write a page of characters following a calligraphy model

【仿办】fǎngbàn 依照办理 act accordingly; follow the same procedure:这种做法各地可以～。This practice can be followed in other places.

【仿单】fǎngdān 介绍商品的性质、用途、使用法的说明书,多附在商品包装内 small book or manual of instructions on the nature, uses and usage of a commodity, usu. put along with the packaging

【仿佛】fǎngfú ❶ 似乎;好像 seemingly; as if:他干起活来～不知道什么是疲倦。He works as if he never knew fatigue. ❷ 像;类似 be more or less the same; be alike:他的模样还和十年前相～。He looks about the same as he did ten years ago.

【仿古】fǎnggǔ 模仿古器物或古艺术品 modelled after an antique; in an ancient style:紫砂～陶器 imitation of ancient pottery|～的唐三彩 imitation of the tricoloured glazed pottery of the Tang Dynasty

【仿冒】fǎngmào 仿造冒充 copy; counterfeit:不法厂商～名牌商品。Lawless manufacturers are given to imitating well-known brands.

【仿若】fǎngruò 仿佛;好像 seem to be; as if:回忆往事,～隔世。In recollection, the past seems to belong to another world.

【仿生学】fǎngshēngxué 研究生物系统的结构、功能等,用来改进工程技术系统的科学。如模拟人脑的结构和功能原理,改善电子计算机。bionics; science of improving engineering technology systems by modelling after living organisms, e. g. computer systems that imitate the structure and function of the human brain to improve the computer's performance

【仿宋】fǎngsòng 印刷字体的一种,依照宋版书上所刻的字体,笔画粗细均匀,有长、方、扁三体 printed typeface imitating a Song-Dynasty script characterized by even strokes; also 仿宋体 fǎngsòngtǐ or 仿宋字 fǎngsòngzì

【仿效】fǎngxiào 模仿(别人的方法、式样等) imitate; follow the example of (methods, styles, etc. of others):艺术贵在创新,不能一味～别人。Do not always imitate others, for innovation is most important in art.

【仿行】fǎngxíng 仿照实行 follow an example; follow suit:这个办法很好,可以参照～。This is a good method that can be followed.

【仿影】fǎngyǐng 练习写毛笔字的时候,放在仿纸下照着写的样字 model characters; model characters to be copied in practising calligraphy

【仿造】fǎngzào 模仿一定的式样制造 copy; be modelled on:这些古瓶都是～的。These antique vases are imitations.

【仿照】fǎngzhào 按照已有的方法或式样去做 imitate; follow; follow the existing practice or method:～办理 handle accordingly; take care (of sth.) in the same manner; follow the same procedure|～苏州园林风格修建花园 build and create a garden following the style of Suzhou gardens

【仿纸】fǎngzhǐ 练习拿毛笔写大字用的纸,多印有格子 paper used for practising calligraphy, usu. printed with squares

【仿制】fǎngzhì 仿造 copy; imitate; be modelled on:～品 replica; copy; imitation

访 fǎng ❶ 访问 visit; call on:～友 call on a friend|有客来～ have visitors ❷ 调查;寻找 seek by enquiry or search; try to get:～查 investigate; go about making enquiries|采～ gather material|明察暗～ conduct a thorough investigation

【访古】fǎnggǔ 寻访古迹 search for ancient relics:河套～ in quest of antiquities at the Great Bend|～寻幽 search for scenes of historical interest and sights of scenic beauty

【访旧】fǎngjiù 访问故旧、故地 visit old friends and/or native place:寻根～go root-seeking; visit one's native place and search for things related to one's ancestors

【访求】fǎngqiú 查访寻求 search for:～善本古籍 search for rare and ancient books

【访谈】fǎngtán 访问并交谈 interview:～录 collection of interviews|登门～ call at sb.'s house

【访问】fǎngwèn 有目的地去探望人并跟他谈话 visit; call on; interview; visit sb. with a purpose and conduct a talk or an interview:～先进工作者 interview an outstanding worker◇我怀着崇敬的心情,～了这座英雄的城市。I visited this heroic city with great reverence.

【访寻】fǎngxún 打听寻找;访求 enquire; search for:～失散的亲人 search for missing relatives|～草药和良方 search for herbal medicines and good remedies

【访员】fǎngyuán 报社外勤记者的旧称 old term for field reporter; field journalist

彷 fǎng [彷佛](fǎngfú) same as 仿佛 fǎngfú ☞ páng on p.1445

纺 fǎng ❶ 把丝、麻、棉、毛等纤维拧成纱,或把纱捻成线 spin; make thread or yarn from wool, cotton, silk, etc. by drawing out and twisting:～纱 yarn manufacture; spinning|～线 spinning|～棉花 spin cotton ❷ 比绸子稀而轻、薄的丝织品 a kind of silk cloth that is thinner and lighter than satin:杭～ Hangzhou silk

【纺车】fǎngchē 手摇或脚踏的有轮子的纺纱或纺线工具 spinning wheel; simple machine for spinning thread on a spindle turned by a large wheel worked by hand or foot

【纺绸】fǎngchóu 一种平纹丝织品,用生丝织成,质地细软轻薄,适宜做夏季服装 soft and thin plain-weave silk fabric made of raw silk, usu. used as a material to make summer clothes

【纺锤】fǎngchuí 纺纱工具,是一个中间粗两头尖的小圆木棒,把棉絮或棉纱的一端固定在上面,纺锤旋转,就把棉絮纺成纱,或把纱纺成线 spindle; rod thick in the middle and thin at the ends on which yarn or thread is twisted or wound by hand in spinning

【纺锭】fǎngdìng ☞ 纱锭 shādìng on p.1665

【纺织】fǎngzhī 把棉、麻、丝、毛等纤维纺成纱或线,织成布匹、绸缎、呢绒等 spinning and weaving; textile production; make cotton, flax, silk and wool into yarn and thread, and then into cloth:～厂 textile mill|～工艺 textile techniques

【纺织品】fǎngzhīpǐn 把棉、麻、丝、毛等纤维经过纺织及其复制加工的产品。包括单纱、股线、机织物、针织物、编织物、毡毯等。textile; fabric; products of cotton, flax, silk and wool manufactured by spinning, weaving and reprocessing, including yarn, thread, machine-woven cloth, braided fabric, felt rugs, etc.

昉 fǎng〈书 *fml.*〉❶ 明亮 bright ❷ 起始 start; begin

舫 fǎng 船 boat:画～ painted pleasure boat|游～pleasure tour boat|石～marble boat

髣 fǎng [髣髴](fǎngfú) same as 仿佛 fǎngfú

fàng(ㄈㄤˋ)

放 fàng ❶ 解除约束,使自由 release; set free; let go:释～ release; set free|把俘虏～回去 release prisoners-of-war ❷ 在一定的时间停止(学习、工作) stop (studying or working) for a certain length of time:～学 (of school) class dismissal at end of day|～工 leave or finish work ❸ 放纵 give way to; let oneself go:～任 let go unchecked|～声高歌 sing heartily|～言高论 have a high-flown talk ❹ 让牛羊等在草地上吃草和活动 put out (sheep and cattle) to pasture; let off for prey:～牛 put cattle out to pasture|～羊 let off sheep to pasture ❺ 把人驱逐到边远的地方 send sb. away to a remote area; send away:～逐 send into exile|流～ exile ❻ 发出 emit; give out:～枪 shoot, discharge (a gun)|～冷箭 make a sneak attack|～光 give out light|玉簪花～出阵阵的清香。The plantain lily gives off wafts of delicate fragrance. ❼ 点燃 light; fire:～火 set on fire|～爆竹 set off firecrackers ❽ 借钱给人,收取利息 lend money for interest:～债 lend money for interest|～款 loan; make loans ❾ 扩展 expand; enlarge; let out:～大 magnify|～宽 relax restrictions|上衣的身长要～一寸 let out an inch on the length of the jacket ❿ (花)开 blossom:百花齐～ a hundred flowers in bloom ⓫ 搁置 lay aside; put aside:这件事情不要紧,先～一～。It is not an urgent matter, and we may put it aside for the moment. ⓬ 弄倒 fell:上山～树 go up the mountain to fell trees ⓭ 使处于一定的位置 place; put; put in a certain place：把书～在桌子上。Put the book on the table. ⑭ 加进去 add; put in：菜里多～点酱油。Put a bit more soya sauce in the dish. ⑮ 控制自己的行动，采取某种态度，达到某种分寸 place oneself under control and moderate one's behaviour and attitude to a certain extent：～明白些。Be sensible. | ～稳重些。Be sedate and steady. | 脚步～轻些。Tread softly.

【放榜】fàngbǎng 发榜 publish a list of successful candidates

【放包袱】fàngbāo·fu〈比喻 *fig.*〉消除思想顾虑 lay down a burden

【放步】fàng//bù 迈开大步 making big strides：～前进 march with big strides

【放黜】fàngchù〈书 *fml.*〉放逐；斥退 dismiss; send away; send into exile

【放达】fàngdá〈书 *fml.*〉言行不受世俗礼法的拘束 unrestrained by customs and rites：纵酒～ act in unrestricted manner and drink to excess | ～不羁 unruly; uninhibited

【放大】fàngdà 使图像、声音、功能等变大 magnify; amplify; enlarge (images, sounds, functions, etc.)：～镜 magnifier; magnifying glass | ～器 amplifier | ～照片 make an enlargement of a photograph; have a photo enlarged

【放大镜】fàngdàjìng 凸透镜的通称 general term for 凸透镜 tūtòujìng

【放大器】fàngdàqì ❶ 能把输入讯号的电压或功率放大的无线电装置，由电子管或晶体管、电源变压器和其他电器元件组成。用在通讯、广播、雷达、电视、自动控制等各种装置中。amplifier; radio device composed of electron tubes, transistors, transformer and other elements for amplifying electrical voltage and power, widely used in communications, broadcasting, radar, television and auto-control equipment ❷ 画图的时候，放大或缩小图形的用具 device used in drawing for enlarging or contracting graphs; also 放大尺 fàngdàchǐ

【放大纸】fàngdàzhǐ 放大相片的感光纸，上面涂有卤化银乳剂，感光程度比印相纸高 enlarging paper; bromide paper; photosensitive paper coated with a silver bromide agent used for enlarging photos, having greater sensitivity than photographic paper

【放贷】fàngdài 贷给款项 provide a loan to; extend credit to

【放胆】fàngdǎn 放开胆量 act boldly and with confidence：你尽管～试验，大家支持你。Go on with confidence in your experimentation, for you have everyone's support. | 他迟疑了一会儿，才～走进屋里。He hesitated for a while before going in courageously.

【放诞】fàngdàn 行为放纵，言语荒唐 wild and uninhibited in speech and behaviour：生性～ have an uninhibited disposition

【放荡】fàngdàng 放纵，不受约束或行为不检点 abandoned; dissolute; dissipated; completely uncontrolled in a way that is immoral：～不羁 unconventional and unrestrained | 生活～ lead a licentious life

【放电】fàng//diàn ❶ 带电体的电荷消失而趋于中性。闪电就是自然界的放电现象。discharge; lose or give off a stored electrical charge: e.g. lightening is a natural discharge of electricity ❷ 电池等释放电能 discharge; remove stored energy from a battery

【放刁】fàng//diāo 用恶劣的手段或态度跟人为难 make difficulties with base means or attitude; act in a rascally manner：～撒泼 be rascally and shrewish

【放定】fàng//dìng 旧俗订婚时，男方给女方送订婚礼物；下定（old custom）a man's family presenting gifts to a woman's family at their engagement（定 *dìng*：指金银首饰等订婚礼物 jewellery and other engagement gifts）

【放毒】fàng//dú ❶ 投放毒物或施放毒气 poison; put poison in food, water, etc. or release poisonous gas ❷〈比喻 *fig.*〉散布、宣扬反动言论 make vicious remarks; spread poisonous ideas

【放飞】fàngfēi ❶ 准许飞机起飞 allow the aircraft to take off ❷ 把鸟撒出去使高飞 release birds：这批信鸽从济南市～，赛程约500公里。The homing pigeons were released in Ji'nan to cover a racing distance of about 500 km. ❸ 使风筝升起 fly a kite：～风筝 fly a kite

【放风】fàng//fēng ❶ 使空气流通 let in fresh air ❷ 监狱里定时放坐牢的人到院子里散步或上厕所叫放风 let prisoners out for exercise or to relieve themselves ❸ 透露或散布消息 leak information; spread news or rumours：有人放出风来，说厂领导要调整。News was spread that the factory leadership was going to be shaken up. ❹〈方 *dial.*〉把风；望风 be on the lookout; act as a lookout

【放歌】fànggē 放声歌唱；纵情高歌 sing loud; sing with abandonment or at the top of one's voice：～一曲 sing a song at the top of one's voice

【放工】fàn//gōng 工人下班 leave work, finish work; knock off：下午五点钟工厂～。The factory knocks off at five o'clock in the afternoon. | 有些事咱们放了工再研究。We will discuss those matters after we knock off.

【放虎归山】fàng hǔ guī shān ☞ 纵虎归山 zòng hǔ guī shān on p. 2558

【放怀】fànghuái ❶ 纵情；尽情 to one's heart's content：～畅饮 drink to one's heart's content | ～大笑 laugh heartily ❷ 放心 be at ease：妻子的病有了好转，我也就～了些。I felt relieved as my wife's illness took a turn for the better.

【放还】fànghuán ❶ 放回(扣押的人、畜等) release (a detained person, livestock, etc.); let go: ～人质 release the hostage ❷ 放到原来的位置 return sth. to its former place: 架上期刊,阅后～原处。Please return the periodicals to their original places on the shelves.

【放荒】fàng//huāng 放火烧山野的草木 make a fire with wood and grass in a mountainous area

【放火】fàng//huǒ ❶ 有意破坏,引火烧毁房屋、粮草、森林等 set fire, to houses, army provisions or woods, etc. maliciously; set fire to; set on fire; commit arson ❷〈比喻 *fig.*〉煽动或发动骚乱事件 agitate or create disturbance

【放假】fàng//jià 在规定的日期停止工作或学习 have a vacation free from work or study; have a holiday or vacation; have a day off: 放了三天假 had three days off | 国庆节～两天 have a two-day holiday during National Day

【放课】fàngkè 下课;放学 dismiss (a class); leave school

【放空】fàng//kōng 运营的车、船等没有载人或载货而空着行驶 (of a truck, ship, etc.) travel unloaded or without passengers: 做好调度工作,避免车辆～ make a good dispatch to avoid having the vehicles travel unloaded

【放空炮】fàng kōngpào〈比喻 *fig.*〉说空话,说了不能兑现 talk big; spout hot air; make empty talk without commitment; indulge in idle boasting: 要说到做到,不能～。Don't talk big. Act on what you say.

【放空气】fàng kōngqì〈比喻 *fig.*〉故意制造某种气氛或散布某种消息(多含贬义 usu. derog.) drop a hint to create a certain atmosphere; spread word; create an impression: 他早就放出空气,说先进工作者非他莫属。He has spread word that he will get the honour of outstanding worker.

【放宽】fàngkuān 使要求、标准等由严变宽 relax restrictions on requirements and standards; relax: ～尺度 relax the requirements | 入学年龄限制适当～。The restrictions on school-age are appropriately relaxed.

【放款】fàng//kuǎn ❶ (银行或信用合作社等)把钱借给用户(of banks or credit cooperatives) loan; make loans ❷ 放债 lend money for interest

【放旷】fàngkuàng〈书 *fml.*〉旷达;放达 be open-minded; defy custom: ～不检 be broad-minded and not care for rituals | 恃才～ ignore, or defy, customs or rules, because one is very aware of and confident in one's abilities

【放浪】fànglàng〈书 *fml.*〉放荡;放纵 unrestrained; dissolute: 行为～ behave in an unrestrained manner

【放浪形骸】fànglàng xínghái 行为放纵,不受世俗礼法的束缚 refuse to be bound by convention; be defiant of conventions

【放冷风】fàng lěngfēng〈比喻 *fig.*〉散布流言飞语 spread slanderous rumours

【放冷箭】fàng lěngjiàn〈比喻 *fig.*〉暗中害人 snipe; stab in the back; injure sb. by underhand means; shoot from a hidden position

【放量】fàng//liàng 尽量(吃、喝) (eat or drink) to the limit of one's capacity; to one's heart's content: 放开量喝酒 drink to one's heart's content | 你～吃吧,有的是。There's lots of food, so eat to your heart's content.

【放疗】fàngliáo 利用放射线(如 X 射线、丙种射线等)治疗恶性肿瘤等症 radiotherapy; treatment for malignant tumours using X-ray, γ-ray, etc.

【放牧】fàngmù 牧放 put out to pasture; graze; herd: ～羊群 go sheepherding; herd sheep

【放盘】fàng//pán (～儿 fàngpánr) 指商店减价出售或增价收买 (of a shop) sell at cut rates or buy at raised prices

【放炮】fàng//pào ❶ 使炮弹发射出去 fire a gun ❷ 点燃引火线,使爆竹爆炸 light the fuse to set off firecrackers ❸ 用火药爆破岩石、矿石等 blast; dynamite rocks or ore with gunpowder: ～开山 dynamite mountains ❹ 密闭的物体爆裂 (of an airtight object) blow out: 车胎～ blowout of a tire ❺〈比喻 *fig.*〉发表激烈抨击的言论 make harsh remarks; shoot off one's mouth: 发言要慎重,不能乱～。Be cautious with your remarks and don't shoot off your mouth.

【放屁】fàng//pì ❶ 从肛门排出臭气 pass gas (from the intestines and through the anus); break wind; fart (not a polite term) ❷〈比喻 *fig.*〉说话没有根据或不合情理(骂人的话 curse) talk nonsense

【放弃】fàngqì 丢掉(原有的权利、主张、意见等) abandon (original rights, views, opinions, etc.); give up; relinquish; abjure; forsake; resign; surrender: ～阵地 abandon one's position | 工作离不开,他只好～了这次进修的机会。He was so busy with his work that he could not but abandon the opportunity to attend advanced studies.

【放青】fàng//qīng 把牲畜放到青草地上吃草 put (cattle, etc.) out to graze

【放青苗】fàng qīngmiáo〈旧时 *old*〉地主或商人在谷物没有成熟的时候,利用农民需要现款的机会,用低价预购谷物,是一种变相的高利贷 buy standing crops dirt cheap; (of landlords or merchants) purchase standing crops at extremely low prices from poor peasants who run short before the harvest

【放情】fàngqíng 尽情;纵情 to one's heart's content; as much as one likes: ～歌唱 sing to one's heart's content | ～丘壑(纵情游山玩水) indulge oneself in mountains and gullies (i.e.

nature)

【放晴】fàng//qíng 阴雨后转晴 clear up (after rain):天已～,人们忙着晒衣服。The people got busy airing their clothes when it cleared up.|等放了晴再走。Leave after it has cleared up.

【放权】fàngquán 把权力交给下属或下属部门 delegate power to lower levels:简政～ streamline administration and delegate power to lower levels

【放任】fàngrèn 听其自然,不加约束或干涉 not interfere; let alone; let go; leave unchecked:～自流 let things drift (or slide)|对错误的行为不能～不管。We cannot let wrongdoing go unchecked.

【放散】fàngsàn (烟、气味等)向外散开 (of smoke, scent, etc.) diffuse; disperse; dissipate

【放哨】fàng//shào 站岗或巡逻 be on sentry or on patrol

【放射】fàngshè 由一点向四外射出 radiate; emit; branch out from the centre:～形 in radiating formation|太阳～出耀眼的光芒。The sun sends forth dazzling rays.

【放射病】fàngshèbìng 病,由各种放射线(如原子弹或氢弹爆炸时放出的射线)破坏人体组织而引起。症状是体温增高,恶心,皮肤和黏膜出血,毛发脱落,白细胞减少等。radiation sickness; sickness produced by overexposure to radiation, e.g. from explosions of an A-bomb or H-bomb, characterized by increased body temperature, nausea, bleeding of skin and mucous membrane, loss of hair, decrease of leukocytes, etc.

【放射线】fàngshèxiàn 某些元素(如镭、铀等)的不稳定原子核衰变时放射出来的有穿透性的粒子束。分为甲种射线、乙种射线和丙种射线,其中丙种射线贯穿力最强。radioactive rays; penetrating stream of particles given off by the spontaneous disintegration of atoms of certain radioactive elements (such as radium and uranium), as alfa, beta, and gamma rays, the last form having the most penetrating capabilities

【放射形】fàngshèxíng 从中心一点向周围伸展出去的形状 radiating formation; a form of branching out from a centre:～道路 roads in a radiating formation

【放射性】fàngshèxìng ❶ 某些元素(如镭、铀等)的不稳定原子核自发地放出射线而衰变成另外的元素的性质 radioactivity; property of certain elements (e.g. radium, uranium, etc.) of giving off rays spontaneously, and in so doing disintegrating into another element ❷ 医学上指由一个痛点向周围扩散的现象 pain spreading from a centre to surrounding parts of the body ◇～影响 radioactive effect

【放射性元素】fàngshèxìng yuánsù 能发出射线而衰变成另一种元素的化学元素,如镭、铀、钚、钫 radiating element; radioactive element; chemical elements that can emit rays and disintegrate into other elements, including radium, uranium, plutonium and francium

【放生】fàng//shēng 把捉住的小动物放掉,特指信佛的人把别人捉住的鱼鸟等买来放掉 free animals from captivity; (of Buddhists) buy captive fish or birds and set them free:～池 pool for freeing captive fish

【放声】fàngshēng 放开喉咙出声 raise one's voice to its utmost; shout (etc.) at the top of one's lungs:～痛哭 cry loudly|～大笑 guffaw; laugh heartily

【放手】fàng//shǒu ❶ 松开握住物体的手 let go; let go one's hold:放开手 let go|他一～,笔记本就掉了。He let go his hold and the notebook dropped to the ground. ❷〈比喻 *fig.*〉解除顾虑或限制 relieve apprehension and restraints; have a free hand; go all out:～发动群众 go all out to mobilize the masses; fully arouse the masses

【放肆】fàngsì (言行)轻率任意,毫无顾忌 wanton; (of words and actions) unbridled:说话注意点,不要太～。Mind what you say, and don't be so careless.

【放松】fàngsōng 对事物的注意或控制由紧变松 relax; slacken; loosen; become less attentive or tense:～警惕 relax one's vigilance|～肌肉 relax one's muscles|～学习,就会落后。You should relax in your studies, or you will lag behind.

【放送】fàngsòng 播送 broadcast; send out:～音乐 broadcast music|～大会实况录音 broadcast a live recording of the conference

【放下屠刀,立地成佛】fàng xià túdāo, lìdì chéng fó 原为佛教徒劝人修行的话,后用来比喻作恶的人只要决心悔改,就会变成好人 drop one's cleaver and become a Buddha; (fig.) salvation will be achieved as soon as one gives up evil

【放像机】fàngxiàngjī 只能用来放录像带而不能录像的机器 videocassette player; videotape player; device for playing but not recording videocassettes

【放血】fàngxiě 医学上指用针刺破静脉,放出血液,或用水蛭放在耳部周围吸血 bloodletting; phlebotomy; opening a vein to remove blood by needle or leech

【放心】fàng//xīn 心情安定,没有忧虑和牵挂 free from pain or worry; set one's mind at rest; rest assured; feel relieved; be at ease:你只管～,出不了错。You can be rest assured that everything will be all right.|看到一切都安排好了,他才放了心。He set his mind at ease after seeing everything had been well arranged.

【放行】fàngxíng (岗哨、海关等)准许通过 let

sb. or sth. pass (sentry, customs, etc.):免税～ tariff-free clearance

【放学】fàng//xué ❶ 学校里一天或半天课业完毕,学生回家 pupils leaving school after classes are over; classes are over; school lets out; get out of school ❷ 指学校里放假 (of a school) have a holiday or vacation

【放眼】fàngyǎn 放开眼界(观看) take a broad view; scan widely:～未来 look toward the future|胸怀祖国,～世界 have one's country or motherland in mind while setting one's view on the whole world|～望去,一派生气勃勃的景象。Looking ahead, one sees a vision full of vigour and growth.

【放羊】fàng//yáng ❶ 把羊赶到野外吃草 put sheep out to pasture ❷〈比喻 *fig.*〉不加管理,任其自由行动 be slack in management and allow for free action:老师没来上课,学生只好～。The teacher did not show up, so the pupils did as they pleased.

【放洋】fàngyáng ❶〈旧时 *old.*〉指出使外国或到外国留学 go abroad as a diplomat or to study ❷〈书 *fml.*〉船只出海航行 ships sailing to the ocean

【放养】fàngyǎng 把鱼虾、白蜡虫、柞蚕或水浮莲、红萍等有经济价值的动植物放到一定的地方使它们生长繁殖 put (fish, shrimp, wax insects, tussah silkworm, water cabbage, red duckweed or other animals or plants of economic value) in a suitable place to breed:～草鱼 breed grass carp|～海带 kelp culture

【放样】fàng//yàng (～儿 fàng//yàngr)在正式施工或制造之前,制作建筑物或制成品的模型,作为样品 loft; make models of buildings or products before formal construction or production

【放印子】fàngyìn·zi 借给别人印子钱 lend in usury; ☞ 印子钱 yìn·ziqián on p.2297

【放映】fàngyìng 利用强光装置把图片或影片上的形象照射在幕上或墙上。一般指电影放映。project; show (a film); throw an image on a screen or a wall, as from a transparent slide or film, usu. referring to showing a film

【放映机】fàngyìngjī 放映电影用的机器,用强光源透过影片上的形象,经过镜头映在银幕上。放映机附带光电设备,把影片上的声带变成声音。projector; machine for throwing an image from a film on a screen through a powerful luminant, with optical electronic equipment to convert the soundtrack into voice

【放淤】fàngyū 把泥水引到地里,使泥土淤积,增加土地的肥力,扩大可耕面积 warp; divert mud water into fields to deposit silt and sediment so as to increase the fertility of the soil and expand arable land

【放债】fàng//zhài 借钱给人收取利息 lend money for interest

【放账】fàng//zhàng same as 放债 fàng//zhài

【放赈】fàngzhèn 向灾民或贫民发放救济物资 distribute relief to victims in a disaster-stricken area:开仓～ open granaries and distribute relief

【放置】fàngzhì 安放 lay up; lay aside:～不用 lay up (machinery, equipment, etc.); lie idle

【放逐】fàngzhú〈古时 *arch.*〉把被判罪的人驱逐到边远地方 exile; banish; send into exile

【放恣】fàngzì〈书 *fml.*〉骄傲放纵,任意胡为 arrogant and self-indulgent; proud and undisciplined

【放纵】fàngzòng ❶ 纵容;不加约束 indulge; let sb. have his way; abandon oneself to sth.:～不管 be indulgent with someone ❷ 不守规矩;没有礼貌 self-indulgent; undisciplined:骄奢～ decadent and undisciplined|～不羁 uninhibited; hedonistic; bohemian

fēi (ㄈㄟ)

飞(飛) fēi ❶ (鸟、虫等)鼓动翅膀在空中活动 fly; flit; (of birds or insects) move through the air by flapping wings:～蝗 flying locusts|鸟～了。The bird flew away. ❷ 利用动力机械在空中行动 fly; aviate; move in the air by using mechanical equipment:～行 flight; aviation|明天有飞机～上海。There is a flight to Shanghai tomorrow. ❸ 在空中飘浮游动 hover or flutter in the air:～云 scudding clouds|～沙走石 flying sands and rolling pebbles|～雪花了。Snowflakes flew about. *or* It was snowing. ❹ 形容极快 swift; fast:～奔 run at full speed|～跑 race|～涨 soar ❺〈方 *dial.*〉非常;极 very:～快 very quick|～灵 very effective ❻ 挥发 disappear through evaporation:盖上瓶子吧,免得香味儿～了。Cover the bottle or the fragrance will disappear.|樟脑放久了,都～净了。The camphor balls evaporated into the air with time. ❼ 意外的;凭空而来的 unexpected; accidental; unfounded; groundless:～灾 unexpected disaster|～祸 unexpected disaster|流言～语 rumour and slander ❽〈方 *dial.*〉same as 飞轮 fēilún ②

【飞白】fēibái 一种特殊的书法,笔画中露出一丝丝的白地,像用枯笔写成的样子 a style of calligraphy characterized by some hollow areas in a stroke, as if done with a half-dry brush or a fast stroke; also 飞白书 fēibáishū

【飞镖】fēibiāo ❶ 旧式武器,形状像长矛的头,投掷出去能击伤人 dart-like weapon, an ancient weapon in the shape of a dart that can be thrown at a target ❷ 一种投掷运动,镖多用木料制成。比赛时,以在一定时间内掷出和收回的飞镖最多者或镖的飞行时间最长者为优胜。darts, throwing game usu. with wood darts, with the party that throws and gets back most darts within a certain period of time or whose dart flies farthest through the air declared as the winner

【飞播】fēibō 用飞机撒种 aerial sowing:～造林 afforestation with aerial sowing|～优良牧草一万多亩 sow more than 10,000 *mu* of high-quality herbage by aircraft

【飞车】fēichē ❶ 骑车或开车飞快地行驶 drive or cycle at high speed:～走壁 stunt cycling ❷ 飞快行驶的车 car driven at high speed:开～是造成交通事故的重要原因之一。Reckless driving is a major cause of traffic accidents.

【飞车走壁】fēi chē zǒu bì 杂技的一种,演员骑着自行车或开着摩托车和特制的小汽车,在口大底小的木制的圆形建筑物内壁上奔驰(acrobatics) stunt cycling, where an acrobat drives a special car or rides a motorcycle along the inner surface of a wooden wall in the shape of a truncated upside-down cone

【飞驰】fēichí (车马)很快地跑(of trains, cars, horses, etc.) speed along:列车～而过。A train sped by.|骏马在原野上～。Steeds raced in the field.

【飞船】fēichuán ❶ 指宇宙飞船 spaceship; spacecraft ❷〈旧时 *old*〉指飞艇 airship

【飞弹】fēidàn ❶ 装有自动飞行装置的炸弹,如导弹 bombs equipped with auto-flight devices, like missiles ❷ 流弹 stray bullet

【飞地】fēidì ❶ 指位居甲省(县)而行政上隶属乙省(县)的土地 land of one province or county enclosed by that of another ❷ 指甲国境内的隶属乙国的领土 enclave; exclave; territory of one country enclosed by that of another

【飞碟】fēidié ❶ 指空中不明飞行物,发光,速度很快,多呈圆形 unidentified flying object (UFO) in the shape of a disc, glowing and moving fast ❷ 射击用的一种靶,形状像碟,用抛靶机抛射到空中 skeet; trapshooting; skeet shooting; disc-shaped object used as target for shooting:～射击(一种体育运动比赛项目) skeet shooting, a sports event

【飞短流长】fēi duǎn liú cháng 造谣生事,搬弄是非 spread fabricated stories and malicious gossip; 飞 also put as 蜚 fēi

【飞蛾投火】fēi é tóu huǒ〈比喻 *fig.*〉自取灭亡 moth darting into a flame — bring destruction upon oneself; seek one's own doom; also 飞蛾扑火 fēi é pū huǒ

【飞归】fēiguī 珠算中两位数除法的一种算法,口诀跟归除不同,比归除简捷 way of doing division with a two-digit divisor on the abacus

【飞红】fēihóng ❶ (脸)很红 (of face) bright red; blush; scarlet; crimson:她一时答不上,急得满脸～。Her face waxed scarlet as the answer evaded her. ❷ (脸)很快变红 (of face) become red quickly:小张～了脸,更加忸怩起来。Xiao Zhang went crimson with embarrassment.

【飞鸿】fēihóng〈书 *fml.*〉❶ 指鸿雁 swan goose:～踏雪(比喻往事留下的痕迹) swan geese leaving tracks on the snow; (fig.) trace left by the past ❷〈比喻 *fig.*〉书信 letter; mail:～传情 love messages carried by the swan goose, i. e. love letters|万里～ letter from afar

【飞花】fēihuā 纺织和弹花时飞散的棉花纤维 cotton bits that fly about in the process of weaving or fluffing

【飞黄腾达】fēihuáng téngdá 韩愈诗《符读书城南》:'飞黄腾踏去,不能顾蟾蜍。'(飞黄 *feihuang*:古代传说中的神马名 holy horse in the legendary) Han Yu's poem *Studying in the South City*: 'Soar like the holy horse, leaving the toad behind.' 后来用飞黄腾达比喻官职、地位上升得很快 (fig.) make rapid advance in one's career; have a meteoric rise

【飞机】fēijī 飞行的工具,由机翼、机身、发动机等构成。种类很多。广泛用在交通运输、军事、农业、探矿、测量等方面。aircraft; airplane; aeroplane; plane; structure designed to travel through the air, composed of wings, body, engine, etc., widely used in transportation, military affairs, agriculture, prospecting and surveying

【飞溅】fēijiàn 向四外溅 splash:钢花～,铁水奔流。Sparks fly, and melted steel flows.

【飞快】fēikuài ❶ 非常迅速 swiftly; very fast; at lightning speed:渔船鼓着白帆,～地向远处驶去。Fishing boats, their white sail hoister, moved at great speed towards distant climes.|日子过得～,转眼又是一年。Time flies — a year has passed at the twinkling of an eye. ❷ 非常锋利 extremely sharp; razor-sharp:镰刀磨得～。Sharpen the sickles till they are as sharp as razors.

【飞来横祸】fēi lái hènghuò 突然发生的意外灾祸 unexpected disaster (that has flown in from nowhere)

【飞灵】fēilíng〈方 *dial.*〉❶ 特别灵活或灵敏 very smart:脑子～ have a sharp brain ❷ 特别灵验 very effective:这药治感冒,～。This medicine is highly effective against colds.

【飞轮】fēilún ❶ 机器上安装的大而重的轮子。利用它的惯性使机器旋转均匀。flywheel; big and heavy wheel for regulating the speed and uniformity of motion of the machine to which it is attached ❷ (～儿 fēilúnr)自行车后轮上装的传动齿轮 freewheel; device in the rear hub of a bicycle

【飞毛腿】fēimáotuǐ ❶ 指跑得特别快的腿 fleet-footed; swift of foot ❷ 指跑得特别快的人 fleet-footed runner

【飞盘】fēipán (～儿 fēipánr)一种投掷的玩具,形状像圆盘子,用塑料制成 frisbee; frisbee disk;

plastic, saucer-shaped disk that sails back and forth between players in a simple game

【飞蓬】fēipéng 多年生草本植物,叶子像柳叶,边缘有锯齿。秋天开花,花外围白色,中心黄色。bitter fleabane (*Erigeron acer*); perennial herb with willow-like leaves, blooming in autumn with flowers white at the edges and yellow in the centre; also 蓬 péng

【飞潜动植】fēi qián dòng zhí 指各种动物和植物 all the animals and plants; all kinds of creatures (飞 *fei*:天空飞的 flying in the sky; 潜 *qian*:水中游的 swimming in the waters)

【飞禽】fēiqín 会飞的鸟类,也泛指鸟类 flying birds; (in a broad sense) birds:~走兽 birds and beasts

【飞泉】fēiquán ❶ 从峭壁上的泉眼喷出的泉水 spring that flows out of a cliffside; cliffside spring ❷ 喷泉 fountain

【飞人】fēirén ❶ 指悬空进行杂技表演 aerial acrobatics:空中~ flying trapeze ❷ 指跳得特别高或跑得非常快的人 fast runner; best sprinter; person who jumps very high or runs very fast:女~woman sprinter | 世界~world-class sprinter

【飞散】fēisàn ❶ (烟、雾等)在空中飘动着散开 (of smoke, mist, etc.) disperse; dissipate:一团浓烟在空中~着,由黑色渐渐变成灰白。A cloud of thick, dark smoke dispersed through the air and gradually turned grey. ❷ (鸟等)飞着向四下散开 scatter; disperse; (of birds) fly away in different directions:麻雀听到枪声惊慌地~了。The sparrows scattered in alarm at the sound of a gun.

【飞沙走石】fēi shā zǒu shí 沙子飞扬,石块滚动。形容风很大。sand flying about and stones hurtling through the air (as in a windstorm):骤然狂风大作,~,天昏地暗。A fierce gale sprang up suddenly, threw sands and pebbles in all directions, and darkened the sky.

【飞身】fēishēn 身体轻快地跳起 vault; jump over agilely in a single movement:~上马 leap onto the horse's back in a flying mount; vault onto the saddle | ~越过壕沟 leap swiftly over the trench

【飞升】fēishēng ❶ 往上升;往上飞 rise; ascend; fly up ❷ 〈旧时 *old*〉指修炼成功,飞向仙境(迷信) (superstition) upon successful completion of certain religious or alchemist regimen, ascend to heaven and achieve immortality

【飞逝】fēishì (时间等)很快地过去或消失 fly; elapse; (of time, or a fast-moving object) slip by or past:时光~。Time flies. | 流星~。A meteor flew by.

【飞鼠】fēishǔ ❶ 哺乳动物,形态和习性均似鼯鼠而体较小,前后肢之间的薄膜宽大多毛 flying squirrel (*Petauristinae*); a kind of mammal resembling the phalanger in habit and appearance with winglike folds of skin attached to the legs and body ❷ 〈书 *fml.*〉蝙蝠 bat

【飞速】fēisù 非常迅速 at full speed:~发展 develop by leaps and bounds; make rapid development | ~前进 run at full speed

【飞腾】fēiténg 迅速飞起;很快地向上升;飞扬 fly swiftly upward; soar:烟雾~。A smoke-laden fog rose quickly and soon filled the air. | 烈焰~ furious flames spewing high into the air

【飞天】fēitiān 〈佛教 *Budd.*〉壁画或石刻中的在空中飞舞的神。梵语称神为提婆,因提婆有'天'的意思,所以汉语译为飞天。Apsaras (literally meaning 'sky flier' because in Sanskrit, god is known as 'deva', a term that means 'sky' among other things); flying gods as found in Buddhist frescoes or stone carvings

【飞艇】fēitǐng 飞行工具,没有翼,利用装着氢气或氦气的气囊所产生的浮力上升,靠螺旋桨推动前进。飞行速度比飞机慢。airship; dirigible; wingless flying vehicle that ascends by the floatage of an airbag containing hydrogen or helium, and is propelled by propellers at speeds slower than those of airplanes

【飞吻】fēiwěn 先吻自己的手,然后向对方挥手,表示吻对方 blow a kiss

【飞舞】fēiwǔ 像跳舞似地在空中飞 flutter; dance in the air:雪花~ snowflakes dancing in the air | 蝴蝶在花丛中~。Butterflies fluttered about among the flowers.

【飞翔】fēixiáng 盘旋地飞,泛指飞 circle in the air; (in a broad sense) hover:展翅~ spread wings and fly | 鸽子在天空~。A pigeon is hovering in the sky.

【飞行】fēixíng (飞机、火箭等)在空中航行 (of aircraft, rockets, etc.) fly; make a flight:~员 pilot | 低空~ low-altitude flight

【飞行器】fēixíngqì 能够在空中飞行的机器或装置的统称,包括气球、飞机、火箭、人造卫星、宇宙飞船等 aircraft; general term for any installation or machine designed to travel through the air, including balloon, airplane, rocket, man-made satellite, space shuttle, etc.

【飞行员】fēixíngyuán 飞机等的驾驶员 pilot; aviator; flyer, person who operates the controls of an aircraft

【飞旋】fēixuán 盘旋地飞 fly in circles:雄鹰在天空~。A hawk is circling in the sky. ◇他那爽朗的笑声不时在我耳边~。His hearty laughter echoes in my ears from time to time.

【飞檐】fēiyán 我国传统建筑檐部形式,屋檐特别是屋角的檐部向上翘起 upturned eaves; flying eaves; shape of eaves in traditional Chinese architecture with the edges turning upward

【飞檐走壁】fēi yán zǒu bì 旧小说中形容练武的人身体轻捷,能在房檐和墙壁上行走如飞 gravity-defying stunt; (of martial-arts masters in old Chinese novels) leap onto roofs and scale walls

【飞眼】fēi//yǎn (～儿 fēi//yǎnr)用眼睛表达意思 make eyes; ogle; use eyes to suggest

【飞扬】fēiyáng ❶ 向上飘起 fly upward; rise: 彩旗～ bunting fluttering in the air | 尘土～ clouds of dust flying up ❷ 形容精神兴奋得意 in high spirits: 神采～ in high spirits; in full feather ‖ also 飞飏 fēiyáng

【飞扬跋扈】fēi yáng bá hù 骄横放肆 arrogant and domineering; unruly; throw one's weight around

【飞鱼】fēiyú 鱼,身体长筒形,胸鳍特别发达,像翅膀,能跃出水面在空中滑翔。产于温带和亚热带海中,我国黄海、东海和南海都有。flying fish (*Exocoetidae*); marine fish in temperate and subtropical seas, such as the Yellow Sea, the East China Sea and the South China Sea of China, having a cylindrical body and wing-like pectoral fins that enable it to jump out of the water and glide through the air

【飞语】fēiyǔ 没有根据的话 groundless gossip; rumours; slander: 流言～ rumour and slander; also 蜚语 fēiyǔ

【飞跃】fēiyuè ❶ 事物从旧质到新质的转化。由于事物性质的不同,飞跃有时通过爆发的方式来实现,有时通过新质要素的逐渐积累和旧质要素的逐渐消亡来实现。不同形式的飞跃都是质变。leap; sudden transition; qualitative change from old properties to new ones, sometimes realized in an explosive way, and sometimes in a gradual way in which new properties accumulate and old ones wither away. In philosophy a leap, no matter what form it takes, entails a qualitative change. ❷〈比喻 *fig.*〉突飞猛进 leap: ～发展 develop by leaps and bounds ❸ 飞腾跳跃;腾空跳跃 fly swiftly and skip: 麻雀在丛林中～。The sparrows fly and skip in the woods. | 你刚才这一～翻身的动作,真有功夫。The leaps and flips you just did were really something.

【飞越】fēiyuè ❶ 飞着从上空越过 fly over or across; overfly: ～大西洋 fly across the Atlantic ❷〈书 *fml.*〉same as 飞扬 fēiyáng ②: 心神～ elated; inspired

【飞灾】fēizāi 意外的灾难 sudden disaster; unexpected calamity: ～横祸 sudden accident; unexpected disaster

【飞贼】fēizéi ❶ 指手脚灵便能很快地登墙上房的贼 cat burglar; nimble and deft burglar able to break into houses by climbing over walls and roofs ❷ 指由空中进犯的敌人 intruding enemy airman; air marauder or pirate

【飞涨】fēizhǎng (物价、水势等)很快地往上涨 (of prices, water level, etc.) soar; shoot up; skyrocket: 物价～。Prices were skyrocketing. | 连日暴雨,河水～。It has rained for days on end, and the river has swollen.

【飞舟】fēizhōu 行驶极快的船 swiftly moving boat: 浪遏～。Waves stayed the speeding boats. | ～竞渡 speed boat race

妃 fēi 皇帝的妾;太子、王、侯的妻 imperial concubine; wife of a prince, king or duke: ～嫔 imperial concubine | 贵～ highest-ranking imperial concubine | 王～ princess consort

【妃嫔】fēipín 妃和嫔,泛指皇帝的妾 (in a broad sense) imperial concubine

【妃色】fēisè 淡红色 light red

【妃子】fēi·zi 皇帝的妾,地位次于皇后 imperial concubine, second in status to the empress

非[1] fēi ❶ 错误;不对(跟'是[1]'相对 as opposed to 'correct') mistake; wrong; error: 是～ right and wrong | 习～成是 accept what is wrong as right and grow accustomed to it | 痛改前～ repent thoroughly of one's misdeeds ❷ 不合于 not conform to; go against; run counter to: ～法 illegal; unlawful; illicit | ～礼 impolite; rude; improper | ～分(fèn) presumptuous; not one's due ❸ 不以为然;反对;责备 censure; oppose; find fault with: ～难 blame; condemn; reproach | ～议 condemn; reproach; censure | 无可厚～ no ground for blame ❹ 不是 not; non-; in-; un-: ～卖品 article not for sale | ～无产阶级思想 non-proletarian ideology | ～司机不得开车。Only (certified) drivers are allowed to operate a car. | 答～所问 give an irrelevant answer | ～笔墨所能形容 indescribable; beggar description ❺ 跟'不'呼应,表示必须 [in combination with 不 bù to express a sense of necessity]: 要想做出成绩,～下苦功不可。Painstaking efforts are absolutely necessary if you want to amount to something. ❻ 必须;偏偏 must; simply; imperative: 不行,我～去(一定要去)! No, I simply must go! ❼〈书 *fml.*〉不好;糟 degenerate; deteriorate: 景况日～。The situation is deteriorating day by day.

非[2] Fēi 指非洲 Africa

【非常】fēicháng ❶ 异乎寻常的;特殊的 extraordinary; uncommon; unusual; special: ～时期 time of emergency | ～会议 extraordinary session ❷ 十分;极 very; highly; extremely; exceedingly: ～光荣 extremely honourable | ～高兴 very pleased | ～努力 work very hard | 他～会说话。He has a smooth (or glib) tongue.

【非但】fēidàn 不但 not only: 他～能完成自己的任务,还肯帮助别人。He can not only complete his own task, but is also willing to help others. | ～我不知道，连他也不知道。I did not know and neither did he.

【非导体】fēidǎotǐ 绝缘体 non-conductor

【非得】fēiděi 表示必须(一般跟'不'呼应 usu. in combination with 不 bù) compelled; must: 棉花长了蚜虫，～打药(不成)。The cotton has got aphids and must be treated with pesticides. | 干这活儿～胆子大(不行)。You've got to be daring to do this job.

【非电解质】fēidiànjiězhì 在水溶液中或在熔融状态下不能形成离子，因而不能导电的化合物。如蔗糖、乙醇、甘油等。anelectrolyte; nonelectrolyte; chemical compound that cannot form ions in aqueous solution or under melting conditions, and so cannot conduct electricity, e.g. sucrose, ethanol, glycerine, etc.

【非独】fēidú 〈书 *fml.*〉不但 not merely: 蜜蜂能传花粉，～无害，而且有益。Bees spread pollen and so are actually useful, not harmful.

【非对抗性矛盾】fēiduìkàngxìng máodùn 不需要通过外部冲突形式去解决的矛盾 non-antagonistic contradiction; contradiction that can be resolved without outside conflict: 人民内部矛盾是～。Internal contradictions among the people are non-antagonistic ones.

【非法】fēifǎ 不合法 unlawful; illegal; illicit; illegitimate: ～收入 illegal income (or earnings); illicit gains | ～活动 illegal activity | ～占据 take illegal possession of something. | 倒卖文物是～的。Reselling cultural relics at a profit is illegal.

【非凡】fēifán 超过一般；不寻常 extraordinary; outstanding; uncommon: ～的组织才能 outstanding (or exceptional) organizational ability | 市场上热闹～。The market is bustling with activity.

【非…非…】fēi… fēi… 既不是…又不是… neither ... nor ...: ～亲～故 be neither kith nor kin; perfect stranger | ～驴～马 neither donkey nor horse

【非分】fēifèn ❶ 不守本分；不安分 assuming; presumptuous; overstep one's bounds: ～之想 inordinate ambition or desire | 不做～的事 do nothing improper ❷ 不属自己分内的 not one's due: ～之财 money not honestly earned

【非…即…】fēi…jí… 不是…就是… either ... or ...; if not ... then ...: ～此～彼 either this or that | ～亲～友 either relative or friend | ～打～骂 if not a beating then a scolding

【非金属】fēijīnshǔ 一般没有金属光泽和延展性、不易导电、传热的单质。除溴以外，在常温下都是气体或固体，如氧、氮、硫、磷等。nonmetal; simple substance without the gloss and ductility of a metal, and with poor electricity and heat conductivity. All nonmetal elements such as oxygen, nitrogen, sulphur and phosphorus are gases or solids under normal temperature except bromine.

【非晶体】fēijīngtǐ 外形和内部原子排列都无定形的固体，如玻璃、松香、沥青、电木。有的物质既可以是晶体又可以是非晶体，如天然石英是晶体，熔化的石英是非晶体。amorphous body; noncrystal; solid with no regular external shape or internal atomic structure, such as glass, resin, pitch and bakelite. Some substances can be both under different external conditions, e.g. natural quartz is a crystal, but becomes amorphous when melted.

【非礼】fēilǐ 不合礼节；不礼貌 impolite; improper; rude: ～举动 improper behaviour; discourteous conduct

【非卖品】fēimàipǐn 只用于展览、赠送等而不出卖的物品 article used as display, gift, etc., but not for sale

【非命】fēimìng 遭受意外的灾祸而死亡叫死于非命 death caused by unexpected disaster

【非难】fēinàn 指摘和责问 blame; reproach; condemn; censure: 遭到～ receive censure (or blame) | 他这样做是对的，是无可～的。His behaviour is right and above criticism.

【非人】fēirén 不属于人应有的 inhuman: ～待遇 inhuman treatment | 过着～的生活 lead a miserable life

【非特】fēitè 〈书 *fml.*〉不但 not only

【非条件刺激】fēitiáojiàn cìjī 能引起机体非条件反射的刺激。如狗吃食物时就分泌唾液，食物就是引起唾液分泌的非条件刺激。unconditioned stimulus; stimulus that can evoke the unconditioned reflex of an organism (e.g. a dog secretes saliva when eating — food is the unconditioned stimulus of saliva secretion); also 无条件刺激 wútiáojiàn cìjī

【非条件反射】fēitiáojiàn fǎnshè 人或其他动物生来就具有的比较简单的反射活动。如手碰着火，就立刻缩回去。unconditioned reflex; simple innate reflections of man or other animals (e.g. a hand immediately pulls back when touched by fire); also 无条件反射 wútiáojiàn fǎnshè

【非同小可】fēi tóng xiǎo kě 形容事情重要或情况严重，不能轻视 no small or trivial matter; important matter or serious situation not to be taken lightly

【非徒】fēitú 不仅(常跟'而且'呼应 usu. in combination with 而且 érqiě) not merely; not only: 溺爱子女，～无益，而且有害。Spoiling a child is not only pointless — it can be harmful as well.

【非笑】fēixiào 讥笑 ridicule; sneer at: 受人～ held up to ridicule

【非刑】fēixíng 在法律规定之外施行的残酷的肉体刑罚 (unlawful) brutal torture; cruel and illegal punishment: ～拷打 torture sb. brutally; subject sb. to brutal torture | 受尽～折磨 suffer much torture

【非议】fēiyì 责备 reproach; condemn; blame; censure: 无可～ beyond (or above) reproach; irreproachable

菲[1] fēi 形容花草美、香味浓 (of flowers and grass) luxuriant and fragrant: 芳～ fragrance of flowers and plants

菲[2] fēi 有机化合物,分子式 $C_{14}H_{10}$。无色晶体,有荧光,是蒽的同分异构体。用来制染料、药品等。phenanthrene; colourless, fluorescent, crystalline organic compound, molecular formula $C_{14}H_{10}$, isomer of anthracene, used to make dyes and medicines ☞ fěi on p. 562

【菲菲】fēifēi 〈书 *fml.*〉❶ 花草茂盛、美丽 (of flowers and grass) luxuriant and beautiful ❷ 花草香气浓郁 aromatic; (of flowers and grass) heady fragrance

【菲林】fēilín 〈方 *dial.*〉胶卷 film; roll of film

啡 fēi ☞ 咖啡 kāfēi on p. 1068 and [吗啡] (mǎfēi) on p. 1291

骓 fēi 〈书 *fml.*〉〈古时 *arch.*〉指车前驾在辕马两旁的马 horses harnessed to both sides of the shaft-horse in front of a cart

F

绯 fēi 红色 red: ～红 bright red; rosy; crimson | 深～ deep (or dark) red

【绯红】fēihóng 鲜红 rosy; crimson; bright red: 两颊～ flush crimson; blush scarlet | ～的晚霞 rosy evening clouds

【绯闻】fēiwén 桃色新闻 sex scandal; amorous affair: 影坛～ sex scandals in film circles

扉 fēi 门扇 door; leaf: 柴～ faggot door ◇ 心～ way of thinking

【扉画】fēihuà 书籍正文前的插图 front illustration placed before the full text of a book

【扉页】fēiyè 书刊封面之内印着书名、著者、出版者等项内容的一页 title page inside a book or periodical cover, with the title, name(s) of author(s), publisher, etc.

蜚 fēi 〈书 *fml.*〉same as 飞 fēi ☞ fěi on p. 562

【蜚短流长】fēi duǎn liú cháng same as 飞短流长 fēi duǎn liú cháng

【蜚声】fēishēng 〈书 *fml.*〉扬名 make a name; establish one's reputation: ～文坛 win renown in literary circles

【蜚语】fēiyǔ same as 飞语 fēiyǔ

霏 fēi 〈书 *fml.*〉❶ 霏霏 fall thick and fast: 雨雪其～。The snow flakes fall thick and fast. ❷ 飘扬;飘散 flutter; diffuse; disperse: 烟～云敛。The smoke drifted away and the clouds dispersed.

【霏霏】fēifēi 〈书 *fml.*〉(雨、雪)纷飞;(烟、云等)很盛 (of rain, snow) drift; fall thick; heavy (of smoke, clouds, etc.): 雨雪～。The snow falls thick and fast. | ～细雨 fine drifty rain | 云雾～ heavy mist

【霏微】fēiwēi 〈书 *fml.*〉雾气、细雨等弥漫的样子 heavy with mist or drizzle: 烟雨～ misty rain

鲱 fēi 鱼,身体侧扁而长,背部灰黑色,两侧银白略带绿色,没有侧线,生活在海洋中。是重要的经济鱼类。Pacific herring (*Clupea pallasi*); important commercial marine fish with long, laterally flat body, dark-grey back, silvery sides tinged with green, and without lateral lines; also 鰊 liàn

féi (ㄈㄟˊ)

肥 féi ❶ 含脂肪多(跟'瘦'相对,除'肥胖、减肥'外,一般不用于人 as opposed to 'thin' or 'slender'; usu. not used to describe a person, except for 'fat', 'obese' or 'lose weight') fat; greasy: ～猪 fat pig | ～肉 fatty meat; fat | 马不得夜草不～。A horse not fed with fodder at night will not get fat. ❷ 肥沃 fertile; rich: 土地很～。The land is rather fertile. ❸ 使肥沃 make fertile; fertilize: ～田粉 soil fertilizer-ammonium sulphate ❹ 肥料 fertilizer; manure; compost: 底～ base manure | 绿～ green manure | 化～ chemical fertilizer | 积～ collect manure; store compost ❺ 收入多;油水多 yielding good profits; profitable; lucrative: ～差 fat job; lucrative post | 活儿～。The job is lucrative. ❻ 指由不正当的收入而富裕 get rich by illegal income ❼ 利益;好处 profit; benefit: 分～ divide up the spoils | 抄～(捞外快) earn extra income ❽ same as 肥大 féidà ①(跟'瘦'相对 as opposed to 'tight'): 棉袄的袖子太～了。The sleeves of the cotton-padded jacket are too wide.

【肥差】féichāi 指从中可多得好处的差事 post or job from which one can gain many benefits

【肥肠】féicháng (～儿 féichángr)指用做食品的猪的大肠 pig's large intestine (used as food): 熘～ stir-fry pig's intestines | 烩～ braised pig's intestines

【肥膪膪】féidādā 形容肥胖的样子 fat; plump

【肥大】féidà ❶ (衣服等)又宽又大 (of clothes, etc.) loose; wide: ～的灯笼裤 loose sweat pants | 这件褂子很～。The coat is very wide. ❷ (生物体或生物体的某部分)粗大壮实 plump; corpulent; (of part or whole of organism) stout and solid: ～的河马 large hippopotamus | 豌豆角很～。The pea pods are very full. ❸ 人体的某一脏器或某一部分组织,由于病变而体积增加 pathological enlargement of an organ or tissues of the human body: 心脏～ hypertrophy of the heart | 扁桃体～ hypertrophy of the tonsil

【肥分】féifèn 肥料中含氮、磷、钾等营养元素的成分,一般用百分数来表示 (usu. percentage of) nitrogen (N), phophorus (P) and potassium (K) nutriments in fertilizer

【肥厚】féihòu ❶ 肥而厚实 plump; fleshy: ～的

手掌 fleshy palm | ～的橡皮树叶子 fleshy leaves of the India rubber tree ❷ 人体的某一脏器或部分组织由于病变而体积增加 (of human organs or tissues) hypertrophy; enlargement: 右心室～ hypertrophic right ventricle ❸ (土层)肥沃而厚(of soil) fertile and thick ❹ 多;优厚 rich; generous; favourable: 油水～ big profit; lucrative | 奖金～ handsome bonus

【肥力】féilì 土壤肥沃的程度 fertility (of soil): 提高土地～ improve the fertility of the soil

【肥料】féiliào 能供给养分使植物发育生长的物质。肥料的种类很多,所含的养分主要是氮、磷、钾三种 fertilizer; manure; substances providing nutrients to boost plant growth. There are a good variety of fertilizers, but nitrogen (N), phophorus (P) and potassium (K) are their main nutrients: 化学～ chemical fertilizer

【肥美】féiměi ❶ 肥沃 fertile; rich: 河流两岸是～的土地。The river is bounded with fertile land on both banks. ❷ 肥壮;丰美 luxuriant; plump; fleshy; fat: ～的牛羊 fat cattle and sheep | ～的牧草 rich pastures ❸ 肥而味美 rich and tasty: ～的羊肉 rich and tasty mutton

【肥胖】féipàng 胖 overweight; obese; corpulent: ～症 obesity; adiposis

【肥缺】féiquē 指收入(主要是非法收入)多的官职 official position with a handsome income (mainly illegal earnings)

【肥实】féi·shi ❶ 肥胖 fat; stout: ～的枣红马 large bay horse ❷ 脂肪多 rich in fat: 这块肉很～。This piece of meat is very fatty. ❸ 富足;有钱 rich; affluent: 他家日子过得挺～。His family leads a rich life.

【肥瘦儿】féishòur ❶ 衣服的宽窄 girth of a garment: 你看这件衣裳的～怎么样? Does this garment fit (me) well? ❷ 〈方 *dial.*〉半肥半瘦的肉 meat that is half fat and half lean: 来半斤～。(I)'ll take half *jin* of meat, half fat and half lean.

【肥水】féishuǐ 〈方 *dial.*〉含有养分的水;液体肥料 water rich in nutrients; liquid fertilizer: ～不流外人田(比喻好处不能让给别人) rich water should stay in one's own fields; (fig.) keep all benefits for one's self.

【肥硕】féishuò ❶ (果实等)又大又饱满 (of fruit, etc.) large and fleshy ❷ (肢体)大而肥胖 (of limbs and body) large and firm

【肥田】féi//tián 采用施肥等措施使土地肥沃 fertilize or enrich the soil (by applying fertilizer or adopting other measures): 草木灰可以～。Plant ashes can be used to fertilize the soil.

【肥田】féitián 肥沃的田地 rich soil; fertile land: ～沃土 fertile land

【肥沃】féiwò (土地)含有较多的适合植物生长的养分、水分 fertile; rich; (of land) containing nutrients and moisture suitable for plants growth: 土壤～ rich soil

【肥效】féixiào 肥料的效力 fertilizer efficacy or effect; manurial effect: ～高 highly effective fertilizer | ～持久 lasting manurial effect

【肥育】féiyù 在宰杀之前的一段时期使猪、鸡等家畜、家禽很快地长肥。通常是喂给大量的精饲料。animal husbandry fattening; making domestic animals and fowl, such as pigs and chickens, grow fat before they are slaughtered, usu. by feeding them large quantities of concentrated feed; also 育肥 yùféi and 催肥 cuīféi

【肥源】féiyuán 肥料的来源,如人畜的粪便、动物的骨头、绿肥作物、榨油后剩下的油饼,以及某些矿物质 source of manure or fertilizer, e.g. human and animal excrement and urine, animal bones, green manure crops, bean dregs left from pressing oil, and some minerals

【肥皂】féizào 洗涤去污用的化学制品,通常制成块状。一般洗涤用的肥皂用油脂和氢氧化钠制成。工业上用重金属或碱土金属盐的肥皂做润滑剂。有的地区叫胰子。soap; chemical product used for washing and cleansing usu. made by treating fat with sodium hydroxide; soap made from heavy metal or alkaline-earth metal salts are used as industrial lubricant; also called 胰子 yí·zi in some places

【肥壮】féizhuàng (生物体)肥大而健壮 (of organism) stout and strong: 禾苗～ healthy seedlings (of cereal crops) | ～的牛羊 thriving herds of cattle and sheep

淝 Féi 淝河,河名,在安徽 Feihe River in Anhui Province; also 淝水 féishuǐ

腓1 féi 腿肚子 calf (of the leg)

腓2 féi 〈书 *fml.*〉病;枯萎 diseased; wither; wilt: 百卉俱～。All the plants have wilted.

【腓肠肌】féichángjī 胫骨后面的一块肌肉,扁平,在小腿后面形成隆起部分 gastrocnemius; flat muscle behind the shin bone that causes the bulge at the back of the shank

【腓骨】féigǔ 小腿外侧的长形骨,比胫骨细而短,有三个棱 fibula; outer long bone in the shank with three ridges, thinner and shorter than the shin bone; (图见 ☞ figure for 骨骼 gǔgé on p.693)

fěi (ㄈㄟˇ)

朏 fěi 〈书 *fml.*〉新月开始发光 gleam of the crescent moon

匪1 fěi 强盗 robber; bandit; gangster; brigand: 盗～ robber; bandit | 土～ brigand; bandit; outlaw | ～徒 robber; gangster; brigand; bandit|～患 banditry; scourge of banditry|剿～ suppress bandits

匪[2] fěi〈书 *fml.*〉非 not; no: 获益～浅 profit immensely; reap no little benefit|～夷所思 fantastic; bizarre; strange; (of ideas, events, etc.) out of the ordinary

【匪帮】fěibāng 有组织的匪徒或行为如同盗匪的反动政治集团 bandit gang; gang of bandits, or reactionary political group engaging in gangster-like activities: 法西斯～ fascist gang

【匪盗】fěidào 盗匪 robber; bandit; brigand

【匪患】fěihuàn 盗匪造成的祸患 banditry; scourge of banditry

【匪祸】fěihuò same as 匪患 fěihuàn

【匪首】fěishǒu 盗匪的头子 bandit chieftain; mob boss

【匪徒】fěitú ❶ 强盗 bandit; robber; brigand; gangster; mobster: 财物被～抢劫一空。Everything was stolen by the robbers. ❷ 危害人民的反动派或坏分子 reactionaries or bad elements who harm people

【匪穴】fěixué 敌人、盗匪盘踞的地方 bandits' den or lair; enemy hideaway: 直捣～ attack the bandits' den

【匪夷所思】fěi yí suǒ sī 指言谈行动超出常情，不是一般人所能想像的 (of speech and movement) out of the ordinary; strange (夷 *yi*: 平常 ordinary)

诽 fěi 毁谤 slander; calumniate: ～谤 slander; calumniate

【诽谤】fěibàng 无中生有，说人坏话，毁人名誉；诬蔑 slander; defame; do sb. down; fabricate malicious remarks about someone to destroy his reputation: 恶意～ malicious slander|～中伤 slander (or malign) sb. viciously

菲 fěi ❶ 古书上指萝卜一类的菜 radish or red turnip (in ancient books) ❷〈书 *fml.*〉菲薄(多用做谦辞 usu. hum.) humble; poor; unworthy: ～礼 my humble gift|～酌 simple meal|～材 my humble (or unworthy) talent

☞ fēi on p. 560

【菲薄】fěibó ❶ 微薄(指数量少、质量次) poor; humble (small quantity or poor quality): 待遇～ poorly paid|～的礼物 humble gift ❷ 瞧不起 belittle; despise; look down upon: 妄自～ unduly belittle oneself; be excessively humble|～前人 despise one's predecessors

【菲敬】fěijìng〈谦辞 *hum.*〉菲薄的礼物 small gift; humble present

【菲仪】fěiyí〈谦辞 *hum.*〉菲薄的礼物 my small (humble, or unworthy) gift

【菲酌】fěizhuó〈谦辞 *hum.*〉不丰盛的酒饭 simple meal and plain drink: 敬备～，恭候光临。We request the pleasure of your company at a simple dinner.

悱 fěi〈书 *fml.*〉想说又不知道怎么说 not know what to say; be at a loss for words

【悱恻】fěicè〈书 *fml.*〉形容内心悲苦 sad at heart; laden with sorrow: 缠绵～ lingering sorrow

棐 fěi〈书 *fml.*〉辅助 support; assist

斐 fěi〈书 *fml.*〉有文采 great literary talent: ～然 splendid; brilliant; striking literary talent

【斐然】fěirán〈书 *fml.*〉❶ 有文采的样子 striking literary talent: ～成章 show striking literary merit or talent ❷ 显著 outstanding; brilliant; splendid: 成绩～ outstanding achievements; illustrious accomplishments|～可观 striking; impressive

榧 fěi 榧子树，常绿乔木，树皮灰绿色，叶子针形，种子有硬壳，两端尖，仁可以吃。木质坚硬，可做建筑材料。Chinese torreya (*Torreya grandis*); evergreen tree having greyish-green bark, needle-shaped leaves, hard-shelled seeds pointed at both ends and with an edible kernel, and hardwood used as a building material; 通称 generally known as 香榧 xiāngfěi

【榧子】fěi·zi ❶ 榧子树 Chinese torreya ❷ 榧子树的种子 Chinese torreya-nut

蜚 fěi 古书上指蝗虫一类的昆虫 insects like locusts in ancient books

☞ fēi on p. 560

【蜚蠊】fěilián 蟑螂 cockroach (*Blatta orientalis*); roach

翡 fěi 古书上指一种有红毛的鸟 a variety of bird with redish feathers in ancient books

【翡翠】fěicuì ❶ 鸟的一属，嘴长而直，有蓝色和绿色的羽毛，飞得很快，生活在水边，吃鱼虾等。羽毛可做装饰品。kingfisher (*Alcedo atthis*); halcyon; bird genus characterized by a long and straight beak, blue and green feathers, fast flight, living by the water, and feeding on fish and shrimp, its feathers used to decorate ornaments ❷ 矿物，成分是 $NaAl(Si_2O_6)$。绿色、蓝绿色或白色中带绿色斑纹，有玻璃光泽，硬度 6—7，可做装饰品。jadeite; glass mineral of green or bluish-green colour, or white with green patches, used to make ornaments. Chemical composition is $NaAl(Si_2O_6)$, hardness 6-7.

篚 fěi〈书 *fml.*〉圆形的竹筐 round bamboo basket

fèi (ㄈㄟˋ)

芾 fèi ☞ 蔽芾 bìfèi on p. 109

☞ fú on p. 594

吠 fèi (狗)叫 bark; yap; yelp: 狂～ howl; bark furiously|鸡鸣犬～。Cocks crow and dogs bark.

【吠形吠声】fèi xíng fèi shēng《潜夫论·贤难》:'一犬吠形,百犬吠声' According to *A Hermit's Discourses·Misfortune of a Virtuous Man*, 'When one dog barks at a shadow all the others join in.'〈比喻 *fig*.〉不明察事情的真伪而盲目附和 slavishly echo others without really knowing whether they are right or wrong; also 吠影吠声 fèi yǐng fèi shēng

肺 fèi 人和高等动物的呼吸器官。人的肺在胸腔中,左右各一,和支气管相连。由心脏出来含有二氧化碳的血液经肺动脉到肺泡内进行气体交换,变成含有氧气的血液,经肺静脉流回心脏。lung; respiratory organ of man and higher animals. Man has a lung on either side of the thoracic cavity, connected by the bronchus. Blood containing carbon dioxide starts from the heart, passes through the pulmonary artery into the pulmonary alveoli, becomes oxygenated through gas exchange, and flows through the pulmonary vein back to the heart. also 肺脏 fèizàng

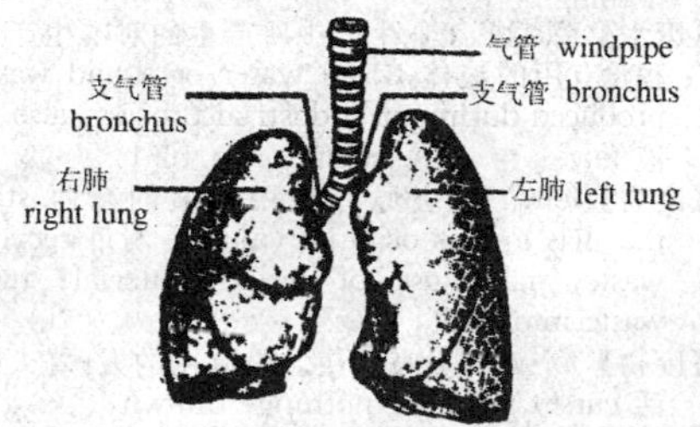

人的肺

Human Lungs

【肺病】fèibìng 肺结核的通称 general term for 肺结核 fèijiéhé

【肺动脉】fèidòngmài 从心向肺输送血液的血管,短而粗,共有两条,从右心室发出,分别进入左右两肺,分为小枝成毛细血管网包住肺泡。肺动脉中的血液含有二氧化碳,颜色暗红。pulmonary artery; two short and thick vessels conveying blood from the right ventricle of the heart to the left and right lungs, where they divide into small branches, forming a blood capillary network around the pulmonary alveoli. Blood in the pulmonary arteries contains carbon dioxide and is dark-red.(图见 ☞ figure for 心 xīn on p. 2126)

【肺腑】fèifǔ ❶ 肺脏 lungs:香沁～refreshing; invigorating ❷〈比喻 *fig*.〉内心 bottom of one's heart:感人～deeply moving; touch one to the depth of one's soul

【肺腑之言】fèifǔ zhī yán 发自内心的真诚的话 earnest; words from the bottom of one's heart

【肺活量】fèihuóliàng 一次尽力吸气后再尽力呼出的气体总量。成年男子正常的肺活量约为3.5—4升,成年女子正常的肺活量约为3升。vital lung capacity; total volume of air expirated after a deep inhalation. Normal lung capacity of an adult male is approximately 3.5-4 litres; and of an adult female, 3 litres.

【肺结核】fèijiéhé 慢性传染病,病原体是结核杆菌。症状是低热,夜间盗汗,咳嗽,多痰,消瘦,有时咯血。pulmonary tuberculosis (TB); chronic infectious disease caused by the tubercle bacillus. Symptoms include low fever, night sweating, cough, phlegm, emaciation and sometimes haemoptysis; 通称 generally known as 肺病 fèibìng

【肺静脉】fèijìngmài 从肺向心输送血液的血管,从左右两肺各发出两条,进入左心房。肺静脉中的血液含有氧气,颜色鲜红。pulmonary vein; two vessels conveying blood from the left and right lungs respectively to the left ventricle of the heart. Blood in the pulmonary veins contains oxygen and is bright red; (图见 ☞ figure for 心 xīn on p. 2126)

【肺痨】fèiláo〈中医 *Chin. med*.〉指肺结核 tuberculosis

【肺泡】fèipào 肺的主要组成部分,位置在最小支气管的末端,略呈半球形,周围有毛细血管网围绕。血液在肺泡内进行气体交换。pulmonary alveolus, major part of the lungs in the form of semi-spherical air cells situated at the end of the finest bronchioles, and covered by in a network of blood capillaries, where gas exchange occurs

【肺循环】fèixúnhuán 心脏收缩的时候,右心室中含有二氧化碳的血液,经过肺动脉流入肺部,在肺内进行气体交换,排出多余的二氧化碳,吸收新鲜的氧气,经过肺静脉流入左心房,再流入左心室。血液的这种循环叫做肺循环。pulmonary circulation. When the heart contracts, blood containing carbon dioxide in the right ventricle of the heart flows through the pulmonary arteries to the lungs, where unnecessary carbon dioxide is released and fresh oxygen absorbed, and continues its flow through the left atrium of the heart and into the left ventricle. This whole process called pulmonary circulation; also 小循环 xiǎoxúnhuán

【肺炎】fèiyán 肺部发炎的病,由细菌、病毒等引起,种类较多。症状是发高热,咳嗽,胸痛,呼吸困难等。pneumonia; inflammation of the lungs caused by bacteria or viruses. There are various types of pneumonia, which is characterized by high fever, cough, pain in the chest, difficult breathing.

【肺叶】fèiyè 肺表面深而长的裂沟把左肺分成两部分,把右肺分成三部分,每一部分叫一个肺叶 lobe of the lung. The left lung is divided into two lobes, the right into three, by long deep furrows on the surface.

【肺脏】fèizàng 肺 lungs

狒 fèi [狒狒]哺乳动物，身体形状像猴，头部形状像狗，毛灰褐色，四肢粗，尾细长。群居，杂食。多产在非洲。baboon (*Papio hamadryas*); African mammal with a body like a monkey's, doglike head, brown fur, thick four limbs, and a long and thin tail. Baboons live in groups and are omnivorous.

废(廢) fèi ❶ 不再使用；不再继续 abandon; abolish; reject; give up: ～除 abolish; abrogate; annul; repeal | 半途而～ give up halfway ❷ 荒芜；衰败 lie waste; decline: ～园 abandoned garden | ～墟 ruins; debris ❸ 没有用的或失去了原来的作用的 waste; useless; disused: ～话 nonsense; rubbish; superfluous words | ～纸 waste paper | ～铁 scrap iron | 修旧利～ repair old equipment and make use of waste materials ❹ 残废 disabled; maimed: ～疾 disability ❺〈书 *fml.*〉废黜 dethrone; depose

【废弛】fèichí (政令、风纪等)因不执行或不被重视而失去约束作用 (of law, custom, etc.) cease to be binding; (of discipline, etc.) become lax (due to unenforcement or regligence): 纪律～。Discipline has become lax.

【废除】fèichú 取消；废止(法令、制度、条约等) (of law or decree, system, treaty, etc.) abolish; annul, abrogate; repeal; blow up: ～农奴制 abolish serfdom | ～不平等条约 abrogate the unequal treaties

【废黜】fèichù ❶〈书 *fml.*〉罢免；革除(官职) banish; demote; dismiss from office ❷ 取消王位或废除特权地位 remove from the throne or a privileged position

【废话】fèihuà ❶ 没有用的话 nonsense; rubbish; superfluous words: ～连篇 reams of rubbish; pages of nonsense; load of garbage | 少说～。No more idle words. ❷ 说废话 talk nonsense: 别～，快干你的事去。Stop that nonsense and get on with your business.

【废旧】fèijiù 废弃的和陈旧的(东西) (of things) scrap; junked; old and useless: ～物资 scrap; waste materials

【废料】fèiliào 在制造某种产品过程中剩下的而对本生产过程没有用的材料 waste; scrap; waste material; materials left over from the manufacturing process, which cannot be used: 造纸厂的～可以制造酒精。The waste materials from a paper mill can be used to produce alcohol.

【废品】fèipǐn ❶ 不合出厂规格的产品 substandard product ❷ 破的、旧的或失去原有使用价值的物品 broken, old and worthless objects: ～收购站 waste recycling station

【废气】fèiqì 工业生产或动力机械运转中所产生的对本生产过程没有用的气体 waste gas or steam from industrial production or emitted during mechanical movement and useless to the production process; ☞ 三废 sānfèi on p. 1651

【废弃】fèiqì 抛弃不用 abandon; discard; cast aside: 把～的土地变成良田 turn abandoned land into fine farmland | 旧的规章制度要一概～。Old rules and regulations should be discarded without exception.

【废寝忘食】fèi qǐn wàng shí 顾不得睡觉，忘记吃饭。形容非常专心努力。work so hard as to forsake food and sleep; also 废寝忘餐 fèi qǐn wàng cān

【废然】fèirán〈书 *fml.*〉形容消极失望的样子 dispirited and disappointed: ～而返 return disappointed | ～而叹 sigh in disappointment

【废热】fèirè 在工业生产中所产生的对本生产过程没有用的热水、热气 waste hot water or heat discharged during an industrial process and useless to it: 利用工厂～取暖 utilize waste heat from a factory to provide heating

【废人】fèirén 因残废而失去工作能力的人。也泛指无用的人。person unable to work due to disablement; (in a broad sense) good-for-nothing

【废水】fèishuǐ 工业生产中所产生的对本生产过程没有用的液体 waste water or liquid waste produced during an industrial process; also 废液 fèiyè; ☞ 三废 sānfèi on p. 1651

【废物】fèiwù 失去原有使用价值的东西 sth. that has lost its original value: ～利用 recycle waste; make use of waste material; turn waste into asset

【废物】fèi·wu〈比喻 *fig.*〉没有用的人(骂人的话 curse) good-for-nothing; dimwit

【废墟】fèixū 城市、村庄遭受破坏或灾害后变成的荒凉地方 ruins; remains of city or village destroyed by natural or man-made disaster: 一片～ ruins | 大地震后，整个城市成了～。The earthquake reduced the city to rubble.

【废学】fèixué 不再继续上学；辍学 discontinue one's studies; drop out of school: 中途～ drop out of school

【废渣】fèizhā 工业生产中所产生的对本生产过程没有用的固态物质 slag; dross; waste residue; solid matter produced during an industrial process, and useless to it; ☞ 三废 sānfèi on p. 1651

【废止】fèizhǐ 取消，不再行使(法令、制度) (law, decree, institution, etc.) abolish; annul; nullify; put to an end: 本条令公布后，以前的暂行条例即行～。All previous interim rules shall be annulled upon the promulgation of this regulations.

【废址】fèizhǐ〈书 *fml.*〉已经毁坏的建筑物的地址 site of a building in ruins: 这里原是清代县衙门的～。This is the previous site of the county magistrate's office in the Qing Dynasty.

【废置】fèizhì 认为没有用而搁在一边 put aside

as useless：这些材料～不用，太可惜了。It is a great pity not to use these materials.

沸 fèi 沸腾 boil; bubble：～水 boiling water | ～油 boiling oil | 扬汤止～stop water from boiling by scooping it out and pouring it back ◇～天震地(形容声音极响) ear-splitting; (of sound) so loud it can be heard in the sky and shake the earth

【沸点】fèidiǎn 液体开始沸腾时的温度。沸点随外界压力变化而改变，压力低，沸点也低。boiling temperature of a liquid, which varies with external pressure, the lower the pressure, the lower the boiling point

【沸反盈天】fèi fǎn yíng tiān 形容喧哗吵闹，乱成一团 hullabaloo; uproar

【沸沸扬扬】fèifèiyángyáng 像沸腾的水一样喧闹，多形容议论纷纷 hubbub; noisy; usu. animated discussion; give rise to much discussion

【沸泉】fèiquán 温度在 80℃ 以上的泉水 near-boiling spring (spring with a temperature of over 80℃)

【沸热】fèirè 火热 boiling hot; steaming hot：～的南风 boiling south wind ◇～的心 extremely warm-hearted

【沸水】fèishuǐ 滚水；开水 boiling water

【沸腾】fèiténg ❶ 液体达到一定温度时急剧转化为气体的现象，这时液体发生汽化，产生气泡 boil; bubble; reach ebullition; phenomenon of the rapid transformation of a liquid into gas at a certain temperature, as the liquid is vaporized, bubbles appear ❷〈比喻 *fig.*〉情绪高涨 exhilaration seething with excitement：热血～ full of excitement ❸〈比喻 *fig.*〉喧嚣嘈杂 noisy and confused：群情激愤，人声～。Public indignation was expressed in a loud hubbub of voices.

【沸腾炉】fèiténglú 锅炉的一种，因烧煤时空气把煤粒吹得上下翻动，像开水沸腾而得名。导热强度高，可烧用劣质煤或矸石。fluosolid furnace; a type of furnace in which culms bounce up and down on the air flow as if boiling, producing high heat and capable of burning inferior coal or waste rock as fuel

费 fèi ❶ 费用 fee; expense; charge：水电～ charges for water and electricity | 医药～ medical costs | 免～ free of charge ❷ 花费；耗费 cost; spend; expend：～心 give great care; take much trouble | 消～ consume | ～了半天工夫 take a long time ❸ 用得多；消耗得多(跟'省'相对 as opposed to 'save') consume too much; be wasteful; expend too quickly：老式汽车～油。Old-style cars consume too much gas. | 走山路～鞋。Walking on mountain paths is wearing on the shoes | 孩子穿衣裳真～。Children wear out clothes quickly. ❹ (Fèi) 姓 a surname

【费工】fèi//gōng 耗费工夫 time-consuming; take time and energy：加工这种零件比较～，一小时怕完不了。Processing this spare part is time-consuming and one hour is probably not enough.

【费话】fèi//huà 耗费言词，多说话 take a lot of talking or explaining：一说他就明白，用不着～。He understands things very quickly, no need for lengthy explanations. | 我费了许多话才把他说服。It took me a lot of explaining to convince him.

【费解】fèijiě (文章的词句、说的话)不好懂 puzzling; obscure; (of spoken or written word) hard to understand：这篇文章词意隐晦，实在～。The language used in this article is so obscure it is quite incomprehensible.

【费劲】fèi//jìn (～儿 fèijìnr) 费力 laboured; showing signs of effort or difficulty：腿脚不好，上楼～。It's hard to walk upstairs with stiff legs. | 费了半天劲，也没有干好。Even after so much effort the result was unsatisfactory.

【费力】fèi//lì 耗费力量 require or need great effort; be strenuous：～劳心 taxing | 他有气喘病，说话很～。He suffers from asthma and his speech is laboured.

【费难】fèi//nán〈方 *dial.*〉感到困难，不容易做 find sth. difficult to do; be hard put to it; give sb. trouble：他学过木匠，打个柜子不～。He has learned carpentry, so making a cupboard should be easy for him. | 让他去介绍经验，他可费了难。It's a challenge for him to talk about his experiences.

【费神】fèi//shén 耗费精神(常用做请托时客套话 polite words used when asking for help) expend effort：这篇稿子您～看看吧。Would you mind going over this article for me?

【费时】fèishí 耗费时间 take time; be time-consuming：这座大楼～一年才建成。It took a whole year to complete this building.

【费事】fèi//shì 事情复杂，不容易办；费工 troublesome; difficult：给同志们烧点水喝，并不～。It's no trouble to boil some water for the comrades. | 洗件衣服，费不了什么事。Washing a single garment is no bother.

【费手脚】fèi shǒujiǎo 费事 need or require much effort：真要把这件事做好，也得费点手脚。Success in this endeavour will take some effort.

【费心】fèi//xīn 耗费心神(多用做请托或致谢时客套话 polite words used when asking for help or expressing thanks) take much trouble; may I trouble you (to do sth.); would you mind (doing sth.)：您要是见到他，～把这封信交给他。Would you mind giving him this letter when you see him? | 这孩子真让人～。This child is really troublesome.

【费用】fèi·yong 花费的钱；开支 cost; expenses：生活～ cost of living | 这几个月家里～太大。

F

Our family expenses have gone way too high these last months.

剕(踋) fèi 〈古代 *arch.*〉砍掉脚的酷刑 punishment consisting of amputation of the feet

痱(疿) fèi ☞ below

【痱子】fèi·zi 皮肤病，暑天皮肤上起的红色或白色小疹，很刺痒，常由出汗多、皮肤不清洁、毛孔被泥垢堵塞引起 prickly heat, a summer skin condition characterized by small itchy red or white pimples usu. caused by heavy perspiration, unclean skin, or clogged pores

【痱子粉】fèi·zifěn 用滑石粉、氧化锌、水杨酸、硫磺、薄荷脑等加香料制成的一种药粉，可用来防治痱子 prickly-heat powder; medicinal powder made from talcum powder, zinc oxide, salicylic acid, sulphur, peppermint and fragrance used to prevent and cure prickly heat

镄 fèi 金属元素，符号 Fm (fermium)。有放射性，由人工核反应获得。fermium (Fm); radioactive metal element obtained through artificial nuclear reactions

篚(籄) fèi 〈书 *fml.*〉竹席 bamboo mat

fēn (ㄈㄣ)

分 fēn ❶ 使整体事物变成几部分或使联在一起的事物离开（跟‘合’相对 as opposed to ‘join’ or ‘combine’）divide; separate; part; split; divide an entirety into several parts, or separate what was joined: ～裂 split; divide; break up | ～散 scatter; disperse; diffuse | ～离 separate; sever | 一个瓜～两半 divide a watermelon in half ❷ 分配 assign; distribute; allot: 这个工作～给你。This job is assigned to you. ❸ 辨别 tell; distinguish; differentiate: ～清是非 distinguish between right and wrong | 不～皂白 make no distinction between black and white (or right and wrong) ❹ 分支；部分 branch (of organization); part: ～会 branch (of society, committee, association, etc.) | ～局 sub-bureau; out-station; minor office | 第三～册 Book Three ❺ 分数 fraction: 约～ reduce a fraction | 通～ reduce fractions to a common denominator ❻ 表示分数 express fractions and percentages: 二～之一 one-half; 50 per cent | 百～之五 five per cent ❼（某些计量单位的）10 分之 1 one-tenth of (certain units of measurement): ～米 decimetre (dm.) | ～升 decilitre (dl.) ❽ 计量单位名称 name of unit of measurement a) 长度，10 厘等于 1 分，10 分等于 1 寸 *fen*, a unit of length (1 *fen* = 1/3 centimetre or 1/10 *cun*) b) 地积，10 厘等于 1 分，10 分等于 1 亩 *fen*, a unit of area (1 *fen* = 0.666 are or 1/10 *mu*) c) 重量，10 厘等于 1 分，10 分等于 1 钱 *fen*, a unit of weight (1 *fen* = 1/2 gramme or 1/10 *qian*) d) 货币，10 分等于 1 角 *fen*, a fractional unit of currency in China (1/10 of a *jiao*) e) 时间，60 秒等于 1 分，60 分等于 1 小时 (of time) minute (= 60 seconds or 1/60 of an hour) f) 弧或角，60 秒等于 1 分，60 分等于 1 度 (of arch or angle) minute (= 60 seconds or 1/60 of a degree) g) 经度或纬度，60 秒等于 1 分，60 分等于 1 度 (of longitude or latitude) minute (= 60 seconds or 1/60 of a degree) h) 利率，年利一分按十分之一计算，月利一分按百分之一计算 of interest rate (1/10 of annual interest rate or 1/100 monthly interest rate) i)（～儿 fēnr）评定成绩等 mark; point: 考试得了一百～ get full marks in the exam | 这场球赛双方只差几～。There is only a difference of a few points between the two sides in the ball game. ❾〈方 *dial.*〉指钞票或十元的人民币 bank note; ten-yuan note: 捞～（赚钱）make money | 赚了十张～ earn 10 ten-yuan notes

☞ fèn on p. 575

【分贝】fēnbèi 计量声音强度或电功率相对大小的单位，它的数值等于音强或功率比值的常用对数的 10 倍。当选定一个基准音强或功率时，分贝数也表示音强或功率的绝对大小。decibel (db); unit of measurement for the relative intensity of sound or electric power, equal to 10 times the common logarithm of the ratio of sound intensity or power. Relative to a base intensity of sound or electric power, the decibel number also indicates the absolute value of the sound intensity or electric power.

【分崩离析】fēn bēng lí xī 形容集团、国家等分裂瓦解 (of a group, country, etc.) disintegrate; crumble; come or fall apart

【分辨】fēnbiàn 辨别 distinguish; differentiate: ～香花和毒草 distinguish fragrant flowers from poisonous weeds | 天下着大雨，连方向也～不清了。The rain is so heavy it's hard to see where we are going.

【分辩】fēnbiàn 辩白 defend oneself (against a charge); offer an explanation: 证据俱在，无需～。The evidence is all here; no explanations are necessary. | 他们说什么就是什么，我不想～。They can say what they like; I will not argue.

【分别】[1] fēnbié 离别 part; leave; say goodbye to each other; bid farewell: 暂时～，不久就能见面。It's only a temporary separation. We'll soon meet again. | 他们～了好多年啦。They have been parted for years.

【分别】[2] fēnbié ❶ 辨别 distinguish; differentiate: ～是非 distinguish right and wrong; tell right from wrong | ～轻重缓急 distinguish priorities ❷ 不同 distinction; difference: ～对待

different treatments|～处理 treat or deal with in different ways|看不出有什么～。No difference is visible. ❸ 分头;各自 respectively; separately:会议商定,几个人～去做动员工作。At the meeting they agreed to fan out and mobilize the people in their respective places.|部队到达前沿,～进入阵地。The troops have each taken up their respective posts after reaching the forward position.

【分兵】fēnbīng 分开或分散兵力 separate or disperse armed forces:～而进 divide troops into separate advancing columns|～把守要隘 divide one's forces to defend strategic passes

【分布】fēnbù 散布(在一定的地区内) be distributed (over an area):人口～图 map of population distribution|商业网点～得不均匀。The commercial outlets are unevenly distributed.

【分餐】fēncān ❶ 集体吃饭的时候,把菜肴分开吃 meal served individually; (when a group of people eat together) each person has a separate portion of food (instead of sharing from common dishes):我因为有病,跟家里人～。Because I am ill, I have my own separate portions at family meal time. ❷ 指把菜肴分开吃的吃饭方式 sharing a meal by dividing the dishes among the eaters:吃～eat individual portions

【分册】fēncè 一部篇幅较大的书,按内容分成若干本,每一本叫一个分册 fascicle long book published in separate parts divided according to content, each called a fascicle

【分成】fēn//chéng (～儿 fēn//chéngr)按成数分钱财、物品等 (money, property, goods, etc.) share; divide into tenths:四六～ four to six split out of 10|三七～ three to seven split out of 10

【分爨】fēncuàn 〈书 *fml.*〉分家过日子 (of brothers) divide the property and live apart:兄弟～。The brothers have now each set up his own establishment.

【分寸】fēn·cun 说话或做事的适当限度 limits for speech or action; sense of appropriateness or proportion:有～ have due sense of proportion|没～ has no sense of propriety|注意说话的～。It's important to pay attention to appropriateness of speech.

【分担】fēndān 担负一部分 share (part of sth.):～任务 share the tasks|～责任 share responsibility for

【分道扬镳】fēn dào yáng biāo 指分道而行 separate and go different ways;〈比喻 *fig.*〉因目标不同而各奔各的前程或各干各的事情 each going his or her own way or doing his or her own business because of different objectives

【分店】fēndiàn 一个商店分设的店 branch of (shop):这家商行去年又开设了两家～。The trading company established two branches last year.

【分队】fēnduì 一般指军队中相当于营到班一级的组织 detachment; troop unit corresponding to a level from platoon to squad

【分发】fēnfā ❶ 一个个地分给 distribute; hand out; issue (to individuals):～慰问品 extend gratitude and appreciation by way of gifts; distribute relief materials ❷ 分派(人员到工作岗位) assign (to post); appoint (to job)

【分肥】fēn//féi 分取利益(一般指不正当的) share ill-gotten gains; divide booty; divide up the spoils

【分付】fēn·fù same as 吩咐 fēn·fù

【分割】fēngē 把整体或有联系的东西分开 separate; (of a whole or of related aspects) cut apart; carve up; break up:民主和集中这两方面,任何时候都不能～开。Democracy and centralism should never be separated from each other.

【分隔】fēngé 在中间隔断 separate; isolate; partition:夫妻～两地。Husband and wife live separately in two places.|垒了一道墙,把一间房子～成两间。The room was partitioned into two by a wall.

【分工】fēn//gōng 分别从事各种不同而又互相补充的工作 engage in different but related work:社会～ social division of labour|～合作 share the work and help one another; divide the work and cooperate|他～抓生产。He is responsible for production.|这几件事,咱们分分工吧。Let's divide up these tasks.

【分管】fēnguǎn 分工管理(某方面工作) be in charge of; assume personal responsibility for (specific job):他～农业。He is in charge of agriculture.|这是老张～的地段。This area is Old Zhang's responsibility.

【分毫】fēnháo 指很少的数量;些微 fraction; iota; of little quantity:～不爽 be correct in every detail|不差～ identical

【分号】[1] fēnhào 标点符号(;),表示一句话中间并列分句之间的停顿 semi-colon, punctuation mark (;) marking the pause between coordinate clauses of a sentence

【分号】[2] fēnhào 分店 branch (of shop, etc.):本店只此一家,别无～。Our shop is the only one bearing this name; there are no branches.

【分红】fēn//hóng ❶ 指人民公社时期社员定期分配工分值 (in the people's communes) periodical distribution of the cash value of workpoints to commune members ❷ 企业分配盈余或利润 (of an enterprise) share surplus or profits; distribute bonuses:年终～ distribute the year-end bonus|按股～ dividends on share; pay dividends to shareholders

【分洪】fēnhóng 为了使某些地区不遭受洪水灾害,在上游适宜地点,把一部分洪水引入别的地方,这种措施叫做分洪 flood diversion; divert some of the flood waters at an appropriate site on the upper reaches of a river so that areas lower down will not be devastated

【分化】fēnhuà ❶ 性质相同的事物变成性质不同的事物；统一的事物变成分裂的事物（of similar of integrated matters）become divided; break up; split up：两极～ polarization; division (of a group, society, etc.) into two opposite extremes｜有些字，古代本是一个，由于后来加上了不同的偏旁，就～成几个。In ancient times, some characters were written in one common form, but later evolved into several different forms as different radicals were added. ❷ 使分化 divide：～瓦解 disintegrate; split; divide and demoralize｜～敌人 split and demoralize the enemy (forces) ❸ 在生物个体发育的过程中，细胞向不同的方向发展，在构造和机能上，由一般变为特殊的现象，例如胚胎时期的某些细胞分化成为肌细胞，另一些细胞分化成为结缔组织（of cells）differentiate; develop in different directions by changing from generalized to specialized structures and functions during the process of development of an organism. For example, in the embryo, some cells differentiate into muscle and others into connective tissue.

【分机】fēnjī 需通过总机才能接通电话的通话装置（telephone）extension; communication device which allows connection through a telephone exchange

【分家】fēn//jiā ❶ 原来在一起生活的亲属把共有的家产分了，各自成家过活（of family members, usu. grown-up and married children）divide up family property and live apart：～单过 split the family property and live apart ❷ 泛指一个整体分开（of an entirety）split up; break up：鞋底和鞋帮分了家。The shoe sole and upper have separated.

【分节歌】fēnjiégē 指用几段歌词配同一曲调的歌曲。各段歌词在字数、韵律方面大致相同。民歌和群众歌曲中常见，如《兰花花》、《绣金匾》、《三大纪律八项注意》等。folk or popular song with several verses set to the same melody, each verse having a similar number of characters and a similar rhyme scheme, e.g. *Lan Huahua*, *Embroidering a Silk Banner with Golden Thread*, *Three Main Rules of Discipline and Eight Points for Attention* of the Chinese People's Liberation Army, etc.)

【分解】fēnjiě ❶ 一个整体分成它的各个组成部分，例如物理学上力的分解，数学上因式的分解等（of a whole）separate into parts; break up; break down; dismantle, e.g. in physics resolution of force, in mathematics resolve into factors ❷ 一种物质经过化学反应而生成两种或两种以上其他物质，如碳酸钙加热分解成氧化钙和二氧化碳 decompose; resolve; break up; split; (of a substance) break up into two or more substances through chemical reaction. For example, when heated, calcium carbonate breaks up into calcium oxide and carbon dioxide. ❸ 排解（纠纷）；调解 mediate; make peace：难以～ difficult to mediate｜让他替你们～～。Let him help you sort things out. ❹ 分化瓦解 disintegrate：做好各项工作，促使敌人内部～。If we do things well we can hasten the enemy's disintegration from within. ❺ 解说；分辩 recount; disclose; defend oneself：且听下回～（章回小说用语）will be disclosed in the following chapter (an expression used in novels written in traditional *zhanghui* style)｜不容他～，就把他拉走了。He was allowed no explanation before being taken away.

【分界】fēn//jiè 划分界限 demarcate; have as the boundary：～线 boundary; line of demarcation｜河北省和辽宁省在山海关～。Hebei and Liaoning provinces are demarcated by Shanhaiguan Pass.

【分界】fēnjiè 划分的界线 dividing line; line of demarcation：赤道是南半球和北半球的～。The equator is the dividing line between the northern and southern hemispheres.

【分界线】fēnjièxiàn ❶ 划分开地区的界线 boundary; line of demarcation：过了河北河南两省的～，就进入了豫北。After crossing the boundary between Hebei and Henan provinces, you will enter the northern part of Henan Province. ❷〈比喻 *fig.*〉界限 bound; dividing line; demarcation line：是非的～不容混淆。Confusing right and wrong is inexcusable.

【分斤掰两】fēn jīn bāi liǎng〈比喻 *fig.*〉过分计较小事 be over-concerned with minor matters

【分镜头】fēnjìngtóu 导演将整个影片或电视片的内容按景别、摄法、对话、音乐、镜头长度等分切成许多准备拍摄的镜头，称为分镜头 storyboard; film director cuts the film or television film into many sequences according to different scenes, filming methods, dialogues, music, length of shot, etc.

【分居】fēn//jū 一家人分开生活 separated; (of married couple) live apart：～另过 live separated｜他们夫妻两地～。The husband and wife live in two separate places.

【分句】fēnjù 语法上指复句里划分出来的相当于单句的部分。分句和分句之间一般有停顿，在书面上用逗号或者分号表示。分句和分句在意义上有一定的联系，常用一些关联词语（连词、有关联作用的副词或词组）来连接，如：天晴了，雪也化了。clause; part of a compound sentence equivalent to a simple sentence usu. divided by a pause indicated by a comma or semicolon. Clauses are associated in meaning and oft. linked by connectives (conjunctions, adverbs or phrases with connective functions), e.g. The sky cleared, and the snow melted away. ☞ 复句 fùjù on p. 611

【分开】fēn//kāi ❶ 人或事物不聚在一起 (of persons or things) be apart; part: 弟兄两人~已经三年了。The two brothers have been apart for three years.|这些问题是彼此~而又联系着的。The problems are separate yet also linked. ❷ 使分开 (cause to) separate or part: 老赵用手~人群，挤到台前。Separating the crowd with his hands, Old Zhao pushed his way to the platform.|这两件事要~解决。The two matters should be resolved separately.

【分类】fēn//lèi 根据事物的特点分别归类 sort out or classify according to their characteristics: 图书~法 classification of books|把文件~存档。File the documents under different classifications.

【分厘卡】fēnlíkǎ ☞ 百分尺 bǎifēnchǐ on p. 40

【分离】fēnlí ❶ 分开 separate; sever: 理论与实践是不可~的。Theory and practice go together.|从空气中~出氮气来 separate nitrogen from air ❷ 别离 leave; part: ~了多年的兄弟又重逢了。The brothers met again after years of separation.

【分力】fēnlì 几个力同时对某物体的作用和另外一个力对该物体的作用效果相同，这几个力就是那一个力的分力 component force; actions of several forces on an object having the same effect as one force, the several forces are called components of the one

【分列式】fēnlièshì 军队等按照不同的兵种或编制排列成一定的队形，依次走正步、行注目礼通过检阅台，这种队形叫分列式 march past; pass in view; ceremonial march; (of troops, etc.) formations of different military branches or units marching in parade step and saluting with the eyes when passing the reviewing stand

【分裂】fēnliè ❶ 整体的事物分开 (of a whole) division; fission: 细胞~ cell division ❷ 使整体的事物分开 split; divide; break up: ~组织 split an organization

【分流】fēnliú ❶ 从干流中分出一股或几股水流注入另外的河流或单独入海 distributary; split-flow; one or several streams of water flowing away from the mainstream, and then into another body of water or into the sea ❷ (人员、车辆等)分别向不同的道路、方向流动 diversion; (of crowds and vehicles) split flow: 人车~ diversions of crowds and vehicles|消费资金~split flows of consumption funds

【分馏】fēnliú 液体中含有几种挥发性不同的物质时，蒸馏液体，使它所含的成分互相分离 fractionation; fractional distillation; separation of a liquid containing several substances with different volatility into ingredients by distillation: ~石油可以得到汽油、煤油等。Gasoline and kerosene can be obtained through the fractionation of oil.

【分袂】fēnmèi 〈书 *fml.*〉离别；分手 part; bid farewell to each other

【分门别类】fēn mén bié lèi 根据事物的特性分成各种门类 put into different categories according to the specific properties: 把收集的标本~地摆列起来 categorize a collection of samples

【分泌】fēnmì ❶ 从生物体的某些细胞、组织或器官里产生出某种物质。如胃分泌胃液，花分泌花蜜，病菌分泌毒素等。secrete; production of a substance in certain cells, tissues or organs of an organism, such as the stomach secreting gastric juices, flowers secreting nectar and germs secreting toxins, etc. ❷ 岩石中的裂隙逐渐被流动的矿物溶液填满。也指这样形成的矿物。(of cracks in rocks) gradually fill up with liquified minerals; minerals thus formed

【分蜜】fēnmì 制糖的一道工序，把熬出来的糖膏里的糖蜜和糖的结晶分离开 extraction of molasses and crystallized sugar from massecuite, a process of sugar production

【分娩】fēnmiǎn ❶ 生小孩儿 childbirth; delivery; labour; parturition ❷ 生幼畜 (of animals) give birth

【分秒】fēnmiǎo 一分一秒。指极短的时间 minute and second; instant (very short time): ~必争 seize every minute and second; not a second to be lost; make the best use of one's time|时间不饶人，~赛黄金。Time flies! Time is money.

【分秒必争】fēn miǎo bì zhēng 一点儿时间也不放松 seize every minute and second; not a second to be lost

【分明】fēnmíng ❶ 清楚 clear; obvious; distinct: 黑白~ clear as black and white; distinct in sharp contrast|爱憎~ know what to love and what to hate; be clear whom to love and whom to hate ❷ 明明；显然 obviously; clearly; plainly; evidently: 他~朝你来的方向去的，你怎么没有看见他？He was clearly walking towards you, how is it you didn't see him?

【分母】fēnmǔ same as 分数 fēnshù ②

【分蘖】fēnniè 稻、麦、甘蔗等植物发育的时候，在幼苗靠近土壤的部分生出分枝。有的地区叫发棵。tiller; (of plants such as rice, wheat, sugarcane, etc.) grow lateral shoots from the base of the stem during its development; also 发棵 fākē in some places

【分派】fēnpài ❶ 分别指定人去完成工作或任务 assign work, task: ~专人负责 assign a specific person to be in charge ❷ 指定分摊；摊派

apportion (money); share (expenses):这次旅游的费用,由参加的人～。Travel expenses for this trip will be shared among the participants.

【分配】fēnpèi ❶ 按一定的标准或规定分(东西) distribute; allocate; allot sth. according to a certain criterium:～宿舍 allot dormitories|～劳动果实 distribute the fruits of labour ❷ 安排;分派 assign:服从组织～ accept an organizational assignment|合理～劳动力 rational disposition of manpower ❸ 经济学上指把生产资料分给生产单位或把消费资料分给消费者。分配的方式决定于社会制度。mode of distribution or allocation of means of production to production units, or means of consumption to consumers, determined by the social system

【分片】fēn//piàn (～儿 fēn//piànr)根据工作需要,把较大的地区或范围划分成若干小的区域或范围 divide a comparatively large area or task into several smaller ones in accordance with the work needs:～包干 sub-divide the task and assign a part to each (individual or group)

【分歧】fēnqí (思想、意见、记载等)不一致;有差别 (of ideas, opinions, records, etc.) difference; divergence; dispute:～点 difference; point of divergence|理论～ theoretical difference|消除～ eliminate (or iron out) differences

【分清】fēn//qīng 分辨清楚 distinguish; tell from or between; draw a clear distinction between:～是非 distinguish between right and wrong|一片汪洋,分不清哪是天哪是水。In the wide expanse the sky is indistinguishable from the water.

【分群】fēn//qún 养蜂业中指新的母蜂产生后两三天内,旧的母蜂和一部分工蜂离开原来的蜂巢,到另一个地方组成新的蜂群 (apiculture) hive off; swarm to form a subcolony — the old queen bee and a number of worker bees leaving the original hive to form a new colony somewhere else two or three days after a new queen bee hatches

【分润】fēnrùn 分享利益(多指金钱 usu. of money) share in the profits or benefits

【分散】fēnsàn ❶ 散在各处;不集中 scatter; decentralize:～活动 carry out individual (or small group) operations; act on one's own|山村的人家住得很～。Families of mountain villages live very scattered. ❷ 使分散 disperse; divert:～注意力 distract (or divert) one's attention; take one's mind off sth. ❸ 散发;分发 distribute; hand out:～传单 distribute leaflets

【分色镜】fēnsèjìng 一种专用镜片,能反射某种色光,而透过其他色光 colour selective mirror, special lens which reflects a certain colour, and allows the other colours through

【分设】fēnshè 分别设置 set up or establish as separate:局下面～三个处。The bureau has three departments under it.

【分身】fēn//shēn 抽出时间去照顾其他方面(多用于否定式 usu. with a negative) spare time (from one's main work to attend to sth. else):难以～hard to be in two places at once|无法～ cannot attend to many things at the same time|一直想去看看您,可总是分不开身。I have been wanting to call on you, but can't find the time.

【分神】fēn//shén 分心 divert sb.'s attention; be distracted:要集中注意力,不要～。Please focus, and not get distracted.|那本书请您～去找一找,我们等着用。Would you mind looking for the book? We are waiting to use it.

【分式】fēnshì 有除法运算,而且除式中含有字母的有理式。如$\frac{1}{x}$,$\frac{a}{b-c^2}$。fraction; rational expression of a fraction containing letters, such as $\frac{1}{x}$ and $\frac{a}{b-c^2}$

【分手】fēn//shǒu 别离;分开 part; part company; say goodbye:我往北走了,咱们在这儿～吧。I'm heading north so we'll say goodbye here.|他们两人合不到一起,早分了手。They did not get along and parted long ago.

【分数】fēnshù ❶ 评定成绩或胜负时所记的分儿的数字 mark; grade; score; point; number recorded when grading, or determining success or failure:三门功课的平均～是87分。The average mark for the three subjects is 87.|鞍马,他得的～是9.5分。He got 9.5 for the pommel horse. ❷ 把一个单位分成若干等份,表示其中的一份或几份的数,是除法的一种书写形式,如$\frac{2}{5}$(读作五分之二),$2\frac{3}{7}$(读作二又七分之三)。在分数中,符号'—'叫做分数线,相当于除号;分数线上面的数叫做分子,相当于被除数,如$\frac{2}{5}$中的2;分数线下面的数叫做分母,相当于除数,如$\frac{2}{5}$中的5。fraction; fractional number; number expressing one or several parts of a unit; a way of writing the operation of division (e.g. $\frac{2}{5}$ and $2\frac{3}{7}$). In a fraction, the symbol '—' is called the fraction line, equivalent to a division sign; the number above it, the numerator, equivalent to a dividend (e.g. 2 in $\frac{2}{5}$); the number below it, the denominator, equivalent to a divisor (e.g. 5 in $\frac{2}{5}$).

【分数线】fēnshùxiàn ❶ ☞ 分数 fēnshù ② ❷

考生被录取的最低分数标准 bottom or floor mark for enrolment eligibility：他的考试成绩超过了本市录取～。His marks for the examination are above the floor mark for enrolment set by the city.

【分水岭】fēnshuǐlǐng ❶ 两个流域分界的山脊或高原 watershed; divide — ridge or high plateau dividing two drainage; also 分水线 fēnshuǐxiàn ❷〈比喻 *fig.*〉不同事物的主要分界 point of division between two conditions, phases, etc.

【分说】fēnshuō 分辩(多用在'不容、不由'等否定语之后 usu. used in the negative, following negative expressions such as 'not allow', 'not tolerate', etc.) defend oneself (against a charge)

【分摊】fēntān 分担(费用) (of expenses) share; apportion; contribute：聚餐的钱，大家～。The cost of the dinner will be shared between us.

【分庭抗礼】fēn tíng kàng lǐ 原指宾主相见，站在庭院的两边，相对行礼。现在用来比喻平起平坐，互相对立。host and guest salute each other from opposite sides of the courtyard; (oft. fig.) stand up to sb. as an equal; make rival claims as an equal

【分头】[1] fēntóu 若干人分几个方面(进行工作) handle separately by several people：～办理 handle separately | 大家～去准备。Everyone made their separate preparations.

【分头】[2] fēntóu 短头发向两边分开梳的式样 hairstyle with a part：他留着～。He has parted hair.

【分文】fēnwén 指很少的钱 little money：～不值 worthless; not worth a farthing; not worth a straw | 身无～ penniless; broke | ～不取 gratis; not take or charge a single cent; free of charge

【分文不取】fēn wén bù qǔ 一个钱也不要(多指应给的报酬或应收的费用 usu. of due reward or charges) gratis; not take or charge a single cent; free of charge：我要是治不好你的病，～。I will not charge you a cent if I cannot cure your disease.

【分析】fēnxī 把一件事物、一种现象、一个概念分成较简单组成部分，找出这些部分的本质属性和彼此之间的关系(跟'综合'相对 as opposed to 'summarize') analyse; separate a matter, phenomenon or concept into simple constituent parts to identify their basic properties and their links：化学～ chemical analysis | ～问题 analyse problems; reason things out | ～目前国际形势 analyse (or size up) the current international situation

【分析语】fēnxīyǔ 语言学上指词与词间的语法关系主要不是靠词本身的形态变化，而是靠词序、虚词等来表示的语言。一般认为汉语是典型的分析语。(linguis.) analytical language; language where grammatical relations are expressed by word order or function words, instead of changes to the word form. Chinese is generally regarded as a typical analytical language.

【分享】fēnxiǎng 和别人分着享受(欢乐、幸福、好处等) share (joy, happiness, benefit, etc.); partake of：晚会中老师也～着孩子们的欢乐。At the evening party the teacher also shared in the joy of the children.

【分晓】fēnxiǎo ❶ 事情的底细或结果(多见于'见'后 oft. used after 'see') outcome; result; solution：究竟谁是冠军，明天就见～。We'll see who is the champion after tomorrow's results. ❷ 明白；清楚 see or understand clearly：问个～ make thorough enquiries; find out the whys and wherefores of sth. | 且看下图，便可～。Look at the diagram below and you'll understand everything. ❸ 道理(多用于否定式 usu. used in the negative) reason：没～的话 unreasonable remark | 这个人好没～，信口乱说。This person is really unreasonable and talks irresponsibly.

【分心】fēn//xīn ❶ 分散注意力；不专心 divert or distract sb.'s attention：孩子的功课叫家长～。Parents are distracted by their children's schoolwork. ❷ 费心 claim attention：～劳神 tax one's mind | 这件事您多～吧。May I trouble you to attend to this matter?

【分野】fēnyě 划分的范围 dividing line; line of demarcation; same as 界限 jièxiàn ①：政治～ political dividing line | 思想～ ideological dividing line

【分阴】fēnyīn 日影移动一分的时间。指极短的时间。time of the shadow cast by the sun moving one *fen*; very short time：惜～ treasure every second; make the best use of every precious moment

【分忧】fēn//yōu 分担别人的忧虑；帮助别人解决困难 share sb.'s worries; help solve difficult problems：～解愁 relieve sb. of daily worries; share and reduce worries | 为国～ contribute to solving difficult national problems; do one's bit for the country in times of trouble or crisis

【分赃】fēn//zāng ❶ 分取赃款赃物 divide the spoils; share the booty or loot：坐地～ take a share of the spoils without participating in the crime ❷〈比喻 *fig.*〉分取不正当的权利或利益 get a share of ill-gotten power or gains

【分张】fēnzhāng〈书 *fml.*〉分手；离别 part company; bid farewell; take leave

【分账】fēnzhàng 按照一定比例分钱财 divide money according to a set ratio：三七～ divide the money 3 to 7

【分针】fēnzhēn 钟表上指示分数的指针，比时针长 minute hand (of watch or clock, longer than the hour hand)

【分支】fēnzhī 从一个系统或主体中分出来的部分 branch (of a system or main body):～机构 branch; affiliate; affiliated agency

【分至点】fēnzhìdiǎn 春分点、秋分点、夏至点、冬至点的合称 general term for the Vernal Equinox, Autumnal Equinox, Summer Solstice and Winter Solstice

【分子】fēnzǐ ❶ same as 分数 fēnshù ② ❷ 物质中能够独立存在并保持本物质一切化学性质的最小微粒,由原子组成 molecule; the smallest independent unit of matter that retains its chemical properties, made up of atoms ☞ fènzǐ on p. 575

【分子量】fēnzǐliàng 分子的相对质量。是一个分子中各原子的原子量的总和,如水(H_2O)的分子量约为18,氢(H_2)的分子量约为2。molecular weight; molecular mass. The sum of all atom weights in a molecule, e. g. the molecular weight of H_2O is 18, of hydrogen, 2.

【分子筛】fēnzǐshāi 用吸附性很强的物质(如硅铝酸盐)塑成的物体。具有许多孔径大小均一的微孔,能有选择的吸附某种小于孔径的分子。用于液体和气体的干燥、分离、净化。molecular sieve; made of a strong absorbent with tiny pores (e. g. siallitic acid salt), which can selectively absorb smaller molecules; used in drying, separation and purification of liquids and gases

【分子式】fēnzǐshì 用元素符号表示物质分子组成的式子,如水的分子式是 H_2O,氧的分子式是 O_2 molecular formula, chemical formula denoting molecular composition, written with chemical element symbols e. g. molecular formula for water is H_2O and oxygen, O_2

芬 fēn 香气 fragrance; perfume:～芳 fragrant; sweet-smelling|清～ faint scent; delicate fragrance

【芬芳】fēnfāng 香;香气 fragrant; sweet-smelling:～的花朵 fragrant flowers|气味～ fragrance; sweet scent|空气里弥漫着桂花的～。The air is filled with the fragrance of sweet-scented osmanthus.

吩 fēn [吩咐](fēn•fù) 口头指派或命令;嘱咐:spoken order; tell; instruct:父亲～大哥务必在月底以前赶回来。Father told my eldest brother he must return by the end of the month.|我们俩做什么,请你～。Please tell us what to do. also 分付 fēn•fù

纷 fēn ❶ 多;杂乱 many; diverse; profuse:～乱 numerous and confused|～飞 swirl in the air; fly about in disorderly fashion ❷ 纠纷 chaos; dispute:排难解～ solve problems and mediate disputes; pour oil on troubled waters

【纷呈】fēnchéng 纷纷呈现 present one after the other or all at once:色彩～ be a riot of colour|戏曲汇演,流派～ opera festival of performances in many styles

【纷繁】fēnfán 多而复杂 numerous and complicated:头绪～ have too many things to take care of; too many loose ends

【纷飞】fēnfēi (雪、花等)多而杂乱地在空中飘扬 (of snow, flowers, etc.) swirl in the air; fly about in a disorderly way:大雪～。It is snowing heavily.|柳絮～。Willow catkins are flying thick and fast. ◇战火～ flames of war rage far and wide

【纷纷】fēnfēn ❶ (言论、往下落的东西等)多而杂乱 profuse; (opinions, falling objects, etc.) numerous and confused:议论～ provoke much discussion|落叶～。Leaves fall in profusion. ❷ (许多人或事物)接二连三地 (of many things or matters) one after another; in quick succession:大家～提出问题。Questions were asked one after the other.

【纷纷扬扬】fēnfēnyángyáng (雪、花、叶等)飘洒得多而杂乱 (of snowflakes, flowers, leaves, etc.) flying or fluttering in confusion:鹅毛大雪～。The air is thick with flying snow flakes.|碎纸～地落了一地。Scraps of paper were strewn all over the ground.

【纷乱】fēnluàn 杂乱;混乱 numerous and messy; chaotic:思绪～ confused state of mind|～的脚步声 hurried footsteps

【纷披】fēnpī 〈书 *fml.*〉散乱张开的样子 spread wildly about:枝叶～。Branches and leaves spread in all directions.

【纷扰】fēnrǎo 混乱 confusion; chaos; turmoil:内心～ one's mind in a turmoil; feel perturbed|世事～。Worldly affairs are full of confusion.

【纷纭】fēnyún (言论、事情等)多而杂乱 (of opinions, events, etc.) diverse and confused:头绪～ have too many things to attend to|众说～,莫衷一是。Opinions differ widely, and there is no consensus at all.

【纷杂】fēnzá 多而乱;纷乱 messy; numerous and disorderly:头绪～ have too many things to attend to|～的思绪 confused state of mind; confused train of thought

【纷争】fēnzhēng 纠纷;争执 quarrel; dispute; wrangle:引起一场～ set off a dispute

【纷至沓来】fēn zhì tà lái 纷纷到来;连续不断地到来 come in a continuous stream; come thick and fast; keep pouring in:顾客～,应接不暇。Customers came streaming in and kept the shop assistants busy.

玢 fēn ☞ 赛璐玢 sàilùfēn on p. 1649 ☞ bīn on p. 134

氛 fēn 气 atmosphere; same as 气象 qìxiàng ③:气～ atmosphere|战～ atmosphere of war

【氛围】fēnwéi 周围的气氛和情调:atmosphere; mood:人们在欢乐的～中迎来了新的一年。People welcomed the new year in a cheerful atmosphere; also 雰围 fēnwéi

棻 fēn〈书 *fml.*〉有香气的木头 fragrant wood

酚 fēn 有机化合物的一类，是芳香烃分子中苯环上的氢原子被羟基取代而成的化合物。特指苯酚。phenol; group of organic chemical compounds obtained when hydrogen atoms on the benzene ring of aromatic hydrocarbon molecules are replaced by a hydroxyl radical

雰 fēn〈书 *fml.*〉雾气；气 mist; air; atmosphere

【雰雰】fēnfēn〈书 *fml.*〉霜雪等很盛的样子(of snow, frost, etc.) thick; heavy：雨雪～。It is snowing heavily.

【雰围】fēnwéi same as 氛围 fēnwéi

𫘜(㖹) 〈方 *dial.*〉未曾 have not：～来过 have never been here

fén (ㄈㄣˊ)

坟(墳) fén 坟墓 grave; tomb：祖～ ancestral grave｜上～ visit a grave (to pay respect to the dead)｜一座～ a tomb (or grave)

【坟地】féndì 埋葬死人的地方；坟墓所在的地方 graveyard; cemetery; burial place

【坟墓】fénmù 埋葬死人的穴和上面的坟头 grave; tomb; pit where the body remains of a dead person are buried and the tumulus above it

【坟山】fénshān〈方 *dial.*〉❶ 用做坟地的山。泛指坟地。grave mound; (in a broad sense) graveyard or cemetery ❷ 高大的坟头 large grave mound ❸ 坟墓或坟地后面的土围子 protective wall behind a grave or cemetery; also 坟山子 fénshān·zi

【坟头】féntóu (～儿 féntóur) 埋葬死人之后在地面上筑起的土堆，也有用砖石等砌成的 tumulus; grave mound (made by heaping earth over the grave or built with bricks and stones, etc.)

【坟茔】fényíng ❶ same as 坟墓 fénmù ❷ same as 坟地 féndì

汾 Fén 汾河，水名，在山西 Fenhe River in Shanxi Province

【汾酒】fénjiǔ 山西汾阳出产的一种白酒 distilled spirits made in Fenyang, Shanxi Province

蚡 fén〈书 *fml.*〉same as 鼢 fén

棼 fén〈书 *fml.*〉纷乱 confused; tangled; ravelled：治丝益～ try to sort silk threads only to tangle them further; (*fig.*) make matters worse; add to the confusion

焚 fén 烧 burn：～香 burn joss sticks (in a temple)｜玩火自～。(He) who plays with fire will get burned.｜忧心如～ burning anxiety

【焚风】fénfēng 气流沿山坡下降而形成的热而干的风。多焚风的地区，空气平常比较干燥，容易发生森林火灾。foehn; hot, dry wind formed by air currents descending along a hillside; air is usu. very dry in areas where the foehn oft. blows, and forest fires are frequent

【焚膏继晷】fén gāo jì guǐ 点燃灯烛来接替日光照明。形容夜以继日地用功读书或努力工作。burn a candle to prolong the day; burn the midnight oil; study or work hard day and night

【焚化】fénhuà 烧掉(尸骨、神像、纸钱等) incinerate; cremate (skeleton, image, paper money, etc.)

【焚毁】fénhuǐ 烧坏；烧毁 destroy by fire; burn down：一场大火～了半个村子的民房。Half the village houses were burnt down in the big fire.

【焚琴煮鹤】fén qín zhǔ hè ☞ 煮鹤焚琴 zhǔ hè fén qín on p. 2507

【焚烧】fénshāo 烧毁；烧掉 burn; set on fire; consume with flames：～毒品 burn narcotics

【焚香】fén//xiāng ❶ 烧香 burn joss sticks (in a temple)：～拜佛 burn joss sticks and prostrate oneself before Buddha ❷ 点燃香 burn incense：～静坐 burn incense and sit in meditation｜～操琴 light incense and play the *guqin* (a stringed musical instrument)

濆 fén〈书 *fml.*〉水边 waterside; water margin

豮 fén〈方 *dial.*〉雄性的牲畜 male domestic animal：～猪 boar

鼢 fén［鼢鼠］(fénshǔ) 哺乳动物，身体灰色，尾短，眼小，在地下打洞，吃甘薯、花生、豆类等植物的地下部分，也吃牧草，对农牧业危害性很大。也叫盲鼠，有的地区叫地羊。zokor (*Spalacidae*), mammal with grey body, short tail and small eyes, which digs underground to feed on the roots of sweet potatoes, peanuts, beans, and forage grass, causing great damage to agriculture and animal husbandry; also 盲鼠 mángshǔ and known as 地羊 dìyáng in some areas

fěn (ㄈㄣˇ)

粉 fěn ❶ 粉末 powder：面～ (wheat) flour｜藕～ lotus root starch｜花～ pollen ❷ 特指化妆用的粉末 powder used as cosmetic：香～ face powder｜涂脂抹～ apply powder and paint; prettify ❸ 用淀粉制成的食品 food stuff made from starch：凉～ bean jelly｜～皮 sheet jelly (made from bean or sweet potato starch) ❹ 特指粉条或粉丝 noodles or vermicelli made from flour, bean, sweet potato starch, etc.：米～ rice-flour noodles｜绿豆～ mung bean flour｜菠菜炒～ bean noodles stir-fried with spinach ❺ 变成粉末 pulverize; turn to powder: ～碎 broken into (or to) pieces|～身碎骨 be smashed to pieces and crushed to pulp; be ground to powder|石灰放得太久,已经～了。Time has turned the lime to powder. ❻〈方 *dial.*〉粉刷 whitewash: 墙刚～过。The wall has just been whitewashed. ❼ 带着白粉的;白色的 white (with white powder): ～蝶 pierid; white butterfly|～连纸 a kind of thin, transparent paper used for tracing ❽ 粉红 pink; rosy: ～色 pink|～牡丹 pink peony|这块绸子是～的。The silk is pink.

【粉笔】fěnbǐ 在黑板上写字用的条状物,用白垩、熟石膏粉等加水搅拌,灌入模型后凝固制成 stick-shape piece of chalk used for writing on blackboard, made by mixing chalk and slaked lime in water, and letting it solidify in moulds

【粉肠】fěncháng (～儿 fěnchángr)用团粉加少量油脂、盐、作料等灌入肠衣做熟的副食品 cooked sausage made from bean starch paste, oil, salt, seasoning, etc.

【粉尘】fěnchén 在燃烧或工业生产过程中产生的粉末状的废物 dustparticles produced from burning or industrial production: ～污染 dust pollution

【粉刺】fěncì 痤疮的通称 general term for 痤疮 cuóchuāng

【粉黛】fěndài〈书 *fml.*〉❶ 妇女化妆用的白粉和青黑色的颜料 (female cosmetics) white powder and black pigment: 不施～ apply no powder and paint ❷ 借指妇女 (beautiful) woman: 六宫～ beautiful women of the palace

【粉蝶】fěndié 蝴蝶的一种,翅白色,有黑色斑点,也有黄色或橙色的。幼虫吃白菜、油菜、萝卜等十字花科蔬菜的叶,是农业害虫。white butterfly (*Pieris brassicae*); butterfly with white wings marked by black, yellow or orange spots, whose larvae feed on the leaves of mustard vegetables, such as Chinese cabbage, rape and turnip, considered an agricultural pest

【粉坊】fěnfáng 做粉皮、粉条、粉丝等食品的作坊 workshop where sheet jelly, starch noodles, bean starch vermicelli, etc. are made

【粉红】fěnhóng 红和白合成的颜色 colour produced from mixing red and white

【粉剂】fěnjì 散剂 powder

【粉连纸】fěnliánzhǐ 一种白色的一面光的纸,比较薄,半透明,可以蒙在字画上描摹 thin, semi-transparent white paper, smooth on one side, used for tracing

【粉末】fěnmò (～儿 fěnmòr)极细的颗粒;细屑 powder: 金属～ powdered metal|研成～ grind into powder

【粉墨登场】fěn mò dēng chǎng 化装上台演戏。今多比喻登上政治舞台(含讥讽意 derog.) put on makeup and go onstage; embark upon a political career

【粉牌】fěnpái 白色的水牌 used in shops, white lacquered board for writing which can be erased

【粉皮】fěnpí (～儿 fěnpír)用绿豆、白薯等的淀粉制成的片状的食品 sheet jelly made from bean or sweet potato starch

【粉扑儿】fěnpūr 扑粉的用具,多用棉质物制成 powder puff, usu. made of cotton

【粉芡】fěnqiàn 芡粉加水搅拌而成的糊状物,供做菜时勾芡用 paste mixture of water and starch for cooking

【粉墙】fěnqiáng 白色的墙(多指用白垩等粉刷过的墙) whitewashed wall; plaster wall (usu. wall whitewashed with chalk, etc.)

【粉砂】fěnshā 土壤中介于沙与黏土之间的细颗粒,捏在手中像面粉,细腻而不粘手。含粉沙的土壤保水能力好,适于种植马铃薯、花生等。silt; fine soil particles between sand and clay, smooth like flour yet not sticky. Silt holds water well and the soil contained in it is suitable for growing potatoes and peanuts.

【粉身碎骨】fěn shēn suì gǔ 身体粉碎(多指为了某种目的而丧生) smashed to pieces and crushed to pulp; be ground to powder (usu. lose one's life in pursuit of some goal)

【粉饰】fěnshì 涂饰表面,掩盖污点或缺点 prettify; gloss over; whitewash stains or shortcomings: ～门面 window dressing|～太平 present a picture of false peace and prosperity

【粉刷】fěnshuā ❶ 用白垩等涂抹墙壁等 whitewash (walls, etc., with chalk or other materials): 房屋～一新。The house looks brand new after a facelift. ❷〈方 *dial.*〉在建筑物的表面抹上泥、石灰、水泥等材料,有时再刷上灰浆或做出各种花纹 cover the surface of buildings with earth, lime, cement, etc., and sometimes with plaster or decoration ❸〈方 *dial.*〉抹在建筑物表面的保护层 layer of protective plaster on the surface of buildings

【粉丝】fěnsī 用绿豆等的淀粉制成的线状的食品 vermicelli; thin noodles made from mung bean starch, etc.

【粉碎】fěnsuì ❶ 碎成粉末 break into pieces: ～性骨折 compound fracture|茶杯摔得～。The cup broke into smithereens. ❷ 使粉碎 grind; pulverize: ～机 grinder; kibbler; pulverizer|～矿石 crush ore ❸ 使彻底失败或毁灭 smash; shatter; crush: ～敌人的进攻 shatter an enemy attack

【粉条】fěntiáo (～儿 fěntiáor)用绿豆、白薯等的淀粉制成的细条状的食品 flat noodles made from bean or sweet potato starch, etc.

【粉线】fěnxiàn 沾着黄、白等颜色粉末的线,裁衣服时用来在衣料上打上线条 tailor's chalk line — thread dipped in yellow or white powder and used to draw straight seam lines on cloth：打～ draw a tailor's chalk line

【粉蒸肉】fěnzhēngròu 米粉肉 pork steamed with ground rice flour

fèn（ㄈㄣˋ）

分[1] fèn ❶ 成分 component; element：水～ moisture content｜盐～ salt; salt content｜养～ nutrient ❷ 职责、权利等的限度 limit of one's right or obligation：本～ one's duty｜过～ excessive; too much; go too far｜恰如其～ appropriate; just right｜非～之想 excessive ambition or desire ❸ 情分；情谊 affection; friendly feeling：看在老朋友的～上，原谅他吧。For old friends' sake, please forgive him. ❹ same as 份 fèn

分[2] fèn〈书 *fml.*〉料想 expect; think; know：自～不能肩此重任 be well aware of one's inability to shoulder such a heavy responsibility; know one's limits

☞ fēn on p. 566

【分际】fènjì ❶ 合适的界限；分寸 proper limits; sense of propriety：说话做事严守～ strictly observe the proper limits of speech and action ❷ 地步 condition; extent; state：想不到他竟胡涂到这个～。I can't believe he can be so confused.

【分量】fèn·liàng 重量 weight：这个南瓜的～不下二十斤。This pumpkin weighs at least twenty *jin*. ◇话说得很有～。These words should not be taken lightly.

【分内】fènnèi 本分以内（within）one's job or duty：关心学生是教师～的事。It is a teacher's duty to care about the students.

【分外】fènwài ❶ 超过平常；特别 especially; particularly：～高兴 particularly happy｜月到中秋～明。The moon at the Mid-autumn Festival is especially bright. ❷ 本分以外 beyond one's duty or job; beyond one's due：他从来不把帮助别人看做～的事。He never thinks helping others is too much.

【分子】fènzǐ 属于一定阶级、阶层、集团或具有某种特征的人 person belonging to a class, stratum, group, or showing certain characteristics：资产阶级～ bourgeois element｜知识～ intellectual; educated person; intelligentsia｜积极～ activist; active member

☞ fēnzǐ on p. 572

份 fèn ❶ 整体里的一部 share; part; portion：股～ share; stock ❷（～儿 fènr）〈量词 *classifier*〉a)用于搭配成组的东西 (a) set：一～儿饭 package meal, food portion｜一～儿礼 gift of cash b)用于报刊、文件等（of newspapers, periodicals, documents, etc.）copy：一～《人民日报》a copy of *People's Daily*｜本合同一式两～，双方各执一～。The contract was done in duplicate, each party holding a copy. ❸ 用在'省、县、年、月'后面，表示划分的单位 [used after 省 shěng，县 xiàn，年 nián，月 yuè to express a unit]：省～ province｜年～ year

〈古 *arch.*〉same as 彬 bīn

【份额】fèn'é 整体中分占的额数 share; portion (of a whole)：把节能所得效益的一定～拨给企业 allocate some share of the benefits from energy-saving to the enterprise

【份儿】fènr ❶ 搭配成整体的东西；整体分成的部分 portion; share：这一～是你的。This is your share. ❷ 地位 position; status：这个团体里没有我的～。I'm a person of no consequence in this organization. ❸〈方 *dial.*〉派头；气势 manner; bearing; face; self-respect：摆～ put on airs; throw one's weight about; be ostentatious and extravagant｜跌～ lose face ❹ 程度；地步 degree; extent：都闹到这～上了，他还当没事儿呢。Things have come to such a sorry pass, yet he acts as if nothing happened.

【份儿饭】fènrfàn 论份儿卖的饭；分成份儿吃的饭 table d'hôte; set meal

【份子】fèn·zi ❶ 集体送礼时各人分摊的钱 share of the expense of a group gift：凑～ get together to buy a gift ❷ 泛指做礼物的现金 (in a broad sense) gift of cash：出～ get together to buy a gift

坋 fèn 古坋（Gǔfèn），地名，在福建 Gufen, a place in Fujian Province

☞ bèn on p. 93

奋（奮） fèn ❶ 鼓起劲来；振作 exert oneself, act vigorously：振～ rouse oneself; feel inspired｜兴～ excited; high spirits｜勤～ diligent; industrious ❷ 摇动；举起 rock; raise; take up; lift：～臂高呼 cheer with uplifted arms｜～笔疾书 take up a pen and write swiftly; wield one's (writing) brush energetically

【奋不顾身】fèn bù gù shēn 奋勇直前，不顾生命 (charge forward) regardless of personal safety

【奋斗】fèndòu 为了达到一定目的而努力干 fight; strive; struggle (for a purpose); work hard：艰苦～ work arduously｜为实现伟大理想而～ strive to realize a great ideal

【奋发】fènfā 精神振作，情绪高涨 energetic and bracing mood：～有为 energetic and promising｜～向上 uplifting; spur sb. on

【奋发图强】fèn fā tú qiáng 振作精神，努力自强 put all efforts in to achieving success; exert all one's strength

【奋飞】fènfēi（鸟）振翅飞翔 (of birds) spread the wings and soar

【奋激】fènjī 兴奋激昂；激奋 elated; roused to enthusiasm：情绪～ in an elated mood

【奋进】fènjìn 奋勇前进 advance boldly; forge ahead courageously：催人～ urge sb. to advance boldly

【奋力】fènlì 充分鼓起劲来 exert oneself to the utmost; do all one can; spare no effort:～拼搏 struggle with all one's might|～抢救落水儿童 exert every ounce of energy to rescue the drowning child

【奋袂】fènmèi〈书 *fml*.〉指感情激动时把袖子一甩,准备行动 roll up one's sleeves for action:～而起 shake one's sleeves and stand up; rise up and be ready for action

【奋勉】fènmiǎn 振作努力 make a determined effort

【奋起】fènqǐ ❶ 振作起来 brace up; exert oneself; rise with energy and determination:～直追 pursue with all one's might|～反击 mount a counter-attack ❷ 有力地举起或拿起来 strongly raise or lift:～铁拳 vigorously shake one's strong fist

【奋勇】fènyǒng 鼓起勇气 dauntless; summon up one's courage and energy:～杀敌 fight the enemy bravely|自告～ volunteer (for sth. difficult or dangerous)

【奋战】fènzhàn 奋勇战斗 fight bravely:浴血～ engage in bloody battle

忿1 fèn same as 愤 fèn

忿2 fèn ☞ 不忿 bùfèn on p.160 and 气不忿儿 qì bù fènr on p.1520

【忿忿】fènfèn same as 愤愤 fènfèn

【忿詈】fènlì〈书 *fml*.〉因愤怒而骂 scold out of anger

偾 fèn〈书 *fml*.〉毁坏;败坏 destroy; spoil; ruin:～事 spoil things

【偾事】fènshì〈书 *fml*.〉把事情搞坏 make a mess of things:胆大而心不细,只能～。Being bold without being carful will only ruin things.

粪(糞) fèn ❶ 从肛门排泄出来的经过消化的食物的渣滓;屎 feces; stool; excrement waste from digested food excreted through the anus:牛～ cow dung|拾～ gather dung|上～ spread manure ❷〈书 *fml*.〉施肥 apply manure:～地 spread manure on farmland|～田 apply manure to the fields ❸〈书 *fml*.〉扫除 clear away:～除 wipe out; thoroughly clean (a place)

【粪便】fènbiàn 屎和尿 excrement and urine; poop; dung; night soil

【粪除】fènchú〈书 *fml*.〉扫除 wipe out; thoroughly clean (a place)

【粪肥】fènféi 用做肥料的人或家畜、鸟类等的粪便 human excrement, animal dung or birds' droppings (used as fertilizer); night soil

【粪箕子】fènjī·zi 盛粪的器具,用荆条、竹篾等编成,形状像簸箕,有提梁 manure scoop; basket shaped like a dustpan with a handle, woven from twigs, bamboo strips, etc. for holding manure; also 粪箕 fènjī

【粪坑】fènkēng ❶ 积粪便的坑 manure pit ❷ 指茅厕坑 latrine‖also 粪坑子 fènkēng·zi

【粪筐】fènkuāng ❶ 拾粪的时候用来盛粪的筐 manure basket ❷ 粪箕子 manure scoop

【粪门】fènmén〈方 *dial*.〉肛门 anus

【粪土】fèntǔ 粪便和泥土 muck; dung and dirt;〈比喻 *fig*.〉不值钱的东西 worthless thing

愤 fèn 因为不满意而感情激动;发怒 anger; indignation; fury; resentment:气～ furious; resentful|义～ righteous indignation; moral indignation|公～ public resentment; popular anger|～世嫉俗 cynical; detest human injustices; loathe the ways of the world

【愤愤】fènfèn 很生气的样子 angry; indignant; furious:～不平 indignant; resentful; feel aggrieved; also 忿忿 fènfèn

【愤恨】fènhèn 愤慨痛恨 indignantly resent; furiously detest:不正之风,令人～。People are indignant and resentful towards social evils.

【愤激】fènjī 愤怒而激动 aroused and indignant; furious:～的情绪 wave of anger

【愤慨】fènkǎi 气愤不平 (righteous) indignation:无比～ immense indignation|无耻行为,令人～。Shameless acts arouse strong indignation.

【愤懑】fènmèn〈书 *fml*.〉气愤;抑郁不平 disgruntled; resentful:～之情,溢于言表 words and expression betray smouldering resentment

【愤怒】fènnù 因极度不满而情绪激动 ire; anger; fury; indignation; wrath:～的人群 indignant crowd|～声讨侵略者的罪行 angrily denounce the crimes of the invaders

【愤然】fènrán 形容气愤发怒的样子 angry; indignant:～离去 leave in anger; walk off in a huff

【愤世嫉俗】fèn shì jí sú 对不合理的社会和习俗表示愤恨憎恶 detest human injustice; loathe the ways of the world; be cynical

鲼 fèn 鱼类的一科,身体扁平,呈菱形,尾部细长像鞭子,有的种类尾部有硬刺。生活在热带和亚热带海洋中。eagle ray (*Myliobatidae*); a family of fish living in tropical and subtropical oceans, with a flat diamond-shaped body, long, thin whip-like tail, some varieties having a hard spike on the tail

瀵 fèn〈书 *fml*.〉水由地面下喷出漫溢 (of underground water) gush out and overflow

【瀵泉】fènquán 从地层深处喷出地表的水,含有氮、磷、钾等元素,用于灌溉,肥效显著 geyser; subterranean water that gushes out of the earth's surface, containing nitrogen, phosphorus, potassium, etc., used for irrigation, with great manurial effect

fēng（ㄈㄥ）

丰[1]（豐） fēng ❶ 丰富 rich; abundant; plentiful:～满 full; plentiful|～盛 rich; abundant; lavish; sumptuous|～收 bumper harvest; big harvest|～衣足食 have ample food and clothing; be well-fed and well-clad ❷ 大 great:～碑 monument; monumental work|～功伟绩 magnificent exploits and great feats; signal or monumental contributions ❸（Fēng）姓 a surname

丰[2] fēng 美好的容貌和姿态 good looks; fine appearance; graceful carriage:～采 graceful bearing; elegant demeanour|～姿 charisma|～韵 graceful bearing

【丰碑】fēngbēi 高大的石碑 tall stone tablet; 〈比喻 *fig.*〉不朽的杰作或伟大的功绩 imperishable masterpiece or great achievement:历史的～ historical monument

【丰采】fēngcǎi same as 风采 fēngcǎi ①

【丰产】fēngchǎn 农业上指比一般产量高 high yield; bumper crop; plenteous harvest:～田 high-yield cropland|～经验 experience in reaping bumper harvests

【丰登】fēngdēng 丰收 bumper harvest:五谷～ abundant harvest of all crops; bumper grain harvest

【丰富】fēngfù ❶（物质财富、学识经验等）种类多或数量大（of material wealth, learning, experience, etc.）rich; plentiful; abundant; wealthy:物产～ large variety of products|～多彩 rich and varied; luxuriant and colourful|～的知识 rich knowledge ❷ 使丰富 enrich: 开展文体活动，～业余生活 develop cultural and sports activities to enrich one's leisure time|通过实践，～工作经验 enrich one's working experience through practice

【丰功伟绩】fēng gōng wěi jì 伟大的功绩 glorious exploits and feats; signal or monumental contributions; also 丰功伟业 fēng gong wěi yè

【丰厚】fēnghòu ❶ 多而厚实 rich and thick:海狸的皮绒毛～。Beaver（fur）is rich and thick. ❷ 丰富;多 rich and generous:收入～ handsome income|～的礼品 generous gift

【丰满】fēngmǎn ❶ 充足 full; plentiful:今年好收成，囤里的粮食都很～。The granaries are full this year from a bumper harvest. ❷（身体或身体的一部分）胖得匀称好看（of the body or part of it）full and rounded; well-developed; full-grown:他比去年生病的时候～多了。He has put on weight and looks much better than last year when he was ill.

【丰茂】fēngmào 茂盛;茂密 luxuriant; lush; profuse:树木丛生，百草～ thick trees and luxuriant grass|大树长出了～的枝叶。The big tree has put out rich piles of foliage.

【丰美】fēngměi 多而好 lush:～的食品 plentiful and good food|水草～的牧场 lush pasture

【丰年】fēngnián 农作物丰收的年头儿 bumper harvest year; year of abundance; good year: 瑞雪兆～。A timely snow foretells a bumper harvest.

【丰沛】fēngpèi（雨水）充足（of rain）plentiful; abundant

【丰饶】fēngráo 富饶 rich and fertile:物产～ rich and fertile in products|辽阔～的大平原 wide, rich and fertile plain

【丰润】fēngrùn（肌肤等）丰满滋润（of skin, flesh, etc.）plump and smooth:两颊～ smooth, round cheeks

【丰赡】fēngshàn〈书 *fml.*〉丰富;充足 rich; abundant; plentiful:内容～rich in content

【丰盛】fēngshèng 丰富（指物质方面）（of materials）rich; abundant; lavish; sumptuous:～的酒席 lavish feast; sumptuous banquet

【丰收】fēngshōu 收成好（跟'歉收'相对 as opposed to 'crop failure' or 'bad harvest'）bumper harvest; big harvest:～年 bumper harvest year|粮食～ reap a bumper grain harvest◇今年的文艺创作获得～。There have been many outstanding artistic and literary creations this year.

【丰硕】fēngshuò（果实）又多又大（多用于抽象事物 oft. in the abstract）（of fruits）plentiful and large; abundant; rich :～的成果 rich reward; great success

【丰衣足食】fēng yī zú shí 形容生活富裕 well-fed and well-clad; ample food and clothing; be well off

【丰盈】fēngyíng ❶（身体）丰满（of the body）full; well developed:体态～ full（or well-rounded）figure ❷ 富裕;丰富 rich; plentiful: 衣食～ample food and clothing; have enough to spare

【丰腴】fēngyú ❶ same as 丰盈 fēngyíng ① ❷ 多而好 rich; plentiful; abundant; fertile:～的酒席 sumptuous feast|牧场水草～ lush（or rich）pasture land

【丰裕】fēngyù 富裕;富足 in plenty; well provided for:生活～ live in plenty; be comfortably off

【丰韵】fēngyùn same as 风韵 fēngyùn

【丰姿】fēngzī same as 风姿 fēngzī

【丰足】fēngzú 富裕;充足 plentiful; abundant: 衣食～plentiful food and clothing

风（風） fēng ❶ 跟地面大致平行的空气流动，是由于气压分布不均匀而产生的 wind; breeze; gale — air current moving approximately parallel to the ground surface, caused by uneven distribution of atmospheric pressure ❷ 借风力吹（使东西干燥或纯净）put out to dry; winnow:～干 air-dry|晒干～净 sun-dried and well winnowed ❸ 借风力吹干

的 air-dried：～鸡 air-dried chicken｜～肉 air-dried meat ❹ 像风那样快 as swift as the wind；speedily：～发 swift as the wind；speedily｜～行 fast；rapidly；vigorously ❺ 风气；风俗 practice；custom；atmosphere：蔚然成～ become prevalent；become customary｜移～易俗 change established (or prevailing) habits and customs；transform old traditions｜不正之～ unhealthy social trends；undesirable social practices ❻ 景象 scene；view：～景 scenery；landscape｜～光 scene；view；sight ❼ 态度 attitude；style：作～ style of work｜～度 manner；bearing；demeanour ❽ (～儿 fēngr)风声；消息 news；information：闻～而动 act without delay on hearing the news；take immediate action｜刚听见一点～儿就来打听 fish for information on getting wind of sth. ❾ 传说的；没有确实根据的 hearsay；rumour：～闻 learn through hearsay；hear through the grapevine；get wind of｜～言～语 canard；slanderous gossip；groundless talk ❿ 指民歌(《诗经》里的《国风》，是古代十五国的民歌) *Folk Songs of States*, a chapter in the classic *The Book of Songs* which collected folksong from 15 states：采～ collect ballads；collect folk songs ⓫〈中医 *Chin. med.*〉指某些疾病 used in names of certain diseases：羊痫～ epilepsy｜鹅掌～ fungal infection of the hand；tinea manuum ⓬(Fēng) 姓 a surname

〈古 *arch.*〉same as 讽 fěng

【风暴】fēngbào ❶ 刮大风而且往往同时有大雨的天气现象 windstorm；storm；tempest ❷〈比喻 *fig.*〉规模大而气势猛烈的事件或现象 large-scale, tumultuous event or phenomenon：革命的～ revolutionary storm

【风泵】fēngbèng 用来抽气或压缩气体的装置 air pump；air compressor；also 气泵 qìbèng

【风波】fēngbō〈比喻 *fig.*〉纠纷或乱子 conflict；disturbance；trouble；rumpus：一场～ a disturbance｜平地～ storm out of the blue｜政治～ political turmoil

【风采】fēngcǎi〈书 *fml.*〉❶ 人的仪表举止(指美好的)；神采 charisma；graceful bearing；elegant demeanour：～动人 very attractive bearing；also 丰采 fēngcǎi ❷ 文采 literary grace or talent

【风餐露宿】fēng cān lù sù 形容旅途或野外生活的艰苦 describing the rigours of travel or outdoor living；also 露宿风餐 lù sù fēng cān

【风操】fēngcāo 风范操守 elegant demeanour and personal integrity

【风铲】fēngchǎn 风动工具，跟风镐相似，用铲子或凿子代替钎子，用来分离岩体上的土壤或铲平铸件的毛边等 pneumatic (air) shovel；pneumatic (air) chipper；pneumatic tool resembling an air pick, used in place of a rock drill to separate soil from rocks or smooth the raw edges of casts

【风潮】fēngcháo 指群众为迫使当局接受某种要求或改变某种措施而采取的各种集体行动 agitation；unrest；popular group action taken to compel the authorities to accede to requests or change certain measures：闹～ agitate (for reform；etc.)｜平息～ calm popular unrest

【风车】fēngchē ❶ 利用风力的动力机械装置，可以带动其他机器，用来发电、提水、磨面、榨油等 windmill — wind-driven machine used to power other devices to produce electricity, lift water, grind wheat, press oil, etc. ❷ 扇车 winnower ❸ 儿童玩具，装有叶轮，能迎风转动 pinwheel — toy with vanes, which turn in the wind

【风尘】fēngchén ❶〈比喻 *fig.*〉旅途劳累 travel fatigue：～仆仆 worn out by a long journey；travel-worn and weary｜满面～(旅途劳累的神色) travel-stained ❷〈比喻 *fig.*〉纷乱的社会或漂泊江湖的境况 social turmoil and uncertainties；hardships of a wandering, unsettled life：～侠士 chivalrous man in times of turmoil｜沦落～(of a woman) fall into prostitution ❸〈书 *fml.*〉〈比喻 *fig.*〉战乱 war：～之警 threat of war

【风驰电掣】fēng chí diàn chè 形容像刮风和闪电那样迅速 swift as the wind and quick as the lightning

【风传】fēngchuán ❶ 辗转流传 spread a rumour：村里～，说他要办工厂。It is rumoured in the village that he is going to start a factory. ❷ 辗转流传的事情 rumour；hearsay：这是～，不一定可靠。This is mere hearsay and not necessarily reliable.

【风吹草动】fēng chuī cǎo dòng〈比喻 *fig.*〉轻微的变故 slight change；hint of disturbance or trouble

【风锤】fēngchuí 手持的锤击工具，用压缩空气做动力。多用于铆工。pneumatic hammer；hand-held percussive tool, driven by compressed air, usu. used for driving rivets

【风挡】fēngdǎng 汽车、飞机等前面挡风的装置 windscreen (or windshield) at the front of a car, plane, etc.：飞机～ windscreen of a plane

【风刀霜剑】fēng dāo shuāng jiàn 寒风像刀子，霜像剑一样刺人的肌肤。形容气候寒冷。也比喻恶劣的环境。wind cuts like a knife and the frost bites like a sword；severely cold weather；(fig.) frosty weather；adverse circumstances；harsh environment

【风灯】fēngdēng ❶ 一种手提或悬挂的能防风雨的油灯 hand-held or hanging storm lantern — type of oil lamp which can withstand wind and rain；also 风雨灯 fēngyǔdēng ❷〈方 *dial.*〉一种家庭里悬挂的装饰品，形状像宫灯 decorative home lantern resembling a palace lantern

【风笛】fēngdí 管乐器，由风囊、吹管和若干簧管组成,流行于欧洲民间 bagpipes; wind instrument composed of wind bag, blowpipe and several reeds, popular in European folk music

【风斗】fēngdǒu (～儿 fēngdǒur)冬季安在窗户上的通气挡风的东西,多用纸糊成 window vent; device made from paper fixed at an angle on a window opening for ventilation in winter

【风度】fēngdù 美好的举止姿态 graceful demeanour; elegant bearing: 有～ have poise; behave with grace and ease | ～翩翩 elegant demeanour; graceful manner or bearing

【风发】fēngfā 原指像风一样迅速,现多指奋发 speedily; (extended meaning) energetic; swift as the wind: 意气～ daring and energetic

【风帆】fēngfān 船帆 sail ◇鼓起生活的～ hoisting the sail on the ship of life

【风范】fēngfàn 〈书 *fml.*〉风度;气派 bearing; demeanour; manner: 大家～ air of a great master; refined manner | 名将～ manner of a famous general

【风风火火】fēngfēnghuǒhuǒ (～的 fēngfēnghuǒhuǒ·de) ❶ 形容急急忙忙、冒冒失失的样子 in a hurry; hastily and rashly; hustling and bustling: 他～地闯了进来。He rushed into the room. ❷ 形容很活跃、有劲头的样子 active; dynamic: ～的战斗年代 hectic war years

【风干】fēnggān 放在阴凉的地方,让风吹干 air-dried; air-dry: ～栗子 air-dried chestnuts | ～腊肉 air-dried bacon | 木材经过～可以防止腐烂。Air-drying can prevent wood from rotting.

【风镐】fēnggǎo 手持的风动工具,用压缩空气推动活塞往复运动,使镐头不断撞击。用于采矿、筑路等。pneumatic pick; air pick; hand-held pneumatic tool in which compressed air pushes a piston back and forth to strike a surface, used in mining and road-building

【风格】fēnggé ❶ 气度;作风 character; integrity: ～高 honourable style | 发扬助人为乐的高尚～ promote the fine quality of taking pleasure in helping others ❷ 一个时代、一个民族、一个流派或一个人的文艺作品所表现的主要的思想特点和艺术特点 style; (of a nation, school or individual literary and artistic works) principal philosophical concerns and artistic style: 艺术～ artistic style | 民族～ national style

【风骨】fēnggǔ ❶ 指人的气概、品格 strength of character ❷ (诗文书画)雄健有力的风格 (of poetry, calligraphy, painting) vigorous style

【风光】fēngguāng 风景;景象 scene; view; sight: 北国～ northern scenery | ～旖旎(yǐnǐ) beautiful (or wonderful) view | 青山绿水～好 wonderful view of green hills and blue waters

【风光】fēng·guang 〈方 *dial.*〉热闹 bustle; excitement; respectable; creditable; dignity; same as 体面 tǐ·miàn②: 儿子有出息,母亲也觉得～。A son's success brings credit to his mother.

【风害】fēnghài 大风造成的灾害 windburn; damage caused by high wind

【风寒】fēnghán 冷风和寒气 cold (wind); chill: 经常用冷水擦身可以抵御～。Rubbing one's body with cold water can ward off the cold.

【风耗】fēnghào 刮风造成的损耗 loss caused by wind: 煤厂安装了喷雾装置,减少了煤炭～。The coal plant installed sprayers to reduce the loss of coal by wind.

【风戽】fēnghù 用风力来带动的汲水灌田的器具 wind-powered or wind-driven waterwheel (for irrigation)

【风花雪月】fēng huā xuě yuè ❶ 原指古典文学里描写自然景物的四种对象,后转喻堆砌词藻而内容贫乏的诗文 wind, flowers, snow and moon; (orig.) subjects in classical literature; flowery, empty poetic prose ❷ 指男女情爱的事 love affair; romance

【风华】fēnghuá 〈书 *fml.*〉风采和才华 charisma and talent: ～正茂 in the flower of youth; in one's prime; at life's full flowering | ～绝代 indescribably beautiful and striking; unusual and outstanding beauty

【风化】[1] fēnghuà 风俗教化 morals; decency: 有伤～ offence against decency

【风化】[2] fēnghuà ❶ 由于长期的风吹日晒、雨水冲刷、生物的破坏等作用,地壳表面和组成地壳的各种岩石受到破坏或发生变化 weathering; process of disintegration or change of the earth's crust and rock due to wind, sunshine, rain and biological erosion over a long period of time ❷ 含结晶水的化合物在空气中失去结晶水 (of a compound containing crystal water) lose water of crystallization through exposure to air

【风火墙】fēnghuǒqiáng 防火墙 fire wall

【风机】fēngjī 鼓风机 air-blower; blower

【风鸡】fēngjī 腌制风干的鸡。鸡杀后不煺毛,除去内脏,在腹内抹上花椒、盐等风干。air-dried chicken — cured by drying, without removing the feathers but cleaning out the stomach, and rubbing the cavity with Chinese prickly ash and salt

【风级】fēngjí 风力的等级。一般分为 13 级,速度每秒 0.2 米以下的风是 0 级风,32.6 米以上的风是 12 级风。wind scale usu. divided into 13 levels, wind speeds below 0.2 metre per second measure 0 on the scale; and over 32.6 metres per second, 12

【风纪】fēngjì 作风和纪律 conduct and discipline: 军容～ (military) discipline; appearance and bearing | 整顿～ tighten discipline

【风纪扣】fēngjìkòu 制服、中山装等的领扣儿。扣上领扣儿显得整齐严肃,所以叫做风纪扣。hook and eye on the collar of a uniform

风级表 Wind Scale Table

风力等级 Wind scale	风速(米/秒) Wind speed (metre/second)	海面情况 Ocean surface features	地面情况 Land features
0	0～0.2	静 calm	静，烟直上。Calm; smoke goes straight up.
1	0.3～1.5	渔船略觉摇动。Fishing boats rock gently.	烟能表示方向，树叶略有摇动。Smoke blown in a direction, leaves shake slightly.
2	1.6～3.3	渔船张帆时，可以随风移动，每小时2～3千米。Fishing boats at full sail move at 2,000-3,000 m. per hour.	人的脸感觉有风，树叶有微响，旗子开始飘动。Wind felt on face, leaves rustle, flags start to flutter.
3	3.4～5.4	渔船渐觉簸动，随风移动，每小时5～6千米。Fishing boats toss gently, advance at 5,000-6,000 m. per hour.	树叶和很细的树枝摇动不息，旗子展开。Leaves and twigs sway continuously, flags extend fully.
4	5.5～7.9	渔船满帆时，船身向一侧倾斜。Fishing boats at full sail tilt to one side.	能吹起地面上的灰尘和纸张，小树枝摇动。Raises dust and loose paper, shakes small branches.
5	8.0～10.7	渔船缩帆(即收去帆的一部分)。Fishing boats take in part of their sail.	有叶的小树摇摆，内陆的水面有小波。Small trees begin to sway, surface of inland waters ruffles.
6	10.8～13.8	渔船加倍缩帆，捕鱼须注意风险。Fishing boats take in more sail, fishing becomes risky.	大树枝摇动，电线呼呼有声，举伞困难。Big branches wave, electric wires hum, umbrellas become hard to use.
7	13.9～17.1	渔船停息港中，在海面上的渔船应下锚。Fishing boats to remain in harbour, and those at sea drop anchor.	全树摇动，迎风步行感觉不便。Entire trees sway, difficult to walk into the wind.
8	17.2～20.7	近港的渔船都停留在港内不出来。All fishing boats return to nearby harbour.	折毁小树枝，迎风步行感到阻力很大。Twigs broken off trees, great difficulty walking against the wind.
9	20.8～24.4	机帆船航行困难。Motor sailing boats advance with difficulty.	烟囱顶部和平瓦移动，小房子被破坏。Chimney tops and plain tiles move, loosened small houses destroyed.
10	24.5～28.4	机帆船航行很危险。dangerous to sail motor sailing boats.	陆地上少见。能把树木拔起或把建筑物摧毁。Uncommon on land trees uprooted and buildings destroyed.
11	28.5～32.6	机帆船遇到这种风极危险 extreme danger to motor sailing boats	陆地上很少，有则必有严重灾害 Rare on land, wide spread damage.
12	大于32.6 above 32.6	海浪滔天 gigantic waves	陆地上绝少见，摧毁力极大 very rare on land, violent destruction

hooking the collar fastening gives a neat and formal demeanour, hence 风纪扣 fēngjìkòu

【风景】fēngjǐng 一定地域内由山水、花草、树木、建筑物以及某些自然现象(如雨、雪)形成的可供人观赏的景象 scenic view in a particular area, composed of mountains, waters, flowers and plants, trees, buildings, and some natural phenomena such as rain or snow:～点 scenic spot|～区 scenic resort; scenic spot|～宜人 attractive (or charming) scenery|秋天的西山,～格外美丽。The scenery of the Western Hills in autumn is very beautiful.

【风镜】fēngjìng 挡风沙的眼镜,玻璃片的四周有棉纱、橡胶或塑料做成的罩子 wind goggles where the lenses are surrounded by a rim made of cotton yarn, rubber or plastic

【风卷残云】fēng juǎn cán yún 大风吹散残存的浮云 strong wind scatters wisps of cloud;〈比喻 *fig.*〉一下子消灭干净 make a clean sweep of sth.

【风口】fēngkǒu 山口、街口、巷口等有风的地方 place where there is a draught, e.g. mountain pass, entrance to a street or lane:身上出汗不要站在～上。Don't stand in the draught when you are sweating.

【风口浪尖】fēng kǒu làng jiān 〈比喻 *fig.*〉社会斗争最为激烈、尖锐的地方 place where social conflict is most acute; in the centre of the storm

【风浪】fēnglàng ❶ 水面上的风和波浪 wind and waves:～大,船颠簸得很厉害。The ship tossed terribly on the rough sea. ❷〈比喻 *fig.*〉艰险的遭遇 hardship; difficult experience:久经～experience many hardships

【风雷】fēngléi 狂风和暴雷 strong wind and cracking thunder;〈比喻 *fig.*〉气势浩大而猛烈的冲击力量 tempest — vast and violent force of impact:革命的～ storm of revolution; revolutionary tempest

【风力】fēnglì ❶ 风的力量 force or power of wind:～发电 wind power (generation) ❷ 风的强度 wind intensity:～三四级 wind speed of three to four on the wind scale; ☞ 风级 fēngjí

【风凉】fēngliáng 有风而凉爽 breezy and cool:大家坐在～的地方休息。Everyone rested in a cool place.

【风凉话】fēngliánghuà 不负责任的冷言冷语 irresponsible and sarcastic remarks:说～ make derisive comments

【风量】fēngliàng 单位时间内空气的流通量,用于表明鼓风机或通风设备的能力,单位是米³/秒 unit of measurement of the flow of air to describe the capacity of bellows or ventilation equipment, expressed in cubic metres/second

【风铃】fēnglíng 佛殿、宝塔等檐下悬挂的铃,风吹时摇动发出声音 aeolian bell; wind bell (hung under the eaves of pagodas or temple buildings, which chime in the wind)

【风流】fēngliú ❶ 有功绩而又有文采的;英俊杰出的 outstanding; distinguished and accomplished:数～人物,还看今朝。For truly great men, look to this age alone. ❷ 指有才学而不拘礼法 talented and free-spirited:～才子 gifted free-thinking scholar|名士～ unconventional and carefree behaviour of talented scholars ❸ 指跟男女间情爱有关的 romantic; dissolute; loose:～案件 romance case|～韵事 romantic (or love) affair

【风流云散】fēng liú yún sàn 形容四散消失 dispersed by the wind and scattered like the clouds — separated and scattered; also 云散风流 yún sàn fēng liú

【风马牛不相及】fēng mǎ niú bù xiāng jí 《左传》僖公四年:'君居北海,寡人居南海,唯是风马牛不相及也 *The Zuo Commentary · Duke Xi 4th Year*: 'You live by the North Sea, I by the South, so we have absolutely nothing to do with each other.' ('风' *feng*:雌雄相引诱 male-female seduction);〈比喻 *fig.*〉两者全不相干 absolutely unconnected; totally irrelevant

【风帽】fēngmào ❶ 御寒挡风的帽子,后面较长,披到背上 cowl-like head covering worn in winter against cold and wind ❷ 连在皮大衣、棉大衣等上面的挡风的帽子 hood; head covering connected to the collar of fur coat or cotton-padded coat to protect from the wind

【风貌】fēngmào ❶ 风格和面貌 characteristic style and features:时代～ ethos; style and feature of the time|民间艺术的～style and features of folk art ❷ 风采相貌 appearance and manner; looks and bearing:～娉婷 (of a woman) have elegant looks and bearing ❸ 景象 view; scene; appearance:远近～,历历在目。Distant views and nearby scenery appear vividly in the mind's eye.

【风门】fēngmén (～儿 fēngménr)冬天在房门外面加设的挡风的门 storm door; additional door installed outside a regular door to keep out the wind in winter; also 风门子 fēngmén·zi

【风靡】fēngmǐ 形容事物很风行,像风吹倒草木 fashionable; in vogue; become popular; sweeping (as the wind flattens grass and trees):～一时 become fashionable for a time|～世界 sweep the world

【风魔】fēngmó same as 疯魔 fēngmó

【风磨】fēngmò 利用风力转动的磨 windmill

【风平浪静】fēng píng làng jìng 没有风浪,水面很平静 wind has abated and the waves have stilled;〈比喻 *fig.*〉平静无事 calm and tranquil

【风起云涌】fēng qǐ yún yǒng ❶ 大风起来,乌云

涌现 rising wind and rolling clouds：～，雷电交加。As the wind rose and clouds raced across the sky, thunder roared and lightning flashed. ❷〈比喻 *fig.*〉事物迅速发展，声势浩大 wide-spread and fast-changing; roll on with full force; (of situation, events, etc.) develop fast with great strength and momentum

【风气】fēngqì 社会上或某个集体中流行的爱好或习惯 general mood or common practice (popular in society or group)：社会～ public (or social) morals｜不良～ unhealthy social atmosphere

【风琴】fēngqín 键盘乐器，外形是一个长方木箱，里面排列着铜簧片，上面有键盘，按键就能压动铜簧片上的开关；下面有踏板，用来鼓动风箱生风，使铜簧片振动发音 organ; rectangular, box-shaped keyboard instrument, lined with copper reeds which open and shut by pressing the keys while pedals below push air through them to produce sounds from vibration

【风情】fēngqíng ❶ 关于风向、风力的情况 information about wind-force and wind direction ❷〈书 *fml.*〉人的仪表举止 bearing; demeanour ❸〈书 *fml.*〉情怀；意趣 thoughts and feelings：别有一番～ unusual thoughts and feelings ❹ 流露出来的男女相爱的感情（常含贬义 usu. derog.）lust; amorous feeling：卖弄～ flirt; trifle with or make eyes at ❺ 指风土人情 lifestyle; local conditions and customs：南国～ lifestyle of the south

【风趣】fēngqù 幽默或诙谐的趣味（多指话或文章 usu. of speech or writing）humour; wit：他讲话很～。He is a witty talker.

【风圈】fēngquān（～儿 fēngquānr）日晕或月晕的通称 general term for solar or lunar halo

【风骚】[1] fēngsāo〈书 *fml.*〉❶ 风指《诗经》中的《国风》，骚指屈原的《离骚》，后来泛称文学 风 *feng*: *Folk Songs of States* from *The Book of Songs*; 骚 *sao*: *Encountering Sorrow* by Qu Yuan; (in a broad sense) literature ❷ 在文坛居于领袖地位或在某方面领先叫领风骚 literary trend-setter; one who holds a leading position in a certain area

【风骚】[2] fēngsāo 指妇女举止轻佻 (of a woman) coquettish; flirtatious：卖弄～ play the coquet

【风色】fēngsè ❶ 刮风的情况 condition of the wind：～突然变了，由南往北刮，而且风势渐渐大起来了。The wind suddenly veered round to the north, and blew harder and harder. ❷〈比喻 *fig.*〉情势 situation; circumstances; how things stand; trend of events：看～ see which way the wind blows; see how things stand; size up the situation｜～不对。Things are not going right.

【风沙】fēngshā 风和被风卷起的沙土 dust storm; sand blown by the wind：漫天的～。The air is full of sand blown by the wind.

【风扇】fēngshàn ❶ 热天取凉的旧式用具，用布制成，吊在梁上，用人力拉动生风 fan; old cooling device for moving the air, made of cloth and hung from the beam, made to wave back and forth by pulling a rope ❷ 电扇 electric fan

【风尚】fēngshàng 在一定时期中社会上流行的风气和习惯 prevailing custom or practice of society at a specific time：时代～ trend of the day｜社会～ social tendency; common practice

【风声】fēngshēng ❶ 刮风的声音 sighing or soughing of the wind：～鹤唳 moan of the wind and cry of the cranes — fearful and apprehensive ❷ 指传播出来的消息 news; word; rumour：走漏～ leak information｜～越来越紧。The situation is getting tense.

【风声鹤唳】fēng shēng hè lì 前秦苻坚领兵进攻东晋，大败而逃，溃兵听到风声和鹤叫，都疑心是追兵（见于《晋书·谢玄传》）。形容惊慌疑惧。moan of the wind and cry of the cranes — fearful and apprehensive (*History of Jin·Biography of Xie Xuan*). During the Former Qin Dynasty (350-394) the troops of general Fu Jian were routed by the Eastern Jin and fled in disorder. The soldiers were so jittery that they thought the moaning of the wind and the cry of cranes were the sounds of the pursuing troops.

【风蚀】fēngshí 地表（如岩石等）被风力逐渐破坏，这种现象在沙漠地区特别显著 wind erosion; phenomenon of the earth's surface (e.g. rocks) being gradually worn away by wind, especially conspicuous in the desert

【风势】fēngshì ❶ 风的势头 wind force：到了傍晚，～减弱。The wind fell at dusk. ❷〈比喻 *fig.*〉情势 how the wind blows; how things stand：探探～再说 first try to find out how things stand (or which way the wind blows)｜他一看～不对，拔腿就跑。He slipped away when he saw trouble was brewing.

【风霜】fēngshuāng〈比喻 *fig.*〉旅途上或生活中所经历的艰难困苦 wind and frost — hardships experienced in life or during a journey：饱经～ weather-beaten

【风水】fēng·shuǐ 指住宅基地、坟地等的地理形势，如地脉、山水的方向等。迷信的人认为风水好坏可以影响其家族、子孙的盛衰吉凶。*fengshui*; geomancy; location of a house, grave, etc., from the perspectives of the geomantic features of surrounding and nearby hills and waters. Superstitious people believe this can affect the fortunes of a family and its descendants：看～ practise *fengshui*｜～宝地（风水好的地方）place with good geomantic potency

【风俗】fēngsú 社会上长期形成的风尚、礼节、习惯等的总和（general term for）long-standing social customs, etiquette, habits, etc.：～人情 local customs

【风俗画】fēngsúhuà 用当时社会风俗及日常生活做题材的绘画 genre; genre painting; paintings of scenes of contemporary customs and everyday life

【风速】fēngsù 风的速度，通常以米/秒、千米/小时为单位 wind speed; wind velocity (usu. measured by metre/second or kilometre/hour)

【风瘫】fēngtān 瘫痪①的通称 general term for 瘫痪 tānhuàn ①; also 疯瘫 fēngtān

【风调雨顺】fēng tiáo yǔ shùn 指风雨适合农时 propitious winds and rains; favourable weather (for agriculture)

【风头】fēng·tou ❶〈比喻 *fig.*〉形势的发展方向或与个人有利害关系的情势 trend; circumstances (esp. those affecting a person's interests)：避避～ lie low until the dust settles | 看～办事 act according to circumstances ❷ 出头露面，显示个人的表现（含贬义 usu. derog.）show off; seek public attention; grab the limelight：出～ show off; seek publicity | ～十足 do the utmost to attract notice

【风土】fēngtǔ 一个地方特有的自然环境（土地、山川、气候、物产等）和风俗、习惯的总称（collect.）natural conditions (such as the land, mountains, rivers, climate, products, etc.) and social customs of a place：～人情 local conditions and customs

【风味】fēngwèi 事物的特色（多指地方色彩 oft local feature）distinctive flavour：～小吃 typical local snack; local delicacy | 家乡～ local flavour | 江南～ flavour of the localities south of the lower Yangtze River | 这首诗有民歌～。This poem has the distinctive flavour of a ballad.

【风闻】fēngwén 由传闻而得知（没有证实）hear; learn through hearsay; get wind of (without proof)：～他要去留学。It is said he will study abroad.

【风物】fēngwù 一个地方特有的景物 scenery (typical of a place)

【风险】fēngxiǎn 可能发生的危险 risk; danger; hazard：担～ assume a risk | 冒着～去搞试验 carry out an experiment in spite of the risks

【风箱】fēngxiāng 压缩空气而产生气流的装置。最常见的一种由木箱、活塞、活门构成，用来鼓风，使炉火旺盛。bellows; wind chest; instrument for producing a current of air to fan a furnace, usu. by drawing in air through a valve into a wooden air chamber and forcing it out with a piston

【风向】fēngxiàng ❶ 风的来向，如从东方吹来的风叫东风，从西北方吹来的风叫西北风 wind direction; how the wind blows (e.g. wind blowing from an easterly is called the east wind; and from the northwest, a northwesterly one) ❷〈比喻 *fig.*〉情势 situation; circumstances：看～行动 act according to circumstances; follow the direction of the prevailing wind

【风向标】fēngxiàngbiāo 指示风向的仪器，一般是安在高杆上的一支铁箭，铁箭可随风转动，箭头指着风吹来的方向 weathervane; weathercock; wind vane; instrument to indicate wind direction; usu. an iron arrow fixed on top of a tall pole, that turns with the wind

【风行】fēngxíng ❶ 普遍流行；盛行 be in fashion or vogue; be popular; become prevalent：～一时 in great vogue for a time | ～全国 popular throughout the country ❷ 形容迅速 fast; rapid; vigorous：雷厉～ do sth. vigorously and speedily

【风雅】fēngyǎ〈书 *fml.*〉❶《诗经》有《国风》、《大雅》、《小雅》等部分，后来用风雅泛指诗文方面的事 sections in *The Book of Songs* entitled '*Guo Feng*' or '*Folk Songs of States*', '*Da Ya*' or '*Epics*', and '*Xiao Ya*' or '*Odes*'. Hence the term, referring to literary pursuits：附庸～ mingle with men of letters and pose as lovers of art and culture ❷ 文雅 elegant; polite; refined：举止～elegant in manner; refined manners

【风言风语】fēng yán fēng yǔ ❶ 没有根据的话；恶意中伤的话 canard; groundless talk; slanderous gossip ❷ 私下里议论或暗中散布某种传闻 privately talk about or spread a rumour：有些人～，说的话很难听。Some people like to gossip and spread scandalous rumours.

【风谣】fēngyáo〈古代 *arch.*〉指民谣或风俗歌谣 ballad; folk rhyme

【风衣】fēngyī 一种挡风的外衣 windcoat; windbreaker; windcheater

【风雨】fēngyǔ ❶ 风和雨 wind and rain; weather：～无阻 stopped by neither wind nor rain — regardless of the weather; rain or shine | ～大作。The storm rages. ❷〈比喻 *fig.*〉艰难困苦 hardships; trials and tribulations; stress and strain：经～，见世面 experience difficulties and meet challenges

【风雨飘摇】fēngyǔ piāoyáo 形容形势很不稳定 (of situation) shaky; precarious; tottering; swaying in the storm

【风雨同舟】fēngyǔ tóngzhou〈比喻 *fig.*〉共同度过困难 in the same storm-tossed boat — stick it out; tide over difficulties together

【风源】fēngyuán ❶ 风的来源 source of wind：查～，治流沙 investigate the source of the wind in order to curb drifting sand dunes ❷ 产生某种风气的根源 root cause of a prevailing practice or popular trend

【风月】fēngyuè ❶ 风和月，泛指景色 view; wind and moon; (in a broad sense) scenery;

～清幽。A quiet and beautiful landscape. ❷指男女恋爱的事情 love affair; romantic liaison:～债 debts from a love affair|～场 circle of social butterflies

【风云】fēngyún ❶风和云 wind and clouds — stormy or unstable situation:天有不测～。In nature, winds and storms may take people unawares. ❷〈比喻 *fig.*〉变幻动荡的局势 changeable or fluid situation:～突变 abrupt change of the weather; sudden change in the situation

【风云人物】fēngyún rénwù 指在社会上很活跃,很有影响的人 influential person; man of the hour

【风韵】fēngyùn 优美的姿态(多用于女子 oft. of a woman) graceful bearing; charm:～犹存 still retain a graceful bearing (manner); keep one's charm; still be attractive; also 丰韵 fēngyùn

【风灾】fēngzāi 暴风、台风或飓风过境造成的灾害 disaster caused by passing windstorm, typhoon or hurricane

【风闸】fēngzhá 机车或其他车辆、机器中用压缩气体做动力的制动装置 pneumatic brake; brake of engine, vehicle or machine operated by compressed air

【风障】fēngzhàng 在菜畦旁边用苇子、高粱秆等编成的屏障,用来挡风,保护秧苗 screen woven from reeds, sorghum stalks, etc., erected around vegetable beds to protect young sprouts from the wind

【风筝】fēng·zheng 一种玩具,在竹篾等做的骨架上糊纸或绢,拉着系在上面的长线,趁着风势可以放上天空 kite; toy consisting of a frame of bamboo strips, etc. covered with paper or silk, flown in the wind at the end of a long string

【风致】fēngzhì〈书 *fml.*〉❶美好的容貌和举止 charm; good looks; graceful bearing:～翩翩 graceful manner or bearing ❷风味;风趣 humour; wit; special flavour:别有～ have a special flavour (or charm)

【风中之烛】fēng zhōng zhī zhú〈比喻 *fig.*〉随时可能死亡的人或随时可能消灭的事物 candle guttering in the wind; (of person or thing) may die or disappear at any moment

【风烛残年】fēng zhú cán nián〈比喻 *fig.*〉随时可能死亡的晚年 old and feeble like a candle guttering in the wind — remaining years of a person's life when death may come anytime (风烛 *fengzhu*: 风中之烛 candle flickering in the wind)

【风姿】fēngzī 风度姿态 charm; charisma; graceful bearing:～秀逸 elegant and calm demeanour|～绰约 (of woman) carry oneself gracefully; have graceful bearing; also 丰姿 fēngzī

【风钻】fēngzuàn ❶凿岩机 rock drill ❷用压缩空气做动力的金属加工工具,用于钻孔 pneumatic drill; tool operated by compressed air, used to bore holes in metal

沣(灃) Fēng 沣河,水名,在陕西 Fenghe River in Shaanxi Province

沨 fēng〈书 *fml.*〉水声 gurgle; sound of flowing water

枫 fēng 枫树,落叶乔木,叶子互生,通常三裂,边缘有锯齿,秋季变成红色,花黄褐色,翅果。树脂可入药。maple (*Acer*); deciduous tree with alternate palmate, three-lobed, serrated leaves which turn red in autumn, yellowish-brown flowers, and winged fruits, its resin used in medicine; also 枫香树 fēngxiāngshù

封[1] fēng ❶古时帝王把爵位(有时连土地)或称号赐给臣子 in imperial times, confer (title, land, etc.) upon:～王 confer the title of prince|分～诸侯 grant titles and lands to the nobles ❷(Fēng)姓 a surname

封[2] fēng ❶封闭 seal; cap:查～ seal up; close down|～河 (of river) frozen over|大雪～山。Heavy snow has sealed the mountain passes.|～住瓶口 seal up the mouth of the bottle|把信～起来 seal (up) a letter ❷(～儿 fēngr)封起来的或用来封东西的纸包或纸袋 wrapper; sealed packet:赏～ gratuity or small gift wrapped in red paper|信～ envelope ❸〈量词 *classifier*〉用于封起来的东西 [used for sth. sealed]:一～信 a letter|一～银子 a packet of silver

【封闭】fēngbì ❶严密盖住或关住使不能通行或随便打开 seal (up); block; cap:大雪～了道路。The road is closed by heavy snow.|用火漆～瓶口 seal a bottle with sealing wax ❷查封 seal off; close (down):～赌场 close a gambling house

【封闭疗法】fēngbì liáofǎ 一种治疗方法,把麻醉剂注射在身体的一定部位,使局部病变的恶性刺激不再传到大脑皮层,对大脑皮层有保护性的抑制作用,从而达到治疗的目的 block therapy; treatment consisting of injecting an anaesthetic into a part of the body to prevent malignant stimuli from local pathological changes spreading to the cerebral cortex, thus producing a protective inhibition in the cortex and effecting a cure

【封存】fēngcún 封闭起来保存 seal up for safekeeping:资料暂时～起来 temporarily seal up the materials for safekeeping

【封底】fēngdǐ 书刊的背面,跟封面③相对的一面 (of bookbinding) back cover (as opposed to 'front cover'); also 封四 fēngsì

【封地】fēngdì 奴隶社会或封建社会君主分给诸侯、诸侯再向下面分封的土地 fief; manor; feudal estate; in the slave or feudal society, land granted by a ruler to his nobles, who then conferred it upon their vassals

【封顶】fēngdǐng ❶ 植株的顶芽停止生长 (of the terminal bud of a plant) stop growing ❷ 建成建筑物顶部 put a roof on：大楼已经按期～。The roof of the large building has been completed on time. ❸ 指限定最高数额 set a maximum rate：奖金不～。There is no ceiling on the bonus.

【封冻】fēngdòng ❶ (江、河等) 水面结冰 (of river, etc.) freeze over ❷ 土地上冻 (of soil) frozen over; frozen hard

【封二】fēng'èr 书刊中指封面③的背面 inside front cover

【封港】fēnggǎng 指由于沉船、施工或冰冻等原因,港口或航道停止通航 closing of port or channel (due to shipwreck, construction, ice, etc.)

【封官许愿】fēng guān xǔ yuàn 为了使别人替自己卖力而答应给以名利地位 offer high position or other favours as a bribe

【封河】fēng//hé 冰封闭了河面 (of river) be frozen over：～期 ice-locked season

【封火】fēng//huǒ 把炉火压住,让它燃烧不旺,但不熄灭 bank a fire

【封建】fēngjiàn ❶ 一种政治制度,君主把土地分给宗室和功臣,让他们在这土地上建国。我国周代开始有这种制度,其后有些朝代也曾仿行。欧洲中世纪君主把土地分给亲信的人,形式跟我国古代封建相似,我国也把它叫做封建。system of holding lands in fief; political system by which a sovereign grants land to royal clansmen and meritorious statesmen as fiefs. In China, the system began in the Zhou Dynasty and was followed by other dynasties. During the Middle Ages, European monarchs granted lands to trusted followers in a form similar to the system of enfeoffment in ancient China, and that is why Chinese historians also call that system 封建. ❷ 指封建主义社会形态 feudalism：反～ anti-feudal｜～剥削 feudal exploitation ❸ 带有封建社会的色彩 feudal; pertaining to feudalism：头脑～ feudal-minded; old-fashioned

【封建割据】fēngjiàn gējù 封建时代拥有武力的人占据部分地区,对抗中央政权,各自为政,形成分裂对抗的局面 feudal separatist rule. In feudal times areas controlled by military strongmen who defied the central political power of the sovereign and created a hostile separatist situation.

【封建社会】fēngjiàn shèhuì 一种社会形态,特征是地主占有土地,农民只有很少土地或全无土地,只能耕种地主的土地,绝大部分产品被地主剥夺。封建社会比奴隶社会前进了一步,农民可以有自己的个体经济,但终身依附土地,实际上仍无人身自由。保护封建剥削制度的权力机关是地主阶级的封建国家。feudal society; social structure characterized by land ownership in the hands of landlords so that peasants had little or none, and had no choice but to cultivate the landlords' fields and hand over most of their produce. Feudal society was an advance over slave society since peasants could engage in some economic activities for private gain, however, they were still bound to the land for life, and had no personal freedom. The feudal state controlled by the landlord class was the power structure that upheld this system of feudal exploitation.

【封建主】fēngjiànzhǔ 封建社会的领主 feudal lord

【封建主义】fēngjiàn zhǔyì 一种社会制度,它的基础是地主占有土地,剥削农民 feudalism; social system based on land ownership by landlords who exploited the peasantry; ☞ 封建社会 fēnjiàn shèhuì

【封疆】fēngjiāng ❶〈书 *fml.*〉疆界 boundary; frontier ❷ 指统治一方的将帅,明清两代指总督、巡抚等 general or marshal in charge; (in the Ming and Qing dynasties) governor or commander：身任～ assume the post of the governor (or commander) of a border province｜～大吏 governor (or commander) of a border province

【封禁】fēngjìn ❶ 封闭 close; seal up; seal off：～府库 seal up the government repository ❷ 查封;禁止 prohibit; ban; forbid：～了一批黄色书刊 ban a number of pornographic books and periodicals

【封镜】fēngjìng 指影片、电视片拍摄工作结束 finish shooting a film or TV movie

【封口】fēng//kǒu (～儿 fēng//kǒur) ❶ 封闭张开的地方(伤口、瓶口、信封口等) seal; close (wound, bottle, envelope, etc.)：这封信还没～。The letter has not been sealed.｜腿上的伤已经～了。The leg wound has closed. ❷ 闭口不谈;把话说死不再改变 refuse to discuss; speak with a tone of finality：他没～,还可以商量。He has not closed the door on discussion.｜人家已经封了口,没法儿再谈了。The final word has been said and no further discussion is possible.

【封口】fēngkǒu (～儿 fēngkǒur) 信封、封套等可以封起来的地方 flap on letter or document envelope that can be sealed：信件的～要粘牢。The letter should be firmly sealed.

【封里】fēnglǐ 书刊中指封二,有时也兼指封三 (of book or magazine) inside front cover; inside back cover

【封门】fēng//mén ❶ 在门上贴上封条,禁止开启 seal off a door to prohibit entry ❷ (～儿 fēng//ménr) 把话说死不再改变 speak with finality; refuse to say more; same as 封口 fēng//kǒu ②：几句话他就封了门儿。He closed the discussion after just a few words. ❸〈方 *dial.*〉〈旧时 *old*〉死了长辈的人家,用白纸把门上的对联或门神像封起来 (of a bereaved family in which an elder has died) cover the couplets and picture of the door-god pasted on the gate with white paper

【封面】fēngmiàn ❶ 线装书指书皮里面印着书名和刻书者的名称等的一页 title page (of traditional thread-bound book); page inside the cover with the title of the book and the name(s) of the engraver(s) ❷ 新式装订的书刊指最外面的一层,用厚纸、布、皮等做成 front and back cover of modern-style bound book or periodical, made of thick paper, cloth, leather, etc. ❸ 特指新式装订的书刊印着书刊名称等的第一面 (of modern-style bound book or periodical) front cover with book title; also 封一 fēngyī

【封皮】fēngpí ❶ same as 封面 fēngmiàn ② ❷ 信封 envelope ❸〈方 *dial.*〉包裹在物品外面的纸等 wrapper; paper wrapping ❹〈方 *dial.*〉封条 strip of paper used for sealing off objects

【封妻荫子】fēng qī yìn zǐ 君主时代功臣的妻子得到封号,子孙世袭官职 hereditary official position and the title bestowed by the ruler on the wife of a meritorious statesman

【封三】fēngsān 书刊中指封四的前一面,就是封底之内的那一面 inside back cover

【封山育林】fēng shān yù lín 保证树林成长的一种措施,对长有幼林或可能生长林木的山地在一定时间里不准放牧、采伐、砍柴 close off hills with woods or young forests to livestock grazing, lumbering and wood-cutting for a period of time to facilitate afforestation

【封禅】fēngshàn〈古代 *arch.*〉帝王上泰山祭祀天地 (of the emperor) offer sacrifices to heaven and earth on Mountain Taishan

【封赏】fēngshǎng ❶〈古代 *arch.*〉帝王把土地、爵位、称号或财物赏赐臣子 (of emperor) award (land, noble rank, title or goods) to an official: ～群臣 award all officials ❷ 指封赏的东西 reward; award: 领～ receive the reward

【封四】fēngsì same as 封底 fēngdǐ

【封锁】fēngsuǒ ❶ (用强制力量)使跟外界联系断绝 blockade; cut off from the external world (by force): 经济～ economic blockade | ～消息 information blackout ❷ (采取军事等措施)使不能通行 close to passage (by military or other action): ～线 blockade; blockade line | ～边境 close (or seal off) the border

【封套】fēngtào 装文件、书刊等用的套子,多用比较厚的纸制成 large envelope or pouch for documents, books, etc., usu. made of thick paper

【封条】fēngtiáo 封闭门户或器物时粘贴的纸条,上面注明封闭日期并盖有印章 paper strip seal; strip of paper pasted on door or other objects bearing official seal and date of their sealing off

【封一】fēngyī same as 封面 fēngmiàn ③

【封斋】fēng//zhāi ❶ 伊斯兰教奉行的一种斋戒,在伊斯兰教历的九月里白天不进饮食 Ramadan. During the ninth month of the Muslim year, Muslims abstain from food and drink between sunrise and sunset. also 把斋 bǎ//zhāi ❷ 天主教的斋戒期,教徒在封斋期内的特定日期必须守斋 Catholic fasting period, when Catholics fast on specific days

【封嘴】fēng//zuǐ ❶ same as 封口 fēngkǒu ②: 先不要～,再考虑一下。Please reconsider before making the final decision. ❷ 使人不说话 silence: 他想封住我的嘴,办不到。He will never be able to shut me up.

砜 fēng 硫酰基与烃基结合而成的有机化合物 sulphone; class of organic chemical compounds containing sulphur acyl and hydrocarbon radicals

疯 fēng ❶ 神经错乱;精神失常 mad; insane; crazy; deranged: 发～ go mad; become insane; be out of one's mind ❷ 指没有约束地玩耍 play without inhibition: 她跟孩子～了一会儿。She played wildly with the child for a while. ❸ 指农作物生长旺盛,但是不结果实 (of agricultural crop) grow tall and thin without bearing fruit: ～长 overgrow; spindle | ～枝 spindling stem | 这些棉花～了。The cotton plants are spindled.

【疯癫】fēngdiān same as 疯 fēng ①

【疯疯癫癫】fēng·fengdiāndiān (～的 fēng·fengdiāndiān·de) 精神失常的样子,常用来形容人言语行动轻狂或超出常态 be mentally deranged; speak or behave in an irrational or abnormal manner

【疯狗】fēnggǒu 患狂犬病的狗 mad dog; rabid dog; ☞ 狂犬病 kuángquǎnbìng on p. 1124

【疯话】fēnghuà 颠三倒四的话;不合常理的话 nonsense; incoherent speech; irrational speech

【疯狂】fēngkuáng 发疯 wild; crazy; insane;〈比喻 *fig.*〉猖狂 frenzied; unbridled: 打退敌人的～进攻 push back the enemy's desperate attack

【疯魔】fēngmó ❶ same as 疯 fēng ① ❷ 入迷;入魔 fascinated; obsessed; infatuated: 他们下棋下～了。They are mad about chess. ❸ 使人迷 fascinate; enchant; hold spellbound: 这场足球比赛几乎～了所有的球迷。The football match held all the fans spellbound. ‖ also 风魔 fēngmó

【疯人院】fēngrényuàn 专门收容精神病人的病院 madhouse; lunatic asylum; mental hospital

【疯瘫】fēngtān same as 风瘫 fēngtān

【疯长】fēngzhǎng ❶ 农作物茎叶发育过旺,不结果实 spindle; (of crops) overgrow without bearing fruit ❷ 花卉枝叶长得很旺,不开花 (of flowering plants) grow excessively without blooming

【疯枝】fēngzhī 农作物植株上不结果实的分枝 (of crops) stem which bears no fruit; also 疯杈 fēngchà

【疯子】fēng·zi 患严重精神病的人 madman; lunatic; maniac

峰(峯) fēng ❶ 山的突出的尖顶 peak; summit: ~峦 ridges and peaks | 高~ lofty peak | 顶~ peak; summit; pinnacle ❷ 形状像山峰的事物 hump; shaped like a peak: 波~ crest of a wave | 驼~ camel's hump | 单~骆驼 dromedary ❸〈量词 *classifier*〉用于骆驼 [used for camels]: 一~骆驼 a camel

【峰巅】fēngdiān 顶峰 summit; peak

【峰回路转】fēng huí lù zhuǎn 形容山峰、道路迂回曲折 (of mountain path) serpentine; winding; full of twists and turns; circuitous

【峰峦】fēngluán 山峰和山峦 ridges and peaks: ~起伏 mountain ridges rise and fall | ~重叠 range upon range of ridges and peaks

【峰年】fēngnián 在一定时期内，自然界中某种活动达到高峰的年度 peak year; period of high activity for natural phenomena: 1980年前后是太阳活动的~。Solar activity reached a peak around 1980.

烽 fēng 烽火 beacon fire: ~燧 nocturnal beacon fire and daytime smoke from burning wolves' dung as alarm signals

【烽火】fēnghuǒ ❶〈古代 *arch.*〉边防报警点的烟火 beacon fire along the border (for giving the alarm) ❷〈比喻 *fig.*〉战火或战争 flames of war: ~连天 flames of war raging all over the land

【烽燧】fēngsuì〈古时 *arch.*〉遇敌人来犯，边防人员点烟火报警，夜里点的火叫烽，白天放的烟叫燧 beacon fire and smoke to give the alarm during a border incursion; 烽 *feng*: fire lit at night; 燧 *sui*: smoke signals sent in daylight

【烽烟】fēngyān 烽火 beacon fire; beacon; flames of war: ~四起 flames of war raging all over the country

葑 fēng 古书上指芜菁 turnip (in ancient books)

☞ fèng on p. 590

锋 fēng ❶ (刀、剑等)锐利或尖端的部分 sharp point or cutting edge (of knife, sword, etc.): 刀~ blade point; knife point | 笔~ tip of a writing brush; firm stroke; vigour of style in calligraphy | 针~相对 tit for tat ◇词~ incisive style of writing; pungent language ❷ 在前列带头的(多指军队 oft. of an army, etc.) van; forefront; leading edge: 前~ vanguard; forward | 先~ vanguard ❸ 锋面 front: 冷~ cold front | 暖~ warm front

【锋镝】fēngdí〈书 *fml.*〉刀刃和箭头，泛指兵器，也比喻战争 blade and arrowhead; (in a broad sense) weapons; (fig.) war: ~余生 survive a war

【锋利】fēnglì ❶ (工具、武器等)头尖或刃薄，容易刺入或切入物体 (of tool, weapon, etc.) sharp point or keen edge for easy piercing or cutting: ~的匕首 keen dagger ❷ (言论、文笔等)尖锐 (of speech, writing, etc.) incisive; biting; caustic: 谈吐~ trenchant style of speaking | ~的目光 keen eyesight

【锋芒】fēngmáng ❶ 刀剑的尖端，多比喻事物的尖利部分 sharp point (of knife or sword); spearhead; (usu. fig.) sharp or most forceful part: 斗争的~指向帝国主义。The struggle was spearheaded against imperialism. ❷〈比喻 *fig.*〉显露出来的才干 show talent: ~外露 display ability ‖ also 锋铓 fēngmáng

【锋铓】fēngmáng same as 锋芒 fēngmáng

【锋面】fēngmiàn 大气中冷、暖气团之间的交界面 weather front; boundary between masses of cold and warm air

蜂(䗬) fēng ❶ 昆虫，种类很多，有毒刺，能蜇人，常成群住在一起 wasp (*Vespula vulgaris*), large family of insects with a poisonous sting, usu. living in groups ❷ 特指蜜蜂 bee (*Apoidea*): ~箱 beehive; hive | ~蜜 honey ❸〈比喻 *fig.*〉成群地 in swarms; flocking: ~起 in large number | ~拥 swarm; flock; gather | ~聚 gather in large numbers; swarm together

【蜂巢】fēngcháo 蜂类的窝，特指蜜蜂的窝 honeycomb; beehive; wasp nest

【蜂巢胃】fēngcháowèi 反刍动物的胃的第二部分，内壁有蜂巢状的构造 reticulum; honeycomb stomach; second part of the stomach of a ruminant, which has honeycomb-like inner lining

【蜂房】fēngfáng 蜜蜂用分泌的蜂蜡造成的六角形的巢，是蜜蜂产卵和储藏蜂蜜的地方 beehive; honeycomb; hexagonal cells made of beeswax secreted by bees, for storage of their eggs and honey

【蜂糕】fēnggāo 用发酵的面粉加糖等蒸的糕，比较松软，切开后断面呈蜂窝状 soft, sweet steamed bread with many holes inside and like a honeycomb

【蜂聚】fēngjù 像蜂群似的聚在一起 gather in crowds, flock together

【蜂蜡】fēnglà 蜜蜂腹部的蜡腺分泌的蜡质，是蜜蜂造蜂巢的材料 beeswax; wax secreted by wax glands on the bee's belly to make the honeycomb; 通称 generally called 黄蜡 huánglà

【蜂蜜】fēngmì 蜜蜂用采集的花蜜酿成的黏稠液体，黄白色，有甜味，主要成分是葡萄糖和果糖。供食用和药用。honey; sweet pale yellow, sticky liquid produced by bees from flower nectar, mainly composed of glucose and fructose, used as food and medicine; also 蜜 mì

【蜂鸟】fēngniǎo 鸟类中最小的一种，大小跟大拇指差不多，羽毛很细，在日光照射下呈现出不同的颜色，嘴细长。吃花蜜和花上的小昆虫。产于南美洲。hummingbird (*Trochilidae*); the smallest known bird about the size of a human thumb, characterized by a long and thin bill, and fine iridescent feathers, feeds on nectar and small insects on flowers, living in South America

【蜂起】fēngqǐ 像蜂飞一样成群地起来 rise up in large numbers：义军～。The army fighting for a just cause gathered in large numbers.

【蜂王】fēngwáng 母蜂 queen bee; queen wasp

【蜂王浆】fēngwángjiāng 王浆 royal jelly

【蜂窝】fēngwō ❶ 蜂巢的通称 general term for 蜂巢 fēngcháo ❷ 像蜂窝似的多孔形态 with the appearance of a honeycomb; containing many spaces or holes：～煤 honeycomb coal briquet | 混凝土构件上的～现象 gas hole in concrete

【蜂窝煤】fēngwōméi 煤末搀适量石灰或黏土加水和匀，用模型压制成的短圆柱形燃料，有许多上下贯通的孔 honeycomb coal briquet; short cylindrical moulded coal block with evenly-spaced holes, made of coal dust mixed with lime or clay, and water, used as fuel by stacking the blocks on top of each other so the holes line up, and the fire can burn upward

【蜂箱】fēngxiāng 用来养蜜蜂的箱子 beehive; box hive; box used to raise bees

【蜂拥】fēngyōng 像蜂群似的拥挤着（走） swarm; flock like bees：～而上 swarm onto; crowd onto | 欢呼着的人群向广场～而来。The cheering crowd swarmed into the square.

鄷 Fēng 姓 a surname

【鄷都】Fēngdū 地名，在四川。今作丰都。Fengdu county in Sichuan Province; present-day 丰都 Fēngdū

【鄷都城】Fēngdūchéng 迷信传说指阴间 (in supernatural tales) hades; inferno; nether world

féng（ㄈㄥˊ）

冯 Féng 姓 a surname

☞ píng on p. 1488

逢 féng ❶ 遇到；遇见 meet; encounter; come across：相～ meet by chance; come across | ～场作戏 join in the fun whenever there is a chance; join in the spirit of the the occasion | 千载难～ extremely rare; once in a blue moon | 每～佳节倍思亲 feel doubly homesick on festive days ❷ (Féng)姓 a surname

【逢场作戏】féng chǎng zuò xì 原指卖艺的人遇到合适的演出场地，就开场表演，后来指遇到机会，偶然玩玩，凑凑热闹 (orig.) street artists perform whenever they encounter a suitable site; join in the fun whenever there is a chance; make the most of whatever amusement is available

【逢集】féngjí 轮到有集市的日子 on market day：黄村是三、六、九～。The 3rd, 6th and 9th of each month is market day in Huangcun Village.

【逢迎】féngyíng 说话和做事故意迎合别人的心意（含贬义 derog.） ingratiate oneself with; make up to; fawn on; curry favour with：百般～ do everything to curry favour | 阿谀～ flatter and toady

缝 féng 用针线将原来不在一起或开了口儿的东西连上 sew; stitch; use needle and thread to join together or close an opening：～件衣裳 sew or make a dress | 鞋开了绽要～上。Sew together a shoe that has split open. | 动过手术，伤口刚～好。The wound has just been sutured after surgery.

☞ fèng on p. 590

【缝补】féngbǔ 缝和补 sew and mend：～衣服 mend clothes | 这件衬衫缝缝补补穿了好多年。The patched and mended shirt has lasted many years.

【缝缝连连】féngféngliánlián 泛指缝补工作 (in a broad sense) sewing and mending：拆拆洗洗、～的活儿，她都很内行。She is very good at unpicking, washing, sewing and mending.

【缝合】fénghé 外科手术上指用特制的针和线把伤口缝上 suture; sew up; (of surgical operation) use a special needle and thread to suture a wound

【缝穷】féngqióng 〈旧时 *old*〉指贫苦妇女以代人缝补衣服谋生 (of poor women) sew and mend clothes for a pittance

【缝纫】féngrèn 指裁剪制作衣服、鞋帽等 cut, sew and tailor (clothes, shoes, caps, etc.)

【缝纫机】féngrènjī 做针线活的机器，一般用脚蹬，也有用手摇或用电动机做动力的 sewing machine; machine for sewing, usu. operated by treadle, hand crank or electric motor

【缝缀】féngzhuì 把一个东西缝在另一个东西上；缝补 patch; stitch together：新战士把领章～在军装的领子上。The new soldiers sewed insignia patches on the collars of their uniforms. | ～破衣服 mend torn clothes

fěng（ㄈㄥˇ）

讽 fěng ❶ 用含蓄的话指责或劝告 satirize; mock; allude or admonish euphemistically：讥～ ridicule; satirize | 嘲～ ridicule; deride; sneer at | 冷嘲热～ burning satire and cold irony ❷ 〈书 *fml.*〉诵读 chant; intone：～诵 chant; read with intonation and feeling

【讽刺】fěngcì 用比喻、夸张等手法对人或事物进

行揭露、批评或嘲笑 satirize; ridicule; mock; expose, criticize or mock a person or thing with analogy and exaggeration: ～画 caricature; satirical cartoon|用话～了他几句。(I) said a few mocking words to him.

【讽谏】fěngjiàn〈书 *fml.*〉用含蓄委婉的话向君主进谏 petition or offer advice to the sovereign in a euphemistic and indirect language

【讽诵】fěngsòng 抑扬顿挫地诵读 chant; read with intonation and expression: ～古诗 chant classic poems

【讽喻】fěngyù 一种修辞手段,用说故事等方式说明事物的道理 parable; allegory; rhetorical device for making a point by telling a story: ～诗 parabolic or allegorical poem

覂 fěng〈书 *fml.*〉(车马)翻 (of cart, horse) overturn: ～驾(翻车)。The cart turned over.

唪 fěng 大声吟诵 chant in a loud voice

【唪经】fěngjīng (和尚、道士)念经 (of Buddhist or Taoist monk) recite or chant scriptures aloud

fèng (ㄈㄥˋ)

凤(鳳) fèng ❶ 凤凰 phoenix: 龙～ dragon and phoenix|鸾～ husband and wife|丹～朝阳。The scarlet phoenix flies towards the sun. ❷ (Fèng)姓 a surname

【凤冠】fèngguān〈古代 *arch.*〉后妃所戴的帽子,上面有用贵金属和宝石等做成凤凰形状的装饰,旧时妇女出嫁也用做礼帽 phoenix coronet (worn by an empress or imperial concubine); head gear decorated with a phoenix-shaped ornament made of precious metal and embossed with gems; (old) bridal headdress: ～霞帔 phoenix coronet and embroidered tassel cape (formerly worn by a woman of high rank)

【凤凰】fènghuáng〈古代 *arch.*〉传说中的百鸟之王,羽毛美丽,雄的叫凤,雌的叫凰。常用来象征祥瑞。phoenix; legendary king of the birds, with beautiful plumage; 凤 fèng being the male and 凰 huáng the female

【凤梨】fènglí ❶ 多年生草本植物,叶子大,边缘有锯齿,花紫色,果实密集在一起,外部呈鳞片状,果肉味甜酸,有很浓的香味。产于热带,我国广东、台湾等地都有出产。pineapple (*Ananas comosus*); tropical perennial plant, grown in Guangdong and Taiwan provinces with large, serrated leaves, purple flowers, and bunched scaly fruits whose flesh is tart and sweet with a strong fragrance ❷ 这种植物的果实 fruit of such plant ‖ also 菠萝 bōluó; 俗称 popular name 菠萝蜜 bōluómì

【凤毛麟角】fèng máo lín jiǎo〈比喻 *fig.*〉稀少而可贵的人或事物 phoenix feathers and unicorn horn — unique and valuable person or object

【凤尾鱼】fèngwěiyú 鲚的通称 general term for 鲚 jì

奉 fèng ❶ 给;献给(多指对上级或长辈 oft. to superiors or elders) give or present with respect: ～献 devote; dedicate; present with respect; offer as a tribute |～上新书一册 present a new book ❷ 接受(多指上级或长辈的 orders, etc. from superiors or elders) receive; accept: ～旨 by decree of the emperor; by imperial edict|～到命令 receive an order ❸ 尊重 esteem; revere; regard with respect: 崇～ worship; believe in |～为圭臬 regard as the standard ❹ 信仰 believe in; espouse (religion): 信～ believe in|素～佛教 faithful belief in Buddhism ❺ 侍候 wait upon; attend to: ～养 support and care for|侍～ care for; look after ❻〈敬辞 *pol.*〉用于自己的举动涉及对方时 [used for one's actions that affect others]: ～托 request sb. to do sth. |～陪 keep sb. company|～劝 offer a piece of advice|～告 inform you; let you know ❼(Fèng) 姓 a surname

【奉承】fèng·cheng 用好听的话恭维人,向人讨好 flatter; fawn upon; ingratiate oneself: ～话 flattery

【奉达】fèngdá〈敬辞 *pol.*〉告诉;表达(多用于书信 usu. in correspondence) inform; express: 特此～。This is to inform you ...; respectfully yours

【奉复】fèngfù〈敬辞 *pol.*〉回复(多用于书信 usu. in correspondence) reply; respond: 谨此～。(at the start of the message) In response to your letter ...; (at the end of the message) So much for my response to your letter.

【奉告】fènggào〈敬辞 *pol.*〉告诉 inform you; let you know: 详情待我回来后当面～。I'll give you the details upon my return.

【奉公】fènggōng 奉行公事 act in the public interest: 克己～ work selflessly for the public interest

【奉公守法】fèng gōng shǒu fǎ 奉行公事,遵守法令 law-abiding

【奉还】fènghuán〈敬辞 *pol.*〉归还 return with thanks: 原物～ return sth. to its original owner|如数～ repay (money, etc.) in full

【奉令】fèng//lìng same as 奉命 fèng//mìng

【奉命】fèng//mìng 接受使命;遵守命令 receive orders; act under orders: ～出发 receive orders to start out; start as ordered

【奉陪】fèngpéi〈敬辞 *pol.*〉陪伴;陪同做某事 accompany; keep sb. company: 恕不～ Sorry, I cannot stay with you. |我还有点急事,不能～了。I cannot stay any longer as I have some urgent business to attend to.

【奉劝】fèngquàn〈敬辞 *pol.*〉劝告 suggest; beseech; offer advice:～你少喝点儿酒。Please do not drink too much.

【奉使】fèngshǐ 奉命出使 be posted as an envoy:～西欧 sent to Western Europe on a diplomatic mission

【奉送】fèngsòng〈敬辞 *pol.*〉赠送 give away free; offer as a gift

【奉托】fèngtuō〈敬辞 *pol.*〉拜托 request sb. to do sth.:这件事只好～您了。I shall have to bother you to take care of this matter.

【奉为圭臬】fèng wéi guīniè 把某些言论或事物当做准则 consider (opinion or action) as the standard; regard as a model; ☞ 圭臬 guī niè on p. 729

【奉献】fèngxiàn ❶ 恭敬地交付;呈献 devote; dedicate; present with respect; offer as a tribute:把青春～给祖国 devote one's youth to the motherland ❷ 奉献出的东西 contribution; dedication; service; same as 贡献 gòngxiàn ②:她要为山区的建设做点～。She wants to contribute her efforts to building up the mountainous area.

F

【奉行】fèngxíng 遵照实行 pursue (policy, etc.):～独立自主的外交政策 pursue an independent foreign policy|～故事(按老规矩办事) act in accordance with established practice; follow tradition

【奉养】fèngyǎng 侍奉和赡养(父母或其他尊亲) support and care for (parents or other older relatives):～二老 support and look after one's parents

【奉迎】fèngyíng ❶ 奉承;逢迎 flatter; fawn on; curry favour with:～上级 curry favour with one's superiors ❷〈敬辞 *pol.*〉迎接 greet; meet:他是专程前来～诸位的。He made a special trip to meet you.

【奉赠】fèngzèng〈敬辞 *pol.*〉赠送 offer as a present; present as a gift

覅 fèng〈方 *dial.*〉不用 no need; not necessary

俸 fèng ❶ 俸禄 salary; pay; stipend:薪～ salary (usu. of ranking government employee) ❷ (Fèng) 姓 a surname

【俸禄】fènglù 封建时代官吏的薪水 in feudal times, official's emolument

葑 fèng 古书上指菰的根 root of wild rice in ancient books

☞ fēng on p. 587

赗 fèng〈书 *fml.*〉❶ 用财物帮助人办丧事 help defray funeral expenses by presenting gifts or money to the bereaved family:赙～ present a funeral gift to a bereaved family ❷ 送给办丧事人家的东西 gift for funeral expenses

缝 fèng (～儿 fèngr) ❶ 接合的地方 seam — where two pieces join together:缭～儿 stitch up a seam|无～钢管 seamless steel tubing ❷ 缝隙 chink; slit; crack; crevice:裂～ crack|门～儿 space between a door and its frame; chink in the door|见～插针 take advantage of the smallest opportunity|床板有道～。There is a crack in the wooden bed boards.

☞ féng on p. 588

【缝隙】fèngxì 裂开或自然露出的狭长的空处 chink; crack; rift; fissure; crevice; split, or natural long and narrow opening:从大门的～向外张望 look out through a chink in the front gate

【缝子】fèng·zi 缝隙 crack; chink; crevice:墙裂了道～。There's a crack in the wall.

fiào (ㄈㄧㄠˋ)

嫑 fiào〈方 *dial.*〉不要 don't:～动气。Don't be angry.

fó (ㄈㄛˊ)

佛 fó ❶ 佛陀的简称 abbr. for 佛陀 Fótuó ❷ 佛教徒称修行圆满的人 one who has attained enlightenment:立地成～ abruptly change one's ways; become an instant saint ❸ 佛教 Buddhism:～寺 Buddhist temple|～家 Buddhist religion; Buddhism|～老 Buddha and Laozi; Buddhism and Taoism ❹ 佛像 image or statue of Buddha:铜～ bronze statue of the Buddha|大殿上塑着三尊～。There are three statues of the Buddha in the hall. ❺ 佛号或佛经 name of the Buddha (Amitabha); Buddhist scripture or sutra; Buddhist sacred literature:念～ pray to the Buddha|诵～ chant Buddhist scriptures

☞ fú on p. 595

【佛典】fódiǎn 佛教的经典 Buddhist scripture or sacred literature

【佛法】fófǎ ❶ 佛教的教义 Buddha's teachings; Buddhist doctrine; Buddhadharma ❷ 佛教徒和迷信的人认为佛所具有的法力 power of Buddha (belief of Buddhists and superstitious people)

【佛光】fóguāng ❶ 佛教徒指佛带来的光明 glory of the Buddha:～普照。The glory of Buddha shines over the whole world. ❷ 佛像头上的光辉 Buddha's halo ❸ 山区的一种自然景象,在与太阳相对方向的云层或雾层上呈现围绕人影的彩色光环,由光线通过云雾区的小水滴经衍射作用而形成 Buddha's halo; anticorona; brocken bow; brocken spectre; natural phenomenon frequent in mountainous areas, when a luminous coloured halo around the shadow of an observer is thrown by the sun onto a cloud or fog bank; created by the diffraction of light through water droplets in mist

【佛号】fóhào 佛的名号,特指信佛的人念的'阿弥陀佛'名号 name of the Buddha, esp. 'Amitabha' chanted by Buddhists: 口诵～ chant the name of the Buddha

【佛教】Fójiào 世界上主要宗教之一,相传为公元前6—前5世纪古印度的迦毗罗卫国(今尼泊尔境内)王子释迦牟尼所创,广泛流传于亚洲的许多国家。西汉末年传入我国。Buddhism; one of the principal religions of the world that is popular in Asian countries, said to be founded by Sakyamuni, prince of the ancient Indian state of Kopilavastu (in present-day Nepal), during the 6th-5th century B.C. Buddhism was first introduced to China towards the end of the Western Han Dynasty.

【佛经】fójīng 佛教的经典 Buddhist scripture; Buddhist sutra; Buddhist sacred literature; also 释典 shìdiǎn; ☞ 释藏 shìzàng on p.1763

【佛龛】fókān 供奉佛像的小阁子,多用木头制成 niche for a statue of Buddha (usu. of wood)

【佛口蛇心】fó kǒu shé xīn 〈比喻 *fig.*〉嘴上说得好听,心肠却非常狠毒 duplicitous; deceitful; hypocritical; have the face of the Buddha but the heart of a viper

【佛老】Fó-Lǎo 佛和老子。也指佛教和道教。Buddha and Laozi; Buddhism and Taoism

【佛门】fómén 指佛教 Buddhism: ～弟子 Buddhist; disciple of the Buddha | ～规矩 Buddhist rules | 皈(guī)依～convert to Buddhism

【佛事】fóshì 指僧尼拜忏的事情 Buddhist ceremony; Buddhist service: 做～hold a Buddhist service

【佛手】fóshǒu ❶ 常绿小乔木,叶子长圆形,花白色。果实鲜黄色,下端有裂纹,形状像半握着的手,有芳香。可入药。fingered citron (*Citrus medica* var. *Sarcodactylis*); Buddha's hand; small fragrant, evergreen shrub with oval leaves, white flowers, bright-yellow fruits with lobes that give the shape of a half open hand. Can be used as medicine. ❷ 这种植物的果实 fruit of such plant

【佛寺】fósì 佛教的庙宇 Buddhist temple

【佛头着粪】fó tóu zhuó fèn 佛的塑像上着了鸟雀的粪便 smear the head of a Buddhist statue with guano; 〈比喻 *fig.*〉好东西上添上不好的东西,把好东西给糟蹋了(含讥讽意 derog.) desecrate; sully; spoil a good thing

【佛陀】Fótuó 佛教徒称释迦牟尼 Buddha (title given by Buddhists to Sakyamuni); 简称 abbr. 佛 fó [梵 Sanskrit: buddha]

【佛像】fóxiàng ❶ 佛陀的像 image or statue of Buddha ❷ 泛指佛教供奉的神像 (in a broad sense) all sacred images worshipped by Buddhists

【佛学】fóxué 指佛教及其研究的学问 Buddhist learning; Buddhist philosophy

【佛牙】fóyá 佛教徒指释迦牟尼遗体火化后留下的牙齿 Buddha's tooth; tooth sarira of Sakyamuni (left after his cremation)

【佛爷】fó·ye 佛教徒对释迦牟尼的尊称 Buddha; honorific title given by Buddhists to Sakyamuni

【佛珠】fózhū (～儿 fózhūr)数珠 beads; rosary

【佛祖】fózǔ 佛教徒指佛和开创宗派的祖师,也专指释迦牟尼 Buddha and founder of a Buddhist sect; (also referring to) Sakyamuni

fǒu (ㄈㄡˇ)

缶 fǒu ❶〈古代 *arch.*〉一种大肚子小口儿的瓦器 earthen utensil with large body and small opening ❷〈古代 *arch.*〉一种瓦质的打击乐器 clay percussion instrument

否 fǒu ❶ 否定 negate; deny: ～决 reject; overrule; veto; vote down | ～认 deny; disavow; repudiate ❷〈书 *fml.*〉表示不同意,相当于口语的'不' [same as 不 bù in spoken language] no; nay ❸〈书 *fml.*〉用在问句尾表示询问 [used at the end of a question]: 知其事～? Do you know about it? ❹'是否、能否、可否'等表示'是不是、能不能、可不可'等意思 [used after 是 shì, 能 néng, 可 kě, etc. to indicate a choice or question]: 明日能～出发,尚待最后决定。Whether or not we will start off tomorrow is yet to be decided.

☞ pǐ on p.1468

【否定】fǒudìng ❶ 否认事物的存在或事物的真实性(跟'肯定'相对 as opposed to 'affirm' or 'uphold')negate; deny the existence or truth of sth.: 全盘～ total negation; reject completely | ～一切 completely negate (or deny) ❷ 表示否认的;反面的(跟'肯定'相对 as opposed to 'affirmative' or 'in favour of') negative; contrary: ～判断 negative judgement

【否决】fǒujué 否定(议案)(proposal) reject; veto; overrule; vote down: 提案被～了。The motion was voted down.

【否决权】fǒujuéquán ❶ 某些国家的元首、上议院所享有的推翻已通过的议案或使其延缓生效的权力 veto; veto power; power held by the head of state, or upper house in some countries to repudiate an adopted proposal, or postpone its effective date ❷ 在会议中少数否决多数的权力。如联合国安全理事会常任理事国享有的否决权。power held by the minority to veto a proposal of the majority, e.g. the veto power of the permanent member states of the United Nations Security Council

【否认】fǒurèn 不承认 deny; disavow; repudiate: 矢口～ flatly deny | ～事实 deny the facts

【否则】fǒuzé 〈连词 *conj.*〉是'如果不这样'的意思 otherwise; if not; or else: 首先必须把场地清理好，～无法施工。The site must be cleared first, or else it will be impossible to start construction.

fū (ㄈㄨ)

夫 fū ❶ 丈夫(zhàng·fu) husband: ～妻 husband and wife | ～妇 husband and wife; married couple | 姐～ older sister's husband; brother-in-law | 姑～ husband of father's sister; uncle by marriage ❷ 成年男子 man: 匹～ ordinary man | 一～守关，万～莫开。One man guarding the pass will stop ten thousand from getting through. ❸ 从事某种体力劳动的人 person engaged in manual labour: 渔～ fisherman | 农～ farmer | 轿～ sedan-chair carrier ❹ 〈旧时 *old*〉服劳役的人，特指被统治阶级强迫去做苦工的人 conscripted labourer; corvée labourer: ～役 coolie; hired hand; conscripted labourer | 拉～ pressgang

☞ fú on p. 593

【夫唱妇随】fū chàng fù suí 〈比喻 *fig.*〉夫妻互相配合，行动一致。也指夫妻和睦。work together as a couple; domestic harmony; also 夫倡妇随 fū chàng fù suí

【夫妇】fūfù 夫妻 husband and wife; married couple: 新婚～ newly-weds; newly married couple

【夫妻】fūqī 丈夫和妻子 husband and wife: 结发～ husband and wife by the first marriage

【夫妻店】fūqīdiàn 由夫妻两人经营的、一般不用店员的小店 mom-and-pop store; small shop run by husband and wife (usu. without employing assistants)

【夫权】fūquán 指封建社会丈夫支配妻子的权力 (in feudal society) authority of the husband over the wife

【夫人】fū·rén 〈古代 *arch.*〉诸侯的妻子称夫人，明清时一二品官的妻子封夫人，后来用来尊称一般人的妻子。现在多用于外交场合。wife; lady; madame; wife of a duke or prince; (in the Ming and Qing dynasties) wife of highest and second highest rank officials; madame, mostly used on diplomatic occasions

【夫役】fūyì ❶ 〈旧时 *old*〉指服劳役、做苦工的人 coolie ❷ 〈旧时 *old*〉指受雇做杂务的人 hired hand; conscripted labourer; also 伕役 fūyì

【夫子】fūzǐ ❶ 〈旧时 *old*〉对学者的尊称 term of address for a scholar: 孔～ Confucius; Master Kong | 孟～ Mencius; Master Meng | 朱～ Master Zhu ❷ 〈旧时 *old*〉学生称老师(多用于书信 oft. in correspondence) form of address to a teacher ❸ 〈旧时 *old*〉妻称夫 my husband ❹ 读古书而思想陈腐的人 (含讥讽意 derog.) pedant (one who reads ancient books and has old-fashioned thinking): 老～ old pedant | 迂～ pedantic old fogey | ～气 pedantry; pedantic attitude

【夫子自道】fūzǐ zì dào 指本意是说别人而事实上却正说着了自己 master's criticisms of others apply to himself; criticism that backfires

伕 fū same as 夫 fū ④

呋 fū ☞ below

【呋喃】fūnán 有机化合物，化学式 C_4H_4O。无色液体，有特殊气味，用来制药品，也是重要的化工原料。furan(C_4H_4O); organic chemical compound in the form of a colourless liquid with a distinct odour, used in pharmaceuticals, also an important industrial chemical

【呋喃西林】fūnánxīlín 药名，有机化合物，化学式 $C_6H_6O_4N_4$。浅黄色粉末，对多种细菌有抑制和杀灭作用，外用可作皮肤、黏膜的消毒剂。nitrofurazone ($C_6H_6O_4N_4$); furacin; name of a medicine, organic chemical compound in the form of a light yellow powder which inhibits and kills many kinds of germs, and can be used as disinfectant on the skin and mucosa [新拉 new Latin: furacilinum]

玞 fū ☞ [珷玞] (wǔfū) on p. 2035

肤(膚) fū 皮肤 skin: 切～之痛 keenly felt pain | 体无完～ cuts and bruises all over the body; covered in injuries

【肤泛】fūfàn 浮浅空泛 skin-deep; superficial; shallow: ～之论 shallow ideas

【肤觉】fūjué 皮肤、黏膜等受外界刺激时所产生的感觉，分为触觉、痛觉、温觉等 dermal sensation; cutaneous sensation; sensation of the skin and mucosa when subject to stimulation, degrees of sensation include touch, pain, heat, etc.

【肤廓】fūkuò 〈书 *fml.*〉内容空洞浮泛，不切合实际 (of content) empty; shallow; unrealistic

【肤皮潦草】fūpí liáocǎo ☞ 浮皮潦草 fúpí liáocǎo on p. 598

【肤浅】fūqiǎn (学识)浅；(理解)不深 (of knowledge or understanding) superficial; (of theory) shallow: ～的认识 superficial knowledge (or understanding) | 我对戏曲的了解很～。I have only a superficial understanding of opera.

【肤色】fūsè 皮肤的颜色 colour of the skin

柎 fū 〈书 *fml.*〉❶ 花萼 calyx ❷ 钟鼓架的腿 leg of a bell or drum stand; foot of a bell or drum rack

砆 fū ☞ [碔砆] (wǔfū) on p. 2035

𫓧 fū 〈书 *fml.*〉铡刀 fodder chopper; hand hay cutter: ～锧 (铡刀和铡刀座) fodder chopper and its stand

麸(麩) fū same as 麸子 fū·zi

【麸子】fū·zi 通常指小麦磨成面筛过后剩下的麦皮和碎屑 (wheat) bran; usu. ground husks of wheat separated from flour meal; also 麸皮 fūpí

趺 fū〈书 *fml*.〉❶ same as 跗 fū ❷ 碑下的石座 pedestal of stone tablet: 石～ stone pedestal | 龟～ tortoise pedestal (supporting a stele)

【趺坐】fūzuò〈书 *fml*.〉佛教徒盘腿端坐,左脚放在右腿上,右脚放在左腿上 sit cross-legged in the lotus posture (as Buddhists do)

跗 fū 脚背 instep: ～骨 tarsus | ～面 instep

【跗骨】fūgǔ 蹠骨和胫骨之间的骨,构成脚跟和脚面的一部分,由七块小骨组成 tarsus; tarsal bones; seven small bones of the foot between the metatarsal and shin bone, forming part of the heel and instep; (图见 ☞ figure for 骨骼 gǔgé on p. 693)

【跗面】fūmiàn 脚面 instep

【跗蹠】fūzhí 鸟类的腿以下到趾之间的部分,通常没有羽毛,表皮角质鳞状 tarsometatarsus (of bird); lower part of a bird's leg which articulates with the toes, usu. featherless and covered by a scaly cuticle

稃 fū 小麦等植物的花外面包着的硬壳 husk; chaff; bran: 内～ bran | 外～ husk; chaff

痡 fū〈书 *fml*.〉病;疲劳过度 exhaustion; fall ill

鄜 Fū 鄜县,地名,在陕西。今已改作富县。Fuxian County in Shaanxi Province; now changed to 富县 Fùxiàn

孵 fū 鸟类伏在卵上,用体温使卵内的胚胎发育成雏鸟。也指用人工的方法调节温度和湿度,使卵内的胚胎发育成雏鸟。hatch; brood; incubate; (of birds) sit on eggs to maintain constant temperature so the embryoes inside develop into nestlings; use artificial methods to adjust temperature and humidity to incubate: ～了一窝小鸡 hatch a brood of chicks

【孵化】fūhuà 昆虫、鱼类、鸟类或爬行动物的卵在一定的温度和其他条件下变成幼虫或小动物 hatch; incubate; eggs of insects, fishes, birds or reptiles change into larvae or young animals with appropriate temperature and other conditions

【孵育】fūyù 孵;孵化 hatch; incubate: 刚～出来的小鸡就会走会啄食。Newly hatched chicks can walk and peck.

敷 fū ❶ 搽上;涂上 apply (powder, ointment, etc.): ～粉 powder | ～药 apply ointment ❷ 铺开;摆开 spread; lay out: ～设 lay; install; lay out ❸ 够;足 sufficient; enough: 入不～出 income insufficient to cover expenditure

【敷陈】fūchén〈书 *fml*.〉详细叙述 elaborate; relate in great detail

【敷料】fūliào 外科上用来包扎伤口的纱布、药棉等 dressing; (surgery) gauze, absorbent cotton, etc. used to dress wounds

【敷设】fūshè ❶ 铺(轨道、管道等) lay out; lay; install (tracks, pipes, etc.): ～电缆 lay electricity cables | ～铁路 lay track ❷ 设置(水雷、地雷等) place; lay (mines, etc.)

【敷衍】fūyǎn〈书 *fml*.〉叙述并发挥 elaborate; expound; develop: ～经文要旨 develop the message of scriptures and important sayings; also 敷演 fūyǎn

【敷衍】fū·yǎn ❶ 做事不负责或待人不恳切,只做表面上的应付 perfunctory; go through the motions; make a show of: ～塞责 perform one's duty in a perfunctory manner; make a show of doing one's duty; muddle through one's work | ～了事 do sth. perfunctorily; muddle through sth.; skimp a job ❷ 勉强维持 just manage; barely get by: 手里的钱还够～几天。The money is barely enough to get by for a few days.

【敷演】fūyǎn same as 敷衍 fūyǎn

fú (ㄈㄨˊ)

夫 fú〈书 *fml*.〉❶〈指示词 *demons*. *pron*.〉那;这 this; that: 独不见～螳螂乎? Did you ignore that praying mantis? ❷〈代词 *pron*.〉他 he: 使～往而学焉 make him go there to study ❸〈助词 *aux*.〉a) 用在一句话的开始 [used at the beginning of a sentence]: ～战,勇气也。Fighting in a battle is a courageous deed. b) 用在一句话的末尾或句中停顿的地方表示感叹 [used at the end of a sentence, or at a pause in the middle of a sentence to express an exclamation]: 人定胜天,信～。It is absolutely true that man is bound to conquer nature. | 逝者如斯～,不舍昼夜。Thus do all things pass, day after day!
☞ fū on p. 592

市 fú same as 韍 fú

弗 fú〈书 *fml*.〉不 not: 自愧～如 be ashamed of one's inferiority; feel one's inferiority keenly; acknowledge one's inferiority

伏[1] fú ❶ 身体向前靠在物体上;趴 lean on; bend over: ～案 bend over one's desk ❷ 低下去 fall; subside; go down: 起～ rise and fall | 此起彼～ as one falls, another rises in succession ❸ 隐藏 hide: 潜～ hide; lie low | ～击 ambush; ambuscade | 昼～夜出 nocturnal; hide by day and come out at night ❹ 初伏、中伏、末伏的统称;伏天 dog days; any of the three nine-day periods constituting the hottest season of the year: 入～ begin (or enter into) the hottest season | 初～ first day of the first period of the hottest season (falling usu. in mid-July) | 三～天 dog days; three nine-day periods constituting the hottest season of the year ❺ 屈服;低头承认;被迫接受 yield; admit (defeat, guilt, etc.); compelled to accept: ～罪 plead guilty | ～诛 be executed ❻ 使屈服;降伏 subdue; overcome; vanquish: 降龙～虎 subdue the dragon and tame the tiger — overcome powerful adversaries ❼ (Fú) 姓 a surname

伏[2] fú 伏特的简称 abbr. for 伏特 fútè

【伏案】fú'àn 上身靠在桌子上(读书、写字) bend over one's desk (reading or writing): ～写作 bend over one's desk writing

【伏笔】fúbǐ 文章里前段为后段埋伏的线索 foreshadow; hint later developments in story, essay, etc.

【伏辩】fúbiàn 〈旧时 *old*〉指认罪的供状或悔过书 written document of repentance; written confession (of guilt, etc.); also 服辩 fúbiàn

【伏兵】fúbīng 埋伏下来伺机攻击敌人的军队 troops in ambush

【伏地】fúdì 〈方 *dial.*〉本地出产或土法制造的 locally-produced: ～小米儿 local millet | ～面 locally grown wheat flour

【伏法】fúfǎ (犯人)被执行死刑 (of criminals) be executeed: 罪犯已于昨天～。The criminal was executed yesterday.

【伏旱】fúhàn 伏天出现的旱情 drought in hottest season: 战胜～ combat the summer drought

【伏击】fújī 用埋伏的兵力突然袭击敌人 ambush; ambuscade: 打～ ambush | 途中遭到～ fall into an ambush on the way

【伏侍】fú·shi same as 服侍 fú·shi

【伏输】fú//shū same as 服输 fú//shū

【伏暑】fúshǔ 炎热的伏天 hottest season; height of summer

【伏特】fútè 电压单位,1安培的电流通过电阻为1欧姆的导线时,导线两端的电压是1伏特。这个单位名称是为纪念意大利物理学家伏特(Conte Alessandro Volta,也译作伏打)而定的。volt; standard measure of electric motive force named after the Italian physicist Conte Alessandro Volta. One volt has the electromotive force required to produce a current of one ampere through resistance of one ohm; also 伏打 fúdǎ; 简称 abbr. 伏 fú

【伏特计】fútèjì 测量电路中两点间电压的仪器 voltmeter; instrument for measuring the potential difference between two points in a circuit; also 电压表 diànyābiǎo or 电压计 diànyājì

【伏特加】fútèjiā 俄罗斯的一种烈性酒 vodka; strong Russian alcoholic liquor [俄 Russian: водка]

【伏天】fútiān 指三伏时期,是一年中最热的时候 dog days; hottest summer days; ☞ 三伏 sānfú on p.1651

【伏帖】fútiē ❶ 舒适 comfortable; at ease: 心里很～ feel at ease; also 伏贴 fútiē ❷ same as 服帖 fútiē ①

【伏贴】fútiē ❶ 紧贴在上面 close fit; adhere fully: 壁纸糊得很～。The wall paper is well pasted. ❷ same as 伏帖 fútiē ①

【伏线】fúxiàn 埋下的线索;伏笔 foreshadow; clue; hint later developments (in a story, essay, etc.)

【伏汛】fúxùn 在伏天里发生的河水暴涨 summer flood

【伏诛】fúzhū 〈书 *fml.*〉伏法 be executed

【伏罪】fú//zuì 承认自己的罪过 plead guilty: 低头～ lower one's head and admit one's guilt; also 服罪 fú//zuì

凫(鳬) fú ❶ 野鸭 wild duck: ～趋雀跃(比喻人欢欣鼓舞) jubilant; elated; in high spirits ❷ same as 浮 fú ②: ～水 swim

【凫茈】fúcí 古书上指荸荠 water chestnut in ancient books

芙 fú ☞ below

【芙蕖】fúqú 〈书 *fml.*〉荷花 lotus

【芙蓉】fúróng ❶ 木芙蓉 cottonrose hibiscus (*Hibisus mutablis*) ❷ 荷花 lotus (*Nymphaea lotus*): 出水～ lotus flower appearing just above the water

芾 fú 〈书 *fml.*〉❶ 草木茂盛 lush; luxuriant ❷ same as 黻 fú。宋朝书画家米芾。Mi Fu, also 米黻 mǐfú, a calligrapher and painter of the Song Dynasty

☞ fèi on p.562

苿 fú [苿苢](fúyǐ) 古书上指车前(草名) Asiatic plantain (*Plantago*); plantago asiatica

扶 fú ❶ 用手支持使人、物或自己不倒 support oneself or sb. else with the hand; support sth. with the hand: ～犁 put one's hand to the plough; follow the plough | ～老携幼 help the aged and lead the young by the hand; bring along both old and young | ～着栏杆 hold on to the railings ❷ 用手帮助躺着或倒下的人坐或立;用手使倒下的东西竖直 straighten; hold up: ～苗 straighten the seedlings flattened by wind or rain | 护士～起伤员,给他换药。The nurse propped up the injured person and changed the bandage. ❸ 扶助 help; assist; lend a hand: ～贫 help the poor; aid a poverty-stricken area; alleviate poverty | ～危济困 help those in distress and peril; help those in danger and relieve those in need; rescue the endangered and succour the poor | 救死～伤 heal the wounded and rescue the dying ❹ (Fú) 姓 a surname

【扶病】fúbìng 带着病(做某件事)(do sth.) in

spite of illness：～出席 attend in spite of illness｜～工作 work in spite of illness

【扶持】fúchí ❶ 搀扶 support；hold up ❷ 扶助；护持 foster；give aid；help sustain：～新办的学校 help (or give aid to) the newly established school｜老人没有子女，病中全靠街坊尽心～。The childless, old man had to rely on the wholehearted care of his neighbours when he fell ill.

【扶乩】fú//jī same as 扶箕 fú//jī

【扶箕】fú//jī 一种迷信活动，在架子上吊一根棍儿，两个人扶着架子，棍儿就在沙盘上画出字句来作为神的指示 planchette writing；superstitious practice where two people hold up a frame with a suspended stick which scratches lines in a container of sand, and these being read as words from the gods；also 扶乩 fú//jī

【扶鸾】fú//luán same as 扶箕 fú//jī

【扶苗】fú//miáo 把倒伏的农作物的苗扶直，使它正常生长 straighten the seedlings (after flattening by wind or rain)

【扶贫】fúpín 扶助贫困户或贫困地区发展生产，改变穷困面貌 help the poor or aid a poverty-stricken area (to develop production and better its circumstances)：做好农村～工作 succeed in helping the rural poor

【扶桑】[1] fúsāng ❶ 古代神话中海外的大树，据说太阳从这里出来 (in ancient mythology) huge mulberry tree beyond the seas from which the sun rises ❷ (Fúsāng)传说中东方海中的古国名，旧时指日本 legendary name of an ancient country beyond the East China Sea, later referring to Japan ‖ also 榑桑 fúsāng

【扶桑】[2] fúsāng ☞ 朱槿 zhūjǐn on p. 2499

【扶手】fú·shou 能让手扶住的东西(如栏杆顶上的横木) handrail；rail；banisters；balustrade (e.g. crossbeam on the top of balusters)

【扶疏】fúshū 〈书 *fml.*〉枝叶茂盛，高低疏密有致 luxuriant and airy：枝叶～。The foliage is luxuriant yet airy.｜花木～。The flowers and trees are luxuriant but well spaced.

【扶梯】fútī ❶ 有扶手的楼梯 staircase with banisters ❷ 〈方 *dial.*〉梯子 ladder

【扶危济困】fú wēi jì kùn 扶助处境危急的人，救济生活困难的人 help those in distress and aid those in peril；help those in danger and relieve those in need；rescue the endangered and succour the poor；also 扶危济急 fú wēi jì jí or 扶危救困 fú wēi jiù kùn

【扶养】fúyǎng 养活 provide for；bring up；foster：把孩子～成人 bring up a child

【扶摇】fúyáo 〈书 *fml.*〉自下而上的旋风 cyclone spiralling upwards

【扶摇直上】fúyáo zhí shàng 形容地位、名声、价值等迅速往上升 skyrocket；(of status, reputation or value) rise quickly；be promoted quickly

【扶掖】fúyè 〈书 *fml.*〉搀扶；扶助 support；help；assist

【扶正】fú//zhèng 〈旧时 *old*〉把妾提到妻的地位叫扶正 elevate a concubine to the status of formal wife

【扶植】fúzhí 扶助培植 foster；cultivate；promote；prop up：～新生力量 foster new emerging forces

【扶助】fúzhù 帮助 help；assist；support：～老弱 help the old and the weak｜～困难户 assist poverty-stricken families

佛 fú same as 拂 fú ③
☞ fó on p. 590

【佛戾】fúlì 〈书 *fml.*〉违背；违反 violate；go against；run counter to

孚 fú 使人信服 inspire confidence (in sb.)：深～众望(很使群众信服) enjoy great popularity；enjoy high prestige

刜 fú 〈书 *fml.*〉用刀砍；击 hit；cut with a knife

苻 fú ❶ same as 莩 fú ❷ (Fú)姓 a surname

茀 fú 〈书 *fml.*〉❶杂草太多 weedy；infested with weeds ❷ 福 bliss；good luck

拂 fú ❶ 轻轻擦过 stroke；caress；touch：春风～面 spring breeze caresses the face ❷ 甩动；抖 whisk；flick：～袖 flick one's sleeve in anger ❸ 〈书 *fml.*〉违背(别人的意图) run counter to；go against (sb.'s wishes)：～逆 go against；run counter to｜～意 contrary to one's wishes；not suit sb.；not appeal to sb.｜～耳(逆耳) jar on the ear
〈古 *arch.*〉same as 弼 bì

【拂尘】fúchén 掸尘土和驱除蚊蝇的用具，柄的一端扎马尾(mǎyǐ) horsetail whisk wand tied with horsetail hairs on one end for brushing off dust and chasing away mosquitoes and flies

【拂拂】fúfú 形容风轻轻地吹动 (of wind) blow gently：凉风～ gentle, cool breeze

【拂逆】fúnì 违背；不顺 go against；run counter to：他不敢～老人家的意旨。He dare not go against the old man's wish.

【拂拭】fúshì 掸掉或擦掉(尘土) wipe off；whisk off (dust)：拿抹布把桌椅～了一遍 dust off the tables and chairs with a cloth

【拂晓】fúxiǎo 天快亮的时候 before dawn：～出发 set off before daybreak

【拂袖】fúxiù 〈书 *fml.*〉把衣袖一甩(旧时衣袖较长)，表示生气 flick one's sleeve in anger (sleeves being longer in old times)：～而去 storm out；leave in a huff；walk out on sb.

【拂煦】fúxù 〈书 *fml.*〉(风)吹来温暖 (of wind) bring warmth：微风～。The breeze is soothingly warm.

【拂意】fúyì 不合心意；不如意 dissatisfactory；be contrary to one's wishes；against one's desires：稍有～，就大发雷霆。He flies into a rage at the slightest dissatisfaction

佛 fú ☞[彷佛](fǎngfú) on p. 551

服 fú ❶ 衣服;衣裳 clothes; garments; dress; attire:制～ uniform|便～ everyday (or informal) clothes; mufti ❷ 丧服 mourning (apparel):有～在身 be in mourning ❸ 穿(衣服) wear (clothes):～丧 be in mourning ❹ 吃(药) take (medicine):～药 take medicine|内～ to be taken orally ❺ 担任(职务);承当(义务或刑罚) honour an obligation; serve a sentence; hold office:～役 be on active service; enlist or serve in the army|～刑 serve a sentence (in prison) ❻ 承认;服从;信服 obey; submit (oneself to); be convinced:～输 admit defeat|心～口～ be completely convinced|你有道理,我算～了你了。What you've said is reasonable. I'm convinced. ❼ 使信服 convince:～众 convince the public|以理～人 convince others by reason ❽ 适应 be used to; be accustomed to; be acclimatized to:不～水土 not used to the local environment ❾ (Fú) 姓 a surname

☞ fù on p. 609

【服辩】fúbiàn same as 伏辩 fúbiàn

【服从】fúcóng 遵照;听从 follow; obey; submit (oneself to); be subordinated to:～命令 follow orders|少数～多数。The minority should submit to the majority.|个人利益～集体利益 subordinate one's own interests to the overall ones

【服毒】fú//dú 吃毒药(自杀) take poison (to commit suicide)

【服老】fúlǎo 承认年老,精力不如人(多用于否定式 usu. in the negative) admit that one is old and not as vigorous as before; be reconciled to one's age and failing health:不～not take one's age lying down; refuse to give in to age; not be reconciled to age and failing health

【服满】fúmǎn 服丧期满 be out of mourning; complete a period of mourning

【服气】fúqì 由衷地信服 be convinced; be won over:两个人都很自负,互不～。They were both too proud to concede anything to each other.

【服软】fú//ruǎn (～儿 fú//ruǎnr) ❶ 服输 admit or acknowledge defeat:不在困难面前～be uncowed by difficulties ❷ 认错 acknowledge or admit a mistake; give in:向老人服个软儿 admit one's mistake to one's elder|他知道是自己错了,可嘴上还不肯～。He knew he was wrong, but wouldn't admit it.

【服丧】fúsāng 长辈或平辈亲属等死后,遵照礼俗,在一定期间内带孝 be in mourning for a period for the death of a kinsman, etc. according to custom

【服色】fúsè 衣服的样式、颜色 style and colour of clothes:民族～ national costume

【服式】fúshì 服装的式样 fashion; dress style:新潮～ latest fashion; trendy dress style

【服侍】fú·shi 伺候;照料 nurse; wait upon; attend to:～父母 care for one's parents|在他病中同志们轮流来～。The comrades took turns nursing him while he was sick. also 伏侍 fú·shi or 服事 fú·shi

【服饰】fúshì 衣着和装饰 dress; attire; clothes and personal adornment:～淡雅 simply but elegantly attired (or dressed)|华丽的～ gorgeous attire and rich ornaments

【服输】fú//shū 承认失败 admit or acknowledge defeat

【服帖】fútiē ❶ 驯服;顺从 docile; compliant; obedient; submissive:他能使劣马变得～。He can tame a wild horse. also 伏帖 fútiē ❷ 妥当;平妥 fitting; neat; well-arranged:事情都弄得服服帖帖。Everything is properly arranged.

【服务】fúwù 为集体(或别人的)利益或为某种事业而工作 serve; work for the interests of a group or other individuals, or for a cause; give or render service to; be in the service of:～行业 service trades (or sector)|为人民～ serve the people|科学为生产～。Science serves production.|他在邮局～了三十年。He has worked in the post office for 30 years.

【服务行业】fúwù hángyè 为人服务、使人生活上得到方便的行业,如饮食业、旅馆业、理发业、修理生活日用品的行业等 service trades (or sector) which provide convenience to people, such as catering, hotel service, hairdressing and repair service

【服务员】fúwùyuán 机关的勤杂人员;旅馆、饭店等服务行业中招待客人的工作人员 janitor in an organization; attendant who serves customers in hotel, restaurant and other service trades

【服刑】fú//xíng 服徒刑 serve a sentence (in prison):服了两年刑 do a two-year sentence|正在劳改农场～ serve a sentence on a reform-through-labour farm

【服药】fú//yào 吃药 take medicine

【服役】fú//yì ❶ 服兵役 be on active service; enlist or serve in the army:他在部队～多年。He has served in the army for many years. ❷〈旧时 *old*〉指服劳役 corvée labour

【服膺】fúyīng〈书 *fml.*〉(道理、格言等)牢牢记在心里;衷心信服(of truth, motto, etc.) keep in mind; be deeply convinced

【服装】fúzhuāng 衣服鞋帽的总称,一般专指衣服 clothing; dress; garment; costume; (collect.) clothes, hat and shoes:～商店 clothing shop|～整齐 neatly dressed|民族～ national costume

【服罪】fú//zuì same as 伏罪 fú//zuì

佛 fú 〈书 *fml.*〉形容忧愁或愤怒 gloomy; depressed; worried; indignant; angry; glowering:～郁(郁闷气愤) depressed; gloomy and indignant; depressed and angry | ～然 glower; look angry or offended

【佛然】fúrán 〈书 *fml.*〉生气的样子 glower; look angry or offended:～作色 glower; flush with anger | ～不悦 peeved; wear an offended expression

绂 fú ❶〈古代 *arch.*〉系印章的丝绳 silk ribbon used to tie a seal ❷〈书 *fml.*〉same as 黻 fú

绋 fú 〈书 *fml.*〉大绳,特指牵引灵柩的大绳 thick (hemp) rope; thick cords fastening the coffin, or used for pulling the hearse:执～ serve as a pallbearer (at a funeral ceremony or procession)

韨(韍) fú ❶〈古代 *arch.*〉祭服前面的护膝围裙,用熟皮做成 knee-length, cured leather apron tied over the ceremonial gown worn for sacrificial rites ❷〈古代 *arch.*〉系玺印的丝绳 silk ribbon attached to the imperial seal

茯 fú [茯苓](fúlíng)寄生在松树根上的真菌,形状像甘薯,外皮黑褐色,里面白色或粉红色。可入药。fuling (*Poris cocos*); parasitic fungus shaped like a sweet potato that lives on the roots of pine trees, having dark-brown skin, and white or pink flesh, and used in medicine

罘 fú 芝罘(Zhīfú),山名,在山东 Zhifu Mountain in Shandong Province

【罘罳】fúsī ❶ 古代的一种屏风,设在门外 screen or latticed partition placed outside the door ❷ 设在屋檐下防鸟雀来筑巢的金属网 metal netting placed under the eaves to prevent birds building nests ‖ also 罦罳 fúsī

氟 fú 气体元素。符号 F (fluorine)。淡黄绿色,剧毒,有强烈的腐蚀性和刺激性。化学性质非常活泼,与氢直接化合能发生爆炸,许多金属都能在氟气里燃烧。含氟的塑料和橡胶,性能特别良好。fluorine (F); pale yellowing-green, extremely toxic and highly corrosive and irritating, as well as highly reactive and explodes when directly combined with hydrogen. Many metals burn in fluorine, and plastic and rubber containing fluorine are high performance materials.

俘 fú ❶ same as 俘虏 fúlǔ ①:～获 capture| 被～be taken prisoner ❷ same as 俘虏 fúlǔ ②:战～ prisoner of war | 遣～(遣返战俘) repatriate prisoners of war

【俘获】fúhuò 俘虏和缴获 capture:～甚众 capture many enemy soldiers; take many prisoners

【俘虏】fúlǔ ❶ 打仗时捉住(敌人) capture; take prisoner:～了敌军师长 capture the enemy division commander ❷ 打仗时捉住的敌人 captive; captured personnel; prisoner of war:释放～ release the captives

郛 fú 〈古代 *arch.*〉指城外面围着的大城 outer wall of a city

洑 fú ❶ 旋涡 whirlpool; eddy; vortex ❷ 水在地面下流 subterranean stream

☞ fù on p.613

祓 fú ❶〈古时 *arch.*〉一种除灾求福的祭祀 sacrificial ceremony to banish misfortune and pray for blessings; exorcistic ceremony ❷〈书 *fml.*〉扫除 general cleaning or cleansing

莩 fú 〈书 *fml.*〉芦苇秆子里面的薄膜 thin membrane inside a rush stalk

☞ piǎo on p.1476

栿 fú 〈书 *fml.*〉房梁 beam

砩 fú 砩石,矿物,成分是氟化钙。现作氟石。fluorite; fluorspar; now also 氟石 fúshí

蚨 fú ☞ 青蚨(qīngfú) on p.1563

浮 fú ❶ 停留在液体表面上(跟'沉'相对 as opposed to 'sink') suspend on liquid surface; float:～萍 duckweed | 油～在水上。Oil floats on water. ◇～云 drifting clouds | 脸上～着微笑。A faint smile played across his face. ❷〈方 *dial.*〉在水里游 swim:他能一口气～到对岸。He can swim across the river with one breath. ❸ 在表面上的 superficial; on the surface:～土 loose surface soil | ～雕 relief sculpture ❹ 可移动的 movable; portable:～财 movable (or portable) property ❺ 暂时的 temporary, provisional; transient:～记 keep a running tally before entering it in the regular accounts; keep a temporary account | ～支 temporary account of expenses ❻ 轻浮;浮躁 heedless; flippant; superficial; impetuous:他人太～,办事不塌实。He is impetuous and cannot be depended upon. ❼ 空虚;不切实 empty; hollow; inflated:～名 empty name; vain glory; bubble reputation | ～夸 be boastful; exaggerate ❽ 超过;多余 exceed; be surplus or redundant:人～于事 overstaffed; redundant; too many people for the job | ～额 surplus volume

【浮报】fúbào 以少报多;虚报 give an exaggerated report of number, amount, or achievement; report inflated figures:～产量 report an inflated output

【浮标】fúbiāo 设置在水面上的标志,用来指示航道的界限、航行的障碍物和危险地区 buoy-anchored float that marks a navigable channel, navigation obstacle or hazard

【浮财】fúcái 指金钱、首饰、粮食、衣服、什物等动产 movable property; portable property (such as money, jewellery, grain, clothes, utensils, furniture, etc.)

【浮尘】fúchén 在空中飞扬或附在器物表面的灰

尘 airborne dust; surface dust; dust on the surface of objects

【浮沉】fúchén 在水中忽上忽下 bob up and down; go up and down; drift along ◇与世～(比喻跟着世俗走,随波逐流)(fig.) follow the trend (or current)|宦海～(旧时比喻官职升降)(fig.) ups and downs of an official career in old times; vicissitudes in the world of officialdom

【浮船坞】fúchuánwù 可以在水上移动并能沉浮的凹形船坞,用来修理船只 floating dock-hollow dock which can be moved about, raised and lowered, used to repair vessels

【浮词】fúcí 不切实际的言词;没有根据的话 verbiage; empty words; groundless remarks:～艳句 empty, flowery talk|满纸～paper covered with verbiage

【浮厝】fúcuò 暂时把灵柩停放在地面上,周围用砖石等砌起来掩盖,以待改葬 place a coffin in a temporary place, and cover it with bricks or stones pending burial

【浮荡】fúdàng ❶ 飘荡 drift; float in the air:歌声在空中～。The sound of singing floats through the air.|小船在湖中～。The small boat drifts about on the lake. ❷ 轻浮放荡 dissolute; loose in morals

【浮雕】fúdiāo 雕塑的一种,在平面上雕出的凸起的形象 bas-relief, form of sculpture in which the figures project slightly above the background

【浮吊】fúdiào 能在水上移动,进行起重作业的船 floating crane; movable platform with a device for lifting heavy weights; also 起重船 qǐzhòngchuán

【浮动】fúdòng ❶ 飘浮移动;流动 float; drift:树叶在水面上～。Leaves are floating on the water. ❷ 上下变动;不固定 fluctuate; variable; rise and fall:～汇率 floating exchange rate|向上～一级工资 raise sb.'s salary by one grade ❸ 不稳定 unsteady:解放前物价飞涨,人心～。Price hikes caused widespread insecurity before Liberation.

【浮动汇率】fúdòng huìlǜ 兑换比例不予以固定,根据外汇市场的供求关系任其自由涨落的汇率 floating exchange rate; variable exchange rate which fluctuates freely in response to supply and demand on the foreign exchange market

【浮泛】fúfàn ❶〈书 *fml.*〉漂浮在水面上 float:轻舟～。A light skiff floated on the water. ❷ 流露 show; reveal; display:她的脸上～着天真的表情。Innocence showed on her face. ❸ 表面的;不切实的 superficial; unsubstantial:言词～ shallow words|～的研究 superficial studies

【浮光掠影】fú guāng lüè yǐng〈比喻 *fig.*〉印象不深刻,好像水面的光和掠过的影子一样,一晃就消逝 passing light and shadow; vague impression which vanishes quickly; fleeting impression

【浮华】fúhuá 讲究表面上的华丽或阔气,不顾实际 vain; showy; flashy; ostentatious:～的装饰品 flashy decorations

【浮滑】fúhuá 轻浮油滑 canny and flippant:～习气 frivolous and cunning ways

【浮记】fújì 商店把账目暂时记在水牌上,泛指账目没有切实结算而暂时记上 keep a tally of a transaction before entering it in the regular accounts; tally sth. for the time being

【浮家泛宅】fú jiā fàn zhái 形容长时期在水上生活,漂泊不定 live a wandering life on the water (for a long period time); dwell on a boat; lead an unsettled life; also 泛家浮宅 fàn jiā fú zhái

【浮夸】fúkuā 虚夸,不切实 boastful; exaggerate:语言～ boastful words|～作风 work style characterized by boasting and exaggeration; prone to boasting and hyperbole

【浮礼儿】fúlǐr〈方 *dial.*〉虚礼 insincere politeness; empty courtesy

【浮力】fúlì 物体在流体中受到的向上托的力。浮力的大小等于被物体所排开的流体的重量。buoyancy; power of supporting a body so that it floats in a liquid, equivalent to the weight of the fluid displaced by it

【浮面】fúmiàn(～儿 fúmiànr) same as 表面[1] biǎomiàn:把～的一层稀泥铲掉 scrape a thin coat of mud off the surface|他～上装出像没事的样子。He looked as if nothing had happened.

【浮名】fúmíng 虚名 empty name; vain glory; bubble reputation:～虚誉 empty name and false reputation|不慕～show no interest in an empty name

【浮皮】fúpí(～儿 fúpír) ❶ 生物体的表皮 cuticle; epidermis; (of an organism) outer skin ❷ 物体的表面 surface

【浮皮潦草】fúpí liáocǎo 形容不认真,不仔细 cursory; casual; perfunctory; superficial and careless; also 肤皮潦草 fūpí liáocǎo

【浮漂】fúpiāo(工作、学习等)不塌实;不认真(of work, study, etc.) negligent; careless; superficial:作风～ sloppy work style

【浮签】fúqiān(～儿 fúqiānr)一端粘在试卷、书册、文稿上,便于揭去的纸签 removable marker pasted on the margin of an examination paper, book or manuscript

【浮浅】fúqiǎn 浅薄;肤浅 superficial; shallow:内容～ superficial (or shallow) content|他对社会的认识很～。He has a shallow understanding of society.

【浮桥】fúqiáo 在并列的船或筏子上铺上木板而成的桥 pontoon; floating bridge; bridge made of boards laid on juxtaposed boats or rafts

【浮生】fúshēng ❶ 指短暂虚幻的人生(对人生的

消极看法）(negative outlook on life) brief and illusory life; fleeting life：～若梦。Life is but a dream. ❷ 浮在水面上生长 grow on water surface：浮萍～在池塘中。The duckweed grows on the surface of the pond.

【浮尸】fúshī 浮在水上的尸体 floating dead body; floating corpse

【浮水】fúshuǐ 在水里游 swim

【浮筒】fútǒng 漂浮在水面上的密闭金属筒，下部用铁锚固定，用来系船或做航标等 float; pontoon; buoy; floating, sealed metal can fixed in place by an iron anchor, used for mooring, or as a buoy

【浮头】fútóu 渔业上指水中缺氧时鱼类把口吻伸出水面呼吸 (of fish) stick its mouth out of the water to breathe because of lack of oxygen in the water

【浮头儿】fútóur〈方 *dial.*〉浮面 surface：筐里～的一层苹果，都是大个儿的。The apples on the top of the basket are big ones.

【浮图】fútú same as 浮屠 fútú

【浮屠】fútú ❶ 佛陀 Buddha ❷〈书 *fml.*〉和尚 Buddhist monk ❸ 塔 pagoda; stupa：七级～ seven-storey pagoda ‖ also 浮图 fútú

【浮土】fútǔ (～儿 fútǔr) ❶ 地表层的松土 loose surface soil ❷ 器物表面的灰尘 dust on objects：掸掉鞋上的～ whisk the dust off the shoes

【浮现】fúxiàn ❶ (过去经历的事情)再次在脑子里显现 (of past experiences) come to mind：往事又～在眼前。The past rose before my eyes again. ❷ 呈现；显露 reveal; show：脸上～出笑容。A smile appeared on (her) face.

【浮想】fúxiǎng ❶ 头脑里涌现的感想 thoughts or ideas flashing across one's mind：～联翩 thoughts crowded one's mind ❷ 回想 recollect; recall：独对孤灯，～起一幕幕的往事。Sitting alone before the lamp, I recalled many scenes from the past.

【浮性】fúxìng 物体在流体表面(如船在水面)或在流体中(如气球在空气中)浮于一定平衡位置的能力 buoyant capacity; ability of an object to float in equilibrium on the surface of a fluid (e.g. boat on water), or in it (balloon in the air)

【浮艳】fúyàn ❶ 浮华艳丽 flashy; gaudy; gorgeous：衣饰～ gorgeously dressed ❷ 辞章华美而内容贫乏 (of writing) affected and vacuous：词句～ florid expressions

【浮游】fúyóu ❶ 在水面上漂浮移动 swim; sail：～生物 plankton ❷〈书 *fml.*〉漫游 roam about; go on a pleasure trip：～四方 roam about the world

【浮游生物】fúyóu-shēngwù 生活在海洋或湖沼中，行动能力微弱，全受水流支配，并且身体较小的动物或植物，如水母、藻类 plankton; tiny forms of plant and animal life, such as jellyfish and algae living in oceans, lakes and marshes, possessing little motor ability, and thus moving with the currents

【浮员】fúyuán 多余的人员 redundant personnel：裁汰～ down-size; cut down redundant personnel

【浮云】fúyún 飘浮的云彩 floating cloud：～蔽日 floating clouds obscure the sun — treacherous court officials deluding the monarch

【浮躁】fúzào 轻浮急躁 impetuous; impulsive：性情～ impetuous temperament

【浮肿】fúzhǒng 水肿的通称 general term for 水肿 shuǐzhǒng

【浮子】fú·zi 鱼漂 (of fishery) float

菔 fú ☞ 莱菔 láifú on p.1144

桴[1] fú ❶〈书 *fml.*〉小筏子 small raft ❷〈方 *dial.*〉房屋大梁上的小梁 tie; small beam attached to the main beam; also 桴子 fú·zi

桴[2]**(枹)** fú〈书 *fml.*〉鼓槌 drumstick：～鼓相应 drum responds to the sticks — cooperate in perfect harmony; work in perfect coordination
☞ 枹 bāo on p.63

【桴鼓相应】fú gǔ xiāng yìng 用鼓槌打鼓，鼓就响起来 drum responds to the drumsticks;〈比喻 *fig.*〉相互应和，配合得很紧密 cooperate in perfect harmony; work in perfect coordination

【桴子】fú·zi ❶〈方 *dial.*〉小筏子 small raft ❷ same as 桴[1] fú ②

符 fú ❶ 符节 tally given by a ruler to a general or envoy as credentials：兵～ tally issued to a commander to prove authorization to move troop | 虎～(虎形的兵符) tiger-shaped tally issued to a general as imperial authorization for troop movement ❷ 代表事物的标记；记号 symbol; sign; mark：～号 symbol; mark; sign | 音～ musical note ❸ 符合(多跟'相'或'不'合用 oft. used with 相 xiāng and 不 bù) match; accord with; tally with：两个数目相～ two figures tally | 他所说的与事实不～。What he said does not tally with the facts. ❹ 道士所画的一种图形或线条，声称能驱使鬼神、给人带来祸福 magic drawing or sign traced by a Taoist priest to invoke or expel spirits, or bring good or ill fortune：护身～ amulet; protective talisman | 画了一张～ draw a magic sign ❺ (Fú) 姓 a surname

【符号】fúhào ❶ 记号；标记 symbol; mark; sign：标点～ punctuation mark | 文字是记录语言的～。Letters are a set of symbols for recording a language. ❷ 佩带在身上表明职别、身份等的标志 insignia

【符号论】fúhàolùn 一种主观唯心主义的理论。认为人的感觉、观念不是外界事物的反映，而仅仅是一些和外界事物没有任何相似之处的记号、符号或象形文字。semiotics; symbol theory; subjective, idealistic theory which proposes that human senses and ideas are merely indicators, symbols or pictographs that do not originate from the external world, and bear no resemblance to it; also 象形文字论 xiàngxíng wénzìlùn

【符合】fúhé (数量、形状、情节等)相合 (of quantity, shape, circumstances, etc.) accord with; tally with; conform to; be in line with:～事实 tally with the reality|这些产品不～质量标准。These products are not up to quality standard.

【符节】fújié 〈古代 *arch.*〉派遣使者或调兵时用做凭证的东西。用竹、木、玉、铜等制成,刻上文字,分成两半,一半存朝廷,一半给外任官员或出征将帅。tally given by a ruler to a general or an envoy as credentials. Tallies were made of bamboo, wood, jade, copper, etc., carved with characters, and split into two halves — one half retained at court, and the other held by an official appointed to a region, or a general going on a campaign.

【符箓】fúlù 符④(总称) general term for 符 fú ④

【符咒】fúzhòu 道教的符和咒语 Taoist magic drawings and incantations

匐 fú ☞ 匍匐 púfú on p.1499

涪 Fú 涪江,发源于四川,流至重庆入嘉陵江 Fujiang River in Sichuan Province, which joins the Jialingjiang River in Chongqing

袱 fú 包裹、覆盖用的布单 cloth-wrapper; covering cloth:包～ cloth-wrapper

艴 fú 〈书 *fml.*〉形容生气 look angry; look offended:～然 be angry; be offended

幅 fú ❶ (～儿 fúr)布帛、呢绒等的宽度 width of cloth, silk, woollen fabric:～面 width of cloth|单～ single width|双～ double width|宽～的白布 white cloth of broad width; extra-wide white cloth ❷ 泛指宽度 (in a broad sense) breadth; width; size: ～度 range; scope; extent; margin|～员 area (of national territory)|振～ amplitude of vibration ❸ (～儿 fúr) 〈量词 *classifier*〉用于布帛、呢绒、图画等 [used for cloth, silk, woollen fabric, paintings, etc.]:一～画 a painting|用两～布做一个床单儿 make a sheet from two widths of cloth.

【幅度】fúdù 物体振动或摇摆所展开的宽度 range of fluctuation; scope; extent; 〈比喻 *fig.*〉事物变动的大小 degree of change:今年小麦增产的～较大。Wheat production increased by a big margin this year.|产品质量有较大～的提高。The product quality has improved considerably.

【幅面】fúmiàn 布帛、呢绒等的宽度 width of cloth, silk, woollen fabric, etc.:～宽 double-width cloth|～窄 single-width cloth

【幅员】fúyuán 领土面积 area (of territory); size (of a country) (幅 *fu*: 宽度 width; 员 *yuan*: 周围 vicinity):～广大 (of a country) have a vast territory|～辽阔 vast territory

罦 fú 〈书 *fml.*〉捕鸟的网 bird net; bird trap

【罦罳】fúsī same as 罘罳 fúsī

辐 fú 车轮中连接车毂和轮辋的一条条直棍儿 spoke; straight rod radiating from a wheel hub to the rim; (图见 ☞ figure for 轮子 lún·zi on p.1275)

【辐辏】fúcòu 〈书 *fml.*〉形容人或物聚集像车辐集中于车毂一样 converge like the spokes of a wheel:车船～。Vehicles and ships converged. also 辐凑 fúcòu

【辐射】fúshè ❶ 从中心向各个方向沿着直线伸展出去 radiate; extend in rays in all directions from a centre:～形 radiation form ❷ 热的传播方式的一种,从热源沿直线向四周发散出去。光线、无线电波等电磁波的传播也叫辐射。radiation; form of heat transmission, in which heat rays are emitted from a source. The emission of electromagnetic waves, such as light and radio waves, is also called radiation.

【辐条】fútiáo same as 辐 fú

蜉 fú [蜉蝣](fúyóu)昆虫的一科。若虫生活在水中一年至五、六年。成虫有翅两对,常在水面飞行,寿命很短,只有数小时至一星期左右。mayfly (*Epheme roptera*); member of the insect family whose nymphs live in water for five or six years and whose imagoes oft. skim water surfaces, on two pairs of wings and have a brief life span from a few hours to about one week

鵩 fú 古书上说的像猫头鹰一类的鸟 bird that resembles an owl, mentioned in ancient literature

鲋 fú ☞ 魴鲋 fángfú on p.550

福 fú ❶ 幸福;福气(跟'祸'相对 as opposed to 'misfortune') luck; happiness; blessing; good fortune :～利 well-being; welfare; material benefits|享～ enjoy oneself; have a good life|造～do good for ❷ 〈旧时 *old*〉妇女行'万福'礼 woman's curtesy:～了一～ make a curtesy ❸ (Fú)指福建 short name for Fujian Province:～橘 tangerine produced in Fujian Province ❹ (Fú)姓 a surname

【福地】fúdì ❶ 道教指神仙居住的地方 (of Taoism) place where immortals live:～洞天 cave inhabited by immortals; beautiful scenic place ❷ 指幸福的地方 place of happiness:身在～不知福。When one grows up in happiness, one fails to appreciate it.

【福分】fú·fen 福气 good fortune; good luck; happy lot:有～ fortunate; lucky|～不浅 be fortunate enough to; have the good fortune to (do sth.)

【福将】fújiàng 指运气好、每战总能获胜的将领。借指做事处处如意的人。fortune's favourite; lucky general who always wins the battle; person who always succeeds

【福晋】fújìn 满族称亲王、郡王等的妻子 wife of a Manchu prince; (Manchu) princely consort

【福利】fúlì ❶ 生活上的利益。特指对职工生活(食、宿、医疗等)的照顾。well-being; material benefits; welfare-provision of food, housing, medical care to employees): ～费 benefits; welfare expense; welfare funds | ～事业 welfare projects or services | 为人民谋～。Work for the well-being of the people. ❷ 使生活上得到利益 bring material benefits to: 发展生产,～人民 promote production to benefit the people; improve the people's livelihood through developing production

【福气】fú·qi 指享受幸福生活的命运 good luck; good fortune; happy lot: 有～ have good fortune | ～大 very fortunate or lucky

【福如东海】fú rú dōng hǎi 福气像东海一样无边无际。用作对人的祝颂(多与'寿比南山'连用 expression of good wishes, usu. followed by 寿比南山 'a life as enduring as the Southern Mountain') happiness as boundless as the sea

【福无双至】fú wú shuāng zhì 幸运的事情不会连续到来(常与'祸不单行'连用 oft. followed by 'misfortune never comes singly') blessings do not come in pairs

【福相】fúxiàng 有福气的相貌 features of the face, or countenance which presage good fortune

【福星】fúxīng 象征能给大家带来幸福、希望的人或事物 mascot; lucky star

【福音】fúyīn ❶ 基督教徒称耶稣所说的话及其门徒所传布的教义 gospel; teachings and sayings of Christ and his apostles ❷〈比喻 *fig.*〉有利于公众的好消息 good news; good tidings: 希望你能带来～。I hope you will bring us good news.

【福音书】Fúyīnshū 指基督教《新约全书》中的《马太福音》、《马可福音》、《路加福音》、《约翰福音》,里面记载传说的耶稣生平事迹和教训 Gospels; story of the life and teachings of Jesus recorded in *The Gospel According to Matthew*, *Mark*, *Luke and John*, in the Christian *New Testament*

【福至心灵】fú zhì xīn líng 运气来了,心思也显得灵巧了 When good fortune comes, one's mind works like magic. *or* Luck brings wisdom.

【福州戏】fúzhōuxì same as 闽剧 mǐnjù

榑 fú [榑桑] (fúsāng) ☞ 扶桑[1] fúsāng on p.595

箙 fú〈书 *fml.*〉盛箭的用具 container for holding arrows; quiver

髴 fú ☞ [髣髴] (fǎngfú) on p.551

蝠 fú 蝙蝠 bat

幞 fú〈书 *fml.*〉❶ 幞头 a kind of scarf worn by men ❷ same as 袱 fú

【幞头】fútóu〈古代 *arch.*〉男子用的一种头巾 a kind of scarf worn by men

黻 fú ❶〈古代 *arch.*〉礼服上绣的半青半黑的花纹 half-blue, half-black patterns embroidered on ceremonial gowns ❷ 同'韨' same as 韨 fú

襆 fú〈书 *fml.*〉❶被单 (bed) sheet ❷ 包扎 wrap: ～被 pack; wrap up clothes and bedding ❸ same as 袱 fú

【襆被】fúbèi〈书 *fml.*〉用袱子包扎衣被,准备行装 pack; wrap up clothes and bedding: ～前往 pack up and go

fǔ (ㄈㄨˇ)

父 fǔ〈书 *fml.*〉❶ 老年男子 (respectful term for) elderly man: 田～ old farmer | 渔～ old fisherman ❷ same as 甫[1] fǔ ①
☞ fù on p.605

甫[1] fǔ ❶〈古代 *arch.*〉加在男子名字下面的美称,如孔丘字仲尼,也称尼甫,后来指人的表字 *fu*, courtesy name for a man (e.g. Kong Qiu took the style name of Zhongni and so was also called Nifu); referring to a person's secondary name: 台～ your name ❷ (Fǔ)姓 a surname

甫[2] fǔ〈书 *fml.*〉刚刚 just, only; only just: 惊魂～定 barely recovered from a fright; still badly shaken | 年～二十 just turned twenty

抚(撫) fǔ ❶ 安慰;慰问 comfort; console: ～问 console | ～恤 comfort and compensate a bereaved family ❷ 保护 protect; nurture; foster: ～养 raise; foster; bring up | ～育 foster; nurture ❸ 轻轻地按着 stroke; press lightly: ～摩 stroke; caress ❹ same as 拊 fǔ

【抚爱】fǔ'ài 照料,爱护 caress; fondle; take care of: ～儿女 cherish one's children

【抚躬自问】fǔ gōng zì wèn ☞ 反躬自问 fǎn gōng zì wèn on p.537

【抚今追昔】fǔ jīn zhuī xī 接触当前的事物而回想过去 contemplate the present and recall the past; recall the past in the light of the present; also 抚今思昔 fǔ jīn sī xī

【抚摸】fǔmō same as 抚摩 fǔmó

【抚摩】fǔmó 用手轻轻按着并来回移动 stroke; caress: 妈妈～着女儿的头发。The mother stroked her daughter's hair.

【抚琴】fǔqín〈书 *fml.*〉弹琴 play the zither

【抚慰】fǔwèi 安慰 comfort; console; soothe:

百般～ do everything to comfort sb.｜～灾民 console the people in a disaster-stricken area

【抚恤】fǔxù（国家或组织）对因公受伤或致残的人员，或因公牺牲以及病故的人员的家属进行安慰并给以物质帮助（of the state or an organization）comfort and compensate the family of an employee who has been injured, disabled or killed in the line of duty

【抚养】fǔyǎng 爱护并教养 foster; raise; rear; bring up：～子女 rear（or bring up）one's children

【抚育】fǔyù ❶ 照料、教育儿童，使健康地成长 care for and educate children to ensure their healthy growth：～孤儿 bring up orphans ❷ 照管动植物，使很好地生长 tend or look after animals or plants so they grow well：～幼畜 tend young animals｜～森林 tend the forest

【抚掌】fǔzhǎng same as 拊掌 fǔzhǎng

拊 fǔ〈书 *fml.*〉拍 clap：～手 clap hands｜～掌 clap hands

【拊膺】fǔyīng〈书 *fml.*〉拍胸，表示悲痛 beat one's chest to express grief：～长叹 beat one's chest and sigh deeply｜～顿足 beat one's chest and stamp one's feet

【拊掌】fǔzhǎng〈书 *fml.*〉拍手 clap hands：～大笑 clap hands and laugh loudly; also 抚掌 fǔzhǎng

斧 fǔ ❶ 斧子 axe; hatchet：板～ broad axe ❷〈古代 *arch.*〉一种兵器 battleaxe, a kind of weapon：～钺 axe and battleaxe

【斧头】fǔ·tóu same as 斧子 fǔ·zi

【斧削】fǔxuē〈书 *fml.*〉斧正 chop with an axe; make corrections

【斧钺】fǔyuè〈书 *fml.*〉斧和钺，古代兵器，用于斩刑。借指重刑 axe and battleaxe; ancient weapons used for execution; capital punishment：甘冒～以陈 state one's opinions at the risk of one's life

【斧凿】fǔzáo ❶ 斧子和凿子 axe and chisel ❷〈比喻 *fig.*〉诗文词句造作，不自然（of literary writing）artificial; affected：～痕 marks of hatchet and chisel — deliberate attempts to embellish a text

【斧正】fǔzhèng〈书 *fml.*〉〈敬辞 *pol.*〉用于请人改文章 submit my humble writing for correction; also 斧政 fǔzhèng

【斧锧】fǔzhì〈古代 *arch.*〉斩人的刑具，像铡刀 executioner's block and axe

【斧子】fǔ·zi 砍竹、木等用的金属工具，头呈楔形，装有木柄 axe; hatchet; tool with metal wedge-shaped head and wooden handle, used for splitting bamboo and cutting wood

府 fǔ ❶〈旧时 *old*〉指官吏办理公事的地方，现在指国家政权机关 seat of government; government office：官～ government (esp. local government)｜政～ government ❷〈旧时 *old*〉官府收藏文书、财物的地方 archive or treasury of (local) government：～库 government repository（for archives, valuables, etc.）❸〈旧时 *old*〉指大官、贵族的住宅，现在也指某些国家元首办公或居住的地方 official residence; mansion：王～ residence（or palace）of a prince｜元首～ residence of the head of state｜总统～ presidential palace ❹〈敬辞 *pol.*〉称对方的家 your home：贵～your residence ❺ 唐朝至清朝的行政区划，比县高一级 prefecture;（from the Tang to the Qing dynasties）administrative division above the county level：开封～ prefecture of Kaifeng｜济南～ prefecture of Ji'nan ❻（Fǔ）姓 a surname

〈古 *arch.*〉same as 腑 fǔ

【府城】fǔchéng〈旧时 *old*〉指府一级的行政机构所在的城市 seat of a prefecture; prefectural capital

【府绸】fǔchóu 一种平纹棉织品，质地细密平滑，有光泽，多用来做衬衣 poplin; plain glossy weave, cotton cloth with fine and smooth texture, usu. used to make shirts

【府邸】fǔdǐ same as 府第 fǔdì

【府第】fǔdì 贵族官僚或大地主的住宅 mansion; mansion house; residence of aristocrats, high officials or wealthy landlords

【府上】fǔ·shàng〈敬辞 *pol.*〉称对方的家或老家 your home; your residence; your native place：改日我一定到～请教。I'll visit your residence to consult you some other day.｜您～是杭州吗？Are you from Hangzhou?

俛 fǔ〈书 *fml.*〉same as 俯 fǔ

☞ miǎn on p. 1337

俯 fǔ ❶ 头低下（跟'仰'相对 as opposed to 'face upward'）bow (one's head); bend forward or down：～首 stoop; bow one's head｜～视 overlook; look down at｜～冲 nose dive ❷〈敬辞 *pol.*〉〈旧时 *old*〉公文书信中用来称对方对自己的行动 [used in official documents or letters] deign to; condescend to：～允 condescend to grant; deign to approve

【俯察】fǔchá〈书 *fml.*〉❶ 向低处看 look down：仰观～ look up and down ❷〈敬辞 *pol.*〉称对方或上级对自己理解（of sb. or one's superior）deign to examine; kindly understand：所陈一切，尚祈～。I hope you will be so kind as to look into what I have described.

【俯冲】fǔchōng（飞机等）以高速度和大角度向下飞（of plane, etc.）dive; nose dive：～轰炸 dive-bombing｜老鹰从天空～下来。The eagle dived from the sky.

【俯伏】fǔfú 趴在地上（多表示屈服或崇敬 in subservience or respect）lie prostrate：～听命 humbly take orders

【俯角】fǔjiǎo 视线在水平线以下时，在视线所在的垂直平面内，视线与水平线所成的角叫做俯角 depression; angle of depression; angle between a horizontal line and a line of vision below it, in the vertical plane

俯角
Angle of Depression

【俯就】fǔjiù ❶〈敬辞 *pol.*〉用于请对方同意担任职务 condescend to take or accept (a position, etc.): 经理一职，尚祈～。I hope you will condescend to accept the position of manager. ❷ 迁就；将就 tolerate; make do with; put up with: 事事～ tolerate everything

【俯瞰】fǔkàn 俯视 overlook; look down at

【俯念】fǔniàn〈敬辞 *pol.*〉称对方或上级体念 (of another or one's superior) kindly bear in mind; be kind enough to consider: ～群情 give sympathetic consideration to public sentiment

【俯拾即是】fǔ shí jí shì 只要弯下身子来捡，到处都是。形容地上的某一类东西、要找的某一类例证、文章中的错别字等很多。not uncommon; (there are so many objects on the ground, examples, or wrongly written Chinese characters in an article that) one only has to stoop to find them; also 俯拾皆是 fǔ shí jiē shì

【俯视】fǔshì 从高处往下看 overlook; look down at: 站在山上～蜿蜒的公路 look down from a hilltop at a meandering road

【俯视图】fǔshìtú 由物体上方向下做正投影得到的视图 vertical view; view of an object from above; bird's-eye view; also 顶视图 dǐngshìtú

【俯首】fǔshǒu ❶ 低下头 bow one's head; stoop: ～沉思 bow one's head in thought ❷〈比喻 *fig.*〉顺从 obey: ～听命 obey submissively; be at sb.'s beck and call

【俯首帖耳】fǔ shǒu tiē ěr 形容非常驯服恭顺（含贬义 derog.）docile and obedient; servile; also 俯首贴耳 fǔ shǒu tiē ěr

【俯卧】fǔwò 脸朝下躺着 lie prostrate; lie on one's stomach: 战士一动也不动地～在地上。The soldier lay on all fours motionless.

【俯卧撑】fǔwòchēng 增强臂力的一种辅助性体育运动。两手和两前脚掌撑地，身体俯卧，连续平起平落。press-up; push-up; exercise to increase arm strength, in which person keeps a prone position with hands and balls of the feet on the ground, and pushes up and down by bending and straightening the arms

【俯仰】fǔyǎng〈书 *fml.*〉❶ 低头和抬头 lower and lift one's head: ～之间 in the twinkling of an eye; in an instant ❷ 指一举一动 action: ～由人 be at sb.'s beck and call

【俯仰由人】fǔ yǎng yóu rén〈比喻 *fig.*〉一切受人支配 completely controlled by another; be at sb.'s beck and call

【俯仰之间】fǔ yǎng zhī jiān 形容时间很短 in the twinkling of an eye; in an instant: ～，船已驶出港口。Very quickly, the ship sailed out of the harbour.

【俯允】fǔyǔn〈敬辞 *pol.*〉称对方或上级允许 (of another or one's superior) condescend to grant; deign to approve: 承蒙～所请，不胜感激。My gratitude knows no bounds at your kind granting of my request.

釜 fǔ〈古代 *arch.*〉指炊事用具，相当于现在的锅 cauldron; boiler; pan; pot: 破～沉舟 break the cauldrons and sink the boats (after crossing a river) — cut off all means of retreat; burn one's boat (or bridges) | ～底抽薪 remove firewood from underneath the cauldron; take drastic measures to deal with a critical situation; fundamental solution

【釜底抽薪】fǔ dǐ chōu xīn 抽去锅底下的柴火 remove firewood from underneath the cauldron;〈比喻 *fig.*〉从根本上解决 take drastic measures to deal with a critical situation; tackle a problem at the root; solve a problem once and for all

【釜底游鱼】fǔ dǐ yóu yú〈比喻 *fig.*〉处在极端危险境地的人 fish swimming in the bottom of a cauldron — person in extreme danger; doomed

辅 fǔ ❶ 辅助 assist; complement; supplement: ～币 fractional currency or money | 相～而行 assist one another along 派个助手～你工作。(I)'ll send an assistant to help with your work. ❷〈书 *fml.*〉国都附近的地方 areas round a national capital: 畿～ environs of a national capital

【辅币】fǔbì 辅助货币的简称 abbr. for 辅助货币 fǔzhù huòbì

【辅弼】fǔbì〈书 *fml.*〉辅佐 assist a ruler in governing a country: ～大臣 official who assists a ruler in governing a country

【辅车相依】fǔ chē xiāng yī《左传》僖公五年：'谚所谓辅车相依、唇亡齿寒者，其虞虢之谓也' *The Zuo Commentary · Duke Xi 5th Year*: 'The relationship between the dukedoms of Yu and Guo is just like the saying that the jaw and the gums cannot do without each other or that without the lips, the teeth will feel the cold.'（辅 *fu*: 颊骨 jaw; 车 *che*: 牙床 gums）;〈比喻 *fig.*〉两者关系密切，互相依存 (of two parties) closely related and interdependent

【辅导】fǔdǎo 帮助和指导 coach; tutor; guide: ～员 counsellor; instructor; assistant | 课外～ after-school tutoring | ～学生学习基础知识 guide students in learning basic knowledge

【辅料】fǔliào ❶ 对产品生产起辅助作用的材料 subsidiary material; supplementary material necessary for the production process：许多轻工业生产需用的原料和～得靠农业供应。Many light industrial products depend on agriculture for raw and supplementary materials. ❷ 指烹饪中的辅助原材料，如做菜用的葱、香菜、木耳等 side cooking ingredients; aromatics; garnish, e.g. scallion, coriander, edible black fungus, etc.

【辅音】fǔyīn 发音时气流通路有阻碍的音，如普通话语音的 b, t, s, m, l 等 consonant; speech sound made by partly or completely obstructing the flow of air through the mouth, e.g. b, t, s, m and l in standard Chinese; also 子音 zǐyīn

【辅助】fǔzhù ❶ 从旁帮助 assist; aid：多加～ offer plenty of assistance｜派个助手～你工作。(I)'ll send an assistant to help with your work. ❷ 辅助性的；非主要的 supplementary; supplemental; subsidiary; auxiliary：～劳动 supplemental labour｜～人员 auxiliaries

【辅助货币】fǔzhù huòbì 在本位货币之外发行的起辅助性作用的币值小的货币，如我国单位为角或分的人民币 fractional currency or money; coins or paper money of a smaller denomination than the basic monetary unit (e.g. *jiao* and *fen* of Renminbi in China); 简称 abbr. 辅币 fǔbì

【辅佐】fǔzuǒ 协助 assist (ruler in governing a country)：～朝政 assist a ruler in handling state affairs

脯 fǔ ❶ 肉干 dried meat：兔～ dried hare meat｜鹿～ dried venison ❷ 蜜饯果干 preserved fruit; candied fruit：果～ candied fruit｜桃～ preserved dried peach｜杏～ preserved apricot

☞ pú on p. 1499

頫 fǔ 〈书 *fml.*〉same as 俯 fǔ

腑 fǔ 〈中医 *Chin. med.*〉把胆、胃、大肠、小肠、三焦和膀胱叫六腑 six hollow organs (gallbladder, stomach, large intestine, small intestine, bladder and sanjiao); ☞ 脏腑 zàngfǔ on p. 2392

滏 fǔ 滏阳河(Fǔyáng Hé)，水名，在河北，与滹沱河会合后叫子牙河 Fuyang River in Hebei Province with the section that joins the Hutuo River called Ziya River

腐 fǔ ❶ 腐烂；变坏 rotten; decay; turn bad：～朽 moulder｜～败 decay; corrupt｜流水不～。Running water does not turn fetid. ❷ 豆腐 tofu; bean curd：～乳 fermented tofu with spices

【腐败】fǔbài ❶ same as 腐烂 fǔlàn ①：不要吃～的食物。Don't eat spoiled food.｜木材涂上油漆，可以防止～。A coat of paint will prevent wood from decaying. ❷ (思想)陈旧；(行为)堕落 (of ideas) outmoded; (of behaviour) degenerate; corrupt：～分子 degenerate; corrupt (or decadent) person ❸ (制度、组织、机构、措施等)混乱、黑暗 (of system, organization, institution, measure, etc.) chaotic; corrupt; fraudulent：政治～ corrupt politics; political corruption

【腐臭】fǔchòu 有机体腐烂后散发的臭味 smelly; putrid; foul odour of rotting organism：一股～难闻的气味 a putrid smell

【腐恶】fǔ'è 腐朽凶恶，也指腐朽凶恶的势力 corrupt and evil; corrupt and evil power

【腐化】fǔhuà ❶ 思想行为变坏(多指过分贪图享乐) (of thought and behaviour) degenerate; decay (from over-indulgence)：生活～ lead a dissipated life｜贪污～graft and corruption ❷ 使腐化堕落 corrupt; corrode; same as 腐蚀 fǔshí ②：封建余毒～了一些人的灵魂。Vestiges of pernicious feudal ideas have corroded some people's mentality. ❸ same as 腐烂 fǔlàn ①：尸体已经～。The corpse has decomposed.

【腐旧】fǔjiù 陈腐；陈旧 stale; outdated：～思想 outmoded thoughts or ideas

【腐烂】fǔlàn ❶ 有机体由于微生物的滋生而破坏 rot; decompose; putrefy; decay in an organism caused by micro-organisms：受伤的地方，肌肉开始～。The flesh around the wound has begun to putrefy. ❷ same as 腐败 fǔbài ②：生活～ lead a decadent (or dissolute) life｜～的灵魂 decadent soul ❸ same as 腐败 fǔbài ③：剥削制度～透顶。The system of exploitation was extremely corrupt.

【腐儒】fǔrú 迂腐不明事理的读书人 pedant; pedantic scholar

【腐乳】fǔrǔ 豆腐乳 fermented bean curd or tofu

【腐生】fǔshēng 生物分解有机物或已死的生物体，并摄取养分以维持生活，如大多数霉菌、细菌等都以这种方式生活 saprophytic, e.g. most fungi and bacteria that feed on organic or dead organisms

【腐蚀】fǔshí ❶ 通过化学作用，使物体逐渐消损破坏，如铁生锈，氢氧化钠破坏肌肉和植物纤维 corrode; etch; gradually destroy by chemical action. (For example, iron rusts, and sodium hydroxide destroys muscle and vegetable fibres.)：氢氟酸～性很强，能～玻璃。Hydrofluoric acid is very corrosive and can disintegrate glass. ❷ 使人在坏的思想、行为、环境等因素影响下逐渐变质堕落 pervert; corrupt; deprave; debauch (under the influence of evil thoughts, behaviour, and environment)：黄色读物会～青少年。Pornography corrupts young people.

【腐蚀剂】fǔshíjì 有腐蚀作用的化学物质，如氢氧化钠、硝酸 corrosive; corrodent; corrosive chemicals, e.g. sodium hydroxide and hydrogen nitrate

【腐熟】fǔshú 不易分解的有机物(如粪尿、秸秆、落叶、杂草)经过微生物的发酵分解,产生有效肥分,同时也形成腐殖质(of compost, etc.) thoroughly decompose (e.g. manure, night-soil, straw, leaf litter and weeds). Matters which resist decay are turned into fertilizer and humus after fermentation and decomposition by micro-organisms.

【腐朽】fǔxiǔ ❶ 木料等含有纤维的物质由于长时期的风吹、雨打或微生物的侵害而破坏 rot; decay; condition of fibrous matter (e.g. wood) after the effect of wind, rain or micro-organic decay over a long period of time: 埋在地里的木桩都~了。The wooden stake buried in the earth has rotted. ❷〈比喻 *fig.*〉思想陈腐、生活堕落或制度败坏(of ideas, living, system) decadent; degenerate; depraved; dissolute; rotten: 思想~ decadent ideology (or ideas)|~的生活 debauchery; dissolute (or depraved) life

【腐殖质】fǔzhízhì 已死的生物体在土壤中经微生物分解而形成的有机物质。黑褐色,含有植物生长发育所需要的一些元素,能改善土壤,增加肥力。humus; dark-brown organic matter formed by dead organisms decomposed by soil micro-organisms, containing elements necessary for plant growth, and capable of improving soil quality and fertility

【腐竹】fǔzhú 卷紧成条状的干豆腐皮 rolls of dried bean milk cream

黼 fǔ〈书 *fml.*〉same as 釜 fǔ

簠 fǔ〈古代 *arch.*〉祭祀时盛谷物的器皿,长方形,有盖,有耳 square sacrificial vessel for grain, with a cover and handles

黼 fǔ〈古代 *arch.*〉礼服上绣的半白半黑的花纹 black and white patterns embroidered on official robes

fù(ㄈㄨˋ)

父 fù ❶ 父亲 father: ~子 father and son|老~ elderly father ❷ 家族或亲戚中的长辈男子 male relative of an older generation: 祖~ grandfather|伯~ paternal uncle|舅~ maternal uncle

☞ fǔ on p. 601

【父辈】fùbèi 跟你父亲同辈的亲友 people of father's generation

【父本】fùběn 植物繁殖过程中亲代的雄性植株 male parent; ☞ 亲代 qīndài on p. 1558

【父老】fùlǎo 一国或一乡的长者 elders (of a country or district): ~兄弟 elders and brethren

【父母】fùmǔ 父亲和母亲 parents; father and mother

【父母官】fùmǔguān〈旧时 *old*〉指地方长官(多指州、县一级的) county magistrate or prefect (regarded by the local people as parents)

【父亲】fù·qin 有子女的男子是子女的父亲 father; man who has a child (or children)

【父权制】fùquánzhì 原始公社后期形成的男子在经济上及社会关系上占支配地位的制度。由于男子所从事的畜牧业和农业在生活中逐渐起决定作用,造成氏族内男子地位的上升与女子地位的下降。又由于对偶制婚姻的出现,子女的血统关系由确认生母转为确认生父。这样就形成了以男子为中心的父系氏族公社。patriarchy; social system formed in the later period of primitive communal society, in which males assumed dominance in economic and social relations. The growing importance of animal husbandry and agriculture carried out by men boosted men's status, to the detriment of the status of women within the clan. With the emergence of paired marriage, blood relationship was reckoned along the line of the biological father instead of the mother, which gave rise to a communal patrilineal clan centred on the male. ☞ 母权制 mǔquánzhì on p. 1373

【父系】fùxì ❶ 在血统上属于父亲方面的 paternal; belonging to the paternal bloodline: ~亲属 paternal relatives; relatives on the paternal side ❷ 父子相承的 patrilineal; paternal line: ~家族制度 patrilineal family system

【父兄】fùxiōng ❶ 父亲和哥哥 father and elder brothers ❷ 泛指家长 (in a broad sense) head of a family

【父执】fùzhí〈书 *fml.*〉父亲的朋友 father's friend

讣 fù ❶ 报丧 announce sb.'s death ❷ 报丧的信 obituary

【讣告】fùgào ❶ 报丧 announce sb.'s death ❷ 报丧的通知 obituary

【讣闻】fùwén 向亲友报丧的通知,多附有死者的事略 obituary; notice on the death of a family member, usu. including a short biography of the deceased; also 讣文 fùwén

付[1] fù ❶ 交给 commit; give; hand or turn over: 交~ turn over|托~ commit sth. to sb.'s care|~表决 put to the vote; take a vote|~诸实施 put into practice; carry out|~之一炬 burn; commit to the flames; set on fire|尽~东流 carried away on the east-flowing stream — all to no avail; come to naught ❷ 给(钱) pay: ~款 pay money; make payment|支~ pay out ❸ (Fù) 姓 a surname

付[2] fù same as 副[2] fù

【付丙】fùbǐng〈书 *fml.*〉(把信件等)用火烧掉 burn (a letter, etc.): 阅后~。After reading this, please burn it immediately. also 付丙丁 fù bǐngdīng (丙丁 *bingding*: 指火 fire)

【付出】fùchū 交出(款项、代价等) pay; expend (sum of money, price, etc.): ~现款 pay in cash|～辛勤的劳动 put in a lot of hard work

【付方】fùfāng 簿记账户的右方，记载资产的减少，负债的增加和净值的增加(跟'收方'相对 as opposed to 'debit side') credit; credit side; right-hand side of a standard account, which records asset reduction, and increases in debt and net worth; also 贷方 dàifāng

【付排】fùpái 稿件交给印刷部门排版(of manuscript) send to the compositor: 书稿已经～，不日即可与读者见面。The manuscript has been sent to the compositor, and will soon be published.

【付讫】fùqì 交清(多指款项 usu. of a bill) paid; pay up: 报费～ pay subscription for a newspaper

【付托】fùtuō 交给别人办理 entrust; put (sth.) in sb.'s charge: ～得人 have entrusted the matter to the right person|胜利地完成了祖国人民～给我们的任务。We have successfully fulfilled the task entrusted to us by the motherland and the people.

【付现】fùxiàn 交付现金 pay in cash; make cash payment: 购物一律要～，不收支票。All purchases must be paid in cash, no checks allowed.

【付型】fùxíng 稿件完成排版、校对后，把活字版制成纸型 turn the type plate into paper mould after composing and proof-reading; make paper moulds or matrices: 书稿已经～，不便再作大的改动。The paper moulds of the manuscript are completed, no more major changes can be made.

【付印】fùyìn ❶ 稿件交付出版社，准备出版 (of manuscript) send to the press ❷ 稿件已完成排版校对过程，交付印刷 turn over to the printing shop after composing and proof-reading: 清样签字后，才能～。The final proof must be signed before it goes to the printing shop.

【付邮】fùyóu 交给邮局递送 post; mail; sent by mail; take to the post

【付与】fùyǔ 拿出；交给 give; pay: 尽力完成时代～我们的使命。We will do our utmost to fulfil the mission conferred on us by our times.

【付账】fù//zhàng 赊购货物后，理发洗澡后，或在饭馆、茶馆吃喝后，付给应付的钱 pay a balance (after relying on credit to shop, get a haircut, go to a bathhouse, eat or drink at a restaurant or tea house)

【付之一炬】fù zhī yī jù 给它一把火，指全部烧毁 burn; commit to the flames; set on fire; turn to ashes; also 付诸一炬 fù zhū yī jù

【付之一笑】fù zhī yī xiào 一笑了之，表示毫不介意 laugh away; dismiss (sth.) with a laugh

【付诸东流】fù zhū dōng liú 把东西扔在东流的水里冲走 drift away on the east-flowing stream; 〈比喻 *fig.*〉希望落空，前功尽弃 wasted efforts; come to naught; lose all previous gains

【付梓】fùzǐ 〈古时 *arch.*〉用木版印刷，在木板上刻字叫梓，因此把稿件交付刊印叫付梓 turn over (a manuscript) for printing; send to press (梓 *zi*: cut wooden blocks for printing)

负 fù ❶ 背 (bēi) shoulder; carry on the back or shoulder: ～荆 bear bramble twigs to express remorse|～重 bear a (heavy) load or weight ❷ 担负 bear; take up: ～责任 take responsibility|身～重任 shoulder an important task ❸ 依仗；倚靠 rely on; have at one's back: ～隅 back to the wall|～险固守 resist resolutely by relying on one's strategic position ❹ 遭受 suffer; sustain: ～伤 be wounded; sustain an injury|～屈 suffer a grievance or injustice ❺ 享有 enjoy: 久～盛名 have long enjoyed a good reputation; have long been famous ❻ 亏欠；拖欠 owe; be indebted: ～债 be in debt; incur debts ❼ 背弃；辜负 fail (in duty, obligation, etc.) disappoint; betray: ～约 break a promise; go back on one's word|忘恩～义 ungrateful|有～重托 disappoint; fail the trust given one ❽ 失败(跟'胜'相对 as opposed to 'win') lose (battle, game, etc.); be defeated: 胜～ victory or defeat; success or failure; outcome (of war, etc.)|～于客队。The home team was defeated by the visiting team. ❾ 小于零的(跟'正'相对 as opposed to 'positive' or 'plus') minus; negative: ～数 negative number|～号 negative sign (－) ❿ 指得到电子的(跟'正'相对 as opposed to 'positive') receive electrons; negative: ～极 negative pole|～电 negative electricity

【负担】fùdān ❶ 承当(责任、工作、费用等) bear; carry; shoulder (a responsibility, work, expense, etc.) ❷ 承受的压力或担当的责任、费用等 burden; load; weight; strain; encumbrance: 思想～ mental burden; weight on one's mind|家庭～ family burden (esp. financial)|减轻～ lighten the load

【负电】fùdiàn 物体得到多余电子时表现出带电现象，这种性质的电叫做负电 negative electricity; electricity present when an object receives a surplus of electrons; also 阴电 yīndiàn

【负荷】fùhè ❶〈书 *fml.*〉same as 负担 fùdān ①: 不克～ unable to bear the load ❷ 动力设备、机械设备以及生理组织等在单位时间内所担负的工作量。也指建筑构件承受的重量。load; performance capacity; (of power and mechanical equipment, organic tissue, etc.) load per unit of time; load that construction components can sustain; also 负载 fùzài or 载荷 zàihè

【负极】fùjí same as 阴极 yīnjí ①

【负荆】fùjīng 战国时，廉颇和蔺相如同在赵国做官。蔺相如因功大，拜为上卿，位在廉颇之上。

廉颇不服，想侮辱蔺相如。蔺相如为了国家的利益，处处退让。后来廉颇知道了，感到很惭愧，就脱了上衣，背着荆条，向蔺相如请罪，请他责罚（见于《史记·廉颇蔺相如列传》）。后来用'负荆'表示认错赔礼。bear bramble twigs to express contrition. Lian Po and Lin Xiangru were officials of the state of Zhao during the Warring States Period. In recognition of his great merit, Lin Xiangru was appointed senior minister, a position which put him above Lian Po in rank. The chagrined Lian Po took every opportunity to slight him. In the interest of the state, Lin Xiangru went out of his way to avoid the conflict. When Lian Po finally realized this he felt very ashamed. He removed his upper garment, put some bramble twigs on his back and went to Lin Xiangru to ask for punishment (*Records of the Historian · Biographies of Lian Po and Lin Xiangru*). 负荆 fùjīng has later been used to mean 'apologize'：～请罪 proffer bramble twigs and ask for a flogging — make a humble and heartfelt apology; express deep contrition

【负疚】fùjiù〈书 *fml.*〉自己觉得抱歉，对不起人 be apologetic; feel guilty; feel conscience-stricken：事情没办好，感到～。(I) feel guilty for not completing the task properly.

【负离子】fùlízǐ 带负电荷的离子。如氯离子 Cl^-、硝酸根离子 NO_3^- 等。anion; ion with negative charge, e.g. chlorine ion (Cl^-), nitrate ion (NO_3^-); also 阴离子 yīnlízǐ

【负利率】fùlìlǜ 低于同期物价上涨幅度的利率 negative interest; interest rate lower than rate of prices increase in the same period

【负面】fùmiàn 坏的、消极的一面；反面 downside; negative：～效果 negative effect｜～影响 unfavourable influence

【负片】fùpiàn 经曝光、显影、定影等处理后的胶片，物像的明暗与实物相反（黑白胶片）或互为补色（彩色胶片），用来印制正片 negative; film treated by exposing, developing, fixing, etc., where black and white are reversed (in black-and-white film) or complementary (in colour film); used to make prints

【负气】fùqì 赌气 (do sth.) in a fit of pique：～出走 leave home in a fit of pique; walk out in a huff

【负屈】fùqū 遭受委屈或冤屈 suffer a grievance or injustice：～含冤 be falsely accused and have no hope of redress

【负伤】fù//shāng 受伤 sustain an injury; be wounded：因公～ injured while on duty; work-related injury｜他在战争中负过伤。He was wounded in battle.

【负数】fùshù 小于零的数，如 －3，－0.25 negative number, such as －3 and －0.25

【负心】fùxīn 背弃情谊（多指转移爱情 esp. in love) untrue; fickle; ungrateful; heartless：～汉 fickle-hearted man

【负隅】fùyú（敌人或盗贼）倚靠险要的地势（抵抗）(of enemy or bandit) (put up a resistance) at a strategic place：～顽抗 put up a desperate resistance with one's back to the wall. also 负嵎 fùyú

【负嵎】fùyú same as 负隅 fùyú

【负约】fùyuē 违背诺言；失约 break a promise; go back on one's word

【负载】fùzài same as 负荷 fùhè ②

【负责】fùzé ❶ 担负责任 be responsible; be in charge of; bear responsibility for; be accountable for：～后勤工作 be in charge of general service｜这里的事由你～。You are responsible for the work here. ❷（工作）尽到应尽的责任；认真塌实 conscientious：他对工作很～。He is very conscientious in his work.

【负债】fù//zhài 欠人钱财 be in debt; incur debts：～累累 be heavily in debt; be over head and ears in debt

【负债】fùzhài 资产负债表的一方，表现营业资金的来源 liabilities; part of a statement of assets and liabilities indicating source of capital; ☞ 资产负债表 zīchǎn fùzhài biǎo on p. 2537

【负重】fùzhòng ❶ 背上背（bēi）着沉重的东西 bear heavy load or weight：～竞走 loaded footrace｜～泅渡 swim across with a load ❷ 承担重任 shoulder an important task：忍辱～ endure humiliation in order to discharge important duties

妇(婦) fù ❶ 妇女 woman：～科 (department of) gynaecology｜～幼 women and children｜～联（妇女联合会）Women's Federation (abbr. for 妇女联合会 fùnǚ liánhéhuì) ❷ 已婚的女子 married woman：少～ young married woman ❸ 妻 wife：夫～ man and wife

【妇道】fùdào〈旧时 *old*〉指妇女应该遵守的行为准则 female virtues; rules of proper female behaviour：克尽～ strictly observe the rules of proper female behaviour｜谨守～ carefully observe the rules of proper female behaviour

【妇道】fù·dao 指妇女 women; womenfolk：～人家 women; womenfolk

【妇科】fùkē 医院中专门治妇女病的一科 (department of) gynaecology

【妇女】fùnǚ 成年女子的通称 general term for woman：～干部 woman cadre｜劳动～ labouring (or working) women

【妇女病】fùnǚbìng 妇女特有的病症，如月经病 women's disease; gynaecological disease, e.g. menstrual disorders

【妇女节】fùnǚjié ☞ 三八妇女节 Sān-Bā Fùnǚ Jié on p. 1650

【妇孺】fùrú 妇幼 women and children：～皆知。Even women and children know.

【妇幼】fùyòu 妇女和儿童 women and children：～卫生 maternity and child care｜～保健站 health centre for women and children

汉 fù 湖汉(Húfù)，地名，在江苏 Hufu, place name, in Jiangsu Province

附(坿) fù ❶ 附带 add; attach; append; enclose; include：～设 affiliate to｜～则 supplementary article (appended to a treaty, decree, etc.)｜～寄照片一张 enclose a photograph｜你给我再～上一笔，让他收到信后就回信。Please add a word in the letter asking him to reply as soon as he receives it. ❷ 靠近 approach; near; be close by：～近 nearby; adjacent; neighbouring｜～在他的耳朵旁边低声说话。A man whispered in his ear. ❸ 依从；依附 attach oneself to; depend on; comply with：～议 second a motion; support a proposal｜～庸 dependency; vassal｜魂不～体 frightened out of one's wits

【附白】fùbái 附上说明 attached explanation：这部书上卷的插画说明印错了，拟在下卷里～订正。There was an error in the caption in the first volume, so a corrigendum is going to be printed in the second volume.

【附笔】fùbǐ 书信、文件等写完后另外加上的话 additional note; postscript (PS) (to a letter, document, etc.)

【附带】fùdài ❶ 另外有所补充的；顺便 supplementary; incidentally; in passing：～条件 additional conditions｜～声明一句 make an incidental announcement ❷ 非主要的 secondary：～的劳动 supplementary labour

【附耳】fù'ěr 嘴贴近别人的耳边（小声说话） whisper in sb.'s ear：～低语 whisper in sb.'s ear｜他们俩～谈了几句。The two whispered a few words to each other.

【附睾】fùgāo 男子和雄性哺乳动物生殖器官的一部分，附于睾丸的后上缘，由许多弯曲的小管构成，功用是储存精子 epididymis; parastata; part of man's and male mammal's reproductive organs, situated on the back upper side of the testis, and consisting of many small, twisting tubes for storing sperm

【附和】fùhè （言语、行动）追随别人（多含贬义 usu. derog.）(of speech or behaviour) echo; chime in with; parrot; toady：随声～ chime in with others to say the right things

【附会】fùhuì 把没有关系的事物说成有关系；把没有某种意义的事物说成有某种意义 see links where there are none; attribute a certain significance where none exists：牵强～ unconvincing; draw a forced analogy｜穿凿～ give strained interpretations and draw far-fetched analogies; also 傅会 fùhuì

【附骥】fùjì 蚊蝇附在好马的尾巴上，可以远行千里 mosquito or fly can ride a thousand *li* on the tail of a good horse;〈比喻 *fig.*〉依附名人而出名 win fame by attaching oneself to a well-known person; ride to success on sb.'s coattails; bask in reflected glory; also 附骥尾 fùjìwěi

【附加】fùjiā ❶ 附带加上；额外加上 add; attach; append：条文后面～两项说明。Two explanatory notes are attached at the end of the document.｜除运费外，还得～手续费。Apart from transport expenses, a service charge has to be added. ❷ 附带的；额外的 additional; appended; attached：～刑 accessory punishment｜～税 surtax; supertax; additional tax; additional duty

【附加刑】fùjiāxíng ☞ 从刑 cóngxíng on p. 325

【附件】fùjiàn ❶ 随同主要文件一同制定的文件 appendix; annex; side document drawn up at the same time as the primary one ❷ 随同文件发出的有关的文件或物品 other document or object distributed with the main document enclosed ❸ 组成机器、器械的某些零件或部件；机器、器械成品附带的零件或部件 accessory; attachment; mechanical spare part or component that goes with a finished product：汽车～ car accessories｜新买的机器没有带～。The new machine has no spare parts attached.

【附近】fùjìn ❶ 靠近某地的 nearby; adjacent; neighbouring：～地区 neighbouring areas; nearby region｜～居民 neighbouring residents ❷ 附近的地方 close by; in the vicinity of：他家就在～，几分钟就可以走到。His house is only a few minutes' walk from here.

【附丽】fùlì〈书 *fml.*〉依附；附着 rely on; adhere to; attach oneself to：无所～ nothing to rely on; no support

【附录】fùlù 附在正文后面与正文有关的文章或参考资料 appendix; related article or information attached to the end of a primary text：词典正文后面有五种～。There are five appendixes (or appendices) to the text of the dictionary.

【附逆】fùnì 投靠叛逆集团 throw one's lot in with the rebels; join the rebels：变节～ treacherous rebellion

【附设】fùshè 附带设置 attached to an institution：这个图书馆～了一个读书指导部。The library also has a department offering reading guidance.

【附属】fùshǔ ❶ 某一机构所附设或管辖的（学校、医院等）subsidiary; auxiliary; attached (school, hospital, etc.)：～小学 attached or affiliated primary school｜～工厂 auxiliary factory ❷ 依附；归属 attached to; affiliated with：这所医院～于医科大学。This hospital is affiliated with (or attached to) the medical university.

【附属国】fùshǔguó 名义上保有一定的主权，但在经济和政治方面以某种形式从属于其他国家的国家 dependency; dependent state; state which retains part of its sovereignty in name, but is in certain ways dependent on another state economically and politically

【附送】fùsòng 附带赠送 give complimentary gifts：在本店购买收录机一台，～录音带两盒。Buy a cassette recorder at our shop and you'll get two cassette tapes for free.

【附小】fùxiǎo 附属小学的简称 abbr. for 附属小学 fùshǔ xiǎoxué

【附议】fùyì 同意别人的提议，作为共同提议人 second a motion; support a proposal：小陈提议选老魏为工会主席，还有两个人～。Xiao Chen proposed to elect Lao Wei president of the trade union, and two other people supported (or seconded) the motion.

【附庸】fùyōng ❶〈古代 *arch.*〉指附属于大国的小国，今借指为别的国家所操纵的国家 vassal; small state subordinate to a large state; dependency; state controlled by another; client state ❷ 泛指依附于其他事物而存在的事物 (in a broad sense) anything that depends on sth. else for its existence; appendage; hanger-on：语言文字学在清代还只是经学的～。During the Qing Dynasty, philology was a mere appendage of the study of Confucian classics.

【附庸风雅】fùyōng fēngyǎ 为了装点门面而结交名士，从事有关文化的活动 (of officials, landlords, merchants, etc.) mingle with men of letters and pose as a lover of culture; pretend to be a connoisseur of art and literature

【附载】fùzǎi 附带记载 appendix; subsidiary note：省委的报告后面还～了三个县委的调查报告。The investigation reports of three county Party committees were appended to the report of the provincial Party committee.

【附则】fùzé 附在法规、条约、规则、章程等后面的补充性条文，一般是关于生效日期、修改程序等的规定 supplementary articles dealing with effective date and revision procedure appended to a law or regulation, treaty, decree, charter, etc.

【附识】fùzhì 附在文章、书刊上的有关记述 notes appended to an article, book or periodical：再版～ supplementary notes to the second edition

【附中】fùzhōng 附属中学的简称 abbr. for 附属中学 fùshǔ zhōngxué

【附注】fùzhù 补充说明或解释正文的文字，放在篇后，或一页的末了，或用括号插在正文中间 notes appended to a book, etc.; annotation; supplementary introduction or explanation to the text, placed at the end of an article or at the bottom of a page, or bracketed in the text

【附着】fùzhuó 较小的物体黏着在较大的物体上 (of a small object) adhere to; stick to; cling to (a large one)：这种病菌～在病人使用过的东西上。The bacteria is found on the things used by the patients.

咐 fù ☞［吩咐］(fēnfù) on p.572

阜 fù〈书 *fml.*〉❶ 土山 earth mound ❷（物资）多 abundant：物～民丰。Products abound and the people live well.

服 fù〈量词 *classifier*〉用于中药；剂 (of Chinese medicine) dose：一～药 a dose of medicine

☞ fú on p.596

驸 fù〈古代 *arch.*〉几匹马共同拉一辆车时，驾辕之外的马叫驸 extra horse harnessed by the side of a team of horses drawing a cart

【驸马】fùmǎ 汉代有'驸马都尉'的官职，后来皇帝的女婿常做这个官，因此驸马成为皇帝的女婿的专称 *fuma*; emperor's son-in-law, a term derived from *fuma duwei* (commandant-escort in charge of horses pulling the imperial carriage, an official title instituted by King Wu of the Han Dynasty), owing to the fact that it later gradually became a common practice for an emperor to confer this title on his son-in-law

赴 fù ❶ 到(某处)去 attend; go to; be bound for：～会 attend a meeting; meet sb. by appointment｜～宴 go to a banquet｜～京 go to Beijing; go to the capital ❷ 在水里游 swim：～水 swim ❸ same as 讣 fù

【赴敌】fùdí〈书 *fml.*〉到战场去跟敌人作战 go to the battlefront to fight

【赴难】fùnàn 赶去拯救国家的危险 step forward to the salvation of one's country; help protect the nation from danger：慷慨～fight heroically for national salvation

【赴汤蹈火】fù tāng dǎo huǒ〈比喻 *fig.*〉不避艰险 be ready to jump into boiling water and plunge into raging fire; go through hell and high water; be ready to risk one's life：为了人民的利益，～，在所不辞。In the interests of the people, we will not flinch from the most hazardous tasks.

【赴约】fùyuē 去和约会的人见面 meet sb. by appointment; keep an appointment

复[1]（複）fù ❶ 重复 repeat; duplicate：～写 duplicate; make carbon copies｜～制 duplicate; reconstruct; reproduce; make a copy of｜～线 double or dual track; multiple track ❷ 繁复 compound; complicated; complex：～姓 compound surname; two-character surname｜～分数 complex fraction｜～比例 compound ratio; double ratio

复[2]（復）fù ❶ 转过去或转回来 turn back and forth; turn over：反～ chop and change; behave capriciously; reverse back and forth｜往～ move back and forth; repeat oneself｜翻来～去 repeated; toss and turn ❷ 回答；答复 answer; reply：～信 reply; respond; write a letter in reply｜敬～ reply with respect | 电～ reply by wire; cable a reply

复[3]（復） fù ❶ 恢复 recover; resume: 光～ recover | 收～ recover; recapture | ～原 restore; rehabilitate; recover from an illness | ～婚 restoration of a marriage; resumption of matrimonial relations; reunion of a couple after divorce ❷ 报复 revenge: ～仇 revenge; avenge

复[4]（復） fù 再；又 again; repeatedly: ～发 recur; have a relapse | ～苏 recovery; resuscitate; come back to life or consciousness | 死灰～燃 resurgence; revival; dying embers glow again | 无以～加 could not be more ...; in the extreme | 一去不～返 (sth.) comes but once; go never to return

【复本】fùběn 同一种书刊收藏不止一部时，第一部以外的称为复本 duplicate copy; when several copies of a work are collected, all those other than the original are duplicate copies

【复本位制】fùběnwèizhì 一国同时用黄金和白银作本位货币的货币制度 bimetallism; monetary system using both gold and silver as the monetary standard of a country

【复辟】fùbì 失位的君主复位。泛指被推翻的统治者恢复原有的地位或被消灭的制度复活。restoration; comeback; restore a dethroned monarch; restore the old order; reinstate an overthrown ruler or revive a defunct system

【复查】fùchá 再一次检查 reexamine; check again: 上次透视发现肺部有阴影，今天去～。A shadow was found on his lungs in the last X-ray, so he went for a reexamination today.

【复仇】fù//chóu 报仇 revenge; avenge: ～雪耻 avenge an insult; take revenge to assuage one's honour

【复出】fùchū 不再担任职务或停止社会活动的人又出来担任职务或参加社会活动（多指名人 usu. of prominent person） return to public life and resume an official position; make a comeback

【复发】fùfā （患过的病）再次发作 recur; have a relapse

【复方】fùfāng ❶〈中医 *Chin. med.*〉指由两个或两个以上成方配成的方子 medicinal compound; compound of two or more prescriptions of herbal medicines: ～丹参片 compound tablet of *danshen*, root of red-rooted salvia (*Salvia miltiorrhiza*) ❷ 西医指成药中含有两种或两种以上药品的 medicine with two or more ingredients; medicinal compound: ～阿司匹林 aspirin compound (APC)

【复分解】fùfēnjiě 两种化合物经过化学反应互相交换成分而生成两种另外的化合物，如氯化钠和硝酸银反应生成硝酸钠和氯化银 double decomposition; process by which two parts of two chemical compounds exchange components to form two new ones, e.g. sodium chloride and silver nitrate reacting to produce sodium nitrate and silver chloride

【复辅音】fùfǔyīn 两个或更多的辅音结合在一起叫复辅音，如俄语 КНИГА（书）中的 КН，英语 spring（春天）中的 spr 等。有的书把塞擦音（如普通话语音的 z，zh，j，c，ch，q）和送气音（如普通话语音的 p，t，k，c，ch，q）也叫做复辅音。consonant cluster; cluster of two or more consonants, such as КН in КНИГА (Russian for 'book') and 'spr' in 'spring'. Some works also define affricates (e.g. z, zh, j, c, ch, q in standard Chinese) and aspirates (e.g. p, t, k, c, ch, q in standard Chinese) as consonant clusters.

【复工】fù//gōng 停工或罢工后恢复工作 return to work (after a strike or stoppage)

【复古】fùgǔ 恢复古代的制度、风尚、观念等 restore ancient systems, customs, ideas, etc.; return to the past; turn back the clock: 学习古代文化，不是为了～，而是古为今用。We study ancient culture to make the past serve the present, not to turn back the clock.

【复归】fùguī 回复到（某种状态） return to the original state; go back to a former condition: 暴风雨过后，湖面～平静。Calm returned to the lake after the storm.

【复果】fùguǒ 果实的一类，由生长在一个花序上的许多花的成熟子房和其他花器官联合发育而成。如菠萝、无花果等的结实。multiple fruit; compound fruit; collective fruit; fruit formed by the coalescence of mature ovaries and other accessory parts of many flowers growing on a single inflorescence, e.g. pineapple and fig; also 聚花果 jùhuāguǒ

【复合】fùhé 合在一起；结合起来 compound; complex; composite: ～词 compound word | ～元音 compound vowel; diphthong or triphthong | ～材料 composite; composite or complex material

【复合词】fùhécí ☞ 合成词 héchéngcí on p. 781

【复合量词】fùhé liàngcí 表示复合单位的量词，如'架次、人次、秒立方米、吨公里' compound classifier (e.g. sortie, person-time, cubic metre per second, and ton kilometre)

【复合元音】fùhé yuányīn 在一个音节里的音值前后不一致的元音，发音时嘴唇和舌头从一个元音的位置过渡到另一个元音的位置，如普通话语音中的 ai，ei，ao，ou，uai，uei 等 compound vowel; diphthong or triphthong; vowel whose value quality varies within a syllable, produced by moving lips and tongue from the position of pronouncing one vowel to that of another, e.g. ai, ei, ao, ou, uai, uei, etc. in standard Chinese

【复核】fùhé ❶ 审查核对 check; cross-check: 把报告里面的数字～一下 check the data in the report ❷ 法院判处死刑案件的特定司法程序。在我国指最高人民法院对于判处死刑的案件做再一次的审核。specific judicial process in cases involving a death sentence. The Supreme People's Court of China makes it a point to review cases in which a death sentence has been passed by a lower court.

【复会】fù//huì 中途停止的会议恢复开会 resume (a session or meeting)

【复婚】fù//hūn 离婚的男女恢复婚姻关系 restoration of a marriage; reunion of a couple after divorce; resumption of matrimonial relations

【复活】fùhuó ❶ 死了又活过来。多用于比喻。(usu. fig.) revive; come back to life: 经过修理,报废的车床又～了。The scrapped lathe was repaired and returned to use. ❷ 使复活 resuscitate; resurrect; revive; bring back to life: 反对～军国主义 oppose the resurgence (or revival) of militarism

【复活节】Fùhuó Jié 基督教纪念耶稣复活的节日,是春分后第一次月圆之后的第一个星期日 Easter; Christian festival in commemoration of the resurrection of Jesus, falling on the first Sunday after the first full moon following the Vernal Equinox

【复交】fùjiāo ❶ 恢复交谊 restore friendship; resume relations ❷ 特指恢复外交关系 re-establish or resume diplomatic relations

【复旧】fù//jiù ❶ 恢复陈旧的习俗、观念、制度等 restore old ways (such as customs, ideas, systems); return to the past ❷ 恢复原来的样子 restore; rehabilitate; return to original state: ～如初 be restored to (one's original state or status)

【复句】fùjù 语法上指能分成两个或两个以上相当于单句的分段的句子,如:梅花才落,杏花又开了|河不深,可是水太冷|明天不下雨,我们上西山去。这三个复句各包含两个分句。同一复句里的分句,说的是有关系的事。一个复句只有一个句终语调,不同于连续的几个单句。sentence with two or more clauses; complex, or compound sentence. (For example, each of the following three complex sentences contains two clauses: Chinese plum flowers have faded but apricot flowers now are in bloom. *or* The river is not deep, but the water is very cold. *or* If it does not rain tomorrow, we will go to the Western Hills.) The clauses of a compound sentence describe related matters. A compound sentence has only one ending intonation, unlike a string of simple sentences. ☞ 分句 fēnjù on p. 569

【复刊】fù//kān (报刊)停刊后恢复刊行 (of magazine or newspaper) resume publication

【复课】fù//kè 停课或罢课后恢复上课 resume classes

【复利】fùlì 计算利息的一种方法,把前一期的利息和本金加在一起算做本金,再计算利息 compound interest; interest that is calculated on the sum both principal and accrued interest

【复名数】fùmíngshù 带有两个或两个以上单位名称的数,如 5 元 8 角、3 丈 5 尺 2 寸等 compound number; quantity expressed in two or more denominations or units, as 5 *yuan* 8 *jiao*, 3 *zhang* 5 *chi* 2 *cun*, etc.

【复明】fùmíng 眼失明后恢复视力 regain one's eyesight; recover lost vision: 白内障患者,有的可以经过手术～。Some people with cataracts regain their eyesight after operations.

【复命】fùmìng 执行命令后回报 report (to one's superiors) on completion of a task

【复赛】fùsài 体育竞赛中初赛后决赛前进行的比赛 intermediary heat; competition after the preliminary trials and before the final

【复审】fùshěn ❶ 再一次审查 reexamine; recheck; cross-check: 稿子初审已过,有待～。The manuscript has gone through the first check and will be cross-checked. ❷ 法院对已审理的案件再一次进行审理 review a case

【复生】fùshēng 复活 revive; bring back to life

【复市】fùshì 商店、集市等罢市或停止营业后恢复营业 reopen a shop or market; resume business etc. (after a strike or stoppage)

【复试】fùshì 有些考试分两次举行,第一次叫做初试,第二次叫做复试(一般是第一次考普通科目,及格后再考专门科目) final round of examinations; some examinations proceed through two stages, the preliminary examination and the final one. The preliminary examination tests general subjects, only those who pass may sit in the final round.

【复述】fùshù ❶ 把别人说过的话或自己说过的话重说一遍 repeat (one's own or another's words) ❷ 语文教学上指学生把读物的内容用自己的话说出来,是教学方法之一 retell; language-teaching method in which student retells a text in his or her own words

【复数】fùshù ❶ 某些语言中由词的形态变化等表示的属于两个或两个以上的数量。例如英语里 book(书,单数)指一本书,books(书,复数)指两本或两本以上的书。plural form; in some languages, form of a word denoting two or more in number (e.g. in English, 'books' is the plural of 'book') ❷ 形如 $a+bi$ 的数叫做复数。其中 a,b 是实数,$i^2=-1$,i 是虚数单位。a 叫做复数的实部,bi 叫做复数的虚部。如 $1-3i$,$5i$ 都是复数。complex number; mathematical expression $a+bi$, in which a and b are real numbers, $i^2=-1$, i is an imaginary number; a is called the real part, and b, the imaginary part, e.g. $1-3i$ and $5i$ are all complex numbers

【复苏】fùsū ❶ 生物体或离体的器官、组织或细胞等在生理机能极度减缓后又恢复正常的生命活动;苏醒过来 resuscitate; revive; return to normal function of an organism organ, tissue or cell, separated from the body, after a period of slowdown in physiological function; come back to life or consciousness：死而～ come back to life ◇大地～，麦苗返青。Wheat seedlings turn green as the earth comes back to life. ❷ 资本主义再生产周期中继萧条之后的一个阶段，其特征是生产逐渐恢复，市场渐趋活跃，物价回升，利润增加等 resurgence; recovery; stage in the cycle of capitalist reproduction after a depression, characterized by gradual resumption of production, market dynamism, rising prices and increasing profits：经济～ economic recovery

【复位】fù//wèi ❶ 脱位的骨关节回复到原来的部位 reset; reduce; put a dislocated joint back into its original position ❷ 失去地位的君主重新掌权 (of deposed monarch) regain the throne; resume power

【复胃】fùwèi 反刍动物的胃 complex stomach (of ruminant); ruminant stomach; stomachus compositus

【复习】fùxí 重复学习学过的东西，使巩固 revise; review what has been learnt：～功课 review one's lessons｜～提纲 revision outline

【复线】fùxiàn 有两组或两组以上轨道的铁道或电车道，相对方向的车辆可以同时通行（区别于'单线' as compared with 'single track'） double or dual track; multiple track (for trains or trams, so vehicles moving in opposite directions may run at the same time)

【复写】fùxiě 把复写纸夹在两张或几张纸之间书写，一次可以写出若干份 duplicate; make carbon copies; place carbon paper between two or more sheets of paper to make duplicate copies

【复写纸】fùxiězhǐ 一种涂着蜡质颜料供复写或打字用的纸 carbon paper; paper covered with a coloured wax layer used for making written or typed duplicates

【复信】fù//xìn 答复来信 reply; write a letter in reply：及时～ timely reply｜收到读者来信后，就立即复了信。Replies were immediately sent out in response to letters from readers.

【复信】fùxìn 答复的信 reply; reply letter：信寄出很久了，还没有收到～。The letter was posted many days ago, but no reply has been received yet.

【复兴】fùxīng ❶ 衰落后再兴盛起来 revival; reinvigoration; renaissance; rejuvenation：民族～ national revival｜文艺～ Renaissance ❷ 使复兴 revive; reinvigorate; rejuvenate：～国家 rejuvenate the country｜～农业 reinvigorate agriculture

【复姓】fùxìng 不止一个字的姓，如欧阳、司马等 compound surname; two-character surname, e. g. Ouyang and Sima

【复学】fù//xué 休学或退学后再上学 go back to school (after absence of leave); resume interrupted studies

【复眼】fùyǎn 昆虫主要的视觉器官，由许多六角形的小眼构成，例如蚂蚁一个复眼由 50 个小眼构成 compound eye (of insects); primary visual organ of insects composed of many little hexagonal eyes (e. g. the compound eye of the ant is composed of 50 little eyes)

【复业】fùyè ❶ 恢复本业 take up one's old occupation; reestablish one's business ❷ 商店停业后恢复营业 reopen; (of shop) resume business after a close-down：饭店停业整顿，年后～。The hotel suspended business in order to reorganize, and will reopen in a year's time.

【复议】fùyì 对已做决定的事做再一次的讨论 reconsider (decision); revisit (issue)：事关大局，厂领导还要～。The issue affects the overall situation, so factory management will reconsider it.

【复音】fùyīn 由许多纯音组成的声音。复音的频率用组成这个复音的基音的频率来表示。一般乐器发出的声音都是复音。complex tone; sound composed of many pure tones, whose frequency is indicated by that of its fundamental tone. Sounds made by common musical instruments are complex tones.

【复音词】fùyīncí 有两个或几个音节的词。如葡萄、服务、革命、共产党等。word with two or more syllables; disyllabic or polysyllabic word e. g. 葡萄 pú·táo，服务 fúwù，革命 gémìng and 共产党 gòngchǎndǎng, etc.

【复印】fùyìn 照原样重印，特指用复印机重印 duplicate; photocopy; xerox; copy on copy machine：～资料 duplicate materials｜～了十份设计图纸 reproduce (or xerox) ten design drawings

【复印机】fùyìnjī 利用光敏导体的静电特性和光敏特性将文件、图片等照原样重印在纸上的机器 duplicator; photocopier; Xerox copier; copy-machine that duplicates documents and photographs on paper by employing the light-sensitive conductors with specific electrostatic and light-sensitive properties

【复元】fù//yuán same as 复原 fù//yuán ①

【复员】fù//yuán ❶ 武装力量和一切经济、政治、文化等部门从战时状态转入和平状态 (of armed forces, and the economic, political and cultural departments, etc.) return to peacetime conditions ❷ 军人因服役期满或战争结束等原因而退出现役 demobilize; demob; (of servicemen) retire from active military service at the completion of the term of service or at the end of a war：～军人 ex-serviceman; demobilized solider｜～回乡 return to one's hometown after demobilization｜他去年从部队复了员。He was demobilized from the army last year.

【复原】fù//yuán ❶ 病后恢复健康 recover from an illness; be restored to health：身体已经～ recover one's health from a disease; also 复元

fù// yuán ❷ 恢复原状 restore; rehabilitate: 被破坏的壁画已无法～。The destroyed murals cannot be restored.

【复圆】fùyuán 日食或月食的过程中,月亮阴影和太阳圆面或地球阴影和月亮圆面第二次外切时的位置关系,也指发生这种位置关系的时刻。复圆是日食或月食过程的结束。fourth contact (of a total eclipse); last contact (of a partial eclipse); end of sun or moon eclipse; position of the moon's shadow in relation to the surface of the sun in a sun eclipse, or the second external tangent of the earth's shadow in relation to the surface of the moon in a moon eclipse, or the time when these positions occur at the end of a sun or moon eclipse; ☞ 食相 shíxiàng on p. 1746

【复杂】fùzá (事物的种类、头绪等)多而杂 (of content, aspects, etc.) complicated; complex; intricate: 颜色～ complex colours | ～的问题 complicated problem (or matter) | ～的人际关系 complicated interpersonal relationship

【复杂劳动】fùzá láodòng 需要经过专门训练,具有一定技术才能胜任的劳动(跟'简单劳动'相对 as opposed to 'simple labour') complex labour; labour that requires expertise acquired through special training

【复诊】fùzhěn 医疗部门指病人经过初诊后再来看病 further consultation after first visit (with doctor); subsequent visit (to doctor)

【复职】fù//zhí 解职后又恢复原职 resume one's post; be reinstated

【复制】fùzhì 仿造原件(多指艺术品)或翻印书籍等(usu. of works of art) duplicate; reproduce; make a copy of (books, etc.): ～品 replica; reproduction | 这些文物都是～的。These cultural artifacts are replicas.

【复种】fùzhòng 在同一块地上,一年播种和收获两次以上的耕作方法 multiple cropping; farming practice of sowing and harvesting more than twice a year on a field

【复壮】fùzhuàng 恢复品种的原有优良特性并提高种子的生活力 rejuvenate; restore original properties of a plant strain and improve its seed viability: 品种～ rejuvenation of seed strain | 某些春播作物进行冬播可以使种子～。The seeds of certain spring-sown crops can be rejuvenated by sowing in winter instead.

洑 fù 在水里游 swim: ～水 swim | ～过河去 swim across the river

☞ fú on p. 597

【洑水】fùshuǐ 在水里游 swim: ～过河 swim across the river

袱 fù ❶ 古代的一种祭祀,后死者附祭于祖庙 ancient sacrificial rite in which people who would die later offer sacrifice at an ancestral temple ❷〈书 *fml.*〉合葬 bury in the same grave; bury together

副1 fù ❶ 居第二位的;辅助的(区别于'正'或'主' as compare with 'chief, prime, principal' or 'principal, main') deputy; assistant; vice-: ～主席 vice-chairman | ～班长 deputy class monitor | ～食品 non-staple food or foodstuffs ❷ 辅助的职务;担任辅助职务的人 assistant post or position; assistant: 团～ subsidiary regimental commander | 二～ second mate ❸ 附带的 complementary; auxiliary; secondary: ～业 sideline; side occupation | ～作用 side-effect; by-effect; secondary action ❹ 符合 fit; correspond to: 名～其实 correspond with reality; in reality as well as in name | 名不～实 name falls short of the reality; in name but not in fact; unworthy of the name

副2 fù 〈量词 *classifier*〉 a)用于成套的东西 set; pair: 一～对联 a pair of antithetical couplets | 一～手套 a pair of gloves | 一～象棋 a set of chess | 全～武装 fully armed; in full battle array; armed to the teeth b)用于面部表情[indicating facial expression]: 一～笑脸 a smiling face | 一～庄严的面孔 solemn looks; a solemn face

【副本】fùběn ❶ 著作原稿以外的誊录本 transcript; transcribed manuscript other than the master copy:《永乐大典》～ transcript of *The Great Encyclopaedia of Emperor Yongle* ❷ 文件正本以外的其他本 duplicate; copy other than the original document: 照会的～ copy of a (diplomatic) note

【副标题】fùbiāotí same as 副题 fùtí

【副产品】fùchǎnpǐn 制造某种物品时附带产生的物品,如炼焦的副产品是苯、蒽、萘等 by-product; side products produced during manufacture, e.g. benzene, anthracene and naphthalene are the by-products of coking; also 副产物 fùchǎnwù

【副词】fùcí 修饰或限制动词和形容词,表示范围、程度等,而不能修饰或限制名词的词,如'都、只、再三、屡次、很、更、越、也、还、不、竟然、居然'等 adverb; word that modifies or restricts a verb or an adjective but not a noun, to indicate limit, degree, etc., e.g. all, only, time and again, repeatedly, very, more, more and more, also, still, not, and even unexpectedly

【副官】fùguān 〈旧时 *old*〉军队中办理行政事务的军官 adjutant; aide-de-camp; army officer in charge of administrative affairs

【副虹】fùhóng ☞ 霓 ní on p. 1405

【副交感神经】fùjiāogǎnshénjīng 植物神经系统的一部分,上部从中脑和延髓发出,下部从脊髓的最下部(骶部)发出,分布在体内各器官里。作用跟交感神经相反,有抑制和减缓心脏收缩,使瞳孔收缩、肠蠕动加强等作用。parasympathetic nerve; part of the automatic nervous system, spreading out from the deutocerebrum and medulla oblongata, and the sacrum, to all organs of the body. Its functions are opposite to the sympathetic system, and it acts to inhibit and reduce heartbeat, contract the pupil of the eye, and strengthen peristalsis of the intestine, etc.

【副教授】fùjiàoshòu 高等学校中职别次于教授的教师 associate professor; teacher of an institute of higher learning whose rank is just below that of professor

【副净】fùjìng 架子花的旧称 (old term for) painted-face actor skilled in traditional Chinese opera

【副刊】fùkān 报纸上刊登文艺作品、学术论文等的专页或专栏 supplement; special page or column publishing literary writings, academic treaties, etc.

【副科】fùkē 所学课程中的次要科目 (in a course of study) minor subject; secondary course:学校设置课程不能重主科,轻～。The school curriculum should not stress major courses at the expense of minor ones.

【副品】fùpǐn 质量没达到标准要求的产品 seconds; products that do not meet the required standards; substandard goods

【副热带】fùrèdài 亚热带 subtropics; subtropical zone; subtropical belt

【副神经】fùshénjīng 第十一对脑神经,从延髓发出,分布在颈部和胸部的肌肉中。主管咽部和肩部肌肉的运动。accessory nerve; either one of the 11th pair of cranial nerves from the spinal cord extending through the muscles of the neck and chest, and controlling movement of the pharynx and shoulder muscles

【副肾】fùshèn 肾上腺 adrenal gland

【副食】fùshí 指下饭的鱼肉蔬菜等 non-staple food; fish, meat and vegetables, eaten with staple starch foods:～品 non-staple food or foodstuffs|～店 grocery; grocer's

【副手】fùshǒu 助手;帮手 assistant; helper

【副题】fùtí 加在文章、新闻等标题旁边或下面作为补充说明的标题 subtitle; subheading; title printed beside or beneath the main title of an article, piece of news, etc. as supplementary explanation; also 副标题 fùbiāotí

【副性征】fùxìngzhēng 人和动物发育到一定阶段表现出来的与性别有关的特征。如男子长胡须、喉结突出、声调低;女子乳房发育、声调高等。secondary sex characteristic; characteristics of human beings and animals specific to each sex at a certain stage of development, e.g. beard growth, protruding Adam's apple, and low voice pitch in men; breast development, high voice pitch, etc. in women

【副修】fùxiū 主修以外,附带学习(某门课程或专业) minor; study in a subject or speciality in addition to the major subject:～课 minor courses

【副业】fùyè 主要职业以外,附带经营的事业,如农民从事的编席、采集药材等 sideline; side occupation; supplementary occupation in addition to the major one, e.g. straw mat-weaving and picking medicinal herbs by farmers

【副油箱】fùyóuxiāng 装在飞机体外的油箱,用来增加飞机的航程,必要时可以抛掉 auxiliary tank; drop tank; fuel tank installed outside the fuselage of an aircraft to increase its flight range, which can be jettisoned if necessary

【副职】fùzhí 副的职位 deputy position:～干部 cadres in deputy positions|担任～ hold the deputy post

【副作用】fùzuòyòng 随着主要作用而附带发生的不好的作用 side effect; harmful or unpleasant effect that occurs simultaneously with the main effect:这种药没有～。The drug has no side effects.

蝜 fù [蝜蝂] (fùbǎn)寓言中说的一种好负重物的小虫(见于唐朝柳宗元《蝜蝂传》) *fuban*, a legendary small insect which excels at carrying heavy weights (recorded in the *Story of Fuban* by Liu Zongyuan of the Tang Dynasty)

赋1 fù (上对下)交给 (from superior to inferior) bestow on; endow with; vest with:～予 entrust; bestow; give

赋2 fù ❶〈旧时 *old*〉指农业税 agricultural tax:田～ land tax|～税 land and other taxes; taxes and levies ❷〈书 *fml.*〉征收(赋税) levy; impose:～以重税 levy heavy taxes (or duties)

赋3 fù ❶ 我国古代文体,盛行于汉魏六朝,是韵文和散文的综合体,通常用来写景叙事,也有以较短的篇幅抒情说理的 *fu*; rhapsody; prose-poetry; descriptive prose interspersed with verse; literary genre very much in vogue through the six dynasties from the Han to the Wei Dynasty, combining verse and prose, oft. for narration or scenic description; some shorter texts were lyrical or analytical ❷ 做(诗、词) compose (verse); write poetry:～诗一首 compose a poem

【赋税】fùshuì 田赋和各种捐税的总称 general term for land and other taxes; taxes and levies

【赋闲】fùxián 晋朝潘岳辞官家居,作《闲居赋》,后来因称没有职业在家闲着为赋闲 (of an official, etc.) be idle; be out of office. Pan Yue, an official of the Jin Dynasty, resigned his government post and stayed at home to write *On the Idle Life*. The expression 赋闲 *fuxian* means 'stay at home unemployed'.

【赋性】fùxìng 天性 inborn nature:～刚强 unyielding by nature; of firm (or strong) character|～聪颖 intelligent by nature

【赋役】fùyì 赋税和徭役 taxes and corvée

【赋有】fùyǒu 具有(某种性格、气质等) possess (naturally); be gifted with; be endowed with (quality, temperament, etc.):劳动人民～忠厚质朴的性格。The labouring people have the qualities of honesty and unpretentiousness.

【赋予】fùyǔ 交给(重大任务、使命等) entrust; bestow; give (an important task, mission, etc.):这是历史～我们的重任。This is the mission history has entrusted on us.

傅[1] fù ❶〈书 *fml.*〉辅助;教导 teach; instruct ❷ 负责教导或传授技艺的人 teacher; instructor:师～ master; teacher ❸ (Fù)姓 a surname

傅[2] fù〈书 *fml.*〉❶ 附着;加上 attach; stick to; adhere to:皮之不存,毛将安～? Without skin, how can the hair grow? ❷ 涂抹;搽 apply; lay on:～粉 dust with powder; powder (one's face)

【傅粉】fù//fěn〈书 *fml.*〉搽粉 apply powder; powder (one's face)

【傅会】fùhuì same as 附会 fùhuì

【傅科摆】fùkēbǎi 用来证明地球自转运动的天文仪器,一根长十几或几十米的金属丝,一端系一个重球,另一端悬挂在支架上。由于地球自转,在北半球,摆动所形成的扇状面按顺时针方向旋转;在南半球则按逆时针方向旋转。因法国科学家傅科(Léon Foucault)发明而得名。Foucault pendulum; astronomical instrument that demonstrates the rotation of the earth, made by hanging a heavy ball at one end of a long metal wire and attaching the other end to a support. The rotation of the earth causes the fan-shaped plane of oscillation to rotate clockwise in the northern hemisphere, counterclockwise in the southern hemisphere. The instrument is named after the French scientist Léon Foucault.

富 fù ❶ 财产多(跟'贫、穷'相对 as opposed to 'needy' and 'poor') rich; wealthy:～裕 prosperous; well off; well-to-do | ～有 rich; wealthy; affluent | ～户 rich (or well-to-do) family | 农村～了。The rural areas have become prosperous. ❷ 使变富 enrich:～国强兵 make one's country prosperous and build up its military might | ～民政策 policy of enriching the people ❸ 资源;财产 wealth; resource:～源 natural resources | 财～ wealth; riches ❹ 丰富;多 plenty; abundant:～饶 fertile; abundant | ～于养分 full of (or rich in) nutrient ❺ (Fù)姓 a surname

【富贵】fùguì 指有钱又有地位 riches and honour; wealth and rank:荣华～ honour and splendour | ～人家 wealthy and influential family

【富贵病】fùguìbìng 俗称需要长期休养和滋补调理的某些慢性病 rich man's disease; chronic illness needing a long period of recuperation and plenty of nourishment

【富国】fùguó ❶ 使国家富足 make one's country prosperous:～裕民 make one's country rich and its people prosperous | ～强兵 make one's country prosperous and build up its military might ❷ 富足的国家 rich country:由于盛产石油,这个国家很快由穷国变成了～。The oil-rich country has quickly been transformed from a poor country into a rich one.

【富豪】fùháo 指有钱又有权势的人 rich and powerful people

【富矿】fùkuàng 品位较高的矿石或矿床 rich ore; high-grade ore

【富丽】fùlì 宏伟美丽 splendid; gorgeous:～堂皇 sumptuous; splendid; gorgeous; grand | 陈设豪华～ luxuriously furnished

【富民】fùmín 使人民富足 make the people prosperous; enrich the people:富国～ make one's country rich and its people prosperous | ～政策 policy of enriching the people

【富农】fùnóng 农村中以剥削雇佣劳动(兼放高利贷或出租部分土地)为主要生活来源的人。一般占有土地和比较优良的生产工具以及活动资本。自己参加劳动,但收入主要是由剥削来的。rich peasant; farmer whose major source of income is from exploitation of wage labour (as well as usury or renting out part of his land), who oft. owns land, good production tools and movable capital. He may work on the land too, but his income comes mainly from exploiting others.

【富强】fùqiáng (国家)出产丰富,力量强大 (of a country) rich and powerful; prosperous and strong:繁荣～ prosperous and strong | 国家～,人民安乐。The country prospers, and its people live in peace and happiness.

【富饶】fùráo 物产多;财富多 fertile; abundant:～之国 richly endowed country | ～的长江流域 fertile Yangtze River valley

【富商】fùshāng 钱财多的商人 rich merchant:～大贾 wealthy merchants

【富实】fù·shí (家产、资财)富足;富裕 (of family property and assets) rich; abundant; well-off:家业～ substantial family property

【富庶】fùshù 物产丰富,人口众多 well-populated and highly productive

【富态】fù·tai〈婉辞 *euph.*〉身体胖 plump; stout:这人长得很～。The person is very plump.

【富翁】fùwēng 拥有大量财产的人 rich man; man of wealth

【富有】fùyǒu ❶ 拥有大量的财产 wealthy; rich; affluent:～的商人 rich merchant ❷ 充分地具有(多指积极方面 usu. in a positive sense) rich in; full of; replete with:～生命力 full of vitality | ～代表性 be typical

【富裕】fùyù ❶ (财物)充裕 (of property) prosperous; well-to-do; well off:日子过得挺～ be quite well-off|农民一天天地～起来。Peasants are becoming better off day by day. ❷ 使富裕 enrich; make rich or prosperous:发展生产,～人民。Develop production to enrich the people.

【富裕中农】fùyù zhōngnóng 上中农 well-to-do middle-peasant

【富余】fù·yu 足够而有剩余 have more than needed; have enough and to spare:～人员 surplus personnel|把～的钱存银行 deposit the spare money in the bank|时间还～,不必着急。There is plenty of time, and we needn't worry.|这里抽水机有～,可以支援你们两台。We have water pumps to spare, and can let you have two.

【富源】fùyuán 自然资源,如森林、矿产等 natural resources, e.g. forests, minerals, etc.

【富足】fùzú 丰富充足 affluent; plentiful; rich; abundant:过着～的日子 lead an affluent life

腹 fù ❶ 躯干的一部分。人的腹在胸的下面。动物的腹在胸的后面。belly; abdomen; stomach; part of the trunk, the human abdomen is below the chest and the stomach of an animal is behind its chest; 通称 generally called 肚子 dù·zi; (图见 ☞ figure for 身体 shēntǐ on p.1701) ❷ 指内心 in the heart; innermost:～案 secret plan; mental plan|～议 keep one's criticism or opinion to oneself ❸ 指鼎、瓶子等器物的中空而凸出的部分 rounded cavity of a vessel or bottle:壶～ belly of a jug|瓶～ body of a bottle

【腹案】fù'àn ❶ 内心考虑的方案 plan under consideration; mental plan:他初步有了个～。He has figured out a preliminary plan. ❷ 指已经拟定而尚未公开的方案 plan that has not been disclosed to the public:这是他们经过半年研究得出的～。This plan has been drawn up after six months of investigation but has not been disclosed to the public yet.

【腹背受敌】fù bèi shòu dí 前面和后面都受到敌人的攻击 exposed to attacks from the front and the rear

【腹地】fùdì 靠近中心的地区;内地 hinterland; interior:深入～ go deep into the hinterland

【腹诽】fùfěi 〈书 *fml.*〉嘴里虽然不说,心里认为不对 consider sth. wrong but not voice it; harbour unspoken criticism; also 腹非 fùfēi

【腹稿】fùgǎo 已经想好但还没写出的文稿 draft worked out in one's mind; mental notes

【腹股沟】fùgǔgōu 大腿和腹部相连的部分 inguen; groin; part of the body where the top of the leg joins with the trunk; also 鼠蹊 shǔxī

【腹面】fùmiàn 动物身上胸部、腹部的那一面 underside; chest and belly of an animal

【腹膜】fùmó 腹腔内包着胃肠等脏器的薄膜,由结缔组织构成 peritoneum; membrane that covers the abdomen and intestines in the abdominal cavity, composed of connective tissue

【腹鳍】fùqí 鱼类腹部的鳍,左右各一,是转换方向和支持身体平衡的器官 ventral fin; pair of fins on the left and right sides of the belly of a fish, used for steering and maintaining stability; (图见 ☞ figure for 鳍 qí on p.1513)

【腹腔】fùqiāng 体腔的一部分,上部有横膈膜和胸腔隔开,下部是骨盆,前部和两侧是腹壁,后部是脊椎和腰部肌肉。胃、肠、胰、肾、肝、脾等器官都在腹腔内。abdominal cavity; part of the body separated by the diaphragm from the thoracic cavity above it, containing the stomach, intestines, pancreas, kidneys, liver and spleen. The lower part of the cavity is lined by the pelvis; the front and the left and right sides, napes; and the rear, vertebra and waist muscle, in which many organs grow.

【腹水】fùshuǐ 腹腔内因病积聚的液体,心脏病、肾炎、肝硬变等疾病都能引起腹水 ascites; accumulation of fluid in the abdominal cavity due to diseases such as heart disease, nephritis, cirrhosis, etc.

【腹泻】fùxiè 指排便次数增多,大便稀薄或呈水状,有的带脓血,常兼有腹痛。由于肠道感染,消化机能障碍而引起。diarrhoea; condition caused by intestinal infection and impaired digestive functions, characterized by excessive frequency and fluidity of fecal evacuations; also 水泻 shuǐxiè; 通称 generally called 拉稀 lāxī, 泻肚 xièdù or 闹肚子 nàodù·zi

【腹心】fùxīn ❶〈比喻 *fig.*〉要害或中心部分 (to the) quick; belly and heart; vital organs; key parts:～之患 disease in one's vital organs; serious hidden trouble or danger ❷〈比喻 *fig.*〉极亲近的人;心腹 confidant; reliable agent; crony; trusted subordinate:言听计从,倚为～ rely on one's trusted subordinate and always follow his advice ❸〈书 *fml.*〉〈比喻 *fig.*〉真心诚意 sincerity; genuine feelings:敢布～ venture to air my opinions|～相照 very sincere

【腹议】fùyì 〈书 *fml.*〉嘴上没说出,心里有看法 keep one's criticism or opinion to oneself

鲋 fù 古书上指鲫鱼 crucian carp (*Carassius auratus*) recorded in ancient books:涸辙之～ fish trapped in a dry rut — person in a desperate situation needing immediate relief

缚 fù 捆绑 tie up; bind fast:束～ tie; bind up; fetter|作茧自～ spin a cocoon around oneself — get into trouble of one's own making|手无～鸡之力 lack the strength to truss a chicken; very weak

赙 fù 〈书 *fml.*〉赙赠 present a gift to a bereaved family:～仪 gift to a bereaved family|～金 money presented to a bereaved family

【赙仪】fùyí 〈书 *fml.*〉向办丧事的人家送的礼

gift presented to bereaved family

【赙赠】fùzèng〈书 *fml*.〉赠送财物给办丧事的人家 present gift to bereaved family

蝮 fù [蝮蛇](fùshé)毒蛇的一种,头部呈三角形,身体灰褐色,有斑纹。生活在山野和岛上,捕食小动物,也能伤害人或家畜。Pallas pit viper (*Agkistrodon halys*); a variety of poisonous snake with a triangular head and striped taupe body, living in mountains, on plains and islands, catching and feeding on small animals, and harmful to man and domestic animals

鳆 fù [鳆鱼](fùyú) same as 鲍鱼[2] bàoyú

覆 fù ❶ 盖住 cover; envelop: ～盖 cover | 被～ coat; coating | 天～地载 all-embracing ❷ 底朝上翻过来;歪倒 overturn; capsize; upset: 颠～ overthrow (a government) | 前车之～,后车之鉴 warning taken from the overturned cart on the road ahead; lesson drawn from others' mistakes ❸ same as 复[2] fù

【覆被】fùbèi 覆盖 cover; overspread; screen: 森林～占全省面积三分之一以上。More than one third of the province's total area is covered by forests.

【覆巢无完卵】fù cháo wú wán luǎn 鸟窝翻落下来不会有完好的鸟蛋 When the nest is overturned no egg stays unbroken.〈比喻 *fig*.〉整体覆灭,个体不能幸免 When the whole is destroyed, no individual is unaffected.

【覆盖】fùgài ❶ 遮盖 cover: 积雪～着地面。The earth is blanketed (or covered) with snow. ❷ 指地面上的植物,对于土壤有保护作用 vegetation; plant cover: 没有～,水土容易流失。Soil erosion is likely to occur when there is no vegetation cover.

【覆盖面】fùgàimiàn ❶ 覆盖的面积 covered area: 森林的～日益减少。The land covered with woods has been shrinking. ❷ 泛指涉及或影响到的范围 (in a broad sense) coverage; involved or affected area: 扩大法制教育的～ extend knowledge of the law to more people

【覆灭】fùmiè 全部被消灭 total ruin; destruction; total collapse: 全军～。The whole army was destroyed.

【覆没】fùmò ❶〈书 *fml*.〉(船)翻而沉没 (of ship) sink ❷ (军队)被消灭 (of troops) be overwhelmed; be destroyed ❸〈书 *fml*.〉same as 沦陷 lúnxiàn ①: 中原～ fall of the Central Plains

【覆盆之冤】fù pén zhī yuān 形容无处申诉的冤枉 grievous wrong that can never be righted; irredeemable wrong (覆盆 *fu pen*: 翻过来放着的盆子,里面阳光照不到 inverted basin into which the sun cannot shine)

【覆水难收】fù shuǐ nán shōu 倒(dào)在地上的水无法再收回 Spilled water cannot be gathered up again.〈比喻 *fig*.〉已成事实的事难以挽回(多用于夫妻离异 oft. referring to a divorced couple) no putting broken pieces back together; *or* What is done cannot be undone.

【覆亡】fùwáng 灭亡 (of an empire, nation, etc.) fall; downfall; collapse

【覆辙】fùzhé 翻过车的道路 track of an overturned cart;〈比喻 *fig*.〉曾经失败的做法 previously unsuccessful method: 重蹈～ take the track of an overturned cart; make the same mistake as others before

馥 fù〈书 *fml*.〉香;香气 fragrance: ～郁 strong fragrance; heavy perfume

【馥馥】fùfù〈书 *fml*.〉形容香气很浓 richly fragrant; strongly scented

【馥郁】fùyù〈书 *fml*.〉形容香气浓厚 strong fragrance; heavy perfume: 芬芳～ beautiful and fragrant | 花朵散发着～的香气。The flowers are sending out a rich, sweet scent.

G

gā (ㄍㄚ)

夹(夾) gā [夹肢窝](gā·zhiwō)腋窝的通称 commonly known as 腋窝 yèwō; also 胳肢窝 gā·zhiwō
☞ jiā on p.925 and jiá on p.931

旮 gā ☞ below

【旮旮旯旯儿】gā·galálár〈方 *dial.*〉所有的角落 all corners; every nook and cranny:～都打扫干净了。Every nook and cranny has been swept clean.

【旮旯儿】gālár〈方 *dial.*〉❶ 角落 nook; corner:墙～ a corner formed by two walls; corner ❷ 狭窄偏僻的地方 out-of-the-way place:山～ a mountain recess|背～ obscure place

伽 gā [伽马射线](gāmǎ shèxiàn)丙种射线 gamma ray; γ ray; also γ 射线 gāmǎ shèxiàn
☞ jiā on p.926 and qié on p.1553

呷 gā [呷呷] same as 嘎嘎(gāgā)
☞ xiā on p.2060

咖 gā [咖喱](gālí)用胡椒、姜黄、番椒、茴香、陈皮等的粉末制成的调味品,味香而辣,色黄 curry; yellow condiment consisting of assorted ground spices such as cayenne pepper, fenugreek, turmeric, and fennel
☞ kā on p.1068

胳 gā [胳肢窝](gā·zhiwō) same as 夹肢窝 gā·zhiwō
☞ gē on p.650 and gé on p.654

嘎 gā〈拟声词 *onom.*〉形容短促而响亮的声音 screech; loud high-pitched sound:汽车～的一声刹住了。The car screeched to a halt.
☞ gá on p.618 and gǎ on p.619

【嘎巴】gābā〈拟声词 *onom.*〉形容树枝等折断的声音 snap; crack; cracking or snapping sound:～一声,树技折成两截儿。Crack! The branch broke in two.

【嘎巴】gā·ba〈方 *dial.*〉黏的东西干后附着在器物上 crust; sticky stuff that adheres to a utensil when dried:饭粒都～在锅底上了。Grains of rice have crusted on the pot.

【嘎巴儿】gā·bar〈方 *dial.*〉附着在器物上的干了的粥、糨糊等 caking; scab; dried porridge or paste that has adhered to a utensil:衣裳上还有粥～。There are scabs of porridge on these clothes.

【嘎嘣脆】gā·bēngcuì〈方 *dial.*〉❶ 很脆 crunchy; very crispy ❷ 形容直截了当;干脆 snappy; straightforward:说话办事～ work and speak in a simple and straightforward manner

【嘎嘎】gāgā〈拟声词 *onom.*〉形容鸭子、大雁等叫的声音 gaggle; quack; quacking sound made by a duck or a goose; also 呷呷 gāgā
☞ gá·ga on p.619

【嘎渣儿】gā·zhār〈方 *dial.*〉❶ 痂 scab ❷ 食物粘在锅上的部分或烤焦、烤黄的硬皮 food that has stuck to a pot, or the scorched, brown skin that forms on food

【嘎吱】gāzhī〈拟声词 *onom.*〉形容物件受压力而发出的声音(多重叠用 usu. reduplicated) creak; squeak; creaking sound of objects that are under great stress:他挑着行李,扁担压得～～的响。He carried the luggage on a shoulder pole that creaked under its weight.

gá (ㄍㄚˊ)

轧 gá〈方 *dial.*〉❶ 挤 press:人～人。People push against one another. ❷ 结交 associate with:～朋友 make friends with sb. ❸ 核算;查对 check:～账 check the accounts
☞ yà on p.2197 and zhá on p.2404

钆 gá 金属元素,符号 Gd (gadolinium)。是一种稀土金属。银白色,磁性强,低温时具有超导性,用于微波技术,也用做原子反应堆的结构材料等。gadolinium (Gd); silvery white magnetic metallic element of the rare earth group with superconductivity at a low temperature, used for microwave technology or as structural material for atomic reactors

尜 gá [尜尜](gá·ga) ❶ (～儿 gár)一种儿童玩具,两头尖,中间大 *ga*; children's toy with a bulging middle and pointed at both ends; also 尜儿 gár ❷ 像尜尜的 spindle-like:～枣 spindle-like jujube|～汤(用玉米面等做的食品) soup made from spindle-like corn noodles ‖ also 嘎嘎 gá·ga

嘎 gá ☞ below
☞ gā on p.618 and gǎ on p.619

【嘎调】gádiào 京剧唱腔里,用特别拔高的音唱某个字,唱出的音叫嘎调 (of Peking Opera) note high-pitched for enunciation of a specific word

【嘎嘎】gá·ga same as 尜尜 gá·ga

☞ gāgā on p.618

噶 gá ☞ below

【噶伦】gálún 原西藏地方政府主要官员 galoin; title of a ranking official of the former local government of Tibet

【噶厦】gáxià 原西藏地方政府,由噶伦四人组成。1959年3月后解散。gaxag; former local government of Tibet consisting of four galoins, disbanded in March 1959

gǎ (ㄍㄚˇ)

尕 gǎ〈方 *dial.*〉❶ 乖僻;脾气不好 cantankerous; cross; crabby:这人~得很,不好说话。This person is not easy-going. ❷ 调皮 puckish; mischievous:~小子 naughty boy

【尕古】gǎ·gu〈方 *dial.*〉(人的脾气、东西的质量、事情的结局等)不好(of man's disposition, the quality of goods, the outcome of an event, etc.) not good

【尕子】gǎ·zi〈方 *dial.*〉调皮的人(有时用来称小孩儿,含喜爱意 sometimes used as nickname for a child) naughty, mischievous person; also 嘎子 gǎ·zi

尕 gǎ〈方 *dial.*〉小 little; small:~娃 a little kid|~李 younger Li

嘎 gǎ same as 尕 gǎ:~古 not good|~子 a naughty guy

☞ gā on p.618 and gá on p.618

【嘎子】gǎ·zi same as 尕子 gǎ·zi

gà (ㄍㄚˋ)

尬 gà ☞ [尴尬] (gāngà) on p.629

gāi (ㄍㄞ)

该[1] gāi ❶ 应当 need; ought to; should:应~ should be|~说的一定要说。What should be said must be said.|你累了,~休息一下了。You're tired and need a break.|~两天干的活儿,一天就干完了。The work that was supposed to take two days has been finished in a day's time. ❷ 应当是;应当(由…来做) be sb.'s turn, duty, or lot:这一回~我了吧!It's my turn now, isn't it?|这个工作~老张来担任。This is a job for Lao Zhang to take on. [注意] **NOTE:** 有时带'着'(·zhe) sometimes followed by 着:今天晚上~着你值班了。It's your turn to be on duty tonight.

❸ 理应如此 deserve punishment; serve sb. right:活~。You deserve it.|~!谁叫他淘气来着。It serves him right; he shouldn't have been so naughty. ❹ 表示根据情理或经验推测必然的或可能的结果 indicate a certain or probable outcome in accordance with reason or experience; will probably; can reasonably or naturally be expected to:天一凉,就~加衣服了。People generally wear more clothes when the weather turns cold.|再不浇水,花都~蔫了。If they are not watered soon, the flowers will wither. [注意] **NOTE:** 用在感叹句中兼有加强语气的作用 also used in exclamatory sentences for emphasis:我们的责任~有多重啊!How weighty our responsibilities are!|要是水泵今天就运到,~多么好哇!It would be wonderful if the pump could arrive today!

该[2] gāi 欠 owe:~账 owe a debt|我~他两块钱。I owe him two yuan.

该[3] gāi 指示词,指上文说过的人或事物(多用于公文 usu. in official document) this; that; the said; the above-mentioned:~地交通便利。The area has convenient communications.|~生品学兼优。The said student has both a good character and fine scholarship.

该[4] gāi same as 赅 gāi

【该博】gāibó same as 赅博 gāibó

【该当】gāidāng 应当 should:大伙儿的事,我~出力,没说的。It's something for everybody and I should do my bit.

【该欠】gāiqiàn 借别人的财物没有还;短欠 owe; be in arrears:我量入为出,从来不~别人的。I live within my means and owe nothing to anyone.

【该死】gāisǐ 表示厌恶、愤恨或埋怨的话 expression of abomination, anger, or complaint:~的猫又叼去一条鱼。That damned cat stole another fish!|真~,我又把钥匙丢在家里了。Oh, no! I've left my key at home again.

【该应】gāiyīng〈方 *dail.*〉❶ 应该 should ❷ same as 该着 gāizháo

【该着】gāizháo 指命运注定,不可避免(迷信) (superstition) predestined by fate; unavoidable:刚一出门就摔了一跤,~我倒霉。I fell over as soon as I walked out of the door. Just my luck!

陔 gāi〈书 *fml.*〉❶ 靠近台阶下边的地方 landing; place underneath the stairs ❷ 级;层 a flight of stairs; layer ❸ 田间的土岗子 earthen mound in the fields

垓[1] gāi〈古代 *arch.*〉数目名,指一万万 a hundred million

垓[2] gāi 垓下 Gāixià,古地名,在今安徽灵璧东南。项羽在这里被围失败。Gaixia, name of an ancient place in today's southeast Lingbi, Anhui Province, where Xiang Yu (232-202 B.C.), the Lord of Chu and his army were besieged and routed

【垓心】gāixīn 战场的中心(多见于旧小说 most-

G

ly in old novels) centre of a battlefield：困在～ be besieged at the centre of the battlefield

荄 gāi 〈书 *fml*.〉草根 grass roots

赅 gāi 〈书 *fml*.〉❶ 兼；包括 include；embrace：举一～百 draw inferences on other cases from one instance｜以偏～全 regard the part as the whole；be lopsided ❷ 完备；全 complete；full：言简意～ impart a profound meaning with only a few words；precise and to the point

【赅博】gāibó 〈书 *fml*.〉渊博 encyclopaedic；erudite；also 该博 gāibó

【赅括】gāikuò 〈书 *fml*.〉概括 summarize；generalize；epitomize

gǎi（ㄍㄞˇ）

改 gǎi ❶ 改变；更改 change；transform：～口 retract what has just been said｜～名 rename｜～朝换代 dynastic changes｜几年之间，家乡完全～了样子了。My hometown has changed beyond recognition over the past few years. ❷ 修改 alter；revise：～文章 have an article revised｜这扇门太大，得往小里～一～。The door is too big and must be altered to make it smaller. ❸ 改正 correct；rectify；put right：～邪归正 give up vice and return to virtue｜有错误一定要～。Any mistakes you have made must be corrected. ❹（Gǎi）姓 a surname

【改扮】gǎibàn 改换打扮，成另外的模样 disguise；change customary dress and take on a false appearance or an assumed identity：为了侦察敌情，他～成一个游街串巷的算命先生。In order to gather intelligence about the enemy, he disguised himself as a fortune-teller, wandering from place to place.

【改编】gǎibiān ❶ 根据原著重写（体裁往往与原著不同）rewrite an original work（usu. into a different genre）；adapt；revise：这部电影是由同名小说～摄制的。This movie has been adapted from a novel of the same title. ❷ 改变原来的编制（多指军队 usu. of a military unit）change the original organizational structure；reorganize：把原来的三个师～成两个师 regroup the previous three divisions into two

【改变】gǎibiàn ❶ 事物发生显著的差别 striking difference or improvement occurring in sb. or sth.：山区面貌大有～。Great changes have taken place in mountainous areas.｜随着政治、经济关系的～，人和人的关系也～了。Along with the improvement in political and economic relations, human relations have also improved. ❷ 改换；更动 change；alter：～样式 change the style｜～口气 alter one's vein of speech｜～计划 revise a plan｜～战略 change the strategy

【改产】gǎi//chǎn 不再生产原来产品而生产别的产品；转产 switch to the manufacture of another line of products

【改朝换代】gǎi cháo huàn dài 旧的朝代为新的朝代所代替。泛指政权更替。replace an old regime with a new one；dynastic changes；change of the times

【改窜】gǎicuàn 窜改 alter；tamper with；falsify

【改道】gǎi//dào ❶ 改变行走的路线 change one's route：此处翻修马路，车辆必须～行驶。The road is under reconstruction, and vehicles must take another route. ❷（河流）改变经过的路线（of a river）change its course：黄河～ change the course of the Yellow River

【改点】gǎi//diǎn 更改原定的时间 reschedule；change the original schedule：列车～运行。The train has a new schedule.

【改订】gǎidìng 修订（书籍文字、规章制度等）reformulate；rewrite（books or regulations）：～计划 draw up a new plan

【改动】gǎidòng 变动（文字、项目、次序等）rehash；change；alter；modify（writing, items, or order）：这篇文章我只～了个别词句。I changed just a few sentences in this essay.｜这学期的课程没有大～。There are no big changes in this semester's curriculum.

【改革】gǎigé 把事物中旧的不合理的部分改成新的、能适应客观情况的 amend and improve by changing old, irrational factors so as to conform to the objective conditions：技术～ technical innovation｜文字～ reform of the written form of a language｜～经济管理体制 restructure the economic management system

【改观】gǎiguān 改变原来的样子，出现新的面目 change the original appearance；take on a new look：这一带防风林长起来，沙漠的面貌就要大大～。The look of the desert will change considerably when the windbreak is established.

【改过】gǎiguò 改正过失或错误 correct one's faults or mistakes：～自新 mend one's ways for a fresh start｜勇于～ have the courage to correct one's mistakes

【改行】gǎi//háng 放弃原来的行业，从事新的行业 give up one's original profession（or occupation, trade）for a new one：张大夫已经～当老师了。Doctor Zhang has quitted his old profession and become a teacher.

【改换】gǎihuàn 改掉原来的，换成另外的 replace one with another：～门庭 upgrade one's family status｜～生活方式 change one's lifestyle｜这句话不好懂，最好～一个说法。This sentence is difficult to understand. You had better try putting it another way.

【改换门庭】gǎihuàn méntíng ❶ 改变门第出身，提高社会地位 upgrade one's family background in order to raise one's social status ❷ 投靠新的主人或势力，以图维持、发展 throw in one's lot with a new master or power in order to maintain status quo or seek development

【改悔】gǎihuǐ 认识错误，加以改正 realize one's faults and mend one's ways：不知～ have no intention of redeeming oneself

【改嫁】gǎi//jià 妇女离婚后或丈夫死后再跟别人结婚 (of a woman) remarry after divorce or the death of her husband

【改建】gǎijiàn 在原有的基础上加以改造，使适合于新的需要（多指厂矿、建筑物等）build on the original basis while adapting to new requirements; reconstruct (of factories or buildings)

【改醮】gǎijiào〈旧时 *old*〉称改嫁 (of a woman) remarry

【改进】gǎijìn 改变旧有情况，使有所进步 ameliorate; improve：～工作 improve one's work | 操作方法有待～。The operating methods need to be improved.

【改口】gǎi//kǒu ❶ 改变自己原来说话的内容或语气 withdraw or modify one's previous remark：他发觉自己说错了，于是连忙～。As soon as he realized that he had made a slip of the tongue, he withdrew his remark. ❷ 改变称呼 change the appellation：叫惯了姐姐，如今要～叫嫂子，真有点别扭。As I used to call her sister, I now find it a bit difficult to call her sister-in-law.

【改良】gǎiliáng ❶ 去掉事物的个别缺点，使更适合要求 discard flaws and make better or more tolerable：～土壤 improve (or ameliorate) the soil | ～品种 improve a breed or a strain ❷ same as 改善 gǎishàn

【改良主义】gǎiliáng zhǔyì 反对从根本上推翻不合理的社会制度，主张在原有社会制度的基础上加以改善的思想 reformism; thought or theory that advocates making improvements to a regime instead of overthrowing it

【改判】gǎipàn 法院更改原来所做的判决 (of court) change the original sentence; commute; amend a judgement

【改期】gǎi//qī 改变预定的日期 change the predetermined date; postpone：会议～举行。The meeting has been put off.

【改日】gǎirì same as 改天 gǎitiān：～登门拜访。I'll call around to your house another day.

【改色】gǎisè ❶ 改变原有的颜色 change the original colour：秋末冬初，林木～。When autumn moves into winter, leaves on the trees turn red and yellow. ❷ 改变神色 change the facial expression：面不～ remain calm

【改善】gǎishàn 改变原有情况使好一些 improve; make the situation better：～生活 improve the livelihood | ～两国邦交 improve the relations between two countries

【改天】gǎitiān 以后的某一天（指距离说话时不很远的一天）some day in the near future：～见。See you later. | 今天我还有别的事，咱们～再谈吧。I've got something else to do today; let's talk it over another time.

【改天换地】gǎi tiān huàn dì 指从根本上改造大自然，也比喻巨大变革 reshape or change nature; great transformation; change the world：治山治水，～ change nature by transforming mountains and taming rivers | 这是一场～的政治斗争。This is a political struggle that could change the world.

【改头换面】gǎi tóu huàn miàn〈比喻 *fig.*〉只改形式，不变内容（贬义 derog.）change the superficial but not the essence; dish sth. up in a new form

【改弦更张】gǎi xián gēng zhāng 琴声不和谐，换了琴弦，重新安上 replace old discordant strings with new ones;〈比喻 *fig.*〉改革制度或变更方法 make a fresh start; turn over a new leaf; start a thorough reform

【改弦易辙】gǎi xián yì zhé 改换琴弦，变更行车道路 change one's strings and course of action;〈比喻 *fig.*〉改变方法或态度 change one's method or attitude; take a new line

【改线】gǎi//xiàn 改变公共交通、电话等的线路 change public transportation routes or telephone lines

【改邪归正】gǎi xié guī zhèng 不再做坏事，走上正路 give up vice and return to virtue; forsake heresy and return to the truth; turn over a new leaf

【改写】gǎixiě ❶ 修改 rewrite：论文在吸收别人意见的基础上，～了一次。This essay has been rewritten on the basis of someone else's comments. ❷ 根据原著重写 rewrite an original work; adapt：把这篇小说～成剧本 adapt this novel for the stage

【改选】gǎixuǎn 当选人任期届满或在任期中由于其他原因而重新选举 re-elect on expiration of term of office, or during the term, for some reason：～工会委员 re-elect a member of the trade union

【改样】gǎi//yàng (～儿 gǎi//yàngr) 改变原来的式样或模样；变样 change in style or appearance：几年没见，您还没～儿。You haven't changed a bit since we last saw you a few years ago.

【改业】gǎi//yè same as 改行 gǎi//háng

【改易】gǎiyì 改动；更换 change; alter：～文章标题 change the title of an article

【改元】gǎiyuán 君主、王朝改换年号，每一个年号开始的一年称'元年' change the designation of an imperial reign; change the title of a reign

【改造】gǎizào ❶ 就原有的事物加以修改或变更，使适合需要 transform; modify or reform the original conditions to conform to requirements：～低产田 transform low-yielding farm-

G

land ❷ 根本上改变旧的、建立新的,使适应新的形势和需要 remould; radically replace the old with the new in order to meet the needs of a new situation: ～思想 remould one's ideology | 劳动能～世界。Labour can recreate the world.

【改辙】gǎi//zhé 〈比喻 *fig.*〉改变办法 change the way

【改正】gǎizhèng 把错误的改为正确的 correct; amend; put right: ～缺点 correct one's mistakes | ～错别字 correct wrongly written and misused characters

【改制】gǎizhì 改变政治、经济等制度 change a political or economic system

【改装】gǎizhuāng ❶ 改变装束 change one's costume or dress: 她这一～,几乎让人认不出来了。She is barely recognizable in this new dress. ❷ 改变包装 change package: 商品～ repack the commodity ❸ 改变原来的装置 change the original installation; re-equip: 为了保证安全,已经将高压保险器～过了。In order to guarantee safety, the high-voltage safety equipment has been refitted.

【改锥】gǎizhuī 装卸螺丝钉用的工具,尖端有十字、扁平等形状,适用于钉帽上有槽纹的螺丝钉 screwdriver; tool with a cross-shaped or compressed end for turning screws; also 螺丝刀 luósīdāo

G

【改组】gǎizǔ 改变原来的组织或更换原有的人员 shake-up; restructure the original organization or change the staff: ～内阁 reshuffle the cabinet

【改嘴】gǎi//zuǐ same as 改口 gǎi//kǒu

胲 gǎi 〈书 *fml.*〉颊上的肌肉 cheek muscle ☞ hǎi on p.754

gài (ㄍㄞˋ)

丐 gài 〈书 *fml.*〉❶ 乞求 beg ❷ 乞丐 beggar ❸ 给;施与 give; grant; bestow

匄 gài 〈书 *fml.*〉same as 丐 gài

芥 gài ☞ below ☞ jiè on p.999

【芥菜】gàicài same as 盖菜 gàicài ☞ jiècài on p.999

【芥蓝菜】gàilán cài 二年生草本植物,叶柄长,叶片短而阔,花白色或黄色。是一种不结球的甘蓝。嫩叶和菜薹是普通蔬菜。cabbage mustard (*Brassica alboglabra*); biennial herbal plant that does not grow to a head, and has long leaf-stalks, short, wide leaves, white or yellow flowers, and leaves and bolt that serve as vegetable

陔(陰) gài 〈方 *dial.*〉❶ 斜靠 lean; recline: 梯子～在墙上。A ladder was leant against the wall. ❷ 依仗 count on; rely on: ～牌头(倚仗别人的面子或势力) rely on sb.'s power and position

钙 gài 金属元素,符号 Ca (calcium)。银白色,化学性质活泼。钙的化合物在建筑工程和医药上用途很广。calcium (Ca); silver-white metallic element with active chemical properties; calcium compound is widely used for architectural engineering and pharmaceutical purposes

【钙化】gàihuà 机体的组织由于钙盐的沉着而变硬。如儿童的骨骼经过钙化变成成人的骨骼,又如肺结核的病灶经过钙化而痊愈。calcify; organism hardened by deposits or secretion of calcium salts; i. e. children's bones calcify into adult's bones; the core of pulmonary tuberculosis is healed through calcification

盖[1](蓋) gài ❶ (～儿 gàir)器物上部有遮蔽作用的东西 cover of a utensil; lid: 锅～ the lid of a wok | 茶壶～儿 teapot lid◇膝～ knee | 天灵～ top of the skull ❷ (～儿 gàir)动物背部的甲壳 shell on the back of an animal: 螃蟹～儿 crab shell | 乌龟～儿 tortoise shell ❸ 〈古时 *arch.*〉把伞叫盖(现在方言还有把伞叫雨盖的) ancient name for an umbrella (still used in some modern dialects): 华～(古代车上像伞的篷子) canopy (over an imperial carriage) ❹ 由上而下地遮掩;蒙上 put a cover on; cover: 遮～ cover | ～盖儿 put a lid on | ～被子 put a quilt on | 撒种后～上一层土 cover the sown seeds with earth◇丑事情想～也～不住。Scandals cannot be covered up. ❺ 打上(印) affix (a seal): ～钢印 affix an embossing seal | ～图章 stamp ❻ 超过;压倒 surpass; top: 他的嗓门很大,把别人的声音都～下去了。His voice was so loud that it drowned out everyone else's. ❼ 〈方 *dial.*〉超出一般地好;非常好 extraordinarily good; super: 昨晚的戏演得真～。It was a wonderful performance last night. ❽ 建筑(房屋) build (houses): 翻～楼房 rebuild a house | 宿舍～好了。The dormitory has been completed. ❾ 耢(lào) leveller; farm tool used to level the fields ❿ (Gài)姓 a surname

盖[2](蓋) gài 〈书 *fml.*〉❶ 大概 approximately; about; around: 此书之印行～在 1902 年。The book was probably printed in 1902. ❷ 承上文申说理由或原因 for; because: 屈原之作《离骚》,～自怨生也。Qu Yuan composed *Encountering Sorrow* out of resentment at his unrecognized talents. ☞ Gě on p.655

【盖菜】gàicài 一年生草本植物,芥(jiè)菜的变种,叶子大,表面多皱纹,叶脉显著,是普通蔬菜 leaf mustard (*Brassica juncea*); annual herbal plant with large, creased, veined leaves that may be eaten as a vegetable; also 芥菜 jiècài

【盖饭】gàifàn 一种论份儿吃的饭,用碗盘等盛米饭后在上面加菜而成 a kind of set meal; bowl of rice served with meat and vegetables on top; also 盖浇饭 gàijiāofàn

【盖棺论定】gài guān lùn dìng 指一个人的是非功过到死后做出结论 final judgement can be passed on a person only when the lid is placed on his coffin; no final assessment can be made of a man until after his death

【盖火】gài·huo 盖在炉口上压火的铁器，圆形，中凸，顶端有小孔 round ironware lid with a hole in its raised centre, used to cover the mouth of a stove

【盖建】gàijiàn 建筑（房屋等）build (a house, etc.)

【盖韭】gàijiǔ 冬天种在阳畦里的韭菜，夜间盖上马粪、麦糠等，白天扒掉 winter leek, planted in a cold frame; covered with horse manure and wheat bran at night that is washed off the following day

【盖帘】gàilián（～儿 gàiliánr）用细秫秸等做成的圆形用具，多用来盖在缸、盆等上面 round kitchen utensil made of thin stalks, used to cover a vat or a basin

【盖帽儿】gài//màor ❶ 篮球运动防守技术之一，指防守队员跳起，打掉进攻队员在头的上部出手投篮时的球 block; defence tactic in a basketball game; blocking a shot ❷〈方 *dial.*〉形容极好 excellent：拔尖～ top-notch

【盖然性】gàiránxìng 有可能但又不是必然的性质 probability; quality or state of being probable but not inevitable

【盖世】gàishì（才能、功绩等）高出当代之上（of talent, achievement, etc.）unparalleled; matchless; peerless：～无双 unequalled｜英名～ illustrious name overshadowing the world

【盖世太保】Gàishìtàibǎo 法西斯德国的国家秘密警察组织。希特勒曾用它在德国国内及占领区进行大规模的恐怖屠杀。也译作盖斯塔波。Gestapo; secret-police organization in Nazi Germany that Hitler employed to carry out terrorist massacres in Germany and its occupied areas [德 German: short form of Geheime Staatspolizei（国家秘密警察 guójiā mìmì jǐngchá）]

【盖头】gài·tou 旧式婚礼新娘蒙在头上遮住脸的红绸布 red kerchief the bride uses to cover her head in a traditional Chinese wedding

【盖碗】gàiwǎn（～儿 gàiwǎnr）带盖儿的茶碗 teacup with lid and saucer：～茶 cup with lid for drinking tea｜细瓷～ fine-ceramic teacup

【盖造】gàizào 建造（房屋等）build (a house, etc.)

【盖子】gài·zi ❶ 器物上部有遮蔽作用的东西 lid; cover; cap; top：茶杯～碎了。The teacup lid smashed. ◇内幕总要揭开，捂～是没有用的。The truth will come to light, so it is useless to try covering up. ❷ 动物背上的甲壳 shell on the back of an animal; carapace; crust

溉 gài〈书 *fml.*〉灌；浇 pour; water：灌～ irrigate

概[1]（槩）gài ❶ 大略 general idea; outline：梗～ gist; abstract｜大～ roughly｜～况 general situation｜～要 summary ❷ 一律 generally; approximately：货物出门，～不退换。Goods sold are not returnable.

概[2] gài ❶ 气度神情 manner of carrying oneself; deportment：气～ lofty quality ❷〈书 *fml.*〉景象；状况 scenery; condition：胜～（优美的景色）beautiful scenery

【概观】gàiguān 概括的观察；概况（多用于书名 oft. used in book titles）general survey; general situation：市场～ general market situation｜《红学～》*A General Survey of Redology*

【概况】gàikuàng 大概的情况 general situation：生活～ general living conditions｜敦煌历史～ survey of the history of Dunhuang

【概括】gàikuò ❶ 把事物的共同特点归结在一起；总括 summarize; generalize; epitomise：各小组的办法虽然都不一样，但～起来不外两种。Different groups have various methods, but these may be generalised into two. ❷ 简单扼要 brief and to the point：他把剧本的故事向大家～地说了一遍。He gave a brief introduction to the scenario.

【概览】gàilǎn 概观（多用于手册一类的书名 usu. used in book titles）general survey：《上海～》*A General Survey of Shanghai*

【概率】gàilǜ 某种事件是同一条件下可能发生也可能不发生，表示发生的可能性大小的量叫做概率。例如在一般情况下，一个鸡蛋孵出的小鸡是雌性或雄性的概率都是 1/2。probability; extent to which an event is likely or unlikely to happen under a given condition, e.g. the probability of a chicken hatched from an egg under normal conditions being either male or female is generally 50%; also called 几率（jīlǜ）；旧称 formerly called 或然率 huòránlǜ

【概略】gàilüè ❶ 大概情况 outline; summary：这只是整个故事的～，详细情节可以看原书。This is just an outline of the story. For the plot in all its detail you can read the book. ❷ 简单扼要；大致 brief; rough：～介绍 brief introduction｜～说明 brief description

【概论】gàilùn 概括的论述（多用于书名 usu. used in book titles）outline; introduction：《地质学～》*An Introduction to Geology*｜《中国文学～》*A General Introduction to Chinese Literature*

【概貌】gàimào 大概的状况 general conditions：沿海城市～ general picture of coastal cities｜地形～ general state of the topography

【概莫能外】gài mò néng wài 一概不能超出这个范围；一概不能例外 without exception; absolutely not allowed to exceed certain limit：这是共同的道理，古今中外，～。This is the common truth to which there is no exception, whether in modern or ancient times, in China or abroad.

【概念】gàiniàn 思维的基本形式之一,反映客观事物的一般的、本质的特征。人类在认识过程中,把所感觉到的事物的共同特点抽出来,加以概括,就成为概念。比如从白雪、白马、白纸等事物里抽出它们的共同特点,就得出'白'的概念。concept; conception; notion; idea; sth. conceived in the mind; abstract or generic idea generalized from particular instances e. g. the concept of the colour 'white' is generalized from the common characteristics of such things as snow, white horses, and white paper

【概念化】gàiniànhuà 指文艺创作中缺乏深刻的具体描写和典型形象的塑造,用抽象概念代替人物个性的不良倾向 generalization; deal in generalities; undesirable tendency to write or speak in abstract terms, with no profound description and specific images:要克服文艺创作中的~倾向。We should overcome the tendency towards generalization in creative writing.

【概述】gàishù 大略地叙述 give a brief account of:当事人~了事态的发展过程。The person involved gave a brief account of the events leading up to this incident.

【概数】gàishù 大概的数目。或者用几、多、来、左右、上下等来表示,如几年、三斤多米、十来天、一百步左右、四十岁上下;或者拿数词连用来表示,如三五个、一两天、七八十人 approximate number; round number expressed with 几 jǐ, 多 duō, 来 lái, 左右 zuǒyòu, 上下 shàngxià, e. g. 3-odd jin of rices, a fortnight, about 100 steps, around 40 years of age; approximation expressed by putting two numerals together, e. g. two to five, a couple of deys, 70 or 80 people

【概算】gàisuàn 编制预算以前对收支指标所提出的大概数字,预算就是在这个数字的基础上,经过进一步的详细计算而编制出来的 budgetary estimate; estimated figure of revenue and expenditure that provides the basis for the formulation of a budget after detailed calculations are made

【概要】gàiyào 重要内容的大概(多用于书名 usu. used in book titles) essentials; outline:《中国文学史~》*Essentials of History of Chinese Literature*

戤 gài〈方 *dial.*〉❶ 冒牌图利 counterfeit ❷ same as 隑 gài

gān(ㄍㄢ)

干[1] gān ❶〈古代 *arch.*〉指盾 shield ❷(Gān)姓 a surname

干[2] gān ❶〈书 *fml.*〉冒犯 offend:~犯 encroach upon ❷ 牵连;涉及 have to do with; be concerned with; be implicated in:~连 be responsible for|~涉 intervene; concern oneself with|这件事与你无~。It has nothing to do with you. *or* This is none of your business. ❸〈书 *fml.*〉追求(职位、俸禄等) seek (official positions, emoluments, etc.):~禄 seek official emoluments

干[3] gān〈书 *fml.*〉水边 waterside; bank:江~ river bank|河~ riverside

干[4] gān 天干 ten Heavenly Stems that designate points in a Chinese era (years, months, days, and hours):~支 Heavenly Stems and Earthly Branches

干[5](乾) gān ❶ 没有水分或水分很少 dry (跟'湿'相对 as opposed to 'wet'):~燥 dry|~柴 a stick|油漆未~ wet paint|衣服晾~了。The washing has dried in the sunshine. ❷ 不用水的 without use of water:~洗 dry cleaning|~馏法 dry distillation ❸(~儿 gānr)加工制成的干的食品 dried food:饼~ biscuit|葡萄~儿 raisin|豆腐~儿 dried bean curd ❹ 空虚;空无所有 empty; hollow:外强中~ outwardly strong but inwardly weak|钱都花~了。The money has been used up. ❺ 只具形式的 merely a matter of form:~笑 hollow laugh|~号(háo) cry aloud but shed no tears; affected wailing ❻ 指拜认的亲属关系 taken into nominal kinship:~妈 godmother|~儿子 adopted son ❼ 徒然;白 in vain; to no purpose; for nothing:~着急 be anxious but unable to do anything|~瞪眼 look on in despair; unable to help|~打雷,不下雨 all thunder but no rain; pay lip service to ❽〈方 *dial.*〉形容说话太直太粗(不委婉)(of speech) excessively vulgar and blunt:你说话别那么~。Don't be so coarse. ❾〈方 *dial.*〉当面说气话或抱怨的话使人难堪 embarrass sb. by making sarcastic remarks or complaining about him to his face:我又~了他一顿。I embarrassed him once again. ❿〈方 *dial.*〉慢待;置之不理 leave sb. out in the cold; give sb. the cold shoulder:主人走了,把咱们~起来了。The host left, leaving us to see to ourselves

☞ gàn on p. 634 and 乾 qián on p. 1537

【干碍】gān'ài 关系;牵连;妨碍 relation; connection; intervention

【干巴】gān·ba ❶ 失去水分而收缩或变硬 dried up; shrivelled; wizened owing to lack of water:枣儿都晒~了。The dates have all shrivelled in the sun. ❷ 缺少脂肪,皮肤干燥 dry skin owing to lack of fat:人老了,皮肤就变得~了。When a person grows old, his or her skin becomes wizened. ❸(语言文字)枯燥,不生动 (of language, writing) dull; uninteresting:话说得~乏味。His words were as dry as dust.

【干巴巴】gānbābā (~的 gānbābā · de) ❶ 干

燥(含厌恶意 derog.) dry：过去～的红土地带，如今变成了米粮川。The parched laterite of yesterday has today become a fertile grain field. ❷ (语言文字)内容不生动，不丰富 (of language, writing) dull; insipid; dry as dust：文章写得～的，读着引不起兴趣。This article is dull, and contains nothing of interest to the reader.

【干板】gānbǎn 表面涂有感光药膜的玻璃片，用于照相 dry plate; glass plate coated with a light-sensitive layer used for photography; also 硬片 yìngpiàn

【干杯】gān//bēi 喝干杯中的酒(用于劝别人喝酒和表示庆祝的场合 when urging sb. to drink, or for a special toast) drink a toast; bottoms up：为客人们的健康而～。Let's drink a toast to the health of our guests.

【干贝】gānbèi 用海产扇贝的肉柱(即闭壳肌)晒干而成的食品 dried scallop (adductor)

【干瘪】gānbiě ❶ 干而收缩，不丰满 dry; shrivelled：墙上挂着一串串辣椒，风吹日晒，都已经～了。Those strings of capsicum hanging on the wall have been dried out by the wind and sun.｜别看他是个～老头儿，力气可大着呢。Although a wizened old man, he still has great physical strength. ❷ (文辞等)内容贫乏，枯燥无味 (of writing) dull; drab; dry as dust

【干冰】gānbīng 固态的二氧化碳，白色，半透明，形状像冰。在常温常压下不经液化直接变成气体，产生低温。用做冷冻剂，也用于人工降雨。dry ice; solidified carbon dioxide usu. in the form of white, translucent blocks that change directly into a gas under normal temperatures and air pressure; used chiefly as a refrigerant and also for artificial rainfall

【干菜】gāncài 晒干或晾干的蔬菜 dried vegetable

【干草】gāncǎo 晒干的草，有时特指晒干的谷草 hay; dried millet straw

【干柴烈火】gān chái lièhuǒ 〈比喻 *fig*.〉一触即发的形势，也比喻情欲正盛的男女 dry wood near a fierce fire — an explosive situation or a man and a woman burning with passion

【干城】gānchéng 〈书 *fml*.〉盾牌和城墙 shield and city wall;〈比喻 *fig*.〉捍卫国家的将士 army that safeguards the nation; defender

【干脆】gāncuì ❶ 直截了当；爽快 clear-cut; straightforward：说话～利落。He speaks simply and straightforwardly. ❷ 索性 simply; just; altogether：那人不讲理，～别理他。Since he is unreasonable, simply leave him alone.

【干打雷，不下雨】gān dǎ léi, bù xià yǔ 〈比喻 *fig*.〉只有声势，没有实际行动 all thunder but no rain — much noise but no action

【干打垒】gāndǎlěi ❶ 一种简易的筑墙方法，在两块固定的木板中间填入黏土夯实 rammed-earth construction ❷ 用干打垒方法筑墙所盖的房 adobe house; house with walls of rammed earth

【干瞪眼】gāndèngyǎn 形容在一旁着急而又无能为力 stand by anxiously, unable to help; look on in despair

【干电池】gāndiànchí 电池的一种 dry battery; ☞电池 diànchí on p. 436

【干犯】gānfàn 冒犯；侵犯 offend; encroach upon：～国法 break the law

【干饭】gānfàn 做熟后不带汤的米饭 cooked rice

【干肥】gānféi 把人的粪尿跟泥土搀在一起晒干而成的肥料 dry manure; fertilizer that is a dried mixture of earth, and human excrement and urine

【干粉】gānfěn 干的粉条和粉丝 dried bean noodless; dried vermicelli made from starch

【干戈】gāngē 泛指武器，比喻战争 weapons of war; (fig.) war：～四起 war started on all sides; a nation torn by war｜大动～ take up arms; go to war｜化～为玉帛 turn hostility into friendship; bury the hatchet; turn swords into ploughshares

【干股】gāngǔ 指不出股金、赚了分红而赔了不受损失的股份 shares that do not require payment of a unit price and that can earn a free dividend

【干果】gānguǒ ❶ 果实的一大类，包括荚果、坚果、颖果和瘦果。通常指外有硬壳而水分少的果实，如栗子、榛子、核桃。fruit with hard husk and little moisture, including legume, nuts, caryopsis, and achene, e.g. chestnut, hazelnut, walnut ❷ 晒干了的水果，如柿饼 dried fruit, e.g. dried persimmon

【干旱】gānhàn 因降水不足而土壤、气候干燥 (of climate or soil) arid due to a shortage of precipitation

【干号】gānháo 不落泪地大声哭叫 cry and sob aloud without shedding tears; also 干嚎 gānháo

【干嚎】gānháo same as 干号 gānháo

【干涸】gānhé (河道、池塘等)没有水了 (of river, pond, etc.) dry up; run dry; have no water

【干花】gānhuā 利用干燥剂等使鲜花迅速脱水而制成的花。这种花可以较长时间保持鲜花原有的色泽和形态。dehydrated flower; dried flower made from a fresh flower by use of a desiccant, retaining its original colour and shape for a long period

【干货】gānhuò 指晒干、风干的果品 dried food and nuts

【干急】gānjí 心里着急而没有办法 be anxious but unable to do anything

【干将】gānjiāng 〈古代 *arch*.〉宝剑名，常跟莫邪并说，泛指宝剑 *ganjiang*, name for a famed ancient double-edged sword oft. mentioned in the same breath as *moya*; (in a broad sense) treasured double-edged sword

G

☞ gànjiàng on p. 634

【干结】gānjié 含液体少，发硬 dry and hard：大便～ constipation

【干净】gānjìng ❶ 没有尘土、杂质等 clean; neat and tidy; free from dust or impurity：孩子们都穿得干干净净的。The children's clothes are neat and tidy. ❷ 形容说话、动作不拖泥带水 (of speaking, act) quick and neat：笔下～ (of writing) concise and to-the-point ❸〈比喻 *fig.*〉一点儿不剩 complete; total：打扫～ a thorough cleaning | 消灭～ eliminate completely

【干酒】gānjiǔ 一种不含糖分的酒，多用葡萄酿成 dry wine; wine that is brewed with grapes and contains no sugar

【干咳】gānké 只咳嗽，没有痰 have a cough, with no sputum; dry cough

【干枯】gānkū ❶ 草木由于衰老或缺乏营养、水分等而失去生机 (of grass and trees) shrivelled because of ageing or lack of water and nutrition：一夜大风，地上落满了～的树叶。After a night of high wind, the ground is covered with withered leaves. ❷ 因缺少脂肪或水分而皮肤干燥 (of skin) wizened because of lack of water or fat ❸ 干涸 dry-up：～的古井 dry-up old well

【干酪】gānlào 牛奶等发酵、凝固制成的食品 cheese; dairy food made by the process of fermentation and concretion of milk

G

【干冷】gānlěng (天气)干燥而寒冷 (of weather) dry and cold

【干礼】gānlǐ 用钱代替礼品送的礼 money presented as gift

【干连】gānlián 牵连 be implicated in; be involved with

【干粮】gān·liáng 预先做好的供外出食用的干的主食，如炒米、炒面、馒头、烙饼等。有的地区也指在家食用的干的面食，如馒头、烙饼等。staple food prepared for a journey, e. g. fried rice, fried noodles, steamed bread, pancakes; in some areas solid pastry, e. g. steamed bread, pancakes

【干裂】gānliè 因干燥而裂开 crack owing to dryness：土地～ dry land | 嘴唇～ parched lips | 在北方，竹器容易～。In northern areas bamboo ware is prone to crack.

【干馏】gānliú 把固体燃料和空气隔绝，加热使分解，如煤干馏后分解成焦炭、焦油和煤气 dry distillation; carbonisation; process whereby solid fuel is placed in a vacuum and decomposed by the action of heat, e. g. coal can be carbonized into coke, tar, and gas; also 碳化 tànhuà

【干亲】gānqīn 没有血缘关系或婚姻关系而结成的亲戚，如干爹、干娘 adoptive kinship, e. g. godparents

【干扰】gānrǎo ❶ 扰乱；打扰 disturb; interfere; obstruct：他正在备课，我不便去～他。Since he is preparing his lessons, I won't disturb him. ❷ 妨碍无线电设备正常接收信号的电磁振荡。主要由接收设备附近的电气装置引起。日光、磁暴等天文、气象上的变化也会引起干扰。radio interference; jam; electromagnetic vibrations that hamper a radio's normal reception of signals, caused by nearby electrical installations or such astronomic or meteorological phenomena as sunshine or a magnetic storm

【干涩】gānsè ❶ 因发干而显得滞涩或不润泽；枯涩 not lenitive; not smooth：～的嘴唇 dry and coarse lips ❷ (声音)沙哑；不圆润 (of voice) raucous：嗓音～ husky voice ❸ 形容表情、动作生硬、做作 (of facial expression, action) blunt; affected：～地一笑 a factitious smile

【干涉】gānshè ❶ 过问或制止，多指不应该管硬管 interfere; intervene; meddle：互不～内政 non-interference in each other's internal affairs ❷ 关涉；关系 relation：二者了无～。There is no relation whatever between the two.

【干尸】gānshī 外形完整没有腐烂的干瘪尸体 mummy; shrivelled but otherwise well preserved corpse with no trace of putrefaction

【干瘦】gānshòu 瘦而干瘪 skinny and wizened; bony

【干爽】gānshuǎng ❶ (气候)干燥清爽 (of weather) dry and salubrious ❷ (土地、道路等)干松；干燥 (of land, road, etc.) dry and in good condition：到处都是雨水，找不到～的地方。There is so much rainwater everywhere; not a dry spot can be found.

【干松】gān·song〈方 *dial.*〉干燥松散 dry and loose：躺在～的草堆上晒太阳 lie on a mound of cut grass and sunbathe

【干洗】gānxǐ 用汽油或其他溶剂去掉衣服上的污垢(区别于用水洗 as compared with 'wash') dry-clean; remove dirt and marks by the use of gasoline or other solvents

【干系】gān·xì 牵涉到责任或能引起纠纷的关系 responsibility or relationship that may cause dispute：～重大 major implication; major involvement

【干笑】gānxiào 不想笑而勉强装着笑 laugh hollowly; force a smile

【干薪】gānxīn ❶ 挂名不工作而领取的薪金 salary drawn for a sinecure ❷ 指不包括其他收入的纯工资 net salary excluding all other incomes

【干谒】gānyè〈书 *fml.*〉有所企图或要求而求见(显达的人) seek favour; seek an interview (with sb. influential or powerful) for some purpose

【干与】gānyù same as 干预 gānyù

【干预】gānyù 过问(别人的事) intervene; interpose; meddle：事涉隐私，不便～。This is your private affair; it is not for us to interfere. also 干与 gānyù

【干哕】gān·yue 要呕吐又吐不出来 feel sick; be nauseated; retch:他一闻到汽油味就～。The smell of gasoline always makes him retch.

【干燥】gānzào ❶ 没有水分或水分很少 dry; arid:沙漠地方气候很～。The desert climate is arid. ❷ 枯燥,没有趣味 dull; uninteresting:演讲生动,听的人不会觉得～无味。An interesting speech never bores the audience.

【干政】gānzhèng 干预政事 intervene in political affairs:宦官～。Eunuchs intervene in state affairs.

【干支】gānzhī 天干和地支的合称。拿十干的'甲、丙、戊、庚、壬'和十二支的'子、寅、辰、午、申、戌'相配,十干的'乙、丁、己、辛、癸'和十二支的'丑、卯、巳、未、酉、亥'相配,共配成六十组,用来表示年、月、日的次序,周而复始,循环使用。干支最初是用来纪日的,后来多用来纪年,现农历的年份仍用干支。10 Heavenly Stems (*jia*, *yi*, *bing*, *ding*, *wu*, *ji*, *geng*, *xin*, *ren*, *gui*) and the 12 Earthly Branches (*zi*, *chou*, *yin*, *mao*, *chen*, *si*, *wu*, *wei*, *shen*, *you*, *xu*, *hai*). Each Heavenly Stem pairs up alternatively with each of the Earthly Branches to form 60 pairs that are used in a recurrent cycle to designate years, months and dates. This system was employed to mark dates in the beginning, but was mostly used to mark years in a later stage, a practice that is still followed in the Chinese lunar calendar.

甘 gān ❶ 甜;甜美(跟'苦'相对 as opposed to 'bitter') sweet; pleasant:～泉 sweet spring water | ～露 sweet dew | 同～共苦 share weal and woe; go through thick and thin together | 苦尽～来 after suffering comes happiness; no sweets without sweat ❷ 自愿;乐意(多为不好的事 usu. of sth. undesirable) willingly; of one's own accord:～愿 be willing | 不～落后 unwilling to fall behind ❸ (Gān)姓 a surname

【甘拜下风】gān bài xià fēng 佩服别人,自认不如 give sb. best; throw in one's hand:您的棋实在高明,我只有～。I have to acknowledge defeat due to your mastery of chess.

【甘草】gāncǎo 多年生草本植物,茎有毛,花紫色,荚果褐色。根有甜味,可入药,又可做烟草、酱油等的香料。liquorice (*Glycyrrhiza uralensis*); perennial herbal plant that has pilous caudex, purple flowers, brown seedpods and sweet root, and can be used for medicine, or for spice in tobacco and soy sauce

【甘结】gānjié 〈旧时 *old*〉交给官府的一种字据,表示愿意承当某种义务或责任,如果不能履行诺言,甘愿接受处罚 written pledge given to the authorities promising a willingness to bear certain responsibilities or perform a certain duty on pain of punishment

【甘居】gānjū 情愿处在(较低的地位) willing to be in an inferior position:～人下 be willing to be second best | ～中游 reconciled to the state of mediocrity

【甘苦】gānkǔ ❶〈比喻 *fig.*〉美好的处境和艰苦的处境 sweetness and bitterness; joys and sorrows:同～,共患难 share the joys and sorrows and go through thick and thin together ❷ 在工作或经历中体会到的滋味,多偏指苦的一面 hardships and difficulties experienced at work:没有搞过这种工作,就不知道其中的～。Those who have never undertaken this type of work have no idea of its difficulties.

【甘蓝】gānlán 二年生草本植物,叶子宽而厚,一般是蓝绿色,表面有蜡质,花黄白色。变种很多,可做蔬菜,如结球甘蓝、花椰菜、苤蓝等。wild cabbage (*Brassica oleracea*); biennial herbal plant that has broad, thick cyan leaves with a waxy surface and yellow and white flowers, and that can be cooked and eaten as a vegetable

【甘霖】gānlín 指久旱以后所下的雨 rain after a long drought; timely rainfall

【甘露】gānlù 甜美的露水 sweet dew

【甘美】gānměi 甜美 sweet:～的果汁 sweet and refreshing juice

【甘泉】gānquán 甜美的泉水 sweet and refreshing spring water

【甘薯】gānshǔ ❶ 一年生或多年生草本植物,蔓细长,匍匐地面。块根,皮色发红或发白,肉黄白色,除供食用外,还可以制糖和酒精。sweet potato (*Ipomoea batatas*); annual or perennial herbal plant that has long, thin vines, and red or white root tubers whose yellowish pulp may be cooked and eaten as a vegetable or used for making sugar and brewing liquor ❷ 这种植物的块根 tuberous root of sweet potato ‖ 通称红薯或白薯,在不同地区还有番薯、山芋、地瓜、红苕(sháo)等名称 generally known as 红薯 hóngshǔ or 白薯 báishǔ; known variously in different areas, such as 番薯 fānshǔ, 山芋 shānyù, 地瓜 dìguā, or 红苕 hóngsháo etc.

【甘甜】gāntián 甜 sweet:～可口 sweet and delicious

【甘味】gānwèi 〈书 *fml.*〉❶ 美味 delicious ❷ 感觉味美 relish delicious food:食不～ have no appetite for food

【甘心】gānxīn ❶ 愿意 do sth. willingly:～情愿 be ready and willing ❷ 称心满意 be reconciled to; resign oneself to; be content with:不拿到金牌决不～。I will not be happy until I win a gold medal.

【甘心情愿】gānxīn qíngyuàn 心甘情愿 willingly and gladly

G

【甘休】gānxiū 情愿罢休；罢手 be willing to give up：善罢～ let it go at that|试验不成功，决不～。If the experiment does not work, we mustn't give up.

【甘于】gānyú 甘心于；情愿 be willing to; be ready to; be happy to：～牺牲 be ready to sacrifice one's life

【甘愿】gānyuàn 心甘情愿 do sth. willingly：～受罚 be ready to be punished

【甘蔗】gān·zhe ❶ 多年生草本植物，茎圆柱形，有节，表皮光滑，黄绿色或紫色。茎含糖质，是主要的制糖原料。sugarcane (*Saccharum spp*); perennial plant that has a large terminal panicle and is widely grown in warm regions as a source of sugar ❷ 这种植物的茎 stem of this plant

【甘之如饴】gān zhī rú yí 感到像糖一样甜，表示甘愿承受艰难、痛苦 enjoy sth. bitter as if it were malt sugar — gladly endure hardship

忏 gān〈书 *fml.*〉干扰 bother; disturb

玕 gān☞ 琅玕 lánggān on p. 1151

杆 gān 杆子(gān·zi) pole：旗～ flagpole ☞ gǎn on p. 629

【杆塔】gāntǎ 架设电线用的支柱的总称。一般用木材、钢筋混凝土或钢铁制成，有单杆、双杆、A形杆、铁塔等。general term for the poles on which to span telegraph lines or electric wires (usu. made of wood, reinforced concrete, or iron and steel), including single poles, twin poles, A-shaped poles, and derricks

【杆子】gān·zi ❶ 有一定用途的细长的木头或类似的东西(多直立在地上，上端较细) pole; long, narrow, usu. cylindrical object of wood or metal erected on the ground for a certain purpose：电线～ pole for telephone or electric power lines ❷〈方 *dial.*〉指结伙抢劫的土匪 bandit; brigand：拉～ draw sb. into a gang|～头儿 brigand chief ☞ gān·zi on p. 629

肝 gān 人和高等动物的消化器官之一。人的肝在腹腔内右上部，分为两叶。主要功能是分泌胆汁，储藏动物淀粉，调节蛋白质、脂肪和碳水化合物的新陈代谢等，还有解毒、造血和凝血作用。liver; digestive organ of man and higher animals, located at the upper right abdomen in the case of human beings; main functions are excreting bile, storing hepatin, and regulating the metabolism of proteins, fats, and carbohydrates; also plays a role in detoxification, blood regeneration, and coagulation. also 肝脏 gānzàng;(图见☞ figure for 消化系统 xiāohuà xìtǒng on p. 2100)

【肝肠】gāncháng 肝和肠，多用于比喻 liver and bowels (usu. used as metaphor)：～欲裂 be so sad that one's liver and bowels are about to split|痛断～ be filled with deep sorrow

【肝肠寸断】gāncháng cùn duàn 形容非常悲痛 be heartbroken; be deeply grieved

【肝胆】gāndǎn ❶〈比喻 *fig.*〉真诚的心 openheartedness; sincerity：～相照 show utter devotion to each other ❷〈比喻 *fig.*〉勇气、血性 heroic spirit; courage：～过人 far surpass others in courage

【肝胆相照】gāndǎn xiāng zhào〈比喻 *fig.*〉以真心相见 treat each other with sincerity

【肝火】gānhuǒ 指容易急躁的情绪；怒气 irascibility：动～ lose one's temper|～旺 hot-tempered; irascible

【肝脑涂地】gān nǎo tú dì 原指战乱中惨死，后用来表示牺牲生命 spill one's liver and brains on the ground — sacrifice one's life for a just cause

【肝气】gānqì ❶〈中医 *Chin. med.*〉指有两肋胀痛、呕吐、腹泻等症状的病 diseases with symptoms such as costal pain, vomiting, and diarrhoea ❷ 容易发怒的心理状态 irritability

【肝儿】gānr 指供食用的猪、牛、羊等动物的肝脏 liver of an animal (such as pig, calf, or sheep) as food

【肝儿颤】gānrchàn〈方 *dial.*〉形容非常害怕 extremely scared; be in fear of

【肝脏】gānzàng 肝 liver

坩 gān〈书 *fml.*〉盛东西的陶器 earthenware

【坩埚】gānguō 熔化金属或其他物质的器皿，一般用黏土、石墨等耐火材料制成。化学实验用的坩埚，用瓷土、铂、镍或其他材料制成。crucible; vessel made of a refractory material (such as porcelain) used for melting and calcining a substance, generally made of clay, graphite, or other fire-resistant materials; crucible used for chemical experiments, made of porcelain clay, platinum, or nickel

苷 gān ☞ 糖苷 tánggān on p. 1867

矸 gān ☞ below

【矸石】gānshí 煤里含的石块，不易燃烧 gangue; uninflammable waste rock in coal

【矸子】gān·zi same as 矸石 gānshí

泔 gān same as 泔水 gān·shuǐ

【泔脚】gānjiǎo〈方 *dial.*〉倒掉的残汤剩菜和刷过锅碗的水 hogwash; the discarded remains of a meal

【泔水】gān·shuǐ 淘米、洗菜、洗刷锅碗等用过的水。有的地区叫潲水。swill; slops; used water (after washing rice, vegetables, or dishes and pans); known in some areas as 潲水 shàoshuǐ

柑 gān ❶ 常绿灌木，开白色小花，果实球形稍扁，果肉多汁，味道甜，果皮粗糙，成熟后黄色。树皮、果皮、叶子、花、种子都入药。mandarin orange (*Citrus reticulata*); ever-green shrub that has white flowers and bears yellow, sweet, succulent, loose-seedcase fruit; its bark, seedcase, leaves, flowers, and seeds can all be used for medicine ❷ 这种植物的果实 mandarin croups ‖ 有的地区叫柑子 known in some areas as 柑子 gān·zi

【柑橘】gānjú 果树的一类,指柑、橘、柚、橙等 oranges, tangerines, and citrus

【柑子】gān·zi 〈方 *dial.*〉柑 mandarin orange

竿 gān 竿子 pole; rod: 钓～ fishing rod | 百尺～头,更进一步 make still further progress

【竿子】gān·zi 竹竿,截取竹子的主干而成 bamboo pole

酐 gān 酸酐的简称 abbr. for 酸酐 suāngān

疳 gān 〈中医 *Chin. med.*〉指小儿面黄肌瘦、腹部膨大的病,多由饮食没有节制或腹内有寄生虫引起 infantile malnutrition due to digestive disturbances or intestinal parasites; also 疳积 gānjī

尴(尲、尶) gān [尴尬] (gāngà) ❶ 处境困难,不好处理 (of the situation one is in) awkward; difficult to deal with: 他觉得去也不好,不去也不好,实在～。To go or not to go, he was in a real quandary. ❷〈方 *dial.*〉(神色、态度)不自然 (of expression, attitude) unnatural; embarrassed: 表情～ look embarrassed

澉 gān 〈书 *fml.*〉干燥 dry

gǎn (ㄍㄢˇ)

杆(桿) gǎn ❶ (～儿 gǎnr) 器物的像棍子的细长部分(包括中空的) shaft or arm of sth.: 钢笔～儿 pen holder | 秤～ weigh beam | 枪～ barrel of a rifle ❷〈量词 *classifier*〉用于有杆的器物 [for long and thin cylindrical object]: 一～秤 a steelyard | 一～枪 a rifle

☞ gān on p. 628

【杆秤】gǎnchèng 秤的一种,秤杆用木头制成,杆上有秤星。称物品时,移动秤锤,秤杆平衡之后,从秤星上可以知道物体的重量。steelyard; balance in which an object to be weighed is suspended from the shorter arm of a level and the weight determined by moving a counterpoise along a graduated scale on the longer arm until equilibrium is attained

【杆菌】gǎnjūn 细菌的一类,杆状或近似杆状,分布广泛,种类很多,如大肠杆菌、布氏杆菌等 bacillus; straight rod-shaped bacterium (such as coliform bacteria, brucella)

【杆子】gǎn·zi same as 杆 gǎn ①: 枪～ barrel of a rifle | 笔～ pen holder; facile writer

☞ gān·zi on p. 628

秆(稈) gǎn (～儿 gǎnr) 某些植物的茎 stalk of some plants: 烟～ tobacco stalk | 麦～儿 wheat straw | 麻～儿 hemp stalk

【秆子】gǎn·zi 某些植物的茎 stalk: 高粱～ sorghum stalk

赶(趕) gǎn ❶ 追 catch up with; overtake: 你追我～ race against each other; try to outdo each other; chase each other | 学先进,～先进 emulate and catch up with the advanced ❷ 加快行动,使不误时间 try to catch; make a dash for; rush for: ～路 hurry along one's journey | ～任务 rush through one's job | 他骑着车飞也似地往厂里～。He got on his bicycle and pedaled like the wind to the factory. ❸ 去;到(某处) go to: ～集 go to market | ～考 go one's way to sit in an exam | ～庙会 attend a temple fair ❹ 驾驭 drive: ～驴 drive a donkey | ～大车 drive a cart ❺ 驱逐 drive away; expel: ～苍蝇 whisk the flies off; brush away a fly ❻ 遇到(某种情况);趁着(某个时机) happen to; find oneself in (a situation); avail oneself of (an opportunity): ～巧 happen to | ～上一场雨 get caught in the rain ❼〈介词 *prep.*〉用在时间词前面表示等到某个时候 till: ～明儿咱们也去。Let's go there another day. | ～年下再回家。I won't be going home until Spring Festival.

【赶不及】gǎn·bu jí 来不及 there's not enough time (to do sth.); it's too late (to do sth.): 船七点开,动身晚了就～了。The ship leaves at seven, and we'll miss it if we start out too late.

【赶不上】gǎn·bu shàng ❶ 追不上;跟不上 be unable to catch up with: 他已经走远了,～了。He's way ahead. We'll never be able to catch up with him now. ◇ 我的功课～他。My school work is not as good as his. | 这里的环境～北京。The environment here compares unfavourably with that of Beijing. ❷ 来不及 not enough time (to do sth.): 离开车只有十分钟,怕～了。The train leaves in ten minutes. I'm afraid we'll be too late. ❸ 遇不着(所希望的事物) be unable to meet with or chance upon (what is expected): 这几个星期日总～好天气。We have had no good weather these past few Sundays.

【赶场】gǎn//cháng 〈方 *dial.*〉 same as 赶集 gǎn//jí

【赶场】gǎn//chǎng (演员)在一个地方表演完毕赶紧到另一个地方去表演 (of a performer) hurry from one place to another for performance

【赶潮流】gǎn cháoliú 〈比喻 *fig.*〉追随社会时尚,做适应形势的事 follow the fashion; jump on the bandwagon

【赶车】gǎn//chē 驾驭牲畜拉的车 drive a cart

【赶得及】gǎn·de jí 来得及 there is still time; be able to do sth. in time; be able to make it: 马上就动身,还～。There's still time if we set out immediately.

【赶得上】gǎn·de shàng ❶ 追得上;跟得上 be able to catch up:你先去吧,我走得快,～你。You go first, I'll catch up with you. ◇你的功课～他吗? Can you keep up with him in your school work? ❷ 来得及 there's still time; be able to do sth. in time:车还没开,你现在去,还～跟他们告别。The train has not yet left, so if you set out right away, you'll still be in time to say goodbye to them. ❸ 遇得着(所希望的事物) be able to meet with or chance upon (what is expected):～好天气,去郊游吧。If the weather is fine, let's go on an outing.

【赶点】gǎn//diǎn ❶ (车、船等)晚点后加快速度,争取正点到达 (of train, ship, etc.) speed up in order to make the scheduled time; be in a hurry ❷ (～儿 gǎndiǎnr)赶上时机 come at an opportune time:你真赶上点儿啦,正缺你一个呢。You have shown up at just the right time; there is just one vacancy. ❸〈方 *dial.*〉掷色子赌博时在一旁叫喊,希望出现某个点数,叫做赶点 hope to throw the right number when playing dice

【赶赴】gǎnfù 赶到(某处)去 hurriedly go to (some place):～现场 hurry to the scene of an incident

【赶工】gǎngōng 为按时或提前完成任务而加快进度 try to get work done on time, or ahead of schedule:日夜～挖水渠 dig a canal day and night

【赶海】gǎn//hǎi〈方 *dial.*〉趁退潮时到海滩去捕捉、拾取各种海洋生物 gather seafood on the beach as the tide ebbs:～人 beach comber

【赶汗】gǎn//hàn〈方 *dial.*〉为治感冒,喝很烫的茶水或喝有发汗作用的流质使出汗 drink very hot tea or other liquid to induce perspiration and treat a cold

【赶集】gǎn//jí 到集市上买卖货物 go to market; go to a fair

【赶脚】gǎnjiǎo 指赶着驴或骡子供人雇用 lead a donkey or mule for hire

【赶街】gǎn//jiē〈方 *dial.*〉same as 赶集 gǎn//jí

【赶紧】gǎnjǐn 抓紧时机,毫不拖延 with haste; without delay or procrastination:他病得不轻,要～送医院。He is seriously ill and should go to hospital immediately. | 天要下雨了,～把晒的衣服收进来。It's about to rain. Hurry up and bring in those clothes that have been drying outside.

【赶尽杀绝】gǎn jìn shā jué 消灭净尽,泛指对人狠毒,不留余地 kill all; ruthlessly exterminate; spare none

【赶考】gǎnkǎo 去参加科举考试 (in feudal dynasties) on one's way to take imperial examinations

【赶快】gǎnkuài 抓住时机,加快速度 at once; quickly:时间不早了,我们～走吧。Time is getting on. Get a move on.

【赶浪头】gǎn làng·tou〈比喻 *fig.*〉紧紧追随时尚,做适应当前形势的事 follow the trend; catch the fad

【赶路】gǎn//lù 为了早到目的地加快速度走路 redouble one's pace in order to make a timely arrival at one's destination:今天好好睡一觉,明天一早起来～。We had better get a good sleep tonight so as to make an early start on our journey tomorrow. | 赶了一天路,走得人困马乏。We were exhausted after a full day on the road.

【赶忙】gǎnmáng 赶紧;连忙 hurriedly; hastily:趁熄灯前～把日记写完。I had better be quick and write my diary before the lights are turned out.

【赶庙会】gǎn miàohuì 到庙会上去买卖货物或游玩 go to a temple fair for shopping or fun

【赶明儿】gǎnmíngr 等到明天,泛指以后;将来 another day; in the future:～我长大了,也要当医生。When I grow up I'm going to be a doctor too.

【赶巧】gǎnqiǎo 凑巧 happen to; it so happened that:上午我去找他,～他不在家。I went to see him this morning, but, as it happened, he was out.

【赶热闹】gǎn rè·nao (～儿 gǎn rè·naor)到热闹的地方去玩 join in the fun:他最不喜欢～,见人多的地方就躲着。He dislikes bustling activity most, and does his best to avoid crowds.

【赶时髦】gǎn shímáo 指迎合当时最流行的风尚 follow the fashion; try to be in style

【赶趟儿】gǎn//tàngr same as 赶得上 gǎn·de shàng:不必今天就动身,明天一早儿去也～。We don't need to set off today; if we leave early tomorrow morning we'll still make it in time. | 再不走可就赶不上趟儿了。We're going to be late unless we hurry up a bit.

【赶圩】gǎn//xū〈方 *dial.*〉same as 赶集 gǎn//jí

【赶鸭子上架】gǎn yā·zi shàng jià〈比喻 *fig.*〉迫使做能力所不及的事情 force a duck to sit on a perch — try to make sb. do sth. beyond his capabilities:我不会唱,你偏叫我唱,不是～吗? I can't sing, and if you insist, it will be like forcing a duck to sit on a perch. also 打鸭子上架 dǎ yā·zi shàng jià

【赶早】gǎnzǎo (～儿 gǎnzǎor)趁早;赶紧 do sth. as early as possible:～把货脱手 sell the goods as soon as possible | 还是～儿走吧,要不就来不及了。We had better leave at once or we'll be late.

【赶嘴】gǎn//zuǐ〈方 *dial.*〉赶上别人正吃东西,也参加同吃 be an uninvited dinner guest

笴 gǎn〈书 *fml.*〉箭杆(gǎn) arrow shaft

敢[1] gǎn ❶ 有勇气；有胆量 bold; courageous; daring：勇～ boldness; bravery | 果～ courageous and resolute ❷ 表示有胆量做某种事情 have guts or pluck enough to do sth.; dare：～作～为 bold and decisive in one's actions | ～想、～说、～干 dare to think, speak, and act ❸ 表示有把握做某种判断 have the confidence to; be certain; be sure：我不～说他究竟哪一天来。I'm not sure on what day he will come. ❹ 〈书 *fml.*〉〈谦辞 *hum.*〉表示冒昧地请求别人 make bold; venture：～问 venture to ask; may I ask | ～请 would you please | ～烦 (I or we) venture to bother you

敢[2] gǎn 〈方 *dial.*〉莫非；怕是；敢是 perhaps; I'm afraid

【敢情】gǎn·qing 〈方 *dial.*〉〈副词 *adv.*〉❶ 表示发现原来没有发现的情况 [used when sth. is discovered or seen for the first time]: why ...; so...; I say ...：哟！～夜里下了大雪啦。Oh! So it snowed heavily last night! ❷ 表示情理明显，不必怀疑 of course; indeed; really：办个托儿所吗？那～好！We're going to run a nursery? That will indeed be wonderful!

【敢是】gǎn·shì 〈方 *dial.*〉莫非；大概是 perhaps; I'm afraid; I venture to ask：这不像是去李庄的道儿，～走错了吧？This doesn't seem to be the way to Lizhuang Village. I'm afraid we might have taken the wrong road.

【敢死队】gǎnsǐduì 军队为完成最艰巨的战斗任务由不怕死的人组成的先锋队伍 dare-to-die corps; suicide squad

【敢许】gǎnxǔ 〈方 *dial.*〉也许；或许 perhaps; probably

【敢于】gǎnyú 有决心，有勇气（去做或去争取）dare to; be bold in; have the courage to：～挑重担 dare to shoulder a heavy burden

【敢自】gǎn·zi 〈方 *dial.*〉same as 敢情 gǎn·qing

感 gǎn ❶ 觉得 feel; sense：身体偶～不适 not feel well; be indisposed; be out of sorts ❷ 感动 move; touch; affect：～人肺腑 be greatly touched | 深有所～ be deeply moved ❸ 对别人好意怀着谢意 be grateful; be obliged：～谢 thank | ～恩 be grateful | ～激 appreciate ❹ 〈中医 *Chin. med.*〉指感受风寒 be affected by cold; catch cold：外～内伤 affection by exogenous pathogenic factors; diseases caused by external factors ❺ same as 感觉 gǎnjué①；情感；感想 sense; feeling; sentiment：美～ appeal; aesthetic attainment | 好～ favor; good impression | 自豪～ sense of pride | 亲切之～ intimacy | 观～ reaction to (or impression of) | 百～交集 all kinds of feelings well up in one's heart ❻ （摄影胶片、晒图纸等）接触光线而发生变化 (oft. film, blueprint paper, etc.) sensitize：～光 light-sensitization

【感触】gǎnchù 跟外界事物接触而引起思想情绪 thoughts and feelings; emotional stirrings：他对此事很有～。He has deep feelings about this matter. | 旧地重游，～万端。On revisiting the place I had visited long ago, I was beset by emotional stirrings.

【感戴】gǎndài 感激而拥护（用于对上级）feel gratitude and respect for (one's superior)

【感到】gǎndào 觉得 feel; sense：从他的话里我～事情有点不妙。From his words, I sensed that not everything in this matter was as it should be.

【感动】gǎndòng ❶ 思想感情受外界事物的影响而激动，引起同情或向慕 be moved by external events; be touched：看到战士舍身救人的英勇行为，群众深受～。The masses were deeply touched by the soldier's heroic sacrifice of his own life in order to save another's. ❷ 使感动 move; touch：他的话～了在座的人。His speech deeply moved everyone present.

【感恩】gǎn//ēn 对别人所给的帮助表示感激 feel grateful; be thankful：～不尽 be extremely grateful | ～图报 be grateful to sb. and seek ways to repay the kindness

【感恩戴德】gǎn ēn dài dé 对别人所给的恩德表示感激 be deeply grateful; be deeply grateful to others for their kindness

【感恩图报】gǎn ēn tú bào 感激他人对自己所施的恩惠而设法报答 be grateful to sb. and seek ways to repay the kindness

【感奋】gǎnfèn 因感动、感激而兴奋或奋发 be moved and inspired; be fired with enthusiasm：胜利的喜讯使人们～不已。Everybody was moved and inspired by the news of the victory.

【感愤】gǎnfèn 有所感触而愤慨 be moved to indignation

【感官】gǎnguān 感觉器官的简称 abbr. for 感觉器官 gǎnjué qìguān

【感光】gǎn//guāng 照相胶片等受光的照射而起化学变化 sensitization; chemical changes caused by the influence of radiant energy, esp. light

【感光片】gǎnguāngpiàn 表面涂有感光药膜的塑料片、玻璃片等 light-sensitive film, plastic or glass plate coated with sensitive layer on the surface

【感光纸】gǎnguāngzhǐ 表面涂有感光药膜的纸，如放大纸、印相纸、晒图纸等 light-sensitive paper; paper coated with a sensitive layer, e.g. bromide paper, photographic paper, blueprinting paper, etc.

【感化】gǎnhuà 用行动影响或善意劝导，使人的思想、行为逐渐向好的方面变化 help sb. who has gone astray to mend his or her ways by persuasion, setting an example, etc.：～失足者 reform those who have gone astray

【感怀】gǎnhuái 有所感触；感伤地怀念 recall

G

with emotion：～诗 emotional poetry｜～身世 recall one's life experiences with deep feeling

【感激】gǎn·jī 因对方的好意或帮助而对他产生好感 be thankful; be appreciative of favour or help received：～涕零 shed grateful tears｜非常～你给我的帮助。I'm extremely grateful for your help.

【感激涕零】gǎn·jī tì líng 因感激而流泪，形容非常感激 shed grateful tears; be moved to tears in gratitude; be extremely thankful

【感觉】gǎnjué ❶ 客观事物的个别特性在人脑中引起的反应，如苹果作用于我们的感官时，通过视觉可以感到它的颜色，通过味觉可以感到它的味道。感觉是最简单的心理过程，是形成各种复杂心理过程的基础。sense; perception; sensation; mental process precipitated by physical stimulation, based on which various complex psychological processes ensue, e.g. when an apple acts on the sense organs, its colour can be seen and its fragrance smelt ❷ same as 觉得 jué·de ①：一场秋雨过后就～有点冷了。I felt a little chilly after a fall of autumn rain. ❸ same as 觉得 jué·de ②：他～工作还顺利。He thinks the job is going smoothly.

【感觉器官】gǎnjué qìguān 感受客观事物刺激的器官，如皮肤、眼睛、耳朵等 sensory organ; organs that sense objective things, i.e. skin, eyes, ears, etc.；简称 abbr. 感官 gǎnguān

【感慨】gǎnkǎi 有所感触而慨叹 sigh with emotion：～万端 be beset with welling emotions

【感慨系之】gǎnkǎi xì zhī 感慨的心情联系着某件事，指对某件事有所感触而不禁慨叹 heave a deep sigh over an emotional issue

【感愧】gǎnkuì 感激并惭愧 feel gratitude and shame：～交加 feel grateful and ashamed

【感喟】gǎnkuì〈书 *fml*.〉有所感触而叹息 sigh with emotion：人事沧桑，～不已 sigh with emotion over the rapid changes occurring in the world

【感冒】gǎnmào ❶ 传染病，病原体是病毒，在身体过度疲劳、着凉、抵抗力降低时容易引起。症状是咽喉发干、鼻塞、咳嗽、打喷嚏、头痛、发烧等。cold; flu; contagious virus caused by fatigue, staying too long in the cold, or low resistance in the body, characterized by a dry throat, inflammation of mucous membranes of respiratory passages, coughing, sneezing, headaches, and fever ❷ 患这种病 catch a cold ‖ also 伤风 shāngfēng

【感念】gǎnniàn 因感激或感动而思念 remember with gratitude; recall with deep emotion：～不忘 always recall sb. with deep emotion

【感佩】gǎnpèi 感激佩服 be grateful and admire：衷心～ be heartily grateful and admire

【感情】gǎnqíng ❶ 对外界刺激的比较强烈的心理反应 emotion; sentiment; strong psychological reaction to outside stimulation：动～ be carried away by one's emotions; get worked up｜～流露 reveal one's feelings ❷ 对人或事物关切、喜爱的心情 affection; love; concern and favour about sb. or sth.：联络～ maintain contact within a relationship or friendship; liaise｜他对农村产生了深厚的～。He has developed a deep affection for the countryside.

【感情用事】gǎnqíng yòng shì 不冷静考虑，凭个人好恶或一时的感情冲动处理事情 be carried away by one's emotions; act impetuously

【感染】gǎnrǎn ❶ 受到传染 be infected：身体不好，容易～流行性感冒。If one is feeling physically low, it is easy to catch the flu. ❷ 通过语言或行为引起别人相同的思想感情 influence; affect; induce the same thoughts and feelings in others by persuasion or actions：～力 appeal｜欢乐的气氛～了每一个人。The joyful atmosphere affected everybody present.

【感人】gǎnrén 感动人 touching; moving：～至深 deeply moving｜生动～ vivid and touching

【感人肺腑】gǎn rén fèi fǔ 使人内心深受感动 touch one to the depths of one's soul; move sb. deeply：言词恳切，～。The sincerity with which this article is written makes it deeply moving to whoever reads it.

【感纫】gǎnrèn〈书 *fml*.〉感激（多用于书信 used in letters）my gratitude

【感伤】gǎnshāng 因感触而悲伤 sad; sorrowful; sentimental：一阵～，潸然泪下。Sorrow welled up in his heart and brought tears to his eyes.

【感世】gǎnshì 对不正的世风、世事有所感慨 heave a sigh at undesirable public morals and unhealthy trends：他的诗文多为～之作。His poetry is mostly an expression of anguish at the bad in the world.

【感受】gǎn shòu ❶ 受到（影响）；接受 be affected by (influenced)：～风寒 be affected by the cold; catch a cold ❷ 接触外界事物得到的影响；体会 taste; experience; feel：生活～ life experiences｜看到经济特区全面迅速的发展，～很深。I was deeply impressed by the rapid development in the special economic zones.

【感受器】gǎnshòuqì 神经系统的末梢组织，能把所感受的外界刺激变成神经兴奋传入中枢神经。如表皮下面的接触、疼痛和温度的感受器等。receptor; distally structured nervous system that, on receiving stimulus, initiates waves of excitation in associated sensory nerve fibres which convey specific impulses to the central nervous system

【感叹】gǎntàn 有所感触而叹息 sigh with emotion

【感叹号】gǎntànhào 叹号 exclamation mark; exclamation point (!)

【感叹句】gǎntànjù 带有浓厚感情的句子，如：

'哎哟!''好哇!''哟!你也来了!'在书面上,感叹句末用叹号 exclamatory sentence, ending with an exclamation mark

【感同身受】gǎn tóng shēn shòu 感激的心情如同亲身受到(恩惠),也泛指给人带来的麻烦,自己也能亲身感受到。多用来代替别人表示谢意。express gratitude for favour extended to or apologize for troubling sb. else as if it were received or caused in person, (said when extending one's gratitude on behalf of a friend) I shall count it as a personal favour

【感悟】gǎnwù 有所感触而领悟:come to realize; realize; grasp 在奋斗中~到人生的真谛。Through personal struggles I've come to see the true meaning of life.

【感想】gǎnxiǎng 由接触外界事物引起的思想反应 impressions; reflections; thoughts:看了这封信,你有何~? What do you think about this letter?

【感谢】gǎnxiè 感激或用言语行动表示感激 thank; express one's gratitude through language or action:再三~a thousand thanks|我很~他的热情帮助。I am truly grateful to him for his help.

【感性】gǎnxìng 指属于感觉、知觉等心理活动的(跟'理性'相对 as opposed to 'rational cognition') perception; mental sensory experience:~认识 perceptual knowledge

【感性认识】gǎnxìng rèn·shi 通过感觉器官对客观事物的片面的、现象的和外部联系的认识。感觉、知觉、表象等是感性认识的形式。感性认识是认识过程中的低级阶段。要认识事物的全体、本质和内部联系,必须把感性认识上升为理性认识。perceptual knowledge; objective, phenomenal awareness of external elements of the environment through sense organs; the initial stage in the course of cognition; an overall, substantial, and internally-related awareness requiring an elevated cognition — rational knowledge. ☞ 理性认识 lǐxìng rèn·shi on p.1182

【感言】gǎnyán 表达感想的话 words that express one's thoughts or feelings:建厂三十五周年~thoughts on the 35th anniversary of the founding of the factory

【感应】gǎnyìng ❶ 某些物体或电磁装置受到电场或磁场的作用而发生电磁状态的变化,叫做感应 induction; process through which an object or an electromagnetic body becomes magnetized when in a magnetic field or in the magnetic flux set up by a magnetomotive force; also known as 诱导 yòudǎo ❷ 因受外界影响而引起相应的感情或动作 response; reaction; feeling or act of response caused by an outside influence:凡是动物都有对外界的刺激发生比较灵敏的~的特性。A keen reaction to outside stimuli is characteristic of all animals.

【感应电流】gǎnyìng diànliú 由电磁感应产生的电流。如日常使用的市电。induction current; faradic current; induced current; current of electricity produced by electromagnetic induction, such as the electricity supplied for household use; also 感生电流 gǎnshēng diànliú or 应电流 yìng·diànliú

【感召】gǎnzhào 感化和召唤 move and inspire:~力 power of influence

【感知】gǎnzhī ❶ 客观事物通过感觉器官在人脑中的直接反映 mental perception experienced through sensory organs ❷ 感觉 feeling:已能~腹中胎儿的蠕动 feel the movements of a fetus

澉 gǎn 澉浦(Gǎnpǔ),地名,在浙江 Ganpu, name of a place in Zhejiang Province

橄 gǎn ☞ below

【橄榄】gǎnlǎn ❶ 常绿乔木,羽状复叶,小叶长椭圆形,花白色,果实长椭圆形,两端稍尖,绿色,可以吃,也可入药 olive (*Canarium albums*); evergreen tree that bears pinnately comprund leaves that are small and in the shape of small ovals, white flowers, and green and oval fruit that is edible and of pharmaceutical value ❷ 这种植物的果实。有的地区叫青果。fruit of olive; known in some regions as 青果 qīngguǒ ❸ 油橄榄的通称 general term for olive trees

【橄榄绿】gǎnlǎnlǜ 像橄榄果实那样的青绿色 olive green

【橄榄球】gǎnlǎnqiú ❶ 球类运动项目之一,球场类似足球场,比赛分两队,每队十一人,球可以用脚踢,用手传,也可以抱球奔跑。有英式和美式两种,规则和记分法有所不同。rugby; American football; game played on a rectangular field between two teams of 11 players each, in which the ball is in the possession of one side at a time and is advanced by running or passing, and in which kicking, dribbling, lateral passing, and tackling are featured ❷ 橄榄球运动使用的球,用皮革制成,形状似橄榄,大小和篮球差不多 inflated leather oval-shaped ball used in the game of American football

【橄榄枝】gǎnlǎnzhī 油橄榄的枝叶,西方用作和平的象征 olive branch — used by the Western people as a symbol of peace

擀(扞) gǎn ❶ 用棍棒来回碾(使东西延展变平、变薄或变得细碎) roll with a stick (to make sth. flat, thin, or to break up into fragments):~面 roll dough; make noodles|~毡子 make a roll of a piece of felt|~饺子皮儿 roll out dumpling wrappers|把盐~一~ roll the salt ❷ 〈方 *dial.*〉来回细擦 polish:先用水把玻璃擦净,然后再~一过儿。When you have finished cleaning the windows with a wet towel, use a dry one to polish them.

G

☞ 扞 hàn on p. 766

【擀面杖】gǎnmiànzhàng 擀面用的木棍儿 rolling pin

【擀毡】gǎn//zhān ❶ 用羊毛、驼毛等擀制成毡子 felt made of wool or camel's hair ❷ 蓬松的绒毛、头发等结成片状 be dishevelled or fluffy as felt：皮袄～ fluffy fur-lined jacket｜头发都～了，快梳一梳吧。Your hair is tousled; perhaps you should comb it.

鳡 gǎn 鱼，身体长而大，青黄色，吻尖，尾鳍分叉。性凶猛，捕食其他鱼类，对淡水养殖业有害。yellowcheek carp (*Elopichthys bambusa*), long, large fish with a pointed mouth, of a ferocious nature and feeding on other types of fish, and therefore harmful to freshwater aquiculture; also 黄钻 huángzuàn

gàn (ㄍㄢˋ)

干[1]**（幹、榦）** gàn ❶ 事物的主体或重要部分 main part：树～ trunk｜骨～ backbone; mainstay ❷ 指干部 government functionary cadre：调～ (of a worker, farmer, etc.) enrolled as a government functionary｜～群关系 relationship between cadres and the masses

干[2]**（幹）** gàn ❶ 做（事）do; work：实～ work energetically｜～活儿 work on sth.｜埋头苦～ bury oneself in work ❷ 能干；有能力的 capable; able：～练 capable and experienced｜～才 capable person ❸ 担任；从事 work as; go in for：他～过厂长。He once acted as factory director. ❹〈方 *dial.*〉事情变坏；糟 (of things) going wrong; involving trouble：要～。It's going wrong.｜～了，钥匙忘在屋里了。Oh no! Disaster! I've left my key in my room.

☞ gān on p. 624

【干部】gànbù ❶ 国家机关、军队、人民团体中的公职人员（士兵、勤杂人员除外）cadre; functionary; officers of government institutions, military, or mass organizations ❷ 指担任一定的领导工作或管理工作的人员 leader; personnel who assume the office of leadership or management：工会～ trade union leaders｜区乡～ leaders of districts and townships

【干部学校】gànbù xuéxiào 培养、训练干部的学校 school for training cadres; cadre school；简称 abbr. 干校 gànxiào

【干才】gàncái ❶ 办事的才能 ability; capability：这个人还有点～。The man is quite capable. ❷ 有办事才能的人 capable person：这位副经理是公关上的～。This deputy manager has great ability in the field of public relations.

【干道】gàndào 行车的主要道路 artery; trunk road

【干掉】gàn//diào 铲除；消灭 kill; get rid of; sweep away

【干架】gàn//jià〈方 *dial.*〉打架；吵架 quarrel; come to blows

【干将】gànjiàng 能干的或敢干的人 capable person; go-getter：得力～ right-hand man｜一员～ a go-getter

☞ gānjiāng on p. 625

【干劲】gànjìn (～儿 gànjìnr) 做事的劲头 energy; drive; vigour; enthusiasm：～儿十足 be full of vigour (or drive)｜鼓足～，力争上游 go all out and aim high

【干警】gànjǐng 公、检、法部门中干部和警察的合称，有时泛指警察 police officer; agents of public security organs; (in a broad sense) policemen

【干练】gànliàn 又有才能又有经验 capable and experienced：他的确是一个精明～的人才。He really is a bright and capable man.

【干流】gànliú 同一水系内全部支流所流注的河流 trunk stream; mainstream; also 主流 zhǔliú

【干吗】gànmá 干什么 why on earth; whatever for：您～说这些话？Why on earth did you say that?｜你问这件事～？What's you up to, enquiring into this like that?

【干渠】gànqú 从水源引水的渠道 trunk canal; main ditch

【干什么】gànshén·me 询问原因或目的[ask for the reason or purpose]：你～不早说呀！Why didn't you say so earlier?｜他老说这些～？Why is he always talking about this? 注意 **NOTE**：询问客观事物的道理，只能用'为什么'或'怎么'，不能用'干什么'或'干吗' when enquiring about the way of things, use 为什么 wèishén·me or 怎么 zěn·me rather than 干什么 gànshén·me or 干吗 gànmá, such as 蜘蛛的丝为什么不能织布？Why can't a spider weave cloth?｜西瓜怎么长得这么大？How come this watermelon has grown so big?

【干事】gàn·shi 专门负责某项具体事务的人员，如宣传干事、人事干事等 personnel in charge of a specific affair (e.g. person in charge of promotion, human resources, etc.)

【干线】gànxiàn 交通线、电线、输送管（水管、输油管之类）等的主要路线（跟'支线'相对 as opposed to 'lateral line'）main line; trunk line; artery of transportation, electricity, or pipeline, e.g. water pipe, oil pipeline

【干校】gànxiào 干部学校的简称 abbr. for 干部学校 gànbù xuéxiào

【干仗】gàn//zhàng〈方 *dial.*〉打架；吵架 come to blows; have a row

旰 gàn〈书 *fml.*〉天色晚；晚上 late at night：宵衣～食 getting up before dawn and eating late — busy with state affairs

绀 gàn 稍微带红的黑色 dark purple; dark red

【绀青】gànqīng 黑里透红的颜色 dark purple;

prune purple; also 绀紫 gànzǐ

淦 Gàn ❶ 淦水，水名，在江西 Ganshui River in Jiangxi Province ❷ (Gàn) 姓 a surname

骭 gàn 〈书 *fml.*〉❶ 小腿 shank ❷ 肋骨 rib

澉 gàn 澉井沟 (Gànjǐnggōu)，地名，在四川忠县 Ganjinggou, name of a place in Zhongxian County, Sichuan Province

赣(灨) Gàn 〈书 *fml.*〉same as 赣 Gàn

赣 Gàn ❶ 赣江，水名，在江西 Ganjiang River, in Jiangxi Province ❷ 江西的别称 another name for 江西 Jiāngxī

〈古 *arch.*〉same as 贡 gòng

【赣剧】gànjù 江西地方戏曲剧种之一，由弋阳腔发展而来，流行于上饶、景德镇等地区 *ganju*; Jiangxi Opera; one of the local operas in Jiangxi Province, stemmed from the Yiyang tune of singing; popular in the Shangrao and Jingdezhen areas

gāng (ㄍㄤ)

冈(岡) gāng 较低而平的山脊 relatively low and evenly ridged hill: 山～ low hill | 景阳～ the Jingyang Ridge

【冈陵】gānglíng 山冈和丘陵 ridges and hills; rolling country

【冈峦】gāngluán 连绵的山冈 serpentive hills: ～起伏 undulating hills

江 Gāng 姓 a surname

扛 gāng ❶ 用两手举(重物) lift (sth. heavy) using both hands: 力能～鼎 (of a man) strong enough to lift an ancient bronze cauldron ❷ 〈方 *dial.*〉抬东西 carry sth. on shoulder

☞ káng on p. 1083

刚[1](剛) gāng ❶ 硬；坚强 (跟'柔'相对 as opposed to 'soft') hard; firm; strong; indomitable: ～强 unyielding | ～直 upright and outspoken | 他的性情太～。He has a very strong character. ❷ (Gāng) 姓 a surname

刚[2](剛) gāng 〈副词 *adv.*〉❶ 恰好 just; exactly: 不大不小，～合适 Just the right size, neither too big nor too small. ❷ 表示勉强达到某种程度；仅仅 barely; only; just: 清早出发的时候天还很黑，～能看出前面的人的背包。It was still dark when I set out in the early morning, so I could just make out the backpack of the person ahead of me. ❸ 表示行动或情况发生在不久以前 only a short while ago; just now: 他～从省里回来。He just came back from the provincial capital. | 那时弟弟～学会走路。That was at the time my younger brother had just learned to walk. ❹ 用在复句里，后面用'就'字呼应，表示两件事紧接 [for use in a compound sentence, followed by 就 jiù to indicate close connection between two events] as soon as: ～过立春，天气就异乎寻常地热了起来。It unusually warmed up as soon as spring began.

【刚愎】gāngbì 倔强固执，不接受别人的意见 headstrong; opinionated: ～自用 be obstinate and self-opinionated

【刚才】gāngcái 指刚过去不久的时间 a moment ago; just now: 他把～的事儿忘了。He forgot what happened just now. | ～他在车间劳动，这会儿开会去了。He was working in the workshop just a moment ago and is now at a meeting.

【刚度】gāngdù 工程上指机械、构件等在受到外力时抵抗变形的能力 (engineering) toughness; stiffness; resistance capability (of machinery or components) against deformation under the impact of outside force

【刚风】gāngfēng same as 罡风 gāngfēng

【刚刚】gāng·gāng 刚[2] just; only; exactly: 不多不少，～一杯。It's just a cup, neither more nor less. | 箱子不大，～装下衣服和书籍。The suitcase is just the right size for clothes and books. | 他～走，你快去追吧！He left just a minute ago; see if you can catch him.

【刚好】gānghǎo ❶ 正合适 just; exactly: 这双鞋他穿着不大不小，～。This pair of shoes fits him perfectly. ❷ 恰巧；正巧 by chance; by coincidence: 他们两个人～编在一个小组里。The two of them just happened to be in the same group. | ～大叔要到北京去，信就托他捎去吧。My uncle happens to be going to Beijing; you can ask him to take your letter along with him.

【刚健】gāngjiàn (性格、风格、姿态等)坚强有力 (of character, style, posture, etc.) vigorous; energetic; robust: 画风～质朴 simple but vigorous style of painting

【刚介】gāngjiè 〈书 *fml.*〉刚强耿介 be bold and honest

【刚劲】gāngjìng (姿态、风格等)挺拔有力 (of posture, style, etc.) bold; vigorous; sturdy: 笔力～ write in a bold hand | 枣树伸出～的树枝。The date tree has sprouted sturdy boughs.

【刚烈】gāngliè 刚强有气节 fiery and forthright; upright and unyielding: 禀性～ of an upright and unyielding disposition

【刚毛】gāngmáo 人或动物体上长的硬毛，如人的鼻毛、蚯蚓表皮上的细毛 (of human or animals) bristle; seta; chaeta

【刚强】gāngqiáng (性格、意志)坚强，不怕困难或不屈服于恶势力 (of character, willpower) firm; staunch; unyielding: ～不屈 keep a stiff upper lip; undaunted; imdomitale

G

【刚巧】gāngqiǎo 恰巧;正凑巧 by chance; by coincidence:你算赶上了,明天~有车进城。You're in luck. It just so happens that there's a bus going to town tomorrow.

【刚柔相济】gāng róu xiāngjì 刚强的和柔和的互相补充,使恰到好处 couple hardness with softness (in dealing with people); temper toughness with gentleness

【刚体】gāngtǐ 物理学上指任何情况下各点之间距离都保持不变,即形状和大小始终不变的物体(phys.) rigid body; objects impermeable to any change in shape or size

【刚毅】gāngyì 刚强坚毅 resolute and steadfast:~的神色 an expression of fortitude

【刚玉】gāngyù 矿物,成分是三氧化二铝,晶体,有玻璃光泽,硬度仅次于金刚石。红色透明的叫红宝石,蓝色透明的叫蓝宝石,是贵重的装饰品。刚玉可用作精密仪器的轴承,也用作研磨材料。corundum; very hard mineral (Al_2O_3) that consists of aluminum oxide of a hardness second only to diamond, occurring in massive and variously coloured crystal form, including ruby of red colour and sapphire of blue colour (both being precious stone), that may be used as an abrasive or as a material for making bearings for precision apparatuses

【刚正】gāngzhèng 刚强正直 upright; honourable; principled:为人~ upright personality

【刚直】gāngzhí 刚正 upright and outspoken:~不阿 be upright and never stooping to flattery

杠 gāng 〈书 *fml*.〉❶ 桥 bridge ❷ 旗杆 flagpole
☞ gàng on p. 639

掆(㨡) gāng 〈书 *fml*.〉same as 扛 gāng

岗(崗) gāng same as 冈 gāng
☞ gǎng on p. 638 and gàng on p. 639

肛 gāng 肛门和肛道的总称 general term for anus and proctodaeum:脱~ rectocele

【肛道】gāngdào 直肠末端通肛门的部分。周围有肛门括约肌围绕。proctodaeum; posterior part of the rectum and surrounded by anal sphincter; also 肛管 gāngguǎn

【肛门】gāngmén 直肠末端的口儿,粪便从这里排出体外 anus; posterior opening of the alimentary canal

纲(綱) gāng ❶ 提网的总绳(多用于比喻 oft. in a figurative way) headrope of a fishing net:~目 detailed outline|提~挈领 take a net by the headrope — concentrated on the main point|~举目张。When the headrope of a fishing net is pulled up, all of its mesh opens. ❷〈比喻 *fig*.〉事物最主要的部分(多指文件或言论 usu. for a document or speech) prime part, guiding principle:~领 outline|大~ general outline|提~ summary ❸ 生物学中把同一门的生物按照彼此相似的特征和亲缘关系再分为若干群,每一群叫一纲,如苔藓植物门分为苔纲和藓纲,脊椎动物亚门分为鱼、鸟、哺乳等纲。纲以下为目。(biol.) class; major category in biological taxonomy, e.g. the class of mammals ❹〈旧时 *old*〉成批运输货物的组织 transportation gang, esp. one transporting large quantities of goods under convoy:盐~ salt transported under convoy; salt convoy|花石~ rock convoy

【纲常】gāngcháng 三纲五常的简称 abbr. for 三纲五常 sāngāng wǔcháng

【纲纪】gāngjì 〈书 *fml*.〉社会的秩序和国家的法纪 social order; state law and legal system; discipline:~有序 kept in good order|~废弛。Disciplines become lax.

【纲举目张】gāng jǔ mù zhāng 纲是网上的大绳子,目是网上的眼,提起大绳子来,一个个网眼就都张开了 once the headrope of a fishing net is pulled up, all of its mesh opens;〈比喻 *fig*.〉文章条理分明,或做事抓住主要的环节,带动次要的环节 once the key link is grasped, everything falls into place

【纲领】gānglǐng ❶ 政府、政党、社团根据自己在一定时期内的任务而规定的奋斗目标和行动步骤 platform; pitch; (of governments, parties, mass organizations) goals to be achieved and measures to be taken within a certain period:政治~ political principle ❷ 泛指起指导作用的原则 programme; guiding principle:~性文件 programmatic document

【纲目】gāngmù 大纲和细目 detailed outline:拟定调查~ work out the outline for an investigation|《本草~》*Compendium of Materia Medica*

【纲要】gāngyào ❶ 提纲 outline; sketch:他把问题写成~,准备在会议上提出讨论。He made an outline of the issues and prepared to present them at the meeting. ❷ 概要(多用做书名或文件名 usu. used in book titles or document names) essentials; compendium:《农业发展~》*The Programme for Agricultural Development*

棡(棡) gāng ☞ 青棡 qīnggāng on p. 1563

矼 gāng 〈书 *fml*.〉石桥 stone bridge

釭 gāng 〈书 *fml*.〉油灯 oil lamp

钢(鋼) gāng 铁和碳的合金,含碳量0.03%~2%,并含有少量的锰、硅、硫、磷等元素。是重要的工业材料。steel; commercial iron that contains carbon of any amount between 0.03 and 2 per cent as an essential alloying constituent, and a small amount of manganese, silicon, sulphur, phosphor, and other elements, and that is an important raw material for industry
☞ gàng on p. 639

【钢板】gāngbǎn ❶ 板状的钢材 steel plate; plate ❷ 汽车上使用的片状弹簧 spring (of a motorcar, etc.) ❸ 誊写钢版的简称 abbr. for 誊写钢版 téngxiě gāngbǎn

【钢包】gāngbāo 盛钢水的钢制容器,内砌耐火砖,钢水由底部的口流出,进行浇铸 molten steel container made of steel and lined with refractory bricks, with a hole at the bottom from which molten steel flows out for casting; also 钢水包 gāngshuǐbāo

【钢镚儿】gāngbèngr 指金属辅币 coin; also 钢镚子 gāngbèng·zi

【钢笔】gāngbǐ 笔头用金属制成的笔。一种是用笔尖蘸墨水写字,也叫蘸水钢笔。另一种有贮存墨水的装置,写字时墨水流到笔尖,也叫自来水笔。pen; metal implement for writing, mainly of two kinds: dip pen and fountain pen, which contains a reservoir that automatically feeds the writing point with ink

【钢材】gāngcái 钢锭或钢坯经过轧制后的成品,如钢板、钢管、型钢等 steel products; steel; rolled steel, e.g. steel plate, steel tube, profiled bar

【钢锭】gāngdìng 把熔化的钢水注入模型,经冷凝而成的块状物。是制造各种钢材的原料。steel ingot; raw material for steel products

【钢管】gāngguǎn 管状的钢材 steel tube (or pipe)

【钢轨】gāngguǐ 铺设轨道所用的钢条,横断面形状像'工'字 rails (for trains, etc.); steel bar having a H-shaped cross section; track; also 铁轨 tiěguǐ

【钢花】gānghuā 指飞溅的钢水 spray (or sparks) of molten steel

【钢化】gānghuà 把玻璃加热至接近软化时急速均匀冷却,以增加硬度 (usu. of glass) toughening; temper glass through a controlled process of sudden cooling that makes it harder

【钢筋】gāngjīn 钢筋混凝土中所用的钢条。按断面形状不同可分为圆钢筋、方钢筋等,按表面形状不同可分为光钢筋、竹节钢筋、螺纹钢筋等。reinforcing bar, including round and square bars in terms of cross section, and glossy, bamboo-like, and whorl bars in terms of surface; also 钢骨 gānggǔ

【钢筋混凝土】gāngjīn hùnníngtǔ 用钢筋做骨架的混凝土。钢筋可以承受拉力,增加机械强度。广泛应用在土建工程上。reinforced concrete; concrete in which steel, in the form of rods, bars, or meshwork, is embedded in such a manner as to make the two materials act together to increase the mechanical intensity of a building; also 钢骨混凝土 gānggǔ hǔnníngtǔ or 钢骨水泥 gānggǔshuǐní

【钢精】gāngjīng 指制造日用器皿的铝 aluminium (as used for utensils):~锅 aluminium pan; also 钢种 gāngzhǒng

【钢口】gāng·kou (~儿 gāngkour) 指刀、剑等刃部的质量 quality of the edge of a knife or a sword:这把菜刀~儿不错。This kitchen knife blade is sharp.

【钢盔】gāngkuī 士兵、消防队员戴的帽子,金属制成,用来保护头部 helmet; hat made of metal, used by soldiers and fire fighters to protect their heads

【钢坯】gāngpī 用钢锭轧制成的半成品,形状比较简单,供继续轧制型钢、钢板、线材等 billet; semi-finished iron or steel, nearly square in a simple shape to be further rolled into sectional steel, steel plate, wire rod, etc.

【钢瓶】gāngpíng 贮存高压氧气、煤气、石油液化气等的钢制瓶 steel cylinder for storing high-pressure oxygen, gas, or liquefied petroleum gas

【钢琴】gāngqín 键盘乐器,体内装有许多钢丝弦和包有绒毡的木槌,一按键盘就能带动木槌敲打钢丝弦而发出声音 piano; stringed percussion instrument with steel wire strings stretched over a sounding board that resonate when struck by felt-covered wooden hammers operated from a keyboard

【钢水】gāngshuǐ 液体状态的钢。钢水一般都铸成钢锭,也可以直接浇铸成铸件。molten steel; steel in a liquid state, used for casting

【钢丝】gāngsī 用细圆钢拉制成的线状成品,粗细不等,是制造弹簧、钢丝绳、钢丝网等的材料 steel wire, the material for making spring, wire rope, and wire mesh

【钢丝锯】gāngsījù 锯的一种,形状像弓,锯条用钢丝制成,上面有细齿,用来在工件上锯出镂空的图案。有的地区叫锼弓子。fret saw; scroll saw; bow-shaped saw for cutting curves or irregular designs; known in some regions as 锼弓子 sōugōng·zi

【钢丝绳】gāngsīshéng 用几根钢丝绞成一股,再由几股绞成的绳,多用做起重的绳索 steel cable made by twisting thinner wires together; wire rope

【钢铁】gāngtiě ❶ 钢和铁的合称,有时专指钢 iron and steel; steel ❷〈比喻 *fig.*〉坚强 strong; firm; staunch:~战士 dauntless fighter

【钢印】gāngyìn 机关、团体、学校、企业等部门使用的硬印,盖在公文、证件上面,可以使印文在纸面上凸起。也指用钢印盖出的印痕。steel seal; embossed stamp; hard scal with raised lettering and design used by an organization, group, school, or enterprise for imprinting its stamp on a document or certificate; also referred to an embossing stamp

【钢渣】gāngzhā 浮在钢水上面的渣滓,是钢内杂质氧化而成的氧化物 slag; dross that floats on molten impure steel, resulting from oxidation during the refining process

【钢纸】gāngzhǐ 用浓氯化锌溶液处理过的特种纸,质地轻而硬,多用做绝缘材料和隔热材料等 vulcanized fibre paper, light but hard, usu. used as insulating or adiabatic material

【钢种】gāngzhǒng same as 钢精 gāngjīng

【钢珠】gāngzhū（～儿 gāngzhūr）滚珠 steel ball (in a ball bearing); ball bearing

缸（瓨） gāng ❶（～儿 gāngr）盛东西的器物，一般底小口大，用陶、瓷、搪瓷、玻璃等烧制而成 vat; jar; crock; container made of pottery, porcelain, porcelain enamel, or glass：水～ water vat｜酒～ wine jar｜小鱼～儿 goldfish bowl ❷ 缸瓦 compound of sand, clay, etc. for making earthenware：～砖 quarry tile｜～盆 glazed earthen basin ❸ 形状像缸的器物 jar-shaped vessel：汽～ cylinder

【缸管】gāngguǎn 陶管的通称 earthen pipe

【缸盆】gāngpén 缸瓦制成的盆 glazed earthen basin

【缸瓦】gāngwǎ 用砂子、陶土等混合而成的一种质料，制成器物时外面多涂上釉、缸、缸盆等就是用缸瓦制造的 compound of sand, clay, etc. used to make earthenware

【缸砖】gāngzhuān 用陶土烧制成的砖，黄色或赤褐色，是耐高温、耐磨和耐侵蚀的建筑材料 clinker (tile); quarry tile, yellow or russet, usu. used as building material, being hard-wearing, corrosion-proof, and high-temperature resistant

【缸子】gāng·zi 喝水或盛东西等用的器物，形状像罐儿 mug; bowl：茶～ tea mug｜糖～ sugar bowl｜玻璃～ glass mug

G

罡 gāng［罡风］(gāngfēng) 道家称天空极高处的风，现在有时用来指强烈的风（Taoism) wind in the empyrean; strong wind; also 刚风 gāngfēng

堽 gāng 堽城屯（Gāngchéng tún)，地名，在山东 Gangcheng, name of a place in Shandong Province

gǎng（ㄍㄤˇ）

岗（崗） gǎng ❶（～儿 gǎngr）same as 岗子 gǎng·zi ①：黄土～儿 loess hill ❷（～儿 gǎngr）same as 岗子 gǎng·zi ②：眉毛脱了，只剩下两道肉～儿。Only his two superciliary ridges can be seen since his eyebrows have fallen out. ❸ 岗位；岗哨 sentry; post：站～ stand guard｜门～ gate sentry

☞ gāng on p. 636 and gàng on p. 639

【岗地】gǎngdì 坡度较平缓的丘陵地带上的旱田 dry land on a gentle slope

【岗警】gǎngjǐng 在站岗的警察 policeman on sentry duty

【岗楼】gǎnglóu 碉堡的一种，上有枪眼，可以居高临下，从内向外射击 military watchtower with embrasures

【岗卡】gǎngqiǎ 为收税或警备而设置的检查站或岗哨 checkpoint for collecting tax, or to keep guard

【岗哨】gǎngshào ❶ 站岗放哨的处所 lookout post ❷ 站岗放哨的人 sentinel

【岗亭】gǎngtíng 为军警站岗而设置的亭子 sentry box; police box

【岗位】gǎngwèi 原指军警守卫的处所，现泛指职位（orig.）sentinel post; (in a broad sense) post; station：坚守工作～ stand fast at one's post

【岗子】gǎng·zi ❶ 不高的山或高起的土坡 hillock; mount：土～ earth hillock ❷ 平面上凸起的一长道 ridge; wale; welt：胸口上肿起一道～。There is a welt on his chest.

吭 gǎng ❶ same as 航 gǎng ❷ 云南德宏傣语地区过去相当于乡一级的行政区划，也用来称乡一级的头人 former administrative division of the township level in Dehong, an area mainly inhabited by the Dai ethnic group in Yunnan Province; title of a township leader

航（䴚） gǎng〈书 *fml.*〉盐泽 tidal salt marsh

港 gǎng ❶ 港湾 port; harbour：军～ military harbour｜～口 harbour｜不冻～ ice-free port ❷ 航空港 airport：飞机离～。The aircraft took off from the airport. ❸ 江河的支流（多用于河流名），如江山港、常山港（都在浙江）branch of a river (usu. used in the name of a river), such as 江山港 Jiāngshāngǎng and 常山港 Chángshāngǎng (both in Zhejiang Province) ❹（Gǎng）指香港 Hong Kong：～币 Hong Kong dollar｜～澳同胞 compatriots from Hong Kong and Macao ❺ 形容具有香港地方的特色 with a flavour of Hong Kong; of a Hong Kong characteristic：打扮得真～ dress in Hong Kong style｜她这一身儿才～呢！This outfit makes her look like someone from Hong Kong.

【港币】gǎngbì 香港地方通行的货币，以圆为单位 Hong Kong dollar; currency of Hong Kong

【港埠】gǎngbù 港口；码头 port; wharf：国际～ international port

【港汊】gǎngchà 河汊子 branching stream：～纵横 network of crisscrossing streams

【港警】gǎngjǐng 港口上维持秩序、保护运输安全的警察 harbour guard; harbour police; police whose duty is to maintain order and protect transportation at a harbour

【港口】gǎngkǒu 在河、海等的岸边设有码头，便于船只停泊、旅客上下和货物装卸的地方。有的港口兼有航空设备。port; harbour; structure built on the banks of a river or on the seashore so that ships may weigh anchor alongside to receive and discharge cargo and passengers; some ports also feature aeronautical facilities

【港湾】gǎngwān 便于船只停泊的海湾，一般有防风、防浪设备 harbour; place where ships may rest secure from storms and waves

【港务】gǎngwù 港口管理工作 management of

the harbour; harbour affairs

【港纸】gǎngzhǐ 〈方 *dial*.〉 same as 港币 gǎngbì

gàng(ㄍㄤˋ)

杠(槓) gàng ❶ 较粗的棍子 thick rod:顶门~ bar with which to lock a gate ❷ 体操器械,有单杠、双杠、高低杠等 gymnastic apparatus; bar, e.g. horizontal bar, parallel bars, asymetrical bars ❸ 机床上的棍状零件 rod-like spare part of a machine tool:丝~ guide screw; leading screw ❹ 出殡时抬送灵柩的工具 stout poles used to carry the coffin in a funeral procession ❺ (~儿 gàngr)批改文字或阅读中作为标记所画的粗直线 thick, straight lines (drawn beside or under words when reading books or correcting assignments):他看过的书都打了不少红~。He has left quite a few red marks on the books he has read. ❻ 把不通的文字或错字用直线划去或标出 cross out; delete:他一面看,一面用红笔在稿子上~了许多杠子。He crossed out many superfluous words and phrases in the draft he proof-read. ❼ (~儿 gàngr)〈比喻 *fig*.〉一定的标准 certain standard

☞ gāng on p.636

【杠房】gàngfáng 〈旧时 *old*〉称出租殡葬用具和代为安排仪杖鼓乐等的铺子 undertaker's store, where funereal utensils are put up for renting, and funerals arranged

【杠夫】gàngfū 〈旧时 *old*〉称殡葬时抬运灵柩的工人 professional coffin bearer

【杠杆】gànggǎn ❶ 简单机械,是一个能绕着固定点转动的杆。绕着转动的固定点叫支点,动力的作用点叫动力点,阻力的作用点叫阻力点。改变三点的两段距离的比率,可以改变力的大小。如剪刀(支点在中间)、铡刀(阻力点在中间)、镊子(动力点在中间)等就属于这一类。lever; bar that can turn around on a fixed point that is used to exert pressure or to sustain weight at one point of its length by the application of force at a second point, and turning it at a third point on a fulcrum that is fixed in one of three positions: between the load and effort, such as in the scissors; with the load between fulcrum and effort, such as in a hand hay cutler; and with the effort applied between load and fulcrum, such as in a pair of tongs ❷〈比喻 *fig*.〉起平衡或调控作用的事物或力量 inducing or compelling force:经济~ economic levers | 发挥金融机构在经济发展中的~作用 give play to the role of financial institutions as levers in economic development

【杠杠】gàng·gang ❶ same as 杠 gàng ⑤:在纸上画了一条~ draw a line on a piece of paper ❷ same as 杠 gàng ⑦:这条法规就是判断合法交易与非法交易的~。This regulation is the standard by which legal and illegal trades are defined. | 这次工资调整,规定了几条~。There are several criteria as regards salary readjustments.

【杠铃】gànglíng 举重器械,在横杠的两端安上圆盘形的金属片,金属片最重的 50 公斤,最轻的 0.25 公斤。金属片外加卡箍,以防止滑出。锻炼或比赛时,可以根据体力调节重量。barbell; bar with adjustable weighted disks (each weighing 0.25kg. at least and 50kg. at most) at each end used for exercise or weightlifting

【杠头】gàngtóu 〈方 *dial*.〉 ❶ 杠夫的头目 head coffin bearer ❷ 爱抬杠(争辩)的人 devil's advocate; person prone to arguing for argument's sake

【杠子】gàng·zi ❶ 较粗的棍子 thick stick; stout carrying pole ❷ same as 杠 gàng ②:盘~ perform on a horizontal bar ❸ same as 杠 gàng ⑤:老师把写错了的字都打上~。The teacher underlined the mis-spelled words.

岗(崗) gàng ☞ below

☞ gāng on p.636 and gǎng on p.638

【岗尖】gàngjiān 〈方 *dial*.〉(~儿 gàngjiānr) ❶ 形容极满 very full:~满的一车土 truck loaded full of earth | 手里端着~一碗米饭 hold a full bowl of rice with two hands ❷ 超出一般的;极好 excellent; super:这是一批~儿的大苹果。The apples in this batch are extraordinarily big.

【岗口儿甜】gàngkǒurtián 〈方 *dial*.〉形容极甜 extremely sweet:哈密瓜~。Hami melons are extremely sweet.

钢(鋼) gàng ❶ 把刀放在布、皮、石头等上面磨,使它快些 sharpen; whet; strop:~刀布 knife-whetting cloth | 把刀~一~ sharpen a knife ❷ 在刀口上加上点儿钢,重新打造,使更锋利 reinforce the edge (of a knife, etc.) by adding steel and re-tempering:这口铡刀该~了。This hay cutter needs to be reinforced.

☞ gāng on p.636

筻 gàng 筻口(Gàngkǒu),地名,在湖南 Gangkou, name of a place in Hunan Province

戆 gàng 〈方 *dial*.〉傻 rash; reckless; same as 愣 lèng ②:~头~脑 muddle-headed

☞ zhuàng on p.2527

【戆大】gàngdà 〈方 *dial*.〉傻瓜 fool; dumbbell

【戆头】gàngtóu 〈方 *dial*.〉傻瓜 fool; dumbbell

gāo(ㄍㄠ)

皋(臯) gāo ❶ 〈书 *fml*.〉水边的高地 highland by a waterside:汉~ a

highland on the bank of the Hanshui River | 江～ river bank ❷ (Gāo)姓 a surname

高 gāo ❶ 从下向上距离大;离地面远(跟'低'相对 as opposed to 'low') tall; high:～楼大厦 tall buildings | 这里地势很～。The terrain here is very high. ❷ 高度 height:那棵树有两丈～。That tree is about seven metres high. | 书桌长四尺,宽三尺,～二尺五。The desk is 1.33 metres in length, one metre in width, and 0.83 metre in height. ❸ 三角形、平行四边形等从底部到顶部(顶点或平行线)的垂直距离 vertical distance between the top and bottom of a triangle or a parallelogram ❹ 在一般标准或平均程度之上 above the average:～速度 high speed | 体温～ have a fever | 见解比别人～ have better understanding than most others ❺ 等级在上的 a notch above; of a high level or degree:～等 higher level | ～级 high-class; advanced ❻〈敬辞 *hon.*〉称别人的事物 your:～见 your opinions | ～论 your views ❼ (Gāo)姓 a surname

【高矮】gāo'ǎi (～儿 gāo'ǎir) 高矮的程度 height:这两棵白杨差不多一样的～。The two white poplars are about the same height.

【高昂】gāo'áng ❶ 高高地扬起 hold high (one's head, etc.):骑兵队伍骑着雄健的战马,～着头通过了广场。The cavalry, mounted on robust war horses, passed through the square with their heads held high. ❷ (声音、情绪)向上高起 (of voice or mood) high; elated; exalted:士气～ be in high morale | 广场上的歌声愈来愈～。The inspiring strains of songs surged across the square. ❸ 昂贵 dear; expensive; exorbitant:价格～ high prices

【高傲】gāo'ào 自以为了不起,看不起人;极其骄傲 supercilious; arrogant; haughty; proud:神态～ having an arrogant manner | ～自大 conceited and self-important

【高倍】gāobèi 倍数大的 high power:～望远镜 high-power telescope

【高拨子】gāobō·zi 徽剧主要腔调之一。京剧、婺剧等剧种也用高拨子。*gaobozi*; major tune of Hui Opera that is also employed in Peking Opera, Wu Opera, etc.; 简称 abbr. 拨子 bō·zi

【高不成,低不就】gāo bù chéng, dī bù jiù 高而合意的,做不了或得不到;做得了、能得到的,又认为低而不合意,不肯做或不肯要(多用于选择工作或选择配偶 oft. used in choosing a job or one's spouse) unfit for a higher post but unwilling to make do with a lower one; be unable to achieve one's heart's desire but unwilling to accept less

【高才生】gāocáishēng 指成绩优异的学生 brilliant student; top student; 才 cái also put as 材 cái

【高层】gāocéng ❶ (楼房等)层数多的 (of building) multi-storey; multi-storeyed:～住宅 multi-storey building | ～建筑 high-rises ❷ 居于上层的 higher level; high-ranking:～岗位 higher leadership post | ～领导 superior leaders | ～人物 ranking official

【高产】gāochǎn ❶ 产量高 with high production:～作物 high-yield crop ❷ 高的产量 high yield; high output:创～ chalk up an all-time high in output | 战高温,夺～ fighting against heat and struggling for a high output

【高超】gāochāo 好得超过一般水平 superb; excellent:见解～ excellent ideas | 技术～ superb skills

【高潮】gāocháo ❶ 在潮的一个涨落周期内,水面上升的最高潮位 high tide; high water ❷〈比喻 *fig.*〉事物高度发展的阶段 upsurge; stage of high-speed development ❸ 小说、戏剧、电影情节中矛盾发展的顶点 (of fiction, drama and film) climax

【高程】gāochéng 从某个基准面起算的某点的高度,如从平均海水面起算的山的高度,从某个测量点所在的平面起算的建筑物的高度 altitude; vertical elevation of an object above a surface, such as the height of a mountain above the average sea level, and the height of a building above the surface from which the survey starts

【高大】gāodà ❶ 又高又大 tall and big:～的建筑 tall and big structure | 身体～ be of tall and sturdy stature ❷ (年岁)大 (多见于早期白话 usu. in early vernacular) aged:老夫年纪～。I am old.

【高档】gāodàng 质量好,价格较高的(商品) (of commodities) high-end; high-grade; superior quality:～家具 high-grade furniture | ～服装 top-of-the-line garment

【高等】gāoděng ❶ 比较高深的 higher; advanced:～数学 higher mathematics ❷ 高级 senior; high-ranking; high-quality; high-level; advanced:～学校 institutions of higher learning; colleges and universities

【高等动物】gāoděng dòngwù 在动物学中,一般指身体结构复杂、组织和器官分化显著并具有脊椎的动物。但在脊椎动物中,对鱼类而言,称四足类(包括两栖类、爬行类、鸟类和哺乳类)为高等动物;对两栖类以下的无羊膜动物而言,则称爬行类以上的羊膜动物为高等动物;对爬行类以下的变温动物而言,则称鸟类和哺乳类恒温动物为高等动物。更狭义的专指哺乳类为高等动物。higher animal; gen. referring to vertebrates that have complex body structures and distinct systems and organs, such as amphibians, reptiles, birds, and mammals; compared with anamnias that fall under the category of amphibians, amniotas are above reptiles and are high animals; compared with poikilothermal animals, homoiotherms are higher animals; in a narrow sense, referring to mammals

G

【高等教育】gāoděng jiàoyù 培养具有专门知识、技能的人材的教育。实施高等教育的学校有大学、专门学院等。higher education for training specialized talent; 简称 abbr. 高教 gāojiào

【高等学校】gāoděng xuéxiào 大学、专门学院和高等专科学校的统称 institutions of higher learning; colleges and universities; 简称 abbr. 高校 gāoxiào

【高等植物】gāoděng zhíwù 指个体发育过程中具有胚胎期的植物,包括苔藓类、蕨类和种子植物。一般有茎、叶的分化和由多细胞构成的生殖器官。旧时的高等植物范围较小,仅指种子植物。higher plant, including bryophytes, ferns, and seed plants; plant that contains an embryonic period during its growth, generally characterized by the differentiation between stalk and leaves and by a multicellular reproductive organ; in old times the scope of higher plants was limited to spermatophytes

【高低】gāodī ❶ 高低的程度 height: 朗诵时,声音的～要掌握好。You should have a good command over the pitch of your voice while enunciating. | 因为离得远,估不出山崖的～。It is difficult to estimate the height of the cliff, owing to its distance. ❷ 高下 relative superiority or inferiority: 两个人的技术水平差不多,很难分出～。The two have equal skills and it is hard to say who is better. ❸ 深浅轻重(指说话或做事 of words or deeds) sense of propriety; discretion: 不知～ not know what is appropriate; have no sense of propriety ❹ 无论如何 on no account; just; simply: 嘴都说破了,老王～不答应。No matter how hard everyone tried to persuade him, Lao Wang would simply not budge an inch. ❺〈方 *dial.*〉到底;终究 at long last: 这本书找了好几天,～找到了。We had looked for the book for a few days before finally finding it.

【高低杠】gāodīgàng ❶ 女子体操器械的一种,用两根木杠一高一低平行地装置在铁制或木制的架上构成(gymnastic apparatus) asymetric bars; a pair of horizontally supported wooden bars above floor level at different heights ❷ 女子竞技体操项目之一,运动员在高低杠上做各种动作 women's gymnastics event on asymmetric bars

【高地】gāodì 地势高的地方,军事上特指地势较高能够俯视、控制四周的地方 highland; upland; elevation; (mil.) altitude: 无名～ unnamed height

【高调】gāodiào (～儿 gāodiàor) 高的调门儿 lofty tone; high-sounding publicity; 〈比喻 *fig.*〉脱离实际的议论或说了而不去实践的漂亮话 high-sounding words that are detached from reality or never acted on: 唱～ impractical argument; high-flown words; say fine-sounding things but take no action

【高度】gāodù ❶高低的程度;从地面或基准面向上到某处的距离;从物体的底部到顶端的距离 altitude; height; extent of elevation above a specified level; distance from the bottom to the top of something standing upright: 飞行的～ flying altitude | 这座山的～是四千二百米。The mountain is 4,200 metres high. ❷ 程度很高的 high degree: ～的劳动热情 in high working spirits | ～评价他的业绩 speak highly of his achievements | 这个问题应该受到～重视。Great importance should be attached to this problem.

【高度计】gāodùjì 利用气压、雷达等来测量高度的仪表,常用于航空和登山 altimeter; instrument designed to measure altitude by using atmospheric pressure, radar, etc.; also 高度表 gāodùbiǎo

【高尔夫球】gāo'ěrfūqiú ❶ 球类运动之一,用棒杆击球,使通过障碍进入小圆洞 golf; game in which a player using special clubs attempts to sink a ball with as few strokes as possible into each of the 9 or 18 successive holes on a course ❷ 这种运动使用的球,用橡皮等制成,比网球小 golf ball; hard dimpled ball used in golf, smaller than a tennis ball, made of rubber

【高风亮节】gāo fēng liàng jié 高尚的品格,坚贞的节操 of noble character and sterling integrity: ～,举世同仰。A noble character and sterling integrity are qualities greatly admired all over the world.

【高峰】gāofēng ❶ 高的山峰 high peak; pinnacle; top: 1960 年 5 月 25 日我国登山队胜利地登上了世界第一～珠朗玛峰。On May 25, 1960, a Chinese mountaineering team successfully reached the summit of Mount Qomolangma, the world's highest peak. ❷〈比喻 *fig.*〉事物发展的最高点 acme; apex, zenith; highest point of the development of sth.: 把革命推向胜利的～。Carry the revolution through to its triumphant end. | 上下班～时间路上比较拥挤。Traffic jams occur at rush hour.

【高高在上】gao gāo zùi shàng 形容领导者不深入实际,脱离群众 (of a leader) lord it over the masses; be far removed from the masses and reality

【高歌】gāogē 放声歌唱 sing heartily: ～一曲 sing a song heartily

【高歌猛进】gāo gē měng jìn 放声歌唱,勇猛前进。形容行进中情绪高涨,斗志昂扬。stride forward singing songs of triumph; advance triumphantly

【高阁】gāogé ❶ 高大的楼阁 high building; high pavilion ❷ 放置书籍、器物的高架子 shelf: 置之～ shelve sth. | 束之～ pigeon-hole sth.

【高跟儿鞋】gāogēnrxié 后跟部分特别高的女鞋 high-heeled shoes

【高贵】gāoguì ❶ 达到高度道德水平的 morally elevated; noble; noble-minded:～品质 noble quality ❷ 极为贵重的 very valuable:服饰～ expensive clothing ❸ 指地位特殊、生活享受优越的 highly privileged; elitist:～人物 honourable person; blue blood

【高寒】gāohán 地势高而寒冷 high and cold:～地带 high and cold area

【高胡】gāohú 高音二胡,一般用钢丝弦 alt-*erhu*; traditional Chinese fiddle, generally with wire strings

【高级】gāojí ❶ (阶段、级别等)达到一定高度的 senior; high-ranking; high-level; high:～神经中枢 higher nerve centre | ～干部 high-ranking official | ～人民法院 Supreme People's Court ❷ (质量、水平等)超过一般的 high-grade; high-quality; advanced:～商品 high-grade commodities | ～毛料 high-grade wool

【高级神经活动】gāojí shénjīng huódòng 大脑皮层的活动。人类的语言、思维和实践活动都是高级神经活动的表现。higher nervous activity; pallium activity, represented by activities involving use of language, thought, and practice

【高级小学】gāojí xiǎoxué 我国实施过的后一阶段的初等教育的学校 senior primary school; 简称 abbr. 高小 gāoxiǎo

【高级中学】gāojí zhōngxué 我国实施的后一阶段的中等教育的学校 senior high school; 简称 abbr. 高中 gāozhōng

【高甲戏】gāojiǎxì 福建地方戏曲剧种之一,流行于该省泉州、厦门、漳州和台湾省等地区 *gaojia* opera; local opera popular in Quanzhou, Xiamen, and Zhangzhou in Fujian Province, and in Taiwan Province; also 戈甲戏 gējiǎxì or 九角戏 jiǔjiǎoxì

【高价】gāojià 高出一般的价格 above-par price; high price:～商品 expensive commodities | ～出售 sold at a high price | ～收购古画 purchase ancient paintings at a high price

【高见】gāojiàn 〈敬辞 *pol*.〉高明的见解 sb.'s brilliant idea or opinion:不知～以为如何? I wonder if you would be kind enough to enlighten us on this matter.

【高教】gāojiào 高等教育的简称 abbr. for 高等教育 gāoděng jiàoyù

【高洁】gāojié 高尚纯洁 noble and unsullied:品行～ decent conduct | ～的情怀 noble mind

【高就】gāojiù 〈敬辞 *pol*.〉指人离开原来的职位就任较高的职位 move up to a higher position (usu. in another place):另有～ land a better job

【高举】gāojǔ 高高地举起 hold high; hold aloft:～火把 hold high a firebrand | 他～着奖杯向观众致意。He held the cup high and greeted the audience.

【高峻】gāojùn (山势、地势等)高而陡 (of mountain, terrain, etc.) high and steep

【高看】gāokàn 看重;重视 value; think highly of; treasure

【高亢】gāokàng ❶ (声音)高而洪亮 (of voice) loud and sonorous; resounding:～的歌声 sonorous singing ❷ (地势)高 (of terrain) high:计划平整七十亩～地 plan to level off 70 *mu* of highland ❸ 〈书 *fml*.〉高傲 supercilious; arrogant; haughty:神态～ in an arrogant manner

【高考】gāokǎo 高等学校招收新生的考试 college entrance examination:参加～ sit in the college entrance exams

【高空】gāokōng 距地面较高的空间 high in the sky; upper air:～飞行 high-altitude flight | ～作业 work high above the ground

【高空作业】gāokōng zuòyè 登上架子、杆子等在高处进行操作。修建高的建筑物或桥梁,架设电线等工程都有这种作业。aerial operation; work high on a ladder or scaffolding, usu. for the construction of high buildings and bridges or when spanning electrical wires

【高栏】gāolán 男子径赛项目之一,规定距离约110米,栏架高106.7厘米 high hurdles; men's and women's track event in which a series of hurdles, 106.7 centimetres high and 110 metres apart, are jumped

【高丽】Gāolí 朝鲜历史上的王朝(公元918—1392)。我国习惯上多沿用来指称朝鲜或关于朝鲜的。Koryo; name of a dynasty in Korea (918-1392):～参 Korean ginseng | ～纸 Korean paper

【高丽纸】gāolízhǐ 用桑树皮制造的白色绵纸,质地坚韧,多用来糊窗户 Korean paper; white, tough tissue paper made of mulberry bark, usu. used for window panes

【高利】gāolì 特别高的利息和利润 very high interest or profits:～盘剥 exploit by charging high interest on a loan | 牟取～ seek exorbitant profits

【高利贷】gāolìdài 索取特别高额利息的贷款 usury; usurious loan:放～ practise usury

【高粱】gāo·liang ❶ 一年生草本植物,叶和玉米相似,但较窄,花序圆锥形,生在茎的顶端,子实红褐色。品种很多,子实供食用外,还可酿酒和制淀粉。Chinese sorghum (*Sorghum vulgare*); annual cultivated plant with leaves similar to corn but narrower, panicles of flowers growing at the top of the stem, bearing reddish brown seeds that are edible and used for brewing liquor or making starch ❷ 这种植物的子实 sorghum seeds ‖ also 蜀黍 shǔshǔ

【高粱米】gāo·liangmǐ 碾去皮的高粱子实 hulled sorghum

【高龄】gāolíng ❶ 〈敬辞 *pol*.〉称老人的年龄(多指六十岁以上 usu. over 60) advanced age; venerable age:他已经到了八十多岁的

～，精神还很健旺。At the venerable age of 80, he is still full of energy. ❷ 岁数较大（就一般标准来说）over age（by general standards）：～孕妇 older pregnant woman

【高岭土】gāolǐngtǔ 纯净的黏土，主要成分是铝和硅的氧化物。白色或灰白色粉末，熔点1,750℃，是陶瓷工业和其他化学工业的原料。因为我国江西景德镇高岭所产的质量最好，所以叫高岭土。kaolin; fine usu. white clay that is an oxide of aluminum and silicon and used in ceramics and other chemical industries, and has a melting temperature of 1,750℃; called Gaoling clay, because China's highest-quality clay is produced in Gaoling, Jiangxi Province

【高炉】gāolú 从矿石提炼生铁的熔炼炉，直立圆筒形，内壁用耐火材料砌成。由顶上的开口装料（矿石、石灰石、焦炭等），铁水从靠近炉底的口流出。blast furnace; large vertical cylindrical furnace for smelting iron from ore, with its interior lined with refactory material, an opening in the top for loading iron ore, limestone and coke, and another opening close to the bottom for discharging molten iron

【高迈】gāomài〈书 *fml.*〉❶（年纪）大；老迈 advanced in years ❷ 高超非凡；超逸 exuberant; outstanding：风神～ an elegant demeanour

【高慢】gāomàn 高傲；傲慢 arrogant; proud：态度～，目中无人 be supercilious with an arrogant attitude

【高帽子】gāomào·zi〈比喻 *fig.*〉恭维的话 flattery：戴～ flatter; give compliments; also 高帽儿 gāomàor

【高门】gāomén 高大的门 tall and big door;〈旧时 *old*〉指显贵的人家 wealthy family：～大户 rich family|～望族 distinguished family

【高妙】gāomiào 高明巧妙 ingenious; masterly：手艺～ masterly craftsmanship

【高明】gāomíng ❶（见解、技能）高超（of ideas, techniques）extraordinary; better than average：主意～ brilliant ideas ❷ 高明的人 wise person：另请～ invite an expert

【高难】gāonán（技巧上）要求高，难度大（technically）highly difficult and challenging：他练的武术有许多～动作。The martial arts he practises include very difficult stunts.

【高能】gāonéng 具有很高能量的 high energy：～粒子 high-energy particle|～食品 high-nutrition food

【高攀】gāopān 指跟社会地位比自己高的人交朋友或结成亲戚（多用于客套话'不敢高攀'等）make friends or claim ties of kinship with someone of a higher social position; polite term oft. in the phrase 'I dare not aspire to have such honour as to....'

【高朋满座】gāo péng mǎn zuò 高贵的宾客坐满了席位，形容来宾很多 great gathering of distinguished guests

【高气压区】gāoqìyāqū 气压比周围高的地区。高气压区内空气往往下沉，天气多晴朗。region of high atmospheric（or barometric）pressure, where the air falls and the sky is clear

【高腔】gāoqiāng 戏曲声腔之一，由弋阳腔与各地民间曲调结合而成，音调高亢，唱法、伴奏乐器和弋阳腔相同，有湘剧高腔、川剧高腔等 style of opera tune that combines *yiyangqiang* and elements of folk tunes of different places, characterized by high-pitched singing, and similar to the *yiyangqiang* in terms of technique and musical accompaniment, such as in the Xiang Opera, Chuan Opera, etc.

【高强】gāoqiáng（武艺）高超 consummate; excellent in（martial arts）

【高跷】gāoqiāo 民间舞蹈，表演者踩着有踏脚装置的木棍，边走边表演。也指表演高跷用的木棍。walking on stilts; folk dance in which two poles each with a rest or strap for the feet are used to elevate the performer above the ground as they walk; stilts

【高热】gāorè same as 高烧 gāoshāo

【高人】gāorén ❶〈书 *fml.*〉same as 高士 gāoshì ❷ 学术、技能、地位高的人 very capable or talented person; man of superior attainments

【高人一等】gāo rén yī děng 比别人高出一等 a cut above other people; elitist：自视～的人往往是浅薄无知的人。Those who think themselves a cut above others are often superficial.

【高山反应】gāoshān fǎnyìng 登上空气稀薄的高山或高原地区而发生的反应。一般健康人在海拔4,000米以上有头痛、头晕、恶心、呼吸困难、心跳加快等症状。altitude sickness; sickness that occurs to a healthy person at an altitude of more than 4,000 metre, where air is rarefied, with such symptoms as headache, light-headedness, nausea, palpitations, and dyspnea due to oxygen deficiency in the blood and tissues; also 高山病 gāoshānbìng

【高山景行】gāo shān jǐng xíng《诗经·小雅·车辖》：'高山仰止，景行行止'（高山：比喻道德高尚；景行：比喻行为光明正大；止：语助词），后来用'高山景行'指崇高的德行 *The Book of Songs·Odes·Cart Shaft Keys*：'You are like mountain high; Like the broad road you go along.' In the lines, 'mountain high' and 'broad road' are used figuratively to mean nobility of character and moral integrity respectively. Hence the phrase, exalted virtue and great moral integrity

【高山流水】gāo shān liú shuǐ《列子·汤问》：'伯牙善鼓琴，钟子期善听。伯牙鼓琴，志在登高山，钟子期曰："善哉，峨峨兮若泰山！"志在流水，钟子期曰："善哉，洋洋兮若江河！"'后来用

G

'高山流水'比喻知音或乐曲高妙。*Lie Zi · Yin Tang's Questions*：'Bo Ya was a good zither-player, and Zhong Ziqi had a good ear for music. When Bo strummed his zither, with his mind on mounting a lofty mountain, Zhong commented, "How delightful! It sounds as grand as Mount Taishan." When Bo meditated on flowing waters, Zhong said, "How delightful! It sounds as vast as the Yellow River and the Yangtze River."' This passage adds new meanings to the phrase 'high mountains and flowing rivers', which is now a figurative expression for 'bosom friends' or 'musical virtuosity'.

【高山族】Gāoshānzú 我国少数民族之一,主要分布在台湾省 Gaoshan (Kaoshan) nationality, or the Gaoshans (Kaoshans), mainly inhabiting Taiwan Province

【高尚】gāoshàng ❶ 道德水平高 noble; lofty; high code of (morality, honour, etc.):～的情操 noble sentiment ❷ 有意义的,不是低级趣味的 significant; not in poor taste:～的娱乐 tasteful entertainment

【高烧】gāoshāo 人的体温在 39℃ 以上叫高烧 high fever; body temperature that is above 39℃; also 高热 gāorè

【高射机关枪】gāoshè-jīguānqiāng 机关枪的一种,装有特种枪架和瞄准器,主要用于射击低空飞行的敌机和空降兵,对空有效射程约 2,000 米 anti-aircraft machine gun; equipped with special gun mounting and gunsight and designed for shooting low-flying enemy planes and paratroops, with an effective range of about 2,000 metres

【高射炮】gāoshèpào 地面上或舰艇上防空用的火炮,用于射击飞机、空降兵和其他空中目标 anti-aircraft gun; artillery installed on earth or aboard a warship to shoot aircaft, paratroops or other airborne targets

【高深】gāoshēn 水平高,程度深(多指学问、技术 of scholarship or skill) advanced; profound:莫测～ be quite beyond one's depth; enigmatic|～的理论 profound theory

【高升】gāoshēng ❶ 职务由低向高提升 be promoted to a higher post:步步～ gradually rise to eminence ❷〈方 *dial.*〉起火(qǐ·huo);双响 get angry

【高师】gāoshī 高等师范学校的简称,包括师范大学、师范学院、师范专科学校、教育学院等 abbr. for higher normal schools, including teachers' universities, normal colleges, junior colleges of education, education institutes, etc.

【高士】gāoshì〈书 *fml.*〉志趣、品行高尚的人,多指隐士 excellent person, usu. referring to a hermit

【高视阔步】gāo shì kuò bù 形容气概不凡或态度傲慢 carry oneself proudly; strut; swagger; prance

【高手】gāoshǒu (～儿 gāoshǒur)技能特别高明的人 past master; master hand; ace:下棋的～ master of chess|他在外科手术上是有名的～。He is a celebrated master hand of surgery.

【高寿】gāoshòu ❶ 长寿 longevity; long life ❷〈敬辞 *pol.*〉用于问老人的年纪 your venerable age:老大爷～啦? May I ask how old you are, grandpa?

【高耸】gāosǒng 高而直 tall and erect; towering:～入云 reach to the sky; soar to the clouds|～的纪念碑 towering monument

【高速】gāosù 高速度 high speed:～发展 develop by leaps and bounds|～公路 expressway; superhighway

【高速公路】gāosù gōnglù 专供汽车高速行驶的公路。道路平直,在和其他道路相交时采用立体交叉。expressway; freeway; high-speed, multi-lane highway for through traffic, with partially or fully controlled access and graded separations at important intersections with other roads

【高抬贵手】gāo tái guì shǒu〈客套话 *pol.*〉多用于请求对方饶恕或通融 [used when requesting some kind of indulgence, such as bending the rules, or a loan] be magnanimous; be generous; not be too hard on sb.

【高谈阔论】gāo tán kuò lùn 漫无边际地大发议论(多含贬义 oft. derog.) indulge in loud and empty talk; talk volubly or bombastically:越是一知半解的人,往往越是喜欢～。Some people like to indulge in loud and empty talk despite having only a smattering of knowledge.

【高汤】gāotāng 煮肉或鸡鸭等的清汤,也指一般的清汤 soup-stock; (chicken or duck) broth; light soup

【高堂】gāotáng ❶ 高大的厅堂 big hall; main hall ❷〈书 *fml.*〉指父母 one's parents

【高挑儿】gāotiǎor〈方 *dial.*〉(身材)瘦长 tall and lanky:细～ thin and tall|～身体 tall, lanky build|～的个子 tall person

【高头大马】gāo tóu dà mǎ ❶ 体形高大的马 big horse ❷〈比喻 *fig.*〉人身材高大 (of a person) tall and big

【高徒】gāotú 水平高的徒弟,泛指有成就的学生 brilliant student:严师出～。A strict teacher never fails to produce a brilliant student.

【高位】gāowèi ❶〈书 *fml.*〉显贵的职位 high position:～厚禄 high post with a salary to match ❷ (肢体)靠上的部位 upper part (of human body):～截肢 amputation of the upper of a limb; high amputation

【高温】gāowēn 较高的温度,在不同的情况下所指的具体数值不同,例如在某些技术上指几千摄氏度以上,在工作场所指 32 摄氏度以上 high temperature; definition of a high temperature varies according to the situation — several thousand °C for certain technologies, and over 32°C for a working environment

【高温作业】gāowēn zuòyè 在温度很高的厂房里进行生产操作 operating under high temperatures; working at a high-temperature workshop

【高屋建瓴】gāo wū jiàn líng 在房顶上用瓶子往下倒水(建:倾倒;瓴:盛水的瓶子),形容居高临下的形势(见于《史记·高祖本纪》)operate from a strategic commanding height; (press upon the dukedoms like) water being poured off a steep roof — sweep down irresistibly from a commanding height (originating from *Records of the Historian · Official Records of Emperor Gaozu*)

【高下】gāoxià same as 上下[1] shàngxià③;优劣(用于比较双方的水平 of a comparison between two parties) superiority or inferiority:两个人的技术难分～。The two of them are equally matched in skills.

【高限】gāoxiàn 指山区生物分布的最高界限(of biological distribution in a mountain area) upper boundary

【高小】gāoxiǎo 高级小学的简称 abbr. for 高级小学 gāojí xiǎoxué

【高校】gāoxiào 高等学校的简称 abbr. for 高等学校 gāoděng xuéxiào

【高效】gāoxiào 效能高的;效率高的 high efficiency; highly active:～灭虫剂 highly effective pesticide

【高薪】gāoxīn 高额的薪金 high salary; high pay:～聘请 hire sb. at a high salary

【高兴】gāoxìng ❶ 愉快而兴奋 glad; happy; cheerful:听说你要来,我们全家都很～。Our entire family was glad to hear that you were coming. ❷ 带着愉快的情绪去做某件事;喜欢 be willing to; be happy to:他就是～看电影,对看戏不感兴趣。He is fond of films but not at all interested in the theatre.

【高血压】gāoxuèyā 成人的动脉血压持续超过140/90毫米水银柱时叫做高血压。有两种类型,一种叫症状性高血压,由某些疾病引起;另一种叫原发性高血压,由大脑皮层功能紊乱引起。通常把后者称为高血压病。hypertension; disease caused by elevation of blood pressure to 140/90 mm. on the mercury column, of two types: symptomatic, which is caused by some other diseases, and primary hypertension, caused by cerebral cortex dysfunction; the latter is generally known as 高血压病 gāoxuèyābìng

【高压】gāoyā ❶ 较高的压强 high pressure ❷ 较高的电压 high voltage ❸ 高气压区 high-pressure atmospheric area ❹ 心脏收缩时血液对血管的压力 maximum pressure; pressure of blood within the vein as the heart contracts ❺ 残酷迫害;极度压制 high-handed persecution; coercion:～政策 high-handed policy|～手段 high-handed means

【高压电】gāoyādiàn 工业上指电压在3,000—11,000伏的电源。通常指电压在250伏以上的电源。high voltage (generally the power at a level of 250 volts or more); (in industry) power between 3,000 and 11,000 volts

【高压锅】gāoyāguō 锅盖装有胶圈的密封锅,多用铝合金制成。加热时锅内气压升高,食物熟得快。pressure cooker, usu. of aluminium alloy, made airtight with a rubber washer for rapid cooking by means of superheated steam under pressure; also 压力锅 yālìguō

【高压脊】gāoyājǐ 在同高度上,高气压中心向外突出的部分,其气压高于其他部分 ridge of high pressure; pressure ridge, the protruding part of the centre of high atmospheric pressure whose pressure is higher than that of other parts at the same altitude; also 高空脊 gāokōngjǐ or 高压楔 gāoyāxiē

【高压线】gāoyāxiàn 输送高压电流的导线 high voltage line (or wire)

【高雅】gāoyǎ 高尚,不粗俗 refined; elegant:格调～ elegant style; tastefulness of presentation

【高扬】gāoyáng ❶ 高高升起或举起 raise high; uplift; soar:情绪～ uplifted spirit|士气～ rising morale ❷ 高度发扬 carry forward; develop:～见义勇为精神。Carry forward the spirit of helping others for a just cause.

【高原】gāoyuán 海拔较高、地形起伏较小的大片平地 plateau; highland; tableland; usu. extensive land area having a relatively level surface that rises sharply above adjacent land on at least one side

【高远】gāoyuǎn 高而深远 high and far:～的蓝天 high and far sky|志向～ lofty aspirations; ambitious

【高瞻远瞩】gāo zhān yuǎn zhǔ 形容眼光远大 look far ahead and aim high; far sighted

【高涨】gāozhǎng (物价、运动、情绪等)急剧上升或发展(of price, movement, enthusiasm, etc.) rise; upsurge; run high

【高招】gāozhāo (～儿 gāozhāor)好办法;好主意 clever idea; brilliant idea:出～ come up with a great idea|就这两下子,没有什么～。That's all he could come up with, nothing particularly ingenious. also 高着 gāozhāo

【高着】gāozhāo same as 高招 gāozhāo

【高枕】gāozhěn 垫高了枕头(睡觉) high pillow:～而卧(形容不加警惕) lying on a high pillow — set one's heart at rest|～无忧 sleep in peace free from anxiety

【高枕无忧】gāo zhěn wú yōu 垫高了枕头睡觉,无所忧虑 shake the pillow and have a good sleep; 〈比喻 *fig.*〉平安无事,不用担扰 sit back and relax; be carefree

【高枝儿】gāozhīr 〈比喻 *fig.*〉高的职位或职位高的人 higher branches; high position or sen-

G

ior official：攀～ play up to one's superiors or betters | 巴～ curry favour with one's superiors

【高中】gāozhōng 高级中学的简称 abbr. for 高级中学 gāojí zhōngxué

【高姿态】gāozītài 指对自己要求严格，而对别人表现出宽容、谅解的态度 lofty stance; magnanimous attitude：你要～，不要和他计较。You should take a magnanimous attitude and not engage in any dispute with him.

【高足】gāozú〈敬辞 *pol.*〉称呼别人的学生 your brilliant disciple; your pupil

【高祖】gāozǔ ❶ 曾祖的父亲 great-great-grandfather ❷〈书 *fml.*〉指始祖或远祖 forefather; remote ancestors

【高祖母】gāozǔmǔ 曾祖的母亲 great-great-grandmother

羔 gāo（～儿 gāor）羔子 lamb; kid; fawn：羊～ lamb | ～儿皮 caracule; lambskin | 鹿～ fawn

【羔皮】gāopí 小羊、小鹿等的毛皮 lambskin; kidskin; kid

【羔羊】gāoyáng 小羊，多比喻天真、纯洁或弱小者 lamb;（oft. fig.）innocent and helpless person; scapegoat：替罪的～ scapegoat; fall guy

【羔子】gāo·zi 小羊，也指某些动物的崽子 lamb; kid; fawn; young animal：兔～ small hare

G

槔(槹) gāo ☞ 桔槔 jiégāo on p. 993

睾 gāo [睾丸] gāowán 男子或某些雄性哺乳动物生殖器官的一部分，在阴囊内，椭圆形，能产生精子。人的睾丸也叫外肾。testis; testicle; typically paired male reproductive gland that produces sperm; also 精巢 jīngcháo

膏 gāo ❶ 脂肪；油 fat; grease; oil：～火 lamp oil | 春雨如～。Rain in spring is as precious as oil. ❷ 很稠的糊状物 paste; cream; ointment：～药 plaster | 梨～ pear syrup | 牙～ tooth paste | 雪花～ vanishing cream ❸ 肥沃 fertile：～壤 fertile soil | ～腴 fertile land ☞ gào on p. 649

【膏肓】gāohuāng ☞ 病入膏肓 bìng rù gāo huāng on p. 143

【膏火】gāohuǒ〈书 *fml.*〉灯火 lights（膏 *gao*：灯油 lamp oil）；〈比喻 *fig.*〉夜间工作的费用（多指求学的费用 usu. cost of private tuition）expense incurred by night work

【膏剂】gāojì〈中医 *Chin. med.*〉指内服的膏状药物 medicinal extract; electuary

【膏粱】gāoliáng 肥肉和细粮，泛指美味的饭菜 fat meat and fine grain; rich food：～子弟（指富贵人家的子弟）sons of the idle rich

【膏血】gāoxuè（人的）脂肪和血液（man's）fat and blood；〈比喻 *fig.*〉用血汗换来的劳动成果 fruits of toil：国家财产是人民的～。The Nation's property is the fruit of the people's industry.

【膏药】gāo·yao 一种中药外用药，用植物油加药熬炼成膏，涂在布、纸或皮的一面，可以较长时间地贴在患处，用来治疮疖、消肿痛等（Chin. med.）medicated plaster; medicine for external use that is pasted on one side of a piece of cloth or paper and applied to the affected part, for the purpose of curing boils, reducing swelling, and easing pain

【膏腴】gāoyú〈书 *fml.*〉肥沃 fertile：～之地 fertile land

【膏泽】gāozé〈书 *fml.*〉❶ 滋润作物的及时雨 timely rain ❷〈比喻 *fig.*〉给予恩惠 kindness; favour：～下民 benefit the people

【膏子】gāo·zi 熬成浓汁服用或外敷的药物 ointment-like medicine for oral or external use

篙 gāo 撑船的竹竿或木杆 punt pole

【篙头】gāo·tou〈方 *dial.*〉篙 punt pole

【篙子】gāo·zi〈方 *dial.*〉❶ 篙 punt pole ❷ 晒衣服用的杆子 pole for hanging clothes on out in the sun

糕(餻) gāo 用米粉、面粉等制成的食品，种类很多，如年糕、蜂糕、蛋糕等 cake; pudding; bread-like food made from a dough or batter that is usu. fried or baked

【糕饼】gāobǐng〈方 *dial.*〉糕点 cakes and pastries

【糕点】gāodiǎn 糕和点心（总称）（collect.）cakes and pastries

【糕干】gāo·gan 一种代乳品，主要用米粉和糖等制成 sweetened rice flour (sometimes fed to infants as a substitute for powdered milk)

櫜 gāo〈书 *fml.*〉❶ 收藏盔甲、弓矢的器具 tool for collecting armour and bows ❷ 储藏 store up

gǎo（《幺ˇ）

杲 gǎo ❶〈书 *fml.*〉明亮 bright：～日 bright sun ❷（Gǎo）姓 a surname

【杲杲】gǎogǎo〈书 *fml.*〉（太阳）很明亮的样子（of the sun）shining brightly：～出日。The bright sun rises into the void. | 秋阳～ bright autumn sun

搞 gǎo ❶ 做；干；从事 do; carry on; be engaged in：～生产 be engaged in production | ～工作 do one's job; work | ～建设 be engaged in construction work ❷ 设法获得；弄 get; get hold of; secure：～点儿水来 go and get some water | ～材料 draw materials ❸ 整治人，使吃苦头 discipline sb.; torment sb.; make sb. do the work：他们合起来～我。They worked together to play tricks on me.

【搞鬼】gǎo//guǐ 暗中使用诡计或做手脚 play tricks; get up to mischief：不怕他～ do not be afraid of his mischief | 你又搞什么鬼？What are you up to?

【搞活】gǎohuó 采取措施使事物有活力 vitalize; enliven:解放思想,~经济。Liberate people's ideas and enliven the economy.

缟 gǎo 古代的一种白绢 fine, white silk used in ancient China

【缟素】gǎosù〈书 *fml.*〉白衣服,指丧服 white mourning apparel

槁(槀) gǎo 干枯 withered:枯~withered

【槁木】gǎomù 枯槁的树干 withered tree:形如~ in the shape of a withered tree

【槁木死灰】gǎomù sǐhuī 枯槁的树干和火灭后的冷灰 rotten trees and cold ashes;〈比喻 *fig.*〉心情冷淡,对一切事情无动于衷 lifeless and complete apathy; living corpse

暠 gǎo〈书 *fml.*〉白 white

☞ hào on p. 780

镐 gǎo 刨土用的工具 pick; pickaxe:鹤嘴~ mattock

☞ hào on p. 780

【镐头】gǎo·tou 镐 pick; pickaxe

稿[1](稾) gǎo〈书 *fml.*〉谷类植物的茎 stalk of grain:~荐 straw mattress

稿[2](稾) gǎo ❶(~儿 gǎor)稿子 draft; sketch:手~ manuscript|定~ finalize a book or text|~纸 manuscript paper|打个~儿 make a sketch|心里也没有个~儿(心中无数) have no well-thought-out plan in mind ❷ 外发公文的草稿 rough draft (of a document); draft:拟~ make a draft|核~ check a draft

【稿本】gǎoběn 著作的底稿 manuscript (of a book, etc.)

【稿酬】gǎochóu same as 稿费 gǎofèi

【稿费】gǎofèi 图书、报刊等出版机构在发表著作、译稿、图画、照片等的时候付给作者的报酬 royalty; payment for a published article, book, translation, photograph, or illustration; contribution fee; author's remuneration

【稿件】gǎojiàn 出版社、报刊编辑部等称作者交来的作品 manuscript; written contribution

【稿荐】gǎojiàn 稻草、麦秸等编成的垫子,用来铺床 straw mattress; pallet

【稿约】gǎoyuē 刊物的编辑部向投稿人说明刊物的性质、欢迎哪些稿件以及其他注意事项的告白,一般写成条文,登载在刊物上 notice to solicit contributors (to a magazine, etc.). Such a notice is oft. carried in a magazine to inform prospective contributors of the characteristcs of the magazine, what kind of contributions are needed, and other points of attention.

【稿纸】gǎozhǐ 供写稿用的纸,多印有一行行的直线或小方格儿 standardized writing paper with squares or lines

【稿子】gǎo·zi ❶ 诗文、图画等的草稿 draft; sketch for writing or painting:写~ draft an article ❷ 写成的诗文 manuscript; contribution:这篇~是谁写的? Who wrote this article? ❸ 心里的计划;谱⑤ idea; plan:心里还没个准~。I do not have a definite plan yet.

藁 gǎo 藁城(Gǎochéng),地名,在河北 Gaocheng, name of a place in Hebei Province

gào(ㄍㄠˋ)

告 gào ❶ 把事情向人陈述、解说 tell; inform; notify:~诉 tell|~知 inform|广~ advertise|报~ report|通~ notice|忠~ advice ❷ 向国家行政司法机关检举、控诉 go to law against sb.; sue; take sb. to court:~状 bring a lawsuit against sb.|到法院去~他 go to court and sue him ❸ 为了某事而请求 ask for; request; solicit:~假 ask for leave|~贷 ask for a loan ❹ 表明 declare; announce:~辞 take leave of; say goodbye to|自~奋勇 offer to undertake; volunteer to do sth. ❺ 宣布或表示某种情况的实现 reach (a particular state):~成 be accomplished|~罄 be exhausted; run out|~一段落 come to the end of a stage; be brought to a temporary close

【告白】gàobái ❶(机关、团体或个人)对公众的声明或启事 public notice or announcement ❷ 说明;表白 express; justify oneself:向朋友~自己的忧虑 express one's worry to friends

【告便】gào//biàn〈婉辞 *euph.*〉向人表示自己将要离开一会儿(多指上厕所) ask permission to be briefly absent (to relieve oneself)

【告别】gào//bié ❶ 离别;分手(一般要打个招呼或说句话 by way of a wave of hand or words of pleasantry) leave; part from:~亲友 part from relatives and friends|他把信交给了队长,就匆匆~了。He hurried off after handing over the letter to the team leader. ❷ 辞行 bid farewell to; say goodbye to:动身的那天清早,我特地去向他~。I specially went to say goodbye to him before setting out that morning. ❸ 和死者最后诀别,表示哀悼 pay one's last respects to the deceased

【告成】gàochéng 宣告完成(较重要的工作)(of a major task or project) completed or accomplished:大功~ be crowned with success

【告吹】gàochuī(事情、交情)宣告破裂;不成功(of a project or relationship) fizzle out; fail

【告辞】gào//cí(向主人)辞别 take leave (of one's host):我怕耽误他的时间,谈了一会儿就~走了。I took my leave after a brief talk so as not to take up too much of his time.

【告贷】gàodài 请求旁人借钱给自己 ask for a loan:四处~ borrow money from everyone|~无门(没处借钱) be unable to get a loan from any source

【告地状】gàodìzhuàng 把自己的不幸遭遇写在纸上铺在街头或用粉笔写在地上,向路人乞求钱财或其他帮助 screeve; write down one's sufferings on the pavement or sidewalk to solicit charity from the passers-by

【告发】gàofā 向公安机关、法院或政府检举揭发 report (an offender) to a public security organ, the court or the government; inform on; lodge an accusation against: 写信～他的违法行为 write a letter in accusation of his illegal behaviour | 尽管多方遮掩，还是被人～了。He was finally reported despite all his efforts to conceal the facts.

【告负】gàofù (体育比赛等)失败 (of sports events, etc.) be defeated: 甲队以0比3～。Team A lost three nil.

【告急】gào//jí 报告情况紧急并请求援救(多指军事、灾害等 of a war, a disaster, etc.) be in a state of emergency; report an emergency; ask for emergency help: 前线～。The frontline units signalled for help. | 灾区～。The disaster-stricken area was in danger. | ～电报 emergency telegraph

【告假】gào//jià 请假 ask for leave: 他家里有事，想告两天假。He asked for two days' leave in order to see to a family matter.

【告捷】gào//jié ❶(作战、比赛等)取得胜利 (in war or games) win victory: 初战～ win the very first battle or game ❷ 报告得胜的消息 report a victory: 向司令部～ report a victory to the command

【告竭】gàojié 指财物、矿藏等净尽 (of property, mineral resources) run out; be used up: 库藏～。The stocks have been used up. | 该地区矿藏由于长期开采，今已～。The mineral resources in this area have run out owing to extended periods of exploitation.

【告戒】gàojiè same as 告诫 gàojiè

【告诫】gàojiè 警告劝戒(多用于上级对下级或长辈对晚辈 mostly of a leader to a subordinate or a person to sb. of the yonnger generation) warn; admonish; exhort: 再三～ repeated exhortation | 谆谆～ admonish sb. earnestly and tirelessly. also 告戒 gàojiè

【告借】gàojiè 请求别人借钱物给自己 ask for a loan: ～无门 be unable to get a loan from any source

【告警】gàojǐng 报告发生紧急情况，请求加强戒备或援助 report an emergency; give (or sound) an alarm: ～电话 alarm telephone

【告绝】gàojué 宣告绝迹 vanish; be stamped out: 匪患～。Banditry has been stamped out.

【告竣】gàojùn 宣告事情完毕(多指较大的工程) (of large, major projects) be completed: 铁路修建工程已全部～。The railway construction project has been completed.

【告劳】gàoláo 向别人表示自己的劳苦 let one's moil or pain be known: 不敢～。I dare not complain about my hardship or misery.

【告老】gào//lǎo 〈旧时 *old*〉官吏年老请求辞职，泛指年老退休 (of an aging official) request to be released of government duties and retire; (in a broad sense) retire on account of age: ～还乡 retire and return to one's hometown

【告密】gào//mì 向有关部门告发旁人的私下言论或活动(多含贬义 oft. derog.) blow the gaff; tip off; secretly inform the relevant departments of sb.'s statements or activities

【告罄】gàoqìng 指财物用完或货物售完 (of properties or goods) run out; be exhausted: 存粮～ be out of stocks of grain

【告饶】gào//ráo 求饶 beg for mercy: 求情～ plead for mercy

【告示】gào·shi ❶ 布告 official notice; bulletin: 安民～ notice to reassure the people ❷〈旧时 *old*〉指标语 slogan; poster: 红绿～ colourful posters

【告送】gào·song 〈方 *dial.*〉告诉；告知 inform; notify; also 告诵 gàosòng

【告诉】gàosù 受害人向法院告发 file a suit: ～到法院 file a suit in court

【告诉】gào·su 说给人，使人知道 tell; let know: 请你～他，今天晚上七点钟开会。Please tell him the meeting is at 7 p.m. tonight.

【告退】gàotuì ❶ 在集会中要求先离去 ask for leave before a meeting is over: 我有点事，先～了。I have something to deal with and must go now. ❷ 从集体中退出 retire from a group: 老队员已先后挂拍～。Old athletes retired one after another. ❸〈旧时 *old*〉指自请辞去职位 quit; resign from office: 年老～resign from office due to age

【告慰】gàowèi 表示安慰；感到安慰 comfort; feel relieved: 请大家加把劲儿，把文集早日印出来，以此～死者在天之灵。Let's work hard to have the collection printed as soon as possible so as to comfort the souls of the deceased.

【告枕头状】gào zhěn·touzhuàng 妻子向丈夫说别人的坏话，叫告枕头状 make complaints in private to one's husband about sb. or sth.

【告知】gàozhī 告诉使知道 inform; notify: 把通信地址～在京的同志。Inform comrades in Beijing about the mailing address.

【告终】gàozhōng 宣告结束 come to an end; end up: 第二次世界大战以德、意、日三个法西斯国家的失败而～。World War II ended with the defeat of the three Fascist countries of Germany, Italy and Japan.

【告状】gào//zhuàng ❶(当事人)请求司法机关审理某一案件 (of a party concerned) go to court against sb. ❷ 向某人的上级或长辈诉说自己或别人受到这个人的欺负或不公正的待遇 lodge a complaint against sb. with his superiors: 就这点小事，干吗到处～? Why did you lodge complaints everywhere over such a trifle?

郜 Gào 姓 a surname

诰 gào ❶〈书 *fml*.〉告诉(用于上对下) admonish (subordinates); issue ❷〈古代 *arch*.〉一种告诫性的文章 written admonition ❸ 帝王对臣子的命令 imperial mandate:～封 conferment of a honorary title on one's ancestors or wife by imperial mandate

【诰封】gàofēng 封建王朝对官员及其先代、妻室授予爵位或称号 conferment of honorary titles on one's ancestors or wife by imperial mandate

【诰命】gàomìng ❶ 帝王对臣子的命令 imperial mandate ❷ 封建时代指受过封号的妇女(多见于早期白话 oft. used in early vernacular) (in feudal times) titled lady

锆 gào 金属元素,符号 Zr (zirconium)。银灰色,质硬,熔点高,耐腐蚀。用来制合金、闪光粉等,也用作真空中的除气剂,紧密压制的纯锆用作核反应堆的铀棒外套。zirconium (Zr); silver grey metallic element with a high melting point, hard and corrosion resisting, used in the making of alloys or as a degasifying agent in a vacuum. When tightly compressed, it is also used as thc coating for uranium bars in a nuclear reactor

膏 gào ❶ 在轴承或机器等经常转动发生摩擦的部分加润滑油 put some lubricant on the friction parts of a bearing or machinery: ～车 lubricate the cart axle|在轴上～点儿油 put some lubricant on the axle ❷ 把毛笔蘸上墨,在砚台边上掭匀 dip a writing brush in ink and smooth it on an ink-stone before writing: ～笔 smooth a wet writing brush on an ink-stone|～墨 dip a writing brush in ink

☞ gāo on p. 646

gē (ㄍㄜ)

戈 gē ❶〈古代 *arch*.〉兵器,横刃,用青铜或铁制成,装有长柄 dagger-axe with a cross blade, made of bronze or iron, with a long handle ❷ (Gē) 姓 a surname

【戈比】gēbǐ 俄罗斯等国的辅助货币 kopeck, auxiliary currency in countries such as Russia

【戈壁】gēbì 蒙古人称沙漠地区,这种地区尽是沙子和石块,地面上缺水,植物稀少 *gobi* desert; Mongolian term for areas covered with gravel lacking water and vegetation

仡 gē [仡佬族] (Gēlǎozú)我国少数民族之一,主要分布在贵州 Gelo (Kelao) people, minority ethnic group living in Guizhou Province

☞ yì on p. 2272

圪 gē ☞ below

【圪垯】gē·da ❶ same as 疙瘩 gē·da ❷ 小土丘 knoll; also 圪塔 gē·da

【圪塔】gē·da same as 圪垯 gē·da

【圪节】gē·jie〈方 *dial*.〉❶ 稻、麦、高粱、竹子等茎上分枝长叶的地方 (of rice, wheat, sorghum and bamboo) joint, where branches and leaves emerge ❷ 两个圪节间的一段 part between two such points ❸ 泛指长条形东西的一段 (in a broad sense) part of anything stick-like:这根棍子断成三～了。This stick has broken into three parts.

【圪蹴】gē·jiu〈方 *dial*.〉蹲 squat on the heels: 老羊倌～在门前石凳上听广播。The old shepherd squatted on the stone seat in front of the gate to listen to the radio.

【圪塄】gē·láo〈方 *dial*.〉角落(也用做地名 also used in place names) corner:炕～corner of a kang|王家～(在陕西) Wangjiagelao (in Shaanxi Province)

【圪针】gē·zhen〈方 *dial*.〉指某些植物枝梗上的刺儿 thorns on the branches of some plants: 枣～jujube thorn

屹 gē [屹嶝] (gē·da) ❶ same as 疙瘩 gē·da ❷ 小土丘 mound; knoll

☞ yì on p. 2273

纥 gē [纥繨] (gē·da) same as 疙瘩 gē·da ②;多用于纱、线、织物等 lump; knot, usu. in yarn, thread, fabric, etc.: 线～ thread knot|包袱～ cloth-wrapped bundle

☞ hé on p. 784

疙 gē ☞ below

【疙疤】gē·ba〈方 *dial*.〉痂 scar:疮～ scar

【疙瘩】gē·da same as 疙瘩 gē·da

【疙瘩】gē·da ❶ 皮肤上突起的或肌肉上结成的硬块 swelling on the skin; pimple; lump ❷ 小球形或块状的东西 lump; knot:面～dough-ball|芥菜～ lump of shepherd's purse|线结成～了。The thread has got tangled (knotted). ❸ 不易解决的问题 knot in one's heart; lump in one's throat:心上的～早去掉了。He has long since got over the hang-up.|解开他们两人中间的～dispel the misunderstanding between the two of them ❹〈方 *dial*.〉〈量词 *classifier*〉:一～石头 a stone|一～糕 a cake ❺〈方 *dial*.〉麻烦;别扭 trouble; not get along well ‖ also 疙疸 gē·da

【疙疙瘩瘩】gē·gedādā (～的 gē·gedādā·de) 不平滑;不顺利 rough; knotty; bumpy:路上净是石头子儿,～的,不好走。The road was so gravely and bumpy that I almost stumbled.|这事情～的,办得很不顺手。It was a tricky problem to deal with. also 疙里疙瘩 gēlǐgēdā

咯 gē ☞ below

☞ kǎ on p. 1069, ·lo on p. 1248 and luò on p. 1280

【咯噔】gēdēng〈拟声词 *onom*.〉:从楼梯上传来了～～的皮靴声。The clops of leather boots against the stairs could be heard.|听说厂里出了事儿,我心里～一下子,腿都软了。When I heard something was wrong in the factory, my heart thumped and my legs turned to jelly. also 格登 gēdēng

【咯咯】gēgē same as 格格 gēgē

【咯吱】gēzhī〈拟声词 *onom.*〉:扁担压得~~地直响。The carrying pole creaked under the load.

饹 gē [饹馇](gē·zha)一种食品,用豆面做成饼形,切成块炸着吃或炒菜吃 food made of bean flour, shaped like a cake, cut into cubes for eating, fried in oil or stir-fried as a dish:绿豆~*gezha* — made of mung bean

☞ ·le on p.1166

格 gē ☞ below

☞ gé on p.653

【格登】gēdēng same as 咯噔 gēdēng

【格格】gēgē〈拟声词 *onom.*〉❶ 形容笑声 sound of laughter; chuckles; ha ha; hee hee:他~地笑了起来。He chuckled. ❷ 形容咬牙声 sound of grinding teeth:牙齿咬得~响 grind one's teeth ❸ 形容机关枪的射击声 sound of a machine gun ❹ 形容某些鸟的叫声 chirping sounds of some birds; also 咯咯 gēgē

哥 gē ❶ 哥哥(elder) brother:大~ eldest brother|二~ second eldest brother ❷ 亲戚中同辈而年纪比自己大的男子 elderly male relative of the same generation:表~ elder cousin ❸ 称呼年纪跟自己差不多的男子(含亲热意) brother, term of endearment for older male acquaintances:李二~ Brother Li'er

【哥哥】gē·ge ❶ 同父母(或只同父、只同母)而年纪比自己大的男子 elder brother (having the same parents or parent) ❷ 同族同辈而年纪比自己大的男子 elder male relative of the same generation:叔伯~elder cousins|远房~ an elder brother of a distant relative

【哥老会】Gēlǎohuì 帮会的一种,清末在长江流域各地活动,成员多数是城乡游民。最初具有反清意识,后来分化为不同支派,常为反动势力所利用。Gelao Society, secret society in the Yangtze river valley in the later years of the Qing Dynasty, the majority of its members being the rural and urban homeless, anti-Qing government at its founding, later divided into many different branches and oft. playing into the hand of reactionary forces

【哥们儿】gē·menr ❶ 弟兄们 brothers:他们家~好几个呢。There are several sons in their family. ❷ 用于朋友间,带亲热的口气[a friendly term of address for friends] pals:他和我是~,俩人好得无话不说。We are best buddies, so we keep no secrets from each other. ‖ also 哥儿们 gēr·men

【哥儿】gēr ❶ 弟弟和哥哥(包括本人) brothers (including oneself):你们~几个? How many of you boys are there altogether in your family?|~俩都是运动员。The two brothers are athletes. ❷ 称有钱人家的男孩子 boys (of rich families):公子~playboy; pampered son of a wealthy or influential family

【哥儿们】gēr·men same as 哥们儿 gē·menr

【哥萨克人】Gēsàkèrén 俄罗斯人的一部分,主要散居在顿河、库班河一带 Cossack; Russians and Kazak people mainly living along the Don and Kuban rivers

胳(肐) gē ☞ below

☞ gā on p.618 and gé on p.654

【胳臂】gē·bei 胳膊 arm

【胳膊】gē·bo 肩膀以下手腕以上的部分 arm; part between shoulder and wrist

【胳膊拧不过大腿】gē·bo nǐng bù·guo dàtuǐ〈比喻 *fig.*〉弱小的敌不过强大的 arm is no match for the thigh — the weaker can't contend with the stronger; also 胳膊扭不过大腿 gè·bo niǔ bù·guo dàtuǐ

【胳膊腕子】gē·bo wàn·zi 腕子 wrist; also 胳膊腕儿 gē·bowànr

【胳膊肘朝外拐】gē·bozhǒu cháowài guǎi〈比喻 *fig.*〉不向着自家人而向着外人 take an outsider's side instead of one's own; also 胳膊肘向外拐 gē·bozhǒu xiàngwài guǎi

【胳膊肘子】gē·bo zhǒu·zi 肘 elbow; also 胳膊肘儿 gē·bozhǒur

鸽 gē 鸽子 dove; pigeon:信~ carrier pigeon

【鸽子】gē·zi 鸟,翅膀大,善于飞行,品种很多,羽毛有白色、灰色、酱紫色等,以谷类植物的种子为食物,有的可以用来传递书信。常用做和平的象征。pigeon (*Columba livia*); dove; a variety of bird with large wings, wonderful flying skill, and feathers ranging in colour from white to grey and dark reddish purple, eating grain, sometimes used for carrying letters, oft. a symbol of peace

袼 gē [袼褙](gē·bei)用碎布或旧布加衬纸裱成的厚片,多用来制布鞋 pieces of old cloth or rags glued together to make cloth shoes

搁 gē ❶ 使处于一定的位置 put:把箱子~在屋子里。Put the suitcase in the room. ❷ 加进去 add; put:豆浆里~点糖。Put some sugar in the soya milk. ❸ 搁置 put aside; leave over; shelve:这件事~一~再办吧。We'll have to shelve matter for the time being.|都是紧急任务,一样也~不下。Everything is urgent; we can leave nothing aside.

☞ gé on p.654

【搁笔】gēbǐ (写作、绘画)停笔;放下笔 lay down the pen or brush; stop writing or painting

【搁浅】gē//qiǎn ❶ (船只)进入水浅的地方,不能行驶 (of ships) run aground; become stranded ❷〈比喻 *fig.*〉事情遭到阻碍,不能进行 reach a deadlock:谈判~。The negotiations have come to a deadlock.

【搁置】gēzhì 放下;停止进行 lay aside; shelve:事情重要,不能~。This matter is too important to be pidgeon-holed.

割 gē ❶ 用刀截断 cut with a knife：～麦子 cut wheat | ～肉 cut meat ❷ 分割；舍弃 cut apart; give up：～地 cede territory | ～爱 give up what one treasures

【割爱】gē'ài 放弃心爱的东西 give up what one cherishes：忍痛～ endure pain silently in giving away what one loves

【割除】gēchú 割掉；除去 cut off; remove; excise：～肿瘤 remove a tumour

【割地】gē//dì 割让领土 cede territory：～求和 cede territory for peace

【割断】gēduàn 截断；切断 sever; cut off：～绳索 cut rope ◇历史无法～。You cannot separate one part of history from the continuum.

【割鸡焉用牛刀】gē jī yān yòng niúdāo 杀个鸡何必用宰牛的刀 no need to use an ox cleaver to kill a chicken;〈比喻 *fig.*〉做小事情不值得用大的力量 trifle is not worth endowing with great value

【割胶】gē//jiāo 把橡胶树干的表皮割开，使胶乳流出来 tap latex by cutting the bark of a rubber tree

【割据】gējù 一国之内，拥有武力的人占据部分地区，形成分裂对抗的局面 nation torn apart by armed separatist forces：封建～feudal warlordism | ～称雄 nation torn apart by rival principalities

【割礼】gēlǐ 犹太教、伊斯兰教的一种仪式，把男性教徒的生殖器包皮割去少许。犹太教在婴儿初生时举行，伊斯兰在童年举行。religious circumcision ceremony in Judaism and Islam, cutting a bit of the foreskin of a male believer's penis, performed on newborn babies in Judaism, and children in Islam

【割裂】gēliè 把不应当分割的东西分割开(多指抽象的事物 usu. abstract facts) cut apart or separate sth. that should not be isolated

【割蜜】gē//mì 旧法养蜂的取蜜法，把蜂巢中储存蜜的部分用刀割下来 (old) bee-keeping practice of cutting off the honey comb in order to get honey

【割漆】gē//qī 把漆树干的表皮割开，使漆树的树脂流出来 tap a lacquer tree for latex to flow out of its inner bark

【割弃】gēqì 割除并抛弃；舍弃 cut off and throw away; give up; abandon：与主题无关的情节，就应～。We should cut out and eliminate those plots irrelevant to the theme.

【割枪】gēqiāng 气割用的带活门的工具，形状略像枪，前端有喷嘴 burning torch; gun-like tool with valve and spray head on the front end, used for gas cutting; also 割炬 gējù

【割让】gēràng 因战败或受侵略，被迫把一部分领土让给外国 be forced to cede territory after being defeated in war or invade

【割舍】gēshě 舍弃；舍去 give up; part with：～旧情 part with an old flame; give up an old-time friendship

【割席】gēxí〈书 *fml.*〉三国时管宁跟华歆同学，合坐一张席读书，后来管宁鄙视华歆的为人，把席割开分坐(见于《世说新语·德行》)。后世指跟朋友绝交。breaking off relations between friends. During the Three Kingdoms Period, Guan Ning and his classmate Hua Xin shared a reading mat, and later Guan Ning was so disgusted with Hua Xin's conduct that he cut the mat and sat separately from Hua (*A New Account of Tales of the World · Virtue*).

【割线】gēxiàn 通过圆周或其他曲线上任意两点的直线 secant, intersecting line across a circle, esp. one intersecting a curve at two or more points

谞 gē〈书 *fml.*〉same as 歌 gē

歌 gē ❶ (～儿 gēr)歌曲 song：民～folk song | 山～儿 folk song sung in the fields during or after work | 唱一个～儿 sing a song ❷ 唱 sing：～者 singer | 高～一曲 sing a song loudly

【歌本】gēběn (～儿 gēběnr)专门刊载歌曲的书，也指专用来抄录歌曲的本子 songbook, or book for collecting songs

【歌唱】gēchàng ❶ 唱(歌)sing：～家 singer | 尽情～ sing to one's heart's content ❷ 用唱歌、朗诵等形式颂扬 praise (through songs, poems, etc.)：～祖国的繁荣富强 sing (in praise) of the prosperity of one's motherland

【歌词】gēcí 歌曲中的词 lyric; words of a song

【歌功颂德】gē gōng sòng dé 歌颂功绩和恩德(多用于贬义 oft. derog.) eulogize sb.'s virtues and achievements; sing the praises of sb.

【歌喉】gēhóu 指唱歌人的嗓子，也指唱的声音 singer's voice; singing voice：～婉转 have a sweet (or beautiful) voice

【歌剧】gējù 综合诗歌、音乐、舞蹈等艺术而以歌唱为主的戏剧 opera; dramatic work that foregrounds singing and synthesizes poetry, music and dance

【歌诀】gējué 为了便于记诵，按事物的内容要点编成的韵文或无韵的整齐句子；口诀 formulas or directions put to rhyme so as to be easy to memorize：汤头～(用汤药成方中的药名编成的口诀) *Recipes in Verse*; *Prescriptions in Rhyme* (using the names of liquid herbal medical preparations)

【歌迷】gēmí 喜欢听歌曲或唱歌而入迷的人 people who love listening to songs or are engrossed by singing

【歌女】gēnǚ 在舞厅等场所以歌唱为业的女子 sing-song girl

【歌片儿】gēpiānr 印有歌曲的纸片 song sheet

【歌谱】gēpǔ 歌曲的谱子 music score of a song; music of a song

【歌曲】gēqǔ 供人歌唱的作品，是诗歌和音乐的结合 song, a mixture of poetry and music

【歌声】gēshēng 唱歌的声音 sound of singing：欢乐的～joyous singing|～四起。Sounds of singing were heard all around.

【歌手】gēshǒu 擅长歌唱的人 singer；vocalist：赛歌会上，～如云。There are a large number of vocalists at the singing contest.

【歌颂】gēsòng 用诗歌颂扬，泛指用言语文字等赞美 sing the praises of；extol；eulogize：～祖国的大好河山 sing the praises of the beautiful rivers and mountains of one's country

【歌坛】gētán 指歌唱界；声乐界 circle of singers：～新秀 a new singing star

【歌舞】gēwǔ 唱歌和舞蹈的合称 song and dance：～团 song and dance ensemble|表演～perform singing and dancing

【歌舞伎】gēwǔjì 日本戏剧的一种，表演时演员不歌唱，只有动作和说白，另由伴奏音乐的人配合演员的动作在后面歌唱 kabuki；popular Japanese dramatic form in which the actors do not sing but speak and act，accompanied by instrumentalists who sing according to the actors' dramatizations

【歌舞剧】gēwǔjù 兼有歌唱、音乐和舞蹈的戏剧 song and dance drama

【歌星】gēxīng 有名的歌唱演员 singing star

【歌谣】gēyáo 指随口唱出，没有音乐伴奏的韵语，如民歌、民谣、儿歌等 ballad；folk song；nursery rhyme，such as folk songs and children's songs

【歌吟】gēyín 歌唱；吟咏 sing；recite a poem

【歌咏】gēyǒng 唱（歌）singing：～队 singing group；chorus|～比赛 singing competition

【歌仔戏】gēzǎixì 台湾省地方戏曲剧种之一，由当地民谣山歌发展而成。流行于台湾和福建芗江（九龙江）一带。福建称之为芗剧。one of Taiwan's local operas，originating from local folk songs popular in Taiwan and Xiangjiang (Jiulongjiang) in Fujian Province；also called Xiang Opera in Fujian

【歌子】gē·zi 歌曲 song：嘴里哼着～hum a tune

gé（ㄍㄜˊ）

革[1] gé ❶ 去了毛并且加过工的兽皮 leather；processed skin of an animal：皮～leather|制～process hides ❷（Gé）姓 a surname

革[2] gé ❶ 改变 change：～新 reform|变～change ❷ 开除；撤除（职务）remove sb. from office；expel：开～expel|～职 dismiss sb. from office

☞ jí on p.904

【革出】géchū 开除出去 expel

【革除】géchú ❶ 铲除；去掉 abolish；get rid of；eliminate：～陋习 eliminate irrational practices ❷ 开除；撤职 expel；dismiss；remove sb. from office

【革故鼎新】gé gù dǐng xīn 去掉旧的，建立新的 discard the old and introduce the new

【革履】gélǚ 皮鞋 leather shoes：西装～in Western dress and leather shoes；be impeccably attired

【革命】gé//mìng ❶ 被压迫阶级用暴力夺取政权，摧毁旧的腐朽的社会制度，建立新的进步的社会制度。革命破坏旧的生产关系，建立新的生产关系，解放生产力，推动社会的发展。revolution — the oppressed classes rise in revolt to seize power，destroy an old decadent social system and build a new advanced society. Revolution can destroy the old relations of production，build new ones，free up productivity，and promote the development of society. ❷ 具有革命意识的 revolutionary nature：工人阶级是最～的阶级。The working class is most dedicated to the cause of the revolution. ❸ 根本改革 revolution：思想～revolution in thought|技术～technological revolution|产业～ industrial revolution

【革命家】gémìngjiā 具有革命思想，从事革命工作，并做出重大贡献的人 revolutionary；one who is engaged in revolutionary work and has made major contributions：鲁迅是伟大的思想家和～。Lu Xun was a great thinker and revolutionary.

【革新】géxīn 革除旧的，创造新的 innovate；improve：技术～technological innovation|～运动 campaign for innovation

【革职】gé//zhí 撤职 remove sb. from office；dismiss sb. from his post：～查办 remove sb. from office and prosecute him|他上个月革了职。He was removed from office last month.

茖 gé［茖葱］（gécōng）多年生草本植物，野生，茎细，叶子长椭圆形，花白色。茎叶可以吃，也可入药。long-rooted garlic（*Allium victorialis*）；wild herbaceous perennial plant having thin stems，long oval leaves and white flowers，with both stems and leaves used for food or medicine.

闷 gé〈书 *fml.*〉❶ 小门 small side door ❷ same as 阁 gé ❸（Gé）姓 a surname

☞ 阖 hé on p.791

阁 gé ❶ 风景区或庭园里的一种建筑物，四方形、六角形或八角形，一般两层，周围开窗，多建筑在高处，可以凭高远望 pavilion；building in scenic spots or gardens，usu. two-storeyed，with four，six or eight corners，and windows built into surrounding walls，usu. built on a vantage point so one can lean over the balcony and look into the distance：亭台楼～ pavilions，terraces and open halls ❷〈旧时 *old*〉指女子的住屋 boudoir：闺～boudoir|出～（of a woman）marry ❸ 指内阁 Cabinet（of a government）：组～ set up a Cabinet ❹〈书 *fml.*〉放东西的架子 shelf：束之高～ put on the shelf

【阁楼】gélóu 在较高的房间内上部架起的一层

矮小的楼 (within an upper room) attic; loft; garret

【阁下】géxià 〈敬辞 *pol*.〉称对方,从前书函中常用,今多用于外交场合 [earlier often in letters, now mostly used on diplomatic occasions] Your Excellency; His or Her Excellency: 大使～ Your Excellency Mr. Ambassador; His Excellency the Ambassador | 首相～ Your Excellency Mr. Prime Minister

【阁员】géyuán 内阁的成员 member of a cabinet

【阁子】gé·zi ❶ 小的木板房子 small wooden house: 板～ small house made of wooden planks ❷ 〈方 *dial*.〉same as 阁楼 gélóu

格[1] gé ❶ (～儿 gér) 格子 squares formed by crossing lines; check: 方～纸 squared paper; graph paper | 把字写在～儿里。Write the characters in the squares. | 四～儿的书架 bookcase with four shelves ❷ 规格;格式 standard; pattern; style: 品～ one's character and morals | ～律 rules and forms of classical poetic composition (with respect to tonal pattern, rhyme scheme, etc.) | 合～ qualified | 别具一～ have a style of its own ❸ 品质;风度 character; bearing: 人～ personality | 风～ style; manner ❹ 〈书 *fml*.〉阻碍;限制 obstruct; bar: ～于成例 be hindered by conventions ❺ (Gé) 姓 a surname

格[2] gé 某些语言中名词(有的包括代词、形容词)的语法范畴,用词尾变化来表示它和别的词之间的语法关系。例如俄语的名词、代词、形容词都有六个格。case; a category in some languages, involving the inflection of nouns (sometimes pronouns and adjectives included), noting the syntactic relation of a word to other words by changes in the suffix, e. g. in Russian, nouns, pronouns and adjectives each have six cases.

格[3] gé 〈书 *fml*.〉推究 examine; study: ～物 study natural phenomena

格[4] gé 打 fight: ～斗 grapple; fist fight | ～杀 kill those who resist

☞ gē on p. 650

【格调】gédiào ❶ 指不同作家或不同作品的艺术特点的综合表现 style; ethos; comprehensive style of different literary or artistic works by different writers or artists: ～高雅 elegant style ❷ 〈书 *fml*.〉指人的风格或品格 moral quality

【格斗】gédòu 紧张激烈地搏斗 grapple; wrestle; fist fight

【格格不入】gé gé bù rù 有抵触,不投合 incompatible with; out of tune with; out of one's element; like a square peg in a round hole

【格局】géjú 结构和格式 pattern; set-up; structure: 经济迅速发展,不断打破旧～,形成新～。In a rapidly developing economy, old patterns are being constantly broken to give way to new ones. | 这篇文章写得很乱,简直不成个～。This article is badly written and without any structure.

【格里历】gélǐlì 公历,因1582年罗马教皇格里哥里(Gregorius)十三世修改而得名 Gregorian calendar, named after Roman Pope Gregorius XIII who amended it in 1582

【格林尼治时间】Gélínnízhì shíjiān 世界时。旧译作格林威治时间。Greenwich mean time (GMT); universal time; also translated as 格林威治时间 Gélínwēizhì shíjiān

【格律】gélǜ 诗、赋、词、曲等关于字数、句数、对偶、平仄、押韵等方面的格式和规则 rules and forms of classical poetic composition (with respect to tonal pattern, rhyme scheme, etc.)

【格杀勿论】gé shā wù lùn 指把行凶、拒捕或违反禁令的人当场打死,不以杀人论罪 legally kill on the spot those who have committed murder, resisted arrest or broken a ban

【格式】gé·shi 一定的规格式样 form; pattern: 公文～ form (or standardized style) of an official document | 书信～ form of a letter

【格外】géwài ❶ 〈副词 *adv*.〉表示超过寻常 especially; particularly; all the more: 久别重逢,大家～亲热。After a long separation, we met with particular affection. | 国庆节的天安门,显得～庄严而美丽。Tian'anmen Square looks especially stately and resplendent on National Day. ❷ 额外;另外 additionally: 卡车装不下,～找了一辆大车。As the truck couldn't hold all the goods, an additional cart was ordered.

【格物】géwù 〈书 *fml*.〉推究事物的道理 investigate principles of matters: ～致知 study natural phenomena in order to acquire knowledge

【格物致知】gé wù zhì zhī 穷究事物的原理法则而总结为理性知识 study natural phenomena in order to acquire knowledge

【格言】géyán 含有劝诫和教育意义的话,一般较为精练,如'满招损,谦受益','虚心使人进步,骄傲使人落后' maxim; motto; sentence for expostulation, usu. very brief, e. g. 'Pride leads to loss, while modesty brings benefit,' 'Modesty helps one go forward, whereas conceit makes one lag behind.'

【格致】gézhì 〈书 *fml*.〉'格物致知'的略语。清朝末年讲西学的人用它做物理、化学等科学的总称。short form of 格物致知 gé wù zhì zhī. In the later years of the Qing Dynasty, people who taught Western learning used this as a general reference for natural sciences such as physics and chemistry.

【格子】gé·zi 隔成的方形空栏或框子 squares formed by crossing lines; check: 打～ square (the page) off | ～布 checked fabric

鬲 gé ❶ 鬲津(Géjīn),水名,发源于河北,流入山东 Gejin, name of a river originating in Hebei Province and flowing into Shandong Province ❷ 胶鬲(Jiāogé),殷末周初人 Jiao Ge, a man living in the last years of the Shang Dynasty and the early years of the Zhou dynasty

☞ lì on p.1192

胳 gé [胳肢](gé·zhi)〈方 *dial.*〉在别人身上抓挠,使发痒 tickle sb.

☞ gā on p.618 and gē on p.650

葛 gé ❶ 多年生草本植物,茎蔓生,上有黄色细毛,叶子大,分成三片,花紫红色。根肥大,叫葛根,可制淀粉,也供药用。茎皮可制葛布。kudzu vine (*Pueraria lobata*); herbaceous perennial plant having tuberous stems with yellow hair, large leaves divided into three parts, reddish purple flowers, fat roots which are used for starch and medicine and the skin of stem for clothes; 通称 generally called 葛麻 gémá ❷ 表面有花纹的纺织品,用丝做经,棉线或麻线等做纬 poplin; fabric of floral pattern woven of silk, cotton or hemp

☞ Gě on p.655

【葛布】gébù 用葛的纤维织成的布,可以做夏季服装等 ko-hemp cloth, used for summer clothes.

【葛藤】géténg〈比喻 *fig.*〉纠缠不清的关系 entangled relations

搁 gé 禁受 bear; stand; endure

☞ gē on p.650

【搁不住】gé·bu zhù 禁受不住 cannot stand:丝织品~揉搓。Silk fabrics do not stand rubbing.

【搁得住】gé·de zhù 禁受得住 stand; bear:再结实的东西,~你这么使吗? Nothing, however durable it is, can stand the way you use them.

蛤 gé ❶ 蛤蜊、文蛤等瓣鳃类软体动物 pelecypod, such as clam ❷ ☞ 蛤蜊 gé·lí

☞ há on p.753

【蛤蚧】géjiè 爬行动物,形似壁虎而大,头大,背部灰色而有红色斑点。吃蚊、蝇等小虫。可入药。gecko (*Gekko gecko*); crawling creature that looks like the house lizard but is bigger, has a big head, a grey back with red spots, eats mosquitoes and flies, and is used for Chinese medicine.

【蛤蜊】gé·lí ❶ 软体动物,长约3厘米,壳卵圆形,淡褐色,边缘紫色。生活在浅海底。clam (*Mactra*); mollusk, 3 cm. long, having a light brown round shell with purple edges, living at the bottom of shallow sea ❷ 文蛤的通称(in general) clams

颌 gé〈书 *fml.*〉口 mouth

☞ hé on p.790

隔(隔) gé ❶ 遮断;阻隔 separate; cut off; partition:一间屋~成两间 partition a room into two|~着一重山 on the other side of a hill|~河相望 face each other across a river ❷ 间隔;距离 be apart from; be at a distance from:~两天再去 go to a place in two days' time|相~很远 at a long distance

【隔岸观火】gé àn guān huǒ〈比喻 *fig.*〉见人有危难不援助而采取看热闹的态度 watch a fire from the other side of the river — look on at sb.'s troubles with indifference

【隔壁】gébì 左右相毗连的屋子或人家 next door:左~next door to the left|~邻居 next-door neighbour

【隔断】géduàn 阻隔;使断绝 cut off; separate; obstruct:高山大河不能~我们两国人民之间的联系和往来。Mountains and seas cannot obstruct relations between our two peoples.

【隔断】gé·duàn 把一间屋子隔成几间的遮挡的东西,如板壁、隔扇等 partition wall or board that separates a room into several spaces

【隔房】géfáng 指家族中不是同一房的 different branches of a family:~兄弟 brothers from different branches of a family

【隔行】géháng 行业不相同 different trades or professions:~不隔理。Trades may differ, but principles are the same.|~如隔山。Different trades are separated as if by mountains.

【隔阂】géhé 彼此情意不通,思想有距离(of feeling and thought) estrangement; misunderstanding:感情~feelings of estrangement|消除~ clear up misunderstanding

【隔绝】géjué same as 隔断(géduàn):音信~never been heard from once again|与世~be cut off from the outside world|降低温度和~空气是灭火的根本方法。The fundamental way to put out a fire is to lower the temperature and cut off the air.

【隔离】gélí ❶ 不让聚在一起,使断绝往来 keep apart ❷ 把患传染病的人、畜和健康的人、畜分开,避免接触 quarantine; isolate people or animals with an infectious disease from healthy people or animals:~病房 isolation ward; quarantine ward

【隔膜】gémó ❶ 情意不相通,彼此不了解 lack of mutual understanding:消除~clear up misunderstanding|两人之间有些~。They are somewhat estranged from each other. ❷ 不通晓;外行 be unfamiliar with:我对这种技术实在~。I know very little about the technique.

【隔墙有耳】gé qiáng yǒu ěr〈比喻 *fig.*〉说秘密的事会有人偷听 walls have ears; beware of eavesdroppers

【隔日】gérì 隔一天 every other day:夜校~上课。The night school has classes every other day.

【隔三差五】gé sān chà wǔ 每隔不久;时常 every now and then; often:她~回娘家看看。She often returns to her parents' home. 差 also put as 岔 chà

【隔山】géshān 指同父异母的兄弟姐妹之间的关系 relationship between half-brothers or half-sisters having the same father：～兄弟 half-brothers with the same father

【隔扇】gé·shan 在房屋内部起隔开作用的一扇一扇的木板墙，上部一般做成窗棂，糊纸或装玻璃 partition inside a room, usu. with upper panels made of paper or glass

【隔世】géshì 隔了一世 it seems as if a whole generation had passed：恍如～ have not the same feelings as today's era｜回念前尘，有如～。When recalling past events, it seems as if a whole generation has passed.

【隔心】géxīn 彼此心里有隔阂；不投合 misunderstanding; not get along：咱俩不～，有什么事你别瞒我。We get along, so don't hide anything from me.

【隔靴搔痒】gé xuē sāo yǎng〈比喻 *fig.*〉说话作文等不中肯，没有抓住解决问题的关键 scratch an itch from outside one's boot — fail to get to the root of the matter; fail to strike home; take totally ineffective measures

【隔夜】gé//yè 隔一夜 of the previous night：～的茶不能喝，快倒了。Don't drink last night's tea. Just throw it away.

【隔音】gé//yīn 隔绝声音的传播 sound insulation：～板 soundproof board

【隔音符号】géyīn fúhào 汉语拼音方案所规定的符号(')，必要时放在 ɑ，o，e 前头，使音节的界限清楚，如：激昂 jī'áng，定额 dìng'é syllable-dividing mark (') regulated by the Scheme for the Chinese Phonetic Alphabet, put before ɑ, o, or e if necessary in order to distinguish different syllables, for example, jī'áng (激昂)，dìng'é(定额)

塥 gé〈方 *dial.*〉沙地。多用于地名，如青草塥（在安徽）。sands; usu. used in place names, e.g. Qingcaoge in Anhui Province

嗝 gé（～儿 gér）❶ 胃里的气体从嘴里出来时发出的声音（多在吃饱后 usu. after a meal）belch; eject gas spasmodically and noisily from the stomach through the mouth ❷ 横膈膜痉挛，吸气后声门突然关闭而发出的一种特殊声音 hiccup; spasm of diaphragm, a particular sound after each breath resulting from sudden closing of the glottis

滆 Gé 滆湖，湖名，在江苏 Gehu lake in Jiangsu Province

槅 gé ❶ 房屋中有窗格子的门或隔扇 latticed door or partition in a room：～门 latticed door ❷ 分层放置器物的架子 set of latticed shelves：～子 a set of latticed shelves｜多宝～ shelves for placing various things, especially curios and antiques

【槅门】gémén 旧式建筑中的一种比较讲究的门，上部做成窗棂，糊纸或装玻璃，对开或中间对开、两边单开 elegant latticed door in old-style architecture, with its upper panels made of paper or glass, in halves that open in the middle, or single leafs on both sides

【槅扇】gé·shan same as 隔扇 gé·shan

鬲 gé〈方 *dial.*〉用力抱 tightly embrace

【鬲犋】géjù〈方 *dial.*〉插犋 two or more farmers share draught animals and farm tools

膈 gé 人或哺乳动物胸腔和腹腔之间的膜状肌肉。收缩时胸腔扩大，松弛时胸腔缩小。(in human beings or mammals) diaphragm; muscular, membranous or ligamentous wall separating two cavities or limiting a cavity, with pleural enlargement when contracting, pleural reduction when loose; also 膈膜 gémó or 横膈膜 hénggémó

☞ gè on p. 657

骼 gé ☞骨骼 gǔgé on p. 693

镉 gé 金属元素，符号 Cd (cadmium)。银白色，质软，延展性强。用来制合金、光电管和核反应堆的中子吸收棒等，也用于电镀。cadmium (Cd); white, ductile and divalent metallic element, for use in the making of certain alloys, phototubes and the neutron-absorbing sticks for nuclear reactors, and also in electroplating

镉 gé ☞［镠镉］(jiāogé) on p. 973

gě（ㄍㄜˇ）

个(個) gě ☞ 自个儿 zìgěr on p. 2545

☞ gè on p. 655

合 gě ❶ 容量单位。10 勺等于 1 合，10 合等于 1 升。a unit of dry measure for grain 1 *ge* = 10 spoons; 10 *ge* = 1 litre ❷ 量粮食的器具，容量是 1 合，方形或圆筒形，多用木头或竹筒制成 container for measuring grain, equal to one *ge*, square or cylindrical, made of wood or bamboo

☞ hé on p. 781

各 gě〈方 *dial.*〉特别（含贬义 derog.）peculiar; queer：这人真～。The man is really queer.

☞ gè on p. 657

哿 gě〈书 *fml.*〉可；嘉 approve; praise

舸 gě〈书 *fml.*〉大船 barge

盖(蓋) Gě 姓 a surname

☞ gài on p. 622

葛 Gě 姓 a surname

☞ gé on p. 654

gè（ㄍㄜˋ）

个[1](個、箇) gè ❶〈量词 *classifier*〉a) 用于没有专用量词的名词（有些名词除了用专用量词之外也能用'个'）[used before nouns without a special classifier of their own (some nouns can also use this instead of using their special classifier)]：三～苹果 three apples|一～理想 one ideal|两～星期 two weeks b)用于约数的前面[preceding an approximate number]：哥儿俩也不过差～两三岁。There's only a difference of two or three years between the two brothers.|一天走～百儿八十里，不在话下。There is no problem to walk eighty or one hundred miles a day. c)用于带宾语的动词后面，有表示动量的作用(原来不能用'个')的地方也用'个'[used between a verb and its object to indicate momentum; orig. 个 gè was not used]：见～面儿，说～话儿。Let's meet and have a talk. d)用于动词和补语的中间，使补语略带宾语的性质(有时跟'得'连用)[used between a verb and its complement sometimes together with 得·de]：吃～饱 eat one's fill|玩儿～痛快 have a wonderful time|笑～不停。keep laughing|雨下～不停。It kept raining.|学了～八九不离十 have basically learned the ropes|扫得～干干净净 give it a thorough cleaning ❷ 单独的 individual：～人 individual|～体 individuality

个²(個、箇) gè ❶ 量词'些'的后缀[used as a suffix after classifier 些 xiē]：那些～花儿 all those flowers|这么些～书哪看得完? How can I finish reading so many books?|有一些～令人鼓舞的消息。There is some inspiring news. ❷〈方 *dial.*〉加在'昨儿、今儿、明儿'等时间词后面，跟'某日里'的意思相近[used after 昨儿 zuór, 今儿 jīnr, 明儿 míngr, etc., similar in meaning to 'on a certain day']

☞ gě on p.655

【个案】gè'àn 个别的、特殊的案件或事例 particular and special case or instance：作～处理 be treated specially

【个别】gèbié ❶ 单个；各个 individual; specific：～谈话 private talk|～处理 be treated specially ❷ 极少数；少有 very few; one or two：这种情况是极其～的。Such instances are very rare.

【个儿】gèr ❶ 身体或物体的大小 size; height; stature：他是个大～。He is very tall.|棉桃的～真不小。What huge cotton balls these are! ❷ 指一个个的人或物[persons or things taken singly]：挨～握手问好 shake hands with each one|买鸡蛋论斤不论～。Eggs are sold by the *jin*, not by the piece. ❸〈方 *dial.*〉够条件的人；有能力较量的对手 qualified person; capable competitors：跟我摔跤，你还不是～。You are not capable enough to wrestle with me.

【个人】gèrén ❶ 一个人(跟'集体'相对 as opposed to 'the collective')individual person：～利益服从集体利益。Personal interests should be subordinated to the collective interests.|集体领导同～负责相结合 combine collective leadership with individual responsibility ❷ 自称，我(在正式场合发表意见时用 used on formal occasions to address oneself when one expresses one's opinion) I：～认为这个办法是非常合理的。In my opinion, this method is very reasonable.

【个人主义】gèrén zhǔyì 一切从个人出发，把个人利益放在集体利益之上，只顾自己，不顾别人的错误思想。个人主义是生产资料私有制的产物，是资产阶级世界观的核心。它的表现形式是多方面的，如个人英雄主义、自由主义、本位主义等。individualism; erroneous trend of thought that places individual interests above that of the collective interests and cares for oneself to the neglect of others. As an outcome of private ownership of means of production, individualism constitutes the core of the bourgeois world outlook, and manifests itself in many forms, such as individualized heroism, liberalism, and compartmentalism.

【个体】gètǐ ❶ 单个的人或生物 individuality; being ❷ 指个体户 self-employed worker

【个体户】gètǐhù 个体经营的农民或工商业者 self-employed farmer or businessperson

【个体经济】gètǐ jīngjì 以生产资料私有制和个体劳动为基础的经济形式 individual economy, based on privately ownership of means of production, and self-employed labour

【个体所有制】gètǐ suǒyǒuzhì 生产资料和产品归个体劳动者所有的制度 individual ownership of means of production and products; ☞ 小生产者 xiǎoshēngchǎnzhě on p.2111

【个头儿】gètóur 身材或物体的大小 size; height：这种柿子～特别大。This type of persimmon is remarkable for its size.

【个位】gèwèi 十进制计数的基础的一位。个位以上有十位、百位等，以下有十分位、百分位等。single digit; basic unit of the decimal system, with tens and hundreds, etc. above it, and tenths percentile and hundredths percentile, etc. below it.

【个性】gèxìng ❶ 在一定的社会条件和教育影响下形成的一个人的比较固定的特性 individual character; individuality; personality：～强 strong character|这个人很有～。This man has an unusual character. ❷事物的特性，即矛盾的特殊性。一切个性都是有条件地、暂时地存在的，所以是相对的。specific characteristic of contradiction; individualities are conditional and temporary, and, therefore, relative

【个展】gèzhǎn 个人作品(多为书法、绘画、雕塑等)展览 (usu. of calligraphy, painting or carving) solo exhibition

【个中】gèzhōng〈书 *fml.*〉其中 therein：～滋味 the feeling of sth.

【个子】gè·zi ❶ 指人的身材，也指动物身体的大小(of a human being or animal) height; build：高～ tall person|矮～ short person|这

只猫～大。This is a very big cat. ❷ 指某些捆在一起的条状物 of tied stick-shaped things：谷～ a bundle of millet | 麦～a sheaf of wheat | 高粱～ a bundle of sorghum

各 gè ❶〈指示词 *demons. pron.*〉a) 表示不止一个 different; various; each; all：世界～国 every country in the world | ～位来宾 every guest b) 表示不止一个并且彼此不同 different; various：～种原材料都备齐了。Various kinds of materials are ready. | ～人回～人的家。Each goes to his or her own home. ❷〈副词 *adv.*〉表示不止一人或一物同做某事或同有某种属性 variously; respectively：左右两侧～有一门。There is a door on either side. | 三种办法～有优点和缺点。Each of the three methods has its strengths and weaknesses. | 双方～执一词。Each sticks to his own argument, and shows no room of a compromise.

☞ gě on p. 655

【各别】gèbié ❶ 各不相同；有分别 distinct; different：对于本质上不同的事物，应该～对待，不应该混为一谈。Things of different natures should be treated differently. ❷〈方 *dial.*〉别致；新奇 out of the ordinary; peculiar：这个台灯式样很～。This desk lamp is quite unusual-looking. ❸ 特别(贬义 derog.) odd; eccentric：这个人真～，为这点小事生那么大的气。He's a really eccentric character, for he became very upset at such a trifling matter.

【各得其所】gè dé qí suǒ 每一个人或事物都得到合适的安顿 each (person or thing) is in a proper place; each is properly provided for; each has a role to play

【各个】gègè ❶ 每个；所有的那些个 each; every; various：～厂矿 each factory and mine | ～方面 various aspects ❷ 逐个 one by one：～击破 destroy one by one

【各就各位】gè jiù gè wèi 各自到各自的位置或岗位上 man your posts; take your marks; on your marks

【各色】gèsè ❶ 各种各样 all kinds：～货物，一应俱全。(The store) is stocked with goods of all kinds. ❷〈方 *dial.*〉特别（贬义 derog.）odd; eccentric：这个人真～，跟谁都说不到一块儿。He is such a queer character; nobody is on good terms with him.

【各行其是】gè xíng qí shì 各自按照自己以为对的去做 each does what he thinks is right; each goes his own way

【各有千秋】gè yǒu qiān qiū 各有各的存在的价值；各有所长；各有特色 each has his or its own merits; each has his or her strong points

【各自】gèzì 各人自己；各个方面自己的一方 each; respective：既要～努力，也要彼此帮助。There must be both individual effort and mutual support. | 工作中出了问题，不能只责怪对方，～要多做自我批评。When something goes wrong in our work, we should make self-criticism instead of blaming others.

【各自为政】gè zì wéi zhèng 按照各自的主张做事，不互相配合；不顾全局，各搞自己的一套 each does things in his own way

虼 gè ☞ below

【虼螂】gèláng 蜣螂 dung beetle

【虼蚤】gè·zao 跳蚤 flea

硌 gè 触着凸起的东西觉得不舒服或受到损伤 (of sth. hard or bulging) press or rub against：～牙(of food) so gritty as to hurt the teeth | ～脚 hurt the foot | 褥子没铺平，躺在上面～得难受。That bumpy mattress was terribly uncomfortable.

☞ luò on p. 1281

【硌窝儿】gèwōr〈方 *dial.*〉指鸡鸭等的蛋因受挤压而蛋壳稍有破损 cracked (duck's or chicken's egg)：～鸡蛋 a cracked egg

铬 gè 金属元素，符号 Cr (chromium)。银灰色，质硬而脆，耐腐蚀。用来制特种钢等，镀在别种金属上可以防锈。chromium (Cr); lustrous, hard, brittle, metallic element, used in alloy steels for its hardness and resistance to corrosion, as in stainless steel and for plating other metals; also 克罗米 kèluómǐ

膈 gè [膈应](gè·yīng)〈方 *dial.*〉讨厌；腻味 dislike; get fed up

☞ gé on p. 655

gěi (ㄍㄟˇ)

给 gěi ❶ 使对方得到某些东西或某种遭遇 give; grant：叔叔～他一支笔。His uncle gave him a pen. | 杭州～我的印象很好。Hangzhou left a very good impression on me. | 我们～敌人一个沉重的打击。We struck a heavy blow at the enemy. ❷ 用在动词后面，表示交与，付出 [after a verb] pass; pay：送～他 give him | 贡献～祖国 contribute to the country 注意 **NOTE**：动词本身有给予意义的，后面可以用'给'，也可以不用'给'；本身没有给予意义的，后面必须用'给' It's flexible to use 给 or not if the verb has the meaning of giving, but 给 must be used if not. 如 e.g.：还(～)他一本书 return his book | 送(～)我一笔 give me a pen | 捎～他一个包袱 bring him a cloth-wrapped bundle | 留～你钥匙 leave the key with you ❸ same as 为 wèi ②：他～我们当翻译。He will act as an interpreter for us. | 医生～他们看病。The doctor treated them. ❹ 引进动作的对象，跟'向'相同 [introduce the object of the verb, same as 向 xiàng]：小朋友～老师行礼。The children saluted their teacher. 注意 **NOTE**：这种用法，普通话有一定限制，有的说法方言里有，普通话里没有，如'车走远了，她还在～我们招手'，普通话用'向'

或'跟'There is a difference between standard Chinese and dialects: in standard Chinese 向 xiàng or 跟 gēn is used instead of 给, while in some dialects, 给 is oft. used. For example: She still waved at us, although the car had driven far away. ❺ 叫;让 let; make a)表示使对方做某件事 enable sb. to do sth.:农场拨出一块地来～他们做试验。The farm set aside a field for them to carry out experiments. b)表示容许对方做某种动作 permit sb. to do sth.:那封信他收着不～看。He kept that letter and did not let us see it. c)表示某种遭遇[indicate a bitter experience]:羊～狼吃了。The sheep was eaten by the wolf.|树～炮弹打断了。The tree was distroyed by the bomb. ❻〈助词 *aux.*〉直接用在表示被动、处置等意思的句子的谓语动词前面,以加强语气[used in a passive sentence to introduce either the doer of the action or the action if the doer is not mentioned]:裤腿都叫露水～湿透了。Our trouser legs were drenched with morning dew.|弟弟把花瓶～打了。My brother broke the vase.|我记性不好,保不住就～忘了。I may forget because of my poor memory.

☞ jǐ on p. 911

【给面子】gěi miàn·zi 照顾情面,使人面子上下得来 do sb. a favour; save sb.'s face:你们俩是老同学,你总得给他点面子。You are old classmates, you'd better help him save face. also 给脸 gěiliǎn

【给以】gěi//yǐ same as 给 gěi ①:职工生病的时候,应当～帮助。(We) should help our workers when they are ill.|对于劳动竞赛中优胜的单位或个人,应该～适当的奖励。Units and individuals that win labour competitions should be given appropriate awards. 注意 NOTE: '给以'后面只说所给的事物(并且多为抽象事物),不说接受的人。要是说出接受的人,'给以'就要改成'给'。给以 is used only when followed by sth. (usu. with an abstract noun as a direct object) rather than sb.; when it is followed by sb., 给以 must be replaced by 给:职工生病的时候,应当给他帮助。When a worker is ill, give him support.|对于劳动竞赛中优胜的单位和个人,应当给他们适当的奖励。Give units and individuals that win labour competitions appropriate awards.

gēn (ㄍㄣ)

根 gēn ❶(～儿 gēnr)高等植物的营养器官,分直根和须根两大类。根能够把植物固定在土地上,吸收土壤里的水分和溶解在水中的养分,有的根还能贮藏养料。root; nutritive organ of higher plant that is classified as tap-root and fibrous root, can fix plant to the ground, absorb water from the earth and dissolve nutrients in the water. Some roots can even store nutriments. ❷〈比喻 *fig.*〉子孙后代 offspring:这孩子是他们家的～。The child is the family heir. ❸(～儿 gēnr)物体的下部或某部分和其他东西连着的地方 root; foot; base:耳～ear|舌～the root of the tongue|墙～the foot of the wall|～基 foundation|～底 foundation ❹(～儿 gēnr)事物的本原;人的出身底细 cause; origin; source:祸～the cause of ruin|寻～seek roots|刨～问底 enquire into the root of the matter|我们是老街坊,彼此都知～知底的。We are old neighbours, so we know each other's background very well. ❺ 根本地;彻底 thoroughly; completely:～究 make a thorough investigation of|～治 cure once and for all|～绝 root out; uproot; wipe out ❻ 依据;作为根本:～据 basis|无～之谈 groundless statement ❼(～儿 gēnr)〈量词 *classifier*〉用于细长的东西[for long, thin objects]:两～筷子 two chopsticks|一～无缝钢管 a seamless steel rod ❽ 方根的简称 abbr. for 方根 fānggēn ❾ 一元方程的解(of an algebraic equation) solution ❿〈化学 *chem.*〉指带电的基 live radical:铵～ammonium radical|硫酸～acid radical

【根本】gēnběn ❶ 事物的根源或最重要的部分 foundation; base:应当从～上考虑解决问题的方法。We should solve a problem by getting at its root. ❷ 主要的;重要的 basic; fundamental; essential:不要回避最～的问题。Don't avoid the basic problem. ❸ 本来;从来 at all; simply:这话我～没说过。I never said that. ❹ 从头到尾;始终;全然(多用于否定式 usu. in the negative) at all; simply:他～就没想到这些问题。He has simply never thought of these problems.|我～就不赞成这种做法。I don't agree with you at all. ❺ 彻底 radically; thoroughly:问题已经～解决。The problem has been settled once and for all.

【根本法】gēnběnfǎ ❶ 指国家的宪法,因一切法律都要根据它来制定 fundamental law; constitution ❷ 有的国家指某些方面的基本法律(in some countries) basic law

【根插】gēnchā 扦插的一种,把植物的根切成几段埋在土中,使生根,成为独立的植物体。某些不易生根的植物如蒲公英可以用这种方法繁殖。cuttage; cutting the root of a plant into several parts and burying them in the earth in order to let them take root and become independent plants. This method is used for some plants that don't easily take root, such as dandelion.

【根除】gēnchú 彻底铲除 thoroughly do away with; eradicate; root out; eliminate:～陋习 eradicate corrupt customs|～血吸虫病 eliminate snail fever

【根底】gēndǐ ❶ 基础 foundation:他的古文～很

好。He has a solid foundation in classical Chinese. ❷ 底细 cause; root: 追问～ get at the root of the matter | 探听～try to find out the cause of sth.

【根雕】gēndiāo 在树根上进行雕刻的艺术，也指用树根雕刻成的工艺品 tree-root carving; handicraft items made from tree roots

【根基】gēnjī ❶ 基础 foundation; basis: 建筑房屋一定要把～打好。We must lay a solid foundation when building a house. ❷〈比喻 *fig.*〉家底 family property accumulated over a long time; assets: 咱们家～差，花钱可不能那样大手大脚。You'd better not spend so extravagantly, for our family is not financially stable.

【根脚】gēn·jiao ❶ 建筑物的地下部分 underground part of a building: 这座房子的～很牢靠。This house has a solid foundation. ❷ 指出身、来历(多见于早期白话 in early vernacular) family background; earlier experience

【根茎】gēnjīng 地下茎的一种，一般是长形，横着生长在地下，外形像根，有节，没有根冠而有顶芽。如莲、芦苇等的地下茎。rhizome; a kind of subterraneous stem, generally long, that grows underground horizontally like a root, having knots and terminal buds but not a crown, e.g. the subterraneous stems of lotus and reeds.

【根究】gēnjiū 彻底追究 make a thorough investigation of sth.; get to the bottom of; probe into: ～事故责任 investigate responsibility for an accident

【根据】gēnjù ❶ 把某种事物作为结论的前提或语言行动的基础 on the basis of; according to; in the light of; in line with: ～气象台的预报，明天要下雨。According to the weather forecast, it's going to rain tomorrow. | ～大家的意见，把计划修改一下。We will revise the plan on the basis of your opinions. ❷ 作为根据的事物 basis; foundation; grounds: 说话要有～。One should avoid making unfounded assertions.

【根据地】gēnjùdì 据以长期进行武装斗争的地方，特指我国在第二次国内革命战争、抗日战争和解放战争时期的革命根据地 base area for a long-term struggle, esp. referring to the revolutionary base areas in China during the Second Revolutionary Civil War, the War of Resistance against Japan and the War of Liberation

【根绝】gēnjué 彻底消灭 stamp out; eradicate; exterminate: ～虫害 stamp out pestilential insects | ～浪费现象 eliminate the phenomenon of waste

【根瘤】gēnliú 生长在豆科植物根部的球状小瘤，由根瘤菌侵入根部形成 root nodule; small globular tumour growing at the root of plants of the bean family, formed by nodule bacteria invading the root

【根毛】gēnmáo 密生在根的尖端的细毛，是根吸收水分和养料的主要部分 root hairs; main part of the root for absorbing water and nourishment

【根苗】gēnmiáo ❶ 植物的根和最初破土长出的部分 root and shoots ❷ 事物的来由和根源 source; cause: 听我细说～。Let me give you the causes in detail. ❸ 指传宗接代的子孙 offspring: 他是这家留下的惟一～。He is the only offspring to carry on the family line.

【根深蒂固】gēn shēn dì gù〈比喻 *fig.*〉基础稳固，不容易动摇 deep-rooted; ingrained; inveterate; also 根深柢固 gēn shēn dǐ gù

【根式】gēnshì 含有开方运算的算式或代数式。如 $\sqrt[n]{a}$(n 为大于 1 的正整数，n 为奇数时，a 为一切实数；n 为偶数时，$a \geqslant 0$)。radical (expression) or algebraic expression with extraction of a root, e.g. $\sqrt[n]{a}$ (Under the condition that 'n' is a positive integer larger than one, if 'n' is an odd number, 'a' is any real number; but if 'n' is an even number, $a \geqslant 0$.)

【根系】gēnxì 主根和全部侧根的总称，一般分直根系和须根系两种 root system; main root and all the branch roots in general, divided into tap root and fibrous root systems

【根由】gēnyóu 来历；缘故 cause; origin: 追问～ make detailed enquiries about the cause of sth.

【根源】gēnyuán ❶ 使事物产生的根本原因 source; origin; root: 寻找事故的～ find out the cause of the accident ❷ 起源(于) originate; stem from: 经济危机～于资本主义制度。Economic crises are endemic to the capitalist system.

【根植】gēnzhí 扎根(多用于比喻 usu. fig.) take root: 只有～于生活，艺术才会有生命力。Only by taking root in real life can art gain vitality.

【根治】gēnzhì 彻底治好(指灾害、疾病) (of a disease) effect a radical cure; (of a disaster) bring under permanent control: ～黄河 harness the Yellow River once and for all | ～血吸虫病 effect a radical cure for snail fever

【根子】gēn·zi ❶ same as 根 gēn ① ❷ same as 根 gēn ④

跟 gēn ❶ (～儿 gēnr) 脚的后部或鞋袜的后部 heel: 脚后～ heel | 高～儿鞋 high-heeled shoes ❷ 在后面紧接着同一方面行动 follow: 他跑得快，我也～得上。He runs fast, but I can still keep up with him. ◇～上形势 keep abreast of the current situation ❸ 指嫁给某人 (of a woman) marry sb.: 他要是不好好工作，我就不～他。If he doesn't work hard, I won't marry him. ❹〈介词 *prep.*〉引进动作的对象 [used to indicate accompaniment, relationship, involvement, etc.]: a) 同 with: 有

G

事要～群众商量。Consult the masses when problems crop up. b)向 towards:你这主意好,快～大家说说。This is a good idea. Why don't you spell it out for us all? ❺〈介词 *prep.*〉引进比较异同的对象;同[used to show comparison] same as:她待我～待亲儿子一样。She treated me like her own son.|高山上的气压～平地上不一样。The atmospheric pressure in the mountains is different from that on the plains.|他的脾气从小就～他爸爸非常相像。From the time he was a child, his temper has been the same as his father's. ❻〈连词 *conj.*〉表示联合关系;和 and:车上装的是机器～材料。There are machines and materials loaded on the vehicle.|他的胳膊～大腿都受了伤。His arm and leg were both injured.

【跟班】gēn//bān 随同某一劳动集体或学习集体(劳动或学习) join a regular shift or class:～干活儿 (of a leading comrade) go to work in a workshop for a specified period of time|～听课 audit a class

【跟班】gēnbān 〈旧时 *old*〉跟随在官员身边供使唤的人 footman of an official; also 跟班儿的 gēnbānr·de

【跟包】gēnbāo ❶〈旧时 *old*〉指专为某个戏曲演员管理服装及做其他杂务 attendant taking care of costumes and running errands for a stage actor ❷ 指做这种工作的人 people who act as an attendant for an actor

【跟差】gēnchāi same as 跟班 gēnbān

【跟从】gēncóng ❶ same as 跟随 gēnsuí:只要你领头干,我一定～你。If you take the lead, I will certainly follow you. ❷〈旧指 *old*〉随从人员 retinue

【跟斗】gēn·dou 〈方 *dial.*〉same as 跟头 gēn·tou

【跟脚】gēnjiǎo 〈方 *dial.*〉❶〈旧指 *old*〉跟随主人出门,照料伺侯 wait upon one's master when he is out:～的 footman ❷ (孩子)跟随大人,不肯离开 (of children) not be willing to leave one's parents ❸ (鞋)大小合适,便于走路 (of shoes) fit well ❹ (～儿 gēnjiǎor)随即(限用于行走之类的动作) follow close upon sb.'s heels:你刚走,他～儿也出去了。He followed you out right after you left.

【跟屁虫】gēnpìchóng (～儿 gēnpìchóngr)指老跟在别人背后的人(含厌恶意 derog.) parasite; toady; hanger-on; refers to those who always follow others

【跟前】gēnqián ❶ (～儿 gēnqiánr)身边;附近 close to; nearby; near:请你到我～来。Please come close to me.|她坐在窗户～的床上。She is sitting on the bed near the window. ❷ 临近的时间 shortly before:春节～ shortly before Spring Festival

【跟前】gēn·qian 身体的近旁(专指有无儿女说) (have a daughter or son living) near or close to oneself:他～只有一个女儿。He has only one daughter living with him.

【跟梢】gēn//shāo 钉梢 shadow sb.; tail sb.

【跟手】gēnshǒu 〈方 *dial.*〉(～儿 gēnshǒur) ❶ 随手 conveniently:他一进屋子,～就把门关上。He closed the door behind him as he entered the room. ❷ 随即 immediately:他接到电报,～儿搭上汽车走了。He received a telegram and immediately left by bus.

【跟随】gēnsuí ❶ same as 跟 gēn②:他从小就～着爸爸在山里打猎。From the time he was a child he used to go hunting with his father in the mountains. ❷ 指随从人员 retinue

【跟趟儿】gēn//tàngr 〈方 *dial.*〉❶ 赶上一般人的水平 catch up to the average:他学习跟上趟儿了。He has caught up with the others now in his studies.|他的认识有点儿跟不上趟儿。His understanding is a bit behind the times. ❷ 来得及 there's still time:吃完饭再去看电影还～。There is still time to go to the movie after dinner.

【跟头】gēn·tou (人、物等)失去平衡而摔倒或向下弯曲而翻转的动作(of people, things, etc. after losing balance) tumble; fall:栽～have a fall|翻～ turn a somersault

【跟尾儿】gēnyǐr 〈方 *dial.*〉随后 follow:你先回家吧,我～就去。You go home first, and I will follow soon.

【跟着】gēn·zhe ❶ same as 跟 gēn ② ❷ 紧接着 tag along; follow in the wake of:听完报告～就讨论。We held a discussion right after hearing the report.

【跟踪】gēnzōng 紧紧跟在后面(追赶、监视) follow the tracks of:～追击 go in hot pursuit of

gén (ㄍㄣˊ)

哏 gén 〈方 *dial.*〉❶ 滑稽;有趣 amusing; comical; funny:这段相声真～。This comic dialogue is really funny.|这孩子笑的样子有点儿～。The way the child laughs is quite funny. ❷ 滑稽有趣的语言或动作 clownish speech or behaviour:逗～ the lead role in a cross-talk performance

gěn (ㄍㄣˇ)

艮[1] gěn 〈方 *dial.*〉(性子)直;(说话)生硬 blunt; straightforward:这个人真～! That fellow is really blunt!|他说的话太～! He was a bit too blunt!

艮[2] gěn 〈方 *dial.*〉(食物)坚韧而不脆 (of food) tough; leathery:发～ become tough|～萝卜不好吃。Tough radishes are not good to eat.

☞ gèn on p. 661

G

gèn (ㄍㄣˋ)

亘(亙) gèn (空间上或时间上)延续不断 (of space or time) extend; stretch: 横～lie across | 绵～stretch in an unbroken chain | ～古 ancient times; antiquity

【亘古】gèngǔ 整个古代;终古 ancient times: ～以来 from remote antiquity | ～至今(从古到今) from time immemorial (until now) | ～未有 no such thing from time immemorial; unheard of; unprecedented

艮 gèn ❶ 八卦之一,卦形是'☶',代表山 one of the Eight Diagrams, symbolized by '☶', indicating mountain; ☞ 八卦 bāguà on p. 22 ❷ (Gèn)姓 a surname
☞ gěn on p. 660

茛 gèn ☞ 毛茛 máogèn on p. 1306

gēng (ㄍㄥ)

更[1] gēng ❶ 改变;改换 change; replace: 变～change | ～改 change | ～衣 change dresses | ～名改姓 change one's whole name | 除旧～新 exchange the old for the new ❷〈书 *fml.*〉经历 experience: 少不～事 inexperienced and easily fooled

更[2] gēng 〈旧时 *old*〉一夜分成五更,每更大约两小时 one of the five two-hour periods into which the night was formerly divided: 打～sound the night watch | 三～半夜 in the dead of night
☞ gèng on p. 663

【更次】gēngcì 指夜间一更(约两小时)长的时间 one of the five two-hour periods into which the night was formerly divided: 睡了约有一个～slept about two hours

【更迭】gēngdié 轮流更换 alternate; change: 人事～personnel changes | 朝代～a change of dynasty

【更定】gēngdìng 改订 reformulate: ～法律 reformulate laws | ～规章制度 reformulate rules and regulations

【更动】gēngdòng 改动;变更 change; alter: 比赛日程有所～。The match schedule has been changed a bit. | 这部书再版时,作者在章节上做了一些～。When the book was reprinted, the author made some changes in some chapters and sections.

【更番】gēngfān 轮流替换 by turns; alternately: ～守护 watch by turns

【更改】gēnggǎi 改换;改动 change; alter: ～时间 change the time | ～名称 change name | 飞往上海的飞机中途遇雾,临时～航线。Due to fog the plane had to change course en route to Shanghai.

【更换】gēnghuàn 变换;替换 change; replace: ～位置 change places | ～衣裳 change one's clothes | ～值班人员 change the operator on duty | 展览馆里的展品不断～。The exhibits in the exhibition hall are being changed all the time.

【更阑】gēnglán 〈书 *fml.*〉更深夜尽;深夜 the dead of the night: ～人静。All is quiet in the dead of night.

【更名】gēngmíng 更换名字或名称 rename; change one's name: ～改姓 change one's name

【更年期】gēngniánqī 人由成年期向老年期过渡的时期。通常女子在 45—55 岁,卵巢功能逐渐减退,月经终止;男子在 55～65 岁,睾丸逐渐退化,精子生成减少。climacteric; menopause; mid-life crisis; change of life from middle to old age, for women, occurring between age 45 to 55, with a gradual diminution of the ovariam function; for men, occurring between age 55 to 65, with gradual degeneration of testicles, and a reduction in sperm

【更仆难数】gēng pú nán shǔ 换了很多人来数,还是数不完,形容人或事物很多 too many to count; innumerable; countless

【更深】gēngshēn 指半夜以后;夜深 second half of the night — the dead of the night: ～人静 deep into the night and all being quiet | ～夜静。In the dead of the night all is quiet.

【更生】gēngshēng ❶ 重新得到生命 regenerate; 〈比喻 *fig.*〉复兴 revive: 自力～ rely on one's own efforts ❷ same as 再生 zàishēng ③: ～布 renewable cloth

【更始】gēngshǐ 〈书 *fml.*〉除去旧的,建立新的;重新起头 make a new beginning: 与民～get rid of the old to make way for the new

【更替】gēngtì 更换;替换 replace: 季节～ the change of seasons | 人员～ replacement of personnel

【更新】gēngxīn ❶ 旧的去了,新的来到;除去旧的,换成新的 replace the old with the new: 万象～。Everything has taken on a new look. | 岁序～end of the old year and beginning of the new year | ～设备 upgrade equipment | ～武器 arms renewal ❷ 森林经过采伐、火灾或破坏后重新长起来(of forest, plants, etc.) renewal after logging, fire or destruction

【更衣】gēngyī ❶ 换衣服 change one's clothes ❷〈婉辞 *euph.*〉指上厕所 go to the toilet

【更易】gēngyì 更改;改动 change; alter: ～习俗 change old-fashioned customs | 这篇稿子～过两三次。This article has been changed a few times.

【更张】gēngzhāng 调节琴弦 tune a stringed instrument; 〈比喻 *fig.*〉变更或改革 change or reform; ☞ 改弦更张 gǎi xián gēng zhāng on p. 621

【更正】gēngzhèng 改正已发表的谈话或文章中有关内容或字句上的错误 make corrections

(of errors in published statements or articles):～启事 notice of correction; errata notice|那篇讲话要～几个字。Several words of that speech need to be corrected.

庚 gēng ❶ 天干的第七位 7th of the Ten Heavenly Stems (天干); ☞ 干支 gānzhī on p. 627 ❷ 年龄 age: 年～age|同～ of the same age ❸ (Gēng)姓 a surname

【庚齿】gēngchǐ 〈书 *fml.*〉年庚;年龄 age

【庚日】gēngrì 用干支来纪日时,有天干第七位'庚'字的日子。夏至三庚数伏,就是指夏至后的第三个庚日开始初伏。When recording the day by the Heavenly Stems and Earthly Branches, the day representing the 7th of the Ten Heavenly Stems is called *gengri*. The dog days begin after the third *gengri* after Summer solstice.

【庚帖】gēngtiě 八字帖 written marriage proposal stating the hour, day, month and year of one's birth

畊 gēng 〈书 *fml.*〉 same as 耕 gēng

耕 gēng ❶ 用犁把田里的土翻松 plough; till: ～田 plough|～种 plough and sow|春～ spring ploughing|深～细作 deep ploughing and intensive cultivation ❷〈比喻 *fig.*〉从事某种劳动 make a living: 笔～earn one's living by writing|舌～ earn one's living by the gift of gab

G

【耕畜】gēngchù 用来耕地的牲畜,主要是牛、马、骡子等 farm animal, mainly bull, horse and mule

【耕地】gēng//dì 用犁把田地里的土翻松 plough; till

【耕地】gēngdì 种植农作物的土地 cultivated land: ～面积 area under cultivation|不能随意占用～。You can't occupy cultivated areas as you like.

【耕读】gēngdú 指既从事农业劳动又读书或教学 study or teach part-time, while farming: ～小学 a primary school under a part-study and part-farming system|～教师 teacher under a part-time teaching and part-time farming system

【耕云播雨】gēng yún bō yǔ 指控制降雨,改造自然,多用于比喻 (oft. fig.) command the clouds and rain: 为文艺园地百花盛开而～。Work hard for a hundred flowers to bloom in the field of literature and art.

【耕耘】gēngyún 耕地和除草,常用于比喻 (oft. fig.) plough and weed; hard work; diligence: 着意～,自有收获。Devotion to one's work will certainly pay off.

【耕种】gēngzhòng 耕地和种植 till; cultivate: 开春了,农民都忙着～土地。At the beginning of spring, farmers are busy cultivating the fields.

【耕作】gēngzuò 用各种方法处理土壤的表层,使适于农作物的生长发育,包括耕、耙、锄等 tillage, cultivation, means of preparing the soil surface in order to grow crops, including ploughing, raking, hoeing, etc.

浭 Gēng 浭水,水名,蓟运河的上游,在河北 Gengshui, name of river that is in the upper reaches of the Ji Canal in Hebei Province

赓 gēng ❶〈书 *fml.*〉继续;连续 continue: ～续 continue ❷ (Gēng)姓 a surname

【赓续】gēngxù 〈书 *fml.*〉继续 continue: ～旧好 renew an old friendship

絙(緪、縆) gēng 〈方 *dial.*〉粗绳索 thick rope

【絙索】gēngsuǒ 〈方 *dial.*〉粗的绳索 thick rope

鹒 gēng ☞ [鸧鹒] (cānggēng) on p. 190

羹 gēng 通常用蒸、煮等方法做成的糊状食物 steamed or boiled thick soup; custard: 豆腐～beancurd custard|鸡蛋～ egg custard

【羹匙】gēngchí 匙子;汤匙 soup spoon; tablespoon

gěng (ㄍㄥˇ)

埂 gěng ❶ (～儿 gěngr)埂子 low bank of earth between fields: 田～儿 rand; baulk ❷ 地势高起的长条地方 long, narrow mound: 再往前走,就是一道小山～。Go further ahead, and you'll come across the narrow strip of a hill. ❸ 用泥土筑成的提防 earth dyke (or embankment): ～堰 ridge|堤～ dam

【埂子】gěng·zi 田地里稍稍高起的分界线,像狭窄的小路 ridge; low bank of earth between fields like a pathway: 地～ field bund

耿 gěng ❶〈书 *fml.*〉光明 bright ❷ 耿直 honest and just; upright ❸ (Gěng)姓 a surname

【耿耿】gěnggěng ❶ 明亮 bright: ～星河 the bright Milky Way ❷ 形容忠诚 devoted; dedicated: ～丹心 upright heart|忠心～loyal and faithful ❸ 形容有心事 having sth. on one's mind: ～不寐 lose sleep over sth.|～于怀 take sth. to heart

【耿介】gěngjiè 〈书 *fml.*〉正直,不同于流俗 straightforward and outstanding — not like ordinary people: 性情～straightforward and outstanding character|～之士 straightforward and outstanding person

【耿直】gěngzhí (性格)正直;直爽 honest and frank; upright: 他是个～人,一向知无不言,言无不尽。He is honest and frank who always speaks his mind without reserve. also 梗直 gěngzhí and 鲠直 gěngzhí

哽 gěng ❶食物堵塞喉咙不能下咽 choke due to food blockage: 慢点吃,别～着。

Eat slowly so that you won't choke. ❷ 因感情激动等原因喉咙阻塞发不出声音 choke (with emotion); feel a lump in one's throat:～咽 choke with sobs|他心里一酸,喉咙～得说不出话来。He felt a pang of sadness, and got so choked up that he couldn't speak.

【哽塞】gěngsè same as 哽 gěng②:她才说了两个字,话便～在嗓子眼儿里了。She spoke only two words and felt a lump in her throat.

【哽噎】gěngyē ❶ 食物堵住食管 gullet blocked by food:他嘴里像有什么东西～住,说不出话来。It was as if his mouth was blocked by something and he couldn't utter a word. ❷ same as 哽咽 gěngyè

【哽咽】gěngyè 哭时不能痛快地出声 choke with sobs; with a lump in one's throat; also 梗咽 gěngyè

绠 gěng〈书 *fml.*〉汲水用的绳子 rope with which to fetch water from a well

【绠短汲深】gěng duǎn jí shēn 吊桶的绳子很短,却要打很深的井里的水 short rope for a deep well;〈比喻 *fig.*〉能力薄弱,任务重大(多用做谦辞 usu. hum.)inadequate ability for a major task

梗 gěng ❶(～儿 gěngr)某些植物的枝或茎 stalk or stem of some plants:花～ flower stem|高粱～儿 sorghum stalk ❷ 挺直 straighten:～着脖子 straightening up one's neck ❸ 直爽 frank; forthright:～直 upright ❹〈书 *fml.*〉顽固 stubborn:顽～ obstinate ❺ 阻塞;妨碍 obstruct; block:～塞 block|从中作～ put a spoke in sb.'s wheel; make things difficult for sb.

【梗概】gěnggài 大略的内容 broad outline; main idea:故事～ gist of a story

【梗塞】gěngsè ❶ 阻塞 block; obstruct; clog ❷ 局部动脉堵塞,血流停止 infarction

【梗死】gěngsǐ 组织因缺血而坏死。多发生于心、肾、肺、脑等器官。infarction, mainly occurring in organs such as the heart, kidney, lungs and brain

【梗咽】gěngyè same as 哽咽 gěngyè

【梗直】gěngzhí same as 耿直 gěngzhí

【梗阻】gěngzǔ ❶ 阻塞 block:道路～jammed passage|山川～ be separated by mountains and rivers ❷ 拦挡 obstruct:横加～unreasonably obstruct or raise obstacles

颈(頸) gěng ☞ 脖颈儿 bógěngr on p. 149 ☞ jǐng on p. 1028

鲠(鯁) gěng ❶〈书 *fml.*〉鱼骨头 fishbone:如～在喉 like having a fishbone caught in one's throat (said of sb. who has sth. he must say) ❷ (鱼骨头等)卡在喉咙里 (of a fishbone) get stuck in one's throat ❸〈书 *fml.*〉正直 upright:～直 upright

【鲠直】gěng zhí same as 耿直 gěngzhí

gèng(ㄍㄥˋ)

更 gèng〈副词 *adv.*〉❶ 更加 more; even more:刮了一夜北风,天～冷了。The weather got even colder after the north wind blew all night. |～好地工作 work harder ❷〈书 *fml.*〉再;又 further; what is more:～上一层楼 strive for further improvement ☞ gēng on p. 661

【更加】gèngjiā〈副词 *adv.*〉表示程度上又深了一层或者数量上进一步增加或减少(of degree or quantity) more; still more; even more:公家的书,应该～爱护。You should take even better care of public books. |天色渐亮,晨星～稀少了。The stars faded as day dawned.

【更其】gèngqí〈书 *fml.*〉same as 更加 gèngjiā

【更上一层楼】gèng shàng yī céng lóu 唐王之涣《登鹳雀楼》诗:'欲穷千里目,更上一层楼。' The poem *Climbing Guanque Tower* written by Wang Zhihuan of Tang says: 'Would you command a prospect of a thousand *li*? Climb yet one storey higher.'〈比喻 *fig.*〉再提高一步 attain a yet higher goal:今年力争生产～。We'll try to attain an even higher goal in production this year.

堩(𡑣) gèng〈书 *fml.*〉道路 road

暅(晅) gèng〈书 *fml.*〉晒。多用于人名。bask, usu. used in people's names

G

gōng(ㄍㄨㄥ)

工[1] gōng ❶ 工人和工人阶级 workers and the working class:矿～miner|钳～fitter|瓦～ tiler|技～ skilled worker|女～ woman worker|～农联盟 worker-peasant alliance ❷ 工作;生产劳动 work; labour:做～work|上～ go to work|加～process|勤～俭学 study under a work-study program|省料又省～save both material and labour ❸ 工程 construction project:动～ come under construction|竣～(of a project) be completed ❹ 工业 industry:化～(化学工业) chemical industry|～交系统 the industrial and communications front ❺ 指工程师 engineer:高～(高级工程师) senior engineer|王～ Engineer Wang ❻ 一个工人或农民一个劳动日的工作 person-day:砌这道墙要六个～。Building this wall will need six person-days. ❼(～儿 gōngr)技术和技术修养 skill; craftsmanship:唱～art of singing|做～ workmanship ❽ 长于;善于 be good at:～诗善画 be well-versed in painting and poetry ❾ 精巧;精致 exquisite; fine:～巧 exquisite|～稳 well chosen

工[2] gōng 我国民族音乐音阶上的一级,乐谱上用做记音符号,相当于简谱的'3' note of the scale in *gongchepu* 工尺谱, corresponding to ‘3’ in numbered musical notation; ☞ 工尺 gōngchě

【工本】gōngběn 制造物品所用的成本 cost (of production):～费 cost of production | 不惜～ at all costs

【工笔】gōngbǐ 国画的一种画法,用笔工整,注重细部的描绘(区别于‘写意’as compared with ‘freehand brushwork’) meticulous brushwork; traditional Chinese realistic painting characterized by fine brushwork and close attention to details

【工兵】gōngbīng 工程兵的旧称 old term for engineering corps

【工厂】gōngchǎng 直接进行工业生产活动的单位,通常包括不同的车间(usu. with different workshops) factory; mill; plant; works

【工场】gōngchǎng 手工业者集合在一起生产的场所(of handicraftsmen) workshop

【工潮】gōngcháo 工人为实现某种要求或表示抗议而掀起的风潮 workers' demonstration or protest movement; strikes

【工尺】gōngchě 我国民族音乐音阶上各个音的总称,也是乐谱上各个记音符号的总称。符号各个时代不同,现在通用是:合、四、一、上、尺、工、凡、六、五、乙。*gongche*, a traditional Chinese musical scale with different symbols used in different periods, those currently in use being *he*, *si*, *yi*, *shang*, *chi*, *gong*, *fan*, *liu*, *wu* and *yi*

G

【工程】gōngchéng ❶ 土木建筑或其他生产、制造部门用比较大而复杂的设备来进行的工作,如土木工程、机械工程、化学工程、采矿工程、水利工程等(civil, mechanical, chemical, mining, water conservancy, etc.) engineering ❷ 泛指某项需要投入巨大人力和物力的工作 project that needs a large quantity of manpower and materials:菜篮子～(指解决城镇蔬菜、副食供应问题的规划和措施) vegetable-basket project (refers to planning and measures to ensure supply of vegetables and food to urban residents)

【工程兵】gōngchéngbīng 担任复杂的工程保障任务的兵种。执行构筑工事、架桥、筑路、伪装、设置和排除障碍物等工程任务。也称这一兵种的士兵。engineer corps (in an army), responsible for construction work, e.g. building bridges, road construction, camouflage work, installation and removal of obstacles; soldiers engaged in such work; 旧称 formerly called 工兵 gōngbīng

【工程师】gōngchéngshī 技术干部的职务名称之一。能够独立完成某一专门技术任务的设计、施工工作的专门人员。engineer; specialist who can independently complete planning and construction of a technical project

【工地】gōngdì 进行建筑、开发、生产等工作的现场 construction site

【工读】gōngdú ❶ 用本人劳动的收入来供自己读书 study relying on one's own income:～生 students who earn their tuition and living by labour ❷ 指工读教育 education for juvenile delinquents

【工读教育】gōngdú jiàoyù 对有较轻违法犯罪行为的青少年进行改造、挽救的教育 education-through-work; education aimed at reforming and redeeming juvenile delinquents

【工段】gōngduàn ❶ 建筑、交通、水利等工程部门根据具体情况划分的施工组织(of architecture, communication, water conservancy, etc.) work section of a construction project ❷ 工厂车间内按生产过程划分的生产组织,由若干生产班组组成 work section; workshop division according to production process

【工房】gōngfáng〈方 *dial.*〉❶ 由国家或集体建造分配给职工或居民居住的房屋;工人宿舍 workers' living quarters, built by the state or collective and distributed to works or residents ❷ 厂房;工棚 factory building; workshed

【工分】gōngfēn 某些集体经济组织计算个人工作量和劳动报酬的单位 workpoint (measurement unit indicating the quantity and quality of labour performed, and the amount of payment earned, in certain collective economic organizations)

【工蜂】gōngfēng 蜜蜂中生殖器官发育不完全的雌蜂,身体小,深黄灰色,翅膀长,善于飞行,有毒刺,腹部有分泌蜡质的蜡腺,两只后脚上有花粉篮。工蜂担任修筑蜂巢,采集花粉和花蜜,哺养幼虫和母蜂等工作,不能传种。worker bee; worker; small in body, deep yellowish grey in colour, good at flying, with long wings and telson, a wax gland in the belly and a pollen basket on the rear legs, responsible for building the honeycomb, collecting pollen and nectar, feeding larvae and the queen bee, but without the ability of reproduction

【工夫】gōng·fū〈旧指 *old*〉临时雇的短工 casual labourer; temporary worker

【工夫】gōng·fu (～儿 gōngfur) ❶ 时间(指占用的时间) time:他三天～就学会了游泳。It took him only three days to learn to swim. ❷ 空闲时间 leisure time:明天有～再来玩儿吧! If you have time tomorrow, please come visit again. ❸〈方 *dial.*〉时候 at that time:我当闺女那～,婚姻全凭父母之命,媒妁之言。When I was a girl, matches were arranged by go-betweens according to the wishes of the parents. also 功夫 gōng·fu

【工会】gōnghuì 工人阶级的群众性组织。最早出现于18世纪中叶的英国,后各国相继建立。一般分为产业工会和职业工会两大类。labour union; first appeared in the mid-18th century in Britain, later spread all over the world, generally divided into industrial unions and professional unions.

【工价】gōngjià 指建筑或制作某项物品用于人工方面的费用(多用于制订计划或计算成本时)

labour cost in construction or manufacturing (usu. for planning or cost calculation)

【工架】gōngjià 戏曲演员表演时的身段和姿势 movements and postures of actors (in traditional operas); also 功架 gōngjià

【工间】gōngjiān 指从上班到下班的工作时间以内的(多用于其间的某种活动 usu. referring to certain activity) between work hours: ~操 work-break exercises|~休息 coffee break

【工间操】gōngjiāncāo 机关和企业中的工作人员每天在工作时间内抽出一定时间来集体做的体操 work-break exercises (for staff members of offices and enterprises)

【工件】gōngjiàn 作件 work-piece; work

【工匠】gōngjiàng 手艺工人 craftsman

【工交】gōngjiāo 工业和交通运输业的合称 industry and communications and transportation: ~系统 industrial and communications circles

【工具】gōngjù ❶ 进行生产劳动时所使用的器具,如锯、刨、犁、锄 tool, instrument, implements of production, e.g. saw, digger, plough, hoe ❷〈比喻 *fig.*〉用以达到目的的事物 instrument; sth. used to reach certain purpose: 语言是人们交流思想的~。Language is an instrument for people to exchange thoughts.

【工具书】gōngjùshū 专为读者查考字义、词义、字句出处和各种事实而编纂的书籍,如字典、词典、索引、历史年表、年鉴、百科全书等 reference book; complied for readers to look up the meaning and source of a word, sentence or fact, e.g. dictionary, index, historical chronology, yearbook, encyclopaedia, etc.

【工楷】gōngkǎi 工整的楷书 (in Chinese calligraphy) neat regular script

【工科】gōngkē 教学上对有关工程学科的统称 (in education) engineering courses

【工矿】gōngkuàng 工业和矿业的合称 industry and mining: ~企业 industrial and mining enterprises

【工力】gōnglì ❶ 本领和力量 skill; craftsmanship: 做到这样是不容易的,必须用很大的~。This is not easy to do without remarkable skill. ❷ 指完成某项工作所需要的人力 human resources (needed for accomplishing certain work)

【工力悉敌】gōnglì xī dí〈书 *fml.*〉指双方本领和力量相等,不分上下 rival each other in artistry or workmanship

【工料】gōngliào ❶ 人工和材料(多用于制订计划或计算成本时 usu. used for planning or cost calculation) labour and materials ❷ 指工程所需的材料 materials for building a project: 购买~ purchase materials

【工龄】gōnglíng 工人或职员的工作年数 (of workers or staff) length of service; seniority

【工农联盟】gōng nóng liánméng 工人阶级和劳动农民在工人阶级政党领导下的革命联合 worker-peasant alliance; revolutionary alliance of workers and peasants under the leadership of the political party of the working class

【工棚】gōngpéng 工地上临时搭起来供工作或住宿用的简便房屋 temporary shed on a construction site

【工期】gōngqī 工程的期限 time limit for a project: 延长~ extend the time limit for a project|~定为一年。The time limit for the project is one year.

【工钱】gōng·qian ❶ 做零活儿的报酬 money paid for odd jobs; charge for a service: 做套衣服要多少~? How much should I pay for having the suit made? ❷〈方 *dial.*〉same as 工资 gōngzī

【工巧】gōngqiǎo 细致,精巧(多用于工艺品或诗文、书画 usu. to describe handicraft, poetic prose, painting, calligraphy, etc.) exquisite; fine

【工区】gōngqū 某些工矿企业部门的基层生产单位 work area; grass-roots unit of an industrial enterprise

【工人】gōng·rén 个人不占有生产资料、依靠工资收入为生的劳动者(多指体力劳动者 usu. manual worker) worker; labourer possessing no means of production goods and making a living by selling his labour for wages

【工人阶级】gōngrén jiējí 不占有任何生产资料、依靠工资为生的劳动者所形成的阶级,是无产阶级革命的领导阶级,代表着最先进的生产力,它最有远见,大公无私,具有高度的组织性、纪律性和彻底的革命性 working class, whose members possess no means of production and make a living by selling labour for wages; leading class of the proletarian revolution, representing the most advanced productivity, and marked for its keenest foresight, selflessness, a high sense of organization and discipline, and a thorough revolutionary character

【工日】gōngrì 一个劳动者工作一天为一个工日 work day

【工伤】gōngshāng 在生产劳动过程中受到的意外伤害 injury suffered on the job: ~事故 industrial accident

【工商业】gōngshāngyè 工业和商业的统称 industry and commerce

【工时】gōngshí 工人工作一小时为一个工时,是工业上计算工人劳动量的时间单位 person-hour; man-hour

【工事】gōngshì 保障军队发扬火力和隐蔽安全的建筑物,如地堡、堑壕、交通壕、掩蔽部等 fortifications; defence works for making full use of firepower and providing cover with safety structures, e.g. bunker, trench, communication trench, shelter, etc.

【工头】gōngtóu (~儿 gōngtóur) 资本家雇用来监督工人劳动的人。也泛指指挥、带领工人劳

G

动的人。foreman; person who supervises workers on behalf of a factory owner; (in a broad sense) person who commands and guides workers' labour.

【工稳】gōngwěn 工整而妥帖(多指诗文 usu. of poetic prose) apt; well chosen:造句～well-worded phrases|对仗～well-chosen antithesis

【工细】gōngxì 精巧细致 exquisite and fine:雕刻～exquisite and fine carving

【工效】gōngxiào 工作效率 work efficiency:提高～raise (or improve) work efficiency

【工薪】gōngxīn same as 工资 gōngzī

【工休】gōngxiū ❶ 指工作一阶段的休息 rest after a period of work:～日 day off; holiday|全体司机放弃～运送旅客。All the drivers gave up their holidays to transporting travellers. ❷ 指工间休息 break:～时,女工们有的聊天,有的打毛衣。During the work-break, some women workers chat and some knit.

【工序】gōngxù 组成整个生产过程的各段加工,也指各段加工的先后次序。材料经过各道工序,加工成成品。work procedure; process in order from raw materials to end products

【工业】gōngyè 采取自然物质资源,制造生产资料、生活资料,或对农产品、半成品等进行加工的生产事业 industry; productive undertaking that turns natural materials into means of production or daily supplies, or processes farm produce and semi-finished products

G

【工业革命】gōngyè gémìng 产业革命 industrial revolution

【工业国】gōngyèguó 现代工业在国民经济中占主要地位的国家 industrialized country; country in which modern industry dominates the national economy

【工业化】gōngyèhuà 使现代工业在国民经济中占主要地位 industrialize

【工蚁】gōngyǐ 生殖器官不发达的蚂蚁,在群体中数量占绝对优势 worker; worker ant; ergate; ant with underdeveloped reproductive system and making up the overwhelming majority of an ant group; ☞ 蚁 yǐ on p. 2269

【工艺】gōngyì ❶ 将原材料或半成品加工成产品的工作、方法、技术等 technological process; method and technology for processing raw materials or semi-finished products into products:～复杂 complicated technological process|～精细 exquisite workmanship ❷ 手工艺 handicraft; handicraft art:～品 works of handicraft

【工艺美术】gōngyì měishù 指工艺品的造型设计和装饰性美术 industrial arts; arts and crafts; applied arts

【工艺品】gōngyìpǐn 手工艺的产品 article of handicraft; handiwork

【工役】gōngyì 〈旧时 *old*〉给机关、学校或官僚、绅士人家做杂事的人 people who do odd jobs in institutions, schools and homes of officials and gentry

【工友】gōngyǒu ❶ 机关、学校的勤杂人员 manual worker such as a janitor, cleaner, etc. in a school or government office ❷ 〈旧时 *old*〉称工人,也用于工人之间的互称 workers; fellow worker

【工于】gōngyú 长于;善于 be good at; be adept at:～心计 adept at scheming; very calculating|他～工笔花鸟。He is adept at meticulously drawing of flowers and birds.

【工余】gōngyú 工作时间以外的 spare time; time outside of work:他利用～时间学习文化知识。He acquired knowledge after work.

【工整】gōngzhěng 细致整齐;不潦草 careful and neat:字写得～极了 neatly lettered

【工致】gōngzhì 精巧细致 exquisite; delicate:这一枝梅花画得很～。This plum-blossom painting is exquisitely done.

【工种】gōngzhǒng 工矿企业中按生产劳动的性质和任务而划分的种类,如钳工、车工、铸工等 types of production work, classified according to the nature and task of productive labour, e.g. bench work, lathe work, foundry work, etc.

【工资】gōngzī 作为劳动报酬按期付给劳动者的货币或实物 wages; pay; salary; money or material objects paid regularly to sb. for his or her work

【工作】gōngzuò ❶ 从事体力或脑力劳动,也泛指机器、工具受人操纵而发挥生产作用 work, referring to manual or mental labour, and, in a broad sense, the productive role of a machine or tool operated by man; operate:积极～work hard|开始～begin to work|铲土机正在～。The spading machine is in operation. ❷ 职业 job:找～look for a job|～没有贵贱之分。There are no differences of social status in work. ❸ 业务;任务 work:～量 amount of work|宣传～ propaganda work|工会～ trade union work|科学研究～ scientific research

【工作服】gōngzuòfú 为工作需要而特制的服装 work overall; boiler suit

【工作面】gōngzuòmiàn ❶ 直接开采矿物或岩石的工作地点,随着采掘进度而移动 work face, on which minerals and rocks are directly extracted, and which progressively shifts with the mining process ❷ 零件上进行机械加工的部位 working surface of components

【工作母机】gōngzuò mǔjī 制造机器和机械的机器,如车床、铣床、刨床和磨床等 machine tools, e.g. lathes, shapers, planers and grinders, etc.; also 机床 jīchuáng and 工具机 gōngjùjī; 简称 abbr. 母机 mǔjī

【工作日】gōngzuòrì ❶ 一天中按规定做工作的时间 workday; working time of a day ❷ 按规定应该工作的日子 working day:本周星期一至星期五是～,星期六和星期天是休息日。This week Monday to Friday are working days and Saturday and Sunday are days off.

【工作证】gōngzuòzhèng 表示一个人在某单位工作的证件 employee's card; I. D. card

弓 gōng ❶ 射箭或发弹丸的器械，在近似弧形的有弹性的木条两端之间系着坚韧的弦，拉开弦后，猛然放手，借弦和弓背的弹力把箭或弹丸射出 bow; apparatus for shooting arrows or balls, with taut string fastened between two ends of a flexible arched strip of wood, operated by pulling back the string and letting it go suddenly, so the arrow or ball is shot with the power of the string and the arching of the bow: ～箭 bow and arrow | 弹～ catapult | 左右开～ shoot first with one hand, then with the other; hit with both hands ❷（～儿 gōngr）弓子 sth. bow-shaped: 弹棉花的绷～儿 bow used to tease cotton ❸ 丈量地亩的器具，用木头制成，形状略像弓，两端的距离是5尺 *gong*; wooden land-measuring divider, bow-shaped, the length between both ends equal to 5 *chi*; also 步弓 bùgōng ❹〈旧时 *old*〉丈量地亩的计算单位，1弓等于5尺 unit of length for measuring land, equal to 5 *chi* ❺ 使弯曲 bend; arch; bow: ～背 arch one's back | ～着腰 bend one's waist | ～着腿坐着 sitting with arched legs ❻（Gōng）姓 a surname

【弓子】gōng·zi 形状或作用像弓的东西 sth. bow-shaped: 胡琴～ bow of the *huqin* instrument | 三轮车上的车～ handle bars of a tricycle

公1 gōng ❶ 属于国家或集体的（跟'私'相对 as opposed to 'private'）public; state-owned; collective: ～款 public funds | ～物 public property | ～事公办。Public business should be strictly attended to. ❷ 共同的；大家承认的 common; general: ～分母 common denominator | ～议 public discussion | ～约 convention; treaty ❸ 属于国际间的 of the world; international: ～海 international waters | ～制 metric system | ～历 Gregorian calendar ❹ 使公开 make public: ～布 announce | ～之于世 make known to the world ❺ 公平；公正 fair; impartial; just: ～买～卖 be fair in buying and selling | 大～无私 selfless | 秉～办理 handle a matter impartially ❻ 公事；公务 public affairs; official business: 办～ handle official business | ～余 after work ❼（Gōng）姓 a surname

公2 gōng ❶ 封建五等爵位的第一等 duke; first rank of the five ranks of nobility in feudal society: ～爵 duke | ～侯 duke and marquis | 王～大臣 princes, dukes and ministers ❷ 对上了年纪的男子的尊称 [respectful term of address for an elderly man]: 诸～ all the gentlemen | 张～ the reverend Mr. Zhang ❸ 丈夫的父亲；公公 husband's father; father-in-law: ～婆 parents-in-law ❹（禽兽）雄性的（跟'母'相对 as opposed to 'female'）male (animal): ～羊 ram | 这只小鸡是～的。This chick is a cock.

【公安】gōng'ān 社会整体（包括社会秩序、公共财产、公民权利等）的治安 public security, including social order, public property and civil rights: ～局 police station; public security bureau | ～人员 public security officer

【公案】gōng'àn ❶ 指官吏审理案件时用的桌子 court desk (used by a judge) ❷ 指疑难案件，泛指有纠纷的或离奇的事情 complicated legal case; much discussed issue; sensational affair: 一桩～ a complicated case | ～小说 short piece of fictional writing that involves the committing of a crime and its subsequent legal handling, the actions of a clever judge often being the focus

【公办】gōngbàn 国家创办 state-run; established by the state: ～学校 public school | ～企业 state-owned enterprise

【公报】gōngbào ❶ 公开发表的关于重大会议的决议、国际谈判的进展、国际协议的成立、军事行动的进行等的正式文告 public service announcement (PSA); communiqué; publicly published formal statements on resolutions made at important meetings, progress of international negotiations, conclusion of international agreements, and progress of military actions: 新闻～ press release; communiqué | 联合～ joint communiqué ❷ 由政府编印的刊物，专门登载法律、法令、决议、命令、条约、协定及其他官方文件 gazette; bulletin, compiled and published by government, focusing on laws, regulations, resolutions, orders, treaties, agreements and other official documents

【公报私仇】gōng bào sī chóu 借公事来报个人的仇 avenge personal wrongs in the name of public interest; abuse public power to retaliate against a personal enemy; also 官报私仇 guān bào sī chóu

【公布】gōngbù（政府机关的法律、命令、文告，团体的通知事项）公开发布，使人家知道（of laws, orders and statements of governmental institutions, and notices of organizations) promulgate; announce; make public: ～于众 make public | ～新宪法 promulgate the new constitution | 食堂的账目每月～一次 publish the cafeteria accounts once a month

【公差】gōngchā 机器制造业中，对机械或机器零件的尺寸许可的误差（of machine-building) tolerance for error

【公差】gōngchāi ❶ 临时派遣去做的公务 official errand; public business: 出～ go on a public trip ❷〈旧时 *old*〉在衙门里当差的人 bailiff in a yamen

【公产】gōngchǎn 公共财产 public property: 侵吞～ gobble up public property

【公称】gōngchēng 机器性能、图纸尺寸等的规格或标准 specifications or standards for machine functions, blueprint dimensions, etc.

【公出】gōngchū 因办理公事而外出 be away on official business: 我要～一个月，家里的事就拜托你了。I'll be away on official business for a month, so I need to ask you to take care of family matters.

【公畜】gōngchù 雄性牲畜，畜牧业上通常指留种用的 male animal; stud (kept for breeding)

【公道】gōngdào 公正的道理 justice: 主持～ uphold justice | ～自在人心。Justice is on everybody's mind.

【公道】gōng·dao 公平；合理 fair; just; reasonable; impartial: 说句～话 be fair | 办事～ be impartial in handling matters | 价钱～ reasonable price

【公德】gōngdé 公共道德 public ethics: 讲～ stress on social morality | 社会～ social ethics

【公敌】gōngdí 共同的敌人 public enemy: 人民～ enemy of the people; public enemy

【公爹】gōngdiē 〈方 *dial.*〉 same as 公公 gōng·gong ①

【公断】gōngduàn ❶ 由非当事人居中裁断 arbitrate by sb. unconcerned: 听候众人～ await the verdict of the public ❷ 秉公裁断 consider and decide impartially: 执法部门自会～。The law enforcement department will certainly take everything into consideration and decide impartially.

G

【公法】gōngfǎ ❶ 西方法学中指与国家利益有关的法律，如宪法、行政法等（区别于'私法' as compared with 'private law'）public law; laws concerned with the national interest, according to Western law, such as constitutional and administrative law ❷ 指调整国际关系的准则 norms for adjusting international relations: 国际～ international public law

【公方】gōngfāng 指公私合营企业中国家的一方（跟'私方'相对 as opposed to 'private party'）state in a joint public-private enterprise: ～代表 representatives of state ownership | ～人员 staff representing state ownership

【公房】gōngfáng 属于公家的房屋 public housing

【公费】gōngfèi 由国家或团体供给的费用 funded by the state or the collective: ～医疗 public health services | ～留学 study abroad on a state scholarship

【公愤】gōngfèn 公众的愤怒 public indignation; popular anger: 激起～ arouse public indignation

【公干】gōnggàn ❶ same as 公事 gōngshì: 有何～? What important business brings you here? ❷ 办理公事 deal with official business: 外出～ go out on official business | 来京～ work on a business trip to Beijing

【公告】gōnggào ❶ same as 通告 tōnggào①: 以上通令，～全体公民周知。The above announcement is made public to all citizens. ❷ 政府或机关团体等向公众发出的通告 public announcement made by the government or other institution

【公公】gōng·gong ❶ 丈夫的父亲 husband's father; father-in-law ❷〈方 *dial.*〉祖父 paternal grandfather ❸〈方 *dial.*〉外祖父 maternal grandfather ❹ 尊称年老的男子 [respectful term of address for an elderly man] grandpa: 刘～ Grandpa Liu | 老～ old grandpa ❺ 对太监的称呼（多见于早期白话 oft. used in early venacular）form of address for a court eunuch

【公共】gōnggòng 属于社会的；公有公用的 public; common: ～卫生 public health | ～汽车 public bus | ～场所 public places | 爱护～财产 take good care of public property

【公共关系】gōnggòng guān·xì 指团体、企业或个人在社会活动中的相互关系（of organizations, enterprises or individuals）PR; public relations in social activities; 简称 abbr. 公关 gōngguān

【公共积累】gōnggòng jīlěi same as 公积金 gōngjījīn

【公共汽车】gōnggòng qìchē 供乘客乘坐的汽车。有固定的路线和停车站。bus; public bus having a regular route and fixed stops

【公股】gōnggǔ 公私合营的工商企业中，国家所有的股份 government share in a joint state-private enterprise

【公关】gōngguān 公共关系的简称 abbr. for 公共关系 gōnggòng guān·xì: ～部门 department of public relations | ～小姐（从事公关工作的女职员）Miss Public Relations

【公馆】gōngguǎn 官员、富人的住宅 mansion (of a rich person or important official)

【公国】gōngguó 欧洲封建时代的诸侯国家，以公爵为国家元首 duchy; European kingdoms in feudal times, with dukes as rulers

【公海】gōnghǎi 各国都可使用的不受任何国家权力支配的海域 high seas; sea areas that any country may use and no country may control

【公害】gōnghài ❶ 各种污染源对社会公共环境造成的污染和破坏 environmental hazard ❷〈比喻 *fig.*〉对公众有害的事物 public hazard: 赌博是一大～。Gambling is a major social ill.

【公函】gōnghán 平行及不相隶属的部门间的来往公文（区别于'便函' as compared with 'informal letter'）official letter between parallel or affiliated departments

【公会】gōnghuì 同业公会 trade council; trade association

【公积金】gōngjījīn 生产单位从收益中提取的用做扩大再生产的资金（of a factory）accumulation fund for expansion of production

【公祭】gōngjì ❶ 公共团体或社会人士举行祭

奠，向死者表示哀悼 public memorial：～死难烈士 public memorial service in honour of martyrs ❷ 这种祭礼 public memorial ceremony：～在哀乐声中开始。The public memorial ceremony began with funeral music.

【公家】gōng·jia 指国家、机关、企业、团体（区别于'私人'as compared with 'private'）state; public; organization：不能把～的东西据为己有。You can't take forcible possession of public property.

【公教人员】gōng jiào rényuán 对机关工作人员和学校教员的合称 government employees and teachers

【公举】gōngjǔ 共同推举 elect by referendum：～代表 elect a representative

【公决】gōngjué 共同决定 referendum：全民～referendum|这件事须经大家讨论～。This matter should be decided by everyone through discussion.

【公开】gōngkāi ❶ 不加隐蔽；面对大家（跟'秘密'相对 as opposed to 'secret'）open; public; transparent：～活动 open activity ❷ 使秘密的成为公开的 make public; come out of the closet：这件事暂时不能～。We cannot make this matter public for the time being.

【公开信】gōngkāixìn 写给个人或集体，但作者认为有使公众知道的必要，因而公开发表的信 open letter to an individual or a collective that the author thinks necessary to make public

【公款】gōngkuǎn 属于国家、机关、企业、团体的钱 public money (or fund) owned by the state, an organization, enterprise or group

【公理】gōnglǐ ❶ 经过人类长期反复实践的考验，不需要再加证明的命题，如：如果 $A=B$, $B=C$，则 $A=C$ generally acknowledged truth, e.g., if $A=B$ and $B=C$, $A=C$ must be correct ❷ 社会上多数人公认的正确道理 truth acknowledged by the majority of the public

【公历】gōnglì 阳历的一种，是现在国际通用的历法。一年 365 天，分为十二个月，一、三、五、七、八、十、十二月为大月，每月 31 天，四、六、九、十一月为小月，每月 30 天，二月是 28 天。因地球绕太阳一周实际为 365.24219 天（太阳年），所以每 400 年中有 97 个闰年，闰年在二月末加一天，全年是 366 天。闰年的计算法是：公元年数能够用 4 整除的是闰年（如 1960 年），能够用 100 整除的是平年（如 1900 年），能够用 100 整除也能用 400 整除的是闰年（如 2000 年）。纪元是从传说的耶稣生年算起。Gregorian calendar; internationally used solar calendar, with 365 days and 12 months a year, with January, March, May, July, August, October and December as solar months of 31 days, April, June, September and November as solar months of 30 days, and February with 28 days. A sun year, i.e., the time it takes for the earth to move round the sun once, is 365.24219 days, so there are 97 leap years every 400 years; in a leap year, 1 day is added to February, then that year is 366 days. Leap years occur in years where the last two digits are evenly divisible by 4(e.g. 1960) or where the whole number evenly divisible by 100 and 400 (e.g. 2000). Non-leap years occur in years evenly divisible by 100 (e.g. 1900). The years began from what is said to be the birth year of Christ. also 格里历 gélǐlì；通称 commonly called 阳历 yánglì

【公立】gōnglì 政府设立 established and maintained by the government; public：～学校 public school

【公例】gōnglì 一般的规律 general rule

【公粮】gōngliáng 农业生产者或农业生产单位每年缴纳给国家的作为农业税的粮食 agricultural tax paid in grain

【公了】gōngliǎo 双方发生纠纷，通过上级或主管部门调解或判决了结（跟'私了'相对 as opposed to 'settle in private'）dispute arbitrated or judged by a higher level or the department in charge

【公路】gōnglù 市区以外的可以通行各种车辆的宽阔平坦的道路 highway, road outside of the downtown area

【公论】gōnglùn 公众的评论 public opinion; verdict of the masses：尊重～respect public opinion|是非自有～。Public opinion will decide what is right and what is wrong.

【公民】gōngmín 具有或取得某国国籍，并根据该国法律规定享有权利和承担义务的人 citizen; sb. having a certain state's nationality and enjoying rights and accepting responsibilities according to the state's laws

【公民权】gōngmínquán 公民根据宪法规定所享受的权利 citizenship; civil rights stipulated by the constitution

【公母俩】gōng·muliǎ 〈方 *dial.*〉夫妻二人 husband and wife：老～的感情可真好。The old couple have a great relationship.

【公墓】gōngmù 公共坟地（区别于一姓一家的坟地 as compared with 'private or family cemetery'）public cemetery

【公派】gōngpài 由国家派遣 state dispatched：～留学 sent by the state to study overseas

【公判】gōngpàn ❶ 公开宣判，就是法院在群众大会上向当事人和公众宣布案件的判决 pronounce a judgement in public ❷ 公众评判 verdict of the public

【公平】gōng·píng 处理事情合情合理，不偏袒哪一方面 fair; just; impartial; equitable：～合理 fair and reasonable|～交易 fair deal|裁判～judge fairly

【公平秤】gōngpíngchèng 商业单位设置的供顾客检验所购商品分量是否准确的标准秤 fair scale; standard scale for commercial units in order to let consumers check the weight of what they've bought

【公婆】gōngpó ❶ 丈夫的父亲和母亲;公公和婆婆 husband's father and mother; parents-in-law ❷〈方 *dial.*〉指夫妻,夫妻两人叫两公婆 husband and wife; couple

【公仆】gōngpú 为公众服务的人 public servant: 社会～ servant of society | 人民～ servant of the people

【公然】gōngrán 公开地;毫无顾忌地 openly; undisguisedly; brazenly: ～作弊 openly practise fraud | ～撕毁协议 brazenly tear up an agreement

【公认】gōngrèn 大家一致认为 generally acknowledge (or recognize); universally accept: 他的刻苦精神是大家～的。His hard-working spirit is generally acknowledged.

【公设】gōngshè 不需要证明就可以认为是真的假设,例如,由一点到另一点可以引一条直线 postulation that can be assumed true without proof, e.g. a straight line can be drawn from any one point to another

【公社】gōngshè ❶ 原始社会中,人们共同生产、共同消费的一种结合形式,如氏族公社等。在阶级社会中也保持了很长一个时期。commune; primitive commune — a system in which people work and consume together, such as a clan commune, and which has been in existence for a long time. ❷ 欧洲历史上的城市自治机关,如法国、意大利等国早期的公社。它是资产阶级政权的初级形式。commune, organ of self-administration in European history, such as the primitive communes in France and Italy, which is the early form of power of the bourgeoisie ❸ 无产阶级政权的一种形式,如法国 1871 年的巴黎公社,我国 1927 年的广州公社 commune, a form of power of the proletariat, e.g. the Paris Commune of 1871, and the Guangzhou Commune in 1927 ❹ 特指人民公社 referring to a people's commune

【公审】gōngshěn 我国人民法院公开审判案件的一种方式,在群众参加下审判有重大社会意义的案件 public (or open) trial by the People's Court in China, usu. for important cases of major social significance

【公使】gōngshǐ 由一国派驻在另一国的次于大使一级的外交代表,全称是特命全权公使 envoy, envoy extraordinary; minister plenipotentiary

【公式】gōngshì ❶用数学符号或文字表示各个数量之间的关系的式子,具有普遍性,适合于同类关系的所有问题。如圆面积公式是 $S=\pi R^2$,长方形面积公式是面积 = 长 × 宽。formula; set form of words for stating or declaring sth. definitively or authoritatively, for indicating procedure to be followed by things of the same kind. For example, the formula for a circle's area is $S=\pi R^2$ and a rectangle's area is length × width. ❷ 泛指可以应用于同类事物的方式、方法(in a broad sense) any fixed or conventional method for doing sth.

【公式化】gōngshìhuà ❶ 指文艺创作中套用某种固定格式来描写现实生活和人物性格的不良倾向 formulism; undesirable trend in art and literature to portray real life and characters according to stereotypes ❷ 指不针对具体情况而死板地根据某种固定方式处理问题 formulistic; stereotyped

【公事】gōngshì ❶ 公家的事;集体的事(区别于'私事'as compared with 'private affairs') public affairs; official business: ～公办 business is business | 先办～,后办私事。Public affairs should come before private ones. ❷〈方 *dial.*〉指公文 official document: 每天上午看～ read official documents every morning

【公输】Gōngshū 姓 a surname

【公司】gōngsī 一种工商业组织,经营产品的生产、商品的流转或某些建设事业等 company; corporation; industrial and commercial organization dealing with manufacturing, distribution of goods or construction work

【公私】gōngsī 公家和私人 public and private: ～兼顾 give concurrent consideration to public and private interests | ～合营 joint state-private ownership

【公私合营】gōngsī héyíng 我国对民族资本主义工商业实行社会主义改造的一种形式,分为个别企业公私合营和全行业公私合营两个阶段 joint state-private ownership (the principal form of state capitalism adopted during the socialist transformation in China, in two phases: individual joint state-private ownership, and corporate joint state-private ownership)

【公诉】gōngsù 刑事诉讼的一种方式,由检察机关代表国家对认为确有犯罪行为、应负刑事责任的人向法院提起的诉讼(区别于'自诉'as compared with 'private prosecution') public prosecution; procuratorial organs lodge legal proceedings against an offender

【公诉人】gōngsùrén 代表国家向法院提起公诉的人 public prosecutor, representing the state

【公孙】Gōngsūn 姓 a surname

【公所】gōngsuǒ ❶〈旧时 *old*〉区、乡、村政府办公的地方 office of the government at district, township and village levels: 区～district office | 乡～township office | 村～village office ❷〈旧时 *old*〉同业或同乡组织办公的地方 office of a trade association or association of fellow provincials: 布业～textile industrial society

【公堂】gōngtáng ❶ 指官吏审理案件的地方 law court: 私设～set up a kangaroo court | 对簿～ confront sb. before a court of law ❷ 指祠堂 ancestral hall (or temple)

【公帑】gōngtǎng〈书 *fml.*〉same as 公款

gōngkuǎn：靡费～ squander public funds

【公推】gōngtuī 共同推举(某人担任某种职务或做某事) recommend sb. for a post or task by consensus：大家～他当代表。He was recommended as the representative by consensus.

【公文】gōngwén 机关相互往来联系事务的文件 official document：～袋 official envelope｜～要求简明扼要。Official documents should be concise and to the point.

【公务】gōngwù 关于国家或集体的事务 public affairs; official business：办理～handle official business｜～人员 government functionary｜～繁忙 busy with official business

【公务员】gōngwùyuán ❶ 政府机关的工作人员 government office worker ❷〈旧时 *old*〉称机关、团体中做勤杂工作的人员 personnel regularly performing certain odd jobs in institutions and organizations

【公物】gōngwù 属于公家的东西 public property：爱护～ take good care of public property

【公心】gōngxīn ❶ 公正之心 fairness：秉持～ uphold justice｜处以～handle sth. with fairness ❷ 为公众利益着想的心意 public spirit：他这样做是出于～。He did this out of public spirit.

【公休】gōngxiū 星期日、节日等集体的休假 public holiday; Sunday and other festivals; official holiday：～日 general holiday

【公演】gōngyǎn 公开演出 perform in public; give a performance：这出新戏将于近期～。This new drama will be staged soon.

【公议】gōngyì 大家在一起评议 have a public or mass discussion

【公益】gōngyì 公共的利益(多指卫生、救济等群众福利事业 usu. regarding health and relief work) public good; public welfare：热心～be public-spirited

【公益金】gōngyìjīn 企业单位、生产单位用来兴办本单位的文化事业和公共福利事业的资金 public welfare fund (of an enterprise, factory, etc.)

【公营】gōngyíng 由国家或地方经营 publicly owned; publicly operated; public：～企业 public-owned enterprise

【公映】gōngyìng (影片)公开放映 (of a movie) publicly show：这部影片即将～。The movie will soon be shown.

【公用】gōngyòng 公共使用；共同使用 for public use; public; common：～电话 public telephone｜～事业 public utilities｜两家～一个厨房。The two families shared a kitchen.

【公用事业】gōngyòng shìyè 城市和乡镇中供居民使用的电报、电话、电灯、自来水、公共交通等企业的统称 public services for urban residents; general term for enterprises concerned with telecommunications, electricity, water supply and public transportation

【公有】gōngyǒu 集体或全民所有 publicly owned; public：～制 public ownership of means of production｜～财产 public property

【公有制】gōngyǒuzhì 生产资料归公共所有的制度。现在我国存在着两种公有制，即社会主义的全民所有制和社会主义的集体所有制。public ownership of the means of production. There are two such systems in China: socialist ownership by all the people and socialist ownership by the collective.

【公余】gōngyú 办公时间以外的时间 leisure hours (after work)：～以写字、画画儿作为消遣 relax by writing and drawing after work

【公寓】gōngyù ❶〈旧时 *old*〉租期较长、房租论月计算的旅馆，住宿的人多半是谋事或求学的 lodging houses for long-term boarders paying by the month, mainly for working people or students ❷ 能容许多人家居住的房屋，多为楼房，房间成套，设备较好 apartment building; complex housing shared by many families, usually with suites of rooms and well-equipped

【公元】gōngyuán 国际通用的公历的纪元，是大多数国家纪年的标准，从传说的耶稣诞生那年算起。我国从 1949 年正式规定采用公元纪年。Christian era, the internationally recognized periodization of eras, with years numbering from what is said to be the birth year of Christ. China formally adopted it in 1949.

【公园】gōngyuán 供公众游览休息的园林 (public) park; place for the public to visit and take a rest

【公约】gōngyuē ❶ 条约的一种名称。一般指三个或三个以上的国家缔结的某些政治性的或关于某一专门问题的条约。convention; generally ralified by three or more countries concerning politics or special issues ❷ 机关、团体或街道居民内部拟订的共同遵守的章程 joint pledge made by institutions, organizations or residents：爱国～ patriotic pledge｜卫生～ public health pledge

【公允】gōngyǔn 公平恰当 just and sound; fair and equitable：持论～ be just and fair in argument

【公债】gōngzhài 国家向公民或外国借的债 public or government bonds; debts that a country owes to its citizens or foreign countries

【公债券】gōngzhàiquàn 公债债权人取本息的证券 public or government; securities with which creditors, can reclaim their capital and interest bond(s)

【公章】gōngzhāng 机关、团体使用的印章 official seal

【公正】gōngzhèng 公平正直，没有偏私 just; fair; impartial; fair-minded：为人～ fair-minded｜～的评价 fair evaluation

【公证】gōngzhèng 法院或被授以权力的机关对于民事上权利义务关系所做的证明，如对合同、遗嘱等都可进行公证 notarise; certify a contract, will, etc.; cause to be certified through a court or a notary public

【公职】gōngzhí 指国家机关或公共企业、事业单位中的正式职务 public office; public employment: 担任～hold public office | 开除～discharge sb. from public service | ～人员 civil servant

【公制】gōngzhì 国际公制的简称 abbr. for 国际公制 guójì gōngzhì

【公众】gōngzhòng 社会上大多数的人;大众 public: ～领袖 leader of the public | ～利益 public interest

【公诸同好】gōng zhū tóng hào 把自己喜爱的东西给有同样爱好的人共同享受 let others with the same taste share things one loves

【公主】gōngzhǔ 君主的女儿 princess

【公助】gōngzhù ❶ 共同资助 finance jointly: 社会～financial support from society ❷ 国家资助 subsidized by the state: 这是一座民办～的学校。This is a school run by the local people and subsidized by the state.

【公转】gōngzhuàn 一个天体绕着另一个天体转动叫做公转。如太阳系的行星绕着太阳转动,行星的卫星绕着行星转动。地球绕太阳公转一周的时间是 365 天 6 小时 9 分 10 秒;月球绕地球公转一周的时间是 27 天 7 小时 43 分 11.5 秒。orbit; revolution — the circling of one heavenly body around another, e.g. in a solar system, planets revolve around the sun, and satellites revolve around the planets. The earth's period of each revolution around the sun is 365 days, 6 hours, 9 minutes and 10 seconds; the moon's period of revolution around the earth is 27 days, 7 hours, 43 minutes and 11.5 seconds.

【公子】gōngzǐ 〈古代 *arch.*〉称诸侯的儿子,后称官僚的儿子,也用来尊称人的儿子 son of a duke in ancient times; son of a high official; also a respectful term for sb. else's son

【公子哥儿】gōngzǐgēr 原称官僚和有钱人家不知人情世故的子弟,后泛指娇生惯养的年轻男子 dandy; pampered, unsophisticated son of a wealthy or influential family; spoiled young men in general

【公子王孙】gōngzǐ wángsūn 〈旧时 *old*〉泛指贵族、官僚的子弟(in a broad sense) sons of princes and nobles; sons of the aristocracy and the rich

功 gōng ❶ 功劳(跟'过'相对 as opposed to 'demerit') meritorious service (or deed); merit; achievement: 立～render meritorious service | 记一大～ cite sb. for outstanding service ❷ 成效和表现成效的事情(多指较大的) result; effect; success: 教育之～the fruits of education | ～亏一篑 fall short of success for lack of a final effort | 大～告成 be crowned with success; ring the bell | 好大喜～ have a fondness for the grandiose ❸ (～儿 gōngr) 技术和技术修养 skill: 唱～singing skill | ～架 movements and postures of actors (in traditional opera) | 基本～basic skill ❹ 一个力使物体沿力的方向通过一段距离,这个力就对物体做了功 work, as accomplished by a force that acts on an object and causes it to move through a distance in the direction of the motion of the force

【功败垂成】gōng bài chuí chéng 快要成功的时候遭到失败(含惋惜意 in a regrettably tone) fail on the verge of success; suffer defeat when victory is within reach

【功臣】gōngchén 有功劳的臣子,泛指对某项事业有显著功劳的人(in a broad sense) person who has rendered outstanding service: 航天事业的～ meritorious staff in the aerospace industry

【功成不居】gōng chéng bù jū 立了功而不把功劳归于自己(语出《老子》二章:'功成而不居') claim no credit for one's service (*Laozi* · *Chapter 2*: 'He accomplishes without claiming merit.')

【功成名就】gōng chéng míng jiù 功业建立了,名声也有了 achieve success and win recognition; also 功成名立 gōng chéng míng lì or 功成名遂 gōng chéng míngsuì

【功德】gōngdé ❶ 功劳和恩德 merits and virtues: 歌颂人民英雄的～extol the merits and virtues of the people's heroes ❷ 指佛教徒行善、诵经念佛、为死者做佛事及道士打醮等(of a Buddhist) charitable and pious deeds, including alms-giving, chanting sutras and praying to the Buddha, holding a Buddhist service for the dead; (of a Taoist) saying mass for departed souls: 做～ hold a Buddhist service

【功底】gōngdǐ 基本功的底子 grounding in basic skills: ～扎实 have a good grounding in basic skills | 他的书法有着深厚的～。He has a good grounding in the basic skills of calligraphy.

【功夫】gōng·fu ❶ 本领;造诣 skill; attainment: 他的诗～很深。He is a poet of great talent. | 这个杂技演员真有～。This acrobat has unmatched skills. ❷ same as 工夫 gōngfū

【功夫茶】gōng·fuchá 福建广东一带的一种饮茶风尚,茶具小巧精致,沏茶、饮茶有一定的程序、礼仪 *gongfu tea*; tea-drinking custom in Fujian and Guangdong provinces, characterized by a small and exquisite tea set, and certain procedures and etiquette in the making and drinking of tea

【功夫片儿】gōng·fupiānr same as 功夫片 gōng·fupiàn

【功夫片】gōng·fupiàn 表现以武打为主的故事片 gongfu (kung fu) movie

【功绩】gōngjì 功劳和业绩 merits and achievements: ～卓著 outstanding merit and achievement | 不可磨灭的～ everlasting merit

【功架】gōngjià same as 工架 gōngjià
【功课】gōngkè ❶ 学生按照规定学习的知识、技能 schoolwork:他在学校里每门～都很好。He does well in every subject at school. ❷ 指教师给学生布置的作业 homework:做完～再看电视。You can watch TV after finishing your homework. ❸ 佛教徒按时诵经念佛等称为做功课(in Buddhism) routine rituals such as chanting sutras and praying to the Buddha
【功亏一篑】gōng kuī yī kuì 伪古文《尚书·旅獒》:'为山九仞,功亏一篑。'堆九仞高的土山,只差一筐土而不能完成。(from the pseudo-historical writing *Classics of Documents·Dog from Lu*) fail to build a mound for want of one final basket of earth;〈比喻 *fig.*〉一件大事只差最后一点儿人力物力而不能成功(含惋惜意 in a regrettable tone) come out in a funk; fall short of success for lack of a final effort
【功劳】gōng·láo 对事业的贡献 contribution:汗马～toil and hardship in the war; do one's bit for a cause or undertaking
【功力】gōnglì ❶ same as 功效 gōngxiào:草药的～不能忽视。The efficacy of herbal medicine should not be ignored. ❷ 功夫和力量 skill and force:他的字苍劲洒脱,颇见～。His writing is vigorous and untrammelled, showing considerable skill.
【功利】gōnglì ❶ 功效和利益 utility; material gain:～显著 distinguished material gain ❷ 功名利禄 rank, fame and riches:追求～seek fame and fortune
【功利主义】gōnglì zhǔyì 主张以实际功效或利益为行为准则的伦理观点 utilitarianism, the ethical doctrine that regards actual results or gains as the norms of conduct
【功令】gōnglìng〈旧时 *old*〉指法令 regulations and laws
【功率】gōnglǜ 功跟完成这些功所用时间的比,即单位时间内所做的功。电能的功率单位有瓦特、千瓦等。机械能的功率单位有千克米/秒、马力等。power; rate of work in unit time; power units of electrical energy including watt and kilowatt, and power units of mechanical energy including kilogmetre/second and horsepower.
【功名】gōngmíng 封建时代指科举称号或官职名位 scholarly honour or official rank (in feudal times):革除～strip sb. of his official rank
【功能】gōngnéng 事物或方法所发挥的有利的作用;效能 function:～齐全 complete in functions|这种药物～显著。This medicine is most effective.
【功效】gōngxiào 功能;效率 efficacy; effect:立见～ immediate effect
【功勋】gōngxūn 指对国家、人民做出的重大贡献,立下的特殊的功劳 meritorious service for the nation and the people:～卓著 distinct exploits|立下不朽～ perform immortal feats
【功业】gōngyè 功勋事业 exploits; achievements:建立～ establish achievements
【功用】gōngyòng 功能;用途 function; use

红 gōng ☞ 女红 nǚgōng on p.1428
☞ hóng on p.802

攻 gōng ❶ 攻打;进攻(跟'守'相对 as opposed to 'defend') attack; take the offensive:围～besiege|～城 attack a city|能～能守 able to charge or hold ground|～下敌人的桥头堡 take the enemy's bridgehead ❷ 对别人的过失、错误进行指责或对别人的议论进行驳斥 accuse:群起而～之 rise together and attack|～其一点,不及其余 attack sb. for a single fault without considering his other qualities ❸ 致力研究;学习 study; major in:他是专～地质学的。He specializes in geology.
【攻城略地】gōng chéng lüèdì 攻占城池,夺取土地 attack cities and seize territories
【攻错】gōngcuò〈书 *fml.*〉《诗经·小雅·鹤鸣》:'他山之石,可以为错。'又:'他山之石,可以攻玉。'(from *The Book of Songs·Odes·Honking Cranes*) 'Stones from other hills may serve to polish the jade of this one'; 后来用'攻错'比喻拿别人的长处补救自己的短处 other people's advice is of help(错 *cuo*:磨刀石 whetstone; grindstone;攻 *gong*:治 polish)
【攻打】gōngdǎ 为占领敌方阵地或据点而进攻 attack to take the enemy's position or stronghold
【攻读】gōngdú 努力读书或钻研某一门学问 pursue; diligently study:～博士学位 pursue a doctorate|～中医经典 study classics of traditional Chinese medical science
【攻关】gōngguān 攻打关口 surmount a fortification;〈比喻 *fig.*〉努力突破科学、技术等方面的难点 tackle key scientific and technical problems:刻苦钻研,立志～study diligently and strive to solve knotty problems|对于重点科研项目,要组织有关人员协作～。For key scientific research projects, we should organize those concerned to work together and solve knotty problems.
【攻击】gōngjī ❶ 进攻 attack; assault:发动～launch an offensive|～敌人阵地 attack the enemy's position ❷ 恶意指摘 accuse; vilify:进行人身～ carry out a personal attack
【攻歼】gōngjiān 攻击并歼灭 wipe out:～被围之敌 wipe out a beseiged enemy
【攻坚】gōngjiān ❶ 攻打敌人的坚固防御工事 assault fortified positions:～战 battle in which fortified positions are stormed ❷〈比喻 *fig.*〉努力解决某项任务中最困难的问题 try to tackle the most difficult part of a task
【攻坚战】gōngjiānzhàn 攻击敌人坚固阵地的战斗 storming of heavily fortified positions
【攻讦】gōngjié〈书 *fml.*〉揭发别人的过失或阴私而加以攻击(多指因个人或派系利害矛盾

usu. conflict between individuals or factions) rake up sb.'s past and attack him; take a swipe at

【攻克】gōngkè 攻下(敌人的据点) capture (an enemy's position)

【攻破】gōngpò 打破;攻下 make a breakthrough; take:~防线 break through defence lines

【攻其不备】gōng qí bù bèi 趁敌人没有防备的时候进攻 strike where or when the enemy is unprepared; take sb. by surprise; catch sb. unawares

【攻取】gōngqǔ 攻打并夺取 storm and capture:~据点 capture a stronghold

【攻势】gōngshì 向敌方进攻的行动或形势 offensive:冬季~ winter offensive|采取~take the offensive ◇这次足球比赛,客队的~非常猛烈。In the football match, the visiting team maintained a powerful offense.

【攻守同盟】gōng shǒu tóngméng ❶ 两个或两个以上的国家为了在战争时对其他国家采取联合进攻或防御而结成的同盟 offensive and defensive alliance between two or more countries in war to coordinate offence or defence operations ❷ 指共同作案的人为了应付追查或审讯而事先约定共同隐瞒、互不揭发的行为 agreement between partners in crime not to give each other away

G

【攻陷】gōngxiàn 攻克;攻占 occupy; capture

【攻心】gōngxīn ❶ 从精神上或心理上瓦解对方 mentally attack; make a psychological attack:~战术 psychological warfare ❷ 俗称因悲痛、愤怒而神志昏迷为'怒气攻心',因浑身溃烂或烧伤而发生生命危险为'毒气攻心'或'火气攻心' be in a coma or remain in a stupor (because of sorrow or hatred); be in danger of dying (from severe burns or gangrene)

【攻占】gōngzhàn 攻击并占领(敌方的据点)attack and occupy (an enemy position)

供 gōng ❶ 供给;供应 supply; feed:~不应求 supply falls short of demand ❷ 提供某种利用的条件(给对方利用) provide sb. with sth. (for the use or convenience of sb.):~读者参考 for readers' reference|~旅客休息 passenger lounge

☞ gòng on p. 679

【供不应求】gōng bù yìng qiú 供应的东西不能满足需求 supply falls short of demand; in short supply

【供稿】gōnggǎo 提供稿件 contribute a piece of writng:本版诗文、照片均由运动会宣传组~。The poems and text and photographs on this page have been provided by the public relations department of the games.

【供给】gōngjǐ 把生活中必需的物资、钱财、资料等给需要的人使用 supply or provide necessary goods and materials, money and means, etc. for people in need:学习用品由训练班免费~。Stationery is freely provided by the training class.

【供给制】gōngjǐzhì 按大致相同的标准直接供给生活资料的分配制度 supply system—a system of payment in kind, providing working personnel and their dependants with the primary necessities of life

【供求】gōngqiú 供给和需求(多指商品 usu. of goods) supply and demand:~关系 the relation between supply and demand|调剂物资,使~平衡 redistribute goods and materials to strike a balance between supply and demand

【供求率】gōngqiúlǜ 社会总商品量与社会有支付能力的需求量之间的比率。它是商品的生产和消费之间的关系在市场上的反映。ratio between total commodity supply and demand which has the ability to pay; a reflection of the relation between commodity production and consumption in the market

【供销】gōngxiāo 供应生产资料和消费品,以及销售各种产品的商业性活动 supply and marketing:~合同 supply and marketing contract|~部门 supply and marketing department

【供销合作社】gōngxiāo hézuòshè 为满足农村生产和生活需要而设立的销售生产工具、生活用品和收购农产品、副业产品的商业机构 rural supply and marketing co-operative that meets the needs of production and daily use by selling production tools and goods for daily use, and purchasing farm produce and sideline products; 简称 abbr. 供销社 gōngxiāoshè

【供需】gōngxū same as 供求 gōngqiú:避免~脱节 avoid discrepancy between supply and demand

【供养】gōngyǎng 供给长辈或年长的人生活所需;赡养 take care of; provide for (one's parents or elders); support:~老人 support elders

☞ gòngyǎng on p. 679

【供应】gōngyìng 以物资满足需要(有时也指以人力满足需要) supply goods and materials (sometimes human resources) to meet the demand:~站 supply station|计划~planned supply|农业用粮食和原料~工业。Agriculture supplies industry with grain and raw materials.|发展生产才能够保证~。Only through developing production can supply be guaranteed.

【供应舰】gōngyìngjiàn 专门担负海上补给、修理任务的军舰 cockboat, responsible for supplying and repairing; refuelling barge; also 补给舰 bǔjǐjiàn

肱 gōng 〈书 *fml*.〉胳膊上从肩到肘的部分,也泛指胳膊 upper arm; arm:股~right-hand man|曲~而枕 sleep with one's head resting on one's bent arm

【肱骨】gōnggǔ 上臂中的长骨,上端跟肩部相连,下端跟尺骨和桡骨相连 humerus; long bone of the upper arm whose upper end connects with the shoulder and whose lower end connects with the ulna and the radius;(图见 ☞ figure for 骨骼 gǔgé on p. 693)

宫[1] gōng ❶ 帝后太子等居住的房屋 imperial palace:～殿 palace | 行～ imperial palace for short stays away from the capital | 故～ Former Imperial Palace; Forbidden City | 东～ Eastern Palace ❷ 神话中神仙居住的房屋 house in which supernatural beings live:天～ heavenly palace | 龙～ Dragon King's palace | 月～ moon palace; the moon | 蟾～ the moon ❸ 庙宇的名称 temple (used in names):碧霞～ Bixia Temple | 雍和～ Lamasary of Peace and Harmony (in Beijing); Yonghe Palace ❹ 人民文化活动或娱乐用的房屋的名称 place for cultural activities and recreation:少年～ children's palace | 民族～ palace for ethnic peoples | 劳动人民文化～ Workers' Cultural Palace ❺ 指子宫 uterus:～颈 cervix of uterus | 刮～ dilatation and curettage | ～外孕 ectopic pregnancy ❻ (Gōng)姓 a surname

宫[2] gōng 〈古 *arch.*〉五音之一,相当于简谱的 '1' note of the ancient Chinese five-tone scale, corresponding to 1 in numbered musical notation; ☞ 五音 wǔyīn on p. 2032

【宫灯】gōngdēng 八角或六角形的灯,每面糊绢或镶玻璃,并画有彩色图画,下面悬挂流苏。原为宫廷使用,因此得名。octagonal or hexagonal palace lantern, with each side pasted with thin, tough silk or glazed glass, painted with colourful pictures, and tassels swinging underneath; palace lantern, which has its origin in the imperial palace

【宫殿】gōngdiàn 泛指帝王居住的高大华丽的房屋 (in a broad sense) imperial palace

【宫调】gōngdiào 中国古乐曲的调式。唐代规定二十八调,即琵琶的四根弦上每根七调。最低的一根弦(宫弦)上的调式叫宫,其余的叫调。后来宫调的数目逐渐减少。元代杂剧,一般只用五个宫(正宫,中吕宫,南吕宫,仙吕宫,黄钟宫)和四个别的弦上的调(大石调,双调,商调,越调)。这是后世所谓九宫。form of ancient Chinese music of the 28 notes of the Tang Dynasty. That is to say, each string of the *pipa* has 7 notes, the note of the lowest string being called *gong*, and the others *diao*; the number of notes were reduced later in Yuan-dynasty operas to 5 *gongs* (*zhenggong*, *zhonglügong*, *nanlugong*, *xianlügong* and *huangzhonggong*) and 4 *diaos* (*dashidiao*, *shuangdiao*, *shangdiao* and *yuediao*). Hence the term, 'nine *gongs*'.

【宫娥】gōng'é same as 宫女 gōngnǚ

【宫禁】gōngjìn ❶ 帝王居住的地方 emperor's living quarters; palace precincts:～重地 important palace precincts ❷ 宫闱的禁令 palace taboos; palace prohibitions

【宫颈】gōngjǐng 子宫颈的简称 abbr. for 子宫颈 zǐgōngjǐng:～癌 carcinoma of cervix and uterus | ～糜烂 cervical erosion

【宫女】gōngnǚ 被征选在宫廷里服役的女子 maid conscripted to provide labour and service in an imperial palace

【宫阙】gōngquè 指宫殿 imperial palace

【宫室】gōngshì 〈古 *arch.*〉房屋的通称,后来特指帝王的宫殿 houses in general in ancient times; later indicating imperial palaces

【宫廷】gōngtíng ❶ 帝王的住所 imperial palace ❷ 由帝王及其大臣构成的统治集团 ruling clique composed of an emperor and his ministers; royal court

【宫廷政变】gōngtíng zhèngbiàn 原指帝王宫廷内发生篡夺王位的事件。现在一般用来指某个国家统治集团少数人从内部采取行动夺取国家政权。palace coup to usurp the throne; now indicating an attempt by a minority in the ruling group to seize state power

【宫闱】gōngwéi 〈书 *fml.*〉 same as 宫廷 gōngtíng ①

【宫刑】gōngxíng 〈古代 *arch.*〉阉割生殖器的残酷肉刑 castration (a punishment in ancient China)

【宫掖】gōngyè 〈书 *fml.*〉宫室;宫廷 palace

恭 gōng 恭敬 respectful:～候 await respectfully | ～贺 congratulate | 洗耳～听 cock one's ears to listen; be all ears

【恭贺】gōnghè 恭敬地祝贺 congratulate:～新禧 Happy New Year

【恭候】gōnghòu 〈敬辞 *pol.*〉等候 await respectfully:～光临。We request the pleasure of your company. | 我们已经～很久了。We have awaited you respectfully for a long time.

【恭谨】gōngjǐn 恭敬谨慎 respectful and cautious:态度～ respectful and cautious in manner

【恭敬】gōngjìng 对尊长或宾客严肃有礼貌 respect for elders or guests

【恭请】gōngqǐng 恭敬地邀请 invite respectfully

【恭顺】gōngshùn 恭敬顺从 respectful and submissive:态度～ respectful and submissive attitude

【恭桶】gōngtǒng 马桶 closestool; nightstool

【恭惟】gōng·wei same as 恭维 gōng·wei

【恭维】gōng·wei 为讨好而赞扬 flatter; compliment:～话 flattery | 曲意～ do everything to flatter sb.; also 恭惟 gōng·wei

【恭喜】gōngxǐ 〈客套话 *pol.*〉祝贺人家的喜事 congratulate:～发财 Congratulations and may you prosper! | ～! ～! ～你们试验成功。Congratulations! Congratulations! I congratulate you on the success of your experiment.

【恭迎】gōngyíng 恭敬地迎接 welcome respectfully

蚣 gōng ☞ 蜈蚣 wú·gōng on p. 2028

躬(躳) gōng ❶ 自身;亲自 personally:反～自问 ask oneself | ～行实践 practise what one preaches | ～逢其盛(亲自参加了盛典或亲身经历了盛世) be present in person on a grand occasion ❷ 弯下(身子) bend forward; bow:～身下拜 bend at the waist

【躬亲】gōngqīn 〈书 *fml*.〉亲自去做 attend to personally:事必～take care of every single thing personally

【躬行】gōng xíng 〈书 *fml*.〉亲身实行 attend to personally:～节俭 personally practise thrift

鸮 gōng 鸟,大小如鸡,羽毛黑褐色,有横纹,嘴尖而长。善走而不善飞,吃昆虫、蜘蛛等,也吃植物的根和种子。产于美洲。tinamou (*Rhynchotus refescens*); bird in the America, the size of a chicken, with black and brown bands of feathers, a long and pointed beak, good at walking but not flying, feeding on insects and spiders as well as roots and seeds of plants

龚(龔) Gōng 姓 a surname

塨 gōng 用于人名,李塨,清初学者 used in person names; Li Gong, a scholar in the early Qing Dynasty

觥 gōng 古代用兽角做的酒器 *gong*; ancient bronze wine vessel in the shape of an animal horn:～筹交错 toast each other

G

【觥筹交错】gōng chóu jiāocuò 形容许多人相聚饮酒的热闹场面 wining and dining with abandon wine cups made of horn and chopsticks lie about, describing a dinner party at which wine flows freely

【觥觥】gōnggōng 〈书 *fml*.〉形容刚直或健壮的样子 upright and outspoken

gǒng (ㄍㄨㄥˇ)

巩(鞏) gǒng ❶ 巩固 consolidate ❷ (Gǒng)姓 a surname

【巩固】gǒnggù ❶ 坚固;不易动摇(多用于抽象的事物 usu. of abstract things) consolidated; rock-firm; stable:基础～solid foundation | 政权～rock-firm political power ❷ 使坚固 consolidate; strengthen:～国防 strengthen national defence | ～工农联盟 strengthen the worker-peasant alliance

【巩膜】gǒngmó 眼球最外层的纤维膜,白色,很坚韧,前面与角膜相连,有保护眼球内部组织的作用 sclera; dense, white fibrous membrane that, with the cornea, forms the external covering of the eyeball; (图见☞ figure for 眼 yǎn on p. 2210)

汞 gǒng 金属元素,符号 Hg (hydrargyrum)。银白色液体,内聚力强,蒸气有剧毒,化学性质不活泼,能溶解许多种金属。用来制药品、温度计、气压计等。通称水银。hydrargyrum (Hg); mercury; heavy, highly toxic silver-white metallic element with inactive chemical properties, capable of dissolving a good variety of metals, used in the making of pharmaceuticals, thermometres, and barometres

拱[1] gǒng ❶ 两手相合,臂的前部上举 cup one hand in the other before the chest (in salutation):～手 pay obeisance by cupping one hand in the other before the chest ❷ 环绕 surround:～卫 surround and protect | 众星～月。Stars twinkle around the bright moon. | 四山环～的大湖 mountain-rimmed large lake ❸ 肢体弯曲成弧形 hunch; arch:～肩缩背 hunch one's shoulders and bow one's back | 黑猫～了～腰。The black cat arched its back. ❹ 建筑物成弧形的 arched:～门 arched door | 连～坝 arched dam

拱[2] gǒng ❶ 用身体撞动别的东西或拨开土地等物体 push with one's body:用身子～开了大门 push the door open with one's body | 猪用嘴～地。Pigs dig up the earth with their snouts. | 蚯蚓从地下～出许多土来。The earthworms wriggled their way out, pushing up a lot of earth. | 一个小孩儿从人群里～出去了。A child elbowed his way out of the crowd. ❷ 植物生长,从土里向外钻或顶 sprout up through the earth:苗儿～出土了。The sprouts are poking up through the earth.

【拱抱】gǒngbào (山峦)环绕;环抱 surround:群峰～ surrounded by cliffs

【拱璧】gǒngbì 〈书 *fml*.〉大璧,泛指珍宝 round flat piece of jade with a hole in its centre; (in a broad sense) treasures:这些藏书对于他来说不啻～。These collections of books are treasures to him.

【拱火】gǒng//huǒ 〈方 *dial*.〉(～儿 gǒng//huǒr)用言行促使人发火或使火气更大 excite sb. to anger through words or action; inflame sb.'s anger:他已经烦得够受的,你就别再～了。Don't provoke him since he is already very angry.

【拱门】gǒngmén 上端是弧形的门,也指门口由弧线相交或由其他对称曲线构成的门 arched door; door consisting of intersecting arched lines or symmetrical curved lines

【拱棚】gǒngpéng 顶部成弧形、上面覆盖塑料薄膜的棚,用于冬季培育花木、蔬菜、秧苗等 greenhouse; arched canopy with a plastic cover, for growing flowers, trees, vegetables and rice roots, etc., in winter

【拱桥】gǒngqiáo 中部高起、桥洞呈弧形的桥 arched bridge:石～ stone arched bridge

【拱让】gǒngràng 拱手相让 give sth. to sb. with both hands:劳动成果怎能～他人? How can you give away the fruits of your labour to other people?

【拱手】gǒng//shǒu 两手在胸前相抱表示恭敬 pay obeisance by cupping one hand in the other before the chest：～相迎 greet sb. by cupping one hand in the other before the chest|～道别 bid farewell to each other with a cupped-hand salute, each asking the other to take good care

【拱卫】gǒngwèi 环绕在周围保卫着 surround and protect：辽东半岛和山东半岛像两个巨人，紧紧环抱着渤海，同时也～着首都北京。Like two giants, the Liaodong Peninsula and the Shandong Peninsula surround the Bohai Sea and protect the capital city Beijing.

【拱券】gǒngxuàn 桥梁、门窗等建筑物上筑成弧形的部分 arch in a bridge, door or window, etc.; also 券 xuàn

珙 gǒng 〈书 *fml.*〉一种玉 a kind of jade

栱 gǒng ☞［枓栱］(dǒugǒng) on p. 472

蛬 gǒng 又 also qióng 古书上指蟋蟀 referring to cricket in ancient books

gòng（ㄍㄨㄥˋ）

共 gòng ❶ 相同的；共同具有的 common; general; identical, the same, alike：～性 common character, general character, generality|～通 generally applicable, applicable to all ❷ 共同具有或承受 share：同甘苦，～患难 share weal and woe, go through thick and thin together ❸ 在一起；一齐 together; in company; at the same time：～鸣 resonance, sympathetic response, sympathy|和平～处 peaceful coexistence ❹ 一共；总计 altogether; in all; amount to：这两个集子～收小说十二篇。There are altogether twelve short stories in these two collections.|全书～十卷。The whole book contains ten volumes. *or* There are ten volumes in the whole book. ❺ 共产党的简称 abbr. for 共产党 gòngchǎndǎng：中～ Communist Party of China

〈古 *arch.*〉same as 恭 gōng; also 供 gōng

【共产党】gòngchǎndǎng 无产阶级的政党。共产党是无产阶级的先锋队，是无产阶级的阶级组织的最高形式。它的指导思想是马克思列宁主义，目的是领导无产阶级和其他一切被压迫的劳动人民，通过革命斗争夺取政权，用无产阶级专政代替资产阶级专政，实现社会主义和共产主义。中国共产党成立于 1921 年 7 月。Communist Party; proletarian political party. The Communist Party is the vanguard of the proletariat and the highest form of the class organization of the proletariat. Its guiding thought is Marxism-Leninism; its aim is to lead the proletariat and all other oppressed working people to seize political power through revolutionary struggle, replace the dictatorship of the bourgeoisie with the dictatorship of the proletariat and achieve socialism and communism. The Communist Party of China was founded on July 1, 1921.

【共产主义】gòngchǎn zhǔyì ❶ 指无产阶级的整个思想体系 whole system of proletarian ideology; ☞ 科学社会主义 kēxué shèhuì zhǔyì on p. 1090 ❷ 人类最理想的社会制度。它在发展上分两个阶段，初级阶段是社会主义，高级阶段是共产主义。通常所说的共产主义，指共产主义的高级阶段。在这个阶段，生产力高度发展，社会产品极大丰富，人们具有高度的思想觉悟，劳动成为生活的第一需要，消灭了三大差别，实行共产主义公有制，分配原则是'各尽所能，按需分配'。communism; the most ideal social system of mankind. It is divided into two stages of development, the primary stage being socialism and the advanced stage being communism. Communism in the general sense refers to the advanced stage, in which the productive force is highly developed, the social products are in great abundance, the people have a high level of political consciousness, work becomes the first need of their life, the three great differences are eliminated, communist public ownership is practised, and the principle of distribution is 'from each according to his ability, to each according to his needs'.

【共产主义青年团】gòngchǎn zhǔyì qīngniántuán 在共产党领导下的先进青年的群众性组织。中国共产主义青年团是党的有力助手，它团结和教育青年一代为共产主义事业而奋斗。Communist Youth League; mass organization of the progressive youth under the leadership of the Communist Party. The Communist Youth League of China is a powerful assistant to the Communist Party; it unites and educates the young generation to fight for the Communist cause. 简称 abbr. 共青团 gòngqīngtuán

【共处】gòngchǔ 相处；共同存在 live together, get along with each other; coexist, exist together：～一室 live in the same room|和平～ peaceful coexistence

【共存】gòngcún 共同存在 coexist, exist together

【共度】gòngdù 共同度过 spend time together; tide over (get over) together：～难关 tide over (overcome, surmount, get over) a difficulty (crisis) together|全国各民族～佳节。The people of different ethnic backgrounds throughout the country celebrate the festival together.

【共犯】gòngfàn ❶ 共同犯罪 joint crime, joint offence ❷ 共同犯罪中的罪犯 joint offenders

【共管】gòngguǎn ❶ 共同管理 joint rule, joint control, joint management：社会治安需要动员全社会的力量齐抓～。The maintenance of the public order calls for the joint efforts of the whole society. ❷ 国际共管的简称 abbr. for 国际共管 guójì gòngguǎn

【共和】gònghé ❶ 历史上称西周从厉王失政到宣王执政之间的十四年为共和。共和元年为公元前 841 年。The intervening fourteen years between the loss of power by King Li and the takeover of the power by King Xuan in the Western Zhou Dynasty is historically called the reign of Gonghe. The first year of the Gonghe reign was 841 B.C. ❷ same as 共和制 gònghézhì

【共和国】gònghéguó 实施共和政体的国家 republic; country in which the republican form of government is adopted

【共和制】gònghézhì 国家元首和国家权力机关定期由选举产生的一种政治制度 republicanism; political system under which the head of state and the organ of state power are elected periodically

【共计】gòngjì ❶ 合起来计算 add up to:～三千万元 total 30 million yuan ❷ 共同计议;共议 discuss together:～大事 discuss an important matter together

【共居】gòngjū 同时存在(多指抽象事物 oft. of sth. abstract) exist simultaneously; exist together; coexist:矛盾的两个方面因一定的条件～于一个统一体中。The two aspects of a contradiction coexist in a single entity.

【共聚】gòngjù 两种或两种以上的单体聚合成高分子化合物。如丁二烯和苯乙烯聚合成丁苯橡胶。copolymerisation; two or more monomers polymerize into a high molecular compound. For example, butadiene and styrene form butadiene styrene rubber by polymerization.

【共勉】gòngmiǎn 共同努力;互相勉励 make joint efforts; encourage each other:提出这一希望,并与你～。I give you this advice as our mutual encouragement.

【共鸣】gòngmíng ❶ 物体因共振而发声的现象,如两个频率相同的音叉靠近,其中一个振动发声时,另一个也会发声 resonance; sound produced in an object by sound or vibrations of a similar frequency from another object. For example, when two tuning forks are brought close to each other, and if one of them is vibrating and emitting a sound, the other produces a sound as well. ❷ 由别人的某种情绪引起的相同的情绪 sympathetic feeling; same feeling aroused by a certain feeling of another person:诗人的爱国主义思想感染了读者,引起了他们的～。The patriotic feelings of the poet affected his readers and aroused their sympathy.

【共栖】gòngqī 两种不同的生物生活在一起,不是相依生存,只对其中一种有利,这种生活方式叫做共栖。如文鸟专在胡蜂窝的附近筑巢,因为胡蜂有毒刺,许多动物不敢接近,文鸟也就得到保护。commensalism; relation between two kinds of organisms in which one obtains food or benefits from the other without damaging or benefiting it. For example, mannikins like to build their nests by wasp honeycombs, because wasps have vicious stings and many animals are afraid of them, thus providing protection to the mannikins.

【共青团】gòngqīngtuán 共产主义青年团的简称 abbr. for 共产主义青年团 gòngchǎn zhǔyì qīngniántuán

【共生】gòngshēng 两种不同的生物生活在一起,相依生存,对彼此都有利,这种生活方式叫做共生。如白蚁肠内的鞭毛虫帮助白蚁消化木材纤维,白蚁给鞭毛虫提供养料,如果分离,二者都不能独立生存。intergrowth; symbiosis; intimate living together of two kinds of organisms, which are interdependent and benefit each other. For example, the flagellate in the intestine of the termite helps to digest wood fibre, while the termite supplies nutriment to the flagellate. Therefore, neither is independent.

【共识】gòngshí 共同的认识 common understanding; consensus; to concur on:经过多次讨论,双方消除了分歧,达成～。The two sides eliminated their differences and reached a common understanding after many discussions.|对国家前途的～使他们成为挚友。The common understanding of the future of the nation brings them together as true friends.

【共事】gòng//shì 在一起工作 work together; be fellow workers:我和他～多年,对他比较了解。I have worked together with him for many years and therefore have a better understanding of him.

【共通】gòngtōng ❶ 通行于或适用于各方面的 applicable to all aspects; generally applicable:～的道理 generally applicable argument ❷ same as 共同 gòngtóng ①:这三篇习作有一个～的毛病。There is a common mistake in the three compositions.

【共同】gòngtóng ❶ 属于大家的;彼此都具有的 belonging to, or shared by all:～点 common ground|～语言 the same opinion|搞好经济建设是全国人民的～心愿。It is the common desire of the people of the whole country to carry out economic construction well. ❷ 大家一起(做) work together:～努力 make joint efforts

【共同市场】gòngtóng shìchǎng 若干国家为了共同的政治、经济利益而组成的相互合作的统一市场 common market; association of countries formed to effect a closer political and economic union, esp. by means of mutual tariff concessions

【共同体】gòngtóngtǐ ❶ 人们在共同条件下结成的集体 community; group of people living together as a social unit and having interests, work, etc. in common ❷ 由若干国家在某一方面组成的集体组织 commonwealth; group of nations associated for the same interests in a certain field

【共同语言】gòngtóng yǔyán 指相同的思想、认识和生活情趣等 common language; same ideas, same understanding and same interests：他俩缺乏～，难以长期在一起生活。As the two of them have no common language, it is difficult for them to live together.

【共性】gòngxìng 指不同事物所共同具有的普遍性质 general character possessed jointly by different things：各种地方戏都有其个性，但作为戏曲又有其～。Each local opera has its own individuality, but it has the general character as an opera.

【共议】gòngyì 共同商议 discuss together：～国是 discuss state affairs together

【共振】gòngzhèn 两个振动频率相同的物体，当一个发生振动时，引起另一个物体振动的现象 resonance; vibration produced in one object by another vibrating object of a similar frequency

【共总】gòngzǒng 一共；总共 altogether; add up to; in all; in the aggregate：这几笔账～多少？How much do all these accounts add up to? *or* How much all these accounts come to?

贡 gòng ❶〈古代 *arch.*〉臣民或属国把物品献给朝廷 paying of tribute to the court by a subject or a vassal state：～奉 to offer as tribute to the court｜～米 rice offered as tribute ❷ 贡品 articles of tribute：进～ pay tribute to ❸ 封建时代称选拔（人才），荐给朝廷 recommend scholars to the imperial court in feudal times：～生 scholars recommended by local governments to the imperial court in feudal times｜～院 place where a provincial or imperial examination was given to scholars in feudal times ❹ (Gòng)姓 a surname

【贡缎】gòngduàn 一种纹路像缎子的棉织品，光滑，有亮光，多用做被面 sateen; glossy and lustrous cotton fabric with satin grains for making quilt cover

【贡奉】gòngfèng 向朝廷或上级贡献物品；进贡 offer articles of tribute to the court or to a leader; pay tribute

【贡品】gòngpǐn〈古代 *arch.*〉臣民或属国献给帝王的物品 articles of tribute offered to an emperor by a subject or vassal state in ancient times

【贡生】gòngshēng 明清两代科举制度中，由府、州、县学推荐到京师国子监学习的人 scholars recommended by local prefecture or county governments to the Imperial College in the capital city under the imperial examination system in the Ming and Qing dynasties

【贡税】gòngshuì〈古代 *arch.*〉臣民向皇室缴纳的金钱、实物等；赋税 tribute and taxes; money or goods paid by subjects to the imperial family in ancient time; also 贡赋 gòngfù

【贡献】gòngxiàn ❶ 拿出物资、力量、经验等献给国家或公众 contribute; dedicate; devote; give goods, or offer one's efforts or experience, to the country or the public：为祖国～自己的一切 contribute all one has to the motherland ❷ 对国家或公众所做的有益的事 valuable thing done to the country or the public：他们为国家做出了新的～。They have made a new contribution to the country.

【贡院】gòngyuàn 科举时代举行乡试或会试的场所 place where a provincial or imperial examination was given under the imperial examination system in ancient times

供[1] gòng ❶ 把香烛等放在神佛或先辈的像（或牌位）前面表示敬奉；祭祀时摆设祭品 present joss sticks and candles before the Buddha, the portrait of an ancestor (or a memorial tablet); lay up offerings at a rite or service：遗像前～着鲜花。Fresh flowers were laid out before the portrait of the deceased. ❷ 陈列的表示虔敬的东西；供品 goods displayed to show reverence; offerings：蜜～ sweetened fried narrow dough strips offered as a sacrifice｜上～ offer a sacrifice; lay offerings on the altar

供[2] gòng ❶ 受审者陈述案情 statement made by the person on trial：～认 confess, confession｜～出作案同伙 give the name of an accomplice ❷ 口供；供词 statement; confession：录～ take down confession｜问不出～来。No confession was obtained.

☞ gōng on p. 674

【供案】gòng'àn 供桌 altar table：雕花～ carved altar table

【供词】gòngcí 受审者所陈述的或所写的与案情有关的话 confession; statement made by sb. on trial during interrogation

【供奉】gòngfèng ❶ 敬奉；供养 present; make offerings to, offer sacrifices to：～神佛 make or present offerings to the God or Buddha｜～父母 provide for one's parents ❷ 以某种技艺侍奉帝王的人 person who waited upon an emperor with a certain skill：老～ old attendant｜内廷～ inner court attendant

【供品】gòngpǐn 供奉神佛祖宗用的瓜果酒食等 offerings; melons, fruits, wine and food offered to the God, the Buddha and ancestors

【供认】gòngrèn 被告人承认所做的事情 defendant admitted what he had done：～不讳 confess candidly; confess everything

【供事】gòng//shì 担任职务 take a post

【供养】gòngyǎng 用供品祭祀（神佛和祖先）make offerings to God, the Buddha and ancestors

☞ gōngyǎng on p. 674

【供职】gòng//zhí 担任职务 hold office; take up a post:在海关～三十年 hold office in the Customs for thirty years

【供状】gòngzhuàng 指书面的供词 written confession

【供桌】gòngzhuō 陈设供品的桌子 altar table; table where offerings are laid

唝 gòng 唝吥(Gòngbù),柬埔寨地名 Kampot, name of a place in Cambodia

☞ hǒng on p. 808

gōu(ㄍㄡ)

勾[1](句) gōu ❶ 用笔画出钩形符号,表示删除或截取 draw a check mark with a pen to delete or take out; cancel; cross out; strike out; tick off: ～销 liquidate; write off|把这篇文章里最精彩的对话～出来 tick off the most interesting dialogues in the article ❷ 画出形象的边缘;描画 delineate; draw; draw the outline of an image: 用铅笔～一个轮廓 draw an outline with a pencil ❸ 用灰、水泥等涂抹砖石建筑物的缝 fill up the joints of brickwork or stonework with mortar or cement; point: ～墙缝 point up a brick wall ❹ 调和使黏 thicken: ～芡 thicken a soup by means of starch ❺ 招引;引 induce; evoke; call to mind: ～引 seduce; entice; lure|～魂 bewitch; enchant; fascinate|这件事～起了我的回忆。This evoked my memories. *or* This brought back my memory. ❻ 结合: ～结 collude with; gang up with|～通 collude with; work hand in glove with ❼ (Gōu)姓 a surname

勾[2](句) gōu〈古代 *arch*.〉称不等腰直角三角形中较短的直角边 name given to the shorter leg of a right triangle in ancient times

☞ gòu on p. 684, 句 gōu on p. 681 and jù on p. 1050

【勾搭】gōu·da 引诱或互相串通做不正当的事 seduce or gang up with each other for an illegitimate purpose: ～一起做坏事 gang up (with someone) to do an unlawful thing|几个人整天勾勾搭搭的,不知要干什么。These guys have ganged up all day long, and you can't tell what they are going to do.

【勾兑】gōuduì 把不同的酒适量混合,并加添调味酒,进行配制 blend different kinds of wine properly and add some seasoning wine to make up a new wine: ～工艺 blending technology

【勾股形】gōugǔxíng〈古代 *arch*.〉称直角三角形 name given to right triangle in ancient China

【勾画】gōuhuà 勾勒描绘;用简短的文字描写 draw the outline of; delineate; sketch; draw; paint; line; give a brief account of: ～脸谱 paint faces for traditional Chinese operas|这篇游记～了桂林的秀丽山水。The travelogue gives a brief description of the beautiful scenery in Guilin.

【勾魂】gōu//hún(～儿 gōuhúnr)招引灵魂离开肉体(迷信)(superstition) snatch the soul from the flesh;〈比喻 *fig*.〉事物吸引人,使心神不定 captivating; enchanting; fascinating; bewitching: 看他那坐立不安的样子,像是被勾了魂似的。He looks so uneasy as if he is possessed.

【勾魂摄魄】gōu hún shè pò 形容事物具有强烈的吸引力,使人心神摇荡,不能自制 captivating; enchanting; fascinating; bewitching; sth. that has such a strong attraction that one is distracted and unable to control oneself

【勾稽】gōujī same as 钩稽 gōujī

【勾结】gōujié 为了进行不正当的活动暗中互相串通、结合 collude; collude with each other secretly to engage in illegal acts: 暗中～ collude with secretly|～官府 collude with the government

【勾栏】gōulán 宋元时称演出杂剧、百戏的场所,后来指妓院 theatre; place where a variety show was given in the Song and Yuan dynasties, or a brothel in the later years; also 勾阑 gōulán

【勾阑】gōulán same as 勾栏 gōulán

【勾勒】gōulè ❶ 用线条画出轮廓;双钩 draw the outline of; sketch the contours of; trace the contour of a stroke, leaving the centre hollow ❷ 用简单的笔墨描写事物的大致情况 give a brief account of; outline: 作品善于～场面,渲染气氛。The work is good at outlining scenes to play up the atmosphere.

【勾连】gōulián ❶ same as 勾结 gōujié: 暗中～ collude with secretely|他们～在一起,干了不少坏事。They have ganged up with each other and done many evil things. ❷ 牵涉;牵连 implicate; involve: 我怀疑这事与他有～。I suspect that he is involved in the matter ‖ also 勾联 gōulián

【勾脸】gōu//liǎn(～儿 gōu//liǎnr)画脸谱 paint the face in traditional operas

【勾留】gōuliú 逗留 stop over; break one's journey at

【勾描】gōumiáo 勾勒描绘 draw: 用细线条把景物的轮廓～出来 draw the contours of the scenery with thin lines

【勾芡】gōu//qiàn 做菜做汤时加上芡粉使汁变稠 thicken a soup by means of starch

【勾通】gōutōng 暗中串通;勾结 collude with secretly; collaborate with; gang up with

【勾销】gōuxiāo 取消;抹掉 cancel; liquidate, write off: 一笔～ write off at one stroke; cancel all debts

【勾心斗角】gōu xīn dòu jiǎo same as 钩心斗角 gōu xīn dòu jiǎo

【勾乙】gōuyǐ 在报刊书籍的某些词句两端，画上形状像'乙'的记号(「」)，表示要抄录下来，作为资料 mark the symbols (「」) like 乙 yǐ at both ends of certain sentences or words in newspapers and books to indicate that they will be taken down as reference materials

【勾引】gōuyǐn ❶ 勾结某种势力，或引诱人做不正当的事 collude with people with certain influence; seduce sb. to engage in illegitimate affairs：他被坏人～，变成了一个小偷。Seduced by a bad person, he has become a thief. ❷ 引动；吸引 arouse; attract：他的话～起我对往事的回忆。His words aroused my memories of the past.

【勾针】gōuzhēn same as 钩针 gōuzhēn

句 gōu 高句骊（Gāogōulí），古国名。又人名用字，句践（Gōujiàn），春秋时越国国王。used in 高句骊（Gāogōulí）Koguryo, the name of an ancient country; also used in the name of a person, e.g. Goujian, name of the king of Yue in the Spring and Autumn Period

☞ jù on p.1050

佝 gōu ☞ below

【佝偻】gōu·lóu 脊背向前弯曲 hunchback; bending forward of the backbone

【佝偻病】gōulóubìng 病，患者多为婴幼儿，由缺乏维生素D，肠道吸收钙、磷的能力降低等引起。症状是头大，鸡胸，驼背，两腿弯曲，腹部膨大，发育迟缓。也叫软骨病。rickets; disease of the skeletal system, chiefly of children, resulting from absence of the normal effect of vitamin D in depositing calcium salts in the bone, and characterized by a softening and, oft., bending of the bones. Its symptoms are big head, chicken chest, hunchback, bending of legs, expanded abdomen and slow development. It is also known as osteomalacia (soft-bone disease).

沟(溝) gōu ❶ 人工挖掘的水道或工事 artificially dug water channel or trench：暗～ underground ditch (trench, channel) | 交通～ communication trench ❷（～儿 gōur）浅槽；和沟类似的洼处 groove; rut; furrow; low-lying place similar to a groove：地面上轧了一道～。A groove was cut on the ground. | 瓦～里流下水来。Water flows down from the gutter. ❸（～儿 gōur）一般的水道 ordinary waterway; gully; ravine：山～ mountain gully | 小河～儿 brook; creek; stream

【沟渎】gōudú〈书 *fml*.〉same as 沟渠 gōuqú

【沟沟坎坎】gougoukǎnkǎn〈比喻 *fig*.〉遇到的困难或障碍 twists and turns; difficulties; obstacles

【沟谷】gōugǔ 径流在地面上冲出的沟。雨季沟中有流水，平时干涸。gully worn on the ground surface by running water. Such a gully has running water in the rainy season, but it is dry in the other seasons.

【沟灌】gōuguàn 灌溉的一种方法，在农作物行间挖沟培垄，把水引到沟里，水从边上渗入土垄 furrow irrigation; method of irrigation in which furrows are dug in the crop fields and water is drawn into the furrows and permeates into the ridges.

【沟壑】gōuhè 山沟；坑：mountain gullies; gully; ravine：～纵横 a maze of gullies

【沟堑】gōuqiàn 壕沟 trench

【沟渠】gōuqú 为灌溉或排水而挖的水道的统称 general term for waterways opened for irrigation or drainage

【沟通】gōutōng 使两方能通连 link up the two sides：～思想 promote mutual understanding | ～两国文化 facilitate the cultural exchange (flow) between the two countries | ～南北的长江大桥 the Yangtze River Bridge that links up the southern and northern provinces

【沟洫】gōuxù〈书 *fml*.〉水道；沟渠 waterway; ditch, channel,

【沟沿儿】gōuyánr 沟渠的边沿儿 banks of a ditch or canal

【沟子】gōu·zi〈方 *dial*.〉same as 沟 gōu

枸 gōu [枸橘]（gōujú）trifoliate orange (*Poncirus trifoliata*); medlar; ☞ 枳 zhǐ on p.2467

☞ gǒu on p.683 and jǔ on p.1048

钩(鉤) gōu ❶（～儿 gōur）same as 钩子 gōu·zi ①：秤～儿 steelyard hook | 钓鱼～儿 fishhook ❷（～儿 gōur）汉字的笔画，附在横、竖等笔画的末端，成钩形，形状是'亅、乛、乚、㇂' hook stroke in Chinese characters at the end of a horizontal or vertical stroke to form the shape of a hook, its forms being '亅、乛、乚、㇂' ❸（～儿 gōur）钩形符号，形状是'√'，一般用来标志内容正确的文字、算式或合格的事物，旧时也用做勾乙或删除的符号 tick; check mark, its form being '√', usu. used to indicate the correct language, a correct mathematical formula or something that has reached the standard, and also used in old times as a symbol for 勾乙 gōuyǐ or deletion ❹ 使用钩子搭、挂或探取 use a hook to hang or pick up something secure with a hook：～住高枝儿采桑叶 catch a tall twig to pick mulberry leaves | 杂技演员用脚～住绳索倒挂在空中。The acrobat hooked his foot into the loop to hang himself upside down in the air. ❺ 探求 seek, search for：～沉 search after | ～玄 probe into ❻ 用带钩的针编织 weaving with a hooked needle：～一个针线包 crochet a sewing kit ❼ 缝纫方法，用针粗缝 sew with large stitches：～贴边 sew on an edging ❽ 说数字时用来代表 9 spoken form for the numeral 9 ❾ (Gōu)姓 a surname

【钩沉】gōuchén 探索深奥的道理或佚失的内容 seek a profound truth or lost writings:《古小说～》*Lost and Found Pieces of Ancient Stories*

【钩秤】gōuchèng 杆秤的一种,装有铁钩,用来挂所称物品 a kind of steelyard with a hook for hanging an object to be weighed

【钩尺】gōuchǐ 测量原木小头横截面直径的尺子,尺端(零点处)有一个钩 ruler with a hook at its end (the zero point) for measuring the diameter of the cross-section of the small end of a log

【钩虫】gōuchóng 寄生虫,成虫线形,很小,乳白色或淡红色,口部有钩,寄生在人的小肠内。虫卵随粪便排出体外。幼虫丝状,钻入人的皮肤,最后进入小肠,吸人血,引起丘疹、贫血等。hookworm; milky white or light pink small parasitic intestinal nematode worm with hooks around the mouth. Its eggs are discharged with the night soil. Its silk-shaped larvae get through the skin of the human body and finally into the small intestine and suck human blood, causing papule, anaemia, etc.

【钩稽】gōujī ❶ 查考 examine; investigate; check; ascertain:～文坛故实 ascertain the past facts of the literary world ❷ 核算 audit ‖ also 勾稽 gōujī

G

【钩心斗角】gōu xīn dòu jiǎo 原指宫室结构精巧工致 originally the exquisite and fine craftsmanship of the construction of the palatial chambers;〈比喻 *fig.*〉各用心机,互相排挤 intriguing to squeeze each other out; 钩 also put as 勾 gōu

【钩玄】gōuxuán〈书 *fml.*〉探求精深的道理 seek the profound truth:～提要 probe into the reasoning of something abstract

【钩针】gōuzhēn (～儿 gōuzhēnr)编织花边等用的带钩的针 crochet hook; hooked needle used to weave laces; also 勾针 gōuzhēn

【钩子】gōu·zi ❶ 悬挂东西或探取东西的用具,形状弯曲 hook; curved piece of metal for hanging or taking sth.:火～poker ❷ 形态像钩子的东西 sth. shaped like a hook:蝎子的～有毒。The sting of a scorpion is poisonous.

缑 gōu ❶〈书 *fml.*〉刀剑等柄上所缠的绳 cord twining the handle of a sword ❷ (Gōu)姓 a surname

篝 gōu〈书 *fml.*〉笼(lóng) cage

【篝火】gōuhuǒ bonfire; campfire 原指用笼子罩着的火,现借指在空旷处或野外架木柴、树枝燃烧的火堆 originally a fire covered by a cage, now an outdoor fire built on firewood and twigs:营火会上燃起熊熊的～。A bright bonfire was built at camp.

【篝火狐鸣】gōu huǒ hú míng《史记·陈涉世家》:'夜篝火,狐鸣呼曰:"大楚兴,陈胜王。"'陈涉准备起义,夜里用笼罩住火,忽隐忽现像磷火,同时还学狐叫,假托狐鬼发动戍卒起事。According to the *Records of the Historian · Hereditary House of Chen She*, 'Seeing the caged fire, a fox cried: "The Great Chu rises with Chen Sheng as its king."' Chen She was ready to revolt. He used cages to cover the fire at night, which flickered like a jack-o-lantern. At the same time, he asked his soldiers to cry like foxes and start the revolt in the name of foxes and ghosts.〈比喻 *fig.*〉策划起义 plan for a revolt

鞲 gōu [鞲鞴] (gōubèi) ☞ 活塞 huósāi on p. 877

gǒu (ㄍㄡˇ)

苟[1] (❷茍) gǒu ❶ 随便 casual:一笔不～ not at all casual | 不～言笑 serious in speech and manner ❷ (Gǒu)姓 a surname

苟[2] gǒu〈书 *fml.*〉假使;如果 if:～无民,何以有君。If there were no subjects, how could there be a king.

【苟安】gǒu'ān 只顾眼前,暂且偷安 live in a moment's peace without taking any measure to avert a looming danger:～一时 be content with a moment's peace

【苟存】gǒucún〈书 *fml.*〉苟且生存 manage to live an animal's life

【苟合】gǒuhé 不正当的结合(指男女间) illicit sexual relations

【苟活】gǒuhuó 苟且图生存 live at the expense of one's principle; to live ignobly:忍辱～ endure humiliation to live ignobly

【苟简】gǒujiǎn〈书 *fml.*〉苟且简略;草率简陋 too brief to be intelligible; unduly simple or brief; slipshod

【苟且】gǒuqiě ❶ 只顾眼前,得过且过 drift along; be resigned to circumstances:～偷安 live in a moment's peace without taking any measure to avert a looming danger ❷ 敷衍了事;马虎 perfunctory; dispose of sth. perfunctorily; careless:因循～ follow routines without thinking about improvement, be perfunctory and unimaginative in handling things | 他做翻译,一字一句都未敢～。In doing translation, he chose every word with great care. ❸ 不正当的(多指男女关系) illicit (sexual relations); improper

【苟全】gǒuquán 苟且保全(生命) keep living for living's sake; barely manage to preserve one's life:～性命 barely manage to survive

【苟同】gǒutóng〈书 *fml.*〉随便地同意 agree without giving serious thought; readily subscribe to (sb.'s view):未敢～ beg to differ;

(I)'ll have to part company with you on that point.

【苟延残喘】gǒu yán cán chuǎn 勉强拖延一口没断的气 be on one's last legs;〈比喻 *fig.*〉勉强维持生存 linger on in a steadily worsening condition; prolong one's life with great difficulty

岣 gǒu 岣嵝(gǒulǒu),山名,就是衡山,在湖南 Goulou, another name of Mount Hengshan in Hunan Province

狗 gǒu 哺乳动物,种类很多,嗅觉和听觉都很灵敏,毛有黄、白、黑等颜色。是一种家畜,有的可以训练成警犬,有的用来帮助打猎、牧羊等。dog (*Canis familiaris*); mammal and domesticated canine, in many breeds and in yellow, white, black and other colours, with keen senses of smell and hearing, commonly kept as house pets and also used for hunting, guarding people or property or grazing sheep, some trained as police dogs. also 犬 quǎn

【狗吃屎】gǒu chī shǐ 身体向前跌倒的姿势(含嘲笑意 derog.)dog eating dung — a heavy fall; fall flat on the face; fall to the ground face down: 摔了个～ fall flat on the face

【狗胆包天】gǒu dǎn bāo tiān 指人胆大妄为(骂人的话 curse) audacious and reckless; extremely audacious; monstrously audacious

【狗苟蝇营】gǒu gǒu yíng yíng ☞ 蝇营狗苟 yíng yíng gǒu gǒu on p. 2303

【狗獾】gǒuhuān 哺乳动物,毛一般灰色,腹部和四肢黑色,头部有三条白色纵纹。趾端有长而锐利的爪,善于掘土,穴居在山野,昼伏夜出。脂肪炼的獾油用来治疗烫伤等。badger (*Nyctereutes procyonoides*); nocturnal mammal with grey hair, black belly, black feet, three white vertical stripes on the head, long and sharp claws for burrowing in hills, and its fat used for treating burns; also 獾 guān

【狗急跳墙】gǒu jí tiào qiáng〈比喻 *fig.*〉走投无路时不顾一切地行动 cornered beast will do something desperate; when cornered, a dog in desperation jumping over the barrier; take a desperate action in a critical situation

【狗皮膏药】gǒupí gāo·yao 药膏涂在小块狗皮上的一种膏药,疗效比一般膏药好。旧时走江湖的人常假造这种膏药来骗取钱财,因而用来比喻骗人的货色。plaster formerly spread on a small piece of dogskin, with a better curative effect than other plasters. Quacks often defrauded other people of their money by selling fake plaster; fraud

【狗屁】gǒupì 指毫无可取的话或文章(骂人的话 curse) horseshit; rubbish; nonsense; shit; meaningless words or articles: 放～ shit|～不通 mere trash; rubbish|～文章 mere trash; rubbish

【狗屎堆】gǒushǐduī〈比喻 *fig.*〉令人深恶痛绝的人 the most disgusting person; the most detestable person

【狗头军师】gǒutóu jūnshī 指爱给人出主意而主意并不高明的人 person who likes to give advice, but not very good advice; person who offers bad advice; inept adviser

【狗腿子】gǒutuǐ·zi 指给有势力的坏人奔走帮凶的人(骂人的话 curse) hired thug; lackey; henchman

【狗尾草】gǒuwěicǎo 一年生草本植物,叶子细长,花序圆柱形,穗有毛 foxtail (*Setaria viridis*); annual herb with long and slender leaves, cylindrical spikes bearing spikelets interspersed with still bristles; also 莠 yǒu

【狗尾续貂】gǒu wěi xù diāo〈比喻 *fig.*〉拿不好的东西接到好的东西后面,显得好坏不相称(多指文学作品) put a dog's tail to a marten's body — complete a masterpiece with poor finishing (of a literary work); dog's tail joined to sable — a wretched sequel to a fine work

【狗熊】gǒuxióng ❶ 黑熊 black bear ❷〈比喻 *fig.*〉怯懦无用的人 coward: 谁英雄,谁～,咱比比! Who is a hero and who is a coward? Let's compare and see!

【狗血喷头】gǒuxuè pēn tóu 形容骂得很凶 pour out a stream of abuses; also 狗血淋头 gǒuxuè lín tóu

【狗咬狗】gǒu yǎo gǒu〈比喻 *fig.*〉坏人之间互相倾轧、争斗 dog-eat-dog; struggle between or among bad persons for power

【狗仗人势】gǒu zhàng rén shì〈比喻 *fig.*〉仗势欺人(骂人的话 curse) like a dog threatening people on the strength of its master's power; be a bully with the backing of a powerful person; take advantage of one's or sb. else's power to bully people

【狗嘴吐不出象牙】gǒuzuǐ tǔ·bu chū xiàngyá〈比喻 *fig.*〉坏人嘴里说不出好话来 no decent words come from the mouth of a bad person; no ivory issues from the mouth of a dog; filthy mouth can't utter decent language; what can you expect from a dog but a bark; also 狗嘴长不出象牙 gǒuzuǐ zhǎng·bu chū xiàngyá

耇(耉) gǒu〈书 *fml.*〉年老;长寿 old age; long life

枸 gǒu [枸杞](gǒu qǐ)落叶灌木,叶子披针形,花淡紫色。果实叫枸杞子(gǒuqǐzǐ),是圆形或椭圆形的浆果,红色,可入药。Chinese wolfberry (*Lycium chinense*); deciduous shrub with pale yellow flowers and red round or ellipse berries; used as a Chinese tonic ☞ gōu on p. 681 and jǔ on p. 1048

笱 gǒu〈方 *dial.*〉竹制的捕鱼器具,鱼进去出不来 bamboo box for catching fish, which allows the fish to swim in but not out.

gòu（ㄍㄡˋ）

勾（句） gòu ❶ same as 够 gòu（多见于早期白话 oft. in early vernacular） ❷（Gòu）姓 a surname
☞ gōu on p. 680，句 gōu on p. 681 and jù on p. 1050

【勾当】 gòu·dàng 事情，今多指坏事情（derog.） business; deal：罪恶～ criminal activities｜从事走私～ engage in smuggling activities

构[1]（構） gòu ❶ 构造；组合 construct; form; compose：～图 composition of a picture; construct｜～词 form a word ❷ 结成（用于抽象事物） form; fabricate; make up：虚～fabricate; make up｜～怨 be at feud; nurse hatred against ❸ 指文艺作品 literary composition：佳～ a good piece of writing

构[2]（構） gòu ☞ 楮 chǔ ❶ on p. 293

【构成】 gòuchéng ❶ 形成；造成 constitute; amount to; give rise to, cause, bring about：眼镜由镜片和镜架～。Glasses are made up of a rim and lenses.｜违法情节轻微，还没有～犯罪。It is a minor offence, which does not constitute a crime. ❷ same as 结构 jiégòu ①：研究所目前的人员～不尽合理。The composition of the staff of the research institute is not yet desirable.

【构词法】 gòucífǎ 由词素构成词的方式 method of building a word from morphemes

【构架】 gòujià 建筑物的框架 architectural structure; frame work;〈比喻 *fig.*〉事物的组织结构 organizational structure of a substance：木～ wooden structure 艺术～ artistic structure

【构件】 gòujiàn ❶ 组成机构的单元，可以是一个零件，也可以是由许多零件构成的刚体 element; component; unit that forms a part of a mechanism, which can be a part or a rigid body composed of many parts ❷ 组成建筑物某一结构的单元，如梁、柱 unit that forms part of a certain structure of a building such as a beam, column, etc.

【构建】 gòujiàn 建立（多用于抽象事物 mostly in abstracts） build, construct：～新的学科体系 build a new system of courses

【构思】 gòusī 做文章或制作艺术品时运用心思 plot or racking brains when writing an article or making a work of art：～精巧 well-conceived｜艺术～ artistic conception

【构图】 gòutú 绘画时根据题材和主题思想的要求，把要表现的形象适当地组织起来，构成协调的完整的画面 composition (of a picture); arrangement of parts of a painting on the basis of its subject matter and theme so as to form a unified, harmonious whole

【构陷】 gòuxiàn 定计陷害，使别人落下罪名 set sb. up; make a false charge against sb.; frame sb. up; plot to make a false charge against sb.; also 搆陷 gōuxiàn

【构想】 gòuxiǎng ❶ same as 构思 gòusī：～巧妙 ingenious conception｜这部小说，～和行文都不高明。This novel is none too satisfactory, either in conception or in execution. *or* This novel is not at all desirable, either in conception or in writing. ❷ 形成的想法 conceived idea：提出体制改革的～ give an idea for the structural reform

【构象】 gòuxiàng 有机化合物分子中，由于碳原子上结合的原子（或原子团）的相对位置改变而产生的不同的空间排列方式 conformation; different arrangement of molecules in an organic chemical compound resulting from the change of the relative position of the atom (or atomic group) combined with carbon

【构造】 gòuzào 各个组成部分的安排、组织和相互关系 arrangement, composition and interrelation of the different parts of a thing：人体～ the structure of a human body｜地层的～ structure of a stratum｜句子的～ structure of a sentence; sentence construction

【构造地震】 gòuzào dìzhèn 地震的一种，由地层发生断层而引起。波及范围广，破坏性很大。世界上 90% 以上的地震属于构造地震。tectonic earthquake; a kind of earthquake cause by the fault of rock strata, which affects large areas and is extremely destructive. More than 90% of the earthquakes occurring in the world are tectonic earthquakes; also 断层地震 duàncéng dìzhèn

【构筑】 gòuzhù 建造；修筑 build; construct：～工事 construct field works

【构筑物】 gòuzhùwù 一般不直接在里面进行生产和生活活动的建筑物，如水塔、烟囱等 building in which people do not live or work, such as a water tower, a chimney, etc.

购（購） gòu 买 buy; purchase：采～ buy, purchase｜统～统销 state monopoly for purchase and marketing｜认～公债 subscribe for treasury bonds

【购买】 gòumǎi 买 buy; purchase：～力 purchasing power｜～年货 shopping for the Spring Festival; go shopping in preparation of the Spring Festival

【购买力】 gòumǎilì ❶ 指个人或机关团体购买商品和支付生活费用的能力 purchasing power; power of an individual or an organization to pay for the goods purchased and cover living expenses ❷ 指单位货币购买商品的能力 power of the unit money for purchasing goods

【购销】 gòuxiāo 商业上的购进和销售 buying and selling in commerce; buying and selling：～两旺 brisk buying and selling

【购置】gòuzhì 购买(长期使用的器物) buy; purchase (oft. durable goods):～图书资料 buy books and reference materials | 为了扩大生产,这家工厂～了一批新设备。The factory has bought a large amount of equipment for expanded production.

诟 gòu〈书 *fml.*〉❶ 耻辱 shame; humiliation ❷ 怒骂;辱骂 revile; talk abusively; use abusive and contemptuous language in speaking:～病 blame; criticize; denounce; castigate

【诟病】gòubìng〈书 *fml.*〉指责 blame; criticize denounce; castigate:为世～ become an object of public denunciation; be denounced by the public

【诟骂】gòumà〈书 *fml.*〉辱骂 revile; abuse; vilify

垢 gòu ❶〈书 *fml.*〉污秽;肮脏 filth; dirt:蓬头～面 with dishevelled hair and a dirty face; unkempt ❷ 脏东西 dirt; filth:油～ grease stain | 牙～ tartar; dental calculus | 泥～ dirt; grime ❸〈书 *fml.*〉耻辱 shame; disgrace; humiliation:含～忍辱 endure humiliation and insult

【垢污】gòuwū 污垢 dirt; filth

姤 gòu〈书 *fml.*〉❶ same as 遘 gòu ❷ 善;美好 good; excellent; fine

冓 gòu〈书 *fml.*〉宫室的深处 secluded place in the palace

够(夠) gòu ❶ 数量上可以满足需要 meet the need in quantity; enough; sufficient; adequate:钱～不～? Do you have enough money? | 老觉得时间不～用。I always find I don't have enough time. ❷ 达到某一点或某种程度 reach a certain point or a certain extent:～格 be qualified | ～结实 strong enough ❸ (用手等)伸向不易达到的地方去接触或拿来 (of a hand) stretch to a certain place; take something from a certain place beyond one's reach:～不着 can't reach | ～得着 can reach

【够本】gòu//běn (～儿 gòu//běnr) ❶ 买卖不赔不赚;赌博不输不赢 make enough money to cover the cost; (of gambling) break even ❷〈比喻 *fig.*〉得失相当 gain balancing the loss

【够格】gòu//gé (～儿 gòu//gér)符合一定的标准或条件 be qualified; be up to standard:他体力差,参加抢险不～。He is too weak to be qualified for the rescue mission.

【够交情】gòu jiāo·qing ❶ 指交情很深 be on very good terms ❷ 够朋友 be a true friend

【够劲儿】gòujìnr 担负的分量极重;程度极高 extremely heavy load; really hard job; (of an onerous task, etc.) almost too much to cope with; an extremely high degree:一头骡子拉这么多煤,真～。It's really an extremely heavy load for the mule to carry so much coal. | 这辣椒辣得真～。This pepper is really hot.

【够朋友】gòu péng·you能尽朋友的情分 deserve to be called a true friend; be a friend indeed; be a true friend

【够呛】gòuqiàng same as 够戗 gòuqiàng

【够戗】gòuqiàng〈方 *dial.*〉十分厉害;够受的 terrible; unbearable; terrible:累得～ awfully tired; also 够呛 gòuqiàng

【够瞧的】gòuqiáo·de 十分厉害;够受的;看不下去 terrible; really; awful; too much; unbearable; cannot stand it:天热得真～,庄稼都晒蔫了。The crop droops in the heat of the scorching sun. | 这个人脾气越来越大,真～。It is really awful to see that man's temper go from bad to worse.

【够受的】gòushòu·de 达到或超过人所能忍受的最大限度,含有使人受不了的意思 to or over the maximum limit of what one can endure; unbearable; hard to bear:干了一天活儿,累得真～。He was completely exhausted from a day's work.

【够味儿】gòuwèir 工力达到相当高的水平;意味深长;耐人寻味 fairly high level of craftsmanship; meaningful; give much food for thought; intriguing; just the right flavour; just the thing:这两句你唱得可真～。The way you sang the last two lines was superb! *or* How superb the way you sang the last two lines!

【够意思】gòu yì·si ❶ 达到相当的水平(多用来表示赞赏 oft. in praise) reach a fairly high level:这篇评论说得头头是道,真～。This commentary is great, and logically presented. ❷ 够朋友;够交情 be a friend indeed; be a true friend; be on good terms; be a true friend:他能抽空陪你玩,就～的了。It's very kind of him to find time to show you around. | 他这样做,有点儿不～。It's unfriendly of him to do it that way.

遘 gòu〈书 *fml.*〉相遇 encounter

彀[1] gòu 张满弓弩 draw a bow to the full:～中 shooting range

彀[2] gòu same as 够 gòu

【彀中】gòuzhōng〈书 *fml.*〉箭能射及的范围 shooting range;〈比喻 *fig.*〉牢笼、圈套 trap; snare:入我～ fall into my trap; ensnared

搆 gòu same as 构 gòu

【搆陷】gòuxiàn same as 构陷 gòuxiàn

雊 gòu〈书 *fml.*〉野鸡叫 cry of a pheasant

媾 gòu〈书 *fml.*〉❶ 结为婚姻 make a marriage:婚～(两家结亲 marriage between two families) marriage ❷ 交好 be on friendly terms:～和 make peace ❸ 交配 mate; copu-

G

late; have sex; have a sexual intercourse: 交～ copulation

【媾和】gòuhé 交战国缔结和约,约束战争状态。也指一国之内交战团体达成和平协议,结束战争。(of belligerent countries) make peace; concluded a peace treaty to end the war; (of belligerent parties in one country) reached a peace agreement to end the war

覯 gòu〈书 *fml.*〉遇见 meet

gū(ㄍㄨ)

估 gū 估计;揣测 estimate; appraise; guess: ～一～这块地能收多少粮食。Can you estimate how many kilogrammes of grain can be harvested from this plot? | 不要低～他的作用。Don't underestimate his role.

☞ gù on p.697

【估产】gū//chǎn 凭生产经验,预先估计农作物等的产量 estimate the yield of a crop in advance by experience in production; appraise the assets; assess

【估堆儿】gū//duīr 估计成堆商品的数量或价格 estimate the quantity, or the value of a pile of goods

【估计】gūjì 根据某些情况,对事物的性质、数量、变化等做大概的推断 make an approximate calculation of the nature, quantity and changes of a thing in the light of certain circumstances; estimate; appraise; reckon: ～他今天会来。I reckon he will come today. | 最近几天～不会下雨。It is not likely to rain in the next few days.

【估价】gū//jià 估计商品的价格 estimate the price of a commodity; appraise; evaluate: 请给这件古董估个价吧。Please estimate the price of this piece of antique.

【估价】gūjià 对人或事物给以评价 evaluate or appraise: 对历史人物的～不能离开历史条件。In evaluating historical personages, we should not forget specific historical conditions.

【估量】gū·liàng same as 估计 gūjì: 难以～的损失 inestimable loss

【估摸】gū·mo same as 估计 gūjì: 我～着他会来。I surmise he will come.

【估算】gūsuàn 大致推算 estimate; appraise; reckon: ～产量 estimate the yield; an estimated yield

苽 gū〈书 *fml.*〉same as 菰 gū

咕 gū〈拟声词 *onom.*〉母鸡、斑鸠等的叫声 clucking of a hen, turtledove; cooing of a pigeon

【咕咚】gūdōng〈拟声词 *onom.*〉重东西落下或大口喝水的声音 sound of a heavy thing falling down or drinking water heavily; thud; splash; plump: 大石头～一声掉到水里去了。The rock fell into the water with a splash. | 他拿起啤酒瓶,对着嘴～～地喝了几口。He took a bottle of beer and drank it with some gulps.

【咕嘟】gūdū〈拟声词 *onom.*〉液体沸腾、水流涌出或大口喝水的声音 sound of boiling, gurgling and gulping water; bubble; gurgle: 锅里的粥～～响。The porridge is boiling in the pot. | 泉水～～地往外冒。The spring kept bubbling up. | 小刘端起一碗水,～～地喝了下去。Xiao Liu took a bowl of water and gulped it down quickly.

【咕嘟】gū·du ❶〈方 *dial.*〉长时间煮 boil for a long time: 把海带～烂了再吃。Eat the kelp after it is cooked and becomes soft. ❷(嘴)撅着;鼓起 pout; purse one's lips: 他生气了,～着嘴半天不说话。He was so angry that he kept silence for a long time with his lips pursed up.

【咕叽】gūjī same as 咕唧 gūjī

【咕唧】gūjī〈拟声词 *onom.*〉水受压力而向外排出的声音 sound of discharging water when under pressure; squelching sound: 他在雨地里走着,脚底下～～地直响。He walked along in the rain, the water squelching under his boots. also 咕叽 gūjī

【咕唧】gū·ji 小声交谈或自言自语 whisper; murmur: 他们俩交头接耳地～了半天。They whispered to each other for a long time. | 他一边想心事,一边儿～。He was murmuring to himself as he thought about something. also 咕叽 gūjī

【咕隆】gūlōng〈拟声词 *onom.*〉雷声、大车声等 sound of thunder, truck, etc.; rumble; rattle; roll: 雷声～～,由远而近。The thunder roared as it drew near from the distance. also 咕隆隆 gūlōnglōng

【咕噜】gūlū〈拟声词 *onom.*〉水流动或东西滚动的声音 sound of flowing water or a rolling object; rumble; roll: 他端起一杯水～一口就喝完了。He took a glass of water, and gulped it down. | 石头～～滚下去了。A rock rolled down. also 咕噜噜 gūlūlū

【咕噜】gū·lu same as 咕哝 gū·nong

【咕哝】gū·nong 小声说话(多指自言自语,并带不满情绪 mostly to oneself, with some displeasure) murmur; mutter; grumble: 他低着头嘴里不知～些什么。He bent his head, murmuring to himself. *or* He murmured to himself, his head hanging low.

呱 gū ☞ below

☞ guā on p.702 and guǎ on p.703

【呱呱】gūgū〈书 *fml.*〉小儿哭声 cry of a baby: ～而泣 mewl

☞ guāguā on p.702

【呱呱坠地】gūgū zhuì dì 指婴儿出生 birth of a

new baby

沽[1] gū〈书 *fml.*〉❶ 买 buy：～酒 buy wine ❷ 卖 sell：待价而～ wait for the right price to sell

沽[2] Gū 天津的别称 another name for Tianjin

【沽名】gūmíng 故意做作或用某种手段谋取名誉 seek fame through affectation or by certain means：～钓誉 fish for fame and compliments｜～之作 work done to seek fame

姑[1] gū ❶（～儿 gūr）父亲的姐妹 father's sister；aunt｜大～ father's elder sister｜二～ father's second sister｜表～ daughter of grandmother's brother ❷ 丈夫的姐妹 husband's sister；sister-in-law：大～子 husband's elder sister｜小～儿 husband's younger sister ❸〈书 *fml.*〉丈夫的母亲 husband's mother；mother-in-law：翁～ wife's mother-in-law ❹ 出家修行或从事迷信职业的妇女 woman who becomes a Buddhist nun or engages in a superstitious profession；nun：尼～ nun｜三～六婆 women whose professions are either illegitimate or disreputable

姑[2] gū〈书 *fml.*〉姑且；暂且 tentatively；for the moment：～置勿论 leave sth. aside for the moment

【姑表】gūbiǎo 一家的父亲和另一家的母亲是兄妹或姐弟的亲戚关系（区别于'姨表' as compared with 'relationship between the children of two sisters'）relationship between the children of a brother and a sister：～亲 cousinship｜～兄弟 male cousins｜～姐妹 female cousins

【姑爹】gūdiē〈方 *dial.*〉same as 姑夫 gū·fu

【姑夫】gū·fu 姑母的丈夫 husband of father's sister；uncle

【姑父】gū·fu same as 姑夫 gū·fu

【姑姑】gū·gu same as 姑母 gūmǔ

【姑舅】gūjiù same as 姑表 gūbiǎo：～兄弟 male children of a brother and a sister｜～姐妹 female children of a brother or a sister

【姑宽】gūkuān 姑息宽容 be sympathetic and forgiving：从严查处，决不～。Investigate the case and handle those involved strictly with no lenience.

【姑老爷】gūlǎo·ye ❶ 岳家对女婿的尊称 respectful form of address for a man used by members of his wife's family ❷ 母亲的姑夫 husband of sister of one's maternal grandfather

【姑姥姥】gūlǎo·lao 母亲的姑母 sister of one's maternal grandfather

【姑妈】gūmā 姑母（指已婚的）father's (married) sister；aunt

【姑母】gūmǔ 父亲的姐妹 father's (married) sister；aunt

【姑奶奶】gūnǎi·nai ❶ 父亲的姑母 sister of one's paternal grandfather；paternal grand-aunt ❷ 娘家称已经出嫁的女儿 married daughter

【姑娘】gūniáng〈方 *dial.*〉❶ same as 姑母 gūmǔ ❷ 丈夫的姐妹 husband's sister；sister-in-law

【姑娘】gū·niang ❶ 未婚的女子 girl ❷ 女儿 daughter

【姑娘儿】gū·niangr〈方 *dial.*〉称妓女 prostitute

【姑婆】gūpó〈方 *dial.*〉❶ 丈夫的姑母 husband's aunt ❷ 父亲的姑母 paternal grand-aunt

【姑且】gūqiě〈副词 *adv.*〉表示暂时地 tentatively；for the moment：此事～搁起。Leave it for the moment.｜我这里有支钢笔，你～用着。I have a pen here. You can use it for the moment.

【姑嫂】gūsǎo 女子和她的弟兄的妻子的合称（嫂兼指弟妇）combined form of address for a woman and her younger brother's wife；sisters-in-law

【姑妄听之】gū wàng tīng zhī 姑且听听（不必信以为真）Let's hear what he is going to say (one doesn't have to believe it)；see no harm in hearing what sb. has to say

【姑妄言之】gū wàng yán zhī 姑且说说（对于自己不能深信不疑的事情，说给别人时常用此语以示保留 expression to be used when relating sth. one is not sure of）Let me tell you sth., but don't take it seriously

【姑息】gūxī 无原则地宽容 excessively tolerant；appease；indulge；tolerate；forgive：对自己的错误不应该有一点儿～。You should never forgive your own mistakes.

【姑息养奸】gūxī yǎng jiān 由于过分宽容而助长坏人坏事 To tolerate evil is to encourage evildoers. *or* To tolerate evil is to abet it.

【姑爷】gū·ye 岳家称女婿 respectful form of address for a man used by members of his wife's family

【姑爷爷】gū·yéye 父亲的姑夫 husband of paternal grand-aunt，also 姑爷 gū·yé

【姑丈】gūzhàng same as 姑夫 gū·fu

【姑子】gū·zi 尼姑 Buddhist nun

孤 gū ❶ 幼年丧父或父母双亡的（of a child）fatherless or orphaned：～儿 orphan ❷ 单独；孤单 alone；lonely；solitary；isolated：～雁 lone or solitary wild goose｜～岛 isolated island｜～掌难鸣。It's impossible to clap with one hand. *or* It's difficult to achieve anything without support. ❸ 封建王侯的自称 I；self-address for 'I' by a feudal monarch

【孤哀子】gū'āizǐ〈旧时 *old*〉儿子死了父亲称孤子，死了母亲称哀子，父母都死了称孤哀子（多用于讣闻 used in obituaries）a boy was called a 'son bereaved of his father' after his father died, a 'son bereaved of his mother' after his

G

mother died, and a 'son bereaved of both parents' after both his father and mother died

【孤傲】gū'ào 孤僻高傲 proud and aloof; aloof and arrogant:～不群 most aloof and arrogant

【孤本】gūběn 指某书仅有一份在世间流传的版本,也指仅存的一份未刊手稿或原物已亡,仅存的一份拓本 only existing copy of a book; only copy extant of an unpublished manuscript; only existing copy of rubbings with its original already lost

【孤雌生殖】gūcí-shēngzhí 某些比较低等的生物的卵未经受精就能发育成新的个体,这种繁殖叫做孤雌生殖。动物中如蚜虫不经过交配就能繁殖,植物中如黄瓜不经过传粉受精就能结果。parthenogenesis; reproduction by the development of an unfertilized ovum, seed, or spore, as in certain insects or algae, it may be induced artificially by chemical or mechanical means. For instance aphid reproduces without mating, and cucumber grows to bear fruits without pollination

【孤单】gūdān ❶ 单身无靠,感到寂寞 live alone and feel lonely:～一人 all alone; all by oneself; a lone soul | 她一个人生活很～。She lives alone and feels very lonely. ❷ (力量)单薄 (of force) weak:势力～ weak and isolated

【孤胆】gūdǎn 单独跟许多敌人英勇作战 fight single-handed against many enemies:～英雄 lone fighter

【孤独】gūdú 独自一个人;孤单 lone soul; all alone; live alone:～的老人 lone old man | 儿女都不在身边,他感到很～。He feels very lonely in the absence of his children.

【孤儿】gū'ér ❶ 死了父亲的儿童 fatherless child; child bereaved of its father:～寡母 a widow and her son ❷ 失去父母的儿童 orphans; children bereaved of parents:孤～院 orphanage

【孤芳自赏】gū fāng zì shǎng 〈比喻 *fig.*〉自命清高,自我欣赏 profess oneself to be above politics and worldly considerations and indulge in self-admiration

【孤负】gūfù same as 辜负 gūfù

【孤高】gūgāo 〈书 *fml.*〉高傲,不合群 haughty and aloof; arrogant; do not go on well with others:性情～ aloof and arrogant | ～不群 very aloof and arrogant

【孤寡】gūguǎ ❶ 孤儿和寡妇 widow and her son:老弱～ the old, weak, widowed and orphaned ❷ same as 孤独 gūdú:～老人 lone old man | 家里只剩下我一个～老婆子。I, an old woman, is the only one left in the family.

【孤拐】gū·guai 〈方 *dial.*〉❶ 颧骨 cheekbone ❷ 脚掌两旁突出的部分 ball of the foot

【孤寂】gūjì 孤独寂寞 lonely; live alone and feel lonely:～难耐 It's difficult to endure loneliness. | 他一个人留在家里,感到十分～。Having been left alone at home, he feels very lonely.

【孤家寡人】gūjiā guǎrén 古代君主自己谦称为孤或寡人('孤家'多见于戏曲),现在用'孤家寡人'比喻脱离群众,孤立无助的人 person who is utterly isolated (oft. in Chinese theatre); Emperors of ancient times called themselves 'I, the Lonely One'; the expression is now used to describe a person who is isolated and can get no support from the masses

【孤军】gūjūn 孤立无援的军队 isolated force:～作战 fight alone without any support from others | ～深入 isolated force penetrating deep into enemy's territory (or occupied area)

【孤苦】gūkǔ 孤单无靠,生活困苦 lone and helpless:～伶仃 orphaned and helpless; alone and uncared for; friendless and wretched | ～无依 lone and helpless | ～的老人 a lonely and helpless old man

【孤苦伶仃】gūkǔ língdīng 形容孤独困苦,无依无靠 orphaned and helpless; alone and uncared for; friendless and wretched; also 孤苦零丁 gūkǔ língdīng

【孤老】gūlǎo ❶ 孤独而年老 lonely and old ❷ 孤独而年老的人 lonely old man:赡养～ provide for a lonely old man

【孤立】gūlì ❶ 同其他事物不相联系 isolated from other things; isolated:湖心有个～的小岛。There is an isolated island in the middle of the lake. | 这个事件不是～的。It is not an isolated incident. ❷ 不能得到同情和援助 be unable to get sympathy and aid:～无援 isolated and cut off from support ❸ 使得不到同情和援助 make it impossible for one to get sympathy and aid; isolate:～敌人 isolate the enemy

【孤立木】gūlìmù 生长在空旷地上的单株树木,树干多弯曲,下部粗,上部细,树冠大,节子较多(区别于'林木' as compared with 'forest') lone tree, esp. one growing in an open space with a bent trunk, the lower part bigger and the upper part smaller, a large crown and many nodes

【孤立语】gūlìyǔ 词根语 inflectionless language

【孤零零】gūlínglíng 形容孤单,无依无靠或没有陪衬 solitary; lone; all alone; helpless:家里只剩下他～一个人。He was left alone in the family. | 山脚下有一间～的小草房。There is a lone thatched hut at the foot of the hill.

【孤陋寡闻】gū lòu guǎ wén 知识浅陋,见闻不广 ignorant and ill-informed

【孤僻】gūpì 孤独怪僻 unsociable and eccentric:性情～ of an uncommunicative and eccentric disposition; uncommunicative and eccentric

【孤身】gūshēn 孤单一人(多指没有亲属或亲属不在身边) alone (having no family members or the family members do not live with him):父母早年去世,只剩下他～一人。After the death of his parents in his early years, he was left alone.

【孤孀】gūshuāng ❶ 孤儿寡妇 widow and her son ❷ 寡妇 widow

【孤行】gūxíng 不顾别人反对而独自行事 do things arbitrarily despite opposition from others: ～己见 follow one's bigoted course; stick stubbornly to one's thinking | 一意～ follow one's course obstinately

【孤掌难鸣】gū zhǎng nán míng 一个巴掌难以拍响 impossible to clap with one hand;〈比喻 *fig.*〉力量单薄,难以成事 difficult to accomplish anything without help

【孤证】gūzhèng 单一的证据或例证 only evidence or example

【孤注一掷】gū zhù yī zhì 把所有的钱一下投做赌注,企图最后得胜 stake all on a single throw; put all one's eggs in one basket;〈比喻 *fig.*〉在危急时把全部力量拿出来冒一次险 risk everything on a single venture

【孤子】gūzǐ ❶ same as 孤儿 gū'ér ❷ ☞ 孤哀子 gū'āizǐ

轱 gū ☞ below

【轱轳】gū·lu same as 轱辘 gū·lu

【轱辘】gū·lu ❶ 车轮子 wheel ❷ 滚动 roll: 油桶～远了。The barrel has rolled away. also 轱轳 gū·lu or 毂辘 gū·lu

骺 gū 〈书 *fml.*〉大骨 big bone

骨 gū ☞ below
☞ gǔ on p. 693

【骨朵儿】gū·duor 没有开放的花朵 bud: 花～ flower bud

【骨碌碌】gūlūlū 形容很快地转动 roll quickly: 他眼睛～地看看这个,又看看那个。His eyes rolled quickly as he looked this way and that.

【骨碌】gū·lu 滚动 roll: 皮球在地上～。The ball is rolling on the ground. | 他一～从床上爬起来。He rolled out of bed.

鸪 gū ☞ 鹁鸪 bógū on p. 150 and [鹧鸪] (zhègū) on p. 2432

罛 gū 〈书 *fml.*〉一种大的渔网 large fishnet

菇 gū 蘑菇 mushroom: 香～dried mushroom | 冬～ dried mushroom picked in winter

菰 gū ❶ 多年生草本植物,生长在池沼里,花单性,紫红色。嫩茎的基部经某种菌寄生后,膨大,做蔬菜吃,叫茭白。wild rice (*Zizania caduciflora*); perennial herbal plant with purplish red unisexual flower growing in water ponds or paddy fields. The base part of its tender stem becomes swollen after a certain kind of bacterium lives on it like a parasite and is an edible vegetable. It is generally called water wild rice; water wild rice stem ❷ same as 菇 gū

蛄 gū ☞ [蟪蛄] (huìgū) on p. 870 and 蝼蛄 lóugū on p. 1253
☞ gǔ on p. 695

菁 gū [菁葖] (gūtū) ❶ 果实的一种,由一个心皮构成,子房只有一个室,成熟时,果皮仅在一面裂开,如芍药、八角的果实 follicle; dry seed pod with a single cavity, that splits open along only one seam to release its seeds, as a Chinese peony, anise pod ❷ same as 骨朵儿 gū·duor

辜 gū ❶ 罪 crime; guilt: 无～ innocent | 死有余～ deserve to die many times for one's crimes; even death would be too good for him; even death would not expiate all his crimes ❷〈书 *fml.*〉背弃;违背 betray; go back on; turn one's back on to, renounce; go against: ～负 let down; disappoint, fail to live up to (one's expectations) | ～恩背义 be forgetful of all favours received; show ingratitude to sb. who has done favours ❸ (Gū)姓 a surname

【辜负】gūfù 对不住(别人的好意、期望或帮助) show ingratitude to (other's good will, expectations or help); let down; fail to live up to; be unworthy of; disappoint: 不～您的期望。We will never let you down. *or* We'll certainly live up to your expectations. also 孤负 gūfù

酤 gū 〈书 *fml.*〉❶ 薄酒;清酒 light wine; rice wine ❷ 买(酒) buy (wine) ❸ 卖(酒) sell (wine)

觚 gū ❶〈古代 *arch.*〉一种盛酒的器具 wine vessel wine vessel; beaker; goblet ❷〈古代 *arch.*〉写字用的木板 wooden writing tablet: 操～(写文章) writing a literary composition ❸〈书 *fml.*〉棱角 edges and corners

毂 gū [毂辘] (gū·lu) same as 轱辘 gū·lu
☞ gǔ on p. 697

箍 gū ❶ 用竹篾或金属条捆紧;用带子之类勒住 bind tightly with a bamboo strip or a metal strip; tie something with a ribbon; bind round; hoop: 用铁环～木桶 bind a wooden bucket with an iron hoop | 他头上～着条毛巾。He had a towel tied around his head. ❷ (～儿 gūr) 紧紧套在东西外面的圈儿 hoop wound tightly around something; hoop; band: 柱子上围了六七道金～。There are six or seven golden hoops around the pillar. | 左胳膊上带着红～儿。There is a red band around the left arm.

【箍眼】gū·yan 〈方 *dial.*〉 same as 眼罩 yǎnzhào ①

【箍嘴】gū·zui 〈方 *dial.*〉笼嘴 muzzle

gǔ (ㄍㄨˇ)

古 gǔ ❶ 古代(跟'今'相对 as opposed to the 'present'); ancient; ancient times; age-old; palaeo-：太～ too ancient | 厚今薄～ stress the present, not the past; emphasize the present, slight the past ❷ 经历多年的 passing many years：～画 ancient painting | ～城 an ancient city | 这座庙～得很。This temple is very old. ❸ 具有古代风格的 with an ancient style：～拙 primitive and crude | ～朴 simple and unsophisticated; of primitive simplicity ❹ 真挚纯朴 sincere and simple：人心不～。Public morality has degenerated. *or* Public morality is not what it used to be. ❺ 古体诗 ancient poetry：五～ five-character-line poem | 七～ seven-character-line poem ❻ (Gǔ) 姓 a surname

【古奥】gǔ'ào 古老深奥，难于理解（多指诗文 oft. of writing）too archaic and abstruse to be understood：行文～ an archaic and abstruse style of writing

【古板】gǔbǎn（思想、作风）固执守旧；呆板少变化（of idea, or style）old-fashioned; inflexible：为人～ unsophisticated; inactive; square; old-fashioned; conservative | 脾气～ old-fashioned and inflexible

【古代】gǔdài ❶ 过去距离现代较远的时代（区别于'近代、现代'）。在我国历史分期上多指 19 世纪中叶以前。period before the modern times and the present times (as opposed to 'modern'); period in Chinese history from remote antiquity down until the mid-19th century ❷ 特指奴隶社会时代（有时也包括原始公社时代）age of slave society (sometimes also including the primitive commune period); ancient times; antiquity

【古道热肠】gǔ dào rè cháng 指待人真挚、热情 sincere; warm-hearted; compassionate

【古典】gǔdiǎn ❶ 典故 classical allusion; literary quotation ❷ 古代流传下来的在一定时期认为正宗或典范的 classical：～哲学 classical philosophy | ～政治经济学 classical political economics

【古典文学】gǔdiǎn wénxué〈古代 *arch.*〉优秀的、典范的文学作品。也泛指古代的文学作品。classical literature; model literary works of ancient times; literary works of ancient times

【古典主义】gǔdiǎn zhǔyì 西欧文学艺术上的一个流派，盛行于 17 世纪，延续到 18 世纪后期。主要特点是模仿古希腊、罗马的艺术形式，尊重传统，崇尚理性，要求均衡、简洁，表现出反宗教权威的精神。但由于模拟多，创造少，不能反映现实。classicism; school of Western European literature and art, prevailing in the 17th century and lasting to the late 18th century, which imitates the artistic forms of ancient Greece and Rome; respects traditions, worships rationalism, calls for balance and simplicity, and opposes the authority of religion, but fails to reflect reality due to its preference of imitation to creativity

【古董】gǔdǒng ❶〈古代 *arch.*〉留传下来的器物，可供了解古代文化的参考 antique; curio; ancient utensils and implements left and uncovered for the understanding of the ancient culture ❷〈比喻 *fig.*〉过时的东西或顽固守旧的人 old-fashioned article or person; old fogey ‖ also 骨董 gǔdǒng

【古都】gǔdū 古代的都城 ancient capital ancient capital city：～洛阳 Luoyang, an ancient capital city

【古尔邦节】Gǔ'ěrbāng Jié 宰牲节 animal-slaughtering day; Islam Corban [古尔邦，阿拉伯 qurbān Corban, from the Arabic word qurbān]

【古方】gǔfāng（～儿 gǔfāngr）古代传下来的药方 ancient prescription; prescription passed down from ancient times

【古风】gǔfēng ❶ 古代的风俗习惯，多指质朴的生活作风 ancient customs; ancient practices; simple life style; antiquities：～犹存。Vestiges of ancient customs are still evident. ❷ same as 古体诗 gǔtǐshī

【古怪】gǔguài 跟一般情况很不相同，使人觉得诧异的；生疏罕见的 eccentric; odd; strange, rare：脾气～ eccentric disposition | 样子～ strange-looking; odd-looking

【古国】gǔguó 历史悠久的国家 country with a long history; ancient country

【古话】gǔhuà 流传下来的古人的话 old saying

【古籍】gǔjí same as 古书 gǔshū

【古迹】gǔjì 古代的遗迹，多指古代留传下来的建筑物 historic site; place of historic interest; ancient buildings：名胜～ famous scenic spots and places of historical interest

【古旧】gǔjiù 古老陈旧 old and worn out; antiquated; archaic：～建筑 ancient building

【古来】gǔlái 自古以来 since time immemorial

【古兰经】Gǔlánjīng 伊斯兰教的经典 *Koran*; sacred book of Islam [古兰，也译作可兰，阿拉伯 Qur'an：Qur'ān in Arabic and translated as 古兰 Gǔlán or 可兰 Kělán in Chinese]

【古老】gǔlǎo 经历了久远年代的 ancient; age-old：～的风俗 ancient (or old) customs | ～的民族 ancient nation

【古朴】gǔpǔ 朴素而有古代的风格 simple and ancient style (of art, architecture, etc.) simple and unsophisticated; of primitive simplicity：建筑风格～典雅。The architectural style is marked for its primitive simplicity and elegance. | 笔力苍劲～ bold and vigorous strokes with ancient and simple style

【古琴】gǔqín 我国很古就有的一种弦乐器，用梧桐等木料做成，有五根弦，后来增加为七根，沿用到现代 ancient Chinese stringed instrument made of parasol wood with five strings and later seven strings, which is still used today; also 七弦琴 qīxiánqín

【古人】gǔrén 泛指古代的人 ancients; our forefathers; ancient people

【古色古香】gǔ sè gǔ xiāng 形容富于古雅的色彩或情调 in graceful ancient colour and style

【古生物】gǔshēngwù 古代动物和古代植物的统称。古代生物的遗体有少数变成化石保存下来,如三叶虫、恐龙、猛犸等。ancient, extinct life; a general term for ancient animals and ancient plants; a few remains of the ancient life have been preserved in the form of fossils, such as trilobite, dinosaur and mammoth

【古诗】gǔshī ❶ same as 古体诗 gǔtǐshī ❷ 泛指古代诗歌 (in a broad sense) ancient poems and songs

【古书】gǔshū 古代的书籍或著作 ancient books or writings

【古体诗】gǔtǐshī 唐代以后指区别于近体诗(律诗、绝句)的一种诗体,有四言、五言、六言、七言等形式,句数没有限制,每句的字数也可以不齐,平仄和用韵都比较自由 a form of pre-Tang poetry with no restriction to the number of lines, each line having four, five, six or seven characters, or the number of characters differing from line to line in one poem, with a free use of tonal patterns and rhymes, as opposed to the 'modern-style' poetry innovated in and after the Tang Dynasty (618-907) with strict tonal patterns and rhyme schemes; also 古诗 gǔshī or 古风 gǔfēng

【古铜色】gǔtóngsè 像古代铜器的深褐色 dark brown colour similar to the ancient bronze ware; bronze-coloured; bronze

【古玩】gǔwán same as 古董 gǔdǒng ①

【古往今来】gǔ wǎng jīn lái 从古代到现在 from ancient times till today; since time immemorial; of all ages; throughout the ages; from time immemorial: 他记得许多～的故事。He remembers many stories of all ages.

【古文】gǔwén ❶ 五四以前的文言文的统称(一般不包括'骈文') general term for the proses written in the classical Chinese literary style before the May Fourth Movement in 1919 (not including the rhythmical proses marked by parallelism and ornateness) ❷ 汉代通行隶书,因此把秦以前的字体叫做古文,特指许慎《说文解字》里的古文(reference in *Discourses on Words and Explanations of Characters* by Xu Sheng) Chinese script used before the Qin Dynasty(221-206 B.C.), different from the official script current in the Han Dynasty (206 B.C.- A.D. 220)

【古文字】gǔwénzì 古代的文字。在我国指古代传下的篆文体系的文字,特指秦以前的文字,如甲骨文和金文。ancient writing, especially pre-Qin writings, such as the inscriptions on bones or tortoise shells of the Shang Dynasty (c.16th-11th century B.C.) and inscriptions on ancient bronze objects

【古物】gǔwù 古代的器物 ancient objects; antiquities

【古昔】gǔxī 〈书 *fml*.〉古时候 ancient times

【古稀】gǔxī 指人七十岁(源于杜甫《曲江》诗句'人生七十古来稀') seventy years of age (Source: 'Man is old enough when he gets on seventy', a line from the poem *Qu Jiang* by Du Fu, a poet of the Tang Dynasty): 年近～ approaching seventy; getting on for seventy

【古训】gǔxùn 指古代流传下来的、可以作为准则的话 old maxim; ancient teachings; teachings passed down from ancient times

【古雅】gǔyǎ 古朴雅致(多指器物或诗文 of material, things, literary works, etc.) of classic beauty and in elegant taste; of classic elegance; of classical simplicity and elegance: 这套瓷器很～。This chinaware is of classical simplicity and elegance.

【古谚】gǔyàn 古代流传下来的谚语 old proverb; proverbs from ancient times: 中国有句～,只要功夫深,铁杵磨成针。An old Chinese proverb says: As long as you work hard, even an iron rod can be ground into a needle.

【古音】gǔyīn ❶ 泛指古代的语音(in a broad sense) ancient speech sounds ❷ 专指周秦时期的语音 speech sounds in the Zhou and Qin Dynasties (11th century-206 B.C.)

☞ 今音 jīnyīn on p.1003

【古语】gǔyǔ ❶ 古代的词语 ancient words; archaism: 书中个别～加了注释。Annotations are given for archaisms in a few cases in the book. ❷ 古话 old saying: ～说,满招损,谦受益。An old saying goes: Arrogance invites losses while modesty brings benefits. *or* One loses by pride and gains by modesty.

【古筝】gǔzhēng 弦乐器,木制长形。唐宋时有十三根弦,后增至十六根,现发展到二十五根弦。*guzheng*; long stringed instrument made of wood, with 13 strings in the Tang and Song Dynasties (618-1279), 16 later, and 25 now; also 筝 zhēng

【古装】gǔzhuāng 古代式样的服装 (跟'时装'相对 as opposed to 'fashion') ancient costume; ancient style of clothing: ～戏 operas in which the actors and actresses wear ancient costumes

【古拙】gǔzhuō 古朴少修饰 looking ancient in an unaffected way; primitive crudity: 这幅画气韵～,可能出自名家之手。The painting is of primitive simplicity and it might have been done by a famous painter. | 这个石刻虽然形式～,但是很有艺术价值。Though primitive and crude in form, this stone carving has very high artistic value.

谷[1] gǔ ❶ 两山或两块高地中间的狭长而有出口的地带(特别是当中有水道的) narrow and long stretch of low-lying land between

G

mountains or hills and usually having a river or stream flowing through it; valley; gorge: 万丈深～ a very deep valley ❷ (Gǔ)姓 a surname

谷[2](**穀**) gǔ ❶ 谷类作物 cereal crops: 百～ all kinds of grain | 五～杂粮 five cereals ❷ 谷子(粟) millet: ～草 millet straw; rice straw | ～穗儿 the ear of rice or millet ❸〈方 *dial*.〉稻或稻谷 unhusked rice ☞ yù on p. 2348

【谷草】gǔcǎo ❶ 谷子(粟)脱粒后的秆,可做饲料 hollow stalks or stems of grain after threshing for fodder; millet straw ❷〈方 *dial*.〉稻草 rice stalks; rice straw

【谷底】gǔdǐ〈比喻 *fig*.〉下降到的最低点;升降中的最低限度 drop to the lowest point; minimum limit for rise or fall: 产品销售量大幅度下降,目前已跌至～。Sales have dropped by a big margin to an all-time low.

【谷地】gǔdì 地面上向一定方向倾斜的低洼地。如山谷、河谷。valley; dale; low-lying land sloping in a certain direction, such as a mountain valley, a river valley

【谷坊】gǔfáng 在沟底修筑的小水坝,用来调整坡度,减缓流速,防止沟底被冲刷 water conservancy dam; small dam built at the bottom of a gully to adjust the gradient, retard the flow and prevent erosion of the bottom

【谷风】gǔfēng 气象学上指白天从谷底吹向山顶的风(meteorol.) wind from a valley blowing to the top of the mountain at daytime

【谷类作物】gǔlèi zuòwù 稻、麦、谷子、高粱、玉米等作物的统称 general term for rice, wheat, millet, sorghum, maize, etc.; cereal crops

【谷神星】gǔshénxīng 太阳系中最大的小行星,直径约 1,000 公里 Ceres; the largest minor planet in the solar system, its diameter being 1,000 km.

【谷物】gǔwù ❶ 谷类作物的子实 seeds of cereal crops; cereal; grain ❷ 谷类作物的通称 general term for the cereal crops

【谷雨】gǔyǔ 二十四节气之一,在 4 月 19,20 或 21 日 Grain Rain; one of the 24 solar terms, falling on April 19, 20 or 21; ☞ 节气 jié·qì on p. 989 and 二十四节气 èrshísì jiéqì on p. 516

【谷子】gǔ·zi ❶ 一年生草本植物,茎直立,叶子条状披针形,有毛,穗状圆锥花序,子实圆形或椭圆形,脱壳后叫小米,是我国北方的粮食作物 millet (*Setaria*); annual herbal plant with a vertical stalk, hairy linear leaves, panicle inflorescence, round or oval seeds; a grain crop in northern China; also 粟 sù ❷ 谷子的没有去壳的子实 unhusked grain; also 粟 sù ❸〈方 *dial*.〉稻的没有去壳的子实 unhusked rice

汩 gǔ〈书 *fml*.〉水流的样子(of running water) gurgle; water gurgles

【汩汩】gǔgǔ 水流动的声音或样子 sound of gurgling water or the way water gurgles: 水车又转动了,河水～地流入田里。The waterwheel is working again, bringing gurgling water from the river into the fields.

【汩没】gǔmò〈书 *fml*.〉埋没 bury; submerge; drown; cover up

诂 gǔ 用通行的话解释古代语言文字或方言字义 explain archaic or dialectal words in current language; use current language to annotate archaic or dialectic works in ancient books: 训～ explanations of words in ancient books | 解～ explanatory notes in ancient books

股[1] gǔ ❶ 大腿 thigh; (图见☞ figure for 身体 shēntǐ on p. 1701) ❷ 某些机关、企业、团体中的组织单位 organizational unit of an office, enterprise or organization (of an office, enterprise, etc.); section: 总务～ general affairs section | 人事～ personnel section ❸ (～儿 gǔr)绳线等的组成部分 component part of a string or thread; strand; ply: 三～儿绳 three-strand rope | 把线捻成～儿。Twist threads into yarn. ❹ (～儿 gǔr)集合资金的一份或一笔财物平均分配的一份 share in a pool of capital or one of several equal parts of property; share in a company or one of several equal parts of property: ～份 a share | 分～ divide into equal parts | 按～均分,每～五百元。Divide equally by share, five hundred yuan for each share. ❺ (～儿 gǔr)〈量词 *classifier*〉a) 用于成条的东西 [for a long and narrow thing]: 一～线 a skein of thread | 一～泉水 a stream of spring water | 上山有两～道。There are two paths up the hill b) 用于气体、气味、力气等 [for gas, smell, strength]: 一～热气 a gush (flow, stream or puff) of hot air | 一～香味 a whiff of fragrance | 一～劲 a burst of energy c) 用于成批的人 [for a group of people]: 两～土匪 two gangs of bandits | 一～敌军 a horde of enemy soldiers; an enemy detachment

股[2] gǔ 我国古代称不等腰直角三角形中较长的直角边 old term for the longer leg of a right triangle

【股本】gǔběn 股份公司用发行股票方式组成的资本。也指其他合伙经营的工商企业的资本或资金。capital stock; capital pooled by a stock company in the form of issuing stocks; capital or funds of an industrial or commercial enterprise pooled by other means

【股东】gǔdōng 股份公司的股票持有人,有权出席股东大会并有表决权。也指其他合伙经营的工商企业的投资人。shareholder; stockholder; holder of a stock from a stock company, who has rights to attend meetings of stockholders and to vote; investor who contributes a fund to an industrial or commercial enterprise

【股匪】gǔfěi 成批的土匪 gangs of bandits

【股分】gǔfèn same as 股份 gǔfèn

【股份】gǔfèn ❶ 股份公司或其他合伙经营的资本单位 share; stock; unit of capital owned by a stock company or other collectively owned businesses ❷ 投入消费合作社的资金的单位 unit of capital fund put into a consumers' cooperative ‖ also 股分 gǔfèn

【股份公司】gǔfèngōngsī 集股经营的企业,公司获得的利润按各个股东拥有的股票额分配 stock company or joint-stock enterprise, with profits distributed proportionately among shareholders

【股份制】gǔfènzhì 以投资入股或认购股票的方式联合起来的企业财产组织形式,按股权多少进行收入分配 joint-stock system; organizational form of enterprise property pooled in the form of investing in stocks or subscribing stocks, its income being distributed by the ownership of stock shares

【股肱】gǔgōng〈书 *fml.*〉〈比喻 *fig.*〉左右辅助得力的人 right-hand man

【股骨】gǔgǔ 大腿中的长骨,是全身最长的骨,上端跟髋骨相连,下端跟胫骨相连 thigh bone; femur; long bone in the thigh; the longest bone in the human body connecting the hip bone above and the shin bone below;(图见 ☞ figure for 骨骼 gǔgé on p. 693)

【股金】gǔjīn 投入股份制企业或消费合作社中的股份资金 money paid to a stock company or a consumers' cooperative for shares; money paid for shares

【股利】gǔlì same as 股息 gǔxī

【股票】gǔpiào 用来表示股份的证券 share; stock; certificate for a stock; share certificate

【股市】gǔshì ❶ 买卖股票的市场 stock market: 香港～ Hong Kong Stock Market ❷ 指股票的行市 stock market quotations; current prices of stocks:～暴跌。The stock prices fall drastically.

【股息】gǔxī 股份公司按照股票的数量分给各股东的利润 dividend profit divided among the stockholders on the basis of their ownership of shares; also 股利 gǔlì

【股子】gǔ·zi same as 股[1] gǔ ⑤

骨 gǔ ❶ same as 骨头 gǔ·tou ① ❷〈比喻 *fig.*〉在物体内部支撑的架子 skeleton; framework: 钢～水泥 reinforced concrete | 船的龙～ keel ❸ 品质;气概 quality; character; spirit:～气 moral integrity | 媚～ obsequiousness | 傲～ lofty and unyielding character | 侠～ chivalrous spirit

☞ gū on p. 689

【骨刺】gǔcì 骨头上增生的针状物,通常引起疼痛或其他神经系统症状 spur; spine-like outgrowth of bone, usually causing pain or other symptoms in the nervous system

【骨董】gǔdǒng same as 古董 gǔdǒng

【骨朵】gǔduǒ〈古代 *arch.*〉兵器,用铁或硬木制成,像长棍子,顶端瓜形。后来只用做仪仗,叫金瓜。weapon made of iron or hard wood in the form of a long stick with a melon-shaped head. It was later used by guard of honour and called golden melon.

【骨干】gǔgàn ❶ 长骨的中央部分,两端跟骨骺相连,里面是空腔 shaft of a long bone with a cavity, linked with the epiphysis at both ends;(图见 ☞ figure for 骨头 gǔ·tou) ❷〈比喻 *fig.*〉在总体中起主要作用的人或事物 backbone, mainstay:～分子 core member; key member; key element | ～企业 key enterprise | 业务～ key member of a professional staff; key member of a business staff; backbone; mainstay

【骨骼】gǔgé 人或动物体内或体表坚硬的组织。分两种,人和高等动物的骨骼在体内,由许多块骨头组成,叫内骨骼;节肢动物、软体动物体外的硬壳以及某些脊椎动物(如鱼、龟等)体表的鳞、甲等叫外骨骼。通常说的骨骼指内骨骼。skeleton; hard skeleton inside or outside the body of a human being or an animal. There are two kinds of skeleton: the skeleton of a human being or other higher animals inside the body, which consists of many bones, is known as endoskeleton, and the hard shells outside the body of arthropod or mollusc and scales of some vertebrate animals (such as fish and tortoise) are called exoskeleton. The skeleton we speak of usually refers to endoskeleton.

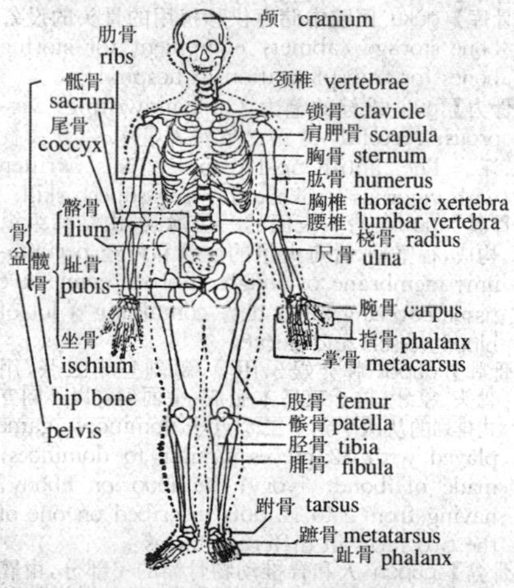

人的骨骼 Human Bone Structure

【骨鲠】gǔgěng〈书 *fml.*〉❶ 鱼骨头 formal fishbone:～在喉 have a fishbone caught in the throat ❷ 耿直 upright; honest and frank;

G

～之气 the moral integrity of an upright official|～之臣 upright official

【骨鲠在喉】gǔgěng zài hóu 鱼骨头卡在喉咙里 having a fishbone caught in one's throat;〈比喻 *fig.*〉心里有话没说出来,非常难受 cannot rest until one speaks out one's mind:～,不吐不快。As if a fishbone has got stuck in my throat, (I) cannot rest until I speak out my mind.

【骨骺】gǔhóu 长骨两端的部分 epiphysis; end part of a long bone which is at first separated from the main part by cartilage, but later fuses with it by ossification; also 骺 hóu;(图见 ☞ figure for 骨头 gǔ·tou)

【骨灰】gǔhuī ❶ 人焚化后骨骼烧成的灰 bone ash; ashes of the dead ❷ 动物骨头烧成的灰,成分以磷酸钙为主,是制磷和过磷酸钙的原料,又可直接用做肥料 bone ash. The composition of animal bone ashes is mainly calcium phosphate, a raw material for making phosphate and calcium superphosphate and also used directly as a fertilizer.

【骨架】gǔjià 骨头架子 skeleton;〈比喻 *fig.*〉在物体内部支撑的架子 framework inside an object:这种猪的～大,而且瘦肉率很高。This kind of pig has a big skeleton and produces a higher percentage of lean meat.|工地上耸立着房屋的～。The framework of a house stands on the construction site.

【骨胶】gǔjiāo 用动物的骨头熬成的胶状物质,可以做黏合剂 bone glue; adhesive matter prepared by boiling from animal bones; adhesive

【骨节】gǔjié 骨头的关节 joints of bones

【骨库】gǔkù 医院中储存供移植用的骨头的设备 bone storage cabinet; equipment for storing bones for transplantation in hospital

【骨力】gǔlì 雄健的笔力 (of handwriting) vigorous; forceful:这副对联写得很有～,功夫很深。The antithetical couplet was written with vigorous strokes, showing superb skill.

【骨膜】gǔmó 骨头表面的一层薄膜,由结缔组织构成,很坚韧,含有大量的血管和神经 periosteum; membrane of tough, fibrous connective tissue covering all bones, containing a lot of blood vessels and nerves

【骨牌】gǔpái 牌类娱乐用具,每副三十二张,用骨头、象牙、竹子或乌木制成,上面刻着以不同方式排列的从两个到十二个点子 dominoes; game played with 32 pieces similar to dominoes, made of bone, ivory, bamboo or ebony, having from 2 to 12 dots inscribed on one of the two faces in different forms

【骨盆】gǔpén 人和脊椎动物骨骼的一部分,由髋骨、骶骨和尾骨组成,形状像盆,有支撑脊柱和保护膀胱等脏器的作用 pelvis; part of the skeleton of a human being or vertebrate animal, composed of the hip bone, sacrum and coccyx in the shape of a basin, supporting the spinal column and protecting the bladder;(图见 ☞ figure for 骨骼 gǔgé)

【骨气】gǔqì ❶ 刚强不屈的气概 unyielding spirit; strength of character; moral integrity:他是个有～的人,宁死也不向恶势力低头。He is a man of integrity and would rather die than yield to a vicious force. ❷ 书法所表现的雄健的气势 powerful strength displayed in calligraphy; strength of calligraphic strokes:他的字写得很有～。His hand writing shows strength in the strokes. *or* His hand writing is very powerful.

【骨肉】gǔròu ❶ 指父母兄弟子女等亲人 flesh and blood; kindred, parents, brothers, sisters and children:～之情 kindred feelings|～团聚 a family reunion|亲生～ one's own flesh and blood; blood relations; one's own children ❷〈比喻 *fig.*〉紧密相连,不可分割的关系 close relations:亲如～ as close as flesh and blood|情同～ kindred feelings

【骨殖】gǔ·shi 尸骨 skeleton (of a human body after decomposition)

【骨瘦如柴】gǔ shòu rú chái 形容非常瘦(多用于人) (of person) extremely thin; reduced to mere shadow lean as a rake; worn to a shadow; mere skeleton; bag of bones; be/become concentration-camp thin

【骨髓】gǔsuǐ 骨头空腔中柔软像胶的物质 marrow; soft, vascular, fatty tissue that fills the cavities of most bones;(图见 ☞ figure for 骨头 gǔ·tou)

【骨炭】gǔtàn 把兽骨密闭、加热、脱脂所得的活性炭,能吸收溶液中的杂质 bone black; animal charcoal; active carbon obtained after heating and degreasing animal bones in airtight condition, and absorbing impurities in the solution

【骨头】gǔ·tou ❶ 人和脊椎动物体内支持身体、保护内脏的坚硬组织,主要成分是炭酸钙和磷酸钙。根据形状的不同,分为长骨、短骨、扁骨等。bone; hard tissue in the body of a human being and vertebrate animals supporting the body and protecting the internal organs, its main composition being calcium carbonate and calcium phosphate; there are long bones, short bones and flat bones ❷〈比喻 *fig.*〉人的品质 character of a person:懒～ lazy bone|硬～ man of great moral integrity ❸〈方 *dial.*〉〈比喻 *fig.*〉话里暗含的不满、讽刺等意思 bitterness; sting:话里有～ a bite to the words

骨骺 epiphysis
骨髓 marrow
骨干 shaft bone
骨骺 epiphysis

骨头 Bone

【骨头架子】gǔ tou·jià·zi ❶ 人或高等动物的骨骼 skeleton of a human being or higher animal ❷ 形容极瘦的人 very thin person

【骨头节儿】gǔ·toujiér〈方 *dial.*〉same as 骨节 gǔjié

【骨血】gǔxuè 骨肉①（多指子女等后代 usu. of one's offspring）flesh and blood：她确是这对夫妇的亲～。She is really the couple's biological child.

【骨折】gǔzhé 由于外伤或骨组织的病变，骨头折断、变成碎块或发生裂纹 bone fracture; break; crack or split in a bone caused by an injury or pathological changes in the bone tissues

【骨子】gǔ·zi 东西里面起支撑作用的架子 frame in an object supporting it; frame; ribs：伞～ umbrella frame; ribs of an umbrella | 扇～ ribs of a fan | 钢条扎成的～ frame made of steel rods

【骨子里】gǔ·zilǐ ❶〈比喻 *fig.*〉内心或实质上 in one's innermost feelings; in substance; in the bones; beneath the surface：他表面上不动声色，～却早有打算。He looked indifferent, but at heart he had his own calculations. ❷〈方 *dial.*〉〈比喻 *fig.*〉私人之间 private, secret：这是他们～的事，你不用管。This is their private affair; don't bother about it. also 骨子里头 gǔ·zi lǐ·tou

牯 gǔ same as 牯牛 gǔniú

【牯牛】gǔniú 公牛 bull

贾 gǔ ❶ 商人（古时'贾'指坐商，'商'指行商）merchant (in ancient times, 贾 *gu* means 'shopkeeper'; 商 *shang* means 'travelling merchant')：商～ merchants | 书～ book dealer; bookseller ❷ 做买卖 do business; engage in trade：多财善～ rich and having business acumen ❸〈书 *fml.*〉买 buy：～马 buy a horse ❹〈书 *fml.*〉招致；招引 bring on; invite; incur; court：～祸 court disaster; invite or bring on trouble, calamity or misfortune; invite trouble ❺〈书 *fml.*〉卖 sell; afford：余勇可～ with courage to spare; very courageous or brave

☞ Jiǎ on p. 932

【贾祸】gǔhuò〈书 *fml.*〉招来祸害 court disaster; invite or bring on trouble, calamity or misfortune; invite trouble：骄贪～ Arrogance and greed invite trouble (or disaster).

【贾人】gǔrén〈书 *fml.*〉做买卖的人 merchant; trader; businessman

眝 gǔ〈方 *dial.*〉瞪大眼睛（表示不满 expressing displeasure）glare

罟 gǔ〈书 *fml.*〉❶ 捕鱼的网 fishnet ❷ 用网捕鱼 fishing with a net

钴 gǔ 金属元素，符号 Co (cobaltum)。银白色，用来制合金和瓷器釉料等，医学上用放射性钴(Co^{60})治疗恶性肿瘤。cobalt (Co); metallic element, silver white, used in the preparation of high-strength alloys, paints and varnishes; steel-grey; a radioactive isotope cobalt-60 (Co^{60}) is used for the treatment of cancer, in research, etc.

【钴鉧】gǔmǔ〈书 *fml.*〉熨斗 iron; flat iron

【钴炮】gǔpào 指用放射性(Co^{60})进行放射治疗的装置 apparatus for radioactive treatment with cobalt-60

羖(羖) gǔ〈书 *fml.*〉公羊 ram

蛄 gǔ ☞ 蝲蛄 làgǔ on p. 1141 and 蝲蝲蛄 làlàgǔ on p. 1141

☞ gū on p. 689

蛊(蠱) gǔ〈古代 *arch.*〉传说把许多毒虫放在器皿里使互相吞食，最后剩下不死的毒虫叫蛊，用来放在食物里害人 *gu*; legendary venomous insect. Legend has it that someone had put many venomous insects in a utensil so that they ate each other and mixed the one that survived, called *gu*, with food to harm people.

【蛊惑】gǔhuò 毒害；迷惑 poison and bewitch; bewitch; confuse：～人心 confuse people; poison the minds of people; resort to demagogy; also 鼓惑 gǔhuò

鹄 gǔ〈书 *fml.*〉射箭的目标；箭靶子 target (in archery)：中～ hit the target

☞ hú on p. 819

【鹄的】gǔdì〈书 *fml.*〉❶ 箭靶子的中心；练习射击的目标 bull's eye; target; centre of the target; target for practise shooting：三发连中～ All the three shots hit the target. ❷ 目的 purpose; aim

馉 gǔ [馉饳](gǔduò) 古时一种面制食品 a kind of food made of wheat flour in ancient times

鼓 gǔ ❶（～儿 gǔr）打击乐器，多为圆筒形或扁圆形，中间空，一面或两面蒙着皮革 percussion instrument consisting of a hollow cylinder or hemisphere with a membrane stretched tightly over the end or ends, played by beating with the hands, sticks, etc drum：铜～ bronze drum | 手～ small drum similar to tambourine played by hands | 花～ flower-drum dance, a folk dance popular in the Yangtze River valley ❷ 形状、声音、作用像鼓的 shape, sound etc. of a drum; thing like a drum：石～ drum-shaped stone | 蛙～ frog drummers (or croaks) | 耳～ eardrum ❸ 使某些乐器或东西发出声音；敲 sound produced by some instruments or things; beat：～琴 play the zither | ～掌 clap hands ❹ 用风箱等扇（风）blow with bellows, etc.：～风 work a bellows; blow with bellows, etc. ❺ 发动；振奋 rouse; agitate：～动 agitate; arouse | ～励 encourage; urge; inspire | ～舞 inspire; encourage; hearten | ～起勇气 pluck up one's courage rouse ❻ 凸起；涨大 bulge; swell：他～着嘴半天没出声。He gaped for a long time without uttering a word.|口袋装得～～的 fill one's pockets till they bulge

【鼓包】gǔ//bāo (～儿 gǔbāor)物体或身体上鼓起疙瘩 swelling on an object or a human body; bulge; swell: 他的脸上鼓了一个包儿。There is a swelling on his face.

【鼓包】gǔbāo (～儿 gǔbāor)物体或身体上的凸起物 a protrusion on an object or on a human body; swelling; lump; bump; bulge; swell: 头上碰了个～。There was a lump on his head after he bumped into something.

【鼓吹】gǔchuī ❶ 宣传提倡 advocate; preach; publicise advocate: ～革命 advocate revolution ❷ 吹嘘 boast; brag; preach; advertise; play up; lavish praise on oneself or others: ～自己如何如何 self-praise

【鼓捣】gǔ·dao〈方 *dial.*〉❶ 反复摆弄 tinker with; fiddle with: 他一边同我谈话，一边～收音机。He toyed with his radio as he talked with me. ❷ 挑拨；设法支使 instigate; egg on; incite; egg on: 一定是他～你去干的。He must have incited you to do it.

【鼓点】gǔdiǎn (～儿 gǔdiǎnr) ❶ 打鼓时的音响节奏 drumbeat ❷ 戏曲中的鼓板的节奏，用来指挥其他乐器 clapper beats which set the tempo and lead the orchestra in traditional Chinese operas ‖ also 鼓点子 gǔdiǎn·zi

【鼓动】gǔdòng ❶ 扇动 fan; flap: 小鸟～翅膀。The bird flaps its wings. ❷ 用语言、文字等激发人们的情绪，使他们行动起来 gird sb. into action with rhetorics; agitate; arouse: 宣传～ propaganda and agitation|经他一～，不少人都去学习气功了。Many people started learning *qigong* through his agitation.

【鼓风机】gǔfēngjī 产生气流的机械，常见的是在蜗牛状的外壳里装着叶轮，用于各种炉灶的送风，建筑物和矿井的通风、排气等 air-blower; blower; mechanical device for producing a current of air; sth. shaped like a snail with vanes inside an outer covering, used to blow air into furnaces, or for ventilation in buildings and for exhaust in mines; also 风机 fēngjī

【鼓风炉】gǔfēnglú 装有鼓风装置的冶炼炉，多用来炼铜、锡、镍等。冶炼炉的鼓风装置也叫鼓风炉。blast furnace; furnace with a blowing device for refining copper, tin, nickel, etc.; also 鼓风炉 gǔfēnglú

【鼓鼓囊囊】gǔ·gunāngnāng (～的 gǔgunāngnāng·de)形容口袋、包裹等填塞得凸起的样子 (of pocket or parcel) bulging: 背包装得～的。The backpack is bulging.

【鼓惑】gǔhuò same as 蛊惑 gǔhuò

【鼓角】gǔjiǎo〈古代 *arch.*〉军队中用来发出号令的战鼓和号角 battle drums and horns, used in an army in ancient times for issuing orders: ～齐鸣。Battle drums were beaten and horns were blown simultaneously.

【鼓劲】gǔ//jìn (～儿 gǔ//jìnr)鼓动情绪，使振作起来；鼓起劲来 rouse one's enthusiasm; brace up: 互相～ encourage each other

【鼓励】gǔlì 激发；勉励 arouse; encourage; urge: 车间主任～大家努力完成增产指标。The workshop director encouraged all to work hard to fulfil the increased production target. |大家的赞扬给了他很大的～。The praises gave him tremendous encouragement.

【鼓楼】gǔlóu drum tower〈旧时 *old*〉城市中设置大鼓的楼，楼内按时敲鼓报告时辰 drum tower in a city, beaten to announce time once in every two hours and twelve times a day

【鼓膜】gǔmó 外听道和中耳之间的薄膜，由纤维组织构成，椭圆形，半透明。内表面与听骨相连，外界的声波震动鼓膜，使听骨发生振动。tympanic membrane; eardrum; thin oval, translucent membrane of fibre tissues, that separates the middle ear from the external ear and vibrates when struck by sound waves; also 耳鼓 ěrgǔ and 耳膜 ěrmó; (图见 ☞ figure for 耳朵 ěr·duo on p. 512)

【鼓弄】gǔ·nong 摆弄 play with; fiddle with; tinker with: 这孩子就喜欢～积木。This child likes to play with building blocks.

【鼓儿词】gǔrcí 大鼓的唱词 lyrics to *dagu* (big drum), a folk singing tune

【鼓舌】gǔ//shé 卖弄口舌，多指花言巧语 wag the tongue (esp. in honeyed talk): 鼓其如簧之舌 talk glibly; wag one's tongue|摇唇～ instigate by talking; incite someone to do evil things by honeyed talk

【鼓师】gǔshī 戏曲乐队中敲击板鼓的人 person in a Chinese opera band who keeps on beating a small drum with two thin sticks; conductor of a Chinese opera band who keeps time on a small drum with two thin drumsticks

【鼓室】gǔshì 中耳的一部分，位于鼓膜和内耳之间，是一个不规则的含气空腔 tympanum; part of the middle ear between the tympanic membrane and the internal ear; irregular cavity with air

【鼓手】gǔshǒu 乐队中打鼓的人 drum player

【鼓书】gǔshū 大鼓(曲艺的一种) *gushu*, versified story sung to the accompaniment of a small drum and other instruments

【鼓舞】gǔwǔ ❶ 使振作起来，增强信心或勇气 inspire; encourage; hearten; brace up: ～人心 encouraging; inspiring; heartening|～士气 boost the morale of the soldiers ❷ 兴奋；振作 exciting; pull oneself together: 令人～ inspiring|欢欣～ be overjoyed; be elated; filled with joy

【鼓乐】gǔyuè 敲鼓声和奏乐声 strains of music to the accompaniment of drumbeats: ～齐鸣 the simultaneous playing of instruments and singing; crescendos of music|～喧天 deafening sounds of musical instruments

【鼓噪】gǔzào〈古代 *arch.*〉指出战时擂鼓呐喊,以壮声势。今泛指喧嚷。roars of drum beating and shouting during battles in ancient times; uproar; make an uproar; raise a hubbub; clamour: ～一时 make a great to-do about sth.

【鼓掌】gǔ//zhǎng 拍手,多表示高兴、赞成或欢迎 clap one's hands to express joy, approval or welcome; applaud: 当中央首长进入会场时,代表们热烈～,表示欢迎。When leaders of the central authorities appeared in the conference hall, the delegates applauded warmly to express their welcome.

【鼓胀】gǔzhàng ❶ 凸起;胀起 bulge; swell: 手背上暴出几条～的青筋。Blue veins stood out on the back of his hand. ❷〈中医 *Chin. med.*〉指由水、气、淤血、寄生虫等原因引起的腹部膨胀的病 tympanites; distension of the abdomen caused by accumulation of fluid, gas or air, or by stasis or parasites; also 膨胀 péngzhàng

轂 gǔ 车轮的中心部分,有圆孔,可以插轴 hub with a round hole for the shaft; (图见 ☞ figure for 轮子 lúnzi on p.1275)

☞ gū on p.689

榾 gǔ [榾柮](gǔduò)〈方 *dial.*〉木头块;树根墩子 wood block; stump

縠 gǔ ☞ 楮 chǔ ① on p.293

嘏 gǔ, 又 also jiǎ〈书 *fml.*〉福 good luck; good fortune; happiness

鹘 gǔ [鹘鸼](gǔzhōu) 古书上说的一种鸟 *guzhou*, bird described in ancient books

☞ hú on p.820

穀[1] gǔ〈书 *fml.*〉❶ 善;好 good: ～旦(吉利的日子) auspicious day ❷ 俸禄 official's salary

穀[2] gǔ same as 谷[2] gǔ

薣 gǔ [薣子](gǔ·zi) 烹饪用具,周围陡直的深锅,一般用沙土烧制,也有铁制的 cooking utensil; deep pot with a straight round wall, usually made of earth or iron: 沙～ earthenware pot | 瓷～ ceramic pot

臌 gǔ 鼓胀 bulge; swell: 水～ dropsy | 气～ distension of the abdomen caused by accumulation of gas due to dysfunction of the spleen or to emotional factors

【臌胀】gǔzhàng same as 鼓胀 gǔzhàng ②

瞽 gǔ〈书 *fml.*〉眼睛瞎 blind: ～者 blind person ❷ 指没有识别能力的 lacking discernment: ～说(不达事理的言论) stupidities

【瞽言】gǔyán〈书 *fml.*〉没有根据或不合情理的话(多用作谦辞 oft. hum.) groundless or unreasonable talk (words): ～刍议 my groundless talk and humble opinion

盬 gǔ〈书 *fml.*〉❶ 盐池 salt pond ❷ 不坚固 infirm, not strong, not solid ❸ 停止 stop, cease

濲 gǔ 濲水(Gǔshuǐ),地名,在湖南 Gushui, a geographical name in Hunan Province; also 谷水 Gǔshuǐ

gù(ㄍㄨˋ)

估 gù [估衣](gù·yi) 出售的旧衣服或原料较次、加工较粗的新衣服 second-hand clothes or new clothes badly tailored and made of inferior quality: ～铺 second-hand clothes shop

☞ gū on p.686

固[1] gù ❶ 结实;牢固 solid; firm; strong: 稳～ solid; firm; stable | 本～枝荣。When the root is firm, the branches flourish. | 基础已～。The foundation is solid. | 大堤要加高、加宽、加～。The dam will be heightened, widened and strengthened. ❷ 坚硬 solid; hard: ～体 solid; solid body | 凝～ solidify; consolidate; strengthen ❸ 坚决地;坚定地 firmly; steadfastly; determinedly; resolutely: ～辞 flatly refuse; firmly decline; resolutely refuse | ～请 insistent request; insistently request | ～守阵地 defend one's position tenaciously ❹ 使坚固 solidify: ～本 solidify the foundation | ～防 strengthen the defensive position ❺〈书 *fml.*〉鄙陋 ill-informed; ignorant: ～陋 ignorant; ill-informed ❻ same as 痼 gù: ～疾 chronic disease | ～习 inveterate habit ❼ (Gù)姓 a surname

固[2] gù〈书 *fml.*〉❶ 本来;原来 originally; in the first place; at first; as a matter of course: ～有 intrinsic; inherent | ～当如此。It should have been so. *or* It is just as it should be. | ～所愿也。It was my old wish. *or* It was just as I originally wished. ❷ 固然 true; it is true that: 坐车～可,坐船亦无不可。True, we can take the train, but we can also take the boat. *or* True, we can go by bus, but we can also go by sea.

【固步自封】gù bù zì fēng same as 故步自封 gù bù zì fēng

【固辞】gùcí〈书 *fml.*〉坚决推辞 resolutely refuse; flatly refuse; firmly decline: ～不就 resolutely refuse to take a post

【固氮】gùdàn 植物通过微生物的作用把空气中的氮转变为植物可以吸收和利用的氨或其他含氮有机物 nitrogen fixation; conversion of atmospheric nitrogen into ammonia or other nitrogeous compounds by bacteria found in the root nodules of legumes and certain other plants, and in the soil

【固定】gùdìng ❶ 不变动或不移动的(跟'流动'相对 as opposed to 'mobile') fixed; regular; not changeable or not movable: ～职业 permanent job | ～资产 fixed assets ❷ 使固定 fix; regularize: 把学习制度～下来 establish a regular schooling system

【固定汇率】gùdìng huìlǜ 指兑换比例只能根据国际协定的规定,在官价上下限的幅度内波动的汇率 fixed (exchange) rate; exchange rate that can fluctuate between the ceiling and the bottom of an official price fixed under an international agreement

【固定价格】gùdìng jiàgé 不变价格 fixed price; constant price

【固定资产】gùdìng zīchǎn 单位价值在规定限额以上,使用期限在一年以上,能作为劳动资料或其他用途的财产,例如厂矿、企业、机关、学校中的房屋、机器、运输设备、家具、图书等(跟'流动资产'相对 as opposed to 'circulating assets') fixed assets; property with its unit value above the set quota and a use period of one year or longer, which can be used as means of labour or for other purposes, such as premises, machinery, transport equipment, furniture, books, etc.

【固定资金】gùdìng zījīn 企业用于购置机器设备、运输工具和其他耐用器材以及修建厂房、职工住宅等的资金。按用途可分为生产固定资金和非生产固定资金(跟'流动资金'相对 as opposed to 'circulation funds') fixed funds; fixed capital; funds with which an enterprise buys machinery, means of transport and other durables or can build premises and workers' housing estates; in two categories: fixed funds for production and fixed funds for non-production

【固陋】gùlòu〈书 *fml.*〉见闻不广 ignorant; ill-informed; provincial

【固然】gùrán〈连词 *conj.*〉❶ 表示承认某个事实,引起下文转折[admitting a certain fact for transition in the context] though; of course; admittedly; no doubt; it is true:这样办~稳当,但是太费事,怕缓不济急。True, it would be safer to do it that way, but it takes too much trouble; I'm afraid that slow action cannot save a critical situation. ❷ 表示承认甲事实,也不否认乙事实 admitting fact A is right, but fact B is also right:意见对,~应该接受,就是不对也可作为参考。If his views are correct, they should be accepted; even if they are not correct, they can also be used as reference.

【固若金汤】gù ruò jīn tāng 形容城池或阵地坚固,不易攻破 city that is so impregnable that it can not be captured by an outside force; strongly fortified; impregnable (金 *jin*:指金属造的城 city made of metal; 汤 *tang*:指滚水的护城河 moat with surging hot water)

【固沙林】gùshālín 在沙荒和沙漠地带为了固定流沙而造的防护林 sand-fixation forest; dune-fixing forest; a protective forest built in a sand covered area or desert to fix shifting sand dunes

【固守】gùshǒu ❶ 坚决地守卫 defend tenaciously; be firmly entrenched in: ~阵地 defend one's position tenaciously | 据险~ take advantage of a natural barrier to put up a strong defence ❷ 主观固执地遵循 follow subjectively and obstinately; stick to: ~成法 stick to the conventional regulations

【固态】gùtài 物质的固体状态。是物质存在的一种形态。solid state of a substance; form of existence of substance

【固体】gùtǐ 有一定体积和一定形状,质地比较坚硬的物体。在常温下,钢、铁、岩石、木材、玻璃等都是固体。solid body; solid; hard substance with a certain length, breadth and thickness, and a certain shape; steel, iron, rock, timber and glass are all solids under constant temperature

【固体潮】gùtǐcháo 由于月球、太阳等的引力而产生的地球固体部分的升降运动 solid tide; rise and fall of the solid part of the earth due to gravitation of the moon or the sun; also 地潮 dìcháo

【固习】gùxí same as 痼习 gùxí

【固有】gùyǒu 本来有的;不是外来的 intrinsic; inherent; innate: ~文化 traditional culture

【固执】gù·zhí ❶ 坚持己见,不肯改变 obstinate; stubborn: 性情~ obstinate

故[1] gù ❶ 事故 accident: 变~ unforeseen event ❷ 缘故;原因 cause; reason: 无~缺勤 be absent without reason | 不知何~ don't know why ❸ 故意;有意 intentionally; on purpose; deliberately: ~作镇静 pretend to be calm | 明知~犯 violate (discipline) knowingly; break a law deliberately ❹ 所以;因此 so; therefore: 因大雨,~未如期起程。It rained heavily, so we did not leave as scheduled. *or* We did not leave as scheduled because of a heavy rain.

故[2] gù ❶ 原来的;从前的;旧的 original; former; old: ~址 former address; the old address | ~乡 native village (town) | 依然~我 be one's old self; remain what one used to be ❷ 朋友;友情 friend; acquaintance; friendship: 亲~ relatives and old friends | 沾亲带~ with blood or marital relationship; having personal connections; close or remote; have ties of kinship or friendship ❸ (人)死亡 (of people) die; dead: 病~ die of illness | 染病身~ die of illness | 父母早~ one's parents died when one was very young; left an orphan when very young | ~友 old friend; former friend

【故步自封】gù bù zì fēng〈比喻 *fig.*〉安于现状,不求进步 oneself to the original place; be content with what it is and do not seek to make progress; stand still and refuse to make progress; be complacent and conservative (故步 *gu bu*:走老步子 old steps; 封 *feng*:限制

住 restrict); 故 also put as 固 gù

【故常】gùcháng〈书 *fml.*〉惯例;旧例 old practice; usual practice: 不依～ not follow the usual practice | 习为～ used to it as an old practice | 囿于～ limited by old practice; hampered by old knowledge

【故此】gùcǐ 因此;所以 so; therefore; hence: 因为天气不好,今天的登山活动～作罢。As the weather is not so good, the mountain climbing activities for today are cancelled.

【故道】gùdào ❶ 从前走过的道路;老路 beaten path; old road ❷ 水流改道后的旧河道 old course after the water flow changed its course: 黄河～ old course of the Yellow River

【故地】gùdì 曾居住过的地方 old haunt: ～重游 revisit an old haunt

【故都】gùdū 过去的国都 former capital

【故而】gù'ér 因而;所以 so; therefore; hence: 听说老人家身体欠安,～特来看望。Hearing that you are not so well, I've come specially to see you.

【故宫】gùgōng 旧王朝的宫殿,特指北京的清故宫 palace of a former dynasty, esp. the Imperial Palace of the Qing Dynasty in Beijing

【故国】gùguó〈书 *fml.*〉❶ 历史悠久的国家 country with a long history ❷ 祖国 motherland ❸ same as 故乡 gùxiāng

【故技】gùjì 老花招;老手法 old trick: ～重演 play one's old trick; also 故伎 gùjì

【故交】gùjiāo〈书 *fml.*〉老朋友 old friend: ～新知 old and new friends

【故旧】gùjiù 旧友(总称) general term for old friends and acquaintances: 亲戚～ relatives and friends

【故居】gùjū 曾居住过的房子 former residence (or home): 鲁迅～ the former residence of Lu Xun

【故里】gùlǐ 故乡;老家 native land; native place; home village; hometown: 荣归～ return to one's hometown with honour

【故弄玄虚】gù nòng xuánxū 故意玩弄使人迷惑的欺骗手段 resort purposely to deceptive means to mystify others; purposely make a mystery of a simple thing; be deliberately mystifying

【故去】gùqù 死去(多指长辈 usu. referring to one's elders) depart; pass away; die: 父亲～快三年了。My father has departed for nearly three years.

【故人】gùrén ❶ 老朋友;旧友 old friend: 过访～ visit an old friend ❷ 死去的人 the dead: 吊祭～ pay a condolence over the dead | 不料一别之后,竟成～。No one would expect that he should have died since our last parting.

【故杀】gùshā 故意杀害(区别于'误杀' as compared with 'manslaughter') premeditated (or wilful) murder; intentional killing

【故实】gùshí ❶ 以往的有历史意义的事实 past fact; incident in former times; historical facts or anecdotes (esp. as holding moral lessons) ❷ 出处;典故 allusion; literary quotation; source

【故世】gùshì 去世 die; pass away; depart

【故事】gùshì 旧日的行事制度;例行的事 established practice; old practice; routine: 虚应～ muddle through routine work | 奉行～(按照老规矩敷衍塞责) follow established practice mechanically; follow the old practice

【故事】gù·shi ❶ 真实的或虚构的用做讲述对象的事情,有连贯性,富吸引力,能感染人 story; tale; attractive account of a happening or connected series of happenings, whether true or fictitious: 神话～ fairy tale | 民间～ folk story ❷ 文艺作品中用来体现主题的情节 plot: ～性 plot

【故事片儿】gù·shipiānr same as 故事片 gù·shipiàn

【故事片】gù·shipiàn 表演故事的影片 feature film

【故书】gùshū ❶ 古书 ancient book ❷ 旧书 old book

【故态】gùtài 旧日的情况或态度 state or attitude of former days

【故态复萌】gùtài fù méng 旧日的习气或老毛病重新出现 get back into the old habit; return to the old practice; slip back into one's old ways

【故土】gùtǔ same as 故乡 gùxiāng: 怀念～ yearn for one's homeland; be homesick | ～难离 find it hard to say goodbye to the homeland; it's hard to leave one's homeland

【故我】gùwǒ 旧日的我 one's old self: 依然～ be one's former self; be still what one used to be

【故习】gùxí 旧习 old habit: 一洗～ get rid of all the old habits

【故乡】gùxiāng 出生或长期居住过的地方;家乡;老家 place where one was born or once lived for a long time; old home; native place; birthplace

【故意】gùyì 有意识地(那样做) consciously; intentionally; deliberately; on purpose: 他～把声音提高,好引起大家的注意 He raised his voice with a purpose to draw everybody's attention. | 他不是～不理你,是没看见你。It's not that he paid no heed to you on purpose, but that he didn't see you.

【故友】gùyǒu ❶ 死去了朋友 departed friend ❷ 旧日的朋友;老朋友 friend of old days; old friend: ～重逢 old friends meet again

【故园】gùyuán same as 故乡 gùxiāng: ～风物依旧。The scenery at my homeland remains unchanged.

【故障】gùzhàng (机械、仪器等)发生的不能顺利运转的情况 breakdown; stoppage; trouble; same as 毛病 máo·bìng①: 发生～。A breakdown occurs. | 排除～ fix a breakdown

【故知】gùzhī〈书 *fml*.〉老朋友；旧友 old friend

【故址】gùzhǐ 旧址 old site; site of historical interest

【故纸堆】gùzhǐduī 指数量很多并且十分陈旧的书籍、资料等 a heap of musty old books and papers

【故智】gùzhì 以前用过的计谋 old scheme; old trick rehashed

顾[1]（顧）gù ❶ 转过头看；看 turn round and look at; look at：环～ look around | 相～一笑 smile at each other knowingly; look at each other with a smile ❷ 注意；照管 attend to; take into consideration; take care of; look after：兼～ give due consideration to both sides | 奋不～身 do something regardless of one's own safety ❸ 拜访 visit; call on; pay a visit to：三～茅庐 visit a thatched hut three times (to solicit the service of a wise man) ❹ 商店或服务行业指前来购买东西或要求服务的 person who buys from or requests service from an establishment：～客 customer ❺（Gù）姓 a surname

顾[2]（顧）gù〈书 *fml*.〉❶ 但是 but; however ❷ 反而 on the contrary; instead

【顾此失彼】gù cǐ shī bǐ 顾了这个，顾不了那个 take care of one thing and miss the other; cannot attend to one thing without neglecting the other; have too many things to take care of at the same time

【顾及】gùjí 照顾到；注意到 take care of; look after; pay heed to; take into account; attend to; give consideration to：无暇～ have no time to attend to | 既要～生产，又要～职工生活 pay attention to both production and the workers' livelihood

【顾忌】gùjì 恐怕对人或对事情不利而有顾虑 scruple; misgiving：无所～ without scruple; have no scruples

【顾家】gù//jiā 顾念家庭，多指照管家务，赡养家属等 look after one's family; look after one's household affairs; support one's family

【顾客】gùkè 商店或服务行业称来买东西或要求服务的人 person who buys or requests service; customer; shopper; client：～至上。Customers First.

【顾怜】gùlián 顾念爱怜 care for and show love for：我这样做全是为了～他。I did this merely to care for and show love for him.

【顾脸】gù//liǎn 顾惜脸面 care for one's face：不～ not care for one's face | 都到这份儿上了，你还顾什么脸。Why should you care for your face since it has got to this pass.

【顾恋】gùliàn 顾念；留恋 care for; yearn for; think of：～老小 care for one's parents and children | ～子女 care for one's children; think of one's children

【顾虑】gùlǜ 恐怕对自己、对人或对事情不利而不敢照自己本意说话或行动 misgiving; apprehension; worry; dare not to speak or act as one wishes for fear that it may be not good for oneself, for others or for things：打消～ dispel one's misgivings (or worries) | ～重重 have no end of worries; be full of misgivings

【顾名思义】gù míng sī yì 看到名称，就联想到它的意义 seeing the name of a thing one thinks of its function (or meaning); just as its name implies; as the term suggests：川剧，～就是流行于四川的地方戏。The Sichuan Opera, as the term suggests, is a local opera popular in Sichuan.

【顾念】gùniàn 惦念；顾及 think of; take care of; think about; be concerned about：承您老人家这样～我们。We are most grateful to you for taking care of us.

【顾盼】gùpàn 向两旁或周围看来看去 look around：左右～ glance right and left

【顾盼自雄】gùpàn zì xióng 形容自以为了不起 feel complacent; look about complacently

【顾全】gùquán 顾及，使不受损害 give consideration to; take care of：～大局 take the interests of the whole into account; consider the situation as a whole; take care of the situation as a whole; take the interests of the whole into consideration | ～面子 save sb.'s face; spare sb.'s feelings

【顾问】gùwèn 有某方面的专门知识，供个人或机关团体咨询的人 adviser; consultant：军事～ military adviser

【顾惜】gùxī ❶ 顾全爱惜 value; care for：～身体 be mindful of one's own health; look after one's health | ～国家财产。take care of the state property ❷ 照顾怜惜 take care of and show sympathy for：大家都很～这个没爹没娘的孩子。Everyone is taking care of this orphan.

【顾绣】gùxiù 指沿用明代顾氏绣法制成的刺绣，所绣花鸟人物形象逼真 Gu school of embroidery; school of traditional embroidery invented by a man surnamed Gu in the Ming Dynasty (1368-1644), in which flowers, birds and figures look very true to life

【顾影自怜】gù yǐng zì lián 望着自己的影子，自己怜惜自己。形容孤独失意的样子。也指自我欣赏。be egocentric; be narcissistic; look at one's shadow and lament one's lot; look at one's reflection and admire oneself

【顾主】gùzhǔ same as 顾客 gùkè

堌 gù 堤。多用于地名 dyke; *Gu*, used for geographical names：青～集（在山东）Qingguji in Shandong | 龙～（在江苏）Longgu in Jiangsu

梏 gù〈古代 *arch*.〉木制的手铐 handcuffs made of wood：桎～ shackles; fetters; handcuffs

崮 gù 四周陡峭,顶上较平的山。多用于地名 hill with a flat top and steep cliffs; *gu*, used for geographical names:孟良～ Menglianggu|抱犊～(都在山东) Baodugu both in Shandong Province

牿 gù〈书 *fml.*〉❶ 绑在牛角上使牛不得顶人的横木 horizontal piece of wood tied on the horns of an ox to prevent it from butting people ❷ 养牛马的圈(juàn) cattle pen

雇(僱) gù ❶ 出钱让人给自己做事 hire, employ:～用 hire|～保姆 hire a maid ❷ 出钱使别人用车、船等给自己服务 hail; rent:～车 hail a car|～船 rent a boat

【雇工】gù//gōng 雇用工人 hire labour; hire hands

【雇工】gùgōng ❶ 受雇用的工人 hired labourer ❷ 指雇农 tenant; farmhand; farm labourer

【雇农】gùnóng 农村中的长工、月工、零工等。他们没有或只有极少量的土地和生产工具,主要依靠出卖劳动力为生。farmhand; farm labourer; farm labourer hired by the year, the month or the day, having no or little land or few production tools and living mainly by selling labour

【雇请】gùqǐng 出钱请人替自己做事 get the services of a person in return for payment:～佣工 hire or employ a labourer or servant; hire or employ (a person)

【雇佣】gùyōng 用货币购买劳动力 purchase labour power with money

【雇佣兵役制】gùyōng bīngyìzhì 某些国家施行的一种招募士兵的制度,形式上是士兵自愿应募,实质上是雇佣 mercenary system; system of recruiting soldiers, especially foreign soldiers in some countries, whereby soldiers volunteer for service in name but are hired in essence

【雇佣观点】gùyōng guāndiǎn 工作中缺乏主人翁思想而采取的拿一分钱干一分活的消极态度 hired-hand mentality; attitude of a person who works only for how much he is paid

【雇佣劳动】gùyōng láodòng 受雇于资本家的工人的劳动。在资本主义制度下,被剥夺了生产资料的劳动者被迫把劳动力当作商品出卖给资本家,为资本家创造剩余价值。wage labour; labour hired by a capitalist. Under the capitalist system, the labourer deprived of means of production is compelled to sell labour as a commodity to the capitalist and create surplus value for the capitalist.

【雇用】gùyòng 出钱让人为自己做事 get the services of a person in return for payment:～临时工 hire a casual labourer

【雇员】gùyuán 被雇用的职员或编制以外的临时工作人员 employee; person hired by another, or by a business firm, to work for wages or salary

【雇主】gùzhǔ 雇用雇工或车船等的人 employer; person who employs; person, a business firm, etc. that hires one or more persons to work for wages or salary or hire a motor vehicle or a boat

锢 gù ❶ 熔化金属堵塞(物体的空隙) plug (cavities of an object) with molten metal; run metal into cracks ❷〈书 *fml.*〉禁锢 hold in custody; imprison:党～ interdiction of party activities by confinement of party members, etc.

【锢露】gù·lou 用熔化的金属堵塞金属物品的漏洞 plug up holes in a metal container with molten metal:～锅 run molten metal into the crack of a pot; also 锢漏 gùlòu

痼 gù 经久难治愈的;长期养成不易克服的 long-lasting or recurrent; inveterate:～疾 an incurable chronic disease|～习 deep-rooted habit; inveterate habit|～癖 addiction; fondness

【痼疾】gùjí 经久难治愈的病 incurable chronic disease:医学越来越发达,很多所谓～都能治好。Thanks to the advances in medical science, many so-called chronic diseases can be cured. *or* Advances in medical science have made it possible to cure many so-called chronic diseases.

【痼癖】gùpǐ 长期养成不易改掉的癖好 long-established fondness for sth. bad

【痼习】gùxí 长期养成不易改掉的习惯 inveterate (or confirmed) habit; also 固习 gùxí

鲴 gù 鱼类的一属,体长 30 厘米左右,侧扁,口小。生活在河流、湖泊中,吃藻类和其他水生植物。silvery chub (*Xenocypris argentea*); a kind of fish with a small mouth, about 30 centimetres long, laterally flat, growing in rivers and lakes and feeding on weeds and other water plants

guā(ㄍㄨㄚ)

瓜 guā ❶ 葫芦科植物,茎蔓生,叶子像手掌,花多是黄色,果实可以吃。种类很多,如西瓜、南瓜、冬瓜、黄瓜等。melon, gourd, etc.; any trailing or climbing plant of the gourd family with palm-like leaves, yellow flowers and edible fruits, including melons, pumpkins, cucumbers, gourds, etc. ❷ 这种植物的果实 fruits of such plants

【瓜代】guādài〈书 *fml.*〉春秋时齐襄公叫连称和管至父两个人去戍守葵丘地方,那时正当瓜熟的季节,就对他们说,明年吃瓜的时候叫人来接替(见于《左传》庄公八年)。后来把任期已满换人接替叫做瓜代。*The Zuo Commentary · Duke Zhuang Eighth Year*: Duke Xiang of the state of Qi in the Spring and Autumn Period asked Lian Cheng and Guan Zhifu to guard a place called Kuiqiu. It was the melon season, and the duke told the two of them that he would appoint someone to replace them during the next melon season. Afterwards, replacement of an official at the expiration of the term of his office was called *guadai*, which literally means 'substitute to the melon-guard'

【瓜分】guāfēn 像切瓜一样地分割或分配,多指分割疆土 carve up, esp. the territory of a defeated country by victors like cutting up a melon

【瓜葛】guāgé 瓜和葛都是蔓生的植物,能缠绕或攀附在别的物体上,比喻辗转相连的社会关系,也泛指两件事情互相牵连的关系 both melon and vine are intertwining climbing plants, which is likened to 'implicated social connections' or implicated affairs:他与此事没有~。He has nothing to do with the matter.

【瓜农】guānóng 以种瓜为主的农民 melon grower; peasant who grows melons

【瓜皮帽】guāpímào (~儿 guāpímàor)像半个西瓜皮形状的旧式便帽,一般用六块黑缎子或绒布连缀制成 skullcap; a kind of skullcap resembling the rind of half a watermelon, usu. made of six pieces of black satin or cotton flannel sewn together

【瓜片】guāpiàn 绿茶的一种。产于安徽六安、霍山一带。*guapian*; green tea produced in Liu'an and Huoshan, Anhui Province

G

【瓜期】guāqī〈书 *fml*.〉指任职期满换人接替的日期 date of replacement for an official at the expiration of his office term; ☞ 瓜代 guādài

【瓜熟蒂落】guā shú dì luò〈比喻 *fig*.〉条件成熟了,事情自然会成功 when a melon is ripe it falls off its stem — things are easily settled once conditions are ripe

【瓜田李下】guā tián lǐ xià 古诗《君子行》:'瓜田不纳履,李下不正冠。'经过瓜田,不弯下身来提鞋,免得人家怀疑摘瓜;走过李树下面,不举起手来整理帽子,免得人家怀疑摘李子。后用'瓜田李下'比喻容易引起嫌疑的地方。From the ancient poem *Gentleman's Etiquette*: 'Don't put on your shoes in a melon patch; don't adjust your cap under a plum tree.' In other words, when you walk past a melon patch, you should not bend your body to put on your shoes so that you will not be suspected of picking a melon; when you walk under a plum tree, you should not raise your hands to adjust your cap so that you will not be suspected of picking plums. The four-character expression has been used to liken sth. that would cause suspicion.

【瓜子】guāzǐ (~儿 guāzǐr)瓜的种子,特指炒熟做食品的瓜子、南瓜子等 melon seeds, esp. the baked watermelon seeds and pumpkin seeds for food

【瓜子脸】guāzǐliǎn 指微长而窄,上部略圆,下部略尖的面庞 oval face; long face with the upper part slightly round and the lower part slightly pointed

呱 guā ☞ below
☞ gū on p.686 and guǎ on p.703

【呱哒】guādā same as 呱嗒 guādā

【呱哒】guā·da same as 呱嗒 guā·da

【呱嗒】guādā ❶〈拟声词 *onom*.〉clip-clop; clack:地是冻硬的,走起来~~地响。The ground is frozen hard and clacks when you walk on it. ❷〈方 *dial*.〉讽刺;挖苦 speak sarcastically or ironically:~人 make sarcastic remarks ‖ also 呱哒 guādā

【呱嗒】guā·da〈方 *dial*.〉❶ 因不高兴而板起(脸) pull a long face:~着脸,半天不说一句话。He pulled a long face for a long time without speaking a word. ❷ 说话(含贬义 derog.) talk foolishly:乱~一阵 talk a lot of nonsense ‖ also 呱哒 guā·da

【呱嗒板儿】guā·dabǎnr ❶ 演唱快板儿等打拍子用的器具,由两块大竹板或若干块小竹板用绳连接而成 bamboo clappers, instrument for beating time in reciting a story to its rhythmic accompaniment ❷〈方 *dial*.〉趿拉板儿(tā·labǎnr) clogs

【呱呱】guāguā〈拟声词 *onom*.〉形容鸭子、青蛙等的响亮的叫声 quacking of a duck; croaking of a frog; cawing of a crow
☞ gūgū on p.686

【呱呱叫】guāguājiào 形容极好 top-notch; great; excellent:他象棋下得~。He plays chess very well. ‖ also 刮刮叫 guāguājiào

【呱唧】guā·ji ❶〈拟声词 *onom*.〉多形容鼓掌的声音 sound of hands being clapped ❷ 指鼓掌 clap hands:欢迎小王唱个歌,大家给他~~。Everyone claps hands to request Xiao Wang to sing a song.

刮[1] guā ❶ 用刀等贴着物体的表面移动,把物体表面上的某些东西去掉或取下来 remove sth. by rubbing over the surface of it with sth. sharp or rough; scrape; shave:~胡子 shave the beard | ~锅 scrape a pot clean | ~垢磨光 scrape the dirt and polish — improve oneself ❷ 在物体表面上涂抹(多用于糨糊一类稠东西) spread over the surface of sth. (paste, etc.); smear with (paste, etc.):~糨子 size; stiffen (cloth) by spreading paste over it ❸ 搜刮(财物) plunder; fleece; extort ❹〈方 *dial*.〉训斥 reprimand; rebuke

刮[2] **(颳)** guā (风)吹(of the wind) blow:又~起风来了! It's blowing again!

【刮鼻子】guābí·zi ❶ 用食指刮对方的鼻子,表示处罚对方(多用在玩牌游戏时) rub the nose of a person with one's forefinger as a punishment (in playing cards) ❷ 刮自己的鼻子,表示使对方感到羞臊或难为情 rub one's own nose to embarrass a person ❸〈方 *dial*.〉〈比

喻 *fig*.〉训斥或斥责 reprimand; rebuke:他让连长狠狠地刮了顿鼻子。The company leader reprimanded him severely.

【刮刀】guādāo 手工工具,条形,横截面有扁平形、半圆形、三角形等不同形状。主要用来刮去工件表面的微量金属,提高工件的外形精度和光洁度。scraper; scraping knife; hand tool, flat, semi-circular or triangular in shape, mainly used to remove a trace of metal from the surface of a workpiece so as to improve the precision and smooth finish of the workpiece

【刮地皮】guā dìpí〈比喻 *fig*.〉搜刮民财 extort money from people; bleed sb. white

【刮宫】guā//gōng 把子宫口扩大,用特制的医疗器械去掉胚胎或子宫的内膜。刮宫手术多用于人工流产。D and C; dilatation of the cervix and curettage of the uterus, mostly used for abortion

【刮刮叫】guāguājiào same as 呱呱叫 guāguājiào

【刮胡子】guāhú·zi〈方 *dial*.〉〈比喻 *fig*.〉训斥 reprimand; rebuke

【刮脸】guā//liǎn 用剃刀等把脸上的胡须和寒毛刮掉 shave; use a shaver to remove the beard and hair from one's face

【刮脸皮】guā liǎnpí〈方 *dial*.〉用手指头在脸上划,表示对方不知羞耻 rub one's own cheek with a finger to shame a person; rub the forefinger against one's own cheek (to indicate scorn for sb.); point the finger of scorn at sb.

【刮目】guāmù 指彻底改变眼光 view things in a completely new light:令人～ be marvelled at|～相看 marvel at a person's progress or achievements

【刮目相看】guāmù xiāng kàn 用新的眼光来看待 treat a person with increased respect; look at a person with new eyes; look at sb. with new eyes; treat sb. with increased respect; also 刮目相待 guāmù xiāng dài

【刮痧】guāshā 民间治疗某些疾病的方法,用铜钱等物蘸水或油刮患者的胸、背等处,使局部皮肤充血,减轻内部炎症 popular folk treatment for certain illnesses by scraping the forehead, neck, chest and back of the patient with a copper coin to cause congestion in the skin vessels to alleviate pain or inflammation

【刮舌子】guāshé·zi 刮除舌面污垢的用具 implement for removing dirt from the surface of the tongue

【刮削】guāxiāo scrape ❶ 用刀子一类的工具把物体表面的东西去掉 remove sth. from the surface of an object with a sharp tool ❷〈比喻 *fig*.〉克扣或盘剥 embezzle or practise usury:～钱财 embezzle money from others

苦 guā [苦蒌](guālóu) same as 栝楼 guālóu

括 guā ☞ 挺刮 tǐng·guā on p. 1914
☞ kuò on p. 1134

胍 guā 有机化合物,化学式 CH_5N_3。无色晶体,容易潮解。用来制磺胺类药物或染料等。guanidine; organic chemical compound, colourless, crystalline, apt to deliquesce, used for making sulphanilamides or dyestuffs

栝 guā ❶ 古书上指桧(guì)树 Chinese juniper as described in ancient Chinese books ❷〈书 *fml*.〉箭末扣弦处 arrow nock; protuberance on the end of an arrow which catches the bowstring
☞ kuò on p. 1134

【栝楼】guālóu ❶ 多年生草本植物,茎上有卷须,叶子心脏形,花白色,雌雄异株,果实卵圆形,黄色,种子长圆形。可入药。Chinese trichosanthes (*Trichosanthes kirilowii*); perennial herbal plant, dioecious, with tendrils on its stem, heart-shaped leaves, white flowers, yellow oval fruits and long and round seeds; used for medicine ❷ 这种植物的果实 fruit of the plant ‖ also 苦蒌 guālóu

埚(緺) guā ❶〈书 *fml*.〉紫青色的绶(丝带) purplish green silk ribbon ❷〈古时 *old*〉女子头发一束为一埚 strand of a lady's hair

锅(騧) guā〈古代 *arch*.〉指黑嘴的黄马 yellow horse with a black mouth

鸹 guā ☞ 老鸹 lǎo·guā on p. 1158

劀 guā〈书 *fml*.〉刮去 scrape off

guǎ(ㄍㄨㄚˇ)

呱 guǎ ☞ 拉呱儿 lā//guǎr on p. 1137
☞ gū on p. 686 and guā on p. 702

剐(剮) guǎ ❶ 割肉离骨,指封建时代的凌迟刑 cut to pieces; dismember a body (a form of capital punishment in ancient times):千刀万～ cut to pieces (a form of capital punishment in ancient times) ❷ 尖锐的东西划破 cut; slit:手上～了一个口子 have a cut on the hand

寡 guǎ ❶ 少;缺少(跟'众、多'相对 as opposed to 'many') few; scant; scant; short of:～欢 unhappy|沉默～言 taciturn; reticent|～不敌众 be hopelessly outnumbered; be overwhelmed by sheer number; fight against hopeless odds|孤陋～闻 ill-informed; ignorant ❷ 淡而无味 bland; tasteless:清汤～水 tasteless clear soup ❸ 妇女死了丈夫 widowed; woman bereaved of her husband:守～ widowed|～居 live as a widow

【寡不敌众】guǎ bù dí zhòng 人少的一方抵挡不住人多的一方 be hopelessly outnumbered; be overwhelmed by sheer number; fight against hopeless odds

【寡妇】guǎ·fu 死了丈夫的妇人 widow; woman who outlived her husband at the time of his death

【寡合】guǎhé〈书 *fml*.〉不易同人合得来 have little intercourse with others: 性情孤僻,落落～ aloofness that keeps others at a distance; unsociable; standoffish

【寡欢】guǎhuān 缺少欢乐,不高兴 joyless; unhappy: 郁郁～ unhappy; depressed; melancholy

【寡酒】guǎjiǔ 渴酒不就菜或无人陪伴叫吃寡酒 drink wine without food or drink wine alone

【寡居】guǎjū 守寡 remain a widow; live alone as a widow: ～多年 remain a widow for many years; live in widowhood for many years

【寡廉鲜耻】guǎ lián xiǎn chǐ 不廉洁,不知羞耻 shameless; have no sense of honour

【寡情】guǎqíng 缺乏情义;薄情 unfeeling; cold-hearted; heartless

【寡人】guǎrén〈古代 *arch*.〉君主自称 self-address for 'I' by a monarch in ancient China; I, your unworthy king

【寡头】guǎtóu 掌握政治、经济大权的少数头子 a few rulers who control the politics and the political power; any of the rulers of an oligarchy; oligarch: 金融～ financial oligarch; financial magnate

G

【寡头政治】guǎtóu zhèngzhì 由少数统治者操纵一切的政治制度,如古代罗马的贵族政权 oligarchy; form of government in which the ruling power belongs to a few persons, such as the ancient Roman aristocratic government

【寡味】guǎwèi 没有滋味;缺乏意味 tasteless; dull; uninteresting: 茶饭～ a tasteless meal | 他的讲话索然～。He gave a dull talk.

【寡言】guǎyán 很少说话;不爱说话 uncommunicative; reticent; not inclined to speak; taciturn: 沉默～ reticent; taciturn, uncommunicative | 憨厚～ honest and reticent; good-natured and taciturn | ～少语 reticent; taciturn

guà (ㄍㄨㄚˋ)

卦 guà 古代的占卜符号,后也指迷信占卜活动所用的器具 divinatory symbols used in ancient times; articles used for divinatory activities: 占～ divine by means of the Eight Diagrams | 打～求签 seek divine guidance by drawing lots

【卦辞】guàcí ☞ 彖辞 tuàncí on p. 1947

诖 guà〈书 *fml*.〉❶ 欺骗 cheat; deceive ❷ 牵累;贻误 implicate; involve; tie down: ～误 suffer by implication; implicate or involve in trouble

【诖误】guàwù 被别人牵连而受到处分或损害 be punished for implication made by sb. else; affect adversely; bungle; also 罣误 guàwù

挂(掛) guà ❶ 借助于绳子、钩子、钉子等使物体附着于某处的一点或几点 attach an object to sth. above with no support from below by means of string, rope, hook or nail; hang; put up: ～钟 wall clock | 把大衣～在衣架上 hang an overcoat on the coat hanger (or clothes rack) | 墙上～着一幅世界地图。A world map is hung on the wall. ◇一轮明月～在天上。The bright moon hangs in the sky. ❷(案件等)悬而未决 unsettled: 这个案子还～着呢。The case is still waiting. *or* The case is not yet settled. ❸ 把耳机放回电话机上使电路断开 hang up; ring off: 电话先不要～,等我查一下。Don't hang up until I find out. ❹ 指交换机接通电话,也指打电话 dial; call, ring up; put a person through to: 请你～总务科。Put me through to the General Affairs Section, please! | 给防汛指挥部～个电话。Give a call to the Flood Control Headquarters. ❺ 钩 hitch; get caught: 她的衣服给钉子～住了。Her dress got caught on a nail. ❻(内心)牵挂 worry; be concerned about; have sth. at heart: 他总是～着家里的事。He always worries about his family. ❼(物体表面)蒙上;糊着: be covered; be coated with: 脸上～了一层尘土。His face was covered with dust. | 瓦器外面～一层釉子。The earthen pot is glazed outside. ❽ 登记 register (at a hospital, etc.): ～失 registered for sth. lost; report the loss of sth. to | ～一个号 register for a number ❾〈量词 *classifier*〉多用于成套或成串的东西 set or string (of things): 一～四轮大车 a four-wheel cart | 十多～鞭炮 a dozen strings of firecrackers

【挂碍】guà'ài 牵挂;牵掣 hold up; impede; worry; be concerned about: 心中没有～ have no worries

【挂表】guàbiǎo〈方 *dial*.〉怀表 pocket watch

【挂不住】guà·bu zhù〈方 *dial*.〉因羞辱而沉不住气 lose temper; lose control of one's feelings: 他受到一点儿批评就～了。He got irritated when he was slightly criticized. *or* He lost temper when he was slightly criticized.

【挂彩】guà//cǎi ❶ 悬挂彩绸,表示庆贺 decorate with coloured silk festoons as a token of celebration: 披红～ be dressed in red and decorated with coloured silk festoons ❷ 作战负伤流血 wounded in action: 在战斗中,几个战士挂了彩。Several soldiers were wounded in action.

【挂车】guàchē 由机车或汽车牵引而本身没有动力装置的车辆 trailer; cart, wagon or van pulled by an engine or a truck for hauling freight, animals, etc.

【挂齿】guàchǐ 说起;提起(常用做客套话 oft. pol.) mention:这点小事,何足～。Such a trifle is not worth mentioning.

【挂锄】guà//chú 指锄地工作结束 put away the hoe (for the winter); finish hoeing

【挂单】guàdān (游方和尚)到庙里投宿 (of a travelling Buddhist monk) lodge in a temple for the night; also 挂褡 guàdān

【挂斗】guàdǒu 拖在汽车、拖拉机等后边装货的较小车辆,没有动力装置 trailer; smaller cart drawn by a motor truck or a tractor for carrying freight

【挂钩】guà//gōu ❶ 用钩把两节车厢连接起来 couple (two railway coaches); articulate ❷〈比喻 *fig.*〉建立某种联系 link up with; establish contact with; get in touch with:基层供销社直接跟产地～。A grass-roots supply and marketing cooperative has established direct contact with the place of production. | 这两个单位早就挂起钩来了。The two organizations have established contact with each other for a long time.

【挂钩】guàgōu 用来吊起重物或把车厢等连接起来的钩 hook for hoisting a heavy thing or a couple that links two railway wagons:吊车～ crane hook | 火车～ railway couple

【挂冠】guàguān〈书 *fml.*〉指辞去官职 resign from office:～归隐 resign from office and live in a hermitage | ～而去。He resigned and returned home.

【挂果】guà//guǒ (果树)结果实 bear fruit:三年成林,五年～。The trees became a forest in three years and began bearing fruits in five years. | 这片苹果树今年第一次挂了果。These apple trees are bearing fruit for the first time this year.

【挂号】guà//hào ❶ 为了确定次序并便于查考而编号登记 register for a number to keep order (at a hospital, etc.):看病要先～。Please register before seeing a doctor. ❷ 重要信件和印刷品付邮时由邮电局登记编号,给收据,叫挂号。挂号邮件如有遗失,由邮电局负责追查。An important letter or printed matter is registered for a serial number when being mailed at a post office. If a registered piece of mail is lost, the post office is responsible for finding it out.

【挂花】guà//huā ❶ (树木)开花 bear flowers:正是梨树～的时候,远远望去一片雪白。The pear tree looks all white in the distance when it is in bloom. ❷ 作战负伤流血 be wounded and bleeding in action:排长～了,班长代替指挥。The platoon leader was wounded and the squad leader replaced him in commanding the action. | 他腿上挂过两次花。He was twice wounded in the leg.

【挂怀】guàhuái 挂念;挂心 worry; have sth. weighing on one's mind; be concerned (or worried) about:区区小事,不必～。Don't worry about such a trifle.

【挂幌子】guà huǎng·zi〈方 *dial.*〉❶ 在商店门前悬挂表示所售货物的标志或象征营业的记号,如颜料店挂漆成五色的小棍,饭铺挂笊篱 business token or symbol for the goods on sale hung in front of a shop, such as a painted stick for a paint shop, a wire strainer for a restaurant ❷〈比喻 *fig.*〉某种迹象显露在外面 tell-tale sign:他刚才准是喝了酒,脸上都～了(指脸红)。He must have drunk wine as he is red in the face.

【挂火】guàhuǒ〈方 *dial.*〉(～儿 guàhuǒr)发怒;生气 be furious; flare up; get angry:有话慢慢说,别～。Take time if you have anything to say, but don't be angry.

【挂记】guà·ji 挂念;惦记 worry about; be concerned about; be anxious about; keep thinking about:你安心工作,家里的事用不着～。Keep your mind on your work, and don't always think about the family.

【挂甲】guàjiǎ 指军人退役 demobilize; retire from military service:～归田 retire from military service and return home ◇女排几位老队员先后～离队。Some old members of the women's volleyball team have retired and left the team.

【挂件】guàjiàn 挂在墙壁上或脖子上的装饰品 pendant; ornament hanging on the wall or around the neck:金～ gold hanging

【挂镜线】guàjìngxiàn 钉在室内四周墙壁上部的水平木条,用来悬挂镜框、画幅等 nailing strip; picture mould; horizontal wood strip nailed on the wall of a room for hanging a mirror, paintings, etc. also 画镜线 huàjìngxiàn

【挂靠】guàkào 机构或组织从属或依附于另一机构或组织叫挂靠 affiliation of an organization to another organization:～单位 affiliated organization | 旅游协会～在旅游局。The Tourist Association is affiliated to the Tourist Bureau

【挂累】guàlěi 牵挂;连累 be implicated; be involved:没有任何～ have nothing to do with ...; not get involved | 受此事～的人很多。Many people were involved in this affair.

【挂历】guàlì 挂在墙上用的月历 monthly calendar hung up on the wall; wall calendar

【挂镰】guà//lián 指一年中最后一茬庄稼的收割工作结束 put away the sickle; complete the year's harvest

【挂零】guàlíng (～儿 guàlíngr)整数外还有零数 odd:这个人看样子顶多不过四十～。This man looks about forty odd at most.

【挂漏】guàlòu same as 挂一漏万 guà yī lòu wàn:～之处,在所难免。Missings in the book can hardly be avoided.

【挂虑】guàlǜ 挂念,不放心 worry about; be

G

concerned about; be anxious about: 家里的事有我照顾呢，你不用～。I'm looking after the family affairs, so you don't have to worry.

【挂面】guàmiàn 特制的面条，丝状或带状，因悬挂晾干得名 fine dried noodles; vermicelli

【挂名】guà//míng (～儿 guà//míngr) 担空头名义，不做实际工作 titular; nominal; only in name: ～差使 nominal job | ～充数 hold a nominal position to make up the number

【挂念】guàniàn 因想念而放心不下 miss someone and worry about him; worry about sb. who is absent: 母亲十分～在外地念书的儿子。The mother worries very much for her son studying in another city.

【挂拍】guàpāi (～儿 guàpāir) ❶ 指乒乓球、羽毛球、网球等运动员结束运动员生活，不再参加正规则训练和比赛 put aside one's bat or racket to end one's life as a professional player in table tennis, badminton, tennis, etc. and stop participating in regular training and competition ❷ 指乒乓球、羽毛球、网球等比赛结束(of a table tennis, badminton or tennis competitions) draw to an end: 全国少年乒乓球赛～。The national juniors' table tennis tournament has closed.

【挂牌】guà//pái ❶ 指医生、律师等正式开业 be inaugurated; opening of a clinic or office by a doctor or a lawyer; hang out one's shingle; put up one's brass plate: 他行医多年，在上海和北京都挂过牌。He practised medicine for many years and opened clinics of his own in both Shanghai and Beijing. ❷ (～儿 guà//páir) 医生、售货员、服务员等工作时胸前佩戴印有姓名、号码等的标牌 name plate pinned on the chest by doctors, nurses, shop clerks and attendants while on duty: ～服务 (said of a doctor or nurse) giving service with one's name card | ～售货 (of a clerk in a department store) sell goods wearing a name plate

【挂屏】guàpíng (～儿 guàpíngr) 贴在带框的木板上或者镶在镜框里的屏条 framed painting or calligraphy; a set of hanging scrolls of painting or calligraphy

【挂气】guà//qì 〈方 *dial.*〉(～儿 guà//qìr) 生气；发怒 get angry: 犯不着为这点小事～。It's not worthwhile getting angry at such a trifling thing!

【挂牵】guàqiān 挂念；牵挂 worry; care about

【挂欠】guàqiàn 赊账 buy on credit

【挂失】guà//shī 遗失票据或证件时，到原发的机关去登记，声明作废 report on the loss of sth. esp. business bill, identification card, etc.; when a bill or a certificate is lost, report it to the issuing organ to declare it invalid.

【挂帅】guà//shuài 掌帅印，当元帅 be in command; assume (or take) command; 〈比喻 *fig.*〉居于领导、统帅地位 assume leadership: 厂长～抓产品质量工作。The factory manager took charge of product quality.

【挂锁】guàsuǒ 一种用时挂在屈戌儿的环孔中的锁 padlock; movable lock with a hinged or pivoting link to be passed through a staple, chain or eye

【挂毯】guàtǎn 壁毯 tapestry

【挂图】guàtú 挂起来看的大幅地图、图表或图画 large wall map; hanging chart; drawing: 教学～ teaching charts

【挂孝】guà//xiào 带孝 wear mourning

【挂鞋】guàxié 指足球、滑冰、田径等运动员结束运动员生活，不再参加正规训练和比赛 (of football players, skaters and other athletes) retire; stop regular training and competition; also 挂靴 guàxuē

【挂心】guàxīn 牵挂在心上；挂念 worry about; be on one's mind: 他～家里，恨不得马上赶回去。He was very much worried about his family. How he wished if he could hurry back home at once.

【挂羊头卖狗肉】guà yángtóu mài gǒuròu 〈比喻 *fig.*〉用好的名义做幌子，实际上做坏事 hang up a sheep's head and sell dog meat; use the name of a good thing as a cover, but actually do an evil thing; try to palm off sth. inferior to what it purports to be

【挂一漏万】guà yī lòu wàn 形容列举不全，遗漏很多 incomplete listing with many missings; for one thing cited, ten thousand things may have been left out; list is far from complete

【挂账】guà//zhàng 赊账 on credit

【挂职】guàzhí ❶ 临时担任某种职务(以进行锻炼) hold a certain temporary position: 这位作家～副县长，深入生活搜集创作素材。This writer took on the position as a deputy county magistrate in order to go deep into the thick of life and gather source material for his novel. ❷ 保留原职务(下放到基层单位工作 when sb. is dispatched to work in a grass-roots unit) reserve one's original position: ～下放 leave one's regular job to work at a grass-roots level with one's original position and pay reserved

【挂钟】guàzhōng 挂在墙上的时钟(区别于'座钟' as compared with the 'table clock') wall clock

【挂轴】guàzhóu (～儿 guàzhóur) 装裱成轴可以悬挂的字画 mounted painting or calligraphy hung on the wall; hanging scroll (of Chinese painting or calligraphy)

结 guà 〈书 *fml.*〉formal 绊住；阻碍 trip; stumble; impede; hinder

罣(罫) guà same as 挂 guà ⑥

【罣误】guàwù same as 诖误 guàwù

褂 guà (～儿 guàr) 褂子 Chinese-style unlined garment; gown: 短～儿 short gown |

小～儿（短的）short gown｜大～儿（长的）long gown｜马～儿 mandarin jacket

【褂子】guà·zi 中式的单上衣 Chinese-style unlined upper garment; short gown

guāi（ㄍㄨㄞ）

乖[1] guāi ❶（小孩儿）不闹；听话 be quiet; obedient; well-behaved：小宝很～，阿姨都喜欢他。The baby is very obedient and quiet, and every nurse likes him. ❷ 伶俐；机警 clever; sharp; shrewd; alert：这孩子嘴～。The child has a honey tongue.｜上了一次当，他也学得～多了。Being fooled once, he has become wiser.

乖[2] guāi〈书 *fml.*〉❶ 违反；背离 violate; go against; run counter to; perverse; contrary to reason：～背 run counter to｜有～人情 not amenable to reason ❷（性情、行为）不正常（of character, behaviour, etc.）irregular; abnormal：～戾｜～谬 absurd; fallacious

【乖舛】guāichuǎn〈书 *fml.*〉❶ 谬误；差错 mistake; error ❷ 不顺遂 unsuccessful：命途～。The course of one's life is not smooth (or successful).

【乖乖】guāiguāi ❶（～儿的 guāiguāir·de）顺从；听话 submissive; obedient; well-behaved; meekly：孩子们都～儿地坐着听阿姨讲故事。The children all sat quietly, listening to the teacher telling stories. ❷ 对小孩儿的爱称 endearing name for a child; little dear; darling

【乖乖】guāi·guai〈叹词 *interj.*〉表示惊讶或赞叹[expressing surprise or admiration] wow：～，外边真冷！Why, it's so cold outside!｜～，这艘船真大！Wow, what a big ship!

【乖蹇】guāijiǎn〈书 *fml.*〉（命运）不好（of luck）bad; ill：时运～ bad luck; ill luck

【乖觉】guāijué 机警；聪敏 alert; clever; quick：～伶俐 clever and quick-witted｜小松鼠～得很，听到一点儿响声就溜跑了。The squirrel is very alert, and runs away at the slightest sound.

【乖剌】guāilà〈书 *fml.*〉违背常情；乖戾：perverse; contrary to reason; run counter to reason｜措置～ handle (or manage, arrange) unreasonably (or improperly)

【乖戾】guāilì（性情、言语、行为）别扭，不合情理（of disposition, utterings, or behaviour）perverse; unreasonable; disagreeable; cantankerous：性情～ bad temper, eccentric｜语多～ perverse words; speak perversely

【乖谬】guāimiù 荒谬反常 absurd; abnormal：这人性情怪僻，行动多有～难解之处。The man is eccentric and acts strangely.

【乖僻】guāipì 怪僻；乖戾 eccentric; unreasonable：性情～ eccentric nature; be unreasonable

【乖巧】guāiqiǎo ❶（言行等）合人心意；讨人喜欢（of words and deeds）agreeable; cute：为人～ a lovely person ❷ 机灵 quick-witted; cute; clever; ingenious：～伶俐 clever and nimble-minded｜又顽皮又～的孩子 naughty and clever child

【乖违】guāiwéi〈书 *fml.*〉❶ 错乱反常 disorderly, deranged; abnormal：寒暑～ abnormal weather ❷ 违背；背离 run counter to ❸ 离别；分离 part; separate

【乖张】guāizhāng ❶ 怪僻，不讲情理 eccentric and difficult; perverse; recalcitrant：脾气～ queer｜行为～ queer behaviour ❷〈书 *fml.*〉不顺 unsuccessful; not smooth：命运～ bad lot

掴（摑）guāi，又 also guó 用巴掌打 slap; box; smack：～了一记耳光 slap a person in the face; box a person on the ear

guǎi（ㄍㄨㄞˇ）

拐[1]（❺柺）guǎi ❶ 转变方向 change direction; turn：那人～进胡同里去了。The man turned into an alley.｜前面不能通行，～回来吧！There's no road ahead. Let's turn back. ❷〈方 *dial.*〉弯曲处；角 corner; turn：墙～ corner formed by two walls｜门～ corner of the gate (or door) ❸ 瘸（qué）limp：他一～一～地走了过来。He limped along. *or* He walked with a limp. ❹ 说数字时用来代表'7' spoken form for the numeral 'seven' ❺ 下肢患病或有残疾的人走路拄的棍子，上端有短横木便于放在腋下拄着走 crutches; staff with a hand grip and a padded crosspiece on top that fits under the armpit

拐[2] guǎi 拐骗 abduct; swindle; kidnap; make off with：诱～ carry off a woman by fraud｜～款潜逃 abscond with funds

【拐棒】guǎibàng（～儿 guǎibàngr）弯曲的棍子 crooked stick

【拐脖儿】guǎibór 弯成直角的铁皮烟筒，用来连接两节烟筒，使互相垂直 pipe elbow, used to connect two pipes to form a right angle

【拐带】guǎidài 用欺骗手段把妇女小孩儿携带远走 kidnap (women or children); abduct abduct women and children：～人口 abduct people

【拐棍】guǎigùn（～儿 guǎigùnr）走路时拄的棍子，手拿的一头多是弯曲的 walking stick with one end bent as a handle

【拐角】guǎijiǎo（～儿 guǎijiǎor）拐弯儿的地方 corner; turning：房子的～有个消火栓。There is a fire hydrant in the corner of the house.｜那个小商店就在胡同的～。That shop is just at the corner of the lane.

【拐卖】guǎimài 拐骗并卖掉（人）kidnap and sell; engage in slavery：～妇女 abduct and sell women and children｜～人口 kidnap and sell people

【拐骗】guǎipiàn 用欺骗手段弄走(人或财物) carry off (a person or property) by fraud:～钱财 swindle money|～儿童 kidnap a child abduct

【拐弯】guǎi//wān (～儿 guǎiwānr) ❶ 行路转方向 turning; turn to a new direction; turn a corner; make a turn:拐了三道弯儿 turn three times|车辆～要慢行。Vehicles are advised to slow down when turning a corner. ❷(思路、语言等)转变方向 change point; change one's opinion to another point of view; pursue a new course:话说得离题太远,不容易拐过弯儿来。He strayed too far away to come back to the point. ❸ same as 拐角 guǎijiǎo

【拐弯抹角】guǎi wān mò jiǎo (～的 guǎiwān mò jiǎo·de) ❶ 沿着弯弯曲曲的路走 walk in a roundabout way ❷〈比喻 *fig.*〉说话、写文章不直截了当 not straightforward in speaking or in writing; talk in a roundabout way; beat around the bush

【拐枣】guǎizǎo ❶ 落叶乔木,叶子卵形或卵圆形,花淡黄绿色,果实近球形,果柄肥厚弯曲,肉质、红褐色,味甜,可以吃。种子扁圆形。果柄、种子、树皮等均可入药。Japanese raisin tree (*Hovenia dulcis*); honey tree; deciduous arbour with oval leaves, pale yellowish green flowers, spherical fruits, thick and curved fruit stalk, reddish brown, sweet and edible flesh, and flat and round seeds; the fruit stalk, seeds, and bark being useful as medicine; also 枳椇 zhǐjǔ and 鸡爪树 jīzhǎoshù ❷ 这种植物的果实和果柄 fruit and its stalk

【拐杖】guǎizhàng same as 拐棍 guǎigùn

【拐子】[1] guǎi·zi 腿脚瘸的人 cripple

【拐子】[2] guǎi·zi ❶ 一种简单的木制工具,形状略像'工'字,两头横木短,中间直木长。把丝纱等绕在上面,拿下来就可以成桄(guàng)。I-shaped spool or reel; wooden roller, usu. with a hole for a spindle from end to end and a rim at either end, upon which thread, silk yarn, etc. is wound ❷ same as 拐[1] guǎi ⑤

【拐子】[3] guǎi·zi 拐骗人口、财物的人 abductor; swindler

guài(ㄍㄨㄞ)

夬 guài《易经》六十四卦的一个卦名 one of the 64 divine symbols in *The Book of Changes*

怪[1](恠) guài ❶ 奇怪 strange; odd; queer; bewildering:～事 a queer thing ❷ 觉得奇怪 find sth. strange; wonder at:大惊小～ make a fuss over ❸ 很;非常 very; quite; rather:～不好意思的 feel rather embarrassed|箱子提着～费劲的。It's quite heavy to carry the suitcase. ❹ 怪物;妖怪(迷信)(superstition) monster; demon; devil being:鬼～ demon; devil; ghost; monster

怪[2](恠) guài 责备;怨;blame; complain:不能～他,只～我没讲清楚。It's not his fault; I'm to blame for not having made it clearer.

【怪不得】[1] guài·bu·de 表示明白了原因,对某种情况就不觉得奇怪 no wonder; so that's why; that explains why:天气预报说今晚有雨,～这么闷热。The weather report says that there will be a rain tonight, no wonder it is so sultry.

【怪不得】[2] guài·bu·de 不能责备;别见怪 not take offence; not to blame:昨天下了那么大的雨,他没有赶到,也～他。He was not to blame for coming late. It rained so heavily yesterday.

【怪诞】guàidàn 荒诞离奇;古怪 odd; fantastic; incredible; absurd; queer; weird; strange:～不经(不经:不正常)weird and uncanny; fantastic; wild; absurd|关于沙漠,曾有许多～的传说。There were many weird legends about the desert.

【怪道】guài·dào〈方 *dial.*〉怪不得;难怪 no wonder; so that's why; that explains why:她是我过去的学生,～觉得很眼熟。She is my former student; no wonder she looks so familiar.

【怪话】guàihuà 怪诞的话,也指无原则的牢骚或议论 cynical remark; grumble; complaint:～连篇 a lot of cynical remarks|背后说～ make cynical remarks behind one's back

【怪谲】guàijué〈书 *fml.*〉怪异荒诞 weird; fantastic

【怪里怪气】guài·liguàiqì(形状、装束、声音等)奇特,跟一般的不同(含贬义 derog.)(of looks, attire, voice, etc.) eccentric; peculiar; queer:戏台上的媒婆总是那么～的。The woman matchmaker on the stage always looks so eccentric (or funny).

【怪模怪样】guài mú guài yàng (～儿的 guài mú guài yàngr·de)形态奇怪 queer-looking; grotesque:她这身打扮土不土,洋不洋,～的。It's queer-looking; the way she is dressed is neither traditional nor Western.

【怪癖】guàipǐ 古怪的癖好 strange hobby

【怪僻】guàipì 古怪 odd:性情～ eccentric

【怪圈】guàiquān〈比喻 *fig.*〉难以摆脱的某种怪现象(多指恶性循环的 oft. vicious cycle) a strange phenomenon hard to get rid of:有些地区总跳不出'越穷越生孩子,越生孩子越穷'的～。Some areas can hardly get out of the vicious circle for people to become 'the poorer the more children they have, and the more children they have, the poorer they become'.

【怪事】guàishì 奇怪的事情 strange thing:咄咄～ sheer absurdity

【怪物】guài·wu ❶ 神话传说中奇形怪状的妖魔,泛指奇异的东西 strange-looking monster in fairy tales; bizarre thing; monster; monstrosity; freak ❷ 称性情非常古怪的人 queer man; eccentric person; queer bird; oddball

【怪异】guàiyì ❶ 奇异 bizarre; monstrous; strange; unusual: 行为～ strange behaviour | ～的声音引起了我的警觉。Strange noises alerted me. ❷ 奇异反常的现象 strange and unusual phenomenon; portent; prodigy: ～丛生 a lot of strange things

【怪怨】guàiyuàn 责怪埋怨 blame: 自己没搞好,不要～别人。You yourself are responsible for the failure. Don't blame others.

【怪罪】guàizuì 责任;埋怨 blame: 这事不要～他。Don't blame him for this. | 要是上面～下来怎么办? What if the higher authorities blame those at the lower level?

guān (ㄍㄨㄢ)

关(關、関) guān ❶ 使开着的物体合拢 shut; close: ～窗户 close the window | 把抽屉～上。Close the drawer. ❷ 使机器等停止运转;使电气装置结束工作状态 turn off; switch off an electrical device: ～机 switch off the machine | ～灯 turn off the light | ～电视 turn off the television set ❸ 放在里面不使出来 shut in; lock up: 鸟儿～在笼子里。The bird is shut up in the cage. | 监狱是～犯人的。A prison is where criminals are jailed. ❹ (企业等)倒闭;歇业 close down; shut a business: 有一年,镇上～了好几家店铺。There was a year in which quite a few shops in the town were closed down. ❺〈古代 *arch.*〉在交通险要或边境出入的地方设置的守卫处所 pass; guard post set up at a strategically located point and frontier point of entrance and exit in ancient times: ～口 strategic pass | ～防 military installation at a strategical point on the border | 山海～ Shanhaiguan Pass | 嘉峪～ Jiayuguan Pass ◇我的责任就是不让废品混过～去。My duty is to prevent rejects from passing the checks. ❻ 城门外附近的地区 area just outside a city gate: 城～ suburban area | 北～ north suburbs | ～厢 neighbourhood outside of a city gate ❼ 门栓 door bolt: 门插～儿 bolt; latch | 斩～落锁 cut down the bolt and padlock ❽ '关上'的简称 short form for 关上 guānshàng ❾ 货物出口和入口收税的地方 place where customs are paid and freight is cleared for entering and leaving: 海～custom house | ～税 customs duty; tariff: ❿〈比喻 *fig.*〉重要的转折点或不容易度过的一段时间 barrier; critical juncture: 难～ barrier; difficulty | 只要突破这一～,就好办了。Once we have got over this difficulty, it will be plain sailing. *or* It will be smooth sailing once you overcome this hurdle. ⓫ 起转折关联作用的部分 key part; crucial part: 机～ organ | ～节 joint | ～键 key ⓬ 牵连;关系 concern; involve: 这些见解很～重要。These views are extremely important. | 此事与他无～。This has nothing to do with him. | 交有～部门处理 leave it to the department concerned ⓭ 发放或领取(工资) give out or draw (pay): ～饷 (of soldiers, policemen, etc.) get paid ⓮ (Guān)姓 a surname

【关爱】guān'ài 关怀爱护 express solicitude for the well-being of: 老师的～使她很受感动。She was greatly moved by the solicitude of the teacher.

【关隘】guān'ài〈书 *fml.*〉险要的关口 pass

【关碍】guān'ài 妨碍;阻碍 obstruct; hinder hamper; impede: 这次事故对公司信誉大有～。The company's prestige was greatly hindered (or injured) by the accident.

【关闭】guānbì ❶ smac as 关 guān ①: 门窗都紧紧～着。The doors and windows were all tightly closed. ◇～机场 close the airport ❷ 企业、商店、学校等歇业或停办(of an enterprise, a shop, a school, etc.) close down; shut down: ～了几所学校。Some schools were closed down.

【关尺】guānchǐ〈旧时 *old*〉海关收税用的标准尺,1关尺合0.358米 customs unit for measuring the length used; one unit equals to 0.358 metre.

【关东】Guāndōng 指山海关以东一带地区,泛指东北各省 area east of Shanhaiguan; (in a broad sense) provinces in northeast China: 闯～ go to northeast China to earn a living; make a difficulty journey to northeast China to eke out a living; also 关外 guānwài

【关东糖】guāndōngtáng 一种麦芽糖,用麦芽和米或杂粮制成,白色或带黄色 northeastern candy; a kind of malt candy made of malt and rice or other cereals, white or yellowish (originating in the Northeast China)

【关防】guānfáng ❶ 防止泄漏机密的措施 security measures: ～严密 tight security measures ❷〈旧时 *old*〉政府机关或军队用的印信,多为长方形 government or army seal (usu. rectangular in shape) ❸〈书 *fml.*〉有驻军防守的关口要塞 guarded fortress at a strategic point

【关乎】guānhū 关系到;涉及 concern; relate to; involve: 调整物价是～人民生活的一件大事。Price adjustment is a matter of vital importance to the life of the people.

【关怀】guānhuái same as 关心 guān//xīn: ～备至 show the utmost solicitude | 亲切～ show loving care for; pay kin attention to | ～青年人的成长 show concern for the growth of the young people

【关键】guānjiàn ❶ 门闩或功能类似门闩的东西 door bolt; door bar ❷〈比喻 *fig.*〉事物最关紧要的部分;对情况起决定作用的因素 crucial part of a matter; decisive factor; key; hinge; crux:摸清情况是解决问题的～。A clear knowledge of the situation is the key to solving the problem.|办好学校～在于提高教育质量。The decisive factor for running the school well is to improve teaching quality. ❸ 最关紧要的 the most crucial:～问题 the most crucial problem|～时刻 the most critical moment

【关节】guānjié ❶ 骨头互相连接的地方。根据构造可分为三种,不动的如头骨的各关节,稍动的如椎骨的关节,活动的如四肢的关节。joint; joint of bones; there are three kinds of joints: the immovable joints of the skull, the slightly movable joints of the vertebra and the movable joints of the limbs ❷ 起关键性作用的环节 crucial link; key (or crucial) link; key (or crucial) point:这是问题～的所在。This is the crucial link to the problem.|认真分析,找出～。Find out the crucial link through a careful analysis. ❸ 指暗中行贿勾通官府或官员的事 bribe an official:打～ practise bribery|暗通～ bribe covertly

【关津】guānjīn〈书 *fml.*〉关口和渡口,也指设在关口或渡口的关卡 pass and ferry; outpost of an tax office at a pass or ferry

【关紧】guānjǐn〈方 *dial.*〉要紧 important; essential

【关口】guānkǒu ❶ 来往必须经过的处所 strategic pass:把守～ guard a strategic pass ❷ 关键的地方;关头 crucial point; juncture

【关里】Guānlǐ same as 关内 Guānnèi

【关连】guānlián same as 关联 guānlián

【关联】guānlián 事物相互之间发生牵连和影响 interrelation among different things; be related; be connected:国民经济各部门是互相～互相依存的。The various sectors of the national economy are interrelated and interdependent.|这可是～着生命安全的大事。This is a matte of vital importance, with life at stake.

【关联词】guānliáncí 在语句中起关联作用的词语。如'因为…所以…'、'一方面…,另一方面…'、'总而言之'等。uninflected word used to connect words, phrases, clauses, sentences, such as 'because ... therefore,' 'on the one hand ..., on the other hand ...,' 'in short,' etc.

【关门】guān//mén ❶〈比喻 *fig.*〉停业(of a shop, etc.) close; close down ❷〈比喻 *fig.*〉把话说死,无商量余地 refuse discussion or consideration ❸〈比喻 *fig.*〉不愿容纳 refuse to admit others:～主义 closed-doorism; exclusionism. ❹ 指最后的 final:～之作 final piece of writing|～弟子 final disciple

【关门】guānmén 关口上的门 gate of a pass

【关内】Guānnèi 指山海关以西或嘉峪关以东一带地区 area to the west of Shanhaiguan or to the east of Jiayuguan

【关卡】guānqiǎ 为收税或警备在交通要道设立的检查站、岗哨 outpost of a tax office or a checkpoint at a vital communication line

【关切】guānqiè ❶ 亲切 considerate; thoughtful:他待人非常和蔼、～。He's very kind and considerate (or thoughtful). ❷ 关心 be deeply concerned about; show one's concern over; feel concern over:感谢同志们对我的～。I'm grateful to you comrades for your deep concern.|对他的处境深表～。We feel deep concern over his circumstances.

【关塞】guānsài 关口上的要塞 frontier fortress

【关山】guānshān 关口和山岳 frontier passes and mountains:～迢递(形容路途遥远) remote passes and mountains

【关上】guānshàng ☞ 寸口 cùnkǒu on p. 337

【关涉】guānshè 关联;牵涉 involve; concern; be related to:他与此案毫无～。He is not at all involved in the case.

【关书】guānshū〈旧时 *old*〉聘请教师或幕僚的文书 contract for employing a teacher or an assistant

【关税】guānshuì 国家对进出口商品所征收的税 tax imposed on import and export goods by a government; customs duty; customs; tariff

【关说】guānshuō〈书 *fml.*〉代人陈说;从中给人说好话 put in a word for sb.; speak in sb.'s favour

【关头】guāntóu 起决定作用的时机或转折点 decisive juncture; turning point; juncture; key moment:紧要～ critical moment|危急～ critical moment (or juncture)

【关外】Guānwài 指山海关以东或嘉峪关以西一带地区 areas to the east of Shanhaiguan or to the west of Jiayuguan

【关系】guān·xì ❶ 事物之间相互作用、相互影响的状态 relation; relationship:正确处理科学技术普及和提高的～ correctly handle the relationship between the popularization of science and technology and the raising of their standards|这个电门跟那盏灯没有～。This switch has nothing to do with that light. ❷ 人和人或人和事物之间的某种性质的联系 connection between or among persons or between a person and a thing; connections; relations; relationship:拉～ try to establish a relationship with somebody; cotton up to; cotton on to|～户 persons or groups having dealings with each other that promote their common interests|同志～ relationship between or among comrades|军民～ relationship between the army and the people|社会～ social connections ❸ 对有关事物的影响或重要性;值得注意

的地方（常跟‘没有、有’连用 oft. used together with 没有 méi·yǒu，有 yǒu）impact on；importance to；sth. worth noting；relevance；bearing；influence；significance：这一点很有～。This matters a lot.｜没有～，修理修理照样儿能用。It doesn't matter. After some repair, it can be used again all the same. ❹ 泛指原因、条件等 cause；condition［usu. used with 由于 yóuyú or 因为 yīn·wèi to indicate cause or reason］：由于时间～，暂时谈到这里为止。Since time is limited, I'll have to stop here this time. ❺ 表明有某种组织关系的证件 document showing identity credentials, membership in or connection with an organization：随身带上团的～。Bring your Youth League credentials with you. ❻ 关联；牵涉 relating to；involve concern；affect；have a bearing on；have to do with：棉花是～到国计民生的重要物资。Cotton is a major material that has an important bearing on the national economy and the people's livelihood.

【关厢】guānxiāng 城门外大街和附近的地区 street and its adjoining area just outside a city gate；neighbourhood outside of a city gate

【关饷】guān//xiǎng （军队）发饷，泛指发工资 pay, esp.（of soldiers）

【关心】guān//xīn （把人或事物）常放在心上；重视和爱护 have sb. or sth. on one's mind；pay great attention to and care for；be concerned about；show solicitude for；care for；be interested in：～群众生活 care for the livelihood of the masses｜这是厂里的大事，希望大家多关点儿心。This is a matter of importance to our factory. I hope that everyone will show more interest in it

【关押】guānyā 把犯罪的人关起来 lock up；imprison；put under detention；put in prison：～犯人 put a criminal in prison

【关于】guānyú ❶〈介词 *prep.*〉引进某种行为的关系者，组成介词结构做状语［used as a relation or function word, such as 'about', 'on', 'with regard to', and 'concerning' that connects an action to form a prepositional construction as an adverbial modifier］：～兴修水利，上级已经做了指示。The higher authorities have issued an instruction on building water conservancy projects. ❷〈介词 *prep.*〉引进某种事物的关系者，组成介词结构做定语（后面要加‘的’），或在‘是…的’式中做谓语［used as a relation or function word that connects a thing to form a prepositional construction as an attribute or a predicate］：他读了几本～政治经济学的书。He read a few books on political economy.｜今天在厂里开了一个会，是～爱国卫生运动的。A meeting was held in the factory concerning the patriotic health campaign. ‖ 注意 **NOTE**：a)表示关涉，用‘关于’不用‘对于’如：～织女星，民间有个美丽的传说。when indicating 'related to' or 'relating to', use 关于 instead of 对于 duìyú, e. g. There is a beautiful legend about the Vega. 指出对象，用‘对于’不用‘关于’ when indicating an object, use 对于 instead of 关于，如：对于文化遗产，我们必须进行研究分析。e. g. Speaking of the cultural legacy, we must make a study and analysis. 兼有两种情况的可以用‘关于’，也可以用‘对于’ in a situation involving both cases, use either 关于 or 对于，如：（对于）订立公约，大家都很赞成。e. g. As to concluding a public agreement, everybody said yes. b)‘关于’有提示性质，用‘关于’组成的介词结构，可以单独作文章的题目 prepositional structure using 关于 can be used as the title of an article, such as：～人生观 On Outlook on Life｜～杂文 On Essays 用‘对于’组成的介词结构，只有跟名词组成偏正词组，才能作题目 prepositional structure using 对于 can be used as the title of an article only when it is combined with a noun to form a word group consisting of a modifier and the word it modifies, such as：对于百花齐放政策的认识 On（Our）Understanding of the Policy of 'Letting a Hundred Flowers Blossom'

【关张】guān//zhāng 指商店停止营业，也指商店倒闭（of a shop）close down；go out of business

【关照】guānzhào ❶ 关心照顾 look after；take care of；keep an eye on：我走后，这里的工作请你多多～。When I'm gone, you'll have to look after the work here. ❷ 互相照应，全面安排 look after each other and make an overall arrangement ❸ 口头通知 notify by word of mouth；tell：你～食堂一声，给开会的人留饭。Tell the cafeteria to save some food for those attending the meeting.

【关中】Guānzhōng 指陕西渭河流域一带 area in the Weihe River basin；the Central Shaanxi Plain；area within the passes

【关注】guānzhù 关心重视 follow with interest；pay close attention to；show solicitude for：多蒙～。Thanks for your concern (or interest).｜这件事引起了各界人士的～。This happening has aroused concern among all walks of life.

【关子】guān·zi 小说、戏剧情节中最紧要、最吸引人的地方 climax in a novel or drama；〈比喻 *fig.*〉事情的关键 key to a thing；☞ 卖关子 mài guān·zi on p. 1296

观（觀） guān ❶ 看 see；look at；watch；observe：～日出 watch the sunrise｜走马～花 look at flowers while riding on horseback；gain a superficial understanding through cursory observation；view flowers from the back of a galloping horse — observe things in a hurry|坐井～天 look at the sky from the bottom of a well — have a very narrow view ❷ 景象或样子 sight; view: 奇～ marvellous spectacle|改～ change the appearance or look of... ❸ 对事物的认识或看法 outlook; view; concept: 乐～ optimism; optimistic view|悲～ pessimism; pessimistic view|世界～ world outlook

☞ guàn on p. 718

【观测】guāncè ❶ 观察并测量(天文、地理、气象、方向等) observe and survey (astronomy, geography, weather, direction): ～风力 observing the wind force ❷ 观察并测度(情况) observe; watch: ～敌情 watch enemy movements

【观察】guānchá 仔细察看(事物或现象) observe carefully; watch; survey: ～地形 survey the terrain|～动静 watch what is going on|～问题 look into a problem; study a problem

【观察家】guānchájiā 政治评论家。通常用做报刊上重要政治评论文章作者的署名。political commentator; political critic, usually used as an undersigned for an important political commentary printed in a newspaper; observer (a pseudonym used by a political commentator)

【观察哨】guāncháshào 观察敌情的哨兵或哨所 sentry; outpost watching enemy movements; also 瞭望哨 liàowàngshào

【观察所】guānchásuǒ 军队作战时,为观察战场而设置的场所,通常设在隐蔽而又视野开阔的地点 observation post; location for watching the battlefield, usu. hidden but having a broad view

【观察员】guāncháyuán 一个国家派遣的列席国际会议的外交代表,依照国际惯例,观察员只有发言权,没有表决权 observer; diplomatic envoy to an international conference, who has the right to make a speech, but no right to vote

【观点】guāndiǎn ❶ 观察事物时所处的位置或采取的态度 viewpoint; point of view; standpoint: 生物学～ biological point of view|纯技术～ (from a) purely technical point of view ❷ 专指政治观点 political viewpoint: 没有正确的立场,就不会有正确的～。Without a correct stand, there cannot be a correct point of view.

【观风】guān//fēng 望风 keep watch; be on the lookout; serve as a lookout

【观感】guāngǎn 看到事物以后所产生的印象和感想 impressions; observations: 代表们畅谈访问农村的～。The delegates talked freely of their impressions of the rural areas they had visited.|就自己～所及,写些通讯。I wrote a news report based on my own observations.

【观光】guānguāng 参观外国或外地的景物、建筑等 visit places and see things of interest, oft. in other countries or other places; go sightseeing; visit; tour: ～客 sightseer; tourist|有不少外宾前来桂林～。Many foreign visitors have come to see Guilin.|他陪同我们在上海各处～了一番。He took us to see all places of interest in Shanghai.

【观看】guānkàn 特意在看;参观;观察 view; watch; observe; visit: ～景物 see sights of interest|～动静 watch what is going on|～足球比赛 watch a football match

【观礼】guān//lǐ (被邀请)参观典礼 attend a ceremony or celebration upon invitation: ～台 reviewing stand; visitors' stand|国庆～ attend National Day celebrations

【观摩】guānmó 观看,多指观看彼此的成绩,交流经验,互相学习 watch, inspect and learn from each other's work: ～演出 demonstrative performance oft. before fellow artists

【观念】guānniàn ❶ 思想意识 ideology sense; idea; concept: 破除旧的传统～ eschew outdated traditional modes of thinking ❷ 客观事物在人脑里留下的概括的形象(有时指表象) image; generalized idea

【观念形态】guānniàn xíngtài 意识形态 ideology

【观赏】guānshǎng 观看欣赏 view and admire: ～名花异草 enjoy famous flowers and exotic grasses|～杂技表演 marvel at an acrobatic show

【观赏鱼】guānshǎngyú 形状奇异,颜色美丽,可供观赏的鱼,如金鱼和热带产的许多小鱼 ornamental fish; fishes of different shapes and colours for ornamentation, such as goldfishes and small tropical fishes; fishes for display

【观赏植物】guānshǎng zhíwù 专门培植来供观赏的植物,一般都有美丽的花或形态比较奇异 ornamental (or decorative) plant; plant cultivated specially for ornament and decoration, usually having beautiful flowers and exotic shapes

【观世音】Guānshìyīn 〈佛教 *Budd.*〉菩萨之一,佛教徒认为是救苦救难之神 Avalokitesvara; Guanyin; one of the Buddhisattvas; Goddess of Mercy; also 观自在 Guānzìzài and 观音大士 Guānyīn dàshì; 俗称 popularly called 观音 guānyīn

【观望】guānwàng ❶ 怀着犹豫的心情观看事物的发展变化 wait and see: 意存～ wait and see intentionally|徘徊～ hesitate; wait for the dust to settle; wait and see; look on (from the sidelines) ❷ 张望 look around: 四下～ look around

【观象台】guānxiàngtái 观测天文、气象、地磁、地震等现象的机构,按其任务的不同,现已分别采用天文台、气象台、地磁台、地震台等名称 observatory; institution for observing astronomical, meteorological, terrestrial magnetic and seismic phenomena, and thus known variously as astronomical observatory, meteorological observatory, terrestrial magnetograph station and seismograph station

【观音土】guānyīntǔ 一种白色的黏土 a kind of white clay; also 观音粉 gānyīnfěn

【观瞻】guānzhān ❶ 具体的景象和景象给人的印象;外观和对外观发生的反应 sth. or an impression it leaves; appearance or response to it:以壮～ make it more impressive|有碍～ eyesore; be repugnant to the eye; be unpleasant to the eye ❷ 瞻望;观赏 look forward; look far ahead; view and admire:楼阁建成后,～者络绎不绝。An endless flow of visitors came to see the pavilion after it was completed.

【观战】guānzhàn 从旁观看战争、战斗,自己不参加。也借指体育竞赛时从旁观看助兴。watch a match or contest; watch a battle; watch other people fight; watch a battle without participating

【观止】guānzhǐ 看到这里就可以不再看了,称赞所看到的事物好到极点 regard what one has seen as perfect and nothing else as worth seeing:叹为～ acclaim something as highest perfection; ☞ 叹观止矣 tàn guān zhǐ yǐ on p. 1861

【观众】guānzhòng 看表演或比赛的人 spectator; viewer; audience:电视～ TV audience|演出结束,～起立鼓掌。The performance ended with a standing ovation from the audience.

纶(綸) guān [纶巾](guānjīn)〈古代 *arch.*〉配有青丝带的头巾 kerchief with a green silk ribbon:羽扇～ (of a commander at a moment of composure) waving a feather fan and wearing a kerchief with a green silk ribbon
☞ lún on p. 1273

官1 guān ❶ 政府机关或军队中经过任命的、一定等级以上的公职人员 person appointed to a position of authority in a government or in the armed forces; government official; officer; office holder:～员 official|武～ military officer; military attache|做～ hold an official position|外交～ diplomatic envoy ❷ 指属于政府的或公家的 of a government; governmental; official:～办 government-run; run or operated by the government|～费 funds from public coffers ❸ 公共的;公用的 public:～大道 public avenue|～厕所 public W. C.; public toilet ❹ (Guān) 姓 a surname

官2 guān 器官 organ (a part of the body):五～ five sense organs (ears, eyes, lips, nose and tongue)|感～ sense organ; sensory organ; senses

【官办】guānbàn 政府开办或经营 run or operated by the government or official organizations:～企业 enterprise run by the government

【官报私仇】guān bào sī chóu 公报私仇 avenge a personal wrong in the name of public interests; abuse public power to retaliate on a personal enemy;

【官兵】guānbīng ❶ 军官和士兵 officers and men:正确处理～关系 correctly handle the relations between officers and men ❷〈旧时 *old*〉指政府的军队 government troops

【官舱】guāncāng〈旧时 *old*〉轮船中的高等舱位 luxury cabin on a passenger ship

【官差】guānchāi ❶ 官府的公务 government business; public errand:出～ go on a public errand; go on official business ❷ 官府的差役 government corvée

【官场】guānchǎng 指官吏阶层及其活动范围(贬义,强调其中的虚伪、欺诈、逢迎、倾轧等特点) officialdom (derog., emphasizing its hypocrisy, fraud, fawning, and endless infighting)

【官倒】guāndǎo ❶ 政府机构或政府工作人员进行的倒买倒卖活动 speculation by government organs or by their employees ❷ 指进行倒买倒卖活动的政府机构或政府工作人员 official speculators

【官邸】guāndǐ 由公家提供的高级官员的住所(区别于'私邸' as compared with 'private house') residence provided by the government to high officials:official residence; official mansion:首相～ prime minister's residence

【官方】guānfāng 政府方面 of or from the government:～消息 news from official sources; government sources|～人士 government officials or sources|～评论 official comment

【官费】guānfèi〈旧时 *old*〉指由政府供给的费用 allowance provided by the government:～生 student sponsored by the government|～留学 study abroad with a government scholarship

【官府】guānfǔ ❶〈旧时 *old*〉称行政机关,特指地方上的 government house, esp. a local one; local authorities; official government house ❷ 称封建官吏 feudal official

【官官相护】guān guān xiāng hù 当官人相互包庇、袒护 officials shied each other; bureaucrats protect each other; officials protect each other; also 官官相卫 guān guān xiāng wèi

【官话】guānhuà ❶ 普通话的旧称。作为汉族共同语的基础方言的北方话也统称官话。Mandarin; official dialect; old term for the official dialect; northern dialect which serves as the basic dialect the common language of the Han nationality (now replaced by 普通话 *putonghua*) ❷ 官腔 bureaucratic jargon

【官宦】guānhuàn〈书 *fml.*〉泛指做官的人 (in a broad sense) official:～人家 official's family

【官家】guānjiā ❶ 指官府或朝廷 government

G

house; imperial court; government authorities ❷〈古代 *arch*.〉对皇帝的称呼 address for the emperor ❸〈旧时 *old*〉官吏 officials

【官价】guānjià 指政府规定的价格 government price; official price (or rate)

【官阶】guānjiē 官员的等级 official rank

【官爵】guānjué 官职爵位 offices and titles; ranks and titles

【官吏】guānlì〈旧时 *old*〉政府工作人员的总称 general term for government officials

【官僚】guānliáo ❶ 官员;官吏 officials; bureaucrats: ❷ 指官僚主义 bureaucracy: 要～ behave like a bureaucrat; act like a bureaucrat

【官僚主义】guānliáo zhǔyì 指脱离实际,脱离群众,不关心群众利益,只知发号施令而不进行调查研究的工作作风和领导作风 work style of the leadership characterized by being divorced from reality and from the masses and paying no attention to their interests, and knowing only to issue orders without making investigations; bureaucracy; bureaucratism

【官僚资本】guānliáo zīběn 官僚资产阶级所拥有的资本 bureaucratic capital; capital owned by the bureaucratic capitalist class; capital owned by the bureaucrat-capitalist class; bureaucratic capital

【官僚资本主义】guānliáo zīběn zhǔyì 半殖民地半封建国家中的买办的、封建的国家垄断资本主义 bureaucratic capitalism; comprador and feudal state monopoly capitalism in a semi-colonial and semi-feudal country

【官僚资产阶级】guānliáo zīchǎn jiējí 半封建半殖民地国家里,勾结帝国主义和地主阶级势力,掌握国家政权,垄断全国经济命脉的买办性的资产阶级 bureaucratic bourgeoisie; comprador capitalist class which controls the state power and monopolizes the national economic lifeline in a semi-colonial and semi-feudal country by colluding with the imperialists and the landlord class forces

【官迷】guānmí 指一心想做官的人 person who is bent on seeking office; person who hankers after public office; office seeker

【官名】guānmíng ❶〈旧时 *old*〉称在乳名以外起的正式名字 formal name given to a person by parents after the infant name; one's formal name (as opposed to infant or pet name) ❷ 官衔 title of an official position

【官能】guānnéng 有机体的器官的功能,例如视觉是眼睛的官能 sense; function of an organ of an organic body; organic function. For instance, the sight is the function of the eyes.

【官能团】guānnéngtuán 有机化合物分子中能够决定有机化合物主要化学性质的原子或原子团。如双键、叁键、羟基、羧基等。function group; atom or atomic group among the molecules of an organic chemical compounds which determines the compound's main chemical properties, such as double bond, triple bond, hydroxyl; carboxyl, etc.; also 功能团 gōngnéngtuán

【官气】guānqì 官僚作风 bureaucratic style of work; bureaucratism: ～十足 full of bureaucratic airs

【官腔】guānqiāng〈旧时 *old*〉称官场中的门面话,今指利用规章、手续等来敷衍推托或责备的话 bureaucratic tone or official jargon; speak in a perfunctory manner; make excuses for not doing anything; reprimand people by making use of regulations and formalities: 打～ talk like a bureaucrat; speak in a bureaucratic manner; bureaucratic tone; official jargon

【官人】guānrén ❶〈书 *fml*.〉有官职的人 person with an official position ❷ 宋朝对一般男子的尊称 [a term of respectful address for a man in the Song Dynasty (960-1279)] ❸ 妻子称呼丈夫(多见于早期白话 oft. in early vernacular) wife's term of address for husband

【官纱】guānshā 浙江杭州、绍兴一带产的一种丝织品,经线用生丝,纬线用熟丝织成,质薄而轻,可做夏衣,旧时多贡内廷,所以叫官纱 official gauze; a kind of silk fabric woven with raw silk as warp and boiled-off silk as weft, thin and light, for making summer dresses; known as official gauze because it was a tribute to the royal family

【官商】guānshāng ❶〈旧时 *old*〉指官办商业,也指从事这种商业的人 government commerce; state-operated commerce; bureaucratic operator of a commercial enterprise ❷ 现指有官僚作风的国营商业部门或这些部门的人员 state commercial departments or their employees handling things in a bureaucratic style

【官书】guānshū ❶〈旧时 *old*〉由官方编修或刊行的书 official book; book compiled or published by a government agency ❷〈书 *fml*.〉指文书;公文 official document

【官署】guānshǔ same as 官厅 guāntīng

【官司】guān·si 指诉讼 suit: 打～ file a suit ◇ 笔墨～(书面上的争辩) written polemics (controversy); battle of words; lawsuit

【官厅】guāntīng〈旧时 *old*〉称政府机关 government offices

【官位】guānwèi 官员的职位;官职 official position

【官衔】guānxián 官员的职位名称 official title

【官样文章】guānyàng-wénzhāng 徒具形式,照例敷衍的虚文滥调 officialese; bureaucratic red tape; mere formalities

【官员】guānyuán 经过任命的、担任一定职务的政府工作人员(现在多用于外交场合 oft. used on diplomatic occasions) official; official appointed to a certain post

【官运】guānyùn 做官的运气 official career; fortunes of officialdom; luck of being an official:～亨通 have a successful official career

【官长】guānzhǎng ❶ 指官吏 government official ❷〈旧时 *old*〉指军官 army officer

【官职】guānzhí 官吏的职位 government post; official position:在封建时代,宰相是最高的～。The prime minister was the highest official in the feudal times.

【官佐】guānzuǒ〈旧时 *old*〉指军官 army officer

冠 guān ❶ 帽子 hat:皇～ crown | 桂～laurels | 衣～整齐 be sloppily dressed | 怒发冲～ bristle with anger ❷ 形状像帽子或在顶上的东西 sth. shaped like a hat or on the top of sth. else; corona; crown:鸡～ cockscomb | 树～ crown of a tree.

☞ guàn on p.718

【冠盖】guāngài〈古代 *arch.*〉官吏的帽子和车盖,借指官吏 official hats and canopies; (metaphor) officials:～相望 constant exchange of visits of ranking officials between nations | ～云集 a large gathering of dignitaries; a large meeting of ranking officials

【冠冕】guānmiǎn ❶ 古代帝王、官员戴的帽子 crown; official hat ❷ 冠冕堂皇; 体面② elegant and stately; high-sounding; ceremonious:尽说些～话有什么用? What's the good of so much high-sounding talk?

【冠冕堂皇】guānmiǎn tánghuáng 形容表面上庄严或正大的样子 superficially dignified or upright; highfalutin; high-sounding

【冠状动脉】guānzhuàng-dòngmài 供给心脏养分的动脉,起于主动脉,分左右两条,环绕在心脏的表面,形状像王冠 coronary artery; one of two arteries supplying blood to the heart, stemming from the aorta, and branching out around the heart to form a crown-shaped network; (图见 ☞ figure for 心 xīn on p.2126)

【冠子】guān·zi 鸟类头上红色的肉质突起 crest; comb; red fleshy outgrowth on the top of the head of a bird:鸡～ cockscomb

矜 guān〈书 *fml.*〉❶ same as 鳏 guān ❷ same as 瘝 guān

☞ jīn on p.1007 and qín on p.1560

莞 guān 指水葱一类的植物 plant like water onion

☞ guǎn on p.715 and wǎn on p.1975

倌 guān (～儿 guānr) ❶ 农村中专管饲养某些家畜的人员 man or boy whose work is tending, feeding and currying domestic animals; keeper of domestic animals; herdsman:羊～儿 shepherd | 猪～儿 swineherd ❷〈旧时 *old*〉某些行业中被雇用专做某种活计的人 hired hand in certain trades:堂～儿 waiter | 磨～儿(磨面的人) miller

棺 guān 棺材 coffin:盖～论定 final judgement can be passed on a person only when the lid is laid on his coffin

【棺材】guān·cai 装殓死人的东西,一般用木材制成 coffin; case or box in which a dead body is buried

【棺椁】guānguǒ 棺和椁,泛指棺材 inner coffin and outer coffin, which are called coffins in a broad sense

【棺木】guānmù same as 棺材 guān·cai

瘝 guān〈书 *fml.*〉病;痛苦 illness; pain:恫～在抱 suffer from illness; confined to illness

鳏 guān 无妻或丧妻的 man who has no wife or has lost his wife; wifeless; widowered:～寡孤独 widowers, widows, orphans and the childless | ～居 live as a widower

【鳏夫】guānfū 无妻或丧妻的人 widower; man who has no wife or has lost his wife; old wifeless man

【鳏寡孤独】guān guǎ gū dú 泛指丧失劳动力而又无依无靠的人 people who have no kith and kin and cannot support themselves

guǎn (ㄍㄨㄢˇ)

莞 guǎn 东莞(Dōngguǎn),地名,在广东 Dongguan, a place in Guangdong Province

☞ guān on p.715 and wǎn on p.1975

馆(舘) guǎn ❶ 招待宾客居住的房屋 place of accommodation for guests, visitors, tourists, etc.:宾～ guesthouse; hotel | 旅～ hotel; inn ❷ 一个国家在另一国家办理外交的人员常驻的处所 official residence or offices for diplomatic envoys and officials; legation or consulate:使～ embassy | 领事～ consulate embassy ❸ (～儿 guǎnr) 某些服务性商店的名称(of service trades) shop:理发～ barber shop; hairdresser's shop | 照相～ photo studio | 饭～儿 restaurant ❹ 储藏、陈列文物或进行文体活动的场所 places for storing goods, displaying exhibits or carrying out sports activities and entertainment:博物～ museum | 天文～ planetarium | 文化～ cultural centre | 图书～ library | 展览～ exhibition hall | 体育～ indoor stadium; gymnasium ❺〈旧时 *old*〉指塾师教书的地方 old-style private school:坐～ teach in a school | 他教过三年～。He taught in a school for three years.

【馆藏】guǎncáng ❶ 图书馆或博物馆等收藏(of a library or a museum) have a collection of:～中外书刊七十万册 have a collection of 700,000 volumes of books and periodicals in Chinese and foreign languages ❷ 图书馆、博物馆等收藏的图书、器物等 books, paintings, articles, etc. in a library or museum collec-

tion

【馆子】guǎn·zi 卖酒饭的店铺 restaurant; eating house: 下～ eat out; eat at a restaurant | 吃～(到馆子里吃东西) eat at a restaurant

琯 guǎn〈古代 *arch.*〉乐器,用玉制成,六孔,像笛 *guan*; flute-like wind instrument of jade with six holes

辖(錧) guǎn〈书 *fml.*〉包在大车毂头上的铁 hub sleeve; iron piece that covers the hub of a cart

筦 guǎn ❶ same as 管 guǎn ❷ (Guǎn)姓 a surname

痯 guǎn〈书 *fml.*〉疲劳;病 fatigue; ailment

管1 guǎn ❶ (～儿 guǎnr)管子 tube; pipe: 钢～ steel tube; steel pipe | 竹～ bamboo pipe | 水～ water pipe | 笔～ penholder | 气～儿 windpipe; trachea ❷ 吹奏的乐器 wind instrument: ～弦乐 orchestral music ❸ 形状像管的电器件 tube-shaped electrical element; valve; tube: 电子管 electron tube | 晶体～ transistor ❹〈量词 *classifier*〉用于细长圆筒形的东西 [for a long, slender cylinder]: 一～毛笔 a writing brush | 两～牙膏 two tubes of toothpaste ❺ (Guǎn)姓 a surname

管2 guǎn ❶ 管理;看管 manage; run; control; look after; take care of; be in charge of: ～账 keep accounts | ～图书 take care of the books in the library | 谁～仓库? Who is in charge of the warehouse? *or* Who keeps the warehouse? | 她能同时～十台机器。She can tend ten machines at the same time. ❷ 管辖 have jurisdiction over; administer: 这个省～着几十个县。This city has jurisdiction over ten counties. ❸ 管教 discipline (children or students): ～孩子 discipline children ❹ 担任(工作) be in charge of: 我～宣传,你～文体。I'll be in charge of publicity and you'll take care of recreation and sports. ❺ 过问 be concerned about; care about; bother about; intervene; mind: ～闲事 mind other's business | 这事我们不能不～。We have to do something about this matter. ❻ 保证;负责供给 guarantee; provide: ～保 guarantee | 不好～换。We guarantee to change it if it is not any good. | ～吃～住 provide food and accommodation ❼〈介词 *prep.*〉作用跟'把'相近,专跟'叫'配合[close in function to 管 guǎn, esp. matching with 叫 jiào] call: 他长得又矮又胖,大家都～他叫小胖子。He is short and fat, so everyone calls him Little Fatty. ❽〈方 *dial.*〉〈介词 *prep.*〉作用跟'向'相近[close in function to 向 xiàng]: ～他借钱 borrow money from him | ～我要东西 ask me for something ❾〈方 *dial.*〉不管;无论 no matter what: 这是国家财产,～什么也不能让它受到损失。This is state property. We must make sure no damage is done to it no matter what happens. ❿〈方 *dial.*〉关涉;牵涉 involve: 他不愿来,～我什么事? I don't care if he wants to come or not.

【管保】guǎnbǎo 完全有把握;保证 be absolutely sure; guarantee: ～成功 be sure to succeed | 有了水和肥,～能多打粮食。With water and fertiliser, I'm sure more grains will be harvested.

【管材】guǎncái 管状的材料,如钢管、陶管等 tubular materials such as steel tubes, ceramic tubes, etc.

【管道】guǎndào 用金属或其他材料制成的管子,用来输送或排除流体(如水蒸气、煤气、石油、水等) pipeline; piping; conduit; tubing; pipes or tubes made of metal or other materials for conveying or drain steam, gas, petroleum, water, etc.

【管段】guǎnduàn 分段管理的地段 section of an area: 这一～的治安状况良好。Security is satisfactory in this part of the area.

【管风琴】guǎnfēngqín 键盘乐器,用几组音色不同的管子构成,由风箱压缩空气通过管子而发出声音 pipe organ; organ; large wind instrument consisting of various sets of pipes which, as they are opened by corresponding keys on one or more keyboards, allow passage to a column of compressed air that causes sound by vibration

【管家】guǎn·jiā ❶〈旧时 *old*〉称呼为地主、官僚等管理家产和日常事务的地位较高的仆人 butler; housekeeper; head servant in charge of property and day-to-day affairs for a landlord or a bureaucrat: 女～ woman housekeeper ❷ 现在指为集体管理财物或日常生活的人 person in charge of collective property or daily life: 大家都说食堂管理员是群众的好～。Everyone claims that the person in charge of the cafeteria is a good housekeeper of the masses.

【管家婆】guǎnjiāpó ❶〈旧时 *old*〉称呼为地主、官僚等管理家务的地位较高的女仆 woman housekeeper; woman head servant in charge of household affairs for a landlord or a bureaucrat ❷ 主妇 housewife

【管见】guǎnjiàn〈谦辞 *hum.*〉浅陋的见识(像从管子里看东西,看到的范围很小)(as if looking through a tube and able to catch only a small part of sth.) my humble opinion; my limited understanding: 略陈～。Let me state my humble opinion briefly.

【管教】[1] guǎnjiào same as 管保 guǎnbǎo

【管教】[2] guǎnjiào ❶ 约束教导 discipline (children or students); correct: 严加～ discipline strictly ❷ 管制并劳教 put under surveillance and reeducation through labour: ～所 house for surveillance and reeducation | 解除～ relieved from surveillance and reeducation through labour

【管界】guǎnjiè ❶ 管辖的地区 area under jurisdiction ❷ 管辖地区的边界 boundary of an area under jurisdiction

【管井】guǎnjǐng 用机械开凿、装上铁管或缸管等而通到深层地下水的井 tube well; deep well dug by machinery and equipped with iron or ceramic tubing

【管窥】guǎnkuī 从管子里看东西 look at sth. through a bamboo tube;〈比喻 *fig.*〉所见片面 have a restricted view:～所及 in my humble opinion

【管窥蠡测】guǎnkuī lícè 从竹管里看天,用瓢来量海水 look at the sky through a bamboo tube and measure the sea with a calabash;〈比喻 *fig.*〉眼光狭窄,见识短浅 restricted in vision and shallow in understanding

【管理】guǎnlǐ ❶ 负责某项工作使顺利进行 in charge of; manage; run; administer; govern; take care of: ～财务 be in charge of financial affairs|～国家大事 administer state affairs ❷ 保管和料理 take care of; look after: ～图书 take care of library books|公园～处 park office ❸ 照管并约束(人或动物) look after; tend and control (people or animals): ～罪犯 keep criminals under control|～牲口 tend draught animals

【管片】guǎnpiàn (～儿 guǎnpiànr)分片管理的地段 area divided for management: 雨季前本～的房屋检修工作已全部完成。Repairs of the houses in the area under our charge have all been finished.

【管钳子】guǎnqián·zi 用来扳动或卡住圆柱形工件的工具 alligator wrench; tool for holding and turning pipes; also 管扳子 guǎnbān·zi

【管区】guǎnqū 管辖的区域 area under jurisdiction

【管事】guǎn//shì ❶ 负责管理事务 run affairs; be in charge ❷(～儿 guǎn//shìr) same as 管用 guǎn//yòng: 这个药很～儿,保你吃了见好。This medicine is very effective. You'll surely get better after taking it.

【管事】guǎnshì 〈旧时 *old*〉称在企业单位或有钱人家里管总务的人 manager; one who manages a business; one who manages affairs or expenditures of a household in old times

【管束】guǎnshù 加以约束,使不越轨 restrain; check; control

【管辖】guǎnxiá 管理;统辖(人员、事务、区域、案件等) administer; manage; have jurisdiction over; exercise control over (personnel, affairs, areas, cases, etc.): ～范围 jurisdiction over|直辖市由国务院直接～。The municipalities are directly under the jurisdiction of the State Council. *or* The municipalities are directly under the State Council

【管弦乐】guǎnxiányuè 用管乐器、弦乐器和打击乐器配合演奏的音乐 orchestral music; music played by an orchestra composed of wind instruments, stringed instruments and percussion instruments

【管线】guǎnxiàn 各种管道和电线、电缆等的总称 general term for pipes, wires and cables: 铺设～ lay pipes and cables

【管押】guǎnyā 临时拘押 take sb. into custody; keep in custody; detain

【管用】guǎn//yòng 有效;起作用 effective: 这种药挺～,吃了就见好。This medicine is very effective. You'll get better after taking it.|学普通话光听不～,必须常讲多练。It's no use if you just listen when you learn *putonghua* of the Chinese language. You must practise speaking it very often.

【管乐器】guǎnyuèqì 指由于管中空气振动而发音的乐器,如笛、箫、号等 wind instrument; instrument sounded by blowing air through it to cause vibration, such as flute, oboe, trumpet, etc.

【管制】guǎnzhì ❶ 强制管理 control: ～灯火 enforce a blackout ❷ 强制性的管理 put (a criminal, etc.) under surveillance: 军事～ military control|交通～ traffic control ❸ 对罪犯或坏分子施行强制管束 put criminals or bad elements under surveillance

【管中窥豹】guǎn zhōng kuī bào 通过竹管子的小孔来看豹,只看到豹身上的一块斑纹(见于《世说新语·方正》) *A New Account of Tales of the World · Righteousness*: Looking at a leopard through a bamboo tube, one can only see a spot on the leopard;〈比喻 *fig.*〉只见到事物的一小部分。有时同'可见一斑'连用,比喻从观察到的部分,可以推测全貌。having a limited view of sth. When used together with 可见一斑 kějiàn yībān, it means 'when you see a part of sth., you can guess the whole of it.'

【管子】guǎn·zi 圆而细长中间空的东西 long and slender hollow cylinder; pipe; tube: 自来水～ tap water pipe

【管自】guǎnzì 〈方 *dial.*〉❶ 径自 straight: 他水也没喝一口,～回家去了。He went straight home so much as drinking any water. ❷ 只管;只顾 by all means; simply: 让他们去商量吧,我们～干。Let them discuss it. We'll go ahead by all means.

鳤 guǎn 鱼,体长 1—2 尺,银白色,圆筒形,鳞小。生活在淡水中。ochetobius (*Ochetobius elongatus*); freshwater fish 30 to 70 cm. long, silver white in colour, cylindrical in shape, with small scales

guàn (ㄍㄨㄢˋ)

毌 guàn 〈书 *fml.*〉same as 贯 guàn

丱 guàn 〈书 *fml.*〉形容儿童束发成两角的样子 child's hair bunched into two horns

G

观(觀) guàn ❶ 道教的庙宇 Taoist temple：道～ Taoist Temple｜白云～ Baiyun (White Cloud) Temple (in Beijing) ❷ (Guàn)姓 a surname

☞ guān on p. 711

贯 guàn ❶ 穿；贯通 pass through; pierce：如雷～耳 reverberate like thunder｜学～古今 be well-versed in both ancient and modern learning; having a thorough knowledge ancient❷ 连贯 continuous：鱼～而入 file in; enter in a single file｜累累如～珠 as numerous as a string of pearls be linked together; follow in a continuous line ❸ 旧时的制钱，用绳子穿上，每一千个叫一贯 (in old times) a string of 1,000 cash：万～家私 private property to the tune of ten thousand strings of cash ❹ 世代居住的地方 place inhabited a family by generations：籍～ birthplace｜乡～ native village ❺〈书 *fml*.〉事例；成例 example; instance; case：一仍旧～ stick to the old practice; follow the old routine ❻ (Guàn)姓 a surname

【贯彻】guànchè 彻底实现或体现(方针、政策、精神、方法等) carry out; carry through; go through with; put into effect; implement：～始终 carry... through to the end; always adhere to｜～增产节约的方针 carry out the policy of increasing production and practising

【贯穿】guànchuān ❶ 穿过；连通 run through; penetrate; connect：这条公路～本省十几个县。This highway runs through a dozen counties. ❷ same as 贯串 guànchuàn：团结互助的精神～在我们整个车间里。Our workshop is permeated with the spirit of unity and mutual help.

【贯串】guànchuàn 从头到尾穿过一个或一系列事物 spread through; run through; permeate：这部小说的各篇各章都～着一个基本思想。A basic idea runs through each chapter of this novel.

【贯口】guànkǒu 指曲艺演员以很快的速度歌唱、背诵唱词或连续叙述许多事物。一般在不换气或不明显地换气的情况下进行。(of a ballad-singing artist) sing or recite words or lines non-stop at a very fast speed, usu. without a change of breath or changing breath distinctly

【贯气】guànqì 迷信的人指风水上地脉贯通，认为这样会走好运 (of superstition) continuous flow of underground waters in geomancy, indicating good luck

【贯通】guàntōng ❶ (学术、思想等方面)全部透彻地了解 have a thorough knowledge of; be well-versed in：融会～ blend what one has learned harmoniously and grasp it thoroughly; have a thorough knowledge｜～中西医学 have a thorough knowledge of both Western and traditional Chinese medicine ❷ 连接；沟通 connect; link up; thread together：上下～ promote mutual understanding between leaders and the rank and file｜武汉长江大桥修成后，京广铁路就全线～了。The whole railway line has been linked up with the completion of the Yangtze River Bridge at Wuhan.

【贯注】guànzhù ❶ (精神、精力)集中 concentrate (one's energy, mind) on：把精力～在工作上 concentrate one's energy on one's work｜他全神～地听着。He listened with rapt attention. ❷ (语意、语气)连贯；贯穿 fluent in meaning; consistent in feeling：这两句是一气～下来的。There is a sense of flow between these two sentences.

冠 guàn ❶〈书 *fml*.〉把帽子戴在头上(古代男子二十岁举行冠礼，表示已成年) put on a hat; come of age (a man began to wear a hat at twenty to show that he had grown up in ancient times)：未～(不到二十岁) (of a boy) under twenty ❷ 在前面加上某种名号或文字 put a title and some words before; precede; crown with：县名前～上省名 put the name of the province before the name of the county ❸ 居第一位 take (or win, capture) the first place; rank first：～军 champion; first place ❹ 指冠军 champion：夺～ win the championship, the title or the first place｜三连～(连续三次获得冠军) win the championship three times on end; become the champion for three consecutive times ❺ (Guàn)姓 a surname

☞ guān on p. 715

【冠军】guànjūn 体育运动等竞赛中的第一名 champion; first place in a competition

【冠军赛】guànjūnsài 锦标赛 championship

掼 guàn〈方 *dial*.〉❶ 扔；摞 throw; toss; cast：～手榴弹 throw a hand grenade｜把棉袄～在床上 throw his cotton-padded clothes onto the bed ❷ 握住东西的一端而摔另一端 thresh; flail：～稻 thresh rice ❸ 跌；使跌 fall; throw down：他～了一个跟头。He had a fall.｜对方抱住他的腰，又把他～倒了。The opponent held him by the waist and threw him down to the ground again.

【掼跤】guàn//jiāo〈方 *dial*.〉摔跤 tumble; trip and fall

【掼纱帽】guàn shāmào〈方 *dial*.〉〈比喻 *fig*.〉因气愤或不满而辞职 throw away one's official's hat in a huff; resign in resentment; quit office

涫 guàn〈书 *fml*.〉沸 boiling

惯 guàn ❶ 习以为常，积久成性；习惯 be used to; be in the habit of：我劳动～了，一天不干活就不舒服。I'm used to physical labour. I'll feel uncomfortable if I don't work in a day. ❷ 纵容(子女)养成不良习惯或作风 indulge; spoil：娇生～养 be addled since childhood|不能～着孩子。Don't spoil the child.

【惯常】guàncháng ❶ 习以为常的；成了习惯的 be used to：从那～的动作上，可以看出他是个熟练的水手。From his habitual movements, it can be seen that he is a skilled sailor. ❷ 经常 often; frequently：～出门的人，知道旅途上的许多不便。A frequent traveller knows how many inconveniences he has on the road. ❸ 平常；平时 usual; at his ordinary times：他恢复了～的镇定。He was his former composed self again.

【惯犯】guànfàn 经常犯罪而屡教不改的罪犯 habitual offender; hardened criminal; recidivist; repeater

【惯匪】guànfěi 经常抢劫的匪徒 hardened bandit; professional brigand; bandit with a record

【惯技】guànjì 经常使用的手段（贬义 derog.）customary tactic; old trick; usual gimmick：～重演 play the same old trick again

【惯家】guàn·jia 指惯于做某种事情的人；老手（多含贬义 oft. derog.）person used to doing sth.; old hand

【惯例】guànlì ❶ 一向的做法；常规 convention; usual practice：打破～ do away with convention; break with usual practice|因循～ follow the beaten track; stick to old ways of doing things|国际～ international practice ❷ 司法上指法律没有明文规定，但过去曾经施行、可以仿照办理的做法或事实 practice or fact that has occurred before and can be followed, but there is no explicit stipulation

【惯量】guànliàng 物体惯性的大小。惯量是用物体质量的大小来表示的，质量大的，惯量也大。inertia, as indicated by the quantity of the mass of matter — the bigger the quantity, the bigger the inertia.

【惯窃】guànqiè 经常盗窃的人 habitual thief; hardened thief

【惯偷】guàntōu same as 惯窃 guànqiè

【惯性】guànxìng 物体保持自身原有运动状态或静止状态的性质，如行驶的机车刹车后不马上停止前进，静止的物体不受外力作用就不变位置，都是由于惯性的作用 inertia; tendency of matter to remain at rest if stationary, or, if moving, to keep movming in the same direction, unless affected by some outside force

【惯用】guànyòng 惯于使用；经常运用 habitually practise; consistently use：～语 customary usage|～伎俩 customary tactics; old tricks

【惯贼】guànzéi same as 惯窃 guànqiè

【惯纵】guànzòng 娇惯放纵 pamper; spoil; indulge：对孩子可不能～。A child should not be indulged.

祼 guàn〈古代 *arch.*〉酌酒灌地的祭礼（ancient rite）libation; spreading wine over the ground in worship

盥 guàn〈书 *fml.*〉❶ 洗（手、脸）wash (hands or face) ❷ 盥洗用的器皿 wash basin

【盥漱】guànshù 洗脸漱口 wash one's face and rinse one's mouth：～室 washroom

【盥洗】guànxǐ 洗手洗脸 wash one's hands and face：～室 washroom

灌 guàn ❶ 浇；灌溉 water; irrigate：引水～田 draw water to irrigate fields ❷ 倒进去或装进去（多指液体、气体或颗粒状物体 oft. liquid, air or particulate matter）pour into; fill：～了一瓶热水 fill a thermos flask with hot water|风雪呼呼地～进门来 The wind whirled, driving snowflakes into the house.|那响亮的声音直往他耳朵里～。The loud noise poured into his ears. ❸ 指录音 record (sound, music, etc. on a tape or disc)：～唱片 make a gramophone record; cut a disc

【灌肠】guàn//cháng 为了清洗肠道、治疗疾病等，把水、液体药物等从肛门灌到肠内 give an enema; clyster; inject water, purgative, medical solution, etc. into the colon through the anus

【灌肠】guàn·chang 一种食品，原来是用肠衣塞肉末和淀粉，现在多用淀粉制成，吃时切成片，用油煎熟 sausage; meat (chopped fine and mixed with starch) or starch stuffed into membranous casings of varying sizes

【灌顶】guàndǐng 佛教的一种仪式，凡继承阇梨位或弟子入门的，须先经师父用水或醍醐灌洒头顶（Buddhist rite）abhiseka; murdhabhisitka; (of a monk) inaugurating a disciple's monkhood by sprinkling or pouring water or cream on his head

【灌溉】guàngài 把水输送到田地里 convey water into the fields; irrigate：～农田 irrigate the fields

【灌溉渠】guàngàiqú 引水灌溉田地的较大的人工水道 man-made waterway to divert irrigation water; irrigation canal; also 灌渠 guànqú

【灌浆】guàn//jiāng ❶ 为了使建筑物坚固，把灰浆浇灌到砌起来的砖块或石块之间的空隙中 use mortar to fill chinks between bricks, tiles or stones to make a building solid; grout ❷ 粮食作物快成熟时，养料通过导管灌到子粒里去。胚乳逐渐发育成浆液状。(of grain) be in the milk; nutrients are supplied to the grains through the ducts when a grain crop is ripening, and the endosperm gradually develops into milk ❸ 通常指疱疹中的液体变成脓，多见于天花或接种的牛痘 form a vesicle (during smallpox or after vaccination); small cavity or sac filled with fluid; usu. the fluid in the blister becomes pus (during smallpox or after vaccination)

【灌录】guànlù 录制（唱片、磁带）record a tape or a gramophone

【灌米汤】guàn mǐ·tang〈比喻 *fig.*〉用甜言蜜

语奉承人迷惑人 lay it on thick; butter sb. up

【灌木】guànmù 矮小而丛生的木本植物，如荆、玫瑰、茉莉等 bush; shrub; a low, woody plant with several stems instead of a single trunk, such as brambles, rose, jasmine, etc.

【灌区】guànqū 指某一水利灌溉工程的受益区域 irrigated area; area benefited from an irrigation project: 韶山～ Shaoshan Irrigated Area

【灌渠】guànqú same as 灌溉渠 guàngàiqú

【灌输】guànshū ❶ 把流水引导到需要水分的地方 divert water to where water is needed; divert water for use elsewhere ❷ 输送(思想、知识等)(of thought, knowledge, etc.) impart; instil into; inculcate; imbue with: ～爱国主义思想 instil patriotism | ～文化科学知识 imbue someone with general and scientific knowledge

【灌音】guàn//yīn 录音 record one's voice; have one's voice recorded

【灌制】guànzhì 用录音设备录制 record sth. with recording equipment: ～唱片 record a gramophone | ～教学磁带 record a teaching tape

【灌注】guànzhù 浇进；注入 pour into: 把铁水～到砂型里，凝固后就成了铸件 pour molten iron into a sand mould to produce a cast piece ◇ 她把心血全部～在孩子的身上。She expended all her painstaking care on her child.

G

瓘 guàn 古书上指一种玉 (in ancient books) a kind of jade

鹳 guàn 鸟类的一属，形状像白鹤，嘴长而直，羽毛灰色、白色或黑色。生活在水边，吃鱼、虾等。较常见的有白鹳。stork (*Ciconiiformes*); bird which looks like a white crane, with a long and straight bill, and grey, white or black feathers, living on the waterside and feeding on fish and shrimps. The white stork is more common.

罐(鑵) guàn ❶ (～儿 guànr) 罐子 jar; pot; tin: 瓦～ earthen jar | 水～儿 water pitcher | 茶叶～儿 tea caddy ❷ 煤矿装煤用的斗车 coal tub

【罐车】guànchē 装运液体物品的货车 vehicle for carrying liquids; tank car; tank truck; tanker

【罐笼】guànlóng 矿井里的升降机，用于运送人员、矿石、材料等 cage elevator; mine elevator for transporting miners, ores, materials, etc.

【罐头】guàn·tou ❶ 〈方 *dial.*〉 same as 罐子 guàn·zi ❷ 罐头食品的简称，是加工后装在密封的铁皮罐子或玻璃瓶里的食品，可以存放较长的时间 canned food; tinned food; processed food preserved in an airtight tin or bottle

【罐子】guàn·zi 盛东西用的大口的器皿，多为陶器或瓷器 large ceramic container pot; jar; pitcher; jug: 空～ empty jar | 两～水 two jugs of water

guāng (ㄍㄨㄤ)

光 guāng ❶ 通常指照在物体上，使人能看见物体的那种物质，如太阳光、灯光、月光等。可见光是波长 0.77—0.39 微米的电磁波。此外还包括看不见的红外光和紫外光。因为光是电磁波的一种，所以也叫光波；在一般情况下光沿直线传播，所以也叫光线。light; electromagnetic radiation that acts upon the retina of the eye, optic nerve, etc., making sight possible; matter that shines over an object, making it visible to the eye, such as sunlight, lamplight, and moonlight. The wavelength of the visible light is a electromagnetic wave 0.77-0.39 micrometres in length. Besides, there are infrared light and ultraviolet light. As light is one of the electromagnetic waves, it is also called light wave. In normal conditions, light is transmitted along a straight line, and is therefore called ray. ☞ 红外线 hóngwàixiàn on p. 804 and 紫外线 zǐwàixiàn on p. 2542 ❷ 景物 sights: 风～ scenery | 春～明媚 sunlit and enchanting spring scenery: ❸ 光彩；荣誉 lustre; splendour; honour; glory: 为国增～ bring honour to the country; do credit to one's country honour ❹ 〈比喻 *fig.*〉 好处 benefit; good; advantage: 沾～ benefit from the support or influence of someone | 叨～ much obliged to you | 借～ excuse me ❺ 〈敬辞 *pol.*〉 表示光荣，用于对方来临 honour; pleasure: ～临 your presence | ～顾 patronize; patronage (used in polite formulas) ❻ 光大 glorify; bring honour to: ～前裕后 to glorify the forefathers and to provide for the descendants ❼ 明亮 bright; lustre: ～明 bright; light; open-hearted | ～泽 lustre ❽ 光滑；光溜 smooth; slippery; glossy; sleek; polished: 磨～ polish | 这种纸很～。This paper is very glossy. ❾ 一点儿不剩；全没有了；完了 nothing left; all gone; used up: 精～ with nothing left | 用～ use up | 把敌人消灭～ wipe out the enemy ❿ (身体)露着 bare: ～膀子 be stripped to the waist | ～着头 bare head; bareheaded ⓫ 只；单 only; alone: 任务这么重，～靠你们两个人恐怕不行。The task is so heavy. I'm afraid it's not enough just for the two of you to do it. ⓬ (Guāng)姓 a surname

【光斑】guāngbān 太阳表面上特别明亮的纤维状斑点，是太阳活动比较剧烈的部分 bright areas visible on the surface of the sun; facula

【光板儿】guāngbǎnr ❶ 磨掉了毛的皮衣服或皮褥子 worn-out fur ❷ 指没有轧上花纹和字的铜元 (in former times) copper coin without a distinctive stamp

【光波】guāngbō same as 光 guāng ①

【光彩】guāngcǎi ❶ 颜色和光泽；光辉: colour

and lustre; lustre; splendour; radiance; brilliance: 大放～ shine with dazzling splendour | 橱窗里面摆着～夺目的各色丝绸。Silk fabrics wreaked a brilliant riot of colour in the shop window. ❷ 光荣 honourable; honoured; glorious; honour: 小张当了劳动模范，咱全村都很～。The whole village felt honoured to have Xiao Zhang named as a model worker.

【光彩照人】guāngcǎi zhàorén 形容人或事物十分美好或艺术成就辉煌，令人注目、敬仰 (of personality, good things, achievements) shine with brilliance or splendour

【光灿灿】guāngcàncàn (～的 guāngcàncàn·de) 形容光亮耀眼 shining; dazzlingly; bright: ～的秋阳 dazzling autumn sun

【光赤】guāngchì (身体)露着 naked; stark naked

【光宠】guāngchǒng 〈书 *fml.*〉(赐给的)荣耀或恩惠 honour or favour (granted)

【光大】guāngdà 〈书 *fml.*〉❶ 使显赫盛大 glorify; carry forward; develop: ～门楣 bring glory to one's family; win honour and distinction for one's family | 发扬～ carry forward ❷ 广大 wide; extensive; vast

【光刀】guāngdāo ❶ 利用激光代替钢制手术刀进行手术的装置 laser scalpel; device for surgical operation using laser instead of steel scalpel ❷ 这种装置的光束 light beam of this device

【光导纤维】guāngdǎo-xiānwéi 一种能够导光的纤维。用玻璃或塑料制成。光线在纤维中可以弯曲传导，并能改变像的形状。用于医疗器械、电子光学仪器、光通讯线路等方面。optical fibre; a kind of fibre capable of conducting light, made of glass or plastic. The light can be conducted in the fibre in a curved way and change the shape of the image. It is used in medical instruments, electron optical instruments, optical fibre communications, etc. also 光学纤维 guāoxué xiānwéi; 简称 abbr. 光纤 guāngxiān

【光电池】guāngdiànchí 利用光的照射产生电能的器件，用光电效应强的物质如硒、氧化铜等制成。摄影上测量光度的光度计就是用光电池做成的。photoelectric cell, whose electric state is changed by the effect of light, made of material with a strong photoelectric effect such as selenium, copper oxide. etc., the photometer used in photography for measuring luminosity is made of photoelectric cells.

【光度】guāngdù ❶ 光源所发的光的强度。通常以烛光为单位。luminosity; intensity of light produced by a light source, usu. using candle light as a unit ❷ 恒星的真实亮度，用整个恒星的表面每秒钟放出的能量来表示 true luminosity of the star, indicated by the energy released by the surface of the whole star per second

【光风霁月】guāng fēng jì yuè 雨过天晴时风清月明的景象 clear moon and a light breeze after a rain; 〈比喻 *fig.*〉开阔的胸襟和坦白的心地，太平清明的政治局面 open and above board; open-hearted and above board; peaceful; uncorrupted political situation; also 霁月光风 jì yuè guāng fēng

【光复】guāngfù 恢复(已亡的国家)；收回(失去的领土) recover (lost territory); restore (old glory, etc.); restore the sovereignty of a conquered nation; recover the lost territory: ～旧物 recover what has been lost (to an invader) | ～河山 recover the lost land

【光杆儿】guānggǎnr ❶ 指花叶尽落的草木或没有叶子衬托的花朵 bare trunk; bare stalk; flower on a bare stalk: ～牡丹 peony on a bare stalk | 高粱被雹子打得成了～。The sorghum was stripped to the stem by a hail. ❷ 〈比喻 *fig.*〉孤独的人或失去群众、没有助手的领导 man who has lost his family; person without a following; leader without a following: ～司令 general without an army; leader without a following; commander without an army | 他家只剩下他一个～。He has been left alone in the family.

【光顾】guānggù 〈敬辞 *pol.*〉称客人来到，商家多用来欢迎顾客 [term of respect for customers patronizing one's shop] welcome

【光怪陆离】guāng guài lù lí 形容现象奇异、色彩繁杂 grotesque and gaudy; grotesque in shape and gaudy in colour; bizarre and motley

【光棍】guāng·gùn ❶ 地痞；流氓 ruffian; hoodlum ❷ 〈方 *dial.*〉指识时务的人 clever (or wise) person: ～不吃眼前亏。A wise man doesn't fight against impossible odds.

【光棍儿】guānggùnr 没有妻子的成年人；单身汉 unmarried man; bachelor: 打～(过单身汉的生活) live a bachelor's life

【光合作用】guānghé- zuòyòng 光化作用的一类，如绿色植物的叶绿素在日光照射下把水和二氧化碳合成有机物质并排出氧气 photosynthesis; production of organic substances and oxygen from carbon dioxide and water occurring in green plant cells supplied with enough light to allow chlorophyll to aid in the transformation of the radiant energy into a chemical form

【光华】guānghuá 明亮的光辉 brilliance; splendour: 日月～ brilliance of the sun and the moon

【光滑】guāng·huá 物体表面平滑；不粗糙 smooth; glossy; sleek; not rough: 皮肤～ smooth skin | 大理石的桌面很～。The surface of the marble table is very smooth.

【光化作用】guānghuà-zuòyòng 物质由于光的照射而产生化学变化的作用，包括光合作用和光解作用两类 photochemical action; chemical action of a substance due to irradiation of the light, including photosynthesis and photolysis

【光环】guānghuán ❶ 某些行星周围明亮的环状物，由冰和铁等构成，如土星、天王星等都有数量不等的光环 aureole; ring of light around a planet, which is composed of ice and iron, such as Saturn, Uranus, etc., each having a different number of rings of light ❷ 发光的环子 luminous ring：霓虹灯组成了象征奥运会的五彩～。The neon lights form the five coloured rings symbolic of the Olympic Games. ❸ 特指神像或圣像头部周围画的环形光辉；灵光② halo; aureole; symbolic ring of light shown around the head of a saint, etc.

【光辉】guānghuī ❶ 闪烁耀目的光 radiance; brilliance; glory：太阳的～ brilliance of the sun ❷ 光明；灿烂 bright, brilliant; magnificent; splendid：～前程 bright future brilliant; magnificent; glorious

【光火】guāng//huǒ 〈方 *dial.*〉发怒；恼怒 flare up; fly into a rage; lose one's temper

【光洁】guāngjié 光亮而洁净 bright and clean：在灯光照耀下，平滑的大理石显得格外～。In the lamp light the smooth marble looks especially bright and clean.

【光洁度】guāngjiédù 〈旧称 *old*〉机器零件、工件等的表面粗糙程度 smooth finish (of the surface of machine parts, work pieces); degree of finish

【光解作用】guāngjiě- zuòyòng 光化作用的一类，如照相材料在可见光的照射下感光，碘化氢在紫外线的照射下分解成氢和碘 photolysis; photochemical action, such as the sensitization of the photographic materials due to the action of a visible light and the decomposition of hydrogen iodide into hydrogen and iodine due to the action of the ultraviolet light

【光景】guāngjǐng ❶ 时光景物 scene：好一派草原～。What a magnificent grassland! ❷ 境况；状况；情景 situation; circumstances; conditions：他家的～还不错。He's quite comfortably off. | 我们俩初次见面的～，我还记得很清楚。I can still clearly remember the scene when we first met. ❸ 表示估计 prospects a)一般的情况 general situation：今天太闷热，～是要下雨。It's stifling. It looks like rain. b)时间或数量(用在表时间或数量的词语后面)[used after time and numerical expressions] about; around：半夜～起了风。A wind sprang up around midnight. | 里面有十几个小孩子，大都只有五六岁～。There are a dozen or so children inside, mostly five or six years old.

【光缆】guānglǎn 由许多根经过技术处理的光导纤维组合而成的缆，用来传输光信号 optical cable; cable with many processed optical fibres used for the transmission of light signals

【光亮】guāngliàng ❶ 明亮 bright：～的窗子 bright window | 这套家具油漆得挺～。This set of furniture has a very shiny coast of paint. ❷ 亮光 light：山洞里一点儿～也没有。There is not a flicker of light in the mountain cave.

【光临】guānglín 〈敬辞 *pol.*〉称宾客来到 presence of a guest; honour sb. with one's presence：敬请～。Your presence is cordially requested. *or* It's a pleasure to have your presence. *or* It's an honour to have your presence. | 欢迎～指导。We welcome you and would appreciate your advice. *or* Your visit and advice would be deeply appreciated.

【光溜】guāng·liu 光滑；滑溜 smooth; glossy; slippery：这种道林纸比电光纸还～。The Dowling paper is even glossier than the glazed paper.

【光溜溜】guāngliūliū (～的 guāngliūliū·de) ❶ 形容光滑 smooth; slippery：她走在～的冰上有点害怕。She was a bit nervous walking on the slippery ice. ❷ 形容地面、物体、身体上没有遮盖的样子 bare; naked：院子里种上点花儿，省得～的不好看。Grow some flowers in the compound to offset the dullness of the bare ground. | 孩子们脱得～的在河里洗澡。The children stripped off their clothes and swam naked in the river.

【光芒】guāngmáng 向四面放射的强烈的光线 rays of light：～万丈 shining with boundless radiance; gloriously radiant; resplendent | ～四射 shining with radiance in all directions

【光明】guāngmíng ❶ 亮光 light：黑暗中的一线～ a streak of light in the darkness ❷ 明亮 bright; promising：这条街上的路灯，一个个都像通体～的水晶球。The street lights in this street all look like bright crystal balls. ❸ 〈比喻 *fig.*〉正义的或有希望的 righteous; promising：～大道 bright road | ～的远景 bright prospect ❹ (胸襟)坦白；没有私心 honest and above board; selfless; openhearted; guileless：～正大 honest; just and upright | ～磊落 selfless; honest and above board; open and above board | 心地～ open-hearted; upright and pure in mind

【光明磊落】guāngmíng lěiluò 形容没有私心，胸怀坦白 selfless; honest and above board; open and above board

【光明正大】guāngmíng zhèngdà 形容襟怀坦白，行为正派 honest; just and upright; just and honourable; open and above board; also 正大光明 zhèngdà guāngmíng

【光能】guāngnéng 光所具有的能 energy of the light

【光年】guāngnián 天文学上的一种距离单位，即以光在 1 年内在真空中走过的路程为 1 光年。光速每秒约 30 万公里，1 光年约等于 94,605 亿公里。light year; unit of distance equal to the distance that light travels in a vacuum in a year, c. 9,460,500,000,000 km.; the speed of the light is 300,000 km. per second

【光谱】guāngpǔ 复色光通过棱镜或光栅后，分解成的单色光按波长大小排成的光带。日光的光谱是红、橙、黄、绿、蓝、靛、紫七色。spectrum; series of coloured bands dispersed and arranged in the order of their respective wavelengths by the passage of white light through a prism or other dispersing device and shading continuously from red (produced by the longest wave visible) through violet (produced by the shortest): the main colours of the spectrum are red, orange, yellow, green, blue, indigo and violet

【光谱仪】guāngpǔyí 把成分复杂的光分解为光谱线的仪器，用棱镜或衍射光栅等构成 spectrograph; instrument for decomposing the complex light into spectrum lines, composed of a prism and a diffraction grating

【光前裕后】guāng qián yù hòu 给前人增光，为后代造福(多用来称颂别人的功业 oft. in praise of one's achievements) bring honour to one's ancestors and prosperity to one's descendants

【光圈】guāngquān 摄影机等光学仪器的镜头中改变通光孔径的大小、调节进入光量的装置 device in the lens of a camera and other optical instruments for changing the diameter of the hole, through which light passes into the lens; diaphragm; aperture; stop; also 光孔 guāngkǒng and 光阑 guānglán

【光荣】guāngróng ❶ 由于做了有利于人民的和正义的事情而被公认为值得尊敬的 respected for doing sth. good for the people and justice; honourable; honoured; glorious: ～之家 honoured family|～牺牲 die a glorious death ❷ 荣誉 honour; glory; credit: ～归于祖国。Glory (honour, credit) goes to the motherland honour.

【光荣榜】guāngróngbǎng 表扬先进人物的榜，榜上列出姓名，有时加上照片和先进事迹 honour roll; roster of honour; roll of names of persons cited for their outstanding deeds, sometimes their photos and brief descriptions attached

【光润】guāngrùn 光滑润泽(多指皮肤 usu. referring to skin) smooth

【光栅】guāngshān 能产生衍射现象的光学器件，光线透过它或被它反射时就形成光谱，一般用玻璃或金属制成，上面刻有很密的平行细纹 grating; diffraction grating; plate of glass or polished metal ruled with a series of very close, equidistant, parallel lines, used to produce a spectrum by the diffraction of reflected or transmitted light

【光闪闪】guāngshǎnshǎn (～的 guāngshǎnshǎn·de)形容光亮闪烁 bright and glistening: ～的珍珠 glistening pearl

【光束】guāngshù 呈束状的光线，如探照灯的光 light beam; beam of light, such as the light from a searchlight

【光速】guāngsù 光波传播的速度，在真空中每秒约 30 万公里，在空气中也与这个数值相近 velocity of light; speed of the transmission of light wave, about 300,000 km. per second in vacuum, and also close to this numerical value in the air

【光趟】guāng·tang 〈方 *dial.*〉光滑；不粗糙 fine and smooth: 席子编得又细密又～。The mat is well woven and feels so smooth.

【光天化日】guāng tiān huà rì 〈比喻 *fig.*〉大家看得很清楚的地方 evidently, obviously: ～之下 in broad daylight; broad daylight; the light of day

【光通量】guāngtōngliàng 单位时间内通过某一面积的光的量。单位是流明。flow of light measured in lumens; luminous flux

【光头】guāng//tóu 头上不戴帽子 bare one's head: 他不习惯戴帽子，一年四季总光着头。He is not used to wearing a hat and goes bareheaded all year round.

【光头】guāngtóu 剃光的头；没有头发的头；秃头 shaved head; head without hair; bald head

【光秃秃】guāngtūtū (～的 guāngtūtū·de)形容没有草木、树叶、毛发等盖着的样子 without the natural or customary covering (grass, leaves, hair, etc.); bare; bald: 冬天叶子全掉了，只剩下～的树枝。All leaves fell in the winter, leaving the branches and twigs bare.

G

【光鲜】guāngxiān ❶ 明亮鲜艳；整洁漂亮 bright and new; clean and beautiful: 衣着～ be dressed in a bright new suit ❷〈方 *dial.*〉光彩；光荣 lustrous; glorious: 总想把事情办得～体面一点儿 always want to handle affairs in a lustrous and respectable way

【光线】guāngxiàn same as 光 guāng ①

【光绪】Guāngxù 清德宗(爱新觉罗载湉)年号(公元 1875—1908) reigning title of Emperor Dezong (Aisin Gioro Zaitian) of the Qing Dynasty, whose reign lasted from 1875 to 1908

【光学】guāngxué 物理学的一个分支，研究光的本性、光的发射、传播和接收规律，以及光跟其他物质的相互作用等 optics; branch of physics dealing with the nature and properties of light and vision, the law of emission, transmission and reception of light, and the interaction between light and other substances

【光学玻璃】guāngxué bō·lí 用来制造光学仪器的高级玻璃，具有良好的光学性能。摄影机、经纬仪、望远镜等的镜头都用光学玻璃制成。optical glass; high-grade glass used to make optical instruments, having good optical properties. The lenses for camera, theodolite and telescope are all made of optical glass.

【光压】guāngyā 射在物体上的光对物体所产生的压力。彗星的尾巴背着太阳就是太阳的光压造成的。light pressure; pressure given to an object by the light shed on the object; the phenomenon in which the tail of a comet points away from the sun is exactly the action of the light pressure of the sun

【光艳】guāngyàn 鲜明艳丽 bright and colourful

【光焰】guāngyàn 光芒；光辉 radiance：万丈～ boundless radiance|～耀目 dazzling to the eye

【光洋】guāngyáng 〈方 *dial*.〉银圆 silver dollar

【光耀】guāngyào ❶same as 光辉 guānghuī ①; brilliant light; brilliance：～夺目 dazzling; dazzlingly brilliant ❷ 荣耀 honour; glory; credit：立功是～的事。It's a glorious thing to render meritorious service. ❸ 光大 glorify; carry forward; develop：～门庭 glorify a family ❹ 光辉照耀(多用于比喻 oft. fig.) shine with brilliance：～史册 shine with brilliance in history

【光阴】guāngyīn ❶ 时间 time available; time：～似箭。Time flies like an arrow. *or* How time flies! |青年时代的～是最宝贵的。Time in the youth is most precious. |一寸～一寸金，寸金难买寸～。An inch of time is an inch of gold, but an inch of gold can hardly buy an inch of time. ❷〈方 *dial*.〉same as 日子 rì·zi ③

G

【光源】guāngyuán 发光(通常指可见光)的物体，如太阳、灯、火等 luminous substance (usu. visible light), such as the sun, lamp, fire, etc.; light source; illuminant

【光泽】guāngzé 物体表面上反射出来的亮光 light reflected from the surface of a substance：脸盘红润而有～。His face is glowing with health.

【光照】guāngzhào ❶ 光线的照射。是生物生长和发育的必要条件之一。illumination, one of the essential conditions for the growth and development of living things illumination ❷ 光辉照耀(多用于比喻 oft. fig.) shine with radiance：～人间 shines over the world; benefit humanity with one's achievements

【光照度】guāngzhàodù 物体单位面积上所得到的光的量，用来表明物体被照亮的程度。单位是勒克斯。intensity of illumination; quantity of light obtained over a unit area of a substance, used for indicating the degree of illumination over the substance; the unit of illumination is lux; luminosity; 简称 abbr. 照度 zhàodù

【光针】guāngzhēn ❶ 利用激光代替毫针进行针灸的装置 laser needle; device using a laser beam as an acupuncture needle ❷ 这种装置的光束 beam produced by such a device; laser needle beam

【光柱】guāngzhù same as 光束 guāngshù：探照灯的～划破长空。The night sky was pierced by searchlight rays.

【光子】guāngzǐ 构成光的基本粒子，具有一定的能量，是光能的最小单位。光子的能量随着光的波长而变化，波长愈短，能量愈大。quantum of light; photon; fundamental particles that form light. A photon has a certain amount of energy and is the smallest unit of light. The energy of a quantum of light varies with the wavelength of the light: the shorter the wavelength, the more energy; also 光量子 guāngliàngzǐ

【光宗耀祖】guāng zōng yào zǔ 指为祖先、宗族增添光彩 glorify or bring honour to one's ancestors or family clan

咣 guāng〈拟声词 *onom*.〉形容撞击振动的声音 banging sound; crash：～的一声，关上了大门。(He) slammed the door shut with a bang. *or* (He) shut the door with a bang.

【咣当】guāngdāng〈拟声词 *onom*.〉形容撞击振动的声音 bang; crash：水缸碰得～～响。The water vats banged against each other.

洸 guāng 浛洸(Hánguāng)，地名，在广东 Hanguang, name of a place in Guangdong

珖 guāng〈书 *fml*.〉一种玉(多用于人名 oft. used in the given name of a person) a kind of jade

桄 guāng [桄榔](guāngláng) ❶ 常绿乔木，羽状复叶，肉穗花序，果实倒圆锥形，有辣味。产在热带地方。茎中的髓可以制淀粉，叶柄的纤维可制绳。gomuti sugarpalm (*Arenga pinnata*); tropical evergreen tree with feather-like compound leaves and spadices, spicy fruit shaped like inverse cones, the pith of its trunk used to make a starch, and the fibres from the leaf-stalk good for making rope ❷ 这种植物的果实 fruit of the tree; sugar palm; gomuti palm; gomuti

☞ guàng on p. 726

胱 guāng ❶ [胱氨酸](guāng'ānsuān)含有二硫键(两个硫原子连接在一起的键)的氨基酸，广泛存在于毛、发、骨、角中 amino acid; containing a disulphide bond (two linked sulphur atoms), widely found in fur, hair, bone, and horn ❷ ☞ 膀胱 pángguāng on p. 1446

guǎng (ㄍㄨㄤˇ)

广[1](廣) guǎng ❶ (面积、范围)宽阔(跟'狭'相对 as opposed to 'narrow') (of area, scope, etc.) wide; vast; extensive：～场 square; plaza|地～人稀 vast (in area) but sparsely populated|这支小调流行很～。The ditty is very popular. ❷ 多 numerous：大庭～众 out in the open; in front of a big crowd; in public; before a large audience ❸ 扩大；扩充 expand; spread：推～ popularize|以～流传 so as to spread it far and wide; so that it may reach far; to make it circulate

广[2]（廣） Guǎng ❶ 指广东、广州 Guangzhou; Guangdong; Canton: ～货 goods from Guangdong 注意 **NOTE:** 广西简称广，限于两广（广东和广西）Guangxi is abbreviated as Guang only in the old term of *liangguang* or 'Two Guangs' (Guangdong and Guangxi) ❷ 姓 a surname

☞ ān on p.8

【广播】guǎngbō ❶ 广播电台、电视台发射无线电波，播送节目。有线电播送节目也叫广播。(of a radio or television station) transmit programmes by sending out radio waves; wired radio programmes; broadcast; be on the air ❷ 指广播电台或有线电播送的节目 radio programme; programme broadcast from a radio station or wired radio station: 听～ listen to the radio ❸〈书 *fml.*〉广泛传扬 widely spread; known far and wide: 诗名～ well-known poet|～儒风 disseminate Confucianism far and wide

【广播电台】guǎngbō diàntái 用无线电波向外播送新闻、报刊文章、科学常识和文艺等节目的机构 radio station; broadcasting station; establishment from which broadcasting of news, newspaper articles, scientific knowledge, literary and art programmes is transmitted by radio waves

【广播段】guǎngbōduàn 无线电广播所使用的波长范围，包括中波、中短波和短波 wave band; specific range of wavelengths of radio broadcasting, including medium wave, mid-short wave, and short wave

【广播剧】guǎngbōjù 专供广播电台播送的戏剧 radio play or drama; play esp. written and produced for broadcasting on the radio

【广播体操】guǎngbō tǐcāo 通过广播指挥做的健身体操，一般有音乐配合 exercises and calisthenics led by radio broadcast with music accompaniment; also 广播操 gǎngbōcāo

【广博】guǎngbó 范围大，方面多（多指学识 of a person's knowledge) extensive, wide: 知识～ with extensive knowledge in many fields; erudite; well-informed

【广场】guǎngchǎng 面积广阔的场地，特指城市中的广阔场地 large, open public area esp. in a city or town; square; plaza: 天安门～ Tian'anmen Square

【广大】guǎngdà ❶（面积、空间）宽阔（of an area or space) vast; wide; extensive: ～区域 vast area|拖拉机在～的田野上耕作。The tractor is working on the extensive fields. ❷（范围、规模）巨大 large-scale; widespread; broad: 有～的组织 have a large-scale organization|掀起～的增产节约运动 launch a large-scale campaign to increase production and practise economy ❸（人数）众多 numerous: ～群众 the broad masses|～干部 the majority of cadres|～读者 the reading public

【广东戏】guǎngdōngxì 粤剧 Guangdong Opera; Cantonese opera

【广东音乐】Guǎngdōng yīnyuè 主要流行于广东一带的民间音乐。演奏时以高胡、扬琴等弦乐器为主，配以笛子、洞箫等。Guangdong music; Cantonese music; folk music popular in Guangdong, mainly performed by high-pitched, two-stringed Chinese fiddles, dulcimers, and other stringed instruments, accompanied by bamboo flutes, *dongxiao* (vertical bamboo flutes), etc.

【广度】guǎngdù（事物）广狭的程度 scope; breadth; range: 向生产的深度和～进军 develop the range and depth of production

【广泛】guǎngfàn（涉及的）方面广，范围大；普遍 wide; broad; extensive; widespread; sweeping; comprehensive; universal: 内容～ covering a wide range of subjects; wide-ranging in content|题材～ a great variety of themess; based on a wide range of sources|～征求群众意见 solicit opinions from all quarters or sides; canvass opinions extensively

【广告】guǎnggào 向公众介绍商品、服务内容或文娱体育节目的一种宣传方式，一般通过报刊、电视、广播、招贴等形式进行 advertisement; pitch; public promotion of a product, service, entertainment or sports programme, generally appearing in the medium of print, television, radio, or posters, etc.

【广货】guǎnghuò 广东出产的百货 goods from Guangdong

【广角镜】guǎngjiǎojìng ❶ same as 广角镜头 guǎngjiǎo-jìngtóu ❷〈比喻 *fig.*〉使视角范围广的事物 sth. that broadens one's vision; eye-opener: 这部书是开阔眼界、增长知识的～。The book is an eye-opener which is both enlightening and nourishing.

【广角镜头】guǎngjiǎo-jìngtóu 镜头的一种，视角比一般镜头广而焦距短，常用于拍摄面积很大的景物 wide-angle, panoramic or pantoscopic lens; camera lens providing wider view of an image than an ordinary lens and at a small focal length, generally used to photograph broad scenes and sights

【广开言路】guǎng kāi yán lù 尽量给下属和群众创造发表意见的条件 make way for free airing of opinions from subordinates or the masses

【广阔】guǎngkuò 广大宽阔 vast; wide; broad; extensive: 视野～ having a broad view|～天地 the vast world|～的国土 vast territory or land

【广袤】guǎngmào〈书 *fml.*〉❶ 土地的长和宽（东西的长度叫'广'，南北的长度叫'袤' expanse from east to west is 广 guǎng, from north to south is 袤 mào) length and breadth of land：～千里 expanse of a thousand miles across ❷ 广阔；宽广 vast；broad；immense：蔚蓝的天空，～无际。The blue sky is boundless.

【广漠】guǎngmò 广大空旷 vast and barren：～的沙滩上，留着潮水退落后的痕迹。On the bare expanse of beach remain traces of the ebbing tides.

【广土众民】guǎng tǔ zhòng mín 广阔的土地和众多的人民 vast territory and large population

【广绣】guǎngxiù 广东出产的刺绣 Guangdong embroidery；also 粤绣 yuèxiù

【广义】guǎngyì 范围较宽的定义（跟'狭义'相对 as opposed to 'narrow sense'）broad sense：～的杂文也可以包括小品文在内。Essays，in a broad sense，may include sketches as well.

【广远】guǎngyuǎn 广阔辽远；广大深远 far and wide；far-reaching and profound：川泽～ stretches of mountains and vast waters｜影响～ having a profound and far-reaching influence

【广种薄收】guǎng zhòng bó shōu 农业上一种粗放的经营方式，大面积播种，单位面积产量较低 extensive farming，which involves extensive cultivation with low per-unit yields

【广州起义】Guǎngzhōu Qǐyì 中国共产党为了挽救第一次国内革命战争的失败，于 1927 年 12 月 11 日在广州举行的武装起义。领导人有张太雷、叶挺、叶剑英等。由工人和革命士兵三万余人组成的起义部队，经过英勇奋战，占领了市内绝大部分地区，建立了工农民主政权——广州公社。后在敌人反扑下失败。Guangzhou Uprising；organized and led by the Communist Party of China on December 11，1927 in the hope of turning the tide after losing the First Revolutionary Civil War. Under the leadership of Zhang Tailei，Ye Ting，Ye Jianying，and others，the uprising troops，composed of over 30，000 workers and revolutionary soldiers，battled gallantly and seized most parts of the city，setting up a democratic government run by workers and peasants，the Guangzhou Commune. Later，under fierce enemy counter-attack，the Guangzhou Uprising failed.

犷（獷） guǎng 〈书 *fml.*〉粗野 uncouth；unrefined；wild；boorish：粗～ rough；rugged｜～悍 rough and ferocious；tough and intrepid

【犷悍】guǎnghàn 粗野强悍 rough，unrefined and ferocious

guàng（ㄍㄨㄤˋ）

桄 guàng ❶ 把线绕在桄子上 wind yarn or thread upon a reel：把线～上 reel the thread ❷（～儿 guàngr）在桄子或拐子上绕好后取下来的成圈的线 reel of thread：线～儿 reels of thread ❸（～儿 guàngr）〈量词 *classifier*〉用于线 unit to measure the quantity of thread wound on a reel：一～线 a reel of thread

☞ guāng on p. 724

【桄子】guàng·zi 竹木制成的绕线器具 cylindrical device made of bamboo or wood on which thread，yarn or wire is wound

逛 guàng 外出散步；闲游；游览 go out for an airing；stroll；wander；roam；ramble；saunter；rove；traipse：闲～ take a leisurely walk；stroll around｜～大街 take a stroll in the street；check out the street；traipse around the streets：东游西～ roam about

【逛荡】guàng·dang 闲逛；游荡（含贬义 derog.）gad about；stroll around；saunter；loiter；loaf about；lounge；gallivant

【逛灯】guàng//dēng 指农历正月十五日夜晚上街观赏花灯（usu. refers to the Lantern Festival，on the 15th of the 1st month of the lunar calendar）walk around the streets or parks；enjoying various lanterns on display

【逛游】guàng·you 闲逛 saunter；roam；gad about

guī（ㄍㄨㄟ）

归（歸） guī ❶ 返回 return；go or come back：～国华侨 returned overseas Chinese｜无家可～ become homeless；have no home to return to ❷ 还给；归还 give back；return sth. to sb.：物～原主 return sth. to its rightful owner ❸ 趋向或集中于一个地方 converge；come together at a certain point：殊途同～ all roads lead to Rome；arrive at the same goal by different routes｜千条河流～大海。All rivers will empty into the sea. *or* A thousand rivers find their way to the sea.｜把性质相同的问题～为一类 classify problems of similar nature into one category ❹ 由（谁负责）be put under sb.'s care；be in sb.'s charge 一切杂事都～这一组管。This group is in charge of miscellaneous tasks. ❺ 属于（谁所有）belong to；attribute sth. to sb. or sth.；accredit sth. to sb.：功劳～大家。I owe it to all of you.｜这些东西～你。You may keep all these things. ❻ 用在相同的动词之间，表示动作并未引起相应的结果［used between identical verbs to indicate absence of any desired response of action］：表扬～表扬，可就是突击任务没分配给我们。Despite of all the praise，we haven't been assigned any crack jobs. ❼ 珠算中一位除数的除法（on the abacus）division with a one-digit divisor ❽（Guī）姓 a surname

【归案】guī//àn 隐藏或逃走的罪犯被逮捕、押解或引渡到有关司法机关，以便审讯结案 arrest, escort or handing over to justice of a criminal, who is either on the run or in hiding, so as to provide for due legal process：捉拿～ arrest sb. and bring him or her to court for trial or punishment

【归并】guībìng ❶ 把这个并到那个里头；并入 incorporate into；merge into：撤消第三组，把人～到第一组和第二组 dismiss the third group and merge the people into the first and second groups ❷ 合在一起；归拢 lump together；put together；add up：把三笔账～起来，一共是五千五百元。The three accounts add up to 5,500 yuan.

【归程】guīchéng 返回来的路程 return journey or trip；homeward journey：在外漂泊数载的游子，终于踏上了～。The man, who had lived in a foreign country for many years, finally set out on a journey home.

【归除】guīchú 珠算中两位或两位以上除数的除法 (on the abacus) division with a divisor of two or more digits

【归档】guī//dàng 把公文、资料等分类保存起来 keep (an official document or data) on file；place (a document) on file；file (a document) away

【归队】guī//duì ❶ 回到原来所在的队伍 rejoin one's unit；return to one's former party ❷ 〈比喻 *fig.*〉回到原来所从事的行业或专业 return to one's former profession：他是学冶金的，毕业后改行做了多年行政工作，现在～了。He is a metallurgy major who did an office job for many years after graduation, but now has taken up his profession again.

【归附】guīfù 原来不属于这一方面的投到这一方面来 come under；submit to the authority of the other side

【归根】guī//gēn 〈比喻 *fig.*〉客居他乡的人最终返回本乡 return to one's native place after a long stay in a foreign land；return home：叶落～。A falling leaf finds its way to its roots. *or* A falling leaf settles at the roots. *or* What comes from the soil will return to the soil. *or* A person who is long separated from home eventually returns.｜认祖～ return to one's ancestral home；pay a visit to one's ancestral home

【归根结底】guī gēn jié dǐ 归结到根本上 in the final or last analysis；ultimately；put it in a nutshell；basically；fundamentally；ultimately；in the end；after all is said and done：～，人民的力量是无敌的，人民的意志是不可违抗的。After all, the force of the people is invincible, and the will of the people irresistible. 底 also put as 柢 dǐ；also 归根结蒂 guī gēn jié dì

【归公】guī//gōng 交给公家 hand sth. over to the state；turn possession over to the state or the collective：一切缴获要～。All captured articles must be turned in (to the army).

【归功】guīgōng 把功劳归于某个人或集体 give credit to sb. (or a collective)；owe sth. to sb.；attribute sth. to sb.：优异成绩的取得～于老师的辛勤教导。The good score can be attributed to the hard work of the teacher.

【归还】guīhuán 把借来的钱或物还给原主 return borrowed money or articles to their rightful owner；give back；revert：向图书馆借书，要按时～。Books borrowed from the library should be returned on time.｜捡到东西要～失主。What is found should be returned to its rightful owner.

【归回】guīhuí 返回；回到 return；go or come back：～故乡 return to one's hometown or homeland｜～祖国 go back to one's country or motherland

【归结】guījié ❶ 总括而求得结论 sum up；conclude；come to a conclusion；put in a nutshell；boil down to：原因很复杂，～起来不外三个方面。The reasons are complex but boil down to three points. ❷ 结局 end (of a story, etc.)：这件事儿总算有了一个～。The matter came to its ultimate end.

【归咎】guījiù same as 归罪 guīzuì：把错误都～于客观原因是不正确的。It's incorrect to ascribe all of one's errors to objective causes.

【归口】guī//kǒu ❶ 按性质分类划归有关部门 sort management tasks and assign them to the relevant departments：～管理 assign control (or management) to specialized departments ❷ 指回到原来所从事的行业或专业 return to the profession one was trained in：他下放到农村十年，～以后感到专业荒疏了许多。After being sent down to work in the countryside for a decade, he felt incompetent upon returning to his former profession.

【归来】guīlái 从别处回到原来的地方 be back to one's original place；return；come back：海外～ return from abroad

【归里包堆】guī·libāoduī 〈方 *dial.*〉总计；拢共 in all；altogether；in total：家里～就我和老伴两个人。There are altogether two people in my family — my wife and I.

【归拢】guī·lǒng 把分散着的东西聚集到一起 put together；gather up：～农具 put the farm tools together｜把散放的书～～。Gather up those books.

【归谬法】guīmiùfǎ ☞ 反证法 fǎnzhèngfǎ on p. 539

【归纳】guīnà ❶ 归拢并使有条理(多用于抽象事物 oft. used abstractly) lead to a concise but well-organized conclusion；induce；infer；draw；sum up；conclude：大家提的意见，～起来主要就是这三点。Your opinions can be summed up into these three points. ❷ 一种推理方法,由一系列具体的事实概括出一般原理(跟'演绎'相对 as opposed to 'deductive method') inductive method; induction; reasoning method, deriving general principles from particular facts or instances

【归宁】guīníng〈书 *fml.*〉回娘家看望父母 (of a married woman) visit her parents; pay a visit to her parents' home

【归期】guīqī 返回的日期 date of return: ～未定。The date of return is not yet set.

【归齐】guīqí〈方 *dial.*〉❶ 到底;结果 in the end; finally: 说了～,今天的事不能怨他。In the end, what happened today is not his fault.|他张罗了好几天,～还是没去成。He had been preparing for the trip for quite some time, but he didn't get to go after all. ❷ 拢共 altogether: 连去带回,～不到一个星期。The round trip took altogether less than a week.

【归侨】guīqiáo 归国的侨民 returned overseas Chinese; overseas Chinese who have returned to China

【归属】guīshǔ 属于;划定从属关系 belong to; come under the jurisdiction of; be affiliated to: 无所～ belong nowhere|～未定 The ownership is not settled yet.

【归顺】guīshùn 归附顺从;向敌对势力屈服 cross over and pledge allegiance; surrender to an enemy force

G

【归宿】guīsù 人或事物最终的着落 end result; destination; final settling place or result for a person or thing: 人生的～ destination of life's journey|导河,开湖,让千山万壑的溪流有了～。Building canals and reservoirs has created a settling place for streams from numerous mountains and valleys.

【归天】guī//tiān〈婉辞 *euph.*〉指人死 go to one's resting place; pass away

【归田】guītián〈书 *fml.*〉指退职回乡 resign and retire to one's native village: 解甲～ retire from military service and return to one's native village; leave military service and resume civilian life|告老～ resign on account of old age and return to one's native village

【归途】guītú 返回的路途 homeward journey; one's way home

【归西】guī//xī〈婉辞 *euph.*〉指人死 pass away (西 *xi*: 西天 the Western Sky, where Heaven is situated)

【归降】guīxiáng 投降 surrender; capitulate

【归向】guīxiàng 向好的一方面靠拢(多指政治上的倾向 oft. politically) turn towards the righteous or winning side: 人心～ inclination of the hearts of the people; swing of popular support; trend of popular feeling

【归心】guīxīn ❶ 回家的念头 desire to return home: ～似箭 with one's heart speeding home like an arrow; can't wait to return home; be anxious to start off on one's way home ❷ 心悦诚服而归附 willingly and sincerely submit to (the authority of sb.); pledge heartfelt allegiance (to sb.): 四海～ allegiance coming from all parts of the country

【归省】guīxǐng〈书 *fml.*〉回家探亲 return to visit one's family

【归依】guīyī ❶ same as 皈依 guīyī ❷〈书 *fml.*〉投靠;依附 depend on: 无所～ homeless; with nobody to depend on; with nothing to live on

【归阴】guī//yīn 指死亡 die (阴 *yin*: 阴间 Hades; land of the dark or the dead)

【归隐】guīyǐn〈书 *fml.*〉回到民间或故乡隐居 retire to one's native place and settle down; withdraw from the society and live in solitude: ～故园 retire to one's native village and live a rural life

【归于】guīyú ❶ 属于(多用于抽象事物 oft. for abstract things) belong to; be attributed to; be subsumed into: 光荣～祖国。Glory to our motherland. ❷ 趋向;趋于 have a tendency toward; be inclined to; end in; lead to: 经过讨论,大家的意见已经～一致了。Discussion led to agreement among all of us.

【归着】guī·zhe same as 归置 guī·zhi

【归真】guīzhēn ❶ 佛教、伊斯兰教指人死 (of Buddhism and Islam) pass into the real world; die ❷ ☞归真返璞 guī zhēn fǎn pú

【归真返璞】guī zhēn fǎn pú 去掉外在的装饰,恢复原来的质朴状态 return to one's original simplicity without any ostentatious adornment; return to one's original self and regain truth from life; return to nature; rediscover one's true self; also 归真返朴 guī zhēn fǎn pǔ

【归整】guī·zhěng same as 归置 guī·zhi: ～家什 put one's house in order

【归置】guī·zhi 整理(散乱的东西);收拾 put in order; tidy up: 把东西～～,马上就要动身了。Put everything in order, since we're starting off right away.

【归总】guīzǒng 把分散的归并到一处;总共 put (separate items, etc.) together; sum up; altogether: 把各小组报的数字～一下。Make a list of all the numbers reported by each group.|说什么大队人马,～才十几个人! What is this so-called big party? There are no more than a dozen or so people here!

【归罪】guīzuì 把罪过归于某个人或集体 put the blame on sb.; blame sth. on sb.; impute guilt to sb.; pin responsibility on sb.: ～于人 blame it on others

圭[1] guī ❶〈古代 *arch.*〉帝王诸侯举行礼仪时所用的玉器,上尖下方 *gui* scepter; jade scepter; jade tablet with pointed top and square bases held by ancient emperors, dukes and princes on ceremonial occasions ❷ 指圭表 gnomon; sundial: ～臬 sundial

圭[2] guī 〈古代 *arch.*〉容量单位，一升的十万分之一 unit of measurement of volume in ancient times, equal to one 100,000th of a litre

【圭表】guībiǎo 我国古代天文仪器，是在石座上平放着一个尺（圭），南北两端各立一个标杆（表）。根据日影的长短可以测定节气和一年时间的长短。sundial; ancient Chinese astronomical instrument, consisting of an elongated dial (*gui*) fixed above a stone with a pole (gnomon) standing on either side of it (north and south), which can be used for measuring, by the shadow of the sun, the solar terms and the length of the year

【圭角】guījiǎo 〈书 *fml.*〉圭的棱角 point of a jade tablet;〈比喻 *fig.*〉锋芒；迹象 talent displayed; noticeable sign: 初露～ the dawning of one's talent | 不露～ display no talent; with no noticeable talent

【圭臬】guīniè 〈书 *fml.*〉指圭表 sundial;〈比喻 *fig.*〉准则或法度 criterion; standard: 奉为～ regarded as the criteria

龟（龜） guī 爬行动物的一科，身体长圆而扁，背部隆起，有坚硬的壳，四肢短，趾有蹼，头、尾巴和四肢都能缩入甲壳内。多生活在水边，吃植物或小动物。常见的有乌龟。tortoise (*Testudinidae*); turtle; terrapin; chelonian; family of reptiles having round flat bodies curved on the backs and hard shells, short limbs and webbed feet, capable of withdrawing their heads, limbs and tails into their carapace, and living near water feeding on plants or small animals. The tortoise is the most commonly seen member of the family.

☞ jūn on p. 1066 and qiū on p. 1581

【龟板】guībǎn 龟甲，中医用做药材 tortoise plastron; tortoise shell, used in traditional Chinese medicine

【龟趺】guīfū 碑的龟形底座 base of a tombstone tablet carved in the shape of a tortoise

【龟甲】guījiǎ 乌龟的硬壳，古人用它来占卜。殷代占卜用的龟甲遗存至今，上面刻着有关占卜的记载。carapace; tortoise shell, used in ancient times for divination; the tortoiseshell from the Yin Dynasty has remained to this day, on which carved divining records can be found; ☞ 甲古文 jiǎgǔwén on p. 932

【龟鉴】guījiàn 〈比喻 *fig.*〉借鉴 sth. serving as an objective lesson or a warning; lesson of the past held up as a mirror to look into in the present and the future (龟 *gui*: 占卜用的龟甲 tortoiseshell for divination; 鉴 *jian*: 镜子 mirror)

【龟镜】guījìng same as 龟鉴 guījiàn

【龟缩】guīsuō 〈比喻 *fig.*〉像乌龟的头缩在甲壳内一样，躲藏在里面不出来 withdraw into passive defence like a turtle; huddle up; hole up: 敌军～在碉堡里。The enemy was holed up in the pillbox.

【龟头】guītóu 阴茎前端膨大的部分 glans; vascular body that forms the end of the penis

【龟足】guīzú 甲壳类动物，身体外形像龟的脚，有石灰质的壳，足能从壳口伸出捕取食物。生活在海边的岩石缝里。pollicipes (*Pollicipes mitella*); crustacean with a body shaped like the foot of a turtle and with a calcareous shell, its feet capable of extending out of its shell to catch prey, living in crevices of littoral rocks; also 石蜐 shíjié

妫（媯、嬀） Guī ❶ 妫水，水名，在北京 Guishui, name of a river in Beijing ❷ 姓 a surname

规（槼） guī ❶ 画圆形的工具 device for forming circles: 圆～ compass | 两脚～ pair of compass points or dividers ❷ 规则；成例 rules; regulation; convention; rut; etiquette: 校～ school regulations | 革除陋～ abolish outmoded regulations ❸ 劝告 admonish; advise; counsel; exhort: ～劝 admonish; provide rules and advice; counsel; exhort | ～勉 provide rules, advice and encouragement ❹ 谋划；打主意 plan; devise; scheme; calculate; cook up: ～划 programme; map out a plan | ～定 stipulate; specify; provide; regulate; fix; rule; prescribe; formulate; ordain

【规避】guībì 设法避开；躲避 evade; dodge; shun; elude; get around; bypass; avoid: 临场～ shun confrontation on the field; shun on-site appearances; dodge a task at the last moment | ～实质性问题 evade the essential issue

【规程】guīchéng 对某种政策、制度等所做的分章分条的规定 procedures; regulations; rules formulated by chapters and articles in a policy, system, etc.: 操作～ rules of operation

【规定】guīdìng ❶ 对某一事物做出关于方式、方法或数量、质量的决定 make (or express) demands or provisions on the pattern, technique, quantity or quality of sth.; stipulate; specify; provide; prescribe; set; formulate; ordain; regulate; rule; fix: ～产品的质量标准 set quality criteria | 不得超过～的日期 no delay beyond the fixed date ❷ 所规定的内容 provisions; stipulations; rules and regulations: 关于职工退职、退休问题，中央已经有了～。The central authorities have made provisions for the resignation and retirement of staff and workers.

【规定动作】guīdìng dòngzuò 某些体育项目（如跳水、体操等）比赛时，规定运动员必须做的整套或单个的动作 compulsory exercises or programme; (of athletic competitions, e.g. div-

G

ing, gymnastics, etc.) compulsory set of movements or single movement

【规范】guīfàn ❶ 约定俗成或明文规定的标准 norms; standards; specifications; established or provided rules or patterns serving as a standard: 语音～ phonetic standard | 道德～ morality; ethics; moral standards ❷ 合乎规范 within the given standards; normal; meets specifications; regular: 这个词的用法不～。This usage of the word is not the norm. ❸ 使合乎规范 standardize; normalize; regulate: 用新的社会道德来～人们的行动 regulate people's conduct under the new social morality

【规范化】guīfànhuà 使合于一定的标准 standardize; normalize: 实行～服务 give standardized service

【规复】guīfù〈书 *fml.*〉恢复(机构、制度等); 收复(失地) restore (an organization, system, etc.); recapture or recover (lost territory): ～约法 restore legislation | ～中原 recover or recapture the Central Plains

【规格】guīgé ❶ 产品质量的标准,如一定的大小、轻重、精密度、性能等 specifications; standards; norms; exact statement of quality criteria for a manufactured product, prescribing the size, weight, precision, properties, etc.: 产品合乎～。The product is up to the standard. ❷ 泛指规定的要求或条件 (in a broad sense) requirement or condition: 接待来宾的～很高。The protocal for receiving guests is of a high standard.

【规划】guīhuà ❶ 比较全面的长远的发展计划 programme; plan; layout; project; blueprint: 制订～ map out, make, draw up and work out a plan or programme | 十年～ ten-year plan ❷ 做规划 draw up a plan; map out a plan: 兴修水利问题,应当全面～。An overall plan should be made for water conservancy construction.

【规谏】guījiàn〈书 *fml.*〉忠言劝戒; 规劝 admonish; advise; exhort

【规诫】guījiè〈书 *fml.*〉规劝告诫 admonish; warn; also 规戒 guījiè

【规矩】guī·ju ❶ 一定的标准、法则或习惯 custom; established practice; established standard, rule or habit: 老～ established rules | 立～ set rules | 守～ observe the rules; abide by the rules; behave oneself | 按～办事 follow the rules ❷ (行为)端正老实; 合乎标准或常理 (of a person's conduct) well-disciplined; honest; proper; decent; conforming to norms: ～人字写得很～。An honest person writes in a neat hand.

【规律】guīlǜ 事物之间的内在的本质联系。这种联系不断重复出现,在一定条件下经常起作用,并且决定着事物必然向着某种趋向发展。规律是客观存在的,是不以人们的意志为转移的,但人们能够通过实践认识它,利用它。norm; law; regular pattern; orderliness; relations inherent in the nature of things that keep recurring and performing the same actions under certain conditions, and thus set unavoidable tendencies in the development of things. Such laws exist objectively, and independently of human will, but people can learn about them and make use of them. also 法则 fǎzé

【规模】guīmó (事业、机构、工程、运动等)所具有的格局、形式或范围 scale; scope; extent; dimensions; setup, pattern or extent of an undertaking, establishment, project, sport, etc.: 粗具～ begin to take shape | ～宏大 on a large scale; broad in scale or scope

【规劝】guīquàn 郑重地劝告,使改正错误 admonish; advise; exhort; warn: 多次～,他仍无悔改之意。He didn't show any repentance in spite of the many warnings.

【规行矩步】guī xíng jǔ bù ❶〈比喻 *fig.*〉举动合乎规矩,毫不苟且 act meticulously in conformity of rules; behave correctly and cautiously ❷〈比喻 *fig.*〉墨守成规,不知变通 stick to established practices; follow the beaten track; get into a rut

【规约】guīyuē ❶ 经过相互协议规定下来的共同遵守的条款 terms of agreement stipulated after negotiations; stipulations: 竞赛～ contest rules | 履行～ fulfil an agreement ❷ 限制,约束 restrict; restrain; set a limit to: 用理智～言行。Let reason rule one's words and deeds.

【规则】guīzé ❶ 规定出来供大家共同遵守的制度或章程 set of rules or regulations prescribed and observed by all: 交通～ traffic regulations or rules | 借书～ library rules | 工厂管理～ managing regulations of a factory ❷ 规律; 法则 law; rule: 自然～ law of nature | 造字～ word formation rules ❸ (在形状、结构或分布上)合乎一定的方式; 整齐 (of form, structure, or set-up) in conformity with a fixed pattern; regular: ～四边形 regular quadrilateral | 这条河流的水道原来很不～。Originally the river's course was quite irregular.

【规章】guīzhāng 规则章程: ～制度 rules and regulations | 法令～ laws and regulations

【规整】guīzhěng 合乎一定的规格; 规矩整齐 in conformity to certain standards; regular; standard; tidy; neat: ～的仿宋字 neat imitation of Song characters | 形制～。The form (or structure) is regular. | 规规整整的四合院 neat and tidy quadrangle

【规正】guīzhèng ❶〈书 *fml.*〉规劝,使改正; 匡正 admonish and correct; put or set right; rectify: 互相～ correct each other | ～风俗 rectify customs ❷ 规整 regular; tidy; neat: 他们围坐成一个不很～的圆圈。They sat in a somewhat irregular circle.

【规制】guīzhì ❶ 规则；制度 rules or regulations; system ❷（建筑物的）规模形制 size and shapc of a building：天安门虽经多次修缮，但～未变。After numerous renovations, the Tian'anmen rostrum still retains its original size, shape and structure.

邽 guī ❶ 下邽（Xiàguī），地名，在陕西 Xiagui, name of a place in Shaanxi ❷（Guī）姓 a surname

皈 guī［皈依］（guīyī）原指佛教的入教仪式，后来泛指虔诚地信奉佛教或参加其他宗教组织（orig.）ceremony of initiating sb. as a Buddhist; in a broad sense, it refers to conversion to Buddhism or another religion or faith

闺 guī ❶〈书 *fml.*〉上圆下方的小门 arched door ❷ 闺房 boudoir; zenana; harem：深～ innermost bedchamber (built at the innermost part of a house in old times) | ～门 door of a boudoir

【闺范】guīfàn ❶ 封建时代指妇女所应遵守的道德规范 moral norms for women in feudal China ❷ 指女子的风范（of a woman）demeanour; bearing; poise：举止端庄，有大家～ graceful and well-bred

【闺房】guīfáng〈旧称 *old*〉女子居住的内室 bedroom of a lady

【闺阁】guīgé same as 闺房 guīfáng

【闺阃】guīkǔn〈旧指 *old*〉妇女居住的地方 women's living quarters

【闺门】guīmén 闺房的门 door of a boudoir

【闺门旦】guīméndàn 戏曲中旦角的一种，演闺阁小姐或天真活泼的年轻姑娘 ingenue; female character in traditional opera playing the role of an unengaged elegant maiden or cheerful girl

【闺女】guī·nü ❶ 没有结婚的女子 girl; maiden ❷ 女儿 daughter

【闺秀】guīxiù〈旧时 *old*〉称富贵人家的女儿 daughter of a wealthy and influential family：大家～ graceful girl or woman from a rich family

珪 guī same as 圭 guī

硅 guī 非金属元素，符号 Si (silicium)。黑灰色晶体或粉末，自然界分布极广，普通的沙子就是不纯的二氧化硅。有单向导电性。用来制合金等，也是重要的半导体材料。silicium (Si); silicon; non-metallic element, usu. a dark crystalline substance or powder, occurring extensively in the earth, also found in sand in the form of silica, a one-way conductive, used in alloys and as a key material in semi-conductors; 旧称 formerly called 矽 xī

【硅肺】guīfèi 一种职业病，由长期吸入含二氧化硅的灰尘引起，病状是呼吸短促，胸口发闷或疼痛，咳嗽，体力减弱，常并发肺结核症 silicosis; occupational disease of the lungs, caused by continued inhalation of silica dust and characterized by a chronic shortness of breath, chest discomfort or pain, coughing, weakness, and combined with the tendency to develop complications of tuberculosis; 旧称 formerly called 矽肺 xīfèi

【硅钢】guīgāng 含硅量高于 0.4% 的合金钢 silicon steel; alloy steel with more than 0.4% silicon; 旧称 formerly called 矽钢 xīgāng

【硅化】guīhuà〈古代 *arch.*〉植物遗体由于其中某些成分被硅酸盐所置换而逐渐变硬，成为化石 silicification; process of the remains of ancient plants being gradually replaced by silicate and converted into solid fossils

傀 guī〈书 *fml.*〉❶ 怪异 unusual; strange; odd：～奇 unusual; peculiar ❷ 独立的样子 stand all by itself：～然独立 stand alone ☞ kuǐ on p. 1130

庬 Guī 古山名，在今河南洛阳西 ancient name of a mountain to the west of present-day Luoyang, Henan Province; ☞ wěi on p. 1997

瑰 guī〈书 *fml.*〉❶ 一种像玉的石头 jade-like stone ❷ 珍奇 rare; marvellous; magnificent：～丽 magnificent | ～异 fantastic

【瑰宝】guībǎo 特别珍贵的东西 rarity; treasure; gem; sth. highly prized for its value or perfection：敦煌壁画是我国古代艺术中的～。The Dunhuang frescoes are gems of ancient Chinese art.

【瑰丽】guīlì 异常美丽 unusually beautiful; magnificent; splendid：江边的夜景是雄伟而～的。The night view along the riverbank is majestic and magnificent. | 这些作品为我们的文学艺术增添了新的～花朵。These works add more splendour to the literature and art of our country.

【瑰奇】guīqí 瑰丽奇异 magnificent and fantastic：～的黄山云海 fantastic ocean of clouds of Mount Huangshan

【瑰伟】guīwěi same as 瑰玮 guīwěi

【瑰玮】guīwěi〈书 *fml.*〉❶（品质）奇特（of a quality）odd; vagarious ❷（文辞）华丽（of a writing style）ornate ‖ also 瑰伟 guīwěi

【瑰异】guīyì same as 瑰奇 guīqí

鲑 guī 鱼类的一科，身体大，略呈纺锤形，鳞细而圆，是重要的食用鱼类。常见的有大麻哈鱼。salmon (*Salmo salar*); family of fish with large bodies shaped slightly like spindles, round fine scales, and seen as an important food fish. Chum is one of the commonly found members of the family. ☞ xié on p. 2122

鬹 guī〈古代 *arch.*〉陶制炊事器具，有三个空心的足 cooker made of clay with three hollow feet

瓌 guī same as 瑰 guī

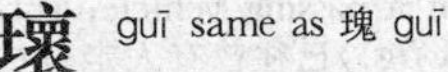

guǐ (ㄍㄨㄟˇ)

氿 guǐ 氿泉，从侧面喷出的泉 fountain that gushes sideways
☞ jiǔ on p.1037

宄 guǐ ☞ 奸宄 jiānguǐ on p.938

轨 guǐ ❶ same as 路轨 lùguǐ ①：钢～ rail｜铁～ rail ❷ same as 轨道 guǐdào ① railroad; railway line; tram road：出～ derail; run off the rails｜无～电车 trolley (bus); trackless tram ❸〈比喻 *fig.*〉办法、规矩、秩序等 course; way; rule; order：常～ regular course; orbit｜越～ deviate; off-track｜步入正～ be put on the right track; be on the right track ❹〈书 *fml.*〉依照；遵循 abide by; adhere to; follow：～于法令 abide by law

【轨道】guǐdào ❶ 用条形的钢材铺成的供火车、电车等行驶的路线 railroad; tram road; road composed of parallel steel rails providing a track for trains, trams, etc. ❷ 天体在宇宙间运行的路线 orbit; path of a celestial body moving round another body; also 轨迹 guǐjì ❸ 物体运动的路线，多指有一定规则的，如原子内电子的运动和人造卫星的运行都有一定的轨道 path; orbit; trajectory; route or course along which an object moves, often regularly; e.g. movement of an electron within an atom and a man-made satellite both follow a certain course ❹ 行动应遵循的规则、程序或范围 rule; procedure; scope of an action; right track：生产已经走上～。Production has been put on track.

【轨道衡】guǐdàohéng 铁路上使用的铺有轨道的地秤 track scale; rail scale; platform scale bearing a track (part of the line of a railway) for weighing loaded cars

【轨度】guǐdù〈书 *fml.*〉法度 law; code of conduct：不循～ transgress the law

【轨范】guǐfàn 行动所遵循的标准 accepted rules for an action; code; standard

【轨迹】guǐjì ❶ 一个点在空间移动，它所通过的全部路径叫做这个点的轨迹 locus; line traced by a point which varies its position according to given laws; such a line is the locus of the point ❷ same as 轨道 guǐdào ② ❸〈比喻 *fig.*〉人生经历的或事物发展的道路 track; path along which a person goes through his or her life, or along which sth. develops：这些诗篇记录了诗人一生的～。These poems are a record of the path of the poet's whole life.｜文章勾勒出汉字发展演变的～。The article outlined the track along which Chinese characters have developed.

【轨辙】guǐzhé 车轮行过留下来的痕迹 marks left by the wheels of a passing vehicle; rut; beaten track;〈比喻 *fig.*〉已往曾有人走过的道路或做过的事情 well-travelled road or sth. already done

【轨枕】guǐzhěn 垫在钢轨下面的结构物，通常用木头或特制的钢筋混凝土制成，用来固定钢轨的位置，并将火车的压力传到道床和路基上 railway sleeper; tie; framework set under the rails of a railroad, oft. made of wood or special concrete, for fixing the rails in place, and spreading the pressure from the train down to the railroad bed and base

庋(庪) guǐ〈书 *fml.*〉❶ 放东西的架子 shelf ❷ 放置；保存 keep; preserve：～藏 store up; preserve

匦 guǐ 匣子 box：票～ ballot box

佹 guǐ〈书 *fml.*〉❶ 乖戾 perverse; unreasonable; freak ❷ 奇异 queer; odd; singular; whimsical; fantastic ❸ 偶然 accidental; fortuitous：～得～失 accidentally gained, accidentally lost

诡 guǐ ❶ 欺诈；奸滑 deceitful; tricky; sly; cunning：～诈 deceitful; fraudulent｜～计 wile; craft; trick ❷〈书 *fml.*〉奇异 weird; bizarre; eerie：～形 weird shape｜～观 strange view｜～异 uncanny

【诡辩】guǐbiàn ❶ 外表上、形式上好像是运用正确的推理手段，实际上违反逻辑规律，做出似是而非的推论 sophistry; sophism; casuistry; quibbling; crafty reasoning that puts on the appearance of appropriate logic, but in effect gives rise to a plausible but fallacious and illogical argument ❷ 无理狡辩 quibble

【诡诞】guǐdàn 虚妄荒诞 unfounded and absurd; surreal：～不经 surreal; incredible

【诡怪】guǐguài 奇异怪诞 fantastic; freakish：行事～ act in a freakish, bizarre manner

【诡计】guǐjì 狡诈的计策 crafty plot; trick; wiles; artifice; ruse; dodgery; intrigue; machination：～多端 be up to all sorts of tricks or dodges; be full of craft; be very crafty; have a lot of tricks up one's sleeve; be foxy and wily; have a whole bag of tricks

【诡谲】guǐjué〈书 *fml.*〉❶ 奇异多变 strange; highly changeable and unpredictable ❷ 离奇古怪 weird; eccentric; bizarre; offbeat：言语～ speak cryptically ❸ same as 诡诈 guǐzhà：为人～ be wily and crafty

【诡秘】guǐmì (行动、态度等)隐秘不易捉摸 (of action, mind, etc.) secretive or elusory; furtive; surreptitious; stealthy：行踪～ furtive in action

【诡奇】guǐqí 诡异 guǐyì：～难测 freakish and unpredictable｜情节～ bizarre plot

【诡异】guǐyì 奇异；奇特 strange; odd; queer; bizarre; fantastic：～的笔调 fantastic and bizarre style of writing｜故事～有趣。The story is fantastically interesting.

【诡诈】guǐzhà 狡诈 cunning; crafty; wily;

treacherous; sly: ～异常 be extremely wily | 阴险～ dangerous and treacherous

垝(陒) guǐ 〈书 *fml*.〉毁坏；坍塌 ruin; collapse: ～垣 wall in ruins

鬼 guǐ ❶ 迷信的人所说的人死后的灵魂 supernatural being; ghost; phantom; spirit; apparition; shade; spook ❷ 称有不良嗜好或行为的人（含厌恶意 derog.）one with bad habits or behaviour: 烟～ chain-smoker | 讨厌～ skunk; wretch | 吝啬～ niggard; screw; miser; skinflint; scrooge; churl ❸ 躲躲闪闪；不光明 stealthy; clandestine; surreptitious: ～头～脑 having a thievish look; furtive; stealthy | ～～祟祟 secretive; sneaky ❹ 不可告人的打算或勾当 sinister plot; dirty trick: 捣～ play a trick | 心里有～ have a guilty conscience ❺ 恶劣；糟糕(限做定语 used as an attributive only) terrible; damnable: ～天气 damnable weather | ～主意 wicked idea; trick | 这～地方连棵草都不长。What a damned place with not even a single blade of grass! ❻ 机灵(多指小孩儿或动物 usu. referring to a child or animal) clever; smart; quick: 这孩子～得很! What a clever boy! ❼ 二十八宿之一 one of the 28 lunar constellations in ancient Chinese astronomy

【鬼把戏】guǐbǎxì ❶ 阴险的手段或计策 sinister plot; treacherous scheme ❷ 暗中捉弄人的手段 mischief; dirty tricks; monkeyshine; monkey tricks

【鬼才】guǐcái 指某种特殊的才能，也指有某种特殊才能的人 wizard; special talent: 文坛～ a literary genius

【鬼点子】guǐdiǎn·zi 坏主意 wicked idea; trick

【鬼斧神工】guǐ fǔ shén gōng 形容建筑、雕塑等技艺的精巧 (of a building, statue, etc.) displaying superb craftsmanship; uncanny workmanship; also 神工鬼斧 shén gōng guǐ fǔ

【鬼怪】guǐguài 鬼和妖怪 ghosts and monsters; spectre; bogey; demon; genie: 妖魔～ bevil forces

【鬼画符】guǐhuàfú ❶ 形容写字随意涂抹，潦草难认 illegible scrawl; scratchy handwriting ❷〈比喻 *fig*.〉虚伪的话 hypocritical talk; false talk

【鬼话】guǐhuà 不真实的话；谎话 falsehood; mendacity; fabricated story; lie: ～连篇 pack of lies

【鬼魂】guǐhún 死人的灵魂(迷信) (superstition) spirit; ghost; spectre; apparition

【鬼混】guǐhùn ❶ 糊里糊涂地生活 muddle along; lead an aimless and irregular life; mess around or about; fool around; hang around or about; piddle: 在外～多年，什么也没学到。After fooling around for many years, he ended up in ignorance. ❷ 过不正当的生活 lead an immoral life: 两人整天在一起～。The two of them lived their aimless life together all day long.

【鬼火】guǐhuǒ 磷火的俗称 popular name for 磷火 línhuǒ

【鬼哭狼嚎】guǐ kū láng háo 形容大声哭叫声音凄厉(含贬义 derog.) wail like a ghost and howl like a wolf — give dreary cries and screams

【鬼脸】guǐliǎn (～儿 guǐliǎnr) ❶ 用厚纸做成的假面具，是一种儿童玩具，多按照戏曲中的脸谱制作 mask made of thick paper that is a toy for children to play with, often designed in patterns of facial makeup in traditional opera ❷ 故意做出来的滑稽的面部表情 funny face; grimace; wry face: 扮～ make a face; make a grimace; grimace; make a wry face; distort one's face | 他把舌头一伸，做了个～。He stuck out his tongue and made a face.

【鬼魅】guǐmèi 〈书 *fml*.〉same as 鬼怪 guǐguài

【鬼门关】guǐménguān 迷信传说中的阴阳交界的关口 (superstition) gates of hell; jaws of death;〈比喻 *fig*.〉凶险的地方 dangerous place; jaws of danger; precipice

【鬼迷心窍】guǐ mí xīn qiào 指受迷惑，犯糊涂 be obsessed; be possessed; be besotted: 我真是～，把坏人当好人。I must have been brainwashed to have thought this bad guy was a decent person.

【鬼神】guǐshén 鬼怪和神灵 ghosts and deities; spirits and gods; supernatural beings: 不信～ disbelieving in supernatural things; godless | ～莫测(形容极其神奇奥妙) as unpredictable as a ghost (supernatural and miraculous)

【鬼使神差】guǐ shǐ shén chāi 好像鬼神暗中差使一样，形容意外地发生某种凑巧的事或不由自主地做出某种意想不到的事 (of things or people) happen or act as if guided by a ghost or deity; unexpected or coincidental happenings; also 神差鬼使 shén chāi guǐ shǐ

【鬼祟】guǐsuì ❶ 偷偷摸摸；不光明正大 underhanded and dishonest; furtive; secretive; covert; surreptitious: 行为～ act sneakily | 只见一个人鬼鬼祟祟地探头探脑。A man was lurching along, popping out his head this way and that. ❷ same as 鬼怪 guǐguài

【鬼胎】guǐtāi 〈比喻 *fig*.〉不可告人的念头 evil idea; evil plot; ulterior motive; dark scheme: 心怀～ brewing a dark scheme

【鬼剃头】guǐtìtóu 斑秃的俗称 popular name for alopecia

【鬼头鬼脑】guǐ tóu guǐ nǎo 形容行为鬼祟 act sneakily; thievishly

【鬼物】guǐwù 鬼；鬼怪 ghost; spectre

【鬼雄】guǐxióng 〈书 *fml*.〉鬼中的雄杰，用于称颂壮烈死去的人 remain a hero even in afterlife; person whose death was tragic but heroic

【鬼蜮】guǐyù ❶ same as 鬼怪 guǐguài ❷ 阴险

害人的 treacherous; viperous: ～伎俩 devilish stratagem; dirty, underhanded tricks; evil tactics; insidious tricks; sinister intrigue

【鬼子】guǐ·zi 对侵略我国的外国人的憎称 term of abuse for foreign invaders

姽 guǐ［姽婳］(guǐhuà)〈书 *fml.*〉形容女子娴静美好 (of a woman) demure and pretty

癸 guǐ 天干的第十位 last of the ten Heavenly Stems; ☞干支 gānzhī on p.627

殷 guǐ same as 簋 guǐ, 见于金文 found in inscriptions on ancient bronze objects

晷 guǐ ❶〈书 *fml.*〉日影 shadow of the sun;〈比喻 *fig.*〉时光 time: 余～ spare time | 焚膏继～ burn a candle to prolong the day; day and night ❷〈古代 *arch.*〉用来观测日影以定时刻的仪器 sundial; ancient instrument to show the time of day by means of the shadow cast by the sun

簋 guǐ〈古代 *arch.*〉盛食物的器具,圆口,两耳 *gui*; ancient food vessel with a round mouth and two handles

guì (ㄍㄨㄟˋ)

柜(櫃) guì ❶ (～儿 guìr)收藏衣物、文件等用的器具,方形或长方形,一般为木制或铁制 cupboard; cabinet; closet for storing clothes, documents, etc., square or rectangular-shaped box made of wood or iron: 衣～ dresser; chest; wardrobe | 碗～儿 (kitchen) cupboards; cabinet | 橱～ cupboard; cabinet | 保险～ safe ❷ 柜房,也指商店 cashier's (office); also refers to a shop: 现款都交了～了。All the cash has been handed in to the cashier's office.

☞ jǔ on p.1047

【柜橱】guìchú 橱柜 cupboard; cabinet

【柜房】guìfáng 商店的账房 (in a shop) cashier's office; cashier's desk; cashier's

【柜上】guì·shang 指柜房,也指商店 cashier's desk; also refers to a shop

【柜台】guìtái 商店营业用的装置,式样像柜而长,用木料、金属或玻璃板制成 (sales) counter; bar; furniture used in a shop, looking like a long cabinet and made of wood, metal or plate glass

【柜子】guì·zi same as 柜 guì ①

炅 Guì 姓 a surname

☞ jiǒng on p.1034

刿(劌) guì〈书 *fml.*〉伤;割 wound; stab; cut

刽(劊) guì〈书 *fml.*〉割断 cut off; chop off

【刽子手】guì·zishǒu ❶〈旧时 *old*〉执行死刑的人 executioner; headsman; hangman ❷〈比喻 *fig.*〉屠杀人民的人 slaughterer; butcher

炔 Guì 姓 a surname

☞ quē on p.1601

贵 guì ❶ 价格高;价值大 (跟'贱'相对 as opposed to 'cheap') expensive; costly; dear: 绸缎比棉布～。Silk is more expensive than cotton. | 春雨～如油。Spring rains are as precious as oil. ❷ 评价高;值得珍视或重视 highly valued; valuable; precious: 宝～ valuable; precious | 可～ valuable; praiseworthy; golden; commendable ❸ 以某种情况为可贵 be treasured in certain respects: 人～有自知之明。It's wise for a person to be aware of his own limits. | 锻炼身体,～在坚持。When it comes to physical exercise, persistence is important. ❹ 地位优越(跟'贱'相对 as opposed to 'base' or 'humble') high-ranking; noble; of exalted position: ～族 nobleman; aristocrat; baron; peer; patrician | ～妇人 lady of noble rank | 达官～人 high officials and important people ❺〈敬辞 *pol.*〉称与对方有关的事物 your: ～姓 your name (surname) | ～国 your country | 高抬～手 (I) beg your forgiveness; be lenient; be kind enough; be generous ❻ (Guì)姓 a surname

【贵宾】guìbīn 尊贵的客人(多指外宾 oft. foreign guests) honoured guest; distinguished guest

【贵妃】guìfēi 次于皇后的地位高的妃子 imperial concubine next to the queen in rank

【贵干】guìgàn〈敬辞 *pol.*〉问人要做什么 (asking about sb.'s errand) your business: 有何～? What auspicious business brings you here?

【贵庚】guìgēng〈敬辞 *pol.*〉问人年龄 your age

【贵贱】guìjiàn ❶ 价钱的高低 cheap or expensive: 管它～,只要看中了,就买了来。Whatever the price, if it caught my eye I bought it. ❷ 地位的高低 high or low social status: 无论～,都以礼相待。Treat everyone courteously, whatever their social status. ❸〈方 *dial.*〉无论如何;反正 in any case; at any rate; anyway; no matter what (happens): 他嫌太累,～不肯去。He fears he will be tired out and won't go no matter what.

【贵金属】guìjīnshǔ 通常指在自然界含量较少,不易开采,因而价格昂贵的金属,包括金、银和铂族元素(钌、铑、钯、锇、铱、铂) precious metals; metals with small natural deposits that cannot be easily mined, and as a result are highly priced, including gold, silver, and the platinum family of metals (ruthenium, rhodium, palladium, osmium, iridium, platinum)

【贵客】guìkè 尊贵的客人 honoured guest; distinguished guest: ～临门。A distinguished guest is visiting.

【贵人】guìrén ❶ 尊贵的人 person of eminence;

达官～ high officials and important people|～眼高。Men of eminence are not easily pleased. ❷〈古代 *arch.*〉皇宫中女官名 worthy lady; woman with a title or position of responsibility in the Chinese imperial palace in ancient times

【贵姓】guìxìng〈敬辞 *pol.*〉问人姓氏 your name (surname)

【贵恙】guìyàng〈敬辞 *pol.*〉称对方的病 your illness or ailment

【贵重】guìzhòng 价值高;值得重视 valuable; valued; precious; costly; golden: ～仪器 valuable instrument|～物品 valuables

【贵胄】guìzhòu〈书 *fml.*〉贵族的后代 descendants of a noble family

【贵子】guìzǐ〈敬辞 *pol.*〉称人的儿子(多含祝福的意思 oft. used in congratulations or greetings) your son: 喜生～。Congratulations on your newborn baby!

【贵族】guìzú 奴隶社会或封建社会以及现代君主国家里统治阶级的上层,享有特权 nobleman; aristocrat; peer; patrician; baron; ruling class in a slave or feudal society as well as in a modern monarchical country, entitled with certain privileges

桂[1] guì ❶ 肉桂 cinnamon; cassia: ～皮 Chinese cinnamon; cassia; cassia bark ❷ 木犀 osmanthus; devilwood: 金～ genus osmanthus|～花 sweet-scented osmanthus; osmanthus flowers ❸ 月桂树 laurel; bay; bay laurel; sweet bay: ～冠 laurel wreath ❹ 桂皮树 cassia-bark tree

桂[2] Guì ❶ 桂江,水名,在广西 Guijiang, name of a river in Guangxi ❷ 广西的别称 another name for Guangxi ❸ (Guì)姓 a surname

【桂冠】guìguān 月桂树叶编的帽子,古代希腊人授予杰出的诗人或竞技的优胜者。后来欧洲习俗以桂冠为光荣的称号。现在也用来指竞赛中的冠军。laurels; wreath of laurel conferred as a mark of honour in ancient Greece upon outstanding poets or victors in athletic contests; later, European people customarily refer to laurels as honour or glory won for great achievement, and now it also refers to winners of contests: 争夺～ contend for distinction

【桂花】guìhuā 木犀的通称 osmanthus flowers (*Osmanthus fragrans*); general term for sweet-scented osmanthus

【桂剧】guìjù 广西地方戏曲剧种之一,流行于广西汉族说北方话的地区 *guiju* opera; local opera of Guangxi, popular among Guangxi's Han community speaking northern dialects

【桂皮】guìpí ❶ 桂皮树,常绿乔木,叶呈卵形,花黄色,果实黑色。树皮可入药或做香料。Chinese cinnamon; cassia-bark tree (Chinese cinnamon tree), evergreen tree with oval leaves, yellow flowers and dark fruit; its bark can be used as a herb or spice ❷ 桂皮树的皮 cinnamon; cassia; cassia-bark ❸ 肉桂树的皮,可入药,也可做香料或制桂油 cinnamon bark, used as a herb as well as a spice or Cassia oil

【桂圆】guìyuán 龙眼 longan

【桂竹】guìzhú 竹子的一种,秆高大,坚韧致密,用作建筑材料,也可制器物。产于台湾省。castillo bamboo (*Phyllostachys bambusoides*); bamboo with a tall stalk, solid and fine textured, used as building material or to make utensils, grown in Taiwan Province; also 筀竹 guìzhú

【桂子】guìzǐ〈书 *fml.*〉same as 桂花 guìhuā: ～飘香。The osmanthus flowers are emitting their delicate fragrance.

桧(檜) guì 常绿乔木,幼树的叶子像针,大树的叶子像鳞片,雌雄异株,雄花鲜黄色,果实球形,种子三棱形 Chinese juniper (*Sabina chinensis*); hermaphrodite evergreen tree with bright yellow staminate flowers, needle-like (in the young) or scale-like leaves (in the full-grown), and triangular seeds; also 刺柏 cìbǎi

☞ huì on p. 869

硊 guì 石硊镇(shíguìzhèn),地名,在安徽 town of Shigui, in Anhui Province

筀 guì [筀竹](guìzhú) same as 桂竹 guìzhú

跪 guì 两膝弯曲,使一个或两个膝盖着地 go down on one or both knees; kneel: 下～ drop down on one's knees; kneel down|～拜 kowtow

【跪拜】guìbài〈旧时 *old*〉一种礼节,跪在地上磕头 kowtow; act of courtesy in China, to kneel and touch the forehead to the ground as an expression of respect, worship or submission

【跪射】guìshè 射击训练和比赛的一种姿势,一条腿跪在地上射击 kneel to shoot; shooting posture in exercise or competition on one knee

鲹(鱥) guì 鱼,身体侧扁,有黑色小点,吻尖,口大。生活在溪流中。minnow (*Phoxinus phoxinus L.*); fish, with a laterally flat body spotted with black, pointed lips and a big mouth, living in brooks and streams

鳜 guì 鳜鱼,口大,鳞片细小,背部黄绿色,全身有黑色斑点。生活在淡水中,是我国的特产。有的地区叫花鲫鱼。mandarin fish (*Siniperca chuatsi*); fish having a big mouth, tiny scales, greenish yellow back with black spots, living in fresh water, a specialty seafood in China; known in some areas as 花鲫鱼 huājìyú

gǔn (ㄍㄨㄣˇ)

衮(袞) gǔn 〈古代 *arch.*〉君王等的礼服 ceremonial dress for royalty：～服 imperial robe; emperor's ceremonial dress |～冕(衮服和冕旒) emperor's ceremonial dress and crown (with jade ornaments hanging at front and back)

【衮服】gǔnfú 天子的礼服 emperor's ceremonial dress

【衮衮】gǔngǔn 〈书 *fml.*〉连续不断;众多 continuous; endless; numerous

【衮衮诸公】gǔngǔn zhū gōng 称居高位而无所作为的官僚 high-ranking officials with mediocre performance

绲 gǔn ❶ 织成的带子 ribbon ❷〈书 *fml.*〉绳 string; cord ❸ 缝纫方法,沿着衣服等的边缘缝上布条、带子等 way of hemming or trimming the edge of a dress, etc., with a narrow band of cloth or ribbon：～边 trim with lace|用红绦子在领口上～一道边儿 bind the edge of the collar with red ribbon

【绲边】gǔnbiān (～儿 gǔnbiānr)在衣服、布鞋等的边缘特别缝制的一种圆棱的边儿 embroidered border or hem; raised half-rolled border along the edge of a dress, garment, shoe, etc.; also 滚边 gǔnbiān

辊 gǔn 机器上能滚动的圆柱形机件的统称 roller; general term for any cylindrical machine part that rolls or rotates; also 罗拉 luólā

【辊子】gǔn·zi 辊 roller

滚(滾) gǔn ❶ 滚动;翻转 roll; tumble; trundle; welter：荷叶上～着亮晶晶的水珠。Some sparkling drops of water rolled on the lotus leaf.|那骡子就地打了个～儿又站起来。The mule weltered in its place and rose. ❷ 走开;离开(含斥责意 in an angry tone) get away; scram：～开 get out; be off; get lost|你给我～! Off with you! *or* Go to hell! *or* Beat it! ❸ (液体)翻腾,特指受热沸腾 (of a liquid) bubble up when heated to a boiling point; boil; seethe：锅里水～了。The water in the pot is boiling. ❹ 使滚动;使在滚动中沾上(东西) roll around to get bigger by picking up thicker layers：～元宵 roll rice dumplings|～雪球 roll a snowball; snowball ◇利～利 usurious loan; compound interest ❺ 缝纫方法 way of sewing, same as 绲 gǔn ③ ❻ (Gǔn)姓 a surname

【滚边】gǔnbiān same as 绲边 gǔnbiān

【滚齿机】gǔnchǐjī 金属切削机床,用来加工齿轮、涡轮和花键轴等的齿形。加工时,工件和滚刀做相对滚动,滚刀一面旋转,一面推进切削。hobbing machine; gear-hobbing machine; metal-cutting lathe, used for forming the teeth of gears, worm wheels and spline shafts; during operation, the work piece and the hob are rolling against each other, with the hob cutting forward while rolling

【滚存】gǔncún 簿记用语,指逐日累计的积存 term of accounting, day-by-day accumulation

【滚蛋】gǔn//dàn 离开;走开(斥责或骂人的话 in an angry tone or curse) away with; get out; scram; beat it; get the hell out; go to hell; get away

【滚刀肉】gǔndāoròu 〈方 *dial.*〉〈比喻 *fig.*〉不通情理、胡搅蛮缠的人 unreasonable troublemaker; nuisance; annoying person

【滚动】gǔndòng 一个物体(多为圆球形或圆柱形)在另一物体上接触面不断改变地移动 (of an object, oft. spherical or cylindrical) move forward on a surface by repeatedly turning over; roll; rotate：车轮～。The wheels are rolling.

【滚动轴承】gǔndòng zhóuchéng 轴承的一种,利用滚珠或滚柱的滚动来代替滑动。摩擦力较小,但承受冲击负荷不及滑动轴承。按构造不同,可分为滚珠轴承、滚柱轴承和滚针轴承。ball bearing; bearing that rotates instead of slides by means of balls or rollers, and with reduced friction, bears a smaller load than sliding bearing; in terms of mechanical structure, divided into ball bearing, roller bearing and needle bearing

【滚翻】gǔnfān 体操动作,全身向前、向后或向侧翻转 gymnastic movement, with body rolling forward, backward or sideways; roll：前～ forward roll|后～ backward roll

【滚肥】gǔnféi 非常肥(多指动物 usu. referring to animals) fat; corpulent; swollen; inflated; bulky; puffy：这头猪喂得～～的。The pig is well-fed and fat.

【滚沸】gǔnfèi (液体)沸腾翻滚 (of liquid) boiling：一锅～的汤 pot of boiling soup ◇～的感情 effusive feelings; burning love; feelings at a boiling point

【滚杠】gǔngàng 机器或简单机械中能转动的圆柱形用具。一般在运输重物时起车轮的作用。rolling bar; roller; cylindrical instrument in a machine or simple mechanical structure that rolls and usually acts like a wheel in the transportation of a heavy load

【滚瓜烂熟】gǔnguā-lànshú 形容读书或背书流利纯熟 read or recite fluently from memory; continuously produce sth. from memory; learn sth. thoroughly by heart; have sth. at one's fingertips

【滚瓜溜圆】gǔnguā-liūyuán 滚圆,多用来形容牲畜肥壮 (of animals) fat and round; roly-poly

【滚滚】gǔngǔn ❶ 形容急速地滚动或翻腾 roll; surge; billow：车轮～ trundling wheels|大江～东去。The river flows and surges eastward.|狂风卷起了～的黄沙。The violent wind blew up rolling clouds of dust. ❷ 形容连续不断 occurring continuously 雷声～ a long roll of thunder; rolls of thunder; rumbling thunder | 财源～。Wealth or money keeps rolling in. *or* Fortune pours in from all sides.

【滚雷】gǔnléi ❶ 声音连续不断的雷 rolling thunder ❷ 从高处滚放的能延时爆炸的地雷 rolling mine; a kind of mine, designed to be rolled down from a high position and detonated by a time fuse

【滚轮】gǔnlún 运动器械的一种,由若干铁棍连接两个大小相同的铁环制成。人在轮里手攀脚登,使环滚动。gyro wheel; hoop; sports apparatus, composed of a certain number of iron bars that are joined with two identical rings, where sb. inside can direct the forward movement of the wheel by using all their limbs; 旧称 formerly called 虎伏 hǔfú

【滚木】gǔnmù 〈古代 *arch.*〉作战时从高处推下以打击敌人的大木头 battle log; heavy log used in ancient battles to be let down from a high position to kill the enemy: ～礌石 battle logs and rocks

【滚热】gǔnrè 非常热(多指饮食或体温 of food or human body) burning; boiling hot; piping hot: 喝一杯～的茶 have a cup of piping hot tea | 他头上～,可能是发烧了。His forehead is so burning hot, he must be running a fever.

【滚水】gǔnshuǐ 正在开着的或刚开过的水 boiling water

【滚烫】gǔntàng same as 滚热 gǔnrè

【滚筒】gǔntǒng 机器上能转动的圆筒形机件的统称 roller; rolling cylinder; general term for any cylindrical part of a machine that rolls or rotates

【滚雪球】gǔn xuěqiú 在雪地上玩的一种游戏,滚动成团的雪,使体积越来越大。也用于比喻。roll a snowball; snowball; winter game played by a rolling snowball, which gets bigger and bigger; also used figuratively

【滚圆】gǔnyuán 非常圆 perfectly round; round as a ball: 腰身～的母牛 round-bellied cow | 两只眼睛睁得～～的。(His) two eyes are wide open.

【滚珠】gǔnzhū (～儿 gǔnzhūr)钢制的圆珠形零件 ball; machine part that is a small steel ball; also 钢珠 gāngzhū; ☞滚珠轴承 gǔnzhū zhóuchéng

【滚珠轴承】gǔnzhū zhóuchéng 滚动轴承的一种,滚珠装在内钢圈和外钢圈的中间,能承受较大的载荷 ball bearing; one form of rolling bearing, with freely revolving balls contained between two steel (inner and outer) rings, and with a large bearing capacity; also 球轴承 qiúzhóuchéng; ☞ 滚动轴承 gǔndòng zhóuchēng

碌(磙) gǔn ❶ 碌子 roller: 石～ stone roller ❷ 用碌子轧 level (the ground, etc.) with a roller: ～地 level the ground with a roller

【碌子】gǔn·zi ❶ 碌碡(liù·zhóu) stone roller ❷ 播种以后把覆土轧紧的农具,通常是圆柱形的石头,中间粗两头略细,装在轴架上 farming tool, usually a cylindrical stone with a thick body that is smaller at the two ends, and is fixed to an axle framework and used to roll along a seeded field ❸ 泛指圆柱形的碾轧器具 any cylindrical roller used for levelling

鲧(鯀) Gǔn 古人名,传说是禹的父亲 name of the father of King Yu, a legendary leader of remote antiquity

gùn (ㄍㄨㄣˋ)

棍[1] gùn (～儿 gùnr) 棍子 stick; rod; wand; baton: 木～ stick; wooden rod | 铁～ iron rod | 小～儿 short stick; small stick

棍[2] gùn 无赖;坏人 scoundrel; rascal; rotten person 恶～ scoundrel; ruffian; hooligan | 赌～ gamester; gambler | 讼～ pettifogger; shyster

【棍棒】gùnbàng ❶ 棍子(总称) (collect.) stick, staff, baton, rod, cudgel, bludgeon or club ❷ 器械体操用具 stick or staff used in gymnastics

【棍儿茶】gùnrchá 用茶树的叶柄或嫩茎制成的低级茶 low-quality tea made of tea-leaf stalks or tender tea stems

【棍子】gùn·zi 用树枝、竹子截成,或用金属制成的圆长条 stick; long slender piece of wood, bamboo or metal

guō (ㄍㄨㄛ)

过(過) Guō 姓 surname
☞guò on p.746

矿(彍、彉) guō 〈书 *fml.*〉拉开弓弦 draw or bend a bow

呙(咼) Guō 姓 surname

埚(堝) guō ☞坩埚 gānguō on p.628

郭 guō ❶ 〈古代 *arch.*〉在城的外围加筑的一道城墙 outer wall of a city; rampart: 城～ inner and outer city walls | 东～ east wall of a city ❷ 物体周围的边或框 rim; frame: 耳～ auricle ❸ (Guō)姓 a surname

涡(渦) Guō 涡河,发源于河南,流入安徽 Guohe, a river originating from Henan Province and flowing into Anhui Province
☞ wō on p.2013

崞 guō 崞县,旧县名,在山西 Guoxian, defunct name of a county in Shanxi Province

聒 guō 声音嘈杂,使人厌烦 unpleasantly noisy: ～噪 noisy; clamorous; raucous | ～耳 strident; jarring

【聒耳】guō'ěr (声音)嘈杂刺耳 (of a sound) grate on one's ears; rasp on the ears; raspy; strident; jarring

【聒噪】guōzào 〈方 *dial.*〉声音杂乱;吵闹 noisy; clamorous; raucous; vociferous

锅(鍋) guō ❶ 炊事用具,圆形中凹,多用铁、铝等制成 pot; wok; cauldron; pan; cooking vessel that is deep and round, made of iron, aluminium, etc.; hollowware; boiler: 一口～ a pot | 铁～ iron pot | 沙～ earthenware pot; casserole; clay pot | 钢精～ aluminium pot or pan ❷ 某些装液体加热用的器具 vessel for heating water or for cooking: ～炉 boiler | 火～ chaffing dish; hotpot ❸ (～儿 guōr) same as 锅子 guō·zi ②: 烟袋～儿 bowl of a pipe; pipe

【锅巴】guōbā ❶ 焖饭时紧贴着锅的焦了的一层饭 brown crust of cooked rice left on the bottom of a cooking vessel; rice crust ❷ 米粟加佐料等烘制成的一种食品 a kind of food made with flavoured roasted rice: 三鲜～ name of a popular dish: three-flavour rice crust; rice crust with three delicacies

【锅饼】guō·bing 一种较硬较大较厚的烙饼 big, hard and thick pancake

【锅伙】guō·huo (～儿 guō·huor) 〈旧时 *old*〉单身工人、小贩等临时组成的集体食宿处,设备简陋 boarding house, simply furnished, in which single workers, peddlers, etc., live temporarily together

【锅盔】guō·kuī 较小的锅饼 small pancake

【锅炉】guōlú 产生水蒸气的装置,由盛水的钢制容器和烧火的装置构成。产生的水蒸气用来取暖或发动蒸汽机、汽轮机。有的锅炉也用来烧热水。boiler; apparatus composed of a steel container and a heater, used to produce steam for heating, starting an engine or a turbine, or supplying boiled water

【锅台】guōtái 灶上面放东西的平面部分 flat top of a kitchen range

【锅贴儿】guōtiēr 在铛(chēng)上加少量的油和水煎熟的饺子 dumplings fried on a pan with a little oil and water; lightly fried dumplings

【锅驼机】guōtuójī 锅炉和蒸汽机连在一起的动力机器,可以带动水车、发电机或其他机械,用煤炭、木柴、重油等做燃料 engine that combines a boiler and a steam engine, to start a water-wheel, generator or other mechanical devices, and fuelled by coal, wood, heavy oil, etc.

【锅烟子】guōyān·zi 锅底上的烟子,可做黑色颜料 soot left on the bottom of a cooking vessel which can be used as black paint

【锅庄】guōzhuāng 藏族的民间舞蹈。在节日或农闲时跳,男女围成圆圈,自右而左,边歌边舞。有些彝族地区也流行这种舞蹈。Tibetan folk dance during festivals or slack farm season, in which men and women form a circle and move from left to right while singing and dancing; also popular in some Yi communities

【锅子】guō·zi ❶〈方 *dial.*〉锅 pot; pan ❷ 某些器物上像锅的部分 pot-like part of a device; bowl: 烟袋～ bowl of a pipe ❸ 火锅 chafing dish; hotpot: 涮～ eat from a hotpot

蝈(蟈) guō [蝈蝈儿](guō·guor)昆虫,身体绿色或褐色,腹部大,翅膀短,善于跳跃,吃植物的嫩叶和花。雄的前翅有发音器,能发出清脆的声音。有的地区称叫哥哥。katydid (*Microcentrum*); long-horned grasshopper; insect, with a green or brown body, a big belly and short wings, capable of swift jumps and living on tender leaves and flowers, the male having stridulating organs on the forewings used for making a loud thrill sound; also known as 哥哥 gē·ge in some places.

guó (ㄍㄨㄛˊ)

国(國、囯) guó ❶ 国家 country; state; nation: ～内 internal (to a nation); domestic; home | 祖～ one's own country; motherland; home country; homeland | 外～ foreign country | 保家卫～ protect our home and defend our country ❷ 代表或象征国家的 standing for or symbolic of a country; of the state; national: ～徽 national emblem | ～旗 national flag | ～花 national flower ❸ 在一国内最好的 among the best within a country: ～手 top-notch person in the country; player on a national sports team | ～色 most beautiful woman in the country; of matchless or peerless beauty ❹ 指本国的,特指我国的 of one's own country, i. e. Chinese: ～产 home-made; domestically produced; made in China | ～术 traditional Chinese martial arts | ～画 traditional Chinese painting | ～药 Chinese herbal medicine ❺ (Guó)姓 a surname

【国宝】guóbǎo ❶ 国家的宝物 national treasure: 传为～ passed down as a national treasure ❷〈比喻 *fig.*〉对国家有特殊贡献的人 people who have made special contributions to the country: 这些老艺术家都是我们的～。These veteran artists are all national treasures.

【国本】guóběn 立国的根本 foundation of a nation; cornerstone of a nation: 民为～。Citizens are the foundation of a country.

【国宾】guóbīn 应本国政府邀请前来访问的外国元首或政府首脑 visiting head or government leader of a foreign country on the invitation of the host government; state guest

【国柄】guóbǐng 〈书 *fml.*〉国家大权 state power; helm of a state

【国策】guócè 国家的基本政策 basic policy of a state; national policy

【国产】guóchǎn 本国生产的 domestically produced; made in the country: ～汽车 home-made automobiles|～影片 domestic film

【国耻】guóchǐ 因外国的侵略而使国家蒙受的耻辱,如割地、签订不平等条约等 national humiliation from a foreign invasion, such as ceding territory, signing an unequal treaty, etc.; national humiliation: 洗雪～ wipe out a national humiliation

【国仇】guóchóu 因国家受到侵略而产生的仇恨 hatred fanned by a foreign invasion; national enmity: ～家恨 national enmity and family hatred

【国粹】guócuì 指我国固有文化中的精华 quintessence or best of Chinese culture

【国道】guódào 由国家统一规划修筑和管理的干线公路,一般跨省和直辖市 state highway; national road; national highway; artery road under unified state planning and management

【国都】guódū 首都 national capital; capital

【国度】guódù 指国家(多就国家区域而言 usu. referring to the land or territory) country: 他们来自不同的～。They are from different countries.

【国法】guófǎ 国家的法纪 state law; law: ～难容 not within the law; punishable by law

【国防】guófáng 一个国家为了保卫自己的领土主权,防备外来侵略,而拥有的人力、物力,以及和军事有关的一切设施 national defence; armies, material resources and all military facilities of a country in defence of its territory and sovereignty against possible foreign invasion: 巩固～ strengthen, reinforce and consolidate national defence|～建设 defence construction; defence buildup

【国防军】guófángjūn 保卫国家的正规军 national defence forces; regular troops in defence of a country

【国父】guófù 〈尊称 *honor.*〉为创建国家建立特殊功勋的领导人 father of a nation; one who made special contributions to the founding of a country

【国歌】guógē 由国家正式规定的代表本国的歌曲。我国国歌是《义勇军进行曲》。national anthem; popular song or hymn designated by a country as representative of the country; the national anthem of China is ‘March of the Volunteers’

【国格】guógé 指国家的体面或尊严(多体现在涉外活动中) national prestige or dignity (in foreign affairs)

【国故】[1] guógù 我国固有的文化(多指语言文字、文学、历史等) culture native to China in terms of language, literature, history, etc.; national cultural heritage: 整理～ sort out our national cultural heritage

【国故】[2] guógù 〈书 *fml.*〉国家遭受的灾荒、瘟疫、战争等重大变故 major happening in a country such as a natural disaster, plague, war, etc.

【国号】guóhào 国家的称号,如汉、唐、宋、元、明等 title of a reigning dynasty, e.g. Han, Tang, Song, Yuan, Ming, etc.

【国花】guóhuā 国家把本国人民喜爱的花作为国家的象征,这种花叫做国花 national flower; popular flower taken by a country as an emblem of the country, hence given the title national flower

【国画】guóhuà 我国传统的绘画(区别于‘西洋画’ as compared with ‘Western painting’) traditional Chinese painting

【国徽】guóhuī 由国家正式规定的代表本国的标志。我国国徽,中间是五星照耀下的天安门,周围是谷穗和齿轮。national emblem; symbol designated by a country to represent the country. China's national emblem shows Tian'anmen bathed in the glow of five stars above it and surrounded by ears of millet and a gear of industry.

G

【国会】guóhuì 议会 Parliament (UK); Congress (US)

【国魂】guóhún 指一个国家国民的特殊的精神 national spirit; soul of a nation

【国货】guóhuò 本国制造的工业品 domestic goods; national goods; native goods of a country

【国籍】guójí ❶ 指个人具有的属于某个国家的身份 nationality; citizenship ❷ 指飞机、船只等属于某个国家的关系(of a plane, a ship, etc.) national identity: 一架中国～大型客机即将起飞。A large Chinese passenger airliner is about to take off.

【国计民生】guójì mín shēng 国家经济和人民生活 national economy and the people's livelihood

【国际】guójì ❶ 国与国之间;世界各国之间 international; the world: ～协定 international agreement|～关系 international relations|～足球锦标赛 International Football Championship|改革开放以来,我国的～地位不断提高。China's international status has been on the rise since the country began reform and opening up to the outside world. ❷ 与世界各国有关的(事物)(of sth.) concerning all countries in the world: ～音标 international phonetic alphabet|～惯例 international standard practice

【国际裁判】guójì cáipàn 经国际体育运动组织

批准,具有在国际体育运动竞赛中担任裁判资格的裁判员 international referee; person who is authorized by an international sport organization and rules on games in international sports competitions

【国际单位制】guójì dānwèizhì 一种计量制度,1960年第十一届国际计量大会通过采用。长度的单位米,质量的单位千克(公斤),电流强度的单位安培等,是国际单位制的基本单位;由基本单位推导出来的单位叫导出单位,如面积的单位平方米,速度的单位米/秒等。international unit system; International System of Units; measurement system approved and adopted by the 11th International Measurement Conference in 1960, with the metre as the basic unit of length, the kilogram for weight, and the ampere for electrical currency; a unit that is derived from the basic unit is called a derived unit, e.g. the unit of square metre for area, and metre per second for speed; 简称 abbr. 国际制 guójì·zhì

【国际儿童节】 Guójì Értóng Jié International Children's Day; ☞ 六一儿童节 Liù-Yī Értóng Jié on p. 1247

【国际法】guójìfǎ 国际公法的简称 abbr. for 国际公法 guójì gōngfǎ

【国际妇女节】 Guójì Fùnǚ Jié International Women's Day; ☞ 三八妇女节 Sān-Bā Fùnǚ Jié on p. 1650

G 【国际歌】Guójì Gē 国际无产阶级革命歌曲。法国鲍狄埃(Eugène Pottier)作词,狄盖特(Pierre Degeyter)配曲 *The Internationale*; revolutionary song of the international proletariat, with words in French by Eugène Pottier, and music by Pierre Degeyter

【国际公法】guójì gōngfǎ 调整各国之间的政治、经济、军事、文化等各种关系的准则的总称。这些准则是由各国通过协议来制定、修改和执行的,没有统一的立法机关和执行机关,它的渊源是国际条约、国际惯例和国标机构的决议。(public) international law; law of nations; general term for the rules regulating the relationships between nations in politics, economy, military affairs, culture, etc., which are established, amended and enforced through negotiations among nations without a centralized legislative or executive body; the set of rules originate from international treaties, practices or decisions of international institutions; 通常简称 popularly shortened as 国际法 guójìfǎ

【国际公制】guójì gōngzhì 一种计量制度,创始于法国,1875年十七个国家的代表在法国巴黎开会议定为国际通用的计量制度。长度的主单位是米,一米等于通过巴黎的子午线的四千万分之一。标准米尺用铂铱合金制成,断面为X形,在0℃时标准米尺上两端所刻的线之间的距离为一米。质量的主单位是公斤,标准公斤的砝码是用铂铱合金制成的圆柱体,在纬度45°的海平面上的重量为一公斤。容量的主单位是升,一升等于一公斤纯水在标准大气压下4℃(密度最大)时的体积。metric system; system of mass and length originating in France in 1875, when representatives from 17 countries had a conference in Paris and established the system by agreement for use throughout the world. The metre as a unit of length equals one forty-millionth of the meridian going through Paris; the standard ruler for the metre is made of an alloy of platinum and iridium with an X-shaped cross section, and at 0℃ the length is one metre between the end marks on the ruler. Standard weight for the kilogramme as a unit mass is a cylinder made of an alloy of platinum and iridium that is one kilogramme at sea level at 45° latitude. The litre is the unit of volume, where one litre is equal to the cubage of one kilogramme of water in standard atmosphere and at 4℃ (at which water has the highest density); also called 米制 mǐzhì; 简称 abbr. 公制 gōngzhì

【国际共管】guójì gòngguǎn 由两个或两个以上的国家共同统治或管理某一地区、国家或某一国家的部分领土 (international) condominium; joint sovereignty or rule by two or more nations of a region, a nation or part of the territory of a nation; 简称 abbr. 共管 gòngguǎn

【国际惯例】guójì guànlì 在国际交往中逐渐形成的一些习惯做法和先例,是国际法的主要渊源之一 international practice; customary actions or precedents developed from the intercourse among nations, also one of the major sources of international law

【国际劳动节】 Guójì Láodòng Jié International Labour Day; ☞ 五一劳动节 Wǔ-Yī Láodòng Jié on p. 2032

【国际联盟】Guójì Liánméng 第一次世界大战后(1920年)成立的国际组织,它标榜以防止世界大战再度发生和解决国际纠纷为目的,实际上只是保护第一次世界大战的战胜国的既得利益,维护既成的国际秩序。第二次世界大战爆发后,联盟无形瓦解,到1946年正式解散。League of Nations; international organization set up after World War I (1920) with the stated aim of preventing any world war from occurring and of settling international disputes, but, in effect, merely ensured protection of those World War I winners' vested interests and maintained the achieved world order; the League virtually fell apart after World War II, and by 1946 it was officially dismissed; 简称 abbr. 国联 Guólián

【国际日期变更线】 guójì rìqī biàngēng xiàn 地球表面上的一条假想线,在地球180°经线附近,稍有弯曲,用作划分相连两日的界线 international dateline; dateline; hypothetical line on the surface of the earth that deflects a little while following the 180th meridian and serves as the division line between two adjacent dates; also 日界线 rìjièxiàn

【国际私法】guójì sīfǎ 国家处理和调整涉及外国公民的民事法律关系的规则的总称。这种关系一般是由于对外贸易和本国人同外国人往来而产生的。private international law; rules concerning a nation's handling or regulating of civil litigations involving foreign citizens, which occurs as a result of foreign trade and intercourse between the citizens of the nation and the foreigners

【国际象棋】guójì xiàngqí 棋类运动的一种,黑白棋子各十六个,分成六种,一王、一后、两象、两车、两马、八兵。棋盘为正方形,由六十四个黑白小方格相间排列而成。两人对下,按规则移动棋子,将(jiāng)死对方的王为胜。chess; board game for 2 players, each with 16 pieces (white or black) in 6 kinds, i.e. 1 king, 1 queen, 2 bishops, 2 castles, 2 knights and 8 pawns, where the chessboard is a big square composed of 64 alternating black or white small squares. The two players move the pieces according to the rules of play and the one who checkmates the opposing king wins.

【国际音标】guójì yīnbiāo 国际语音学会制定的标音符号。初稿在1888年发表,后来经过不断的修改,内容逐渐完备,各种语言常用的音都有适当的符号。形式以拉丁字母的小楷为主,加以补充。在各种音标中,是通行范围较广的一种。international phonetic alphabet (IPA); phonetic symbols formulated by the International Phonetic Association; the first draft went to print in 1888 and was perfected after constant modifications, with the speech sounds of all languages corresponding with appropriate symbols written in regular script of Latin letters with supplements; among various phonetic systems, it is the most widely used

【国际制】guójìzhì 国际单位制的简称 abbr. for 国际单位制 guójì dānwèizhì

【国际主义】guójì zhǔyì 马克思主义关于国际无产阶级团结的思想,是国际共产主义运动的指导原则之一 internationalism; Marxist belief in international proletarian unity and one of the guiding principles for the international communist movement

【国际纵队】guójì zòngduì 指1936—1939年西班牙内战期间,许多国家的工人、农民等为支援西班牙人民反对佛朗哥反动军队和德意法西斯武装干涉所组成的志愿军。后泛指为反对侵略,不同国籍的人志愿组成的军队。International Brigades. During the Spanish Civil War of 1936-1939, some workers and peasants from many countries organized into an armed force of volunteer soldiers to support the Spanish people in their struggle against Francisco Franco and his reactionary army, and the fascist troops from Germany and Italy. It also refers to any multi-national army of volunteers from different countries for the purpose of resisting invasion.

【国家】guójiā ❶ 阶级统治的工具,是统治阶级对被统治阶级实行专政的暴力组织,主要由军队、警察、法庭、监狱等组成。国家是阶级矛盾不可调和的产物和表现,它随着阶级的产生而产生,也将随着阶级的消灭而自行消亡。state; nation; country; apparatus by which the ruling class exercises dictatorship over the ruled, mainly composed of the army, police, courts and prisons. The state is a result and manifestation of irreconcilable class contradictions; it originates out of class and will disappear with class as well ❷ 指一个国家的整个区域 complete territory of a country

【国家裁判】guójiā cáipàn 国家级裁判员的简称,是经我国体育运动组织批准的最高一级裁判员的称号 national referee (for basketball, football, etc.); national judge (for track and field); national umpire (for volleyball, badminton, tennis, baseball, pingpong, etc.); short form for a referee at the national level, and the title for a top-ranking referee authorized by a sports organization in China

【国家机关】guójiā jīguān ❶ 行使国家权力、管理国家事务的机关。包括国家权力机关、国家行政机关、审判机关、检察机关和军队等。如我国的全国人民代表大会、国务院、地方各级人民代表大会和人民政府、各级人民法院、人民检察院、公安机关等。state organ; state agency; government office; organ that carries out state power and runs state affairs, including organ of state power, organ of administration, judicial organ, procuratorial organ, military armies, etc., e.g. the National People's Congress, the State Council, the people's congresses at local levels, the people's governments at all levels, the people's courts at all levels, the people's procuratorates at all levels, the public security organs at all levels in China; also 政权机关 zhèngquán jīguān (organ of state power) ❷ 特指中央一级机关 referring in particular to a top-level organ at the central level

【国家所有制】guójiā suǒyǒuzhì 生产资料和产品归国家所有的制度,它的性质因社会制度的不同而不同 state ownership; system where the state is the owner of the means of production and its products, and varies in nature under different social systems

【国交】guójiāo 国家与国家间的外交关系 diplomatic relations between nations

【国脚】guójiǎo 指人选国家队的足球运动员 football player on the national team

【国教】guójiào 某些国家明文规定的本国所信仰的正统宗教 state religion; orthodox religion explicitly stipulated by a state for its people to follow

【国界】guójiè 相邻国家领土的分界线 national boundary or border; line separating adjoining countries: 划定～(of a country) draw the boundary line

【国境】guójìng ❶ 一个国家行使主权的领土范围 national territory; territory over which a country exercises its sovereignty ❷ 指国家的边境 national border or boundary: 偷越～ cross the border illegally|～检查站 border inspection station; border checkpoint

【国剧】guójù 指一个国家的广为流行的传统剧种,如我国的京剧 popular traditional opera of a country, such as Peking Opera of China

【国君】guójūn 君主国家的统治者 monarch

【国库】guókù 金库的通称 exchequer; general term for natural treasury or state treasury

【国库券】guókùquàn 国家银行发行的一种债券 treasury bond (TB); treasury bill; T-bill; treasury stock; bond issued by a state bank; 简称 abbr. 库券 kùquàn

【国力】guólì 国家在政治、经济、军事、科学技术等方面所具备的实力 national power; national strength; national strength in politics, economy, military affairs, science and technology: 增强～ enhance national strength|～强大 great national strength.

【国立】guólì 由国家设立的(用于学校、医院等 of a school, hospital, etc.) state-run; state-maintained; national: ～大学 national university

【国联】Guólián 国际联盟的简称 abbr. for 国际联盟 Guójì Liánméng

【国门】guómén 〈书 *fml.*〉指国都的城门,也指边境 gateway of a country; border: 拒敌于～之外 keep the enemy beyond the borders|产品走出～,打入国际市场。The products have made their way beyond the border and into the world market.

【国民】guómín 具有某国国籍的人是这个国家的国民 people of a nation; nationals; citizens, people having the citizenship of a nation

【国民党】guómíndǎng 1912 年 8 月,孙中山在中国同盟会的基础上,合并统一共和党、国民共进会、国民公党等几个党派组建的资产阶级政党 Kuomintang(KMT); bourgeois party established by Sun Yat-sen by incorporating his Chinese Revolutionary League with the United Republican Party, National Co-Progress Union, National Public Party, etc., in August 1912

【国民经济】guómín jīngjì 一个国家的生产、流通、分配和消费的总体,包括各个生产部门和为生产服务的流通部门,如工业、农业、建筑业、交通运输业、商业等,也包括文化、教育、科学研究、医药卫生等非生产部门 national economy; overall activity of a country in production, circulation, distribution and consumption, including various production sectors and circulation sectors serving production, e.g. industry, agriculture, building, communications and transport, commerce, etc., as well as non-production sectors like culture, education, scientific research, medicine, etc.

【国民收入】guómín shōurù 一个国家国民经济各个生产部门在一个时期内新创造的价值的总和。就是从一个时期内的社会总产品的价值中,减去生产上消耗掉的生产资料的价值后剩余的部分。national income; sum total of the value produced by the various economic sectors of a national economy over a given period of time, calculated by subtracting the value of the means of production consumed during the production from the value of the gross national product over that period

【国难】guónàn 国家的危难,特指由外国侵略造成的国家灾难 national crisis, esp. one caused by foreign aggression

【国戚】guóqī 帝王的外戚 relatives on the emperor's (or king's) mother's side, or on the empress' (or queen's) side: 皇亲～ relatives of the emperor

【国旗】guóqí 由国家正式规定的代表本国的旗帜。我国国旗是五星红旗。national flag; flag officially designated by a nation to represent itself. The national flag of China is the Five-Star Red Flag.

【国情】guóqíng 一个国家的社会性质、政治、经济、文化等方面的基本情况和特点。也特指一个国家某一时期的基本情况和特点。national conditions; state of a country; general social, political, economic and cultural conditions and features of a nation: 适合～ conform to the general conditions in the nation|熟悉～ be familiar with the general conditions of the country

【国庆】guóqìng 开国纪念日。我国国庆是 10 月 1 日。National Day; anniversary of the founding of a country. The National Day of China falls on October 1.

【国人】guórén 指本国的人 compatriots; fellow countrymen; countrymen

【国丧】guósāng 指皇帝、皇后、太上皇、太后的丧事 funeral affairs of a deceased emperor, empress, or emperor's father or mother

【国色】guósè 〈书 *fml.*〉在一国内容貌最美的女子 prettiest woman in a country; woman with matchless beauty: 天姿～ the most graceful and beautiful woman

【国殇】guóshāng 〈书 *fml.*〉为国牺牲的人 those who die for their country; martyrs who died for the national cause

【国史】guóshǐ ❶ 一国或一个朝代的历史 history of a nation or dynasty ❷ 古代的史官 official historian or historiographer (of ancient times)

【国事】guóshì 国家大事 state affairs; national

affairs

【国事访问】guóshì fǎngwèn 一国元首或政府首脑接受他国邀请而进行的正式访问 state visit; official visit by the head of a country to another country on invitation

【国势】guóshì ❶ same as 国力 guólì: ～强大 great national power | ～蒸蒸日上。National strength is growing day by day. ❷ 国家的形势 state of affairs in a country: ～危殆。The nation is in a critical situation.

【国是】guóshì 〈书 *fml.*〉国家大计 important matters of a country; state affairs: 共商～ discuss state affairs

【国手】guóshǒu 精通某种技能(如医道、棋艺等)在国内数第一流的人,也指入选国家队的选手 top-notch expert of a nation; master; one who excels in a trade or skill (e.g. medicine, chess, etc.) and is first-rate in the country; also a player who is recruited onto a national team

【国书】guóshū 一国派遣或召回大使(或公使)时,由国家元首写给驻在一国元首的文书。大使(或公使)只有在向所驻国呈递国书以后,才能得到国际法所赋予的地位。letter of credence; credentials; official letter written by the head of a country to the head of another to dispatch or recall an ambassador (or envoy). An ambassadors (or envoy) will not have the status granted by international law until he presents his credentials to the host country

【国术】guóshù 指我国传统的武术 traditional Chinese martial arts

【国泰民安】guó tài mín ān 国家太平,人民生活安定 The country is peaceful and the people have a stable life.

【国帑】guótǎng 〈书 *fml.*〉国家的公款 national funds; state finances: 盗用～ embezzle national funds | 消耗～ deplete national funds

【国体】guótǐ ❶ 表明国家根本性质的国家体制,是由社会各阶级在国家中的地位来决定的。我国的国体是工人阶级(经过共产党)领导的,以工农联盟为基础的无产阶级专政。state system; system that shows the fundamental nature of a state, and is identified by the status of various social classes within the state. The Chinese state system is proletarian dictatorship led by the working class (through the Communist Party) and based on the alliance of workers and peasants ❷ 国家的体面 national prestige or dignity

【国统区】guótǒngqū 抗日战争和解放战争时期称国民党政府统治的地区 KMT (Kuomintang)-controlled areas during the Anti-Japanese War (1937-1945) and the War of Liberation (1946-1949)

【国土】guótǔ 国家的领土 national territory or land: 收复～ recover lost national territory

【国王】guówáng 〈古代 *arch.*〉某些国家的统治者;现代某些君主制国家的元首 king (of an ancient country or a modern monarchic country)

【国威】guówēi 国家的声威 national prestige; national power or influence: 大振～ boost the national prestige

【国文】guówén ❶ 本国的文字,旧时指汉语汉文 national language; old reference to Chinese language; Mandarin ❷〈旧时 *old*〉指中小学的语文课 Chinese (as a subject of learning in a primary or middle school)

【国务】guówù 国务的事务;国事 state affairs: ～会议 state conference

【国务卿】guówùqīng ❶ 民国初年协助大总统处理国务的人 official who assisted the president in handling state affairs during the early Republican years in China ❷ 美国国务院的领导人,由总统任命 Secretary of State; head of the State Department of the United States of America, appointed by the President

【国务委员】guówù wěiyuán 我国国务院组成人员,相当于副总理 State Councillor; member of the State Council in China, equivalent to Vice Premier

【国务院】guówùyuàn ❶ 我国最高国家权力机关的执行机关,即最高国家行政机关,也就是中央人民政府,由总理、副总理、国务委员、各部部长、各委员会主任等人员组成。国务院对全国人民代表大会和它的常务委员会负责并报告工作。State Council (in China); executive department of the supreme organ of state power, which is the top state administrative organ or the Central People's Government, composed of Premier, Vice Premiers, State Councillors, and Ministers in charge of various Ministries and Commissions. The State Council is responsible for, and report its work to, the National People's Congress. ❷ 民国初年的内阁,以国务总理为首 cabinet of the Republic of China in its early years, headed by the State Premier ❸ 美国政府中主管外交兼管部分内政的部门,主管者称国务卿 State Department; government department of the United States of America in charge of foreign relations and certain internal affairs under the leadership of the Secretary of State

【国学】guóxué ❶ 称我国传统的学术文化,包括哲学、历史学、考古学、文学、语言学等 study of Chinese culture; Chinese national culture; studies of traditional Chinese culture including philosophy, history, archaeology, literature, and linguistics ❷〈古代 *arch.*〉指国家设立的学校,如太学、国子监 imperial college in ancient China, e.g. National University, and Directorate of Education

【国宴】guóyàn 国家元首或政府首脑为招待国宾或在重要节日招待各界人士而举行的隆重宴会

state banquet; grand and ceremonious banquet hosted by a head of a state or government in honour of state guests or representatives from various sectors of the nation on important occasions

【国药】guóyào 中药 traditional Chinese medicine; Chinese herbal medicine

【国医】guóyī 中医 traditional Chinese medical science; traditional Chinese medicine; practitioner of traditional Chinese medicine

【国音】guóyīn 〈旧时 *old*〉指国家审定的汉语标准音 standard Chinese pronunciations approved by the state

【国营】guóyíng 由国家投资经营，在我国有中央国营和地方国营两种形式 state-run; invested and operated by the state; state-run enterprises in China operate at two levels: central and local: ～农场 state-run farm | ～企业 state-run enterprise | 这家商站是～的。The shop is state-run.

【国有】guóyǒu 国家所有 state-owned; national: ～化 nationalization | ～企业 state-owned enterprise | 土地～ nationalization of land; state ownership of land | 铁路～ nationalization of the railway; state ownership of the railway

【国语】guóyǔ ❶ 指本国人民共同使用的语言。在我国是汉语普通话的旧称。Mandarin (former term for *putonghua* or standard Chinese); official national language of a country ❷ 〈旧时 *old*〉指中小学的语文课 Chinese (as a subject of learning in a primary or middle school)

【国乐】guóyuè 指我国传统的音乐 traditional Chinese music

【国运】guóyùn 〈书 *fml.*〉国家的命运 national destiny or fortune: ～昌隆。Fate smiles at the nation.

【国葬】guózàng 以国家名义为有特殊功勋的人举行的葬礼 state burial, held for sb. who has made special contribution to his or her country

【国贼】guózéi 危害国家或出卖国家主权的败类 traitor; person who has done great damage to or committed treaon against his or her country

【国债】guózhài 国家所欠的债务 national debt; treasury bond

【国子监】guózǐjiàn 我国封建时代最高的教育管理机关，有的朝代兼为最高学府 imperial academy; highest educational administration in feudal China, which was concurrently the highest institution of education in some dynasties

掴(摑) guó '掴'(guāi)的又音 also pronounced 掴 guāi

帼(幗) guó ☞ 巾帼 jīnguó on p.1002

涸(漍) guó 北涸(Běiguó)，地名，在江苏 Beiguo, name of a place in Jiangsu Province

腘(膕) guó 膝部的后面。腿弯曲时腘部形成一个窝，叫腘窝。popliteal area; back of the knee joint; hollow of the knee; ham; area behind the knee joint; when the leg is bent, it forms a hollow behind the knee joint, and the area is called 腘窝 guówō; (图见 ☞ figure for 身体 shēntǐ on p.1701)

虢 Guó ❶ 周朝国名。西虢在今陕西宝鸡东，后来迁到河南陕县东南。东虢在今河南郑州西北。Guo, a state in the Zhou Dynasty; the state of West Guo was east of present-day Baoji, Shaanxi Province before it was moved to the southeast of Shanxian County, Henan Province, while the state of East Guo was located to the northwest of present-day Zhengzhou, Henan Province ❷ (Guó)姓 a surname

馘(聝) guó 〈古代 *arch.*〉战争中割掉敌人左耳计数献功。也指割下的左耳。(in ancient battles) number of severed left ears of enemy troops as a measure of a fighter's merit in war; also the left ears cut off so

漍 guó 〈书 *fml.*〉水流声 murmuring sound of flowing water: 溪水～～ babbling stream

guǒ (ㄍㄨㄛˇ)

果[1] guǒ ❶ (～儿 guǒr) same as 果实 guǒshí ①: 水～ fruit | 开花结～ yield blossoms and bear fruit; bloom and fructify ❷ 事情的结局；结果（跟'因'相对 as opposed to 'cause') result; consequence; outcome; upshot; effect: 成～ gain; fruit; harvest; achievement | 前因后～ cause and effect; causation ❸ (Guǒ)姓 a surname

果[2] guǒ 果断 determined; resolute; decisive; firm: ～敢 resolute and daring; decisive and courageous

果[3] guǒ 果然 really; as expected; sure enough: 如～ if; in case; supposing; in the event that | ～不出所料。It just happened as expected; as expected.

【果报】guǒbào 因果报应，是起源于佛教的一种宿命论 (fatalism originating in Buddhism) karma; reap what you sow; preordained fate; retribution; retributive justice; judgement: ～不爽。Retributive justice never fails.

【果不其然】guǒ ·bu qí rán 果然(强调不出所料) just as expected; indeed: 我早说要下雨，～，下了吧！I told you it was going to rain, and indeed it's raining! also 果不然 guǒ ·bu rán

【果丹皮】guǒdānpí 一种用干、鲜红果或制作红果脯、苹果脯等的下脚料为原料制成的食品 haw roll; food made from fresh or dried haw, or remnant portion from preserved haw, apples, etc.

【果冻儿】guǒdòngr 用水果的汁和糖加工制成的半固体食品 fruit jelly; fruit gelatin; soft, semi-solid food made of juice and sugar

【果断】guǒduàn 有决断;不犹豫 resolute; decisive; firm: 他处理问题很～。He is quick and firm in decision-making.

【果饵】guǒ'ěr 糖果点心(总称)(general term for) sweets and pastries

【果粉】guǒfěn 某些植物(如苹果、冬瓜等)的果实成熟后表皮上覆盖的一层白色粉末 white powder covering the outer skin of the fruit of some plant when ripe, e.g. apple, white gourd, etc.

【果脯】guǒfǔ 用桃、杏、梨、枣等水果加糖或蜜制成的食品的统称(general term for) preserved fruit; candied fruit; food made of fruit such as peach, apricot, pear, date, etc., with sugar or honey

【果腹】guǒfù 〈书 *fml.*〉吃饱肚子 fill one's stomach; satisfy one's hunger: 食不～ be poorly fed; be famished for food; lead a life of starvation; never have enough to eat

【果干儿】guǒgānr 水果经晾晒或烘干而制成的食品的统称(general term for) dried fruit; food made by dehydrating fresh fruit by sunning or baking; also 果子酒 guǒ·zijiǔ

【果敢】guǒgǎn 勇敢并有决断 courageous and determined; resolute and daring: 勇猛～的战士 a lion-hearted and determined soldier | 他的指挥还不够～。He is not resolute and daring enough as a commander.

【果酱】guǒjiàng 用水果加糖、果胶制成的糊状食品 jam; soft food made of fruit with sugar and pectin; also 果子酱 guǒ·zijiàng

【果酒】guǒjiǔ 用水果发酵制成的酒 fruit wine; beverage made of fermented fruit juice; also 果子酒 guǒ·zijiǔ

【果决】guǒjué 果敢坚决 firm in decision-making; (sb.) of strong resolution; decisive: 办事～ possess a decisive manner; operates in a decisive and determined way

【果料儿】guǒliàor 加在甜点心上的青丝、红丝、松仁、瓜子仁、葡萄干儿等物品的总称(general term for) ingredients such as shredded red plum, shredded green plum, pine nut, melon seeds, raisins, etc., used in cakes and in pastries

【果绿】guǒlǜ 浅绿 light green

【果木】guǒmù same as 果树 guǒshù

【果农】guǒnóng 栽培果树,从事果品生产的农民 fruit grower; orchard worker; orchardman; orchardist

【果盘】guǒpán (～儿 guǒpánr)专用于盛放果品的盘子 fruit tray

【果皮】guǒpí 植物果实的皮,分内果皮、中果皮和外果皮三层,一般所指的是外果皮(fruit) peel; rind; pericarp; skin of a fruit, divided into the inner, middle and outer skin, usu. referring to the outer skin

【果品】guǒpǐn 水果和干果的总称 general term for both fresh and dried fruit: ～店 fruit store | 干鲜～ fresh and dried fruit

【果儿】guǒr 〈方 *dial.*〉鸡蛋(chicken) egg: 卧～(把去壳的鸡蛋整个放在汤里煮) poached egg (shelled hard-boiled egg cooked in boiling soup) | 甩～(把去壳的鸡蛋搅匀后撒在汤里) egg-drop (shelled and beaten egg stirred into boiling soup)

【果然】guǒrán ❶〈副词 *adv.*〉表示事实与所说或所料相符 really; indeed; as expected: ～名不虚传。He really deserves his reputation. | 他说要下雪,～下雪了。He said it was going to snow, and indeed it snowed. ❷〈连词 *conj.*〉假设事实与所说或所料相符 if indeed; if really: 你～爱她,就该帮助她。If you really loved her, you should help her.

【果肉】guǒròu 水果可以吃的部分,一般是中果皮,如桃儿的果肉就是核和外层薄皮之间的部分 flesh of a fruit; pulp; sarcocarp; edible part of fruit, usu. referring to the middle, e. g. the edible part of a peach is between the stone and the outer skin (peel)

【果实】guǒshí ❶ 植物体的一部分,花受精后,子房逐渐长大,成为果实。有些果实可供食用。fruit; ripened reproductive body of a seed plant, developed from the ovary after the fecundation of the flower ❷〈比喻 *fig.*〉经过斗争或劳动得到的胜利品或收获 gains; fruits; sth. gained or harvested after struggling or labouring: 劳动～ fruits of labour

【果树】guǒshù 果实主要供食用的树木,如桃树、苹果树等 fruit tree; tree that bears fruit for eating, e.g. peach tree, apple tree

【果穗】guǒsuì 指某些植物(如玉米、高粱)的聚集在一起的果实 ear of grain; spike; fruit or seeds in clusters such as maize (corn), broomcorn (sorghum)

【果糖】guǒtáng 有机化合物,是蔗糖、甜菜糖等的组成物质,化学式 $C_6H_{12}O_6$。白色结晶,味甜。水果和蜂蜜中含有果糖。fructose ($C_6H_{12}O_6$); levulose; fruit sugar; organic chemical compound, component of saccharose, beet sugar, etc.; sweet white crystals occurring in many fruits and in honey; also 左旋糖 zuǒxuántáng

【果园】guǒyuán 种植果树的园地 orchard; also 果木园 guǒmùyuán

【果真】guǒzhēn same as 果然 guǒrán: 这一次劳动竞赛二组～夺到了红旗。As expected, Group Two won the red pennant in the labour competition. | ～是这样,那就好办了。If it's really the case, things will be easy.

【果汁】guǒzhī 用鲜果的汁水制成的饮料 fruit juice

G

【果枝】guǒzhī ❶ 果树上结果实的枝 fruit-bearing shoot; fruit branch ❷ 棉花植株上结棉桃的枝 boll-bearing branch of a cotton plant

【果子】guǒ·zi ❶ 指可以吃的果实 edible fruit ❷ same as 馃子 guǒ·zi

【果子酱】guǒ·zijiàng same as 果酱 guǒjiàng

【果子酒】guǒ·zijiǔ same as 果酒 guǒjiǔ

【果子露】guǒ·zilù 在蒸馏水中加入果汁制成的饮料 fruit syrup or concentrate; drink made of distilled water with fruit juice

菓 guǒ same as 果[1] guǒ ①，用于水菓、红菓儿等，occurring in 水菓 shuǐguǒ，红菓儿 hóngguǒ, etc.

馃 guǒ same as 馃子 guǒ·zi

【馃子】guǒ·zi ❶ 一种油炸的面食 deep-fried doughnut ❷〈方 *dial.*〉旧式点心的统称 general term for traditional cakes and pastry; also 果子 guǒ·zi

椁(槨) guǒ〈古代 *arch.*〉套在棺材外面的大棺材 outer coffin: 棺～ inner and outer coffins

蜾 guǒ [蜾蠃](guǒluǒ) 一种寄生蜂 parasitic wasp; ☞螟蛉 mínglíng on p.1359

裹 guǒ ❶ (用纸、布或其他片状物)缠绕;包扎 bind; wrap: 包～ wrap up; bind up; enfold in; pack in|～腿 leggings|用绷带把伤口～好 dress a wound; bind up a wound; wrap a bandage around a wound ❷ 包裹好的东西 package; bundle; parcel: 大包小～ all the bundles, big or small ❸ 为了不正当的目的把人或物夹杂在别的人或物里面 mix sb. or sth. into another group of people or things with ulterior motives; make away with: 土匪逃跑时～走了村子里的几个人。The bandits carried off some villagers when they retreated. ❹〈方 *dial.*〉吸(奶) suck (milk): 小孩儿一生下来就会～奶。A baby is able to suck at the breast right after birth.

【裹脚】guǒ//jiǎo〈旧时 *old*〉一种陋习,用长布条把女孩子的脚紧紧地缠住,为使脚纤小,而造成脚骨畸形 foot-binding; vile practice in feudal China of binding a girl's feet with long bands of cloth to prevent growth in order to make the feet very small, resulting in deforming the feet

【裹脚】guǒ·jiao〈旧时 *old*〉妇女裹脚用的长布条 cloth for foot-binding; bandages used in foot-binding; long narrow band of cloth used to bind a woman's feet; also 裹脚布 guǒ·jiaobù

【裹乱】guǒ//luàn〈方 *dial.*〉加入其中扰乱;搅扰 mess up; disturb; derange; upset: 他正在写文章,不许去～。He is writing an article, so don't disturb him.

【裹腿】guǒ·tui 缠在裤子外边小腿部分的布条,旧时士兵行军时多打裹腿 puttee; leggings; leg coverings of bands of cloth binding the outer trousers from the ankles to the knees, esp. worn by marching soldiers in old days

【裹胁】guǒxié 用胁迫手段使人跟从(做坏事) force sb. to take part in (evil doings); coerce; also 裹挟 guǒxié

【裹挟】guǒxié ❶ (风、流水等)把别的东西卷入,使随着移动(of winds, currents, etc.) carry away; carry things along their route of motion: 河水～着泥沙,滚滚东流。The river water rolled to the east, carrying mud and sand along with it. ❷ (形势、潮流等)把人卷进去,迫使其采取某种态度 (of circumstances, trends, etc.) sweep sb. along; engulf; involve; draw sb. into ❸ same as 裹胁 guǒxié

【裹扎】guǒzā 包扎 wrap up; dress: ～伤口 dress a wound

【裹足不前】guǒ zú bù qián 停步不进(多指有所顾虑) hesitate to proceed

guò (ㄍㄨㄛˋ)

过(過) guò ❶ 从一个地点或时间移到另一个地点或时间;经过某个空间或时间 go through (space or time); pass; cross: ～来 come over|～去 go up to; go over to|～河 cross a river|～桥 pass or go over a bridge|～年 celebrate the New Year (or Spring Festival)|～节 celebrate a festival|日子越来越好～了。Life is getting better and better. ❷ 从甲方转移到乙方 transfer: ～户 transfer of names; transfer of ownership from one person to another|～账 transfer (an item) to a ledger; post (up) ❸ 使经过(某种处理) undergo; go through; go over: ～罗 sift; sieve|～筛子 sift; sieve; riddle|～滤 filter; filtrate|～淋 filter; filtrate|～磅 weigh|～秤 weigh|～油肉 meat cooked only briefly in hot frying oil|～数儿 count ❹ 用眼看或用脑子回忆 look at; view; call to mind; go over: ～目 look at; view|把昨天的事在脑子里～了一遍 review, recall or go through one more time what happened yesterday in one's mind ❺ 超过(某个范围和限度) exceed; go beyond; overstep: ～分 going too far; excessive; going to excess|～期 be overdue; expire|～犹不及 too much is as bad as not enough; going beyond is as bad as falling short|树长得～了房。The tree has grown above the roof of the house. ❻〈书 *fml.*〉探望;拜访 visit: ～访 pay a visit ❼〈方 *dial.*〉去世 pass away; die: 老太太～了好几天了。The old woman passed away a few days ago. ❽ 过失 (跟'功'相对 as opposed to 'merit') demerit; fault; error; slip; lapse: ～错 mistake; fault|记～ give a demerit to sb.|勇于改～ have the courage to mend one's ways ❾ 用在动词加'得'的后面,表示胜过或通过的意思 [used after a verb plus 得] better than; deserve: 干起活儿来,他抵得～两三个人。When it comes to work, he outdoes two people.|这种人我们信得～。Such a person deserves our trust. *or* Such people we can trust. ⑩〈方 *dial.*〉传染 contagious: 这个病～人。This disease is contagious.

过(過) ·guo ❶ 用在动词后,表示完毕[used after a verb to indicate the completion of an action]: 吃～饭再走。Please go after you have the meal.|杏花和碧桃都已经开～了。The apricot and peach trees have finished blooming. ❷ 用在动词后,表示某种行为或变化曾经发生,但并未继续到现在[used after a verb to indicate a past action or state]: 他去年来～北京。He was in Beijing last year.|我们吃～亏,上～当,有了经验了。We were fooled and suffered a loss, and we've learned a lesson from it.

☞ Guō on p. 737

【过半】guòbàn 超过总数的一半 more than half; over half: 时间～,任务～。When half of the time has passed, over half of the task is done.

【过磅】guò//bàng 用磅秤称 weigh (on scales)

【过不去】guò ·bu qù ❶ 有阻碍,通不过 cannot get through or get by; cannot make it through; be impassable: 大桥正在修理,这里～。The bridge is under renovation, and there is no thoroughfare from here. ❷ 为难 be hard on; make things difficult for: 请放心,他不会跟你～的。Rest assured. He won't give you a hard time. ❸ 过意不去;抱歉 feel sorry; be apologetic: 让他白跑一趟,心里真有点～。I feel sorry for having caused him a fruitless trip.

【过场】guòchǎng ❶ 戏曲中角色上场后,不多停留,就穿过舞台从另一侧下场 (of a traditional opera role) cross the stage without much stopping or acting ❷ 戏剧中用来贯串前后情节的简短表演 (between the acts of a play) interlude ❸ ☞ 走过场 zǒu guòchǎng on p. 2560

【过程】guòchéng 事情进行或事物发展所经过的程序 course of events; process: 认识～ the process of learning|生产～ process of production|到了新地方要有一个适应的～。It takes some getting used to when you go to a new place. *or* There is a process of adaptation one has to go through in a new environment.

【过秤】guò//chèng 用秤称 weigh (on the steelyard or scales): 这筐苹果还没～。The basket of apples has not been weighed yet.

【过从】guòcóng〈书 *fml.*〉来往;交往 engage in social intercourse (with sb.); associate: 两人～甚密。They keep close contact with each other.

【过错】guòcuò 过失 fault; error; blame; offence; same as 错误 cuòwù ②

【过当】guòdàng 超过适当的数量或限度 exceed the proper limits; be improper; be inappropriate: 防卫～ exceed the proper limits of self-defence|药剂用量～ take an overdose of medicine

【过道】guòdào ❶ 新式房子由大门通向各房间的走道 corridor ❷ 旧式房子连通各个院子的走道,特指大门所在的一间或半间屋子 passageway; doorway; passage

【过得去】guò ·de qù ❶ 无阻碍,通得过 be able to pass or get through: 这条胡同儿很宽,汽车～。The lane is wide enough for a car to get through. ❷ (生活)不很困难 (of living conditions) passable; not hard ❸ 说得过去 not too bad; tolerable; okay: 准备一些茶点招待客人,也就～了。It's okay just to treat the guests with some tea and snacks. ❹ 过意得去(多用于反问 oft. used in rhetorical questions) feel at ease: 看把您累成那个样子,叫我心里怎么～呢? How can I feel at ease when I have tired you out so?

【过电】guò//diàn 电流通过(身体);触电 be electrified; get an electric shock

【过冬】guò//dōng 度过冬天 pass the winter; winter; hibernate; overwinter: 这件薄棉袄能过得了冬天吗? Can you ride out the winter in such a thin jacket?|大雁每年都来这儿～。Every year wild geese fly here to pass the winter.

【过冬作物】guòdōng zuòwù 越冬作物 winter crop

【过度】guòdù 超过适当的限度 too much; over the limit; excess: ～疲劳 overworked; overtired|～兴奋 overexcited

【过渡】guòdù 事物由一个阶段或一种状态逐渐发展变化而转入另一个阶段或另一种状态 (of things) passing from one stage or state to another; transition; interim: ～时期 transition; interim; transitional period|～地带 transitional zone

【过渡内阁】guòdù nèigé 看守内阁 caretaker cabinet; caretaker government; interim cabinet; transitional government; also 过渡政府 guòdù zhèngfǔ

【过房】guòfáng〈方 *dial.*〉same as 过继 guòjì

【过访】guòfǎng〈书 *fml.*〉访问 pay or make a visit; make or pay a call

【过分】guò//fèn (说话、做事)超过一定的程度或限度 (of speech or action) beyond or over the limit; to excess; to a fault; going too far; (of sth.) be excessive; be undue; overshoot the mark: ～谦虚,就显得虚伪了。Too much modesty may appear hypocritical.|这幅画虽然画得不够好,但你把它说得一文不值,也未免～了。It's true the painting is not that good, but you are going too far by describing it as worthless.

【过付】guòfù 双方交易,由中人经手交付钱或货物 make business deals through a broker or go-between

【过关】guò//guān 通过关口,多用于比喻(oft. fig.)pass a barrier or test: 过技术关 be approved technically; be technically up to standard; meet the technical requirements|蒙混～ muddle through; bluff it out|产品质量不合标准就不能～。The products can't pass if the quality fails to reach the standard.

【过关斩将】guò guān zhǎn jiàng 〈比喻 *fig.*〉竞赛中战胜对手,进入下一轮比赛,在前进中克服困难 beat one's opponent and go into the next round of competition; overcome difficulties in the course of progress

【过河拆桥】guò hé chāi qiáo 〈比喻 *fig.*〉达到目的以后,就把曾经帮助过自己的人一脚踢开 spurn one's benefactor after fulfilling an objective; destroy the bridge after crossing the river; kick down the ladder

【过后】guòhòu ❶ 往后 afterwards; later: 这件事暂且这么决定,有什么问题,～再说。Let's make a temporary settlement here; then if anything comes up, we will handle it later. ❷ 后来 at a later time: 我先去通知了他,～才来通知你的。I first went to tell him, and then came to inform you.

【过户】guò//hù 房产、车辆、记名有价证券等在买卖、继承或赠与时,依照法定手续更换物主姓名(of property, vehicles, stocks and bonds, etc.) transfer of ownership from one person to another in conformity with certain legal procedures; transfer of names

【过话】guò//huà 〈方 *dial.*〉(～儿 guò//huàr) ❶ 交谈 converse; talk: 我们俩不太熟,只见面打个招呼,没有过～儿。We don't know much about each other, and haven't really talked except for exchanging greetings. ❷ 传话 send word; deliver a message: 请你替我过个话儿,就说明天我不去找他了。Would you please send word that I'm not going to meet him tomorrow?

【过活】guòhuó 生活;过日子 make a living; lead a life; get along: 那时,一家人就靠父亲做工～。At that time the whole family lived on the father's wages.

【过火】guò//huǒ (说话、做事)超过适当的分寸或限度 go beyond the proper limit; go too far; go to extremes; overdo: 这话说得有点～。It's going a bit far to say that.

【过激】guòjī 过于激烈 ultra; radical; extreme: ～的言论 radical remarks

【过继】guòjì 把自己的儿子给没有儿子的兄弟、堂兄弟或亲戚做儿子;没有儿子的人以兄弟、堂兄弟或亲戚的儿子为自己的儿子 have one's son adopted by a relative without a son; (of a person without a son) adopt the son of a relative

【过家伙】guò jiā·huo same as 打出手 dǎ chūshǒu① on p. 347

【过奖】guòjiǎng 〈谦辞 *hum.*〉过分地表扬或夸奖(用于对方赞扬自己时 in response to a compliment) overpraise; lay it on thick: 您～了,我不过做了该做的事。You're laid it on thick — I've just done what I should.

【过街老鼠】guò jiē lǎoshǔ 〈比喻 *fig.*〉人人痛恨的坏人 person hated by everyone; much-hated person

【过街楼】guòjiēlóu 跨在街道或胡同上的楼,底下可以通行 overhead projection of a building spanning a street or a lane

【过街天桥】guò jiē tiānqiáo 为了行人横穿马路而在马路上空架设的桥 overpass; overbridge; flyover; (for the convenience of pedestrians) passage or bridge that crosses above a roadway or thoroughfare

【过节】guò//jié ❶ 在节日进行庆祝等活动 celebrate a festival or holiday ❷ 指过了节日 indicating the completion of such celebrations: ～后咱们就开始做新的工作。Let's start our new work after the holidays.

【过节儿】guò·jiér 〈方 *dial.*〉❶ 待人接物时所应重视的礼节或手续 rituals or formalities one should respect in social life ❷ 嫌隙 grudge; gulf: 你们之间的～,你也有不是的地方。You have to take part of the blame for the gulf between you. ❸ 细节;琐事 detail; trifle: 这虽是小～,但也不能忽视。This may be a trifling matter, but it cannot be ignored.

【过境】guò//jìng 通过国境或地区管界 pass through the territory of a country or region; make a transit: ～税 transit duty|台风～。The typhoon is passing into the region.

【过客】guòkè 过路的客人;旅客 passing traveller; passer-by

【过来】guò//·lái 从另一个地点向说话人(或叙述的对象)所在地来 come over; come up: 车来了,赶快～吧! The bus is coming. Hurry up!|那边有只小船～了。A small boat came over from that side.

【过来】//·guò//·lái ❶ 用在动词后,表示时间、能力、数量充分(多跟'得'或'不'连用 oft. used with 得·de or 不 bù)[used after a verb to indicate a sufficiency of time, ability or amount] can manage; can handle; can deal with: 活儿不多,我一个人干得～。It's not much work, so I can manage alone.|这几天我忙不～。I can't manage it alone in the next few days. ❷ 用在动词后,表示来到自己所在的地方 [used after a verb to indicate a movement toward the speaker]: 捷报从四面八方飞～。News of the victory kept pouring in from all around.|敌人几次三番想冲过桥来,都叫我们给打退了。The enemy tried several times to charge from the other end of the bridge, but each time we fought them back. ❸ 用在动词后,表示正面对着自己［used after a verb to indicate sth. facing oneself］：他转过脸来,我才认出是位老同学。I didn't recognize him as one of my former classmates until he turned around. ❹ 用在动词后,表示回到原来的、正常的状态［used after a verb to indicate coming round to the original state］：醒～了 come to｜觉悟～了 become enlightened; become aware of; come to the realization｜他真固执,简直劝不～。He is too stubborn to come round.｜爬到山顶,大家都累得喘不过气来。All of us were quite out of breath when we got to the top of the mountain.

【过来人】guò·láirén 对某事曾经有过亲身经历和体验的人 old hand; person who has experience：你是～,当然明白其中的道理。As an experienced person, you ought to know why.

【过礼】guò//lǐ ❶ 旧俗,结婚前男家把彩礼送往女家（old custom）（groom's family）deliver betrothal gifts to the bride's family ❷ 指以礼相见;行礼 pay respects to; greet; salute

【过量】guò//liàng 超过限量 excessive：饮酒～ drink to excess; go on a binge｜～施肥对作物生长不利。Overfertilization is harmful to the growth of crops.

【过淋】guòlín same as 过滤 guòlǜ：把煎好的药用纱布～一下。Filtrate the decocted herbs through a piece of gauze.

【过录】guòlù 把一个本子上的文字抄写在另一个本子上 copy from one notebook or account to another：从流水账～到总账上 record day-to-day accounts in the general ledgers｜把这三种批注用不同颜色的笔～到一个本子上。Copy the three memos into another book in different colours.

【过路】guòlù 途中经过某个地方 pass by on one's way：我是个～的人,对这儿的情况不了解。I'm just a passer-by and don't know much about the place.

【过路财神】guòlù cáishén〈比喻 *fig.*〉暂时经手大量钱财而没有所有权和支配权的人 temporary god of wealth — one who handles large sums of money for a short time but has no legal possession or standing

【过虑】guòlǜ 忧虑不必忧虑的事 be over-anxious; worry unnecessarily about：你～了,情况没那么严重。Don't be so worried; things are not that bad.

【过滤】guòlǜ 使流体通过滤纸或其他多孔材料,把所含的固体颗粒或有害成分分离出去 filter; filtrate; pass liquid through a filter or other porous material to separate the fluid from suspended particles or harmful impurities

【过滤嘴】guòlǜzuǐ 一种起过滤作用的烟嘴儿,用泡沫塑料等材料制成,安在香烟的一头。也指带过滤嘴的香烟。filter tip（of cigarette）; cigarette end made of foam, plastic, etc., that contains a material to filter the smoke; also refers to a cigarette with a filter tip

【过门】guòmén（～儿 guòménr）女子出嫁到男家 marry into a family;（of a girl）move into husband's house on the wedding day：刚～的新媳妇 newly-wed woman

【过门儿】guòménr 唱段或歌曲的前后或中间,由器乐单独演奏的部分,具有承前启后的作用 prelude or interlude; independent instrumental music that precedes, follows or comes in the middle of an aria or song, serving as overture or interlude between parts of a performance

【过敏】guòmǐn ❶ 有机体对某些药物或外界刺激的感受性不正常地增高的现象 allergy; allergic reaction;（of organisms）abnormally high sensitivity to certain medicines or external irritation：药物～ drug allergy ❷ 过于敏感 oversensitive：你不要～,没人说你坏话。Don't be so sensitive — no one has said anything against you.

【过目】guò//mù 看一遍(多用来表示审核 mostly in examination and verification) look over：名单已经排好,请过一下目。Here is the list for your perusal.

【过目成诵】guò mù chéng sòng 看了一遍就能背诵出来,形容记忆力强 be able to recite sth. after reading it once; have a good memory

【过年】guò//nián ❶ 在新年或春节期间进行庆祝等活动 celebrate the New Year or Spring Festival ❷ 指过了新年或过了春节 after the New Year or the Spring Festival：这事不急,等过了年再说。There is no hurry; let's wait until after the New Year.

【过年】guò·nian 明年 next year：这孩子～该上学了。The boy is going to start school next year.

【过期】guò//qī 超过期限 exceed the time limit; be overdue：～作废 invalid after the expiry date

【过谦】guòqiān 过分谦虚(指推让) showing too much modesty by declining：这个会由你来主持最合适,不必～了。You are the best person to become the chair, so don't be so modest.

【过去】guòqù 时间词,现在以前的时间(区别于'现在、将来' as compared with 'present and future') past; former; previous; time earlier than the present time：～的工作只不过像万里长征走完了第一步。The work done in the past is like the first step made in a long march of ten thousand miles.

【过去】guò//·qù ❶ 离开或经过说话人(或叙述的对象)所在地向另一个地点去［leave or pass by where a speaker or a listener is and go toward another place］go over; pass by：你在这里等着,我～看看。Stay here and wait, and let me go have a look.｜门口刚～一辆汽车。A car just passed by outside the gate. ❷〈婉辞 *euph.*〉死亡(后面要加'了' followed by 了 ·le) die; pass away: 他祖父昨天夜里～了。His grandfather passed away last night.

【过去】//·guò//·qù ❶ 用在动词后,表示离开或经过自己所在的地方 [used after a verb to indicate a motion away from or past the speaker]: 我对准了球门一脚把球踢～。I sent the ball toward the goal with a hard kick. | 老乡又送～几床被子给战士们盖。The villagers sent over some more quilts for the soldiers. ❷ 用在动词后,表示反面对着自己 [used after a verb to indicate turning the back of sth. towards the speaker]: 我把信封翻～,细看邮戳上的日子。I turned over the envelope and examined the date stamped on it. ❸ 用在动词后,表示失去原来的、正常的状态 [used after a verb to indicate loss of a normal or original state]: 病人晕～了。The patient fainted. ❹ 用在动词后,表示通过 [used after a verb to indicate success of an action]: 蒙混不～了 fail to find a way out of a muddle ❺ 用在形容词后,表示超过(多跟'得'或'不'连用) [used after an adjective plus 得 · de or 不 bù to indicate superiority or inferiority]: 鸡蛋还能硬得过石头去? Can an egg be harder than a stone? | 天气再热,也热不过乡亲们的心去。Warm as the day may get, it could never match the warm hearts of these people.

G

【过儿】guòr 〈方 *dial.*〉〈量词 *classifier*〉遍 times: 这衣服洗了三～了。The coat has been washed three times. | 我把书温了好几～。I've reviewed the book several times.

【过热】guòrè 〈比喻 *fig.*〉事物发展的势头猛,超过了应有的限度 overheated; superheated: 经济发展～ overheated economic growth

【过人】guòrén 超过一般人 be superior to the common run: 聪明～ extraordinarily intelligent | 他在工作中表现出了～的才智。He has proven to be exceptionally capable and perceptive in work.

【过日子】guò rì·zi 生活;过活 lead a life; get by; get along; live: 小两口儿和和气气地～。The young couple lead a harmonious life.

【过筛子】guò shāi·zi ❶ 使粮食、矿石等通过筛子,进行挑选 put (flour, ore, etc.) through a sieve or riddle in order to separate the fine from the coarse particles; sift; sieve; sift out; screen; riddle; bolt ❷〈比喻 *fig.*〉选择 prioritize; carefully select; go over carefully; scan: 先把该解决的问题过一下筛子。Let's go over the urgent problems first.

【过晌】guòshǎng 〈方 *dial.*〉 same as 过午 guòwǔ

【过甚】guòshèn 过分;夸大(多指说话) exaggerate; overstate: 言之～ stated in exaggerated language; exaggeration | ～其词 stretch the facts; give an exaggerated account; overstate the case

【过生日】guò shēng·ri 在生日这一天,举行庆祝活动 celebrate a birthday; have a birthday party

【过剩】guòshèng ❶ 数量远远超过限度,剩余过多 excess; surplus: 精力～ excessively energetic; overenergetic ❷ 供给远远超过需要或市场购买力 amount of supply over and above what is demanded by or beyond the purchasing power of the market: surplus; oversupply: 生产～ overproduction

【过失】guòshī 因疏忽而犯的错误 fault; error; demerit; slip; blunder; lapse; misstep; negligence

【过时】guò//shí ❶ 过了规定的时间 past the appointed time: ～不候 no waiting after the set time ❷ 过去流行现在已经不流行;陈旧不合时宜 out-of-date; outdated; outmoded; demoded; unfashionable; obsolete; out of fashion; antiquated: 他穿着一件～的长袍。He is wearing an outdated long gown.

【过世】guò//shì 去世 die; pass away

【过手】guò//shǒu 经手办理(特指钱财) deal with or handle (esp. money): 他～的钱,从未出过差错。He has never made a single mistake in all his dealings with money.

【过数】guò//shù (～儿 guòshùr) 清点数目 count; check the amount: 这是货款,你过一下数。Here is the money from the loan; please count it.

【过堂】guò//táng 〈旧时 *old*〉指诉讼当事人到公堂上受审问 (of a litigant) appear in court to be tried; be tried; be interrogated

【过堂风】guòtángfēng (～儿 guòtángfēngr)通过穿堂、过道或相对的门窗的风 draught; current of air moving through a passageway or two opposite windows or doors

【过天】guòtiān 〈方 *dial.*〉改天 some other day

【过厅】guòtīng 旧式房屋中,前后开门,可以由中间通过的厅堂。现在楼房卧室之间的过道也有叫过厅的。(of an old Chinese house) hallway; (of a present-day apartment building) passageway or hallway (to a bedroom); foyer; lobby

【过头】guò//tóu (～儿 guò//tóur) 超过限度;过分 go beyond the limit; carry (sth.) too far; overdo: 说～话,做～事 go too far in words and deeds | 他对自己的估计有点儿～。He has overestimated himself.

【过屠门而大嚼】 guò túmén ér dà jué 〈比喻 *fig.*〉心中羡慕而不能如愿以偿,用不实际的办法安慰自己 feast oneself in imagination at the butcher's door — feed oneself on unfulfilled dreams or illusions; fan a vain ambition (屠门 *tumen*: 肉铺 butcher's)

【过往】guòwǎng ❶ 来去 come and go; pass: ～客商 passing merchants or businessmen | 今

天赶集，路上～的人很多。There is a fair today, and the traffic is heavy along the way. ❷ 来往；交往 associate with; contact; engage social intercourse with：他们俩是老同学，～很密。They are former classmates who keep in close contact with each other.

【过望】guòwàng 超过自己原来的希望 more than expected; beyond one's expectations：大喜～ be delighted with the unexpected outcome; be overjoyed

【过问】guòwèn 参与其事；参加意见；表示关心 get involved in; concern oneself with; take an interest in; bother about：～政治 be concerned with politically | ～生产 attend to production | 水泥堆在外面无人～。The cement has been left out there and forgotten by everybody.

【过午】guòwǔ 中午以后 afternoon：上午他不在家，请你～再来吧。He is not at home in the mornings; please come back in the afternoon.

【过细】guòxì 仔细 meticulous; careful：～检查一遍 make a careful check; examine sth. closely | 要～地做工作 work with meticulous care

【过心】guòxīn〈方 *dial.*〉❶ 多心 oversensitive; suspicious：我直话直说，你别～。I am going to be straightforward with you, so don't get oversensitive. ❷ 知心 intimate; understanding：咱俩是～的朋友，有什么话不能说？We are close friends. What is it that we cannot say to each other?

【过眼】guò//yǎn same as 过目 guò//mù

【过眼云烟】guò yǎn yúnyān〈比喻 *fig.*〉很快就消失的事物 transient; ephemeral; short-lived; transitory; fleeting; passing; fugacious; also 过眼烟云 guò yǎn yānyún

【过夜】guò//yè ❶ 度过一夜(多指在外住宿) stay overnight (away from home); put up for the night; stay overnight：在工地～ spend the night at the worksite ❷ 隔夜 of the previous evening or night：不喝～茶。Don't drink tea from the previous day.

【过意不去】guò yì bù qù 心中不安(抱歉) feel guilty, sorry and apologetic：这本书借了这么多日子才还你，真有点～。I'm really sorry to return the book after so many days. also 不过意 bù guòyì

【过瘾】guò//yǐn 满足某种特别深的癖好，泛指满足爱好 satisfy the urge of a hobby; do sth. to one's heart's content; enjoy oneself to the full：这段唱腔优美，听起来真～。This aria is a great joy to listen to.

【过硬】guò//yìng 禁受得起严格的考验或检验 (of a quality or skill) stand to the stiffest test; have a perfect command of sth.; be really up to the mark：过得硬 be well up to the standard; highly competitive or competent | 技术～ (of a person) be skilful; (of a product) be well up to technical standards | ～本领 perfect skill

【过犹不及】guòyóubùjí 事情办得过火，就跟做得不够一样，都是不好的 going too far is as bad as not going far enough; too much is as bad as not enough; going beyond is as bad as falling short

【过于】guòyú〈副词 *adv.*〉表示程度或数量过分；太 too (much); over; excessively; unduly：～劳累 overworked; overtired | ～着急 over-anxious | ～乐观 over-optimistic

【过誉】guòyù 过分称赞(多用做谦辞 usu. to show modesty) over-praise; unearned praise：您如此～，倒叫我惶恐了。I'm afraid I don't really deserve your praise. | 人们称赞他是人民的公仆，并非～。It's not an unearned praise for him to be acclaimed as a selfless public servant of the people.

【过逾】guò·yu 过分；过甚 excessive; too much：小心没～。You can never be too careful.

【过载】guòzài ❶ 超载 overload ❷ 把一个运输工具上装载的东西卸下来，装到另一个运输工具上 transfer (or be transferred) from one conveyance to another; tranship; also 过儎 guòzài

【过儎】guòzài same as 过载 guòzài ②

【过账】guò//zhàng 过去指商业上把账目由甲账转入乙账，现在簿记上指把传票、单据记在总账上或把日记账转登在分类账上 post; transfer items (as from a daybook to a ledger); (of a past commercial practice) transfer items from account A to account B; (in present-day bookkeeping) record (in the general ledgers) slips and bills, or original entries of a daybook

H

hā (ㄏㄚ)

哈[1] hā ❶ 张口呼气 breathe out (with the mouth open); exhale with parted lips; blow one's breath out: ～了一口气 breathe out a puff of air ❷〈拟声词 *onom.*〉形容笑声(大多叠用 usu. repeated) sound of laughing: ～～大笑 ha ha; laugh heartily; roar with laughter ❸〈叹词 *interj.*〉表示得意或满意(大多叠用 usu. repeated) expressing self-pride or satisfaction: ～～,我猜着了。Aha, I guessed right. | ～～,这回可输给我了。Aha, for once I've beat you.

哈[2] (䱽) hā ☞ 哈腰 hā//yāo ☞ hǎ on p. 753 and hà on p. 753

【哈哈】hā·ha ☞ 打哈哈 dǎ hā·ha on p. 348

【哈哈镜】hāhājìng 用凹凸不平的玻璃做成的镜子,照起来奇形怪状,引人发笑 distorting mirror; magic mirror; mirror made of glass with an uneven surface that distorts images in a strange and funny way

【哈哈儿】hā·har〈方 *dial.*〉可笑的事 sth. funny; ridiculous matter; joke: 这真是个～。This is really ridiculous. | 闹了个～ make a fool of oneself; make oneself a laughing stock

【哈喇】[1] hā·la 食油或含油食物日久味道变坏 rank and sour; stale; (of edible oil or oily food) tasting or smelling unpleasant after being stored for a long time: 点心～了,不能吃了。The snacks have gone rancid and are inedible.

【哈喇】[2] hā·la 杀死(多见于早期白话 oft. in early vernacular) kill; put sb. to death

【哈喇子】hālá·zi〈方 *dial.*〉流出来的口水 dribble; drivel; drool

【哈里发】hālǐfā ❶ 穆罕默德逝世(公元 632)后,伊斯兰教国家政教合一的领袖的称呼 caliph; calif; kalif; khalif(a); theocratic leader of an Islamic nation, regarded as successor to Muhammad after his death in A. D. 632 ❷ 我国伊斯兰教对在寺院中学习伊斯兰经典的人员的称呼 Islamic caliph; Chinese Muslim term of address for those studying Islamic scriptures at a mosque [阿拉伯 Arabic: khalīfah]

【哈密瓜】hāmìguā ❶ 甜瓜的一大类,品种很多,果实较大,果肉香甜,多栽培于新疆哈密一带 saccharinus (*Cucumis melo var*); Hami melon; major type of muskmelon with multiple varieties, large fruit with sweet pulp, grown mainly in the Hami region in the Xinjiang Uygur Autonomous Region of China ❷ 这种植物的果实 Hami melon (fruit)

【哈尼族】Hānízú 我国少数民族之一,分布在云南 Hani people; Hanis; one of China's minority ethnic peoples living in Yunnan Province

【哈气】hā//qì 张口呼气 breathe out with parted lips; breathe out (with mouth open): 他把手放在嘴边哈了一口气。He put his hands around his mouth and breathed out a puff of air.

【哈气】hāqì ❶ 张口呼出来的气 air coming out of the lungs; breath (through an open mouth) ❷ 指凝结在玻璃等上面的水蒸气 water vapour that forms on windows, etc.

【哈欠】hā·qian 困倦时嘴张开,深深吸气,然后呼出,是血液内二氧化碳增多,刺激脑部的呼吸中枢而引起的生理现象 yawn; take (usu. involuntarily) a deep breath with the mouth wide open, as when sleepy or bored — a physiological phenomenon caused by increased carbon dioxide in the blood stimulating the respiratory centre in the brain: 打～ yawn; give a yawn

【哈萨克族】Hāsàkèzú ❶我国少数民族之一,主要分布在新疆、甘肃 Kazak (Kazakh) people; Kazaks (Kazakhs); one of China's minority ethnic peoples living mainly in the Xinjiang Uygur Autonomous Region and Gansu Province ❷ 哈萨克斯坦共和国人数最多的民族 the largest ethnic group in the Republic of Kazakhstan

【哈腰】hā//yāo ❶ 弯腰 stoop; bend one's back: 一～把钢笔掉在地上了。As I bent over, my fountain pen fell to the ground. ❷ 稍微弯腰表示礼貌(不及鞠躬郑重) bow slightly as a form of greeting (not as solemn as a deep bow): 点头～ bow and scrape; bow unctuously

铪 hā 金属元素,符号 Hf (hafnium)。银白色,熔点高。用于制高强度高温合金,也用作 X 射线管的阴极,在核反应堆中做中子吸收剂。hafnium (Hf); silvery metallic element with a high-melting point, used to make high-intensity alloy, and as negative poles in X-ray tube and as neutron absorber in nuclear reactors

há（ㄏㄚˊ）

虾(蝦) há［虾蟆］(há·má) same as 蛤蟆 há·má
☞ xiā on p. 2060

蛤 há ☞ below
☞ gé on p. 654

【蛤蟆】há·má 青蛙和蟾蜍的统称 general term for frog and toad; also 虾蟆 há·má

【蛤蟆夯】há·mahāng 用电动机作动力的夯,工作时铁砣转动,把夯带动跳起向前移动,砸实地基。工作方式像蛙跳。load rammer or tamper; frog rammer; portable power-driven rammer which, following the revolving of an iron wheel, jumps upward and then forward in a movement akin to that of a frog to ram a foundation home

【蛤蟆镜】há·majìng 镜架较大的太阳镜的俗称。镜片略呈蛤蟆眼睛形状。frog sunglasses; popular name for sunglasses with a relatively large frame and lenses that resembles somewhat frogs' eyes

hǎ（ㄏㄚˇ）

哈 hǎ ❶〈方 *dial.*〉斥责 scold:～他一顿 give him a good scolding or lecturing ❷ (Hǎ) 姓 a surname
☞ hā on p. 752 and hà on p. 753

【哈巴狗】hǎ·bagǒu ❶ (～儿 hǎ·bagǒur)一种体小毛长腿短的狗。供玩赏。pug; Pekinese dog, also Pekingese; a breed of small pet dog with long silky hair and short legs; also 狮子狗 shī·zigǒu or 巴儿狗 bārgǒu ❷〈比喻 *fig.*〉驯顺的奴才 toady; sycophant; lackey; obsequious flunkey

【哈达】hǎdá 藏族和部分蒙古族人表示敬意和祝贺用的长条丝巾或纱巾,多为白色,也有黄、蓝等色 katag; *hada*; long piece of silk (oft. white, sometimes yellow or blue) used as a welcome gift by the Tibetans and some Mongolians

奤 hǎ 奤夿屯(Hǎbātún),地名,在北京市 name of a place in Beijing
☞ 呔 tǎi on p. 1853

hà（ㄏㄚˋ）

哈 hà ☞ below
☞ hā on p. 752 and hǎ on p. 753

【哈巴】hà·ba〈方 *dial.*〉走路时两膝向外弯曲 bend one's knees outward while walking

【哈什蚂】hà·shimǎ 蛙的一种,身体灰褐色,生活在阴湿的地方。雌性的腹内有脂肪状物质,叫哈什蚂油,可入药。哈什蚂是我国特产之一,主要产在东北各省。Chinese forest frog (*Rana temporaria chensinensis*); special breed of frog found mainly in Northeast China, that has a light brown body and lives in dark damp places; the oviduct fat in females' abdomen can be used as medicine when dried [满 Manchu term]

hāi（ㄏㄞ）

咍 hāi〈书 *fml.*〉❶ 讥笑 ridicule; satirize; sneer at:为众人所～ lay oneself open to ridicule; make one a laughing stock ❷ 欢笑;喜悦 rejoice; laugh happily:欢～ laugh happily ❸ same as 咳 hāi

咳 hāi〈叹词 *interj.*〉表示伤感、后悔或惊异 expressing sadness, regret or surprise:～!我怎么这么糊涂! Oh no! How stupid I was! | ～!真有这种怪事儿! Hey, that's really strange!
☞ ké on p. 1091

嗨 hāi［嗨哟］(hāiyō)〈叹词 *interj.*〉做重体力劳动(大多集体操作)时呼喊的声音 (voice made usu. collectively while doing heavy manual labour) heave ho; hey-ho; yo-heave-ho:加油干呐,～! Give it your best, heave ho!
☞ 嘿 hēi on p. 795

hái（ㄏㄞˊ）

还(還) hái〈副词 *adv.*〉❶ 表示现象继续存在或动作继续进行;仍旧 (of a phenomenon or action) still; yet; still in existence or in progress; just yet:十年没见了,她～那么年轻。I hadn't seen her for ten years, and she still looks so young. | 半夜了,他～在工作。It's already midnight, and he is still working. ❷ 表示在某种程度之上有所增加或在某个范围之外有所补充 even more (than a certain degree or scope); still more; also; too; as well; in addition:今天比昨天～冷。It is even colder today than yesterday. | 改完作业,～要备课。After correcting and grading the students' homework, he still has to prepare for tomorrow's lessons. ❸ 用在形容词前,表示程度上勉强过得去(一般是往好的方面说)[usu. in a positive way, used before an adjective] passably; fairly:屋子不大,收拾得倒～干净。The room is small, but it's kept quite tidy. ❹ 用在上半句话里,表示陪衬,下半句进而推论,多用反问的语气;尚且 [used in the first half of a sentence to set off the inference or extrapolation contained in the second half, usu. in a rhetorical question] even:你～搬不动,何况我呢? If you can't move it, how can I? ❺ 表示对某件事

物,没想到如此,而居然如此 [indicating that sth. quite unexpected has happened] unexpectedly; beyond expectations: 他~真有办法。You've got to admit he really is resourceful. ❻ 表示早已如此 as early as: ~在几年以前,我们就研究过这个方案。We discussed the plan several years ago.

☞ huán on p. 843

【还是】hái·shi ❶ same as 还 hái①: 尽管今天风狂雨大,他们~照常出工。They went out to work despite the strong wind and heavy rain today. ❷ same as 还 hái⑤: 没想到这事儿~真难办。I didn't expect it to be so difficult. ❸ 表示希望,含有'这么办比较好'的意思 (expressing hope) had better: 天气凉了,~多穿点儿吧。It's getting cold, you'd better put on more clothes. ❹ 用在问句里,表示选择,放在每一个选择的项目的前面,不过第一项之前也可以不用'还是' [used in a question to express selection among several choices, placed before each choice except the first where it is optional] or: 你~上午去? ~下午去? Will you go in the morning or in the afternoon? | 去看朋友,~去电影院,~去滑冰场,他一时拿不定主意。He hesitates as to whether he should visit a friend, go to the cinema, or go skating.

孩 hái (~儿 háir) 孩子 child: 小~儿 child; kid | 女~儿 little girl

【孩儿】hái'ér 父母称呼儿女或儿女对父母自称 (多见于早期白话 usu. in early vernacular) [parents addressing their children] my child; my son; my daughter; [self-reference when talking to one's parents] I; me

【孩提】háití 〈书 *fml*.〉儿童;幼儿 child; infant

【孩童】háitóng same as 儿童 értóng: 三尺~ small kid; young child

【孩子】hái·zi ❶ same as 儿童 értóng: 小~ child; baby | 男~ boy ❷ same as 子女 zǐnǚ: 她有两个~。She has two children.

【孩子气】hái·ziqì ❶ 孩子似的脾气或神气 childishness; childish air: 他一脸的~。He still looks so childish. ❷ 脾气或神气像孩子 childish; behaving or looking like a child: 他越来越~了。He has grown increasingly childish.

【孩子头】hái·zitóu (~儿 hái·zitóur) ❶ 爱跟孩子们玩的大人 adult who is very popular with children ❷ 在一群孩子中充当头头儿的孩子 leader of a group of children

骸 hái ❶ 骸骨 bones of a body; skeleton: 四肢百~ all the limbs and bones ❷ 借指身体 body: 形~ human body | 病~ ailing body | 遗~ remains (of the dead); corpse; (dead) body

【骸骨】háigǔ 人的骨头(多指尸骨) human bones (of the dead); skeleton

hǎi (厂万)

胲 hǎi 有机化合物的一类,是羟胺的烃基衍生物的统称 hydroxylamine; group of organic compounds including all the alkyl derivatives of hydroxylamine

☞ gǎi on p. 622

浬 hǎilǐ,又 also lǐ,海里旧也作浬 old term for nautical mile

海 hǎi ❶ 大洋靠近陆地的部分,有的大湖也叫海,如青海、里海 (the parts of the ocean close to the continent) sea; (sometimes) big lake, e.g. the Qinghai Lake, and the Caspian Sea ❷〈比喻 *fig*.〉连成一大片的很多同类事物 expanse; sea; great number or quantity of people or things coming together: 人~ sea of faces; huge crowd of people | 火~ sea of flames; sea of fire ❸ 大的(器皿或容量等) extra large; immense; of great capacity: ~碗 extra-large bowl | ~量 magnanimity ◇夸下~口 make a promise one can never fulfil; talk big ❹〈古代 *arch*.〉指从外国来的 foreign; from overseas: ~棠 Chinese flowering crabapple | ~枣 date palm ❺〈方 *dial*.〉极多(后面一般跟'了、啦'等 usu. followed by 了 ·le, 啦 ·la, etc.) countless; numerous: 街上的人可~啦! There were countless people on the streets. ❻〈方 *dial*.〉漫无目标地 randomly; aimlessly; everywhere: ~骂 shout at no one in particular | 她丢了枝笔,~找。She looked high and low for her lost pen. ❼〈方 *dial*.〉毫无节制地 with no limit or restraint: ~吃~喝 eat and drink to one's heart's content; squander money on food and drink ❽ (Hǎi) 姓 a surname

【海岸】hǎi'àn 邻接海洋边缘的陆地 seacoast; coast; seashore; land bordering the sea

【海岸线】hǎi'ànxiàn 陆地和海洋的分界线 coastline; beachline; shoreline; dividing line between the land and the ocean

【海拔】hǎibá 以平均海水面做标准的高度 elevation; height above sea level; also 拔海 báhǎi

【海报】hǎibào 戏剧、电影等演出或球赛等活动的招贴 playbill, poster, notice; placard announcing or advertising a play, film, sports event, etc.

【海滨】hǎibīn 海边;沿海地带 seashore; seaside; strand: ~浴场 bathing beach | ~城市 seaside city

【海菜】hǎicài 泛指海洋里出产的供食用的植物 edible seaweed; edible plants from the sea

【海产】hǎichǎn ❶ 海洋里出产的 obtained from or produced in the sea: ~植物 marine plants ❷ 海洋里出产的动植物,如海蜇、海藻等 marine products; edible plants and animals from the sea, e.g. jellyfish and marine algae

【海潮】hǎicháo 海洋潮汐。指海洋水面定时涨落的现象。(sea) tide; regular flow and ebb of the sea

【海程】hǎichéng 船只在海上航行的路程 voyage; distance travelled by sea：再有半天的～，我们就可到达目的地了。Half a day's voyage more and we will arrive at our destination.

【海带】hǎidài 褐藻的一种，生长在海底的岩石上，形状像带子，含有大量的碘质，可用来提制碘、钾等。中医入药时叫昆布。kelp (*Laminaria japonica*); honey wrack; any of various belt-shaped brown algae that grow on rocks on the seabed and is used as a source of potash and iodine; called 昆布 kūnbù in Chinese traditional medicine

【海岛】hǎidǎo 海洋中的岛屿 island (in the sea)

【海盗】hǎidào 出没在海洋上的强盗 pirate; sea-rover

【海底捞月】hǎi dǐ lāo yuè〈比喻 *fig.*〉根本做不到，白费力气 try to scoop the moon from the bottom of the sea; try to make the impossible possible; strive for the impossible or illusory; cry for the moon; fruitless attempt; vain effort; also 水中捞月 shuǐ zhōng lāo yuè

【海底捞针】hǎi dǐ lāo zhēn〈比喻 *fig.*〉极难找到 fish for a needle in the ocean; search for a needle in a haystack; very difficult to find; also 大海捞针 dà hǎi lāo zhēn

【海防】hǎifáng 在沿海地区和领海内布置的防务 coastal defence; defence along coastal regions and within one's territorial waters

【海匪】hǎifěi same as 海盗 hǎidào

【海风】hǎifēng ❶ 海上刮的风 sea breeze; sea wind ❷ 气象学上指沿海地带白天从海洋吹向大陆的风 wind blowing from ocean to land during the daytime in coastal regions

【海港】hǎigǎng 沿海停泊船只的港口，有军港、商港、渔港等 seaport; harbour (for mooring boats and ships; including naval port, trade port, fishing port, etc.)

【海沟】hǎigōu 深度超过 6,000 米的狭长的海底凹地。两侧坡度陡急，分布于大洋边缘。如太平洋的菲律宾海沟、大西洋的波多黎各海沟等。tectogene; fosse; oceanic trench; submarine trench; narrow ditch on the seafloor over 6,000 metres deep, that has steep slopes and is found at the edges of oceans, e.g. the Philippine Trench of the Pacific Ocean, the Puerto Rico Trench of the Atlantic Ocean, etc.

【海狗】hǎigǒu 哺乳动物，四肢短，像鳍，趾有蹼，尾巴短，毛紫褐色或深黑色，雌的毛色淡。生活在海洋中，能在陆地上爬行。它的阴茎和睾丸叫做腽肭(wànà)脐，可入药。毛皮珍贵。fur seal; ursine seal (*Callorhinus ursinus*); marine mammal that is able to crawl on land, with broad flat limbs like flippers, a short tail, and puce or rich black hair (lighter on females). The ursine seal's pelt is valuable, and its penis and testis, called *wanaqi* in Chinese, can be used as medicine; also 腽肭兽 wànàshòu or 海熊 hǎixióng

【海关】hǎiguān 对出入国境的一切商品和物品进行监督、检查并照章征收关税的国家机关 customhouse; customs; department of government that monitors and inspects all commodities and goods entering or leaving a country and collects duties according to law

【海涵】hǎihán〈敬辞 *pol.*〉大度包容(用于请人原谅时) be magnanimous enough to forgive or tolerate (sb.'s errors or shortcomings)：由于条件简陋，招待不周，还望～。Please forgive us for our poor hospitality due to our humble conditions.

【海魂衫】hǎihúnshān 水兵穿的横的蓝白条纹相间的汗衫，圆领，长袖 striped sailor's shirt; collarless and buttonless sailor's shirt or pullover with long sleeves and horizontal blue and white stripes

【海货】hǎihuò 指市场上出售的海产品 seafood; marine products sold on the market

【海疆】hǎijiāng 指沿海地区和沿海海域 coastal areas and territorial seas：万里～ vast territorial seas

【海椒】hǎijiāo〈方 *dial.*〉same as 辣椒 làjiāo

【海禁】hǎijìn 指禁止外国人到中国沿海通商和中国人到海外经商的禁令。明清两代都有过这种禁令。ban on maritime trade or relations with foreign countries, as during the Ming (1368-1644) and Qing (1644-1911) dynasties

【海军】hǎijūn 在海上作战的军队，通常由水面舰艇、潜艇、海军航空兵、海军陆战队等兵种及各专业部队组成 navy; naval force; part of a country's military force that is organised for fighting at sea, usually consisting of branches such as the naval surface-vessel unit, naval submarine unit, naval air force and marine corps, as well as specialised forces

【海军呢】hǎijūnní 用粗毛纱织成的呢子，原料、织物组织、色泽和麦尔登呢相似，但质地稍差，常用来做制服等 navy cloth; woollen cloth made of roving that is similar to melton in source material, fabric and colour, but of inferior quality, usually used to make uniforms

【海口】[1] hǎikǒu ❶ 河流通海的地方 estuary; mouth of a river where it flows into the sea ❷ 海湾内的港口 seaport in a bay

【海口】[2] hǎikǒu 漫无边际地说大话叫夸海口 talk big; boast about what one can do

【海枯石烂】hǎi kū shí làn 直到海水枯干，石头粉碎。形容经历极长的时间（多用于誓言，反衬意志坚定，永远不变 usu. in an oath expressing firm will and unchanging fidelity) even if the seas should run dry and the rocks crumble — no matter what happens and for how long; (I shall love you) till seas run dry and rocks melt away：～，此心不移。The seas may run dry and the rocks may crumble, but my heart will always remain loyal.

【海况】hǎikuàng ❶ 指海区的温度、海水成分、浮游生物组成等情况 sea or marine conditions; state of the sea, such as temperature, composition of the seawater, plankton composition, etc. ❷ 指海面在风的作用下波动的情况，根据波浪的大小有无，分为 0—9 共 10 级。wave conditions on the sea as influenced by the wind, divided into 10 scales (0-9) based on the presence and degree of waves; ☞ 海况表 Table of Sea Conditions

【海阔天空】hǎi kuò tiān kōng 形容大自然的广阔，也比喻想像或说话毫无拘束，漫无边际 as boundless as the sea and the sky; (fig.) endless vast; unrestrained and far-ranging (speaking or imaginary); discursive：两人都很健谈，～，聊起来没个完。They were both talkative and had a rambling chat about everything under the sun.

【海蓝】hǎilán 像大海那样的蓝颜色 sea blue

【海里】hǎilǐ 计量海洋上距离的长度单位，一海里等于 1,852 米。旧也作浬。nautical mile; sea mile; admiralty mile; measure of distance on the sea (1,852 metres); formerly also 浬 lǐ

【海量】hǎiliàng ❶〈敬辞 *pol.*〉宽宏的度量 magnanimity：对不住的地方，望您～包涵。I hope you will be magnanimous enough to excuse any inappropriate behaviour on my part. ❷ 指很大的酒量 enormous capacity for liquor：您是～，不妨多喝几杯。You can hold your liquor, so a few more drinks won't put you out.

【海岭】hǎilǐng 海底的山脉。一般较陆地的山脉高而长，两侧较陡。ocean ridge; ridge at the bottom of the ocean with steep sides, usually taller and longer than those on the land; also 海脊 hǎijǐ

【海流】hǎiliú ❶ ☞ 洋流 yángliú on p. 2222 ❷ 泛指流动的海水 (in a broad sense) ocean current; flowing seawater

【海路】hǎilù 海上运输的航线 sea-lane; seaway; sea route

【海轮】hǎilún 专在海洋上航行的轮船 seagoing (or oceangoing) vessel

【海螺】hǎiluó 海里产的螺的统称。个儿一般较大，壳可以做号角或手工艺品。conch; sea snail; whelk; large type of shellfish with a spiral shell, which can be made into horns or handicrafts

海况表 Table of Sea Conditions

海况等级 Scale	海面征状 Signs on the Sea Surface
0	海面光滑如镜 glassy and calm
1	波纹 ripples
2	波浪很小，波峰开始破裂，但浪花不是白色，而是玻璃色的 small waves with the ridges starting to crack, with the spray being, transparent not white
3	波浪不大，但很触目，波峰破裂，其中有些地方形成白色浪花——白浪 small but quite eye-catching waves with cracking ridges and whitecaps in some parts
4	波浪具有很明显的形状，到处形成白浪 waves in notable shapes and whitecaps everywhere
5	出现高大波峰，有浪花的波顶占了波峰上很大的面积，风开始削去波峰上的浪花 huge ridges mostly covered by spray on the crest, which is constantly razed by wind
6	波峰上被风削去的浪花开始沿波浪斜面伸长成带状，有时波峰出现风暴波的长波形状 spray razed off by wind starting to spread along the wave slant, and sometimes developing into the shape of a long storm wave on the ridge
7	风削去的浪花带布满了波浪的斜面，并且有些地方达到波谷 wind-razed spray entirely covering the wave slant and reaching the troughs of the wave in some parts
8	稠密的浪花带布满了波浪斜面，海面因而变成白色，只在波底有些地方才没有浪花 wave slant fully covered with dense spray with the exception of only a few parts at the troughs, turning the sea entirely white
9	整个海面布满了稠密的浪花层，空气中充满了水滴和飞沫，能见度显著降低 sea entirely covered by a thick layer of spray with splattered drops and spindrifts filling the air, with an obvious deterioration in visibility

【海洛因】hǎiluòyīn 有机化合物，白色晶体，有苦味，有毒，用吗啡制成。医药上用做镇静、麻醉剂。常用成瘾。作为毒品时，叫白面儿。heroin; diamorphine; (slang) scag; smack; snow; bitter, poisonous white crystalline organic compound made from morphine, used medically as a tranquilliser and a narcotic but extended use is addictive; nicknamed 白面儿 báimiànr when used as hard drugs

【海米】hǎimǐ 海产的小虾去头去壳之后晒干而成的食品 dried shrimp, with head and shell removed, used as food

【海绵】hǎimián ❶ 低等多细胞动物，种类很多，多生在海底岩石间，单体或群体附在其他物体上，从水中吸取有机物质为食物。有的体内有柔软的骨骼。sponge; kinds of multicellular marine animals of lower life form, mostly living among rocks on the seabed, clinging to other objects alone or in a colony, and absorbing organic substances from the water as food, some having an internal soft skeleton ❷ 专指海绵的角质骨骼 keratose skeleton of sponges ❸ 用橡胶或塑料制成的多孔材料，有弹力，像海绵 elastic porous foam rubber, or plastic, sponge: ～底球鞋 sponge-insole shoes | ～球拍 foam-rubber or sponge ping-pong racket

【海面】hǎimiàn 海水的表面 sea surface; sea level

【海难】hǎinàn 船舶在海上所发生的灾难，如失火、沉没等 marine or maritime perils; perils of the sea, e.g. fire, shipwreck, etc.

【海内】hǎinèi 古人认为我国疆土四面环海，因此称国境以内为海内 within the four seas; throughout the country; People in ancient China believed that the country was surrounded by seas on the four sides, thus the phrase: 风行～ prevalent throughout the country; popular all over the country | ～孤本 only extant copy (of a book) in the country

【海派】hǎipài 以上海为代表的京剧表演风格。泛指在某方面具有上海特色的 Shanghai school of Peking Opera; of Shanghai style in a certain manner: ～川菜 Shanghai-style Sichuan cuisine | ～服装 Shanghai fashion

【海盆】hǎipén 深度在3,000—6,000米之间的海底盆地，除海岭和海沟外，底部平缓。海盆面积占海洋总面积的70%以上。ocean basin; sea basin; basin at the bottom of the ocean 3,000-6,000 metres deep, which is generally flat except for ridges and trenches, and represents over 70% of the total ocean area

【海侵】hǎiqīn 地面下沉时，海水淹没陆地 encroachment of the sea into low-lying land; advance of the sea; also 海进 hǎijìn

【海区】hǎiqū 海洋上的一定区域。根据军事需要划定的海区，范围一般用坐标标明。sea area designated for military purposes, the scope of which is usually marked on a coordinate system

【海参】hǎishēn 棘皮动物的一纲，身体略呈圆柱状，体壁多肌肉，口和肛门在两端，口的周围有触手。种类很多，生活在海底，吃各种小动物。是珍贵的食品。sea cucumber (*Holothurioidea*); bêche-de-mer; sea slug; trepang; class of echinoderm with a cylindrical body, muscle-filled wall, tentacle-fringed mouth on one end of the body and anus on the other, the greater variety of which live on the seabed and feed themselves on various kinds of small animals; an expensive delicacy

【海蚀】hǎishí 海水的冲击和侵蚀 marine erosion; lashing of waves

【海市蜃楼】hǎi shì shèn lóu ❶ 大气中由于光线的折射作用而形成的一种自然现象。当空气各层的密度有较大的差异时，远处的光线通过密度不同的空气层就发生折射或全反射，这时可以看见在空中或地面以下有远处物体的影像。这种现象多在夏天出现在沿海一带或沙漠地方。古人误认为蜃吐气而成，所以叫海市蜃楼。mirage; castles in the air; optical phenomenon that is often observed in summer in coastal regions or deserts, that gives a mirror-like illusion of distant places or objects in the air or below the ground level, due to extreme variations in density among different layers of air, which causes refraction or total reflection when distant rays pass through such layers. People in ancient China believed that the phenomenon was caused by the air breathed out by a big clam (蜃). also 蜃景 shènjǐng ❷〈比喻 *fig.*〉虚幻的事物 illusion; mirage; sth. illusory like a mirage; an unattainable vision

【海事】hǎishì ❶ 泛指一切有关海上的事情。如航海、造船、验船、海运法规、海损事故处理等。(in a broad sense) maritime affairs such as navigation, ship building, ship testing, maritime regulations, settlement of sea damage cases, etc. ❷ 指船舶在海上航行或停泊所发生的事故，如触礁、失火等 marine accident (of a ship sailing or anchored at the sea), e.g. striking a reef or catching fire

【海誓山盟】hǎi shì shān méng 男女相爱时所立的誓言和盟约，表示爱情要像山和海一样永恒不变 couple's pledge of love as long-lasting as the mountains and the seas; (make) a solemn pledge of love; (exchange) solemn vows and pledges; (swear) an oath of mutual love and fidelity; also 山盟海誓 shān méng hǎi shì

【海兽】hǎishòu 生活在海洋中的哺乳动物，如海豚、鲸等 sea animal; marine mammal, e.g. dolphin, whale, etc.

【海损】hǎisǔn ❶ 货物在海运中受到的损失 average; damage to goods in ocean shipping ❷ 船舶在海上航行中受到损坏 sea damage; marine loss; damage to ships at sea

【海獭】hǎitǎ 哺乳动物，身体圆而长，前肢比后肢短，趾有爪，尾巴短而扁，毛深褐色。生活在近岸的海洋中。毛皮很珍贵。sea otter (*Enhydra lutris*); offshore mammal with a long round body, clawed feet, longer forelegs and shorter hindlegs, short and flat tail, and dark brown fur, for which it is considered valuable; 通称 commonly known as 海龙 hǎilóng

【海滩】hǎitān 海边的沙滩 beach; sea beach

【海棠】hǎitáng ❶ 落叶小乔木，叶子卵形或椭圆形，花白色或淡粉红色。果实球形，黄色或红色，味酸甜。Chinese flowering crabapple (*Malus spectabilis*); cherry-apple tree; deciduous arbour with oval or elliptic leaves, white or light pink flowers, yellow or red round fruits which taste sweet and sour ❷ 这种植物的果实 plum-leaf crab; Chinese flowering crabapple

【海塘】hǎitáng 防御海潮的堤 seawall (against a sea tide)

【海图】hǎitú 航海用的标明海洋情况的图 sea (marine, nautical) chart; chart marking the conditions of the sea to facilitate navigation

【海涂】hǎitú 河流或海流夹杂的泥沙在地势较平的河流入海处或海岸附近沉积而形成的浅海滩。低潮时，其较高部分露出海面。修筑围堤，挡住海水可以垦殖。shoal; tidal land; tidal flat; tidal marsh; shallow beach in flat estuaries of a river or near the seashore, which are created by deposits of silt brought by river or ocean currents, with higher parts rising above the water during low tide, and which can be reclaimed by building dykes to ward off seawater; 简称 abbr. 涂 tú

【海豚】hǎitún 哺乳动物，身体长达一丈，鼻孔长在头顶上，背部青黑色，有背鳍，腹部白色，前肢变为鳍。生活在海洋中，吃鱼、乌贼、虾等。dolphin (*Delphinus delphis*); delphis; porpoise; popularly known as sea hog; marine mammal around one *zhang* (3.33 metres) in length, that has nostrils on top of its head, dark blue back, dorsal fins, white belly and fin-like forelegs, and eats fish, cuttlefish, shrimp, etc.; 通称 commonly known as 海猪 haǐzhū

【海豚泳】hǎitúnyǒng 游泳的一种姿势，也是游泳项目之一，是蝶泳的变形，两臂的动作跟蝶泳相同，两腿同时上下打水，因像海豚游水的姿势而得名。有时也叫蝶泳。dolphin butterfly stroke; dolphin fishtail; dolphin (swimming); style of swimming and a swimming event that originates from the butterfly stroke, with both arms moving upward and outward at the same time as the feet kick up and down, named for its resemblance to the movement of the dolphin; sometimes called butterfly stroke

【海外】hǎiwài 国外 overseas; abroad: 销行～be sold all over the world | ～奇闻 unfounded, absurd story; ☞ 海内 hǎinèi

【海外奇谈】hǎiwài qítán 指没有根据的、稀奇古怪的谈论或传说 tall-tale; traveller's tale; fantastic tale; strange story from across the sea; unfounded, absurd story or legend

【海湾】hǎiwān 海洋伸入陆地的部分 bay; gulf; part of the sea mostly surrounded by land

【海碗】hǎiwǎn 特别大的碗 very big bowl

【海王星】hǎiwángxīng 太阳系九大行星之一，按离太阳由近而远的次序计为第八颗，绕太阳公转周期约 164.8 年，自转周期约 22 小时。光度较弱，肉眼看不见。Neptune, the 8th in order from the sun among the nine planets of our solar system, with an or bital cycle of 164.8 years around the sun and a rotation time of 22 hours, invisible to the naked eye for its relatively weak luminosity; (图见 ☞ figure for 太阳系 tàiyángxì on p. 1855)

【海味】hǎiwèi 海洋里出产的食品(多指珍贵的 usu. expensive delicacy) seafood; choice seafood: 山珍～ rare dainties from the mountains and the seas; all sorts of delicacies

【海峡】hǎixiá 两块陆地之间连接两片海洋的狭窄水道 strait; channel; gullet; pass; fretum; narrow passage of water (between two pieces of land) connecting two seas

【海鲜】hǎixiān 供食用的新鲜的海鱼、海虾等 fresh seafood, e.g. sea fish, shrimp, etc.

【海象】hǎixiàng 哺乳动物，身体大，颜色深褐或灰黄，皮上没有毛，眼小，没有耳郭，上颌有两个特别长的牙。生活在海洋中，也能在陆地上行动。长牙可以做象牙的代用品。walrus (*Odobenus rosmarus*); morse; elephant seal; large, dark brown or greyish yellow marine mammal that has no fur nor auricles, and has small eyes and two extra-long teeth on its upper jaw which can serve as a substitute for ivory tusks; also capable of moving on land

【海啸】hǎixiào 由海底地震或风暴引起的海水剧烈波动。海水冲上陆地，往往造成灾害。seaquake; tsunami; bore; seismic sea wave; tidal wave; strong sea wave caused by an earthquake under the sea, or a storm, capable of bringing about disaster when seawater rushes onto the land

【海寻】hǎixún 计量海洋水深的长度单位，国际公制 1 海寻等于 1.852 米(1/1,000 海里)。旧也作浔。nautical fathom; length measurement for measuring the depth of seawater, with one nautical fathom equal to 1.852 metre or 1/1,000 sea mile; formerly also 浔 xún

【海盐】hǎiyán 用海水晒成或熬成的盐，是主要的食用盐 sea salt; bay salt; major type of edible salt obtained by drying seawater in the sun or boiling it

【海蜒】hǎiyán 幼鳀(tí)加工制成的鱼干 dried

processed young anchovy; ☞ 鳀 tí on p.1883

【海晏河清】hǎi yàn hé qīng ☞ 河清海晏 hé qīng hǎi yàn on p.788

【海洋】hǎiyáng 海和洋的统称 general term for seas and oceans; ocean

【海洋权】hǎiyángquán 沿海国家对距离海岸线一定宽度的海域及其资源的所有权 marine rights; maritime rights; ownership by a coastal nation of the sea area, within a certain distance from its coastline, and the resources therein

【海洋生物】hǎiyáng shēngwù 生活在海洋中的动物和植物 marine organisms; halobios; animals and plants living in the ocean

【海洋性气候】hǎiyángxìng qìhòu 近海地区受海洋影响明显的气候，全年和一天内的气温变化较小，空气湿润，降水量多，分布均匀 maritime (or marine) climate; climate in maritime regions notably influenced by the ocean, with humid air and an evenly distributed large amount of rainfall, and without much variation in temperature throughout the day and the year

【海洋学】hǎiyángxué 研究海水的性质、海浪和潮汐等现象以及海水与海中生物关系的学科 oceanography; oceanology; thalassography; oceanics; study of the properties of seawater and phenomena such as oceanic waves and tides as well as the relationship between seawater and other marine life forms

【海鱼】hǎiyú 生活在海里的鱼，如带鱼、黄鱼等 marine fish; saltwater fish; sea fish, such as cutlass fish, yellow croaker, etc.

【海域】hǎiyù 指海洋的一定范围（包括水上和水下）maritime space; sea area (including the area both above and below the water surface)

【海员】hǎiyuán 在海洋轮船上工作的人员的通称 seaman; sailor; mariner; seafarer; (general term for) people working on seagoing vessels

【海运】hǎiyùn 海洋上的运输 sea transportation; sea transport; ocean shipping; ocean carriage

【海葬】hǎizàng 处理死人遗体的一种方法，把尸体投入海洋 sea-burial; form of burial by throwing the corpse into the sea

【海战】hǎizhàn 敌对双方海军兵力在海洋上进行的战役或战斗 sea warfare; naval battle; battle or armed conflict between two enemy naval troops on the sea

【海蜇】hǎizhé 腔肠动物，身体半球形，青蓝色，半透明，上面有伞状部分，下面有八条口腕，口腕下端有丝状器官。生活在海中，靠伞状部分的伸缩而运动。伞状部分叫海蜇皮，口腕叫海蜇头，可以吃。jellyfish (*Rhopilema esculentum*); madusa; bluish, translucent, semi-circular coelenterate, with an umbrella-like top part, from the underside of which hangs tentacle suckers with filamentous organs attached at the bottom, living in the sea and swimming by alternately opening and shutting the umbrella, which is called the jellyfish tegument, while the tentacles are called jellyfish head, both edible

【海子】hǎi·zi 〈方 *dial.*〉湖 lake

醢 hǎi 〈书 *fml.*〉❶ 肉、鱼等制成的酱 minced fish, etc., or meat paste ❷ 剁成肉酱 cut into mince

hài（ㄏㄞˋ）

亥 hài 地支的第十二位 last of the 12 Earthly Branches; ☞ 干支 gānzhī on p.627

【亥时】hàishí 旧式计时法指夜间九点钟到十一点钟的时间 period of the day from 9 p.m. to 11 p.m. (based on the old chronometric method)

核 hài 〈书 *fml.*〉痛苦；愁苦 pain; anxiety; distress; misery

骇 hài 惊吓；震惊 frighten; shock; amaze; be astonished; be shocked: 惊涛～浪 stormy waves; turbulent waters | ～人听闻 monstrous; astounding; shocking

【骇怪】hàiguài 惊讶；惊诧 be shocked; be astonished

【骇怕】hàipà same as 害怕 hài//pà

【骇然】hàirán 惊讶的样子 gasping with astonishment; be struck dumb with amazement: ～失色 turn pale with astonishment; be flabbergasted | ～不知所措 be struck dumb and helpless

【骇人听闻】hài rén tīng wén 使人听了非常吃惊（多指社会上发生的坏事 oft. on hearing about sth. evil）astounding; shocking; appalling; terrifying; horrifying; shocking to the ear

【骇异】hàiyì 惊讶；惊异 be shocked; be astonished

氦 hài 气体元素，符号 He (helium)。无色无臭无味，在大气中含量极少，化学性质极不活泼。可用来填充灯泡和霓虹灯管，也用来制造泡沫塑料。液态的氦常用做冷却剂。helium (He); colourless, odourless inert gaseous element found in rare amounts in the atmosphere, used to fill light bulbs and neon tubes, and to produce foam. Liquid helium is often used as a refrigerant. 通称 commonly known as 氦气 hàiqì

害 hài ❶ 祸害；害处 harm; damage; disadvantage; calamity (跟'利、益'相对 as opposed to 'benefit, advantage'): 灾～ disaster; calamity | 虫～ insect pests | 为民除～ rid the people of a scourge | 吸烟对身体有～。Smoking is bad for one's health. ❷ 有害的 harmful; destructive; injurious (跟'益'相对 as opposed to 'beneficial')：～虫 pest|～鸟 harmful bird ❸ 使受损害 do harm to; impair; cause trouble to：～人不浅 do people great harm; cause (inflict) deep injury to sb.|你把地址搞错了，～得我白跑了一趟。You gave me the wrong address and made me go all that way for nothing. ❹ 杀害 kill; murder：遇～ be killed or assassinated ❺ 发生疾病 contract; or suffer from (an illness)：～眼 suffer from eye trouble or disease|～了一场大病 contract a serious illness; fall seriously ill; be seized by a severe illness ❻ 发生不安的情绪 feel uneasy (ashamed, afraid, etc.)：～羞 be shy|～怕 be afraid

〈古 *arch.*〉same as 曷 hé

【害病】hài//bìng same as 生病 shēng//bìng

【害虫】hàichóng 对人有害的昆虫。有的传染疾病，如苍蝇、蚊子，有的危害农作物，如蝗虫、螟虫、棉蚜。pest; vermin; varmint; injurious (or destructive) insects that either spread disease (e.g. flies and mosquitoes) or destroy crops (e.g. locusts, snout moth's larvae, cotton aphids, etc.)

【害处】hài·chu 对人或事物不利的因素；坏处 harm; damage; disadvantage

【害口】hài//kǒu〈方 *dial.*〉same as 害喜 hài//xǐ

【害鸟】hàiniǎo 以农作物或果树的果实和种子为主要食物的鸟类，如斑鸠。此外有些鸟吃鱼苗，也是害鸟，如翠鸟。harmful (destructive, pernicious) bird; birds that mainly eat crops or fruits and fruit seeds (e.g. turtledove), or eats fish (e.g. kingfisher)

【害怕】hài//pà 遇到困难、危险等而心中不安或发慌 scary; be afraid (in the face of difficulties or risks); be scared; have a dread of; be in fear of; have (get) cold feet：～走夜路 be afraid to go out at night|洞里阴森森的，叫人～。The charnel cave is spooky.

【害群之马】hài qún zhī mǎ〈比喻 *fig.*〉危害集体的人 black sheep; rotten apple in the barrel; pests of society; evil horse of the herd — one who brings disgrace on or constitutes a danger to one's group

【害人虫】hàirénchóng〈比喻 *fig.*〉害人的人 pest; vermin; evil creature; annoying person

【害臊】hài//sào same as 害羞 hài//xiū

【害兽】hàishòu 损害农作物，破坏森林、草原，危害家畜、家禽或传染疾病的各种兽类，如鼠、獾、狼、野猪、黑熊等 vermin; varmint; harmful (or destructive) creature that either destroys crops and forests, endanger livestock and poultry or spreads epidemics, e.g. mouse, badger, wolf, boar, black bear, etc.

【害喜】hài//xǐ 因怀孕而恶心、呕吐、食欲异常。有的地区说害口。suffer from morning sickness; (of pregnant women) feel sick, vomit or exhibit unusual food cravings; also 害口 hàikǒu in some regions

【害羞】hài//xiū 因胆怯、怕生或做错了事怕人嗤笑而心中不安；怕难为情 be bashful; be shy; feel uneasy or nervous out of timidity, shyness or fear of being laughed at for one's mistakes：她是第一次当众讲话，有些～。This was the first time that she ever spoke before a crowd, so she was a bit nervous.|你平时很老练，怎么这会儿倒害起羞来了？How come an experienced person like you feels shy now?

【害眼】hài//yǎn 患眼病 have eye trouble

嗐 hài〈叹词 *interj.*〉表示伤感、惋惜、悔恨等 [expressing sadness, regret or remorse]：～！他怎么病成这个样子。Oh dear, how come he is so seriously ill?

hān（ㄏㄢ）

顸 hān〈方 *dial.*〉same as 粗 cū①：这线太～，换根细一点儿的。This thread is too thick. Please give me a finer one.

【顸实】hān·shi〈方 *dial.*〉(物体)粗而结实 thick and solid：把挺～的一根棍子弄折了 break a thick and sturdy stick

犴 hān〈方 *dial.*〉驼鹿 elk; moose

蚶 hān same as 蚶子 hān·zi

【蚶田】hāntián 沿海养殖蚶子的田 clam breeding ground; clam-bed; field for breeding blood clams along the coast

【蚶子】hān·zi 软体动物，壳厚而坚硬，外表淡褐色，有瓦垄状的纵线，内壁白色，边缘有锯齿。肉可食。blood clam (*Arca anadara*); type of mollusk with a thick, hard hazel shell resembling rows of roof tiles, white inside, saw-toothed edge, and edible meat; also 瓦垄子 wǎlǒng·zi or 瓦楞子 wǎléng·zi

酣 hān ❶ 饮酒尽兴 (drink, etc.) to one's heart's content：～饮 be given to heavy drinking|半～ half drunk; somewhat tipsy|酒～耳热 heated with wine ❷ 泛指尽兴、畅快 (in a broad sense) merry and lively：～歌 sing to one's heart's content; sing lustily|～睡 sleep soundly

【酣畅】hānchàng same as 畅快 chàngkuài：喝得～ be merry and lively with drink|睡得很～ be sound asleep

【酣梦】hānmèng 酣畅的睡梦；熟睡 sweet dream; sound sleep; deep sleep

【酣眠】hānmián same as 熟睡 shúshuì

【酣然】hānrán 酣畅的样子 merrily (drunk); sound (asleep)：～大醉 be merrily drunk; be as drunk as a lord|～入梦 fall into a deep sleep

【酣睡】hānshuì same as 熟睡 shúshuì

【酣饮】hānyǐn same as 畅饮 chàngyìn

【酣战】hānzhàn 激烈战斗 hard-fought battle;

fierce battle：两军～ two armies locked in fierce battle

憨 hān ❶ 傻；痴呆 foolish；silly：～痴 idiotic；stupid | ～笑 simper；smile fatuously ❷ 朴实；天真 straightforward；naive；ingenuous；innocent：～直 honest and upright | ～厚 simple and honest | ～态可掬 charmingly naive ❸（Hān）姓 a surname

【憨厚】hān·hòu 老实厚道 straightforward and good-natured；simple and honest：心地～ be simple and honest in nature

【憨实】hānshí 憨厚老实 simple and honest；straightforward and good-natured：为人纯朴～ be honest and unsophisticated

【憨态】hāntài 天真而略显傻气的神态 air of charming naivety：～可掬 charmingly naive

【憨笑】hānxiào 傻笑；天真地笑 smile fatuously；simper；smile naively

【憨直】hānzhí 憨实直爽 honest and straightforward

【憨子】hān·zi 〈方 *dial.*〉傻子；傻瓜 fool；blockhead；simpleton

鼾 hān 睡着时粗重的呼吸 snore；deep and noisy breathing while asleep：～声 sound of snoring | 打～ snore

【鼾声】hānshēng 打呼噜的声音 the sound of snoring：～如雷 snore thunderously

【鼾睡】hānshuì 熟睡而打呼噜 be sound asleep and snoring

hán（ㄏㄢˊ）

邗 hán 邗江（Hánjiāng），地名，在江苏 Hanjiang，name of a county in Jiangsu Province

汗 hán 可汗（kèhán）的简称 abbr. for 可汗 kèhán；king of ancient mongol tribes

☞ hàn on p.766

邯 hán 邯郸（Hándān），地名，在河北 name of a place in Hebei Province

【邯郸学步】Hándān xué bù 战国时有个燕国人到赵国都城邯郸去，看到那里的人走路的姿势很美，就跟着人家学，结果不但没学会，连自己原来的走法也忘掉了，只好爬着回去（见于《庄子·秋水》）。后来用'邯郸学步'比喻模仿别人不成，反而丧失了原有的技能。learn the Handan walk — lose the ability one already has in trying to acquire a new trick (originally from the parable in *Zhuangzi · Autumn Floods* about a man from the state of Yan, who went to Handan, capital of the state of Zhao, and, taking a fancy to the graceful way the local people walked, began to learn the ropes, but, before he could master what the Handan people had to teach him, he forgot his own way of walking and had to crawl all the way back home)；attempt to walk like a swan, the crow loses its own gait；imitate sb. without success, and lose one's own individuality

含 hán ❶ 东西放在嘴里，不咽下也不吐出 keep or hold (sth.) in the mouth (neither swallowing nor spitting it out)：～一口水 hold water in one's mouth | ～着青果 hold a Chinese olive in one's mouth ❷ 藏在里面；包括在内；容纳 contain：～着眼泪 with tears in one's eyes | 这种梨～水分很多。These pears are very juicy. | 工龄满三十年以上（～三十年）者均可申请。Anyone who has worked 30 years or more is eligible to apply. ❸ 带着某种意思、情感等，不完全表露出来 harbour；hold or nurse (certain idea, feeling, etc.), without expressing：～怒 with suppressed anger | ～羞 bashful | ～笑 with a smile

【含苞】hánbāo 裹着花苞 in bud：～待放 (of buds) ready to burst into bloom；(of a girl, etc.) in early puberty

【含悲】hánbēi 怀着悲痛或悲伤 be filled with deep sorrow：～忍泪 hold back one's sorrow and choke down one's tears | ～饮泣 sob pitifully

【含垢忍辱】hán gòu rěn rǔ 忍受耻辱 endure contempt and insults；bear shame and humiliation with patience；eat dirt；eat humble pie；be patient under ignominy；passively swallow every insult；silently endure all disgrace and humiliation

【含恨】hán//hèn 怀着怨恨或仇恨 nurse a grievance or hatred；hold a grudge；be full of resentment：～终生 die holding onto a lifelong regret | ～离开了人世 die unavenged

【含胡】hán·hu same as 含糊 hán·hu

【含糊】hán·hu ❶ 不明确；不清晰 ambiguous；vague：～其辞 equivocate；prevaricate；talk ambiguously | 他的话很～，不明白是什么意思。He was so vague, that I don't know what he really meant. ❷ 不认真；马虎 careless；perfunctory：这事一点儿也不能～。We'll have to handle the matter with meticulous care. ❸ 示弱（多用于否定 mostly used in the negative）display a white feather；show one's weakness or cowardice：要比就比，我绝不～。Let's have a contest if you want, since I'm not one to turn tail. ‖ also 含胡 hán·hu

【含混】hánhùn 模糊；不明确 indistinct；ambiguous；vague：～不清 unclear and inarticulate | 言辞～，令人费解 speak so ambiguously as to be barely intelligible

【含量】hánliàng 一种物质中所包含的某种成分的数量 content；quantity of an ingredient contained in a substance：这种食品的脂肪～很高。This kind of food has a high fat contents.

【含怒】hán//nù 有怒气而没有发作 with suppressed anger

【含情】hánqíng 脸上带着或内心怀着情意、情感(多指爱情 usu. of lovers) exude love; cherish affection or tender feelings (for sb. or sth.): ～脉脉; languishing; (soft eyes) exuding tenderness and love; (of young women in love) full of silently conveyed tenderness; full of tender affection; very much enamored

【含沙射影】hán shā shè yǐng 传说水中有一种叫蜮的怪物,看到人的影子就喷沙子,被喷着的人就会得病 legend has it that *yu*, a river monster, sprays sand from its mouth at the shadows of people, who then fall ill as a result;〈比喻 *fig.*〉暗地里诽谤中伤 make allusions and innuendoes about sb.; attack by innuendo; insinuate; name the lime tree and really mean the acacia

【含笑】hán//xiào 面带笑容 smilingly; wear a smile; smile; with a smile: ～点头 nod with a smile|～于九泉 smile in the underworld — one who has nothing to regret in life; smile in one's grave; die contented; go happily into the netherworld

【含辛茹苦】hán xīn rú kǔ 经受艰辛困苦 endure hardship and eat bitterness; undergo all sorts of hardships and deprivations; suffer untold hardships and privations; endure suffering (茹 *ru*:吃 eat); also 茹苦含辛 rú kǔ hán xīn

【含羞】hán//xiū 脸上带着害羞的神情 bashfully; with a shy look: ～不语 be silent with shame; be too shy to speak; withdraw into one's shell|～而去 leave with shame

【含蓄】hánxù ❶ same as 包含 bāohán: 简短的话语,却～着深刻的意义。His words are few but pregnant with profound meaning. ❷(言语、诗文)意思含而不露,耐人寻味 (of remarks, writings) implicit; veiled ❸(思想、感情)不轻易流露 (of ideas, feelings) reserved: 性格～ reserved in nature ‖ also 涵蓄 hánxù

【含血喷人】hán xuè pēn rén〈比喻 *fig.*〉捏造事实,诬赖别人 make slanderous accusations (charges) against others; make vicious attacks; hurt sb. with malicious words; throw dirt (mud) at sb.; venomously slander sb.; slur sb.'s good name

【含饴弄孙】hán yí nòng sūn 含着糖逗小孙子。形容老年人闲适生活的乐趣。play with one's grandchildren while chewing maltose; spend one's remaining years happily in the company of grandchildren; enjoy a happy and leisurely old age; lead a carefree life in one's old age

【含义】hányì (词句等)所包含的意义 (of words, sentences, etc.) meaning; implication; import; message: ～深奥 with profound implications; also 涵义 hányì

【含意】hányì (诗文、说话等)含有的意思 (of poems, remarks, etc.) implied meaning: 猜不透她这话的～。I don't know what she could have been driving at with this remark.

【含英咀华】hán yīng jǔ huá〈比喻 *fig.*〉琢磨和领会诗文的要点和精神 relish the beauty and joy of literature; enjoy the beauty of words; study and grasp the essence of sth.

【含冤】hán//yuān 有冤未申 suffer an injustice; suffer a wrong; be the victim of a false or unjust charge: ～而死 die uncleared of a false charge; die with one's name uncleared

【含蕴】hányùn 含有(某种思想、感情等);包含 bear (certain ideas, feelings, etc.); contain: 一番话～着丰富的哲理。His remarks contained a wealth of philosophical implications.

函(圅) hán ❶〈书 *fml.*〉匣;封套 case; casket; envelope: 石～ stone casket|镜～ case for a mirror|这部《全唐诗》分成十二～。This set of *Complete Tang Poetry* comes in twelve cases. ❷ 信件 letter: 公～ official letter|来～ incoming letter|～授 teach by correspondence|～购 mail order

【函电】hándiàn 信和电报的总称 general term for letter and telegram

【函告】hángào 用书信告诉 inform by letter: 行期如有变化,当及时～。I shall write to you in time should my date of departure change.

【函购】hángòu 用通信方式向生产或经营的单位购买 purchase by mail; mail order: ～电视英语教材 purchase TV English textbooks by mail|开展～业务 start a mail-order service

【函件】hánjiàn same as 信件 xìnjiàn

【函授】hánshòu 以通信辅导为主的教学方式(区别于'面授' as compared with 'instruct directly') teach mainly through correspondence; give a correspondence course: ～生 a correspondence (postal) course student|～教材 correspondence textbooks

【函授教育】hánshòu jiàoyù 以通讯方式开展教学的教育。学生以自学函授教材为主,并由函授学校给以辅导和考核。correspondence education; education conducted via correspondence, where students study the correspondence textbooks mainly by themselves while the correspondence school provides tutorship and examinations

【函数】hánshù 在某一变化过程中,两个变量 x、y,对于某一范围内的 x 的每一个值,y 都有确定的值和它对应,y 就是 x 的函数。这种关系一般用 $y=f(x)$ 来表示。function; two variables x and y related to each other so that for each value assumed by x there is a value determined for y, and y is called a function of x, usu. expressed in the equation $y=f(x)$

【函索】hánsuǒ 用通信方式索取(宣传品、资料等) request (brochures, ads, etc.) by letter: 本公司备有产品说明书,～即寄。A catalogue of our products is available upon request.

浛 hán 浛洸(Hánguāng),地名,在广东 Hanguang, name of a place in Guangdong Province

琀 hán〈书 *fml.*〉死者口中所含的珠玉 jade piece put in the mouth of the dead upon burial

晗 hán〈书 *fml.*〉天将明 dawn; daybreak

焓 hán 热学上表示物质系统能量状态的一个状态参数。数值等于系统的内能加上压强与体积的乘积。enthalpy; total heat; heat content; sensible heat; thermodynamic parameter used to express energy status of the physical system, equivalent to the sum of the internal energy of the system plus the product of its volume, multiplied by the pressure exerted on it by its surroundings; also 热函 rèhán

涵 hán ❶ 包含;包容 contain: ～养 virtue of patience|海～ be magnanimous enough to forgive or tolerate (sb.'s errors or shortcomings) ❷ 指涵洞 culvert: 桥～(桥和涵洞) bridges and culverts

【涵洞】hándòng 公路或铁路与沟渠相交的地方使水从路下流过的通道,作用和桥类似,但一般孔径较小 culvert; transverse drain or waterway, as under a road or railway, that functions like a bridge to facilitate the flow of water, but generally with smaller openings

【涵盖】hángài 包括;包容 cover; encompass; contain; embody: 作品题材很广,～了社会各个领域。The book has a broad theme which covers all walks of life.

【涵管】hánguǎn ❶ 用来砌涵洞等的管子 culvert pipe; pipes for making culverts ❷ 管状的涵洞 pipe-shaped culvert

【涵容】hánróng〈书 *fml.*〉包容;包涵 excuse; forgive; bear with: 不周之处,尚望～。Please forgive us for being such poor hosts.

【涵蓄】hánxù same as 含蓄 hánxù

【涵养】hányǎng ❶ 能控制情绪的功夫 self-restraint; ability to control oneself; virtue of patience; same as 修养 xiūyǎng②: 很有～ know how to exercise self-control; never allow oneself to be provoked ❷ 蓄积并保持(水分等) conserve (water, etc.); (water) retention: 用造林来～水源 conserve water through afforestation|改良土壤结构,～地力 improve soil structure to conserve soil fertility

【涵义】hányì same as 含义 hányì

【涵闸】hánzhá 涵洞和水闸的总称 general term for culvert and sluice

韩(韓) Hán ❶ 周朝国名,在今河南中部和山西东南部 Han, state in the Zhou Dynasty, in present-day central Henan Province and southeast Shanxi Province ❷ 姓 a surname

寒 hán ❶ 冷(跟'暑'相对 as opposed to 'hot') cold; frigid; chilly: ～冬 cold winter|～风 chilly wind|天～地冻。The weather is cold and the ground is frozen.|受了一点～ catch a slight cold; catch a chill ❷ 害怕;畏惧 be stricken with terror; tremble with fear: 心～ be bitterly disappointed|胆～ be terrified; be stricken with panic ❸ 穷困 poor; needy: 贫～ impoverished; poverty-stricken

【寒蝉】hánchán ❶ 天冷时不再叫或叫声低微的蝉 cicada in cold weather (which can no longer make any or much noise): ～凄切 plaintive droning of a cicada in cold weather|噤若～ as silent as a cicada in cold weather — keep quiet out of fear ❷ 蝉的一种,身体小,黑色,有黄绿色的斑点,翅膀透明。雄的有发音器,夏末秋初时在树上叫。a kind of small black cicada with transparent wings and yellowish green flecks; the male ones have sound organs and sing loudly in the trees towards the end of summer and beginning of fall

【寒潮】háncháo 从北方寒冷地带向南方侵袭的冷空气,寒潮过境时气温显著下降,时常带来雨、雪或大风,过境后往往发生霜冻 cold spell; polar outbreak; cold-air outbreak; cold air invading the south from the cold regions in the north, typically bringing about a sudden drop in temperature and often also rain, snow or strong winds as it passes by, and frost immediately after

【寒伧】hán·chen same as 寒碜 hán·chen

【寒碜】hán·chen ❶ 丑陋;难看 ugly; unsightly; shabby: 这孩子长得不～。This child is not at all bad-looking. ❷ 丢脸;不体面 disreputable; disgraceful; shameful: 全班同学就我不及格,真～! I was the only one in the class who failed the exam. What a disgrace! ❸ 讥笑,揭人短处,使失去体面 ridicule; make fun of; put to shame: 你这是存心～我。You mean to put me to shame, don't you? |叫人～了一顿 be ridiculed by sb.

【寒窗】hánchuāng〈比喻 *fig.*〉艰苦的读书生活 cold window — hard conditions under which a poor scholar studies: 十年～ ten years' of study in straitened circumstances; long years of hard study (of a student or a scholar)

【寒带】hándài 南极圈、北极圈以内的地带,气候寒冷。近两极的地方,半年是白天,半年是黑夜。frigid zone; cold zone; zones within the Antarctic and the Arctic Circles with frigid weather, and areas near the two poles that have long days for half the year and long nights for the other half

【寒冬】hándōng 寒冷的冬天;冬季 cold or freezing winter; winter

【寒冬腊月】hán dōng làyuè 指农历十二月天气最冷的时候。泛指寒冷的冬季。the jaws of

winter (12th month of the lunar calendar); (in a broad sense) severe winter; dead of winter; freezing winter

【寒光】hánguāng 使人感觉寒冷或害怕的光(多形容刀剑等反射的光) chilling light or gleam oft. referring to reflected light (of a sword, moonlight, etc.); pallid light (of the moon); dazzling gleam (of a sword): 刺刀闪着～。The bayonets had a deathly gleam. | 眼睛射出两道凶狠的～。The fierce glare in his eyes chills one to the bone.

【寒假】hánjià 学校中冬季的假期,在一二月间 winter vacation during a school year, usu. between January and February

【寒螀】hánjiāng 古书上说的一种蝉 a kind of cicada (referred to in ancient books)

【寒噤】hánjìn 因受冷或受惊而身体颤动 shiver or shudder (with cold or fear); tremble: 打～ have (get) the shivers; experience a chill shooting through oneself

【寒苦】hánkǔ 贫穷困苦 destitute; poverty-stricken; in difficult financial straits: 家境～ (come from) a destitute family; with one's family in straitened circumstances

【寒来暑往】hán lái shǔ wǎng 炎夏过去,寒冬来临。指时光流逝。passing of summer and coming of winter; passage of time; year in, year out

【寒冷】hánlěng same as 冷 lěng①: 气候～ have a cold climate | ～的季节 the cold season

【寒流】hánliú ❶ 从高纬度流向低纬度的洋流。寒流的水温比它所到区域的水温低。cold ocean current flowing from high latitudes to low latitudes, with lower water temperatures than those in the destination zones ❷ 指寒潮 cold wave

【寒露】hánlù 二十四节气之一,在10月8日或9日 Cold Dew, the 17th of the 24 solar terms that falls on October 8 or 9; ☞ 节气 jié·qi on p. 989 and 二十四节气 èrshísì jiéqì on p. 516

【寒毛】hán·máo 人体皮肤表面上的细毛 fine hair or down on the surface of human skin; (图见 ☞ figure for 皮肤 pífū on p. 1464)

【寒门】hánmén 〈书 *fml.*〉❶ 贫寒的家庭。旧时多用来谦称自己的家。(usu. hum. in old times) my poor family; my humble family ❷ 微贱的家庭 humble family; lowly family: 出身～ be born into a humble family; be of lowly origins

【寒气】hánqì ❶ 冷的气流 cold; cold air; cold draught: ～逼人。There is a nip in the air. ❷ 指因受冻而产生的冷的感觉 chill one feels as a result of exposure to cold weather: 喝口酒去去～ drink some liquor to take the chill off the body

【寒峭】hánqiào 〈书 *fml.*〉形容冷气逼人 chilly; icy: 北风～ piercing north wind

【寒秋】hánqiū same as 深秋 shēnqiū

【寒热】hánrè ❶〈中医 *Chin. med.*〉指身体发冷发烧的症状 chills and fever ❷〈方 *dial.*〉same as 发烧 fā//shāo

【寒色】hánsè 给人以寒冷感的颜色,如青、绿、紫 cold or cool colour; colour that makes one feel cool or cold, e.g. blue, green, purple

【寒舍】hánshè 〈谦辞 *hum.*〉对人称自己的家 my humble home; my humble abode: 请光临～一叙。May I invite you to my humble home for a chat?

【寒食】Hánshí 节名,在清明前一天。古人从这一天起,三天不生火做饭,所以叫寒食。有的地区清明叫寒食。Cold Food Festival, beginning on the day before Qingming or Pure Brightness (usu. on April 5 or 6), when only cold food was served for three days in ancient times; in some areas, it is another name for Qingming

【寒士】hánshì 〈书 *fml.*〉贫穷的读书人 poor scholar; scholar of little means

【寒暑】hánshǔ ❶ 冷和热 cold and heat: ～表 thermometer ❷ 冬天和夏天,常用来表示整个一年 winter and summer — a whole year: ～易节 with seasonal changes; with the passage of time | 经历了十五个～才完成这部书稿。He spent a total of 15 years writing this book.

【寒暑表】hánshǔbiǎo 测量气温的一种温度计,表上刻度通常分华氏、摄氏两种 thermometer; instrument for measuring atmospheric temperature, usually based either on the calibrations of Fahrenheit or of Centigrade (Celsius)

【寒素】hánsù 〈书 *fml.*〉❶ 清贫 impoverished; poor; destitute: 家世～ be from an impoverished family ❷ 清贫的人 poor people; people of limited means or humble origins: 拔擢～ promote people of humble origins ❸ 朴素;简陋 simple; plain; crude: 衣装～ plainly dressed

【寒酸】hánsuān ❶ 形容穷苦读书人的不大方的姿态 (as of a poor scholar) shabby and miserable: ～相 look shabby and miserable | ～气 an air of shabbiness ❷ 形容简陋或过于俭朴而显得不体面 too simple to be respectable, too shabby to be handsome: 穿得太～了 be shabbily dressed

【寒腿】hántuǐ 腿部的风湿性关节炎 rheumatism in the legs

【寒微】hánwēi 指家世、出身贫苦,社会地位低下 of low station; of humble origins: 出身～ be of humble origins

【寒心】hán//xīn ❶ 因失望而痛心 be bitterly disappointed; be disillusioned: 孩子这样不争气,真叫人～。It is bitterly disappointing to have such a child who has always let us down. ❷ 害怕 be afraid; be fearful

【寒星】hánxīng 指寒夜的星斗 stars on a cold night: ～点点 twinkling stars on the cold night|～闪烁。Stars were twinkling on that frozen night.

【寒暄】hánxuān 见面时谈天气冷暖之类的应酬话 exchange of pleasantries; engage in small talk about the weather; pass the time of day: 宾主～了一阵，便转入正题。After exchanging pleasantries, host and guest got down to business.

【寒衣】hányī 御寒的衣服，如棉衣、棉裤等 winter clothing, e.g. cotton-padded coat and trousers, etc.

【寒意】hányì 寒冷的感觉 feel of cold: 深秋的夜晚，风吹在身上，已有几分～。There was quite a nip in the air as the late-autumn wind rose in the evening.

【寒战】hánzhàn same as 寒噤 hánjìn: 一阵冷风吹来，她禁不住打了个～。She couldn't help shivering as a gust of cold wind rose. also 寒颤 hánzhàn

【寒颤】hánzhàn same as 寒战 hánzhàn

hǎn（ㄏㄢˇ）

罕 hǎn ❶ 稀少 rarely; seldom: 希～ cherish|～见 rarely seen|～闻 rarely or seldom heard of|～有 rarely found|人迹～至 show little trace of human habitation ❷ (Hǎn) 姓 a surname

【罕觏】hǎngòu 〈书 *fml.*〉难得遇见 rarely encountered; meet rarely

【罕见】hǎnjiàn 难得见到；很少见到 seldom seen; rare: 人迹～ show little trace of human habitation|～的奇迹 rarely seen miracle

【罕有】hǎnyǒu 很少有 very rare; unusual; exceptional: 古今～ rarely ever found

喊 hǎn ❶ 大声叫 shout; cry out; yell: ～口号 shout slogans ❷ 叫(人) call (sb.): 你去～他一声。Go and give him a shout. ❸〈方 *dial.*〉称呼 address (sb.); call: 论辈分他要～我姨妈。He should call me 'aunt' based on our positions in the family hierarchy.

【喊话】hǎn//huà 在前沿阵地上对敌人大声宣传或劝降 shout propaganda to enemy troops across the frontline

【喊叫】hǎnjiào 大声叫 shout; cry out: 大声～ shout; scream

【喊嗓子】hǎn sǎng·zi 戏曲演员锻炼嗓子，不用乐器伴奏，多在空旷的地方进行 train (or exercise) one's voice by shouting or singing loudly (as traditional opera singers do in an open space early in the morning, unaccompanied by instruments)

【喊冤】hǎn//yuān 诉说冤枉 cry out grievances: ～叫屈 cry out one's grievances; complain loudly about an alleged injustice

㘎（闞）hǎn 〈书 *fml.*〉虎叫声 (of a tiger) roar; growl

☞ 阚 Kàn on p. 1082

hàn（ㄏㄢˋ）

汉[1]（漢）Hàn ❶ 朝代，公元前 206—公元 220，刘邦所建 Han Dynasty (206 B.C.-A.D. 220), established by Liu Bang; ☞ 西汉 Xī Hàn on p. 2042 and 东汉 Dōng Hàn on p. 463 ❷ same as 后汉 Hòu Hàn ② ❸ 元末农民起义领袖陈友谅所建的政权（公元 1360-1363）Han Regime (1360-1363) established by the peasant uprising led by Chen Youliang in the late Yuan Dynasty ❹ 汉族 Han ethnic group: ～人 Han people; the Hans|～语 Chinese (language) ❺(hàn) 男子 man: 老～ old man|好～ brave fellow; real man|英雄～ hero; brave man|彪形大～ strapper

汉[2]（漢）hàn 指银河 Milky Way; Silver River: 银～ Milky Way; Silver River

【汉白玉】hànbáiyù 一种白色的大理石，可以做建筑和雕刻的材料 white marble, used as building and carving material

【汉堡包】hànbǎobāo 夹牛肉、乳酪等的圆面包 (translit. of hamburger) bun with a patty of ground meat, cheese, etc. in between

【汉调】hàndiào 汉剧的旧称 old name for Hubei Opera

【汉奸】hànjiān 原指汉族的败类，后泛指投靠侵略者、出卖国家民族利益的中华民族的败类 traitor (of China); quisling (of China); orig. a traitor to the Han people; later used to refer to Chinese who threw themselves into the lap of an aggressor and betrayed the interest of the Chinese nation

【汉剧】hànjù 湖北地方戏曲剧种之一，腔调以西皮、二黄为主，流行于湖北全省和河南、陕西、湖南的部分地区，历史较久，对京剧的形成有很大的影响 *Hanju* Opera; Hubei opera, with a long history and with *xipi* and *erhuang* (two major types of music in traditional Chinese opera) as its main melodic patterns; popular throughout Hubei Province and parts of Henan, Shaanxi and Hunan provinces, and having a major influence to the rise of Peking Opera; 旧称 also 汉调 hàndiào in former times

【汉民】Hànmín 指汉族人 Han people; the Han

【汉人】Hànrén ❶ 汉族；汉族人 the Han; Han people ❷ 指西汉、东汉时代的人 people of the Han Dynasty (206 B.C.-A.D. 220)

【汉文】Hànwén ❶ same as 汉语 Hànyǔ: ～翻译 translation into and from Chinese|译成～ translate into Chinese ❷ same as 汉字 Hànzì: 学写～ learn to write Chinese

【汉姓】hànxìng ❶ 汉族的姓 used by the Han people ❷ 特指非汉族的人所用的汉族的姓

Han surnames adopted by other ethnic groups

【汉学】hànxué ❶ 汉代人研究经学着重名物、训诂，后世因而称研究经、史、名物、训诂、考据之学为汉学 study of Chinese classics; Han Dynasty school of classical philology, including the study of Confucianist classics, history, naming and description of objects, explanations of words in ancient books and textual research, so named because people of the Han Dynasty were known for their particular emphasis on the names and descriptions of objects and the explanations of words in the study of classical literature ❷ 外国人指研究中国的文化、历史、语言、文学等方面的学问 Sinology; study outside China of Chinese culture, history, language and literature

【汉语】Hànyǔ 汉族的语言，是我国的主要语言。现代汉语的标准语是普通话。Chinese; language spoken by the Han people, the major language spoken in China; standard contemporary Chinese language is Putonghua; ☞ 普通话 pǔtōnghuà on p. 1501

【汉语拼音方案】Hànyǔ Pīnyīn Fāng'àn 给汉字注音和拼写普通话语音的方案，1958 年 2 月 11 日第一届全国人民代表大会第五次会议批准。这方案采用拉丁字母，并用附加符号表示声调，是帮助学习汉字和推广普通话的工具。*pinyin*; Scheme for the Chinese Phonetic Alphabet; formally adopted on 11 February 1958, at the 5th Session of the 1st National People's Congress, using the Latin alphabet with some additional symbols to indicate tones; *pinyin* is a helpful tool for learning Chinese characters and popularising standard Chinese

【汉子】hàn·zi ❶ 男子 man; fellow ❷〈方 *dial.*〉丈夫 husband

【汉字】Hànzì 记录汉语的文字。除极个别的例外，都是一个汉字代表一个音节。Chinese (written) character; with a few exceptions, one Chinese character corresponds to one syllable

【汉族】Hànzú 我国人数最多的民族，分布在全国各地 Han nationality, or the Han; China's main nationality, distributed all over the country

扞[1] hàn same as 捍 hàn

扞[2] hàn [扞格](hàngé)〈书 *fml.*〉互相抵触 mutual conflict: ～不入 incompatible with; out of tune with

☞ 擀 gǎn on p. 633

闬 hàn〈书 *fml.*〉❶ 里巷的门 gate to an alley or lane; entrance gate to a block of houses ❷ 墙垣 wall

汗 hàn 人或高等动物从皮肤排泄出来的液体，是皮肤散热的主要方式 sweat; perspiration; fluid excreted through the pores of the skin of humans or higher animal forms

☞ hán on p. 761

【汗斑】hànbān same as 汗碱 hànjiǎn

【汗褂儿】hànguàr same as 汗衫 hànshān ①

【汗碱】hànjiǎn 汗干后留在衣帽等上面的白色痕迹 sweat stain; white stain left on clothes or hats when sweat has dry

【汗津津】hànjīnjīn (～的 hànjīnjīn·de)形容微微出汗的样子 sweaty; damp (wet) with sweat: ～的头发 sweaty hair | 脸上～的 sweaty face

【汗孔】hànkǒng 汗腺在皮肤表面的开口，汗从这里排泄出来 pore; openings of the sweat glands on the surface of the skin through which sweat may pass; also 毛孔 máokǒng

【汗淋淋】hànlīnlīn (～的 hànlīnlīn·de)形容汗水往下流的样子 dripping with perspiration; soaked with sweat: 他跑得浑身～的。He was dripping with sweat from running all the way.

【汗流浃背】hàn liú jiā bèi 汗水湿透了背上的衣服。形容汗出得很多。perspire all over; sweat profusely; sweat streaming down and drenching one's back — be soaked with sweat

【汗马功劳】hàn mǎ gōngláo 指战功。也泛指大的功劳。distinctions won in battle; war exploits; (in a broad sense) grand contributions or meritorious services (汗马 *han ma*: 将士骑马作战，马累得出汗 sweating horses carrying sweating warriors)

【汗漫】hànmàn〈书 *fml.*〉❶ 广泛，无边际 wide-ranging; rambling; wide of the mark: ～之言 irrelevant remarks; rambling talk ❷ 形容水势浩荡 vast and mighty flow of water

【汗毛】hànmáo same as 寒毛 hán·máo

【汗牛充栋】hàn niú chōng dòng 形容书籍极多 enough books to make a pack-ox sweat or to fill a house to the rafters — an immense collection of books (汗牛 *han niu*: 用牛运输，牛累得出汗 make the ox carrying the books perspire; 充栋 *chong dong*: 堆满了屋子 fill a house to the rafters)

【汗青】hànqīng ❶〈古时 *arch.*〉在竹简上记事，采来青色的竹子，要用火烤得竹板冒出水分才容易书写，因此后世把著作完成叫做汗青 sweating green bamboo strips — completion of a literary undertaking (referring to the ancient practice of sweating green bamboo strips on the fire before writing on them) ❷ same as 史册 shǐcè

【汗衫】hànshān ❶ 一种上身穿的薄内衣 T-shirt; thin undershirt ❷〈方 *dial.*〉衬衫 shirt; vest

【汗水】hànshuǐ 汗 (指较多的 esp. in large amounts) perspiration: ～湿透衣衫 with one's shirt soaked in sweat

【汗褟儿】hàntār〈方 *dial.*〉夏天贴身穿的中式小褂 Chinese-style singlet or vest

【汗腺】hànxiàn 皮肤中分泌汗的腺体。汗腺受交感神经的支配，分泌量随外界温度和心理状态的变化而增减。sweat gland; tubular glands in the human skin that are manipulated by sympathetic nerves and secrete perspiration in quantities that rise and fall with changes in the temperature outside and one's psychological state; (图见 ☞ figure for 皮肤 pífū on p. 1464)

【汗颜】hànyán 因羞惭而出汗。泛指惭愧 perspire from embarrassment or shame; blush with shame; feel ashamed: 深感～ feel humbled|～无地(羞愧得无地自容) be a humbling experience; can find no place to hide oneself from shame; feel too ashamed to show one's face

【汗液】hànyè same as 汗 hàn

【汗珠子】hànzhū·zi 成滴的汗 beads of sweat; also 汗珠儿 hànzhūr

【汗渍】hànzì 汗迹 sweat stain: 衬衣上留下一片片～。The shirt was left with patches of sweat stains.

旱 hàn ❶ 长时间没有降水或降水太少(多跟'涝'相对 usu. opposed to 'flood') drought; dry spell; long period of time with no rainfall or too little rainfall: ～灾 drought; severe drought causing famine|天～ dry weather|防～ prevent against drought|抗～ combat drought|庄稼～了。The crops dried up. ❷ 跟水无关的 not related to water: ～烟 tobacco (smoked in a long-stemmed Chinese pipe)|～伞 parasol|～冰 roller-skating ❸ 非水田的；陆地上的 dryland; land other than paddy fields: ～地 dry farmland|～稻 upland rice; dry rice|～獭 marmot|～船 land boat ❹ 指陆地交通 on land; by land: ～路 overland route|起～ take an overland route (usu. on foot)

【旱魃】hànbá 传说中引起旱灾的怪物 *hanba*, legendary demon of drought: ～为虐。The drought demon ran amok. *or* There was a severe drought.

【旱船】hànchuán ❶〈方 *dial.*〉园林中形状略像船的临水房屋 boat-shaped waterfront house in a garden ❷ 民间舞蹈'跑旱船'所用的船形道具 boat float; model boat used as a stage prop in some folk dances

【旱道】hàndào〈方 *dial.*〉(～儿 hàndàor) same as 旱路 hànlù

【旱稻】hàndào 种在旱地里的稻，抗旱能力比水稻强，根系比较发达，叶片较宽，米质软，光泽少 dry rice; upland rice; rice planted in dry land, with a well-developed root system, broad leaves, soft-textured grains that have little lustre; more capable of resisting drought than paddy rice; also 陆稻 lùdào

【旱地】hàndì same as 旱田 hàntián

【旱季】hànjì 不下雨或雨水少的季节 dry season; season with little or no rainfall

【旱井】hànjǐng ❶ 在水源缺少的地方为了积蓄雨水而挖的口小肚大的井 water-retention well; wide at the bottom and narrow at the top, usu. found in places with a severe shortages of water ❷ 像井的深洞，冬天用来贮藏蔬菜等 dry well; deep hole used to store vegetables in the winter

【旱涝保收】hàn lào bǎo shōu 不管发生旱灾还是涝灾，都能保证收成 ensure stable yields despite drought or excessive rain;〈比喻 *fig.*〉无论出现什么情况都能得到好处 gain benefit whatever happens; ensure a safe income

【旱路】hànlù 陆地上的交通路线 overland route

【旱桥】hànqiáo 横跨在经常没有水的山谷、河沟或城市交通要道上空的桥 viaduct; overpass; flyover; bridge over an often dry valley, brook or over the trunk lines of a city

【旱情】hànqíng (某个地区)干旱的情况 damage caused by drought; ravages of drought: 由于连日降雨，～已得到缓解。The drought has eased up thanks to several days of rain.

【旱伞】hànsǎn same as 阳伞 yángsǎn

【旱獭】hàntǎ 哺乳动物，全身棕灰色或带黄黑色，前肢的爪发达，善于掘土，成群穴居，有冬眠的习性。皮可制衣帽。旱獭是鼠疫杆菌的主要传播者。marmot (*Marmota Blumenbach*); tarabagan; brown-grey or slightly yellow-black hibernating mammal that has well-developed forelegs for digging the earth, living in burrows in colonies, and a major vector of yersinia pestis, its pelt used to make coats and hats; also 土拨鼠 tǔbōshǔ

【旱田】hàntián ❶ 土地表面不蓄水的田地，如种小麦、杂粮、棉花、花生等的田地 dry farmland; dry land; land with no water stored on the surface of the earth, e. g. land for planting wheat, coarse cereal, crops, cotton, peanut, etc. ❷ 浇不上水的耕地 non-irrigated land

【旱象】hànxiàng 干旱的现象 signs of drought: ～严重 signs of severe drought

【旱鸭子】hànyā·zi 指不会游泳的人(含诙谐意 hum.)duck raised on dry land; non-swimmer

【旱烟】hànyān 装在旱烟袋里吸的烟丝或碎烟叶 cut tobacco; chopped leaf tobacco (smoked in a long-stemmed Chinese pipe)

【旱烟袋】hànyāndài 一种吸烟用具，一般在细竹管的一端安着烟袋锅儿，可以装烟，另一端安着玉石、翡翠等的嘴儿，可以衔在嘴里吸。tobacco pipe; long-stemmed Chinese bamboo pipe, usu. with a bowl for filling with tobacco leaves, and a tip made of jade, jadeite, etc., at the other end, to be held in the mouth when smoking; 通称 commonly known as 烟袋 yāndài

【旱灾】hànzāi 由于长期干旱缺水造成作物枯死或大量减产的灾害 drought; severe damage to crops, or great reduction in yields, due to a long period of drought

垾 hàn 小堤,多用于地名 small dyke; mostly used in place names: 中~(在安徽) Zhonghan, name of a place in Anhui Province

捍 hàn 保卫;防御 defend; guard: ~卫 protect|~御 guard against

【捍卫】hànwèi same as 保卫 bǎowèi: ~领空 defend national airspace|~主权 uphold state sovereignty

【捍御】hànyù〈书 *fml.*〉保卫;抵御 defend; guard; protect: ~边疆 defend national frontiers|~外侮 guard against foreign invasion

悍 hàn ❶ 勇猛 brave; bold; dauntless: 强~ intrepid; valiant; resolute|一员~将 a brave warrior ❷ 凶狠;蛮横 fierce and malicious; ferocious: 凶~ fierce and tough; ferocious

【悍然】hànrán 蛮横的样子 outrageously; brazenly; flagrantly: ~不顾 in gross defiance (disregard) of; fly in the face (teeth) of|~撕毁协议 flagrantly scrap an agreement

【悍勇】hànyǒng 强悍勇敢 intrepid; dauntless: ~好斗 intrepid and bellicose; brave and pugnacious

菡 hàn [菡萏](hàndàn)〈书 *fml.*〉荷花 lotus

焊(銲、釬) hàn 用熔化的金属把金属工件连接起来,或用熔化的金属修补金属器物 weld; solder; join metalwork by melting metal, or repair metal ware with melted metal: ~接 weld; solder|电~ electric welding|~洋铁壶 weld a tin teakettle

【焊工】hàngōng ❶ 金属焊接工作 welding; soldering ❷ 做焊接工作的工人 welder; solderer

【焊剂】hànjì 焊接时用的粒状、粉状或糊状的物质,能清除金属工件焊接部分表面的杂质,防止氧化,使容易焊接,如松香等 flux; solder; welding flux; welding fluid; soldering flux; granule, powder or paste-like substance (e.g. rosin) applied to surfaces of metal pieces to be joined by welding, soldering, or brazing, to facilitate the flowing of solder or prevent the formation of oxides, etc.; also 焊药 hànyào

【焊接】hànjiē ❶ 用加热、加压等方法把金属工件连接起来。如气焊、电焊、冷焊等。weld; solder; braze; seal; join (metals) by applying heat or pressure, e.g. gas welding, electric welding, cold welding, etc. ❷ 用熔化的焊锡把金属连接起来 join metals with melted soldering tin

【焊镴】hànlà ❶ 软焊料 soft solder; fine solder; ☞ 焊料 hànliào ❷〈方 *dial.*〉same as 焊锡 hànxī

【焊料】hànliào 焊接时用来填充工件接合处的材料。分软焊料和硬焊料两种。软焊料熔点较低,质软,也叫焊镴,如铅锡合金(焊锡)。硬焊料熔点较高,质硬,如铜锌合金。solder; welding flux; soldering flux; any of various fusible alloys used to join metallic parts, including soft solders, with low melting points and soft in quality (also 焊镴 hànlà, e.g. alloys of lead and tin), and hard solders, with high melting points and hard in quality (e.g. alloys of copper and zinc)

【焊钳】hànqián 电焊用的工具,有两个柄,形状像钳子。作用是夹住电焊条,作为电焊时的一个电极。hawkbill; electrode-holder or pliers; pinch welder; welding tongs; soldering tongs; tool with two handles that resembles a pair of pliers, used in electric welding to hold the welding rod in place and functioning as an elctrode

【焊枪】hànqiāng 气焊用的带活门的工具,形状略像枪,前端有喷嘴 (welding) blowpipe; welding torch; welding gun; gun-shaped tool for gas welding, with a valve and a nozzle at the front end; also 焊炬 hànjù

【焊丝】hànsī 气焊或电焊时熔化填充在工件接合处的金属丝。焊丝的表面不涂防氧化作用的焊剂。solder wire; welding stick; wire that is melted to fill the joints of metalwork during gas welding or electric welding, the surface of which is free of oxidation-proof welding flux

【焊条】hàntiáo 气焊或电焊时熔化填充在焊接工件的接合处的金属条。焊条的材料通常跟工件的材料相同。welding rod; solder stick; filler rod; metal pencil; solder club; metal strip that is melted to fill the joint of metalwork during gas welding or electric welding, usu. of the same material as the piece to be welded

【焊锡】hànxī 锡铅合金,熔点较低,用于焊接铁、铜等金属物件 soldering tin; tin solder; fusible alloy of tin and lead with a low melting point, used to join metallic parts such as iron and lead; also called 白镴 báilà;有的地区叫锡镴 in some areas known as 锡镴 xīlà

睅 hàn〈书 *fml.*〉眼睛瞪大突出 (of eyes) wide open and protruding

颔 hàn〈书 *fml.*〉❶ 下巴 chin ❷ same as 点头 diǎn//tóu: ~首 nod

【颔联】hànlián 律诗的第二联(三、四两句),一般要求对仗 third and fourth lines of a *lüshi* poem forming a symmetrical couplet

【颔首】hànshǒu〈书 *fml.*〉same as 点头 diǎn//tóu: ~微笑 nod smilingly|~赞许 nod approvingly; give an approving nod

蔊 hàn [蔊菜](hàncài)一年生草本植物,叶形变化很大,基部叶子分裂多,茎部叶子长椭圆形,花小,黄色,结角果。全草中医入药。marsh cress (*Rorippa islandica*); yellow water cress; annual herb that varies greatly in leaf shape (splitting basal leaves and long oval leaves at the stalk) and has small yellow flowers and siliques; used whole as a type of Chinese traditional medicine

撖 Hàn 姓 a surname

暵 hàn〈书 *fml.*〉❶ 晒干 dry by exposing to the sun ❷ 干枯 wither; become dry

熯 hàn〈方 *dial.*〉❶ 焙 bake over a slow fire ❷ 用极少的油煎 fry with little oil; sauté ❸ 蒸 steam

翰 hàn〈书 *fml.*〉原指羽毛,后来借指毛笔、文字、书信等 (orig.) quill; (later referred to) a writing brush, writing, letters, etc.: 挥～ wield one's writing brush; write (with a brush) | ～墨 brush and ink | 书～ writings and letters

【翰林】hànlín 唐以后皇帝的文学侍从官,明清两代从进士中选拔 imperial academician; member of the Imperial Academy from the Tang Dynasty (618-907) onward, chosen from among successful candidates in the highest imperial examination during the Ming (1368-1644) and Qing (1616-1911) dynasties.

【翰墨】hànmò〈书 *fml.*〉笔和墨。借指文章书画等。brush and ink — writing, painting, calligraphy, etc.

撼 hàn 摇;摇动 shake: 摇～ shake violently | 震～天地 shake heaven and earth; shake the world | 蚍蜉～大树,可笑不自量。A tiny insect that tries to shake a mighty tree is ludicrously ignorant of its own weakness.

【撼动】hàndòng 摇动;震动 shake; vibrate: 一声巨响,～山岳。The loud explosion shook the mountains and hills. | 这一重大发现,～了整个世界。This major discovery shook the whole world.

【撼天动地】hàn tiān dòng dì 形容声音响亮或声势浩大 shake heaven and earth — very loud sound or high-spirited atmosphere; cause a great sensation: 喊杀声～ earthshaking shouts of 'charge forward' | ～的革命风暴 earthshaking revolutionary storm

憾 hàn 失望;不满足 disappointment; regret: 缺～ imperfection; disappointment | 遗～ regret | ～事 matter for regret | 引以为～ consider it as a matter for regret; deem it regrettable

【憾然】hànrán 失望的样子 disappointed: 不胜～ very disappointed

【憾事】hànshì 认为不完美而感到遗憾的事情 matter for regret: 终身～ regret for life; lifelong regret

瀚 hàn〈书 *fml.*〉广大 vast; immense: 浩～ vast; immense

【瀚海】hànhǎi〈书 *fml.*〉指沙漠 vast desert: ～无垠 endless desert

hāng (厂尢)

夯(碎) hāng ❶ 砸实地基用的工具或机械,有木夯、石夯、铁夯、蛤蟆夯等 rammer; tamper; tool or device used to pound the ground to make it hard and solid, e. g. wood rammer, stone rammer, iron rammer, load rammer, etc.: 打～ ram; tamp ❷ 用夯砸 ram; tamp; pound: ～实 pound (the earth) to make it solid | ～地 ram the ground | ～土 ram the earth ❸〈方 *dial.*〉用力打 strike heavily; pound; buffer; thrash: 举起拳头向下～ raise one's fist and pound | 用大板来～ strike with a big plank ❹〈方 *dial.*〉用力扛 carry sth. heavy on one's shoulder

☞ bèn on p. 93

【夯歌】hānggē 打夯时唱的歌 rammers' work chant

【夯砣】hāngtuó 夯接触地面的部分,用石头或金属做成 heavy end of a rammer (usu. made of stone or metal), which touches the ground

háng (厂尢́)

亢 háng same as 吭 háng

☞ kàng on p. 1084

行 háng ❶ 行列 line; row: 双～ double rows | 第五～ the fifth line | 杨柳成～ lined with rows of willows ❷ 排行 seniority among brothers and sisters: 您～几? Where do you come among your brothers and sisters? | 我～三。I'm the third child in my family. ❸ 行业 trade; profession; line of business: 内～ connoisseur | 同～ people of the same trade or profession | 在～ be expert at; be in one's line | 懂～ know the ropes | 改～ switch to a new profession | 各～各业 all walks of life; all trades and professions | 干一～,爱一～ love whatever job one takes up ❹ 某些营业机构 business firm: 商～ trading company; commercial firm | 银～ bank | 车～ car dealer; bicycle dealer ❺〈量词 *classifier*〉用于成行的东西[for things in a line]: 一～字 a line of characters | 几～树 rows of trees | 两～眼泪 two streams of tears

☞ hàng on p. 772, héng on p. 797 and xíng on p. 2143

【行帮】hángbāng 同一行业的人为了维护自己的利益而结成的小团体 guild; trade association; association of persons of the same trade or pursuits, formed to protect mutual interests

【行辈】hángbèi same as 辈分 bèi·fen: 他～比我大。He ranks senior to me in the clan.

【行车】hángché 〈方 dial.〉☞ 天车 tiānchē on p.1888
☞ xíngchē on p.2144

【行当】háng·dang ❶（～儿 háng·dangr）same as 行业 hángyè：他是哪一个～上的？What profession is he in? *or* What's his line? ❷ 戏曲演员专业分工的类别，主要根据角色类型来划分，如京剧的生、旦、净、丑 type of role in traditional Chinese opera, e.g. male role, female role, painted role and clown in Peking Opera

【行道】háng·dao 〈方 dial.〉 same as 行业 hángyè
☞ xíngdào on p.2144

【行东】hángdōng 商行、作坊的业主 proprietor; owner of a trading company or a workshop

【行贩】hángfàn（～儿 hángfànr）贩卖货物的小商人；小贩 peddler; vendor

【行规】hángguī 行会所制定的各种章程，由同行业的人共同遵守 guild regulations; regulations set down by a guild, that are to be abided by everyone in the trade

【行话】hánghuà 某个行业的专门用语（一般人不大理解）professional jargon; cant (generally difficult for outsiders to understand)

【行会】hánghuì 〈旧时 *old*〉城市中同行业的手工业者或商人的联合组织。每一个行会都有自己的行规。guild; union of craftsmen or businessmen of the same trade in the cities, each with its own regulations

【行货】hánghuò 加工不精细的器具、服装等商品 crudely made goods; common stock

【行家】háng·jia ❶ 内行人 expert; master hand; connoisseur; specialist：老～ old hand; veteran ❷〈方 *dial.*〉在行（用于肯定式 used in the affirmative）be expert at; be a dab hand at：您对种树挺～呀！You are quite an expert at planting trees!

【行间】hángjiān ❶〈书 *fml.*〉行伍之间 in the ranks of the army ❷ 行与行之间 between the lines; between the rows：字里～ between the lines｜栽种向日葵～的距离要宽。Leave a wide space between the rows when planting sunflowers.

【行距】hángjù 相邻的两行之间的距离，通常指两行植株之间的距离 spacing; row spacing; line width; usually space between two rows of plants; array pitch; row pitch

【行款】hángkuǎn 书写或排印文字的行列款式 format; form and arrangement of lines in calligraphy or printing

【行列】hángliè 人或物排成的直行和横行的总称 rank; horizontal and vertical lines of people or things：他站在～的最前面。He stood in the very front line of the formation. ◇这家工厂经过整顿，已经进入了同类企业的先进～。The factory has joined the ranks of advanced enterprises in the industry after a good shake-up.

【行情】hángqíng 市面上商品的一般价格。也指金融市场上利率、汇率、证券价格等的一般情况。prices of goods on the market; quotations on the market; mood of a market; financial market conditions including interest rates, exchange rates and stock quotations：摸～ size up the market conditions｜熟悉～ get familiar with the market｜～看涨。The market is strong (or bullish). *or* Market prices are expected to rise.

【行市】háng·shi 市面上商品的一般价格 quotations (on the market); prices：～看好。The market is picking up.｜摸准～ find out which way the market is going

【行伍】hángwǔ〈旧时 *old*〉称军队的行列。泛指军中。lines and rows of troops; the ranks; (in a broad sense) the army：投身～ join the army; enlist｜～出身（当兵出身）rise through the ranks; army background

【行业】hángyè 工商业中的类别。泛指职业。categories of industry and commerce; (in a broad sense) trade; profession; industry：饮食～ food industry｜服务～ service trades

【行业语】hángyèyǔ same as 行话 hánghuà

【行院】hángyuàn 金、元时代指妓女或优伶的住所。有时也指妓女或优伶。house for prostitutes or opera performers in the Jin (1115-1234) and Yuan(1206-1368) dynasties; sometimes referring to prostitutes or opera performers; also 衏衙 hángyuàn

【行栈】hángzhàn 代人存放货物并介绍买卖的行业 broker's storehouse; place providing both storage and brokerage services to merchants

【行子】háng·zi〈方 *dial.*〉称不喜爱的人或东西 a disliked person or thing：我不稀罕这～。I have no interest in this thing at all.

吭 háng 喉咙 throat：引～高歌 sing at the top of one's voice; sing lustily
☞ kēng on p.1101

迒 háng〈书 *fml.*〉❶ 野兽的脚印或车轮的痕迹 (of animals or wheels) track; pug ❷ 道路 trail; path

杭 Háng ❶ 指杭州 refer to 杭州 Hángzhōu ❷ 姓 a surname

【杭纺】hángfǎng 指杭州出产的一种纺绸 soft plain-weave silk fabric made in Hangzhou; Hangzhou plain silk

【杭育】hángyō〈拟声词 *onom.*〉重体力劳动（大多集体操作）时呼喊的声音 heave ho; yo-heave-ho; hey-ho; chanted collectively by manual workers when doing heavy manual work

绗 háng 用针线固定面儿和里子以及所絮的棉花等，缝时针孔疏密相间，线大部分藏在夹层中间，正反两面露出的都很短 sew with regularly spaced long stitches to attach the cover and underside, as well as the cotton wadding in between, with the thread mostly hidden in the interlining and barely visible on both sides: ～棉袄 sew the wadded jacket with long stitches | ～被子 sew on the quilt cover with long stitches

绗 háng [绗绗] (hángyuàn) same as 行院 hángyuàn

航 háng ❶ 船 boat; ship ❷ 航行 navigate (by water or air); sail; fly: ～海 navigation | ～空 aviation | ～线 route | ～向 course (of a ship or a plane); desired track | ～程 voyage; flight | 领～ pilotage; pilot a ship

【航班】hángbān 客轮或客机航行的班次。也指某一班次的客轮或客机。scheduled flight (of a plane) or voyage (of a passenger liner); flight or voyage number; passenger liner or passenger plane of a scheduled number

【航标】hángbiāo 指示船舶安全航行的标志 buoy; navigation marker; marker that guides ships to navigate safely: ～灯 beacon; navigation light

【航测】hángcè 航空摄影测量。在飞机上利用特制的摄影机连续对地面照相,根据摄取的相片绘制地形图。air survey; aerial survey; the process of taking a series of photographs of the earth with a special-purpose camera on a plane, and making relief maps accordingly

【航程】hángchéng 指飞机、船只航行的路程 voyage; passage; range; flight; distance travelled: ～万里 voyage (or flight) of ten thousand *li*

【航船】hángchuán ❶ 江浙一带定期行驶于城镇之间的载客运货的木船 (in Jiangsu and Zhejiang Provinces) wooden boat that plies regularly between inland towns ❷ 泛指航行的船只 (in a broad sense) steamboat or ship (that sails on a river or sea); seafaring vessel

【航次】hángcì ❶ 船舶、飞机出航编排的次第 sequence of voyages or flights; voyage or flight number ❷ 出航的次数 number of voyages or flights made

【航道】hángdào 船舶或飞机安全航行的通道 channel; sea lane; fairway; course; passage: 主～ main channel | 疏浚～ dredge a channel | 开辟新的～ open an air (or a sea) route

【航海】hánghǎi 驾驶船只在海洋上航行 sail; navigate by sea: ～家 navigator; voyager; seafarer | ～日志 logbook; log

【航空】hángkōng ❶ 指飞机在空中飞行 aviation; air navigation: ～事业 aviation undertakings | ～公司 airways; airline company | 民用～ civil aviation ❷ 跟飞机飞行有关的 related to airplanes or air transport: ～信 airmail | ～母舰 aircraft carrier

【航空兵】hángkōngbīng 装备有各种军用飞机,在空中执行任务的部队的统称 air force; air unit; military force equipped with various kinds of aircraft and assigned tasks to be performed in the air

【航空港】hángkōnggǎng 固定航线上的大型机场 airport; large airport on a regular route

【航空母舰】hángkōng mǔjiàn 作为海军飞机海上活动基地的大型军舰。通常与若干艘巡洋舰、驱逐舰、护卫舰等编成航空母舰编队,远离海岸机动作战。按任务和所载飞机的不同,分为攻击航空母舰、反潜航空母舰等。carrier; aircraft carrier; large naval vessel designed as a mobile air base for fighting at sea, typically in formation with cruisers, destroyers and frigates; divided into attack aircraft carrier, antisubmarine aircraft carrier, etc., based on their purposes and the types of planes on-board

【航空器】hángkōngqì 指在大气层中飞行的飞行器,如气球、飞艇、飞机等 aircraft; aerobat; aerostat; aerial craft; airborne craft; machine or device that is capable of atmospheric flight, e. g. air balloon, airship, airplane, etc.

【航空信】hángkōngxìn 由飞机运送的信 airmail; airmail letter; air letter

【航路】hánglù 船只、飞机航行的路线 air or sea route: ～畅通。The air (or sea) route is clear.

【航模】hángmó 飞机和船只的模型 model of airplanes and ships; model plane; model ship: ～表演 exhibition of model ships and planes | ～比赛 competition of model ships and planes

【航速】hángsù 航行的速度 speed of a ship or plane; navigational speed

【航天】hángtiān ❶ 指人造卫星、宇宙飞船等在地球附近空间或太阳系空间飞行 space flight; astronautic flight; flight of man-made satellite or spacecraft near the Earth or within the solar system ❷ 跟航天有关的 aerospace; of or related to the Earth's atmosphere and space beyond: ～技术 space technology; astronautical technology | ～事业 astronautical undertakings

【航天飞机】hángtiān fēijī 兼有航空和航天功能的空中运载工具。利用助推火箭垂直起飞,然后启动轨道飞行器进行轨道航行,返回地面时滑翔降落。可以重复使用。shuttlecraft; space shuttle; space plane; aerospace plane; reusable space vehicle for aviation and aerospace purposes that takes off vertically with the assistance of a booster rocket, then activates an orbiter to start an orbital manoeuvre, and finally glides to a landing when returning to the earth

【航务】hángwù 有关船舶、飞机运输的业务 navigational matters; matters related to shipping by water; and air

【航线】hángxiàn 水上和空中航行路线的统称 pathway; air or shipping line; air or sea route; flight course: 开辟新～ open a new navigation or air line

【航向】hángxiàng 航行的方向。也用于比喻。course (of a ship or plane); (fig.) intended direction; desired course: 偏离～ deviate from the desired course | 拨正～ get back on course | 指引革命～ steer a revolutionary course

【航行】hángxíng 船在水里或飞机在空中行驶 sail; fly; navigate by water; navigate by air

【航运】hángyùn 水上运输事业的统称,分内河航运、沿海航运、远洋航运 shipping by water, including inland navigation, coastal shipping and oceangoing voyage

颃 háng ☞ 颉颃 xiéháng on p. 2122

hàng (厂尢)

行 hàng ☞ 树行子 shù hàng·zi on p. 1788
☞ háng on p. 769, héng on p. 797 and xíng on p. 2143

沆 hàng〈书 *fml.*〉形容大水 vast expanse of water

【沆瀣】hàngxiè〈书 *fml.*〉夜间的水气 evening mist

【沆瀣一气】hàng xiè yī qì 唐朝崔瀣参加科举考试,考官崔沆取中了他。于是当时有人嘲笑说,'座主门生,沆瀣一气'(见于钱易《南部新书》)。后来比喻臭味相投的人结合在一起。*New Book in the South* by Qian Yi: During the Tang Dynasty (618-907), a man by the name of Cui Xie sat in an imperial examination, and was matriculated by an examiner named Cui Hang. Hence the sarcastic remark: 'Examiner Hang and examinee Xie are from the same family'. (derog.) act in collusion with; practise nepotism; wallow in the mire with; work hand in glove with sb.; collaborate in evildoing; like attracts like; birds of a feather flock together

巷 hàng same as 巷道 hàngdào
☞ xiàng on p. 2097

【巷道】hàngdào 采矿或探矿时在地面或地下挖掘的大致成水平方向的坑道,一般用于运输和排水,地下的也用于通风 tunnel; gallery; horizontal passageway dug on the earth surface or underground, for mining or prospecting purposes, usually used for transport and drainage, with underground tunnels also used for ventilation

hāo (厂幺)

蒿 hāo same as 蒿子 hāo·zi

【蒿子】hāo·zi 通常指花小、叶子作羽状分裂、有某种特殊气味的草本植物 wormwood (*Artemisia absinthium*); artemisia; herb with small flowers, pinnate leaves and a particular smell

【蒿子秆儿】hāo·zigǎnr 茼蒿的嫩茎叶,做蔬菜时叫蒿子秆儿 tender leaves and stems of the crown daisy chrysanthemum (used as a vegetable)

薅 hāo ❶ 用手拔(草等) pull up (weeds, etc.): ～苗(间苗) thin out seedlings ❷〈方 *dial.*〉揪 pull; tug; drag: 一把把他从座位上～起来。Pull him up from the seat with one jerk.

【薅锄】hāochú 除草用的短柄小锄 weeding hoe; a short-handled hoe for weeding

嚆 hāo [嚆矢](hāoshǐ) 带响声的箭 arrow with a whistle attached; 〈比喻 *fig.*〉事物的开端或先行者 forerunner; harbinger; precursor: 人造地球卫星的发射是人类星际旅行的～。The launching of a man-made earth satellite was the precursor for interstellar travel by humankind.

háo (厂幺)

号(號) háo ❶ 拖长声音大声叫唤 howl; yell; utter a long, loud wailing cry: 呼～ cry out in distress | ～叫 shriek; scream ◇ 北风怒～。The north wind is howling. ❷ 大声哭 wail: 哀～ cry piteously
☞ hào on p. 778

【号叫】háojiào 大声叫 howl; yell: 她一面哭,一面～着。She howled as she cried.

【号哭】háokū 连喊带叫地大声哭 wail; express grief or pain by long, loud cries: ～不止 keep wailing

【号丧】háo//sāng 旧俗,家中有丧事,来吊唁的人和守灵的人大声干哭,叫号丧 howl at a funeral; an old custom of crying loud without tears at a funeral by mourners and those keeping vigil beside the coffin

【号丧】háo·sang〈方 *dial.*〉哭(骂人的话 curse) howl as if at a funeral; weep: 谁也没欺负你,你～什么! No one has bullied you. Why do you howl as if someone's died?

【号咷】háotáo same as 号啕 háotáo

【号啕】háotáo 形容大声哭 wail; cry loudly: ～大哭 cry loudly | ～痛哭 weep and wail; also 号咷 háotáo, 嚎啕 háotáo or 嚎咷 háotáo

蚝(蠔) háo 牡蛎 oyster

【蚝油】háoyóu 用牡蛎的肉制成的浓汁,供调味用 oyster sauce; thick juice made by boiling oyster meat, used as seasoning

毫 háo ❶ 细长而尖的毛 fine long hair: 狼～笔 writing brush made of weasel hair | 羊～笔 writing brush made of goat hair ❷ 指毛笔 writing brush: 挥～ flourish a writing brush in one's hand; write or draw a picture (with a brush) ❸ 秤或戥子上用手提的绳 one of the two or three loops on a steelyard for hanging from the user's hand：头～ first loop ｜二～ second loop ❹ 一点儿（只用于否定式 only used in the negative）in the least；at all：～不足怪 not at all surprising｜～无头绪 no clue at all ❺（某些计量单位的）千分之一 milli-：～米 millimetre（mm.）｜～升 millilitre（ml.）｜～克 milligram（mg.）❻ 计量单位名称 *hao*，a unit of measurement a)长度，10 丝等于 1 毫，10 毫等于 1 厘 a unit of length（＝1/3 decimillimetre）；10 *si* is equal to 1 *hao*，and 10 *hao* 1 *li*. b)重量，10 丝等于 1 毫，10 毫等于 1 厘 a unit of weight（＝0. 005 gramme）；10 *si* is equal to 1 *hao*，and 10 *hao* is equal to 1 *li*. ❼〈方 *dial.*〉货币单位，即角 a monetary unit，same as 角 jiǎo

【毫发】háofà〈书 *fml.*〉毫毛和头发 soft hair on body and hair on head；〈比喻 *fig.*〉极小的数量（多用于否定式 usu. used in the negative）the least bit；the slightest：～不爽 not deviating a hair's breadth；without the slightest error｜不差～ be perfectly accurate

【毫分】háofēn 分毫 fraction；iota：不差～ just right；without the slightest error

【毫厘】háolí 一毫一厘。形容极少的数量。the least bit；an iota：～不爽 without the slightest error｜失之～，谬以千里。An error the breadth of a single hair can lead you astray by a thousand miles.

【毫毛】háomáo 人或鸟兽身上的细毛。多用于比喻。（oft. fig.）soft hair on the body of humans，birds or animals：不准你动他一根～。You are not allowed to touch a hair of his.

【毫末】háomò〈书 *fml.*〉毫毛的梢儿 the tip of a hair；〈比喻 *fig.*〉极微小的数量或部分 an extremely small amount or part：～之差 the smallest difference｜～之利 a petty profit

【毫无二致】háo wú èr zhì 丝毫没有两样；完全一样 identical；without the slightest difference；just the same

【毫洋】háoyáng〈旧时 *old*〉广东、广西等地区通行的本位货币 the basic monetary unit in Guangdong and Guangxi provinces

【毫针】háozhēn 针刺穴位用的针，根据粗细和长短的不同分为若干型号 filiform needle used in acupuncture；acupuncture needle，divided into several types according to thickness and length

【毫子】háo•zi ❶〈旧时 *old*〉广东、广西等地区使用的一角、二角、五角的银币，二角的最常见 silver coin of Guangdong and Guangxi Provinces in denominations of 1，2，and 5 *jiao*，the most common being the denomination of 2 *jiao* ❷ same as 毫 háo⑦

嗥（嘷） háo（豺狼等）大声叫（of a jackal or wolf）howl

【嗥叫】háojiào 号叫（多指豺狼等 of a jackal or wolf）howl

貉 háo 义同'貉'（hé），专用于'貉绒、貉子' same as 貉 hé，used in 貉绒 háoróng and 貉子 háo•zi

☞ hé on p. 791 and mò 貊 on p. 1368

【貉绒】háoróng 拔去硬毛的貉子皮，质地轻软，是珍贵的毛皮 raccoon fur with hard hair removed，which is light and soft，very precious

【貉子】háo•zi 貉的通称 general term for 貉 hé

豪 háo ❶ 具有杰出才能的人 a person of extraordinary powers or endowments：英～ heroes｜文～literary giant；great writer ❷ 气魄大；直爽痛快，没有拘束的 bold and unconstrained；forthright；unrestrained：～放 bold and unconstrained｜～爽 bold and uninhibited ｜～迈 heroic；bold and generous ｜～言壮语 brave words；proud words◇～雨 torrential rain ❸ 指有钱有势 despotic；bullying：～门 rich and powerful family；wealthy and influential clan｜～富 powerful and wealthy ❹ 强横 arrogant；rude and unreasonable：～强 despotic；tyrannical｜巧取～夺 secure（belongings，rights，etc.）by force or trickery

【豪放】háofàng 气魄大而无所拘束 bold and unconstrained：～不羁 bold and free-wheeling ｜性情～ a bold and uninhibited character｜文笔～ write in a bold and uninhibited style

【豪富】háofù 有钱有势。也指有钱有势的人。powerful and wealthy；（rich and powerful）person

【豪横】háohèng 强横；仗势欺人 despotic；bullying

【豪横】háo•heng〈方 *dial.*〉性格刚强有骨气 firm；staunch；unyielding

【豪华】háohuá ❶（生活）过分铺张；奢侈 luxurious（living）；extravagant ❷（建筑、设备或装饰）富丽堂皇；十分华丽（of architecture，equipment or furnishing）posh；sumptuous；magnificent：～的客厅 a magnificent sitting room｜～型轿车 a deluxe car｜室内摆设非常～。The interior furnishings are exceptionally sumptuous.

【豪杰】háojié 才能出众的人 hero；person of exceptional ability：英雄～ heroes and outstanding figures

【豪举】háojǔ 指有魄力的行动。也指阔绰的行动。bold move；munificent act

【豪迈】háomài 气魄大；勇往直前 heroic；bold and generous：气概～ heroic spirit｜～的事业 heroic undertaking

【豪门】háomén 指有钱有势的家庭 rich and powerful family；wealthy and influential clan：～大族 powerful families and great clans ｜～子弟 sons of the rich｜～出身 come from a rich and powerful family

【豪气】háoqì 英雄气概；豪迈的气势 heroism；heroic spirit

【豪强】háoqiáng ❶ same as 强横 qiánghèng ❷ 指依仗权势欺压人民的人 despot; bully; a person exercising power abusively, oppressively or tyrannically: 剪除～ get rid of bullies

【豪情】háoqíng 豪迈的情怀 lofty sentiments: ～壮志 lofty sentiments and high aspirations

【豪绅】háoshēn 指地方上依仗封建势力欺压人民的绅士 despotic gentry; local tyrants and evil gentry who, relying on feudal power, oppressed the common people

【豪爽】háoshuǎng 豪放直爽 bold and uninhibited, liberated: 性情～ a bold and uninhibited character

【豪侠】háoxiá ❶ 勇敢而有义气 gallant; brave and chivalrous: ～之士 gallant man ❷ 勇敢而有义气的人 gallant man: 江湖～ vagrant chivalrons man

【豪兴】háoxìng 好的兴致;浓厚的兴趣 exhilaration; exuberant spirits; keen interest: ～尽消。Their exuberant spirit has all diminished. | 老人吟诗作画的～不减当年。The old man has maintained a keen interest in composing poetry and painting pictures as ever before.

【豪言壮语】háo yán zhuàng yǔ 气魄很大的话 brave words; proud words

【豪饮】háoyǐn 放量饮酒 drink with abandon; drink heavily

【豪雨】háoyǔ 大雨 torrential rain: 一夜～。The downpour lasted a whole night.

【豪语】háoyǔ 豪迈的话 brave words; bold promises

【豪猪】háozhū 哺乳动物,全身黑色,自肩部以后长着许多长而硬的刺,刺的颜色黑白相杂,穴居,昼伏夜出 porcupine (*Hystrix hodgsoni*); black mammal with stiff, sharp black-and-white erectile bristles mingled with its fur, dwells in caves, inactive by day and active at night; also 箭猪 jiànzhū

【豪壮】háozhuàng 雄壮 grand and heroic: ～的事业 a grand and heroic cause | ～的声音 a firm, strong voice

【豪族】háozú 指有钱有势的家族 rich and powerful family; wealthy and influential clan

壕 háo ❶ 护城河 moat: 城～ city moat ❷ 壕沟 trench: 战～ entrenchment | 防空～ air-raid dugout | 沟满～平。The trenches and ditches are filled with water.

【壕沟】háogōu ❶ 为作战时起掩护作用而挖掘的沟 trench; ditch dug in the ground to give troops shelter from enemy fire ❷ 沟;沟渠 ditch; canal

【壕堑】háoqiàn same as 堑壕 qiànháo

嚎 háo ❶ 大声叫 howl: 一声长～ give a long howl | 狼～ howl of a wolf ❷ same as 号 háo ②: ～啕 cry loudly

【嚎春】háochūn 有些动物发情时发出叫声,因多在春季,所以叫嚎春 spring howl; certain animals cry when they are in heat, mostly in spring, so it is called a spring howl

【嚎咷】háotáo same as 号啕 háotáo

【嚎啕】háotáo same as 号啕 háotáo

濠 háo 护城河 moat: 城～ city moat

hǎo (厂ㄠˇ)

好 hǎo ❶ 优点多的;使人满意的 (跟'坏'相对 as opposed to 'bad') good; fine; nice: ～人 a nice person | ～东西 a good thing | ～事情 a happy event | ～脾气 good temper | 庄稼长得很～。The crops are doing very well. ❷ 用在动词前,表示使人满意的性质在哪方面 [used before verbs to express satisfaction] be good to; be easy to: ～看 good-looking | ～听 pleasant to listen to | ～吃 delicious; good to eat ❸ 友爱;和睦 friendly; kind: 友～ friendly | ～朋友 a good friend | 他跟我～。He is kind to me. ❹ (身体)健康;(疾病)痊愈 be in good health; get well: 您～哇! How are you? | 他的病～了。He is well (or all right) now. ❺ 用于套语[used in polite expressions]: ～睡。Have a sound sleep. | 您～走。Take care on your way. ❻ 用在动词后头,表示完成或达到完善的地步 [used after verbs to indicate finishing or finishing satisfactorily]: 计划订～了。The plan has been worked out. | 功课准备～了。The lessons have been prepared. | 外边太冷,穿～了衣服再出去。It is very cold outside, so dress properly before going out. | 坐～吧,要开会了。Take your seats, please. The meeting is going to begin. ❼ 表示赞许、同意或结束等语气 [used at the beginning of a sentence or a clause, to express agreement, approval, ending, etc.]: ～,就这么办。OK, it's settled. | ～了,不要再说了。All right, no need to say any more. ❽ 反话,表示不满意 [used at the beginning of a sentence or a clause, to express disapproval]: ～,这一下可麻烦了。Well, we're in trouble now. ❾ 容易 [used before verbs] be easy to: 那个歌儿～唱。That song is easy to sing. | 这问题很～回答。This question is very easy to answer. ❿ 便于 be better to; in order to; so that: 地整平了～种庄稼。Level the ground so as to grow crops. | 告诉我他在哪儿,我～找他去。Tell me his whereabouts so that I can go see him. ⓫ 〈方 *dial.*〉应该;可以 may; can; should: 我～进来吗? May I come in? | 时间不早了,你～走了。It's getting late. You ought to get going. ⓬ 用在数量词、时间词前面,表示多或久 [used before indefinite numbers or time words] quite a few: ～多 so many | ～久 so long | ～几个 quite a few | ～一会儿 quite a long time | ～大半天 quite a while ⓭ 用在形容词、动词前,表示程度深,并带感叹语气[used before adjectives or verbs to show high degree, with exclamatory force] very; quite; so:～冷 so cold|～香 so fragrant|～漂亮 so beautiful|～面熟 look so familiar|～大的工程! What a huge project! |原来你躲在这儿,害得我～找! Why, you are hiding here, making me look for you everywhere! ⓮ 用在形容词前面问数量或程度,用法跟'多'相同[used before adjectives to inquire about quantity or degree, same as the usage of 多 duō]:哈尔滨离北京～远? How far is Harbin from Beijing?

☞ hào on p.778

【好比】hǎobǐ 表示跟以下所说的一样;如同 can be compared to; may be likened to; be just like:批评和自我批评就～洗脸扫地,要经常做。Criticism and self-criticism should be conducted regularly, like washing our faces and sweeping the floor.

【好不】hǎobù〈副词 *adv.*〉用在某些双音形容词前面表示程度深,并带感叹语气,跟'多么'相同[used before some two-character adjectives to show high degree, with exclamatory force, same as 多么 duō·me] very; quite; so: 人来人往,～热闹。What a busy place it is, with so many people coming and going. 注意 **NOTE:** 这样用的'好不'都可以换用'好','好热闹'和'好不热闹'的意思都是很热闹,是肯定的。但是在'容易'前面,用'好'或'好不'意思都是否定的,如'好容易才找着他'跟'好不容易才找着他'都是'不容易'的意思。好不 hǎobù used in this way can all be substituted by 好 hǎo. 好热闹 hǎo rènào and 好不热闹 hàobù rènào both mean 'very brisk', and are affirmative, but 好 or 好不 used before 容易 róngyì are both negative. For instance, 好容易才找着他 and 好不容易才找着他 both mean 'It is not at all easy to find him.'

【好处】hǎo·chu ❶ 对人或事物有利的因素 good; benefit; advantage:喝酒过量对身体没有～。Excessive drinking is not good for the health. ❷ 使人有所得而感到满意的事物 gain; profit: 他从中得到不少～。He has gained quite a lot from this. |给他点～他就晕头转向了。Give him a little inducement and he is thrown into confusion.

【好处费】hǎochùfèi 托人办事时付给的额外费用 pickings;extra money paid for a favour

【好歹】hǎodǎi ❶ 好坏 good and bad; what's good and what's bad:这人真不知～。This person cannot tell good from bad. ❷(～儿 hǎodǎir)指危险(多指生命危险 usu. risking life) mishap; disaster; risk:万一她有个～,这可怎么办? What if something should happen to her? ❸ 不问条件好坏,将就地(做某件事) no matter in what way; anyhow; make do with (sth.):时间太紧了,～吃点儿就行了! Time is pressing, we'll order whatever there is. ❹ 不管怎样;无论如何 in any case; at any rate; anyhow:她要是在这里,～也能拿个主意。If she were here she would give us some advice at any rate.

【好端端】hǎoduānduān (～的 hǎoduānduān·de)形容情况正常、良好 in perfectly good condition; when everything is all right:～的,怎么生起气来了? Why are you angry when everything is perfectly all right? |～的公路,竟被糟蹋成这个样子。A perfectly good highway has been damaged like this.

【好多】hǎoduō ❶ 许多 a good many; a good deal; a lot of:～人 a lot of people|～东西 many things ❷〈方 *dial.*〉多少(问数量) how many; how much:今天到会的人有～? How many people came to the meeting today?

【好感】hǎogǎn 对人对事满意或喜欢的情绪 good opinion; favourable impression:有～ be well disposed towards sb.; have a good opinion of sb.|产生～ take a liking to sb.

【好过】hǎoguò ❶ 生活上困难少,日子容易过 be well off; be in easy circumstances:她家现在～多了。Her family has a much easier time now. ❷ 好受 feel well:他吃了药,觉得～一点儿了。He felt a bit better after taking the medicine.

【好汉】hǎohàn 勇敢坚强或有胆识有作为的男子 brave man; true man; hero:英雄～ heroes|～做事～当。A true man has the courage to accept the consequences of his own actions.

【好好儿】hǎohāor (～的 hǎohāor·de) ❶ 形容情况正常;完好 in perfectly good condition; when everything is all right:那棵百年老树,至今还长得～的。That hundred-year-old tree is still growing well. |～的一支笔,叫他给弄折了。He broke a perfectly good pen. ❷ 尽力地;尽情地;耐心地 all out; to one's heart's content; be patient:大家再～想一想。Everyone think it over again carefully. |我真得～谢谢他。I'll really have to thank him. |咱们～地玩儿几天。Let's spend a few days enjoying ourselves to our hearts' content. |你～跟他谈,别着急。Talk to him nicely. Don't worry.

【好好先生】hǎohǎo xiān·sheng 一团和气、与人无争,不问是非曲直、只求相安无事的人 Mr. Agreeable; Mr. Goody-goody; one who tries not to offend anybody (oft. at the expense of principle)

【好话】hǎohuà ❶ 有益的话 good advice:他们说的都是～,你别当作耳旁风。They are giving good advice, and you should not turn a deaf ear to it. ❷ 赞扬的话;好听的话 a good word; word of praise:～说尽,坏事做绝。Say every fine word and do every foul deed. ❸ 求情的话;表示歉意的话 words to beg for mercy; words to apologise:向他说了不少～,他就是不答应。A lot of fine words were said to plead with him, but he still did not consent.

【好几】hǎojǐ ❶ 用在整数的后面表示有较多的零数［added after a whole number］quite a few：他已经三十～了。He's well over 30. ❷ 用在数量词、时间词前面表示多［used before a measure word, a time word］quite a few; a good few：～倍 quite a few folds｜～千两银子 quite a few thousand taels of silver｜咱们～年没见了。We haven't seen each other for quite a few years.

【好家伙】hǎojiā·huo〈叹词 *interj*.〉表示惊讶或赞叹（express surprise or admiration）good god; good lord; good heavens：～，他们一夜足足走了一百里！Good lord, they walked a hundred *li* overnight!｜～，你们怎么干得这么快呀！Good heavens, how is that you have proceeded so quickly!

【好景】hǎojǐng 美好的景况 good times：～不常。Good times don't last long.

【好久】hǎojiǔ 很久；许久 a long time：我站在这儿等他～了。I have been standing here for a long time, waiting for him.｜～没收到她的来信了。I haven't got a letter from her for a long time.

【好看】hǎokàn ❶ 看着舒服；美观 good-looking; look nice：这花布做裙子穿一定很～。This piece of cotton print would surely make a very beautiful skirt. ❷ 脸上有光彩；体面 honoured; proud：儿子立了功，做娘的脸上也～。My son has won distinction; as his mother, I share the honour. ❸ 使人难堪叫做要人的好看 in an embarrassing situation; on the spot：你让我上台表演，这不是要我的～吗？Me, on the stage? Do you want me to make a fool of myself?

【好赖】hǎolài same as 好歹 hǎodǎi①③④

【好力宝】hǎolìbǎo 蒙古族的一种曲艺，流行于内蒙古自治区，原为民间歌手自拉自唱，现在有独唱、对唱、重唱、合唱等形式，有时还夹有快板节奏的说白，用四胡或马头琴伴奏 ballad of the Mongolian people, popular in the Inner Mongolia Autonomous Region. Originally a solo by a folk singer, with musical accompaniment by himself, it has developed into multiple forms such as solo, antiphonal singing, an ensemble of two or more singers, with each singing one part, and chorus. Sometimes the songs have parts spoken to the rhythm of bamboo clappers, and the musical accompaniment is done with a *sihu* (a four-stringed bowed instrument) or a *matouqin* (a bowed stringed instrument with a scroll carved like a horse's head); also 好来宝 hǎoláibǎo

【好脸】hǎoliǎn（～儿 hǎoliǎnr）和悦的脸色 smiling face：你一天到晚没个～，是谁得罪你啦？You always pull a long face. Who has offended you?

【好评】hǎopíng 好的评价 be well-judged; favourable comment; high opinion：这次演出获得观众的～。The performance is well received by the audience.

【好气儿】hǎoqìr 好态度（多用于否定式 usu. in the negative）good humour; good temper：老人看见别人浪费财物，就没有～。Seeing any waste of money or materials would get the old man into a bad mood.

【好儿】hǎor ❶ 恩惠 favour; kindness：人家过去对咱有过～，咱不能忘了。They were kind to us, and we should never forget their kindness. ❷ 好处 benefit; advantage：这事要是让他知道了，还会有你的～？If he gets to know about it, you'll get into trouble, won't you? ❸ 指问好的话 regards; kind wishes, greeting：见着你母亲，给我带个～。When you see your mother, give her my best regards.

【好人】hǎorén ❶ 品行好的人；先进的人 good (or fine) person; advanced person：～好事 fine people and fine deeds ❷ 没有伤、病、残疾的人 healthy person ❸ 老好人 soft person who tries to get along with everyone (oft. at the expense of principle)：她只想做个～，连说句话也怕得罪人。She's out to please everyone, and she takes care that whatever she says offends no one.

【好人家】hǎorénjiā（～儿 hǎorénjiār）清白的人家 decent family; respectable family

【好日子】hǎorì·zi ❶ 吉利的日子 auspicious day ❷ 办喜事的日子 wedding day：你们的～定在哪一天？Which day have you chosen as your wedding day? ❸ 美好的生活 good days; happy life：这几年他才过上～。He has been living a happy life only in recent years.

【好容易】hǎoróngyì 很不容易（才做到某件事）not at all easy (to accomplish sth.)：跑遍了全城，～才买到这本书。I just managed to get hold of a copy of this book after running around the entire city. ☞ 好不 hǎobù

【好生】hǎoshēng〈方 *dial*.〉❶ 多么；很；极 quite; very; exceedingly：这个人～面熟。This person looks quite familiar.｜老太太听了，心中～不快。Hearing that, the old woman felt very unhappy. ❷ 好好儿地 carefully; properly：有话～说 say it properly｜～要（好好儿地玩儿）enjoy oneself to one's heart's content

【好声好气】hǎo shēng hǎo qì（～的 hǎo shēng hǎo qì·de）语调柔和，态度温和 gently; in a kindly manner：人家～地劝他，他倒不耐烦起来。People persuaded him in a kindly manner, but he became impatient.

【好事】hǎoshì ❶ 好事情；有益的事情 good deed; good turn：好人～ fine people and fine deeds ❷ 指僧道拜忏、打醮等事 Taoist or Buddhist rites (performed to save the souls of the dead) ❸ 指慈善的事情 an act of charity; good works ❹〈书 *fml*.〉喜庆事 happy event; joyous occasion

☞ hàoshì on p.779

【好事多磨】hǎoshì duō mó 好事情在实现、成功前常常会经历许多波折 the road to happiness (or success) is strewn with setbacks

【好手】hǎoshǒu 精于某种技艺的人;能力很强的人 good hand; past master: 游泳～ good swimmer|论烹调,他可是一把～。When it comes to cooking, he is a good hand.

【好受】hǎoshòu 感到身心愉快;舒服 feel better; feel more comfortable: 出了身汗,现在～多了。I felt much better after breaking into a sweat.|你别说了,他心里正不～呢! Don't say any more; he's already feeling rather bad.

【好说】hǎoshuō ❶〈客套话 *pol*.〉用在别人向自己致谢或恭维自己时,表示不敢当[used in answer to praises or thanks]: ～,～! 您太夸奖了。It's very good of you to say so, but I don't deserve such praise. *or* You flatter me. I wish I could deserve such compliments. ❷ 表示同意或好商量 no problem: 关于参观的事,～。As for the visit, no problem.|只要你没意见,她那边就～了。As long as you have no objection, there is no problem with her.

【好说歹说】hǎo shuō dǎi shuō 用各种理由或方式反复请求或劝说 try every possible way to persuade sb.: 我～,他总算答应了。He finally agreed, but only after I had pleaded with him in every possible way.

【好说话儿】hǎo shuōhuàr 指脾气好,容易商量、通融 easygoing; good-natured; open to persuasion: 他这人～,你只管去。He is open to persuasion, so just go ahead.

【好似】hǎosì same as 好像 hǎoxiàng

【好天儿】hǎotiānr 指晴朗的天气 fine day; lovely weather

【好听】hǎotīng ❶(声音)听着舒服;悦耳 (of sound) pleasant to hear; melodious: 这段曲子很～。This is a very pleasant melody. ❷(言语)使人满意 (language) agreeable to the hearer: 话说得～,但还要看行动。What he says is nice to hear, but we have to see his actions.

【好玩儿】hǎowánr 有趣;能引起兴趣 amusing; interesting

【好像】hǎoxiàng 有些像;仿佛 seem; be like: 他们俩一见面就～是多年的老朋友。The two of them were as intimate as close old friends the moment they came together.|静悄悄的,～屋子里没有人。It is so quiet. It seems there is no one in the room.|他低着头不作声,～在想什么事。He lowered his head and kept silent, as if having something on his mind.

【好笑】hǎoxiào 引人发笑;可笑 laughable; funny; ridiculous

【好些】hǎoxiē 许多 many; quite a lot (of); a good deal of: 他在这里工作～年了。He has been working here for a good many years.

【好心】hǎoxīn 好意 good intention; kindness: 一片～ with the best of intentions

【好性儿】hǎoxìngr 好脾气 good-natured

【好样儿的】hǎoyàngr·de 有骨气、有胆量或有作为的人 person of integrity, courage or action; fine example; great fellow

【好意】hǎoyì 善良的心意 kindness; good intention: 好心～ well-meaning intention|一番～ goodwill|谢谢你对我的～。Thank you for your kindness to me.

【好意思】hǎoyì·si 不害羞;不怕难为情(多用在反诘句中 mostly used in retort) how can one have the face (or nerve) to do sth.: 做了这种事,亏他还～说呢! Fancy his doing that sort of thing and then having the nerve to talk about it!

【好在】hǎozài 表示具有某种有利的条件或情况 fortunately; luckily; have the advantage of: 我有空再来,～离这儿不远。I'll come again when I'm free, since luckily I'm not far from here.

【好转】hǎozhuǎn 向好的方面转变 take a turn for the better; take a favourable turn; improve: 病情～。The patient is on the mend.|局势～。The situation took a favourable turn.

【好自为之】hǎo zì wéi zhī 自己妥善处置,好好干 look out for yourself

郝 Hǎo 姓 a surname

hào(厂幺)

号[1](號) hào ❶ 名称 name: 国～ title of a reigning dynasty|年～ reign title (a designation for the years when an emperor was on the throne) ❷ 原指名和字以外另起的别号,后来也泛指名以外另起的字 style name; alias; literary name; sobriquet: 苏轼字子瞻,～东坡。Su Shi, styled Zizhan, was also known by his literary name Dongpo ('Eastern Slope').|孔明是诸葛亮的～。Kongming was Zhuge Liang's alternative name. ❸ 商店 business house: 商～ shop|银～ banking house|分～ branch (of a shop)|宝～ your firm ❹(～儿 hàor)标志;信号 mark; sign; signal: 记～ mark; sign|问～ question mark|加减～ plus and minus signs|暗～儿 secret signal|击掌为～ signal by clapping ❺(～儿 hàor)排定的次第 assigned number: 挂～ register|编～ serial number ❻(～儿 hàor)表示等级 size: 大～ large size|中～ medium size|

H

小～ small size | 五～铅字 type No. 5 ❼ 种；类 kind; sort; type：这～人甭理他。Don't bother with that sort of person. | 这～生意不能做。You can't do this kind of business. ❽（～儿 hàor）指某种人员 personnel：病～ sick personnel | 伤～ the wounded | 彩～ soldier wounded in action ❾（～儿 hàor）表示次序（多放在数字后 used after a numeral to mark the order）：a）一般的 general：第三～简报 No. 3 Bulletin | 门牌二～ House No. 2 b）特指一个月里的日子 date in a month：五月一～是国际劳动节。May 1st is International Labour Day. ❿〈量词 *classifier*〉a）用于人数［for number of people］：今天有一百多～人出工。Over a hundred people went to work today. b）（～儿 hàor）用于成交的次数 for business deals：一会儿工夫就做了几～买卖。Several deals were clinched in a short time. ⓫ 标上记号 make a mark on：～房子 mark the houses | 把这些东西都～一～。Have all these items marked. ⓬ 切（脉搏）feel (the pulse)：～脉 feel the pulse

号[2]**（號）** hào ❶ 号令 order：发～施令 issue orders ❷ 号筒 anything used as a horn ❸ 军队或乐队里所用的西式喇叭 any brass wind instrument used in an army or a band ❹ 用号吹出的表示一定意义的声音 bugle call：起床～ reveille; taps | 集合～ a bugle call to fall-in | 冲锋～ a bugle call to charge

☞ háo on p. 772

【号兵】hàobīng 军队中管吹号的士兵 bugler; trumpeter for troops

【号称】hàochēng ❶ 以某种名号著称 be known as：四川～天府之国。Sichuan is known as the land of plenty. ❷ 对外宣称；名义上称做 claim to be：敌人的这个师～一万二千人，实际上只有七八千。The enemy division claimed it had 12,000 people, but actually it had only 7,000 to 8,000.

【号房】hàofáng〈旧时 *old*〉指传达室或做传达工作的人 janitor; gatekeeper; gate house; janitor's room

【号角】hàojiǎo〈古时 *arch.*〉军队中传达命令的管乐器，后世泛指喇叭一类的东西 bugle; horn; trumpet; wind instrument used by ancient armies to convey orders ◇石油大会战的～吹响了。The clarion call for the great battle for oil exploration has been sounded.

【号坎儿】hàokǎnr〈旧时 *old*〉车夫、轿夫、搬运工等所穿的有号码的坎肩儿 numbered singlet worn by rickshaw pullers, sedan-chair bearers or porters

【号令】hàolìng ❶ 军队中用口说或军号等传达命令：verbal command; call made on a bugle：～三军 command the three armed services ❷ 特指战斗时指挥战士的命令：order to soldiers issued in wartime：发布～ issue orders

【号码】hàomǎ（～儿 hàomǎr）表示事物次第的数目字 number to indicate the order of sth. in a series：门牌～ house number | 电话～ telephone number

【号脉】hào//mài same as 诊脉 zhěn//mài

【号炮】hàopào 为传达信号而放的炮 signal gun

【号手】hàoshǒu 吹号的人 bugler; trumpeter

【号筒】hàotǒng〈旧时 *old*〉军队中传达命令的管乐器，筒状，管细口大，最初用竹、木等制成，后用铜制成 trumpet, a wind instrument used to convey orders to troops; first made of bamboo or wood, and later of copper

【号头】hàotóu ❶（～儿 hàotóur）same as 号码 hàomǎ ❷〈方 *dial.*〉指一个月的特定的一天 a specific date in a month

【号外】hàowài 报社因需要及时报道某重要消息而临时增出的小张报纸，因在定期出版的报纸顺序编号之外，所以叫号外 extra edition; special edition of a newspaper, containing important or breaking news that is not covered in the regular issues

【号衣】hàoyī〈旧时 *old*〉兵士、差役等所穿的带记号的衣服 marked livery or army uniform for soldiers or runners in a yamen

【号召】hàozhào 召唤（群众共同去做某事）call; appeal (the masses to join forces to do sth.)：响应～ respond to a call | ～全厂职工积极参加义务劳动。All the workers and staff members of the factory are called upon to take an active part in volunteer labour.

【号志灯】hàozhìdēng 铁路上用的手提的信号灯 portable signal lamp used by rail workers

【号子】[1] hào·zi ❶〈方 *dial.*〉记号；标志 mark; sign; signal ❷ 指监狱里关押犯人的房间，每个房间有统一编排的号码 cell; a numbered room for prisoners in a prison

【号子】[2] hào·zi 集体劳动中协同使劲时，为统一步调、减轻疲劳等所唱的歌，大都由一人领唱，大家应和 a work song to synchronise movements and alleviate fatigue, with one person leading and the others responding in chorus

好 hào ❶ 喜爱（跟'恶'wù相对 as opposed to 'dislike'）like; love; be fond of：嗜～ hobbies | ～学 be fond of learning; be eager to learn | ～动脑筋 like to use one's head | ～吃懒做 be fond of eating and averse to work; be gluttonous and lazy | 他这个人～表现自己。He likes to show off. ❷ 常容易（发生某种事情）be liable to：刚会骑车的人～摔跤。A beginner is liable to tumble off the bicycle.

☞ hǎo on p. 774

【好大喜功】hào dà xǐ gōng 指不管条件是否许可，一心想做大事，立大功（多含贬义 oft. derog.）crave for greatness and success; have a fondness for the grandiose (in disregard of the actual conditions)

【好高务远】hào gāo wù yuǎn 不切实际地追求过高的目标 reach for what is beyond one's grasp; aim too high; 务 also put as 骛 wù

【好客】hàokè 指乐于接待客人,对客人热情 be hospitable; keep an open house

【好奇】hàoqí 对自己所不了解的事物觉得新奇而感兴趣 be curious; be inquisitive; be full of curiosity: ～心 curiosity | 孩子们～,什么事都想知道个究竟。Children are curious, and want to get to the heart of a matter, whatever it may be.

【好强】hàoqiáng 要强 eager to do well in everything: 她是个～的姑娘,从来不肯落后。She is eager to do well in everything, and refuses to lag behind others.

【好色】hàosè (男子)沉溺于情欲,贪恋女色 love woman's beauty; be fond of women: ～之徒 lecher; libertine

【好善乐施】hào shàn lè shī 喜欢做善事,乐于拿财物帮助人 philanthropic; be devoted to charitable work; also 乐施好善 lè shī hào shàn

【好尚】hàoshàng 爱好和崇尚 one's likes or preferences; what is valued or held in esteem: 各有～。Everyone has his or her own hobbies.

【好胜】hàoshèng 处处都想胜过别人 love to outshine others; seek to keep others down: ～心 desire to outshine others | 争强～ seek to keep others down

【好事】hàoshì 好管闲事;喜欢多事 meddlesome; officious
☞ hǎoshì on p.776

【好为人师】hào wéi rén shī 喜欢以教育者自居,不谦虚 like to lecture people; be given to laying down the law

【好恶】hàowù 喜好和厌恶,指兴趣 likes and dislikes; tastes: ～不同 different tastes | 不能从个人的～出发来评定文章的好坏。One should not pass judgement on an article according to one's own tastes.

【好逸恶劳】hào yì wù láo 贪图安逸,厌恶劳动 love ease and hate work

【好整以暇】hào zhěng yǐ xiá 形容虽在百忙之中,仍然从容不迫 remain calm and composed while handling pressing affairs

昊 hào 〈书 *fml.*〉❶ 广大无边 vast and boundless ❷ 指天 sky; heaven

耗[1] hào ❶ 减损;消耗 consume; cost: 点灯～油 consuming oil by lighting a lamp | 锅里的水快～干了。The pot is boiling dry. ❷ 〈方 *dial.*〉拖延 dawdle; waste time: 你别～着了,快走吧。Stop dawdling and get going.

耗[2] hào 坏的音信或消息 bad news: 噩～ sad news of the death of sb. beloved | 死～ news of sb.'s death | 音～ news; message; information

【耗费】hàofèi same as 消耗 xiāohào: ～时间 expend time | ～人力物力 consume human and material resources

【耗竭】hàojié 消耗净尽 exhaust; use up: 兵力～ be drained of military strength | 物资～ exhaust resources

【耗神】hàoshén 消耗精力 take up one's energy: ～费力 take up one's energy and strength

【耗损】hàosǔn 消耗损失 consume; waste; lose: ～精神 take up one's energy | 减少粮食的～ reduce the wastage of grain

【耗资】hàozī 耗费资财 cost (a large sum of money): 工程～上亿。The project costs 100 million yuan.

【耗子】hào·zi 〈方 *dial.*〉same as 老鼠 lǎo·shǔ

浩 hào ❶ 浩大 great; vast; grand: ～繁 vast and numerous ❷ 多 many; much: ～博 extensive; wide-embracing | ～如烟海 vast as the open sea; a tremendous amount (of literature, data, etc.)

【浩博】hàobó 非常多;丰富 extensive; wide-embracing: 征引～ quote copiously (to support one's thesis); be well documented

【浩大】hàodà (气势、规模等)盛大;巨大 (of momentum, plan, etc.) very great; huge; vast: 声势～ momentous; powerful and dynamic | 工程～ a huge (or vast) project

【浩荡】hàodàng ❶ 水势大 (the flow of water) vast and mighty: 江水～ the mighty river | 烟波～ a vast expanse of misty rolling waters ❷ 形容广阔或壮大 vast and mighty: 军威～ awesome military might | 春风～。The spring wind blows with mighty power. | 游行队伍浩浩荡荡地通过天安门。The paraders marched past Tian'anmen Rostrum in an endless procession.

【浩繁】hàofán 浩大而繁多;繁重 vast and numerous: 卷帙～ a vast literature of books and volumes | ～的开支 heavy expenditure

【浩瀚】hàohàn ❶ 形容水势盛大 a vast body of water: 湖水～ a vast expanse of lake | ～的大海 a boundless sea ❷ 形容广大;繁多 vast; numerous: 典籍～ a vast accumulation of ancient literature | ～的沙漠 a vast stretch of desert

【浩劫】hàojié 大灾难 great calamity; catastrophe: 空前～ an unheard-of calamity | 惨遭～ suffer from a horrible disaster

【浩茫】hàománg 〈书 *fml.*〉广阔无边 vast; extensive; boundless: ～的大地 boundless land ◇心事～ be laden with anxiety; be weighed down with care

【浩淼】hàomiǎo 形容水面辽阔 (of water) extending into the distance; vast: 烟波～ a vast expanse of misty rolling waters; also 浩渺 hàomiǎo

【浩渺】hàomiǎo same as 浩淼 hàomiǎo

【浩气】hàoqì 浩然之气;正气 noble spirit; moral force: ～长存。A noble spirit will never perish.｜～凛然 inspiring awe by one's noble spirit

【浩然】hàorán〈书 *fml*.〉❶ 形容广阔，盛大 great; vast; grand: 江流～ a torrential river｜洪波～ a sweep of rolling waves ❷ 形容正大刚直 upright and outspoken: ～之气 noble spirit; moral force

【浩然之气】hàorán zhī qì 正大刚直的精神 noble spirit; moral force

【浩如烟海】hào rú yān hǎi 形容文献、资料等非常丰富 vast as the open sea; a tremendous amount (of literature, data, etc.)

【浩叹】hàotàn 大声叹息 heave a deep sigh; sigh deeply

【浩特】hàotè 蒙古族牧人居住的自然村，也指城市 *hot*; Mongolian for 'village' or 'city'［蒙: Mongolian］

淏 hào〈书 *fml*.〉水清 clear water

皓（**皜**）hào ❶ 白；洁白 white: ～首 hoary head｜明眸～齿 bright eyes and white teeth ❷ 明亮 bright; luminous: ～月 bright moon

【皓首】hàoshǒu〈书 *fml*.〉白头（指年老 referring to old age）hoary head: ～穷经（钻研经典到老）continue to study the classics into one's old age

【皓月】hàoyuè 明亮的月亮 bright moon: ～当空 a bright moon hanging in the sky

鄗 Hào 古县名，在今河北柏乡北 name of an ancient county, to the north of present-day Baixiang County, Hebei Province

滈 Hào 滈河，水名，在陕西长安县 Hao River, name of an ancient river, in present-day Chang'an county, Shaanxi Province

暠 hào〈书 *fml*.〉same as 皓 hào

☞ gǎo on p. 647

镐 Hào 周朝初年的国都，在今陕西西安西南 Hao, capital of the early Zhou Dynasty, to the southwest of present-day, Shaanxi Province

☞ gǎo on p. 647

皞 hào〈书 *fml*.〉明亮 bright

澔 hào〈书 *fml*.〉same as 浩 hào

颢 hào〈书 *fml*.〉白而发光 white and luminous

灏 hào〈书 *fml*.〉❶ same as 浩 hào ❷ same as 皓 hào

hē（ㄏㄜ）

诃[1] hē same as 呵[2] hē

诃[2] hē［诃子］(hēzǐ) ❶ 常绿乔木，叶子卵形或椭圆形。果实像橄榄，可以入药。产于我国云南、广东一带，以及印度、缅甸、马来亚等地。myrobalan (*Terminalia chebula*); evergreen tree with egg-shaped or oval leaves, and dive-like fruit that can be used as an ingredient in traditional Chinese medicine, growing in China's Yunnan and Guangdong provinces, as well as in India, Myanmar and Malaya ❷ 这种植物的果实 the seeds of myrobalan ‖ also 藏青果 zàngqīngguǒ

呵[1] hē 呼(气)；哈(气) breathe out (with the mouth open): ～一口气 a puff｜一气～成 get sth. done at one go｜他一边写，一边～手。As he wrote, he kept blowing on his hands to warm them.

呵[2]（**訶**）hē 呵斥 scold: ～责 berate; excoriate

呵[3] hē same as 嗬 hē

☞ ā on p. 1, á on p. 2, ǎ on p. 2, à on p. 2, 啊·a on p. 2 and kē on p. 1088

【呵斥】hēchì 大声斥责 berate; excoriate: 受了一通～。He was berated. also 呵叱 hēchì

【呵呵】hēhē〈拟声词 *onom*.〉形容笑声 the sound of laughter; hee hee; ha ha; hee haw: ～大笑 laugh loudly｜～地笑了起来 roar with laughter

【呵喝】hēhè〈书 *fml*.〉为了申斥、恫吓或禁止而大声喊叫 shout to rebuke, threaten or prohibit

【呵护】hēhù〈书 *fml*.〉❶ same as 保佑 bǎoyòu ❷ 爱护；保护 to baby sb.; take good care of: ～备至 baby sb. or be babied in every possible way

【呵欠】hē·qian〈方 *dial*.〉same as 哈欠 hā·qian

【呵责】hēzé same as 呵斥 hēchì

喝[1]（**欱**）hē ❶ 把液体或流食咽下去 drink; to take in or suck up (liquid or liquid food): ～水 drink water｜～茶 drink tea｜～酒 drink alcohol｜～粥 drink porridge ◇～风 against the wind ❷ 特指喝酒 drink alcohol: 爱～ be fond of drinking｜～醉了 be drunk｜遇上高兴的事总要～两口。One should drink a little when something happy happens.

喝[2] hē same as 嗬 hē

☞ hè on p. 791

【喝闷酒】hē mènjiǔ 烦闷时一人独自饮酒叫喝闷酒 drink alcohol alone when one is unhappy

【喝墨水】hē mòshuǐ (～儿 hē mòshuǐr) 指上学读书 drink ink — go to school: 他没喝过几年墨水。He's had only a few years of schooling.

【喝西北风】hē xīběifēng 指没有东西吃，挨饿 drink the northwest wind; live on air; have nothing to eat; starve

嗬 hē〈叹词 *interj*.〉表示惊讶 ah; oh (to express surprise): ～，真不得了！Oh, how terrible!｜～，这小伙子真棒！Ah! what a fine young chap!

蠚 hē〈方 *dial*.〉蜇 zhē (of bees, wasps, etc.) sting

hé (ㄏㄜˊ)

禾 hé ❶ 禾苗。特指水稻的植株。standing grain; rice plants ❷ 古书指粟 (as recorded in ancient books) millet; foxtail millet

【禾场】héchǎng 〈方 *dial.*〉打稻子或晒稻子等用的场地 threshing floor; sunning ground

【禾苗】hémiáo 谷类作物的幼苗 seedlings of cereal crops

合¹ hé ❶ 闭;合拢 close; shut: ～上眼 close the eyes | 笑得～不上嘴 grin from ear to ear ❷ 结合到一起;凑到一起;共同 (跟'分'相对 as opposed to 'separate') join; combine: ～办 join forces; pool efforts | 同心～力 unite and make a common effort ❸ 全 whole: ～村 the whole village | ～家团聚 a reunion of the whole family ❹ 符合 suit; agree: ～情～理 fair and reasonable; fair and sensible | 正～心意 be to one's liking (or taste) ❺ 折合;共计 be equal to; add up to: 一公顷～十五市亩。One hectare is equal to fifteen *mu*. | 这件衣服连工带料～多少钱? How much does this coat cost, material, tailoring and all? ❻〈书 *fml.*〉应当;应该 proper; ought to: 理～声明。I deem it appropriate to make a statement. ❼〈量词 *classifier*〉旧小说中指交战的回合 (in ancient novels) passage at arms; round; bout: 大战三十余～ fight over 30 bouts ❽ 在太阳系中,当行星运行到与太阳、地球成一直线,并且地球不在太阳与该行星之间的位置时,叫做合 conjunction; in the solar system, when another planet, the earth and the sun are in a straight line, and the earth is not in between. ❾ (Hé) 姓 a surname

合² hé 我国民族音乐音阶上的一级,乐谱上用做记音符号,相当于简谱的'5̣' note of the scale in 工尺谱 (gōngchěpǔ), a traditional Chinese musical notation, corresponding to '5̣' in the numbered musical notation. ☞ 工尺 gōngchě on p. 664

☞ gě on p. 655

【合抱】hébào 两臂围拢(多指树木、柱子等的粗细) (of a tree, pillar, etc.) circumference big enough to wrap one's arms around: 院里有两棵～的大树。In the yard there are two trees wide enough to fill a person's arm.

【合璧】hébì 指把不同的东西放在一起而配合得宜。也指两种东西摆在一起对比参照。(of two different things) combine harmoniously; match well: 诗画～ a good combination of poetry and painting | 中西～ a good combination of Chinese and Western elements

【合并】hébìng ❶ 结合到一起 merge; amalgamate; ～机构 merge organizational structures | 这三个提议～讨论。The three proposals will be discussed together. ❷ 指正在患某种病的同时又发生(另一种疾病) (of an illness) be complicated by another illness: 麻疹～肺炎 pneumonia resulting from measles

【合不来】hé·bu lái 性情不相投,不能相处 not get along well; be incompatible

【合不着】hé·bu zháo 〈方 *dial.*〉不上算;不值得 not worthwhile: 跑这么远的路去看一场戏,实在～。It's not worth going all that way to watch a performance.

【合唱】héchàng 由若干人分几个声部共同演唱一首多声部的歌曲,如男声合唱、女声合唱、混声合唱等 chorus; a group of people singing a songs together in different parts, e.g. a male chorus, female chorus, mixed chorus

【合成】héchéng ❶ 由部分组成整体 compose; compound: ～词 compound word | 合力是分力～的。Resultant force is composed of components. ❷ 通过化学反应使成分比较简单的物质变成成分复杂的物质 synthetise; synthesise; combine substances into a compound through chemical reaction

【合成词】héchéngcí 两个以上的词素构成的词 compound word; word composed of two or more base morphemes, 合成词可以分为两类 compound words fall into two categories: a) 由两个或两个以上词根合成的,如'朋友、庆祝、火车、立正、照相机、人行道' word composed of two or more roots, such as 朋友 péng·you, 庆祝 qìngzhù, 火车 huǒchē, 立正 lìzhèng, 照相机 zhàoxiàngjī and 人行道 rénxíngdào b) 由词根加词缀构成的,如'桌子、瘦子、花儿、木头、甜头、阿姨'。前一类也叫复合词,后一类也叫派生词。words composed of roots and affixes, such as 桌子 zhuō·zi, 瘦子 shòu·zi, 花儿 huā'ér, 木头 mù·tou, 甜头 tián·tou and 阿姨 āyí. The former are called compounds, and the latter are called derivatives.

【合成洗涤剂】héchéng xǐdíjì 洗涤用品,用化学合成方法制成。除家庭洗涤用以外,也用于纺织、印染、制革等工业。synthetic detergent; detergent made by synthesis; I in addition to domestic detergents, there are also those used in the textile, printing and dyeing, and hide-processing industries; 通称 generally called 洗涤剂 xǐdíjì

【合成洗衣粉】héchéng xǐyīfěn 洗涤用品,用化学合成方法制成粉粒状,用于洗涤衣服、织物等 synthetic washing powder; laundry powder made by synthesis, used to wash clothes and fabrics, etc.; 通称 generally called 洗衣粉 xǐyīfěn

【合成纤维】héchéng xiānwéi 高分子化合物,是用煤、石油、天然气、乙炔等为原料合成的纤维,如涤纶、锦纶、维纶。合成纤维强度高,耐磨,可制绳索、传送带、轮胎的帘布等,也用来做纺织品。synthetic fibre; macromolecular compounds that are fibres synthesised from such raw materials as coal, petroleum, natural gas and ethyne, including polyester, polyamide and polyvinyl fibres. Synthetic fibres, of high intensity and wear-resistance, can be used to make ropes, conveyance belts, and cord fabric for tires, as well as to make textiles.

【合成橡胶】héchéng xiàngjiāo 高分子化合物,用石油、天然气、煤、电石等为原料合成。种类很多,如丁苯橡胶,异戊橡胶等。synthetic rubber;macromolecular compounds that are synthesised from such raw materials as petroleum, natural gas, coal and calcium carbide, coming in many varieties, e.g. butadiene styrene rubber, and isovaleric rubber

【合得来】hé·de lái 性情相合,能够相处 get along well; be compatible

【合得着】hé·de zháo 〈方 *dial.*〉上算;值得 paying; worthwhile

【合度】hédù 合乎尺度;合适;适宜 right; proper; appropriate

【合法】héfǎ 符合法律规定 legal; lawful; legitimate; rightful:~权利 legitimate right; lawful right|~地位 legal status|~斗争 legal struggle|合理~rational and legal

【合该】hégāi 理应;应该 should; ought to:~如此。It should be so.

【合格】hégé 符合标准 qualified; up to standard:质量~ up to standard|检查~ qualified after inspection|产品完全~。The products are fully qualified.

【合共】hégòng same as 一共 yīgòng:两个班~八十人。The two classes have altogether 80 students.

【合股】hégǔ 若干人聚集资本(经营工商业) pool capital; form a partnership (to run a business):~经营 run a business in partnership

【合乎】héhū 符合;合于 conform with (or to); correspond to; accord with; tally with:~事实 tally with the facts|~规律 be in conformity with the norms|~要求 fulfil requirements

【合欢】héhuān ❶(相爱的男女)欢聚 conjugal happiness;sexual compatibility ❷落叶乔木,树皮灰色,羽状复叶,小叶对生,白天张开,夜间合拢。花萼和花瓣黄绿色,花丝粉红色,荚果扁平。木材可以做家具。silktree Alizzia(*Albizzia julibrissin*); deciduous tree having silver bark, bipinnate leaves that open in the daytime and close at night, yellowish-green calyx and petals, pink filaments, flat pods, and timber that is used to make furniture; also 马缨花 mǎyīnghuā

【合伙】héhuǒ (~儿 héhuǒr)合成一伙(做某事) form a partnership:~经营 run a business in partnership|~干坏事 gang up and do evil

【合击】héjī 几路军队共同进攻同一目标 make a joint attack on: 分进~ concerted attack by converging columns

【合计】héjì 合在一起计算;总共 amount to; add up to; total:两处~六十人。The two places add up to 60 people.

【合计】hé·ji ❶盘算 think over; figure out:他心里老~这件事。He kept thinking it over. ❷商量 consult:大家~~这事该怎么办。Let's put our heads together and see what's to be done.

【合剂】héjì 由两种或两种以上的药物配制而成的水性药剂,如镇咳用的复方甘草合剂 mixture; liquid medicine composed of two or more drugs, such as Compound Liquorice which is an antitussive

【合家】héjiā 全家 the whole family:~欢乐 gaiety of the whole family

【合家欢】héjiāhuān 一家大小合摄的相片儿 family group photo

【合脚】hé//jiǎo (鞋、袜)适合脚的大小和肥瘦 (of shoes or socks) fit; be of proper size and shape for one's feet

【合金】héjīn 由一种金属元素跟其他金属或非金属元素熔合而成的、具有金属特性的物质。一般合金的熔点比组成它的各金属低,而硬度比组成它的各金属高。alloy; metal formed of a mixture of metals, or of metal and another substance. In general, the melting point of the alloy is lower than those of the various metals that compose the alloy, but the hardness is higher.

【合卺】héjǐn 〈书 *fml.*〉成婚(卺是瓢,把一个匏瓜剖成两个瓢,新郎新娘各拿一个饮酒,是旧时成婚时的一种仪式)(of bride and bridegroom) drink the nuptial cup; go through the marriage ceremony (卺 *jin* refers to two dippers carved out of a gourd which are used as wine containers for bride and bridegroom)

【合口】hé//kǒu 疮口或伤口长好(of a wound or sore) heal

【合口】hékǒu 适合口味 (of a dish) be to one's taste:咸淡~ neither salty nor bland|味道~ be to one's taste

【合口呼】hékǒuhū ☞ 四呼 sìhū on p.1821

【合饹】hé·le same as 饸饹 hé·le

【合理】hélǐ 合乎道理或事理 rational; reasonable; equitable:~使用 rational utilization|~密植 rational close planting|他说的话很~。What he said is quite reasonable.

【合理化】hélǐhuà 设法调整改进,使更合理 rationalize; reorganize (a process, industry, etc.) in order to make it more rational:~建议 rationalization proposal

【合力】hélì ❶一起出力 join forces; pool efforts:同心~ unite and make a common effort ❷一个力对某物体的作用和另外几个力同时对该物体的作用的效果相同,这一个力就是那几个力的合力 resultant force; when the force on an object is equal to that of several other forces on the object, this force is the resultant force of the other forces

【合流】héliú ❶(河流)汇合在一起 flowing together; confluence:运河和大清河在天津附近～。The Grand Canal and the Daqing River meet near Tianjin. ❷〈比喻 *fig*.〉在思想行动上趋于一致 collaborate; work hand in glove with sb. ❸ 学术、艺术等方面的不同流派融为一体 different schools (of thought, art, etc.) merge into one

【合龙】hé//lóng 修筑堤坝或桥梁等从两端施工,最后在中间接合,叫做合龙 closure (of a dam, dyke, bridge, etc., that is built from both ends); join the two sections of a bridge, dam, etc.

【合拢】hé//lǒng 合到一起;闭合 close up; join together:～书本 close the book|心里焦急烦躁,到半夜也合不拢眼。I was restless with anxiety, and could not close my eyes even at midnight.

【合谋】hémóu 共同策划(进行某种活动) conspire; connive; plot together:～作案 conspire to commit a crime

【合拍】hé//pāi 符合节奏 in time; in step;〈比喻 *fig*.〉协调一致 in harmony:两个人思路～。Their two strains of thought are in harmony.

【合拍】hépāi ❶ 合作拍摄(电影、电视等) coproduction in the making of films or television programmes ❷ 在一起拍照(相片) take photos together

【合情合理】hé qíng hé lǐ 合乎情理 fair and reasonable; fair and sensible

【合群】héqún ❶ (～儿 héqúnr)跟大家关系融洽,合得来 get on well with others; be sociable:她性情孤僻,向来不～。She is of an uncommunicative and eccentric disposition, and has never been sociable. ❷ 结成团体,互助合作 be gregarious and help

【合扇】héshàn〈方 *dial*.〉same as 合叶 héyè

【合身】hé//shēn (～儿 hé//shēnr)(衣服)适合身材 fit;to have the proper size or shape for a figure:这套衣服做得比较～。This set of clothes fits quite well.

【合十】héshí〈佛教 *Budd*.〉一种敬礼方式,两掌在胸前对合 place the open palms together before one's chest, as a salute (十 *shi*:十指 the ten fingers):双手～ place the two open palms together

【合时】héshí 合乎时尚;合乎时宜 fashionable; in vogue:穿戴～dress fashionably|这话说得不大～。What you said is inappropriate.

【合式】héshì ❶ 合乎一定的规格、程式 up to certain specifications, patterns or formulas ❷ same as 合适 héshì

【合适】héshì 符合实际情况或客观要求 suitable; appropriate; becoming; right:这双鞋你穿着正～。This pair of shoes fits you beautifully.|这个字用在这里不～。This isn't the right word to use here.

【合数】héshù 在大于1的整数中,除了1和这个数本身,还能被其他正整数整除的数,如4,6,9,15,21 composite number; an integral number larger than 1 that can be divided without a remainder by another positive integer other than itself or 1, such as 4, 6, 9, 15 and 21.

【合算】hésuàn ❶ 所费人力物力较少而收效较大 paying; worthwhile; lower cost but higher yield:适于种花生的地用来种棉花,当然不～。It is not worthwhile to grow cotton on a plot that is suitable for growing peanuts. ❷ same as 算计 suànjì ②:去还是不去,得仔细～～。You should figure out whether it is worthwhile going or not.

【合体】hé//tǐ same as 合身 hé//shēn

【合体】hétǐ 汉字按结构可分独体、合体。合体是由两个或更多的独体合成的,如'解'由'刀、牛、角'合成,'横'由'木'和'黄'合成。compound character; Chinese characters are composed of single characters and compound characters; a compound character is composed of two or more single characters, e. g. 解 jiě is composed of 刀 dāo,牛 niú and 角 jiǎo; and 横 héng is composed of 木 mù and 黄 huáng.

【合同】hé·tong 两方面或几方面在办理某事时,为了确定各自的权利和义务而订立的共同遵守的条文 contract;a binding agreement between two or more persons or parties to define the rights and responsibilities of each person or party:产销～ a contract for production and marketing

【合同工】hé·tonggōng 以签订劳动合同的办法招收的工人 contract worker;a worker recruited by signing a labour contract

【合围】héwéi ❶ 四面包围(敌人或猎物等) surround (enemy or prey) from four sides ❷ 合抱 a circumference enough to wrap one's arms around:树身粗壮,五人才能～。The tree trunk is so thick that it takes five persons to put their arms around it.

【合心】hé//xīn same as 合意 hé//yì:这件衣服挺～。This dress fits well.|这事办得正合他的心。This matter is being handled to his satisfaction.

【合眼】hé//yǎn ❶ 指睡觉 sleep; close one's eyes:他一夜没～。He didn't get a wink of sleep last night.|忙了一夜,到早上才合了合眼。He was busy all night and did not sleep until morning. ❷ 指死亡 die

【合演】héyǎn 共同表演;同台演出 appear together in the same play, dance, etc.; co-star:他们两个人曾～过《兄妹开荒》。The two of them co-starred in *Brother and Sister Reclaiming Wasteland*.

【合叶】héyè 由两片金属构成的铰链,大多装在门、窗、箱、柜上面 hinge; piece of metal on which a lid, door, window or gate turns or swings as it opens and closes; also called 合页

héyè;有的地区叫合扇 in some place known as 合扇 héshàn

【合宜】héyí same as 合适 héshì:他担任这个工作倒很～。He's just the right man for the job.

【合议庭】héyìtíng 由审判员或审判员和陪审员共同审理案件时组成的审判庭 collegial panel; collegiate bench (of judges, or of a judge and peoples' assessors)

【合意】hé//yì 合乎心意;中意 suit; be to one's liking (or taste):你的想法正合他的意。Your idea is just to his liking.

【合营】héyíng 共同经营 jointly operate; joint operation:公私～joint state-private ownership|中外～ Sino-foreign joint management|～企业 joint venture

【合影】hé//yǐng 若干人合在一块儿照相 take a group photograph (or picture):～留念 have a group photo taken to mark the occasion

【合影】héyǐng 若干人合在一块儿照的相片 group photo (or picture):这张～是我们毕业时照的。This is a group photo we took upon graduation.

【合用】héyòng ❶ 共同使用 share:两家～一个厨房。Two families share a kitchen. ❷ 适合使用 of use:绳子太短,不～。The rope is too short to be of any use.

【合约】héyuē 合同(多指条文比较简单的 oft. esp. one with simple clauses) contract

【合葬】hézàng 人死后同葬一个墓穴,特指夫妻死后同葬在一个墓穴里 (of husband and wife) be buried in the same grave

【合照】hézhào ❶ 若干人一起照相 take a group photograph (or picture):～一张照片 have a group photograph taken ❷ 若干人合在一块儿照的相片 group photo (or picture)

【合辙】hé//zhé (～儿 hé//zhér) ❶ 若干辆车的车轮在地上轧出来的痕迹相合 fit in the tracks; 〈比喻 *fig.*〉一致 in agreement:两个人的想法一样,所以一说就～儿。Since the two of them had similar ideas, the moment they started talking they found themselves in complete agreement. ❷ (戏曲、小调)押韵(of drama, ditty) rhyme:快板～儿,容易记。The words of *kuaibanr* (monologue to the accompaniment of bamboo clappers) are easy to memorize because they rhyme.

【合资】hézī 双方或几方共同投资(办企业) pool capital; enter into partnership (to run an enterprise):～经营 joint operation|中外～企业 joint venture with Chinese and foreign capital

【合子】hézǐ 生物体进行有性繁殖时,雌性和雄性生殖细胞互相融合形成的一个新细胞。合子逐渐发育,成为新的生物体。zygote; a cell formed by the union of two gametes, a male and a female, growing gradually to become a new organism

【合子】hé·zi ❶ 类似馅儿饼的一种食品 a kind of meat pie ❷ same as 盒子 hé·zi

【合奏】hézòu 几种乐器或按种类分成的几组乐器,分别担任某些声部,演奏同一乐曲,如管乐合奏 instrumental ensemble; musical ensemble composed of several instruments or several groups of instruments, either constituting an organic whole or producing a single effect, e.g. a wind instrument ensemble

【合作】hézuò 互相配合做某事或共同完成某项任务 cooperate; collaborate; work together:分工～share the work and help one another|技术～technological co-operation

【合作化】hézuòhuà 用合作社的组织形式,把分散的个体劳动者和小私有者组织起来 cooperation; (a movement to) organize individual labourers and small proprietors into cooperatives

【合作社】hézuòshè 劳动人民根据互助合作的原则自愿建立起来的经济组织。合作社按照经营业务的不同,可以分为生产合作社、消费合作社、供销合作社、信用合作社等。co-operative; co-op; economic organization organized on a voluntary basis and on the principle of mutual help and cooperation; in terms of business lines, they are divided into production, consumption, supply and marketing, and credit co-operatives

纥 hé ☞ 回纥 Huíhé on p.860
☞ gē on p.649

何 hé ❶ 〈疑问代词 *interrog. pron.*〉a)什么 what:～人 who|～物 what|～事 for what reason b)哪里 where:～往 whither|从～而来? Where from? c)为什么 why:吾～畏彼哉? Why should I be afraid of him? ❷ 表示反问 [rhetorical question]:～济于事? Of what avail is it? |～足挂齿? Is it worth mentioning? |谈～容易 easier said than done|有～不可? Why not? ❸ (Hé) 姓 a surname 〈古 *arch.*〉same as 荷 hè

【何必】hébì 用反问的语气表示不必 [used in rhetorical questions] there is no need; why:既然不会下雨,～带伞! Since it's not going to rain, why bring an umbrella?

【何不】hébù 用反问的语气表示应该或可以,意思跟'为什么不'相同 [used in rhetorical questions to express 'should' or 'could'] why not:既然有事,～早说? If you had something on your mind, why didn't you say earlier? |他也进城,你～搭他的车一同去呢? He's also going into town, why don't you get a lift in his car?

【何曾】hécéng 用反问的语气表示未曾 [used in rhetorical questions to express 'never'] ever:这些年来,他～忘记过家乡的一草一木? When has he ever forgotten a single blade of grass or single tree of his hometown all these years?

【何尝】hécháng 用反问的语气表示未曾或并非

[used in rhetorical questions to express 'never'] ever so:我～不想去,只是没工夫罢了? Not that I don't want to go, but have I got the time?

【何啻】 héchì 〈书 *fml.*〉用反问的语气表示不止 [used in rhetorical questions to express 'more than'] can it be any less than: 今昔生活对比,～天壤之别! There's a world of difference in living standards between the past and the present.

【何等】 héděng ❶ 什么样的 what kind:你知道他是～人物? Do you know what kind of person he is? ❷ 用感叹的语气表示不同寻常;多么[used in exclamations to express 'extraordinary'] what; how:这是～巧妙的技术! What consummate skill! |他们生活得～幸福! How happily they are living! *or* Aren't they leading a happy life?

【何妨】 héfáng 用反问的语气表示不妨 [used in rhetorical questions] why not; might as well: ～试试? Why not have a try? *or* You might as well have a try. |拿出来叫人们见识一下,又～呢? Why not take it out and let others have a look?

【何故】 hégù 为什么;什么原因 why; for what reason:他～至今未到? Why hasn't he come yet?

【何苦】 hékǔ 何必自寻苦恼,用反问的语气表示不值得 [used in rhetorical questions] why bother; is it worth the trouble:你～在这些小事上伤脑筋? Why bother about such trifles? |冒着这么大的雨赶去看电影,～呢? Going to the movies in this heavy rain — is it worth it? also 何苦来 hékǔlái

【何况】 hékuàng 〈连词 *conj.*〉用反问的语气表示更进一层的意思[used in rhetorical questions] much less; let alone:他在生人面前都不习惯讲话,～要到大庭广众之中呢? He is too shy to speak in front of a stranger, let alone a large audience.

【何乐而不为】 hé lè ér bù wéi 用反问的语气表示很可以做或很愿意做[used in rhetorical questions] why not do it; one would be only too glad to do it:储蓄对国家对自己都有好处,～? Putting your saving in a bank is beneficial to both the state and the individual — why not do it?

【何其】 héqí 多么(多带有不以为然的口气) [used in exclamations to express disapproval] what; how:～糊涂。What a fool! |～相似。What a striking likeness!

【何去何从】 hé qù hé cóng 指在重大问题上采取什么态度,决定做不做或怎么做 (when faced with an important question) what course to follow; what attitude to take; what decision to make

【何如】 hérú ❶ 怎么样 how about; What do you say of sth. or sb.?:你先试验一下,～? How about you trying it out first? ❷ 怎样的 what kind of:我还不清楚他是～人。I do not yet know what kind of person he is. ❸ 用反问的语气表示不如[used in rhetorical questions] wouldn't it be better:与其靠外地供应,～就地取材,自己制造。Wouldn't it be better if we make it by using local materials than relying on outside supplies.

【何首乌】 héshǒuwū 多年生草本植物,茎细长,能缠绕物体,叶子互生,秋天开花,白色。根块状,可入药。multiflower knotweed (*Polygonum multiflorum*); perennial herb, with thin long stems that climb around other things, has alternate leaves, with white flowers in autumn; its root tuber can be used as an ingredient for traditional Chinese medicine; also 首乌 shǒuwū

【何谓】 héwèi 〈书 *fml.*〉❶ 什么叫做;什么是 what is meant by:～灵感? What is meant by inspiration? |～幸福? What is meant by happiness? ❷ 指什么;是什么意思(后面常带'也'字 oft. followed by 也 yě) what is the meaning of:此～也? What does it mean? *or* What do you mean?

【何须】 héxū 用反问的语气表示不须要 [used in rhetorical questions to express unnecessity] what is the need:详情我都知道了,～再说! I know all the details, what is the need of repeating? |从这里走到车站,～半个钟头? Does one need half an hour to walk from here to the station?

【何许】 héxǔ 〈书 *fml.*〉何处 where; what kind of; what:～人(原指什么地方人,后来也指什么样的人) what sort of person (orig. used to ask where the person comes from, later also used to ask what sort of person he or she is)

【何以】 héyǐ ❶〈书 *fml.*〉用什么 how:～教我。How to educate me? |～为生。What do you live on? ❷ 为什么 why:既经说定,～变卦? It has already been settled. What makes you change your mind?

【何在】 hézài 〈书 *fml.*〉在哪里 where:理由～? What is the reason for it?

【何止】 hézhǐ 用反问的语气表示超出某个数目或范围 [used in rhetorical questions] far more than:这个风景区方圆～十里。This scenic area has a circumference far more than 10 *li*. |厂里的先进人物～这几个? Are the advanced figures in this factory not far more than these few?

诃 hé 〈书 *fml.*〉和谐。多用于人名。in harmony (mostly used for people's names)

和[1] (龢) hé ❶ 平和;和缓 gentle; mild; kind:温～ warm; lukewarm|柔～ soft; gentle|～颜悦色 have a kind face; have a genial expression ❷ 和谐;和睦 harmonious; on good terms:～衷共济 work together with one accord (in time of difficulty)|弟兄不～。The brothers are estranged. ❸ 结束战争或争执 peace; end hostilities between those who have been at war or in a state of enmity:讲～settle a dispute|媾～ make peace ❹（下棋或赛球）不分胜负(of sports) draw; tie:～棋 a draw in chess|～局 draw; tie; tied game|末了一盘～了。The last game of chess ended in a draw. ❺（Hé）姓 a surname

和2 hé ❶ 连带 together with:～盘托出 reveal everything; hold nothing back|～衣而卧（不脱衣服睡觉）sleep without undressing ❷〈介词 *prep.*〉表示相关、比较等[used to indicate relationship, comparison, etc.]:他～大家讲他过去的经历。He told us his past experience.|柜台正～我一样高。The counter is just the same height as I. ❸〈连词 *conj.*〉表示联合;跟;与 and:工人～农民都是国家的主人。Workers and peasants are all masters of the country. ❹ 加法运算中,一个数加上另一个数所得的数,如 6+4=10 中,10 是和 sum; the result of adding numbers, e.g. 6+4=10, 10 is the sum; also 和数 héshù

和3 Hé 指日本 refer to Japan:～服 kimono ☞ hè on p.791, hú on p.817, huó on p.875 and huò on p.884

【和蔼】hé'ǎi 态度温和,容易接近 kindly; affable; amiable:～可亲 affable and genial|慈祥～的笑容 a kindly and amiable smile

【和畅】héchàng 温和舒畅 (of wind) gentle and pleasant:春风～ a gentle and pleasant spring breeze

【和风】héfēng 温和的风。多指春风。soft breeze (esp. in spring):～丽日 gentle breeze and bright sun|～拂面 a gentle breeze caressing one's face

【和风细雨】hé fēng xì yǔ〈比喻 *fig.*〉方式和缓,不粗暴 like a gentle breeze and light rain; in a gentle and mild way

【和服】héfú 日本式的服装 kimono; loose robe with wide sleeves and a broad sash, traditionally worn as an outer garment by Japanese people

【和光同尘】hé guāng tóng chén 指不露锋芒、与世无争的处世态度(见于《老子》第四章 *Laozi · Chapter Four*):'(The way) merges with the brilliant, and becomes one with the dust.' swim with the tide

【和好】héhǎo ❶ 和睦 harmony; concord; amity:兄弟～ fraternal harmony ❷ 恢复和睦的感情 become reconciled:～如初 be on good terms again|重新～ restore good relations

【和缓】héhuǎn ❶ 平和;缓和 gentle; mild:态度～ adopt a mild attitude|药性～。This medicine is quite mild.|口气～ talk in a mild tone|局势～了。The situation has eased up. ❷ 使和缓 ease up; relax:～一下气氛 relieve the tension a little

【和会】héhuì 战争双方为了正式结束战争状态而举行的会议。一般在休战之后举行。peace conference; conference held by two warring sides to end the conflict, generally held after an armistice

【和解】héjiě 不再争执或仇视,归于和好 become reconciled:双方～。The two parties have become reconciled.

【和局】héjú（下棋或赛球）不分胜负的结果 tied game; draw; tie:三盘棋却有两盘是～。Two of the three chess games ended in a draw.

【和乐】hélè 和睦快乐 happy and harmonious:～的气氛 happy and harmonious atmosphere|一家大小,～度日。The whole family leads a happy life.

【和美】héměi 和睦美满 harmonious:～的家庭 harmonious family|小两口儿日子过得挺～。The young couple are living together in perfect harmony.|和和美美地过日子 live happily together

【和睦】hémù 相处融洽友爱;不争吵 harmony; concord; amity:家庭～ family harmony; domestic peace|～相处 live in harmony

【和暖】hénuǎn 暖和 pleasantly warm; genial:天气～ warm, genial weather|～的阳光 genial sunshine

【和盘托出】hé pán tuō chū〈比喻 *fig.*〉全部说出或拿出来,没有保留 lay all the cards on the table; make a clean breast of it

【和平】hépíng ❶ 指没有战争的状态 peace; state of freedom from war or violence:～环境 peaceful environment|保卫世界～ safeguard world peace ❷ 温和;不猛烈 mild; not severe:药性～。The medicine is mild. ❸ 平静;宁静 calm; tranquil:听了这番话,他心里～了一些。Hearing this, he calmed down a little.

【和平鸽】hépínggē 象征和平的鸽子。西方传说古代洪水后,坐在船里的挪亚(Noah)放出鸽子,鸽子衔着橄榄(齐墩果)树枝回来,证实洪水已经退去(见于《旧约·创世记》八章)。后世就用鸽子和橄榄枝象征和平,并把象征和平的鸽子的图画或模型叫做和平鸽。dove of peace; the symbol of peace (*The Old Testament · Genesis viii*); According to the Bible, after the flood, Noah, sitting in the ark, released a dove, which brought an olive branch back to prove the flood had receded. Later, the dove and olive branch were made symbols of peace, and pictures or models depicting the dove as a symbol of peace are called 'doves of peace'.

【和平共处】hépíng gòngchǔ 指不同社会制度的国家,用和平方式解决彼此争端,在平等互利的基础上,发展彼此间经济和文化联系 peaceful coexistence; countries of different social systems settle disputes peacefully and develop economic and cultural relations based on equality and mutual benefit

【和平共处五项原则】hépíng gòngchǔ wǔ xiàng yuánzé 我国倡导的处理社会制度不同国家相互关系的重要原则。即:1.互相尊重主权和领土完整;2.互不侵犯;3.互不干涉内政;4.平等互利;5.和平共处。the Five Principles of Peaceful Coexistence; important principles advocated by China to handle relations between countries of different social systems including: (1) mutual respect for territorial integrity and sovereignty; (2) mutual non-aggression; (3) non-interference in each other's internal affairs; (4) equality and mutual benefit; and (5) peaceful coexistence

【和平谈判】hépíng tánpàn 交战双方为了结束战争而进行的谈判 peace negotiations; peace talks; talks held by two sides of a war for ending the conflict

【和棋】héqí 下棋不分胜负的终局 draw in chess or other board games

【和气】hé·qi ❶ 态度温和 gentle; friendly; polite; amiable: 对人～ be friendly with people ❷ 和睦 harmonious; friendly: 和和气气 polite and amiable | 他们彼此很～。They are very friendly with each other. ❸ 和睦的感情 friendship: 咱们别为小事儿伤了～。Don't let small things hurt our friendship.

【和洽】héqià 和睦融洽 harmonious; on friendly terms: 相处～ get along well with each other

【和亲】héqīn 封建王朝与边疆少数民族统治集团结亲和好 (of some feudal dynasties) attempt to cement relations with rulers of minority nationalities in the border areas by marrying daughters of the imperial family to them: ～政策 the policy of cementing friendly relation through political marriages

【和善】héshàn 温和善良;和蔼 kind and gentle; genial: 态度～ be amiable | 性情～ of a gentle and amiable disposition

【和尚】hé·shang 出家修行的男佛教徒 Buddhist monk

【和尚头】hé·shangtóu 俗指剃光的头;光头(guāngtóu) shaven head; bare one's head

【和声】héshēng ❶ 语调温和 mild tone: 她说话总是～细气的。She always speaks gently. ❷ 指同时发声的几个乐音的协调的配合 harmony; the combination of simultaneous musical notes in a chord

【和事老】héshìlǎo 调停争端的人。特指无原则地进行调解的人。peacemaker, esp. one who is more concerned with stopping the bickering than settling the issue

【和顺】héshùn 温和顺从 gentle and amiable: 性情～ of gentle and amiable disposition

【和谈】hétán same as 和平谈判 hépíng tánpàn

【和婉】héwǎn 温和委婉 tactful; (of speech) mild and roundabout: 语气～ in a tactful tone

【和文】héwén 日本文 written Japanese language

【和谐】héxié 配合得适当和匀称 harmonious; having the parts agreeably related: 音调～ in perfect harmony; melodious; tuneful | 这张画的颜色很～。The colours of this painting match quite well. ◇～的气氛 a harmonious atmosphere

【和煦】héxù 温暖 genial; pleasantly warm: 春风～。The spring breeze is warm and gentle. | ～的阳光 genial sunshine

【和颜悦色】hé yán yuè sè 形容态度和蔼可亲 have a kind face; be all smiles and sweetness; have a genial expression

【和议】héyì 交战双方关于恢复和平的谈判 peace talks; talks held by two warring sides to restore peace

【和易】héyì 态度温和,容易接近 unassuming; amiable: ～近人 amiable and easy of approach | 性情～ of amiable disposition

【和约】héyuē 交战双方订立的结束战争、恢复和平关系的条约 peace treaty; treaty signed by two warring sides to end a war and restore peace

【和悦】héyuè 和蔼愉悦 affable and pleasant: 神情～ look amiable and pleasant

【和衷共济】hé zhōng gòng jì 〈比喻 *fig.*〉同心协力,共同克服困难 work together with one accord (in time of difficulty)

郃 hé 郃阳(Héyáng),地名,在陕西。今作合阳。Heyang, name of place in Shaanxi Province; now written as 合阳 Héyáng

劾 hé 揭发罪状 expose sb.'s misdeeds or crimes: 弹～ impeach (a public official) | 参～ present a memorial to the emperor impeaching an official

河 hé ❶ 天然的或人工的大水道 river; natural or artificial stream of water flowing in a channel: 江～ rivers | ～流 water course | 内～ inland river | 运～ canal | 护城～ city moat ❷ 指银河系 the Milky Way galaxy: ～外星系 anagalactic nebula; extragalactic nebula ❸ (Hé)特指黄河 esp. refer to the Yellow River: ～西 west of the Yellow River | ～套 the Great Bend of the Yellow River

【河浜】hébāng 〈方 *dial.*〉小河 creek; streamlet

【河北梆子】Héběi bāng·zi 河北地方戏曲剧种之一,由清乾隆年间传入河北的秦腔和山西梆子逐渐演变而成 Hebei clapper opera; local opera in Hebei Province, evolved from Shanxi opera and Shanxi clapper opera, introduced into Hebei during the reign of Emperor Qianlong of the Qing Dynasty; ☞ 梆子腔 bāng·ziqiāng on p. 57

【河槽】hécáo same as 河床 héchuáng

【河汊子】héchà·zi 大河旁出的小河 tributary;

a branch of a river

【河川】héchuān 大小河流的统称（general term for）rivers and creeks

【河床】héchuáng 河流两岸之间容水的部分 riverbed；ground over which a river usually flows；also 河槽 hécáo or 河身 héshēn

【河道】hédào 河流的路线，通常指能通航的河 river course；the route of a river, often referring to a navigable river：疏通～ dredge a river

【河防】héfáng ❶ 防止河流水患的工作。特指黄河的河防 flood-prevention work done on rivers, esp. on the Yellow River：～工程 flood-prevention project ❷ 指黄河的军事防御 military defence on the Yellow River：～部队 the Yellow River garrison | ～主力 the main force of the Yellow River garrison

【河肥】héféi 做肥料用的江河、湖泊或池塘中的淤泥 river fertilizer；silt in rivers, lakes or ponds used as fertiliser

【河工】hégōng ❶ 治理河道、防止水患的工程。特指治理黄河的工程。river conservancy works, esp. for the Yellow River ❷ 治河工人 river conservancy workers

【河沟】hégōu 小水道 brook；stream

【河谷】hégǔ 河流两岸之间低于地平面的部分，包括河床和两边的坡地 river valley；stretch of land between riverbanks, including riverbed and slopes

【河汉】héhàn〈书 *fml*.〉❶ same as 银河 yínhé ❷〈比喻 *fig*.〉不着边际、不可凭信的空话。转指不相信或忽视（某人的话）unrelated words；hollow talk；farfetched words（as far off as the Milky Way）；regard as farfetched words：幸毋～斯言。I hope you will not take this as wild talk.

【河口】hékǒu 河流流入海洋、湖泊或其他河流的地方 estuary；stream outlet；the place where a stream enters a larger body of water, such as an ocean, lake or another river

【河流】héliú 地球表面较大的天然水流（如江、河等）的统称 rivers；a natural stream of water of considerable volume on the surface of the earth

【河漏】hé·lou ☞［饸饹］（hé·le）on p. 789

【河马】hémǎ 哺乳动物，身体肥大，头大，长方形，嘴宽而大，尾巴短，皮厚无毛，黑褐色。大部分时间生活在水中，头部露出水面。产于非洲。hippopotamus（*Hippopotamus amphibius Linnaeus*）；hippo；river horse；large herbivorous blackish-brown mammal with an extremely large rectangular head, wide mouth, short tail, and hairless thick hide, most of the time living in water, with its head exposed above the water surface；of African origin

【河漫滩】hémàntān 河两岸由洪水带来的泥沙淤积而成的可耕平地 alluvial flat；river flat；washland；arable land silted up by floods along riverbanks

【河南梆子】Hénán bāng·zi 豫剧 Henan clapper opera；another name for 豫剧 yùjù

【河南坠子】Hénán zhuì·zi 曲艺坠子的通称 ballad singing to the accompaniment of the *zhuiqin*（坠琴），popular in Henan Province

【河清海晏】hé qīng hǎi yàn 黄河的水清了，大海也平静了。用来形容天下太平。The Yellow River is clear and the sea is calm. The world is at peace. also 海晏河清 hǎi yàn hé qīng

【河曲】héqū 河流弯曲的地方 meander；bend of a river

【河渠】héqú 河和渠。泛指水道。rivers and canals；（in a broad sense）waterways：兴水利，开～ undertake water conservancy projects, and build rivers and canals

【河山】héshān 指国家的疆土 rivers and mountains；land；territory：锦绣～a land of splendour | 大好～ beautiful rivers and mountains；one's beloved country

【河身】héshēn same as 河床 héchuáng

【河滩】hétān 河边水深时淹没、水浅时露出的地方 wash；river flat；a piece of land washed by the river, which was submerged during the flood season and exposed during dry season

【河套】hétào ❶ 围成大半个圈的河道。也指这样的河道围着的地方。the bend of a river；land surrounded by the bend of a river ❷（Hétào）指黄河从宁夏横城到陕西府谷的一段。过去也指黄河的这一段围着的地区；现在则指黄河的这一段和贺兰山、狼山、大青山之间的地区。Great Bend of the Yellow River；section of the Yellow River between Hengcheng of Ningxia Hui Autonomous Region and Fugu of Shaanxi Province；（in the past）the area surrounded by this section of the Yellow River；the area between this section of the Yellow River and the Helan Mountains, Langshan Mountains and the Daqing Mountains

【河豚】hétún 鱼，头圆形，口小，背部黑褐色，腹部白色，鳍常为黄色。肉味鲜美。卵巢、血液和肝脏有剧毒。我国沿海和某些内河有出产。globefish（*Tetrodontidae*）；balloonfish；puffer；fish with a round head, small mouth, blackish-brown back, white abdomen, and yellow fins；its ovaries, blood and liver are hypertoxic；found in China's coastal areas and certain inland rivers；also 鲀 tún

【河外星系】héwài-xīngxì 在银河系以外的恒星的集合体，距离地球在数百万光年以上。河外星系是和银河系相当的恒星系。anagalactic nebula；extragalactic nebula；an aggregate of fixed stars outside the Milky Way, millions of light-years from the earth；anagalactic nebula is a stellar system similar to the Milky Way; 旧称 formerly also 河外星云 héwài xīngyún

【河网】héwǎng 纵横交错的许多水道所构成的整体 a network of waterways: ～化 build a network of waterways | ～如织 be crisscross rivers

【河西走廊】Héxī-zǒuláng 甘肃西北部祁连山以北、合黎山和龙首山以南、乌鞘岭以西的狭长地带,东西长约 1,000 公里,南北宽约 100—200 公里,因在黄河之西而得名 Hexi Corridor; a long and narrow area of 1,000 km from east to west and 100-200 km. from north to south in northwestern Gansu Province, north of the Qilian Mountains, south of the Heli Mountain and Longshou Mountain, and west of the Wuqiao Mountain; so called because it lies west of the Yellow River

【河鲜】héxiān 供食用的新鲜的河鱼、河虾等 fresh water fish and shrimp used for food

【河沿】héyán (～儿 héyánr) 河流的边沿 riverbank; riverside

【河鱼】héyú 生活在河里的鱼,如鲫鱼、鲢鱼、鲤鱼等 freshwater fish; river fish, such as crucian carp, silver carp, carp, etc.

【河运】héyùn 内河运输 river transport

曷 hé 〈书 *fml*.〉❶ 怎么 how; why ❷ 何时 when

饸 hé [饸饹](hé·le)用饸饹床子(做饸饹的工具,底有漏孔)把和(huó)好的荞麦面、高粱面等轧成的长条,煮着吃 *hele* noodles, made from buckwheat, sorghum flour, etc., by using a noodle press with holes at the bottom, boiled before serving; also 合饹 hé·le and 河漏 hé·lou

阂 hé 阻隔不通 cut off from; not in communication with: 隔～estrangement; misunderstanding; barrier

盍(盇) hé 〈书 *fml*.〉何不 why not: ～往视之? Why not go and see it?

荷[1] hé 莲 lotus

荷[2] Hé 指荷兰 the Netherlands (Holland) ☞ hè on p. 791

【荷包】hé·bāo ❶ 随身携带、装零钱和零星东西的小包 pouch; small bag (for carrying money and odds and ends) ❷ 指衣服上的兜儿 pocket (in a garment)

【荷包蛋】hé·bāodàn 去壳后在开水里煮熟或在滚油里煎熟的整个儿的鸡蛋 poached or fried eggs (with the shell removed)

【荷尔蒙】hé'ěrméng 激素的旧称 hormone; old name for 激素 jīsù

【荷花】héhuā ❶ 莲的花 lotus flower ❷ 莲 lotus

【荷塘】hétáng 种莲的池塘 lotus pond; pond for growing lotus

核[1] hé ❶ 核果中心的坚硬部分,里面有果仁 pit; stone; the hard central portion of drupaceous fruit (such as peach), with a kernel inside: 桃～ peach-pit; peach-stone | 杏～ apricot-pit ❷ 物体中像核的部分 nucleus; the central part of a substance: 菌～sclerotium | 细胞～cell nucleus ❸ 指原子核、核能、核武器等 atomic nucleus; nuclear energy; nuclear weapon: ～装置 nuclear device | ～讹诈 nuclear blackmail

核[2] **(覈)** hé ❶ 仔细地对照考察 examine; check: 审～ verify | ～算 assess | ～实 check | ～准 examine and approve ❷ 〈书 *fml*.〉真实 true: 其文直,其事～。The article is straightforward, and the facts are true. ☞ hú on p. 819

【核查】héchá 审查核实 check; examine and verify: 对案情认真～ examine and verify the details of a case | ～了工厂的固定资产 check the fixed assets of a factory

【核弹】hédàn 原子弹、氢弹等原子武器的统称 common name for nuclear weapons such as the atomic bomb and hydrogen bomb

【核弹头】hédàntóu 指作为导弹或炮弹弹头的原子弹,或作为导弹弹头的氢弹等 nuclear warhead; atomic bomb used as projectile nose of missiles or artillery shells, or hydrogen bomb used as projectile nose of missiles

【核电站】hédiànzhàn 利用原子能发电的机构 nuclear power plant; power plant using nuclear energy to generate electricity

【核定】hédìng 核对审定 check and ratify; appraise and decide: ～资金 check and ratify funds | ～产量 check and ratify output

【核对】héduì 审核查对 double check; examine and check: ～账目 check accounts | ～事实 check the facts

【核讹诈】hé'ézhà 凭借拥有的核武器进行威胁恫吓 nuclear blackmail; threaten or intimidate depending on nuclear weapons

【核发】héfā 核准后发给 approve and issue: ～驾驶执照 approve and issue a driving license

【核反应】héfǎnyìng 带电粒子、中子或光子与原子核相互作用,使核的结构发生变化,形成新核,并放出一个或几个粒子 nuclear reaction; mutual action between charged particles, neutrons or photons and atomic nuclei causes structural changes in the nucleus and forms a new nucleus, and releases one or more particles

【核反应堆】héfǎnyìngduī same as 原子反应堆 yuánzǐ fǎnyìngduī

【核辐射】héfúshè ❶ 指放射性原子核放射阿尔法、贝塔、伽马射线 nuclear radiation; radioactive atomic nucleus radiating alpha, beta and gamma rays ❷ 指阿尔法、贝塔、伽马射线。通常也包括中子射线 alpha, beta and gamma rays, usu. including neutron rays

【核果】héguǒ 液果的一种。外果皮很薄。中果皮多汁,是食用部分。内果皮是坚硬的壳,里面包着种子。如桃、梅、李等。drupe; fleshy fruit with very thin epicarp, juicy, edible mesocarp and a hard endocarp containing the seed, such as peach, different plums, etc.

【核计】héjì 核算 assess; calculate:～成本 assess the cost

【核减】héjiǎn 审核后决定减少 examine (a budget, etc.) and make cuts:～经费 cut funds after examination

【核力】hélì 核子之间的相互作用力。在距离不超过原子核的大小时,这种力才起作用。nuclear forces; interactive force among the nuclei that works only when the distance is within an atomic nucleus

【核能】hénéng 原子能。因原子能是原子核裂变或聚变时释放出来的,所以也叫核能。atomic energy; energy released from nuclear fission or nuclear fusion; also nuclear energy

【核潜艇】héqiántǐng 用原子能做动力的潜艇。能长时间地连续地在水中进行战斗活动。nuclear-powered submarine, which can operate in water continuously for a long period of time

【核燃料】héránliào 用来在原子反应堆中进行核裂变,同时产生原子能的放射性物质,主要的有铀、钚、钍等 nuclear fuel; mainly composed of uranium, plutonium and thorium, used for nuclear fission in a nuclear reactor, while producing radioactive substances

【核实】héshí 审核是否属实 verify; check:～情况 check the situation|～数据 check the data

【核算】hésuàn 企业经营上的核查计算 examine and calculate; assess; business accounting:～成本 work out the costs|资金～ accounting of capital

【核桃】hé·tao ❶ 核桃树,落叶乔木,羽状复叶,小叶椭圆形,核果球形,外果皮平滑,内果皮坚硬,有皱纹。木材坚韧,可以做器物,果仁可以吃,可以榨油,也可以入药。walnut tree(*Juglans*), deciduous tree, with small, oval pinnate compound leaves, and ball-like nuts; the epicarp of the drupe is smooth, and the endocarp is hard and wrinkled; the timber is hard, used for making utensils, and the kernel is edible and pressed to obtain oil, and also used as an ingredient in traditional Chinese medicine. ❷ 这种植物的果实 the fruit of this plant. also 胡桃 hútáo

【核武器】héwǔqì 利用核子反应所放出的能量造成杀伤和破坏的武器,包括原子弹、氢弹、中子弹和放射性战剂等 nuclear weapon; weapon that uses energy released by nuclear reaction to kill and destroy, including atomic bomb, hydrogen bomb, neutron bomb, and radioactive agent; also 原子武器 yuánzǐ wǔqì

【核心】héxīn 中心;主要部分(就事物之间的关系说)(of the relationship between things) nucleus; core; kernel:领导～the core of the leadership|～小组 the nucleus group|～工事 the core fortifications|～作用(play) a key role

【核战争】hézhànzhēng 用核武器进行的战争(区别于'常规战争'as compared with 'conventional war') nuclear war; warfare using nuclear weapons

【核装置】hézhuāngzhì 能发生核子反应的装置。多指原子弹和氢弹。nuclear device; device that can produce a nuclear reaction; usu. refers to atomic bomb and hydrogen bomb

【核准】hézhǔn 审核后批准 examine and approve; check and approve:施工计划已经审计部门～。The construction plan has been examined and approved by the auditing department.

【核资】hézī 核查资金、资产:check up on funds and assets:清产～ general checkup on enterprise assets

【核子】hézǐ 构成原子核的基本粒子,即质子和中子的统称 nucleon; basic particles that comprise an atomic nucleus, i.e. proton and neutron

盉 hé〈古代 *arch.*〉温酒的铜制器具,形状像壶,有三条腿 *he*; three-legged bronze vessel for heating liquor, similar to a kettle in shape

菏 hé 菏泽(Hézé),地名,在山东 Heze, name of a place in Shandong Province

龁 hé〈书 *fml.*〉咬 bite

盒 hé (～儿 hér) ❶ same as 盒子 hé·zi ①:饭～儿 lunch box|铅笔～儿 pencil box|火柴～儿 match box ❷ same as 盒子 hé·zi ②:花～ firework box

【盒带】hédài 盒式录音带或录像带 audio or video cassette tape

【盒饭】héfàn 装在盒子里出售的份儿饭 box lunch; set meal sold in boxes

【盒子】hé·zi ❶ 盛东西的器物,一般比较小,用纸糊成或用木板、金属、塑料等制成,大多有盖,间或是抽屉式 box; case; casket; small containers made of paper, wood, metal or plastic, mostly with a lid, some like drawers ❷ 一种烟火,外形像盒子 a kind of fireworks, which looks like a box ❸ 指盒子枪 Mauser pistol

【盒子枪】hé·ziqiāng〈方 *dial.*〉same as 驳壳枪 bókéqiāng; also 盒子炮 hé·zipào

涸 hé〈书 *fml.*〉干涸 dry up:～辙 dry rutin

【涸辙之鲋】hé zhé zhī fù 在干涸了的车辙里的鲋鱼(鲫鱼)(见于《庄子·外物》see *Zhuangzi·External Things*) a fish stranded in a dry rutin;〈比喻 *fig.*〉处在困境中急待救援的人 person in a desperate situation

颌 hé 构成口腔上部和下部的骨头和肌肉组织。上部叫上颌,下部叫下颌。jaw; one of the two bony structures and muscles that

form the framework of the mouth; the upper part is called the upper jaw, and the lower part is called the lower jaw
☞ gé on p.654

【颌下腺】héxiàxiàn 下颌部的唾液腺,左右各一 salivary glands, at the lower jaw, with one on the left and one on the right; ☞ 唾液腺 tuòyèxiàn on p.1962

貉 hé 哺乳动物,毛棕灰色,两耳短小,两颊有长毛横生。栖息在山林中,昼伏夜出,吃鱼虾和鼠兔等小动物。是一种重要的毛皮兽。raccoon-dog (*Nyctereutes procyonoides*); carnivorous mammal with brownish-grey hair, small short ears, and long hairs on its cheeks, lives in woods, hides by day and comes out at night, eating fish, shrimp and small animals such as rats and rabbits; is an important animal for its fur; 通称 commonly called 貉子 háo·zi, also 狸 lí
☞ háo on p.773 and 貊 mò on p.1368

阖(阖) hé ❶ 全;总共 entire; whole:~家 the whole family|~城 the whole town ❷ 关闭 shut; close:~户 close the door
☞ 阁 gé on p.652

【阖第】hédì same as 阖府 héfǔ

【阖府】héfǔ 〈敬辞 *pol.*〉称对方全家 your whole family

鹖 hé 古书上说的一种善斗的鸟 a kind of fighting bird mentioned in ancient books

【鹖鸡】héjī same as 褐马鸡 hèmǎjī

翮 hé ❶ 鸟羽的茎状部分,中空透明 shaft of a feather, which is hollow and transparent; quill ❷ 〈书 *fml.*〉指鸟的翅膀 wings (of a bird):振~高飞 flap the wings and soar high into the sky

鞨 hé ☞ [靺鞨](Mòhé) on p.1368

hè(ㄏㄜˋ)

吓(嚇) hè ❶ 恐吓;恫吓 threaten; intimidate ❷ 〈叹词 *interj.*〉表示不满 showing disapproval:~,怎么能这样呢? Hey, how could you do that?
☞ xià on p.2069

和 hè ❶ 和谐地跟着唱 join in singing:曲高~寡。Highbrow songs find few singers. — too highbrow to be popular|一唱百~。When one starts singing, the others join in — meet with general approval. ❷ 依照别人的诗词的题材和体裁做诗词 compose a poem in reply, using the same theme and rhyme scheme:奉~一首 write a poem in reply (to one sent by a friend, etc.)
☞ hé on p.786, hú on p.817, huó on p.875 and huò on p.884

【和诗】hè//shī 指作诗与别人互相唱和。也指这种唱和的诗。an exchange of poems (i.e. one person writing a poem and another writing one in reply, both using the same rhyme scheme); poems exchanged in this way

佫 Hè 姓 a surname

贺 hè ❶ 庆祝;庆贺 celebrate; congratulate:祝~ congratulate|道~congratulate|~喜 offer congratulations|~信 congratulatory letter|~词 message of congratulation|~电 congratulatory telegram ❷ (Hè) 姓 a surname

【贺词】hècí 在喜庆的仪式上所说的表示祝贺的话 greetings; speech (or message) of congratulations; congratulations

【贺电】hèdiàn 祝贺的电报 message of congratulations; congratulatory telegram

【贺函】hèhán same as 贺信 hèxìn

【贺卡】hèkǎ 祝贺亲友新婚、生日或节日用的纸片,一般印有祝贺文字和图画 greeting card; card to congratulate a friend on a wedding, birthday, holiday, etc., generally printed with congratulatory text and pictures

【贺礼】hèlǐ 祝贺时赠送的礼物 gift presented at occasions of celebration or congratulation

【贺年】hè//nián (向人)庆贺新年 extend New Year greetings:~片 New Year card

【贺喜】hè//xǐ same as 道喜 dào//xǐ

【贺信】hèxìn 祝贺的信 congratulatory letter; letter of congratulation; also 贺函 hèhán

荷 hè ❶ 背(bēi)或扛 carry on one's shoulder or back:~锄 carry a hoe on one's shoulder|~枪实弹 carry loaded rifles — ready for an emergency ❷ 〈书 *fml.*〉承当 bear (a burden); take (responsibility):~天下之重任 shoulder important responsibilities for the country ❸ same as 负担 fùdān ②:肩负重~ be charged with important tasks ❹ 承受恩惠(多用在书信里表示客气 oft. in correspondence) be accorded kindness:感~ be thankful for; feel gratitude for|为~ (the above) would be a great kindness
☞ hé on p.789

【荷枪实弹】hè qiāng shí dàn 扛着枪,子弹上膛。指军队、警察等处于戒备状态。(of soldiers or policemen) carry loaded rifles and ready for an emergency

【荷载】hèzài ❶ 指作用在物体上的外力 external force acted on an object ❷ 承载;承重 bear a load, bear a weight

【荷重】hèzhòng 建筑物能够承受的重量 load; weight a building can bear

喝 hè 大声喊叫 shout loudly:吆~ cry out|~问 shout a question to|大~一声 give a loud shout
☞ hē on p.780

【喝彩】hè//cǎi 大声叫好 acclaim; cheer; shout 'bravo!':齐声~ cheer in chorus; cheer with one accord|全场观众都喝起彩来。All the audience cheered in chorus.

【喝倒彩】hè dàocǎi 喊倒好儿 hoot; boo; make catcalls; ☞ 倒好儿 dàohǎor on p.396

【喝道】hèdào 封建时代官员出门时,前面引路的差役喝令行人让路 (of yamen runners, lictors, etc. in old times) clear the road for the procession of an official by going in the front and shouting to the crowd to give way

【喝令】hèlìng 大声命令 shout an order (or command)

【喝问】hèwèn 大声地问 shout a question: 严词～ shout a question in strong terms

猲 hè 〈书 *fml.*〉 ❶ 喘息恐惧的样子 frightened panting ❷ 威胁;吓唬 threaten; intimidate

☞ xiè on p.2124

愒 hè 〈书 *fml.*〉吓唬 scare: 虚～ bluff and bluster | 恐～ threaten; intimidate

☞ kài on p.1079 and qì on p.1525

赫¹ hè ❶ 显著;盛大 conspicuous; grand: 显～ illustrious; celebrated | 烜～ of great renown and influence ❷ (Hè) 姓 a surname

赫² hè 赫兹的简称 abbr. for 赫兹 hèzī

【赫赫】hèhè 显著盛大的样子 illustrious; very impressive: ～有名 distinguished; illustrious

【赫然】hèrán ❶ 形容令人惊讶或引人注目的事物突然出现 impressively; awesomely: 巨幅标语～在目。The huge slogan catches the eye impressively. ❷ 形容大怒 terribly angry: ～而怒 get into a terrible temper; fly into a violent rage

【赫哲族】Hèzhézú 我国少数民族之一,分布在黑龙江 Hezhen (Hoche) people; one of the minority peoples in China inhabiting Heilongjiang Province

【赫兹】hèzī 频率单位,一秒钟振动一次是一赫兹。这个单位名称是为纪念德国物理学家赫兹 (Heinrich Rudolf Hertz) 而定的。hertz; international unit of frequency, equal to one cycle per second, named after German physicist Heinrich Rudolf Hertz; 简称 abbr. 赫 hè

褐 hè ❶ 〈书 *fml.*〉粗布或粗布衣服 coarse cloth or clothing: 短～ short clothing ❷ 像栗子皮那样的颜色 brown; the colour of the chestnut shell: ～铁矿 limonite; brown iron ore

【褐马鸡】hèmǎjī 鸟,体长约一米,羽毛大部分黑褐色,尾羽基部白色,末端黑而有紫蓝色光泽,是我国特有的珍禽 brown-eared pheasant (*Crossoptilon mantchuricum*); bird, with a body about one metre long, most of its feathers dark brown, and its tail feathers basically white with a purplish-blue lustre at the tip. It is a rare bird species unique to China; also 鹖鸡 hèjī

【褐煤】hèméi 煤的一种,一般褐色,有的灰黑色,含水分较多。除做燃料外,还用来提炼汽油、煤油、焦油等。lignite; brown coal; a kind of coal, generally brown in colour, sometimes grayish-black, containing extra moisture; besides being used as fuel, gasoline, kerosene and tar, can also be extracted from it

鹤 hè 鸟类的一属,头小颈长,嘴长而直,脚细长,羽毛白色或灰色,群居或双栖,常在河边或海岸捕食鱼和昆虫。常见的有白鹤、灰鹤等。crane (*Gruidae*); bird genus, with small head and long neck, long straight bill, long thin legs, and white or grey feathers, living in groups or in pairs, and often catching fish and insects on riversides or sea coasts. The common species are the white crane and grey crane.

【鹤发童颜】hè fà tóng yán 白白的头发,红红的面色。形容老年人气色好,有精神。white hair and ruddy complexion; healthy in old age; hale and hearty; also 童颜鹤发 tóng yán hè fà

【鹤立鸡群】hè lì jī qún 〈比喻 *fig.*〉一个人的才能或仪表在一群人里头显得很突出 like a crane standing among chickens; stand head and shoulders above others; outstanding in talent and appearance among people

【鹤嘴镐】hèzuǐgǎo 挖掘土石用的工具,镐头两头尖,或一头尖一头扁平,中间装着木把 pick; pickaxe; mattock; implement with two pointed picks, or one flat blade and one pick, set at right angles to the handle, used to dig stones or earth; 通称 generally called 洋镐 yánggǎo

翯 hè [翯翯]〈书 *fml.*〉形容羽毛洁白润泽 (of feathers) white and sleek

壑 hè 山沟或大水坑 gully; big pool: 丘～ hills and ravines | 沟～ ravine; gully | 千山万～ innumerable mountains and valleys ◇ 欲～难填 greed is a valley that can never be filled; avarice knows no bounds

hēi (ㄏㄟ)

黑 hēi ❶ 像煤或墨的颜色,是物体完全吸收日光或与日光相似的光线时所呈现的颜色 (跟'白'相对 as opposed to 'white') black; the colour of coal or pitch, or sth. that absorbs all sunlight or sunlight-like rays: ～板 blackboard | ～白分明 with black and white sharply contrasted; in sharp contrast | 白纸～字 (written) in black and white ❷ 黑暗 dark: 天～了。It's dark. | 屋子里很～。It's very dark in the room. ❸ 秘密;非法的;不公开的 secret; illegal; shady: ～市 black market | ～话 cant | ～户 unregistered household; illegal shop | ～社会 the underworld ❹ 坏;狠毒 wicked; sinister: ～心 black heart; evil mind ❺ 象征反动 reactionary: ～帮 reactionary gang ❻ (Hēi) 姓 a surname

【黑暗】hēi'àn ❶ 没有光 dark; without light: 山

洞里一片～。It's pitch dark in the cave. ❷〈比喻 *fig.*〉(社会状况)落后;(统治势力)腐败 (of social conditions) backward; (of ruling forces) corrupt:～势力 forces of darkness; reactionary forces|～统治 dark rule; reactionary rule

【黑白】hēibái ❶ 黑色和白色 black and white:～片 black-and-white film|～分明 with black and white sharply contrasted ❷〈比喻 *fig.*〉是非、善恶 right and wrong; good and evil:～不分 make no distinction between black and white|颠倒～ confuse black and white|混淆～ mix up black and white

【黑白片儿】hēibáipiānr same as 黑白片 hēibáipiàn

【黑白片】hēibáipiàn 没有彩色的影片(区别于'彩色片' as compared with 'colour film') black-and-white film

【黑板】hēibǎn 用木头或玻璃等制成的可以在上面用粉笔写字的黑色平板 blackboard; large, smooth, and dark board of wood, glass and other materials on which to write or draw with chalk

【黑板报】hēibǎnbào 工厂、机关、团体、学校等办的报,写在黑板上,内容简短扼要 blackboard newspaper; blackboard bulletin; newspaper run by factories, institutes, groups or schools, written with brief contents on blackboards

【黑帮】hēibāng 指社会上暗中活动的犯罪团伙和其他反动集团或其成员 cabal; reactionary gang; sinister gang; members of criminal groups or other reactionary groups:～头目 ringleader|～分子 gangsters

【黑不溜秋】hēi·buliūqiū〈方 *dial.*〉(～的 hēi·buliūqiū·de)形容黑得难看 swarthy; having a dark complexion

【黑沉沉】hēichénchén (～的 hēichénchén·de) 形容黑暗(多指天色 of the sky) gloomy; overcast

【黑道】hēidào (～儿 hēidàor) ❶ 夜间没有亮光的道路 dark road:拿着电筒,省得走～。Take a torch, or you'll be groping your way in the dark. ❷ 指不正当的或非法的行径 dark deeds; illegal activities:～买卖 illegal dealings ❸ 指流氓盗匪等结成的黑社会组织 underworld organizations formed by hooligans and bandits:～人物 underworld elements

【黑灯瞎火】hēidēng-xiāhuǒ 形容黑暗没有灯光 dark; unlit:楼道里～的,下楼时注意点儿。It's dark in the passageway, so take care when you go downstairs. also 黑灯下火 hēidēng-xiàhuǒ

【黑地】hēidì 指没有登记在国家地亩册子上的田地 unregistered land

【黑店】hēidiàn 杀人劫货的客店(多见于早期白话 oft. early vernacular) an inn run by brigands

【黑洞洞】hēidòngdōng (～的 hēidòngdōng·de) 形容黑暗 pitch-dark:隧道里头～的,伸手不见五指。It's so dark in the tunnel that you cannot see your hand in front of you.

【黑洞】hēidòng 演变到最后阶段的恒星。由中子星进一步收缩而成,有巨大的引力场,使得它所发射的任何电磁波都无法向外传播,变成看不见的孤立天体,人们只能通过引力作用来确定它的存在,所以叫做黑洞。black hole; fixed star in the last stage of evolution, formed from a neutron star undergoing contraction, its huge gravitational field preventing any electromagnetic wave from escaping, so it becomes an invisible, isolated celestial body. People can determine its existence only through its gravitational action, thus its name, black hole. also 坍缩星 tānsuōxīng

【黑豆】hēidòu 子实表皮黑色的大豆。多做牲口的饲料。black soya bean, mostly used as animal feed

【黑非洲】Hēi Fēizhōu 指非洲撒哈拉大沙漠以南的广大地区。居民绝大多数是黑人。Black Africa; the vast area south of the Sahara Desert in Africa, where the majority of the inhabitants are dark skinned

【黑钙土】hēigàitǔ 暗黑色的土壤,在我国主要分布在东北、西北地区。腐殖质含量高,养分丰富,是肥沃的土壤之一。black earth; chernozem; dark soil, mainly distributed in northeastern and northwestern China, with a high content of humus and rich nutrients, a fertile soil

【黑更半夜】hēigēng-bànyè (～的 hēigēng-bànyè·de)指深夜 in the dead of night; in the still of the night; in the middle of the night

【黑咕隆咚】hēi·gulōngdōng (～的 hēi·gulōngdōng·de)形容很黑暗 very dark; pitch-dark:天还～的,他就起来了。He got up when it was still pitch-dark.|屋里拉上了窗帘,～的。The room is pitch-dark with the window curtains drawn.

【黑管】hēiguǎn same as 单簧管 dānhuángguǎn

【黑光】hēiguāng 指紫外线 black light; invisible ultraviolet ray

【黑锅】hēiguō ☞ 背黑锅 bēi hēiguō on p.77

【黑糊糊】hēihūhū (～的 hēihūhū·de) ❶ 形容颜色发黑 black; blackened:一个～的沙罐 a blackened earthen jar|两手油泥,～的 hands dirty with grease ❷ 光线昏暗 dusky; rather dark:天～的。The sky is gloomy.|屋子里～的。It's rather dark in the room. ❸ 形容人或东西多,从远处看模糊不清 indistinctly observable in the distance:远处是一片～的树林。A dark smudge of trees loomed in the distance.|路旁站着～的一片人。On the roadside there stood a dense crowd of people. ‖ also 黑乎乎 hēihūhū

【黑户】hēihù 指没有户口的住户。也指没有营业执照的商号。unregistered household; unregistered resident; shop without a license; illegal shop

【黑话】hēihuà ❶ 帮会、流氓、盗匪等所使用的暗语 bandits' argot; thieves' cant ❷ 指反动而隐晦的话 double-talk; malicious words

【黑货】hēihuò 指漏税或违禁的货物 contraband; smuggled goods

【黑胶绸】hēijiāochóu 一种涂有薯莨汁液的平纹丝织品，适于做夏季衣料。主要产于广东。a rust-coloured variety of summer silk; gambiered Guangdong silk; a plain fabric coated with juice of dye yam (dioscorea cirrhosa), suitable for making summer clothes, and mainly produced in Guangdong Province. also so 莨绸 liángchóu or 拷绸 kǎochóu

【黑口】hēikǒu 线装书书口的一种格式，版口中心上下端所刻的线条，粗阔的叫大黑口，细狭的叫小黑口（区别于'白口[1]' as compared with 白口[1] báikǒu）a pattern on the foredge of thread-bound books, the lines on the upper and lower foredges; the thick lines are called 大黑口 dàhēikǒu, and the thin lines are called 小黑口 xiǎohēikǒu

【黑马】hēimǎ 〈比喻 *fig.*〉实力难测的竞争者或出人意料的优胜者 black horse; rival whose strength is unfathomable; unexpected winner

【黑茫茫】hēimángmáng（～的 hēimángmáng·de）形容一望无边的黑（多用于夜色 usu. of night scenes) a boundless stretch of darkness：～的夜空 vast dark sky｜眼前～的一片，分不清哪儿是荒草，哪儿是道路。Before our eyes is a boundless stretch of darkness, where we cannot distinguish the weeds from the road.

【黑蒙蒙】hēimēngmēng（～的 hēimēngmēng·de）形容光线昏暗，看不清楚 dim, dusky, difficult to make out：部队趁着～的夜色急速前进。The troops made a rapid march under the cover of night.

【黑名单】hēimíngdān 反动统治者或反革命集团等为进行政治迫害而开列的革命者和进步人士的名单 blacklist; a list of names of revolutionaries and progressive personages made by reactionary rulers or counterrevolutionary cliques for the purpose of persecution

【黑幕】hēimù 黑暗的内幕 inside story of a plot, shady deal, etc.

【黑钱】hēiqián 指以贪污受贿或敲诈勒索等非法手段得来的钱 ill-gotten money, money got through embezzlement, taking bribes, extortion, blackmail or other illegal methods

【黑枪】hēiqiāng ❶ 非法暗藏的枪支 illegally possessed firearms ❷ 乘人不备暗中射出的枪弹 a shot fired from a hiding-place：挨～ be shot from a hiding-place｜打～ snipe; fire shots from a hiding-place

【黑黢黢】hēiqūqū（～的 hēiqūqū·de）形容很黑 pitch-dark：深夜，屋外～的，什么也看不见。In the deep of the night it is pitch-dark outdoors. One can see nothing at all.

【黑热病】hēirèbìng 寄生虫病，病原体是黑热病原虫（旧称利什曼原虫），由白蛉传染。症状是发烧，鼻和牙龈出血，肝、脾肿大，贫血，白细胞减少等。kala-azar; visceral leishmaniasis; infection with a species of Leishmania from sand flies, with symptoms being fever, bleeding of nose and gums, swelling of the liver and spleen, anaemia, and a reduce white-blood-cell count

【黑人】Hēirén 指黑种人 Black people; person with dark skin

【黑人】hēirén ❶ 姓名没有登记在户籍上的人 unregistered resident ❷ 躲藏起来不敢公开露面的人 persons who hide and dare not appear in public

【黑色火药】hēisè huǒyào 用75%的硝酸钾、10%的硫和15%的木炭混合制成的火药，黑色，粒状，爆炸时烟雾很大。供军用、猎用和爆破用，也用来做花炮。黑色火药是我国唐朝时发明的。gunpowder; mixture of 75 per cent potassium, 10 per cent sulphur and 15 per cent charcoal, in the form of black particles, produces thick smoke when exploding; used for military, hunting and explosive purposes, and also in making fireworks. It was invented in China during the Tang Dynasty (618-907).

【黑色金属】hēisè jīnshǔ 工业上铁、锰和铬的统称。包括钢和其他以铁为主的合金。ferrous metal; general name for iron, manganese and chromium, including steel and alloys with iron as the main contents

【黑色素】hēisèsù 皮肤、毛发和眼球的虹膜所含的一种色素。这些组织的颜色的深浅由所含黑色素的多少而定。melanin; pigment in the skin and hair and in the sclera of the eyeball. The shades of colour of these tissues are determined by the amount of melanin they contain.

【黑社会】hēishèhuì 指社会上暗中进行犯罪活动的各种黑暗势力，如反动帮会，流氓、盗窃集团，走私、贩毒团伙等 underworld; social sphere beneath the level of ordinary life, especially the world of organized crime, such as gangs of reactionaries, hooligans, thieves, smugglers and drug traffickers, etc.

【黑市】hēishì 暗中进行的不合法买卖的市场 black market; market where illicit trade of commodities takes place：～交易 black market operations

【黑手】hēishǒu 〈比喻 *fig.*〉暗中进行阴谋活动的人或势力 a vicious person manipulating sb. or sth. from behind the scenes; evil backstage manipulator

【黑糖】hēitáng 〈方 *dial.*〉红糖 brown sugar

【黑陶】hēitáo 新石器时代的一种陶器，表面漆黑光亮 black pottery; pottery painted black, dating back to the late Neolithic Age

【黑陶文化】hēitáo wénhuà ☞ 龙山文化 Lóngshān wénhuà on p. 1249

【黑体】hēitǐ ❶ 排版、印刷上指笔画特别粗，撇捺等不尖的字体（区别于'白体' as compared with 'regular type'）boldface; heavy-faced type in composition and printing, in Chinese meaning thick strokes and the left-falling and right-falling strokes not pointed at the end ❷ 对照射在上面的白光能够全部吸收的理想物体。一个中空的不透明物体，表面留一透光小孔，这个小孔就十分近似于黑体的表面。blackbody; an ideal body or surface that completely absorbs all radiating energy falling upon it, with no reflection. Leaving a small hole on the surface of a hollow opaque object closely approximates to the surface of a blackbody. also 绝对黑体 juéduì hēitǐ

【黑头】hēitóu 戏曲中花脸的一种，因勾黑脸谱而得名。起初专指扮演包公的角色，后来指偏重唱工的花脸。black-face role; painted-face role in traditional opera whose make-up is largely done in black; originally referring to the role of Lord Bao; referring to painted-face roles with much singing

【黑土】hēitǔ 黑色的土壤，在我国主要分布在东北地区。腐殖质含量高，养分丰富，是肥沃的土壤之一。chernozem; black earth; mainly distributed in northeast China, with high contents of humus and rich nutrients, a fertile soil

【黑窝】hēiwō 〈比喻 *fig.*〉坏人隐藏或干坏事的地方 den; place where evil or immoral activities go on: 掏～ wipe out a den of evil-doers

【黑瞎子】hēixiā·zi 〈方 *dial.*〉same as 黑熊 hēixióng

【黑匣子】hēixiá·zi 飞行记录仪。装在座舱里，用来记录飞机飞行中的各种资料。飞机失事后，可依其记录分析失事原因。black box; flight recorder; electronic device installed in the cockpit of a plane to record various flight data, to be analysed in case of an aviation accident to determine the cause of the accident.

【黑下】hēi·xia 〈方 *dial.*〉same as 黑夜 hēiyè

【黑心】hēixīn ❶ 阴险狠毒的心肠 black heart; evil mind: 起～ cherish evil intentions ❷ 心肠阴险狠毒 sinister; insidious: ～的家伙 an insidious scoundrel

【黑信】hēixìn same as 匿名信 nìmíngxìn

【黑猩猩】hēixīng·xing 哺乳动物，直立时高可达一米半，毛黑色，面部灰褐色，无毛，眉骨高。生活在非洲森林中，喜欢群居，吃野果、小鸟和昆虫。是和人类最相似的高等动物。chimpanzee (*Pan troglodytes*); primate mammal, whose upright height can reach 1.5 metres, with black hair and a greyish-brown face with no hair and a high superciliary ridge, living in groups in the forests of Africa, and eating wild fruits, birds and insects. It is a higher species of animal, the most similar to human beings.

【黑熊】hēixióng 哺乳动物，身体肥大，尾巴短，脚掌大，爪有钩，胸部有新月形白斑，其余部分黑色，会游泳，能爬树，也能直立行走。胆可入药。black bear (*Euarctos americanus*); mammal, with a sturdy fat body, short tail, big paws with hooked claws, a white crescent on its chest, while the rest of its body is black; can swim, climb trees and walk erect on its hind legs; its gallbladder used as ingredient in traditional Chinese medicine; also 狗熊 gǒuxióng; 有的地区叫黑瞎子 in some localities also called 黑瞎子 hēixiā·zi

【黑魆魆】hēixūxū（～的 hēixūxū·de）形容黑暗 dark: 洞里～的，什么也看不见。It is pitch-dark in the cave, and nothing is observable.

【黑压压】hēiyāyā（～的 hēiyāyā·de）形容密集的人，也形容密集的或大片的东西 a dense or dark mass of: 广场上～的站满了人。The square was filled with a dense crowd. | 远处～的一片，看不清是些什么东西。One couldn't make out what the dark mass was from a distance. also 黑鸦鸦 hēiyāyā

【黑眼珠】hēiyǎnzhū（～儿 hēiyǎnzhūr）眼球上黑色的部分 pupil; the black part of the eyeball

【黑夜】hēiyè 夜晚；夜里 night: 白天～不停地施工。Construction is going on day and night.

【黑油油】hēiyōuyōu（～的 hēiyōuyōu·de）形容黑得发亮 jet-black; shiny black: ～的头发 shiny black hair | ～的土地 black land; also 黑黝黝 hēiyōuyōu

【黑黝黝】hēiyōuyōu（～的 hēiyōuyōu·de）❶ same as 黑油油 hēiyōuyōu ❷ 光线昏暗，看不清楚 dim; dark: 四周～的，没有一点儿光。It's dark all around, without a spark of light. | 一片～的松林 a stretch of dark pine forest. also 黑幽幽 hēiyōuyōu

【黑鱼】hēiyú 乌鳢的通称 common name for 乌鳢 wūlǐ

【黑枣】hēizǎo ❶ 落叶乔木，叶子椭圆形，花暗红色或绿白色。果实球形或椭圆形，黄色，贮藏一个时期后变成黑褐色，可以吃，味甜。dateplum persimmon (*Diospyros lotus*); deciduous tree with oval leaves, dark-red or greenish-white flowers, and spherical or oval fruit that are yellow and turn blackish-brown after prolonged storage, edible and sweet ❷ 这种植物的果实 the fruit of this plant ‖ also 软枣 ruǎnzǎo ❸〈方 *dial.*〉被枪毙叫吃黑枣（含诙谐意 humor）be executed by shooting is called 'eating dateplum persimmon'

【黑种】Hēizhǒng 指主要分布在非洲的尼格罗—澳大利亚人种 the black race; Negroid (Australoid) people, mainly living in Africa

【黑子】hēizǐ ❶〈书 *fml.*〉黑色的痣 black mole (on the skin) ❷ ☞ 太阳黑子 tàiyáng hēizǐ on p. 1855

嘿(嗨) hēi 〈叹词 *interj.*〉❶ 表示招呼或提起注意 [used to call attention]

hey; why:～,老张,快走吧! Hey, Old Zhang, hurry up! |～! 我说的你听见没有? Hey! Did you hear what I said? ❷ 表示得意 [used to show pride or satisfaction]:～,咱们生产的机器可实在不错呀! Hey, the machine we made is really not bad. ❸ 表示惊异 [used to express surprise]:～,下雪了! Hey, it's snowing! |～,这是什么话! Why, what do you mean by saying that!

☞ mò on p. 1368 and 嗨 hāi on p. 753

【嘿嘿】hēihēi 〈拟声词 *onom.*〉形容笑声 sound of laughter; ha ha

hén (ㄏㄣˊ)

痕 hén 痕迹 mark; trace:泪～ tear stains|刀～ a mark left by a knife-cut|伤～ scar; bruise|裂～ rift; crack; fissure

【痕迹】hénjì ❶ 物体留下的印儿 mark; trace stain:车轮的～ wheel tracks|白衬衣上有墨水～。The white shirt has ink stains on it. ❷ 残存的迹象 vestige; traces of what once existed:这个山村,旧日的～几乎完全消失了。The old traces of this mountain village have almost totally disappeared.

hěn (ㄏㄣˇ)

很 hěn 〈副词 *adv.*〉表示程度相当高 very; very much; quite:～快 very fast|～不坏 not bad at all|～喜欢 like (sb. or sth.) very much|～能办事 very capable|好得～ great; very good|大家的意见～接近。People's opinions are very similar. |我～知道他的脾气。I am very familiar with his disposition.

狠[1] hěn ❶ 凶恶;残忍 ruthless; relentless:凶～ fierce and malicious|～毒 vicious; venomous ❷ 控制感情,下定决心 suppress (one's feelings); harden (the heart):～着心把泪止住。I will harden my heart and hold back my tears. ❸ 坚决 firm; resolute; severe:～抓业务 keep a firm hand on professional work ❹ 严厉;厉害 severe; sternly:对自己人要和,对敌人要～ be gentle to people on one's own side, and be severe to the enemy|～～打击各种犯罪分子 take vigorous measures to crack down on various criminals

狠[2] hěn same as 很 hěn

【狠毒】hěndú 凶狠毒辣 vicious; venomous:心肠～ with vicious intent|阴险～的家伙 an insidious and vicious villain

【狠命】hěnmìng 用尽全力;拼命 go all out; for all one's worth:～追赶 go all out to run after|～往人堆里挤 squeeze through the crowd for all one's worth

【狠心】hěn//xīn 下定决心不顾一切 harden one's heart; make a painful decision:狠一狠心 harden one's heart|狠了心 make a painful decision

【狠心】hěnxīn ❶ 心肠残忍 cruel; heartless; callous:～的人 cruel man ❷ 极大的决心 be determined:下～离开了他。I make a painful decision to dump him.

hèn (ㄏㄣˋ)

恨 hèn ❶ 仇视;怨恨 hate; have a grudge against sb.; be angry that...:～入骨髓 hate sb. to the marrow of one's bones|～之入骨 bear a bitter hatred for sb. ❷ 悔恨;不称心 regretful; unsatisfactory:～事 a regretful matter|遗～ eternal regret

【恨不得】hèn·bu·de 急切希望(实现某事);巴不得 one wishes one could; one would if one could; be dying to:他～长出翅膀来一下子飞到北京去。He wishes he could have wings to fly to Beijing. also 恨不能 hèn·bunéng

【恨人】hènrén 〈方 *dial.*〉使人生气;让人怨恨 make one angry; irritating:他又把饭做煳了,真～! The rice he cooked is burnt again. Really irritating!

【恨入骨髓】hèn rù gǔsuǐ 形容痛恨到了极点 hate sb. to the marrow of one's bones; also 恨之入骨 hèn zhī rùgǔ

【恨事】hènshì 憾事 regretful matter:引为～ regard it as a matter to regret

【恨铁不成钢】hèn tiě bù chéng gāng 〈比喻 *fig.*〉对人要求严格,希望他变得更好 wish iron could simply transform into steel — be anxious for sb. to improve

hēng (ㄏㄥ)

亨[1] hēng ❶ 顺利 go smoothly:～通 go smoothly; be prosperous ❷ (Hēng)姓 a surname

〈古 *arch.*〉same as 烹 pēng

亨[2] hēng 亨利的简称 abbr. for 亨利 hēnglì

【亨利】hēng lì 电感单位,电路中电流强度在1秒钟内的变化为1安培、产生的电动势为1伏特时,电感就是1亨利。这个单位名称是为纪念美国物理学家亨利 (Joseph Henry) 而定的。henry; actual SI unit of inductance, equal to the self-inductance of a circuit, or the mutual inductance of two circuits, in which the variation of one ampere per second results in an induced electromotive force of one volt; named after American physicist Joseph Henry; 简称 abbr. 亨 hēng in Chinese and 'h' in English

【亨通】hēngtōng same as 顺利 shùnlì:万事～。Everything is going smoothly. |他这几年青云直上,官运～。In recent years he has had a successful official career and a meteoric rise.

哼 hēng ❶ 鼻子发出声音 groan; snort: 痛得～了几声 groan with pain ❷ 低声唱或吟哦 hum; croon: 他一边走一边～着小曲儿。He was humming a tune as he walked along. | 这几首诗是在旅途上～出来的。These poems were chanted on the journey.

☞ hng on p. 800

【哼哧】hēngchī 〈拟声词 *onom.*〉形容粗重的喘息声 puff hard: 他累得～～地直喘气。He was huffing from toiling so hard.

【哼哈二将】Hēng-Hā èr jiàng 佛教的守护庙门的两个神,形象威武凶恶,《封神演义》把他们描写成有法术的监督押运粮草的官,一个鼻子里哼出白气,一个口中哈出黄气。后多用来比喻有权势者手下得力而盛气凌人的人(如果碰巧是两个)。也比喻狼狈为奸的两个人。(of Buddhism) Marshals Heng and Ha; two fierce-looking divinities guarding a temple gate. In the novel *Canonization of the Gods* the two are portrayed as army provision escorts with divine power. Heng, the 'Snorter,' exhales white vapour from his nostrils while Ha, the 'Blower,' blows yellow gas out of his mouth. Later they have become a metaphor for any pair of overbearing men who have the favour of a powerful master or act in collusion with each other.

【哼唧】hēng·ji 低声说话、歌唱或诵读 mutter; croon; hum: 他～了半天,也没说明白。He hummed and hawed for a long while but still did not make himself understood. | 他一边劳动,一边～着小曲儿。He hums a tone while working.

【哼儿哈儿】hēngrhār 〈拟声词 *onom.*〉形容鼻子和嘴发出的声音(多表示不在意 expressing a 'who cares?' mentality or attitude) be a 'Yes, sir' type of person; hum and haw: 他总是～的,问他也没用! He always hums and haws, so there is no use asking him!

【哼唷】hēngyō 〈叹词 *interj.*〉做重体力劳动(大多集体操作)时发出的有节奏的声音 heave ho!; yo-heave-ho!; yo-ho!; rhythmic sound uttered while doing heavy physical labour (mostly in a collective operation)

啈 hēng 〈叹词 *interj.*〉表示禁止 to express prohibition

☞ hèng on p. 800

脝 hēng ☞ 膨脝 pénghēng on p. 1459

héng (ㄏㄥˊ)

行 héng ☞ 道行 dào·héng on p. 400

☞ háng on p. 769, hàng on p. 772 and xíng on p. 2143

恒(恆) héng ❶ 永久;持久 permanent; lasting: 永～ eternal; perpetual | ～心 perseverance ❷ 恒心 perseverance: 有～ persist | 持之以～ persevere ❸ 平常;经常 usual; common; constant: ～态 constant state | ～言 common saying | 人之～情 what is natural and normal in human relationships ❹ (Héng) 姓 a surname

【恒产】héngchǎn 指田地房屋等比较固定的产业;不动产 real estate; immovable property; immovables; properties in the form of buildings and land

【恒齿】héngchǐ 人或哺乳动物的乳齿脱落后长出的牙齿。恒齿脱落后不再生牙齿。permanent teeth; second set of teeth of a mammal or human being that follows the milk teeth, typically lasting into old age; also 恒牙 héngyá

【恒等式】héngděngshì 所含的未知量用任意数代替,等号两边的数值永远相等的式子。如 $\cos^2 x + \sin^2 x = 1, (a+b)^2 = a^2 + 2ab + b^2$。identical equation; identity; an equation that is satisfied for all values of the symbols, e. g. $\cos^2 x + \sin^2 x = 1, (a+b)^2 = a^2 + 2ab + b^2$

【恒定】héngdìng 永恒固定 constant

【恒河沙数】Héng Hé shā shù 形容数量极多,像恒河里的沙子一样(原是佛经里的话,恒河是印度的大河) innumerable; countless; as numerous as the sands of the Ganges (a quotation from Buddhist scriptures, the Ganges being a big river in India)

【恒久】héngjiǔ 永久;持久 permanent; lasting; enduring: ～不变 everlasting

【恒量】héngliàng same as 常量 chángliàng

【恒温】héngwēn 相对稳定的温度 constant temperature

【恒温动物】héngwēn dòngwù 能自动调节体温,在外界温度变化的情况下,能保持体温相对稳定的动物,如鸟类和哺乳类 homoiothermal (or warm-blooded) animal; animals that can regulate their body temperature and have a relatively constant body temperature relatively independent of their surroundings, such as birds and mammals; also 常温动物 chángwēn dòngwù, 温血动物 wēnxuè dòngwù or 热血动物 rèxuè dòngwù

【恒心】héngxīn 长久不变的意志 perseverance; constancy of purpose: 学习要有～。One should have perseverance in one's studies.

【恒星】héngxīng 本身能发出光和热的天体,如织女星、太阳。过去认为这些天体的位置是固定不动的,所以叫做恒星。实际上恒星也在运动。fixed star; celestial body that can emits light and heat, e. g. Vega and the sun. In the past these stars were considered to be at a fixed position, thus the name; in fact, 'fixed stars' are also in motion.

【恒星年】héngxīngnián 地球绕太阳一周实际所需的时间,也就是从地球上观测,以太阳和某一个恒星在同一位置上为起点,当观测到太阳再

H

回到这个位置时所需的时间。一恒星年等于365天6小时9分10秒。sidereal year; time it takes for the earth to complete one revolution in its orbit around the sun as measured with a certain star as reference. One sidereal year equals 365 days, 6 hours, 9 minutes and 10 seconds of solar time.

【恒星系】héngxīngxì 由无数恒星组成的集合体，如银河系和河外星系 stellar system; galaxy; complex consisting of countless fixed stars, such as the Milky Way and extragalactic nebula; 简称 abbr. 星系 xīngxì

姮 héng [姮娥] Héng'é〈书 *fml*.〉嫦娥 another name for 嫦娥 Cháng'é

珩 héng〈古代 *arch*.〉佩玉上面的横玉，形状像古代的磬 top gem of a girdle-pendant (as worn by aristocrats and high officials in ancient China, in the shape of an ancient chime stone)

【珩磨】héngmó 用若干油石或砂条组成磨具，在工件内作旋转或往复运动。可使工件达到很高的精度和光洁度。hone; use a grinding apparatus made of several oilstones or abrasive bars that, rotates or reciprocates inside a workpiece to render a high degree of precision and finish

桁 héng 檩(lǐn)purlin

【桁架】héngjià 房屋、桥梁等的架空的骨架式承重结构 truss; an assemblage of pieces (e. g. beams) forming a rigid framework that bears the load of a house or bridge, etc.

鸻 héng 鸟类的一属，体形较小，嘴短而直，前端略膨大，翅膀的羽毛长。只有前趾，没有后趾。多群居在海滨。plover (*Charadriidae*); a genus of shore-dwelling birds that have short straight bills a bit swollen at the tips, stout compact build, and long feathers on the wings, and front claws but no hind claws.

横 héng ❶ 跟地面平行的（跟'竖、直'相对 as opposed to 'perpendicular' and 'vertical') horizontal; parallel to the horizon: ～额 horizontal inscribed board | ～梁 crossbeam ❷ 地理上东西向的（跟'纵[1]'相对 as opposed to 'from north to south' or 'from south to north') transverse; from east to west or from west to east: 黄河～贯本省。The Yellow River flows across this province from west to east. ❸ 从左到右或从右到左的（跟'竖、直、纵[1]'相对 as opposed to 'perpendicular,' 'from top to bottom', or 'from bottom to top') crosswise; sideways; from left to right, or from right to left: ～写 write from left to right or vice versa | 一队飞机～过我们的头顶。A flight of aircraft flew over our head in a row. ❹ 跟物体的长的一边垂直的（跟'竖、直、纵[1]'相对 as opposed to 'perpendicular' or 'verticle') at a right angle to the longer side of an object: ～剖面 cross-section | 人行～道 zebra crossing; pedestrian crosswalk ❺ 使物体成横向 place sth. crosswise or horizontally: 把扁担～过来。Put the carrying pole in a horizontal position. ❻ 纵横杂乱 unrestrained; turbulent: 蔓草～生 overgrown with creepers | 老泪～流 tears flowing from the eyes of an old person ❼ 蛮横；凶恶 violent; fierce; flagrant: ～加阻拦 willfully obstruct | ～行霸道 ride roughshod over; trample on; tyrannize; domineer 注意 **NOTE**: 与'横'(hèng) ① 义相近，但只用于成语或文言词中 semantically similar to 横 hèng ① but used only in idioms or classical Chinese ❽（～儿 héngr）汉字的笔画，平着由左向右，形状是'一' horizontal stroke (in a Chinese character) ❾〈方 *dial*.〉横竖；反正 in any case; anyway: 我～不那么办！I'm not doing that no matter what! | 事情是你干的，我～没过问。You did this, so it has nothing to do with me. ❿〈方 *dial*.〉横是 most likely; probably: 今天下雨，他～不来了。It's raining today, so he most likely won't come.

☞ hèng on p. 800

【横标】héngbiāo 横幅标语 horizontal banner: 巨幅～ huge horizontal banner

【横波】héngbō ❶〈书 *fml*.〉形容眼神流动。也比喻女子的眼睛 glances; (fig.) eyes of women: ～一笑 smile while casting amorous glances ❷ 介质质点振动方向与传播方向垂直的机械波 transverse wave; wave in which a rippling effect moves in a direction perpendicular to the direction of the advance of the wave

【横冲直撞】héng chōng zhí zhuàng 乱冲乱闯 push one's way by shoving or bumping; dash around madly; barge about; charge about; also 横冲直闯 héng chōng zhí chuǎng

【横倒竖歪】héng dǎo shù wāi 形容东西放得纵横杂乱 in disorder; higgledy-piggledy: 几条破板凳～地放在屋子里。Several shabby wooden benches lay in the room higgledy-piggledy.

【横笛】héngdí ☞ 笛 dí ① on p. 415

【横渡】héngdù 从江河等的这一边过到那一边 cross a river, etc.: ～长江 cross the Yangtze River

【横队】héngduì 横的队形 row: 三列～ a three-deep row

【横幅】héngfú 横的字画、标语、锦旗等 banner; streamer; horizontal scroll of painting or calligraphy: 一条(张、幅)～ a horizontal scroll of calligraphy

【横膈膜】hénggémó ☞ 膈 gé on p. 655

【横亘】hénggèn（桥梁、山脉等）横跨；横卧（of a bridge or mountain range) span; lie across;

大桥～在广阔的水面上。A bridge spans the vast river.|两县交界的地方～着几座山岭。Several mountains lie across the border of the two counties.

【横贯】héngguàn（山脉、河流、道路等）横着通过去（of mountains, rivers, roads) pass through from east to west, or from west to east; traverse: 陇海铁路～我国中部。The Lianyungang-Lanzhou Railway traverses the middle part of China from east to west.

【横加】héngjiā 不讲道理，强行施加 do sth. to sb. unreasonably, forcibly, wilfully, etc.:～指责 make unwarranted charges|～阻挠 wilfully obstruct

【横结肠】héngjiécháng 结肠的一部分，上端与升结肠相连，横过胃的下面，下端与降结肠相连 transverse colon; part of the colon extending transversely beneath the stomach, with its upper end linked with ascending colon and its lower end linked with the descending colon; （图见 ☞ figure for 消化系统 xiāohuà xìtǒng on p. 2100）

【横流】héngliú ❶ 形容泪水往四下流 tears streaming down: 老泪～ (of an old person) in tears ❷ 水往四处乱流; (of water) overflow; inundate: 洪水～ the flood inundates ◇物欲～ the overflow of material desires

【横眉】héngméi 形容怒目而视的样子 frown in anger; scowl:～竖眼 with a frown and angry eyes; darting fierce looks of hate

【横眉怒目】héng méi nù mù 怒视的样子。多用来形容强横或强硬的精神。with frowns and angry eyes; darting fierce looks of hate; unyielding or arrogant; also 横眉努目 héng méi nǔ mù or 横眉立目 héng méi lì mù

【横批】héngpī 同对联相配的横幅 horizontal scroll bearing an inscription (usu. hung over a door and flanked by two vertical scrolls that form a couplet)

【横披】héngpī 长条形的横幅字画 horizontal wall inscription; a horizontal hanging scroll

【横剖面】héngpōumiàn 从垂直于物体的轴心线的方向切断物体后所呈现出的表面，如圆柱体的横剖面是一个圆形 cross (or transverse) section; cutting or piece of sth. cut off at right angles, e.g. the cross-section of a cylinder is a circle. also 横断面 héiduànmiàn or 横切面 héngqiēmiàn

【横七竖八】héng qī shù bā 形容纵横杂乱 in disorder; at sixes and sevens; higgledy-piggledy: 地上～地堆放着各种农具。The ground was cluttered with all sorts of farm tools.

【横肉】héngròu 使相貌显得凶恶的肌肉 facial muscles that make one look ferocious: 一脸～ look ugly and ferocious

【横扫】héngsǎo ❶ 扫荡；扫除 sweep across or over; sweep away: ～千军 sweep away a thousand troops ❷ 目光迅速地左右移动着看 sweep one's eyes over: 他把会场～了一遍也没找到他。He swept his eyes over the audience but did not find him.

【横生】héngshēng ❶ 纵横杂乱地生长 grow wild: 蔓草～be overgrown with weeds ❷ 意外地发生 happen unexpectedly: ～枝节 occurrence of unexpected difficulties; deliberately complicate an issue|～是非。A dispute unexpectedly broke out. ❸ 层出不穷的表露 be overflowing with; be full of: 妙趣～ full of wit and humour

【横生枝节】héngshēng zhījié〈比喻 *fig.*〉意外地插进了一些问题使主要问题不能顺利解决 occurrence of unexpected difficulties; deliberately complicate an issue so as to obstruct the smooth solution of the main problem

【横是】héng·shi〈方 *dial.*〉〈副词 *adv.*〉表示揣测；大概 probably; most likely: 他～快四十了吧？He's getting on forty, I suppose? |天又闷又热，～要下雨了。It's so muggy, it will probably rain.

【横竖】héng·shù 反正（表示肯定）(expressing affirmation) in any case; anyway: 他～要来的，不必着急。No need to worry, he'll be coming anyway.

【横挑鼻子竖挑眼】héng tiāo bí·zi shù tiāo yǎn〈比喻 *fig.*〉多方挑剔 find fault in a petty manner; pick holes in sth.; nitpick

【横纹肌】héngwénjī 由细长圆柱形细胞组成的肌肉，细胞上横列着许多明暗相间的条纹。横纹肌的两端附着在骨骼上，它的活动受人的意志支配。striated muscle; striped muscle; skeletal muscle; muscle connected at either or both extremities with a bone, and consisting of elongated, multinucleated, transversely striated skeletal muscle fibres, with its movements under the control of the brain; also 随意肌 suíyìjī or 骨骼肌 gǔgéjī

【横向】héngxiàng ❶ 平行的；非上下级之间的 horizontal; non-verticle: ～比较 horizontal comparison|～交流 horizontal exchange|～协作 horizontal coordination|～经济联合 horizontal economic collaboration ❷ 指东西方向 from east to west, or from west to east: 京广铁路是纵向的，陇海铁路是～的。The Beijing-Guangzhou Railway runs from north to south, while the Lianyungang-Lanzhou Railway runs from east to west.

【横心】héng//xīn 下决心不顾一切 steel one's heart; become desperate: 这一次他可是横了心了。He became desperate this time.

【横行】héngxíng 行动蛮横；倚仗势力做坏事 run wild; run amok; be on a rampage: ～不法 run wild|～无忌 run amok

【横行霸道】héngxíng bàdào 仗势胡作非为，蛮不讲理 ride roughshod over; trample on; tyrannize; domineer

【横痃】héngxuán 由下疳引起的腹股沟淋巴结肿

胀、发炎的症状 bubo; swelling of a lymph node in the groin caused by chancres; a venereal disease

【横溢】héngyì ❶（江河等）泛滥（of a river）overflow; be in flood：江河～ turbulent waters overflowing the riverbanks ❷（才华等）充分显露（of talent, enthusiasm, etc.）exuberant; brimming; overflowing：才思～ brimming with talent and wit

【横征暴敛】héng zhēng bào liǎn 强征捐税，搜刮人民财富 extort excessive (or heavy) taxes and levies; levy exorbitant taxes on the people

【横直】héngzhí〈方 *dial*.〉〈副词 *adv*.〉反正；横竖（héng·shù）in any case; anyway

衡 héng ❶ 秤杆。泛指称重量的器具。graduated arm of a weighing apparatus; weighing apparatus ❷ 称重量 weigh：～器 weighing apparatus ❸ 衡量 judge：～情度理 consider the circumstances and judge by common sense; all things considered ❹〈书 *fml*.〉平；不倾斜 level; even：平～ balance｜均～ equilibrium ❺（Héng）姓 a surname

【衡量】héng·liáng ❶ 比较；评定 weigh; measure; judge：～得失 weigh up the gains and losses ❷ 考虑；斟酌 consider; deliberate：你～一下这件事该怎么办。Will you please consider what to do about this matter?

【衡器】héngqì 称重量的器具，如秤、天平 weighing apparatus, e.g. steelyard, balance, weigh scale

蘅 héng ☞ 杜蘅 dùhéng on p. 481

hèng（ㄏㄥˋ）

啈 hèng 发狠的声音［sound indicating exasperation］grunt; growl
☞ hēng on p. 797

横 hèng ❶ 粗暴；凶暴 harsh and unreasonable; perverse：蛮～ rude and unreasonable｜强～ tyrannical; arrogant｜～话 harsh, unreasonable words ❷ 不吉利的；意外的 ominous; unexpected：～事 an untoward accident｜～祸 unexpected calamity; sudden misfortune
☞ héng on p. 798

【横暴】hèngbào 强横凶暴 perverse and violent：～不法 violent and unlawful｜～的行为 an outrageous manner

【横财】hèngcái 意外得来的钱财（多指用不正当的手段得来的）ill-gotten wealth (or gains)：发～ get rich by foul means; have a windfall

【横祸】hènghuò 意外的祸患 unexpected calamity; sudden misfortune：惨遭～ meet an unexpected calamity

【横蛮】hèngmán same as 蛮横 mánhèng

【横逆】hèngnì 横暴的行为 perverse and unreasonable manner; outrageous manner

【横事】hèngshì 凶事；横祸 unlucky incident; untoward accident

【横死】hèngsǐ 指因自杀、被害或意外事故而死亡 die a violent death; meet with sudden death; died of suicide

hm（ㄏㄇ）

噷 hm［h 跟单纯的双唇鼻音拼合的音］〈叹词 *interj*.〉表示申斥或不满意［expressing disapproval or reproach］humph：～你还闹哇！Humph, you are still making a fuss!｜～，你骗得了我？Humph, how can you cheat me?

hng（ㄏㄤ）

哼 hng［h 跟单纯的舌根鼻音拼合的音］表示不满意或不相信［expressing disapproval or suspicion］humph：～，你信他的！Humph! How can you believe what he said?
☞ hēng on p. 797

hōng（ㄏㄨㄥ）

吽 hōng〈佛教 *Budd*.〉咒语用字 hum; word used in an incantation

轰（轟、❸揈） hōng ❶〈拟声词 *onom*.〉bang; boom：突然～的一声，震得山鸣谷应。With a sudden bang, the echo of the explosion reverberated in the valley. ❷（雷）鸣；（炮）击；（火药）爆炸（of thunder）rumble;（of artillery）bombard;（of bombs, fireworks etc.）explode：～炸 attack with bombs｜～击 shell; bombard｜雷～电闪。Thunder rumbled and lightning flashed. ❸ 赶；驱逐 shoo away; drive off：～麻雀 shoo away the sparrows｜他摇着鞭子～牲口。He wields a whip to shoo livestock.｜把他～出去。Throw him out.

【轰动】hōngdòng 同时惊动很多人 cause a sensation; make a stir：～全国 cause a sensation throughout the country｜～一时 create a furore; make a great stir; cause a great sensation｜全场～ make a stir in the audience (or in the hall); also 哄动 hōngdòng

【轰赶】hōnggǎn 驱赶；驱逐 shoo away; drive off：～牲口 drive off livestock｜～苍蝇 whisk the flies off

【轰轰烈烈】hōnghōnglièliè 形容气魄雄伟，声势浩大 vigorous; dynamic; on a grand and spectacular scale：～地做一番事业 engage in an undertaking on a grand and spectacular scale｜开展了～的群众运动 launch a vigorous mass movement

【轰击】hōngjī ❶ 用炮火攻击 shell; bombard;

～敌人阵地 shell enemy positions ❷ 用质子、中子、甲种射线或阴极射线等撞击元素的原子核等 direct a stream of particles, such as neutrons and protons, against the atomic nuclei of an element to produce nuclear transformations

【轰隆】hōnglōng〈拟声词 *onom.*〉形容雷声、爆炸声、机器声等 rumble; roll; boom; clang; the sound of thunder, explosions or machines: 炮声～～直响。The cannons boomed. |～一声巨响,房子倒塌下来。With a deafening boom, the house collapsed.

【轰鸣】hōngmíng 发出轰隆轰隆的巨大声音 thunder; roar: 礼炮～。The gun salute roared.

【轰然】hōngrán 形容大声 with a loud crash (or bang): ～大笑 roar with laughter |～作响 rumble; boom

【轰响】hōngxiǎng 轰鸣 roar; rumble: 马达～。The motors roared.

【轰炸】hōngzhà 从飞机上对地面或水上各种目标投掷炸弹 attack with bombs; drop bombs; bomb targets on the ground or water (from an airplane): 轮番～ bomb in waves

【轰炸机】hōngzhàjī 用来从空中对地面或水上目标进行轰炸的飞机,有装置炸弹、导弹等的专门设备和防御性的射击武器,载重量大,飞行距离远 bomber; airplane designed for bombing targets on the ground or water surface, with special equipment, such as bombs, missiles and defensive guns, with a great loading capacity and long-distance flight capability

哄 hōng ❶〈拟声词 *onom.*〉形容许多人大笑声或喧哗声 guffaws; roars of laughter or noise ❷ 许多人同时发出声音 hubbub; noise; uproar: ～动 cause a sensation; make a stir |～传 (of rumours) circulate widely

☞ hǒng on p. 808 and hòng on p. 808

【哄传】hōngchuán 纷纷传说 (of rumours) circulate widely: 四处～ circulate widely | 这消息很快就～开了。It was not long before the news was widely circulated.

【哄动】hōngdòng same as 轰动 hōngdòng

【哄抢】hōngqiǎng 许多人拥上去抢购或抢夺(财物) (of a crowd of people) make a mad rush to purchase goods; scramble for (property)

【哄然】hōngrán 形容许多人同时发出声音 boisterous; uproarious: 舆论～。There was a public outcry. |～大笑 burst into uproarious laughter

【哄抬】hōngtái 投机商人纷纷抬高(价格) (of profiteers) drive up (prices): ～物价 drive up prices

【哄堂】hōngtáng 形容全屋子的人同时大笑 roomful of people laughing at the same time: ～大笑。The whole room is rocking with laughter.

訇 hōng ❶ 形容大声 loud noise: ～然 with a loud noise |～的一声 with a loud crash ❷

☞ 阿訇 āhōng on p. 1

烘 hōng ❶ 用火或蒸汽使身体暖和或者使东西变熟、变热或干燥 dry, heat or cook (sth.) by the fire or with steam; dry or warm (one's body) by the fire or with steam: ～箱 oven |～手 warm one's hands by the fire | 把湿衣服～一～ dry wet clothes by the fire ❷ 衬托 set off: ～衬 set off by contrast |～托 throw into sharp relief

【烘焙】hōngbèi 用火烘干(茶叶、烟叶等) cure (tea or tobacco leaves, etc.)

【烘衬】hōngchèn 烘托;陪衬 set off by contrast; bring into sharp relief

【烘烘】hōnghōng〈拟声词 *onom.*〉形容火着得旺的声音 the sound of a roaring fire: 炉火～ roaring stove fire

【烘笼】hōnglóng (～儿 hōnglóngr) 竹片、柳条或荆条等编成的笼子,罩在炉子或火盆上,用来烘干衣物 basketwork frame put over an oven or brazier for drying clothes

【烘染】hōngrǎn 烘托渲染 set off by contrast and exaggerate: 他把自己所听到的,加上许多～之词,活灵活现地讲给大家听。He gave a vivid description of what he had heard, adding many exaggerated details.

【烘托】hōngtuō ❶ 国画的一种画法,用水墨或淡的色彩点染轮廓外部,使物象鲜明 (in traditional Chinese painting) add shading around an object to make it stand out ❷ 写作时先从侧面描写,然后再引出主题,使要表现的事物鲜明突出 (in writing) provide a foil for a character or an incident in a literary work; achieve the effect of prominence through contrast ❸ 泛指陪衬,使明显突出 (in a broad sense) set off by contrast; throw into sharp relief: 蓝天～着白云。The blue sky is set off by white clouds. | 红花还要绿叶～。The red flowers need green leaves to set them off.

【烘箱】hōngxiāng 用加热的方法把潮湿物品中水分去掉的箱形装置,多用于工业 oven; box-like device for baking, heating or drying, mostly used in industry

【烘云托月】hōng yún tuō yuè〈比喻 *fig.*〉从侧面加以点染以烘托所描绘的事物 paint clouds to set off the moon; provide a foil for a character or an incident in a literary work

薨 hōng 君主时代称诸侯或大官等的死 (of feudal lords or high officials) die; pass away: ～逝 pass away

hóng (ㄏㄨㄥˊ)

弘 hóng ❶ 大 great; grand; magnificent: ～图 great plan; grand prospect |～愿 great aspirations; noble ambition |～旨 main theme; main idea of an article; 现多作宏 now usu. written as 宏 hóng ❷ 扩充;光大 enlarge; expand: 恢～ broad; extensive ❸ (Hóng) 姓 a surname

【弘论】hónglùn same as 宏论 hónglùn

【弘图】hóngtú same as 宏图 hóngtú

【弘扬】hóngyáng 〈书 *fml*.〉发扬光大 carry forward; develop; enhance: ～祖国文化 develop the culture of the motherland. also 宏扬 hóngyáng

【弘愿】hóngyuàn same as 宏愿 hóngyuàn

【弘旨】hóngzhǐ same as 宏旨 hóngzhǐ

【弘治】Hóngzhì 明孝宗(朱祐樘)年号(公元1488—1505) Hongzhi, the reign title of Emperor Xiaozong (Zhu Youtang) from 1488 to 1505 during the Ming Dynasty

红 hóng ❶ 像鲜血或石榴花的颜色 red; colour of blood or the pomegranate flower: ～枣 red dates | ～领巾 red scarf ❷ 象征喜庆的红布 red cloth, bunting, etc., used on festive occasions: 披～ drape a band of red silk over sb.'s shoulders (as a token of honour) | 挂～ hang up red streamers ❸ 象征顺利、成功或受人重视、欢迎 symbol of success or importance attached to sb., or sth., or of popularity: ～运 good luck | 开门～ make a good beginning | 满堂～ all-round victory; success in every field | 他唱戏唱～了。He achieved stardom as an opera actor. ❹ 象征革命或政治觉悟高 revolutionary; high level of political consciousness: ～军 Red Army | 又～又专 both red and expert; both politically conscious and professionally competent ❺ 红利 bonus; dividend: 分～ draw dividends; share profits

☞ gōng on p. 673

【红案】hóng'àn (～儿 hóng'ànr) 炊事分工上指做菜的工作(区别于'白案' as compared with 'white board cooking') 'red-(chopping)-board cooking' — a division of kitchen work that deals with making meat and vegetable dishes

【红白喜事】hóng bái xǐshì 男女结婚是喜事,高寿的人病逝的丧事叫喜丧,统称红白喜事。有时也说红白事。泛指婚丧。weddings and funerals; weddings are 'red happy events' (when people wear red), and funerals for those who have lived a long life and died naturally are 'white happy events' (when people wear white); also 红白事 hóngbáishì

【红榜】hóngbǎng 指光荣榜,因多用红纸写成,所以叫红榜 honour roll (or board) written on red paper

【红包】hóngbāo (～儿 hóngbāor) 包着钱的红纸包儿,用于馈赠或奖励等 red paper envelope containing money as a gift, tip, or bonus: 送～ give bonus | 发～ issue bonuses

【红宝石】hóngbǎoshí 红色透明的刚玉,硬度大,用来做首饰和精密仪器的轴承等 ruby; precious stone that is a red transparent corundum, which is very hard, used to make jewelry and bearings for precision instruments.

☞ 刚玉 gāngyù on p. 636

【红不棱登】hóng·bulēngdēng (～的 hóng·bulēngdēng·de) 红(含厌恶意 disagreeably) reddish in colour: 这件蓝布大褂染得不好,太阳一晒变得～的。This blue jacket was badly dyed and has turned reddish after exposure to the sun.

【红茶】hóngchá 茶叶的一大类,是全发酵茶。色泽乌黑油润,沏出的茶色红艳,具有特别的香气和滋味。black tea; main category of tea that is dark in colour from complete fermentation of the leaves before firing; this tea when brewed is red in colour, with a special fragrance and taste

【红潮】hóngcháo ❶ 害羞时两颊上泛起的红色 blush; flush; reddening of the face from shyness ❷ 指月经 red tide; red water; menstruation

【红尘】hóngchén 指繁华的社会。泛指人世间。the world of mortals; (in a broad sense) human society: 看破～ see through the vanity of the world; be disillusioned with the mortal world

【红蛋】hóngdàn 用颜料染红的鸡蛋,旧俗生孩子的人家用来分送亲友 red egg; egg dyed red on the happy occasion of the birth of a child, and given as gifts to friends and relatives

【红灯区】hóngdēngqū 指某些城市中妓院、舞厅、酒吧、夜总会等集中的地区 red-light district; a district in which prostitution houses, ballrooms, pubs and night clubs are clustered

【红点颏】hóngdiǎnké 鸟,歌鸲(qú)的一种。羽毛褐色,雄的喉部鲜红色,叫的声音很好听。mynah (*Luscinia calliope*); bird having brown feathers, the male being cardinal red at the throat and having a pleasant chirp; 通称 generally called 红靛颏儿 hóngdiànkér

【红豆】hóngdòu ❶ 红豆树,乔木,羽状复叶,小叶长椭圆形,圆锥花序,花白色,荚果扁平,种子鲜红色。产在亚热带地方。red bean shrub (*Abrus precatorius*); Indian licorice; rosary pea; subtropical shrub that has pinnately compound oval leaves, panicles, white flowers and flat legumes, and bears cardinal-red seeds ❷ 这种植物的种子。古代文学作品中常用来象征相思。seeds of the rosary pea, oft. used to symbolize love in ancient literature, hence the variant name 'lovesickness seeds'; also 相思子 xiāngsīzǐ

【红骨髓】hónggǔsuǐ 含有很多血管和神经的红色骨髓,有造血功能。婴儿的骨髓都是红骨髓,成人长骨骨腔的红骨髓变为黄骨髓。red marrow; reddish bone marrow that contains many blood vessels and nerves and is the centre of blood-cell production; an infant's marrow is reddish and turns yellow with maturity

【红光满面】hóng guāng mǎn miàn 形容人的脸色红润,有光泽 (of sb.'s face) glowing with health; in the pink of health; also 满面红光 mǎn miàn hóng guāng

【红果儿】hóngguǒr〈方 *dial.*〉same as 山里红 shān•lihóng

【红火】hóng•huo 形容旺盛、兴隆、热闹 flourishing; prosperous; lively: 五月的石榴花越开越～。Pomegranate flowers blossom with increasing vibrancy through the month of May. | 她家的日子越过越～。Her family is becoming better and better off. | 小店办得日趋～。The shop has prospered with each passing day. | 联欢晚会节目很多,开得很～。That evening's party offered many activities and was a roaring success.

【红货】hónghuò〈旧时 *old*〉指珠宝一类的贵重物品 jewellery; treasures such as pearls and jewels: ～铺 jewellery store

【红教】Hóngjiào 藏族地区喇嘛教的一派。8 世纪到 9 世纪盛行。Red Hats; Rnyingma Sect; prevailing Lamaist cult in Tibet in the 8th and 9th centuries

【红净】hóngjìng 戏曲中净角的一种,专演红色脸谱的人物 red-face role; painted-face role in traditional Chinese opera with makeup largely in red

【红角】hóngjué (～儿 kóngjuér)指受广大观众欢迎的演员 very popular actor or actress; star

【红军】Hóngjūn ❶ 第二次国内革命战争时期中国共产党领导下的革命军队,全称中国工农红军 the Red Army (short form for the Chinese Workers' and Peasants' Red Army); revolutionary army under the leadership of the Communist Party of China during the period of the second revolutionary civil war (1928-1937); ☞ 中国工农红军 Zhōngguó Gōng Nóng Hóngjūn on p.2481 ❷ 指 1946 年以前的苏联军队 Soviet army before 1946

【红利】hónglì ❶ 指企业分给股东的利润或分给职工的额外报酬 dividend for shareholders; extra pay for employees in an enterprise ❷ 参加集体生产单位的个人所得的额外收益 bonus; an individual's extra income from participating in collective production

【红脸】hóng//liǎn ❶ 指害羞 blush: 这小姑娘见了生人就～。This girl often blushes when meeting strangers. ❷ 指发怒 flush with anger; get angry: 我们俩从来没红过脸。We have never gotten angry with each other.

【红领巾】hónglǐngjīn ❶ 红色的领巾,代表红旗的一角,少年先锋队员的标志 red scarf, which symbolises a corner of the red flag and is an emblem of the Young Pioneers ❷ 指少先队员 Young Pioneer

【红绿灯】hónglǜdēng 指挥车辆通行的信号灯,多设在城市的交叉路口,红灯指示停止,绿灯指示前进 traffic light; traffic signals set at intersections for controlling traffic (red light signals 'stop', and green light signals 'go')

【红毛坭】hóngmáoní〈方 *dial.*〉same as 水泥 shuǐní

【红帽子】hóngmào•zi ❶ 在白色恐怖时期,进步人士被反动派指为共产党员或与共产党有联系,叫做被戴上红帽子 red cap — anyone branded a Communist or a Communist sympathiser before Liberation was said to wear a 'red cap' ❷ 称火车站上装卸货物、搬运行李的工人,他们工作时头戴红色帽子 (railway) redcap; porters who wear red caps at work at a railway station

【红模子】hóngmú•zi 供儿童练习毛笔字用的纸,印有红色的字,用墨笔顺着红字的笔画写 copy sheet; sheet of paper with characters printed in red, for children learning calligraphy to trace over with a brush

【红木】hóngmù 紫檀一类的木材,多为红色或褐色,质地坚硬,大多用来做贵重的家具 padauk (*Pterocarpus*); mahogany; a kind of rosewood that is red or brown and has a hard character, usu. used to make precious furniture

【红男绿女】hóng nán lǜ nǚ 指穿着各种漂亮服装的青年男女 gaily dressed young men and young women

【红娘】Hóngniáng《西厢记》中崔莺莺的侍女,促成了莺莺和张生的结合。后来用做媒人的代称。maid in the play *Romance of the Western Chamber*, whose intercession helps bring about the union of the lovers, her mistress Yingying and the young scholar Zhang Sheng; later used as an alternative name for a go-between or matchmaker

【红牌】hóngpái 红色的硬纸片。某些球类比赛中裁判员用来处罚严重犯规的球员。足球比赛中被出示红牌的球员须立即退出赛场,同时不得参加下一场或几场球赛。red card; warning card used in some ball games by the referee to punish players who commit flagrant fouls. Players at football games who are warned with a red card have to leave the game immediately and are not allowed to participate in the game that follows.

【红盘】hóngpán (～儿 hóngpánr)〈旧时 *old*〉(商业用语) 指春节后开始营业时的价格 (business) new-year price quotation

【红皮书】hóngpíshū ☞ 白皮书 báipíshū on p.36

【红票】hóngpiào ❶〈旧时 *old*〉戏剧或杂技等的演出者赠送给人的免费入场券 free admission ticket given by performers for theatrical or acrobatic show ❷〈旧时 *old*〉戏剧演出以较高价格售出的票(多为硬性摊派 usu. apportioned compulsively) drama tickets sold at high prices

【红扑扑】hóngpūpū（～的 hóngpūpū·de）形容脸色红 flushed；rosy-faced：喝了几杯酒，脸上～的。After a few drinks his face became flushed.

【红葡萄藤】hóngpú·táoténg 落叶藤本植物，叶子阔卵形，有细长的叶柄，聚伞花序，浆果成熟时蓝黑色。秋天叶子变成红色。茎和根可入药。Boston ivy (*Parthenocissus tricuspidata*); woody vine with 3-lobed leaves that turn red in autumn, slim leafstalks, and cymes bearing dark-blue baccas, and caudex and roots that can be used for medicine; also 爬墙虎 páqiánghǔ

【红旗】hóngqí ❶ 红色的旗子，是无产阶级革命的象征 red flag or banner (oft. a symbol of the proletarian revolution)：～飘飘 red flag fluttering in the wind ❷ 竞赛中用来奖励优胜者的红色旗子 red flag used as encouragement for winners of a competition ❸〈比喻 *fig.*〉先进 advanced：～手 pioneer；bannerman|～单位 advanced unit

【红契】hóngqì〈旧时 *old*〉指买田地房产时经过纳税而由官厅盖印的契约（区别于'白契' as compared with 'title deeds without tax seals'） red-sealed title deeds; real-estate transaction documents with government tax seals

【红青】hóngqīng 黑里透红的颜色 dark purple; also 绀青 gànqīng

【红区】hóngqū 第二次国内革命战争时期共产党建立的农村根据地 Red area; base area established by the Communist Party of China in rural areas during the Second Revolutionary Civil War

【红壤】hóngrǎng 红色的土壤，在我国主要分布在长江以南和台湾地区。铁铝含量高，酸性强，养分少。red soil; red earth, with a high content of iron and aluminum, strong acidity, and few nutrients; around China it is mainly found in Taiwan and the area south of the Yangtze River; also 红土 hóngtǔ

【红热】hóngrè 某些物质加高温（500—1,200℃）后发出暗红色至橙红色的光亮，这种状态叫做红热。如果温度继续升高，就由红热转为白热。red heat; the state in which a substance becomes red-hot and glows crimson or orange red at a high temperature (500-1,200℃), and turns a incandescent white if the temperature continues to rise

【红人】hóngrén（～儿 hóngrénr）称受宠信的人 favourite; favourite person of sb. in power

【红润】hóngrùn 红而滋润（多指皮肤 usu. of skin）ruddy; rosy：孩子的脸像苹果一样～。The child's cheeks are as rosy as an apple.

【红色】hóngsè ❶ 红的颜色 colour red ❷ 象征革命或政治觉悟高 red; symbol of revolution or high political consciousness：～政权 red political power|～根据地 revolutionary base

【红烧】hóngshāo 一种烹调方法，把肉、鱼等加油、糖略炒，并加酱油等作料，焖熟使成黑红色 red cook; cooking style in which meat or fish is stir-fried with oil and sugar, and, with soy sauce and other seasonings added, stewed until it turns dark red：～肉 pork braised in soy sauce|～鲤鱼 red-cooked carp

【红苕】hóngsháo〈方 *dial.*〉same as 甘薯 gānshǔ

【红生】hóngshēng 戏曲中扮演勾红脸人物的生角 painted-face role of common people in traditional Chinese opera whose makeup is largely red

【红十字会】Hóngshízìhuì 一种国际性的志愿救济团体，救护战时病伤军人和平民，也救济其他灾害的受难者。1864 年日内瓦公约规定以在白地儿上加红十字作为它的标志。Red Cross; international organization whose main purpose is to voluntarily rescue and assist wounded combatants and civilians during wars or victims of other disasters. At the Geneva Convention of 1864, a red cross on a white background was chosen as the symbol of the Red Cross.

【红薯】hóngshǔ 甘薯的通称 common name for 甘薯 gānshǔ

【红糖】hóngtáng 糖的一种，褐黄色、赤褐色或黑色，用甘蔗的糖浆熬成，含有砂糖和糖蜜。供食用。有的地区叫黑糖或黄糖。brown sugar; soft sugar derived from the syrup of sugarcane, containing gooey granulated sugar, used for food, and can be brown, russet, or dark in colour; also called 黑糖 hēitáng or 黄糖 huángtáng in some regions

【红彤彤】hóngtōngtōng（～的 hóngtōngtōng·de）形容很红 glowing; bright red：～的火苗 glowing red flames|～的晚霞 bright-red sunset glow|脸上晒得～的。His face is aglow and deeply tanned from exposure to the sun. also 红通通 hóngtōngtōng

【红头文件】hóngtóu-wénjiàn 指党政领导机关（多指中央一级）下发的文件，因版头文件名称多印成红色，故称红头文件 red document; document issued by the Party or leading department of the state (oft. at the central government level), with a title printed in red, hence the term

【红土】hóngtǔ ❶ same as 红壤 hóngrǎng ❷ same as 红土子 hóngtǔ·zi

【红土子】hóngtǔ·zi 一种颜料，暗红色或淡红色，用赤铁矿研细而成，用来绘画，也用于建筑方面 wine or rosy pigment ground from hematite and used for painting or architecture; also 铁丹 tiědān or 红土 hóngtǔ

【红外线】hóngwàixiàn 波长比可见光长的电磁波，波长 0.77—1,000 微米，在光谱上位于红色光的外侧。易于被物体吸收，穿透云雾的能力比可见光强。具有很强的热能，工业上用做烘烤的热源，也用于通讯、探测、医疗等。infrared radiation; electromagnetic wave with a wavelength (0.77-1,000 microns) longer than that of visible light, lying outside the visible spectrum's red end, easily attracted by objects, having strong thermal energy and a stronger ability than visible light to penetrate clouds and mists, used for industry, telecommunications, exploration, and medical science; also 红外光 hóngwàiguāng or 热线 rèxiàn

【红细胞】hóngxìbāo 血细胞的一种，比白细胞小，圆饼状，红色，没有细胞核，含血红蛋白，产生在红骨髓中。作用是输送氧气到各组织并把二氧化碳带到肺泡内。red blood cell; smaller than white cell, round-shaped, with haemoglobin but no nucleolus, produced in red marrow, with the function of conveying oxygen to all the tissues and bringing carbon dioxide to the alveoli; also 红血球 hóngxuèqiú

【红心】hóngxīn〈比喻 *fig.*〉忠于无产阶级革命事业的思想 red heart; heart loyal to the cause of proletarian revolution：一颗～为人民 with a red heart and always loyal to the people

【红星】hóngxīng ❶ 红色的五角星 five-pointed red star ❷ 指非常受欢迎的明星 popular actor or actress：影视～ movie star

【红学】hóngxué 指研究古典小说《红楼梦》的学问 Red-ology; studies of *Hongloumeng* (*A Dream of Red Mansions*); Hongloumeng scholarship：～家 Hongloumeng scholar

【红血球】hóngxuèqiú same as 红细胞 hóngxìbāo

【红颜】hóngyán 指貌美的女子 pretty woman

【红眼】hóng//yǎn ❶ 指发怒或发急 become infuriated; see red：输红了眼 flare up after repeated losses (or defeat) ❷ 眼红 be envious; be jealous of

【红眼病】hóngyǎnbìng ❶ 病，因急性结膜炎而眼白发红 red eye; disease where the eyes turn red because of acute contagious conjunctivitis; 俗称 popularly called 红眼 hóngyǎn ❷ 羡慕别人有名或有利而心怀忌妒的毛病 envy; jealousy; painful or resentful awareness of advantages enjoyed by others, along with a desire to possess the same advantages

【红艳艳】hóngyànyàn (～的 hóngyànyàn·de) 形容红得鲜艳夺目 brilliant red：～的杜鹃花 bright red azaleas

【红样】hóngyàng 用红笔批改过的校样 proof sheet with mark-up or corrections in red pen

【红叶】hóngyè 枫树、黄栌、槭树等的叶子秋天变成红色，叫红叶 red autumnal leaves (of maple trees, smoke tree, acer tree, etc. in autumn)

【红缨枪】hóngyīngqiāng 一种旧式兵器，在长柄的一端装有尖锐的金属枪头，枪头和柄相连的部分装饰着红缨 red-tassel spear; old-fashioned weapon with a sharp medal spearhead at the end of a long handle and decorated with a red tassel

【红云】hóngyún〈比喻 *fig.*〉脸上呈现的红晕 become red in the face：两颊泛起～ both cheeks flushed

【红运】hóngyùn 好运气 good luck：走～ have a spate of good luck; also 鸿运 hóngyùn

【红晕】hóngyùn 中心浓而四周渐淡的一团红色 blush; flush：脸上泛出～ one's face blushing scarlet

【红妆】hóngzhuāng same as 红装 hóngzhuāng

【红装】hóngzhuāng〈书 *fml.*〉❶ 妇女的红色装饰。泛指妇女的艳丽装束。women's red clothes; (in a broad sense) women's gorgeous attire ❷ 指青年妇女 young woman ‖ also 红妆 hóngzhuāng

吰 hóng ☞ [噌吰] (chēnghóng) on p.244

闳 hóng ❶〈书 *fml.*〉巷门 gate of a lane ❷〈书 *fml.*〉宏大 great; grand ❸ (Hóng) 姓 a surname

【闳中肆外】hóng zhōng sì wài 形容文章内容丰富，文笔豪放 (of writings) rich in content and bold and unconstrained in writing style

宏 hóng ❶ 宏大 great; grand：～伟 magnificent｜～图 grand prospect; great plan｜～愿 great aspirations｜宽～ generous; broad-minded ❷ (Hóng) 姓 a surname

【宏大】hóngdà 巨大；宏伟 great; grand：规模～ on a grand scale｜～的志愿 high aspirations

【宏富】hóngfù 丰富 abundant; rich：采摭～ rich collection｜征引～ copious quotations

【宏观】hóngguān ❶ 不涉及分子、原子、电子等内部结构或机制的（跟'微观'相对 as opposed to 'microscopic'）macroscopic; with no reference to internal elements such as molecules, atoms, or electrons：～世界 macroscopic world｜～观察 macroscopic observation ❷ 指大范围的或涉及整体的 large scale; sth. as a whole：～经济 macro-economy｜对市场进行～调控 carry out macroeconomic controls on the market

【宏观经济学】hóngguān jīngjìxué 以整个国民经济活动作为研究对象的经济学 macroeconomics; study of economics in terms of an entire system, esp. with reference to general levels of output and income and to the interrelations among sectors of the economy

【宏观世界】hóngguān shìjiè 不涉及分子、原子、电子等结构的物质世界 macrocosm; material world with no reference to such structures as molecules, atoms, or electrons

【宏丽】hónglì 宏伟壮丽；富丽 magnificent; grand; majestic：～的建筑物 grand building

【宏论】hónglùn 见识广博的言论 informed opinion; intelligent view：大发～ spell out one's informed opinion in detail; also 弘论 hónglùn

【宏赡】hóngshàn〈书 *fml.*〉(学识等)丰富 (of knowledge, scholarship) erudite: 学力～ broad and profound scholarship

【宏图】hóngtú 远大的设想;宏伟的计划 long-range blueprint; great plan; grand prospect: ～大略 great plan with broad outlines|大展～ create a grand prospect; also 弘图 hóngtú or 鸿图 hóngtú

【宏伟】hóngwěi (规模、计划等)雄壮伟大 (of scale, plan, etc.) grand; magnificent: 气势～ imposing manner|～的蓝图 grand blueprint

【宏扬】hóngyáng same as 弘扬 hóngyáng

【宏愿】hóngyuàn 伟大的志愿 great aspirations; noble ambition: 改造自然的～ great aspirations to reshape nature; also 弘愿 hóngyuàn

【宏旨】hóngzhǐ 大旨;主要的意思 main theme; leading idea: 无关～ unrelated to the main idea; also 弘旨 hóngzhǐ

纮 hóng〈古代 *arch.*〉帽子上的带子,用来把帽子系在头上 sash used to tie a hat to one's head

泓 hóng〈书 *fml.*〉❶ 水深而广 (of water) deep and broad ❷〈量词 *classifier*〉清水一道或一片叫一泓 a stream or body of water: 一～清泉 a clear spring|一～秋水 an expanse of limpid water in autumn

荭 hóng [荭草](hóngcǎo)一年生草本植物,茎高达 3 米,叶子阔卵形,花红色或白色,果实黑色。供观赏。prince's feather (*Polygonum orientale*); annual plant with caudexes as high as 3 metres, broad leaves, red or white flowers, and dark fruit, used for appreciation and ornamentation

虹 hóng 大气中一种光的现象,天空中的小水珠经日光照射发生折射和反射作用而形成的弧形彩带,由外圈至内圈呈红、橙、黄、绿、蓝、靛、紫七种颜色。出现在和太阳相对着的方向。rainbow; arc or circle displaying concentric bands in the colours of the spectrum (from inner to outer: red, orange, yellow, green, blue, indigo, violet), formed opposite the sun by the refraction and reflection of the sun's rays through raindrops, spray, or mist; also 彩虹 cǎihóng

☞ jiàng on p. 964

【虹膜】hóngmó 眼球前部含色素的环形薄膜,由结缔组织细胞、肌纤维等构成,当中是瞳孔。眼球的颜色是由虹膜所含色素的多少决定的。iris; the opaque contractile diaphragm made up of connective tissue cells and muscle fibres and perforated by the pupil, forming the coloured portion of the eye; 旧称 formerly called 虹彩 hóngcǎi; (图见 ☞ figure for 眼 yǎn on p. 2210)

【虹吸管】hóngxīguǎn 使液体产生虹吸现象所用的弯管,呈倒 U 字形而一端较长,使用时管内要预先充满液体 siphon; tube bent in the shape of an inverted 'U' to form two legs of unequal length by which a liquid can be transferred to a lower level over an intermediate elevation due to atmospheric pressure; 通称 commonly called 过山龙 guòshānlóng

【虹吸现象】hóngxī-xiànxiàng 依靠大气压强,液体从较高的地方通过虹吸管,先向上再向下流到较低地方去的现象 siphonage; phenomenon of atmospheric pressure forcing a liquid up the shorter branch of a siphon, while the excess of weight of the liquid in the longer branch, once filled, causes continuous flow

铉 hóng 形容金属撞击的声音(多用于人名 oft. used in personal names) (of metal) clang; clatter; clink

竑 hóng〈书 *fml.*〉广大 large; vast

洪 hóng ❶ 大 big; vast: ～水 flood|～钟 large bell|～炉 great furnace|～量 generosity ❷ 指洪水 flood: 防～ prevent or control flood|蓄～ store floodwater|分～ flood diversion|山～暴发。Mountain torrents swept down. ❸(Hóng) 姓 a surname

【洪帮】Hóng Bāng 从天地会发展出来的一个帮会,流行于长江流域和珠江流域一带。清末曾参加反清斗争,后来有些派别被反动势力所利用。the Hong Bang; secret society derived from the Heaven and Earth Society, popular in the Yangtze and Zhujiang river valleys and active in the struggle against the rule of the late Qing Dynasty (1616-1911). Some of its factions later played into the hands of reactionary powers.

【洪大】hóngdà (声音等)大 loud: ～的回声 resounding echoes

【洪峰】hóngfēng 河流在涨水期间达到最高点的水位。也指涨达最高水位的洪水。flood peak; the highest water level to which a river rises; flooding at the highest water level

【洪福】hóngfú 大福气 great blessing: ～齐天 limitless blessing; also 鸿福 hóngfú

【洪荒】hónghuāng 混沌蒙昧的状态。借指太古时代 chaotic state; primeval times: ～时代 primeval ages|～世界 chaotic world

【洪亮】hóngliàng (声音)大;响亮 (of voice) sonorous; loud and clear: ～的回声 loud and clear echoes|嗓音～ a sonorous voice

【洪量】hóngliàng ❶ 宽宏的气量 magnanimity; generosity ❷ 大的酒量 great capacity for liquor

【洪流】hóngliú 巨大的水流 mighty torrent; powerful current: 春暖雪融的时候,～的冲刷力特别猛烈。The torrents of the spring thaw have a powerful scouring force. ◇时代～ powerful current of the times

【洪炉】hónglú 大炉子。陶冶和锻炼人的环境 great furnace; environment in which one's character and disposition are nurtured and tempered:革命的～ mighty crucible of revolution

【洪水】hóngshuǐ 河流因大雨或融雪而引起的暴涨的水流 flood; rise and overflow of a body of water due to heavy rain or melting snow:～泛滥 overrunning flood; flowage

【洪水猛兽】hóngshuǐ měngshòu 〈比喻 *fig.*〉极大的祸害 fierce floods and savage beasts; great scourges

【洪武】Hóngwǔ 明太祖(朱元璋)年号(公元1368—1398) Hongwu: title of the reign (1368-1398) of Emperor Taizu (Zhu Yuanzhang) of the Ming Dynasty (1368-1644)

【洪熙】Hóngxī 明仁宗(朱高炽)年号(公元1425) Hongxi, title of the reign (1425) of Emperor Renzong (Zhu Gaochi) of the Ming Dynasty

【洪灾】hóngzāi 洪水造成的灾害 disaster caused by floods

【洪钟】hóngzhōng 〈书 *fml.*〉大钟 large bell:声如～ have a stentorian (or sonorous) voice

翃(翝) hóng〈书 *fml.*〉飞 fly

铁 hóng 〈书 *fml.*〉弩弓上射箭的装置 the device on a bow for shooting an arrow

虹 hóng 鱼类的一属,身体扁平,略呈方形或圆形,尾呈鞭状,有毒刺。生活在我国沿海,吃无脊椎动物和小鱼。stingray (*Dasyatis zugei*); fish with a square- or round-shaped flat body, a whip-like tail, a poisonous serrated spine at the base of the tail, living along China's coast and feeding on invertebrates and small fish

鸿 hóng ❶ 鸿雁 swan; goose:～毛 goose feather ❷〈书 *fml.*〉指书信 letter:来～(来信) a letter received ❸ 大 great; grand:～图 grand plan|～儒 great Confucian scholar ❹ (Hóng) 姓 a surname

【鸿福】hóngfú same as 洪福 hóngfú

【鸿沟】Hónggōu 〈古代 *arch.*〉运河,在今河南境内,楚汉相争时是两军对峙的临时分界 Honggou, an ancient canal in today's Henan Province, which served as a temporary boundary during the war between the Chu and the Han armies during the Warring States Period;〈比喻 *fig.*〉明显的界线 wide gap:我们之间并不存在不可逾越的～。There is no unbridgeable gulf between us.

【鸿鹄】hónghú 天鹅。因飞得很高,所以常用来比喻志向远大的人。swan (*Anseres*), oft. used to compare with a person of noble aspirations:～高翔 a soaring swan|～之志 lofty ambitions

【鸿毛】hóngmáo 鸿雁的毛 goose feather; 〈比喻 *fig.*〉事物轻微或不足道 sth. very light or insignificant:死有重于泰山,有轻于～。Death befalls all people alike, but the loss of some is heavier than Mount Taishan, of others, lighter than a feather.

【鸿门宴】Hóngményàn 公元前206年刘邦攻占秦都咸阳,派兵守函谷关。不久项羽率四十万大军攻入,进驻鸿门(今陕西临潼东),准备进攻刘邦。刘邦到鸿门跟项羽会见。酒宴中,项羽的谋士范增让项庄舞剑,想乘机杀死刘邦。刘邦在项伯、樊哙等人的护卫下乘隙脱逃(见于《史记·项羽本纪》)。后来用'鸿门宴'指加害客人的宴会。In 206 B.C., Liu Bang attacked and occupied Xianyang, capital of the state of Qin, and had troops stationed at the Hangu Pass. Soon after, his rival Xiang Yu led 400,000 troops to camp at Hongmen, east of today's Lintong in Shaanxi Province, where he made preparations for attacking Liu Bang. At Hongmen, Xiang Yu offered a feast for Liu Bang, at which Xiang Yu's advisor, Fan Zeng, asked Xiang Zhuang to perform a sword dance, and make an attempt on Liu's life. However, aided by Xiang Bo and Fan Kuai, Liu Bang escaped unscathed. (*Records of the Historian · Official Records of Xiang Yu*) Thus the phrase Hongmen Feast — a meeting contrived as a deadly trap.

【鸿蒙】hóngméng 〈书 *fml.*〉古人认为天地开辟之前是一团混沌的元气,这种自然的元气叫做鸿蒙 (ancient belief) vital principle in nature prior to creation; primeval atmosphere of nature:～初辟 primeval atmosphere of nature first created; also 鸿濛 hóngméng

【鸿篇巨制】hóng piān jù zhì 指规模宏大的著作 monumental work; magnum opus

【鸿儒】hóngrú 〈书 *fml.*〉渊博的学者 erudite person; a learned scholar

【鸿图】hóngtú same as 宏图 hóngtú

【鸿雁】hóngyàn ❶ 鸟,羽毛紫褐色,腹部白色,嘴扁平,腿短,趾间有蹼。吃植物的种子,也吃鱼和虫。群居在水边,飞时一般排列成行,是一种冬候鸟。swan goose (*Anser cygnoides*); wild goose; winter migratory bird that has purple brown feathers, a white belly, a flat beak, short legs and webbed feet, eats plant seeds, fish and worms, lives in large groups on the waterside and flies in formation; also 大雁 dàyàn ❷〈书 *fml.*〉〈比喻 *fig.*〉same as 书信 shūxìn

【鸿运】hóngyùn same as 红运 hóngyùn

【鸿爪】hóngzhǎo ☞ 雪泥鸿爪 xuění hóngzhǎo on p. 2180

渱 hóng same as 荭 hóng

葒 hóng ☞ 雪里葒 xuělǐhóng on p. 2180
☞ hòng on p. 808

黉(黌) hóng 〈古代 *arch*.〉学校 school

【黉门】hóngmén 〈古代 *arch*.〉学校 school：～学子 school students | ～秀才 scholars

hǒng (ㄏㄨㄥˇ)

哄 hǒng ❶ 哄骗 fool; humbug：你这是～我，我不信。You must be kidding. I don't believe it. ❷ 哄逗。特指看(kān)小孩儿或带小孩儿 keep (esp. a child) in good humour; coax：奶奶～着孙子玩儿。The old lady kept her grandson in good humour.

☞ hōng on p. 801 and hòng on p. 808

【哄逗】hǒngdòu 用言语或行动引人高兴 coax; keep (esp. a child) in good humour through words or actions：～孩子 coax children

【哄弄】hǒng·nòng 〈方 *dial*.〉欺骗；要弄 cheat; humbug; hoodwink

【哄骗】hǒngpiàn 用假话或手段骗人 cheat; humbug; deceive with or other evil means：你这番话～不了人。Your words are mere much humbug.

嗊 hǒng 罗嗊曲，词牌名 *Luohongqu*; name of a tune to which Chinese *ci* poems are composed

☞ gòng on p. 680

hòng (ㄏㄨㄥˋ)

讧 hòng 〈书 *fml*.〉争吵；混乱 quarrel; chaos：内～ internal conflict

哄(閧) hòng 吵闹；开玩笑 uproar; horseplay：起～ create a disturbance | 一～而散 break up in an uproar

☞ hōng on p. 801 and hǒng on p. 808

【哄闹】hòngnào 许多人同时喧闹 horse around; bustle：会场上一片～声。The meeting place was bustling with noise.

澒 hòng [澒洞](hòngdòng)〈书 *fml*.〉弥漫无际 endlessly pervasive

蕻 hòng ❶〈书 *fml*.〉茂盛 luxuriant; flourishing ❷〈方 *dial*.〉某些蔬菜的长茎 stem of some vegetables：菜～ vegetable stems

☞ hóng on p. 807

hōu (ㄏㄡ)

齁1 hōu [齁声](hōushēng) 打呼噜的声音 grunt; sound of snoring

齁2 hōu ❶ 太甜或太咸的食物使喉咙不舒服 sickeningly sweet or salty：这个菜咸得～人。This dish is much too salty. ❷〈方 *dial*.〉非常(多表示不满意 usu. implying dissatisfaction) very; awfully：～咸 awfully salty | ～苦 very bitter | ～酸 very sour | 天气～热。It's awfully hot.

hóu (ㄏㄡˊ)

侯 hóu ❶ 封建五等爵位的第二等 second of the five ranks of nobility in feudal China：～爵 marquis | 公～ duke ❷ 泛指达官贵人 (in a broad sense) nobleman or high official：～门似海 (of a rich man's home) be inaccessible to the common people ❸ (Hóu) 姓 a surname

☞ hòu on p. 814

喉 hóu 介于咽和气管之间的部分，由甲状软骨、环状软骨和会厌软骨等构成。喉是呼吸器官的一部分，喉内有声带，又是发音器官。

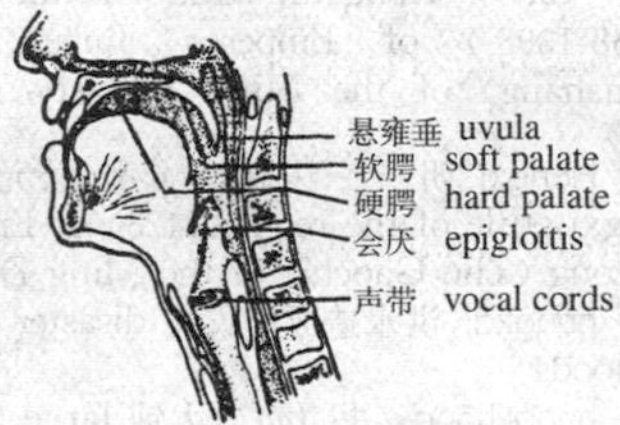

人的喉 Human Larynx

larynx; throat; the part between pharynx and trachea, composed of thyroid cartilage, cricoid cartilage and epiglottic cartilage, one of the respiratory organs and also a speech organ containing the vocal cords; also 喉头 hóutóu

【喉擦音】hóucāyīn 声带靠近，气流从中挤出而发出的辅音，例如上海话的'好、鞋'等字起头的音，国际音标分别用[h]和[ɦ]来表示 guttural fricative; consonant characterized by frictional passage of expended breath through a narrowing at some point of the vocal tract, such as the opening consonants of 好 hǎo and 鞋 xié in Shanghai dialect, denoted by [h] or [ɦ] in the international phonetic alphabet

【喉结】hóujié 男子颈部由甲状软骨构成的隆起物 Adam's apple; laryngeal protuberance; protrusion composed of thyroid cartilage on man's neck; also 结喉 jiéhóu

【喉咙】hóu·lóng 咽部和喉部的统称 common name for pharynx and throat

【喉塞音】hóusèyīn 声带紧闭，然后突然打开而发出的辅音，例如上海话的'一、十、百'等字收尾的音，国际音标用[ʔ]来表示 glottal stop; consonant characterized by interruption of breathing during speech by the closure of the glottis, such as the ending consonants of 一 yī, 十 shí and 百 bǎi in Shanghai dialect, denoted by [ʔ] in the international phonetic alphabet

【喉舌】hóushé 泛指说话的器官。多比喻代为发表言论的工具或人 (in a broad sense) mouthpiece; (fig.) spokesperson：我们的报纸是人民的～。Our newspaper is the mouthpiece of the people.

【喉头】hóutóu 喉 larynx; throat

猴 hóu ❶ (～儿 hóur)哺乳动物，种类很多，形状略像人，身上有毛，多为灰色或褐色，有尾巴，行动灵活，好群居，口腔有储存食物的颊囊，以果实、野菜、鸟卵和昆虫为食物。monkey (*Cercopithecidae*); long-tailed primate mammal with grey or brown fur on the body, a pouch in the cheek for storing food, agile in action, often living in groups, and feeding on fruits, wild herbs, bird eggs and insects; 通称 generally called 猴子 hóu•zi ❷〈方 *dial.*〉乖巧；机灵(多指孩子) (of children) clever and naughty: 这孩子多～啊！What a naughty child! ❸〈方 *dial.*〉像猴似的蹲着 squat on the heels like a monkey: 他～在台阶上嗑瓜子儿。He squatted on the step and cracked melon seeds between his teeth.

【猴年马月】hóu nián mǎ yuè ☞ 驴年马月 lǘ nián mǎ yuè on p. 1264

【猴皮筋儿】hóupíjīnr same as 橡皮筋 xiàngpíjīn; also 猴筋儿 hóujīnr

【猴儿精】hóurjīng〈方 *dial.*〉❶ 形容人很精明 astute; shrewd: 这小子～～的。This guy is very shrewd. ❷〈比喻 *fig.*〉机灵而顽皮的人 shrewd and mischievous person

【猴戏】hóuxì ❶ 用猴子耍的把戏，猴子穿衣服、戴假面，模仿人的某些动作 monkey show; show by a performing monkey which wears clothes and imitates human gestures ❷ 指以孙悟空为主角的戏曲表演 performance of the Monkey King in traditional opera

【猴子】hóu•zi 猴的通称 general term for 猴 hóu

睺 hóu ☞ 罗睺 luóhóu on p. 1277

瘊 hóu [瘊子](hóu•zi)疣(yóu)的通称 common name for 疣 yóu

骺 hóu ☞ 骨骺 gǔhóu on p. 694

篌 hóu ☞ [箜篌](kōnghóu) on p. 1105

糇(餱) hóu〈书 *fml.*〉干粮 preserved food: ～粮 solid food

hǒu (ㄏㄡˇ)

吼 hǒu ❶ (猛兽 of beasts of prey)大声叫 roar; howl: 牛～ roar of an ox | 狮子～ the roar of a lion ❷ 发怒或情绪激动时大声叫喊 shout; cry out in anger or agitation: 狂～ shout crazily | 大～一声 howl ❸ (风、汽笛、大炮等)发出很大的响声 (of winds, sirens, guns, etc.) shriek; loud noise: 北风怒～。The north wind howled violently. | 汽笛长～了一声。The siren shrieked loud and long.

【吼叫】hǒujiào 大声叫；吼 roar; howl; shout: 狮子～着扑上去。The lion pounced with a roar. | 人们愤怒地～起来。People shouted in anger.

【吼声】hǒushēng 大的呼喊声；巨大的响声 roaring; tremendous noise: ～震天 thunderous roaring

犼 hǒu 古书上说的一种吃人的野兽，形状像狗 *hou*, legendary dog-like man-eater (in ancient books)

hòu (ㄏㄡˋ)

后[1](後) hòu ❶ 在背面的(指空间，跟'前'相对 of space, as opposed to 'front') behind; back; rear: ～门 back door | 村前村～ in front of and behind the village; all across the village ❷ 未来的；较晚的(指时间，跟'前'、'先'相对 of time, as opposed to 'early', 'forward') after; afterwards; later: ～天 the day after tomorrow | 日～ in the future | ～辈 offspring; younger generation | 先来～到 in order of arrival ❸ 次序靠近末尾的(跟'前'相对 as opposed to 'first') last: ～排 back row | ～十五名 the last 15 (in ranking) ❹ 后代的人。指子孙等。offspring: 无～ childless; have no offspring

后[2] hòu ❶ 君主的妻子 wife of a king or emperor: 皇～ empress | ～妃 empress and imperial concubines ❷〈古代 *arch.*〉称君主 sovereign: 商之先～ king of the Shang Dynasty ❸ (Hòu)姓 a surname

【后半晌】hòubànshǎng〈方 *dial.*〉(～儿 hòubànshǎngr) afternoon

【后半天】hòubàntiān (～儿 hòubàntiānr)下午 afternoon

【后半夜】hòubànyè 从半夜到天亮的一段时间 second half of the night; wee hours; also 下半夜 xiàbànyè

【后备】hòubèi 为补充而准备的(人员、物资等) reserve; personnel or materials ready for supplement: ～军 reserve force | ～力量 reserve forces | 精打细算，留有～ careful calculation and strict budgeting to keep sth. in reserve

【后备军】hòubèijūn ❶ 预备役军人的总称 general term for reservists ❷ 指某些职业队伍的补充力量 supplementary force for some professional teams: 产业～ industrial reserve force

【后辈】hòubèi ❶ 后代。指子孙。offspring; posterity ❷ 同行中年轻的或资历浅的人 (among people of the same profession) juniors; younger generation

【后边】hòu•bian (～儿 hòu•bianr) same as 后面 hòu•mian

【后步】hòubù 说话做事时为了以后伸缩回旋而留的地步 leeway; room for manoeuvre: 话不要说绝，得给自己留个～。We'd better not speak in absolute terms, and must leave ourselves sufficient room for manoeuvre.

【后尘】hòuchén〈书 *fml.*〉走路时后面扬起来的尘土 dust kicked up by sb. walking in front;〈比喻 *fig.*〉别人的后面 follow another's footprints:步人～ follow the trail of sb.

【后代】hòudài ❶ 某一时代以后的时代 later periods (in history); later ages:这些远古的事,大都是～人们的推测。These stories of remote antiquity are mostly based on people's speculations in later periods. ❷ 后代的人。也指个人的子孙 later generations; descendants; posterity:我们要为～造福。We should create benefits for our future generations.|这家人没有～。This family has no descendants.

【后爹】hòudiē same as 继父 jìfù

【后盾】hòudùn 指背后的支持和援助力量 sth. or sb to fall back on; backing; backup force; support and aid:坚强的～ powerful backing

【后发制人】hòu fā zhì rén 先退让一步,使自己处于有利的地位后,再制服对方 make a concession to obtain an advantageous position and gain control by striking only after the opponent has struck

【后方】hòufāng ❶ 远离战线的地区(跟'前线'、'前方'相对 as opposed to 'frontage' or 'frontline') rear; area far from the battlefront ❷ 后面;后头 behind; back:在我舰的～,发现一艘潜艇。A submarine was found behind our ship.

【后福】hòufú 未来的或晚年的幸福 future blessings; blessings in one's old age:大难不死,必有～。Surviving a major disaster must mean future blessings.

【后父】hòufù same as 继父 jìfù

【后跟】hòugēn (～儿 hòugēnr)鞋或袜挨近脚跟的部分 heel:鞋～heel of a shoe|袜子～heel of a sock

【后宫】hòugōng ❶ 君主时代妃嫔住的宫室 imperial harem; palace of the imperial concubines ❷ 指妃嫔 imperial concubines

【后顾】hòugù ❶ 回过头来照顾 turn back (to take care of sth.):无暇～ have no time to look after things one has left behind|～之忧 fear of disturbance at the rear ❷ 指回忆 look back (on the past):～与前瞻 look back on the past and ahead to the future

【后顾之忧】hòu gù zhī yōu 需要回过头来照顾的忧患。泛指来自后方的或家里的忧患。fear of disturbance at the rear; (in a broad sense) trouble back at home:孩子入托了,解除了家长上班的～。With the child enrolled in a nursery, working parents are free from worry.

【后果】hòuguǒ 最后的结果(多用在坏的方面 usu. in the negative) fallout; consequence; aftermath:～堪虑。The consequences are worrisome.|检查制度不严,会造成很坏的～。A lax checking system may have serious consequences.

【后汉】Hòu Hàn ❶ same as 东汉 Dōng Hàn ❷ 五代之一,公元 947-950,刘知远所建 the Later Han Dynasty (947—950), founded by Liu Zhiyuan during the Five Dynasties Period; ☞ 五代 Wǔ Dài on p. 2029

【后话】hòuhuà 在叙述的过程中,指留待以后再说的事情 part of a story to be recounted later; part of a story that is to come:这是～,暂且不提。That's the later part of the story, so no more for now.

【后患】hòuhuàn 以后的祸患 future trouble:～无穷 endless trouble in the future|根绝～ dig up the root of (or remove the cause of) future trouble

【后悔】hòuhuǐ 事后懊悔 regret; repent:～莫及 too late to repent|事前要三思,免得将来～。We should think carefully before taking any action so that we won't regret it in the future.

【后悔药】hòuhuǐyào ☞吃后悔药 chī hòuhuǐyào on p. 256

【后会有期】hòu huì yǒu qī 以后还有相见的时候(多用于离别时安慰对方 usu. used to comfort the other side on departing) We shall meet again some day. See yon again.

【后婚儿】hòuhūnr 称再嫁的妇女 remarried woman

【后记】hòujì 写在书籍、文章等后面的短文,用以说明写作目的、经过或补充个别内容 postscript (added to a finished book, etc.), stating the purpose and process of writing a book; supplementary contents

【后继】hòujì 后面继续跟上来;后来接续前头(的) successors; sb. or sth. that follows:～有人。There is no lack of successors. *or* There's another generation to carry on with the cause.|前赴～ advance wave upon wave

【后脚】hòujiǎo ❶ 迈步时在后面的一只脚 rear foot (in walking):前脚一滑,～也站不稳。As the front foot slipped, the rear foot became unsteady. ❷ 与前脚连说时表示在别人后面(时间上很接近)[used with 'front foot'] close behind (in time):我前脚进大门,他～就赶到了。Immediately after I stepped in the house, he arrived.

【后金】Hòu Jīn 明代建州左卫(在今辽宁新宾一带)都指挥使爱新觉罗·努尔哈赤于公元1616 年建立金国,自称金国汗。历史上称为后金,以与12、13 世纪的金代相区别。Later Jin; Kingdom of Jin, established in 1616 by Aisin-Gioro Nurhachi, governor of Zuowei in Jianzhou (today's Xinbin in Liaoning Province) of the Ming Dynasty (1368-1644), who ascended the throne and proclaimed himself Khan (king) of what is historically known as the Later Jin, different from the Jin Dynasty (1115-1234)

【后襟】hòujīn 上衣、袍子等背后的部分 back of a Chinese robe or jacket

【后进】hòujìn ❶ 学识或资历较浅的人 juniors：提携～ guide and support juniors ❷ 进步比较慢、水平比较低的 backward; lagging behind; less advanced：～班组 laggard group ❸ 指进步比较慢、水平比较低的人或集体 those who trail behind：学先进，帮～ learn from the advanced and help those trailing behind

【后劲】hòujìn ❶ 显露较慢的作用或力量 delayed effect; after-effect：这酒～大。This wine has a strong after-effect. ❷ 用在后一阶段的力量 reserve strength; stamina：他～足，最后冲刺时超过了所有的对手。With plenty of stamina, he shot ahead of all other runners at the last dash.

【后晋】Hòu Jìn 五代之一，公元 936—947，石敬瑭所建 Later Jin Dynasty (936-947), founded by Shi Jingtang during the Five Dynasties Period; ☞ 五代 Wǔ Dài on p. 2029

【后景】hòujǐng 画面上衬托在主体后面的景物 background (of a picture)

【后来】hòulái ❶ 指在过去某一时间之后的时间 later; afterwards; the comparative of 'late'：他还是去年二月里来过一封信，～再没有来过信。I haven't heard from him since last February when he wrote me. 注意 **NOTE**：'后来'跟'以后'的分别 Pay attention to the difference between 后来 hòulái and 以后 yǐhòu a)'以后'可以单用，也可以作为后置成分，'后来'只能单用，例如只能说'七月以后'，不能说'七月后来' 以后 yǐhòu can be used on its own or after a phrase; while 后来 hòulái can only be used on its own, as yon can say '七月以后' but not '七月后来' b)'以后'可以指过去，也可以指将来，'后来'只指过去，例如只能说'以后你要注意'，不能说'后来你要注意' 以后 yǐhòu implies either the past or the future while 后来 hòulái only implies the past ❷ 后到的；后成长起来的 afterwards; later：～人 successors｜～居上 the latecomers surpass the old-timers

【后来居上】hòu lái jū shàng 后起的超过先前的 the latecomers surpass the old-timers

【后浪推前浪】hòu làng tuī qián làng 〈比喻 *fig.*〉后面的事物推动前面的事物，不断前进 the rear waves drive on those ahead — the new excels the old

【后脸儿】hòuliǎnr 〈方 *dial.*〉指人或东西的背面 back; reverse side：前面走的那个人，看～好像张老师。The person walking ahead of me looked from the back like teacher Zhang.｜怎么把钟的～朝前摆着？Why did you set the reverse side of the clock to the front?

【后梁】Hòu Liáng 五代之一，公元 907—923，朱温（后改名全忠）所建 Later Liang Dynasty (907-923), founded by Zhu Wen during the Five Dynasties Period; ☞ 五代 Wǔ Dài on p. 2029

【后路】hòulù ❶ 军队背后的运输线或退路 communications lines to the rear; route of retreat：抄～ attack from the rear ❷（～儿 hòulùr）〈比喻 *fig.*〉回旋的余地；后步 room for manoeuvre; a way of escape

【后妈】hòumā same as 继母 jìmǔ

【后门】hòumén（～儿 hòuménr）❶ 房子、院子等后面的门 back door (or gate) of a house (or compound) ❷〈比喻 *fig.*〉通融的、舞弊的途径 backdoorism; clout for accommodation or embezzlement：走～ secure advantages through influence｜开～ backdoor deal; let in by the back door

【后面】hòu·mian（～儿 hòu·mianr）❶ 空间或位置靠后的部分 at the back; in the rear; behind (in space or position)：房子～有一个花园。There's a garden behind the house.｜前面坐满了，～还有座位。The front seats have been occupied, but there are still some available at the back. ❷ 次序靠后的部分；文章或讲话中后于现在所叙述的部分 (in a speech, article) later (in order)：关于这个问题，～还要详细说。I'll give the details about this issue later.

【后母】hòumǔ same as 继母 jìmǔ

【后脑】hòunǎo 脑的一部分，位于脑颅的后部，由脑桥、延髓和小脑构成 hindbrain; rhombencephalon; part of the brain at the back of pericranium, composed of pons, medulla and cerebella

【后脑勺儿】hòunǎosháor〈方 *dial.*〉脑袋后面突出的部分 back of the head; also 后脑勺子 hòunǎosháo·zi

【后年】hòunián 明年的明年 the year after next

【后娘】hòuniáng same as 继母 jìmǔ

【后怕】hòupà 事后感到害怕 fear after an event; lingering fear：想起那次海上遇到的风暴，还有些～。Whenever I recall that storm I encountered at sea, I become really scared.

【后期】hòuqī 某一时期的后一阶段 later stage; later period：十九世纪～ late 19th century｜抗日战争～ later stage of the War of Resistance against Japan

【后起】hòuqǐ 后出现的或新成长起来的（多指人才 oft. people of talent）new arrivals; younger generation：～之秀 an up-and-coming youngster; a promising young person｜他们大多是球坛上～的好手。They are the younger generation of talented ball players.

【后起之秀】hòu qǐ zhī xiù 后出现的或新成长起来的优秀人物 up-and-coming youngster; promising young person

【后勤】hòuqín 指后方对前方的一切供应工作。也指机关、团体等的行政事务性工作。rear service (for the front); logistics; administrative affairs of institutions and organizations

【后鞧】hòuqiū 套车时拴在驾辕牲口屁股周围的

皮带、帆布带等 leather or canvas strap, used for harnessing a draught animal to a cart

【后儿】hòur same as 后天 hòutiān; also 后儿个 hòur·ge

【后人】hòurén ❶ 后代的人 later generation: 前人种树,～乘凉。Earlier generations plant trees, while later generations enjoy the shade. ❷ same as 子孙 zǐsūn

【后任】hòurèn 在原来担任某项职务的人去职后继任这个职务的人 successor (to a post)

【后厦】hòushà 房屋后面的廊子 back veranda: 前廊～ front corridor and back veranda

【后晌】hòushǎng 〈方 *dial.*〉 same as 下午 xiàwǔ

【后晌】hòu·shang 〈方 *dial.*〉 same as 晚上 wǎn·shang: ～饭 supper

【后身】hòushēn ❶ (～儿 hòushēnr)身体后边的部分 back of a person: 我只看见～,认不清是谁。I couldn't make out who he was as I only saw his back. ❷ (～儿 hòushēnr)上衣、袍子等背后的部分 back of a garment: 这件衬衫～太长了。The back of this shirt is too long. ❸ (～儿 hòushēnr)房屋等的后边 back of a building: 房～有几棵枣树。There are several jujube trees at the back of the house. ❹ 人或动物来世转生的人或动物(迷信)(superstition) reincarnation of humans or animals ❺ (机构、制度等)由早先的一个转变而成的另一个(有的只是改变名称)(of an institution, system, etc.) successor: 八路军、新四军的～是中国人民解放军。The Chinese People's Liberation Army is the successor to the Eight Route Army and the New Fourth Army.

【后生】hòu·shēng 〈方 *dial.*〉 ❶ 青年男子 young man: 好～ good young man ❷ 年轻 having a youthful appearance: ～家(年轻人) young guy | 他长得～,看不出是四十多岁的人。He's over forty but looks much younger.

【后生可畏】hòushēng kě wèi 指青年人是新生的力量,很容易超过他们的前辈 the young are to be regarded with awe; the younger generations are a newly rising force tending to surpass their elders

【后世】hòushì ❶ same as 后代 hòudài ①:《诗经》和《楚辞》对～的文学有很大的影响。*The Book of Songs* and *the Elegies of Chu* have a great influence on the literature of later generations. ❷ same as 后裔 hòuyì ❸ 〈佛教 *Budd.*〉指来世 next life

【后事】hòushì ❶ 以后的事情 what happened afterwards: 前事不忘,～之师。Past experience, if not forgotten, is a guide for the future. | 欲如～如何,且听下回分解。If you want to know what happened afterwards, read the next chapter. ❷ 指丧事 funeral affairs: 准备～ get ready for a funeral | 料理～ deal with funeral affairs

【后手】hòushǒu ❶ 〈旧时 *old*〉指接替的人 successor ❷ 〈旧时 *old*〉指接受票据的人 bill receiver ❸ 下棋时被动的形势(跟'先手'相对 as opposed to 'at an advantage') at a disadvantage in a chess game: ～棋 at a disadvantage in a chess game | 这一着儿一走错,就变成～了。By this false move you've forced yourself into the defensive. ❹ (～儿 hòushǒur) same as 后路 hòulù ②

【后首】hòushǒu 〈方 *dial.*〉 ❶ 后来 afterwards; later: 当时没有听懂,～一想才明白了。I didn't understand at the moment, but I figured it out later after thinking it over. ❷ 后头;后面 behind; back; in the rear

【后嗣】hòusì 指子孙 descendants

【后台】hòutái ❶ 剧场中在舞台后面的部分。演出的艺术工作属于后台的范围。backstage; backstage work ❷ 〈比喻 *fig.*〉在背后操纵、支持的人或集团 backstage (backroom) support; person or group engaged in behind-the-scene manipulation and support

【后台老板】hòutái lǎobǎn 原指戏班子的班主,借指背后操纵、支持的人或集团 boss of a theatrical troupe; behind-the-scenes backer

【后唐】Hòu Táng 五代之一,公元 923—936,李存勖(xù)所建 Later Tang Dynasty (923-936), founded by Li Cunxu during the Five Dynasties Period; ☞ 五代 Wǔ Dài on p. 2029

【后天】[1] hòutiān 明天的明天 day after tomorrow

【后天】[2] hòutiān 人或动物离开母体后单独生活和成长的时期(跟'先天'相对 as opposed to 'innate') postnatal; acquired; the period in which humans or animals live independently after birth: 先天不足,～失调 be congenitally deficient, and lack proper care after birth

【后头】hòu·tou ❶ same as 后面 hòu·mian ①: 楼～有一片果树林。There's an orchard behind the building. ❷ same as 后面 hòu·mian ②: 怎样预防的问题,～还要细谈。We'll discuss later the details of the question about prevention. ❸ 〈方 *dial.*〉same as 后来 hòulái ①

【后退】hòutuì 向后退;退回(后面的地方或以往的发展阶段) draw back; fall back; retreat (to the rear or to a previous stage of development): ～两步 fall back two steps | 怎么成绩没提高,反而～了? How could your grades fall back instead of advancing?

【后卫】hòuwèi ❶ 军队行军时在后方担任掩护或警戒的部队 rear guard ❷ 篮球、足球等球类比赛中主要担任防御的队员 (of ball games like basketball, football) defender; linebacker; fullback; guard

【后效】hòuxiào 后来的效果;后来的表现 later effect; later performance: 略示薄惩,以观～。Give a light punishment, and see how he behaves in the future.

【后心】hòuxīn 脊背当中的部位 centre of the

back

【后行】hòuxíng 后进行;以后进行 carry out as a second step; carry out later

【后续】hòuxù ❶ 接着来的 follow-up:~部队 follow-up troops ❷〈方 *dial.*〉续娶;续弦 remarry after the death of one's wife

【后学】hòuxué 后进的学者或读书人(常用做谦辞 oft. used as a modest term to refer to oneself when addressing an elder) young or junior scholar or student

【后遗症】hòuyízhèng ❶ 某种疾病痊愈或主要症状消退之后所遗留下的一些症状。后遗症有的消退得很慢,有的终生不消退。sequela; aftereffect of disease or injury that may disappear or recover very slowly, or, in some cases, remain for the rest of one's life ❷〈比喻 *fig.*〉由于做事情或处理问题不认真、不妥善而留下的消极影响 after-effect; aftermath

【后尾儿】hòuyǐr 最后的部分;后边 very rear part; behind:车~ rear end of a vehicle|船~ stern|他走得慢,落在~了。He was very slow on the road and fell behind.

【后裔】hòuyì 已经死去的人的子孙 descendant (of a dead person); offspring

【后影】hòuyǐng (~儿 hòuyǐngr)从后边看到的人或东西的形状 shape of a person or thing as seen from the back:那人一下就跑过去了,只看见一个~儿。I only vaguely saw his back as the guy dashed away.

【后援】hòuyuán 援军,泛指支援的力量 reinforcements; backup force; backing

【后院】hòuyuàn (~儿 hòuyuànr) ❶ 正房后面的院落 backyard ❷〈比喻 *fig.*〉后方或内部 rear; home front:~起火(比喻内部闹矛盾或后方出了麻烦事) internal contradictions occur; trouble in the backyard

【后账】hòuzhàng ❶ 不公开的账 accounts kept secret; hidden accounts ❷ 以后再算的账,多指事后追究责任的事 turn back to account for sth.; look into sb.'s responsibility after sth. happened:只要自己行得正,不怕别人算~。Don't be afraid of being investigated, as long as you're well behaved.

【后罩房】hòuzhàofáng〈方 *dial.*〉四合院中正房后边跟正房平行的一排房屋 posterior house; row of houses behind and parallel to the main rooms in a courtyard

【后肢】hòuzhī 昆虫或有四肢的脊椎动物长在身体后部的两条腿 hind legs (of insects or vertebrates)

【后周】Hòu Zhōu 五代之一,公元 951—960,郭威所建 Later Zhou Dynasty (951-960), founded by Guo Wei during the Five Dynasties Period; ☞ 五代 Wǔ Dài on p. 2029

【后缀】hòuzhuì 加在词根后面的构词成分,如'作家、科学家'里的'家','规范化、绿化'里的'化','人民性、党性'里的'性' suffix, such as jiā in zuòjiā (writer) and kēxuéjiā (scientist); huà in guīfànhuà (regulation) and lǜhuà (afforestation), and xìng in rénmínxìng (popular appeal) and dǎngxìng (Party spirit)

【后坐】hòuzuò 弹头射出时枪炮向后运动 fall back under pressure; the recoil of a gun upon firing; the act or action of recoiling:~力 recoil

【后坐力】hòuzuòlì 指枪弹、炮弹射出时的反冲力 recoil; backlash

郈 Hòu 姓 a surname

厚 hòu ❶ 扁平物上下两面之间的距离大(跟'薄'相对 as opposed to 'thin') thick; having relatively great depth or extent from one surface to its opposite:~木板 thick wooden plank|~棉衣 heavy cotton-padded coat|嘴唇很~ thick lips ❷ 厚度 depth; thickness:下了两寸~的雪。Two inches of snow fell. ❸(感情)深 (of love; relationship) deep; profound:深情~谊 deep affection and a profound relationship|交情很~ profound friendship ❹ 厚道 kind; magnanimous:宽~ generous|忠~ honest and tolerant ❺(利润)大;(礼物价值)大 large; generous (of gifts; value):~利 big profit or high interest|~礼 generous gifts ❻(味道)浓 rich or strong (in flavour):酒味很~。The wine has a mellow taste. ❼(家产)富有;殷实 rich (in family property):家底儿~ (of a family) wealthy ❽ 优待;推崇;重视 favour; stress; highly value:~此薄彼 say turkey to one and buzzard to another|~今薄古 treasure the present and overlook the past ❾(Hòu)姓 a surname

【厚爱】hòu'ài 称对方对自己深切的喜爱或爱护 great favour and good care granted by others:承蒙~。I'm indebted to you for your kindness.

【厚薄】hòubó ❶ 厚度 thickness:这块板子的~正合适。This plate is just the right thickness. ❷ 指重视与轻视,优待与慢待,亲近与疏远 treasure (one) and overlook (another); prefer and slight; intimacy and alienation:都是朋友,为何要分~? There should be no differences in how we treat our friends.

【厚薄规】hòubóguī 测量两个接合面的间隙的量具,由不同厚度(一般为 0.01—0.50 毫米)的金属薄片组成 feeler gauge; thickness gauge; an instrument to measure the clearance between two joint faces, composed of metal chips of different thickness (gen. 0.01-0.50 mm.); also 塞尺 sāichǐ

【厚此薄彼】hòu cǐ bó bǐ 重视或优待一方,轻视或慢待另一方。指对人或事不同等看待。unequal treatment of sb. or sth.; favour one and be prejudiced against the other; favour one and discriminate against the other

【厚待】hòudài 优厚地对待;优待 treat sb. kindly:人家这样~咱们,心里实在过意不去。We

really appreciate their kindness toward us.

【厚道】hòu·dao 待人诚恳,能宽容,不刻薄 honest and tolerant:为人～ behave honestly and tolerantly|他是个～人。He's an honest and kind person.

【厚度】hòudù 扁的物体上下两面之间的距离 thickness; distance between the top and bottom surfaces of a flat object

【厚墩墩】hòudūndūn (～的 hòudūndūn·de)形容很厚 very thick:～的棉大衣 a heavily padded overcoat

【厚古薄今】hòu gǔ bó jīn 指在学术研究上,重视古代,轻视现代(in academic research and study) stress the past to the neglect of the present

【厚今薄古】hòu jīn bó gǔ 指在学术研究上,重视现代,轻视古代(in academic research and study) stress the present to the neglect of the past

【厚礼】hòulǐ 丰厚的礼物 generous gifts:赠以～ present a generous gift

【厚利】hòulì 大的利润或高的利息 big profit or high interest:赚取～ make a large profit

【厚实】hòu·shi ❶ 厚 thick:这布挺～。This cloth is rather thick and durable.|炕上厚厚实实地铺着一层稻草。The platform bed is covered with a thick layer of straw. ❷ 宽厚结实 thick and strong:～的肩膀 big and strong shoulders ❸ 深厚扎实 solid; down-to-earth:武功～ accomplished in martial arts|学术基础～ solid academic grounding ❹〈方 *dial.*〉忠厚诚实 honest and sincere:为人～ conduct honestly and sincerely|心眼～ be kind of heart ❺ 丰富;富裕 abundant; rich:家底～ family with substantial resources

【厚望】hòuwàng 很大的期望 great expectations:寄予～ place high hopes on

【厚颜】hòuyán 脸皮厚,不知羞耻 brazen-faced; audacious:～无耻 impudent; brazen; shameless

【厚谊】hòuyì 深厚的情谊 profound friendship:深情～ deep affection and profound friendship

【厚意】hòuyì 深厚的情意 kind thought; kindness:多谢各位的～。Thank you for your kindness.

【厚遇】hòuyù 优厚的待遇 handsome pay and nice accommodation; high wages and good benefits

【厚葬】hòuzàng 用隆重的仪式安葬。也指耗费大量钱财办理丧事。bury in pomp and pageantry; a lavish funeral

【厚重】hòuzhòng ❶ 又厚又重 thick and heavy:～的棉帘子 thick and heavy cotton curtains ❷ 丰厚 rich and generous:～的礼物 generous gifts ❸〈书 *fml.*〉敦厚持重 kind and dignified:为人～笃实 treat others kindly and sincerely

侯 hòu 闽侯(Mǐnhòu),地名,在福建 Minhou, name of a place in Fujian Province ☞ hóu on p. 808

垕 hòu ❶ same as 厚 hòu ①—⑧ ❷ 神垕(Shénhòu),地名,在河南 Shenhou, name of a place in Henan Province

逅 hòu ☞ [邂逅](xièhòu) on p. 2125

候[1] hòu ❶ 等待 wait; await:～车 wait for the bus|你稍～一会儿,他马上就来。Please wait a moment, he'll be right here. ❷ 问候;问好 inquire after; greet:致～ pay one's respect to|敬～起居。How's your life going?

候[2] hòu ❶ 时节 time; season:时～ time|气～ weather|～鸟 migratory bird ❷〈古代 *arch.*〉五天为一候,现在气象学上仍沿用 every five days; a term still used in meteorology today:～温 five-day air temperature ❸ (～儿 hòur)情况 condition; state:征～ sign; symptom|火～ duration and degree of heating, cooking, smelting, etc.; level of attainment

【候补】hòubǔ 等候递补缺额 be a candidate (for a vacancy); be an alternate:～委员 alternate committee member

【候场】hòuchǎng 等候上场(演出)(of an actor or actress) wait to go onstage:演员按时到后台～。The performers waited backstage as scheduled.

【候车】hòuchē 等候乘车 wait for a train, bus, etc.:～室 waiting room

【候虫】hòuchóng 随季节而生或鸣叫的昆虫,如夏天的蝉、秋天的蟋蟀等 insects that are born or chirp seasonally, e.g. cicada in summer, cricket in autumn, etc.

【候风地动仪】hòufēng dìdòngyí 我国东汉时天文学家张衡创制的世界上最早的地震仪 seismograph as invented by the Eastern Han astronomer Zhang Heng in A.D. 132, the earliest of its kind in the world; 简称 abbr. 地动仪 dìdòngyí

【候光】hòuguāng〈书 *fml.*〉〈敬辞 *pol.*〉等候光临(多用于请帖 usu. used in invitations) await the honour of your presence:洁樽～。We have had the wine goblets cleaned, and await your presence.

【候教】hòujiào〈敬辞 *pol.*〉等候指教 await your instructions:本星期日下午在舍下～。I'll be expecting you at my place Sunday afternoon.

【候鸟】hòuniǎo 随季节的变更而迁徙的鸟,如杜鹃、家燕、鸿雁等 migratory bird; e.g. cuckoo, barn swallow, wild goose, etc. ☞ 冬候鸟 dōnghòuniǎo on p. 464 and 夏候鸟 xiàhòuniǎo on p. 2069

【候审】hòushěn (原告、被告)等候审问(plaintiff or defendant) await trial:出庭～ appear in court and await trial

【候温】hòuwēn 每候(五天)的平均气温 average air temperature of every five days

【候选人】hòuxuǎnrén 在选举前预先提名作为选举对象的人 candidate; one that is nominated or qualified for a position to be elected

【候诊】hòuzhěn (病人)门诊时等候诊断治疗 (of patients) wait to see the doctor: ～室 waiting room (in a hospital)

堠 hòu 〈古代 *arch.*〉瞭望敌方情况的土堡 watchtower, for overseeing an enemy's situation

鲎[1] (鱟) hòu 节肢动物,头胸部的甲壳略呈马蹄形,腹部的甲壳呈六角形,尾部呈剑状,生活在海底 king crab (*Limulus polyphemus L.*); marine arthropod with a broad horseshoe-shaped cephalothorax, hexagonal belly, and blade-shaped tail, living on the seabed; 俗称 popularly known as 鲎鱼 hóngyú

鲎[2] (鱟) hòu 〈方 *dial.*〉虹 rainbow

鲘 hòu 鲘门(Hòumén),地名,在广东 Houmen, name of a place in Guangdong Province

hū (ㄏㄨ)

乎[1] hū 〈书 *fml.*〉〈助词 *aux.*〉❶ 表示疑问,跟'吗'相同 [express doubt, equivalent to 吗·ma]: 王侯将相宁有种～? Does nobility really have a future? ❷ 表示选择的疑问,跟'呢'相同 [express questioning, equivalent to 呢·ne]: 然～? 否～? Is that so? Isn't it? ❸ 表示揣度,跟'吧'相同 [express estimation, equivalent to 吧·ba]: 成败兴亡之机,其在斯～? Does not success or failure hinge on this?

乎[2] hū ❶ 动词后缀,作用跟'于'相同 [verb suffix, used similarly to 于 yú]: 在～ lies in | 无须～ unnecessary | 出～意料 unexpectedly | 合～规律 in accordance with law | 超～寻常 be out of the ordinary ❷ 形容词或副词后缀 [suffix of an adjective or adverb]: 巍巍～ towering; lofty | 郁郁～ depressed | 迥～不同 widely different | 确～重要 very important indeed

乎[3] hū 〈书 *fml.*〉〈叹词 *interj.*〉跟'啊'相同 [exclamation similar to 啊 ā]: 天～! Oh, heavens!

戏(戲、戲) hū ☞ 於戏 wūhū on p. 2017 ☞ xì on p. 2055

怃[1] (憮) hū 〈方 *dial.*〉覆盖 cover: 小苗让草～住了,赶快锄吧! Let's start hoeing at once — the young shoots are almost choked with weeds.

怃[2] (憮) hū 〈书 *fml.*〉❶ 宽大;大 broad; large ❷ 傲慢;怠慢 arrogant; give sb. the cold shoulder

呼[1] hū ❶ 生物体把体内的气体排出体外(跟'吸'相对 as opposed to 'inhale') (of an organism) breathe out; exhale discharge air: ～吸 breathe; exhale and inhale | ～出一口气 exhale a breath ❷ 大声喊 shout; cry out: ～声 shout | 欢～ cheer; acclaim | ～口号 shout slogans | 大声疾～ appeal in a loud voice ❸ 叫;叫人来 call: 直～其名 address sb. disrespectfully by name | 一～百诺 a hundred people respond when one gives a single call | ～之即来,挥之即去 be ready to come and go at one's beck and call ❹(Hū) 姓 a surname

呼[2] hū 〈拟声词 *onom.*〉: 北风～～地吹。The north wind is whistling.

【呼哧】hūchī 〈拟声词 *onom.*〉形容喘息的声音 sound of panting: ～～地喘着粗气 puff and blow; also 呼蚩 hūchī

【呼蚩】hūchī same as 呼哧 hūchī

【呼风唤雨】hū fēng huàn yǔ 使刮风下雨。原指神仙道士的法力,现在比喻能够支配自然。有时也比喻进行煽动性的活动。summon wind and rain — powers of immortals and Daoist priests; (fig.) be able to manipulate nature; stir up trouble

【呼喊】hūhǎn 喊;嚷 call out; shout: 大声～ shout at the top of one's voice | ～口号 shout slogans

【呼号】hūháo 因极端悲伤而哭叫;因处于困境需要援助而叫喊 wail; cry out in distress; (of sb. in a predicament) call for aid: 仰天～ look up at the sky and cry out in distress | 奔走～ go hither and thither campaigning for a cause

【呼号】hūhào ❶ 无线电通讯中使用的各种代号,有时专指广播电台的名称的字母代号 call sign; call letters; codes used in radio communications ❷ 某些组织专用的口号,如中国少年先锋队的呼号是:'准备着,为共产主义事业而奋斗!' motto; catchword (of an organization), e. g. the motto of the Chinese Young Pioneers: 'Get ready, and we'll struggle for the Communist cause!'

【呼唤】hūhuàn ❶ 召唤 call; shout to: 祖国在～我们! Our motherland is calling us! ❷ 呼喊 exclaim; yell out: 大声～ yell loudly

【呼叫】hūjiào ❶ 电台上用呼号叫对方 call sb. by using telecommunications signals: 勇敢号! 勇敢号! 我在～! *Courage*! *Courage*! I'm calling! | 船长! 管理局在～我们。Captain, the administrative bureau is calling us. ❷ 呼喊 shout; call out: 高声～ shout loudly

【呼救】hūjiù 呼叫求救 call for help: 落水儿童大声～。The child who fell into water yelled for help. | 情况危急,赶快通过电台向总部～。The situation is urgent, we should send radio SOS signals right away to headquarters for help.

【呼啦】hūlā 〈拟声词 *onom.*〉: 红旗被风吹得～

～地响。The red flag is flapping in the wind. also 呼喇 hūlā and 呼啦啦 hūlālā

【呼喇】hūlā same as 呼啦 hūlā

【呼噜】hūlū〈拟声词 *onom.*〉wheeze：他气管炎犯了，嗓子里～～老响。He's a bit wheezy due to an attack of tracheitis.

【呼噜】hū·lu 睡着时由于呼吸受阻而发出的粗重的呼吸声；鼾声 snore；rough，hoarse noise of breathing during sleep：打～ snore away

【呼朋引类】hū péng yǐn lèi 招引同类的人。多指坏人结成一伙做坏事。summon one's cohorts；gang up（for evil deeds）

【呼扇】hū·shān ❶（片状物）颤动（of flat，thin things）shake：跳板太长，走在上面直～。The springboard was too long，so it shook as I walked on it. ❷ 用片状物扇风 fan：他满头大汗，摘下草帽不停地～。His head soaked with sweat，so he took off his straw hat and fanned himself with it. ‖ also 唿扇 hū·shān

【呼哨】hūshào 把手指放在嘴里用力吹时，或物体迅速运动时，发出的尖锐的像哨子的声音 whistle；shrill clear sound produced by the forcible expulsion of breath through the lips with the fingers inside the mouth，or a sound produced by an object due to its quick movement：打～ give a whistle｜一声～。A whistle was heard. also 唿哨 hūshào

【呼声】hūshēng ❶ 呼喊的声音 cry；shout：～动天 earth-shaking shout ◇此次联赛，北京队夺冠～最高。The Beijing Team is the most likely to win the championship in the league matches. ❷ 指群众的意见和要求 opinions and requirements of the masses：倾听群众的～ listen to the voice of the masses

【呼天抢地】hū tiān qiāng dì 大声叫天，用头撞地。形容极度悲痛。lament to heaven and knock one's head on the ground — in utter anguish

【呼吸】hūxī ❶ 生物体与外界进行气体交换。人和高等动物用肺呼吸，低等动物靠皮肤呼吸，植物通过表面的组织进行气体交换。breathe；respire. Organisms exchange air with the environment. Human beings and higher animals breathe through lungs，lower animals breathe through the skin，plants breathe through their surface tissue. ❷〈书 *fml.*〉一呼一吸 an inhalation and an exhalation；〈比喻 *fig.*〉极短的时间 an instant：成败在～之间。Success or failure just happens in an instant.

【呼吸道】hūxīdào 人或高等动物呼吸空气的通路，包括鼻腔、咽、喉、气管和支气管 respiratory tract；passage for human beings' and higher animals' breathing functions，consisting of the nasal cavity，pharynx，throat，trachea and bronchia

【呼吸相通】hūxī xiāng tōng〈比喻 *fig.*〉思想一致，利害相关 share the same sentiments and fate；be bound together by common interests：～，患难与共 share the same fate and go through thick and thin together

【呼啸】hūxiào 发出高而长的声音 whistle；scream；whizz：北风～。The north wind is howling.｜炮弹从头顶上～而过。A bullet whizzed past over my head.

【呼延】Hūyán 姓 a surname

【呼幺喝六】hū yāo hè liù ❶ 掷色子时的喊声（幺、六是色子的点子）。泛指赌博喧哗声。play at dice；shout out numbers while throwing dice；（fig.）make a lot of noise during gambling ❷〈方 *dial.*〉形容盛气凌人的样子 shouting left and right — arrogant

【呼应】hūyìng 一呼一应，互相联系或照应 echo；work in concert with：前后～。The end works in concert with the beginning.｜遥相～ echo each other at a distance

【呼吁】hūyù 向个人或社会申述，请求援助或主持公道 appeal；call on：奔走～ rush about in appeal｜～各界人士捐款赈济灾区 appeal for donations from people from all walks of life to the relief of disaster-stricken areas

【呼之欲出】hū zhī yù chū 指人像等画得逼真，似乎叫他一声他就会从画里走出来。泛指文学作品中人物的描写十分生动。（of a lifelike portrait）seem ready to come out at one's beckoning；（in a broad sense）vivid portrayal of characters in a literary work

忽[1] hū 不注意；不重视 neglect；overlook；ignore：～略 omit｜～视 overlook｜疏～ neglect

忽[2] hū 忽而 suddenly；all of a sudden；now...，now ...：天气～冷～热。The weather keeps blowing hot and cold.｜油灯被风吹得～明～暗。In the wind the oil lamp now brightened，now dimmed. *or* The oil damp flickered in the wind.

忽[3] hū ❶（某些计量单位的）十万分之一 one-100,000th（of some measuring units）：～米 0.00001 metre ❷ 计量单位名称 a unit of measurement：a）长度，10 忽等于 1 丝（of length）10 *hu* is equal to 1 *si* b）重量，10 忽等于 1 丝（of weight）10 *hu* is equal to 1 *si*

【忽地】hūdì 忽然；突然 suddenly；all of a sudden：灯～灭了。The light suddenly went out.｜～下起雨来。It rained suddenly.

【忽而】hū'ér 忽然（大多同时用在意义相对或相近的动词、形容词等前头 oft. used simultaneously before verbs or adjectives of opposite or similar meanings）suddenly；now...，now...：～说，～笑 now talk，now burst out langhing｜湖上的歌声～高，～低。The singing over the lake surged and abated.

【忽忽】hūhū ❶ 形容时间过得很快［used in describing the passing of time］fast；quickly：离开杭州，～又是一年。A year has slipped by since I left Hangzhou. ❷〈书 *fml.*〉形容失意或迷惘 perplexed or frustrated: ～不乐 downhearted | ～如有所失 distracted as if sth. has been lost

【忽律】hūlǜ same as 猢狸 hūlǜ

【忽略】hūlüè 没有注意到;疏忽 neglect; overlook: 只追求数量,～了质量 stress quantity to the neglect of quality

【忽然】hūrán〈副词 *adv.*〉表示来得迅速而又出乎意料;突然 suddenly; all of a sudden; quickly and unexpectedly: 他正要出去,～下起大雨来了。Just as he was going out, it suddenly started pouring.

【忽闪】hūshǎn 形容闪光(of light) flash: 闪光弹～一亮,又～一亮。The flare flashed now and then.

【忽闪】hū•shan 闪耀;闪动(of eyes, etc.) sparkle; flash: 小姑娘～着大眼睛看着妈妈。The little girl, her big eyes flashing, stared at her mother.

【忽视】hūshì 不注意;不重视 ignore; overlook; neglect: 不应该强调一方面而～另一方面 Don't stress one aspect to the neglect of another. | ～安全生产,后果将不堪设想。There will be disastrous consequences if production safety is overlooked.

【忽悠】hū•you〈方 *dial.*〉same as 晃动 huàngdòng: 大旗叫风吹得直～。The flag fluttered in the wind. | 渔船上的灯火～～的。Lights flickered on the fishing boats.

轷 Hū 姓 a surname

烀 hū 用少量的水,盖紧锅盖,加热,半蒸半煮,把食物弄熟 stew in shallow water: ～白薯 stewed sweet potato

唿 hū ☞ below

【唿扇】hū• shān same as 呼扇 hū•shān

【唿哨】hūshào same as 呼哨 hūshào

猢 hū [猢狸](hūlǜ)指鳄鱼(见于《水浒》) reference to crocodile (see *Outlaws of the Marsh*); also 忽律 hūlǜ

滹 hū [滹浴](hù// yù)〈方 *dial.*〉洗澡 bathe; have (or take) a bath

惚 hū ☞ 恍惚 huǎng•hū on p. 855

嘑 hū〈书 *fml.*〉same as 呼 hū

滹 hū 滹沱河(HūtuóHé),水名,在河北,与滏阳河会合后叫子牙河 Hutuo River, in Hebei Province, but the section that joins the Fuyang River is called Ziya River

糊 hū 用较浓的糊状物涂抹缝子、窟窿或平面 plaster; daub thick paste in a seam or hollow or on a surface: 用灰把墙缝～上 plaster up cracks in the wall | 往墙上～了一层泥 spread a layer of mud on the wall

☞ hú on p. 820 and hù on p. 825

hú (ㄏㄨˊ)

囫 hú ☞ below

【囫囵】húlún 完整;整个儿 whole: ～觉 sound sleep | ～吞枣 swallow a date whole

【囫囵觉】hú•lunjiào 整夜不被惊醒的睡眠;整宿(xiǔ)的觉 uninterrupted sleep; good night's sleep: 她每天夜里起来给孩子喂奶,换尿布,没睡过一个～。She's been waking up every night to feed her baby and change diapers, and hasn't had one good night's rest.

【囫囵吞枣】húlún tūn zǎo 把枣儿整个儿吞下去 swallow a date whole; 〈比喻 *fig.*〉读书等不加分析地笼统接受 lap up information without digesting it; read without understanding

和 hú 打麻将或斗纸牌时某一家的牌合乎规定的要求,取得胜利 win and complete a set in mahjong

☞ hé on p. 786, hè on p. 791, huó on p. 875 and huò on p. 884

狐 hú ❶ 哺乳动物的一属,外形略像狼,面部较长,耳朵三角形,尾巴长,毛通常赤黄色。性狡猾多疑,昼伏夜出,吃野鼠、鸟类、家禽等。毛皮可做衣物。较常见的是草狐和赤狐。fox (*Vulpes bowdich*); a mammal of the dog family, related to wolves, with a longer face, triangular ears, a long bushy tail, and helvolus fur that makes an ideal material for clothing, having a cunning and suspicious character, resting during the day and coming out at night, eating field mice, birds and poultry; 通称 commonly called 狐狸 hú•li ❷ (Hú) 姓 a surname

【狐臭】húchòu 由于腋窝、阴部等部位的皮肤内汗腺分泌异常而产生的刺鼻臭味 body odour (B. O.); bromhidrosis; repulsive odour caused by unusual secretions of the sweat glands of the skin at the armpits or private parts; also 胡臭 húchòu or 狐臊 húsāo

【狐假虎威】hú jiǎ hǔ wēi 老虎捉到一只狐狸,要吃它。狐狸说:'上天命令我做百兽的王,你吃了我就违背了天意。如果你不信,就跟我一块儿走,百兽见了我没有一个不逃跑的。'老虎依了它的话,跟它一块儿走,果然各种走兽见了都逃跑了。老虎不知道百兽是怕自己,还真以为是怕狐狸(见于《战国策•楚策》)。比喻倚仗别人的势力来欺压人。fox borrows the tiger's fierceness (by walking in the latter's company); like a donkey in a lion's hide; bully people by flaunting one's powerful connections. According to *Intrigues of the Warring States • Intrigues of Chu*, a tiger caught a fox and was about to eat it. The fox said, 'God has made me the king of all the beasts. You'll go against God's will if you take my life. Don't you believe that? Come with me and you'll see beasts running away upon coming across me.' The tiger then walked together with the fox and just as the fox had said, various beasts ran away as soon as they saw the fox. The tiger did not realize that the beasts were actually frightened of him, not the fox.

【狐狸】hú·li 狐的通称 general term for 狐 hú

【狐狸精】hú·lijīng 指妖媚迷人的女子(骂人的话 curse) seductive woman

【狐狸尾巴】hú·li wěi·ba 传说狐狸变成人形后，尾巴会经常露出来。后来用狐狸尾巴比喻终究要暴露出来的坏主意或坏行为。fox's tail (legend has it that the fox's tail eventually reappears after the fox turns into a human); commonly used to compare evil intentions or actions that will be finally revealed

【狐媚】húmèi 用媚态迷惑人 bewitch by cajolery; entice by flattery

【狐朋狗友】hú péng gǒu yǒu〈比喻 *fig.*〉品行不端的朋友 a gang of scoundrels; evil cohorts

【狐肷】húqiǎn 毛皮业上指狐狸的胸腹部和腋下的毛皮 belly hair and armpit hair of a fox

【狐群狗党】hú qún gǒu dǎng〈比喻 *fig.*〉勾结在一起的坏人 a pack of rogues; a gang of scoundrels; also 狐朋狗党 hú péng gǒu dǎng

【狐死首丘】hú sǐ shǒu qiū〈古代 *arch.*〉传说狐狸如果死在外面，一定把头朝着它的洞穴(见于《礼记·檀弓上》) Ancient legend has it that when a fox dies somewhere else, it turns its head in the direction of its den. (*The Book of Rites·Tan Gong* (*I*));〈比喻 *fig.*〉不忘本或怀念故乡 longing for home or mindful of one's origins

【狐疑】húyí same as 怀疑 huáiyí ①：满腹～ be full of misgivings; be very suspicious | ～不决 undecided; be unable to make up one's mind

弧 hú ❶ 圆周上任意两点间的部分 arc; of a curved line (as out of a circle or ellipse) ❷〈古代 *arch.*〉指弓 bow：弦木为～(用弦绷在树枝上做成弓) bow made by setting a string on a tree branch

【弧度】húdù 平面角的度量单位。圆心角所对的弧长和半径相等，这个角就是一弧度角。radian; a unit of plane angular measurement that is equal to the angle at the centre of a circle subtended by an arc equal in length to the radius; 旧称 formerly called 弪 jìng

【弧光】húguāng 电弧所发出的光。光度很强，带蓝紫色。arc; arc light; sustained luminous discharge of electricity across a gap in a circuit or between electrodes, emitting intense royal purple light

【弧光灯】húguāngdēng 用碳质电极产生的电弧做光源的照明用具。这种灯能发出极强的光，可以做探照灯，也可以用于电影的制片和放映。arc lamp (light); electric lamp that produces an arc of light when a current passes between two incandescent electrodes surrounded by gas, used as a searchlight or for making and projecting films; also 炭精灯 tànjīngdēng

胡[1] Hú ❶〈古代 *arch.*〉泛称北方和西方的少数民族 ethnic minorities inhabiting the northern and western part of China：～人 Tartars; Mongols ❷(hú)〈古代 *arch.*〉称来自北方和西方少数民族的(东西)。也泛指来自国外的(东西) goods introduced from the minority-inhabited northern and western areas or foreign countries：～琴 *huqin* fiddle; two-stringed Chinese violin | ～桃 walnut | ～椒 pepper ❸ 姓 a surname

胡[2] hú〈副词 *adv.*〉表示随意乱来 recklessly, wantonly, outrageously：～闹 run wild | ～说 talk nonsense

胡[3] hú〈书 *fml.*〉疑问词，为什么；何故 why：～不归？Why not return?

胡[4](鬍) hú same as 胡子 hú·zi ①：～须 whiskers

【胡扯】húchě 闲谈；瞎说 talk nonsense; chatter idly：两个人～了一通。The two of them chattered idly for a while. | ～，世上哪有这种事！Nonsense! It can't happen in this world!

【胡臭】húchòu same as 狐臭 húchòu

【胡蝶】húdié same as 蝴蝶 húdié

【胡豆】húdòu same as 蚕豆 cándòu

【胡匪】húfěi〈方 *dial.*〉〈旧时 *old*〉称土匪 bandit; also 胡子 hú·zi

【胡蜂】húfēng 昆虫，头胸部褐色，有黄色斑纹，腹部深黄色，中间有黑褐色横纹。尾部有毒刺，能蜇人。以花蜜和虫类为食物。wasp (*Vespa mandarinia*); hornet; insect that has a brown head and a chest with yellow stripes, a deep yellow belly embellished with dark brown grains across, and a poisonous sting at the tail that can hurt people, and that eats caterpillars, bugs, and nectar; 通称 commonly called 马蜂 mǎfēng

【胡话】húhuà 神志不清时说的话 raving; wild and irrational talk：他烧得直说～。He was raving and delirious with fever.

【胡笳】hújiā 我国古代北方民族的一种乐器，类似笛子 nomadic flute; a musical instrument like the flute, used by northern tribes in ancient China

【胡椒】hújiāo ❶ 常绿藤本植物，叶子卵形或长椭圆形，花黄色。果实小，球形，成熟时红色。未成熟果实干后果皮变黑，叫黑胡椒；成熟的果实去皮后色白，叫白胡椒。有辣味，是调味品，又可入药。pepper (*Piper nigrum*); an evergreen jointed climbing shrub with ovate or oblong ovate leaves, yellow flowers, and small, round fruit which turns red when ripe; usu. used as pungent condiment or material for medicine; the immature pepper seed with the black husk still on is known as black pepper; the ripe pepper seed after the black husk is removed is known as white pepper ❷

这种植物的果实 pepper seed; fruit of a pepper

【胡搅】hújiǎo ❶ 瞎搗乱;扰乱 nag, badger ❷ 狡辩;强辩 hassle; wrangle

【胡搅蛮缠】hú jiǎo mán chán 不讲道理,胡乱纠缠 argue on and on in an annoying way; pester sb. with unreasonable demands

【胡来】húlái ❶ 不按规程,任意乱做 mess things up; fool with sth.:既然不会,就别～。Don't fool with it if you don't know how to do it. ❷ 胡闹;胡作非为 run wild; act irresponsibly or recklessly:放规矩些,不许～。Behave and don't act recklessly.

【胡噜】hú·lu〈方 *dial.*〉❶ 抚摩 rub:他的头碰疼了,你给他～～。He's knocked his head against something — rub it for him. ❷ 用拂拭的动作把东西除去或归拢在一处 sweep (away); gather together:把瓜子皮儿～到簸箕里 sweep the melon-seed shells into a dustpan | 把棋子都～到一堆儿 gather the chess pieces together ❸ 应付;办理 handle; deal with:事太多,一个人还真～不过来。It's really hard for one person to deal with so many things at the same time.

【胡乱】húluàn ❶ 马虎;随便 carelessly; casually; at random:～涂上几笔 draw a few strokes casually | ～吃了两口就走了 leave after a hasty meal ❷ 任意;没有道理 wildly; at will:他话还没听完,就～批评一气。He criticized the speech wildly without even finishing listening to it. | 粮食不能～糟蹋。We should not waste grain carelessly.

【胡萝卜】húluó·bo ❶ 二年生草本植物,羽状复叶,开白色小花,果实长圆形。根长圆锥形,肉质,有紫红、橘红、黄色等多种,是常见的蔬菜。carrot (*Daucus carota*); biennial herbal plant that has pinnately compound leaves and white flowers and bears oval fruits; its root, conic in shape and mauve, orange or yellow in colour, are common vegetables ❷ 这种植物的根 root of this plant

【胡闹】húnào 行动没有道理;无理取闹 shenanigans; run wild; be mischievous; make trouble:任意～ make trouble unscrupulously

【胡琴】hú·qin (～儿 hú·qinr)弦乐器,在竹弓上系马尾毛,放在两弦之间拉动。有京胡、二胡等。general term for certain two-stringed bowed instruments, such as *erhu* and *jinghu*

【胡说】húshuō ❶ 瞎说 talk nonsense or drivel:信口～ make irresponsible remarks ❷ 没有根据的或没有道理的话 nonsense; drivel; unsubstantial or irrational words:这纯属～,不必理会。It's just nonsense. Forget it.

【胡说八道】hú shuō bā dào same as 胡说 húshuō

【胡思乱想】hú sī luàn xiǎng 没有根据或不切实际地瞎想 given to flights of fancy; give way to foolish fancies; let one's imagination run away

【胡桃】hútáo same as 核桃 hé·tao

【胡同】(衚衕) hú·tòng (～儿 hú·tòngr)巷;小街道。注意 **NOTE**:用做巷名时,'同'字轻声不儿化。lane; alley; When appearing in the name of an alleyway, it is pronounced hú·tong, not hú·tongr.

【胡涂】hú·tu same as 糊涂 hú·tu

【胡须】húxū same as 胡子 hú·zi ①

【胡言】húyán ❶ same as 胡说 húshuō:～乱语 talk nonsense; rave ❷ 胡话 nonsense:一派～ all nonsense

【胡诌】húzhōu 随口瞎编;胡说 fabricate wild tales; cook up (tales):顺嘴～ speak thoughtlessly | ～一气 cook up a story

【胡子】hú·zi ❶ 嘴周围和连着鬓角长的毛 beard, moustache or whiskers ❷〈方 *dial.*〉胡匪 bandit

【胡子拉碴】hú·zilāchā (～的 hú·zilāchā·de)形容满脸胡子未加修饰 unshaven; stubbly beard; bristly unshaven chin

【胡作非为】hú zuò fēi wéi 不顾法纪或舆论,任意行动 act wildly in defiance of the law or public opinion; commit all kinds of outrages; run amuck

壶(壺) hú ❶ 陶瓷或金属等制成的容器,有嘴儿,有把儿或提梁,用来盛液体,从嘴儿往外倒 kettle; pot; ceramic or metallic container that has a handle and a mouth from which liquid is poured out:茶～ teapot | 酒～ flagon | 喷～ watering can ❷ (Hú)姓 a surname

核 hú [核儿](húr) same as 核[1](hé)①②,用于某些口语词,如'梨核儿、煤核儿、冰核儿' used for some colloquial words Chinese such as 梨核儿 (pear core), 煤核儿(partly burnt coals or briquettes), and 冰核儿(ice cube) ☞ hé on p.789

斛 hú 旧量器,方形,口小,底大,容量本为十斗,后来改为五斗 cubic measure used in former times, small at the mouth and large at the bottom, with a capacity originally equal to 10 *dou* (斗), and later reduced to 5 *dou*

葫 hú [葫芦](hú·lu) ❶ 一年生草本植物,茎蔓生,叶子互生,心脏形,花白色。果实中间细,像两个球连在一起,表面光滑,可做器皿,也供玩赏。bottle gourd (*Lagenaria Siceraria*); calabash; annual cauline plant that has intergrown heart-shaped leaves, white flowers, and smooth fruit that looks like two balls connected, oft. used as ornaments, vessels or utensils ❷ 这种植物的果实 fruit of the gourd

搰 hú〈书 *fml.*〉❶ 掘 dig ❷ 搅浑 disturb

鹄 hú ☞ 天鹅 tiān'é on p.1888
☞ gǔ on p.695

【鹄立】húlì〈书 *fml.*〉直立 stand erect:瞻望～

stand erect and look forward

【鹄望】húwàng〈书 *fml*.〉直立而望。形容盼望等待。eagerly look forward to; expect on tiptoe

猢 hú [猢狲](húsūn) 猕猴的一种,身上有密毛,生活在我国北方山林中 monkey, a kind of macaque that has bushy chaetae and mostly lives in the mountain forests of north China

馇 hú 粥类 thick congee; thick gruel; porridge

【馇口】húkǒu 勉强维持生活 keep body and soul together; eke out a living: 养家～ support a family|摆小摊赚几个钱～ eke out a living by running a small business stall. also 糊口 húkǒu

湖 hú ❶ 被陆地围着的大片积水 lake; a large expanse of water surrounded by land: 太～ Taihu Lake|洞庭～ Dongting Lake ❷(Hú) 指浙江湖州 short form for 湖洲 Huzhou (a city in Zhejiang Province): ～笔 writing brushes produced in Huzhou|～绉 Huzhou crepe (textile) ❸(Hú) 指湖南、湖北 a name referring to the provinces of Hunan and Hubei: ～广 Hunan and Hubei as one province during the Ming Dynasty; Hunan, Hubei, Guangdong and Guangxi as one province during the Yuan Dynasty

【湖笔】húbǐ 浙江湖州制造的毛笔 writing brush produced in Huzhou, Zhejiang Province

【湖光山色】hú guāng shān sè 湖和山相映衬的秀丽景色 beautiful scenery of mountains silhouetted in a lake

H

【湖广】Húguǎng 指湖北、湖南,原是明代省名。元代的湖广包括两广在内,明代把两广划出,但仍用旧名。name referring to today's Guangdong and Guangxi provinces, originally the name of a province in which today's Hunan and Hubei were included during the Yuan Dynasty but excluded during the Ming Dynasty

【湖绿】húlǜ 淡绿色 light green

【湖泊】húpō 湖的总称 general term for 湖 hú

【湖色】húsè 淡绿色 light green

【湖田】hútián 在湖泊地区开辟的水田,四周修筑围埝 shoaly land; paddy field reclaimed from a lake, surrounded by low banks

【湖泽】húzé 湖泊和沼泽 lakes and marshes

【湖绉】húzhòu 浙江湖州出产的有皱纹的丝织品 a type of wrinkled silk fabric produced in Huzhou, Zhejiang Province

瑚 hú ☞ 珊瑚 shānhú on p. 1672

煳 hú 食品经火变焦发黑;衣物等经火变黄、变黑 (of food) burned (scorched) black due to the cooking fire; (of clothes) turn brown or dark due to fire: ～锅巴 burned rice crust|饭烧～了。The rice is burnt.|衣服烤～了。The dress got seared.

鹕 hú ☞ [鹈鹕](tíhú) on p. 1882

斛 hú 蒲式耳的旧称 old name for bushel

鹘 hú 隼 (sǔn) falcon
☞ gǔ on p. 697

槲 hú 落叶乔木或灌木,叶子略呈倒卵形,花黄褐色,结坚果,球形,木材坚硬。树皮可以做黑色染料。叶子和果实可入药。Mongolian oak (*Quercus dentate*); deciduous arbour or shrub that has reverse-oval leaves, russet-brown flowers and hard timber, and bears ball-shaped nuts; its bark can be used as black dye, and its leaves and fruits can be used for medicine

【槲栎】húlì 落叶乔木,茎高近30米,叶子长椭圆形,边缘有波状的齿,背面有白毛,果实长椭圆形 oriental white oak (*Quercus aliena*); deciduous arbour that has a trunk nearly 30 metres high and oblong oval leaves with undulating edges and white capillus on the back, bearing oblong oval fruits; also 青冈 qīnggāng

蝴 hú ☞ below

【蝴蝶】húdié 昆虫,翅膀阔大,颜色美丽,静止时四翅竖立在背部,腹部瘦长。吸花蜜。种类很多,有的幼虫吃农作物,是害虫,有的幼虫吃蚜虫,是益虫。butterfly (*Rhopalocera*); slender-bodied insect with four oft. brightly coloured broad wings that stand erect on the back when at rest, and usu. sucking nectar for food; some are pests because their grubs eat crops, and some are beneficial because they eat budworms; 简称 abbr. 蝶 dié; also 胡蝶 húdié

【蝴蝶结】húdiéjié 形状像蝴蝶的结子 bowknot; butterfly knot; bow-tie

【蝴蝶瓦】húdiéwǎ same as 小青瓦 xiǎnqīngwǎ

【蝴蝶装】húdiézhuāng 图书装订法的一种,有字的纸面相对折叠,中缝的背面用胶或糨糊粘连,再以厚纸包裹做书面。展开时,两边向外,像蝴蝶的双翅,故名。method of bookbinding in which the pages are folded on the side with words printed, bound together with glue on the back of the central seams and finally packed with thick paper for the cover; when spread, the book looks like the wings of a butterfly, hence the term

衚 hú [衚衕](hú·tòng) ☞ 胡同 hú·tòng on p. 819

糊1 hú 用黏性物把纸、布等粘起来或粘在别的器物上 paste; stick with paste: ～信封 make an envelope|～墙 wallpaper|～顶棚 paste a sheet of paper over a ceiling joist; paper ceiling|～风筝 make a kite

糊2 hú same as 煳 hú

糊³ hú same as 馏 hú
☞ hū on p.817 and hù on p.825

【糊糊】hú·hu〈方 *dial.*〉用玉米面、面粉等熬成的粥 thick porridge made of corn flour or flour:稀～ gruel|棒子～ corn porridge

【糊口】húkǒu same as 馏口 húkǒu

【糊涂】hú·tu ❶ 不明事理;对事物的认识模糊或混乱 muddled; confused; bewildered:他越解释,我越～。The more he explained, the more confused I became. ❷ 内容混乱的 messy; chaotic:～账 chaotic accounts|一塌～ in a complete mess ❸〈方 *dial.*〉模糊 blurred; indistinct ‖ also 胡涂 hú·tu

【糊涂虫】hú·tuchóng 不明事理的人(骂人的话 curse) blunderer; bungler

【糊涂账】hú·tuzhàng 混乱不清的账目 chaotic accounts:一笔～ a chaotic account

縠 hú〈书 *fml.*〉有皱纹的纱 crepe yarn

鹘 hú ☞ [鹈鹕](tíhú) on p.1883

觳 hú [觳觫](húsù)〈书 *fml.*〉因恐惧而发抖 shiver out of fear

hǔ (ㄏㄨˇ)

虎¹ hǔ ❶ 哺乳动物,毛黄色,有黑色的斑纹。听觉和嗅觉都很敏锐,性凶猛,力气大,夜里出来捕食鸟兽,有时伤害人。tiger(*Panthera tigris*); carnivorous mammal with a black striped tawny coat, a keen sense of hearing and olfaction, strong and fierce, preying and feeding on birds and animals at night, sometimes molesting humans as well; 通称 commonly called 老虎 lǎohǔ ❷〈比喻 *fig.*〉勇猛威武 brave; vigorous:～将 brave general|～～有生气 vigorous and lively ❸〈方 *dial.*〉露出凶相 look ferocious:～起脸 take a fierce look ❹ (Hǔ) 姓 a surname

虎² hǔ same as 唬 hǔ
☞ hù on p.824

【虎背熊腰】hǔ bèi xióng yāo 形容人的身体魁梧强壮 have a tiger's back and a bear's waist — tough and stocky

【虎贲】hǔbēn〈古代 *arch.*〉指勇士;武士 knight; warrior

【虎彪彪】hǔbiāobiāo 形容壮实而威风 strapping; strong and vigorous:～的小伙子 a strapping young fellow

【虎步】hǔbù ❶ 矫健威武的脚步 sturdy and vigorous steps:迈着～,噔噔噔地走上台来 step onto the stage with firm strides like those of a tiger ❷〈书 *fml.*〉形容举止威武,也指称雄于一方 with vigour; rule the roost:～关中 rule the Central Shaanxi Plain

【虎符】hǔfú〈古代 *arch.*〉调兵用的凭证,用铜铸成虎形,分两半,右半存朝廷,左半给统兵将帅。调动军队时须持符验证。tiger-shaped copper tally divided into two halves, with the right kept at the court and the left issued to a general as imperial authorization for troop movement

【虎将】hǔjiàng 勇猛善战的将领 brave general

【虎劲】hǔjìn (～儿 hǔjìnr) 勇猛的劲头儿 dash; dauntless drive:他干起活来真有股子～儿。He always does his work full of drive and daring.

【虎踞龙盘】hǔ jù lóng pán 像虎蹲着,像龙盘着。形容地势险要。'盘'也作蟠。forbidding strategic location; also 龙盘虎踞 lóng pán hǔ jù

【虎口】¹ hǔkǒu〈比喻 *fig.*〉危险的境地 tiger's mouth — the jaws of death:～脱险 be out of danger|逃离～ escape from the throes of death

【虎口】² hǔkǒu 大拇指和食指相连的部分 part of the hand between the thumb and the index finger

【虎口拔牙】hǔ kǒu bá yá〈比喻 *fig.*〉做十分危险的事 pull a tooth from the tiger's mouth — dare the greatest danger

【虎口余生】hǔ kǒu yú shēng〈比喻 *fig.*〉经历大难而侥幸保全生命 be saved from the tiger's mouth — have a narrow escape from death; be snatched from the jaws of death

【虎狼】hǔláng〈比喻 *fig.*〉凶狠残暴的人 tiger and wolf — cruel and ruthless:～之辈 cruel and ruthless group (of people)|～之心 voracious and wolfish heart

【虎皮宣】hǔpíxuān 有浅色斑纹的红、黄、绿等色的宣纸 red, yellow or green *xuan* paper with faint stripes

【虎魄】hǔpò same as 琥珀 hǔpò

【虎气】hǔqì 形容有气势 full of vigour:小伙子方脸大眼,瞧着挺～。With a square face and shining eyes, the young man looks full of vigour.

【虎钳】hǔqián same as 老虎钳 lǎohǔqián ①

【虎生生】hǔshēngshēng (～的 hǔshēngshēng·de)形容威武而有生气 forceful and lively:～的大眼睛 radiant big eyes|他看着这群～的年轻人,心里特别高兴。He was extremely pleased to see this group of dynamic young people.

【虎视】hǔshì ❶ 贪婪而凶狠地注视 cast a greedy eye on:～中原 covet the central plains ❷ 威严地注视 glare at:战士们～着山下的敌人,抑制不住满腔怒火。The soldiers glared at the enemy at the foot of the hill, their bosoms bursting with flames of fury.

【虎视眈眈】hǔ shì dāndān 形容贪婪而凶狠地注视 eye covetously and menacingly

【虎势】hǔ·shi〈方 *dial.*〉形容健壮 strong:这小伙子膀大腰粗的,长得真～。The young man is strongly built, with broad shoulders and a thick waist. also 虎实 hǔ·shi

【虎头虎脑】hǔ tóu hǔ nǎo 形容健壮憨厚的样子

（多指儿童 usu. of a child）look strong and good-natured：小家伙儿～的，非常可爱。This little boy is lovely, strong and good-natured.

【虎头蛇尾】hǔ tóu shé wěi 〈比喻 *fig.*〉做事有始无终，起初声势很大，后来劲头很小 start off okay, then hurtle downhill fast; tiger's head and a snake's tail — a fine start and a poor finish; in like a lion, out like a lamb

【虎威】hǔwēi 指武将的威风。也指威武的气概。（of a military officer）valiant and awe-inspiring

【虎穴】hǔxué 〈比喻 *fig.*〉危险的境地 dangerous spot：龙潭～ extremely dangerous place｜不入～，不得虎子。A faint heart never conquers.

【虎穴龙潭】hǔ xué lóng tán ☞ 龙潭虎穴 lóng tán hǔ xué on p. 1249

【虎牙】hǔyá 俗称突出的犬牙 protruding canine tooth

【虎跃龙腾】hǔ yuè lóng téng ☞ 龙腾虎跃 lóng téng hǔ yuè on p. 1249

浒 hǔ 水边 waterside
☞ xǔ on p. 2165

【浒湾】Hǔwān 地名，在河南 name of a place in Henan Province
☞ Xǔwān on p. 2165

唬（虎）hǔ 虚张声势、夸大事实来吓人或蒙混人 frighten or deceive sb. by making a false show of strength or exaggerating the facts：～人 bluff sb.｜差一点儿叫他～住了 be all but intimidated by him
☞ xià on p. 2069

琥 hǔ ［琥珀］(hǔpò)〈古代 *arch.*〉松柏树脂的化石，成分是 $C_{10}H_{16}O$。淡黄色、褐色或红褐色的固体，质脆，燃烧时有香气，摩擦时生电。用来制造琥珀酸和各种漆，也可做装饰品，可入药。amber; yellowish, brownish or orange translucent fossil resin ($C_{10}H_{16}O$) that is of a fragile texture, emits an aroma when burnt, produces electricity when rubbed, and is used chiefly in making amber acid, various paints, ornamental objects, or medicine; also 虎魄 hǔpò

hù（ㄏㄨˋ）

互 hù 互相 mutually; each other：～访 exchange visits｜～通有无 make up for each other's deficiencies; each makes up what the other lacks｜～不干涉 mutual non-interference｜～敬～爱 respect and love each other

【互补】hùbǔ ❶ 互为补角 be at an supplementary angle to each other ❷ 互相补充 mutually complement：沿海和内地互通有无，～互利。By supplying what the other needs, the coastal and hinterland areas complement and benefit each other.

【互感】hùgǎn 由于电路中电流的变化，而在邻近的另一电路中产生感生电动势的现象 mutual inductance; electromotive force induced in an electric circuit due to voltaic changes in a neighbouring circuit; also 互感应 hùgǎnyìng

【互惠】hùhuì 互相给予好处 reciprocal; mutually beneficial：平等～ equality and mutual benefit｜～待遇 reciprocal treatment｜～关税 reciprocal preferential tariff

【互见】hùjiàn ❶（两处或几处的文字）相互说明补充（of what is written in two or more places）cross-reference ❷（两者）都有；同时存在（of two contrasting elements）exist side by side：瑕瑜～ have defects as well as merits

【互利】hùlì 互相有利 mutually beneficial; of mutual benefit：平等～ equality and mutual benefit

【互让】hùràng 彼此谦让 yield to each other; give in to each other：互谅～ understand and yield to each other

【互溶】hùróng 一般指两种液体（如水和酒精）能以任何比例互相溶解（generally of two liquids, e.g. water and alcohol）mutually dissolvable in any proportion

【互生】hùshēng 叶序的一种，茎的每个节上只长一个叶子，相邻的两个叶子长在相对的两侧，如杨树、桃树等的叶子 alternation, a kind of phyllotaxy in which each of the stem nodes bears only a single leaf, with two nearby leaves growing on the two opposite sides, e.g. the leaves of poplar and peach

【互通】hùtōng 互相沟通、交换 mutually communicate; exchange：～消息 mutual communication of information｜～有无 each supplies what the other needs; supply (or meet) each other's needs

【互相】hùxiāng 〈副词 *adv.*〉表示彼此同样对待的关系 mutually; each other：～尊重 mutually respect｜～帮助 help each other｜～支持 support each other

【互训】hùxùn（两处或几处的文字）相互注释（of what is written at two or more places）mutually annotate

【互质】hùzhì 两个正整数只有公约数 1 时，它们的关系叫做互质。如 3 和 11 互质。relatively prime; the relationship between two positive integers which have no common divisor except 1, i.e. 3 and 11 are relatively prime with each other

【互质数】hùzhìshù 只有公约数 1 的两个正整数叫做互质数，如 4 和 5，7 和 8 relatively prime numbers; co-prime numbers; two positive integers that have no common divisor except 1, i.e. 4 and 5, or 7 and 8 are relatively prime numbers

【互助】hùzhù 互相帮助 help each other：～合作 mutual aid and cooperation｜～小组 mutual-aid groups

【互助会】hùzhùhuì 经济上互相帮助的群众性组

织，多由基层工会组织领导 non-governmental organizations committed to mutual financial aid, mostly led by labour unions at the grass-roots level

【互助组】hùzhùzǔ ❶ 在生产、工作或学习上互相帮助的小集体 mutual aid group; group organized for mutual aid in production, work, or study ❷ 我国农业合作化的初级形式，由若干户农民自愿组织起来，在劳动力、农具、牲畜等方面进行互助合作 mutual-aid team, an elementary form of organization in China's agricultural cooperative movement, in which several peasant families shared labour hands, farming tools, draught animals, etc.

户 hù ❶ 门 door：门～ door｜夜不闭～。Doors are not bolted at night. ❷ 人家；住户 household; family：～籍 household register｜专业～ specialized household; house of special trade｜全村好几百～。There are several hundred households in the whole village. ❸ 门第 family status：门当～对 be well matched in social and economic status for marriage ❹ 户头（bank) account：存～ depositor｜账～ account｜开个～ open an account ❺ (Hù) 姓 a surname

【户籍】hùjí 地方民政机关以户为单位登记本地区内居民的册子。转指作为本地区居民的身份。census register; household register; registration of residents on a household basis by local civil administrative authorities; also the identity of residents in an area

【户口】hùkǒu ❶ 住户和人口，例如旧时称某一地有若干户，若干口 number of households and total population ❷ 户籍 registered permanent residence; residence registration：报～ apply for a residence permit｜迁～ change one's residence registration

【户口簿】hùkǒubù 记载住户成员的姓名、籍贯、年龄、职业等内容的册子 (permanent) residence booklet, which records names, birthplaces, ages, professions, etc. of members of a family; also 户口本儿 hùkǒuběnr

【户枢不蠹】hù shū bù dù 门的转轴不会被虫蛀蚀 a door hinge never becomes worm-eaten; 〈比喻 *fig.*〉经常运动着的东西不易被腐蚀 constant activity staves off decay：流水不腐，～。Running water never goes stale and a door hinge never becomes worm-eaten.

【户头】hùtóu 会计部门称账册上有账务关系的个人或团体 account; individuals or groups which keep financial business contacts with banks or accounting departments：开～ open an account｜这个～很久没有来提款了。This account has not been withdrawn from for a long time.

【户限】hùxiàn 〈书 *fml.*〉门槛(kǎn) threshold：～为穿（形容进出的人很多) threshold worn low by visitors — an endless flow of visitors

【户牖】hùyǒu 〈书 *fml.*〉门窗 door and window; same as 门户 ménhù ①

【户长】hùzhǎng 〈方 *dial.*〉same as 户主 hùzhǔ

【户主】hùzhǔ 户籍上一户的负责人 head (person-in-charge) of a registered household

冱(沍) hù 〈书 *fml.*〉❶ 冻 frozen：～寒 cold ❷ 闭塞 out-of-the-way

护(護) hù ❶ 保护；保卫 protect; guard; shield：爱～ take good care of｜～路 patrol and guard a road or railway｜～航 convoy｜～林 protect a forest ❷ 袒护；包庇 be partial to; shield：～短 shield a fault｜官官相～ bureaucrats (officials) shield one another

【护岸】hù'àn 保护海岸、河岸等使不受波浪冲击的建筑物，多用石块或混凝土筑成 bank revetment; usu. built with rocks or concrete, to protect seashores or riverbanks from being lashed by waves

【护岸林】hù'ànlín 栽种在渠道、河流两岸使免受冲刷的防护林 protective forest belt along an embankment

【护壁】hùbì same as 墙裙 qiángqún

【护兵】hùbīng 随从官吏的卫兵 (an official's) bodyguard

【护城河】hùchénghé 人工挖掘的围绕城墙的河，古代为防守用 city moat; used as a defence work in ancient times

【护持】hùchí ❶ 保护维持 shield and sustain：交通要道要派专人～。Specialists should be dispatched to protect and maintain the trunk transportation lines. ❷ 爱护照料 take good care of：她像姐姐似的～我。She took good care of me, as if she were my own sister.

【护从】hùcóng ❶ 跟随保卫 follow and protect ❷ 跟随保卫的人 follower and guard

【护犊子】hù dú·zi 〈方 *dial.*〉〈比喻 *fig.*〉庇护自己的孩子(含贬义 derog.) shield the shortcomings or faults of one's child

【护短】hù//duǎn 为自己(或与自己有关的人)的缺点或过失辩护 shield a shortcoming or fault of oneself (or sb. related)：孩子有了错误，做家长的不应～。Parents should not shield their children's faults.

【护耳】hù'ěr 保护耳朵使不受冻的用品 ear-muffs; ear-flaps

【护法】hùfǎ ❶ 卫护佛法 safeguard Buddhist doctrine ❷ 卫护佛法的人。后来指施舍财物给寺庙的人。one who safeguards Buddhist doctrine, later referring to one who donates money and property to a temple ❸ 卫护国法 protect state law

【护封】hùfēng 包在图书外面的纸，一般印着书名或图案，有保护和装饰的作用 book jacket; paper cover of a book, printed with the book's title or a design, for protection and decoration

【护符】hùfú same as 护身符 hùshēnfú

【护航】hùháng 护送船只或飞机航行 escort;

convoy (a ship or an aircraft):～舰 escort vessel|专机有战斗机～。The private plane was escorted by fighter planes.

【护驾】hùjià same as 保驾 bǎo//jià

【护栏】hùlán ❶ 设置在路边或人行道与车道之间的铁栅栏 iron railing by the roadside or between a roadway and the sidewalk ❷ 起保护作用的栏杆 guardrail; protective railing (fence):草地周围有～。The lawn is surrounded by a protective fence.

【护理】hùlǐ ❶ 配合医生治疗,观察和了解病人的病情,并照料病人的饮食起居等 nurse; observe and understand a patient's state, and attend to a patient's daily needs to facilitate medical treatment:～员 nurse|～病人 nursing a patient ❷ 保护管理,使不受损害 tend and protect (against damage):～林木 tend the wood|精心～小麦越冬 take good care of the wheat through the winter

【护林】hùlín 保护森林 protect a forest:～防火 fire prevention and forest protection

【护坡】hùpō 河岸或路旁用石块、水泥等筑成的斜坡,用来防止河流或雨水冲刷 water conservancy; transportation slope protection; slopes along riverbanks, roadsides, etc., covered with rocks and cements to prevent erosion by river or rain

【护身符】hùshēnfú ❶ 道士或巫师等所画的符或念过咒的物件,迷信的人认为随身佩带,可以驱邪免灾 amulet; protective talisman; charm (as an ornament), oft. inscribed with a magic incantations or symbols to protect the wearer against evil (such as disease or witchcraft) ❷〈比喻 *fig.*〉保护自己、借以避免困难或惩罚的人或事物 person or thing that protects one from misery, punishment or censure; a shield ‖ also 护符 hùfú

【护士】hù·shi 医疗机构中担任护理工作的人员 (in a medical institution) nurse

【护送】hùsòng 陪同前往使免遭意外(多指用武装保护 usu. under armed protection) escort; convoy:～伤员 escort wounded soldiers|～粮草 escort grain and vegetables|～出境 escort sb. across the border

【护腿】hùtuǐ 保护小腿的用品 shinguard; an article for protecting the shins

【护卫】hùwèi ❶ 保护;保卫 protect; guard:在保安人员的～下安全抵达机场。He safely arrived at the airport under the protection of security guards. ❷ 执行护卫任务的武装人员 bodyguard; armed personnel executing a protective mission

【护卫舰】hùwèijiàn 以火炮和反潜武器为主要装备的轻型军舰。用于护航、反潜、巡逻、布雷、支援部队登陆等。装有导弹的护卫舰叫导弹护卫舰。frigate; corvette; escort vessel; light-duty warship mainly armed with artillery and anti-submarine weapons, used for escorting warships, anti-submarine actions, patrolling, laying mines, and helping troops with landing. One that is equipped with guided missiles is known as 'guided-missile frigate'.

【护卫艇】hùwèitǐng same as 炮艇 pàotǐng

【护膝】hùxī 保护膝部的用品 kneepad; kneecap; an article for protecting the knees

【护养】hùyǎng ❶ 护理培育 cultivate; nurse; rear:～秧苗 breed seedlings|精心～仔猪 carefully rear piglets ❷ 养护 maintain:～公路 maintain a highway

【护佑】hùyòu 保护;保佑 protect; bless:～一方 bless and protect a region

【护照】hùzhào ❶ 国家主管机关发给出国执行任务、旅行或在国外居住的本国公民的证件,证明其国籍和身份 passport; formal document that is issued by an authorized institution of a country to its citizens, usu. necessary for exit from and re-entry into a country, and that testifies to his or her nationality and identity while working, travelling, or living in a foreign country ❷〈旧时 *old*〉因出差、旅行或运输货物向主管机关领取的凭证 certificate or document of identification issued by authorities institution for going out on business, travelling, or transporting goods

沪(滬) Hù 上海的别称 Hu, another name for Shanghai

【沪剧】hùjù 上海的地方戏曲剧种,由上海滩簧发展而成 Shanghai opera; local opera of Shanghai, developed from a local folk art form

枑 hù ☞[梐枑](bìhù) on p.107

虎 hù [虎不拉](hù·bulā)〈方 *dial.*〉伯劳 shrike

☞ hǔ on p.821

岵 hù〈书 *fml.*〉多草木的山 verdant wooded hill

怙 hù〈书 *fml.*〉依靠 rely on:失～(指死了父亲) loss of one's father to death

【怙恶不悛】hù è bù quān 坚持作恶,不肯悔改 be steeped in evil and refuse to repent; remain impenitent

【怙恃】hùshì〈书 *fml.*〉❶ 依仗;凭借 rely on ❷《诗经·小雅·蓼莪》:'无父何怙,无母何恃。'后来用'怙恃'为父母的代称。another name for parents, derived from *The Book of Songs · Odes · Tall Is the Knot-weed*: 'Whom am I going to rely on without my father? And whom am I going to depend on without my mother?':少失～ one's parents died in one's childhood

戽 hù ❶ 戽斗。也泛指汲水灌田的农具。bailing bucket; farm tool for bailing and irrigation:风～ air scoop ❷ 汲(水灌田) bail (water to irrigate fields):～水机 scooping machine|～水抗旱 bail water to ward off a drought

【戽斗】hùdǒu 汲水灌田的旧式农具,形状略像斗,两边有绳,两人引绳,提斗汲水 bailing bucket; old farm tool for bailing water and irrigating fields, in the shape of a dipper, with a rope on either sides to be drawn by a person for lifting the tool and drawing up water

祜 hù〈书 *fml.*〉福 blessing; bliss

笏 hù〈古代 *arch.*〉君臣在朝廷上相见时手中所拿的狭长板子,用玉、象牙或竹制成,上面可以记事 tablet, usu. made of jade, ivory, or bamboo, sometimes with writing on it, held before the breast by officials as a badge when received in audience by the emperor

瓠 hù same as 瓠子 hù·zi

【瓠果】hùguǒ 指浆果中属于瓜类的果实,由子房和花托一起发育而成,如西瓜、黄瓜、南瓜等 any of the edible gourds that become ripe as their ovaries and thalami grow, e.g. watermelon, cucumber, pumpkin, etc.

【瓠子】hù·zi ❶ 一年生草本植物,茎蔓生,花白色,果实细长,圆筒形,表皮淡绿色,果肉白色,可做蔬菜 calabash gourd (*Lagenaria siceraria*); annual cauline plant with white flowers and long, columnar fruit which has a light-green peel and white pulp, and eaten as a vegetable ❷ 这种植物的果实。有的地区叫蒲瓜。fruit of this plant, also known as 蒲瓜 púguā in some areas

扈 hù ❶〈书 *fml.*〉随从 retinue:~从 entourage; retinue ❷(Hù) 姓 a surname

【扈从】hùcóng〈书 *fml.*〉❶ 帝王或官吏的随从 retinue of an emperor or high official ❷ 随从;跟随 escort; follow:随驾~ escort the imperial carriage|~大帅西征 follow the commander on an expedition to the west

楛 hù 古书上指荆一类的植物,茎可制箭杆 (in ancient books referring to) thorny plant, whose stem can be used for making arrows

☞ kǔ on p. 1115

鄠 Hù 鄠县,在陕西。今作户县。Huxian county, in Shaanxi Province

糊 hù 样子像粥的食物 paste; porridge-like food:面~ flour paste|芝麻~ sesame congee|辣椒~ chilli paste

☞ hū on p. 817 and hú on p. 820

【糊弄】hù·nong〈方 *dial.*〉❶ 欺骗;蒙混 fool; deceive; palm sth. off on (sb.):说老实话,别~人。Be honest and don't try to fool others. ❷ same as 将就 jiāng·jiu:衣服旧了些,~着穿吧。The clothes are a bit old, but you'll have to make do with them.

【糊弄局】hù·nongjú〈方 *dial.*〉(~儿 hù·nongjúr)敷衍蒙混的事情 be slipshod in work; muddle through one's work:他马马虎虎拾掇一下就走了,这不是~吗? He carelessly tidied up and then left — how slipshod he is!

鹱 hù 鸟类的一科,身体大,嘴的尖端略呈钩状,趾间有蹼。会游泳和潜水,生活在海岸边,吃鱼类和软体动物。shearwater (*Puffinus*); any of numerous oceanic birds that have large bodies, hook-like beaks and webfeet, can swim and dive, and live on the seashore and feed on fish and mollusk

鳠 hù 鱼,身体细长,灰褐色,有黑色小点,无鳞,口部有四对须。生活在淡水中。spotted longbarbel catfish (*Mystus guttatus*); fresh-water fish with a slim, dust-coloured body, with black dots, but no scales, and four pairs of palpus near the mouth

huā (ㄏㄨㄚ)

化 huā same as 花² huā:~钱 spend money; cost money|~工夫 put in one's time doing sth.; spend time; take time

☞ huà on p. 835

【化子】huā·zi same as 花子 huā·zi

花¹ huā ❶ (~儿 huār)种子植物的有性繁殖器官。花由花瓣、花萼、花托、花蕊组成,有各种颜色,有的长得很艳丽,有香味 flower; shoot of the sporophyte of a seed plant modified for reproduction, having leaves, calyces, thalami, and pistils, some featuring splendid colours and emitting fragrance:一朵~儿 a flower ❷ (~儿 huār)可供观赏的植物 plant cultivated for ornamentation:~木 flowers and trees|~盆儿 flowerpot|~儿匠 gardener|种~儿 grow flowers ❸ (~儿 huār)形状像花朵的东西 anything resembling a flower:灯~儿 snuff|火~ spark|雪~儿 snowflake ❹ 烟火的一种,以黑色火药加别种化学物质制成,在夜间燃放,能喷出许多火花,供人观赏 fireworks; made of black powder and other explosive or flammable substances, for producing a dazzling display of sparks at night:~炮 fireworks and firecrackers|礼~ gun salute|放~ let off firecrackers ❺ (~儿 huār)花纹 design; decorative pattern:白地蓝~儿 blue flowers on a white background|这被面~儿太密。The design on this quilt cover is too busy. ❻ 用花或花纹装饰的 coloured; flower-decorated:~圈 wreath|~篮 floral basket|~灯 festive lantern|~车 festooned vehicle|~布 printed cloth ❼ 颜色或种类错杂的 multicoloured; coloured; variegated:~白 grizzled|~猫 spotted kitty|~~绿绿 showy; gaudy ❽ (眼睛)模糊迷乱 blurred; dim:眼~ have blurred vision|昏~ dim-sighted ❾ 衣服磨损或要破没破的样子 (of clothes) worn and torn but not

yet worn-out：袖子都磨～了。The sleeves are threadbare. ⑩ 用来迷惑人的；不真实或不真诚的 attractive but unreal or insincere：～招儿 tricky；disguise｜～账 padded accounts｜～言巧语 sweet words；alluring speech ⑪〈比喻 *fig.*〉事业的精华 cream；essence：文艺之～ the cream of literature and art｜革命之～ the essence of revolution ⑫〈比喻 *fig.*〉年轻漂亮的女子 pretty young women：校～ school beauty｜交际～ social butterfly ⑬ 指妓女或跟妓女有关的 used metaphorically for courtesans or prostitutes：～魁 the most popular courtesans｜～街柳巷 red-light district｜寻～问柳 be in on a racket ⑭ 指棉花 cotton：轧～gin cotton｜弹～ fluff cotton｜～纱布 cotton yarn and cloth ⑮（～儿 huār）指某些小的颗粒、块、滴等 small grains，pieces，or drops：泪～ teardrops｜油～儿 oil slicks｜葱～ chopped onion ⑯ 指某些幼小动物 pup：蚕～ silkworms｜鱼～ fry ⑰（～儿 huār）痘 smallpox：天～ smallpox｜种～儿 pox vaccination｜出过～儿 already had smallpox ⑱ 作战时受的外伤 wound：挂了两次～ have been wounded twice in action ⑲（Huā）姓 a surname

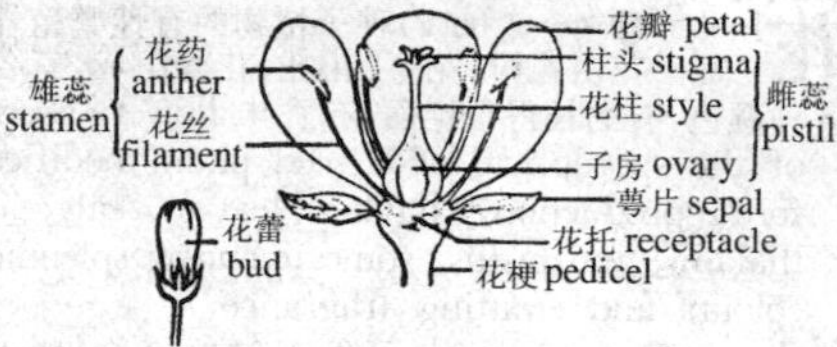

花 Flower

花² huā 用；耗费 spend；expend：～费 spend｜～钱 spend money｜～时间 take time｜该～的～，该省的省 spend what should be spent and save what should be saved

【花把势】huābǎ·shi 指有经验的花农或花匠。泛指擅长种花的人。gardener；experienced florist

【花白】huābái（须发）黑白混杂（of hair or beard）grey；grizzled：～胡须 grey beard｜才四十岁的人头发都～了。He's just turned 40 but his hair is already greying.

【花瓣】huābàn 花冠的组成部分之一，构造和叶子相似，但细胞里含有各种不同的色素，所以有各种不同的颜色 petal；one of the modified leaves of a corolla of a flower，with varied pigments contained in the cell，hence petals of different colours；（图见 ☞ figure for 花 huā）

【花苞】huābāo 苞¹的通称 common name for 苞¹ bāo

【花被】huābèi 花萼和花冠的统称，有保护花蕊和引诱昆虫的作用 perianth；general term for calyces and corolla，which protect pistils and lure insects

【花边】huābiān ❶（～儿 huābiānr）带花纹的边缘 decorative border；border or edge with decorative patterns：瓶口上有一道蓝色的～。There is a blue floral border around the mouth of the vase. ❷（～儿 huābiānr）手工艺品，编织或刺绣成各种花样的带子，通常用做衣服的镶边 lace；ornamental braid or embroidery for edging and trimming coats or uniforms ❸（～儿 huābiānr）〈印刷用语 *print.*〉文字图画的花纹边框 fancy borders in printing：～新闻 fancy news ❹〈方 *dial.*〉银圆的俗称 nickname for silver dollar

【花不棱登】huā·bulēngdēng（～的 huā·bulēngdēng·de）形容颜色错杂（含厌恶意 derog.）extravagantly fancy；loud；flashy；gaudy：这件衣服～的，我不喜欢。This dress is too flashy (or loud) for me.

【花草】huācǎo 指供观赏的花和草 flowers and plants for ornamentation

【花插】huāchā ❶ 插花用的底座，一般放在浅口的水盆里 base for cut flowers，usu. set in a shallow basin ❷ 供插花用的各种形状的瓶子 any container for cut flowers

【花插着】huā·chā·zhe 交叉；交错 crisscross：大人、孩子～坐在树阴下听评书。Adults and children listened to storytelling while sitting scattered in the shade of a tree.

【花茶】huāchá 用茉莉花等鲜花熏制的绿茶 scented tea；green tea scented with fresh flowers (e.g. jasmine，etc.)；also 香片 xiāngpiàn

【花车】huāchē 举行喜庆典礼或迎接贵宾时特别装饰的汽车、火车或马车 festooned vehicle；specially decorated car，train or carriage for festive celebrations or welcoming a distinguished guest

【花池子】huāchí·zi 庭园中四周矮栏围绕、中间种植花草的地方 flowerbed；place in a courtyard surrounded by low fences，with flowers and grass planted inside

【花丛】huācóng 丛生在一起的花 flowering shrubs；flowers in clusters：蝴蝶在～中飞来飞去。Butterflies are flying around the flowering shrubs.

【花搭着】huā·dā·zhe 种类或质量不同的东西错综搭配 interspersed；diversified；arrange in pairs or groups things that differ in variety and quality：细粮粗粮～吃 diversify one's diet by eating both fine and coarse grain

【花旦】huādàn 戏曲中旦角的一种，扮演性格活泼或放荡泼辣的年轻女子 *huadan*，one of the main types of the *dan* or female role in Chinese opera，traditionally the role for a perky，bold and unconventional young woman

【花灯】huādēng 用花彩装饰的灯。特指元宵节供观赏的灯。festive lanterns (as displayed during the Lantern Festival)：闹～ merry-making during the Lantern Festival | 看～ tour a festive lantern show

【花灯戏】huādēngxì 流行于云南、四川等地的地方戏，由民间玩耍花灯的歌舞发展而成，跟花鼓戏相近 lantern opera; local opera popular in Yunnan and Sichuan provinces, developed from folk songs and dances depicting people playing with festive lanterns; similar to flower-drum opera

【花点子】huādiǎn·zi ❶ 欺骗人的狡猾手段、计策等 deceit; artifice ❷ 不切实际的主意 unrealistic ideas

【花雕】huādiāo 上等的绍兴黄酒，因装在雕花的坛子里而得名 engraved crock; high-grade Shaoxing wine stored in an engraved crock, hence its name

【花朵】huāduǒ 花[1]①(总称)(collect.) flowers: 这株牡丹的～特别大。This peony is especially large. ◇儿童是祖国的～。Children are the flowers of our country.

【花萼】huā'è 花的组成部分之一，由若干萼片组成，包在花瓣外面，花开时托着花冠 calyx; external, usu. green or leafy, part of a flower consisting of sepals and supporting the corolla in blossom; 简称 abbr. 萼 è

【花儿】huā'ér 甘肃、青海、宁夏一带流行的一种民间歌曲 a kind of folk song, popular in Gansu, Qinghai and Ningxia

【花房】huāfáng 养花草的温室 greenhouse provinces; hothouse (for growing flowers and plants)

【花肥】huāféi ❶ 在棉花、油菜等作物开花期施的肥，能促使多开花结果，提高产量 fertilizers for crops (cotton, rapeseed, etc.) in anthesis for a high yield ❷ 指给盆栽观赏植物施的肥 fertilizers for potted flowers

【花费】huāfèi 因使用而消耗掉 spend; expend; cost: ～金钱 spend money | ～时间 take time | ～心血 take pains

【花费】huā·fei 消耗的钱 expenditure; expenses; money spent: 这次搬家要不少～。This move will cost a large sum.

【花粉】huāfěn ❶ 花药里的粉粒，多是黄色的，也有青色或黑色的。每个粉粒里都有一个生殖细胞。pollen; a mass of microspores in the anther of a seed plant, mostly yellow and sometimes also cyan or black, with each grain consisting of a single reproductive cell ❷〈中医 *Chin. med*〉指栝楼根制成的淀粉 starch of the root of the Mongolian snakegourd

【花粉篮】huāfěnlán 工蜂后足上由硬毛围成的器官，用来携带花粉 organ surrounded with bristles on the back leg of a worker bee, used for carrying pollen

【花岗岩】huāgāngyán ❶ 火成岩的一种，在地壳上分布最广，是岩浆在地壳深处逐渐冷却凝结成的结晶岩体，主要成分是石英、长石和云母。一般是黄色带粉红的，也有灰白色的。质地坚硬，色泽美丽，是很好的建筑材料。granite; very hard natural igneous rock formation of a visibly crystalline texture, formed essentially of quartz, isinglass, and orthoclase or microcline, and often yellow tinted with pink or grey, used as a building material; 通称 commonly called 花岗石 huāgāngshí ❷〈比喻 *fig.*〉顽固不化 incorrigibly obstinate; unyielding firmness: ～脑袋 a granite-like skull; ossified thinking

【花梗】huāgěng 花的柄，是茎的分枝，构造和茎相同 pedicel; branch of a flower's stem, with the same structure as the stem; (图见 ☞ figure for 花 huā)

【花骨朵】huāgū·duo 花蕾的通称 common name for 花蕾 huālěi

【花鼓】huāgǔ 一种民间舞蹈，一般由男女两人对舞，一人敲小锣，一人打小鼓，边敲打，边歌舞 flower-drum, folk dance with a man beating a small gong and a woman playing a small drum while dancing

【花鼓戏】huāgǔxì 流行于湖北、湖南、安徽等省的地方戏曲剧种，由民间歌舞花鼓发展而成 flower-drum opera, developed from the flower-drum folk dance, popular in Hunan, Hubei and Anhui provinces

【花冠】[1] huāguān 花的组成部分之一，由若干花瓣组成。双子叶植物的花冠一般可分为合瓣花冠和离瓣花冠两大类。corolla; part of the flower consisting of several petals; the corollas of dicotyledons are classified into gamopetalous corolla and choripetalous corolla

【花冠】[2] huāguān〈旧时 *old*〉妇女出嫁时戴的装饰华丽的帽子 ornamental crown worn by a bride on her wedding day

【花棍舞】huāgùnwǔ ☞ 霸王鞭[1] bàwáng biān on p. 31

【花好月圆】huā hǎo yuè yuán〈比喻 *fig.*〉美好团聚(多用做新婚的颂词 oft. used as a congratulatory message for sb.'s marriage) blooming flowers and a full moon — pleasant reunion

【花和尚】huāhé·shang 指不守戒规(如喝酒、吃肉等)的和尚 monks who violate religious discipline (e.g. drinking alcohol or eating meat)

【花红】[1] huāhóng ❶ 落叶小乔木，叶子卵形或椭圆形，花粉红色。果实球形，像苹果而小，黄绿色带微红，是常见的水果。Chinese pear-leaved crabapple (*Malus asiatica* var. *rinki*); a deciduous arbour with oval leaves and pink flowers, bearing globular fruit like small apples, in yellow-green with a bit of red; a common fruit ❷ 这种植物的果实 fruit of this plant ‖ also 林檎 línqín or 沙果 shāguǒ

【花红】[2] huāhóng ❶ 指有关婚姻等喜庆事的礼物 gift for a wedding or other happy event: ～彩礼 betrothal gifts ❷ same as 红利 hónglì ❸ same as 赏钱 shǎng·qián

【花红柳绿】huā hóng liǔ lǜ ❶ 形容春天花木繁

茂艳丽的景色 red flowers and green willows — a beautiful spring scene ❷ 形容颜色鲜艳多彩 colourful; splendid colours：姑娘们一个个打扮得～。The girls were all colourfully dressed.

【花花肠子】huā·hua-cháng·zi 〈方 *dial*.〉〈比喻 *fig*.〉狡猾的心计 cunning; trickery; deceit：那家伙～可多了。That guy is full of cunning.

【花花搭搭】huā·huadādā (～的 huā·huadādā·de) ❶ 花搭着 interspersed; diversified; alternate：米饭、面食～地换着样儿吃 eat rice and wheat products alternately ❷ 形容大小、疏密不一致 irregular; varied in size and density：天气虽然还冷，树上已经～地开了些花儿了。It's still cold, but flowers have come out here and there on the trees. | 地太干，高粱苗出得～的。Because of the dry soil, the young sorghum plants grew irregularly.

【花花公子】huāhuā-gōngzǐ 指富贵人家中不务正业，只知吃喝玩乐的子弟 playboy; dandy; coxcomb; fop; man from a wealthy or noble family who lives a life devoted chiefly to the pursuit of pleasure

【花花绿绿】huāhuālǜlǜ (～的 huāhuālǜlǜ·de) 形容颜色鲜艳多彩 colourful; brightly coloured：墙上贴着～的年画。Hung on the wall were New-Year paintings in bright colours. | 姑娘们穿得～的，在广场上跳舞。The girls, colourfully dressed, danced in the square.

【花花世界】huāhuā-shìjiè 指繁华地区或灯红酒绿、寻欢作乐的场所。也泛指人世间。(含贬义 derog.) busy area or location of debauchery and gaiety; also the dazzling human world with its myriad temptations

【花环】huāhuán ❶ 用鲜花或纸花扎成的环状物，多用来表演舞蹈、迎接贵宾等 garland; floral hoop; ring of fresh or paper flowers used to adorn a dance or welcome distinguished guests ❷ same as 花圈 huāquān

【花卉】huāhuì ❶ same as 花草 huācǎo ❷ 以花草为题材的中国画 paintings of flowers and plants in a traditional Chinese style

【花会】huāhuì ❶ 一种民间体育和文艺活动，多在春节期间举行，节目有高跷、狮子舞、龙灯、旱船、中幡等等 popular sport and cultural activity, usu. held during the Spring Festival, featuring such traditional performances as stilt walking, lion dances, dragon lanterns, land boats, and flag sports, etc. ❷ 花卉展销大会。有的地方在花会期间同时进行土特产展览交易，有的还演出民间戏曲，表演民间武术等。flower exhibition (show); in some places, flower shows take place alongside exhibition fairs of local products, as well as performances of traditional operas or martial arts

【花甲】huājiǎ 指六十岁（用干支纪年，错综搭配，六十年周而复始 using items from the Heavenly Stems and Earthly Branches respectively to form 60 unique pairs to represent a cycle of 60 years) age of 60：～之年 60 (years of age) | 年逾～ over 60 years old; in one's sixties

【花架】huājià 专用来摆放盆花的架子 special shelf for holding potted flowers

【花架子】huājià·zi ❶ 指花哨而不实用的武术动作 showy postures or movements in martial arts ❷〈比喻 *fig*.〉外表好看但缺少实用价值的东西。也指形式主义的做法 thing that is showy but of little practical value; formalistic method of work：工作要讲实效，不要做表面文章，摆～。In our work we should go after real efficiency rather than put on a show.

【花椒】huājiāo ❶ 落叶灌木或小乔木，枝上有刺，果实球形，暗红色。种子黑色，可以做调味的香料，也可入药。Chinese prickly ash (*Zanthoxylun bungeanum*); deciduous shrub or arbour that has thorns on the branches, bears globular, dark-red fruit, and yields black seeds used as a spice or for medicine. ❷ 这种植物的种子 seeds of Chinese prickly ash

【花轿】huājiào 旧俗结婚时新娘所坐的装饰华丽的轿子 (old custom) sedan chair for a bride at her wedding

【花街柳巷】huā jiē liǔ xiàng 指妓院较集中的地方 streets of ill-repute; red-light district

【花镜】huājìng 矫正花眼用的眼镜，镜片是凸透镜 presbyopic glasses

【花卷】huājuǎn (～儿 huājuǎnr) 一种蒸熟吃的面食，多卷成螺旋状 fancy-shaped (braided, twisted) steamed wheaten food

【花魁】huākuí 百花的魁首。多指梅花。旧时也比喻有名的妓女。in old times queen of flowers — an epithet for the plum blossom; referring to a famous courtesan in old times

【花篮】huālán (～儿 huālánr) ❶ 装着鲜花的篮子，祝贺时用做礼物，有时吊丧、祭奠也用 a basket of flowers as a congratulatory gift; sometimes for funerals, or memorial occasions ❷ 装饰美丽的或编制有图案的篮儿 gaily decorated basket

【花蕾】huālěi 没有开放的花 (flower) bud; incompletely open flower; (图见 ☞ figure for 花 huā); 通称 commonly called 花骨朵 huāgū·duo

【花里胡哨】huā·lihúshào (～的 huā·lihúshào·de) ❶ 形容颜色过分鲜艳繁杂(含厌恶意 derog.) gaudy; garish; showy：穿得～的 be gaudily dressed ❷〈比喻 *fig*.〉浮华，不实在 without substantial worth

【花脸】huāliǎn 净[2]的通称。因必须勾脸谱而得名，有铜锤、黑头、架子花等区别。popular term for 净[2] jìng; painted-face role, so named because characters in this category all have their faces painted, sub-divided into 铜锤 tóngchuí, 黑头 hēitóu, 架子花 jià·zihuā, etc.

【花翎】huālíng 清代官吏礼帽上的孔雀翎，根据品级不同有单眼、双眼、三眼的区别 tail feather of a peacock as adornment on the hat of an imperial official of the Qing Dynasty, classified into single-, double- and triple-eye according to the official's grade (眼 *yan*：孔雀翎端的圆形纹理 eye-shaped pattern towards the tip of a peacock feather)

【花令】huālìng 植物开花的季节 flowering season：养蜂必须随着～迁移蜂箱。Bee hives should be taken to where there are different flowering seasons of different plants.

【花柳病】huāliǔbìng same as 性病 xìngbìng

【花露水】huālùshuǐ 稀酒精中加香料制成的化妆品 toilet water (*eau de cologre*); cosmetic fragrance made of watery alcohol with added scent

【花蜜】huāmì ❶ 花朵分泌出来的甜汁，能引诱蜂蝶等昆虫来传播花粉 nectar; sweet liquid that is secreted by the nectaries of flowers, and lures bees and butterflies to spread pollen ❷ 指蜂蜜 honey

【花面狸】huāmiànlí 哺乳动物，身体比家猫细长，全身灰色，鼻部和眼部有白纹，耳部有白色环纹。生活在山林中，吃果实、谷物、小鸟等。毛皮可用来制衣帽。masked civet (*Viverra civetta*); gem-faced civet; long-bodied mammal, entirely grey, having white veins near its nose, eyes, and ears, living in mountain forests, and eating fruit, corn, and small birds; its fur can be used to make clothes and hats; also 果子狸 guǒ·zilí or 青猺 qīngyáo

【花苗】huāmiáo ❶ 花[1]②的幼苗 flower seedling ❷〈方 *dial.*〉棉花的幼苗 cotton seedling

【花名册】huāmíngcè 人员名册 register (of names); membership roster; muster roll

【花木】huāmù 供观赏的花和树木 flowers and trees (in parks or gardens for appreciation)

【花呢】huāní 指表面起条、格、点等花纹的一类毛织品 fancy suiting; first-grade wool woven with patterns of stripes, lattices, dots, etc.

【花鸟】huāniǎo 以花、鸟为题材的中国画 traditional Chinese flower-and-bird painting

【花农】huānóng 以种植花木为业的农民 flower grower

【花盘】huāpán ❶ 花托顶部膨大扁平呈盘状的部分 flower disc; large, flat part on the top of the thalamus ❷ 装在机床主轴上的圆盘形夹具，常用来固定形状较复杂的工件 faceplate; disc chuck; disc-shaped clamp fixed with its face at right angles to the live spindle of a lathe to which the work is attached

【花炮】huāpào 烟火和炮仗 fireworks and firecrackers

【花瓶】huāpíng (～儿 huāpíngr) 插花用的瓶子。放在室内，作装饰品。flower vase; vase for holding flowers for indoor decoration

【花圃】huāpǔ 种花草的园地 flower nursery

【花期】huāqī 植物开花的时间 florescence; flowering period：梅花的～在冬季。The florescence of the plum blossom is in winter.｜这种月季～特别长。This kind of the Chinese rose has an extra-long florescence.

【花旗】huāqí 指美国，由美国国旗的形象得名 star-spangled banner, referring to the United States

【花扦儿】huāqiānr 连枝折下来的鲜花或人工制成的绢花、纸花 fresh flowers picked with stems attached; or artificial silk or paper flowers

【花枪】huāqiāng ❶ 旧式兵器，像矛而较短 (of old style weapon) short spear ❷ same as 花招儿 huāzhāor ②：耍～ play tricks

【花腔】huāqiāng ❶ 有意把歌曲或戏曲的基本腔调复杂化、曲折化的唱法 coloratura; florid ornamental tune in Chinese opera singing ❷〈比喻 *fig.*〉花言巧语 guileful talk; sweet words：耍～ speak guilefully

【花墙】huāqiáng 上半段砌成镂空花样的墙 lattice wall; wall with the upper part hollowed out in decorative patterns

【花圈】huāquān 用鲜花或纸花等扎成的圆形的祭奠物品 wreath; circle of fresh or paper flowers, etc., used funerals or sacrificial occasions：献～ present a wreath (to a deceased person)

【花拳绣腿】huā quán xiù tuǐ 指姿势好看而搏斗时用处不大的拳术 showy but not practical martial arts; showy but impractical skill

【花儿洞子】huārdòng·zi 一半在地面以下的养花的温室 semi-underground hothouse for growing flowers

【花儿匠】huārjiàng ❶ 称以种花、卖花为业的人 florist; gardener; person who lives on growing and selling flowers ❷ 称制作花扦儿的人 person engaged in flower pruning

【花儿样子】huāryàng·zi 绣花用的底样 flower pattern to do embroidery work on

【花儿针】huārzhēn 绣花用的细针 fine needle for embroidery

【花容月貌】huā róng yuè mào 形容女子美丽的容貌 flower-like features and moon-like face — a pretty woman

【花蕊】huāruǐ 花的雄蕊和雌蕊的统称 stamen or pistil

【花色】huāsè ❶ 花纹和颜色 design and colour：这布的～很好看。This cloth's design and colour are lovely. ❷ 同一品种的物品从外表上区分的种类 (of merchandise) variety of designs, sizes, colours, etc.：～品种 variety of colours and designs｜灯具～繁多 a great variety of lamps and lanterns

【花纱布】huāshābù 棉花、棉纱、棉布的合称 collective name for cotton, cotton yarn and cloth

【花哨】huā·shao ❶ 颜色鲜艳多彩(指装饰) colourful; garish; gaudy: 穿着过于～ gaudily dressed ❷ 花样多;变化多 unusually varied; changeable: 鼓点子敲得又响亮又～ beat the drum loudly with a lot of flourish | 电视上的广告越来越～。The TV commercials have become richer and more varied.

【花生】huāshēng ☞ 落花生 luò·huashēng on p.1282

【花生豆儿】huāshēngdòur 〈方 *dial.*〉 same as 花生米 huāshēngmǐ

【花生酱】huāshēngjiàng 把花生米炒熟、磨碎制成的糊状食品 peanut butter

【花生米】huāshēngmǐ 落花生的果实去壳后剩下的种子。供食用,可以榨油。shelled peanut, for eating or extracting oil; also 花生仁儿 huāshēngrénr

【花生油】huāshēngyóu 用花生米榨的油,含脂肪较多,供食用,也是制造肥皂、化妆品等的原料 peanut oil; oil squeezed from the peanut kernel, rich in fat, usu. used for food or for making soup or cosmetics

【花市】huāshì 集中出售花卉的集市 flower market

【花事】huāshì 指花卉开花的情况 blossoming season (of a flower): ～已过。The blossoming season is already over. | 当年,～最盛的去处就数西山了。In those years the best place for enjoying flowers in bloom should be the West Mountains.

【花饰】huāshì 装饰性的花纹 ornamental design

【花束】huāshù 成束的花 bouquet; a bunch of flowers

【花说柳说】huā shuō liǔ shuō 〈方 *dial.*〉说虚假而动听的话 use flattery; use sweet but insincere words

【花丝】huāsī 雄蕊的下部,多为丝状,作用是支撑花药 filament; threadlike anther-bearing stalk of a stamen; (图见 ☞ figure for 花 huā)

【花坛】huātán 种植花卉的土台子,四周有矮墙,或堆成梯田形式,边缘砌砖石,用来点缀庭园等 (raised) flowerbed; flower terrace, used to embellish a courtyard

【花天酒地】huātiān jiǔ dì 形容沉湎于吃喝嫖赌的荒淫腐化生活 decadent; indulge in wine and women, and gambling

【花厅】huātīng 某些住宅中大厅以外的客厅,多盖在跨院或花园中 reception room or parlour (of a residential compound), usu. in a garden or side courtyard

【花头】huā·tou 〈方 *dial.*〉 ❶ same as 花纹 huāwén ❷ same as 花招儿 huāzhāor: 出～ hatch a trick ❸ 新奇的主意或办法 novel idea or method: 这些人里面就数他～最多。He has the most novel ideas among these people. ❹ 奥妙的地方 where the secret is: 这种游戏看起来简单,里面的～还真不少。This kind of game looks easy but contains a lot of tricks.

【花团锦簇】huā tuán jǐn cù 形容五彩缤纷、十分华丽的形象 scene (or image) of splendid colours and magnificence

【花托】huātuō 花的组成部分之一,是花梗顶端长花的部分。有些植物的果实是由花托发育而成的,如苹果和梨。receptacle; end of the flower stalk which bears the floral organ; some plants (e.g. apple, pear, etc.) bear fruits from a receptacle; (图见 ☞ figure for 花 huā)

【花纹】huāwén (～儿 huāwénr)各种条纹和图形 figure; decorative patterns: 贝壳上面有绿色的～。The shell features green stripes on the surface. | 他能织各种～的席子。He can weave mats of different patterns.

【花线】huāxiàn ❶ 电线的一种,由许多根很细的金属丝合为一股,用绝缘材料套起来后,再将两股(或三股)拧在一起,通常用做没有固定位置的用电设备(如台灯、电熨斗等)的电源线 flex; flexible cord; electrical cord of two or three wires twisted together, each made up of several slender metal threads and covered with insulating material, usu. used as a power cord for mobile electrical appliances (e.g. table lamp, electrical iron, etc.); also 软线 ruǎnxiàn ❷ 〈方 *dial.*〉绣花用的彩色丝线 coloured thread for embroidery

【花项】huā·xiàng 〈方 *dial.*〉花钱的项目 items of expenditure: 没有什么～,要不了这么多的钱。There are few expenses to cover, and this much money is not needed.

【花消】huā·xiao ❶ 花费(钱) spend (money): 他的工资也就只够他一个人～的。His salary is only enough to support himself. ❷ 开支的费用 expense; cost: 人口多,～也就大些。A large family generally has greater expenses. ❸ 〈旧时 *old*〉称买卖产业或商品时的佣金或捐税 commission or tallage for trading properties or commodities ‖ also 花销 huā·xiao

【花信】huāxìn same as 花期 huāqī

【花须】huāxū 指花蕊 stamen or pistil

【花序】huāxù 花在花轴上排列的方式,分有限花序和无限花序两大类,前者如聚伞花序,后者如总状花序、穗状花序、伞形花序 inflorescence; mode of development and arrangement of flowers on an axis, which can be classified into definite inflorescence (e.g. cyme) and indefinite inflorescence (e.g. raceme, spica, umbel)

【花絮】huāxù 〈比喻 *fig.*〉各种有趣的零碎新闻(多用做新闻报道的标题 oft used in title of news report) tidbits (of news); interesting sidelights: 大会～ sidelights of a meeting | 赛场～ sidelights on a playing area

【花押】huāyā 〈旧时 *old*〉公文契约上的草书签名 cursive signature on a document or contract：画～ sign a document

【花芽】huāyá 发育后长成花朵的芽，通常比同株植物的叶芽肥大 flower bud, usu. hypertrophic compared with the leaf bud of the same plant

【花言巧语】huā yán qiǎo yǔ ❶ 指虚假而动听的话 blandishments; fancy words and fine promises; sweet talk; sweet but insincere words：他的那套～，我早有领教。I learned his game of flattery long ago. ❷ 说虚假而动听的话 sweet-talk sb. into doing sth.; flatter; speak fine words：他整天～，变着法儿骗人。He always utters fine words, just to deceive people.

【花眼】huāyǎn 老视眼的通称 general term for 老视眼 lǎoshìyǎn

【花样】huāyàng（～儿 huāyàngr）❶ 花纹的式样。也泛指一切式样或种类。variety; decorative pattern：～繁多 a great variety｜～翻新 innovations in pattern or design｜～滑冰 figure skating ❷ 绣花用的底样，多用纸剪成或刻成（usu. paper or cut) master pattern for embroidery ❸ same as 花招儿 huāzhāor：玩～ play tricks｜这又是他闹的什么新～。I wonder what he's up to now.

【花样刀】huāyàngdāo 冰刀的一种，装在花样滑冰冰鞋的底下，刀口中间有槽，头部弯曲有齿，尾部直而较短 skate with a metal runner attached for ice and figure skating; It has a slot in the middle, a dentiform lead end curving upwards, and a short straight back end.

【花药】huāyào ❶ 雄蕊的上部，长在花丝的顶端，呈囊状，里面有花粉 anther; saccate upper part of a stamen that develops and contains pollen and is usu. borne on a stalk;（图见 ☞ figure for 花 huā）❷ 治花卉病虫害的药 chemical for treating flower diseases and insect pests

【花椰菜】huāyēcài 二年生草本植物，叶子大。花呈块状，黄白色，是蔬菜。cauliflower (*Brassia oleracea* var. *botrytis*); biennial herbal plant bearing lumpy off-white fruit and broad leaves, often eaten as vegetable; 通称 generally called 菜花 càihuā；有的地区叫花菜 in some places known as 花菜 huācài

【花园】huāyuán（～儿 huāyuánr）种植花木供游玩休息的场所 garden; flower garden; also 花园子 huāyuán·zi

【花账】huāzhàng 浮报的账目 padded accounts or bills：开～ pad the accounts; padded accounts

【花障】huāzhàng（～儿 huāzhàngr）有花草攀附的篱笆 fence padded (or trellis) climbing with flowers

【花招】huāzhāo（～儿 huāzhāor）❶ 练武术时，变化灵巧、姿势好看的动作（不一定是真工夫）。泛指巧妙的陪衬手法。showy movements in martial arts; (in a broad sense) ingenious complementary manouver ❷ 欺骗人的狡猾手段、计策等 trick; game; cunning tact in deception：耍～ play tricks｜玩弄～ fiddle with tricks‖ also 花着 huāzhāo

【花着】huāzhāo same as 花招 huāzhāo

【花朝】huāzhāo 农历二月十二日（也有人说是二月初二或二月十五日），相传为百花生日，所以叫花朝 legendary birthday of flowers, which falls on the 12th of the 2nd lunar month (also said to be the 2nd or 15th of the 2nd lunar month)

【花枝招展】huāzhī zhāozhǎn 形容妇女打扮得十分艳丽 (of women) be gorgeously dressed

【花轴】huāzhóu 生长花的茎 floral axis; also 花茎 huājìng

【花烛】huāzhú 旧式结婚新房里点的蜡烛，上面多用龙凤图案等做装饰 candles with dragon and phoenix patterns used in an old-fashioned bridal chamber on a wedding night：洞房～ wedding ceremony｜～夫妻（旧时指正式结婚的夫妻）old term for legally married husband and wife

【花柱】huāzhù 雌蕊的一部分，在子房和柱头之间，形状像细长的管 style; part of the pistil and filiform prolongation of a plant ovary, bearing a stigma at its apex;（图见 ☞ figure for 花 huā）

【花砖】huāzhuān 表面光洁，有彩色花纹的砖，主要用来墁地 ornamental tiles for flooring

【花子】huā·zi same as 乞丐 qǐgài; also 化子 huā·zi

【花子儿】huāzǐr ❶ 供观赏的花草的种子 flower seeds ❷〈方 *dial.*〉指棉花子 cotton seeds

砉 huā〈拟声词 *onom.*〉形容迅速动作的声音 noise descriptive of sth. done with a splash：乌鸦～的一声从树上直飞起来。The crow flew swiftly out of the tree.

☞ xū on p.2161

哗（嘩） huā〈拟声词 *onom.*〉：铁门～的一声拉上了。The iron gate was pulled to with a clang.｜流水～～地响。The flowing water gurgled.

☞ huá on p.833

【哗啦】huālā〈拟声词 *onom.*〉：～一声，墙倒了。The wall fell with a crash.｜雨～～地下。The rain kept splashing down.

huá（ㄏㄨㄚˊ）

划[1] huá 拨水前进 paddle; row：～船 row a boat｜～桨 paddle

划[2] huá 合算 pay; be to one's profit：～得来 be worth it｜～不来 be not worth it｜～得着 be worth it｜～不着 be not worth it

划[3]**（劃）** huá 用尖锐的东西把别的东西分开或在表面上刻过去、擦过去 scratch or cut the surface of sth. with a sharp object：～玻璃 cut glass｜～根火柴 strike a match｜手上～了一个口子 a scratch on the hand

☞ huà on p. 837 and ·huai on p. 842

【划不来】huá·bu lái 不合算；不值得 be not worth it; does not pay：为这点儿小事跑那么远的路～。It doesn't pay to walk such a long way for a trifle.

【划得来】huá·de lái 合算；值得 pay; be worth it：花这么点儿钱，解决那么多问题，～！It pays to solve so many problems by spending a little money!

【划拉】huá·la〈方 *dial*.〉❶ 用拂拭的方式除去或取去；扫；掸 sweep; brush away; whisk away or off：把身上的泥土～掉 brush dirt off one's body｜你没事把里外屋～～。If you are free, you'd better sweep the house and the outside. ❷ 寻找；设法获取 look for; try to get：从仓库里～些旧零件凑合着用。Look for some old spare parts in the storehouse to make do with. ❸ same as 搂 lōu ①：在山上～干草 rake up hay on the hill ◇～几个钱花 earn some extra money ❹ 随意涂抹；潦草写字 scrawl; scribble

【划拳】huá//quán 饮酒时两人同时伸出手指并各说一个数，谁说的数目跟双方所伸手指的总数相符，谁就算赢，输的人喝酒 finger-guessing game played by two drinkers, who each extend a number of fingers and announce a number at the same time; The man whose announced number tallies with the sum of fingers extended by both sides is declared the winner, and the loser takes a drink：～行令 play a drinking game; also 豁拳 huá//quán or 搳拳 huá//quán

【划算】huásuàn ❶ 计算；盘算 calculate; weigh：～来，～去，半夜没有合上眼。I was wide awake until midnight weighing the pros and cons. ❷ 上算；合算 be to one's profit; pay：这块地还是种麦子～。It pays to grow wheat on this field.

【划子】huá·zi 用桨拨水行驶的小船 small rowboat

华[1]**（華）** huá ❶ same as 光彩 guāngcǎi ①；光辉 magnificent; splendid：～美 gorgeous｜～丽 magnificent｜～灯 colourfully decorated lantern｜光～ brilliance; bright ❷ 出现在太阳或月亮周围的彩色光环，内紫外红 corona, colourful ring of light appearing around the sun or the moon, purple inside and red outside ❸ 繁盛 prosperous：繁～ flourishing｜荣～ glory ❹ 精华 best part：英～ beauty and adornment｜才～ talent ❺ 奢侈 flashy; extravagant：浮～ showy｜奢～ luxurious ❻ 指时光 time：韶～ glorious youth｜似水年～。Time passes like flowing water. ❼（头发）花白(of hair) grizzled; grey：～发 grey hair ❽〈书 *fml*.〉〈敬辞 *pol*.〉用于跟对方有关的事物 your：～翰 your esteemed letter｜～诞 your birthday｜～宗（称人同姓）your namesake (addressing people with the same surname)

〈古 *arch*.〉same as 花 huā

华[2]**（華）** huá 泉水中的矿物质由于沉积而形成的物质 matter formed by mineral sediment in spring water：钙～ adarce｜矽～ siliceous sinter

华[3]**（華）** Huá ❶ 指中国 China：～夏 Huaxia, ancient name for China｜～北 northern China｜～南 southern China｜驻～大使 ambassador to China ❷ 汉（语）Chinese (language)：～俄词典 Chinese-Russian dictionary ❸ 姓 a surname（应读 Huà，近年也有读 Huá 的 pronounced Huà and also Huá in recent years）

☞ Huà on p. 838

【华北】Huáběi 指我国北部河北、山西、北京市、天津市一带地区 northern China, including Hebei and Shanxi provinces, and the Municipalities of Beijing and Tianjin

【华表】huábiǎo〈古代 *arch*.〉宫殿、陵墓等大建筑物前面做装饰用的巨大石柱，柱身多雕刻龙凤等图案，上部横插着雕花的石板 *huabiao*; paired ceremonial columns erected in front of a palace, tomb, etc., usu. carved with dragon and phoenix patterns, with a transverse engraved stone slab on its top

【华达呢】huádání 密度较小，带有斜纹的毛织品或棉织品，质地柔软结实，适宜于做制服 gabardine; firm, densely woven fabric of wool or cotton with a twill weave, suitable for making uniforms

【华诞】huádàn〈书 *fml*.〉〈敬辞 *pol*.〉称人的生日 your birthday

【华灯】huádēng 雕饰华美或光华灿烂的灯 colourfully decorated lantern：～初上 when the evening lights are lit｜长安街上～齐放。Bright lamps light up Chang'an Street.

【华东】Huádōng 指我国东部地区，包括山东、江苏、浙江、安徽、江西、福建、台湾七省和上海市 Eastern China, including Shandong, Jiangsu, Zhejiang, Anhui, Jiangxi, Fujian and Taiwan provinces, and Shanghai Municipality

【华而不实】huá ér bù shí 只开花不结果 produce flowers but bear no fruit;〈比喻 *fig*.〉外表好看，内容空虚 flashy, without substance; superficially clever

【华尔街】Huá'ěr Jiē 美国纽约的一条街，有许多垄断组织和金融机构的总管理处设在这里。常用做美国财阀的代称。Wall Street; street in New York City, US, where many monopolies and financial head offices are located, synonymous to American financial magnates

【华尔兹】huá'ěrzī 交际舞的一种，起源于奥地利民间的一种 3/4 拍舞蹈。用圆舞曲伴奏，舞时两人成对旋转，分快步和慢步两种。waltz; ballroom dance of Austrian origin, in moderately fast triple metre, in which the dancers revolve in continual circles, taking one step to each beat, alternating a fast step and a slow step

【华发】huáfà 〈书 *fml*.〉花白的头发 grey hair

【华盖】huágài ❶〈古代 *arch*.〉帝王所乘车子上伞形的遮蔽物 canopy; umbrella-like cover on an imperial carriage ❷ 古星名。迷信的人认为运气不好,是有华盖星犯命,叫交华盖运。但据说和尚华盖罩顶是走好运。*Huagai*, ancient name of a constellation that in superstition angurs ill for lay people but well for monks

【华工】huágōng 〈旧时 *old*〉在国外做工的中国工人 overseas Chinese labourers

【华贵】huáguì ❶ 华丽珍贵 luxurious; sumptuous; costly:～的地毯 luxurious carpet ❷ 豪华富贵 wealthy:～之家 wealthy family

【华翰】huáhàn 〈书 *fml*.〉〈敬辞 *pol*.〉称对方的书信 your esteemed letter

【华里】huálǐ 市里的旧称 old name for *li*, a unit of distance (about 1/2 km.)

【华丽】huálì 美丽而有光彩 magnificent; resplendent; gorgeous:服饰～gorgeously dressed and richly ornamented|宏伟～的官殿 magnificent palace

【华美】huáměi same as 华丽 huálì

【华南】Huánán 指我国南部地区,包括广东、广西和海南 South China, including Guangdong, Guangxi and Hainan provinces

【华侨】huáqiáo 旅居国外的中国人 overseas Chinese

【华人】huárén ❶ 中国人 Chinese ❷ 指取得所在国国籍的中国血统的外国公民 foreign citizens of Chinese descent:美籍～ American Chinese

【华氏温标】Huáshì wēnbiāo 温标的一种,规定在一个标准大气压下,纯水的冰点为 32 度,沸点为 212 度,32 度至 212 度之间均匀分成 180 份,每份表示 1 度。这种温标是德国物理学家华兰海特(Gabriel Daniel Fahrenheit)制定的。Fahrenheit (F), temperature scale devised by German physicist Gabriel Daniel Fahrenheit in which 32 ℉ represents the freezing point and 212 ℉ the boiling point; between 32° and 212°, there are 180 calibrations, each representing one degree F

【华氏温度】Huáshì wēndù 华氏温标的标度,用符号'°F'表示 Fahrenheit thermometer, using the symbol ℉

【华文】Huáwén 指中文 the Chinese language:～学校 Chinese-language school|～报纸 Chinese-language newspaper

【华西】Huáxī 指我国长江上游地区四川一带 West China, covering the upper reaches of the Yangtze River, including Sichuan Province and the Chongqing Municipality

【华夏】Huáxià 我国的古称 an ancient name for China

【华严宗】huáyánzōng 〈佛教 *Budd*.〉我国佛教宗派之一,因依《华严经》创立宗派而得名 Huayan Sect; school of Buddhism in China based on the *Huayan Scriptures* (*Garland Sutra* or *Buddhavatamsaka-mahavaipulya Sutra*)

【华裔】huáyì ❶ 指我国和我国的四邻 China and its neighbouring countries ❷ 华侨在侨居国所生并取得侨居国国籍的子女 foreign citizen of Chinese origin

【华语】Huáyǔ 指汉语 Chinese (language)

【华章】huázhāng 〈书 *fml*.〉华美的诗文(多用于称颂 usu. for praise) your beautiful writing

【华中】Huázhōng 指我国长江中游湖北、湖南一带 Central China, covering the middle reaches of the Yangtze River, including Hunan and Hubei provinces

【华胄】[1] huázhòu 〈书 *fml*.〉贵族的后裔 descendants of a nobleman

【华胄】[2] huázhòu 〈书 *fml*.〉华夏的后裔,指汉族 Chinese people, referring to Han people

哗(嘩、譁)

huá 喧哗;喧闹 noise; clamour:～然 in an uproar|～笑 roar with laughter|～变 mutiny|寂静无～ silent and still; very quiet

☞ huā on p.831

【哗变】huábiàn (军队)突然叛变 (army) mutiny

【哗然】huárán 形容许多人吵吵嚷嚷 in an uproar:举座～。All those present made an uproar.|舆论～。There was a public outcry.

【哗众取宠】huá zhòng qǔ chǒng 用言论行动迎合众人,以博得好感或拥护 sansationalism; try to please the public with claptrap

骅(驊)

huá [骅骝](huáliú)〈书 *fml*.〉赤色的骏马 fine red horse

铧(鏵)

huá 犁铧 ploughshare

猾

huá 狡猾 cunning; crafty:奸～ mean and crafty|～吏 crafty, wicked officials

滑

huá ❶ 光滑;滑溜 slippery; smooth:又圆又～的小石子 smooth, round pebbles|长满青苔的路～得很。The road covered with moss is very slippery ❷ 滑动;滑行 slip; slide:～冰 skating|～雪 skiing|～了一跤 slip and fall ❸ 油滑;狡诈 cunning; crafty; slippery:耍～ act in a slick way|～头～脑 a cunning person ❹ 用搪塞或瞒哄的方法混过去 slip through by dodging or deception:这次查得很严,想～是～不过去的。You cannot hope to slip through the inspection since this time it will be really strict. ❺ (Huá) 姓 a surname

【滑冰】huá//bīng ❶ 体育运动项目之一。穿着冰鞋在冰上滑行。比赛分花样滑冰(做出各种姿势和花样)和速度滑冰两种。skating; sport, sliding on ice wearing skates; two forms: figure skating and speed skating ❷ 泛指在冰上滑行 sliding on ice

【滑不唧溜】huá•bujīliū〈方 *dial*.〉(～的 huá•bujīliū•de)形容很滑(含厌恶意 disgustingly) slippery：刚下过雨，地上～的不好走。The road was slippery after the rain. also 滑不唧 huá•bujī or 滑不唧唧 huá•bujījī

【滑车神经】huáchē shénjīng 第四对脑神经，从中脑发出，分布在眼球周围的肌肉中，主管眼球的运动 trochlear nerve; either one of the fourth pair of cranial nerves, consisting of motor fibres that innervate the superior oblique muscle of the upper part of the eyeball

【滑动】huádòng 一个物体在另一物体上接触面不变地移动，如滑冰时冰刀在冰上的运动 slide, where one thing keeps moving on another, like an ice-skate blade moving on the ice

【滑竿】huágān (～儿 huágānr)一种旧式的交通工具，在两根长竹竿中间，架上类似躺椅的坐位，讲究的形似轿子而无顶，都由两个人抬着走 litter; or palanquin, usu. made of bamboo poles and carried by two people. A more elaborate version consists of a topless couch and two long shafts.

【滑稽】huá•jī (在古书中念 gǔjī pronounced gǔjī in ancient books) ❶(言语、动作)引人发笑 (of speech or movement) funny; amusing：这个丑角的表演非常～。The clown gave a very funny performance. ❷ 曲艺的一种，流行于上海、杭州、苏州等地，和北方相声相近 a kind of *quyi* (Chinese folk art forms, including balladeering, story-telling, comic dialogues, clapper talk, cross-talk, etc.) popular in Shanghai, Hangzhou and Suzhou, and similar to comic cross-talk in North China

【滑稽戏】huájīxì 一种专门以滑稽手段来表现人物的剧种，流行于上海、江苏和浙江的部分地区 a kind of farce, depicting characters through humour, popular in Shanghai, Jiangsu and parts of Zhejiang; also 滑稽剧 huájījù

【滑精】huájīng〈中医 *Chin. med*.〉指无梦而遗精 spermatorrhoea; involuntary emission

【滑溜】huáliū 烹调方法，把肉、鱼等切好，用芡粉拌匀，再用油炒，加葱、蒜等作料，再勾上芡，使汁变稠 sáute; cooking method whereby, slice meat or fish is mixed with starch, fried with oil, added with seasonings such as Chinese onion and garlic, and thickened with starch before serving：～鱼片 sautéd fish slices with gravy | ～里脊 sauté fillet with thick gravy

【滑溜】huá•liu 光滑(含喜爱意)(praise) slick; smooth; slippery：缎子被面摸着挺～。This silk feels very smooth.

【滑轮】huálún 简单机械，是一个装在架子上的周缘有槽的轮子，能穿上绳子或链条，多用来提起重物 pulley; simple mechanism consisting of a wheel with a grooved rim for carrying a cord or chain, which turns in a frame or block, and serves to change direction or transmit force, as when one end of the line is pulled to raise a weight at the other end; 通称 generally called 滑车 huáchē

【滑轮组】huálúnzǔ 由定滑轮和动滑轮组成的滑轮装置 assembly pulley, consisting of a fixed pulley and movable pulley

【滑腻】huánì 光滑细腻(多形容皮肤)(of the skin) satiny; velvety

【滑坡】huápō ❶ 指地表斜坡上大量的土石整体地向下滑动的自然现象。速度快的滑坡会产生巨响，并发出火光。滑坡对建筑物、公路、铁路、农田、森林会造成很大破坏。landslide; downward falling or sliding of a mass of soil, detritus, or rock down a steep slope. High-speed landslide may give off a deafening sound and emit sparks, causing extensive damage to buildings, roads, railways, fields and forests. ❷〈比喻 *fig*.〉下降；走下坡路 slide down a slope; fall down：质量～。There has been a decline in quality. | 经营不善，旅游业出现～。The tourism industry declined due to poor management.

【滑润】huárùn 光滑润泽 well lubricated：肌肤～ well-moisturised skin

【滑膛】huátáng 没有膛线的枪膛或炮膛 bore of a gun or cannon without rifling：～炮 shotgun

【滑梯】huátī 儿童体育活动器械，在高架子的一面装上梯子，另一面装上斜的滑板，儿童从梯子上去，从斜板滑下来 children's slide; elevated frame with a ladder to climb on on one side and a smooth chute to slide down on the other

【滑头】huátóu ❶ 油滑不老实的人 slippery fellow：老～ an old slippery fellow ❷ 油滑，不老实 slippery：这家伙～得很。The guy is very slippery.

【滑头滑脑】huá tóu huá nǎo 形容人油滑，不老实 crafty; artful; slick

【滑翔】huáxiáng 某些物体不依靠动力，而利用空气的浮力和本身重力的相互作用在空中飘行 glide; move through the air without engine power, solely through the action of air currents and gravity or by momentum already acquired

【滑翔机】huáxiángjī 没有动力装置，构造简单而轻便的飞行器，有翅膀，用于飞行训练和航空体育运动。一般用飞机、汽车或弹性绳索等来牵引它上升，然后借上升气流在空中滑翔。glider; motorless, heavier-than-air aircraft with wings, for gliding from a higher to a lower level by the action of gravity or from a lower to a higher level by the action of air currents, used for flight training and sport

【滑行】huáxíng ❶ 滑动前进 slide; coast：他穿着冰鞋在冰上快速～。He skated on the ice at a fast speed. ❷ 机动车行驶时，把离合器分开或用空挡使传动装置脱离发动机，靠惯性前进 (of vehicles) taxi; move under its own power by using a clutch or neutral gear to uncouple a gearbox from an engine

【滑雪】huá//xuě 脚登滑雪板，手拿滑雪杖在雪地上滑行 ski, wearing skis and holding ski poles

【滑雪板】huáxuěbǎn 滑雪时固定在滑雪鞋上的长条形薄板，前端稍微翘起 skis; a pair of long strips with boots fixed on top and ends slightly curved up

【滑雪衫】huáxuěshān〈方 *dial.*〉一种像夹克的冬季上衣，原多为登山、滑雪时所穿，所以叫滑雪衫 ski suit, originally worn while climbing and skating

【滑音】huáyīn 音乐上指从一个音向上或向下滑到另一个音的演唱或演奏的方法 portamento; sing or play from one note gliding up or down to another note

搳 huá［搳拳］(huá//quán) same as 划拳 huá//quán

鲳 huá 鱼类的一属，身体侧扁，头部略尖，有须一对，尾鳍分叉。生活在淡水中。skin carp (*Hemibarbus labeo*); fish with flat body, slightly pointed head, pair of feelers, and divided tail and fin, and living in fresh water

豁 huá［豁拳］(huá//quán) same as 划拳 huá//quán

☞ huō on p. 875 and huò on p. 886

huà（ㄏㄨㄚˋ）

化[1] huà ❶ 变化；使变化 change; turn; transform：～脓 suppurate | ～名 assumed name | ～装 (put on) makeup | 顽固不～ be set in one's way | 泥古不～ stick stubbornly to old rules | ～整为零 break up the whole into parts | ～险为夷 transform danger into safety ❷ 感化 convert; influence：教～ train in good manners | 潜移默～ imperceptible influence; exert a subtle influence on sb.'s character or way of thinking ❸ 熔化；融化 melt; dissolve：～冻 melt | ～铁炉 cupola | 太阳一出来，冰雪都～了。The ice and snow melted away when the sun came out. ❹ 消化；消除 digest：～食 digest | ～痰止咳 (capable of) preventing phlegm from forming and stopping a cough ◇食古不～ follow the beaten path ❺ 烧化 cremate; burn：焚～ cremate | 火～ cremate ❻ (僧道)死 (of a Buddhist monk or Taoist priest) die：坐～ (of a Buddhist monk) die in a sitting position, with legs crossed | 羽～ (of a Taoist) die ❼ 指化学 short for chemistry：理～ physics and chemistry | ～工 chemical industry | ～肥 chemical fertilizer ❽〈后缀 *suffix.*〉加在名词或形容词之后构成动词，表示转变成某种性质或状态 [used as a suffix for a noun or an adjective to indicate sth. or sb. is becoming or made to have that attribute]：绿～ make the land green by planting trees, flowers, etc. | 美～ beautify | 恶～ worsen | 电气～ electrification | 机械～ mechanization | 水利～ bring all farmland under irrigation

化[2] huà (僧道)向人求布施 (of Buddhist a monk or Taoist priest) beg for alms：募～ (of a Buddhist monk or Taoist priest) collect alms | ～缘 (of Buddhist a monk or Taoist priest) beg for alms | ～斋 beg for alms from door to door

☞ huā on p. 825

【化除】huàchú 消除(多用于抽象事物 usu. abstract things) eliminate; dispel; remove：～成见 dispel prejudices | 一经解释，疑虑～ clear up doubts after explanation

【化冻】huà//dòng 冰冻的江河、土地等融化 (of frozen river, earth, etc.) thaw; melt

【化肥】huàféi 化学肥料的简称 abbr. for 化学肥料 huàxué féiliào

【化干戈为玉帛】huà gān gē wéi yù bó〈比喻 *fig.*〉把战争或争斗变为和平、友好 put away the sword; bury the hatchet; make peace

【化工】huàgōng 化学工业的简称 abbr. for 化学工业 huàxué gōngyè

【化合】huàhé 两种或两种以上的物质经过化学反应而生成另一种物质，如氢与氧化合成水 chemical combination; two or more substances turn into another substance after chemical reaction, e.g. hydrogen and oxygen compounded into water

【化合价】huàhéjià 一定数目的一种元素的原子跟一定数目的其他元素原子化合的性质。通常以氢的化合价等于1为标准，其他元素的化合价就是该元素的一个原子相化合(或置换出)的氢原子数。valence; relative combining capacity of an atom or group compared with that of the standard hydrogen atom. The chloride ion, Cl^-, with a valence of one, has the capacity to unite with one atom of hydrogen or its equivalent. also called 原子价 yuánzǐjià; 简称 abbr. 价 jià

【化合物】huàhéwù 由不同种元素组成的纯净物，有固定的组成和性质，如氧化镁、氯酸钾等 chemical compound, consisting of different elements, fixed in structure and nature, such as magnesium oxide, potassium chlorate, etc.

【化解】huàjiě 解除；消除 resolve; eliminate：～矛盾 resolve contradictions | 心中的疑虑难以～。It's difficult to dispel misgivings.

【化境】huàjìng 幽雅清新的境地；极其高超的境界(多指艺术技巧等 usu. referring to artistic skill, etc.) sublimity; perfection：身入～ reach perfection | 他的水墨山水已达～。He has achieved virtuosity in ink-and-water landscape painting.

【化疗】huàliáo 用化学药物治疗恶性肿瘤 chemotherapy for treating cancer

【化名】huà//míng 为了使人不知道真实姓名而用别的名字 use an assumed name：他原叫张杰，～王成。His name is Zhang Jie, alias Wang Cheng.

【化名】huàmíng 为了使人不知道真实姓名而用的假名字 alias; assumed name：他原叫张杰，王成是他的～。His name is Zhang Jie, Wang Cheng is his assumed name.

【化募】huàmù same as 募化 mùhuà

【化脓】huà//nóng 人或动物体的组织因细菌感染等而生脓（of human being or animal organs) fester; suppurate

【化身】huàshēn ❶〈佛教 *Budd.*〉称佛或菩萨暂时出现在人间的形体 incarnation ◇这本小说的主人公正是作者自己的～。The hero of this novel is a portrait of the author himself. ❷ 指抽象观念的具体形象 embodiment：旧小说里把包公描写成正义的～。The honest and upright official Lord Bao was often described in old novels as justice incarnate.

【化生】huàshēng ❶ 机体的一种组织由于细胞生活环境改变或理化因素刺激，在形态和机能上变为另一种组织的过程，是机体的一种适应现象。如支气管黏膜的柱状上皮组织长期受刺激变为鳞状上皮组织。metaplasia; transformation of one type of tissue into another, as the body adapts itself to a changed living environment for cells or responds to stimulations from a certain physicochemical factor, such as the columnar epithelial tissue of bronchial mucosa transformed into lepidote epithelial tissue after long stimulation ❷〈书 *fml.*〉化育生长 give birth and foster growth：天地～万物。From heaven and earth come all things in this world.

【化石】huàshí〈古代 *arch.*〉生物的遗体、遗物或遗迹埋藏在地下变成的跟石头一样的东西。研究化石可以了解生物的演化并能帮助确定地层的年代。fossil; remains, impression or trace of a living thing from a former geologic age, buried underground and petrified, for studying the evolution of life and helping determine the age of stratra

【化外】huàwài〈旧时 *old*〉指政令教化达不到的偏远落后的地方 outside the pale of civilization：～之民 people outside the pale of civilization|～之邦 states outside the pale of civilization

【化纤】huàxiān 化学纤维的简称 abbr. for 化学纤维 huàxué xiānwéi

【化险为夷】huà xiǎn wéi yí 使危险的情况或处境变为平安 turn danger into safety; head off disaster

【化形】huàxíng 指神话传说中妖魔鬼怪变化形状（of demons and ghosts in legend) transformation of appearance

【化学】huàxué ❶ 研究物质的组成、结构、性质和变化规律的科学，是自然科学中的基础学科之一 chemistry; one of the basic natural sciences, the science that deals with the composition, structure, properties and rules of change of substances and various elementary forms of matter ❷ 赛璐珞的俗称 poplular name for celluloid：这把梳子是～的。This comb is made of celluloid.

【化学变化】huàxué biànhuà 物质变化中生成其他物质的变化，如木材燃烧放出光和热剩下灰，铁在潮湿空气中生锈等。发生化学变化时，物质的组成和化学性质都改变。chemical change, in which one substance turns into another, such as burned wood becoming ash after releasing light and heat, iron rusting in wet air, etc. When a chemical transformation occurs, the composition and chemical nature of the substance will change too.

【化学电池】huàxué diànchí 把化学能转变为电能的装置。主要部分是电解质溶液和浸在溶液中的正、负电极。使用时用导线接通两极，得到电流。chemical battery; device for turning chemical energy into electrical energy, mainly consisting of electrolytes and positive and negative electrodes soaking in a solution; when in use, the two electrodes are electrically connected to produce an electric current

【化学反应】huàxué fǎnyìng 物质发生化学变化而产生性质、成分、结构与原来不同的新物质的过程 chemical reaction; process in which one substance is turned into another with different properties, composition and structure

【化学方程式】huàxué fāngchéngshì 用化学式表明化学反应的式子。化学方程式中，反应物的化学式写在左边，生成物的化学式写在右边，中间用等号连接，各元素在两侧的原子数相等。如 $N_2 + 3H_2 = 2NH_3$。chemical equation; symbolic representation showing the type and amount of the elementary materials and products of a reaction in which the chemical formula of the elementary materials is on the left, and that of the product is on the right, with both connected by an equal sign, and having equal atomicity of each element on both sides, such as $N_2 + 3H_2 = 2NH_3$; also 化学反应式 huàxué fǎnyìngshì; 简称 abbr. 方程式 fāngchéngshì

【化学肥料】huàxué féiliào 以空气、水、矿物等为原料，经过化学反应或机械加工制成的肥料，肥分多，见效快，通常用做追肥。有氮肥、磷肥、钾肥及微量元素肥料等。chemical fertilizer; fertilizer made of gas, water, minerals, etc. through chemical reaction or mechanical treatment, characterised by rich nutriment and rapid effectiveness, usu. used for topsoil application; including nitrogenous fertilizer, phosphate fertiliser, potassic fertiliser and trace elements, etc.; 简称 abbr. 化肥 huàféi

【化学分析】huàxué fēnxī 确定物质化学成分或组成的方法。根据分析要求不同，可分为定性分析和定量分析。chemical analysis; determine the chemical composition of a matter by qualitative analysis or quantitative analysis or both

【化学工业】huàxué gōngyè 利用化学反应生产

化学产品的工业，包括基本化学工业和塑料、合成纤维、石油、橡胶、药剂、染料等各种工业 chemical industry; industry producing chemical products via chemical reaction, including primary chemical industry for the production of plastics, combined fibres, petroleum, rubber, pharmacenticals, and dyes；简称 abbr. 化工 huàgōng

【化学键】huàxuéjiàn 分子中相邻原子之间通过电子而产生的相互结合的作用。化学结构式中用短线（—）表示。chemical bond; attraction between atoms in a molecule or crystalline structure; in a chemical structural formula, represented by a hyphen

【化学能】huàxuénéng 物质进行化学反应时放出的能，如物质燃烧时放出的光和热、化学电池放出的电 chemical energy; energy given out by a substance in a chemical reaction, e. g. a burning substances emit heat and light, and chemical batteries produce electricity

【化学平衡】huàxué pínghéng 可逆反应中，正反应和逆反应速度相等，反应混合物里各组成成分百分含量保持不变的状态 chemical equilibrium; state where reversible reaction, positive reaction and backward reaction have the same speed and the mixture of the reactions remains unchanged in composition ratios

【化学式】huàxuéshì 用化学符号表示物质化学组成的式子，包括分子式、实验式（最简式）、结构式、示性式、电子式等 chemical formula; formula expressing chemical composition of substances by chemical symbols, including molecular formula, experimental formula (fraction in lowest terms), constitutional formula, rational formula, and electronic type, etc.

【化学武器】huàxué wǔqì 利用毒剂大规模杀伤破坏的一种武器，包括毒剂和施放毒剂的各种武器弹药。也指喷火或发烟的军用器械等。chemical weapons; weapons of mass destruction that make use of toxic agents and various weapons and munitions for discharging them; also referring to weapons for ejecting fire or smoke

【化学纤维】huàxué xiānwéi 用高分子化合物为原料制成的纤维。用天然的高分子化合物制成的叫人造纤维，用合成的高分子化合物制成的叫合成纤维。chemical fibre; fibre made of a polymer compound; those made of natural polymers (compounds) are called artificial fibre, those made of synthetic polymers (compounds), synthetic fibre; 简称 abbr. 化纤 huàxiān

【化学性质】huàxué xìngzhì 物质在发生化学变化时表现出来的性质，如酸性、碱性、化学稳定性等 chemical property; property that a substance reveals during chemical reaction, such as acidity, alkalinity, chemical stability, etc.

【化学元素】huàxué yuánsù 具有相同核电荷数（即相同质子数）的同一类原子的总称 chemical element; same kind of atom with the same nuclear charge; 简称 abbr. 元素 yuánsù

【化验】huàyàn 用物理的或化学的方法检验物质的成分和性质 chemical examination for testing the composition and nature of a substance：～员 laboratory technician | 药品～ drug test | ～大便 have one's stools examined

【化雨春风】huàyǔ chūnfēng ☞ 春风化雨 chūnfēng huàyǔ on p. 310

【化育】huàyù 滋养；养育 rear; bring up：阳光雨露，～万物。Sunlight, rain and dew nourish all things on earth.

【化缘】huà//yuán 僧尼或道士向人求布施（of a Buddhist monk or nun or Taoist priest) beg for alms

【化斋】huà//zhāi 僧道挨门乞讨饭食（of a Buddhist monk or Taoist priest) beg for a meal from door to door; also 打斋 dǎ zhāi or 打斋饭 dǎ zhāifàn

【化妆】huà//zhuāng 用脂粉等使容貌美丽 make up with rouge, powder, etc.

【化妆品】huàzhuāngpǐn 化妆用的物品，如脂粉、唇膏、香水等 cosmetics, including rouge, powder, lipstick, perfume, etc.

【化装】huà//zhuāng ❶ 演员为了适合所扮演的角色的形象而修饰容貌（of actor) put on makeup for a stage role ❷ 改变装束、容貌；假扮 disguise oneself：～舞会 fancy dress ball | 他～成乞丐模样。He disguised himself as a beggar.

划[1]（劃）huà ❶ 划分 delimit; differentiate：～界 delimit a boundary | ～定范围 delimit scope ❷ 划拨 transfer; assign：～付 transfer money | ～款 transfer money | ～账 transfer an account ❸ 计划 plan：筹～ plan and prepare | 策～ plan

划[2]（劃）huà same as 画[2] huà ☞ huá on p. 831 and ·huai on p. 842

【划拨】huàbō ❶（款项或账目）从某一单位或户头转到另一单位或户头 transfer (money or accounts) from one account to another, or from one unit to another：这笔款子由银行～。The money will be transferred through the bank. ❷ 分出来拨给 assign; allocate：～钢材 allocate steel | ～物资 allocate goods and materials

【划策】huàcè 出主意；筹谋计策 plan; scheme：出谋～ give advice and suggestions; also 画策 huàcè

【划分】huàfēn ❶ 把整体分成几部分 divide：～行政区域 divide a country into administrative regions ❷ same as 区分 qūfēn：～阶级 classify a population into classes | ～人民内部矛盾和敌我矛盾 differentiate contradictions among the people, and contradictions between ourselves and the enemy

【划粉】huàfěn 裁剪衣服时用来划线的粉块 tailor's chalk

【划价】huà//jià（医院药房）计算患者药费和其他医疗费用，把款额写在处方上 have a prescription priced (in a hospital dispensary)

【划时代】huàshídài 开辟新时代（多做定语用 usu. as attribute）epoch-making：～的作品 work that is a landmark in history｜～的事件 epoch-making event｜～的文献 epoch-making document

【划一】huàyī ❶ 一致；一律 standardized; uniform：整齐～ neat and uniform ❷ 使一致 standardize：～体例 standardize the layout

【划一不二】huà yī bù èr ❶ 不二价；照定价不折不扣 unalterable; fixed price ❷（做事）一律；刻板 uniform; stereotyped：写文章，可长可短，没有～的公式。There are no hard-and-fast rules for the length of a piece of writing.

华(華) Huà ❶ 华山，山名，在陕西 Mount Huashan in Shaanxi Province ❷ 姓 a surname（近年也有读 Huá 的 also pronounced Huá in recent years）
☞ huá on p.832

画¹(畫) huà ❶ 用笔或类似笔的东西做出图形 draw or paint with a brush, pen, etc.：～山水 paint mountains and rivers｜～人像 draw a portrait｜～画儿 draw a picture ❷（～儿 huàr）画成的艺术品 drawing; painting; picture：年～ New Year picture｜壁～ mural painting｜油～ oil painting｜风景～ landscape painting ❸ 用画儿装饰的 be decorated with paintings or pictures：～屏 painted screen｜～堂 hall decorated with paintings｜～栋雕梁 painted pillars and carved beams (of a magnificent building)

画²(畫、劃) huà ❶ 用笔或类似笔的东西做出线或作为标记的文字 draw or mark with a brush, pen, etc.：～线 draw a line｜～押 make one's cross｜～到 register one's attendance at a meeting or at the office｜～十字 make a cross ❷ 汉字的一笔叫一画 stroke (of a Chinese character)：笔～ stroke｜'天'字四～。The character 天 is made up of four strokes. ❸〈方 *dial.*〉汉字的一横叫一画 horizontal stroke (in Chinese characters)

【画板】huàbǎn 绘画用的板子，画画时画纸钉在上面 drawing board, with drawing paper nailed to it when painting or drawing

【画报】huàbào 以刊登图画和照片为主的期刊或报纸 pictorial; illustrated magazine or newspaper：《儿童～》*Children's Pictorial*

【画笔】huàbǐ 绘画用的笔 brush; painting brush

【画饼充饥】huà bǐng chōng jī〈比喻 *fig.*〉借空想安慰自己 draw cakes to allay hunger — feed on illusions

【画布】huàbù 画油画用的布，多为麻布 canvas for painting, usu. hemp cloth

【画册】huàcè 装订成本子的画 picture album; album of paintings

【画策】huàcè same as 划策 huàcè

【画到】huà//dào same as 签到 qiān//dào

【画地为牢】huà dì wéi láo 在地上画一个圈儿当做监狱 draw a circle on the ground to serve as a prison;〈比喻 *fig.*〉只许在指定的范围之内活动 restrict sb.'s activities to a designated area or sphere

【画舫】huàfǎng 装饰华美专供游人乘坐的船 gaily painted pleasure-boat for tourists

【画符】huà//fú 道士做符箓（Taoism）draw magic figures or incantations：～念咒 draw magic figures and chant

【画幅】huàfú ❶ 图画（总称）(collect.) picture; painting ◇美丽的田野是天然的～。The beautiful open country is a veritable painting worked by nature. ❷ 画的尺寸 size of a picture：～虽然不大，所表现的天地却十分广阔。The picture is small but shows broad vistas.

【画稿】huà//gǎo 负责人在公文稿上签字或批字表示认可 (of a person in certain position) put down one's signature or comment on an official document to show approval

【画稿】huàgǎo（～儿 huàgǎor）图画的底稿 rough sketch (for a painting)

【画工】huàgōng ❶ 以绘画为职业的人 commercial painter ❷ 指绘画的技法 painting skill：～精细 fine painting skill; also 画功 huàgōng

【画供】huà//gòng 犯人在供状上画押，表示承认上面记录的供词属实 sign a written confession to a crime

【画虎类狗】huà hǔ lèi gǒu《后汉书·马援传》：'画虎不成反类狗' *History of Later Han·Biography of Ma Yuan*, try to draw a tiger and end up with the likeness of a dog;〈比喻 *fig.*〉模仿得不到家，反而弄得不伦不类 attempt sth. over-ambitious and end in failure; also 画虎类犬 huà hǔ lèi quǎn

【画夹】huàjiā 绘画用的夹子，较大较硬，绘画时画纸铺在上面 portfolio; big and solid painting folder

【画家】huàjiā 擅长绘画的人 painter; artist

【画架】huàjià 绘画用的架子，有三条腿，绘画时把画板或蒙画布的框子斜放在上面 easel; three-legged stand for supporting an artist's drawing board or framed canvas at a slanted angle

【画匠】huàjiàng 绘画的工匠。旧时也指缺乏艺术性的画家。artisan-painter; inferior painter

【画境】huàjìng 图画中的境界 picturesque scene：风景优美，如入～。The beautiful scenery makes one feel as though in a landscape painting.

【画镜线】huàjìngxiàn same as 挂镜线 guàjìngxiàn

【画具】huàjù 绘画用的工具，如画笔、画板、画架等 painter's paraphernalia, such as brush, drawing board, easel, etc.

【画卷】huàjuàn ❶ 成卷轴形的画 picture scroll ❷〈比喻 *fig.*〉壮丽的景色或动人的场面 magnificent scenery or stirring scene

【画廊】huàláng ❶ 有彩绘的走廊 painted corridor ❷ 展览图画照片的走廊 picture gallery

【画龙点睛】huà lóng diǎn jīng 传说梁代张僧繇(yóu)在金陵安乐寺壁上画了四条龙，不点眼睛，说点了就会飞掉。听到的人不相信，偏叫他点上。刚点了两条，就雷电大发，震破墙壁，两条龙乘云上天，只剩下没有点眼睛的两条(见于唐张彦远《历代名画记》)。Legend has it that Zhang Sengyou of the Liang Dynasty drew four dragons on the wall of Anle Temple in Jinling and stopped without painting the pupils in their eyes, saying that if he did the dragons would fly away. Compelled by some skeptics, he dipped pupils into the eyes of two of the dragons. Lightning accompanied by peals of thunder broke through the wall immediately, and the two dragons flew into the sky, while the other two dragons without pupils remained. (*Stories of Famous Paintings of All Generations* by Zhang Yanyuan of the Tang Dynasty);〈比喻 *fig.*〉作文或说话时在关键地方加上精辟的语句，使内容更加生动传神 bring a picture of a dragon to life by putting pupils into its eyes — add the touch that brings a work of art to life; add the finishing touch; add an apt word to clinch the point

【画眉】huàméi 鸟，身体棕褐色，腹部灰白色，头、后颈和背部有黑褐色斑纹，有白色的眼圈。叫的声音很好听，雄鸟好斗。hwa-mei (*Garrulax canorus*); thrush bird, usually dull brown, with grey-white belly, black and brown stripes on the head, nape and back, and white eyes and lovely singing; the male is bellicose

【画面】huàmiàn 画幅、银幕、屏幕等上面呈现的形象 tableau; general appearance of a picture, screen: ～清晰 clear tableau

【画皮】huàpí 传说中妖怪伪装美女时披在身上的人皮，可以取下来描画(见于《聊斋志异·画皮》) painted human skin. Legend has it that human skins used by monsters to disguise themselves as human beings can be taken off and used for drawing. (*Strange Stories from a Chinese Studio · Painted Human Skin*);〈比喻 *fig.*〉掩盖狰狞面目或丑恶本质的美丽外表 pretty disguise or mask of an evildoer

【画片儿】huàpiànr same as 画片 huàpiàn

【画片】huàpiàn 印制的小幅图画 miniature reproduction of a painting

【画屏】huàpíng 用图画装饰的屏风 painted screen

【画谱】huàpǔ ❶ same as 画帖 huàtiè ❷ 鉴别图画或评论画法的书 a book on the art of drawing or painting

【画蛇添足】huà shé tiān zú 蛇本来没有脚，画蛇添上脚(见于《战国策·齐策》) draw a snake and add feet to it (*Intrigues of the Warring States · Intrigues of Qi*);〈比喻 *fig.*〉做多余的事，反而不恰当 ruin the effect by adding sth. superfluous

【画师】huàshī ❶ same as 画家 huàjiā ❷ 以绘画为职业的人 artisan-painter

【画十字】huà shízì ❶ 不识字的人在契约或文书上画个'十'字代替签字 mark an × (on a document in place of a signature, by sb. who cannot write) ❷ 基督教徒祈祷时一种仪式，用右手从额上到胸前，再从一肩到另一肩画个'十'字形，纪念耶稣被钉在十字架上 make the sign of the cross with the right hand from the forehead to the chest and then from one shoulder to another shoulder, in memory of Christ's death on the cross

【画室】huàshì 绘画用的房间 studio

【画坛】huàtán 绘画界 art circle

【画帖】huàtiè 临摹用的图画范本 book of model paintings or drawings

【画图】huà//tú 画图形(多指图样或地图) draw designs, maps, etc.: ～员 designer

【画图】huàtú 图画(多用于比喻 oft. fig.) picture: 这些诗篇构成了一幅农村生活的多彩的～。These poems present a colourful picture of country life.

【画外音】huàwàiyīn 电影、电视等指不是由画面中的人或物体直接发出的声音 (of film or TV) off-screen voice or narration

【画像】huà//xiàng 画人像 draw a portrait: 给他画个像 draw a portrait for him

【画像】huàxiàng 画成的人像 portrait: 一幅鲁迅先生的～ a portrait of Mr. Lu Xun

【画行】huà//xíng〈旧时 *old*〉主管人在公文稿上写一'行'字，表示认可 (a person in charge) write the character 行 xíng on a document to show approval

【画押】huà//yā 在公文、契约或供词上画花押或写'押'字、'十'字，表示认可 put a signature (or mark) on a document or contract to show approval: 签字～ make an X or sign one's signature

【画页】huàyè 书报里印有图画或照片的一页 page with illustrations (in a book or magazine)

【画院】huàyuàn〈古代 *arch.*〉供奉内廷的绘画机构，宋徽宗时代(公元 1101—1125)的最著名，画法往往以工细为特点。后来称这种风格为画院派。现在的某些绘画机构也叫做画院。imperial art academy, notably that of Emperor Huizong (徽宗) of the Song Dynasty (1101-1125), whose style of painting was characterized by delicate brushwork and close attention to detail. Some art academies today also call themselves *huayuan*.

【画展】huàzhǎn 绘画展览会 art exhibition; exhibition of paintings

【画知】huà//zhī 在知单上自己的名字下面写一'知'字,表示已经知道 write the character 知 zhī (know) under one's name on an invitation list to indicate that one has been sent the invitation

【画轴】huàzhóu 裱后带轴的图画(总称)(collect.) painted scroll; scroll painting: 仕女~ scroll painted with female figures | 山水~ scroll of landscape painting

【画字】huà//zì 〈方 *dial.*〉 same as 画押 huà//yā; (多指画一个'十' oft. making a cross as signature)

话 huà ❶ (~儿 huàr)说出来的能够表达思想的声音,也指把这种声音记录下来的文字 words; remark; talk; spoken words expressing meaning, including the written records of speech: 讲~ talk | 会~ conversation | 土~ local dialect | 这两句~说得不妥当。These two sentences are not suitable. ❷ 说;谈 talk about; speak about: ~别 say a few parting words | ~家常 chitchat; engage in smalltalk

【话把儿】huàbàr same as 话柄 huàbǐng

【话白】huàbái ❶ 戏曲中的说白 spoken part of an opera ❷ 〈旧时 *old*〉评书演员登台后,先念上场诗,接着拍醒木,再说几句引入正书的话,叫做话白 prelude; short monologue leading to the story proper, spoken by a storyteller after he ascends the stage, recites a poem and smacks his wooden block to call attention

【话本】huàběn 宋代兴起的白话小说,用通俗文字写成,多以历史故事和当时社会生活为题材,是宋元民间艺人说唱的底本。今存《清平山堂话本》、《全相平话五种》等。*huaben* stories; printed versions of prompt-books used by popular storytellers in Song and Yuan times (salient features: use of the vernacular loaded with the stock expressions of professional storytellers; liberal admixture of colloquialisms and archaisms; frequent inclusion of rhymed passages, idioms, or poems for narrative or descriptive purposes; a routine preamble before the feature story). Extant books include: *Colloquial Tales from Mount Qingping Studio* and *Five Popular Stories with Complete Illustratiuns*.

【话别】huà//bié 离别前聚在一块儿谈话 say goodbye; say a few parting words: 临行~,不胜依依 reluctant to part when saying goodbye

【话柄】huàbǐng 被人拿来做谈笑资料的言论或行为 handle; subject of ridicule: 留下~leave behind a subject for ridicule

【话茬儿】huàchár 〈方 *dial.*〉 ❶ 话头 thread of discourse: 我刚说到这儿,她就接上了~。When I had spoken up to that point, she took up the thread. ❷ 口风;口气 tone of one's speech: 听他的~,这件事好办。Judging from what he says, that can be easily done.

【话锋】huàfēng 话头 thread of conversation; topic of discourse: 把~一转 change the subject | 避开~ avoid the topic (of conversation)

【话旧】huàjiù 跟久别重逢的朋友谈往事;叙旧 talk over old times

【话剧】huàjù 用对话和动作来表演的戏剧 modern drama; stage play

【话口儿】huàkǒur 〈方 *dial.*〉口气;口风 tone; implied meaning: 听他的~是不想去的意思。From his tone, he was reluctant to go.

【话里有话】huà·li yǒu huà 话里暗含有别的意思 There's more to what is actually said or spoken.

【话说】huàshuō ❶ 旧小说中常用的发语词 it is said that ... (an opening phrase used in traditional stories and novels) ❷ 说;讲述 talk about:《~长江》*A Random Talk About the Yangtze River*

【话题】huàtí 谈话的中心 subject of a talk; topic of conversation: ~转了 change the subject (of a conversation) | 换个~接着说 shift to another topic

【话筒】huàtǒng ❶ 发话器 microphone ❷ 微音器的通称 telephone transmitter ❸ 向附近许多人大声讲话用的类似圆锥形的筒 megaphone to amplify speech; also 传声筒 chuánshēngtǒng

【话头】huàtóu (~儿 huàtóur)谈话的头绪 thread of conversation: 打断~ interrupt sb.

【话务员】huàwùyuán 使用交换机分配电话线路的工作人员 telephone operator

【话匣子】huàxiá·zi 〈方 *dial.*〉 ❶ 原指留声机,后来也指收音机 (orig.) gramophone; later also referring to radio ❷ 〈比喻 *fig.*〉话多的人 chatterbox

【话音】huàyīn (~儿 huàyīnr) ❶ 说话的声音 voice (in speech): ~未落,只听外面一声巨响。He had hardly finished speaking when there came a huge bang outside. ❷ 言外之意 implication: 听他的~儿,准是另有打算。His tone suggests that he has something else in mind.

【话语】huàyǔ 言语;说的话 words; what one says: 天真的~ naive words | 他~不多,可句句中听。His words are few, but everything he says makes good sense.

桦(樺) huà 双子叶植物的一属,落叶乔木或灌木,树皮白色、灰色、黄色或黑色,叶子互生。在我国多产于东北地区。白桦、黑桦就是这一属的植物。birch (*Betula*); dicotyledon, deciduous tree or machaka, having white, grey, yellow or black bark and alternate leaves, widely found in northeast China, including silver birch and black birch

婳(嫿) huà ☞［姽婳］(guǐhuà) on p.734

huái（ㄏㄨㄞˊ）

怀(懷) huái ❶ 胸部或胸前 bosom：掩着～ cover one's chest｜小孩儿睡在妈妈～里。The baby slept in its mother's arms. ❷ 心怀；胸怀 mind：壮～ great aspirations｜襟～ heart｜正中下～ fit in exactly with one's wishes or desires ❸ 思念；怀念 think of; yearn for：～乡 yearn for one's native place｜～友 think of a friend｜～古 meditate on the past ❹ 腹中有(胎) conceive (a child)：～胎 be pregnant｜～孕 become pregnant ❺ 心里存有 keep in mind：～恨 nurse hatred｜不～好意 harbour evil designs｜少～大志 harbour lofty ambitions when young ❻ (Huái) 姓 a surname

【怀抱】huáibào ❶ 抱在怀里 hold or carry in the arms：～着婴儿 carry a baby in one's arms ❷ 胸前 bosom：睡在母亲的～里 sleep in mother's arms ◇回到祖国的～ return to the embrace of one's homeland ❸ 心里存有 cherish：～着远大的理想 cherish lofty ideals ❹〈书 *fml.*〉心胸；打算 ambition; wish：别有～ have another ambition ❺〈方 *dial.*〉(～儿 huáibàor)指婴儿时期 babyhood

【怀表】huáibiǎo 装在衣袋里使用的表，一般比手表大 pocket watch, bigger than a wristwatch

【怀才不遇】huái cái bù yù 有才能而得不到施展的机会 have unrecognized talents

【怀春】huáichūn〈书 *fml.*〉指少女爱慕异性 (of a young girl) have thoughts of love

【怀古】huáigǔ 追念古代的事情（多用做有关古迹的诗题 oft. used in titles of poems that are reflections on historical events) meditate on the past：～伤今 meditate on the past and feel sad about the present｜赤壁～ Recalling Antiquity at Red Cliff

【怀鬼胎】huái guǐtāi〈比喻 *fig.*〉心里藏着不可告人的事或念头 have evil intentions; harbour sinister designs

【怀恨】huái//hèn 心里怨恨；记恨 nurse a hatred：～在心 nurse a hatred

【怀旧】huáijiù 怀念往事和旧日有来往的人 nostalgia; feeling of fondness for sth. in the past or old acquaintances

【怀恋】huáiliàn same as 怀念 huáiniàn：～故园风物 think fondly of one's former home

【怀念】huáiniàn 思念 cherish the memory of; think of：～故乡 yearn for one's hometown｜～亲人 think of one's kinsfolk

【怀柔】huáiróu 用政治手段笼络其他的民族或国家，使归附自己 (of feudal rulers) pacify; make a show of conciliation in order to bring a nation or state under control：～政策 policy of control through conciliation; policy of pacification

【怀胎】huái//tāi 怀孕 be (or become) pregnant：十月～ ten months of pregnancy

【怀想】huáixiǎng 怀念 think about with affection：临风～，遐思悠悠 thinking facing the wind — far away in one's reveries

【怀疑】huáiyí ❶ 疑惑；不很相信 doubt; suspect：他的话叫人～。What he said is doubtful.｜对于这个结论谁也没有～。Nobody doubted the conclusion. ❷ 猜测 doubt：我～他今天来不了。I doubt if he will come today.

【怀孕】huái//yùn 妇女或雌性哺乳动物有了胎 (of women or female mammals) be pregnant

徊 huái ☞［徘徊］(páihuái) on p.1439 ☞ huí on p.863

淮 Huái 淮河，发源于河南，流经安徽，入江苏 Huai River, originating in Henan Province and flowing through Anhui and Jiangsu provinces

【淮北】Huáiběi 指淮河以北的地区。特指安徽的北部。area north of the Huai River, particularly northern Anhui Province

【淮海】Huái-Hǎi 指以徐州为中心的淮河以北及海州（现在的连云港西南）一带的地区 Huaihai, area north of the Huai River with Xuzhou as the hub and Haizhou area (southwest of today's Lianyungang)

【淮剧】huáijù 江苏地方戏曲剧种之一，原名江淮戏，流行于淮阴、盐城等地 Huai opera, originally known as Jianghuai opera, popular in Huaiyin and Yancheng in northern Jiangsu Province

【淮南】Huáinán 指淮河以南、长江以北的地区，特指安徽的中部 the area south of the Huai River and north of the Yangtze River, central Anhui Province in particular

槐 huái ❶ 槐树，落叶乔木，羽状复叶，花淡黄色，结荚果，圆筒形。花蕾可以制黄色染料。花、果实以及根上的皮都入中药。pagoda tree; Chinese scholar tree (*Sophora japonica*); a deciduous tree, with feather-like compound leaves, light yellow flowers, round legumes. Its buds can be used to make a yellow dye, and its flowers, legumes and root bark are used as ingredients in traditional Chinese medicine. ❷ (Huái) 姓 a surname

踝 huái 小腿与脚之间部位的左右两侧的突起，是由胫骨和腓骨下端的膨大部分形成的 ankle; (in human beings) joint between the foot and the leg, formed by the tibia and the inflated part of the perinea

☞ 内踝 nèihuái on p.1399 and 外踝 wàihuái on p.1968；(图见 ☞ figure for 身体 shēntǐ on p.1701)

【踝子骨】huái ·zigǔ〈方 *dial.*〉内踝和外踝的统

称 general term for internal malleolus and external malleolus

耰 huái [耰耙](huái·bà)东北地区一种翻土的农具 a kind of harrow used in northeast China

huài (ㄏㄨㄞˋ)

坏(壞) huài ❶ 缺点多的;使人不满意的(跟'好'相对 as opposed to 'good') bad; harmful:工作做得不～。The work was pretty well done. ❷ 品质恶劣的;起破坏作用的 bad; evil:～人～事 evildoers and bad deeds ❸ 变成不健全、无用、有害 on the fritz; go on the blink; go bad; ruin; spoil:水果～了。The fruit has gone bad.|玩具摔～了。The toy crashed and broke. ❹ 使变坏 go bad; spoil:吃了不干净的食物容易～肚子。It is easy to have an upset stomach after eating food that is not clean.|成事不足,～事有余 spoil rather than accomplish things ❺ 表示身体或精神受到某种影响而达到极不舒服的程度,有时只表示程度深(of degrees of discomfort of the body or spirit) extremely; badly; awfully; very:饿～了 very hungry|气～了 be beside oneself with rage|忙～了 be dead busy|这件事可把他乐～了。This incident made him wild with joy. ❻ 坏主意 evil idea:使～ play a dirty trick|一肚子～ full of tricks

☞ 坯 pī on p.1462

【坏处】huài·chu 对人或事物有害的因素 harm; disadvantage:这么做一点～也没有。There's no harm at all in doing it.

【坏蛋】huàidàn same as 坏人 huàirén (骂人的话 curse)

【坏东西】huàidōng·xi same as 坏人 huàirén

【坏分子】huàifènzǐ 指盗窃犯、诈骗犯、杀人放火犯、流氓和其他严重破坏社会秩序的坏人 bad element; referring to thief, swindler, murderer, arsonist, hooligan or other evil people who cause major damage to social order

【坏话】huàihuà ❶ 不对的话;不入耳的话 unpleasant words:不能光听颂扬,好话～都要听。You should listen to criticisms as well as praises. ❷ 对人对事不利的话 malicious remarks; vicious talk:有话当面讲,不要在背后说人～。Don't speak ill of others behind their backs.

【坏疽】huàijū 坏死的一种,机体的大块组织坏死后,受腐败菌的作用变成黄绿色或黑色 gangrene; necrosis or death of soft tissue due to obstructed circulation, turning into yellow, green or black

【坏人】huàirén ❶ 品质恶劣的人 bad person ❷ 坏分子 evildoer

【坏事】huài//shì 使事情搞糟 mess up; make things worse:照他说的做,非～不可。Following his words will only mess things up.

【坏事】huàishì 坏事情;有害的事情 bad thing; evil deed:坏人～ evildoer and bad deed

【坏水】huàishuǐ 〈方 *dial.*〉(～儿 huàishuǐr)〈比喻 *fig.*〉狡诈的心计;坏主意 wicked idea; evil idea:一肚子～ full of wicked ideas

【坏死】huàisǐ 机体的局部组织或细胞死亡。坏死后原有的功能丧失。形成坏死的原因很多,如局部血液循环断绝,强酸、强碱等化学药品对局部组织的破坏。necrosis; death of a circumscribed part of animal or plant tissue, resulting in loss of original functions. The reasons for necrosis vary, such as blockage of local blood circulation and damage to local tissue by powerful acids, alkalis or other chemicals.

【坏账】huàizhàng 会计上指确定无法收回的账 bad debt

·huai (·ㄏㄨㄞ)

划(劃) ·huai ☞ [刨划] (bāi·huai) on p. 31

☞ huá on p.831 and huà on p.837

huān (ㄏㄨㄢ)

欢(歡、懽) huān ❶ 快乐;高兴 joyous; merry; jubilant:～喜 happy|～乐 merry|～迎 welcome|～送 see off|～呼 cheer ❷ 喜爱,也指所喜爱的人(多指情人 usu. referring to one's sweetheart) love; loved one:～心 love|新～ new sweetheart ❸〈方 *dial.*〉起劲;活跃 vigorously; with great drive; in full swing:火着得很～。The fire is burning merrily.|雨越下越～。It's raining harder and harder.|文娱活动搞得挺～。Recreational activities are in full swing.

【欢蹦乱跳】huān bèng luàn tiào 形容健康、活泼、生命力旺盛 healthy-looking and vivacious:幼儿园里的孩子个个都是～的。All the children in the kindergarten were healthy and lively. also 活蹦乱跳 huó bèng luàn tiào

【欢畅】huānchàng 高兴,痛快 elated; thoroughly delighted:心情～ elated

【欢歌】huāngē ❶ 欢乐地歌唱 joyously sing:尽情～ joyously sing to the best one can ◇汽笛在～。The siren is joyously wailing. ❷ 欢乐的歌声 merry singing:～笑语 merry singing and laughter|远处传来了青年们的阵阵～。The young people's happy singing was heard from a distance.

【欢呼】huānhū 欢乐地呼喊 hail; cheer; acclaim:热烈～ warmly cheer|～胜利 hail the victory

【欢聚】huānjù 快乐地团聚 happy reunion:～一

堂 have a joyous gathering

【欢快】huānkuài 欢乐轻快 cheerful and light-hearted：～的心情 in a cheerful mood｜～的乐曲 a lively melody

【欢乐】huānlè 快乐（多指集体的 usu. of a collective）happy；joyous：广场上～的歌声此起彼伏。Merry songs one after another from the square rose.

【欢闹】huānnào ❶ 高兴地闹着玩 play joyfully：孩子们在操场上～。The children are romping on the playing grounds. ❷ 喧闹 cacophony：～的锣鼓声、鞭炮声响成一片。Gongs and drums and firecrackers burst forth in a joyful cacophony.

【欢洽】huānqià 欢乐而融洽 friendly；congenial：两情～ friendly mutual relationship｜两人谈得十分～。The two of them talked very congenially.

【欢声】huānshēng 欢呼的声音 cheers：～雷动。Cheers resounded like peals of thunder.

【欢实】huān·shi〈方 *dial.*〉起劲；活跃 lively；full of vigour：你看，孩子们多～啊！Look! How lively the children are!｜机器转得挺～。The machine is working at full strength. also 欢势 huān·shi

【欢送】huānsòng 高兴地送别（多用集会方式 usu. in a collective fashion）see off；send off：～会 farewell meeting｜前来～的人很多。There are many people present to see them off.

【欢腾】huānténg 欢喜得手舞足蹈 jubilation；great rejoicing：喜讯传来，人们立刻～起来。There was mass rejoicing at the good news.

【欢天喜地】huān tiān xǐ dì 形容非常欢喜 with boundless joy

【欢喜】huānxǐ ❶ 快乐；高兴 joyful；happy；delighted：满心～ be filled with joy｜欢欢喜喜过春节 spend a joyful Spring Festival｜她掩藏不住心中的～。She failed to contain the joy in her heart. ❷ 喜欢；喜爱 have a weakness for；be fond of：他～打乒乓球。He likes to play table tennis.｜他很～这个孩子。He is very fond of the child.

【欢笑】huānxiào 快活地笑 laugh heartily：室内传出阵阵～声。Peals of laughter were heard from the room.

【欢心】huānxīn 对人或事物喜爱或赏识的心情 favourite；have a liking or love (for sb. or sth.)：讨人～ win people's favour｜这孩子人小嘴甜，最得爷爷奶奶的～。The honey-tongued child is the favourite of the grandparents.

【欢欣】huānxīn 快乐而兴奋 joy；elation：～鼓舞 be filled with exultation

【欢颜】huānyán〈书 *fml.*〉快乐的表情；笑容 happy appearance：强作～ force oneself to look happy

【欢迎】huānyíng ❶ 很高兴地迎接 welcome；greet：～大会 welcome meeting｜～贵宾 welcome distinguished guests ❷ 乐意接受 readily accept：～你参加我们的工作。You're welcome to join us in our work.｜新产品很受消费者的～。The new product has been well received by customers.

【欢悦】huānyuè 欢乐喜悦 happy；joyous：满心～ happy in mind｜～的笑声 happy laugh

【欢跃】huānyuè same as 欢腾 huānténg

讙（嚾） huān〈书 *fml.*〉❶ 喧哗 noisy ❷ same as 欢 huān

獾（貛） huān 狗獾 badger

驩 huān〈书 *fml.*〉same as 欢 huān

huán（ㄏㄨㄢˊ）

还（還） huán ❶ 返回原来的地方或恢复原来的状态 return；go or come back；resume an earlier state：～家 go home｜～乡 return to one's native place｜～原 return to an original condition or form｜～俗（of Buddhist monks and nuns or Taoist priests）resume secular life ❷ 归还 give back；return：偿～ pay back｜～书 return books ❸ 回报别人对自己的行动 give or do sth. in return：～嘴 answer back｜～手 strike back｜～击 fight back｜～价 counter-offer｜～礼 return a salute；present a gift in return｜以牙～牙，以眼～眼 a tooth for a tooth, an eye for an eye ❹ (Huán) 姓 a surname

☞ hái on p. 753

【还报】huánbào 报答；回报 return；retribution

【还本】huán//běn 归还借款的本金 repayment of principal (or capital)：～付息 repay capital with interest

【还魂】huán//hún ❶ 死而复活（迷信）（superstition）revive after death ❷〈方 *dial.*〉same as 再生 zàishēng ③：～纸 recycled paper｜～橡胶 recycled rubber

【还击】huánjī same as 回击 huíjī

【还价】huán//jià（～儿 huán//jiàr）买方因嫌货价高而说出愿付的价格 counter-offer；counter-bid：讨价～ bargaining

【还口】huán//kǒu 回嘴 retort；answer back：骂不～not answer back when insulted｜他自知理亏，怎么说他也不～。Knowing he was in the wrong, he didn't answer back no matter what was said.

【还礼】huán//lǐ ❶ 回答别人的敬礼 return a salute：连长敬了一个礼，参谋长也举手～。The company commander saluted, and the chief of staff returned the salute. ❷ 回赠礼品 send a present in return

【还情】huán//qíng 报答别人的恩情或美意 repay a favour

【还手】huán//shǒu 因被打或受到攻击而反过来

打击对方 strike (or hit) back：打不～ do not hit back even when being struck｜无～之力 have no strength to hit back

【还俗】huán//sú 僧尼或出家的道士恢复普通人的身份(of Buddhist monks and nuns or Taoist priests) resume secular life

【还席】huán//xí (被人请吃饭之后)回请对方吃饭 give a return dinner：明天晚上我～，请诸位光临。It will be my treat tomorrow evening, please come for dinner.

【还阳】huán//yáng 死而复活(迷信) (superstitious) return to life from the nether world

【还原】huán//yuán ❶ 事物恢复原状 return to an original condition or form ❷ 指含氧物质被夺去氧。也泛指物质在化学反应中得到电子或电子对偏近。如氧化铜和氢气加热后生成铜和水。还原和氧化是伴同发生的。reduction; deoxidize, or refers to gaining an electron or a close electron pair in a chemical change, e.g., copper oxide and hydrogen become copper and water after heating; reduction and oxidation develop in tandem.

【还愿】huán//yuàn ❶ (求神保佑的人)实践对神许下的报酬 fulfil a vow to a deity ❷〈比喻 *fig.*〉实践诺言 fulfil one's promise

【还债】huán//zhài 归还所欠的债 pay one's debts; repay a debt

【还账】huán//zhàng 归还所欠的债或偿付所欠的货款 pay one's debts; settle accounts

【还嘴】huán//zuǐ same as 回嘴 huí//zuǐ

环(環) huán ❶ (～儿 huánr)圆圈形的东西 ring; hoop：耳～ earring｜花～ garland｜铁～ iron hoop ❷ 指射击、射箭比赛中射中环靶的环数，射中靶心，一般以十环计，离靶心远的，所得环数依次递减 target; shooting mark divided by 10 centric circles, the farther from the bull's-eye, the less the score：三枪打中了二十八～ hit 28 points with three rifles ❸ 环节 link：从事科学研究，搜集资料是最基本的一～。Data collection is the most basic link in scientific research. ❹ 围绕 surround; encircle：～绕 surround｜～球 round the world｜～城铁路 a railway encircling the city ❺ (Huán)姓 a surname

【环靶】huánbǎ 当中一个圆点，外面套着若干层圆圈的靶子 round (bull's-eye) target in sports

【环保】huánbǎo 环境保护的简称 abbr. for 环境保护 huánjìng bǎohù

【环抱】huánbào 围绕(多用于自然景物 usu. of natural scenery) surround; encircle：群山～ be mountain-rimmed; nestling among the hills｜青松翠柏，～陵墓。The tomb is surrounded by green pine and cypress.

【环衬】huánchèn 指某些书籍封面后、扉页前的一页，一般不印任何文字 lining paper; a blank page between the front cover and title page of some books

【环岛】huándǎo 指交叉路口中心的高出路面的圆形设置 traffic circle

【环顾】huángù〈书 *fml.*〉向四周看；环视 look about (or around)：～左右 look around｜～四座 look around at all the people present

【环合】huánhé 环绕(多用于自然景物 usu. of natural environment) surround：四面竹树～，清幽异常。With bamboo and trees on all sides, the place is sequestened in the exceptional peace and quiet of rural repose.

【环节】huánjié ❶ 某些低等动物如蚯蚓、蜈蚣等，身体由许多大小差不多的环状结构互相连接组成，这些结构叫做环节，能伸缩 segment; connected ring-like structures of similar sizes that form the body of some lower animals, such as earthworm and centipede, extendible and contractible ❷ 指互相关联的许多事物中的一个 link; sector：主要～ key link｜薄弱～ the weak link

【环节动物】huánjié dòngwù 动物的一门，身体长而柔软，由许多环节构成，表面有像玻璃的薄膜，头、胸、腹不分明，肠子长而直，前端为口，后端为肛门，如蚯蚓、水蛭等 annelid; any segmented worm of the phylum Annelida such as earthworm, and leech, having a long and soft segmented body covered with glassy thin film, and indistinguishable head, chest and belly; the front end of its long and straight intestine serving as the mouth, and its rear end, the anus

【环境】huánjìng ❶ 周围的地方 environment; surroundings; circumstances：～优美 beautiful environment｜～卫生 sanitation ❷ 周围的情况和条件 surroundings; conditions：客观～ objective conditions｜工作～ work environment

【环境保护】huánjìng bǎohù 有关防止自然环境恶化，改善环境使之适于人类劳动和生活的工作 environmental protection; 简称 abbr. 环保 huánbǎo

【环境污染】huánjìng wūrǎn 由于人为的因素，环境受到有害物质的污染，使生物的生长繁殖和人类的正常生活受到有害影响 pollution of the environment; environmental pollution caused by man-made factors that harm both reproduction of organisms and normal human life

【环流】huánliú 流体的循环流动，由流体各部分的温度、密度、浓度不同，或由外力的推动而形成 circulation of fluid, formed by differences in temperature, density and concentration of the fluid or outside forces：全球大气～ atmospheric circulation of the whole globe

【环球】huánqiú ❶ 围绕地球 round the world：～旅行 go world trotting; travel round the world ❷ same as 寰球 huánqiú

【环绕】huánrào 围绕 surround; encircle：村庄四周有竹林～。The village is surrounded by bamboo trees.

【环生】huánshēng 一个接一个地发生(of sth. bad) occur one after another：险象～ signs of danger appearing everywhere

【环视】huánshì 向周围看 look around：～四周 look around

【环卫】huánwèi 指关于环境卫生的 environmental sanitation：～工人 sanitation worker｜～部门 public sanitation department

【环线】huánxiàn 环行路线 loop line：地铁～ subway loop line｜沿～行驶 drive along the loop line

【环行】huánxíng 绕着圈子走 going in a ring：～电车 circular-route tram｜～公路 ring road｜～一周 make a circuit

【环形】huánxíng 圆环。也指这样的形状。annular; ring-like shape

【环形交叉】huánxíng jiāochā 平面交叉的一种。两条或两条以上的道路相交时，通过交叉路口的车辆一律绕环岛单向环形行驶，再转入所去的道路。roundabout; intersection of two or more roads where vehicles crossing have to circle the roundabout in a single direction and then continue on their way

【环形山】huánxíngshān 月球、火星等表面上最突出的一种结构。山呈环形，四周高起，中间平地上又常有小山，多由陨星撞击而形成。crater; the most prominent structure resulting from meteor impacts on the surface of the moon and Mars, with mountains skirting a flatland in the middle that is often studded with small hills

【环宇】huányǔ same as 寰宇 huányǔ

【环志】huánzhì 戴在候鸟身上的金属或塑料环形标志，上面刻有国名、单位、编码等标记，用做研究候鸟迁徙规律的依据 metal or plastic, ring mark attached to the body of a migratory bird with names of country and organization and number on it, used for studying the migratory patterns of birds

【环状软骨】huánzhuàng ruǎngǔ 人的喉部下方的软骨，呈环形，上连甲状软骨，下连气管 cricoid, soft bone below the throat, ring-like, connecting thyroid cartilage on the top and its windpipe on the end

【环子】huán·zi 圆圈形的东西 ring; link：门～ knocker

郇 Huán 姓 a surname
☞ Xún on p. 2187

萑 huán 多年生草本植物，地下茎粗壮，叶子心脏形，花白色带紫色条纹，果实椭圆形。全草入药。*Hypericum patulum*; a kind of violet, herbaceous perennial, leafy-stemmed plant having white flowers with purple stripes, heart-shaped leaves, and round fruit, used as herbal medicine

洹 Huán 洹河，水名，在河南。过去叫安阳河。Huanhe, a river in Henan Province, formerly called 安阳河 Ānyánghé

桓 Huán 姓 a surname

萑 huán 萑苻泽（Huánfú Zé），春秋时郑国泽名。据记载，那里常有盗贼聚集出没。Huanfu Ze, a pond in the state of Zheng during the Spring and Autumn Period, where banditry was rampant according to records

貆 huán〈书 *fml*.〉❶ 幼小的貉 young raccoon dog ❷ 豪猪 porcupine
〈古 *arch*.〉same as 獾 huān

锾 huán〈古代 *arch*.〉重量单位，一锾等于六两 *huan*, unit of weight that is equal to 6 *liang*

圜 huán ☞ 转圜 zhuǎnhuán on p. 2519
☞ yuán on p. 2365

阛 huán［阛阓］（huánhuì）〈书 *fml*.〉街市 street market

澴 Huán 澴河，水名，在湖北 Huanhe, a river in Hubei Province

寰 huán 广大的地域 extensive region：～宇 globe; earth; whole world｜～海 sea｜人～ humanity; world of man

【寰球】huánqiú 整个地球；全世界 earth; whole world; also 环球 huánqiú

【寰宇】huányǔ〈书 *fml*.〉寰球；天下 globe; earth; whole world：声震～ enjoy a global reputation; also 环宇 huányǔ

嬛 huán ☞ 琅嬛 lánghuán on p. 1151

缳 huán〈书 *fml*.〉❶ 绳索的套子 noose：投～（上吊）hang oneself ❷ 绞杀 strangle：～首 hang (as punishment)

瓛（瓛） huán 玉圭的一种，多用于人名 *huan*, a kind of jade, usu. used in names

轘 huán 轘辕（Huányuán），关名，在河南轘辕山 Huanyuan, name of a pass in Huanyuanshan Mountain, Henan Province
☞ huàn on p. 849

鹮 huán 鸟类的一科，身体大，嘴细长而弯曲，腿长。生活在水边。ibis (*Threskiornithiclae*); bird having a big body, curved long thin mouth, and long legs, and living by water

鬟 huán 妇女梳的环形的发髻 bun of hair：云～ high rings

huǎn（ㄏㄨㄢˇ）

缓 huǎn ❶ 迟；慢 slow; unhurried：迟～ slow｜～步 walk slowly｜～不济急。Slow action cannot save an urgent situation. ❷ 延缓；推迟 delay; postpone; put off：～办 postpone doing sth.｜～期 postpone a deadline｜这事～几天再说。Let's put it off for a couple of days. ❸ 缓和；不紧张 not tense; relaxed：～冲 buffer｜～急 degree of urgency ❹ 恢复正常的生理状态 recuperate; come to：昏过去又～过来 revive after coma｜蔫了的花，浇上水又～过来了。The withered flowers revived after being watered.

【缓兵之计】huǎn bīng zhī jì 使敌人延缓进攻的计策。借指使事态暂时缓和同时积极设法应付的策略。measures to stave off an attack; stratagem to gain a respite

【缓不济急】huǎn bù jì jí 指行动或办法赶不上迫切需要 slow action cannot save a critical situation: 临渴掘井，～。It is too late to dig a well when one is already thirsty.

【缓冲】huǎnchōng 使冲突缓和 buffer; cushion: ～地带 buffer zone | ～作用 cushioning effect

【缓和】huǎnhé ❶（局势、气氛等）变和缓（of situation, mood, etc.）relax; mitigate; ease up: 紧张的心情慢慢～下来了。My nervous mind gradually relaxed. ❷ 使和缓 ease; reach a détente: ～空气 ease the atmosphere | ～紧张局势 ease a tense situation

【缓急】huǎnjí ❶ 和缓和急迫 greater or lesser urgency: 分别轻重～ in order of importance and urgency ❷ 急迫的事；困难的事 emergency: ～相助 help each other in case of need

【缓颊】huǎnjiá 〈书 *fml.*〉为人求情 intercede for sb.; put in a good word for sb.

【缓解】huǎnjiě ❶ 剧烈、紧张的程度有所减轻；缓和 relieve; alleviate; ease: 病情～ alleviate the patient's condition | 展宽马路后，交通阻塞现象有了～。Traffic congestion was eased after the road was widened. ❷ 使缓解 alleviate: ～市内交通拥挤状况 alleviate traffic congestion within the city

【缓慢】huǎnmàn 不迅速；慢 slow: 行动～ slow in movement

【缓坡】huǎnpō 和水平面所成角度小的地面；坡度小的坡 gentle slope

【缓期】huǎnqī 把预定的时间向后推 suspend; put off a deadline: ～执行 suspend a sentence temporarily | ～付款 delay (or defer) payment

【缓气】huǎn//qì 恢复正常呼吸（多指极度疲劳后的休息 usu. referring to rest after extreme tiredness) get breathing space; have a respite; take a breather: 乘胜追击，不给敌人～的机会。Advance on the crest of a victory and give no respite to one's adversary.

【缓限】huǎnxiàn 延缓限期 suspend; put off a deadline: 予以通融，～三天。Please make an exception in my favour and put off the deadline for three days.

【缓泻】huǎnxiè 用药物润滑肠壁、软化粪便使大便通畅 mild purgative; also 轻泻 qīngxiè

【缓行】huǎnxíng ❶ 慢慢地走或行驶 walk or drive slowly: 拄杖～ walk slowly and carry a big stick | 车辆～ slow drive ❷ 暂缓实行 postpone implementation of a plan, etc.: 计划～ postpone a plan

【缓刑】huǎnxíng 对犯人所判处的刑罚在一定条件下延期执行或不执行。缓刑期间，如不再犯新罪，就不再执行原判刑罚，否则，就把前后所判处的刑罚合并执行。probation; temporary conditional suspension of a sentence; criminal who does not commit a new crime during probation is not required to serve the original sentence, but if he does he will serve a combined sentence

【缓醒】huǎn·xing 〈方 *dial.*〉失去知觉之后又恢复过来 revive; regain consciousness; come to; come round

【缓役】huǎnyì 缓期服兵役 deferment (of conscription)

【缓征】huǎnzhēng 缓期征收或征集 postpone the imposition of a tax or levy

huàn（ㄏㄨㄢˋ）

幻 huàn ❶ 没有现实根据的；不真实的 unreal; imaginary; illusory: 虚～ unreal | 梦～ dream | ～想 fancy ❷ 奇异地变化 magical; changeable: ～术 magic | 变～莫测 change unpredictably

【幻灯】huàndēng ❶ 利用强光和透镜的装置，映射在白幕上的图画或文字 slide show: 放～ show slides | 看～ watch a slide show ❷ 幻灯机 slide projector

【幻灯机】huàndēngjī 放映幻灯的装置，主要由光源、透镜和机箱构成 slide projector, mainly consisting of a light source, lens and case; also 幻灯 huàndēng

【幻化】huànhuà 奇异地变化 magically change: 雪后的山谷，～成一个奇特的琉璃世界。The snow changed the valley into a magical frozen world.

【幻景】huànjǐng 虚幻的景象；幻想中的景物 illusion; mirage

【幻境】huànjìng 虚幻奇异的境界 dreamland; fairyland: 走进原始森林，好像走进了童话的～。Entering the virgin forest, one felt as if in a fairyland.

【幻觉】huànjué 视觉、听觉、触觉等方面，没有外在刺激而出现的虚假的感觉。患有某种精神病或在催眠状态中的人常出现幻觉。hallucination; illusion, delusion, etc.; something that deceives by producing a false or misleading impression of reality without external stimulation. Those who suffer a mental disease, or those in hypnosis often have delusions.

【幻梦】huànmèng 虚幻的梦；幻想 illusion; dream: 一场～ an idle dream | 从～中醒悟过来 wake up from an idle dream

【幻灭】huànmiè （希望等）像幻境一样地消失 (of hope, etc.) vanish into thin air

【幻术】huànshù same as 魔术 móshù

【幻想】huànxiǎng ❶ 以社会或个人的理想和愿望为依据，对还没有实现的事物有所想像 imagine; dream: 科学～ scientific imagination | ～成为一名月球上的公民 dream of becoming a resident on the moon ❷ 这样的想像 illusion; fancy：一个美丽的～ a beautiful illusion

【幻象】huànxiàng 幻想出来的或由幻觉产生的形象 mirage; phantom; phantasm

【幻影】huànyǐng 幻想中的景象 unreal image

奂(奐) huàn 〈书 *fml*.〉 ❶ 盛；多 abundant; plentiful ❷ 文采鲜明 brilliant

宦 huàn ❶ 官吏 official：～海 official circles ❷ 做官 fill an office：仕～ fill an office｜～游 leave home and take up government employment ❸ 宦官 eunuch ❹ (Huàn) 姓 a surname

【宦官】huànguān 君主时代宫廷内侍奉帝王及其家属的人员，由阉割后的男子充任 eunuch; man castrated to serve the emperor and his family in imperial palace in the ancient times; also 太监 tàijiàn

【宦海】huànhǎi 〈比喻 *fig*.〉 官吏争夺功名富贵的场所；官场 official circles：～沉浮 ups and downs of officialdom; the vicissitudes of an official career｜～风波 disturbance in official circles

【宦途】huàntú 〈书 *fml*.〉指做官的生活、经历、遭遇等；官场 official career：～失意 official career full of frustrations

【宦游】huànyóu 〈书 *fml*.〉为求做官而出外奔走 go from place to place seeking an official post：～四方 wander about seeking office

换 huàn ❶ 给人东西同时从他那里取得别的东西 exchange; barter; trade：交～ exchange｜调～ change ❷ 变换；更换 change：～车 change buses｜～人 substitution of players｜～衣服 change one's clothes ❸ 兑换 exchange; convert

【换班】huàn//bān (工作人员)按时轮流替换上班 (of workers) change shifts：日班和夜班的工人正在～。Day-time and night-time workers are changing shifts now.

【换茬】huàn//chá 一种农作物收获后，换种另一种农作物 change of crops

【换代】huàndài ❶ 改变朝代 change of dynasty or regime：改朝～ ❷ 指产品在结构、性能等方面比原来的有明显的改进和发展 (of a product's structure and property) upgrade; regenerate：～产品 replace the older generations of products with new ones｜加快产品的更新～ accelerate the development of new models and new products

【换防】huàn//fáng 原在某处驻防的部队移交防守任务，由新调来的部队接替 relieve a garrison army and replace it with new troops

【换个儿】huàn//gèr 互相调换位置 change places：咱俩换个个儿坐。Let's change places.｜这两个抽屉大小不一样，不能～。The two drawers are not the same size, so they are not interchangeable.

【换工】huàn//gōng 农业生产单位之间或农户之间在自愿基础上互相换着干活 exchange labour between agricultural units and farm households on a voluntary basis

【换季】huàn//jì (衣着)随着季节而更换 change garments according to the season：眼看就热了，～衣服要准备好。It's becoming warmer now, so we should take out all the clothes for the new season.

【换肩】huàn//jiān 把挑的担子或扛的东西从一个肩移到另一个肩上 shift the carrying pole onto the other shoulder

【换届】huànjiè 领导机构一届期满后另行改选或调任 replace or re-elect when a term of office expires：～选举 re-election (when the current term expires)

【换马】huànmǎ 〈比喻 *fig*.〉撤换担负某项职务的人(含贬义 derog.) change horses (midway); have sb. replaced (before his term is over)

【换脑筋】huàn nǎojīn 指改造思想或改变旧的观念 change one's way of thinking

【换气扇】huànqìshàn 安在墙壁或窗户上，排除室内污浊气体，保持空气清新的电风扇 ventilation fan on the wall or window for removing dirty air; also 排风扇 páifēngshàn

【换钱】huàn//qián ❶ 把整钱换成零钱或把零钱换成整钱；把一种货币换成另一种货币 break a bill or note; get change; change coins into bills; change money (from one currency into another) ❷ 把东西卖出得到钱 sell：破铜烂铁也可以～。Scrap iron can be sold for money.

【换亲】huànqīn 两家互娶对方的女儿做媳妇 (of two families) take each other's daughters as daughters-in-law

【换取】huànqǔ 用交换的方法取得 exchange (or barter) sth. for; get in return：用工业品～农产品 exchange (or barter) industrial products for farm produce

【换算】huànsuàn 把某种单位的数量折合成另一种单位的数量 conversion

【换汤不换药】 huàn tāng bù huàn yào 〈比喻 *fig*.〉只改变形式，不改变内容 same medicine under a different name — same old stuff with a different label; change in form but not in content (or essence); old wine in new bottles

【换帖】huàn//tiě 〈旧时 *old*〉朋友结拜为异性兄弟时，交换写着姓名、年龄、籍贯、家世的帖儿 exchange cards with personal and family details when becoming sworn brothers：～弟兄 sworn brothers

【换文】huàn//wén (国家与国家之间)交换文书 (between states) exchange of notes (or letters)

【换文】huànwén 国家与国家之间就已经达成协议的事项而交换的内容相同的文书。一般用来补充正式条约或确定已达成的协议，如建立外交关系的换文，处理边界问题的换文等。copies of an agreement between states; memorandum of understanding on a specific issue, generally supplementing a formal treaty or confirming an agreement reached, e.g. on establishing diplomatic relations or deadling with boundary issues

【换洗】huànxǐ 更换并洗涤(衣服、床单等) change and wash (clothes, linen, etc.):衣服要勤～。Clothes should be frequently changed and washed.|这次出门,就带了几件～的衣服。I just took a few changes of clothes for this trip.

【换血】huàn//xiě〈比喻 *fig.*〉调整、更换组织、机构等的成员 reorganization by introduction of fresh personnel

【换牙】huàn//yá 乳牙逐一脱落,恒牙逐一生出来。一般人在六岁到八岁时开始换牙,十二岁到十四岁时全部乳牙被恒牙所代替。(of a child) grow permanent teeth, usu. starting between 6 to 8 years old; By 12 to 14 all milk teeth are replaced by permanent teeth.

【换言之】huàn yán zhī〈书 *fml.*〉换句话说 in other words

唤 huàn 发出大声,使对方觉醒、注意或随声而来 call out; summon:呼～ call out|～醒 wake up|～起 arouse

【唤起】huànqǐ ❶ 号召使奋起 arouse:～民众 arouse the masses of the people ❷ 引起(注意、回忆等)(of attention and memory) call; draw; recall:这封信～了我对往事的回忆。The letter evoked old memories.

【唤头】huàn·tou 街头流动的小贩或服务性行业的人(如磨刀的、理发的)用来招引顾客的各种响器 percussion tool (used by itinerant knife sharpeners, barbers, etc., to attract customers)

【唤醒】huànxǐng ❶ 叫醒 awaken; wake up:他把我从睡梦中～。He woke me up from a deep sleep. ❷ 使醒悟 arouse:～民众 arouse the people

涣 huàn 消散 dissolve; vanish:～散 slack

【涣涣】huànhuàn〈书 *fml.*〉形容水势盛大(of water) overflowing

【涣然】huànrán 形容嫌隙、疑虑、误会等完全消除 (of misgivings, doubts, etc.) melt away; disappear; vanish:～冰释 disappear; vanish; melt away (like ice)

【涣散】huànsàn ❶(精神、组织、纪律等)散漫;松懈 (of morale, organization, discipline, etc.) lax; slack:士气～ low morale|精神～ be demoralized ❷ 使涣散 sap:～军心 sap the army's morale|～组织 be lax in organization

浣(澣) huàn ❶ 洗 wash:～衣 wash clothes|～纱 rinse yarn ❷ 唐代定制,官吏十天一次休息沐浴,每月分为上浣、中浣、下浣,后来借作上旬、中旬、下旬的别称 in the Tang Dynasty, officials could take a day off for rest and bathing every ten days and three times a month; later indicating any of the three ten-day intervals of a month

患 huàn ❶ 祸害;灾难 trouble; peril; disaster:～难 trials and tribulations|水～ flood|防～未然 take preventive measures ❷ 忧虑 worry:忧～ worry|～得～失 worry about personal gains and losses ❸ 害(病) contract; suffer from:～病 suffer from an illness; fall ill|～者 patient

【患处】huànchù 长疮疖或受外伤的地方 injured or affected part (of a patient's body)

【患得患失】huàn dé huàn shī《论语·阳货》:'其未得之也,患得之;既得之,患失之。'指对于个人的利害得失斤斤计较。*Analects·Yang Huo*: 'Before they get their posts, they are constantly afraid of not being able to secure them; and after they have obtained their posts, they are constantly afraid of losing them.' be swayed by considerations of gains while experiencing losses, and be swayed by considerations of losses while making gains; obsession with personal gains and losses

【患难】huànnàn 困难和危险的处境 trials and tribulations; adversity; trouble:同甘苦,共～ share hardships and dangers|～之交(共过患难的朋友) friends in adversity; tested friends

【患难与共】huànnàn yǔ gòng 在不利处境中,共同承受困难或灾祸 go through thick and thin together; share weal and woe

【患者】huànzhě 患某种疾病的人 sufferer; patient:肺结核～ person suffering from tuberculosis

焕 huàn 光明;光亮 shining; glowing:～发 shine

【焕发】huànfā ❶ 光彩四射 shine; glow:精神～ full of vim and vigour|容光～ one's face glowing with health ❷ 振作 irradiate:～激情 irradiate passion|～革命精神 radiate a revolutionary spirit

【焕然】huànrán 形容有光彩 shining:～一新 take on an altogether new aspect

【焕然一新】huànrán yī xīn 形容出现了崭新的面貌 take on an altogether new aspect:店面经过装饰,～。The shop took on an entirely new look after a facelift.

逭 huàn〈书 *fml.*〉逃;避 evade; get away from:罪实难～。One cannot evade responsibility or guilt.

睆 huàn〈书 *fml.*〉❶ 明亮 bright ❷ 美好 beautiful

痪 huàn ☞ 瘫痪 tānhuàn on p.1858

㬇 Huàn 姓 a surname

豢 huàn same as 豢养 huànyǎng

【豢养】huànyǎng 喂养(牲畜) feed; groom;

keep;〈比喻 *fig*.〉收买并利用 buy over and make use of

漶 huàn ☞ 漫漶 mànhuàn on p.1301

鲩 huàn ☞ 草鱼 cǎoyú on p.195

擐 huàn〈书 *fml*.〉穿 wear; put on:～甲执兵 put on armour and take up arms|躬～甲胄 put on armour

轘 huàn〈古代 *arch*.〉一种用车分裂人体的酷刑 cruel torture in ancient times, execution by tearing the body apart by lassoing a person's limbs to several carts and driving the carts in opposite directions

☞ huán on p.845

huāng(ㄏㄨㄤ)

肓 huāng ☞ 病入膏肓 bìng rù gāo huāng on p.143

荒 huāng ❶ 荒芜 waste:地～了。The land lies waste. ❷ 荒凉 desolate; barren:～村 deserted village|～郊 desolate place outside town|～岛 wild island ❸ 荒歉 famine; crop failure:～年 famine year|备～ prepare against crop failure ❹ 荒地 wasteland:生～ virgin soil|熟～ abandoned cultivated land|开～ reclaim wasteland|垦～ reclaim wasteland ❺ 荒疏 neglect; out of practice:别把功课～了。Don't neglect your lessons.|多年不下棋,～了。It's such a long time since I played chess the last time, I'm getting rusty. ❻ 严重的缺乏 shortage; scarcity:粮～ grain shortage|煤～ coal shortage|房～ housing shortage ❼ 不合情理 unreasonable:～谬 absurd|～诞 fantastic ❽〈方 *dial*.〉不确定的 uncertain:～信 unconfirmed information|～数儿 rough figure ❾〈书 *fml*.〉迷乱;放纵 indulge:～淫 dissolute

【荒草】huāngcǎo 野草 weeds:～丛生 overgrown with weeds

【荒村】huāngcūn 荒僻的村落 deserted village

【荒诞】huāngdàn 极不真实;极不近情理 fantastic; absurd; incredible:～不经 preposterous|～无稽 fantastic|情节～ incredible plot

【荒地】huāngdì 没有开垦或没有耕种的土地 wasteland; uncultivated (or undeveloped) land

【荒废】huāngfèi ❶ 该种而没有耕种 leave uncultivated; lie waste:村里没有一亩～的土地。Not a single *mu* of land in the village lies waste. ❷ 荒疏 neglect practice:～学业 neglect one's studies ❸ 不利用;浪费(时间) fall into disuse; waste time:他学习抓得很紧,从不～一点工夫。He studied hard, never wasting a single moment.

【荒古】huānggǔ 太古 remote antiquity:～世界 world of remote antiquity

【荒寂】huāngjì 荒凉寂静 desolate and still:四周空旷～。It is bleak and quiet open country all round.|～的山谷 a bleak and quiet valley

【荒凉】huāngliáng 人烟少;冷清 bleak and desolate:一片～ scene of desolation

【荒乱】huāngluàn 指社会秩序极端不安定 great social disorder:～年月,民不安生。The people have no peace of life in times of turmoil.

【荒谬】huāngmiù 极端错误;非常不合情理 absurd; preposterous:～绝伦 absolutely preposterous|～的论调 ridiculous formulation

【荒漠】huāngmò ❶ 荒凉而又无边无际 desolate and boundless:～的草原 desolate and boundless grasslands ❷ 荒凉的沙漠或旷野 bleak and boundless desert; wilderness:渺无人烟的～ uninhabited wilderness|变～为绿洲 turn a wilderness into an oasis

【荒年】huāngnián 农作物收成很坏或没有收成的年头儿 famine (or lean) year

【荒僻】huāngpì 荒凉偏僻 desolate and out-of-the-way:～的山区 desolate mountain area

【荒歉】huāngqiàn 农作物没有收成或收成很坏 famine; crop failure

【荒时暴月】huāng shí bào yuè 指年成很坏或青黄不接的时候 time of scarcity; lean year; hard times

【荒疏】huāngshū (学业、技术)因平时缺乏练习而生疏 rusty; (study or skill) out of practice:因病休学,功课都～了。I'm getting rusty with lessons as I have lost schooltime due to illness.

【荒数】huāngshù〈方 *dial*.〉(～儿 huāngshùr)大约的、不确定的数目 approximate number

【荒唐】huāng·táng ❶ (思想、言行)错误到使人觉得奇怪的程度 (of thought, words and action) absurd; preposterous:～之言 preposterous words|～无稽 frivolous and unfounded|这个想法毫无道理,实在～。This idea is unreasonable and preposterous. ❷ (行为)放荡,没有节制 dissipated; loose; intemperate

【荒无人烟】huāng wú rén yān 十分荒凉,没有人家 desolate and uninhabited

【荒芜】huāngwú (田地)因无人管理而长满野草 (fields) go out of cultivation:田园～。The land was allowed to go to waste.

【荒信】huāngxìn〈方 *dial*.〉(～儿 huāngxìnr)不确定的或没有证实的消息 unconfirmed news

【荒野】huāngyě 荒凉的野外 wilderness; wilds

【荒淫】huāngyín 贪恋酒色 dissolute; licentious; debauched:～无耻 lead a life of luxury and debauchery

【荒原】huāngyuán 荒凉的原野 wasteland; wilderness:过去沙碱为害的～,变成了稻浪翻滚的良田。A gravelly, alkaline wasteland has been turned into fine paddy fields.

塃 huāng〈方 *dial*.〉开采出来的矿石 ore

慌 huāng 慌张 flurried; flustered; confused: 惊～ alarmed|恐～ panic|心～ be flustered|～手～脚 do sth. in a confused manner|沉住气,不要～。Keep calm. Don't panic!

慌 ·huang 表示难以忍受(用做补语,前面加'得' used after 得 ·de as a complement) awfully; unbearably: 疼得～ unbearably painful|累得～ be tired out; be dog-tired|闷得～ bored beyond endurance

【慌促】huāngcù 慌忙急促 in a hurry: 临行～,把东西忘在家里了。I was in such a hurry that I left my things at home.

【慌乱】huāngluàn 慌张而混乱 flurried; alarmed and bewildered: 脚步～ flurried pace|心中一点也不～ not be at all alarmed and bewildered

【慌忙】huāngmáng 急忙;不从容 in a great rush: ～之中,把衣服都穿反了。In a hurry, I wore my clothes the wrong side out.

【慌神儿】huāng//shénr 心慌意乱 in a flutter; mentally confused: 考试时不能～。Be sure to remain cool-headed during the examination.|越～,越容易出错。The more you panic, the more easily you make mistakes.

【慌手慌脚】huāng shǒu huāng jiǎo (～的 huāng shǒu huāng jiǎo ·de)形容做事慌张忙乱 in a rush; in a flurry

【慌张】huāng·zhāng 心里不沉着,动作忙乱 flurried; flustered; confused: 神色～ look flurried (or flustered)

huáng(ㄏㄨㄤˊ)

皇 huáng ❶〈书 *fml*.〉盛大 grand; magnificent ❷ 君主;皇帝 monarch; emperor: ～宫 imperial palace|三～五帝 Three Emperors and Five Sovereigns (in ancient China) ❸ (Huáng) 姓 a surname
〈古 *arch*.〉same as 遑 huáng

【皇朝】huángcháo 封建王朝 feudal dynasty

【皇储】huángchǔ 确定的继承皇位的人 crown prince; designated heir to the throne

【皇帝】huángdì 最高封建统治者的称号。在我国皇帝的称号始于秦始皇。emperor; in China, the title of emperor started with Qinshihuang, the founding father of the Qin Dynasty

【皇甫】Huángfǔ 姓 a surname

【皇宫】huánggōng 皇帝居住的地方 imperial palace

【皇冠】huángguān 皇帝戴的帽子,多用来象征皇权 imperial crown, symbolizing imperial power

【皇后】huánghòu 皇帝的妻子 empress

【皇皇】[1] huánghuáng same as 惶惶 huánghuáng

【皇皇】[2] huánghuáng same as 遑遑 huánghuáng

【皇皇】[3] huánghuáng 形容堂皇,盛大 grand; splendid: ～文告 grand statement|～巨著 monumental work; magnum opus

【皇家】huángjiā same as 皇室 huángshì

【皇历】huáng·li same as 历书 lìshū; also 黄历 huáng·li

【皇粮】huángliáng ❶〈旧时 *old*〉指官府的粮食;公粮 public grain ❷ 借指国家供给的资金、物资 funds, goods, etc. provided by the government

【皇权】huángquán 指皇帝的权力 imperial power (or authority)

【皇上】huáng·shang 我国封建时代称在位的皇帝 emperor; His Majesty; Your Mejesty

【皇室】huángshì ❶ 皇帝的家族 imperial family (or house) ❷ 指朝廷 court: 效忠～ loyal to the court

【皇太后】huángtàihòu 皇帝的母亲 empress dowager

【皇太子】huángtàizǐ 皇帝的儿子中已经确定继承皇位的 crown prince

【皇天】huángtiān 指天;苍天 Heaven (personified); High Heaven: ～后土 Heaven and Earth (personified and apostrophized, esp. in a spoken vow)|～不负苦心人。Providence doesn't let down a man who does his best.

【皇天后土】huáng tiān hòu tǔ 指天和地。古人认为天地能主持公道,主宰万物。Heaven and Earth (personified and apostrophized, esp. a spoken vow), in the belief of ancient people that Heaven and Earth upheld justice

【皇位】huángwèi 皇帝的地位 throne: 继承～ succeed the throne

【皇子】huángzǐ 皇帝的儿子 son of an emperor

【皇族】huángzú 皇帝的家族 people of imperial lineage; imperial kinsfolk

黄[1] huáng ❶ 像丝瓜花或向日葵花的颜色 yellow, like the flowers of towel gourd or sunflower ❷ 指黄金 gold: ～货 gold|～白之物 gold and silver ❸ (～儿 huángr)指蛋黄 yolk: 双～蛋 egg with two yolks ❹ 象征腐化堕落,特指色情 pornographic: 查禁～书 ban pornographic books ❺ (Huáng)指黄河 Yellow River: 治～ harness the Yellow River|～泛区 area formerly flooded by the Yellow River ❻ (Huáng) 指黄帝,我国古代传说中的帝王 Huangdi; Yellow Emperor: 炎～子孙 descendants of Yandi and Huangdi ❼ (Huáng) 姓 a surname

黄[2] huáng 事情失败或计划不能实现 fail; fizzle out; come to nothing; fall through: 买卖～了。The deal is off.

【黄斑】huángbān 眼球视网膜正中央的一部分,略呈圆形,黄色。黄斑正对瞳孔,物体的影像正落在这一点上时,看得最清楚。yellow spot; central part of the retina, nearly round, straight to the pupil, image are the clearest right on this spot; (图见 ☞ figure for 眼 yǎn on p. 2210)

【黄包车】huángbāochē〈方 *dial.*〉same as 人力车 rénlìchē ②

【黄骠马】huángbiāomǎ 一种黄毛夹杂着白点子的马 horse having a yellow coat with white spots

【黄表纸】huángbiǎozhǐ 迷信的人祭神用的黄色的纸 yellow paper for sacrificial use

【黄柏】huángbò same as 黄檗 huángbò

【黄檗】huángbò 落叶乔木,树皮淡灰色,羽状复叶,小叶卵形或卵状披针形,开黄绿色小花,果实黑色。木材坚硬,可以制造枪托,茎可以制黄色染料。树皮可入药。cork tree (*philodendron*); deciduous tree having light grey bark, pinniform compound oval leaves that are either leaflets or lanceolate, small yellow and green flowers, and black fruit, its timber useful for making gunstock, its stems for making yellow dyestuff, and its bark for medicine; also 黄柏 huángbò

【黄菜】huángcài〈方 *dial.*〉用打散了的鸡蛋摊成的菜叫摊黄菜,溜成的菜叫溜黄菜 dishes made from scrambled eggs

【黄灿灿】huángcàncàn(～的 huángcàncàn·de)形容金黄而鲜艳 golden; bright yellow:麦苗绿油油,菜花～ green wheat seedlings and golden rape flowers

【黄巢起义】Huáng Cháo Qǐyì 黄巢所领导的唐末农民大起义。公元 875 年,黄巢发动起义,起义军提出'均平'的政治口号。公元 881 年,起义军攻下唐都长安,建立了农民革命政权,国号大齐,也叫齐。后来起义虽被唐王朝所镇压,但却导致了唐王朝的迅速灭亡。Huang Chao Uprising; major peasant uprising that began in 875 AD under Huang Chao's leadership, with the political slogan of 'equality'. In 881, this peasant army sacked Chang'an, the capital of the Tang Dynasty, and established the regime of Daqi or Qi. Although put down by the Tang court, it precipitated the rapid fall of the dynasty.

【黄疸】huángdǎn 病人的皮肤、黏膜和眼球的巩膜发黄的症状,由血液中胆红素增高而引起。某些肝炎有这种症状。jaundice; symptom where the patient's skin, and the tunica mucosa and sclera of the eyes turn yellow, resulting from the rise of bilirubin in the blood, oft. seen in cases of hepatituse; 通称 generally called 黄病 huángbìng

【黄道】huángdào 地球一年绕太阳转一周,我们从地球上看成太阳一年在天空中移动一圈,太阳这样移动的路线叫做黄道。它是天球上假设的一个大圆圈,即地球轨道在天球上的投影。黄道和赤道平面相交于春分点和秋分点。ecliptic; great circle formed by the intersection of the plane of the earth's orbit with the celestial sphere; the apparent annual path of the sun in the heavens; the ecliptic and equatorial plane intersect at the vernal point and the autumnal equinox

【黄道带】huángdàodài 黄道两旁各宽八度的范围。日、月、行星都在带内运行。zodiac; imaginary star belt in the heavens, extending 8° on each side of the ecliptic, within which are the apparent paths of the sun, moon, and principal planets

【黄道吉日】huángdào jírì 迷信的人认为宜于办事的好日子 a propitious (or auspicious) date; also 黄道日 huángdàorì

【黄道十二宫】huángdào shí'èrgōng〈古代 *arch.*〉把黄道带分为十二等份,叫做黄道十二宫,每宫包括一个星座。它们的名称,从春分点起,依次为白羊、金牛、双子、巨蟹、狮子、室女、天秤、天蝎、人马、摩羯、宝瓶、双鱼。由于春分点移动,现在十二宫和十二星座的划分已不一致。12 signs of the zodiac in ancient astronomy, each containing a constellation, starting from the vernal equinox point: Aries, Taurus, Gemini, Cancer, Leo, Virgo, Libra, Scorpio, Sagittarius, Capricorn, Aquarius, and Pisces; due to the movement of the vernal equinox point, current zodiac signs are different from the old ones

【黄澄澄】huángdēngdēng(～的 huángdēngdēng·de)形容金黄色 glistening yellow; golden:谷穗儿～的 golden ears of wheat|～的金质奖章 shiny gold medal

【黄帝】Huángdì ☞ 炎黄 Yán-Huáng on p. 2205

【黄豆】huángdòu 表皮黄色的大豆 soybean

【黄骨髓】huánggǔsuǐ 含有很多脂肪细胞的黄色骨髓,缺乏造血功能。存在于成人长骨骨腔内。yellow marrow; containing many adipocytes, lacking the function of making blood, in the long bone osseous of adults

【黄瓜】huáng·gua ❶ 一年生草本植物,茎蔓生,有卷须,叶子互生,花黄色。果实圆柱形,通常有刺,成熟时黄绿色,是普通蔬菜。cucumber (*Cucumis sativus*); annual grass plant, having a trailing stem, tendrils, alternate leaves, yellow flowers, and thorny cylindrical fruit, turning yellowish green when mature, used as a common vegetable ❷ 这种植物的果实 fruit of the plant ‖ 有的地区叫胡瓜 in some places also called 胡瓜 húguā

【黄花】huánghuā ❶ 指菊花 chrysanthemum (*Chrysanthemum morifolium*) ❷(～儿 huánghuār)金针菜的通称 general term for 金针菜 jīnzhēncài ❸ 指没有经过性交的(青年男女) virgin:～后生 virgin boy|～女儿 virgin

【黄花女儿】huánghuānǚr 处女的俗称 popular term for 处女 chǔnǚ

【黄昏】huánghūn 日落以后天黑以前的时候 dusk

【黄昏恋】huánghūnliàn 指老年男女之间的恋爱 love between an elderly couple

【黄酱】huángjiàng 黄豆、面粉等发酵后制成的酱,呈红黄色 salted and fermented soy paste, reddish yellow

【黄教】Huángjiào 藏族地区喇嘛教的一派，14 世纪末宗喀巴所创，是喇嘛教中最大的教派 Dgelugs-pa; Gelug Sect; Yellow Sect (leading sect of Lamaism in Tibet, founded by Tsong-kha-pa towards the end of the 14th century, so called due to the colour of their hats)

【黄巾起义】Huángjīn Qǐyì 东汉末年张角领导的大规模农民起义。张角创立太平道，组织民众，进行活动，公元 184 年发动起义，头裹黄巾为标志，故称黄巾军。起义失败后，余部仍坚持斗争二十多年，沉重打击了东汉王朝的统治。Yellow Turban Rebellion, large-scale peasant uprising in the warring years towards the end of the Eastern Han Dynasty, under the leadership of Zhang Jiao. Zhang set up the Taiping Society to engage in anti-government activities, and launched the uprising in A. D. 184, with members wearing a yellow turban. After its failure, the survivors of the uprising struggled on for more than 20 years and dealt a heavy blow to the rule of the Eastern Han Dynasty.

【黄金】huángjīn ❶ 金[1]④的通称 general term for 金[1] jīn ④ ❷〈比喻 *fig.*〉宝贵 precious：～时代 golden age | ～地段 golden section | 电视广播的～时间 primetime item on TV and radio

【黄金分割】huángjīn fēngē 把一条线段分成两部分，使其中一部分与全长的比等于另一部分与这部分的比，比值为$\frac{\sqrt{5}-1}{2}=0.618\cdots$，这种分割称为黄金分割，因这种比例在造型上比较美观而得名 golden section; ratio between two portions of a line, or two dimensions of a plane figure, in which the lesser of the two is to the greater as the greater is to the sum of both: a ratio of approximately 0.618 to 1.000, named for its beautiful shape; also 中外比 zhōngwàibǐ

【黄金时代】huángjīn shídài ❶ 指政治、经济或文化最繁荣的时期 (of politics, economy and culture) golden age ❷ 指人一生中最宝贵的时期 prime of one's life

【黄猄】huángjīng 指某些小型的麂类 muntjac (*Munticus muntjac*); ☞ 麂 jǐ on p. 912

【黄酒】huángjiǔ 用糯米、大米、黄米等酿造的酒，色黄，含酒精量较低 yellow rice or millet wine, made of polished glutinous rice, husked rice and yellow rice, etc., with low alcohol content

【黄口小儿】huáng kǒu xiǎo ér 指婴儿，多用来讥诮无知的年轻人 baby — ignorant youth, callow young fellow (黄口 *huang kou*：雏鸟的嘴 the mouth of young bird)

【黄蜡】huánglà 蜂蜡的通称 general term for 蜂蜡 fēnglà

【黄鹂】huánglí 鸟，身体黄色，自眼部至头后部黑色，嘴淡红色。叫的声音很好听，吃森林中的害虫，对林业有益。oriole (*Oriolidae*); bird having yellow body, black from eyes to the back of the head, and a pale red mouth, a good singer, eats pests in forests, beneficial to forestry; also 鸧鹒 cānggēng or 黄莺 huángyīng

【黄历】huáng·li same as 皇历 huáng·li

【黄连】huánglián 多年生草本植物，茎高三四寸到一尺多，羽状复叶，花小，白色。根茎味苦，可入药。rhizome of Chinese goldthread (*Coptis chinensis*); herbaceous perennial, with stem height from 3 or 4 *cun* to over 1 *chi*, having pinniform compound leaves, small white flowers, bitter tasting root and stem, used for medicine

【黄连木】huángliánmù 落叶乔木，羽状复叶，小叶披针形，花单性，雌雄异株，果实球形，紫色。种子可以榨油，树皮和叶子可以制栲胶。鲜叶有香味，可以提制芳香油。有的地区叫楷(jiē)树。Chinese pistache (*Pistacia chinensis*); deciduous tree, having pinniform compound leaves, lanceolate leaflets, separate flowers, dioecy, purple round fruit; its seeds can be used for extracting oil, bark and leaves, for making tannin extract, fragrant fresh leaves, for refining perfume oil; called 楷树 jiēshù in some places

【黄粱梦】huángliángmèng 有个卢生，在邯郸旅店中遇见一个道士吕翁，卢生自叹穷困。道士借给他一个枕头，要他枕着睡觉。这时店家正煮小米饭。卢生在梦中享尽了一生荣华富贵。一觉醒来，小米饭还没有熟(见于唐沈既济《枕中记》)。A young scholar by the name of Lu Sheng met a Taoist priest surnamed Lü in an inn. When Lu Sheng complained about his poverty, Lü lent him a pillow to sleep on. At that time, the innkeeper was cooking a meal of millet. In his dream, Lu Sheng enjoyed a lifetime of power and wealth. He woke up to find the millet still being cooked (see *A Dream of the Pillow* by Shen Jiji of the Tang Dynasty). Thus the phrase, golden millet dream, referring to vanished dream or evanescence of life. also 黄粱美梦 huángliáng měimèng; 一枕黄粱 yī zhěn huángliáng

【黄龙】Huánglóng 黄龙府，金国的地名，在今吉林农安。宋金交战时，岳飞曾经说要直捣黄龙府。后来泛指敌方的要地。Huanglongfu, name of a place in the Kingdom of Jin, in today's Nong'an of Jilin Province. During the war between the Song Dynasty and Jin, Yue Fei, a famous Song general, said he would defeat the enemy and capture its capital city of Huanglong. (in a broad sense) enemy's strategic point：直捣～ storm the enemy's den | 痛饮～ drink to one's heart's content after storming the enemy capital

【黄栌】huánglú 落叶灌木，叶子互生，卵形或倒卵形，秋季变红，花单性和两性同株共存，果实肾脏形。木材黄色,可以制染料。smoke tree (*Cotinus coggygria*); deciduous tree having oval or reversed oval alternate leaves which turn red in the autumn, coexisting single and hermaphrodite flowers, kidney-shaped fruit, yellow wood, used for making dyestuff

【黄毛丫头】huángmáo yā·tou 年幼的女孩子(含戏谑或轻侮意 with a playful or scornful sense) chit of a girl; silly little girl

【黄梅季】huángméijì 春末夏初梅子黄熟的一段时期,这段时期我国长江中下游地方连续下雨,空气潮湿,衣服等容易发霉 rainy season, in late spring and early summer, with continuous rain in areas along the middle and lower reaches of the Yangtze River, when clothes go mouldy easily; also 黄梅天 huángméitiān

【黄梅戏】huángméixì 安徽地方戏曲剧种之一,流行于该省中部,因主要曲调由湖北黄梅传入而得名 Huangmei opera; opera popular in central Anhui Province, named after its derivation from Huangmei in Hubei Province; also 黄梅调 huángméidiào

【黄梅雨】huángméiyǔ 黄梅季下的雨 intermittent drizzle in the rainy season in the middle and lower reaches of the Yangtze River; also 梅雨 méiyǔ or 霉雨 méiyǔ

【黄米】huángmǐ 黍子去了壳的子实,比小米稍大,颜色很黄,煮熟后很黏 glutinous millet; shelled seeds of broomcorn millet, slightly bigger than millet, deep yellow and very sticky after being cooked

【黄牛】huángniú ❶ 牛的一种,角短,皮毛黄褐色,或黑色,也有杂色的,毛短。用来耕地或拉车,肉供食用,皮可以制革。ox (*Bos taurus*); cattle having short horns, yellow and brown or black or variegated hide and short hair, serving as a draught animal in ploughing and driving, its meat used for food, its fur for leather-making ❷〈方 *dial.*〉指恃力气或利用不正当手法抢购物资以及车票、门票后高价出售而从中取利的人 ticket scalper:～党 scalpers of tickets ❸〈方 *dial.*〉指言而无信的人 person who fails to keep promises

【黄牌】huángpái 黄色的牌子。体育比赛中,运动员、教练员等严重犯规,裁判员出示黄牌予以警告。yellow card; in sports, referees warn players or coaches who grossly violate rules by showing them a yellow card ◇交通管理部门向发生重大交通事故的单位亮～。The traffic authorities issued a warning to a unit after one of its drivers had caused a major traffic accident.

【黄袍加身】huáng páo jiā shēn 五代后周时,赵匡胤在陈桥驿发动兵变,部下给他披上黄袍,推拥为皇帝。后来用'黄袍加身'指政变成功,夺得政权。take the throne; seize political power after a coup. During the Later Zhou of the Five Dynasties, Zhao Kuangyin launched a coup and was draped in imperial yellow robes by his supporters.

【黄皮书】huángpíshū ☞ 白皮书 báipíshū on p. 36

【黄芪】huángqí 多年生草本植物,羽状复叶,小叶长圆形,有毛茸,开淡黄色小花。根可入药。membranous mik vetch (*Astragalus membranaceus*); herbaceous perennial plant having pinniform compound leaves, long and round and hairy leaflets, light yellow flowers, and root used for medicine

【黄泉】huángquán 地下的泉水。指人死后埋葬的地方,迷信的人指阴间 (superstitious) underworld; Yellow Springs — the world of the dead: ～之下 under the Yellow Springs — in death | 命赴～ go to the Yellow Springs — die

【黄壤】huángrǎng 黄色的土壤,在我国主要分布在四川、贵州、广西等省区。铁的含水氧化物含量高,酸性强,养分较丰富。yellow earth, mainly found in Sichuan, Guizhou and Guangxi in China, with a high content of aqueous oxide, strong acidity, and rich nutrients

【黄色】huángsè ❶ 黄的颜色 yellow ❷ 象征腐化堕落,特指色情 decadent; pornographic:～小说 pornographic novel | ～录像 pornographic record

【黄色炸药】huángsè zhàyào 烈性炸药,成分是三硝基甲苯,黄色结晶 trinitrotoluene (TNT), powder in yellow crystals; also 梯恩梯 tī'ēntī

【黄鳝】huángshàn 鱼,身体像蛇而无鳞,黄褐色,有黑色斑点。生活在水边泥洞里。ricefield eel (*Monopterus albus*); fish, looking like a snake but without scales, yellow-brown with black spots, living in mud holes by water; also called 鳝鱼 shànyú

【黄熟】huángshú 谷类作物成熟时,子实内部变硬,植株大部分变成黄色,不再生长,叫黄熟 yellow maturity; when grain crops become mature, their seeds turn hard and the stalks turn yellow and do not grow anymore

【黄鼠狼】huángshǔláng same as 黄鼬 huángyòu

【黄汤】huángtāng 指黄酒(骂人喝酒时说 offens. to curse drinkers) yellow stuff, referring to yellow rice or millet wine

【黄糖】huángtáng〈方 *dial.*〉same as 红糖 hóngtáng

【黄体】huángtǐ 卵巢里由许多黄色颗粒状细胞形成的内分泌腺体。卵巢每次排卵后有黄体出现,妊娠后,黄体发育增大,所分泌的激素有使子宫黏膜增厚,抑制子宫收缩,促进乳腺分泌等作用。corpus luteum; ductless gland developed within the ovary by the reorganization of a Graafian follicle following ovulation. After conception, the corpus luteum enlarges and secretes a hormone that can thicken the uterine mucosa, restrain uterosystole and promote breast secretion.

【黄土】huángtǔ 砂粒、黏土和少量方解石的混合物，灰黄或黄褐色，用手搓捻容易成粉末。我国西北地区是世界有名的黄土地带，土层厚度一般20—30米。loess; usu. yellowish and calcareous, loamy deposit formed by wind, that turns out to be a mixture of sand, clay and a little calcite, easy to turn to powder by rubbing between the fingers; Northwest China is world-famous for its cover of loess that runs 20 to 30 metres deep

【黄癣】huángxuǎn 头癣的一种，在头部发生黄色斑点或小脓疱，有特殊的臭味，结痂后，毛发脱落，痊愈后留下疤痕，不生毛发。北方叫秃疮或癞，南方叫瘌痢。favus; skin disease, esp. of the scalp, characterized by dry yellow encrustation with an unpleasant odour. Where scabs form after the favus is gone; hair is lost and never grows again; called 秃疮 tūchuāng or 癞 lài in the north; 瘌痢 là·lì in the south

【黄烟】huángyān 〈方 *dial.*〉 same as 旱烟 hànyān

【黄猺】huángyáo same as 青鼬 qīngyòu

【黄莺】huángyīng same as 黄鹂 huánglí

【黄油】huángyóu ❶ 从石油中分馏出来的膏状油脂，黄色或褐色，黏度大，多用做润滑油 grease, fractionated from petroleum, yellow or brown, terribly sticky, usu. used as lubricant ❷ 从牛奶或奶油中提取的淡黄色固体，主要成分为脂肪，是一种食品 butter; a type of food, fatty substance that becomes separated as a whitish or yellowish soft solid when milk or cream is agitated or churned

【黄鼬】huángyòu 哺乳动物，身体细长，四肢短，尾蓬松，背部棕灰色。昼伏夜出，主要捕食鼠类，有时也吃家禽。是一种毛皮兽，尾毛可制毛笔。yellow weasel (*Mustela sibirica*); nocturnal mammal with a long, slender body, short limbs, fluffy tail, brown grey back, feeding chiefly on small rodents, its tail fur used for making brushes; also called 黄鼠狼 huángshǔláng; 有的地区叫黄皮子 in some places called 黄皮子 huángpí·zi

【黄鱼】huángyú ❶ 鱼类的一属，身体侧扁，尾巴狭窄，头大，侧线以下有分泌黄色物质的腺体。生活在海中。分大黄鱼和小黄鱼两种。yellow croaker (*Pseudosciaena*); fish having a flat-sided body, narrow tail, big head, and glands under a side line that can secret a yellow substance, living in the ocean, divided into big croaker and small croaker; also called 黄花鱼 huánghuāyú ❷〈旧时 *old*〉指轮船水手、汽车司机等为捞取外快而私带的旅客 extra passengers sailors or drivers give a ride to for extra money to fill their own pocket ❸〈方 *dial.*〉指金条 gold piece

【黄账】huángzhàng 〈方 *dial.*〉收不回来的账 bad debt

【黄纸板】huángzhǐbǎn 用稻草、麦秸等制成的一种纸板，黄色，质地粗糙，多用来制作纸盒。俗称马粪纸。strawboard; yellow board made from rice and wheat straw, of a coarse texture, usu. used for making paper boxes, with a vulgar name of 马粪纸 mǎfènzhǐ (paper of horse's shit)

【黄种】Huángzhǒng 蒙古人种 Mongoloid race

凰 huáng ☞ 凤凰 fènghuáng on p. 589

隍 huáng 没有水的城壕 dry moat outside a city: 城～ town god

喤 huáng [喤喤]〈书 *fml.*〉❶ 形容钟鼓声大而和谐 (of bell or drum sound) resonant and harmonious: 钟鼓～ resounding music of bells and drums ❷ 形容小儿啼哭声洪亮 sound of child bawling

遑 huáng 〈书 *fml.*〉闲暇 leisure: 不～ have no time for

【遑遑】huánghuáng 〈书 *fml.*〉匆忙 in a hurry; also 皇皇 huánghuáng

【遑论】huánglùn 〈书 *fml.*〉不必论及；谈不上 let alone; to say nothing of: 生计无着，～享乐。It's a problem making a living, let alone enjoying life.

徨 huáng ☞ [彷徨] (pánghuáng) on p. 1445

馆 huáng ☞ [张馆] (zhānghuáng) on p. 2415

湟 Huáng 湟水，水名，发源于青海，流入甘肃 Huangshui, a river with its source in Qinghai Province and flowing into Gansu Province

惶 huáng 恐惧 fear; trepidation: ～恐 terrified | 惊～ panic

【惶惶】huánghuáng 恐惧不安 alarmed; in a state of anxiety; on tenterhooks: 人心～ popular anxiety | ～不可终日 in a constant state of anxiety; be on tenterhooks; also 皇皇 huánghuáng

【惶惑】huánghuò 疑惑畏惧 perplexed and alarmed: 他整天～不安。He has been perplexed and uneasy all day and all night.

【惶遽】huángjù 〈书 *fml.*〉惊慌 frightened: 神色～ look scared

【惶恐】huángkǒng 惊慌害怕 panic-stricken: 万分～ be seized with fear | ～不安 in a state of trepidation

【惶然】huángrán 恐惧不安的样子 frightened and uneasy: ～不知所措 be tied up in knots; be alarmed and confused

【惶悚】huángsǒng 〈书 *fml.*〉 same as 惶恐 huángkǒng: ～不安 in flutter

煌 huáng 明亮 bright; brilliant: 辉～ brilliant

【煌煌】huánghuáng 形容明亮 bright; brilliant: 明星～。The stars are twinkling brightly.

锽 huáng 〈古代 *arch.*〉一种兵器 a kind of weapon

【锽锽】 huánghuáng 〈书 *fml.*〉形容钟鼓声 sound of bells and drums

潢[1] huáng 〈书 *fml.*〉积水池 pool

潢[2] huáng 染纸 dye or colour paper：装～ decorate；decoration

璜 huáng 〈书 *fml.*〉半璧形的玉 semi-circular jade pendant

蝗 huáng 蝗虫 locust (*Locusta*)：～灾 plague of locusts | 灭～ wipe out locusts

【蝗虫】 huángchóng 昆虫，种类很多，口器坚硬，前翅狭窄而坚韧，后翅宽大而柔软，善于飞行，后肢很发达，善于跳跃。主要危害禾本科植物，是农业害虫。有的地区叫蚂蚱。locust (*Locusta*)；insect with a great variety, having stiff mouthparts, narrow and tough front wings, wide and soft rear wings, good at flying and jumping due to its well-developed hind legs, harmful to agriculture, particularly to grasses; also called 蚂蚱 mà·zha in some places

【蝗蝻】 huángnǎn 蝗虫的若虫，形状像成虫而翅膀很短，身体小，头大 nymph of the locust, like the adult locust but with shorter wings, small body, big head; also 跳蝻 tiàonǎn

【蝗灾】 huángzāi 成群的蝗虫吃掉大量农作物的茎叶造成的灾害 plague of locusts

篁 huáng 〈书 *fml.*〉竹林，泛指竹子 bamboo grove：幽～ secluded bamboo grove | 修～（长竹子）tall bamboo

艎 huáng ☞ [艅艎] (yúhuáng) on p. 2341

磺 huáng 硫磺（用于合成词 used in compound word) sulphur：硝～（硝石和硫磺）nitre and sulphur

镄 huáng same as 簧 huáng

癀 huáng [癀病] (huángbìng) 〈方 *dial.*〉牛、马、猪、绵羊等家畜的炭疽病（disease of domestic animals such as cow, horse, pig and sheep, etc.) anthrax

蟥 huáng ☞ 蚂蟥 mǎhuáng on p. 1292

簧 huáng ❶ 乐器里用铜或其他质料制成的发声薄片 reed (in a musical instrument) made of copper or other materials ❷ 器物上有弹力的机件 spring：弹～ spring | 锁～ lock spring | 闹钟的～拧断了。The main spring of the alarm clock is broken.

鳇 huáng 鱼类的一属，大的体长可达5米，有5行硬鳞，嘴很突出，半月形，两旁有扁平的须。夏季在江河中产卵，过一段时间后，回到海洋中生活。sturgeon (*Huso dauricus*); fish as large as five metres long, having five rows of hard scales, a prominent crescent moon-shaped mouth, and flat feelers on both sides, spawning in rivers in summer and swimming back to the sea afterwards

huǎng（ㄏㄨㄤˇ）

怳 huǎng ☞ [惝怳] (chǎnghuǎng) on p. 222

恍 huǎng ❶ 恍然 all of a sudden：～悟 suddenly realize what has happened ❷ 仿佛（与'如、若'等连用 used together with 如 rú, 若 ruò, etc.) seem; as if：～如梦境 as if in a dream | ～如隔世 there seems to be a gap of a whole generation; (said on finding things greatly changed) feel as if in another world

【恍忽】 huǎng·hū same as 恍惚 huǎng·hū

【恍惚】 huǎng·hū ❶ 神志不清；精神不集中 absent-minded; in a trance：精神～ be stoned; be in a trance ❷（记得、听得、看得）不真切；不清楚 dimly; faintly; seemingly：我～听见他回来了。I was faintly aware that he had entered the room. ‖ also 恍忽 huǎng·hū

【恍然】 huǎngrán 形容忽然醒悟 all of a sudden：～大悟 suddenly see the light; suddenly realize what has happened

【恍如隔世】 huǎng rú gé shì 好像隔了一世。多用来形容对时间的变迁、事物的变化的感慨。there seems a whole generation had elapsed (said on finding things greatly changed)

【恍悟】 huǎngwù 忽然醒悟 suddenly realize what has happened

晃 huǎng ❶（光芒）闪耀 dazzle：太阳～得眼睛睁不开。The shining sun is dazzling me, so I cannot open my eyes. ❷ 很快地闪过 flash past：虚～一刀 make a feint | 窗外有个人影儿一～就不见了。A figure flashed past the window and disappeared.

☞ huàng on p. 856

【晃眼】 huǎngyǎn ❶ 光线过强，刺得眼睛不舒服 dazzling：摄影棚内强烈的灯光直～。The strong light in the film studio is dazzling. ❷ 形容极短的时间；瞬间 twinkling：刚才还看见他在这儿，怎么～就不见了？I saw him here just now. How could he have disappeared in a wink of the eye?

谎 huǎng ❶ 谎话 lie：说～ tell a lie | 撒～ lie | 漫天大～ monstrous lie ❷ 说谎话 tell a lie：～报 lie about sth. | ～称 falsely claim

【谎报】 huǎngbào 故意不真实地报告 lie about sth.; spread disinformation; spread a canard：～军情 make a false report about the (military) situation | ～成绩 give a false account of one's achievements

【谎花】 huǎnghuā（～儿 huǎnghuār）不结果实的花，如南瓜、西瓜等的雄花 fruitless flower, e.g. male flowers of pumpkin and watermelon plants

【谎话】 huǎnghuà 不真实的、骗人的话；假话 lie; falsehood：～连篇 a pack of lies

【谎价】 huǎngjià（～儿 huǎngjiàr）出售货物时所要的高于一般的价钱 inflated price

【谎信】huǎngxìn 〈方 *dial.*〉（～儿 huǎngxìnr）same as 荒信 huāngxìn

【谎言】huǎngyán same as 谎话 huǎnghuà：戳穿～ expose a lie

幌 huǎng 〈书 *fml.*〉帷幔 heavy curtain

【幌子】huǎng·zi ❶ 商店门外表明所卖商品的标志 shop sign; signboard ❷〈比喻 *fig.*〉进行某种活动时所假借的名义 pretence; cover：打着开会的～游山玩水 sightseeing under the pretence of attending a convention

huàng（ㄏㄨㄤˋ）

晃[1]（搖）huàng 摇动；摆动 shake; sway：摇头～脑 shake one's head｜风刮得树枝直～。The free branches kept swaying in the wind.

晃[2] Huàng 晃县，旧县名，在湖南 Huangxian county, an old county name in Hunan Province

☞ huǎng on p. 855

【晃荡】huàng·dang ❶ 向两边摆动 shake; sway：小船在水里直～。The small boat is rocking in the water.｜桶里水很满，一～就撒出来了。The bucket was so full that it overflowed at the slightest movement. ❷ 闲逛；无所事事 saunter; loaf：他在河边～了一天。He loafed along the river for the whole day.｜正经事儿不做，一天到晚瞎～。Loaf around all day long without doing anything serious.

【晃动】huàngdòng 摇晃；摆动 rock; sway：小树被风吹得直～。The sapling is swaying in the wind.

【晃悠】huàng·you same as 晃荡 huàng·dang：树枝来回～。The branches of the trees are swaying.｜老太太晃晃悠悠地走来。The old woman was tottering along.

滉 huàng 〈书 *fml.*〉水深而广（of water）deep and vast

榥 huàng 〈书 *fml.*〉帷幕、屏风之类 curtain; screen

皝 huàng 用于人名，慕容皝，东晋初年鲜卑族的首领，建立前燕国 used in names, such as in Murong Huang, leader of the Xianbei people in the early years of the Eastern Jin Dynasty who established the Kingdom of Former Yan

huī（ㄏㄨㄟ）

灰 huī ❶ 物质经过燃烧后剩下的粉末状的东西 ash：炉～ ashes from a stove｜烟～ tobacco ash｜柴～ firewood ash｜～烬 ashes｜～肥 ash manure ❷ 尘土；某些粉末状的东西 dust; powder：青～ graphite powder｜把桌子上的～掸掉。Brush the dust off the table. ❸ 特指石灰 lime：～墙 plastered wall｜～顶 plastered roof｜抹～ apply mortar ❹ 像木柴灰的颜色，介于黑色和白色之间 grey：银～ silver-grey｜～鼠 squirrel ❺ 消沉；失望 disheartened; discouraged：心～意懒 lose heart completely

【灰暗】huī'àn 暗淡；不鲜明 murky grey; gloomy：天色～ gloomy sky｜前途～ gloomy future

【灰白】huībái 浅灰色 greyish white：～的炊烟 greyish-white smoke from kitchen chimneys｜头发～ greying hair

【灰不溜丢】huī·buliūdiū 〈方 *dial.*〉（～的 huī·buliūdiū·de）形容灰色（含厌恶意 unpleasantly）grey and dull; also 灰不溜秋 huī·bu liūqiū

【灰尘】huīchén 尘土 dust; dirt：打扫～ sweep the dust

【灰沉沉】huīchénchén（～的 huīchénchén·de）形容灰暗（多指天色 usu. of the sky）gloomy; leaden：天空～的，像是要下雨的样子。It's gloomy and looks like rain.

【灰顶】huīdǐng 抹（mò）石灰而不盖瓦的房顶 plastered roof

【灰分】huīfèn 物质燃烧后剩下的灰的重量与原物质重量的比值，叫做这种物质的灰分。如 100 千克的煤，燃烧后剩灰 25 千克，这种煤的灰分就是 25%。ash ratip; ratio of the remnant powdery residue after burning to the original matter, e. g. 1,000 kg. of coal leaves behind 25 kg. of ash after burning, so the ash ratio is 25 per cent

【灰膏】huīgāo 除去渣滓沉淀后呈膏状的熟石灰。是常用的建筑材料。slaked lime, an often-used building material

【灰光】huīguāng 农历每月月初，月球被地球阴影遮住的部分现出的微光。灰光是地球反射的太阳光照亮了月球，再反射回地球而形成的。发灰光的部分和娥眉月形成一个整圆。grey light; at the beginning of each lunar month, part of the moon that is in the earth's shadow radiates a grey light. The sunlight reflected off the earth lights the moon and this again reflects on the earth, thus forming the grey light. The part radiating grey light and the crescent moon make up a full moon.

【灰化土】huīhuàtǔ 枯萎凋落的枝叶被真菌分解而成的土壤，灰白色，在我国主要分布于东北、西北的部分林区。这种土壤酸性强，含腐殖质少，缺乏养分。podzol; soil rendered grayish white by fallen leaves decomposed by fungus and thus becoming highly acidic, containing little humus and lacking nutrients, mainly in the forests of northeast and northwest China

【灰浆】huījiāng ❶ 石灰、水泥或青灰等加水拌和而成的浆，用来粉刷墙壁 mortar; mixture of lime, cement or greenish lime and water, used for whitewashing walls ❷ ☞ 砂浆 shājiāng on p. 1665

【灰烬】huījìn 物品燃烧后的灰和烧剩下的东西 ashes:化为～ be reduced to ashes

【灰溜溜】huīliūliū(～的 huīliūliū·de) ❶ 形容颜色暗淡(含厌恶意 unpleasantly) dull grey:屋子多年没粉刷,～的。The room is dingy because it has not been whitewashed for many years. ❷ 形容神情懊丧或消沉 gloomy; dejected:他挨了一顿训斥,～地走出来。He walked out, looking dejected after the dressing-down. | 不知什么原因,他这阵子显得～的。He recently looked a little crestfallen for unknown reasons.

【灰蒙蒙】huīmēngmēng(～的 huīmēngmēng·de)形容暗淡模糊(多指景色)(of a scene) be all grey; dusky; overcast:～的夜色 a dusky night scene | 一起风沙,天地都变得～的。The sky was overcast when the wind and the sand rose.

【灰棚】huīpéng〈方 *dial*.〉❶ 堆草木灰的矮小的房子 straw-ash shed ❷(～儿 huīpéngr)灰顶的小房子 mortar-roofed hut

【灰色】huīsè ❶ 像木柴灰的颜色 grey; ashy ❷〈比喻 *fig*.〉颓废和失望 pessimistic; gloomy:～的作品 a literary work pessimistic in tone | ～的心情 feel dejected ❸〈比喻 *fig*.〉态度暧昧 obscure; ambiguous

【灰头土脸儿】huītóu-tǔliǎnr〈方 *dial*.〉(～的 huītóu-tǔliǎnr·de) ❶ 满头满脸沾上尘土的样子 head and face covered with dust:他扬完了场,闹了个～。He got himself dusty all over after he went winnowing. ❷ 形容神情懊丧或消沉 dejected; depressed:你高高兴兴地去了,可别弄得～地回来。You must go cheerfully and not come back crestfallen.

【灰土】huītǔ 尘土 dust:车后卷起一片～。The car raised a cloud of dust as it drove by.

【灰心】huī//xīn(因遭到困难、失败)意志消沉 lose heart; be discouraged:～丧气 down in the dumps | 不怕失败,只怕～。Failure is not dreadful, but losing heart is.

【灰质】huīzhì 脑和脊髓的灰色部分,主要由神经细胞组成 grey matter in the brain and the spinal cord, mainly consisting of subnucleus

㧑(撝、㩣) huī〈书 *fml*.〉指挥 command

诙 huī〈书 *fml*.〉❶ 戏谑 banter; crack jokes ❷ 嘲笑 laugh at

【诙谐】huīxié 说话有风趣,引人发笑 humorous; jocular:谈吐～ be witty in conversation

虺 huī [虺虺](huītuí)〈书 *fml*.〉疲劳生病(多用于马 of horses) fall ill due to fatigue; also 虺隤 huīkuì

☞ huǐ on p. 864

挥 huī ❶ 挥舞 wave; wield:～手 wave (one's hand) | ～拳 shake one's fist | ～刀 wield a sword | 大笔一～ a stroke of the pen ❷ 用手把眼泪、汗珠儿等抹掉 wipe off:～泪 shed tears | ～汗 wipe off one's sweat ❸ 指挥(军队) command (an army):～师东进 command an army to march eastward ❹ 散出;散 scatter; disperse:～发 volatile | 发～ bring into play | ～金如土 throw gold about like dirt

【挥斥】huīchì〈书 *fml*.〉❶ 指摘;斥责 criticize; scold ❷(意气)奔放 bold and unrestrained

【挥动】huīdòng same as 挥舞 huīwǔ:～手臂 wave one's arm | ～皮鞭 wield a whip

【挥发】huīfā 液体在常温下变为气体向四周散布,如醚、酒精、石油等都能挥发 volatilize; liquid turns into gas and spreads under ordinary temperatures, e.g. ether, alcohol, petroleum, etc.

【挥发油】huīfāyóu 容易挥发的油类。有时专指汽油。volatile oil; sometimes indicating gas

【挥戈】huīgē 挥动着戈。形容勇猛进军 brandish one's weapons; advance boldly:～跃马 brandish one's weapon on horseback | ～东进 march eastward

【挥毫】huīháo〈书 *fml*.〉指用毛笔写字或画画儿 wield one's writing brush; write or draw a picture (with a brush):～泼墨 take up a brush and paint | 对客～ write (with a brush) in the presence of a guest

【挥霍】huīhuò ❶ 任意花钱 squander; spend freely:～无度 spend without restraint | ～钱财 squander money ❷〈书 *fml*.〉形容轻捷、洒脱 lively; free and easy:运笔～ write or paint freely and easily

【挥金如土】huī jīn rú tǔ 形容任意挥霍钱财,毫不在乎 squander; spend money like water; throw money about like dirt

【挥洒】huīsǎ ❶ 洒(泪、水等) sprinkle (water); shed (tears):～热血 shed one's blood (for a worthy cause) ❷〈比喻 *fig*.〉写文章、画画儿运笔不拘束 write or paint in an untrammelled style:～自如 write or paint with facility | 随意～ write or paint freely ❸〈书 *fml*.〉洒脱自然 free and unrestrained:风神～ free and graceful demeanour

【挥师】huīshī 指挥军队 command an army:～北上 command an army to march north

【挥手】huī//shǒu 举手摆动 wave one's hand:～告别 wave farewell | ～示意 wave a greeting

【挥舞】huīwǔ 举起手臂(连同拿着的东西)摇摆(while holding sth.) wave; wield; brandish:孩子们～着鲜花欢呼。Children are waving flowers cheerfully.

咴 huī [咴儿咴儿](huīrhuīr)〈拟声词 *onom*.〉形容马叫的声音(of horse) neigh; whinny

恢 huī 广大;宽广 extensive; vast:～弘 broad

【恢复】huīfù ❶ 变成原来的样子 recover; regain:秩序～了 ordered a return to normalcy | 健康已完全～ fully recover ❷ 使变成原来的样子;把失去的收回来 restore; reinstate; rehabilitate：～原状 resume original shape|～失地 restore lost land

【恢弘】huīhóng〈书 *fml*.〉❶ 宽阔；广大 broad；extensive：气度～ broad-minded；magnanimous ❷ same as 发扬 fāyáng；carry on：～士气 boost morale ‖ also 恢宏 huīhóng

【恢宏】huīhóng same as 恢弘 huīhóng

【恢恢】huīhuī〈书 *fml*.〉形容非常广大 extensive；vast：天网～，疏而不漏（形容作恶者一定受到惩罚）。The net of heaven has its meshes，but it lets nothing through — evildoers can never escape punishment.

【恢廓】huīkuò〈书 *fml*.〉❶ same as 宽宏 kuānhóng：～的胸襟 broad-mindedness ❷ 扩展 expand；spread；extend：～祖业 expand one's ancestral achievement

袆（褘） huī 袆衣，古时王后的一种祭服 mourning robe for an empress in ancient times

珲 huī 瑷珲（Àihuī），地名，在黑龙江。今作爱辉。Aihui，a place name in Heilongjiang Province，currently 爱辉 Àihuī；known as 'Aigun' when the unequal 1858 Sino-Russian Treaty was signed there

☞ hún on p. 873

豗 huī ☞ 喧豗 xuānhuī on p. 2170

晖 huī 阳光 sunshine；sunlight：春～ spring sunshine|朝～ dawning|斜～ slanting rays of the sun

【晖映】huīyìng same as 辉映 huīyìng

辉（煇） huī ❶ 闪耀的光彩 brightness；splendour：光～ lustre；glow|晚霞的余～ last rays of the evening sun ❷ 照耀 shine：～映 reflect|星月交～。The moon and the stars are shining together.

【辉煌】huīhuáng 光辉灿烂 brilliant；splendid；glorious：灯火～ brightly lit|金碧～ dazzlingly magnificent ◇战果～ brilliant victory of war，endeavour，etc.|～的成绩 outstanding achievement

【辉映】huīyìng 照耀；映射 shine；reflect：灯光月色，交相～。The lamplight and the moon mingle and add radiance and beauty to each other.|绚丽的晚霞～着大地。The beautiful sunset glow adds radiance and beauty to the land. also 晖映 huīyìng

翚 huī ❶〈书 *fml*.〉飞翔 fly ❷ 古书中指一种有五彩羽毛的野鸡 a kind of pheasant known for its beautiful multi-hued plumage (mentioned in ancient texts)

麾 huī ❶〈古代 *arch*.〉指挥军队的旗子 standard of a commander ❷〈书 *fml*.〉指挥（军队） command (army)：～军前进 command an army to march forward

【麾下】huīxià〈书 *fml*.〉❶ 指将帅的部下 under sb.'s command ❷〈敬辞 *pol*.〉称将帅 (a respectful term of address) general；commander

徽[1] huī ❶ 表示某个集体的标志；符号 emblem；badge；insignia：国～ national emblem|团～ Youth League badge|校～ school badge|～章 badge ❷ 美好的 fine；glorious：～号 glorious title

徽[2] Huī 指徽州（旧府名，府治在今安徽歙县） Huizhou，an ancient prefecture with its seat of government in present-day Shexian in Anhui Province：～墨 Huizhou ink stick (orig. produced in Huizhou，and considered the best of its kind)

【徽调】huīdiào ❶ 徽剧所用的腔调。包括吹腔、高拨子、二黄、西皮等。清代传到北京，对京剧腔调的形成有很大的影响。Anhui tune；musical style of Anhui opera including such tunes as *chuiqiang*，*gaobozi*，*erhuang* and *xipi*，which spread to Beijing in the Qing Dynasty and had a major impact on the emergence of the vocal style of Peking Opera ❷ 徽剧的旧称 old name for 徽剧 huījù

【徽号】huīhào 美好的称号 title of honour；good name：同学送给他'诗人'的～。His classmates call him 'poet'.

【徽记】huījì same as 标志 biāozhì：飞机上的～ insignia on a plane

【徽剧】huījù 安徽地方戏曲剧种之一，流行于该省和江苏、浙江、江西等地区 Anhui opera，popular in Jiangsu，Zhejiang and Jiangxi provinces，as well as Anhui；旧称 formerly known as 徽调 huīdiào

【徽墨】huīmò 徽州出产的墨 Huizhou ink stick (originally produced in Huizhou，a prefecture in present-day Anhui Province，considered the best of its kind)

【徽章】huīzhāng 佩带在身上用来表示身份、职业等的标志，多用金属制成 badge；insignia，indicating identity and occupation，usu. made of metal

隳（隓） huī〈书 *fml*.〉毁坏 destroy

☞ 堕 duò on p. 502

huí（ㄏㄨㄟˊ）

回[1]（囘、囬、❶迴、廻） huí ❶ 曲折环绕 circle；wind：～旋 circle around|巡～ do the rounds|迂～ circuitous|～形针 (paper) clip|峰～路转。The path winds along mountain ridges. ❷ 从别处到原来的地方；还 return；go back：～家 go back home|～乡 return to one's hometown|送～原处 return to where one came from ❸ 掉转 turn around：～头 turn back one's head|～过身来 turn around ❹ 答复；回报 answer；reply：～信 write back|～敬 retaliate ❺ 回禀 report back (to one's superior) ❻ 谢绝（邀请）；退掉（预定的酒席等）；辞去（伙计、佣工） decline (an invitation)；cancel (a reservation); dismiss (an employee) ❼〈量词 classifier〉指事情、动作的次数 [indicating frequency of occurrence, time]: 来了一～ have been here once | 听过两～ have heard twice | 那是另一～事。That's a different matter. ❽〈量词 classifier〉说书的一个段落,章回小说的一章 chapter: 一百二十～抄本《红楼梦》*A Dream of Red Mansions* in a hand-copied version with 120 chapters

回[2](囘、囬) Huí ❶ 回族 Hui people: ～民 people of the Hui ethnic group ❷ 姓 a surname

【回拜】huíbài same as 回访 huífǎng

【回报】huíbào ❶ 报告(任务、使命等执行的情况) report back on what has been done ❷ 报答;酬报 repay; requite: 做好事不图～ do good not for reciprocation ❸ 报复 retaliate; get one's own back: 你这样恶意攻击人家,总有一天会遭到～的。One day you will pay for your spiteful attacks on others.

【回避】huíbì ❶ 让开;躲开 evade; dodge; avoid: ～要害问题 evade the crucial question ❷ 侦破人员或审判人员由于同案件有利害关系或其他关系而不参加该案的侦破或审判 withdraw; if the judge is a (of an investigator or judege) withdraw of his or her own accord for being an interested party to the case or having some other relationship with it

【回禀】huíbǐng〈旧时 old〉指向上级或长辈报告 report back (to one's superior): ～父母 report back to one's parents

【回驳】huíbó 否定或驳斥别人提出的意见或道理 refute another's advice or argument: 当面～ refute sb. immediately to his face | 据理～ refute sb. on just grounds

【回采】huícǎi 修建巷道后进行采掘、装运等,叫做回采 extraction

【回茬】huíchá 一年内一茬农作物收获后复种的那一茬 second crop (of a year): ～麦 wheat as a second crop of a given year

【回肠】[1] huícháng 小肠的一部分,上接空肠,下连盲肠,形状弯曲 ileum; third and lowest division of the small intestine, extending from the jejunum to the cecum; (图见 ☞ figure for 消化系统 xiāohuà xìtǒng on p.2100)

【回肠】[2] huícháng〈书 *fml.*〉形容内心焦虑,好像肠子在旋转 worried like ileum spinning: ～九转 with anxiety gnawing at one's heart; weighed down with grief

【回肠荡气】huí cháng dàng qì 形容文章、乐曲等十分动人 (of music, poems, etc.) soul-stirring; also 荡气回肠 dàng qì huí cháng

【回潮】huí//cháo ❶ 已经晒干或烤干的东西又变湿 (of dried things) get damp again: 连下几天雨,晒好的粮食又～了。The dried grain got damp again after it rained for days on end. ❷〈比喻 *fig.*〉已经消失了的旧事物、旧习惯、旧思想等重新出现 resurgence (of old things, habits and thoughts, etc.): 近几年,一些地方的迷信活动又～了。There has been a revival of superstitious practices in some places in recent years.

【回嗔作喜】huí chēn zuò xǐ 由生气变为高兴 anger give way to joy; cease to be angry and begin to smile; one's angry face relaxes into a smile

【回程】huíchéng 返回的路程 return trip: ～车 return bus

【回春】huíchūn ❶ 冬天去了,春天到来 return of spring: 大地～ return of spring ❷〈比喻 *fig.*〉医术高明或药物灵验,能把重病治好 revive; bring back to life: 妙手～ (of a doctor) bring the dying back to life | ～灵药 a miraculous cure

【回答】huídá 对问题给予解释;对要求表示意见 answer; reply; response: ～不出来 fail to answer a question | 满意的～ satisfactory answer

【回单】huídān (～儿 huídānr) same as 回条 huítiáo

【回荡】huídàng (声音等)来回飘荡 echo; resound; reverberate: 歌声在大厅里～。The songs respound in the hall.

【回电】huí//diàn 接到电报或信件后用电报回复 wire back: 赶快给他回个电。Please wire him back immediately.

【回电】huídiàn 回复的电报 return cable: 收到一个～ receive a return cable

【回跌】huídiē (商品价格)上涨后又往下降 (of prices) go down after a rise: 物价～。Prices began to fall again.

【回返】huífǎn 往回走;返回 come or go back: ～家乡 return to one's native place | ～路程 return trip

【回访】huífǎng 在对方来拜访以后去拜访对方 pay a return visit

【回复】huífù ❶ 回答;答复(多指用书信) reply a letter: ～群众来信 reply letters from the masses ❷ 恢复(原状) return (to a normal state): ～常态 return to a normalcy

【回顾】huígù 回过头来看 review; retrospect; look back ◇～过去,瞻望未来 recall the past and look hopefully into the future

【回光返照】huí guāng fǎn zhào 指太阳刚落到地平线下时,由于反射作用而发生的天空中短时发亮的现象 momentary glow in the sky produced by reflection after the sun sets;〈比喻 *fig.*〉人临死之前精神忽然兴奋的现象。也比喻旧事物灭亡之前暂时兴旺的现象 short-lived burst of energy just before death; sudden spurt of activity prior to collapse; (of sth. old) temporary flourishing before fading away

【回光镜】huíguāngjìng 用于聚光灯、车灯等照明装置中的凹面镜 concave mirror used in illumination equipment such as spotlights and vehicle lights

【回归】huíguī 回到(原来地方);归回 return; go back to (the original place):～自然 return to nature; go back to nature|～祖国 return to one's motherland; revert to the sovereignty of a country|这个研究单位独立几年后,又～科学院了。After being left to go alone for several years, the institute has once again be placed under the leadership of the Academy of Sciences.

【回归带】huíguīdài ☞ 热带 rèdài on p.1612

【回归年】huíguīnián 太阳中心连续两次经过春分点所需要的时间。一个回归年等于365天5小时48分46秒。tropical year; solar year; time between one vernal equinox and the next. One tropical year equals about 365 days, 5 hours, 48 minutes and 46 seconds. also 太阳年 tàiyángnián

【回归线】huíguīxiàn 地球上赤道南北各23°26′处的纬度圈。北边的叫北回归线,南边的叫南回归线。夏至时,太阳直射在北纬23°26′;冬至时,太阳直射在南纬23°26′。太阳直射的范围限于这两条纬线之间,来回移动,所以叫回归线。imaginary lines of latitude drawn around the earth at 23°26′north and south of the equator, respectively called the tropics of Cancer and Capricorn. At the Summer Solstice, the sun shines down vertically over latitude 23° 26′ N at the Winter Solstice, over latitude 23°26′ S. Between the tropics the sun shines down vertically at least once a year.

【回锅】huí//guō 重新加热(已熟的食品) (cooked food) heat up; re-heat:把这碗菜回回锅再吃。Heat up this dish; again before serving it.

【回合】huíhé 旧小说中描写武将交锋时一方用兵器攻击一次而另一方用兵器招架一次叫一个回合。现在也指双方较量一次 round; bout; (in old-style fiction) an attack and parry between two warriors; timed period of contest:拳击赛进行到第十个～仍不分胜负。Even at the 10th round of the boxing match, the winner was still unclear.

【回纥】Huíhé 我国古代少数民族,主要分布在今鄂尔浑河流域。唐时曾建立回纥政权。Huihe (Ouigour), ancient ethnic people living mainly in the E'erhun River valley. During the Tang Dynasty, it established a Huihe state. also 回鹘 Huíhú

【回鹘】Huíhú same as 回纥 Huíhé

【回护】huíhù 袒护;包庇 shield; protect; partial to; be biased towards; favour:你老这样～他,他越发放纵了。Your favouratism only encourages him to act without restraint.

【回话】huí//huà 回答别人问话(旧时用于下对上 of subordinate to superior in the old times) reply; answer an inquiry from one's superior

【回话】huíhuà (～儿 huíhuàr)答复的话(多指由别人转告的 oft. through sb. else) reply; answer:我一定来,请你带个～给他。I will come, so please let him know.

【回还】huíhuán 回到原来的地方 return; go back to the original place:～故里 return home|一去不～ go away and never return

【回环】huíhuán 曲折环绕 wind; zigzag:溪水～。The creek winds along.

【回回】Huí·hui 〈旧时 *old*〉称回民 Hui ethnic people; Huis

【回火】huí//huǒ ❶ 把淬火后的工件加热(不超过临界温度),然后冷却,使能保持一定的硬度,增加韧性 tempering; impart strength and toughness to a metal work piece by heating it (to below its critical temperature) and cooling it again; also 配火 pèihuǒ ❷ 氧炔吹管等的火焰向反方向燃烧 (of flame from oxyacetylene blowpipe) flareback burn in the opposite direction

【回击】huíjī 受到攻击后,反过来攻击对方 counterattack; fight back:奋力～ make a powerful counterattack

【回见】huíjiàn 〈客套话 *pol.*〉用于分手时,表示回头再见面 so long; see you later; see you soon; goodbye

【回教】Huíjiào 我国称伊斯兰教 Islam

【回敬】huíjìng 回报别人的敬意或馈赠 return a compliment or gift; give sth. in return:～你一杯。Let me toast you in return.

【回绝】huíjué 答复对方,表示拒绝 decline; refuse; reject:一口～ refuse resolutely|～了他的不合理要求 reject his unreasonable demand

【回空】huíkōng (车船等)回程不载旅客或货物 (of vehicles or ships, etc.) return empty; return without either passengers or cargo:～车 empty lorry on the return|～的船 empty ship on the return voyage

【回口】huí//kǒu 〈方 *dial.*〉same as 回嘴 huí//zuǐ

【回扣】huíkòu 经手采购或代卖主招揽顾客的人向卖主索取的佣钱。这种钱实际上是从买主支付的价款中扣出的,所以叫回扣。有的地区也叫回佣(huíyòng)。kick back; rake-off; sales commission; money paid to a sales person or agent for soliciting clients, which actually comes out of the purchase price; also called 回佣 huíyòng in some places

【回来】huí//·lái 从别处到原来的地方来 return to the original place; come back:他刚从外地～。He has just returned to town.|他每天早晨出去,晚上才～。He leaves home every morning and comes back at nightfall.

【回来】//·huí//·lái 用在动词后,表示到原来的地方来[used after a verb to express the sense of returning] back:跑～ run back|把借出的书要～ get the borrowed book back

【回廊】huíláng 曲折环绕的走廊 winding corridor

【回老家】huí lǎojiā 指死去(多含诙谐意 oft.

humor.) die; pass away

【回礼】huí//lǐ ❶ 回答别人的敬礼 return a salute:首长向站岗的卫兵回了个礼。The senior officer returned a salute to the sentry. ❷ 回赠礼品 present a gift in return gift

【回礼】huílǐ 回赠的礼品 return gift:一份～ a return gift

【回历】Huílì 伊斯兰教历 Moslem Calendar

【回流】huíliú 流过去或流出去的又流回;倒流 (of flowing water) flow back; return; inverse flow; flow out and back again:河水～ backflowing river water◇人才～ return of skilled people

【回笼】huí//lóng ❶ 把冷了的馒头、包子等放回笼屉再蒸 heat up cold, steamed buns, stuffed buns, etc. by putting them back into a steamer ❷ 在社会上流通的货币回到发行的银行 (of currency in circulation) return to the issuing bank:货币～ withdraw currency from circulation

【回炉】huí//lú 重新熔化(金属);重新烘烤(烧饼之类) melt down (metal) again; bake (buns, etc.) again:废铁～ melt down scrap iron | ～重造 recast by putting a workpiece back in the melting furnace◇落榜考生～补课。Students who failed the examination will take refresher courses.

【回禄】Huílù 〈书 *fml*.〉传说中的火神名,多借指火灾 God of Fire in Chinese legend:～之灾 fire disaster | 惨遭～ suffer great losses in a fire

【回路】huílù ❶ 返回去的路 retreat; return road; the way back:～已被截断。The retreat was cut off. ❷ 电流通过器件或其他介质后流回电源的通路。通常指闭合电路。return circuit; path for an electric current to return to its source after passing through electric articles or insulating media; usu. a closed circuit

【回落】huíluò (水位、物价等)上涨后下降 (of water level, price, etc.) subside; drop fall after rising:水位已～到警戒线以下。The water level has fallen below the warning line.

【回马枪】huímǎqiāng 回过头来给追击者的突然袭击 sudden attack on one's pursuer; back thrust:杀～ give sb. a backthrust; fire a Parthian shot; swing round and catch sb. off guard

【回门】huí//mén 结婚后若干日内(有的当天,有的三天,多则一月)新夫妇一起到女家拜见长辈和亲友,叫做回门 (of newlyweds) return together to the bride's home to call on her relatives after the wedding (on the same day of the wedding, or three days or a month after)

【回民】Huímín 指回族人 ethnic Hui group; the Hui people

【回眸】huímóu 回过头看(多指女子 usu. of women) look back; glance back:～一笑 look back with a smile

【回目】huímù 章回小说每一回的标题。也指章回小说标题的总目录。couplet title of a chapter in a serial novel; table of contents of a serial novel

【回念】huíniàn 回想;回顾 recall; retrospect; reminisce; call to mind:～往事 recall the past

【回暖】huínuǎn 天气由冷转暖 (of weather) turn warm; become warm after a cold spell

【回聘】huípìn 对已离开职位的人员重新加以聘用 re-employ one who has left a post:～退休人员 re-employ sb. in retirement; also 返聘 fǎnpìn

【回棋】huí//qí same as 悔棋 huǐ//qí

【回迁】huíqiān 搬离后又搬回原住地 move back to the place from where one moved away:新楼建好后,居民纷纷～。The residents moved back after the new building was completed.

【回青】huí//qīng 返青 revive; turn green:麦苗～。The wheat seedlings are turning green.

【回请】huíqǐng 被人请后(如请吃饭等),还请对方 return an invitation; invite sb. to a meal in return

【回去】huí//·qù 从别处到原来的地方去 go back; return; go back to where one comes from:离开家乡十年,一次也没～过。He has never once returned home since he left ten years ago.

【回去】//·huí//·qù 用在动词后,表示到原来的地方去 [used after a verb to express a sense of returning] back:跑～ run back | 把这支笔给他送～。Return this pen to him.

【回绕】huírào 曲折环绕 wind; zigzag:这里泉水～,古木参天。In this place, springs form winding streams, and ancient trees tower into the sky.

【回煞】huíshà 迷信的人认为人死若干日后,灵魂要回家一次,叫做回煞 superstitious belief that the soul of the deceased returns home several days after death

【回身】huí//shēn 转身 turn around:回过身来 turn around | 他放下东西,～就走了。He put down the things, turned on his heel and left.

【回神】huí//shén (～儿 huí//shénr)从惊诧、恐慌、出神等状态中恢复正常 recover from surprise, shock, terror, reverie, etc.:等他回过神儿来,报信的人早已跑远了。When he recovered from the shock, the messenger was long gone.

【回升】huíshēng 下降后又往上升 recover; pick up; rise again after a fall:产量～。The output rose. | 物价～。Prices recovered. | 气温～。The temperature has risen again.

【回生】[1] huíshēng 死后再活过来 resurrect; come back to life:起死～ resurrect

【回生】[2] huíshēng 对前一阶段已经学会的东西又感到生疏 rusty; feel out of practice; unfamiliar with something learned before: 几天不练琴，手指就～。Just a few days without practice on the instrument and the fingers become stiff.

【回声】huíshēng 声波遇到障碍物反射回来再度被听到的声音 echo; repetition of sound produced by reflection of sound waves from an obstructing surface: 山谷中响起他叫喊的～。The valley echoed with his shouts.

【回师】huíshī 作战时把军队往回调动 pull troops back in battle

【回收】huíshōu ❶ 把物品(多指废品或旧货)收回利用 retrieve; reclaim; collect (mostly scrap and junk) to be recycled: ～余热 recycle waste heat | ～废旧物资 retrieve waste material ❷ 把发放或发射出的东西收回 recover what has been issued or launched: ～贷款 recover loans | ～人造卫星 retrieval or recovery of a satellite

【回手】huíshǒu ❶ 把手伸向身后或转回身去伸手 extend the hand behind the back or turn round and stretch out the hand: 走出了屋子，～把门带上 leave the room and close the door behind ❷ 还手；还击 hit back; return an attack; counterattack: 打不～ refrain from hitting back when attacked

【回首】huíshǒu ❶ 把头转向后方 look back: 屡屡～，不忍离去 keep looking back as one is reluctant to leave ❷〈书 *fml.*〉same as 回忆 huíyì: ～往事 recall the past

【回书】huíshū〈书 *fml.*〉答复的信 letter of reply

【回溯】huísù same as 回忆 huíyì: ～过去，瞻望未来 recall the past and look hopefully into the future

【回天】huítiān 形容力量大，能扭转很难挽回的局面 powerful; powerful enough to change a desperate situation for the better: ～之力 power to reverse a desperate situation | ～乏术 unable to reverse a desperate situation

【回填】huítián 土石方工程上指把挖起来的土重新填回去(in construction) backfill; soil used for refilling an excavation: ～土 backfill | ～的时候要逐层夯实。The backfill must be rammed tight layer by layer.

【回条】huítiáo (～儿 huítiáor) 收到信件或物品后交来人带回的收据 receipt; note that acknowledges receipt of letter or article

【回帖】huítiě (～儿 huítiěr)〈旧 *old*〉收款人收到邮电局汇款时，盖章后交邮电局寄回汇款人的凭证 return receipt; receipt for postal remittance that is stamped by the payee and sent back to the remitter

【回头】huí//tóu ❶把头转向后方 turn round; turn one's head; look back: 一～就看见了。I saw it once I turned round. | 请你回过头来。Turn round, please. ❷ 回来；返回 come back; return: 一去不～ go away and never return ❸ 悔悟；改邪归正 repentant; repent; give up evil and return to good: 败子～ repentant libertine; return of the prodigal son; turn over a new leaf | 现在～还不算晚。It is not too late to change yet.

【回头】huítóu 少等一会儿；过一段时间以后 after a while; a moment later; minutes later: 你先吃饭，～再谈。Eat first. We'll talk later. | 我先走了，～见! I must get going now. See you later!

【回头客】huítóukè 商店、饭馆、旅馆等指再次光顾的顾客 frequenter; regular customer; customer who frequently patronizes a shop, restaurant or hotel

【回头路】huítóulù〈比喻 *fig.*〉倒退的道路或已经走过的老路 backtrack; road of retrogression, or road already taken once

【回头人】huítóurén〈方 *dial.*〉指再嫁的寡妇 widow who remarries

【回头是岸】huí tóu shì àn 佛教说'苦海无边，回头是岸' from the Buddhist saying: 'The sea of bitterness is boundless, but turn round and the shore is at hand.';〈比喻 *fig.*〉罪恶虽大，只要悔改，就有出路 repentance will bring salvation no matter how monstrous the crimes; it is never too late to mend one's ways

【回味】huíwèi ❶ 食物吃过后的余味 aftertaste; taste remaining after food has been eaten ❷ 从回忆里体会 re-experience through memories; ponder over memories of the past

【回文诗】huíwénshī 一种诗体。可以倒着或反复回旋地阅读。如诗句'池莲照晓月，幔锦拂朝风'，倒读就是'风朝拂锦幔，月晓照莲池'。多属文字游戏。palindromic verse; usu. in word games; poem that can be read forwards and backwards, e.g. '池莲照晓月，幔锦拂朝风', which can be read backwards as'风朝拂锦幔，月晓照莲池'

【回席】huí//xí same as 还席 huán//xí

【回戏】huí//xì (戏曲)临时因故不能演出 (of Chinese theatre) temporarily cancel a performance for unexpected circumstances

【回翔】huíxiáng 盘旋地飞 wheel; circle round in the air: 鹰在空中～。The eagle is circling in the sky.

【回响】huíxiǎng ❶ same as 回声 huíshēng: 歌声在山谷中激起了～。The valley echoed with singing. ❷ same as 响应 xiǎngyìng: 增产节约的倡议得到了全厂各车间的～。The call to improve output by cutting waste drew a warm response from every workshop in the factory.

【回想】huíxiǎng 想(过去的事) recall; reminisce; think about (the past): ～不起来 fail to recall | ～起不少往事 remember many things from the past

【回销】huíxiāo 返销 sell a product to where it was produced:～粮 grain resold to the place that grew it

【回心转意】huí xīn zhuǎn yì 改变态度,不再坚持过去的成见和主张(多指放弃嫌怨,恢复感情 usu. overcoming grudges and reestablishing positive feelings) change one's mind; have a change of heart; come around; change one's attitude and give up one's prejudices and opinions

【回信】huí//xìn 答复来信 write back; write in reply:希望早日～ look forward to hearing from you soon|给他回了一封信 write him a reply

【回信】huíxìn ❶ 答复的信 letter in reply:给哥哥写了一封～ reply by letter to one's brother ❷(～儿 huíxìnr)答复的话 words in reply; verbal reply:事情办妥了,我给你个～儿。I'll send word to you when the matter is settled.

【回形针】huíxíngzhēn same as 曲别针 qūbiézhēn

【回修】huíxiū 返工修理 return for repairs; repair shoddy work:～活儿 work to be done over again

【回叙】huíxù ❶ 倒叙 flashback; cut back:作品在这里插入一段～。A flashback is inserted in the narrative here. ❷ 叙说过去的事情 relate past events:～往事 describe past events

【回旋】huíxuán ❶ 盘旋;绕来绕去地活动 circle; go round and round:飞机在上空～着。The plane is circling overhead.|～的地区很大 much room for manoeuvre ❷ 可进退;可商量 room for flexibility; room for discussion:留点儿～的余地,别把话说死了。Don't be too categorical, but leave some room for discussion.

【回旋曲】huíxuánqǔ 乐曲形式之一,特点是表现基本主题的旋律屡次反复 rondo; musical form where the principal theme recurs

【回血】huí//xuè 静脉注射时,针头扎进血管后回流进针管少量的血 tiny amount of blood that flows back into the intravenous drip tube when the needle pierces a blood vessel

【回忆】huíyì 回想 call to mind; recall; reminisce; recollect:～过去 recall the past|童年生活的～ recollections of childhood

【回忆录】huíyìlù 一种文体,记叙个人所经历的生活或所熟悉的历史事件 reminiscence; memoirs; recollections; literary form recording personal experiences, or historical events known to the writer

【回音】huíyīn ❶ same as 回声 huíshēng:礼堂～大,演奏效果差一些。The echo in the hall affected the quality of the performance. ❷ 答复的信;回话 reply letter; message in response:我连去三封信,但一直没有～。I've written him three times but haven't heard anything in reply.|不管行还是不行,请给个～。Please send me word no matter whether things work out or not.

【回应】huíyìng 回答;答应 answer; respond:叫了半天,也不见有人～。I called for a long time but nobody answered.

【回佣】huíyōng〈方 *dial.*〉same as 回扣 huíkòu

【回游】huíyóu same as 洄游 huíyóu

【回赠】huízèng 接受赠礼后,还赠对方礼物 present a gift in return; send a present in return:～一束鲜花 send a bouquet of flowers in return

【回涨】huízhǎng (水位、物价等)下降后重新上涨 rebound; (of water level, price, etc.) rise again after a fall

【回执】huízhí ❶ same as 回条 huítiáo ❷ 向寄件人证明某种邮件已经递到的凭据,由收件人盖章或签字交邮局寄回给寄件人 return receipt; receipt stamped or signed by receiver and posted back to the sender as proof that mail has been received

【回转】huízhuǎn ❶ 返回 return; go back:～故里 return to one's hometown ❷ 掉转 turn round:～身去 turn round|他～马头向原地跑去。He turned the horse around and galloped back to where he had started.

【回转仪】huízhuǎnyí 利用陀螺高速旋转时轴的方向恒定不变的特性而制成的一种装置,轮船上用来指示方向,军事上用来瞄准目标 gyroscope; gyro; apparatus consisting of a rotating wheel so mounted that its axis is capable of maintaining the same absolute direction, used to determine direction for a ship, and aim artillery

【回族】Huízú 我国少数民族之一,主要分布在宁夏、甘肃、青海、河南、河北、山东、云南、安徽、新疆、辽宁及北京等地 Hui ethnic minority people, or the Huis, mainly distributed in the Ningxia Hui Autonomous Region, Gansu, Qinghai, Henan, Hebei, Shandong, Yunnan, Anhui, the Xinjiang Uygur Autonomous Region, Liaoning and Beijing

【回嘴】huí//zuǐ 受到指责时进行辩驳;挨骂时反过来骂对方 retort; answer or talk back; scold or curse back:他自知理亏,无论你怎么说,都不～。He knew he was in the wrong, so no matter what was said, remained silent.

茴 huí [茴香](huíxiāng) ❶ 多年生草本植物,叶子分裂成丝状,花黄色。茎叶供食用,果实长椭圆形,可以做调味香料。果实榨的油叫茴香油,供药用。fennel (*Foeniculum vulgare*); perennial plant with fine linear leaves and yellow flowers. The stem and leaf are edible and the oval-shaped fruit is aromatic and used in cooking. Fennel oil, extracted from the fruit, is used in medicine ❷〈方 *dial.*〉same as 八角 bājiǎo ②

徊 huí ☞ 低徊 dīhuí on p. 411
☞ huái on p. 841

回

洄 huí 〈书 *fml*.〉水流回旋 (of water) whirl; twirl

【洄游】huíyóu 海洋中一些动物(主要是鱼类)因为产卵、觅食或季节变化的影响,沿着一定路线有规律地往返迁移 (of marine animals, mainly fish) migrate regularly to and from one habitat to another along the same route for spawning, feeding or because of seasonal changes; also 回游 huíyóu; ☞ 季节洄游 jìjié huíyóu on p. 919 and 生殖洄游 shēngzhí huíyóu on p. 1719

蛔(蚘、蛕) huí same as 蛔虫 huíchóng

【蛔虫】huíchóng 寄生虫,形状像蚯蚓,白色或米黄色,成虫长约 4—8 寸,雌虫较大。能附着在人的肠壁上引起蛔虫病,进入肝脏、胆道等还会造成其他疾病 roundworm (*Ascaris lumbricoides*); ascarid; bellyworm; white or pale yellow worm shaped like an earthworm, the adults 4-8 *cun* long and the female being larger than the male, adhering to the intestinal wall in humans, and causing ascariasis. Its presence in the liver and the bile duct may lead to other diseases.

鮰 huí 古书上指鮠鱼(wéiyú) term for white catfish (*Ictalurus catus*) in ancient books

huǐ (ㄏㄨㄟˇ)

虺 huǐ 古书上说的一种毒蛇 a kind of poisonous snake mentioned in ancient books ☞ huī on p. 857

【虺虺】huǐhuǐ 〈书 *fml*.〉打雷的声音 sound of thunder

悔 huǐ 懊悔;后悔 regret; remorse; repent; rue: ～悟 repent | 追～ regret; be penitent | 忏～ repent; confess

【悔不当初】huǐ bù dāngchū 后悔当初不该这样做或没有那样做 regret having done sth. or not having done sth.: 早知如此,～。Had I known earlier it would be like this, I wouldn't have acted as I did.

【悔改】huǐgǎi 认识错误并加以改正 realize and correct one's error: 他已表示愿意～。He has expressed his repentance and willingness to mend his ways.

【悔过】huǐguò 承认并追悔自己的错误 admit one's mistake and repent; be repentant: ～自新 repent of one's past misdemeanors and start afresh; repent and turn over a new leaf; repent and make a fresh start | 诚恳～ sincerely regret one's errors; be sincerely contrite

【悔恨】huǐhèn 懊悔 remorse: ～不已 regret deeply; be filled with bitter remorse

【悔婚】huǐ//hūn 订婚后一方废弃婚约 break of marriage engagement; jilt

【悔棋】huǐ//qí 棋子下定后收回重下 retract a move in a chess game; also 回棋 huí//qí

【悔悟】huǐwù 认识到自己的过错,悔恨而醒悟 realize one's mistakes and show repentance; repent

【悔罪】huǐ//zuì 悔恨自己的罪恶 show remorse for one's crime; show repentance: 有～表现 show signs of remorse

毁(❷燬、❸譭) huǐ ❶ 破坏;糟蹋 damage; sabotage; demolish; ruin; lay waste to: ～灭 exterminate; extinguish | 销～ destroy; ruin | 好好儿的一本书,让你给～了。The book was in good condition, and now you have ruined it. ❷ 烧掉 burn away; burn off; burn out; burn up: 烧～ burn off; burn out | 焚～ burn away ❸ 毁谤;说别人坏话 slander; smear; vilify; obloquy; sling mud on sb.; speak ill of others: ～誉 slander | 诋～ vilify; calumniate ❹ 〈方 *dial*.〉把成件的旧东西改成别的东西(多指衣服 oft. clothes) refashion; make something out of old clothes: 用一件大褂给孩子～两条裤子。Make two pairs of trousers for the child out of an overcoat.

【毁谤】huǐbàng same as 诽谤 fěibàng

【毁害】huǐhài 毁坏 destroy; bane; cause damage to; same as 祸害 huòhài ③: 这一带常有野兽～庄稼。This area is frequented by wild beasts that often destroy crops.

【毁坏】huǐhuài 损坏;破坏 damage; ruin; sabotage: 不许～古迹。Damaging historical sites is forbidden. | ～他人名誉 ruin the reputation of sb. else

【毁家纾难】huǐ jiā shū nàn 捐献全部家产,帮助国家减轻困难 donate all one's possessions to help alleviate a national crisis (纾 *shu*: 缓和 alleviate, relieve)

【毁灭】huǐmiè 摧毁消灭 destroy; exterminate: ～罪恶势力 destroy evil forces | 遭到～性打击 suffer a crushing or devastating blow

【毁弃】huǐqì 毁坏抛弃 scrap; destroy and throw away

【毁容】huǐ//róng 毁坏面容 disfigure; deface; deform

【毁伤】huǐshāng 破坏;伤害 damage; harm; hurt; injure

【毁损】huǐsǔn 损伤;损坏 spoil; mangle; impair: 不得～公共财物。No damaging public property.

【毁誉】huǐyù 毁谤和称赞;说坏话和说好话 praise or blame; praise or condemn: ～参半 equal parts of censure and praise; get both praise and blame; receive a mixed reception | 不计～indifferent to praise or blame

【毁约】huǐ//yuē 撕毁共同商定的协议、条约、合同等 break one's promise; go back on one's word; scrap an agreement, treaty or contract

huì(ㄏㄨㄟˋ)

卉 huì 各种草(多指供观赏的)的总称 general term for various kinds of plants (usu. ornamental):花～ flowers and plants|奇花异～ exotic flowers and rare grasses

汇[1](滙、匯、❷❸彙) huì ❶ 汇合 converge; join:百川所～。One hundred rivers converge. |～成巨流 converge into a mighty river ❷ 聚集;聚合 collect; gather together:～报 report; give an account of sth.|～印成书 collect and compile materials into a book ❸ 聚集而成的东西 collection; assemblage:词～ vocabulary|总～ collection; complete inventory

汇[2](滙、匯) huì ❶ 通过邮电局、银行等把甲地款项划拨到乙地 transfer funds from one place to another through post office, bank, etc.:电～ wire transfer; telegraphic money order|～款 remit money|～给他一笔路费 remit his travel expenses ❷ 指外汇 foreign currency:换～convert one currency into another |创～ earn foreign exchange by exports

【汇报】huìbào 综合材料向上级报告,也指综合材料向群众报告 summarize information and data to report to one's superior or the public:听～ listen to a report|～处理结果 give an account of the results

【汇编】huìbiān ❶ 把文章、文件等汇总编排在一起 compile; put articles or documents together:～成书 compile into a book ❷ 编在一起的文章、文件等(多用做书名 usu. in book titles) compilation; collection; articles and documents collected together:法规～ collection of statutes|资料～ collection of materials

【汇兑】huìduì 银行或邮局根据汇款人的委托,把款项汇交指定的收款人 remittance; money sent through bank or post office to recipient

【汇费】huìfèi 银行或邮局办理汇款业务时,按汇款金额所收的手续费 remittance fee; transaction fee charged by bank or post office based on the amount remitted; also 汇水 huìshuǐ

【汇合】huìhé (水流)聚集;会合(of water) converge; join:小河～成大河。Small creeks converge into a big river.◇人民的意志～成一支巨大的力量。The will of the people converged into a mighty force.

【汇集】huìjí 聚集 collect; gather:～材料 collect data|把资料～在一起研究 gather materials for study|游行队伍从大街小巷～到天安门广场上。The processions came down the streets and lanes to congregate on Tian'anmen Square. also 会集 huìjí

【汇价】huìjià same as 汇率 huìlǜ

【汇聚】huìjù same as 会聚 huìjù

【汇款】huì//kuǎn 把款汇出 remit money:他到邮局～去了。He went to the post office to remit money.

【汇款】huìkuǎn 汇出或汇到的款项 remittance; money sent or received:收到一笔～ receive a remittance

【汇流】huìliú 水流等会合(of water) converge; join:数条小溪在这里～成河。Several streams converge here to form a river.

【汇拢】huìlǒng 聚集;聚合 assemble; gather; come together:几股人群～一起。Several crowds joined together.|～群众的意见 gather and sort out opinions from the public

【汇率】huìlǜ 一个国家的货币兑换其他国家的货币的比例 exchange rate; ratio at which the unit of currency of one country can be exchanged for the unit of currency of another country; also 汇价 huìjià

【汇票】huìpiào 银行或邮局承办汇兑业务时发给的支取汇款的票据 draft; bill of exchange; money order; written order for payment of specified sum, issued by bank or post office

【汇水】huìshuǐ same as 汇费 huìfèi

【汇演】huìyǎn same as 会演 huìyǎn

【汇展】huìzhǎn (商品等)汇集在一起展览(of merchandise) exhibit; be on display:南北糕点～ exhibition of speciality cakes and sweetmeats from southern and northern China|名牌时装～ fashion show

【汇总】huìzǒng (资料、单据、款项等)汇集到一起 gather or collect (materials, receipts and funds):等各组的资料到齐后～上报 submit a full report after data from each group have been collected; present an itemized report to one's superiors

会[1](會) huì ❶ 聚合;合在一起 gather; congregate; assemble:～合 congregate; assemble|～齐 join together|～诊 medical consultation|～审 joint hearing; joint review ❷ 见面;会见 meet; see:～面 meet|～客 receive a guest|昨天没有～着他。I tried but didn't meet him yesterday. ❸ 有一定目的的集会 rally; assemblage; assembly; congregation; gathering with a specific purpose:晚～ evening party|舞～ dance party; ball|开～ hold a meeting|报告～ meeting; lecture|晚上有一个～。There's going to be a meeting tonight. ❹ 某些团体 association; society; organization:工～ workers' union|妇女联合～ women's union ❺ 庙会 temple fair:赶～ go to a temple fair ❻ 民间朝山进香或酬神求年成时所组织的集体活动,如香会、迎神赛会等 popular gathering at a temple to pray for a bumper harvest, e.g. gathering of worshippers, festival to pacify the spirits ❼ 民间一种小规模经济互助组织,入会成员按期平均交款,分期轮流使用 small credit association, where members regularly contribute an equal amount to a common fund and draw from it by turns ❽ 主要的城市 main city：都～ capital；metroplis｜省～ provincial capital ❾ 时机 chance；opportunity：机～ chance；opportunity｜适逢其～ happen to be present ❿〈书 *fml*.〉恰巧；正好 happen；coincide with；it happens...：～有客来。At that moment，a guest happened to visit. ⓫〈书 *fml*.〉应当 ought to；should：长风破浪～有时。There should come a time when you can display all your talents.

会²（會） huì ❶ 理解；懂得 understand；grasp：体～ realize；grasp｜误～ misunderstanding｜心领神～ readily take a hint or cue；taut understanding｜只可意～，不可言传 can be felt but not expressed；inexpressible in words ❷ 熟习；通晓 familiar with；acquainted with：～英文 know English｜～两出京戏 able to sing a few airs from Peking Opera ❸ 表示懂得怎样做或有能力做（多半指需要学习的事情）able to；can；know how to do sth. or be able to do sth.（esp. sth. learned）：我不～滑冰。I cannot skate.｜这孩子刚～走路，还不大～说话。The baby has just learned to walk but hasn't learned to speak yet. ❹ 表示擅长 good at；excel at；skilled in：能说～道 has a glib tongue｜～写～画的人倒不太讲究纸的好坏。One who writes and paints well does not pay much attention to the quality of the paper. ❺ 表示有可能实现 likely to；sure to：他不～不来。He's sure to come.｜树上的果子熟了，自然～掉下来。When the fruit is ripe，it will automatically fall. ☞ 注意 a)，b) and c) of 能 néng in the NOTE on p.1402

会³（會） huì 付账 pay a bill：我～过了。I have paid the bill.

会⁴（會） huì ☞ 会儿 huìr and 会子 huì·zi ☞ kuài on p.1118

【会标】huìbiāo 代表某个集会的标志 logo；mascot；emblem of a specific gathering

【会餐】huì∥cān 聚餐 dine together：节日～ group meal to celebrate a festival

【会操】huì∥cāo 指会合举行军事或体育方面的操演 joint drill or practice；come together for joint military drill or sports practice：下午两点在大操场～。There will be a joint drill session on the sports field at two o'clock this afternoon.

【会场】huìchǎng 开会的场所 venue；place for a meeting

【会钞】huì∥chāo same as 会账 huì∥zhàng

【会车】huìchē 相向行驶的列车、汽车等同时在某一地点交错通过（of trains or motor vehicles going in opposite directions）cross each other at a certain place

【会党】huìdǎng 清末以反清复明为宗旨的一些原始形式的民间秘密团体的总称。如哥老会、三合会等。general term for certain secret primitive societies that rose in force towards the end of the Qing Dynasty to overthrow the Qing Dynasty and re-establish the Ming Dynasty，e.g. Gelao Society and Sanhe Society

【会道门】huìdàomén（～儿 huìdàoménr）会门和道门的合称 collective term for superstitious sects and secret societies

【会典】huìdiǎn 记载某一朝代法令制度的书籍，多用做书名，如《明会典》collection；book that records the laws and regulations of a specific dynasty，usu. in book titles，e.g. *The Code of Ming*

【会费】huìfèi 会员按期向所属组织交的钱。会员按期向所属组织交的钱 membership dues a member regularly pays to the organization he or she belongs to

【会攻】huìgōng 联合进攻 joint attack；concerted attack：兵分两路，～匪巢。The troops approaches the bandit's lair along two routes and launched a combined attack.

【会馆】huìguǎn 同省、同府、同县或同业的人在京城、省城或大商埠设立的机构，主要以馆址的房屋供同乡、同业聚会或寄寓 guild；guild hall；institution established in a capital，provincial capital or major commercial port by people coming from the same province，prefecture，county or in the same trade，to provide accommodation for fellow countrymen and traders

【会合】huìhé 聚集到一起 join；congregate；assemble；converge；meet：两军～后继续前进。The two armies joined forces and marched on.｜黄浦江在吴淞口与长江～。The Huangpu and the Yangtze rivers converge at the Wusong Estuary.

【会话】huìhuà same as 对话 duìhuà ①（多用于学习别种语言或方言时 usu. for learning a foreign language or a dialect）

【会徽】huìhuī 代表某个集会的标志 logo；emblem of a gathering：全国运动会～ logo of the National Games

【会集】huìjí same as 汇集 huìjí

【会见】huìjiàn 跟别人相见 interview；meet with sb.：～亲友 meet one's relatives and friends｜友好的～ friendly meeting

【会聚】huìjù 聚集 assemble；get together；congregate；also 汇聚 huìjù

【会考】huìkǎo same as 统考 tǒngkǎo

【会客】huì∥kè 和来访的客人见面 receive a visitor；receive a guest：～室 reception room

【会门】huì∥mén（～儿 huì∥ménr）某些封建迷信的组织 organization based on superstitious beliefs

【会面】huìmiàn same as 见面 jiàn∥miàn

【会期】huìqī ❶ 开会的日子 time fixed for a conference；date of a meeting：～定在九月一

日。The meeting will be held on September 1. ❷ 开会的天数 duration of a meeting:～三天。The meeting is scheduled to last three days.

【会齐】huì//qí 聚齐 assemble; get together:各村参加集训的民兵后天到县里～。The militiamen from all the villages due to undergo military training will assemble in the county seat the day after tomorrow.

【会旗】huìqí 某些集会的旗帜 flag of a meeting; conference flag:主席台上高悬着绘有骏马和弓箭的那达慕～。Hunging above the rostrum is the Nadam Fair flag emblazoned with a steed and arrow.

【会儿】huìr 指很短的一段时间 a moment; a while; a short time:一～ a moment|这～ at this moment|等～ wait a moment|用不了多大～。It won't take long.

【会商】huìshāng 双方或多方共同商量 consult; discuss; hold bilateral or multilateral discussion or negotiation:～大计 hold consultations on major issues

【会审】huìshěn ❶ 会同审理(案件等) conduct a joint trial or hearing ❷ 会同审查 joint review:～施工图纸 jointly review the blueprints of a construction project

【会师】huì//shī 几支独立行动的部队在战地会合(of two or more armies) combine forces; several independent military units join forces on a battlefield:胜利～ join forces in victory ◇各地革新能手在首都～。Innovators and those with creative talent from all over the country converged on the capital.

【会试】huìshì 明清两代各省举人参加的科举考试,每三年在京城举行一次 during the Ming and Qing dynasties imperial examination held once every three years in the capital for those candidates successful in the provincial examination

【会首】huìshǒu 〈旧时 *old*〉民间各种叫做会的组织的发起人 sponsor of a popular unofficial organization or society; also 会头 huìtóu

【会水】huì//shuǐ 会游泳 know how to swim:他从小就～。He knew how to swim since he was very young.

【会谈】huìtán 双方或多方共同商谈 bilateral or multilateral talks:两国～ talks between two countries

【会堂】huìtáng 礼堂(多用做建筑物名称 usu. part of the name of a building) assembly hall; conference hall; meeting hall; hall:科学～ Hall of Science|人民大～ the Great Hall of the People

【会通】huìtōng 〈书 *fml.*〉融会贯通 achieve thorough understanding through mastery of all relevant materials; achieve mastery through comprehensive study

【会同】huìtóng 跟有关方面会合起来(办事) (handle matters) conjointly; jointly with relevant departments:这事由商业局～有关部门办理。This matter will be dealt with conjointly by the commercial bureau and the other departments concerned.

【会务】huìwù 集会或会议的事务 affairs associated with a conference; day-to-day managing of a conference:主持～ be in charge of day-to-day conference business|～工作 conference administration

【会晤】huìwù 会面;会见 meet; meet with:两国领导人～ summit meeting; meeting of senior leaders of two countries|～当地知名人士 meet local celebrities

【会衔】huìxián (两个或两个以上的机关)在发出的公文上共同具名 joint signature; (of two or more institutions) jointly sign an official document

【会心】huìxīn 领会别人没有明白表示的意思 understanding; knowing; perceptive; insightful; understand implied meaning:别有～ very perceptive|～的微笑 an understanding smile

【会演】huìyǎn 各地或各单位的文艺节目集中起来,单独或同台演出。具有汇报、互相学习、交流经验的作用。drama festival; solo or joint performances by actors from different places and troupes for the purpose of displaying their skills, learning from each other and exchanging experiences; also 汇演 huìyǎn

【会厌】huìyàn 喉头上前部的树叶状的结构,由会厌软骨和黏膜构成。呼吸或说话时,会厌向上,使喉腔开放;咽东西时,会厌向下,盖住气管,使东西不至进入气管内。epiglottis; leaf-shaped structure in the upper front part of the throat, consisting of cartilage and mucous membrane. When breathing or speaking, the epiglottis rises to let the windpipe open, during swallowing, and drops to cover the glottis and prevent food from entering the trachea; (图见 ☞ figure for 人的喉 rén·dehóu on p.808)

【会厌软骨】huìyàn ruǎngǔ 构成会厌的软骨,形状扁平,像树叶,下部附着在结喉的内壁上 epiglottic cartilage; flat, leaf-shaped cartilage forming the epiglottis; its lower end attached to the inside of the Adam's apple at one end

【会要】huìyào 记载某一朝代各项经济政治制度的书籍,多用做书名,如《唐会要》(used in book titles) book of economic and political structures during certain dynasties, e.g. *Economic and Political Structures of the Tang Dynasty*

【会议】huìyì ❶ 有组织有领导地商议事情的集会 meeting; conference; organized gathering for discussion and consultation:全体～ plenary session|厂务～ factory management meeting|工作～ working session ❷ 一种经常商讨

并处理重要事务的常设机构或组织 congress; council; conference; standing body that meets regularly to discuss and make decisions on important matters: 中国人民政治协商～ Chinese People's Political Consultative Conference | 部长～ council of ministers

【会意】[1] huìyì 六书之一。会意是说字的整体的意义由部分的意义合成,如'公'字、'信'字。'背私为公','公'字由'八'字和'厶'(私)字合成,'八'表示'违背'的意思,跟'自私'相反叫'公'。'人言为信','信'字由'人'字和'言'字合成,表示人说的话有信用。combined meaning; associative compound; one of the six categories of Chinese characters; A Chinese character consists of several elements, which combine to give meaning. For example, 公 gōng comprises 八 meaning 'against', and 厶 meaning 'selfish', so 公 means 'altruistic'. 信 xìn consists of 人 meaning 'human being' and 言 meaning 'speak', or 'speech', so 信 means 'words of a human being are trustworthy'.

【会意】[2] huìyì same as 会心 huìxīn

【会阴】huìyīn 肛门与外生殖器之间的部分 perineum; area between the anus and the external genitalia

【会友】huìyǒu ❶ 指同一个组织的成员 fellow member of the same organization ❷〈书 *fml.*〉结交朋友 make friends with: 以文～ make friends through literary or academic exchanges

【会元】huìyuán 明清两代称会试考取第一名的人(in the Ming and Qing dynasties) candidate who comes first in the highest imperial examination

【会员】huìyuán 某些群众组织或政治组织的成员 member of a mass or political organization: 工会～ trade unionist; member of a trade union

【会战】huìzhàn ❶ 战争双方主力在一定地区和时间内进行的决战 decisive battle between two main rival forces at a specific place within a specific period ❷〈比喻 *fig.*〉集中有关力量,突击完成某项任务 launch a mass campaign; pool the efforts of all those concerned to finish a task quickly: 石油大～ great campaign to discover and drill oil

【会账】huì//zhàng (在饭馆、酒馆、茶馆、澡堂、理发馆等处)付账(多指一人给大家付账) foot the bill for; pay for; treat (others in restaurant, pub, teahouse, bathhouse, or barber's); also 会钞 huìchāo

【会诊】huì//zhěn 几个医生共同诊断疑难病症(of several doctors) medical consultation for difficult cases; multi-specialty consultation: 他的病明天由内科医生～。Doctors from the department of internal medicine will consult on his disease tomorrow.

【会众】huìzhòng ❶ 到会的人;参加开会的人 participants; attendees; audience at a meeting; ❷〈旧时 *old.*〉指参加某些会道门等组织的人 members of sect or secret society

【会子】huì·zi 指一段时间 a while; a period of time; a moment; some time: 说～话儿 talk for a while | 喝了～茶 have some tea | 来了～了,该回去了。I've been here for a while. I must go now.

讳(諱) huì ❶ 因有所顾忌而不敢说或不愿说;忌讳 avoid saying; regard as taboo; dare not say: 隐～ hide; cover up; avoid mentioning | 直言不～ speak frankly; talk straight; call a spade a spade ❷ 忌讳的事情 taboo; prohibition; restriction: 犯了他的～了。You talked about something that is taboo to him. ❸〈旧时 *old*〉不敢直称帝王或尊长的名字,叫讳。也指所讳的名字。deferential practice of avoiding addressing or mentioning the emperor or a senior person directly by the name; the name thus being avoided: 名～ (forbidden) name

【讳疾忌医】huì jí jì yī 怕人知道有病而不肯医治(of a sick person) refuse to be treated for fear that others will know about one's illness;〈比喻 *fig.*〉掩饰缺点,不愿改正 cover up one's mistakes and refuse to correct them; refuse to face up to one's errors

【讳忌】huìjì same as 忌讳 jì·huì: 毫不～ hold nothing back; speak straight from the shoulder | 不知～ know no taboo

【讳莫如深】huì mò rú shēn 紧紧隐瞒 carefully guard a secret; hide from others; hold back; not breathe a word to a soul

【讳言】huìyán 不敢或不愿说 dare not or will not speak up: 无可～ hold nothing as taboo; hold nothing back

荟(薈) huì〈书 *fml.*〉草木繁盛 (of grass and trees) luxuriant

【荟萃】huìcuì (英俊的人物或精美的东西)会集;聚集(of distinguished people or beautiful objects) gather together; assemble: ～一堂 gather together in one hall | 人才～ gathering of talented people

哕(噦) huì〈书 *fml.*〉鸟鸣声 chirp; twitter

☞ yuě on p. 2369

【哕哕】huìhuì〈书 *fml.*〉铃声 ringing of bells

浍(澮) Huì 浍河,水名,发源于河南,流入安徽 Hui River, which rises in Henan Province and flows into Anhui Province

☞ kuài on p. 1121

诲 huì 教导;诱导 teach; instruct: 教～ instruction; advice | ～人不倦 teach tirelessly; teach with tireless zeal

【诲人不倦】huì rén bù juàn 教育人极有耐心,不知疲倦 teach with zeal and patience; be never tired of admonishing others

【海淫海盗】huì yín huì dào 引诱人做奸淫、盗窃的事 entice sb. to promiscuity and theft; stir up the base passions; propagate sex and violence

绘(繪) huì same as 画[1] huà ①:描～ describe; portray; delineate|～画 painting; drawing|～图 charting; map-making; drafting

【绘画】huìhuà 造型艺术的一种,用色彩、线条把实在的或想像中的物体形象描绘在纸、布或其他底子上。从使用的工具和材料来分,有油画、水彩画、墨笔画、木炭画等。painting; drawing; visual plastic art in which colours and lines expressing real or imaginary images are traced on paper, cloth or other materials; It is divided into several categories: oils, watercolours, ink painting, charcoal drawing, etc. based on the implements and materials used.

【绘声绘色】huì shēng huì sè ☞ 绘影绘声 huì yǐng huì shēng

【绘事】huìshì 〈书 *fml.*〉关于绘画的事情 all that is associated with drawing and painting

【绘图】huìtú 绘制图样或地图等 chart; sketch; draw a pattern; draft a design; draw a map

【绘影绘声】huì yǐng huì shēng 形容叙述、描写生动逼真 describe or narrate vividly; give a lifelike portrayal; give a vivid account; also 绘声绘影 huì shēng huì yǐng and 绘声绘色 huì shēng huì sè

【绘制】huìzhì 画(图表) draw (charts and diagrams):～工程设计图 make a design drawing of an engineering project

恚 huì 〈书 *fml.*〉怨恨 grudge; resentment:～恨 hatred; enmity

桧(檜) huì 用于人名,秦桧,南宋奸臣 used in names of people, e. g. Qin Hui, a treacherous court official of the Southern Song Dynasty

☞ guì on p. 735

贿 huì ❶〈书 *fml.*〉财物 property; wealth ❷ 贿赂 bribe:行～ commit bribery|受～ take a bribe|纳～ take a bribe|索～ ask for a bribe

【贿赂】huìlù ❶ 用财物买通别人 grease sb.'s hand; tip; bribe; influence or corrupt sb. with a bribe:～上司 bribe one's superior ❷ 用来买通别人的财物 bribe; material benefit given to influence judgment or conduct:接受～ take a bribe

【贿赂公行】huìlù gōng xíng 公开行贿受贿 openly give or take a bribe; open bribery

【贿选】huìxuǎn 用财物买通选举人使选举自己或跟自己同派系的人 buy votes; practise bribery during election; get elected by bribery; bribe voters to vote for oneself or for someone of one's faction

烩(燴) huì ❶ 烹饪方法,炒菜后加少量的水和芡粉 braise; culinary technique of adding a small amount of cornstarch mixed with water just before serving dish:～虾仁 braised shrimp meat|～什锦 braised mixed vegetables ❷ 烹饪方法,把米饭等和荤菜、素菜混在一起加水煮 simmer; cook rice with meat, vegetables and water:～饭 simmering meat, vegetables and rice with water|～饼 shredded pancake simmered with meat, and vegetables

彗(篲) huì (旧读 formerly pronounced suì)〈书 *fml.*〉扫帚 broom

【彗星】huìxīng 绕着太阳旋转的一种星体,通常在背着太阳的一面拖着一条扫帚状的长尾巴,体积很大,密度很小 comet; celestial body moving about the sun, often with a long broom-like tail flowing away from the sun; large in volume but with a low density; 通称 popular known as 扫帚星 sào•zhouxīng; (图见 ☞ figure for 太阳系 tàiyángxì on p. 1855)

晦 huì ❶ 农历每月的末一天 last day of a lunar month:～朔 period from the last day of a lunar month to the first day of the next one ❷ 昏暗;不明显 dark and gloomy; not obvious:～涩 obscure|～暝 dark and gloomy|隐～ obscure; veiled ❸ 夜晚 night:风雨如～ wind and rain sweeping across a gloomy sky; grim situation ❹〈书 *fml.*〉隐藏 hide; cover up:～迹 cover one's tracks|韬～ conceal one's true features or intentions; cover up

【晦暗】huì'àn 昏暗;暗淡 dark and gloomy; dim; shadowy:天色～ dark and gloomy sky◇心情～ gloomy; moody; in low spirits; downcast

【晦明】huìmíng 〈书 *fml.*〉❶ 夜间和白天 day and night ❷ 昏暗和晴朗 dark and bright

【晦暝】huìmíng 〈书 *fml.*〉昏暗 dusky; dim; murky:风雨～。Driving rain cast a gloomy pall. also 晦冥 huìmíng

【晦气】huì•qì ❶ 不吉利;倒霉 unlucky; out of luck; down on one's luck; hapless; unfortunate:真～,刚出门就遇上大雨。What rotten luck! It started to pour the moment we went out. ❷ 指人倒霉或生病时难看的气色 look poorly when ill or things are going badly:满脸～。Misfortune was written all over his face.

【晦涩】huìsè (诗文、乐曲等的含意)隐晦不易懂 (of meaning of poetry or prose, music, etc.) hard to understand; obscure; dubious; abstruse; cryptic:文字～ obscure language

【晦朔】huìshuò 〈书 *fml.*〉从农历某月的末一天到下月的第一天。也指从天黑到天明。period from the last day of a lunar month to the first day of the next one; also period from dusk to dawn

秽(穢) huì ❶ 肮脏 dirty; grimy; unclean:污～ filthy; foul ❷ 丑恶; 丑陋 ugly; abominable; heinous; ignominious:～行 dirty trick; debauched behaviour; immoral conduct; scandalous conduct|自惭形～ feel unworthy of; sense of inferiority or inadequacy

【秽迹】huìjì 〈书 *fml*.〉丑恶的事迹 scandal; dirty business

【秽气】huìqì 难闻的气味;臭气 stench; stink; offensive smell; foul smell

【秽土】huìtǔ same as 垃圾 lājī

【秽闻】huìwén 〈书 *fml*.〉丑恶的名声(多指淫乱的名声 usu. for promiscuous behaviour) infamous reputation; ill repute:～四播 notorious for immoral behaviour|～远扬 widely known for scandalous and licentious conduct

【秽行】huìxíng 〈书 *fml*.〉丑恶的行为(多指淫乱的行为 usu. licentious behaviour) debauch behaviour; immoral conduct

【秽语】huìyǔ 淫秽的话 obscene words; lewd speech:市井～ vulgar market talk; vulgar and crude language

惠 huì ❶ 给予的或受到的好处;恩惠 favour; kindness; courtesy:小恩小～ small gifts and favours|施～于人 bestow favour on sb.|受～无穷 benefit immensely from sb. or sth. ❷ 给人好处 benefit; kindness:平等互～ equality and mutual benefit ❸ 〈敬辞 *pol*.〉用于对方对待自己的行动 [complimentary reference to sb.'s acts toward oneself]:～临 your gracious presence|～顾 your patronage|～存 please retain ❹ (Huì) 姓 a surname 〈古 *arch*.〉same as 慧 huì

【惠存】huìcún 〈敬辞 *pol*.〉请保存(多用于送人相片、书籍等纪念品时所题的上款 oft. inscribed on photograph, book or other memento) please keep; to so-and-so, as a souvenir

【惠风】huìfēng 〈书 *fml*.〉和风 breeze; gentle wind:～和畅。A breeze is gently blowing.

【惠顾】huìgù same as 惠临 huìlín (多用于商店对顾客 usu. a shop addressing its customer) your patronage:家具展销,敬请～。Your patronage is solicited at the furniture exhibition.

【惠及】huìjí 〈书 *fml*.〉把好处给予某人或某地 bestow benefit on sb. or a place; bring benefit to:～远方 kindness extends far and wide

【惠临】huìlín 〈敬辞 *pol*.〉指对方到自己这里来 your gracious presence; complimentary reference to sb.'s presence at one's place:日前～,失迎为歉。I apologize for not meeting you when you honoured me with a visit the other day.

【惠允】huìyǔn 〈敬辞 *pol*.〉指对方允许自己(做某事) kindly permit; be kind enough to permit (action)

【惠赠】huìzèng 〈敬辞 *pol*.〉指对方赠予(财物) kind gift of money or material help

喙 huì 〈书 *fml*.〉❶ 鸟兽的嘴 bill; beak of a bird; snout of an animal:长～ long beak|短～ short snout ❷ 借指人的嘴 human mouth:百～莫辩 cannot explain away|不容置～(不容许插嘴) permit no interruption

翙(翽) huì [翙翙] 〈书 *fml*.〉鸟飞的声音 flying sound of brid(s)

阓 huì ☞ [阛阓] huánhuì on p. 845

缋 huì 〈书 *fml*.〉same as 绘 huì

殨(㱮) huì (疮 sore) 溃烂 fester:～脓 fester
☞ 溃 kuì on p. 1130

蔧 huì (旧读 formerly pronounced suì) ☞ 王蔧 wánghuì on p. 1981

嘒 huì 〈书 *fml*.〉形容微小 tiny

僡 huì 〈书 *fml*.〉same as 惠 huì

慧 huì 聪明 clever; smart; bright; intelligent; brilliant:智～ wisdom|聪～ intelligent|～心 wisdom

【慧根】huìgēn 〈佛教 *Budd*.〉指能透彻领悟佛理的天资。借指人天赋的智慧。ability to thoroughly grasp the meaning of Buddhist doctrines; innate intelligence

【慧黠】huìxiá 〈书 *fml*.〉聪明而狡猾 shrewd; clever and cunning:～过人 more clever and cunning than others

【慧心】huìxīn 原是佛教用语,指能领悟佛理的心。今泛指智慧。(in a broad sense) wisdom; (orig.) Buddhist term for an enlightened mind able to comprehend Buddhist doctrines

【慧眼】huìyǎn 原是佛教用语,指能认识到过去未来的眼力今泛指敏锐的眼力 sharp eyes; insight; discernment; (orig.) Buddhist term, insight into past and future:独具～ have exceptional insight|～识英雄 discernment will recognize talent

蕙 huì 多年生草本植物,叶子丛生,狭长而尖,初夏开花,黄绿色,有香味,生在山野 orchid(*Cymbidium faberi*); perennial epiphytic or terrestrial mountain plant with narrow, long, pointed leaves and fragrant, greenish-yellow flowers, blooms in early summer

槥 huì 〈书 *fml*.〉粗陋的小棺材 crudely made small coffin

潓 Huì 古水名 name of an ancient river

憓 huì 〈书 *fml*.〉same as 惠 huì

靧 huì 〈书 *fml*.〉洗脸 wash face

蟪 huì [蟪蛄](huìgū) 蝉的一种,吻长,身体短,黄绿色,有黑色条纹,翅膀有黑斑 a variety of cicada (*Platypleura kaempferi*), with long mouth parts, short, greenish-yellow, black-striped body and black-spotted wings

hūn (ㄏㄨㄣ)

昏 hūn ❶ 天刚黑的时候；黄昏 dusk; twilight：晨～dawn and dusk ❷ 黑暗；模糊 dark; dim; vague：～暗 dim｜～黄 dull yellow｜～花 dim-sighted｜天～地暗 dark all around ❸ 头脑迷糊；神志不清 muddled; confused：～庸 fatuous｜～头～脑 muddle-headed ❹ 失去知觉 lose consciousness：～厥 faint; fall into a swoon; fall down in a faint｜～迷 be in a coma; comatose

〈古 *arch.*〉same as 婚 hūn

【昏暗】hūn'àn 光线不足；暗 dim; dark：灯光～dim light｜太阳下山了，屋里渐渐～起来。The sun set behind the hills and the room gradually got dark.

【昏沉】hūnchén ❶ 暗淡 pale; murky：暮色～murky twilight ❷ 头脑迷糊，神志不清 dazed; dizzy; befuddled：喝醉了酒，头脑～。He felt dizzy when he got drunk.

【昏黑】hūnhēi 黑暗；昏暗 dark; dusky：夜色～dark night｜～的小屋 a little, dark room

【昏花】hūnhuā （眼光）模糊（多指老年人）(of sight, usu. of elderly person) dim：老眼～dim-sighted from age

【昏黄】hūnhuáng 暗淡模糊的黄色（用于天色、灯光等 of sky, light, etc.）pale or dull yellow; dim：月色～ pale moon; faint moonlight

【昏厥】hūnjué 因脑部贫血引起供氧不足而短时间失去知觉。心情过分悲痛、精神过度紧张、大出血、直立过久、心脏疾患等都能引起昏厥。faint; short loss of consciousness due to lack of oxygen to the brain; Fainting may also be caused by excessive grief, nervousness, massive hemorrhage, standing too long, and heart disease. also 晕厥 yūnjué

【昏君】hūnjūn 昏庸的帝王 fatuous and self-indulgent ruler

【昏聩】hūnkuì 眼花耳聋 dim-sighted and deaf;〈比喻 *fig.*〉头脑糊涂，不明是非 muddle-headed; unable to tell right from wrong：神志～muddle-headed; dazed｜～无能 muddle-headed and incompetent; fatuous and incompetent

【昏乱】hūnluàn ❶ 头脑迷糊，神志不清 confused; dazed; befuddled：思路～befuddled; confused ❷〈书 *fml.*〉政治黑暗，社会混乱 political corruption and social chaos

【昏迷】hūnmí 因大脑功能严重紊乱而长时间失去知觉。严重的外伤、脑出血、脑膜炎等都能引起昏迷。stupor; coma; prolonged unconsciousness due to serious brain malfunction, caused by severe trauma, cerebral hemorrhage, meningitis, etc.

【昏睡】hūnshuì 昏昏沉沉地睡 lethargy; narcoma; lethargic sleep：病人仍处在～状态。The patient remains in a state of unconsciousness.

【昏天黑地】hūn tiān hēi dì ❶ 形容天色昏暗 in total darkness; pitch-dark; dim; dark sky：到了晚上，～的，山路就更不好走了。At night, it is very dark and the mountain path becomes even more treacherous. ❷ 形容神志不清 disoriented; delirious; unconscious：当时我流血过多，觉得～的。At the time, I felt dizzy from excessive loss of blood. ❸ 形容生活荒唐颓废 dissipated; decadent; loose and profligate life-style：你可不能跟这帮人～地鬼混了。You must stop associating with people who lead such dissipated lives. ❹ 形容打斗或吵闹得厉害 fight or quarrel fiercely：吵得个～have a fierce quarrel ❺ 形容社会黑暗或秩序混乱 social decadence or social chaos

【昏头昏脑】hūn tóu hūn nǎo 形容头脑迷糊，神志不清 nonplused; dizzy; muddle-headed; confused and disoriented：他一天到晚忙得～的，哪顾得这件事。He is so busy all day that he has no time to deal with the matter. also 昏头涨脑 hūn tóu zhàng nǎo

【昏星】hūnxīng 我国古代指日落以后出现在西方天空的金星或水星 old name for Venus or Mercury which appear in the western sky after sunset

【昏眩】hūnxuàn 头脑昏沉，眼花缭乱 dizzy; giddy; dazed; with spinning head and dazzled eyes：一阵～，便晕倒在地。His head spun and he fell on the ground in a faint.

【昏庸】hūnyōng 糊涂而愚蠢 fatuous; muddle-headed; confused and stupid：老朽～ fatuousness of old age

荤 hūn ❶ 指鸡鸭鱼肉等食物（跟'素'相对 as opposed to 'vegetarian'）meat foods, e.g. chicken, duck and fish, etc.：～菜 meat dish｜三～一素 three meat dishes and one vegetable dish｜她不吃～。She doesn't eat meat. *or* She's a vegetarian.｜饺子馅儿是～的还是素的？Is the stuffing for the dumplings meat or vegetable? ❷ 佛教徒称葱蒜等有特殊气味的菜 (Buddhist) for strong-smelling vegetable, e.g. scallion, and garlic, etc.：五～five kinds of pungent vegetables ❸ 指粗俗的、淫秽的 vulgar; coarse; uncouth; lewd; foul：～话 obscene language｜～口 coarse and vulgar words in *quyi* performance

☞ xūn on p. 2184

【荤菜】hūncài 用鸡鸭鱼肉等做的菜 meat dishes prepared with chicken, duck or fish, etc.

【荤话】hūnhuà 指粗俗下流的话；脏话 obscene words; vulgar remarks; foul language; cuss-word

【荤口】hūnkǒu 曲艺表演中指低级、粗俗的话（区别于'净口' as compared with 'clean mouth'）foul mouth; coarse and vulgar words in *quyi* performance

【荤腥】hūnxīng 指鱼肉等食品 meat or fish：老

人家常年吃素，不沾～。The old man only eats vegetables and never touches meat.

【荤油】hūnyóu 指食用的猪油 lard; pork fat

阍 hūn〈书 *fml.*〉❶ 看门 guard the entrance; keep the door: ～者（看门的人）gatekeeper; janitor ❷ 门（多指宫门 usu. of palace）door; gate: 叩～ knock on the door

惛 hūn〈书 *fml.*〉糊涂 slow-witted; muddled

婚 hūn ❶ 结婚 marry: 未～ unmarried | 新～ newly married ❷ 婚姻 marriage; wedding: ～约 engagement | 结～ get married | 离～ divorce

【婚变】hūnbiàn 家庭中婚姻关系的变化。多指夫妻离异或有外遇。change marital relations, usu. due to estrangement or adultery

【婚嫁】hūnjià 泛指男女婚事（in a broad sense）marriage

【婚检】hūnjiǎn 指结婚前的身体检查 physical check-up before getting married

【婚礼】hūnlǐ 结婚仪式 wedding ceremony; wedding: 举行～ hold a wedding

【婚恋】hūnliàn 结婚和恋爱 fall in love and get married: 云南各民族有着不同的～风情。Each ethnic group in Yunnan Province has different customs for courting and marriage.

【婚龄】hūnlíng ❶ 结婚的年龄 duration of a marriage: 他俩的～已有50年。They've been married for 50 years. ❷ 法定的结婚年龄 legal marriageable age; come of age for marriage: 他俩今年刚够～。They've just come of age for marriage this year.

【婚配】hūnpèi 结婚（多就已婚未婚说 usu. a reference to a person's marital status）married: 子女两人，均未～。Both son and daughter are unmarried.

【婚纱】hūnshā 结婚时新娘穿的一种特制的礼服 wedding dress; gown specially made for a bride for the wedding ceremony

【婚事】hūnshì 有关结婚的事 marriage; wedding: 办～ arrange a wedding; make preparations for a wedding | ～新办 wedding arranged in a new way

【婚书】hūnshū〈旧 *old*〉结婚证书 marriage certificate; marriage lines

【婚俗】hūnsú 有关婚姻的习俗 marriage customs: 不同民族有不同的～。Different ethnicities have different marriage customs.

【婚外恋】hūnwàiliàn 指与配偶以外的人发生恋情 affair; extramarital love; fall in love with someone other than one's spouse

【婚姻】hūnyīn 结婚的事；因结婚而产生的夫妻关系 matrimony; marriage; wedlock; live as husband and wife after marriage: ～法 marriage law | ～自主 marry of one's free will | 他们的～十分美满。They have a very happy marriage.

【婚姻法】hūnyīnfǎ 规定有关婚姻和家庭制度的法律 marriage law; law dealing with issues of marriage and family

【婚约】hūnyuē 男女双方对婚姻的约定 engagement; agreement of marriage between man and woman

棔 hūn 古书上指合欢树 albizzia（*Albizzia*）in ancient books

hún（ㄏㄨㄣˊ）

浑 hún ❶ 浑浊 muddy; turbid; murky: ～水 muddy water | 把水搅～ stir water to muddy it ❷ 糊涂；不明事理 muddle-headed; unintelligent; tardy: ～人 stupid person | ～头～脑 addle-brained; foolish ❸ 天然的：natural: ～朴 simple and natural | ～厚 simple and vigorous | ～金璞玉 unrefined gold and uncut jade; gold and jade in a natural state ❹ 全；满 whole; complete; full; total: ～身 the whole body | ～似 resemble completely ❺（Hún）姓 a surname

【浑蛋】húndàn 不明事理的人（骂人的话 curse）bastard; scoundrel; skunk; also 混蛋 húndàn

【浑噩】hún'è 形容无知无识、糊里糊涂 ignorant; foolish; confused: ～麻木 dull and apathetic; buzzed

【浑古】húngǔ 浑厚古朴 simple and vigorous: 所刻印章疏密有致，苍劲～。The inscription on the seal is out in simple, vigorous strokes that are well spaced.

【浑厚】húnhòu ❶ 淳朴老实 simple and honest: 天性～born an honest person; honest by nature ❷（艺术风格等）朴实雄厚；不纤巧（of artistic style, etc.）simple and powerful: 笔力～ vigorous brushwork ❸（声音）低沉有力（of voice）deep and sonorous: 嗓音～ rich, sonorous voice; resonant voice

【浑浑噩噩】húnhún'è'è 形容混沌无知的样子 muddle-headed and ignorant

【浑家】húnjiā same as 妻子 qī·zi（多见于早期白话 mostly in early vernacular）

【浑金璞玉】hún jīn pú yù ☞ 璞玉浑金 pú yù hún jīn on p. 1500

【浑朴】húnpǔ 浑厚朴实 simple and guileless; unsophisticated; unadorned: 字体～ handwriting in a simple and natural style | 风俗～ plain and simple customs

【浑球儿】húnqiúr〈方 *dial.*〉same as 浑蛋 húndàn; also 混球儿 húnqiúr

【浑然】húnrán ❶ 形容完整不可分割 inseparable; indispensable; integral: ～一体 a complete whole; integrated mass; unified entity | ～天成 integral whole ❷ 完全地；全然 entirely; purely; wholly; comprehensively: ～不觉 completely in the dark; entirely unaware | ～不理 totally ignore

【浑如】húnrú 完全像；很像 be in complete likeness; resemble exactly; be very much alike: 蜡像做得～真人一样。The wax figures are lifelike.

【浑身】húnshēn 全身 from head to toe; all over: ～是汗 covered all over with sweat | ～是胆(形容胆量极大) brave; every inch a hero (embodiment of valour) | 使出～解数 do sth. for all one's worth; try everything; do one's level best; do all one can

【浑水摸鱼】hún shuǐ mō yú〈比喻 *fig.*〉趁混乱的时机攫取利益 take advantage from a chaotic situation to further one's interests; 浑 also put as 混 hún

【浑说】húnshuō 胡说;乱说 drivel; prattle; blether; talk nonsense: 信口～ make an impudent remark; wag one's tongue too freely; talk irresponsibly

【浑似】húnsì 非常像;酷似 resemble exactly; be very much alike

【浑天仪】húntiānyí ❶ same as 浑仪 húnyí ❷ same as 浑象 húnxiàng

【浑象】húnxiàng 我国古代的一种天文仪器,相当于现代的天球仪 celestial globe; astronomical instrument in ancient China, similar to the modern celestial sphere; also 浑天仪 húntiānyí

【浑仪】húnyí 我国古代测量天体位置的仪器 armillary sphere; in ancient China, astronomical instrument used to determine the position of a celestial body; also 浑天仪 húntiānyí

【浑圆】húnyuán 很圆 perfectly round: ～的珍珠 a perfectly round pearl | ～的月亮 full moon

【浑浊】húnzhuó same as 混浊 hùnzhuó

珲 hún〈书 *fml.*〉一种玉 a kind of jade
☞ huī on p. 858

【珲春】Húnchūn 地名,在吉林 Hunchun, name of a place in Jilin Province

馄 hún [馄饨](hún·tún)面食,用薄面片包馅儿,通常是煮熟后带汤吃 wonton; kind of dumpling made with thin wrappers, usu. served in soup

混 hún same as 浑 hún ①②
☞ hùn on p. 873

【混蛋】húndàn same as 浑蛋 húndàn

【混球儿】húnqiúr same as 浑球儿 húnqiúr

【混水摸鱼】hún shuǐ mō yú same as 浑水摸鱼 hún shuǐ mō yú

魂 hún ❶ (～儿 húnr) same as 灵魂 línghún ① ❷ 指精神或情绪 spirit; mood: 梦～萦绕 miss badly; pine for; yearn for | 神～颠倒 infatuated with; head over heels in love; enchanted with; obsessed with ❸ 特指崇高的精神 lofty spirit: 国～spirit of a country | 民族～national spirit; spirit of a people

【魂不附体】hún bù fù tǐ 形容恐惧万分 scared to death; scared out of one's wits; greatly frightened

【魂不守舍】hún bù shǒu shè 灵魂离开了躯壳。形容精神恍惚、心神不定。也形容惊恐万分。absent-minded; in a trance; terrified; be out of one's wits

【魂飞魄散】hún fēi pò sàn 形容非常惊恐 in panic; half dead from terror

【魂灵】hún·líng (～儿 hún·língr) same as 灵魂 línghún ①

【魂魄】húnpò 迷信的人指附在人体内可以脱离人体存在的精神 soul; superstitious belief of a spiritual essence inhabiting the body, which also exists separate from it

【魂牵梦萦】hún qiān mèng yíng 形容思念情切 miss very much; long for; pine for: 他认出了这正是失散多年、日夜～的儿子。He recognized the boy as his long-lost son whom he had yearned for day and night.

hùn (ㄏㄨㄣˋ)

诨 hùn 戏谑;开玩笑 joke; jest: ～名 nickname | 打～ crack a joke; make fun of

【诨号】hùnhào same as 诨名 hùnmíng

【诨名】hùnmíng same as 外号 wàihào

圂 hùn〈书 *fml.*〉厕所 toilet; bath room; water closet (W.C.)

混 hùn ❶ 搀杂 mix; blend; mingle: ～合 mix together | ～为一谈 confuse sth. with sth. else; lump or jumble together ❷ 蒙混 pass for: ～充 pass off as; palm off as | 鱼目～珠 pass off fish eyes as pearls ❸ 苟且地生活 dawdle on; muddle along; drift along: ～日子 scrape by | ～了半辈子 muddle away half of one's life without achieving anything ❹ 胡乱 carelessly; thoughtlessly: ～出主意 make thoughtless suggestions
☞ hún on p. 873

【混充】hùnchōng 蒙混冒充 pretend to be; palm sth. or sb. off as: ～内行 pass oneself off as an expert

【混沌】hùndùn ❶ 我国传说中指宇宙形成以前模糊一团的景象 chaos; primeval state of the universe according to Chinese legend: ～初开 when the earth was first separated from the heavens ❷ 形容糊里糊涂、无知无识的样子 muddle-headed and ignorant; dull and confused

【混纺】hùnfǎng ❶ 用不同类别的纤维混合在一起纺织。常用化学纤维和天然纤维或不同的化学纤维混纺。混纺可以节约较贵重的原料,或使纺织品具有某种新的性能。blending; fabric woven from different kinds of fibres, usually a mix of synthetic and natural fibres. Blending saves raw materials or gives a fabric new characteristics. ❷ 混纺的纺织品 blend fabric

【混合】hùnhé ❶ 搀杂在一起 mix; blend; mingle: 男女～双打 (of sports event) mixed doubles | 客货～列车 passenger and freight train ❷ 两种或两种以上的物质搀和在一起,相互间不

发生化学反应，各自保持原有的化学性质 blend; mingle; mix; two or more substances mixed together without any chemical reaction and each retains its original chemical properties

【混合面儿】hùnhémiànr 抗日战争时期华北、东北沦陷区作为粮食配售的一种用玉米心、豆饼、糠秕等混合磨成的粉 mixed flour; mixture of ground corncob, bean cake, chaff etc., used as grain substitute and sold in Japanese-occupied North and Northeast China during the War of Resistance against Japan (1937-1945)

【混合物】hùnhéwù 由两种或两种以上的单质或化合物混合而成的物质，没有固定的组成，各成分仍保持各自原有的性质。如空气是氮气、氧气、二氧化碳、惰性气体等的混合物。mixture; mixture of two or more simple substances or chemical compounds, in varying proportions that retain their own properties, e.g., the atmosphere is a mixture of nitrogen gas, oxygen, carbon dioxide, inert gas, etc.

【混混儿】hùn·hunr 〈方 *dial.*〉流氓；无赖 rascal; scoundrel

【混迹】hùnjì 〈书 *fml.*〉隐蔽本来面目混杂在某种场合 hide one's identity and mingle with others; undeserved status: ～江湖 occupy a social position of which one is unworthy

【混交】hùnjiāo 两种或两种以上的树木混生在一起 two or more species of trees growing together; mixed growth of varying tree species: 带状～ banded growth of different species of trees | 松树和栎树～ mixed woods of pine and oak

【混乱】hùnluàn 没条理；没秩序 confusion; chaos; disarray: 思想～ ideological confusion; confused thinking | 秩序～ in disorder; chaotic

【混凝土】hùnníngtǔ 一种建筑材料，用水泥、砂、石子和水按比例拌和而成，具有耐压、耐水、耐火、可塑性等性能 concrete; building material made by mixing cement, sand, gravel and water in certain proportions, resulting in a pressure-resistant, water-resistant, fire-resistant substance which can be molded

【混世魔王】hùn shì mówáng 〈比喻 *fig.*〉扰乱世界、给人民带来严重危害的恶人 human fiend; devil incarnate; evil person who wreaks havoc

【混事】hùn//shì 只以取得衣食为目的而从事某种职业；谋生（含贬义 derog.）work only to feed and clothe oneself; make a living; scrape a living

【混同】hùntóng 把本质上有区别的人或事物同样看待 confuse; mix up; treat different things and people as the same

【混为一谈】hùn wéi yī tán 把不同的事物混在一起，说成是同样的事物 mix up; confuse; confuse one thing with another; lump or jumble things together

【混淆】hùnxiáo ❶ 混杂；界限模糊（多用于抽象事物 usu. the abstract）obscure; blur: 真伪～ confuse the real with the sham ❷ 使混淆；使界限模糊 confuse; blur; mix up: ～黑白 mix black and white | ～是非 confuse right and wrong

【混血儿】hùnxuè'ér 指不同种族的男女相结合所生的孩子 person of mixed blood; half-breed; person whose parents are of different races

【混一】hùnyī 不同的事物混合成为一体 amalgamate; combine or coalesce different things into one

【混杂】hùnzá 混合搀杂 mix; mingle: 鱼龙～ mix the eyeballs of a fish with pearls; mix the bad with the good

【混战】hùnzhàn 目标不明或对象常变的战争或战斗 tangled warfare; shifting battle; fighting without a clear goal or against changing adversaries; chaotic warfare: 军阀～ tangled warfare among warlords | 一场～ chaotic struggle

【混账】hùnzhàng 言语行动无理无耻（骂人的话 curse）(of words and behaviour) unreasonable and shameful: ～话 impudent remark; vile rubbish | ～小子 scoundrel; bastard; son of a bitch

【混浊】hùnzhuó （水、空气等）含有杂质，不清洁，不新鲜 (of water, atmosphere, etc.) muddy; turbid; unclear; foul; bleary; cloudy; containing particle, dirty and tainted

溷 hùn 〈书 *fml.*〉❶ 混乱 chaotic: ～浊 muddy; murky ❷ 厕所 bathroom; toilet; lavatory; water closet (W.C.)

【溷浊】hùnzhuó 〈书 *fml.*〉same as 混浊 hùnzhuó

慁（慁） hùn 〈书 *fml.*〉❶ 忧患 worry ❷ 扰乱 disturb; make trouble

huō（ㄏㄨㄛ）

耠 huō 用耠子翻松（土壤）till (land) with a hoe: ～地 hoeing; hoe the land

【耠子】huō·zi 翻松土壤用的农具，比犁轻巧，多用于中耕。也用来开沟播种。hoe; ground-breaking implement, lighter than the plough and used to intertill or open a furrow for sowing

騞（剨） huō 〈书 *fml.*〉东西破裂的声音 crashing sound; searing sound

锪 huō 一种金属加工方法。用专门的刀具对工件上已有的孔进行加工，刮平端面或切出锥形、圆柱形凹坑。ream; use reamer (metal processing and cutting tool) to finish a hole drilled in metal, e.g. smoothing the surface or opening up conical or cylindrical indentations

劐 huō ❶ 用刀尖插入物体然后顺势拉(lá)开 slit or cut with the point of a knife: 把鱼肚子～开 slit open the fish belly | 用刀一～，绳

子就断了。The knife sliced the rope in two. ❷ same as 耠 huō

嚄 huō〈叹词 *interj*.〉表示惊讶[used to express surprise]:～! 好大的鱼! Wow! What a big fish!

☞ huò on p. 886 and ǒ on p. 1431

豁1 huō 裂开 breach; break; slit:～了一个口子。There's a crack.|纽襻儿～了。The button loop broke.

豁2 huō 狠心付出很高的代价;舍弃 sacrifice; give up; pay an extremely high price for:～出三天工夫也得把它做好。Even if it takes us three whole days, we must get it done.

☞ huá on p. 835 and huò on p. 886

【豁出去】huō·chu·qu 表示不惜付出任何代价 spare no effort; pay a high price for; sacrifice everything for:事已至此,我也只好～了。With things as they are, I have no choice but to give it my all.

【豁口】huōkǒu (～儿 huōkǒur) same as 缺口 quēkǒu:城墙～ breach in the city wall|碗边有个～。There is a chip on the edge of the bowl.|北风从山的～吹过来。The north wind blew through the mountain pass.

【豁子】huō·zi〈方 *dial*.〉❶ same as 豁口 huōkǒu:碗上有个～。The edge of the bowl is chipped. ❷ 指豁嘴的人 person with a harelip

【豁嘴】huōzuǐ (～儿 huōzuǐr) ❶ same as 唇裂 chúnliè ❷ 指唇裂的人 one with a harelip

攉 huō 把堆积的东西倒出来。特指把采出的煤、矿石等铲起来倒到另一个地方或容器中 remove heaped materials; esp. shovel coal, ore, etc. from one place into another or to a container:～土 shovel earth|～煤机 mechanical coal shovel

huó(ㄏㄨㄛˊ)

和 huó 在粉状物中加液体搅拌或揉弄使有黏性 add liquid to powder and stir or knead to make viscous:～面 knead dough|～泥 mix earth with water|～点儿水泥把窟窿堵上。Mix some cement to plug up the hole.

☞ hé on p. 786, hè on p. 791, hú on p. 817 and huò on p. 884

活1 huó ❶ 生存;有生命(跟'死'相对 as opposed to 'dead') live; living; be alive:～人 living person|～到老,学到老 never too old to learn; learn as long as one lives|鱼在水里才能～。The fish can only live in water. ❷ 在活的状态下 alive; living:～捉 catch sth. alive ❸ 维持生命;救活 keep alive; save:养家～口 support one's family|～人一命 save sb.'s life ❹ 活动;灵活 movable; flexible; agile:～水 flowing water|～结 slipknot; bowknot|～页 loose-leaf; detachable page|～塞 piston ❺ 生动活泼;不死板 spirited; dynamic; lifelike:～气 lively atmosphere|～跃 active|这一段描写得很～。This paragraph contains a lively description. ❻ 真正;简直 exactly; simply:～现 lifelike; real|这孩子说话～像个大人。The child speaks just like an adult.

活2 huó (～儿 huór) ❶ 工作(一般指体力劳动的,属于工农业生产或修理服务性质的 usu. physical work, e.g. industrial or agricultural production or repair and maintenance) work:细～ fine work|重～heavy work|庄稼～ farm work; farming|干～儿 work; take a job ❷ 产品;制成品 product; finished product:出～儿 productive; efficient|箱子上配着铜～ a trunk decorated with copper trimming|这一批～儿做得很好。This batch of products is of high quality.

【活版】huóbǎn 活字版 typography; letterpress:～印刷术 technology of typographic printing

【活宝】huóbǎo 指可笑的人或滑稽的人(一般含贬义 usu. derog.) clown; joker; funny person

【活报剧】huóbàojù 反映时事新闻的短小活泼的戏剧,可以在街头演出 follies; living newspaper drama; poster drama; street skit, usually comical and based on current events

【活蹦乱跳】huó bèng luàn tiào same as 欢蹦乱跳 huān bèng luàn tiào

【活便】huó·bian〈方 *dial*.〉❶ 灵活;活动 dexterous; nimble; agile; deft:手脚～ dexterous and quick ❷ 方便;便利 convenient:事情还是这么办比较～。Things will go smoother this way.|开两个门进出～一点。Opening two doors will make entry and exit more convenient.

【活茬】huóchá〈方 *dial*.〉(～儿 huóchár) same as 农活 nónghuó

【活地图】huódìtú 指对某地区地理情况很熟悉的人 walking map; one very familiar with the geography of a certain area

【活地狱】huódìyù〈比喻 *fig*.〉黑暗悲惨的社会环境 hell on earth; living hell; oppressive and miserable social circumstances

【活动】huó·dòng ❶ (肢体)动弹;运动(of limbs) move about; exercise:坐久了应该站起来～～。One should get up and move about after sitting for a long time.|出去散散步,～一下筋骨。Let's go for a walk to limber up. ❷ 为某种目的而行动 purpuseful action:这一带常有游击队～。The guerrillas are quite active in this area. ❸ 动摇;不稳定 shaky; unsteady:这个桌子直～。The desk is shaky.|门牙～了。The incisor is getting loose. ❹ 灵活;不固定 movable; flexible; mobile:～模型 movable model|～房屋 movable room|条文规定得比较～。The regulations are flexible. ❺ 为达到某种目的而采取的行动 manoeuvre; activities carried out for a specific objective: 野外～ activity in the open | 文娱～ entertainment; amusements | 体育～ sports; sporting activity | 政治～ political activity ❻ 指钻营、说情、行贿 take actions to secure gain, put in a word for sb., and commit bribery: 他为逃避纳税四处～。He played every trick to avoid paying taxes.

【活动家】huódòngjiā 在政治生活、社会生活中积极活动并有较大影响的人 activist; public figure; one who is influential and active in public and political life

【活泛】huó·fan ❶ 能随机应变;灵活 quick-witted; flexible; agile: 心眼～ intelligent; smart | 脑筋不～ slow-witted ❷ 指经济宽裕 ample; well-to-do: 钱你先用着,等手头～了再还我。Please take the money now, and pay me back when you are in better circumstances.

【活佛】huófó ❶ 喇嘛教中用转世制度继位的上层喇嘛 Living Buddha; senior lama selected in accordance with the rules of incarnation in Lamaism ❷ 旧小说中称济世救人的僧人 (in traditional fiction) chivalrous monk

【活该】huógāi ❶ 表示应该这样,一点也不委屈(有值不得怜惜的意思) get one's deserts; serve one right (undeserving of sympathy): ～如此。Serves him right. ❷〈方 *dial.*〉应该;该当(含命中注定意) (be predestined) should; fated: 我～有救,碰上了这样的好医生。I was fated to be saved, having such a good doctor.

【活化】huóhuà 使分子或原子的能量增强。如把普通木炭放在密闭器中加热,变成吸附能力较强的活性炭。activate; make a molecule or an atom more active, e.g. heating ordinary charcoal in a closed container to change it into strongly absorpbent activated carbon

【活化石】huóhuàshí 指某些在地质年代中曾繁盛一时,广泛分布,而现在只限于局部地区,数量不多,有可能灭绝的生物。如大猫熊和水杉。living fossil; living organisms that thrived over a wide area in past geological eras but now live in small pockets on the verge of extinction, e.g. the giant panda and metasequoia (redwood); also 孑遗生物 jiéyí shēngwù

【活话】huóhuà (～儿 huóhuàr) 不很肯定的话 vague message; open-ended remark; noncommittal words: 他临走的时候留下个～儿,说也许下个月能回来。He said vaguely before he left that he might come back next month.

【活活】huóhuó (～儿的 huóhuór·de) ❶ 在活的状态下(多指有生命的东西受到损害 usu. of damage to living thing) while still alive: ～打死 be beaten to death | ～气死 die of fury ❷ 简直,表示完全如此或差不多如此 simply; completely; almost: 瞧你这个样子,～是个疯子! Look at yourself, quite mad!

【活火】huóhuǒ 有焰的火 blaze; burn with flames

【活火山】huóhuǒshān 在人类历史时期经常或周期性地喷发的火山 active volcano; volcano which erupts frequently or regularly throughout human history

【活计】huó·ji ❶ 过去专指手艺或缝纫、刺绣等,现在泛指各种体力劳动 (formerly referring to) handiwork; e.g. sewing or embroidery; manual labour: 针线～ needlework | 地里的～快干完了。Farm work is almost finished. ❷ 做成的或待做的手工制品 completed or unexecuted handiwork: 她拿着～给大家看。She showed her work to everybody.

【活检】huójiǎn 医学上指对活体组织进行检验 (med.) biopsy; excision of living tissue for diagnostic study

【活见鬼】huójiànguǐ 形容离奇或无中生有 sheer nonsense; utterly impossible; simply absurd: 书明明放在桌子上,怎么忽然不见了,真是～! I know I put the book on the table, but now it's gone. How weird!

【活校】huójiào 按照原稿校对,同时检查原稿有无错误、缺漏,叫活校(区别于'死校' as compared with 'proofread against original text only') proofread against original text while checking the latter for mistakes and omissions

【活结】huójié 一拉就开的绳结(区别于'死结' as compared with 'fast knot') slipknot; bowknot; a knot that can be undone by pulling

【活局子】huójú·zi〈方 *dial.*〉圈套;骗局 snare; trap; hoax

【活口】huókǒu ❶ 命案发生时在场而没有被杀死,可以提供线索或情况的人 living witness to a crime; survivor of a murder attempt; one who survives a murder and may provide clues or information ❷ 指可以提供情况的俘虏、罪犯等 prisoner or criminal who can furnish information

【活扣】huókòu (～儿 huókòur) same as 活结 huójié

【活劳动】huóláodòng 物质资料生产过程中消耗的劳动(跟'物化劳动'相对 as opposed to 'material labour') human labour; living labour consumed during the process of material production

【活力】huólì 旺盛的生命力 vitality; vigour; energy: 身上充满了青春的～ full of youth and vitality; lively and spirited

【活灵活现】huó líng huó xiàn 形容描述或模仿的人或事物生动逼真 (of imitation or description of people or things) vivid; lifelike; also 活龙活现 huó lóng huó xiàn

【活路】huólù ❶ 走得通的路 through path: 遇见白杨树向右转是一条～。When you see a poplar tree, turn right and the road will take you out. ❷〈比喻 *fig.*〉行得通的方法 workable method: 他提出的技术革新方案,大家觉得

是条～。Everyone agreed that his plan for technological innovation is workable. ❸〈比喻 *fig.*〉能够生活下去的办法 way out; means of subsistence：得找条～，不能等着挨饿。We must do something and not just wait and starve.

【活路】huó·lu 泛指各种体力劳动（in a broad sense) various kinds of physical labour; manual labour：粗细～他都会干。He can do all kinds of work, skilled or unskilled.｜家里～忙，我抽不开身。I have no time now because there's too much to do at home.

【活络】huóluò〈方 *dial.*〉❶（筋骨、器物的零件等）活动（of bones, parts of a machine) loose; shaky：人上了年纪，牙齿也有点～了。With age, one's teeth become loose.｜板凳腿～了，你抽空修一修。The stool legs are wobbly, please find time to repair them. ❷ 灵活；不确定 nimble; animated; flexible; noncommittal; uncertain：头脑～ quick-witted; smart｜眼神～ vivacious expression｜他说得很～，不知道究竟肯不肯去。He was rather vague so I don't know whether he is going.

【活埋】huómái 把活人埋起来弄死 bury sb. alive

【活卖】huómài 房地产出卖后，卖主保留赎回的权利叫活卖 sale of estate with the seller reserving the right to redeem it

【活门】huómén 阀[2]的通称 general term for 阀[2] fá

【活命】huó//mìng ❶ 维持生命 earn a living; eke out a living; scrape along：他在旧社会靠卖艺～。In pre-1949 China, he made a living as a street entertainer. ❷〈书 *fml.*〉救活性命 save one's life：～之恩 owe someone one's life

【活命】huómìng 生命；性命 life：留他一条～ spare his life

【活泼】huó·po ❶ 生动自然；不呆板 lively; vivacious; vivid and natural：天真～的孩子 innocent and lively children｜这篇报道，文字～。This report is written in vivid language. ❷ 指单质或化合物容易与其他单质或化合物发生化学变化 (of simple substance or compound) chemically reactive

【活菩萨】huópú·sa〈比喻 *fig.*〉心肠慈善、救苦救难的人 living Buddha; one who shows compassion for the suffering and the needy

【活期】huóqī 存户随时可以提取的 current account; account from which a depositor can withdraw money any time：～储蓄 current deposit; demand deposit｜这笔存款是～的。This deposit goes into my current account.

【活气】huóqì 生气；活力 vitality; vigour; energy：这里荒无人烟，没有一点～。The place is deserted and quite still.｜车水的车水，插秧的插秧，田里充满了一片～。The field comes alive with people transplanting rice and manning the waterwheel to irrigate the paddy.

【活契】huóqì 出卖房地产时所立的契约，上面规定房地产可以赎回的，叫活契 conditional real estate sales document that allows the seller to redeem the property identified in the document

【活钱儿】huóqiánr ❶ 指现钱 cash; ready money：他节假日外出打工，挣些～。He got a job over the holidays to make some money.｜把鸡蛋卖了，换几个～使。Sell the eggs for some cash. ❷ 指工资外的收入 grey income; extra income：他每月除工资外，还有些～。He has other income in addition to his monthly salary.

【活塞】huósāi 汽缸或唧筒里往复运动的机件，通常圆饼形或圆柱形。在发动机汽缸里，活塞的作用是把蒸汽或燃料爆发的压力变为机械能。piston; disk-like or cylindrical part moving back and forth within a tube or a pump. In the air cylinder of an engine, a piston functions to change the pressure produced by steam or fuel combustion into mechanical power. also 鞲鞴 gōubèi

【活生生】huóshēngshēng（～的 huóshēngshēng·de）❶ 实际生活中的；发生在眼前的 real; living：～的事实 real fact｜～的例子 living example｜这篇小说里的人物都是～的，有血有肉的。The characters in the story are vivid and lifelike. ❷ same as 活活 huóhuó ①：包办的婚姻把她～地断送了。The arranged marriage has literally snuffed out her young life.

【活食】huóshí（～儿 huóshír）指某些动物吃的活的蚯蚓、蚂蚱、兔子、小鱼等 live food for animals, e. g. earthworms, grasshoppers, rabbits, fish, etc.

【活受罪】huóshòuzuì 活着而遭受苦难，表示抱怨或怜悯（大多是夸张的说法 usu. as exaggerated expression of complaint or sympathy) have a hell of a life; lead a miserable life：要我这五音不全的人登台唱歌，简直是～！It's agonizing for a lousy singer like me to get up on stage to sing!

【活水】huóshuǐ 有源头而常流动的水 running water; water flowing from a source：挖条渠把～引进湖里 dig a ditch to divert the flowing water into the lake

【活体】huótǐ 自然科学指具有生命的物体，如活着的动物、植物、人体及其组织 live thing or substance; in natural science, living being e.g. animal, plant, the human body and its parts

【活脱儿】huótuōr（相貌、举止）跟脱胎一样十分相像(of look, gesture) bear a remarkable resemblance; be strikingly alike：他长得～是他爷爷。He looks just like his grandfather.

【活现】huóxiàn 逼真地显现 appear vividly; come alive：神气～ cocksure; high and mighty|他的形象又～在我眼前了。His image once again appeared vividly in my mind's eye.

【活像】huóxiàng 极像 be a spitting image of sb.; look exactly like; be an exact replica; as like as two peas:这孩子长得～他妈妈。The child is the spitting image of its mother.

【活性炭】huóxìngtàn 吸附能力很强的炭,把硬木、果壳、骨头等放在密闭容器中烧成炭再增加其孔隙后制成。防毒面具中用来过滤气体,工业上用来脱色、使溶液纯净,医药上用来吸收胃肠中的毒素、细菌或气体。activated carbon; highly absorbent carbon produced by burning hard wood, shells and bones in a closed container and increasing its porousness. It is used in gas masks to filter air, in industry for decolorization and purification, in medicine to absorb toxins, bacteria or gases in the gastrointestinal tract.

【活血】huóxuè〈中医 *Chin. med.*〉指使血脉畅通 invigorate blood circulation:舒筋～relax muscles and invigorate blood circulation; soothe the sinews and quicken the blood

【活阎王】huóyán•wang〈比喻 *fig.*〉极凶恶残忍的人 tyrant; brutal and cruel person; devil incarnate

【活页】huóyè 书页等不装订成册,可以随意分合的 loose-leaf; unbound pages of a book which can be put together or separated at will:～文选 loose-leaf volume of literary anthology|～笔记本 loose-leaf notebook

【活跃】huóyuè ❶ 行动活泼而积极;气氛蓬勃而热烈 brisk; active; dynamic:他是文体～分子。He is active in sporting and recreational activities.|学习讨论会开得很～。The seminar is very lively. ❷ 使活跃 enliven; animate; invigorate:～部队生活 liven up servicemen's life|～农村经济 stimulate or revitalize the rural economy

【活质】huózhì 最基本的有生命的物质,主要由蛋白质组成,有细胞结构和非细胞结构两种 bioplasm; most basic living substance mainly composed of protein with or without cell structure

【活捉】huózhuō 活活地抓住。多指在作战中抓住活的敌人。capture alive, usu. an enemy in battle

【活字】huózì 印刷上用的金属或木质的方柱形物体,一头铸着或刻着单个反着的文字或符号,排版时可以自由组合 movable type or letter; movable font; metallic or wooden block inscribed with a reversed single character or symbol on one side that can be used freely in typesetting

【活字版】huózìbǎn 用金属、木头等制成的活字排成的印刷版。也指用活字排版印刷的书本。block of type composed of movable metallic or wooden fonts; book printed from movable type

【活字典】huózìdiǎn 指字、词等知识特别丰富的人。泛指对某一方面情况非常熟悉能随时提供情况、数据等的人。walking dictionary; erudite person; sb. with extensive knowledge of words and phrases; one who is very familiar with something and able to provide information and data at any time

【活字印刷】huózì yìnshuā 采用活字排版的印刷。是我国北宋庆历(1041—1048)年间毕昇首先发明的。movable-type printing; letter press; printing method invented by Bi Sheng during the Qingli reign (1041-1048) of the Northern Song Dynasty.

【活罪】huózuì 活着所遭受的苦难 bitter sufferings; life's hardships or suffering:受～ have a terrible life

huǒ(ㄏㄨㄛˇ)

火 huǒ ❶(～儿 huǒr)物体燃烧时所发的光和焰 fire; light and flame caused by burning:～光 fire light|～花 spark|灯～ light|点～ light a fire ❷ 指枪炮弹药 firearms; ammunition:～器 firearm|～力 firepower; fire|～网 fire net|军～ firearms and ammunition|走～(of firearm) discharge accidentally ❸ same as 火气 huǒqì ③:上～ suffer from excessive internal heat|败～ relieve internal heat ❹形容红色 red as fire; red colour:～鸡 turkey|～腿 ham ❺〈比喻 *fig.*〉紧急 urgent; pressing:～速 at top speed|～急 urgent; pressing ❻(～儿 huǒr)〈比喻 *fig.*〉暴躁或愤怒 rage; fury; wrath:～性 hot temper|冒～ get angry|心头～起 fly into a rage|他～儿了。He lost his temper. *or* He flared up. ❼兴旺;兴隆 prosperous; thriving; flourishing:买卖很～。Business is brisk. ❽同 same as '伙' huǒ ❾(Huǒ)姓 a surname

【火把】huǒbǎ 用于夜间照明的东西,有的用竹篾等编成长条,有的在棍棒的一端扎上棉花,蘸上油 torch; light to illuminate at night, made of a stick or rod with one end tied with fuel-soaked cotton

【火把节】Huǒbǎ Jié 彝、白、傈僳、纳西、拉祜等族的传统节日。一般于农历六月二十四日举行。届时人们举行斗牛、赛马、摔跤等各种娱乐活动,夜里燃点火把,奔驰田间,驱除虫害,并饮酒歌舞。Torchlight Festival; traditional festival of ethnic minority peoples such as the Yis, Bais, Lisus, Naxis and Lahus. The festival usually falls on the 24th day of the 6th lunar month, with activities including bull-fighting, horseracing, and wrestling. At night, revellers light torches and run about in the fields to chase off insects, and then gather to drink, sing and dance.

【火伴】huǒbàn ☞ 伙伴 huǒbàn on p. 883
【火棒】huǒbàng 游艺用的短棒，一端钉有许多层布，成球形，蘸上酒精，点着后在黑暗处挥舞，使火光呈各种曲线形 fire stick; short stick bound with a ball of cloth at one end soaked in alcohol, lit and waved in the dark to trace flaming curves in the air
【火暴】huǒbào 〈方 *dial.*〉❶ 暴躁；急躁 fiery; impatient：～性子 have a fiery temper; hot-tempered ❷ 旺盛；热闹；红火 prosperous; thriving; exuberant：牡丹开得真～。The peonies are in full bloom.｜这一场戏的场面很～。This scene in the play is full of action and excitement.｜日子越过越～。Our life is getting better and better.‖ also 火爆 huǒbào
【火爆】huǒbào same as 火暴 huǒbào
【火并】huǒbìng 同伙决裂，自相杀伤或并吞 open fight between factions; intramural strife; factional fight; falling out between partners heading to mutual injury or defeat of one party
【火柴】huǒchái 用细小的木条蘸上磷或硫的化合物制成的取火的东西。现在常用的是安全火柴。match; short, slender piece of wood or other material tipped with a phosphorus or sulphur compound that produces fire when struck; usu. safety match
【火场】huǒchǎng 失火的现场 site of a fire
【火车】huǒchē 一种重要的交通运输工具，由机车牵引若干节车厢或车皮在铁路上行驶 train; major form of transport made up of a locomotive pulling a number of carriages along a railroad
【火车头】huǒchētóu ❶ 机车的通称 locomotive; general term for engine ❷〈比喻 *fig.*〉起带头作用或领导作用的人或事物 person or matter that plays a leading role
【火炽】huǒchì 旺盛；热闹；紧张 white-hot; exuberant; tense; bustling with excitement：石榴花开得真～。The pomegranates are blooming luxuriantly.｜篮球赛到了最～的阶段。The basketball match has reached the most exciting stage.
【火刀】huǒdāo 〈方 *dial.*〉same as 火镰 huǒlián
【火电】huǒdiàn 火力发电的简称 abbr. for 火力发电 huǒlì fādiàn
【火夫】huǒfū ❶〈旧时 *old*〉指机器间或锅炉房中烧锅炉的工人 worker who tends the boiler ❷〈旧时 *old*〉指军队、机关、学校的厨房中挑水、煮饭的人 cook; person who fetches water and cooks for the military, an organization or school; also 伙夫 huǒfū
【火罐儿】huǒguànr 拔罐子使用的小罐儿 (Chin. med.) small cupping jar or glass used in treatment
【火光】huǒguāng 火发出的光 flame; blaze：～冲天。Flames soared and licked the sky.
【火锅】huǒguō (～儿 huǒguōr)金属或陶瓷制成的用具，锅中央有炉膛，置炭火，使菜保持相当热度，或使锅中的汤经常沸腾，把肉片或蔬菜等放在汤里，随煮随吃。也有用酒精、石油液化气等做燃料的。用电加热的叫电火锅。hotpot; chafing dish; metal or porcelain cooking utensil with a hollow center for burning charcoal to keep food warm or boil soup. Diners dip slices of meat or vegetable in the hot soup to cook. Ethyl alcohol, liquid gas or electricity can be also used as heating fuel. Pots using electricity are called electric hotpots.
【火海】huǒhǎi 指大片的火 sea of flames：太阳的表面像个～。The surface of the sun is like a sea of flames.｜阵地上打成一片～。The battlefield became a sea of fire and wreckage.
【火海刀山】huǒ hǎi dāo shān ☞ p. 390 刀山火海 dāo shān huǒ hǎi
【火红】huǒhóng ❶ 像火一样红 fiery; flaming; as red as fire：～的太阳 the flaming sun ❷ 形容旺盛或热烈 prosperous; brisk; ardent：～的青春 dynamism and enthusiasm of youth｜日子过得～ lead an active, busy life
【火候】huǒ·hou (～儿 huǒ·hour) ❶ 烧火的火力大小和时间长短 duration and amount of heat：烧窑炼铁都要看～。Temperature is key in a firing kiln or iron-smelter.｜她炒的菜，作料和～都很到家。She knows just the right ingredients as well as heat time for cooking. ❷〈比喻 *fig.*〉修养程度的深浅 level of accomplishment or sophistication：他的书法到～了。He has learned the ropes of calligraphy. ❸〈比喻 *fig.*〉紧要的时机 critical moment; crucial moment：这儿正缺人，你来得正是～。We're short of hands here and you've arrived at just the right moment.
【火花】[1] huǒhuā 迸发的火焰 spark：烟火喷出灿烂的～。The fireworks exploded in a riot of colours. ◇生命的～ dynamism of life
【火花】[2] huǒhuā (～儿 huǒhuār)火柴盒上的图案 design on a matchbox cover
【火花塞】huǒhuāsāi 内燃机上的点火装置，形状像塞子，装在汽缸盖上，通过高压电时能产生火花，使汽缸里的燃料爆发。有的地区叫电嘴。spark plug; ignition plug; ignition equipment in an internal combustion engine, shaped like a cork and installed on the lid of the cylinder; high-voltage current in the plug lights spark that causes the fuel in the cylinder to explode. also called 电嘴 diànzuǐ in some places
【火化】huǒhuà same as 火葬 huǒzàng
【火浣布】huǒhuànbù 用石棉织成的布，能耐火 fire-resistant cloth woven from asbestos
【火急】huǒjí 非常紧急 urgent; pressing; imminent：十万～ posthaste; most urgent
【火急火燎】huǒ jí huǒ liǎo 形容非常焦急 ex-

tremely worried; terribly anxious: 听说发生了事故,他心里～的。He was distraught at the news of the accident.

【火剪】huǒjiǎn ❶ 生火时夹煤炭、柴火的用具,形状像剪刀而特别长 fire-tongs; tongs; instrument shaped like long scissors, used to hold coal or firewood when making a fire; also 火钳 huǒqián ❷ 烫发的用具,形状像剪刀 curling tongs; curling irons; scissor-shaped instrument for curling hair

【火箭】huǒjiàn 利用反冲力推进的飞行器,速度很快,用来运载人造卫星、宇宙飞船等,也可以装上弹头制成导弹 rocket; high-speed, flying object propelled by recoil forces, used to carry man-made satellite, space shuttle, etc. into orbit, can be equipped with a warhead to become a missile

【火箭弹】huǒjiàndàn 用火箭炮、火箭筒等发射的弹药,由弹头、推进装置和稳定装置构成,有时专指弹头 warhead; rocket projectile; rocket shell; ammunition-filled shell together with propulsion and stablization equipment

【火箭炮】huǒjiànpào 利用火箭的反冲力把炮弹发射出去的一种火炮。有多管式、滑轨式等。rocket gun; any weapon that uses rocket propulsion to propel a shell over a certain distance, e.g. multi-barrel, slidable-orbital rocket launchers, etc.

【火箭筒】huǒjiàntǒng 单人使用的发射火箭弹的轻型武器,圆筒形。装有红外线瞄准镜,发射时无后坐力,用于摧毁近距离的装甲目标和坚固工事。rocket launcher; bazooka; cylindrical-shaped, recoiless, portable rocket launcher with infrared gunsight, can be handled by a single person and penetrate armoured targets and solid works at a short distance

【火井】huǒjǐng 指能喷出天然气的井 gas well; well that spouts natural gas

【火警】huǒjǐng 失火的事件(包括成灾的和不成灾的) fire (catastrophic and otherwise); fire alarm: 报～ report a fire|～电话 fire number

【火镜】huǒjìng 指凸透镜(因为可以用来取火) convex lens (can be used to start a fire)

【火酒】huǒjiǔ 〈方 *dial.*〉 same as 酒精 jiǔjīng

【火居道士】huǒjū dào·shi 不出家,可娶妻的道士 Taoist-monk who does not join a temple and need not remain celibate

【火具】huǒjù 点火和引爆的器材的总称,包括拉火管、导火索、雷管等 collective term for ignition apparatus or equipment, including lanyard, blasting fuse and detonator; also 火工品 huǒgōngpǐn

【火炬】huǒjù same as 火把 huǒbǎ: ～接力赛 torch-relay race

【火炕】huǒkàng 设有烟道,可以烧火取暖的炕 brick bed built with a flue so it can be heated

【火坑】huǒkēng 〈比喻 *fig.*〉极端悲惨的生活环境 abyss of suffering; dire straits: 跳出～escape from a living hell

【火筷子】huǒkuài·zi 夹炉中煤炭或通火的用具,用铁制成,形状像两根筷子,一端由铁链子连起来 fire poker; tongs; implement for holding charcoal or coal in an oven, or poking the fire, made of two long, iron rods like chopsticks and connected with an iron chain at one end

【火辣辣】huǒlālā (～的 huǒlālā·de) ❶ 形容酷热 burning; scorching: 太阳～的。The sun is scorching hot. ❷ 形容因被火烧或鞭打等而产生的疼痛的感觉 searing, stinging pain caused by burning or whipping: 手烫伤了,疼得～的。I burnt my hand and it hurts badly. ❸ 形容激动情绪(如兴奋、焦急、暴躁、害羞等) (of mood) excited; anxious; furious; shy: 我心里～的,恨不得马上赶到工地去。I'm terribly anxious and cannot wait to get to the work site. |脸上～的,羞得不敢抬头。She blushed furiously and lowered her head in embarassment. ❹ 形容动作、性格泼辣;言词尖锐 (of behaviour or character) bold and resolute; (of language) sharp; acerbic: ～的性格 a bold and resolute character |～的批评 sharp criticism

【火老鸦】huǒlǎoyā 〈方 *dial.*〉大火时飞腾的火苗 leaping flames of raging fire

【火犁】huǒlí 〈方 *dial.*〉农业上用的拖拉机 tractor for farm use

【火力】huǒlì ❶ 利用煤、石油、天然气等做燃料获得的动力 thermal power; power obtained from burning coal, oil and natural gas ❷ 弹药发射或投掷后所形成的杀伤力和破坏力 fire; destructive capability of ammunition launched or fired ❸ 指人体的抗寒能力 ability of the human body to resist cold: 年轻人～旺。Young people can stand the cold better.

【火力点】huǒlìdiǎn 轻重机枪、直接瞄准火炮等配置和发射的地点 firing point; place from where light or heavy machine guns and cannon can fire directly; also 发射点 fāshèdiǎn

【火力发电】huǒlì fādiàn 用煤、煤气、汽油、柴油等做燃料产生动力而发电 thermal power generating; electricity generated from the power of burning coal, liquid gas, petroleum and diesel, etc.

【火力圈】huǒlìquān 在一个区域内各种火力所及的范围 range of firepower; field of fire

【火镰】huǒlián 取火的用具,用钢制成,形状像镰刀,打在火石上,发出火星,点着火绒 sickle-shaped steel object used for striking flint to produce sparks that ignite tinder to raise a fire

【火亮】huǒliàng 〈方 *dial.*〉(～儿 huǒliàngr) 小的火光 small light: 炉子里一点～也没有了。There is not a spark in the oven.

【火龙】huǒlóng ❶ 形容连成一串的灯火或连成一线的火焰 fiery dragon; long string of lights or flame: 大堤上的灯笼火把像一条～。The line of lanterns and torches on the bank resembled a fiery dragon. | ～乘着风势迅速延伸。Fanned by the wind, the fire spread rapidly. ❷〈方 *dial*.〉从炉灶通向烟囱的倾斜的孔道 flue; sloping duct connecting the kitchen stove to the chimney

【火笼】huǒlóng〈方 *dial*.〉烘篮 handwarmer; portable bamboo basked brazier

【火炉】huǒlú (～儿 huǒlúr) same as 炉子 lú·zi; also 火炉子 huǒlú·zi

【火轮船】huǒlúnchuán〈旧时 *old*〉称轮船 steam ship; also 火轮 huǒlún

【火冒三丈】huǒ mào sān zhàng 形容怒气特别大 furious; fly into a rage; flare up

【火媒】huǒméi same as 火煤 huǒméi

【火煤】huǒméi (～儿 huǒméir)指引柴、纸煤儿等引火用的东西 wood, paper or coal bits used as kindling; also 火媒 huǒméi

【火苗】huǒmiáo (～儿 huǒmiáor)火焰的通称 general term for 火焰 huǒyàn; also 火苗子 huǒmiáo·zi

【火磨】huǒmò 用电动机或内燃机带动的磨 electric mill; milling machine driven by electricity or internal combustion engine

【火捻】huǒniǎn (～儿 huǒniǎnr) ❶ 火煤 kindling ❷ 用纸裹火硝等做成的引火的东西 fuse; tinder made of saltpetre wrapped in paper for kindling

【火炮】huǒpào same as 炮 pào ①

【火盆】huǒpén 盛炭火等的盆子,用来取暖或烘干衣物 fire pan; brazier; basin for holding burning charcoal, used for heating or drying clothes

【火拼】huǒpīn same as 火并 huǒbìng

【火漆】huǒqī 用松脂和石蜡加颜料制成的物质,稍加热就熔化,并有黏性,用来封瓶口、信件等 sealing wax; sticky substance made of turpentine, olefin and dye, which melts easily and is used as a sealant for bottles or letters; also 封蜡 fēnglà

【火气】huǒqì ❶ 怒气;暴躁的脾气 fury; anger; hot temper:压不住心头的～ can hardly contain one's anger; cannot hold back one's rage ❷ 指人体中的热量 body heat:年轻人～足,不怕冷。Young people's blood is thicker and they can stand the cold better. ❸〈中医 *Chin. med*.〉指引起发炎、红肿、烦躁等症状的病因 internal heat, regarded as the cause of inflammation, turgescence and restlessness

【火器】huǒqì 利用炸药等的爆炸或燃烧性能起破坏作用的武器,如枪、炮、火箭筒、手榴弹等 firearm; weapon that uses the explosive or combustible power of dynamite to eject a destructive projectile, e. g. gun, cannon, bazooka and grenade, etc.

【火钳】huǒqián same as 火剪 huǒjiǎn ①

【火枪】huǒqiāng 装火药和铁砂的旧式枪,现多用于打猎 flintlock; firelock; old-style gun with powder and small shot as ammunition, now mostly used for hunting

【火墙】huǒqiáng ❶ 中间有通热气的烟道、可以取暖的墙 hollow wall with flues carrying warm air, built for heating ❷ same as 火网 huǒwǎng

【火情】huǒqíng 失火时火燃烧的情况 fire conditions:～严重 serious fire

【火热】huǒrè ❶ 像火一样热 fiery; burning hot:～的太阳 burning sun ❷ 形容感情热烈 fervent; ardent; passionate:～的心 fervent heart | 他那～的话语感动了在场的每一个人。His enthusiastic words moved everyone present. ❸ 亲热 intimate; affectionate:谈得～ have an intimate talk | 两个人打得～。The two of them are very close. ❹ 紧张激烈 intense; fierce:～的斗争 fierce fight; intense strife

【火绒】huǒróng 用火镰和火石取火时引火的东西,用艾草等蘸硝做成 tinder; highly flammable material consisting of moxa and nitre used for catching a spark when flint and steel are struck to light a fire

【火肉】huǒròu〈方 *dial*.〉火腿肉 ham

【火色】huǒsè〈方 *dial*.〉same as 火候 huǒ·hou:看～ see if the fire is suitable for cooking | 拿稳了～ be sure that the fire is just right for cooking

【火山】huǒshān 因地球表层压力减低,地球深处的岩浆等高温物质从裂缝中喷出地面而形成的锥形高地。火山由火山锥、火山口、火山通道组成。volcano; conical mountain formed by high-temperature lava deep in the earth, expelled through a vent in the earth's crust, due to a drop in pressure of the crust. A volcano consists of a volcanic cone, a crater and volcanic passage. ☞ 活火山 huóhuǒshān on p. 876, 死火山 sǐhuǒshān on p. 1818 and 休眠火山 xiūmián huǒshān on p. 2156

【火山地震】huǒshān dìzhèn 地震的一种,由火山爆发而引起。波及范围和破坏性都较小。volcanic earthquake; earthquake caused by volcanic eruption, usu. affecting a limited area and causing limited damage

【火伤】huǒshāng 因接触火焰的高温而造成的烧伤 burn caused by high temperature flames

【火上加油】huǒ shàng jiā yóu〈比喻 *fig*.〉使人更加愤怒或使事态更加严重 aggravate; intensify; add fuel to the flame; intensify anger; aggravate a situation; also 火上浇油 huǒ shàng jiāo yóu

【火烧】huǒ·shao 表面没有芝麻的烧饼 baked wheat flour cake without sesame on the top

【火烧火燎】huǒ shāo huǒ liǎo (～的 huǒ shāo huǒ liǎo·de)〈比喻 *fig*.〉身上热得难受或心中十分焦灼 unbearably hot; extremely anxious; burning with anxiety; filled with anxiety

【火烧眉毛】huǒ shāo méi·mao〈比喻 *fig*.〉非

常急迫 imminent; urgent; pressing:～眼下急。It's extremely urgent.|这是～的事儿,别这么慢条斯理的。This is a matter of utmost urgency, so please hurry up.

【火烧云】huǒshāoyún 日出或日落时出现的赤色云霞 red clouds at sunrise or sunset

【火舌】huǒshé 比较高的火苗 tongues of fire; leaping flames

【火绳】huǒshéng 用艾、草等搓成的绳,燃烧发烟,用来驱除蚊虫,也可以引火 kindling cord; cord of plaited mugwort and grass, which produces smoke that repels insects and can also be used as kindling

【火石】huǒshí ❶ 燧石的通称 general term for 燧石 suìshí ❷ 用铈、镧、铁制成的合金,摩擦时能产生火花。通常用于打火机中。alloy of cerium, lanthanum and iron, which produces sparks when struck; usu. used in a lighter

【火势】huǒshì 火燃烧的情势 intensity of a fire:～已得到控制。The fire is under control.

【火树银花】huǒ shù yín huā 形容灿烂的灯火或烟火 fire-spitting trees and silver-petalled flowers; bright display of lights or fireworks; splendid sea of lights or dazzling display of fireworks

【火速】huǒsù 用最快的速度(做紧急的事)(do sth. urgent) at top speed; posthaste; lose no time in doing sth.:～行动 act at top speed|任务紧急,必须～完成。It's an urgent task and must be finished as soon as possible.

【火炭】huǒtàn 燃烧中的木炭或木柴 burning charcoal or wood

【火塘】huǒtáng〈方 *dial.*〉室内地上挖成的小坑,四周垒砖石,中间生火取暖 fire pit; small pit dug in the floor, lined with brick and stone, for burning a fire for warmth

【火烫】huǒtàng ❶ 非常热;滚烫 scalding; burning hot:他正在发烧,脸上～。He's got a high fever and his face is burning. ❷ 用烧热的火剪烫发 curl hair with heated iron tongs

【火头】huǒtóu ❶ (～儿 huǒtóur) 火焰 flame; fire:油灯的～儿太小。The flame of the oil lamp is too low. ❷ (～儿 huǒtóur) same as 火候 huǒ·hou ①:～儿不到,饼就烙不好。Without enough heat, the cakes will not bake properly. ❸ same as 火主 huǒzhǔ ❹ (～儿 huǒtóur) same as 怒气 nùqì:你先把～压一压,别着急。Calm down and take it easy!

【火头军】huǒtóujūn 近代小说戏曲中称军队中的炊事员(现代用做戏谑的话 now humor. in contemporary fiction and skite) army cook; one who cooks for others

【火头上】huǒtóu·shang 发怒的时候 at the height of anger:他正在～,等他消消气再跟他细说。He's very angry now, so talk to him after he calms down.

【火腿】huǒtuǐ 腌制的猪腿。浙江金华和云南宣威出产的最有名。ham; salted leg of pork; The most famous ham is produced in Jinhua, Zhejiang Province and Xuanwei, Yunnan Province.

【火网】huǒwǎng 弹道纵横交织的密集火力 cross fire; heavy gunfire where the lines of fire cross one another; also 火力网 huǒlìwǎng

【火险】huǒxiǎn ❶ 火灾的保险 fire insurance ❷ 失火的危险 fire danger:～隐患 hidden fire danger

【火线】huǒxiàn ❶ 作战双方对峙的前沿地带 battlefront; frontline in a battle ❷ 电路中输送电的电源线。在市电上指对地电压大的导线,在直流电路中指接正极的导线。live wire; power line; in city power supply, the conducting wire with higher-potential to ground; in direct current, conducting wire connected to the positive electrode

【火星】[1] huǒxīng 太阳系九大行星之一,按离太阳由近而远的次序计为第四颗,比地球小,公转周期约 687 天,自转周期约 24 小时 37 分 Mars, one of the nine planets in the Solar system, the 4th closest to the sun, smaller than the earth. It takes the Mars 687 days to revolve around the sun and 24 hours and 37 minutes to complete one rotation on its own axis.(图见 ☞ figure for 太阳系 tàiyángxì on p.1855)

【火星】[2] huǒxīng (～儿 huǒxīngr) 极小的火 spark:铁锤打在石头上,迸出不少～。Sparks flew when the hammer hit the rock.◇他气得两眼直冒～。His eyes flashed with fury.

【火性】huǒxìng 急躁的、容易发怒的脾气 quick temper; hot temper; easily angered; also 火性子 huǒxìng·zi

【火眼】huǒyǎn〈中医 *Chin. med.*〉指急性结膜炎 pinkeye; acute conjunctivitis

【火眼金睛】huǒ yǎn jīn jīng《西游记》第七回写孙悟空被放在八卦炉里锻炼,他那一双被炉烟熏红的眼叫做火眼金睛,能识别各种妖魔鬼怪借指能洞察一切的眼力。piercing eyes; penetrating insight. In Chapter Seven of the novel *Journey to the West*, Monkey King is imprisoned in the Eight-Diagram Stove to be tempered. The smoke makes his eyes red, thus the term 火眼金睛, and he is able to recognize all sorts of demons and ghosts. It refers to peretrating eyes or deep insight.

【火焰】huǒyàn 燃烧着的可燃气体,发光,发热,闪烁而向上升。其他可燃体如石油、蜡烛、木材等,燃烧时先产生可燃气体,所以也有火焰。flame; tongue of fire. Rising blaze and heat from burning gas. Combustible substances such as oil, candle wax and wood produce burning vapor when ignited which also produce flames. also 火苗 huǒmiáo

【火焰喷射器】huǒyàn pēnshèqì flamethrower; ☞ 喷火器 pēnhuǒqì on p.1457

【火药】huǒyào 炸药的一类。爆炸时有的有烟,如黑色火药,有的没有烟,如硝酸纤维素。gunpowder; powder; explosive, e.g. charcoal gunpowder, which produce smoke on explosion, and cellulose nitrate, which is smokeless

【火药味】huǒyàowèi (～儿 huǒyàowèir)〈比喻 *fig.*〉强烈的敌意或激烈的冲突气氛 hostile; confrontational; antagonistic; smell of gunpowder; bellicose atmosphere: 他今天的发言带～。He made a very aggressive speech today. | 辩论会上～很浓。The debate was highly confrontational.

【火印】huǒyìn 把烧热的铁器或铁质的图章烙在木器、竹片等物体上而留下的标记 brand; mark left by hot iron object or seal on wooden or bamboo articles

【火油】huǒyóu〈方 *dial.*〉same as 煤油 méiyóu

【火灾】huǒzāi 失火造成的灾害 fire disaster; conflagration: 防止森林～。Forest fires should be prevented.

【火葬】huǒzàng 处理死人遗体的一种方法,用火焚化尸体 cremation; funeral rite to reduce a dead body to ashes by fire

【火针】huǒzhēn 一种针刺疗法,将针尖烧红,迅速刺入一定部位的皮下组织,并立即拔出 hot-needle acupuncture; form of needle therapy. A red hot needle tip is quickly stuck into subcutaneous tissue at a specific point, and then immediately withdrawn. also 燔针 fánzhēn, 淬针 cuìzhēn and 烧针 shāozhēn

【火纸】huǒzhǐ ❶ 涂着硝的纸,容易燃烧,多用做火煤儿 touch paper; paper smeared with nitre and easy to ignite, often used for kindling ❷〈方 *dial.*〉迷信的人祭奠死人时烧的纸 ritual paper money burned for the dead

【火中取栗】huǒ zhōng qǔ lì 一只猴子和一只猫看见炉火中烤着栗子,猴子叫猫去偷,猫用爪子从火中取出几个栗子,自己脚上的毛被烧掉,栗子却都被猴子给吃了(见于法国拉·封登[Jean de La Fontaine]的寓言) pull chestnuts out of the fire; be a cat's paw; according to a fable by French writer Jean de La Fontaine, a monkey and a cat saw roasting chestnuts in a stove. The monkey asked the cat to steal them, so the cat pulled some out of the fire, burning the fur on its paws, but the monkey got to eat all the chestnuts.〈比喻 *fig.*〉冒危险给别人出力,自己上了大当,一无所得 be duped into taking risks for sb. else without any benefit to oneself

【火种】huǒzhǒng 供引火用的火 kindling spark; spark ◇革命的～ seeds of revolution; sparks of revolution

【火烛】huǒzhú 泛指可以引起火灾的东西 (in a broad sense) anything that could cause a fire: 小心～。Flammable, be ware!

【火主】huǒzhǔ 引起火灾的人家 place where a fire starts; person responsible for starting a fire

【火柱】huǒzhù 柱状的火焰 column of flame

【火箸】huǒzhù〈方 *dial.*〉same as 火筷子 huǒkuài·zi

【火砖】huǒzhuān 耐火砖 refractory brick; fire brick; brick that withstand high heat

伙[1](火) huǒ 伙食 mess; board; meals; food: 起～cook meals | 包～ get or supply meals at a fixed rate; board

伙[2](火、夥) huǒ ❶ 同伴;伙计 partner; companion: ～伴 companion | ～友 partner ❷ 由同伴组成的集体 partnership; company: 合～ join together | 入～ enter into partnership | 成群搭～ band together; throng; form crowds ❸〈量词 *classifier*〉用于人群 group; crowd; band; gang: 一～人 a group of people | 分成两～divide into two groups | 三个一群,五个一～ in twos and threes; in small groups ❹ 共同;联合 combine; join: ～同 join together | ～办 join in some action | 几个人～着干。Several people work together.

【伙伴】huǒbàn〈古代 *arch.*〉兵制十人为一火,火长一人管炊事,同火者称为火伴,现在泛指共同参加某种组织或从事某种活动的人,写作伙伴 partner; companion; pal; chum. In ancient military practice, 10 soldiers formed a group to use a cooking fire (火 huǒ). One soldier of each group was solely responsible for cooking and was titled fire head (火头 huǒtóu); the others were called fire companions (伙伴 huǒbàn). It refers to people who join the same organization or take part in the same activity, written as 伙伴.

【伙房】huǒfáng 学校、部队等集体中的厨房 kitchen of a school or a military unit

【伙夫】huǒfū same as 火夫 huǒfū ②

【伙耕】huǒgēng 共同耕种 collaborate to cultivate land: 他们～了十来亩地。Together they cultivated more than ten *mu* of land.

【伙计】huǒ·ji ❶ 合作的人;伙伴(多用来当面称对方 form of address oft. used face-to-face) partner; pal; business associate: ～,咱得加快干。Guys, let's hurry up. ❷〈旧时 *old*〉指店员或长工 salesman; shop assistant; hired hand: 当年我在这个店当～。I once worked as a shop assistant in this store.

【伙食】huǒ·shí 饮食,多指部队、机关、学校等集体中所办的饭食 mess; food; meals; mostly prepared for a group in a military unit, government organization or school: ～费 board expenses; money for meals | 改善～ improve the quality of food; have better food

【伙同】huǒtóng 跟别人合在一起(做事)(work) with others; join together: 老王～几个退休工人办起了农机修理厂。Old Wang and some other retired workers set up a repair shop for farm equipment.

【伙种】huǒzhòng same as 伙耕 huǒgēng

【伙子】huǒ·zi same as 伙[2] huǒ ③: 他们是一～。

H

They belong to the same group.

钬 huǒ 金属元素，符号 Ho (holmium)。是一种稀土金属。holmium (Ho), a rare-earth metal

漷 huǒ 漷县，在北京市通州区 Huoxian, name of a place in Tongzhou District, Beijing

夥1 huǒ 〈书 *fml.*〉多 much; many; numerous; a great deal: 获益甚～ gain much from; benefit greatly from

夥2 huǒ same as 伙2huǒ

huò（ㄏㄨㄛˋ）

或 huò ❶ 或许；也许 perhaps; maybe; probably: 慰问团已经起程，明日上午～可到达。The delegation coming to convey greetings and appreciation has set off and is expected to arrive tomorrow morning. ❷ same as 或者 huòzhě ②: ～多～少 more or less｜不解决桥～船的问题，过河就是一句空话。Without a boat or a bridge, there is no way to cross the river.｜他生怕我没听清～不注意，所以又嘱咐了一遍。He repeated his advice for fear I had not heard or was not paying attention. ❸〈书 *fml.*〉某人；有的人 someone; some people: ～告之曰。Somebody told him that... ❹〈书 *fml.*〉稍微 a little; a bit; slightly; in some sort: 不可～缺 absolutely necessary; indispensable｜不可～忽 essential; absolutely necessary

【或然】huòrán 有可能而不一定 probably: ～性 probability

【或然率】huòránlǜ 概率的旧称 previous term for 概率 gàilǜ

【或许】huòxǔ same as 也许 yěxǔ: 他没来，～是病了。He didn't come, so maybe he's ill.

【或则】huòzé same as 或者 huòzhě ②（大多叠用 oft. used repeatedly）: 天晴的日子，老人家～到城外散步，～到河边钓鱼。On sunny days, the old man either took a walk in the city suburbs or went fishing in the river.

【或者】huòzhě ❶ same as 或许 huòxǔ: 你快走，～还赶得上车。If you hurry, you may still catch the bus. ❷〈连词 *conj.*〉用在叙述句里，表示选择关系 [used in a narrative sentence to express a choice]: 你们叫我杨同志～老杨都行，可别再叫我杨科长。You may call me Comrade Yang or Old Yang, but don't call me Director Yang.｜这本书～你先看，～我先看。Either of us can read the book first.

和1 huò 粉状或粒状物搀和在一起，或加水搅拌使成较稀的东西 mix; blend; mix powder or particles with water: ～药 mix medicine｜藕粉里～点儿糖。Add a little sugar to the lotus root powder.

和2 huò〈量词 *classifier*〉指洗东西换水的次数或一剂药煎的次数 number of rinses or decoctions: 衣裳已经洗了三～。The clothes have been rinsed three times.｜二～药 second decoction of herbs

☞ hé on p. 786, hè on p. 791, hú on p. 817 and huó on p. 875

【和弄】huò·nong〈方 *dial.*〉❶ same as 搅拌 jiǎobàn ❷ same as 挑拨 tiǎobō

【和稀泥】huò xīní〈比喻 *fig.*〉无原则地调解或折中 appease; smooth things over; mediate at the expense of principle

货 huò ❶ 货币；钱 money; currency: 通～ currency ❷ 货物；商品 goods; commodity: 百～ daily necessities｜南～ goods from the south｜订～ order goods｜销～ sell goods｜～真价实 quality goods at a fair price; value for money｜奇～可居 rare commodity worth hoarding for a better price ❸ 指人（骂人的话 curse）person: 笨～ stupid person; fool｜蠢～ blockhead; idiot｜好吃懒做的～ lazybones; idler ❹〈书 *fml.*〉出卖 sell: ～卖 sell

【货币】huòbì 充当一切商品的等价物的特殊商品。货币是价值的一般代表，可以购买任何别的商品。money; currency; special commodity that serves as a medium of exchange for all commodities. Money is a general measure of value and can purchase any commodity.

【货舱】huòcāng 船或飞机上专用于装载货物的舱 cargo bay on a plane; cargo hold; area on aircraft or ship specifically for storing cargo

【货场】huòchǎng 车站、商店、仓库等储存或临时堆放货物的场地 storage area; space to store or temporarily stack goods in a station, a shop or warehouse

【货车】huòchē 主要用来载运货物的车辆 lorry; truck; freight train; freight car; vehicle used primarily to transport goods

【货船】huòchuán 主要用来载运货物的船 freighter; cargo ship; cargo vessel; vessel primarily for transporting cargo

【货柜】huòguì ❶ 摆放货物的柜台 showcase; counter for displaying goods ❷〈方 *dial.*〉same as 集装箱 jízhuāngxiāng

【货机】huòjī 主要用来载运货物的飞机 cargo aircraft; air freighter; aircraft primarily for transporting cargo

【货架子】huòjià·zi ❶ 商店里放货物的架子 store rack shelves in a shop for displaying goods ❷ 指自行车的座子后面的架子 metal frame fixed to a bicycle behind the seat

【货款】huòkuǎn 买卖货物的款子 payment for goods

【货郎】huòláng 在农村、山区或城市小街僻巷流动地贩卖日用品的人，有的也兼营收购 itinerant peddler; street vendor; person who travels from place to place selling daily necessities in rural and mountainous areas, and small urban streets and alleys; some also engage in procurement: ～担(货郎装货物的担子) peddler's wares carried on a shoulder pole

【货郎鼓】huòlánggǔ 货郎招揽顾客用的手摇小鼓,形状跟拨浪鼓相同而比较大 peddler's drum; small rattle-drum used by peddlers to attract customers

【货轮】huòlún 主要用来载运货物的轮船 freighter; cargo ship; cargo vessel; vessel primarily for transporting cargo

【货票】huòpiào 运输企业承运货物时开给托运人的票据,是托运人或收货人提货的凭证 cargo claim check; receipt from transportation company to customer upon receiving goods to be freighted; used by customer to claim the goods

【货品】huòpǐn 货物。也指货物的品种 goods or types of goods: ～丰富 abundant goods; a variety of goods

【货色】huòsè ❶ 货物(就品种或质量说)(in terms of variety or quality) goods: ～齐全。Goods of every description are available.|上等～ first-class goods; quality goods ❷ 也指人或思想言论、作品等(多含贬义 usu. derog.) lousy; poor stuff; referring to a person, thoughts, speech or works

【货声】huòshēng 小贩等叫卖的声音或做某些修补工作的人走街串巷招揽主顾的吆喝声 hawk; signature calls of itinerant peddlers or repairmen to attract customers

【货损】huòsǔn 货物在运输过程中发生的损坏 freight damage; damage to cargo during transportation: ～严重 serious damage to freight|禁止野蛮装卸,减少～。Rough handling during loading and unloading is forbidden in order to reduce damages.

【货摊】huòtān (～儿 huòtānr)设在路旁、广场上的售货处 stall; stand; vending stand set up by the road or in a square: 摆～ sell goods at a stall

【货梯】huòtī 主要用来运载货物的电梯 freight elevator; freight or goods

【货位】huòwèi ❶ 铁路运输上可装满一车皮的货物量,叫一货位 car load; quantity of goods which will fill one railway freight car ❷ 车站、商店、仓库等储存或临时堆放货物的位置 storage space; place to store or temporarily stack goods in station, shop or warehouse

【货物】huòwù 供出售的物品 goods; commodity; merchandise

【货样】huòyàng 货物的样品 sample; sample goods

【货源】huòyuán 货物的来源 source of goods; supply of goods: ～充足 an ample supply of goods|开辟～ open up new sources of goods|扩大～ increase the supply of goods

【货运】huòyùn 运输企业承运货物的业务 freight transport; shipment of goods; cargo service of a transport company

【货栈】huòzhàn 营业性质的堆放货物的房屋或场地 warehouse; rented storage space building or area rented out for storage

【货真价实】huò zhēn jià shí 货物不是冒牌的,价钱也是实在的。原是商人招揽生意的用语。现在引申为实实在在,一点不假。real; genuine goods at a fair price; originally used by merchants to attract customers; (of goods or other things) true to the name

【货殖】huòzhí 〈古 *arch.*〉指经营商业和工矿业 engage in trade and mining

【货主】huòzhǔ 运输部门称所运货物的主人 owner of cargo; consignor or consignee of cargo

获(❶❷獲、❸穫) huò ❶ 捉住;擒住 seize; catch: 捕～ catch|俘～ capture ❷ 得到;获得 acquire; attain; obtain: ～胜 win|～利 gain profits|～奖 win a prize|～罪 be sentenced|～救 be saved|不劳而～ reap without sowing ❸ 收割 harvest; reap: 收～ harvest; gather in

【获得】huòdé 取得;得到(多用于抽象事物 usu. abstract things) obtain; acquire; win; access; achieve: ～好评 win acclaim; earn favourable comments|～宝贵的经验 gain valuable experience|～显著的成绩 score great achievements; be highly successful

【获救】huòjiù 得到挽救 be saved; be rescued: 食物中毒的民工均已～。All workers who suffered from food poisoning were saved.

【获取】huòqǔ 取得;猎取 obtain; gain; acquire: ～情报 acquire information|～利润 gain profits

【获释】huòshì 得到释放,恢复自由 be released; be set free; regain freedom: ～出狱 be released from prison

【获悉】huòxī 得到消息知道(某事) be informed; get to know; learn of something: 日前～,他已南下探亲。We learned the other day that he had gone south to visit his parents.

【获知】huòzhī same as 获悉 huòxī: ～你已康复出院,大家都十分高兴。We're delighted to know that you are better and out of hospital.

【获致】huòzhì 获得;得到 gain; obtain; acquire; achieve: 产权纠纷～解决。The quarrel over property rights has been settled.

【获准】huòzhǔn 得到准许 gain or obtain a permission; get the greenlight; get the nod: 开业申请业已～。Our application for a business permit has been approved.

祸(禍) huò ❶ 祸事;灾难(跟'福'相对 as opposed to 'good fortune') misfortune; disaster; calamity; catastrophe: 车～ traffic accident|闯～ get into trouble|大～临头 imminent disaster|～不单行。Misfortunes never come singly. ❷ 损害 harm; injure; damage: ～国殃民 disastrous; ruinous

【祸不单行】huò bù dān xíng 表示不幸的事接连发生 misfortune does not come singly; mishaps always come in battalions; it never rains but it pours

【祸端】huòduān〈书 *fml.*〉祸根 source of disaster; cause of damage; apple of discord

【祸根】huògēn 祸事的根源;引起灾难的人或事物 root of trouble; person or matter that causes disaster: 留下～ lay the seeds for future trouble|铲除～ get rid of the root of trouble

【祸国殃民】huò guó yāng mín 使国家受害,人民遭殃 ruinous; extremely destructive; disastrous; bring disaster to the country and calamities to the people

【祸害】huò·hai ❶ 祸事 havoc; disaster; catastrophe: 黄河在历史上经常引起～。In its history, the Yellow River often wreaked havoc on the people. ❷ 引起灾难的人或事物 scourge; bane; person or matter that causes damage ❸ 损害;损坏 damage; destroy: 野猪～了一大片庄稼。Wild boar have destroyed a large patch of crops.

【祸患】huòhuàn 祸事;灾难 mishap; trouble; disaster; calamity: 消除～eradicate disasters

【祸乱】huòluàn 灾难和变乱;祸事 chaos; turmoil; social upheaval: ～不断 incessant social upheavals|～临头 imminent calamity

【祸起萧墙】huò qǐ xiāoqiáng 祸乱发生在家里 trouble within a family; trouble in one's backyard;〈比喻 *fig.*〉内部发生祸乱 internal strife

【祸事】huòshì 危害性大的事情 disaster; calamity; mishap

【祸首】huòshǒu 引起祸患的主要人物 chief culprit; chief offender; person who causes trouble: 罪魁～ringleader; arch criminal

【祸水】huòshuǐ〈比喻 *fig.*〉引起祸患的人或事 person or event that causes a disaster

【祸祟】huòsuì 迷信的人指鬼神带给人的灾祸 disaster caused by ghosts and spirits

【祸胎】huòtāi same as 祸根 huògēn

【祸心】huòxīn 作恶的念头 malicious; evil intent: 包藏～ harbour vicious intentions

【祸殃】huòyāng same as 灾祸 zāihuò: 招惹～ invite disaster; court disaster

惑 huò ❶ 疑惑;迷惑 perplexed; puzzled; bewildered: 惶～ puzzled and fightened|大～不解 bewildered; baffled; unable to make head or tail of sth.; be all at sea|智者不～。A wise man always keeps a clear mind. ❷ 使迷惑 confuse; baffle; delude: ～乱 befuddle|～人耳目 confuse one's mind|谣言～众 spread rumours to baffle people

【惑乱】huòluàn 使迷惑混乱 befuddle; confuse; delude: ～人心 confuse and poison people's minds|～军心 undermine troop morale

膗 huò same as 臛 huò

霍 huò ❶ 霍然 suddenly; all of a sudden ❷ (Huò) 姓 a surname

【霍地】huòdì〈副词 *adv.*〉表示动作突然发生 suddenly; all of a sudden: ～闪开 dodge aside quickly|～立起身来 spring to one's feet; stand up suddenly

【霍霍】huòhuò ❶〈拟声词 *onom.*〉: 磨刀～ sound of knives being sharpened ❷ 闪动 flash; sparkle: 电光～。The lightning flashed.

【霍乱】huòluàn ❶ 急性肠道传染病,病原体是霍乱弧菌。症状是腹泻,呕吐,大便很稀,像米泔水,四肢痉挛冰冷,休克。患者因脱水而眼窝凹陷,手指、脚趾干瘪。cholera; acute, infectious disease characterized by profuse diarrhea, vomitting, cramps, cold limbs, coma and dehydration; victim's eyes sink into their sockets and fingers and toes shrivel from dehydration. ❷〈中医 *Chin. med.*〉泛指有剧烈吐泻、腹痛等症状的胃肠疾患 acute gastroenteritis; intestinal disease characterized by profuse diarrhea, vomitting and stomach ache

【霍然】huòrán ❶〈副词 *adv.*〉突然 suddenly; quickly; all of a sudden: 手电筒～一亮。The flashlight lit suddenly. ❷〈书 *fml.*〉疾病迅速消除(of a disease) be cured quickly: 病体～ be restored to health quickly; recover from illness quickly

【霍闪】huòshǎn〈方 *dial.*〉same as 闪电 shǎndiàn

嚯 huò〈书 *fml.*〉❶ 大呼;大笑 cry out; shout at the top of one's voice; laugh loudly ❷〈叹词 *interj.*〉表示惊讶 oh; wow; exclamation of surprise

☞ huō on p. 875 and ǒ on p. 1431

鳠 huò 鱼类的一属,身体长形,侧扁,牙齿呈绒毛状,头上的鳞圆形,其他部分的鳞呈栉状。生活在海洋中。white wat (*Wak sina*); a genus of sea fish with long, flat body, villus-like teeth, round scales on the top of the head and comb-teeth-like squamas on other parts of its body

臛 huò〈书 *fml.*〉红色或青色的可作颜料的矿物,泛指好的彩色 red or black mineral used to make pigment; general term for high quality colour: 丹～ red; scarlet

豁 huò ❶ 开阔;开通;通达 clear; open; open-minded; sanguine: ～然 clear; open|～达 sanguine; optimistic|显～ bright and clear; obvious; conspicuous ❷ 免除 exempt; waive: ～免 exempt from; waive; absolve

☞ huá on p. 835 and huō on p. 875

【豁达】huòdá 性格开朗;气量大 cheerful; optimistic; generous: 胸襟～ generous; broad-minded|～大度 open-minded and magnanimous

【豁朗】huòlǎng (心情)开朗(of mood) elated; sanguine: 他觉得天地是那么广阔,心里是那么

～。He felt the boundless sky matched his elation.

【豁亮】huòliàng ❶ 宽敞明亮 spacious and bright：这间房子又干净又～。This room is clean, bright and spacious. ❷（嗓音）响亮（of voice）loud；sonorous；resonant

【豁免】huòmiǎn 免除（捐税、劳役等）exempt from（taxes or corvee）

【豁然】huòrán 形容开阔或通达 wide and open；magnanimous：～开朗 be suddenly enlightened；suddenly understand｜～贯通 suddenly see the whole thing in a clear light｜～醒悟 suddenly realize；suddenly become aware of

镬 huò ❶〈方 *dial.*〉锅 pot；pan；boiler ❷ 古代时大锅（in ancient time）cauldron；huge pot：斧锯鼎～（指古代残酷的刑具）hatchet，saw，tripod and cauldron — ancient instruments of torture

【镬子】huò·zi〈方 *dial.*〉锅 pot；pan；boiler

藿 huò〈书 *fml.*〉豆类作物的叶子 leaves of pulses

嚯 huò ❶〈叹词 *interj.*〉表示惊讶或赞叹［expression of surprise or admiration］oh；wow：～，原来你们也在这儿！Why，you're here，too！❷〈拟声词 *onom.*〉：～～大笑 guffaw；laugh heartily

蠖 huò ☞ 尺蠖 chǐhuò on p. 262

貛 huò［貛狮狓］（huòjiāpí）哺乳动物，体形像长颈鹿，但小得多，毛赤褐色，臀部与四肢有黑白相间的横纹。生活在非洲原始森林中，吃树叶。okapi（*Okapia johnstoni*）；mammal resembling the giraffe，but smaller，with reddish fur marked with black and white stripes on its rump and legs，living in virgin forests of Africa and eating tree leaves.

臛 huò〈书 *fml.*〉肉羹 meat broth

J

jī(ㄐㄧ)

几[1] jī(～儿 jīr)小桌子 small table: 茶～儿 tea table; coffee table | 窗明～净 (of a room or houses) spotlessly clean

几[2](幾) jī〈书 *fml.*〉几乎;近乎 almost; nearly; virtually: 歼灭敌军,～三千人。Nearly 3,000 enemy troops were wiped out.

☞ jǐ on p.910

【几案】jī'àn 条案,也泛指桌子 long table; table in general

【几乎】jīhū ❶ 将近于;接近于 close to; virtually: 今天到会的～有五千人。Close to 5,000 were present at the meeting today. ❷ 差点儿② all but; almost: 不是你提醒我,我～忘了。I all but forgot had you not reminded me. | 两条腿一软,～摔倒。My legs buckled, and I almost fell to the ground. also 几几乎 jījīhū

【几率】jīlǜ same as 概率 gàilǜ

讥(譏) jī 讥讽 deride: ～笑 make fun of; jeer | ～刺 taunt | 反唇相～ answer back sarcastically

【讥嘲】jīcháo same as 讥讽 jīfěng: ～的笔调 (of writing) bantering tone

【讥刺】jīcì same as 讥讽 jīfěng

【讥讽】jīfěng 用旁敲侧击或尖刻的话指责或嘲笑对方的错误、缺点或某种表现 criticize or laugh at sb.'s mistake, shortcoming or conduct by innuendo or with sarcasm: ～的口吻 sarcastic tone

【讥诮】jīqiào 冷言冷语地讥讽 deride; mock

【讥笑】jīxiào 讥讽和嘲笑 chaff; sneer: 别人有缺点要热情帮助,不要～。Let's reach out with a warm heart to those who have shortcomings — on no account should we make fun of them.

击(擊) jī ❶ 打;敲打 strike; beat: ～鼓 beat a drum | ～掌 applaud; clap one's hands | 旁敲侧～ make oblique reference to; by innuendo ❷ 攻打 attack: 袭～ raid; attack | 游～ guerrilla warfare | 声东～西 make a feint to the east while attacking in the west ❸ 碰;接触 contact; touch: 冲～ onslaught | 撞～ slam into ◇目～(亲眼看见) eye-witness (see with one's eyes)

【击败】jībài 打败 defeat; beat: ～对手,获得冠军 become the champion after beating one's opponent

【击毙】jībì 打死(多指用枪 oft. with a gun) shoot dead

【击发】jīfā 射击时用手指扳动扳机 pull the trigger of a gun

【击毁】jīhuǐ 击中并摧毁 hit and smash: ～敌方坦克三辆。(Our troops) destroyed three enemy tanks. | 建筑物被雷电～。The building was destroyed by a thunderbolt.

【击剑】jījiàn 体育运动项目之一,比赛时运动员穿着特制的保护服装,用剑互刺或互劈 art or sport of swordplay, with bouts taking place between two athletes wearing protective gear attacking each other using the sabre, the foil or the epee

【击节】jījié 打拍子,表示得意或赞赏 beat time; clap and applaud: ～叹赏(形容对诗文、音乐等的赞赏) show admiration for a piece of music or a poem by clapping one's hands to the rhythm of it

【击溃】jīkuì 打垮;打散 rout; thrash: ～敌军一个师 put an enemy division to rout

【击落】jīluò 打下来(天空的飞机等) down; shoot down (an airplane, etc.)

【击破】jīpò 打垮;打败 crush; defeat: 各个～ defeat (enemy troops, etc.) one at a time

【击赏】jīshǎng〈书 *fml.*〉击节称赏;赞赏 admire; applaud rhythmically (during a concert or recital)

【击水】jīshuǐ ❶ 拍打水面 pat water surface; (of a swimmer) strike the water with both arms: 举翼～ raise the oars to strike the water surface ❷ 指游泳 swim

【击掌】jīzhǎng ❶ 拍手 clap one's hands: ～称好 applaud | ～为号 signal by clapping hands ❷ 双方相互拍击手掌,表示对所立誓言,永不反悔 (of two persons) clap each other's hands by way of an oath: ～为盟 clap each other's hands to vow alliance

叽(嘰) jī〈拟声词 *onom.*〉chirp: 小鸟～～叫。Little birds are chirp ing incessantly.

【叽咕】jī·gu 小声说话 whisper: 他们两个叽叽咕咕,不知在说什么。The two of them are whispering about who knows what. also 唧咕 jī·gu

【叽叽嘎嘎】jī·jigāgā〈拟声词 *onom.*〉形容说笑声等 cackle: 他们～地嚷着笑着。They made a lot of noise, cackling and laughing. also 唧唧嘎嘎 jī·jigāgā

【叽叽喳喳】jī·jizhāzhā same as 唧唧喳喳 jī·jizhāzhā

【叽里旮旯儿】jī·ligālár 〈方 *dial.*〉各个角落；到处 everywhere; every nook and cranny：他的工作室里，～都是昆虫标本。His studio is littered with insect samples.

【叽里咕噜】jī·ligūlū 〈拟声词 *onom.*〉形容说话别人听不清楚或听不懂。也形容物体滚动的声音。talk indistinctly or inaudibly; sth. rolling about：他们俩～地说了半天。The two of them jabbered for a long time.｜石头～滚下山去。Rocks went rolling down the mountain.

【叽里呱啦】jī·liguālā 〈拟声词 *onom.*〉形容大声说话 sound of loud talk or chatter：～说个没完 babble loudly and interminably

饥[1] jī 饿 hungry：～餐渴饮 eat when hungry and drink when thirsty｜如～似渴 hungry and thirsty for or after (knowledge, etc.)

饥[2]**(饑)** jī 饥荒① famine; crop failure：连年大～major crop failures for years on end

【饥不择食】jī bù zé shí 〈比喻 *fig.*〉急需的时候顾不得选择 hunger finds no fault with the cookery; a hungry person is not choosy about what he eats

【饥肠】jīcháng 〈书 *fml.*〉饥饿的肚子 empty stomach：～辘辘（形容非常饥饿）(of one's belly or stomach) rumble with hunger

【饥饿】jī'è 饿 hunger：～难忍 unbearable hunger

【饥饿线】jī'èxiàn 饥饿的境地 on the verge of starvation

【饥寒】jīhán 饥饿和寒冷 hunger and cold：～交迫（形容生活极其贫困）live in hunger and cold; poverty-stricken

【饥荒】jī·huang ❶ 庄稼收成不好或没有收成 crop failure ❷ 经济困难；周转不灵 be hard up; have difficulty making ends meet：家里闹～。My family is running short of money. ❸ 债 debt：拉～ incur a debt

【饥馑】jījǐn 〈书 *fml.*〉same as 饥荒 jī·huang ①

【饥民】jīmín 因饥荒挨饿的人 famine refugee：赈济～ provide relief to those on the verge of starvation

【饥色】jīsè 因受饥饿而表现出来的营养不良的脸色 look of malnutrition：面带～look hungry

玑(璣) jī ❶ 〈书 *fml.*〉不圆的珠子 pearl that is not perfectly round：珠～ pearls ❷ 古代的一种天文仪器 armillary sphere, an ancient astronomical instrument

圾 jī ☞垃圾 lājī on p.1136

芨 jī ☞芨芨草 jījīcǎo below and 白芨 báijī on p.34

【芨芨草】jījīcǎo 多年生草本植物，叶子狭而长，花淡绿色。生长在碱性土壤的草滩上，是良好的固沙耐碱植物。可作饲料，又可编织筐、篓、席等。splendid achnatherum (*Achnatherum splendens*); perennial plant with long and narrow leaves and light-green flowers growing on alkaline marshes. An alkali-resistant plant ideal for sand-fixation purposes, it can also be used as fodder or basketry material. also 枳机草 zhǐjīcǎo

机(機) jī ❶ 机器 machine：缝纫～ sewing machine｜打字～ typewriter｜插秧～ rice transplanter｜拖拉～ tractor ❷ 飞机 aircraft：客～ passenger plane｜运输～ air freighter｜僚～ wing plane｜～群 air fleet ❸ 事情变化的枢纽；有重要关系的环节 turning point; crucial point：事～ confidential matter｜生～ gleam of hope｜转～ turn for the better ❹ 机会；时机 opportunity; chance：乘～ take the opportunity to do sth.｜随～应变 adapt to the changing circumstances｜～不可失 not to let an opportunity slip through one's fingers ❺ 生活机能 organic：有～体 organism｜无～化学 inorganic chemistry ❻ 重要的事务 major affair：日理万～ have one's hands full handling a myriad of tasks ❼ 心思；念头 intention; idea：动～ motive｜心～ calculating; cunning｜杀～ murderous intention ❽ 能迅速适应事物的变化的；灵活 adaptable; flexible：～智 clever; sharp｜～警 vigilant; quick-witted

【机变】jībiàn 〈书 *fml.*〉随机应变 flexible：善于～ adept at coping with changing situations

【机舱】jīcāng ❶ 轮船上装置机器的地方 (of ships) engine room ❷ 飞机内载乘客装货物的地方 (of aircraft) passenger or cargo compartment; cabin

【机场】jīchǎng 飞机起飞、降落、停放的场地 airport; tract of land with facilities for the landing, takeoff and shelter of aircraft

【机车】jīchē 用来牵引车厢在铁路上行驶的动力车。有蒸汽机车、电力机车、内燃机车等。steam, electric or diesel engine or locomotive, a self-propelled vehicle for pulling trains along a railway; 通称 popularly called 火车头 huǒchētóu

【机床】jīchuáng 工作母机，也特指金属切削机床 machine tool, esp. metal-cutting machine tool

【机电】jīdiàn 机械和电力设备的统称 general term for machinery and electrical equipment：～产品 mechanical and electrical products

【机动】[1]jīdòng 利用机器开动的 power-driven; motorized：～车 motor vehicle

【机动】[2]jī dòng ❶ 权宜（处置）；灵活（运用）handle sth. as one sees fit; flexible in using or disposing of sth.：这笔经费你们可以～使用。You may use this fund flexibly. ❷ 准备灵活

运用的 in reserve; for emergency use: ~费 money reserved for emergencies | ~力量 reserved force

【机帆船】jīfānchuán 有动力装置的帆船 motor sailboat; motorized junk

【机房】jīfáng ❶〈旧时 *old*〉设置织机从事手工纺织的房屋 room which houses hand-operated looms ❷ 泛指安装机器的房屋 (in a broad sense) room with a machine installed in it

【机耕】jīgēng 用机器耕地 mechanical ploughing: ~地 farmland ploughed by tractors; tractor-ploughed farmland

【机工】jīgōng 机械工人 mechanic; machine worker

【机构】jīgòu ❶ 机械的内部构造或机械内部的一个单元 mechanism; unit of the internal structure of a machine, or part of it: 传动~ transmission mechanism | 液压~ hydraulic mechanism ❷ 泛指机关、团体或其他工作单位 government department, institution or other workaday organization: 外交~ diplomatic mission | 这个~已经撤销了。This organization has been abolished. ❸ 机关、团体等的内部组织 internal organization of a government department, institution, etc.: ~庞大 cumbersome organizational structure | 调整~ institutional restructuring

【机关】jīguān ❶ 整个机械的关键部分 central part of a machinery: 摇动水车的~,把河水引到田里。Turn the crank of the waterwheel to pump water into the fields. ❷ 用机械控制的 machine-controlled: ~枪 machine-gun | ~布景 machine-operated stage scenery ❸ 办理事务的部门 functioning department: 行政~ administrative department | 军事~ military unit | ~工作 office work ❹ 周密而巧妙的计谋 scheme; stratagem; trick: 识破~ see through a trick | ~用尽 leave no stone unturned; for all one's calculations and scheming

J

【机关报】jīguānbào 国家机关、政党或群众组织出版的报纸和刊物 organ; official newspaper or journal of a government (or government department), political party or mass organization

【机关刊物】jīguān kānwù 国家机关、政党或群众组织出版的刊物 official journal of a government (or one of its departments), political party or mass organization

【机关枪】jīguānqiāng 装有枪架、能自动连续发射的枪,分为轻机关枪、重机关枪、高射机关枪等几种 machine-gun; automatic gun giving continuous fire, often hoisted upon a stand, including sub-machine gun, heavy machine-gun, and anti-aircraft machine-gun; 简称 abbr. 机枪 jīqiāng

【机灌】jīguàn 用机器抽水灌溉 motor-pumped irrigation

【机徽】jīhuī 漆在飞机身上表明飞机所属的标志 logo painted on the body of an aircraft

【机会】jī·huì 恰好的时候;时机 opportunity; chance: 错过~ miss a good opportunity | 千载一时的好~ once-in-a-lifetime opportunity

【机会主义】jīhuì zhǔyì 工人运动中或无产阶级政党内部的反马克思主义思潮。机会主义有两种。一种是右倾机会主义,其主要特点是牺牲工人阶级长远的、全局的利益,贪图暂时的、局部的利益,反对革命,以至向反革命势力投降。一种是'左'倾机会主义,其主要特点是不顾客观实际的可能性,不注意斗争的策略,采取盲目的冒险行动。opportunism; anti-Marxist ideological trend in the workers' movement or a proletarian party. Opportunism falls in two categories: rightist opportunism, characterized mainly by the tendency to sacrifice the long-term, overall interests of the working class in return for temporary, partial interests, and run so far as to oppose revolution or even capitulate to the anti-revolutionary forces; leftist opportunism, marked chiefly by the propensity to take adventurist actions by ignoring actual conditions and throwing overboard all strategies and tactics.

【机件】jījiàn 组成机器的各个零件 component part of a machine

【机井】jījǐng 用水泵汲水的深水井。这种井用机械开凿。well dug deep into the ground with a machine, with water drawn from it with a pump

【机警】jījǐng 对情况的变化觉察得快;机智敏锐 highly perceptive; nimble-minded: ~的目光 alert eyes

【机具】jījù 机械和工具的统称 machines and tools

【机理】jīlǐ ☞机制[2] jīzhì ①②③

【机灵】[1] jī·ling 聪明伶俐;机智 smart; intelligent: 这孩子怪~的。The child is quite smart. also 机伶 jī·ling

【机灵】[2] jī·ling same as 激灵 jī·ling

【机米】jīmǐ 用机器碾出的大米。现在一般指用机器碾出的籼米。machine-husked rice; long-shaped rice husked with a machine

【机密】jīmì ❶ 重要而秘密 sth. so important that it has to be hidden from the knowledge of others: ~文件 classified or confidential document ❷ 机密的事 sth. to be kept hidden: 保守国家的~ guard state secrets

【机敏】jīmǐn 机警灵敏 alert and resourceful: 反应~ quick to react | ~过人 exceptionally nimble-witted

【机谋】jīmóu〈书 *fml.*〉能迅速适应事物变化的计谋 stratagem; artifice; scheme

【机能】jīnéng 细胞组织或器官等的作用和活动能力 physiological function and activity of cells, tissues or organs: 人体~ functions of the human body

【机器】jī·qì 由零件装成、能运转、能变换能量或产生有用的功的装置。机器可以作为生产工具,能减轻人的劳动强度,提高生产率。installation put together with component parts, capable of converting one kind of energy into another or providing useful work. Used as a production tool, machine can lessen labour intensity and raise labour productivity.

【机器翻译】jī·qì fānyì 利用电子计算机一类的装置把一种语言文字译成另一种语言文字 machine translation; method to translate one written language into another by using such equipment as computers

【机器脚踏车】jī·qì jiǎotàchē 〈方 *dial*.〉摩托车 motorcycle

【机器人】jī·qìrén 一种自动机械,由电子计算机控制,能代替人做某些工作 robot; automatic machine controlled by a computer to replace man in carrying out a series of actions; also 机械人 jīxièrén

【机器油】jī·qìyóu 涂在机器的轴承或其他摩擦部分的各种润滑油 lubricating oil; lubricant; substance for lessening friction in the bearings and other working parts of a mechanism

【机枪】jīqiāng 机关枪的简称 abbr. for 机关枪 jīguānqiāng

【机巧】jīqiǎo 灵活巧妙 adroit: 应对~ respond to a situation adroitly

【机群】jīqún 编队飞行的一群飞机 air fleet; air armada

【机体】jītǐ 具有生命的个体的统称,包括植物和动物,如最低等最原始的单细胞生物、最高等最复杂的人类 organism; general term for any form of animal or plant life, such as the most primitive unicellular organism, and the highest and most complex organism, the human being; also 有机体 yǒujī·tǐ

【机务】jīwù 指机器或机车的使用、维修、保养等方面的事务 affairs concerning the use, repair and maintenance of a machine or locomotive: ~段 maintenance section | ~员 maintenance worker

【机械】jīxiè ❶ 利用力学原理组成的各种装置。杠杆、滑轮、机器以及枪炮等都是机械。installation put together according to principles of mechanics, such as lever, pulley, machine, and arms ❷〈比喻 *fig*.〉方式拘泥死板,没有变化;不是辩证的 mechanical; rigid; not dialectical: 工作方法太~ mechanical work method

【机械波】jīxièbō 机械振动在介质中的传播过程。如水波、声波等。mechanical wave, the process in which mechanical vibration is transmitted through a medium

【机械化】jīxièhuà 广泛使用机器装备以代替或减轻体力劳动,提高效能 mechanization, referring to use of machines to replace or alleviate physical labour and increase efficiency: 农业~ farm mechanization | ~部队 mechanized troops

【机械论】jīxièlùn 机械唯物主义 mechanical materialism

【机械能】jīxiènéng 机械运动具有的能,包括动能和势能 mechanical energy, including both kinetic energy and potential energy

【机械手】jīxièshǒu 能代替人手做某些动作的机械装置,种类很多 mechanical arm; manipulator; any mechanical device with the capabilities of the human hand

【机械唯物主义】jīxiè wéiwù zhǔyì 形而上学的唯物主义,十七世纪和十八世纪盛行于欧洲。它肯定世界是物质的和运动的,同时用机械力学原理来解释一切现象和过程,用孤立的、片面的观点观察世界,把自然界和社会的变化过程归结为数量增减、位置变更,把运动看作是外力的推动,否认事物运动的内部原因、质的变化和发展的飞跃。mechanical materialism; metaphysical materialism in vogue in Europe during the 17th and 18th centuries. While conceding that the world is material and in motion, mechanical materialists follow the principles of mechanics in interpreting all the phenomena and processes, observe the world from an isolated and unilateral point of view, attribute the changing processes of nature and society to changes in quantity and position, regard motion as the result of external force, and negate the internal causes for the motion of things as well as their qualitative change and leap of development. also 机械论 jīxièlùn

【机械效率】jīxiè xiàolǜ 机械所做的有用功和总功的比值,通常用百分数表示 mechanical efficiency; ratio of the useful work of a machine to the total amount of work it has performed

【机械运动】jīxiè yùndòng 物体之间或物体中各点之间相对位置改变的运动,是物质最简单、最基本的运动形式,如机械运转、车辆行驶等 mechanical movement; movement between objects or of a given object that results in the shift of the relevant positions of various points, the simplest and most fundamental form of matter's movement, such as the working of a maching and the driving of a vehicle

【机修】jīxiū 机器维修 machine maintenance and repair: ~工 maintenance worker

【机要】jīyào 机密重要的 confidential: ~工作 confidential work | ~部门 confidential department | ~秘书 confidential secretary

【机宜】jīyí 针对客观情势处理事务的方针、办法等 guideline or way of doing things designed to handle affairs in light of actual situation: 面授~ advise sb. face-to-face

【机油】jīyóu 机器油。特指用于内燃机等的自动润滑系统中的润滑油。engine oil; machine oil, esp. lubricant applied to the automatic lubricating mechanism of an internal combustion engine

【机遇】jīyù 境遇；时机；机会（多指有利的 oft. favourable) opportune time; opportunity; luck：难得的～ rare opportunity; windfall

【机缘】jīyuán 机会和缘分 good luck or chance：～凑巧 as luck would have it

【机制】[1] jīzhì 用机器制造的 machine-made：～纸 machine-made paper | ～煤球 machine-made (egg-shaped) briquettes

【机制】[2] jīzhì ❶ 机器的构造和工作原理，如计算机的机制 mechanism; structure and operational principle of a machine, such as that of a computer ❷ 有机体的构造、功能和相互关系，如动脉硬化的机制 structure and function, and the relationship between them, in an organism, such as the mechanism of arteriosclerosis ❸ 指某些自然现象的物理、化学规律。如优选法中优化对象的机制。physical and chemical law governing a natural phenomenon, such as the mechanism of objects in optimization ‖ also 机理 jīlǐ ❹ 泛指一个工作系统的组织或部分之间相互作用的过程和方式 process and methodology of interaction between the organizations or departments of a given operational system：市场～ market mechanism | 竞争～ competition mechanism

【机智】jīzhì 脑筋灵活，能够随机应变 nimble-minded; capacity to adapt oneself to changed situation：英勇～的战士 brave and resourceful soldier

【机杼】jīzhù ❶〈书 *fml.*〉指织布机 loom ❷〈比喻 *fig.*〉诗文的构思和布局 conception and composition of a poem or a piece of writing：自出～ break new ground for oneself

【机子】jī·zi ❶ 指某些机械或装置，如织布机、电话机等 machinery or installation, such as loom and telephone set ❷ 枪上的扳机 trigger

【机组】jīzǔ ❶ 由几种不同机器组成的一组机器，能够共同完成一项工作。如汽轮机、发电机和其他附属设备组成汽轮发电机组。unit or set of machines put together to tackle a task, such as generating set, which consists of a steam turbine, a generator and ancillary equipment ❷ 一架飞机上的全体工作人员 aircrew; crew

乩

jī ☞扶乩 fú//jī on p.595

肌

jī 肌肉 muscle：平滑～ smooth or involuntary muscle | ～肤 muscle and skin

【肌肤】jīfū〈书 *fml.*〉肌肉和皮肤 muscle and skin

【肌腱】jījiàn 腱 tenden

【肌理】jīlǐ〈书 *fml.*〉皮肤的纹理 skin texture：～细腻 fine-textured skin

【肌肉】jīròu 人和动物体内的一种组织，由许多肌纤维集合构成。上面有神经纤维，在神经冲动的影响下收缩，引起器官运动。可分为横纹肌、平滑肌和心肌三种。muscle; tissue that consists of fascicles (or bundles of muscle fibrils) in the body of a human being or animal. The nerve fibres on the muscle contract under the impact of nerve impulses, causing movement in an organ. Classified into striated muscle, smooth muscle and cardiac muscle (myocardium). also 筋肉 jīnròu

【肌体】jītǐ 指身体，也用来比喻组织机构 human body; organism; (fig.) organizational structure

【肌纤维】jīxiānwéi 构成肌肉的细而长的细胞，呈纤维状。许多肌纤维组成一个肌束，许多肌束组成一块肌肉。muscle fibre or fibril; long and slim fibre-shaped cells that form the muscle. Many muscle fibrils combine to form a fascicle, or bundle of fibres, and many fascicles form a muscle.

禨(禨)

jī〈书 *fml.*〉福；祥 good fortune; bliss

矶(磯)

jī 水边突出的岩石或石滩 rock protruding over the water：钓～ protruding rock for angling | 燕子～（在江苏）Swallow Crag (Yanziji, name of a place in Jiangsu Province) | 采石～（在安徽）Quarry Crag (Caishiji, name of a place in Anhui Province)

鸡(鷄、雞)

jī 家禽，品种很多，嘴短，上嘴稍弯曲，头部有肉质的冠。翅膀短，不能高飞。chicken, of diverse breeds, a domestic fowl with a fleshy cockscomb, a short beak whose upper mandible is slightly crooked, and wings that are too short for flying; also 家鸡 jiājī

【鸡雏】jīchú 幼小的鸡 chick

【鸡蛋里挑骨头】jīdàn·li tiāo gǔ·tou〈比喻 *fig.*〉故意挑毛病 look for a bone in an egg; nitpick

【鸡飞蛋打】jī fēi dàn dǎ 鸡飞走了，蛋也打破了 the hen has flown away and the eggs in the coop are broken;〈比喻 *fig.*〉两头落空，毫无所得 all is lost

【鸡公车】jīgōngchē〈方 *dial.*〉独轮手推车 wheelbarrow

【鸡冠】jīguān 鸡头上高起的肉冠 cockscomb; also 鸡冠子 jīguān·zi

【鸡黄】jīhuáng〈方 *dial.*〉孵出不久的小鸡，身上有淡黄色的毛 newly-hatched chick, with its body covered with light yellow down

【鸡奸】jījiān 指男人与男人之间发生性行为 sodomy; buggery; also 要奸 jījiān

【鸡口牛后】jī kǒu niú hòu《战国策·韩策》：'宁为鸡口，无为牛后。' 'Better be a chicken's head than a cow's rump', quoted from *Intrigues of the Warring States · Intrigues of Han*;〈比喻 *fig.*〉宁愿在局面小的地方当家作主，不愿在局面大的地方任人支配 rather rule the roost in a small place than be manipulated by someone else in a large place; also 鸡尸牛从 jī shī niú cóng（尸 *shi*：主 be the boss）

【鸡肋】jīlèi 〈书 *fml.*〉鸡的肋骨,吃着没味,扔了可惜 chicken ribs — of little taste and yet wasteful to throw away;〈比喻 *fig.*〉没有多大价值、多大意思的事情(见于《三国志·魏书·武帝纪》注)things of little value or interest (see footnotes in *Records of Three Kingdoms · Kingdom of Wei · Biography of Emperor Wu*)

【鸡零狗碎】jī líng gǒu suì 〈比喻 *fig.*〉事物零零碎碎,不成片段 in bits and pieces; fragmentary

【鸡毛掸子】jīmáo dǎn·zi 掸灰尘的用具,把鸡毛扎在藤或竹竿的一端制成。有的地区叫鸡毛帚。feather duster, fashioned by fastening chicken feathers to one end of a cane or bamboo pole, known in some areas as 鸡毛帚 jīmáozhǒu

【鸡毛店】jīmáodiàn 〈旧时 *old*〉最简陋的小客店。没有被褥,垫鸡毛取暖。small inn that is all but unfurnished, with the floor of its rooms covered with chicken feathers as makeshift bedding

【鸡毛蒜皮】jīmáo suànpí 〈比喻 *fig.*〉无关紧要的琐事 chicken feathers and garlic skins; trivialities; trifles

【鸡毛信】jīmáoxìn 过去须要火速传递的紧急公文、信件,就插上鸡毛,叫鸡毛信 (old) chicken-feather letter; message with a chicken feather attached as a sign of urgency

【鸡毛帚】jīmáozhǒu 〈方 *dial.*〉鸡毛掸子 feather duster

【鸡鸣狗盗】jī míng gǒu dào 战国时,齐国孟尝君被秦国扣留。他的一个门客装做狗夜里潜入秦宫,偷出本已献给秦王的狐白裘献给秦王的爱姬,才得释放。孟尝君深夜到函谷关,城门紧闭,他的另一个门客学公鸡叫,骗开城门,才得脱险逃回齐国(见于《史记·孟尝君列传》)。后来用'鸡鸣狗盗'比喻微不足道的技能。According to *Records of the Historian · Biographies of Lord Mengchan*, during the Warring States Period, Lord Mengchan of the state of Qi was detained by the state of Qin, and he was released only after one of his hangers-on disguised himself as a dog, sneaked into the Qin palace, made away with the white fox-fur coat that Lord Mengchan had already presented to the king of Qin as a gift, and bribed the king's favourite concubine with it. On another occasion, Lord Mengchan arrived at Hangu Pass at midnight, only to see the gate of the pass closed, and only after another hanger-on of his hoodwinked the guards into opening the gate by aping the cockadoodledoo of a cock was he able to escape and return to the safety of his home state. The phrase 'crow like a cock and snatch like a dog' has since been used to refer to mean or petty tricks.

【鸡皮疙瘩】jīpí gē·da 因受冷或惊恐等皮肤上形成的小疙瘩,样子和去掉毛的鸡皮相似 goose-flesh; rough condition of the skin, resembling that of a plucked goose, induced by cold or fear

【鸡犬不宁】jī quǎn bù níng 形容搅扰得很厉害,连鸡狗都不得安宁 turmoil, in which even fowls and dogs are not left in peace

【鸡犬升天】jī quǎn shēng tiān 传说汉代淮南王刘安修炼成仙,连鸡狗吃了剩下的仙药也都升了天(见于汉代王充《论衡·道虚》)。后来用'鸡犬升天'比喻一个人得势,同他有关系的人也跟着沾光。According to a legend in the *Discourses Weighed in the Balance · On Falsehood* by Wang Chong of the Han Dynasty, when Liu An, the Prince of Huainan, achieved immortality after taking the pills of immortality he had acquired by practising alchemy, even his chickens and dogs ascended heaven after eating the pills he had left behind. (fig.) When a man attains the Tao (enlightenment), even his pets ascend to heaven; when a man acquires an influential position, all his friends and relations benefit from association with him.

【鸡尸牛从】jī shī niú cóng ☞鸡口牛后 jī kǒu niú hòu

【鸡尾酒】jīwěijiǔ 用几种酒加果汁、香料等混合起来的酒,多在饮用时临时调制 cocktail; mixed drink of liquor and juice and other flavourings, often prepared impromptu

【鸡瘟】jīwēn 鸡的各种急性传染病。特指鸡新城疫。chicken pest; virus-induce acute contagious diseases of chickens, esp. Newcastle disease

【鸡心】jīxīn ❶ 上圆下尖近似心脏的形状 heart-shaped:～领 V-neck ❷ 指一种鸡心形的首饰 heart-shaped pendant

【鸡新城疫】jīxīnchéngyì 鸡瘟的一种,由滤过性病毒引起。症状是鸡冠变成紫色或紫黑色,口鼻流黏水,排黄绿色的稀粪,腿麻痹不能起立,多数死亡。Newcastle disease (*Avian pneumoencephalitis*); serious disease of birds and fowls, chickens included, induced by the filterable virus. Among the symptoms are cockscomb turning purple or purplish dark, mouth and nose running with mucus, yellowish green watery increment and paralysis of limbs. Most of the chickens die once infested with this disease.

【鸡胸】jīxiōng 因佝偻病形成的胸骨突出像鸡的胸脯的症状 pigeon breast; chicken breast; disease in human beings caused by rachitis, with the breastbone protruding like that of a chicken or pigeon

【鸡血石】jīxuèshí 带红色斑点或全红色的昌化石,是珍贵的制印章的材料 bloodstone; heliotrope; variety of chalcedony with small bloodlike spots or red jasper scattered through it, a precious material for seal carving

【鸡眼】jīyǎn 皮肤病,脚掌或脚趾上角质层增生而形成的小圆硬块,样子像鸡的眼睛,局部有压痛 corn; horny callosity of the epidermis in the shape of a chicken eye, usu. with a central core, formed on the toes or feet, and feel sore to the touch; also 肉刺 ròucì

【鸡杂】jīzá (～儿 jīzár) 鸡的肫、肝、心等做食物时叫鸡杂 giblets, the gizzard, liver, heart, and the like, of a chicken, used as food

【鸡子】jī·zi〈方 *dial.*〉鸡 chicken

【鸡子儿】jī·zǐr 鸡蛋 egg

【鸡㙡】jīzōng 蕈的一种,菌盖圆锥形,中央凸起,熟时微黄色,可食用 *Collybia albuminosa*, a kind of mushroom with a dome-like cap, turning slightly yellow when cooked

其 jī 用于人名,郦食其(Lì Yìjī),汉朝人 ji, used as part of a person's name; Li Yiji, a man of the Han Dynasty

☞ qí on p.1509

奇 jī ❶ 单的;不成对的(跟'偶'相对 as opposed to 'even') odd:～数 odd number|～偶 disparity ❷〈书 *fml.*〉零数 fractional amount:五十有～ fifty odd

☞ qí on p.1509

【奇零】jīlíng〈书 *fml.*〉零数 odd lots; small amount in addition to what is counted or specified; also 畸零 jīlíng

【奇数】jīshù 不能被 2 整除的整数,如 1,3,5,−7。正的奇数也叫单数。odd number, such as 1,3,5, or −7, leaving a remainder of 1 when divided by 2. A positive odd number is also known in Chinese as 单数 dānshù.

畟 jī [畟奸](jījiān) same as 鸡奸 jījiān

咭 jī same as 叽 jī

剞 jī [剞劂](jījué)〈书 *fml.*〉❶ 雕刻用的弯刀 graver; carving knife ❷ 雕版;刻书 engraving; block-print

J

唧 jī 喷射(液体)(liquid) spurt; squirt:～筒 pump|～他一身水。Water squirted all over him.

【唧咕】jī·gu same as 叽咕 jīgū

【唧唧】jījī〈拟声词 *onom.*〉形容虫叫声等 sound of chirping insects

【唧唧嘎嘎】jī·ji gāgā same as 叽叽嘎嘎 jī·ji gāgā

【唧唧喳喳】jī·jizhāzhā〈拟声词 *onom.*〉形容杂乱细碎的声音 succession of quick, inarticulate sounds; twitter; chattering:小鸟儿～地叫。Little birds are chattering. also 叽叽喳喳 jī·jizhāzhā

【唧哝】jī·nong 小声说话 talk in a low voice; whisper:贴着耳根～了好一会 whisper in sb's ear for a while|他们俩在隔壁唧唧哝哝商量了半天。The two of them whispered conspiringly in the room next door.

【唧筒】jītǒng 泵 pump

积(積) jī ❶ 积累 accumulate:～少成多 many a little or pickle makes a mickle; many drops make a shower|日～月累 by slow but steady accumulation ❷ 堆积 pile up:～木 building blocks|～土成山 mountain built of heaped-up earth|货物山～ goods piled up like a small hill ❸ 长时间积累下来的 long-standing; long-pending:～习 deep-seated habit|～弊 age-old malpractice ❹〈中医 *Chin. med.*〉指儿童消化不良的病 indigestion in infants and children:食～ dyspepsia|奶～(of a baby) indigestion caused by improper breastfeeding|捏～ chiropractic; therapy of massage to adjust the segments of the spinal column|这个孩子有～了。The child is suffering digestive disorder. ❺ 乘积的简称 abbr. for 乘积 chéngjī

【积案】jī'àn 长期积压而未了结的案件 long-pending case:清理～ clear the docket|～如山 huge accumulation of unsolved cases

【积弊】jībì 积久相沿的弊病 engrained malpractice; long-standing abuse:清除～ uproot all forms of old malpractice

【积不相能】jī bù xiāng néng〈书 *fml.*〉素来不和睦 be always at variance or loggerheads

【积储】jīchǔ same as 积存 jīcún

【积存】jīcún 积聚储存 lay up:每月～一点钱,以备他用 save a little money on a monthly basis for future use

【积德】jī//dé 迷信的人指为了求福而做好事。泛指做好事。superstitious practice of performing good deeds for one's own good; (in a broad sense) performing of good deeds:～行善 do good deeds and dispense charities

【积非成是】jī fēi chéng shì 长期沿袭下来的谬误,会被认为是正确的 lie or wrong idea passed down from over a long time can be mistaken for truth

【积肥】jī//féi 积攒肥料 collect manure

【积分】jīfēn 参加若干场比赛累计所得的分数 accumulated points:在足球联赛中,北京队～暂居第二。By accumulated points in the soccer competition, Beijing ranks second for the time being.

【积愤】jīfèn 郁积在心中的愤慨 pent-up anger:倾吐胸中的～ air one's pent-up grievances

【积极】jījí ❶ 肯定的;正面的(跟'消极'相对,多用于抽象事物 as opposed to 'negative', oft. used for sth. abstract) positive:起～作用 play a positive role|从～方面想办法 think about how to do it in a positive way ❷ 进取的;热心的(跟'消极'相对 as opposed to 'passive') progressive, enthusiastic:～分子 active element|他对于社会工作一向很～。He has always been very keen on social work.

【积极分子】jījí fènzǐ ❶ 政治上要求进步,工作上积极负责的人 person who is progressive politically and works hard with a sense of responsibility ❷ 在体育、文娱及社会活动等方面比较积极的人 active element in sports, cultural and recreational events, and social work

【积极性】jījíxìng 进取向上、努力工作的思想和表现 enthusiasm; ardour: 调动广大群众的～。Arouse the enthusiasm of the masses.

【积聚】jījù 积累① gather; accumulate: 把～起来的钱存入银行 deposit the savings in the bank

【积劳】jīláo〈书 *fml*.〉长期经受劳累 be habitually overworked: ～成疾 fall ill from constant overwork

【积累】jīlěi ❶（事物）逐渐聚集 gather; accumulate: ～资金 accumulate funds | ～材料 gather materials | ～经验 gain experience ❷ 国民收入中用在扩大再生产的部分 accumulation; part of the national income to be used for production expansion

【积累基金】jīlěi jījīn 指国民收入中用于扩大再生产、进行非生产性基本建设和建立物资储备的那部分基金 accumulation fund, referring to the fund laid aside from the national revenue for expanding production, carrying out nonproductive capital construction and establishing material reserves

【积木】jīmù 儿童玩具，是一套大小和形状不相同的木块，大多是彩色的，可以用来摆成多种形式的建筑物的模型 building blocks; toy bricks; children's toy consisting of a set of wood blocks of varying sizes and shapes, most of them being colourful, that can be put together to form a variety of architectural structures

【积年】jīnián〈书 *fml*.〉多年 for many years: ～旧案 unsolved cases piled up over the years

【积年累月】jī nián lěi yuè 形容经历时间很长 year in, year out; for years on end

【积欠】jīqiàn ❶ 累次欠下 have one's debts piling up: 还清了～的债务 clear up all one's outstanding debts ❷ 积累下的亏欠 outstanding debts; arrears: 清理～ clear up all the debts

【积善】jī//shàn 积德 accumulate good and charitable deeds: ～之家 charitable family

【积食】jī//shí〈方 *dial*.〉停食（多指儿童）(of children) suffer indigestion

【积温】jīwēn 在一定时期内，每日的平均温度和某给定温度的差的总和 cumulative temperature; sum total of the differences between the average daily temperature and the given temperature during a certain period of time

【积习】jīxí 长期形成的习惯（多指不良的 usu. bad) old habit: ～甚深 deep-rooted habit | ～难改。Old habits die hard.

【积蓄】jīxù ❶ 积存 save; lay aside: ～力量 build up one's strength ❷ 积存的钱 savings: 月月都有～ salt away part of one's salary every month

【积压】jīyā 长期积存，未作处理 keep long in stock; overstock: ～物资 materials kept in stock ◇～在心中的疑问 doubt that's been bothering one for a long time

【积羽沉舟】jī yǔ chén zhōu 羽毛虽轻，堆积多了也可以把船压沉（见于《战国策·魏策一》）enough feathers can sink a boat (see *Intrigues of the Warring States · Intrigues of Wei* (*I*));〈比喻 *fig*.〉细微的事物积累多了也可以产生巨大的作用 tiny things may gather into a mighty force

【积郁】jīyù 郁结 piled-up grievances: ～成疾 break down from constant worries | 发泄～在心中的不满 give vent to one's pent-up grievances

【积攒】jīzǎn 一点一点地聚集 save (or collect) bit by bit: ～肥料 accumulate manure piecemeal | 多年省吃俭用，～了一笔钱 save an amount of money by living a Spartan life for many years

【积重难返】jī zhòng nán fǎn 指长期形成的不良的风俗、习惯不易改变 bad old practices die hard; ingrained habits are hard to change

【积铢累寸】jī zhū lěi cùn ☞ 铢积寸累 zhū jī cùn lěi on p. 2500

笄 jī〈古代 *arch*.〉束发用的簪子 hairpin: 及～(of a child) come of age

屐 jī ❶ 木头鞋 clogs: 木～ clogs ❷ 泛指鞋 shoes: ～履 shoes

姬 jī ❶〈古代 *arch*.〉对妇女的美称 complimentary term for women ❷〈古代 *arch*.〉称妾 name for a concubine: 侍～ concubine | ～妾 concubines ❸〈旧时 *old*〉称以歌舞为业的女子 woman living on singing and dancing: 歌～ sing-song girl ❹（Jī）姓 a surname

基 jī ❶ 基础 base; foundation: 房～ foundation of a house | 地～ foundation | 路～ road bed ❷ 起头的；根本的 primary; fundamental: ～层 grassroots | ～数 base number ❸ 化合物分子中所含的一部分原子，被看做是一个单位时叫做基，如羟基、氨基 radical, an element, an atom, or a group of these forming part of a compound, such as hydroxyl and amino (amino-group)

【基本】jīběn ❶ 根本 foundation: 人民是国家的～。The people are the foundation of a nation. ❷ 根本的 fundamental: ～矛盾 fundamental contradiction | ～原理 underlying principle ❸ 主要的 main; essential: ～条件 essential condition | ～群众 people to rely on ❹ 大体上 by and large; on the whole: 质量～合格。The quality is up to standard on the whole. | 大坝工程已经～完成。Engineering work of the big dam has been basically completed.

【基本词汇】jīběn cíhuì 词汇中最主要的一部分，生存最久、通行最广、构成新词和词组的能力最强，如'人、手、上、下、来、去'等 basic vocabulary; basic word-stock, referring to such words as 人 rén (man), 手 shǒu (hand), 上 shàng (up), 下 xià (down), 来 lái (come) and 去 qù (go), which are the oldest and most popular and most often used to form new words and new phrases

【基本单位】jīběn dānwèi ☞ 国际单位制 guójì dānɡwèizhì on p. 740

【基本法】jīběnfǎ 根本法 basic law

【基本功】jīběngōng 从事某种工作所必须掌握的基本的知识和技能 basic training; basic skill; essential technique; basic knowledge or skill essential to doing a job or fulfilling a task

【基本建设】jīběn jiànshè ❶ 国民经济各部门增添固定资产的建设,如建设厂房、矿井、铁路、桥梁、农田水利、住宅以及安装机器设备,添置船舶、机车、车辆、拖拉机等 capital construction; projects conducted in different sectors of the national economy for increasing fixed assets, such as the construction of factory buildings, mines, railways, bridges, farmland irrigation works, housing, the installation of machines and equipment, as well as the purchase of ships, rolling stock, vehicles, tractors, etc.; 简称 abbr. 基建 jījiàn ❷〈比喻 *fig.*〉对全局有重大作用的工作 undertakings of fundamental importance:购置图书资料是研究所的一项～。The purchase of books and reference materials is of primary importance to a research institute.

【基本粒子】jīběn lìzǐ 构成物体的比原子核更简单的物质,包括电子、正电子、质子、中子、光子、介子、超子、变子、反粒子等 elementary particle; subatomic particles simpler than atomic nucleus, including electron, positive electron, proton, neutron, photon, mesotron, hyperon, varitron, and anti-particle; also 粒子 lìzǐ

【基本矛盾】jīběn máodùn 规定事物发展全过程的本质,并规定和影响这个过程其他矛盾的存在和发展的矛盾 basic contradiction, which determines the nature of the entire development process of matters, and which also determines and impacts the existence and development of other contradictions in the process

【基本上】jīběn·shang ❶ 主要地 mainly:这项任务,～要靠第一车间来完成。Workshop No. 1 was counted on to tackle the lion's share of the task. ❷ 大体上 in the main:一年的任务,到十月份已经～完成。By October the task for the year has been fulfilled in the main.

【基层】jīcéng 各种组织中最低的一层,它跟群众的联系最直接 grassroots level, which is at the bottom rung of an organizational structure and which maintains the most direct contact with the masses:～单位 grassroots unit|～干部 cadre at the basic (or grassroots) level|深入～ go down to the grassroots

【基础】jīchǔ ❶ 建筑物的根脚 foundation of a building ❷ 事物发展的根本或起点 basis; starting point:～知识 basic knowledge|在原有的～上提高 seek improvement on the basis of what has been achieved ❸ ☞ 经济基础 jīngjì jīchǔ on p. 1019

【基础代谢】jīchǔ dàixiè 人或动物在清醒而安静的情况下,不受运动、食物、神经紧张、外界温度改变等影响时总的能量消耗 basal metabolism; total energy turnover of the human or animal body in a conscious and reposed situation, free from the impact of movement, food, nervousness, and changes in environmental temperature

【基础教育】jīchǔ jiàoyù 国家规定的对儿童实施的初等教育 elementary education; state-mandated primary education for children

【基础科学】jīchǔ kēxué 研究自然现象的基本理论,作为应用科学的基础的科学 basic science, scientific research of the basic theories behind natural phenomena, serving as the basis for applied sciences

【基础课】jīchǔkè 高等学校中,使学生获得有关学科的基本概念、基本规律的知识和技能的课程,是学生进一步学习专门知识的基础 basic course (of a college curriculum), referring to a course of higher education that enables students to acquire the knowledge and skills concerning the basic concepts and norms of related disciplines of learning; school course designed to lay a foundation for further studies of professional knowledge

【基地】jīdì 作为某种事业基础的地区 base:军事～ military base|工业建设～ industrial base

【基点】jīdiǎn ❶ 作为开展某种活动的基础的地方 base:以产棉乡为～推广棉花生产新技术 popularize a new cotton production technology centring on cotton-growing townships ❷ 基础 ②basis; starting point:通过调查研究弄清情况是解决问题的～。The basis for solving the problem lies in gaining a clear idea about the situation through research.

【基调】jīdiào ❶ 音乐作品中主要的调,作品通常用基调开始或结束 fundamental key; main key that marks the beginning or end of a piece of music ❷ 主要精神;基本观点 keynote; basic point:这部作品虽然有缺点,但它的～是鼓舞人向上的。For all its drawbacks, the basic tone of this work is encouraging and uplifting.

【基督】Jīdū〈基督教 *Christ.*〉称救世主 Christ, the Messiah; ☞ 救世主 Jiùshìzhǔ on p. 1041 [希腊 Greek: christos]

【基督教】Jīdūjiào 世界上主要宗教之一,公元 1 世纪产生于亚细亚的西部地区,奉耶稣为救世主。公元 4 世纪成为罗马帝国的国教,公元 11 世纪分裂为天主教和东正教。公元 16 世纪宗教改革以后,又陆续从天主教分裂出许多新的教派,合称新教。我国所称基督教,多指新教。Christianity; major worldwide religion that emerged in West Asia in the 1st century and worships Christ as the Messiah. It became the national religion of the Roman Empire during the 4th century, and split into Catholicism and Orthodoxy during the 11th century. After a 16th-century religious reform, many new churches emerged from Catholicism, which are collectively known as Protestantism. The Christianity referred to in China is on most occasions Protestantism.

【基肥】jīféi 在作物播种或移栽前施的肥。厩肥、堆肥、绿肥等迟效肥料适于做基肥。base manure; base fertilizer, which is applied to the farmland prior to sowing and transplantation. Among the suitable base fertilizers are barnyard manure, compost, green manure, and other slow-acting fertilizers. also 底肥 dǐféi

【基干】jīgàn 基础;骨干 backbone; core:~民兵 core members of the militia

【基价】jījià 计算各个时期的平均物价指数时,用来作为基础的某一固定时期的物价 base price; price of a given period employed as the basis upon which to calculate the average price index of different periods

【基建】jījiàn 基本建设的简称 abbr. for 基本建设 jīběn jiànshè:~工程 capital construction project | ~投资 investment in capital construction

【基金】jījīn 为兴办、维持或发展某种事业而储备的资金或专门拨款。基金必须用于指定的用途,并单独进行核算。如教育基金、福利基金等。foundation; fund; stock of money set apart for a special purpose, such as establishing, maintaining or developing a certain sideline occupation. A fund should be used for a specific purpose and the accounts are settled independently. Examples are education fund and welfare fund.

【基诺族】Jīnuòzú 我国少数民族之一,分布在云南 Jinos, a minority ethnic people inhabiting various parts of Yunnan Province

【基期】jīqī 统计中计算指数或发展速度等动态指标时,作为对比基础的时期,如 1986 年同 1984 年对比物价指数时,1984 年为基期(statistics) base period, which provides the background for the calculation of indices, growth rates and other dynamic economic indicators. For instance, when the price index of 1986 is compared with that of 1984, the year 1984 is the base period.

【基色】jīsè same as 原色 yuánsè

【基石】jīshí ❶ 做建筑物基础的石头 foundation stone; cornerstone ❷〈比喻 *fig.*〉基础或中坚力量 staunch force; mainstay:工农联盟是我国现代化建设的~。The worker-peasant alliance is the cornerstone of China's modernization drive.

【基数】jīshù ❶ 一、二、三…一百、三千等普通整数,区别于第一、第二、第三…第一百、第三千等序数 cardinal number, denoting quantity (one, two, three ... 100, 3,000, etc.) as opposed to an ordinal number (first, second, third ... 100th, 3,000th, etc.) ❷ 作为计算标准或起点的数目 base; base number that serves as the criterion or starting point of calculation

【基态】jītài 原子、原子核等所具有的各种状态中能量最低、也最稳定的状态 ground state; state of the least energy and utmost stability of an atom, a neutron, etc.

【基体】jītǐ 由两种或两种以上不同物质制成的材料或物品中,作为主体部分的物质叫做基体 matrix; substance constituting the major part of a compound or object made of two or more materials

【基线】jīxiàn 测量时作为基准的线段 surveying and drawing datum line

【基业】jīyè 事业发展的基础 foundation on which to build:创立~ lay the foundation for a cause, an undertaking, a career, etc.

【基因】jīyīn 生物体遗传的基本单位,存在于细胞的染色体上,作直线排列 gene; basic unit of heredity transmitted in the chromosome. Genes are arrayed in a straight line.

【基因工程】jīyīn gōngchéng ☞ 遗传工程 yíchuán gōngchéng on p. 2263

【基音】jīyīn 复音中频率最低部分的声音。是声音的最主要成分,由发声体整体振动所产生。fundamental tone; ground note; note with the lowest frequency in a complex tone. Produced through the vibration of the entire body of articulation, the ground note is the major component of a voice.

【基于】jīyú same as 根据 gēnjù ①:~以上理由,我不赞成他的意见。Based on the aforementioned reasons, I take exception to his opinion.

【基质】jīzhì ❶ 植物、微生物从中吸取养分借以生存的物质,如营养液等 stroma; material such as nutritive liquid that provides life-sustaining nutrition for a plant or micro-organism ❷ 混合物中作为溶剂或起类似溶剂作用的成分 element in a compound that serves as solvent or plays the role as a solvent:凡士林是许多种药膏的~。Vaseline is the substratum of many kinds of medicine and ointment.

【基准】jīzhǔn 测量时的起算标准。泛指标准。surveying and drawing datum; (in a broad sense) standard

靰(鞿) jī 〈书 *fml.*〉马缰绳 reins; halter

J

期（朞） jī〈书 *fml*.〉一周年；一整月 one full year or month：～年 a whole year｜～月 a whole month
☞ qī on p.1506

赍（齎） jī〈书 *fml*.〉❶ 怀着；抱着 cherish；hold：～志而殁（志未遂而死去）die with one's ambition unfulfilled ❷ 把东西送给人 present sth. as a gift

【赍恨】jīhèn〈书 *fml*.〉抱恨 have regret gnawing at one's heart：～而亡 die a remorseful death｜机遇若失，将～终身。A good opportunity lost can become a lifelong regret.

【赍赏】jīshǎng 赏赐 bestow a reward

犄 jī ☞ below

【犄角】jījiǎo〈方 *dial*.〉（～儿 jījiǎor）❶ 物体两个边沿相接的地方；棱角 meeting place of two converging lines or surfaces：桌子～ corner of a table ❷ 角落 corner：屋子～ corner of a house

【犄角】jī·jiao〈方 *dial*.〉牛、羊等头上长出的坚硬的东西 horn；one of the bony，often curved and pointed，hollow，paired growths on the upper part of the head of certain ungulate mammals such as cattle and goats：牛～ ox horn

嵇 Jī 姓 a surname

缉 jī 缉拿 seize；arrest：～私 anti-smuggling｜通～ order the arrest of a fugitive
☞ qī on p.1507

【缉捕】jībǔ 缉拿 arrest：～在逃凶手 pursue a murderer at large

【缉查】jīchá 搜查 search；ransack：挨户～ door-to-door search

【缉毒】jīdú 检查贩卖毒品的行为，缉捕贩卖毒品的人 crack down on narcotic trafficking；track and arrest drug dealers

【缉获】jīhuò 拿获；查获 nab；seize；capture：～罪犯 arrest a criminal｜～走私货物 seize smuggled goods

【缉拿】jīná 搜查捉拿（犯罪的人）arrest；apprehend：～归案 bring (a criminal) to justice

【缉私】jīsī 检查走私行为，缉捕走私的人 crack down on smuggling；seize smugglers or smuggled goods

畸 jī ❶ 偏 lopsided；unbalanced：～轻～重 attach too much weight to one and too little weight to another ❷ 不正常的；不规则的 irregular；abnormal：～变 abnormal change｜～形 distortion ❸〈书 *fml*.〉数的零头 odd lots：～零 fractional amount

【畸变】jībiàn ❶ 不正常变化 aberrant；abnormal change ❷ same as 失真 shī// zhēn ②

【畸零】jīlíng ❶ same as 奇零 jīlíng ❷ 孤零零 lonely：～人 lonely person｜～无侣 companionless

【畸轻畸重】jī qīng jī zhòng 偏轻偏重 attach too much weight to this and too little to that；lopsided；now too much，now too little

【畸形】jīxíng ❶ 生物体某部分发育不正常 deformity；malformation：～发育 deformed maturity ❷ 泛指事物发展不正常，偏于某一方面（in a broad sense）lopsided；unbalanced；abnormal：我国产业地区分布的～状况正在改变。The lopsided geographical distribution of industry in China is being changed.

跻（躋） jī〈书 *fml*.〉登；上升 ascend；mount：使中国科学～于世界先进科学之列。Find a niche for China's science among the world's most advanced.

【跻身】jīshēn 使自己上升到（某种行列、位置等）；置身 ascend；find oneself in (a position，situation，etc.)：～文坛 find one's way into the literary world｜～前八名 rank among the top eight

锜 jī ☞［镃锜］(zījī) on p.2539

禨 jī〈书 *fml*.〉衣服的褶儿 wrinkle on clothes

箕 jī ❶ 簸箕 dustpan：～踞 sit with one's legs stretched out (in a casual manner) ❷ 簸箕形的指纹 loop of a fingerprint：斗～ fingerprint ❸ 二十八宿之一 *Ji*，the 7th of the 28 constellations (consisting of four stars in the shape of a sieve in Sagittarius) ❹（Jī）姓 a surname

【箕斗】jīdǒu〈书 *fml*.〉❶ 箕宿和斗宿。泛指群星。*Ji* and *Dou*，two of the 28 constellations；stars (in general) ❷《诗经·小雅·大东》：'维南有箕，不可以簸扬；维北有斗，不可以挹酒浆'。后来用'箕斗'比喻虚有其名。*The Book of Songs · Odes · Great Eastern States*：In the south there is a Winnowing Fan，/ But it cannot be used to sift grain；/ In the north there is a Dipper，/ But it cannot ladle wine. The phrase means 'have an undeserved reputation'. ❸ 手指印；斗箕 fingerprint；loop of a fingerprint：验明～ check and verify a fingerprint

【箕踞】jījù〈书 *fml*.〉古人席地而坐，随意伸开两腿，像个簸箕，是一种不拘礼节、傲慢不敬的坐法（arch.）sit on the floor with one's legs stretched out — a casual manner or gesture；oft. interpreted as being impolite

稽[1] jī ❶ 查考 check：～查 investigate｜无～之谈 nonsense；unfounded theory，story，etc.｜有案可～ on record；verifiable ❷ 计较 argue：反唇相～ recriminate；argue ❸（Jī）姓 a surname

稽[2] jī〈书 *fml*.〉停留；拖延 delay；procrastinate：～留 hold up；delay｜～延 postpone；put off
☞ qǐ on p.1520

【稽查】jīchá ❶ 检查（走私、偷税、违禁等活动）

check (to prevent smuggling, tax evasion, etc.) ❷ 担任这种检查工作的人 official engaged in such work; customs officer

【稽核】jīhé 查对计算(多指账目) check; examine; audit (accounts)

【稽考】jīkǎo 〈书 *fml.*〉查考 ascertain; verify: 无可～ unascertainable

【稽留】jīliú 〈书 *fml.*〉停留 delay: 因事～,未能如期南下。He failed to go south on time because he was occupied.

【稽延】jīyán 〈书 *fml.*〉拖延 delay; procrastinate: ～时日 considerably delayed

觭 jī 〈书 *fml.*〉单数 odd number; same as 奇 jī

齑(齏) jī 〈书 *fml.*〉❶ 调味用的姜、蒜或韭菜碎末儿 finely chopped ginger, garlic, etc., used as seasoning ❷ 细;碎 fine; powdery: ～粉 fine powder; broken bits; (be ground to) dust

【齑粉】jīfěn 〈书 *fml.*〉细粉;碎屑 fine powder; broken bits: 化为～ reduce to powder

畿 jī 国都附近的地区 environs of a capital city: 京～ vicinity of the capital city | ～辅 capital and vicinity

【畿辅】jīfǔ 〈书 *fml.*〉国都附近的地方 capital and vicinity

墼 jī ☞ 炭墼 tànjī on p. 1862

激 jī ❶ (水)因受到阻碍或震荡而向上涌 swash; surge; dash 江水冲到礁石上,～起六七尺高。The water smashed into the reef and dashed up that surged two metres above the surface of the river. ◇～起了一场风波 cause a commotion ❷ 冷水突然刺激身体使得病 fall ill from getting wet: 他被雨水～着了。He caught a chill after being drenched in the rain. ❸ 〈方 *dial.*〉用冷水冲或泡食物等使变凉 chill sth. by putting it in cold water: 把西瓜放在冰水里～一～ chill a watermelon in cold water ❹ 使发作;使感情冲动 stir up (emotions or feelings); excite: 刺～ evoke; simulate; incite | 劝将不如～将。To persuade a general does no better than to goad him on. ❺ (感情)激动 touched; moved: 感～ feel grateful | ～于义愤 stirred by righteous indignation ❻ 急剧;强烈 fierce; sharp; violent: ～战 fierce battle | ～流 rapids | 偏～ extreme

【激昂】jī'áng (情绪、语调等)激动昂扬 excited and indignant; roused: ～慷慨 impassioned | 群情～。Public feeling was surging.

【激昂慷慨】jī'áng kāngkǎi ☞ 慷慨激昂 kāngkǎi jī'áng on p. 1083

【激变】jībiàn 急剧变化 drastic change: 形势～。The situation changed drastically.

【激磁】jīcí 线圈内因有电流通过,受到激发而产生磁场 (of electric current going through a coil) excite an electric magnetic field: ～线圈 magnetizing coil | ～电流 magnetizing electric current; also 励磁 lìcí

【激荡】jīdàng ❶ 因受冲击而动荡 surge; rage: 海水～。The sea is surging. | 感情～ seethe with irrepressible feelings ❷ 冲击使动荡 agitate: ～人心 heart-stirring

【激动】jīdòng ❶ (感情)因受刺激而冲动 excite: 情绪～ excited; ablaze with excitement ❷ 使感情冲动 move: ～人心 moving ❸ 激荡 seethe (with excitement, etc.)

【激发】jīfā ❶ 刺激使奋发 arouse; stimulate: ～群众的积极性 fire the masses with enthusiasm (for doing sth.) ❷ 使分子、原子等由能量较低的状态变为能量较高的状态 excite; raise an atom, molecule, and the like, from a low-energy state to an excited one

【激奋】jīfèn 激动振奋 stirring: 精神～ in high spirits | ～人心 keep the morale high

【激愤】jīfèn 激动而愤怒 indignant; be stirred to anger: 群情～。Popular feelings are running high. also 激忿 jīfèn

【激光】jīguāng 某些物质原子中的粒子受光或电的激发,由低能级的原子跃迁为高能级原子,当高能级原子的数目大于低能级原子的数目,并由高能级跃迁回低能级时,就放射出相位、频率、方向等完全相同的光,这种光叫做激光。颜色很纯,能量高度集中,广泛应用在工业、军事、医学、探测、通讯等方面。laser; acronym derived from the term 'light amplification by stimulated emission of radiation'. Excited by light or electricity, the particles in an atom or molecule leap to higher energy levels; and when atoms at higher energy levels outnumber those at lower energy levels while returning to a lower level, they give off light of a wholly coherent wavelength, frequency, direction, etc. Such a stimulated emission, marked for its purity of colour and high concentration of energy, is widely used in industry, war, medicine, surveying and telecommunications. also 莱塞 láisè

【激光器】jīguāngqì 产生激光的装置,有固体、液体、气体、半导体等几种类型。根据工作方式不同又分为连续激光器和脉冲激光器。laser; device designed to emit laser, coming in solid, liquid, gaseous, and semi-conducting types. In terms of work method, there are also continuous and pulse laser devices. also 莱塞 láisè

【激化】jīhuà ❶ (矛盾)向激烈尖锐的方面发展 intensify or sharpen (a contradiction): 避免矛盾～ prevent contradictions from getting out of control ❷ 使激化 aggravate: ～矛盾 aggravate a contradiction

【激活】jīhuó 刺激有机体内某种物质,使其活跃地发挥作用 activate; stimulate certain substance in an organism and make it active: 某些植物成分能～细胞免疫反应。Some plant elements can activate cellular immunization response.

【激将】jījiàng 用刺激性的话或反面的话鼓动人去做(原来不愿做或不敢做的事) prod (or goad) sb. by ridicule, sarcasm, etc. into doing sth.:~法 means of goading sb. on|请将不如~。It's better to prod than implore a person (to do sth.).

【激进】jījìn 急进 radical:~派 radical|观点~ radical point of view

【激剧】jījù ❶ 激烈 intense; acute:看样子他是在~地进行思想斗争。He seems to be in intense soul-searching at the moment. ❷ 急剧 rapid:~发展 rapid development

【激浪】jīlàng 汹涌急剧的波浪 raging waves:~滔滔 torrential waters

【激励】jīlì 激发鼓励 encourage; inspire:~将士 spur the officers and men on

【激烈】jīliè ❶(动作、言论等)剧烈 (of movement, language) intense:百米赛跑是一项很~的运动。The 100-metre sprint is a strenuous sport.|大家争论得很~。We were locked in heated argument. ❷(性情、情怀)激奋,刚烈 (of temperament, emotion) uplifting; unyielding:壮怀~ cherishing lofty aspirations

【激灵】jī·ling〈方 *dial.*〉受惊吓猛然抖动 give a start:他吓得一~就醒了。He woke up with a start. also 机灵 jī·ling

【激流】jīliú 湍急的水流 rapids; turbulent current

【激酶】jīméi 具有刺激作用的酶。某些酶从细胞中分泌出来以后,必须经过激酶的刺激才有作用。kinase; substance that causes a zymogen to change into an enzyme. Some zymogens secreted from cells can be activated only with the stimulation of kinase.

【激怒】jīnù 刺激使发怒 infuriate; enrage:他这一说更把赵大叔~了。What he said threw Uncle Zhao into a rage.

【激切】jīqiè〈书 *fml.*〉(言语)激烈而直率(of language) impassioned; vehement:言辞~ impassioned wording

【激情】jīqíng 强烈激动的情感 passion; fervour:创作~ urge to write a literary work or create a work of art, etc.|~满怀 impassioned

【激赏】jīshǎng〈书 *fml.*〉极其赞赏 high acclaim; greatly admire:~不已 shower praise and appreciation on sb.

【激素】jīsù 内分泌腺分泌的物质。直接进入血液分布到全身,对肌体的代谢、生长、发育和繁殖等起重要调节作用。包括甲状腺素、肾上腺素、胰岛素等。hormone; substance produced in endocrine glands that enters the blood and spreads all over the human or animal body to play an important role in regulating metabolism, growth and reproduction. Among the hormones are thyroxine, adrenalin, and insulin. 旧称 formerly known as 荷尔蒙 hé'ěrméng

【激扬】jīyáng ❶ 激浊扬清 drain away dirt and bring in fresh water:指点江山,~文字。Pointing to our mountains and rivers,/Setting people afire with our words. ❷ 激动昂扬 inspired:~的欢呼声 spirited cheers ❸ 激励使振作起来 inspire:~士气 boost the morale

【激越】jīyuè (声音、情绪等)强烈、高亢 high-pitched:雄浑~的军号声 loud and ringing bugle sound|感情~ in the throes of emotion

【激增】jīzēng (数量等)急速地增长 increase rapidly

【激战】jīzhàn 激烈战斗 pitched battle:~一场,不分胜负。The fierce battle ended up without a winner.

【激浊扬清】jī zhuó yáng qīng 冲去污水,让清水上来 drain dirt mud and bring in fresh water;〈比喻 *fig.*〉抨击坏人坏事,奖励好人好事 dispel evil and usher in good; eliminate vice and exalt virtue; also 扬清激浊 yáng qīng jī zhuó

羁(覊) jī〈书 *fml.*〉❶ 马笼头 bridle; headstall:无~之马 unbridled horse ❷ 拘束 restrain; control:~绊 fetters|放荡不~ dissolute; uninhibited ❸ 停留;使停留 stay; detain:~旅 stay long in a strange place|~留 stop over

【羁绊】jībàn〈书 *fml.*〉缠住了不能脱身;束缚 trammels; yoke:挣脱~ break the fetters|冲破旧习惯势力的~ break the fetters of old ideas

【羁勒】jīlè〈书 *fml.*〉束缚 manacles:摆脱礼教的~ smash the shackles of old rites

【羁留】jīliú ❶(在外地)停留 stay (in a strange place); stop over ❷ 羁押 keep in custody; detain

【羁旅】jīlǚ〈书 *fml.*〉长久寄居他乡 stay long away from home:~异乡 live in a place that is not one's hometown

【羁縻】jīmí〈书 *fml.*〉❶ 笼络(藩属等) pacify (a vassal state, etc.) ❷ 羁留 stay; stop over; be held up (in a place)

【羁押】jīyā〈书 *fml.*〉拘留;拘押 detain; take into custody

jí(ㄐㄧˊ)

及[1] jí ❶ 达到 reach, amount to:波~ impact; exert an impact on|普~ popularize|~格 pass an exam, a test, etc.|目力所~ as far as the eye can see|由表~里(analyze or dissect matter) from external to internal|将~十载。Nearly a decade has passed. ❷ 赶上 be in time for:~时 timely|~早 at an early date|望尘莫~ trailing too far behind to catch up ❸ 比得上 match:论学习,我不~他。

In study I am no comparison with him. ❹〈书 *fml*.〉推及；顾及 take into account; take care of：老吾老，以～人之老。I care for other people's elders as I care for my own.｜攻其一点，不～其余 attack sb. for a minor fault while ignoring his or her strengths ❺(Jí)姓 a surname

及[2] jí〈连词 *conj*.〉连接并列的名词或名词性词组[connect juxtaposed nouns or noun phrases]and; as well as：图书、仪器、标本～其他 books, instruments, samples and other things 注意 **NOTE：** 用'及'连接的成分多在意义上有主次之分，主要的成分放在'及'的前面。This character is used to join two or more nouns, with the one following it subordinate in meaning.

【及第】jídì 科举时代考试中选。特指考取进士，明清两代只用于殿试前三名。pass the imperial examination for civil servants, esp. the highest imperial exam which came up with only three successful candidates during the Ming and Qing dynasties：状元～ become the Number-One Scholar in the highest imperial examination

【及格】jí//gé（考试成绩）达到规定的最低标准 pass; pass a test, examination, etc.

【及冠】jíguàn〈书 *fml*.〉指男子年满二十岁，到了成年）(of a young man) come of age（冠 *guan*：古代男子二十岁举行冠礼，戴上成年人戴的帽子 In ancient China, when a man turned 20, a ceremony would be held to crown him with the hat only an adult was entitled to wear.）

【及笄】jíjī〈书 *fml*.〉指女子年满十五岁（of a girl) come of age（笄 *ji*：束发用的簪子。古时女子满十五岁把头发绾起来，戴上簪子 In ancient China girls at 15 began to wear their hair bound up and held in place by a pin.）

【及龄】jílíng 达到规定的年龄 reach an eligible age：～儿童已全部入学。All the school-age children are attending school.

【及门】jímén〈书 *fml*.〉正式拜师求学的 come under the tutelage of a teacher：～弟子 disciple directly taught by a master｜～之士 scholar who has finished his studies under a private tutor

【及时】jíshí ❶正赶上时候，适合需要 timely; in time：～雨 timely rain; timely help｜～播种 sow in good time ❷不拖延；马上；立刻 promptly; without delay：有问题就～解决。Problems should be solved when and where they occur.

【及时雨】jíshíyǔ ❶指在农作物需要雨水时下的雨 timely rain：这场～缓解了旱情。It rained just in time to alleviate the draught. ❷〈比喻 *fig*.〉能在紧急关头解救危难的人或事物 help rendered in the nick of time; timely help

【及早】jízǎo 趁早 at an early date; before it is too late：生了病要～治。When you are ill, see the doctor as soon as possible.

【及至】jízhì〈连词 *conj*.〉表示等到出现某种情况 up to; until：～上了岸，才知道是个荒岛。We did not know it was a barren isle until we went ashore.

伋 jí 人名用字。孔伋，字子思，孔子的孙子。Ji, a character used in names. Kong Ji, whose style name was Zisi, was a grandson of Confucius.

吉 jí ❶吉利；吉祥（跟'凶'相对 as opposed to 'ominous', 'unpropitious'）auspicious; propitious：凶多～少 promise more evil than good; in for trouble｜万事大～。All went well. ❷(Jí)姓 a surname

【吉卜赛人】Jíbǔsàirén 原来居住在印度西北部的居民，10世纪时开始向外迁移，流浪在西亚、北非、欧洲、美洲等地，多从事占卜、歌舞等职业 Gypsy; nomadic people who began to leave their home in northwest India during the 10th century and migrate to west Asia, north Africa, Europe and the Americas, most of them living a vagrant life on fortune-telling, singing and dancing. also 茨冈人 Cígāngrén

【吉光片羽】jíguāng piàn yǔ〈古代 *arch*.〉传说，吉光是神兽，毛皮为裘，入水数日不沉，入火不焦。'吉光片羽'指神兽的一小块毛皮，比喻残存的珍贵的文物。tiny bit of the fur from the body of the celestial animal Jiguang; (fig.) fragment of a priceless artifact. Legend has it that the fur that covered Jiguang's body neither sank even after being soaked in water for days nor got scotched when thrown into a fire：～，弥足珍贵 rare and precious relic

【吉剧】jíjù 吉林地方戏曲剧种，在曲艺二人转的基础上吸收东北其他民间歌舞和地方戏曲逐步发展而成 Jilin opera, indigenous theatrical genre of Jilin Province in northeast China, involved into its present form by drawing on folk songs and dances and local operas of northeast China on the basis of *errenzhuan* (song-and-dance duet)

【吉利】jílì 吉祥顺利 auspicious; propitious：～话 lucky adage

【吉普车】jípǔchē 轻型越野汽车，能适应高低不平的道路 jeep; light-duty cross-country automobile, made for travelling on rugged roads

【吉期】jíqī 吉日。特指结婚的日子。red-letter day, esp. wedding day

【吉庆】jíqìng 吉祥 auspicious occasion：～话 words and phrases meant for an auspicious occasion｜平安～ safety and happiness

【吉人天相】jí rén tiān xiàng〈旧时 *old*〉迷信的人认为好人有上天保佑（多用作遭遇危险或困难时的安慰语）heaven stands by the good man; by an old superstition, a good man is always protected by heaven, an adage of self-gratification when in danger or difficulty

【吉日】jírì 吉利的日子 auspicious day; lucky day:～良辰 happy day

【吉他】jítā 六弦琴 guitar; six-stringed musical instrument

【吉祥】jíxiáng 幸运;吉利 fortunate, promising:～如意 good luck

【吉祥物】jíxiángwù 某些大型运动会上用来象征吉祥的标记,多选用动物图案或模型 mascot; mostly in the image of an animal, serving as an auspicious logo for big sports competitions

【吉星】jíxīng 迷信的人指显示吉兆的星。借指能带来吉祥的人或事物 (of superstition) lucky star; person or thing that brings good luck:～高照 be blessed by a lucky star

【吉凶】jíxiōng 好运气和坏运气;吉利和凶险 good or ill luck:～未卜 one's fate in the balance; uncertain whether one will have good or bad fortune

【吉言】jíyán 吉利的话 auspicious words

【吉兆】jízhào 吉祥的预兆 good omen; propitious sign

岌 jí〈书 *fml.*〉山高的样子(of a mountain) towering; high

【岌岌】jíjí〈书 *fml.*〉❶ 形容山势高耸(of a mountain) lofty; towering ❷ 形容十分危险,快要倾覆或灭亡 in grave danger; in a critical condition:～可危 in imminent danger|～不可终日 gripped by constant fear

汲 jí ❶ 从下往上打水 fetch water:从井里～水 draw water from a well ❷ (Jí)姓 a surname

【汲汲】jíjí〈书 *fml.*〉形容心情急切,努力追求 anxious; avid:～于富贵 crave wealth and power

【汲取】jíqǔ 吸取 draw:～经验 draw on experience|～营养 draw nutrition

J 【汲引】jíyǐn〈书 *fml.*〉引水 fetch water;〈比喻 *fig.*〉举荐提拔 recommend sb. for promotion

伋 jí same as 急 jí

级 jí ❶ 等级 level; rank:高～ senior|上～ higher up|县～ county level|～差 differential|三～工 third-grade worker ❷ 年级(of school) grade:留～ fail to advance to the next higher grade|同～不同班 in the same grade but not the same class ❸ 台阶儿 step:石～stone step ❹〈量词 *classifier*〉用于台阶、楼梯等 step:十多～台阶 flight of a dozen or so steps

【级别】jíbié 等级的区别;等级的高低次序 rank; level; grade; scale:干部～ rank of a cadre|举重比赛已决出三个～的名次。Results have been announced for three categories of the weightlifting competition.

【级差】jíchā 等级之间的差别程度 differential:工资～ wage differential

【级任】jírèn 中小学校里设过的负责管理一个班级的教师(of primary and secondary schools) class master:～老师 teacher in charge of a grade

极(極) jí ❶ 顶点;尽头 apex; extremity:登峰造～ reach the acme; come to a head|无所不用其～(用尽可能使用的各种手段)go to every extreme; leave no stone unturned ❷ 地球的南北两端;磁体的两端;电源或电器上电流进入或流出的一端 pole:南～ South Pole; Antarctic Pole|北～ North Pole; Arctic Pole|阴～ negative pole|阳～ positive pole ❸ 尽;达到顶点 last; utmost:～力 spare no effort; do one's utmost|～目四望 take in a panoramic view from a high point|物～必反。Things turn into their opposites when they reach the extreme.|～一时之盛 achieve unprecedented prosperity; unmatched pageantry and throng ❹ 最终的;最高的 sheer; supreme:～度 extremely|～端 extreme|～量 maximum dosage ❺〈副词 *adv.*〉表示达到最高度 extremely; to the greatest extent:～重要 of cardinal importance|～少数 a handful of

注意 **NOTE**:'极'也可做补语,但前头不能用'得',后面一般带'了',如'忙极了'。极 can also be used as a complement; it cannot be preceded by 得·de and is oft. followed by 了·le, as in 忙极了 mángjí·le.

【极地】jídì 极圈以内的地区 polar region

【极点】jídiǎn 程度上不能再超过的界限 limit:高兴到了～ feel extremely happy

【极顶】jídǐng ❶ 山的最高处;山顶 top of a mountain; mountaintop:泰山～ summit of Mount Taishan ❷ 极点 extreme:他对你佩服到～。He is knocked out with admiration for you. ❸ 达到极点的 extreme:～聪明 absolutely clever|～糊涂 hopelessly muddleheaded

【极度】jídù ❶ 程度极深的 extreme; exceeding:～兴奋 beside oneself with joy|～的疲劳 bone-tired ❷ 极点 limit:他的忍耐已经到了～。He has reached the limit of patience.

【极端】jíduān ❶ 事物顺着某个发展方向达到的顶点 extreme:看问题要全面,不要走～。Take a balanced point of view — don't go to extremes. ❷ 达到极点的 utter:～兴奋 utterly happy|～困难 extremely hard

【极光】jíguāng 在高纬度地区,高空中大气稀薄的地方出现的一种光的现象。由太阳发出的高速带电粒子受地球磁场影响,进入两极附近,激发高空中的原子和分子而引起。通常是弧状、带状或幕状,微弱时白色,明亮时黄绿色,有时还有红、灰、紫、蓝等色。aurora or polar lights; radiant emission from the rarefied upper atmosphere that occurs sporadically over places of high latitudes in the form of luminous arcs, bands, screens, or the like, turning white when waning and yellowish green when bright, looking red, grey, purple and blue occasionally, caused by the bombardment of the atmosphere with charged solar particles being guided along the earth's magnetic lines of force

【极口】jíkǒu 在言谈中极力(称道、赞扬或抨击、抗辩等)(praise, speak, condemn, etc.) in the highest possible terms:～称扬 speak highly of|～诋毁 defame sb. or sth. with utmost causticity

【极乐世界】jílè shìjiè 佛经中指阿弥陀佛所居住的国土。佛教徒认为居住在这个地方,就可获得光明、清净和快乐,摆脱人间一切烦恼。(of Buddhism) Land of Ultimate Bliss, where Amitabha lives. Buddhists believe that once one has found home in this land one will gain sunshine, peace of mind, and happiness and be free from all worries. also 西天 xītiān

【极力】jílì 用尽一切力量;想尽一切办法 do one's utmost; spare no effort:～设法 rack one's brains for a way out|～克服困难 exert oneself to overcome difficulties

【极量】jíliàng ❶ 医学上指在一定时间内,病人服药或注射药水最大限度的剂量 maximum dosage of medication by oral administration or injection for a patient during a given period of time ❷ 泛指作为极限的数量(in a broad sense) maximum amount or quantity

【极目】jímù 用尽目力(远望) stretch one's eyes to look afar:～远眺 gaze far into the distance

【极品】jípǐn〈书 *fml.*〉❶ 最上等的(物品) highest grade; best quality:～狼毫(一种毛笔) writing brush of the best quality, made of hair from weasel's tail|关东人参号称～。Ginseng from northeast China is the best anywhere in the world. ❸ 最高的官阶 top-ranking:官居～ be an official of the highest rank

【极其】jíqí〈副词 *adv.*〉非常;极端 most; extremely; very:劳动是～光荣的事情。Physical labour is something of the utmost glory. |受到了～深刻的教育 be educated in a profound way

【极圈】jíquān 地球上 66°34′的纬线所形成的圈 polar circle, at 66°34′degrees north or south latitude

【极权】jíquán 指统治者依靠暴力行使统治权力,人民毫无自由 totalitarian government, maintained by violence and depriving the people of freedom:～统治 totalitarian rule

【极为】jíwéi〈副词 *adv.*〉表示程度达到极点 exceptionally:～勇敢 extremely brave|～不满 utterly dissatisfied|～贫困 dire poverty

【极限】jíxiàn ❶ 最高的限度 limit; maximum; ceiling:轮船的载重已经达到了～。The ship is already carrying full capacity of load. ❷ 如果变量 x 逐渐变化,趋近于定量 a,即它们的差的绝对值可以小于任何已知的正数时,定量 a 叫做变量 x 的极限。可写成 $x \to a$,或 $\lim x = a$。如数列 $\frac{1}{2}, \frac{2}{3}, \cdots, n/n+1$ 的极限是 1,写做 $\lim\limits_{n\to\infty} \frac{n}{n+1} = 1$。limit. If the variable x changes gradually and becomes sufficiently close to the definite quantity a, that is, the absolute value of their difference has become smaller than any known positive number, the definite quantity a is the limit of the variable x. For instance, the limit of the number sequence $\frac{1}{2}, \frac{2}{3}, \cdots, n/n+1$ is 1, hence $\lim\limits_{n\to\infty} \frac{n}{n+1} = 1$

【极限量规】jíxiàn liángguī same as 界限量规 jièxiàn liángguī

【极刑】jíxíng 指死刑 capital penalty:处以～ sentence sb. to death

【极意】jíyì 用尽心思;尽心 do one's utmost; rack one's brains:～奉承 go to extremes in currying favour with sb. |～模仿 try one's best to imitate

【极昼】jízhòu 极圈以内的地区,每年总有一个时期太阳不落到地平线以下,一天 24 小时都是白天,这个时期叫做极昼 polar day, the time of the year in regions within the polar circles when the sun remains above the horizon 24 hours a day

庋 jí〈书 *fml.*〉门闩 door bolt

即[1] jí ❶ 靠近;接触 approach; come into contact:若～若离 maintain a lukewarm relationship; keep sb. at arm's length; half-hearted|可望而不可～ tantalizing; within sight but without reach ❷ 到;开始从事 assume; undertake:～位 (of an emperor) ascend the throne ❸ 当下;目前 at present; in the immediate future:～日 (as of) today|～期 soon|成功在～。Success is coming in sight. ❹ 就着(当前环境) be prompted by the occasion:～景生情 recall old memories at the sight of sth.

即[2] jí〈书 *fml.*〉❶ 就是 the same as; mean; namely:荷花～莲花。*Hehua* (lotus) is the same as *lianhua* (lotus). |非此～彼。It must be either this or that. ❷ 就;便 prompt; at once:一触～发 touch-and-go situation; imminent|招之～来 be on call at any hour|闻过～改 correct one's mistake as soon as it is pointed out ❸ 即使 even; even if:～无他方之支援,也能按期完成任务。We can fulfil the task on time even without outside support. ☞就[2] jiù on p.1041

【即便】jíbiàn same as 即使 jíshǐ

【即或】jíhuò same as 即使 jíshǐ

【即将】jíjiāng 将要;就要 soon; be about to; be on the point of:理想～实现。(My) dream will soon come true. |展览会～闭幕。The exhibition is drawing to an end.

【即景】jíjǐng〈书 *fml.*〉就眼前的景物(作诗文或绘画)(of a literary or artistic work) inspired by what one sees:～诗 extempore poem|农村～rural vistas|西湖～a glimpse of the West Lake

【即景生情】jí jǐng shēng qíng 对眼前的情景有所感触而产生某种思想感情 be touched at what one sees

【即刻】jíkè 立刻 at once; immediately:～出发 start at once

【即令】jílìng 即使 even; even if; even though

【即日】jírì ❶ 当天 this or that very day:本条例自～起施行。This act shall come into effect as of the day of its promulgation. ❷ 最近几天;近日 in the next few days:本片～放映。The film will be shown in the next few days.

【即若】jíruò〈书 *fml.*〉即使 even if; even though

【即时】jíshí 立即 immediately; forthwith:～投产 go into production right away

【即食】jíshí 立即可以食用的(of food) instant:～面(方便面) instant noodles

【即使】jíshǐ〈连词 *conj.*〉表示假设的让步[expression supposition] even; even if; even though; though:～我们的工作取得了很大的成绩,也不能骄傲自满。We cannot afford to sit on our laurels even if we have made big achievements.|～你当时在场,恐怕也没有别的办法。There was little you could have done even if you had been there. 注意 **NOTE**: '即使'所表示的条件,可以是尚未实现的事情,也可以是与既成事实相反的事情。The condition indicated by this conjunction may be either sth. that has not happened or sth. that is opposite to the actual situation.

【即事】jíshì 对眼前的事物、情景有所感触而创作 write out of inspiration:～诗 impromptu or extempore poem

【即位】jí//wèi〈书 *fml.*〉❶ 就位 ascend the throne ❷ 指开始做帝王或诸侯 assume the position of an emperor or duke

【即席】jíxí〈书 *fml.*〉❶ 在宴会或集会上(at a banquet or gathering) do sth. impromptu or extemporaneous:～讲话 speak off the cuff; speak impromptu; make an impromptu (or extemporaneous) speech|～赋诗 improvise a poem ❷ 入席;就位 take one's seat (at a dinner table, etc.)

【即兴】jíxìng 对眼前景物有所感触,临时发生兴致而创作 do sth. without preparation or at the inspiration of what one sees:～之作 improvisation|～表演 improvise a performance

佶 jí〈书 *fml.*〉健壮 robust and sturdy

【佶屈聱牙】jíqū áoyá (文章)读起来不顺口(of a piece of writing) difficult to read or comprehend (佶屈 *jiqu*:曲折 complicated; 聱牙 *aoya*:拗口 difficult to read); same as 诘屈聱牙 jíqū áoyá

诘 jí [诘屈聱牙] same as 佶屈聱牙 jíqū áoyá

☞ jié on p. 990

亟 jí〈书 *fml.*〉急迫地 urgently; anxiously; earnestly:～待解决(of a problem) demanding prompt solution|～须纠正 must be speedily put right

☞ qì on p. 1525

【亟亟】jíjí〈书 *fml.*〉急迫;急忙 in a hurry; in haste:～奔走 go on errands in a hurry|不必～no need to hurry

革 jí〈书 *fml.*〉(病)危急 (of an illness) in a critical condition

☞ gé on p. 652

笈 jí〈书 *fml.*〉❶ 书箱 book chest; satchel 负～从师 carry a book case and leave home to pursue studies ❷ 书籍;典籍 book; document

急 jí ❶ 想要马上达到某种目的而激动不安;着急 agitated by the desire to get sth. done; impatient; anxious:～着要走 cannot wait to go|眼都～红了。(One's) eyes become bloodshot because of anxiety. ❷ 使着急 make restless or anxious; worry:火车快开了,他还不来,实在～人。The train was about to move but he was nowhere to be seen — I was so worried. ❸ 容易发怒;急躁 ill-tempered; quick-tempered:～性子 quick temper|没说上三句话他就～了。Our conversation hadn't gone far before he lost his patience. ❹ 很快而且猛烈;急促 rapid and violent:～雨 pelting rain|～转弯 sharp turn; sudden turnabout|水流很～。The water flows turbulently.|炮声甚～。Guns were rumbling in a barrage.|话说得很～talk a blue streak ❺ 急迫;紧急 urgency; emergency:～事 urgent matter|～件 emergency mail|～中生智 hit upon an idea on the spur of the moment ❻ 紧急严重的事情 urgent matter:告～appeal for emergency help|救～come to sb.'s rescue|当务之～task of top priority ❼ 对大家的事或别人的困难,赶快帮助 be eager to help those in need:～公好义 public-spirited; zealous for the common weal|～人之难(nàn) eager to help those in need

【急巴巴】jíbābā 急迫的样子 anxious; impatient

【急变】jíbiàn 紧急的事变 sudden turn of events; emergency or crisis

【急病】jíbìng 急症 acute disease:生～come down with an acute disease|害～contract a disease that calls for immediate treatment

【急茬儿】jíchár〈方 *dial.*〉紧急的事情 urgent matter; emergency case:这是～,可不能耽误

了。This is an emergency case that has to be attended to at once.

【急赤白脸】jí·chibáiliǎn 〈方 *dial.*〉(～的 jí·chibáiliǎn·de)心里着急,脸色难看 so agitated as to look ugly in the face:两个人～地吵个没完。The two never stopped quarrelling, fuming and red in the face. also 急扯白脸 jí·chebáiliǎn

【急匆匆】jícōngcōng (～的 jícōngcōng·de)非常匆忙的样子 in a great hurry; hastily:～走来一个人。A man came in haste.

【急促】jícù ❶ 快而短促 hurried; rapid:呼吸～short of breath|～的脚步声 hurried footsteps ❷ (时间)短促 (of time) short; pressing:时间很～,不能再犹豫了。Time is running out. Stop hesitating or dithering.

【急电】jídiàn 需要赶紧拍发和递送的电报 urgent telegram; urgent cable

【急风暴雨】jí fēng bào yǔ 急剧而猛烈的风雨,多用来形容声势浩大的革命运动 violent storm; hurricane; tempest; influential large scale revolutionary movement

【急公好义】jí gōng hào yì 热心公益,爱帮助人 zealous for the common weal; public-spirited; philanthropic

【急功近利】jí gōng jìn lì 急于求目前的成效和利益 eager for instant success and benefit

【急火】[1] jíhuǒ 指烧煮东西时的猛火 quick and ranging fire:～煮不好饭。You can't do rice to a turn in a haste.

【急火】[2] jíhuǒ 因着急而产生的火气 pent-up anxiety:～攻心 burning with anxiety

【急急巴巴】jí·jibābā (～的 jí·jibābā·de)形容急忙 hastily; in a hurry:他的任务还没完成,为什么要～地叫他回来? He hasn't fulfilled his task yet. Why want him back in such a hurry?

【急急风】jíjífēng 戏曲打击乐的一种打法,节奏很快,多用来配合紧张、急速的动作 playing a percussion instrument in rapid succession, a technique oft. used to accentuate tense and rapid movement in opera

【急急如律令】jí jí rú lǜ lìng 立即遵照命令。本是汉代公文用语,后来道士念咒驱使鬼神,末尾照例用这句话。hurry up and act on my instruction: a Han-dynasty document-writing jargon that has become an incantation used by a Taoist priest to conclude a preach to exorcize evil spirits

【急件】jíjiàn 须要很快送到的紧急文件 urgent document or dispatch

【急进】jíjìn 急于改革和进取 radical:～派 radicals

【急救】jíjiù 紧急救治 first aid; emergency treatment:～危重病人 put a patient critically ill under emergency treatment

【急救包】jíjiùbāo 装有急救药品及消过毒的纱布、绷带等的小包,供急救伤病员时使用 first-aid dressing; kit containing medicine and dressing to render emergency aid or treatment before regular medical service can be obtained

【急就章】jíjiùzhāng 为了应付需要,匆忙完成的作品或事情(原为书名,也叫《急就篇》,汉代史游作) hurriedly-written essay; hasty work; improvisation, which originated in a book entitled *A Collection of Stories Written in a Hurry* by the Han-dynasty author Shi You

【急剧】jíjù 急速;迅速而剧烈 rapid; sharp; sudden:气温～下降。Temperature plunged all of a sudden.

【急遽】jíjù 急速 rapid; sharp; sudden

【急口令】jíkǒulìng 〈方 *dial.*〉绕口令 tongue-twister

【急流】jíliú 湍急的水流 torrent; rapid stream; rapids:～滚滚 surging torrent|渡过～险滩 sweep over rapids and shoals

【急流勇退】jí liú yǒng tuì 〈旧时 *old*〉〈比喻 *fig.*〉仕途顺利的时候毅然退出官场,现也比喻在复杂的斗争中及早抽身 step down resolutely at the height of one's official career;(fig) extricate oneself from a complicated struggle

【急忙】jímáng 心里着急,行动加快 in a hurry; in haste; hurriedly; hastily:听说厂里有要紧事儿,他～穿上衣服跑出门去。He hurriedly put on his coat and ran out of the door upon learning something urgent had happened in the factory.|急急忙忙赶着去上班 make haste and rush off to work

【急难】jí//nàn 〈书 *fml.*〉热心地帮助别人摆脱患难 be anxious to help (those in grave danger):扶危～succour those in peril and help the distressed|急人之难 extend a hand to people in trouble

【急难】jínàn 危急患难 misfortune; adversity:～之中见人心。Adversity reveals a man's heart. *or* In a misfortune it's easy to tell a true friend from a false one.

【急迫】jípò 马上需要应付或办理,不容许迟延 urgent; pressing; imperative:情况～。The matter is urgent.|～的任务 emergency task; task that tolerates no delay

【急起直追】jí qǐ zhí zhuī 马上行动起来,迅速赶上进步较快的人或发展水平较高的事物 rouse oneself to catch up; do one's utmost to overtake

【急切】jíqiè ❶ 迫切 eager; impatient:需要～in urgent need|～地盼望成功 look forward on tiptoe to success ❷ 仓促 in a hurry; in haste:～间找不着适当的人。It's impossible to find the right person on such short notice.

【急如星火】jí rú xīng huǒ 形容非常急迫 extremely pressing; most urgent; post-haste

【急事】jíshì 急需办理的事;紧急的事情 matter in need of immediate attention; urgent matter

【急速】jísù 非常快 at a quick speed; at full throttle:火车～地向前飞奔。The train sped forward at full throttle.

【急湍】jítuān ❶ 很急的水流 swift (or rushing) current ❷ 湍急 turbulent; foamy:～的溪流 swift stream

【急弯】jíwān ❶ 道路突然转折的地方 sharp turn:前有～,行车小心。Drivers be careful — sharp turn ahead. ❷ 车、船、飞机等行进方向的突然改变 make a sharp turn:战斗机拐了个～,向西南飞去。The fighter made a sharp southwest turn and flew away.

【急务】jíwù 紧急的事务 urgent task:当前～ current pressing task

【急先锋】jíxiānfēng〈比喻 *fig.*〉在行动上积极领头的人 one who is eager to take the lead in doing sth.; daring vanguard

【急行军】jíxíngjūn 部队执行紧急任务时进行的快速行军 forced march; march conducted by troops on an emergency mission at a faster pace than usual

【急性】jíxìng ❶ 发作急剧的、变化快的(病) acute:～阑尾炎 acute appendicitis ❷ (～儿 jíxìngr)急性子 impetuous

【急性病】jíxìngbìng ❶ 发病急剧、病情变化很快、症状较重的疾病,例如霍乱、急性阑尾炎等 acute (opposed to chronic) disease; swift and severe attack of a disease, such as cholera and acute appendicitis ❷〈比喻 *fig.*〉不顾客观实际、急于求成的毛病 impetuosity, pertaining to the propensity for sudden and rash action in disregard of actual conditions

【急性子】jíxìng·zi ❶ 性情急躁 of impatient disposition; impetuous:～人 impatient person ❷ 性情急躁的人 impetuous person:他是个～,总要一口气把话说完。As an impatient man, he always says what he wants to say in one breath.

J

【急需】jíxū 紧急需要 crying need; be badly in need of:～处理 (of sth.) need to be handled immediately | 以应～ meet a crying need

【急眼】jí//yǎn〈方 *dial.*〉❶ 发火;发脾气 get angry; fly into a rage:人家这么两句话就把你惹～啦。How come you get angry at such slight provocation? ❷ 着急;急 worried; anxious:他一～,连话都说不出来了。His words fail him when he gets worried.

【急用】jíyòng 紧急需用(多指金钱方面 oft. of money) urgent need:节约储蓄,以备～ be thrift and save up for a rainy day

【急于】jíyú 想要马上实现 anxious; impatient:～求成 be rash for success; impatient for getting things done | 他～回厂,准备今天就走。He wants to go today because he can't wait to be back in his factory.

【急躁】jízào ❶ 碰到不称心的事情马上激动不安 irritable; irascible:性情～irascible temperament | 一听说事情弄糟了,他就～起来了。As soon as he heard that things had gone wrong, he got very irritable. ❷ 想马上达到目的,不做好准备就开始行动 impetuous; rash; impatient:～冒进 advance impetuously | 别～,大家商量好再动手。Don't get impatient. Wait until we have come up with a way out.

【急诊】jízhěn 指病情严重,需要马上诊治 emergency call; emergency treatment:～室 emergency room | 看～make an emergency call to the doctor

【急症】jízhèng 突然发作来势很猛的病症 sudden attack (of illness); acute disease; emergency case

【急智】jízhì 在紧急情况下突然想出来的应付办法 nimbleness of mind in dealing with emergencies; quick-wittedness

【急中生智】jí zhōng shēng zhì 在紧急中想出好的应付办法 hit upon a plan in desperation; suddenly hit on a way out of a predicament

【急骤】jízhòu 急速 hurried; flurried:～的脚步声 sound of a flurry of footsteps

【急转直下】jí zhuǎn zhí xià (形势、剧情、文笔等)突然转变,并且很快地顺势发展下去(of the course of events in a situation, opera, story, etc.) take a sudden turn and then develop rapidly

姞 Jí 姓 a surname

疾[1] jí ❶ 疾病 disease; sickness; illness:积劳成～ fall ill from overwork ❷ 痛苦 pain; suffering:～苦 distress ❸ 痛恨 hate; abhor:～恶如仇 abhor evildoers as if they were personal enemies

疾[2] jí 急速;猛烈 fast; quick:～风 high wind | ～驰 whirl; speed | ～走 walk quickly; scamper | 大声～呼 make a clarion call to awaken the public to sth; call out with loud voice to sb.

【疾病】jíbìng 病(总称)(general term for) disease:预防～disease prevention | ～缠身 be ridden with diseases

【疾步】jíbù 快步 walk quickly; at a fast pace:～行走 walk like shooting forward

【疾驰】jíchí (车马等)奔驰 (of a vehicle, a horse, etc) speed; rumble by:汽车～而过。Automobiles whirled past.

【疾恶如仇】jí è rú chóu 恨坏人坏事像痛恨仇敌一样 hate evil like an enemy; also 嫉恶如仇 jí è rú chóu

【疾风】jífēng ❶ 气象学上指 7 级风 (meteorol.) force seven wind; moderate gale; ☞ 风级 fēngjí on p. 579 ❷ 猛烈的风 strong wind:～劲草 strength of the grass put to test by the high wind | ～迅雨 strong wind and pelting rain

【疾风劲草】jí fēng jìng cǎo 在猛烈的大风中,只有坚韧的草才不会被吹倒 sturdy grass withstands high winds — strength of character is tested in a crisis;〈比喻 *fig.*〉在大风浪或艰苦危急之中,只有立场坚定、意志坚决的人才经得起考验 Only those who are steadfast and strong-willed can stand the test of trials and tribulations. also 疾风知劲草 jí fēng zhī jìng cǎo

【疾患】jíhuàn〈书 *fml.*〉病 illness; ailment

【疾苦】jíkǔ (人民生活中的)困苦 suffering; hardship:关心群众的～ be concerned about the weal and woe of the people

【疾驶】jíshǐ (车辆等)快速行驶(of vehicles, etc.)drive at a fast speed:～而去 speed past

【疾首蹙额】jí shǒu cù é 形容厌恶、痛恨的样子 with aching head and knitted brows — frowning in disgust; with abhorrence(疾首 *ji shou*:头痛 headache;蹙额 *cu e*:皱眉 knitted brows)

【疾书】jíshū 迅速地书写 scribble rapidly:奋笔～ set pen to paper and scribble in rapid strokes

【疾言厉色】jí yán lì sè 说话急躁,神色严厉。形容发怒时的神情。harsh words and stern looks; angry look — severe countenance and harsh voice

棘 jí ❶ 酸枣树 sour jujube; thorn bush ❷ 泛指有刺的草木 thorny plants; brambles:披荆斩～ blaze a new trial by breaking through brambles and thorns; open a path through all manner of obstacles ❸ 刺;扎 prick:～手 thorny; sticky

【棘刺】jícì 豪猪等脊背上长的硬而长的刺。泛指动植物体上的针状物。bristle on the back of a porcupine, etc.; (in a broad sense) prickle or thorn grown on animal or plant

【棘轮】jílún 一种轮状零件,通常是有齿的。棘轮和棘爪、连杆等组成间歇运动机构。ratchet; toothed wheel provided with a pawl that fits between its teeth and links it with a connecting rod to allow intermittent movement

【棘皮动物】jípí dòngwù 无脊椎动物的一门,外皮一般具有石灰质的刺状突起,身体球形、星形或圆棒形,生活在海底,运动缓慢或不运动,如海星、海胆、海参、海百合等 echinoderm; invertebrate such as starfish (*Asteroidea*), heart urchin (*Echinoidea*), brittle-star (*Ophiuroidea*) and sea lily (*Ptilocrinus*), with its skin covered with prickle-like calcarious outgrowths, its body in the shape of a ball, star or rod, inhabiting the bottom of the sea, slow in movement or motionless

【棘手】jíshǒu 形容事情难办,像荆棘刺手 thorny; troublesome; knotty:～的问题 knotty problem; hard nut to crack|这件事情非常～。This is a sticky business.

【棘爪】jízhuǎ 拨动棘轮做间歇运动的零件。棘爪由连杆带动做往复运动,从而带动棘轮做单向运动。pawl; piece of metal fit into the teeth of a ratchet and linked to a connecting rod, so that when the connecting rod moves back and forth in sync with the pawl, the ratchet is driven in a one-way movement

殛 jí〈书 *fml.*〉杀死 kill:雷～ struck dead by lightning

戢 jí ❶〈书 *fml.*〉收敛;收藏 restrain; put away:～翼(of a bird) fold its wings|～怒 restrain one's anger|～兵 cease hostilities; put arms away and declare armistice ❷(Jí)姓 a surname

集 jí ❶ 集合;聚集 gather; collect:汇～put together|齐～congregate|～思广益 draw on collective wisdom and absorb all useful ideas; pool the wisdom of everyone|惊喜交～do not know whether to cry or laugh ❷ 集市 rural fair; market:赶～go to a local fair ❸ 集子 collection; anthology:诗～collection of poem|文～collected writings|全～complete collection|地图～album of atlas ❹ 某些篇幅较长的著作或作品中相对独立的部分 volume; part:《康熙字典》分为子、丑、寅、卯等十二～。The *Kangxi Dictionary* comes in 12 categories, such as *Zi*, *Chou*, *Yin* and *Mao*.|影片上下两～,一次放映。The movie is in two parts but it is shown in one stretch。|三十～电视连续剧 30-episode serial television play ❺'集合'[2]的简称 abbr. for 集合[2] jíhé ❻(Jí)姓 a surname

【集部】jíbù 我国古代图书分类的一大部类。包括各种体裁的文学著作。literature; one of the traditional categories of Chinese books and writings, including various genres of literary works; also 丁部 dīngbù; ☞ 四部 sìbù on p.1820

【集成】jíchéng 同类著作汇集在一起(多用做书名 usu. part of a book title) collection:《丛书～》*A Collection of Book Series*|《中国古典戏曲论著～》*Collected Essays on Classical Chinese Theatre*

【集成电路】jíchéng-diànlù 在同一硅片上制作许多晶体管和电阻,并将它们联成一定的电路,完成一定的功能,这种电路称为集成电路。具有体积小,耐震,耐潮,稳定性高等优点。广泛应用于电子计算机、测量仪器和其他方面。integrated circuit; small chip of silicon incorporating large numbers of transistors and resistive elements into a circuit to perform certain functions, characterized by small size, shock and humidity resistance, and high stability, widely used in computers, metres and apparatuses, and other fields

【集大成】jí dàchéng 集中某类事物的各个方面,达到相当完备的程度 pool all that is good; synthesize; culmination of sth.; give concentrated expression to:这是一部～的优秀著作。This is an overall outstanding work.

【集合】[1] jíhé ❶ 许多分散的人或物聚在一起 assemble; muster; get together: 全校同学已经在操场～了。All the students of the school have assembled on the playground. ❷ 汇集 collect: ～各种材料,加以分析。Put various materials together for an analysis.

【集合】[2] jíhé 数学上指若干具有共同属性的事物的总体。如全部整数就成一个整数的集合,一个工厂的全体工人就成一个该工厂全体工人的集合。(of mathematics) set; assemblage and aggregation; collection of objects or elements classed together. For example, a collection of integers is regarded as a set of integers, and all the workers of a factory is the factory's worker assemblage. 简称 abbr. 集 jí

【集会】jíhuì 集合在一起开会 assembly; rally

【集结】jíjié 聚集。特指军队等集合到一处。(esp. of troops) mass; concentrate: ～待命 assemble and await orders|～兵力 muster the troops

【集锦】jíjǐn 编辑在一起的精彩的图画、诗文等(多用做标题 usu. part of a book title) collection of choice specimens: 图片～gleanings of fine pictures | 邮票～ collection of superb stamps

【集句】jíjù 摘取前人的诗句拼成的诗(多为律诗)。词也有集句而成的。poem (oft. one of eight lines each containing five or seven characters; sometimes a *ci* poem) composed of lines from different poets of former times

【集聚】jíjù 集合;聚合 collect; assemble: 人们～在老槐树下休息。People spent their time of leisure under the old Chinese scholar tree.

【集刊】jíkān 学术机构刊行的成套的、定期或不定期出版的论文集 collection of papers (of an academic institution) published regularly or irregularly:《红楼梦研究～》*Collected Essays on 'A Dream of Red Mansions'*

【集拢】jílǒng 聚集 gather: 场院中～了一群人。A crowd gathered in the yard.

【集录】jílù (把资料)收集、抄录在一起或编印成书 collect and compile, or print a compilation (of reference materials)

【集权】jíquán 政治、经济、军事大权集中于中央 centralization of state power; centralization of political, economic and military power in the hand of the central authorities

【集日】jírì 有集市的日子 market day: 这个镇的～是每旬的三六九。Market day in this town falls on the 3rd, 6th and 9th days of each of the three 10-day periods of a month.

【集散地】jísàndì 本地区货物集中外运和外地货物由此分散到区内各地的地方 distribution centre, where local goods are collected for outbound shipping and the goods that have been shipped in are distributed to surrounding areas

【集市】jíshì 农村或城市中定期买卖货物的市场 country fair; market: ～贸易 country fair trade

【集思广益】jí sī guǎng yì 集中众人的智慧,广泛吸收有益的意见 draw on collective wisdom and absorb all useful ideas; pool the wisdom of the entire group of people

【集体】jítǐ 许多人合起来的有组织的整体(跟'个人'相对) collective: ～生活 collective life|～领导 collective leadership|个人利益服从～利益。Individual interests come second to those of the collective.

【集体经济】jítǐ jīngjì 以生产资料集体所有制和共同劳动为基础的经济形式 collective economy, a mode of economy based on collective ownership of means of production and collective labour

【集体所有制】jítǐ suǒyǒuzhì 社会主义所有制的低级形式,主要的生产资料、产品等归生产者集体所有 collective ownership, the primary mode of socialist ownership, under which major means of production, products, etc. are owned by a collective of labourers

【集体舞】jítǐwǔ ❶ 多人共同表演的舞蹈,常用乐器伴奏 collective dance, performed by a group of people to the accompaniment of musical instruments; also 群舞 qúnwǔ ❷ 形式比较自由、动作比较简单的群众娱乐性的舞蹈 group dance, a form of dance, simple of both form and movement, for mass entertainment

【集体主义】jítǐ zhǔyì 一切从集体出发,把集体利益放在个人利益之上的思想,是社会主义、共产主义的基本精神 collectivism, the idea of doing everything by proceeding from the interests of the collective and placing the interests of the collective above those of individuals; basic spirit of socialism and communism

【集团】jítuán 为了一定的目的组织起来共同行动的团体 clique, circle and bloc, organization put together for common purpose and action

【集团军】jítuánjūn 军队的一级编组,辖若干个军或师 group army, a military unit composed of several armies or divisions

【集训】jíxùn 集中到一个地方训练 assemble for training: 干部轮流～。Cadres take turns to assemble at a place for a term of training. |运动员提前一个月～。The athletes are assembled one month ahead of schedule.

【集腋成裘】jí yè chéng qiú 狐狸腋下的皮虽然很小,但是聚集起来就能缝成一件皮袍 the bits of fur from the axillae of many foxes, once put together, make a robe;〈比喻 *fig.*〉积少成多 many a little makes a mickle

【集邮】jí//yóu 收集和保存各种邮票,也包括与邮政有关的各种封、片、戳等用品 stamp collecting; philately; collection and study of postage stamps, as well as objects associated with the postal service, such as stamped envelopes, postal cards and postmarks

【集邮册】jíyóucè 一种特制的用于集邮的本子

stamp album; also 插册 chācè

【集约】jíyuē ❶ 农业上指在同一土地面积上投入较多的生产资料和劳动，进行精耕细作，用提高单位面积产量的方法来增加产品总量（跟‘粗放’相对）。这种经营方式叫做集约经营。intensive (as opposed to ‘individual’) farming; mode of farming, whereby relatively more means of production and labour are put in the same amount of land for intensive and meticulous cultivation, so that per-unit yield can be increased to raise the total farm output ❷ 泛指采用现代化管理方法和科学技术，加强分工、协作，提高资金、资源使用效率的经营方式 intensive operation; general term for any mode of management whereby modern managerial expertise and science and technology are employed, and the division of labour and cooperation are intensified, so as to increase the efficiency of use of funds and resources

【集运】jíyùn 集中起来运输 bulk transport; containerized transport：～木材 bulk transportation of timber

【集镇】jízhèn 以非农业人口为主的比城市小的居住区 town; market town; referring to residential area that is smaller than a city, with a population dominated by non-agricultural residents

【集中】jízhōng 把分散的人、事物、力量等聚集起来；把意见、经验等归纳起来 concentrate, centralize and assemble scattered people, objects, and strength; summarize opinions or experience：～兵力 concentrate the troops｜～资金 pool funds｜精神～concentrate one's mind

【集中营】jízhōngyíng 帝国主义国家或反动政权把政治犯、战俘或掳来的非交战人员集中起来监禁或杀害的地方 concentration camp; (of an imperial country or reactionary government) putting political prisoners, prisoners of war, or non-combat captives together at a place for imprisonment or execution

【集注】[1] jízhù （精神、眼光等）集中 focus：代表们的眼光都～在大会主席台上。All eyes of the delegates to the conference were focused on the rostrum.

【集注】[2] jízhù 汇集前人关于某部书的注释再加上自己的见解进行注释，多用做书名（usu. part of a book title) collected commentaries; variorum, i.e, incorporation of one's own opinions with footnotes written by predecessors to a book; also 集解 jíjiě or 集释 jíshì

【集装箱】jízhuāngxiāng 具有一定规格、便于机械装卸、可以重复使用的装运货物的大型容器，形状像箱子，多用金属材料制成。有的地区叫货柜。container; large, box-like (mostly metal) receptacle of standard design that facilitates mechanical loading and unloading, made to be repeated use for the transportation of goods; known in some areas as 货柜 huòguì

【集资】jízī 聚集资金 raise funds; pool money：～经营 raise funds to start a business

【集子】jí·zi 把许多单篇著作或单张作品收集在一起编成的书 collection; collected works; anthology：这个～里一共有二十篇小说。This is a collection of 20 novellas.

蒺 jí［蒺藜］(jí·lí) ❶ 一年生草本植物，茎平铺在地上，羽状复叶，小叶长椭圆形，开黄色小花，果皮有尖刺。种子可入药。puncture vine (*Tribulus terrestris*); annual herb with stem lying on the ground, pinnate compound ovate leaflets, tiny yellow flowers, thorny fruit, and seeds that are of medical value ❷ 这种植物的果实 fruit of puncture vine ‖ also 蒺蔾 jí·lí

楫 jí 桨 oar：舟～ vessels

辑 jí ❶ 编辑；辑录 collect; compile; edit ❷ 整套书籍、资料等按内容或发表先后次序分成的各个部分 (of a series of books) part; volume; division：新闻简报第一～ Newsletter No.1｜这部丛书分为十～，每～五本。This set of books consists of ten parts, and each part comes in five volumes.

【辑录】jílù 把有关的资料或著作收集起来编成书 compile; put related materials or works together in the form of a book

【辑佚】jíyì ❶ 辑录前人或今人通行的集子以外的散佚的文章或作品 compile the writings of an ancient or contemporary writer that are not found in known books：～并印行古籍数十种。Several dozen books of formerly scattered ancient writings have been compiled and published. ❷ 辑佚而编成的书或文章（多用做书名）book thus put together：《鲁迅著作～》*A Compilation of Unpublished Works by Lu Xun* ‖ also 辑逸 jíyì

嵴 jí 山脊 mountain or hill ridge

嫉 jí ❶ 忌妒 jealous; envious：～贤妒能 jealous of the good and envious of the able; jealous of sb. better than oneself ❷ 憎恨 hate：～恶如仇 hate injustice like poison; abhor evils like one's personal enemies

【嫉妒】jídù same as 忌妒 jì·du

【嫉恶如仇】jí è rú chóu same as 疾恶如仇 jí è rú chóu

【嫉恨】jíhèn 因忌妒而愤恨；憎恨 jealous rage; envy and hate; hatred born of jealousy

【嫉贤妒能】jí xián dù néng 对品德、才能比自己强的人心怀怨恨嫉妒 be envious of people of worth and ability

蕺 jí 蕺菜 see below

【蕺菜】jícài 多年生草本植物，茎上有节，叶子互生，心脏形，花小而密，结蒴果。茎和叶有鱼腥气。全草入药。cardate houttuynia (*Hout-*

tuynia cordata); perennial plant with a knotted stem, heart-shaped alternate leaves, close clusters of small flowers, bearing capsules, and both stem and leaves smelling of fish, used wholly as a medicine; also 鱼腥草 yúxīngcǎo

踖 jí ☞ 蹴踖 cùjí on p. 330

瘠 jí 〈书 *fml.*〉❶(身体)瘦弱 lean; thin and weak ❷ 瘠薄 barren; poor; lean: ～土 poor soil; lean soil | ～田 barren land

【瘠薄】jíbó (土地)缺少植物生长所需的养分、水分;不肥沃 barren; (of land) lack of nutrition needed for the growth of plants; unproductive

【瘠田】jítián 不肥沃的田地 infertile land

鹡 jí [鹡鸰](jílíng)鸟类的一属,最常见的一种,身体小,头顶黑色,前额纯白色,嘴细长,尾和翅膀都很长,黑色,有白斑,腹部白色。吃昆虫和小鱼等,是保护鸟。wagtail (*Motacilla*); black-crested common bird under human protection, with small black body marked by white dots and white belly, white forehead, long and slim beak, long tail and wings, feeding on insects and small fish

藉 jí ❶〈书 *fml.*〉践踏;侮辱 tread on; trample underfoot; insult ❷ (Jí)姓 a surname

☞ jiè on p. 1002

蹐 jí 〈书 *fml.*〉小步 make small steps

籍 jí ❶ 书籍;册子 book; record: 古～ ancient book ❷ 籍贯 native place: 原～ place of origin ❸ 代表个人对国家、组织的隶属关系 membership: 国～ nationality | 党～ party membership | 学～ registration of one's name on a school roll ❹ (Jí)姓 a surname

【籍贯】jíguàn 祖居或个人出生的地方 place of one's ancestral home or birth; native place

【籍没】jímò 〈书 *fml.*〉登记并没收(家产) make a list of sb.'s property and confiscate it

jǐ (ㄐㄧˇ)

几(幾) jǐ ❶ 询问数目(估计数目不太大) how many (with a small number anticipated): 来了～个人? How many people have come here? | 你能在家住～天? For how many days can you stay home? ❷ 表示大于一而小于十的不定的数目 a few; several; some: ～本书 a few books | 十～岁 a little older than ten | ～百人 several hundred people

☞ jī on p. 888

【几曾】jǐcéng 用反问的语气表示未曾;几时曾经 (in a rhetorical question) when; at what time (past tense): 在他重病期间,我～安睡过一夜。When did I have a single night's good sleep when he was so ill?

【几次三番】jǐ cì sān fān 一次又一次;屡次 time and again: 朋友们～地劝说,他都当成了耳旁风。Time and again his friends' persuasions fell on deaf ears.

【几多】jǐduō 〈方 *dial.*〉❶〈疑问代词 *interrog. pron*〉a) 询问数量 how many; how much: ～人? How many people are there? | 这袋米有～重? How much does this sack of rice weigh? b) 表示不定的数量 who knows how much: 在他身上,父母不知花费了～精力,～钱财。Who knows how much energy and money his parents have spent on him. ❷ 多么 how: 这孩子～懂事! How well-behaved the child is!

【几何】jǐhé ❶〈书 *fml.*〉多少 how much; how many: 价值～? How much is its worth? | 曾～时 it does not take long for sth. or sb. to...; only a short while ago ❷几何学的简称 abbr. for 几何学 jǐhéxué

【几何体】jǐhétǐ 空间的有限部分,由平面和曲面所围成。如棱柱体、正方体、圆柱体、球体。solid; body or magnitude of three dimensions consisting of plains and /or curved surfaces, such as prism, square cube, circular cylinder and spheroid; also 立体 lìtǐ

【几何图形】jǐhé túxíng 点、线、面、体或它们的组合 geometric figure, referring to point, line, surface, solid, or their combination; 简称 abbr. 图形 túxíng

【几何学】jǐhéxué 研究空间图形的形状、大小和位置的相互关系的学科 geometry; branch of mathematics concerned with the properties and relations of points, lines, surfaces and solids

【几经】jǐjīng 经过多次 several times; time and again: ～波折 after a lot of bother | ～交涉 through repeated negotiations; after making repeated representations

【几儿】jǐr 〈方 *dial.*〉哪一天 what date: 你～来的? When did you get here? | 今儿是～? What's the date today?

【几时】jǐshí 什么时候 what time; when: 你们～走? What time are you leaving? | 你～有空儿过来坐吧。Come when you are free.

【几许】jǐxǔ 〈书 *fml.*〉多少 how much; how many: 不知～。No one knows how much it is.

己 jǐ ❶ 自己 oneself: 知～知彼 know oneself and know the other party | 舍～为人 make personal sacrifices for the interests of others | 严于律～ be strict with oneself ❷ 天干的第六位 *Ji*, the 6th of the 10 Heavenly Stems; ☞ 干支 gānzhī on p. 627

【己方】jǐfāng 自己这一方面 one's own party; one's own side

【己见】jǐjiàn 自己的意见 one's own opinions (idea, view, suggestion): 各抒～ each airs (expresses, presents) his own view | 固执～ stick to (cling to) one's own view; stubborn

【己任】jǐrèn 自己的任务 one's own task (duty, assignment):以天下为～ regard it as one's own duty to defend the national interests; regard the national affairs as one's own

纪 Jǐ 姓(近年也有读 Jì 的 also pronounced Jì in recent years) a surname

☞ jì on p.915

虮(蟣) jǐ 虮子 see below

【虮子】jǐ·zi 虱子的卵 egg of a louse; nit; young louse

挤(擠) jǐ ❶(人、物)紧紧靠拢在一起;(事情)集中在同一时间内 jam; squeeze; press closely together; handle many things at the same time:～做一团 be closely pressed together; be packed | 屋里～满了人。The room is closely packed. *or* The room is jammed with people. | 事情全～在一块儿了。The matters are all packed together. *or* The matters have all cropped up at the same time. ❷ 在拥挤的环境中用身体排开人或物 squeeze (into, out, through); elbow one's way (into, out, through):人多～不进来。There are too many people for us to get in. ❸ 用压力使从孔隙中出来 exert pressure to get sth. out:～牛奶 milk; milk a cow | ～牙膏 squeeze toothpaste from a tube ◇～时间学习 find time to study ❹ 排斥;排挤 expel; repel; reject; squeeze out:我的名额被～掉了。My name was taken out.

【挤兑】jǐduì 许多人到银行里挤着兑现 many people make a run on the bank

【挤对】jǐ·dui〈方 *dial.*〉逼迫使屈从 force sb. into submission:他不愿意,就别～他了。Don't push him if he doesn't like it.

【挤咕】jǐ·gu〈方 *dial.*〉挤(眼) wink at; make eyes at:眼睛里进去了沙子,一个劲儿地～。(He) kept winking as a sand particle got into one of his eyes.

【挤眉弄眼】jǐ méi nòng yǎn 用眉眼示意 make eyes at; wink at:几个人都对他～,叫他别去。A few people winked at him, signalling him not to go.

【挤牙膏】jǐ yágāo〈比喻 *fig.*〉说话不爽快,经别人一步一步追问,才一点儿一点儿说 squeeze toothpaste from a tube — tell the truth reluctantly; be forced to tell the truth bit by bit

【挤轧】jǐyà 排挤倾轧 jossle and jockey (for position):互相～ jockeying with each other for (power, position, etc.)

【挤占】jǐzhàn 强行挤入并占用 take sth. by force:～耕地 take sb.'s farmland by force

济(濟) Jǐ 济水,古水名,发源于今河南,流经山东入渤海。现在黄河下游的河道就是原来的济水的河道。今河南济源,山东济南、济宁、济阳,都从济水得名。Ji River, an ancient river that rises in Henan and runs through Shandong into the Bohai Sea. The present course of the lower reaches of the Yellow River was the original course of the Ji River; Jiyuan in Henan, and Ji'nan, Ji'ning and Jiyang in Shandong all derived their names from the Ji River.

☞ jì on p.919

【济济】jǐjǐ 形容人多 many people:人才～ galaxy; assembly of brilliant people | ～一堂 gathering of many people

【济济一堂】jǐjǐ yītáng 形容许多有才能的人聚集在一起 many brilliant or talented people coming together

给 jǐ ❶ 供给;供应 supply; provide:补～ supplies | 配～ ration | 自～自足 self-sufficient ❷ 富裕充足 ample:家～户足。Families have ample supplies and people live in contentment.

☞ gěi on p.657

【给付】jǐfù 付给(应付的款项等) pay (amounts payable):按保险条例～保险金 pay insurance money according to insurance regulations

【给水】jǐshuǐ 供应生产或生活用水 water supply; supply water for production and drinking

【给养】jǐyǎng 指军队中人员的伙食、牲畜的饲料以及炊事燃料等物资 provisions for the army, including food, animal fodder, cooking fuels, etc.:补充～ replenish the provisions

【给予】jǐyǔ〈书 *fml.*〉给(gěi) give:～帮助 give help | ～同情 express (give, show) one's sympathy; also 给与 jǐyǔ

脊 jǐ ❶ 人或动物背上中间的骨头;脊柱 spine; backbone:～髓 spinal cord | ～椎 vertebra ❷ 物体上形状像脊柱的部分 part of sth. in the shape of a ridge:山～ mountain ridge | 屋～ ridge of a roof | 书～ spine of a book

【脊背】jǐbèi same as 背¹ bèi ①

【脊梁】jǐ·liang 脊背 back

【脊梁骨】jǐ·lianggǔ same as 脊柱 jǐzhù

【脊檩】jǐlǐn 架在屋架或山墙上面最高的一根横木 ridgepole; horizontal timber or beam at the ridge of a roof, to which the upper ends of the rafters are attached; also 大梁 dàliáng or 正梁 zhèngliáng;(图见☞ figure for 房子 fáng·zi on p.550)

【脊鳍】jǐqí 背鳍 dorsal fin

【脊神经】jǐshénjīng 连接在脊髓上的神经。共分31对,分布在躯干、腹侧面和四肢的肌肉中。主管颈部以下的感觉和运动。spinal nerve; nerve that is linked with the spinal cord. There are altogether 31 pairs, distributed in the muscles of the trunk, the sides of the abdomen and the four limbs. They control the senses and movements of the parts below the neck.

【脊髓】jǐsuǐ 人和脊椎动物中枢神经系统的一部分，在椎管里面，上端连接延髓，两旁发出成对的神经，分布到四肢、体壁和内脏。脊髓的内部有一个H形灰色神经组织，主要由神经细胞构成，外层为白色神经组织，由神经纤维构成。脊髓是许多简单反射的中枢。spinal cord; part of the central nervous system of a human being and other vertebrate, which is found in the spinal canal and connects the medulla oblongata at its upper end. Pairs of nerves extend from the cord to the four limbs, body wall and internal organs. In the cross section, the spiral cord appears as a white oval with a grey, butterfly-shaped area in the centre. The white matter consists of myelinated (sheathed) fibres; the grey matter contains cell bodies, unsheathed motor-neurons fibres. The spinal cord is the centre of many simple reflexes.

【脊髓灰质炎】jǐsuǐ huīzhìyán 急性传染病，由病毒侵入血液循环系统引起，部分病毒可侵入神经系统。患者多为一至六岁儿童，主要症状是发热，全身不适，严重时肢体疼痛，发生瘫痪。通称小儿麻痹症。poliomyelitis; polio; acute infectious disease, esp. of children, caused by a virus inflammation of the grey matter of the spinal cord; part of the viruses may affect the nervous system. Most of the sufferers are children between one and six in age; it is accompanied by a fever, pains and sometimes paralysis of muscle groups that sometimes atrophy, oft. with resulting permanent deformities; 通称 generally known as 小儿麻痹症 xiǎo'ér mábìzhèng

【脊索】jǐsuǒ 某些动物身体内部的支柱，略呈棒形，由柔软的大细胞构成。高等动物的脊柱是由胚胎时期的脊索变化而成的，低等动物(如文昌鱼)的脊索终生不变。notochord; elongated, rod-shaped structure composed of large, soft cells, forming the primitive supporting axis of the body. The spinal column of higher animals is developed from a similar structure in the embryonic stages, but it remains unchanged for life in lower animals (such as lancelet).

【脊索动物】jǐsuǒ dòngwù 动物的一个门，包括原索动物和脊椎动物 chordate, a phylum of the animal world, including protochordates and vertebrates

【脊柱】jǐzhù 人和脊椎动物背部的主要支架。人的脊柱由33个椎骨构成，形状像柱子，在背部的中央，中间有椎管，内有脊髓。脊柱分为颈、胸、腰、骶、尾五个部分。有的地区叫脊梁骨。spinal column; vertebral column; spine; backbone; main supporting frame of the back of a human being and vertebrates. The spinal column of a human being, made up of 33 vertebrae, looks like a column in the centre of the back, with a spinal canal containing a spinal cord in it. It consists of five parts: the cervical vertebrae, thoracic vertebrae, lumbar vertebrae, sacral vertebrae and coccygeal vertebrae. also called 脊梁骨 jǐ·lianggǔ in some places

【脊椎】jǐzhuī ❶ 脊柱 spinal column ❷ 椎骨 vertebra

【脊椎动物】jǐzhuī dòngwù 有脊椎骨的动物，是脊索动物的一个亚门。这一类动物一般体形左右对称，全身分为头、躯干、尾三个部分，躯干又被横膈膜分成胸部和腹部，有比较完善的感觉器官、运动器官和高度分化的神经系统。包括鱼类、两栖动物、爬行动物、鸟类和哺乳动物等五大类。vertebrate; animal with vertebra and a subphylum of the chordate. The bodily form of a vertebrate is generally symmetrical and is divided into the head, the trunk and the tail (limbs), and the trunk is also divided into the chest and the abdomen. It has fairly complete sense organs, locomotive organs and a nervous system with high differentiation. It includes fishes, amphibious animals, reptiles, birds and mammals.

【脊椎骨】jǐzhuīgǔ 椎骨的通称 general term for 椎骨 zhuīgǔ

掎 jǐ 〈书 *fml.*〉❶ 牵住；拖住 restrain; take hold of ❷ 牵引；拉 draw; pull

【掎角之势】jǐ jiǎo zhī shì 〈比喻 *fig.*〉作战时分兵牵制或合兵夹击的形势 divide forces to contain or assemble forces to attack the enemy in fighting battles

鱾 jǐ 鱼类的一属，身体侧扁，略呈椭圆形，头小而钝，口小。生活在海底岩石间。*Girella punctatea*; a kind of flat, oval fish with a small and blunt head, and a small mouth, living among rocks at the bottom of the sea

戟 jǐ ❶ 古代兵器，在长柄的一端装有青铜或铁制成的枪尖，旁边附有月牙形锋刃 halberd; ancient weapon with a pointed bronze or iron head fitted on one end of a long handle and a sharp crescent blade ❷〈书 *fml.*〉刺激 stimulate

麂 jǐ 哺乳动物的一属，是小型的鹿，雄的有长牙和短角。腿细而有力，善于跳跃，毛棕色，皮很柔软，可以制革。muntjac (*Muntiacus*); mammal, the small jungle deer of Southeast Asia and the East Indies, the males having short horns, long, sharp tusk-like canine teeth, slender and strong legs that are good for leaping, brown hair, and soft hide that is a good material for leather making; 通称 generally called 麂子 jǐ·zi

jì (ㄐㄧˋ)

计 jì ❶ 计算 calculate; compute; count; number: 核～ assess; calculate | 共～ total; add up to; total amount comes to|不～其数 countless; innumerable; numerous|数以万～ numbering tens of thousands; by the tens of thousands; countless ❷ 测量或计算度数、时间等的仪器 instrument for measuring number of degrees, time, etc.:时～ timer|体温～ thermometer|血压～ sphygmomanometer|晴雨～ barometer ❸ 主意;策略;计划 idea; tactics; plan:～策 plan; stratagem|巧～ artful plan; tactful scheme|缓兵之～ plan to gain a respite; stalling tactics|眉头一皱,～上心来。An idea comes to mind as soon as one knits the brows.|百年大～ project of lasting importance ❹ 做计划;打算 plan; intend; make a plan:设～ devise; design|为加强安全～,制定了工厂保卫条例。In order to tighten security, the factory has formulated security rules. ❺ 计较;考虑 give thought to; give consideration to:不～成败 give no thought to success or failure|无暇～及 have no time to think of ❹ (Jì)姓 a surname

【计策】jìcè 为对付某人或某种情势而预先安排的方法或策略 plan; scheme; method or stratagem adopted in advance to cope with a certain person or a certain situation

【计程车】jìchéngchē 〈方 *dial.*〉小型出租汽车 taxi

【计酬】jìchóu 计算报酬 remunerate; calculate payment:按劳～ pay according to work done

【计划】jìhuà ❶ 工作或行动以前预先拟定的具体内容和步骤 plan; programme or scheme for making, doing or arranging sth.:科研～ scientific research plan|五年～ Five-Year Plan ❷ 做计划 make a plan:先～一下再动手。Make a plan before (you) start.

【计划经济】jìhuà jīngjì 按照统一计划管理的国民经济 central planning; planned economy; national economy managed according to a unified plan

【计价】jìjià 计算价钱 price; valuate:～器 fee register|～标准 pricing criteria|按质～ pricing according to quality

【计件工资】jìjiàn gōngzī 按照生产的产品合格件数或完成的作业量来计算的工资 piece rate wage; payment calculated on the basis of a prescribed number of pieces of goods produced or of work done

【计较】jìjiào ❶ 计算比较 calculate and compare:斤斤～ be calculating; argue about every trifle, detail, ounce, etc.|他从不～个人的得失。He never gave any thought to personal gains or losses. ❷ 争论 argue; dispute:我不同你～,等你气平了再说。I won't argue with you for the moment. Let's wait and talk it over until you get calm. ❸ 打算;计议 intend; discuss:此事暂且不论,日后再作～。Leave it aside for the moment. We'll discuss it afterwards.

【计量】jìliàng ❶ 把一个暂时未知的量与一个已知的量做比较,如用尺量布,用体温计量体温 measure; calculate; compare an unknown quantity with a known quantity, e.g. using a ruler to measure cloth or a thermometer to measure temperature ❷ 计算 calculate:影响之大,是不可～的。The influence is inestimable.

【计谋】jìmóu 计策;策略 scheme; stratagem:有～ crafty; artful

【计日程功】jì rì chéng gōng 可以数着日子计算进度。形容在较短期间就可以成功。progress can be estimated by counting the number of days; have the completion of a project well in sight

【计时工资】jìshí gōngzī 按照劳动时间多少和技术熟练程度来计算的工资 time wage; payment calculated on the basis of work time and skill

【计数】jìshù 统计(数目);计算 count; calculate:不可～ countless|难以～ countless; difficult to count; too many to count

【计数】jì//shù 数(shǔ)事物的个数;统计数目 count the number of sth.:～器 counter|～单位 counting unit

【计数器】jìshùqì 能自动计数的仪器。种类很多,根据机械、光电、电磁等不同原理制成,在科学研究和生产技术中广泛应用。counter; instrument for automatic counting; different counters made on the basis of different principles of mechanics, photo-electricity and electromagnetism and widely used in scientific research and production

【计算】jìsuàn ❶ 根据已知数通过数学方法求得未知数 count; calculate; obtain an unknown number from a known number by mathematical method:～人数 count the number of people|～产值 calculate the output value ❷ 考虑;筹划 consider; plan:做事没个～,干到哪儿算哪儿。In the absence of a plan, we have no choice but to make shift and see what happens next. ❸ 暗中谋划损害别人 plot, scheme:当心被小人～。Beware of a villain's plot.

【计算尺】jìsuànchǐ 根据对数原理制成的一种辅助计算用的工具,由两个有刻度的尺构成,其中一个嵌在另一个尺的中间并能滑动,把两个尺上一定的刻度对准,即能直接求出运算的结果。应用于乘、除、乘方、开方、三角函数及对数等运算上。slide rule; supplementary tool for calculation made on the principle of logarithm, consisting of a ruler with a central sliding piece, both parts being marked with various number scales, used to find product, quotient, involution, square root, trignometric function, logarithm, etc. rapidly; also 算尺 suànchǐ

【计算机】jìsuànjī 能进行数学运算的机器。有的用机械装置做成，如手摇计算机；有的用电子元件做成，如电子计算机。computer; machine for performing mathematical operations, made either of mechanisms, such as a hand-operated computer, or of electronic components, such as an electronic computer

【计算机病毒】jìsuànjī bìngdú 计算机软件中故意设计来破坏正常程序的程序 computer virus; programme in the computer software designed to destroy the normal programme; also 电脑病毒 diànnǎo bìngdú

【计算中心】jìsuàn zhōngxīn 配备有通用电子计算机，进行各种类型科学计算、工程设计、数据处理等的服务机构 computing centre; service institution equipped with multi-purpose electronic computers for all types of scientific computations, project designing and data processing

【计议】jìyì 商议 discuss; deliberate; consult：从长～ take time to discuss it carefully; need careful consideration｜他们～着生产竞赛的办法。They are discussing the rules for an emulation campaign in production.

记 jì ❶ 把印象保持在脑子里 keep one's impression in mind; bear in mind; remember; memorize：～忆 memory; recollection｜～性 memory｜～得 remember｜～不清 can't remember it clearly｜好好～住 keep it in mind; bear it in mind; memorize it; commit to memory; learn by heart ❷ 记录；记载；登记 record; take notes; register; jot down：～事 record of facts; account of events; chronicle of events｜～账 keep accounts｜摘～ excerpts; extracts; take notes｜～一大功 record a major merit ❸ 记载、描写事物的书或文章（常用做书名或篇名 oft. used for the title of a book or an article) record; book or article describing events：日～ diary; daily record of events｜笔～ notes｜游～ travel notes｜《岳阳楼～》*Notes of Yueyang Tower* ❹（～儿 jìr）标志；符号 mark; symbol; sign：标～ sign; mark; symbol｜钤～ official seal; chop｜暗～儿 secret mark ❺ 皮肤上的生下来就有的深色的斑 birthmark; born dark-coloured spot on the skin：左边眉毛上有个黑～ a black birthmark on the left eyebrow ❻〈方 *dial.*〉〈量词 *classifier*〉（多用于某些动作的次数 number of certain action)：打一～耳光 a slap in the face; slap someone in the face; a slap on the cheek｜一～劲射，足球应声入网。A powerful kick sent the ball straight into the net.

【记仇】jì//chóu 把对别人的仇恨记在心里 bear grudges against; keep grudges against someone in mind：他这个人从来不～。He never bears grudges.｜我说了他几句，他就记了仇。I gave him some scolding, and he harboured bitter resentment.

【记得】jì·de 想得起来；没有忘掉 remember; not forget：他说的话我还～。I still remember what he said.｜这件事不～是在哪一年了。I don't remember in which year this incident occurred.

【记分】jì//fēn（～儿 jì//fēnr）记录工作、比赛、游戏中得到的分数 keep the score in a match or a game; record work points; record students' marks：～员 scorekeeper

【记工】jì//gōng 记录工作时间或工作量 record the work time or the amount of work

【记功】jì//gōng 登记功绩，作为一种奖励 register a merit as an award：～一次。A merit was registered.

【记挂】jìguà〈方 *dial.*〉惦念；挂念 miss; keep thinking of; be concerned about：好好养病，不要～厂里的事。Take good rest and nourishment to regain your health. Don't keep thinking of your work in the factory.

【记过】jì//guò 登记过失，作为一种处分 register a demerit as a punishment：记了一次过。A demerit was registered.

【记号】jì·hao 为引起注意，帮助识别、记忆而做成的标记 mark; sign; mark or sign that attracts one's attention or helps someone recognize or remember sth.：联络～ mark for contact｜有错别字的地方，请你做个～。Mark down if there is a wrongly written word.

【记恨】jì·hèn 把对别人的怨恨记在心里 bear grudges：～在心 bear grudges｜咱们俩谁也别～谁。The two of us should not bear each other any grudges.

【记录】jìlù ❶ 把听到的话或发生的事写下来 keep tabs on sth.; record; put down what is heard or what happens; take notes; keep the minutes：～在案 place sth. on record ❷ 当场记录下来的材料 minutes; notes：会议～ minutes of a meeting ❸ 做记录的人 note-taker：推举他当～。He was recommended as the note-taker. ❹ 在一定时期、一定范围以内记载下来的最高成绩 record; best result recorded at a specific time or on a specific occasion：打破～ break a record; smash a record｜创造新的世界～ set a new world record; create a new world record ‖ also 纪录 jìlù

【记录片儿】jìlùpiānr 记录片 documentary film; also 纪录片儿 jìlùpiānr

【记录片】jìlùpiàn 专门报道某一问题或事件的影片 documentary; documentary film; special film on a certain problem or a certain event; also 纪录片 jìlùpiàn

【记名】jìmíng 记载姓名，表明权利或责任的所在 registered; put down one's name to indicate one's right or responsibility：～证券 registered securities; inscribed securities｜无～投票 secret ballot

【记念】jìniàn same as 纪念 jìniàn

【记念】jì·niàn 惦记；挂念 be concerned about;

miss; keep thinking of:心里～着家乡的亲人 keep thinking of the relatives in one's homeland

【记取】jìqǔ 记住(教训、嘱咐等) remember; bear (keep) in mind (lesson, advice, etc.)

【记认】jìrèn ❶ 辨认 identify; recognize:她穿着一条黄裙子,最好～。She wears a yellow skirt and is easily recognizable.|这个字形体特别,容易～。This character is written in a strange form, and is easy to recognize. ❷〈方 *dial*.〉指便于记住和识别的标志 mark for easy identification:借来各家的椅子要做个～,将来不要还错了。The chairs borrowed from different families should be marked so that they will not be returned wrongly.

【记事】jì//shì ❶ 把事情记录下来 record; keep a record of:～册 notebook ❷ 记述历史经过 chronicle of historical events

【记事儿】jìshìr 指小孩儿对事物已经有记忆的能力 ability of children to begin to remember things:二十年前我跟妈妈到过上海,那时还不～,所以毫无印象。I was so young and didn't remember things when I went to Shanghai with my mother twenty years ago, so I have no impression at all.

【记述】jìshù 用文字叙述;记载 narrate; recount; record:～往事 account of past events|那篇文章对此事有翔实的～。That article gives a full and accurate account of the event.

【记诵】jìsòng 默记和背诵;熟读 commit to memory and be able to recite; learn by heart:他从小就～了许多古代诗文。He learnt many ancient poems and pieces of prose by heart.

【记性】jì·xing 记忆力 memory:～好 have a good memory|没～ have a poor (or short) memory

【记叙】jìxù 记述 narrate; narration:～文 narrative writing|～体 narrative style

【记叙文】jìxùwén 泛指记人、叙事、描写景物的文章 piece of writing narrating events or describing people or scenery; narrative writing

【记要】jìyào same as 纪要 jìyào

【记忆】jìyì ❶ 记住或想起 remember:小时候的事情有些还能～起来。I can still remember some of what happened in the childhood. ❷ 保持在脑子里的过去事物的印象 memory:～犹新 remain fresh in one's memory

【记忆力】jìyìlì 记住事物的形象或事情的经过的能力 memory; faculty of memory:～强 powerful (long, good, strong) memory|～弱 poor (short) memory

【记载】jìzǎi ❶ 把事情写下来 put down in writing; record:据实～ put down the facts; record the facts|回忆录～了当年的战斗历程。The memoirs have recorded the fighting course of those years. ❷ 记载事情的文章 record; account:我读过一篇当时写下的～。I've read an account written at that time.

【记者】jìzhě 通讯社、报刊、广播电台、电视台等采访新闻和写通讯报道的专职人员 journalist; reporter; correspondent; professional news writer in a news agency, newspaper, a radio and a television station

伎 jì ❶ same as 技 jì ❷〈古代 *arch*.〉称以歌舞为业的女子 professional female dancer or singer

【伎俩】jìliǎng 不正当的手段 illicit means; trick; manoeuvre; intrigue:骗人的～ deceptive trick

齐(齊) jì〈书 *fml*.〉❶ 调味品 seasonings; dressings; condiments; flavourings ❷ 合金 (此义今多读 oft. pronounced qí in this meaning) alloy

☞ qí on p.1508

纪[1] jì 纪律 discipline:军～ military discipline|政～ government discipline|风～ discipline; conduct and discipline|违法乱～ violate law and discipline

纪[2] jì ❶ 义同'记',主要用于'纪念、纪年、纪元、纪传'等,别的地方多用'记' [same as 记 jì, chiefly used in 纪念 jìniàn,纪年 jìnián,纪元 jìyuán,纪传 jìzhuàn, etc.; 记 jì is oft. used in other phrases] ❷〈古时 *arch*.〉以十二年为一纪,今指更长的时间 *ji*; 12 years were counted as one *ji* in ancient times, but it is longer today:世～ age; epoch; century|中世～ Middle Ages ❸ 地质年代分期的第三级。根据生物在地球上出现和进化的顺序划分。各纪延续的时间长短不同,如寒武纪延续了八千万年,侏罗纪延续了三千万年。跟纪相应的年代地层单位叫做系(xì)。period; third stage of geologic time divisions based on the sequence of the evolutionary stages in plant and animal development. The time differs from period to period, e.g., the Cambrian period lasted for 80,000,000 years and the Jurassic period lasted 30,000,000 years. The stratigraphic system corresponding to the period is called 系 xì.

☞ Jǐ on p.911

【纪纲】jìgāng〈书 *fml*.〉法度 law; rules and regulations

【纪检】jìjiǎn 纪律检查 discipline inspection:～工作 discipline inspection work

【纪录】jìlù same as 记录 jìlù

【纪录片儿】jìlùpiānr same as 记录片儿 jìlùpiānr

【纪录片】jìlùpiàn same as 记录片 jìlùpiàn

【纪律】jìlǜ 政党、机关、部队、团体、企业等为了维护集体利益并保证工作的正常进行而制定的要求每个成员遵守的规章、条文 rules, regulations and articles formulated by the political parties, government organs, army, organizations and enterprises to safeguard the collective interests and ensure the normal work order and obeyed by every member：～严明 highly disciplined；strictly disciplined；vigorously disciplined｜遵守～ obey discipline；observe discipline；keep discipline

【纪年】jìnián ❶ 记年代，如我国过去用干支纪年，从汉武帝到清末又兼用皇帝的年号纪年，公历纪年用传说的耶稣生年为第一年 way of numbering the years，e.g.，China designated the years by the Heavenly Stems and Earthly Branches in the past and the years of the reigns of the emperors simultaneously from Emperor Wu of the Han Dynasty（206 B.C.-A.D. 220）down to the end of the Qing Dynasty in 1911；years in the Gregorian calendar have been numbered with the birth year of Christ as the first year ❷ 史书体裁之一，依照年月先后排列历史事实，如《竹书纪年》form of writing historical records；chronological arrangement of events，such as the *Bamboo Annals*

【纪念】jìniàn ❶ 用事物或行动对人或事表示怀念 cherish the memory of some person or event by sth. or some action；commemorate：用实际行动～先烈 cherish the memory of the martyrs through concrete actions；commemorate the martyrs through concrete actions ❷ 用来表示纪念的（物品）commemorative；memorial：～品 commemorative articles｜～碑 monument｜～塔 memorial tower ❸ 纪念品 souvenir；keepsake：这张照片给你做个～吧。This photo (or picture) is for you as a keepsake. ‖ also 记念 jìniàn

【纪念碑】jìniànbēi 为纪念有功绩的人或重大事件而立的石碑 stone tablet erected to honour a merited person or an important event：人民英雄～ Monument to the People's Heroes

【纪念币】jìniànbì 为纪念重大事件、著名人物、珍贵物品而发行的一种特殊的货币。一般用金、银等贵重金属铸成。special coin issued to honour an important event，a noted person or a precious good，usually made of gold，silver or other precious metals

【纪念册】jìniàncè 有纪念性质的册子，多请人在上面题写文字 autograph book；autograph album，on which people present on an occasion are requested to write autographs

【纪念馆】jìniànguǎn 为纪念有卓越贡献的人或重大历史事件而建立的陈设实物、图片等的房屋 museum；memorial hall；building erected to display articles and photographs in memory of a distinguished person or an important historic event：鲁迅～ Lu Xun Museum｜南昌起义～ Nanchang Uprising Museum

【纪念品】jìniànpǐn 表示纪念的物品 souvenir；keepsake；memento；commemorative article

【纪念日】jìniànrì 发生过重大事情值得纪念的日子，如国庆日、中国共产党成立纪念日、国际劳动节 commemoration day；day to honour an important historic event，such as National Day，an anniversary of the founding of the Communist Party of China，International Labour Day

【纪念邮票】jìniàn yóupiào 邮政部门为纪念国内、国际上重要人物、重大事件或其他纪念性内容而发行的邮票 commemorative stamp；stamp issued by the posts administration to commemorate an important person at home or abroad，an important event or commemorative activities

【纪念章】jìniànzhāng 表示纪念的徽章 souvenir badge；pin

【纪实】jìshí ❶ 记录真实情况 record of actual events；on-the-spot report：～文学 investigative literature；reportage ❷ 指记录真实情况的文字（多用于标题 mostly used for titles）writing recording an actual event：《植树活动～》'Record of Tree Planting Activities'

【纪事】jìshì ❶ 记录事实 record of facts：～诗 narrative poem ❷ 记载某些事迹、史实的文字（多用于书名 mostly used for book titles）writings that record certain events and historical facts：《唐诗～》*Records on Tang Poetry*

【纪事本末体】jìshìběnmòtǐ 我国传统史书的一种体裁，以重要事件为纲，自始至终有系统地把它记载下来。创始于南宋袁枢的《通鉴纪事本末》。form of traditional Chinese historical writing in which every chapter is dedicated to the systematic recording of a particular historic event from beginning to end，first introduced by Yuan Shu in the Southern Song Dynasty（1127-1279）in his *Topically Arranged Chronological Mirror for Aid in Government*

【纪行】jìxíng 记载旅行见闻的文字、图画（多用于标题 mostly used for titles）travelogue；writings and photographs recording what is seen and heard during travels；travel notes：《延安～》*Travelogue on Yan'an*

【纪要】jìyào 记录要点的文字 summary；writings recording the main points；summary of minutes：新闻～ news summary｜会谈～ summary of talks；also 记要 jìyào

【纪元】jìyuán 纪年的开始，如公历以传说的耶稣出生那一年为元年 era；epoch；beginning of an era，e.g.，the Gregorian calendar adopted the birth year of Christ as its first year

【纪传体】jìzhuàntǐ 我国传统史书的一种体裁，主要以人物传记为中心，叙述当时的史实。'纪'是帝王本纪，列在全书的前面，'传'是其他人物的列传。创始于汉代司马迁的《史记》。form of writing traditional historical records in China，mainly centred on biographies narrating the historical facts of the times. 纪 jì are the biographical sketches of emperors arranged at the beginning of the book，followed by 传 zhuàn, the biographies of other people. The first of its kind was *Records of the Historian*, created by Sima Qian in the Han Dynasty (206 B.C.-A.D.220).

芰 jì 古书上指菱 ancient name for water caltrop

技 jì 技能;本领 skill; ability; trick: ~术 skill; technique|~巧 skill; trick; technique; craftsmanship|绝~ superb skill; superb craftsmanship; unique skill; consummate skill|黔驴~穷 Guizhou donkey at the end of its tether; one who has exposed his limited ability; from the story of a donkey brought to Guizhou which first frightened a tiger but was immediately overpowered when the latter discovered its real ability|无所施其~ no place for displaying one's skill

【技法】jìfǎ 技巧和方法 skill and technique: 雕塑~ sculpture; art of carving wood, chiselling stone, casting metal, moulding clay or wax, etc. into three-dimensional representations, as statues, figurines, forms, etc.|~纯熟 consummate skill; perfect skill

【技工】jìgōng 有专门技术的工人 worker with a special skill; skilled worker

【技工学校】jìgōng xuéxiào 培养某种专业技术工人的中等学校 secondary technical school; secondary school for training workers in certain trades and industries; 简称 abbr. 技校 jìxiào

【技击】jìjī 用于搏斗的武术 art of attack and defence; martial art; *wushu* adapted to man-to-man combat: 精于~ have a good mastery of attack and defence skills

【技能】jìnéng 掌握和运用专门技术的能力 ability to grasp and use special skills; technical ability: 基本~ basic skills|~低下 poor technical ability

【技巧】jìqiǎo ❶ 表现在艺术、工艺、体育等方面的巧妙的技能 skill; technique; craftsmanship; ingenious skill displayed in arts, art crafts, sports, etc.: 运用~ use techniques or skills|绘画~ painting technique|熟练的~ good skill; consummate skill ❷ 指技巧运动: ~比赛 acrobatic gymnastics competition

【技巧运动】jìqiǎo yùndòng 体操运动项目之一。动作以翻腾、抛接、造型等为主,并配有徒手操和舞蹈动作,有单人、双人、三人、四人等项。acrobatic gymnastics; sport event whose movements include somersault, tossing and receiving, forming patterns, etc. as well as bare-handed exercises and dancing movements, including singles, pairs, trios, quartets etc.

【技师】jìshī 技术人员的职称之一,相当于初级工程师或高级技术员的技术人员 technician; one of the technical titles for technicians, equivalent to a junior engineer or a senior technician

【技士】jìshì 技术人员的职称之一,低于工程师 one of the technical titles for technicians; title lower than engineer

【技术】jìshù ❶ 人类在利用自然和改造自然的过程中积累起来并在生产劳动中体现出来的经验和知识,也泛指其他操作方面的技巧 technology; technique; skill; experience and knowledge accumulated in the course of utilizing and transforming nature and displayed in production and work; (in a broad sense) skills in operations: 钻研~ perfect one's skill; master technique|~先进 technologically advanced ❷ 指技术装备 technology; technological equipment: ~改造 technical transformation; technological transformation

【技术革命】jìshù gémìng 指生产技术上的根本变革,例如从用体力、畜力生产改为用蒸汽做动力生产,用手工工具生产改为用机器生产 technological revolution; fundamental change in production and technology, such as the replacement of physical labour and animals with steam power and the replacement of hand tools with machines in production

【技术革新】jìshù géxīn 指生产技术上的改进,如工艺规程、机器部件等的改进 technical innovation; technological innovation; technical improvement in production, such as the improvement of a technical process, a machine part, etc.; also 技术改革 jìshù gǎigé

【技术科学】jìshù kēxué 应用科学 applied science

【技术性】jìshùxìng 有关技术方面的 technical; related to technique; of a technical nature: ~问题 technical matters|这种工作,~要求较高。This job is highly technical.

【技术学校】jìshù xuéxiào 培养某种专业技术人员的中等学校,如铁路技术学校、邮电技术学校 technical school; secondary school for training technicians in certain trades, such as railway technical school, posts and telecommunications technical school; 简称 abbr. 技校 jìxiào

【技术员】jìshùyuán 技术人员的职称之一,在工程师的指导下,能够完成一定技术任务的技术人员 technician; title for technicians; technician who can fulfil certain technical assignments under the guidance of an engineer

【技术装备】jìshù zhuāngbèi 生产上用的各种机械、仪器、仪表、工具等设备 technical equipment; technological equipment; equipment used in production, including machines, instruments, meters, tools, etc.

【技术作物】jìshù zuòwù 经济作物 industrial crops; cash crops

【技校】jìxiào 技术学校和技工学校的简称 abbr. for 技术学校 jìshù xuéxiào or 技工学校 jìgōng xuéxiào

【技痒】jìyǎng 有某种技能的人遇到机会时极想

施展 itch for action, esp. in the case of a person with a special skill and an urge to exercise his skill when he has a chance: 他看别人打球,不觉～。He itched to have a try when he saw people playing basketball.

【技艺】jìyì 富于技巧性的表演艺术或手艺 artistry; skill: ～高超 highly skilled | 精湛的～ perfect skill; superb skill

系(繫) jì 打结;扣 tie; fasten; button up; tie up; do up: ～鞋带 tie shoe laces | ～着围裙 wear a kitchen apron | 把领扣儿～上 button up your collar ☞ xì on p.2057

忌 jì ❶ 忌妒 be jealous of; jealousy; envy: ～刻 jealous and acrid | 猜～ be suspicious and jealous of ❷ 怕 fear; dread; scruple: 顾～ scruple; misgiving | ～惮 scruple; fear; dread ❸ 认为不适宜而避免 avoid; shun; abstain from: ～嘴 avoid certain food (when ill) | ～生冷 avoid uncooked and cold food ❹ 戒除 give up: ～烟 give up smoking; quit smoking | ～酒 give up alcohol; abstain from wine

【忌辰】jìchén 先辈去世的日子(旧俗这一天忌举行宴会或从事娱乐,所以叫忌辰) death anniversary; anniversary of the death of a parent, ancestor, or anyone else held in esteem (according to an old custom, no banquet or entertainment should be arranged on this day)

【忌惮】jìdàn 〈书 *fml.*〉顾忌;畏惧 scruple; fear; dread: 肆无～ have no scruples; without any scruple

【忌妒】jì·du 对才能、名誉、地位或境遇等比自己好的人心怀怨恨 resentment or grudge against someone who has better ability, reputation, position or circumstances: ～心 jealousy; envy | ～人 be jealous of someone

【忌讳】jì·huì ❶ 因风俗习惯或个人理由等,对某些言语或举动有所顾忌,积久成为禁忌 taboo; misgivings about some words or actions for customs, habits or personal reason: 过年过节～说不吉利的话。Inauspicious words are banned when celebrating the New Year or a festival. ❷ 对某些可能产生不利后果的事力求避免 avoid sth. for fear of its possible bad consequences: 在学习上,最～的是有始无终。The first taboo in study is to start something without carrying it through. ❸ 〈方 *dial.*〉指醋 vinegar

【忌刻】jìkè 对人忌妒刻薄 jealous and acrid; jealous and mean; jealous and malicious; also 忌克 jìkè

【忌口】jì//kǒu 因有病或其他原因忌吃不相宜的食品 be on a diet; avoid certain food (as when one is ill or for some other reason); also 忌嘴 jì//zuǐ

【忌日】jìrì ❶ 忌辰 anniversary of the death of a parent, ancestor or anyone else held in esteem ❷ 迷信的人指不宜做某事的日子 (superstition) day when sth. should be avoided

【忌嘴】jì//zuǐ same as 忌口 jì//kǒu

际(際) jì ❶ 靠边的或分界的地方 border; boundary; edge: 边～ limit; boundary; margin | 分～ mark a boundary | 天～ horizon | 一望无～ boundless; stretch as far as one can see; spread from horizon to horizon ❷ 里边;中间 inside: 脑～ in one's mind | 胸～ in one's heart; in one's mind ❸ 彼此之间 between; among: 国～ international | 星～旅行 interplanetary travel ❹ 时候 occasion: 正当革命胜利之～ on the occasion of the victory of the revolution ❺ 正当(指时机、境遇) on the occasion of: ～此盛会 on the occasion of this grand gathering ❻ 遭遇 one's lot; circumstances: 遭～ one's lot | ～遇 opportunity

【际会】jìhuì 际遇;遇合 opportunity; chance: 风云～ gathering of heroes or talented people

【际涯】jìyá 〈书 *fml.*〉边际 boundary; limit: 渺无～ boundless

【际遇】jìyù 〈书 *fml.*〉遭遇(多指好的) opportunity; luck

妓 jì 妓女 prostitute: 娼～ prostitute; whore; streetwalker | 狎～ visit a brothel; patronize a prostitute

【妓女】jìnǚ 以卖淫为业的女人 prostitute; whore; streetgirl; woman who sells sexual favour for money

【妓院】jìyuàn 妓女卖淫的处所 brothel

季 jì ❶ 一年分春夏秋冬四季,一季三个月 season; year is divided into four seasons: spring, summer, autumn and winter; a season has three months ❷ (～儿 jìr) 季节 season: 雨～ rainy season | 旺～ brisk season | 西瓜～儿 watermelon season ❸ 指一个时期的末了 end of a period: 清～(清朝末年) last years of the Qing Dynasty | ～世 declining years of a dynasty; years of decadence ❹ 指一季的第三个月 third month of a season: ～春 third month of spring; ☞ 孟 mèng on p. 1327 and 仲 zhòng on p. 2491 ❺ 在弟兄排行里代表第四或最小的 fourth or the youngest brother: 伯仲叔～ the first, second, third and fourth brothers | ～弟 fourth or youngest brother ❻ (Jì) 姓 a surname

【季度】jìdù 以一季为单位时称为季度 quarter: ～预算 quarterly budget | 这本书预定在第二～出版。This book will come off the press in the second quarter.

【季风】jìfēng 随季节而改变风向的风,主要是海洋和陆地间温度差异造成的。冬季由大陆吹向海洋,夏季由海洋吹向大陆。monsoon; wind which changes its direction from season to season, mainly due to temperature difference between the sea and the land blowing from the land to the sea in winter and from the sea to the land in summer

【季风气候】jìfēng qìhòu 指受季风影响较显著的地区的气候。特点是夏季受海洋气流影响，高温多雨，冬季受大陆气流影响，低温干燥。monsoon climate; climate in areas heavily affected by monsoons, which is characterized by high temperature and rainfalls arising from the air current from the sea in summer and low temperature and dryness arising from the air current from the land in winter

【季候】jìhòu〈方 *dial.*〉季节 season：隆冬～ mid-winter season

【季节】jìjié 一年里的某个有特点的时期 characteristic period of the year：～性 seasonal｜农忙～ busy farming season｜严寒～ cold season

【季节工】jìjiégōng 因季节性的需要而雇用的临时工 seasonal worker

【季节洄游】jìjié huíyóu 海洋中某些鱼类每年春夏两季随暖流北游，秋冬两季随寒流南游，这种现象叫季节洄游 seasonal migration; phenomenon in which some sea fishes migrate to the north with the warm current in spring and summer and to the south with the cold current in autumn and winter

【季军】jìjūn 体育运动等竞赛中的第三名 third place winner in a sports competition

【季刊】jìkān 每季出版一次的刊物 quarterly; quarterly publication

【季世】jìshì〈书 *fml.*〉末世；末叶 declining years of a dynasty：殷周～ declining years of the Yin and Zhou dynasties (12th century B.C.-2nd century B.C.)

剂(劑) jì ❶ 药剂；制剂 pharmaceutical preparation or other chemical preparation：针～ injection｜麻醉～ anaesthesia; narcotic ❷ 指某些起化学作用或物理作用的物质 substance which produces a chemical or physical action：杀虫～ insecticide｜冷冻～ coolant ❸（～儿 jìr）剂子 small pieces of dough：面～儿 small cut pieces of dough ❹〈量词 *classifier*〉用于若干味药配合起来的汤药 dose; decoction of medicinal ingredients：一～药 a dose of medicine; also 服 fù

【剂量】jìliàng 医学上指药品的使用分量。也指化学试剂和用于治疗的放射线等的用量。dosage; exact amount of medicine given or taken at one time; amount of chemical reagent and of radiation delivered to a given part of the body

【剂型】jìxíng 药物制成的形状，例如片状、丸状、膏状等 form of a drug (e.g. pill, bolus, plaster, etc.)

【剂子】jì·zi 做馒头、饺子等的时候，从和好了的长条形的面上分出来的小块儿 small pieces cut from a long strip of dough for making dumplings and buns

垍 jì〈书 *fml.*〉坚硬的土 hard soil; hard clay

荠(薺) jì 指荠菜 shepherd's purse; edible wild plant：其甘如～ as sweet as the shepherd's purse

☞ qí on p.1511

【荠菜】jìcài 一年或多年生草本植物，叶子羽状分裂，裂片有缺刻，花白色。嫩叶可以吃。全草入药。shepherd's purse (*Capsella bursa-pastoris*); annual or perennial herb having pinnate and incised leaves and white flowers, its tender leaves being edible and the whole plant useful as a traditional Chinese medicine

哜(嚌) jì〈书 *fml.*〉尝(滋味) taste

【哜哜嘈嘈】jì·jicáocáo〈拟声词 *onom.*〉形容说话声音又急又乱 jabber：屋里面～，不知他们在说些什么。They are jabbering in the room, and you don't know what they are talking about.

迹(跡、蹟) jì ❶ 留下的印子；痕迹 mark; trace：足～ footprint; footmark｜血～ blood stain｜笔～ handwriting｜踪～ trace ❷ 前人遗留的事物(主要指建筑或器物) remains; ruins; vestige：古～ site of historical interest｜陈～ thing of the past｜事～ deed; achievement｜史～ historical site; historical relics ❸ 形迹 movements and expression; act; outward sign; indication：～近违抗(行动近乎违背、抗拒上级指示) act verging on defying an order from the higher authorities

【迹地】jìdì 林业上指采伐之后还没重新种树的土地 slash (in forest land); land without planting new trees after felling

【迹象】jìxiàng 指表露出来的不很显著的情况，可借以推断事物的过去或将来 sign; indication; sth. which is not very clearly shown but can indicate what has happened or what is going to happen：～可疑 signs arouse suspicion｜从～看，这事不像是他做的。Signs show that he is not likely to do it.

洎 jì〈书 *fml.*〉到；及 up to (a point or a period of time)：自古～今 from ancient times up to now, since ancient times｜～乎近世 until recent time

济(濟) jì ❶ 过河；渡 cross a river：同舟共～ in the same boat ❷ 救；救济 aid; relieve; help：接～ give money to; give material (financial) help to｜缓不～急。Slow action cannot save a critical situation. ❸(对事情)有益；成 be of help; benefit：无～于事 be of no help; be no good; of no avail; to no avail; to no effect｜假公～私 use public office for personal gain

☞ Jǐ on p.911

【济贫】jìpín 救济贫苦的人 help the poor; relieve the poor：赈灾～ relieve the poor people in a disaster-stricken area

【济世】jìshì 救济世人 benefit mankind; do good to society:行医～ practise medicine to benefit mankind; practise medicine to help people|～安民 benefit society and pacify the people

【济事】jìshì 能成事;中用(多用于否定 usu. used in the negative) be of help (or use):人多了浪费,人少了不～。Too many people are a waste; too few people are of no help.

既 jì ❶ 已经 already:～成事实 *fait accompli*; fact already accomplished; *de facto*; accomplished fact|～得利益 vested interest|～往不咎 let bygones be bygones; forgive someone's past deeds; no postmortems ❷ 既然 since; now that:～来之,则安之。Since you are already here, please stay and make yourself at home.|～要当运动员,就要刻苦训练。Now that you are a sportsman, you should train hard. ❸〈书 *fml*.〉完了;尽 finished; be over:食～ finish a meal ❹〈连词 *conj*.〉跟'且、又、也'等副词呼应,表示两种情况兼而有之 [used correlatively with the adverbs 且 qiě,又 yòu,也 yě, etc. to show both situations are available] both ... and ...; as well as:～高且大 tall and big|～聪明又用功 both clever and hardworking|～要有周密的计划,也要有切实的措施。There should be a well-prepared plan—plus feasible measures.

【既而】jì'ér〈书 *fml*.〉〈时间副词 *adv. of time*〉用在全句或下半句的头上,表示上文所说的情况或动作发生之后不久 [used at the beginning of a complete sentence or the latter half of a sentence to show soon after the occurrence described in the preceding paragraph]:～雨霁,欣然登山。The rain having stopped, we started climbing up the mountain in high spirits.

【既然】jìrán〈连词 *conj*.〉用在上半句话里,下半句话里往往用副词'就、也、还'跟它呼应,表示先提出前提,而后加以推论 [for use in the first half of a sentence; used correlatively with 就 jiù,也 yě, and 还 hái when appearing in the latter half of the sentence to show that a premise is followed by an inference] since; as; now that:～知道做错了,就应当赶快纠正。Since you know you've made a mistake, you should correct it immediately.|你～一定要去,我也不便阻拦。Since you insist on going, I am not in a position to stop you.

【既是】jìshì 既然 since; as; now that:～他不愿意,那就算了吧。Since he doesn't want to do it, he doesn't need to.

【既往不咎】jì wǎng bù jiù 对过去的错误不再责备 forgive someone's past misdeeds; not censure someone for his past misdeeds; also 不咎既往 bù jiù jì wǎng

【既望】jìwàng〈书 *fml*.〉指望日的次日,通常指农历每月十六日 day following the full moon; 16th day of a lunar month

勣 jì〈书 *fml*.〉功绩 merit; achievement

觊(覬) jì〈书 *fml*.〉希望;希图 wish to; covet

【觊觎】jìyú〈书 *fml*.〉希望得到(不应该得到的东西) wish to get (what one should not get); covet

继(繼) jì ❶ 继续;接续 continue; follow; succeed:～任 succeed someone to a position (in a post)|中～线 main line; trunk line|前赴后～ advance wave upon wave; one steps into the breach as another falls|相～落成 be completed one after another ❷ 继而 then; afterwards:初感头晕,～又吐泻 feel dizzy and then begin vomiting and diarrhoea

【继承】jìchéng ❶ 依法承受(死者的遗产等) inherit (legacy of the dead, etc.):～权 right of inheritance; right of succession; right to inherit; right to succeed|～人 heir; inheritor; successor ❷ 泛指把前人的作风、文化、知识等接受过来 carry on; carry forward:～优良传统 carry forward the fine traditions; uphold the fine traditions|～文化遗产 inherit the cultural legacy ❸ 后人继续做前人遗留下来的事业 carry on the lifework of the deceased:～先烈的遗业 carry on the work (cause) left behind by the martyrs

【继承权】jìchéngquán 依法或遵遗嘱承受死者遗产等的权利 right to inherit the property of the deceased according to law or the will; right of inheritance; right of succession

【继承人】jìchéngrén ❶ 依法或遵遗嘱继承遗产等的人 heir; inheritor; person who inherits or is legally entitled to inherit, through the natural action of the law, another's property upon the other's death; anyone who receives property of a deceased person either by will or by law ❷ 君主国家中指定或依法继承王位的人 person who is entitled to succeed to the throne either by appointment or by law in a monarchy:王位～ successor to the throne

【继而】jì'ér〈副词 *adv*.〉表示紧随着某一情况或动作之后 then; afterwards:人们先是一惊,～哄堂大笑。The people were first surprised, but then the whole room burst into laughter.|先是领唱的一个人唱,～全体跟着一起唱。The leading singer soloed first, then the others joined in.

【继父】jìfù 妇女带着子女再嫁,再嫁的丈夫是她原有的子女的继父 stepfather; woman is remarried with her children, and the new husband is the stepfather of her children

【继母】jìmǔ 男子已有子女后续娶,续娶的妻子是他原有的子女的继母 stepmother; man having his own children is remarried, and the new wife is the stepmother of his original children

【继配】jìpèi 指在元配死后续娶的妻子 second wife (taken after the death of one's first wife); also 继室 jìshì

【继任】jìrèn 接替前任职务 succeed sb. in a post

【继室】jìshì same as 继配 jìpèi

【继嗣】jìsì〈书 *fml.*〉❶ 过继 adopt a son ❷ 继承者 heir

【继往开来】jì wǎng kāi lái 继承前人的事业，并为将来开辟道路 carry forward the cause of the predecessors and forge ahead into the future

【继武】jìwǔ〈书 *fml.*〉接上前面的足迹 follow the footsteps of;〈比喻 *fig.*〉继续前人的事业 carry on the unfinished work of one's predecessor

【继续】jìxù ❶（活动）连下去；延长下去；不间断 continue; go on: ～不停 nonstop; without a break|～工作 continue with one's work|大雨～了三昼夜。It kept raining heavily for three days and nights. *or* It rained heavily for three days and nights. ❷ 跟某一事有连续关系的另一事 be follow-through on sth.; continuation: 中国革命是伟大的十月革命的～。The Chinese revolution is a continuation of the great October Revolution.

【继子】jìzǐ ❶ 过继来的儿子 adopted son ❷ 后夫或后妻原有的儿子 stepson

偈 jì 佛经中的唱词 gatha; sloka; librettor in Buddhist scripture [偈陀之省，梵 abbreviation of 偈陀 jìtuó, Sanskrit: gatha, 颂 sòng]

☞ jié on p. 994

徛 jì〈方 *dial.*〉站立 stand

祭 jì ❶ 祭祀 perform a memorial service for: ～坛 sacrificial altar|～祖宗 offer sacrifices to ancestors ❷ 祭奠 offer a sacrifice to: 公～死难烈士 hold a public memorial ceremony for the martyrs ❸ 使用（法宝）wield (a magic wand)

☞ Zhài on p. 2408

【祭奠】jìdiàn 为死去的人举行仪式，表示追念 hold a memorial ceremony for the deceased: ～英灵 hold a memorial ceremony for the martyrs

【祭礼】jìlǐ ❶ 祭祀或祭奠的仪式 sacrificial rites; memorial ceremony ❷ 祭祀或祭奠用的礼品 sacrificial offerings

【祭祀】jì·sì〈旧俗 *old*〉备供品向神佛或祖先行礼，表示崇敬并求保佑 offer sacrifices to gods or ancestors in reverence and for blessings

【祭坛】jìtán 祭祀用的台 sacrificial altar

【祭文】jìwén 祭祀或祭奠时对神或死者朗读的文章 funeral oration; elegiac address

【祭灶】jì//zào〈旧俗 *old*〉腊月二十三或二十四日祭灶神 offer sacrifices to the Kitchen God on the 23rd or 24th of the 12th lunar month

悸 jì〈书 *fml.*〉因害怕而心跳得厉害 throb with terror; palpitate: ～动 palpitate with terror; palpitate from nervousness|惊～ palpitate with fear|心有余～ have a lingering fear

寄 jì ❶ 原指托人递送，现在专指通过邮局递送 post; mail; send by mail: ～信 send a letter; post a letter; mail a letter|～钱 remit money; send money by mail|包裹已经～走了。The parcel has been sent by post. ❷ 付托；寄托 entrust; deposit; place: ～存 deposit; check; leave with|赋诗～怀 compose a poem to express one's feelings|～希望于青年 place hope on the youth ❸ 依附别人；依附别的地方 depend on; attach oneself to: ～食 live at sb. else's expenses|～居 live temporarily with sb.|～人篱下 live under sb. else's roof ❹ 认的（亲属）adopted: ～父 adopted father|～母 adopted mother|～儿 adopted son|～女 adopted daughter

【寄存】jìcún 寄放 deposit; check; leave with: 小件行李～处 left-luggage office; checkroom|把大衣～在衣帽间 check one's overcoat at the cloakroom

【寄存器】jìcúnqì 电子计算机中用来在操作时暂时存储信息的部件 computer register; computer part for storing information temporarily during operation

【寄递】jìdì 邮局递送邮件 deliver mails

【寄放】jìfàng 把东西暂时付托给别人保管 leave with; leave in the care of: 把箱子～在朋友家 leave a suitcase with a friend

【寄费】jìfèi 邮资 postage

【寄籍】jìjí 指长期离开本籍，居住外地，附于外地的籍贯（区别于'原籍' as compared with 'native place'）live away from one's birthplace

【寄居】jìjū 住在他乡或别人家里 live away from home: ～青岛 live in Qingdao|她从小就～在外祖父家里。She lived with her maternal grandfather from childhood.

【寄卖】jìmài 委托代为出卖物品或受托代卖 put up goods for sale in a secondhand shop; consign goods for sale on commission: ～行 consignment shop|收音机放在信托商店里～ put a radio set on sale in a commission shop; also 寄售 jìshòu

【寄名】jìmíng〈旧俗 *old*〉叫幼童认僧尼为师或认他人为义父母，以求长寿，叫做寄名 become sb.'s foster child; become apprenticed to a monk or nun without tonsuring

【寄情】jìqíng 寄托情怀 give expression to one's feelings; express one's feelings: ～山水 express one's feelings for the scenery

【寄人篱下】jì rén lí xià〈比喻 *fig.*〉依靠别人过活 live under another's roof; depend on sb. for a living

【寄生】jìshēng ❶ 一种生物生活在另一种生物

的体内或体表，并从寄主取得养分，维持生活。如动物中的蛔虫、蛲虫、跳蚤、虱子；植物中的菟丝子。parasitism; plant or animal that lives on or in an organism of another species from which it derives sustenance or protection without benefit to, and usu. with harmful effects, on the host, such as roundworm, pinworm, flea, louse among animals, and Chinese dodder among plants ❷ 指自己不劳动而靠剥削别人生活 parasitic; living at the expense of others：～阶级 parasitic classes｜～生活 parasitic life

【寄生虫】jìshēngchóng ❶ 寄生在别的动物或植物体内或体表的动物，如跳蚤、虱子、蛔虫、姜片虫、小麦线虫。寄生虫从寄主取得养分，有的并能传染疾病，对寄主有害。parasite; animal that lives on or in an animal of another species or a plant, such as flea, louse, roundworm, fasciolopsiasis, wheat nematode. Parasites derive sustenance from their hosts, and some even cause infection to the hosts, usu. with harmful effects on the hosts. ❷〈比喻 *fig.*〉能劳动而不劳动、依靠剥削为生的人 hanger-on; parasite; person who lives at the expense of others without making any useful contribution in return

【寄售】jìshòu same as 寄卖 jìmài

【寄宿】jìsù ❶ 借宿 lodge：我暂时～在一个朋友家里。I lodge at a friend's house for the time being. ❷（学生）在学校宿舍里住宿（区别于'走读' as compared with students travelling between school and home）boarding（student）：～生 boarding student｜～学校 boarding school

【寄宿生】jìsùshēng 在学校宿舍里住宿的学生 boarding student; resident student; boarder

【寄托】jìtuō ❶ 托付 entrust to the care of sb. else; leave with sb.：把孩子～在邻居家里 entrust one's child or pet to the care of a neighbour ❷ 把理想、希望、感情等放在（某人身上或某种事物上）place（ideal, hope, feeling, etc.）on; find sustenance in：～哀思 give expression to one's grief｜作者把自己的思想、情感～在剧中主人公身上。The writer concentrated his own thoughts and feelings on the hero in the play.

【寄养】jìyǎng 托付给别人抚养或饲养 entrust one's child or pet to the care of sb. else; ask sb. to bring up one's child or to take care of one's pet：她从小～在姑母家。She was left from childhood in the care of her aunt.｜我出门这几天，把猫～在邻居家里。I put my cat under the care of a neighbour during the days when I was away.

【寄予】jìyǔ ❶ 寄托 place（hope, etc.）on：国家对于青年一代～极大的希望。The country places great hope on the youth. ❷ 给予（同情、关怀等）show（sympathy, solicitude, etc.）; give; express：～无限同情 show boundless sympathy to‖also 寄与 jìyǔ

【寄寓】jìyù〈书 *fml.*〉❶寄居 lodge at：～他乡 live in a place other than one's homeland ❷ same as 寄托 jìtuō ②：小说～着作者对劳动人民的深切同情。The novel gives expression to the author's sympathy for the working people.

【寄主】jìzhǔ 寄生物所寄生的生物，例如人就是蛔虫的寄主 host（of a parasite）; plant or animal on which the parasite lives, e.g. humans as the host of roundworms; also 宿主 sùzhǔ

寂 jì ❶ 寂静 quiet; silent; still：沉～ quiet｜～寥 solitary and lonesome｜～无一人 quiet and deserted｜万籁俱～。All is quiet and still. ❷ 寂寞 lonely; lonesome; solitary：枯～ dull and lonely｜孤～ solitary and still

【寂静】jìjìng 没有声音；很静 quiet; still; silent：～无声 quiet and still

【寂寥】jìliáo〈书 *fml.*〉寂静；空旷 solitary and lonesome; still, lonely; desolate

【寂寞】jìmò ❶ 孤单冷清 lonely; lonesome：晚上只剩下我一个人在家里，真是～。I was the only person left in the house. How lonely I was. ❷ 清静；寂静 quiet; still; silent：～的原野 quiet open country; quiet field

【寂然】jìrán〈书 *fml.*〉形容寂静的样子 silent; still; quiet

绩 jì ❶ 把麻纤维披开接续起来搓成线 split the hemp fibre and twist it into thread：纺～ spin｜～麻 spin hemp ❷ 功业；成果 achievement; accomplishment：成～ results｜功～ achievement; merits｜劳～ merits and accomplishments｜战～ military successes, military exploits

【绩效】jìxiào 成绩；成效 results：～显著 notable results

惎 jì〈书 *fml.*〉❶ 怨恨；忌刻 grudge; resentment; jealous and acrid ❷ 教；指点 teach; instruct

塈 jì〈书 *fml.*〉❶ 涂屋顶 paint the roof ❷ 休息 take a rest; rest ❸ 取 take

蓟[1] jì ☞ 大蓟 dàjì on p.357

蓟[2] Jì 古地名，在今北京城西南，曾为周朝燕国国都 Ji, geographical name of an ancient place to the southwest of the present-day Beijing, once the capital city of the State of Yan in the Zhou Dynasty（11th century B.C.- 3rd century B.C.）

霁（霽） jì〈书 *fml.*〉❶ 雨后或雪后转晴 clear up after rain or snow：雪～。It's stopped snowing and is clearing up.｜光风～月 clear moon and light breeze after a rain; like a light breeze and a clear moon-open and above board; open-hearted and above board ❷ 怒气消散 calm down after being angry：色～ calm down after losing temper｜～颜 calm down after a fit of anger; appear mollified

跽 jì〈书 *fml.*〉双膝着地，上身挺直 kneel on the ground with the torso straight

穊 jì〈书 *fml.*〉稠密 dense：深耕～种 deep ploughing and close planting

鲚（鱭） jì 鱼，体侧扁，长约 3—4 寸，无侧线，头小而尖，尾尖而细。生活在海洋中，春季或初夏到河中产卵。anchovy（*Engraulis mordax*）; long-tailed anchovy; fish about three to four *cun* long, with a flat body, small head and pointed tail, living in the sea and spawning in the rivers in spring or early summer; 通称 generally called 凤尾鱼 fèngwěiyú

漈 jì〈书 *fml.*〉水边 waterside

暨 jì ❶〈书 *fml.*〉和；及；与 and ❷〈书 *fml.*〉到；至 up to; till：～今 up to now; till today ❸（Jì）姓 a surname

稷 jì ❶〈古代 *arch.*〉称一种粮食作物，有的书说是黍一类的作物，有的书说是谷子（粟）millet; grain crop in ancient times; some books say it is broomcorn millet, some books say it is millet ❷〈古代 *arch.*〉以稷为百谷之长，因此帝王奉祀为谷神 millet was the foremost of all cereals in ancient times, and emperors worshipped it as the God of Grains：社～ country; state; God of the Land and the God of Grains

鲫 jì 鲫鱼，体侧扁，头部尖，中部高，尾部较窄，生活在淡水中，是常见的食用鱼 crucian carp（*Carassius auratus*）; common food fish with a laterally flat body, a pointed head, a narrow tail and a big belly; it lives in fresh water

髻 jì 在头顶或脑后盘成各种形状的头发 hair coiled in various forms and worn on the top or back of the head：发～ bun; knot｜抓～ one of the twisted knots of hair on either side of the head｜蝴蝶儿～ bow knot; butterfly-shaped hair bun

冀¹ jì〈书 *fml.*〉希望；希图 hope; long for; look forward to：希～ hope for; wish for｜～求 seek for; hanker after｜～盼 look forward to｜～其成功 look forward to the success of sb. or sth.

冀² Jì ❶ 河北的别称 another name for Hebei Province ❷ 姓 a surname

【冀图】jìtú 希图 try to; long for：～东山再起 hope for a comeback

【冀望】jìwàng〈书 *fml.*〉希望 hope for; long for

穄 jì 穄子 similar to millet

【穄子】jì·zi ❶ 一年生草本植物，形状跟黍子相似，但子实不黏 broom corn millet（*Panicum miliaceum*），annual herb which looks like millet but is not glutinous ❷ 这种植物的子实 its grains ‖ also 糜子 méi·zí

罽 jì〈书 *fml.*〉用毛做成的毡子一类的东西 sth. like a woollen felt：～帐 felt tent｜～幕 felt curtain

鳖 jì ☞ 白鳖豚 báijìtún on p. 34

檵 jì［檵木］（jìmù）常绿灌木或小乔木，叶子椭圆形或卵圆形，花淡黄色，结蒴果，褐色。枝条和叶子可以提制栲胶，种子可以榨油。Chinese loropetalum（*Loropetalum chinense*），evergreen shrub or small arbor with oval or egg-shaped leaves, yellowish flowers and brown capsules, whose twigs and leaves can be used to extract tannin and whose seeds can be used to extract oil

鰶 jì 鱼，体长 5—6 寸，侧扁，背部灰绿色，两侧银白色。组成背鳍的鳍条中最后一根特别长。生活在我国沿海。gizzard shad（*Dorosoma cepedianum*）; a kind of fish, five or six *cun* long with a laterally flat body, greyish green back, silver sides, the last bone of its dorsal fin being particularly long, and living in China's coastal waters

骥 jì〈书 *fml.*〉❶ 好马 thoroughbred horse：按图索～ find a horse according to a drawing; look for a horse with the aid of a picture; try to locate sth. by following up a clue ❷〈比喻 *fig.*〉贤能 able and virtuous person

jiā（ㄐㄧㄚ）

加 jiā ❶ 两个或两个以上的东西或数目合在一起 add; plus; two or more things or numbers are joined or united：二～三等于五。Two plus three makes five. *or* Two and three is five.｜功上～功 one merit after another ❷ 使数量比原来大或程度比原来高；增加 increase; make the number bigger or the degree higher：～大 enlarge｜～强 strengthen｜～快 quicken; accelerate｜～速 increase the speed, make it faster｜～多 increase｜～急 more urgent｜～了一个人 have one more person ❸ 把本来没有的添上去 put in; add; append：～符号 put in a mark｜～注解 append notes to ❹ same as 加以 jiāyǐ：不～考虑 will not consider｜严～管束 bring sb. or sth. under strict control 注意 **NOTE**：'加'跟'加以'用法不同之点是'加'多用在单音状语之后。The difference between 加 and 加以 jiāyǐ in usage is that 加 is usu. used after a single-character adverb. ❺（Jiā）姓 a surname

【加班】jiā//bān 在规定以外增加工作时间或班次 work overtime; time beyond the established limit：～加点 work for longer hours;

work extra shifts or extra hours|～费(加班得到的报酬) overtime; pay for overtime work; overtime pay; pay for extra hours

【加倍】jiā//bèi ❶ 增加跟原有数量相等的数量 double; redouble: 产量～ double the output|～偿还 double the repayment ❷ 指程度比原来深得多 put in more efforts: ～努力 redouble one's efforts|～的同情 increased sympathy

【加点】jiā//diǎn 在规定的工作时间终了之后继续工作一段时间 work extra hours: 加班～ work extra shifts and extra hours

【加法】jiāfǎ 数学中的一种运算方法。最简单的是数的加法,即两个或两个以上的数合成一个数的计算方法。addition; method of mathematical operations; the simplest is the addition of figures, namely, the calculating method of adding two or more numbers into another number

【加封】jiā//fēng 贴上封条 put up a strip of paper to seal a door; seal up (a door, document, etc.)

【加封】jiāfēng 封建时代指在原有的基础上再封给(名位、土地等) (of feudal years) grant additional titles and fiefs (to a noble man)

【加工】jiā//gōng ❶ 把原材料、半成品等制成成品,或使达到规定的要求 process; turn raw materials or semi-finished products into products according to required standards: 来料～ processing with materials supplied by a customer|～成型 processing and forming|面粉～厂 flour mill ❷ 指做使成品更完美、精致的各种工作 art of making a finished product perfect and exquisite: 技术～ technical improvement|艺术～ artistic improvement

【加固】jiāgù 使建筑物等坚固 reinforce; consolidate: ～堤坝 strengthen the dam (dyke)|～楼房 reinforce a building

【加紧】jiājǐn 加快速度或加大强度 catch up; step up; speed up; intensify: ～生产 step up production|～训练 intensify training|～田间管理工作 intensify field management

【加劲】jiā//jìn (～儿 jiā//jìnr)增加力量;努力 redouble one's effort; put more energy into; make a greater effort: ～工作 work still harder

【加剧】jiājù 加深严重程度 aggravate; exacerbate: 病势～。The patient's condition is getting worse.|矛盾～。The contradictions are sharpening.

【加快】jiākuài ❶ 使变得更快 accelerate; quicken; speed up; become quicker: ～建设进度 accelerate the construction|他～了步子,走到队伍的前面。He quickened his steps until he found himself walking in the van of the contingent. ❷ 铁路部门指持有慢车车票的旅客办理手续后改乘快车 passenger holding a slow train ticket changes to an express train after going through necessary formalities

【加料】jiā//liào 把原料装进操作的容器之中;添加原料 feed in raw material: ～工人 feeding worker|自动～ automatic feeding

【加料】jiāliào 原料比一般用得多,质量比一般好的(制成品) finished product which is made by using more raw materials and thus acquires better quality

【加仑】jiālún 英美制容量单位,英制 1 加仑等于 4.546 升,美制 1 加仑等于 3.785 升 gallon; unit of liquid measure equaling to four quarts (3.785 litres) in the United States, and 4.546 litres in Britain

【加码】jiā//mǎ ❶ (～儿 jiā//mǎr)指提高商品价格 raise the price of commodities; overcharge ❷ 指增加赌注 raise the stakes in gambling ❸ 提高数量指标 raise the quota: 层层～ raise the quota at each level

【加盟】jiāméng 加入某个团体或组织 become a member of an alliance or union: 因有世界一流球星～,该队实力大增。The team is much stronger with the participation of some top players in the world.

【加冕】jiā//miǎn 某些国家的君主即位时所举行的仪式,把皇冠戴在君主头上 coronation; ceremony of crowning a sovereign in some countries

【加农榴弹炮】jiānóng-liúdànpào 兼有加农炮和榴弹炮弹道特点的火炮,主要用来射击较远距离目标和破坏工程设施 howitzer; short cannon, larger than a mortar, firing shells in a high trajectory, chiefly used to shoot at targets in the distance and destroy military works; 简称 abbr. 加榴炮 jiāliúpào

【加农炮】jiānóngpào 炮身长、初速大、弹道低伸的火炮,多用于直接瞄准射击,以及射击远距离的目标 cannon; gun; gun with a long barrel, a fast primary speed and a low trajectory, more used to shoot at targets in the distance

【加强】jiāqiáng 使更坚强或更有效 strengthen; enhance; augment; reinforce: ～团结 strengthen unity|～领导 strengthen leadership|～爱国主义教育 improve the education on patriotism; give more education on patriotism

【加热】jiā//rè 使物体的温度增高 heat up; increase the temperature of sth.

【加人一等】jiā rén yī děng 高出别人一等。形容学问、才能等出众。cut above sb.; have better knowledge and talent than others

【加入】jiārù ❶ 加上;搀进去 add; mix; put in: ～食糖少许 add a little sugar ❷ 参加进去 join; accede to: ～工会 join a trade union|～足球队 join a football team

【加塞儿】jiā//sāir 为了取巧而不守秩序,插进排好的队列里 jump in; push into a queue out of turn; jump a queue

【加深】jiāshēn 加大深度;变得更深 deepen: ～了解 get a deeper understanding; increase understanding|矛盾～。The contradiction has deepened.

【加速】jiāsù ❶ 加快速度 quicken; accelerate; expedite; speed up: 火车正在～运行。The train is running faster. ❷ 使速度加快 hasten; accelerate: ～其自身的灭亡 hasten its own destruction

【加速度】jiāsùdù 速度的变化与发生这种变化所用的时间的比，即单位时间内速度的变化 acceleration; ratio between the time taken for changing a speed and the time consumed in the occurrence of such a change

【加速器】jiāsùqì 用人工方法产生高速运动粒子的装置，是研究原子核和基本粒子性质的工具，如静电加速器、回旋加速器、直线加速器、同步加速器等 accelerator; apparatus that accelerates charged particles to high energies; tool for studying atomic nucleus and elementary particles, such as betatron, electrostatic accelerator, cyclotron, linear accelerator, synchrotron

【加委】jiāwěi 〈旧时 *old*〉主管机关对所属单位或群众团体推举出来的公职人员办理委任手续 formality of competent authorities for the appointment of a public official recommended by an affiliated department or by a nongovernmental organization

【加压釜】jiāyāfǔ 工业上在高压下进行化学反应的设备，有的附有搅拌或传热装置 compression cauldron; industrial equipment for chemical reaction under high pressure, some with a mixing or heat conduction device; also 热压釜 rèyāfǔ or 高压釜 gāoyāfǔ

【加以】jiāyǐ ❶ 用在多音的动词前，表示如何对待或处理前面所提到的事物[used before a polysyllabic verb to indicate that the action is directed towards sth. or sb. mentioned earlier in the sentence]: 施工方案必须～论证。Feasibility studies must be done on the construction plan. |发现问题要及时～解决。Problems should be solved immediately after they are discovered. 注意 **NOTE**: '加以'跟'予以'不同之处是'予以'可以用在一般名词之前，表示给与，如'予以自新之路'，'加以'没有这种用法。The difference between 加以 and 予以 yǔyǐ is that 予以 can be used before a noun to indicate 给与 jǐyǔ, such as 予以自新之路 yǔyǐ zìxīn zhī lù, and that 加以 cannot be used this way. ❷ 〈连词 *conj.*〉表示进一步的原因或条件[for further reason or condition]: 他本来就聪明，～特别用功，所以进步很快。He is clever, and moreover, he is very diligent, so he has made fast progress.

【加意】jiāyì 特别注意；非常留意 with special care; with close attention: ～保护 protect with special care|～经营 manage the business with special attention

【加油】jiā//yóu ❶ 添加燃料油、润滑油等 refuel; fill sth. with lubricant: ～站 gas station ❷ (～儿 jiā//yóur)〈比喻 *fig.*〉进一步努力；加劲儿 make more efforts: ～干 work harder; work with more vigour|大家为运动员鼓掌～。The crowd encouraged the players with applause. *or* The crowd cheered the players on.

【加之】jiāzhī 〈连词 *conj.*〉表示进一步的原因或条件[indicating a further reason or condition] moreover; furthermore: 天气闷热，～窗外车马声不断，简直无法休息。It is sultry, and moreover, there are endless noises of carts and horses outside the window, making it impossible to take a rest.

【加重】jiāzhòng 增加重量或程度 make or become heavier; increase the weight of: ～负担 increase the burden; add to the burden|～语气 speak with emphasis|病势～ patient's condition being worse|责任～了 have greater responsibility

夹(夾、❷挾) jiā ❶ 从两个相对的方面加压力，使物体固定不动 press from both sides; place in between; sandwich: ～菜 pick up food with chopsticks|用钳子～住烧红的铁 grip a piece of red-hot iron with a pair of tongs ❷ 胳膊向胁部用力，使腋下放着的东西不掉下 carry sth. under one's armpit: ～着书包 carry one's school bag under one's armpit|～起铺盖卷儿 carry one's bedroll under one's armpit ❸ 处在两者之间 be wedged between two things; in between: 两座大山～着一条小沟 two high mountains with a small gully lying in between; small gully lies between two high mountains|你在左，我在右，他～在中间。You are on the left, I'm on the right, and he is sandwiched between us. |把信～在书本里 put the letter in between the pages of a book ❹ 夹杂；搀杂 mix; mingle; intersperse: ～在人群里 be mingled with a crowd|风声～着雨声 wind accompanied by a rain|白话～文言，念起来不顺口。The vernacular mixed with classical Chinese does not read smoothly. ❺ 夹子 folder; clip; clamp; pin: 文件～ document folder

☞ gā on p. 618 and jiá on p. 931

☞ 挟 xié on p. 2120

【夹板】jiābǎn 用来夹住物体的板子，多用木头或金属制成 pair of splints; boards for pressing sth. or holding things together, mostly made of wood or metal

【夹板气】jiābǎnqì 指来自对立的双方的责难 be blamed by two opposing sides; state of being between two fires: 受～ be caught between two fires

【夹层】jiācéng 双层的墙或其他片状物，中空或

夹着别的东西 double layer; double-layered wall or a plate with sth. sandwiched inside: ～墙 double-layered wall | ～玻璃 laminated glass

【夹层玻璃】jiācéng bō·lí 安全玻璃的一种，在两层玻璃之间夹聚乙烯等塑料薄片黏合而成。这种玻璃破碎时，碎片不会飞散，多用在汽车、飞机等交通工具的门窗上。sandwich glass; laminated glass; a kind of safety glass; double-layered glass with polyethylene sandwiched and stuck between them, which is more used for the doors and windows of motor vehicles, airplanes and other means of transport

【夹带】jiādài ❶ 藏在身上或混杂在其他物品中间偷偷携带 carry secretly; smuggle: 严禁～危险品上车。Dangerous goods are strictly prohibited on vehicles. ❷ 考试时作弊，暗中携带的与试题有关的材料 notes smuggled into an examination hall

【夹道】jiādào ❶ (～儿 jiādàor) 左右都有墙壁等的狭窄道路 narrow lane; passageway ❷ (许多人或物) 排列在道路的两边 line both sides of a street: ～欢迎 line both sides of the street to welcome someone | 松柏～ road flanked by pines and cypresses on both sides

【夹缝】jiāfèng (～儿 jiāfèngr) 两个靠近的物体中间的狭窄空隙 crack; crevice; narrow space between two adjacent things: 书掉在两张桌子的～里。The book fell into the narrow space between two desks.

【夹肝】jiāgān 〈方 *dial.*〉牛、羊、猪等动物的胰腺作为食物时叫夹肝 pancreas of ox, sheep or pig when used for food

【夹攻】jiāgōng 从两方面同时进攻 attack from both sides; converging attack; pincer attack: 左右～ attack from left and right | 内外～ attack from within and without

【夹棍】jiāgùn 〈旧时 *old*〉一种刑具，用两根木棍做成，行刑时用力夹犯人的腿 instrument for torture or punishment, which is made of two wooden rods, used to press the legs of a criminal

【夹击】jiājī 夹攻 converging attack; pincer attack: 两面～ attack from both sides | 前后～ attack from both the front and the rear

【夹剪】jiājiǎn 夹取物件的工具，用铁制成，形状像剪刀，但没有锋刃，头上较宽而平 tweezers; tongs; instrument for seizing or lifting objects, made of iron, shaped like scissors with broad and flat heads, but without sharp blades

【夹具】jiājù 用来固定工件的装置 fixture; jig; clamping apparatus; also 卡具 qiǎjù

【夹克】jiākè 一种长短只到腰部，下口束紧的短外套 jacket: ～衫 jacket | 皮～ leather jacket; also 茄克 jiākè

【夹批】jiāpī 在书籍、文稿的文字行间所写的批注 inter-linear annotations and comments in a book or writing

【夹七夹八】jiā qī jiā bā 混杂不清，没有条理(多指说话) incoherent; confused; cluttered (with irrelevant remarks): 她～地说了许多话，我也没听懂是什么意思。She rambled on at great length but I couldn't make head or tail of what she said.

【夹生】jiāshēng (食物) 没有熟透 (of food) half-baked; half-cooked: ～饭 half-baked rice ◇这孩子不用功，学的功课都是～的。This child is not diligent; the lessons he has learned are all half-baked.

【夹生饭】jiāshēngfàn ❶ 半生不熟的饭 half-cooked rice ❷ 〈比喻 *fig.*〉开始做没有做好再做也很难做好的事情，或开始没有彻底解决以后也很难解决的问题 job not thoroughly done or a problem not thoroughly solved

【夹丝玻璃】jiāsī bō·lí 安全玻璃的一种，把金属网铸在玻璃中间。这种玻璃破碎时不会散落，多用在建筑物的天窗上 wired glass; a kind of safety glass which contains a metal netting cast inside and is used usu. in the skylights of buildings

【夹馅】jiāxiàn (～儿 jiāxiànr) 里面有馅儿的 stuffed (pastry, etc.): ～馒头 stuffed bun | ～烧饼 sandwiched cake

【夹心】jiāxīn (～儿 jiāxīnr) 夹馅 with filling: ～饼干 sandwich biscuits | ～糖 sweets with filling

【夹杂】jiāzá 搀杂 be mixed up with; be mingled with: 脚步声和笑语声～在一起。Footsteps are mingled with laughter.

【夹注】jiāzhù 夹在正文字句中间的字体较小的注释文字 interlinear annotations; interlinear notes

【夹子】jiā·zi 夹东西的器具 clip; tongs; tweezers: 头发～ hair clips; hairpin | 皮～ wallet | 讲义～ teaching materials folder | 把文件放在～里 put documents in a folder

伽 jiā [伽倻琴] (jiāyēqín) 朝鲜族的弦乐器，有些像筝 plucked stringed instrument, used by the Korean people
☞ gā on p. 618 and qié on p. 1553

茄 jiā ❶ 古书上指荷花的茎 stem of the lotus flower described in ancient books ❷
☞ 茄克 jiākè and 雪茄 xuějiā on p. 2180
☞ qié on p. 1553

【茄克】jiākè same as 夹克 jiākè

佳 jiā 美；好 good; fine; beautiful: ～句 good sentence | ～音 good news | 成绩甚～ get excellent marks; achieve very good results | 身体欠～ not feel well

【佳宾】jiābīn same as 嘉宾 jiābīn

【佳话】jiāhuà 流传一时，当做谈话资料的好事或趣事 talk of the town; deed praised far and wide; story on everybody's lips: 传为～ become the talk of the town | 千秋～ story passed down throughout the ages

【佳节】jiājié 欢乐愉快的节日 happy festive time; festival:中秋～ joyous Mid-Autumn Festival|每逢～倍思亲。More than ever we think of the parents or children (also close friends) far away on a happy festival.

【佳境】jiājìng ❶ 风景优美的地方 enjoyable or pleasant scenic sites:西山～ beautiful scenic sites of the Western Hills ❷ 美好的境界;美好的意境 good state of mind:渐入～ have a better state of mind; become more and more delightful

【佳丽】jiālì ❶ (容貌、风景等)美丽;美好(of looks, scenery, etc.) beautiful ❷〈书 *fml*.〉美貌的女子 beautiful woman

【佳酿】jiāniàng 美酒 good wine; excellent wine:名酒～ good wine with a famous brand

【佳偶】jiā'ǒu〈书 *fml*.〉感情融洽、生活美满的夫妻;美好的配偶 happily married couple

【佳期】jiāqī ❶ 结婚的日期 wedding (or nuptial) day ❷ 相爱着的男女幽会的日期、时间 date of a rendezvous between a man and a woman

【佳人】jiārén〈书 *fml*.〉美人 beautiful woman; beauty:才子～ marriage between a brilliant man and a beautiful woman; ideal couple; gifted scholars and beautiful women|绝代～ beauty of beauties; peerless beauty

【佳肴】jiāyáo 精美的菜肴 delicacies:～美酒 delicious food and excellent wine

【佳音】jiāyīn〈书 *fml*.〉好消息 good news; welcome news:静候～ wait for the news of your success

【佳作】jiāzuò 优秀的作品 good piece of writing; excellent work:影视～ good film and TV production

珈 jiā ☞ [獾㹢狓](huòjiāpí) on p. 887

迦 jiā 用于译音,也用于专名 *jia*, character used in proper names and in rendering some foreign names

珈 jiā〈古代 *arch*.〉妇女的一种首饰 ornament for women

枷 jiā〈旧时 *old*〉套在罪犯脖子上的刑具,用木板制成 cangue; large wooden yoke fastened about the neck as a punishment for crimes:披～带锁 wear the cangue with a lock

【枷锁】jiāsuǒ 枷和锁链 yoke; chains; shackles; fetters;〈比喻 *fig*.〉所受的压迫和束缚 oppression and restriction:精神～ spiritual shackles|挣脱封建～ shake off the yoke of feudalism

浃(浹) jiā〈书 *fml*.〉透;遍及 wet through:汗流～背 stream with sweat

痂 jiā 伤口或疮口表面上由血小板和纤维蛋白凝结而成的块状物,伤口或疮口痊愈后自行脱落 scab; crust of congealed platelet and protein fibre that forms over a sore or wound during healing, and fall off automatically when it heals

家 jiā ❶ 家庭;人家 family; household:他～有五口人。There are five people in his family.|张～和王～是亲戚。The Zhangs and the Wangs are relatives. ❷ 家庭的住所 home:回～ go home|这儿就是我的～。This is my home.|我的～在上海。My home is in Shanghai. ❸ 借指部队或机关中某个成员工作的处所 work place for a certain member in an army unit or a government office:我找到营部,刚好营长不在～。I went to the battalion headquarters, but the battalion commander was not in. ❹ 经营某种行业的人家或具有某种身份的人 person or family engaged in a certain trade:农～ farmer|渔～ fisherman|船～ boatman; shipowner; person who owns a boat or a ship and makes a living as a boatman or a shipowner|东～ proprietor; boss; master; family for which a servant works|行(háng)～ expert; specialist ❺ 掌握某种专门学识或从事某种专门活动的人 specialist; person who has a certain special knowledge or is engaged in certain special business:专～ expert; specialist|画～ painter|政治～ statesman; politician|科学～ scientist|艺术～ artist|社会活动～ social activist ❻ 学术流派 school; school of thought:儒～ Confucianists|法～ Legalists|百～争鸣 contention of one hundred schools of thought; let one hundred schools of thought contend|一～之言 one school of thought ❼ 指相对各方中的一方 one side; one party:上～ person who sits on the left|下～ person who sits on the right|公～ state; public; organization; collective|两～下成和棋。The two sides played to a draw in the chess game. ❽〈谦辞 *hum*.〉用于对别人称自己的辈分高或年纪大的亲属 [used when speaking of relatives older than oneself] I; my:～父 my father|～兄 my elder brother ❾ 饲养的(跟'野'相对 as opposed to 'wild') domestic:～畜 domestic animals|～禽 poultry|～兔 rabbit|～鸽 pigeon ❿〈方 *dial*.〉饲养后驯服 domesticated:这只小鸟已经养～了,放了它也不会飞走。This bird has been domesticated. It will not fly away if you release it. ⓫〈量词 *classifier*〉用来计算家庭或企业 [for families and business establishments]:一～人家 one family|两～饭馆 two restaurants|三～商店 three shops ⓬(Jiā) 姓 a surname

家 ·jia〈后缀 *suffix*〉❶ 用在某些名词后面,表示属于那一类人 [used after certain nouns to indicate a specific group of people]:女人～ women|孩子～ children|姑娘～ girls|学生～ students ❷〈方 *dial*.〉用在男人的名字或排行后面,指他的妻 [used after a man's name or designation of order of seniority to

J

indicate his wife]：秋生～Qiusheng's wife|老三～ Lao San's wife; third son's wife

☞ ·jie on p. 1002

【家财】jiācái 家庭的钱财；家产 family property：万贯～ family property worth of ten thousand strings of cash

【家蚕】jiācán 昆虫，幼虫灰白色，吃桑叶，蜕皮四次，吐丝做茧，变成蛹，蛹变成蚕蛾。蚕蛾交尾产卵后就死去。幼虫吐的丝是重要的纺织原料。silkworm (*Bombyx mori*); moth caterpillar of greyish white colour that feeds on mulberry leaves, casts off its skin four times and produces cocoons of silk fibre, is a major textile material, becoming chrysalis and then turning into moth, which dies after mating and ovipositing; also 桑蚕 sāngcán

【家产】jiāchǎn 家庭的财产 family property：继承～ inherit family property; obtain a family inheritance

【家长里短】jiā cháng lǐ duǎn 〈方 *dial.*〉(～儿 jiā cháng lǐ duǎnr) 指家庭日常生活琐事 domestic trivia：谈谈～儿 have chitchat

【家常】jiācháng 家庭日常生活 daily life of a family; domestic trivia：～话 small talk; chitchat|～便饭 homely food, everyday family fare|拉～ have a chitchat|她们俩谈起～来。The two of them chitchatted.

【家常便饭】jiācháng biànfàn ❶ 家庭日常的饭食 ordinary simple meal; homely food ❷〈比喻 *fig.*〉经常发生、习以为常的事情 common occurrence; routine：他太忙了，加班熬夜是～。He is too busy, and overtime and night work is common place for him. ‖ also 家常饭 jiācháng fàn

【家丑】jiāchǒu 家庭内部的不体面的事情 family scandal; skeleton in the cupboard (or closet)：～不可外扬。The disgrace of a family scandal should never be spread without. *or* Don't wash your dirty linen in public.

【家畜】jiāchù 人类为了经济或其他目的而驯养的兽类，如猪、牛、羊、马、骆驼、家兔、猫、狗等 domestic animals; livestock; animals raised by humans for money or other purposes, such as pig, ox, sheep, horse, camel, rabbit, cat, dog, etc.

【家慈】jiācí 〈书 *fml.*〉〈谦辞 *hum.*〉对人称自己的母亲 my mother

【家当】jiā·dàng (～儿 jiā·dàngr) 家产 family belongs; family property：置～ buy household necessities|好不容易才挣下这份～。It's not easy to have earned money for these family belongings.

【家道】jiādào 家境 family financial situation：～小康 be comfortably off|～殷实 be well-off; well-off family|～中落。The family fortunes declined. *or* The family fortunes were at a low ebb.

【家底】jiādǐ (～儿 jiādǐr) 家里长期积累起来的财产 family property accumulated over a long time; resources：～厚 with substantial family resources; financially strong family|～薄 without substantial family resources; not financially solid

【家电】jiādiàn 家用电器的简称 abbr. for 家用电器 jiāyòng diànqì：～产品 electrical household appliances|～维修部 electrical household appliances service shop

【家丁】jiādīng 〈旧时 *old*〉大地主或官僚家里雇来保护自己并供差使的仆役 retainer of a big family; person hired to serve the families of a big landlord or bureaucrat

【家法】jiāfǎ ❶〈古代 *arch.*〉学者师徒相传的学术理论和治学方法 theories and research methods handed down from master to pupil ❷ 封建家长统治本家或本族人的一套法度 family rules; domestic rules and discipline exercised by the head of a feudal household and family ❸ 封建家长责打家人的用具 rod for punishing children or servants in a feudal household

【家访】jiāfǎng 因工作需要到人家里访问 (of a teacher or factory leader) visit the parents of schoolchildren or young workers：通过～，深入了解学生的情况 get a deeper understanding of the students through visits to their families

【家父】jiāfù 〈谦辞 *hum.*〉对人称自己的父亲 my father

【家鸽】jiāgē 鹁鸽(bógē) pigeon

【家馆】jiāguǎn 〈旧时 *old*〉设在家里的教学处所，聘请教师教自己的子弟 family school (formerly a private school maintained by a rich family for the education of its own children and the children of its relatives)

【家规】jiāguī 家庭中的规矩 domestic discipline and family rules：国有国法，家有～。The state has laws while a family has rules.

【家伙】jiā·huo ❶ 指工具或武器 tool; utensil; weapon ❷ 指人(含轻视或戏谑意 derog. or humor.) fellow; guy：你这个～真会开玩笑。What a joker you are! ❸ 指牲畜 referring to domestic animals：这～真机灵，见了主人就摇尾巴。What a clever thing it is! It wags its tail whenever it sees its master. ‖ also 傢伙 jiā·huo

【家给人足】jiā jǐ rén zú 家家户户丰衣足食 each family is provided for and every person is well-fed and well-clothed; all live in plenty

【家计】jiājì 家庭生计 family livelihood：维持～ earn a family livelihood; make a family livelihood|～艰难 find it hard to make ends meet in a family; poor family livelihood

【家家户户】jiājiāhùhù 每家每户；各家各户 each and every family; every household：～都打扫得很干净。Every family has made their house clean and tidy.

【家教】jiājiào 家长对子弟进行的关于道德、礼节的教育 family education; upbringing: 有～ well brought up; properly brought up | 没～ ill-bred; not properly brought up

【家景】jiājǐng same as 家境 jiājìng

【家境】jiājìng 家庭的经济状况 family's financial situation; family circumstances: ～贫寒 family in straitened circumstances | ～优裕 well-off family

【家居】jiājū 没有就业,在家闲着 stay idle at home; be unemployed

【家具】jiā·jù 家庭用具,主要指床、柜、桌、椅等 furniture, such as bed, wardrobe, table, desk, chairs, etc.; also 傢具 jiā·jù

【家眷】jiājuàn 指妻子儿女等(有时专指妻子) one's wife and children (sometimes one's wife only)

【家口】jiākǒu 家里人;家中人口 members of a family; number of people in a family: ～不多 not many family members | 养活～ support one's family

【家累】jiālěi 家庭生活负担 family burden: 没有～ have no family burden | 上有老,下有小,～不轻。He has quite a big family burden with parents above and children below.

【家门】jiāmén ❶ 家庭住所的大门,借指家 gate of one's house; one's home: 工作单位离～不远,上班方便。I work not far away from my home, so it's easy for me to go to work. | 新媳妇娶进了～ take a new wife; bring the daughter-in-law into one's home ❷〈书 *fml*.〉称自己的家族 one's own clan or family: 辱没～ disgrace one's family ❸〈方 *dial*.〉本家 member of one's own clan or family: 他是我的～堂兄弟。He's my cousin on my father's side. ❹ 指个人的家世、经历、家庭成员及经济状况等 personal family's social background, experience, family members and financial situation; family situation: 自报～ state one's own family situation

【家母】jiāmǔ〈谦辞 *hum*.〉对人称自己的母亲 my mother

【家谱】jiāpǔ 家族记载本族世系和重要人物事迹的书 family tree; genealogical tree; genealogy

【家雀儿】jiāqiǎor〈方 *dial*.〉麻雀(鸟名) sparrow

【家禽】jiāqín 人类为了经济或其他目的而驯养的鸟类,如鸡、鸭、鹅等 poultry; domestic birds bred by humans for money or other purposes, such as chicken, duck, goose, etc.

【家人】jiārén ❶ 一家的人 family members: ～团聚 family reunion ❷〈旧称 *old*〉仆人 servant

【家什】jiā·shi 用具;器物;家具 family belongings; utensils, furniture: 食堂里的～擦得很干净。The kitchen furnishings have all been wiped clean. | 锣鼓～打得震天价响。The sky reverberates with a flourish of gongs and drums. also 傢什 jiā·shi

【家世】jiāshì〈书 *fml*.〉家庭的世系;门第 family background; genealogy, pedigree; family status

【家事】jiāshì ❶ 家庭的事情 family matters; domestic affairs: 一切～,都是两个人商量着办。All family affairs are handled after discussion between the two of them. ❷〈方 *dial*.〉家境 family's financial situation

【家室】jiāshì ❶ 家庭;家眷(有时专指妻子 sometimes referring to the wife only) family; family member; wife: 无～之累 have no family burden | 已有～ be married; get married ❷〈书 *fml*.〉房舍;住宅 house

【家书】jiāshū same as 家信 jiāxìn: 代写～ write a letter home for someone

【家塾】jiāshú〈旧时 *old*〉把教师请到家里来教自己的子弟读书的私塾,有的兼收亲友子弟 family school; private school where a teacher is employed to teach one's children at home, sometimes also admitting children of one's relatives and friends

【家属】jiāshǔ 家庭内户主本人以外的成员,也指职工本人以外的家庭成员 family members; (family) dependants

【家私】jiāsī 家产 family property: 万贯～ family property worth of ten thouand strings | 变卖～ sell family property

【家庭】jiātíng 以婚姻和血统关系为基础的社会单位,包括父母、子女和其他共同生活的亲属在内 family; household; social unit based on marital and blood relationship, consisting of parents, the children they rear and other relatives

【家庭妇女】jiātíng fùnǚ 只做家务而没有就业的妇女 housewife; woman whose duty is to manage a household and take care of household affairs

【家徒四壁】jiā tú sì bì 家里只有四堵墙。形容十分贫穷。have nothing but the bare walls in one's house; be utterly destitute; also 家徒壁立 jiā tú bì lì

【家务】jiāwù 家庭事务 household duties: 操持～ manage household affairs | ～劳动 housework; household chores

【家乡】jiāxiāng 自己的家庭世代居住的地方 hometown; native place

【家小】jiāxiǎo 妻子和儿女,有时专指妻子 wife and children; sometimes wife only: 丢下～无人照料 leave one's wife and children uncared-for (neglected, not looked after) | 未娶～ remain unmarried

【家信】jiāxìn 家庭成员间彼此往来的信件 letter home; letter from home; letters exchanged between or among family members: 平安～ family letter telling all is well

【家兄】jiāxiōng〈谦辞 *hum*.〉对人称自己的哥哥 my elder brother

J

【家学】jiāxué〈书 *fml.*〉❶ 家庭里世代相传的学问 learning handed down in a family:～渊源。The family has a long tradition of learning. ❷ 家塾 family school

【家严】jiāyán〈书 *fml.*〉〈谦辞 *hum.*〉对人称自己的父亲 my father

【家燕】jiāyàn 燕的一种,身体小,背部羽毛黑色,有光泽,腹部白色,颈部有深紫色圆斑,多在屋檐下筑窝 house swallow; swallow with black, lustrous feathers on the back, white belly and dark purple round spots around the neck, oft. building nests under eaves; 通称 popularly known as 燕子 yàn•zi

【家养】jiāyǎng 人工饲养(区别于'野生' as compared with 'wild') domestic

【家业】jiāyè ❶ 家产 family property; property:重建～(usu. after a disaster) rebuild a family, factory, etc.|继承～ inherit family property ❷〈书 *fml.*〉家传的事业或学问 work and learning handed down in a family

【家用】jiāyòng ❶ 家庭中的生活费用 family expenses; housekeeping money:贴补～ help out with the family expenses|供给～ provide for the family ❷ 家庭日常使用的 for household use:～电器 electrical appliances for household use|～小商品 small commodities for household use

【家用电器】jiāyòng diànqì 日常生活中使用的各种电气器具,如电视机、录音机、洗衣机、电冰箱等 electrical home appliances; electrical household appliances, such as TV sets, tape recorders, washers, fridges, etc.; 简称 abbr. 家电 jiādiàn

【家喻户晓】jiā yù hù xiǎo 每家每户都知道 known to every household; widely known; known to all

【家园】jiāyuán ❶ 家中的庭园。泛指家乡或家庭。home; homeland; (in a broad sense) native village or household:返回～ return to one's homeland|重建～ rebuild one's village or town ❷〈方 *dial.*〉家中园地上出产的 produced in the family garden:～茶叶 tea from one's family garden

【家贼】jiāzéi 指偷盗自家财物的人 thief within a house

【家宅】jiāzhái 住宅。也指家庭。house; family:一人出事,闹得～不宁。One member being in trouble, the whole house had no peace.

【家长】jiāzhǎng ❶ 家长制之下的一家中为首的人 patriarch; head of a family ❷ 指父母或其他监护人 parent or guardian of a child:学校里明天开～座谈会。There will be a parents' meeting in our school tomorrow.

【家长制】jiāzhǎngzhì 奴隶社会和封建社会的家庭组织制度,产生于原始公社末期。作为家长的男子掌握经济大权,在家庭中居支配地位,其他成员都要绝对服从他。patriarchal system; organizational system of a family in the slave society and feudal society, first seen in the declining years of the primitive communes, with man as the patriarch who controlled the financial power and held the dominant position in the family, and the other members having to obey him unconditionally

【家政】jiāzhèng 指家庭事务的管理工作,如有关家庭生活中烹调、缝纫、编织及养育婴幼儿等 household management; home economics, such as cooking, sewing, knitting, weaving, raising children, etc.

【家种】jiāzhòng ❶ 人工种植 household cultivation:把野生药材改为～ household cultivation of wild medicinal herbs ❷ 自己家里种植的 cultivated at home:～蔬菜 vegetables grown at family gardens

【家资】jiāzī 家财;家产 family property; family resources:～耗尽 exhaustion of family resources

【家子】jiā•zi 家庭;人家 household; family:这～有八口人,相处得很和睦。There are eight people in this family, and they live in harmony.|那边好几～都是新搬来的。Quite a few families over there have just moved in.

【家族】jiāzú 以血统关系为基础而形成的社会组织,包括同一血统的几辈人 clan; family; social organization based on blood lineage, including several generations of the same blood lineage

笳 jiā 胡笳 reed instrument used by the northern tribes in ancient China

袈 jiā [袈裟](jiāshā)和尚披在外面的法衣,由许多长方形小块布片拼缀制成 cassock; long robe worn by Buddhist monks; patchwork outer vestment worn by a Buddhist monk [梵 Sanskrit: kaṣāya]

葭 jiā〈书 *fml.*〉初生的芦苇 young shoot of a reed

【葭莩】jiāfú〈书 *fml.*〉芦苇茎中的薄膜 membrane of a reed stem;〈比喻 *fig.*〉关系疏远的亲戚 tenuous relationship:～之亲 distant relatives

跏 jiā [跏趺](jiāfū)盘腿而坐,脚背放在股上,是佛教徒的一种坐法 sit cross-legged with the instep on the thigh (as the Buddhists do when in meditation)

筴(筞、梜) jiā〈古代 *arch.*〉指箸;筷子 chopsticks

☞ cè on p. 197

傢 jiā see below

【傢伙】jiā•huo same as 家伙 jiā•huo

【傢具】jiā•jù same as 家具 jiā•jù

【傢什】jiā•shi same as 家什 jiā•shi

嘉 jiā ❶ 美好 good; fine; great; excellent:～宾 distinguished guest; honoured guest|～礼(婚礼) wedding ❷ 夸奖;赞许 praise;

J

commend:～奖 commend; cite|～纳(赞许并采纳) praise and accept; accept with admiration|其志可～ one's ideal (or aspiration) is praiseworthy ❸ (Jiā)姓 a surname

【嘉宾】jiābīn 尊贵的客人 honoured guest; distinguished guest:～如云 great number of distinguished guests|～满座 houseful of distinguished guests; also 佳宾 jiābīn

【嘉奖】jiājiǎng ❶ 称赞和奖励 commend; cite:通令～ issue an order of commendation|～有功人员 commend the people who have performed distinguished services ❷ 称赞的话语或奖励的实物 praises and awards:最高的～ highest award

【嘉靖】Jiājìng 明世宗(朱厚熜)年号(公元1522—1566) Jiajing, the title of the reign of Emperor Shizong (Zhu Houcong) (1522-1566) of the Ming Dynasty

【嘉勉】jiāmiǎn〈书 *fml.*〉嘉奖勉励 praise and encourage:函电～ letter or telegraph of citation

【嘉庆】Jiāqìng 清仁宗(爱新觉罗颙琰)年号(公元1796—1820) Jiaqing, the title of the reign of Emperor Renzong (Aisin Gioro Yongyan) (1796-1820) of the Qing Dynasty

【嘉许】jiāxǔ〈书 *fml.*〉夸奖;赞许 praise; approve:品学兼优,深得师长～ earn a teacher's praise for one's good character and scholarship

【嘉言懿行】jiā yán yì xíng〈书 *fml.*〉有教育意义的好言语和好行为 wise words and noble deeds of an educational value

镓 jiā 金属元素,符号 Ga (gallium)。银白色,质软。用作制光学玻璃、真空管、半导体等的原料,也用来制高温温度计。gallium (Ga); metallic element, silver white in colour and soft in texture, used for making optical glass, vacuum tubes, transistors, as well as high-temperature thermometer

麚 jiā〈书 *fml.*〉牡鹿 stag

jiá(ㄐㄧㄚˊ)

夹(夾、裌、袷) jiá 双层的(衣被等) double-layered; lined:～袄 lined jacket|～被 lined quilt|这件衣服是～的。This is a lined jacket.

☞ gā on p.618, jiā on p.925 and 袷 qiā on p.1526

郏(郟) Jiá ❶ 郏县,地名,在河南 Jiaxian, geographical name of a place in Henan ❷ 姓 a surname

荚(莢) jiá 一般指豆类植物的果实 pod; usu. the fruit of beans:豆～ bean pod|皂～ Chinese honey locust|槐树～ pod of the Chinese scholar tree

【荚果】jiáguǒ 干果的一种,由一个心皮构成,成熟时裂成两片,如豆类的果实 pod; legume; a kind of dry fruit, as the fruit of beans, a seed vessel developed from a single carpel enclosing one or more seeds and usu. splitting along two sutures at maturity

恝 jiá〈书 *fml.*〉无动于衷;不经心 indifferent; unconcerned

【恝然】jiárán〈书 *fml.*〉冷漠不在意的样子 indifferent; unconcerned:～置之 be indifferent; be unconcerned|～而去 leave indifferently

【恝置】jiázhì〈书 *fml.*〉淡然置之,不加理会 disregard; neglect

戛(戞) jiá〈书 *fml.*〉轻轻地敲打 knock gently:～击 tap lightly

【戛戛】jiájiá〈书 *fml.*〉❶ 形容困难 difficult; hard going:～乎难哉! How difficult it is! ❷ 形容独创 original:～独造 have great originality

【戛然】jiárán〈书 *fml.*〉❶ 形容嘹亮的鸟鸣声 loud cry of a bird:～长鸣 long and loud cries ❷ 形容声音突然中止 (of sound, etc.) cease abruptly; come to an abrupt end:～而止 stop abruptly

铗(鋏) jiá〈书 *fml.*〉❶ 冶铸用的钳 pincers; tongs:铁～ iron pincers; iron tongs ❷ 剑 sword:长～ long sword ❸ 剑柄 hilt of a sword

颊(頰) jiá 脸的两侧从眼到下颌的部分 cheek; part of the face between the nose and ear and below the eyes:两～ checks

【颊囊】jiánáng 仓鼠等啮齿动物和猿猴的口腔内两侧的囊状构造,用来暂时贮存食物 cheek pouch; pouch-like structure in the cheek of hamster and other rodents, monkeys, etc., used for holding food temperarily; also 颊嗛 jiáqiǎn

蛱(蛺) jiá [蛱蝶](jiádié)蝴蝶的一类,成虫赤黄色,幼虫灰黑色,身上有很多刺。有的吃麻类植物的叶子,对农作物有害。vanessid (*Nymphalidae*); butterfly whose caterpillar is reddish yellow and whose lava is greyish black with many stings, some feeding on the leaves of hemp, ramie, flax, etc., and therefore being harmful to crops

跲 jiá〈书 *fml.*〉绊倒 trip down

jiǎ(ㄐㄧㄚˇ)

甲[1] jiǎ ❶ 天干的第一位 *Jia*, the 1st of the 10 Heavenly Stems; ☞ 干支 gānzhī on p.627 ❷ 居第一位 be first, rank first:～等 first rate|桂林山水～天下。The mountains and waters of Guilin are the finest under heaven. ❸ (Jiǎ)姓 a surname

甲[2] jiǎ ❶ 爬行动物和节肢动物身上的硬壳 shell; carapace; horny covering of reptiles and arthropods: 龟～ turtle shell | ～壳 shell ❷ 手指和脚趾上的角质硬壳 nail; horny growth at the ends of the fingers or toes of a human: 指～ nail ❸ 围在人体或物体外面起保护作用的装备,用金属、皮革等制成 protective equipment of metal or leather worn around a human body or a thing: 盔～ armour | 装～车 armoured car

甲[3] jiǎ 旧时的一种户口编制 unit of civil administration consisting of 10 households in the old society; ☞ 保甲 bǎojiǎ on p. 66

【甲板】jiǎbǎn 轮船上分隔上下各层的板(多指最上面即船面的一层 oft. referring to the main deck) deck; a platform separating different floors of a steamboad

【甲兵】jiǎbīng 〈书 *fml*.〉❶ 铠甲和兵器。泛指武备、军事。armour and weaponry; (in a broad sense) military equipment ❷ 披坚执锐的士卒 soldier in armour

【甲部】jiǎbù 经部 Classics (one of the four traditional library divisions)

【甲虫】jiǎchóng 鞘翅目昆虫的统称,身体外部有硬壳,前翅是角质,厚而硬,后翅是膜质,如金龟子、天牛、象鼻虫等 beetle (*Coleoptera*); any of a large order of insects with biting mouthparts, hard shells outside the body and the thick and hard front horny wings that cover the membranous hind wings when the hind wings are folded, such as scarab, longhorned beetle, weevil, etc.

【甲骨文】jiǎgǔwén 〈古代 *arch*.〉刻在龟甲和兽骨上的文字,内容多是殷人占卜的记录,现在的汉字就是从甲骨文演变下来的 inscriptions on bones or tortoise shells of the Shang Dynasty (c. 16th-11th century B.C.), from which the current Chinese language has developed

【甲壳】jiǎqiào 虾、蟹等动物的外壳,由壳质、石灰质及色素等形成,质地坚硬,有保护身体的作用 crust; shell; hard protective outer shell of shrimp, crab, etc., formed of chitin, lime and pigments

【甲壳动物】jiǎqiào dòngwù 节肢动物的一类,全身有硬的甲壳,头部和胸部结合成头胸部,后面是腹部。头胸部前端有大小两对触角,足的数目不等。生活在水中,用鳃呼吸。虾和蟹是最常见的甲壳动物。crustacean; any of a subphylum of arthropods, including shrimps, crabs, barnacles and lobsters, that usu. live in the water, breathe through gills, and have a hard outer shell, two pairs of feelers, different number of pairs of legs, jointed head and chest, and abdomen

【甲午战争】Jiǎwǔ Zhànzhēng 1894—1895 年,日本发动的并吞朝鲜侵略中国的战争。因为 1894 年是甲午年,所以称甲午战争。Sino-Japanese War of 1894-1895, launched by Japan to annex Korea and invade China

【甲鱼】jiǎyú 鳖 soft-shelled turtle

【甲种粒子】jiǎzhǒng lìzǐ 某些放射性物质衰变时放射出来的氦原子核,由两个中子和两个质子构成,质量为氢原子的四倍,速度每秒可达两万公里,带正电荷。穿透力不大,能伤害动物的皮肤。alpha particle; positive charged particle given off by certain radioactive substances which consists of two protons and two neutrons (a helium nucleus) and is converted into an atom of helium by the acquisition of two electrons, its mass being four times that of an atom of hydrogen with a speed of 20,000 kilometres per second and having little piercing power but harmful to the skin of animals; also 阿尔法粒子 ɑ'ěrfǎ lìzǐ

【甲种射线】jiǎzhǒng shèxiàn 放射性物质衰变时放射出来的甲种粒子流 alpha ray; stream of alpha particles, radiated by a radioactive matter as it decays; also 阿尔法射线 ɑ'ěrfǎ shèxiàn

【甲胄】jiǎzhòu 〈书 *fml*.〉盔甲 armour

【甲状软骨】jiǎzhuàngruǎngǔ 颈部前面的方形软骨,左右各一,在颈部的正前方连接在一起,下部跟环状软骨相连。男性的特别突出,叫喉结。thyroid cartilage; Adam's apple; square cartilage at the front part of the throat, one on each side and joined together, the lower part linked with the cricoid (ring-shaped cartilage) of the larynx, seen chiefly in men; also 喉结 hóujié

【甲状腺】jiǎzhuàngxiàn 内分泌腺之一,在甲状软骨下面的两侧,分左右两叶,彼此相连,能分泌甲状腺素。甲状腺素是含碘的化合物,有促进新陈代谢、增加血糖等作用。thyroid gland; one of the endocrine glands, located on the two sides under the thyroid cartilage and joined with each other secreting thyroxine, a chemical compound containing iodine which helps to promote metabolism and increase blood sugar

【甲子】jiǎzǐ 用干支纪年或计算岁数时,六十组干支字轮一周叫一个甲子 *jiazi*, a cycle of sixty years; ☞ 干支 gānzhī on p. 627

岬 jiǎ ❶ 岬角(多用于地名 usu. used as part of a place name) cape; promontory: 成山～(也叫成山角,在山东) Chengshanjia (also named Chengshanjiao, in Shandong Province) ❷ 两山之间 narrow passage between mountains

【岬角】jiǎjiǎo 突入海中的尖形陆地 cape; promontory

胛 jiǎ 肩胛 shoulder blade: ～骨(肩胛骨) scapula; either of two flat, triangular bones in the back of the shoulders of humans

贾 Jiǎ 姓 a surname
〈古 *arch*.〉same as 价(價)jià
☞ gǔ on p. 695

【贾宪三角】Jiǎ Xiàn sānjiǎo 杨辉三角 Jia Xian

triangle; Yang Hui triangle; Pascal's triangle

钾 jiǎ 金属元素,符号 K (kalium)。银白色,质软。化学性质极活泼,容易氧化,燃烧时发出紫色光,遇水剧烈反应,放出氢气,同时燃烧起火。在工农业中用途很广。potassium (K); soft, silver-white metallic chemical element that oxidizes rapidly when exposed to air, gives out purple light when burning, and emits hydrogen and burns at the same time when meeting water, widely used in industry and agriculture

【钾肥】jiǎféi 含钾的肥料,能促使作物的茎秆坚韧,提高产量,如氯化钾、硫酸钾、草木灰等 potash fertilizer; fertilizer containing potassium, that helps to toughen the stems of the crops and increase output, such as: potassium chloride, potassium sulphate, plant ash, etc.

假 jiǎ ❶ 虚伪的;不真实的;伪造的;人造的(跟'真'相对 as opposed to 'true') false; fake; sham; phoney; artificial:～话 lie; falsehood|～发 wig|～山 small artificial hill|～证件 fraudulent certificate, fake credentials; fake card|～仁～义 pretended benevolence and righteousness; hypocrisy ❷ 假定 suppose; assume; grant; presume:～设 supposition; hypothesis; assumption|～说 postulate; hypothesis ❸ 假如 if; in case:～若 if; supposing; in case|～使 if; in case; supposing that ❹ 借用 borrow; avail oneself of:久～不归 keep putting off returning sth. one has borrowed; appropriate sth. borrowed for one's own use|～公济私 jobbery; use public office for private gain ◇不～思索 without thinking; without hesitation; readily

☞ jià on p. 937

【假扮】jiǎbàn 为了使人错认而装扮成跟本人不同的另一种人或另一个人;化装:disguise oneself as; dress up as:他～什么人,就像什么人。He looks just like what he disguise himself as.

【假充】jiǎchōng 装出某种样子;冒充 pretend to be; pose as:～正经 pretend to be honest|～内行 pretend to be an expert

【假道学】jiǎdàoxué 表面上正经,实际上很坏的人;伪君子 hypocrite; sanctimonious person

【假定】jiǎdìng ❶ 姑且认定 suppose; assume; grant; presume; putative:～他明天起程,后天就可以到达延安。Supposing he leaves tomorrow, he will be in Yan'an the day after tomorrow. ❷ 科学上的假设,从前也叫假定 scientific hypothesis, called 假定 jiǎdìng in the past; ☞ 假设 jiǎshè

【假根】jiǎgēn 由单一的细胞发育而成的根,形状像丝,没有维管束,作用与根相同,如苔藓植物的根 rhizoid; silk-like root without vascular bundle, developed from a single cell, such as the root of the bryophyte

【假公济私】jiǎ gōng jì sī 假借公事的名义,取得私人的利益 jobbery; use public office for private gain

【假果】jiǎguǒ 果实的食用部分不是子房壁发育而成,而是花托或萼发育而成的叫做假果,如梨、苹果、无花果、桑葚等 pseudocarp; spurious fruit, such as pear, apple, fig, mulberry, etc., whose edible part is developed from the receptacle or calyx, not from the ovary

【假借】jiǎjiè ❶ 利用某种名义、力量等来达到目的 make use of an excuse or force to achieve one's goal:～名义,招摇撞骗 go swindling by falsification of sb. else's name ❷ 六书之一。许慎《说文解字叙》:'假借者,本无其字,依声托事。'假借是说借用已有的文字表示语言中同音而不同义的词。例如借当小麦讲的'来'作来往的'来',借当毛皮讲的'求'作请求的'求'。phonetic loan characters; character adopted to represent homophones; one of the six categories of Chinese characters which, according to Xu Shen's *Discourses on Words and Explanations of Characters · Narration*, borrows its sense from another character identical in sound but of different in form, e.g. 来 lái (wheat) for 来 lái (come), 求 qiú (fur) for 求 qiú (entreat) ❸〈书 *fml*.〉宽容 tolerant; lenient:针砭时弊,不稍～。Don't be tolerant at all when criticizing a prevailing mistake.

【假冒】jiǎmào 冒充 pass oneself off as; palm off (a fake as genuine):认清商标,谨防～。Identify (or recognize) the brand, and beware of imitations.

【假寐】jiǎmèi〈书 *fml*.〉不脱衣服小睡 catnap; doze:凭几～ take a nap by the tea table|闭目～ close one's eyes for a catnap

【假面具】jiǎmiànjù ❶ 仿照人物或兽类脸形制成的面具,古代演戏时化装用,后多用做玩具 mask, stage property worn by an actor as make-up, oft. used as a toy ❷〈比喻 *fig*.〉虚伪的外表 false appearance; false front

【假名】jiǎmíng 日本文所用的字母,多借用汉字的偏旁。楷书叫片假名,草书叫平假名。*kana*. Most of the letters used in the Japanese script are borrowed from the basic structural parts of Chinese characters: the portion used in the printing scrip (the regular script) is called *katakana* and the portion used in the writing scrip (letters in Japanese executed swiftly and with strokes flowing together) is called *hiragana*.

【假模假式】jiǎ·mojiǎshì 装模作样 insincere; hypocritical; also 假模假样 jiǎ·mojiǎyàng

【假撇清】jiǎpiēqīng〈方 *dial*.〉假装自己清白,跟坏事无关 pretend innocence

【假仁假义】jiǎ rén jiǎ yì 虚假的仁义道德 pretended benevolence and righteousness; hypocrisy

【假如】jiǎrú 如果 if; supposing; in case:～明天不下雨,我一定去。I'll go if it doesn't rain

J

tomorrow.

【假若】jiǎruò 如果 if; supposing; in case:～你遇见这种事,你该怎么办? What will you do if you come across such a thing?

【假嗓子】jiǎsǎng·zi 歌唱时使用的非本嗓发出的嗓音 *falsetto*; artificial way of singing

【假山】jiǎshān 园林中用石块(大多是太湖石)堆砌而成的小山 rockery; rocks (mostly *taihu* rocks) arranged for growing a rock garden

【假设】jiǎshè ❶ 姑且认定 suppose; assume; grant; presume:这本书印了十万册,～每册只有一个读者,那也就有十万个读者。100,000 copies of this book are printed, if each copy has only one reader, it will receive a readership of 100,000. ❷ 虚构 fictitious:故事情节是～的。The story is fictitious. ❸ 科学研究上对客观事物的假定的说明,假设要根据事实提出,经过实践证明是正确的,就成为理论 hypothesis; explanations for the hypothesis in scientific research; if a hypothesis based on facts proves correct through practice, it becomes a theory

【假使】jiǎshǐ 如果 if; in case; in the event that:～你同意,我们明天一清早就出发。We'll leave early tomorrow morning if you agree.

【假释】jiǎshì 在一定条件下,把未满刑期的犯人暂时释放。假释期间,如不再犯新罪,就认为原判刑罚已经执行完毕,否则,就把前后所判处的刑罚合并执行。release on parole (or on probation); temporary release of a prisoner whose sentence has not expired, on condition of future good behaviour. If the prisoner does not commit a new crime during parole, the original sentence is regarded as already being executed, otherwise the two sentences will be consolidated.

【假手】jiǎ//shǒu 利用别人做某种事来达到自己的目的 make use of someone else to achieve one's own purpose; do sth. through sb. else; make a cat's paw of sb.:～于人 (achieve one's end) through the instrumentality of sb. else

【假说】jiǎshuō same as 假设 jiǎshè ③

【假死】jiǎsǐ ❶ 因触电、癫痫、溺水、中毒或呼吸道堵塞等,引起呼吸停止,心脏跳动微弱,面色苍白,四肢冰冷,叫做假死。婴儿初生,由于肺未张开,不会啼哭,也不出气,也叫假死。如果及时抢救,大都可以救活。suspended animation; phenomenon of temporary cessation of breathing, faint heartbeat, pale face and cold limbs resulting from electrical shock, epilepsy, drowning, poisoning and blocking up of the respiratory tract. Some babies are born without crying or breathing because their lungs fail to start working. Such cases are also called suspended animation, but most of them can live if emergency treatment is given on time. ❷ 某些动物遇到敌人时,为了保护自己,装成死的样子 play dead; feign death; play possum; some animals feign death in order to protect themselves when encountering an enemy

【假托】jiǎtuō ❶ 推托 on the pretext of:他～家里有事,站起来先走了。He rose and left on the pretext of having something to do at home. ❷ 假冒 under the name of sb. else:他～经理的名义签订合同。He signed a contract under the name of the manager. ❸ 凭借 by means of; through the medium of:寓言是～故事来说明道理的文学作品。Fable is a literary genre using story to show truth.

【假想】jiǎxiǎng 想像;假设② imagination; hypothesis; supposition:～敌 imaginary enemy; hypothetical enemy | ～的故事结局 fictitious ending of the story

【假想敌】jiǎxiǎngdí 军事演习时所设想的敌人 imaginary enemy; hypothetical enemy; enemy imagined for military exercises

【假相】jiǎxiàng same as 假象 jiǎxiàng

【假象】jiǎxiàng 跟事物本质不符合的表面现象 false appearance:擦亮眼睛,不要被～所迷惑。Sharpen your vigilance and don't be misled by appearances. *or* Be watchful, don't be misled by appearances. also 假相 jiǎxiàng

【假象牙】jiǎxiàngyá 〈旧称 *old*〉赛璐珞 celluloid

【假小子】jiǎxiǎo·zi 指性格泼辣、举止大胆奔放像男子的女孩子 tomboy

【假惺惺】jiǎxīng·xīng 虚情假意的样子 hypocritically; unctuously

【假牙】jiǎyá 牙齿脱落或拔除后镶上的牙,多用瓷或塑料等制成 dental prosthesis; false tooth; denture

【假意】jiǎyì ❶ 虚假的心意 unction; insincerity; hypocrisy:虚情～ pretended affection; insincerity; hypocrisy; insincere; hypocritical ❷ 故意(表现或做出) pretend; put on:他～笑着问,'刚来的这位是谁呢?' He put on a smile and asked:'Who is there?'

【假造】jiǎzào ❶ 模仿真的造假的 forge; counterfeit:～证件 forge a certificate ❷ 捏造 invent; fabricate:～理由 invent an excuse

【假装】jiǎzhuāng 故意做出某种动作或姿态来掩饰真相 pretend; feign; simulate; make believe:他继续干着手里的活儿,～没听见。He continued his work at hand and pretended not to hear it. | ～糊涂 pretend to play fool

【假座】jiǎzuò 借用(某个场所) borrow (a place):～俱乐部举办联谊会 hold a party in the club

斝(斚) jiǎ 古代盛酒的器具,圆口,三足 *jia*, an ancient wine vessel with a round mouth and three legs

嘏 jiǎ 嘏的又音 another pronunciation for 嘏 gǔ

檟 jiǎ 古书上指楸树或茶树 Chinese catalpa or tea tree in ancient books

榎 jiǎ 〈古 *arch*.〉 same as 檟 jiǎ

瘕 jiǎ 〈书 *fml*.〉 肚子里结块的病 lump in the abdomen

jià (ㄐㄧㄚˋ)

价(價) jià ❶ 价格 price：物～ price｜调～ price adjustment; adjust prices｜物美～廉 good in quality and cheap in price; good and cheap｜无～之宝 priceless treasure; invaluable asset ❷ 价值 value：等～交换 exchange at equal value ❸ 化合价的简称 valence：氢是一～的元素。Hydrogen is a one-valence element.

☞ jiè on p. 998 and ·jie on p. 1002

【价格】jiàgé 商品价值的货币表现，如一件衣服卖五十元人民币，五十元就是衣服的价格 price, e.g. if a dress sells at 50 yuan, 50 yuan is the price of the dress

【价款】jiàkuǎn 买卖货物时收付的款项 cost; money paid for sth. purchased or received for sth. sold

【价码】jiàmǎ (～儿 jiàmǎr)价目；价钱 list price; marked price：标明～ mark (goods) with a price tag; have goods clearly priced

【价目】jiàmù 标明的商品价格 marked price; list price：～表 price list

【价钱】jià·qian 价格 price：～公道 fair price

【价值】jiàzhí ❶ 体现在商品里的社会必要劳动。价值量的大小决定于生产这一商品所需的社会必要劳动时间的多少。不经过人类劳动加工的东西，如空气，即使对人们有使用价值，也不具有价值。value; socially necessary labour embodied in a commodity, whose value is determined by the socially necessary labour and the time consumed in the production of it. A thing that consumes no human labour, as air, has no value even if it has use value to the humans. ❷ 积极作用 positive effect; worth; value：这些资料很有参考～。These data have great reference value.｜粗制滥造的作品毫无～。Works done in a slipshod way are of no value.

【价值规律】jiàzhí guīlǜ 商品生产的基本经济规律。依照这个规律，商品的交换是根据两个商品所包含的社会必要劳动量(价值量)相等而相互交换。law of value; fundamental economic law guiding commodity production, by which two commodities containing equal socially necessary labour (magnitude of value) are exchanged

【价值量】jiàzhíliàng 指体现在商品中的社会必要劳动量 magnitude of value; necessary social labour content as represented in commodities

【价值形式】jiàzhí xíngshì 商品价值的表现形式，也就是交换价值。一个商品的价值不能由这个商品自身来表现，而必须在同另一种商品交换时，通过所交换的一定数量的商品才能表现出来。如一丈布可以交换二斗米，二斗米就是一丈布的价值形式或交换价值。form of value; form in which the price of a commodity is manifested; value of exchange; price of a commodity is manifested not in the commodity itself but in exchange with a given quantity of another commodity. For example, one *zhang* (3.33 metres) of cloth can be exchanged for two decilitres of rice; thus two decilitres of rice is the form of value or exchange value for one *zhang* of cloth.

驾 jià ❶ 使牲口拉(车或农具) harness; draw (a cart, etc.)：两匹马～着车 cart drawn by two horses｜～着牲口耕地 harness cattle to plough the fields ❷ 驾驶 drive：～车 drive a car｜～飞机 pilot a plane◇腾云～雾 mount the clouds and ride the mist — speed across the sky ❸ 指车辆，借用为敬辞，称对方 vehicle; (pol.) you：车～ Emperor; His Majesty｜大～ your gracious presence; carriage for a sovereign or emperor｜劳～ excuse me｜挡～ refuse to receive visitors; stop visitors from entering a place or calling on someone ❹ 特指帝王的车，借指帝王 imperial carriage; emperor：晏～ death of an emperor｜～崩(帝王死去) death of an emperor; (of an emperor) pass away; die

【驾到】jiàdào 〈敬辞 *pol*.〉称客人来到 arrival of a visitor

【驾临】jiàlín 〈敬辞 *pol*.〉称对方到来 your arrival; your esteemed presence：敬备菲酌，恭候～。Your presence is cordially requested at a simple meal.

【驾凌】jiàlíng 凌驾 place oneself above

【驾轻就熟】jià qīng jiù shú 驾轻车，就熟路 drive a light carriage on a familiar road; 〈比喻 *fig*.〉对事情熟习，做起来容易 handle a job with ease because of previous experience; do a familiar job with ease

【驾驶】jiàshǐ 操纵(车、船、飞机、拖拉机等)使行驶 drive (a vehicle); pilot (a ship or plane)：～员 driver; pilot｜～舱 control cabin; cockpit; pilot's compartment

【驾驭】jiàyù ❶ 驱使车马行进 drive (a cart, horse, etc.)：这匹马不好～。This horse is hard to control. ❷ 使服从自己的意志而行动 control; master; bring under one's control：～自然 tame nature ‖ also 驾御 jiàyù

【驾御】jiàyù same as 驾驭 jiàyù

【驾辕】jià//yuán 驾着车辕拉车 (of a horse) pull a cart or carriage from between the shafts; be hitched up

J

架 jià ❶ (～儿 jiàr)架子① frame; rack; shelf; stand: 房～ framework of a house| 书～ bookcase; bookshelves | 衣～儿 coat hanger; clothes rack | 脚手～ scaffold; scaffolding ❷ 支撑;支起 prop up; support; put up; erect: ～桥 build a bridge|～电线 put up wires|梯子～在树旁。Put up the ladder against the tree. ❸ 招架 fend off; ward off; withstand: 拿枪～住砍过来的刀 ward off a sword thrust with a spear ❹ 绑架 kidnap: 他爹被下山的土匪～走了。His father was kidnapped by the bandits coming down from the mountain. ❺ 搀扶 support; prop; help: 连搀带～ support and help|～着伤员慢慢走 help a wounded soldier to walk slowly ❻ 殴打或争吵的事 fight; quarrel: 打～ fight| 吵～ quarrel |劝～ try to stop people from fighting each other; mediate; try to reconcile parties to a quarrel ❼〈量词 *classifier*〉a)用于有支柱的或有机械的东西 [for things with support or with machines]: 一～机器 a machine| 几～飞机 several planes| 三～钢琴 three pianos b)〈方 *dial.*〉用于山,相当于'座' [when used for mountains, it is equivalent to 座 zuò]: 一～山 a mountain

【架不住】jià·bu zhù〈方 *dial.*〉❶ 禁不住;受不住 cannot sustain (the weight); cannot stand (the pressure); cannot stand up against: 双拳难敌四手,好汉～人多。Two fists cannot stand up against four hands, and a strong and brave man cannot stand up against too many people. |老大娘开始还有些怀疑,～大家七嘴八舌地一说,也就相信了。At first, the old lady had some suspicion, but was convinced after everybody had put a word in. ❷ 抵不上 be no match for: 你们虽然力气大,～她们会找窍门。You may have more strength, but these women folks know better how to do it.

【架次】jiàcì〈复合量词 *compound classifier*〉表示飞机出动或出现若干次架数的总和。如一架飞机出动三次为三架次,三架飞机出动一次也是三架次。又如在一天内飞机出动三次,第一次三架,第二次六架,第三次九架,那一天总共出动十八架次。sortie; total number of missions flown by military planes in one day; e.g. it is three sorties if one plane flying three missions or three planes each flying one mission. If three groups of planes are dispatched in one day, three planes in the first group, six planes in the second group and nine planes in the third group, the planes fly a total of 18 sorties that day.

【架得住】jià·de zhù〈方 *dial.*〉禁得住;受得住 can bear, stand or endure; be able to bear, stand or endure: 有的小学给学生留的家庭作业太多,孩子怎能～? Some primary schools leave too much homework to the pupils. How can the children cope with it?

【架构】jiàgòu ❶ 建造;构筑 build; construct ❷ 框架;支架 framework; frame ❸〈比喻 *fig.*〉事物的组织、结构、格局 organization; structure; pattern: 市场～ market structure| 故事～庞大。The structure of the story is massive.

【架空】jiàkōng ❶ 房屋、器物下面用柱子等撑住而离开地面 built on stilts: 竹楼是～的,离地约有六七尺高。The bamboo huts are built on stilts, about six or seven *chi* (1/3 metre) from the ground. ❷〈比喻 *fig.*〉没有基础 having no foundation; impracticable; unpractical: 没有相应的措施,计划就会成为～的东西。Unless (we) adopt necessary measures the plan will come to nothing. ❸〈比喻 *fig.*〉表面推崇,暗中排挤,使失去实权 turn sb. into a mere figurehead

【架设】jiàshè 支起并安设(凌空的物体) erect or build (above ground or water level, as on stilts or posts): ～桥梁 put up (erect, built) a bridge|～电线 put up power line

【架势】jià·shi ❶ 姿势;姿态 posture; stance; manner: 双方摆开～准备较量。The two sides assumed their postures, ready for a trial of strength. |看他走路的～像是个军人。He walks in the gait of an armyman. ❷〈方 *dial.*〉势头;形势 condition; situation: 看她病的～是不行了。Her condition looks not so good. |看今春这～,雨水少不了。As it is, there will be a lot of rainfall this spring. ‖ also 架式 jià·shi

【架秧子】jiàyāng·zi〈方 *dial.*〉哄闹;起哄 noise; create disturbance; boo; hoot: 起哄～ create disturbance by hooting

【架子】jià·zi ❶ 由若干材料纵横交叉地构成的东西,用来放置器物、支撑物体或安装工具等 frame; stand; rack; shelf; anything made of parts fitted together according to a design; basic or skeletal structure around which a thing is built and that gives the thing its shape; framework, case, stand, grating, etc. for holding or displaying various things: 花瓶～ flower vase stand| 骨头～ skeleton| 保险刀的～ safety razor stand ❷〈比喻 *fig.*〉事物的组织、结构 framework, skeleton, outline: 写文章要先搭好～。Make an outline before you start writing. ❸ 自高自大、装腔作势的作风 airs; haughtiness: 官～ bureaucratic airs| 拿～ put on airs| 那位局长一点儿～都没有。That bureau director has no airs. ❹ 架势;姿势 posture; stance: 锄地有锄地的～,一拿锄头就看出他是内行。Hoeing calls for its own posture. When he holds a hoe, he shows he is a dab hand.

【架子车】jià·zichē 一种用人力推拉的两轮车。用木料等做车架,上面铺木板、竹板或薄铁板制成。handcart; two-wheeled cart pushed or pulled by one person, consisting of a wooden frame covered with some wood or bamboo planks, and sometimes with a thin steel sheet

【架子工】jià·zigōng ❶ 专门搭、拆脚手架的工种 job for erecting or removing scaffolds ❷ 做这种工作的建筑工人 scaffolder; worker doing such work

【架子花】jià·zihuā 戏曲中花脸的一种,因偏重做工和工架而得名 *jiazihua*, a male role in Chinese opera with heavy makeup, and named for its emphasis on acting and posture

【架子猪】jià·zizhū 已长大但没有养肥的猪。有的地区叫壳郎猪。feeder pig; also known as 壳郎猪 ké·langzhū in some areas

假 jià 按照规定或经过批准暂时不工作或不学习的时间 holiday; vacation; leave of absence; furlough; day or a period of time set aside by law or with approval for suspension of work, business or study: 请～ ask for leave | 暑～ summer vacation | 病～ sick leave | 婚～ wedding leave | 春节有三天～ three-day holiday for the Spring Festival; three days off for the Spring Festival

☞ jiǎ on p. 933

【假期】jiàqī 放假或休假的时期 vacation; holiday; period of leave

【假日】jiàrì 放假或休假的日子 holiday; day off

【假条】jiàtiáo (～儿 jiàtiáor)写明请假理由和期限的纸条子 slip of paper asking for leave; application for leave; leave permit; doctor's certificate for sick leave

嫁 jià ❶ 女子结婚(跟'娶'相对 as opposed to 'take a woman as wife') marrying of a woman: 出～ be married off | 改～ be married to another man | ～人 (of a woman) marry; marry off; get married | ～女儿 marry off a girl ❷ 转移(罪名、损失、负担等) shift (a crime, loss, burden, etc.): 转～ shift on to; remarry; marry again | ～祸于人 shift the misfortune onto sb. else; put the blame on sb. else

【嫁接】jiàjiē 把要繁殖的植物的枝或芽接到另一种植物体上,使它们结合在一起,成为一个独立生长的植株。嫁接能保持植物原有的某些特性,是常用的改良品种的方法。grafting; shoot or bud of one plant or tree to be inserted into the stem or trunk of another, where it continues to grow, becoming a permanent part, a common technique designed to preserve certain original properties of the plant and improve the strains of plants

【嫁妆】jià·zhuang 女子出嫁时,从娘家带到丈夫家去的衣被、家具及其他用品 dowry; trousseau; clothes, bed quilts, furniture and other articles a woman take to the home of her husband when she gets married; also 嫁装 jià·zhuang

稼 jià ❶ 种植(谷物) sow (grain): 耕～ ploughing and sowing | ～穑 sowing and reaping ❷ 谷物 cereals: 庄～ crops

【稼穑】jiàsè 〈书 *fml.*〉种植和收割。泛指农业劳动。sowing and reaping; (in a broad sense) farming; farm work: ～艰难 toil and hardship of farm work; toil and hardship of a farmer's life

jiān (ㄐㄧㄢ)

戋(戔) jiān [戋戋]〈书 *fml.*〉少;细微 scant; small; tiny: 为数～ insignificant amount; very small amount; little bit | ～微物 very tiny thing

尖 jiān ❶ 末端细小;尖锐 tiny end; sharp: 把铅笔削～了 sharpen a pencil | ～下巴颏儿 pointed chin ❷ 声音高而细 high-pitched; shrill; piercing: ～声～气 in a shrill voice | ～嗓子 shrill voice ❸ (耳、目、鼻子)灵敏 sharp; acute; keen: 眼～ sharp eyes | 耳朵～ have sharp ears; be sharp-eared | 他鼻子～得很,有一点异味都闻得出。He has a sharp nose and can sense even a little offensive smell. ❹ 使嗓音高而细 scream: 她～着嗓子喊。She screamed at the top of her voice. ❺ (～儿 jiānr)物体锐利的末端或细小的头儿 point; tip; top: 笔～儿 tip of a pen | 针～儿 tip of a needle | 刀～儿 tip of a knife | 塔～ pinnacle of a pagoda ❻ (～儿 jiānr)出类拔萃的人或物品 best of its kind; pick of the bunch; cream of the crop: ～儿货 top notch person | 姐妹三个里头就数她是个～儿。She is top-notch among the three sisters. ❼〈方 *dial.*〉吝啬;抠门儿 stingy: ～抠 stingy | 这人可～了,一点儿亏也不吃。This man is very stingy, and never loses anything. ❽ 尖刻 acrimonious; caustic; biting: 他嘴～,说话不留情面。He speaks with biting sarcasm, and never spares the feelings of others.

【尖兵】jiānbīng ❶ 行军时派出的担任警戒任务的分队 point: ～班 point platoon ❷〈比喻 *fig.*〉工作上走在前面开创道路的人 trailblazer; pathbreaker; pioneer; vanguard: 我们是地质战线上的～。We are pioneers on the geological front.

【尖刀】jiāndāo〈比喻 *fig.*〉作战时最先插入敌人阵地的 first group of soldiers thrust into the enemy's position in fighting a battle: ～连 vanguard company | ～组 vanguard group | ～部队 vanguard force

【尖顶】jiāndǐng 顶端;顶点 pinnacle

【尖端】jiānduān ❶ 尖锐的末梢;顶点 pointed end; acme; peak ❷ 发展水平最高的(科学技术等) most advanced; sophisticated: ～科学 most advanced branches of science; frontiers of science | ～技术 most advanced technology |

J

～产品 highly sophisticated products

【尖刻】jiānkè 尖酸刻薄 acrimonious; caustic; biting: 语言～ speak with biting sarcasm | 他为人～。He is acrimonious to people.

【尖厉】jiānlì 形容声音高而刺耳 high and piercing voice: 哨声～ piercing whistle | 寒风～地呼啸着。The cold wind whistled piercingly.

【尖利】jiānlì ❶ 尖锐;锐利 sharp; keen; cutting: 笔锋～ write in an incisive style; write with cutting words | 他的眼光非常～,一眼就看出对方的畏怯。He has a sharp sight and sees the timidness of his opponent at first glance. ❷ same as 尖厉 jiānlì

【尖溜溜】jiānliūliū 〈方 *dial.*〉(～的 jiānliūliū · de)形容尖细或锋利 sharp; pointed: ～的嗓子 shrill voice

【尖脐】jiānqí ❶ 螃蟹腹下面的甲是尖形的(雄蟹的特征,区别于'团脐' as compared with 'the round abdomen of a female crab') narrow triangular abdomen of a male crab ❷ 指雄蟹 male crab

【尖锐】jiānruì ❶ 物体有锋芒,容易刺破其他物体的;锋利① sharp-pointed: 把锥子磨得非常～。Sharpen an awl by grinding. ❷ 认识客观事物灵敏而深刻;敏锐 penetrating; incisive; sharp; keen: 眼光～ sharp eye; keen eye | 他看问题很～。He sees things with a keen (or sharp) eye. ❸ (声音)高而刺耳 shrill; piercing: ～的哨声 shrill sound of a whistle | 子弹发出～的啸声。The bullet whistled. ❹ (言论、斗争等)激烈 intense; acute; sharp: ～的批评 acute criticism | 进行了～的斗争 wage a sharp struggle

【尖酸】jiānsuān 说话带刺,使人难受 acrid; acrimonious; tart: ～刻薄 acrimonious | 气量狭小,口角～ be narrow-minded and quarrels in an acrimonious tone

【尖团音】jiāntuányīn 尖音和团音的合称。尖音指 z、c、s 声母拼 i、ü 或 i、ü 起头的韵母,团音指 j、q、x 声母拼 i、ü 或 i、ü 起头的韵母。有的方言中分别'尖团',如把'尖、千、先'读作 ziān、ciān、siān,把'兼、牵、掀'读作 jiān、qiān、xiān。普通话语音中不分'尖团',如'尖=兼'jiān,'千=牵'qiān,'先=掀'xiān。昆曲所谓尖团音范围还要广些,z、c、s 和 zh、ch、sh 的分别也叫尖团音,如'灾'zāi 是尖音,'斋'zhāi 是团音,'三'sān 是尖音,'山'shān 是团音。sharp and rounded sounds; combined term for sharp sound and rounded sound; sharp sounds are the consonants z, c, s combined with vowels beginning with i, ü or i, ü, while the rounded sounds are the consonants of j, q, x combined with vowels beginning with i, ü or i, ü. In some dialects, the two categories are differentiated, e.g. 尖,千,and 先 are read as ziān, ciān, and siān, 兼,牵 and 掀 are read as jiān, qiān, and xiān. In the common speech of the Chinese language, the two are not differentiated, such as 尖 = 兼 for jiān, 千 = 牵 for qiān, and 先 = 掀 for xiān. In the *kunqu* opera, the range of the so-called sharp and rounded sounds is still broader; the difference between z, c, s and zh, ch, sh is also called 'sharp and rounded sounds'. For instance, 灾 zāi is a sharp sound, 斋 zhāi is a rounded sound, 三 sān is a sharp sound, and 山 shān is a rounded sound.

【尖音】jiānyīn ☞ 尖团音 jiāntuányīn

【尖子】jiān·zi ❶ 尖⑤ point; tip; top ❷ 尖⑥ best of its kind; pick of the bunch; cream of the crop: 他是我们班的～,名次总不出前三名。He's one of the top students in the class, and always ranks among the top three. ❸ 戏曲中指忽然高亢的唱腔 sudden rise in pitch (in opera singing)

【尖嘴薄舌】jiān zuǐ bó shé 形容说话尖酸刻薄 have a caustic and biting tongue

【尖嘴猴腮】jiān zuǐ hóu sāi 形容人面部瘦削,相貌丑陋 have a mouth that sticks out and a chin like an ape's; have a wretched look

奸[1] jiān ❶ 奸诈 wicked; evil; treacherous: ～笑 sinister smile; malicious smile | ～计 treacherous plot; wicked scheme | 老～巨猾 shrewd and crafty, crafty old scoundrel ❷ 不忠于国家或君主的 unfaithful to the country or the sovereign: ～臣 disloyal and cunning minister; treacherous court official ❸ 出卖国家、民族或阶级利益的人 traitor: 汉～ Chinese traitor | 内～ hidden traitor; secret enemy agent within one's ranks | 为党除～ ferret out enemy agents hidden in the party ❹ 自私;取巧 self-seeking and wily: 藏～耍滑 harbour treachery and play fast and loose | 这个人才～哪,躲躲闪闪不肯出力。This man is really sly. He evasively refuses to exert himself.

奸[2] **(姦)** jiān 奸淫 illicit sexual relations: 通～ have illicit adultery | 强～ rape

【奸臣】jiānchén 指残害忠良或阴谋篡夺帝位的大臣 disloyal and cunning minister; treacherous court official

【奸宄】jiānguǐ 〈书 *fml.*〉坏人(由内而起叫奸,由外而起叫宄) evildoer (an evildoer within is called 奸 jiān, and a malefactor from without 宄 guǐ)

【奸滑】jiānhuá same as 奸猾 jiānhuá

【奸猾】jiānhuá 诡诈狡猾 treacherous; crafty; deceitful; also 奸滑 jiānhuá

【奸计】jiānjì 奸诈的计谋 evil plot: 中了～ be taken in

【奸佞】jiānnìng 〈书 *fml.*〉❶ 奸邪谄媚 crafty and fawning: ～小人 crafty and fawning small man ❷ 奸邪谄媚的人 crafty sycophant: ～专权。A crafty sycophant monopolizes the power.

【奸商】jiānshāng 用投机倒把、囤积居奇等不正当手段牟取暴利的商人 unscrupulous merchant; profiteer; merchant who profiteers by the illicit means of speculation, hoarding and cornering

【奸徒】jiāntú 奸险的人 crafty person

【奸污】jiānwū 强奸或诱奸 rape or seduce

【奸细】jiān·xi 给敌人刺探消息的人 spy; enemy agent

【奸险】jiānxiǎn 奸诈阴险 wicked and crafty; treacherous; malicious: 为人～狠毒 be crafty, wicked and vicious

【奸笑】jiānxiào 阴险地笑 sinister (or villainous) smile: 满脸～ have a sinister smile on one's face

【奸邪】jiānxié 〈书 *fml.*〉 ❶ 奸诈邪恶 crafty and evil; treacherous ❷ 奸诈邪恶的人 crafty and evil person: ～当道 crafty evildoers in power

【奸雄】jiānxióng 用奸诈手段取得大权高位的人 person who achieves high position by unscrupulous scheming: 乱世～ treacherous pretender in an age of chaos

【奸淫】jiānyín ❶ 男女间不正当的性行为 illicit sexual relations; adultery ❷ 奸污 rape: ～掳掠 rape, loot and pillage; rape and loot

【奸贼】jiānzéi 奸险的人;奸臣 traitor; conspirator; treacherous minister

【奸诈】jiānzhà 虚伪诡诈 fraudulent; crafty; treacherous

歼(殲) jiān 歼灭 annihilate; wipe out; destroy: ～匪 wipe out the bandits | 围～ surround and annihilate | ～敌五千 annihilate 5,000 enemy troops | 聚而～之 annihilate en masse

【歼击】jiānjī 攻击和歼灭 attack and wipe out: ～逃敌 wipe out the fleeing enemy

【歼击机】jiānjījī 一种主要用来在空中歼灭敌机和其他空袭兵器的飞机,装有机关枪、机关炮和导弹等武器。速度快,爬升迅速,操纵灵便。旧称驱逐机或战斗机。fighter plane; fighter; pursuit plane; small, fast and manoeuvrable airplane for aerial combat, equipped with machine guns and cannons, missiles, etc. formerly called 驱逐机 qūzhújī or 战斗机 zhàndòujī

【歼灭】jiānmiè 消灭(敌人) annihilate; wipe out; destroy: 集中优势兵力,各个～敌人 concentrate a superior force to wipe out the enemy forces one by one

【歼灭战】jiānmièzhàn 消灭全部或大部敌人的战役或战斗 battle of annihilation

坚(堅) jiān ❶ 硬;坚固 hard; solid; firm; strong: ～冰 solid ice; hard ice | ～城 heavily fortified city | ～不可破 impregnable; invulnerable | ～如磐石 as firm as a rock ❷ 坚固的东西或阵地 fortification; stronghold: 攻～ storm a fortified position | 披～执锐 wear armour and hold weapons; in full combat-readiness | 无～不摧 be all-conquering; overrun all fortifications ❸ 坚定;坚决 firmly; steadfastly: ～信 firmly believe | ～守阵地 hold one's position; stick to one's position; defend one's position successfully ❹ (Jiān)姓 a surname

【坚壁】jiānbì 藏起来使不落到敌人的手里(多指藏物资) hide supplies to prevent the enemy from seizing them; place in a cache; cache: 把粮食～起来 hide grain from the enemy

【坚壁清野】jiānbì qīngyě 作战时采用的一种对付入侵之敌的策略,坚守据点,转移周围的人口、牲畜、财物、粮食,毁掉战地附近的房屋、树木等,使敌人既攻不下据点,也抢不到东西 fortify the defence works and leave nothing usable to the invading enemy; strengthen the defences and clear the fields; tactic of coping with an invading enemy force; hold fast to the fortification, evacuate the residents, animals, property and food grains and destroy the houses and trees in the vicinity of the battlefield so that the invading enemy force cannot capture the fortification nor seize anything

【坚不可摧】jiān bù kě cuī 非常坚固,摧毁不了 indestructible; impregnable; indomitable

【坚持】jiānchí 坚决保持、维护或进行 keep plugging away; persist in; persevere in; uphold; insist on; stick to; adhere to: ～原则 adhere to the principle | ～己见 hold on to one's own views | ～不懈 persistent, unremitting; persevering | ～工作 persist in one's work

【坚定】jiāndìng ❶ (立场、主张、意志等)稳定坚强;不动摇 (of stand, opinion, will, etc.) firm; staunch; steadfast: ～不移 steadfast; unswerving; unshakable; unflinching; firm | 各级领导要～地贯彻群众路线。The leadership at all levels should adhere to the mass line steadfastly. ❷ 使坚定 make firm: ～立场 firm stand | ～信念 firm conviction; firm belief; unshakable faith

【坚固】jiāngù 结合紧密,不容易破坏;牢固;结实 firm; solid; sturdy; strong: 阵地～ strong position; impregnable position | ～耐用 sturdy and durable

【坚果】jiānguǒ 干果的一种,果皮很坚硬,果实里只有一个种子,如栗子、橡子等 nut; dry, one-seeded fruit of trees or shrubs, consisting of a kernel, oft. edible, in a hard and woody or tough and leathery shell, more or less separable from the seed itself, such as walnut, acorn, etc.

【坚决】jiānjué (态度、主张、行动等)确定不移;不犹豫 (of attitude, opinion, act, etc.) firm; resolute; determined: 态度～ determined attitude; firm position|认识了错误就~改正。Correct your mistake determinedly once you have seen it.|~抓好安全生产的各项工作 resolutely grasp all aspects of work related to production safety

【坚苦】jiānkǔ 坚忍刻苦 steadfast and assiduous

【坚苦卓绝】jiānkǔ zhuōjué (在艰难困苦中)坚忍刻苦的精神超越寻常 (under hard and difficult circumstancs) showing utmost fortitude; extremely hard and arduous; extremely steadfast and arduous

【坚强】jiānqiáng ❶ 强固有力,不可动摇或摧毁 strong; firm; staunch:意志~ strong will|~不屈 firm and unyielding ❷ 使坚强 strengthen:丰富自己的知识,~自己的信心。Broaden one's knowledge and strengthen one's confidence.

【坚忍】jiānrěn (在艰苦困难的情况下)坚持而不动摇 (in face of difficulties) steadfast and persevering:~不拔的意志 indomitable will; strong will

【坚韧】jiānrèn 坚固有韧性 tough and tensile; firm and tenacious:质地~ tensile in quality

【坚实】jiānshí ❶ 坚固结实 solid; substantial:~的基础 solid foundation ❷ 健壮 strong; robust:身体~ strongly built; robust

【坚守】jiānshǒu 坚决守卫;不离开 stick to; hold fast to; stand fast:~阵地 hold fast to one's position; hold one's ground|~岗位 stand fast to one's post

【坚挺】jiāntǐng ❶ 坚强有力;硬而直 strong:~的身架 (man of) sturdy build|枝条上有~的刺。There are hard thorns on the twig. ❷ 价格呈上升趋势或稳定(多用于货币)(of a currency) strong and stable:价格~ strong prices

【坚信】jiānxìn 坚决相信 firmly believe:~我们的事业一定要胜利。We firmly believe that we will succeed in our cause.

【坚毅】jiānyì 坚定有毅力 firm and persistent; unswerving determination; with inflexible will:性格~ firm character; strong character|~的神态 firm expression

【坚硬】jiānyìng 非常硬 hard; solid:~的山石 solid rock

【坚贞】jiānzhēn 节操坚定不变 faithful; constant:~不屈 remain faithful and unyielding

间(間) jiān ❶ 中间 between; among:彼此~ each other|同志之~ among comrades|居~调停 mediate a dispute between two sides ❷ 一定的空间或时间里 within a definite time or space:田~ in the fields|人~ in the world|晚~ in the evening|一刹那~ in an instant ❸ 一间屋子;房间 room:里~ inner room|车~ workshop|衣帽~ cloakroom ❹〈量词 *classifier*〉房屋的最小单位 bay:一~卧室 one-bay bedroom; one bedroom|三~门面 three-bay shop front

☞ jiàn on p.952 and 闲(閒) xián on p.2074

【间冰期】jiānbīngqī 两个冰期之间相对温暖的时期 interglacial stage; interglacial

【间不容发】jiān bù róng fà 中间容不下一根头发 not a hair's breadth apart or away;〈比喻 *fig.*〉与灾祸相距极近,情势极其危急 disaster is imminent; critical situation

【间架】jiānjià 本指房屋的结构形式,借指汉字书写的笔画结构。也指文章的布局。framework of a house; form of a Chinese character; structure of an essay

【间距】jiānjù 两者之间的距离 distance between two points:从足迹的前后~可以知道动物四肢或躯体的长短。From the distance between the footprints one can tell the length of the limbs or of the body of an animal.

【间量】jiān·liang〈方 *dial.*〉(~儿 jiān·liangr) 房间的面积 floor space of a room:这间屋子~儿太小。The room is too small.

【间脑】jiānnǎo 脑的一部分,在大脑两半球的中间,由许多形状不规则的灰质块和神经纤维构成。间脑包括丘脑和下丘脑。diencephalon; part of the brain between the two hemispheres of the cerebrum, which is composed of many grey matters of irregular shapes and nerve fibres, and includes thalami and hypothalamus

☞ 丘脑 qiūnǎo on p.1581

【间奏曲】jiānzòuqǔ 戏曲或歌剧中在两幕(或场)之间演奏的小型器乐曲 entr'acte; intermezzo

浅(淺、濺) jiān [浅浅]〈书 *fml.*〉形容流水声 sound of flowing water

☞ qiǎn on p.1539 and 溅 jiàn on p.957

肩 jiān ❶ 肩膀 shoulder:两~ shoulders|并~ shoulder to shoulder; side by side; (图见☞ figure for 身体 shēntǐ on p.1701) ❷ 担负 take on; undertake; shoulder; bear:身~大任 shoulder heavy responsibilities ❸〈方 *dial.*〉扛(káng) carry sth. on one's shoulder:~着鱼叉 carry a fish fork on the shoulder|~起扁担上路 start a journey with a carrying-pole on the shoulder

【肩膀】jiānbǎng (~儿 jiānbǎngr)人的胳膊或动物前肢或躯干相连的部分 shoulder; joint connecting the arm or forelimb with the body ◇~儿硬(能担负重大责任) having tough shoulders (can shoulder great responsibilities)|溜~(不负责任) sloping shoulders (not responsible); having no sense of responsibility

【肩负】jiānfù 担负 take on; undertake; shoulder; bear:我们~着建设社会主义的伟大任务。We are entrusted with the great task of building socialism.

【肩胛】jiānjiǎ ❶ 肩膀 shoulders ❷ 医学上指肩膀的后部(med.) back of the shoulders

【肩胛骨】jiānjiǎgǔ 人体胸背部最上部外侧的骨头,左右各一,略呈三角形。肩胛骨、锁骨和肱骨构成肩关节。scapula; shoulder blade; flat, triangular bones in the back of the shoulders on the outerside of the top part of the human back and chest; scapula, clavicle (collar bone) and humerus (bone of the upper arm) form the shoulder joints; also 胛骨 jiǎgǔ or 琵琶骨 pí·pagǔ in some areas; (图见 ☞ figure for 骨骼 gǔgé on p. 693)

【肩摩毂击】jiān mó gǔ jī 肩膀和肩膀相接触,车轮和车轮相碰撞。形容行人车辆非常拥挤。shoulder to shoulder and hub to hub — crowded with people and vehicles; also 摩肩击毂 mó jiān jī gǔ

【肩摩踵接】jiān mó zhǒng jiē ☞ 摩肩接踵 mó jiān jiē zhǒng on p. 1363

【肩头】jiāntóu ❶ 肩膀上 on the shoulders: ～的担子不轻 load on the shoulders is not light ❷〈方 *dial.*〉肩膀 shoulders: 两个～不一般高。The two shoulders are not equally high.

【肩窝】jiānwō (～儿 jiānwōr)肩膀上凹下的部分 hollow part of a shoulder

【肩章】jiānzhāng 军人或某些部门的工作人员佩带在制服的两肩上用来表示行业、级别等的标志 shoulder badge; epaulette

艰(艱) jiān 困难 difficult; hard: ～苦 arduous; hard | ～深 difficult to understand; abstruse | 物力维～ shortage of material power; scarce in resources

【艰巨】jiānjù 困难而繁重 arduous; formidable; difficult and heavy: ～的任务 enormity of a task; arduous task | 这个工程非常～。This is a very difficult project. *or* This is a formidable project.

【艰苦】jiānkǔ 艰难困苦 arduous; difficult; hard; tough: ～奋斗 arduous struggle; hard struggle | 环境～ difficult circumstances | ～的岁月 difficult years | ～的工作 arduous work; difficult work; tough job; difficult job

【艰苦卓绝】jiānkǔ zhuójué 形容斗争十分艰苦,超出寻常 extreme hardship and difficulty

【艰难】jiānnán 困难 difficult; hard: 行动～ walk with difficulty | 生活～ live in straitened circumstances | 不畏～险阻 fear no hardships nor dangers

【艰涩】jiānsè (文词)晦涩,不流畅,不易理解 (of diction) obscure; hard to understand; not smooth

【艰深】jiānshēn (道理、文词)深奥难懂 (of reasoning or diction) difficult to understand; abstruse: 文字～ abstruse language | ～的哲理 abstruse philosophy

【艰危】jiānwēi 艰难危险(多指国家、民族) difficulties and dangers (confronting a nation): 处境～ in a difficult situation; in a dangerous situation; in peril; in danger | 形势日益～。The situation is getting more difficult and dangerous.

【艰险】jiānxiǎn 困难和危险 hardships and dangers: 不避～ brave hardships and dangers | 路途～ difficult road; difficult and dangerous journey

【艰辛】jiānxīn 艰苦 hardships: 历尽～,方有今日。The good life today would not be possible without the fill of hardships yesterday.

监(監) jiān ❶ 从旁察看;监视 supervise; inspect; watch: ～考 oversee an examination or test | ～察 supervise ❷ 牢狱 prison; jail: 收～ put into prison; be imprisoned; be jailed | 探～ visit a prisoner
☞ jiàn on p. 955

【监测】jiāncè 监视检测 monitor: ～卫星 monitoring satellite | 环境～ monitoring of the environment | 空气污染～ monitor air pollution

【监察】jiānchá 监督各级国家机关和机关工作人员的工作并检举违法失职的机关或工作人员 supervise; control; supervise the work of the state organs and their staff and single out organs or staff members that have violated law or neglected their duties

【监场】jiān//chǎng 监视考场,使应考的人遵守考试纪律 invigilate

【监督】jiāndū ❶ 察看并督促 supervise; superintend; control: ～执行 exercise supervision | 接受～ accept supervision ❷ 做监督工作的人 supervisor: 舞台～ stage supervisor

【监犯】jiānfàn 监狱中的犯人 prisoner; convict; inmate

【监工】jiān//gōng 在厂矿或工地监督工作 supervise; oversee; oversee work in a factory or on a work site

【监工】jiāngōng 做监工工作的人 overseer; supervisor

【监管】jiānguǎn 监视管理 supervise; keep watch on: ～犯人 keep watch on criminals; supervise prisoners

【监规】jiānguī 监狱中要求犯人遵守的各项规定 prison regulations; prison rules: 违反～ break prison rules; offend prison rules

【监护】jiānhù ❶ 法律上指对未成年人、精神病人等的人身、财产以及其他一切合法权益的监督和保护 guardianship; custody; guarding, protecting and taking care of the property and other legitimate rights and interests of minors, the mentally retarded, etc. ❷ 仔细观察并护理 monitoring and nursing: ～病人 observe and nurse a patient | 新生儿～ observation and nursing of a newborn

【监护人】jiānhùrén 法律上指负责监护的人 (leg.) guardian

【监禁】jiānjìn 把犯人押起来,限制他的自由 take into custody; imprison; put in jail (or prison)

【监考】jiān//kǎo 监视应考的人,使遵守考试纪律 invigilate

【监考】jiānkǎo 做监考工作的人 invigilator

【监控】jiānkòng ❶ 监测和控制(机器、仪表的工作状态或某些事物的变化等) monitor and control (the performance of machines, instruments, etc.) ❷ 监督控制 supervise and control: 实行物价～ exercise price supervision and control

【监牢】jiānláo 监狱 prison; jail

【监视】jiānshì 从旁严密注视、观察 keep watch on; keep a lookout over: 跟踪～ keep track of and watch on | 瞭望哨远远～着敌人。The lookout post keeps watch on the enemy from afar.

【监守】jiānshǒu 看管 have custody of; guard; take care of: 选举时票箱由专人～。The ballot box is specially guarded during the election.

【监守自盗】jiānshǒu zì dào 盗窃自己所看管的财物 steal what is entrusted to one's care; turn from custodian to thief

【监听】jiāntīng 利用无线电等设备对别人的谈话或发出的无线电信号进行监督 monitor; monitor sb's conversations or radio signals by means of radio transmission devices

【监外执行】jiān wài zhíxíng 指法院对具有某种法定原因(如患有严重疾病,怀孕或正在哺乳自己的婴儿)的犯人暂不羁押,而交付一定机关监管 execute (a sentence) outside prison; court does not detain a criminal temporarily for some legal reason (such as serious illness, pregnancy or sb. breast-feeding own infant) and hand over him or her to a certain department for supervision

【监押】jiānyā ❶ 监禁;关押 put in jail; put in prison; imprison; jail: ～罪犯 put a criminal in prison ❷ 押解 escort: 法警～犯人去受审。The bailiff escorted a criminal to the court for trial.

【监狱】jiānyù 监禁犯人的处所 prison; jail

【监制】jiānzhì 监督制造(商品);监督摄制(影片、电视片) supervise the manufacture of (a commodity); supervise the production of (a film, telefilm)

兼 jiān ❶ 两倍的 double; twice: ～程 travel at double speed | ～旬 twenty days ❷ 同时涉及或具有几种事物 simultaneously; concurrently: ～而有之 have both | ～收并蓄 take in everything; incorporate things of different nature | 品学～优 have good character and scholarship | ～听则明,偏信则暗。You will know the truth if you listen to both sides, and be cheated if you heed to only one side. *or* Listen to both sides and you will be enlightened; heed to only one side and you will be benighted. | 他是副厂长～总工程师。He is deputy factory director and concurrently chief engineer.

【兼备】jiānbèi 同时具备几个方面 have both ... and ...: 德才～ have both good moral character and professional ability; have both ability and political integrity | 文武～ be adept with both the pen and the sword | 形神～ have both the form and the spirit

【兼并】jiānbìng 把别的国家的领土并入自己的国家或把别人的产业并为己有 annex (territory, property, etc.)

【兼差】jiānchāi 〈旧时 *old*〉称兼职 do two or more jobs concurrently

【兼程】jiānchéng 一天走两天的路;以加倍的速度赶路 travel at double speed: ～前进 advance on (or at) the double | 日夜～ travel night and day

【兼顾】jiāngù 同时照顾几个方面 give due consideration to all the quarters concerned: 统筹～ make overall planning and give consideration to the interests of all sides | 公私～ take both public and private interests into account

【兼毫】jiānháo 用羊毫和狼毫在一起制造的毛笔(羊毫较软,狼毫较硬,兼毫适中) Chinese writing brush made of a mixture of goat's and yellow weasel's hair (the goat's hair is too soft, the yellow weasel's hair is too hard, and the mixture of the two is just good)

【兼课】jiān//kè 在本职以外兼任教课工作 do some teaching apart from one's main occupation; hold two or more teaching jobs at the same time

【兼任】jiānrèn ❶ 同时担任几个职务 hold two or more posts concurrently: 总务主任～学校工会主席 serve concurrently as director of general affairs and chairman of the school trade union ❷ 不是专任的 part-time: ～教员 part-time teacher

【兼容】jiānróng 同时容纳几个方面 compatible; capable of living together or getting along well together (with); work well together; combine well: ～并包 all-inclusive | 善恶不能～ good and evil can never be mutually containing

【兼容并包】jiān róng bìng bāo 把各个方面或各种事物都容纳进去 all-embracing; all-inclusive

【兼收并蓄】jiān shōu bìng xù 把内容不同、性质相反的东西都吸收进来 incorporate things of different nature; take in everything; also 兼容并蓄 jiān róng bìng xù

【兼祧】jiāntiāo 〈书 *fml.*〉宗法制度下一个男子兼做两房或两家的继承人 be appointed heir to one's uncle as well as to one's father; under the patriarchal clan system, a man can be appointed heir to two families or two branches of one clan

【兼之】jiānzhī 加以② furthermore; besides; in addition; moreover: 人手不多,～期限迫近,紧张情形可以想见。There are not many people, and moreover, the deadline is getting close, so the strain is obvious.

【兼职】jiān//zhí 在本职之外兼任其他职务

moonlight; hold two or more posts concurrently:身兼数职 hold several posts|～教师 part-time teacher

【兼职】jiānzhí 在本职之外兼任的职务 concurrent post; part-time job:辞去～ resign one's concurrent job

菅 jiān ❶ 多年生草本植物,叶子细长而尖,花绿色,结颖果,褐色 villous themeda (*Themeda gigantea* var. *villosa*); perenial herbal plant with slender and pointed leaves, green flowers and brown caryopsis ❷ (Jiān) 姓 a surname

笺(牋、❷❸椾) jiān ❶ 注解 annotation; commentary:～注 notes and commentary ❷ 写信或题词用的纸 stationery; writing paper:信～ letter paper|便～ notepaper; memo; memo pad ❸ 信札 letters:～札(书信) letters; correspondence

【笺注】jiānzhù 古书的注释 notes and comments to ancient texts

渐 jiān〈书 *fml.*〉❶ 浸 soak; be saturated with:～染 be imperceptibly influenced ❷ 流入 flow into:东～于海 flow east and empty into the sea

☞ jiàn on p.956

【渐染】jiānrǎn〈书 *fml.*〉因接触久了而逐渐受到影响 be imperceptibly influenced as a result of long contact

犍 jiān 指犍牛 bullock:老～ old bullock

☞ qián on p.1537

【犍牛】jiānniú 阉割过的公牛。犍牛比较驯顺,容易驾驭,易于肥育。bullock; castrated bull, which tends to be more docile and easy to harness or fatten

湔 jiān〈书 *fml.*〉洗 wash:～洗 wash; remove (stain, etc.)|～雪 redress (a wrong); remove (a stain)

【湔洗】jiānxǐ〈书 *fml.*〉❶ 洗濯 wash ❷ 除去(耻辱、污点等) remove (humiliation, stain, etc.):～前罪 redeem a crime

【湔雪】jiānxuě〈书 *fml.*〉洗雪 wipe out; remove; redress:～冤屈 redress a wrong

缄 jiān 封闭(常用在信封上寄信人姓名后 oft. used after the sender's family name on the envelope) seal; close:王～ from Wang|上海刘～ from Liu in Shanghai

【缄口】jiānkǒu〈书 *fml.*〉闭着嘴(不说话) keep one's mouth shut; hold one's tongue:～不语 hold one's tongue and say nothing

【缄默】jiānmò 闭口不说话 keep silent; be reticent:保持～ keep silent|～无言 keep silent; hold one's tongue and say nothing

瑊 jiān〈书 *fml.*〉瑊玏 beautiful stone like jade

【瑊玏】jiānlè〈书 *fml.*〉像玉的美石 jade-like beautiful stone

蒹 jiān 古书上指芦苇一类的植物 plant similar to reed described in ancient books

椾 jiān〈书 *fml.*〉same as 笺 jiān

搛 jiān(用筷子)夹 pick up with chopsticks:～菜 pick up food with chopsticks

煎 jiān ❶ 烹饪方法,锅里放少量油,加热后,把食物放进去使表面变黄(cooking method) fry in shallow oil without stirring; put a little oil in the pan, heat it, put in the food and fry it until its surface turns yellow:～鱼 fry fish|～豆腐 fry bean curd ❷ 把东西放在水里煮,使所含的成分进入水中 simmer in water; decoct; put things into a cooking pot and boil them until their essences are dissolved in the water:～茶 cook tea|～药 decoct medicinal herbs ❸〈量词 *classifier*〉煎中药的次数 (of herb medicine) decoction:头～first decoction|二～ second decoction|这病吃一～药就好。Take one decoction and you will be all right.

【煎熬】jiān'áo〈比喻 *fig.*〉折磨 suffering; torture; torment:受尽～ suffer severely; be severely tortured

【煎饼】jiān·bing 用高粱、小麦或小米等浸水磨成糊状,在鏊子上摊匀烙熟的薄饼 pancake; thin, flat cake of sorghum, wheat or millet batter baked on a griddle

缣 jiān〈书 *fml.*〉细绢 fine silk

【缣帛】jiānbó 古代一种质地细薄的丝织品。古人在纸发明以前常在缣帛上书写文字。fine silk fabric produced in ancient times, on which ancient people used to write before paper was invented

鲣(鰹) jiān 鱼,身体纺锤形,侧扁,两侧有数条浓青色纵线,嘴尖。生活在热带海洋中。oceanic bonito (*Katsuwonus pelamis*); skipjack (tuna); spindle-like and laterally flat fish with some dark green vertical lines on both sides of the body and a pointed mouth, living in tropical seas

鹣 jiān 鹣鹣,古代传说中的比翼鸟 legendary bird with one eye and one wing (so that a pair must unite in order to fly)

【鹣鲽】jiāndié〈书 *fml.*〉〈比喻 *fig.*〉恩爱的夫妻 devoted couple:～情深 be deeply in love

熸 jiān〈书〉❶ 火熄灭 extinction of a fire ❷ 军队溃败 defeat of an army; be defeated; be routed

鞬 jiān 马上盛弓箭的器具 quiver (for arrows) on a horse; case for holding arrows on a horse

鞯(韉) jiān ☞ 鞍鞯 ānjiān on p.12

鳒 jiān 鱼,身体长卵圆形,一般两眼都在身体的左侧,也有在右侧的,上方的眼睛靠近头顶,有眼的一侧黄褐色,无眼的一侧白色。主要产在我国南海地区。spiny-rayed flounder (*Psettodes erumei*); big-mouthed flounder; fish living mainly in the South China Sea having a long, oval body with both eyes on the left and yellow side and no eyes at all on the right and white side (sometimes vice versa) and the upper eye close to the top of the head

櫼 jiān〈书 *fml*.〉木片楔子(xiē·zi) wooden wedge

jiǎn (ㄐㄧㄢˇ)

囝 jiǎn〈方 *dial*.〉❶ 儿子 son ❷ 儿女 child ☞ 囡 nān on p. 1387

规 jiǎn〈书 *fml*.〉same as 茧 jiǎn

拣[1](**揀**) jiǎn 挑选 choose; select; pick out: ～选 select; choose | ～择 select; choose | 挑肥～瘦 pick the fat or choose the lean; choose whatever is to one's liking | 时间有限,请～要紧的说。As time is limited, please choose the important points to make. *or* As time is limited, please say what you think is most important.

拣[2](**揀**) jiǎn same as 捡 jiǎn

【拣选】jiǎnxuǎn 选择 select; choose: ～上等药材 select top-quality medicinal herbs

【拣择】jiǎnzé 挑选;选择 select; choose: ～吉日 choose an auspicious date

枧[1] jiǎn same as 笕 jiǎn

枧[2] jiǎn〈方 *dial*.〉指肥皂 soap: 番～(洗衣服用的肥皂) laundry soap | 香～(香皂) toilet soap; perfumed soap

茧[1](**繭**) jiǎn 某些昆虫的幼虫在变成蛹之前吐丝做成的壳,通常是白色或黄色的。蚕茧是缫丝的原料。cocoon; silky or fibrous case which the larvae of certain insects spin about themselves for shelter during the pupa stage, usu. white or yellow; silkworm cocoon is a raw material for spinning silk

茧[2](**繭**) jiǎn same as 趼 jiǎn

【茧绸】jiǎnchóu 柞丝绸的旧称 old term for 柞丝绸 zuòsīchóu

【茧子】[1] jiǎn·zi〈方 *dial*.〉蚕茧 silkworm cocoon

【茧子】[2] jiǎn·zi same as 趼子 jiǎn·zi

柬 jiǎn 信件、名片、帖子等的统称 card; note; letter: 书～ letter | ～札 letters | ～帖 invitation card; note; short letter | 请～ invitation card

俭(**儉**) jiǎn 俭省 thrifty; frugal: 勤～ diligent and frugal; hardworking and frugal | 节～ thrifty | 省吃～用 live frugally; live a frugal life | ～以养廉。Frugality makes honesty.

【俭朴】jiǎnpǔ 俭省朴素 thrifty and simple; economical: 服装～ dress simply | 生活～ lead a thrifty and simple life

【俭省】jiǎnshěng 爱惜物力;不浪费财物 economical; thrifty; careful management of one's money and resources: 精打细算,过日子～ live a frugal and simple life through careful management of one's money

【俭约】jiǎnyuē〈书 *fml*.〉俭省 thrifty; economical

捡(**撿**) jiǎn 拾取 pick up; collect; gather; glean (a reaped field): ～柴 gather firewood | ～了东西要送交招领处。Send it to the Lost and Found Service when you pick up something.

【捡漏】jiǎn//lòu 检修房顶漏雨的部分 repair the leaky part of a roof; plug a leak in the roof

【捡漏儿】jiǎn//lòur〈方 *dial*.〉抓住别人的漏洞;抓把柄 seize on one's loopholes; seize on one's handle

【捡破烂儿】jiǎn pòlànr 捡取别人扔掉的废品 pick odds and ends from refuse heaps

【捡拾】jiǎnshí 拾取 pick up; collect: 在海滩上～贝壳 pick shells on a sea beach

【捡洋落儿】jiǎn yánglàor〈方 *dial*.〉原指捡拾外国人丢弃的物品,后泛指得到意外的财物或好处 pick up goods left by foreigners; (in a broad sense) get unexpected property or benefit

笕 jiǎn 引水的长竹管,安在檐下或田间 bamboo water pipe laid under the eaves of a house or in a field

检(**檢**) jiǎn ❶ 查 check up; inspect; examine: ～验 check up; examine | ～阅 review | 体～ physical examination | ～字表 index ❷ 约束;检点 restrain oneself; be careful in one's conduct: 行为不～ be careless in one's conduct | 言语失～ be careless in speaking ❸ same as 捡 jiǎn ❹ (Jiǎn) 姓 a surname

【检波】jiǎnbō 从经过调制的高频振荡电流中分离出调制信号,叫做检波 demodulation; detection; process of recovering at the receiver a signal that has been modulated on a carrier wave

【检测】jiǎncè 检验测定 test; examine; check up: 质量～ check on the quality; quality check

【检查】jiǎnchá ❶ 为了发现问题而用心查看 check up; inspect; examine: ～身体 have a health check; have a medical checkup | ～工作 check up on work ❷ 翻检查考(书籍、文件等) look over and study (books, documents, etc.）❸ 检讨 ① self-criticism：口头～ oral self-criticism|犯了错误要做～。Make a self-criticism if you've made a mistake.

【检察】jiǎnchá 〈书 *fml.*〉检举核查；考察 procuratorial work；report to the authorities and check；investigation

【检察院】jiǎncháyuàn 指审查批准逮捕、审查决定起诉、出席法庭支持公诉的国家机关。在我国，人民检察院有时也简称检察院。procuratorate；state organ which examines，and approves arrests，examines and decides on law suits，attends court hearings and supports public prosecution. In China，the People's Procuratorate is called the Procuratorate for short.

【检场】jiǎnchǎng ❶〈旧时 *old*〉戏曲演出时，在不闭幕的情况下，在舞台上布置或收拾道具 rearrange the property onstage without lowering the curtain in an opera production ❷ 做检场工作的人 property man making stage rearrangement

【检点】jiǎndiǎn ❶ 查看符合与否；查点 examine；check：～行李 check the luggage|～人数 check the number of people present ❷ 注意约束（自己的言语行为）be cautious（about what one says or does）：说话失于～ be carcless about one's words|糖尿病人对饮食尤要多加～。Diabetics should be particularly careful about their diet.

【检定】jiǎndìng 检查鉴定 examine and determine：药品～ test drugs|～计量器具 test and appraise the measuring instruments|教师资格～考试 teacher accreditation examination

【检举】jiǎnjǔ 向司法机关或其他有关国家机关和组织揭发违法、犯罪行为 inform against（an offender）；accuse（an offender）；report（an offence）to the judicial authorities or other competent state organs

【检录】jiǎnlù 比赛前给运动员点名并带领入场 call the roll of contestants in athletic events：～员 register；registrar|～处 registration office；registration desk；registry

【检票】jiǎn//piào 检验车船票、选票等 ticket inspection；inspect the tickets，votes，etc.

【检视】jiǎnshì 检验查看 inspect：～现场 inspect the scene（of an incident，a crime，etc.）；inspect a site

【检束】jiǎnshù 检点，约束 restrain：行为有所～ restrain one's behaviours

【检索】jiǎnsuǒ 查检寻找（图书、资料等）refer to；look up：数据～ data retrieval|资料按音序排列便于～。For the convenience of reference，the materials are *pinyin* alphabetized.

【检讨】jiǎntǎo ❶ 找出缺点和错误，并做自我批评 make a self-criticism：书面～ written self-criticism|工作～ review one's work|生活～会 self-criticism meeting ❷ 总结分析；研究 sum up and analyse；study：原稿不在手边，一时无从～。The original scrip not being at hand，it's impossible to make a review for the moment.

【检修】jiǎnxiū 检查并修理（机器、建筑物等）overhaul；examine and repair（machine，building，etc.）：～设备 overhaul the equipment|～工具 examine and repair tools|～房屋 examine and repair a house

【检验】jiǎnyàn 检查验看 test；examine；inspect：～汽车机件 inspect the motor engines and parts|实践是～真理的唯一标准。Practice is the sole criterion for testing truth.|商品～ commodity inspection

【检疫】jiǎnyì 防止传染病在国内蔓延和国际间传播的预防措施。如对传染病区来的人或货物、船只等进行检查和消毒，或者采取隔离措施等。quarantine；preventive measure to keep contagious diseases from spreading at home and abroad. For example，persons，freight，vessels found to have been infested with contagious diseases are kept in isolation for sterilization.

【检阅】jiǎnyuè ❶ 高级首长亲临军队或群众队伍的面前，举行检验仪式 review（troops，etc.）；inspect；high-ranking officials or officers attend a ceremony to review a military parade or a mass parade：～仪仗队 review the guard of honour ❷ 翻检阅读 look over and read：～书稿 look over and read the manuscripts of a book

【检字法】jiǎnzìfǎ 字典或其他工具书里文字排列次序的检查方法。检查汉字常用的有部首检字法、音序检字法、笔画检字法、四角号码检字法等。way in which Chinese characters are arranged and are to be located as in a dictionary or other reference books；indexing system for Chinese characters. There are four ways in indexing Chinese characters：indexing by radicals，indexing by pronunciation，indexing by strokes and indexing by four-corner numbers.

趼(繭) jiǎn 趼子 callus

【趼子】jiǎn·zi 手掌或脚掌上因摩擦而生成的硬皮 callus；part of the skin of a palm or sole，which is hardened and thickened by rubbing；also 茧子 jiǎn·zi or 老趼 lǎojiǎn

减(減) jiǎn ❶ 从总体或某个数量中去掉一部分 subtract：削～ cut down|裁～ reduction；cut|～员 reduce the staff|偷工～料 do shoddy work and use inferior material；scamp work and stint material|五～三是二。Five minus three is two. *or* Three from five is two. ❷ 降低；衰退 reduce；decrease；cut：～色 fade；pale；lose colour；lose lustre；impair the excellence of|工作热情有增无～ work with ever increasing zeal|人虽老了，干活还是不～当年！Although he is old，he works as energetically as he did before.

【减产】jiǎn//chǎn 产量减少;减少生产 reduction of output; drop in production:粮食～grain output drops; cut or drop in the grain production|采取～措施,降低库存 adopt output-control measures to cut down the grain stock (or reserve)

【减低】jiǎndī 降低 reduce; lower; bring down; cut; go down; fall:～物价 reduce prices; cut down prices|～速度 lower the speed; slow down

【减法】jiǎnfǎ 数学中的一种运算方法。最简单的是数的减法,即从一个数减去另一个数的计算方法。subtraction; mathematical process of finding the difference between two numbers or quantities; the simplest process is subtraction of numbers, namely, the process of subtracting a number from another number

【减肥】jiǎn//féi 指采取节制饮食、增加锻炼等办法减轻肥胖的程度 lose weight; slim:～茶 weight-losing tea|～健美操 pound-shedding exercises

【减河】jiǎnhé 为了减少河流的水量,在原来河道之外另开的通入海洋、湖泊、洼地或别的河流的河道 water conservancy distributary; cut an additional canal to the sea, a lake, a low-lying land or another river apart from the original course in order to reduce the flow of a river

【减缓】jiǎnhuǎn (程度)减轻;(速度)变慢 retard; slow down:老年人新陈代谢～。Metabolism in old people invariably slows down.

【减免】jiǎnmiǎn 减轻或免除(捐税、刑罚等) reduce or remit (taxation, etc.); reduction of or exemption from (taxation); mitigate or annul (a punishment)

【减轻】jiǎnqīng 减少重量、数量或程度 abate; decrease; reduce; lighten; ease; alleviate; mitigate:～负担 lighten the burden; reduce the burden|病势～。The patient's condition has eased. *or* The patient's condition is getting better.

【减弱】jiǎnruò (气势、力量等)变弱 weaken; abate:风势～。The wind has subsided.|兴趣～ become less interested|凝聚力～了。The organization is losing its rallying power among its staff.

【减色】jiǎnsè 指事物的精彩程度降低 lose lustre; mar the excellence of; detract from the merit of:原定的一些节目不能演出,使今天的晚会～不少。Some items on the programme were cancelled, greatly spoiling the performance this evening.

【减少】jiǎnshǎo 减去一部分 par down; reduce; decrease; lessen; cut down:～人员 reduce the staff|～麻烦。It takes less trouble to do something.|工作中的缺点～了。There are fewer mistakes in our work.

【减速】jiǎn//sù 降低速度 slow down; decelerate; retard:～行驶 drive at a reduced speed

【减损】jiǎnsǔn 减少;减弱 reduce; weaken:虽经磨难,而斗志丝毫没有～。Sapped the hardships, the morale is not at all sapped.

【减缩】jiǎnsuō 缩减 reduce; cut down; retrench:～课时 reduce class hours; reduce the number of class periods

【减退】jiǎntuì (程度)下降;减弱(of degree) drop; go down:近年视力有些～。My eyesight has been failing these years.|雨后,炎热～了许多。The heat abated considerably after the rain.

【减刑】jiǎn//xíng 法院根据犯人在服刑期间改恶从善的程度,依法把原来判处的刑罚减轻 reduce a penalty; reduce a sentence; commute (or mitigate) a sentence; court reduces the sentence passed on a convict in the light of his conduct during his term of imprisonment

【减削】jiǎnxuē 削减 cut down; reduce:～经费 cut down the funds (or outlay)

【减员】jiǎn//yuán ❶ 由于伤病、死亡等原因而人员减少(多指部队 oft. in an armed force) depletion of numbers as a result of casualties and illnesses ❷ 裁减人员 cut down on the size of a staff

剪 jiǎn ❶ 剪刀 scissors; shears; clippers ❷ 形状像剪刀的器具 instruments in the shape of scissors:夹～ tweezers; tongs|火～ fire-tongs ❸ 用剪刀等使东西断开 cut (with scissors); clip; trim:～裁 tailor clothing; cut out dresses|～纸 paper-cuts|～指甲 trim one's nails|～羊毛 shear a sheep|～几尺布做衣服 buy several *chi* of cloth for making clothes ❹ 除去 wipe out; exterminate:～除 wipe out; exterminate; annihilate|～灭 annihilate; wipe out|～草除根 cut the grass and remove its root; cut the weeds and dig the roots; wipe out all and everything; stamp out the source of trouble

【剪报】jiǎn//bào 把报纸上有参考价值的文字剪下来 newspaper clipping

【剪报】jiǎnbào 从报纸上剪下来的文章等 clippings:她积累的～有两万多张。She has collected more than 20,000 clippings.

【剪裁】jiǎncái ❶ 缝制衣服时把衣料按照一定尺寸剪断裁开 cut out (a garment); tailor ❷ 〈比喻 *fig.*〉做文章时对材料的取舍安排 cut out unwanted material (from a piece of writing); prune:把情节复杂的小说改编成电影是需要很好地加以～的。Adapting a novel with a complicated plot to a film calls for a good deal of pruning.

【剪彩】jiǎn//cǎi 在新造车船出厂、道路桥梁首次通车、大建筑物落成或展览会等开幕时举行的仪式上剪断彩带 cut the ribbon to inaugurate a car, ship, building, an exhibition or to open a new road or bridge to traffic

【剪除】jiǎnchú 铲除(恶势力);消灭(坏人) wipe out; annihilate; exterminate:～奸宄 wipe out malefactors or evildoers

【剪床】jiǎnchuáng 剪金属薄板用的机床。所用的刀具由两片合成,刀片的一边有刃,作用跟剪刀相同。shearing machine; machine tool made up of a pair of shears for cutting sheet metal,functioning in the same way as scissors

【剪刀】jiǎndāo 使布、纸、绳等东西断开的铁制器具,两刃交错,可以开合 scissors; shears;iron tool for cutting cloth,paper,rope and string, etc., consisting of two blades joined in a cross so that they can be opened or shut freely

【剪刀差】jiǎndāochā 一般指工业品的价格比农业品的价格高时,两者之间的差额。用统计图来表示这种差额时,图上形成剪刀张开的形状,因此称为剪刀差。scissors movement of prices; scissors differential (or difference); price scissors; difference between industrial products and agricultural products when the price of the former is higher than that of the latter. When a statistical table or chart is used to indicate the difference, the figure of a pair of open scissors is found on it, hence the name of scissors difference.

【剪辑】jiǎnjí ❶ 影片、电视片的一道制作工序,按照剧本结构和创作构思的要求,把拍摄好的许多镜头和声带,经过选择、剪裁、整理,编排成结构完整的影片或电视片 film montage; film editing; process of film or telefilm production as required by the structure and conception. Large footages of shots and sound tapes produced are arranged into a complete film or telefilm through selection, cutting and editing. ❷ 经过选择、剪裁,重新编排,也指这样编排的作品 select, cut and rearrange a work; work produced through such process:～照片 photo montage|新闻图片～ news photo editing|话剧录音～ highlights of a live recording of a play

【剪接】jiǎnjiē 剪辑① film montage; film editing

【剪灭】jiǎnmiè 剪除;消灭 wipe out; exterminate; annihilate:～群雄 eliminate the warlords

【剪票】jiǎn//piào 铁路或公路上查票时,用钳状器具在车票的边缘剪出缺口,表示经过查验 punch a ticket at a railway station, in the train or a coach

【剪贴】jiǎntiē ❶ 把资料从书报上剪下来,贴在卡片或本子上 paste newspaper clippings in a scrapbook or on cards ❷ 一种手工工艺,用彩色纸等剪成人或东西的形象,贴在纸或别的东西上 handcraft art; cutting coloured paper into figures and paste them on a sheet of paper or other things

【剪影】jiǎnyǐng ❶ 照人脸或人体、物体的轮廓剪纸成形。也指剪出的作品。paper-cut silhouette; cut the silhouette of a human face, a human body or an object out of a paper ❷ 〈比喻 *fig*.〉对于事物轮廓的描写 outline; sketch:京华～ sketch of life of Beijing

【剪纸】jiǎnzhǐ 民间工艺,用纸剪成人物、花草、鸟兽等的形象。也指剪成的工艺品。paper-cut; folk art of cutting figures, flowers, birds, animals, etc. out of paper

【剪纸片儿】jiǎnzhǐpiānr 剪纸片 paper-cut film

【剪纸片】jiǎnzhǐpiàn 美术片的一种,把人、物的表情、动作、变化等剪成许多剪纸,再用摄影机拍摄而成 paper-cut film; animated film of paper-cuts showing the expressions, movements and changes of human beings and objects

【剪子】jiǎn·zi 剪刀 scissors; shears; clippers

硷(礆、鹼) jiǎn same as 碱 jiǎn

揃 jiān 〈书 *fml*.〉剪断;分割 cut into two pieces; separate

睑[1](瞼) jiǎn 〈书 *fml*.〉眼睑;眼皮 eyelid

睑[2](瞼) jiǎn 唐代南诏地区的行政单位,大致与州相当 *jian*, an administrative unit in the Nanzhao area in the Tang Dynasty (618-907), equivalent to a prefecture

锏 jiǎn 〈古代 *arch*.〉兵器,金属制成,长条形,有四棱,无刃,上端略小,下端有柄 mace; ancient long weapon made of metal with four edges and no blades, the upper end smaller and the lower end fixed with a handle

☞ jiàn on p. 956

裥 jiǎn 〈方 *dial*.〉衣服上打的褶子 pleat

睐 jiǎn 〈书 *fml*.〉明亮(多用于人名 oft. used for a given name) brightness

简[1] jiǎn ❶ 简单(跟'繁'相对 as opposed to 'complex') simple; brief:～便 simple and convenient; handy|～体 simplified form|言～意赅 in concise words; concise and comprehensive; compendious|删繁就～ remove the superfluities and make it simple; simplify by weeding out superfluities; reduce to bare essentials ❷ 使简单;简化 simplify:精兵～政 better troops and simpler administration; better staff and simplier administration ❸ (Jiǎn)姓 a surname

简[2] jiǎn ❶ 古代用来写字的竹片 bamboo slips used for writing on in ancient times:～札 letters; correspondence|～册 books|银雀山竹～ Yinqueshan bamboo slips ❷ 信件 letter:书～ letters|小～ informal letter

简[3] jiǎn 〈书 *fml*.〉选择 (人才) select; choose (talents):～拔 select|～任 select for appointment

【简板】jiǎnbǎn 打击乐器,用两片一尺多长的木板或竹板制成。用作戏曲或道情的伴奏。clappers; percussion instrument made up of two pieces of wood or bamboo clappers, each about 33 cm. long, used in Chinese opera or chanting folk tales as an accompaniment

【简报】jiǎnbào 内容比较简略的报道 bulletin; brief report: 新闻～ news bulletin | 工作～ work bulletins

【简本】jiǎnběn 内容、文字较为简单的或较原著简略的版本 concise edition

【简编】jiǎnbiān 内容比较简略的著作。也指某一著作的简本(多用做书名 usu. used in book titles) short course; concise edition:《中国通史～》*A Concise History of China*

【简便】jiǎnbiàn 简单方便 simple and convenient; handy: ～算法 simple algorithm | 使用方法～。It's easy to use or operate. | 做事要周到,不要光图～ be careful in doing anything instead of just seeking simplicity and convenience

【简称】jiǎnchēng ❶ 较复杂的名称的简化形式。如中专(中等专业学校)、奥运会(奥林匹克运动会)。abbreviated form of a complicated name; abbreviation; e.g. 中专 zhōngzhān is the abbreviation of 中等专业学校 zhōngděng zhuānyè xuéxiào and 奥运会 Aòyùnhuì is the abbreviation of 奥林匹克运动会 Aòlínpǐkè Yùndònghuì ❷ 简单地称呼 call sth. for short: 化学肥料～化肥。化学肥料 huàxué féiliào is called 化肥 huàféi for short.

【简单】jiǎndān ❶ 结构单纯;头绪少;容易理解、使用或处理 simple; uncomplicated: 情节～ simple plot | ～扼要 brief and to the point | 这种机器比较～。This type of machine is simply constructed. | 他简简单单说了几句话。He said something briefly. ❷ (经历、能力等)平凡(多用于否定式 oft. used in the negative) (of experience, ability, etc.) commonplace; ordinary: 李队长主意多,有魄力,可真不～。Team Leader Li is no ordinary person. He is full of ideas and has daring and resolution. ❸ 草率;不细致 oversimplified; casual; careless; rash: ～从事 take rash action

【简单机械】jiǎndān jīxiè 杠杆、轮轴、滑轮、斜面、螺旋和劈的总称,是复杂机械的基础 simple machinery; general term for lever, pulley, wheel and axle, oblique plane (bevel), screw and wedge, which are the foundation for complex machinery

【简单劳动】jiǎndān láodòng 不需要经过专门训练,一般劳动者都能胜任的劳动(跟'复杂劳动'相对 as opposed to 'complex work') simple work; work that does not require special training and everyone can do

【简单商品生产】jiǎndān shāngpǐn shēngchǎn 以个体所有制和个体劳动为基础,为交换或出卖而进行的产品生产 simple commodity production; production of goods for exchange or sale, which is based on individual ownership and individual work; also 小商品生产 xiǎoshāngpǐn shēngchǎn

【简单再生产】jiǎndān zàishēngchǎn 按原有生产规模进行的再生产 simple reproduction; reproduction carried on the original production scale; ☞ 再生产 zàishēngchǎn on p. 2387

【简短】jiǎnduǎn 内容简单,言词不长 brief: 话说得很～。The remark is rather pithy. | 壁报的文章要～生动。The articles on the wall newspaper should be brief and lively.

【简古】jiǎngǔ 〈书 *fml.*〉简略古奥;单纯古朴 laconic and classic: 文笔～ write in a laconic and classic style

【简化】jiǎnhuà 把繁杂的变成简单的 simplify: ～手续 simplify the procedure; simplify the formalities | 力求～ do one's best to simplify

【简化汉字】jiǎnhuà Hànzì ❶ 简化汉字的笔画,如把'禮'简化为'礼','動'简化为'动'。同时精简汉字的数目,在异体字里选定一个,不用其余的,如在'勤、懃'里选用'勤',不用'懃',在'劫、刼、刧、刦'里选用'劫',不用'刼、刧、刦'。simplify Chinese characters, i.e. reduce the number of strokes and eliminate complicated variants, such as 禮 lǐ simplified as 礼 lǐ and 動 dòng simplified as 动 dòng. At the same time, the number of Chinese characters is also reduced, i.e., if one character has two or more variants, only one is chosen, such as 勤 qín for 勤 qín and 懃 qín and 劫 jié for 劫 jié, 刼,刧 and 刦 jié. ❷ 经过简化的汉字,如'礼''动'等 simplified Chinese characters, such as 礼 lǐ and 动 dòng

【简化字】jiǎnhuàzì 简化汉字② simplified Chinese characters

【简洁】jiǎnjié (说话、行文等)简明扼要,没有多余的内容(of speech, writing, etc.) succinct; terse; pithy; laconic: 文笔～ written in a pithy style | 话语～ speak briefly

【简捷】jiǎnjié ❶ 直截了当 simple and direct; forthright; also 简截 jiǎnjié ❷ 简便快捷 simple and quick: 算法～ simple and quick method of calculation

【简截】jiǎnjié same as 简捷 jiǎnjié ①

【简介】jiǎnjiè ❶ 简要地介绍 brief introduction; synopsis; summarized account ❷ 简要介绍的文字 summary: 中国民航事业～ A Brief Introduction to China's Civil Aviation

【简况】jiǎnkuàng 简要的情况;概况 brief description; brief account; general situation; general information: 介绍候选人～ give a brief account of the candidates

【简括】jiǎnkuò 简单而概括 brief but comprehensive; compendious: ～的总结 brief summary | 把意见～地谈一下 make one's comments briefly

【简历】jiǎnlì 简要的履历 résumé; biographical notes; curriculum vitae

【简练】jiǎnliàn（措辞）简要；精练（of wording）terse；succinct；pithy：文字～ succinct language｜用词～ write in a succinct style

【简陋】jiǎnlòu（房屋、设备等）简单粗陋；不完备（of house, facility, etc.）simple and crude：设备～ simple and crude equipment｜～的工棚 crude work shed

【简略】jiǎnlüè（言语、文章的内容）简单；不详细（of language, content of writing）simple；brief；sketchy：～地说明 explain in a few words｜叙述过于～，不能说明问题。The account he gave is too sketchy to explain anything.

【简慢】jiǎnmàn 怠慢失礼 negligent（in attending to one's guest）；treat a guest impolitely or coolly：今天～你啦 treat you too coolly today｜～得很，请多多原谅。I'm very sorry for my impoliteness.

【简明】jiǎnmíng 简单明白 simple and clear；concise：～扼要 brief and to the point｜他的谈话～有力。His speech is concise and forceful

【简朴】jiǎnpǔ（语言、文笔、生活作风等）简单朴素（of language, writing, lifestyle, etc.）simple and unadorned；plain：陈设～ simply furnished｜衣着～ be simply dressed

【简谱】jiǎnpǔ 用阿拉伯数字 1、2、3、4、5、6、7 及附加符号做音符的乐谱 numbered musical notation using Arabic figures 1, 2, 3, 4, 5, 6, 7 and additional symbols

【简任】jiǎnrèn 民国时期文官的第二等，在特任以下，荐任以上 simple appointment；second rank of the four-echelon civil service during the Republic of China before 1949, below 'special appointment' and above 'recommended appointment'

【简省】jiǎnshěng 把繁杂的、多余的去掉；节省 get rid of the superfluities；simplify；reduce；save：～手续 simplify the formalities｜～费用 cut down the expenses

【简缩】jiǎnsuō 精简 condense；simplify；reduce：各种报表的数量应该尽量～。The number of all report forms should be reduced as far as possible.

【简体】jiǎntǐ ❶ 笔画经简化后变得比较简单的 simplified forms（of Chinese characters）：～字 simplified Chinese character ❷ 指简体字 simplified Chinese character：'車'的～是'车'。The simplified form of 車 che is 车 chē.

【简体字】jiǎntǐzì 用简体写法写出的汉字，如刘（劉）、灭（滅）等 simplified Chinese character, such as 刘(劉) Liú，灭(滅) miè, etc.

【简写】jiǎnxiě 指汉字的简体写法，如'刘'是'劉'的简写，'灭'是'滅'的简写 write a Chinese character in simplified form, e.g. 刘 liú is the simplified form for 劉 liú, and 灭 miè is the simplified form for 滅 miè

【简讯】jiǎnxùn 简短的消息 news in brief：时事～ brief news on current affairs｜科技～ brief news on science and technology

【简要】jiǎnyào 简单扼要 concise and to the point；brief：叙述～ brief description；brief account；brief narration｜～的介绍 brief introduction；briefing

【简易】jiǎnyì ❶ 简单而容易的 simple and easy：～办法 simple and easy method ❷ 设施简陋的 simply constructed；simply equipped；unsophisticated：～公路 simply-built highway｜～楼房 economy building

【简约】jiǎnyuē ❶ 简略 brief；concise；sketchy：文字～ in concise words｜构图～ simple in composition ❷ 节俭 frugal：生活～ live a frugal life

【简则】jiǎnzé 简要的规则 general regulations；general rules

【简章】jiǎnzhāng 简要的章程 general regulations：招生～ general regulation for enrolment

【简直】jiǎnzhí〈副词 *adv.*〉❶ 表示完全如此（语气带夸张 tone of exaggeration）simply；at all：屋子里热得～呆不住。The room is so hot that no one can stay in it.｜街上的汽车一辆跟着一辆，～没个完。The street is filled with an endless stream of automobiles. ❷〈方 *dial.*〉索性 simply：雨下得那么大，你～别回去了。It is raining so heavily. You simply don't have to go home.

【简装】jiǎnzhuāng（商品）包装简单（区别于'精装'② as compared with 'de luxe packing'）（of commodity）simple packing：～奶粉 simply packed milk powder

谫(譾) jiǎn〈书 *fml.*〉浅薄 shallow

【谫陋】jiǎnlòu〈书 *fml.*〉浅陋 shallow and ignorant：学识～ be possessed of meagre knowledge

戬 jiǎn〈书 *fml.*〉❶ 剪除；消灭 wipe out；annihilate ❷ 福；吉祥 bliss；blessedness

碱(鹼、堿) jiǎn ❶ 电解质电离时所生成的阴离子全部是氢氧根离子的化合物。能跟酸中和生成盐和水，水溶液有涩味，可使石蕊试纸变蓝。如氢氧化钠、氢氧化钾等。alkali；chemical compound produced when all the negative ions derived from the ionization of an electrolyte are ions with hydroxide radicals, capable of being neutrolized with acid to produce salt and water, its aqueous solution being puckery and able to turn the litmus paper blue, such as sodium hydroxide and potassium hydroxide ❷ 含有 10 个分子结晶水的碳酸钠，无色晶体，用作洗涤剂，也用来中和发面中的酸味 soda；sodium carbonate with 10-molecule crystal water, a colourless crystal, used as detergent or to neutralize the acidity of fermented dough ❸ 被盐碱侵蚀 alkalized：这间房子的墙都～了。The walls of this room are alkalized.

J

【碱地】jiǎndì ☞ 盐碱地 yánjiǎndì on p. 2207

【碱荒】jiǎnhuāng 荒废的盐碱地 waste alkaline land：改造～，种植水稻 improve the waste alkaline land and turn it into paddy fields

【碱土】jiǎntǔ 含碳酸钠、重碳酸钠较多、呈强碱性反应的土壤 alkali soil; soil containing sodium carbonate or sodium bicarbonate, with strong alkaline reaction

翦 jiǎn ❶ same as 剪 jiǎn ❷（Jiǎn）姓 a surname

蹇 jiǎn ❶〈书 *fml.*〉跛 crippled ❷〈书 *fml.*〉不顺利 unlucky; unfortunate：命运多～ ill fate; bad lot ❸〈书 *fml.*〉指驴。也指驽马。donkey or inferior horse ❹（Jiǎn）姓 a surname

謇 jiǎn〈书 *fml.*〉❶ 口吃；言辞不顺畅 stuttering ❷ 正直 upright; honest

㓺 jiǎn〈书 *fml.*〉same as 剪 jiǎn

鬋 jiǎn〈书 *fml.*〉❶ 下垂的鬓发 hanging hair on the temples ❷ 剪须发 get a shave and a haircut

瀽 jiǎn〈方 *dial.*〉泼（水）；倾倒（液体）splash water; pour out liquid

jiàn（ㄐㄧㄢˋ）

见[1]**（見）** jiàn ❶ 看到；看见 see; catch sight of; clap eyes on sb. or sth.：罕～ rare; rarely seen｜眼～是实。What one sees is true.｜喜闻乐～ love to see and hear｜视而不～ turn a blind eye to; look and see nothing; ignore ❷ 接触；遇到 meet with; be exposed to：这种药怕～光。This medicine is not to be exposed to daylight.｜冰～热就化。Ice melts with heat. ❸ 看得出；显现出 show evidence of; appear to be：～效 become effective; be effective in doing sth.; produce desired results｜病已～好。The patient's condition is getting better.｜日久～人心。It takes time to know a person. ❹ 指明出处或需要参看的地方 refer to; see; *vide*：～上 see above｜～右图 see the picture on the right｜～本书附录 refer to the book's appendix｜～《史记·项羽本纪》。See *Records of the Historian · Official Records of Xiang Yu*. ❺ 会见；会面 meet; call on; see：接～ receive｜他要来～你。He wants to see you. *or* He'll call on you. ❻ 对于事物的看法；意见 view; opinion：主～ one's own view; one's personal view; ideas or thoughts of one's own｜成～ prejudice; fixation; bias｜～解 view; idea; opinion｜固执己～ stick to one's own view ❼（Jiàn）姓 a surname

见[2]**（見）** jiàn〈书 *fml.*〉〈助词 *aux.*〉❶ 用在动词前面表示被动［used before a verb to indicate the passive］：～重于当时 be held in esteem by one's contemporaries｜～笑于人 be laughed at; become a laughing stock of others ❷ 用在动词前面表示对我怎么样［used before a verb in polite requests］：～告 let me know; inform me｜～示。Your comments are requested. *or* Please give your comments.｜～教。Your advice is kindly requested.｜～谅 excuse me; pardon me; forgive me

☞ 现 xiàn on p. 2080

【见报】jiàn//bào 在报纸上刊登出来 be printed in newspapers：这篇文章明天就可以～。This article will appear in tomorrow's newspapers. *or* This article will be printed in tomorrow's newspapers.

【见背】jiànbèi〈书 *fml.*〉〈婉辞 *euph.*〉指长辈去世（of one's parents）pass away

【见不得】jiàn·bu·dé ❶ 不能遇见（遇见就有问题）not to be exposed to; unable to stand：雪～太阳。Snow is not to be exposed to the sun. ❷ 不能让人看见或知道 not fit to be seen or revealed：不做～人的事。Don't do anything you are ashamed of. ❸〈方 *dial.*〉看不惯；不愿看见 cannot bear the sight of; frown upon：我～懒汉。I can't stand that sluggard. *or* I can't bear to see that sluggard.

【见长】jiàncháng 在某方面显示出特长 be good at; be expert in：先生学贯古今，尤以诗词～。My teacher is well-versed in both ancient and modern learning, and poetry in particular.
☞ jiànzhǎng on p. 952

【见得】jiàn·dé 看出来；能确定（只用于否定式或疑问式 only used in the negative or in questions）seem; appear：怎么～他来不了？How do you know he can't come? ☞ 不见得 bù jiàn·dé on p. 162

【见地】jiàndì 见解 insight; judgement：很有～ have keen insight; show sound judgement｜～很高 have good judgement

【见方】jiànfāng 用在表长度的数量词后，表示以该长度为边的正方形 square (used after a numeral-classifier indicating length to show a square with that length as the side)：这间屋子有一丈～。This room is one *zhang* (3.33 metres) square.

【见风是雨】jiàn fēng shì yǔ〈比喻 *fig.*〉只看到一点迹象，就轻率地信以为真 take wind as the indication of rain; jump to a conclusion at the mere sight of a little sign

【见风转舵】jiàn fēng zhuǎn duò ☞ 看风使舵 kàn fēng shǐ duò on p. 1081

【见缝插针】jiàn fèng chā zhēn〈比喻 *fig.*〉尽量利用一切可以利用的空间或时间 stick in a pin wherever there's room — make use of every bit of space or time

【见怪】jiànguài 责备；怪（多指对自己）mind; take offence; blame：事情没给您办好，请不要

～。Please don't blame me for not handling the affair well for you.

【见鬼】jiàn//guǐ ❶〈比喻 *fig*.〉离奇古怪 fantastic; preposterous; absurd：真是见了鬼，怎么一转眼就不见了？Isn't it funny that (he) has disappeared in an instant? ❷ 指死亡或毁灭 go to hell：让这些害人虫～去吧！To hell with these evil creatures!

【见好】jiànhǎo（病势）有好转（of a patient's condition) get better

【见机】jiànjī 看机会；看形势 as the opportunity arises; as befits the occasion; according to circumstances：～行事 act as the opportunity arises; do as one sees fit

【见教】jiànjiào〈客套话 *pol*.〉指教(我) favour me with your advice; instruct me：有何～？Is there any advice you can give me?

【见解】jiànjiě 对事物的认识和看法 view; opinion; understanding：～正确。The view is correct.｜他对中医理论有独到的～。He has original views on the theory of traditional Chinese medicine.

【见老】jiànlǎo（相貌）显出比过去老 look older; be aged：他这两年～多了。He looks much older than two years ago.

【见礼】jiàn//lǐ 见面行礼 salute or greet sb. upon meeting him：连忙上前～ make haste and step forward to greet someone

【见谅】jiànliàng〈客套话 *pol*.〉表示请人谅解（多用于书信 oft. used in letters) excuse me; forgive me：敬希～。I sincerely hope you'll forgive me.

【见猎心喜】jiàn liè xīn xǐ 原指爱打猎的人见别人打猎，自己也很兴奋 thrill to see one's favourite sport and itch to have a go; hunter becomes very excited when he sees others go hunting;〈比喻 *fig*.〉看见别人演的技艺或做的游戏正是自己以往所喜好的，不由得心动，想来试一试 have one's interest revived in one's old favourite sport upon seeing others doing the same sport

【见面】jiàn//miàn 彼此对面相见 meet; see：跟这位老战友多年没～了。It's many years since I last saw this old comrade-in-arms. ◇思想～ each stating frankly what's on his mind to the other

【见面礼】jiànmiànlǐ 初次见面时赠送的礼物（多指年长对年幼的 oft. from a senior person to a junior person) present given to someone on their first meeting

【见轻】jiànqīng（病势）显出好转（of illness) take a turn for the better; take a favourable turn; get better

【见仁见智】jiàn rén jiàn zhì《易经·系辞上》：'仁者见之谓之仁，智者见之谓之智。'指对于同一个问题各人有各人的见解。opinions differ; *The Book of Changes · Great Treatise* (*I*)：'The virtuous sees virtue and the wise sees wisdom' — different people have different views on the same question

【见世面】jiàn shìmiàn 在外经历各种事情，熟悉各种情况 experience the world and get to know various circumstances：经风雨，～ stand tests in the real world

【见识】jiàn·shi ❶ 接触事物，扩大见闻 widen one's knowledge; enrich one's experience：到各处走走，～～也是好的。It's a good idea to go around and gain more experience. ❷ 见闻；知识 knowledge; experience; sense; scope; sensibleness：长～ widen one's knowledge; broaden one's horizons｜～广 have wide experience

【见所未见】jiàn suǒ wèi jiàn 见到从来没有看到过的。形容事物十分稀罕。see what one has never seen before; see what is rarely seen; sth. rare

【见天】jiàntiān（～儿 jiàntiānr）每天 everyday：他～早上出去散步。He goes out for a walk every morning.

【见外】jiànwài 当外人看待 regard sb. as an outsider：你对我这样客气，倒有点～了。The way you give me this kind of formality makes me think I'm an outsider.｜请随便些，不要～。Just make yourself at home, please. *or* Don't stand on ceremony, please.

【见危授命】jiàn wēi shòu mìng 在危亡关头勇于献出生命 be ready to give one's life for one's country when it is in peril

【见微知著】jiàn wēi zhī zhù 见到一点苗头就能知道它的发展趋向或问题的实质 from the first symptoms one can see what is going to happen; from the first small beginnings one can see how things will develop; recognize the whole through observing the part

【见闻】jiànwén 见到和听到的事 what is seen and heard; knowledge; information：～广 well-informed; knowledgeable; intelligent｜增长～ increase one's knowledge; gain knowledge

【见习】jiànxí 初到工作岗位的人在现场实习 learn on the job; be on probation：～技术员 technician on probation

【见效】jiànxiào 发生效力 become effective; produce the desired result：～快 produce quick results; produce a quick effect｜这药吃下去就～。This medicine produces an instant effect.

【见笑】jiànxiào ❶ 被人笑话（多用做谦辞 oft. hum.) be laughed at：写得不好，～，～。Excuse me for my poor writing. ❷ 笑话(我) incur ridicule (by one's poor performance)：这是我刚学会的一点粗活儿，您可别～。Don't laugh at me. I've just learnt this bit of unskilled work.

【见新】jiàn//xīn〈方 *dial*.〉修理装饰旧房屋、器物，使像新的 make an old house, implements, etc. anew by redecoration: 把门面油漆一下,见见新。Paint the front of the shop to make it anew.

【见义勇为】jiàn yì yǒng wéi 看到正义的事情奋勇地去做 be ready to do whatever one sees right; be ready to take up the cudgels for a just cause

【见异思迁】jiàn yì sī qiān 看见不同的事物就改变原来的主意。指意志不坚定,喜爱不专一。change one's mind the moment one sees sth. new; be inconstant

【见于】jiànyú 指明文字出处或可以参看的地方 see or refer to a source: '背私为公'~《韩非子·五蠹篇》。For 'give up the private interests for the public interests', refer to *Hanfeizi · Five Vermin*.

【见长】jiànzhǎng 看着比原来高或大 grow perceptibly: 一场春雨后,麦苗~了。The wheat sprouts grew perceptibly after a spring rain. | 孩子的个头~。The child has grown perceptibly.

☞ jiàncháng on p. 950

【见证】jiànzhèng ❶ 当场目睹可以作证的 witness; testimony: ~人 witness; eyewitness ❷ 指见证人或可作证据的物品 witness: 他亲眼看见的,可以做~。What he saw with his own eyes can serve as witness. ◇历史是最好的~。History is the most forceful witness.

【见罪】jiànzuì 〈书 *fml*.〉见怪;怪罪 take offence; blame; forgive, excuse: 招待不周,请勿~。Forgive me for my poor hospitality.

件 jiàn ❶〈量词 *classifier*〉用于个体事物(for individual matters or things): 一~事 a matter; a thing | 两~衣裳 two dresses; two suits of clothes ❷ (~儿 jiànr)指可以一一计算的事物 item; piece: 铸~ castings | 工~ work pieces | 零~儿 spare parts | 案~ cases ❸ 文件 documents: 来~ message, parcel, letter or document received | 急~ urgent document or dispatch | 密~ restricted (or confidential) document or dispatch

间(閒) jiàn ❶ (~儿 jiànr)空隙 space in between; opening: 乘~ seize an opportunity; seize a fleeting chance | 当~儿 in the middle ❷ 嫌隙;隔阂 grudge; feeling of animosity; enmity; ill will; mental barrier; estrangement: 亲密无~ be on very intimate terms with each other ❸ 隔开;不连接 separate: ~隔 partition; interval | 黑白相~ black alternating with white; in black and white check ❹ 挑拨使人不和;离间 sow discord: 反~计 stratagem of sowing distrust or discord among one's enemies ❺ 拔去或锄去(多余的苗) thin out (seedlings): ~萝卜苗 thin out the turnip seedlings

☞ jiān on p. 940 and 闲(閒) xián on p. 2074

【间壁】jiànbì ❶ 隔壁 next door; next-door neighbour ❷〈方 *dial*.〉把房间隔开的简易墙壁 simply-built wall separating a room

【间道】jiàndào 〈书 *fml*.〉偏僻的或抄近的小路 bypath; shortcut

【间谍】jiàndié 被敌方或外国派遣、收买,从事刺探军事情报、国家机密或进行颠覆活动的人 spy; person employed by a government to get secret information about the affairs, plans, armed forces, etc. of another government or to engage in activities to subvert such a government

【间断】jiànduàn (连续的事情)中间隔断不连接 (of sth. that should be continuous) be disconnected; be interrupted: 试验不能~。An experiment or test cannot be interrupted. | 他每天都去锻炼身体,从没有~过。He has kept doing physical exercises every day without interruption.

【间伐】jiànfá 为加速林木生长或为防止病虫害等,有选择地砍伐部分树木 selective tree felling to accelerate the growth of trees and forests or to prevent forest plant diseases and insect pests

【间隔】jiàngé ❶ 事物在空间或时间上的距离 interval; intermission: 菜苗~匀整。The vegetable seedlings are evenly spaced. ❷ 隔开;隔绝 separate; completely cut off; isolate: 两个疗程之间要~一周。There should be an interval of one week between two periods of treatment. | 彼此音讯~ have not heard from each other; there is no communication between them

【间隔号】jiàngéhào 标点符号(·),表示外国人或某些少数民族人名内各部分的分界,也用来表示书名与篇(章、卷)名或朝代与人名之间的分界 separation dot; punctuation mark separating the parts of the name of a person in a foreign country or a person of some ethnic minority in China, or separating the title of a book from a chapter or a volume title, or a dynasty name from a person's name

【间或】jiànhuò 偶然;有时候 occasionally; now and then; sometimes; once in a while: 大家聚精会神地听着,~有人笑一两声。Everybody listened with full attention, with occasional chuckles from the floor.

【间接】jiànjiē 通过第三者发生关系的(跟'直接'相对 as opposed to 'direct') indirect; have relations with someone through a third party: ~传染 indirect infection | ~选举 indirect election | ~经验 indirect experience

【间接经验】jiànjiē jīngyàn 从书本或别人的经验中取得的经验(跟'直接经验'相对 as opposed to 'direct experience') indirect experience; experience obtained from books or from someone else

【间接税】jiànjiēshuì 从出售商品(主要是日用品)或服务性行业中征收的税。这种税不由纳税人负担,间接由消费者等负担,所以叫间接税。indirect tax; tax collected from the sale of commodities (chiefly consumer's goods) or from service trades. This tax is not paid by taxpayers, but indirectly by consumers, hence indirect tax.

【间接推理】jiànjiē tuīlǐ 由两个以上的前提推出结论的推理 mediate inference; conclusion inferred on the basis of two or more premises; ☞ 三段论 sānduànlùn on p. 1650

【间接选举】jiànjiē xuǎnjǔ 由选民选出代表，再由代表选举上一级代表的选举制度 indirect election; election system under which the voters elect their representatives for the election of representatives at a higher level

【间苗】jiàn//miáo 为了使作物的每棵植株有一定的营养面积，按照一定的株距留下幼苗，把多余的苗去掉 gapping; thin out seedlings (or young shoots); ensure that every plant of a crop has a certain area of nourishment, the plants should be properly spaced, and the unnecessary plants are taken away

【间日】jiànrì〈书 *fml.*〉隔一天 every other day

【间色】jiànsè 两种原色配合成的颜色，如红和黄配合成的橙色，黄和青配合成的绿色 assorted colours; multi-coloured; colour blended from two primary colours, e.g. red and yellow are into orange, and yellow and dark green blend into light green

【间隙】jiànxì 空隙 interval; gap; space: 利用工作～学习 find free time from work to study | 利用玉米地的～套种绿豆 interplant mung bean in the corn (or maize) fields

【间歇】jiànxiē 动作、变化等每隔一定时间停止一会儿 intermittence; intermission: 心脏病患者常常有～脉搏。Sufferers of heart disease often have intermittent pulse.

【间杂】jiànzá 错杂 be intermingled; be mixed: 红白～ red mixed with white; red and white intermingled

【间作】jiànzuò 在一块耕地上间隔地种植两种或两种以上作物。如玉米和绿豆两种作物间作，就是在两行玉米之间种一行或两行绿豆。intercropping; interplanting; two or more crops are grown in the same field in alternate rows; if maize (corn) and mung bean are intercropped, a row or two rows of mung bean are grown between two rows of maize; also 间种 jiànzhòng

谗(譖) jiàn〈书 *fml.*〉巧言；能言善辩 cunning words; deceitful talk; fine words; sweet words; eloquent and glib in argument

饯[1](餞) jiàn 饯行 give a farewell dinner: ～别 give a farewell dinner

饯[2](餞) jiàn 浸渍（果品）preserve (fruits): 蜜～ preserved fruits

【饯别】jiànbié 饯行 give a farewell dinner: ～宴会 farewell banquet; farewell dinner

【饯行】jiànxíng 设酒食送行 give a farewell dinner: 为代表团～ give a farewell dinner to a delegation

建[1] jiàn ❶ 建筑 build; construct; erect: 新～ newly built; build a new building | 扩～ expanded ❷ 设立；成立 establish; set up; found: ～国 founding of a new country | ～都 found a capital; establish a capital | ～军 army founding; found an army; build an army ❸ 提出；首倡 propose; advocate: ～议 suggest; propose; suggestion; proposal

建[2] Jiàn ❶ 建江，就是闽江，在福建 Jianjiang River, or Minjiang River, in Fujian Province ❷ 指福建 Fujian Province: ～兰 sword-leaved cymbidium, a fragrant species of orchid originally grown in Fujian | ～漆 lacquerware produced in Fujian

【建安】Jiàn'ān 汉献帝（刘协）年号（公元 196—220）Jian'an, the title of the reign (196-220) of Emperor Xiandi (Liu Xie) of the Han Dynasty

【建白】jiànbái〈书 *fml.*〉提出（建议）；陈述（主张）propose; suggest; make a proposal; make a suggestion; state one's view

【建材】jiàncái 建筑材料 building materials: ～工业 building materials industry

【建都】jiàn//dū 建立首都；把首都设在某地 found a capital; establish a capital; make (a place) the capital

【建国】jiàn//guó ❶ 建立国家 found (or establish) a state: ～功臣 person who makes an outstanding contribution to the founding of a nation ❷ 建设国家 build up a country: 勤俭～ build up a country through thrift and hard work; build a country thriftily and industriously

【建交】jiàn//jiāo 建立外交关系 establish diplomatic relations

【建兰】jiànlán 多年生草本植物，叶子丛生，条状披针形，夏秋季开花，淡黄绿色，有紫色条纹，气味清香，是观赏植物 sword-leaved cymbidium (*Cymbidium ensifolium*); fragrant species of orchid originally grown in Fujian; ornamental perennial herbal plant with luxuriant growth of its leaves in clusters, bearing yellowish green flowers with purple stripes in summer and autumn; also 兰花 lánhuā; 俗称 popularly called 兰草 láncǎo

【建立】jiànlì ❶ 开始成立 build; establish; set up; found: ～政权 establish a political power | ～新的工业基地 set up a new industrial base; establish a new industrial centre ❷ 开始产生；开始形成 form; establish; found: ～友谊 build or form friendship | ～邦交 establish diplomatic relations

【建漆】jiànqī 福建出产的一种漆，由生漆和树脂清漆加工制成。也指用这种漆制造的漆器。

lacquer produced in Fujian, which is prepared from raw lacquer and resin varnish; Fujian lacquerware; lacquerware made of such lacquer

【建设】jiànshè 创立新事业;增加新设施 build (a new cause); construct (new facilities):经济～ economic construction|组织～ organizational building|～家园 build the homeland|～现代化强国 build up a powerful modern country ◇思想～ ideological education

【建树】jiànshù ❶ 建立(功绩) make a contribution; contribute:～了不朽的功勋 perform an immortal deed ❷ 建立的功绩 attainment; achievement:在事业上颇有～ big achievement in one's own career

【建文】Jiànwén 明惠帝(朱允炆[wén])年号(公元1399—1402) Jianwen, the title of the reign (1399-1402) of Emperor Huidi (Zhu Yunwen) of the Ming Dynasty

【建议】jiànyì ❶ 向集体、领导等提出自己的主张 propose; suggest; recommend to a collective or leadership:我～休会一天。I suggest that the meeting be adjourned for one day. ❷ 向集体、领导等提出的主张 make a proposal to a collective or leadership:合理化～ rationalization proposal

【建元】jiànyuán 开国后第一次建立年号;也泛指建国 designate the title of a reign for the first time after the founding of a new dynasty; founding of a new dynasty or a new country

【建造】jiànzào 建筑;修建 build; construct; make:～房屋 build houses|～花园 build a garden

【建制】jiànzhì 机关、军队的组织编制和行政区划等制度的总称 organizational system; general term for the organizational systems of the government, the armed forces and the administrative regionalization

J

【建筑】jiànzhù ❶ 修建(房屋、道路、桥梁等) build (house, road, bridge, etc.); construct; erect:～桥梁 build a bridge; construct a bridge|～铁路 build a railway; construct a railway|这座礼堂～得非常坚固。This auditorium is solidly built. ◇不能把自己的幸福～在别人的痛苦上。You can't base your own happiness on the suffering of others. ❷ 建筑物 building; structure:古老的～ ancient building ◇上层～ superstructure

荐[1](薦) jiàn ❶ 推举;介绍 recommend:举～ recommend|推～ recommend|～人 recommend a person ❷〈书 *fml.*〉献;祭 offer sacrifices

荐[2](薦) jiàn〈书 *fml.*〉❶ 草 grass; straw ❷ 草垫子 straw mat:草～ straw mat

【荐骨】jiàngǔ 骶(dǐ)骨 sacrum

【荐举】jiànjǔ 介绍;推荐 propose someone for an office; recommend:～人才 recommend people of special abilities

【荐任】jiànrèn 民国时期文官的第三等,在简任以下,委任以上 recommended appointment; third grade of civil officials during the period of the Republic of China, under 'simple appointment', above 'appointment'

【荐头】jiàn·tou〈方 *dial.*〉〈旧时 *old*〉以介绍佣工为业的人 employment agent; person whose occupation is to recommend servants, employees:～行 employment agency|～店 employment shop

【荐引】jiànyǐn〈书 *fml.*〉荐举;引荐 recommend; introduce

【荐椎】jiànzhuī 骶(dǐ)骨 sacrum

贱(賤) jiàn ❶ (价钱)低(跟'贵'相对 as opposed to 'expensive') cheap; low-priced; inexpensive:～卖 sell cheap|～价 cheap; low prices|菜～了。The vegetables are cheaper. ❷ 地位低下(跟'贵'相对 as opposed to 'noble') lowly; humble:贫～ poor and lowly; in straitened and humble circumstances|卑～ lowly; mean and low ❸ 卑鄙;下贱 mean; base; despicable; contemptible:～骨头 miserable wretch; despicable person; good-for-nothing; poor wretch ❹〈谦辞 *hum.*〉称有关自己的事物[term of self-address] my:(您)贵姓?～姓王。What's your family name? My family name is Wang.

【贱骨头】jiàngǔ·tou ❶ 指不自尊重或不知好歹的人(骂人的话 curse) despicable person; good-for-nothing; one who does not deserve respect from others or who does not know what's good for oneself ❷ 指有福不会享而甘愿受苦的人(含戏谑意 oft. humor.) miserable wretch; poor wretch; person who does not know how to enjoy happiness and is destined to suffering

【贱货】jiànhuò ❶ 不值钱的货物 cheap goods ❷ 指下贱的人(骂人的话 curse) miserable (or contemptible) wretch

【贱民】jiànmín ❶〈旧时 *old*〉指社会地位低下,没有选择职业自由的人(区别于'良民'① as compared with 'law-abiding people') people of the lowest social stratum, who had no freedom to choose jobs ❷ 印度种姓之外的社会地位最低下的阶层 untouchables; Pariah; lowest caste in India; ☞ 种姓 zhǒngxìng on p.2489

犖 jiàn ❶ 斜着支撑 prop up (in a slanting way):打～拨正(房屋倾斜,用长木头支起弄正) erect long logs to keep a dilapidated house from collapse ❷ 用土石挡水 keep water off by piling up earth and stone

剑(劍、劒) jiàn〈古代 *arch.*〉兵器,长条形,一端尖,两边有刃,安有短柄。现在击剑运动用的剑,剑身是长而宽的钢条,无刃,顶端为一小圆球。sword; sabre;

ancient hand weapon having a long, sharp-pointed blade with a sharp edge on both sides, set in a hilt; swords used in the modern fencing sport having long and broad steel strips with round ball tips but no sharp edges

【剑拔弩张】jiàn bá nǔ zhāng 形容形势紧张,一触即发 with swords drawn and bows bent; at daggers drawn; very critical situation

【剑客】jiànkè〈旧指 *old*〉精于剑术的人;剑侠 (in old novels) chivalrous swordsman

【剑眉】jiànméi 较直而末端翘起的眉毛 straight eyebrows slanting upwards and outwards; dashing eyebrows

【剑术】jiànshù 武术或击剑运动中用剑的技术 swordsmanship; fencing skills

【剑侠】jiànxiá 精于剑术的侠客(多见于旧小说 oft. in old novels) chivalrous swordsman

浒 jiàn 北浒(Běijiàn),越南地名 Bac Kan, name of a place in Vietnam

涧 jiàn 山间流水的沟 ravine:溪~ creek|山~ brook; ravine; gully

监(監) jiàn ❶〈古代 *arch.*〉官府名 name of an ancient office:钦天~ Board of Astronomy|国子~ Imperial College, the highest educational administration in feudal China ❷ (Jiàn)姓 a surname

☞ jiān on p.941

【监本】jiànběn 历代国子监刻印的书 books cut and printed by the Imperial Colleges in all dynasties

【监利】Jiànlì 地名,在湖北 Jianli, name of a place in Hubei Province

【监生】jiànshēng 明清两代称在国子监(封建时代国家最高学校)读书或取得进国子监读书资格的人。清代可以用捐纳的办法取得这种称号。student of or one who is qualified to enrol in the Imperial College in the Ming and Qing dynasties. One could also get the title by making a donation in the Qing Dynasty.

健 jiàn ❶ 强健 healthy; strong:~康 healthy; in good health|~全 sound; perfect ❷ 使强健 strengthen; amplify; toughen; invigorate:~身 keep fit; make strong|~胃 be good for the stomach; aid digestion ❸ 在某一方面显示的程度超过一般;善于 be strong in; be good at:~谈 good talker|~忘 forgetful; have a bad memory

【健步】jiànbù 善于走路;脚步轻快有力 walk with fleety, vigorous strides:~如飞 walk quickly; walk as if on wings; walk fast and vigorously

【健存】jiàncún 健在 be still living and in good health; be still in good health:许多同辈相继去世,~的屈指可数了。Many people of the same generation have passed away, those still living and in good health can be counted on fingers.

【健儿】jiàn'ér 称体魄强健而富有活力的人(多指英勇善战或长于体育技巧的青壮年) valiant fighter; outstanding athlete; person of strong physique and brimming with youthful vigour:空军~ valiant fighters in the air force|体坛~ athlete; outstanding athlete

【健将】jiànjiàng ❶ 称某种活动中的能手 master sportsman; top-notch player ❷ 运动员等级中最高一级的称号,由国家授予 title of the highest honour conferred on an athlete by the state

【健康】jiànkāng ❶ (人体)生理机能正常,没有缺陷和疾病 (of the human body) good health; strong physique; be in good health:恢复~ recover one's health|使儿童~地成长 ensure the healthy growth of the children; make the children grow healthily ❷ (事物)情况正常,没有缺陷 healthy; sound; in normal condition; perfect:各种课外活动~地开展起来 encourage the development of extra-curricular activities|促进汉语规范化,为祖国语言的纯洁~而奋斗 promote the standardization of the Chinese language and strive for its purity and health

【健美】jiànměi 健康而优美 healthy and fit; strong and handsome; vigorous and graceful:~的体魄 strong physique

【健美运动】jiànměi yùndòng 一种使身体强健、肌肉发达的体育运动。主要用哑铃、杠铃、扩胸器等进行锻炼。body-building; sport of strengthening the body and developing the muscles; practice of lifting weights and performing certain specific callisthenics, as sit-ups and push-ups, to develop a strong body

【健全】jiànquán ❶ 强健而没有缺陷 sound; perfect:身心~ sound in mind and body|头脑~ sound mind ❷ (事物)完善,没有欠缺 perfect; complete:设施~ well-equipped; have every necessary facility ❸ 使完备 strengthen; amplify; perfect:~基层组织 amplify the root-level organization|~生产责任制度 improve the production responsibility system

【健身】jiànshēn 使身体健康 keep fit; work out; keep in good health:~操 callisthenics|健身房 fitness centre|饭后散步也是一种~活动。It's also an exercise to take a walk after a meal.

【健身房】jiànshēnfáng 专门为体育锻炼而建筑或装备的屋子 gym; room or building equipped for workouts

【健谈】jiàntán 善于说话,经久不倦 be good at talking; be a good talker; be a brilliant conversationalist

【健忘】jiànwàng 容易忘事 forgetful; having a bad memory

【健旺】jiànwàng 身体健康,精力旺盛 healthy and vigorous:精神~ full of vigour|年纪虽老,但人还~。Being advanced in age, he is still full of vigour.

【健在】jiànzài 健康地活着(多指上年纪的人 of a person of advanced age) still in good health:父母都～。One's parents are still in good health.

【健壮】jiànzhuàng 强健 healthy and strong; robust:身体～ be physically fit|牧草肥美,牛羊～ rich pastures and thriving herds

舰(艦) jiàn 排水量在 500 吨以上的军用船只;军舰 warship; naval vessel; man-of-war; military vessel with a displacement of 500 tons or above:～队 fleet|主力～ capital ship|巡洋～ cruiser|驱逐～ destroyer|航空母～ aircraft carrier

【舰队】jiànduì ❶ 担负某一战略海区作战任务的海军兵力,通常由水面舰艇、潜艇、海军航空兵、海军陆战队等部队组成 fleet; naval force; a number of warships under one command in a definite strategical area of operation, usu. composed of surface vessels, submarines, airplanes and marines ❷ 根据作战、训练或某种任务的需要,以多艘舰艇临时组成的编队 any group of warships acting together for operation, training or a certain assignment

【舰日】jiànrì 一艘军舰在海上活动一天叫一个舰日 a day a warship spends at sea

【舰艇】jiàntǐng 各种军用船只的总称 warships; naval vessels

【舰只】jiànzhī 舰(总称) warships; naval vessels

渐 jiàn 逐步;逐渐 gradually; by degrees:天气～冷。It's getting cold. *or* The weather is getting cold.|歌声～远。The singing is getting farther and farther.
☞ jiān on p.943

【渐变】jiànbiàn 逐渐的变化 gradual change

【渐次】jiàncì〈书 *fml*.〉渐渐 gradually; one after another:雨声～停息。The rain gradually subsided.

【渐渐】jiànjiàn〈副词 *adv*.〉表示程度或数量的逐步增减 gradually; by degrees; little by little:过了清明,天气～暖起来了。The weather is getting warm after Pure Brightness sets in.|十点钟以后,马路上的行人～少了。The number of pedestrians gradually dwindled after ten p. m.|站台上的人群向～远去的火车招着手。The crowd on the platform waved their hands to the departing train.

【渐进】jiànjìn 逐渐前进、发展 advance gradually; progress step by step:循序～ advance gradually in an orderly way

【渐悟】jiànwù〈佛教 *Budd*.〉指必须不断排除障碍,渐渐觉悟真理。泛指渐渐领悟。gradual awakening to the truth; gradually grasp the truth by removing obstacles from time to time; (in a broad sense) gradual comprehension

谏 jiàn〈书 *fml*.〉规劝(君主、尊长或朋友),使改正错误 remonstrate with (one's monarch, superior or friend); expostulate with:进～ submit an admonition; remonstrate with|直言敢～ speak bluntly to admonish|从～如流 follow good advice as naturally as a river follows its course; readily accept good advice

【谏诤】jiànzhèng〈书 *fml*.〉直爽地说出人的过错,劝人改正 criticize someone's faults frankly and urge him to correct them

楗 jiàn〈书 *fml*.〉❶ 插门的木棍子 wooden rod for locking a door ❷ 堵塞河堤决口所用的竹木土石等材料 bamboo, wood, earth, rock, etc. used to block a dyke breach

瞷(瞯) jiàn〈书 *fml*.〉窥视 peep; spy out

践(踐) jiàn ❶ 踩 trample; tread:～踏 trample on ❷ 履行;实行 act on; carry out:实～ practise; put into practice; carry out; live up to|～约 live up to one's word; perform a contract; keep a promise; keep an appointment; keep one's word

【践诺】jiànnuò〈书 *fml*.〉履行诺言 keep one's promise (or word)

【践踏】jiàntà ❶ 踩 tread on; trample underfoot:不要～青苗。Keep off the young seedlings. ❷〈比喻 *fig*.〉摧残 wreck; devastate:凭借势力～乡邻 take advantage of one's power to ravage neighbours

【践约】jiàn//yuē 履行约定的事情(多指约会) keep a promise; keep an appointment

【践祚】jiànzuò〈书 *fml*.〉即位;登基 ascend the throne

锏 jiàn 嵌在车轴上的铁条,可以保护车轴并减少摩擦 iron rod set in the axle, which protects the axle and reduces friction
☞ jiǎn on p.947

毽 jiàn (～儿 jiànr) 毽子 shuttlecock

【毽子】jiàn·zi 游戏用具,用布等把铜钱或金属片包扎好,然后装上鸡毛。游戏时,用脚连续向上踢,不让落地。shuttlecock; game in which a person keeps kicking a shuttlecock upward and prevents it from falling to the ground. The shuttlecock is made of a coin covered in cloth and fitted with cock feathers.

腱 jiàn 连接肌肉与骨骼的结缔组织,白色,质地坚韧 tendon; sinew; white, tough tissue which connects muscle and bone; any of the inelastic cords of tough, fibrous connective tissue in which muscle fibres end and by which muscles are attached to bones or other parts; also 肌腱 jījiàn

【腱鞘】jiànqiào 包着长肌腱的管状纤维组织,手和足部最多,有约束肌腱和减少摩擦的作用 tendon sheath; tubular fibrous tissue mostly found in the hands and feet, which wraps the long tendon or sinew, helps to restrict the tendon and reduces friction

【腱子】jiàn·zi 人身上或牛羊等小腿上肌肉发达的部分 calf; (beef or mutton) shank

溅(濺) jiàn 液体受冲击向四外射出 splash; spatter: ～了一身泥 be spattered with mud

☞ 浅 jiān on p. 940

【溅落】jiànluò 重物从高空落入江河湖海中。特指人造卫星、宇宙飞船等返回地球时,落入海洋。splash down; sth. heavy splashing down from air into a river, lake or sea, esp. soft landing of man-made satellites, spaceship, etc. on the sea, permitting recovery

鉴(鑒、鑑) jiàn ❶ 镜子(古代用铜制成) mirror (made of bronze or brass in ancient times) ❷ 照 reflect; mirror: 水清可～。The water is so clear that you can see your reflection in it. ❸ 仔细看;审察 inspect; scrutinize; examine: ～别 distinguish; differentiate; discriminate | ～定 appraise; appraisal ❹ 可以作为警戒或引为教训的事 warning; object lesson: 引以为～ take it as a warning | 前车之覆,后车之～。The overturn of the cart ahead serves as a warning to those behind. ❺ 旧式书信套语,用在开头的称呼之后,表示请人看信 [usu. used in the opening phrase in letters]: 惠～ [a conventional phrase used after the salutation in a letter] for your gracious perusal; be kind enough to read (the following letter) | 台～。[a form used after the name in the salutation of a business letter] Dear Mr. so-and-so; May I draw your attention to the following. | 钧～。[a conventional phrase used in the salutation in formal letters addressed to a superior] I wish to draw Your Excellency's attention.

【鉴别】jiànbié 辨别(真假好坏) distinguish; differentiate; discriminate (truth from falsehood, good from evil): ～古画 distinguish ancient paintings | ～真伪 discriminate the true from the false; tell the true from the false

【鉴定】jiàndìng ❶ 鉴别和评定(人的优缺点) appraisal (of a person's strong and weak points): ～书 certificate of appraisal | 自我～ self-examination ❷ 评定人的优缺点的文字 appraise; identify; authenticate: 写～ write an appraisal | 一份～ a document of appraisal ❸ 辨别并确定事物的真伪、优劣等 determine the authenticity, quality, etc. of sth.: ～碑帖 examine rubbings from stone inscriptions | ～出土文物的年代 determine the date of an unearthed cultural relic

【鉴定人】jiàndìngrén 受侦察、审判机关委托,运用专门知识或技能对案件的专门事项进行鉴别和判断的人 appraiser; person who makes an appraisal of and judgement on a special incident involved in a case by taking advantage of his professional knowledge and skill upon the request of a judicial organ

【鉴戒】jiànjiè 可以使人警惕的事情 warning; object lesson: 引为～ take warning from

【鉴赏】jiànshǎng 鉴定和欣赏(艺术品、文物等) appreciate (works of art, relics, etc.): ～字画 appreciate calligraphy and painting

【鉴于】jiànyú 觉察到;考虑到 considering that; in view of; seeing that: ～党在国家和社会生活中的领导地位,党更加需要向党的一切组织和党员提出严格的要求。In view of the leading place of the Party in the state and social life, the Party must more than ever set strict demands on all its organizations and members. 注意 **NOTE**: 用在表示因果关系的偏句里,前边一般不用主语 usu. without a subject when used at the beginning of a clause expressing causality

键 jiàn ❶ 使轴与齿轮、皮带轮等连接并固定在一起的零件,一般是用钢制的长方块,装在被连接的两个机件上预先制成的键槽中 key; a device, usu. a rectangular steel piece, inserted in prefabricated grooves to lock together mechanical parts, such as shafts and gears or belt pulleys ❷〈书 *fml.*〉插门的金属棍子 bolt; metal bar that slides into a socket and is used to fasten doors and gates ❸ 某些乐器、打字机或其他机器上,使用时按动的部分 key; button or lever of a musical instrument, typewriter or other machines, to be pressed with the finger: 琴～ key on a piano, accordion, and other musical instruments | ～盘 keyboard ❹ 在化学结构式中表示元素原子价的短横线 bond; hyphen (-) representing the valence of an element in a structural formula

【键槽】jiàncáo 机器上安装键的槽子,多在轴和轮上,一般为长条形 keyway; key slot; key seat; long, narrow slot for a key in a shaft or a wheel

【键盘】jiànpán 钢琴、风琴、打字机等上面安着很多键的部分 (of a piano, an accordion, a typewriter, etc.) keyboard; fingerboard

【键盘乐器】jiànpái yuèqì 指有键盘装置的乐器,如风琴、钢琴等 keyboard instrument, such as organ, piano, etc.

槛(檻) jiàn ❶ 栏杆 banisters; balustrade ❷ 关禽兽的木笼;囚笼 wooden cage for animals: 兽～ animals cage | ～车(古代运送囚犯的车) (of ancient times) prisoners' van

☞ kǎn on p. 1081

僭 jiàn〈书 *fml.*〉超越本分。古时指地位在下的冒用地位在上的名义或礼仪、器物。assume; usurp; overstep one's authority; (in ancient times) referring to an inferior illegally using the title, ceremony or articles designated for a superior: ～号(冒用帝王的称号)

usurp the title of an emperor | ～越 (超越本分,冒用在上的名义或物品) overstep one's authority (illegally assume the title or use the articles designated for a superior)

踺 jiàn [踺子] (jiàn·zi) 体操运动等的一种翻身动作 somersault; gymnastic stunt performed by turning the body forward and backward, and heels over head

箭 jiàn ❶ 古代兵器,长约二三尺的细杆装上尖头,杆的末梢附有羽毛,搭在弓弩上发射。现代射箭运动用的箭一般用钢、铝合金、塑料等制成。arrow; ancient weapon mounted on a slender shaft 2 to 3-*chi*-long, pointed at one end and feathered at the other, for shooting from a bow. Arrows used in modern archery are usu. made of steel, aluminium alloy or plastic ❷ 指箭能射到的距离 distance covered by an arrow after shooting: 一～之遥 as far as an arrow reaches | 半～多路 very near; a few minutes' walk

【箭靶子】 jiànbǎ·zi 练习射箭时用做目标的东西 target for archery

【箭步】 jiànbù 一下子蹿得很远的脚步 sudden big stride forward: 他一个～蹿上月台。He leapt up to the platform with a big stride.

【箭垛子】 jiànduǒ·zi ❶ 女墙 battlements ❷ 箭靶子 target for archery

【箭楼】 jiànlóu 城楼,周围有供瞭望和射箭用的小窗 embrasured watchtower over a city gate

【箭头】 jiàntóu (～儿 jiàntóur) ❶ 箭的尖头 arrowhead ❷ 箭头形符号,常用来指示方向 arrow sign to indicate a direction or position

【箭在弦上】 jiàn zài xián shàng 〈比喻 *fig.*〉事情已经到了不得不做或话已经到了不得不说的时候 high time to shoot the arrow already fitted to the bowstring; do sth. that has to be done: ～,不得不发 arrow fitted to the bowstring cannot avoid being discharged — one cannot but go ahead; one has reached the point of no return

【箭竹】 jiànzhú 竹子的一种,秆高约3米,深紫色,嫩枝叶是猫熊爱吃的食物 arrow bamboo (*Sinarundinaria nitida*); a kind of bamboo, about three metres tall, and dark purple in colour, its tender leaves being a favourite food for pandas

【箭镞】 jiànzú 箭前端的尖头,多用金属制成 metal arrowhead

jiāng (ㄐㄧㄤ)

江 jiāng ❶ 大河 river: 长～ Yangtze River | 珠～ Pearl River | 黑龙～ Heilongjiang ❷ (Jiāng) 指长江 Yangtze River: ～汉 region encompassing part of the basins of the Yangtze River and its tributary Hanjiang River in Hubei Province; Jianghan Plain (plain of the Yangtze and Hanjiang rivers) | ～淮 Jianghuai Plain (the plain covering part of the Yangtze and Huai river volleys) | ～南 south of the Yangtze River | ～左 region east of the Yangtze River ❸ (Jiāng) 姓 a surname

【江北】 Jiāngběi ❶ 长江下游以北的地区,就是江苏、安徽两省靠近长江北岸的一带 region north of the lower Yangtze River reaches, including part of Jiangsu and Anhui north of the Yangtze River ❷ 泛指长江以北 (in a broad sense) north of the Yangtze River

【江东】 Jiāngdōng 长江在芜湖、南京之间为西南、东北走向,古代是南北往来主要渡口所在的江段,习惯上称自此以下的南岸地区为江东。也指三国时吴国孙权统治下的全部地区。region east of the Yangtze River, a geographical term derived from the fact that the section of the Yangtze between Wuhu in Anhui and Nanjing in Jiangsu flows southwest and northeast where all the major ferries for south-north traffic were located in ancient times, making the region south of the Yangtze river look like it is east of it; also the whole region under the rule of Sun Quan, founder of the Wu Kingdom (222-280) during the Three Kingdoms Period

【江防】 jiāngfáng ❶ 防止江河水患的工作。特指长江的江防。flood prevention along the rivers, esp. along the Yangtze River ❷ 指长江的军事防御 military defence of the Yangtze River: ～工事 fortifications along the Yangtze River

【江河日下】 jiāng hé rì xià 江河的水天天向下游流 rivers flowing downstream on a daily basis; 〈比喻 *fig.*〉情况一天天坏下去 go from bad to worse; be on the decline

【江湖】 jiānghú 〈旧时 *old*〉泛指四方各地 all places in the country; every corner: 走～ go from place to place for making a living | 闯～ scrape a living by roaming from one place to another | 流落～ lead a vagrant life

【江湖】 jiāng·hú 〈旧时 *old*〉指各处流浪靠卖艺、卖药等生活的人。也指这种人所从事的行业。people living a vagrant life as fortune-teller, quack doctor, entertainers, etc.; profession or trade of sb. who is always travelling: ～艺人 itinerant entertainer

【江湖骗子】 jiānghú piàn·zi 原指闯荡江湖靠卖假药等骗术谋生的人 swindler; charlatan

【江郎才尽】 Jiāngláng cái jìn 南朝江淹年少时以文才著称,晚年诗文无佳句,人们说他才尽了。后来用'江郎才尽'比喻才思枯竭。legend has it that Jiang Yan of the Southern Dynasties showed brilliance as a poet at an early age and became widely known as Prodigy Jiang, but he produced nothing of note in his later years. Thus 'Prodigy Jiang used up his literary talent' becomes a set phrase to mean 'at the end of one's resources'.

【江蓠】jiānglí ❶ 红藻的一种，暗红色，细圆柱形，有不规则的分枝。生在海湾浅水中。可用来制造琼脂。*Gracilaria verrucosa*; a kind of red alga, dark red, thin and cylindrical, having irregular branches, living in shallow water in bays, used for making agar ❷ 古书上说的一种香草 fragrant plant mentioned in ancient books

【江轮】jiānglún 专在江河中行驶的轮船 river steamer

【江米】jiāngmǐ 糯米 polished glutinous rice

【江米酒】jiāngmǐjiǔ 糯米加曲酿造的食品，甘甜，酒味淡 fermented glutinous rice, sweet in taste and low in alcohol content; also 酒酿 jiǔniàng or 醪糟 láozāo

【江米纸】jiāngmǐzhǐ 糯米纸 glutinous rice paper

【江南】Jiāngnán ❶ 长江下游以南的地区，就是江苏、安徽两省的南部和浙江省的北部 region south of the lower Yangtze River, including southern Jiangsu and Anhui and northern Zhejiang ❷ 泛指长江以南 (in a broad sense) south of the Yangtze River

【江山】jiāngshān 江河和山岭，多用来指国家或国家的政权 rivers and mountains; landscape; territory; land; country; mostly referring to state or sovereignty; state power: ～如此多娇 land with such superb beauty and grandeur | 打～fight for supreme power

【江天】jiāngtiān 江河水面上的广阔空际 sky over a river: 万里～wide expanse of sky over a river

【江豚】jiāngtún 哺乳动物，生活在江河中，形状很像鱼，没有背鳍，头圆，眼小，全身黑色。吃小鱼和其他小动物。cowfish (*Neomeris phocaenoides*); black finless porpoise; mammal shaped like a fish, with round head and small eyes, black in colour, without a dorsal fin, living in rivers, feeding on small fish and other small animals; 通称 generally called 江猪 jiāngzhū

【江洋大盗】jiāngyáng dàdào 在江河海洋上抢劫行凶的强盗 one who robs at sea or on a river; pirate; freebooter; sea wolf; corsair; buccaneer

【江珧】jiāngyáo 软体动物，壳略呈三角形，表面苍黑色。生活在海岸的泥沙里。pen shell (*Atrina pectinata*); mollusc, soft-bodied animal with a triangular shell, living in seaside wet sands

【江珧柱】jiāngyáozhù 江珧的闭壳肌干制后叫江珧柱，是珍贵的食品。干贝通常也叫江珧柱。dried adductor of a pen shell, a highly-valued seafood; another name for 干贝 gānbèi

茳 jiāng [茳芏](jiāngdù) 多年生草本植物，茎呈三棱形，叶子细长，花绿褐色。茎可用来织席。*Cyperus malaccensis* var. *brevifolius*; perennial plant with long narrow leaves and greenish brown flowers, whose stem, triangular in cross-section, can be used for weaving mats

将(將) jiāng ❶〈书 *fml.*〉搀扶；领；带 support; bring; take: 出郭相扶～ help each other on the way out of town ❷ 保养 take care of: ～养 rest and recuperate | ～息 rest; recuperate ❸〈方 *dial.*〉(牲畜)繁殖；生 (of animals) give birth; breed; propagate; reproduce: ～羔 give birth to a lamb ❹〈书 *fml.*〉做(事) deal with or handle (affairs); act: 慎重～事 handle matters with care; act carefully ❺ 下象棋时攻击对方的'将'或'帅' (in chess game) attack the opponent's king; check ❻ 用言语刺激 verbally push someone to act; challenge; prod; spur: 他做事稳重，你～他没用。He is discrete in handling things. It's no use trying to egg him on. ❼〈介词 *prep.*〉拿⑧(多见于成语或方言 oft. used in idioms or dialects) with; by; by means of: ～功折罪 expiate one's sin by good service; atone for one's misdeeds by doing good | ～鸡蛋碰石头 dash an egg against a stone; bang one's head against a brick wall ❽〈介词 *prep.*〉把²[used to introduce the object before a verb]: ～他请来 send for him; ask him to come over | ～门关上 shut the door ❾ 将要 be going to; be about to; will; shall: 船～启碇。The ship is about to weigh anchor. ❿ 又；且(叠用) (used in reiteration) besides; and; also: ～信～疑 half believe; skeptical; believe partially ⓫〈方 *dial.*〉〈助词 *aux.*〉用在动词和'进来、出去'等表示趋向的补语中间 [used between a verb and a directional complement like 'in' or 'out']: 走～进去 go inside | 打～起来 get into a fight ⓬ (Jiāng) 姓 a surname

☞ jiàng on p. 964 and qiāng on p. 1543

【将次】jiāngcì〈书 *fml.*〉将要；快要 on the point of; be about to

【将错就错】jiāng cuò jiù cuò 事情既然做错了，索性顺着错误做下去 leave a mistake uncorrected and make the best of it; make the best of a bad bargain

【将计就计】jiāng jì jiù jì 利用对方的计策向对方使计策 turn sb.'s trick against him; beat sb. at his own game; counterplot

【将近】jiāngjìn (数量等)快要接近(of number) close to; near; approximately; almost: anywhere near; anything like: ～掌灯时分 towards darkness; when it's almost dark | 中国有～四千年的有文字可考的历史。China has nearly 4,000 years of recorded history.

【将就】jiāng·jiu 勉强适应不很满意的事物或环境 accept unsatisfactory events or conditions reluctantly; make do with; do without; make the best of; put up with: ～吃一点儿 make do with some food | 衣服稍微小一点，你～着穿吧！

The coat is a bit short for you, just make do with it.

【将军】jiāng//jūn ❶ 将⑤(in a chess game) check ❷〈比喻 *fig.*〉给人出难题,使人为难 put sb. on the spot; embarrass; baffle: 他当众将了我一军,要我表演舞蹈。He embarrassed me in public by asking me to dance.

【将军】jiāngjūn ❶ 将(jiàng)级军官 general (officer rank) ❷ 泛指高级将领(in a broad sense) high-ranking military officers

【将军肚】jiāngjūn dù 指男子因发胖而形成的向前腆起的腹部(含戏谑意 humor.) protruding belly on a fat man; pot-belly; pot; big belly; beer belly

【将来】jiānglái 时间词,现在以后的时间(区别于'过去、现在' as compared with 'past' or 'present')future: 这些资料要妥为保存,以供~参考。File these materials properly for future reference.

【将息】jiāngxī 将养 rest; recuperate: 大病初愈,一定要好好~。You have barely recovered from a major ailment and must rest properly.

【将心比心】jiāng xīn bǐ xīn 拿自己的心去比照别人的心。指遇事设身处地替别人着想。compare one's feeling with other's; put oneself in sb. else's place or shoes; have empathy for sb. else's feelings

【将信将疑】jiāng xìn jiāng yí 有些相信,又有些怀疑 take sth. with a grain of salt; half believe; skeptical; have doubts; regard with a guarded optimism: 我说了半天,他还是~。After all I said, he still remained skeptical.

【将养】jiāngyǎng 休息和调养 rest and recuperate: 医生说再~两个礼拜就可以好了。The doctor said he should recuperate for another two weeks.

【将要】jiāngyào〈副词 *adv.*〉表示行为或情况在不久以后发生[of an event or action to take place in near future] be going to; will; shall: 他~来北京。He will come to Beijing soon.

姜[1](**薑**) jiāng ❶ 多年生草本植物,根茎黄褐色,叶子披针形,穗状花序,花冠黄绿色,通常不开花。根茎有辣味,是常用的调味品,也可入药。ginger (*Zingiber officinale*); perennial herbaceous plant with a yellowish brown, pungent rhizome, lanceolate leaves, spike inflorescence and yellowish green corollas that usu. do not bloom, oft. used as a seasoning as well as in medicine ❷ 这种植物的根茎 rhizome of the ginger plant

姜[2] Jiāng 姓 a surname

【姜黄】jiānghuáng ❶ 多年生草本植物,叶子很大,根茎椭圆形,深黄色,开黄花。根茎入药,也可以做黄色染料。turmeric (*Curcuma longa*); perennial herbaceous plant with large leaves, dark yellow, fleshy rhizome, yellow flowers. Its rootstock can be used as medicine, or as a yellow dye. ❷ 形容像姜似的黄颜色(of sth.) having the colour of ginger: 病人脸色~,气息微弱。The patient's complexion is yellow and breath is weak.

豇 jiāng [豇豆](jiāngdòu) ❶ 一年生草本植物,茎蔓生,叶子由三个菱形小叶合成,花淡紫色。果实为圆筒形长荚果,种子呈肾脏形。嫩荚是普通的蔬菜。cowpea (*Vigna unguiculata*) annual herbaceous trailing plant, with diamond-shaped ternate leaves, lavender flowers, bearing long cylindrical pods with kidney-shaped seeds. The young pods are an ordinary vegetable. ❷ 这种植物的荚果或种子 cowpea pod; cowpea seed

浆(**漿**) jiāng ❶ 较浓的液体 thick liquid: 豆~soya-bean milk | 泥~slop; slurry | 纸~paper pulp | 粉~starchy liquid | 牛痘~small pox serum ❷ 用粉浆或米汤浸纱、布或衣服使干后发硬发挺 starch; dip cloth or clothing in liquid starch or rice-water to stiffen it after drying: ~洗 wash and starch | 衬衫领子要~一下。The shirt collar must be starched.

☞ 糨 jiàng on p. 965

【浆果】jiāngguǒ 液果的一种,中果皮和内果皮都是肉质,水分很多,如葡萄、番茄等的果实 berry; pulpy fruit, with fleshy, juicy mesocarp and endocarp, such as the grape and tomato

【浆洗】jiāngxǐ 洗并且浆 wash and starch: 衣服~得很干净。The clothes are washed and starched clean.

【浆液】jiāngyè 机体内浆膜分泌的液体,无色,透明,有润滑作用 serous fluid; colourless, clear liquid secreted by the serous membranes of the body, acts as a lubricant

僵(❶**殭**) jiāng ❶ 僵硬 stiff; rigid; numb: ~尸 corpse | 手脚都冻~了。Hands and feet went numb with cold. | 百足之虫,死而不~。An insect with a hundred feet may die, but will never stiffen. ❷ 事情难于处理,停滞不进 refuse to budge; deadlock; impasse; stagnation; standstill: 大家一时想不出适当的话,情形非常~。No one could think of anything appropriate to say, and things remained deadlocked. | 不要把事情弄~了,以致无法解决。Don't let things get into an impasse. ❸〈方 *dial.*〉收敛笑容,使表情严肃 unsmiling; serious: 他~着脸。He kept a straight face.

【僵持】jiāngchí 相持不下 in a stalemate; deadlocked; reach an impasse: 双方~了好久。For a long time, neither side would budge an inch.

【僵化】jiānghuà 变僵硬;停止发展 ossify; petrify; fossilize; rigid; inflexible: 骄傲自满只能使思想~。Arrogance and conceit lead to rigid thinking.

【僵局】jiāngjú 僵持的局面 deadlock; impasse; stalemate; logjam: 陷入～reach an impasse or deadlock; come to a standstill | 打破～break a deadlock; resolve a stalemate

【僵尸】jiāngshī 僵硬的死尸。常用来比喻腐朽的事物。stiff corpse; (fig.)(of things) mouldy; rotton; decayed

【僵死】jiāngsǐ 僵硬而失去生命力 dead as mutton; stone dead; rigid; ossified

【僵硬】jiāngyìng ❶(肢体)不能活动(of limbs) stiff; stark; ankylosis: 他的两条腿～了。His legs have stiffened. ❷ 呆板;不灵活 rigid; stiff; inflexible; inelastic; stark: 工作方法～work in a mechanical and rigid way

【僵直】jiāngzhí 僵硬,不能弯曲 stiff; unbending: 手指冻得～。(My) fingers are frozen stiff.

螀(螿) jiāng ☞ 寒螀 hánjiāng on p.764

缰(韁) jiāng 缰绳 rein; halter; trace: 信马由～ride with lax reins | 脱～的野马 wild runaway horse; unbroken horse

【缰绳】jiāng·shéng 牵牲口的绳子 rein; halter; trace; rope for curbing a draught animal

鳉(鱂) jiāng 鱼类的一科,头部扁平,腹部突出,口小。生活在淡水中。killifish (*Fundulus*); cyprinodont fish (*Cyprinodontidae*); cyprinodont; family of fish with a flat head, protruding stomach and small mouth, living in fresh water

礓 jiāng ❶ [礓礤儿](jiāngcār)〈方 *dial.*〉台阶 steps ❷ ☞ 砂礓 shājiāng on p.1665

疆 jiāng ❶ 边界;疆界 boundary; border; confines: 边～borderland; frontier; border area; frontier region | ～域 territory ❷ (Jiāng)指新疆 Xinjiang: 南～(新疆天山以南的地区) South Xinjiang (area to the south of the Tianshan Mountains in Xinjiang)

【疆场】jiāngchǎng 战场 battlefield; battleground: 驰骋～gallop across the battlefield

【疆界】jiāngjiè 国家或地域的边界 boundary; border; confines

【疆土】jiāngtǔ 疆域;领土 territory

【疆埸】jiāngyì〈书 *fml.*〉❶ 田边 edge of field ❷ 边境 border

【疆域】jiāngyù 国家领土(着重面积大小)(area of) national territory; domain

jiǎng (ㄐㄧㄤˇ)

讲(講) jiǎng ❶ 说 speak; tell; say; talk; relate; deliver oneself of: ～故事 tell a tale; relate a story | 他高兴得话都～不出来了。He could not speak for excitement. ❷ 解释;说明;论述 explain; make clear; interpret; represent: ～书 lecture about a book | 这个字有几个～法。There are several explanations for this Chinese character. | 这本书是～气象的。The book is on meteorology. ❸ 商量;商议 discuss; negotiate; confer: ～价儿 bargain ❹ 就某方面说;论 as far as sth. is concerned; as to; concerning; with regard to; in terms of: ～技术他不如你,～干劲儿他比你足。He does not match you in terms of skills, but he is more motivated. ❺ 讲求 pay attention to; stress; strive for; be particular about: ～卫生 be particular about hygiene | ～团结 emphasize solidarity | ～速度 strive for speed

【讲法】jiǎng·fa ❶ 指措词 way of saying; wording; diction; phraseology; verbiage ❷ 指意见;见解;解释 opinion, standpoint; interpretation; statement; version; explanation: 这种～过于牵强。This statement is far-fetched. | 这句话可有好几种～。This sentence can be interpreted several ways. ☞ 说法 shuō·fa on p.1809

【讲稿】jiǎnggǎo (～儿 jiǎnggǎor)讲演、报告或教课前所写的底稿 draft or text of a speech, report or lecture; lecture notes

【讲古】jiǎnggǔ 讲述过去的传说、故事 recount legends and stories of the past: 孩子们围坐树下听老人～。The children sat around under a tree to listen to legendary tales and stories told by an old man.

【讲和】jiǎng//hé 结束战争或纠纷,彼此和解 make peace after war or dispute; settle a dispute; become reconciled; put up the sword

【讲话】jiǎng//huà ❶ 说话;发言 speak; talk; address: 他很会～。He is a good talker. | 这次座谈会没有一个不～的。Every one spoke at the seminar. | 来宾也都讲了话。All the guests gave speeches too. ❷ 指责;非议 blame; criticize; censure: 你这样搞特殊,难怪人家要～了。With all the privileges you enjoy, small wonder people pick fault with you.

【讲话】jiǎnghuà ❶ 讲演的话 speech; talk; address: 他的～代表了多数人的要求。His speech represented the views of most people. ❷ 一种普及性的著作体裁(多用做书名 oft. used in book titles) talks; discourses; style of writing aimed at popularizing a difficult subject:《形式逻辑～》*An Introduction to Formal Logic* or *A Talk on Formal Logic*

【讲价】jiǎng//jià (～儿 jiǎng//jiàr)讨价还价 bargain; haggle (over price)

【讲价钱】jiǎng jià·qian ❶ 讲价 bargain; haggle over price: 他买东西从不～。He never bargains when shopping. ❷〈比喻 *fig.*〉在接受任务或举行谈判时提出要求和条件 make terms; raise demands or terms when negotiating or accepting a task

【讲解】jiǎngjiě 解释;解说 explain; expound;

J

explicate：～员 docent；tour guide；lecturer｜他指着模型给大家～。He pointed to the model while explaining to everyone.

【讲究】jiǎng·jiu ❶ 讲求；重视 pay attention to；stress；strive for；be particular about：～卫生 be particular about hygiene｜我们一向～实事求是。We always stress seeking truth from facts. ❷（～儿 jiǎng·jiur）值得注意或推敲的内容 deserving of attention or careful study：翻译的技术大有～。The art of translation deserves careful study. ❸ 精美 exquisite；delicate；superb；tasteful：房间布置得很～。The room is furnished with great taste.

【讲课】jiǎng//kè 讲授功课 teach；lecture；prelect：他在我们学校～。He teaches at our school.｜上午讲了三堂课。(I) taught three classes this morning.

【讲理】jiǎng//lǐ ❶ 评是非曲直 reason (with sb.)；argue：咱们跟他～去。Let's go and reason with him. ❷ 遵从道理 consistent with reason；governed by sound thinking；reasonable；sensible；rational：蛮不～utterly unreasonable｜他是个～的人。He is a sensible man.

【讲论】jiǎnglùn ❶ 谈论；议论 talk about；discuss：她从不在背地里～别人。She never talks about other people behind their backs. ❷ 论述 deal with：这是一本～戏剧的书。This is a book on drama.

【讲盘儿】jiǎng//pánr〈方 *dial.*〉商谈价钱或条件 negotiate about price or terms；also 讲盘子 jiǎng//pán·zi

【讲评】jiǎngpíng 讲述和评论 comment on；appraise；critique：～作文 comment on a composition｜文章～critique an article

【讲情】jiǎng//qíng 替人求情，请求宽恕 intercede for sb.；appeal on behalf of sb. for forgiveness

J

【讲求】jiǎngqiú 重视某一方面，并设法使它实现，满足要求；追求 pay attention to；stress；strive for；be particular about：办事要～效率。All work must stress efficiency.｜要～实际，不要～形式。Emphasis should be put on practical result rather than form.

【讲师】jiǎngshī 高等学校中职别次于副教授的教师 instructor；lecturer；prelector；docent；college or university academic rank inferior to associate professor

【讲史】jiǎngshǐ 我国古代民间流行的口头文学形式，主要讲述历史上朝代兴亡和战争的故事，篇幅较长，如《三国志平话》、《五代史平话》等 form of oral folk literature from ancient times，mainly recounting stories of wars，and the rise and fall of dynasties，e. g. *Popular Stories of the Three Kingdoms*，*Popular Stories of the Five Dynasties*，etc.

【讲授】jiǎngshòu 讲解传授 lecture；instruct；teach；impart：～数学课 teach mathematics

【讲述】jiǎngshù 把事情或道理讲出来 explain events or principles；give an account of；narrate；relate；tell of：～事情经过 give an account of events｜～机械原理 explain the fundamentals of mechanics

【讲台】jiǎngtái 在教室或会场的一端建造的高出地面的台子，人在上面讲课或讲演 podium；platform；dais；stand；raised portion of floor in a classroom or meeting place，for speaker or instructor to stand on

【讲坛】jiǎngtán 讲台；泛指讲演讨论的场所 platform；rostrum；any forum for public discussion

【讲习】jiǎngxí ❶ 讲授和学习 lecture and study：～班 study group；seminar ❷ 研习 study；research：～学问 study knowledge

【讲学】jiǎng//xué 公开讲述自己的学术理论 give lectures；deliver lectures；discourse publicly on academic or theoretical topics：应邀出国～go abroad to give lectures on invitation｜他在这里讲过学。He has lectured here.

【讲演】jiǎngyǎn 对听众讲述有关某一事物的知识或对某一问题的见解 lecture；speech；talk；prelection：登台～take the floor；mount the podium to deliver a speech｜他的～很生动。He gave a lively speech.

【讲义】jiǎngyì 为讲课而编写的教材 teaching materials；lecture sheets

【讲座】jiǎngzuò 一种教学形式，多利用报告会、广播、电视或刊物连载的方式进行 series of lectures for teaching purposes，usu. given at meetings，over the radio，television or in journal installments：汉语拼音～lectures on Chinese Phonetic Alphabet (or Chinese *pinyin*)

奖(奬) jiǎng ❶ 奖励；夸奖 reward；praise；commend；encourage；put a premium on：褒～praise and honour｜嘉～commend｜有功者～。The meritorious will be rewarded. ❷ 为了鼓励或表扬而给予的荣誉或财物等 honour or material reward given as incentive or in recognition；award；prize；bonus；reward；encouragement：得～win，obtain or get a prize；be awarded a prize｜发～give a prize；present an award；issue a reward｜一等～first prize；first award

【奖杯】jiǎngbēi 发给竞赛优胜者的杯状奖品，一般用金属制成 cup awarded to winner of a competition，usu. made of metal；pot；trophy

【奖惩】jiǎngchéng 奖励和惩罚 rewards and punishments；rewards and penalties：～分明 be fair in handing out rewards and punishments｜～制度 system of rewards and penalties

【奖金】jiǎngjīn 作奖励用的钱 money given as an incentive；bonus；prize；premium；reward；prix；stakes；dividend

【奖励】jiǎnglì 给予荣誉或财物来鼓励 encourage and reward with honour or money; reward; award; offer or put a premium on: 物质～material incentive; material reward|～先进生产者 reward advanced workers

【奖牌】jiǎngpái 发给竞赛优胜者的金属牌，有金牌、银牌、铜牌等 medal; flat piece of metal given as an award to winners in a competition, graded into gold, silver, bronze, etc.

【奖品】jiǎngpǐn 作奖励用的物品 objects given as reward; prize; award; trophy

【奖券】jiǎngquàn 一种证券，上面编着号码，按票面价格出售。开奖后，持有中奖号码奖券的，可按规定领奖。lottery ticket; numbered ticket sold at face value so that when the winning number is announced, the one with the corresponding ticket claims a reward

【奖赏】jiǎngshǎng 对有功的或在竞赛中获胜的集体或个人给予奖励 award; reward

【奖售】jiǎngshòu ❶ 用奖励的方法鼓励出售产品 prize sale; reward sale ❷ 作为奖励而售给 sell sth. as a reward: 这些名牌自行车是～卖粮食较多的农户的。These brand-name bicycles are for sale to those farmers who sold more grain than others.

【奖学金】jiǎngxuéjīn 学校、团体或个人给予学习成绩优良的学生的奖金 scholarship; fellowship; exhibition; financial aid granted by an individual, school or organization to a student for outstanding academic achievement

【奖掖】jiǎngyè〈书 *fml.*〉奖励提拔 reward and promote; encourage by promoting and rewarding: ～后进 encourage those who lag behind to catch up by offering incentives

【奖挹】jiǎngyì〈书 *fml.*〉same as 奖掖 jiǎngyè

【奖章】jiǎngzhāng 发给受奖人佩带的徽章 medal; decoration; badge given to recipient of an award

【奖状】jiǎngzhuàng 为奖励而发给的证书 certificate of merit; citation; diploma; commendation

桨(槳) jiǎng 划船用具，多为木制，上半圆柱形，下半扁平而略宽 oar; implement for rowing a boat, usu. made of wood, consisting of a pole with a broad blade at one end

蒋(蔣) Jiǎng 姓 a surname

耩 jiǎng 用耧来播种 sow with a drill: ～地 drill a field|～豆子 plant beans in drills; also 耧播 lóubō

【耩子】jiǎng·zi〈方 *dial.*〉耧 drill (used to sow seeds in furrows)

膙 jiǎng [膙子](jiǎng·zi)〈方 *dial.*〉趼(jiǎn)子 callosity; callus: 两手磨起了～。(My) hands callused.

jiàng(ㄐㄧㄤˋ)

匠 jiàng ❶ 工匠 craftsman; artisan; workman; handicraftsman; tradesman; artificer; smith: 铁～blacksmith|铜～coppersmith|木～carpenter; joiner|瓦～bricklayer; tiler; plasterer|石～stoneman; stonemason; stonecutter|能工巧～master craftsman; skilled craftsman ❷〈书 *fml.*〉指在某方面很有造诣的人 person highly skilled in some area; master: 宗～great master (in literature or art)|文学巨～literary giant

【匠人】jiàngrén〈旧指 *old*〉手艺工人 craftsman; artisan

【匠心】jiàngxīn〈书 *fml.*〉巧妙的心思 ingenuity; craftsmanship: 独具～outstanding ingenuity|～独运 demonstrate inventiveness; show ingenuity

降 jiàng ❶ 落下(跟'升'相对 as opposed to 'ascend') fall; drop; go down; come down: ～落 come down; descend; land; touch down; alight|～雨 rainfall|温度下～drop in temperature ❷ 使落下;降低(跟'升'相对 as opposed to 'raise') lower; reduce; cut; cut down; bring down: ～价 lower, reduce or cut the price|～级 demote; degrade; drop in ranking ❸ (Jiàng)姓 a surname
☞ xiáng on p. 2093

【降班】jiàng//bān (学生)降级;留班 (of student) be put down a grade; repeat the same grade

【降半旗】jiàng bànqí 下半旗 at half-mast (flag); hoist, fly or hang a flag at half-mast

【降尘】jiàngchén 颗粒较大，不能在空中长时间飘浮的粉尘 fallen dust; heavier particles of dust which cannot remain suspended for long in the air; also 落尘 luòchén

【降低】jiàngdī 下降;使下降 drop; recede; come down; lower; reduce; cut: 温度～了。The temperature dropped.|～物价 cut, bring down or reduce prices|～要求 moderate one's demands

【降幅】jiàngfú (价格、利润、收入等)降低的幅度 (of prices, profits, income, etc.) range of decrease: 商品零售价平均～2.5%。Retail prices of commodities have fallen by an average margin of 2.5%.

【降格】jiàng//gé 降低标准、身份等 lower one's standards or status; degrade: ～以求 settle for (sth. less than best)

【降级】jiàng//jí 从较高的等级或班级降到较低的等级或班级 demote; degrade; drop from higher rank of grade to lower one

【降价】jiàng//jià 降低原来的定价 reduce, lower, cut or bring down the price: 滞销货物～处理 sell slow-selling goods at reduced prices

【降结肠】jiàngjiécháng 结肠的一部分，上端与横结肠相连，向下行，在左髂骨附近与乙状结肠相连 descending colon; part of the colon that descends from the transverse colon and joins the sigmoid colon near left ilium;（图见 ☞ figure for 消化系统 xiāohuà xìtǒng on p.2100）

【降解】jiàngjiě ❶ 有机化合物分子中的碳原子数目减少，分子量降低 degradation;（of organic compound) decrease of carbon atoms in a molecule leading to a decline in molecular weight ❷ 高分子化合物的大分子分解成较小的分子（of a macromolecular compound) breakdown of macromolecules into smaller molecules

【降临】jiànglín 来到 befall; arrive; come: 夜色～。Night fell. | 大驾～your gracious presence

【降落】jiàngluò 落下；下降着落 land; alight; descend; touch down: 飞机～在跑道上。The plane landed on the runway.

【降落伞】jiàngluòsǎn 凭借空气阻力使人或物体从空中缓慢下降着陆的伞状器具 parachute; umbrella-shaped apparatus used to retard a free fall from the sky

【降旗】jiàng//qí 把旗子降下 lower the flag

【降生】jiàngshēng 出生；出世（多指宗教的创始人或其他方面的有名人物 usu. of founder of a religion, or other prominent persons) be born; come into the world

【降水】jiàngshuǐ 从大气中落到地面的固体或液体形式的水，主要有雨、雪、霰、雹等 precipitation; any form of water, solid or liquid, such as rain, snow, sleet, hail, that falls from the atmosphere to the earth's surface

【降温】jiàng//wēn ❶ 降低温度。特指用喷水或喷冷空气等方法使高温厂房和车间等温度降低。lower the temperature, esp. in a workshop by means of spraying water or blowing cool air: 防暑～lower the temperature to prevent heatstroke ❷ 气温下降 drop in temperature ❸〈比喻 *fig.*〉热情下降或事物发展的势头减弱 decline in enthusiasm or momentum; cool down: 抢购热已～。The buying spree has cooled down.

J

虹 jiàng 义同'虹'(hóng)，限于单用 same as 虹 hóng in meaning, used alone
☞ 虹 hóng on p.806

将(將) jiàng ❶ 将官；将领；泛指军官 rank of general; commander;（in a broad sense) military officer: 少～major general | 全军～士 all officers and men ❷〈书 *fml.*〉带(兵) command (troops); lead: 韩信～兵，多多益善。When Han Xin is in command, the more troops the better.
☞ jiāng on p.959 and qiāng on p.1543

【将才】jiàngcái 领导、指挥军队的才能。也指有将才的人。ability to lead or command troops; man with leadership talent

【将官】jiàngguān 将级军官，低于元帅，高于校官 rank of general military rank above colonel but below marshal

【将官】jiàng·guan same as 将领 jiànglǐng

【将领】jiànglǐng 高级的军官 general; high-ranking officer: 陆军～senior officers of the army

【将令】jiànglìng 军令（多见于早期白话 mostly in early vernacular Chinese) military order

【将门】jiàngmén 将帅之家 family of a general: ～虎子 capable young man from a distinguished family

【将士】jiàngshì 将领和士兵的统称 officers and soldiers; commanders and fighters: ～用命（军官和士兵都服从命令）。Both officers and men obey orders conscientiously.

【将帅】jiàngshuài 泛指军队的高级指挥官（in a broad sense) senior commanding officer: ～之才 makings of a good commander; talent of a good general

【将校】jiàngxiào 将官和校官。泛指高级军官。generals and field officers;（in a broad sense) high-ranking officers

【将指】jiàngzhǐ〈书 *fml.*〉手的中指；脚的大趾 middle finger; big toe

洚 jiàng〈书 *fml.*〉大水泛滥 flood; inundate; overflow; be in spate; deluge: ～水（洪水）flood; floodwater

绛 jiàng 深红色 deep red; crimson

【绛紫】jiàngzǐ 暗紫中略带红的颜色 deep purple tinged with red; dark reddish purple; also 酱紫 jiàngzǐ

弶 jiàng〈书 *fml.*〉❶ 捕捉老鼠、鸟雀等的工具 mousetrap; snare; catcher; instrument to catch mice, birds, etc. ❷ 用弶捕捉 catch in a trap

强(強、彊) jiàng 强硬不屈；固执 stubborn; unyielding; unbending; self-willed; obstinate: 倔～unbending; obdurate; obstinate
☞ qiáng on p.1543 and qiǎng on p.1547

【强嘴】jiàngzuǐ 顶嘴；强辩 answer back; talk back; reply defiantly; also 犟嘴 jiàngzuǐ

酱(醬) jiàng ❶ 豆、麦发酵后，加上盐做成的糊状调味品 thick sauce or paste made from fermented soya beans or wheat flour and flavoured with salt: 黄～soya paste | 甜面～sweet flour paste | 炸～fried soya paste ❷ 用酱或酱油腌的(菜)；用酱油煮的(肉) vegetable marinated in soya sauce or soya paste; meat stewed in soya sauce: ～萝卜 pickled radish | ～肘子 pork joint simmered in brown sauce ❸ 用酱或酱油腌(菜) marinate or pickle (vegetable) in soya paste or soya sauce: 把萝卜～一～marinate the radish in soya sauce ❹ 像酱的糊状食品 paste；jam：芝麻～sesame butter｜花生～peanut butter｜果子～jam｜辣椒～chilli pepper paste

【酱菜】jiàngcài 用酱或酱油腌制的菜蔬 pickles；vegetables pickled in soya sauce or soya paste

【酱豆腐】jiàngdòu·fu 豆腐乳 fermented bean curd

【酱坊】jiàngfáng same as 酱园 jiàngyuán

【酱缸】jiànggāng 制造和储存酱、酱油、酱菜所用的缸 jar or vat for making and storing soya bean paste, soya sauce or pickled vegetables

【酱色】jiàngsè 深赭色 dark brown；dark reddish brown

【酱油】jiàngyóu 用豆、麦和盐酿造的咸的液体调味品 soya sauce；soya；condiment made from fermented soya beans, flour and salt

【酱园】jiàngyuán 制造并出售酱、酱油、酱菜等的作坊、商店 workshop or shop that makes and sells soya bean paste, soya sauce and pickles

【酱紫】jiàngzǐ same as 绛紫 jiàngzǐ

犟(㢡) jiàng 固执；不服劝导 obstinate；stubborn；self-willed；hell-bent；immovable；opinionated；pertinacious：脾气～unbending；headstrong；as stubborn as a mule

【犟劲】jiàngjìn 顽强的意志、劲头 tenacity：他～一上来，谁也劝不住。No one can stop him when his mind is made up.

【犟嘴】jiàngzuǐ same as 强嘴 jiàngzuǐ

糨(浆、糡) jiàng 液体很稠 (of a liquid) thick：大米粥熬得太～了。The porridge is too thick.

☞浆 jiāng on p. 960

【糨糊】jiàng·hu 用面粉等做成的可以粘贴东西的糊状物 sticky paste made from flour, water, used as an adhesive

【糨子】jiàng·zi 糨糊 paste：打～mix paste

jiāo (ㄐㄧㄠ)

艽 jiāo ☞ 秦艽 qínjiāo on p. 1560

交[1] jiāo ❶ 把事物转移给有关方面 hand over sth. to sb.；deliver；hand in；turn over：～活 turn over a finished item｜～税 pay tax｜～公粮 deliver grain to the state (as tax in kind)｜把任务～给我们这个组吧。Leave the task to our team. ❷ 到(某一时辰或季节)(of a time or season) set in；come：～子时 around midnight｜明天就～冬至了。Tomorrow is the winter solstice.｜～九的天气 coldest days of winter ❸ (时间、地区)相连接 (of points in time or places) meet；join：～界 (of places) contiguous｜春夏之～time of the year when spring gives way to summer｜太行山在河北、山西两省之～。The Taihang Mountains are located on the boundary between the provinces of Hebei and Shanxi. ❹ 交叉 cross；intersect：两直线相～于一点。Two straight lines intersect at one point. ❺ 结交；交往 associate with；befriend；mix with：～朋友 make friends；develop friendships｜建～establish diplomatic relations ❻ 友谊；交情 friendship；friendly relationship：绝～break up with sb.；break off relations with sb.；break off with sb.；sever, cut off or discontinue a relationship｜一面之～mere acquaintance；casual acquaintance ❼ (人)性交；(动植物)交配 have sexual intercourse (between humans)；mate；copulate；breed (of animals)：～媾 sexual intercourse；coition；copulation｜杂～cross-breeding；hybridism ❽ 互相 mutual；reciprocal；each other：～换 exchange；swap；commute｜～流 exchange；communicate；intercourse；give-and-take｜～易 business；deal；transaction；trade｜～谈 talk (with each other)；converse；chat ❾ 一齐；同时(发生) together；simultaneously：风雪～加 snowing and blowing hard；snowy and windy；snowstorm｜饥寒～迫 cold and hungry｜惊喜～集 pleasant surprise；feelings of surprise mixed with joy

交[2] jiāo same as 跤 jiāo

【交白卷】jiāo báijuàn (～儿 jiāo báijuànr) ❶ 考生不能回答试题，把空白试卷交出去 hand in a blank examination paper without answering any questions ❷〈比喻 *fig.*〉完全没有完成任务 utterly fail to complete a task：咱们必须把情况摸清楚，不能回去～。We must find out about things here so we won't go back empty-handed.

【交班】jiāo//bān 把工作任务交给下一班 hand over to the next shift；change shift

【交办】jiāobàn 交给某人办理(多指上级对下级 usu. of sb. in authority to a subordinate) entrust sth. to sb.；assign sb. a task：这是上级～的任务。This is a task from the superiors.

【交保】jiāo//bǎo 司法机关将人犯交付有信用的保人，保证他不逃避侦查和审判，随传随到 post bail；bail out；hand over a criminal to a trustworthy person, or bailsman, who provides bail to guarantee the criminal's availability for further investigation or trial：～释放 release on bail

【交杯酒】jiāobēijiǔ 旧俗举行婚礼时新婚夫妇饮的酒，把两个酒杯用红丝线系在一起，新婚夫妇交换着喝两个酒杯里的酒 (old wedding custom) wine drunk by the bride and groom at a wedding, served in two cups tied together with a red silk thread, which the newly-weds switch around

【交兵】jiāobīng〈书 *fml.*〉交战 be at war；in a state of belligerence；wage a war；engage in battle：两国～two countries at war

【交叉】jiāochā ❶ 几个方向不同的线条或线路互相穿过 cross; intersect; intercross; criss-cross; place where different lines or routes intersect: ～火力网 crossfire coverage|立体～桥 flyover; overpass; interchange|公路和铁路～intersection of highway and railway ❷ 有相同有不同的;有相重的 similar yet not identical; overlapping: ～的意见 overlapping views|～学科 overlapping fields of learning; cross-disciplinary science ❸ 间隔穿插 alternate; stagger; take turns: ～作业 work alternately

【交差】jiāo//chāi 任务完成后把结果报告上级 report back to one's superior after accomplishing a task: 事情不办好,怎么回去～? How can we report back when things are unfinished?

【交错】jiāocuò〈书 *fml.*〉交叉;错杂 interlock; interlace; criss-cross; intersect; alternate: 犬牙～interlocking; jigsaw-like|纵横～的沟渠 labyrinth of ditches; criss-crossing canals and ditches; interlacing canals and ditches

【交代】jiāodài ❶ 把经手的事务移交给接替的人 hand over; turn over; transfer; transfer work at hand to a replacement: ～工作 hand over work (to one's successor) ❷ 嘱咐 tell; give instructions; enjoin; exhort: 他一再～我们要注意工程质量。He repeatedly exhorted us to pay attention to the quality of the project. ❸ 把事情或意见向有关的人说明;把错误或罪行坦白出来 make clear; brief; account for; explain or clarify to people concerned; confess (error or crime): ～政策 explain a policy; clarify a policy|～问题 admit one's faults; also 交待 jiāodài

【交待】jiāodài ❶ same as 交代 jiāodài③ ❷ 完结(指结局不如意的)(含诙谐意 humor.) come to an unpleasant end: 要是飞机出了事,这条命也就～了。If the plane crashes, I will be a goner.

【交道】jiāodào 指交际来往的事 contact; dealings; come-and-go: 打～have dealings with; handle; deal with|我和他曾有过几次～。I once had some dealings with him.

【交底】jiāo//dǐ (～儿 jiāo//dǐr) 交代事物的底细 let in on the secret of sth.; reveal one's real intentions: 你不向我～,我自然不明白其中奥妙。If you keep something back from me, naturally I won't understand all the subtleties.

【交点】jiāodiǎn 线与线、线与面相交的点 intersection; intersection point; point of intersection of lines or line and surface

【交锋】jiāo//fēng 双方作战 cross swords; engage in battle: 敌人不敢和我们～。The enemy dare not risk engaging us. ◇这两支足球劲旅将在明日～。The two strong football teams will confront each other tomorrow.

【交付】jiāofù 交给 pay; consign (a task) to sb.; entrust sb. with (a task); hand over; deliver: ～定金 place a down payment|～任务 consign a task to sb.|新楼房已经～使用。The new building is already in use.

【交感神经】jiāogǎn-shénjīng 从胸部和腰部的脊髓发出的神经,在脊柱两侧形成串状的交感神经节,再由交感神经节发出神经纤维分布到内脏、腺体和血管的壁上。作用跟副交感神经相反,有加强和加速心脏收缩,使瞳孔扩大,使肠蠕动减弱等作用。sympathetic nerve; sympathetic system; nerves extending from the thoracic and lumbar regions of the spinal cord, and forming clusters of ganglia on each side of the spine. Nerve fibres from the ganglia extend to the inner organs, the glands and the vascular system. They function in opposition to the parasympathetic system to strengthen and accelerate systolic heart, dilate the pupil of the eye and diminish intestinal peristalsis, amongst others.

【交割】jiāogē ❶ 双方结清手续(多用于商业) change hands; settle or complete a business transaction: 这笔货款业已～。The money for this consignment has already been paid. ❷ 移交;交代 hand over; turn over; transfer; deliver: 工作都～清了。The work has been completely transferred.

【交工】jiāo//gōng 施工单位把已完成的工程移交给建设单位 hand over by the construction unit of a completed project to the contracting unit

【交媾】jiāogòu 性交 sexual intercourse; copulation; coitus

【交关】jiāoguān ❶ 相关联 related to: 性命～matter of life and death; of vital importance ❷〈方 *dial.*〉非常;很 rather; very: 上海今年冬天～冷。This winter it was rather cold in Shanghai. ❸〈方 *dial.*〉很多 many: 公园里人～。There are so many people in the park.

【交好】jiāohǎo 互相往来,结成知己或友邦 meet and establish friendship; (of states) be on friendly terms: 两国～。The two countries are on friendly terms.|～有年 be on good terms for years

【交合】jiāohé ❶ 连接在一起 link; combine: 悲喜～ be happy and sad at the same time|两旁行道树,枝叶～。Branches and leaves of the trees on either side of the street interweave with one another. ❷指性交 sexual intercourse

【交互】jiāohù ❶ 互相 each other; mutual; one another: 教师宣布答案之后,就让同学们～批改。After he announced the answers, the teacher let the students correct each other's papers. ❷ 替换着 alternately; in turn: 他两手～地抓住野藤,向山顶上爬。He clutched the creeping vine, and climbed hand over hand towards the top of the cliff.

【交还】jiāohuán 归还；退还 give back; return; restore; retrocede：文件阅后请及时～。Please read the document and return immediately.

【交换】jiāohuàn ❶ 双方各拿出自己的给对方；互换 exchange; interchange; swap; commute：～纪念品 exchange souvenirs|～意见 exchange views|两队～场地。The two teams changed sides. ❷ 以商品换商品；买卖商品 exchange of goods; barter; business exchange; commodity exchange

【交换机】jiāohuànjī 设在各电话用户之间，能按通话人的要求来接通电话的机器。交换机有人工的和自动的两大类。(telephone) exchange; switchboard; apparatus that connects individual telephones and puts through a telephone conversation on demand. There are two types of switchboard, manual and automatic.

【交换价值】jiāohuàn jiàzhí 某种商品和另一种商品互相交换时的量的比例，例如一把斧子换二十斤粮食，二十斤粮食就是一把斧子的交换价值。商品的交换价值是商品价值的表现形式。exchange value; ratio between quantities of commodities in an exchange, e. g. if one axe can be exchanged for 20 *jin* of grain, then that is the exchange value of one axe. Exchange value is the expression of commodity value.

【交汇】jiāohuì (水流、气流等)聚集到一起；会合 (of water or air currents) confluence; converge; join; meet：长江口因为咸水和淡水～，鱼类资源极为丰富。The mouth of the Yangtze River is rich in fish resources because of the confluence of salty and fresh water.

【交会】jiāohuì 会合；相交 meet; converge; intersect：郑州是京广、陇海两条铁路的～点。Zhengzhou is where the Beijing-Guangzhou and Lanzhou-Lianyungang railways intersect.

【交火】jiāo//huǒ 交战；互相开火 open fire; exchange fire; fight

【交集】jiāojí (不同的感情、事物等)同时出现 (of different feelings or things) mix; mingle; occur simultaneously：百感～experience mixed feelings|惊喜～feelings of surprise mixed with joy; joyful surprise|雷雨～thunder storm

【交际】jiāojì 人与人之间的往来接触；社交 socialize; communication：语言是人们的～工具。Language is a means of communication for human beings.|他不善于～。He is not good at socializing.

【交际花】jiāojìhuā 在社交场中活跃而有名的女子(含轻蔑意 derog.) social butterfly; hetaera; party girl

【交际舞】jiāojìwǔ 一种社交性的舞蹈，男女两人合舞 ballroom dance; social dance; also 交谊舞 jiāoyìwǔ

【交加】jiāojiā (两种事物)同时出现或同时加在一个人身上(of two things) occur simultaneously; accompany each other：风雪～snowstorm|惊喜～feelings of surprise mixed with joy|拳足～alternate punches with kicks; beat up

【交接】jiāojiē ❶ 连接 join; connect：夏秋～的季节 when summer changes into autumn ❷ 移交和接替 hand over and take over：新上任的保管和老保管办理～手续。The new custodian has completed hand-over procedures with the former one. ❸ 结交 associate with; mix with; make friends with：他～的朋友也是爱好京剧的。The friends he mixes with are also fond of Peking Opera.

【交结】jiāojié ❶ 结交；交往 associate with; mix with; make friends with：～朋友 make friends|他在文艺界～很广。He has a large circle of friends in the world of art and literature. ❷〈书 *fml*.〉互相连接 interconnect：～盘错 intertwine; intermingle

【交界】jiāojiè 两地相连，有共同的疆界(of two or more places) have a common boundary; contiguous：云南省南部跟越南、老挝和缅甸～。Yunnan Province borders on Vietnam, Laos and Myanmar in the south.

【交九】jiāojiǔ 进入从冬至开始的'九'enter the nine periods (of nine days each) following the winter solstice; ☞九 jiǔ ② on p. 1036

【交卷】jiāo//juàn (～儿 jiāo//juànr) ❶ 应考的人考完交出试卷(of examinee) hand in an examination paper ❷〈比喻 *fig*.〉完成所接受的任务 fulfil one's task; discharge one's mission：这事交给他办，三天准能～。Give him the task and he is sure to finish it in three days.

【交口】jiāokǒu ❶ 众口同声(说) speak with one voice; chorus; say sth. in unison：～称誉 praise sb. with one voice; praise unanimously ❷〈方 *dial*.〉交谈 converse; talk：他们久已没有～。They haven't spoken for a long time.

【交困】jiāokùn 各种困难同时出现 beset by difficulties：内外～be beset by difficulties at home and abroad|上下～。Everyone is facing difficulties.

【交流】jiāoliú ❶ 交错地流淌 cross-flow：涕泪～cry and snivel|河港～river that flows into a bay ❷ 彼此把自己有的供给对方 swap; exchange; interchange; communicate; interflow：物资～exchange of goods and materials|文化～cultural exchange|～工作经验 exchange work experience

【交流电】jiāoliúdiàn 方向和强度作周期性变化的电流。现在使用的交流电，一般是方向和强度每秒改变 50 次。alternating current (AC); electric current which reverses direction and magnitude at regular intervals. The currently used AC is at 50 cycles per second.

【交纳】jiāonà 向政府或公共团体交付规定数额的金钱或实物 hand in; render; pay (to the state or public organization): ～会费 pay membership dues|～膳费 pay for meals|～农业税 pay agricultural taxes

【交配】jiāopèi 雌雄动物发生性的行为;植物的雌雄生殖细胞相结合(in animals) mating; copulation; (in plants) amphimixis

【交迫】jiāopò (不同的事物)同时逼迫 (of different things) assail at the same time; harass: 饥寒～assailed by hunger and cold|贫病～beset by poverty and disease

【交情】jiāo·qing 人与人互相交往而发生的感情 friendship; friendly relations; fellowship: ～深 on intimate terms|他们之间很有～。They are intimate friends.

【交融】jiāoróng 融合在一起 mix; blend; mingle: 水乳～blend like water and milk; in harmony with; in tune with; in favour with; compatible

【交涉】jiāoshè 跟对方商量解决有关的问题 discuss in order to solve a problem; negotiate; bargain; make representations (to sb. about sth.); take up (sth. with sb.): 办～take up the matter (with sb.)|你去～一下,看能不能提前交货。You go and talk to them to see whether the delivery can be made early.

【交手】jiāo//shǒu 双方搏斗 fight hand to hand; hand-to-hand combat; clash; come to grips; wrestle with; grapple with: 他俩交过三次手都不分高下。They have come to grips on three occasions and neither has won.

【交谈】jiāotán 互相接触谈话 come in contact and talk; converse; chat: 亲切地～talk warmly; talk heart-to-heart|他们用英语～起来。They began to converse in English.

【交替】jiāotì ❶ 接替 give place to; replace; supersede: 新旧～。The new replaces the old. ❷ 替换着;轮流 alternately; one after another; in turn; by turns: 循环～go in a cycle; rotate|儿童的作业和休息应当～进行。Children should alternate homework and rest.

【交通】jiāotōng ❶ 往来通达 connected; linked; come and go: 阡陌～criss-cross paths leading in all directions ❷ 各种运输和邮电事业的总称 general term for transportation and postal services ❸ 抗日战争和解放战争时期指通信和联络工作(in the War of Resistance against Japan and the War of Liberation) communication; liaison ❹ 指交通员 liaison man; underground messenger ❺〈书 *fml.*〉结交;勾结 associate with; collude with; collaborate with: ～权贵 associate with the rich and powerful|～官府 collaborate with government officials

【交通车】jiāotōngchē 机关、团体等为公务来往而定时行驶的大型汽车或火车 office bus; shuttle bus; regular train; regular bus or train service provided by a government office, organization, etc. for the purpose of official business

【交通岛】jiāotōngdǎo 道路中间的圆形小平台,警察站在上面指挥交通,有时也用白漆划线表示 traffic island; circular platform or area marked out by white, painted lines at road junctions for policemen to stand on to direct traffic

【交通工具】jiāotōng gōngjù 运输用的车辆、船只和飞机等 means of transportation; vehicle, ship or aircraft used for transport

【交通壕】jiāotōngháo 阵地内连接堑壕和其他工事以供交通联络的壕沟。在重要地段上有射击设施。communication trench; on the battlefield, trench that provides for communication between defence trenches and other fortifications and is equipped with firearms in important sections; also 交通沟 jiāotōnggōu

【交通线】jiāotōngxiàn 运输的路线,包括铁路线、公路线、航线等 lines of communication; communication routes, including railways, highways and air routes

【交通员】jiāotōngyuán 抗日战争和解放战争中担任通讯联络工作的人员(in the War of Resistance against Japan and the War of Liberation) liaison man; underground messenger

【交头接耳】jiāo tóu jiē ěr 彼此在耳朵边低声说话 whisper to each other; speak in each other's ears; speak head to head

【交往】jiāowǎng 互相来往 associate; contact: 我跟他没有～。I have no contact with him.|他不大和人～。He rarely associates with anyone. *or* He is unassociable.

【交尾】jiāowěi 动物交配(of animals) mate; pair; couple; copulate

【交恶】jiāowù 互相憎恨仇视 fall foul of each other; become enemies; regard each other with enmity: 两国～。The two countries regarded each other with hostility. *or* Hostility flared up between the two nations.

【交相辉映】jiāo xiāng huī yìng (各种光亮、彩色等)相互映照 (of bright lights or colours) add radiance and beauty to each other; enhance each other's beauty: 星月灯火,～。Stars, moon and lights enhance each other's brilliance.

【交响乐】jiāoxiǎngyuè 由管弦乐队演奏的大型乐曲,通常由四个乐章组成,能够表现出多样的、变化复杂的思想感情 symphony; symphonic music; sinfonia; extended piece of music for symphony orchestra, usu. in four movements, expressing varied and complex emotions

【交卸】jiāoxiè 〈旧时 *old*〉官吏卸职,向后任交代

(of official) hand over official duties to one's successor

【交心】jiāo//xīn 把自己内心深处的想法无保留地说出来 lay one's heart bare; open one's heart (to sb.): 通过～,他们相互间加深了了解。After heart-to-heart talks, they now understand each other better.

【交椅】jiāoyǐ ❶〈古代 *arch.*〉椅子,腿交叉,能折叠 folding chair: 坐第一把～(指当大头领,现比喻当第一把手) occupy the first chair; be in command; (now fig.) be the No. 1 leader ❷〈方 *dial.*〉椅子(多指有扶手的) armchair

【交易】jiāoyì 买卖商品 business (deal); bargain; trade; (business) transaction; deal; swap; traffic; exchange: ～市场 market | 做了一笔～ complete a transaction ◇不能拿原则做～ never barter away principles

【交易所】jiāoyìsuǒ 进行证券或商品交易的市场,所买卖的可以是现货,也可以是期货。通常有证券交易所和商品交易所两种。exchange; bourse; place where securities and commodities (spot goods or futures) are bought and sold; usu. referring to stock exchange and commodity exchange

【交谊】jiāoyì 交情;友谊 friendship; friendly relations; companionship

【交游】jiāoyóu 〈书 *fml.*〉结交朋友 make friends: ～很广 have many friends; have a large circle of friends

【交战】jiāo//zhàn 双方作战 (of two sides) be at war; fight a war: ～国 belligerent countries; nations at war

【交战国】jiāozhànguó 实际上已交战或彼此宣布处于战争状态的国家 belligerent countries (states, nations or powers); nations at war; countries already at war or declared to be in a state of war

【交账】jiāo//zhàng ❶ 移交账务 hand over the accounts ❷〈比喻 *fig.*〉向有关的人交代自己承担的事情 account for a task entrusted to one: 把你冻坏了,我怎么向你哥～。If you catch cold, what will I say to your brother?

【交织】jiāozhī ❶ 错综复杂地合在一起 intertwine; mingle; interweave; interlace: 各色各样的烟火在天空中～成一幅美丽的图画。Colourful fireworks mingled to form a beautiful picture in the sky. ❷ 用不同品种或不同颜色的经纬线织 interweave with warps and wefts of different texture or colours: 棉麻～ mixed weave of cotton with linen | 黑白～ interweave black with white

郊 jiāo 城市周围的地区 suburbs; outskirts; surrounding areas of a city: 四～ suburbs; outskirts | ～外 countryside around a city; outskirts | ～野 countryside | ～游 outing; excursion

【郊区】jiāoqū 城市周围在行政管辖上属这个城市的地区 suburbs; outskirts; *banlieue*; outlying areas of a city under its jurisdiction

【郊外】jiāowài 城市外面的地方(对某一城市说) outskirts; environs; *faubourg*; countryside around a city: 古都～名胜很多。There are a lot of scenic spots around the ancient capital.

【郊野】jiāoyě 郊区旷野 country areas outside a city; countryside

【郊游】jiāoyóu 到郊外游览 outing; excursion; excursion to the outskirts

茭 jiāo 〈书 *fml.*〉喂牲口的干草 hay; dried grass used for fodder

【茭白】jiāobái 菰的嫩茎经某种病菌寄生后膨大,做蔬菜吃叫茭白 wild rice stem; young stem of wild rice which thickens when parasitized by certain bacteria; called *jiaobai* when eaten as a vegetable

峧 jiāo 地名用字 character used in place names: ～头(在浙江) Jiaotou (in Zhejiang Province)

浇[1](澆) jiāo ❶ 让水或别的液体落在物体上 pour (liquid); sprinkle (water): ～水 sprinkle; water | 大雨～得全身都湿透了。(He) was drenched in the downpour. ❷ 灌溉 irrigate; water: 车水～地 lift water by waterwheel to irrigate ❸ 浇灌① cast; pour; mould: ～铸 casting; moulding | ～铅字 type casting; type founding | ～版 casting

浇[2](澆) jiāo 〈书 *fml.*〉刻薄 unkind; mean; harsh: ～薄 unkind; mean

【浇薄】jiāobó 〈书 *fml.*〉(人情、风俗)刻薄;不淳厚 (of relationships, customs) harsh; mean; decadent: 人情～ impersonal relationship | 世风～。There are scarcely any public morals to speak of these days.

【浇灌】jiāoguàn ❶ 把流体向模子内灌注 pour; mould: ～混凝土 pour concrete ❷ 浇水灌溉 irrigate; water

【浇冷水】jiāo lěngshuǐ 〈比喻 *fig.*〉打击别人的热情 cast a damper over; dampen enthusiasm; discourage; pour cold water on others' enthusiasm; also 泼冷水 pō lěngshuǐ

【浇漓】jiāolí 〈书 *fml.*〉(风俗等) 不朴素敦厚 (of customs, etc.) unkind; sophisticated; mean: 世道～,人心日下。The ways of the world are harsh and going from bad to worse, and so is the human heart.

【浇头】jiāo·tou 〈方 *dial.*〉加在盛好的面条或米饭上面的菜 sauce with meat or vegetables, poured over noodles or rice

【浇注】jiāozhù 把金属熔液、混凝土等注入(模型等) cast; teem; pour melted metal, concrete, etc. into a mould

【浇铸】jiāozhù 把熔化了的金属等倒入模型,铸成物件 cast; pour melted metal, etc. into a mould to produce a cast

【浇筑】jiāozhù 土木建筑工程中指把混凝土等材料灌注到模子里制成预定形体(of a construction project) pour concrete into a mould to form an expected shape：～大坝 pour concrete to build a dam

娇(嬌) jiāo ❶(女子、小孩、花朵等)柔嫩、美丽可爱(of women, girls, flowers, etc.) tender; delicate; pretty; lovely：～娆 enchantingly beautiful | 嫩红～绿 tender blossoms and delicate leaves ❷ 娇气 delicate; fragile; squeamish; effeminate：才走几里地,就说腿酸,未免太～了。This person is really very soft to start complaining about tired legs after walking just a few *li*. ❸ 过度爱护 spoil; coddle; pamper; over-indulge：～生惯养 spoilt; brought up by indulgent parents; be over-indulged | 别把孩子～坏了。Don't spoil the child.

【娇宠】jiāochǒng 娇惯宠爱 spoil; over-indulge; pamper; coddle：对孩子不能过于～。Don't indulge your children too much.

【娇滴滴】jiāodīdī ❶ 形容娇媚 delicately pretty; sweetly affected：～的声音 charming, affected voice ❷ 形容过分娇气的样子 too delicate; frail

【娇儿】jiāo'ér 心爱的儿子。也泛指心爱的幼小儿女。beloved son; (in a broad sense) darling young son or daughter

【娇惯】jiāoguàn 宠爱纵容(多指对幼年儿女) pamper; spoil; coddle; over-indulge (young children)：别把孩子～坏了。Don't spoil your child.

【娇贵】jiāo·gui ❶ 看得贵重,过度爱护 spoil; coddle; pamper; value and cherish excessively：这点雨还怕,身子就太～啦！You have been far too coddled if this little rain frightens you! ❷(物品)贵重而容易损坏(of object) valuable and fragile：仪表～,要小心轻放。The meters are delicate, please handle them with care.

【娇客】jiāokè ❶ 指女婿 son-in-law ❷ 娇贵的人 pampered person

【娇媚】jiāomèi ❶ 形容撒娇献媚的样子 coquettish; flirtatious ❷ 妩媚 lovely; charming; sweet：舞姿～graceful and charming dance movements

【娇嫩】jiāo·nen 柔嫩 tender and lovely; delicate：～的鲜花 delicate flowers | 她的身体也太～,风一吹就病了。She is too delicate and falls ill at the slightest breeze.

【娇气】jiāo·qì ❶ 意志脆弱、不能吃苦、习惯于享受的作风 delicate; squeamish; fragile; effeminate ❷ 指物品、花草等容易损坏(of objects, plants, etc.) fragile

【娇娆】jiāoráo〈书 *fml.*〉娇艳妖娆 enchanting and beautiful; fascinating：体态～graceful carriage

【娇柔】jiāoróu 娇媚温柔 pretty and tender; delicate and adorable

【娇生惯养】jiāo shēng guàn yǎng 从小被宠爱纵容 pampered and indulged since childhood

【娇娃】jiāowá ❶ 美丽的少女 pretty young girl ❷〈方 *dial.*〉指娇生惯养的孩子 spoilt child：这帮大城市来的～都经受了艰苦的考验。These pampered children from large cities all have withstood the test of hardship.

【娇小】jiāoxiǎo 娇嫩小巧 petite; delicate; cute：～的女孩子 petite young girl | ～的野花 delicate little wild flowers

【娇小玲珑】jiāoxiǎo línglóng 小巧灵活 delicate and supple; small and dainty：身材～small and dainty figure

【娇羞】jiāoxiū 形容少女害羞的样子(of young girls) shy; bashful; blushing; shamefaced

【娇艳】jiāoyàn 娇嫩艳丽 delicate and charming; tender and beautiful：～的桃花 delicate and charming peach blossoms

【娇养】jiāoyǎng (对小孩)宠爱放任,不加管教 pamper or spoil (a child)

【娇纵】jiāozòng 娇养放纵 over-indulge; spoil; pamper：～孩子,不是爱他而是害他。To over-indulge a child is to ruin him, not love him.

姣 jiāo〈书 *fml.*〉相貌美 beautiful; handsome：～好 beautiful; graceful; charming

骄(驕) jiāo ❶ same as 骄傲 jiāo'ào ①：戒～戒躁 guard against arrogance and rashness | 胜不～,败不馁 be neither conceited by success, nor downcast by failure ❷〈书 *fml.*〉猛烈 intense：～阳 scorching sun; blazing sun

【骄傲】jiāo'ào ❶ 自以为了不起,看不起别人 arrogant; cocky; conceited; vainglorious; be opinionated and look down on others：～自满 proud and conceited; arrogant and complacent | 虚心使人进步,～使人落后。Modesty leads to advancement; pride comes before a fall. ❷ 自豪 be proud of; take pride in：我们都以是炎黄子孙而感到～。We take pride in being the descendants of the Yellow and Red Emperors. ❸ 值得自豪的人或事物 object or person worthy of pride：古代四大发明是中国的～。The four great ancient inventions are the pride of China.

【骄横】jiāohèng 骄傲专横 arrogant and high-handed; overbearing：～一时 wax arrogant in an unbridled manner

【骄矜】jiāojīn〈书 *fml.*〉骄傲自大;傲慢 self-important; egotistic; haughty：面有～之色 haughty expression

【骄慢】jiāomàn 傲慢 arrogant; haughty; overweening; pompous：为人～be haughty | 态度～arrogant manner

【骄气】jiāo·qì 骄傲自满的作风 overbearing airs; arrogant attitude

【骄奢淫逸】jiāo shē yín yì 骄横奢侈,荒淫无度 haughty and decadent; proud and dissolute; wallow in luxury and pleasure; extravagant and dissipated

【骄阳】jiāoyáng〈书 *fml*.〉强烈的阳光 blazing sun; scorching sun:～似火 scorching sun

【骄躁】jiāozào 骄傲浮躁 arrogant and rash:～情绪 arrogance and impulsiveness

【骄子】jiāozǐ 受宠爱的儿子,多用于比喻(usu. fig.) favourite son:天之～God's favourite; darling of the gods; unusually lucky person|时代的～darling of the time

【骄纵】jiāozòng 骄傲放纵 arrogant and wilful

胶(膠) jiāo ❶ 某些具有黏性的物质,用动物的皮、角等熬成或由植物分泌出来,也有人工合成的。通常用来黏合器物,如鳔胶、桃胶、万能胶,有的供食用或入药,如果胶、阿胶。glue; gum; mucus; gelatin; adhesive substance obtained by boiling animal hide and horns, etc., also secreted by plants or made synthetically, e.g. isinglass, peach gum, all-purpose adhesive, usu. used to stick objects together, some being edible and used in medicine, e.g. pectin and donkey-hide gelatin ❷ 用胶粘 stick or fasten with glue:～柱鼓瑟 stubbornly follow the old ways; incapable of flexibility|镜框坏了,把它～上。The frame is broken, glue it together. ◇不可～于成规。Don't be so set on established rules. ❸ 像胶一样黏的 adhesive (like glue); sticky; gummy; mucous; viscous:～泥 clay ❹ 指橡胶 rubber:～皮 rubber|～鞋 rubber overshoes; sneakers; rubber-soled shoes|～布 adhesive tape

【胶版】jiāobǎn 胶印的印刷底版 offset plate

【胶布】jiāobù ❶ 涂上黏性橡胶的布,多用于包扎电线接头 adhesive tape; tape coated on one side with an adhesive, used to wrap around spliced electric wires ❷ 橡皮膏 adhesive plaster

【胶带】jiāodài 用塑料制成的磁带 magnetic tape made of plastic

【胶合】jiāohé 用胶把东西粘在一起 glue together

【胶合板】jiāohébǎn 用多层木质单板黏合、压制成的板材。层数多为单数,各层的木纹纵横交错。强度大,节约木材,广泛用于建筑工程和制造家具等。plywood; veneer board; plyboard; laminated board; board made by gluing together (usu. an odd number) of layers of wood veneers with the veins of one crossing those of another. Plywood is strong, saves wood, and is widely used in construction and the manufacture of furniture.

【胶结】jiāojié 糨糊、胶等半流体干燥后变硬黏结在一起 cement; glue; hardening and cementing of thick paste or glue, etc.

【胶卷】jiāojuǎn (～儿 jiāojuǎnr)成卷的照相胶片 film; roll of camera film

【胶木】jiāomù 橡胶和多量硫磺加热制成的硬质材料,多用做电器的绝缘材料,也用来制其他日用品 bakelite; hard substance made by heating a mixture of rubber and a large quantity of sulphur, mostly used as insulating material for electric appliances, and to make other articles of daily use

【胶囊】jiāonáng 医药上指用明胶制成的囊状物,把味苦或刺激性大的药粉按剂量装入胶囊中,便于吞服 capsule; (in pharmaceuticals) spherical gelatinous case in which a dose of bitter or irritating medicinal powder is enclosed for easy swallowing

【胶泥】jiāoní 含有水分的黏土,黏性很大 wet, glutinous clay

【胶皮】jiāopí ❶ 硫化橡胶的通称 general term for 硫化橡胶 liúhuà xiàngjiāo ❷〈方 *dial*.〉人力车② rickshaw

【胶片】jiāopiàn 涂有感光药膜的塑料片,用于摄影 film; thin plastic strip coated with a photosensitive emulsion used for photography; also 软片 ruǎnpiàn

【胶乳】jiāorǔ ❶ 割开橡胶树树皮后流出的白色乳状液体,是制造橡胶的原料 latex; milky sap that drips from the cut of a rubber tree, and is the raw material for rubber ❷ 树脂粉末悬浮在水中而成的乳状液,用来制合成橡胶或某些不易加工的产品,如胶线、薄膜等 latex; emulsion of resin globules in water used to make synthetic rubber or certain unprocessible goods, such as rubber thread, membrane, etc.

【胶水】jiāoshuǐ (～儿 jiāoshuǐr)粘东西用的液体的胶 mucilage; glue; sticky liquid used for adhesion

【胶体溶液】jiāotǐ róngyè 溶胶 colloid solution

【胶鞋】jiāoxié 用橡胶制成的鞋。有时也指橡胶底布面的鞋。rubber overshoes; galoshes; rubbers; rubber-soled shoes

【胶靴】jiāoxuē 用橡胶制成的靴子 galoshes; boots made of rubber

【胶印】jiāoyìn 用胶版印刷。印版不直接和纸张接触,先把油墨从印版移印到有弹性的胶布面,由胶布面转印到纸上。offset printing; offset; process of printing by indirect image transfer, using a plate which makes an inked impression on a rubber-blanketed cylinder, which in turn transfers it to the paper

【胶粘剂】jiāozhānjì 黏合剂 adhesive

【胶柱鼓瑟】jiāo zhù gǔ sè〈比喻 *fig*.〉固执拘泥,不能变通 obdurate; stubbornly stick to old ways and be incapable of flexibility (柱 *zhu*: 瑟上调弦的短木。柱被粘住,就不能调整音高 short tuning pegs of the *se*, a stringed instrument, which cannot be tuned when the pegs are stuck):情况变了,办法也要改进,不能～。Our methods must be adapted to the changed situation, and we should avoid stubbornness.

【胶着】jiāozhuó〈比喻 *fig.*〉相持不下,不能解决 deadlocked; in a stalemate: ～状态 deadlock; stalemate; in an impasse

教 jiāo 把知识或技能传给人 teach; instruct; tutor; impart knowledge or skill to others: ～唱歌 teach sb. to sing|～小孩儿识字 teach a child how to read and write|师傅把技术～给徒弟。The master passes on a skill to his apprentice.
☞ jiào on p.981

【教书】jiāo//shū 教学生学习功课 teach school; teach; teach lessons to students: ～先生 teacher|他在小学里～。He teaches primary school.

【教书匠】jiāoshūjiàng 指教师(含轻蔑意 derog.) pedagogue; teach-book-smith

【教学】jiāo//xué 教书 teach; teach school
☞ jiàoxué on p.982

鸡 jiāo [鸡鹊](jiāojīng)古书上说的一种水鸟 aquatic bird mentioned in ancient books

椒 jiāo 指某些果实或种子有刺激性味道的植物 any of several plants bearing spicy, pungent fruits or seeds: 花～Chinese prickly ash; Sichuan pepper|辣～chilli pepper; red pepper|秦～thin, long hot pepper

【椒盐】jiāoyán(～儿)把焙过的花椒和盐轧碎制成的调味品 spiced salt; Sichuan pepper-salt; condiment made by grinding toasted Sichuan peppercorns with salt: ～排骨 spareribs with spiced salt|～月饼 moon cakes with pepper-salt flavoured fill

蛟 jiāo same as 蛟龙 jiāolóng

【蛟龙】jiāolóng〈古代 *arch.*〉传说中指兴风作浪、能发洪水的龙 legendary flood dragon; mythical dragon capable of summoning storms and floods

焦1 jiāo ❶ 物体受热后失去水分,呈现黄黑色并发硬、发脆 singe; burn; state of browning, hardening and crisping of objects after being heated and dehydrated: 树烧～了。The trees are burnt. ◇舌敝唇～talk until one's tongue and lips are parched ❷ 焦炭 coke: 煤～coking coal|炼～coke ❸ 着急 anxious; worried: ～急 anxious; worried stiff; in a sweat|心～worried; impatient ❹〈中医 *Chin. med.*〉指身体的某些部位 certain places on the body; ☞ 上焦 shàngjiāo on p.1682, 下焦 xiàjiāo on p. 2065 and 中焦 zhōngjiāo on p.2482 ❺ (Jiāo)姓 a surname

焦2 jiāo 焦耳的简称 abbr. for 焦耳 jiāo'ěr

【焦愁】jiāochóu 焦急忧愁 extremely worried: 母亲为他的病昼夜～。Mother is worrying about his illness day and night.

【焦点】jiāodiǎn ❶ 某些与椭圆、双曲线或抛物线有特殊关系的点。如椭圆的两个焦点到椭圆上任意一点的距离的和是一个常数。focal point; focus; point that has a special relationship with an ellipse, hyperbola or parabola. For example, the sum of the distances between either focal point of an ellipse and any point on the ellipse is constant ❷ 平行光线经透镜折射或曲面镜反射后的会聚点 focal point; focus; point at which parallel rays of light refracted through a lens or reflected from a concave mirror converge ❸〈比喻 *fig.*〉事情或道理引人注意的集中点 centre of interest or activity; central issue; focus: 争论的～ focus of controversy; point at issue

【焦耳】jiāo'ěr 功、能量和热的单位,1牛顿的力使其作用点在力的方向上位移1米所作的功,就是1焦耳。1焦耳等于10^7尔格。这个单位名称是为纪念英国物理学家焦耳(James Prescott Joule)而定的。joule; unit of work, energy or heat equal to the work done when a force of one newton acts through a distance of one metre. One joule is equal to 10^7 ergs, named after the British physicist James Prescott Joule. 简称 abbr. 焦 jiāo

【焦黑】jiāohēi 物体燃烧后呈现的黑色 blacken by fire; be charred black

【焦化】jiāohuà 指有机物质碳化变焦。特指煤的高温干馏并同时收回化工产品。carbonization of organic matter; esp. coal carbonization; pyrogenation

【焦黄】jiāohuáng 黄而干枯的颜色 sallow; brown; dry and brown: 面色～sallow complexion|～的豆荚 dry, brown beanpod

【焦急】jiāojí 着急 anxious; worried; agitated; in a stew; in a sweat; be in a fret; impatient: ～万分 be stewed up with anxiety|心里～be worried or anxious

【焦距】jiāojù 曲面镜的顶点或薄透镜的中心到主焦点的距离 focal length; focal distance; focus; foci; distance from the summit of a convex or concave mirror or the centre of a lens to its prime focus

【焦渴】jiāokě 非常干渴 terribly thirsty; parched with thirst: ～难耐 unbearably thirsty

【焦枯】jiāokū (植物)干枯(of plants) shrivelled; withered; dried up: 久旱不雨,禾苗～。The seedlings are withered from the long drought.

【焦雷】jiāoléi 声音响亮的雷 thunderclap; thunderbolt

【焦虑】jiāolǜ 焦急忧虑 agitated; anxious; have worries and misgivings: ～不安 on tenderhooks; anxious|万分～tormented by anxiety

【焦煤】jiāoméi 烟煤的一种,炼焦时结焦性强,单独用这种煤炼的焦强度高,块大,但块过大不易从炉中出焦 coking coal; soft coal, used for coking, with the coke obtained exclusively from such coal being highly intensified and in chunks so large as to be likely to clog the outlet of the furnace; also 主焦煤 zhǔjiāoméi

【焦炭】jiāotàn 一种固体燃料，质硬，多孔，发热量高。用煤高温干馏而成。多用于炼铁。coke; solid fuel, hard and porous, with high heating value, obtained from the destructive distillation of bituminous coal, oft. used for making steel

【焦头烂额】jiāo tóu làn é〈比喻 *fig.*〉十分狼狈窘迫 in a terrible fix; in a wretched plight; utterly exhausted

【焦土】jiāotǔ 烈火烧焦的土地。指建筑物、庄稼等毁于炮火之后的景象。earth scorched by fire; ravages of war (ruins of buildings, crops, etc. from gunfire)

【焦心】jiāoxīn 着急 anxious; worried：至今没有接到儿子来信，真叫人～。I am so worried at still not hearing from my son.

【焦油】jiāoyóu 煤焦油和木焦油的统称 general term for coal tar and wood tar; 旧称 formerly called 滘 tǎ

【焦枣】jiāozǎo 一种焦而脆的枣，将枣去核，用火烤干而成。有的地区叫脆枣。crisp jujube; roasted stoned Chinese jujube; known as 脆枣 cuìzǎo in some places

【焦躁】jiāozào 着急而烦躁 restless with anxiety; fretful; impatient; in a fuss：～不安 on pins and needles; in a lather | 心里～ upset; worried

【焦砟】jiāozhǎ 烟煤或煤球燃烧后凝成的块状物 hard fragments left from the burning of soft coal or briquettes

【焦炙】jiāozhì 形容心里像火烤一样焦急 burning with anxiety：心情～万分 extremely anxious

【焦灼】jiāozhuó 非常着急 deeply worried：～不安 worried and bothered

跤 jiāo 跟头 fall：跌～fall; tumble | 摔了一～have a fall

僬 jiāo [僬侥](jiāoyáo)〈古代 *arch.*〉传说中的矮人 mythological pygmy

鲛 jiāo 鲨鱼 shark

蕉 jiāo 指某些有像芭蕉那样的大叶子的植物 plant with large sheath leaves like those of plantain：香～banana | 美人～canna
☞ qiáo on p.1550

【蕉农】jiāonóng 以种植香蕉为主的农民 banana farmer; farmer who cultivates bananas

镠 jiāo [镠辖](jiāogé)〈书 *fml.*〉交错 intersect; interlace

嶕 jiāo [嶕峣](jiāoyáo)〈书〉高耸 lofty; high

礁 jiāo ❶ 礁石 reef; skerry ❷ 由珊瑚虫的遗骸堆积成的岩石状物 coral ridge or mound formed from skeletons of anthozoan animals

【礁石】jiāoshí 河流、海水中距水面很近的岩石 reef; rock (near the surface of a body of water)

鹪 jiāo [鹪鹩](jiāoliáo)鸟，体长约三寸，羽毛赤褐色，略有黑褐色斑点，尾羽短，略向上翘。以昆虫为主要食物。wren (*Troglodytes troglodytes idius*); bird, measuring about three *cun* long, with reddish-brown plumage, dark brown spots and a short, erect tail, and feeding on insects

jiáo (ㄐㄧㄠˊ)

矫(矯) jiáo same as 矫情 jiáo·qing
☞ jiǎo on p.976

【矫情】jiáo·qing〈方 *dial.*〉指强词夺理，无理取闹 unreasonable; argumentative; quibble about words and argue for the sake of arguing：这个人太～。This person is too contentious. | 犯～be difficult
☞ jiǎoqíng on p.976

嚼 jiáo 上下牙齿磨碎食物 chew; munch; masticate; crush food between lower and upper teeth：细～慢咽 chew well and swallow slowly; eat slowly ◇ 咬文～字 speak like a book; play with words; mince words; pay excessive attention to wording
☞ jiào on p.983 and jué on p.1063

【嚼裹儿】jiáo·guor〈方 *dial.*〉指生活费用 daily expenses：辛苦一年，挣的钱刚够～。The earnings from a year of hard work could barely cover daily expenses. also 缴裹儿 jiǎo·guor

【嚼舌】jiáoshé ❶ 信口胡说；搬弄是非 gossip; blabber; wag one's tongue or jaws; tell tales; sow discord; make mischief (between ...); make irresponsible remarks and distort the truth：有意见当面提，别在背后～。Say what's on your mind, don't gossip behind people's backs. ❷ 无谓地争辩 argue without purpose：没工夫跟你～。I've no time to argue with you. ‖ also 嚼舌头 jiáoshé·tou and 嚼舌根 jiáoshé·gen

【嚼用】jiáo·yong〈方 *dial.*〉生活费用 daily expenses：人口多，～大。A large family requires a large daily budget.

【嚼子】jiáo·zi 为便于驾驭，横放在牲口嘴里的小铁链，两端连在笼头上 bit (of a briddle); metal mouthpiece of a bridle, connected to the headstall at both ends, to control draught animal

jiǎo (ㄐㄧㄠˇ)

角[1] jiǎo ❶ 牛、羊、鹿等头上长出的坚硬的东西，一般细长而弯曲，上端较尖 horn; one of the hard structures projecting from the head of certain mammals, e.g. cattle, sheep, deer, etc., usu. long, thin and curved with a pointed tip: 牛～ox horn | 鹿～antler ❷〈古时 *arch.*〉军中吹的乐器 army bugle; horn: 号～bugle ❸ 形状像角的东西 horn-shaped object: 皂～Chinese honey locust | 菱～water caltrop ❹ 岬角。多用于地名。(usu. in a place name) cape; headland; promontory: 镇海～(在福建)Cape of Zhenhai (in Fujian) ❺ (～儿 jiǎor)物体两个边沿相接的地方;角落 corner; place where two edges meet to form an angle: 桌子～儿 corner of a table or desk | 墙～儿 foot of a wall | 拐～儿 corner | 东南～south-easterly direction◇英语～English corner ❻ 从一个点引出两条射线所形成的,或从一条直线上展开的两个平面或从一点上展开的多个平面所形成的图形 angle; figure formed by two lines diverging from a common point, or that formed by two planes or several planes diverging from a common line or point: 直～right angle | 锐～acute angle | 两面～dihedral angle | 多面～polyhedral angle ❼〈量词 *classifier*〉四分之一 quarter: 一～饼 a quarter of a pancake ❽ 二十八宿之一 one of the 28 constellations

角2 jiǎo 我国货币的辅助单位,一角等于一圆的十分之一 *jiao*; fractional unit of currency in China, equal to one tenth of a yuan

角3 jiǎo same as 饺 jiǎo
☞ jué on p. 1058

【角暗里】jiǎo'àn·li〈方 *dial.*〉角落。指偏僻的地方。corner; remote place

【角尺】jiǎochǐ 一种检验或画线用的工具,两边互成直角。木工用的曲尺也叫角尺。angle square; square; instrument with two sides perpendicular to each other for drawing lines or checking a right angle; also carpenter's try square

J

【角度】jiǎodù ❶ 角的大小。通常用度或弧度来表示。angle; space between two lines or planes that intersect, measured in degrees or radians ❷ 看事情的出发点 point of view; angle; way of looking at things: 如果光从自己的～来看问题,意见就难免有些片面。Approaching the problem solely from your own point of view will certainly lead to bias.

【角钢】jiǎogāng 断面呈 L 形的条状钢材,分等边的和不等边的两种 angle iron; angle bar; L-beam; rolled bar of iron with an L-shaped cross-section with the two arms being either equilateral or unequilateral; 俗称 commonly known as 角铁 jiǎotiě or 三角铁 sānjiǎotiě

【角弓反张】jiǎogōng-fǎnzhāng 头和颈僵硬、向后仰、胸部向前挺、下肢弯曲的症状,常见于脑膜炎、破伤风等病 opisthotonos; tetanic spasm in which the head and neck bend rigidly backwards, the chest thrusts forwards and the lower limbs are contorted, occurring frequently in cases of meningitis, tetanus, etc.

【角果】jiǎoguǒ 干果的一种,由两个心皮构成,成熟时果皮由基部向上裂开。如油菜、白菜、荠菜等的果实。dry fruit, composed of two carpels which split open from the base up when ripe, e.g. rape seed, and the seeds of Chinese cabbage and shepherd's purse

【角楼】jiǎolóu 城角上供瞭望和防守用的楼 turret; corner tower; watchtower at the corner of a city wall

【角落】jiǎoluò ❶ 两堵墙或类似墙的东西相接处的凹角 corner; angle; nook; where two walls or flat surfaces meet: 他找遍了屋子的每个～,也没有找到那块表。He searched every nook and cranny in the room, but did not find the watch. | 院子的一个～长着一棵桃树。A peach tree grows in one corner of the courtyard. ❷ 指偏僻的地方 remote place: 他的事迹传遍了祖国的每一个～。His story spread to every corner of the country.

【角门】jiǎomén 整个建筑物的靠近角上的小门。泛指小的旁门。side gate; corner postern; (in a broad sense) postern gate; also 脚门 jiǎomén

【角膜】jiǎomó 黑眼珠表面的一层透明薄膜,由结缔组织构成,向前凸出,没有血管分布,有很多神经纤维,感觉非常灵敏,后部与巩膜相连 cornea; transparent convex anterior coat covering the pupil, formed by connective tissue, having no blood vessels but many nerve fibres, extremely sensitive and continuous with the sclera; (图见 ☞ figure for 眼 yǎn on p. 2210)

【角膜接触镜】jiǎomó jiēchù jìng 眼镜的一种,镜片用高分子材料制成,很薄,直接贴附在眼球角膜上,以达到矫正视力的作用 contact lens; thin 'glasses' made of a polymer, fitted over the cornea of the eye to correct various vision defects; 通称 commonly known as 隐形眼镜 yǐnxíng-yǎnjìng

【角票】jiǎopiào 票面以角为单位的纸币的统称 Renminbi banknotes of one, two or five *jiao* denomination; also 毛票 máopiào

【角速度】jiǎosùdù 物体转动时在单位时间内所转过的角度。匀速转动的物体,角速度 = 转过的角度/时间。angular velocity; change of angular displacement within a unit of time. For a steadily rotating object, the angular velocity equals the degree of angle rotated divided by time.

【角台】jiǎotái 棱台 frustum of a pyramid

【角质】jiǎozhì 某些动植物体表皮的一层组织,质地坚韧,是由壳质、石灰质等构成的,有保护内部组织的作用 cutin; tough tissue constiting one layer of the cuticle of certain plants and animals, composed of chitin, lime, etc., and serving as protection for inner tissues

【角子】jiǎo·zi〈方 *dial.*〉〈旧时 *old*〉通用的一角和两角的小银币 silver coin of one or two *jiao* in common circulation

侥(僥) jiǎo [侥幸](jiǎoxìng)由于偶然的原因而得到成功或免去灾害lucky; by luck; by a fluke; succeed or avoid disaster by chance: 心存～want to try one's luck|～心理 mentality to leave things to chances; dependence on luck; also 僥倖 jiǎoxìng or 徼倖 jiǎoxìng

☞ yáo on p. 2228

佼 jiǎo〈书 *fml.*〉美好 handsome; beautiful

【佼佼】jiǎojiǎo〈书 *fml.*〉胜过一般水平的 above average; outstanding: 庸中～outstanding among the mediocre

挢(撟) jiǎo〈书 *fml.*〉❶ 抬起;举起;翘起 lift; raise: ～首高视 raise one's head and look up ❷ same as 矫[1] jiǎo ①

狡 jiǎo 狡猾 crafty; foxy; cunning: ～计 guile; trick; wiles

【狡辩】jiǎobiàn 狡猾地强辩 quibble; give false arguments: 事实胜于～。Facts speak louder than sophisms.

【狡猾】jiǎohuá 诡计多端,不可信任 crafty; cunning; tricky; also 狡滑 jiǎohuá

【狡滑】jiǎohuá same as 狡猾 jiǎohuá

【狡计】jiǎojì 狡猾的计谋 guile; trick; wiles; stratagem; ruse

【狡狯】jiǎokuài〈书 *fml.*〉狡诈 deceitful; crafty; cunning: 故弄～(故意迷惑人)use artifice and guile (to deliberately baffle)

【狡赖】jiǎolài 狡辩抵赖 deny (with fallacious arguments): 百般～deny by every means

【狡兔三窟】jiǎo tù sān kū 狡猾的兔子有三个窝 wily hare has three burrows;〈比喻 *fig.*〉藏身的地方多 have more than one hiding place

【狡黠】jiǎoxiá〈书 *fml.*〉same as 狡诈 jiǎozhà

【狡诈】jiǎozhà 狡猾奸诈 deceitful; cunning; crafty: 阴险～treacherous and false; insidious and deceitful

饺 jiǎo (～儿 jiǎor) 饺子 dumpling: 水～儿 boiled dumplings | 烫面～儿 steamed dumplings

【饺子】jiǎo·zi 半圆形的有馅儿的面食 dumpling (crescent-shaped wheat dough wrapper with meat and vegetable filling)

绞 jiǎo ❶ 把两股以上条状物扭在一起(of two or more strands) twist into one; wring; entangle: 铁索是用许多铁丝～成的。An iron cable is twisted from several iron strands. ◇好多问题～在一起,闹不清楚了。It's hard to get a clear idea when the issues are entangled like that. ❷ 握住条状物的两端同时向相反方向转动,使受到挤压;拧 twist; wring; turn the ends of an elongated object in opposite directions to squeeze: 把毛巾～干 wring (out) the towel ◇～尽脑汁 rack, tax or cudgel one's brains; task one's mind ❸ 用绞刀切削 ream: ～孔 ream a hole ❹勒死;吊死 hang (by the neck): ～杀 kill by hanging; hang|～架 gallows; gibbet|～索 bowstring; rope ❺ 把绳索一端系在轮上,转动轮轴,使系在另一端的物体移动 wind; raise or move a load by turning a horizontal cylinder so that a line attached to the load winds around the cylinder: ～车 winch; windlass|～盘 winch; windlass; capstan|～着辘轳打水 raise water by winding a windlass ❻〈量词 *classifier*〉用于纱、毛线等 skein; hank: 一～纱 a hank of yarn

【绞包针】jiǎobāozhēn 缝麻袋等大型包裹用的一种铁针,较粗而长,略呈弯形 long, thick, curved needle for sewing jute bags

【绞车】jiǎochē 卷扬机的通称 general term for 卷扬机 juǎnyángjī

【绞刀】jiǎodāo 金属切削工具,用来使工件上原有的孔光洁或使直径扩大 reamer; metal cutting tool, used to polish or enlarge holes or bores

【绞架】jiǎojià 把人吊死的刑具,在架子上系着绞索 gallows; gibbet; apparatus for execution with rope tied to a cross beam

【绞脸】jiǎo//liǎn〈旧时 *old*〉妇女整容时用绞在一起的细线一张一合去掉脸上的寒毛 (of a married woman) depilate facial hair; remove fine hair from the face by rolling two twisted threads over the skin

【绞脑汁】jiǎo nǎozhī 费思虑;费脑筋 rack, cudgel or tax one's brains

【绞盘】jiǎopán 利用轮轴的原理制成的一种起重机械。船上起锚和用绳索牵引重物等都用绞盘。capstan; apparatus used for hoisting weights, also used on ships to weigh anchor and pull loads with cables

【绞杀】jiǎoshā ❶ 用绳勒死 hang; put to death by suspending by the neck ❷〈比喻 *fig.*〉压制、摧残使不能存在或发展 strangle; throttle; snuff out: ～革命 strangle the revolution|～新生事物 smother innovation

【绞手】jiǎoshǒu 一种手工工具,有两个把儿,用以卡住丝锥、绞刀等工具对工件进行切削 diestock; manual tool with two handles for holding dies (tap, reamer, etc.) to cut or shape: 板牙～diestock

【绞索】jiǎosuǒ 绞刑用的绳子 noose; a piece of rope that is formed into a circle at one end, so that if the other end is pulled the circle becomes smaller, used for killing sb. by hanging

【绞刑】jiǎoxíng 死刑的一种,用绳子勒死 gallows; gibbet; garrotte; noose; death by hanging

铰 jiǎo ❶ 剪③ cut with scissors: 用剪子～ cut with scissors ❷ same as 绞 jiǎo ③ ❸ 指铰链 hinge: ～接 hinge; articulate

【铰接】jiǎojiē 用铰链连接 join with a hinge; articulate: ～式无轨电车 articulated trolley-

J

bus

【铰链】jiǎoliàn 连接机器、车辆、门窗、器物的两个部分的装置或零件，所连接的两部分或其中的一部分能绕着铰链的轴转动 hinge; flexible joint; jointed device that holds together two parts of a machine, vehicle, door, window or utensil so that one can swing relative to the other

矫[1]（矯） jiǎo ❶ 矫正 correct; rectify; remedy; redress: ～枉过正 overcorrect; overcompensate ❷（Jiǎo）姓 a surname

矫[2]（矯） jiǎo 强壮；勇武 strong; powerful; brave: ～健 strong and vigorous | ～若游龙 as vigorous as a flying dragon; as strong and brave as a lion

矫[3]（矯） jiǎo 假托 pretend; feign: ～饰 dissemble | ～命 counterfeit an order; issue false orders

☞ jiáo on p. 973

【矫健】jiǎojiàn 强壮有力 strong and vigorous: 身手～brisk and dynamic | ～的步伐 vigorous strides

【矫捷】jiǎojié 矫健而敏捷 vigorous and nimble; brisk; agile: 他飞速地攀到柱顶，像猿猴那样～。He climbed to the top of the pole as swiftly as a monkey.

【矫命】jiǎomìng 〈书 *fml*.〉假托上级命令 counterfeit an order; issue false orders

【矫情】jiǎoqíng 〈书 *fml*.〉故意违反常情，表示高超或与众不同 be deliberately unconventional; deliberately run counter to customary practice and remain aloof or different

☞ jiáo·qing on p. 973

【矫揉造作】jiǎo róu zào zuò 形容过分做作，极不自然 affectation; pretension; extreme affectation and artificiality

【矫饰】jiǎoshì 故意造作来掩饰 feign in order to conceal; dissemble

【矫枉过正】jiǎo wǎng guò zhèng 纠正偏差做得过了头 exceed the proper limits in righting a wrong; hypercorrect; overcorrect; overdo; too far east is west: 应该纠正浪费的习惯，但是一变而为吝啬，那就是～了。Extravagance should be corrected, but turning into parsimony would be going too far.

【矫形】jiǎoxíng 用外科手术把人体上畸形的部分改变成正常状态，如矫正畸形脊柱、关节等 orthopaedics; orthopedics; branch of surgery concerned with the correction of body deformities, e. g. those of the spine and joints

【矫正】jiǎozhèng 改正；纠正 correct; rectify; remedy; redress; straighten out; put right; set right: ～发音 correct sb.'s pronunciation | ～错误 correct a mistake | ～偏差 rectify a deviation

【矫治】jiǎozhì 矫正并医治（斜视、口吃等缺陷）correct and cure (such defects as strabismus, stammering, etc.): ～口吃 correct and cure stammer | 对视力减退的学生进行药物～。Give medication to students with poor eyesight.

皎 jiǎo ❶ 白而亮 clear and bright: ～洁 bright and clear | ～月 luminous moon; bright moon ❷（Jiǎo）姓 a surname

【皎皎】jiǎojiǎo 形容很白很亮 very bright; glistening white: ～的月光 clear, bright and silvery moonlight

【皎洁】jiǎojié （月亮等）明亮而洁白（of the moon, etc.）bright and white; silvery; white and luminous

脚（腳） jiǎo ❶ 人或动物的腿的下端，接触地面支持身体的部分 foot; lower extremity of the vertebrate leg, supporting the body in direct contact with the ground when standing or walking: ～面 instep | ～背 instep（图见 ☞ figure for 身体 shēntǐ on p. 1701）❷ 东西的最下部 lowest part; base; foot: 墙～foot of a wall | 山～foot of a hill | 高～杯 goblet ❸ 指跟体力搬运有关的 involving manual portage: ～夫 stevedore; porter | ～行 portage agent | ～力 porter; strength of one's legs

☞ jué on p. 1062

【脚板】jiǎobǎn 脚掌 sole (of foot)

【脚背】jiǎobèi 脚掌的反面 instep; upper part of foot opposite from the sole; also 脚面 jiǎomiàn

【脚本】jiǎoběn 表演戏剧、曲艺，摄制电影等所依据的本子，里面记载台词、故事情节等 script; scenario; text of a play, traditional *quyi*, film, etc. providing spoken lines, plot, etc.

【脚脖子】jiǎobó·zi 〈方 *dial*.〉脚腕子 ankle

【脚步】jiǎobù ❶ 指走路时两脚之间的距离 footstep; footfall; step; pace; distance between feet when walking: ～大 big step ❷ 指走路时腿的动作 footstep; footfall; way of walking: 放轻～walk softly; lighten one's step | 嚓嚓的～声 sound of shuffling feet

【脚踩两只船】jiǎo cǎi liǎng zhī chuán 〈比喻 *fig*.〉因为对事物认识不清或存心投机取巧而跟两方面都保持联系 straddle the fence; temporize; maintain contact with both sides either because of lack of information or out of opportunism; have a foot in either camp; hedge one's bets; run after two hares; also 脚踏两只船 jiǎo tà liǎng zhī chuán

【脚灯】jiǎodēng ❶ 安装在舞台口边缘向内照射的一排灯 footlights; row of lights at the foot of theatre stage that illuminate the set and actors ❷ 贴近地面安设的灯，便于黑暗中行走 ground light; light set on the ground to assist walking in the dark

【脚蹬子】jiǎodēng·zi 某些机器或机械上专供踏脚的部件 pedal; treadle

【脚底】jiǎodǐ 脚掌 sole (of foot): ～起了茧。

I've got calluses on the soles of my feet. also 脚底板 jiǎodǐbǎn

【脚夫】jiǎofū ❶〈旧称 *old*〉搬运工人 stevedore; porter ❷〈旧称 *old*〉赶着牲口供人雇用的人 person who is hired to transport goods on his own donkey or mule

【脚根】jiǎogēn same as 脚跟 jiǎogēn

【脚跟】jiǎogēn 脚的后部 heel; calcaneus ◇立定～(站得稳,不动摇)gain one's footing; keep one's footing (take a firm stand without yielding); also 脚根 jiǎogēn

【脚孤拐】jiǎogū·guai〈方 *dial.*〉大趾和脚掌相连向外突出的地方 metatarsal bone; protruding part of foot where big toe joins with sole

【脚行】jiǎoháng〈旧称 *old*〉搬运业或搬运工人 portage service or porters

【脚后跟】jiǎohòu·gen 脚跟 heel

【脚迹】jiǎojì 脚印 footmark; footprint; track; trail; pug mark

【脚尖】jiǎojiān (～儿 jiǎojiānr)脚的最前部分 tiptoe; tip of toe: 踮着～走 walk on tiptoe; tiptoe

【脚劲】jiǎojìn〈方 *dial.*〉(～儿 jiǎojìnr)两腿的力气 strength of one's legs: 妈妈的眼睛不如从前了,可是～还很好。Mother's eyesight is failing, but her legs are still strong.

【脚扣】jiǎokòu 套在鞋上爬电线杆子用的一种弧形铁制用具 climber; crampon; climbing iron; curved iron clasp attached to a shoe to prevent slipping when climbing a telegraph pole

【脚力】jiǎolì ❶ 两腿的力气 strength of one's legs: 他一天能走八九十里,～很好。He's got strong legs and can cover 80 *li* or more a day. ❷〈旧称 *old*〉搬运工人 porter ❸ 脚钱 payment to a porter ❹〈旧时 *old*〉给前来送礼的夫役的赏钱 tip paid to messenger who delivers gifts

【脚镣】jiǎoliào 套在犯人脚腕子上使不能快走的刑具,由一条铁链连着两个铁箍做成 manacles; shackles; fetters; metals used for encircling or confining the ankles of a prisoner so as to prevent free motion, usu. composed of two rings connected by a chain

【脚炉】jiǎolú 冷天烘脚用的小铜炉,状圆而稍扁,有提梁,盖上有许多小孔,炉中燃烧炭墼、锯末或砻糠 foot warmer; foot stove; round, flattish bronze stove with a carrying handle and a perforated cover that burns charcoal, sawdust or rice chaff, for warming the feet in winter

【脚轮】jiǎolún 安在提包、箱笼、沙发腿、床腿底下的小轮子 caster; roller; truckle; trundle; small wheel fixed to the bottom of a handbag, suitcase, sofa leg, bed leg, etc.

【脚门】jiǎomén same as 角门 jiǎomén

【脚面】jiǎomiàn 脚背 instep

【脚盆】jiǎopén 洗脚用的盆 foot basin; basin for washing the feet

【脚片】jiǎopiàn〈方 *dial.*〉脚 foot

【脚蹼】jiǎopǔ 一种潜水的用具,仿照动物的蹼,用橡胶或塑料压制而成,戴在脚上,以增加拨水的能力 flipper; fin; rubber or plastic paddle-like device, resembling an animal fin, worn on the feet to aid in swimming or diving

【脚气】jiǎoqì ❶ 由于缺乏维生素 B_1 而引起的疾病。症状是患者疲劳软弱,小腿沉重,肌肉疼痛萎缩,手足痉挛,头痛,失眠,下肢发生水肿,心力衰竭等。beriberi; disease caused by a deficiency of thiamine and characterized by debilitating fatigue, heaviness in the legs, muscle pain and atrophy, convulsions of the hands and feet, headache, insomnia, swelling in the lower limbs, heart failure, etc. ❷ 脚癣的通称 general term for 脚癣 jiǎoxuǎn

【脚钱】jiǎo·qian 指付给搬送东西的人的工钱 payment to a porter

【脚手架】jiǎoshǒujià 为了建筑工人在高处操作而搭的架子 scaffold; scaffolding; staging; framework erected around or on a building for the construction workers to stand on

【脚踏车】jiǎotàchē〈方 *dial.*〉自行车 bicycle; bike; push bike

【脚踏两只船】jiǎo tà liǎng zhī chuán ☞脚踩两只船 jiǎo cǎi liǎng zhī chuán

【脚踏实地】jiǎo tà shídì 形容做事塌实认真 down-to-earth; solid and earnest; do things conscientiously and reliably

【脚腕子】jiǎowàn·zi 小腿和脚连接的部分 ankle; joint where the shin meets the foot; also 脚腕儿 jiǎowànr

【脚下】jiǎoxià ❶ 脚底下 under one's feet ❷〈方 *dial.*〉目前;现时 at present; right now: ～是农忙季节,要合理使用劳力。It's harvesting season now, so we must make rational use of manpower. ❷〈方 *dial.*〉临近的时候 soon in time; imminent; at hand: 冬至～。The Beginning of Winter is drawing near.

【脚心】jiǎoxīn 脚掌的中央部分 arch; central part of the sole of a foot

【脚癣】jiǎoxuǎn 皮肤病,病原体是一种霉菌,多发生在脚趾之间。症状是起水泡,奇痒,抓破后流黄水,严重时溃烂。tinea pedis; athlete's foot; ringworm of the foot; contagious fungal skin infection caused by a species of mycete that usu. affects the feet, esp. the skin between the toes, and is characterized by itching, blisters which secrete yellowish fluid when broken, and ulcerate in serious cases; 通称 generally known as 脚气 jiǎoqì

【脚丫子】jiǎoyā·zi〈方 *dial.*〉脚 foot; also 脚鸭子 jiǎoyā·zi

【脚印】jiǎoyìn (～儿 jiǎoyìnr)脚踏过的痕迹 footprint; footmark; track; trail; pug (footprint of animal); mark left by stepping

【脚掌】jiǎozhǎng 脚接触地面的部分 sole of the

foot

【脚爪】jiǎozhǎo 〈方 *dial.*〉动物的爪子(of animal) paw; claw; talon; unguis

【脚指头】jiǎozhǐ·tou same as 脚趾 jiǎozhǐ

【脚趾】jiǎozhǐ 脚前端的分支 toe; terminal digit of the foot

【脚注】jiǎozhù 列在一页末了的附注 footnote; note added at the foot of a page

【脚镯】jiǎozhuó 套在脚腕子上的环形装饰品,多用金、银、玉等做成。舞蹈用的脚镯系有小铃铛。anklet; bangle; leglet; ring worn around the ankle as an ornament, usu. made of gold, silver, jade, etc. For dancing, small bells are attached to the anklet.

搅(攪) jiǎo ❶ 搅拌 stir; mix up; whisk; whip; beat up; churn up: 茶汤~匀了。The roasted millet flour has been mixed with boiling water to become a nice paste. | 把粥~一~。Give the porridge a stir. ❷ 扰乱;打扰 disturb; upset; mess up; disorder: ~扰 disturb; annoy; upset; harass | 胡~ wrangle; pester; be mischievous; make a nuisance of oneself

【搅拌】jiǎobàn 用棍子等在混合物中转动、和弄,使均匀 stir; mix up; whisk; whip; beat up; churn up: ~箱 mixing box | ~种子 stir the seeds | ~混凝土 mix cement with sand, gravel, pebbles, etc.; make concrete

【搅拌机】jiǎobànjī 搅拌材料用的机器,通常指混凝土搅拌机 concrete mixer; cement mixer

【搅动】jiǎo//dòng ❶ 用棍子等在液体中翻动或和弄 stir; mix; agitate: 用铁锹在泥浆池里~ puddle the slurry with a spade ❷ 搅扰;搅乱 disturb; mess up; spoil; tousle: 嘈杂的声音~得人心神不宁。The cacophony of sounds is annoying and agitating.

【搅浑】jiǎo//hún 搅动使浑浊(多用于比喻 oft. fig.) stir muddy; puddle; roil: 把水~ muddle the waters; muddle things up

【搅混】jiǎo·hun 〈方 *dial.*〉混合;搀杂 mix; blend; mingle: 歌声和笑声~成一片。Songs and laughter filled the air.

【搅和】jiǎo·huo 〈方 *dial.*〉❶ 混合;搀杂 mingle by stirring: 惊奇和喜悦的心情~在一起 mixture of joy and surprise ❷ 扰乱 mess up; ruin; spoil: 事情让他~糟了。He has messed things up.

【搅局】jiǎo//jú 扰乱别人安排好的事情 spoil or upset things; upset sb.'s apple cart; upset someone else's arrangements

【搅乱】jiǎoluàn 搅扰使混乱;扰乱 disturb; disorder; mess up; tousle; subvert; shuffle; scramble; ruffle; unsettle; disarrange; disorganize: ~人心 cause confusion among people; cause unease in people's hearts | ~会场 make trouble at the meeting; cause a stir at the meeting

【搅扰】jiǎorǎo (动作、声音或用动作、声音)影响别人使人感到不安(of movement or sound, or by movement and sound) disturb; annoy; bother; upset: 姐姐温习功课,别去~她。Your sister is doing her homework, leave her alone.

筊 jiǎo 〈书 *fml.*〉用竹子编的绳索 rope plaited from bamboo

湫 jiǎo 〈书 *fml.*〉低洼 low-lying
☞ qiū on p. 1582

【湫隘】jiǎo'ài 〈书 *fml.*〉低洼狭小 narrow and low-lying: 街巷~ narrow and low-lying streets and lanes

敫 Jiǎo 姓 a surname

剿(勦) jiǎo 剿灭;讨伐:(send armed forces to) suppress; put down: 围~ encircle and annihilate | ~匪 suppress bandits
☞ chāo on p. 228

【剿除】jiǎochú same as 剿灭 jiǎomiè

【剿灭】jiǎomiè 用武力消灭 exterminate; wipe out; annihilate by armed force: ~土匪 defeat and wipe out the bandits

儌 jiǎo [儌倖](jiǎoxìng) same as 侥幸 jiǎoxìng

徼 jiǎo 〈书 *fml.*〉求 beg; request; seek; entreat
☞ jiào on p. 983

【儌倖】jiǎoxìng same as 侥幸 jiǎoxìng

缴 jiǎo ❶ 交纳;交出(指履行义务或被迫)(of an obligation or under compulsion) pay; hand over; hand in: 上~ turn in | ~费 pay a bill | ~枪不杀。Those who lay down their arms will be spared. ❷ 迫使交出(多指武器) capture (arms); compelled to hand over (weapons): ~了敌人的枪 disarm the enemy; capture the enemy's arms
☞ zhuó on p. 2535

【缴裹儿】jiǎo·guor ☞ 嚼裹儿 jiáo·guor on p. 973

【缴获】jiǎohuò 从战败的敌人或罪犯等那里取得(武器、凶器等) capture (weapons from an enemy or a criminal); seize: ~敌军大炮三门 seize three enemy cannons

【缴纳】jiǎonà 交纳 pay; hand over: ~公粮 hand in grain tax | ~税款 pay tax

【缴销】jiǎoxiāo 缴回注销 hand in for cancellation: 汽车报废时应将原牌照~。When a car is scrapped, its licence plate should be handed in and cancelled.

【缴械】jiǎo//xiè ❶ 迫使敌人交出武器 compel the enemy to disarm: 把敌人~disarm the enemy | 缴了敌人的械 capture an enemy's arms; disarm an enemy ❷ 被迫交出武器 surrender one's weapons; lay down one's arms: ~投降 lay down one's arms and surrender

皦 jiǎo ❶ 〈书 *fml.*〉(珠玉)纯白;明亮(of jade, pearls) pure white; brilliant ❷ 〈书

fml.〉清白；清晰 pure; clean; clear ❸（Jiǎo）姓 a surname

jiào（ㄐㄧㄠˋ）

叫[1]（呌）jiào ❶ 人或动物的发音器官发出较大的声音，表示某种情绪、感觉或欲望 cry; shout; yell; bray; loud voice by human beings or high sound by animals to express mood, emotion or desire：鸡～crowing of a cock｜蝈蝈儿～（of katydid）make trilling sounds｜拍手～好 applaud and cheer｜大～一声 give a loud cry; shout out ◇汽笛连声～。The steam whistle blows without pause. ❷ 招呼；呼唤 call; ask for：外边有人～你。Someone outside is asking for you.｜把他们都～到这儿来。Ask them all to come.｜电话～通了。The call is put through. ❸ 告诉某些人员（多为服务行业）送来所需要的东西 ask for service：～车 get a taxi; call a taxi｜～两个菜 order two dishes ❹（名称）是；称为 call; name：这～不锈钢。This is called stainless steel.｜您怎么称呼？——我～王勇。What's your name? My name is Wang Yong. ◇那真～好！That's really great!｜这～什么打枪呀？瞧我的。You call that shooting? Let me show you. ❺〈方 *dial.*〉雄性的（某些家畜和家禽）male (domestic animal or poultry)：～驴 jackass｜～鸡 cock; rooster

叫[2]（呌）jiào ❶ 使；命令 make; order; ask：～他早点回去 tell him to return early｜要～穷山变富山 turn a bare hill into a fertile one ❷ 容许或听任 allow; permit; let：他不～去，我就不去。If he doesn't let me go, I won't. ❸ same as 被[3] bèi ①：他～雨淋了。He was caught in the rain.｜你把窗户打开点儿，别～煤气熏着。Keep the window ajar so the gas does not poison you.

【叫板】jiàobǎn 戏曲中把道白的最后一句节奏化，以便引入到下面的唱腔上去。用动作规定下面唱段的节奏也叫叫板。（in traditional 'theatre'）speak rhythmically the last sentence of a spoken part to lead into a vocal passage; use movements to mark the beat of the next vocal passage

【叫春】jiàochūn 指猫发情时发出叫声（of cat）give off a mating call

【叫喊】jiàohǎn 大声叫；嚷 cry; shout; yell; roar; clamour; howl：高声～shout at the top of one's voice｜～的声音越来越近。The sound of shouting came nearer.

【叫好】jiào//hǎo（～儿 jiào//hǎor）对于精彩的表演等大声喊'好'，以表示赞赏 applaud; shout 'bravo!'; shout 'well done'; cheer an outstanding performance

【叫号】jiāo//hào（～儿 jiào//hàor）❶ 呼唤表示先后次序的号 call out a number in a series (of a waiting patient, etc.)：看病的人都坐在门外等候医生～。All registered patients are waiting outside for the doctor to call their number. ❷〈方 *dial.*〉喊号子 sing a work song：几个小伙子叫着号把大木头抬起来。A few young fellows lifted the big log chanting a work song. ❸〈方 *dial.*〉用言语向对方挑战或挑衅 provoke with words; verbally challenge：他这样说简直是在～。He is just defying me by saying things like this.｜甭～，这点问题难不倒人。Don't try daring me, there's nothing difficult here.

【叫化子】jiàohuā·zi same as 叫花子 jiàohuā·zi

【叫花子】jiàohuā·zi 乞丐 beggar; panhandler; also 叫化子 jiàohuā·zi

【叫唤】jiào·huan ❶ 大声叫 cry out; call out：疼得直～cry out with pain ❷（动物）叫（of animal）cry; call：牲口～cries of draught animals｜小鸟儿在树上叽叽喳喳地～。Birds are chirping in the tree.

【叫魂】jiào//hún（～儿 jiào//húnr）迷信认为人患某些疾病是由于灵魂离开身体所致，呼唤病人的名字能使灵魂回到人的身上，治好疾病，这种做法叫做叫魂 call back the spirit of the sick. According to superstitious beliefs, certain diseases are caused when the spirit leaves the body, so a cure is effected by saying the name of the sick person in order to call back the spirit.

【叫鸡】jiàojī〈方 *dial.*〉公鸡 cock; rooster

【叫劲】jiào//jìn same as 较劲 jiào//jìn

【叫绝】jiào//jué 称赞事物好到极点 applaud sth. outstanding, sing the praises of：拍案～slap the table and shout 'bravo'

【叫苦】jiào//kǔ 诉说苦处 complain of suffering; moan and groan：～不迭 have endless complaints; string of complaints

【叫苦连天】jiào kǔ lián tiān 不断叫苦，形容痛苦得很 complain incessantly and bitterly

【叫驴】jiàolǘ 公驴 jackass

【叫骂】jiàomà 大声骂人 shout curses

【叫卖】jiàomài 吆喝着招揽主顾 peddle; hawk; huckster; sell one's wares by crying them in the street：沿街～peddle; hawk; huckster

【叫门】jiào//mén 在门外叫里边的人来开门 call at the door to be let in; knock at the door

【叫名】jiàomíng ❶（～儿 jiàmíngr）名称 name; term：活字本是版本方面的～。Movable type edition is a term in bibliography. ❷〈方 *dial.*〉在名义上 nominal：这孩子～十岁，其实还不到九岁。The child is said to be ten, but actually he is not yet nine.

【叫屈】jiào//qū 诉说受到冤屈 complain of being wronged; protest against injustice done to oneself：鸣冤～cry out about one's grievances

【叫嚷】jiàorǎng 喊叫 shout; clamour; rave; howl; break out

【叫嚣】jiàoxiāo 大声叫喊吵闹 clamour; raise a

hue and cry; hoot; make a tumult: 疯狂～ furious clamour

【叫啸】jiàoxiào 呼啸 whistle; roar: 江水在峡谷中奔腾～。The river surges and roars through the gorge.

【叫真】jiào//zhēn same as 较真 jiào//zhēn

【叫阵】jiào//zhèn 在阵前叫喊,挑战 challenge an opponent to fight; throw down the gauntlet

【叫子】jiào·zi 〈方 *dial.*〉哨儿 whistle

【叫座】jiàozuò (～儿 jiàozuòr) (戏剧或演员)能吸引观众,看的人多 (of play or performer) draw a large audience; appeal to the audience; be a box-office success: 这出戏连演三十几场,很～。The play has run for over 30 successive performances and has drawn a large audience.

【叫做】jiàozuò (名称)是;称为 be called; be known as; be entitled: 这东西～三角板。This is called a set square. | 跟纬线垂直的线～经线。The yarn at right angles to the woof is called the warp.

峤(嶠) jiào 〈书 *fml.*〉山道 mountain path

☞ qiáo on p. 1549

觉(覺) jiào 睡眠(指从睡着到睡醒)sleep; period from falling asleep to waking up: 午～afternoon nap | 好好地睡一～ have a good sleep | 一～醒来,天已经大亮。The day was already bright when he awoke.

☞ jué on p. 1059

珓 jiào 〈书 *fml.*〉占卜用具,用蚌壳、竹片或木片制成 divination instrument made of clam shells, bamboo or wood; also 杯珓 bēijiào

校 jiào ❶ 订正;校对 check; proofread; proof; collate; emend: ～改 read and correct proofs | ～勘 collate | ～稿子 proofread manuscripts | ～样 proof; proof sheet ❷ same as 较[1] jiào: ～场 drill ground

☞ xiào on p. 2115

【校本】jiàoběn 根据不同版本校勘过的书本 collated edition (of a book)

【校场】jiàochǎng 〈旧时 *old*〉操演或比武的场地 drill ground; ground for military drill and competition; also 较场 jiàochǎng

【校雠】jiàochóu 〈书 *fml.*〉校勘 collate

【校点】jiàodiǎn 校订并加标点 edit and punctuate: ～古籍 collate ancient books

【校订】jiàodìng 对照可靠的材料改正书籍、文件中的错误 revise; mend; check against the authoritative text

【校对】jiàoduì ❶ 核对是否符合标准 check against a standard; calibrate: 一切计量器都必需～合格才可以发售。All measuring instruments must be calibrated before being put on sale. ❷ 按原稿核对抄件或付印样张,看有没有错误 proofread; proof; check copy or proof against original manuscript for errors ❸ 做校对工作的人 proofreader: 他在印刷厂当～。He is a proofreader in a printing house.

【校改】jiàogǎi 校对并改正错误 read and correct proofs

【校勘】jiàokān 用同一部书的不同版本和有关资料加以比较,考订文字的异同,目的在于确定原文的真相 collate; scrutinize comparatively; compare different editions of a book with related documents to note points of agreement or disagreement, and identify the original text

【校勘学】jiàokānxué 研究校勘的学问,是整理古书的专业知识 textual criticism; study of manuscripts or printings to determine the most authoritative form of a text, specialized branch dealing with the bibliography of ancient books

【校样】jiàoyàng 书刊报纸等印刷品印刷前供校对用的样张 proof; proof sheet

【校阅】jiàoyuè ❶ 审阅校订(书刊内容)review and revise (proofs of books or magazines) ❷ 〈书 *fml.*〉检阅 inspect; review: ～三军 review troops of the three armed services | ～阵法 inspect battle array

【校正】jiàozhèng 校对订正 proofread and correct; correct; rectify; revise; emend: ～错字 correct misprints | 重新～炮位 realign the emplacement

【校注】jiàozhù 校订并注释 check against the authoritative text and annotate

【校准】jiào//zhǔn 校对机器、仪器等使准确 calibration; adjusting

轿(轎) jiào 轿子 sedan: 花～bridal sedan chair | 抬～ carry a sedan chair

【轿车】jiàochē ❶ 〈旧时 *old*〉供人乘坐的车,车厢外面套着帷子,用骡、马等拉着走 horse or mule-drawn covered carriage ❷ 供人乘坐的、有固定车顶的汽车 bus or car: 大～bus; coach | 小～car; limousine; sedan

【轿子】jiào·zi 旧时的交通工具,方形,用竹子或木头制成,外面套着帷子,两边各有一根杆子,由人抬着走或由骡马驮着走 sedan; sedan chair; old-fashioned means of transportation consisting of a square structure made of bamboo or wood, covered with a cloth with a horizontal pole on either side, carried by people, horses or mules: 坐～sit in a sedan; go by sedan chair | 抬～carry a sedan chair

较[1] jiào ❶ 比较 compare: ～量 have a contest; compete; stack up against; cross swords | ～一～劲儿 have a trial of strength; compete | 工作～前更为努力 work even harder than before | 用～少的钱,办～多的事 achieve the most with the least money ❷ 〈书

fml.〉计较 haggle; quibble; be particular about: 锱铢必～haggle over every penny; quibble over trifles

较[2] jiào〈书 *fml*.〉明显 obvious; evident; clearly seen; marked: 彰明～著 obvious; conspicuous; striking; prominent; pronounced; in the foreground | 二者～然不同。The two are clearly different.

【较比】jiàobǐ〈方 *dial*.〉〈副词 *adv*.〉表示具有一定程度；比较 comparatively; relatively; fairly; quite: 这间屋子～宽绰。The room is more spacious. | 这里的气候～热。The weather here is quite hot.

【较场】jiàochǎng same as 校场 jiàochǎng

【较劲】jiào//jìn (～儿 jiào//jìnr) ❶ 比力气；较量高低 match one's strength with; have a contest with; match strength to see who is better: 他们几个你追我赶，暗中较上了劲儿。They always try to outdo each other in a secret competition. ❷ 作对；闹别扭；对着干 set oneself against; be at odds with; disobliging; contrary: 这天真～，你越是需要雨，它越是不下。The weather is so disobliging; the more you need rain, the less it falls. ❸ 指特别需要发挥作用或使用力气 require special effort: 眼下是三夏时期，正是～的时候。Now is the summer season of farming, and we must put our shoulders to the wheel. ‖ also 叫劲 jiào//jìn

【较量】jiàoliàng ❶ 用竞赛或斗争的方式比本领、实力的高低 get a shot at sb.; have a contest; compete; stack up against; cross swords; bout: ～枪法 compete in marksmanship ❷〈方 *dial*.〉计较 haggle; quibble; argue; be particular about

【较为】jiàowéi〈副词 *adv*.〉表示有差别，但程度不很深(多用于同类事物相比较 oft. when comparing similar things) a little more; slightly: 这会儿他觉得～舒服些。He now felt a bit more comfortable. | 这样做～安全。It's comparatively safer to do things this way.

【较真】jiào//zhēn〈方 *dial*.〉(～儿 jiào//zhēnr)认真 serious; earnest: 他办事很～儿。He does things seriously. also 叫真 jiào//zhēn

【较著】jiàozhù〈书 *fml*.〉显著 obvious; evident; conspicuous: 彰明～obvious; conspicuous; striking; prominent; pronounced; in the foreground

窌 jiào〈书 *fml*.〉地窖 cellar

教[1] jiào ❶ 教导；教育 teach; instruct: 管～discipline | 请～ask for advice; consult | 受～be taught (by sb.); be a student of | 因材施～teach students in accordance with their aptitude ❷ 宗教 religion: 佛～Buddhism | 伊斯兰～Islam | 信～believe in a religion | 在～be a follower (of a religion) ❷(Jiào) 姓 a surname

教[2] jiào same as 叫[2] jiào
☞ jiāo on p.972

【教案】[1] jiào'àn 教师在授课前准备的教学方案，内容包括教学目的、时间、方法、步骤、检查以及教材的组织等等 teaching plan; lesson plan; plan; teacher's plan drawn up before a lesson, including purpose, time allotment, steps and procedures, learning assessment and the ordering of teaching materials, etc.

【教案】[2] jiào'àn 清末指因外国教会欺压人民而引起的诉讼案件，也指人民反抗教会欺压而引起的外交事件(in the late Qing Dynasty) court case resulting from foreign missionaries browbeating and oppressing ordinary people; also diplomatic incident caused by popular Chinese resistance against foreign missionary heavy handedness

【教本】jiàoběn 教科书 textbook

【教鞭】jiàobiān 教师讲课时指示板书、图片用的棍儿 pointer; rod; stick used by a teacher to point to a blackboard or picture

【教材】jiàocái 有关讲授内容的材料，如书籍、讲义、图片、讲授提纲等 teaching material, e. g. textbooks, lecture sheets, pictures, teaching outlines, etc.

【教程】jiàochéng 专门学科的课程(多用做书名 usu. used in book titles) course of study; tutorial: 近代史～ course in modern history | 政治经济学～ course in political economy

【教导】jiàodǎo 教育指导 teach; instruct; give guidance to; inculcate; indoctrinate; enlighten: ～处 instructor's office | ～有方 effective teaching

【教导员】jiàodǎoyuán 政治教导员的通称 general term for political instructor

【教范】jiàofàn 军事上指技术方面的基本教材，如射击教范、维护修理教范等(mil.) manual on basic skills, e. g. marksmanship, maintenance and repairs, etc.

【教父】jiàofù ❶ 基督教指公元 2—12 世纪在制订或阐述教义方面有权威的神学家 church father; (Christianity) theologians in 2nd-12th centuries A. D. whose works laid down authoritative doctrines of the church ❷ 天主教、正教及新教某些教派新入教者接受洗礼时的男性监护人 godfather; (of Catholic and Eastern Orthodox churches, and some Protestant sects) man who serves as sponsor at baptism of a neophyte

【教改】jiàogǎi 教育改革 education(al) reform

【教工】jiàogōng 学校里的教员、职员和工人的合称 collective term for faculty, administrative and non-teaching staff (of a school)

【教官】jiàoguān 军队、军校中担任教练的军官 drillmaster; instructor; officer who holds the position of a drillmaster in an army or military academy

【教规】jiàoguī 宗教要求教徒遵守的规则 canon; (Hinduism and Buddhism) dharma; religious rules believers are required to observe

【教化】jiàohuà〈书 *fml.*〉教育感化 educate and persuade; enlighten and influence

【教皇】jiàohuáng 天主教会的最高统治者,由枢机主教选举产生,任期终身,驻在梵蒂冈 Pope; pontiff; Holy Father; head of the Roman Catholic Church, elected by cardinal bishops for life who resides in the Vatican

【教会】jiàohuì 天主教、东正教、新教等教派的信徒的组织 kirk; ecclesia; Catholic, Orthodox, or Protestant church

【教诲】jiàohuì〈书 *fml.*〉教训;教导 teaching; instruction; edification: 谆谆~earnest teachings

【教具】jiàojù 教学时用来讲解说明某事某物的模型、实物、图表和幻灯等的总称(collect.) teaching aid; realia

【教科书】jiàokēshū 按照教学大纲编写的为学生上课和复习用的书 textbook

【教练】jiàoliàn ❶ 训练别人掌握某种技术或动作(如体育运动和驾驶汽车、飞机等) train; drill; coach: ~车 learner-driven vehicle | ~工作 coaching | ~得法 effective coaching ❷ 从事上述工作的人员 coach; instructor; drillmaster: 足球~football coach

【教龄】jiàolíng 教师从事教学工作的年数 teaching seniority; years a teacher spends in teaching; length of service as a teacher

【教令】jiàolìng 军队中通常以命令形式颁发的带试验性的原则规定,如飞行教令、步兵武器实弹射击教令等 military term referring to trial instructions issued as orders for flight training, infantry artillery training with live ammunition, etc.

【教门】jiàomén ❶ (~儿 jiàoménr)指伊斯兰教 Islam; Mohammedanism ❷ 教派 sect; denomination; church

J

【教母】jiàomǔ 天主教、正教及新教某些教派新入教者接受洗礼时的女性监护人 godmother; (in Catholic and Eastern Orthodox churches, and some Protestant sects) woman who serves as sponsor at baptism of a neophyte

【教派】jiàopài 某种宗教内部的派别 sect; denomination; church

【教区】jiàoqū 天主教主教管辖的宗教事务行政区。新教的一些教会也用来作为宗教事务行政区的名称。parish; deanery; ecclesiastical district in Roman Catholic Church; some Protestant churches also have similar administrative districts

【教师】jiàoshī 教员 teacher; schoolteacher; instructor; master; pedagogue; preceptor; schoolmaster: 人民~ teacher of the people

【教士】jiàoshì 基督教会传教的神职人员 priest; clergyman; Christian missionary; reverend; gownsman; cassock; christian clergy who spread religious teachings

【教室】jiàoshì 学校里进行教学的房间 classroom; schoolroom; school room in which class are conducted

【教授】jiàoshòu ❶ 对学生讲解说明教材的内容 instruct; teach: ~数学 teach mathematics | ~有方 teach in the right way ❷ 高等学校中职别最高的教师 professor; prof

【教唆】jiàosuō 怂恿指使(别人做坏事) instigate; abet; put sb. up to sth.; incite; set on; egg on: ~犯 abettor; instigator

【教堂】jiàotáng 基督教徒举行宗教仪式的场所 church; temple; cathedral; fane; ecclesia; place of Christian worship and rites

【教条】jiàotiáo ❶ 宗教上的信条,只要求信徒信从,不容许批评怀疑 dogma; doctrine; creed; tenet; doxy; body of religious principles presented for unqualified acceptance or belief ❷ 只凭信仰,不加思考而盲目接受或引用的原则、原理 dogma; doctrine; principles accepted or applied blindly and thoughtlessly, based on sheer belief ❸ 指教条主义 doctrinairism; dogmatism

【教条主义】jiàotiáo zhǔyì 主观主义的一种,不分析事物的变化、发展,不研究事物矛盾的特殊性,只是生搬硬套现成的原则、概念来处理问题 dogmatism; doctrinairism; form of subjectivism, characterized by arrogant and stubborn adherence to existing rules or concepts without considering the changing or particular nature of things

【教廷】jiàotíng 天主教会的最高统治机构,设在罗马城梵蒂冈 Vatican; Holy See; highest authority of the Roman Catholic Church with its seat in the Vatican, Rome

【教头】jiàotóu 宋代军队中教练武艺的人,后来也泛指传授技艺的人。现也指体育运动的教练员。(含诙谐意) (Song Dynasty military) drillmaster; general term for instructor of a skill; (humor.) sports coach

【教徒】jiàotú 信仰某一种宗教的人 follower or believer of a religion

【教务】jiàowù 学校中跟教学活动有关的行政工作 school administration; administrative duties linked to educational activities in school: ~处 Office of Academic Affairs; Office of the Provost

【教习】jiàoxí ❶ 教员的旧称 an old term for teacher; instructor ❷〈书 *fml.*〉教授(学业); 教练 ① teach; train: ~书法 teach calligraphy | ~水军 train the navy

【教学】jiàoxué 教师把知识、技能传授给学生的过程 teaching; education

☞ jiāo//xué on p. 972

【教学相长】jiào xué xiāng zhǎng 通过教学,不但学生得到进步,教师自己也得到提高 teaching benefits teachers as well as students

【教训】jiào·xun ❶ 教育训戒 teach sb. a lesson; lecture sb. (for wrongdoing); scold; moralize; indoctrinate: ~孩子 scold a child

❷ 从错误或失败中取得的知识 lesson; message drawn from a mistake or failure: 接受～,改进工作 learn from a mistake and improve one's work

【教研室】jiàoyánshì 教育厅、局和学校中研究教学问题的组织 department or section for pedagogic research; staff room

【教研组】jiàoyánzǔ 研究教学问题的组织,规模比教研室小 teaching and research group, smaller than a teaching and research section

【教养】jiàoyǎng ❶ 教育培养 bring up; educate; breed; cultivate; nurture: ～子女 educate one's children; discipline one's children ❷ 指一般文化和品德的修养 breeding; upbringing; education; cultivation; culture; discipline: 有～ be well educated; well brought up

【教养员】jiàoyǎngyuán 幼儿园负责全面教育儿童的人员 kindergarten teacher; person providing overall education for young children in a kindergarten

【教义】jiàoyì 某一种宗教所信奉的道理 religious doctrine; creed; tenet; doxy; teaching

【教益】jiàoyì 受教导后得到的益处 benefit gained from sb.'s teaching; enlightenment: 希望大家对我们的工作提出批评,使我们能够得到～。We welcome criticism from everyone so that we may benefit from it.

【教育】jiàoyù ❶ 培养新生一代准备从事社会生活的整个过程,主要是指学校对儿童、少年、青年进行培养的过程 education; schooling; education and preparation of the younger generation for future participation in society world, primarily referring to instruction given to children, teenagers and youths in educational institutions ❷ 用道理说服人使照着(规则、指示或要求等)做 expound; educate; guide; reasoned argument used to persuade sb. to follow rules, instructions or requests, etc.: 说服～persuade and enlighten

【教员】jiàoyuán 担任教学工作的人员 teacher; instructor; teaching staff; facultyman: 中学～middle school teacher

【教正】jiàozhèng〈书 *fml*.〉指教改正(把自己的作品送给人看时用的客套话 expression used when presenting one's work to sb.) give advice and comment: 送上拙著一册,敬希～。With the compliments of the author, who looks forward to your comments.

【教职员】jiàozhíyuán 学校里的教员和职员的合称 collective term for teaching and administrative staff in an educational institution

【教主】jiàozhǔ 某一宗教的创始人,如释迦牟尼是佛教的教主 hierarch; founder of a religion, e. g. Sakyamuni was the founder of Buddhism

窖 jiào ❶ 收藏东西的地洞或坑 cellar or pit used for storage; vault: 花儿～flower cellar | 白菜～ Chinese cabbage cellar | 白薯都已经入了～。The sweet potatoes are stored in the cellar. ❷ 把东西收藏在窖里 store sth. in a cellar or pit: 把白薯～起来。Store the sweet potatoes in the cellar.

【窖藏】jiàocáng 用窖储藏 store in a cellar or pit; cache; hoard: 保存白薯的最好办法是～。The best way to keep sweet potatoes is to store them in a root cellar.

【窖肥】jiàoféi〈方 *dial*.〉沤肥 ② make compost; compost

滘 jiào〈方 *dial*.〉分支的河道。多用于地名,如道滘、双滘墟(都在广东) tributary of a river, oft. used in place names, such as Daojiao and Shuangjiaoxu (both in Guangdong)

斠 jiào ❶〈古时 *arch*.〉平斗斛的器具 strickle; instrument used for levelling grain to the rim of a measure ❷〈书 *fml*.〉校订 check against the authoritative text

酵 jiào 发酵 ferment; leaven

【酵母】jiàomǔ 真菌的一种,黄白色,圆形或卵形,内有细胞核、液泡等。酿酒、制酱、发面等都是利用酵母引起的化学变化。yeast; saccharomyces; sour dough; leaven; barm; type of fungus, yellowish white, in a round or oval shape, containing nucleus, vacuoles, etc., used in the production of alcoholic beverages, soya bean paste and leavened dough, etc.; also 酵母菌 jiàomǔjūn or 酿母菌 niàngmǔjūn

【酵子】jiào·zi〈方 *dial*.〉含有酵母的面团 sour dough; leavening; also 引酵 yǐnjiào

㬭 jiào〈方 *dial*.〉只要 if only; provided

漖 jiào same as 滘 jiào: 东～(在广东) Dongjiao (in Guangdong)

噍 jiào〈书 *fml*.〉嚼;吃东西 chew; eat

【噍类】jiàolèi〈书 *fml*.〉能吃东西的动物,特指活着的人 living beings; human beings; animals that eat, esp. live humans

嗷 jiào〈书 *fml*.〉same as 叫 jiào

徼 jiào〈书 *fml*.〉❶ 边界 boundary ❷ 巡查 patrol

☞ jiǎo on p. 978

藠 jiào [藠头] (jiào·tou) 薤 (xiè) Chinese onion (*Allium bakeri*)

醮 jiào ❶〈古代 *arch*.〉结婚时用酒祭神的礼 libation at a wedding ceremony: 再～(再嫁)(of a woman) remarry ❷ 打醮 perform a Taoist ritual

嚼 jiào ☞倒嚼 dǎojiào on p. 393
☞ jiáo on p. 973 and jué on p. 1063

皭 jiào〈书 *fml*.〉洁白;干净 pure white; spotlessly clean

jiē (ㄐㄧㄝ)

节(節) jiē ☞ below
☞ jié on p.989

【节骨眼】jiē·guyǎn 〈方 *fml.*〉(～儿 jiē·guyǎnr) 〈比喻 *fig.*〉紧要的、能起决定作用的环节或时机 key link; critical moment; nick of time: 眼看就要停工待料了,就在这～上,赶运的原料来了。We were about to stop work for lack of raw materials, and in the nick of time, the stuff was rushed in.|做工作要抓住～儿,别乱抓一气。You should focus on key aspects in your work instead of trying to do every thing at once.

【节子】jiē·zi 木材上的疤痕,是树木的分枝砍去后在干枝上留下的疤 knot; node; knar; round cross-section left on a tree where a stem or branch is cut off

阶(階、堦) jiē ❶ 台阶 steps; stairs: ～梯 ladder ❷ 等级 rank: 官～official rank

【阶层】jiēcéng ❶ 指在同一个阶级中因社会经济地位不同而分成的层次。如农民阶级分成贫农、中农等。stratum; hierarchy; levels within a social class distinguished by different economic status, such as poor peasants, middle peasants within the peasant class ❷ 指由不同阶级出身,因某种相同的特征而形成的社会集团,如以脑力劳动为主的知识分子 stratum; rank; social stratum whose members come from different social classes but who share a common feature, e. g. intellectuals who are mainly engaged in mental work

【阶乘】jiēchéng 从 1 到 n 的连续自然数相乘的积,叫做阶乘,用符号 n! 表示。如 5! =1×2×3×4×5。规定 0! =1。factorial; product of all the positive integers from 1 to a given number, expressed as n!. For example, 5! =1×2×3×4×5, where 0! =1.

【阶段】jiēduàn 事物发展进程中划分的段落 stage; phase; period: 大桥第一～的工程已经完成。The first stage of the bridge project has been completed.

【阶地】jiēdì 河流、湖泊、海洋等岸边呈阶梯状的地貌 terrace; step-like land formation on the margin of river, lake or sea

【阶级】jiējí ❶〈书 *fml.*〉台阶 steps; stairs ❷〈旧指 *old*〉官职的等级 official rank ❸ 人们在一定的社会生产体系中,由于所处的地位不同和对生产资料关系的不同而分成的集团,如工人阶级、资产阶级等 class; (in a specific system of social production) groupings of people who vary in their relations to the means of production and social position, e. g. the working class, and the bourgeoisie

【阶级斗争】jiējí dòuzhēng 被剥削阶级和剥削阶级、被统治阶级和统治阶级之间的斗争 class struggle, that between the exploited and the exploiting classes, between the ruled and the ruling classes

【阶级性】jiējíxìng 在有阶级的社会里人的思想意识所必然具有的阶级特性。这种特性是由人的阶级地位决定的,反映着本阶级的特殊利益和要求。class character; class nature; in a class society, the ideology intrinsic to those belonging to a certain class, determined by their class status and mirroring the particular interests and demands of that class

【阶梯】jiētī 台阶和梯子 stairs; ladder; 〈比喻 *fig.*〉向上的凭借或途径 means of advancement; stepping stone

【阶下囚】jiēxiàqiú 〈旧时 *old*〉指在公堂台阶下受审的囚犯,泛指在押的人或俘虏 prisoner; captive; prisoner on trial at the foot of the steps of a tribunal

疖(癤) jiē same as 疖子 jiē·zi

【疖子】jiē·zi 皮肤病,由葡萄球菌或链状菌侵入毛囊内引起。症状是局部出现充血硬块,化脓,红肿,疼痛。furuncle; boil; skin condition caused by staphylococcal or streptococcic incursion of the hair follicle and characterized by local congestive hardening, festering, and painful red inflammation

皆 jiē 都,都是 all; each and every: 比比～是 ubiquitous; found everywhere; seen all around|放之四海而～准 universally true

【皆大欢喜】jiē dà huān xǐ 大家都很满意、很高兴 everyone is happy; to the happiness of all; all are satisfied

结 jiē 长出(果实或种子) bear (fruit or seed); produce: 树上～了不少苹果。The tree has borne many apples.|这种花～子儿不～? Does this flower produce seeds? |园地里的南瓜、豆荚～得又大又多。This vegetable garden has produced many large pumpkins and beans.
☞ jié on p.991

【结巴】jiē·ba ❶ 口吃的通称 general term for 口吃 kǒuchī; stutter: 他～得厉害,半天说不出一句整话。He stammers badly, and has difficulty saying a full sentence. ❷ 口吃的人 stammerer; stutterer

【结果】jiē//guǒ 长出果实 bear fruit: fructify: 开花～blossom and bear fruit
☞ jiéguǒ on p.992

【结实】jiē·shi ❶ 坚固耐用 solid; durable; stout: 这双鞋很～。This pair of shoes is strong. ❷ 健壮 strong; sturdy; burly: 他的身体～。He is a sturdy man.

接 jiē ❶ 靠近;接触 approach; be close to; border on; come into contact with; in touch with: 邻～ abut upon; adjoin; neighbour (on); proximity|～近 come close to;

J

near; approach; approximate | 交头～耳 speak in each other's ears; whisper in each other's ears ❷ 连接;使连接 connect; join; link: ～电线 connect the electric wires | ～纱头 join thrums | 这一句跟上一句～不上。This sentence doesn't follow the last one. | 这部影片上下两集～着演。The two parts of the film are shown without a break. ❸ 托住;承受 catch; take hold of; support: ～球 catch a ball | 书掉下来了,赶快用手～住。The books are falling, catch them! ❹ 接受 receive; take; accept: ～见 receive; interview | ～待 receive; (of a place) be open to; admit | ～到来信 receive a letter ❺ 迎接 meet; welcome: 到车站～人 meet sb. at the station ❻ 接替 take over; succeed: ～事 start new work; accept a post: | 谁～你的班? Who will succeed you? ❼ (Jiē) 姓 a surname

【接班】jiē//bān (～儿 jiē//bānr) ❶ 接替上一班的工作 take one's turn on duty; take over work from sb. on a rotating schedule: 我们下午三点～,晚十一点交班。Our shift begins at 3 p.m. and ends at 11 p.m. ❷ 指接替前辈人的工作、事业 succeed; follow in the steps of; carry on a cause or project left by a predecessor: 老工人张师傅退休了,由他女儿接了班。The elderly worker Master Zhang retired, and his daughter took his place.

【接茬儿】jiē//chár 〈方 *dial.*〉❶ 接着别人的话头说下去;搭腔 pick up the thread of a conversation; chime in; chop in; get in a word: 他几次跟我说到老王的事,我都没～。He brought up Lao Wang several times but I did not take him up on it. ❷ (一件事完了)紧接着做另外一件事 subsequently; after; follow on immediately after: 随后他们～商量晚上开会的事。They then went on to discuss the meeting scheduled for the evening.

【接长不短】jiē cháng bù duǎn 〈方 *dial.*〉形容时常,隔不多久 often; at short intervals; frequently: 几位老人～聚会欢谈。The old men often get together to chat.

【接触】jiēchù ❶ 挨上;碰着 come into contact with; get in touch with: 皮肤和物体～后产生的感觉就是触觉。Contact between the skin and an object produces the sense of touch. ◇他过去从没有～过书本。He has never touched a book before. ❷ (人跟人)接近并发生交往或冲突 come into contact with; interact with; engage: 领导应该多跟群众～。Leaders are supposed to interact frequently with common people. | 先头部队已经跟敌人的前哨～。The vanguard has engaged the enemy outpost.

【接待】jiēdài 招待 receive; play host to; welcome; take in; (of place) admit; be open to: ～室 reception room | ～来宾 receive guests or visitors

【接地】jiēdì ❶ 为了保护人身或设备的安全,把电力电讯等装置的金属底盘或外壳接上地线 ground connection; ground; earth; connection between the metal chassis or cover of an electrical device and the earth to ensure safety ❷ 接上地线,利用大地作电流回路 connection of an electric conductor with the ground to make a closed circuit

【接二连三】jiē èr lián sān 一个接着一个,形容接连不断 one after another; in quick succession; in quick procession; in a row; repeatedly; continuously: 喜讯～地传来。Announcements of good news followed in quick succession.

【接防】jiē//fáng (部队)接替原在某地驻守的部队的防务 relieve a garrison; relieve

【接风】jiēfēng 请刚从远道来的人吃饭 give a welcome dinner for a visitor from afar: 设宴～give a dinner of welcome; throw a reception of welcome | ～洗尘 give a dinner of welcome

【接羔】jiē//gāo 照顾羊、鹿等产羔 assist at the birth of a sheep, doe, etc.; deliver (a lamb or fawn)

【接管】jiēguǎn 接收并管理 take over control; ～政权 take over political power; come to power | ～财务 take over financial affairs

【接轨】jiē//guǐ 连接路轨 connect the rails: 新建的铁路已全线～铺通。The whole railway has been laid and connected. ◇调整汇率,和国际～adjust our exchange rate in line with international ones

【接合】jiēhé 连接使合在一起 join

【接火】jiē//huǒ (～儿 jiē//huǒr) ❶ 开始用枪炮互相射击 start to exchange fire: 先头部队跟敌人～了。The advanced detachment has started to exchange fire with the enemy. ❷ 内外电线接通,开始供电 provide electricity by connecting to a source: 电灯安好了,但是还没～。The lights are in place, but have yet to be connected to the power source.

【接济】jiējì 在物质上援助 give material assistance to; give financial help to; supply: ～粮草 supply grain and forage; supply provender | ～物资 supply relief goods and materials | 他经常～那些穷困的青年。He often gives financial help to poor young men.

【接见】jiējiàn 跟来的人见面 receive; interview; give an interview to: ～外宾 receive foreign guests | ～与会代表 meet with the conference representatives

【接界】jiējiè 交界 have a common boundary; border on: 这个车站临近两省～的地方。The station is near the common border of the two provinces.

【接近】jiējìn 靠近;相距不远 be close to; near; approach; approximate: ～群众 be in close contact with the masses | 时间已～半夜。It's close to midnight. | 这项技术已～世界先进水平。This technique is approaching the advanced world level. | 大家的意见已经很～，没有多大分歧了。All of us see pretty much eye to eye with little disagreement.

【接境】jiējìng 交界 have a common boundary; contiguous; border: 山西东部同河北～。Shanxi borders on Hebei in the east.

【接客】jiē//kè ❶ 接待客人 receive guests ❷ 指妓女接待嫖客(of a prostitute) receive or sleep with a patron

【接力】jiēlì 一个接替一个地进行 operate by relay: ～赛跑 relay race; relay | ～运输 relay transport

【接力棒】jiēlìbàng 接力赛跑时使用的短棒，用木料或金属等制成 relay baton; baton made of wood or metal passed in a relay race

【接力赛跑】jiēlì sàipǎo 径赛项目之一，由每队四名运动员一个接一个传递接力棒跑完一定距离。有 400 米、800 米、1,600 米接力，和 1,000 米、1,500 米异程接力赛(各人所跑的距离不等)及穿梭(迎面)接力等。relay race; relays; track event, race in which each of the four members of a team runs only a set part of the distance and is then relieved by another member of the team after passing the baton. Relay races are run at the 400, 800 and 1,600 m. distances; there are also the 1,000 or 1,500 m. variable relay (each team member runs a different distance), and shuttle relays (face-to-face relay)

【接连】jiēlián 一次跟着一次；一个跟着一个 running; on end; in a row; in succession; repeatedly; one after the other: ～不断 continuously; incessantly; in rapid succession | 他～说了三次。He repeated it three times running.

J

【接龙】jiē//lóng ☞ 顶牛儿[2] dǐng//niúr on p. 455

【接目镜】jiēmùjìng ☞ 目镜 mùjìng on p. 1377

【接纳】jiēnà ❶ 接受(个人或团体参加组织、参加活动等) admit (into an organization); accept (as a member): 他被～为工会会员。He was admitted into the trade union. | 展览会每天～上万人参观。The exhibition admits tens of thousands of visitors every day. ❷ 采纳 adopt; accept; take: 他～了大家的意见。He took our advice.

【接盘】jiēpán same as 受盘 shòupán

【接气】jiē//qì 连贯(多指文章的内容 oft. of the content of a piece of writing) coherent; consistent: 这一段跟下一段不很～。This paragraph does not connect well with the next one.

【接洽】jiēqià 跟人联系，洽谈有关事项 take up a matter with; arrange business with; consult with; contact sb. for business arrangement: ～工作 talk business; take up business matters

【接腔】jiē//qiāng 接着别人的话来说 answer; respond; take up (a cue, hint, etc.); follow on previous comment: 他说完话，大家谁也没有～。After he spoke, no one said anything.

【接亲】jiē//qīn 男方到女方家中迎娶新娘(of bridegroom) go to the bride's home to escort her to the wedding

【接壤】jiērǎng 交界 border on; contiguous to; adjoin: 河北西部和山西～。The western part of Hebei borders on Shanxi.

【接任】jiērèn 接替职务 take over a job; replace; succeed: 校长一职已由原教务主任～。The president has been replaced by the former dean of academic affairs.

【接墒】jiēshāng 下雨或浇水后，上下湿土相接，土壤中所含水分能满足农作物出苗或生长的需要 (of soil) wet through after rain or watering, so that seeds can sprout or crops can grow

【接生】jiē//shēng 帮助产妇分娩 deliver a child; practise midwifery: ～员 midwife

【接事】jiēshì 接受职务并开始工作 take over a job and start to work

【接收】jiēshōu ❶ 收受 receive; accept: ～来稿 receive articles (submitted for publication); receive manuscripts or contributions | ～无线电信号 receive radio signals ❷ 根据法令把机构、财产等拿过来 take over according to law or order (an organization, property, etc.): ～逆产 take possession of a traitor's property ❸ 接纳 admit; recruit; affiliate: ～新会员 recruit new members

【接手】jiēshǒu 接替 take over: 他走后，俱乐部工作由你～。You will take over his work in the club after he leaves.

【接受】jiēshòu 对事物容纳而不拒绝 accept; take on; undertake: ～任务 accept a task or assignment | ～考验 face up to a test | ～教训 learn a lesson | 虚心～批评 be open to criticism

【接穗】jiēsuì 嫁接植物时用来接在砧木上的枝或芽 scion; graft; twig or shoot grafted to another growing plant; ☞ 砧木 zhēnmù on p. 2437

【接榫】jiē//sǔn ❶ 连接榫头 connect tenons ❷ 〈比喻 *fig.*〉前后衔接 coherent; joining: 这篇文章在前后～的地方没处理好，显得太散。The article is loosely crafted and poor in coherence.

【接谈】jiētán 接见并交谈 meet and talk with: 负责人跟来访的群众～。The person in charge met and talked with the visitors.

【接替】jiētì 从别人那里把工作接过来并继续下去；代替 take over; replace; succeed; supercede: 上级已派人去～他的工作。A new appointee has been sent to take over his work.

【接头】jiē//tóu ❶ 使两个物体接起来 connect;

join ❷ 接洽；联系 contact；get in touch with：领导上叫我来跟你～。I'm sent to contact you. ❸ 熟悉某事的情况 be familiar with；be up on：我刚来，这件事我还不～。I'm a newcomer and know little about this matter.

【接头儿】jiē·tóur 两个物体的连接处 connection；junction；joint：这条床单有个～。The sheet has a seam in it.

【接吻】jiē//wěn 亲嘴 kiss；smooch

【接物镜】jiēwùjìng ☞ 物镜 wùjìng on p.2037

【接线】jiē//xiàn 用导线连接线路 wiring；connection

【接线】jiēxiàn 电器上用来接电源或连接各电器元件的导线 connecting cord (or line or cable)

【接线员】jiēxiànyuán 话务员 telephone operator

【接续】jiēxù 接着前面的；继续 continue；follow：请您～讲下去。Please take up where you left off.

【接应】jiēyìng ❶ 配合自己一方的人行动 reinforce；back up；coordinate with：你们先冲上去，二排随后～。You go first, and the second platoon will back you up. ❷ 接济；供应 give material assistance；supply：粮草～不上。Army provisions are in short supply.

【接援】jiēyuán 接应援助（多用于军队 oft. military）reinforce

【接站】jiē//zhàn 到车站接人 meet sb. at the station：派专车负责～send a car to pick sb. up at a station

【接着】jiē·zhe ❶ 用手接 catch：我往下扔，你在下面～。I'll drop it and you catch it. ❷ 连着（上面的话）；紧跟着（前面的动作）follow (a speech, action)；carry on：我讲完了你～讲。I'll speak first and then you follow.｜这本书，你看完了我～看。I will read the book after you.

【接踵】jiēzhǒng〈书 *fml.*〉后面的人的脚尖接着前面的人的脚跟。形容人多，连接不断。follow on sb.'s heels；crowded；one after another：摩肩～(of people) jostle each other in a crowd｜～而来 come one after another；come close on the heels；follow on the heels of sb. (or sth.)

【接种】jiēzhòng 把疫苗注射到人或动物体内，以预防疾病，如种痘 vaccinate；immunize；introduce bacteria into the human or animal body to create immunity to a specific disease

秸(稭) jiē 农作物脱粒后剩下的茎 straw；stalk of threshed grain：麦～wheat straw｜秋～sorghum stalk｜豆～bean stalk

【秸秆】jiēgǎn 农作物脱粒后剩下的茎 straw；stalk of threshed grain

痎 jiē 古书上指一种疟疾 malaria recorded in ancient books

揭 jiē ❶ 把粘在别的物体上的片状物成片取下 peel off；remove；take off；strip off, remove sth. in strips or flakes that has been stuck to sth. else：～下墙上的画 peel the picture off the wall｜～下粘在手上的膏药 take off a plaster from the hand ❷ 把覆盖或遮挡的东西拿开 uncover；unveil；remove a covering or shield：～幕 inaugurate；unveil；undrape｜～锅盖 remove the pot lid ❸ 揭露 expose；disclose；uncover；unmask：～底 reveal the inside story ❹〈书 *fml.*〉高举 raise；hoist：～竿而起 rise in arms；bear arms against；raise the standard of revolt ❺（Jiē）姓 a surname

【揭榜】jiē//bǎng ❶ 考试后出榜；发榜 announce the results of an examination；publish a list of successful examinees ❷ 揭下写有招聘或招标等内容的榜，表示应征 take down a job or tender announcement to indicate willingness to respond

【揭不开锅】jiē·bukāi guō 指断炊 go hungry；have nothing in the pot；have nothing to eat in the house

【揭穿】jiēchuān 揭露；揭破 expose；lay bare；show up；disclose；debunk：～阴谋 uncover a plot｜～谎言 expose a lie｜～他的老底 disclose his past；bring his past to light｜假面具被～了 unmask sb.；see through sb.'s disguise；strip off a disguise of sb.

【揭疮疤】jiē chuāngbā〈比喻 *fig.*〉揭露人的短处 expose sb.'s weakness；touch sb. to the quick；touch sb. on the raw；rub salt into sb.'s wound；reopen old sores

【揭底】jiē//dǐ（～儿 jiē//dǐr）揭露底细 reveal the inside story：他很怕人家揭他的底。He is afraid his secret will be revealed.

【揭短】jiē//duǎn（～儿 jiē//duǎnr）揭露人的短处 show up sb.'s faults；disclose sb.'s weaknesses：不该当众揭他的短。You shouldn't have talked about his failings in public.

【揭发】jiēfā 揭露（坏人坏事）expose；bring to light；disclose；uncover：～罪行 expose his crime｜检举～impeach and expose

【揭盖子】jiē gài·zi〈比喻 *fig.*〉揭露矛盾或问题 disclose problems and contradictions；take the lid off；lift the lid；bring sth. into the open；bring to light

【揭竿而起】jiē gān ér qǐ 汉代贾谊《过秦论》：'斩木为兵，揭竿为旗。'后用'揭竿而起'指人民起义 *Essay on the Faults of Qin* by Jia Yi of the Han Dynasty：'Chop down trees to arm the soldiers and hoist the banner on a bamboo pole.' The phrase has later been used to refer to popular uprising.

【揭露】jiēlù 使隐蔽的事物显露 expose；lay bare；unveil；uncover；disclose what has been hidden：～矛盾 expose contradictions｜～问题的本质 uncover the crux of the problems｜阴谋被～出来。The plot is laid bare.

【揭秘】jiēmì 揭露秘密 reveal a secret; unveil a mystery; divulge a secret: 这段历史公案有待～。This historical legal case remains a mystery.

【揭幕】jiēmù ❶ 在纪念碑、雕像等落成典礼的仪式上,把蒙在上面的布揭开 unveil a monument, a statue, etc., at an opening ceremony; undrape; inaugurate ❷〈比喻 *fig.*〉重大活动的开始 (of important event) open; start: 展览会～。The exhibition opens.｜国际排球锦标赛～。The International Volleyball Tournament begins.

【揭破】jiēpò 使掩盖着的真相显露出来 prick a bubble; unveil; unmask; lay bare; disclose a hidden truth: ～诡计 expose (his) deception

【揭示】jiēshì ❶ 公布(文告等) announce; post; promulgate: ～牌 notice board ❷ 使人看见原来不容易看出的事物 reveal; throw (shed or cast) light on what was not obvious: ～客观规律 throw light on the objective laws

【揭帖】jiētiě〈旧时 *old*〉指张贴的启事(多指私人的) (personal) notice; announcement

【揭晓】jiēxiǎo 公布(事情的结果) announce; make known; publish: 录取名单还没有～。The enrolment list hasn't been announced.｜乒乓球赛的结果已经～。The results of the table tennis competition has been announced.

喈 jiē [喈喈]〈书 *fml.*〉❶ 形容声音和谐 (of sound) harmonious: 钟鼓～。Bells and drums resounded harmoniously. ❷ 鸟鸣声 chirp; twitter: 鸡鸣～。Roosters are crowing.

嗟 jiē〈书 *fml.*〉叹息 sigh; groan; suspiration; suspire; yammer; lament: ～叹 heave a sigh; sigh

【嗟悔】jiēhuǐ〈书 *fml.*〉叹息悔恨 lament; regret: ～无及 too late for regrets and lamentations

J

【嗟来之食】jiē lái zhī shí 春秋时齐国发生饥荒,有人在路上施舍饮食,对一个饥饿的人说'嗟,来食',饥饿的人说,我就是不吃'嗟来之食',才到这个地步的。终于不食而死(见于《礼记·檀弓》)。今泛指带有侮辱性的施舍。contemptuous handout; food handed out in contempt; handout. According to *The Book of Rites · Tan Gong*, a famine had struck the state of Qi during the Spring and Autumn Period, and a person offered alms to a famine victim by the road, saying, 'Hey, come and eat.' The man replied that he was starving now because he had refused to accept food handed out with contempt, and he eventually died of hunger.

【嗟叹】jiētàn〈书 *fml.*〉叹息 heave a sigh; sigh: ～不已 endless sighs

街 jiē ❶ 街道;街市 street; downtown street: ～头 street corner; street｜大～小巷 streets and lanes｜上～买东西 go shopping in town; go shopping｜～上很热闹。The streets are bustling with activity. ❷〈方 *dial.*〉集市 country fair; bazaar: 赶～ go to a fair; go to market

【街道】jiēdào ❶ 旁边有房屋的比较宽阔的道路 street ❷ 关于街巷居民的 neighbourhood; residential district: ～工作 neighbourhood service; community work (or service)

【街灯】jiēdēng 路灯 street lamp; street light

【街坊】jiē·fang 邻居 neighbour: 我们是～。We are neighbours.

【街垒】jiēlěi 用砖、石、车辆、装了泥沙的麻袋等在街道或建筑物间的空地上堆成的障碍物 street barricade: ～战 fight on the barricades

【街门】jiēmén 院子临街的门 street door; courtyard door opening on to a street

【街面儿上】jiēmiànr·shang〈方 *dial.*〉❶ 市面 business: 一到春节,～特别热闹。Business booms during the Spring Festival. ❷ 指附近街巷 neighbourhood: 他在这儿住了几十年,～都知道他。He has been living here for decades and everyone in the neighbourhood knows him.

【街市】jiēshì 商店较多的市区 downtown streets; city streets with many shops

【街谈巷议】jiē tán xiàng yì 大街小巷里人们的谈论 street gossip; town talk

【街头】jiētóu 街;街上 street; street corner: 十字～crossroads; four-way intersection

【街头巷尾】jiē tóu xiàng wěi 指大街小巷 streets and lanes

【街心】jiēxīn 街道的中央部分 crossroads: ～花园 garden at a street intersection; parkway

湝 jiē [湝湝]〈书 *fml.*〉形容水流动 (of water) running; flowing: 淮水～。The Huai River flows on and on.

楷 jiē〈方 *dial.*〉黄连木 Chinese pistache ☞ kǎi on p. 1078

䥣 jiē〈方 *dial.*〉割稻用的刀,刃有细齿 sickle; knife with toothed blade for harvesting rice

jié (ㄐㄧㄝˊ)

孑 jié〈书 *fml.*〉单独;孤单 lonely; all alone: ～立 lonely; without company｜～身 solitary; alone

【孑孓】jiéjué 蚊子的幼虫,是蚊子的卵在水中孵化出来的,体细长,游泳时身体一屈一伸 wiggler; wriggler; larva or pupa of mosquito hatched in water, with a long narrow body that moves by twisting and turning; 通称 popularly called 跟头虫 gēn·touchóng

【孑然】jiérán〈书 *fml.*〉形容孤独 solitary; lonely; alone: ～一身 all alone in the world

【孑遗】jiéyí〈书 *fml.*〉遭受兵灾等大变故多数人死亡后遗留下的少数人 survivor; small

number of people who survive war, massacre, natural disaster, etc.

【孑遗生物】jiéyí shēngwù 活化石 living fossil

节[1](節) jié ❶ 物体各段之间相连的地方 joint; node; knot; gnarl; place at which separate parts join together: 竹～ bamboo joint | 关～joint ❷ 段落 division; section; part: ～拍 metre; time; tempo; beat; pace | 音～syllable ❸〈量词 *classifier*〉用于分段的事物或文章 section; length; stanza: 两～火车 two railway coaches (or carriages or compartments) | 四～甘蔗 four segments of a sugar cane | 上了三～课。(He) has taken three classes. | 第三章第八～ Section Eight, Chapter Three ❹ 节日;节气 festival; red-letter day; holiday; seasonal division of the year under the traditional Chinese calendar: 五一国际劳动～May Day | 春～Spring Festival | 清明～Clear and Bright Day | 过～celebrate a festival or holiday ❺ 删节 abridge: ～选 excerpt; extract | ～录 excerpt; extract ❻ 节约;节制 economize; save; restrain; abstain: ～电 save electricity; economize on electricity | ～煤 save coal; economize on coal | ～育 birth control | 开源～流 increase earnings and cut expenses ❼ 事项 item; matter: 细～detail | 礼～courtesy; ceremony | 生活小～trifles ❽ 节操 moral integrity; high moral principle: 气～moral integrity | 变～turn coat; apostasy; treachery; make a political recantation | 保持晚～keep one's integrity in one's later years | 高风亮～sterling integrity; high principles; upright and noble character ❾ (Jié) 姓 a surname

节[2] jié 航海速度单位,每小时航行一海里的速度是一节 knot; unit of navigation speed, equal to one nautical mile per hour

☞ jiē on p. 984

【节哀】jié'āi〈书 *fml.*〉抑制哀痛,不使过分(多用于劝慰死者家属 expression of consolation to the bereaved) restrain one's grief

【节本】jiéběn 书籍经过删节的版本 expurgated edition; abbreviated version:《金瓶梅》～abridged edition of *The Plum in a Gold Vase*

【节操】jiécāo〈书 *fml.*〉气节操守 moral integrity; high moral principle

【节点】jiédiǎn 电路中联接三个或三个以上支路的点 panel point; node; nodal point

【节妇】jiéfù〈旧时 *old*〉指坚守贞节,丈夫死后不改嫁的妇女 widow who maintains her chastity and does not remarry

【节假日】jiéjiàrì 节日和假日的合称 collective term for festivals and holidays

【节俭】jiéjiǎn 用钱等有节制;俭省 thrifty; frugal; economical; abstemious

【节减】jiéjiǎn 节省减少(费用) reduce; curtail; cut (expenditure): ～经费 cut expenses

【节礼】jiélǐ 过节时赠送的礼物 present given on a festival; holiday gift

【节理】jiélǐ 岩石受力所产生的裂缝,通常指岩层中的裂隙 joint; pressure fracture or crack in a rock mass

【节烈】jiéliè 封建礼教上指妇女守节或殉节(of a woman, esp. widow in feudal society) rigorously chaste according to feudal ethics

【节令】jiélìng 某个节气的气候和物候 climate and other natural phenomena specific to a season: ～不正 not in the right season | 端午节吃粽子,应应～。Glutinous rice dumplings are eaten during the Dragon Boat Festival, as befits the occasion.

【节录】jiélù ❶ 从整篇文字里摘取重要的部分 excerpt; extract; excerpt important parts from a complete text: 这篇文章太长,只能～发表。We can only publish excerpts from the original article which is too long. ❷ 摘录下来的部分 excerpt; extract; snippet; cento: 这里发表的是全文,不是～。The published article is a complete version, not an extract. | 这一篇是读者来信的～。This piece features excerpts from readers' letters.

【节律】jiélǜ 某些物体运动的节奏和规律 rhythm and pattern of movement

【节略】jiélüè ❶ 概要;摘要 excerpt; outline; abstract; brief; digest; abbreviation; summary: 讲演稿的～excerpts of a speech ❷ 省略 omit; leave out; cut out; pass over: 文章的后一部分～了。The latter part of the article has been cut. ❸ 外交文书的一种,用来说明事实、证据或有关法律的问题,不签字也不用印,重要性次于照会 memorandum; aide-memoire; position paper; diplomatic communication setting forth the major points of a proposed discussion or agreement concerning certain facts, evidence or law, unsigned, not sealed; of lesser significance than a diplomatic note

【节目】jiémù 文艺演出或广播电台、电视台播送的项目 programme; item (on programme); number: ～单 programme; playbill | 文艺～artistic and cultural number | 今天晚会的～很精彩。The programme for this evening's show is excellent.

【节能】jiénéng 节约能源 save energy; energy conservation: ～措施 energy conservation measures

【节拍】jiépāi 音乐中每隔一定时间重复出现的有一定强弱分别的一系列拍子,是衡量节奏的单位。如 2/4、3/4、4/4、3/8、6/8 等。metre; time; beat; tempo; pace; specific rhythm determined by the number of heavy and light beats and the time value assigned to each note in a measure, such as 2/4, 3/4, 4/4, 3/8, and 6/8 time

【节气】jié·qi 根据昼夜的长短、中午日影的高低等,在一年的时间中定出若干点,每一点叫一个节气。节气表明地球在轨道上的位置，也就是太阳在黄道上的位置。通常也指每一点所在的那一天。solar term; day marking one of the 24 seasonal divisions established according to the length of the day and the sun's shadow at noon; the position of the earth on its orbit and the sun on the ecliptic; ☞ 二十四节气 èrshísì jiéqì on p. 516

【节日】jiérì ❶ 纪念日，如五一国际劳动节等 day of commemoration, such as May Day ❷ 传统的庆祝或祭祀的日子，如清明节、中秋节等 traditional holiday or festival; red-letter day; fete day (such as Clear and Bright Day, Mid-Autumn Festival)

【节省】jiéshěng 使可能被耗费掉的不被耗费掉或少耗费掉 economize; save; cut down on; retrench; use sparingly; pinch: ～时间 save time|～劳动力 save labour|～开支 cut down (on) expenses

【节食】jiéshí 减少食量；节制饮食 diet; eat moderately; go on a diet; be on a diet

【节外生枝】jié wài shēng zhī〈比喻 *fig.*〉在问题之外又岔出了新的问题 raise obstacles; deliberately complicate an issue; branch off; (of new problems) crop up unexpectedly

【节下】jié·xia 指节日或接近节日的日子 on or around a certain holiday or festival

【节选】jiéxuǎn 从某篇文章或某本著作中选取某些段落或章节 excerpts; extracts

【节衣缩食】jié yī suō shí 省吃省穿，泛指节俭 economize on food and clothing; (in a broad sense) be thrifty; be frugal

【节余】jiéyú ❶ 因节约而剩下 save: 每月能～三五十元。Thirty to fifty yuan can be saved every month. ❷ 指节余的钱或东西 surplus; savings; money or things saved: 把全部～捐给了灾区。All the savings were donated to the disaster-stricken areas.

【节育】jiéyù 节制生育 birth control

【节约】jiéyuē 节省(多用于较大的范围)(oft. used in a larger scope) practise thrift; economize; save: 增产～ increase output and practise thrift|～时间 save time

【节肢动物】jiézhī-dòngwù 无脊椎动物的一门，身体由许多环节构成，一般分头、胸、腹三部分，表面有壳质的外骨骼保护内部器官，有成对而分节的腿。种类很多，如蜈蚣、蜘蛛、蜂、蝶、虾、蟹等。arthropod; tardigrade; family of invertebrates whose bodies, divided into the three parts of head, chest and belly, have many segments and pairs of legs, and are protected by a chitinous exoskeleton, of many kinds, e.g. centipedes, spiders, bees, butterflies, shrimps, crabs, etc.

【节制】jiézhì ❶ 指挥管辖 control; command: 这三个团全归你～。You will have control of all the three regiments. ❷ 限制或控制 check; restriction; control: 饮食有～，就不容易得病。If you are careful about your diet, you are not likely to fall ill.

【节奏】jiézòu ❶ 音乐中交替出现的有规律的强弱、长短的现象 rhythm; cadence; measure or beat of music produced by strong and weak, and long and short musical notes interchanging systematically: ～明快 lively rhythm ❷〈比喻 *fig.*〉均匀的、有规律的工作进程 rhythmically: 工作要有～地进行。Work should be done rhythmically.

讦 jié〈书 *fml.*〉斥责别人的过失；揭发别人的阴私 sb.'s past misdeeds: 攻～ expose sb.'s past misdeeds

劫[1](刦、刧、刼) jié ❶ 抢劫 loot; rob; plunder; raid: 打～ plunder|～夺 rob and capture|打家～舍 loot a neighbourhood; plunder ❷ 威逼；胁迫 coerce; compel: ～持 hijack

劫[2] jié 灾难 calamity; disaster; misfortune: 浩～ great calamity; catastrophe|遭～ encounter calamity|～后余生 be a survivor of a disaster [劫波之省，梵 abbreviation of 劫波 jiébō, Sanskrit: kalpa]

【劫持】jiéchí 要挟；挟持 abduct; hold under duress; hijack: ～飞机 hijack an airplane

【劫夺】jiéduó 用武力夺取(财物或人) seize (a person or his property) by force: ～资源 seize resources

【劫难】jiénàn 灾难；灾祸 disaster: 历经～ have one's fill of adversities

【劫数】jiéshù 佛教徒所谓注定的灾难 inexorable doom; predestined fate: ～难逃 cannot escape destiny

【劫狱】jié//yù 从监狱里把被拘押的人抢出来 break into a jail and rescue a prisoner

劼 jié〈书 *fml.*〉❶ 谨慎 prudent ❷ 努力 hardworking; assiduous

杰(傑) jié ❶ 才能出众的人 outstanding person: 豪～ hero|俊～ outstanding talent ❷ 杰出 outstanding: ～作 great work

【杰出】jiéchū (才能、成就)出众 (of talent and achievement) outstanding; remarkable; prominent: ～人物 outstanding figure

【杰作】jiézuò 超过一般水平的好作品 masterpiece; great work

疌 jié〈书 *fml.*〉迅速 prompt; quick; same as 捷 jié

诘 jié〈书 *fml.*〉诘问 heckle: 盘～ closely question|反～ rebut; refute

☞ jí on p. 904

【诘难】jiénàn〈书 *fml.*〉责难 blame

【诘问】jiéwèn〈书 *fml.*〉追问；责问 closely question; interrogate; cross-examine

絜 jié same as 洁 jié; 多用于人名 oft. used in personal names

拮 jié［拮据］(jiéjū)缺少钱，境况窘迫 lack of money：手头～ go short of money

洁(潔) jié 清洁 clean：整～ clean and tidy|纯～ pure|～白 pure white

【洁白】jiébái 没有被其他颜色染污的白色 spotlessly white; pure white：～的床单 pure white sheet ◇～的心灵 pure mind; innocence

【洁净】jiéjìng same as 干净 gānjìng ①

【洁癖】jiépǐ 过分讲究清洁的癖好 unhealthy obsession with cleanliness; mysophobia

【洁身自好】jié shēn zì hào 指保持自身纯洁，不同流合污。也指怕招惹是非，只关心自己，不关心公众事情。refuse to be contaminated by evil; preserve one's purity; mind one's own business in order to keep out of trouble

结 jié ❶ 在条状物上打疙瘩或用这种方式制成物品 tie; knit; knot; weave：～绳 tie a rope|～网 weave a net|～彩 adorn with festoons ❷ 条状物打成的疙瘩 knot made from strips：打～ knot|活～ slip-knot|死～ fast knot|蝴蝶～ butterfly knot ❸ 发生某种关系；结合 have a kind of connection：～晶 crystallize|～仇 start a feud; become enemies|集会～社 rally and form an association|～成硬块 solidify into a lump|～为夫妻 become a couple ❹ 结束；了结 end; get things done：～账 settle accounts|归根～底 in the final analysis|你去一次不就～了吗？Why don't you just go there and have it settled? ❺〈旧时 *old*〉保证负责的字据 written pledge; receipt：保～ keep receipts|具～ sign a guarantee

☞ jiē on p. 984

【结案】jié//àn 对案件做出判决或最后处理，使其结束 wind up a case

【结拜】jiébài 因为感情好或有共同目的而相约为兄弟姐妹 become sworn brothers or sisters

【结伴】jié//bàn（～儿 jié//bànr）跟人结成同伴；搭伴儿 go with：结个伴儿 have sb. for company|～远行 go or travel in a group|～赶集 go to the fair in a group

【结彩】jié//cǎi 用彩色绸布、纸条或松枝等结成美丽的装饰物 festoon; adorn or decorate with colourful festoons：悬灯～ be decorated with lanterns and colourful streamers|国庆节，商店门前都结着彩，喜气洋洋。On National Day shops are decorated with colourful streamers.

【结肠】jiécháng 大肠的中段，分为升结肠、横结肠、降结肠和乙状结肠四个部分 colon; middle section of the large intestine, including the colon ascendens, transverse colon, colon descendens and sigmoid colon; ☞ 升结肠 shēngjiécháng on p. 1712, 横结肠 héngjiécháng on p. 799, 降结肠 jiàngjiécháng on p. 627 and 乙状结肠 yǐzhuàng jiécháng on p. 2266

【结仇】jié//chóu 结下仇恨 start a feud; become enemies

【结存】jiécún 结算后余下(款项、货物) cash on hand; balance：将进货栏数字加上前一天的～，减去当天销货，记入当天～栏 add the numbers in the new stock column to the previous day's balance, then deduct the sales made on the day, and record them in the day's balance column

【结党营私】jié dǎng yíng sī 结合成党派以谋取私利 form a clique to pursue selfish interests; gang up for selfish purposes

【结缔组织】jiédì-zǔzhī 人和动物体内具有支持、营养、保护和连接机能的组织，由细胞和不具有细胞结构的活质构成。如骨、软骨、韧带等。connective tissue; tissues in human and animal bodies that support, nourish, protect and connect the body, made of cells and non-cell living tissues, e. g. bone, cartilage, ligament, etc.

【结发夫妻】jiéfà fūqī〈旧时 *old*〉指初成年结婚的夫妻（结发是束发的意思，指初成年）。也泛指第一次结婚的夫妻。couple who got married when they had just come of age; (in a broad sense) husband and wife by a first marriage (结发 *jiefa*: bundling one's hair, a token of coming of age)

【结构】jiégòu ❶ 各个组成部分的搭配和排列 structure; composition; construction：文章的～ structure of an essay|语言的～ language structure|原子～ construction of an atom ❷ 建筑物上承担重力或外力的部分的构造 structure; construction：砖木～ brick and wood structure|钢筋混凝土～ reinforced concrete structure

【结构式】jiégòushì 用元素符号通过价键相互连接表示分子中原子的排列顺序和结合方式的式子，在一定程度上反映分子的结构和化学性质。如分子式为 C_2H_6O 的化合物有两种，用结构式表示，分别为 structural formula; chemical formula that uses the symbols of elements connected by valence bonds to show how the atoms and bonds in a molecule are arranged and to reflect to a certain degree the structure of a molecule and its chemical properties, e. g. C_2H_6O represents two kinds of chemical compounds, whose structural formulas are respectively written as follows:

```
    H  H
    |  |
H—C—C—OH  (乙醇 ethanol)
    |  |
    H  H

   H      H
   |      |
H—C—O—C—H  (甲醚 methand)
   |      |
   H      H
```

【结关】jié//guān 指国际航行船舶于出口前办完海关手续、结清应付的各种款项，海关准许离港出航 customs clearance; (of international ships) get approval for departure from customs by going through all formalities and settling all kinds of payments for the exit

【结果】[1] jiéguǒ 在一定阶段,事物发展所达到的最后状态 result; outcome of development: 优良的成绩,是长期刻苦学习的~。Good grades are the results of long years of hard study.|经过一番争论,~他还是让步了。After a heated argument he finally gave in.

【结果】[2] jiéguǒ 将人杀死 kill somebody (多见于早期白话 oft. in early vernacular)
☞ jiē//guǒ on p.984

【结合】jiéhé ❶ 人或事物间发生密切联系 close relation between people or things: 理论~实际 combine theory with practice ❷ 指结为夫妻 become a couple

【结合能】jiéhénéng 两个或几个自由状态的粒子结合在一起时释放的能量。自由原子结合为分子时放出的能量叫做化学结合能,分散的核子组成原子核时放出的能量叫做原子核结合能。binding energy; energy produced by two or several free particles when combined. When two free atoms combine to become a molecule, the energy produced is called 'chemical binding energy'; when scattered nucleons combine to become atomic nucleus, the energy produced is called 'binding energy of nucleus'.

【结核】jiéhé ❶ 肺、肾、肠、淋巴结等组织由于结核杆菌的侵入而形成的病变 tubercle; pathological changes caused by tubercle bacilli on the tissues of lungs, kidneys, intestines, lymph nodes, etc. ❷ 指结核病 tuberculosis ❸ 可以溶解的矿物凝结在一块固体核周围形成的球状物,如钙质结核、铁质结核等 nodule; soluble minerals centring around a solid mass to form a ball-like substance, e.g. calcium nodule, iron nodule, etc.

【结核病】jiéhébìng 慢性传染病,病原体是结核杆菌。各个器官都能发生,人的结核病以肺结核为多,还有骨结核、肠结核等。除人外,牛等家畜也能感染。tuberculosis; chronic infectious disease of human beings and such domestic animals as cattle, caused by the tubercle bacillus attacking the body, most oft. in the human lungs, bones, intestines, etc.

【结喉】jiéhóu 喉结 Adam's apple

【结汇】jiéhuì 企业或个人按照外汇管理规定向银行买进或卖出外汇 settlement of exchange; (of an enterprise or an individual) buy and sell foreign currency through the bank in line with foreign exchange regulations

【结婚】jié//hūn 男子和女子经过合法手续结合成为夫妻 marry; get married; be married: ~证书 certificate of marriage|~登记 marriage registration

【结伙】jié//huǒ ❶ 跟人结成一伙 form a gang; gang up: 成群~ gang up ❷ 法律上指两人及两人以上预先通谋犯罪的组织 complicity; criminal group of two or more who together plan to commit crimes

【结集】jiéjí 把单篇的文章编在一起;编成集子 collect articles, etc., into a volume; compile a book of selections: ~出版 publish a selection

【结集】jiéjí (军队)调动到某地聚集 concentrate; mass: ~兵力 assemble the troops|在这个地区~了三个师。Three divisions are concentrated in this area.

【结交】jiéjiāo 跟人往来交际,使关系密切 make friends with; associate with: ~朋友 make a friend

【结焦】jiéjiāo 煤炭在隔绝空气的条件下加热,经过不完全燃烧,炼成焦炭 coke; coking; burn coal incompletely in isolation from air to produce coke

【结晶】jiéjīng ❶ 物质从液态(溶液或熔化状态)或气态形成晶体 crystallize; (of substances) become crystal from a liquid or gaseous state ❷ ☞ 晶体 jīngtǐ on p.1023 ❸〈比喻 *fig*.〉珍贵的成果 precious result; crystallization: 劳动的~ fruits of labour

【结晶体】jiéjīngtǐ ☞ 晶体 jīngtǐ p.1023

【结局】jiéjú 最后的结果;最终的局面 final result; outcome; ending: ~出人意料 unexpected ending|悲惨的~ tragic ending

【结论】jiélùn ❶ 从前提推论出来的判断 verdict; conclusion made from premises and inferences; also 断案 duàn//àn ❷ 对人或事物所下的最后的论断 final conclusion or judgement made about a person or event

【结盟】jié//méng 结成同盟 form an alliance; ally; align: 不~国家 non-aligned nations

【结膜】jiémó 从上下眼睑内面到角膜边缘的透明薄膜 conjunctiva; transparent membrane formed from the upper and lower eyelids to the edge of cornea; also 结合膜 jiéhémó; (图见 ☞ figure for 眼 yǎn on p.2210)

【结幕】jiémù 多幕剧中结尾的一幕。现用来比喻事情的高潮或结局。last act; final act; ending; final result; grand finale

【结亲】jiéqīn ❶ 结婚 get married; marry ❷ 两家因定亲结婚而成为亲戚 (of two families) become related by marriage

【结球甘蓝】jiéqiú gānlán 二年生草本植物,叶子大,平滑,层层重叠结成球状,花黄色。是普通的蔬菜。cabbage (*Brassica oleracea* var. *capitata*); biennial herb having yellow flowers and layers of smooth, big leaves that form a ball, a common vegetable; 通称 generally called 圆白菜 yuánbáicài or 洋白菜 yángbáicài; 不同地区有卷心菜、包心菜等名称 in some areas also called 卷心菜 juǎnxīncài, 包心菜 bāoxīncài, etc.

【结社】jiéshè 组织团体 organize; form an association

【结石】jiéshí 某些有空腔的器官及其导管内，由于有机物和无机盐类的沉积而形成的坚硬物质。如胆道(包括肝胆管、胆囊、胆总管)结石、泌尿器官各部的结石。stone; calculus; abnormal concretion in the body, usu. formed of organic substances and inorganic salts and found in organs like the billiary duct (including hepatic ducts, gallbladder and choledochus) and the urinary system

【结识】jiéshí 跟人相识并来往 get acquainted with sb.; get to know sb.: 这次出访，～了许多国际友人。We made acquaintances with many foreign friends on this trip.

【结束】jiéshù ❶ 发展或进行到最后阶段，不再继续 end; finish; conclude; wind up; close; make an end of sth.: 秋收快要～了。The harvest will come to an end. | 代表团～了对北京的访问。The delegation ended its visit to Beijing. ❷ 装束；打扮（多见于早期白话 oft. in early vernacular) dress up

【结束语】jiéshùyǔ 文章或正式讲话末了带有总结性的一段话 concluding remarks of an article or a formal speech

【结算】jiésuàn 把一个时期的各项经济收支往来核算清楚。有现金结算和非现金结算（只在银行转账）两种。settle accounts; close or wind up an account; clear the accounts of the revenues and expenditures over a period of time, through two ways, cash settlement and non-cash settlement (transactions through the bank only)

【结尾】jiéwěi 结束的阶段 ending; winding-up stage: ～工程 winding-up work of a project | 文章的～写得很精彩。The article has an exciting ending.

【结业】jié//yè 结束学业（多指短期训练的 usu. of short-term training) complete a course; wind up one's studies: ～考试 final examination | ～典礼 graduation ceremony

【结义】jiéyì 结拜 become sworn brothers or sisters

【结余】jiéyú ❶ 结算后余下 cash surplus; surplus; balance: 这个月～二十元钱。This month we have a 20 yuan surplus. ❷ 结算后余下的钱 money left after settling accounts

【结语】jiéyǔ 结束语 concluding remarks

【结缘】jié//yuán 结下缘分 form ties (of affection, friendship, etc.); become attached to: 他年轻的时候就和音乐结了缘。He became attached to music while a young man.

【结怨】jié//yuàn 结下仇恨 contract enmity; incur hatred

【结扎】jiézā 外科手术上，用特制的线把血管扎住，制止出血，或把输精管、输卵管等扎住，使管腔不通 ligation; ligature; bind blood vessels with a special cord to check bleeding during surgical operations, or tie the spermaduct and oviducts to block them

【结账】jié//zhàng 结算账目 settle (or square) accounts; balance the book: 饭后～，连酒带饭一百多元。The food and wine ran up a bill of more than 100 yuan.

【结子】jié·zi same as 结 jié ②

桔 jié ☞ below
☞ jú on p.1047

【桔槔】jiégāo 井上汲水的一种工具，在井旁树上或架子上挂一杠杆，一端系水桶，一端坠大石块，一起一落，汲水可以省力 well-sweep; sweep for drawing water out of a well; wooden apparatus or structure with a lever, one end of which is tied to a bucket and the other a stone that will go up and down to save energy when people draw water

【桔梗】jiégěng 多年生草本植物，叶子卵形或卵状披针形，花暗蓝色或暗紫白色，供观赏。根可入药。root of balloon flower (*Platycodon grandiflorum*); perennial herb having egg-shaped or egg-shaped lanceolate leaves, dark blue or dark purplish white flowers, and roots with medicinal value

倢 jié 〈书 *fml.*〉❶ same as 捷 jié ❷ same as 婕 jié

【倢伃】jiéyú same as 婕妤 jiéyú

桀 Jié 夏朝末代君王，即癸，相传是个暴君 Jie, i.e. Gui, last ruler of the Xia Dynasty (around.21st-16th century B.C.), traditionally considered a tyrant
〈古 *arch.*〉same as 杰(傑) jié

【桀骜】jié'ào 〈书 *fml.*〉倔强 contumacy; restiveness; stubbornness: ～不驯(性情倔强不驯顺) stubborn and intractable; obstinate and unruly

【桀犬吠尧】Jié quǎn fèi Yáo《汉书·邹阳传》记载，邹阳从狱中上书：'桀之犬可使吠尧'，桀的狗向尧狂吠，比喻走狗一心为它的主子效劳。*History of Han · Biography of Zou Yang*: Zou Yang wrote in prison to the emperor: 'The tyrant Jie's cur yapped at the sage king Yao.' The phrase depicts a lackey following whatever order is given by his master.

【桀纣】Jié-Zhòu 桀和纣，相传都是暴君。泛指暴君。Jie and Zhou, last rulers of the Xia and Shang dynasties respectively who were both despotic kings; (in a broad sense) despotic monarch

捷[1](**捷**) jié 快 prompt; nimble; quick: 敏～ agile | ～足先登。The swift-footed arrive first. *or* It's the early bird that catches the worm.

捷[2](**捷**) jié 战胜 victory; triumph: 我军大～。Our army won a great victory. | 连战连～ emerge triumphant through a succession of battles

【捷报】jiébào 胜利的消息 news of victory; report of a success: ～频传。News of victory keeps pouring in.

【捷径】jiéjìng 近路 shortcut;〈比喻 *fig*.〉能较快地达到目的的巧妙手段或办法 ingenious means or way to quickly reach one's destination or goal:另寻～ take another shortcut

【捷足先登】jié zú xiān dēng〈比喻 *fig*.〉行动敏捷,先达到目的 the swift-footed arrive first; early bird catches the worm

蛣(蠘) jié 节肢动物,体长一寸左右,呈细杆状,胸部有脚七对,第二对特别大。生活在海藻上。stick insect (*Phasmidae*); walking-stick; arthropod about one *cun* long in the form of a thin stick, having seven pairs of legs at its chest with the second being especially large, and living among algae; also 麦秆虫 màigǎnchóng or 海藻虫 hǎizǎochóng

偈 jié〈书 *fml*.〉勇武 brave; martial
☞ jì on p.921

袺 jié〈书 *fml*.〉用衣襟兜着 use the front of one's jacket as a bag

婕 jié [婕妤](jiéyú)〈古代 *arch*.〉女官名,是帝王妃嫔的称号 official title conferred upon an accomplished imperial concubine; also 倢伃 jiéyú

絜 jié〈书 *fml*.〉same as 洁 jié
☞ xié on p.2122

颉 jié 用于人名 used in a person's name
☞ xié on p.2122

楬 jié〈书 *fml*.〉用做标志的小木桩 small pile of wood as a mark

睫 jié 睫毛 eyelash; lash:目不交～ not sleep a wink

【睫毛】jiémáo 眼睑上下边缘的细毛。有阻挡灰尘、昆虫等侵入眼内及减弱强烈光线对眼睛的刺激等作用。eyelash; lash; fine hairs at the edge of the eyelids, with the function of preventing dust and insects from entering the eyes and alleviating the irritation of strong sunlight to the eyes

蜐 jié ☞ 石蜐 shíjié on p.1736

截 jié ❶ 切断;割断(长条形的东西) cut (sth. shaped like a strip); sever:～头去尾 cut the beginning and the end|把木条～成两段 cut a wood stick into two pieces ❷ (～儿 jiér)〈量词 *classifier*〉段 section; chunk; length:一～儿木头 a piece of wood|话说了半～儿 pause in the middle of a sentence ❸ 阻拦 stop; check; stem:～留 withhold|快把马～住,别让它跑了。Stop the horse and don't let it run away. ❹ 截止 by (a specified time); up to:～至昨天,已有三百多人报名。Up to yesterday more than 300 people had entered their names.

【截长补短】jié cháng bǔ duǎn〈比喻 *fig*.〉用长处补短处 take from the long to add to the short; draw on the strength of one to offset the weakness of the other:我们要彼此～,共同提高。We should give full play to our abilities to make up for our shortcomings and make progress together.

【截断】jié//duàn ❶ 切断 cut off; block:高温的火焰能～钢板。A flame at high temperature can cut a steel plate. ❷ 打断;拦住 cut short; interrupt:电话铃声～了他的话。He was interrupted by the ringing of the telephone.

【截稿】jiégǎo 截止收稿 stop accepting incoming articles or contributions:～日期 deadline for contributions; closing date

【截获】jiéhuò 中途夺取到或捉到 intercept and capture:～对方密电 intercept and capture the coded message from the enemy|一辆走私车被海关～。A smuggler's truck was captured by the customs.

【截击】jiéjī 在半路上截住打击(敌人) intercept:～敌人的增援部队 intercept the enemy's reinforcements

【截流】jiéliú 在水道中截断水流,以提高水位或改变水流的方向 dam a river; cut the flow of a river to increase the water level or change the direction of flow:～工程 river damming project

【截留】jiéliú 扣留所经手的(物品、款项等) intercept and hold on to; retain for one's own use; withhold:～税款 withhold tax funds|文稿被～。The essay was retained.

【截门】jiémén 阀的一种,一般安在管道中间,把手多呈环状,旋紧时管道阻塞 pipe valve; one type of valve, generally fixed in the middle of a conduit, having a ring-shaped handle and used to block the conduit when tightened

【截面】jiémiàn ☞ 剖面 pōumiàn on p.1496

【截取】jiéqǔ 从中取(一段) cut off a section of sth.:～文章开头的几句 quote the first few sentences of an essay

【截然】jiérán 形容界限分明,像割断一样 sharply; completely:～不同 completely different; as different as black and white; poles apart|普及工作和提高工作是不能～分开的。The work of popularization and enhancement cannot be completely separated.

【截瘫】jiétān 下肢全部或部分瘫痪,多由脊髓疾病或外伤引起 paraplegia; complete or partial paralysis of the lower half of the body, oft. caused by illness or damage to the spinal cord

【截肢】jié//zhī 医学上指四肢的某一部分发生严重病变或受到创伤而无法医治时,把这一部分肢体割掉 amputate; cut a limb that has suffered serious pathological changes or is incurably damaged

【截止】jiézhǐ (到一定期限)停止 end; close (by a specified time):报名在昨天已经～。Registration closed yesterday.

【截至】jiézhì 截止到(某个时候) by (a specified time); up to:报名日期～本月底止。The closing date for registration is by the end of this month.

【截子】jié·zi 截② section; chunk; length: 活儿干了半～。Half of the work has been finished. | 走了一大～山路。(They) covered a long stretch of the mountain path. | 他的外语比你差一大～哪。Your English is far better than his.

榤 jié 〈书 *fml.*〉鸡栖息的横木 wooden bar on which chickens roost

碣 jié 石碑 stele; monument; stone tablet: 墓～ tombstone | 残碑断～ crumbling monuments and dilapidated walls; desolate scene

鲒 jié 古书上说的一种蚌 freshwater mussel (as recorded in ancient books)

竭 jié ❶ 尽 exhaust; use up: ～力 do one's utmost; use every ounce of one's energy; try by every possible means | 力～声嘶 be hoarse and exhausted; shout oneself hoarse; shout oneself blue in the face | 取之不尽,用之不～ inexhaustible ❷ 〈书 *fml.*〉干涸 dry; dry up: 枯～ dried up; exhausted | 山崩川～ mountains collapsing and rivers drying up

【竭诚】jiéchéng 竭尽忠诚;全心全意 wholeheartedly; with all one's heart: ～帮助 help wholeheartedly | ～拥护 give wholehearted support | ～为读者服务 serve the readers wholeheartedly

【竭尽】jiéjìn 用尽 use up; exhaust: ～全力 pull out the stops; spare no effort; exert one's utmost; do all one can

【竭蹶】jiéjué 〈书 *fml.*〉原指走路艰难,后用来形容经济困难 (orig.) walk with difficulty; destitute; impoverished: ～状态 impoverished state | 财政～ financial difficulties

【竭力】jiélì 尽力 do one's utmost; use every ounce of one's energy; try by every possible means: 尽心～ try one's best | 我们一定～完成任务。We must try our best to fulfil the task.

【竭泽而渔】jié zé ér yú 排尽湖中或池中的水捉鱼 drain the pond to get all the fish; 〈比喻 *fig.*〉取之不留余地,只顾眼前利益,不顾长远利益 kill the goose that lays the golden eggs

羯¹ jié 羯羊 wether

羯² Jié 我国古代民族,是匈奴的一个别支,居住在今山西省东南部,东晋时曾在黄河流域建立过后赵国(公元 311-334) Jie people; branch of the Huns (Xiongnus) living in the southeast of present-day Shanxi Province, who founded the State of Later Zhao (311-334) in the Yellow River valley during the Eastern Jin Dynasty

【羯鼓】jiégǔ 我国古代的一种鼓。两面蒙皮,腰部细。据说来源于羯族。Jie drum; a type of drum in ancient China, covered with leather, narrow in the middle and said to come from the Jie people

【羯羊】jiéyáng 阉割了的公羊 wether

jiě (ㄐㄧㄝˇ)

姐 jiě ❶ 姐姐 elder sister; big sister: 大～ eldest sister | 二～ second elder sister | ～妹 sisters ❷ 亲戚中同辈而年纪比自己大的女子(一般不包括可以称做嫂的人) woman of the same generation who is older than oneself (but generally not including the wife of one's elder brother): 表～ elder female cousin (on the maternal side) | 远房～ distantly related elder sister ❸ 称呼年轻的女子 form of address for a young woman: 杨三～ Third Sister Yang

【姐夫】jiě·fu 姐姐的丈夫 elder sister's husband; brother-in-law

【姐姐】jiě·jie ❶ 同父母(或只同父、只同母)而年纪比自己大的女子 elder sister; older girl or woman having the same parents or parent ❷ 同族同辈而年纪比自己大的女子(一般不包括可以称做嫂的人 usu. not including sister-in-law) girl or woman who is of the same generation as one but older in age: 叔伯～ elder female cousin (on the paternal side)

【姐妹】jiěmèi ❶ 姐姐和妹妹 elder sister and younger sister a) 不包括本人 excluding the person specified: 她没有～,只有一个哥哥。She has no sisters, but an elder brother. b) 包括本人 inclusive of the person specified: 她们～俩都是先进生产者。The two sisters are both excellent workers. | 她就～一个(没有姐姐或妹妹)。She is the only sister. ❷ 弟兄姐妹;同胞 brothers and sisters; compatriots

【姐儿】jiěr 〈方 *dial.*〉same as 姐妹 jiěmèi ①b and ②: 你们～几个? How many sisters are there in your family? | ～仨里头就数她最会说话。She is the best talker among the three sisters.

【姐儿们】jiěr·men 姐妹们 sisters

【姐丈】jiězhàng 姐夫 elder sister's husband; brother-in-law

毑 jiě ☞ 娭毑 āijiě on p. 4

解(觧) jiě ❶ 分开 separate; divide: ～剖 anatomy | 瓦～ disintegrate; collapse; crumble | 难～难分 be inextricably involved (in a dispute); be locked (in a struggle) ❷ 把束缚着或系着的东西打开 untie; undo: ～扣儿 undo the button | ～衣服 untie the clothes ❸ 解除 free; remove; relieve: ～职 dismiss from office; relieve sb. of his post | ～渴 quench one's thirst | ～乏 recover from fatigue; refresh oneself ❹ 解释 interpret; explain: ～说 explain verbally | ～答 answer | 注～ notes ❺ 了解;明白 understand; comprehend: 令人不～ puzzling | 通俗易～ popular and easy to understand ❻ 解手 release oneself：大～ defecate｜小～ urinate ❼ 代数方程式中未知数的值，例如 $x+16=0$，$x=-16$，-16就是 $x+16=0$ 这个方程的解 solution；answer to an algebra equation，e.g. $x+16=0$，and $x=-16$，so -16 is the solution for the equation ❽ 演算方程式；求方程式中未知数的值 solve the problem in an equation；find the unknown number in an equation

☞ jiè on p.1002 and xiè on p.2125

【解饱】jiěbǎo〈方 *dial.*〉（东西）吃下去耐饥 (of food) hunger-allaying

【解馋】jiě//chán 在食欲上得到了满足（多指吃到想吃到的食物）satisfy a craving for one's favourite food：这一顿包子真～。The steamed stuffed bun really satisfied my craving for good food.

【解嘲】jiě//cháo 用言语或行动来掩饰被别人嘲笑的事情 try to explain things away when being ridiculed：自我～ find excuses to console oneself｜聊以～ make a lame attempt to explain things away when ridiculed；in a feeble attempt to silence jeers

【解愁】jiě//chóu 排解忧愁或愁闷 get rid of one's worries

【解除】jiěchú 去掉；消除 remove；relieve；get rid of：～警报 sound the all-clear｜～顾虑 free one's mind of misgivings｜～武装 disarm｜～职务 remove sb. from his post；relieve sb. of his office

【解答】jiědá 解释回答（问题）answer；explain：《几何习题～》*The Key to Geometry Questions*｜他无法～我的提问。He cannot answer my question.

【解冻】jiě//dòng ❶ 冰冻的江河、土地融化 thaw；unfreeze：一到春天，江河都～了。Once spring comes，all the rivers thaw.｜拖拉机翻耕～的土地。Tractors are ploughing the thawed land.◇两国关系开始～。The relations between the two countries began to thaw. ❷ 解除对资金等的冻结 stop a freeze on funds，etc.

【解毒】jiě//dú ❶ 中和机体内有危害的物质 detoxify；detoxicate ❷〈中医 *Chin. med.*〉指解除上火、发热等症状 relieve internal heat or fever

【解饿】jiě//è 消除饿的感觉 satisfy one's hunger：饼干不～。Biscuits cannot satisfy (my) hunger.

【解乏】jiě//fá 解除疲乏，恢复体力 recover from fatigue：穿着棉衣睡觉不～。Sleeping in a cotton-padded coat cannot relieve fatigue.

【解放】jiěfàng ❶ 解除束缚，得到自由或发展 liberate；emancipate：～思想 emancipate minds｜～生产力 liberating the productive forces ❷ 推翻反动统治，在我国特指1949年推翻国民党统治 liberation，esp. referring to China's Liberation from the rule of the Kuomintang in 1949：～前 before Liberation｜～那年我才15岁。In the year of Liberation，I was only 15 years old.

【解放军】jiěfàngjūn 为解放人民而组织起来的军队，特指中国人民解放军 liberation army；Chinese People's Liberation Army

【解放区】jiěfàngqū 推翻了反动统治、建立了人民政权的地区，特指抗日战争和解放战争时期，中国共产党领导的军队从敌伪统治和国民党统治下解放出来的地区 liberated area；area where the reactionary rule is overthrown and a people's government is set up；esp. referring to areas liberated by the army under the leadership of the Chinese Communist Party from Japanese occupation during the War of Resistance against Japan or the Kuomintang rule during the War of Liberation

【解放战争】jiěfàng zhànzhēng 被压迫的民族或阶级为了争取解放而进行的战争，特指我国第三次国内革命战争 liberation war of an oppressed nation or class；War of Liberation (1945-1949)，the Third Revolutionary Civil War of China

【解雇】jiě//gù 停止雇用 discharge；dismiss；fire

【解恨】jiě//hèn 消除心中的愤恨 vent one's hatred；have one's hatred slaked

【解甲归田】jiě jiǎ guī tián 指军人离开军队，回家务农 take off one's armour and return to the land；be demobilized and return to farming

【解禁】jiě//jìn 解除禁令 lift a ban

【解救】jiějiù 使脱离危险或困难 save；rescue；deliver：～危难 deliver from danger and disaster｜～受灾的同胞 rescue the disaster-stricken compatriots

【解决】jiějué ❶ 处理问题使有结果 solve；resolve；settle：～困难 overcome a difficulty；find the way out of a predicament｜～问题 solve a problem；settle a question (or an issue)；work out a solution｜～矛盾 resolve contradictions ❷ 消灭（坏人）wipe out (evildoers)：残余匪徒全给～了。In that battle we finished off all the enemy troops.

【解渴】jiě//kě 消除渴的感觉 quench one's thirst：热天喝酸梅汤最～。The sweet-and-sour plum juice is the best to quench thirst in hot weather.｜喝杯茶解解渴。Drinking a cup of tea can quench your thirst.

【解铃系铃】jiě líng xì líng 法眼和尚问大家：'老虎脖子上的金铃谁能解下来？'大家回答不出。正好泰钦禅师来了，法眼又问这个问题。泰钦禅师说：'系上去的人能解下来。'（见于《指月录》）Monk Fayan asked，'Who can untie the golden bell on the neck of the tiger?' No one was able to offer an answer，but just at the moment，Monk Taiqin came and Fayan asked the question again. Taiqin answered, 'The one who tied it can untie it.' (See *Album of Zhiyue*.)〈比喻 *fig.*〉由谁惹出来的麻烦还由谁去解决 Whoever started the trouble should end it. also 解铃还须系铃人 jiě líng hái xū xì líng rén

【解码】jiěmǎ 用特定方法把数码还原成它所代表的内容或将电脉冲信号转换成它所表示的信息、数据等的过程。解码在无线电技术和通讯等方面广泛应用。decipher; decode; process of using methods widely used in radio technology, communications, etc. to convert numerals back into the context they represent, or electric pulse codes into information and data, etc.

【解闷】jiě//mèn (～儿 jiě//mènr) 排除烦闷 divert oneself from boredom; amuse: 闲着没事,看小说解解闷儿 divert oneself from boredom by reading novels when there is nothing to do

【解民倒悬】jiě mín dào xuán《孟子·公孙丑上》:'万乘之国行仁政,民之悦之,犹解倒悬也。'后用'解民倒悬'比喻把人民从困苦危难的处境中解救出来。*Mencius·Gongsun Chou* (*I*): 'A country with 10,000 chariots adopts policies of benevolence and the people will be overjoyed as if they were saved from being suspended in midair upside down.' The phrase has later been used to mean 'relieve people of their worries and sufferings' or 'deliver people out of their misery'.

【解难】jiě//nán 解决困难或疑难 overcome difficulties; work out a puzzle: 释疑～。Unravel the difficult points, and work out the puzzle.

【解难】jiě//nàn 解除危难 remove danger, and tide over difficulties: 排忧～ relieve sb. of worries and help solve their problems | 消灾～ eliminate calamities, and tide over difficulties

【解囊】jiěnáng 解开口袋,指拿出财物来(帮助人) open one's purse to help sb. with money: 慷慨～ be generous enough to help others with money | ～相助 help sb. generously with money

【解聘】jiě//pìn 解除职务,不再聘用 dismiss an employee

【解剖】jiěpōu ❶ 为了研究人体或动植物体各器官的组织构造,用特制的刀、剪把人体或动植物体剖开 dissect; cut open the body of a human being, animal or plant with special knives and scissors to study the tissue structure of every organ inside ❷〈比喻 *fig.*〉分析;剖析 analyse; criticize: 严于～自己 be strict in criticizing oneself ideologically; be strict in appraising oneself

【解气】jiě//qì 消除心中的气愤 vent one's spleen; work off one's anger

【解劝】jiěquàn 劝解;安慰 soothe; mollify; comfort

【解散】jiěsàn ❶ 集合的人分散开 dismiss: 队伍～后,大家都在操场上休息喝水。After they were dismissed, the soldiers rested and drank water on the drill ground. ❷ 取消(团体或集会) disband an organization; call off (a rally)

【解释】jiěshì ❶ 分析阐明 explain; expound; interpret: 经过无数次的研究和实验,这种自然现象才得到科学的～。Only after numerous studies and experiments was this natural phenomenon explained in a scientific way. ❷ 说明含义、原因、理由等 construe; explain implications, reasons or causes: ～词句 explain a word or sentence | ～误会 clear up a misunderstanding

【解手】[1] jiě//shǒu (～儿 jiě//shǒur) 排泄大便或小便 relieve oneself; go to the toilet (or lavatory)

【解手】[2] jiě//shǒu〈书 *fml.*〉分手 part company

【解说】jiěshuō 口头上解释说明 explain orally; comment: 讲解员给观众～这种机器的构造和性能。An interpreter was explaining to the visitors the structure and performance of this type of machine.

【解体】jiětǐ ❶ 物体的结构分解 disintegrate ❷ 崩溃;瓦解 disintegrate; collapse; crumble: 联盟～。The alliance fell apart. | 封建经济～。The feudal economy collapsed.

【解脱】jiětuō ❶〈佛教用语 *Budd.*〉摆脱苦恼,得到自在 free or extricate oneself ❷ 摆脱 shake off; free oneself from: 诸事纷扰,使他难以～。He cannot free himself from so much confusion. ❸ 开脱 absolve: 为人～罪责 absolve sb. from guilt

【解围】jiě//wéi ❶ 解除敌军的包围 force an enemy to raise a siege; rescue sb. from a siege ❷ 泛指使人摆脱不利或受窘的处境 help sb. out of a predicament; save sb. from embarrassment: 要不是你来～,我还真下不了台。If not for your help, I would have suffered real embarrassment.

【解悟】jiěwù 在认识上由不了解到了解 come to understand

【解吸】jiěxī 使所吸收或吸附的气体或溶质放出,如用活性炭吸附二氧化氮后,加热或降压使二氧化氮逸出 let out an absorbed gas or solute, e.g. release nitrogen dioxide absorbed by active carbon by heating or reducing pressure

【解析几何】jiěxī jǐhé 用代数方法解决几何学问题的学科。解析几何中,用坐标表示点,用坐标间的关系表示和研究空间图形的性质。analytic geometry; discipline of learning using algebraic methods to solve geometric problems. In analytic geometry, coordinates are used to denote points, and the relations between coordinates are used to represent and study the nature of spatial patterns.

【解严】jiě//yán 解除戒严状态 declare the end of martial law; lift a curfew

【解疑】jiě//yí ❶ 消除疑虑 get rid of worries: 经他一说，我才解了疑。His remarks helped me get rid of my worries. ❷ 解释疑难 explain difficult points: 词典可以为读者释难～。Dictionaries can help readers explain difficult points.

【解颐】jiěyí〈书 *fml*.〉开颜而笑 break into a smile（颐 *yí*：面颊 face）

【解忧】jiě//yōu 排解心中的忧愁 allay sorrow; assuage grief: 排难～ tide over difficulties and allay misgivings

【解约】jiě//yuē 取消原来的约定 terminate an agreement; cancel (or rescind) a contract

【解职】jiě//zhí 解除职务；免职 dismiss from office; discharge; relieve sb. of his post: 因工作不力而被～。He was relieved of his post because of slackness in his work.

檞 jiě 檞树，一种木质像松的树 a kind of tree similar to pine

jiè（ㄐㄧㄝˋ）

介[1] jiè ❶ 在两者当中 in between: ～绍 introduce | 媒～ media | 这座山～于两县之间。The mountain lies between two counties. ❷ 介绍 introduce: 内容简～ brief introduction to the contents ❸ 存留；放在（心里）take to heart: ～意 mind | ～怀 mind ❹（Jiè）姓 a surname

介[2] jiè 甲 armour: ～胄 armour | ～虫 scale insect

介[3] jiè〈书 *fml*.〉耿直；有骨气 upright: 耿～ honest and frank

介[4] jiè 古戏曲剧本中，指示角色表演动作时的用语，如笑介、饮酒介等 term used in ancient play scripts to describe movements in a performance, e. g. laughing, drinking wine, etc.

【介词】jiècí 用在名词、代词或名词性词组的前边，合起来表示方向、对象等的词，如'从、自、往、朝、在、当（方向、处所或时间），把、对、同、为（对象或目的），以、按照（方式），比、跟、同（比较），被、叫、让（被动）' preposition; word that precedes a noun, pronoun or noun phrase to express direction, object, etc., e.g. 从 cóng, 自 zì, 往 wǎng, 朝 cháo, 在 zài, and 当 dāng (indicating direction, location or time); 把 bǎ, 对 duì, 同 tóng and 为 wèi (indicating objects or purposes); 以 yǐ, 按照 ànzhào (indicating methods), 比 bǐ, 跟 gēn, 同 tóng (indicating comparison), and 被 bèi, 叫 jiào and 让 ràng (indicating passive voice)

【介怀】jiè//huái 介意 mind: 毫不～ not mind at all

【介壳】jièqiào 蛤、螺等软体动物的外壳，主要由石灰质和色素构成，质地坚硬，有保护身体的作用 shell; testa; exterior skin of molluscs, such as clams and snails, etc., composed mainly of lime and pigment substances, and of a very hard texture to protect the body

【介入】jièrù 插进两者之间干预其事 intervene; interpose; get involved: 不～他们两人之间的争端。Don't get involved in the dispute between those two.

【介绍】jièshào ❶ 使双方相识或发生联系 introduce; present: ～信 letter of introduction; reference (letter) | ～人 one who introduces or recommends sb.; referee; sponsor | 我给你～一下，这位是张先生。Let me introduce a new friend to you, this is Mr. Zhang. ❷ 引进；带入（新的人或事物）recommend; suggest: ～入会 be recommended to a club | 中国京剧已被～到许多国家。The Peking Opera has been introduced to many countries. ❸ 使了解或熟悉 clue sb. on sth. or sb.; let know; brief: ～情况 let (sb.) in on the situation | ～先进经验 give a briefing on advanced experience

【介意】jiè//yì 把不愉快的事记在心里；在意（多用于否定词后 oft. in the negative）take offence; mind: 刚才这句话我是无心中说的，你可别～。I didn't mean to say it on purpose, so I hope you will not take offence.

【介音】jièyīn 韵母中主要元音前面的元音，普通话语音中有'i、u、ü'三个介音，例如'天'tiān 的介音是'i'，'多'duō 的介音是'u'，'略'lüè 的介音是'ü' medial or semivowel of a final; i, u and ü being the three semivowels in standard Chinese, as in 天 tiān, 多 duō and 略 lüè; ☞ 韵母 yùnmǔ on p. 2381

【介质】jièzhì 一种物质存在于另一种物质内部时，后者就是前者的介质；某些波状运动（如声波、光波等）借以传播的物质叫做这些波状运动的介质 medium; substance in which another substance exists, or substance through which certain undulant waves (e. g. sound waves, light waves, etc.) transmit; also 媒质 méizhì

【介子】jièzǐ 质量介于质量轻的基本粒子（如电子）和质量重的基本粒子（如核子）之间的基本粒子。种类较多，性质不稳定，有的带正电，有的带负电，有的不带电，能用来轰击原子核，引起核反应。meson; mesotron; elementary particle existing between a light-mass elementary particle (e.g. an electron) and a heavy-mass elementary particle (e. g. a nucleon), of various types, unsteady in nature, some carrying a positive electrical charge, some negative, and still some without electrical charge, used to bombard the atomic nucleus to cause nuclear reaction

价 jiè〈书 *fml*.〉称被派遣传送东西或传达事情的人 person who is dispatched to deliver things or convey a message
☞ jià on p. 935 and ·jie on p. 1002

戒 jiè ❶ 防备;警惕 guard against: ～心 vigilance; wariness | ～备 guard; take precautions; be on the alert | ～骄～躁 guard against arrogance and rashness; be on one's guard against conceit and impetuosity ❷ same as 诫 jiè ❸ 戒除 give up; drop; quit: ～烟 quit smoking ❹ 指禁止做的事情 exhort; admonish; warn: 开～ break an abstinence | 杀～ prohibition against taking life ❺〈佛教 *Budd.*〉戒律 commandments: 受～ ordination ❻ 戒指 (finger) ring: 钻～(镶钻石的戒指) diamond ring

【戒备】jièbèi ❶ 警戒防备 guard; take precautions; be on the alert: ～森严 tight security ❷ 对人有戒心而加以防备 be on the alert; be wary: 你对他应有所～。You should be wary of him.

【戒尺】jièchǐ〈旧时 *old*〉教师对学生施行体罚时所用的木板 ferule; teacher's ruler for beating pupils

【戒除】jièchú 改掉(不良嗜好) give up (a bad habit); drop; stop: ～烟酒 stop smoking and drinking

【戒刀】jièdāo〈旧时 *old*〉僧人所佩带的刀,按戒律只用来割衣物,不许杀生 monk's knife, meant to be used only to cut clothes and objects, and not for killing, according to Buddhist commandments

【戒牒】jièdié ☞ 度牒 dùdié on p. 482

【戒忌】jièjì ❶ same as 禁忌 jìnjì ① ❷ 对忌讳的事情存有戒心 be wary of violating taboos

【戒惧】jièjù 警惕和畏惧 vigilance and fear: ～心理 vigilant and fearful mentality

【戒律】jièlǜ 多指有条文规定的宗教徒必须遵守的生活准则 religious discipline; commandment: 犯～ break religious discipline | 清规～ all the regulations

【戒条】jiètiáo same as 戒律 jièlǜ

【戒心】jièxīn 戒备之心;警惕心 vigilance; wariness: 存有～ keep a wary eye on sb.

【戒严】jiè//yán 国家遇到战争或特殊情况时,在全国或某一地区内采取非常措施,如增设警戒、组织搜查、限制交通等 enforce martial law; impose a curfew; cordon off an area; adopt extraordinary measures in a country or an area in times of war or under special conditions, e. g. increased security, thorough searches, traffic restrictions, etc.

【戒指】jiè·zhi (～儿 jiè·zhir) 套在手指上做纪念或装饰用的小环,用金属、玉石等制成 (finger) ring; ring worn on a finger as a sign of commemoration or as ornamentation, made of metal, jade, precious stone, etc.

芥 jiè ❶ 芥菜 leaf mustard: ～末 mustard | ～子 mustard seed ❷ 小草,比喻轻微纤细的事物 grass, referring to sth. very small: 草～ trifle; mere nothing; trash | 纤～ minute; tiny; very small

☞ p. 622 gài

【芥菜】jiècài 一年或二年生草本植物,开黄色小花,果实细长。种子黄色,有辣味,磨成粉末,叫芥末,用做调味品。芥菜变种很多,形态各异,按用途分为叶用芥菜(如雪里红),茎用芥菜(如榨菜)和根用芥菜(如大头菜)。mustard (*Brassica*); annual or biannual herb having small yellow flowers, long thin fruit, and spicy yellow seeds that are ground into powder and used as a spice, of various strains, in different shapes and divided into leaf mustards like potherb mustard, stem mustards for preserved pickles, and root mustards like kohlrabi

☞ gàicài on p. 622

【芥蒂】jièdì〈书 *fml.*〉梗塞的东西 obstruction;〈比喻 *fig.*〉心里的嫌隙或不快 ill feeling; unpleasantness; grudge: 经过调解,两人心中都不再有什么～了。Ill feelings between them evaporated through mediation.

【芥末】jiè·mo 调味品,芥子研成的粉末,味辣 mustard; ground mustard seeds; also 芥黄 jièhuáng

【芥子】jièzǐ 芥菜的种子 mustard seed

【芥子气】jièzǐqì 有机化合物,化学式 $(C_2H_4Cl)_2S$。无色油状液体,有芥末或大蒜味。有剧毒,能引起皮肤溃烂,战争中曾用做毒气。mustard gas; organic chemical compound whose chemical formula is $(C_2H_4Cl)_2S$, a colourless, poisonous oily liquid with a mustard or garlic smell, which can cause skin cankers and once used in war as a poisonous gas

玠 jiè〈书 *fml.*〉大的圭 a kind of large elongated pointed tablet of jade held in the hands of ancient rulers on ceremonial occasions

届 jiè ❶ 到(时候) fall due: ～期 on the appointed date ❷〈量词 *classifier*〉略同于'次',用于定期的会议或毕业的班级等 similar to 'time', used for regular meetings, graduating classes, etc.: 第二～全国人民代表大会 Second National People's Congress | 本～毕业生 this year's graduates

【届满】jièmǎn 规定的担任职务的时期已满 at the expiration of one's term of office: ～离任 resign at the expiration of one's term of office

【届期】jièqī 到预定的日期 when the day comes; on the appointed date: ～务请光临。Your presence is requested for the occasion.

【届时】jièshí 到时候 when the time comes; at the appointed time; on the occasion: ～务请出席。You are supposed to be present on the occasion.

界 jiè ❶ 界限 boundary; demarcation line; dividing line; limits; bounds: 地～ land

J

boundaries|边～ boundary|省～ provincial border|国～ national boundaries|山西和陕西以黄河为～。The boundary between Shanxi and Shaanxi is the Yellow River. ❷ 一定的范围 scope; extent: 眼～ field of vision; outlook|管～ jurisdiction; precinct ❸ 职业、工作或性别等相同的一些社会成员的总体 circles; collective reference to people of the same profession, trade or sex: 文艺～ art circles|科学～ scientific circles|妇女～ women's circles|各～人士 people from all walks of life ❹ 指大自然中动物、植物、矿物等的最大的类别 (of flora and fauna and mineral ores) primary division; kingdom: 无机～ inorganic world|有机～ organic world ❺ 年代地层单位的第二级,跟界相应的地质年代叫做代。界以下为系。erathem; second level in the division in stratigraphy, corresponding to 'era' in geochronology where below 'erathem' is 'system'

【界碑】jièbēi 在交界的地方树立的碑,用做分界的标志 boundary tablet; boundary marker

【界标】jièbiāo 分界的标志,如界碑、界石等 boundary tablet; boundary marker

【界尺】jièchǐ 画直线用的木条,没有刻度 non-graduated ruler

【界定】jièdìng 划定界限;确定所属范围 decide; define: 两个单位的分工要有明确的～。The division of labour between the two departments should be well defined.|是优是劣自有客观标准来～。The good or bad of it will be judged with objective yardsticks.

【界河】jièhé 两国或两地区分界的河流 boundary river

【界面】jièmiàn 物体和物体之间的接触面 place where two objects come into contact

【界山】jièshān 两国或两地区分界的山 mountain serving as a dividing line between two countries or two regions

J

【界石】jièshí 用做分界标志的石碑或石块 boundary stone or tablet

【界说】jièshuō 定义的旧称 (old) definition

【界限】jièxiàn ❶ 不同事物的分界 demarcation line; dividing line; bounds: 划清～ draw a clear line of demarcation|～分明。The limits are obvious. ❷ 尽头处;限度 limit; end: 殖民主义者的野心是没有～的。The wild ambitions of the colonists were insatiable.

【界限量规】jièxiàn liángguī 量具的一种,有两个测量端,分别表示两个不同的尺寸,工件能通过其中一端而不能通过另一端即为合格品。测量轴或凸形工件的叫卡规;测量孔眼或凹形工件的叫塞规。limit gauge; type of gauge having two ends representing two different measurements, so that a product is regarded as up to standard when it passes through one end but not the other. Callipers are used to measure axes or protruding workpieces, while plug gauges are used to measure eyelets or concave workpieces. also 极限量规 jíxiàn liángguī or 量规 liángguī

【界线】jièxiàn ❶ 两个地区分界的线 boundary line: 跨越～cross a boundary line ❷ 不同事物的分界;界限① demarcation line; dividing line; limits; bounds ❸ 某些事物的边缘 boundary line: 标出房基地～ mark out the boundary line for the foundations of a building

【界桩】jièzhuāng 在交界地方树立的桩子,用做分界的标志 boundary marker

疥 jiè 疥疮 scabies

【疥虫】jièchóng 寄生虫,体很小,椭圆扁平,身上有毛,有四对脚,脚上有吸盘。寄生在人的皮肤下,引起疥疮。sarcoptic mange mite (*Sarcoptes*); tiny, flat, oval-shaped, hairy parasite, having four pairs of legs each having a sucker, living underneath human skin and causing scabies

【疥疮】jièchuāng 传染性皮肤病,病原体是疥虫,多发生在手腕、手指、臂部、腹部等部位。症状是局部起丘疹而不变颜色,非常刺痒。scabies; contagious skin disease caused by sarcoptic mites, mostly found on wrists, fingers, arms, bellies, etc., with severe itching and the eruption of papules without changing skin colour

【疥蛤蟆】jièhá·ma 蟾蜍的通称 general term for 蟾蜍 chánchú

诫 jiè 警告;劝告 warn; admonish: 告～ admonition|规～ persuade

蚧 jiè ☞ 蛤蚧 géjiè on p.654

借[1] jiè ❶ 暂时使用别人的物品或金钱;借进 borrow (things or money): 向图书馆～书 borrow a book from the library|跟人～钱 borrow money from sb.|把笔～给我用一下。Could you lend me your pen? ❷ 把物品或金钱暂时供别人使用;借出 lend: ～书给他 lend him a book|～钱给人 lend money to others

借[2] (**藉**) jiè ❶ 假托 on the pretext of: ～故 find an excuse|～端 use sth. as a pretext ❷ 凭借;利用 make use of; take advantage of (an opportunity, etc.): ～助 have the aid of; draw support from|～手(假手) ask for a favour|～着灯光看书 read under a lamp

【借词】jiècí 从另一种语言中吸收过来的词 loanword; loan; word borrowed from another language; ☞ 外来语 wàiláiyǔ on p.1969

【借代】jièdài 修辞方式,不直接把所要说的事物名称说出来,而用跟它有关系的另一种事物名称代替它。如'红领巾参加植树劳动'中的'红领巾'就是代替'少先队员'。transferred epithet; rhetorical device of saying the name of an object indirectly by using the name of another object to replace it, e.g. 'The Red Scarves took part in planting the trees', in which 'Red Scarves' refers to the 'Young Pioneers'

【借贷】jièdài ❶ 借(钱) borrow money: ~无门 find no one to borrow money from ❷ 指簿记或资产表上的借方或贷方 debit and credit sides in an accountant's book or asset chart

【借刀杀人】jiè dāo shā rén 〈比喻 *fig.*〉自己不出面,利用别人去害人 kill sb. by another's hand; use another to harm a person

【借调】jièdiào 一个单位临时借用另一单位的工作人员,而不改变其隶属关系 temporarily transfer; (of a person) transfer from one work unit to another without changing his or her administrative affiliation

【借读】jièdú 没有本地区正式户口的中、小学生在本地区中、小学就读,叫做借读。没有某校学籍的学生,因故在某校就读,也叫借读。study at a school on a temporary basis, either because the student lacks a local registered permanent residence or has not registered as a student

【借端】jièduān 借口某件事 use as a pretext: ~生事 find an excuse to make trouble; avail oneself of a pretext to stir up trouble | ~推托 use a pretext to plead

【借方】jièfāng ☞ 收方 shōufāng on p. 1765

【借风使船】jiè fēng shǐ chuán 〈比喻 *fig.*〉借用别人的力量以达到自己的目的 sail the boat with the help of the wind — achieve one's ends through the agency of sb. else; also 借水行舟 jiè shuǐ xíng zhōu

【借古讽今】jiè gǔ fěng jīn 假借评论古代某人某事的是非,影射现实 use the past to disparage the present

【借故】jiègù 借口某种原因 find an excuse: ~拖延 find an excuse to stall for time | 他不愿意再跟他们谈下去,就~走了。He was unwilling to talk with them any more, and found an excuse and left.

【借光】jiè//guāng ❶ 分沾他人的利益、好处;沾光 get benefits from other people: 能来这里参观,是借了他哥的光。It is due to his elder brother's help that he can visit here. ❷〈客套话 *pol.*〉用于请别人给自己方便或向人询问 excuse me: ~让我过去。Would you mind stepping to one side, please? | ~,百货大楼在哪儿? Excuse me, but can you tell me where the department store is?

【借花献佛】jiè huā xiàn fó 〈比喻 *fig.*〉拿别人的东西做人情 borrow a flower and present it to the Buddha as a gift — make a gift of sth. belonging to sb. else

【借火】jiè//huǒ (~儿 jiè//huǒr) 吸烟时向别人借用引火的东西或利用别人点燃的烟来引火 ask for a light (for a cigarette)

【借鉴】jièjiàn 跟别的人或事相对照,以便取长补短或吸取教训 (used in comparison with other people or events) use as a reference; draw lessons from; draw on the experience of: 可资~。(Wc) can use it as a reference.

【借景】jièjǐng 园林艺术中指借取园外之景或使园内各风景点互相衬托,联成一体 borrow or use the scenery of the surroundings to set off the scenic spots in a garden

【借镜】jièjìng sane as 借鉴 jièjiàn

【借据】jièjù 借用别人的钱或器物时所立的字据,由出借的人保存 IOU (I owe you); receipt for a loan of money or things

【借口】jièkǒu ❶ 以(某事)为理由(非真正的理由) use as an excuse or pretext: 不能~快速施工而降低工程质量。We cannot reduce the engineering quality on the excuse of accelerating the construction. ❷ 假托的理由 excuse; pretext: 别拿忙做~而放松学习。Don't slacken your studying under the pretext of being too busy.

【借款】jiè//kuǎn 向人借钱或借钱给人 loan; borrow or lend money; ask for or offer a loan

【借款】jièkuǎn 借用的钱 money borrowed; loan: 一笔~ a sum of money borrowed; a loan grant

【借尸还魂】jiè shī huán hún 迷信传说人死以后灵魂可能借别人的尸体复活 (superstition) (of a dead person's soul) find reincarnation in sb. else's corpse; 〈比喻 *fig.*〉某种已经消灭或没落的思想、行为、势力等假托别的名义重新出现 (of discarded or waning thoughts, behaviour, forces, etc.) revive in a new guise

【借宿】jiè//sù 借别人的地方住宿 stay overnight at sb. else's place; put up for the night: 勘探队在老乡家里~了一夜。Members of the prospecting team stayed for the night in the homes of some villagers.

【借题发挥】jiè tí fāhuī 借谈论另一个题目来表达自己真正的意思 discuss another subject to express one's own ideas; seize on an incident to exaggerate matters

【借条】jiètiáo (~儿 jiètiáor) 便条式的借据 IOU (I owe you); receipt for a loan

【借位】jiè//wèi 减法运算中,被减数的某一位数不够减时向前一位借一,化成本位的数量,然后再减 borrow ten for subtraction; when the minuend in a subtraction operation is too small to be subtracted, one can borrow (ten) from the preceding digit and use it together with the minuend to do the subtraction

【借问】jièwèn 〈敬辞 *pol.*〉用于向人打听事情 may I ask: ~这里离城还有多远? May I ask how far it is from here to the town?

【借以】jièyǐ 作为凭借,以便做某事 so as to; for the purpose of; by way of: 略举几件事实,~证明这项工作的重要性。Provide a few facts in order to prove the importance of the

J

work.

【借用】jièyòng ❶ 借别人的东西来使用 borrow; have the loan of: ～一下你的铅笔。May I use your pencil? ❷ 把用于某种用途的事物用于另一种用途 use sth. for another purpose: '道具'这个名词原来指和尚念经时所用的东西,现在～来指演戏时所用的器物。The Chinese term *daoju* originally meant the ritual objects a monk used when chanting incantations, but today it means 'stage property'.

【借喻】jièyù 比喻的一种,直接借比喻的事物来代替被比喻的事物,被比喻的事物和比喻词都不出现。如'天下乌鸦一般黑','乌鸦'比喻旧时官吏。metonymy; borrowed analogy; borrowed figure of speech; type of metaphor that directly uses figurative object to refer to the thing to be compared without mentioning the name of the latter or using comparison words. For instance, in the sentence 'Crows are black the world over', the word 'crows' is a metaphor for corrupt officials in old times.

【借阅】jièyuè 借图书、资料等来阅读 borrow books or reading materials: ～图书要如期归还。(You) must return the borrowed books on time.

【借债】jiè//zhài 借钱 borrow money; raise (or contract) a loan

【借账】jiè//zhàng same as 借债 jiè//zhài

【借支】jièzhī 先期支用工资 ask for an advance on one's pay

【借重】jièzhòng 指借用其他的(力量)(多用做敬辞 oft. pol.) rely on sb. for support; enlist sb.'s help: ～一切有用的力量 rely on all useful forces | 敝公司以后～您的地方还很多,还要常来麻烦您。Our company will need a lot more of your help in the future. I'm afraid we'll come to trouble you quite often.

J

【借助】jièzhù 靠别的人或事物的帮助 fall back on; have the aid of; draw support from: 要看到极远的东西,就得～于望远镜。If you want to see something extremely far away, you must have the aid of a telescope.

骱 jiè 〈方 *dial.*〉骨节与骨节衔接的地方 connection between bone joints: 脱～(脱臼) dislocation (of a bone)

解(觧) jiè 解送 send sb. under guard: 起～ (of a prisoner) be sent (somewhere) under guard | 押～ send (a criminal or captive) under escort | 把犯人～到县里。The prisoner has been escorted to the county seat.
☞ jiě on p. 995 and xiè on p. 2125

【解差】jièchāi 〈旧时 *old*〉押送犯人的人 guard escorting prisoners

【解送】jièsòng 押送(财物或犯人) send under guard

【解元】jièyuán 明清两代称乡试考取第一名的人(during the Ming and Qing dynasties) the first on a list of successful candidates who passed the imperial examination at the provincial level

褯 jiè [褯子](jiè·zi)〈方 *dial.*〉尿布 diaper; napkin; nappy

藉 jiè ❶〈书 *fml.*〉垫在下面的东西 mat; mattress ❷ 垫;衬 place sth. underneath: 枕～ lie or fall down together higgledy-piggledy ❸ same as 借[2] jiè
☞ jí on p. 910

·jie (ㄐㄧㄝ)

价(價) ·jie ❶〈方 *dial.*〉〈助词 *aux.*〉用在否定副词后面加强语气 [used after a negative adverb to indicate emphasis]: 不～! No way! | 甭～! Nope! | 别～! No! 注意 **NOTE:** 跟否定副词单独成句,后面不再跟别的成分。If the word 价 ·jie forms an independent sentence together with a negative adverb, it will not be followed by other words. ❷ 某些副词的后缀 [added to certain adverbs as a suffix]: 成天～忙 be busy all day long | 震天～响。The sound is deafening.
☞ jià on p. 935 and jiè on p. 998

家 ·jie same as 价·jie, 如'整天家、成年家' e.g. all day long; all year round
☞ jiā on p. 927

jīn (ㄐㄧㄣ)

巾 jīn 擦东西或包裹、覆盖东西的小块的纺织品 a piece of cloth (as used for a towel, scarf, kerchief, etc.): 手～ (hand or face) towel | 毛～ towel | 头～ scarf; kerchief | 围～ scarf; muffler | 领～ scarf; neckerchief | 枕～ towel used to cover a pillow

【巾帼】jīnguó 巾和帼是古代妇女戴的头巾和发饰,借指妇女 woman's headdress in ancient times; woman: ～英雄 heroic woman; heroine | ～丈夫(有男子气概的女子) heroine

【巾箱本】jīnxiāngběn 本子特小,可以放在巾箱中的古书(巾箱,古时装头巾或手巾的小箱子) very small book which can be stored in a scarf box (巾箱 *jinxiang* meaning small box to store scarves or kerchiefs in ancient times)

斤[1](❶觔) jīn ❶ 重量单位。旧制 1 斤等于 16 两,市制 1 斤后改 10 两,合 500 克 *jin*; unit of weight in the past, where 1 *jin* was equal to 16 *liang* and later changed to be equal to 10 *liang*; now 1 *jin* is equal to 500 g. ❷ 加在某些以重量计算的物名后作总称 [affixed to the name of sth. measured by the weight to form a general reference]: 煤～ coal | 盐～ salt

斤[2] jīn〈古代 *arch.*〉砍伐树木的工具 tool used for felling trees in ancient times

【斤斗】jīndǒu〈方 *dial.*〉跟头 somersault

【斤斤】jīnjīn 过分计较(琐细的或无关紧要的事物) be particular (about small matters):不要～于表面形式,应该注重实际问题。Don't be particular about appearances;(we) should pay more attention to practical problems.

【斤斤计较】jīnjīn jìjiào 形容过分计较微小的利益或无关紧要的事情 haggle over every ounce; be calculating

【斤两】jīnliǎng 分量(多用于比喻 oft. fig.) weight:他的话很有～。What he said should not be taken lightly. *or* What he said carried a lot of weight.

今 jīn ❶ 现在;现代(跟'古'相对 as opposed to 'ancient') modern; present-day:当～ nowadays|～人 modern people|厚～薄古。Stress the present, not the past.|古为～用。Make the past serve the present. ❷ 当前的(年、天及其部分) of today; of this year:～天 today|～晨 this morning|～春 this spring ❸〈书 *fml.*〉此;这 from now on; henceforth:～番 this time; these days|～次 this time

【今草】jīncǎo 草书的一种,是由章草结合楷书发展而成的,六朝时为与章草区别,叫今草 *jincao*; cursive hand, developed from a combination of the *zhangcao* cursive hand and the regular script, and thus called so as to distinguish from *zhangcao* in the Six Dynasties Period

【今后】jīnhòu 从今以后 from now on; in the days to come; henceforth; hereafter; in future:～更要加倍努力。I will work harder in future.

【今年】jīnnián 说话时的这一年 this year

【今儿】jīnr〈方 *dial.*〉今天 today:～晚上我值班。I will be on duty this evening. also 今儿个 jīnr·ge

【今人】jīnrén 现代的人;当代的人 modern people; contemporaries; people of our era

【今日】jīnrì 今天 this day; today:从上海来的参观团预定～到达。The delegation from Shanghai is due to arrive today.

【今生】jīnshēng 这一辈子 this life:～今世 this age

【今世】jīnshì ❶ 当代 contemporary age; present time:～英杰 hero of the present time; hero of this age ❷ 今生 this life

【今天】jīntiān ❶ 说话时的这一天 this day; today:～的事不要放到明天做。You should not put off till tomorrow what you can do today. ❷ 现在;目前 present time or age; today:～的中国已经不是解放前的中国了。China today is no longer what it was before liberation.

【今文】jīnwén 汉代称当时通用的隶字。那时有人把口传的经书用隶字记录下来,后来叫做今文经。modern script; another name for *lishu*, the official script popularly used during the Han Dynasty. People then call the classics passed down orally and later written down in modern script, *jinwenjing*, or classics in modern script.

【今昔】jīnxī 现在和过去 present and past; today and yesterday:～对比 compare the present with the past

【今译】jīnyì 古代文献的现代语译文 modern translation; modern-language version:古籍～modern-language version of ancient books

【今音】jīnyīn ❶ 现代的语音 modern pronunciation of Chinese characters ❷ 指以《切韵》、《广韵》等韵书为代表的隋唐音,跟以《诗经》押韵、《说文》谐声等为代表的'古音'(周秦音)区别 Sui- and Tang-dynasty pronunciation of the Chinese language based on the books *Rhyming and Tuning* (Sui Dynasty) and *Comprehensive Phonology* (Song Dynasty), as distinguished from the classical (Zhou- and Qin-dynasty) pronunciation represented by *The Book of Songs* and *Discourses on Words*

【今朝】jīnzhāo ❶〈方 *dial.*〉今天① today; this day ❷ 今天② present time or age; today:数风流人物,还看～。For truly great men, look to this present age alone.

衿 jīn〈书 *fml.*〉联结衣襟的带子 belt that binds clothes

金[1] jīn ❶ 金属,通常指金、银、铜、铁、锡等 metal; usu. referring to gold, silver, copper, iron, tin, etc.:五～ hardware; tools, pans and other things for household use|合～ alloy ❷ 钱 money:现～ cash|基～ fund ❸〈古时 *arch.*〉金属制的打击乐器,如锣等 ancient percussion instruments made of metal such as gongs:～鼓 gold drum|鸣～收兵 beat the gong and recall the troops; call off a battle ❹ 金属元素,符号 Au (aurum)。黄色,质软,延展性强,化学性质稳定。是贵重金属,用来制造货币、装饰品等。aurum (Au); gold; precious metal that is yellow, soft, highly malleable and chemically stable, and used to make coins, jewellery, etc.; 通称 commonly known as 金子 jīn·zi or 黄金 huángjīn ❺〈比喻 *fig.*〉尊贵、贵重 valuable:～口玉言 gold mouth and jaded words — precious words; pearls; utterances that carry great weight|乌～墨玉(煤炭) coal ❻ 像金子的颜色 golden:～色纽扣 golden buttons|～漆盒子 gold-lacquered box ❼(Jīn) 姓 a surname

金[2] Jīn 朝代,公元 1115—1234,女真族完颜阿骨打所建,在我国北部 Jin Dynasty (1115-1234), founded by Akutta (1069-1123), chieftain of the Nüzhen tribes, in north China

【金榜】jīnbǎng 科举时代俗称殿试录取的榜 list

of successful candidates in the imperial examinations: ～题名 succeed in the imperial examinations

【金镑】jīnbàng 英国等国本位货币'镑'的别称 another name for the pound of Britain, Ireland, etc.

【金本位】jīnběnwèi 用黄金做本位货币的货币制度 gold standard; currency system with gold as its money standard

【金笔】jīnbǐ 笔头用黄金的合金,笔尖用铱的合金制成的高级自来水笔 gold-nib pen; quality fountain pen, the nip of which is made of gold alloy or iridium alloy

【金币】jīnbì〈古代 *arch.*〉泛指金属货币,现在指用黄金作主要成分铸造的货币(in a broat sense) coin; gold coin

【金碧辉煌】jīnbì-huīhuáng 形容建筑物等异常华丽,光彩夺目(of a building, etc.) splendid in green and gold; resplendent and magnificent

【金箔】jīnbó 用金子捶成的薄片或涂上金粉的纸片,用来包在佛像或器物等外面做装饰 gold leaf; gold foil; thin gold flake; paper covered with a layer of gold powder, used to decorate the exterior of Buddhist statues or wares

【金不换】jīn·buhuàn 形容十分可贵 not to be exchanged even for gold; invaluable; priceless: 浪子回头～。A prodigal who returns is more precious than gold.

【金灿灿】jīncàncàn (～的 jīncàncàn·de)形容金光耀眼(of sheen) bright golden: ～的阳光洒满大地。The sun's golden rays lit up the earth.

【金蝉脱壳】jīnchán tuō qiào〈比喻 *fig.*〉用计脱逃而使对方不能及时发觉 slip out of a predicament like a cicada shedding its skin; escape by cunning manoeuvres

【金城汤池】jīn chéng tāng chí 金属造的城,滚水的护城河,形容坚固不易攻破的城池 ramparts of metal and a moat of boiling water; impregnable fortress

【金疮】jīnchuāng〈中医 *Chin. med.*〉指刀枪等金属器械所造成的伤口 metal-inflicted wound; incised wound

【金额】jīn'é 钱数(of money) amount; sum

【金饭碗】jīnfànwǎn〈比喻 *fig.*〉待遇非常优厚的职位 gold rice bowl; job with handsome pay

【金刚】jīngāng〈方 *dial.*〉某些昆虫(如苍蝇)的蛹(of insects such as the fly) pupa

【金刚】Jīngāng〈佛教 *Budd.*〉称佛的侍从力士,因手拿金刚杵(古印度兵器)而得名 vajrabodhisattva; Buddha's warrior attendant holding a vajra (an ancient Indian weapon) in his hand

【金刚努目】Jīngāng nǔ mù 形容面目凶恶 glare like a temple door-god; look ferocious; also 金刚怒目 Jīngāng nù mù

【金刚砂】jīngāngshā ❶ 指碳化硅,纯的为无色晶体,硬度很大,质脆。工业上用做研磨材料。carborundum; silicon carbide; emery; corundum. Pure silicon carbide is in the form of colourless crystal, hard and brittle, and used as an abrasive in industry. ❷ 用做磨料的金刚石、刚玉、碳化硅等的统称 general term for 金刚石 jīngāngshí, 刚玉 gāngyù, 碳化硅 tànhuàguī, etc. used as abrasive ‖ also 钢砂 gāngshā

【金刚石】jīngāngshí 矿物,碳的同素异形体,多为正八面体结晶,纯净的无色透明,有光泽,有极强的折光力,是已知最硬的物质。用做高级切削和研磨材料等。diamond; mineral that is the allotrope of carbon, mostly in octahedral crystals, pure, colourless, transparent, shiny, of strong refractive ability, the hardest of all known substances, and used as an advanced cutting and abrading material; also 金刚钻 jīngāngzuàn

【金刚钻】jīngāngzuàn same as 金刚石 jīngāngshí

【金糕】jīngāo 山楂糕 haw jelly

【金工】jīngōng 金属的各种加工工作的总称(collect.) metalworking; metal processing

【金瓜】jīnguā ❶ 南瓜的一种,果实成熟后果皮为金黄色或红黄色 a kind of golden or reddish yellow pumpkin ❷ 古代一种兵器,棒端呈瓜形,金色。后来用做仪仗。ancient weapon with a pumpkin-like head and of a golden colour, later used for ceremonial purposes

【金龟】jīnguī 乌龟(爬行动物) tortoise

【金龟子】jīnguīzǐ 昆虫,有许多种,身体黑绿色或其他颜色,有光泽,前翅坚硬,后翅呈膜状。幼虫叫蛴螬,是农业害虫。有的地区叫金壳郎。scarab (*Scarabaeus sacer*); chafer; dor; dorbeetle; cockchafer; tumblebug; insects of many different kinds and pests to farm crops, either dark green or in other shiny colours, having hard front wings and gauze-like rear wings, its larva (called 蛴螬 qícáo in Chinese) being a pest; also called 金壳郎 jīn·kelàng in some regions

【金贵】jīn·guì 珍贵;贵重 valuable: 东西越稀少越～。The more rare something is, the more valuable it becomes. | 这里水比油还～。Here, water is more valuable than oil.

【金衡】jīnhéng 英美重量制度,用于金、银等贵重金属(区别于'常衡、药衡' as compared with 'avoirdupois weight and apothecaries' weight') troy weight; troy; weight unit for gold, silver and other valuable metals, used in Britain and the US

【金晃晃】jīnhuānghuāng same as 金煌煌 jīnhuānghuāng

【金煌煌】jīnhuānghuāng (～的 jīnhuānghuāng·de)形容像黄金一样发亮的颜色 golden: ～的琉璃瓦 golden glazed tiles; also 金晃晃 jīnhuānghuāng

【金黄】jīnhuáng 黄而微红略像金子的颜色

golden yellow; golden: ～色头发 golden hair|麦收时节，田野里一片～。The fields turn golden everywhere during the wheat harvest.

【金婚】jīnhūn 欧洲风俗称结婚五十周年为金婚 golden wedding; day marking the 50th anniversary of a couple's marriage

【金鸡独立】jīn jī dú lì 指用一条腿站立的姿势 standing on one leg like a rooster (a posture in Chinese boxing)

【金奖】jīnjiǎng 指一等奖；最高奖 top prize; first prize (多以金杯等为奖品 oft. a golden trophy or medal)

【金科玉律】jīn kē yù lǜ〈比喻 *fig.*〉不能变更的信条或法律条文 golden rule; unalterable precious precept; important principle or law that should always be observed

【金口玉言】jīnkǒu-yùyán 封建社会称皇帝讲的话，后来也用来泛指不能改变的话 golden mouth and pearl words, a reference to an emperor's remarks during the feudal society; precious words; utterances that carry great weight

【金库】jīnkù 保管和出纳国家预算资金的机关 national or state treasury; exchequer; 通称 commonly called 国库 guókù

【金兰】jīnlán 原指牢固而融洽的友情（语本《易经·系辞》'二人同心，其利断金；同心之言，其臭如兰'），后来用做结拜为兄弟姐妹的代称 solid and harmonious friendship; originally from *The Book of Changes·Great Treatise*: 'If two people are of the same mind, their strength can cut gold; having one heart is as good as the fragrance of orchids.' (fig.) sworn brothers or sisters: ～谱 genealogical records of sworn brothers (each keeping a copy)|义结～ become sworn brothers

【金莲】jīnlián (～儿 jīnliánr)〈旧时 *old*〉指缠足妇女的脚 golden lilies; men's laudatory term for women's bound feet

【金銮殿】jīnluándiàn 唐代宫内有金銮殿，后来旧小说戏曲中泛称皇帝上朝理政的殿 throne room; Hall of Golden Chimes, popular name for the emperor's audience hall

【金迷纸醉】jīn mí zhǐ zuì ☞ 纸醉金迷 zhǐ zuì jīn mí on p. 2467

【金牛座】jīnniúzuò 黄道十二星座之一 Taurus; one of the 12 constellations in the zodiac; ☞ 黄道十二宫 huángdào shí'èrgōng on p. 851

【金瓯】jīn'ōu 金属的杯子 golden goblet; 〈比喻 *fig.*〉完整的疆土，泛指国土 territorial integrity; (in a broad sense) national territory: ～无缺 unimpaired territorial integrity

【金牌】jīnpái 奖牌的一种，奖给第一名 gold medal: 荣获～ win a gold medal

【金钱】jīnqián 货币；钱 money

【金钱松】jīnqiánsōng 落叶乔木，树干通直高大，树冠呈圆锥形，叶子条形，花单性，雌雄同株，球果卵形。木材耐腐蚀，供建筑和制器物等用。树形优美，秋季叶呈金黄色，是著名的观赏树之一。golden larch (*Pseudolarix amabilis*); deciduous arbour that is a hermaphrodite, having a tall straight trunk, a conical crown, strip-shaped leaves, unisexual flowers, and egg-shaped cones, its wood being rot resistant and good material for architecture and woodwork. Elegantly shaped, its leaves turning golden in autumn, it is a well-known ornamental tree.

【金枪鱼】jīnqiāngyú 鱼，身体纺锤形，长约一米，头尖，鳞细。生活在海洋中，肉供食用。tuna (*Thunnus thynnus*); tunny; fish usu. about one metre long with a spindle-shaped body, pointed head and fine scales, and living in the sea, its meat commonly used as food

【金秋】jīnqiū 指秋季 golden autumn: ～季节 autumn season|～菊展 chrysanthemum exhibition in autumn

【金融】jīnróng 指货币的发行、流通和回笼，贷款的发放和收回，存款的存入和提取，汇兑的往来等经济活动 finance; banking; economic activities including distribution and circulation of a currency and withdrawal of it from circulation, the granting and retrieving of loans, deposit and withdrawal of savings, conversion of currencies, etc.

【金嗓子】jīnsǎng·zi 指音色清脆、圆润悦耳的歌喉 golden voice; beautiful voice

【金闪闪】jīnshǎnshǎn (～的 jīnshǎnshǎn · de) 形容金光闪烁 shining: ～的奖杯 shining trophy

【金石】jīnshí ❶〈书 *fml.*〉金属和石头 metal and stone; 〈比喻 *fig.*〉坚硬的东西 sth. extremely hard: 精诚所至，～为开(意志坚决，能克服一切困难)。Absolute sincerity can move even a heart of stone. ❷ 金指铜器和其他金属器物，石指石制器物等，这些东西上头多有文字记事，所以把这类历史资料叫做金石 inscriptions on bronzeware, other metal objects and stone tablets

【金属】jīnshǔ 具有光泽、延展性和容易导电、传热等性质的单质。除汞以外，在常温下都是固体，如金、银、铜、铁、锰、锌等。metal; substance possessing lustre and malleability, and highly conductive of electricity, heat, etc. Except for mercury, all the metals are in a solid state under normal temperatures, e.g. gold, silver, copper, iron, manganese, zinc, etc.

【金属探伤】jīnshǔ tànshāng 利用探伤器检验金属制件内部缺陷（如隐蔽的裂纹、砂眼、杂质等）crack detection; metal defect detection; using a defect detector to find defects, e.g. cracks, sand holes, impurities, etc., in a metal workpiece; ☞ 探伤 tànshāng on p. 1863

【金丝猴】jīnsīhóu 哺乳动物，身体瘦长，毛灰黄色，鼻孔向上，尾巴长，背部长毛达一尺多。生活在高山的大树上，是我国特产的一种珍贵动

J

物。golden monkey (*Rhinopithecus roxellanae*); snub-nosed monkey; mammal with a long thin body, greyish yellow fur, an upturned nose, long tail, and hair more than 33 cm. long on its back, living in big trees in high mountains, a valuable animal native to China

【金松】jīnsōng 常绿大乔木,高达 40 米,大叶轮生,扁条形,嫩枝上的小叶鳞片状,树冠呈狭圆锥形,是著名的观赏树之一 golden pine (*Sciadopitys verticillata*); well-known ornamental evergreen tree that grows up to 40 metres high, having big verticillate leaves in the shape of flat strips, scale-shaped small leaves on tender twigs, and conical tree crowns

【金田起义】Jīntián Qǐyì 1851 年洪秀全、杨秀清等在广西桂平金田村领导的农民起义 Jintian Peasant Uprising, led by Hong Xiuquan and Yang Xiuqing in 1851 in Jintian Village in Guiping, Guangxi; ☞ 太平天国 Tàipíng Tiānguó on p. 1854

【金汤】jīntāng '金城汤池'的略语 abbr. for 金城汤池 jīn chéng tāng chí: 固若~ strongly fortified; impregnable; invulnerable

【金条】jīntiáo 铸成长条状的黄金,一般每条重十两,也有五两或二十两的 gold bar; gold that is cast in bars, generally weighing 10 *liang*, sometimes five *liang* or 20 *liang* apiece

【金文】jīnwén 古代铜器上铸的或刻的文字,通常专指殷周秦汉铜器上的文字 inscriptions on ancient bronzeware; esp. inscriptions on the bronzeware of the Shang, Zhou, Qin and Han dynasties; also 钟鼎文 zhōngdǐngwén

【金乌】jīnwū 〈书 *fml*.〉指太阳(传说太阳中有三足乌) Golden Crow; the sun. (Legend has it that there is a three-legged crow on the sun.): ~西坠。The sun is setting in the west.

J

【金星】[1] jīnxīng 太阳系九大行星之一,按离太阳由近而远的次序计为第二颗,绕太阳公转周期约 224.7 天,自转周期约 243 天,自东向西逆转。金星是各大行星中离地球最近的一个。Venus; one of the nine planets in the solar system, the second closest to the sun and the closest to the earth, taking 224.7 days to orbit once around the sun and 243 days to complete a rotation on its axis from east to west; (图见 ☞ figure for 太阳系 tàiyángxì on p. 1855)

【金星】[2] jīnxīng ❶ 金黄色的五角星 golden star: ~勋章 golden-star medal ❷ 头晕眼花时所感到的眼前出现的像星的小点 flashes of light that one appears to see as from dizziness: 我跑得上气不接下气,眼前直冒~。I was out of breath when running, and I seemed to see stars before my eyes.

【金鱼】jīnyú 鲫鱼经过人工长期培养形成的变种,身体的颜色有红、黑、蓝、红白花等许多种,是著名的观赏鱼 goldfish (*Carassius auratus*); variation of crucian carp developing after extended artificial breeding, a well-known ornamental fish red, black, blue, red-white, etc. in colour

【金玉】jīnyù 〈书 *fml*.〉泛指珍宝(in a broad sense) gold and jade; 〈比喻 *fig*.〉华美贵重 valuable; precious: ~良言 golden sayings; invaluable advice | ~其外,败絮其中(外表很华美,里头一团糟) rubbish coated in gold and jade; fair without, foul within

【金圆券】jīnyuánquàn 国民党政府在 1948 年发行的一种纸币 a kind of cash issued in 1948 in China by the Kuomintang government

【金针】jīnzhēn ❶〈书 *fml*.〉缝纫、刺绣用的金属针 metal needle used for sewing and embroidery ❷ 针灸用的针,古时多用金、银或铁制成,现在多用不锈钢制成 acupuncture needle, originally made of gold, silver or iron, and now of stainless steel; ☞ 毫针 háozhēn on p. 773 ❸ 用做食物的金针菜的花 dried day-lily flower

【金针菜】jīnzhēncài ❶ 多年生草本植物,叶子丛生。花筒长而大,黄色,有香味,早晨开放傍晚凋谢,可以做蔬菜。day lily (*Hemerocallis*); perennial herb having thick leaves, long large fragrant yellow flowers that blossom in the morning, wither in the evening, and are edible ❷ 这种植物的花 day-lily flowers ‖ 通称 generally called 黄花 huánghuā or 黄花菜 huánghuācài

【金枝玉叶】jīn zhī yù yè 〈旧 *old*〉指皇族,也指出身高贵的公子小姐 golden branches and jade leaves; people of imperial lineage; royalty

【金子】jīn·zi 金[1] ④ 的通称 general term for 金[1] jīn ④

【金字塔】jīnzìtǎ 〈古代 *arch*.〉埃及、美洲的一种建筑物,是用石头建成的三面或多面的角锥体,远看像汉字的'金'字。埃及金字塔是古代帝王的陵墓。pyramid; architectural structure in ancient Egypt and the Americas, made of stone in the shape of a three-faceted or multi-faceted pyramid, similar in shape to the Chinese character 金 jīn, hence its Chinese name. The pyramids of Egypt were ancient royal tombs.

【金字招牌】jīnzì zhāopái 商店用金粉涂字的招牌,也指商店资金雄厚、信誉卓著 gold-lettered signboard of a store; (of a store) abundant in capital and having good credit; 〈比喻 *fig*.〉向人炫耀的名义或称号 vainglorious title

津[1] jīn ❶ 唾液 saliva; spit; sputum: ~液 body fluid; saliva | 生~止渴 help produce saliva and slake thirst ❷ 汗 sweat; perspiration: 遍体生~ perspire all over ❸ 润泽 moist; damp

津[2] jīn 渡口 ferry crossing, ford: ～渡 ferry crossing; ford|关～ ferry crossing; ford|要～ford of strategic importance

【津津】jīnjīn ❶ 形容有滋味;有趣味: ～有味 with relish; with gusto; with keen pleasure|～乐道(很感兴趣地谈论) take delight in talking about; dwell upon with great relish ❷(汗、水)流出的样子(of sweat, water) drip; drop: 汗～ sweating|水～ dripping with water

【津梁】jīnliáng〈书 *fml.*〉渡口和桥梁 ferry and bridge;〈比喻 *fig.*〉用做引导的事物或过渡的方法、手段 help; aid; sth. used as a guide or transient way or method

【津贴】jīntiē ❶ 工资以外的补助费,也指供给制人员的生活零用钱 financial aid; subsidy; allowance ❷ 给津贴;补助 provide allowance: 每月～他一些钱 provide him with an allowance every month

【津要】jīnyào〈书 *fml.*〉❶ 水陆冲要的地方 key location: 扼守～ defend a place with strategic importance ❷〈比喻 *fig.*〉显要的地位 key post: 身居～ be in a key position

【津液】jīnyè〈中医 *Chin. med.*〉对体内一切液体的总称,包括血液、唾液、泪液、汗液等,通常专指唾液 body fluid; saliva; general term for all kinds of liquids in the body, including blood, saliva, tears, sweat, etc., but usu. referring to saliva

衿 jīn ❶ same as 襟 jīn ❷〈书 *fml.*〉系(jì)衣裳的带子 girdle

矜 jīn ❶ 怜悯;怜惜 pity; sympathize with ❷ 自尊自大;自夸 self-important; conceited: 不～不伐(不自大自夸) be neither arrogant nor boastful|毫无骄～之气 not conceited ❸ 慎重;拘谨 restrained; reserved: ～持 restrained; reserved

☞ guān on p. 715 and qín on p. 1560

【矜持】jīnchí 拘谨;拘束 self-conscious; restrained; reserved: 他第一次上台发言,显得有点～。He looked self-conscious when he took the podium for the first time.

【矜夸】jīnkuā 骄傲自夸 conceited and boastful: 力戒～ guard against being conceited and boastful

筋(觔) jīn ❶ 肌肉 muscle: ～骨 muscles and bones ❷(～儿 jīnr)肌腱或骨头上的韧带 tendon; sinew: 牛蹄～儿 tendon of ox hoof ❸ 可以看见的皮下静脉管 veins that stand out under the skin: 青～ blue veins ❹(～儿 jīnr)像筋的东西 anything resembling a tendon or vein: 叶～ leaf veins|钢～ reinforcing bar|铁～ iron bar|橡皮～儿 rubber band

【筋道】jīn·dao〈方 *dial.*〉❶ 指食物有韧性,耐咀嚼 chewy: 抻面吃到嘴里挺～。Hand-pulled noodles are chewy. ❷ 身体结实(多指老人 oft. referring to an elderly person) strong: 老人的身子骨儿倒很～。The old man is in pretty good shape.

【筋斗】jīndǒu〈方 *dial.*〉跟头 somersault

【筋骨】jīngǔ 筋肉和骨头,也泛指体格 muscles and bones; build; physique: 学武术可以锻炼～。Practising *wushu* strengthens the physique.

【筋节】jīnjié ❶ 肌肉和关节 muscles and joints ❷〈比喻 *fig.*〉文章或言辞重要而有力的转折承接处 vital links in a speech or essay

【筋疲力尽】jīn pí lì jìn 形容非常疲劳,一点力气也没有了 be run ragged; spent; exhausted; played out; worn out; tired out; all in; deadbeat; dog-tired; also 精疲力竭 jīng pí lì jié

【筋肉】jīnròu 肌肉 muscle

禁 jīn ❶ 禁受;耐 bear; stand: 弱不～风 too weak to withstand a gust of wind; extremely delicate; fragile|这双鞋～穿。The shoes are durable. ❷ 忍住 endure: 不～ cannot endure

☞ jìn on p. 1016

【禁不起】jīn·bu qǐ 承受不住(多用于人 oft. of a person) be unable to stand (tests, trials, etc.): ～考验 fail to stand up to rigorous tests

【禁不住】jīn·bu zhù ❶ 承受不住(用于人或物 of people or things) be unable to bear or endure: 这种植物～霜冻。This plant is unable to bear the frost.|你怎么这样～批评? How come you cannot stand a bit of criticism? ❷ 抑制不住;不由得 cannot help doing sth.; cannot refrain from: ～笑了起来 cannot help laughing

【禁得起】jīn·de qǐ 承受得住(多用于人 oft. of a person) be able to stand (tests, trials, etc.): 青年人要～艰苦环境的考验。Young people should be able to withstand the test of hardships.

【禁得住】jīn·de zhù 承受得住(用于人或物 of people or things) be able to bear or endure: 河上的冰已经～人走了。The ice on the river is thick enough to walk on.

【禁受】jīnshòu 受;承受 bear; stand; endure: ～考验 stand tests|～不住打击 cannot stand any attack

襟 jīn ❶ 上衣、袍子前面的部分 front of a garment: 大～ front of a garment|对～ paralleled front of a garment ❷ 指连襟 brothers-in-law whose wives are sisters: ～兄 husband of wife's elder sister|～弟 husband of wife's younger sister ❸ 指胸襟 bosom: ～抱 bosom|～怀 mind

【襟怀】jīnhuái 胸襟;胸怀 bosom; heart; (breadth of) mind: ～坦白 open-hearted and above board; honest and straightforward

jǐn (ㄐㄧㄣˇ)

仅(僅) jǐn 仅仅 only; merely; alone: 不～如此 in addition; not only | 绝无～有 one and only; only one of its kind; unique

☞ jìn on p. 1010

【仅见】jǐnjiàn 极其少见 rarely seen: 规模之大是历史上所～的。It is on a scale so grand as to be rarely seen in history.

【仅仅】jǐnjǐn 〈副词 *adv.*〉表示限于某个范围,意思跟'只'相同而更强调 [similar in meaning to 只 zhǐ but more emphatic] only; merely; alone: 这座大桥～半年就完工了。The bridge was completed in only half a year.

【仅只】jǐnzhǐ 仅仅 only; merely: 他家～养猪一项,就收入几千元。Raising pigs alone earned his family several thousand yuan.

尽[1](儘) jǐn ❶ 力求达到最大限度 to the greatest extent: ～早 as early as possible; at the earliest possible date | ～着平生的力气往外一推 push it out with all one's strength | ～可能地减少错误 avoid mistakes as much as possible ❷ 表示以某个范围为极限,不得超过 be within the limits of: ～着三天把事情办好。Get the job done in three days. ❸ 让某些人或事物尽先 give priority to sb.; use sth. first: 先～旧衣服穿 wear old clothes before buying new ones | 单间房间不多,～着女同志住。As there are not enough single rooms, let's give women comrades first priority. ❹ 用在表示方位的词前面,跟'最'相同 [used before a word indicating orientation, and similar in meaning to 最 zuì]: ～前头 the furthest point in front | ～北边 northernmost part

尽[2](儘) jǐn 〈方 *dial.*〉尽自 keep on doing sth.: 这些日子～下雨。It has been always raining these days. | 事情已经过去了,～责备他也无益。What happened, so there is no point to keep on blaming him.

☞ jìn on p. 1011

【尽管】jǐnguǎn ❶〈副词 *adv.*〉表示不必考虑别的,放心去做 feel free to; not hesitate to: 有意见～提,不要客气。Feel free to offer your opinions. | 你有什么困难～说,我们一定帮助你解决。If you have any difficulties, don't hesitate to ask us for help. ❷〈方 *dial.*〉〈副词 *adv.*〉老是;总是 always: 有病早些治,～耽搁着也不好。If you are ill, you should go to the hospital as early as possible. *or* Always neglecting health problems is not good. ❸〈连词 *conj.*〉表示姑且承认某种事实,下文往往有'但是、然而'等表示转折的连词跟它呼应,反接上文 [usu. followed by 但是 dànshì and 然而 rán'ér, to express a shift in meaning] although; even if: ～他不接受我的意见,我有意见还要向他提。Even if he doesn't listen to me, if I have sth. to say I'll say it anyway. | ～以后变化难测,然而大体的估计还是可能的。Even though future changes are hard to predict, it is possible to make rough estimations.

【尽快】jǐnkuài 尽量加快 as quickly (soon or early) as possible: 使新机器～投入生产 put new machines into production as quickly as possible | ～地制订出新的年度计划。Work out a new annual work plan as soon as possible.

【尽量】jǐnliàng 〈副词 *adv.*〉表示力求在一定范围内达到最大限度 to the best of one's ability; as far as possible: 把你知道的～报告给大家。Tell us as much as you know. | 工作虽然忙,学习的时间仍然要～保证。Although you are busy with your work, you should still arrange enough time to study.

☞ jìnliàng on p. 1011

【尽让】jǐnràng 〈方 *dial.*〉使别人占先;推让 give way to sb. else; let sb. else take precedence: 他们在一起处得很好,凡事彼此都有个～。They get along very well and are always ready to accommodate each other.

【尽先】jǐnxiān 尽量放在优先地位 give first priority to: ～照顾老年人 give first priority to senior citizens | ～生产这种农具 give first priority to producing this kind of farm tool

【尽早】jǐnzǎo 尽可能地提前 as early as possible: 用毕,请～送回。Please return it as soon as you have finished using it.

【尽自】jǐn·zi 〈方 *dial.*〉老是;总是 always; all the time: 她心里乐滋滋的～笑。She is so happy she laughs all the time. | 要想办法克服困难,别～诉苦。Stop complaining all the time, and try your best to overcome difficulties.

卺 jǐn 〈古代 *arch.*〉举行婚礼时用做酒器的瓢 nuptial wine cup; wine cup used at a wedding: 合～ get married

紧(緊) jǐn ❶ 物体受到几方面的拉力或压力以后所呈现的状态(跟'松[2]'相对,②③④⑥同 as opposed to 'loose[2]', and same in ②③④⑥) (of an object worked on by pulling or pressures from several directions) tight; taut; close: 绳子拉得很～。The rope is pulled taut. | 鼓面绷得非常～。The surface of the drum has been stretched extremely tight. ❷ 物体因受外力作用变得固定或牢固 tighten; become tight by outside force: 捏～笔杆 hold a pen tight in one's hand | 把螺丝钉往～里拧一拧 tightened a screw ◇ 眼睛～盯住他 stare hard at him | ～记着别忘了。Make sure to remember it. ❸ 使紧 tighten: ～了一下腰带 tighten one's belt | ～一～弦 tighten the string | ～一～螺丝钉。Tighten a screw. ❹ 非常接近，空隙极小 very narrow; small; tight: 抽屉～，拉不开。The drawer is too tight to open.｜这双鞋太～，穿着不舒服。The shoes are too cramped, and uncomfortable to wear.｜他住在我的～隔壁。He lives next door to my room. ◇全国人民团结～。The whole nation is closely united. ❺ 动作先后密切接连；事情急 urgent; pressing; tense; (of actions) follow closely behind: ～催 press sb. to do sth.｜一个胜利～接着一个胜利。One victory followed another in quick succession.｜他～赶了几步，追上老张。He quickened his pace and caught up with Lao Zhang.｜风刮得～，雨下得急。The wind is blowing hard, and it is raining heavily.｜任务很～。The task is urgent.｜抓～时间。Hurry up. ❻ 经济不宽裕；拮据 hard up; short of money: 这个月用项多一些，手头显得～一点。I spent quite a lot this month, so I am a bit short of money.

【紧巴巴】jǐnbābā (～的 jǐnbābā·de) ❶ 形容物体表面呈现紧张状态 tight: 衣服又瘦又小，～地贴在身上。The coat was tight and small, and I had to squeeze my body into it.｜没洗脸，脸上～的。I haven't washed my face, so it feels tight. ❷ 形容经济不宽裕；拮据 hard up; short of money: 日子过得～ be in financial straits

【紧绷绷】jǐnbēngbēng (～的 jǐnbēngbēng·de) ❶ 形容绷或捆扎得很紧 tightly drawn: 皮带系(jì)得～的 with a belt fastened tight ❷ 形容心情很紧张或表情不自然 (of one's mind) nervous; (of one's facial expression) taut: 脸～的，像很生气的样子。(He) wears a taut face as if he were angry.

【紧凑】jǐncòu 密切连接，中间没有多余的东西或空隙 compact; terse; well-knit: 这所房子的格局很～，所有的地面都恰当地利用了。The house is compactly laid out, and the entire floor space has been well used.｜这部影片很～，没有多余的镜头。The film has a well-knit plot without unnecessary scenes.

【紧箍咒】jǐngūzhòu《西游记》里唐僧用来制伏孙悟空的咒语，能使孙悟空头上套的金箍缩紧，使他头疼，因此叫紧箍咒 Incantation of the Gold Hoop; originally recited by the Monk Tang in the novel *Journey to the West* to tighten up the gold hoop fastened to the head of the Monkey King and give him a headache, so as to keep him under control; 〈比喻 *fig.*〉束缚人的东西 sth. that inhibits sb.

【紧急】jǐnjí 必须立即采取行动、不容许拖延的 urgent; pressing; critical: ～集合 emergency muster｜～措施 pressing measures｜～关头 state of emergency｜任务～ urgent task｜战事～ in the thick of war

【紧急状态】jǐnjí zhuàngtài 非常紧张的形势，一般指国家面临战争的状态 urgent situation; state of emergency; generally referring to a country facing war

【紧邻】jǐnlín 紧挨着的邻居 close neighbour; next-door neighbour

【紧锣密鼓】jǐn luó mì gǔ 锣鼓点敲得很密。多比喻公开活动前的紧张的舆论准备。vehement beating of drums and gongs; oft. used figuratively to mean intense publicity preceding a public event; also 密锣紧鼓 mì luó jǐn gǔ

【紧密】jǐnmì ❶ 十分密切，不可分隔 close together; inseparable: ～结合 closely linked｜～联系 close contact｜～地团结在一起 be closely united ❷ 多而连续不断 rapid and intense: 枪声十分～。There was intense firing.｜～的雨点 rapid and intense raindrops

【紧迫】jǐnpò 没有缓冲的余地；急迫 pressing; urgent; imminent: ～感 feeling of urgency; sense of urgency｜任务～。The task is urgent.｜形势十分～。The situation is critical.

【紧俏】jǐnqiào (商品)销路好，供不应求 (of consumer goods) in great demand but short supply: ～货 goods in great demand｜～物资 materials in short supply

【紧缺】jǐnquē (物资等)因短缺而供应紧张 in short supply; badly needed: 商品～ goods in short supply｜资金～ badly needed funds

【紧身儿】jǐn·shenr 穿在里面的瘦而紧的上衣 close-fitting undergarments; skintight clothes

【紧缩】jǐnsuō 缩小；压缩 reduce; retrench; tighten; downsize; rationalize: ～开支 cut down expenses; retrench; curtail outlay｜～机构 reduce staff

【紧要】jǐnyào 紧急重要；要紧 critical; crucial; vital: ～关头 critical moment (or juncture); crucial moment｜无关～ nothing important

【紧张】jǐnzhāng ❶ 精神处于高度准备状态，兴奋不安 nervous; keyed-up: 第一次登台，免不了有些～。(You) will naturally feel the jitters at your first stage appearance. ❷ 激烈或紧迫，使人精神紧张 tense; intense; strained: ～的劳动 intense work｜～动人的情节 intense and exciting plot｜球赛已经进入～阶段。The football match is entering a decisive stage.｜工作～。The work has really been hectic. ❸ 供应不足，难于应付 in short supply; tight: 粮食～。The food is in short supply.｜电力～。The power is in great demand.

【紧着】jǐn·zhe 加紧 speed up; press on with; hurry: 你写得太慢了，应该～点儿。You write too slowly. Please hurry up.｜下星期一就要演出了，咱们得～练。We will give a performance next Monday. Let's hurry up and practise.

堇 jǐn ☞ below

【堇菜】jǐncài 多年生草本植物，叶子略呈肾脏形，边缘有锯齿，花瓣白色，有紫色条纹 violet

(*Viola*); perennial herb having kidney-shaped, saw-edged leaves, and purple-striped white flower petals; also 堇堇菜 jǐnjǐncài

【堇色】jǐnsè 浅紫色 violet colour

锦 jǐn ❶ 有彩色花纹的丝织品 brocade; colourfully patterned silk: 蜀～ brocade made in Sichuan|壮～ brocade of the Zhuang people ❷ 色彩鲜明华丽 bright and beautiful: ～霞 rose-tinted clouds|～缎 brocade and satin

【锦标】jǐnbiāo 授给竞赛中优胜者的奖品,如锦旗、银盾、奖杯等 prize; trophy; title; award given to the winner of a competition

【锦标赛】jǐnbiāosài 获胜的团体或个人取得锦标的体育运动比赛,如国际乒乓球锦标赛 championship competition; championships, such as the World Table Tennis Championships

【锦缎】jǐnduàn 表面有彩色花纹的丝织品,可做服装和装饰品等 brocade and satin; silk fabric with colourful patterns, used to make clothes and decorations

【锦鸡】jǐnjī 鸟,形状和雉相似,雄的头上有金色的冠毛,颈橙黄色,背暗绿色,杂有紫色,尾巴很长,雌的羽毛暗褐色。多饲养来供玩赏。golden pheasant (*Chrysolophus pictus*); bird similar in shape to a pheasant, having a golden aigrette, orange neck, dark green back tinted with purple, and a long tail for the male and dark brown feathers for the female, oft. raised for enjoyment

【锦葵】jǐnkuí 二年生或多年生草本植物,叶子肾脏形,夏天开花,紫红色。供观赏。mallow (*Malva sylvestris*); high mallow; ornamental biennial or perennial herb having kidney-shaped leaves and purple red flowers that blossom in summer

【锦纶】jǐnlún 合成纤维的一种,由二元酸和二元胺缩聚而成。强度高,耐磨,耐腐蚀,弹性大。用来制袜子、衣物、绳子、渔网、降落伞、轮胎帘布。polyamide fibre; synthetic fibre composed of a compressed diacid base and a diamine, intensive, durable, erosion-resistant and elastic, used to make socks, clothes, ropes, fishing nets, parachutes, tyre cord, etc.; also 尼龙 nílóng

【锦囊妙计】jǐnnáng miàojì 旧小说上常描写足智多谋的人,把可能发生的事变以及所应付的办法预先用纸条写好装在锦囊里,嘱咐办事的人在遇到紧急情况时拆看,并依计行事。现在比喻能及时解决紧急问题的办法。wise counsel concealed in brocade. In old fiction, a resourceful person would often write predictions about future events on a strip of paper and wrap it up in a piece of brocade, and tell the person in charge to open it at the critical moment and act accordingly. (fig.) instructions for dealing with an emergency; wise counsel

【锦旗】jǐnqí 用彩色绸缎制成的旗子,授给竞赛或生产劳动中的优胜者,或者送给团体或个人,表示敬意、谢意等 silk banner; banner made of colourful silk as an award to the winner of a competition or those who excel in production or labour, or presented to an organization or a person as a sign of respect, gratitude, etc.

【锦上添花】jǐn shàng tiān huā 〈比喻 *fig.*〉使美好的事物更加美好 add flowers to the brocade; make what is good even better

【锦心绣口】jǐn xīn xiù kǒu 形容文辞优美 beautiful writing; also 锦心绣腹 jǐn xīn xiù fù

【锦绣】jǐnxiù 精美鲜艳的丝织品 as beautiful as brocade; 〈比喻 *fig.*〉美丽或美好 beautiful; splendid: ～山河 land of splendour; land of charm and beauty; beautiful land|～前程 glorious future

谨 jǐn ❶ 谨慎;小心 careful; cautious; circumspect: 勤～ diligent; hardworking; industrious|～记在心 bear in mind|～守规程 strictly adhere to the rules ❷ 郑重;恭敬 solemnly; sincerely: ～启 sincerely yours|～领 allow me to accept|～具 allow me to present|我们～向各位代表表示热烈的欢迎。We wish to extend to you all our warmest welcome.

【谨饬】jǐnchì 〈书 *fml.*〉谨慎 prudent; careful; cautious; circumspect

【谨防】jǐnfáng 小心地防备 guard against; beware of: ～扒手。Beware of pickpockets.|～假冒。Beware of imitations.|～上当。Beware of swindlers.

【谨慎】jǐnshèn 对外界事物或自己的言行密切注意,以免发生不利或不幸的事情 prudent; careful; cautious; circumspect: 小心～。Please be careful and prudent.

【谨小慎微】jǐn xiǎo shèn wēi 对琐细的事情过分小心谨慎,以致流于畏缩 overcautious in handling small matters; overcautious

【谨严】jǐnyán 谨慎严密 careful and precise: 治学～ careful and exact scholarship|文章结构～。The article is compact and carefully constructed.

馑 jǐn ☞ 饥馑 jījǐn on p. 889

廑(厪) jǐn 〈书 *fml.*〉same as 仅 jǐn ☞ qín on p. 1561

瑾 jǐn 〈书 *fml.*〉美玉 jade

槿 jǐn ☞ 木槿 mùjǐn on p. 1374

jìn (ㄐㄧㄣˋ)

仅(僅) jìn 〈书 *fml.*〉将近 nearly; approximately: 士卒～万人。The

soldiers numbered nearly 10,000.

☞ jǐn on p.1008

尽(盡) jìn ❶ 完 exhausted; finished: 取之不~ inexhaustible|知无不言,言无不~。Say all you know, and say it without reserve.|想~方法节约资财。Try all possible means to save funds and resources. ❷〈书 *fml.*〉死亡 die; pass away: 自~ commit suicide|同归于尽 perish together; end up in common ruin ❸ 达到极端 to the utmost; to the limit: ~头 with all one's heart|~善~美 acme of perfection; perfect|山穷水~ where the hills and streams end; at the end of one's rope ❹ 全部用出 use up; exhaust: ~心 with all one's heart|~力 do all one can; try one's best|~其所有 give everything one has; give one's all|人~其才,物~其用。Human, land and material resources should be used to the best advantage. ❺ 用力完成 try one's best; put to the best use: ~职 fulfil one's duty|~责任 do one's duty; discharge one's responsibilities ❻ 全;所有的 all; exhaustive: ~人皆知 be known to all; be common knowledge|~数收回 all have been returned

☞ jǐn on p.1008

【尽力】jìn//lì 用一切力量 do all one can; try one's best: ~而为 do one's best; do everything in one's power|我一定~帮助你。We'll do our best to help you.

【尽量】jìnliàng 达到最大限度 (drink or eat) to the full: 喝了半斤白酒,还没~。He drank half a *jin* of liquor, but said that he still hadn't drunk to the full.

☞ jǐnliàng on p.1008

【尽情】jìnqíng 尽量由着自己的情感,不加拘束 in abandon; to one's heart's content; as much as one likes: ~欢笑 laugh heartily|~发泄 vent one's spleen; express one's discontent as much as one likes|孩子们~地唱着、跳着。The children are singing and dancing to their hearts' content.

【尽然】jìnrán 完全这样(用于否定式 in the negative) entirely so: 未必~ not exactly so; not exactly the case|你以为他说的都是事实?不~吧。Do you think what he said is true? Not exactly.

【尽人皆知】jìn rén jiē zhī 人人都知道 known to all; be common knowledge: 那是~的事。That is a matter known to all.|他的事迹,在厂里~。His achievement is known to all in the factory.

【尽人事】jìn rén shì 尽力做人所能做到的事 do what one can; do all that is humanly possible

【尽善尽美】jìn shàn jìn měi 非常完美,没有缺陷 acme of perfection; perfect

【尽数】jìnshù 全数;全部 total number; whole amount: 欠款~归还 pay the debt in full

【尽头】jìntóu 末端;终点 end: 胡同的~有一所新房子。There is a new house at the end of the lane.|研究学问是没有~的。There is no limit to learning.

【尽心】jìn//xīn (为别人)费尽心思 with all one's heart: ~竭力 do sth. with all one's heart and all one's might|对老人你们也算尽到心了。You have been taking care of the elders with all your heart.

【尽兴】jìnxìng 兴趣得到尽量满足 to one's heart's content; enjoy oneself to the fullest: 改天咱们再~地谈吧。We will find another day for a hearty talk.|游览了一天,他们还觉得没有~。They have been travelling for the whole day, but they think they still haven't enjoyed themselves to the fullest.

【尽责】jìn//zé 尽力负起责任 do one's duty; discharge one's responsibility; do one's bit: 尽职~。Perform one's duty well.

【尽职】jìn//zhí 尽力做好本职工作 fulfil one's duty: ~尽责 fulfil one's duty|在班主任工作中,他非常~。He has always been a conscientious schoolmaster.

【尽忠】jìn//zhōng ❶ 竭尽忠诚 be utterly loyal: ~报国 be utterly loyal to the country ❷ 指竭尽忠诚而牺牲生命 be faithful until death: 为国~ lay down one's life for one's country

进(進) jìn ❶ 向前移动(跟'退'相对 as opposed to 'retreat') advance; move forward; move ahead: 推~ put forward|跃~ leap|~军 march; advance|~一步 go a step further; further|更~一层。Make progress and reach another level. ❷ 从外面到里面(跟'出'相对 as opposed to 'exit') enter; come in; go into; get into: ~入 enter|~门 enter the gate|~屋来 enter the room|~工厂当学徒 be an apprentice in a factory ❸ 收入 income: ~款 income|~货 stock with goods ❹ 呈上 submit: ~奉 submit|~言 offer a piece of advice or an opinion ❺ 用在动词后,表示到里面[used after a verb] in; into: 走~会场 walk into a meeting hall|把衣服放~箱子里去。Put the clothes into the box. ❻ 平房的一宅之内分前后几排的,一排称为一进 any of several rows of houses in an old-style residential compound

【进逼】jìnbī (军队)向前逼近 close in on; advance on; press on towards: 步步~ advance on closely

【进兵】jìnbīng 军队向执行战斗任务的目的地行进 dispatch troops to attack (a place); (of troops) march on: ~中原。Dispatch troops to attack the central plains.

【进补】jìnbǔ 吃有滋补作用的食物、药物补养身体 take a tonic or nourishing food to build up one's health: 冬令~。Take a tonic or nourishing food to build up one's health in winter.

【进步】jìnbù ❶（人或事物）向前发展，比原来好（of people or things） advance; progress; improve：虚心使人～，骄傲使人落后。Modesty helps one go forward, whereas conceit makes one lag behind. ❷ 适合时代要求，对社会发展起促进作用的（socially） progressive：～思想 progressive ideas | ～人士 progressive figures

【进餐】jìn//cān 指吃饭〈*fml*.〉 have a meal：按时～have meals on time

【进谗】jìnchán〈书 *fml*.〉在上级或长辈面前说人坏话 say sth. against sb. in front of a superior or elder：乘机～ seize the opportunity to say sth. against sb.

【进程】jìnchéng 事物发展变化或进行的过程 course; process; progress：历史的～course of history | 革命的～course of revolution

【进尺】jìnchǐ 采矿、钻探等工作的进度，通常以米为单位计算 footage; amount of work in mining, drilling, or tunnelling, usu. measured by the metre：钻机钻探的年～ annual drilling footage | 隧道掘进日～十米。The daily tunnelling footage is 10 metres.

【进出】jìnchū ❶ 进来和出去 come and go; in and out：住在大院的人由这个门～。People living in the yard pass in and out through this gate. ❷ 收入和支出（business） turnover：这个商店每天有好几万元的～。This store has a daily turnover of tens of thousands of yuan.

【进抵】jìndǐ（军队）前进到达某地（of troops） reach; arrive at：我部不日可望～江岸。Our troops will reach the riverside within days.

【进度】jìndù 工作等进行的速度 rate of progress (or advance)：～表 progress chart | 工程的～大大地加快了。Construction of a project has vastly picked up speed.

【进而】jìn'ér 继续往前；进一步 and then; after that：先提出计划，～提出实施措施。A plan should be put forward first, and then specific measures can be worked out.

【进发】jìnfā（车船或人的集体）出发前进 set out; start：列车向北京～。The train set out for Beijing. | 各小队分头～。Each group will set out separately.

【进犯】jìnfàn（敌军向某处）侵犯（of enemy troops） intrude into; invade

【进攻】jìngōng ❶ 接近敌人并主动攻击 close in and attack; assault; offensive：向山头上的敌人～ launch an attack against the enemy on the top of a hill | ～敌军盘踞的要塞。Launch an attack against the fort the enemy is entrenched in. ❷ 在斗争或竞赛中发动攻势 attack in a struggle; turn up the heat in a competition：快速～到对方篮下 quickly attack under the basket of the other team

【进贡】jìn//gòng ❶ 封建时代藩属对宗主国或臣民对君主呈献礼品 pay tribute to a suzerain or emperor ❷ 给人送礼求方便（含讥讽意 ironic） grease (or oil) sb.'s palm

【进化】jìnhuà 事物由简单到复杂，由低级到高级逐渐发展变化 evolution; (of a thing) develop and change from simple to complex, from low to advanced

【进化论】jìnhuàlùn ☞ 达尔文主义 Dá'ěrwén zhǔyì on p. 344

【进货】jìn//huò 商店为销售而购进货物 stock (a shop) with goods; lay in a stock of merchandise; replenish one's stock：进了一批货 lay in a new stock of goods

【进击】jìnjī（军队）进攻；攻击（of troops） advance; attack：向敌军～ advance on the enemy ◇富有开拓～精神 be full of pioneering and enterprising spirit

【进见】jìnjiàn 前去会见（多指见首长） call on (one's leader, boss, etc.); have an audience with

【进军】jìnjūn 军队出发向目的地前进（of troops） march; advance：红军渡过乌江，向川滇边境～。The Red Army crossed the Wujiang River and advanced towards the border between Sichuan and Yunnan provinces. | ～的号角响了。The bugle to advance sounded. ◇向科学～ march towards the modernization of science; scale new heights in science

【进口】jìn//kǒu ❶（船只）驶进港口（of ships） sail into a port ❷ 外国或外地区的货物运进来 import：～货 import goods | ～成套设备 import sets of equipment

【进口】jìnkǒu（～儿 jìnkǒur）进入建筑物或场地所经过的门或口儿 entrance

【进款】jìnkuǎn 指个人、家庭、团体等的收入 income; earnings (of. sb., a household, or organization)

【进来】jìn//·lái 从外面到里面来 come in; get in; enter：你～，咱们俩好好谈谈心。Come in please, and let's have a good talk. | 门开着，谁都进得来；门一关，谁也进不来。If the door is open, anyone can come in, but if it is shut, no one can.

【进来】//·jìn//·lái 用在动词后，表示到里面来 [used after a verb] in：烟冲～了。The smoke rushed in. | 他从街上跑～。He ran in from the street. | 窗户没糊好，风吹得～。The paper of the window is badly papered, so the wind can blow in. | 我刚看见从外面走进一个人来。I saw a man come in just now.

【进门】jìn//mén ❶ 走进门 go through a door; cross the threshold：他个儿高，～要低头。He is so tall he has to bend when going through the door. ❷〈比喻 *fig*.〉初步得到门径；入门 learn the rudiments of a subject; make it through the door ❸ 指女子出嫁到男家（of a woman) get married and go to live with the man's family：她是刚～的儿媳妇。She is a newly married daughter-in-law.

【进取】jìnqǔ 努力向前；立志有所作为 keep forging ahead；be eager to make progress；be enterprising：～心 enterprising spirit；initiative；gumption | 人要有～的精神。People should always keep making progress.

【进去】jìn//·qù 从外面到里面去 enter：你～看看，我在门口等着你。You go in and have a look, while I wait for you at the gate. | 我有票，进得去；他没票，进不去。I have a ticket, so I can enter；since he doesn't, he cannot.

【进去】//·jìn//·qù 用在动词后，表示到里面去 [used after a verb] in：把桌子搬～ carry the table in | 瓶口很大，手都伸得～。The mouth of the bottle is large enough to put a hand in. | 胡同太窄，卡车开不～。The lane is too narrow to let a truck in. | 从窗口递进一封信去。A letter was delivered through the window.

【进入】jìnrù 进到某个范围或某个时期里 enter；get into：～学校 enter a school | ～新阶段 enter a new phase ◇～角色 get inside the character that one is playing；get into a role；live one's part

【进深】jìn·shēn 院子、房间等的深度 depth or length of a house, yard, room, etc.：院子的～有多少？How about the depth of the house?

【进食】jìnshí 吃饭 take food；have a meal：按时～是个好习惯。Having meals on time is a good habit.

【进士】jìnshì 科举时代称殿试考取的人 successful candidate in the highest imperial examinations

【进退】jìntuì ❶ 前进和后退 advance and retreat：～自如 free to advance or retreat (in a battle or game)；have room for manoeuvre | ～两难 be in a dilemma ❷ 应进而进，应退而退，泛指言语行动恰如其分 sense of propriety：不知～have no sense of propriety

【进退两难】jìn tuì liǎng nán 进退都不好，形容处境困难 be torn between advancing and retreating；be in a dilemma

【进退维谷】jìn tuì wéi gǔ 进退两难 dilemma；between the devil and the deep blue sea (谷 *gu*：〈比喻 *fig.*〉困难的境地 difficult situation)

【进位】jìnwèi 加法中每位数等于基数时向前一位数进一，例如在十进位的算法中，个位满十，在十位中加一，百位满十，在千位中加一 carry；enter a number into another column when doing addition operations. For example, in decimal operations, when the ones' place goes over ten, carry one to the tens' place；when the tens' place goes over ten, carry it to the hundreds' place；when the number in the hundreds' place goes over ten, carry it to the thousands' place.

【进香】jìn//xiāng 佛教徒、道教徒到圣地或名山的庙宇去烧香朝拜，特指从远道去的 (of Buddhist and Taoist believers) make a pilgrimage；travel to a remote sacred place or temple in a famous mountain to burn incense sticks and pay homage to the Buddha or Taoist saints

【进项】jìn·xiang 收入的钱 income；earning：农民的～普遍有了增加。Generally, the farmers' incomes have increased.

【进行】jìnxíng ❶ 从事(某种活动) carry out；execute；conduct；wage：～讨论 carry on a discussion | ～工作 conduct work | ～教育和批评 carry out education and criticism | 会议正在～。The meeting is underway. 注意

NOTE：'进行'总是用在持续性的和正式、严肃的行为，短暂性的和日常生活中的行为不用'进行'，例如不说'进行午睡'、'进行叫喊'。The phrase 进行 is used esp. to describe ongoing formal and serious actions, not short-term or everyday activities, e.g. one doesn't say 进行午睡 jìnxíng wǔshuì and 进行叫喊 jìnxíng jiàohǎn. ❷ 前进 be in progress；be underway；go on：～曲 march

【进行曲】jìnxíngqǔ 适合于队伍行进时演奏或歌唱的乐曲，节奏鲜明，结构严整，由偶数拍子构成，如《解放军进行曲》等 march；music with a strong regular rhythm in even beats, which is written for marches, e.g. *March of the People's Liberation Army*

【进修】jìnxiū 为了提高政治或业务水平而进一步学习（多指暂时离开职位，参加一定的学习组织 oft. on leave from one's position for a set time) engage in advanced studies；take a refresher course；take part in advanced study to improve one's political awareness or work efficiency

【进言】jìn//yán 向人提出意见（尊敬或客气的口气）offer one's advice or opinion (in a respectful or polite tone)：大胆～ make bold to offer an opinion | 向您进一言。Let me give you a piece of advice.

【进一步】jìn yī bù 表示事情的进行在程度上比以前提高 go a step further；further：～实现农业机械化 further realize the mechanization of agriculture | ～加速实现四个现代化的步伐 accelerate the realization of the four modernizations

【进益】jìnyì ❶〈书 *fml.*〉指学识修养的进步 make progress (in study, etc.) ❷ 指经济收入；收益 income；profit：你一年有多少～？How much a year do you earn?

【进展】jìnzhǎn （事情）向前发展 (of sth.) make progress；make headway：～神速 advance at a miraculous pace|推广工作有～。Progress has been made in popularizing (the new skill).

【进占】jìnzhàn 进兵占领 march on and occupy (a certain place): ～边关。March on and take the pass on the border.

【进账】jìnzhàng 指收入;进款 income; receipts: 每月有两三百元的～。The monthly income is two or three hundred yuan.

【进驻】jìnzhù (军队)开进某一地区驻扎下来 (of troops) enter and be stationed in; enter and garrison

近 jìn ❶ 空间或时间距离短(跟'远'相对 as opposed to 'far') near; close: ～郊 outskirts of a city|～日 recently|～百年史 history of the last century|靠～ close|附～ nearby|歌声由远而～。The singing can be heard approaching from the distance.|现在离国庆节很～了。National Day is drawing near. ❷ 接近 approaching; approximately; close to: ～似 be similar to|平易～人 amiable and easy of approach|年～三十 coming on thirty|两人年龄相～。They are nearly the same age.|～朱者赤,～墨者黑。He who stays near vermilion gets stained red, and he who stays near ink gets stained black — one takes on the colour of one's company. ❸ 亲密;关系密切 intimate; closely related: 亲～ intimate|～亲 close relatives ❹〈书 *fml.*〉浅近;浅显 easy to understand: 言～旨远 simple words but deep meaning; simple in language but profound in meaning

【近便】jìn·bian 路比较近,容易走到 close and convenient: 从小路走要～一些。It is close and convenient to go by the narrow path.

【近代】jìndài ❶ 过去距离现代较近的时代,在我国历史分期上多指 19 世纪中叶到五四运动之间的时期 modern times; age that was close to the present; (in Chinese history) the period from the mid-19th century to the May 4th Movement of 1919 ❷ 指资本主义时代 capitalist times

【近道】jìndào 距离短的道路(多就比较而言 oft. in comparison) shortcut: 走～ take the shortcut

【近地点】jìndìdiǎn 月球或人造地球卫星绕地球运行的轨道上离地球最近的点 perigee; point closest to the earth on the orbit of the moon or a man-made satellite

【近东】Jìndōng 指亚洲西南部和非洲东北部,包括亚洲的阿拉伯半岛、土耳其、伊拉克、叙利亚、约旦、黎巴嫩、巴勒斯坦、以色列,非洲的埃及和苏丹 Near East; region encompassing Southwest Asia and Northeast Africa, including Arabian Peninsula, Turkey, Iraq, Syria, Jordan, Lebanon, Palestine, Israel of Asia, and Egypt and Sudan of Africa

【近古】jìngǔ 最近的古代,在我国历史分期上多指宋元明清(到 19 世纪中叶)这个时期 age of recent antiquity; (in Chinese history) period of the Song, Yuan, Ming and Qing dynasties (10th to mid-19th centuries)

【近海】jìnhǎi 靠近陆地的海域 coastal waters; inshore; offshore: ～航行 offshore voyage|利用～养殖海带 inshore kelp-farming

【近乎】jìn·hu ❶ 接近于 close to; little short of: 脸上露出一种～天真的表情。A seemingly naive expression appeared on (his) face. ❷〈方 *dial.*〉(～儿 jìn·hur)关系亲密 intimate; friendly: 套～ cotton up to sb.|他和小王拉～。He tried to be friendly with Xiao Wang.|两个人越谈越～。They seemed to become more friendly with each other the more they talked.

【近郊】jìnjiāo 城市附近的郊区 outskirts of a city; suburbs; environs: 北京～ suburbs of Beijing; suburban Beijing

【近景】jìnjǐng ❶ 近距离的景物 scenery close by ❷ 当前的景象 present situation; current condition: ～规划 plan for the immediate future

【近况】jìnkuàng 最近一段时间的情况 recent developments; how things stand: 不知他的～如何。I don't know how things have been with him lately.

【近来】jìnlái 指过去不久到现在的一段时间 recently; of late; lately: ～天气有些反常。The weather has been somewhat unusual recently.|他～工作很忙。He has been busy lately.

【近邻】jìnlín 挨得较近的邻居 close neighbour: 远亲不如～。Close neighbours are more helpful than close relatives living afar.

【近路】jìnlù 近道 shortcut

【近旁】jìnpáng 附近;旁边 nearby; near: 屋子～种着许多竹子。Many bamboo plants grow near the house.

【近期】jìnqī 最近的一个时期 in the near future: 这部影片将于～上映。The film will be showing very soon.

【近前】jìnqián 附近;跟前 nearby; near: 走到～才认出是他。Only when I came close did I recognize it was him.

【近亲】jìnqīn 血统关系比较近的亲戚 close relative; near relations: ～之间不可结婚。Marriage is not allowed between close relatives.

【近情】jìnqíng 合乎人情;近乎情理 reasonable: ～近理 reasonable and fair|这样做太不～了。It is unreasonable and unfair to do it that way.

【近人】jìnrén ❶ 近代的或现代的人 person of modern times or contemporary ❷〈书 *fml.*〉跟自己关系比较近的人 one's close associate

【近日点】jìnrìdiǎn 行星或彗星绕太阳公转的轨道上离太阳最近的点 perihelion; point closest to the sun in the orbit of a planet or comet

【近世】jìnshì 近代 modern times

【近视】jìnshì ❶ 视力缺陷的一种,能看清近处的东西,看不清远处的东西。近视是由于眼球的晶状体和网膜的距离过长或晶状体折光力过强,使进入眼球的影像不能正落在网膜上而落在网膜的前面。myopia; near-sightedness; short-sightedness; vision defect where one can see things close up but cannot clearly see things in the distance, caused by an excessive distance between the lens of the eyeball and the retina or by an excessively strong refraction of the lens, making images fall on the front of, instead of on, the retina ❷〈比喻 *fig.*〉眼光短浅 short-sighted

【近水楼台】jìn shuǐ lóu tái 宋代俞文豹《清夜录》引宋人苏麟诗,'近水楼台先得月' From *Records on a Clear Night* by Yu Wenbao of the Song Dynasty, quoting the Song-dynasty poet Su Lin's line: 'A waterside pavilion gets the moonlight first.'〈比喻 *fig.*〉因接近某人或某事物而处于首先获得好处的优越地位 be in an advantageous position because of one's close relations to sb. or sth.; be in a favourable position

【近似】jìnsì 相近或相像但不相同 approximate; similar: 这两个地区的方音有些～。The accents of the two regions are somewhat similar.

【近似值】jìnsìzhí 计算上接近准确值的数值叫做近似值,如 3.1416 是圆周率值的近似值 approximate value; approximation; approximate result adequate for a given purpose, such as 3.1416, the ratio of the circumference of a circle to its diameter

【近体诗】jìntǐshī 唐代形成的律诗和绝句的通称(区别于'古体诗'),句数、字数和平仄、用韵等都有比较严格的规定(as compared with 'classical-style poetry') modern-style poetry, referring to innovations in classical poetry during the Tang Dynasty (618-907), marked by strict tonal patterns and rhyme schemes

【近因】jìnyīn 直接促成结果的原因(区别于'远因' as compared with 'remote cause') immediate cause

【近战】jìnzhàn ❶ 敌对双方近距离作战 fight at close quarters; close combat: 善于～ be good at close combat ❷ 近距离的战斗 close combat

【近朱者赤,近墨者黑】jìn zhū zhě chì, jìn mò zhě hēi〈比喻 *fig.*〉接近好人使人变好,接近坏人使人变坏(见于晋代傅玄《太子少傅箴》) he who lies with dogs will rise with fleas; he who stays near vermilion gets stained red, and he who stays near ink gets stained black (*Admonitions from the Junior Mentor of the Crown Prince* by Fu Xuan of the Jin Dynasty)

妗 jìn ☞ below

【妗母】jìnmǔ〈方 *dial.*〉舅母 aunt; wife of one's mother's brother

【妗子】jìn·zi ❶ 舅母 aunt; wife of one's mother's brother ❷ 妻兄、妻弟的妻子 wife of one's wife's brother: 大～ wife of wife's elder brother | 小～ wife of wife's younger brother

劲(勁、劤) jìn ❶ (～儿 jìnr) 力气 strength; energy: 用～ use more energy | 手～儿 strength of one's hand ❷ (～儿 jìnr) 精神;情绪 vigour; spirit; drive; zeal: 鼓足干～,力争上游 go all out, and aim high | 我就喜欢青年人的那股冲(chòng)～儿。I like the vigour the young people display. ❸ (～儿 jìnr) 神情;态度 air; manner; expression: 瞧他那股骄傲～儿。Look at his arrogant ways. ❹ 趣味 interest; relish; gusto: 下棋没～,不如打球去。Playing chess is not as fun as playing basketball.

☞ jìng on p. 1030

【劲头】jìntóu (～儿 jìntóur) ❶ 力量;力气 strength; energy: 战士们身体好,～儿大,个个都像小老虎。The soldiers are strong and full of vigour, all like little tigers. ❷ 积极的情绪 vigour; spirit; drive; zeal: 看他那股兴高采烈的～儿。Look, how happy and excited he is. | 他们学习起来～十足。They study with enthusiasm.

荩[1](藎) jìn same as 荩草 jìncǎo

荩[2](藎) jìn〈书 *fml.*〉忠诚 loyal; faithful; staunch: 忠～ faithful | ～臣 loyal minister

【荩草】jìncǎo 一年生草本植物,叶子卵状披针形,花灰绿色或带紫色,颖果长圆形。茎和叶可以做黄色染料,纤维可以造纸。hispid arthraxon (*Arthraxon hispidus*); annual herb having egg-shaped lanceolate leaves, greyish green flowers sometimes tinted purple, and oval caryopses, its stems and leaves used to make yellow dye, and its fibres used to make paper

浕(濜) Jìn 浕水,水名,在湖北 Jinshui, name of a river in Hubei Province

晋[1](晉) jìn ❶ 进 enter; advance: ～见 call on ❷ 升;升级 promote: ～级 promote | ～升 promote to a higher position | 加官～爵 be promoted to a higher office and rank

晋[2](晉) Jìn ❶ 周朝国名,在今山西、河北南部及陕西中部、河南西北部 Jin, name of a state of the Zhou Dynasty, occupying parts of what are now northern Shanxi and Hebei, central Shaanxi, and northwestern Henan ❷ 朝代,公元 265—420,

J

司马炎所建 Jin Dynasty (265-420), founded by Sima Yan; ☞ 西晋 Xī Jìn on p. 2042 and 东晋 Dōng Jìn on p. 463 ❸ 后晋 Later Jin Dynasty ❹ 山西的别称 another name for Shanxi Province ❺ 姓 a surname

【晋级】jìn//jí 升到较高的等级 formal rise in rank; be promoted

【晋见】jìnjiàn 进见 call on (sb. holding high office); have an audience with

【晋剧】jìnjù 山西地方戏曲剧种之一，由蒲剧派生而成。流行于该省中部地区。Shanxi opera; local opera derived from the *puju* opera and popular in central Shanxi Province; also 山西梆子 Shānxī bāng·zi and 中路梆子 zhōnglù bāng·zi

【晋升】jìnshēng 提高(职位、级别) promote to higher office: ～中将 promote to lieutenant general|～一级工资。(He) received a raise by one grade.

【晋谒】jìnyè 〈书 *fml.*〉进见；谒见 call on (sb. holding high office); have an audience with

赆(贐、賮) jìn 〈书 *fml.*〉临别时赠送的财物 parting gift: ～仪 farewell presents

烬(燼) jìn 物体燃烧后剩下的东西 cinder: 灰～ ashes|余～ ruins

浸(❸寖) jìn ❶ 泡在液体里 soak; seep; immerse: ～种 soak seeds|放在开水里～一～ immerse in boiling water ❷ 液体渗入或渗出 (of liquid) seep: 衣服让汗～湿了。(His) clothes were soaked with sweat.|红砂岩一年四季往外～水。Water seeps from the red sandstone all year round. ❸ 〈书 *fml.*〉逐渐 gradually; increasingly: 友情～厚。The friendship gradually deepened.

【浸沉】jìnchén 沉浸 soak; immerse

【浸没】jìnmò ❶ 淹没；漫过去 soak; immerse ❷ 沉浸 soak; immerse: 人们正～在快乐之中。People are overcome with joy.

【浸泡】jìnpào 放在液体中泡 soak; immerse: ～棉籽 soak cottonseed

【浸染】jìnrǎn ❶ 逐渐沾染或感染 be contaminated; be gradually influenced ❷ 液体渗入而使染上颜色等 soak; (of liquid) soak in and dye sth.; dip-dye: 血水～了白衬衣。(His) white shirt was gradually soaked in the blood.

【浸润】jìnrùn ❶ (液体)渐渐渗入 (of liquid) soak; infiltrate: 墨水滴到纸上，慢慢～开来。The ink dropped onto the paper, gradually soaking it. ❷ 〈书 *fml.*〉指谗言逐渐发生作用 (of rumour, slanderous remarks, erc.) sink in; gradually influence; affect little by little: ～之谮 insidious slander which gradually sink in ❸ 指液体与固体接触时，液体附着在固体表面上的现象 adhesion; physical attraction or joining of liquid on the surface of a solid object ❹ 医学上指由于细菌等侵入或由于外物刺激，有机体的正常组织发生白细胞等聚集的现象 (med.) infiltration; (of normal tissues in an organism) concentration of white cells due to an attack of germs or external stimuli

【浸透】jìntòu ❶ 泡在液体里以致湿透 soak; saturate; steep; infuse: 他穿的一双布鞋被雨水～了。His cloth shoes got soaked with rain. ❷ 液体渗透 soak; saturate; steep; infuse: 汗水～了衬衫。His shirt was soaked with sweat. ❸ 〈比喻 *fig.*〉饱含(某种思想感情等) be full of (thoughts, emotions, etc.): 这些诗篇～着诗人眷念祖国的深情。The poems were infused with the poet's deep love for his motherland.

【浸种】jìn//zhǒng 为了使种子发芽快，在播种前用温水或冷水浸一定时间 seed soaking; soaking seed in warm or cold water for a period of time so as to make the seeds sprout quickly

【浸渍】jìnzì 用液体泡 soak; ret; macerate: 把原料捣碎，放在石灰水里～，再加蒸煮，变成糜烂的纸浆。Pound the materials, soak them in lime water, cook and steam them, and turn them into paper pulp.

琎(璡) jīn 像玉的石头。多用于人名。a kind of stone like jade, oft. used in a person's name

唫 jìn 〈书 *fml.*〉闭口不言 keep silent ☞ 吟 yín on p. 2289

祲 jìn 〈古代 *arch.*〉迷信称不祥之气；妖气 (superstition) evil things

靳 jìn ❶ 〈书 *fml.*〉吝惜，不肯给予 be stingy; grudge ❷ (Jìn) 姓 a surname

禁 jìn ❶ 禁止 prohibit; forbid; ban: ～赌 ban gambling|严～烟火。Smoking is prohibited.|严～走私 ban smuggling ❷ 监禁 be placed in confinement: ～闭 imprison; detain ❸ 法令或习俗所不允许的事项 taboo; what is forbidden by law or custom: 犯～ violate a ban|违～品 contraband|入国问～ on entering a country, enquire about its customs ❹ 〈旧时 *old*〉称皇帝居住的地方 forbidden area; quarters where an emperor lives: ～中 central forbidden area|宫～ palace prohibitions ☞ jīn on p. 1007

【禁闭】jìnbì 把犯错误的人关在屋子里让他反省，是一种处罚 confinement; locking a wrongdoer in a room as a punishment: 关～ be placed in confinement|～三天 be placed in confinement for three days

【禁地】jìndì 禁止一般人去的地方 forbidden area; restricted area; out-of-bounds area

【禁锢】jìngù ❶ 封建时代统治集团禁止异己的人做官或不许他们参加政治活动 (of the ruling class) bar dissidents from holding office or taking part in political activities in feudal times ❷ 关押；监禁 keep in custody; imprison：～犯人 keep prisoners behind bars ❸ 束缚；强力限制 confine；shackle：这些陈规陋习成了～人们精神的枷锁。Outdated rules and regulations have shackled people's minds.

【禁忌】jìnjì ❶ 犯忌讳的话或行动 taboo：旧时的许多～大都与迷信有关。Most taboos in the past were connected with superstition. ❷ 指医药上应避免某类事物（med.）contraindication：～油腻 abstain from greasy food

【禁绝】jìnjué 彻底禁止 totally prohibit；completely ban：～卖淫嫖娼 completely ban prostitution|～吸食毒品 totally prohibit drugs

【禁军】jìnjūn〈古代 *arch.*〉称保卫京城或宫廷的军队 imperial guards

【禁例】jìnlì 禁止某种行为的条例 prohibitory regulations；prohibitions

【禁令】jìnlìng 禁止从事某项活动的法令 prohibition；ban：解除～ lift a ban|违反～ violate a ban

【禁脔】jìnluán〈比喻 *fig.*〉独自占有而不容别人分享的东西 piece of meat for one's exclusive consumption；one's exclusive domain：视为～ regard as one's exclusive domain

【禁区】jìnqū ❶ 禁止一般人进入的地区 out-of-bounds area；forbidden zone；restricted zone ❷ 因其中动植物或地面情况在科学或经济方面有特殊价值而受到特别保护的地区 preserve；reserve；nature reserve；area under special protection because of the scientific or economic value of its flora，fauna or geographic conditions ❸ 医学上指因容易发生危险而禁止动手术或针灸的部位（med.）forbidden zone；places on the body that forbid surgical operation or acupuncture because of dangers easily arising in these places ❹ 在某些球类比赛中，罚球区以内的地方 penalty area in certain types of ball games

【禁书】jìnshū 禁止刊行或阅读的书籍 banned book

【禁欲】jìnyù 抑制性欲或抑制一般享受的欲望 be ascetic；suppress sensual enjoyment

【禁止】jìnzhǐ 不许可 prohibit；ban；forbid：厂房重地，～吸烟。Smoking is prohibited in the workshop.|～车辆通行。No thoroughfare. *or* Closed to traffic.

【禁制品】jìnzhìpǐn 非经特别许可不得制造的物品 banned products；articles not to be manufactured except by special permit

【禁子】jìn·zi〈旧时 *old*〉称在牢狱中看守罪犯的人 jailer；also 禁卒 jìnzú

【禁阻】jìnzǔ 禁止；阻止 prohibit；ban；forbid；prevent；stop

搢 jìn〈书 *fml.*〉❶ 插 insert ❷ 摇 swing

【搢绅】jìnshēn same as 缙绅 jìnshēn

溍 Jìn 古水名 name of an ancient river

缙 jìn〈书 *fml.*〉赤色的帛 red silk

【缙绅】jìnshēn〈古代 *arch.*〉称有官职的或做过官的人 government official；retired government official；also 搢绅 jìnshēn

瑨 jìn〈书 *fml.*〉像玉的石头 jade-like stone

墐 jìn〈书 *fml.*〉❶ 用泥涂塞 paint or fill with mud ❷ same as 殣① jìn

觐 jìn 朝见(君主)；朝拜(圣地) present oneself before（a monarch）；go to court；have an audience with：～见 present oneself before（a monarch）；go to court；have an audience with|朝～ present oneself before（a monarch）

【觐见】jìnjiàn〈书 *fml.*〉朝见（君主）present oneself before（a monarch）；go to court；have an audience with

殣 jìn〈书 *fml.*〉❶ 掩埋 bury ❷ 饿死 starve to death

噤 jìn ❶〈书 *fml.*〉闭口不做声 keep silent：～声 keep silent|～若寒蝉 as silent as a cicada in cold weather — keep quiet out of fear ❷ 因寒冷而发生的哆嗦 shiver；tremble with cold：寒～ shiver with cold

【噤若寒蝉】jìn ruò hánchán 形容不敢做声 as silent as a cicada in cold weather；keep quiet out of fear

jīng（ㄐㄧㄥ）

坙（巠） jīng〈书 *fml.*〉水脉 veins of river

茎（莖） jīng ❶ 植物体的一部分，由胚芽发展而成，下部和根连接，上部一般都生有叶、花和果实。茎能输送水、无机盐和养料到植物体的各部分去，并有贮存养料和支持枝、叶子、花、果实等生长的作用。常见的有直立茎、缠绕茎、攀援茎、匍匐茎等多种。stem of a plant；stalk developing from a sprout，connected with the root at its lower portion，while leaves，flowers and fruit grow on its upper portion. A stem can transport water，inorganic salts and nutrients to every part of the plant，as well as store nutrients and support twigs，leaves，flowers and fruit to grow. Common varieties include strict stems，vines，climbing stems，and stolons. ❷ 像茎的东西 sth. resembling a stem or stalk：阴～ penis|刀～（刀把）handle of a knife|剑～（剑柄）handle of a sword ❸〈书 *fml.*〉〈量词 *classifier*〉用于长条形的东西［used for long，narrow things］：数～小草 a few small blades of grass|数～白发 a few white hairs

京[1] jīng ❶ 首都 capital of a country：～城 capital of a country|～师 capital of a country ❷（Jīng）指我国首都北京 Beijing，capital of China：～剧 Peking Opera|～腔

Beijing accent | ～味儿 Beijing flavour ❸ (Jīng) 姓 a surname

京[2] jīng 〈古代 *arch.*〉数目名，指一千万 ten million

【京白】jīngbái 京剧中指用北京话念的道白 parts in the Peking Opera spoken in Beijing dialect

【京白梨】jīngbáilí 北京地区产的白梨。果实皮薄，肉厚，味甜多汁，香味浓郁。a kind of fragrant, sweet and juicy pear produced in the Beijing area, with a thin peel and thick flesh

【京城】jīngchéng 指国都 capital of a country

【京都】jīngdū 京城 capital of a country

【京二胡】jīng'èrhú 胡琴的一种，和二胡相似，音响介于京胡二胡之间，用于京剧伴奏等 a type of Chinese fiddle similar to the two-stringed *erhu*, producing a musical sound between the *jinghu* and the *erhu*, and used to accompany Peking Opera singing; also 嗡子 wēng·zi

【京官】jīngguān 〈旧时 *old*〉称在京城供职的官员 official with a post in the capital

【京胡】jīnghú 胡琴的一种，形状跟二胡相似而较小，琴筒用竹子做成，发音较高，主要用于京剧伴奏 *jinghu*; Peking Opera fiddle; two-stringed, bamboo-bowed instrument similar to but smaller than the *erhu*, with a high register, used mainly to accompany Peking Opera singing

【京华】jīnghuá 首都 capital of a country: 誉满～ well-known throughout the capital

【京畿】jīngjī 〈书 *fml.*〉国都及其附近的地方 capital city and its environs

【京剧】jīngjù 我国全国性的主要剧种之一。清中叶以来，以西皮、二黄为主要腔调的徽调、汉调相继进入北京，徽汉合流演变为北京皮黄戏，即京剧。Peking Opera; one of the main national operas in China. Beginning from the mid-Qing Dynasty, the Anhui and Hubei melodies composed mainly of the *xipi* and the *erhuang* tones found their way to Beijing and their fusion resulted in the birth of the *pihuang* opera of Beijing, or Peking Opera. also 京戏 jīngxì

【京派】jīngpài 京剧的一个流派，以北京的表演风格为代表 Beijing school of the Peking Opera

【京腔】jīngqiāng 指北京语音 Beijing accent

【京师】jīngshī 〈书 *fml.*〉首都 capital of a country

【京味】jīngwèi (～儿 jīngwèir)北京风味；北京地方特色 special flavour of Beijing; Beijing specialties: ～小吃 Beijing specialty snacks | ～十足的电视剧 TV play rich in Beijing flavour

【京戏】jīngxì same as 京剧 jīngjù

【京油子】jīngyóu·zi 指久住北京老于世故而油滑的人 Beijing sharper; worldly and slippery person who has lived in Beijing for a long time

【京韵大鼓】jīngyùn dàgǔ 曲艺，大鼓的一种，形成于北京，流行北方各地 storytelling in Beijing dialect with drum accompaniment, developed in Beijing and popular in northern China

【京族】Jīngzú ❶ 我国少数民族之一，分布在广西 Jing (Ching) people, or Jings (Chings), one of China's ethnic minority peoples, living in the Guangxi Zhuang Autonomous Region ❷ 越南人数最多的民族 most populous ethnic people in Vietnam

泾(涇) jīng ❶〈方 *dial.*〉河沟 river; brook; stream ❷(Jīng) 泾河，发源于宁夏，流入陕西 Jinghe River, originating in the Ningxia Hui Autonomous Region and flowing through Shaanxi Province

【泾渭分明】Jīng Wèi fēnmíng 泾河水清，渭河水浑，泾河的水流入渭河时，清浊不混，比喻界限清楚 as different as the waters of the Jinghe and Weihe rivers; water of the Jinghe River is clear while the Weihe is muddy, so when the former flows into the latter, the two do not mix; (fig.) categorically different

经[1]**(經)** jīng ❶ (旧读 formerly pronounced jìng)织物上纵的方向的纱或线(跟'纬'相对 as opposed to 'woof') warp; lengthwise yarn or thread on a piece of fabric: ～纱 warp | ～线 warp ❷〈中医 *Chin. med.*〉指人体内气血运行通路的主干 channels; arteries for blood circulation in the human body ❸ 经度 longitude: 东～ longitude east | 西～ longitude west ❹ 经营；治理 manage; deal in; engage in: ～商 engage in trade or business | 整军～武 build up a country's military strength ❺〈书 *fml.*〉上吊 hang (oneself): 自～ hang oneself ❻ 历久不变的；正常 constant; regular: ～常 often | 不～之谈(荒唐无稽的话) unfounded statement; sheer nonsense ❼ 经典 classic: 本草～ *Compendium of Materia Medica* | 佛～ sutra; Buddhist scripture | 古兰～(伊斯兰教的经典) *Koran* (of Islam) ❽ 月经 menses; menstruation: 行～ menstruate | ～血不调 erratic menstruation ❾(Jīng) 姓 a surname

经[2]**(經)** jīng ❶ 经过 pass through; undergo; experience: ～年累月 year in year out | 几～周折 after a lot of twists and turns | 这件事是～我手办的。I am the one who handled the matter. | ～他一说，我才知道。I came to know about it after he mentioned it. ❷ 禁(jīn) 受 stand; bear; endure: ～不起 cannot stand | ～得起考验 can stand the test

☞ jìng on p. 1031

【经闭】jīngbì 妇女月经停止的现象，有生理状态的，也有病理状态的。妇女在妊娠期、授乳期，或生殖器发育不健全以及由于疾病造成的子宫机能损害等，都会引起经闭。amenorrhoea;

abnormal absence of menstruation due to either physiological changes or illness, or resulting from pregnancy, breast-feeding, underdevelopment of genitals, as well as damage to the uterus functions caused by illness; also 闭经 bìjīng

【经部】jīngbù 我国古代图书分类的一大部类。包括四书、五经等儒家经典和文字、音韵、训诂方面的著作。classics; major category in the classification of traditional Chinese books that includes such Confucian classics as the Four Books and the Five Classics, as well as works concerning language, phonology and textual exegesis; also 甲部 jiǎbù; ☞ 四部 sìbù on p. 1820

【经常】jīngcháng ❶ 平常;日常 day-to-day; everyday; daily: ～费 running expense | 积肥是农业生产中的～工作。Collecting manure is day-to-day work in farming. ❷ 常常;时常 frequently; constantly; regularly; often: 他俩～保持联系。The two of them regularly keep in touch with each other. | 要～注意环境卫生。Be sure to keep the area clean at all times.

【经幢】jīngchuáng 刻有佛的名字或经咒的石柱子,柱身多为六角形或圆形 stone pillar inscribed with the names of the Buddhas or incantations, oft. hexagonal or round in shape

【经典】jīngdiǎn ❶ 指传统的具有权威性的著作 religious classic: 博览～ read classics extensively ❷ 泛指各宗教宣扬教义的根本性著作 religious scriptures ❸ 著作具有权威性的 classical: 马列主义～著作 Marxist-Leninist classics; classical works of Marxism-Leninism | ～作家 classical writer

【经度】jīngdù 地球表面东西距离的度数,以本初子午线为 0°,以东为东经,以西为西经,东西各 180°。通过某地的经线与本初子午线相距的度数,就是该地的经度。longitude; angular distance east or west from the first meridian measured in digrees, to the east of which is called the longitude east (180°), and to the west, the longitude west (180°). The longitudinal degrees of a place is derived from the angular distance between its longitude and the first meridian. ☞ 经线 jīngxiàn

【经费】jīngfèi (机关、学校等)经常支出的费用 (of government organs, schools, etc.) expenditure; outlay

【经管】jīngguǎn 经手管理 be in charge of: 财务工作设专人～。A person was appointed specially in charge of financial affairs. | 由～人签字盖章 signed by the person in charge

【经过】jīngguò ❶ 通过(处所、时间、动作等) pass; go through (place, time, movement, etc.): 从北京坐火车到广州要～武汉。A trip from Beijing to Guangzhou by train goes through Wuhan. | 屋子～打扫,干净多了。The room became much cleaner after sweeping. | 这件事情是～领导上缜密考虑的。The matter was carefully considered by the leadership. ❷ 过程;经历② process; experience: 厂长向来宾报告建厂～。The director told his visitors about how his factory was built. | 说说你探险的～。Tell us something about your experience in the exploration.

【经籍】jīngjí 〈书 *fml.*〉❶ 经书 scripture; sutra ❷ 泛指图书(多指古代的 oft. referring to ancient books) (in a broad sense) books

【经纪】jīngjì ❶ 筹划并管理(企业);经营 manage (a business): 不善～ bad at management ❷ 经纪人 broker; middleman; agent ❸ 〈书 *fml.*〉料理 handle; look after: ～其家 be the homemaker for one's family

【经纪人】jīngjìrén ❶ 为买卖双方撮合从中取得佣金的人 broker; middleman; agent; person who gets a commission by acting as a go-between in a deal ❷ 在交易所中代他人进行买卖而取得佣金的人 broker; middleman; agent; person who gets a commission by buying and selling for sb. else

【经济】jīngjì ❶ 经济学上指社会物质生产和再生产的活动 economy; term of economics denoting the production and reproduction activities of a society ❷ 对国民经济有利或有害的 being good or bad for the national economy: ～作物 cash crop; industrial crop | ～昆虫 economic insect ❸ 个人生活用度 financial condition; income: 他家～比较宽裕。His family is relatively well-off. ❹ 用较少的人力、物力、时间获得较大的成果 economical; thrifty; getting more results with less labour, material and time: 作者用非常～的笔墨写出了这一场复杂的斗争。The writer wrote about the complicated struggle with an unusual economy of words. ❺ 〈书 *fml.*〉治理国家 govern the country; run or manage a country: ～之才 ability to run a country

【经济核算】jīngjì hésuàn 企业经营管理的一种方式,用货币来衡量经济活动中的劳动消耗、物资消耗和劳动的经济效果,要求最充分、最合理地使用全部劳动力、机器设备、原料、材料和资源等,使它们能够发挥最大的经济效果 economic accounting; business accounting; business management method for an enterprise, using a currency to measure the consumption of labour and materials and the economic results, and demanding the most reasonable and ample use of all the labour force, machinery, equipment, raw materials, and resources, in order to achieve the greatest economic results

【经济基础】jīngjì jīchǔ 社会发展一定阶段上的社会经济制度,即社会生产关系的总和,它是上层建筑的基础 economic base; economic basis; social and economic system, that is, the sum total of all socio-economic relations during a certain stage of social development, which is the basis of the superstructure; 简称 abbr. 基础 jīchǔ; ☞ 上层建筑 shàngcéng jiànzhù on p. 1680

【经济昆虫】jīngjì kūnchóng 在经济意义上有利或有害的昆虫,有利的如蚕、蜜蜂、白蜡虫等,有害的如蝗虫、蚜虫、红铃虫等 economic insect; economically beneficial or damaging insect. Silkworms, bees and wax insects are among the beneficial insects while locusts, plant louses, pink bollworms, etc. fall into the category of economic pests.

【经济林】jīngjìlín 生产木材、油料、干果或其他林产品的树林。狭义的经济林不包括生产木材的树林。economic forest; woods that yield timber, oilseeds, dried fruit or other forest products. In a narrow sense, an economic forest doesn't include forests that produce timber.

【经济特区】jīngjì tèqū 实行特殊的经济政策和经济管理体制的地区 special economic zone; zone that adopts special economic policies and economic management systems

【经济体制】jīngjì tǐzhì 整个国民经济的管理制度、管理形式、管理方法的总称 economic structure; general term for the system, form and methodology of a national economy as a whole

【经济危机】jīngjì wēijī 指资本主义社会再生产过程中发生的生产过剩的危机,具体表现是:大量商品找不到销路,许多企业倒闭,生产下降,失业增多,整个社会经济陷于瘫痪和混乱状态。经济危机是资本主义生产方式基本矛盾发展的必然结果,具有周期性。economic crisis; crisis of overproduction during the course of reproduction in a capitalist society, characterized by the loss of markets for a large quantities of commodities, the bankruptcy of many enterprises, decreasing production, increasing unemployment, and total paralysis and chaos of society and the economy. The economic crisis is the inevitable cyclical result of the development of basic contradictions existing in the capitalist mode of production. also 经济恐慌 jīngjì kǒnghuāng

【经济效益】jīngjì xiàoyì 经济活动中劳动耗费同劳动成果之间的对比,反映社会再生产各个环节对人力、物力、财力的利用效果 economic performance; economic results; economic effectiveness; economic efficiency; balance of labour and its results in economic activities, which reflects efficiency of society's use of human, material and financial resources in various links of reproduction; also 经济效果 jīngjì xiàoguǒ

【经济学】jīngjìxué ❶ 研究国民经济各方面问题的学科的总称。包括政治经济学、部门经济学、会计学、统计学等。economics; general term for subjects that study a national economy, including political economy, departmental economics, accounting, statistics, etc. ❷ 政治经济学的简称 abbr. for 政治经济学 zhèngzhì-jīngjìxué

【经济杂交】jīngjì zájiāo 两个或两个以上不同品种的家畜(或家禽)进行杂交,所得的第一代杂种生长快,容易饲养和育肥。这种杂交只进行一代,不继续繁殖。commercial cross-breeding; cross-breeding of two or more breeds of livestock or poultry, with the first generation of hybrids being quick in growth and easy to feed and be fattened. This kind of commercial cross-breeding takes place only for one generation alone.

【经济制度】jīngjì zhìdù 指人类社会发展一定阶段上的生产关系的总和。也指一定社会经济部门或一个方面的具体制度,如工业经济制度、农业经济制度等。economic system; sum total of all relations of production during a certain stage in the development of human society; also referring to specific system for an economic department or aspect of society, e. g. industrial economic system, agricultural economic system, etc.

【经济作物】jīngjì zuòwù 供给工业原料的农作物,如棉花、烟草、甘蔗等 industrial crop; cash crop; crop that provides raw materials for industry, e. g. cotton, tobacco, sugar cane, etc.; also 技术作物 jìshù zuòwù

【经久】jīngjiǔ ❶ 经过很长的时间 prolonged: 掌声～不息。Prolonged applause erupted. ❷ 经过较长时间不变 durable; able to stand wear and tear; remain unchanged after a long period of time: ～耐用 durable

【经理】jīnglǐ ❶ 经营管理 handle; manage: 这家商店委托你～。You'll be entrusted with the management of this shop. ❷ 某些企业的负责人 manager; director

【经历】jīnglì ❶ 亲身见过、做过或遭受过 go through; undergo; see the action of: 他一生～过两次世界大战。He saw action in two world wars in his lifetime. ❷ 亲身见过、做过或遭受过的事 personal experience: 生活～ life experiences

【经纶】jīnglún 〈书 *fml*.〉整理过的蚕丝 combed silk thread; 〈比喻 *fig*.〉规划、管理政治的才能 statecraft; statesmanship; talent for politics: 大展～ put one's talent for politics to full use | 满腹～ belly full of essays; full of wisdom and acumen

【经络】jīngluò 〈中医 *Chin. med*.〉指人体内气血运行通路的主干和分支 main and collateral channels, regarded as a network of passages, through which vital energy and blood circulate

【经脉】jīngmài 〈中医 *Chin. med*.〉指人体内气血运行的通路 passages through which vital energy circulates and bodily functions are regulated

【经贸】jīngmào 经济、贸易的合称 economy and trade：～公司 trading company｜～活动 economic relations and trade

【经年累月】jīng nián lěi yuè 经历很多年月，形容时间很长 for years and years; year in, year out：他是个海员，～在海上。As a seaman, he has worked on the seas for years and years.

【经期】jīngqī 妇女行经的时间，每次约为三天至五天 periods; women's menstrual period lasting three to five days each

【经纱】jīngshā 织布时同梭的运动方向垂直的纱 warp; a series of threads extended lengthwise on a loom and crossed by the woof

【经商】jīng//shāng 经营商业 engage in trade; be in business：弃农～ abandon farming to engage in trade｜～多年 be in business for many years

【经史子集】jīng shǐ zǐ jí 我国传统的图书分类法，把所有图书划分为经、史、子、集四大类，称为四部。经部包括儒家经传和小学方面的书。史部包括各种历史书，也包括地理书。子部包括诸子百家的著作。集部包括诗、文、词、赋等。classical works, historical works, philosophical works, and belles-lettres; four traditional divisions of a Chinese library. Classical works refer to Confucian classics and philology; historical works refer to books on history and geography; philosophical works refer to works of various schools of the thought and their exponents in the period spanning from the pre-Qin times to the early years of the Han Dynasty; and belles-lettres refer to poetry and prose.

【经手】jīng//shǒu 经过亲手(办理) handle sth. in person：～人 person handling a transaction, particular job, etc.｜这件事是他～的。He's the one handling this matter.

【经受】jīngshòu 承受；禁受 undergo; experience; withstand; stand; weather：～考验 experience trials｜～多次打击 undergo many blows

【经售】jīngshòu 经手出卖 sell on commission; deal in; distribute; sell：本书由新华书店总～。This book is exclusively distributed by the Xinhua Bookstore.

【经书】jīngshū 指《易经》、《书经》、《诗经》、《周礼》、《仪礼》、《礼记》、《春秋》、《论语》、《孝经》等儒家经传，是研究我国古代历史和儒家学术思想的重要资料 Confucian classics, referring to *The Book of Changes*, *Classics of Documents*, *The Book of Songs*, *The Rituals of Zhou*, *Book of Etiquette and Ceremonial*, *The Book of Rites*, *The Spring and Autumn Annals*, *The Analects*, and *The Book of Filial Piety*, which are essential materials for studying ancient Chinese history and Confucianism

【经天纬地】jīng tiān wěi dì 指谋划天下之事，多用来形容人才能极大 have heaven and earth under one's control; possess great ability：～之才 person of great ability

【经痛】jīngtòng ☞ 痛经 tòngjīng on p.1928

【经纬度】jīngwěidù 经度和纬度的合称。某地的经纬度即该地的地理坐标。latitude and longitude; referring to the geographical coordinates of a place

【经纬仪】jīngwěiyí 测量角度用的仪器，由绕水平轴旋转的望远镜、垂直刻度盘和水平刻度盘等构成。广泛应用在天文、地形和工程测量上。theodolite; transit; surveyor's instrument for measuring horizontal and vertical angles, consisting of a telescope that can revolve horizontally, a vertical graduated disc and a horizontal graduated disc, widely used in surveying, in astronomy, geography and engineering

【经线】jīngxiàn ❶ 编织品或织布机上的纵线 warp; a series of threads extended lengthwise in a fabric or in a loom ❷ 假定的沿地球表面连接南北两极而跟赤道垂直的线。也叫子午线。国际上习惯用英国格林尼治天文台原址的子午线作本初子午线。meridian (line); imaginary great circle passing through the two poles of the earth and intersecting the equator at right angles; also called meridian line; internationally, the meridian line that passes through the former site of the Greenwich Observatory in Britain is customarily regarded as the prime meridian; ☞ 经度 jīngdù

【经销】jīngxiāo 经售 sell on commission; deal in; distribute

【经心】jīngxīn 在意；留心 careful; mindful; conscientious：漫不～ careless

【经学】jīngxué 把儒家经典当作研究对象的学问，内容包括哲学、史学、语言文字学等 study of Confucian classics, including philosophy, historiography, linguistics, etc.

【经血】jīngxuè 〈中医 *Chin. med.*〉称月经 menses; menstruation

【经验】jīngyàn ❶ 由实践得来的知识或技能 experience; knowledge or skill obtained through practice; (do sth. by) rule of thumb：他对嫁接果树有丰富的～。He has rich experience in grafting fruit trees. ❷ 经历①；体验 sth. gone through; experience; anything observed or lived through：这样的事，我从来没～过。I have never experienced such things.

【经意】jīngyì 经心；留意 careful; mindful：毫不～ careless

【经营】jīngyíng ❶ 筹划并管理(企业等) manage (an enterprise, etc.); operate; run; engage in：～商业 engage in commerce｜～畜牧业 engage in animal husbandry｜苦心～ take great pains to build up (an enterprise) ❷ 泛

指计划和组织 (in a broad sense) plan and organize:这个展览会是煞费～的。It took great pains to plan and organize this exhibition.

【经由】jīngyóu 路程经过(某些地方或某条路线) via; by way of:从北京出发～南京到上海 go from Beijing to Shanghai by way of Nanjing

【经院哲学】jīngyuàn zhéxué 欧洲中世纪在学院中讲授的以解释基督教教义为内容的哲学,实际上是一种神学体系。由于采用烦琐的抽象推理的方法,所以也叫烦琐哲学。scholasticism; philosophy on the Christian doctrine taught in college in medieval Europe, which is actually a theological system; also known as eclectic philosophy for its adoption of abstract syllogisms

【经传】jīngzhuàn 原指经典和古人解释经文的传。泛指比较重要的古书。Confucian canon; classical works; classics; Confucian classics and commentaries on them, (in a broad sense) ancient books of major importance:不见～ not be found in the classics; unknown

荆 jīng ❶ 落叶灌木,叶子有长柄,掌状分裂,花小,蓝紫色。枝条可用来编筐、篮等。chaste tree (*Vitex agnus-castus*); deciduous shrub with palmately lobed leaves on a long stalk, bearing small, bluish-purple flowers, its branches used to weave baskets ❷ (Jīng) 姓 a surname

【荆棘】jīngjí 泛指山野丛生的带刺小灌木 thornbush; thistle and thorn; bramble; (in a broad sense) wild thorny undergrowth

【荆棘载途】jīngjí zài tú 沿路都是荆棘 path overgrown with brambles;〈比喻 *fig.*〉环境困难,障碍极多 path beset with difficulties and obstructions

【荆条】jīngtiáo 荆的枝条,性柔韧,可编制筐篮、篱笆等 twigs of the chaste tree (used for weaving baskets, fences, etc.)

J

菁 jīng ☞ below

【菁华】jīnghuá 精华 essence; cream; quintessence

【菁菁】jīngjīng〈书 *fml.*〉草木茂盛 lush; luxuriant

猄 jīng ☞ 黄猄 huángjīng on p. 852

旌 jīng ❶古代一种旗杆顶上用彩色羽毛做装饰的旗子 feather-decked banner hoisted on a mast in aucient times ❷〈书 *fml.*〉表扬 praise; commend:～表 confer honours on sb. |以～其功 to make known one's merits

【旌表】jīngbiǎo 封建统治者用立牌坊或挂匾额等表扬遵守封建礼教的人(of an emperor) confer honours on the virtuous and the worthy (e. g. a loyal subject, filial son, or virtuous widow), usu. by ordering monuments to be erected or inscribed boards to be put up

【旌旗】jīngqí 各种旗子 banners and flags:～招展 flags flutter

惊(驚) jīng ❶ 由于突然来的刺激而精神紧张 start; be frightened; become nervous due to sudden stimuli:～喜 pleasantly surprised|胆战心～ tremble with fear ❷ 惊动 surprise; shock; alarm:～扰 alarm; agitate|打草～蛇 beat the grass and startle a snake; act rashly and alert the enemy ❸ 骡马因害怕而狂跑不受控制 shy; stampede; sudden, headlong flight of frightened animals, esp. horses and mules:马～了。The horse shied.

【惊诧】jīngchà 惊讶诧异 surprised; amazed; astonished:这是意料中的事,我们并不感到～。It was expected, so we are not surprised.

【惊动】jīngdòng 举动影响旁人,使吃惊或受侵扰 alarm; alert; disturb:娘睡了,别～她。Mom is asleep, don't disturb her.

【惊愕】jīng'è〈书 *fml.*〉吃惊而发愣 stunned; stupefied

【惊弓之鸟】jīng gōng zhī niǎo 被弓箭吓怕了的鸟 bird that starts at the mere twang of a bowstring;〈比喻 *fig.*〉受过惊恐见到一点动静就特别害怕的人 badly frightened person

【惊骇】jīnghài〈书 *fml.*〉惊慌害怕 frightened; panic-stricken

【惊慌】jīnghuāng 害怕慌张 alarmed; scared; panic-stricken:～失措 frightened out of one's wits; seized with panic|神色～ look flustered

【惊惶】jīnghuáng same as 惊慌 jīnghuāng

【惊魂】jīnghún 惊慌失措的神态 state of being frightened:～稍定 barely recovered from fright

【惊悸】jīngjì 因惊慌而心跳得厉害 heart palpitating with fear

【惊厥】jīngjué 因害怕而晕过去 faint from fear

【惊恐】jīngkǒng 惊慌恐惧 alarmed and panicky; terrified; panic-stricken; seized with terror:～失色 pale with fear|～万状 in a great panic; convulsed with fear

【惊雷】jīngléi 使人震惊的雷声,多用于比喻 sudden clap of thunder (oft. fig.)

【惊奇】jīngqí 觉得很奇怪 wonder; be surprised; be amazed:这里的变化之大,令人～。The great changes that have taken place here take everyone by surprise. |眼里射出～的目光。(His) eyes are sparkling with wonder.

【惊扰】jīngrǎo 惊动扰乱 alarm; agitate:自相～ alarm one's own group; create a disturbance within one's ranks

【惊人】jīngrén 使人吃惊 astonishing; amazing; alarming:～的消息 surprising news|～的成就 astonishing (or amazing) achievements|数字大得～。The number is alarmingly big.

【惊世骇俗】jīng shì hài sú 因言行异于寻常而使人震惊 (of unusual words and deeds) scandalize the public; also 惊世震俗 jīng shì zhèn sú

【惊叹】jīngtàn 惊讶赞叹 wonder at; marvel at; exclaim (with admiration):精巧的工艺品令人～不已。The exquisite arts and crafts won everybody's admiration.

【惊叹号】jīngtànhào 叹号 exclamation mark (!)

【惊涛骇浪】jīng tāo hài làng ❶ 凶猛而使人害怕的波涛 terrifying waves; stormy sea:船在～中前进。The ship navigates on a stormy sea. ❷〈比喻 *fig.*〉险恶的环境或遭遇 perilous position or circumstance

【惊天动地】jīng tiān dòng dì ❶ 形容声音特别响亮(of sound) shaking heaven and earth:～一声巨响 earth-shaking crash ❷ 形容声势浩大或事业伟大(of a force or event) earth-shaking; world-shaking:～的伟业 magnificent and earth-shaking feat

【惊喜】jīngxǐ 惊和喜;又惊又喜 pleasantly surprised:～交集 joy and astonishment intermingled|～不已 in endless happy astonishment

【惊吓】jīngxià 因意外的刺激而害怕 frighten; scare; sudden fear or panic:孩子受了～,哭起来了。The child got a shock and began to cry.

【惊险】jīngxiǎn (场面、情景)危险,使人惊奇紧张 (of a scene or situation) alarmingly dangerous; breathtaking; thrilling:～小说 thriller|搏斗场面十分～。The scene of combat is extremely thrilling.

【惊心动魄】jīng xīn dòng pò 形容使人感受很深,震动很大 soul-stirring; profoundly affecting

【惊醒】jīngxǐng ❶ 受惊动而醒来 wake up with a start:突然从梦中～ wake up suddenly with a start from a dream ❷ 使惊醒 rouse suddenly from sleep; awaken:别～了孩子。Don't wake the child.

【惊醒】jīng•xing 睡眠时容易醒来 sleep lightly; be a light sleeper:他睡觉很～,有点儿响动都知道。He's a light sleeper; the slightest noise disturbs him.

【惊讶】jīngyà 感到很奇怪;惊异 surprised; amazed; astonished; astounded:～的目光 surprised look|人们对他的举动感到十分～。People are surprised by his behaviour.

【惊疑】jīngyí 惊讶疑惑 surprised and bewildered:他脸上露出～的神色。He looks surprised and bewildered.

【惊异】jīngyì 惊奇诧异 surprised; amazed; astonished; astounded:令人～ surprising

【惊蛰】jīngzhé 二十四节气之一,在3月5,6或7日 Waking of Insects, one of the 24 solar terms, falling on March 5, 6, or 7, when life stirs after the winter sleep; ☞ 节气 jié•qi on p. 989 and 二十四节气 èrshísì jiéqì on p. 516

晶 jīng ❶ 光亮 brilliant; glittering:～莹 sparkling and crystal-clear; glittering and translucent|亮～～glittering ❷ 水晶 quartz; (rock) crystal:茶～citrine; yellow quartz|墨～smoky quartz ❸ 晶体 any crystalline substance:结～ crystallize

【晶体】jīngtǐ 原子、离子或分子按一定空间次序排列而成的固体,具有规则的外形。如食盐、石英、云母、明矾等。crystal; solidified form of a substance (e.g. salt, quartz, mica and alum) in which the atoms, ions or molecules are arranged in a definite pattern that is repeated regularly in three dimensions; also 结晶体 jiéjīngtǐ or 结晶 jiéjīng

【晶体管】jīngtǐguǎn 用锗、硅等晶体制成的电子管。优点是体积小、不怕震、耗电少,在无线电技术中用来整流、检波、放大等。transistor; electronic device composed of semiconductive material, e.g. germanium, silicon, etc. that controls current flow without the use of a vacuum and has the advantage of being compact, durable, and requiring little power, used in radio technology for rectification, detection and amplification

【晶莹】jīngyíng 光亮而透明 sparkling and crystal-clear; glittering and translucent:草上的露珠～发亮。The grass glistened with dewdrops.

【晶状体】jīngzhuàngtǐ 眼球的一部分,形状和作用跟凸透镜相似,受睫状肌的调节而改变凸度,能使不同距离的物体的清晰影像投射在视网膜上 crystalline lens; part of the eyeball, its shape and function similar to convex lens. Controlled by the ciliary muscle, it enables images of objects at different distances to reflect clearly on the retina. also 水晶体 shuǐjīngtǐ; (图见 ☞ figure for 眼 yǎn on p. 2210)

腈 jīng 有机化合物的一类,是烃基和氰基的碳原子连接而成的化合物 nitrile; organic compound of cyanide containing the group CN, which on hydrolysis yields an acid with the elimination of ammonia

【腈纶】jīnglún 合成纤维的一种,用丙烯腈合成。耐光,耐腐蚀,柔软蓬松像羊毛。用来纺毛线(或与羊毛混纺),制造人造毛皮和经常接触阳光的纺织品,如窗帘,帐篷布等。acrylic fibre; synthetic fibre synthetized from acrylic nitrile, light- and corrosion-resistant, and as soft as sheep's wool, used to spin woollen yarn, and to make artificial fur or textiles that are oft. exposed to sunlight, e g. window curtains or tarpaulins

鹡 jīng ☞ [䴔鹡](jiāojīng) on p. 972

睛 jīng 眼珠儿 eyeball:目不转～ look with a fixed gaze; regard with rapt attention|定～一看 look fixedly|画龙点～ bring a picture of a dragon to life by putting in the pupils of its eyes; add a touch that brings a work of art to life; add the finishing touches; add an apt word to clinch the argument

粳(稉、秔) jīng 粳稻 round-grained non-glutinous rice; japonica rice

【粳稻】jīngdào 稻的一种,茎秆较矮,叶子较窄,深绿色,米粒短而粗。round-grained non-glutinous rice; japonica rice; crop with short stalks, narrow, dark-green leaves, and round-grained rice

【粳米】jīngmǐ 粳稻碾出的米 polished round-grained, non-glutinous rice

兢 jīng [兢兢业业](jīngjīngyèyè)小心谨慎,认真负责 cautious and conscientious:他工作一向~,任劳任怨。He'd been doing his job conscientiously regardless of criticism for many years.

精 jīng ❶ 经过提炼或挑选的 refined; selected; choice:~盐 refined salt|~金 refined gold ❷ 提炼出来的精华 essence; extract:酒~ ethyl alcohol|鱼肝油~ extract of cod-liver oil ❸ 完美;最好 perfect; excellent:~彩 brilliant; splendid; wonderful|~益求~ constantly improve sth.; keep improving ❹ 细(跟'粗'相对 as opposed to 'coarse')meticulous; fine; precise:~密 precise|~确 accurate|~巧 exquisite; ingenious ❺ 机灵心细 smart; sharp; clever; shrewd:~明 astute; shrewd; sagacious|~干 keen-witted and capable|这孩子比大人还~。This child is smarter than an adult. ❻ 精通 skilled; conversant; proficient:博而不~ have wide but not expert knowledge; know a bit about everything|~于针灸 skilled in acupuncture ❼ 精神;精力 energy; spirit:聚~会神 concentrate one's attention|~疲力尽 exhausted; worn out; tired out; spent ❽ 精液;精子 sperm; semen; seed:遗~ spermatorrhea; seminal emission|受~ be fertilized ❾ 妖精 goblin; spirit; demon:修炼成~ become a spirit through self-cultivation ❿〈方 *dial.*〉用在某些形容词前面,表示'十分'、'非常'[used before certain adjectives] extremely; very:~瘦 very thin|雨把衣服淋得~湿。The clothes have been soaked through in the rain.

【精兵】jīngbīng 训练有素、战斗力强的士兵 select troops; crack troops:~猛将 crack troops and valiant generals|率~十万 lead 100,000 crack troops

【精兵简政】jīng bīng jiǎn zhèng 缩小机构,精简人员 better troops and simpler administration; better staff and simpler administration; streamlined administration

【精彩】jīngcǎi ❶(表演、展览、言论、文章等)优美;出色(of a performance, exhibition, speech, article, etc.) brilliant; splendid; wonderful:晚会的节目很~。The programme for the evening party is wonderful.|在大会上,很多代表做了~的发言。Many delegates made brilliant speeches at the conference. ❷〈书 *fml.*〉神采;精神 demeanour; mien; spirit

【精巢】jīngcháo ❶ 动物产生精子的生殖腺 spermary; male reproductive glands that produce sperm ❷ 睾丸 testis; testicle

【精诚】jīngchéng〈书 *fml.*〉真诚 absolute sincerity; good faith:~合作 sincerely cooperate|~所至,金石为开。Complete sincerity can affect even metal and stone.

【精赤】jīngchì (身体)裸露,毫无遮盖 stark naked; without a stitch of clothing:上身脱得~ stripped to the waist; barechested

【精虫】jīngchóng 人的精子的俗称 popular name for spermatozoa

【精粹】jīngcuì 精练纯粹 succinct; pithy; terse:文章要写得短而~。Articles should be short and pithy.

【精打细算】jīng dǎ xì suàn (在使用人力物力上)仔细地计算 careful calculation and strict budgeting (in the use of human and material resources)

【精当】jīngdàng (言论、文章等)精确恰当(of speech or article) precise and appropriate:用词~ precise and appropriate wording; masterly choice of words

【精到】jīngdào 精细周到 precise and penetrating:安排~ careful arrangement|这个道理,在那篇文章里发挥得十分~。This idea has been expounded thoroughly in that article.

【精雕细镂】jīng diāo xì lòu 精心细致地雕刻 carve meticulously;〈比喻 *fig.*〉做事认真细致 work at sth. with the care and precision of a sculptor; work at sth. with great care; also 精雕细刻 jīng diāo xì kè

【精读】jīngdú 反复仔细地阅读 intensive reading; read carefully and thoroughly:有些重要文章需要~。Some important articles need to be read carefully and thoroughly.

【精干】jīnggàn 精明强干 keen-witted and capable:他年纪虽轻,却是很~老练。Although young, he is capable and experienced.|选了些~的小伙子做侦察员。Several keen-witted and capable young men were selected as scouts.

【精耕细作】jīng gēng xì zuò 细致地耕作 intensive and meticulous farming; intensive cultivation

【精怪】jīngguài 迷信传说里所说多年的鸟兽草木等变成的妖怪 goblins; spirits; demons; (in mythology and legends) demons transformed from birds, beasts, grass or trees after years of cultivation

【精光】jīngguāng ❶ 一无所有;一点儿不剩 with nothing left; up; clean:一碗菜吃得~。A bowl of vegetables was eaten up.|杂技团的票,不到一个钟头就卖得~。All the tickets for the acrobatic troupe sold out in less than an hour. ❷ 光洁 bright and clean; shiny:司机把汽车擦得~发亮。The driver polished the bus to a high sheen.

【精悍】jīnghàn ❶（人）精明能干 capable and vigorous：办事～ be capable and vigorous in handling affairs ❷（文笔等）精练犀利（of a piece of writing）pithy and poignant：笔力～ pithy and poignant style of writing

【精华】jīnghuá ❶（事物）最重要、最好的部分 cream；essence；quintessence：取其～，去其糟粕 select the essence and discard the dross｜展览会集中了全国工艺品的～。The exhibition has brought together the cream of China's arts and crafts. ❷〈书 *fml.*〉光华；光辉 brilliance；splendour：日月之～ brilliance of the sun and the moon

【精简】jīngjiǎn 去掉不必要的，留下必要的 retrench；simplify；cut；reduce：～节约 simplify administration and practise economy｜～机构 simplify（or streamline）an administrative structure｜～内容 reduce the contents

【精力】jīnglì 精神和体力 energy；vigour；vim：～充沛 full of vim and vigour；vigorous；energetic｜～旺盛 vigorous｜耗费～ consume energy and strength

【精练】jīngliàn（文章或讲话）扼要，没有多余的词句（of writing or speech）concise，without redundant words and expressions；succinct；terse：语言～ succinct language｜他的文章写得很～。His articles are concise and succinct. also 精炼 jīngliàn

【精炼】jīngliàn ❶ 提炼精华，除去杂质 refine；purify；reduce to a pure state：原油送到炼油厂去～。The crude oil is shipped to a refinery for refining. ❷ same as 精练 jīngliàn

【精良】jīngliáng 精致优良；完善 excellent；superior；of the best quality：制作～ of excellent workmanship｜装备～ well-equipped

【精灵】jīng·ling ❶ 鬼怪 spirit；demon ❷〈方 *dial.*〉机警聪明；机灵（of a child）clever；smart；intelligent：这孩子真～，一说就明白了。This child is really clever，and understands immediately what he is told.

【精美】jīngměi 精致美好 exquisite；elegant：包装～beautifully packaged｜我国～的工艺品在国际上享有盛名。The arts and crafts of our country enjoy high prestige in the world.

【精密】jīngmì 精确细密 precise；accurate：～仪器 precision instrument｜～的观察是科学研究的基础。Accurate observation is the foundation of scientific research.

【精妙】jīngmiào 精致巧妙 exquisite：书法～ write in a beautiful script｜～的手工艺品 exquisite handicrafts

【精明】jīngmíng 精细明察，机警聪明 astute；shrewd；sagacious：～强干 intelligent and capable；able and efficient｜～的小伙子 bright young fellow

【精明强干】jīngmíng qiánggàn 形容人精细明察，办事能力很强 intelligent and capable；able and efficient

【精囊】jīngnáng 男子和雄性动物生殖器的一部分，形状像囊，左右各一。精囊的分泌物是精液的一部分。seminal vesicles；part of the male genital organs in the shape of a bag，with one on the left and one on the right. The secretions of the seminal vesicles are part of the seminal fluid.

【精疲力竭】jīng pí lì jié ☞ 筋疲力尽 jīn pí lì jìn on p.1007

【精辟】jīngpì（见解、理论）深刻；透彻（of view or theory）penetrating；incisive：～的分析 penetrating analysis｜论述十分～。The exposition is quite brilliant.

【精品】jīngpǐn 精良的物品；上乘的作品 fine works（of art）；quality goods；articles of fine quality：艺术～ art treasures

【精巧】jīngqiǎo（技术、器物构造等）精细巧妙（of technology，structure of an object，etc.）exquisite；ingenious：制作～ exquisitely manufactured｜构思～ ingeniously conceived

【精确】jīngquè 非常准确；非常正确 accurate；exact；precise：～的计算 accurate calculation｜～地分析 analyse accurately｜论点～，语言明快。The argument is clear-cut，and the language is lucid and lively.

【精肉】jīngròu〈方 *dial.*〉瘦肉（多指猪肉 usu. pork）lean meat

【精锐】jīngruì（军队）装备优良，战斗力强 crack；（of troops）well-equipped and highly combat effective：～部队 crack troops；select troops

【精深】jīngshēn（学问或理论）精密深奥（of learning or theory）profound：博大～ have extensive knowledge and profound scholarship｜学术造诣～ profound academic achievement

【精神】jīngshén ❶ 指人的意识、思维活动和一般心理状态 spirit；mind；consciousness；thinking，motivating，feeling part of man，as distinguished from the body：～面貌 mental attitude；mental outlook｜～错乱 mentally deranged；insane｜～上的负担 mental burden ❷ 宗旨；主要的意义 essence；gist；spirit：领会文件的～ try to understand the thrust of the document

【精神】jīng·shen ❶ 表现出来的活力 vigour；vitality；drive：～焕发 be in high spirits；one's spirits rise｜振作～ bestir oneself；summon up one's energy ❷ 活跃；有生气 spunky；lively；spirited；vigorous；smart：越干越～。The longer one works，the more energetic one becomes.｜这孩子大大的眼睛，怪～的。The child with big eyes is certainly full of life.

【精神病】jīngshénbìng 人的大脑功能紊乱而突出表现为精神失常的病。症状多为感觉、知觉、

J

记忆、思维、感情、行为等发生异常状态。mental disease; mental disorder; psychosis; mental derangement characterized by gross distortion or disorganization of a person's mental capacity, emotional response, and capacity to recognize reality, communicate, and relate to others, to the degree of interfering with the capacity to cope with the ordinary demands of everyday life

【精神分裂症】jīngshén fēnlièzhèng 精神病的一种,症状多为发生幻觉和妄想,沉默,独自发笑,思想、感情和行为不协调等 schizophrenia; type of psychosis characterized mostly by delusions and hallucinations, withdrawal, laughter to oneself, and disorder of feeling, thought, conduct, etc.

【精神衰弱】jīngshén shuāiruò 精神病的一种,患者常有不安全感,缺乏信心,犹疑不决,对某些事物特殊惧怕,不能控制自己,明知某种想法不合实际、某种动作毫无意义,但非想、非做不可。如因为怕脏而经常反复地洗手。psychasthenia; a type of psychosis characterized by feelings of panic, lack of confidence, hesitance, and fear of certain things, loss of self-control, and obsessive thinking or actions, e.g. washing one's hands repeatedly

【精神损耗】jīngshén sǔnhào ☞ 无形损耗 wúxíng sǔnhào on p. 2025

【精神头儿】jīng·shentóur 表现出来的活力和劲头 vigour; energy; vim:他一聊起天儿来,~可大了。He becomes energetic when it comes to chatting.

【精神文明】jīngshén wénmíng 人类社会历史实践过程中所创造的精神财富,包括思想、教育、道德、风尚和科学、文化等 spiritual civilization; spiritual wealth created through the social practices of human history, including ideology, education, ethics, fashion, science, culture, etc.

J

【精审】jīngshěn 〈书 *fml.*〉(文字、计划、意见等)精密周详 (of writings, plans, opinions, etc.) accurate and comprehensive; carefully thought out:释义~ accurate and comprehensive explication of meaning

【精髓】jīngsuǐ 〈比喻 *fig.*〉精华 marrow; pith; quintessence

【精通】jīngtōng 对学问、技术或业务有透彻的了解并熟练地掌握 be proficient in (learning, skill, or profession); have a good command of; master:~医理 have a profound knowledge of medicine

【精微】jīngwēi ❶ 精深微妙 profound and subtle:博大~ have extensive knowledge and profound scholarship ❷ 精深微妙的地方;奥秘 subtleties; mysteries:探索宇宙的~ explore the mysteries of the universe

【精卫填海】jīngwèi tián hǎi 古代神话,炎帝的女儿在东海淹死,化为精卫鸟,每天衔西山的木石来填东海(见于《山海经·北山经》)。后来用精卫填海比喻有深仇大恨,立志必报。也比喻不畏艰难,努力奋斗。According to an ancient legend, after Emperor Yan's daughter was drowned in the Eastern Sea, she turned into the bird Jingwei, who pecked twigs and pebbles from the Western Mountains in an effort to fill up the sea (*Book of Mountains and Seas · Northern Lands Beyond the Sea*). The phrase is used figuratively to mean dogged determination to take revenge or to achieve one's goal.

【精细】jīngxì ❶ 精密细致 meticulous; fine:这一座象牙雕像,手工十分~。This ivory sculpture shows fine workmanship. | 他遇事冷静,考虑问题特别~。He is calm, and thinks matters over very carefully. ❷ 精明细心 smart and careful:为人~ be circumspect

【精心】jīngxīn 特别用心;细心 meticulously; painstakingly; elaborately:~制作 manufacture elaborately | ~治疗 treat with the best of care | ~培育良种 painstakingly cultivate fine breeds

【精盐】jīngyán 经过加工,没有杂质的食盐 refined salt; table salt

【精液】jīngyè 男子和雄性动物生殖腺分泌的含有精子的液体 seminal fluid; semen; penile ejaculation, containing spermatozoa; mixture of the secretions of the genital glands of men or male animals

【精益求精】jīng yì qiú jīng (学术、技术、作品、产品等)好了还求更好 constantly improve sth.; hone (learning, skills, works, products, etc.) to excellence

【精英】jīngyīng ❶ 精华 essence; cream:很多出土的文物,都是我国古代文化的~。Many unearthed cultural relics are the finest specimens of ancient Chinese culture. ❷ 出类拔萃的人 salt of the earth; flower; outstanding figures:象棋~ chess master | 当代青年的~ flower of modern youth

【精湛】jīngzhàn 精深 consummate; exquisite:技术~ consummate skill; superb technique | ~的艺术 exquisite art

【精制】jīngzhì 在粗制品上加工;精工制造 make with extra care; refine:~品 highly finished products | 在生橡胶里加硫磺~,就成普通的橡胶。Adding sulphur to raw rubber and refining it produces ordinary rubber.

【精致】jīngzhì 精巧细致 nifty; fine; exquisite; delicate:~的花纹 fine patterns | 展览会上的工艺品件件都很~。The arts and crafts displayed at the exhibition are all very exquisite.

【精忠】jīngzhōng (对国家、民族)极其忠诚 utterly loyal (to one's nation or people):~报国 serve one's country with unreserved loyalty

【精装】jīngzhuāng ❶ 书籍的精美的装订,一般指封面或书脊上包布的(区别于'平装' as compared with 'paperback') (of books) clothbound; hardback; hardcover: ～本 deluxe edition ❷ (商品)包装精致的(区别于'简装' as compared with 'simple packing') (of commodities) deluxe packing: ～香烟 deluxe cigarette

【精壮】jīngzhuàng 强壮 able-bodied; strong: ～的小伙子 strong lad

【精子】jīngzǐ 人和动植物的雄性生殖细胞,能运动,与卵结合而产生第二代。人的精子产生于睾丸,形状像蝌蚪。semen; sperm; spermatozoon; male gamete or sex cell that can move, and can produce a new generation after conjugating with an ovum; man's sperm, composed of a head and a tail like a tadpole, produced in the testes

鲸 jīng 哺乳动物,种类很多,生活在海洋中,胎生,形状像鱼,体长可达30多米,是现在世界上最大的动物,前肢形成鳍,后肢完全退化,尾巴变成尾鳍,鼻孔在头的上部,用肺呼吸。肉可以吃,脂肪可以制油,用于医药和其他工业。俗称鲸鱼。whale (*Cetacea*); viviparous aquatic mammal that lives in the sea and superficially resembles a large fish, whose body can reach 30 metres long. It is the largest living animal in the world, whose forelegs have evolved into fins, whose hind legs have totally degenerated and whose tail has changed into the caudal fin. With its nostrils on the upper of its head, the whale breathes with lungs. Its nostrils situated on the upper part of the head, and it breathes with lungs; its meat is edible, and its fat can be used to produce oil, and is used in pharmaceuticals and other industries. 俗称 popularly called 鲸鱼 jīngyú

【鲸鲨】jīngshā 鱼,体长可达20米,是现代最大的一种鱼。灰褐色或青褐色,有许多黄色斑纹。口宽大,牙小。性温顺,吃浮游生物和小鱼。皮可以制革,肝熬的油供工业上用。whale shark (*Rhincodon typus*); largest fish in modern times, having a body as much as 20 metres long, greyish or bluish brown with yellow stripes, wide mouth, and small teeth, gentle in nature, living on plankton and small fish, its hide used to make leather, and the oil from its liver used in industry

【鲸吞】jīngtūn 像鲸鱼一样地吞食,多用来比喻吞并土地等 swallow up like a whale; (fig.) annex (territory): 蚕食～ nibble away like a silkworm or swallow like a whale — seize another country's territory through piecemeal encroachment or wholesale annexation

麖 jīng ☞ 水鹿 shuǐlù on p.1800

鯖 jīng ☞ [鼩鯖] (qújīng) on p.1590

jǐng (ㄐㄧㄥˇ)

井[1] jǐng ❶ 从地面往下凿成的能取水的深洞,洞壁多砌上砖石 well; pit or hole sunk in the earth to reach a supply of water, oft. lined by a brick or stone wall: 水～ water well | 一口～ a well | 双眼～ twin wells ❷ 形状像井的东西 sth. in the shape of a well: 矿～ mine shaft; mine pit | 油～ oil well | 盐～ salt well | 竖～ vertical shaft | 探～ exploratory shaft | 渗～ filter well | 天～ small courtyard ❸ 古制八家为一井,后借指人口聚居的地方或乡里 unit of the census register in ancient China, consisting of eight households; later referring to a neighbourhood or a community: 乡～ native place; home village | 市～ marketplace; town | ～邑 native town | 背～离乡 leave one's native place; be away from home ❹ 二十八宿之一 *jing*, one of the 28 constellations into which the celestial sphere was divided according to ancient Chinese astronomy ❺ (Jǐng) 姓 a surname

井[2] jǐng 形容整齐 neat; orderly: ～然 orderly | ～～有条 in perfect order; shipshape; methodical

【井底之蛙】jǐng dǐ zhī wā 井底下的青蛙只能看到井口那么大的一块天 frog in a well (that can see only a tiny patch of sky no bigger than the mouth of the well); 〈比喻 *fig.*〉见识狭小的人 person with limited vision

【井灌】jǐngguàn 用井水灌溉农田 well irrigation; irrigate farmland with well water

【井架】jǐngjià 矿井、油井等井口竖立的金属架,用来装置天车、支撑钻具等 petroleum derrick; headframe; headgear; pithead frame; metal frame at the opening of an oil well or mine pit, used to install overhead travelling cranes or support drilling apparatus

【井井有条】jǐngjǐng yǒu tiáo 形容条理分明 in perfect order; shipshape; methodical

【井喷】jǐngpēn 钻石油井时地下的高压油、天然气等突然从井口喷出 petroleum blowout; high-pressure oil or natural gas blowing out suddenly from the opening of an oil well during the drilling process

【井然】jǐngrán 〈书 *fml.*〉形容整齐的样子 orderly; neat and tidy; shipshape; methodical: 秩序～ in perfect order | 条理～ well-organized | ～不紊 in an orderly way

【井水不犯河水】jǐngshuǐ bù fàn héshuǐ 〈比喻 *fig.*〉两不相犯 well water does not intrude into river water; none may encroach upon the precincts of another

【井台】jǐngtái (～儿 jǐngtáir) 井口周围高出地面的部分 raised platform around a well

【井田制】jǐngtiánzhì 我国奴隶社会时期的土地制度。奴隶主为计算自己封地的人小和监督奴隶劳动，把土地划分成许多方块，因像'井'字形，所以叫做井田制。well-field system; land system supposed to have existed in slave society, according to which arable lands in a fief were divided into units of nine squares, like the Chinese character 井 jǐng, thus its name

【井筒】jǐngtǒng ❶ 从水井口到井底的筒状四壁或空间 tube-shaped space from the mouth to the bottom of a well ❷ 采矿、修建长隧道和地下铁道时开凿的联系地面和地下巷道的通道 pit shaft; channel linking earth's surface and underground tunnels during construction of a mine, long tunnel or subway

【井盐】jǐngyán 打井汲取溶有盐质的地下水制成的食盐。我国四川、云南等地都有出产。well salt; salt extracted from salty groundwater from a well. China's Sichuan and Yunnan provinces produce well salt.

阱(穽) jǐng 捕野兽用的陷坑 trap; pitfall; pit for catching animals：陷～ trap

汫 jǐng 汫洲(Jǐngzhōu)，地名，在广东 Jingzhou, name of a place in Guangdong Province

刭(剄) jǐng〈书 *fml*.〉用刀割脖子 cut (or slit) the throat：自～ commit suicide by cutting one's throat

肼 jǐng 有机化合物，化学式 H_2NNH_2。无色油状液体，有类似氨的刺激性气味，有剧毒，腐蚀性强，燃烧时发出紫色光。用来制药，也用做火箭燃料。hydrazine (H_2NNH_2); organic compound in the form of a colourless oily liquid, with a strong odour, hyper-toxic, corrosive, and giving out a purple light when burned, used in pharmaceuticals and also as rocket fuel; also 联氨 lián'ān

颈(頸) jǐng 颈项 neck：长～鹿 giraffe◇曲～甑 retort；(图见 ☞ figure for 身体 shēntǐ on p.1701)
☞ gěng on p.663

【颈联】jǐnglián 律诗的第三联(五、六两句)，一般要求对仗 third pair of couplets (the 5th and 6th lines) of a regulated verse, that are required to be in parallel structure

【颈项】jǐngxiàng 脖子 neck

【颈椎】jǐngzhuī 颈部的椎骨，共有 7 块，较小的第一颈椎和第二颈椎的构造与其他颈椎不同，称为寰椎和枢椎 cervical vertebra; with seven segments, the first and the second vertebra, called 寰椎 huánzhuī and 枢椎 shūzhuī, smaller and different from the other cervical vertebrae in structure；(图见 ☞ figure for 骨骼 gǔgé on p.693)

景[1] jǐng ❶ (～儿 jǐngr)景致；风景 view; scenery; scene：雪～ snow scene｜西湖十～ 10 sights of the West Lake ❷ 情形；情况 situation; condition：远～ distant view｜背～ background ❸ 戏剧、电影、电视的布景和摄影棚外的景物(in a broad sense) indoor setting and outdoor scenery (of a drama, TV play or film)：内～ indoor setting; indoor scene｜外～ outdoor scene ❹ 剧本的一幕中因布景不同而划分的段落 scene (of a play)：第三幕第一～ Act III, Scene 1 ❺ (Jǐng) 姓 a surname
〈古 *arch*.〉same as 影 yǐng

景[2] jǐng 尊敬；佩服 admire; revere; respect：～慕 esteem; revere｜～仰 admire

【景点】jǐngdiǎn 供游览的风景点 scenic spot：旅游～ tourist spot

【景观】jǐngguān ❶ 指某地或某种类型的自然景色 landscape; natural scenery of a place or landform：草原～prairie landscape｜黄山以它独特的～吸引着游客。Mount Huangshan attracts tourists with its unique scenery. ❷ 泛指可供观赏的景物 (in a broad sense) spectacle; sight：街头雕塑也是这个都市的～之一。Street sculptures are a spectacle in this metropolis.

【景况】jǐngkuàng 情况；境况 situation; circumstances：我们的～越来越好。Things are getting easier and easier for us.

【景慕】jǐngmù〈书 *fml*.〉景仰 esteem; revere; admire：他怀着～的心情参观鲁迅博物馆。He visited the Lu Xun Museum in esteem and awe.

【景片】jǐngpiàn 舞台布景的构件，上面绘有表示墙壁、门窗、山坡、田野等的图形和景物 flat; piece of stage property painted with a wall, windows and doors, mountain slopes, fields, etc.

【景颇族】Jǐngpōzú 我国少数民族之一，分布在云南 Jingpo (Chingpaw) people; Jingpos (Chingpaws), one of China's ethnic minorities inhabiting Yunnan Province

【景气】jǐngqì 指生产增长、失业减少、信用活跃等经济繁荣现象。泛指兴旺。thriving conditions, featuring growth in production, decrease in unemployment, and active credit; (in a broad sense) prosperity; boom

【景区】jǐngqū 供游览的风景区 scenic area：开辟新～ develop new scenic areas

【景色】jǐngsè 景致 scenery; view; scene; landscape：～迷人。The scenery is enchanting.｜日出的时候～特别美丽。The view of the sunrise is particularly beautiful.

【景深】jǐngshēn〈摄影用语 *photog*.〉指用摄影机拍摄某景物时，可保持该景物前后的其他景物成像清晰的范围，使用小光圈、短焦距和适当地利用暗影，都可以得到较好的景深 depth of field; range of distances measured along the optical axis of an image-forming device, as a lens, throughout which objects are imaged with satisfactory definition on a given plane perpendicular to the axis. An ideal depth of field can be obtained through adjusting aperture and focal length, and by proper use of shade.

【景泰】Jǐngtài 明代宗(朱祁钰)年号(公元1450—1456) reign title of Emperor Daizong (Zhu Qiyu) during the 1450-1456 period of the Ming Dynasty

【景泰蓝】jǐngtàilán 我国特种工艺品之一，用紫铜做成器物的胎，把铜丝掐成各种花纹焊在铜胎上，填上珐琅彩釉，然后烧成。明代景泰年间在北京开始大量制造，珐琅彩釉多用蓝色，所以叫景泰蓝。cloisonné enamel; cloisonné; a type of Chinese handicraft, with enamel applied and fired in raised cells (as of soldered copper wires) on a red copper background. Cloisonné were made in large quantities in Beijing during the Jingtai reign of the Ming Dynasty, and the enamel used was mostly of a blue colour, thus its name

【景物】jǐngwù 可供观赏的景致和事物 scenery: 山川秀丽，～宜人。The landscape is beautiful, and the scenery is attractive.

【景象】jǐngxiàng 现象；状况 scene; sight; picture: 太平～ peaceful scene | 一派欣欣向荣的～ picture of prosperity

【景仰】jǐngyǎng 佩服尊敬；仰慕 respect and admire; hold in deep respect: ～先生的为人 hold in deep respect the way you conduct yourself

【景遇】jǐngyù 景况和遭遇 circumstances; one's lot: ～不佳 in straitened circumstances

【景致】jǐngzhì 风景 view; scenery; scene: 西山有几处好～。There are several good sights in the Western Hills.

儆 jǐng 让人自己觉悟而不犯过错 warn; admonish; put on guard against evil: ～戒 warn; admonish; exhort | 以～效尤 warn others against following a bad example; as a warning to others

憬 jǐng 〈书 *fml.*〉醒悟 awake; come to understand: 闻之～然 come to understand it after hearing the news

【憬悟】jǐngwù 〈书 *fml.*〉醒悟 wake up to reality; come to see the truth or one's error, etc.

璟 jǐng 〈书 *fml.*〉玉的光彩 lustre of jade

警 jǐng ❶ 戒备 guard; take precautions: ～惕 on guard against; watch out for; be vigilant | ～戒 warn; admonish ❷ (感觉)敏锐 alert; vigilant: 机～ alert | ～觉 vigilance; alertness ❸ 使人注意(情况严重)；告戒 warn; alarm: ～报 alarm | ～告 warn; caution; admonish | ～世 admonish the world | 惩一～百 punish one to warn a hundred; make an example of sb. ❹ 危险紧急的情况或事情 alarm; emergency: 火～ fire alarm | 报～ report to the police ❺ 警察的简称 abbr. for 警察 jǐngchá: 民～ people's police | 武～ armed police | 交通～ traffic police

【警报】jǐngbào 用电台、汽笛、喇叭等发出的将有危险到来的通知或信号 alarm; warning; alert; signal or notice by radio, siren or loudspeaker to warn of danger: 防空～ air-raid warning; air-raid siren | 台风～ typhoon warning | 降温～ warning of a drop in temperature

【警备】jǐngbèi 警戒防备 guard; garrison: ～森严 be heavily guarded

【警察】jǐngchá 国家维持社会秩序和治安的武装力量。也指这种武装力量的成员。police; policeman; policewoman; governmental armed force, or body of persons, established and maintained for keeping social order

【警车】jǐngchē 警察执行公务用的车辆 police car; police van

【警笛】jǐngdí (～儿 jǐngdír) ❶ 警察用于示警的哨子 police whistle ❷ 发警报的汽笛 siren (to signal alarm)

【警告】jǐnggào ❶ 提醒，使警惕 warn; caution ❷ 对有错误或不正当行为的个人、团体、国家提出告诫，使认识所应负的责任 admonish; warn an individual (or organization or country) against specific faults, and remind them of their due responsibilities ❸ 对犯错误者的一种处分 warning (as a disciplinary measure)

【警官】jǐngguān 警察官员 police officer

【警棍】jǐnggùn 警察执行任务时使用的特制棍棒 police baton; truncheon

【警号】jǐnghào ❶ 报警的信号 warning signal: 警灯闪闪，～呜呜。Red lights on the police cars flash, and sirens wail. ❷ 警察佩戴在警服上的有编号的徽章 badge bearing serial number worn by a policeman

【警戒】jǐngjiè ❶ 告诫人使注意改正错误 warn; admonish; also 警诫 jǐngjiè ❷ 军队为防备敌人的侦察和突然袭击而采取保障措施 be on the alert against; guard against (an enemy reconnaissance or raid); keep a close watch on: ～哨 outpost guards | 加强～ enhance precautionary measures

【警戒色】jǐngjièsè 某些动物在进化过程中形成的能起警告敌害、保护自身作用的鲜艳色彩 warning (or aposematic) coloration; colour or arrangement of colours adopted by an animal during the evolutionary process that serves to make it conspicuous and thus warn a possible enemy against an attack

【警句】jǐngjù 简练而涵义深刻动人的语句 aphorism; epigram; short, pointed sentence expressing a wise or clever observation or a general truth

【警觉】jǐngjué 对危险或情况变化的敏锐感觉 vigilance; alertness; keen sense of danger or a change in situation: 提高～ heighten vigilance | 高度的～性 sharp vigilance

【警力】jǐnglì 警察的力量(指人员多少 number of policemen) police forces: ～不足。The police forces are inadequate.

【警犬】jǐngquǎn 受过训练,能帮助人侦查、搜捕、巡逻警戒的狗 police dog; dog specially trained to assist police to reconnoitre, search and patrol

【警世】jǐngshì 警戒世人,使醒悟 warn or admonish the world:～之作 work that admonishes the world

【警惕】jǐngtì 对可能发生的危险情况或错误倾向保持敏锐的感觉 be on guard against (possible danger or erroneous tendencies); watch out for; be vigilant:提高～,保卫祖国。Enhance our vigilance, and defend our motherland.

【警卫】jǐngwèi ❶ 用武装力量实行警戒、保卫 keep watch over so as to protect from danger and defend:～连 security company ❷ 指执行这种任务的人(security) guard; bodyguard:门口有～把守。The gate is controlled by security guards.

【警醒】jǐngxǐng ❶ 睡眠时易醒、睡不熟 sleep lightly:他睡觉最～不过。He is a very light sleeper. ❷ 警戒醒悟 vigilant; watchful; alert:鉴往知来,值得我们～。Reviewing the past and predicting the future, it is worthwhile for us to be vigilant. also 警省 jǐngxǐng

【警钟】jǐngzhōng 报告发生意外或遇到危险的钟,多用于比喻 alarm bell; bell that warns of danger or trespass; wake-up call; (oft. fig.) tocsin:这件事给那些麻痹大意的人敲了～。This event sounds the alarm for those who are offguard.

jìng (ㄐㄧㄥˋ)

劲(勁) jìng 坚强有力 strong; powerful; sturdy:强～ strong | 刚～ bold; sturdy | 疾风～草。Sturdy grass withstands high winds.

☞ jìn on p. 1015

【劲拔】jìngbá 〈书 *fml*.〉雄健挺拔 tall and straight:苍松～。Sturdy pines stand tall and straight.

【劲敌】jìngdí 强有力的敌人或对手 formidable adversary; strong opponent (or contender)

【劲旅】jìnglǚ 强大而有实力的队伍 strong contingent; crack force

径(徑、❶❷❸逕) jìng ❶ 狭窄的道路;小路 footpath; path; track:山～ mountain path | 曲～ winding path ❷〈比喻 *fig*.〉达到目的的方法 way; means to an end; method:捷～ shortcut | 门～ access; key; way ❸ 径直 straight; directly; straightaway:～行办理 deal with a matter straightaway | ～自答复 reply without consulting anyone | 取道武汉,～回广州。Go straight back to Guangzhou via Wuhan. ❹ 直径的简称 abbr. for 直径 zhíjìng:口～ bore; calibre | 半～ radius | ～尺(直径一尺) diameter of one chi

【径流】jìngliú 降水除蒸发的、被土地吸收的和被拦堵的以外,沿着地面流走的水叫径流。渗入地下的也可以形成地下径流。runoff. Rain, in excess of the amount absorbed by the ground and lost in evaporation, that runs off is called surface runoff; and that seeps into the ground and runs off is called groundwater runoff.

【径情直遂】jìng qíng zhí suì 随着意愿顺利地获得成功 (of things) run as smoothly as one would wish

【径赛】jìngsài 田径运动中各种赛跑和竞走项目比赛的总称 general term for track events; athletic sports performed on a track, such as running, heel-and-toe walking race, etc.

【径庭】jìngtíng (旧读 formerly pronounced jìngtìng)〈书 *fml*.〉相差很远 very different:大有～ widely divergent | 大相～ entirely different

【径行】jìngxíng 直接进行;径自 proceed directly; straight away:厂商希望能～进口自己所需的产品。The factories and stores hope that they can directly import the products they need.

【径直】jìngzhí〈副词 *adv*.〉❶ 表示直接向某处前进,不绕道,不在中途耽搁 (advance) straight; directly; straightaway, non-stop:登山队员～地攀登主峰。The mountaineers made straight for the summit. | 客机～飞往昆明,不在重庆降落。The plane will fly direct to Kunming, without stopping at Chongqing. ❷ 表示直接进行某件事,不在事前费周折 straight; directly; straightaway:你～写下去吧,等写完了再讨论。Just go on writing, and discuss it when you've finished.

【径自】jìngzì〈副词 *adv*.〉表示自己直接行动 without leave; without consulting anyone:他没等会议结束就～离去。He left abruptly in the middle of the meeting.

净[1](淨) jìng ❶ 清洁;干净 clean:～水 clean water | 脸要洗～。One's face must be washed clean. ❷ 擦洗干净 make sth. clean:～一～桌面儿。Clean the top of the table. ❸ 没有余剩 with nothing left:细收～打 harvest carefully and thresh thoroughly | 碗里的水没喝～。The water in the bowl has not been drunk up. ❹ 纯 net:～重 net weight | ～利 net profit ❺〈副词 *adv*.〉表示单纯而没有别的;只 all; all the time:书架上～是科技书籍。The bookshelves are full of books on science and technology. | 这几天～下雨。It's been raining these last few days. | 别～说些没用的话。Don't engage in such useless talk all the time.

净[2](淨) jìng 戏曲角色行当,扮演性格刚烈或粗暴的男性人物 painted-face role; one of the main roles in traditional opera, representing a man of virile or rough character; 通称 generally called 花脸 huāliǎn

【净产值】jìngchǎnzhí 生产单位、生产部门或整个国民经济在一定时期内新创造的价值 net output value; newly created value in a given period of time by a production unit, a production department, or the entire national economy

【净化】jìnghuà 清除杂质使物体纯净 purify; eliminate material impurities or imperfections:～污水 purify sewage|～城市空气 purify the air of the city ◇～心灵 purify one's soul|～社会风气 purify public morality

【净尽】jìngjìn 一点儿不剩 completely used up; with nothing left:消灭～utterly annihilate

【净角】jìngjué (～儿 jìngjuér) same as 净[2] jìng

【净口】jìngkǒu 曲艺表演中指去掉低级、庸俗的语言(区别于'荤口' as compared with 'dirty language') clean language; *quyi* performance without vulgar, indecent language

【净利】jìnglì 企业总收入中除去一切消耗费用和税款、利息等所剩下的利润(区别于'毛利'as compared with 'gross profit') net profit; excess of income over expenditure, taxes and interest, as in a business

【净手】jìng//shǒu ❶〈方 *dial.*〉洗手 wash one's hands:净一净手 wash one's hands|净净手 wash one's hands ❷〈婉辞 *euph.*〉指排泄大小便 relieve oneself

【净桶】jìngtǒng〈婉辞 *euph.*〉马桶 nightstool; closestool; commode

【净土】jìngtǔ ❶〈佛教 *Budd.*〉认为佛、菩萨等居住的世界,没有尘世的污染,所以叫净土 Pure Land (the world resided by Buddhas and Bodhisattvas, free from worldly contamination) ❷ 泛指没有受污染的干净地方 (in a broad sense) unpolluted place

【净余】jìngyú 除去用掉的剩余下来的(钱或物) (of money or resources) net balance; remainder; surplus; amount that remains when use or need is satisfied

【净值】jìngzhí 生产部门在一定时期内投入生产的活劳动所新创造的价值,是总产值减去物质消耗后的余额 net worth; net value; newly created value by a production department through investment in live labour for a given period of time, which is what remains of gross production after deducting material costs

【净重】jìngzhòng 货物除去包装的封皮、盛器或牲畜家禽等除去毛皮或毛的重量(区别于'毛重' as compared with 'gross weight') net weight; weight of goods after deducting all tare or the like; weight of livestock or domestic poultry excluding their hides or feathers

弪(弳) jìng 弧度的旧称 old term for 弧度 húdù

经(經) jìng 织布之前,把纺好的纱或线密密地绷起来,来回梳整,使成为经纱或经线 warping; arrange (yarns or threads) so as to form a warp:～纱 warp yarn

☞ jīng on p. 1018

胫(脛) jìng 小腿 shin

【胫骨】jìnggǔ 小腿内侧的长骨,上端和下端膨大,中部的横断面为三角形 shin bone; tibia; the inner and usu. larger of the two bones of the shank, which is bigger at the upper and lower ends, and has a middle part with a triangular cross section; (图见 ☞ figure for 骨骼 gǔgé on p. 693)

倞 jìng〈书 *fml.*〉强 strong

☞ liàng on p. 1210

痉(痙) jìng [痉挛](jìngluán)肌肉紧张,不自然地收缩。多由中枢神经系统受到刺激引起。convulsion; spasm; abnormal violent and involuntary contraction of the muscles, mostly caused by stimulation of the central nervous system

竞(競) jìng ❶ 竞争;竞赛 compete; contend; vie:～走 heel-and-toe walking race|～技 sports; athletics ❷〈书 *fml.*〉强劲 strong; forceful:南风不～。The south wind is not strong.

【竞渡】jìngdù ❶ 划船比赛 boat race:龙舟～dragon-boat regatta ❷ 渡过江湖等的水面的游泳比赛 swimming race across a river or a lake:游泳健儿～昆明湖。The swimmers compete on the Kunming Lake.

【竞技】jìngjì 指体育竞赛 sports; athletics:～场 arena|～状态不佳 not in good form; out of form; off one's game

【竞技体操】jìngjì tǐcāo 体操运动项目之一。男子项目有自由体操、单杠、双杠、吊环、鞍马、跳马等,女子有自由体操、平衡木、高低杠、跳马等。competitive gymnastics, including men's items (free-style exercises, horizontal bar, parallel bars, rings, pommelled horse, and vaulting horse) and women's items (free-style exercises, balance beam, uneven bars, and vaulting horse)

【竞赛】jìngsài 互相比赛,争取优胜 contest; competition; emulation; race:体育～ athletic contest (or competition)|劳动～ labour emulation drive

【竞相】jìngxiāng 互相争着(做) compete; vie:～逃命 vie with each other in fleeing for one's life|～吹捧 vie with each other in flattery|～压价出售 vie with each other in underselling

【竞选】jìngxuǎn 候选人在选举前进行种种活动争取当选 enter into an election; campaign; run for:参加总统～ run for the presidency|发表～演说 deliver an election speech

【竞争】jìngzhēng 为了自己方面的利益而跟人争

J

胜 compete; strive for an objective:贸易～competition in trade|～激烈 scrimmage; fierce competition|自由～ free competition

【竞走】jìngzǒu 径赛项目之一,走时两脚不得同时离地,脚着地时膝关节不得弯曲 heel-and-toe walking race; track event featuring a stride in which the heel of one foot touches the ground before the toe of the other foot leaves the ground, and the knee joints should not bend when the foot touches the ground

竟[1] jìng ❶ 完毕 finish; complete:未～之业 unaccomplished cause; unfinished task ❷ 从头到尾;全 throughout; whole:～日 whole day; throughout the day|～夜 whole night; throughout the night ❸〈书 *fml.*〉终于 in the end; eventually:有志者事～成。Where there's a will, there's a way.

竟[2] jìng〈副词 *adv.*〉表示出于意料之外 unexpectedly; actually:真没想到他～敢当面撒谎。Who would have thought that he had the audacity to tell a barefaced lie.|都以为他一定不答应,谁知他～答应了。Everyone thought he would never agree, so who would have expected that he did.

【竟然】jìngrán 竟[2] unexpectedly; to one's surprise; actually:这样宏伟的建筑,～只用十个月的时间就完成了。To think that such a magnificent building was completed within 10 months!

【竟日】jìngrì〈书 *fml.*〉终日;整天 whole day; all day long:～游乐 amuse oneself all day long

【竟至】jìngzhì 竟然至于;竟然达到 actually go so far as to:～如此之多 actually so much (or so many)

【竟自】jìngzì 竟然 unexpectedly; to one's surprise; actually:虽然没有人教他,他摸索了一段时间,～学会了。Though nobody taught him, he learnt it all by himself by trial and error.

婧 jìng〈书 *fml.*〉女子有才能 (of a woman) be gifted

靓 jìng〈书 *fml.*〉妆饰;打扮 dress up; make up

☞ liàng on p. 1210

【靓妆】jìngzhuāng〈书 *fml.*〉美丽的妆饰 (of a woman) gorgeously dressed

敬 jìng ❶ 尊敬 respect:～重 deeply respect; revere; honour|～爱 respect and love|～仰 revere; venerate|致～ salute|肃然起～ be filled with deep veneration ❷ 恭敬 respectfully:～请指教。Kindly give us your advice.|～谢不敏。I'm truly sorry but I cannot do it. ❸ 有礼貌地送上(饮食或物品) offer (food, drinks or other objects) politely:～烟 offer a cigarette (to a guest)|～酒 propose a toast|～茶 serve tea|～你一杯。(when toasting) To your health! ❹(Jìng) 姓 a surname

【敬爱】jìng'ài 尊敬热爱 respect and love:～父母 respect and love one's parents|～的张老师 respected Teacher Zhang

【敬辞】jìngcí 含恭敬口吻的用语,如'请问、借光'等 term of respect or polite expression such as 'May I request', 'Excuse me', etc.

【敬而远之】jìng ér yuǎn zhī 表示尊敬,但不愿接近 stay at a respectful distance from sb.

【敬奉】jìngfèng ❶ 虔诚地供奉(神佛) piously worship (deities or the Buddha) ❷ 恭敬地献上 offer respectfully; present politely:～锦缎一匹 present a bolt of brocade with due respect

【敬服】jìngfú 敬重佩服 respect and admire:他为人正直,让人～。He is respected and admired for his uprightness.|人们都～先生的人品才学。People all admire the teacher's talent and scholarship.

【敬告】jìnggào〈敬辞 *pol.*〉告诉 beg to inform:～读者 notice to readers

【敬贺】jìnghè〈敬辞 *pol.*〉祝贺 congratulate with respect; send respectful greetings to

【敬候】jìnghòu ❶〈敬辞 *pol.*〉等候 await respectfully:～回音。We are awaiting your response.|～光临。We await your arrival. ❷ 恭敬地问候 greeting with respect:～起居。(I wish) you good health.

【敬酒不吃吃罚酒】jìng jiǔ bù chī chī fá jiǔ〈比喻 *fig.*〉好好地劝说不听,用强迫的手段却接受了 refuse a toast only to drink a penalty; submit to sb.'s pressure after first turning down his request; be constrained to do what one at first refused to

【敬老院】jìnglǎoyuàn 养老院 home for the aged; old folks' home; seniors' home

【敬礼】jìng//lǐ ❶ 立正、举手或鞠躬行礼表示恭敬 salute; show respect or recognition by assuming a prescribed position or gesture, such as standing at attention, raising one's hand, or bowing:向老师敬个礼。Salute the teachers. ❷〈敬辞 *pol.*〉用于书信结尾 salutations [used at the end of a letter]

【敬慕】jìngmù 尊敬仰慕 respect and admire

【敬佩】jìngpèi 敬重佩服 esteem; admire

【敬畏】jìngwèi 又敬重又畏惧 hold in awe and veneration; revere:令人～ awe-inspiring

【敬献】jìngxiàn 恭敬地献上 offer respectfully; present politely:向烈士陵墓～花圈 lay a wreath at a martyr's tomb

【敬谢不敏】jìng xiè bù mǐn 表示推辞做某件事的客气话 [a polite expression to decline a request] I beg to be excused; I'm sorry, but I'm afraid I can't; (不敏 *bu min*:没有才能 inability)

【敬仰】jìngyǎng 敬重仰慕 revere; venerate:他是青年们～的导师。He is a teacher loved and venerated by the youth.

【敬业】jìngyè 专心致力于学业或工作 study or work diligently:～精神 dedication; dedicated professionalism

【敬意】jìngyì 尊敬的心意 respect; tribute:他让我转达对你的～。He asked me to give you his regards.

【敬重】jìngzhòng 恭敬尊重 deeply respect; revere; honour

靖 jìng ❶ 没有变故或动乱;平安 quiet; peaceful; tranquil; free from civil disturbance:地方安～。The localities are peaceful. ❷ 使秩序安定;平定(变乱) make tranquil; pacify; suppress (a rebellion):～边 pacify the border region|～乱 suppress a rebellion ❸ (Jìng) 姓 a surname

【靖康】Jìngkāng 宋钦宗(赵桓)年号(公元1126—1127) reign title of Emperor Qinzong (Zhao Huan, reigning 1126-1127) of the Song Dynasty

静 jìng ❶ 安定不动 still(跟'动'相对 as opposed to 'dynamic'):～止 static; motionless; at a standstill|安～ quiet|风平浪～。The wind has dropped and the waves have subsided. ❷ 没有声响 quiet; silent:寂～ silent|清～ quiet|夜～更深 in the still of night ❸ 使平静或安静 calm:～下心来 calm down|请大家～一～。Please be quiet. ❹ (Jìng) 姓 a surname

【静场】jìng//chǎng 剧场、电影院等演出结束后,观众退出 empty the theatre (i. e. see to it that the audience leaves the theatre after the end of a performance or show)

【静电】jìngdiàn 不流动的电荷,如摩擦所产生的电荷 static electrical charges, as those resulting from friction

【静电感应】jìngdiàn gǎnyìng 导体接近带电体时,导体表面产生电荷的现象。这时导体两端的电荷相等而正负相反。electrostatic induction; phenomenon of producing electrical charges when a conductor is exposed to the influence of a charged object, at which time the electrical charges at the two ends of the conductor are balanced and in opposite polarity

【静电计】jìngdiànjì 测量电荷量大小的仪器 electrometer; device for measuring differences of potential by means of electrostatic forces

【静观】jìngguān 冷静地观察 watch quietly:在一旁～ watch quietly from the sidelines|～事态的发展 watch quietly the development of the situation

【静脉】jìngmài 把血液送回心脏的血管。静脉中的血液含有较多的二氧化碳,血色暗红。vein; tubular branching vessels that carry blood from the capillaries towards the heart; blood in veins containing more carbon dioxide and thus being dark red

【静脉曲张】jìngmài-qūzhāng 静脉扩张、伸长或弯曲的症状。多由下肢静脉的血液回流受阻,压力增高引起。患者小腿发胀,沉重,容易疲劳。varix; varicosis; dilated, enlarged or distorted veins, caused by backflow obstruction in the lower limbs. Varicose-veins sufferers feel swelling and a sense of heaviness in the lower legs, and tire easily.

【静谧】jìngmì 〈书 *fml.*〉安静 quiet; still; tranquil:～的园林 quiet garden

【静摩擦】jìngmócā 接触物体之间保持相对静止时的摩擦 static friction; friction that keeps contacting objects static

【静默】jìngmò ❶ 寂静;没有声音 quiet; become silent:会场上又是一阵～。Another spell of silence fell upon the meeting room. ❷ 肃立不做声,表示悼念 stand in silent tribute:～三分钟 observe three minutes' silence

【静穆】jìngmù 安静庄严 solemn and quiet:气氛～ solemn and quiet atmosphere|～的灵堂 quiet and solemn mourning hall

【静悄悄】jìngqiāoqiāo (～的 jìngqiāoqiāo·de) 形容非常安静没有声响 very quiet:夜深了,四周～的。In the dead of night, it was very quiet on all sides.

【静态】jìngtài ❶ 相对静止状态;非工作状态 static state; inactive state:～工作点 inactive operating point|～电流 inactive current ❷ 从静态来考察研究的 study sth. in a static state:～分析 static analysis

【静物】jìngwù 用做绘画、摄影对象的静止的物体,如水果、鲜花、器物等 still life; inanimate subject matter for painting or photography:～画 still-life pictures|～写生 paint still life|～摄影 still-life photography

【静心】jìng//xīn 心情平静;使心神安定 calm the mind; quieten down:～读书 banish distracting thoughts from mind and study|你快出去,让我静静心。You go out now, and let me have some peace of mind.

【静养】jìngyǎng 安静地休养 rest quietly to recuperate; convalesce:你这病需要～一段时间。With your ailment, you need to rest quietly for some time to recuperate.

【静园】jìng//yuán 公园在规定时间停止开放,游人退出 clearing out the park (i. e. time for visitors to leave the park after it closes for the day)

【静止】jìngzhǐ 物体不运动 static; motionless; at a standstill:一切物体都在不断地运动,它们的～和平衡只是暂时的,相对的。All objects are in continuous motion, and their state of rest and balance is only temporary and relative.

【静坐】jìngzuò ❶ 排除思虑,闭目安坐,是气功疗法采用的一种方式 banish all distracting thoughts from the mind and sit still; a form of *qigong* therapy ❷ 为了达到某种要求或表示抗议安静地坐着 sit-down; sit-in; sit quietly to force compliance with demands or to protest：～示威 sit-in demonstration；sit-down protest

境 jìng ❶ 疆界；边界 border；boundary：国～ national territory｜入～ enter a country；cross the border ❷ 地方；区域 place；area；territory：渐入佳～(of a situation) be improving；be getting better｜如入无人之～ like entering an unpeopled land；smashing all resistance；meeting no resistance ❸ 境况；境地 condition；situation；circumstances：家～family financial situation；family circumstances｜处～ situation one finds oneself in｜事过～迁。That was then；it is now.

【境地】jìngdì ❶ 生活上或工作上遇到的情况 conditions in one's life or work；circumstances：处于孤立的～ be in conditions of isolation ❷ same as 境界 jìngjiè ②

【境界】jìngjiè ❶ 土地的界限 boundary ❷ 事物所达到的程度或表现的情况 extent reached；plane attained；state；realm：思想～ ideological level｜他的演技已经达到出神入化的～。His performance skills have reached the acme of perfection.

【境况】jìngkuàng 状况(多指经济方面的 usu. financial) condition；circumstances：近年家庭～略有好转。In recent years the financial situation of (his) family has changed slightly for the better.

【境域】jìngyù ❶ same as 境地 jìngdì ❷ same as 境界 jǐngjiè

【境遇】jìngyù 境况和遭遇 circumstances；one's lot

獍 jìng 古书上说的一种像虎豹的兽，生下来就吃生它的母兽 *jing*，legendary animal，similar to the tiger or leopard，that eats its own mother immediately after its birth

镜 jìng ❶ 镜子① looking glass；mirror：穿衣～ full-length mirror｜波平如～。The water surface is as smooth as a mirror. ❷ 利用光学原理制成的帮助视力或做光学实验用的器具，镜片一般用玻璃制成 lens；optical device made of transparent material (usu. glass) for aiding eyesight or optical experiments：花～ presbyopic glasses｜眼～儿 eyeglasses；spectacles｜凹～concave lens｜凸～convex lens｜望远～ telescope｜三棱～ triangular prism

【镜花水月】jìng huā shuǐ yuè 镜中的花，水里的月 flowers in a mirror or the moon in the water；〈比喻 *fig.*〉虚幻的景象 illusion；mirage

【镜框】jìngkuàng (～儿 jìngkuàngr)在用木头、石膏、塑料等做成的框子中镶上玻璃而制成的东西，用来装相片或字画等 picture frame；frame made of wood，plaster，plastic，etc.，for pictures or photographs，oft. with a glass cover

【镜片】jìngpiàn 光学仪器或眼镜等上的透镜 lens；piece of transparent material in an optical device，eyeglass，etc.

【镜台】jìngtái 装有镜子的梳妆台 dressing table；table fitted with drawers and a mirror in front of which one sits to dress and groom oneself

【镜头】jìngtóu ❶ 摄影机或放映机上，由透镜组成的光学装置。用来在胶片或幕上形成影像。camera lens；optical device composed of lenses on a camera or a film projector for forming an image on film or screen ❷ 照相的一个画面 shot；single photographic exposure ❸ 拍摄影片或电视片时从摄影机开始转动到停止时所拍下的一系列画面 take；scene；motion picture or television episode or sequence

【镜匣】jìngxiá 盛梳妆用品的匣子，其中装有可以支起来的镜子 dressing case；wooden case，with a mirror，that holds toiletry articles

【镜箱】jìngxiāng ❶ 指照相机的暗箱 camera bellows；camera obscura ❷ 盥洗室内设置的装有长方形镜子的箱状设备 dressing case；wooden case，with a mirror，that holds toiletry articles in a bathroom

【镜子】jìng·zi ❶ 有光滑的平面，能照见形象的器具，古代用铜铸厚圆片磨制，现在用平面玻璃镀银或镀铝做成 mirror；looking glass；polished or smooth surface that forms images by reflection，made of polished copper in ancient times，and glass plated with silver or aluminium in modern times ❷ 眼镜 eyeglasses；spectacles

jiōng (ㄐㄩㄥ)

坰 jiōng 〈书 *fml.*〉野外 outermost suburbs

駉 jiōng 〈书 *fml.*〉❶ 马肥壮 (of horses) plump and strong：～～牡马 fat and strong male horse ❷ 骏马 fine horse；steed

扃 jiōng 〈书 *fml.*〉❶ 自外关闭门户用的门闩、门环等 bolt，latch，etc.，for fastening a door from the outside ❷ 门；门扇 door；door leaf ❸ 关门 shut the door

jiǒng (ㄐㄩㄥˇ)

冏 jiǒng 〈书 *fml.*〉❶ 光 light ❷ 明亮 bright

炅 jiǒng 〈书 *fml.*〉❶ 日光 sunlight ❷ 明亮 bright

☞ Guì on p. 734

迥 jiǒng 〈书 *fml.*〉❶ 远 far；distant：山高路～。The mountains are high and the roads long. ❷ 差得远 vastly different：～异 totally different｜病前病后～若两人。(He) doesn't look like the same person after his illness.

【迥然】jiǒngrán 形容差别很大 far apart；vastly

different：一个沉着，一个急躁，他俩的性格～不同。One is composed, and the other irritable. The two of them have totally different temperaments.

洞 jiǒng〈书 *fml*.〉❶ 远 far ❷（水）深而阔 (of water) deep and vast

絅(褧) jiǒng〈书 *fml*.〉罩在外面的单衣 unlined outer garment

炯 jiǒng〈书 *fml*.〉明亮 bright：～然 shining

【炯炯】jiǒngjiǒng 形容明亮（多用于目光 of eyes) bright; shining：目光～ flashing eyes｜两眼～有神 have a pair of bright and piercing eyes

炅 jiǒng〈书 *fml*.〉日光 sunlight

颎 jiǒng〈书 *fml*.〉火光 flame; blaze

窘 jiǒng ❶ 穷困 in straitened circumstances; hard up：家境很～ with one's family in straitened circumstances ❷ 为难 awkward; embarrassed; ill at ease：我事前没做准备，当时很～。I did not get ready beforehand, and was caught in an awkward situation. ❸ 使为难 embarrass; disconcert：用话来～他。Say something to embarrass him.

【窘促】jiǒngcù〈书 *fml*.〉窘迫 poverty-stricken

【窘境】jiǒngjìng 十分为难的处境；困境 awkward situation; predicament; plight：陷入～ land oneself in a predicament; be put in a tight spot; be cornered｜摆脱～ extricate oneself from a predicament

【窘况】jiǒngkuàng 非常困难又无法摆脱的境况 awkward situation; predicament; plight; difficult, perplexing or trying situation

【窘迫】jiǒngpò ❶ 非常穷困 poverty-stricken; very poor：生计～live in poverty ❷ 十分为难 hard-pressed; embarrassed; in a predicament：处境～ find oneself in a predicament

【窘态】jiǒngtài 受窘时的神态 embarrassed look：他被大家笑得红了脸，站也不是，坐也不是，显出一副～。He flushed at the uproarious laughter, and in his embarrassment he was at a loss whether to sit or stand.

jiū（ㄐㄧㄡ）

勼 jiū〈书 *fml*.〉聚集 assemble; gather

纠1 jiū 缠绕 entangle：～纷 dispute｜～缠 get entangled

纠2 jiū 集合 gather together：～合 gather together｜～集 get together; muster

纠3 jiū ❶〈书 *fml*.〉督察；检举 supervise; inform against：～察 maintain order at a public gathering｜～举 accuse; inform against ❷ 纠正 correct; rectify：～偏 rectify a deviation; correct an error｜有错必～。Every wrong will be righted.

【纠察】jiūchá ❶ 在群众活动中维持秩序 maintain order at a public gathering：～队 pickets ❷ 在群众活动中维持秩序的人 persons who maintain order at a public gathering：担任～ serve as pickets

【纠缠】jiūchán ❶ 绕在一起 get entangled; be in a tangle：问题～不清。The problem has become very complicated. ❷ 捣麻烦 nag; pester：～不休 endless quibbling over sth.｜我还有事，别再～了。I'm busy. Stop pestering me.

【纠纷】jiūfēn 争执的事情 dispute; issue：调解～ mediate a dispute

【纠葛】jiūgé 纠缠不清的事情；纠纷 entanglement; dispute：他们之间有过～。There was once a dispute between them.

【纠合】jiūhé 集合；联合（多用于贬义 oft. derog.) gather together：～党羽，图谋不轨 gather together one's followers for criminal purposes; also 鸠合 jiūhé

【纠集】jiūjí 纠合（含贬义 derog.) get together; muster; gang up; also 鸠集 jiūjí

【纠结】jiūjié 互相缠绕 intertwine; entangle：藤蔓～。Rattans and vines intertwine.

【纠偏】jiū//piān 纠正偏向或偏差 rectify a deviation; correct an error

【纠正】jiūzhèng 改正（缺点、错误）correct (an error); put right; redress：～姿势 correct sb.'s posture｜～偏差 rectify a deviation｜不良倾向已得到～。The harmful trend has been rectified.

鸠 jiū 斑鸠、雉鸠等的统称 general term for turtle-doves

【鸠合】jiūhé same as 纠合 jiūhé

【鸠集】jiūjí same as 纠集 jiūjí

【鸠形鹄面】jiū xíng hú miàn 形容人因饥饿而很瘦的样子 gaunt and emaciated — referring to a navicular abdomen and protruding chest (鸠形 *jiu xing*：腹部低陷，胸骨突起 body of a turtle-dove; 鹄面 *hu mian*：脸上瘦得没有肉 bone face)

【鸠占鹊巢】jiū zhàn què cháo ☞ 鹊巢鸠占 què cháo jiū zhàn on p. 1604

究 jiū ❶ 仔细推求；追查 study carefully; go into; investigate：研～ study; research｜追～prosecute｜深～ go into (a matter) seriously; get to the bottom of (a matter) ❷〈书 *fml*.〉到底；究竟 actually; really; after all：此事～应如何办理？How should this matter actually be dealt with?

【究办】jiūbàn 追查惩办 investigate and deal with：依法～ investigate a case and deal with it according to law

【究根儿】jiū//gēnr 追问事情的来龙去脉；追究根源 enquire about the origin of (a matter); get to the bottom of (a matter)：这事已经了

结，不必～了。This matter has already been settled. No need to enquire into its origins.

【究诘】jiūjié〈书 *fml.*〉追问结果或原委 interrogate; cross-examine

【究竟】jiūjìng ❶ 结果；原委 outcome; what actually happened：大家都想知道个～。Everybody wants to know what actually happened. ❷〈副词 *adv.*〉用在问句里，表示追究［used in questions to press for an exact answer］actually; exactly：～是怎么回事？What's all this about exactly? | 你～答应不答应？Do you agree or not actually? 注意 **NOTE**：是非问句（如'你答应吗？'）里不用'究竟'。It should not be used in a simple question as 'Do you agree?' which calls for, instead of pressing for, an answer. ❸〈副词 *adv.*〉毕竟；到底 after all; anyway; finally：她～经验丰富，说的话很有道理。After all, she is very experienced, and there is a lot of sense in what she says.

【究问】jiūwèn 追究；追问 question closely; make a detailed enquiry：此事不予～。This matter has not been properly investigated.

赳 jiū［赳赳］(jiūjiū) 健壮威武的样子 valiant; gallant：～武夫 stalwart, martial man | 雄～，气昂昂 valiant and spirited; full of mettle

阄(鬮) jiū (～儿 jiūr) 抓阄时卷起或揉成团的纸片 lots; slips of paper crumpled into balls and used as ballots to determine a question through chance; ☞ 抓阄儿 zhuā//jiūr on p. 2514

揪 jiū 紧紧地抓；抓住并拉 hold tight; seize：～耳朵 hold sb. tightly by the ear | ～着绳子往上爬 hold the rope tightly to climb up | 把他～过来。Haul him over here.

J

【揪辫子】jiū biàn·zi〈比喻 *fig.*〉抓住缺点，作为把柄 seize sb.'s queue — seize upon sb.'s mistakes or shortcomings; capitalize on sb.'s vulnerable spot; also 抓辫子 zhuā biàn·zi

【揪揪】jiū·jiu〈方 *dial.*〉❶（衣物、织品等）不平整（of clothes, fabrics, etc.）creased; crumpled：衣服没熨，还～着呢。The dress has not been ironed, and is full of creases. ❷（心情）不舒展 feel depressed：村里这么一闹腾，我心里也～着。With such a fuss being made in the village, I feel uncomfortable.

【揪痧】jiū//shā 民间治疗某些疾病的方法，通常用手指揪颈部、咽喉部、额部等，使局部皮肤充血以减轻内部炎症 popular treatment for certain diseases by repeatedly pinching the patient's neck, throat or forehead, etc., to achieve decongestion and reduce inflammation

【揪心】jiū//xīn 放不下心；担心；挂心 anxious; worried：这孩子真让人～。This child really makes me worried.

啾 jiū see below

【啾唧】jiūjī〈拟声词 *onom.*〉形容虫、鸟等细碎的叫声 chirping of birds or insects

【啾啾】jiūjiū〈拟声词 *onom.*〉形容许多小鸟一齐叫的声音。也形容凄厉的叫声。chirping of birds; piteous cry

樛 jiū〈书 *fml.*〉树木向下弯曲 tree bending downward

鬏 jiū (～儿 jiūr) 头发盘成的结 hair bun; knot; chignon; knot of hair

jiǔ (ㄐㄧㄡˇ)

九 jiǔ ❶ 数目，八加一后所得 nine, one more than eight; ☞ 数字 shùzì on p. 1791 ❷ 从冬至起每九天是一个'九'，从一'九'数起，二'九'、三'九'，一直数到九'九'为止 each of the nine nine-day periods beginning from the day after the Winter Solstice：数～ beginning of the nine nine-day periods following the Winter Solstice | 冬练三～，夏练三伏。Practise even during the coldest days of winter and the hottest days of summer. | ～尽寒尽。Winter ends with the passing of the ninth nine-day period. ❸ 表示多次或多数 many; numerous：～霄 empyrean; heaven | ～泉 Nine Springs — the nether world; grave | 三弯～转 many twists and turns | ～死一生 narrow escape from death; survival after many perils

【九重霄】jiǔchóngxiāo ☞ 重霄 chóngxiāo on p. 272

【九鼎】jiǔdǐng ❶ 古代传说夏禹铸了九个鼎，象征九州，成为夏、商、周三代传国的宝物 nine tripods. According to ancient legend, King Yu of the Xia Dynasty had nine tripods cast as symbols of the nine parts of China, which were handed down to the Shang and Zhou dynasties as symbols of imperial authority. ❷〈比喻 *fig.*〉分量极重 weighty; weigh heavily：一言～ solemn pledge

【九宫】jiǔgōng ☞ 宫调 gōngdiào on p. 675

【九宫格儿】jiǔgōnggér 练习汉字书法用的方格纸，每个大格再用'井'字形交叉的线分成九个小格 squared paper for practising Chinese calligraphy, where each big square is divided into nine smaller squares like the Chinese character 井 jǐng

【九九歌】jiǔjiǔgē ☞ 小九九 xiǎojiǔjiǔ on p. 2108

【九九归一】jiǔ jiǔ guī yī 转来转去最后又还了原 when all is said and done; in the last analysis; after all：～，还是他的话对。All things considered, what he says is right. also 九九归原 jiǔ jiǔ guī yuán

【九流三教】jiǔ liú sān jiào ☞ 三教九流 sān jiào jiǔ liú on p. 1653

【九牛二虎之力】jiǔ niú èr hǔ zhī lì〈比喻 *fig*.〉很大的力量 strength of nine bulls and two tigers; tremendous effort

【九牛一毛】jiǔ niú yī máo〈比喻 *fig*.〉极大的数量中微不足道的一部分 a single hair out of nine ox hides; a drop in the ocean

【九泉】jiǔquán 指人死后埋葬的地方,迷信的人指阴间 Nine Springs; nether world; grave:～之下 after death|含笑～ smile in one's grave

【九死一生】jiǔ sǐ yī shēng 形容经历极大危险而幸存 narrow escape from death; survival after many perils

【九天】jiǔtiān 较高的天空 highest heavens; heaven:～九地(一个在天上,一个在地下,形容差别极大) as far apart as heaven and earth

【九霄】jiǔxiāo 天空的最高处,〈比喻 *fig*.〉极高或极远的地方 highest heavens; heaven; faraway place:豪情冲～ sentiments as lofty as heaven

【九霄云外】jiǔ xiāo yún wài 形容远得无影无踪 beyond the highest heavens; far, far away:他把我们的忠告抛到了～。He has cast our advice to the winds.

【九一八事变】Jiǔ-Yībā Shìbiàn 1931 年 9 月 18 日夜,日本帝国主义大规模武装侵略中国东北的事件。19 日日军侵占沈阳,同时在吉林、黑龙江等省区发动进攻。由于当时国民政府对日本侵略军采取不抵抗政策,致使四个多月内,东北全境沦陷,1945 年日本投降,东北领土才全部收复。September 18th Incident (the seizure of Shenyang in 1931 by the Japanese invaders, as a step towards their occupation of the entire northeast China). On the night of September 18, 1931, Japanese troops invaded Shenyang, and also attacked Jilin and Heilongjiang provinces. The Kuomintang government of the time adopted a policy of non-resistance, and as a result, within four months all of northeast China was occupied and was not regained until Japan surrendered in 1945.

【九州】jiǔzhōu 传说中的我国上古行政区划,后用作'中国'的代称 nine divisions of China in remote antiquity; poetic name for China

久 jiǔ ❶ 时间长(跟'暂'相对 as opposed to 'temporary') for a long time; long:～别重逢 meet again after a long separation; reunite after a long departure|～经锻炼 be seasoned ❷ 时间的长短 of a specified duration:你来了有多～? How long have you been here? |这座古墓考古队发掘了两个月之～。The archaeological team has been excavating this ancient tomb for as long as two months.

【久别】jiǔbié 长时间地分别 long separation; long years of departure:～重逢 meet again after a long separation; reunite after long years of departure

【久而久之】jiǔ ér jiǔ zhī 经过了相当长的时间 in the course of time; with the lapse of time; as time passes:机器要不好好养护,～就要生锈。Without proper maintenance, the machine will become rusty over time.

【久假不归】jiǔ jiǎ bù guī 长期借去,不归还 put off indefinitely returning sth. one has borrowed; appropriate sth. borrowed

【久久】jiǔjiǔ 许久;好久(用做状语)[used as adv.] for a long, long time:心情激动,～不能平静。(He) was so excited; it took him a long time to calm down.

【久留】jiǔliú 长时间地停留 stay long:此地不宜～。It is not suitable to stay here very long.

【久违】jiǔwéi〈客套话 *pol*.〉好久没见 I haven't seen you for ages:～了,这几年您上哪儿去啦? I haven't seen you for ages. Where have you been over the past few years?

【久仰】jiǔyǎng〈客套话 *pol*.〉仰慕已久(初次见面时说)[to sb. upon first meeting] I've long looked forward to meeting you.

【久已】jiǔyǐ 很久以前已经;早就 for a long time; long since:这件事我～忘了。I have long since forgotten it.

【久远】jiǔyuǎn 长久 far back; ages ago; remote:年代～ of the remote past; age-old; time-honoured

氿 jiǔ 东氿(Dōngjiǔ),西氿(Xījiǔ),湖名,都在江苏宜兴 Dongjiu and Xijiu, names of lakes in Yixing, Jiangsu Province
☞ guǐ on p. 732

玖[1] jiǔ '九'的大写 nine (used for the numeral 九 jiǔ on cheques, etc., to avoid mistakes or alterations); ☞ 数字 shùzì on p. 1791

玖[2] jiǔ〈书 *fml*.〉像玉的浅黑色石头 pale black jade-like stone

灸 jiǔ 中医的一种治疗方法,用燃烧的艾绒熏烤一定的穴位 moxibustion; therapeutic technique in traditional Chinese medicine, of applying ignited mugwort floss over specific acupoints

韭(韮) jiǔ 韭菜 fragrant-flowered garlic; (Chinese) chives

【韭菜】jiǔcài 多年生草本植物,叶子细长而扁,花白色。是普通蔬菜。(Chinese) chives (*Allium odorum*); fragrant-flowered garlic; herbaceous perennial with long, flat leaves and white flowers, a common vegetable

【韭黄】jiǔhuáng 冬季培育的韭菜,颜色浅黄,嫩而味美 hothouse chives; chives grown in winter, pale yellow, tender and delicious

酒 jiǔ ❶ 用粮食、水果等含淀粉或糖的物质经过发酵制成的含乙醇的饮料,如葡萄酒、白酒等 alcoholic drink; wine; liquor; spirits; drinks that contain alcohol made of fermented substances that contain starch or sugar extracted from grain or fruits, e. g. wine and spirits ❷(Jiǔ)姓 a surname

J

【酒吧】jiǔbā 西餐馆或西式旅馆中卖酒的地方 bar; counter at which alcoholic beverages are served in a Western-style restaurant or hotel; also 酒吧间 jiǔbājiān

【酒菜】jiǔcài ❶ 酒和菜 food and drink ❷ 下酒的菜 food to go with wine or liquor

【酒店】jiǔdiàn ❶ 酒馆 wineshop; public house; pub ❷ 较大而设备较好的旅馆(多作名称用 usu. used in names of hotels) hotel

【酒馆】jiǔguǎn (～儿 jiǔguǎnr)卖酒和酒菜等的铺子 public house; pub: 下～ go and drink in a pub; also 酒馆子 jiǔguǎn·zi

【酒鬼】jiǔguǐ 好(hào)酒贪杯的人(骂人的话 curse) wine bibber; toper

【酒酣耳热】jiǔ hān ěr rè 形容酒兴正浓 warmed with wine; mellow with drink

【酒花】jiǔhuā ☞ 啤酒花 píjiǔhuā on p. 1467

【酒会】jiǔhuì 形式比较简单的宴会,用酒和点心待客,不排席次,客人到场、退场都比较自由 cocktail party; informal or semi-formal party or gathering at which wines and snacks are served, where no fixed seats are arranged, and guests can come and go at will

【酒家】jiǔjiā 酒馆,现多用做饭馆名称 (now oft. used in names of restaurants) wineshop; tavern

【酒浆】jiǔjiāng〈书 *fml.*〉酒 wine

【酒精】jiǔjīng 乙醇的通称 common name for 乙醇 yǐchún

【酒力】jiǔlì 饮酒后,酒对人的刺激作用 effects of alcohol: 不胜～ cannot bear the effects of alcohol

【酒帘】jiǔlián same as 酒望 jiǔwàng

【酒量】jiǔliàng 一次能喝多少酒的限度 capacity for liquor: ～大 have great capacity for wine | 他～不行,喝一口就脸红。He is not a good drinker, and his face turns red with a single sip of wine.

【酒令】jiǔlìng (～儿 jiǔlìngr)饮酒时所做的可分输赢的游戏,输了的人罚饮酒 drinkers' wager game, in which losers are punished by having to drink wine: 行～ play drinkers' wager games | 出个～儿 determine the topic for drinkers' wager game

【酒母】jiǔmǔ same as 酒曲 jiǔqū

【酒囊饭袋】jiǔ náng fàn dài〈比喻 *fig.*〉无能的人 wineskin and rice-bag; good-for-nothing

【酒酿】jiǔniàng 江米酒 fermented glutinous rice

【酒钱】jiǔ·qian〈旧时 *old*〉给服务员或临时服务者的小费 tip; sum of money tendered for a service performed or anticipated

【酒曲】jiǔqū 酿酒用的曲 distiller's yeast

【酒肉朋友】jiǔròu péngyǒu 指只在一起吃喝玩乐、不干正经事的朋友 wine-and-meat friends; fair-weather friends

【酒色】jiǔsè 酒和女色 wine and women; sensual pursuits: 沉湎～abandon oneself to wine and women; indulge in sensual pursuits | ～之徒 voluptuary

【酒食】jiǔshí 酒和饭菜 food and drink

【酒水】jiǔshuǐ ❶ 酒和汽水等饮料 beverages; drinks such as wine and soda water, etc.: 餐厅备有二十多种～。The restaurant provides more than 20 kinds of beverages. ❷〈方 *dial.*〉指酒席 banquet: 办了两桌～。Two banquet tables have been prepared.

【酒肆】jiǔsì〈书 *fml.*〉酒馆 wineshop; public house; pub: 茶楼～ teahouse and wineshop

【酒嗉子】jiǔsù·zi〈方 *dial.*〉细而高的盛酒用的器皿,口向外张开,颈细,底大,没有柄,多用锡或陶瓷制成 wine flask; slim, handleless wine container made of tin or porcelain, with a thin neck, open mouth, and wide base

【酒徒】jiǔtú 好(hào)酒贪杯的人 winebibber; toper

【酒望】jiǔwàng〈旧时 *old*〉酒店的幌子,用布做成 wineshop sign in the form of a streamer, made of cloth; also 酒望子 jiǔwàng·zi or 酒帘 jiǔlián

【酒涡】jiǔwō same as 酒窝 jiǔwō

【酒窝】jiǔwō (～儿 jiǔwōr)笑时颊上现出的小圆窝 dimple; slight natural indentation in the cheek when one smiles; also 酒涡 jiǔwō

【酒席】jiǔxí 请客或聚餐用的酒和整桌的菜 feast; banquet; elaborate meal for numerous people in honour of a person or event

【酒兴】jiǔxìng 饮酒的兴致 elation caused by intoxication; rapture from wine: ～正浓 be buoyant with drunken elation

【酒药】jiǔyào 酿制黄酒或江米酒用的曲 yeast for brewing rice wine or fermented glutinous rice

【酒靥】jiǔyè〈方 *dial.*〉same as 酒窝 jiǔwō

【酒意】jiǔyì 将要醉的感觉或神情 tipsy feeling: 有了几分～be slightly tipsy; be mellow

【酒糟】jiǔzāo 造酒剩下的渣滓 distillers' grains

【酒渣鼻】jiǔzhābí 慢性皮肤病,鼻子尖出现鲜红色斑点,逐渐变成暗红色,鼻部结缔组织增长,皮脂腺扩大,成小硬结,能挤出皮脂分泌物 acne rosacea; brandy nose; chronic skin disease characterized by red spots on the tip of the nose, which gradually turn dark red, the growth of connective tissues of the nose and expansion of sebaceous glands, forming deep-seated papules and pustules, from which sebaceous secretions can be squeezed out; also 酒糟鼻 jiǔzāobí

【酒盅】jiǔzhōng (～儿 jiǔzhōngr)小酒杯 small handleless wine cup; also 酒钟 jiǔzhōng

jiù (ㄐㄧㄡˋ)

旧(舊) jiù ❶ 过去的;过时的 (跟'新'相对 as opposed to 'new') past; bygone; old: ～时代 former times | ～经验 old experience|～社会 old society|不要用～脑筋对待新事物。Don't approach new situations with old-fashioned ideas. ❷ 因经过长时间或经过使用而变色或变形的(跟'新'相对 as opposed to 'new') used; worn; old:～书 old books|～衣服 used clothes|窗纱～了。The window screen has become worn. ❸ 曾经有过的;以前的 former; one-time:张家口是～察哈尔省省会。Zhangjiakou used to be the capital of former Chahar Province. ❹ 老交情;老朋友 old friendship; old friend:怀～ remember past times or old acquaintances|念～ keep old friendships in mind; remember old friends|亲戚故～ relatives and old friends

【旧案】jiù'àn ❶ 历时较久的案件 court case of long standing:积年～都已经清理完毕。Court cases of many years' standing have all been cleared. ❷ 过去的条例或事例 old regulations; former practices:优抚工作暂照～办理。The work of giving preferential treatment and privileges to disabled servicemen and family members of revolutionary martyrs and servicemen will be temporarily handled in accordance with former practices.

【旧病】jiùbìng 历时较久、时犯时愈的病;宿疾 old illness; old chronic complaint:～复发 have a recurrence of an old illness; have an attack of a recurrent sickness; have a relapse

【旧部】jiùbù 旧日的部属 former subordinates

【旧地】jiùdì 曾经去过或生活过的地方 once visited or inhabited place:～重游 revisit a once familiar place

【旧调重弹】jiù diào chóng tán 〈比喻 *fig.*〉把陈旧的理论、主张重新搬出来 harp on the same string; rehash the same old tune; reiterate hackneyed theory or views; also 老调重弹 lǎo diào chóng tán

【旧都】jiùdū 故都 former capital

【旧观】jiùguān 原来的样子 former appearance; former state:迥非～ entirely different from what it used to be

【旧国】jiùguó 旧都(古称都城为国) former capital; old capital (capital was called 国 guó in ancient times)

【旧好】jiùhǎo 〈书 *fml.*〉❶ 指过去的交谊 old friendship:重修～ renew cordial relations; become reconciled; bury the hatchet ❷ 指旧交;老朋友 old acquaintance; old friend

【旧家】jiùjiā 〈书 *fml.*〉指久居某地而有声望的人家 notable families that live long in a locality:～子弟 descendants of notable families

【旧交】jiùjiāo 老朋友 old acquaintance; old friend

【旧教】jiùjiào 16 世纪欧洲宗教改革后,称天主教为旧教 Catholicism, called 'old religion' after the Reformation in Europe in the 16th century

【旧居】jiùjū 从前居住过的住所 former residence; old home

【旧历】jiùlì same as 农历 nónglì ①

【旧例】jiùlì 过去的事例或条例 old regulations; former practices:沿用～ continue to follow old regulations

【旧梦】jiùmèng 〈比喻 *fig.*〉过去经历过的事 old dream; past experience:重温～ revive an old dream; relive a past experience

【旧年】jiùnián 〈方 *dial.*〉去年 last year

【旧情】jiùqíng 旧日的情谊 old or former friendships; former affection:不忘～ do not forget old friendships

【旧日】jiùrì 过去的日子 former days; old days:想起～的情景 remember the scene of old days

【旧诗】jiùshī 指用文言和传统格律写的诗,包括古体诗和近体诗 classical poetry; poetry composed following the rules and forms of classical poetic composition with respect to tonal pattern, rhyme scheme, etc., including ancient-style poetry and modern-style poetry

【旧石器时代】Jiùshíqì Shídài 石器时代的早期,也是人类历史的最古阶段。这时人类使用的工具是比较粗糙的打制石器,生产上只有渔猎和采集。Old Stone Age; Paleolithic Period; early period of the Stone Age, also the remotest period of humanity, during which humans used coarse stone implements, and lived by fishing, hunting and gathering

【旧时】jiùshí 过去的时候;从前 old times; old days

【旧式】jiùshì 旧的、过时的式样或形式 old-fashioned; old style:～长袍 old-fashioned robe|～家具 old-style furniture|～婚礼 old-style wedding

【旧事】jiùshì 已往的事 old matter or affair; past event:～重提 bring up a matter of the past

【旧书】jiùshū ❶ 破旧的书 second-hand book; used (or old) book ❷ 古书 ancient book; ancient text

【旧俗】jiùsú 长期流传下来的风俗习惯;旧有的习俗 old customs; folk ways passed down through the ages

【旧闻】jiùwén 指社会上过去发生的事情,特指掌故、逸闻、琐事等 old folklore, esp. anecdotes and trifles; short narratives of interesting, amusing or biographical anecdotes

【旧物】jiùwù ❶ 先代的遗物,特指典章文物 past heritage, esp. decrees and documents ❷ 指原有的国土 lost territory:光复～ recover what has been lost (to an invader)

【旧习】jiùxí 旧的习惯或习俗 old habits or customs:～难改。Old habits are hard to change.|陈规～ outmoded regulations and old customs

【旧学】jiùxué 指我国未受近代西方文化影响前固有的学术 old Chinese learning (as distinct from the new or Western learning)

【旧业】jiùyè 曾从事过的行业 old trade or profession：重操～ resume one's old profession; take up one's old trade again

【旧雨】jiùyǔ 〈书 *fml.*〉〈比喻 *fig.*〉老朋友（杜甫《秋述》：'卧病长安旅次，多雨，…常时车马之客，旧，雨来，今，雨不来。'后人就把'旧'和'雨'联用作老朋友讲）old friend (from Du Fu's *Autumn Account*: 'I am confined to bed during my stay in Chang'an /And it is often rainy, . . . /Friends used to come in on rainy days /But nowadays they don't come when it is raining.' The two characters 旧 jiù and 雨 yǔ are combined to refer to 'old friend'.)：～重逢 meeting of old friends

【旧章】jiùzhāng 过去的典章制度；老规矩 past regulations; old rules：更定～ revise the old regulations｜率由～ observe the old rules

【旧账】jiùzhàng 旧日欠的账 old debt; old score; 〈比喻 *fig.*〉以前的过失、嫌怨等 score; previous errors; old grudge：不要算～。Don't quibble over an old grudge.

【旧址】jiùzhǐ 已经迁走或不存在的某个机构或建筑的旧时的地址 site of an organization or a building that has been moved elsewhere or is no longer in existence

【旧制】jiùzhì 旧的制度。特指我国过去使用的一套计量制度。old system; esp. the old system of weights and measures in China

臼 jiù ❶ 舂米的器具，用石头或木头制成，中部凹下 mortar; stone or wooden vessel in which rice is pounded with a pestle ❷ 形状像臼，中间凹下的 any mortar-shaped thing：～齿 molar teeth

【臼齿】jiùchǐ 位置在口腔后方两侧的牙齿，齿冠上有疣状的突起，适于磨碎食物。人类的臼齿上下颌各六个。molar tooth; tooth adapted to grinding by having a broad rounded or flattened (though oft. ridged or tuberculated) surface, including the posterior pairs (three in each jaw on each side in adults); 通称 commonly known as 槽牙 cáoyá; (图见 ☞ figure for 齿 chǐ on p.263)

咎 jiù ❶ 过失；罪过 fault; blame：引～自责 hold oneself responsible for a mistake｜～有应得 deserve one's punishment ❷ 责备 censure; punish; blame：既往不～ let bygones be bygones; do not censure sb. for his past misdeeds ❸ 〈书 *fml.*〉凶 bad fortune：休～（吉凶）good or ill luck

【咎由自取】jiù yóu zì qǔ 遭受责备、惩处或祸害是自己造成的 have only oneself to blame (for reprimand, punishment or calamity)

疚 jiù 〈书 *fml.*〉对于自己的错误感到内心痛苦 remorse; gnawing distress arising from a sense of guilt over past wrongs：负～ feel apologetic; have a guilty conscience｜内～于心 feel compunction; have qualms of conscience; be conscience-stricken

柩 jiù 装着尸体的棺材 coffin with a corpse in it：棺～ bier｜灵～ coffin containing a corpse

柏 jiù 柏树，就是乌桕 Chinese tallow tree

厩（廐、㕊）jiù 马棚，泛指牲口棚 stable; cattle-shed; pen：～肥 barnyard manure

【厩肥】jiùféi 家畜的粪尿和垫圈的干土、杂草等混在一起沤成的肥料。也叫圈（juàn）肥，有的地区叫圊（qīng）肥。barnyard manure; material that fertilizes land, made of refuse from stables and barnyards, e.g. livestock excreta with litter; also 圈肥 juànféi; called 圊肥 qīngféi in some areas

救（捄）jiù ❶ 援助使脱离灾难或危险 rescue; save; help sb. out of confinement, danger, or evil：～命 save sb.'s life｜挽～ rescue｜营～ succour｜搭～ rescue｜抢～ salvage｜一定要把他～出来。We must rescue him. ❷ 援助人、物使免于（灾难、危险）free (sb. or sth.) from (danger, disaster); relieve (distress, etc.)：～亡 save the nation from destruction｜～荒 send relief to a famine area｜～灾 provide disaster relief; help people tide over a natural disaster｜～急 help sb. to cope with an emergency

【救兵】jiùbīng 情况危急时来援助的军队 relief troops; reinforcements：搬～call in reinforcements

【救国】jiù//guó 拯救祖国，使免于危亡 save the nation (from destruction)：～救民 national salvation｜抗日～运动 movement to resist Japanese aggression and save the country

【救护】jiùhù 援助伤病人员使得到适时的医疗，泛指援助有生命危险的人 give first-aid; rescue; relieve a sick or injured person：～队 ambulance corps｜～车 ambulance｜～伤员 give first-aid to the wounded

【救荒】jiù//huāng 采取措施，度过灾荒 send relief to a famine area; help to tide over a crop failure：～作物 disaster-alleviation crops｜～运动 movement to tide over a crop failure｜生产～tide over a crop failure through production

【救火】jiù//huǒ 在失火现场进行灭火和救护工作 fight a fire; try to put out a fire：～车 fire engine｜消防队员正在～。The firemen are fighting the fire.

【救急】jiù//jí 帮助解决突然发生的伤病或其他危难 help sb. to cope with an emergency; help meet an urgent need

【救济】jiùjì 用金钱或物资帮助灾区或生活困难的人 extend relief to (a disaster area or people in difficulties); relieve the distress of：～费 relief fund｜～粮 relief grain; relief food｜～难民 give relief to refugees

【救苦救难】jiù kǔ jiù nàn 拯救在苦难中的人

help the needy and relieve the distressed

【救命】jiù//mìng 援助有生命危险的人 save sb.'s life：～恩人 benefactor to whom one owes one's life | 治病～ cure diseases to save lives

【救生】jiùshēng 救护生命 save life (esp. sb. from drowning)：水上～ lifesaving in the water | ～设备 lifesaving device; life preserver

【救生圈】jiùshēngquān 水上救生设备的一种，通常是用软木或其他轻质材料做成的圆环，外面包上帆布并涂上油漆。供练习游泳用的救生圈也可用橡胶制成，内充空气，叫橡皮圈。life buoy; ring-shaped life preserver, oft. made of cork or other light material, covered with canvass and coated with paint. A life buoy for swimming can also be made of rubber filled with air, called 橡皮圈 xiàngpíquān.

【救生艇】jiùshēngtǐng 在轮船、军舰或港口设置的小船，用来营救水上遇难的人 lifeboat; strong buoyant boat designed for use in saving lives at sea; boat carried by a ship for emergency

【救生衣】jiùshēngyī 水上救生设备的一种，通常是用布包裹软木等轻质材料做成的背心 life jacket; life preserver in the form of a buoyant vest, oft. made of light materials such as cork covered with cloth; also 救生服 jiùshēngfú

【救世主】Jiùshìzhǔ 基督教徒对耶稣的称呼。基督教认为耶稣是上帝的儿子，降生为人，是为了拯救世人。Saviour; Redeemer; saviour acknowledged by Christians. According to Christianity, Jesus is the son of God, and he was born to bring salvation to human beings.

【救死扶伤】jiù sǐ fú shāng 救活将死的，照顾受伤的 heal the wounded and rescue the dying：～，是医务人员的职责。To heal the wounded and rescue the dying is the responsibility of medical workers.

【救亡】jiùwáng 拯救祖国的危亡 save the nation from destruction：～图存 save the nation from doom and ensure its survival

【救星】jiùxīng〈比喻 *fig.*〉帮助人脱离苦难的集体或个人 liberator; emancipator; saviour; individual or group that saves people from danger or destruction

【救应】jiù·ying 救援；接应 aid and support; reinforce

【救援】jiùyuán 援救 rescue; come to sb.'s help

【救灾】jiù//zāi ❶ 救济受灾的人民 provide disaster relief; send relief to a disaster area; help people tide over a natural disaster：放粮～ provide relief grain ❷ 消除灾害 eliminate calamities：防洪～ control flood to avoid calamities

【救治】jiùzhì 医治使脱离危险 bring a patient out of danger; treat and cure：全力～伤员。Spare no efforts to rescue the wounded.

【救助】jiùzhù 拯救和援助 help sb. in danger or difficulty; succour

就[1] jiù ❶ 凑近；靠近 come near; move towards：迁～ accommodate oneself to; yield to | 避难～易 shirk the difficult and take the easy; take the easy way out; choose the easier of the two alternatives | ～着灯看书 read a book by the light of a lamp ❷ 到；开始从事 undertake; engage in; enter upon：～位 take one's place | ～业 obtain employment | ～寝 go to bed; retire for the night | ～学 go to school, attend school | ～职 assume office ❸ 被；受 suffer; be subjected to：～歼 be annihilated; be wiped out | ～擒 be seized; be captured ❹ 完成；确定 accomplish; make：成～ accomplish; achieve | 功成业～ (of a person's career) crowning success | 生铁铸～的，不容易拆掉。Cast of iron, it is not easily dismantled. ❺ 趁着（当前的便利）take advantage of; accommodate oneself to：～便 at sb.'s convenience | ～近 (do or get sth.) nearby | ～手儿 while you are at it ❻ 一边儿是菜蔬、果品等，一边儿是主食或酒，两者搭着吃或喝 (dishes, fruit, etc.) be eaten (or drunk) with (staple food or wine); go with：花生仁儿～酒 have peanuts with one's drinks ❼〈介词 *prep.*〉表示动作的对象或范围 with regard to; concerning; on：他们～这个问题进行了讨论。They had a discussion on this question.

就[2] jiù〈副词 *adv.*〉❶ 表示在很短的时间以内 at once; right away：我～来。I'll come right away. | 您略候一候，饭～好了。Just wait a little while, please. The meal will be ready in a minute. ❷ 表示事情发生得早或结束得早 as early as; already：他十五岁～参加革命了。He joined the revolution when he was only 15 years old. | 大风早晨～住了。The gale had already stopped by morning. ❸ 表示前后事情紧接着 as soon as; right after：想起来～说。Speak up as soon as you think of something. | 卸下了行李，我们～到车间去了。As soon as we unloaded our luggage, we went to the workshop. ❹ 表示在某种条件或情况下自然怎么样（前面常用'只要、要是、既然'等或者含有这类意思 oft. preceded by conjunctions like 只要 zhǐyào，要是 yào·shi，既然 jìrán, etc.）[indicating a natural result under certain conditions or circumstances] in that case; then：只要用功，～能学好。As long as one works hard, one can learn it well. | 他要是不来，我～去找他。If he does not come, then I will go and find him. | 谁愿意去，谁～去。Anyone who is willing to go can go. ❺ 表示对比起来数目大，次数多，能力强等 as much as; as many as：你们两个小组一共才十个人，我们一个小组～十个人。There are 10 people altogether in your two groups,

but there are as many members in just one group of ours. | 他三天才来一次，你一天～来三次。He comes here once every three days, while you come here three times a day. | 这块大石头两个人抬都没抬起来，他一个人～把它背走了。Two people working together were not strong enough to lift this big rock, but he just carried it away alone on his back. ❻ 放在两个相同的成分之间，表示容忍[used between two identical elements to express resignation]：大点儿～大点儿吧，买下算了。Even though it's a little too big, just buy it. ❼ 表示原来或早已是这样 begin with; as is expected：街道本来～不宽，每逢集市更显得拥挤了。The street is not wide, to begin with, and it becomes more crowded on market days. | 我～知道他会来的，今天他果然来了。I knew he would come, and he came today as expected. ❽ 仅仅；只 only; merely; just：以前～他一个人知道，现在大家都知道了。He used to be the only one to know this, now it is known to all. ❾ 表示坚决 (indicating determination) just; simply：我～不信我学不会。I simply refused to believe that I couldn't learn it. | 我～做下去，看到底成不成。I just continue to do it, to see whether it will succeed or not. ❿ 表示事实正是如此 exactly; precisely：那～是他的家。That is precisely his home. | 这人～是他哥哥。This person is precisely his elder brother. | 幼儿园～在这个胡同里。The kindergarten is exactly in this alley.

就[3] jiù 〈连词 *conj.*〉表示假设的让步，跟'就是'相同[indicating a supposition, same as 就是[2] jiùshì]：你～送来，我也不要。Even if you send it to me, I won't accept it.

【就伴】jiù//bàn 做伴；搭伴 keep sb. company; accompany sb.：我想跟你～进城。I want to go to the city together with you.

【就便】jiù//biàn (～儿 jiù//biànr) 顺便 at sb.'s convenience; while you're at it：你上街～把这封信发了。Mail this letter for me when you go out.

【就餐】jiùcān 到吃饭地方去吃饭 have a meal in a dining room, etc.; eat; dine：他们几个在机关食堂～。They are to dine in the canteen of the institution.

【就此】jiùcǐ 就在此地或此时 at this point; here and now; thus：～前往 proceed from here | 文章～结束。So much for this article.

【就道】jiùdào 〈书 *fml.*〉上路；动身 set out on a journey; start off (or out)：束装～ pack up and start out | 来信催促立即～。A letter has arrived urging (me) to start out at once.

【就地】jiùdì 就在原处(不到别处) on the spot：～正法 execute (a criminal) on the spot | ～取材，～使用。Use materials where they are acquired.

【就读】jiùdú 在某个学校读书 attend school：早年曾～于清华大学。(He) attended Tsinghua University in his early years.

【就范】jiùfàn 听从支配和控制 submit; yield to (governance or authority); give in：迫使～ compel sb. to submit

【就合】jiù·he 〈方 *dial.*〉❶ 凑合；迁就 accommodate oneself to; yield to：你别～他。Don't give in to him. | 买包方便面，～着吃一顿算了。Buy a pack of instant noodles and make it a meal. ❷ 蜷曲；不舒展 huddle up; draw (oneself) together

【就歼】jiùjiān 被歼灭 be eliminated：残敌全部～。All the remnants of the enemy have been wiped out.

【就教】jiùjiào 请教；求教 go to sb. for advice or instructions：移樽～ take one's wine cup and go to sb.'s table to ask his advice — go to sb. for advice | ～于专家 go to experts for advice

【就近】jiùjìn 在附近(不上远处) (do or get sth.) nearby; close at hand：蔬菜、肉类等副食品～都可买到。All the non-staple foods, such as vegetables and meat, are available close at hand.

【就里】jiùlǐ 内部情况 inside information; inside story：不知～ not be in the know

【就擒】jiùqín 被捉住 be seized; be captured：束手～ allow oneself to be seized without putting up a fight; wait for capture with one's hands tied

【就寝】jiùqǐn 上床睡觉 retire for the night; go to bed：按时～ go to bed on time

【就任】jiùrèn 担任(某种职务) take up a post; take office：～总统 take office as president

【就势】jiùshì 顺着动作姿势上的便利(紧接着做另一个动作) make use of momentum (to take another action)：他把铺盖放在地上，～坐在上面。He put his bedroll on the ground and sat on it.

【就是】[1] jiùshì ❶ 用在句末表示肯定(多加'了') [oft. used with 了 ·le, at the end of a sentence to give force to a statement]：我一定办到，你放心～了。I promise to get it done. Don't worry. ❷ 单用，表示同意[used alone to express agreement] yes, that's right; exactly; precisely：～，～，您的话很对。Yes, yes, you are quite right. 注意 **NOTE**：其他'就'和'是'合用的情况，参看'就[2]'。For other combined usages of 就 jiù and 是 shì, see 就[2] jiù.

【就是】[2] jiùshì 〈连词 *conj.*〉表示假设的让步，下半句常用'也'呼应[indicating a supposition, used correlatively with 也 yě] even if：为了祖国，我可以献出一切，～生命也不吝惜。For our motherland I would never balk at any personal sacrifice, even if it meant my life. | ～在日常生活中，也需要有一定的科学知

识。Even in daily life certain scientific knowledge is needed.

【就事】jiùshì 找到职业前往任事 take up office; assume a post

【就事论事】jiù shì lùn shì 根据事情本身情况来评论是非得失 deal with a matter on its own merits; judge a thing in its own context; judge the case as it stands

【就手】jiù//shǒu (～儿 jiù//shǒur)顺手;顺便 while you're at it:出去～儿把门带上。Close the door on your way out.

【就算】jiùsuàn 即使 even if; granted that:～有困难,也不会太大。Even if there are obstacles, it won't be too difficult.

【就位】jiùwèi 到自己应到的位置上 be seated; take one's place:主席团～。Members of the presidium, please be seated.

【就绪】jiùxù 事情安排妥当 be in order; be ready:大致～。Preparations are more or less completed.|一切布置～。Everything is ready.

【就学】jiùxué〈旧指 *old*〉学生到老师所在的地方去学习,今指进学校学习 go to school; attend school:～于北京大学 attend Peking University

【就业】jiù//yè 得到职业;参加工作 obtain employment; take up an occupation; get a job:劳动～ labour and employment|～人数逐年增加。The number of employees is increasing year by year.

【就医】jiù//yī 病人到医生那里请他诊疗 seek medical advice; see the doctor:每天来门诊部～的病人很多。Many patients go to the clinic for medical advice every day.

【就义】jiùyì 为正义事业而被杀害 be executed for championing a just cause; die a martyr:从容～ go to one's death unflinchingly; die a hero's death

【就诊】jiù//zhěn 就医 seek medical advice; go to a doctor

【就正】jiùzhèng 请求指正 solicit comments (on one's writing):现将拙文公开发表,以～于读者。Now I'll publish my article and request readers to offer their criticism.

【就职】jiù//zhí 正式到任(多指较高的职位) assume office (usu. high positions):～演说 inaugural speech|宣誓～ take the oath of office; be sworn in

【就中】jiùzhōng ❶ 居中(做某事) between:～调停 mediate between ❷ 其中 among:这件事他们三个人都知道,～老王知道得最清楚。The three of them all know about this, but of all of them Lao Wang knows the matter the most clearly.

【就坐】jiù//zuò 坐到坐位上 take one's seat; be seated:按顺序～。Take your seats in due order. also 就座 jiù//zuò

舅 jiù ❶ 舅父 mother's brother; maternal uncle:大～ eldest uncle|二～ second uncle ❷ 妻的弟兄 wife's brother:妻～ brother-in-law ❸〈书 *fml.*〉丈夫的父亲 husband's father:～姑(公公和婆婆) parents-in-law

【舅父】jiùfù 母亲的弟兄 mother's brother; maternal uncle

【舅舅】jiù·jiu same as 舅父 jiùfù

【舅妈】jiùmā same as 舅母 jiù·mu

【舅母】jiù·mu 舅父的妻子 wife of mother's brother

【舅嫂】jiùsǎo 妻子的弟兄的妻子 wife of wife's brother; sister-in-law

【舅子】jiù·zi 妻子的弟兄 wife's brother; brother-in-law:大～ eldest brother-in-law|小～ younger brother-in-law

僦 jiù〈书 *fml.*〉租赁 rent:～屋 rent a house

鹫 jiù ☞ 雕[2] diāo on p. 445

·jiu (·ㄐㄧㄡ)

蹴 ·jiu ☞ 圪蹴 gē·jiu on p. 649
☞ cù on p. 331

jū (ㄐㄩ)

车(車) jū 象棋棋子的一种 chariot, one of the pieces in Chinese chess
☞ chē on p. 231

且 jū ❶〈书 *fml.*〉〈助词 *aux.*〉相当于'啊'[equivalent to 啊·a]oh:狂童之狂也～。Oh how crazy the young fool is! ❷ 用于人名,如范雎,也作范且[used in the name of a person, e.g. 范雎 fànjū, also written as 范且 fànjū]
☞ qiě on p. 1554

苴 jū[苴麻](jūmá)大麻的雌株,所生的花都是雌花,开花后结实 hemp; female plant of hemp, which bears female flowers and fruits; also 种麻 zhǒngmá

拘 jū ❶ 逮捕或拘留 arrest; detain:～捕 arrest; take into custody|～押 detain ❷ 拘束 restrain; restrict; constrain:～谨 overcautious; reserved|无～无束 unrestrained ❸ 不变通 inflexible:～泥 be a stickler for (form, etc.); rigidly adhere to (formalities, etc.) ❹ 限制 limit:多少不～。No limit is set on quantity.|不～一格 not stick to one pattern; not limited to one type or style

【拘板】jū·bǎn〈方 *dial.*〉(举动或谈话)拘束呆板;不活泼(of action or speech) stiff; formal:待人接物有些～。(He) has a rather stiff manner.|自己人随便谈话,不必这么～。You're among friends, don't be so formal.

【拘捕】jūbǔ 逮捕 arrest; take into custody

【拘传】jūchuán 法院、检察机关或公安机关对传唤不到案的被告人，签发拘票，强制到案 summon sb. for questioning; people's courts, procuratorates or public security departments may sign and issue a warrant to summon a defendant for questioning

【拘管】jūguǎn 管束；限制 keep in custody：严加～ keep sb. in strict control

【拘谨】jūjǐn （言语、行动）过分谨慎；拘束 over-cautious; reserved：他是个～的人，从不和人随便谈笑。He is reserved and withdrawn, never talking and laughing casually with others.

【拘禁】jūjìn 把被逮捕的人暂时关起来 incarcerate; take into custody

【拘礼】jūlǐ 拘泥礼节 be punctilious; stand on ceremony：熟不～ be too familiar with each other to stand on ceremony

【拘留】jūliú ❶ 公安机关对需要受侦查的人的一种紧急措施，把他在规定时间内暂时押起来 detain; hold in custody; intern; emergency measure taken by the public security department for a person under investigation, to be held in custody for a given period of time ❷ 把违反治安管理的人短期关在公安机关拘留所内，是一种行政处罚 detention; as an administrative punishment, a violator of public security being kept for a short period of time in a house of detention run by the public security department

【拘挛】jūluán ❶ 肌肉收缩，不能伸展自如 cramps; spasms; involuntary and abnormal muscular contractions ❷〈书 *fml.*〉拘泥 rigidly adhere to：～章句 insist on a textual interpretation

【拘挛儿】jū·luanr〈方 *dial*〉（手脚）冻僵，屈伸不灵（of hands and feet） frozen stiff; numb with cold

【拘泥】jū·nì ❶ 固执；不知变通 be a stickler for (form, etc.); rigidly adhere to (formalities, etc.)：～成说 rigidly adhere to accepted theories ❷ 拘束；不自然 constrained; awkward; ill at ease：～不安 ill at ease

【拘票】jūpiào 法院、检察机关或公安机关签发的强制被告或有关人到案的凭证 arrest warrant; warrant; precept issued by courts, procuratorates or public security departments to summon the accused or persons concerned

【拘牵】jūqiān〈书 *fml.*〉束缚 restrain; confine：～于成规 confined to conventions

【拘束】jūshù ❶ 对人的言语行动加以不必要的限制；过分约束 over-restrain (one's speech or action); restrict：不要～孩子的正当活动。Don't restrict the proper activities of children. ❷ 过分约束自己，显得不自然 constrained; awkward; ill at ease：她见了生人，显得有点～。She looks ill at ease in the presence of strangers.

【拘押】jūyā same as 拘禁 jūjìn

【拘役】jūyì 一种短期剥夺犯人自由并使其服劳役的刑罚 criminal detention; punishment involving deprivation of freedom and forced labour

【拘囿】jūyòu 拘泥；局限 rigidly adhere to：不为旧说～ not confined to accepted theories

【拘执】jūzhí 拘泥 rigid; inflexible：这些事儿可以变通着办，不要过于～。We should be flexible in dealing with these matters, and not be so rigid.

狙 jū ❶ 古书里指一种猴子 a kind of monkey mentioned in ancient texts ❷〈书 *fml.*〉窥伺 watch for：～击 snipe

【狙击】jūjī 埋伏在隐蔽地点伺机袭击敌人 snipe; shoot at exposed individuals of an enemy force when not in action, from a concealed vantage point：～手 sniper

泃 Jū 泃河，水名，在河北东北部、北京东部 Juhe, the name of a river in northeastern Hebei Province, to the east of Beijing

居 jū ❶ 住 reside; dwell; live：～民 resident; inhabitant｜分～ (of a married couple) be separated; live apart ❷ 住的地方；住所 residence; house：迁～ change one's dwelling place｜民～ local-style dwelling houses｜故～ former residence (or home) ❸ 在（某种位置） be (in a certain position); occupy (a place)：～左 on the left｜～首 rank first ❹ 当；任 assert; claim：～功 claim credit｜以专家自～ claim to be an expert ❺ 积蓄；存 store up; lay by：～积 hoard｜奇货可～ rare commodity worth hoarding ❻〈书 *fml.*〉停留；固定 stay put; be at a standstill：变动不～ always changing｜岁月不～。Time and tide wait for no one. ❼ 用作某些商店的名称（多为饭馆） [usu. used in names of restaurants] restaurant：同和～ Tonghe Restaurant｜沙锅～ Casseroles Restaurant ❽ (Jū)姓 a surname

【居安思危】jū ān sī wēi 处在安定的环境而想到可能会出现的危难 think of danger in times of safety; be vigilant in peacetime

【居多】jūduō 占多数 be in the majority：他的文章，关于文艺理论方面的～。Most of his writings are on theories of literature and art.

【居高临下】jū gāo lín xià 处在高处，俯视下面。形容处于有利的地位。occupy a commanding position (or height); in a favourable position

【居功】jūgōng 认为某件事情的成功是由于自己的力量；自认为有功劳 think the success of a matter is due to one's own efforts; claim credit for oneself：～自傲 become arrogant because of one's achievements; claim credit and put on airs

【居积】jūjī〈书 *fml.*〉积累（财物）；囤积 accumulate (wealth)：不善～ not good at accumulating wealth｜～致富 amass a fortune

【居家】jūjiā 住在家里 live at home; run a household：～过日子 keep house (economically and efficiently)

【居间】jūjiān 在双方中间(说合、调解)(mediate) between two parties:～调停 mediate between two parties; act as a mediator

【居留】jūliú 停留居住 reside:～证 residence certificate; residence permit|～权 right of residence|他在外国～了五年。He resided abroad for five years.

【居留权】jūliúquán 一国政府根据本国法律规定给予外国人的在本国居留的权利 right of residence (given to an alien by the government of a country, according to the laws of that country)

【居民】jūmín 固定住在某一地方的人 resident; inhabitant:街道～ residents of the neighbourhood|城镇～residents of cities and towns; urban residents

【居民点】jūmíndiǎn 居民集中居住的地方 residential area

【居奇】jūqí 看成是很少有的奇货,留着卖大价钱 hoard and speculate:囤积～ hoarding and cornering; hoarding and profiteering

【居然】jūrán〈副词 *adv.*〉❶ 表示出乎意料;竟然 unexpectedly; actually; to one's surprise:我真没想到他～会做出这种事来。I never thought he would do such a thing. ❷〈书 *fml.*〉表示明白清楚;显然 clear; obviously:～可知 abundantly clear

【居丧】jūsāng〈书 *fml.*〉守孝 be in mourning

【居士】jūshì 不出家的信佛的人 lay Buddhist

【居室】jūshì 居住的房间 room:这套房有三～,还有一个过厅。This apartment has three rooms and a hallway.

【居所】jūsuǒ 居住的处所;住所 residence; living place:～狭小。The living space is narrow.

【居停】jūtíng ❶ 停留下来住下 stop and stay (at a place when travelling) ❷〈书 *fml.*〉寄居之处的主人 landlord; host (原称'居停主人',后来简省为'居停' formely known as 居停主人 jūtíng zhǔ·rén and later abbreviated as 居停)

【居心】jū//xīn 怀着某种念头(多用于贬义 oft. derog.) harbour (evil) intentions:～不善 harbour evil intentions|是何～? What are (you) plotting?

【居心叵测】jū xīn pǒ cè 存心险恶,不可推测 with hidden intent; with ulterior motives

【居于】jūyú 处在(某个地位) occupy (a certain position):～领导地位 in leading position|该省粮食产量～全国之首。That province ranks first nationwide in terms of grain output.

【居中】jūzhōng ❶ 在中间;居间(mediate) between two parties:～调停 mediate between two parties|～斡旋 mediate a dispute ❷ 当中 be placed in the middle:两旁是对联,～是一幅山水画。On either side is a couplet scroll, and in the middle is a landscape painting.

【居住】jūzhù 较长时期地住在一个地方 reside; dwell; live in a place for a long time:他家一直～在北京。His family has always lived in Beijing.

驹 jū ❶ 少壮的马 fine horse:千里～ fine colt; young man of great promise ❷(～儿 jūr)驹子 foal:小驴～儿 foal of a donkey

【驹子】jū·zi 初生或不满一岁的骡、马、驴 foal, the young of a mule, horse or donkey, esp. under one year of age:马～ colt

挶 jū〈书 *fml.*〉❶ 抬土的器具 implement for transporting earth ❷ 握持 hold

俱 Jū 姓 a surname
☞ jù on p.1051

罝 jū〈书 *fml.*〉捉兔子的网。泛指捕野兽的网。net for catching hare; (in a broad sense) net for catching animals

疽 jū〈中医 *Chin. med.*〉指局部皮肤肿胀坚硬而皮色不变的毒疮 subcutaneous ulcer; deep-rooted ulcer; phlegmon; acute suppurative inflammation of subcutaneous connective tissues

椐 jū〈书 *fml.*〉走山路乘坐的东西 litter used on mountain paths

掬(匊) jū 两手捧(东西) hold with both hands:～水 scoop up some water with both hands ◇笑容可～(笑容露出来,好像可以用手捧住,形容笑得明显) be radiant with smiles (as if they could be scooped up with both hands)|憨态可～charmingly naive

据 jū ☞ 拮据 jiéjū on p.991
☞ jù on p.1052

琚 jū ❶ 古人佩带的一种玉 jade pendant in ancient times ❷(Jū)姓 a surname

趄 jū ☞ 趑趄 zījū on p.2538
☞ qiè on p.1556

椐 jū 古书上说的一种小树,枝节肿大,可以做拐杖 small trees, mentioned in ancient texts, with swelling knots that can be used to make walking sticks

跔 jū〈书 *fml.*〉腿脚因寒冷而痉挛 (of legs) twitch (because of coldness)

锔(锯) jū 用锔子连合破裂的陶瓷器等 mend (broken crockery, etc.) with clamps:～盆 mend a basin with clamps|～缸 mend a jar with clamps|～锅 mend a pot with clamps|～碗儿的 crockery mender
☞ jú on p.1047
☞锯 jù on p.1052

【锔子】jū·zi 用铜或铁打成的扁平的两脚钉,用来连接破裂的陶瓷等器物 clamp; copper or iron device bent at the ends and used to mend broken ceramic utensils

腒 jū〈书 *fml.*〉干腌的鸟肉 dried and preserved bird's meat

雎 jū 用于古人名,如范雎、唐雎,都是战国时人 *ju*, used as a personal name in ancient times, e.g. Fan Ju and Tang Ju, both from the Warring States Period

【雎鸠】jūjiū 古书上说的一种鸟 waterfowl mentioned in ancient texts; osprey; turtledove; mallard

鮈 jū 鱼类的一属,身体小,侧扁或圆筒形,有须一对,背鳍一般没有硬棘。生活在温带淡水中。gudgeon (*Gobio gobio*); genus of freshwater fish living in the temperate zone, small, flat or cylindrical in shape, having a pair of feelers, and no hard spines on its dorsal fin

裾 jū 〈书 *fml.*〉❶ 衣服的大襟 full front of a Chinese gown ❷ 衣服的前后部分 full front and back of a Chinese gown

鞠[1] jū ❶〈书 *fml.*〉抚养;养育 rear; bring up:～养 rear | ～育 bring up ❷〈书 *fml.*〉弯曲 bow:～躬 bow ❸ (Jū) 姓 a surname

鞠[2] jū 古代的一种球 ball used for play in ancient times:蹴～ kick a ball

【鞠躬】jū//gōng 弯身行礼 bow:～道谢 bow in thanks | 行了个～礼 salute by making a bow | 深深地鞠个躬 make a deep bow; bow low

【鞠躬】jūgōng 〈书 *fml.*〉小心谨慎的样子 in a discreet and scrupulous manner:～如也 with one's body bent | ～尽瘁 bend oneself to a task and exert oneself to the utmost; spare no effort in the performance of one's duty

【鞠躬尽瘁】jūgōng jìn cuì《三国志·蜀志·诸葛亮传》注引《汉晋春秋》诸葛亮表:'鞠躬尽力,死而后已'('力'选本多作'瘁')。指小心谨慎,贡献出全部精力。bend one's back to a task until one's dying day; give one's all till one's heart stops beating. *Records of Three Kingdoms·Kingdom of Shu·Biography of Zhuge Liang*, quoting an *Annals of Han and Jin* note on memorials of Zhuge Liang: 'bend myself to a task and exert to the utmost until my dying day.'

【鞠养】jūyǎng 〈书 *fml.*〉抚养;养育 rear; bring up:～之恩 kindness of nurturing

鞫 jū 〈书 *fml.*〉用斗、勺等舀取 ladle out with a *dou* measure or a ladle

鞫 jū 〈书 *fml.*〉审问 interrogate:～问 interrogate | ～讯 make a judicial investigation | ～审 examine and judge a case

jú (ㄐㄩˊ)

局[1] jú ❶ 棋盘 chessboard:棋～ game of chess as it develops ❷ 下棋或其他比赛一次叫一局 game; set; innings:下了一～棋 play a game of chess | 打了个平～end in a draw ❸ 形势;情况;处境 situation; state of affairs:结～final result; outcome; ending | 战～ war situation | 顾全大～ take the interests of the whole into account; consider the situation as a whole | 当～者迷。Blunt are those concerned. *or* When it is one's turn to move, one is easily confused. ❹ 人的器量 largeness or smallness of mind; extent of one's tolerance of others:～量 tolerance | 器～ intellectual and spiritual capacity | ～度 tolerance; forbearance ❺ 称某些聚会 gathering:饭～ dinner party; feast | 赌～ gambling party; gambling den ❻ 圈套 ruse; trap:骗～ fraud; hoax; swindle ❼ 拘束 limit; confine:～促 narrow; cramped | ～限 limit; confine

局[2] jú ❶ 部分 part; portion:～部 part ❷ 机关组织系统中按业务划分的单位(一般比部小,比处大) bureau; office; a unit in a system, lower than a ministry and higher than a department:冶金～bureau of metallurgy | 商业～bureau of commerce ❸ 办理某些业务的机构 organizations dealing in certain businesses:邮～ post office | 电话～ telephone bureau ❹ 某些商店的名称 [used in shop names] shop:书～ bookshop

【局部】júbù 一部分;非全体 part; portion:～麻醉 local anaesthesia | ～地区有小阵雨。There will be light showers in parts of the region.

【局促】júcù ❶ 狭小 narrow; cramped:房间太～,走动不便。This room is rather cramped; there's little space to move freely. ❷〈方 *dial.*〉(时间)短促 (of time) short:三天太～,恐怕办不成。I'm afraid three days are not long enough for us to get it done. ❸ 拘谨不自然 feel or show constraint:～不安 ill at ease ‖ also 侷促 júcù or 跼促 júcù

【局度】júdù 〈书 *fml.*〉气度 tolerance; forbearance

【局蹐】jújí same as 跼蹐 jújí

【局量】júliàng 〈书 *fml.*〉器量;气度 tolerance; forbearance

【局面】júmiàn ❶ 一个时期内事情的状态 aspect; phase; situation (within a given period):稳定的～ stable situation | 生动活泼的政治～ lively and vigorous political situation ❷〈方 *dial.*〉规模 scope; scale:这家商店～虽不大,货色倒齐全。Though this store is not large, goods of every description are available here.

【局内人】júnèirén 原指参加下棋的人,泛指参与其事的人 person in the middle of a chess game; person in the know; (in a broad sense) insider:此事非～不得而知。No one should know of this matter except for the insiders. also 局中人 júzhōngrén

【局骗】júpiàn 设圈套骗人 swindle:～财物 swindle sb. out of sth.

【局势】júshì (政治、军事等)一个时期内的发展

情况 political or military situation：～平稳。The situation is stable.|～越来越严重。The situation is becoming more and more serious.

【局外】júwài 棋局之外，指与某事无关 not involved in a chess game; not related to sth.：～人 person not in the know; outsider|置身～ stay aloof from the affair; refuse to be drawn into the matter

【局外人】júwàirén 指与某事无关的人 person not in the know; outsider：～不得而知 unknown to outsiders

【局限】júxiàn 限制在某个范围内 limit; confine：～性 limitations|提倡艰苦朴素，不能只～在生活问题上。Advocacy of hard work and plain living should not be confined to trifling matters of everyday life.

【局子】jú·zi ❶〈旧时 *old*〉指警察局，现指公安局 police station; now referring to public security bureau ❷ 指镖局、拳局等 professional establishment that provided armed escorts ❸ 圈套(多见于早期白话 usu. used in early vernacular) trap

侷 jú［侷促］same as 局促 júcù

桔 jú popular form for 橘 jú
☞ jié on p. 993

菊 jú ❶ 菊花 chrysanthemum：墨～ black chrysanthemum|赏～ appreciate chrysanthemums ❷ (Jú) 姓 a surname

【菊花】júhuā ❶ 多年生草本植物，叶子有柄，卵形，边缘有缺刻或锯齿。秋季开花。经人工培育，品种很多，颜色、形状和大小变化很大。是观赏植物。有的品种可入药。chrysanthemum (*Chrysanthemum morifolium*); herbaceous perennial, with handled, oval-shaped, runcinate leaves, that blossoms in autumn. Artificial cultivation has come up with many varieties that are greatly different in colour, shape and size with some varieties used in traditional Chinese medicine. ❷ 这种植物的花 blossoms of this plant

【菊坛】jútán 指戏曲界；梨园 (多指京剧界 usu. referring to Peking Opera circles) theatre world; Pear Garden

焗 jú〈方 *dial.*〉❶ 烹调方法，利用蒸汽使密闭容器中的食物变熟 steam food in a sealed container：盐～鸡 salted steamed chicken ❷ 因空气不流通或气温高湿度大而感到憋闷 feel smothered; be stifled (because of poor ventilation, high temperature and humidity)

锔 jú 金属元素，符号 Cm (curium)。银白色，有放射性，由人工核反应获得。人造卫星和宇宙飞船上用它作热电源。curium (Cm); metallic radioactive element artificially produced from nuclear reaction, used as a pyroelectrical source for man-made satellites and space shuttles
☞ jū on p. 1045

湨 Jú 湨河，水名，在河南 Juhe, the name of a river in Henan Province

鶪 jú 古书上指伯劳 name for a shrike in ancient books

跼 jú〈书 *fml.*〉腰背弯曲 (of the back) croaching

【跼促】júcù same as 局促 júcù

【跼蹐】jújí〈书 *fml.*〉❶ 形容畏缩不安 uneasy ❷ 狭隘；不舒展 narrow; limited ‖ also 局蹐 jújí

橘 jú ❶ 橘子树，常绿乔木，树枝细，通常有刺，叶子长卵圆形，果实球形稍扁，果皮红黄色，果肉多汁，味道甜。果皮、种子、树叶等中医都入药。tangerine (*Citrus reticulata*); evergreen tree with thin, thorned branches, oval leaves, ball-shaped, slightly flat fruit with reddish-orange peel. The meat of the fruit is juicy and sweet, and its peel, seeds and leaves can be used in traditional Chinese medicine. ❷ 这种植物的果实 fruit of this plant：蜜～tangerine

【橘柑】júgān〈方 *dial.*〉橘子 tangerine

【橘红】júhóng ❶〈中医 *Chin. med.*〉指柑橘类干燥的外果皮，可入药 dried tangerine peel, which can be used as ingredients in traditional Chinese medicine ❷ 像红色橘子皮那样的颜色 tangerine (colour); reddish-orange

【橘黄】júhuáng 比黄色略深像橘子皮的颜色 orange (colour); colour of tangerine peel, which is slightly darker than yellow

【橘络】júluò 橘皮和橘瓣中间的网络形的纤维。中医入药。tangerine pith, which can be used as an ingredient in traditional Chinese medicine

【橘子】jú·zi ❶ 橘子树 tangerine tree ❷ 橘子树的果实 fruit of the tangerine tree

jǔ (ㄐㄩˇ)

弆 jǔ〈书 *fml.*〉收藏；保藏 keep; store; collect：藏～ collect

枸 jǔ［枸柳］(jǔliǔ) ☞ 元宝枫 yuánbǎofēng on p. 2356
☞ guì on p. 734

咀 jǔ 嚼 chew：含英～华(比喻琢磨和领会文章的要点) (fig.) relish the joys of literature
☞ 嘴 zuǐ on p. 2568

【咀嚼】jǔjué ❶ 用牙齿磨碎食物 masticate; chew; crush, grind or gnaw with teeth ❷〈比喻 *fig.*〉对事物反复体会 mull over; ruminate; chew the cud：诗句的意境，耐人～。The intense mood of the poem is thought provoking.

沮 jǔ ❶〈书 *fml.*〉阻止 stop; prevent：～其成行 stop sb. from going ❷ (气色)败坏 turn gloomy, turn glum：～丧 dejected, depressed

☞ jù on p.1051

【沮遏】jǔ'è〈书 *fml.*〉阻止 prevent

【沮丧】jǔsàng ❶ 灰心失望 dejected; depressed; dispirited; disheartened: 神情～ look depressed ❷ 使灰心失望 depress; dispirit; dishearten: ～敌人的精神 demoralize the enemy

莒 Jǔ 莒县,地名,在山东 Juxian County, in Shandong Province

枸 jǔ [枸橼](jǔyuán)香橼 citron

☞ gōu on p.681 and gǒu on p.683

矩(榘) jǔ ❶ 画直角或正方形、矩形用的曲尺 carpenter's square; square: ～尺 carpenter's square ❷ 法度;规则 rules; regulations: 循规蹈～ observe rules docilely; conform to convention; toe the line

【矩尺】jǔchǐ ☞ 曲尺 qūchǐ on p.1587

【矩形】jǔxíng 对边相等(通常邻边不相等),四个角都是直角的四边形 rectangle; parallelogram of all right angles, equal opposite sides (usu. unequal adjoining sides); also 长方形 chángfāngxíng

【矩矱】jǔyuē〈书 *fml.*〉规矩;法度 rules; regulations

举(舉、擧) jǔ ❶ 往上托;往上伸 lift; raise; hold up: ～重 weightlifting | ～手 raise one's hand | 高～着红旗 hold high the red flag ❷ 举动 act; deed; move: 义～ magnanimous act undertaken for the public good | 壮～ magnificent feat; heroic undertaking | 一～一动 every act and every move | 一～两得 gain two ends at once; kill two birds with one stone ❸ 兴起;起 start: ～义 start a revolt | ～兵 call out the troops | ～火 light a fire ❹〈书 *fml.*〉生(孩子) give birth to (a child): ～一男 give birth to a boy ❺ 推选;选举 elect; choose: 推～ elect | ～代表 elect representatives | 公～他做学习组长。He was elected by public nomination as the head of the study group. ❻ 举人的简称 abbr. for 举人 jǔrén: 中～ pass the imperial examination at the provincial level | 武～ (formerly) military officer of second degree in imperial examinations ❼ 提出 cite; enumerate: ～例 give an example | 列～ list; enumerate ❽〈书 *fml.*〉全 whole; entire: ～座 all those present | ～家南迁。The whole family moves southward. | ～国欢腾。The whole nation is jubilant. | ～世闻名 of world renown; world-famous

【举哀】jǔ'āi 丧礼用语,指高声号哭 wail in mourning

【举案齐眉】jǔ àn qí méi 后汉梁鸿的妻子孟光给丈夫送饭时,总是把端饭的盘子举得高高的(见于《后汉书·梁鸿传》)。后人用来形容夫妻相敬。holding the tray level with the brow — husband and wife treating each other with courtesy. When Meng Guang, wife of Liang Hong, served meals to her husband, she always held the tray level with her brow (see *History of Later Han · Biography of Liang Hong*).

【举办】jǔbàn 举行(活动);办理(事业) conduct (activities); hold; run (an undertaking): ～展览会 hold (or put on) an exhibition | ～学术讲座 give academic lectures | ～训练班 conduct a training course | ～群众福利事业 conduct welfare projects for the masses

【举报】jǔbào 向有关单位检举报告(坏人坏事) report (an offender to the department concerned); inform against: ～违法犯罪行为 report illegal activities and crimes

【举步】jǔbù〈书 *fml.*〉迈步 take a step: ～维艰 have difficulty in taking a step

【举措】jǔcuò 举动;措施 move; act: ～失当 make an ill-advised move | 新～ new measures

【举动】jǔdòng 动作;行动 movement; move; act; activity: ～缓慢 move slowly | 近来他有什么新的～? Has he engaged in any new activities recently?

【举发】jǔfā 检举;揭发(坏人、坏事) report (an offender); inform against

【举凡】jǔfán〈书 *fml.*〉凡是(下文大多列举) ranging from ... to ...; all ... such as: 戏曲表演的手法,内容非常丰富,～喜、怒、哀、乐、惊、恐、愁、急等感情的流露,全都提炼出一套完整的程式。The methods of expression are diverse in theatrical performance. A complete set of stylized moves have been summarized to express all emotions, e.g. joy, anger, grief, happiness, surprise, fear, worry, and anxiety.

【举国】jǔguó 整个国家;全国 whole nation: ～欢腾。The whole nation is jubilant. | ～一致 national unanimity | ～上下 whole nation from top to bottom; from the leaders of the nation to all the people

【举火】jǔhuǒ〈书 *fml.*〉❶ 点火 light a fire: ～为号 light a beacon ❷ 专指生火做饭 light the kitchen fire; light the stove

【举架】jǔjià〈方 *dial.*〉指房屋的高度 height of a house: 这间房子～矮。This house is quite low.

【举荐】jǔjiàn 推荐(人) recommend (sb.): ～德才兼备的人来校任教。Recommend people of both professional ability and moral integrity to teach at this school.

【举例】jǔ//lì 提出例子来 give an example: ～说明 illustrate with examples

【举目】jǔmù 抬起眼睛(看) raise the eyes; look: ～远眺 look into the distance | ～无亲 be away from all one's kin; be a stranger in a strange land; have no one to turn to (for help)

【举棋不定】jǔ qí bù dìng〈比喻 *fig.*〉做事犹豫不决 hesitate about (or over) what move to make; be unable to make up one's mind; vacillate; shilly-shally (棋 *qí*: 棋子 piece)

【举人】jǔrén 明清两代称乡试考取的人 successful candidate in the imperial examination at the provincial level in the Ming and Qing dynasties

【举世】jǔshì 整个世间;全世界 throughout the world; universally: ～闻名 of world renown; world-famous | ～瞩目 attract worldwide attention; become the focus of world attention | ～无双 unrivalled; matchless

【举事】jǔshì〈书 *fml*.〉发动武装暴动 stage an uprising; rise in insurrection

【举手之劳】jǔ shǒu zhī láo 形容事情很容易办到;不费事 turn of the hand; as easy as turning one's hands over

【举行】jǔxíng 进行(集会、比赛等) hold (a meeting, contest, etc.): ～会谈 hold talks | ～球赛 hold a ball game | 展览会在文化宫～。The exhibition is being held at the Cultural Palace.

【举要】jǔ//yào 列举大要,多用做书名,如《唐宋文举要》list of main points, mainly used in titles of books, e.g. *Essential Tang and Song Prose*

【举一反三】jǔ yī fǎn sān 从一件事情类推而知道许多事情 draw inferences about other cases from one instance

【举债】jǔzhài〈书 *fml*.〉借债 borrow money; raise (or contract) a loan: ～度日 eke out an existence on borrowed money

【举止】jǔzhǐ 指姿态和风度;举动 bearing; manner; mien: ～大方 have poise; have an easy manner; be gentle of mien | 言谈～ speech and deportment

【举重】jǔzhòng 体育运动项目之一。运动员以抓举、挺举两种举法举起杠铃。weightlifting; sports item where athletes lift barbells in two forms: snatch, or clean and jerk

【举足轻重】jǔ zú qīng zhòng 所处地位重要,一举一动都关系到全局 hold the balance; prove decisive (to the whole situation)

钼 jǔ [钼铻] (jǔyǔ)〈书 *fml*.〉same as 龃龉 jǔyǔ

☞ chú on p. 291

椇 jǔ ❶ ☞ 枳椇 zhǐjǔ on p. 2467 ❷〈古代 *arch*.〉祭祀用的架子,用来放置宰杀的牲口 sacrificial stand, used to set slaughtered animals in ancient sacrificial rites

筥 jǔ〈书 *fml*.〉圆形的竹筐 round rice-washing bamboo basket

蒟 jǔ see below

【蒟酱】jǔjiàng ❶ ☞ 蒌叶 lóuyè on p. 1253 ❷ 用蒌叶果实做的酱,有辣味,供食用 betel pepper paste; thick and hot-tasting sauce made of betel pepper, used as a condiment

【蒟蒻】jǔruò ☞ 魔芋 móyù on p. 1365

榉(櫸) jǔ ☞ 山毛榉 shānmáojǔ on p. 1669

龃 jǔ [龃龉] jǔyǔ〈书 *fml*.〉上下牙齿不齐。upper and lower teeth not meeting properly;〈比喻 *fig*.〉意见不合 disagreement; discord: 双方发生～。The two parties quarrelled. also 钼铻 jǔyǔ

踽 jǔ [踽踽]〈书 *fml*.〉形容一个人走路孤零零的样子(walk) alone: ～独行 walk alone

jù (ㄐㄩˋ)

巨(❶鉅) jù ❶ 大;很大 huge; tremendous; gigantic: ～款 enormous amount of money | ～轮 large wheel | ～幅画像 huge portrait | 为数甚～ huge sum ❷ (Jù) 姓 a surname

【巨变】jùbiàn 巨大的变化 great changes; tremendous change: 这几年家乡的面貌发生了～。In recent years great changes have taken place in the outlook of my hometown.

【巨擘】jùbò〈书 *fml*.〉大拇指 thumb;〈比喻 *fig*.〉在某一方面居于首位的人物 authority in a certain field: 医界～ leading medical authority

【巨大】jùdà (规模、数量等)很大 (of scale, amount) huge; tremendous; enormous; gigantic; immense: 耗资～ cost huge sums of money | ～的工程 giant project | ～的成就 tremendous achievement

【巨额】jù'é 很大的数量(指钱财) huge amount; huge sum: ～贷款 huge loan | ～资金 enormous amount of money | 为国家创造了～财富 create a huge amount of wealth for the country

【巨匠】jùjiàng 泛称在科学或文学艺术上有极大成就的人 great master; consummate craftsman; giant (in the fields of science, literature or art): 文坛～ literary giant

【巨流】jùliú 巨大的水流 mighty current;〈比喻 *fig*.〉巨大的时代潮流 mighty trend of the times: 历史～ mighty historical current

【巨轮】jùlún ❶ 巨大的车轮,多用于比喻(oft. used figuratively) large wheel: 历史的～滚滚向前。The wheel of history rolls on. ❷ 载重量很大的轮船 large ship: 万吨～ 10,000-ton ship

【巨人】jùrén ❶ 身材高大异于常人的人 giant; colossus ❷ 童话里指比一般人高大,而往往有神力的人物 giant; magic figures in fairy tales that are bigger than ordinary people ❸〈比喻 *fig*.〉有巨大影响和贡献的人物 giant; influential figures who have made great contributions: 一代～ giant of the times

【巨头】jùtóu 政治、经济界等有较大势力的头目 magnate; tycoon: 金融～ financial magnate; shark of high finance; financial tycoon

【巨万】jùwàn 形容钱财数目极大 millions; myriads; huge amount (of money):家私～ enormous family property|耗资～cost huge sums of money

【巨细】jùxì 大的和小的(事情) big and small (matters):事无～all matters, big and small|～毕究 let nothing pass unnoticed

【巨蟹座】jùxièzuò 黄道十二星座之一 one of the 12 constellations of the zodiac; ☞ 黄道十二宫 huángdào shí'èrgōng on p. 851

【巨星】jùxīng ❶ 天文学上指光度大、体积大、密度小的恒星 (astron.) giant star; fixed star of large luminosity, large size, and small density ❷〈比喻 *fig.*〉杰出的人 giant; outstanding personage:影坛～ film superstar|～陨落 death of a giant star

【巨眼】jùyǎn〈书 *fml.*〉指见识多,善于鉴别 great eyes; insightful; good at differentiating things:～识人 good judge of talent

【巨制】jùzhì 指伟大的作品,也指规模大的作品 great work; monumental work:鸿篇～ a monumental work

【巨著】jùzhù 篇幅长或内容精深的著作 monumental work; work of profundity

【巨子】jùzǐ 在某方面卓有成就、有声望的人物 magnate; tycoon; giant:文坛～literary giant|实业界～ business tycoon

句 jù ❶ 句子 sentence:语～sentence|词～words and phrases|造～ make a sentence ❷〈量词 *classifier*〉用于语言(of language) sentence:三～话不离本行 can hardly say three sentences without talking shop; talk shop all the time|写了两～诗 write two lines of verse

☞ gōu on p. 681

【句点】jùdiǎn 句号 full stop; period

【句读】jùdòu 古时称文词停顿的地方叫句或读(dòu)。连称句读时,句是语意完整的一小段,读是句中语意未完,语气可停的更小的段落。period and comma; sentences and phrases. In ancient times the pauses in a sentence were called 句 jù or 读 dòu. When the two characters are used together, 句 refers to a longer pause with a complete sense, while 读 refers to a shorter pause without a complete meaning.

【句法】jùfǎ ❶ 句子的结构方式 sentence structure:这两句诗的～很特别。The sentence structure of these two lines of verse is very special. ❷ 语法学中研究词组和句子的组织的部分(gram.) syntax; pattern in which words are put together to form phrases, clauses or sentences

【句号】jùhào 标点符号(。),表示一个陈述句完了 full stop; full point; period; point used to mark the end of a declarative sentence

【句子】jù•zi 用词和词组构成的、能够表达完整的意思的语言单位。每个句子都有一定的语调,表示陈述、疑问、祈使或感叹的语气。在连续说话时,句子和句子中间有一个较大的停顿。在书面上每个句子的末尾用句号、问号或叹号。sentence; grammatically self-contained speech unit consisting of a word or a syntactically related group of words that expresses an assertion, a question, a command, a wish or an exclamation. In speaking it is phonetically distinguished by various patterns of stress, pitch, and pauses; and in writing it concludes with appropriate end punctuation, such as a period, a question mark or an exclamation mark.

【句子成分】jù•zi chéngfèn 句子的组成部分,包括主语、谓语、宾语、补语、定语、状语六种 sentence elements; parts of a sentence, including subject, predicate, object, complement, attribute, and adverbial clauses

讵 jù〈书 *fml.*〉岂,表示反问 [used in rhetorical questions]:～料突然生变。Who could have expected such a sudden change? |～知天气骤寒。Who could have expected that the weather would turn cold so suddenly?

苣 jù ☞ 莴苣 wō•jù on p. 2012

☞ qǔ on p. 1591

拒 jù ❶ 抵抗;抵挡 resist; repel:抗～ resist; defy|～敌 resist the enemy; keep the enemy at bay ❷ 拒绝 refuse; reject:来者不～ refuse nobody; refuse nobody's request or offer|～不执行 refuse to implement|～谏饰非 reject representations and gloss over errors; reject criticisms and whitewash one's mistakes

【拒捕】jùbǔ (罪犯)抗拒逮捕 (of criminal) resist arrest

【拒谏饰非】jù jiàn shì fēi 拒绝别人的规劝,掩饰自己的错误 reject representations and gloss over errors; reject criticisms and whitewash one's mistakes

【拒绝】jùjué 不接受(请求、意见或赠礼等) refuse (a request, opinion or offer); reject; turn down; decline:～诱惑 reject temptation|～贿赂 reject bribes|无理要求遭到～。Unreasonable demands are rejected.

【拒聘】jùpìn 拒绝接受聘请 turn down an offer of job

具[1] jù ❶ 用具 utensil; tool; implement:农～ farm tools|文～ stationery|家～ furniture|雨～ rain gear|卧～ bedding|餐～ table ware; dinner set ❷〈书 *fml.*〉才干;才能 talent; ability:才～ capability; ability|干城之～ heroic defender of the nation ❸〈书 *fml.*〉〈量词 *classifier*〉用于棺材、尸体和某些器物 [for coffins, corpses and certain instruments or machines]:座钟一～ a desk clock

具[2] jù ❶ 具有 possess; have:～备 possess; have; be provided with|初～规模 begin to take shape|略～轮廓 begin to take shape ❷〈书 *fml.*〉备;办 provide; furnish:～呈

submit a memo to a superior | ～结 sign an undertaking | 敬～菲酌 allow me to cordially invite you to a simple dinner with wine ❸〈书 *fml.*〉陈述;写出 state; write down: ～名 put one's name (to a document, etc.); affix one's signature | 条～时弊 list the ills of the times

【具保】jùbǎo 指找人担保 find surety: ～释放 release on surety

【具备】jùbèi 具有;齐备 possess; have; be provided with: ～条件 satisfy the conditions | 青年必须～建设祖国和保卫祖国的双重本领。Young people should have the dual talents to both build and defend the motherland.

【具结】jù//jié〈旧时 *old*〉对官署提出表示负责的文件 sign an undertaking: ～完案 enter into a bond on closing a case | ～领回失物 sign a receipt for restored lost property

【具名】jù//míng 在文件上署名 put one's name (to a document, etc.): 由双方共同～ signed by both parties

【具体】jùtǐ ❶ 细节方面很明确的;不抽象的;不笼统的 concrete; particular: ～化 concretize | ～计划 detailed plan | 深入群众,～地了解情况。Go deep among the masses and learn where things stand. | 事件的经过,他谈得非常～。He talked in detail about the course of the incident. ❷ 特定的 specific: ～的人 specific person | 你担任什么～工作? What is your specific job? ❸ 把理论或原则结合到特定的人或事物上(后面带'到' followed by the word 到 dào) concretize a theory or principle in terms of a specific person or matter: 贯彻增产节约的方针～到我们这个单位,应该采取下列各种有效措施。To carry out the principle of increasing production and practising economy in our unit, the following effective measures should be taken.

【具体而微】jù tǐ ér wēi 内容大体具备而形状或规模较小 small but complete; miniature

【具体劳动】jùtǐ láodòng 按一定形式和目的创造使用价值的劳动,如木工做家具,纺织工人纺纱织布等(跟'抽象劳动'相对 as opposed to 'abstract labour') concrete labour; labour that creates use value according to given forms and aims, e.g. a carpenter makes furniture, or a textile worker spins thread and weaves cloth, etc.

【具文】jùwén 指徒有形式而无实际作用的规章制度 mere formality; dead letter; regulations and rules that have no practical functions: 一纸～ a mere scrap of paper

【具有】jùyǒu 有(多用于抽象事物 oft. sth. immaterial) have; possess: ～信心 be confident | ～伟大的意义 of great significance

炬 jù 火把 torch: 火～ torch | 目光如～ eyes blazing like torches; eyes ablaze with anger; looking ahead with wisdom

沮 jù [沮洳] (jùrù) 由腐烂植物埋在地下而形成的泥沼 marsh; swamp; mire; morass; wet spongy earth formed by rotten plants

☞ jǔ on p. 1047

钜[1] jù〈书 *fml.*〉❶ 硬铁 hard iron ❷ 钩子 hook

钜[2] jù same as 巨 jù ①

秬 jù〈书 *fml.*〉黑黍子 black millet

俱 jù〈书 *fml.*〉全;都 all; complete: 百废～兴。All neglected tasks are being undertaken. *or* All that was left undone is now being undertaken. | 面面～到 attend to each and every aspect of a matter

☞ Jū on p. 1045

【俱乐部】jùlèbù 进行社会、文化、艺术、娱乐等活动的团体和场所 club; association of persons for a common cause, e.g. social, cultural, artistic or recreational activities; meeting place of a club

【俱全】jùquán 齐全;完备 complete in all varieties: 一应～。Everything needed is there. | 样样～。Everything necessary is available. | 麻雀虽小,五脏～。A sparrow may be small, but it has all the vital organs — small but complete.

倨 jù〈书 *fml.*〉傲慢 haughty; arrogant: 前～后恭 first supercilious and then deferential; change from arrogance to humility

【倨傲】jù'ào 骄傲;傲慢 haughty; arrogant: ～无礼 arrogant and rude | 此人态度～,大家都不理他。This man is so arrogant, no one speaks to him.

粔 jù [粔籹] (jùnǔ)〈古代 *arch.*〉一种用油炸或煎的面食 deep-fried or fried wheaten food

剧[1] (劇) jù ❶ 戏剧 theatrical work; drama; play; opera: 演～ stage a drama | 话～ modern drama | 独幕～ one-act play ◇惨～ tragic event | 丑～ farce ❷ (Jù) 姓 a surname

剧[2] (劇) jù 猛烈;厉害 acute; severe; intense; fierce: ～烈 violent | ～痛 acute pain | ～饮 drink to one's heart's content | ～变 sweeping changes; drastic change | 病势加～。(His) disease worsened.

【剧本】jùběn 戏剧作品,由人物对话或唱词以及舞台指示组成 script; scenario; theatrical writing consisting of dialogue or libretto and stage directions

【剧变】jùbiàn 剧烈的变化 violent or drastic change: 形势发生～。The situation has changed dramatically.

【剧场】jùchǎng 供演出戏剧、歌舞、曲艺等用的场所 theatre; place where plays, operas and other performances are staged

【剧烈】jùliè 猛烈 violent; acute; severe:饭后不宜做～运动。It is inadvisable to take strenuous exercise after a meal.

【剧目】jùmù 戏剧的名目 programme; list of plays:传统～ traditional play|保留～ repertory; repertoire

【剧情】jùqíng 戏剧的情节 plot:～介绍 synopsis of a play

【剧团】jùtuán 表演戏剧的团体,由演员、导演和其他有关人员组成 troupe; performance troupe consisting of actors, directors and other relevant personnel

【剧务】jùwù ❶ 指剧团里有关排演、演出的各种事务 stage management; different kinds of affairs concerning troupe rehearsal and performance ❷ 担任剧务工作的人 stage manager

【剧院】jùyuàn ❶ 剧场 theatre; playhouse ❷ 用作较大剧团的名称 name of a big troupe:北京人民艺术～ Beijing People's Art Troupe|青年艺术～ Youth Art Troupe

【剧照】jùzhào 戏剧中某个场面或电影、电视中某个镜头的照片 stage photo; still; photo capturing a scene from a play, a film or a TV drama

【剧种】jùzhǒng ❶ 戏曲的种类,如京剧、汉剧、川剧、越剧、豫剧等 type or genre of traditional Chinese opera, such as Peking Opera, Hubei opera, Sichuan opera, Shaoxing opera, and Henan opera ❷ 戏剧艺术的种类,如话剧、戏曲、歌剧、舞剧等 genre of performing art, such as modern drama, traditional Chinese opera, opera and dance drama

据(據) jù ❶ 占据 occupy; hold:盘～ occupy|～为己有 seize by force; take forcible possession of ❷ 凭借;依靠 rely on; depend on:～点 stronghold|～险固守 defend by relying on a natural barrier ❸ 按照;依据 according to; in line with; on the grounds of:～理力争 argue strongly on just grounds|～实报告 report on the basis of facts ❹ 可以用做证明的事物 evidence; proof; certificate:凭～ evidence; proof|证～ evidence; proof; testimony|字～ written pledge|论～ reasoning; argument|票～ documents such as receipts, bills, vouchers, invoices, etc.|事出有因,查无实～。There must be something behind it, but investigations have failed to reveal any evidence.

☞ jū on p. 1045

【据点】jùdiǎn 军队用作战斗行动凭借的地点 stronghold; strongpoint; fortified point on which a troop relies during military operations:攻占敌军两个～ conquer the enemy's two strongholds

【据守】jùshǒu 占据防守 guard; hold and defend:凭险～ defend by resorting to strategically located place of difficult access|～阵地 defend one's position

【据说】jùshuō 据别人说 it is said; as the story goes; allegedly:～今年冬天气温偏高。It is said that the temperature this winter is higher than average.

【据闻】jùwén 听说;据说 I hear; it is said; as the story goes

【据悉】jùxī 根据得到的消息知道 it is reported that:～,今年入境旅游、观光的人数已超过千万。The number of tourists to the country has reportedly exceeded ten million.

距[1] jù 距离 distance:行(háng)～ row spacing|株～spacing between two plants|两地相～不远。The two places are not far from each other.|～今已有十年。That was ten years ago.

距[2] jù 雄鸡、雉等的腿的后面突出像脚趾的部分 spur; protruding toe-like part on the rear side of a rooster's or pheasant's leg

【距离】jùlí ❶ 在空间或时间上相隔 space distance; time interval:天津～北京约有一百二十公里。Tianjin is about 120 km. from Beijing.|现在～唐代已经有一千多年。The Tang Dynasty dates back to more than 1,000 years ago. ❷ 相隔的长度 distance or space between; interval:等～ equal spacing|拉开一定的～ withdraw a distance from ◇他的看法和你有～。His opinion differs from yours.

惧(懼) jù 害怕;恐惧 be afraid of; be scared of; dread:畏～ fear; dread|毫无所～ undaunted; intrepid; dauntless; fearless|连我也～他三分。Even I am a bit afraid of him.

【惧内】jùnèi〈书 *fml.*〉怕老婆 henpecked

【惧怕】jùpà 害怕 fear; dread:～困难 be daunted by difficulties|我们不～任何敌人。We fear no enemy.

【惧色】jùsè 畏惧的神色 look of fear:他面对凶恶的敌人毫无～。As he confronted the ferocious enemy, he showed no sign of fear.

犋 jù 牵引犁、耙等农具的畜力单位,能拉动一种农具的畜力叫一犋,有时是一头牲口,有时是两头或两头以上 unit of animal power of one or more draft animals, strong enough to pull a plough or a harrow or any other farm implements

飓 jù [飓风](jùfēng)气象学上指12级风 hurricane; gale on the 12th scale in meteorology; ☞ 风级 fēngjí on p. 579

虡(簴) jù〈古代 *arch.*〉悬挂钟或磬的架子两旁的柱子 two posts supporting a stand from which bells or percussion instruments are suspended

锯 jù ❶ 拉(lá)开木料、石料、钢材等的工具,主要部分是具有许多尖齿的薄钢片 saw; any of various tools having a thin steel blade with a sharp, usu. toothed edge, used for cutting wood, stone or steel:拉～ saw|电～

electric saw|手～ hand saw|一把～ a saw ❷ 用锯拉(lá) cut with a saw:～树 saw a tree|～木头 saw wood

☞ 锔 jū on p.1045

【锯齿】jùchǐ (～儿 jùchǐr)锯条上的尖齿 saw tooth

【锯床】jùchuáng 金属切削机床,用来锯金属材料。加工时金属材料固定在工作台上,条锯或圆盘锯做往复或旋转运动去锯。sawing machine; metal-cutting machine tool used to cut metal materials, where the metal is fixed to a work table and cut with a slat saw that moves back and forth or a circular saw that turns

【锯末】jùmò 锯木头、竹子等时掉下来的细末 sawdust; fine particles that fall from wood or bamboo as it is sawed

【锯条】jùtiáo 锯的主要部分,长条形薄钢片,上面有许多尖齿 saw blade; long, thin strip of steel with sharp, toothed edge

【锯子】jù·zi 锯① saw

聚 jù 聚集 assemble; gather; congregate:～会 get together|～沙成塔。Enough grains of sand piled up make a pagoda. *or* Many a little makes a mickle.|大家～在一起商量商量。Let's get together and talk it over.|明天星期日,咱们找个地方～～。Tomorrow is Sunday. Let's find a place to hold a gathering.

【聚宝盆】jùbǎopén 传说中装满金银珠宝而且取之不尽的盆 treasure trove; legendary receptacle for inexhaustible treasures of gold, silver, pearls and precious stones;〈比喻 *fig.*〉资源丰富的地方 place abundant in natural resources; cornucopia; horn of plenty

【聚变】jùbiàn ☞ 热核反应 rèhé-fǎnyìng on p.1613

【聚餐】jù//cān 为了庆祝或联欢大家在一起吃饭 dine together on festive occasions; have a dinner party to celebrate sth.

【聚光灯】jùguāngdēng 装有凸透镜,可以调节光束焦点的灯。用于舞台或摄影等的照明。spotlight; light with a convex lens that can adjust the focus of a beam of light, used for stage lighting or photography

【聚光镜】jùguāngjìng ❶ 使光线聚成光束的凸透镜 convex mirror that condenses light into one beam ❷ 使平行光线聚集的凹面镜 concave mirror that brings together parallel light

【聚合】jùhé ❶ 聚集到一起 aggregate; congregate; get together ❷ 指单体合成变为分子量较大的化合物。生成的高分子化合物叫聚合物。polymerize; (of monomers) combine to form a polymer, a macromolecule compound with heavier molecular weight; ☞ 缩聚 suōjù on p.1842

【聚合果】jùhéguǒ 果实的一类,由一朵花内聚生的多个成熟子房和花托联合发育而成。如草莓、莲、八角等的果实。*Rosaceae*; composite fruit; fruit growing from multilocular ovaries and receptacles on a flower, such as the strawberry, lotus and anise; also 聚生果 jùshēngguǒ

【聚花果】jùhuāguǒ 复果 collective fruit; multiple or compound fruit

【聚会】jùhuì ❶ (人)会合;聚集(of people) get together; congregate; assemble:老同学～在一起很不容易。It is not easy for old classmates to come together for a gathering. ❷ 指聚会的事 party; get-together; social gathering:明天有个～,你参加不参加? There's a get-together tomorrow. Are you coming?

【聚积】jùjī 一点一滴地凑集;积聚 accumulate; collect; build up

【聚集】jùjí 集合;凑在一起 convene; gather; assemble; collect:～力量 build up strength|～资金 raise funds|广场上～了很多人。A large crowd of people gathered in the square.

【聚歼】jùjiān 把敌人包围起来消灭 round up and exterminate; annihilate en masse

【聚焦】jùjiāo 使光或电子束等聚集于一点 focus; focalize; bring light or electric beam to a directional focus:～成像 focusing and image formation

【聚精会神】jù jīng huì shén 集中精神;集中注意力 in rapt attention; be all attention:同学们～地听老师讲课。The class listened to the teacher in rapt attention.

【聚居】jùjū 集中地居住在某一区域 inhabit a region; live in a compact community:少数民族～的地方 regions where ethnic minority peoples live

【聚敛】jùliǎn 重税搜刮(民财) amass wealth by heavy taxation; plunder; extort

【聚拢】jùlǒng 聚集 assemble; get together

【聚落】jùluò 人聚居的地方;村落 settlement; village:原始～ primitive settlement

【聚齐】jù//qí (在约定地点)集合 gather (at an appointed place); assemble:参观的人八时在展览馆门口～。Visitors are to assemble at the gate of the exhibition hall at eight o'clock.

【聚沙成塔】jù shā chéng tǎ〈比喻 *fig.*〉积少成多 enough grains of sand piled up make a pagoda; many a little makes a mickle

【聚生】jùshēng 聚集在一起生长 grow together; cluster:草莓和莲的果实都是～的。The strawberry and lotus bear composite fruits.

【聚首】jùshǒu〈书 *fml.*〉聚会 gather; meet:～一堂 gather together; have a grand gathering

【聚珍版】jùzhēnbǎn 清代乾隆三十八年(1773年)用活字版印《四库全书》里一部分善本书,这种版本称为聚珍版 rare editions of books in the *Complete Library of Four Branches of Books*, set with the movable type and printed in 1773, the 38th year of the Qianlong reign of the Qing Dynasty

【聚众】jùzhòng 纠集一伙人 mob; gather a crowd:～闹事 gather together as a mob to make trouble

窭(窶) jù〈书 *fml.*〉贫穷 poor; destitute; impoverished:贫～ poverty-stricken

踞 jù ❶ 蹲或坐 crouch; squat:龙盘虎～ coiling dragon and crouching tiger — occupy a strategic stronghold ❷ 盘踞;占据 be entrenched; hold; occupy

屦(屨) jù〈古时 *arch.*〉用麻、葛等制成的鞋 sandals made of hemp or kudzu

遽 jù ❶ 匆忙;急 hurriedly; hastily:匆～ in a hurry|情况不明,不能～下定论。The situation is till not clear. Don't jump to any hasty conclusions. ❷ 惊慌 frightened; alarmed:惶～ panic-stricken

【遽然】jùrán〈书 *fml.*〉突然 suddenly; abruptly:～离去 leave abruptly

澽 Jù 澽水,水名,在陕西 Jushui, name of a river in Shaanxi Province

瞿 jù〈书 *fml.*〉惊视;惊恐四顾 look around in panic

☞ Qú on p. 1590

镰 jù ❶ 古乐器,像钟 ancient musical instrument, shaped like a bell ❷ same as 虡 jù

醵 jù〈书 *fml.*〉大家凑钱 pool money:～金 collect money|～资 raise funds

juān (ㄐㄩㄢ)

捐 juān ❶ 舍弃;抛弃 abnegate; cast away; relinquish; abandon:～弃 give up; forsake; discard|～生(舍弃生命) sacrifice one's life|～躯 die for a cause ❷ 捐助 give; donate:～献 contribute|～钱 donate; subscribe|募～ collect donations; solicit donations ❸ 税收的一种名称 levy; another name for tax:车～ tax on cars|上了一笔～ pay a sum of tax

J

【捐款】juān//kuǎn 捐助款项 contribute; donate; subscribe:向灾区～ make a donation to a disaster area|～办学 contribute money to set up a school

【捐款】juānkuǎn 捐助的款项 contribution; donation; subscription:把～寄给灾区 mail the donations to the disaster area

【捐弃】juānqì〈书 *fml.*〉抛弃 abandon; forsake; discard:～前嫌 bury old grudges

【捐躯】juānqū (为崇高的事业)牺牲生命 (for a noble cause) sacrifice one's life; lay down one's life:为国～ sacrifice one's life for one's motherland

【捐输】juānshū〈书 *fml.*〉捐献 contribute; donate:解囊～ open one's purse to donate; donate all one has

【捐税】juānshuì 捐和税的总称 taxes and levies

【捐献】juānxiàn 拿出财物献给(国家或集体) contribute; donate (money or property to the state or an organization):他把全部藏书～给图书馆。He donated his whole collection of books to the library.

【捐赠】juānzèng 赠送(物品给国家或集体) contribute; donate (to the state or an organization):～图书 donate books

【捐助】juānzhù 拿出财物来帮助 offer financial or material assistance; contribute; donate:～灾区人民 offer assistance to the relief of people in a disaster-stricken area

【捐资】juān//zī 捐助资财 donate money and property:～兴学 donate money to set up a school|踊跃～ enthusiastically donate

涓 juān〈书 *fml.*〉细小的流水 tiny stream:～埃 insignificant; negligible|～滴 tiny drop; dribble; driblet

【涓埃】juān'āi〈书 *fml.*〉细小的水流和尘埃 trickle of water and speck of dust;〈比喻 *fig.*〉微小 tiny; insignificant:略尽～之力 make what little contribution one can; do one's bit

【涓滴】juāndī〈书 *fml.*〉极少量的水 tiny amount of water; tiny drop;〈比喻 *fig.*〉极少量的钱或物 tiny amount of money or stuff:～不漏 watertight; leak proof|～归公(属于公家的收入全部缴给公家) turn in every cent of public money; hand over everything in the public treasury

【涓涓】juānjuān〈书 *fml.*〉细水慢流的样子 (of water) trickle sluggishly:～清泉 sluggish trickle of spring water

娟 juān〈书 *fml.*〉美丽 beautiful; pretty; fair:～秀 graceful

【娟秀】juānxiù〈书 *fml.*〉秀丽 beautiful; pretty; fair:字迹～ beautiful handwriting; graceful hand|眉目～ pretty; of delicate features

圈 juān ❶ 用栅栏把家禽家畜围起来 enclose in a pen; pen in:把鸡～起来 herd the chickens into the pen ◇别让暑气～在心里。Don't let summer heat accumulate in your body. ❷ 把人关起来 lock up; put in jail; imprison:孩子总～在家里不好。It is not good practice to confine children to the home.

☞ juàn on p. 1056 and quān on p. 1595

朘 juān〈书 *fml.*〉❶ 剥削 exploit ❷ 减少 reduce; decrease; cut down

☞ zuī on p. 2568

【朘削】juānxuē〈书 *fml.*〉剥削 exploit:～民众 exploit the people

鹃 juān ☞ 杜鹃 dùjuān on p. 481

镌(鐫) juān〈书 *fml.*〉雕刻 engrave; inscribe:～刻 engrave; inscribe|～石 engrave a stone

【镌刻】juānkè 雕刻 engrave; inscribe:大殿柱子上～着一副对联。A couplet is inscribed on two pillars in the hall.

蠲 juān ❶〈书 *fml.*〉免除 exempt; remit:～除 get rid of; abolish|～免 remit; exempt ❷积存(多见于早期白话 oft. in early vernacular) store up; stockpile

【蠲除】juānchú〈书 *fml.*〉免除 annul; abolish:～旧例 abolish old practices

【蠲免】juānmiǎn〈书 *fml.*〉免除(租税、罚款、劳役等) remit or exempt from (taxes, fines or servitude)

juǎn (ㄐㄩㄢˇ)

卷(捲、❹餞) juǎn ❶把东西弯转裹成圆筒形 roll up; curl; furl:把竹帘子～起来 roll up the bamboo screen|～起袖子就干 roll up one's sleeves and set to work immediately|烙饼～大葱 pancakes with green onions wrapped in it ❷一种大的力量把东西撮起或裹住 sweep along, up or off; pull up; carry along:风～着雨点劈面打来。The gale swept right in the face, carrying the rain with it.|汽车～起尘土,飞驰而过。A car sped past, raising a cloud of dust behind it.◇她立刻～入了群众运动的热潮里。She was immediately swept along with the surging tide of the mass movement. ❸(～儿 juǎnr)裹成圆筒形的东西 cylindrical mass of sth.; roll:铺盖～儿 bedding roll; bedroll; roll of bedding|把书裹成一个～儿寄出去。Roll up the book and send it through the post office. ❹(～儿 juǎnr)卷子(juǎn·zi)roll; spool; reel:花～儿 steamed twisted roll|金银～儿 yellow and white steamed rolls prepared with millet or maize and wheat flour ❺(～儿 juǎnr)〈量词 *classifer*〉用于成卷儿的东西 roll; spool; reel:一～纸 a roll of toilet paper|一～铺盖 a roll of bedding

☞ juàn on p. 1055

【卷尺】juǎnchǐ 可以卷起来的软尺 tape measure; band tape:钢～ steel tape|皮～ leather tape

【卷帘门】juǎnliánmén 用许多条形铝合金材料并排连接制成的门,开门时,门像竹帘一样向上卷起 roll-up door; door made of hinged parallel horizontal aluminium strips that is opened by rolling it up like a bamboo screen

【卷铺盖】juǎn pū·gai〈比喻 *fig.*〉被解雇或辞职,离开工作地点 pack up and quit; be fired; be sacked

【卷舌元音】juǎnshé yuányīn 把舌尖卷起来,使舌面和舌尖同时起作用而发出的元音,例如普通话中的 er(儿 ér、耳 ěr、二 èr) retroflex; speech sound produced by rolling up the tip of one's tongue and making it and the tongue surface work together, such as 儿 ér, 耳 ěr and 二 èr, all pronounced as 'er'

【卷逃】juǎntáo(家里的或本单位的人或者经管的人)偷了全部钱财而逃跑(of a family member, a staff worker or a person in charge) abscond with valuables; run away with valuables

【卷土重来】juǎn tǔ chóng lái〈比喻 *fig.*〉失败之后重新恢复势力 stage or launch a comeback after regaining one's strength(卷土 *juan tu*:卷起尘土,形容人马奔跑 raise a cloud of dust, used to describe men running and horses galloping)

【卷心菜】juǎnxīncài〈方 *dial.*〉结球甘蓝 cabbage

【卷须】juǎnxū 某些植物用来缠绕或附着其他物体的器官。有的卷须是从茎演变而成的,如葡萄的;有的卷须是从叶子演变而成的,如豌豆的。tendril; twisting, thread-like plant organs that entwine or cling to other objects. Some tendrils, such as those of the grapevine, develop from stems, and others, such as the pea vine, from leaves.

【卷烟】juǎnyān ❶香烟 cigarette ❷雪茄 cigar

【卷扬机】juǎnyángjī 一种起重装置,由卷筒、钢丝绳等构成,常用于采矿业和建筑工地 hoist; hoister; apparatus made of reels and steel wires for lifting heavy or cumbersome objects, oft. used in the mining industry or on building sites; 通称 general term for 绞车 jiǎochē

【卷子】juǎn·zi 一种面食品,和(huó)面制成薄片,一面涂上油盐,再卷起蒸熟 steamed roll; food prepared from a thin slice of dough, of which one side is spread with oil and salt before it is rolled up and steamed

☞ juàn·zi on p. 1056

卷 juǎn〈书 *fml.*〉卷袖子 roll up one's sleeves

☞ juàn on p. 1056

锩 juǎn 刀剑的刃弯曲(of the edge of a sword or knife) be turned

juàn (ㄐㄩㄢˋ)

卷 juàn ❶书本 book:～帙 volume|手不释～ always have one's nose in a book; be an avid reader ❷〈古时 *arch.*〉书籍写在帛或纸上,卷起来收藏,因此书籍的数量论卷,一部书可以分成若干卷,每卷的文字自成起讫,后代仍用来指全书的一部分:～一 Volume One|第一～ First Volume|上～ Volume One|藏书十万～ collection of 100,000 books ❸(～儿 juànr)卷子(juàn·zi) examination paper:答～ examination paper|交～儿 hand in an examination paper ❹ 机关里保存的文件 documents kept in a government department：～宗 archive；file；dossier｜调～ send for sb.'s file or examination papers｜查～ look through the files

☞ juǎn on p.1055

【卷次】juàncì 书刊分卷的次序 series number of a book or a periodical

【卷帙】juànzhì〈书 *fml.*〉书籍（就数量说 in terms of number）book；volume；tome：～浩繁 vast collection of books

【卷轴】juànzhóu〈书 *fml.*〉指裱好带轴的书画等 mounted calligraphic work or painting

【卷轴装】juànzhóuzhuāng 图书装订法的一种，把纸粘连成长幅，用木棒、象牙、玉石等做轴，从左到右卷成一束 scroll binding；bookbinding method，whereby pages are pasted into a long scroll that winds from left to right on a wood，ivory or jade rod

【卷子】juàn·zi ❶ 考试写答案的薄本子或单页纸；试卷 answer sheet；examination paper：发～ hand out or distribute examination papers｜改～ mark examination papers ❷ 指可以卷起来的古抄本 hand-copied scroll；codex：敦煌～ hand-copied Dunhuang scrolls

☞ juǎn·zi on p.1055

【卷宗】juànzōng ❶ 机关里分类保存的文件 file；dossier；archive ❷ 保存文件的纸夹子 folder

帣 juàn〈书 *fml.*〉囊 bag；purse

☞ juǎn on p.1055

隽(雋) juàn ❶〈书 *fml.*〉隽永 meaningful ❷（Juàn）姓 a surname

☞ 俊 jùn on p.1067

【隽永】juànyǒng〈书 *fml.*〉（言语、诗文）意味深长（of speech，poem or article）meaningful：语颇～，耐人寻味。These remarks are meaningful and thought-provoking.

【隽语】juànyǔ 隽永的话语 meaningful words：～箴言 thought-provoking apothegm

倦 juàn ❶ 疲乏 weary；tired：疲～ tired；fatigued｜人有点～，想睡觉。I am a little tired；I think I'll go to sleep. ❷ 厌倦 be sick of；be tired of；feel bored：孜孜不～indefatigably｜诲人不～ teach tirelessly；teach with tireless zeal

【倦怠】juàndài 疲乏困倦 tired and sleepy：～无力 languid

【倦容】juànróng 疲倦的脸色 tired look：面带～ wear a tired expression

【倦色】juànsè same as 倦容 juànróng

【倦游】juànyóu〈书 *fml.*〉游玩的兴趣已尽 be weary of wandering and sightseeing：～归来 return home satiated after a pleasure excursion

狷(獧) juàn〈书 *fml.*〉❶ 狷急 impatient；rash ❷ 狷介 upright；incorruptible

【狷急】juànjí〈书 *fml.*〉性情急躁 hot-tempered；impatient

【狷介】juànjiè〈书 *fml.*〉性情正直，不肯同流合污 upright；incorruptible：～之士 upright person；honest person

桊 juàn（～儿 juànr）穿在牛鼻子上的小木棍儿或小铁环 small wooden stick or iron ring pierced through the nose of an ox：牛鼻～儿 nose halter for leading an ox

绢 juàn 质地薄而坚韧的丝织品，也指用生丝织成的一种丝织品 fine，hard wearing silk；fabric woven out of raw silk

【绢本】juànběn 字画写在绢上或画在绢上的 silk scroll；calligraphic work or painting done on silk：这两幅山水都是～。These two landscape paintings were done on silk.

【绢花】juànhuā 一种手工艺品，用各种颜色的绢仿制的花卉 silk flower；flowers made of silk in different colours；also 京花 jīnghuā

【绢子】juàn·zi〈方 *dial.*〉手绢儿 handkerchief

鄄 Juàn 鄄城，地名，在山东 Juancheng，name of a place in Shandong Province

圈 juàn ❶ 养猪羊等牲畜的建筑，有棚和栏 shed or pen to raise pigs，sheep，etc.：猪～sty｜羊～ fold ❷（Juàn）姓 a surname

☞ juān on p.1054 and quān on p.1595

【圈肥】juànféi ☞ 厩肥 jiùféi on p.1040

【圈养】juànyǎng 关在圈里饲养 rear livestock in a shed：～牲畜 raise livestock in a sty

眷(❷睠) juàn ❶ 亲属 relatives：～属 family dependant｜家～ family dependant｜亲～ relatives｜女～ womenfolk of a family ❷〈书 *fml.*〉关心；怀念 care；think of；be concerned about：～顾 show concern for｜～注 show loving care for；show solicitude for｜～恋 have tender feelings for；have deep affection for

【眷顾】juàngù〈书 *fml.*〉关心照顾 show concern for；take care of

【眷眷】juànjuàn〈书 *fml.*〉念念不忘；依恋不舍 have tender feelings for；yearn for；long for：～之情 cannot bear to part from（a loved one）；be reluctant to part from sb.

【眷恋】juànliàn〈书 *fml.*〉（对自己喜爱的人或地方）深切地留恋 nostalgic；be sentimentally attached to（a person or a place）：～旧物 have tender feelings for old things｜～故园 cherish deep affection for one's hometown

【眷念】juànniàn〈书 *fml.*〉想念 think fondly of；feel nostalgic about：～故土 be homesick｜～亲人 miss one's family

【眷属】juànshǔ ❶ 家眷；亲属 family dependant；relative ❷ 特指夫妻 specifically used for husband and wife：愿天下有情人终成～。May all lovers under heaven unite in wedlock.

【眷注】juànzhù〈书 *fml.*〉关怀 care; concern: 深承～。I am most grateful for your kind solicitude.

眳 juàn [眳眳]〈书 *fml.*〉侧目而视 give a sidelong glance; look askance

罥 juàn〈书 *fml.*〉挂 hang; put up

juē（ㄐㄩㄝ）

屩（屫、跻） juē〈书 *fml.*〉草鞋 sandal; straw sandals

☞ 跻 qiāo on p.1548

撅[1] juē ❶ 翘起 stick up: ～嘴 pout one's lips | ～着尾巴 stick up the tail ❷ 当面使人难堪；顶撞 embarrass sb. openly; answer back; contradict: ～人 contradict sb. openly | 他平白地～了我一顿。He embarrassed me for no reason at all.

撅[2]（撧） juē 折(zhé) break: ～一根柳条当马鞭 break a willow twig and use it as a horse whip

噘 juē same as 撅[1] juē ①, 用于'噘嘴' used in the phrase 噘嘴 juē//zuǐ

jué（ㄐㄩㄝˊ）

孓 jué ☞ 孑孓 jiéjué on p.988

决[1]（決） jué ❶ 决定 decide; determine: 表～ decide by vote; vote | 判～ sentence; make a court decision; pass a judgement | 犹豫不～ hesitate | ～一雌雄 have a showdown with sb.; fight it out ❷ 一定（用在否定词前面 used before a negative word) definitely; certainly; under any circumstances: ～不退缩 never yield to sth. or sb. | ～无异言 have no disagreement whatsoever ❸ 决定最后胜败 decide the final result: ～赛 finals | ～战 decisive battle | 今日乒乓球赛要～出前三名。Today's table tennis match will decide the first three winners. ❹ 执行死刑 execute (a person); carry out a death sentence: 枪～ execute by a firing squad | 处～ put to death | 立～ immediately carry out a death sentence

决[2]（決） jué 决口 (of a dyke, etc.) be breached; burst: 溃～ burst a dam

【决策】juécè ❶ 决定策略或办法 make policy; make a strategic decision: 运筹～ devise strategies ❷ 决定的策略或办法 strategy; decision of strategic importance: 明智的～ wise decision

【决雌雄】jué cíxióng 决定胜负、高下 fight to see who is the stronger; fight it out

【决定】juédìng ❶ 对如何行动做出主张 decide; make up one's mind; resolve: 领导上～派他去学习。His leader decided to send him away to study. | 这件事情究竟应该怎么办，最好是由大家来～。It would be best if all of us decided how to deal with this matter. ❷ 决定的事项 decision; resolution: 这个问题尚未做出～。A decision has yet to be made regarding this issue. *or* No resolution of this problem has been made. | 组长们回去要向本组传达这项～。On their return, group leaders must let this resolution be known to each group member. ❸ 某事物成为另一事物的先决条件；起主导作用 (of sth.) be the prerequisite (of sth. else); determine; decide: 存在～意识。Man's social being determines his consciousness. | 这件事～了他未来的生活道路。This incident has decided his future life path. ❹ 客观规律促使事物一定向某方面发展变化 decide; determine; (of sth.) change or develop in a certain direction due to objective laws: ～性 decisiveness | ～因素 decisive factor; determinant

【决定性】juédìngxìng 对产生某种结果起决定作用的性质 decisiveness; determining or having the power to determine the outcome: ～的胜利 decisive victory | 在生产中起～作用的是人。Man plays the decisive part in production.

【决斗】juédòu ❶ 过去欧洲流行的一种风俗，两人发生争端，各不相让，约定时间地点，并邀请证人，彼此用武器对打 duel; custom popular in Europe until the mid-19th century when two men, along with their witnesses, or 'seconds', would settle a point of honour by arranging combat at a fixed time and place ❷ 泛指进行你死我活的斗争 (in a broad sense) life-and-death struggle; decisive struggle

【决断】juéduàn ❶ 拿主意；做决定 make a decision: 无从～unable to make a decision | 请您最后～。It's up to you to make the final decision. ❷ 决定事情的魄力 resolve; resolution; determination: 他做事很有～。He is a man of determination.

【决计】juéjì ❶ 表示主意已定 decide; make up one's mind: 无论如何，我～明天就走。I am determined to leave tomorrow, no matter what. ❷ 表示肯定的判断 definitely; certainly: 这样办～没错儿。This method is absolutely foolproof.

【决绝】juéjué ❶ 断绝关系 break off; cut off; sever: 与不良嗜好～ be determined to break oneself of bad habits | ～一切往来 break off all relations ❷ 非常坚决 firm; resolute: 态度～ resolute attitude | 话说得十分～。His words are resolutely spoken.

【决口】jué//kǒu（河堤）被水冲出缺口 (of a dyke) be breached by floods; burst

【决裂】juéliè（谈判、关系、感情）破裂 (of nego-

J

tiation, relationship and feeling) break up; rupture: 自她和我～之后,再没有见过面。We have not met since she broke off with me.|五四时代的青年开始和封建主义的传统～。During the May 4th Movement, the youth began to break away from feudal traditions.

【决然】juérán〈书 *fml*.〉❶ 形容很坚决 firmly; resolutely; determinedly: 毅然～ resolutely and determinedly|～返回 resolutely return ❷ 必然;一定 definitely; inevitably; surely; undoubtedly: 东张西望,道听途说,～得不到什么完全的知识。One can never acquire real knowledge by flitting around and listening to hearsay.

【决赛】juésài 体育运动等竞赛中决定名次的最后一次或最后一轮比赛 finals; final match or final round of matches in a sport which decides the positions in a competition

【决胜】juéshèng 决定最后的胜负 decide the final outcome; determine the victory: ～千里之外 ensure a victory a thousand *li* away

【决死】juésǐ 敌我双方你死我活的(斗争) life-and-death struggle between two contending parties: ～战 cut-throat battle|～的斗争 life-and-death struggle; last-ditch fight

【决算】juésuàn 根据年度预算执行的结果而编制的年度会计报告 final accounts; final accounting of revenue and expenditure, compiled according to the implementation of an annual budget

【决心】juéxīn ❶ 坚定不移的意志 determination; resolution: ～书 statement of one's determination; written pledge to show one's determination|下定～ make up one's mind; resolve ❷ 一心一意,坚定不移地 steadfast; resolute: ～钻研学问 be determined to study hard

J

【决一死战】jué yī sǐ zhàn 不怕牺牲,对敌人作你死我活的战斗 fight a life-and-death battle; fight to the finish

【决议】juéyì 经一定会议讨论通过的决定 resolution; statement or opinions discussed and passed by an assembly

【决意】juéyì 拿定主张;决计① have one's mind made up; be determined: 他～明天一早就动身。He made up his mind to set off tomorrow morning.

【决战】juézhàn 敌对双方使用主力以决胜负的战役或战斗 decisive battle; decisive engagement; battle between major forces of two contending sides to determine victory or defeat

诀1 jué ❶ 就事物主要内容编成的顺口押韵的、容易记忆的词句 rhymed formula; rhyming, easy-to-remember words and sentences that relate the main content of an event: 口～ pithy formula in rhyme|歌～ formulas put into verse ❷ 诀窍 knack; know-how: 秘～ secret of success; key to success|妙～ clever way of doing sth.; knack

诀2 jué 分别 bid farewell; part: ～别 bid farewell|永～ part never to meet again; part for ever; be separated by death

【诀别】juébié 分别(多指不再见的离别 usu. with the implication that there is little chance of meeting again) bid farewell; part

【诀窍】juéqiào (～儿 juéqiàor)关键性的方法 secret of success; key to success; tricks of the trade: 炒菜的～主要是拿准火候儿。By and large, the secret to cooking lies in the control and duration of the heat.

【诀要】juéyào 诀窍 secret of success: 深得其中～ have a profound knowledge of the art of sth.

抉 jué〈书 *fml*.〉剔出;挖出 pick out; single out: ～择 choose; make a choice

【抉择】juézé 挑选;选择 choose; opt for: 从速作出～ make a hasty choice

【抉摘】juézhāi〈书 *fml*.〉❶ 抉择 choose: ～真伪 choose between the true and the fake ❷ 揭发指摘 expose and condemn: ～弊端 expose and castigate malpractice

角1 jué (～儿 juér) ❶ 角色 role; part; character: 主～ leading or principal role; main character|配～ supporting role; co-star|他在这出戏里扮演哪个～儿? What is his role in this play? ❷ 行当② type of role: 丑～ clown|旦～ female role ❸ 主要演员 leading actor or actress: 名～ star; famous actor or actress

角2 jué 竞赛;斗争 competition; contend; fight: ～斗 wrestle|口～ quarrel

角3 jué〈古代 *arch*.〉盛酒的器具,形状像爵 *jue*; ancient three-legged wine cup

角4 jué〈古代 *arch*.〉五音之一,相当于简谱的'3' note of the ancient Chinese five-tone scale, corresponding to 3 in numbered musical notation; ☞ 五音 wǔyīn on p. 2032

角5 Jué 姓 a surname
☞ jiǎo on p. 974

【角斗】juédòu 搏斗比赛 wrestle: ～场 wrestling ring

【角力】juélì 比赛力气 have a trial of strength; wrestle

【角色】juésè ❶ 戏剧或电影、电视中,演员扮演的剧中人物 role; part; character (in drama, movie or TV show) ❷〈比喻 *fig*.〉生活中某种类型的人物 certain type of character in life

【角逐】juézhú ❶ 武力竞争 contend; tussle; enter into rivalry; compete by force: 群雄～ tussle among warlords ❷ 泛指竞争或竞赛 (in a broad sense) compete; contest: 两队在绿茵场上展开激烈～。The two teams are competing fiercely in this match.

駃 jué [駃騠](juétí) ❶ ☞ 驴骡 lúluó on p. 1264 ❷ 古书上说的一种骏马 steed recorded in ancient books

玦 jué 〈古时 *arch.*〉佩带的玉器,半环形,有缺口 penannular jade ring worn as an ornament in ancient China

珏(瑴) jué 〈书 *fml.*〉合在一起的两块玉 two pieces of jade fitted together

砄 jué 〈书 *fml.*〉石头 stone; rock

鴂 jué 古书上指伯劳 shrike recorded in ancient books

【鴂舌】juéshé 〈书 *fml.*〉〈比喻 *fig.*〉语言难懂 (of language) difficult to understand; hardly intelligible

觉(覺) jué ❶ (人或动物的器官)对刺激的感受和辨别 (of human or animal organs) sense; feel; discern certain provocative things: 视～ visual sense, sense of sight | 听～ sense of hearing | 不知不～ unconsciously | 下了雪,～出冷来了。It becomes colder after a fall of snow. ❷ 睡醒 wake; awake: 大梦初～ wake up after a long dream ❸ 觉悟 become aware; wake up to: ～醒 awaken | 自～自愿 of one's own free will; voluntarily

☞ jiào on p. 980

【觉察】juéchá 发觉;看出来 sense; realize; (it) dawn on sb. that ...: 日子长了,她才～出他耳朵有些聋。As time passed by, it dawned on her that he was hard of hearing.

【觉得】jué·de ❶ 产生某种感觉 feel: 游兴很浓,一点也不～疲倦。Having such a lively interest in the excursion, (he) did not feel at all tired. ❷ 认为(语气较不肯定)(in an unassured tone) think; feel: 我～应该先跟他商量一下。I think we should first consult him.

【觉悟】juéwù ❶ 由迷惑而明白;由模糊而认清;醒悟 consciousness; awareness; understanding: 政治～ political consciousness; political understanding | 经过学习,大家的～都提高了。Having been through a period of study, everyone has gained a higher degree of understanding. | 他终于～到蛮干是不行的。It finally dawned on him that acting recklessly does not work. ❷ 〈佛教 *Budd.*〉指领悟教义的真谛 awakening; enlightenment; grasping the essence of Buddhist doctrines

【觉醒】juéxǐng 醒悟;觉悟 awaken; be aroused

鴂 jué ☞「鹈鴂」(tíjué) on p. 1882

绝 jué ❶ 断绝 cut off; break off; sever: ～交 sever relations | ～缘 be isolated from | 隔～ be separated from | 络绎不～ endless flow of sth. ❷ 完全没有了;穷尽;净尽 exhausted; used up; finished: 斩尽杀～ exterminate; wipe out | 法子都想～了。All possible ways have been tried. ❸ 走不通的;没有出路的 desperate; hopeless; unworkable: ～地 desperate situation; extremely dangerous place | ～壁 precipice | ～处逢生 escape by the skin of one's teeth; unexpectedly survive a desperate situation ❹ 气息中止;死亡 be breathless; die; perish; demise: 气～ stop breathing | 悲恸欲～ be so sorrowful as to desire death ❺ 独一无二的;没有人能赶上的 unique; superb; matchless: ～技 superb skill | 他的书画可称双～。In both calligraphy and paintings he may be regarded as being peerless. ❻ 极;最 extremely; most: ～早 extremely early | ～大多数 most; overwhelming majority | ～大部分 most part ❼ 绝对(用在否定词前面 used in the negative) absolutely; by no means; on any account: ～无此意 have absolutely no such intentions ❽ 绝句 four-line poem with a strict tonal pattern and rhyme scheme: 五～ five-character, four-line poem | 七～ seven-character, four-line poem

【绝版】jué//bǎn 书籍毁版不再印行 out of print

【绝笔】juébǐ ❶ 死前最后所写的文字或所作的字画 swan song; last article, calligraphic work or painting done before one's death ❷ 〈书 *fml.*〉指最好的诗文或字画 best poem, article, calligraphic work or painting: 堪称～ can be considered a superb work of art

【绝壁】juébì 极陡峭不能攀援的山崖 precipice; overhanging or extremely steep, inaccessible mass of rock: 悬崖～ precipitous cliffs

【绝唱】juéchàng ❶ 指诗文创作的最高造诣 acme of literary perfection: 千古～ poetic masterpiece throughout the ages ❷ 死前最后的歌唱 swan song, legendary last song of a swan before its death; farewell appearance or work: 明星已经去世,这盒录音带成了她的～。As the singing star has passed away, this cassette is now her swan song.

【绝代】juédài 〈书 *fml.*〉当代独一无二 unique among one's contemporaries; peerless: 才华～ unrivalled talent | ～佳人 beauty of beauties; woman of unsurpassed beauty; matchless beauty

【绝倒】juédǎo 〈书 *fml.*〉形容大笑,前仰后合 rock with laughter; roar with laughter: 诙谐百出,令人～。People split their sides at the fast-flowing stream of humour.

【绝地】juédì ❶ 极险恶的地方 dangerous place: 这里左边是悬崖,右边是深沟,真是个～。Precipitous cliffs to the left and a fathomless valley to the right make here an extremely dangerous place. ❷ same as 绝境 juéjìng ②: 陷于～ fall into a hopeless situation

【绝顶】juédǐng ❶ 极端;非常 extremely; utterly: ～聪明 extremely intelligent ❷ 〈书 *fml.*〉

最高峰 zenith; acme; pinnacle: 会当凌～，一览众山小。When I had climbed to its utmost pinnacle,/The surrounding mountains all were dwarfed.

【绝对】juédui ❶ 没有任何条件的；不受任何限制的（跟'相对'相对 as opposed to 'relative'）absolute; unconditional; unlimited: ～真理 absolute truth | ～服从 obey unconditionally; absolutely comply with | 反对～平均主义 be absolutely opposed to egalitarianism ❷ 只以某一条件为根据，不管其他条件的 on the basis of one condition to the exclusion of all others; absolute: ～值 absolute value | ～温度 absolute temperature | ～高度 absolute altitude ❸ 完全；一定 absolutely; perfectly; definitely: ～正确 absolutely correct | 这些我都检查过，～没有错儿。I have checked all these and there are absolutely no mistakes. ❹ 最；极 most; extremely: 我们的同志～大多数都是好同志。The majority of our comrades are good.

【绝对高度】juédui gāodù 以平均海水面做标准的高度 absolute altitude; height of a thing above sea level

【绝对零度】juédui língdù 热力学温标的零度，就是 -273.15℃ absolute zero; zero degree on the thermometric scale in thermodynamics, equal to -273.15℃

【绝对湿度】juédui shīdù 单位体积空气中所含水蒸汽的质量，叫做空气的绝对湿度 absolute humidity; ratio of the mass of water vapour to the volume of moist air within which it is contained

【绝对温度】juédui wēndù 以 -273.15℃ 为起点计算的温度（-273.15℃ 是最低的温度），用 K 来表示 absolute temperature; temperature measured or calculated on an absolute scale, which is marked by K (-273.15℃ being the lowest temperature)

【绝对真理】juédui zhēnlǐ 指无数相对真理的总和 absolute truth; summation of countless relative truths; ☞ 相对真理 xiāngduì zhēnlǐ on p. 2087

【绝后】jué//hòu ❶ 没有后代 without offspring; with no descendants ❷ 今后不会再有 never to be seen again: 空前～ unprecedented and unrepeatable

【绝户】jué·hu ❶ same as 绝后 jué//hòu ① ❷ 指没有后代的人或人家 childless person or family

【绝活】juéhuó（～儿 juéhuór）最拿手而有特色的本领；绝技 unique skill; consummate skill: 一定要把师傅的～学到手。We must study and learn the consummate skills of our master.

【绝技】juéjì 别人不易学会的技艺 unique skill; consummate skill: 身怀～ have unique skills

【绝迹】jué//jì 断绝踪迹；完全不出现 disappear; be extinct; be stamped out: 由于乱伐森林，这里的稀有野生动物～了。Owing to the reckless depredation of forests, many species of rare wild animals have become extinct altogether. | 天花在我们这儿已经～。Smallpox has been stamped out in our area.

【绝交】jué//jiāo（朋友间或国家间）断绝关系 (as between friends or countries) break off; dissociate; sever: 断然～ break off relations | ～多年。Their relations were severed years ago.

【绝经】juéjīng 因卵巢功能衰退或遭受破坏而停止月经。女子生理性绝经一般发生在 45—50 岁之间。menopause; permanent cessation of menstruation either owing to the natural functional deterioration of the ovaries, or to damage caused otherwise. Physical menopause usu. occurs in women between the ages of 45 and 50.

【绝境】juéjìng ❶〈书 *fml.*〉与外界隔绝的境地 isolated condition; out-of-the-way place ❷ 没有出路的境地 hopeless situation; impasse; blind alley: 濒于～ face an impasse

【绝句】juéjù 旧诗体裁之一，一首四句。每句五个字的叫五言绝句，每句七个字的叫七言绝句。quatrain; old-style poem of four lines, each containing five to seven characters; there are hence penta-syllabic and hepta-syllabic quatrains

【绝口】juékǒu ❶ 住口（只用在'不'后 used only after 不 bù）stop talking: 赞不～ give unstinted praise; praise profusely ❷ 因回避而不开口 keep one's mouth shut so as to avoid unnecessary trouble; avoid all mention of sth.: 他～不提此事。He has never uttered a single word on this matter.

【绝粒】juélì〈书 *fml.*〉断绝饮食 fast; abstain from food

【绝路】jué//lù 断绝了出路 block the way out; leave no way out: 这个办法要是还不行，那可就绝了路了。If this still does not work, there is no other way.

【绝路】juélù 走不通的路；死路 road to ruin; blind alley; dead end; impasse: 走上～ come to a dead end or an impasse

【绝伦】juélún〈书 *fml.*〉独一无二；没有可以相比的 unsurpassed; unequalled; unrivalled; peerless; matchless; beyond compare: 荒谬～ height of absurdity; utterly preposterous | 聪颖～ incomparably intelligent

【绝门】juémén ❶ 没有后代的人家 childless family: ～绝户 family without offspring ❷（～儿 juéménr）〈比喻 *fig.*〉没有人从事的工作、事业等 job or trade no one engages in: 这个行当快成～了。This trade is going to die out. ❸（～儿 juéménr）绝技；绝招 superb skill; consummate skill: 这一手是他的～。This is his superb skill. ❹（～儿 juéménr）形容一般人想像不到或做不出来 unexpected; unimaginable: 他在这件事上做得太～啦！His handling of this matter was unheard of!

【绝密】juémì 极端机密的;必须绝对保密的(文件、消息等)(document and information) top-secret; confidential:～材料 top-secret materials|此事～,切勿外传。This is top secret and strictly between you and me.

【绝妙】juémiào 极美妙;极巧妙 extremely clever; excellent; perfect:～的音乐 excellent music|～的讽刺 superb irony

【绝命书】juémìngshū 指自杀前写的遗书 suicide note

【绝情】jué//qíng 不讲人情;断绝情谊 have no consideration for others' feelings; be heartless; be cruel:～忘义 be heartless and ungrateful|同志之间不要说这种～的话。Don't make such heartless remarks to your comrades.

【绝热过程】juérè-guòchéng 气体迅速膨胀或迅速被压缩而使其来不及跟周围物体交换热量的过程 adiabatic process; process of quickly dilating or compressing gas so that it has no time to exchange heat with surrounding objects

【绝色】juésè〈书 *fml.*〉绝顶美貌(指女子)(of a woman) extremely beautiful; of unrivalled beauty; dazzling:～佳人 beauty of beauties; dazzling beauty

【绝食】jué//shí 断绝饮食(表示抗议或自杀)(as a token of protest or suicide) fast; go on a hunger strike; abstain from food

【绝世】juéshì 绝代 peerless; unmatched; unrivalled:～珍品 peerless treasure|～佳作 masterpiece; unsurpassed excellent work

【绝收】juéshou 完全没有收成 no harvest; total crop failure

【绝嗣】jué//sì〈书 *fml.*〉没有子孙 without offspring or issue

【绝望】jué//wàng 希望断绝;毫无希望 hopeless; beyond hope; in total despair; in desperation:感到～ feel hopeless|～的呼喊 desperate shout

【绝无仅有】jué wú jǐn yǒu 极其少有 only one of its kind; unique:这种奇事是～的。This is a real miracle.

【绝响】juéxiǎng〈书 *fml.*〉本指失传的音乐,后来泛指传统已断的事物 lost art; inimitable art; anything that has lost its tradition:经过努力发掘,这种已成～的技艺后继有人了。After continuous efforts and exploration, qualified successors are now able to carry on this long-lost craft.

【绝续】juéxù 断绝和延续 continue or discontinue; survive or perish:存亡～的关头(生死存亡的关键时刻) critical moment of life or death

【绝学】juéxué〈书 *fml.*〉❶ 失传的学问 lost learning ❷ 高明而独到的学问 profound and original learning; unique scholarship:高才～ of great talent and profound knowledge

【绝艺】juéyì 卓绝的技艺;绝技 consummate art; superb skill:身怀～ have superb skills|传授～ pass on superb skills to sb.

【绝育】jué//yù 采取结扎输精管或输卵管等方法使人失去生育能力 sterilization; causing a person to lose their capacity to reproduce by ligating the spermaduct or oviduct

【绝缘】juéyuán ❶ 跟外界或某一事物隔绝,不发生接触 be isolated from; cut all ties with sth.; have no contact with the outside world or certain thing ❷ 隔绝电流,使不能通过。具有极高电阻的物质可以用来绝缘。insulate; prevent the passage of electricity. Material of high resistance can be used as insulant.

【绝缘体】juéyuántǐ 极不容易传导热或电的物体,分为热的绝缘体(如土、气体、橡胶)和电的绝缘体(如陶瓷、云母、油脂、橡胶) insulator; material that inhibits conduction of heat or electricity, divided into two categories: one of heat insulators, such as earth, gas and rubber, and one of electricity insulators, such as pottery, porcelain, mica, grease and rubber; also 非导体 fēidǎotǐ

【绝缘子】juéyuánzǐ 一种用瓷或玻璃制成的电器零件,呈椭圆体形、鼓形、圆柱形等。用来固定导体并使这个导体与其他导体绝缘。insulator; porcelain or glass electrical part, with a shape either oval, drum-like or cylindrical, used to fix a conductor and also to insulate it from other conductors; 俗称 popularly known as 瓷瓶 cípíng

【绝早】juézǎo 极早 extremely early:～动身 set off extremely early

【绝招】juézhāo (～儿 juézhāor) ❶ 绝技 unique skill ❷ 一般人想像不到的手段、计策 unexpectedly tricky measure or stratagem ‖ also 绝着 juézhāo

【绝着】juézhāo (～儿 juézhāor) same as 绝招 juézhāo

【绝症】juézhèng 指现在无法治好的疾病 incurable disease; fatal illness:身患～ suffer from a fatal illness

【绝种】jué//zhǒng 某种生物因不能适应新环境等而逐渐稀少,终于灭绝,例如恐龙 (of a species) become extinct; die out owing to a failure to adapt to a new environment, e.g. the dinosaur

倔 jué 义同'倔'(juè),只用于'倔强' having the same meaning as 倔 juè, used only in the phrase 倔强 juéjiàng

☞ juè on p.1063

【倔强】juéjiàng (性情)刚强不屈 (of character) stubborn; unbending; tenacious:性格～ of a tenacious character|他有股～劲儿。He is a man of tenacity. also 倔犟 juéjiàng

桷 jué〈书 *fml.*〉方形的椽子 square rafter

掘 jué 刨;挖 dig:～井 dig a well|～土 dig earth|发～ excavate; unearth

【掘进】juéjìn 在采矿等工程中,开凿地下巷道,叫做掘进。包括打眼、爆破、通风、清除碎石、安装巷道支柱等。drive through; tunnel; (in mining) dig an underground tunnel, including drilling, exploding, ventilating, removing gravel and installing lane-way pillars

【掘土机】juétǔjī 挖土用的机器,由起重装置和土斗构成,常用来进行大量土方挖掘工程,也用于露天矿开采 bulldozer; excavator; power shovel; large, usu. mobile, earth-moving machine with a boom and a hinged bucket for excavating and mining out in the open; also 电铲 diànchǎn

崛 jué 〈书 *fml.*〉崛起 rise abruptly

【崛起】juéqǐ〈书 *fml.*〉❶(山峰等)突起(of a mountain top, etc.) rise abruptly:平地上～一座青翠的山峰。A verdant mountain arises abruptly on the plain. ❷兴起 rise to prominence:太平军～于广西桂平金田村。The Taiping troops rose in revolt in Jintian Village, Guiping, Guangxi. ◇为人才～创造条件 create conditions for the upsurge of talented people

脚(腳) jué same as 角[1] jué
☞ jiǎo on p. 976

觖 jué 〈书 *fml.*〉不满足;不满意 dissatisfied; discontented

【觖望】juéwàng〈书 *fml.*〉因不满意而怨恨 be resentful due to dissatisfaction

厥[1] jué 失去知觉,不省人事;晕倒;气闭 faint; lose consciousness; fall into a coma:痰～ faint owing to phlegm blocking the respiratory passage|昏～ syncope; faint

厥[2] jué 〈书 *fml.*〉❶其;他的 his or her; its; their:～后 after that; thereafter|～父 his or her father|大放～词 talk a lot of nonsense ❷乃;才 only then:左丘失明,～有《国语》。Only when Zuoqiu Ming lost his sight did he start to compile his *Remarks of Monarchs*.

傕 jué 〈书 *fml.*〉用于人名。李傕,东汉末人。jue, used in a person's name, such as Li Jue, who lived towards the end of the Eastern Han Dynasty

劂 jué ☞ [剞劂] (jījué) on p. 894

谲 jué 〈书 *fml.*〉❶欺诈 cheat; trick; swindle:正而不～ honest and never up to any tricks; upright ❷奇特;怪异 bizarre; strange; odd:诡～ strange and volatile; treacherous; eccentric and wild; crafty; cunning; tricky

【谲诈】juézhà 奸诈 cunning; crafty:虚伪～ hypocritical and cunning|～多端 extremely crafty

蕨 jué 多年生草本植物,生在山野草地里,根茎长,横生地下,复叶,羽状分裂,下面有繁殖器官,用孢子繁殖。嫩叶供食用,根茎可以制淀粉。全株入药。brake fern (*Pteridium aquilinum* var. *latiusculum*); perennial herbaceous plant growing on mountains having a long spreading rhizome and pinnated leaves, and reproducing through spores. Its tender leaves are edible and its rhizome produces starch. It can be used in medicine.

【蕨类植物】juélèi zhíwù 植物的一大类,草本,很少木本,有真正的根,有茎和叶子,茎有维管束,叶子通常较小,用孢子繁殖,生长在森林和山野的阴湿地带,如蕨、石松等 pteridophyte; family of plant such as fern and wolf's claw, mostly herbaceous, occasionally woody, with real roots, vascular stems, usu. small leaves, reproducing through spores, and growing in the forests and mountains of dark and humid regions

獗 jué ☞ 猖獗 chāngjué on p. 214

潏 Jué 潏水,水名,在湖北 Jueshui River in Hubei Province

橛(橜) jué (～儿 juér)橛子 short wooden stake; wooden pin; peg:钉上一个小木～儿 knock in a small wooden stake

【橛子】jué·zi 短木桩 short wooden stake; wooden pin; peg

噱 jué 〈书 *fml.*〉大笑 loud laughter:可发一～ make sb. laugh loudly
☞ xué on p. 2179

镢 jué 〈书 *fml.*〉箱子上安锁的纽 knob on a trunk for installing a lock

爵[1] jué 爵位 rank of nobility; peerage:公～ duke|封～ confer a title of nobility on sb.

爵[2] jué 〈古代 *arch.*〉饮酒的器皿,有三条腿 goblet; wine vessel with three legs and a loop handle

【爵禄】juélù 〈书 *fml.*〉爵位和俸禄 rank and salary; title of nobility and the emolument that goes with it

【爵士】juéshì 欧洲君主国最低的封号,不世袭,不在贵族之内 knight; lowest rank conferred by European monarchs, neither hereditary nor part of the aristocracy

【爵士乐】juéshìyuè 一种舞曲音乐,二十世纪初产生于美国 jazz; dance music that first emerged in the United States in the early 20th century

【爵位】juéwèi 君主国家贵族封号的等级 rank or title of nobility within a monarchy

蹶(蹷) jué 摔倒 fall;〈比喻 *fig.*〉失败或挫折 setback; failure:一～不振 fail to recover from a setback; collapse after a single setback
☞ juě on p. 1063

矍 jué〈书 *fml.*〉惊视的样子 look shocked; look surprised

【矍铄】juéshuò〈书 *fml.*〉形容老年人很有精神的样子 (of an old man) hale and hearty

嚼 jué 义同'嚼'(jiáo),用于某些复合词和成语 having same meaning as 嚼 jiáo, used in some compound phrases and idioms: 咀～ chew; masticate; ruminate | 过屠门而大～ pass by a butcher's shop and start munching; feed on illusions

☞ jiáo on p. 973 and jiào on p. 983

爝 jué [爝火] (juéhuǒ)〈书 *fml.*〉火把;小火 torch; small fire

攫 jué 抓;夺 seize; grab: ～取 seize; snatch | ～为己有 grab sth. by force; take possession of; appropriate

【攫取】juéqǔ 掠夺 plunder; rob; pillage; swoop; rake in

镢(鐝) jué〈方 *dial.*〉镢头 pick; pickaxe

【镢头】jué·tou〈方 *dial.*〉刨土用的一种农具,类似镐(gǎo) pick; pickaxe; farming tool for digging

juě (ㄐㄩㄝˇ)

蹶 juě [蹶子] (juě·zi) 骡马等用后腿向后踢叫尥(liào)蹶子 (of donkeys, horses, etc.) kick out hind leg

☞ jué on p. 1062

juè (ㄐㄩㄝˋ)

倔 juè 性子直,态度生硬 gruff; surly; blunt: ～头 surly person | ～脾气 rebellious temper; unyielding temper

☞ jué on p. 1061

【倔巴】juè·ba〈方 *dial.*〉倔 gruff; surly: 这人有点～。This person is rather surly.

【倔头倔脑】juè tóu juè nǎo 形容说话、行动生硬的样子 blunt of manner and gruff of speech

jūn (ㄐㄩㄣ)

军 jūn ❶ 军队 armed forces; army; troops: 我～ our troops | 陆～ infantry; ground force; army | 解放～ People's Liberation Army (PLA) | 参～ join the army | 裁～ disarmament | ～地两用人才 people competent in military and productive skills ◇生产大～ labour army; contingent of labour forces | 劳动后备～ labour reserves ❷ 军队的编制单位,下辖若干师 army; unit of military force with several divisions under its command: 第一～ First Army | 敌人的兵力估计有两个～。It is estimated that the enemy troops consist of two armies.

【军备】jūnbèi 军事编制和军事装备 military organization and armament; arms: 裁减～ disarmament | 扩充～ engage in arms expansion

【军操】jūncāo 军事操练 military drill

【军车】jūnchē 军用机动车辆 military vehicle

【军刀】jūndāo〈旧时 *old*〉军人用的长刀 soldier's sword; sabre; scimitar

【军队】jūnduì 为政治目的服务的武装组织 armed forces; army; troops; armed organization established to serve political purposes

【军阀】jūnfá ❶〈旧时 *old*〉拥有武装部队,割据一方,自成派系的人 warlord; military commander with his own armed forces, who exercises administrative power over a region independently: 北洋～ Northern Warlords ❷ 泛指控制政治的反动军人 (in a broad sense) reactionary military man who controls politics

【军法】jūnfǎ 军队中的刑法 military criminal code; military law: 违反军纪者将按～处置。Those who flout military discipline will be court-martialed.

【军费】jūnfèi 国家用于军事方面的经费 military expenditure

【军服】jūnfú 军人穿的制服 military uniform; army uniform

【军港】jūngǎng 军用舰船专用的港口。通常有各种防御设施。naval port; port esp. established for military ships, usu. with different kinds of defence facilities

【军工】jūngōng ❶ 军事工业 defence industry ❷ 军事工程 military project

【军功】jūngōng 战功;武功 military merit; military exploit: ～章 medal for military merit

【军官】jūnguān 被授予尉官以上军衔的军人的统称。也指军队中排长以上的干部。officer; general term of address for army officer holding the rank of lieutenant or above, or above the rank of platoon leader

【军管】jūnguǎn 军事管制的简称 abbr. for 军事管制 jūnshì guǎnzhì

【军国主义】jūnguó zhǔyì 某些帝国主义国家为了加紧对外侵略,把国家置于军事控制之下,实行法西斯军事独裁,强迫人民接受军事训练,向人民灌输侵略思想,使政治、经济、文化等为侵略战争服务的反动政策 militarism; reactionary policy adopted by an imperialist country for the purpose of foreign invasion, including placing the whole country under military control, exercising fascist military dictatorship, imposing mandatory military training on the people, instilling ideas of aggression in its people, and putting political, economic and cultural activities in the service of warmongering

【军号】jūnhào 军用的一种喇叭,用来传达简短号令、发布警报等 bugle; brass wind instrument used to pass short orders and signal

J

alarms

【军徽】jūnhuī 军队的标志。中国人民解放军的军徽是五角红星镶金黄色边，当中嵌金黄色的'八一'两字。army emblem. The emblem of the People's Liberation Army of China is a red five-pointed star with gilded edge, and with the two golden characters 八一（meaning 'August 1st'）at its centre.

【军婚】jūnhūn 指夫妻一方为现役军人的婚姻 marriage where one or both partners are in the military service

【军火】jūnhuǒ 武器和弹药的总称 general term for arms and ammunition; ammunitions：～库 arsenal

【军机】jūnjī ❶ 军事机宜 military plan：贻误～ delay or frustrate the fulfilment of a military plan ❷ 军事机密 military secret：泄漏～ leak a military secret

【军籍】jūnjí 原指登记军人姓名等的簿册，转指军人的身份（orig.）books that keep accounts of the names of soldiers; later referring to a person's identity of servicemen

【军纪】jūnjì 军队的纪律 military discipline：～严明 strict and impartial military discipline

【军舰】jūnjiàn 有武器装备能执行作战任务的军用舰艇的统称，主要有战列舰、巡洋舰、驱逐舰、航空母舰、潜艇、鱼雷艇等 warship; naval vessel; general term for armed ships that participate in wars, including warships, cruisers, chasers, aircraft carriers, submarines, torpedo boats, etc. also 兵舰 bīngjiàn

【军阶】jūnjiē 军衔的等级 military rank; grade

【军垦】jūnkěn 部队开荒搞生产 reclamation of wasteland by an army unit：～农场 army farm; army reclamation farm

【军礼】jūnlǐ 军人的礼节 military salute：行～ give a military salute; salute

【军力】jūnlì 兵力 military strength

【军粮】jūnliáng 供应部队食用的粮食 army provisions; grain for the army

【军龄】jūnlíng 军人在军队中已服役的年数 seniority in military service

【军令】jūnlìng 军事命令 military order：～状 military pledge | ～如山。Military orders must be obeyed unconditionally. *or* A military order has the momentum of an avalanche.

【军令状】jūnlìngzhuàng 戏曲和旧小说中所说接受军令后写的保证书，表示如不能完成任务，愿依军法受罚（in old novels and dramas）military pledge; guarantee written by a warrior after receiving a military order, in which he expresses his willingness to be court-martialed should he fail to carry out the mission

【军旅】jūnlǚ〈书 *fml.*〉军队，也指军事 army; troop; military affairs：～生涯 life in the army

【军马】jūnmǎ ❶ 军用的马 army horse：～场 army horse ranch; army horse-breeding farm ❷〈书 *fml.*〉兵马，泛指军队 troops; soldiers：各路～ all military units; various forces

【军民】jūnmín 军队和人民 army and people; soldiers and civilians; military and civilian：～鱼水情。The army and the people are as close to each other as fish and water.

【军品】jūnpǐn 军用物品（区别于'民品'as compared with 'civilian products'）military products; products for military use

【军棋】jūnqí 棋类游艺的一种。有陆军棋和陆海空军棋，棋子按照军职和军械定名。两人对下，双方按照规则走棋，最后以夺得对方军旗者为胜。military chess; infantry or infantry-navy-airforce military chess, in which the chess pieces are marked with military ranks and names of weapons, played by two persons, with the player who seizes the army flag of the other side declared as the winner

【军旗】jūnqí 军队的旗帜。中国人民解放军军旗为红地儿，左上角缀金黄色五角星和'八一'两字。army flag; colours; ensign. The military banner of the People's Liberation Army, which is red, and in its upper left corner bears a yellow five-pointed star and the two characters 八一（meaning 'August 1st'）

【军情】jūnqíng 军事情况 military movement; war situation：刺探～ collect military intelligence; spy on military movements

【军区】jūnqū 根据战略需要划分的军事区域。设有领导机构，统一领导该区域内军队的作战、训练、政治、后勤，以及卫戍、兵役、民兵等工作。military area command; military area divided according to strategic demands, with a body of leadership in charge of the army's campaigning, drilling, politics, logistics, defence, military service and militias in the area

【军权】jūnquán 兵权 military leadership; military power

【军人】jūnrén 有军籍的人；服兵役的人 soldier; serviceman; army man

【军容】jūnróng 指军队和军人的外表、纪律、威仪等 soldier's discipline, appearance and bearing：整饬～ strengthen army discipline and maintain the required standards of appearance and bearing | ～严整。Army discipline and its standards of appearance and bearing are strictly observed.

【军师】jūn·shī ❶〈古代 *arch.*〉官名。掌管监察军务。military counsellor; army adviser; title of a military official in charge of military affairs ❷〈旧时 *old*〉小说戏曲中所说在军中担任谋划的人，现泛指给人出主意的人（in stories and dramas）person who works out plans and strategies; present use refers to a person who puts forward ideas：狗头～ inept adviser; vicious adviser | 你要下象棋，我来给你当～。I'll serve as your adviser if you want to play Chinese chess.

【军士】jūnshì 高于兵,低于尉官的军人 noncommissioned officer, of a rank higher than private and lower than lieutenant

【军事】jūnshì 与军队或战争有关的事情 military affairs:～工作 military work|～行动 military movement|～基地 military base|～科学 military science

【军事法庭】jūnshì fǎtíng 军队系统中的专门法庭,或由军事机关临时组织的审判机构 military tribunal; military court; special military court or temporary judicial organ set up by the relevant military organs

【军事管制】jūnshì guǎnzhì 国家在战争或其他特殊情况下采取的一种措施,由军事部门暂时接管特定的单位、局部地区,以至国家政权 martial law; measure taken by a country at war or in other special circumstances, allowing the army to temporarily take control of a designated unit, area, and sometimes even of state power

【军事基地】jūnshì jīdì 为军事上的进攻或防守而驻扎军队并储备军火和军事物资的地区 military base; area where troops are stationed and ammunitions and military *matériel* stored

【军事科学】jūnshì kēxué 研究战争和战争指导规律的科学 military science; research into war and military strategies

【军事体育】jūnshì tǐyù 有关军事知识和技能的体育运动,如跳伞运动、航空模型运动、摩托车运动等 military sports; sports concerning military knowledge and skills, such as parachuting, model aircraft competition and motorcycling

【军属】jūnshǔ 现役军人的家属 soldier's dependants; armyman's family

【军团】jūntuán 我国红军时期相当于集团军的编制单位。某些国家的军团相当于我国的军。army group, unit of the Chinese Red Army in the 1930s; army group in some countries, equivalent to army in China

【军务】jūnwù 军队的事务;军事任务 military affairs; military tasks:～繁忙 be busy with military affairs|督理～ supervise military affairs

【军衔】jūnxián 区别军人等级的称号。如元帅、将官、校官、尉官等。military rank, such as marshal, general, captain, lieutenant, etc.

【军饷】jūnxiǎng 军人的薪俸和给养 soldier's pay and provisions

【军校】jūnxiào 专门培养军事干部的学校 military school; military academy

【军械】jūnxiè 各种枪械、火炮、弹药及其备件、附件等的统称 ordnance; armaments; general term for a variety of guns, cannons, ammunitions, accessories, etc.

【军心】jūnxīn 军队的战斗意志 army morale:振奋～ boost or heighten the soldiers' morale|动摇～ shake the army's morale

【军需】jūnxū ❶ 军队所需要的一切物资和器材。特指给养、被服等。military supplies such as equipment, provisions and clothing ❷〈旧时 *old*〉军队中指办理军需业务的人员 quartermaster; officer responsible for the troops' food, clothing, and equipment

【军训】jūnxùn 军事训练 military training

【军医】jūnyī 军队中有军籍的医生 medical officer; military surgeon

【军营】jūnyíng 兵营 military camp; barracks

【军用】jūnyòng 军事上使用的 for military use; military:～物资 military supplies|～地图 military map|～飞机 warplane; military aircraft

【军邮】jūnyóu 军队系统里的邮政 army postal service; army post or mail

【军乐】jūnyuè 俗称用管乐器和打击乐器演奏的音乐,因为军队中常用而得名 martial or military music, usu. performed with brass, wind and percussion instruments:～队 military band; marching band

【军政】jūnzhèng ❶ 军事和政治 military affairs and politics ❷ 军事上的行政工作 military administration ❸ 指军队和政府 army and government

【军种】jūnzhǒng 军队的基本类别。一般分为陆军、海军、空军三个军种。每一军种由几个兵种组成。armed services, usu. divided into infantry, navy and air force, each being further divided into several arms of services

【军装】jūnzhuāng 军服 military uniform; army uniform; uniform

均 jūn ❶ 均匀 equal; even:平～ average; balanced|～摊 share equally|分得不～ unevenly distributed ❷ 都;全 all; without exception:老幼～安。All the family is safe and sound.|各项工作～已布置就绪。All the work has been completed.

〈古 *arch.*〉same as 韵 yùn

【均等】jūnděng 平均;相等 equal; impartial; fair:机会～ equal opportunity

【均分】jūnfēn 平均分配 share and share alike; share out between (or among):大伙～。It is shared out.

【均衡】jūnhéng 平衡 balance; equilibrium:国民经济～地发展。The national economy develops in a balanced way.|走钢丝的演员举着一把伞,保持身体的～。The tightrope walker kept her balance by holding aloft an umbrella.

【均势】jūnshì 力量平衡的形势 balance of power; equilibrium of forces; equilibrium; parity:形成～ strike a balance of power|保持～ keep a balance of power

【均摊】jūntān 平均分摊 share equally:费用按

J

户～ share the expenses equally among all the households

【均匀】jūnyún 分布或分配在各部分的数量相同；时间的间隔相等 even; distributed in a balanced way; equal interval of time, etc.: 今年的雨水很～。Rainfall has been well distributed this year. | 钟摆发出～的声音。Sound of regular ticking issued from the swinging pendulum of a clock. | 把马料拌得均均匀匀的。Mix the horse fodder thoroughly.

【均沾】jūnzhān 大家平均分享(利益) (of people) share (profits, benefits, etc.) equally: 利益～ equal share of profits

龟(龜) jūn [龟裂](jūnliè) ❶ same as 皲裂 jūnliè ❷ 裂开许多缝子；呈现出许多裂纹 (of land) split with many cracks; (of skin) chap: 天久不雨，田地～。There has been no rain for so long that the earth is full of cracks.

☞ guī on p. 729 and qiū on p. 1581

君 jūn ❶ 君主 monarch; sovereign; supreme ruler: 国～ monarch | ～臣 monarch and his subjects ❷ 对人的尊称 [polite term of address]: 张～ Mr. Zhang | 诸～ gentlemen

【君临】jūnlín 〈书 *fml.*〉原指君主统辖，后泛指统治或主宰 orig. referring to the governance of a monarch and later meaning rule or domination: ～天下 rule supreme | ～一切 dominate everything

【君权】jūnquán 君主的权力 monarchical power; royal prerogative

【君主】jūnzhǔ 〈古代 *arch.*〉国家的最高统治者；现代某些国家的元首。有的称国王，有的称皇帝。monarch; sovereign; emperor; king; now the head of state

【君主国】jūnzhǔguó 由君主做元首的国家 monarchical state; monarchy

J

【君主立宪】jūnzhǔ lìxiàn 用宪法限制君主权力的政治制度，是资产阶级专政的一种形式 constitutional monarchy; monarchy in which the power of the ruler is restricted to that granted by the constitution and laws of the nation

【君主专制】jūnzhǔ zhuānzhì 君主独揽国家政权，不受任何限制的政治制度 autocratic monarchy; absolute monarchy; political system in which a monarch possesses exclusive state power without restriction

【君子】jūnzǐ 〈古代 *arch.*〉指地位高的人，后来指人格高尚的人 man of high rank; man of honour; man of virtue: 正人～ man of noble character | 以小人之心度～之腹。A lowly man uses himself as a yardstick when sizing up a man of noble character.

【君子国】jūnzǐguó 传说中人人都有很高的道德的地方 Land of Gentlemen, legendary state where all are of a noble character

【君子兰】jūnzǐlán 多年生草本植物，根肉质，叶子宽带形，伞形花序，花漏斗状，红黄色，供观赏 kaffir lily (*Clivia miniata*); perennial herbaceous plant with succulent roots, broad, band-shaped leaves, umbrella-shaped inflorescence and funnel-shaped yellowish red flowers

【君子协定】jūnzǐ xiédìng 指国际间不经过书面上共同签字只以口头上承诺或交换函件而订立的协定，它和书面条约具有相同的效力。借指彼此之间互相信任的约定。gentleman's agreement; agreement on the basis of mutual understanding; agreement guaranteed only by pledged words or correspondence, but as valid as a written agreement; also 绅士协定 shēnshì xiédìng

钧 jūn ❶ 古代的重量单位，三十斤是一钧 ancient unit of weight, equal to 15 kilogrammes: 雷霆万～之势 momentum of an avalanche; strength as powerful as that of a thunderbolt | 千～一发 a hundred weight hanging by a hair; imminent peril ❷ 制陶器所用的转轮 potter's wheel; throwing wheel ❸ 〈书 *fml.*〉〈敬辞 *pol.*〉用于有关对方的事物或行为(对尊长或上级用) [term used to address one's elders or superiors] you; your: ～座 Your Excellency; Your Honour | ～鉴。I beg to inform you. | ～启 Yours sincerely; Sincerely yours

莙 jūn [莙荙菜](jūndácài)一年或二年生草本植物，叶有长柄，花绿色。叶子嫩时可做蔬菜。spinach beet (*Beta vulgaris* var. *cicla*); annual or biennial herbaceous plant with green flowers and long-stemmed leaves that are used as vegetable when tender

菌 jūn 低等生物的一大类，以寄生或腐生方式摄取营养，种类很多 bacterium; fungus; a large class of low organisms, may be parasitic or saprophytic, and of many varieties

☞ jùn on p. 1067

【菌落】jūnluò 单个菌体或孢子在固体培养基上生长繁殖后形成的肉眼可见的微生物群落 colony of bacteria; visible growth of micro-organisms developed from a single bacterium or a single spore, usu. in a solid culture medium

皲 jūn [皲裂](jūnliè)皮肤因寒冷干燥而开裂 (of skin) chapped from cold or dryness

筠 jūn 筠连(Jūnlián)，地名，在四川 Junlian, name of a place in Sichuan Province

☞ yún on p. 2377

鲪 jūn 鱼类的一属，身体长形，侧扁，口大而斜，尾鳍呈圆形。生活在海中。gopher rock cod (*Sebastodes*); sea fish with a long, flat body, large slanting mouth and a round tail fin

麇(麏) jūn 古书上指獐子 river deer; roe recorded in ancient books

☞ qún on p. 1606

jùn（ㄐㄩㄣˋ）

俊（❷隽、儁） jùn ❶ 相貌清秀好看 cute; handsome; pretty; beautiful:～秀 pretty; of delicate beauty|～俏 pretty and charming|这个孩子长得好～呀! What a pretty child! ❷ 才智出众的 outstanding; talented:～杰 person of outstanding talent; hero|英～ handsome|～士 outstanding personage

☞ 隽 juàn on p. 1056

【俊杰】jùnjié 豪杰 person of exceptional ability; hero:识时务者为～。The person who understands the times is a hero.

【俊美】jùnměi 俊秀 pretty; handsome; beautiful:容貌～ look pretty

【俊俏】jùnqiào（相貌）好看（of appearance）pretty and charming:模样～ look pretty and charming

【俊秀】jùnxiù 清秀美丽 pretty; of delicate features:容貌～ delicate features

郡 jùn 古代的行政区划,比县小,秦汉以后,郡比县大 prefecture; administrative division, smaller than a county before the Qin and Han dynasties, and larger than a county after:～县 prefecture and county|会稽～ Huiji Prefecture|秦分天下为三十六～。There were 36 prefectures in the Qin Dynasty.

捃（攟、擴） jùn〈书 *fml.*〉拾取 pick up

峻 jùn ❶（山）高大（of mountains）high:险～ precipitous; perpendicular|高山～岭 high and steep mountains ❷ 严厉 harsh; severe; stern:严～ grave; serious; severe|严刑～法 strict laws and severe punishments; draconian law

【峻拔】jùnbá（山）高而陡（of a mountain）high and steep:山势～。The mountains are high and precipitous.

【峻急】jùnjí〈书 *fml.*〉❶ 水流急（of water currents）torrential; rapid; swift ❷ 性情严厉急躁 impetuous; severe and impatient

【峻峭】jùnqiào 形容山高而陡（of mountains）high and steep; lofty and precipitous:山势～。The mountains are high and precipitous.

馂 jùn〈书 *fml.*〉吃剩下的食物 eat leftovers

浚（濬） jùn 挖深;疏通（水道）dredge:疏～ dredge|～渠 dredge a canal|～河 dredge a river|～泥船 dredger

☞ Xùn on p. 2190

骏 jùn 好马 fine horse; steed

【骏马】jùnmǎ 跑得快的马;好马 fine horse; steed

珺 jùn〈书 *fml.*〉一种美玉 a kind of fine jade

菌 jùn 蕈（xùn）mushroom

☞ jūn on p. 1066

【菌子】jùn·zi〈方 *dial.*〉蕈（xùn）mushroom

焌 jùn〈书 *fml.*〉用火烧 burn

☞ qū on p. 1589

畯 jùn 古代管农事的官 official in charge of farming in ancient times

竣 jùn 完毕 complete; finish:完～ be completed|告～ be accomplished|～工（of a project）be completed|～事（of a task）be completed

【竣工】jùngōng 工程完成（of a project）be completed:～验收 be completed, checked and accepted|提前～ be completed ahead of time|即将～ be about to be completed|全部～。All has been completed.

寯 jùn〈书 *fml.*〉same as 俊 jùn

K

kā (ㄎㄚ)

咔 kā〈拟声词 *onom*.〉:～的一声关上抽屉。The drawer was closed with a clack.
☞ kǎ on p.1069

【咔吧】kābā same as 喀吧 kābā

【咔嚓】kāchā same as 喀嚓 kāchā

【咔哒】kādā same as 喀哒 kādā

咖 kā ☞ below
☞ gā on p.618

【咖啡】kāfēi ❶ 常绿小乔木或灌木,叶子长卵形,先端尖,花白色,有香味,结浆果,深红色,内有两颗种子。种子炒熟制成粉,可以作饮料。产在热带和亚热带地区。coffee (*Coffee arabica*, *C. canephora*, *C. liberica*, etc.); small evergreen tree or shrub with long oval leaves in tropical and subtropical areas, carrying bouquets of fragrant, white flowers and bearing a kind of cherry that turns deep red when mature and contains two seeds that, after being roasted and ground, provide material for brewing a drink ❷ 咖啡种子制成的粉末 coffee; powder made of the ground seeds of the coffee shrub ❸ 用咖啡种子的粉末制成的饮料 coffee; drink made from roasted and ground coffee seeds

【咖啡碱】kāfēijiǎn 有机化合物,化学式 $C_8H_{10}O_2N_4 \cdot H_2O$,白色有光泽的柱状结晶体,有苦味。多含在咖啡、可可的种子和茶叶中。可做兴奋剂和利尿剂等。caffeine; caffeinum; organic chemical compound ($C_8H_{10}O_2N_4 \cdot H_2O$) in glossy, white columnar crystals with a bitter taste, which is mostly found in coffee and cocoa seeds and tea leaves and can be used as stimulant and diuretic

【咖啡色】kāfēisè 深棕色 colour of coffee; dark brown

【咖啡厅】kāfēitīng 单独开设的或宾馆中附设的出售咖啡及其他饮料的地方 coffee bar; cafě; facility that operates independently or in affiliation to a hotel to sell coffee and other drinks

喀 kā〈拟声词 *onom*.〉呕吐、咳嗽的声音 noise made in coughing or vomiting

【喀吧】kābā〈拟声词 *onom*.〉snap; crack click:～一声,棍子撅成两截。The stick broke into two with a crack. also 咔吧 kābā

【喀嚓】kāchā〈拟声词 *onom*.〉cracking or snapping sound:～一声,树枝被风吹折(shé)了。The branch was broken by the wind with a snap. *or* The branch snapped in the wind. also 咔嚓 kāchā

【喀哒】kādā〈拟声词 *onom*.〉click:～一声,放下了电话筒。The phone was hung up with a click. also 咔哒 kādā

【喀秋莎】kāqiūshā 火箭炮的一种 Katyusha; multi-barrel rocket launcher [俄 Russian: катюша]

【喀斯特】kāsī tè 指岩溶。由亚得里亚海岸的喀斯特(Karst)高地而得名。Karst; limestone formation named after der Karst, a plateau with this landform on the shore of the Adriatic Sea

揢 kā 用刀子刮 scrape with a knife

kǎ (ㄎㄚˇ)

卡 kǎ ❶ 卡路里的简称 abbr. for 卡路里 kǎlùlǐ ❷ 卡片 card:资料～reference index cards|年历～calendar cards|病历～medical records ❸ 录音机上放置盒式磁带的仓式装置 holder in a recorder or player for the cassette, a compact case enclosing a length of audio tape:双～录音机 double-cassette recorder ❹ 卡车 truck:十轮～ten-wheeled truck; ten-wheeler
☞ qiǎ on p.1526

【卡宾枪】kǎbīnqiāng 枪的一种,枪身较短,能自动退壳和连续射击,有效射程较步枪近 carbin; short firearm that can eject bullet shells automatically and fire continuously, with a shorter effective range than rifle

【卡车】kǎchē 运输货物、器材等的载重汽车 lorry; truck; heavy-duty automobile for transporting goods and equipment

【卡尺】kǎchǐ 游标卡尺的简称 abbr. for 游标卡尺 yóubiāo kǎchǐ

【卡带】kǎdài 盒带 cassette tape:音乐～music tape|一盒～ a cassette tape

【卡规】kǎguī 一种测量轴或凸形工件的量具 limit gauge; standard measure for the diameter of a shaft or convex body; ☞界限量规 jièxiàn liángguī on p.1000

【卡介苗】kǎjièmiáo 一种预防结核病的疫苗,除能预防结核病外,还有防治麻风病的作用。这种疫苗是法国科学家卡默特（Albert Calmette）和介林（Camille Guérin）两人首先制成的，所以叫卡介苗。BCG（Bacillus Calmette-Guerin）；anti-tuberculosis vaccine that can also be used to treat and prevent leprosy；named after Albert Calmette and Camille Guerin，the two French scientists who first invented it

【卡拉 OK】kǎlā'ōukèi 20 世纪 70 年代中期由日本发明的一种音响设备，日语是'无人乐队'的意思。它可以供人欣赏机内预先录制的音乐，还可以供人在该机的伴奏下演唱。karaoke (meaning 'empty orchestra' in Japanese)，a kind of stereo equipment invented in Japan in the 1970s for people to listen to music recorded in it or sing popular songs against the equipment's pre-recorded backing [卡拉，日 Japanese：から；OK，译自英 abbr. transliteration from English：orchestra]

【卡路里】kǎlùlǐ 热量单位，使 1 克水的温度升高 1℃ 所需要的热量 calorie；unit of heat energy needed to raise the temperature of one gramme of water one degree Celsius；简称 abbr. 卡 kǎ [法 French：calorie]

【卡片】kǎpiàn 用来记录各种事项以便排比、检查、参考的纸片 card；rectangular piece of thick stiff paper for indexing，checking or reference purposes：资料～reference cards|～目录 card catalogue；card index

【卡其】kǎqí same as 咔叽 kǎjī

【卡钳】kǎqián 用来测量或比较作件内外直径或两端距离的量具。两个脚可以开合，开口的尺寸可用另外的钢尺量出。callipers；compasses with bowed legs that can be opened or closed to measure，with the assistance of a steel ruler，the diameter and internal dimensions，and the distance between the two ends of a convex body

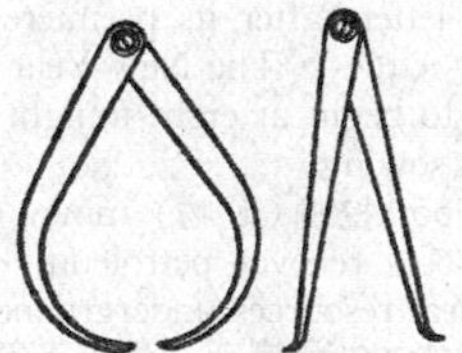

卡 钳 Callipers

【卡特尔】kǎtè'ěr 资本主义垄断组织的形式之一。生产同类商品的企业为了垄断市场，获取高额利润，通过在商品价格、产量和销售等方面订立协定而形成的同盟。参加者在生产上、商业上和法律上仍保持独立性。cartel，form of capitalist monopoly in which manufacturers sign a written agreement on the prices，output and sales of certain commodities to form an alliance in order to monopolize the market and seize high profits，with the participants remaining independent in production，business and legality [法 French：cartel]

【卡通】kǎtōng ❶ 动画片 cartoon ❷ 漫画 caricature

佧 kǎ [佧佤族]（Kǎwǎzú）佤族的旧称 old name for 佤族 Wǎzú

咔 kǎ ☞ below
☞ kā on p. 1068

【咔叽】kǎjī 一种质地较密较厚的斜纹布。也译作卡其。khaki；stout twilled cotton cloth；also transliteration of 卡其 kǎqí

咯 kǎ 使东西从咽头或气管里出来 cough sth. up from the throat or trachea：～血 haemoptysis；spit blood|把鱼刺～出来。Cough up the fishbone.

☞ gē on p. 649，·lo on p. 1248 and luò on p. 1280

【咯血】kǎ//xiě 喉部或喉以下呼吸道出血经口腔排出。咯出的血液鲜红色，常带有泡沫。见于肺结核、肺炎、支气管扩张、肺癌等病或胸部外伤。spit blood；haemoptysis；symptom of tuberculosis，pneumonia，bronchiectasis，lung cancer or chest injury，with bright red，oft. foamy，blood being coughed up from the throat or the respiratory tract

胩 kǎ 烃基和异氰基的化合物，无色液体，有恶臭 carbylamine；isocyanide；compound of the hydrocarbon radical and the isocyano group，in the form of a colourless liquid with a stench；also 异腈 yìjīng

kāi（ㄎㄞ）

开[1]（開）kāi ❶ 使关闭着的东西不再关闭；打开 open；switch on：～门 open the door|～锁 unlock；open a lock|～箱子 open a box|不～口 keep one's mouth shut ❷ 打通；开辟 open up；reclaim：～路 blaze a trail；cut out a path|～矿 open up a mine|墙上～了个窗口 build a window into the wall|～了三千亩水田。(They) reclaimed 3，000 *mu* of paddy fields from wasteland. ❸（合拢或连接的东西）展开；分离 unfold；detach：桃树～花了。The peach trees were blossoming.|扣儿～了。The knot has come undone.|两块木板没粘好，又～了。The glue failed to hold the two planks tight；They ripped once again. ❹（河流）解冻（of a river）thaw：河～了。The river thawed. ❺ 解除（封锁、禁令、限制等）lift；rescind（blockade，embargo，limitation，etc.）：～戒 break an abstinence|～禁 lift a ban|～斋 resume a meat diet；end of Ramadan|～释 release (a prisoner)；be acquitted ❻ 发动或操纵（枪、炮、车、船、飞机、机器等）rev up；start；operate（a gun，cannon，vehicle，ship，plane，machine，etc.）：～枪 open fire|～汽车 drive a car|～拖拉机 rev up a tractor|火车～了。The train has started. ❼（队伍）开拔（of an army）depart；set out：昨天～来两团人，今天又～走了。The

two regiments that had arrived yesterday left today. ❽ 开办 establish:～工厂 run a factory|～医院 open a hospital ❾ 开始 begin; start:～工 start operation; begin production|～学 begin a new school year; school begins|～演 begin a performance ❿ 举行(会议、座谈会、展览会等)hold (a meeting, symposium and exhibition, etc.):～会 attend a meeting; hold a meeting|～运动会 hold a sports meet|～欢送会 give a farewell party ⓫ 写出(多指单据、信件等);说出(价钱)make out (a receipt, letter, etc.); announce (a price; etc.):～价 state a price|～发票 make out an invoice|～药方 write out a prescription|～清单 issue a complete list of expenses (inventory, payments, etc.)|～介绍信 write out a letter of introduction ⓬ 支付;开销(工资、车费)pay (wages, fares):～薪 pay a salary|～饷 pay wages ⓭〈方 *dial.*〉开革;开除 sack; fire:过去资本家随便～掉我们工人。In the past the capitalists could fire us workers at will. ⓮ (液体)受热而沸腾 boil:水～了。The water is boiling. ⓯ 摆上(饭菜、酒席)serve a meal; lay the table:～饭 serve a meal|～席 throw a banquet|～三份客饭。A meal for three, please. ⓰〈方 *dial.*〉吃 eat up:他把包子都～了。He ate up all the steamed stuffed buns. ⓱ 用在动词或形容词后 [used after a verb or adjective]: a)表示扩大或扩展 extend; spread:喜讯传～了。The good news has spread out. b)表示开始并继续下去 start and keep going:下了两天雨,天就冷～了。It got cold after two days of rain.|天还没亮,大家就干～了。Every body began to work before the daybreak. ⓲ 指十分之几的比例 percentage:三七～ (of one's performance) be 70 per cent merits and 30 per cent demerits; be largely sound ⓳ 印刷上指相当于整张纸的若干分之一 book or paper size, given by folding a sheet of paper for a specified number of times:三十二～纸 32 mo ⓴ (Kāi) 姓 a surname

开²(開) kāi 开金中含纯金量的计算单位(二十四开为纯金) karat or carat; measure of purity of gold (pure gold being 24 karat):十四～金的笔尖 14-carat gold pen nib

开(開) //·kāi用在动词后 [used after a verb]: a)表示分开或离开[indicating separation or dissemination] open:拉～pull (two persons) apart|躲～get out of the way|把门开～push the door open|窗户关得紧,打不～。The window was shut so tightly it wouldn't budge. b)表示容下 big enough:这个屋子小,人多了坐不～。This room is not big enough for so many people to sit in it.|这张大床,三个孩子也睡～了。This bed is large enough for three children.

【开拔】kāibá (军队)由驻地或休息处出发(of troops) set out; move:第三天拂晓前,部队～了。On the third day the troops set out before dawn.

【开办】kāibàn 建立(工厂、学校、商店、医院等) start or run (a factory, school, store, hospital, etc.)

【开本】kāiběn 拿整张印书纸裁开的若干等份的数目做标准来表明书刊本子的大小叫开本,如十六开本、三十二开本等(of a book) format; book size, such as 16 mo and 32 mo

【开笔】kāi//bǐ ❶〈旧时 *old*〉指开始学做诗文 write poems or compositions for the first time in one's life:他八岁～,九岁就成了篇。He began to learn how to write at eight and was already coming up with wholesome compositions by the time he turned nine. ❷〈旧时 *old*〉指一年中开始写字 start practising calligraphy for the first time in a year:新春～ start writing when the new year begins ❸ 指开始写某一本书或某篇文章 start writing a book or an article

【开编】kāibiān 开始编写;开始编辑 start compiling or editing:这部词典已经～。Compilation has begun on this dictionary.

【开标】kāi//biāo 拆开标单,通常由招标人召集投标人当众举行 open tenders; ceremony at which a tenderer opens the tenders in front of all the bidders and announces the winner

【开播】kāibō ❶ 广播电台、电视台正式播放节目(of a radio or TV station) begin broadcasting:庆祝电视二台～五周年。Celebrate the 5th anniversary of the inauguration of Channel Two of our TV station. ❷ 某一节目开始播放 première of a radio or television programme:这部电视连续剧～后收到不少观众来信。This TV serial has received many viewers' letters after its première.|春节联欢晚会今晚八点～。The New Year's Gala Party is set to begin at eight tonight. ❸ 开始播种 begin sowing

【开采】kāicǎi 挖掘(矿物) mine; extract; exploit:～石油 recover petroleum|～地下资源 tap natural resources underground

【开场】kāichǎng 演剧或一般文艺演出等开始,也比喻一般活动开始 (of a performance, action, etc.) begin; start:他们到了剧院,～已很久了。The play had already begun by the time they arrived at the theatre.|群众大会上,他总是带头发言,话虽不多,倒能给会议做个很好的～。He was always the first to take the floor whenever there was a mass rally, and his speech, though sparing of words, often made a good beginning for such a meeting.

【开场白】kāichǎngbái 戏曲或某些文艺演出开场时引入本题的道白 prologue (of a play); opening or introductory speech;〈比喻 *fig*〉文

章或讲话等开始的部分 beginning of an article or a speech

【开车】kāi//chē ❶ 驾驶机动车 drive an automobile:路滑,～要注意安全。The road is slippery. Be careful when you drive. ❷ 泛指开动机器 rev up a machine; start a machine; set a machine in motion

【开诚布公】kāi chéng bù gōng 诚意待人,坦白无私 be frank; put one's cards on the table; wear one's heart on one's sleeve

【开诚相见】kāi chéng xiāng jiàn 跟人接触时,诚恳地对待 meet each other in sincerity; open one's heart to sb.

【开秤】kāi//chèng 开始交易(多用于收购季节性货物的商业 oft. seasonal commodities)(of a purchasing station) start purchasing:果品收购站已经～收购西瓜了。The fruit purchasing station has begun purchasing watermelons.

【开初】kāichū 开始;起初 at first; at the outset:～他们互不了解,日子一久,也就熟了。They knew little of each other when they first met, but became familiar as time went by.

【开除】kāichú 机关、团体、学校等将成员除名使退出集体 expel; discharge:～党籍 expel sb. from the party|～学生两名。Two students were sent down.|他被公司～了。His name was taken off the company's books.

【开锄】kāi//chú 一年中开始锄地(of farmers) begin tilling for a farming season

【开创】kāichuàng 开始建立;创建 start; initiate:～新局面 bring about a new situation|～历史新纪元 open a new chapter in history|这家老店～于上世纪末。This old store was established towards the end of the last century.

【开春】kāi//chūn (～儿 kāi//chūnr)春天开始;进入春天(一般指农历正月或立春前后 usu. referring to the first month of the lunar year) beginning of spring:开了春,天气就暖和起来了。It begins to warm up when spring sets in.

【开打】kāidǎ 戏曲中演员表演搏斗 acrobatic stunt in an opera

【开裆裤】kāidāngkù 幼儿穿的裆里有口的裤子 open-seat or split pants (for toddlers)

【开刀】kāi//dāo ❶ 执行斩刑(多见于早期白话 oft. in early vernacular) behead; decapitate:～问斩 execution by decapitation ❷〈比喻 *fig.*〉先从某个方面或某个人下手 make sth. or sb. the first target of attack, criticism, etc. ❸ 医生用医疗器械给病人做手术 perform a medical operation; operate

【开导】kāidǎo 以道理启发劝导 help sb. see the point; enlighten:孩子有缺点,应该耐心～。The child has some faults, but you've got to try to bring him along patiently.

【开倒车】kāi dàochē〈比喻 *fig.*〉违反前进的方向,向后退 back the car; turn back the wheel of history:要顺应历史潮流,不能～。Follow the trend of the times — on no account should you go against it.

【开道】kāi//dào ❶ 在前引路 clear the way:鸣锣～beat gongs to clear the way ❷〈方 *dial.*〉让路 make way

【开吊】kāidiào 办丧事的人家在出殡以前接待亲友来吊唁(of a bereaved family) receive visitors who come to offer condolences

【开动】kāidòng ❶ (车辆)开行;(机器)运转 start; set in motion:～机车 set the locomotive in motion|轰隆隆机器～了。The machine started running at full throttle.◇～脑筋 turn sth. over in one's mind; use one's brains ❷ 开拔前进 move; march:队伍休息了一会就～了。The troops were on the move again after a short rest.

【开冻】kāi//dòng 冰冻的江河、土地融化(of river, land, etc.) thaw; unfreeze

【开端】kāiduān (事情)起头;开头 beginning; start:良好的～good beginning

【开恩】kāi//ēn 请求人宽恕或施与恩惠的用语 [pleading for forgiveness or a big favour] Have mercy please! I beg your grace!

【开尔文】kāi'ěrwén 热力学温度单位,1开尔文是水的三相点热力学温度的1/273.16。这个单位名称是为纪念英国物理学家开尔文(Lord Kelvin)而定的。Kelvin; unit of thermodynamic temperature, with its zero degree equaling −273.16 degrees Celsius; named after the British physicist Lord Kelvin (1824-1907)

【开发】kāifā ❶ 以荒地、矿山、森林、水力等自然资源为对象进行劳动,以达到利用的目的;开拓 develop; open up; exploit (natural resources, such as wasteland, mine, forest, and hydropower):～荒山 reclaim barren mountains|～黄河水利 harness the Yellow River for water conservancy purposes|～边疆 develop frontier regions ❷ 发现或发掘人才、技术等供利用 develop; tap talent or develop technology for constructive purposes:～先进技术 develop advanced technology|人才～中心 intellectual development centre; human resources centre

【开发】kāi·fa 支付;分发 pay; hand out:～车钱 pay travelling expenses|～喜钱 hand out luck money among well-wishers

【开饭】kāi//fàn ❶ 把饭菜摆出来准备吃 serve a meal ❷ 食堂开始供应饭菜 mealtime; (of a cafeteria) begin to serve a meal

【开方】[1] kāi//fāng (～儿 kāi//fāngr)开药方 write out a prescription; also 开方子 kāi fāng·zi

【开方】[2] kāi//fāng 求一个数的方根的运算,如81开4次方得±3 extraction to determine the root of a quantity; For instance, the root of the number 81 extracted for four times is ±3

【开房间】kāi fángjiān〈方 *dial.*〉租用旅馆的房间 rent a room in a hotel

【开放】kāifàng ❶(花)展开(of flowers) come into bloom:百花～flowers in full bloom ❷解除封锁、禁令、限制等 lift a ban, restriction, etc.:公园每天～。The park is open every day.|图书馆～时间每天上午八时至下午六时。The library opens at 8:00 a.m. and closes at 6:00 p.m.|机场关闭了三天,至今日才～。The airport opened today after a close-down of three days. ❸性格开朗 outgoing:性格～of an outgoing disposition

【开赴】kāifù (队伍)开到(某处)去(of troops) march to; bound for:～工地 head for the construction site|～前线 march to the front

【开革】kāigé 开除;除名 expel; discharge

【开工】kāi//gōng ❶(工厂)开始生产(of a factory) begin production ❷(土木工程)开始修建(of civil engineering project) come under construction

【开关】kāiguān ❶电器装置上接通和截断电路的设备 switch; device for making and breaking the connection in an electric circuit; 通称 generally known as 电门 diànmén ❷设在流体管道上控制流量的装置,如油门开关、气门开关 valve; device for controlling the passage of fluid through a pipe, such as oil valve and gas valve

【开光】kāi//guāng ❶神佛的偶像雕塑完成后,选择吉日,举行仪式,揭去蒙在脸上的红绸,开始供奉 consecrate; consecration; ceremony held on an auspicious day to unveil a newly finished statue of the Buddha for people to worship ❷借指人理发、剃头或刮脸(含诙谐意 humor.) have one's hair or facial hair cut or shaved

【开锅】kāi//guō 锅中液体煮沸(of a pot) boil:柴湿火不旺,烧了半天还没有～。The fire was feeble because the firewood was wet, and after what seemed an eternity the water was still not boiling.

【开国】kāiguó 指建立新的国家(在封建时代指建立新的朝代) found a state:～元勋 founding fathers of a nation|～大典 grand ceremony to mark the founding of a new political power

【开航】kāi//háng ❶新开辟的或解冻的河道开始行船;新开辟的民航线开始有飞机航行(of a waterway newly opened or having thawed out) open to navigation; (of a new airline) open to air traffic ❷(船只)开行;起航 (of a boat) set sail; (of an aircraft) take off

【开河】[1] kāi//hé 河流解冻 (of a frozen river) thaw out

【开河】[2] kāi//hé 开辟河道 dig a canal

【开后门】kāi hòumén (～儿 kāi hòuménr)〈比喻 *fig.*〉利用职权给予不应有的方便和利益 backdoor; offer or take unjustifiable benefits by abusing sb.'s power or clout

【开户】kāi//hù 单位或个人跟银行建立储蓄、信贷等业务关系(of an organization or individual) open a savings deposit or credit account with a bank

【开花】kāi//huā (～儿 kāi//huār) ❶生出花朵;花蕾开放 blossom; bloom:～结果(of a plant or tree) blossom and bear fruit; (of an endeavour) come to fruition ❷〈比喻 *fig.*〉像花朵那样破裂开 split (like a flower blooming):～儿馒头 split-top steamed bread|这只鞋～儿了。The shoe has split open.|炮弹在敌人的碉堡上开了花。The bomb exploded on the enemy's pillbox. ❸〈比喻 *fig.*〉心里高兴或脸露笑容 feel happy; smile from ear to ear:心里开了花 burst with joy|乐开了花 feel elated ❹〈比喻 *fig.*〉经验传开或事业兴起(of experience) spread or a cause begin to grow:全面～spread all over a place|遍地～thrive everywhere

【开花弹】kāihuādàn 榴弹的旧称 old name for 榴弹 liúdàn

【开化】kāihuà ❶由原始的状态进入有文化的状态 progress from barbarity to civilization ❷冰、雪开始融化 thaw; unfreeze

【开怀】kāihuái 心情无所拘束,十分畅快 to one's heart's content:～畅饮 drink with abandon; have a hearty drink

【开怀儿】kāi//huáir 指妇女第一次生育(of a woman) give birth to the first baby:没开过怀儿(没有生过孩子) has never given birth to a baby

【开荒】kāi//huāng 开垦荒地 reclaim wasteland

【开会】kāi//huì 若干人聚在一起议事、联欢、听报告等 hold or attend a meeting

【开荤】kān//hūn ❶(信奉佛教等宗教的人)解除吃素的戒律或已满吃斋的期限,开始肉食 (of a person with a religious belief) begin or resume a meat diet; end a meatless diet ❷指经历某种新奇的事情 have a novel experience

【开火】kāi//huǒ (～儿 kāi//huǒr) ❶放枪发炮,开始打仗 open fire; being a battle:前线～了。Fighting has started at the frontline. ❷〈比喻 *fig.*〉进行抨击 attack; assail:向官僚主义～combat bureaucratism

【开伙】kāi//huǒ ❶办伙食 run a mess or cafeteria:刚开学,学校还没有～。The new semester has just begun; the school cafeteria is not open yet. ❷供应伙食 provide food:这个学校的食堂只是中午有饭,早上晚上都不～。The canteen of this school only offers lunch, no breakfast or supper.

【开豁】kāihuò ❶宽阔;爽朗 open and clear:雾气一散,四外都显得十分～。With the mist gone, a vast panorama came to stay. ❷(思想、胸怀)开阔 (of idea, mind) enlightened:听了报告,他的心里更～了。After hearing the report, he became more positive about the situation. *or* The report broadened his horizons.

【开机】kāi//jī ❶ 开动机器 set a machine in motion ❷ 指开始拍摄(电影、电视剧等) start shooting (a movie, TV play, etc.)

【开价】kāi//jià (～儿 kāi//jiàr)说出价格;要价 state or quote a price:～太高 overquote

【开架】kāijià ❶ 指由读者直接在书架上选取图书(of a library or bookstore) open stack:～借阅 open the stacks to readers ❷ 指由顾客直接在货架上选取商品 open shelves (as in a supermarket, from which customers select goods):～售货 open-shelf sales

【开间】kāijiān ❶〈方 *dial.*〉旧式房屋的宽度单位,相当于一根檩的长度(约一丈左右) bay; standard width of a room in an old-style house (about 10 *chi* or the length of a purlin):单～one-bay house; a house about 10 *chi* wide|双～double-bay house; one-room house about 20 *chi* wide ❷ 房间的宽度 width of a room:这间房子～很大。The room is rather wide.

【开讲】kāijiǎng 开始讲课或开始说书 begin a lecture or story-telling

【开奖】kāijiǎng 在有奖活动中,通过一定的形式,确定获奖的等次和人员 draw lottery in public and announce the winner:有奖储蓄当众～。The winner of deposit with lottery will be announced publicly.

【开交】kāijiāo 结束;解决(多用于否定 oft. in the negative) finish; resolve:忙得不可～ be up to one's neck in work

【开胶】kāi//jiāo 用胶黏合的东西裂开 come unglued; come unstuck:三合板～就没法用了。The plywood becomes useless once it comes unglued.|这双运动鞋没穿一个月就开了胶。I had worn this pair of sneakers for barely a month when they came unglued.

【开解】kāijiě 开导劝解(忧愁悲痛的人) console; comfort (a worried or sad person):大家说了些～的话,她也就想通了。She finally came to her senses after we said a lot to console her.

【开戒】kāi//jiè 原指宗教徒解除戒律,借指一般人解除生活上的禁忌,如吸烟、喝酒等(of a religious follower) break an abstinence; break a taboo in daily life, such as smoking, drinking, etc.

【开金】kāijīn 含黄金的合金 gold alloy:～首饰 alloyed gold jewellery
☞ 开[2] kāi

【开禁】kāijìn 解除禁令 lift a ban

【开镜】kāijìng 指影片、电视片开拍 start shooting a movie, television play, etc:这部影片拟于九月～,年底停机。This movie starts shooting in September and will be finished towards the end of the year.

【开局】kāijú ❶(下棋或赛球)开始 opening (of a chess or ball game, etc.):这盘棋刚～。This chess game has just got underway. ❷(下棋或赛球)开始的阶段 beginning of a chess or ball game:～不太顺利,后来逐渐占了上风。After what seemed a rough start the team gradually gained the upper hand.

【开具】kāijù 写出(多指内容分项的单据、信件等);开列 write out (a certificate, letter, etc.):～清单 write out a detailed list

【开卷】kāijuàn ❶〈书 *fml.*〉打开书本,借指读书 open a book; read:～有益。Reading is a rewarding experience. *or* Reading enriches the mind. ❷ 一种考试方法,参加考试的人可自由查阅有关资料(区别于'闭卷' as compared with 'closed-book exam') open-book exam, in which examinees are allowed to consult reference materials

【开掘】kāijué ❶ 挖 dig:～新的矿井 open up a new mine ❷ 文艺上指对题材、人物思想、现实生活等深入探索并充分表达出来(of creative writing) explore and depict a subject matter, character, reality, etc.

【开课】kāi//kè ❶ 学校开始上课 school begins; begin classes ❷ 设置课程,也指教师(主要是高等学校的教师)担任某一课程的教学(chiefly in college) give a course; teach a subject:这学期他开了两门课。He taught two courses this semester.|为了提高教学质量,教师～要做充分的准备。To raise teaching quality, teachers should make full preparations before offering a course.|下学期开哪几门课,教研室正在研究。The teaching research office is studying what courses to offer next term.

【开垦】kāikěn 把荒地开辟成可以种植的土地 open up or reclaim wasteland:～山地 bring barren hills under cultivation

【开口】kāi//kǒu ❶ 张开嘴说话 start to talk:没等我～,他就抢先替我说了。Before I could open my mouth, he went ahead and said it all for me. ❷ 开刃儿 add cutting edge to a new knife

【开口饭】kāikǒufàn〈旧时 *old*〉把以表演戏曲、曲艺等为职业叫做吃开口饭 performing art, esp. the profession of ballad-singing and story-telling

【开口呼】kāikǒuhū ☞ 四呼 sìhū on p.1821

【开口跳】kāikǒutiào 武丑的别名 another term for 武丑 wǔchǒu

【开口销】kāikǒuxiāo 销子的一种。呈⊂形,穿入螺栓轴等的孔中后,将穿出的部分向两侧叉开,用来固定螺栓或使轴上的轮子不至脱落 split pin; metal cotter pin in the shape of ⊂, passed through a hole and held in place by its gaping slit end, for the purpose of fastening a screw bolt or preventing a wheel from falling off a shaft

【开口子】kāi kǒu·zi ❶ 指堤岸被河水冲破 (of

a dyke) break; burst ❷ 指在某方面破例或放松限制 break with precedent; stretch a rule or regulation: 这样照顾，向无先例，我不能开这个口子。There is no precedent for such preferential treatment; I don't think I can give the go-ahead to it.

【开快车】kāi kuàichē 〈比喻 *fig*.〉加快工作、学习速度 step on the gas; speed up: 又要～，又要保证质量。We should speed up and guarantee quality at the same time.

【开矿】kāi//kuàng 开采矿物 open up a mine; exploit a mine

【开阔】kāikuò ❶（面积或空间范围）宽广（of area or space) wide; vast: ～的广场 wide square | 雄鹰在～的天空中翱翔。Eagles hovered and soared high in the sky. ❷（思想、心胸）开朗（of idea, mind) magnanimous; open-minded: 他是一个思想～而又活泼愉快的人。He is broad-minded and vivacious. ❸ 使开阔 broaden: ～眼界 broaden one's horizons | ～路面 widen a road | ～胸襟 broaden one's mind

【开阔地】kāikuòdì 军事上指没有树林、山丘等遮挡的大片平地（military term referring to) open terrain; open ground, i.e. vast expanse of land clear of forests, hills and other things that may block the view

【开朗】kāilǎng ❶ 地方开阔，光线充足（of a place) spacious and with plenty of light: 豁然～become bright open all of a sudden; suddenly see the light ❷（思想、心胸、性格等）乐观、畅快，不阴郁低沉（of idea, mind, character, etc.) sanguine; optimistic: 胸怀～，精神焕发 be optimistic and cheerful

【开犁】kāi//lí ❶ 一年中开始耕地 start the year's ploughing ❷ same as 开墒 kāi//shāng

【开例】kāi//lì 做出不合规定或尚无规定的事情，让别人可以援例 create a precedent: 如果从你这里～，以后事情就不好办了。If we allow you to set this precedent, it will make things difficult in future.

【开镰】kāi//lián 指一茬庄稼成熟，开始收割 start harvesting

【开脸】kāi//liǎn ❶ 旧俗女子临出嫁改变头发的梳妆样式，去净脸和脖子上的寒毛，修齐鬓脚，叫做开脸（old custom for a bride-to-be in preparation for her wedding) remove fine hairs on the face and neck and tidy up the hairline at the temples ❷ 雕塑工艺中指雕刻人物的脸部（of sculpture) carve the face of a statue

【开列】kāiliè 一项一项写出来 draw up; list: ～名单 draw up a name list | 按照～的项目进行 work through a list of assignments

【开裂】kāiliè 出现裂缝 crack; fracture: 木板～。The wooden planks fractured.

【开路】kāilù ❶ 开辟道路 open up a road; blaze a trail: 逢山～，遇水架桥 cut paths through the mountains and build bridges across the rivers ❷ 在前引路 lead the way; blaze a trail: ～先锋 trailblazer; pioneer ❸ 电路中的开关呈开启状态或去掉一个负载，使电流不能构成回路的电路 open circuit; interruption of electric current by switching off the circuit or unloading one of the loads from it; also 断路 duànlù

【开绿灯】kāi lǜdēng 〈比喻 *fig*.〉准许做某事 give the green light; give the go-ahead: 不能给不合格产品上市～。On no account should we give the green light to shoddy products.

【开锣】kāi//luó ❶ 戏曲开演 strike up the band to start a theatrical performance: ～戏（开锣后的第一出戏）first arias on an operatic programme | 我们进了剧院，离～的时候还早。We got to the theatre long before the performance started. ❷〈比喻 *fig*.〉某项活动开始（多用于体育竞赛 oft. of a sporting event) come underway: 举重锦标赛月底～。The weightlifting championships will take place at the end of this month.

【开门】kāi//mén ❶ 敞开门，多用于比喻 open the door; openness (oft. used in a figure of speech): ～整风 open-door rectification of Party style ❷ 指营业开始(of a store) begin a day's business: 银行九点才～。The bank is not open until nine.

【开门红】kāiménhóng 〈比喻 *fig*.〉在一年开始或一项工作开始时就获得显著的成绩 make a good beginning: 争取新学年～。Let's get off to a good start in the new semester.

【开门见山】kāi mén jiàn shān 〈比喻 *fig*.〉说话写文章直截了当 come straight to the point: 这篇文章～，一落笔就点明了主题。This essay comes straight to the point right at the beginning.

【开门揖盗】kāi mén yī dào 开了门请强盗进来 open the door to robbers;〈比喻 *fig*.〉引进坏人来危害自己 invite disaster by letting in evildoers

【开蒙】kāi//méng 〈旧时 *old*〉私塾教儿童开始识字或学习；儿童开始识字或学习 teach a beginner in a private school; start schooling: 请王老师给他～。(We) will ask Mr. Wang to be his first teacher. | 他六岁开的蒙。He started school at six.

【开明】kāimíng 原意是从野蛮进化到文明，后来指人思想开通，不顽固保守 progress from barbarism to civilization; enlightened: ～士绅 enlightened gentry | 思想～liberal-minded

【开幕】kāi//mù ❶ 一场演出、一个节目或一幕戏开始时打开舞台前的幕 curtain rises: 现在七点，戏恐怕已经～了。It's seven now. (I)'m afraid the performance has already begun. ❷（会议、展览会等）开始(of a meeting, exhibition, etc.) open; inaugurate: ～词 opening speech | ～典礼 opening ceremony

【开拍】kāipāi 开始拍摄(电影、电视剧等)'Camera!'; start shooting (a film, television play, etc.):这部影片由去年初～,直至今年底才停机。This movie started shooting early last year, which did not finish until the end of this year.

【开盘】kāi//pán (～儿 kāi//pánr)指证券、黄金等交易市场营业开始,第一次报告当天行情 report the opening quotations of the day on an exchange or gold market

【开炮】kāi//pào ❶ 发射炮弹(of artillery) open fire:向敌军阵地～bomb the enemy front with artillery ❷〈比喻 *fig.*〉提出严厉的批评 level harsh criticism at sb.

【开辟】kāipì ❶ 打开通路;创立 open up; start:～航线 open an air or sea route ❷ 开拓发展 pioneer; create and develop:～工作 get work started and going on|～边疆 open up the frontiers ❸ 古代神话,盘古氏开天辟地,简称开辟,指宇宙的开始 separation of earth from heaven by Pan Gu, a hero in Chinese mythology, which marked the beginning of the universe

【开篇】kāipiān ❶ 弹词演唱故事之前先弹唱的一段唱词,自为起讫,作为正书的引子,也可以单独表演。江苏、浙江有些地方戏曲演出前,有时附加内容与正戏无关的唱段,也叫开篇。如越剧开篇、沪剧开篇。introductory song in *tanci* (storytelling in a southern dialect to the accompaniment of stringed instruments). In some local opera genres in Jiangsu and Zhejiang provinces, an introductory song oft. has nothing to do with the theme of the opera to be performed in its wake, this being the case with the Shanghai and Shaoxing operas. ❷ 指著作的开头 beginning of a written work

【开瓢儿】kāi//piáor〈方 *dial.*〉指脑袋被打破(多含诙谐意 oft. humor.) break one's head; get a cut in one's head

【开票】kāi//piào ❶ 投票后打开票箱,统计候选人所得票数 open the ballot box and count the ballots ❷ 开发票;开单据 make out an invoice, receipt, voucher, etc.

【开启】kāiqǐ ❶ 打开 open:这种灭火器的开关能自动～。This kind of fire extinguisher switches on automatically.|～闸门 open a sluice gate; open a valve ❷ 开创 initiate:～一代新风 herald in a new work style, lifestyle, etc.

【开腔】kāi//qiāng 开口说话 start to say sth.:大家都还没说话,他先～了。He started talking before anyone else.

【开窍】kāi//qiào (～儿 kāi//qiàor) ❶ (思想)搞通 have one's ideas straightened out:思想开了窍,工作才做得好。You can do a good job only after you have thought it over. ❷ (儿童)开始长见识(of a child) begin to know things ❸〈方 *dial.*〉开眼(含讥讽意 satirical) open one's eyes; broaden one's mind

【开缺】kāi//quē〈旧时 *old*〉指官员因故去职或者死亡,职位一时空缺,准备另外选人充任(of an official quitting a post or passing away) make a vacancy available

【开刃儿】kāi//rènr 新的刀、剪等在使用前抢(qiǎng)、磨使刃锋利 sharpen a new knife or a new pair of scissors before use

【开赛】kāisài 开始比赛(of a competition) begin:亚洲杯足球赛～。The Asian Cup Soccer Competition kicked off.|少年戏曲、曲艺比赛今天上午～。The teenagers' theatrical and *quyi* competition began this morning.

【开山】kāi//shān ❶ 因采石、筑路等目的而把山挖开或炸开 cut into a mountain (for quarrying, paving a road, etc.):～劈岭 open up one mountain after another ❷ 指在一定时期开放已封的山地,准许进行放牧、采伐等活动 open a closed mountain to animal husbandry, lumbering, etc. for a period of time ❸〈佛教用语 *Budd.*〉指最初在某个名山建立寺院 build the first temple on a famous mountain

【开山】kāi·shān same as 开山祖师 kāishān zǔshī

【开山祖师】kāishān zǔshī 原是佛教用语,指最初在某个名山建立寺院的人,后来比喻首创学术技艺的某一派别或首创某一事业的人 orig. a Buddhist term referring to the founding father of the first temple on a famous mountain or of a religious sect; (fig.) initiator of a school of thought, discipline of learning, field of endeavour, etc.; also 开山祖 kāishānzǔ

【开衫】kāishān (～儿 kāishānr) 开襟的针织上衣 cardigan:男～ men's cardigan|女～ women's cardigan

【开墒】kāi//shāng 耕地时,先用犁开出一条沟来,以便顺着这条沟犁地 plough the first furrow as a guideline; also 开犁 kāi//lí

【开设】kāishè ❶ 设立(店铺、作坊、工厂等) open (a shop, workshop, factory, etc.); set up ❷ 设置(课程) offer (a course in college, etc.):～公共关系课 offer a public relations course

【开始】kāishǐ ❶ 从头起;从某一点起 begin; start:新的一年～了。A new year has begun.|今天从第五课～。Let's begin today's class from Lesson Five. ❷ 着手进行 set about doing sth.:～一项新的工作 set about a new task|提纲已经定了,明天就可以～写。With the outline set, (we) can begin writing tomorrow. ❸ 开始的阶段 initial stage; outset:一种新的工作,～总会遇到一些困难。One is bound to come across one difficulty or another at the beginning of a new job.

【开氏温标】Kāishì wēnbiāo 热力学温标。因这种温标是英国物理学家开尔文制定的,所以也叫开氏温标。Kelvin scale; a scale of

thermodynamic temperature with absolute zero as zero, so named because it was initiated by the British physicist Lord Kelvin (1824-1907)

【开市】kāi//shì ❶ 商店、作坊等过了休息的日子，或有季节性的商店、作坊等到了营业的季节，开始营业 (of a shop or workshop) reopen after a cessation or at the beginning of a business season ❷ 商店每天第一次成交 (of a shop) conduct the first transaction to begin a day's business

【开释】kāishì 释放(被拘禁的人) acquit; set free (a prisoner):～出狱 be acquitted and released from prison|无罪～be set free as being innocent

【开首】kāishǒu 〈方 *dial.*〉开始；起头 beginning; outset:文章～就点出全文主题。The article came right to its theme at the beginning.

【开涮】kāishuàn 〈方 *dial.*〉戏弄(人)；开玩笑 poke fun at; tease

【开水】kāishuǐ 煮沸的水 boiling water; boiled water

【开司米】kāisīmǐ ❶ 山羊的绒毛，纤维细而轻软，是优良的毛纺原料。原指克什米尔地方所产的山羊绒毛。cashmere; fine soft wool that makes a fine textile material. The term originated in a breed of Himalayan goat from Kashmir in Asia. ❷ 用这种绒毛制成的毛线或织品 woollen yarn or textile product fashioned out of this kind of wool

【开台】kāitái 戏曲开演 begin a theatrical performance:～锣鼓 a flourish of gongs and drums that serve as prelude to a theatrical performance|戏已～。The performance has begun.

【开膛】kāi//táng 剖开胸腔和腹腔(多指家禽、家畜的) cut open the chest (of a pig, chicken, etc.):～母鸡 dressed hen|猪煺毛后就～。The pig will be eviscerated after its hair is removed.

【开天窗】kāi tiānchuāng ❶ 〈比喻 *fig.*〉梅毒患者鼻部溃烂 festering of the nose of a syphilis patient ❷ 〈旧时 *old*〉政府检查新闻，禁止发表某些报道或言论，报纸版面上留下成块空白，叫开天窗 leave a blank in a newspaper as a result of government censorship

【开天辟地】kāi tiān pì dì 古代神话说盘古氏开辟天地后才有世界，因此用'开天辟地'指有史以来 beginning of history; according to Chinese mythology, the world came into being after Pan Gu separated earth from heaven, hence the phrase

【开庭】kāi//tíng 审判人员在法庭上对当事人及其他有关的人进行审问和讯问 open a court session; call the court to order for interrogation and hearing

【开通】kāitōng ❶ 使原来闭塞的(如思想、风气等)不闭塞 remove obstacles from; dredge; clear:～风气 enliven social morale|～民智 cultivate public wisdom ❷ 交通、通讯等线路开始使用(of communication and telecommunication line) open to traffic; open:国内卫星通信网昨天～。The domestic satellite telecommunications network went into operation yesterday.|这条公路已经竣工并～使用。This highway has been completed and opened to traffic.

【开通】kāi·tong ❶ (思想)不守旧；不拘谨固执 (idea) open-minded; liberal; enlightened:思想～liberal-minded|老人学了文化，脑筋更～了。The old man became more open-minded after he had learned how to read and write. ❷ 使开通 enlighten:让他多到外面去看看，～～他的思想。Let's help him broaden his horizons by giving him more opportunities to go out and see what's happening out there.

【开头】kāi//tóu (～儿 kāi//tóur) ❶ 事情、行动、现象等最初发生 begin; start:我们的学习刚～，你现在来参加还赶得上。We've only just begun our study. You can easily catch up. ❷ 使开头 cause to begin:请你先开个头儿? Would you make a start, please?

【开头】kāitóu (～儿 kāitóur)开始的时刻或阶段 in the beginning:～我们都在一起，后来就分开了。We were together in the beginning but were separated later.|这篇文章～就表明了作者的意向。The author made his point right at the beginning of his article.

【开脱】kāituō 推卸或解除(罪名或对过失的责任) absolve; exonerate:～罪责 absolve sb. from guilt or blame|不要为他～。Don't try to find excuses for him.

【开拓】kāituò ❶ 开辟；扩展 open up:～边疆 develop frontier regions|～处女地 tread on uncharted territory ◇这一年短篇小说的创作道路～得更广阔了。The year saw short-story writing embark on a broader avenue. ❷ 采掘矿物前进行的修建巷道等工序的总称 tunnel a mining pit to facilitate the tapping of mineral deposits

【开外】kāiwài 超过某一数量；以外(多用于年岁 oft. of one's age) over; above; on the wrong side of:这位老人，看上去有七十～了，可是精神还很健旺。The old man looks to be on the wrong side of 70, but is still in pretty good shape.|南北四十里，东西六十里～。The place extends 40 *li* south and north and 60-plus *li* east and west.

【开玩笑】kāi wánxiào ❶ 用言语或行为戏弄人 crack a joke; joke; make fun of:他是跟你～的，你别认真。Take it easy. He was only joking.|随便开两句玩笑。(He)'s only kidding. ❷ 用不严肃的态度对待；当做儿戏 flippant; disrespectful about a serious matter:这事关系许多人的安全，可不是～的事情。With the safety of so many people at stake, this is no laughing matter.

【开胃】kāiwèi ❶ 增进食欲 whet or stimulate the appetite：这药吃了能～。This medicine can improve your appetite. ❷〈方 *dial*.〉same as 开心②

【开线】kāi//xiàn 衣物等的缝合处因线断而裂开(of clothing, etc.) come loose at the seams; come unsewn：裤裆开了线了。The trousers came apart at the crotch.

【开销】kāi·xiāo ❶ 支付(费用) pay (expenses)：你带的钱一路够～吗？Have you brought enough money to cover the expenses of the trip? ❷ 支付的费用 expense：住在这儿，～不大，也很方便。Living is cheap and convenient here.

【开小差】kāi xiǎochāi (～儿 kāi xiǎochāir) ❶ 军人私自脱离队伍逃跑(of a soldier) desert; go A. W. O. L. ❷〈比喻 *fig*.〉思想不集中 absent-minded; wool-gathering：用心听讲，思想就不会～。Your mind won't wonder if you listen carefully.

【开心】kāixīn ❶ 心情快乐舒畅 exult; feel happy; rejoice：同志们住在一起，说说笑笑，十分～。The comrades felt real happy living under the same roof and talking and laughing merrily together. ❷ 戏弄别人，使自己高兴 amuse oneself at sb.'s expense; make fun of sb.：别拿他～。Don't make fun of him!

【开心丸儿】kāixīnwánr 宽心丸儿 words of comfort

【开行】kāixíng 开动车或船使行驶(of a boat or vehicle) start：火车已经～，站上欢送的人们还在挥手致意。The train had started and the well-wishers on the platform were still waving their hands.

【开学】kāi//xué 学期开始 school opens; term begins：～典礼 school-opening ceremony

【开言】kāi//yán 开口说话(多用于戏曲中 oft. used in an opera) begin to talk

【开颜】kāiyán 脸上现出高兴的样子 smile; beam：更喜岷山千里雪，三军过后尽～。Minshan's thousand *li* of snow joyously crossed, /The Three Armies march on, each face glowing.

【开眼】kāi//yǎn 看到美好的或新奇珍贵的事物，增加了见识 open one's eyes; widen one's view or horizons：这样好的风景，没来逛过的，来一趟也～。This beautiful scenery is indeed an eye-opener for those who have the opportunity to come and have a look.｜快把那几幅名画拿出来，让大家开开眼。Hurry up and let us have the good fortune of seeing those famous paintings.

【开演】kāiyǎn (戏剧等)开始演出(of a play, movie, etc.) begin：准时～begin a performance on time｜电影～了十分钟他才来。He showed up ten minutes after the movie started.

【开洋】kāiyáng〈方 *dial*.〉same as 虾米 xiā·mi ①(多指较大的 usu. larger ones)

【开业】kāi//yè 商店、企业或律师、私人诊所等进行业务活动(of a shop, enterprise, law firm, private clinic, etc.) start business：～行医 open a private clinic｜公司近日～。The company will begin business in a few days.

【开夜车】kāi yèchē 为了赶时间，在夜间继续学习或工作叫做开夜车 work late into the night; work overtime at night; burn the midnight oil：开了一个夜车，才把这篇稿子赶了出来。Only by staying up all night did (he) finish writing the article.

【开印】kāiyìn (书报、图片等)开始印刷 go to the press; start printing：本报今日三点十分～。This newspaper went to the press at ten past three today.

【开映】kāiyìng (电影)开始放映(of a movie show) begin

【开元】Kāiyuán 唐玄宗(李隆基)年号(公元713—741) Kaiyuan, title of the 713-741 reign of Li Longji (685-772) of the Tang Dynasty (608-907), who was posthumously known as Emperor Xuanzong

【开园】kāi//yuán 园子里瓜、果等成熟，开始采摘(of an orchard or melon garden) start picking

【开源节流】kāi yuán jié liú〈比喻 *fig*.〉在财政经济上增加收入，节省开支 increase revenue and curtail expenditure; tap new sources of economic growth while reducing costs

【开凿】kāizáo 挖掘(河道、隧道等) dig a canal; cut a tunnel：这条铁路沿线共～了十几条隧道。A dozen or so tunnels were built on this railway.

【开斋】kāi//zhāi ❶ 指吃素的人恢复吃荤(of sb. on a vegetarian diet) start eating meat again ❷ 伊斯兰教徒结束封斋(of Muslim) end of Ramadan

【开斋节】Kāizhāi Jié 伊斯兰教的节日。伊斯兰教历九月封斋后的第二十九天黄昏时，如果望见新月，第二天就过开斋节，否则就推迟一天。(Islam) 'Id al-Fitr; Lesser Bairam. It falls on the day immediately after the 29th day of Ramadan, if the crescent moon is observed on the 29th; otherwise it is postponed for a day.

【开展】kāizhǎn ❶ 使从小向大发展；使展开 cause to develop; unfold：～批评与自我批评 carry out criticism and self-criticism｜～科学技术交流活动 carry out exchanges in science and technology ❷ 从小向大发展 develop; launch：植树造林活动已在全国～起来。A tree-planting and afforestation campaign has been launched across the nation. ❸ 展览会开始展出(of an exhibition) begin：一年一度的春节花展明天～。The annual Spring Festival Flower Show will be unveiled tomorrow. ❹

开朗;开豁 open-minded; politically progressive:思想～be open-minded

【开战】kāi//zhàn 打起仗来 make war ◇向自然界～ declare war on nature's harsh conditions

【开绽】kāizhàn (原来缝着的地方)裂开 rip at a seam:鞋～了。The shoe split at the seams.

【开张】kāi//zhāng ❶ 商店等设立后开始营业 open a business; begin doing business:择日～ begin business on a selected day|这家药店明日～。The new pharmacy opens tomorrow. ❷ 经商的人指每天第一次成交 conclude the first transaction to start a day's business ❸〈比喻 *fig.*〉某种事物开始(of certain activity) come underway

【开张】kāizhāng〈书 *fml.*〉❶ 开放;不闭塞 be open (to the outside world) ❷ 雄伟开阔 grand and wide: 气势～ grand and imposing momentum

【开仗】kāi//zhàng ❶ 开战 make war; open hostilities ❷〈方 *dial.*〉打架 come to blows

【开账】kāi//zhàng ❶ 开列账单 make out a bill ❷ 支付账款(多用于吃饭、住旅馆等 used at a restaurant, hotel, etc.) foot a bill

【开征】kāizhēng 开始征收(捐税) begin to levy or collect a tax

【开支】kāizhī ❶ 付出(钱) pay; foot a bill:不应当用的钱,坚决不～。Don't spend a penny where unnecessary. ❷ 开支的费用 expense; expenditure; spending:节省～ cut down on expenses ❸〈方 *dial.*〉发工资 pay (salary or wage)

【开宗明义】kāi zōng míng yì《孝经》第一章的篇名,说明全书宗旨,后来指说话作文一开始就说出主要的意思 straight to the point; in the first place; first of all; title of Chapter One of *The Book of Filial Piety*; (of a speech or composition) clarify the purpose or theme from the very beginning

【开罪】kāizuì 得罪 annoy; irk; upset

揩 kāi 擦;抹 rub; wipe:～汗 wipe away the sweat|把桌子～干净。Wipe the table clean.

【揩拭】kāishì 擦拭 clean; wipe:用抹布～桌面 clean a table with a rag

【揩油】kāi//yóu〈比喻 *fig.*〉占公家或别人的便宜 freeload; get petty gains at the expense of the government or someone else

锎 kāi 金属元素,符号 Cf (californium)。有放射性,由人工核反应获得。californium (Cf), synthetic radioactive metallic element

kǎi (ㄎㄞˇ)

剀(剴) kǎi [剀切](kǎiqiè)〈书 *fml.*〉❶ 跟事理完全相合 true and pertinent:～详明 true and clear in every detail ❷ 切实 in real earnest:～教导 teach earnestly

凯(凱) kǎi ❶ 胜利的乐歌 triumphant strains; victorious:～歌 song of victory|～旋 triumphant homecoming|奏～而归 return in triumph ❷ (Kǎi) 姓 a surname

【凯歌】kǎigē 打了胜仗所唱的歌 song of triumph; paean:高唱～而归 return with a song of victory

【凯旋】kǎixuán 战胜归来 triumphant return

垲(塏) kǎi〈书 *fml.*〉地势高而且干燥(of topography) high and dry:爽～ high and cool

闿(闓) kǎi〈书 *fml.*〉开启 open

恺(愷) kǎi〈书 *fml.*〉快乐;和乐 merry; jovial

铠(鎧) kǎi 铠甲(suit of) armour:铁～ iron armour|首～helmet

【铠甲】kǎijiǎ〈古代 *arch.*〉军人打仗时穿的护身服装,多用金属片缀成 suit of armour; protective garment fashioned by sewing metal pieces together

蒈 kǎi 有机化合物,是莰的同分异构体,天然的蒈尚未发现 carane; organic chemical compound that is the isomer of camphene. Natural carane is yet to be found.

慨(❷ 嘅) kǎi ❶ 愤激 exasperation:愤～ indignant ❷ 感慨 sigh with emotion:～叹 heave an emotional sigh ❸ 慷慨 generous:～允 ready consent

【慨然】kǎirán ❶ 感慨地 with deep feeling:～长叹 heave a long sigh of regret ❷ 慷慨地 generously:～相赠 give (as of a present) generously|～应允 promise unstintingly

【慨叹】kǎitàn 有所感触而叹息 deplore with sighs:不胜～sigh with regret|～不已 overcome with regret

【慨允】kǎiyǔn 慷慨地应许 readily consent; kindly promise:～捐助百万巨资 donate a whopping million yuan

楷 kǎi ❶ 法式;模范 model; pattern:～模 fine example ❷ 楷书 (of Chinese calligraphy) regular script:小～regular scrip in small characters|正～regular script

☞ jiē on p. 988

【楷模】kǎimó 榜样;模范 model; paragon; example:光辉的～illustrious example

【楷书】kǎishū 汉字字体的一种,就是现在通行的汉字手写正体字,它是由隶书演变来的(of Chinese calligraphy) regular script, the standard form of writing evolved from the official script; also 正楷 zhèngkǎi

【楷体】kǎitǐ ❶ same as 楷书 kǎishū ❷ 指拼音字母的印刷体 block letter

锴 kǎi〈书 *fml.*〉好铁 iron of fine quality; choice iron

kài (ㄎㄞˋ)

忾(愾) kài 〈书 *fml.*〉愤恨 hatred:同仇敌～share a bitter hatred of the enemy

欬 kài 〈书 *fml.*〉咳嗽 cough

愒 kài 〈书 *fml.*〉贪 greedy; insatiable
☞ hè on p.792 and qì on p.1525

kān (ㄎㄢ)

刊(栞) kān ❶〈古时 *arch.*〉指书版雕刻,现在也指排印出版 block-print; print; publish:～行 print and distribute|创～ launch a magazine or newspaper|停～(of a periodical) stop publication ❷ 刊物,也指在报纸上定期出的有专门内容的一版 periodical; column in a newspaper:周～ weekly|月～ monthly|副～ supplement (to a newspaper, journal, etc.) ❸ 削除;修改 delete; correct:～误 correction|～谬补缺 correct mistakes and make up for deficiencies

【刊本】kānběn 刻木 block-printed edition:原～ original or master copy of a block-printed edition|宋～Song-dynasty block-printed edition

【刊布】kānbù 〈书 *fml.*〉通过印刷品来公布 publish (in print)

【刊登】kāndēng 刊载 publish in a newspaper or magazine; carry:～广告 carry an advertisement|～消息 carry news

【刊刻】kānkè 刻(木板书) cut or inscribe printing blocks

【刊落】kānluò 〈书 *fml.*〉删除;删削 strike out; delete:～文字 strike out redundant words|～陈言 delete platitudes

【刊授】kānshòu 以刊物辅导为主的教学方式 teach a course through a periodical

【刊头】kāntóu 指报纸、刊物上标出名称、期数等项目的地方(of a newspaper or magazine) masthead:～题字 masthead inscription|～设计 masthead design

【刊物】kānwù 登载文章、图片、歌谱等定期的或不定期的出版物 publication:定期～periodical|内部～periodical for limited circulation|文艺～literary journal

【刊行】kānxíng 出版发行(书报)(of books and newspapers) print and publish:此书年内将～问世。The book will be available by the end of the year.

【刊印】kānyìn 刻板印刷或排版印刷 cut blocks and print; compose and print

【刊载】kānzǎi 在报纸刊物上登载 publish (in a newspaper or magazine); carry:报纸上～了许多有关技术革新的文章。The newspaper carried quite a few articles about technical renovation.

看 kān ❶ 守护照料 look after; take care of; tend:～门 look after a house|一个工人可以～好几台机器。One worker can operate several machines at the same time. ❷ 看押;监视;注视 keep under surveillance; keep an eye on
☞ kàn on p.1081

【看财奴】kāncáinú 守财奴 penny-pincher; niggard

【看管】kānguǎn ❶ same as 看守 kānshǒu ②:～犯人 guard prisoners ❷ 照管 look after; attend to:～行李 look after the luggage

【看护】kānhù ❶ 护理 nurse:～病人 nurse the sick ❷〈旧时 *old*〉称护士 hospital nurse

【看家】kān//jiā ❶ 在家或在工作单位看守、照管门户 look after the house; mind the house ❷ 指本人特别擅长、别人难以胜过的(本领) stock-in-trade; one's trademark or skill:～戏 reserved play of a troupe or actor|～的武艺 one's trademark martial-arts skill

【看家狗】kānjiāgǒu 看守门户的狗,旧时常用来指官僚、地主等家里的管家一类的人 watchdog; guard dog; also referring to custodian in the service of an aristocrat, landlord, etc.

【看家戏】kānjiāxì 某个演员或剧团特别擅长的戏剧 actor or troupe's trademark play or opera

【看青】kān//qīng 看守正在结实还未成熟的庄稼,以防偷盗或动物损害 keep an eye on ripening crops (against theft or animal damage)

【看守】kānshǒu ❶ 负责守卫、照料 watch; look after:～山林 guard a forest|～门户 look after an estate (esp. in the owner's absence) ❷ 监视和管理(犯人) watch over prisoners ❸ 称监狱里看守犯人的人 jailer; warder

【看守内阁】kānshǒu nèigé 指某些国家议会通过对内阁不信任案后,在新内阁组成前,继续留任,处理日常工作的原内阁,或另外组成的临时内阁 caretaker cabinet; government cabinet which, after being voted non-confident by parliament, is retained or replaced by a newly formed temporary cabinet to run the government's routine work pending the formation of a new cabinet; also 看守政府 kānshǒu zhèngfǔ, 过渡内阁 guòdù nèigé or 过渡政府 guòdù zhèngfǔ

【看守所】kānshǒusuǒ 临时拘押未决犯的机关 detention house; lockup for suspects awaiting trial

【看押】kānyā 临时拘押 take into custody; detain:～俘虏 detain prisoners-of-war|把那个犯罪分子～起来。Take the criminal into custody.

勘 kān ❶ 校订;核对 proofread; collate:～误 correct errors in a printed work|校～collate ❷ 实地查看;探测 go fact-finding (to a place); survey:～探 prospect|～查 inspect; reconnoitre|～验 examine; inspect

【勘测】kāncè 勘察和测量 survey:～地形 topographical survey

【勘察】kānchá 进行实地调查或查看(多用于采矿或工程施工前 usu. for engineering or other purposes) reconnoitre; geological prospecting:～现场 on-the-spot survey|～地形 topographical survey; also 勘查 kānchá

【勘探】kāntàn 查明矿藏分布情况,测定矿体的位置、形状、大小、成矿规律、岩石性质、地质构造等情况 explore; prospect a region for mineral resources by verifying its geographical distribution, geological position, shape, size and metallogenetic pattern, as well as the local rock formation and geological structure

【勘误】kānwù 作者或编者更正书刊中文字上的错误 correct errors in a newly printed book or periodical:～表 errata; corrigenda

【勘正】kānzhèng 校正(文字) proofread

龛(龕) kān 供奉神佛的小阁子 niche; shrine:佛～niche enshrined with a Buddhist statue or figurine

【龛影】kānyǐng 用钡餐在X射线下检查胃或肠的溃疡时,溃疡部位被钡剂填充在荧光屏或X光照片上形成的阴影 niche; (of a barium-meal X-ray examination) location or image of a stomach or intestine ulcer projected on-screen or shown in a photograph

堪 kān ❶ 可;能 may; can:～当重任 be capable of shouldering important tasks; can hold a post of great responsibility|不～设想 unimaginable ❷ 能忍受 bearable:难～unbearable|狼狈不～in sore strait; thoroughly crestfallen|不～一击 cannot sustain a single blow

【堪布】kānbù ❶ 掌管戒律的喇嘛 kanpu; lama in charge of discipline in a lamasery ❷ 喇嘛寺的主持人 abbot of a lamasery ❸ 原西藏地方政府的僧官名 kanpu, theocratic title of the former local government of Tibet

【堪达罕】kāndáhǎn 〈方 *dial.*〉驼鹿 elk (*Alces alces*); moose [蒙 Mongolian]

【堪舆】kānyú 〈书 *fml.*〉风水 geomancy; *fengshui*

戡 kān 用武力平定(叛乱) put down; suppress:～乱 crack down on a riot|～平叛乱 put down on an insurrection

【戡乱】kānluàn 平定叛乱 suppress a rebellion

kǎn (ㄎㄢˇ)

坎[1] (❸埳) kǎn ❶ 八卦之一,卦形是'☵',代表水 one of the Eight Trigrams in the shape of '☵' that represents water; ☞八卦 bāguà on p.22 ❷ (～儿 kǎnr) 田野中自然形成的或人工修筑的像台阶形状的东西 bank; ridge:土～儿 earthen bank|田～儿 elevated path on the edge of a patch of farmland ❸〈书 *fml.*〉低洼的地方;坑 pit; pothole

坎[2] kǎn 坎德拉的简称 abbr. for 坎德拉 kǎndélā

【坎德拉】kǎndélā 发光强度单位,一个光源发出频率为540×10¹²赫兹的单色辐射,并且在这个方向上的辐射强度为1/683瓦特每球面度时的发光强度就是一坎德拉。candela; unit of luminous measurement, the luminous intensity in a given direction of a source that emits monochromatic radiation of frequency 540×10^{12} hertz and that has a radiant intensity in that direction of (1/683) watt per steradian; 简称 abbr. 坎 kǎn

【坎肩】kǎnjiān (～儿 kǎnjiānr)不带袖子的上衣(多指夹的,棉的,毛线织的)(cotton or woollen, usu. padded or lined) sleeveless jacket

【坎坷】kǎnkě ❶ 道路、土地坑坑洼洼 bumpy:～不平 rough and bumpy ❷〈书 *fml.*〉〈比喻 *fig.*〉不得志 full of frustrations:半世～life of trepidations and dashed hopes

【坎壈】kǎnlǎn〈书 *fml.*〉困顿;不得志 in straitened circumstances:一生～a life full of frustations

【坎炁】kǎnqì 中药上指脐带 (Chin. med.) umbilical cord

【坎儿】[1] kǎnr 指最紧要的地方或时机;当口儿 critical juncture:这话说到～上了。This remark has hit the nail on its head.|事情正处在～上。Things are coming to a head.

【坎儿】[2] kǎnr same as 侃儿 kǎnr

【坎儿井】kǎnrjǐng 新疆一带的一种灌溉工程,从山坡上直到田地里挖成一连串的井,再把井底挖通,连成暗沟,把山上溶化的雪水和地下水引来浇灌田地 karez; irrigation system in Xinjiang, consisting of wells arrayed from mountain slopes to the fields, with their bottoms connected by underground channels to divert mountain runoffs and subterranean water for irrigation

【坎土曼】kǎntǔmàn 维吾尔族用于锄地、挖土等的农具,用铁制成 a kind of iron mattock used by the Uygur people as a hoeing and digging tool

【坎子】kǎn·zi 地面高起的地方 raised ground; rise:土～mound

侃[1] kǎn〈书 *fml.*〉❶ 刚直 upright and outspoken ❷ 和乐的样子 amiable; pleasant

侃[2] kǎn〈方 *dial.*〉闲谈;闲扯 chat idly:两人～到深夜。The two of them chatted deep into the night.

【侃大山】kǎn dàshān〈方 *dial.*〉漫无边际地聊天;闲聊 shoot the bull; also 砍大山 kǎn dàshān

【侃侃】kǎnkǎn〈书 *fml.*〉形容说话理直气壮,从容不迫 with assurance and composure:～而谈 speak with great ease and confidence

【侃儿】kǎnr 〈方 *dial.*〉隐语；暗语 code word; enigmatic language：调（diào）～ exchange in enigmatic language; speak code words｜这是他们那一行的～。This is the jargon of their trade. same as 坎儿 kǎnr

砍 kǎn ❶ 用刀斧猛力把东西断开 slash; hack; chop：～柴 cut firewood｜把树枝～下来 cut or lop off a branch ❷ 削减；取消 cut; reduce：～价 bargain｜从计划中～去一些项目 delete some projects from the plan ❸〈方 *dial.*〉把东西扔出去打 throw sth. at：拿砖头～狗 throw a brick at a dog ❹ same as 侃² kǎn

【砍大山】kǎn dàshān same as 侃大山 kǎn dàshān

【砍刀】kǎndāo 砍柴用的刀，刀身较长，刀背较厚，有木柄 chopper; long knife with a thick back and wooden handle, for use in chopping firewood

【砍伐】kǎnfá 用锯、斧等把树木的枝干弄下来或把树木弄倒 fell trees; lumber

【砍头疮】kǎntóuchuāng 通常指生在脖子后部的痈 malignant boil or carbuncle on the neck; also 砍头痈 kǎntóuyōng

莰 kǎn 有机化合物，是蒈的同分异构体，白色结晶，有樟脑的香味，容易挥发，化学性质不活泼 camphane; bornane; volatile white crystalline organic compound that is the isomer of carane, with the aromatic smell of camphor and inactive chemical property

欿 kǎn 〈书 *fml.*〉❶ 不自满 not complacent：～然（不自满的样子）look modest ❷ 忧愁；不得意 dejected, pensive; in low spirit

槛（檻） kǎn 门槛；门限 threshold; doorsill ☞ jiàn on p. 957

顑 kǎn [顑颔]（kǎnhàn）〈书 *fml.*〉形容饥饿 famished

轗 kǎn [轗轲]（kǎnkě）〈书 *fml.*〉same as 坎坷 kǎnkě

kàn（ㄎㄢˋ）

看 kàn ❶ 使视线接触人或物 see; watch; look at：～书 reading｜～电影 see a film; go to the cinema ❷ 观察并加以判断 consider; judge：我～他是个可靠的人。In my opinion he is a reliable person.｜你～这个办法好不好？What do you think of this method? ❸ 访问 pay a visit; call on：～望 drop in on sb.｜～朋友 call on a friend ❹ 对待 treat; regard：～待 look upon｜另眼相～ look at sb. with new eyes; change one's attitude towards sb. ❺ 诊治（of a doctor）treat：王大夫把我的病～好了。Doctor Wang cured my disease. ❻ 照料 look after：照～ take care of｜衣帽自～ look after your own clothes ❼ 用在表示动作或变化的词或词组前面，表示预见到某种变化趋势，或者提醒对方注意可能发生或将要发生的某种不好的事情或情况[follow a verb or verbal phrase to indicate sth. that is going to happen, or as a warning] look out; be careful：别跑！～摔着！Don't run, or you'll fall to the ground.｜～饭快凉了，快吃吧。Look, the food's getting cold! Hurry up and eat it. ❽ 用在动词或动词结构后面，表示试一试（前面的动词常用重叠式）[follow a verb or verbal clause to indicate a pending action, with the preceding verb oft. in reiterative locution] try and see：想想～。Think it over.｜找找～。Let's try to find it.｜等一等～。Let's wait and see.｜评评理～ have it out｜先做几天～。Let's do it for a few days and see what'll happen.

☞ kān on p. 1079

【看病】kàn//bìng ❶（医生）给人治病（of a doctor）see a patient：王大夫不在家，他给人～去了。Doctor Wang is not at home. He's gone out to see a patient. ❷ 找医生治病；就诊（of a patient）see a doctor：我下午到医院～去。I'll go and see the doctor in the afternoon.

【看不起】kàn·bu qǐ 轻视 look down on; scorn; despise：别～这本小字典，它真能帮助我们解决问题。Don't look down on this little dictionary. It really solves our problems.

【看茶】kànchá 〈旧时 *old*〉吩咐仆人端茶招待客人的用语（adressing a servant）'Bring a cup of tea to my guest!'

【看承】kànchéng 〈书 *fml.*〉看顾照料 look after; attend to

【看穿】kàn//chuān 看透 see through：～了对方的心计 see through sb.'s mind

【看待】kàndài 对待 look on or upon; regard; treat：把他当亲兄弟～。Treat him as a brother.

【看得起】kàn·de qǐ 重视 have a good opinion of; think highly of：你要是～我，就给我这个面子。Give me an opportunity if you trust me.

【看跌】kàndiē（市场上股票、商品价格）有下跌的趋势（of share value, market prices）be expected to fall

【看法】kàn·fǎ 对客观事物所抱的见解 point of view; way of looking at things：谈两点～。Let me give you two opinions.｜两人～一致。The two of them are of the same opinion.

【看风色】kàn fēngsè 〈比喻 *fig.*〉观望情势 see which way the wind blows; see how things stand：～行事 try to find out how the wind blows before taking acton; also 看风头 kàn fēng·tou and 看风向 kàn fēngxiàng

【看风使舵】kàn fēng shǐ duò 〈比喻 *fig.*〉跟着情势转变方向（贬义 derog.）sail with the wind; see how the cat jumps; take one's cue from changing conditions; also 见风转舵 jiàn fēng zhuǎn duò

【看顾】kàngù 照应;照顾 take care of; look after:这位护士～病人很周到。The nurse is very attentive to her patients.

【看好】kànhǎo ❶(事物)将要出现好的势头 (sth.) turn for the better; look promising:旅游市场的前景～。The future of the tourist market looks promising.|经济前途～。The economy is expected to pick up. ❷认为某人或某事物将在竞争或竞赛中占上风 expect sb. to win:这场比赛,人们～火车头队。Before the match, most people expected the Locomotives to win.

【看见】kàn//·jiàn 看到 catch sight of; see:看得见 get a view of sth.|看不见 unable to see anything|从来没～过这样的怪事。Never have (I) seen anything so weird.

【看开】kàn//kāi 不把不如意的事情放在心上 do not take sth. undesirable to heart:看得开 sustain sth. bad with composure|看不开 take sth. too much to heart|对这件事,你要～些,不要过分生气。Don't get too upset because there was little you could do about what happened.

【看客】kànkè〈方 *dial.*〉观众 spectator; viewer; audience

【看破】kàn//pò 看透 see through:～红尘 see through the vanity of the world; disillusioned

【看破红尘】kàn pò hóngchén 看穿人世间的一切,指对生活不再有所追求 be disillusioned with the mundane world

【看齐】kànqí ❶整队时,以指定人为标准排齐站在一条线上 dress the ranks; bring a group of people into line ❷拿某人或某种人作为学习的榜样 emulate:向先进工作者～。Emulate the advanced workers.

【看轻】kànqīng 轻视 belittle; look down on:不要～环保工作。Don't look down upon environmental protection work.

【看上】kàn//·shàng 看中 take a liking to; take to:看不上 look down upon|看得上 take a fancy to sb. or sth.|她～了这件上衣。She settled on this coat.

【看台】kàntái 建筑在场地旁边或周围,供观众看表演的台(多指运动场上的观众席) bench seats; stands; rows of seats beside or surrounding a stadium, gymnasium, etc. for spectators to sit or stand on

【看透】kàn//tòu ❶透彻地了解(对手的计策、用意等) (of sb.'s trick, intention, etc.) gain an insight into:这一着棋我看不透。I don't quite understand this move. ❷透彻地认识(对方的缺点或事物的没有价值、没有意义) see through (sb.'s shortcoming or sth.'s lack of value or meaning):这个人我～了,没有什么真才实学。I've seen through him; He's not a man of real learning.

【看望】kàn·wàng 到长辈或亲友处问候起居情况 visit; see; drop in on:～父母 see one's parents|～老战友 call on an old comrade-in-arms

【看相】kàn//xiàng 观察人的相貌、骨骼或手掌的纹路等来判断命运好坏(迷信)(superstition) tell sb.'s fortune by reading his or her face, palm lines, etc.

【看笑话】kàn xiào·hua 拿别人不体面的事当做笑料 amuse oneself by watching sb.; make a fool of himself or herself; watch the fun; have a good laugh at:大家都在看他的笑话。Everybody waited to have a good laugh at him.|这件事情,我们要特别小心,不要给人家～。We've got to be very careful on this matter, not to make a laughing stock of ourselves.

【看涨】kànzhǎng (市场上股票、商品价格)有上涨的趋势(of share value and market prices) be expected to rise:黄金继续～。Gold price continued to go up.|股票～。The stock market looks bullish.

【看中】kàn//zhòng 经过观察,感觉合意 take a fancy to; settle on:看得中 take a liking to|看不中 be unimpressed by what one sees|你～哪个就买哪个。Just buy whatever you like.

【看重】kànzhòng 很看得起;看得很重要 regard as important; value; set store by:～知识 set great store by knowledge|青年大都热情有为,我们要～他们。Most of the young people are in good spirits and promising. We should pay due respect to them.

【看座】kàn//zuò〈旧时 *old*〉吩咐仆人或跑堂的等给客人安排座位的用语(addressing a servant, waiter, etc.) 'Find a seat for the guest!'

【看做】kànzuò 当做 look upon as; regard as:不要把人家的忍让～软弱可欺。Don't take their forbearance for weakness and try to bully them.

衎 kàn〈书 *fml.*〉❶快乐 jovial ❷刚直 upright

埳 kàn 赤埳(Chìkàn),地名,在台湾省 Chikan, name of a place in Taiwan Province

嵌 kàn 赤嵌(Chìkàn),地名,在台湾省 Chikan, name of a place in Taiwan Province
☞ qiàn on p.1541

墈 kàn〈方 *dial.*〉高的堤岸。多用于地名,如墈上(在江西)。kan, meaning 'high dyke', oft. used in a place name, such as Kanshang in Jiangxi Province

阚 Kàn 姓 a surname
☞ 嘣 hǎn on p.765

磡 kàn〈方 *dial.*〉山崖。多用于地名,如王磡头、槐花磡(都在浙江)。kan, meaning 'bluff', oft. used in a place name, such as

Wangkantou and Huaihuakan of Zhejiang Province

瞰(❷瞷) kàn ❶ 从高处往下看;俯视 look down from a height; overlook:鸟～a bird's-eye view ❷〈书 *fml.*〉窥;视 peep at; steal a look at

kāng(ㄎㄤ)

闶 kāng [闶阆](kāngláng)〈方 *dial.*〉建筑物中空廓的部分 open space in a building:这井下面的～这么大啊! How spacious it is at the bottom of the well! also 闶阆子 kānglángˑzi

☞ kàng on p.1085

康[1] kāng ❶ 健康;安康 healthy:～宁 safe and sound|～乐 congenial peace|～强 robust ❷〈书 *fml.*〉富足;丰盛 affluent; abundant:～年(丰年)good year|小～well-off ❸(Kāng)姓 a surname

康[2] kāng〈书 *fml.*〉same as 糠 kāng

【康拜因】kāngbàiyīn 联合机。特指联合收割机。combine; harvester

【康采恩】kāngcǎi'ēn 资本主义垄断组织的形式之一。它由不同经济部门的许多企业,包括工业企业、贸易公司、银行、运输公司和保险公司等联合组成。目的在于垄断销售市场、争夺原料产地和投资场所,以攫取高额利润。它操纵经济命脉,控制国家机器,决定国家的对内对外政策。concern; form of capitalist monopoly composed of industrial enterprises, trading companies, banks, shipping companies, insurance companies, etc. for the purpose of monopolizing the market, scrambling for raw-material supplying areas and sites of investment, and seize high profits. A concern also manipulates key branches of a national economy, controls the state apparatus, and decides domestic and foreign state policies. [德 German: Konzern]

【康复】kāngfù 恢复健康 recuperate:病体～ recover from an illness

【康健】kāngjiàn same as 健康 jiànkāng ①:身体～ enjoy good health

【康乐】kānglè 安乐 happy and peaceful

【康乐球】kānglèqiú 一种游艺项目,在周围高起、四角有圆洞的盘上摆好些像棋子形状的球,玩时按一定规则用杆子把自己的球先全部撞进圆洞者为胜 caroms; game played on a table by striking chess-like balls with a rod into the pockets in the table's four corners; The player who is the first to strike all his or her balls into the pockets wins. also 克郎球 kèlángqiú and 克郎棋 kèlángqí

【康宁】kāngníng〈书 *fml.*〉健康安宁 healthy and carefree

【康平纳】kāngpíngnà 指资本主义制度下生产集中和企业联合的一种形式,它是生产社会化向高级阶段发展的产物。也译作联合制。combine; form born of concentration of production and cooperation between enterprises under the capitalist system; also transliteration of 联合制 liánhézhì [拉丁 Latin: combinatus]

【康衢】kāngqú〈书 *fml.*〉宽阔平坦的大路 thoroughfare

【康泰】kāngtài〈书 *fml.*〉健康;平安 healthy and well:全家～。Wish you and your family peace and good health.|身体～ hale and hearty

【康熙】Kāngxī 清圣祖(爱新觉罗玄烨)年号(公元 1662—1722) Kangxi, title of the 1662-1722 reign of Aisin-Gioro Xuanye, or Emperor Shengzu of the Qing Dynasty

【康庄大道】kāngzhuāng-dàdào 宽阔平坦的大路 broad road; main road;〈比喻 *fig.*〉光明美好的前途 bright and good future

慷(忼) kāng ☞ below

【慷慨】kāngkǎi ❶ 充满正气,情绪激昂 full of enthusiasm and fervour:～陈词 present one's views with deep feeling and enthusiasm ❷ 不吝惜 unstinting; generous:～无私的援助 generous aid|～解囊(毫不吝啬地拿出钱来帮助别人) loosen one's purse strings generously; help sb. generously with money

【慷慨激昂】kāngkǎi jī'áng 形容情绪、语调激动昂扬而充满正气 impassioned; vehement and with deep feeling; also 激昂慷慨 jī'áng kāngkǎi

【慷他人之慨】kāng tārén zhī kǎi 指拿别人的财物来做人情或挥霍 rob Peter to pay Paul; be generous at the expense of sb. else

槺 kāng ☞ 榔槺 lángˑkāng on p.1151

糠(穅) kāng ❶ 稻、谷子等作物子实的皮或壳(多指脱下来的) chaff; bran; husk:米～rice husk|～菜半年粮(形容生活贫困) spend six months a year eating nothing but chaff and grass; on the verge of starvation ❷ 发空,质地变得松而不实(多指萝卜因失掉水分而中空 usu. of a radish) spongy:～心儿 spongy in the middle|萝卜～了。This radish has gone.

【糠秕】kāngbǐ 秕糠 chaff; worthless stuff

鱇 kāng ☞ [鮟鱇](ānkāng) on p.12

káng(ㄎㄤˊ)

扛 káng 用肩膀承担物体 carry sth. on the shoulder; shoulder:～枪 shoulder a gun; bear arms|～着锄头 carry a hoe on one's shoulder ◇这个任务你一定要～起来。You've got to shoulder this task.

☞ gāng on p. 635

【扛长工】káng chánggōng 做长工；扛活 work as a farmhand; be a long-term hired hand; also 扛长活 káng chánghuó

【扛大个儿】káng dàgèr〈方 *dial.*〉指在码头、车站上用体力搬运重东西 work as a stevedore at a dock or railway station：～的 porter; bearer

【扛活】káng//huó 指给地主或富农当长工 make a living as a farmhand for a landlord or rich peasant

kàng（ㄎㄤˋ）

亢 kàng ❶ 高 high：高～ resounding; booming ❷ 高傲 haughty：不～不卑 neither servile nor overbearing; neither humble nor pert ❸ 过度；极；很 excessive; extreme：～旱 severe drought｜～奋 feverish ❹ 二十八宿之一 Kang, one of the 28 constellations（二十八宿）into which the celestial sphere was divided in ancient Chinese astronomy（consisting of four stars in the shape of a bent bow in Virgo）❺（Kàng）姓 a surname

☞ háng on p. 769

【亢奋】kàngfèn 极度兴奋 extremely excited; overwrought：精神～ run an adrenaline high; in agitation

【亢旱】kànghàn 长久不下雨，干旱情形严重；大旱 prolonged dry spell; severe drought

【亢进】kàngjìn 生理机能超过正常的情况。如胃肠蠕动亢进、甲状腺机能亢进等。hyperfunction, such as hyperenterocinesia, hyperthyroidism, etc.

伉 kàng ❶〈书 *fml.*〉对等；相称（指配偶）（of a spousal relationship）good match; match; fit：～俪 husband and wife ❷〈书 *fml.*〉高大 high; mighty ❸（Kàng）姓 a surname

【伉俪】kànglì〈书 *fml.*〉夫妻 married couple; husband and wife：～之情 connubial affection

抗 kàng ❶ 抵抗；抵挡 resist; combat; fight：顽～ put up a stubborn fight｜～灾 fight against a disaster｜～日战争 War of Resistance against Japan｜皮袍子旧点没关系，只要能挡风～冻就行。It doesn't matter how worn-out the fur coat has become, so long as it can protect me from wind and cold. ❷ 拒绝；抗拒 refuse; defy：～命 disobey｜～租 refuse to pay rent ❸ 对等 contend with; be a match for：～衡 rival; contend with｜分庭～礼 treat sb. defiantly; stand up to sb. defiantly; treat each other on an equal footing

【抗暴】kàngbào 抵抗和反击暴力的压迫 fight against brutal suppression：～斗争 struggle against violent repression

【抗辩】kàngbiàn 不接受责难而作辩护 counterplea; demurrer

【抗丁】kàng//dīng〈旧时 *old*〉民众抗拒统治者抓壮丁（of the people）rise against government conscription

【抗毒素】kàngdúsù 外毒素侵入后，机体内所产生的能中和外毒素的物质 antitoxin; substance formed in the body that counteracts a specific toxin

【抗旱】kàng//hàn 在天旱时，采取水利措施，使农作物不受损害 combat a drought：积极～ take active anti-drought measures

【抗衡】kànghéng 对抗，不相上下 contend with; match：对方实力强大，无法与之～。The opponent is too powerful to be challenged.

【抗洪】kàng//hóng 发生洪水时，采取措施避免造成严重灾害 fight or combat a flood：～救灾 combat a flood and relieve the victims

【抗婚】kànghūn 抗拒包办的婚姻 refuse to accept a marriage arranged by one's parents

【抗击】kàngjī 抵抗并且反击 fight back：～敌人 resist enemy troops

【抗拒】kàngjù 抵抗和拒绝 resist; defy：奋力～ do all one can to resist｜～命令 disobey an order

【抗捐】kàng//juān 拒绝交纳捐税 refuse to pay a levy or tax

【抗菌素】kàngjūnsù 抗生素的旧称 old term for 抗生素 kàngshēngsù

【抗涝】kàng//lào 在雨水过多时，采取措施，使农作物不受或少受损害 take measures to protect farm crops from water-logging or reduce the loss incurred by excessive rain：做好防汛～工作 make good preparations against flooding and water-logging

【抗粮】kàng//liáng 拒绝交纳粮食 resist grain levy

【抗命】kàngmìng 拒绝接受命令；违抗命令 defy orders; disobey

【抗日战争】Kàng Rì Zhànzhēng 中国人民抗击日本帝国主义侵略的民族解放战争，从 1937 年 7 月 7 日日寇向我国北平（今北京）西南卢沟桥驻防的军队进攻起，到 1945 年 8 月 15 日日本无条件投降止 War of Resistance against Japan（1937-1945）; national war of liberation waged by the Chinese people against Japanese imperialist invaders from July 7, 1937, the day the Japanese enemy launched a surprise attack on the Chinese army at Lugouqiao（Marco Polo Bridge）in southwest Beijing, to August 15, 1945, when Japan declared unconditional surrender

【抗生素】kàngshēngsù 某些微生物或动植物所产生的能抑制另一些微生物的生长繁殖的化学物质。种类很多，常用的有青霉素、链霉素、金霉素、氯霉素等，多用来治疗人或家畜的传染病。也用作催肥剂、消毒剂、杀虫剂等。antibiotic; substance produced by micro-organisms or made synthetically that can inhibit or destroy susceptible micro-organisms. Among the common antibiotics are penicillin, streptomycin, aureomycin and chloromycetin, which are used to treat contagious diseases in humans and animals. Antibiotics are also used as fattening agents, disinfectants and insecticides. 旧称 old name 抗菌素 kàngjūnsù

【抗属】kàngshǔ 指抗日战争时期,在中国共产党领导下坚持抗日的军政人员的家属 family dependent of military and civilian personnel who persisted in the War of Resistance against Japan (1937-1945) under the leadership of the Communist Party of China

【抗税】kàng//shuì 拒绝履行纳税义务 refuse to pay taxes

【抗诉】kàngsù 检察院对法院的判决或裁定提出重新审理的诉讼要求 counter-appeal; appeal against a court ruling or arbitration

【抗体】kàngtǐ 人或动物的血清中,由于病菌或病毒的侵入而产生的具有抵抗或杀死病毒、病菌作用的蛋白性物质。抗体只能跟相应的抗原起作用,如伤寒患者体内所产生的抗体只能对伤寒杆菌起作用。antibody; any of a class of proteins (immunoglobulins) produced in human or animal serum to counteract or kill a virus. However, an antibody can only act against a relevant antigen; for example, the antibody produced in the body of a typhoid patient can only respond to typhoid bacillus.

【抗议】kàngyì 对某人、某团体、某国家的言论、行为、措施等表示强烈的反对 protest; lodge a protest against (the statement, behaviour, measure, etc. of a person, organization or country)

【抗御】kàngyù 抵抗和防御 resist and guard against: ~外侮 resist foreign aggression | ~灾害 cope with natural adversities

【抗原】kàngyuán 进入人或动物体的血液中能使血清产生抗体并与抗体发生化学反应的有机物质。一定种类的抗原只能促使血清中产生相应的抗体。antigen; foreign organic substance (e.g. a toxin) which induces and chemically reacts to an antibody in the serum of a human or animal body. A certain antigen can only produce a relevant antibody in the serum.

【抗灾】kàng//zāi 灾害发生时,采取措施,减轻灾害造成的损失 fight natural calamities; take measures to minimize the losses incurred by a disaster

【抗战】kàngzhàn 抵抗外国侵略的战争,在我国特指1937—1945年反抗日本帝国主义侵略的战争 war of resistance against foreign aggression. In China this refers to the 1937-1945 War of Resistance against Japan.

【抗震】kàngzhèn ❶(建筑物、机器、仪表等)具有承受震动的性能(of a building, machine, meter and apparatus, etc.) anti-seismic capability ❷ 对破坏性地震采取防御措施,尽量减轻生命财产的损失 take precautions against an earthquake; fight an earthquake

【抗争】kàngzhēng 对抗;斗争 take a stand against; resist: 据理~retort with reasoning; try to convince sb. by reasoning

囥 kàng〈方 *dial.*〉藏 hide

阆 kàng〈书 *fml.*〉高大 tall and big
☞ kāng on p. 1083

炕 kàng ❶ 北方人用土坯或砖砌成的睡觉用的长方台,上面铺席,下面有孔道,跟烟囱相通,可以烧火取暖 *kang*; heatable bed; oblong platform built of adobe or brick and covered with a mat, with a fire raised underneath for heating purposes and with the smoke thus produced discharged from a narrow passage to a chimney ❷〈方 *dial.*〉烤 bake or dry by the heat of a fire: 白薯还在炉子边上~着呢。The sweet potatoes are still baking on the stove. | 把湿褥子在热炕头上~一~。Dry the wet padded mattress on the heated *kang*.

【炕梢】kàngshāo (~儿 kàngshāor) 炕离灶远的一头 further end of a *kang* from the stove

【炕头】kàngtóu (~儿 kàngtóur) 炕靠近灶的一头 warmer end of a *kang*: 热~ warmly heated *kang*

【炕席】kàngxí 铺炕的席 *kang* mat

【炕桌儿】kàngzhuōr 放在炕上使用的矮小桌子 small, short-legged table for use on a *kang*; *kang* table

钪 kàng 金属元素,符号 Sc (scandium)。是一种稀土金属。银白色,质软,用来制特种玻璃、轻质耐高温合金。scandium (Sc); rare soft silver-white metal element existing naturally in rare earth, ideal for the making of glass and light heat-resistant alloys

kāo (丂幺)

尻 kāo 古书上指屁股(in ancient books) buttocks; bottom

【尻子】kāo·zi〈方 *dial.*〉屁股 hips

kǎo (丂幺ˇ)

考[1](攷) kǎo ❶ 提出难解的问题让对方回答 give a test or quiz: ~问 question; examine orally | ~~妈妈。Let me ask Mum a question. | 他被我~住了。He was baffled by my question. ❷ 考试 exam: 期~ term exam | 他~上大学了。He has passed the college entrance exams. ❸ 检查 check; inspect: ~察 inspect; make a fact-finding inspection tour | ~勤 check on work attendance ❹ 推求;研究 infer; study: 思~ponder; deliberate | ~古 archaeology

考[2] kǎo〈书 *fml.*〉(死去的)父亲 one's deceased father: 先~my deceased father | ~妣 deceased parents

【考妣】kǎobǐ 〈书 *fml.*〉(死去的)父亲和母亲 one's deceased parents:如丧～(像死了父母一般) as if one's parents had died; pathetic anxiety

【考查】kǎochá 用一定的标准来检查衡量(行为、活动) examine; check (against a certain standard and activity):～学生的学业成绩 check students' academic performance

【考察】kǎochá ❶ 实地观察调查 inspect; make an on-the-spot investigation:他们到各地～水利工程。They went on a fact-finding tour of water conservancy projects in various places. ❷ 细致深刻地观察 observe and study:进行科学研究工作,必须勤于～和思索,才能有成就。Only by diligent study and deliberation can you amount to something in scientific research.

【考场】kǎochǎng 举行考试的场所 exam hall or room

【考点】kǎodiǎn 举行考试的地点 venue of an exam:这次考试全市共设二十多个～,三百个考场。The city has designated 300 exam rooms at 20-odd sites for this round of exams.

【考订】kǎodìng 考据订正 examine and correct; textual research

【考分】kǎofēn (～儿 kǎofēnr)考试后评定的分数 marks (in a test); points

【考古】kǎogǔ ❶ 根据古代的遗迹、遗物和文献研究古代历史 engage in archaeological studies ❷ 考古学 archaeology

【考古学】kǎogǔxué 根据发掘出来的或古代留传下来的遗物和遗迹来研究古代历史的科学 archaeology; study of ancient history through the excavation of sites and the analysis of physical remains and documents

【考官】kǎoguān 〈旧时 *old*〉政府举行考试时担任出题、监考、阅卷等工作的官员 examiner for imperial examinations whose task is to set exam papers, monitor the exam hall and judge the exam papers

【考核】kǎohé 考查审核 examine; check; assess (sb.'s proficiency):定期～ routine check|～干部 check on and assess work performance of government functionaries

【考绩】kǎojì 考查工作人员的成绩 assess the work of an employee

【考究】kǎo•jiu ❶ 查考;研究 examine closely; peruse:这问题很值得～。This problem is worth probing. ❷ same as 讲究 jiǎng•jiu ①:衣服只要穿着暖和就行,不必多去～。There is no need to be picky about what you wear so long as it can keep you warm. ❸ 精美 exquisite; fine:这本书的装潢很～。This book is tastefully designed.

【考据】kǎojù 考证 textual criticism; textual research

【考卷】kǎojuàn 考试的卷子 exam paper

【考量】kǎo•liáng 考虑;思量 deliberate; think over:这件事我已经～过了,就照你的意思办吧。I have thought it over and decided to follow your idea.

【考虑】kǎolǜ 思索问题,以便做出决定 think over; consider:这个问题让我～一下再答复你。Let me think it over before giving you an answer.|你做这件事,有点儿欠～。It was kind of careless of you to do this.

【考评】kǎopíng 考核评议 assess and evaluate:通过～决定干部的聘任 appoint a functionary after an evaluation of his or her credentials|主管部门要定期对企业进行～。The leading authorities are required to assess and evaluate the enterprises at regular intervals.

【考期】kǎoqī 考试的日期 date of an exam

【考勤】kǎoqín 考查工作或学习的出勤情况 check on work attendance:～簿 attendance record

【考区】kǎoqū 统考中分区考试时设置考场的地区 subdivision of a regional or national exam

【考取】kǎo//qǔ 投考被录取 pass an entrance exam; enroll in a school or college after passing an entrance exam:他～了师范大学。He was admitted to a normal university.

【考生】kǎoshēng 报名参加入学考试的学生 examinee; candidate for a school or college entrance examination

【考试】kǎoshì 通过书面或口头提问的方式,考查知识或技能 exam; test; testing of proficiency or knowledge of candidates for a qualification by written or oral questions

【考释】kǎoshì 考证并解释古文字 philological studies of ancient texts; textual research

【考题】kǎotí 考试的题目 exam questions; exam paper

【考问】kǎowèn 为了难倒对方而问;考察询问 examine orally; question:我～～你。Let me see if you can answer my questions.|我被他～住了。I was baffled by his questioning.

【考验】kǎoyàn 通过具体事件、行动或困难环境来检验(是否坚定、忠诚或正确) test (to show sb.'s firmness of stand, loyalty or sense of judgment); trial:革命战争～了他。He stood the test of the revolutionary war.|我们的队伍是一支久经～的队伍。Ours is a long-steeled army.

【考语】kǎoyǔ 〈旧时 *old*〉指对公职人员的工作或其他方面的表现所做的评语 written appraisal of the work and other credentials of an official

【考证】kǎozhèng 研究文献或历史问题时,根据资料来考核、证实和说明 textual criticism; textual research

拷 kǎo 拷打 flog; beat; torture:～问 torture sb. during an interrogation

【拷贝】kǎobèi 用拍摄成的电影底片洗印出来供放映用的胶片 copy; also 正片 zhèngpiàn

K

【栲绸】kǎochóu 黑胶绸 rust-coloured summer silk; gambiered Guangdong silk
【拷打】kǎodǎ 打(指用刑)torture:严刑～subject sb. to severe torture
【栲纱】kǎoshā 香云纱 gambiered Guangdong gauze
【拷问】kǎowèn 拷打审问 torture sb. during interrogation; interrogate with torture

栲 kǎo 栲树,常绿乔木,叶子长圆状披针形,果实球形,表面有短刺。木材坚硬致密,可做船橹、轮轴等,树皮含鞣酸,可以制染料和栲胶。evergreen chinquapin (*Castanopsis*); evergreen tree with oval, lanceolate leaves, bearing ball-shaped nuts that are covered with short thorns. For its hard and compact texture, chinquapin wood makes an ideal material for the making of oars and wheel shafts, and its bark, which contains tannic acid, is a material for making dyeing stuff and tannin extract.

【栲栳】kǎolǎo 用柳条编成的容器,形状像斗 round-bottomed wicker basket in the shape of a dipper; also 筹筹 kǎolǎo or 笆斗 bādǒu

烤 kǎo ❶ 将物体挨近火使熟或干燥 bake; roast; toast:～肉 roast meat|～白薯 baked sweet potato|把湿衣裳～干 dry wet clothes by a fire ❷ 将身体挨近火或高温处取暖 warm oneself by a fire or other sources of heat:～火 keep oneself warm by a fire

【烤电】kǎo//diàn 用透热疗法治疗 diathermia; diathermy; production of heat in body tissues by electric currents for therapeutic purposes
【烤麸】kǎofū 食品,用面筋蒸熟制成 steamed gluten
【烤火】kǎo//huǒ 靠近火取暖 warm oneself by a fire:～费(发给职工用于冬天取暖用的钱) heating allowance; money issued to employees to cover winter house heating expenses
【烤蓝】kǎolán 发蓝 enamel; blue baking finish on a metal object
【烤箱】kǎoxiāng 用来烘烤食物等的箱形装置 oven; heated chamber or compartment for baking, roasting, heating, drying, etc.
【烤鸭】kǎoyā 挂在特制的炉子里烤熟的填鸭 roast duck; roasting force-fed ducks by hanging them over the fire in a specially designed wood-fuelled oven
【烤烟】kǎoyān 在特设的烤房中烤干的烟叶,颜色黄,弹性较大,是香烟的主要原料。也指制造烤烟的烟草。flue-cured tobacco; practice of curing tobacco leaves by smoking in special ovens so that they become more resilient and turn bright yellow before they are supplied as the major raw material for the making of cigarettes

筹 kǎo [筹筹](kǎolǎo) same as 栲栳 kǎolǎo

kào(丂幺)

铐 kào ❶ 手铐 handcuffs:镣～handcuffs and chains ❷ 给人戴上手铐 put handcuffs on sb.; handcuff sb.:把犯人～起来。Handcuff the criminal.

【铐子】kào·zi 〈方 *dial.*〉手铐 handcuffs

犒 kào 犒劳 reward:～赏 reward|～师 reward an army

【犒劳】kào·láo ❶ 用酒食等慰劳 reward with food and drink:～将士 feast the officers and men of an army ❷ 指慰劳的酒食等 rewarded food and drink:吃～(享受犒劳) enjoy rewarded food and drink
【犒赏】kàoshǎng 犒劳赏赐 reward a victorious army, etc. with bounties:～三军 feast and reward soldiers of three armed services

靠[1] kào ❶ (人)坐着或站着时,让身体一部分重量由别人或物体支持着;倚靠 lean against; lean on:～枕 back cushion|～垫 cushion|两人背～背坐着。The two of them leaned back to back against each other.|～着椅子打盹儿 lean against a chair for a nap ❷ (物体)凭借别的东西的支持立着或竖起来(of sth.) lean or stand against:扁担～在门背后。The shoulder pole stood behind the door.|你把梯子～在墙上。Lean the ladder against the wall, please. ❸ 接近;挨近 stand by the side of; get near; come up to:～拢 close in; draw near|船～岸。The ship was coming to anchor by the shore. ❹ 依靠 rely on; depend on:～劳动生活 make a living by doing physical labour.|学习全～自己的努力。(You)'ve got to rely on your own efforts in your studies. ❺ 信赖 trust:可～dependable; reliable|他很～得住。He is a trustworthy person.

靠[2] kào 戏曲中古代武将所穿的铠甲(in traditional opera) stage armour (made of silk, with embroidered back and front):扎～put on stage armour

【靠把】kàobǎ 戏曲表演作战时,演员穿铠甲开打的(in traditional opera) fight between armoured characters:～戏 military plays featuring warriors or ranking generals in full armour|～武生 *wusheng* actors wearing stage armour; also 靠背 kàobèi

【靠背】[1] kàobèi 椅子、沙发等供人背部倚靠的部分 back of a chair, sofa, etc.
【靠背】[2] kàobèi same as 靠把 kàobǎ
【靠边】kào//biān (～儿 kào//biānr) ❶ 靠近边缘;靠到旁边 keep to the side:行人～走。Pedestrians keep to the side of the road. ❷ 〈方 *dial.*〉〈比喻 *fig.*〉近乎情理;挨边 sound reasonable; sensible:这话说得还～儿。That sounds more like it.
【靠边儿站】kàobiānrzhàn 站到旁边去 step

aside;〈比喻 *fig.*〉离开职位或失去权力(多指被迫的 oft. forced to) step down from one's post

【靠不住】kào·bu zhù 不可靠;不能相信 unreliable; unbelievable:这话～。This story is unbelievable.

【靠得住】kào·de zhù 可靠;可以相信 credible; reliable:这个消息～吗? Is the information reliable?

【靠垫】kàodiàn 半躺着或坐着时靠在腰后的垫子,例如沙发靠垫 back cushion, such as those placed on a sofa

【靠耩】kàojiǎng 为了加宽播幅、适当密植,用耧在靠近耩过的地方再耩一次 extend sown acreage by re-ploughing the edges of a farm plot; also 靠耧 kàolóu

【靠近】kàojìn ❶ 彼此间的距离近 near; close to:两人坐得十分～。The two of them sat quite close together.|～沙发的墙角里有一个茶几。A coffee table lay near the sofa in the corner of the room. ❷ 向一定目标运动,使彼此间的距离缩小 draw near; move towards:轮船慢慢地～码头了。The ship is drawing near the dock.

【靠拢】kàolǒng 挨近;靠近 draw close; close up:大家～一点。Close up please, everybody.

【靠旗】kàoqí 戏曲中扎靠的武将背后插的三角形绣旗(in traditional Chinese opera) embroidered silk pennants strapped over a warrior's back

【靠山】kàoshān〈比喻 *fig.*〉可以依靠的有力量的人或集体 backing; clout

【靠手】kàoshǒu 椅子边上的扶手 armrest

【靠枕】kàozhěn 半躺半坐时靠在腰后的枕头 back cushion

【靠准】kào//zhǔn〈方 *dial.*〉(～儿 kào//zhǔnr) 可靠 reliable; credible:这个消息不～。This information is implausible.|他很～,有要紧的事可以交给他办。He is reliable. Come to him when there is something the matter.

熇(焅) kào 用微火使鱼、肉等菜的汤汁变浓或耗干 stew; cook fish, meat, etc. over a mild fire and make the soup simmer until it thickens or dries

K

kē (ㄎㄜ)

𠰢 kē [𠰢旮](kē·lā) same as 坷垃 kē·lā

坷 kē ☞ below
☞ kě on p.1095

【坷垃】kē·lā〈方 *dial.*〉土块 clod:土～ earth clod|打～break clods; also 坷拉 ké·lā

【坷拉】kē·lā same as 坷垃 kē·lā

苛 kē ❶ 苛刻;过于严厉 harsh; stringent; exacting:～求 demanding|对方提出的条件太～了。The terms the other party proposed are too harsh. ❷ 烦琐 over-elaborate:～礼(烦琐的礼节)tedious ritual|～捐杂税 exorbitant taxes and excessive levies

【苛察】kēchá〈书 *fml.*〉苛刻烦琐,显示精明 smart to a fault; hairsplitting

【苛待】kēdài 苛刻地对待 treat sb. harshly; hard upon:～下级 treat one's subordinates naggingly

【苛捐杂税】kējuān záshuì 指繁重的捐税 exorbitant taxes and excessive levies

【苛刻】kēkè (条件、要求等)过高,过于严厉;刻薄(of condition, requirement, etc.) harsh; severe; exacting:对方提出的条件～,使人难以接受。The terms they have advanced are too harsh to be acceptable.

【苛求】kēqiú 过严地要求 make excessive demands on sb.; be overcritical:不要～于人。Don't be too demanding when dealing with people.

【苛细】kēxì〈书 *fml.*〉苛刻烦琐 hairsplitting; exacting

【苛杂】kēzá 苛捐杂税 exorbitant taxes and excessive levies:免除～lift exorbitant levies

【苛责】kēzé 过严地责备 criticize severely; excoriate

【苛政】kēzhèng 指残酷压迫、剥削人民的政治 tyrannical government:～猛于虎。Tyranny is fiercer than a tiger.

匼 kē 古代的一种头巾 muffler in ancient times

【匼河】Kēhé 地名,在山西 Kehe, the name of a place in Shanxi Province

【匼匝】kēzā〈书 *fml.*〉周围环绕 encircle; skirt

呵 kē 呵叻(Kēlè),泰国地名 Nakhon Ratchasima, the name of a city in Thailand
☞ ā on p.2, á, ǎ and à on p.2; 啊·a on p.2 and hē on p.780

珂 kē〈书 *fml.*〉❶ 像玉的石头 jade-like stone ❷ 马笼头上的装饰 ornament on a horse's halter

【珂罗版】kēluóbǎn 印刷上用的一种照相版,把要复制的字、画的底片,晒制在涂过感光胶层的玻璃片上做成,多用于印制美术品 collotype; photomechanical process of printing from the negative of a work of calligraphy or painting reproduced on a glass plate coated with light-sensitive gelatin, a technique used mostly for the reproduction of a work of art; also 珂𤥭版 kēluóbǎn

【珂𤥭版】kēluóbǎn same as 珂罗版 kēluóbǎn

柯 kē ❶〈书 *fml.*〉草木的枝茎 stalk or branch; bough:枝～ foliage|交～错叶 leaves piling up on intertwined branches ❷〈书 *fml.*〉斧子的柄 axe-handle; helve:斧～ handle of an axe ❸ (Kē) 姓 a surname

【柯尔克孜族】Kē'ěrkèzīzú 我国少数民族之一,主要分布在新疆 Kirgiz (Khalkhas); Khalkhas; minority ethnic people inhabiting the Xinjiang Uygur Autonomous Region

轲 kē 用于人名,孟子,名轲,战国时人 Ke, a Chinese character that appears in a given name, Meng Ke (c. 372-c. 289 B.C.), a man of the Warring States Period, known in English as Mencius
☞ kě on p. 1095

科[1] kē ❶ 学术或业务的类别 branch of learning or vocational endeavour: ～目 item; curricular subject | 文～liberal arts; humanities | 理～sciences | 专～vocational study; specialty | 牙～dental department | 妇～ gynaecology ❷ 行政机构按工作性质分设的办事部门 subdivision of an administrative department; section; department: ～员 staff member | 秘书～secretarial office | 财务～accounting department ❸ 科举考试,也指科举考试的科目 imperial exam; subject of an imperial exam: ～场 site of an imperial exam | 登～pass the imperial civil exam; become a successful candidate in an imperial exam | 开～取士 hold an imperial examination to select civil officials ❹ 科班 regular school training; school of Chinese opera: 坐～ receive professional training in an opera school | 出～ graduate from an opera school ❺ 生物学上把同一目的生物按照彼此相似的特征再分为若干群,叫做科,如松柏目有松科、杉科、柏科等,鸡形目有雉科、松鸡科等。科以下为属。family; major division or subdivision of an order or suborder in the classification of plants and animals. The order of pines and cypresses, for instance, consists of such families as *Pinaceae*, *Taxodiaceae* and *Cupressaceae*; and the suborder *Galliformes* includes *Phasianidae* and *Tetraonidae*; a family consists of several genera

科[2] kē 〈书 *fml.*〉 ❶ 法律条文 clause; law: 金～玉律 infallible law; final say | 作奸犯～violate the law and commit crimes; run afoul of law ❷ 判定(刑罚) mete out (a penalty): ～刑 pass a sentence | ～罪 convict sb. and impose a punishment | ～以罚金 impose a fine

科[3] kē 古典戏曲剧本中,指示角色表演动作时的用语,如笑科、饮酒科等(of the scenario of a classical Chinese drama) direction to remind an actor of what to do next onstage, e.g., laughing, or drinking

【科白】kēbái 戏曲中角色的动作和道白(of classical Chinese theatre) what a character does and says on-stage

【科班】kēbān (～儿 kēbānr)〈旧时 *old*〉招收儿童,培养成为戏曲演员的教学组织。常用来比喻正规的教育或训练。opera school; (oft. fig.) regular school training: ～出身 be a professional by training

【科场】kēchǎng 科举时代举行考试的场所 imperial examination hall

【科处】kēchǔ 判决处罚 impose a punishment; pass a sentence: ～徒刑 sentence sb. to a term of imprisonment | 附加刑既可以单独使用,又可以与主刑合并～。An accessory penalty may be applied independently or combined with the principal penalty.

【科第】kēdì 科举制度考选官吏后备人员时,分科录取,每科按成绩排列等第,叫做科第 grade candidates in the imperial exams

【科幻】kēhuàn 科学幻想 science fiction: ～小说 science fiction

【科技】kējì 科学技术 science and technology: 高～hi-tech | ～资料 scientific and technological information | ～工作者 scientist and technicians

【科甲】kējiǎ 汉唐两代考选官吏后备人员分甲、乙等科,后来因称科举为科甲(of the Han and Tang dynasties) top grade in the imperial exams: ～出身(清代称考上进士、举人的人为科甲出身) used to be a successful candidate of the imperial exams; palace graduate; (of the Qing Dynasty) used to de a successful candidate in the highest imperial or provincial imperial exams

【科教】kējiào 科学教育 science and education: ～片 science education film | ～战线 science and education circles

【科教片儿】kējiàopiānr same as 科教片 kējiàopiàn

【科教片】kējiàopiàn 科学教育影片的简称 abbr. for 科学教育影片 kēxué jiàoyù yǐngpiàn

【科举】kējǔ 从隋唐到清代的封建王朝分科考选文武官吏后备人员的制度。唐代文科的科目很多,每年举行。明清两代文科只设进士一科,考八股文,武科考骑射、举重等武艺,每三年举行一次。imperial examination by which Chinese feudal dynasties from the Sui to the Qing selected candidates for civil and military posts. In the Tang Dynasty there were more civil categories than before in such exams, which were held on an annual basis. During the Ming and Qing dynasties, they were held once in three years. The civil examination featured writing, which involved the writing of an eight-episode essay, and was designed to select palace graduates. The military examination featured martial arts, including horsemanship, archery and weightlifting.

【科盲】kēmáng 指缺乏科学常识的成年人 science illiterate; grown-ups who know little about science

【科目】kēmù ❶ 按事物的性质划分的类别(多指关于学术或账目的) course; subject in a curriculum or accounting book ❷ 科举考试分科取士的名目 titles of successful candidates in imperial exams

【科普】kēpǔ 科学普及 popular science; science popularization:～读物 popular science books

【科室】kēshì 企业或机关中管理部门的各科、各室的总称 administrative or technical office:～人员 office staff; administrative personnel

【科学】kēxué ❶ 反映自然、社会、思维等的客观规律的分科的知识体系 science; branch of knowledge reflecting systematized observation of nature, society, or ways of thinking ❷ 合乎科学的 scientific:～种田 scientific farming|这种说法不～。This theory is unscientific.|革命精神和～态度相结合 combine revolutionary spirit with scientific attitude

【科学共产主义】kēxué gòngchǎn zhǔyì 马克思主义的三个组成部分之一,即科学社会主义 scientific communism or socialism, one of three component parts of Marxism

【科学家】kēxuéjiā 从事科学研究工作有一定成就的人 scientist; person who is well-accomplished in scientific research

【科学教育影片】kēxué jiàoyù yǐngpiàn 介绍科学知识的影片 popular science film; science and educational film; 简称 abbr. 科教片 kējiàopiàn

【科学社会主义】kēxué shèhuì zhǔyì 马克思主义的三个组成部分之一。是关于阶级斗争,特别是关于无产阶级革命和无产阶级专政的学说。它根据辩证唯物主义和历史唯物主义的理论,论证了社会主义的胜利和资本主义的灭亡是不以人们意志为转移的客观规律,并提出从资本主义到共产主义的整个过渡时期必须实行无产阶级专政,从而使社会主义从空想变成了科学。scientific socialism (one of three component parts of Marxism), the theory on class struggle, esp. the proletarian revolution and the proletarian dictatorship. On the basis of dialectical materialism and historical materialism, the theory of scientific socialism explains that the victory of socialism and the elimination of capitalism are an objective law independent of man's will, and that proletarian dictatorship should be instituted throughout the period of transition from capitalism to communism, thereby turning socialism from utopia to science. also 科学共产主义 kēxué gòngchǎn zhǔyì

【科学院】kēxuéyuàn 规模较大的从事科学研究的机关,有综合性质的和专门性质的两种 academy of sciences; large organization engaged in scientific research work either comprehensively or in a particular field

【科研】kēyán 科学研究 scientific research:～计划 research plan|推广～成果 popularize scientific research results

牁 kē 牂牁(Zāngkē),古代郡名,在今贵州境内 Zangke, name of an ancient prefecture in present-day Guizhou Province

砢 kē [砢碜](kē·chen)〈方 *dial.*〉寒碜 shabby; unpresentable

疴 kē (旧读 formerly pronounced ē)〈书 *fml.*〉病 illness:沉～(重病)grave and debilitating disease|养～recuperate

棵 kē〈量词 *classifier*〉多用于植物[oft. of plants]:一～树 a tree|一～草 a cluster of grass|一～牡丹 a peony|几～烟卷 several cigarettes

【棵儿】kēr 植株大小的程度(of a plant) size:这棵花～小。This flower is quite small.|拣～大的菜拔。Pick and pull out the bigger vegetables.

【棵子】kē·zi〈方 *dial.*〉植物的茎和枝叶(多指庄稼的 oft. farm crop) stalk; stem:青～green stalk|树～tree sapling's stalk|玉米～长得很高。Corn stalks can grow very tall.

颏 kē 脸的最下部分,在嘴的下面 chin; front of the lower jaw; 通称 generally known as 下巴 xià·ba or 下巴颏儿 xià·bakēr
☞ ké on p. 1092

嗑 kē〈方 *dial.*〉(～儿 kēr)话,有时特指现成的话 words, esp. trite topics:唠～have a chat|他的嘴老不闲着,～真多。He's so talkative; It seems he never runs out of words.
☞ kè on p. 1099

稞 kē [稞麦](kēmài)青稞 highland barley; *qingke* barley (a farm crop of Tibet and Qinghai)

窠 kē 鸟兽昆虫的窝 nest; burrow:狗～doghouse; kennel|蜂～beehive; hive|鸟在树上做～。Birds make their nests in trees.

【窠臼】kējiù〈书 *fml.*〉现成格式;老套子(多指文章或其他艺术品 usu. of writing or artistic creation) beaten track; set pattern:不落～original; break from set practices|摆脱前人的～,独创一格 eschew the patterns set by the predecessors and create a style of one's own

榼 kē〈古时 *arch.*〉盛酒的器具 wine vessel

颗 kē〈量词 *classifier*〉多用于颗粒状的东西[of small and round things]:一～珠子 a pearl|一～黄豆 a soya bean|一～子弹 a bullet|一～牙齿 a tooth|一～～汗珠子往下掉。Beads of sweat kept dripping down.

【颗粒】kēlì ❶ 小而圆的东西(of bean, pearl, etc.) small and round; pellet:珍珠的～大小不一。These pearls are uneven in size.|这个玉米棒子上有多少～? How many grains are there on this corn cob? ❷ (粮食)一颗一粒 grain:～无收 complete crop failure|精收细打,～归仓。Every grain to the granary.

磕(搕) kē ❶ 碰在硬东西上 knock (against sth. hard):碗边儿～掉一块。The edge of the bowl was chipped.|脸上～破了块皮 graze one's face ❷ 磕打 rap:～烟袋锅子 rap the ashes out of a pipe; empty out a pipe|～掉鞋底的泥 knock mud off the shoes

【磕巴】kē·ba〈方 *dial.*〉❶ 口吃 stutter; stammer:说话～speak with a slight stutter; stammer ❷ 口吃的人 stammerer

【磕打】kē·da 把东西(主要是盛东西的器物)向地上或较硬的东西上碰,使附着的东西掉下来 knock sth. out of a vessel, container, etc.:他～了一下烟袋锅儿。He knocked his pipe.|抽屉里的土太多,拿到外边去～～吧! Take the drawer out of the room and knock the dirt out of it.

【磕磕绊绊】kē·kebànbàn ❶ 形容路不好走或腿脚有毛病而行走不灵便(of a road) bumpy; rough; (of a person) limp ❷ 形容事情遇到困难、挫折,不称心,不顺利 obstacle; setback; no smooth sailing

【磕磕撞撞】kē·kezhuàngzhuàng 形容因匆忙或酒醉而走起路来东倒西歪(of hurry or drunk) stumble; stagger along

【磕碰】kēpèng ❶ 东西互相撞击 knock against; collide with; bump against:还是买几个塑料的盘子好,禁得起～。(We)'d better buy a few plastic plates, which stand jostling better than anything else.|这一箱瓷器没包装好,一路磕磕碰碰的,碎了不少。Because of poor packaging, quite a few pieces in this box of porcelain were allowed to bump against each other and got broken on its way here. ❷〈方 *dial.*〉人和东西相撞 collide; bump against:衣架放在走廊里,晚上走路的时候总是～。The clothes-rack is rather out of the place in the corridor — people walking by in the night always run into it. ❸〈比喻 *fig.*〉冲突 clash; squabble:几家住一个院子,生活上出现一点～是难免的。Petty bickering is inevitable when several families live in houses within the same courtyard.

【磕碰儿】kē·pengr〈方 *dial.*〉❶ 器物上碰伤的痕迹 dent; chip (in a utensil):花瓶口上有个～。There is a dent in the rim of the vase. ❷〈比喻 *fig.*〉挫折 setback; reverse:不能遇到点～就泄气。Don't lose heart at a slight setback.

【磕头】kē//tóu 旧时的礼节,跪在地上,两手扶地,头近地或着地 kowtow; age-old Chinese custom of kneeling, with both hands on the floor, and touching the ground with the forehead in worship or submission; act obsequiously

【磕头碰脑】kē tóu pèng nǎo ❶ 形容人多而相挤相碰或东西多而人跟东西相挤相碰(of a place crowded with people or a room full of furniture) bump against each other; (of a crowd) push and bump:一大群人～地挤着看热闹。A large crowd was packed solidly and jostling for a look at the excitement. ❷ 指经常碰见、往来 rub elbows (with one another):都住在一条街上,成天～的,低头不见抬头见。People living in the same street bump into each other all the time. ❸〈比喻 *fig.*〉发生冲突;闹矛盾 conflict; squabble:老人家热心肠,街坊四邻有个～的事,他都出面调停。The old man is so warm-hearted, he never hesitates to settle a dispute whenever it occurs in the neighbourhood.

【磕膝盖】kēxīgài〈方 *dial.*〉(～儿 kēxīgàir)膝盖 knee

【磕牙】kēyá〈方 *dial.*〉闲谈;斗嘴 chitchat; banter:闲～have a chitchat|～聊天儿 shoot the bull

瞌 kē ☞below

【瞌眬】kē·chòng〈方 *dial.*〉瞌睡 sleep; doze:打～ doze off; nod off

【瞌睡】kēshuì 由于困倦而进入睡眠或半睡眠状态;想睡觉 dozy; somnolent:打～take a catnap|夜里没睡好,白天～得很。I felt drowsy during the day today because I hadn't slept well last night.

【瞌睡虫】kēshuìchóng ❶ 旧小说中指能使人打瞌睡的虫子(in old stories) sleep-inducing insect ❷ 指爱打瞌睡的人(含讥讽意 satirical) sleepy person

蝌 kē ☞below

【蝌蚪】kēdǒu 蛙或蟾蜍的幼体,黑色,椭圆形,像小鱼,有鳃和尾巴。生活在水中,用尾巴运动、逐渐发育生出后肢、前肢,尾巴逐渐变短而消失,最后变成蛙或蟾蜍。tadpole; larva in its aquatic stage, black in colour, oval in shape, looking like a fry with gills and tail, moving about in the water by wagging its tail, and becoming a frog or toad when its tail gradually shortens and disappears and its limbs have appeared and grown

【蝌子】kē·zi〈方 *dial.*〉蝌蚪 tadpole:蛤蟆～toad tadpole

髁 kē 骨头上的突起,多在骨头的两端 condyle; rounded process at either end of a bone, forming an articulation with another bone

ké (ㄎㄜˊ)

壳(殼) ké (～儿 kér) 义同壳(qiào) same as 壳 qiào in meaning:贝～sea shell|脑～skull|鸡蛋～儿 egg shell|子弹～儿 bullet shell

☞ qiào on p.1551

【壳郎猪】ké·langzhū〈方 *dial.*〉架子猪 feeder pig

咳 ké 咳嗽 cough:干～dry cough|百日～whooping cough|连～带喘 asthmatic cough

☞ hāi on p.753

【咳嗽】ké·sou 喉部或气管的黏膜受到刺激时迅速吸气,随即强烈地呼气,声带振动发声 cough; expel air from the lungs suddenly, invoking an involuntary harsh noise from the vocal chords, when the mucous membrane of the throat or trachea has been irritated

揢 ké 〈方 *dial*.〉❶ 卡住 get stuck; wedge: 抽屉～住了,拉不开。The drawer's stuck. It won't open.｜这双鞋又小又瘦,穿着～脚。This pair of shoes are too small. They cramp my feet. ❷ 刁难 create difficulties; make things difficult: ～人 make things difficult for sb.

颏 ké ☞ 红点颏 hóngdiǎnké on p. 802 and 蓝点颏 lándiǎnké on p. 1147
☞ kē on p. 1090

kě（ㄎㄜˇ）

可[1] kě ❶ 表示同意 approve: 许～ permit｜认～ consent｜不加～否 noncommittal; decline to comment ❷ 表示许可或可能,跟'可以'的意思相同(限于熟语或正反对举)[indicating admission or possibility, same as 可以 kěyǐ in meaning] can; may: 两～。It works either way.｜～见 thus; it is clear or evident that...｜牢不～破 unbreakable｜～大～小(of sth.) may be big or small, as one sees fit ❸ 表示值得 worth (doing): ～爱 lovable｜～贵 noble; precious｜这出戏～看。The play is worth seeing. 注意 **NOTE**: a) 多跟单音动词组合 [oft. used in combination with a monosyllabic verb] b)'可'有表示被动的作用,整个组合是形容词性质,如'这孩子很可爱','他非常可靠'。唯有'可怜'表示被动的作用时,是形容词性质,如'这个人可怜';表示主动的作用时,是动词性质,如'我很可怜她'。[When used in passive voice, the word 可 becomes part of an adjective phrase, such as in 'The child is so lovable' and 'He is so reliable.' The only exception is the phrase 可怜 kělián in passive voice it serves as an adjective, such as in 'This man is so pitiable,' and in active voice it is a verb, such as in 'I take great pity on her.'] ☞ d and e of NOTE in 能 néng on p. 1402 ❹ 〈书 *fml*.〉大约 about: 年～二十 about 20 years of age｜长～七尺 about 7 *chi* in length ❺ 〈方 *dial*.〉可着 go as far as possible: ～劲儿(do sth.) to the best of one's ability｜疼得他～地打滚儿。He rolled on the ground in excruciating pain. ❻ (病)好;痊愈(多见于早期白话 oft. in early vernacular) be up and about once again; fully recovered ❼ (Kě) 姓 a surname

可[2] kě 〈副词 *adv*.〉❶ 表示转折,意思跟'可是'相同 [indicating a turn in meaning] but; yet; however: 别看他年龄小,志气～不小。He is so young, but he has high aspirations. ❷ 表示强调 so; such (emphasis): 她待人～好了,谁都喜欢她。She treats people so well that everybody likes her.｜昨儿夜里的风～大了。Last night the wind was so ferocious.｜记着点儿,～别忘了。Mind you don't forget it.｜大家的干劲～足了。Everybody is so enthusiastic.｜你～来了,让我好等啊! You've come at long last. I was practically worn out waiting for you. ❸ 用在反问句里加强反问的语气 [in a rhetorical question for emphasis] ever; on earth: 这件事我～怎么知道呢? How on earth can I know?｜都这样说,～谁见过呢? Everybody says so, but who has ever seen it? ❹ 用在疑问句里加强疑问的语气 [in a question for emphasis]: 这件事他～愿意? Is he really willing to do it?｜你～曾跟他谈过这个问题? Have you ever talked to him about this problem?

可[3] kě 适合 fit; suit: ～人意 just what one wants｜这回倒～了他的心了。He's had his wish fulfilled this time.
☞ kè on p. 1095

【可爱】kě'ài 令人喜爱 lovable; likable; lovely: 孩子活泼～。The child is so cute.

【可悲】kěbēi 令人悲伤;使人痛心 sad; lamentable: 结局～ tragic ending

【可比价格】kěbǐ-jiàgé 不变价格 constant price

【可鄙】kěbǐ 令人鄙视 contemptible; despicable; mean: ～的剽窃行为 despicable plagiarism｜自私自利是最～的。Selfishness is most deplorable.

【可不】kěbù 表示附和赞同对方的话(expressing agreement) 'Right!'; 'Exactly!': 您老有七十岁了吧? ～,今年五月就整七十啦! 'You are 70, aren't you?' 'Exactly. I'll turn 70 in May.' also 可不是 kěbù · shi

【可操左券】kě cāo zuǒ quàn 古代称契约为券,用竹做成,分左右两片,立约的人各拿一片,左券常用作索偿的凭证。'可操左券'比喻成功有把握。have sth. in the bag; be sure to succeed; 券 quàn means 'contract' in ancient times, which consisted of two pieces of bamboo, held respectively by the two signing parties, the left piece being used as proof for demanding compensation. The phrase has since come to mean 'certainty of success.'

【可耻】kěchǐ 应当认为羞耻 shameful; disgraceful; ignominious: 节约光荣,浪费～。It is commendable to be thrifty and shameful to waste.

【可丁可卯】kě dīng kě mǎo (～儿 kě dīng kě mǎor) ❶ 就着某个数量不多不少或就着某个范围不大不小 exactly: 每月工资总是～,全部花光。(He) never fails to squander all of his monthly salary before the next pay day. ❷ 指严格遵守制度,不通融 be observant to the letter; meticulous: 他办事～,从不给人开后门儿。He is so strict with his work that he never stretches the rules in anyone's favour. ‖

also 可钉可铆 kě dīng kě mǎo

【可锻铸铁】kěduàn-zhùtiě 用白口铸铁经过热处理后制成的有韧性的铸铁。有较高的强度和可塑性，广泛应用于机器制造业。malleable iron; cast iron heat-treated to become elastic enough to be extended or shaped by hammering or rolling, widely used in machine-building industry; also 马铁 mǎtiě and 玛钢 mǎgāng

【可歌可泣】kě gē kě qì 值得歌颂，使人感动得流泪。指悲壮的事迹使人非常感动。stirring; heroic and moving; so heroic and touching as to bring people to tears

【可观】kěguān ❶ 值得看 worth seeing：这出戏大有～。This play is worth seeing. ❷ 指达到比较高的程度 considerable; impressive：规模～sizeable scale | 三万元这个数目也就很～了。Thirty thousand yuan is a considerable sum.

【可贵】kěguì 值得珍视或重视 valuable; praiseworthy; commendable：难能～(of sth.) hard to come by and unusually valuable | ～的品质 fine quality | 这种精神是十分～的。This spirit is highly commendable.

【可好】kěhǎo 正好；恰巧 as luck would have it; by a happy coincidence：我正想找他来帮忙，～他来了。I was just about to ask him for help when he showed up.

【可恨】kěhèn 令人痛恨；使人憎恨 hateful; detestable; abominable：他这是明知故犯，你说～不～? Isn't it annoying that he made the mistake purposely?

【可见】kějiàn 可以看见；可以想见 it is thus obvious that; it shows; that proves; so：由此～，这次事故是因为思想麻痹造成的。It is thus clear that the accident was caused by negligence.

【可见度】kějiàndù 物体能被看见的清晰程度。可见度的大小主要决定于光线的强弱及介质传播光线的能力。visibility; mainly dependent on given conditions of light and a medium's light-transmitting ability

【可见光】kějiànguang 肉眼可以看见的光，即从红到紫的光波 visible light; light that is perceptible to the eye, i.e., the visible spectrum that extends from red to purple

☞ 光 guāng ① on p. 720

【可卡因】kěkǎyīn 从古柯树叶中提取的一种药物，化学式 $C_{17}H_{21}O_4N$。白色结晶状粉末，有使血管收缩的作用，可以做局部麻醉药。Cocaine ($C_{17}H_{21}O_4N$); white crystalline powder capable of contracting blood veins, for local anaesthesis; also 古柯碱 gǔkējiǎn

【可靠】kěkào ❶ 可以信赖依靠 reliable; dependable; trustworthy：他忠诚老实，为人很～。He is honest and faithful, and very reliable. ❷ 真实可信 truthful：这个消息～不～? Is the news reliable?

【可可】kěkě ❶ 可可树，常绿乔木，叶子卵形，花冠带黄色，花萼粉色，果实卵形，红色或黄色。种子炒熟制成粉可以做饮料，榨的油可供药用。产在热带地区。cocoa (*Cocos nucifera*); evergreen tropical tree with oval leaves, yellowish corollas and pink calyxes, whose red or yellow egg-shaped seeds are baked and ground to make drinks. The oil extracted from the seeds can be used for pharmaceutical purposes. ❷ 可可树种子制成的粉末 cocoa; powder made from crushed cocoa beans ❸ 用可可树种子的粉做成的饮料 cocoa; drink made from powdered cocoa beans ‖ also 蔻蔻 kòukòu

【可可儿的】kěkěr·de〈方 *dial.*〉恰巧；不迟不早，正好赶上 by chance; fortunately; it so happened：我刚出门，～就遇着下雨。It so happened that the moment I stepped out of the door it started to rain.

【可口】kěkǒu (～儿 kěkǒur)食品、饮料味道好或冷热适宜(of food) mouth-watering; toothsome; delectable; palatable：吃着家乡风味的菜，觉得很～。Eating these dishes, prepared in the style of my hometown, was a most delectable experience.

【可兰经】Kělánjīng same as 古兰经 Gǔlánjīng

【可怜】kělián ❶ 值得怜悯 pitiful; pitiable; poor：他刚三岁就死了父母，真是个～的孩子! What a poor child, having lost both his parents at only three! ❷ 怜悯 have pity on; pity：对这种一贯做坏事的人，绝不能～他。On no account should we show mercy to such a hardened evildoer. ❸ (数量少或质量坏到)不值得一提(of quantity or quality) meagre; wretched; miserable; pitiful：少得～a mere pittance | 知识贫乏得～hopelessly deficient knowledge

【可怜巴巴】kěliánbābā (～的 kěliánbābā·de) 形容可怜的样子 piteous; woeful：小姑娘又黄又瘦，～的。How piteous the little girl is, so lean and so haggard! | 儿子眼里含着泪，～地瞅着他。His son, in tears, looked at him with woebegone eyes.

【可怜虫】kěliánchóng〈比喻 *fig.*〉可怜的人(含鄙视意 scornful) pitiful creature; wretch

【可怜见】kěliánjiàn (～儿 kěliánjiànr)值得怜悯 pitiable; poor; pathetic; miserable：这小孩子小小年纪就没了爹娘，怪～的。The child, who lost his parents at such a young age, deserves all our sympathy.

【可能】kěnéng ❶ 表示可以实现 possible; likely：～性 possibility | 团结国内外一切～团结的力量 unite with all the forces that can be united with at home and abroad | 提前完成任务是完全～的。It is entirely possible for the task to be fulfilled ahead of schedule. ❷ 能成为事实的属性；可能性 possibility; probability:

根据需要和～安排工作 arrange work where necessary and possible | 事情的发展不外有两种～。Judging from the way things go, there will be only two possibilities for the future of this matter. ❸ 也许;或许 perhaps; probably: 他～开会去了。Maybe he has gone to the meeting. | 天～要下雪。It looks like snowing.

【可逆反应】kěnì-fǎnyìng 在一定条件下,既可向生成物方向进行,同时也可向反应物方向进行的化学反应。在化学方程式中常用⇌来表示。reversible reaction; chemical reaction in either one of two opposite directions — the resultant or the reactant; in a chemical formula ⇌ is the indication of it

【可巧】kěqiǎo 恰好;凑巧 as luck would have it; by a happy coincidence: 母亲正在念叨他,～他就来了。Mother was just talking about him when he turned up.

【可取】kěqǔ 可以采纳接受;值得学习或赞许 desirable; advisable: 他的意见确有～之处。There is something desirable in his suggestion. | 我以为临阵磨枪的做法不～。It's no use sharpening your spear just before a battle, so to speak.

【可人】kěrén〈书 *fml.*〉❶ 有长处可取的人;能干的人 person with apparent strengths or admirable qualities ❷ 可爱的人;意中人 desirable person; sweetheart ❸ 可人意;使人满意 likable; satisfactory; agreeable: 楚楚～(of a young woman) of delicate beauty; graceful and charming | 风味～agreeable taste

【可身】kěshēn〈方 *dial.*〉(～儿 kěshēnr) 可体 (of clothing) fit sb. like a glove; fit nicely: 这件大衣长短、肥瘦都合适,穿着真～。The overcoat fits me perfectly.

【可是】kěshì ❶〈连词 *conj.*〉表示转折,前面常常有'虽然'之类表示让步的连词呼应[indicating transition, oft. preceded by such conjunctions as 'though'] but; yet; however: 大家虽然很累,～都很愉快。We were bone-tired, but felt happy. ❷ 真是;实在是 indeed; really: 她家媳妇那个贤惠,～百里挑一。Her daughter-in-law is one in a hundred in terms of personality and ability.

【可塑性】kěsùxìng ❶ 固体在外力作用下发生形变并保持形变的性质,多指胶泥、塑料、大部分金属等在常温下或加热后能改变形状的特性 plasticity; (of mud, plastics, metal, etc.) capability of being molded under normal atmospheric temperature or heat and retaining the shape thus molded ❷ 生物体在不同的生活环境影响下,某些性质能发生变化,逐渐形成新类型的特性 (of an organism) formative; capability of developing new cells or tissue by cell division and differentiation under the impact of a different living environment

【可体】kětǐ 衣服的尺寸跟身材正好合适;合身 be a good fit; fit nicely

【可望而不可即】kě wàng ér bù kě jí 只能够望见而不能够接近,形容看来可以实现而实际难以实现 within sight but beyond reach; unattainable; inaccessible; 即 jí also put as 及 jí

【可谓】kěwèi〈书 *fml.*〉可以说 one may well say; it may be said; it may be called

【可恶】kěwù 令人厌恶;使人恼恨 obnoxious; repulsive; abhorrent: 在别人背后搬弄是非,～透了。It is utterly detestable to sow discord behind one's back.

【可惜】kěxī 令人惋惜 what a pity; it's too bad: 机会很好,～错过了。A good opportunity was wasted. What a pity!

【可惜了儿的】kěxīliǎor·de〈方 *dial.*〉令人惋惜 it's a pity: 材料白白糟蹋了,怪～。It's a pity the material has been laid to waste.

【可喜】kěxǐ 令人高兴;值得欣喜 gratifying; heartening: ～可贺 heartening and laudable | 取得了～的进步 have made encouraging progress

【可笑】kěxiào ❶ 令人耻笑 ridiculous; absurd; funny: 幼稚～naive and laughable ❷ 引人发笑 funny: 滑稽～amusing in a silly way | 说到～的地方,连他自己也忍不住笑了起来。He himself couldn't help laughing when he came to the funny part.

【可心】kě//xīn 恰合心愿;合意 satisfactory; to the satisfaction (or liking) of: ～如意 to one's liking | 买了件～的皮夹克。(He) bought a leather jacket he really liked.

【可行】kěxíng 行得通;可以实行 practical; viable: 方案切实～。The plan is feasible.

【可疑】kěyí 值得怀疑 suspicious; doubtful: 形迹～look suspicious

【可以】[1] kěyǐ ❶ 表示可能或能够 can; may: 不会的事情,用心去学,是～学会的。You can learn what you don't know if you set your heart on it. | 这片麦子已经熟了,～割了。The wheat in this field is ripe enough for harvesting. ❷ 表示许可[indicating permission]: 你～走了。You may go. ☞ NOTE d and e of 能 néng on p. 1042

【可以】[2] kěyǐ ❶ 好;不坏 passable; not bad: 这篇文章写得还～。This article is pretty good. ❷ 厉害 terrible; awful: 你这张嘴真～! What a sharp tongue you've got! | 天气实在热得～。It is awfully hot.

【可意】kěyì 称心如意 satisfactory; up to one's standard: 这套房子你住得还～吗? Are you happy with your apartment?

【可憎】kězēng 令人厌恶;可恨 hateful; detestable; abominable: 面目～repugnant looks

【可着】kě·zhe 就着某个范围不增减;尽(jǐn)着 manage to make do: ～劲儿干 work to the best of one's ability | ～嗓子叫唤 shout at the top of one's voice | ～这块布料,能做什么就做什么。You'll have to make do with this piece of cloth.

【可知论】kězhīlùn 主张世界是可以认识的哲学学说 theory of knowability of the universe

坷 kě ☞ 坎坷 kǎnkě on p.1080

☞ kē on p.1088

岢 kě 岢岚(Kělán),地名,在山西 Kelan, the name of a place in Shanxi Province

轲 kě ☞ [轗轲](kǎnkě) on p.1081

☞ kē on p.1089

渴 kě ❶ 口干想喝水 thirsty; athirst:解～quench one's thirst|又～又饿 thirsty and hungry|临～掘井 dig a well when feeling thirsty; make hasty preparation ❷ 迫切地 eager:～望 yearn for; look forward to|～念 miss; long for; carry a torch for

【渴慕】kěmù 非常思慕 think of sb. with respect; admire:～已久 admire sb. greatly for a long time|大家怀着～的心情访问了这位劳动模范。We called on the model worker with deep admiration.

【渴念】kěniàn 渴想 long for; yearn for; miss sb. very much:～远方的亲人 miss one's loved ones who are far away

【渴盼】kěpàn 迫切地盼望 eagerly look forward to; earnestly hope:离散几十年的亲人～早日团圆。After decades of separation, the family members could not wait for a happy reunion.

【渴求】kěqiú 迫切地要求或追求 eagerly yearn for; hunger after:～进步 earnestly strive for progress

【渴望】kěwàng 迫切地希望 hanker after; long for; yearn for:～和平 long for peace|同学们都～着和这位作家见面。My classmates were eager to meet the writer.

【渴想】kěxiǎng 非常想念 pine for; miss sb. very much

kè (ㄎㄜˋ)

可 kè [可汗](kèhán)古代鲜卑、突厥、回纥、蒙古等族最高统治者的称号 khan; title for the ruler of the Xianbei (Sienpi), Tujue (Turk), Uygur and Mongol people in ancient times

☞ kě on p.1092

克[1](❸❹剋、尅) kè ❶ 能 can; able to; capable of:～勤～俭 practise diligence and thrift|不～分身 have one's hands full doing sth.; cannot replicate oneself ❷ 克服;克制 restrain:～己 self-restraint; self-abnegation|以柔～刚 overcome the tough with the mild ❸ 攻下据点;战胜 conquer; subjugate:～复 recapture; recover|～敌 beat or defeat an enemy|攻必～invincible ❹ 消化 digest; absorb:～食 help digestion|～化 digest

克[2](剋、尅) kè 严格限定(期限) set a time limit:～期 schedule|～日 set a deadline. also 刻 kè

☞ 剋(尅) kēi on p.1099

克[3] kè 国际单位制、公制的质量单位,1克等于1千克(公斤)的千分之一 gramme, 1 gramme equals one-thousandth of 1 kg. [法 French: gramme]

克[4] kè ❶ 藏族地区容量单位,1克青稞约重25市斤 *ke*, Tibetan unit of volume or dry measure (1 *ke* equals approximately 12.5 kg. of *qingke* barley) ❷ 藏族地区地积单位,播种1克(约25市斤)种子的土地称为1克地,1克约合1市亩 *ke*, a Tibetan unit of land area (an acreage of land large enough for the sowing of 12.5 kg. of seeds), equal to about 1 *mu*

【克敌制胜】kè dí zhì shèng 打败敌人,取得胜利 vanquish (or conquer) an enemy and emerge victorious

【克服】kèfú ❶ 用坚强的意志和力量战胜(缺点、错误、坏现象、不利条件等) overcome (difficulties, shortcomings, etc.); correct (a mistake):～急躁情绪 overcome impetuosity; rein in one's rashness|～不良习气 overcome undesirable tendencies|群策群力,～重重困难 overcome one difficulty after another by collective wisdom and effort ❷ 克制;忍受(困难) put up with (difficulty):这儿的生活条件不太好,请诸位～一下。Living conditions here are not so good. Please try to put up with it.

【克复】kèfù 经过战斗而夺回(被敌人占领的地方) recover; recapture:～失地 recover lost territory

【克格勃】kègébó 原苏联'国家安全委员会'的俄文(Комитет государственной безопасности)缩写(КГБ)的音译。也指克格勃的人员。KGB; transliteration of the Russian term for the former Soviet State Security Committee; also KGB member

【克化】kèhuà 〈方 *dial.*〉消化(食物) digest (food)

【克己】kèjǐ ❶ 克制自己的私心;对自己要求严格 restrain oneself:～奉公 exercise self-restraint and be dedicated to the public interest ❷ 商店自称货价便宜,不多赚钱(oft. a store's proclamation) cut-rate sales ❸ 节俭;俭省 be thrifty; be frugal:自奉～ live a spartan life

【克己奉公】kè jǐ fèng gōng 严格要求自己,奉行公事 be restrict with oneself and dedicated to one's public duty; work selflessly for the public interest

【克扣】kèkòu 私自扣减应该发给别人的财物,据为己有 embezzle part of what should be issued to others:～粮饷 dock soldiers' living allowances

【克拉】kèlā 宝石的重量单位,1克拉等于200毫克,即0.2克 karat, unit of weight for diamond; 1 carat equals 0.2 gramme [法 French: carat]

【克郎球】kèlángqiú same as 康乐球 kānglèqiú

【克朗】kèlǎng 瑞典、挪威、冰岛、丹麦等国家的本位货币 Krona, unit of money in Sweden, Norway, Iceland and Denmark, etc.

【克里姆林宫】Kèlǐmǔlín Gōng 俄国沙皇的宫殿,在莫斯科市中心。十月革命后是原苏联最高党政机关的所在地。常用做原苏联官方的代称。Kremlin; imperial palace of Tsarist Russia in downtown Moscow, converted into the site of the supreme Party and government headquarters of the former Soviet Union after the October Revolution of 1917; synonymous to the former Soviet government [从俄 Russian: Кремль]

【克期】kèqī 约定或限定日期 set a date; set a time limit:~完工 set a deadline for the completion of a project|~送达 deliver a message, etc., on time. also 刻期 kèqī

【克勤克俭】kè qín kè jiǎn 既能勤劳,又能节俭 industry and frugality:~是我国人民的优良传统。Industry and frugality is a fine tradition of the Chinese people.

【克日】kèrì same as 克期 kèqī:~动工 start a project on a chosen date. also 刻日 kèrì

【克食】kèshí 帮助消化食物 facilitate digestion:山楂能~。Haws help digestion.

【克丝钳子】kèsī-qián•zi 一种手工工具,钳柄上包有绝缘保护套,电工常用,主要用来剪断导线或金属丝 combination pliers; cutting pliers; electrician's tool for cutting lead or other metal wires, with both handles covered with insulating sheaths

【克星】kèxīng 迷信的人用五行相生相克的道理推论,认为有些人的命运是相克的,把相克的人叫做克星 jinx; nemesis; natural enemy; According to the theory of the relationship of mutual promotion and restraint between the Five Elements in Chinese horoscope, some people are ill-matched in their lives' destinations and therefore should never come together in marriage or other relationships. Thus a man may be regarded as the nemesis of a woman; and vice versa ◇ 猫头鹰是鼠类的~。The owl is a natural enemy of mice and rats.

【克制】kèzhì 抑制(多指情感 oft. one's emotions) restrain; exercise restraint:采取~的态度 show restraint (in handling a matter)|他很能~自己的情感,冷静地对待一切问题。He knows perfectly about how to control his own feelings and always stays cool in handling problems.

刻 kè ❶ 用刀子在竹、木、玉、石、金属等物品上雕成花纹、文字 carve; cut; engrave patterns, inscriptions, etc., with a knife in bamboo, wood, jade, metal, etc.:雕~carve; sculpt|篆~engrave a seal|~石 carve an inscription on a stone|~字 engrave letters (for block printing); cut stencils|~图章 engrave a seal ❷ 古代用漏壶记时,一昼夜共一百刻。*ke*, unit of time measured in ancient times by the regulated flow of water through a clepsydra; with a day and night divided into 100 *ke*; ☞ 漏壶 lòuhú on p.1255 ❸ 用钟表计时,以十五分钟为一刻 quarter (of an hour):下午五点一~开车。The bus or train sets off at a quarter past five in the afternoon. ❹ 时间 time:顷~in no time|立~at once|即~immediately|此~at this moment ❺ 形容程度极深 to the highest degree or extent:深~profound|~苦 very diligent; hardworking ❻ 刻薄 harsh:尖~sarcastic; acrimonious|苛~harsh; extremely demanding ❼ same as 克^{2}kè

【刻板】kèbǎn ❶ 在木板或金属板上刻字或图(或用化学方法腐蚀而成),使成为印刷用的底版 cut, or use chemical erosion to prepare, blocks for printing; carve printing blocks; also 刻版 kèbǎn ❷〈比喻 *fig.*〉呆板没有变化 stiff; inflexible:别人的经验是应该学习的,但是不能~地照搬。Other people's experience is to be learned from, but it is not to be mechanically copied.

【刻本】kèběn 用木刻版印成的书籍 block-printed edition:宋~ of a book Song-dynasty block-printed edition

【刻薄】kèbó (待人、说话)冷酷无情;过分的苛求 unkind; harsh; mean:尖酸~caustic

【刻不容缓】kè bù róng huǎn 片刻也不能拖延。形容形势紧迫。afford no delay; demand immediate attention; of great urgency

【刻毒】kèdú 刻薄狠毒 venomous; spiteful:为人~malicious person; mean and spiteful in dealing with other people|~的语言 noxious remark

【刻度】kèdù 量具、仪表等上面刻画的表示量(如尺寸、温度、电压等)的大小的条纹 graduation (on a vessel or instrument) for the measurement of length, temperature, voltage, etc.

【刻工】kègōng ❶ 雕刻的技术 skill of a carver; carving skill:~精细 exquisite chisel work ❷ 从事雕刻工作的工人 sculptor; engraver; carver

【刻骨】kègǔ〈比喻 *fig.*〉感念或仇恨很深,牢记不忘 deeply ingrained; heartfelt:~铭心 engraved on one's bones and heart; unforgettable|~的仇恨 inveterate hatred; deep-seated hatred

【刻骨铭心】kè gǔ míng xīn〈比喻 *fig.*〉牢记在心上,永远不忘(多用于对别人的感激 oft. a debt of gratitude) inscribe in one's heart; also 镂骨铭心 lòu gǔ míng xīn or 铭心刻骨 míng xīn kè gǔ

【刻画】kèhuà ❶ 刻或画 engrave or draw:不得在古建筑物上~。No graffiti on ancient buildings. ❷ 用文字描写或用其他艺术手段表现(人物的形象、性格)(of sb.'s image, character) depict; portray:～入微 depict sb. or sth. in minute detail|鲁迅先生成功地～了阿Q这个形象。Lu Xun vividly portrayed the character of Ah Q.

【刻苦】kèkǔ ❶ 肯下苦功夫;很能吃苦 assiduous; hardworking:～钻研 study assiduously|学习～study hard ❷ 俭朴 simple and frugal:他生活一向很～。He has always lived a frugal life.

【刻期】kèqī same as 克期 kèqī

【刻日】kèrì same as 克日 kèrì

【刻书】kèshū 指刻版印刷出版书籍。旧时有书商刻书、官府刻书和私人刻书等。cut blocks for printing a book; carve printing blocks. In times of yore block-printed books were made by booksellers, governments or individuals.

【刻丝】kèsī same as 缂丝 kèsī

【刻下】kèxià 目前;眼下 at present; at the moment:～家里有事,暂时不能离开。I can't leave now because something has just happened in my family.

【刻写】kèxiě 把蜡纸铺在誊写钢版上用铁笔书写 use a stylus to cut a piece of waxed paper in preparation for producing mimeographed copies:～蜡纸 waxed paper; stencil

【刻意】kèyì 用尽心思 take pains; be meticulous about:～求工 seek perfection sedulously; be a scrupulous craftsman|～经营 spare no pains in managing a business

【刻舟求剑】kè zhōu qiú jiàn 楚国有个人过江时把剑掉在水里,他在船帮上剑落的地方刻上记号,等船停下,从刻记号的地方下水找剑,结果自然找不到(见于《吕氏春秋·察今》) nick the boat to seek the sword; *Lü's Spring and Autumn Annals·On Current Affairs* by Lü Buwei goes as follows: A man from the state of Chu dropped his sword in the river while aboard a boat. He immediate made a notch on the side of the boat. When the boat reached the bank, he jumped into the river from where he marked the boat and, of course, failed to retrieve his sword.〈比喻 *fig.*〉拘泥成例,不知道跟着情势的变化而改变看法或办法 do sth. in disregard of changed circumstances

恪 kè〈书 *fml.*〉谨慎而恭敬 scrupulous and respectful:～守 observe law or rules to the letter|～遵 obey (orders, rules, etc.) with respect|～尽职守 carry out one's duties with dedication

【恪守】kèshǒu〈书 *fml.*〉严格遵守 scrupulously abide by (a treaty, promise, etc.):～中立 observe strict neutrality|～不渝 strictly abide by (a promise, agreement, etc.)

客 kè ❶ 客人(跟'主'相对 as opposed to 'host') guest:宾～ guest|请～give sb. a treat|会～receive a visitor; meet friends|家里来～了。I've got a visitor at home. ❷ 旅客 passenger:～车 passenger train|～店 hotel; inn ❸ 寄居或迁居外地 go and live in a place other than one's homeland:～居 live away from one's homeland|～籍 second home place|作～他乡 be a settler in a strange place ❹ 客商 travelling merchant:珠宝～vagrant jeweller ❺ 顾客 client; customer:乘～passenger|～满(of a hotel) fully booked or occupied ❻ 对某些奔走各地从事某种活动的人的称呼 person who goes from place to place in pursuit of sth.:说～lobbyist|政～politician|侠～knight-errant ❼ 在人类意识外独立存在的 objective; independent of human consciousness:～观 objective|～体 object ❽〈方 *dial.*〉〈量词 *classifier*〉用于论份儿出售的食品、饮料 portion of food, drink for sale:一～蛋炒饭 one rice fried with egg|三～冰激凌 three ice creams

【客帮】kèbāng〈旧时 *old*〉称从外地来的成伙的商贩 travelling merchants from other localities

【客舱】kècāng 船或飞机中用于载运旅客的舱(of a boat or aircraft) passenger cabin

【客场】kèchǎng 体育比赛中,主队所在的场地对客队来说叫客场(of a sports game) the opponent team's home court or ground

【客车】kèchē 铁路、公路上载运旅客用的车辆。铁路上的客车还包括餐车、邮车和行李车。bus; passenger train (complete with dining, postal and luggage carriages)

【客串】kèchuàn 非专业演员临时参加专业剧团演出,也指非本地或本单位的演员临时参加演出(of an amateur actor) play a part in professional performance; be a guest performer

【客店】kèdiàn 规模小设备简陋的旅馆 inn; caravanserai; hostel

【客队】kèduì 体育比赛中,被邀请来参加比赛的外单位或外地、外国的代表队叫客队(of a sports game) visiting team

【客饭】kèfàn ❶ 机关团体的食堂里临时给来客开的饭 meal specially prepared for visitors at a canteen ❷ 饭馆、火车、轮船等处论份儿卖的饭 meal sold in portions in a hotel, on a train, or aboard a passenger ship

【客贩】kèfàn 称往来各地贩运货物的商贩 travelling merchant

【客房】kèfáng 供旅客或来客住宿的房间 guestroom

【客观】kèguān ❶ 在意识之外,不依赖主观意识而存在的(跟'主观'相对 as opposed to 'subjective') objective:～存在 objective reality or existence|～事物 things that exist independent of human consciousness|～规律 objective law or principle ❷ 按照事物的本来面目去考察,不加个人偏见的(跟'主观'相对 as opposed to subjective) study things objectively or without personal bias: 他看问题比较～。He looks at things objectively.

【客观唯心主义】kèguān wéixīn zhǔyì 唯心主义的一个派别，主张有不依赖人的意识而存在的'精神'或'理'，认为物质世界是这种'精神'或'理'的体现或产物 objective idealism; school of idealism maintaining that there exists a 'spirit' or 'reason' independent of human will and that the material world is the embodiment or outcome of it

【客官】kèguān 〈旧时 *old*〉店家、船家等对顾客、旅客的尊称 sir; mister; respectful address to a customer at a shop or to a guest at a hotel

【客户】kèhù ❶〈旧时 *old*〉指以租佃为生的人家 tenant; farmer who makes a living tilling the land for a landlord ❷〈旧时 *old*〉指外地迁来的住户 non-native resident; immigrant ❸ 工厂企业或经纪人称来往的主顾；客商 client; customer: 这次展销的新产品受到国内外～的欢迎。The new products on display during the exhibition caught the fancy of clients from at home and abroad.

【客机】kèjī 载运旅客的飞机 passenger plane

【客籍】kèjí ❶ 寄居的籍贯（区别于'原籍' as compared with 'place of origin'）one's place of abode as an immigrant ❷ 寄居本地的外地人 settler; immigrant

【客家】Kèjiā 指在 4 世纪初（西晋末年）、9 世纪末（唐朝末年）和 13 世纪初（南宋末年）从黄河流域逐渐迁徙到南方的汉人，现在分布在广东、福建、广西、江西、湖南、台湾等省区 Hakkas; people of the ethnic Han background who migrated from the Yellow River basin to south China during the early 4th century (towards the end of the Western Jin Dynasty), the late 9th century (towards the end of the Tang Dynasty) and the early 13th century (towards the end of the Southern Song Dynasty), whose descendants are found in Guangdong, Fujian, Guangxi, Jiangxi, Hunan and Taiwan

【客居】kèjū 在外地居住；旅居 live abroad; live away from home: 二十岁时告别故乡，以后一直～成都。(He) left his hometown at the age of 20, and has since lived in Chengdu.

【客流】kèliú 运输部门指在一定时间内，向一定方向流动的旅客 passenger flow; flow of passengers: ～量 volume of passenger flow | 调查～变化 study changes in passenger flow

【客轮】kèlún 载运旅客的轮船 passenger ship or liner

【客票】kèpiào 旅客乘火车、飞机、轮船等的票（of train, airline, ship）passenger ticket

【客气】kè·qi ❶ 对人谦让、有礼貌 polite; courteous: ～话 pleasantries | 不～地回绝了他。He was refused flatly. ❷ 说客气的话；做客气的动作 speak or behave deferentially: 您坐，别～。Sit down, and don't stand on ceremony. | 他～了一番，把礼物收下了。He accepted the gift after courteously declining it at first.

【客卿】kèqīng 〈古代 *arch.*〉指在本国做官的其他诸侯国的人 person from a feudal state serving in the court of another state

【客人】kè·rén ❶ 被邀请受招待的人；为了交际或事务的目的来探访的人（跟'主人'相对 as opposed to 'host'）guest; visitor; person entertained by invitation or paying a sociality or business visit ❷ 旅客 guest (at a hotel, etc.); traveller ❸ 客商 travelling merchant

【客商】kèshāng 往来各地运货贩卖的商人 travelling merchat: 过往～ travelling merchant | 各国～齐集广州交易会。The Guangzhou Commodities Fair brought together merchants from different countries around the world.

【客死】kèsǐ 〈书 *fml.*〉死在他乡或外国 die in a place far away from one's home; die abroad: ～异域 die in a foreign land

【客岁】kèsuì 〈书 *fml.*〉去年 last year

【客堂】kètáng 〈方 *dial.*〉接待客人用的房间 drawing room; parlour

【客套】kètào ❶ 表示客气的套语 pleasantries; polite formalities; civilities: 我们是老朋友，用不着讲～。As old friends we don't need to stand on ceremony. ❷ 说客气话 make polite remarks: 见了面，彼此～了几句。They exchanged pleasantries with each other when they met.

【客套话】kètàohuà 表示客气的话，如'劳驾、借光、慢走、留步'等 polite expressions or formalities (such as 劳驾 láo // jià, 借光 jiè // guāng, 慢走 mànzǒu, 留步 liúbù, etc.)

【客体】kètǐ ❶ 哲学上指主体以外的客观事物，是主体认识和实践的对象（philosophical term referring to）object; objective things, as opposed to the subject, that may be perceived and practised by the subject ❷ 法律上指主体的权利和义务所指向的对象，包括物品、行为等（legal term referring to）object; target of a subject's right and duty, including articles, actions, etc.

【客厅】kètīng 接待客人用的房间 drawing room; parlour; living room; room for receiving guests

【客土】kètǔ ❶ 为改良本处土壤而从别处移来的土 soil brought in to improve the original ❷〈书 *fml.*〉寄居的地方；异乡 foreign land; residence away from home: 侨居～ live in a foreign land

【客星】kèxīng 我国古代指新星和彗星 nova and comet, as known in ancient China ☞ 新星 xīnxīng on p. 2135 and 彗星 huìxīng on p. 869

【客姓】kèxìng 指聚族而居的村庄中外来户的姓，如王家庄中的张姓、李姓 surname different from that of other families in a village (e.g. the surname Zhang 张 or Li 李 in a Wang family village)

【客运】kèyùn 运输部门载运旅客的业务 passenger transport; passenger traffic:增加车次,缓和～紧张状况 ease the strain on passenger transport by increasing the number of trains

【客栈】kèzhàn 设备简陋的旅馆,有的兼供客商堆货并代办转运 inn; hostel that also offer goods storage or transport services

【客座】kèzuò ❶ 宾客的坐位 guest seat ❷ 指应邀在外单位或外地、外国不定期讲学、演出等而不在编制的 lecture or perform on invitation in units, places, or countries other than one's own at irregular intervals:～教授 guest professor|～演员 guest actor|～研究员 visiting researcher

课1 kè ❶ 有计划的分段教学 class; teaching period:上～ attend a class|下～ finish a class|星期六下午没～ have no class on Saturday afternoon ❷ 教学的科目 subject; course:主～ major course|语文～ Chinese|这学期共有五门～。(We) have five courses this term. ❸ 教学的时间单位 unit of time for teaching:一节～ a class ❹ 教材的段落 lesson; passage from some teaching material:这本教科书共有二十五～。This textbook contains 25 lessons. ❺ 行政机构按工作性质分设的办事部门 division or subdivision of an administrative unit; section:秘书～ secretariat|会计～ accounting section

课2 kè ❶〈旧指 *old*〉赋税 tax:国～ state tax|完粮交～ pay the grain tax ❷ 征收(赋税) levy; collect; impose:～税 collect taxes

课3 kè 占卜的一种 a divination session:起～ divine|卜～ art of divination

【课本】kèběn 教科书 textbook:数学～ mathematics textbook

【课表】kèbiǎo 课程表 school timetable; class schedule

【课程】kèchéng 学校教学的科目和进程 curriculum; schedule (or calendar) of courses and offered by an educational institution:～表 class schedule|安排～ set a curriculum

【课卷】kèjuàn 学生的书面作业 (students') written homework

【课目】kèmù ❶ 课程的项目 items in a curriculum ❷ 军事训练中进行讲解和训练的项目 items in military drill

【课时】kèshí 学时 class hour; period:我担任两班的语文课,每周共有十六～。I teach 16 Chinese classes a week for two classes.

【课室】kèshì 教室 classroom; schoolroom

【课堂】kètáng 教室在用来进行教学活动时叫课堂,泛指进行各种教学活动的场所 classroom; place for teaching activities:～讨论 classroom discussion|～作业 classwork

【课题】kètí 研究或讨论的主要问题或亟待解决的重大事项 issue; topic for study or discussion; problem to be resolved:科研～ research topic

【课外】kèwài 学校上课以外的时间 extracurricular; after school:～作业 homework|～活动 extracurricular activities|～辅导 instruction after class

【课文】kèwén 教科书中的正文(区别于注释和习题等 as compared with notes and exercises, etc.) text proper:朗读～ read a text aloud

【课业】kèyè 功课;学业 lessons; schoolwork:要好好用功,不可荒废～。Study hard and never neglect schoolwork.

【课余】kèyú 上课时间以外的 after class; after school:～时间 after-school time

氪 kè 气体元素,符号 Kr (kryptonum)。无色,无臭,无味,大气中含量极少,化学性质很不活泼。能吸收 X 射线,用作 X 射线的屏蔽材料等。krypton (Kr); colourless, odourless, flavourless, and relatively inert gaseous element that is rarely found in the atmosphere and can absorb X-rays, oft. used as material for screening X-rays

骒 kè 雌性的(骡、马) jenny:～马 mare

缂 kè [缂丝](kèsī) ❶ 我国特有的一种丝织手工艺。织时先架好经线,按照底稿在上面描出图画或文字的轮廓,然后对照底稿的色彩,用小梭子引着各种颜色的纬线,断断续续地织出图画或文字,同时衣料或物品也一起织成。brocade; traditional Chinese method of weaving in which craftspeople weave decorative patterns or figures together with fine silk and colour threads, and a piece of textile comes into being when the patterns or characters are finished ❷ 用缂丝法织成的衣料或物品 fabric woven as above ‖ also 刻丝 kèsī

嗑(齣) kè 用上下门牙咬有壳的或硬的东西 crack sth. between the teeth:～瓜子儿 crack melon seeds|老鼠把箱子～破了。A rat has eaten a hole in the box.
☞ kē on p.1090 and 齣 qiā on p.1526

锞 kè 锞子 small ingot of gold or silver:金～ gold ingot|银～ silver ingot

【锞子】kè·zi〈旧时 *old*〉作货币用的小金锭或银锭 small ingot of gold or silver as currency

溘 kè〈书 *fml.*〉忽然;突然 suddenly:～然 suddenly|～逝(称人死亡) pass away; die

【溘然】kèrán〈书 *fml.*〉忽然;突然 suddenly:～长逝 pass away; die

窸 kè〈书 *fml.*〉same as 恪 kè

kēi (ㄎㄟ)

剋(尅) kēi ❶ 打;打架 beat:挨了一顿～,鼻青脸肿的 be beaten black and blue|吵着吵着,俩人动手～起来了。The two of them kept quarrelling and finally came to blows. ❷ 骂;申斥 scold:你做错了事,妈妈～

你几句还不应该吗？Shouldn't mom scold you a bit since you've made a mistake?

☞ 克 kè on p. 1095

【剋架】kēi//jià〈方 *dial.*〉打架 come to blows; fight; scuffle

kěn（ㄎㄣˇ）

肯[1]（肎） kěn 附着在骨头上的肉 flesh attached to bone：中～ be to the point｜～綮 bone joints

肯[2] kěn ❶ 表示同意 agree; consent：首～ nod assent; agree｜我劝说了半天，他才～了。It took me a long time to talk him into agreeing. ❷ 表示主观上乐意；表示接受要求 be willing to; be ready to：～虚心接受意见 be ready to listen to criticism with an open mind｜我请他来，他怎么也不～来。I invited him to come, but he said no, period. ❸〈方 *dial.*〉表示时常或易于 often; tend to：这几天～下雨。It's been raining often these past few days.

【肯定】kěndìng ❶ 承认事物的存在或事物的真实性（跟'否定'相对 as opposed to 'negate'）affirm; confirm; acknowledge the existence or truth of sth.：～成绩 acknowledge the achievement ❷ 表示承认的；正面的（跟'否定'相对 as opposed to 'negative'）positive; affirmative：～判断 positive assessment｜我问他赞成不赞成，他的回答是～的（＝赞成）。I asked him whether or not he agreed, and his answer was in the affirmative. ❸ 一定；无疑问 definitely; undoubtedly：情况～是有利的。The situation is undoubtedly in our favour. ❹ 确定；明确 definite; sure：他今天来不来还不能～。I'm not sure whether he will come today.｜请给一个～的答复。Please give me a definite answer.

【肯綮】kěnqìng〈书 *fml.*〉筋骨结合的地方 bone joints；〈比喻 *fig.*〉最重要的关键 most important juncture; key points：深中～ to the point

垦（墾） kěn 翻土；开垦（荒地）cultivate (land); reclaim (wasteland)：～地 land reclamation｜～荒 reclaim wasteland

【垦覆】kěnfù 在树木的行间挖沟，种植绿肥，并逐年覆土，使老树更新 dig a ditch between rows of trees and fill it with green manure and earth every year in order to revitalize the trees

【垦荒】kěnhuāng 开垦荒地 reclaim wasteland; bring wasteland under cultivation; open up virgin soil

【垦区】kěnqū 规模较大的开荒生产的地区 reclamation area; large area of land under reclamation

【垦殖】kěnzhí 开垦荒地，进行生产 reclaim and cultivate wasteland：～场 reclaimed field

【垦种】kěnzhòng 开垦种植 reclaim and cultivate：那里有大片可以～的沙荒地。There is a large expanse of gravelly wasteland suitable for reclamation.

恳（懇） kěn ❶ 真诚；诚恳 earnestly; sincerely：～求 implore｜～托 make a sincere request｜～谈 talk sincerely｜勤～ zealous and earnest ❷ 请求 request; entreat; beseech：转～ pass on a request｜敬～ respectfully request

【恳切】kěnqiè 诚恳而殷切 earnest; sincere：言词～ speak in an earnest tone｜情意～ show sincere feeling｜～地希望得到大家的帮助 sincerely hope for help from everybody

【恳请】kěnqǐng 诚恳地邀请或请求 invite or request in real earnest：～出席 earnestly request sb.'s presence｜～原谅 request sb.'s pardon in real earnest

【恳求】kěnqiú 恳切地请求 implore; entreat; beseech：我～他不要这样做。I implored him not to do so.

【恳谈】kěntán 恳切地交谈 talk sincerely; have a heart-to-heart conversation：～会 talkfest

【恳托】kěntuō 恳切地托付 sincerely commit to sb.'s care; earnestly entrust：～你把这件衣服带给他。Would you please take this clothing to him?

【恳挚】kěnzhì（态度或言词）诚恳真挚（of attitude or uttering）earnest; sincere：～的期望 sincere expectation｜词意～动人 express oneself in moving words

啃（齦） kěn 一点儿一点儿地往下咬 nibble; gnaw：～骨头 gnaw a bone｜～老玉米 nibble at an ear of corn ◇～书本 delve into books

☞ 齦 yín on p. 2291

【啃青】kěnqīng〈方 *dial.*〉❶ 指庄稼未完全成熟就收下来吃 harvest and eat crops that are not fully mature ❷ 指牲畜吃青苗（of livestock）eat young crops

kèn（ㄎㄣˋ）

掯 kèn〈方 *dial.*〉❶ 按；压 press：～住牛脖子 hold an ox's neck in place ❷ 刁难 make things difficult for sb.：勒～ obstruct; create difficulties ❸（眼里）含；噙（of eyes）contain：～着泪花 hold back one's tears

裉（褃） kèn 上衣靠腋下的接缝部分 armpit (of clothing)：抬～（上衣从肩头到腋下的尺寸）measurement of clothing between the shoulder and the armpit｜煞～（把裉缝上）sew up the seams of armpits (of clothing)

kēng (ㄎㄥ)

阬 kēng 〈书 *fml.*〉 same as 坑 kēng

坑 kēng ❶ (～儿 kēngr) 洼下去的地方 hole; pit; hollow; place sunken or depressed below an adjacent floor area: 泥～ mud pit | 弹～ crater | 刨个～儿 dig a hole | 一个萝卜一个～。Each radish has a hole of its own. ❷ 地洞; 地道 tunnel; pit: ～道 tunnel | 矿～ mine ❸ 〈古时 *arch.*〉指活埋人 bury alive: ～杀 execute sb. by burying him alive | 焚书～儒 burn books and bury Confucian scholars alive ❹ 坑害 entrap; cheat: ～人 entrap sb. | 她被人～了。She got double-crossed. ❺ (Kēng) 姓 a surname

【坑道】 kēngdào ❶ 开矿时在地下挖成的通道 mine tunnel ❷ 互相通连的地下工事, 用来进行战斗、隐蔽人员或储藏物资 tunnel; web of interconnected underground passageways for defence or storage purposes

【坑害】 kēnghài 用狡诈、狠毒的手段使人受到损害 entrap; lead sb. into a trap by guileful, vicious means; scheme to harm: 不法商人销售伪劣商品～消费者。Illegal merchants harm consumers by selling fake and inferior commodities.

【坑井】 kēngjǐng 坑道和矿井 mine pit

【坑坑洼洼】 kēng·kengwāwā (～的 kēng·kengwāwā·de) 形容地面或器物表面高一块低一块 full of bumps and hollows; bumpy; rough: 路面～, 车走在上面颠簸得厉害。The car bumped along the rough road.

【坑蒙】 kēngmēng 坑害, 蒙骗 swindle; blindfold; bluff and deceive: 以次充好, ～顾客 deceive customers by passing substandard products for fine products

【坑木】 kēngmù 矿井里用做支柱的木料 mine timber; pit prop

【坑骗】 kēngpiàn 用欺骗的手段使人受到损害 entrap; cheat: 有的小贩漫天要价, ～外地游客。Some peddlers overpriced their goods and cheated travellers from out of the town.

【坑气】 kēngqì 沼气 marsh gas

【坑子】 kēng·zi same as 坑 kēng ①: 水～ puddle

吭 kēng 出声; 说话 utter a sound or a word: 一声不～ say not a word | 有什么需要帮忙的事儿, 你就～一声。Give me a yell if you need help.

☞ háng on p. 770

【吭哧】 kēng·chi ❶ 因用力而不自主地发出声音 huff and puff: 他背起一麻袋粮食～～地走了。He heaved a sack of foodstuff onto his back and staggered off from the strain. ◇他～了好几天才写出这篇作文。He toiled a long time over his composition. ❷ 形容说话吞吞吐吐 hem and haw; stumble over one's words: 他～了半天我也没有听明白。He hemmed and hawed for quite a while, but I still could not understand.

【吭气】 kēng//qì (～儿 kēng//qìr) 吭声 utter a sound or a word: 我怕老人知道了不高兴, 一直没敢～。I dared not say a word for fear that the old man would be displeased by the news. | 不管你怎么追问, 他就是不～。He remained tight-lipped no matter how closely you questioned.

【吭声】 kēng//shēng (～儿 kēng//shēngr) 出声; 说话 (多用于否定式 oft. in negative form) utter a sound or a word: 任凭她说什么你也别～。Don't utter any word no matter what she says. | 他受了很多累, 可是从来也不吭一声。He'd been put to a lot of trouble but never complained.

硁(硜、磬) kēng 〈书 *fml.*〉 敲打石头的声音 sound of striking a stone

【硁硁】 kēngkēng 〈书 *fml.*〉 形容浅薄固执 shallow and obstinate: ～自守 adhere stubbornly to one's own opinion | ～之见 (谦辞, 称自己的见解) (hum.) in my point of view

铿(鏗) kēng 〈拟声词 *onom.*〉 形容响亮的声音 sound of clanging or clattering: 铁轮大车走在石头路上～～地响。The iron wheels of the big cart clattered along the cobbled road.

【铿锵】 kēngqiāng 形容有节奏而响亮的声音 rhythmic and sonorous sound: ～悦耳 sonorous and pleasant | ～有力的歌声 rhythmic and dynamic singing | 这首诗读起来音调～。This poem reads rhythmically and sonorously.

【铿然】 kēngrán 〈书 *fml.*〉 形容声音响亮有力 (of sound) loud and clear: 铃声～ clear ring | 溪水奔流, ～有声。The brook rushed on, gurgling and babbling.

kōng (ㄎㄨㄥ)

空 kōng ❶ 不包含什么; 里面没有东西或没有内容; 不切实际的 empty; hollow; void; unrealistic: ～箱子 empty box | ～想 idle dream | ～谈 indulge in empty talk | ～话 idle talk | ～着手去的, 什么都没带 go (somewhere) empty-handed | 把房子腾～了 empty out a room | 操场上～无一人。There isn't a single soul on the playground. ❷ 天空 sky; air: 晴～ clear sky | 高～ upper air | 当～ high above in the sky | 领～ airspace | ～中楼阁 mirage; castle in the air | 对～射击 anti-aircraft fire ❸ 没有结果的; 白白地 for nothing; in vain; without results: ～忙 make fruitless efforts | 落

～ come to nothing; suffer a loss | ～跑一趟 make a journey for nothing; make a wasted trip

☞ kòng on p.1106

【空包弹】kōngbāodàn 一种没有弹头的枪弹或炮弹，通常用于礼炮或部队演习 blank cartridge; bullet or shell without warhead, oft. used for gun salutes or military exercises

【空肠】kōngcháng 小肠的一部分，上端与十二指肠相连，下端连回肠。因为空肠的消化和吸收力强，蠕动快，肠内常呈排空状态，所以叫空肠。jejunum; section of the small intestine that is connected with the duodenum at the upper end and with the ileum at the lower end, wriggles fast and has strong digestive and absorptive capacity; (图见 ☞ figure for 消化系统 xiāohuà xìtǒng on p.2100)

【空城计】kōngchéngjì 小说《三国演义》中的故事。蜀将马谡失守街亭后，魏将司马懿率兵直逼西城，诸葛亮无兵迎敌，但沉着镇定，大开城门，自己在城楼上弹琴。司马懿怀疑设有埋伏，引兵退去。后来用'空城计'泛指掩饰力量空虚，骗过对方的策略。stratagem of the empty city, based on a story in *Romance of Three Kingdoms*: After defeating Ma Su, a general of the state of Shu, and seizing Jieting from him, Sima Yi, a general of the state of Wei, led his troops on an expedition to Xicheng. Lacking a strong enough military force to meet the approaching enemy, Zhuge Liang, prime minister of the state of Shu, had the city gate widely opened and, mounting the city wall, played the zither with deliberate composure. Suspecting an ambush, Sima Yi and his troop beat a hasty retreat. The phrase is now used to refer to the stratagem of presenting a bold front to conceal one's weakness so as to deceive an opposing force.

【空挡】kōngdǎng 汽车或其他机器的变速齿轮所在的一个位置，在这个位置上，从动齿轮与主动齿轮不相连接 neutral gear; position of the gears of a vehicle or any machine at which the driving gear is disconnected from the driven gear

【空荡荡】kōngdàngdàng (～的 kōngdàngdàng·de) 空落落 empty; deserted: 同学们都回家了，教室里～的。The classroom was looked deserted after all the students had gone home.

【空洞】[1] kōngdòng 物体内部的窟窿，如铸件里的砂眼、肺结核病人肺部形成的窟窿等 cavity; hollow in an object, e.g. sand hole of a casting, pulmonary cavity in a TB patient, etc.

【空洞】[2] kōngdòng 没有内容或内容不切实 devoid of content; impractical: ～无物 utter lack of substance; devoid of content | ～的说教 unpractical sermon

【空洞洞】kōngdòngdòng (～的 kōngdòngdòng·de) 形容房屋、场地等很空，没有人或没有东西 (of house, grounds, etc.) empty: 人都下地干活去了，村子里～的。The village was deserted as all the villagers were labouring in the fields. | 房间里～的，连张桌子也没有。The room is empty, without even a single table.

【空乏】kōngfá ❶ 穷困 poverty-stricken; impoverished ❷ 空虚而乏味 empty and tasteless: ～的生活 dull life

【空翻】kōngfān 一种体操动作，身体腾空向前或向后翻转一周或一周以上 flip; somersault; gymnastic act in which the athlete flips forward or backward in a complete circles, bringing the feet over the head, and landing finally on the feet

【空泛】kōngfàn 内容空洞浮泛，不着边际 vague and general; not specific: ～的议论 vague and general opinions | 八股文语言干瘪，内容～。Stereotypical writing is dull and devoid of content.

【空房】kōngfáng ❶ 没放东西或无人居住的房子 empty house; vacant room ❷ 丈夫外出，妻子一人住在家里，叫守空房 woman staying alone at home while her husband is away

【空腹】kōngfù ❶ 空着肚子，没有吃东西 on an empty stomach: ～抽血化验 fasting blood test ❷〈书 *fml.*〉〈比喻 *fig.*〉人没有学问 (of person) lacking in knowledge: ～高心 (指并无才学而盲目自大) lacking in talent but very ambitious

【空谷足音】kōng gǔ zú yīn 在空寂的山谷里听到人的脚步声 (《庄子·徐无鬼》:'夫逃虚空者，……闻人足音跫然而喜矣') sound of footsteps in a deserted valley. (*Zhuangzi · Xu Wugui*: 'The man who hides in a secluded, quiet place is pleased to hear the sound of steps.'); 〈比喻 *fig.*〉难得的音信、言论或事物 rare message, saying, or thing

【空喊】kōnghǎn 只是口头上叫嚷，并无实际行动 loud empty talk: ～口号 shouting of empty slogans | ～一阵有什么用? What's the use of all this empty talk?

【空耗】kōnghào 白白地消耗 endeavour to do nothing; waste: ～时间 waste time | ～精力 waste energy

【空话】kōnghuà 内容空洞或不能实现的话 empty talk; idle talk; hollow, unrealistic words: ～连篇 pages and pages of empty verbiage | 说～解决不了实际问题。Uttering hollow words cannot solve practical problems.

【空怀】kōnghuái 适龄的母畜交配或人工授精后没有怀孕 female livestock of baby-bearing age that fail to conceive through mating or artificial fertilization

【空幻】kōnghuàn 空虚而不真实；虚幻 visionary; illusory

【空际】kōngjì 空中 in the sky; in the air: 峰顶的纪念碑高耸～。The monument soars into the sky from the mountain top. | 广场上掌声

和欢呼声洋溢～。Clapping and cheering prevailed over the square.

【空寂】kōngjì 空旷而寂静；寂寥 quiet and deserted：～的山野 deserted mountain｜湖岸～无人。It's quiet on the banks of the lake, with no one around.

【空架子】kōngjià·zi 只有形式，没有内容的东西（多指文章、组织机构等 usu. referring to a piece of writing, an organization, etc.）mere skeleton; bare outline without content

【空间】kōngjiān 物质存在的一种客观形式，由长度、宽度、高度表现出来。是物质存在的广延性和伸张性的表现 space; objective form of the existence of matter, reflected in length, width, and height, with extensive properties of the existence of matter：三维～ three-dimensional space

【空间通信】kōngjiān tōngxìn 以人造卫星、宇宙飞船或星体为对象的无线电通信。包括卫星通信、空间站与地面站的通信以及空间站之间的通信等。space communications; radio communications targeted at man-made satellites, spacecraft, and planets as objects, between satellites, between a space station and a ground station, or between space stations

【空间图形】kōngjiān túxíng ❶ 几何图形 geometrical graphics ❷ 特指立体图形 solid figure

【空间站】kōngjiānzhàn ❶ 一种围绕地球航行的载人航天器，设置有完善的通信、计算等设备，能够进行天文、生物和空间加工等方面的科学技术研究 space station; manned spacecraft revolving around the earth and serving as a base for scientific observation and technological research in astronomy, biology, and space processing ❷ 设置在月球、行星或宇宙飞船等上面的空间通信设施 space-communication equipment installed on the moon, planets, or in spacecraft ‖ also 航天站 hángtiānzhàn

【空降】kōngjiàng 利用飞机、降落伞由空中着陆 airborne; land by air with the use of aircraft or parachute：～部队 airborne forces

【空姐】kōngjiě 空中小姐的简称 abbr. for 空中小姐 kōngzhōng xiǎojiě

【空军】kōngjūn 在空中作战的军队，通常由各种航空兵部队和空军地面部队组成 air force, usu. composed of different types of flying forces and ground forces

【空空如也】kōngkōng rúyě 空空的什么也没有（见于《论语·子罕》）absolutely empty, a phrase originating in *Analects·Zi Han*：有些人喜欢夸夸其谈，其实肚子里却是～。Some people have glib tongues but empty heads.

【空口】kōngkǒu ❶ 不就饭或酒（而吃菜蔬或果品）；不就菜蔬或果品（而吃饭、饮酒）eat dishes without rice or wine; eat rice or drink wine with nothing to go with it ❷ 不拿出事实或采取措施，只是嘴说 prattle; speak without quoting facts or taking action：这事～是说不明白的。Merely talking without stating facts cannot make this matter clear.｜光～说不行，得真抓实干。Speaking is far from enough, we should also take action.

【空口说白话】kōng kǒu shuō bái huà 形容光说不做，或只是嘴说而没有事实证明 make empty promises; pay mere lip service

【空口无凭】kōng kǒu wú píng 只是嘴说而没有真凭实据 mere verbal statement without conclusive evidence

【空旷】kōngkuàng 地方广阔，没有树木、建筑物等（of place）open and spacious, not covered with trees or buildings：～的原野 expanse of open country｜砍掉了这棵树，院里显着～点ル。After the tree was cut down, the courtyard seems more spacious.

【空灵】kōnglíng 灵活而不可捉摸 flexible and unpredictable：～的笔触 natural and unrestrained strokes｜这～的妙景难以描绘。It's hard to depict a wonderful scene like this.

【空论】kōnglùn 空洞的言论 empty talk：不切实际的～ impractical talk｜少发～，多做实事。Less talk, more action.

【空落落】kōngluòluò（～的 kōngluòluò·de）空旷而冷冷清清 spacious and desolate：落了叶子的树林子～的。The leafless forest looked desolate.｜他送走孩子回到家来，心里觉得～的，像少了点什么似的。After seeing his child off, he returned home, feeling very empty, like something was missing.

【空门】[1] kōngmén 指佛教，因佛教认为世界是一切皆空的（Budd.）door to nirvana：遁入～（出家为僧尼）enter the door to nirvana and become a monk or nun

【空门】[2] kōngmén（～ル kōngménr）指某些球类比赛中因守门员离开而无人把守的球门（of some ball games）free goal; empty net; goal left unguarded by the goalkeeper：面对～却把球踢飞了 kick out the ball in front of an empty net

【空濛】kōngméng〈书 *fml.*〉形容迷茫 hazy; misty：山色～。The hills were shrouded in mist.｜烟雨～ misty rain

【空名】kōngmíng 和实际情况不相符合的名义；虚名 undeserved reputation; empty fame; dummy：他在学会只挂个～，不担任具体职务。He is just a nominal association member.

【空难】kōngnàn 飞机等在空中飞行时发生的灾难，如失火、坠毁等 air disaster; aviation accident（e.g. fire, crash, etc.）

【空气】kōngqì ❶ 构成地球周围大气的气体。无色，无味，主要成分是氮气和氧气，还有极少量的氡、氦、氖、氩、氪、氙等惰性气体和水蒸气、二氧化碳等。air; mixture of invisible, colourless, and odourless gases (e.g. nitrogen, oxygen, vapour, carbon dioxide, plus a small quantity of inert gases including radon, helium, neon, argon, krypton, and xenon) that surrounds the earth ❷ 气氛 atmosphere: 学习～浓厚 serious atmosphere of study | 不要人为地制造紧张～。Don't create a tense atmosphere.

【空气锤】kōngqìchuí 利用压缩空气产生动力的锻锤 pneumatic drill; air hammer; forging hammer that produces power through compressed air; also 气锤 qìchuí

【空气轴承】kōngqì zhóuchéng 轴承的一种,利用包围在轴四周的压缩空气来支承轴,摩擦力小,转速很高 air bearing; bearing supported by compressed air around it, with little frictional force and high rotary speed

【空前】kōngqián 以前所没有 unprecedented: 盛况～ unprecedented grand occasion | 生产力得到了～发展。Productivity has developed at an unprecedented rate.

【空前绝后】kōng qián jué hòu 以前没有过,以后也不会有。多用来形容非凡的成就或盛况。unprecedented and unrepeatable; having no precedent, usu. used to describe a remarkable achievement or a grand occasion

【空勤】kōngqín 航空部门指在空中进行的各种工作(区别于'地勤'as compared with 'ground duty') flight duty; refers to all the types of work in the air of the aviation industry

【空身】kōngshēn (～儿 kōngshēnr) 指身边没有携带东西 carry no luggage; carry nothing: 他连换洗衣服都没带,就～儿去了广州。He went to Guangzhou, taking nothing with him, not even a change of clothes.

【空驶】kōngshǐ (机动车辆等)没有载货或载客而空着行驶 (of motor vehicles, etc.) run without carrying goods or passengers

【空手道】kōngshǒudào 日本的一种拳术,源于中国少林寺的技击。不使用器械进行格斗,分为进攻和防御两部分。karate; Japanese 'empty-handed' wrestling art that stems from the martial arts of China's Shaolin Temple, without using weapons, and divided into attack and defense

【空疏】kōngshū 〈书 *fml.*〉(学问、文章、议论等)空虚;空洞 (of learning, writing, discussion, etc.) empty; lacking in substance: 才学～ poor in scholarship

【空谈】kōngtán ❶ 只说不做;有言论,无行动 indulge in talk without taking action: 提倡实干,切忌～。Don't indulge in empty talk while practical action is called for. ❷ 不切合实际的言论 empty talk; idle talk; prattle: 纸上～ written prattle | 那些所谓的道理不过是娓娓动听的～。Those so-called principles are merely smooth-spoken but empty words.

【空调】kōngtiáo ❶ 空气调节,调节房屋、机舱、船舱、车厢等内部的空气温度、湿度、洁净度、气流速度等,使达到一定的要求 air-condition; control and adjust the humidity, temperature, cleanliness and speed of air in a house, engine room, cabin, or a carriage, etc., to meet certain requirements: ～机 air-conditioner | ～设备 air-conditioning system ❷ 指这种用途的装置 air-conditioner; air-conditioning system: 安装～ install an air-conditioner

【空头】kōngtóu ❶ 从事投机交易的人预料货价将跌而卖出期货,伺机买进相抵,这种人叫空头(因为卖出的货尚未买进,所以叫'空头';跟'多头'相对 as opposed to 'long position') (on the stock exchange) bear; oversold position; shortseller; person engaged in speculation, possessing no goods or property after selling out in anticipation of a fall in prices; ☞ 买空卖空 mǎi kōng mài kōng on p. 1294 ❷ 指有名无实,不发生作用 nominal; phony: ～人情 nominal friendship; lip service; empty favour | ～政治家 armchair politician

【空头支票】kōngtóu zhīpiào ❶ 因票面金额超过存款余额或透支限额而不能生效的支票 bad cheque; dud (or rubber) cheque; cheque returned by a bank because of insufficient funds in the payer's account ❷ 〈比喻 *fig.*〉不实践的诺言 empty promise; lip service

【空投】kōngtóu 从飞机上投下 air-drop; paradrop: 飞往灾区～救灾物资 fly to a stricken area to air-drop relief supplies

【空文】kōngwén ❶ 说空话的文章;没有实用价值的文章 idle essay; article of no substance or use ❷ 有名无实的规章条文 ineffective law or rule: 一纸～ a mere scrap of paper

【空袭】kōngxí 用飞机、导弹等进行袭击 air raid; attack by aircraft or missile

【空想】kōngxiǎng ❶ 凭空设想 indulge in fantasy; daydream: 不要闭门～,还是下去调查一下情况吧。Stop daydreaming, it's better to go down to the grass-roots and see how things stand there. ❷ 不切实际的想法 unrealistic thoughts; fantasy; daydream: 离开了客观现实的想像就成为～。Imagination becomes empty fantasies once it is divorced from reality.

【空心】kōng//xīn 树干髓部变空或蔬菜中心没长实 (of trees, vegetables, etc.) become hollow inside: 老槐树～了。The old locust tree has become hollow inside. | 大白菜空了心了。The Chinese cabbages have gone spongy inside.

【空心】kōngxīn 东西的内部是空的 hollow: ～坝 hollow dam | ～面 macaroni
☞ kòngxīn on p. 1107

【空心菜】kōngxīncài same as 蕹菜 wèngcài

【空心砖】kōngxīnzhuān 中心空的砖。这种砖有较好的保暖和隔音性能,用在不受压力的部分,可以减轻建筑物的重量并节约材料 hollow brick; effective in heat and sound insulation, and used for non-bearing walls to lighten the weight of the building and economize on materials

【空虚】kōngxū 里面没有什么实在的东西；不充实 hollow; void：后方～。The rear is weakly defended.｜精神～ be spiritually barren

【空穴来风】kōng xué lái fēng 有了洞穴才有风进来(见于宋玉《风赋》)'An empty hole invites the wind', a proverb first found in *Ode to Winds* by the poet Song Yu of the Warring States Period;〈比喻 *fig*.〉消息和传说不是完全没有原因的 weakness lends wings to rumours

【空域】kōngyù 指空中划定的一定范围 airspace：战斗～ combat airspace｜搜索～ search airspace

【空运】kōngyùn 用飞机运输 transport by air; airlift：～救灾物资 airlift relief supplies (to a stricken area)

【空战】kōngzhàn 敌对双方的飞机在空中进行的战斗 air battle; aerial combat (between fighting planes of hostile parties)

【空中】kōngzhōng ❶ 天空中 in the air; in the sky; aerial ❷ 指通过无线电信号传播而形成的 airborne; transmitted by radio signals：～信箱 airmail box｜～书场 storyteller's open air arena

【空中楼阁】kōng zhōng lóu gé 指海市蜃楼，多用来比喻虚幻的事物或脱离实际的理论、计划等 castles in the air; mirage; (fig.) far-fetched theory, plan, etc.

【空中小姐】kōngzhōng xiǎojiě 指客机上的女乘务员 air stewardess; 简称 abbr. 空姐 kōngjiě

【空钟】kōng·zhong same as 空竹 kōngzhú

【空竹】kōngzhú 用竹木制成的玩具，在圆柱的一端或两端安上周围有几个小孔的圆盒，用绳子抖动圆柱，圆盒就迅速旋转，发出嗡嗡的声音 diabolo; toy in which a round box, dotted with several holes, is set at one end of a bamboo cylinder or both ends of it and when played with using a string, the box revolves quickly and produces a buzzing sound through its holes

【空转】kōngzhuàn ❶ 机器在没有负载时运转 (of a motor, etc.) idle; race ❷ 由于摩擦力太小或车轮转速急剧增加，机车或汽车等的动轮在轨道上或路面上滑转而不前进 spin; (of a wheel) turn without moving forward (because of little frictional force or suddenly increased speed of rotation)

倥 kōng [倥侗](kōngtóng)〈书 *fml*.〉蒙昧无知 benighted; unenlightened

☞ kǒng on p.1106

崆 kōng 崆峒(Kōngtóng)，山名，在甘肃。又岛名，在山东。Kongtong Mountain, in Gansu Province; Kongtong Island, in Shandong Province

悾 kōng [悾悾]〈书 *fml*.〉形容诚恳 sincere; pure-hearted

箜 kōng [箜篌](kōnghóu)〈古代 *arch*.〉弦乐器，分卧式、竖式两种，弦数因乐器大小而不同，最少的五根弦，最多的二十五根弦 *konghou*; plucked stringed instrument that can be either horizontal or vertical and has a different number of strings, between 5 and 25, according to size

kǒng (ㄎㄨㄥˇ)

孔 kǒng ❶ 洞；窟窿；眼儿 hole; opening; aperture：鼻～ naris｜毛～ pore｜胃穿～gastric perforation｜这座石桥有七个～。This stone bridge has seven arches.｜水银泻地，无～不入。The mercury leaked and made its way to every nook and corner. ❷〈方 *dial*.〉〈量词 *classifier*〉用于窑洞 [for cave-dwellings]：一～土窑 a cave-dwelling ❸ (Kǒng) 姓 a surname

【孔道】kǒngdào 通往某处必经的关口 pass; narrow passage providing the only access to a certain place：交通～ traffic pass

【孔洞】kǒngdòng 窟窿(多指在器物上人工做的 usu. man-made in a utensil) opening or hole

【孔方兄】kǒngfāngxiōng 指钱，因旧时的铜钱有方形的孔(诙谐兼含鄙视意 humor., derog.) money; named after the square hole in coins in ancient times

【孔径】kǒngjìng 机件上圆孔的直径或桥孔、涵洞等的跨度 aperture; diameter of a round hole, span of a bridge opening, or a culvert, etc.

【孔孟之道】Kǒng Mèng zhī dào 孔子和孟子的思想和主张，指儒家学说 doctrines of Confucius and Mencius; Confucianism

【孔庙】Kǒngmiào 纪念和祭祀孔子的庙 Confucian temple; temple for commemorating and offering sacrifices to Confucius

【孔明灯】kǒngmíngdēng 利用热空气比重较轻能上升的原理制成的一种纸灯，上部没有口，灯心烧着后，热空气充满在里边，使灯升到空中去。相传是三国时诸葛亮发明的，亮字孔明，所以叫孔明灯。Kongming Lamp; paper lamp based on the principle that hot air can rise due to its light-specific gravity. There is no opening at the top of the lamp so that when lit, the lamp becomes inflated with hot air and rises to the sky. The lamp is said to be invented by Kongming (another name for Zhuge Liang), prime minister of the state of Shu during the Three Kingdoms Period, hence the name.

【孔雀】kǒng·què 鸟，头上有羽冠，雄的尾巴的羽毛很长，展开时像扇子。常见的有绿孔雀和白孔雀两种。成群居住在热带森林中或河岸边，吃谷类和果实等。多饲养来供玩赏，羽毛可以做装饰品。peafowl (*Pavo cristatus*); peacock; bird with a crest of upright plumules, the male having a greatly elongated tail that can be lifted and spread at will into a shimmering fan shape. The most commonly seen are green and white peacocks which live in groups in tropical forests or on riverbanks and eat cereal and fruit, oft. reared as an ornamental fowl whose feathers are used for decoration.

【孔隙】kǒngxì 窟窿眼儿;缝儿 small opening; hole; slot

【孔穴】kǒngxué 窟窿眼儿;孔洞 hole; cavity

【孔眼】kǒngyǎn 小孔;眼儿 eyelet; small hole: 叶子上有虫吃的～。Wormholes can be found on leaves. | ～大小不同的筛子 screens with meshes of different sizes

恐 kǒng ❶ 害怕;畏惧 be afraid of; dread: ～慌 panic | 惊～ frightened | 有恃无～ be emboldened in the knowledge that one has strong backing | 诚惶诚～ in fear and trepidation ❷ 使害怕 terrify; frighten: ～吓 intimidate ❸ 恐怕 perhaps; probably; be afraid: ～难胜任 be afraid that one is not up to a job, task, etc. | 他不出席～有原因。There is probably some reason for his absence.

【恐怖】kǒngbù 由于生命受到威胁而引起的恐惧 terror; horror; dread (caused by threat): 白色～ white terror | ～手段 terrorism | ～分子(进行恐怖活动的人) terrorist

【恐吓】kǒnghè 以要挟的话或手段威胁人;吓唬 threaten; intimidate; bluster by threatening words or actions: ～信 threatening letter

【恐慌】kǒnghuāng 因担忧、害怕而慌张不安 panic due to worry or fear: ～万状 utter panic | 断水断电的消息引起了人们的～。People panicked at the news of water cut-off and power cut.

【恐惧】kǒngjù 惧怕 fear; dread: ～不安 be frightened and restless

【恐龙】kǒnglóng 〈古代 *arch.*〉爬行动物,在中生代最繁盛,种类很多,大的长达30米,在中生代末期灭绝 dinosaur (*Saurischia* or *Ornithischia*); various large terrestrial carnivorous or herbivorous reptiles (some estimated to be 30 metres long) of remote antiquity, which became extinct in the late Mesozoic era

【恐怕】kǒngpà 〈副词 *adv.*〉❶ 表示估计兼担心 fear; dread; be afraid of: ～他不会同意。(I)'m afraid he won't agree. | 这样做,效果～不好。(I)'m afraid this won't work. ❷ 表示估计 perhaps; probably; maybe: 他走了～有二十天了。It's been maybe 20 days since he left.

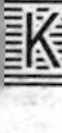

倥 kǒng [倥偬](kǒngzǒng)〈书 *fml.*〉❶ (事情)急迫匆忙 (of matters) pressing; urgent: 戎马～ at a moment of military emergency ❷ 穷困 poverty-stricken; go broke
☞ kōng on p. 1105

kòng (ㄎㄨㄥˋ)

空 kòng ❶ 腾出来;使空 leave empty or blank: 文章每段开头要～两格。Leave two spaces blank at the beginning of each paragraph of an article. | ～出一天时间参观游览。Leave a day for sightseeing. | 把前面几排座位～出来。Please leave the front few rows of seats vacant. ❷ 没有被利用或里面缺少东西 unoccupied; vacant: ～白 blank; vacancy | ～地 open space (ground) | 车厢里～得很。There are many vacant seats in the carriage. ❸ (～儿 kòngr)尚未占用的地方或时间 unoccupied space or time; empty space; opening; same as 空子 kòng·zi ①: 填～ fill in the blanks | 屋里堆得连下脚的～儿都没有。The room is fully occupied, with no more space even for planting one's feet. | 抽～儿到我这儿来一趟。Come over when you have time. ❹ same as 控[3] kòng
☞ kōng on p. 1101

【空白】kòngbái (版面、书页、画幅等上面)空着,没有填满或没有被利用的部分 (of layout of a page, book or painting) blank space: 版面上还有块～,可以补一篇短文。We can fill that space with a short article. ◇～点 blank spot | 这项新产品为我国工业填补了一项～。This new product has filled up a blank in our national industry.

【空白点】kòngbáidiǎn 工作没有达到的方面或部分 blank; gap; part of work to be expected: 消灭计划生育宣传的～ fill gaps in family-planning work

【空当】kòngdāng (～儿 kòngdāngr)空隙 space; gap; interval: 趁这～,你去了解一下。You'd better go and study the situation during this break. | 书架摆满了书,没有～。The bookshelf was packed with books, and there's no extra space. also 空当子 kòngdāng·zi

【空地】kòngdì ❶ 没有被利用的土地 vacant lot; open space; unused land: 门前有一块～可以种菜。There's a patch of open ground in front of the gate, suitable for growing vegetables. ❷ (～儿 kòngdìr)空着的地方;空隙 empty space; spacing: 屋角还有点～,正好放一个小柜。There's still an empty space at the corner of the room, right for putting a small cabinet.

【空额】kòng'é 空着的名额 vacancy: 吃～ claim more money by falsely reporting the number of employees | 编制已满,没有～了。The quota of staff has been fulfilled; there's no vacancy.

【空缺】kòngquē ❶ 空着的职位;缺额 vacant position; vacancy: 还有一个副主任的～。There's still a vacant position for deputy director. ❷ 泛指事物中空着的或缺少的部分 gap; (in a broad sense) empty or missing part of sth.: 填补～ fill a gap

【空日】kòngrì 某些历法中不记日月的日子,如傣族历法中除夕和次年元旦之间的一天或两天 (on some calendars) days not recorded by month and date, i. e. one or two days between the last day of the year and the following New Year's Day in the calendar of the Dai ethnic group

【空隙】kòngxì ❶ 中间空着的地方;尚未占用的时间 interval; empty space; unoccupied time: 农作物行间要有一定的～。There should be specific gaps between the rows of a crop in the field.|工人们利用生产～加紧学习。The workers studied hard during production intervals. ❷ same as 空子 kòng·zi ②

【空暇】kòngxiá same as 空闲 kòngxián ②

【空闲】kòngxián ❶ 事情或活动停下来,有了闲暇时间 free; break (from a matter or an activity): 等师傅～下来,再跟他谈心。The next time the master is free, you can have a heart-to-heart talk with him. ❷ 空着的时间;闲暇 free time; spare time; leisure: 他一有～就练习书法。He practises calligraphy whenever he has spare time. ❸ 空着不用;闲置 idle; be left unused: 充分利用～设备 make the most of idle equipment

【空心】kòngxīn (～儿 kòngxīnr)没吃东西,空着肚子 on an empty stomach: 这剂药～吃。This dose of medicine should be taken on an empty stomach.|先吃点菜垫一垫,免得待会儿喝～酒。Eat a bit first, so as not to drink on an empty stomach.

☞ kōngxīn on p.1104

【空余】kòngyú 空闲 free; vacant; unoccupied: ～房屋 unoccupied room|～时间 free time; spare time

【空子】kòng·zi ❶ 尚未占用的地方或时间 unoccupied place or time; gap; opening: 找了个～往里挤 find a gap and squeeze in|抽个～到我们这里看一看。Do find time to come visit us. ❷ 可乘的机会(多指做坏事的 oft. for doing sth. bad) chance or opportunity: 钻～ avail oneself of loopholes; seize every opportunity (to stir up trouble)

控[1] kòng 告发;控告 accuse; charge: ～诉 condemn|指～ accuse|被～ be charged|上～ appeal

控[2] kòng 控制 control; dominate: 遥～ remote control

控[3] kòng ❶ 使身体或身体的一部分悬空或处于失去支撑的状态 suspend; keep part of the body hanging in mid-air or in a certain position unsupported: 腿都～肿了 legs become swollen after keeping them in one place for too long|枕头掉了,～着脑袋睡着 keep sleeping with one's head unsupported after the pillow has fallen ❷ 使容器口儿(或人的头)朝下,让里边的液体慢慢流出 turn a container upside down to let the liquid trickle out: 把瓶里的油～干净。Turn the bottle upside down to empty it of oil. ‖ also 空 kòng

【控告】kònggào 向国家机关、司法机关告发(违法失职或犯罪的个人或集体) charge; accuse (an individual or collective of an offence through the judiciary)

【控购】kònggòu 控制社会集团购买 control purchases by government-sponsored institutions: ～指标 quota of commodity-purchase controls|～商品 commodities under purchase control

【控股】kòng//gǔ 指掌握一定数量的股份,以控制公司的业务 hold a certain amount of shares to gain control of a company's business

【控诉】kòngsù 向有关机关或公众陈述受害经过,请求对于加害者做出法律的或舆论的制裁 accuse; denounce; complain; make a statement of one's suffering to a relevant institutions or community to obtain judicial or community punishment of an offender: ～大会 accusation meeting|～旧社会 condemn the old society

【控制】kòngzhì ❶ 掌握住不使任意活动或越出范围;操纵 control; dominate; command (in order to avoid wilful activities or movement beyond the domain): ～数字 control figures|自动～ automatic control ❷ 使处于自己的占有、管理或影响之下 control; get (sth. or sb.) under one's hold, management, or influence: 殖民地的经济为宗主国所～。The economy of colonies is dominated by their overlords.|102 高地已完全～在我军手中。Highland No. 102 has fallen completely under the control of our troops.|制高点的火力～了整片开阔地。The fighting force at a commanding elevation controlled the entire expanse of the open ground.

【控制数字】kòngzhì shùzì 对整个国民经济计划或某项工作规定其大致范围的数字 control figures; figures that prescribe the general scope of an overall plan for the national economy or a certain project

鞚 kòng 〈书 *fml.*〉马笼头 halter

kōu (ㄎㄡ)

芤 kōu 古书上指葱 onion; scallion in ancient books

【芤脉】kōumài 〈中医 *Chin. med.*〉指重按时中间无而两边有的脉搏,好像手指按葱管的感觉。多见于大出血。hollow pulse; pulse, when pressed hard, that feels like a scallion between fingers, common in patients suffering from excessive bleeding

抠(摳) kōu ❶ 用手指或细小的东西从里面往外挖 dig, or dig out, with a finger or sth. pointed: 把掉在砖缝里的豆粒～出来 dig out the beans from the furrows ❷ 雕刻(花纹) carve; cut (with patterns): 在镜框边上～出花儿来 carve a design into a picture frame ❸ 不必要的深究；向一个狭窄的方面深求 go into (a matter) in unnecessary earnest; delve into sth. with hair-splitting attention：～字眼儿 puzzle over words and phrases｜死～书本儿 delve mechanically into books ❹ 吝啬 stingy; miserly：这个人～得很，一分钱都舍不得花。He is stingy to even spend a single penny.

【抠门儿】kōuménr〈方 *dial.*〉吝啬 stingy; miserly：这人真～，几块钱也舍不得出。How stingy he is! He even hates to spend a few bucks.

【抠搜】kōu·sou ❶ same as 抠 kōu ① ❷ 吝啬 stingy：这人真～，像个守财奴。This person is really stingy — just like a miser. ❸ 磨蹭 move slowly; dawdle：你这么抠抠搜搜的，什么时候才办完？If you dawdle like this, when will you ever be able to finish?

【抠唆】kōu·suo same as 抠搜 kōu·sou

【抠字眼儿】kōu zìyǎnr 在字句上钻研或挑毛病 pay too much attention to wording; find fault with the choice of words

弧（彄）kōu〈书 *fml.*〉弓弩两端系弦的地方 notch at both ends of a bow for tying a bowstring

眍（瞘）kōu 眼珠子深陷在眼眶里边 (of the eyes) sink in; become sunken：他病了一场，眼睛都～进去了。His illness made him look sunken-eyed.

【眍䁖】kōu·lou same as 眍 kōu

kǒu（ㄎㄡˇ）

口 kǒu ❶ 人或动物进饮食的器官，有的也是发声器官的一部分 mouth; human or animal's organ for taking food and uttering sounds; 通称 generally called 嘴 zuǐ ❷ 指口味 taste：～轻 light taste — hate salty and spicy food｜～重 strong taste — love salty and spicy food ❸ 指人口 people; population：户～ registered permanent residence｜家～ households and population｜拖家带～ be tied down by one's family ❹ (～儿 kǒur) 容器通外面的地方 opening (of a container); mouth：瓶子～儿 mouth of a bottle｜碗～儿 rim of a bowl ❺ (～儿 kǒur) 出入通过的地方 entrance：出～ exit｜入～ entrance｜门～儿 gate｜海～ entrance to the sea｜关～ pass｜胡同～儿 entrance to an alley ❻ 长城的关口，多用做地名，也泛指这些关口 pass; gateway of the Great Wall (usu. used as part of a place name)：～外 area north of Zhangjiakou, Hebei Province｜喜峰～ Xifeng Pass｜古北～ Gubei Pass｜～蘑 mushroom｜西～羊皮 Xikou sheepskin ❼ (～儿 kǒur) same as 口子[2] kǒu·zi ②：伤～ wound｜衣服撕了个～儿。A hole was torn in the jacket. ❽ 性质相同或相近的单位形成的管理系统 department; system involving sections of identical or similar character：归～ reside with a line of occupation｜财贸～ financial and trade circles ❾ 刀、剑、剪刀等的刃 blade; edge of a sword, knife, scissors, etc.：刀卷～了。The edge of the knife has turned. ❿ 指马、驴、骡等的年龄（因可以由牙齿的多少看出来）age of a draught animal (to be told from the number of teeth)：六岁～ six years of age｜这匹马～还轻。This horse is still young. ⓫〈量词 *classifier*〉：一家五～人 a family of five｜三～猪 three pigs｜一～钢刀 a steel sword｜一～井 a well｜一～缸 a jar

【口岸】kǒu'àn 港口 port：通商～ trading port｜～城市 port city

【口碑】kǒubēi〈比喻 *fig.*〉群众口头上的称颂（称颂的文字有很多是刻在碑上的 as compared with words of praise mostly inscribed on stone tablets）public praise; word-of-mouth：～载道 be praised everywhere｜～甚佳 enjoy a sterling reputation

【口碑载道】kǒubēi zài dào 形容到处都是群众称颂的声音 be praised wherever one goes; win popular praise

【口北】Kǒuběi 长城以北的地方，主要指张家口以北的河北省北部和内蒙古自治区中部 area north of Zhangjiakou, including the northern part of Hebei Province and the central part of the Inner Mongolia Autonomous Region; also 口外 Kǒuwài

【口布】kǒubù 餐巾 napkin

【口才】kǒucái 说话的才能 eloquence：有～ eloquent speaker｜他～好，说起故事来有声有色。Eloquent, he made the story come alive.

【口沉】kǒuchén〈方 *dial.*〉口重 be fond of salty and spicy food

【口称】kǒuchēng 口头上说 claim to be; profess：～支持我，背地里却在拆我的台。He claimed to support me but privately undermined my work.

【口吃】kǒuchī 说话时字音重复或词句中断的现象。是一种习惯性的语言缺陷。stutter; stammer; habitual handicap in language ability characterized by involuntary disruption of speech or spasmodic repetition of vocal sounds; 通称 generally called 结巴 jiē·ba

【口齿】kǒuchǐ ❶ 说话的声音；说话的本领 sound of speaking; ability to speak：～清楚（咬字儿正确）have clear enunciation｜～伶俐（说话流畅）speak eloquently and fluently ❷ 指马、驴、骡等的年龄 age (of a draught animal)

【口臭】kǒuchòu 嘴里发出难闻的气味。引起这种症状的主要原因是龋齿、齿槽化脓、慢性口炎、消化不良等。bad breath; halitosis; condition of fetid breath mainly caused by decayed teeth, gingivitis, chronic stomatitis, indigestion, etc.

【口传】kǒuchuán 口头传授 instruct orally:～心授 oral teaching inspires true understanding|民间艺人大都用～的方法来教徒弟。Most folk artists teach their apprentices through oral instruction.

【口疮】kǒuchuāng 口炎、口角炎等的统称 aphtha; general term for stomatitis, commissural cheilitis, etc.

【口袋】kǒu·dai (～儿 kǒu·dair) ❶ 用布、皮等做成的装东西的用具 bag; sack; container made of cloth or leather:面～ flour sack|纸～儿 paper bag ❷ 衣兜 pocket:这件制服上有四个～儿。This uniform has four pockets.

【口淡】kǒudàn 〈方 *dial.*〉same as 口轻[1] kǒuqīng

【口风】kǒu·fēng 指话中透露出来的意思 one's intention or view as revealed by what one says:你先探探他的～,看他是不是愿意去。Sound him out and see whether he wants to go.

【口服】[1] kǒufú 口头上表示信服 profess to be convinced:～心不服 pretend to be convinced

【口服】[2] kǒufú 内服 take orally

【口福】kǒufú 能吃到好东西的福气(含诙谐意 humor.) gourmet's luck; luck to get sth. very nice to eat:～不浅 good luck to eat delicious food|很有～ very lucky in enjoying food

【口赋】kǒufù 〈古代 *arch.*〉每户按人口缴纳的税 tax paid by each household on a per-capita basis; also 口算 kǒusuàn, 口钱 kǒuqián and 丁口钱 dīngkǒuqián

【口腹】kǒufù 指饮食 food:～之欲 desire for good food|不贪～ not indulge one's appetite

【口感】kǒugǎn 食物吃到嘴里时的感觉 taste (of food):这种面条吃起来～好,营养也较丰富。These noodles not only have a nice chewy flavour but are rich in nutrients as well.

【口供】kǒugòng 受审者口头陈述的与案情有关的话 affidavit; confession; statement made by the accused under examination:问～ interrogate the accused|不轻信～ not readily believe the affidavit

【口号】kǒuhào ❶ 供口头呼喊的有纲领性和鼓动作用的简短句子 slogan; sound byte; brief phrase or sentence used in advertising or promotion:呼～ shout slogans|标语～ posters and slogans ❷〈旧指 *old*〉口令 ② watchword

【口红】kǒuhóng 化妆品,用来涂在嘴唇上使颜色红润 lipstick; solid waxy cosmetic in stick form for reddening the lips

【口惠】kǒuhuì 〈书 *fml.*〉口头上许给人好处(并不实行) lip service; empty promise:～而实不至 make a promise and not keep it; pay lip service

【口技】kǒujì 杂技的一种,运用口部发音技巧来模仿各种声音 vocal mimicry; vocal imitation; acrobatic skill of imitating a sound by vocal performance

【口碱】kǒujiǎn 〈方 *dial.*〉出产在西北地区的碱,过去多以张家口、古北口一带为集散地 alkali, produced in Northwest China, with sales outlets mostly in Zhangjiakou and Gubeikou in Hebei Province

【口角】kǒujiǎo 嘴边 corner of the mouth:～流涎 slobber|～生风(形容说话流利) speak fluently

☞ kǒujué

【口紧】kǒujǐn 说话小心,不乱讲;不随便透露情况或答应别人 close-mouthed; tight-lipped; not readily reveal news or make promises

【口径】kǒujìng ❶ 器物圆口的直径 bore; calibre; diameter of the round mouth of an object:天文台装有～130毫米折射望远镜,供人们观察星空。The observatory is equipped with a 130-mm.-bore refracting telescope for people to observe the sky. ❷ 泛指要求的规格、性能等 (in a broad sense) requirements; specifications:螺钉与螺母的～不合。The screw does not match the nut. ❸〈比喻 *fig.*〉对问题的看法和处理问题的原则 line of action; point of view on issues or principles:开会统一～ have a meeting to give line of action|咱俩说的～要一致。Both of us must speak along the same lines. *or* Both of us must say the same thing about what happened.

【口诀】kǒujué 根据事物的内容要点编成的便于记诵的语句 pithy mnemonic formula (oft. in rhyme); mnemonic rhyme:珠算～ abacus rhymes

【口角】kǒujué 争吵 quarrel; bicker; wrangle:不要为了一点小事儿就和人家～起来。Don't bicker with them over trifles.

☞ kǒujiǎo

【口口声声】kǒu·koushēngshēng 形容不止一次地陈说、表白或把某一说法经常挂在口头 say again and again; keep on saying:他～说不知道。He kept on pleading ignorance.

【口粮】kǒuliáng 原指军队中按人发给的粮食,后来泛指各个人日常生活所需要的粮食(military) grain rations; grain necessary for daily diet

【口令】kǒulìng ❶ 战斗、练兵或做体操时以简短的术语下达的口头命令 (in warfare, military training, or physical exercises) word of command:喊～ shout code words ❷ 在能见度不良的情况下识别敌我的一种口头暗号,一般以单词或数字表示 password; code words; countersign; oral signs used to distinguish warring sides in a situation of poor visibility, usu. in words or numbers:问～ ask for the password|对～ exchange code words

【口马】kǒumǎ 口北出产的马 horse native to the area north of Zhangjiakou

【口蜜腹剑】kǒu mì fù jiàn 嘴上说的很甜,肚子里却怀着害人的坏主意。形容人阴险。honey-mouthed but dagger-hearted; honey on one's lips but murder in one's heart; hypocritical and malignant

【口蘑】kǒumó 蕈的一种,多生在牧场的草地上,有白色肥厚的菌盖。供食用,味鲜美。张家口一带出产的最著名。a kind of dried mushroom, mostly growing in meadows, whose white, fleshy pileus is delicious (the best known are those from Zhangjiakou)

【口气】kǒu·qì ❶ 说话的气势 manner of speaking:他的~真不小。He talked big. ❷ 言外之意;口风 what is actually meant; implication:探探他的~ ascertain sb.'s opinions|听他的~,好像对这件事感到为难。Judging by the way he spoke, he seemed to be in an awkward situation. ❸ 说话时流露出来的感情色彩 tone; note:严肃的~ serious tone|诙谐的~ humorous tone|埋怨的~ note of complaint

【口器】kǒuqì 节肢动物口两侧的器官,有摄取食物及感觉等作用 mouthpart (of an insect); structure or appendage near the mouth (of an arthropod) esp. when adapted for use in gathering food or sensory perception

【口腔】kǒuqiāng 口内的空腔,由两唇、两颊、硬腭、软腭等构成。口腔内有牙齿、舌、唾腺等器官。oral cavity, consisting of lips, cheeks, hard palate, and soft palate, inside of which are teeth, tongue and salivary glands

【口琴】kǒuqín 一种乐器,一般上面有两行并列的小孔,里面装着铜制的簧,用口吹小孔发出声响 mouth organ; harmonica; musical instrument that has two parallel rows of holes above each other and copper reeds inside, and that emits sound from the holes when blown with the mouth

【口轻】[1] kǒuqīng ❶ 菜或汤的味不咸 (of dishes or soups) not too salty:我喜欢吃~的,请你少放点儿盐。I prefer food that's not too salty. Please don't put too much salt in it. ❷ 指人爱吃味道淡一些的饮食 be fond of food that is not too salty:他~。He's fond of food that is not too salty.

K

【口轻】[2] kǒuqīng (驴马等)年龄小 (of a horse, donkey, etc.) young:~的骡子 young mule; also 口小 kǒuxiǎo

【口若悬河】kǒu ruò xuán hé 形容能言善辩,说话滔滔不绝 let loose a stream of eloquence; be eloquent; speak volubly

【口哨儿】kǒushàor 双唇合拢,中间留一小孔(有的把手指插在口内),使气流通过而发出的像吹哨子的声音 whistling sound made through rounded lips:吹~ whistle

【口舌】kǒushé ❶ 因说话而引起的误会或纠纷 dispute or misunderstanding caused by gossip:~是非 disputes and quarrels ❷ 指劝说、争辩、交涉时说的话 talk sb. around (when persuading, contesting, or negotiating):指导员费了很多的~,才说服他躺下来休息。It took the instructor a lot of talking to convince him to lie down and rest.

【口实】kǒushí 〈书 *fml.*〉假托的理由;可以利用的借口 cause for gossip; excuse:贻人~ give occasion for talk

【口试】kǒushì 考试的一种方式,要求应试人口头回答问题(区别于'笔试' as compared with 'written examination') oral examination; oral test

【口是心非】kǒu shì xīn fēi 指嘴里说的是一套,心里想的又是一套,心口不一致 say yes and mean no; say one thing and mean another

【口授】kǒushòu ❶ 口头传授(还没有文字记录的歌曲、方技等)(of songs, medical and fortune-telling skills, etc., without written records) teach or instruct orally:我国许多地方戏曲都是由民间艺人世代~而保存下来的。Many of the Chinese local operas have been preserved by folk artists who have passed them down from generation to generation by word of mouth. ❷ 口头述说而由别人代写 dictate:~作战命令 dictate a fighting command

【口述】kǒushù 口头叙述 give an oral account:他~,由秘书记录。He dictated, and the secretary recorded.

【口水】kǒushuǐ 唾液的通称 (general term for) saliva; spit; drool:流~ slobber

【口算】kǒusuàn ❶ 边心算边说出运算结果 add a sum orally ❷ ☞ 口赋 kǒufù

【口谈】kǒután 口头述说 state orally:~和平 verbal call for peace

【口条】kǒu·tiáo 用做食品的猪舌或牛舌 pig or ox tongue (as food):酱~ braised ox tongue

【口头】kǒutóu 用说话方式来表达的 oral; in words a)区别于'思想'或'行动' [as compared with 'thought' or 'action']:他只是~上答应你。He only gave you a verbal promise. b)区别于'书面' [as compared with 'written']:~汇报 oral report|~翻译 interpretation|~文学 oral literature

【口头】kǒu·tou 〈方 *dial.*〉味道(专指吃生的瓜果) flavour; taste (of fruit):这个西瓜的~很好。This watermelon tastes good.

【口头禅】kǒutóuchán 原指有的禅宗和尚只空谈禅理而不实行,也指借用禅宗常用语作为谈话的点缀。今指经常挂在口头的词句。pet phrase; tag; cliche; catch phrases. (orig.) Monks study Chan doctrines but don't practise them, or merely pay lip services to Chan phrases.

【口头文学】kǒutóu wénxué 口耳相传,没有书面记载的民间文学 oral literature; folk tales, ballads, etc., handed down orally

【口头语】kǒutóuyǔ (~儿 kǒutóuyǔr)说话时经常不自觉地说出来的词句 pet phrase:'瞧着办'三个字几乎成了他的~。The words 'I'll watch and do' have become his pet phrase.

【口外】Kǒuwài same as 口北 Kǒuběi

【口腕】kǒuwàn 某些低等动物(如水母)生在口旁的器官,有捕食的作用 oral arms; organs near the mouth of some lower animals (e.g. jellyfish) used for catching food

【口味】kǒuwèi (～儿 kǒuwèir) ❶ 饮食品的滋味 flavour or taste of food: 这个菜的～很好。This dish is tasty. ❷ 各人对于味道的爱好 one's taste: 食堂里的菜不对我的～。The dishes served in the dining hall are not to my taste. ◇豫剧最合他的～。Henan opera suits his taste best.

【口吻】kǒuwěn ❶ 某些动物(如鱼、狗等)头部向前突出的部分,包括嘴、鼻子等 muzzle; snout; protruding jaws and nose of some animals (e.g. fish, dog, etc.) ❷ same as 口气 kǒu·qì ③: 玩笑的～ jocular tone | 教训人的～ in a lecturing tone

【口误】kǒuwù ❶ 因疏忽而说错了话或念错了字 stumble; make a mistake in speaking or wording due to carelessness ❷ 因疏忽而说错的话或念错的字 misspoken words or sentences due to carelessness

【口香糖】kǒuxiāngtáng 糖果的一种,用人心果树分泌的胶质加糖和香料制成,只可咀嚼,不能吞下 chewing gum; sweetened and flavoured insoluble resin (as a preparation of chicle) for chewing

【口小】kǒuxiǎo same as 口轻[2] kǒuqīng

【口信】kǒuxìn (～儿 kǒuxìnr) 口头转告的话;口头传递的消息 oral message: 请你给我家里捎个～,说我今天不回家了。Please send word to my family that I'm not going back home tonight.

【口形】kǒuxíng 人的口部的形状,语音学上特指在发某个声音时两唇的形状 degree of lip-rounding

【口型】kǒuxíng 指说话或发音时的口部形状 shape of the mouth as one speaks or produces a sound

【口血未干】kǒu xuè wèi gān 古人订立盟约时要在嘴上涂上牲畜的血。'口血未干'指订立盟约不久(多用于订立盟约不久就毁约)。(orig.) before the blood of the sacrifice is dry on one's lips (when forming an alliance); soon after an alliance is formed (usu. refers to breaking an agreement)

【口译】kǒuyì 口头翻译(区别于'笔译' as compared with 'written translation') oral interpretation

【口音】kǒuyīn 发音时软腭上升,阻住鼻腔的通道,气流专从口腔出来的叫做口音,对鼻音(口腔不通气,鼻腔通气)和鼻化元音(口腔鼻腔都通气)而言。普通话语音中 m,n,ng 三个是鼻音,ng 尾韵儿化以后前面的元音变成鼻化元音,其余都是口音,如 a,e,o,b,p,f 等。oral speech sounds; sounds produced through the oral cavity when the soft palate rises and blocks the passage of the nasal cavity (as different from nasal sounds and nasal vowels). In *putonghua*, m, n, and ng are nasal sounds, a vowel preceding a combination of ng and r becomes a nasalized vowel, and the others, such as a, e, o, b, p, and f, are oral speech sounds.

【口音】kǒu·yin ❶ 说话的声音 voice: 听他的～,好像是山东人。I could tell from his accent that he came from Shandong Province. ❷ 方音 accent: 有～(说话带方音) speak with an accent | ～很重 strong accent

【口语】kǒuyǔ ❶ 谈话时使用的语言(区别于'书面语' as compared with 'written language') spoken language ❷〈书 *fml.*〉毁谤的话 slander; calumny

【口谕】kǒuyù〈旧指 *old*〉上司或尊长口头的指示 verbal instructions (from one's superior)

【口占】kǒuzhàn〈书 *fml.*〉❶ 不打草稿,口头述说出来 dictate: ～电文 dictate message for a telegram ❷ 指即兴作诗词,不打草稿,随口吟诵出来 improvise (a poem): ～一绝 improvise a *jueju* (or quatrain)

【口罩】kǒuzhào (～儿 kǒuzhàor) 卫生用品,用纱布等制成,罩在嘴和鼻子上,防止灰尘和病菌侵入 gauze mask (worn over nose and mouth to prevent infection from dust or pathogenic bacteria); surgical mask

【口重】kǒuzhòng ❶ 菜或汤的味咸 salty: 我知道你爱吃～的,所以多搁了些酱油。I know you like salty dishes, so I put more soya sauce. ❷ 指人爱吃味道咸一些的饮食 be fond of salty food: 我～。I'm fond of salty food.

【口诛笔伐】kǒu zhū bǐ fá 用语言文字宣布罪状,进行声讨 condemn both in speech and in writing

【口子】[1] kǒu·zi〈量词 *classifier*〉指人 person: 你们家有几～? How many people are there in your family?

【口子】[2] kǒu·zi ❶ (山谷、水道等)大的豁口 (of valleys, canals, etc.) large opening; hole: 山谷的～上有一座选矿厂。There's an ore dressing mill at the entrance to the valley. ❷ (人体、物体的表层)破裂的地方 (of human body or the surface of an object) cut; tear: 不小心手上拉(lá)了一个～。I cut my hand carelessly.

kòu (ㄎㄡˋ)

叩(❶ 敂) kòu ❶ 敲;打 knock; tap: ～门 knock at the door ❷ 磕头 kowtow: ～首 kowtow | ～头 kowtow | ～谢 express one's heartfelt thanks ❸〈书 *fml.*〉询问;打听 enquire; ask: 略～生平 ask about one's life experience | ～以文义 enquire about an meaning of the article

【叩拜】kòubài 叩头下拜,一种旧式的礼节 kowtow; traditional etiquette of kneeling and touching the forehead to the ground in token of homage, worship, or deep respect

【叩打】kòudǎ 敲;打 knock; tap; rap:他用指头轻轻地～着房门。He tapped on the door with his fingers.

【叩阍】kòuhūn 〈书 *fml.*〉官吏、百姓到朝廷诉冤 lodge a complaint with the imperial court:～无门(无处申冤) not know where to air one's grievances

【叩见】kòujiàn 〈书 *fml.*〉进见;拜见 visit; call on

【叩首】kòushǒu 磕头 kowtow:三跪九～ kowtow to sb. incessantly

【叩头】kòu//tóu 磕头 kowtow

【叩谢】kòuxiè 磕头感谢,泛指表示深切的谢意 kowtow in thanks; (in a broad sense) offer earnest thanks:登门～ call at sb.'s house to express earnest thanks

【叩诊】kòuzhěn 〈西医 *W. med.*〉用手指或锤状器械叩击人体一定部位,借以诊断疾病 percussion; diagnostic act or technique of tapping the surface of a body part with fingers or a hammer-like tool to listen and learn about the condition of the part beneath

扣(❼釦) kòu ❶ 套住或搭住 buckle; button up:～扣子 do up the buttons; button up|把门～上 latch the door ❷ 器物口朝下放置或覆盖别的东西 place a cup, bowl, etc., upside down; cover with an inverted cup, bowl, etc.:把碗～在桌子上 turn the bowl upside down on the table|用盘子把碗里的菜～住,免得凉了。Cover the dish with a plate to keep it from getting cold. ❸〈比喻 *fig.*〉安上(罪名或不好的名义) label; brand sb. with unwarranted or unfavourable labels:～帽子 put a label on sb. ❹ 扣留;扣押 detain; take into custody; arrest:把犯人～起来 detain a criminal ❺ 从原数额中减去一部分 deduct (from an amount):～除 deduct|～分 deduct marks|不折不～ one hundred per cent; pure and simple|打九～(减去十分之一) give a 10 per cent discount ❻ (～儿 kòur) same as 扣子 kòu·zi ①:绳～儿 knot (in a rope)|系(jì)一个活～儿 tie (or make) a slipknot ❼ (～儿 kòur) same as 扣子 kòu·zi ②:衣～ clothes button ❽ 用力朝下击打 smash or spike (a ball):～球 slam dunk, smash a ball ❾ same as 筘 kòu:丝丝入～ all threads are closely knit together; done with meticulous care ❿ 螺纹的一圈叫一扣 loop of thread (on a screw):拧了三～ drive in a screw in three twists

【扣除】kòuchú 从总额中减去 deduct:～损耗 deduct loss|～伙食费还有节余。There's still a surplus after the deduction of the cost of meals.

【扣发】kòufā ❶ 扣下(工资、奖金等)不发给(of salary, bonus, etc.) deprive; withhold:～事故责任者当月奖金 deprive that month's bonus from the person responsible for the accident ❷ 扣住(文件、稿件等)不发出或不发表(of an article, document, etc.) keep from being published:～新闻稿 withhold a news release

【扣留】kòuliú 用强制手段把人或财物留住不放 detain; hold in custody; arrest:由于违章,交通警～了他的驾驶证。The traffic officer suspended his driving license because of a traffic violation.

【扣帽子】kòu mào·zi 对人或事不经过调查研究,就加上现成的不好的名目,如'落后分子'、'官僚主义'等 lable; put an unwarranted, unfavourable label, such as 'laggard' and 'bureaucratist' on sb. or sth.

【扣人心弦】kòu rén xīnxián 形容诗文、表演等有感染力,使人心情激动(of literature, performance, etc.) exciting; breath-taking; appealing

【扣题】kòutí 围绕主题;切题 keep to the subject:作文要～。When writing a composition, make sure to keep to the subject.

【扣头】kòu·tou 打折扣时扣除的金额 discount; amount of money deducted at a discount

【扣压】kòuyā 把文件、意见等扣留下来不办理 withhold (a manuscript from publication or an opinion from action)

【扣押】kòuyā 拘留;扣留 detain; hold in custody:犯人已被～。The suspect is being held in custody.

【扣眼】kòuyǎn (～儿 kòuyǎnr)套住纽扣的小孔 buttonhole

【扣子】kòu·zi ❶ 条状物打成的疙瘩 knot ❷ 纽扣 button ❸ 章回小说或说书在最紧要、热闹时突然停顿的地方。扣子能引起人对下一段情节的关切。abrupt break in a story to create suspense; point of high suspense

寇 kòu ❶ 强盗或外来的侵略者(也指敌人) robber; invader (also referring to enemy):～仇 foe|海～ pirate|外～(从国外入侵的敌人) foreign invaders ❷ 敌人来侵略 invade:入～ invade|～边 invade the border ❸ (Kòu) 姓 a surname

【寇仇】kòuchóu 仇敌 enemy; foe:视若～ regard sb. as one's foe

筘(簆) kòu 织布机上的主要机件之一,形状像梳子,用来确定经纱的密度,保持经纱的位置,并把纬纱打紧 reed; device on a loom resembling a comb, used to space warp yarns evenly; also 杼 zhù

蔻 kòu ☞ below

【蔻丹】kòudān 染指甲的油 Cutex; nail polish

【蔻蔻】kòukòu same as 可可 kěkě

㲃 kòu 〈书 *fml.*〉初生的小鸟儿 fledgeling

kū（ㄎㄨ）

矻 kū [矻矻]〈书 *fml.*〉勤劳不懈的样子 diligent; industrious; assiduous：孜孜～ hard-working|～终日 work from sun-up to sundown

刳 kū〈书 *fml.*〉剖开；挖空 hollow out：～木为舟 hollow out a tree trunk to make a canoe; fashion a canoe out of a tree trunk

枯 kū ❶（植物等）失去水分（of plants, etc.）lose water; wither：～萎 wither|～槁 withered|～草 withered grass|～骨 skeleton ❷（井、河流等）变得没有水（of wells, rivers, etc.）be dried up：～井 dried-up well|海～石烂 the seas run dry and the rocks crumble ❸ 肌肉干瘪（of muscle）dry and shrivelled：～瘦的手 shrivelled hands ❹ 没有生趣；枯燥 dull; uninteresting：～坐 sit in boredom; sit idle ❺〈方 *dial.*〉芝麻、大豆、油茶等榨油后的渣滓 dregs of sesame, soya bean, or camellia after extraction：菜～ dregs of canola after extraction|茶～ sasangua cake|麻～ dregs of sesame after oil extraction

【枯肠】kūcháng〈书 *fml.*〉〈比喻 *fig.*〉写诗作文时贫乏的思路 impoverished mind (for writing)：搜索～，不成一句 rack one's brains but not come up with a single sentence

【枯干】kūgān 干枯；枯槁 dried up; withered; wizened：河流～。The river is dried up.

【枯槁】kūgǎo ❶（草木）干枯（of plants）withered：～禾苗 withered seedlings ❷（面容）憔悴（of face）haggard：形容～look haggard

【枯骨】kūgǔ 尸体腐烂后剩下的骨头 dry bones (of a person long dead)

【枯黄】kūhuáng 干枯焦黄 withered and yellow：～的禾苗 withered stalks|过了中秋，树叶逐渐～。The leaves begin to turn yellow and wither after mid-autumn.

【枯寂】kūjì 枯燥寂寞 bored and lonely：～的生活 boring and lonely life|他们人多，虽然在沙漠中行进，也不感到～。They travelled in a large group, so they didn't feel bored or lonely while passing through the desert.

【枯焦】kūjiāo 焦枯；干枯 withered; shrivelled：久旱不雨，禾苗～。The seedlings of the cereal crops have withered because of the drought.

【枯竭】kūjié ❶（水源）干涸；断绝（of water sources）dry up; be cut off：水源～。The source has dried up.|河道～。The riverbed has dried up. ❷ 体力、资财等用尽；穷竭（of physical energy, assets, etc.）spent; exhausted：精力～ tire out; physically spent|资源～ run out of resources

【枯井】kūjǐng 干枯没有水的井 dry well

【枯木逢春】kū mù féng chūn〈比喻 *fig.*〉重获生机 get a new lease of life

【枯荣】kūróng 荣枯 ups and downs

【枯涩】kūsè ❶ 枯燥不流畅 dull and heavy：文字～ dull and heavy style (of writing) ❷ 干燥不滑润 dry and coarse：两眼～ dry and scratchy eyes

【枯瘦】kūshòu 干瘪消瘦 emaciated; skinny：～的手 skinny hands|～如柴 be as thin as a lath; be all skin and bones

【枯水期】kūshuǐqī 河流处于最低水位的时期 dry season; period when a river is at its lowest water level

【枯萎】kūwěi 干枯萎缩 withered：荷叶完全～了。The lotus leaves have all withered.

【枯朽】kūxiǔ 干枯腐烂 withered and rotten：这颗老树已经～了。This old tree has become withered and rotten.

【枯燥】kūzào 单调，没有趣味 dry and dull; uninteresting：生活～ lead a dull life|～无味 dry as dust

哭 kū 因痛苦悲哀或感情激动而流泪，有时候还发出声音 cry; weep; express deep sorrow or agitation by shedding tears：～泣 weep|～诉 complain tearfully|放声大～ cry loudly

【哭鼻子】kū bí·zi 哭（含诙谐意 humor.）cry; snivel：输了不许～。If you lose, don't go snivelling.

【哭哭啼啼】kū·kutítí 没完没了地哭 weep and wail; cry without end

【哭灵】kū//líng 在灵柩或灵位前痛哭 cry bitterly in front of a coffin or sacrificial tablet

【哭泣】kūqì（轻声）哭 sob; weep; cry softly：低声～ weep in a low voice

【哭腔】kūqiāng ❶ 戏曲演唱中表示哭泣的行腔 weeping tune; tunes that express weeping (in traditional Chinese opera) ❷（～儿 kūqiāngr）说话时带哭泣的声音 speak with a trace of weeping

【哭穷】kū//qióng 口头上向人叫苦装穷 go about telling people how hard up one is (which one is not); complain of being hard up

【哭丧】kū//sāng 号丧（háo//sāng）wail at a funeral

【哭丧棒】kūsāngbàng 旧俗出殡时孝子拄的棍子，上面缠着白纸（old custom）staff wrapped with white paper, used by the son of the deceased in a funeral procession

【哭丧着脸】kū·sang·zhe liǎn 心里不痛快，脸上流露出很不高兴的样子 with displeasure written on one's face

【哭诉】kūsù 哭着诉说或控诉 complain tearfully; accuse while weeping; sob out：她向大伙～自己的遭遇。Between sobs she told of her sufferings before the crowd.

【哭天抹泪】kū tiān mǒ lèi 哭哭啼啼的样子（含厌恶意 derog.）wailing and whining; crying piteously

【哭笑不得】kū xiào bù dé 哭也不是,笑也不是。形容处境尴尬,不知如何是好。not know whether to laugh or to cry; find sth. both funny and annoying; be in an awkward dilemma and at a loss

堀 kū 〈书 *fml.*〉❶ same as 窟 kū ❷ 穿穴 bore a hole

啰(圐) kū [啰喻](kūlüè)蒙语指围起来的草场,现多用于村镇名称(Mongolian language) enclosed pasture (presently used as part of place names):马家~(在内蒙古)也译作库伦 Majia Village, in Inner Mongolian; also transliteration of 库伦 kùlún

窟 kū ❶ 洞穴 cave; hole:石~ grotto; rock cave|山~ mountain cave|狡兔三~ a wily rabbit has three burrows — elaborate precautions made for self-protection ❷ 某种人聚集或聚居的场所 den; place of gathering for a certain group of people:匪~ bandits' lair|盗~ thieves' den|赌~ gambling den|贫民~ slum area

【窟窿】kū·long ❶ 洞;孔 hole; cavity:冰~ ice hole|老鼠~ mouse-hole|鞋底磨了个大~wore a big hole in the sole of one's shoe ❷〈比喻 *fig.*〉亏空 deficit; debt ❸〈比喻 *fig.*〉漏洞、破绽 loophole; flaw:堵住税收工作中的~ plug up loopholes in taxation

【窟窿眼儿】kū·longyǎnr 小窟窿;小孔 small hole:这块木头上有好些虫蛀的~。There are a lot of worm-holes in this piece of wood.

【窟穴】kūxué 洞穴;巢穴(多指坏人隐藏的地方)(for evildoers) den; lair; hideout

【窟宅】kūzhái 巢穴,多指盗匪盘踞的地方 bandits' lair

骷 kū [骷髅](kūlóu)干枯无肉的死人头骨或全副骨骼 withered skull; human skeleton

kǔ(ㄎㄨˇ)

苦 kǔ ❶ 像胆汁或黄连的味道(跟'甘'相对 as opposed to 'sweet') bitter:~胆 gallbladder|这药~极了。This medicine tastes very bitter. ❷ 难受;痛苦 hardship; suffering; pain:~笑 forced smile|艰~ hardship|愁眉~脸 furrow; put on a long face|~日子过去了 hard times are over|~尽甘来 after suffering comes happiness ❸ 使痛苦;使难受 cause sb. so much pain; give sb. a hard time:一家五口都仗着他养活,可~了他了。Having to support a family of five, he had a really hard time. ❹ 苦于 suffer from; be troubled by:~旱 suffer from drought|~夏 lose appetite and weight in the summer ❺ 有耐心地;尽力地 painstakingly; doing one's utmost:~劝 earnestly advise|~干 work hard|~思 wrack one's brain|勤学~练 study and train hard ❻〈方 *dial.*〉除去得太多;损耗太过 cut off too much; be worn out:指甲剪得太~了 trim one's nails too short|这双鞋穿得太~了,不能修理了。This pair of shoes is worn out beyond repair.

【苦熬】kǔ'áo 忍受着痛苦度(日子) endure the years:~岁月 go through years of suffering and hardship

【苦差】kǔchāi 艰苦的差事;没有什么好处可得的差事 hard and unprofitable job:出了一趟~ be back from a hard business trip

【苦楚】kǔchǔ 痛苦(多指生活上受折磨 usu. from living) suffering; misery; distress:满腹~,无处倾诉 be full of misery but find no place to pour it out

【苦处】kǔ·chu 所受的痛苦 suffering; hardship; difficulty:这些~,向谁去说? To whom can I pour out these sufferings of mine?

【苦胆】kǔdǎn 胆囊的通称 common name for 胆囊 dǎnnáng

【苦迭打】kǔdiédǎ '政变'的音译(Chinese transliteration) coup d'état [法 French: coup d'État]

【苦工】kǔgōng ❶〈旧社会 *pre-1949*〉被迫从事的辛苦繁重的体力劳动 hard (manual) work; hard labour ❷〈旧社会 *pre-1949*〉被迫做苦工的体力劳动者 coolie

【苦功】kǔgōng 刻苦的功夫 hard work; painstaking effort:语言这东西不是随便可以学好的,非下~不可。The mastery of language is not easy and requires painstaking effort.

【苦瓜】kǔguā ❶ 一年生草本植物,开黄花。果实长圆形或卵圆形,两头尖,表面有许多瘤状突起,熟时橘黄色,略有苦味,可做蔬菜 bitter gourd (or melon); annual herbal plant that bears yellow flowers and oval-shaped pointed-ended fruit with small strumae and a bitter flavour, which can be eaten as a vegetable ❷ 这种植物的果实 fruit of this plant ‖ 有的地区叫癞瓜 in some places also called 癞瓜 làiguā

【苦果】kǔguǒ〈比喻 *fig.*〉坏的结果;使人痛苦的结果 bad consequences:自食~ reap what one has sown

【苦海】kǔhǎi 原是佛教用语,后来比喻很困苦的环境(of Buddhism) abyss of misery; (fig.) very difficult dilemma:脱离~climb out of the abyss of misery

【苦害】kǔhài〈方 *dial.*〉损害;使受害 harm; damage

【苦寒】kǔhán ❶ 极端寒冷;严寒 bitter cold:气候~ bitterly cold weather ❷ 贫寒;寒苦 poor; poverty-stricken:世代~ be poor for generations

【苦活儿】kǔhuór 劳苦而报酬少的工作 hard and unprofitable job:干~ do a hard and poorly paid job

【苦尽甘来】kǔ jìn gān lái〈比喻 *fig.*〉艰苦的境况过去,美好的境况到来 after suffering comes happiness; also 苦尽甜来 kǔ jìn tián lái

【苦境】kǔjìng 痛苦艰难的境地 hard and difficult circumstances

【苦口】kǔkǒu ❶ 不辞烦劳，反复恳切地说 (admonish) in earnest: ～相劝 earnestly advise (or exhort) | ～婆心 advise with earnest words and good intentions ❷ 引起苦的味觉 bitter to the taste: 良药～利于病。Good medicine tastes bitter but is effective.

【苦口婆心】kǔ kǒu pó xīn 劝说不辞烦劳，用心像老太太那样慈爱。形容怀着好心再三恳切劝告。persuade (or admonish) earnestly and patiently

【苦力】kǔlì 帝国主义者到殖民地或半殖民地奴役劳动者，把出卖力气干重活的工人叫做苦力 coolie; unskilled labourer or porter indentured by imperialists in a colony or semi-colony

【苦闷】kǔmèn 苦恼烦闷 depressed; dejected; feeling low: 心情～ be depressed

【苦命】kǔmìng 不好的命运；注定受苦的命(迷信) (superstition) cruel fate; ill-fated life: ～人 luckless person

【苦难】kǔnàn 痛苦和灾难 misery; pain; tribulation: ～深重 be in deep distress; be in the depth of misery | ～的日子 days of suffering | 永远不能忘记旧社会的～。Never forget the misery of the old society

【苦恼】kǔnǎo 痛苦烦恼 vexed; worried: 自寻～ worry oneself | 为此事他～了好几天。He has been worried about this for quite a few days.

【苦肉计】kǔròujì 故意伤害自己身体，骗取敌方信任，以便借机行事的计谋 ruse of self-injury (inflicting an injury on oneself to win the confidence of the enemy)

【苦涩】kǔsè ❶ 又苦又涩的味道 bitter and astringent ❷ 形容内心痛苦 pained; agonized; anguished: ～的表情 pained look | 他～地笑了笑。He forced a smile.

【苦水】kǔshuǐ ❶ 因含有硫酸钠、硫酸镁等矿物质而味道苦的水 bitter water (containing such minerals as sodium sulphate, magnesium sulphate, etc.) ❷ 因患某种疾病而从口中吐出的苦的液体，通常是消化液和食物的混合物 gastric secretion, bile, etc., rising to the mouth (oft. as a result of some disease) ❸〈比喻 *fig.*〉心中藏的痛苦 suffering: 在控诉大会上倒～ pour one's sufferings out at an accusation meeting

【苦思冥想】kǔ sī míng xiǎng 深沉地思索 think hard; rack one's brains

【苦痛】kǔtòng 痛苦 pain

【苦头】kǔtóu (～儿 kǔtóur) 稍苦的味道 bitter taste: 这个井里的水带点～儿。Water from this well has a slightly bitter taste.

【苦头】kǔ·tóu (～儿 kǔ·tóur) 苦痛；磨难；不幸 suffering; misery: 吃尽～ endure untold suffering | 什么～我都尝过了。I have experienced all kinds of misery.

【苦夏】kǔxià 指夏天食量减少，身体消瘦。有的地区叫疰夏。lose appetite and weight in the summer; also called 疰夏 zhùxià in some places

【苦笑】kǔxiào 心情不愉快而勉强做出笑容 forced smile; wry smile in distress

【苦心】kǔxīn ❶ 辛苦地用在某些事情上的心思或精力 trouble taken; painstaking efforts: 煞费～ take a lot of trouble | 一片～ trouble and pain taken for a good cause ❷ 费尽心思 extend much care and thought: ～研究 study painstakingly | ～经营 take great pains to build up (an enterprise, etc.)

【苦心孤诣】kǔ xīn gū yì 费尽心思钻研或经营 drive oneself mercilessly to attain sth. that is unattainable for others (孤诣 *gu yi*: 别人所达不到的 sth. unattained by others)

【苦行】kǔxíng 某些宗教徒的修行手段，故意用一般人难以忍受的种种痛苦来折磨自己 ascetics; ascetic practices; practising strict self-denial as a measure of personal and esp. spiritual discipline

【苦行僧】kǔxíngsēng 用苦行的手段修行的宗教徒 disciplinant; believer of a religion who cultivates himself through ascetic practices

【苦刑】kǔxíng 酷刑 excruciating pain: 受～ suffer from excruciating pain

【苦役】kǔyì〈旧时 *old*〉统治者强迫人民从事的艰苦繁重的体力劳动 hard labour imposed by overlords: 服～ do corvée labour

【苦于】kǔyú ❶ 对于某种情况感到苦恼 be afflicted (by a disadvantage): ～力不从心 be distressed by one's own ability not being equal to one's ambition ❷ 表示相比之下更苦些 be harder off than; be worse off than: 半自耕农，其生活～自耕农。The semi-land-owning peasants were worse off than the land-owner peasants.

【苦雨】kǔyǔ 连绵不停的雨；久下成灾的雨 too much rain: 凄风～ chilly wind and continuous rain (that inspires sadness in one's mind)

【苦战】kǔzhàn 艰苦地奋战 wage an arduous struggle; struggle hard: 通宵～ work hard all night

【苦衷】kǔzhōng 痛苦或为难的心情 pain; feeling of pain or embarrassment: 你应该体谅他的～。You should make allowances for his difficulties.

【苦主】kǔzhǔ 指人命案件中被害人的家属 family members of a murder victim

楛 kǔ〈书 *fml.*〉粗劣；不坚固；不精致 rough; of poor quality

☞ hù on p. 825

kù (ㄎㄨˋ)

库[1] kù ❶ 储存大量东西的建筑物 warehouse; storehouse; structure for housing a large amount of goods：水～ reservoir | 国～ state treasury | 材料～ warehouse for raw materials | 入～put into storage ❷（Kù）姓 a surname

库² kù 库仑的简称 abbr. for 库仑 kùlún

【库藏】kùcáng 库房里储藏 have in storage：清点～物资 check the amount of goods in storage | ～图书三十万册 store a collection of 300,000 books

☞ kùzàng

【库存】kùcún 指库中现存的现金或物资 stock；reserve；money or materials kept in stock：清点～ make an inventory of all the stock

【库缎】kùduàn 一种提花缎子，因清代宫廷入库收藏而得名 reserve satin；jacquard satin, selected for the imperial collection of the Qing Dynasty

【库房】kùfáng 储存财物的房屋 storehouse；storeroom

【库锦】kùjǐn 用金线、银线和彩色绒线织成花纹的锦 tinselled brocade

【库仑】kùlún 电量的实用单位。电流强度为1安培时，1秒钟内通过导体横截面的电量为1库仑。1库仑等于3×10^9静电单位的电量。这个单位名称是为纪念法国物理学家库仑（Charles de Coulomb）而定的。coulomb（C），named after the French physicist Charles de Coulomb；unit of electric charge equal to the quantity of electricity transferred by a current of one ampere in one second；one coulomb equals 3×10^9 electrostatic unit of electricity；简称 abbr. 库 kù

【库仑计】kùlúnjì 用来测定电量的装置，和电解池的装置相同。使用时，保持电流强度不变，测出通电时间和析出物的质量，就可以算出电流强度。coulometre；apparatus for measuring the amount of electricity passing through a conductor by the amount of electrolysis produced

【库伦】kùlún ☞［唠喻］（kūlüè）on p. 1114

【库券】kùquàn 国库券的简称 abbr. for 国库券 guókùquàn

【库容】kùróng 水库、仓库、冷库等的容积 storage capacity（of a reservoir, warehouse, freezer, etc.）

【库藏】kùzàng〈书 *fml.*〉仓库 warehouse；storehouse

☞ kùcáng

绔 kù 同'裤'，用于'纨绔' same as 裤 kù, as used in 纨绔 wánkù；☞ 纨绔 wánkù on p. 1972

袴 kù same as 裤 kù

喾（嚳） Kù 传说中的上古帝王名 Emperor Ku, legendary Chinese ruler of remote antiquity

裤 kù 裤子 trousers；pants：短～ shorts；short pants | 棉～ cotton-padded trousers | 毛～ wool pants | 灯笼～ knickers；pantalets

【裤衩】kùchǎ（～儿 kùchǎr）短裤（多指贴身穿的）underpants；undershorts；underwear：三角～ briefs

【裤裆】kùdāng 两条裤腿相连的地方 crotch（of trousers）

【裤兜】kùdōu（～儿 kùdōur）裤子上的口袋 trouser pocket

【裤管】kùguǎn〈方 *dial.*〉裤腿 trouser legs；also 裤脚管 kùjiǎoguǎn

【裤脚】kùjiǎo ❶（～儿 kùjiǎor）裤腿的最下端 bottom of a trouser leg ❷〈方 *dial.*〉裤腿 trouser legs

【裤头】kùtóu〈方 *dial.*〉（～儿 kùtóur）裤衩 underpants：游泳～ bathing trunks

【裤腿】kùtuǐ（～儿 kùtuǐr）裤子穿在两腿上的筒状部分 trouser legs

【裤线】kùxiàn 指裤腿前后正中从上到下熨成的褶子 creases（of trousers）

【裤腰】kùyāo 裤子的最上端，系腰带的地方 waist of trousers, the very top of the trousers where the belt is fastened

【裤子】kù·zi 穿在腰部以下的衣服，有裤腰、裤裆和两条裤腿 trousers；pants；outer garment covering each leg separately and usu. extending from the waist to the ankle：一条～ a pair of trousers

酷 kù ❶ 残酷 cruel；oppressive：～刑 torture；cruel punishment | ～吏 cruel official ❷ 程度深的；极 very；extremely：～热 extremely hot；brutal heat | ～寒 bitter cold | ～似 be the very image of | ～肖 closely resemble

【酷爱】kù'ài 非常爱好 ardent love；be very fond of：～书法 be very fond of calligraphy | ～音乐 be keen on music

【酷吏】kùlì〈书 *fml.*〉滥用刑罚、残害人民的官吏 official who brutally abuses and tortures people

【酷烈】kùliè〈书 *fml.*〉❶ 残酷 cruel；fierce：中国人民在反动统治时期遭受的苦难极为～。The Chinese people suffered severe tribulations before liberation. ❷（香气）很浓（of fragrance）heady：异香～ heady fragrance ❸ 炽烈 burning fiercely：～的阳光 scorching sunshine

【酷虐】kùnüè 残酷狠毒 cruel and ferocious；ruthless；savage：～成性 cruel and ferocious by nature

【酷热】kùrè（天气）极热（of weather）extremely hot：～的盛夏 extremely hot summer

【酷暑】kùshǔ 极热的夏天 intense heat wave of summer；sweltering summer heat

【酷似】kùsì 极像 be the very image of；be exactly like：她长得～母亲。She looks exactly like her mother.

【酷肖】kùxiào〈书 *fml.*〉酷似 closely resemble；be the very image of；be exactly like：～其父 closely resemble one's father

【酷刑】kùxíng 残暴狠毒的刑罚 cruel（or savage) torture：～逼供 extort a confession by cruel torture

kuā（ㄎㄨㄚ）

夸（誇） kuā ❶ 夸大 exaggerate；overstate；boast：～口 talk big｜她把一点小事～得比天还大。She's making a mountain out of a molehill. ❷ 夸奖 praise：人人都～小兰劳动好，学习好。Everyone praised Xiaolan for her good performance in both labour and study.

【夸大】kuādà 把事情说得超过了原有的程度 exaggerate；overstate；magnify；enlarge or increase，esp. beyond the original extent or the truth：～缺点 magnify one's shortcomings｜～成绩 overstate one's achievements｜～其词 puff sth. up

【夸大其词】kuādà qí cí 说话或写文章不切实际，扩大了事实 make an overstatement in speaking or writing；exaggerate；词 cí also written as 辞 cí

【夸诞】kuādàn〈书 *fml.*〉言谈虚夸，不切实际 exaggerating to an incredible extent；boastful：～之词，不足为信。The exaggeration is not worth believing.

【夸父追日】Kuāfù zhuī rì《山海经·海外北经》记载古代神话，有个夸父，为了追赶太阳，渴极了，喝了黄河、渭河的水还不够，又往别处去找水，半路上就渴死了。他遗下的木杖，后来变成一片树林，叫做邓林。后来用'夸父追日'比喻决心大或不自量力。Kua Fu's race with the sun. According to an ancient myth in *Book of Mountains and Seas · Northern Lands Beyond the Sea*, a man called Kua Fu, feeling extremely thirsty from chasing after the sun, drank up all the water in the Yellow and Weihe rivers, but that was still not enough. He travelled elsewhere seeking water but died from thirst midway. Later people use this phrase as a metaphor for a person with a strong will or who overestimates himself.

【夸海口】kuā hǎikǒu 漫无边际地说大话 brag about；talk big

【夸奖】kuājiǎng 称赞 praise；commend：谁都～他做了一件好事。Everybody praised him for his good deed.

【夸克】kuākè 组成质子、中子等基本粒子的更小的粒子 quark；very small particle constituent of elementary particles like protons and neutrons

【夸口】kuā//kǒu 说大话 boast；brag；talk big：你别～，先做给大家看看。Cut all the boasting，just show us how to do it.

【夸夸其谈】kuākuā qí tán 说话或写文章浮夸，不切实际（of speaking or writing）indulge in exaggeration；indulge in verbiage

【夸示】kuāshì 向人显示或吹嘘（自己的东西、长处等）lavish praise on oneself；boast

【夸饰】kuāshì 夸张地描绘 give an exaggerated account（or description）：文笔朴实，没有半点～。The article was written in a simple style，without a hint of exaggeration.

【夸耀】kuāyào 向人显示（自己有本领、有功劳、有地位势力等）；炫耀 brag about；show off；flaunt（one's abilities，achievements，or an advantageous position）：他从不在人面前～自己。He never brags about himself.

【夸赞】kuāzàn 夸奖 speak highly of；commend；praise：人们都～她心灵手巧。Everyone praised her for being clever and adept.

【夸张】kuāzhāng ❶ 夸大；言过其实 exaggerate；overstate ❷ 修辞手段，指为了启发听者或读者的想像力和加强所说的话的力量，用夸大的词句来形容事物。如'他的嗓子像铜钟一样，十里地都能听见'。［a figure of speech］ hyperbole；extravagant exaggeration in an attempt to inspire the reader's or listener's imagination and strengthen the power of the words；e.g. 'His voice is as loud as a bronze bell that can even be heard 10 miles away.' ❸ 指文艺创作中突出描写对象某些特点的手法（in literary creation）hyperbole；technique of highlighting the features of the object of description

【夸嘴】kuā//zuǐ 夸口 boast；brag；talk big

姱 kuā〈书 *fml.*〉美好 beautiful

kuǎ（ㄎㄨㄚˇ）

侉（咵） kuǎ〈方 *dial.*〉❶ 语音不正，特指口音跟本地语音不同（speak）with an accent（esp. a non-local accent）❷ 粗大；不细巧 big and clumsy；unwieldy：几年不见，长成个～大个儿。I haven't seen you for several years，and you've grown into a strapping young man.｜这个箱子太～了，携带不方便。The suitcase is too big and clumsy to carry.

【侉子】kuǎ·zi〈方 *dial.*〉指口音跟本地语音不同的人 person who speaks with a different accent

垮 kuǎ 倒塌；坍下来 collapse；fall；break down：洪水再大也冲不～坚固的堤坝。No matter how severe the flood water gets，it won't burst through the solid dyke. ◇别把身体累～了。Don't work too hard and wear yourself down.｜打～了敌人 defeat the enemy

【垮台】kuǎ//tái〈比喻 *fig.*〉崩溃瓦解 fall from power；collapse

kuà（ㄎㄨㄚˋ）

挎 kuà ❶ 胳膊弯起来挂住或钩住东西 carry sth. on the arm：～着篮子 with a basket on one's arm | 两个女孩子～着胳膊向学校走去。Two girls went to school arm in arm. ❷ 把东西挂在肩头、脖颈或腰里 tote; carry sth. over one's shoulder, around one's neck or waist: ～着照相机 have a camera slung over one's shoulder; be camera-toting

【挎包】kuàbāo (～儿 kuàbāor) 带子较长的可以挂在肩膀上背的袋子 satchel; small bag with a shoulder strap

【挎斗】kuàdǒu (～儿 kuàdǒur) 安装在摩托车、自行车后侧的斗形装置,可供人乘坐 sidecar; cup-shaped device attached to the side of a motorcycle or bicycle for a passenger

胯 kuà 腰的两侧和大腿之间的部分 hip; laterally projecting region of each side of the lower or posterior part of the mammalian trunk, formed by the lateral parts of the pelvis and upper part of the femur, together with the fleshy parts covering them: ～下 crotch | ～骨 hipbone

【胯裆】kuàdāng 两条腿的中间;裆 crotch; parting of two legs

【胯骨】kuàgǔ 髋骨的通称 common name for hipbone

跨 kuà ❶ 抬起一只脚向前或向左右迈(一大步) stride (forward or sideways): ～进大门 step through a doorway | 向左～一步 take a step to the left ❷ 两腿分在物体的两边坐着或立着 bestride; straddle; stand or sit with legs wide apart: ～在马上 mount a horse ◇铁桥横～长江两岸。An iron bridge sits astride the Yangtze River. ❸ 超越一定数量、时间、地区等的界限 outstrip; go beyond (a certain amount, time, region, etc.): ～年度 span the years | ～地区 transregional | ～行业 beyond trade boundaries ❹ 附在旁边的 attached on the side: ～间 aisle | ～院儿 side courtyard

【跨度】kuàdù ❶ 房屋、桥梁等建筑物中,梁、屋架、拱券两端的支柱、桥墩或墙等承重结构之间的距离 span; spread or extent between abutments, supports, or walls (on a bridge, house, etc.) ❷ 泛指距离 (in a broad sense) distance; limited space: 时间～大 tremendous span of time

【跨国公司】kuà guó gōngsī 通过直接投资、转让技术等活动,在国外设立分支机构或与当地资本合股拥有企业的国际性公司 transnational corporation; international corporation that sets up branches abroad or establishes joint ventures through direct investment, technology transfer, or shareholding in foreign countries; also 多国公司 duō guó gōngsī

【跨栏】kuàlán 田径运动项目之一,在规定的竞赛距离内每隔一定距离摆设栏架,运动员要依次跨过栏架跑到终点 hurdle race; track event in which a series of hurdles, set at regular distances, must be jumped over until the athlete reaches the finish line

【跨年度】kuà niándù (任务、计划、预算等) 跨着两个年度;越过一个年度进入另一个年度 (of tasks, plans, or budgets) go beyond the year; straddle two years: ～工程 project straddling two years | ～预算 budget to be carried over to the next year

【跨院儿】kuàyuànr 正院旁边的院子 side courtyard

【跨越】kuàyuè 越过地区或时期的界限 stride across; leap over; cut across; span: ～障碍 surmount an obstacle | ～长江天堑 conquor the deep chasm of the Yangtze River | ～了几个世纪 span several centuries

kuǎi (ㄎㄨㄞˇ)

㧟[1] **(擓)** kuǎi 〈方 *dial.*〉用指甲抓;搔 scratch: ～痒痒 scratch an itch | ～破了皮 have scratched (and injure) the skin

㧟[2] **(擓)** kuǎi 〈方 *dial.*〉❶ same as 挎 kuà ①: ～着小竹篮 tote a small bamboo basket on one's arm ❷ 舀 (yǎo) ladle; dip; scoop: 从桶里～一勺水 scoop a ladle of water from a barrel

蒯 kuǎi ❶ 蒯草,多年生草本植物,叶子条形,花褐色。生长在水边或阴湿的地方。茎可用来编席,也可造纸。wool grass; perennial herbal plant that has long narrow leaves and brown flowers and a stem to be used for weaving mats or making paper, and grows by water or in sunless wet places ❷ (Kuǎi) 姓 a surname

kuài (ㄎㄨㄞˋ)

凷 kuài 〈书 *fml.*〉土块 clod

会 (會) kuài 总计 sum total: ～计 accounting

☞ huì on p. 866

【会计】kuài·jì ❶ 监督和管理财务的工作,主要内容有填制各种记账凭证,处理账务,编制各种有关报表等 accounting; system of recording, summarizing and verifying business and financial transactions, involving the work of filling out certificates for keeping accounts, handling accounting matters, and making financial statements ❷ 担任会计工作的人员 accountant; one who is in charge of accounting

【会计师】kuàijìshī ❶ 企业、机关中会计人员的职务名称之一 certified accountant; chief accountant; chartered accountant; one of the professional titles for accountants of enterprises or institutions ❷ 〈旧时 *old*〉由政府发给执照并受当事人委托执行会计业务的自由职业

者，主要职务是查核账目，设计会计制度等 government-licensed private accountant who checks accounts and works out an accounting system for clients

块(塊) kuài ❶ (~儿 kuàir)成疙瘩或成团儿的东西 piece; lump; chunk: 糖~儿 hard candy (or fruit drops); lumps of sugar|~煤 lump of coal|把肉切成~儿 cut the meat into cubes ❷〈量词 *classifier*〉用于块状或某些片状的东西 [for sth. shaped like chunks or lumps]: 两~香皂 two cakes of soap|三~手表 three wristwatches|一~桌布 a tablecloth|一~试验田 an experimental plot (of land) ❸〈量词 *classifier*〉用于银币或纸币，等于'圆' [for silver dollars or certain paper money; equivalent to yuan] buck: 三~钱 three yuan

【块儿八毛】 kuài·er-bāmáo 一元钱或比一元钱略少 a yuan or slightly less; also 块儿八角 kuài·er-bājiǎo

【块根】 kuàigēi 根的一种，呈块状，无定形，如甘薯供食用的部分就是块根 root tuber; lump-shaped root of indefinite form, e. g. the edible part of sweet potato

【块规】 kuàiguī 检验工具或工件长度的用具，是厚度精确的长方形金属块。块规是各种量具的检验标准。一套块规由各种厚度的块规组成，应用时可以拼成各种尺寸。gauge block; slip gauge; rectangular metal device of an accurate thickness for examining the length of a tool or a workpiece. It sets the standards by which various measuring tools are tested. A set of gauges is composed of gauge blocks of different thickness, which can be assembled for selected sizes. also 量块 liàngkuài

【块茎】 kuàijīng 地下茎的一种，呈块状，含有大量的淀粉和养料，上面有凹入的芽眼，如马铃薯供食用的部分就是块茎 stem tuber; lump-shaped underground stem that contains a lot of starch and nourishment, and is dotted with eyes at the top, e. g. the stem tuber of potato

【块垒】 kuàilěi〈书 *fml.*〉〈比喻 *fig.*〉郁积在心中的气愤或愁闷 gloom; depression; suppressed indignation

【块儿】 kuàir ❶ 个儿 height; stature ❷〈方 *dial.*〉处；地方 place: 这一带我熟得很，哪~都去过。I'm quite familiar with this place, for I've been to every corner.|你哪~摔痛了? Which part of your body was hurt?|我在这~工作好几年了。I've been working here for quite a few years now.

【块头】 kuàitóu 指人的胖瘦 (physical) build: 大~big burly person

快 kuài ❶ 速度高；走路、做事等费的时间短(跟'慢'相对 as opposed to 'slow') fast; quick; rapid; swift: ~车 express train; express bus|~步 quick steps|多~好省 greater, faster, better, and more economical|他进步很~。He has made rapid progress. ❷ 快慢的程度 rate; speed: 这种汽车在柏油路上能跑多~? How fast can this car go on a tarry road? ❸ 赶快；从速 hurry up; make haste: ~来帮忙 come over quickly and give me a hand|~送医院抢救 send sb. immediately to the hospital for emergency treatment ❹ 快要；将要 soon; be about to: 你再等一会儿，他~回来了。Please wait for a little longer, he'll be back soon.|他从事教育工作~四十年了。He's been engaged in educational work for nearly forty years. ❺ 灵敏 quick-witted; nimble; clever: 脑子~ quick-witted; have a quick mind|眼疾手~ sharp of eye and deft of hand ❻ (刀、剪、斧子等)锋利(跟'钝'相对 as opposed to 'blunt') (of knife, scissors, axe, etc.) sharp: 菜刀不~了，你去磨一磨。The kitchen knife is no longer sharp, go and have it sharpened. ❼ 爽快；痛快；直截了当 straightforward; forthright; plain-spoken: ~人~语 straightforward talk from an honest person ❽ 愉快；高兴；舒服 pleased; happy; gratified: ~感 pleasant sensation; delight|拍手称~ clap for joy|大~人心 affording general satisfaction ❾〈旧时 *old*〉指专管缉捕的差役 yamen runner or officer charged with making arrests: 捕~ runner arresting criminals|马~ servant

【快板儿】 kuàibǎnr 曲艺的一种，词儿合辙押韵，说时用竹板打拍，节奏较快 clapper talk; folk art form in which a performer delivers comic rhymes or monologue to the accompaniment of bamboo clappers

【快报】 kuàibào 机关团体等自办的小型的、能及时反映情况的报纸或墙报 noticeboard; bulletin board; bulletin of an organization for timely reflection on the internal situation and the dissemination of information

【快步流星】 kuàbù liúxīng 大步流星 with vigorous strides

【快餐】 kuàicān 预先做好的能够迅速提供顾客食用的饭食，如汉堡包、盒饭等 quick meal; fastfood; takeout; snack; pre-cooked meal (e. g. hamburger, box meal, etc.) that can be served swiftly to customers

【快车】 kuàichē 中途停站较少，全程行车时间较短的火车或汽车(多用于客运 oft. used in passenger transport) express train or bus; passenger train or bus that travels at high speed with few or no stops along the way

【快当】 kuài·dang 迅速敏捷；不拖拉 quick; prompt: 她做起事来又细心又~。She's quick and careful in her work.

【快刀斩乱麻】 kuài dāo zhǎn luàn má〈比喻 *fig.*〉用果断的办法迅速解决复杂的问题 solve a complicated problem swiftly and resolutely

【快感】 kuàigǎn 愉快或痛快的感觉 pleasant

sensation; delight：好的电视节目能给人以～。A good television programme usually delights the viewers.

【快活】kuài·huo 愉快；快乐 happy; merry; cheerful：提前完成了任务，心里觉得很～。I felt very happy about accomplishing the task ahead of schedule.

【快件】kuàijiàn ❶ 运输部门把托运的货物分为快件、慢件两种，运输速度较慢、运费较低的叫慢件，运输速度较快、运费较高的叫快件。快件一般凭火车票办理托运手续，物品随旅客所乘列车同时运到。express goods, parcels and luggage; transportation departments (in the railway system, airport, etc.) sorts the freight and luggage as express or regular — the regular ones are transported at a comparatively slow speed with lower freight charges, while the express ones are transported at high speed with higher freight charges. Express luggage is usu. consigned on railway ticket to reach the destination at the same time as the passenger. ❷ 邮政部门指快速递送的邮件 (of postal service) express mail; express package

【快捷】kuàijié （速度）快；（行动）敏捷 fast (speed); nimble (action)：动作～ nimble in action｜他迈着～的步伐走在最前头。He walked at the very front, taking quick steps.

【快乐】kuàilè 感到幸福或满意 happy; joyful; cheerful：～的微笑 happy smile｜祝您生日～。Happy birthday to you.

【快马加鞭】kuài mǎ jiā biān 对快跑的马再打几鞭子，使它跑得更快 spur on a flying horse to full speed;〈比喻 *fig.*〉快上加快 redouble one's speed; at top speed

【快慢】kuàimàn 指速度 speed：这条轮船的～怎么样？What's the speed of this steamer? *or* How fast can this steamer sail?

【快慢针】kuàimànzhēn 调节钟表计时快慢的装置。利用改变游丝的有效长度来调节摆轮运动周期。regulator (in a timepiece); device that regulates the timekeeping of a clock or watch by changing the effective length of the hair-springs

【快门】kuàimén 摄影机中控制曝光时间的装置，由薄金属片或不透光的布帘构成。拍照时快门的开启时间可以是数秒、一秒、几分之一秒以至千分之一秒。(camera) shutter; mechanical device that limits the passage of light; esp. a camera attachment that exposes the film or plate by opening and closing an aperture. The period of opening a shutter can be several seconds, one second, a fraction of a second, or even a thousandth of a second.

【快人快语】kuài rén kuài yǔ 爽快的人说爽快的话，指人性格直爽 straight talk from a straightforward person

【快事】kuàishì 令人痛快满意的事 event that gives great satisfaction or pleasure; delight：好友相逢，畅叙别情，实为一大～。It's really a delightful experience for good friends to meet again after a long separation and share their experiences and feelings.

【快手】kuàishǒu（～儿 kuàishǒur）指做事敏捷的人 quick worker; deft hand

【快书】kuàishū 曲艺的一种，用铜板或竹板伴奏，词儿合辙押韵，说时节奏较快，有山东快书、竹板快书等 quick-patter; clapper ballad; folk art form in which the performer tells stories accompanied by rhythmic bamboo or copper clappers

【快速】kuàisù 速度快的；迅速 fast; quick; high-speed：～照相机 high-speed camera｜～炼钢 high-speed steel smelting｜～行军 forced march｜～育肥 speed fattening

【快艇】kuàitǐng 汽艇 speedboat; motor boat; mosquito boat

【快慰】kuàiwèi 痛快而心里感到安慰；欣慰 feel pleased with and derive comfort from sth.; be pleased：得知近况，不胜～ be extremely pleased with news about sb.'s recent situation

【快信】kuàixìn 邮政部门指需要快速投递的信件 express letter

【快性】kuài·xing〈方 *dial.*〉性情爽快 frank disposition：他是个～人，想到什么就说什么。He is straightforward and readily speaks his mind.

【快婿】kuàixù〈书 *fml.*〉指为岳父岳母所满意的女婿 satisfying son-in-law：乘龙～ ideal son-in-law

【快讯】kuàixùn 指迅速采访、刊出或播发的消息 newsflash; flash

【快要】kuàiyào〈副词 *adv.*〉表示在很短的时间以内就要出现某种情况 soon; before long; in a very short time：开水～用完了，再烧一壶去。The boiled water is about to run out. Go and boil another kettle of water.｜国庆节～到了。It'll soon be National Day.｜她长得～跟妈妈一样高了。She has grown to be almost as tall as her mother.

【快意】kuàiyì 心情爽快舒适 pleased; comfortable：微风吹来，感到十分～。A gentle breeze was blowing, and (I) felt refreshed.

【快鱼】kuàiyú same as 鲙鱼 kuàiyú

【快嘴】kuàizuǐ 指不加考虑、有话就说或好传闲话的人 one who readily voices his thoughts; one who is quick to speak his mind without careful consideration, or is keen on spreading gossip

侩(儈) kuài〈旧指 *old*〉以拉拢买卖从中取利为职业的人 middleman; broker; commission merchant：市～ sordid merchant｜牙～ broker｜驵～(zǎngkuài) horse dealer

郐(鄶) Kuài ❶ 周朝国名,在今河南密县东北 Kuai, state during the Zhou Dynasty, in today's northeastern Mixian County, Henan Province ❷ (Kuài)姓 a surname

哙(噲) kuài〈书 *fml.*〉咽下去 swallow

狯(獪) kuài〈书 *fml.*〉狡猾 crafty:狡~ cunning

浍(澮) kuài〈书 *fml.*〉田间的水沟 ditch in the fields

☞ Huì on p.868

脍(膾) kuài〈书 *fml.*〉❶ 切得很细的鱼或肉 ground meat; meat chopped into small pieces; minced meat ❷ 把鱼、肉切成薄片 cut meat or fish into thin pieces:~鲤 sliced carp

【脍炙人口】kuài zhì rén kǒu 美味人人都爱吃 delicious roast meat enjoying wide popularity;〈比喻 *fig.*〉好的诗文或事物,人们都称赞 (of a piece of good writing, event, etc.) win universal praise; enjoy great popularity (炙 *zhi*:烤熟的肉 roast meat)

筷 kuài 筷子 chopsticks:牙~(象牙筷子) ivory chopsticks|碗~ bowls and chopsticks

【筷子】kuài·zi 用竹、木、金属等制的夹饭菜或其他东西的细长棍ㄦ chopsticks; slender sticks (usu. in pairs) made of bamboo, wood, or metal for lifting food to the mouth:一双~ a pair of chopsticks|象牙~ ivory chopsticks|竹~ bamboo chopsticks|火~(夹炭火用的) metal chopsticks for lifting charcoal from fire

鲙(鱠) kuài [鲙鱼](kuàiyú) 鳓 (lè) Chinese herring (*Ilisa elongata*); also 快鱼 kuàiyú

kuān (ㄎㄨㄢ)

宽(寬) kuān ❶ 横的距离大;范围广(跟'窄'相对 as opposed to 'narrow') wide; broad:~银幕 wide-screen|这条马路很~。This road is very wide.|他为集体想得周到,管得~。He is thoughtful towards the collective and readily takes care of almost everything. ❷ 宽度 width:我国国旗的~是长的三分之二。The width of the national flag of China is two-thirds its length.|这条河有一里~。This river is one *li* wide. ❸ 放宽;使松缓 relax; relieve; ease:~限 extend the time limit|~心 feel relieved|听说孩子已经脱险,心就~了一半。(I) was greatly relieved to learn that the child was out of danger. ❹ 宽大;不严厉;不苛求 generous; lenient:~容 tolerant|从~处理 handle leniently ❺ 宽裕;宽绰 comfortably off; well-off:他虽然手头比过去~多了,但仍很注意节约。He's still budget-conscious, although he's much better-off than before. ❻ (Kuān) 姓 a surname

【宽敞】kuān·chang 宽阔;宽大 roomy; spacious; commodious:这间屋子很~。This room is very spacious.

【宽畅】kuānchàng (心里)舒畅 free from worry; happy:胸怀~ happy mood

【宽绰】kuān·chuo ❶ 宽阔;不狭窄 spacious; commodious:~的礼堂 spacious auditorium|人口不多,虽然只两间房子,倒也宽宽绰绰的。Since the family is not large, the two houses are spacious enough for it. ❷ (心胸)开阔 (of mind) relaxed; relieved:听了他的话,心里显着~多了。When (I) heard him say that, I felt greatly relieved. *or* I felt a great load taken off my mind when I heard what he said. ❸ 富余 comfortably off; well-off:人民的生活越来越~了。People's lives have become better and better off.

【宽打窄用】kuān dǎ zhǎi yòng 订计划的时候打得宽裕一些,而实际使用的时候节约一些 budget liberally and spend sparingly

【宽大】kuāndà ❶ 面积或容积大 large (in area or dimension):袍袖~ oversized robe sleeves|~豁亮的客厅 spacious and bright living room ❷ 对人宽容厚道 lenient; magnanimous; generous:心怀~ magnanimous-minded ❸ 对犯错误或犯罪的人从宽处理 show leniency (towards an offender or a criminal):~政策 policy of leniency|~处理 lenient treatment

【宽贷】kuāndài 宽容;饶恕 pardon; forgive:如果再犯,决不~。Any reconviction will never be forgiven.

【宽待】kuāndài 宽大对待 treat with leniency; be lenient in dealing with:~俘虏 give lenient treatment to prisoners of war; treat prisoners of war leniently

【宽度】kuāndù 宽窄的程度;横的距离(长方形多指两条长边之间的距离) width; breadth; (of a rectangle) distance between the two longer sides

【宽泛】kuānfàn (内容、意义)涉及的面宽 (of meaning or content) wide in range:这个词的涵义很~。This word has many different meanings.

【宽广】kuānguǎng 面积或范围大 broad; extensive; vast:~的原野 broad expanse of wilderness|道路越走越~。As (we) walked along, the road became wider and wider.

【宽和】kuānhé 宽厚和易 generous and easy-going:待人~ treat others generously|性情~ generous and easy-going in disposition

【宽宏】kuānhóng (度量)大 magnanimity:~大量 magnanimous; also 宽洪 kuānhóng

【宽宏大量】kuānhóng dàliàng 形容人度量大 broad-minded; magnanimous (宏 also put as 洪 hóng); also 宽宏大度 kuānhóng dàdù

【宽洪】kuānhóng ❶ (嗓音)宽而洪亮 resonant (voice):~的歌声 resonant singing ❷ same as

宽宏 kuānhóng

【宽厚】kuānhòu ❶ 宽而厚 thick and broad:～的胸膛 broad and strong chest ❷(待人)宽容厚道 tolerant and generous; honest and kind ❸(声音)浑厚 deep and vigorous (voice):唱腔高亢～ resounding and vigorous singing

【宽假】kuānjiǎ 〈书 *fml.*〉宽贷;宽恕 pardon; forgive

【宽解】kuānjiě 使宽心;解除烦恼 ease sb.'s anxiety; relieve sb. of his trouble:母亲生气的时候,姐姐总能设法～。Whenever my mother got angry, my sister could always find a way to calm her down.

【宽旷】kuānkuàng 宽广空旷 extensive; vast:～的草原 extensive grasslands

【宽阔】kuānkuò ❶ same as 宽 kuān① and 阔 kuò①:～无垠 vast and boundless|～平坦的林阴大道 smooth and broad avenue ❷(思想)开朗,不狭隘 open-minded:思路～ broad-minded

【宽让】kuānràng 尽让别人,不争执;宽容忍让 tolerate and give in; modestly defer to others and not dispute

【宽饶】kuānráo 宽恕;饶恕 forgive; show mercy; give quarter:依法惩治,决不～ punish (criminals) according to the law without any mercy

【宽容】kuānróng 宽大有气量,不计较或追究 tolerant; lenient:大度～ magnanimous and tolerant

【宽赦】kuānshè 宽大赦免;宽恕 pardon; excuse; absolve

【宽舒】kuānshū ❶ 舒畅 happy; entirely free from worry:心境～ have ease of mind; feel happy ❷ 宽敞舒展 spacious and comfortable:街道用大石铺成,平整～。The slabstone-paved street is level and comfortable.

【宽恕】kuānshù 宽容饶恕 tolerate and pardon; forgive

【宽松】kuān·sōng ❶ 宽绰;不拥挤 spacious; not crowded:列车开动以后,拥挤的车厢略为～了一些。After the train started off, the carriage became less crowded. ❷ 宽畅 feel relieved; be free from worry:她听了同事们劝慰的话,心里～多了。She felt relieved after being consoled by her colleagues. ❸ 放松 ease:～一下紧张的情绪 ease feelings of tension ❹ 宽舒;松快 spacious and comfortable:～和谐的环境 comfortable and harmonious environment ❺ 宽裕 well-off:日子过好了,手头～了。With life getting better steadily, people have more money to spare. ❻(衣服)肥大 (of clothes) loose; oversized:～衫 loose blouse|～式的连衣裙 loose one-piece dress

【宽慰】kuānwèi 宽解安慰 comfort; console:她用温和的话语～着妈妈。She comforted her mother with gentle words.

【宽限】kuān//xiàn 放宽限期 extend a time limit:我们借的东西还要用,请他～几天。Please ask him to extend the deadline for a few more days since we still need to use the borrowed items.

【宽心】kuān//xīn 解除心中的焦急愁闷 feel relieved; free from worry; relieve sb. of his or her trouble:大家去陪她玩玩,让她宽宽心。Let's stay with her and have fun, and get her to relax.

【宽心丸儿】kuānxīnwánr 〈比喻 *fig.*〉宽慰人的话 consolatory words; words said to put people at ease; also 开心丸儿 kāixīnwánr

【宽衣】kuān//yī 〈敬辞 *pol.*〉用于请人脱衣 take off your coat:屋里热,请～。It's hot inside, please take off your coat.

【宽银幕电影】kuānyínmù diànyǐng 电影的一种,银幕略作弧形,比普通电影的银幕宽,使观众看到的画面大而完整,并有身临其境的感觉。这种电影的配音多是立体声。wide-screen film; film that is specially projected on an extra-wide arched screen, designed to present wide and complete images and give the audience a feeling of being personally at the scene

【宽宥】kuānyòu 〈书 *fml.*〉宽恕;饶恕 pardon; forgive

【宽余】kuānyú ❶ 宽阔舒畅 spacious and comfortable ❷ 宽裕 well-off:他近两年手头～多了。He's been much better-off in the last two years.

【宽裕】kuānyù 宽绰富余 well-to-do; be comfortably off; prosperous:人民的生活一天天～起来。People are getting better off with each passing day.|时间很～。There's plenty of time yet.

【宽窄】kuānzhǎi 面积、范围大小的程度 width; breadth; size

【宽展】kuānzhǎn 〈方 *dial.*〉❶(心里)舒畅 (of mind) happy; free from worry:听他们一说,心里～多了。I felt relieved by their words. ❷(地方)宽阔 (of place) broad; wide:～的广场 broad square ❸ 宽裕 well-off:手头不～ not in easy circumstances|日子过得相当～ lead a quite well-off life

【宽纵】kuānzòng 宽容放纵;不加约束 indulge:不要～自己,要求自己越严,进步就越快。Don't be so self-indulgent. The stricter you are with yourself, the greater your progress.

髋(髖) kuān [髋骨](kuāngǔ)组成骨盆的大骨,左右各一,形状不规则,是由髂骨、坐骨和耻骨合成的 hipbone; innominate bone; large flaring bone that makes up the lateral half of the pelvis in mammals, composed of the ilium, ischium and pubis, which are consolidated into one bone in adults; 通称 common name for 胯骨 kuàgǔ; (图见 ☞ figure for 骨骼 gǔgé on p. 693)

kuǎn（ㄎㄨㄢˇ）

款[1]（欵）kuǎn ❶ 诚恳 sincere：～留 cordially urge a guest to stay｜～曲 heartfelt feelings ❷ 招待；款待 receive with hospitality；entertain：～客 entertain guests

款[2]（欵）kuǎn ❶ 法令、规章、条约等条文里分的项目，通常在条下分款，款下分项 clause；article；section of an article in a law，code or treaty，etc.：第二条第一～ Article 2，clause 1 ❷ same as 款项 kuǎnxiàng ①；钱 money；funds：现～ cash｜公～ public funds｜存～ savings；deposit｜汇～ remittance ❸（～儿 kuǎnr）书画上题的作者或赠送对象的姓名 name of the sender or recipient inscribed on a painting or a piece of calligraphy presented as a gift：上～ name of the recipient｜下～ name of the donor｜落～ colophon；inscribe a gift ❹（～儿 kuǎnr）款式 style；pattern；design：这是刚出厂的新～风衣。This newly designed windbreaker is just off the assembly line.｜橱窗里摆着各～鞋帽。Shoes and caps of different designs could be found inside the shop window. ❺〈量词 *classifier*〉：两～风衣 two windbreakers｜五～西式点心 five Western pastries

款[3]（欵）kuǎn〈书 *fml.*〉same as 敲 qiāo ①：～门 knock at a door｜～关 visit a customs house

款[4]（欵）kuǎn〈书 *fml.*〉缓；慢 slow；leisurely：～步 slow steps｜点水蜻蜓～～飞。Dragonflies fly leisurely as they frolicked with the water surface.｜清风徐来，柳丝～摆。The soft，slender willow twigs sway gentally in the breeze.

【款步】kuǎnbù 缓慢地步行 walk with deliberate steps：～向前 step forward deliberately｜～漫游 wander leisurely

【款待】kuǎndài 亲切优厚地招待 treat cordially；entertain：～客人 entertain guests｜盛情～ show hospitality；entertain hospitably

【款额】kuǎn'é 经费或款项的数额 amount of money

【款留】kuǎnliú 诚恳地挽留（宾客）cordially urge（a guest）to stay

【款洽】kuǎnqià 亲切融洽 cordial and harmonious：情意～ cordial and harmonious affection

【款曲】kuǎnqū〈书 *fml.*〉❶ 殷勤应酬 hospitable social intercourse：不善与人～ not good at socializing ❷ 殷勤的心意 heartfelt feelings：互通～express feelings of mutual affection or friendship

【款式】kuǎnshì 格式；样式 pattern；style；design：～新颖 brand-new design｜这个书柜的～很好。The bookcase is of a good design.

【款项】kuǎnxiàng ❶ 为某种用途而储存或支出的钱（多指机关、团体等进出的数目较大的钱 oft. referring to large sums used by organizations，groups，etc.）sum of money；fund；money deposited or expended for certain purposes ❷（法令、规章、条约等）条文的项目 sections and clauses（in laws，regulations，treaties，etc.）

【款识】kuǎnzhì ❶ 钟、鼎等器物上所刻的文字 inscription on a bell，ancient cooking vessel，etc. ❷ 书信、书画上面的落款 colophon on a letter，article，painting，or piece of calligraphy

【款子】kuǎn·zi same as 款项 kuǎnxiàng ①；钱 sum of money：汇来一笔～ receive a sum of money by remittance

窾 kuǎn〈书 *fml.*〉空 empty

kuāng（ㄎㄨㄤ）

匡 kuāng ❶〈书 *fml.*〉纠正 rectify；correct：～谬 correct mistakes ❷〈书 *fml.*〉救；帮助 assist；save：～助 help｜～我不逮（帮助我所做不到的）help me to overcome my shortcomings ❸〈方 *dial.*〉粗略计算；估计 roughly estimate：～一～ make a guess；give a rough estimate｜～计 roughly estimate｜～算 roughly calculate ❹ 料想（多见于早期白话 oft. in early vernacular）think；reckon：不～ not expect ❺（Kuāng）姓 a surname

【匡扶】kuāngfú〈书 *fml.*〉匡正扶持；辅佐 correct and assist：～汉室 assist the Han Dynasty

【匡计】kuāngjì 粗略计算 calculate roughly；estimate：以每亩增产六十斤～，全村能增产粮食十来万斤。A rough calculation based on an increase of 30 kg. per *mu* puts the total increase in the grain output at 50，000 kg. for the village as a whole.

【匡救】kuāngjiù 挽救而使回到正路上来 rescue；save（put sb. or sth. back on the right track）

【匡谬】kuāngmiù 纠正错误 correct mistakes：～正俗 correct mistakes and rectify unhealthy tendencies

【匡算】kuāngsuàn 粗略计算 roughly estimate：据初步～，今年棉花将增产百分之十二。According to an rough estimate，cotton output will go up by 12 per cent this year.

【匡正】kuāngzhèng 纠正；改正 rectify；correct：～时弊 correct the maladies of the times

【匡助】kuāngzhù 辅助；扶助 help；assist

劻 kuāng［劻勷］（kuāngráng）〈书 *fml.*〉急迫不安的样子 terrified；also 俇儴 kuāngráng

俇 kuāng［俇儴］（kuāngráng）〈书 *fml.*〉same as 劻勷 kuāngráng

诓 kuāng 诓骗；哄骗 deceive；hoax：～人 deceive people

【诓骗】kuāngpiàn 说谎话骗人 lie to cheat sb.；

deceive

哐 kuāng 〈拟声词 *onom.*〉形容撞击震动的声音 crash; bang; sound of a crash or vibration:～的一声,脸盆掉在了地上。The basin fell with a crash.

【哐当】kuāngdāng 〈拟声词 *onom.*〉形容器物撞击的声音 crash; bang; sound of a crash:～一声,门被踢开了。The door was kicked open with a bang.

【哐啷】kuānglāng 〈拟声词 *onom.*〉形容器物撞击的声音 crash; bang; sound of a crash:他回身把门～一声关上了。He turned around and banged the door shut.

洭 Kuāng 洭河,水名,在广东 Kuanghe River in Guangdong Province

恇 kuāng 〈书 *fml.*〉害怕;惊慌 be scared; be fearful of:～惧 be frightened|～怯 be fearful of; be afraid of

筐 kuāng (～儿 kuāngr) 用竹篾、柳条、荆条等编的容器 basket; container woven with bamboo strips, wicker, twigs of the chaste tree, etc.:抬～ carry a basket|粪～ manure basket|编竹～儿 weave bamboo baskets|两～土 two baskets of earth

【筐子】kuāng·zi 筐(多指较小的) (small) basket:菜～ small vegetable basket

kuáng (ㄎㄨㄤˊ)

狂 kuáng ❶ 精神失常;疯狂 mad; crazy:发～ go crazy; out of one's mind ◇丧心病～ lose one's mind; go insane; be seized with crazy ideas ❷ 猛烈;声势大 violent:～风 fierce wind|～奔的马 galloping horse ❸ 纵情地、无拘束地(多指欢乐 mostly out of joy) unrestrained; heartily:～喜 jubilant|～欢 carnival ❹狂妄 arrogant; overbearing:～言 overbearing words|你这话可说得有点儿～。What you've just spoken sounds a bit arrogant.

【狂暴】kuángbào 猛烈而凶暴 violent and wild:性情～ violent disposition|～的北风 fierce wind from north

【狂奔】kuángbēn 迅猛地奔跑 run wildly:战马～ galloping war horses ◇洪水～而来。Flood water surged at a furious speed.

【狂飙】kuángbiāo 急骤的暴风 hurricanes;〈比喻 *fig.*〉猛烈的潮流或力量 raging tide or force

【狂草】kuángcǎo 草书的一种,笔势连绵回绕,字形变化繁多 wild cursive hand (an erratic type of cursive hand in Chinese calligraphy, the characters oft. being illegible)

【狂潮】kuángcháo 汹涌的潮水 rushing tide;〈比喻 *fig.*〉声势浩大的局面 mighty trend

【狂放】kuángfàng 任性放荡 unruly or unrestrained:性情～ unrestrained disposition

【狂吠】kuángfèi 狗狂叫,借指疯狂地叫喊(骂人的话 curses) bark furiously; shout crazily

【狂风】kuángfēng ❶ 猛烈的风 fierce wind:～暴雨 fierce wind and torrential rain ❷ 气象学上指10级风 (meteorol.) force 10 gale; ☞ 风级 fēngjí on p. 579

【狂欢】kuánghuān 纵情欢乐 revelry; carnival; hearty carous:～之夜 a night of revelry

【狂澜】kuánglán 巨大的波浪 huge waves;〈比喻 *fig.*〉动荡不定的局势或猛烈的潮流 turbulent situation or violent tide:力挽～ make vigorous efforts to save a critical situation

【狂怒】kuángnù 极端愤怒 furious; in an extreme rage

【狂气】kuáng·qi 狂妄自傲的样子 arrogance; conceit

【狂犬病】kuángquǎnbìng 急性传染病,病原体是狂犬病毒,常见于狗、猫等家畜,人或其他家畜被患狂犬病的狗或猫咬伤时也能感染。家畜患狂犬病时,症状是食欲不振,看见水就恐惧,狂叫,痉挛,碰到人畜或其他物体就咬,最后全身麻痹而死亡。人患狂犬病时,症状是精神失常,恶心、流涎,看见水就恐怖,肌肉痉挛,呼吸困难,最后全身瘫痪而死亡。hydrophobia; rabies; acute infectious disease caused by rabies virus (hydrophobin), oft. in domestic animals such as dogs or cats. Humans and other animals can be infected through the bite of a rabid dog or cat. The symptoms in domestic animals include loss of appetite, fear of water, reckless weeping, convulsions, uncontrollable biting, and finally death from general paralysis, while the symptoms in people include mental instability, nausea, drooling, fear of water, muscle convulsions, laboured breathing, and finally death from general paralysis. also 恐水病 kǒngshuǐbìng

【狂热】kuángrè 一时所激起的极度热情 demented; fanatic; extreme fervour:宗教～ religious fanaticism|小资产阶级的～性 fanaticism of the petty bourgeoisie

【狂人】kuángrén ❶ 疯狂的人 madman; maniac ❷ 极端狂妄自大的人 extremely arrogant person

【狂涛】kuángtāo 汹涌的波涛 surging waves;〈比喻 *fig.*〉浩大的声势 tremendous momentum or impetus

【狂妄】kuángwàng 极端的自高自大 insolent; overbearing:～自大 arrogant and conceited|态度～disdainful

【狂喜】kuángxǐ 极端高兴 wild with joy:他们相见时～地拥抱起来。They hugged each other as soon as they met, wild with joy.

【狂想】kuángxiǎng ❶ 幻想 illusion:～曲 capriccio ❷ 妄想 extravagant hope

【狂想曲】kuángxiǎngqǔ 一种富于幻想或叙事性的器乐曲,根据民歌或民间舞曲的主题改编而成 capriccio; fancy or chronicle instrumental music adapted from folk songs or folk-dance music

【狂笑】kuángxiào 纵情大笑 laugh wildly; laugh boisterously

【狂言】kuángyán 狂妄的话 ravings; wild talk: 口出～ rant wildly

【狂躁】kuángzào 非常焦躁,不沉着 manic; unsteady: 要沉住气,不要～。Be calm, and don't fuss.

诳 kuáng ❶ 欺骗;骗 cheat; deceive: ～语 deceptive words | 你别～我。Don't cheat me. ❷〈方 *dial.*〉谎 lie: 说～ lie | 扯了个～ tell a lie

【诳语】kuángyǔ 骗人的话 lies; falsehood; also 诳话 kuánghuà

鵟 kuáng 鸟,外形像老鹰,但尾部羽毛不分叉,全身褐色,尾部稍淡。吃鼠类,是益鸟。buzzard (*Accipitridae*); useful bird that looks like a vulture but does not have separated tail feathers, is brown all over and lighter at the tail, regarded as a valuable bird, for it preys on mice. also 土豹 tǔbào

kuǎng (ㄎㄨㄤˇ)

夼 kuǎng〈方 *dial.*〉洼地,多用于地名,如大夼、刘家夼、马草夼(都在山东) marsh, mostly used in place names, e.g. Dakuang 大夼, Liujiakuang 刘家夼, Macaokuang 马草夼, all in Shandong Province

kuàng (ㄎㄨㄤˋ)

廾 kuàng (旧读 formerly pronounced gǒng)〈书 *fml.*〉same as 矿 kuàng

邝(鄺) Kuàng 姓 a surname

圹(壙) kuàng ❶ 墓穴 pit for a coffin; grave: ～穴 grave | 打～ dig a grave ❷〈书 *fml.*〉原野 fields

【圹埌】kuànglàng〈书 *fml.*〉形容原野空旷辽阔,一望无际 boundless field

纩(纊) kuàng〈书 *fml.*〉丝绵 silk floss; silk wadding

旷(曠) kuàng ❶ 空而宽阔 empty and vast: ～野 vast wilderness | 地～人稀 vast and sparsely populated area ❷ 心境开阔 free from worry and pettiness: ～达 broad-minded | 心～神怡 be carefree and joyous ❸ 耽误;荒废 neglect; waste: ～课 skip school | ～工 be absent from work without leave | ～日废时 time-consuming; waste time ❹ 相互配合的两个零件(如轴和孔、键和键槽等)的间隙大于所要求的范围;衣着过于肥大,不合体 (of the clearance between two parts of a set, e.g. axis and hole, key and key slot, etc.) loose; beyond the required bounds; (of clothes) loose-fitting: 车轴～了。The axle came loose. | 螺丝～了。The screw has come loose. | 这双鞋我穿着太～了。This pair of shoes is too loose-fitting on me. ❺ (Kuàng) 姓 a surname

【旷达】kuàngdá〈书 *fml.*〉心胸开阔,想得开 broad-minded; big-hearted: 胸襟～ broad-minded

【旷代】kuàngdài〈书 *fml.*〉当代没人比得上 unrivalled; peerless; with no match in one's generation: ～文豪 unrivalled writer

【旷荡】kuàngdàng ❶ 空阔;宽广 spacious; vast: ～的草原 vast grassland ❷ (思想、心胸)开朗 (of thought, mind, etc.) sanguine: 心怀～ open-minded

【旷废】kuàngfèi 耽误,荒废 neglect; waste: ～学业 neglect one's studies

【旷费】kuàngfèi 浪费 waste: ～时间 waste time

【旷工】kuàng//gōng (职工)不请假而缺勤 (of employees) be absent from (or miss) work without leave

【旷古】kuànggǔ ❶ 自古以来(都没有) (never) since ancient times; from time immemorial: ～未闻 unheard-of; unprecedented ❷ 远古;往昔 remote antiquity

【旷课】kuàng//kè (学生)不请假而缺课 (of students) be absent from school without leave; cut classes; skip school; play truant

【旷日持久】kuàng rì chí jiǔ 多费时日,拖得很久 long and drawn-out; prolonged; long-lasting

【旷世】kuàngshì〈书 *fml.*〉❶ 当代没有能相比的 unparalleled or matchless in one's time: ～功勋 achievement unparalleled of the time ❷ 历时久远 (of time) long lasting: ～难成之业 undertaking or cause that cannot be accomplished for a long time to come

【旷野】kuàngyě 空旷的原野 wilderness

【旷远】kuàngyuǎn ❶ 空旷辽远 vast and extending far into the distance: 江面浩渺～。The river, a vast expanse of water, extends far into the distance. ❷〈书 *fml.*〉久远 far back; ages ago; remote: 年代～ of the remote past; age-old

【旷职】kuàng//zhí (工作人员)不请假而缺勤 (of working staff) be absent from duty without leave or good reason

况[1](況) kuàng ❶ 情形 condition; situation: 情～ situation | 状～ condition | 概～ general situation | 盛～ grand occasion | 近～ recent situation ❷ 比方 compare: 比～ draw an analogy | 以古～今 draw parallels from history ❸ (Kuàng) 姓 a surname

况[2](況) kuàng〈书 *fml.*〉况且;何况 moreover; besides; furthermore

【况且】kuàngqiě〈连词 *conj.*〉表示更进一层 moreover; in addition; besides: 上海地方那么大,～你又不知道他的地址,一下子怎么能找到他呢? How do you expect to find him quickly, since Shanghai is so big? Besides, you don't have his address.

【况味】kuàngwèi〈书 *fml.*〉境况和情味 circumstance; condition and situation: 个中～，难以尽言。It's hard to state every detail of the situation.

矿(礦、鑛) kuàng (旧读 formerly pronounced gǒng) ❶ 矿床 ore (or mineral) deposit ❷ 指矿石 ore: 黄铁～ iron pyrites|辉锑～ stibnite ❸ 开采矿物的场所 mine; where mineral ores are mined: 铁～ iron mine|煤～ coal pit

【矿藏】kuàngcáng 地下埋藏的各种矿物的总称 mineral resources; general term for various minerals underground: 我国的～很丰富。China is rich in mineral resources.

【矿层】kuàngcéng 地层中作层状分布的矿物 strata of ores; minerals in stratiform distribution

【矿产】kuàngchǎn 地壳中有开采价值的物质，如铜、云母、煤等 mineral products; valuable substances in the earth's crust e. g. copper, mica, coal, etc.

【矿床】kuàngchuáng 地表或地壳里由于地质作用形成的并在现有条件下可以开采和利用的矿物的集合体 ore deposit; mineral deposit; aggregation of exploitable and useful minerals formed during the geologic process on the surface or crust of the earth; also 矿体 kuàngtǐ

【矿灯】kuàngdēng 矿井里用的特制的照明用具的统称 miner's lamp; illuminative device specially designed for use in mines

【矿工】kuànggōng 开矿的工人 miner

【矿浆】kuàngjiāng 磨细的矿石和水的混合物 ore pulp; mixture of ground ores and water

【矿井】kuàngjǐng 为采矿而在地下修建的井筒和巷道的统称 mine shaft or pit; well-shaft or tunnel built underground for mining

【矿警】kuàngjǐng 维护矿区治安的警察 mine police; police in charge of security in mining areas

【矿坑】kuàngkēng 开矿挖掘的坑和坑道 pit (dug for mining)

【矿脉】kuàngmài 填充在岩石裂缝中成脉状的矿床，常跟地层形成一定角度。金、银、铜、钨、锑等常产于矿脉中。mineral vein; lode; nervation ore deposit that fills the gaps between rocks, and forms at a certain angle with the stratum. Gold, silver, copper, tungsten, antimony, etc. are oft. found in mineral veins

【矿苗】kuàngmiáo ☞ 露头 lùtóu on p. 1264

【矿区】kuàngqū 采矿的地区 mining area

【矿泉】kuàngquán 含有大量矿物质的泉。一般是温泉，有盐泉、铁质泉、硫磺泉等。有些矿泉可以用来治疗疾病。mineral spring; spring water that contains large amounts of mineral substances, e.g. hot springs, salt springs, ferrugimous springs, sulphur springs, etc. Some kinds of mineral spring water can help treat illnesses.

【矿泉水】kuàngquánshuǐ 含有溶解的矿物质或较多气体的水 mineral water, containing dissolved mineral substances or extra gas

【矿砂】kuàngshā 从矿床中开采的或由贫矿经选矿加工制成的砂状矿物 ore sand; sand-form mineral, exploited from an ore deposit, or selected and dressed from lean ores

【矿山】kuàngshān 开采矿物的地方，包括矿井和露天采矿场 mine; places of mining, including shafts and open-air stopes

【矿石】kuàngshí ❶ 含有有用矿物并有开采价值的岩石 ore; rock that contains useful and exploitable minerals ❷ 在无线电收音机上特指能做检波器的方铅矿、黄铁矿等 galena or iron pyrites, used for making radio detectors

【矿物】kuàngwù 地壳中存在的自然化合物和少数自然元素，具有相对固定的化学成分和性质。大部分是固态的(如铁矿石)，有的是液态的(如自然汞)或气态的(如氦)。mineral; natural chemical compound and natural trace element that exists in the earth's crust and has comparatively steady chemical components and properties, mostly solid (e. g. iron ore), some liquid (e. g. natural mercury) or gas (e. g. helium)

【矿业】kuàngyè 开采矿物的事业 mining industry

【矿源】kuàngyuán 矿产资源 mineral resources: 勘察～ explore and survey mineral resources|踏遍青山找～ travel all across the mountain looking for mineral resources

【矿渣】kuàngzhā 矿山开采、选矿及加工冶炼过程中产生的废物 slag; scoria; dross resulting from mining, separation, and processing

【矿柱】kuàngzhù 地下采矿过程中保留下来的矿体，用来支撑顶板，也有保护巷道和地面建筑物的作用 ore pillar; body of ore left in the process of underground mining, used to support the roof and protect tunnels and aboveground buildings

贶 kuàng〈书 *fml.*〉赠；赐 present as a gift; grant

纩 kuàng〈书 *fml.*〉same as 纩 kuàng

框[1] kuàng ❶ 嵌在墙上为安装门窗用的架子 frame or casing set in the wall for installing a door or window ❷ (～儿 kuàngr) 镶在器物周围起约束、支撑或保护作用的东西 frame, circle, or sth. that binds a utensil on all its edges to restrict, support, or protect the utensil: 镜～儿 mirror frame

框[2] kuàng (旧读 formerly pronounced kuāng) ❶ 框框 set pattern ❷ 在文字、图片的周围加上线条 draw a circle around words or pictures: 把这几个字～起来 circle these words ❸ 约束；限制 restrict; restrain: 不能～得太死 cannot make rigid restrictions

【框架】kuàngjià ❶ 建筑工程中，由梁、柱等联结而成的结构 (of a construction project) framework; structure composed of beams and pillars: 完成主体～工程 complete the framework of the main part of a project ❷〈比喻 *fig.*〉事物的组织、结构 organization or structure of sth.: 这部长篇小说已经有了一个大致的～。This full-length novel already has got a general outline.

【框框】kuàng·kuang ❶ 周围的圈 frame; circle: 他拿红铅笔在图片四周画了个～。He drew a circle around the picture with a red pencil. ❷ (事物)固有的格式；传统的做法；事先划定的范围 (of sth.) restriction; convention; set pattern: 突破旧～的限制 break through old ways of doing things

【框图】kuàngtú 方框图的简称 abbr. for 方框图 fāngkuàngtú

【框子】kuàng·zi 框(多指较小的) (small) frame; rim: 眼镜～ rims of glasses | 玻璃～ glass frame

眶 kuàng 眼的四周；眼眶子 eye socket; rim of the eye: 热泪满～ eyes brimming with tears | 眼泪夺～而出。The tears gushed out.

kuī (ㄎㄨㄟ)

亏(虧) kuī ❶受损失；亏折 suffer loss; deficit: ～本 lose money in business | 盈～ profit and loss | ～损 financial loss | 做生意～了。(He) lost money in business. ❷欠缺；短少 insufficient; shortage: 血～ anaemia | 理～ inadequate reason; unreasonable | 功～一篑 fail to achieve success for lack of one last effort ❸亏负 disappoint; treat unfairly: ～心 feel guilty | 人不～地，地不～人。Good harvest comes from well-tended farmland. | 你放心吧，我～不了你。Rest assured that I'll be fair with you. ❹ 多亏；幸亏 due to; thanks to: ～他提醒我，我才想起来。I'd have forgotten about it if he had not reminded me. ❺ 反说，表示讥讽 [expression of irony]: 这样不合理的话，倒～你说得出来。How could you make such unreasonable remarks. | ～你还是哥哥，一点也不知道让着弟弟。What an elder brother you are, being so mean to your younger brother.

【亏本】kuī//běn (～儿 kuī//běnr) 损失本钱；赔本 lose one's capital; lose money in business; be in the red: 做买卖亏了本 lose money in business; run a business at a loss | 工厂经营得好，不会～。(We) won't lose money if the factory is run well.

【亏产】kuīchǎn 没有达到原定生产数量；欠产 fail to reach a production target; fall short of the production quota: 上半年～原煤 500 多万吨。Raw coal output for the first six months fell five million tons short of the quota. | 改进管理制度，变～为超产 improve the managing system and turn losses into profits

【亏秤】kuī//chèng ❶ 用秤称东西卖时不给够分量 give short measure: 无论老人、小孩儿去买东西，他从不～。He never gives short measure to his customers, be they old or young. ❷ 折秤 (shé//chèng) lose weight: 青菜水分大，一放就会～。As the greens have a high water content, they will lose weight after being stored.

【亏待】kuīdài 待人不公平或不尽心 treat unfairly; treat shabbily: 你放心吧，我一定不～他。Don't worry, I won't treat him shabbily.

【亏得】kuī·de ❶ 多亏 fortunately; luckily; thanks to: ～厂里帮助我，才渡过了难关。Thanks to the help from the factory, I overcame the difficulties. ❷ 反说，表示讥讽 say sth. opposite to express sarcasm: 这么长时间才借给我，～你还记得。Fancy you still remembering to lend it to me after such a long time.

【亏短】kuīduǎn 数量不足；缺少 not enough in amount or number; deficient; short: ～分量 give short measure | 账上～1,000 元 1,000 yuan short in the accounts

【亏负】kuīfù ❶ 辜负 fail to live up to; fail to measure up to; let sb. down: 他～了大家的期望。He failed to live up to everyone's expectations. ❷ 使吃亏 cause sb. to be shortchanged; let sb. down: 大家没有～你的地方。Nobody has done anything unfair to you.

【亏耗】kuīhào 损耗 wastage; spoilage; loss through natural processes: 这批水果运输时间长，～很大。This batch of fruit suffered a lot of spoilage in its long course of transportation.

【亏空】kuī·kong ❶ 支出超过收入，因而欠人财物 have a deficit; be in debt: 没有精打细算，上月～了 100 元。(We) had a deficit of 100 yuan last month due to poor planning. ❷ 所欠的财物 debt; deficit: 过日子要是精打细算，就拉不了～。If you plan your budget carefully, you won't get into debt.

【亏累】kuīlěi 一次又一次地亏空 sustain repeated losses; repeatedly come up with deficits: 由于经营不善，这个商店连年～。The store suffered repeated losses over the years due to bad management.

【亏欠】kuīqiàn 亏空 have a deficit; be in arrears; be in debt

【亏折】kuīshé 损失(本钱) lose money in business; lose one's capital: ～血本 lose all that one has invested

【亏蚀】kuīshí ❶ 指日蚀和月蚀 eclipse of the sun or moon ❷ 亏本 lose money in business; lose one's capital: 资金～ loss of funds ❸ 损

耗 wastage; loss; wear and tear: 瓜果在运输途中总要有～。Melons and fruit always suffer natural losses in the course of transportation.

【亏损】kuīsǔn ❶ 支出超过收入;亏折 loss; deficit: 企业经营不善,～很大。The enterprise suffered great losses due to bad management. ❷ 身体因受到摧残或缺乏营养以致虚弱 fragility; debility; weakness caused by injury to the body or lack of nourishment: 气血～ deficiency in vital energy and circulation

【亏心】kuī//xīn 感觉到自己的言行违背正理 have a guilty conscience; feel guilty because one's words or acts have been unreasonable or unjust: 你说这话,真～! Don't you feel guilty for saying that! | 为人不做～事,半夜敲门心不惊。When one doesn't do anything to feel guilty for, one doesn't fear midnight knocks at the door. *or* A clear conscience sleeps through thunder.

刲 kuī〈书 *fml.*〉割 cut; reap

岿(巋) kuī ☞ below

【岿然】kuīrán〈书 *fml.*〉高大独立的样子 towering; lofty: ～不动 steadfastly stand one's ground | ～独存 stand steadfast on one's own; stand alone

【岿巍】kuīwēi〈书 *fml.*〉形容高大矗立的样子 towering; lofty: 山峰～ lofty mountain peaks

悝 kuī 用于人名,李悝,战国时政治家 *kui*, used in a person's name; Li Kui, a statesman of the Warring States Period ☞ lǐ on p. 1180

盔 kuī ❶ 盔子 helmet ❷ 军人、消防人员等用来保护头的金属帽子 metal hat soldiers and firefighters wear to protect their heads: ～甲 suit of armour | 钢～ steel helmet | 铝～ aluminium helmet ❸ (～儿 kuīr)形状像盔或半个球形的帽子 any helmet-shaped hat: 头～ cyclist's helmet | 白～ white helmet | 帽～儿 helmet-like hat

【盔甲】kuījiǎ〈古代 *arch.*〉打仗穿的服装,盔保护头,甲保护身体,用金属或皮革制成 suit of armour; metal or leather costume worn in battles, consisting of a helmet for protecting the head and armour for the body

【盔头】kuī·tou 戏曲演员扮演角色时戴的帽子,着重于装饰性,按剧中人物的年龄、性别、身份、地位的不同而分别使用 hat worn by a role in a traditional Chinese opera, mainly for ornamentation. Different hats are used for roles that are different in age, gender, identity and status.

【盔子】kuī·zi 像瓦盆而略深的容器,多用陶瓷制成 pottery vessel that looks like a basin but is a bit deeper

窥(闚) kuī ❶ 从小孔或缝隙里看 peep; peer through a small aperture; spy: 管中～豹 peep through a tube to get a full picture of the leopard ❷ 暗中察看 observe on the sly; watch in the dark: ～探 spy upon; pry about | ～测 watch; spy out

【窥豹一斑】kuī bào yī bān〈比喻 *fig.*〉只见到事物的一小部分 see only one spot on a leopard; narrow view of sth.; ☞ 管中窥豹 guǎn zhōng kuī bào on p. 717

【窥测】kuīcè 窥探推测 watch; spy on: ～动向 spy on others' activities

【窥察】kuīchá 偷偷地看;窥探 watch on the sly; spy on; pry into: ～地形 secretly map out the topography | ～敌人的动静 spy upon the enemy's movements

【窥度】kuīduó 暗中猜度 surmise in secret; conjecture quietly and in private

【窥见】kuījiàn 看出来或觉察到 peek; get or catch a glimpse of; detect: 从这首诗里可以～作者的广阔胸怀。From the poem one can catch a glimpse of the poet's breadth of vision.

【窥视】kuīshì 窥探 look into; peek; peep at; spy on: ～敌情 spy on the enemy activities | 探头向门外～ peep outside the door

【窥视镜】kuīshìjìng 安在门上,可以从门内看清门外情况的装置。有的地区叫门镜、猫眼儿。peephole; spyhole; installation fixed on a door for one to look out from inside the door; also called 门镜 ménjìng and 猫眼儿 māoyǎnr in some places.

【窥伺】kuīsì 暗中观望动静,等待机会(多含贬义 oft. derog.) lie in wait for; be on watch for

【窥探】kuītàn 暗中察看 pry into; pry about: ～虚实 pry into others' situations

kuí (ㄎㄨㄟˊ)

奎 kuí ❶ 二十八宿之一 one of the 28 constellations ❷ (Kuí) 姓 a surname

逵 kuí〈书 *fml.*〉道路 thoroughfare; road

馗 kuí same as 逵 kuí

隗 Kuí 姓 a surname ☞ Wěi on p. 1997

葵 kuí 指某些开大花的草本植物 certain herbaceous plants with big flowers: 锦～ high mallow (*Malvaceae*) | 蜀～ hollyhock (*Althaea rosea*) | 向日～ sunflower

【葵花】kuíhuā 向日葵 sunflower (*Helianthus annuus*)

【葵花子】kuíhuāzǐ (～儿 kuíhuāzǐr)向日葵的种子,可以吃,也可以榨油 sunflower seeds, which are edible and also used to extract oil

【葵扇】kuíshàn 用蒲葵叶制成的扇子 palm-leaf fan; 俗称 popular name for 芭蕉扇 bājiāoshàn

揆 kuí 〈书 *fml.*〉❶ 推测揣度 conjecture; speculate; estimate: ～其本意 make a guess about sb.'s true intentions | ～情度理 consider the circumstances and judge by common sense; weigh the pros and cons ❷ 准则;道理 guideline; rule; principle; criterion: 古今同～。The principle has been the same since ancient times. ❸ 管理;掌管 manage; run; supervise; administer; be in charge: 总～百事 be in charge of all things ❹ 指宰相,后来指相当于宰相的官 premier; any official of similar rank: 首～ prime minister | 阁～(内阁的首席长官) premier (head of the cabinet)

【揆度】kuíduó 〈书 *fml.*〉估量;揣测 estimate; weigh up; speculate; conjecture: ～得失 estimate losses and gains

【揆情度理】kuí qíng duó lǐ 按照一般情理推测揣度 consider the circumstances and judge by common sense; weigh the pros and cons

喹 kuí [喹啉](kuílín) 有机化合物,化学式 $C_6H_4(CH)_3N$。无色液体,有特殊臭味。用来制药,也可制染料。quinoline ($C_6H_4(CH)_3N$), liquid organic compound that is colourless and has a characteristic foul smell, used for medicinal purposes, and for making dyestuff

骙 kuí [骙骙] 〈书 *fml.*〉形容马强壮 (of horses) strong

暌 kuí 〈书 *fml.*〉隔开;分离(人跟人或跟地方) (persons or persons from a place) block off; curtain off; separate: ～离 depart; part with | ～隔 seclude; be away from; be aloof from | ～违 separate

【暌别】kuíbié 〈书 *fml.*〉分别;离别 leave each other; part with: ～多日。It is some time since we last saw each other. | ～经年 be separated for years

【暌隔】kuígé 〈书 *fml.*〉暌离 be parted from; be separated from: 故乡山川,十年～。It has been ten years since I bade farewell to the mountains and rivers of my homeland.

【暌离】kuílí 〈书 *fml.*〉离别;分离 leave each other; part: ～有年。We have been apart for years.

【暌违】kuíwéi 〈书 *fml.*〉分离;不在一起(旧时书信用语 used in correspondences in ancient times) separate; part: ～数载。It's been years since we last saw each other.

魁 kuí ❶ 为首的;居第一位的 chief; principal; leading: ～首 chief; head | 罪～ chief criminal; arch-criminal | 夺～ win the championship; come first | 花～ queen of the flowers; the most beautiful woman ❷ (身体)高大 (of build) tall and burly: ～梧 big and tall; stalwart | ～伟 strongly built; of a strong build; burly ❸ same as 魁星 kuíxīng ①

【魁岸】kuí'àn 〈书 *fml.*〉魁梧 big and tall; stalwart: 身体～ of a strong, tall build

【魁首】kuíshǒu ❶ 指在同辈中才华居首位的人 ringleader; person who is head and shoulders above others; brightest and best; number one: 文章～ outstanding writer of the time | 女中～ most outstanding woman ❷ 首领 chieftain; headman; leader

【魁伟】kuíwěi 魁梧 tall and strong; stalwart: 身材～ be of a strong build

【魁梧】kuí·wú (身体)强壮高大 (of build) tall and strong; burly: 这个战士宽肩膀,粗胳膊,身量很～。The soldier has a tall and strong build with broad shoulders and big arms.

【魁星】kuíxīng ❶ 北斗七星中成斗形的四颗星。一说指其中离斗柄最远的一颗。four stars in the bowl of the Big Dipper, or the one at the tip of the bowl ❷ (Kuíxīng) 我国神话中所说的主宰文章兴衰的神。旧时很多地方都有魁星楼、魁星阁等建筑物。god that governs literature and writing in Chinese mythology. In ancient times, there were many pavilions built to honour the god, such as the Pavilion of Kuixing and the Tower of Kuixing.

【魁元】kuíyuán 〈书 *fml.*〉❶ 在同辈中才华居首位的人;魁首 person who is head and shoulders above their peers; ringleader; brightest and best ❷ 第一名 come first; win the first prize: 秋试得中～ come first in the autumn imperial examination

戣 kuí 〈古代 *arch.*〉戟一类的兵器 weapon like the halberd; halbert

睽 kuí 〈书 *fml.*〉❶ same as 暌 kuí ❷ 违背;不合 go against; run counter to; breach; disagree

【睽睽】kuíkuí 形容注视 stare; gaze: 众目～ under the watchful eyes of the people; in the spotlight; in the public eye

【睽异】kuíyì 〈书 *fml.*〉(意见)不合 (of views) be in disagreement; be at variance

蝰 kuí [蝰蛇](kuíshé) 毒蛇的一种,体长1米多,背部淡蓝带灰色或褐色,背脊有黑色的链状条纹,身体两侧有不规则的斑点,腹部黑色,多生活在森林或草地里,吃小鸟、蜥蜴、青蛙等 viper (*Viperidae*); venomous snake, usu. over one metre long, having a black chain pattern on its back, irregular dots on both sides of its bluish grey or brown body, and a black belly, usu. living in forests or grasslands, feeding on birds, lizards, frogs, etc.

櫆 kuí 〈书 *fml.*〉北斗星 Big Dipper

夔¹ kuí 〈古代 *arch.*〉传说中一种像龙的独脚怪兽 dragon-like monopode animal in ancient legends

夔² Kuí ❶ 夔州,旧府名,府治在今重庆奉节 Kuizhou, name of a prefecture in ancient China, whose seat is located in present-day

Fengjie County in Chongqing Municipality ❷ 姓 a surname

kuǐ（ㄎㄨㄟˇ）

傀 kuǐ ☞ below
☞ guī on p.731

【傀儡】kuǐlěi ❶ 木偶戏里的木头人 chump; puppet; klutz; wooden figure in puppet show ❷〈比喻 *fig*.〉受人操纵的人或组织(多用于政治方面 oft. in politics) puppet; marionette; stooge; person or organization under others' control：～政权 puppet regime

【傀儡戏】kuǐlěixì 木偶戏 puppet show; puppet play

跬 kuǐ〈书 *fml*.〉一只脚迈出去的距离;半步 half a step：～步 take half a step

【跬步】kuǐbù〈书 *fml*.〉半步 half a step：～不离 follow closely behind; keep close to|～千里(比喻做事只要努力不懈,总可以获得成功) cover a thousand *li* in small steps (unremitting efforts will lead to great successes in a figurative sense)

魄 kuǐ［魄磊］(kuǐlěi)〈书 *fml*.〉❶ 成堆的石块 pile of stones; heap of stones ❷〈比喻 *fig*.〉心中郁积的不平之气;块垒 pent-up indignation; discontentment; dissatisfaction

kuì（ㄎㄨㄟˋ）

匮 kuì〈书 *fml*.〉缺乏 lack; be deficient; be short of：～乏 be short of|～竭 be deficient; dry up
〈古 *arch*.〉same as 柜 guì

【匮乏】kuìfá〈书 *fml*.〉(物资)缺乏;贫乏 (of supplies) be short of; be deficient：药品～ shortage of medicine|极度～ serious shortage in the supply|不虞～ no need to worry about the shortage of supplies

【匮竭】kuìjié〈书 *fml*.〉贫乏,以至于枯竭 poor; impoverished; deficient：精力～ exhausted|被困山谷,粮食～。Stranded in the valley, (they) ran out of food.

【匮缺】kuìquē〈书 *fml*.〉缺乏 lack; be short of; be empty of; be devoid of：器材～ be in short supply of equipment|能源～ be devoid of an energy source

蒉 kuì〈书 *fml*.〉盛土的草包 straw sack for holding earth

喟 kuì〈书 *fml*.〉叹气 sigh; heave a sigh：～叹 sigh with deep feeling|感～ sigh with feeling

【喟然】kuìrán〈书 *fml*.〉叹气的样子 sigh：～长叹 sigh deeply; heave a deep sigh|～太息 heave a deep sigh

【喟叹】kuìtàn〈书 *fml*.〉因感慨而叹气 sigh with emotion：～不已 cannot help or stop sighing

馈(餽) kuì 馈赠 present a gift：～送 present a gift to sb.|～以鲜果 make a present of fresh fruit

【馈送】kuìsòng 馈赠 present; make a present of

【馈线】kuìxiàn 发射机和天线之间的传输线 feed line; feeder; transmission line linking a transmitter and an antenna

【馈赠】kuìzèng 赠送(礼品) present (a gift)：带些土产～亲友。Bring some local specialties as gifts for your relatives and friends.

溃 kuì ❶ (水)冲破(堤坝) (of water) break through (a dam or a dyke)：～堤 burst dyke|～决 burst ❷〈书 *fml*.〉突破(包围) break through an encirclement：～围 break through an encirclement ❸ 溃败;溃散 be defeated; be routed：～兵 defeated army|～退 retreat in chaos|～不成军 be utterly routed ❹ 肌肉组织腐烂 (of muscle tissue) rot; decompose：～烂 fester; ulcerate
☞ 殨 huì on p.870

【溃败】kuìbài (军队)被打垮 (of an army) be utterly defeated; be thoroughly routed：敌军～南逃。The defeated army fled southward.

【溃不成军】kuì bù chéng jūn 军队被打得七零八落,不成队伍,形容打仗败得很惨 (of troops) be utterly routed; break and scatter after a series of defeats

【溃决】kuìjué 大水冲开(堤坝) (of flood waters) burst through (a dyke, dam, etc.)：～成灾。The broken dam resulted in a flood.

【溃烂】kuìlàn 伤口或发生溃疡的组织由于病菌的感染而化脓 fester; ulcerate; canker; rankle：伤口已经～化脓。The wound has festered.

【溃乱】kuìluàn 崩溃混乱 break down in utter confusion：敌军全线～。The enemy was routed and thrown into utter confusion on the battlefront.

【溃灭】kuìmiè 崩溃灭亡 crumble and fall; collapse：旧世界必定～。The old world is doomed to fall apart.

【溃散】kuìsàn (军队)被打垮而逃散 (of troops) be routed and dispersed

【溃逃】kuìtáo (军队)被打垮而逃跑 (of troops) escape in disorder; flee pell-mell; flee helter-skelter：闻风～ escape in disorder at the news

【溃退】kuìtuì (军队)被打垮而后退 (of troops) be defeated and retreat in confusion; beat hasty retreat：敌军狼狈～。The enemy troops beat a retreat in utter confusion.

【溃围】kuìwéi〈书 *fml*.〉突破包围 break through an encirclement：乘势～ take advantage of a situation to break through an encirclement|～而逃 break through an encirclement and flee

【溃疡】kuìyáng 皮肤或黏膜的表皮坏死脱落后形成的缺损。形成溃疡的原因是物理性刺激(如烧灼、重压等)、化学性刺激(如酸、碱等)或生物性刺激(如细菌、霉菌)等。ulcer; abscess; lesion of the skin or mucous membrane due to the necrosis and desquamation of the cuticle, usu. resulting from physical irritations such as cauterizing and cuts, chemical irritants such as acid and alkali, or biological agents such as bacteria and mildew

愦 kuì〈书 *fml.*〉糊涂;昏乱 muddle-headed; confused; befuddled: 昏～ muddled-headed; befuddled|～乱 dazed and confused

【愦乱】kuìluàn〈书 *fml.*〉昏乱 dazed and confused; befuddled

愧(媿) kuì 惭愧 ashamed; abashed; with a stricken conscience: 羞～ ashamed|问心无～ be not ashamed of|～不敢当(感到惭愧,承当不起) (I)'m flattered but I honestly don't deserve it.

【愧汗】kuìhàn〈书 *fml.*〉因羞愧而流汗,形容羞愧到了极点 be so ashamed as to break into a sweat; feel extremely ashamed: 忆及往事,不胜～。(I) cannot help feeling ashamed when I recall the past.

【愧恨】kuìhèn 因羞愧而自恨 ashamed and remorseful; remorseful: 他明白了自己的不对,内心深自～。When he realized his mistake, he felt bitterly remorseful.

【愧悔】kuìhuǐ 羞愧悔恨 ashamed and regretful: ～不及 feel extremely ashamed too late|提起这些事,～难言。(I) feel too ashamed and regretful for words at the mention of these affairs.

【愧疚】kuìjiù 羞愧不安 remorseful and uneasy: ～的心情 guilty feeling|内心深感～ feel extremely guilty

【愧领】kuìlǐng 领受别人的情谊、馈赠时说的客套话[express humble acceptance when receiving a gift or kindness]: 您的心意,我们～啦。We humbly accept your kindness.

【愧色】kuìsè 惭愧的脸色 guilty look; look of shame: 面带～ look guilty; look ashamed

【愧痛】kuìtòng 因羞愧而感到痛苦 feel agonized with shame: 脸上流露出～的表情。His face is wreathed in agony and shame.

【愧怍】kuìzuò〈书 *fml.*〉惭愧 ashamed; abashed; guilty

褙 kuì〈方 *dial.*〉❶(～儿 kuìr)用绳子、带子等拴成的结 knot: 活～儿 slip-knot|死～儿 fast-knot ❷ 拴;系(jì) tie; fasten; do up; button up: ～个褙儿 tie a knot|把牲口～上 tie up the cattle to a pole

聩 kuì〈书 *fml.*〉聋 hearing impaired; deaf; hard of hearing: 发聋振～ rouse those who do not hear or listen

篑 kuì〈书 *fml.*〉盛土的筐子 basket for holding earth: 功亏一～ fail for want of a final effort

kūn (ㄎㄨㄣ)

坤 kūn ❶ 八卦之一,卦形是'☷',代表地, symbol for earth in the Eight Trigrams; ☞ 八卦 bāguà on p. 22 ❷ 指女性的 female; feminine: ～造 bride|～宅 family of the bride|～表 women's watch|～车 women's bicycle|～鞋 women's shoes

【坤包】kūnbāo 妇女用的挎包、手提包等,一般比较小巧 lady's handbag, generally small and exquisite

【坤表】kūnbiǎo 女式手表,比较小巧 small and exquisite women's wristwatch

【坤角儿】kūnjuér〈旧时 *old*〉指戏剧女演员 actress

【坤伶】kūnlíng same as 坤角儿 kūnjuér

【坤造】kūnzào ❶〈旧时 *old*〉指婚姻中的女方 woman in a marriage; bride ❷〈旧时 *old*〉指女子的生辰八字 date of birth and the eight characters concerning the life of a woman

【坤宅】kūnzhái〈旧时 *old*〉指婚姻中的女家 wife's family

昆 kūn〈书 *fml.*〉❶ 哥哥 elder brother: ～仲 form of address for one's brothers|～季 brothers ❷ 子孙;后嗣 offspring; descendant: 后～ descendant; child

【昆布】kūnbù 中药上指海带 term for kelp in traditional Chinese medicine

【昆虫】kūnchóng 节肢动物的一纲,身体分头、胸、腹三部。头部有触角、眼、口器等。胸部有足三对,翅膀两对或一对,也有没翅膀的。腹部有节,两侧有气孔,是呼吸器官。多数昆虫都经过卵、幼虫、蛹、成虫等发育阶段。如蜜蜂、蚊、蝇、跳蚤、蝗虫、蚜虫等。insect; hexapod; any animal of the class *Insecta*, having a body divided into three parts — head, thorax and abdomen — with the head consisting of antennae, eyes and mouth, thorax of three pairs of legs, one or two pairs of wings, or no wings, and the abdomen of femurs and respiratory spiracles on both sides; most insects grow through three stages: egg, pupae, and imago; e.g. bee, mosquito, fly, flea, locust, aphid, etc.

【昆季】kūnjì〈书 *fml.*〉兄弟(xiōngdì) brothers

【昆腔】kūnqiāng 戏曲声腔之一,元代在江苏昆山产生。明代至清中叶以前非常流行,对许多剧种的形成和发展都有影响。*kunqiang* tone; melodies that originated in Kunshan, Jiangsu Province, in the Yuan Dynasty, and were popular in the Ming and mid-Qing dynasties, and exerted a great influence on the shaping and development of many other operas; also 昆曲 kūnqǔ or 昆山腔 kūnshānqiāng

K

【昆曲】kūnqǔ ❶ 流行于江苏南部（南昆）及北京、河北（北昆）等地的地方戏曲剧种，用昆腔演唱 *kunqu*, opera using *kunqiang* melodies and popular in southern Jiangsu Province (southern *kunqu* opera), Beijing and Hebei Province (northern *kunqu* opera); also 昆剧 kūnjù ❷ same as 昆腔 kūnqiāng

【昆仲】kūnzhòng〈书 *fml.*〉对别人兄弟（xiōngdì）的称呼 form of address for one's brothers

崑 kūn 崑崙（Kūnlún），山名，在新疆、西藏和青海。今作昆仑。Kunlun Mountains; a group of mountains stretching across the Xinjiang Uygur Autonomous Region, Tibet and Qinghai Province; today written as 昆仑 Kūnlún

堃 kūn same as 坤 kūn（多用于人名 oft. used in a person's name）

裈（幝、裩） kūn〈书 *fml.*〉裤子 trousers

琨 kūn〈书 *fml.*〉一种美玉 a kind of jade

焜 kūn〈书 *fml.*〉明亮 bright

髡（髠） kūn〈古代 *arch.*〉剃去男子头发的刑罚 shave a man's head (a punishment in ancient times)

鹍（鵾） kūn 鹍鸡，古书上指像鹤的一种鸟 chicken; refers to a crane-like bird in some ancient books

锟 kūn 锟铻（Kūnwú），古书上记载的山名。所产的铁可以铸刀剑，因此锟铻也指宝剑。mountain recorded in some ancient books, said to be rich in iron suitable for casting swords, thus 锟铻 became the synonym for sword

醌 kūn 有机化合物的一类，是芳香族母核的两个氢原子各由一个氧原子所代替而成的化合物 quinone; a class of aromatic compounds

鲲 kūn〈古代 *arch.*〉传说中的一种大鱼 huge fish in ancient legends

【鲲鹏】kūnpéng〈古代 *arch.*〉传说中的大鱼和大鸟。也指鲲化成的大鹏鸟（见于《庄子·逍遥游》）。big fish and big bird in ancient legends; enormous legendary bird transformed from a gigantic fish (from *Zhuangzi · Transcendent Bliss*)

kǔn（ㄎㄨㄣˇ）

捆（綑） kǔn ❶ 用绳子等把东西缠紧打结 tie; bind; bundle up with rope: ～行李 bundle up one's luggage | 把麦子～起来。Bundle up the wheat. ❷（～儿 kǔnr）捆成的东西 bundle; bunch: 韭菜～儿 bunch of leeks ❸（～儿 kǔnr）〈量词 *classifier*〉用于捆起来的东西 bundle; bunch: 一～柴火 a bundle of firewood

【捆绑】kǔnbǎng 用绳子等捆（多用于人 usu. a person）tie up with rope; truss up; bind

【捆扎】kǔnzā 把东西捆在一起，使不分散 tie up; bundle up: 把布袋口儿～好。Tie up the cloth bag. | 这批货物运送的时候，应该妥为包装～。The goods should be packed properly for transport.

【捆子】kǔn·zi same as 捆 kǔn ②: 把芦苇扎成～ bundle up the reeds

阃 kǔn〈书 *fml.*〉❶ 门坎 threshold ❷ 指妇女居住的内室 women's quarters: ～闱 women's quarters ❸ 借指妇女 women: ～范（女子的品德规范）virtues of a woman; women's propriety

悃 kǔn〈书 *fml.*〉真心诚意 sincere: ～诚 sincerity; sincere intentions | 聊表谢～。It's just a token of my sincere gratitude.

【悃愊】kǔnbì〈书 *fml.*〉至诚 utter sincerity: ～无华 honest and simple; sincere and honest

壸（壼） kǔn〈书 *fml.*〉宫里的路 paths in an imperial palace

kùn（ㄎㄨㄣˋ）

困（❺❻ 睏） kùn ❶ 陷在艰难痛苦中或受环境、条件的限制无法摆脱 be stranded; be trapped; be stricken; be unable to break free from a state of pain, or from limitations of circumstance: 为病所～ be stricken by illness | 想当年当（dàng）无可当，卖无可卖，真把我给～住了。In those days, I was in such dire straits that I had nothing to mortgage or trade in. ❷ 控制在一定范围里；围困 keep (sb.) within a certain area; besiege; hold in check; pin down: ～守 defend against a siege; withstand a siege | 把敌人～在山沟里。Pin down the enemy in the valley. ❸ 困难 difficulty: ～苦 hardship and privation | ～厄 dire straits; distress ❹ 疲乏 exhausted; fatigued: ～乏 tired; fatigued | ～顿 worn out; exhausted ❺ 疲乏想睡 sleepy out of tiredness; drowsy: 你～了就先睡。Go to bed first if you're sleepy. ❻〈方 *dial.*〉睡 sleep: ～觉 sleep | 天不早了，快点～吧。It's getting late. Go to bed now!

【困惫】kùnbèi〈书 *fml.*〉非常疲乏 tired out; exhausted: ～不堪 be in a state of utter exhaustion; be worn out; be dog-tired

【困顿】kùndùn ❶ 劳累到不能支持 worn out; exhausted: 终日劳碌，十分～。I feel exhausted after working all day long. ❷（生计或境遇）艰难窘迫 in financial straits or difficulties: 漂泊在外，～潦倒。Leading a wandering life away from home, one is often frustrated and poor.

【困厄】kùn'è（处境）艰难窘迫 dire straits; distress: 从艰难～中闯出一番事业 lift (oneself) out of dire straits and carve out a successful future

【困乏】kùnfá ❶ 疲乏 tired; fatigued: 走了一天路，大家都～了。Everyone felt exhausted after a long day's journey. ❷〈书 *fml.*〉(经济、生活)困难 financial difficulties: 连年歉收，百姓～。The last few years' poor harvests have left people in dire straits.

【困惑】kùnhuò 感到疑难，不知道该怎么办 perplexed; puzzled; confused: ～不解 feel puzzled|这个问题一直～着他们。This problem has been perplexing them the whole time.

【困觉】kùn//jiào〈方 *dial.*〉睡觉 sleep

【困境】kùnjìng 困难的处境 difficult position; predicament; straits: 陷入～ fall into dire straits; find oneself in a tight corner; land oneself in a fix|摆脱～ extricate oneself from a difficult position|处于～ be in a difficult position

【困窘】kùnjiǒng ❶ 为难 be embarrassed; feel awkward: 他～地站在那里，一句话也说不出来。He stood there, embarrassed and unable to utter one word. ❷ 穷困 poverty-stricken; destitute: 家境～ be in destitute family circumstances|～的生活 poverty-stricken life

【困倦】kùnjuàn 疲乏想睡 drowsy; exhausted and sleepy: 一连忙了几天，大家都十分～。Everybody felt exhausted and sleepy after several hectic days.

【困苦】kùnkǔ (生活上)艰难痛苦 hardship; tribulation: 生活～ lead a hard life|～的日子过去了。The days of hardship are gone.

【困难】kùn·nan ❶ 事情复杂，阻碍多 difficulty: 克服～ overcome difficulties ❷ 穷困，不好过 financial difficulty; dire straits: 生活～ live in dire straits; difficult life|～补助 relief; subsidies to those in difficult circumstances

【困扰】kùnrǎo 围困并搅扰 annoy; disturb; perplex; haunt: 游击队四处出击，～敌军。The guerrillas attacked from all directions to confuse the enemy.|这几天被一种莫名的烦乱所～。An indescribable restlessness has been haunting me the last few days.

【困人】kùnrén 使人困倦 inducing drowsiness (in people): ～的天气 drowsy weather

【困守】kùnshǒu 在被围困的情况下坚守(防地) defend against a siege; stand a siege: ～孤城 defend an isolated city

【困兽犹斗】kùn shòu yóu dòu〈比喻 *fig.*〉陷于绝境的人(多指坏人)虽然走投无路，还要顽强抵抗 (usu. of a villain) put up a desperate fight even after falling into a trap

kuò (ㄎㄨㄛˋ)

扩(擴) kuò 扩大 expand; enlarge; extend: ～充 expand; strengthen; augment|～展 expand; develop|～散 spread; diffuse|～建 extend; enlarge|～音机 loudspeaker; microphone; audio amplifier

【扩版】kuòbǎn 报刊扩大版面或增加版数 (of a newspaper or magazine) enlarge the format; increase the number of pages: 晚报将于7月1日～，由四版增为八版。The evening newspaper will increase its number of pages from four to eight starting from July 1.

【扩编】kuòbiān 扩大编制(多用于军队 usu. troops) expand the organization; increase the size of troops: ～队伍 increase the size of the troops

【扩充】kuòchōng 扩大充实 expand; strengthen; enlarge; augment: ～内容 enrich the contents|～设备 procure more equipment; augment one's stock of equipment|教师队伍在不断～。The team of teachers has been expanding.

【扩大】kuòdà 使(范围、规模等)比原来大 enlarge; expand; increase (sphere, scale, etc.): ～生产 expand production|～战果 exploit a victory; press home one's advantage|～眼界 broaden one's horizons; widen one's vision or outlook|～影响 extend one's influence|～耕地面积 expand the acreage of cultivated land

【扩大化】kuòdàhuà 把实际的范围或数量凭空地扩大起来 broaden the scope; exaggerate sth. with no reason at all

【扩大再生产】kuòdà zàishēngchǎn 扩大原有规模的再生产 repeated production on an extended scale; extended or expanded production; ☞ 再生产 zàishēngchǎn on p.2387

【扩建】kuòjiàn 把厂矿企业建筑等的规模加大 expand the scale of a factory, mine, building, etc.: ～厂房 expand the workshop|大力～工业基地 vigorously expand the industrial base

【扩军】kuòjūn 扩充军备 engage in arms expansion

【扩散】kuòsàn 扩大分散出去 spread; diffuse; proliferate: ～影响 extend influence|毒素已～到全身。The toxin has spread to every part of the body.|浓烟～到村庄的上空。Heavy smoke has risen into the sky above the village.

【扩胸器】kuòxiōngqì 体育运动用的一种辅助器械，上面装有弹簧，练习时用双手把它拉开，能增强胸部和臂部肌肉的力量 chest expander; chest developer; sports equipment with strong springs to be stretched with both hands to build up the strength of chest and arm muscles; also 拉力器 lālìqì

【扩音机】kuòyīnjī 用来扩大声音的装置，用于有线广播 loudspeaker; microphone; audio amplifier

【扩印】kuòyìn 放大洗印(照片) enlarge (a photo)：～机 photo processing equipment｜～彩色照片 enlarge a colour photo

【扩展】kuòzhǎn 向外伸展；扩大 extend; expand; develop：～马路 expand a road｜五年内全省林地将～到一千万亩。The forests in the province will expand to 10 million *mu* in five years.

【扩张】kuòzhāng 扩大（势力、疆土等）expand; enlarge; extend; spread (influence, territory, etc.)：向外～ outward expansion｜这种药能使血管～。This medicine can dilate blood vessels.

括 kuò ❶ 扎；束 tighten up; bundle; contract：～约肌 sphincter (muscle) ❷ 包括 include：总～ sum up; put it in a nutshell｜概～ summarize; sum up ❸ 对部分文字加上括号 bracket：把这几个字用括号～起来。Put these words in brackets.

☞ guā on p. 703

【括号】kuòhào ❶ 算术式或代数式中表示几个数或项的结合关系和先后顺序的符号，形式有()、[]、{}三种，分别叫做小括号、中括号、大括号或圆括号、方括号、花括号。中括号用在小括号的外层，大括号用在中括号的外层，运算时先从小括号内的式子算起。parentheses; brackets; symbols to indicate relations and order of numbers and variables in arithmetic and algebra equations, in the forms of ()、[]、{}, respectively called 小括号 (round parentheses), 中括号 (square brackets), 大括号 (brace brackets) or 圆括号 (round parentheses), 方括号 (square brackets), or 花括号 (brace brackets); in solving mathematical problem, the order of operation is that one does what is in the round parentheses first, then the square brackets and lastly the brace brackets. ❷ 标点符号，最常用的形式是圆括号，与数学上的小括号相同，还有方括号([])、六角括号(〔〕)、方头括号(【】)等几种，主要表示文中注释的部分 above used as punctuation, parentheses being the most common; also brackets like [], 〔〕 and 【】, mainly used to indicate explanations in a text

【括弧】kuòhú ❶ 小括号 round parentheses; small bracket; ☞ 括号 kuòhào ① ❷ same as 括号 kuòhào ②。有时也指引号。sometimes also referring to quotation marks

【括约肌】kuòyuējī 肛门、膀胱口、幽门等处的环状肌肉，能收缩和舒张，收缩时使肛门、膀胱口、幽门等关闭，舒张时使它们开放 constrictor muscle; sphincter; ring-like muscle around the anus, the orifice of the bladder, or the pylorus, etc., which constricts to close, and relaxes to open

栝 kuò ☞ [檃栝] (yǐnkuò) on p. 2295

☞ guā on p. 703

逅(适) kuò 〈书 *fml.*〉疾速（多用于人名 usu. used in a person's name) sharpness

☞ 适 shì on p. 1761

蛞 kuò ☞ below

【蛞蝼】kuòlóu 古书上指蝼蛄 mole cricket, as referred in ancient books

【蛞蝓】kuòyú 软体动物，身体圆而长，没有壳，表面多黏液，头上有长短触角各一对，眼长在长触角上。背面淡褐色或黑色，腹面白色。昼伏夜出，吃植物的叶子，危害蔬菜、果树等农作物。slug (*Limax*); mollusc without a shell; any animal having a long or round, soft and fleshy body, sticky grume on its surface, a pair of long antennae with eyes and a pair of short antennae. Its back is pale brown or black, and its belly is white. Resting during the day and active at night, it feeds on leaves of plants, and thus is harmful to vegetables, fruit trees and other crops. also 鼻涕虫 bítìchóng; 有的地区叫蜒蚰 known as 蜒蚰 yányóu in some places.

筈 kuò 〈书 *fml.*〉箭尾扣弦的部分 tail of an arrow to be pressed against the bow string

阔(濶) kuò ❶ （面积）宽；宽广 wide; broad; vast：广～ broad｜辽～ vast｜海～天空 the wide sea and the vast sky; boundless sea and sky; unrestrained and far-ranging ◇～别 be separated for a long time｜高谈～论 indulge in oratory; declaim; mouth high-sounding words; hold forth ❷ 阔绰；阔气；有钱 free with one's money; have the appearance of wealth：摆～ show off one's wealth｜他～起来了。He appears to be getting rich.

【阔别】kuòbié 长时间的分别 be separated for a long time：～多年 have not seen each other for years

【阔步】kuòbù 迈大步 take big strides：～前进 advance with giant strides｜昂首～ stride with one's chin up; stride proudly ahead

【阔绰】kuòchuò 排场大，生活奢侈 ostentatious; extravagant; liberal with money

【阔佬】kuòlǎo 有钱的人 rich man; also 阔老 kuòlǎo

【阔气】kuò·qi 豪华奢侈 luxurious; extravagant; lavish：摆～ display or parade one's wealth

【阔人】kuòrén 有钱的人 member of a rich family; wealthy person

【阔少】kuòshào 有钱的人家的子弟 young man from a wealthy family

【阔野】kuòyě 广阔的原野 vast expanse of open country：一望无垠的～ boundless expanse of open country

【阔叶树】kuòyèshù 叶子的形状宽阔的树木，如白杨、枫树等 broadleaf tree, e.g. poplar, maple, etc.

廓 kuò ❶ 广阔 wide; extensive: 寥～ vast; boundless | ～落 vast and serene ❷ 扩展; 扩大 expand; enlarge; spread: ～大 expand; extend | ～张 expand; spread ❸ 物体的外缘 contour; outline of an object: 轮～ contour; outline | 耳～ rim of the ear

【廓落】kuòluò 〈书 *fml.*〉空阔寂静的样子 vast and serene; extensive and tranquil: ～的夜空 vast and serene night sky

【廓清】kuòqīng ❶ same as 澄清 chéngqīng②; 肃清 clarify; purify; purge; clean up: ～天下 clean up the country; bring peace and unity to the country | ～邪说 dispel heresy ❷ 清除 clear away; remove; clean out; eliminate: ～障碍 clear away obstacles | ～道路 clear the path

【廓张】kuòzhāng 〈书 *fml.*〉扩散; 扩大 expand; enlarge; spread: 吵闹声不断～开去。The noise of quarrelling kept spreading.

鞹(鞟) kuò 〈书 *fml.*〉去毛的兽皮 animal skin with the hair removed; hairless hide; hairless pelt

K

L

lā（ㄌㄚ）

奋 lā ☞［旮旯］(kē·lā) on p. 1088

垃 lā［垃圾］(lājī) 脏土或扔掉的破烂东西 rubbish; garbage; junk ◇清除社会～do away with social dregs; rid society of undesirable elements

拉¹ lā ❶ 用力使朝自己所在的方向或跟着自己移动 pull; draw; tug; drag:～锯 pull a saw|～纤 track a boat|你把车～过来。Pull the cart over here. ❷ 用车载运 transport by vehicle; haul:套车去～肥料 get a cart ready for the manure|平板车能～货，也能～人。A flatbed tricycle can be used to carry goods or people. ❸ 带领转移（多用于队伍 oft. troops to a place）move:把二连～到河那边去。Move No. 2 Company over to the other side of the river. ❹ 牵引乐器的某一部分使乐器发出声音 play (a musical instrument):～胡琴 play the *huqin*, a two-stringed Chinese fiddle|～小提琴 play the violin|～手风琴 play the accordion ❺ 拖长；使延长 drag out; draw out; space out:～长声音说话 speak with a drawl|快跟上，不要～开距离！Hurry up! Don't fall behind. ❻〈方 *dial.*〉抚养 bring sb. up:他母亲很不容易地把他～大。His mother had a tough time bring him up. ❼ 帮助 give (or lend) a helping hand; help:人家有困难，咱们应该～他一把。We should help him when he is in trouble. ❽ 牵累；拉扯 drag in; implicate:自己做的事，为什么要～上别人？It was all your own doing. Why drag in others? ❾ 拉拢；联络 win sb. over:～关系 try to gain clout with (sb. with power or influence)|～交情 cotton up to sb. ❿ 组织（队伍、团伙等）organize; put (people, a team, etc.) together; band:～队伍 recruit an army|～帮结伙 bang together ⓫ 招揽 recruit:～买卖 seek business opportunities|～生意 solicit business deals ⓬〈方 *dial.*〉闲谈 chat:～话 strike up a conversation|～家常 engage in small talk

拉² lā 排泄(大便) defecate:～屎 go to stool; shit|～肚子 come down with diarrhoea ☞ lá on p. 1139, lǎ on p. 1139 and là on p. 1139

【拉巴】lā·ba〈方 *dial.*〉❶ 辛勤抚养 take great pains to bring up (a child):再苦再累也要把孩子～大。I've got to bring my children up no matter how difficult and tiresome it is. ❷ 扶助；提拔 help; support; promote:求大哥～我们一把。Give us a hand, Big Brother!

【拉帮结伙】lā bāng jié huǒ 拉起一帮人结成集团 gang up; band together; recruit people to form a faction; also 拉帮结派 lā bāng jié pài

【拉鼻儿】lā//bír 指鸣汽笛 sound a steam whistle

【拉场子】lā chǎng·zi ❶ 指艺人在街头空地招引观众围成场子，进行表演(of a performing artist) put on a show in a street corner or market place ❷ 指撑场面或打开局面 give publicity to sb. or sth.:请客～throw a dinner for publicity purposes

【拉扯】lā·che ❶ same as 拉 lā ①:你～住他，别让他再出去。Hold him back and don't let go of him again. ❷ 辛勤抚养 scrape and scratch to bring up (a child):屎一把，尿一把，大妈才把你～大。It took your aunt so much trouble to bring you up beginning from the days you were in swaddling clothes. ❸ 扶助；提拔 gloom; prepare sb. for a career, position, etc.:师傅见他有出息，愿意特别～他一把。His master finds him promising and is willing to give him special help. ❹ 勾结；拉拢 gang up with; rope in ❺ 牵扯；牵涉 implicate; drag in:你自己做事自己承当，不要～别人。Be a man and take the blame for what you've done. Don't drag other people in. ❻ 闲谈 chat:李大嫂急着要出门，无心跟他～。Elder Sister Li was in no mood to chat with him because she was in such a hurry to go outdoors.

【拉床】lāchuáng 金属切削机床，用来加工孔眼或键槽。加工时，一般工件不动，拉刀做直线运动切削。broaching machine; machine using the repeated rectilinear motion of an elongated, tapered cutting tool to shape and enlarge grooves or holes in a piece of metal

【拉大片】lā dàpiān same as 拉洋片 lā yángpiān

【拉大旗，作虎皮】lā dàqí, zuò hǔpí〈比喻 *fig.*〉打着某种旗号以张声势，来吓唬人、蒙骗人 hoist the banner of a great cause to hoodwink people; deck oneself out to intimidate others

【拉倒】lādǎo 算了；作罢 forget about it; leave it at that; drop it:你不去就～。Since you don't want to go, let's forget about it.

【拉丁】lā//dīng ❶〈旧时 *old*〉军队抓青壮年男子当兵 enlist able-bodied men by forced conscription ❷ same as 拉夫 lā//fū

【拉丁字母】Lādīng zìmǔ 拉丁文(古代罗马人所用文字)的字母。一般泛指根据拉丁文字母加以补充的字母,如英文、法文、西班牙文的字母。汉语拼音方案也采用拉丁字母。Latin alphabet; Roman alphabet; alphabetical scrip used by people in the Roman Empire for the writing of Latin, later adopted, with modifications and additions of letters, by English, French, Spanish, and other languages. The Latin alphabet has also been adopted as the scheme of the Chinese Phonetic Alphabet.

拉丁字母表
Latin Alphabet

大写 upper case	小写 lower case	名称 * transli-teration	大写 upper case	小写 lower case	名称 * transli-teration
A	a	a	N	n	nê
B	b	bê	O	o	o
C	c	cê	P	p	pê
D	d	dê	Q	q	qiu
E	e	e	R	r	ar
F	f	êf	S	s	ês
G	g	gê	T	t	tê
H	h	ha	U	u	wu
I	i	yi	V	v	vê
J	j	jie	W	w	wa
K	k	kê	X	x	xi
L	l	êl	Y	y	ya
M	m	êm	Z	z	zê

* 按照汉语拼音方案的规定。
Transliteration based on *pinyin* (phonetic system of Chinese)

【拉肚子】lā dù·zi 指腹泻 suffer from diarrhoea; have loose bowels

【拉夫】lā//fū〈旧时 *old*〉军队抓老百姓充当大役 pressgang; force people into military service

【拉杆】lāgān (～儿 lāgānr) ❶ 安装在机械或建筑物上起牵引作用的杆形构件,如自行车闸上的长铁棍 pull rod, such as the long iron stick fixed on a bicycle brake; drag link; draw bar; tension link ❷ 由不同直径的管状物套接而成的杆,能拉长或缩短 telescopic pole that can be compressed or extended to adjust its length:～支架 compressible stand|～天线 telescopic antenna

【拉钩】lā//gōu (～儿 lā//gōur)两人用右手食指或小拇指互相钩着拉一下,表示守信用,不反悔 (of two persons) hook up the index or little fingers of each other's right hands and give them a pull in token of good faith

【拉呱儿】lā//guǎr〈方 *dial.*〉same as 闲谈 xiántán:歇着的时候,几个老头儿就凑到一起～。During the break the old men huddled together for a chat.

【拉关系】lā guān·xi 跟关系较疏远的人联络、拉拢,使有某种关系(多含贬义 oft. derog.) try to establish a relationship with sb.; cotton up to

【拉后腿】lā hòutuǐ〈比喻 *fig.*〉利用亲密的关系和感情牵制别人的行动 hold sb. back; be a drag on sb.; be a hindrance to sb; also 扯后腿 chě hòutuǐ

【拉祜族】Lāhùzú 我国少数民族之一,分布在云南 Lahu people; the Lahus; ethnic minority people inhabiting Yunnan Province

【拉花儿】lāhuār 一种彩色纸花,可以拉成长串,多在节日、喜庆时悬挂 paper garland, for use on festive occasions

【拉饥荒】lā jī·huang 欠债 incur a debt; get into debt

【拉家带口】lā jiā dài kǒu 带着一家大小(多指受家属的拖累 oft. in the sense of being tied down by one's family) with mouths to feed; have a family to provide for; also 拖家带口 tuō jiā dài kǒu

【拉架】lā//jià 拉开打架的人,从中调解 settle a brawl by separating the brawlers

【拉交情】lā jiāo·qing 拉拢感情;攀交情(多含贬义 oft. derog.) try to form ties with; cotton up to

【拉脚】lā//jiǎo (～儿 lā//jiǎor)用大车载旅客或为人运货 transport persons or haul goods by cart

【拉近乎】lā jìn·hu 跟不熟识的人拉拢关系,表示亲近(多含贬义 oft. derog.)cotton up to sb. (oft. a stranger); also 套近乎 tào jìn·hu

【拉锯】lā//jù 两个人用大锯一来一往地锯东西 work a two-handed saw;〈比喻 *fig.*〉双方来回往复 be locked in a seesaw struggle:～式 in a seesaw fashion|～战 seesaw battle

【拉客】lā//kè ❶(饭馆、旅馆等)(of a restaurant or a hotel)招揽顾客或旅客 solicit diners or guests ❷(三轮车、出租汽车等)载运乘客(of a pedicab, taxi, etc.) take on passengers ❸ 指招引嫖客(of a prostitute) solicit patrons

【拉亏空】lā kuī·kong 欠债 be in debt; get into debt

【拉拉队】lālāduì 体育运动比赛时,在旁边给运动员呐喊助威的一组人 cheering squad; rooters; a group of people shouting encouragement to a team at a sports competition

【拉力】lālì ❶ 拉拽的力量 pulling force ❷ 物体所承受的拉拽的力 tension

【拉力器】lālìqì 扩胸器 chest-developer; chest-expander

【拉练】lāliàn 野营训练。多指部队离开营房,在长途行军和野营过程中,按照战时要求,进行训练。camp and field training; (oft. of troops) field training during a long march or camping away from the barracks

【拉链】lāliàn (～儿 lāliànr) same as 拉锁 lāsuǒ

【拉拢】lā•lǒng 为对自己有利,用手段使别人靠拢到自己方面来 win sb. over; rope in: ～人 woo and corrupt sb. | ～感情 win sb. over by currying favour with him or her

【拉买卖】lā mǎi•mai 招揽生意 canvass business orders; drum up trade

【拉毛】lāmáo 用机器把驼绒坯等表面的毛纱拉成毛绒状,使成为柔软绒面的工艺 nap; gig; use a machine to raise the short fuzzy ends of fibers so as to form a downy coating on a piece of cloth; ～围巾 nap scarf; also 拉绒 lāróng

【拉面】lāmiàn 〈方 *dial.*〉 same as 抻面 chēnmiàn

【拉皮条】lā pítiáo 撮合男女发生不正当的关系 pimp; person who brings men and women together in illicit sexual relationship

【拉偏手儿】lā piānshǒur 指拉架时有意偏袒一方 be partial to one side when settling a brawl; also 拉偏架 lā piānjià

【拉平】lā//píng 使有高有低的变成相等 draw even; even up: 甲队反攻频频得手,双方比分逐渐～。The score gradually evened up as team A scored repeatedly in a surge of counter-attacks.

【拉纤】lā//qiàn ❶ 在岸上用绳子拉船前进 tow a boat ❷ 为双方介绍、说合并从中谋取利益 act as a go-between; make a match: 说媒～ serve as a matchmaker | 这笔生意是他拉的纤。It was with his arrangement that this deal was made possible.

【拉山头】lā shāntóu 指组织人马,结成宗派 form a faction

【拉手】lā•shou 安装在门窗或抽屉等上面便于用手开关的木条或金属物等 wooden or metal handle of a door, window, drawer, etc.

【拉丝】lāsī same as 拔丝 básī ①

【拉锁】lāsuǒ (～儿 lāsuǒr)一种可以分开和锁合的链条形的金属或塑料制品,用来缝在衣服、口袋或皮包等上面 zipper; slide fastener; metal or plastic device consisting of two parallel rows of parts to interlock or part two pieces of cloth, plastic, etc., by the motion of a slide; also 拉链 lāliàn

【拉套】lā//tào ❶ 在车辕的前面或侧面拉车(of an extra animal) help pull a cart: 这匹马是～的。This horse is a sidekick to the one hitched up to pull the cart from between the shafts. ❷ 〈方 *dial.*〉〈比喻 *fig.*〉帮助别人,替人出力 help sb. the best one can

【拉稀】lā//xī 腹泻的通称 general term for 腹泻 fùxiè

【拉下脸】lāxià liǎn ❶ 指不顾情面 not spare sb.'s sensibilities: 他办事大公无私,对谁也能～来。He is perfectly fair and impartial and never tries to spare anybody's feelings. ❷ 指露出不高兴的表情 look displeased; pull a long face; put on a stern expression: 他听了这句话,立刻～来。At the remark a look of resentment clouded his face.

【拉下水】lā xià shuǐ 〈比喻 *fig.*〉引诱人和自己一起做坏事 pull sb. into the water — get sb. involved in a conspiracy, etc.; drag sb. into the mire; make an accomplice of sb.; corrupt sb.

【拉线】lā//xiàn 〈比喻 *fig.*〉从中撮合 act as a middleman: 他俩交朋友是我拉的线。I brought the two of them together for their first date.

【拉秧】lā//yāng 瓜类和某些蔬菜过了收获期,把秧子拔掉 uproot plants after their edible portions have been harvested

【拉洋片】lā yángpiān 一种民间文娱活动,在装有凸透镜的木箱中挂着各种画片,表演者一面拉换画片,一面说唱画片的内容。观众从透镜里可以看到放大的画面。peepshow; exhibited display of pictures fixed in a wooden box, to be viewed through a small hole fixed with a magnifying lens, with the performer pulling the pictures while narrating the content usu. in the form of ballad-singing; also 拉大片 lā dàpiān

【拉杂】lāzá 没有条理;杂乱 rambling; jumbled; ill-organized: 这篇文章写得太～,使人不得要领。This article is so ill-organized that no one could make head or tail of it. | 我拉拉杂杂谈了这些,请大家指教。I think I'll stop my random talk and ask for your advice.

【拉账】lā//zhàng 欠债 run up bills; get into debt: 拉了一屁股账 run up heavy debt

啦 lā ☞below
☞ •la on p.1141

【啦呱儿】lā//guǎr same as 拉呱儿 lā//guǎr

【啦啦队】lālāduì same as 拉拉队 lālāduì

喇 lā ☞ 呼喇 hūlā on p.816 and 哇喇 wālā on p.1964
☞ lá on p.1139 and lǎ on p.1139

邋 lā [邋遢](lā•tā)不整洁;不利落 slovenly; sloppy: ～鬼 dragletail; sluggard | 办事真～ slovenly ways of doing things

lá (ㄌㄚˊ)

旯 lá ☞旮旯儿 (gālár) on p.618

拉(剌) lá 刀刃与物件接触,由一端向另一端移动,使物件破裂或断开;割 slash; slit; cut; make a gash in:把皮子~开 slit a piece of leather|手上~个口子 cut one's hand; get a cut in the hand

☞ lā on p. 1136, lǎ on p. 1139 and là on p. 1139.

☞ 剌 là on p. 1139

砬(磖) lá 砬子,多用于地名,如红石砬(在河北) mountain crag; often used in a place name, such as Hongshila (in Hebei Province)

【砬子】lá·zi〈方 *dial.*〉山上耸立的大岩石,多用于地名,如白石砬子(在黑龙江) mountain crag; often used in a place name, such as Baishi Lazi (in Heilongjiang Province)

揦 lá [揦子](lá·zi)〈方 *dial.*〉玻璃瓶 glass bottle

喇 lá ☞哈喇子 (hālá·zi) on p. 752

☞ lā on p. 1138 and lǎ on p. 1139

lǎ (ㄌㄚˇ)

拉 lǎ ☞半拉 bànlǎ on p. 53 and [虎不拉] (hù·bulǎ) on p. 824

☞lā on p. 1136, lá on p. 1139 and là on p. 1139

【拉忽】lǎ·hu〈方 *dial.*〉马虎 negligent; careless:这人太~,办事靠不住。This guy is unreliable because he is so forgetful.

喇 lǎ ☞below

☞ lā on p. 1138 and lá on p. 1139

【喇叭】lǎ·ba ❶ 管乐器,上细下粗,最下端的口部向四周张开,可以扩大声音 trumpet; wind instrument fashioned out of a curved brass tube with a narrow mouthpiece and an outspread wide end for amplifying the sound ❷ 有扩音作用的、喇叭筒状的东西 loudspeaker; trumpet-shaped electrical device that allows sounds or voices to be heard loudly at a distance:汽车~ (of a car) horn|无线电~(扬声器) radio speaker

【喇叭花】lǎ·bahuā 牵牛花的通称 general term for 牵牛花 qiānniúhuā

【喇嘛】lǎ·ma 喇嘛教的僧人,原为一种尊称。lama; honourary title for a Tibetan Buddhist monk [藏 Tibetan]

【喇嘛教】Lǎ·majiào 在我国西藏、内蒙古等地区流行的一种宗教。公元7世纪佛教传入西藏以后,搀入了本地固有的宗教成分,为了区别于一般的佛教,称为喇嘛教。Lamaism; a school of Buddhism that has incorporated elements of the indigenous *Bon* religion after it found its way into Tibet during the 7th century, enjoying wide popularity in Tibet, Inner Mongolia and some other regions in China

là (ㄌㄚˋ)

拉[1] là same as 落(là)

拉[2] là [拉拉蛄](làlàgǔ) same as 蝲蝲蛄 làlàgǔ

☞ lā on p. 1136, lá on p. 1139 and lǎ on p. 1139

剌 là〈书 *fml.*〉乖戾;乖张 brusque; nasty:乖~ peevish

☞ 拉 lá on p. 1139

【剌戾】làlì〈书 *fml.*〉(性情、言语、行为)别扭,不合情理 (of temperament, language, behaviour) disagreeable:秉性~ of a surly temperament

落 là ❶ 遗漏 missing; left out; unaccounted for:这里~了两个字,应该添上。Two words are missing here and should be added. ❷ 把东西放在一个地方,忘记拿走 leave behind; forget to bring along:我忙着出来,把书~在家里了。I was in such a hurry to go that I left my book behind at home. ❸ 因为跟不上而被丢在后面 fall behind; trail:大家都努力干,谁也不愿意~在后面。We worked real hard, for nobody wanted to lag behind.

☞ lào on p. 1163, luō on p. 1276 and luò on p. 1281

腊(臘、臈) là ❶ 古代在农历十二月里合祭众神叫做腊,因此农历十二月叫腊月 *layue*, the 12th lunar month, 腊 là being the ceremony held in this month at which people in ancient times offer sacrifices to the gods, hence the name of the month ❷ 冬天(多在腊月)腌制后风干或熏干的(鱼、肉、鸡、鸭等) preserve fish, meat, chicken, duck, etc., by air-drying or smoking, a household chore usu. done in the 12th lunar month of the year:~肉 cured meat|~鱼 preserved fish|~味 cured meat ❸ (Là)姓 a surname

☞ xī on p. 2048

【腊八】Làbā (~儿 Làbār)农历十二月(腊月)初八日。民间在这一天有喝腊八粥的习俗。the eighth day of the twelfth lunar month (marked by eating *laba* porridge)

【腊八粥】làbāzhōu 在腊八这一天,用米、豆等谷物和枣、栗、莲子等干果煮成的粥。起源于佛教,传说释迦牟尼在这一天成道,因此寺院每逢这一天煮粥供佛,以后民间相沿成俗。*laba* porridge; rice porridge with beans, nuts and dried fruit, originally prepared by monasteries and temples to celebrate the anniversary of Sakyamuni's achievement of Enlightenment on the 8th day of the 12th lunar month. Eating *laba* porridge on that day has long been a Chinese tradition.

【腊肠】làcháng (~儿 làchángr)熟肉食的一种,

猪的瘦肉泥加肥肉丁和淀粉、作料，灌入肠衣，再经煮和烤制成 sausage; minced pork and fat and starch seasoned and often mixed with other ingredients, encased in a length of cylindrical skin, to be boiled or roasted before eating

【腊梅】làméi ❶ 落叶灌木，叶子对生，卵形，开花以后才长叶子。冬季开花，花瓣外层黄色，内层暗紫色，香味浓。供观赏。wintersweet (*Chimonanthus praecox*); ornamental shrub blooming in winter in heavily sweet flowers whose layer of darkish purple petals are skirted by a layer of yellow petals ❷ 这种植物的花 wintersweet flower

【腊日】làrì 〈古时 *arch*.〉岁终祭祀百神的日子，一般指腊八 day of winter sacrifice, which usu. falls on the 8th day of the 12th lunar month

【腊味】làwèi 腊鱼、腊肉、腊肠、腊鸡等食品的总称 general term for fish, meat, sausages, chicken, etc. that have been cured by air-drying or smoking

【腊月】làyuè 农历十二月 the 12th month of the lunar year; the 12th moon

蜡(蠟) là ❶ 动物、矿物或植物所产生的油质，具有可塑性，能燃烧，易熔化，不溶于水，如蜂蜡、白蜡、石蜡等。用做防水剂，也可做蜡烛。wax , including beewax, white wax and paraffin wax; substance secreted by some animals or plants or obtained from certain minerals that is plastic, inflammable, and not dissolvable in water, used for the making of waterproof materials and candles ❷ 蜡烛 candle: 点上一支～。Light a candle.

☞ zhà on p. 2406

【蜡白】làbái (脸)没有血色；煞白 (of complexion) drained of blood; ashen; look pale (with fright)

【蜡板】làbǎn ❶ 粘附在蜜蜂腹部腹面成对的蜡质片状物 small wax scale on the belly of a bee ❷ 制白蜡的工具 tool for making white wax

【蜡版】làbǎn 用蜡纸打字或刻写成的供油印的底版 mimeograph stencil cut and ready for mimeographing

【蜡笔】làbǐ 颜料搀在蜡里制成的笔，画画儿用 colour crayon; wax crayon; stick of coloured wax used for drawing

【蜡床】làchuáng 制白蜡的工具 tool for making white wax

【蜡果】làguǒ 一种工艺品，用蜡制成的各种蔬菜、水果 wax fruit; object of art fashioned out of wax and in the shape of vegetable or fruit

【蜡花】làhuā (～儿 làhuār) 蜡烛点了一些时候之后烛心结成的像花一样的东西 snuff; charred part of a candle-wick that usu. looks like a flower

【蜡黄】làhuáng 形容颜色黄得像蜡 wax yellow; waxen; sallow: ～色的琥珀 waxen amber | 病人面色～。The patient has a sallow complexion.

【蜡泪】làlèi 蜡烛燃烧时流下的蜡烛油 wax guttering; dripping of a burning candle

【蜡扦】làqiān (～儿 làqiānr) 上有尖钉下有底座可以插蜡烛的器物 candlestick; holder of one or several candles

【蜡染】làrǎn 一种染花布的工艺。用熔化的黄蜡在白布上绘制图案，染色后煮去蜡质，现出白色图案。wax printing; batik, a technique of hand-dyeing raw cloth on which dye-repellent wax is used to draw patterns, which present themselves to the eye when the dyeing has finished and the wax removed

【蜡台】làtái 上面有槽用来插蜡烛的器物 candlestick

【蜡丸】làwán (～儿 làwánr) ❶ 用蜡做成的圆形外壳，内装药丸，古代也在蜡壳里面放传递的机密文书 ball-shaped wax encasement for the preservation of a pill or, as it happened in ancient times, for the concealment of a secret letter or document ❷ 外面包有蜡皮的丸药 wax-coated pill

【蜡像】làxiàng 用蜡做成的人或物的形象 wax figure; waxwork

【蜡纸】làzhǐ ❶ 表面涂蜡的纸，用来包裹东西，可以防潮 wax paper; moistureproof material for wrapping up sth. ❷ 用蜡浸过的纸，刻写或打字后用来做油印底版 stencil paper; stencil to be cut or typed with a text for mimeographing

【蜡烛】làzhú 用蜡或其他油脂制成的供照明用的东西，多为圆柱形 candle; solid, usu. cylindrical mass of wax or other fatty substance with an axially embedded wick that is burned to provide light

瘌 là ☞below

【瘌痢】là·lì 〈方 *dial*.〉same as 黄癣 huángxuǎn; also 鬎鬁 là·lì

【瘌痢头】là·lìtóu 〈方 *dial*.〉❶ 长黄癣的脑袋 favus-infested scalp ❷ 指长黄癣的人 person affected with favus on the scalp

辣 là ❶ 像姜、蒜、辣椒等有刺激性的味道 pungent; hot; hot and pungent taste of such pediments as ginger, onion, and pepper: 酸甜苦～sour, sweet, bitter and hot; bittersweet taste of life ❷ 辣味刺激(口、鼻或眼) (of smell or taste) hot and stinging: ～眼睛 make one's eyes sting | 他吃到一口芥末，～得直缩脖子。He ate a bit of mustard, and was so irritated by its sharp and stinging hotness that he pulled in his neck. ❸ 狠毒 vicious; ruthless: 心狠手～vicious and ruthless | 口甜心～sweet-mouthed and wicked-hearted

【辣乎乎】làhūhū (～的 làhūhū·de) 形容辣的感觉 peppery; hot: 芥菜疙瘩～的。The pickled rutabaga tastes rather hot. ◇他想起自己的错

误,心里不由得一阵～地发烧。The feeling of shame came gnawing at his insides as he thought of his past mistakes.

【辣酱】làjiàng 用辣椒、大豆等制成的酱 thick chilli sauce; chilli paste

【辣椒】làjiāo ❶ 一年生草本植物,叶子卵状披针形,花白色。果实大多像毛笔的笔尖,也有灯笼形、心脏形等,青色,成熟后变成红色,一般都有辣味,供食用。hot pepper(*Capsicum frutescens*); chilli; plant of the genus *Piper*, with oval-shaped lanceolate leaves and white flowers, bearing berries in a variety of shapes (a Chinese writing brush's tip, lantern, heart, etc.) that turn red when ripe; hot aromatic condiment from the dried berries of pepper ❷ 这种植物的果实 fruit of this plant ‖有的地区叫海椒 known in some regions as 海椒 hǎijiāo

【辣手】làshǒu ❶ 毒辣的手段 ruthless method; vicious device:下～deal a vicious blow; lay murderous hands on sb. ❷〈方 *dial*.〉手段厉害或毒辣 vicious; ruthless ❸ 棘手;难办 thorny; troublesome; knotty:这件事真～。This is a hard nut to crack.

【辣丝丝】làsīsī (～儿的 làsīsīr·de)形容有点儿辣 a little bit hot

【辣酥酥】làsūsū (～的 làsūsū·de)形容有点儿辣 hot and a little numbing

【辣子】là·zi ❶ same as 辣椒 làjiāo ❷〈比喻 *fig*.〉泼辣、厉害的妇女 spicy girl

蝲 là ☞below

【蝲蛄】làgǔ 甲壳类动物的一属,形状似龙虾而小,第一对足呈螯状。生活在淡水中,是肺吸虫的中间宿主。crayfish (*Cambaroides*); small lobster-like freshwater crustacean with a pair of pincers, serving as the intermediate host of the lung fluke

【蝲蝲蛄】làlàgǔ 蝼蛄的通称 general term for 蝼蛄 lóugū; also 拉拉蛄 lālàgǔ

鯻 là 鱼,身体侧扁,灰白色,有黑色纵条纹,口小。生活在近海。tigerfish (*Therapon theraps Cuvier et Valenciennes*); grunt; fish with small mouth and flat, grayish white body with vertical black strips, found in coastal waters

瘌 là same as 瘌 là
☞ lài on p. 1145

【瘌痢】là·lì same as 瘌痢là·lì

鬎 là [鬎鬁](là·lì)same as 瘌痢 là·lì

镴(鑞) là 锡和铅的合金 solder; alloy of tin and lead; 通称 popularly known as 焊锡 hànxī or 锡镴 xīlà

·la (·ㄌㄚ)

啦 ·la 助词,'了'(·le)和'啊'(·a)的合音,兼有'了'② 和'啊'的作用 fusion of the sounds 了·le and 啊·a and thus acquiring the meanings of both words to express exclamation and interrogation:二组跟咱们挑战～! Group Two has really challenged us to a contest.|他真来～? Has he really come?
☞ lā on p. 1138

鞡 ·la ☞[靰鞡](wù·la) on p. 2040

lái (ㄌㄞ)

来[1](來) lái ❶ 从别的地方到说话人所在的地方(跟'去[1]'① 相对 as opposed to 'go') come; arrive:～往 come and go; to and fro|～宾 distinguished visitor|～信 incoming letter; letter received|从县里～了几个同志。Some comrades have just arrived from the county seat. ❷(问题、事情等)发生;来到 take place; occur:问题～了。There is a problem here.|开春以后,农忙～了。The busy farm season comes when spring sets in. ❸ 做某个动作(代替意义更具体的动词)[used in place of a more specific verb]do:胡～ act like a fool|～一盘棋 play a game of chess|～一场篮球比赛 play a basketball game|你歇歇,让我～。Why don't you take a rest and let me take over.|何必～这一套? Don't give me that. ❹ 跟'得'或'不'连用,表示可能或不可能[used with 得·de or 不 bù to indicate possibility or impossibility]:他们俩很谈得～。The two of them hit it off real nicely.|这个歌我唱不～。I don't know how to sing this song. ❺ 用在另一动词前面,表示要做某件事[proceed a verb to indicate an intention to do sth.]:你～念一遍。Come on, read it.|大家～想办法。Everybody here, please think about how to do it. ❻ 用在另一动词或动词结构后面,表示来做某件事[used after a verb or verbal phrase to indicate what one has come for]:我们贺喜～了。We've come to congratulate you.|他回家探亲～了。He has gone home to see his parents. ❼ 用在动词结构(或介词结构)与动词(或动词结构)之间,表示前者是方法、方向或态度,后者是目的[inserted between two verbs or verbal phrases or between a propositional phrase and a verb or verbal phrase so that the former indicates the way of doing things and the latter the purpose]:他摘了一个荷叶～当雨伞。He picked a lotus leaf and used it as an umbrella.|你又能用什么理由～说服他呢? What reasons do you have to convince him? ❽ 来着[indicate what happened in the past]:这话我多会儿说～? When on earth did I say that? ❾ 未来的 future, next:～年 next year|～日方长。There will be plenty of time. ❿ 从过去到现在 up to the present:从～ always; all along|向～all along; always|近～recently|别

～无恙。How have you been since we saw each other last. | 二千年～over the last two thousand years; ☞以来 on p. 2268 ⓫ 用在‘十、百、千’等数词或数量词后面表示概数 [used after round numbers such as 十 shí, 百 bǎi and 千 qiān to indicate approximation]: 十～天 about a fortnight | 五十～岁 in one's fifties | 三百～人 three hundred and more people | 三斤～重 a little more than three *jin* in weight | 二里～地 a couple of two *li* away ⓬ 用在‘一、二、三’等数词后面，列举理由 [used after numerals — yī, 二 èr, 三 sān, etc. to reel off reasons or points of argument]: 他这次进城，一～是汇报工作，二～是修理机器，三～是采购图书。He came to town this time for three purposes: first, report on his work; second, have the machine repaired; and third, buy some books. ⓭ (Lái) 姓 a surname

来[2]**(來)** lái 诗歌、熟语、叫卖声里用做衬字 [used as a syllable filler in folk ballads]: 正月里～是新春。With first lunar month comes the new year. | 不愁吃～不愁穿。We are not worried about food or clothing. | 黑白桑葚～大樱桃。See what I've got here — white and black mulberries, and real large cherries!

来(來) //·lái ❶ 用在动词后，表示动作朝着说话人所在的地方 [used after a verb, indicating motion towards the speaker] hither; here: 把锄头拿～。Hand the hoe over please. | 各条战线传～了振奋人心的消息。Heartening news keeps pouring in from different fronts. ❷ 用在动词后，表示结果或估量 [used after a verb to indicate result or estimation]: 信笔写～scribble along on the spur of a brainwave | 一觉醒～wake up after a sound sleep | 说～话长。It's a long story. | 看～今年超产没有问题。It looks there will be no problem for us to overfulfil the output plan. | 想～你是早有准备的了。You have long prepared for this, I suppose?

【来宾】láibīn 来的客人，特指国家、团体邀请的客人 guest; visitor: 接待～receive guests | 各位～。Ladies and gentlemen, and our distinguished guests!

【来不得】lái ·bu·de 不能有；不应有 won't do; be impermissible: 知识的问题是一个科学问题，～半点的虚伪和骄傲。This is a matter of science, which permits no dishonesty.

【来不及】lái ·bu jí 因时间短促，无法顾到或赶上 there's not enough time (to do sth.); it's too late (to do sth.): 还有一个钟头就开车，～出城看他去了。The train is going to leave in an hour, so I've got no time to go out of town to see him.

【来潮】lái//cháo ❶ 潮水上涨 tide comes in ◇心血～be carried away by one's whims ❷ 指女子来月经 menstruate; have a period

【来得】[1] lái·de 胜任 competent; equal to: 粗细活儿她都～。She can cope with any kind of farmwork. | 他说话有点儿口吃，笔底下倒～。He speaks with a stammer, but he writes well.

【来得】[2] lái·de (相比之下)显得 [indicate the result of a comparison] as; come out as: 海水比淡水重，因此压力也～大。Sea water is heavier than freshwater, so its pressure is greater, too. | 下棋太沉闷，还是打球～痛快。Playing chess is too boring, and a ball game is far more exciting.

【来得及】lái ·de jí 还有时间，能够顾到或赶上 there's still time; be able to do sth. in time; be able to make it: 电影是七点开演，现在刚六点半，你马上去还～。The movie starts at seven. You can still make it because it's only half past six now.

【来电】lái//diàn ❶ 打来电报或电话 incoming telegram; your telegram or telephone call: 各界～祝贺。Cable congratulations kept coming in from various walks of life. ❷ 电路断开后接通，恢复供电 power supply resumes after a blackout: ～了，这下不用摸黑了。The power is on again, so that we don't need to grope about in the dark.

【来电】láidiàn 打来的电报 incoming telegram: ～收到，货款不日即可汇出。Your telegram received, the loan is coming your way in a few days' time.

【来访】láifǎng 前来访问 come to visit; come to call: 报社热情接待～的读者。All the readers who come to vent their grievances are warmly received at the press.

【来复枪】láifùqiāng 〈旧时 *old*〉指膛内刻有来复线的步枪 rifle; gun with a long rifled barrel, and fired from shoulder levle

【来复线】láifùxiàn same as 膛线 tángxiàn

【来稿】lái//gǎo 编辑、出版单位指作者投来稿件 incoming manuscript; your manuscript: 上月共～350 篇。A total of 350 manuscripts have been received last month.

【来稿】láigǎo 编辑、出版单位指作者投来的稿件 manuscript received by an editor or publisher: 编辑部收到很多～。The editorial department has received large numbers of manuscripts.

【来归】láiguī ❶ 归顺；归附 come over and pledge allegiance ❷ 〈古代 *arch.*〉称女子出嫁(从夫家方面说 as from the groom's side) join a man in marriage

【来函】láihán 〈书 *fml.*〉same as 来信 láixìn: ～敬悉。It is with due respect that I have received Your Excellency's letter.

【来鸿】láihóng 〈书 *fml.*〉same as 来信 láixìn: 远方～a letter from afar

【来回】láihuí ❶ 在一段距离之内去了再回来

make a round trip; make a return journey; go to a place and come back:从机关到宿舍～有一里地。It's one *li* from the workshop to our quarters and back. ❷（～儿 láihuír）往返一次 round trip:从北京到天津，一天可以打两个～儿。One day is enough to make two round trips between Beijing and Tianjin. ❸ 来来去去不止一次 come and go repeatedly:大家抬着土筐～跑。Guys ran back and forth carrying soil baskets in pairs. | 织布机上的梭～地动。The shuttle flies back and forth on the loom.

【来回来去】lái huí lái qù 指动作或言语来回不断地重复 back and forth; over and over again:他～地走着。He paced up and down the floor. | 他怕别人不明白，总是～地说。He repeated himself over and over again lest the listener should not understand.

【来火】lái//huǒ（～儿 lái//huǒr）指生气 flare up; get angry:他一听这话就来了火。He flew off the handle as soon as he heard it.

【来件】láijiàn 寄来或送来的文件或物件 document or parcel received

【来劲】lái//jìn ❶（～儿 lái//jìnr）有劲头儿 full of enthusiasm; in high spirits:他越干越～。The longer he worked at it, the more enthusiastic he became. ❷ 使人振奋 exhilarating; exciting; thrilling:这样伟大的工程，可真～！What a magnificent project! How thrilling!

【来客】láikè 来访的客人 guest; visitor:欢迎远方～ welcome a guess from afar

【来历】láilì 人或事物的历史或背景 origin; source; antecedents; background; past history:查明～trace to the source; ascertain a person's background | ～不明 of unknown origin; (of persons) of dubious background | 提起这面红旗，可大有～。There is a long history to this red flag.

【来临】láilín 来到；到来 come around; arrive; set in; approach:暴风雨即将～。A storm is in the offing. | 每当春天～，这里就成了花的世界。When spring comes around, this place becomes a world of flowers.

【来龙去脉】lái lóng qù mài 山形地势像龙一样连贯着。本是迷信的人讲风水的话，后来比喻人、物的来历或事情的前因后果。(geomancy) shape of a mountain or topography (in comparison of a dragon); (fig.) sequence of events

【来路】láilù ❶ 向这里来的道路 incoming road; approach:洪水挡住了运输队的～。The flood blocked the incoming road of the transportation team ❷ same as 来源 láiyuán:断了生活～cut off sb.'s source of income

【来路】lái·lu same as 来历 láilì:～不明的人 person of dubious background; unidentified person

【来路货】láilùhuò〈方 *dial.*〉进口货 imported goods

【来年】láinián 明年 the coming year; next year:估计～的收成会比今年好。It is estimated that the harvest this year will do better than last year.

【来去】láiqù ❶ 往返 back and forth:～共用了两天时间。The round trip took two days altogether. ❷ 到来或离去 come and go:～自由 free to come and go ❸〈方 *dial.*〉交往 exchange; contact:两家互不～。The two families don't have anything to do with each other.

【来人】láirén 临时派来取送东西或联系事情的人 bearer; messenger:收条儿请交～带回。Please give the bearer the receipt so that it can be brought back.

【来人儿】láirénr〈方 *dial.*〉〈旧时 *old*〉称买卖、租赁、雇用等事的介绍人 broker; intermediary

【来日】láirì 未来的日子；将来 days to come; future:～方长 there is plenty of time ahead; the day is yet to come for sb. or sth.

【来日方长】láirì fāng cháng 未来的日子还很长。表示事有可为，或劝人不必急于做某事。there is a long future before sb.; be patient, as the day of success is yet to come

【来生】láishēng 指人死了以后再转生到世上来的那一辈子(迷信) (superstition) life after death; afterlife

【来世】láishì same as 来生 láishēng

【来事】láishì ❶〈方 *dial.*〉(～儿 láishìr) 处事(多指处理人与人之间的关系) know how to deal with people:他头脑灵活，挺会～的。He is a smart guy who knows how to deal with people. ❷〈方 *dial.*〉行；可以(多用于否定式 oft. in the negative) all right; will do:这样做不～。This won't work. ❸〈书 *fml.*〉将来的事情 future events:～难以预卜。It is hard to foretell what is going to happen in the future.

【来势】láishì 动作或事物到来的气势 force with which sth. breaks out; oncoming force:～汹汹 bear down menacingly; break in on sb. or sth. furiously | 海潮～很猛。The tide of the sea came rolling with a vengeance.

【来书】láishū〈书 *fml.*〉same as 来信 láixìn

【来头】lái·tou ❶（～儿 lái·tour）same as 来历 láilì(多指人的资历或背景 oft. referring to one's qualifications or background):这个人～不小。This guy has powerful backing. ❷ 来由；原由(多指言语有所为而发 oft. sb.'s remark) motive behind; cause:他这些话是有～的，是冲着咱们说的。He didn't say all that without a reason. It was meant for us. ❸ same as 来势 láishì:对方～不善，要小心应付。The man has an axe to grind, so let's be careful in dealing with him. ❹（～儿 lái·

tour)做某种活动的兴趣 interest; fun:棋没有什么～,不如打球。Chess being no fun, I'd rather play a ball game.

【来往】láiwǎng 来和去 come and go:大街上～的人很多。The street is crowded with people going in both directions.|翻修路面,禁止车辆～。Road under repair. No thoroughfare. *or* No Through Traffic.|车站上每天都有不少来来往往的旅客。Every day the railway station is thronged with arriving and departing passengers.

【来往】lái·wang 交际往来 exchange; hand around with:两家经常～。The two families see each other a lot.

【来文】láiwén 送来或寄来的文件 incoming document; document received

【来向】láixiàng 来的方向(of sb. or sth.) incoming direction:根据风的～调整扬场机的位置 adjust the winnower's position against the wind

【来项】lái·xiang 收入的钱;进项 income; receipts:他家最近增加了～。His family has recently found some new ways to make more money.

【来信】lái//xìn 寄信来或送信来:deliver a letter; send a letter:到了那里请来一封信。Write to us as soon as you get there.

【来信】láixìn 寄来或送来的信件 incoming letter; letter received:人民～letters from the people|～收到了。I have received your letter.

【来意】láiyì 到这里来的意图 purpose of coming (to a place):说明～make clear what one has come for

【来由】láiyóu 缘故;原因 reason; cause:这些话不是没有～的。These remarks are certainly not without reason.

【来源】láiyuán ❶ 事物所从来的地方;事物的根源 source; origin:经济～source of income。❷(事物)起源;发生(后面跟'于' followed by 于 yú) originate; stem from:神话的内容也是～于生活的。Mythology stems from real life.

【来者】láizhě ❶ 将来出现的事或人 things to come; generations to come:～犹可追。What is past is beyond help. *or* What is to come may yet to be saved. ❷ 到来的人或物 any person or thing that comes or has come:～不拒。All visitors are welcome; refuse nobody's request or offer

【来着】lái·zhe〈助词 *aux*.〉表示曾经发生过什么事情[used at the end of affirmative sentences or special questions, indicating a past action or state]:你刚才说什么～? What were you saying just now?|他去年冬天还回家～。He was home only last winter.|你忘记小时候爸爸怎么教导咱们～。You've forgot, haven't you, how Dad taught us when we were children.

莱(萊) lái ❶〈书 *fml*.〉藜 lamb's-quarters (*Chenopodium album*) ❷〈古时 *arch*.〉指郊外轮休的田地,也指荒地 fields lying fallow in rotation; wasteland

【莱菔】láifú 萝卜 radish (*Rhaphanus sativus*)

【莱塞】láisè ❶ 激光 laser ❷ 激光器 laser; maser for amplifying radiation of frequencies within or near the range of visible light

崃(崍) lái 邛崃(Qiónglái),山名,在四川 Qionglai, name of a mountain in Sichuan Province

徕(徠、倈) lái ☞ 招徕 zhāolái on p.2421

☞ lài on p.1144

涞(淶) lái 涞水(Láishuǐ)、涞源(Láiyuán),地名,在河北 Laishui and Laiyuan, names of places in Hebei Province

梾(棶) lái [梾木](láimù)落叶乔木,单叶对生,阔卵形,花黄白色,核果椭圆形,紫色。种子榨的油可以制肥皂和润滑油。树皮和叶子可制栲胶或紫色染料。large-leaved dogwood (*Cornus macrophylla*); deciduous tree with paired simple leaves in the shape of a broad oval, yellowish white flowers, purple olive-shaped nuts that contain a kind of oil for the making of soap and lubricant, and both bark and leaves useful for the making of tannin extract or purple dyestuff; also 灯台树 dēngtáishù

鹈(鶆) lái [鹈鹕](lái'ǎo) 美洲鸵 rhea [新拉 new Latin: Rhea]

铼(錸) lái 金属元素,符号 Re (rhenium)。银白色,质硬,机械性能好,电阻高。用来制电极、热电偶、耐高温和耐腐蚀的合金,也用作催化剂。Rhenium (Re), a silver-coloured rare metallic element whose hard texture and excellent mechanical property make it an ideal material for the making of electrodes, thermocouples and refractory and corrosion-resistant alloys. Rhenium is also used as a catalyst.

lài (为劳)

徕(徠) lài〈书 *fml*.〉慰劳 bring gift to or send best wishes to:劳～(慰勉) award sb. in recognition of service rendered

☞ lái on p.1144

赉(賚) lài〈书 *fml*.〉赏赐 grant; bestow; confer:赏～give a reward; bestow a favour

睐(睞) lài〈书 *fml*.〉❶ 瞳人不正 squint ❷ 看;向旁边看 look at; look at sb. or sth. sideways:青～favour; good graces

赖[1] lài ❶ 依赖;依靠 hinge on; depend on:仰～be dependent on|完成任务,有～于大家的努力。Only with everybody's hard work can this task be fulfilled. ❷ 指无赖 rascally; shameless: 耍～act shamelessly; make a scene|～皮 never-do-well; rascal ❸ 留在某处不肯走开 outstay one's welcome or hospitality; hang on in a place: 孩子看到橱窗里的玩具,～着不肯走。At the sight of the toys on display in the window, the child did not want to go away. ❹ 不承认自己的错误或责任; 抵赖 deny one's error or responsibility; go back on one's word: ～债 repudiate a debt; refuse to acknowledge and pay a debt|～婚 breach one's promise of marriage|事实俱在,～是～不掉的。There's no denying the facts. ❺ 硬说别人有错误; 诬赖 accuse sb. of doing sth. fraudulently; frame sb. up: 自己做错了,不能～别人。It's all your fault, so don't shift the blame on someone else. ❻ 责怪 blame: 大家都有责任,不能～哪一个人。Everybody is to blame for it — on no account should the responsibility be shifted on a particular person. ❼ (Lài) 姓 a surname

赖[2] lài 不好; 坏 no good; poor: 好～in any case; good or/and bad|今年庄稼长得真不～。The crops are doing real fine this year.|不论好的～的我都能吃。I can eat anything, good or bad.

【赖词儿】làicír 〈方 *dial.*〉抵赖或诬赖的话 lie; pack of lies

【赖婚】lài//hūn 订婚后反悔不履行婚约 repudiate a marriage contract

【赖皮】làipí ❶ 无赖的作风和行为 rascally; shameless; unreasonable: 耍～act shamelessly ❷ 耍无赖 make a scene: 别在这儿～了,快走吧! Get lost and don't make a spectacle of yourself here.

【赖学】lài//xué 〈方 *dial.*〉逃学 play truant; cut class

【赖账】lài//zhàng 欠账不还,反而抵赖(不承认欠账或说已还清等) repudiate a debt; go back on one's word ◇你说的话要算话,不能～。Mean what you said. Don't ever try to break your promise.

【赖子】lài·zi 要无赖的人 rogue; scoundrel

濑 lài 〈书 *fml.*〉湍急的水 swift current; rapids

癞 lài ❶ 麻风 leprosy ❷ 〈方 *dial.*〉黄癣 favus of the scalp

☞ là on p.1141

【癞瓜】làiguā 〈方 *dial.*〉苦瓜 bitter gourd (*Momordica charantia*)

【癞蛤蟆】làihá·ma 蟾蜍的通称 general term for 蟾蜍 chánchú

【癞皮狗】làipígǒu 〈比喻 *fig.*〉卑鄙无耻的人 mangy dog; loathsome creature

【癞子】lài·zi ❶ 黄癣 favus: 长了一头～favus-infested calp ❷ 头上长黄癣的人 person affected with favus of the scalp

籁 lài ❶ 古代的一种箫 *lai*, traditional Chinese musical pipe ❷ 从孔穴里发出的声音,泛指声音 sound emitting from a hole; (in a broad sense) sound; noise: 万～俱寂。All is quiet. *or* Silence reigns everywhere.

·lai (·ㄌㄞ)

唻(啰) ·lai 〈方 *dial.*〉〈助词 *aux.*〉❶ 用在疑问句(特指问、正反问)的末尾,相当于'呢' [equivalent to 呢·ne, used at the end of an interrogative sentence]: 你们敲锣打鼓的干什么～? What on earth are you beating drums and gongs for? |人～? 怎么找不到了? Where's everybody? Why can't I find you? |你们都有了,我～? Everybody has got his share, where's mine? ❷ 相当于'啦' [equivalent to 啦·la]: 解放前放牛娃可苦～。The lot was real miserable for a child cowherd before liberation. ❸ 相当于'来着' [equivalent to 来着 lái·zhe]: 娘是怎么嘱咐你～,怎么都忘了? What did Mum tell you? Don't you remember?

lán (ㄌㄢˊ)

兰(蘭) lán ❶ same as 兰花 lánhuā ❷ same as 兰草 láncǎo ❸ 古书上指木兰 lily magnolia, as mentioned in ancient books: ～桨 oar made of lily magnolia wood ❹ (Lán) 姓 a surname

【兰草】láncǎo ❶ 佩兰 fragrant thoroughwort (*Eupatorium fortunei*) ❷兰花的俗称 popular name for 兰花 lánhuā

【兰花】lánhuā ❶多年生草本植物,叶子丛生,条形,先端尖,春季开花,淡绿色,味芳香,供观赏。花可制香料。orchid (*Cymbidium goeringii*); perennial plant with narrow, pointed leaves growing in a cluster, blooming in spring, with light blue, fragrant flowers, which are appreciated for their beauty and used for making perfume; also 春兰 chūnlán ❷ same as 建兰 jiànlán ‖ 俗称 popularly called 兰草 láncǎo

【兰花指】lánhuāzhǐ 拇指和中指相对拳曲、其余三个手指翘起的姿势 orchid fingers; lady's hand gesture with the tips of the thumb and the middle finger touching and the other three fingers raised (usu. made on the stage to show delicacy and grace); also 兰花手 lánhuāshǒu

【兰谱】lánpǔ 结拜盟兄弟时互相交换的帖子,上面写着自己家族的谱系(兰味香,比喻情投意合,《易经·系辞》:同心之言,其臭如兰) genealogical records exchanged by those who have sworn brotherhood (The fragrance of orchid is a token of likemindedness. *The Book of Changes·Great Treatise*: 'The oath of like-minded people is as fragrant as the orchid flower.')

【兰若】lánrě 寺庙 temple; monastery [梵 Sanskrit: Āraṇ yakaḥ; 阿兰若 Āranya:树林,寂静处 forest; quiet place]

【兰章】lánzhāng〈书 *fml.*〉美好的文辞(多用于称颂 usu. polite) Your Excellency's beautiful writings

岚 lán 山里的雾气 haze; vapour; mist: 山～ mountain haze | 晓～morning fog

【岚烟】lányān 山间雾气 mountain mist

拦(攔) lán ❶ 不让通过;阻挡 bar; block; hold back: 前面有一道河～住了去路。A river blocked our way. | 你愿意去就去吧,家里决不～你。Go head if that's where you want to go, and as your family members (we) won't hold you back. | 他刚要说话,被他哥哥～回去了。He was about to speak when his elder brother stopped him. ❷ 当;正对着(某个部位) direct; right at: ～头一棍 head-on blow | ～腰斩断 cut sth. right in the middle; dam (a river) right in the middle

【拦挡】lándǎng 不使通过;使中途停止 hurdle; block: 路上有障碍物～,车辆过不去。The vehicles could not get through because of the roadblocks.

【拦道木】lándàomù 拦挡行人、车辆等的横杆或横木,多设在与铁路交叉的公路口 road fence; roadblock; crossbar installed at a railway intersection

【拦柜】lánguì 柜台 counter; also 栏柜 lánguì

【拦河坝】lánhébà 拦截河水的建筑物,多筑在河身狭窄、地基坚实的地方 dam; barrier to obstruct the flow of water, esp. one built on solid ground and across a river's narrow section

【拦洪坝】lánhóngbà 拦截洪水的建筑物 dam for holding back floodwater; dam for flood control

【拦击】lánjī 拦住并袭击 intercept and attack: ～敌人 block an enemy's offensive

【拦劫】lánjié 拦住并抢劫 waylay and rob; mug: ～商船 pirate a merchant ship | 半路遭遇匪徒～be ambushed and plundered on the road by bandits

【拦截】lánjié 中途阻挡,不让通过 intercept: ～洪水 harness a flood | ～歹徒 intercept the ruffians

【拦路】lán//lù 拦住去路 block the way: ～抢劫 waylay; stick sb. up

【拦路虎】lánlùhǔ 过去指拦路打劫的匪徒,现在指前进道路上的障碍和困难 robbery; hurdle; hindrance; road-blocking tiger; (of old times) bandits living on road

【拦网】lánwǎng 排球队员拦阻球网上方对方打过来的球 volleyball block; hindering of an opponent's ball from above the net

【拦蓄】lánxù 修筑堤坝把水流拦住并蓄积起来 retain (water); impound: ～山洪 impound floodwater; confine excessive mountain runoffs in a reservoir

【拦腰】lányāo 从半中腰(截住、切断等) hold by the waist; (cut across) in the middle: ～抱住 seize sb. by the waist from behind | 大坝把黄河～截断。The dam cut the river in the middle.

【拦阻】lánzǔ 阻挡 block; hold back; obstruct

栏(欄) lán ❶ 栏杆 fence; railing; balustrade; hurdle: 石～stone balustrade | 桥～ railing of a bridge | 凭～远望 lean against the railing and look as far as one's eye can see ❷ 养家畜的圈 pen; shed: 牛～cowshed | 用干土垫～cover the floor of a cattle pen with dry earth to keep it dry ❸ 报刊书籍在每版或每页上用线条或空白隔开的部分,有时也指性质相同的一整页或若干页 column; division of a newspaper or magazine page with lines or blank space, sometimes referring to a regular feature article that occupies one or several pages: 左～left column | 专～special column | 广告～classified (page or column) | 书评～book review ❹ 表格中区分项目的大格儿 (of a form) column with a list of items to be filled in: 备注～'notes' column | 这一～的数字还没有核对。The figures in this column are yet to be checked. ❺ 专供张贴布告、报纸等的装置 billboard: 布告～advertisement board | 宣传～bulletin board

【栏杆】lángān 桥两侧或凉台、看台等边上起拦挡作用的东西 railing; banisters; balustrade: 桥～railing of a bridge | 石～stone balustrade; also 阑干 lángān

【栏柜】lánguì same as 拦柜 lánguì

【栏目】lánmù 报纸、杂志等版面上按内容性质分成的标有名称的部分 heading or title of a column in a newspaper, magazine, etc.: 小说～column of fiction | 每逢寒暑假,报纸增设《假期生活》～。The newspaper opens a 'Holiday Life' column during summer and winter vacations every year.

婪 lán ☞贪婪 tānlán on p. 1857

阑[1] lán ❶ same as 栏 lán ① ❷ same as 拦 lán

阑[2] lán〈书 *fml.*〉❶ 将尽(of time) drawing to an end: 岁～year-end | 夜～人静 All is quiet in the dead of night. ❷ 擅自(出入) act without permission: ～出 go out or leave without permission | ～入 trespass

【阑干】lángān ❶〈书 *fml.*〉纵横交错;参差错落 across; crisscross: 星斗～star-spangled sky ❷ same as 栏杆 lángān

【阑入】lánrù〈书 *fml.*〉❶ 擅自进入不应进去的地方 trespass; enter a place that is forbidden to one ❷ 搀杂进去 interpolate; adulterate; bring in extraneous matters

【阑珊】lánshān〈书 *fml.*〉将尽;衰落 drawing to an end; waning:春意～amidst the wane of spring|意兴～losing interest in sth.

【阑尾】lánwěi 盲肠下端蚯蚓状的突起,一般长约7-9厘米。人的阑尾在消化过程中没有作用。管腔狭窄,囊状,病菌容易繁殖而引起发炎。vermiform appendix; appendix; small outgrowth of tissue 7-9 cm. in length, forming a tube-shaped sac attached to the lower end of the large intestine that plays no role whatsoever in man's digestion process. In the shape of a narrow and blind tube, the appendix provides a breeding ground for bacteria and is liable to inflammation.(图见☞figure for 消化系统 xiāohuà xìtǒng on p.2100)

【阑尾炎】lánwěiyán 病,多由于病菌、寄生虫或其他异物侵入阑尾引起。主要症状是右下腹疼痛、恶心、呕吐等。appendicitis; inflammation of the appendix caused by the intrusion of bacteria, parasite or other alien matter, major symptoms being ache in the lower right abdomen, nausea and vomitting; 俗称 popular known as 盲肠炎 mángchángyán

蓝(藍) lán ❶ 像晴天天空的颜色 azure; blue:蔚～azure ❷ 蓼蓝 indigo plant ❸(Lán)姓 a surname

【蓝宝石】lánbǎoshí 蓝色透明的刚玉,硬度大,用来做首饰和精密仪器的轴承等 sapphire; transparent blue precious stone that is hard enough for the making of jewelry and the bearings for precision apparatuses; ☞刚玉 gāngyù on p.636

【蓝本】lánběn 著作所根据的底本 original version of a book; master copy; writing upon which later work is based

【蓝点鲅】lándiǎnbà 鲅鱼 Spanish mackerel (*Scomberomorus niphonius*)

【蓝点颏】lándiǎnké 鸟,身体大小和麻雀相似,羽毛褐色。雄的喉部天蓝色,叫的声音很好听。bluethroat (*Luscinia svecica svecica*); bird the size of a sparrow. The male bluethroat features a blue-coloured throat sings in a pleasant warbling sound. 通称 popular term for 蓝靛颏儿 lándiànkér

【蓝靛】lándiàn 靛蓝的通称 generally term for 靛蓝 diànlán

【蓝晶晶】lánjīngjīng(～的 lánjīngjīng·de)蓝而发亮,多用来形容水、宝石等(oft. of water and precious stones) bright blue

【蓝领】lánlǐng 某些国家或地区指从事体力劳动的工人,他们劳动时一般穿蓝色工作服 blue-collar; manual labourer; worker engaged in physical labour wearing a blue overall

【蓝缕】lánlǚ same as 褴褛 lánlǚ

【蓝皮书】lánpíshū ☞白皮书 báipíshū on p.36

【蓝青官话】lánqīng-guānhuà 方言地区的人说的普通话,夹杂着方音,旧时称为蓝青官话 blue and green Mandarin; Mandarin spoken with a provincial accent; referred to in old times as 蓝青官话(蓝青 *lanqing*:比喻不纯粹 impure in a figurative way)

【蓝田猿人】Lántián yuánrén 中国猿人的一种,大约生活在60多万年以前,化石在1963年发现于陕西蓝田。也叫蓝田人。Lantian Man (*Sinanthropus lantienensis*), primitive man of over 600,000 years ago whose fossil remains were found in Lantian, Shaanxi Province, in 1963

【蓝图】lántú ❶ 用感光后变成蓝色(或其他颜色)的感光纸制成的图纸 blueprint; photographic print of the final stage of an engineering plan in white on a blue (or other) background ❷〈比喻 *fig.*〉建设计划 construction plan:国家建设的～ blueprint for national reconstruction

【蓝盈盈】lányīngyīng〈方 *dial.*〉(～的 lányīngyīng·de)形容蓝得发亮 bright blue:～的天空 blue and glittering sky; also 蓝莹莹 lányīngyīng

谰 lán〈书 *fml.*〉❶ 诬赖 calumniate; slander ❷ 抵赖 refuse to admit a guilt; disavow having done sth.

【谰言】lányán 诬赖的话;没有根据的话 calumny; slander:无耻～ audacious slander

澜 lán 大波浪;波浪 billows; waves:波～surf; waves|微～ripples|力挽狂～strive to save the situation; make one's best to turn the tide|推波助～make a stormy sea stormier; add fuel to the flames; lend a helping hand to

褴(襤) lán [褴褛](lánlǚ)(衣服)破烂 ragged; shabby:衣衫～in rags; also 蓝缕 lánlǚ

篮(籃) lán(～儿 lánr)❶ 篮子 basket:竹～bamboo basket|网～basket with netting|花～儿 flower basket ❷ 装置在篮球架子上为投球用的铁圈和网子(of basketball) basket:投～儿 shoot a basketball ❸ 指篮球 basketball:男～men's basketball|女～women's basketball

【篮球】lánqiú ❶ 球类运动项目之一,把球投入对方防守的球架铁圈中算得分,得分多的获胜 basketball, game in which players move the ball across the court by dribbling and passing to score points by throwing it into the opposing teams basket, with the team scoring more points declared a winner ❷ 篮球运动使用的球,用牛皮做壳,橡胶做胆,也有全用橡胶制成的 basketball; round ball made from cowhide or rubber, with a inflatable bladder in it

【篮坛】lántán 指篮球界 basketball circles:这是一支世界～劲旅。This team is one of the strongest contenders in world basketball.

【篮子】lán·zi 用藤、竹、柳条、塑料等编成的容

器，上面有提梁 basket; container made of interwoven rattan, bamboo slips, wicker, plastics, etc., with a handle over it: 菜～vegetable basket | 草～grass basketry

斓 lán ☞斑斓 bānlán on p. 48

镧 lán 金属元素，符号 La (lanthanum)。是一种稀土金属。银白色，质软，在空气中容易氧化。用于制备钐、铕和镱，镧的化合物用来制光学玻璃等。Lanthanum (La), a soft, silver-white rare earth metal that is used in the manufacture of alloys or catalysts with samarium, europium, ytterbium and lanthanum for the making of optical glass

襕(襴) lán 〈古时 *arch.*〉上下衣相连的服装 dress; overall

籣(韊) lán 〈古时 *arch.*〉盛弩矢的器具 arrow container; quiver

lǎn (ㄌㄢˇ)

览(覽) lǎn 看 look at; see; view: 游～go sightseeing; travel | 展～exhibit; show | 浏～run one's eye over; thumb or leaf through | 阅～read | 一～无余 take in everything at one glance; get a panoramic view

【览胜】lǎnshèng 〈书 *fml.*〉观赏胜景或游览胜地 visit scenic spots: 到黄山～go sightseeing on Mount Huangshan

揽(攬) lǎn ❶ 用胳膊围住别人，使靠近自己 gather sb.'s body into one's arms; take into one's arms: 母亲把孩子～在怀里。The mother clasped the child to her bosom. ❷ 用绳子等把松散的东西聚拢到一起，使不散开 tie a rope around sth.: 把车上的柴火～上点。Put a rope round the faggot on the cart. ❸ 拉到自己这方面或自己身上来 take on; take upon oneself; canvass: 包～undertake the whole thing; take on sth. as a whole | ～买卖 canvass for business orders | 他把责任都～到自己身上了。He took all the responsibility on himself. ❹ 把持 seize; grasp; monopolize: 独～大权 arrogate power to oneself

【揽承】lǎnchéng 应承；承揽 agree to do a job (usu. on a contractual basis)

【揽工】lǎngōng 〈方 *dial.*〉指做长工 work as a farmhand

【揽活】lǎn//huó (～儿 lǎn//huór) 承揽活计 hunting for work opportunity: 他在外面揽了许多活儿。He took on a lot of work out there.

【揽总】lǎnzǒng (～儿 lǎnzǒngr) 全面掌握(工作)；总揽 assume overall responsibility; take overall charge of work or task

缆(纜) lǎn ❶ 拴船用的铁索或许多股拧成的粗绳 hawser; mooring rope; cable: 解～(开船) cast off; set sail ❷ 许多股拧成的像缆的东西 thick rope; cable; 钢～steel cable | 电～power cable ❸ 用绳索拴(船) fasten (a boat) with a rope or cable: ～舟 moor a boat | 把船～住。Moor the ship before landing.

【缆车】lǎnchē ❶ 在斜坡上沿轨道上下行驶的运输设备。用缆绳把车厢系在电动机带动的绞车上，转动绞车，缆车行驶。cable car; small cabin suspended on a cable by which it is drawn up and down a mountainside by a motorized windlass ❷ 指索道上用来运输的设备 cableway equipment

【缆绳】lǎnshéng 许多股棕、麻、金属丝等拧成的粗绳 cable; rope; stout cord made by twisting together strands of hemp, flax, metal wire, etc.

【缆索】lǎnsuǒ same as 缆绳 lǎnshéng

榄(欖) lǎn 指橄榄树的果实 olive fruit

罱 lǎn ❶ 捕鱼或捞水草、河泥的工具，在两根平行的短竹竿上张一个网，再装两根交叉的长竹柄做成，两手握住竹柄使网开合 a kind of net stretched on two parallel short bamboo bars, to be hand-manipulated with the aid of two crossed long bamboo poles attached to it, for fishing or dredging up river sludge ❷ 用罱捞 dredge up: ～河泥 dredge up sludge from a river | ～泥船 a boat used in collecting river sludge for manure

漤(灠) lǎn ❶ 用盐或其他调味品拌(生的鱼、肉、蔬菜) mix (raw fish, meat, or vegetables) with salt or other seasonings ❷ (柿子)放在热水或石灰水里泡，除去涩味 soak (a persimmon) in hot water or limewater to take away its harsh, puckery taste until it becomes soft and ripe: ～柿子 treat persimmons with limewater, etc. to remove its astrigent taste

壈(壈) lǎn ☞坎壈 kǎnlǎn on p. 1080

懒(嬾) lǎn ❶ 懒惰(跟'勤'相对 as opposed to 'diligent') lazy; sluggish; tired: 腿～be disinclined to move about; unwilling to go visiting people or seeing things | 好吃～做 love food but hate work ◇人勤地不～。Where man is diligent, the soil is fertile. ❷ 疲倦；没力气 sluggish; languid: 身子发～，大概是感冒了。I feel weak — probably I've come down with a cold.

【懒虫】lǎnchóng 懒惰的人（骂人或含诙谐意味的话 curse or humor.）lazybones

【懒怠】lǎn•dai ❶ same as 懒惰 lǎnduò ❷ 没兴趣；不愿意(做某件事) too lazy to; be disinclined to: 身体不好，话也～说了。I don't feel like talking because I don't feel well.

【懒得】lǎn•de 厌烦；不愿意(做某件事) be tired of doing or unwilling to do sth.: 天太热，我～

上街。It's too hot. I don't want to go shopping.

【懒惰】lǎnduò 不爱劳动和工作；不勤快 be unwilling to work; lazy：这人太～了，在家里什么事都不愿意干。He's so lazy he doesn't do anything at home.

【懒骨头】lǎngǔ·tou 懒惰的人（骂人的话 curse）loafer; slugabed

【懒汉】lǎnhàn 懒惰的人 sluggard; idler; lazybones

【懒汉鞋】lǎnhànxié 鞋口有松紧带，便于穿、脱的布鞋 lazybones' shoes; cloth shoes with elastic gussets (making them easy to slip on and off); also 懒鞋 lǎnxié

【懒猴】lǎnhóu 猴的一种，比家猫略小，头圆，耳小，眼大而圆，四肢粗短，白天在树上睡觉，夜间活动 slender loris (*Nycticebus coucang*); small, slow-moving nocturnal primate slightly smaller than a cat, with a round head, small ears, large and round eyes, and short limbs

【懒散】lǎnsǎn 形容人精神松懈，行动散漫；不振作 lethargic; indolent：他平时～惯了，受不了这种约束。As a happy-go-lucky man by habit, he won't allow himself to be restrained like that.

【懒洋洋】lǎnyāngyāng (～的 lǎnyāngyāng·de) 没精打采的样子 languid; listless

làn（ㄌㄢˋ）

烂（爛） làn ❶ 某些固体物质组织破坏或水分增加后松软 soft; mashed; pappy：～泥 mud; slush; mire｜牛肉煮得很～。The beef was cooked so well that it melts in the mouth. ❷ 腐烂 rot; decompose：～梨可以做酒。Rotten pears can be used to brew wine.｜樱桃和葡萄容易～。Cherries and grapes are perishables. ❸ 破碎；破烂 tattered; worn out：～纸 scrap paper｜破铜～铁 scrap iron and copper｜衣服穿～了。The clothes are worn out. ❹ 头绪乱 chaotic; disordered; messy：～账 messy accounts｜～摊子 awful mess ❺ 表示程度极深 thoroughly; utterly：～醉 dead drunk｜～熟 well-cooked; have sth. at one's fingertips

【烂糊】làn·hu 很烂（多指食物 oft. referring to food) mashed; pulpy：老年人吃～的好。It's good for old people to have food cooked to a pulp.

【烂漫】lànmàn ❶ 颜色鲜明而美丽 in a riot of colour; bright-coloured; brilliant：山花～ flowers wreaked a riot of colour over the mountain ❷ 坦率自然，毫不做作 unaffected; natural：天真～innocent and naive ‖ also 烂熳 lànmàn or 烂缦 lànmàn

【烂熳】lànmàn same as 烂漫 lànmàn

【烂泥】lànní 稀烂的泥 mud; slush：～坑 muddy pond｜一摊～a quagmire of mud

【烂熟】lànshú ❶ 肉、菜等煮得十分熟(of food) thoroughly cooked ❷ 十分熟悉；十分熟练 have or know sth. off pat：台词背得～learn one's lines off pat

【烂摊子】làntān·zi 〈比喻 *fig.*〉不易收拾的局面或混乱难于整顿的单位 shambles; awful mess; in a terrible mess

【烂污】lànwū 〈方〉❶ 稀屎 watery faeces ❷ 指行为放荡不端（多指女人 of woman) promiscuous; loose：～货 bitch

【烂账】lànzhàng ❶ 头绪混乱没法弄清楚的账目 messy accounts ❷ 指拖得很久、收不回来的账 uncollectable debts

【烂醉】lànzuì 大醉 dead drunk：～如泥 be dead drunk; be as drunk as a lord

滥（濫） làn ❶ 泛滥 overflow; flood ❷ 过度；没有限制 excessive; indiscriminate：宁缺毋～ rather go without than have sth. shoddy; better to accept fewer than merely to make up a number｜～用职权(of a government functionary) abuse one's power

【滥调】làndiào (～儿 làndiàor) 叫人腻烦的、不切实际的言词或论调 truism; cliché：陈词～ hoary platitude; hackneyed words

【滥觞】lànshāng 〈书 *fml.*〉江河发源的地方，水少只能浮起酒杯。今指事物的起源。headwater, where there is only enough for a wine cup to float on it; origin; beginning

【滥套子】làntào·zi 文章中浮泛不切实际的套语或格式 clichés; stereotype; hackneyed phrases

【滥用】lànyòng 胡乱地或过度地使用 abuse; misuse; use indiscriminately：行文～方言。Too much dialect is used in the text.｜～职权 abuse one's authority or position (for personal gain and fame)

【滥竽充数】làn yú chōng shù 齐宣王用三百人吹竽，南郭先生不会吹，混在中间充数（见于《韩非子·内储说上》）*Hanfeizi · Inner Repository of Persuasions*：Once, Duke Xuan of Qi summoned an ensemble to play music for him. Among the 300 players was Nan Guo, a gentleman who did not know how to play the *yu*, a windpipe, but who went there pretending he could play it. 〈比喻 *fig.*〉没有真正的才干，而混在行家里面充数，或拿不好的东西混在好的里面充数 (of incompetent people or inferior goods) be there just to make up the number; mess up the number with sth. inferior

lāng（ㄌㄤ）

啷 lāng [啷当](lāngdāng)〈方 *dial.*〉❶ 左右；上下（用于表示年龄 of one's age) more or less：他才二十～岁，正是年轻力壮的时候。

At around 20, he is in the prime of his life. ❷（～儿的 lāngr·de）列举后煞尾 and so on; and whatnot：他穿得挺讲究，洋服、大氅、皮鞋～的样样全新。He was dressed impeccably — Western suit, overcoat, and leather shoes — everything he wore was brand new.

láng（ㄌㄤˊ）

郎 láng ❶〈古代 *arch.*〉官名 official title in imperial times：侍～ vice-minister｜员外～ counsellor ❷ 对某种人的称呼 [used in forming nouns showing sb.'s status]：货～ migrant vendor｜放牛～ cowherd｜女～ girl ❸ 女子称丈夫或情人 [used by a woman in addressing her husband or lover] darling：～君 my darling｜情～ boyfriend ❹〈旧时 *old*〉称别人的儿子 sb.'s son：大～ your elder son｜令～ your son ❺（Láng）姓 a surname
☞ làng on p. 1151

【郎才女貌】láng cái nǚ mào 男的才华出众，女的姿容出色。形容男女双方非常相配。brilliant young scholar and beautiful woman — good match

【郎当】[1] lángdāng same as 锒铛（lángdāng）

【郎当】[2] lángdāng ❶（衣服）不合身；不整齐（of clothes）loose-fitting; ill-fitting; untidy：衣裤～ be shabbily dressed ❷ 颓唐的样子 crestfallen; dejected：看他走起路来郎郎当当的。See the way he walks — he looks so sloppy. ❸ 形容不成器 down-and-out

【郎舅】lángjiù 男子和他妻子的弟兄的合称 man and his wife's brother

【郎猫】lángmāo 雄猫 tom-cat

【郎中】lángzhōng ❶〈古代 *arch.*〉一种官职（official title）director of a section or bureau ❷〈方 *dial.*〉〈中医 *Chin. med.*〉医生 physician trained in herbal medicine; doctor in traditional Chinese medicine

狼 láng 哺乳动物，形状和狗相似，面部长，耳朵直立，毛黄色或灰褐色，尾巴向下垂。昼伏夜出，性残忍而贪婪，吃兔、鹿等，也伤害人畜，对畜牧业有害。毛皮可以制衣褥等。wolf（*Canis lupus*）; wild flesh-eating yellow or tawny-grey mammal that looks like a dog, with a long face, erect ears, and drooping tail; hiding in the daytime and coming out at night. The wolf is destructive to animal husbandry because it is vicious and greedy and preys on rabbits, dear, draught animals and human beings, but it's hide is a material for making clothing and bedding.

【狼狈】lángbèi 传说狈是一种兽，前腿特别短，走路时要趴在狼身上，没有狼，它就不能行动，所以用'狼狈'形容困苦或受窘的样子 legend has it that 狈 bèi was an animal whose forelegs were so short that it could not move about without crouching over the wolf. Hence the term, which means to cut a sorry figure of oneself, in a difficult position or in a tight corner：十分～ in a very awkward position｜今天外出遇到大雨，弄得～不堪。We were caught in the rain when we were out; it really got us flustered.

【狼狈为奸】lángbèi wéi jiān 互相勾结做坏事 act in collusion（or cahoots）with each other

【狼奔豕突】láng bēn shǐ tū 狼和猪东奔西跑 run like wolves and rush like boars — tear about like wild beasts;〈比喻 *fig.*〉成群的坏人乱窜乱撞（of bad elements）flee in panic; collide right and left when fleeing for life

【狼疮】lángchuāng 皮肤病，病原体是结核杆菌，多发生在面部，症状是皮肤出现暗红色的结节，逐渐增大，形成溃疡，结黄褐色痂，常形成瘢痕 lupus; ulcerous skin disease caused in the face by tubercle bacillus, characterized by brownish nodular tubercles that result in scars

【狼狗】lánggǒu 狗的一个品种，形状像狼，性凶猛，嗅觉敏锐。多饲养来帮助打猎或牧羊。wolfhound; shepherd dog; ferocious large dog that looks like a wolf and has an acute sense of smell, usu. bred for hunting or sheep herding

【狼毫】lángháo 用黄鼠狼的毛做成的毛笔 writing brush made of weasel's hair：小楷～ weasel's hair brush for the writing of small characters in regular scrip

【狼藉】lángjí〈书 *fml.*〉乱七八糟；杂乱不堪 in disorder; in a mess：声名～（形容人的名誉极坏）have a bad name; gain notoriety; notorious; disreputable｜杯盘～ with wine cups and dishes lying about in disorder;（of a table）cluttered up with dishes and cups; also 狼籍 lángjí

【狼头】láng·tou same as 榔头 láng·tou

【狼吞虎咽】láng tūn hǔ yàn 形容吃东西又猛又急 devour ravenously; wolf down; gobble up

【狼心狗肺】láng xīn gǒu fèi〈比喻 *fig.*〉心肠狠毒或忘恩负义 with the heart of a wolf; rapacious as a wolf and savage as a cur; brutal and cold-blooded; heartless and ungrateful.

【狼烟】lángyān〈古代 *arch.*〉边防报警时烧狼粪升起的烟，借指战火 war; smoke of wolves dung burnt as a sign of warning at border posts：～滚滚 alarms of war keep pouring in｜～四起 war alarms raised everywhere

【狼烟四起】lángyān sì qǐ 四处有报警的烽火，指边疆不平靖 smoke signals rising on all fronts; warnings of war keep pouring in from everywhere

【狼主】lángzhǔ 旧小说、戏曲中称北方民族的君主（in Chinese traditional fiction and theatre）tribe head; king of a northern nomadic kingdom

【狼子野心】láng zǐ yě xīn〈比喻 *fig.*〉凶暴的

人用心狼毒 as savage as a wolf in disposition; wild and evil ambition

阆 láng ☞[闶阆](kāngláng) on p.1083
☞ làng on p.1151

琅(瑯) láng〈书 *fml.*〉❶ 一种玉石 a kind of jade ❷ 洁白 pure white

【琅玕】lánggān〈书 *fml.*〉像珠子的美石 pearl-like stone

【琅嬛】lánghuán〈书 *fml.*〉神话中天帝藏书的地方(mythology) where the Lord of Heaven stores his books; also 嫏嬛 lánghuán

【琅琅】lángláng〈拟声词 *onom.*〉金石相击的声音、响亮的读书声音等 tinkling or jingling sound; metallic sound; sound of sb. reading loudly

桹 láng [桹桹]〈书 *fml.*〉〈拟声词 *onom.*〉木头相撞击的声音 sound of wood being struck

廊 láng 廊子 porch; corridor; veranda: 走～ corridor | 长～long corridor; arcade | 前～后厦(of a traditional Chinese house) having a veranda in the front and a portico in the rear

【廊庙】lángmiào〈书 *fml.*〉指朝廷 imperial court

【廊檐】lángyán 廊顶突出在柱子外边的部分 eaves of a veranda

【廊子】láng·zi 屋檐下的过道或独立的有顶的过道 corridor; porch; veranda

嫏 láng [嫏嬛](lánghuán) same as 琅嬛 lánghuán

榔 láng ☞ below

【榔槺】láng·kāng 器物长大,笨重,用起来不方便 bulky; cumbersome

【榔头】láng·tou 锤子(多指比较大的 oft. of a large size) hammer; also 狼头 láng·tou or 鎯头 láng·tou

硠 láng〈书 *fml.*〉水石撞击声 sound of water pounding on rocks

锒 láng [锒铛](lángdāng) ❶〈书 *fml.*〉铁锁链 iron chains: ～入狱(被铁锁链锁着进监狱) be put in chains and thrown into prison ❷ 形容金属撞击的声音 clanking or clanging sound: 铁索～ clanking of an iron chain ‖ also 郎当 láng·dāng

稂 láng 古书上指狼尾草 Chinese pennisetum (*Pennisetum alopecuroides*)

【稂莠】lángyǒu 稂和莠,都是形状像禾苗而妨害禾苗生长的杂草 pennisetum and green bristlegrass; weeds that affect the growth of a farm crop;〈比喻 *fig.*〉坏人 scoundrel; bad people

鎯 láng [鎯头](láng·tou) same as 榔头 láng·tou

螂(蜋) láng ☞ 螳螂 (tángláng) on p.1868, 蜣螂 (qiāngláng) on p.1543, [蟑螂](zhāngláng) on p.2417 and 蛇螂 gèláng on p.657

lǎng(ㄌㄤˇ)

朗 lǎng ❶ 光线充足;明亮 light; bright: 明～ bright and clear | 晴～ sunny; fine | 开～ sanguine; optimistic | 天～气清。The sky is sunny, and the air clear. ❷ 声音清晰响亮(of voice) resonant; loud and clear: ～诵 read in a loud and clear voice | ～读 read aloud

【朗读】lǎngdú 清晰响亮地把文章念出来 read aloud; read loudly and clearly: ～课本 read the text loudly

【朗朗】lǎnglǎng ❶〈拟声词 *onom.*〉形容清晰响亮的声音 sound of reading aloud: 书声～ reading loudly and clearly | 笑语～ chat merrily amidst peals of laughter ❷ 形容明亮 bright: ～星光 bright stars | ～乾坤。All is sunny and peaceful in this part of the world.

【朗生】lǎngshēng same as 囊生 nángshēng

【朗声】lǎngshēng 高声;大声 in a clear loud voice: ～大笑 laugh loudly

【朗诵】lǎngsòng 大声诵读诗或散文,把作品的感情表达出来 read aloud with expression; recite; declaim: 诗歌～会 poem recital party

烺 lǎng〈书 *fml.*〉明朗。多用于人名。bright and cheerful; oft. used in a person's name

塱(朗) lǎng 元塱(Yuánlǎng),地名,在香港。今作元朗。Yuen Long, name of a place in Hong Kong, now written as 元朗 Yuánláng

閬 lǎng 閬梨(Lǎnglí),地名,在湖南 Langli, name of a place in Hunan Province

làng(ㄌㄤˋ)

郎 làng ☞屎壳郎 shǐ·kelàng on p.1750
☞ láng on p.1150

埌 làng ☞扩埌 kuànglàng on p.1125

莨 làng [莨菪](làngdàng) 多年生草本植物,根茎块状,灰黑色,叶子互生,长椭圆形,花紫黄色,结蒴果。有毒。种子和根、茎、叶都入药。(black) henbane (*Hyoscyamus niger*); solanaceous herb having stem tubers and hairy foliage of oval and alternate leaves, bearing capsules, and possessing narcotic and poisonous properties, with both seeds, roots and leaves used as a medicinal herb
☞ liáng on p.1203

崀 làng 崀山(Làngshān),地名,在湖南 Langshan, name of a place in Hunan Province

阆 làng 阆中(Làngzhōng),地名,在四川 Langzhong, name of a place in Sichuan Province
☞ láng on p.1153

【阆苑】làngyuàn〈书 *fml.*〉传说中神仙居住的地方,诗文中常用来指宫苑(mythology) abode

of immortals; (in poetry) palace

浪 làng ❶ 波浪 wave; billow; breaker: 风平～静。The wind is fair and the sea calm. *or* The wind dropped, and the waves subsided. *or* All is tranquil and quiet. | 乘风破～ride the winds and break the waves; sail through wind and waves; brave winds and waves | 白～滔天 white breakers leaping skywards ❷ 像波浪起伏的东西 sth. undulating; wavy: 麦～billowing wheat field in the wind | 声～clamour; din ❸ 没有约束; 放纵 unrestrained; dissolute: 放～licentious | ～费 wasteful ❹〈方 *dial*.〉逛 stroll; roam

【浪潮】làngcháo〈比喻 *fig*.〉大规模的社会运动或声势浩大的群众性行动 tide; wave mass campaign: 改革的～tide of reform

【浪船】làngchuán 儿童体育活动器械,用木制的船挂在架下,坐在上面,可以来回摇荡 swingboat; children's sports apparatus consisting of a wooden boat suspended from a stand so that those aboard it may swing it to and fro

【浪荡】làngdàng ❶ 到处游逛,不务正业;游荡 loiter; loaf about: 终日～loaf about day in, day out ❷ 行为不检点;放荡 dissolute; dissipated: ～公子 loafer; never-do-well

【浪费】làngfèi 对人力、财物、时间等用得不当或没有节制(of manpower, material, time, etc.) waste; squander; chuck away: 反对～,提倡节约 combat waste and encourage economy

【浪花】lànghuā ❶ 波浪激起的四溅的水 spray of breaking waves ❷〈比喻 *fig*.〉生活中的特殊片段或现象 tidbits in one's life: 生活的～gleanings from workaday life

【浪迹】làngjì 到处漂泊,没有固定的住处 wander about; roam about: ～江湖 wander from place to place | ～天涯 trot the world; go world-trotting; ramble about the country

【浪漫】làngmàn ❶ 富有诗意,充满幻想 romantic: 富有～色彩 be imbued with a romantic aura ❷ 行为放荡,不拘小节(常指男女关系而言 oft. referring to man-woman relationship) unconventional; bohemian; loose

【浪漫主义】làngmàn zhǔyì 文学艺术上的一种创作方法,运用丰富的想像和夸张的手法,塑造人物形象,反映现实生活。浪漫主义有几种类型,如消极的浪漫主义和积极的浪漫主义。前者粉饰现实或留恋过去;后者能突破现状,预示事物发展的方向。Romanticism; style of literature and art using imagination and exaggeration in the portrayal of characters and real life, of several types, such as negative Romanticism and positive Romanticism, the former given to nostalgia and whitewashing reality while the latter devoted to eschewing status quo and point out the way of development of things

【浪木】làngmù 体育运动器械。用一根长木头挂在架下,人在上面用力使木头摇荡,顺势来回做各种动作 swing log; sports apparatus consisting of a log suspended horizontally so that a rider standing on it may swing it and performing a variety of stunts; also 浪桥 làngqiáo

【浪桥】làngqiáo same as 浪木 làngmù

【浪涛】làngtāo 波涛 billows: ～滚滚 billowing waves

【浪头】làng·tou ❶ 涌起的波浪 wave: 风大,～高。The wind is strong and the waves surge high. ❷〈比喻 *fig*.〉潮流 trend of the times: 赶～chasing the fad

【浪游】làngyóu 漫无目标地到处游逛 ramble; roam about aimlessly: ～四方 travel from place to place

【浪子】làngzǐ 游荡不务正业的青年人;二流子 prodigal; loafer; wastrel: ～回头 return of the prodigal son

【浪子回头金不换】làngzǐ huítóu jīn bù huàn 指做了坏事的人改过自新后极为可贵 A prodigal is appreciated more than anything else if he mends his ways.

哴 làng〈方 *dial*〉same as 晾 liàng ①②

蒗 làng 宁蒗(Nínglàng),彝族自治县,在云南 Ninglang, Yi autonomous county in Yunnan Province

lāo(ㄌㄠ)

捞(撈) lāo ❶ 从水或其他液体里取东西 scoop up from a liquid; dredge up; fish for; drag for: 打～fish for sth. from water | ～饭 half-boiled, half-steamed rice | ～鱼 net fish ❷ 用不正当的手段取得 get by improper means: 趁机～一把 grab while the grabbing is good ❸〈方 *dial*.〉顺手拉或拿 make off with sth. in passing

【捞本】lāo//běn(～儿 lāo//běnr)赌博时赢回输掉的本钱,泛指采取办法把损失了的补偿上(多含贬义 oft. derog.) win back lost wagers; recover one's losses; recoup oneself

【捞稻草】lāo dàocǎo 快要淹死的人,抓住一根稻草,想借此活命(as of a drowning man struggling for his life) clutch at a straw;〈比喻 *fig*.〉在绝境中作徒劳无益的挣扎 mount a futile struggle under dire circumstances

【捞摸】lāo·mo 在水里寻找,借指攫取非分利益 feel about in water — try to gain sth. underserved

【捞取】lāoqǔ ❶ 从水里取东西 scoop sth. up from water: 塘里的鱼可以随时～。The fish in the pond can be netted anytime you want. ❷ 用不正当的手段取得 angle for; take possession of sth. by hook or by crook: ～暴利 scramble for exorbitant profit

【捞着】lāo//zháo 得到机会(做某事) get the

opportunity (of doing sth.)：那天的联欢会，我没～参加。I missed the get-together of the other day.

láo（ㄌㄠˊ）

劳（勞）láo ❶ 劳动 work; labour：按～分配 to each according to his work; get paid according to work done｜不～而获 reap without sowing ❷ 烦劳（请别人做事所用的客气话）(polite term used when asking a favour of sb.) put sb. to the trouble of：～驾 may I trouble you; will you be so kind as (to do sth.)｜～您走一趟。Will you do me a favour by running an errand for me? ❸ 指劳动者 labourer：～资双方 between labour and capital; between workers and the owner of a factory ❹ 劳苦；疲劳 fatigue; toil：任～任怨 work hard and bear no grudges about it; bear all the hardships without complaint｜积～成疾 break down from constant overwork ❺ 功劳 exploit; meritorious deed：勋～ distinctive service｜汗马之～ distinctions won in battle; war exploits ❻ 慰劳 give award in recognition of sb.'s hard work; reward：犒～award somebody with a gift｜～军 award soldiers for their distinctive service ❼（Láo）姓 a surname

【劳保】láobǎo ❶ 劳动保险的简称 abbr. for 劳动保险 láodòng bǎoxiǎn ❷ 劳动保护的简称 abbr. for 劳动保护 láodòng bǎohù

【劳步】láobù〈敬辞 *pol.*〉用于谢人来访 thanks for coming：您公事忙，千万不要～。You are busy with office work, so don't bother to come.

【劳瘁】láocuì〈书 *fml.*〉辛苦劳累 exhausted from hard work; worn out：不辞～be unsparing of oneself; make nothing of hard work

【劳动】láodòng ❶ 人类创造物质或精神财富的活动 work; labour：体力～manual labour｜脑力～mental labour ❷ 专指体力劳动 physical labour; manual labour：～锻炼 school oneself through manual labour ❸ 进行体力劳动 do physical labour：他～去了。He's out doing manual labour.

【劳动】láo•dong〈敬辞 *pol.*〉烦劳 cause sb. trouble (by asking a favour)：～您跑一趟。May I trouble you to make a trip?

【劳动保护】láodòng bǎohù 为了保护劳动者在劳动过程中的安全和健康而采取的各种措施 labour safety; measure taken to protect the safety and health of those doing physical labour; 简称 abbr. 劳保 láobǎo

【劳动保险】láodòng bǎoxiǎn 工人、职员在患病、年老、丧失工作能力或其他特殊情况下享受生活保障的一种制度 labour insurance; system to insure the life of a worker or employee against illness, old age, loss of work ability, or other circumstances; 简称 abbr. 劳保 láobǎo

【劳动布】láodòngbù 用较粗的棉纱、棉线织成的斜纹布，质地紧密厚实，坚实耐穿，多用来做工作服 denim; hard-wearing cotton twill fabric oft. used for the making of work overalls

【劳动对象】láodòng duìxiàng 政治经济学上指在劳动中被采掘和加工的东西。它可以是自然界原来有的，如地下矿石；也可以是加过工的原材料，如棉花、钢材等。subject of labour; (in political economics) things to be mined or processed in the course of labour, which may be a natural resource such as underground mineral ores, or semi-finished raw materials such as cotton and rolled steel

【劳动改造】láodòng gǎizào 我国对判处徒刑的犯罪分子实行的一种措施，强迫他们劳动，在劳动中改造他们成为新人 reform (of convicts) through labour; measure taken to subject convicted criminals to compulsory manual labour in order to transform them into constructive members of society; 简称 abbr. 劳改 láogǎi

【劳动教养】láodòng jiàoyǎng 我国对违反法纪而又可以不追究刑事责任的有劳动力的人实行强制性教育改造的一种措施，对他们采取劳动生产和政治思想教育相结合的方针，帮助他们学习劳动生产技术，树立爱国守法和劳动光荣的观念 re-education through labour; measure taken to subject an able-bodied person who has violated law but whose offence does not merit criminal prosecution to compulsory manual labour, along with political and ideological education, so as to help him or her learn production skills and become a patriotic, law-abiding citizen who regards it an honour to do physical labour; 简称 abbr. 劳教 láojiào

【劳动节】Láodòng Jié 五一劳动节的简称 abbr. for 五一劳动节 Wǔ-Yī Láodòng Jié

【劳动力】láodònglì ❶ 人用来生产物质资料的体力和脑力的总和，即人的劳动能力 labour force; workforce; labour ❷ 相当于一个成年人所具有的体力劳动的能力，有时指参加劳动的人 capacity of a grownup for physical labour; labourer：全～able-bodied labourer｜半～semi-able-bodied labourer｜辅助～labour doing auxiliary work

【劳动模范】láodòng mófàn 我国授予在生产建设中成绩卓著或有重大贡献的先进人物的一种光荣称号 labour hero; model worker; honourary title conferred on sb. who has distinguished himself or herself in production or construction work, or who has made major a contribution; 简称 abbr. 劳模 láomó

【劳动强度】láodòng qiángdù 劳动的紧张程度。也就是在单位时间内劳动力消耗的程度。labour intensity; amount of labour consumed per unit time

【劳动日】láodòngrì 计算劳动时间的单位，一般以八小时为一个劳动日 workday; working day (generally lasting for 8 hours)

【劳动生产率】láodòng shēngchǎnlǜ 单位时间内劳动的生产效果或能力,用单位时间内所生产的产品数量或单位产品所需要的劳动时间来表示 labour productivity; productivity; productive effect or capacity of labour per unit time, indicated either by the amount of products produced per unit time or the amount of time needed for the production of a set number or amount of products; also 生产率 shēngchǎnlǜ

【劳动手段】láodòng shǒuduàn 劳动资料的旧称 former term for 劳动资料 láodòng zīliào

【劳动条件】láodòng tiáojiàn 指劳动者在劳动过程中所必需的物质设备条件,如有一定空间和阳光的厂房、通风和除尘装置、安全和调温设备以及卫生设施等 working conditions; equipment and other material conditions needed by a labourer in doing physical labour, for example, factory building with adequate space and sunshine, ventilation and dusting installation, safety and temperature-moderating installation, and sanitary facilities

【劳动者】láodòngzhě 参加劳动并以自己的劳动收入为生活资料主要来源的人,有时专指参加体力劳动的人 labourer; worker; person who takes part in labour and who lives on the incomes from his or her labour

【劳动资料】láodòng zīliào 人用来影响和改变劳动对象的一切物质资料的总和,包括生产工具、土地、建筑物、道路、运河、仓库等等,其中起决定作用的是生产工具。从前叫劳动手段。means of labour, referring to all the materials — tools, land, buildings, roads, canals, warehouses, etc., with production tools playing a decisive role — man uses to influence and change the objects of his labour; formerly termed as 劳动手段 láodòng shǒuduàn

【劳顿】láodùn 〈书 *fml.*〉劳累 fatigued; wearied: 旅途～ fatigued by a journey; travel-worn

【劳乏】láofá 疲倦;劳累 fatigued; weary

【劳烦】láofán 〈方 *dial.*〉烦劳 trouble sb. to do sth.: ～尊驾 Would you please ... | ～您走一趟。May I trouble you to make a trip?

【劳方】láofāng 指私营工商业中的职工一方 labour (as opposed to capital or management) in private industry and commerce

【劳改】láogǎi 劳动改造的简称 abbr. for 劳动改造 láodòng gǎizào: ～犯 convict serving a sentence of reform through labour | ～农场 reform-through-labour farm; reformatory

【劳改犯】láogǎifàn 指正在进行劳动改造的犯罪分子 convicted prisoner serving a sentence of reform through labour

【劳工】láogōng ❶ 指工人 labourer; worker: ～运动 labour movement ❷〈旧时 *old*〉指被抓去做苦工的人 coolie

【劳绩】láojì 功劳和成绩 merits and accomplishments: ～卓著 outstanding performance in work

【劳驾】láo//jià 〈客套话 *pol.*〉用于请别人做事或让路 may I trouble you ...; would you please: ～,把那本书递给我。May I trouble you to pass that book, please? | 劳您驾,替我写封信吧! Would you be so kind as to write a letter for me? | ～,请让让路。Excuse me, would you move over a bit?

【劳教】láojiào 劳动教养的简称 abbr. for 劳动教养 láodòng jiàoyǎng: ～人员 person subjected to reeducation in a reformatory | ～农场 reform-through-labour farm

【劳金】láojīn 店主或地主等付给店员或长工的工钱 pay; wage paid by a shop proprietor to a clerk or a landlord to a farmhand

【劳倦】láojuàn 疲劳;疲倦 fatigued; tired: 不辞～make nothing of fatigue | 他连续工作了一整天也不觉得～。He worked for an entire day without feeling tired.

【劳军】láo//jūn 慰劳军队 greet an army with pleasantries and gifts

【劳苦】láokǔ 劳累辛苦 hard work: ～大众 toiling masses; labouring people | 不辞～be unsparing of oneself

【劳苦功高】láo kǔ gōng gāo 做事勤苦,功劳很大 have worked hard and with high distinction

【劳累】láolèi ❶ 由于过度的劳动而感到疲乏 tired; run-down; overworked: 工作～ fatigue from overwork ❷〈敬辞 *pol.*〉指让人受累(用于请人帮忙做事) cause sb. trouble: ～你去一趟。I'm sorry but I have to trouble you to make the trip.

【劳力】láolì ❶ 体力劳动时所用的气力 labour; labour force ❷ 有劳动能力的人 able-bodied person: 农忙季节要特别注意合理安排～。During the peak of the farming season please pay due attention to properly arranging your labour force. ❸〈书 *fml.*〉从事体力劳动 be engaged in physical labour; work with one's brawn (as opposed to 'one's mind')

【劳碌】láolù 事情多而辛苦 work hard; toil: 终日～work all day long

【劳民伤财】láo mín shāng cái 既使人民劳苦,又浪费钱财 exhaust the people and drain the treasury; waste manpower and money

【劳模】láomó 劳动模范的简称 abbr. for 劳动模范 láodòng mófàn

【劳神】láo//shén ❶ 耗费精神 tax one's mind; bother; trouble: 你身体不好,不要多～。You're not feeling well, so don't work too hard. ❷〈客套话 *pol.*〉用于请人办事 raising a polite request: ～代为照顾一下。Please take care of it for me.

【劳师】láo//shī 〈书 *fml.*〉慰劳军队 visit an

army with gifts of food, wine, money, etc.

【劳师动众】láo shī dòng zhòng 原指出动大批军队,现多指动用大批人力(含小题大做之意 make a fuss over sth. small) (orig.) move a large number of troops; belabour the people; use too many people

【劳什子】láoshí·zi〈方 *dial.*〉使人讨厌的东西 nuisance; also 牢什子 láoshí·zi

【劳损】láosǔn 因疲劳过度而损伤 strain:腰肌～muscular strain|脏腑～strain of one's internal organs

【劳务】láowù 指不以实物形式而以劳动形式为他人提供某种效用的活动 labour and service:～市场 labour market|出口～export of labour and service|～输出 export of labour services

【劳务费】láowùfèi 指提供劳动服务所取得的报酬 commission; service charge

【劳心】láoxīn ❶ 费心;操心 take a lot of trouble; give a lot of care:不为小事～。Don't give too much care to trifles. ❷〈书 *fml.*〉从事脑力劳动 do mental labour; work with one's mind ❸〈书 *fml.*〉忧心 anxiety; worry

【劳燕分飞】láo yàn fēn fēi 古乐府《东飞伯劳歌》:'东飞伯劳西飞燕。'后世用'劳燕分飞'比喻人别离。according to the ancient *yuefu* song, *Song of the Shrike Flying East*, 'While the shrike flew east, the swallow was bound for the west.' Later generations have used this line as a metaphor for a couple parting from each other like birds flying in different directions.

【劳役】láoyì ❶ 指强迫的劳动 penal servitude; forced labour:服～be sentenced to corvée labour ❷ 指(牲畜)供使用(of draught animal) of use:这个村共有十七头能～的牛。The village had 17 oxen that could be used.

【劳资】láozī 指私营企业中的工人和资产占有者(of a private firm) labour and capital

【劳作】láozuò ❶〈旧时 *old*〉小学课程之一,教学生做手工或进行其他体力劳动(of a primary school course) handiwork or other forms of physical labour ❷ 劳动,多指体力劳动 do manual labour:农民们都在田间～。The farmers were working in the fields.

牢 láo ❶ 养牲畜的圈 sty; coop; enclosure for animals:亡羊补～mend the fold after losing some sheep of the flock ❷〈古代 *arch.*〉祭祀用的牲畜 sacrificial animal; same as 牺牲 xīshēng ①:太～(原指牛、羊、猪三牲,后也专指祭祀用的牛)(of former days) religious sacrifice that consists of an ox, a sheep and a pig; sacrificial ox ❸ 监狱 prison; jail:监～dungeon|坐～be locked up in a jail; be imprisoned ❹ 牢固;经久 firm; fast; durable:～不可破 too strong to be broken; indestructible|把车床固定～hold a machine tool fast (to the floor)|多温习几遍,就能记得更～。The more you review the lesson, the better you remember it.

【牢不可破】láo bù kě pò 坚固得不可摧毁(多用于抽象事物 oft. used for sth. abstract) so strong as to be indestructible:我们的友谊是～的。Our friendship is unbreakable.

【牢房】láofáng 监狱里监禁犯人的房间 prison cell

【牢固】láogù 结实;坚固 firm; secure:基础～solid foundation|～的大坝挡住了洪水。The dam was so solidly built that it withstood the excessive water.

【牢记】láojì 牢牢地记住 keep firmly in mind; remember well:～在心 bear sth. in mind|～老师的教导 bear a teacher's instruction in mind

【牢靠】láo·kao ❶ 坚固;稳固 sturdy; durable:这套家具做得挺～。This set of furniture was made to last. ❷ 稳妥可靠 reliable:办事～be dependable in getting things done

【牢笼】láolóng ❶ 关住鸟兽的东西 cage (for birds or animals);〈比喻 *fig.*〉束缚人的事物 bonds:冲破旧思想的～shake off the bonds of old ideas ❷ 骗人的圈套 trap; snare:堕入～fall into a trap; be entrapped ❸〈书 *fml.*〉用手段笼络 win over:～诱骗 decoy ❹ 束缚 shackle:不为旧礼教所～smash the shackles of old rites

【牢骚】láo·sāo ❶ 烦闷不满的情绪 complaint; grumble:发～bitching|满腹～have a grudge against everyting; have a bellyful of complaints ❷ 说抱怨的话 complain; grumble:～了半天 grumble about sth. for a long time

【牢什子】láoshí·zi same as 劳什子 láoshí·zi

【牢实】láo·shí 牢固结实 firm and solid; secure and steady:基础～ firm and secure foundation|～的铁门 solid iron door

【牢稳】láowěn 稳妥可靠 safe; reliable:重要文件放在保险柜里比较～。It's safer to keep important papers in a strongbox.

【牢稳】láo·wen (物体)稳定,不摇晃(of objects) stable; secure; firm:机器摆放得很～。The machine is secured firmly on the floor.

【牢狱】láoyù 监狱 prison; jail

埗(埗) láo ☞ 圪埗 gē·láo on p.649

唠(嘮) láo [唠叨](láo·dao) 说起来没完没了;絮叨 be garrulous; chatter:唠唠叨叨 babble on and on|～半天 chatter interminably

☞ lào on p.1163

崂(嶗) Láo 崂山,山名,在山东 Laoshan, name of a mountain in Shandong Province; also 劳山 Láoshān

铹(鐒) láo 金属元素,符号 Lr (lawrencium)。有放射性,由人工核反应获得。lawrencium (Lw), a synthetic, radioactive metallic element obtained from man-made nuclear reaction

痨（癆） láo 痨病 consumptive disease; tuberculosis; consumption: 肺～ tuberculosis; TB | 肠～ tuberculosis of the intestines | 干血～ (type of tubercular disease found in women) emaciation caused by blood disorder

【痨病】 láobìng 〈中医 *Chin. med.*〉指结核病 tuberculosis; TB

簩（簩） láo ☞[篤簩竹] (sīláozhú) on p. 1817

醪 láo 〈书 *fml.*〉❶ 浊酒 wine with dregs; undecanted wine ❷ 醇酒 mellow wine

【醪糟】 láozāo（～儿 láozāor）江米酒 fermented glutinous rice; glutinous rice wine

lǎo（ㄌㄠˇ）

老 lǎo ❶ 年岁大（跟'少'或'幼'相对 as opposed to 'young'）old: ～人 old people | ～大爷 uncle; grandpa | 他六十多岁了，可是一点也不显～。He is in his sixties, but he doesn't look his age. ❷ 老年人（常用做尊称 oft. used as a respectful term of address）elderly person: 徐～ Venerable Xu | 敬～院 senior citizens' home | 扶～携幼 (on a journey) take the old folk by the arm and lead the children along ❸〈婉辞 *euph.*〉指人死（多指老人，必带'了' oft. of old people, with the character 了 ·le attached）pass away; die: 隔壁前天～了人了。Someone next door died the day before yesterday. ❹ 对某些方面富有经验；老练 seasoned; proven: ～手 proven expert; old hand | ～于世故 be worldly-wise ❺ 很久以前就存在的（跟'新'相对，下⑥同 as opposed to 'new'; same as ⑥）old: ～厂 old factory | ～朋友 old friend | ～根据地 former revolutionary base area | 这种纸烟牌子很～了。This cigarette brand is nothing new. ❻ 陈旧 dated; antiquated: ～脑筋 old-fashioned way of thinking | ～机器 outdated machine | 这所房子太～了。This house is too old. ❼ 原来的original; unchanged; same: ～脾气 the same old temperament | ～地方 the same old place ❽（蔬菜）长得过了适口的时期（跟'嫩'相对 as opposed to 'tender'）(of vegetable) grown so much as to be palatable; overgrown; tough: 油菜太～了。The rape has grown too large to be palatable. ❾（食物）火候大（跟'嫩'相对 as opposed to 'underdone'）overcooked; well done: 鸡蛋煮～了。The eggs were overdone. | 青菜不要炒得太～。Don't overcook the cabbage. ❿（某些高分子化合物）变质（of certain macromolecular compounds）deteriorate; age: ～化 ageing | 防～剂 antioxidant; antideteriorant ⓫（某些颜色）深（of certain colours）dark; deep: ～绿 dark green | ～红 deep red ⓬ 长久 for long: ～主顾 long-time patron | 老张近来很忙吧，～没见他了。Old Zhang must be very busy, as we haven't seen him for a while. ⓭ 经常 often; regularly: 人家～提前完成任务，咱们呢！The other guys are always fulfilling their tasks ahead of time; how about us? ⓮ 很；极 rather; very: ～早 rather early | ～远 very far away | 太阳已经～高了。The sky hangs rather high in the sky. ⓯ 排行在末了的（of seniority）youngest: ～儿子 youngest son | ～闺女 youngest daughter | ～妹子 youngest sister ⓰ 前缀，用于称人、排行次序、某些动植物名[as prefix of a person's name to indicate seniority, or before an animal or plant]: ～王 Lao Wang; Old Wang | ～三 Third Child | ～虎 tiger | ～玉米 corn ⓱ (Lǎo) 姓 a surname

【老媪】 lǎo'ǎo 〈书 *fml.*〉年老的妇女 old woman

【老八板儿】 lǎobābǎnr 〈方 *dial.*〉拘谨守旧，也指拘谨守旧的人 stick-in-the-mud; old fogy

【老八辈子】 lǎobābèi·zi 形容古老、陈腐 moribund; outdated: 这是～的话了，没人听了。Such ideas are so behind the times that no one would take them seriously.

【老白干儿】 lǎobáigānr 〈方 *dial.*〉白干儿 sorghum liquor; white spirit

【老百姓】 lǎobǎixìng 人民；居民（区别于军人和政府工作人员 as opposed to serviceman and civil servant）common people; ordinary people; civilian

【老板】 lǎobǎn ❶ 私营工商业的财产所有者；掌柜的 shopkeeper; proprietor; boss ❷〈旧时 *old*〉对著名戏曲演员或组织戏班的戏曲演员的尊称 respectful term of address for opera star or troupe leader

【老板娘】 lǎobǎnniáng 老板的妻子 shopkeeper's wife; proprietress

【老半天】 lǎobàntiān 指相当长的一段时间；好久 for what seems to be an eternity; for a long time: 怎么才来，我们等你～了。How could you come so late — we've been waiting for you for an awfully long time.

【老伴】 lǎobàn（～儿 lǎobànr）老年夫妇的一方 (of an old married couple) my old gal; husband or wife

【老鸨】 lǎobǎo 鸨母 woman running a brothel; procuress; madam; also 老鸨子 lǎobǎo·zi

【老辈】 lǎobèi ❶（～儿 lǎobèir）前代；前辈 the older generation: 他家～都是木匠。Members of the older generation of his family were carpenters. ❷ 年长或行辈较高的人 elders; old folks

【老本】 lǎoběn（～儿 lǎoběnr）最初的本钱 principal; capital

【老鼻子】 lǎobí·zi 〈方 *dial.*〉多极了（后边带'了'字 followed by 了·le）an awful lot: 今年

收的白菜可～了。An awful lot of Chinese cabbages have been harvested this year.

【老表】lǎobiǎo ❶ 表兄弟 male cousin (on the maternal side or on the paternal aunt's side) ❷〈方 *dial.*〉对年龄相近的、不相识的男人的客气称呼 polite form of address to a male stranger

【老病】lǎobìng ❶（～儿 lǎobìngr）经久难治的病；没有完全治好、经常发作的病 chronic illness; old trouble：天一冷，～就犯。An old illness tends to relapse whenever it gets cold. ❷ 指人年老多病 old and sick; ageing and declining：我～无能，多亏他处处关照我。Being sick and weak, I'm lucky having him to take good care of me.

【老伯】lǎobó 对父亲的朋友或朋友的父亲的敬称。也用来尊称老年男子。(respectful term of address for a friend of one's father, the father of one's friend, or an old man) uncle

【老布】lǎobù〈方 *dial.*〉土布 homespun, plain cloth

【老财】lǎocái〈方 *dial.*〉财主（多指地主 oft. referring to a landlord) moneybags

【老苍】lǎo·cāng（相貌）苍老（of one's looks) old and wizened：他虽然六十多岁了，可不显得～。He is not old and wizened at all though he's already in his sixties.

【老巢】lǎocháo 鸟的老窝 nest; den; lair〈比喻 *fig.*〉匪徒盘踞的地方 bandits' den：捣毁土匪的～wipe out a bandits' den

【老成】lǎochéng 经历多，做事稳重 young but mature; experienced; steady：少年～ young but steady|～持重 mature and coolheaded

【老成持重】lǎochéng chízhòng 阅历多，办事稳重 experienced and prudent

【老诚】lǎochéng 老实诚恳；诚实 guileless; honest and sincere：～忠厚 genuine and tolerent|他是个～孩子，从来不说谎话。He is an honest boy and never lies.

【老粗】lǎocū（～儿 lǎocūr）指没有文化的人（多用为谦辞 oft. in self-deprecation) uneducated person; rough and ready chap

【老搭档】lǎodādàng 经常协作或多年在一起共事的人 old partner; old workmate; sidekick

【老大】lǎodà ❶〈书 *fml.*〉年老（of age) old：少壮不努力，～徒伤悲。Idly young, needy old. *or* One who does not work hard in his youth will be grieved when he grows old. ❷ 排行第一的人（in order of seniority) number one ❸〈方 *dial.*〉木船上主要的船夫，也泛指船夫 captain of a boat; (in a broad sense) boatman ❹ 很；非常（多见于早期白话 oft. in early vernacular) greatly; very：心中～不忍 feel extremely reluctant

【老大不小】lǎo dà bù xiǎo 指人已经长大，达到或接近成年人的年龄 have grown up and be no longer a child：他～的了，还跟孩子似的。He is a grown-up now but he behaves like a child.

【老大难】lǎodànán 形容问题错综复杂，难于解决 knotty old problem：～单位 unit beset with problems|～问题 hard nut to crack|这个班秩序乱，成绩差，是全校有名的～班级。Known for its chaos and poor grades, this is a notorious problem class in the school.

【老大娘】lǎodà·niáng 对年老妇女的尊称（多用于不相识的 polite form of address to an old woman, esp. a stranger) aunty; granny

【老大爷】lǎodà·yé 对年老男子的尊称（多用于不相识的 polite form of address to an old man, esp. a stranger) uncle; grandpa

【老旦】lǎodàn 戏曲中旦角的一种，扮演年老的妇女（of traditional Chinese opera) *laodan*; role of an old woman

【老当益壮】lǎo dāng yì zhuàng 年纪虽老，志向更高、劲头儿更大 old, but none the less vigorous and active; in fine fettle; fit as a fiddle

【老道】lǎodào 道士 Taoist priest

【老到】lǎo·dao（做事）老练周到 seasoned; experienced; mature

【老底】lǎodǐ（～儿 lǎodǐr）❶ 内情；底细 sb.'s past; sb.'s unsavoury background：揭～ drag the skeleton out of sb.'s closet ❷ 指祖上留下的财产；老本 family assets left by ancestors：他家～儿厚。His family is rather wealthy.|几年功夫他就把～儿败光了。In a few years' time he frittered away all he had inherited.

【老弟】lǎodì 称比自己年纪小的男性朋友（familiar form of address to a man much younger than oneself) young man; young fellow; my boy

【老调】lǎodiào ❶ 指说过多次使人厌烦的话；陈旧的话 hackneyed theme; platitude ❷ 河北地方戏曲剧种之一，流行于保定地区 *laodiao*, local opera of Hebei, esp. in and around Baoding; also 直隶梆子 zhílìbāng·zi

【老掉牙】lǎodiàoyá 形容事物、言论等陈旧过时（of things, theories, etc.) worn out; dilapidated

【老豆腐】lǎodòu·fu ❶ 北方小吃。豆浆煮开后点上石膏或盐卤凝成块（比豆腐脑儿老些），吃时浇上麻酱、韭菜花、辣椒油等调料 firm tofu (as opposed to 'jellied bean curd'); coagulated curd made by the action of gypsum or bittern to soya bean milk; soft, bland, white cheese-like food made from curdled soybean milk, seasoned with sesame jam, pickled chives flowers, chili oil, etc. when being served ❷〈方 *dial.*〉北豆腐 firm tofu; northern-style bean curd

【老坟】lǎofén 祖坟 ancestral grave

【老夫】lǎofū〈书 *fml.*〉年老的男子自称 old I (used by an old man)

【老夫子】lǎofūzǐ ❶〈旧社会 *pre-*1949〉称家馆或私塾的教师 private school teacher; family

tutor in China ❷ 清代称幕宾(Qing Dynasty) aide; advisor ❸ 称迂阔的不爱活动的知识分子 bookish person, esp. old-fashioned bookworm

【老赶】lǎogǎn〈方 *dial.*〉❶ 指没见过世面 inexperienced in the ways of the world; green; raw: 你真～，连这个也不懂。How can you be so green as to know nothing about such things? ❷ 指没见过世面的人；外行的人 greenhorn; fool; blockhead: 别把我当～。Don't take me for a fool.

【老干部】lǎogànbù 年纪大的或资格老的干部，特指1949年10月1日以前参加革命的干部 veteran cadre, esp. he or she who joined the revolution prior to October 1, 1949

【老疙瘩】lǎogē·da〈方 *dial.*〉指最小的儿子或女儿 pet baby of the family; one's youngest child

【老公】lǎogōng〈方 *dial.*〉same as 丈夫 zhàng·fu

【老公】lǎo·gong 太监 eunuch

【老公公】lǎogōng·gong ❶〈方 *dial.*〉小孩子称呼年老的男人(children's term of address to an old man) Grandpa ❷〈方 *dial.*〉丈夫的父亲 husband's father; father-in-law ❸〈旧时 *old*〉太监 eunuch

【老姑娘】lǎogū·niang ❶ 年纪大了还没结婚的女子 spinster ❷ 最小的女儿 youngest daughter

【老古董】lǎogǔdǒng ❶ 陈旧过时的东西 antique; old-fashioned idea ❷〈比喻 *fig.*〉思想陈腐或生活习惯陈旧的人 stick-in-the-mud; fuddy-duddy

【老鸹】lǎo·guā〈方 *dial.*〉same as 乌鸦 wūyā

【老光】lǎoguāng 指老视眼 presbyopic: 他戴着一副～眼镜。He wears a pair of presbyopic glasses.

【老汉】lǎohàn ❶ 年老的男子 old man ❷ 年老的男子自称 I (used by an old man): ～今年八十整。I am 80 this year.

【老好人】lǎohǎorén 脾气随和，待人厚道，不得罪人的人 benign and uncontentious person who is indifferent to matters of principle; one who tries never to offend anybody

【老狐狸】lǎohú·li〈比喻 *fig.*〉非常狡猾的人 old fox; crafty scoundrel

【老虎】lǎohǔ ❶ 虎的通称 general term for 虎 hǔ ❷ 指大量耗费能源或原材料的设备 equipment that consumes an unusual amount of energy or raw material: 煤～coal-consuming machine | 电～power-consuming equipment ❸ 指有大量贪污、盗窃或偷漏税行为的人 avaricious embezzler, thief or tax evader ❹〈比喻 *fig.*〉凶恶的人 bad-tempered person: 母～ hellcat; shrew

【老虎凳】lǎohǔdèng 旧时的残酷刑具。是一条长凳，让人坐在上面，两腿平放在凳子上，膝盖紧紧绑住，然后在脚根下垫砖瓦，垫得越高，痛苦越大。(of old times) rack, a bench-like instrument of torture to which a victim is stripped down and his knees are tightly tied so that bricks can be wedged under his heels. The more bricks inserted, the more painful the victim feels.

【老虎钳】lǎohǔqián ❶ 钳工等用来夹住工件的工具，装在钳床上，有较大的钳口，用柄扳动螺丝杆旋紧 vice; device attached to a workbench, with two jaws between which an object may be clamped by moving one jaw by means of a screw leaving the handles free to work on it; also 台钳 táiqián or 虎钳 hǔqián ❷ 手工工具，钳口有刃，多用来起钉子或夹断钉子和铁丝 pliers; pincer pliers; pincers with flat, usu. serrated surfaces for removing or cutting nails or wire

【老虎灶】lǎohǔzào〈方 *dial.*〉烧开水的一种大灶，也指出售热水、开水的地方 kitchen range for boiling water; where hot water or boiled water is sold

【老花眼】lǎohuāyǎn 老视眼的通称 generally term for 老视眼 lǎoshìyǎn

【老化】lǎohuà ❶ 橡胶、塑料等高分子化合物，在光、热、空气、机械力等的作用下，变得黏软或硬脆 ageing, referring to rubber, plastics, or any other macromolecular compound becoming sticky and soft or hard and fragile under the impact of light, heat, air, and mechanical force ❷ 指在一定范围内老年人的比重增长(of population) ageing; becoming old: 人口～ ageing population | 领导班子～ leading members of an institution getting too old ❸ 知识等变得陈旧过时(of knowledge, etc.) become outdated: 知识～ old-fashioned knowledge

【老话】lǎohuà ❶ 流传已久的话 old saying; saying; adage: '世上无难事，只怕有心人'，这是很有道理的一句～。There is a meaningful old Chinese saying: 'Nothing in the world is difficult for one who sets his mind on it.' ❷ (～儿 lǎohuàr) 指说过去事情的话 remarks about the old days: ～重提 rehash an old remark, topic, etc. | 咱们谈的这些～，年轻人都不大明白了。What we are saying about the old days is somewhat incomprehensible to young people.

【老皇历】lǎohuáng·li〈比喻 *fig.*〉陈旧过时的规矩 outdated ways of doing things: 情况变了，不能再照～办事。The old ways of doing things do not work any more, because the situation is different now.

【老黄牛】lǎohuángniú〈比喻 *fig.*〉老老实实勤勤恳恳工作的人 willing ox — person who is diligent and conscientious in work

【老几】lǎojǐ ❶ 排行第几 order of seniority among siblings ❷ 用于反问，表示在某个范围内数不上、不够格(多用于自谦或轻视别人 in rhetorical questions to express disparagement)：我不行，在他们中间我算～？Who am I among them? *or* I'm a nobody among them.

【老骥伏枥】lǎo jì fú lì 曹操《步出夏门行》：'老骥伏枥，志在千里。烈士暮年，壮心不已。' *Though the Tortoise Live Long* by Cao Cao: 'An old war-horse may be stabled,/Yet still it longs to gallop a thousand *li*.'〈比喻 *fig*.〉有志的人虽年老而仍有雄心壮志 aged hero still cherishes high aspirations

【老家】lǎojiā ❶ 在外面成立了家庭的人称故乡的家庭 native place; old home ❷ 指原籍 birthplace：我～是湖南。Hunan is my birthplace.

【老家儿】lǎojiār〈方 *dial*.〉指父母及尊亲 parents; grandparents

【老家贼】lǎojiāzéi〈方 *dial*.〉麻雀(鸟名) sparrow

【老奸巨猾】lǎo jiān jù huá 形容十分奸诈狡猾 old crafty person; wild old fox; old hand at trickery and deception

【老茧】lǎojiǎn same as 老趼 lǎojiǎn

【老趼】lǎojiǎn 趼子 callus; also 老茧 lǎojiǎn

【老江湖】lǎojiāng·hu 指在外多年，很有阅历，处世圆滑的人 well-travelled, worldly-wise person; sb. who has seen much of the world

【老将】lǎojiàng 年老的将领；宿将(多用于比喻 oft. fig.) old general; veteran general; old hand; veteran; old-timer：～出马，一个顶俩。An old hand going into action can do the job of two.

【老景】lǎojǐng 老年时的境况 life and circumstances in old age：～凄凉 have a miserable old age|～堪怜 pitiable life in old age

【老境】lǎojìng ❶ 老年时代 old age：渐入～getting on in years ❷ 老年时的境况 life and circumstances in old age：他的～倒也平顺。He lead a rather peaceful life in old age.

【老酒】lǎojiǔ〈方 *dial*.〉酒，特指绍兴酒 wine; esp. Shaoxing rice wine

【老辣】lǎolà ❶ 老练狠毒 shrewd and ruthless：手段～viciousness of a hardened scoundrel ❷ 圆熟泼辣 mellow; full maturity：画风质朴淳厚、～苍劲。The painting is marked for its unaffected simplicity yet there is no lack of full-rounded mellowness and vitality about it.

【老老】lǎo·lao same as 姥姥 lǎo·lao

【老老少少】lǎolǎoshàoshào 指年老和年少的一群人 old and young; people at different ages

【老例】lǎolì 旧规矩；旧习惯 precedence; old practice

【老脸】lǎoliǎn ❶〈谦辞 *hum*.〉年老人指自己的面子(of an old person) this old face of mine; my own reputation ❷ 厚脸皮 thick-skinned person

【老练】lǎoliàn 阅历深，经验多，稳重而有办法 seasoned; experienced：他年纪不大，处事却很～。He is quite young, yet he handle things with a sure hand.

【老林】lǎolín 没有开发的森林 virgin forest：深山～heavily wooded remote mountains

【老龄】lǎolíng same as 老年 lǎonián：～化 ageing problem|～大学 senior citizens' college

【老路】lǎolù ❶ 以前走过的那条旧道路 old road ❷〈比喻 *fig*.〉旧办法、旧路子 old rut; beaten track

【老妈子】lǎomā·zi 指女仆 old amah; maid servant; also 老妈儿 lǎomār

【老马识途】lǎo mǎ shí tú 管仲跟随齐桓公去打仗，回来时迷失了路途。管仲放老马在前面走，就找到了道路(见于《韩非子·说林》)。According to *Hanfeizi · Forest of Commentaries*, Guan Zhong lost his way on his return from a battle under the command of Duke Huan of Qi, but he eventually found his way home by letting his mount, an old horse, lead the way.〈比喻 *fig*.〉有经验，能带领新手工作 an old hand is a good guide

【老迈】lǎomài 年老(常含衰老意 oft. senile) old; aged

【老帽儿】lǎomàor〈方 *dial*.〉指不懂行而又带傻气的人 wooden spoon; moron; half scholar

【老米】lǎomǐ〈方 *dial*.〉陈米 old, stale rice

【老面】lǎomiàn〈方 *dial*.〉面肥 leaven; leavening dough

【老面皮】lǎomiànpí〈方 *dial*.〉厚脸皮，指人不知道羞耻 cheeker; boldface; hussy

【老谋深算】lǎo móu shēn suàn 周密的筹划、深远的打算。形容人办事精明老练。scheming and calculating; circumspect and far-sighted; experienced and astute

【老衲】lǎonà〈书 *fml*.〉年老的僧人，也用做老僧人的自称 old monk; (of a monk referring to oneself) this old monk

【老奶奶】lǎonǎi·nai ❶ 曾祖母 paternal great grandmother ❷ 小孩子尊称年老的妇人(of children addressing an old woman) granny

【老蔫儿】lǎoniānr〈方 *dial*.〉指不爽朗、不爱讲话、不善交际的人 clam; man of few words; taciturnist

【老年】lǎonián 六七十岁以上的年纪 old age; person over 60 years of age

【老年斑】lǎoniánbān 寿斑 age pigment

【老年间】lǎoniánjiān 从前；古时候 former times; ancient times

【老娘】lǎoniáng ❶ 老母亲 old mother ❷〈方 *dial*.〉已婚中年或老年妇女的自称(含自负意 of a harridan referring to herself) I, your old mother

【老娘】lǎo·niang ❶〈旧称 *old*〉收生婆 midwife ❷〈方 *dial*.〉外祖母 maternal grandmother

【老娘们儿】lǎoniáng·menr〈方 *dial*.〉❶ 指已婚女子 married woman; housewife：虽然我是

个～，我的见识可不比你们男人低。Though I'm only a housewife, I'm by no means beneath you men in terms of knowledge. ❷ 指成年妇女（含贬义 derog.）woman：你们～，少管这些闲事。You women! Stop nosing about in other people's business. *or* You women mind your own business. ❸ 指妻子 wife：他～病了。His wife is sick.

【老牛破车】lǎo niú pò chē〈比喻 *fig.*〉做事慢慢腾腾，像老牛拉破车一样 like an old ox tugging at a broken-down cart — making slow progress

【老牛舐犊】lǎo niú shì dú〈比喻 *fig.*〉父母疼爱子女 old cow licking her calf — parent doting on his or her child; parental love; dote on one's children

【老农】lǎonóng ❶ 年老而有农业生产经验的农民 old farmer; skilled farmer：向～学习种植技术 learn cultivation skills from veteran farmers ❷ 泛指农民 farmer：～卖的菜价廉物美。Vegetables sold by farmers are good in quality and low in price.

【老牌】lǎopái（～儿 lǎopáir）❶（货品）创制多年，质量好，被人信任的 established brand; well-known brand：～产品 brand-name product ❷〈比喻 *fig.*〉资格老，人所公认的 old hand：～殖民主义 old-line colonialism

【老派】lǎopài（～儿 lǎopàir）❶ 举止、气派陈旧 antiquated; outmoded：他穿着绸子裤，裤脚系着带儿，未免太～了。He looked so overfangled in silk trousers with both legs laced up at the bottom. ❷ 指举止、气派陈旧的人 old-fashioned person; conservative

【老婆】lǎo·po same as 妻子 qī·zi

【老婆婆】lǎopó·po〈方 *dial.*〉❶ 小孩子称呼年老的妇人（of children addressing an old woman）granny ❷ 丈夫的母亲 husband's mother; mother-in-law

【老婆儿】lǎopór 年老的妇女（含亲热意 with an overtone of intimacy）old woman

【老婆子】lǎopó·zi ❶ 年老的妇女（含厌恶意 with a derogative overtone）old biddy ❷ 丈夫称妻子（用于年老的 of an old husband addressing his old wife）my old woman

【老气】lǎo·qì ❶ 老成的样子 old-mannish：别看他年纪小，说话倒很～。He talks like an old man despite his young age. ❷ 形容服装等的颜色深暗、样式陈旧（of clothes）drab and old-fashioned：她打扮得既不～，也不花哨。The way she attires herself is neither old-fashioned nor gaudy.

【老气横秋】lǎo qì héng qiū ❶ 形容人摆老资格，自以为了不起的样子 act in a self-important way; arrogance stemmed from one's seniority ❷ 形容人没有朝气，暮气沉沉的样子（of a person who is not really very old）looking surprisingly listless

【老前辈】lǎoqiánbèi 对同行里年纪较大、资格较老、经验较丰富的人的尊称 senior; elder

【老亲】lǎoqīn ❶ 多年的亲戚 old relative：～旧邻 old relatives and long-time neighbours ❷ 年老的父母 old parents。

【老区】lǎoqū 指老解放区 former liberated area

【老拳】lǎoquán 拳头（用于打人时）（striking）fist：饱以～（用拳头足足地打他一顿）beat somebody up with one's hands

【老人】lǎo·rén ❶ 老年人 elder; oldster; greybeard ❷ 指上了年纪的父母或祖父母 aged parents; aged grandparents：你到了天津来封信，免得家里～惦记着。Don't forget to write your old folks at home when you arrive in Tianjin.

【老人家】lǎo·ren·jia ❶〈尊称 *honor.*〉年老的人 elderly：您～you｜他～he｜这两位～在一起干活二十多年了。The two old men have worked together for more than twenty years. ❷ 对人称自己的或对方的父亲或母亲 parent：你们～今年有七十了吧？Your parents are seventy this year, aren't they?

【老人星】lǎorénxīng 南部天空的一颗星，亮度仅次于天狼星。我国南方可以看到它在近地平线处出现。古人认为它象征长寿，也称它为南极老人星或寿星。Canopus; star second only to the Sirius in terms of luminosity that raises near the horizon and can be observed close to the horizon in south China; also 南极老人星 nánjí lǎorénxīng or 寿星 shòuxīng as a symbol of longevity

【老弱残兵】lǎo ruò cán bīng〈比喻 *fig.*〉由于年老、体弱以及其他原因而工作能力较差的人 old, weak and wounded troops; the old and the weak; those who on account of old age, illness, etc. are no longer active or efficient

【老三届】lǎosānjiè 指 1966、1967、1968 年三届的初、高中毕业生 junior or senior middle school graduate of 1966, 1967, or 1968

【老少】lǎoshào 老年人和少年人 old and young：～无欺 do fair business｜一家～大团圆 whole family in a happy reunion

【老身】lǎoshēn 老年妇女的自称（多见于早期白话 oft. in early vernacular）（old woman's self-effacing term of address）I

【老生】lǎoshēng 戏曲中生角的一种，扮演中年以上男子，在古典戏中挂髯口（胡须）。分文武两门。*laosheng*; bearded old or middle-aged gentleman of maturity and integrity in Chinese opera. The role of *laoshen* falls into two categories, *wensheng* (scholar, statesman, etc.) and *wuseng* (one with a military career); also 须生 xūshēng

【老生常谈】lǎo shēng cháng tán 原指老书生的平凡议论，今指很平常的老话 home truth; truism

【老师】lǎoshī〈尊称 *honor.*〉传授文化、技术的人。泛指在某方面值得学习的人。teacher; one who teaches, esp. one who is hired to teach knowledge or skills; (in a broad sense) one who deserves to learn from

【老师傅】lǎoshī·fu 〈尊称 *honor*.〉擅长某种技能的年纪大的人(of a skilled craftsman or worker) master

【老实】lǎo·shi ❶ 诚实 veracious; genuine; honest to goodness: 忠诚～faithful and high-minded | 当～人,说～话,办～事。Be an honest person in word and deed. ❷ 规规矩矩;不惹事 well behaved; law-fearing: 这孩子很～,从来不跟人吵架。The child is well behaved and he never quarrels. ❸〈婉辞 *euph*.〉指不聪明 simple-minded; naive; easily taken in

【老实巴交】lǎo·shibājiāo 形容人老实、本分 honest to goodness; taciturn and shy: 他是个～的人,从不惹事生非。A timid man, he never asks for trouble.

【老式】lǎoshì (～儿 lǎoshìr)陈旧的形式或样子 medieval; old style: ～家具 old-fashioned furniture; antique furniture

【老视眼】lǎoshìyǎn 年老的人由于眼球的调节能力减退而形成的视力缺陷。用凸透镜制成的眼镜可以矫正。presbyopia; inability of the eye to focus sharply on a nearby object, resulting from the loss of elasticity of the crystalline lens with advancing age, which can be amended by wearing convex glasses; 通称 popularly known as 花眼 huāyǎn or 老花眼 lǎohuāyǎn

【老手】lǎoshǒu (～儿 lǎoshǒur)对于某种事情富有经验的人 proven master; go-getter; old hand 斲轮～ expert wheelwright | 开车的～ veteran driver

【老寿星】lǎoshòu·xing ❶ 对高寿人的尊称(honor.) venerable man; venerable lady ❷ 称被祝寿的老年人 old person on his or her birthday

【老鼠】lǎo·shǔ 鼠的通称,多指家鼠 rat (*Rattus*); mouse, oft. referring to home mouse

【老鼠过街,人人喊打】lǎo·shǔ guò jiē, rén rén hǎn dǎ 形容危害人的人和事人人都痛恨 rat running across the street, with everybody shouting, 'Kill it!'; (sb. or sth.) hated by everyone

【老死】lǎosǐ 由于年老体衰而死亡(区别于'病死' as compared with 'die of disease') die of a natural cause; die a natural death

【老死不相往来】lǎo sǐ bù xiāng wǎng lái 形容相互之间一直不发生联系 grow old and die without having had any dealings with each other — never be in contact with each other

【老宋体】lǎosòngtǐ ☞ 宋体字 sòngtǐzì on p. 1826

【老太婆】lǎotàipó 老年的妇女 carline

【老太太】lǎotài·tai ❶〈尊称 *honor*.〉年老的妇女 old lady; Venerable Madam ❷〈尊称 *honor*.〉别人的母亲(也对人称自己的母亲或婆婆、岳母) your mother; his mother; my mother; my mother-in-law

【老太爷】lǎotàiyé ❶〈尊称 *honor*.〉年老的男子 elderly gentleman; Respected Sir ❷〈尊称 *honor*〉别人的父亲(也对人称自己的父亲或公公、岳父) term of address for the father of sb. else, or one's own father or father-in-law

【老态龙钟】lǎotài lóngzhōng 形容年老体弱、行动不灵便的样子 senile; doddering; shake or tremble as from old age

【老汤】lǎotāng ❶ 炖过多次鸡、鸭、肉等的陈汤 preserved sauce; sauce repeatedly used for braising chicken, duck, meat, etc. ❷〈方 *dial*.〉腌咸菜泡菜的陈汤 brine, oft. with spices, left from previous round of pickling

【老套子】lǎotào·zi 陈旧的习俗或工作方法 stereotype; slick method

【老天爷】lǎotiānyé 迷信的人认为天上有个主宰一切的神,尊称这个神叫老天爷。现多用来表示惊叹。Superstitious people believe that there is a god in heaven who is in control of everything — the Heavenly Lord. It is oft. used as an exclamation, e.g. My goodness!; Good Heavens!; Good Gracious! God! Heavens!: ～,这是怎么回事儿! My Goodness, what is going on?

【老头儿】lǎotóur 年老的男子(多含亲热意 with a undertone of intimacy) old chap; geezer

【老头儿鱼】lǎotóuryú 鮟鱇(ānkāng)的通称 general term for 鮟鱇 ānkāng

【老头子】lǎotóu·zi ❶ 年老的男子(多含厌恶意 oft. derog.) old fogy; old codger ❷ 妻子称丈夫(用于年老的 wife's term of address for her old husband) my old man ❸ 帮会中人称首领(of a secret society) chief

【老外】lǎowài ❶ 外行 layman; raw hand; amateurish: 一看你这架式就是个～。A look at the way you act, and I know you are an amateur. ❷ 指外国人 foreigner

【老顽固】lǎowán·gù 思想极守旧,不肯接受新事物的人 old fogy; troglodyte

【老窝】lǎowō ❶ 鸟、兽长期栖息的处所(of birds) nest; (of wild animals) den; lair ❷〈比喻 *fig*.〉坏人盘踞的地方(of bad people) lair: 端敌人的～destroy the base of an enemy

【老倭瓜】lǎowōguā〈方 *dial*.〉南瓜 pumpkin

【老弦】lǎoxián 京胡、二胡等乐器上用的粗弦(of *jinghu*, or Peking Opera fiddle, or *erhu*, a traditional Chinese fiddle) thick string

【老乡】lǎoxiāng ❶ 同乡 fellow provincial; fellow townsman; fellow villager: 听你口音,咱们好像是～。Maybe we are fellow provincials, judging from your accent. ❷ 对不知姓名的农民的称呼(friendly form of address to a farmer) buddy

【老相】lǎo·xiàng 相貌显得比实际年龄老 look one's age: 他长得有点儿～,才四十出头,就满脸皱纹了。He really looks his age — he's just a little more than forty yet he's got all the wrinkles in his face.

【老小】[1] lǎoxiǎo 老人和小孩儿,泛指家属或从老人到小孩儿所有的人 grownups and children; one's family:全村～the whole village, old and young|一家～the whole family

【老小】[2] lǎoxiǎo 老婆(多见于早期白话 oft. in early vernacular) wife:娶了～(of a man) get married

【老兄】lǎoxiōng 男性的朋友或熟人相互间的尊称 (familiar form of address between male friends) old chap; buddy

【老羞成怒】lǎo xiū chéng nù 因羞愧到了极点而发怒 turn embarrassment into anger; be shamed into anger

【老朽】lǎoxiǔ ❶ 衰老陈腐 decrepitude; dotage:昏庸～fatuous|～无能 senile and useless ❷〈谦辞 *hum*.〉老年人自称(of an old man) I

【老鸦】lǎoyā〈方 *dial*.〉乌鸦 crow

【老腌儿】lǎoyānr〈方 *dial*.〉用盐腌得很久的 long-pickled:～咸菜 mellowed pickles|～鸡蛋 pickled egg

【老眼昏花】lǎo yǎn hūn huā 指老年人视力模糊 dim-sighted as from advancing age

【老爷】lǎo·ye ❶〈旧社会 *pre*-1949〉对官吏及有权势的人的称呼,现在用时含讽刺的意思 (old term of address to sb. rich and powerful that has become derogative today) master; bureaucrat; lord:干部是人民的勤务员,不是人民的'～'。A government functionary is a civil servant, not someone who lords it over the people. ❷〈旧社会 *pre*-1949〉官僚、地主人家的仆人等称男主人(old respectful term of address to a master by a servant) Sir; Master ❸ 外祖父 maternal grandfather ❹ 指陈旧的、式样老的(车、船等) old-fashioned (vehicle, boat, etc.):～车 old-style car|～船 old-style boat

【老爷们儿】lǎoyé·menr〈方 *dial*.〉❶ 指成年男子 man:谁家的～不干活,光让老娘们儿去干? Who's the guy who does not work and leaves it all to his wife ❷ 指丈夫(zhàng·fu) husband:她～在外地做买卖。Her husband is away doing business.

【老爷爷】lǎoyé·ye ❶ 曾祖父 great grandfather ❷ 小孩子尊称年老的男子(child's term of address of an old man) grandpa

【老爷子】lǎoyé·zi〈方 *dial*.〉❶〈尊称 *honor*.〉年老的男子 venerable old man ❷ 对人称自己的或对方的年老的父亲 my old father; your old father

【老一套】lǎoyītào 陈旧的一套,多指没有改变的习俗或工作方法 conventionality; the same old stuff; the same old story; also 老套 lǎotào

【老鹰】lǎoyīng 鸟,猛禽类,嘴蓝黑色,上嘴弯曲,脚强健有力,趾有锐利的爪,翼大善飞。吃蛇、鼠和其他鸟类。hawk (*Accipitridae*); eagle; any of the birds of prey of the family *Accipitridae*, having a bluish dark hooked bill, strong legs, sharp claws, and large wings, and preying on snakes, rats, and smaller birds; also 鸢 yuān

【老营】lǎoyíng ❶〈旧时 *old*〉指军队长期居住的营房 old barracks ❷〈旧时 *old*〉指歹人、匪徒等长期盘踞的地方 bandits' lair

【老油子】lǎoyóu·zi 处世经验多而油滑的人 sly old fish; trickster; also 老油条 lǎoyóutiáo

【老于世故】lǎo yú shì gù 形容富有处世经验(多含贬义 oft. derog.) know what one is about; know the ways of the world; be worldly-wise

【老玉米】lǎoyù·mi〈方 *dial*.〉玉米 maize; Indian corn; corn; corn ear

【老妪】lǎoyù〈书 *fml*.〉年老的妇女 old woman

【老丈】lǎozhàng〈书 *fml*.〉〈尊称 *honor*.〉年老的男子 old gentleman

【老账】lǎozhàng ❶ 旧账 old debts; long-standing debts:陈年～long-standing debts|～未还,又欠新账。While old debts are still unpaid, new ones are incurred. ❷〈比喻 *fig*.〉已经过了很久的事 old scores:不要翻过去的～了。Don't bring up old scores.

【老者】lǎozhě 年老的男子 old man

【老着脸皮】lǎo·zhe liǎnpí 不顾羞耻 unabashedly; unblushingly

【老子】lǎo·zi ❶ 父亲 father ❷ 骄傲的人自称(一般人只用于气忿或开玩笑的场合 said in anger or for fun) (of an arrogant man) I, your father:～就是不怕,他还能吃了我! I'm afraid of nothing. Can he eat me up!

【老字号】lǎozì·hao 开设年代久的商店 old name in business; old firm; old shop:这是一家有近百年历史的～。This store has a history of nearly a hundred years.

【老总】lǎozǒng ❶〈旧社会 *pre*-1949〉对一般军人的称呼(old form of address to a soldier) Sir ❷〈尊称 *honor*.〉中国人民解放军的某些高级领导人(多和姓连用)[used after a surname as an affectionate form of address to a general or high-ranking PLA commander] chief; marshal; general

佬 lǎo 成年的男子(含轻视意 derog.) man; guy; fellow:阔～moneybags; rich man

拷 lǎo〈方 *dial*.〉绰(chāo);抓取 snatch; grab:天一亮,他就～起锄头出去了。He grabbed a hoe and went out as soon as day broke.

姥 lǎo ☞below
☞ mǔ on p.1373

【姥姥】lǎo·lao ❶ 外祖母 maternal grandmother; grandma ❷〈方 *dial*.〉收生婆 midwife ‖ also 老老 lǎo·lao

【姥爷】lǎo·ye same as 老爷 lǎo·ye ③

栳 lǎo ☞栲栳 (kǎolǎo) on p.1087

铑 lǎo 金属元素,符号 Rh (rhodium)。银白色,质硬。常镀在探照灯等的反射镜上,也用来制热电偶和铂铑合金等。rhodium (Rh);

silvery metallic element of a hard texture, oft. used to electroplate the reflector of a searchlight, and make thermoelectric couples and platinum-rhodium alloy

笼 lǎo ☞[箸笼](kǎolǎo) on p.1087

潦 lǎo〈书 *fml.*〉❶ 雨水大 heavy rain ❷ 路上的流水、积水 puddles on roads

☞ liáo on p.1213

lào(ㄌㄠˋ)

络 lào 义同'络'(luò) same as 络 luò in meaning

☞ luò on p.1280

【络子】lào·zi ❶ 依照所装的物件的形状,用线结成的网状的小袋子 string bag made in the shape of an object to be encased in it ❷ 绕线绕纱的器具,多用竹子或木条交叉构成,中有小孔,安装在有轴的座子上,用手摇动旋转 spindle; spinning wheel, esp. one made of chiasmas of bamboo slips or wooden sticks and fixed on a shaft for the spinning of yarn or threads

唠(嘮) lào〈方 *dial.*〉说;谈(话) talk; chat:有话慢慢～。Let's take our time and talk it over.|大家在一起～得很热闹。Everybody had a good time chatting together.|有什么问题,咱们～～吧。Let's have a heart-to-heart talk about whatever problem is on your mind.

☞ láo on p.1155

【唠扯】lào·chě〈方 *dial.*〉闲谈;聊天儿 chatter; chew the bag:来,咱们坐下～～。Come on, let's sit down and have a nice chat.|几个人在屋里～起来。They went into the room and began nattering right away.

【唠嗑】lào//kē〈方 *dial.*〉(～儿 lào//kēr)闲谈;聊天儿 shoot the breeze; chit-chat:没事的时候,几个人就凑在一块儿～。When they did not have anything particular to do they would huddle together to shoot the breeze.|昨天我跟我大哥唠了会儿嗑。Yesterday I chattered with my elder brother for a while.

烙 lào ❶ 用烧热了的金属器物烫,使衣服平整或在物体上留下标志 brand; iron; use of a heated iron to press wrinkles from fabric or burn a mark on the surface of an object to indicate identity or ownership:～印 brand|～衣服 press clothes ❷ 把面食放在烧热的铛或锅上加热使熟 bake in a pan:～馅儿饼 bake stuffed cakes

☞ luò on p.1280

【烙饼】làobǐng 烙成的饼(饼内一般加油盐) flapjack; pancake made of dough seasoned with oil and salt

【烙花】lào//huā 一种工艺,用烧热的铁扦子,在扇骨、梳篦、芭蕉扇和木制家具等上面,烫出各种图案、花纹 pyrograph, the art of burning designs and patterns on fans, combs, wooden furniture, etc. by using a heated iron spike; also 烫花 tànghuā

【烙铁】lào·tie ❶ 烧热后可以烫平衣服的铁器,底面平滑,上面或一头儿有把儿(bàr) flat iron; iron; iron appliance with a handle and a weighted flat bottom, used when heated to press wrinkles from fabric ❷ 焊接时熔化焊镴用的工具,一端有柄,另一端为紫铜制成的头,有刃 soldering iron; instrument with a handle and a bladed copper head for melting and applying solder

【烙印】làoyìn ❶ 在牲畜或器物上烫的火印,作为标记 brand, mark left on an animal or utensil to indicate ownership or identity;〈比喻 *fig.*〉不易磨灭的痕迹 indelible mark:时代～the brand of the times ❷ 用火烧铁在牲畜或器物上烫成痕迹 brand left by a heated iron on an animal or object;〈比喻 *fig.*〉深刻地留下印象 lasting impression:这些艺术形象,将～在小观众的心头,长时期地起着教育作用。These artistic images will be deeply engraved on the minds of young viewers and serve as an eye-opener for a long time to come.

涝(澇) lào ❶ 庄稼因雨水过多而被淹(跟'旱'相对 as opposed to 'drought')(of crops) waterlogging:防旱防～ take precautious measures against drought and waterlogging|庄稼～了。The crops were waterlogged. ❷ 因雨水过多而积在田地里的水 floodwater; excessive water in the fields:排～drain off the floodwater

【涝害】làohài 因雨水过多农作物被淹而引起的植物体的破坏和死亡 damages done to farm crops by floodwater

【涝灾】làozāi 因涝害而造成大量减产的灾害 disastrous crop failure caused by waterlogging

落 lào 义同'落'(luò) ①②⑥⑨⑩,用于下列各条 same as 落 luò ①②⑥⑨⑩ in meaning, confined to use in the following entries

☞ là on p.1139, luō on p.1276 and luò on p.1281

【落包涵】lào bāo·han〈方 *dial.*〉受埋怨;受责难 incur sb.'s displeasure; draw the ire of sb.:帮他半天忙,还落一身包涵。I helped him a great deal only to draw his ire.

【落不是】lào bù·shi 被认为有过失而受责难 be blamed for doing sth. wrong:他怕～,不想多管这件事。He didn't want to be involved with the business any more, for fear he should be blamed for anything going wrong.|跟他跑里跑外忙了半天,反落一身不是。(I) got nothing but reproach for running about with him all this time.

【落汗】lào//hàn 身上的汗水消下去 stop sweating:累了半天,等落了汗再接着干吧。We

have worked hard for hours, so let's take a rest and go on with our work when we've stopped sweating.

【落价】lào//jià (～儿 lào//jiàr)降价;减价(of price) go down; drop; cut

【落架】lào//jià〈方 *dial.*〉房屋的木架倒塌(of the wooden framework of house) collapse;〈比喻 *fig.*〉家业败落(of family fortune) decline

【落炕】lào//kàng〈方 *dial.*〉病得不能起床 be bedridden; be laid up

【落儿】làor〈方 *dial.*〉生活上的着落(指钱财等,只用在'有、没有'后边 of money, etc., used after 有 yǒu or 没有 méi·yǒu) means of support:有～(富足) be well-off|没～(穷困) be poor; also 落子 lào·zi

【落忍】làorěn〈方 *dial.*〉心里过意得去(常用于否定式 oft. in the negative) not feel apologetic:老麻烦人,心里怪不～的。It makes me feel real bad to be such a bother to others.

【落色】lào//shǎi 布匹、衣服等的颜色逐渐脱落;退色(of fabric, clothing) discolour; fade

【落枕】lào//zhěn ❶ 睡觉时脖子受寒,或因枕枕头的姿势不合适,以致脖子疼痛,转动不便 have a stiff neck (caused by cold or awkward sleeping posture) ❷ (头)枕着枕头 touch the pillow; hit the sack:因白天太劳累,晚上～就着。Because I overworked during the day, I fell asleep the moment I hit the sack at night.

【落子】[1] lào·zi ❶〈方 *dial.*〉指莲花落等曲艺 *laozi*; genre of ballad-singing that includes *lianhualao*:～馆 *laozi* club ❷ 评剧的旧称 old name for 评剧 píngjù:唐山～Tangshan *pingju*

【落子】[2] lào·zi same as 落儿 làor

耢(耮) lào ❶ 平整土地用的一种农具,长方形,用藤条或荆条编成。功用和耙差不多,通常在耙过以后用耢进一步平整土地,弄碎土块。basketry rake; farm tool that is usu. employed in the wake of an iron rake to level the farmland and break the clods more finely; also 耱 mò or 盖 gài ❷ 用耢平整土地 level land with basketry rake

酪 lào ❶ 用牛、羊、马的乳汁做成的半凝固的食品 junket; semi-solid food made from cattle, goat or horse milk:奶～cheese ❷ 用果子或果子的仁做的糊状食品 fruit jelly:杏仁～almond jelley|核桃～walnut cream

嫪 lào 用于人名,嫪毐(Lào'ǎi),战国时秦国人 for use in a person's name: Lao Ai, a man of the state of Qin during the Warring States Period

lē(ㄌㄜ)

肋 lē [肋脦](lē·de,又 also lē·te)〈方 *dial.*〉(衣服)不整洁,不利落(of clothes) sloppy; untidy

☞ lèi on p.1169

嘞 lē [嘞嘞](lē·le)〈方 *dial.*〉唠叨 blabbering; garrulous; chattering:瞎～shoot the breeze|你穷～什么? What are you blabbering for?|少～两句行不行? Shut up, will you? *or* Cut out the garbage, will you?

☞ ·lei on p.1171

lè(ㄌㄜˋ)

仂 lè〈书 *fml.*〉余数 complement of a number; remainder

【仂语】lèyǔ 词组 word group; phrase

艻 lè [萝艻](luólè) same as 罗勒 luólè

叻 Lè 指新加坡(我国侨民称新加坡为石叻、叻埠)Singapore, as referred to by overseas Chinese:～币 Singaporean dollar

乐(樂) lè ❶ 快乐 delight; merry; pleasure:欢～happiness|～事 pleasure; delight|～不可支 outright glee|心里～得像开了花。My heart swelled with happiness. ❷ 乐于 be happy to; take delight in:～此不疲 never get tired of doing sth. ❸ 笑 laugh; to amuse:他说了个笑话把大家逗～了。His joke amused everyone. ❹ (Lè)姓(与 Yuè 不同姓 different from Yuè) a surname

☞ yuè on p.2371

【乐不可支】lè bù kě zhī 形容快乐到了极点 overjoyed; outright glee

【乐不思蜀】lè bù sī Shǔ 蜀汉亡国后,后主刘禅被安置在魏国的都城洛阳。一天,司马昭问他想念不想念西蜀,他说'此间乐,不思蜀'(见《三国志·蜀志·后主传》注引《汉晋春秋》)。后来泛指乐而忘返。According to an *Annals of Han and Jin* annotation on *Records of Three Kingdoms·Kingdom of Shu·Biography of the Last Emperor*, after the kingdom of Shu was eliminated, Liu Shan, the last Shu Emperor, was resettled in Luoyang, the capital of the Kingdom of Wei. One day, when Sima Zhao, the commander of Wei, asked Liu if he missed his homeland of Shu, the latter answered, 'I'm so happy here that I don't think I miss my homeland of Shu.' From this story is derived the phrase: be so abandoned to pleasure as to forget home.

【乐此不疲】lè cǐ bù pí 因喜欢做某件事而不知疲倦。形容对某事特别爱好而沉浸其中。be on sth. without feeling tired of it; delight in sth. and never get tired of it; also 乐此不倦 lè cǐ bù juàn

【乐得】lèdé 某种情况或安排恰合自己心意,因而顺其自然 might as well; be only too glad to:主席让他等一会儿再发言,他也～先听听别人的意见。When the chairman asked him to wait for a little while before taking the floor, he was only too happy to hear what the others might have to say first.

【乐观】lèguān 精神愉快,对事物的发展充满信心(跟'悲观'相对 as opposed to 'pessimistic')sanguine; optimistic:～情绪 optimism|不要盲目～。Don't be too optimistic. *or* Don't be too happy too early.

【乐呵呵】lèhēhē 形容高兴的样子 cheerful; joyful; buoyant; full of cheer; full of joy:老远就看见他～地向这边走来。He saw him coming here cheerfully in the distance.

【乐和】lè·he〈方 *dial.*〉快乐(多指生活幸福 oft. referring to life) contented:日子过得挺～ lead a happy life|人们辛苦了一年,春节的时候都愿意～～。After a year's hard work, people want to have a good time during Spring Festival.

【乐极生悲】lè jí shēng bēi 快乐到了极点的时候,发生悲痛的事情 when joy reaches its height, sorrow comes in its turn; extreme joy begets sorrow

【乐趣】lèqù 使人感到快乐的意味 delight; pleasure; joy:工作中的～是无穷的。There is endless joy in work.|只有乐观的人才能随时享受生活中的～。Only optimistic people can feel the joys of life whenever they want to.

【乐儿】lèr〈方 *dial.*〉same as 乐子 lè·zi

【乐善好施】lè shàn hào shī 爱做好事,喜欢施舍 be philanthropic; prodigal of benefactions

【乐事】lèshì 令人高兴的事情 pleasure; delight:人生～ joy of life|赏心～ things one enjoys doing

【乐陶陶】lètáotáo 形容很快乐的样子 happy; joyful, cheerful; full of cheers:船家生活～,赶潮撒网月儿高。Happy is the life of a boatman, out fishing when the tide is in and the moon is high.

【乐天】lètiān 安于自己的处境而没有任何忧虑 be happy with one's lot; be content with one's lot; be happy-go-lucky; be optimistic:～派 happy-go-lucky person; optimist; easy-going person

【乐天知命】lè tiān zhī mìng 相信宿命论的人认为自己的一切都由命运支配,于是安于自己的处境,没有任何忧虑 be content with one's lot. Fatalists believe that every happening in their life is determined by fate and is inevitable. Therefore, they are always content with their circumstances and have no worries.

【乐土】lètǔ 安乐的地方 happy land; paradise

【乐意】lèyì ❶ 甘心愿意 be willing to; be ready to:这件事只要你～办,保险办得好。If you are willing to do this, I'm sure you can do it well. ❷ 满意;高兴 ① pleased; happy:你的话说得太生硬,他听了有些不～。You spoke too stiffly, that's why he was somewhat unhappy.

【乐于】lèyú 对于做某种事情感到快乐 be happy to do sth.; take delight in doing:～助人 be happy to help others; be ready to help others

【乐园】lèyuán ❶ 快乐的园地 playground; amusement park:儿童～ children's play ground; children's amusement park ❷〈基督教 *Christ.*〉指天堂或伊甸园 paradise; Eden

【乐滋滋】lèzīzī (～的 lèzīzī·de)形容因为满意而喜悦的样子 contented; pleased:他听得心里～的,把原来的烦恼事儿都忘了。He was quite pleased to hear it and forgot all his worries.

【乐子】lè·zi〈方 *dial.*〉❶ 快乐的事 fun; pleasure:下雨天出不了门儿,下两盘棋,也是个～。Since we can't go out because of the rain, it's also a fun to play chess. ❷ 惹人笑的事(含有幸灾乐祸的意思 at the cost of sb.'s misfortune or mischance) ridicule; laughing-stock; laughable matter:他摔了一跤,把端着的金鱼缸也砸了,这个～可真不小。He fell and broke the goldfish bowl, causing a lot of laughter.

玏 lè ☞ 瑊玏 jiānlè on p.943

泐 lè〈书 *fml.*〉❶ 石头顺着纹理裂开 splitting of a rock along its veins ❷ 书写 write a letter:手～ a personal letter ❸ same as 勒² lè

勒¹ lè ❶〈书 *fml.*〉带嚼子的马笼头 bridle ❷ 收住缰绳不让骡马等前进 rein in:悬崖～马 rein in at the brink of the precipice; stop before it is too late ❸ 强制;逼迫 force; coerce:～令 order|～派 force someone to pay levies or do unpaid labour (or corvée)|～索 extort; blackmail ❹〈书 *fml.*〉统率 command:亲～六军 command the army personally

勒² lè〈书 *fml.*〉雕刻 carve; engrave:～石 stone carving|～碑 carve on a stone tablet

勒³ lè 勒克斯的简称 abbr. for 勒克斯 lèkèsī ☞ lēi on p.1166

【勒逼】lèbī 强迫;逼迫 force; coerce

【勒克斯】lèkèsī 照度单位,1 流明的光通量均匀分布在 1 平方米面积上的照度,就是 1 勒克斯 lux; metre-candle; unit of illumination, equal to one lumen per square metre or to the illumination of a surface uniformly one metre distant from a point source of one candela; 简称 abbr. 勒 lè

【勒令】lèlìng 用命令方式强制人做某事 order; compel by order:～停业 be ordered to close down; be ordered to stop doing business; be ordered to suspend business|～搬迁 be ordered to move out; order someone to move out

【勒派】lèpài 强行摊派 apportion a levy arbitrarily; force someone to pay levies, or do corvée (or unpaid labour)

【勒索】lèsuǒ 用威胁手段向别人要财物 extort; blackmail:敲诈～ extort; blackmail|～钱财 extort money from someone

【勒抑】lèyì ❶ 指用压力迫使降低售价 force down the selling price ❷ 勒索压制 blackmail and suppress

【勒诈】lèzhà 勒索敲诈 extort; blackmail:～钱财 extort money from someone

簕 lè ☞ below

【簕榄】lèdǎng 常绿灌木或乔木,枝上有刺,羽状复叶,小叶长圆形,花淡青色,蒴果紫红色,种子黑色,可提制芳香油。根可入药。ailanthus prickly ash (*Zanthoxylum ailanthoides*); evergreen shrub or tree with thorny twigs, small oblong bipinnate leaves, pale green flowers, purple-red capsules, black seeds that are used for extracting aromatic oils, and root that is used for Chinese medicine

【簕竹】lèzhú 竹子的一种,高达 15 米左右,叶子披针形,背面有稀疏的短毛 a kind of bamboo, about 15 metres tall, with lanceolate leaves and thin, short hair on the back

鳓 lè 鳓鱼,身体侧扁,银白色,头小,鳃孔大,无侧线。生活在海中。slender shad (*Ilisha elongata*); silver-white sea fish having a laterally flat body without lateral lines, a small head and big gill slit, also 鲙(快)鱼 kuàiyú, 白鳞鱼 báilínyú or 曹白鱼 cáobáiyú

•le (•ㄌㄜ)

了 •le〈助词 *aux.*〉❶ 用在动词或形容词后面,表示动作或变化已经完成 [used after a verb or an adjective to indicate the completion of an action or a change] a)用于实际已经发生的动作或变化 [used after an action that has taken place or sth. that has changed]:这个小组受到～表扬。This group has been commended.|水位已经低～两米。The water level has dropped by two metres. b)用于预期的或假设的动作 [used for an anticipated or presupposed action]:你先去,我下～班就去。You'll go first, and I'll go there after work.|他要知道～这个消息,一定也很高兴。He will also be very happy if he hears this news. ❷ 用在句子的末尾或句中停顿的地方,表示变化或出现新的情况 [used at the end of a sentence or a pause in the middle of a sentence to indicate a change or a new situation] a)表示已经出现或将要出现某种情况 [indicating that sth. has happened or is about to happen]:下雨～。It's raining.|春天～,桃花都开～。It's spring, and the peach trees are all in bloom.|他吃了饭～。He has had his meal.|天快黑～,今天去不成～。It's getting dark, and we can't go there today. b)表示在某种条件之下出现某种情况 [indicating a certain situation under certain conditions] 天一下雨,我就不出门～。I won't go out once it rains.|你早来一天就见着他～。You would have seen him if you had come one day earlier. c)表示认识、想法、主张、行动等有变化 [indicating a change in one's understanding, idea, view or action]:我现在明白他的意思～。I have now understood what he meant.|他本来不想去,后来还是去～。He didn't want to go at first, but he went later. d)表示催促或劝止 [indicating a request or a command]:走～,走～,不能再等～! Let's go. We can't wait any longer.|好～,不要老说这些事～! Stop. Don't keep talking of these things!

☞ liǎo on p. 1213

饹 •le [饸饹] (hé•le) on p. 789

☞ gē on p. 650

lēi (ㄌㄟ)

勒 lēi ❶ 用绳子等捆住或套住,再用力拉紧;系紧 tighten up; tie or strap sth. tight:行李没有捆紧,再～一～。The luggage is too loose. Tighten it up a bit.|中间再～根绳子就不会散了。Put another string around it in the middle, and it will not break up.|袜带儿太紧,～得腿肚子不舒服。The suspenders are too tight. They cut into the calves. ❷〈方 *dial.*〉强制;逼迫 force; coerce:他硬～着大伙儿在地里种烟草。He forced everyone to grow tobacco in the fields.

☞ lè on p. 1165

【勒掯】lēi•kèn〈方 *dial.*〉强迫或故意为难 force sb. to do sth.; make things difficult for sb.

léi (ㄌㄟˊ)

累(纍) léi ☞ below

☞ lěi on p. 1168 and lèi on p. 1170

【累累】[1] léiléi〈书 *fml.*〉憔悴颓丧的样子 haggard; gaunt:～若丧家之狗 be wretched as a stray cur; also 儽儽 léiléi

【累累】[2] léiléi〈书 *fml.*〉接连成串 clusters of; heaps of:果实～ fruit growing in close clusters; trees hanging heavy with fruit

☞ lěilěi on p. 1169

【累赘】léi•zhui ❶ (事物)多余、麻烦;(文字)不简洁 (of things) cumbersome; troublesome; (of writing) wordy; verbose:这段话显得有些～。This paragraph is too wordy. ❷ 使人感到多余或麻烦 burdensome; cumbersome:我不想再～你们了,明天就回乡下去。I don't want to be burdensome to you any longer. I'll leave for the countryside tomorrow. ❸ 使人感到多余、麻烦的事物 encumbrance; burden;

nuisance：行李带多了，是个～。Too much luggage is a burden. ‖ also 累坠 léi·zhui

雷 léi ❶ 云层放电时发出的响声 thunder：打～ thunder crashes；it thunders｜春～ spring thunder ❷ 军事上用的爆炸武器 mine：地～（land）mine｜水～（submarine mine）｜鱼～ torpedo｜布～ lay mines｜扫～ sweep mines ❸（Léi）姓 a surname

【雷暴】léibào 由积雨云产生的雷电现象，有时伴有阵雨或冰雹 thunderstorm；storm accompanied by thunder and lightning resulting from cumulonimbus，sometimes also accompanied by downpour or hail

【雷场】léichǎng 布设许多地雷的地段 minefield

【雷池】Léichí 古水名，在今安徽望江。东晋时庾亮写给温峤的信里有'足下无过雷池一步'的话，是叫温峤不要越过雷池到京城（今南京）来（见于《晋书·庾亮传》）。现在只用于'不敢越雷池一步'这个成语中，比喻不敢越出一定的范围。ancient name of a river in present-day Wangjiang，Anhui Province. According to *History of Jin·Biography of Yu Liang*，in a letter to Wen Jiao in the Eastern Jin Dynasty（317-420），Yu Liang wrote：'You must not go over the Leichi River by one step'，advising Wen Jiao not to cross Leichi and go to the capital city（Nanjing of today）. From this is derived the phrase '不敢越雷池一步 bùgǎn yuè Léichí yībù'（dare not to cross Leichi by one step — dare not go one step beyond the prescribed limit）.

【雷达】léidá 利用极短的无线电波进行探测的装置。无线电波传播时遇到障碍物就能反射回来，雷达就根据这个原理，把无线电波发射出去再用接收装置接收反射回来的无线电波，这样就可以测定目标的方向、距离、大小等，接收的电波映在指示器上可以得到探测目标的影像。雷达在使用上不受气候条件的影响，广泛应用在军事、天文、气象、航海、航空等方面。radar；device using ultra-short radio waves for detection. When a radio wave is transmitted，it is reflected back if it comes across an obstacle. It is based on this principle that a radar transmits the radio wave and uses a receiving device to receive the reflected radio wave to determine the direction，distance and size of an object. When the received radio wave is reflected on an indicator，the detected object is obtained. Radar is widely used for military purposes，in astronomy，meteorology，navigation，aviation，etc.，and is not affected by weather conditions.

【雷达兵】léidábīng 以雷达为基本装备的部队。也称这一部队的士兵。radarman；radar operator

【雷打不动】léi dǎ bù dòng 形容坚定，不可动摇 not to be shaken by thunder；（of an arrangement or plan）not to be altered under any circumstances：他每天早晨坚持跑步，～。He persists in jogging every morning，an exercise not to be stopped for him under any circumstances.

【雷电】léidiàn 雷和闪电的合称 thunder and lightning

【雷动】léidòng（声音）像打雷一样（of sound）thunderous：掌声～thunderous applause｜～的欢呼声响彻云霄。Thunderous cheers resounded through the skies.

【雷公】Léigōng 神话中管打雷的神 Thunder God in mythology

【雷管】léiguǎn 弹药、炸药包等的发火装置。一般用雷汞等容易发火的化学药品装在金属管里制成 detonator；detonating cap；blasting cap；primer；usually made of a metal tube filled with mercury fulminate and other flammable chemicals

【雷击】léijī 雷电发生时，由于强大电流的通过而杀伤或破坏（人、畜、树木或建筑物等）be struck by lightning；sudden discharge of atmospheric electricity between cloud and earth when a lightning occurs，which may cause injury and death to humans and animals，and damage to trees，buildings，etc.

【雷厉风行】léi lì fēng xíng 像雷一样猛烈，像风一样快。形容执行政策法令等严格而迅速。powerful like thunderbolt and fast like lightning —（when implementing regulations，policies，etc.）vigorous and speed

【雷鸣】léimíng ❶ 打雷 thunder：～电闪。It's thundering and lightning. ❷ 像打雷那么响（多用于掌声 oft. of applause，cheers）thunderous：掌声～ thunderous applause

【雷声大，雨点小】léishēng dà，yǔdiǎn xiǎo〈比喻 *fig.*〉话说得很有气势或计划订得很大而实际行动却很少 loud thunder but small raindrops；much said but little done；much talk but little action

【雷霆】léitíng ❶ 雷暴；霹雳 thunderclap；thunderbolt ❷〈比喻 *fig.*〉威力或怒气 thunder-like power or rage；wrath：～万钧 mighty power｜大发～（大怒）fly into a rage；boil with rage

【雷霆万钧】léitíng wàn jūn〈比喻 *fig.*〉威力极大 as powerful as a thunderbolt：排山倒海之势，～之力 with the momentum of an avalanche and the force of a thunderbolt

【雷同】léitóng 指随声附和，也指不该相同而相同（旧说打雷时，许多东西都同时响应）（phrase derived from the old saying that whenever the thunder bolt strikes，it is echoed in unison by the multitude of things in nature）echo what sb. else has said；identical；exactly the same；similar；lack in originality

【雷雨】léiyǔ 伴有雷电的雨，多发生在夏天的下午 thunderstorm；rain accompanied by thunder，often occurring in summer afternoons

【雷阵雨】léizhènyǔ 伴有雷电的阵雨 thunder

shower; shower accompanied by thunder

蘽(虆) léi 〈书 *fml.*〉土筐 earth basket

嫘 léi 用于人名,嫘祖(Léizǔ),传说中黄帝的妻子,发明养蚕 used in names, as in 嫘祖 Lei Zu, wife of the legendary Yellow Emperor and reputed discoverer of sericulture

缧 léi [缧绁](léixiè)〈书 *fml.*〉捆绑犯人的绳索,借指牢狱 rope used to tie up a criminal; fetters; bonds; shackles; prison: 身陷～ be in jail

㹎 léi 〈书 *fml.*〉牡牛 bull

擂 léi ❶ 研磨 pestle; pound: ～钵 mortar ❷ 打 beat: ～了一拳 give a punch; deal someone a blow with the fist

☞ lèi on p. 1170

檑 léi 〈古代 *arch.*〉作战时从高处推下大块木头,以打击敌人 push large logs down a high altitude to strike at invading enemy troops in battles

【檑木】léimù 〈古代 *arch.*〉作战时从高处往下推以打击敌人的大块木头 large logs used and pushed downward from a high altitude in battles to strike invading enemy soldiers

礌(礧) léi ❶〈古代 *arch.*〉作战时从高处推下石头,以打击敌人 push large stones from a high altitude to hit invading enemy soldiers in battles ❷〈书 *fml.*〉击 strike

【礌石】léishí 〈古代 *arch.*〉作战时从高处往下推以打击敌人的大块石头 large stones pushed downward from a high altitude in battles to strike invading enemy soldiers

镭 léi 金属元素,符号 Ra (radium)。银白色,质软,有放射性。用来治疗恶性肿瘤,镭盐和铍粉的混合制剂可制成中子源。radium (Ra); soft, silver-white, radioactive metallic element which is used in the preparation of a mixture of radium and beryllium powder in neutron sources and in the treatment of cancer and other diseases

羸 léi 〈书 *fml.*〉❶ 瘦 thin; skinny: ～弱 skinny and weak; thin and weak ❷ 疲劳 tired; fatigued; weary: ～惫 tired out; exhausted

【羸顿】léidùn 〈书 *fml.*〉❶ 瘦弱困顿 feeble and tired out ❷ 疲惫困顿 tired out; exhausted

【羸弱】léiruò 〈书 *fml.*〉瘦弱 thin and weak; frail

罍 léi 〈古时 *arch.*〉一种盛酒的器具,形状像壶 ancient urn-shaped drinking vessel

儽 léi [儽儽] ☞ 累累[1](léiléi) on p. 1166

欙 léi 〈古代 *arch.*〉走山路乘坐的器具 litter; ancient carrier in climbing mountain roads

lěi (ㄌㄟˇ)

耒 lěi ❶ 古代的一种农具,形状像木叉 fork-like farm tool used in ancient China ❷〈古代 *arch.*〉农具'耒耜'上的木柄 handle of the farm tool

【耒耜】lěisì 〈古代 *arch.*〉一种像犁的农具,也用做农具的统称 plough-like farm tool used in ancient China; also a general term for farm tools

诔 lěi ❶〈古时 *arch.*〉叙述死者事迹表示哀悼(多用于上对下 oft. a junior person) pronounce a eulogy over the dead ❷ 这类哀悼死者的文章 funeral eulogy; dirge

垒[1](壘) lěi 用砖、石、土块等砌或筑 build by laying bricks, stones, earth, etc.: ～猪圈 build a pigsty | ～一道墙 build a wall | 把井口～高点 build the mouth of the well a bit higher

垒[2](壘) lěi ❶ 军营的墙壁或工事 wall of a barrack or rampart: 壁～ barrier; rampart | 深沟高～ deep ditch and high wall; strong fortifications | 两军对～ two armies pitted against each other ❷ 棒球、垒球运动的守方据点 baseball, softball base: 跑～ base running; run for a base

【垒球】lěiqiú ❶ 球类运动项目之一,球场呈直角扇形,四角各设一垒(守方据点) softball; ball game played on a field with four bases forming a diamond-shaped circuit ❷ 垒球运动使用的球,比棒球略大些。里面用丝或其他纤维缠成硬团,外面包着软皮。softball; ball used for the game, slightly larger than the baseball: it is a hard mass of silk or other fibres covered by soft rawhide

累[1](纍) lěi ❶ 积累 accumulate; pile up: 日积月～ accumulate day after day, month after month; accumulate over a long period | 成千～万 tens of thousands ❷ 屡次;连续 time and again; again and again; repeatedly; continuously: ～教不改 refuse to mend one's ways despite repeated warning | 连篇～牍 publish articles one after another; redundant; lengthy and tedious | 欢聚～日 have a happy gathering for days on end ❸ same as 垒[1] lěi

累[2] lěi 牵连 involve: 牵～ involve | 连～ implicate; get someone into trouble; involve

☞ léi on p. 1166 and lèi on p. 1170

【累次】lěicì 屡次 time and again; repeatedly: ～三番 time and again; repeatedly

【累犯】lěifàn 指被判处有期徒刑以上刑罚,服刑完毕或者赦免后,在一定期限内又犯必须判处有期徒刑以上刑罚的人 recidivist; recidivism;

criminal with old records; habitual criminal (offender); accumulative offence; person who is sentenced to another fixed-term imprisonment or more serious penalties after serving out a term

【累积】lěijī 层层增加;积聚 accumulate:～资料 accumulate data|～财富 accumulate wealth|前八个月完成的工程量～起来,已达到全年任务的90%。The work done in the first eight months amounts to ninety per cent of the annual quota.

【累及】lěijí 连累到 implicate; involve; drag in:～无辜 involve the innocent

【累计】lěijì 加起来计算;总计 total; add up; grand total:一场球打下来,～要跑几十里呢。Playing of a ball game amounts to running dozens of kilometres.

【累进】lěijìn 以某数为基数,另一数与它的比值按等差数列(如1%,2%,3%,4%)、等比数列(如1%,2%,4%,8%)或其他方式逐步增加,叫做累进 progression; sequence of numbers, each of which is obtained from its predecessor by the same rule, either by the arithmetic method (1%,2%,3%,4%) or by geometric method (1%,2%,4%,8%):～率 graduated rates |～税 progressive tax; progressive taxation

【累累】lěilěi ❶ 屡屡 again and again; many times:～失误 make repeated mistakes ❷ 形容累积得多 innumerable; countless:罪行～have a long criminal record; have committed countless crimes。

☞ léiléi on p.1166

【累卵】lěiluǎn 一层层堆起来的蛋,比喻局势极不稳定,随时可能垮台 a stack of eggs liable to collapse any moment; precarious; precarious situation:危如～ as precarious as a stack of eggs liable to collapse any moment

【累年】lěinián 连年 for years in succession; year after year:～丰收 have bumper harvests for years on end (or year after year)

【累世】lěishì 数世;接连几个世代 for many generations; generation after generation:～之功 monumental feat |～侨居海外 live abroad for many generations; reside overseas for many generations

磊 lěi ☞ below

【磊磊】lěilěi 〈书 *fml*.〉形容石头很多[heap of stones; innumerable stones]:怪石～ innumerable strange stones|～涧中石 countless stones in the brook

【磊落】lěiluò ❶ (心地)正大光明 open and upright:光明～ open and aboveboard|～的胸怀 open-hearted and upright ❷〈书 *fml*.〉多而错杂的样子 innumerable and inter-mixed; plenty of:山岳～ a lot of mountains|巨岩～,石径崎岖。There are innumerable monoliths and a rugged rocky path.

蕾 lěi 花蕾 flower bud; bud:～铃 cotton bud and boll|护苗保～ protect the seedlings and flower buds

【蕾铃】lěilíng 棉花的花蕾和棉铃 cotton bud and boll

儡 lěi ☞ 傀儡(kuǐlěi) on p.1130

藟 lěi ❶ 藤 vine:葛～ oriental grape (*Vitis flexuosa*); a variety of grapevine ❷〈书 *fml*.〉缠绕 tangle; twine ❸〈书 *fml*.〉same as 蕾 lěi

瘟 lěi 〈中医 *Chin. med*.〉指皮肤上起的小疙瘩 small swelling on the skin in Chinese traditional medicine

瘟 lěi ☞ 痞瘟 pēilěi on p.1452

灅 Lěi 古水名,上游为今桑干河,中游为今永定河,下游为今海河 ancient name of a river, its upper reaches being present-day Sanggan River, middle reaches the Yongding River and lower reaches the Haihe River

lèi (ㄌㄟˋ)

肋 lèi 胸部的侧面 rib; costal region:两～ both sides of the chest|左～ left side of the chest|右～ right side of the chest

☞ lē on p.1164

【肋骨】lèigǔ 人或高等动物胸壁两侧的长条形的骨。人有十二对肋骨,形状扁而弯,后接脊柱,前连胸骨,有保护胸腔内脏的作用。有的地区叫肋巴骨(lèi·bagǔ)或肋条。rib; long, flat bones on the two sides of the chest wall of humans or vertebrates; any of the arched bones attached posteriorly to the vertebral column and enclosing the chest cavity. In humans there are twelve pairs of such bones; known as 肋巴骨 lèi·bagǔ or 肋条 lèi·tiáo in some places; (图见 ☞ figure for 骨骼 gǔgé on p.693)

【肋膜】lèimó 胸膜 pleura

【肋条】lèi·tiáo 〈方 *dial*.〉❶ same as 肋骨 lèigǔ ❷ 作为食品的带肉的肋骨 pork ribs:～肉 spareribs

泪(淚) lèi 眼泪;泪液 tears:～痕 tear stains|～如雨下 tears falling like rain ◇烛～ melt wax running down the side of a candle after burning; guttering of a candle

【泪痕】lèihén 眼泪流过后所留下的痕迹 tear stains:满脸～ face bathed in tears

【泪花】lèihuā (～儿 lèihuār)含在眼里要流还没有流下来的泪珠 tears in one's eyes:两眼含着～ eyes with tears

【泪涟涟】lèiliánlián 形容不断流泪的样子 in

tears; tears keep coming to one's eyes

【泪人儿】lèirénr 形容哭得很厉害的人 in tears; all tears:哭得成了个～了 be all tears

【泪水】lèishuǐ 眼泪 tear; teardrop

【泪汪汪】lèiwāngwāng (～的 lèiwāngwāng·de)形容眼里充满了泪水 brimming with tears

【泪腺】lèixiàn 眼眶外上方分泌泪液的腺体,略呈椭圆形,受副交感神经纤维的支配 lachrymal gland; oval gland outside the eye socket, which, controlled by the parasympathetic nerve, produces tears

【泪眼】lèiyǎn 含着眼泪的眼睛 tearful eyes:～模糊 eyes blurred by tears

【泪液】lèiyè 眼内泪腺分泌的无色透明液体。泪液有保持眼球表面湿润,清洗眼球的作用。tear; colourless, transparent fluid secreted by the lachrymal gland, which keeps the surface of the eyeballs moist and cleans the eyeballs; 通称 generally known as 眼泪 yǎnlèi

【泪珠】lèizhū (～儿 lèizhūr)一滴一滴的眼泪 teardrop

类(類) lèi ❶ 许多相似或相同事物的综合;种类 kind; type; class; category; synthesis of many similar or identical things:分～ classify; categorize | 同～ the same kind ❷ 类似 similar; analogous:～人猿 anthropoid; ape | 画虎不成反～狗。Try to draw a tiger but end up with the likeness of a dog — attempt something too ambitious and end in failure.

【类比】lèibǐ 一种推理方法,根据两种事物在某些特征上的相似,做出它们在其他特征上也可能相似的结论。如光和声都是直线传播,有反射、折射和干扰现象等,由于声呈波动状态,因而推出光也呈波动状态。类比推理是一种或然性的推理,其结论是否正确还有待实践证明。analogy; inference from certain admitted resemblances between two or more things to a possible further similarity between them. For example, light and sound are both transmitted rectilinearly with reflection, refraction and interference. As sound moves like waves, it is therefore inferred that light also moves like waves. Analogy is an inference based on probability, whether its conclusion is correct or not is to be proved by practice.

【类别】lèibié 不同的种类;按种类的不同而做出的区别 classification; category:这一章讨论土壤的～。This chapter discusses the classification of soil. | ～一栏中填写商品种类的名称。Fill the names of the different kinds of commodities in the category column.

【类固醇】lèigùchún 甾 steroids

【类乎】lèi·hu 好像;近于 seem; be like:这个故事很离奇,～神话。This fantastic story sounds like a fairy tale.

【类群】lèiqún 具有某些共同特性的动植物群体(多指同一物种中再细分的不同种类) fauna or flora; animal or plant group with common characteristics (which can be further classified)

【类人猿】lèirényuán 外貌和举动较其他猿类更像人的猿类,如猩猩、黑猩猩、大猩猩、长臂猿等 anthropoid (ape); any of certainly highly developed primates resembling a human, as the chimpanzee, gorilla, orangutan, gibbon, etc.

【类书】lèishū 摘录各种书上有关的材料并依照内容分门别类地编排起来以备检索的书籍,例如《太平御览》、《古今图书集成》reference book with entries arranged in the form of a dictionary or according to subjects; book class of works combining to some extent the characteristics of encyclopaedias and concordances, embracing the whole field of literature, methodically arranged according to subjects, and each heading giving extracts from former works on the subject in question, e. g. *Imperial Digest of the Taiping Reign* and the *Compendium of Ancient and Modern Books*

【类似】lèisì 大致相像 similar (to); analogous (to):找出犯错误的原因,避免再犯～的错误 find out the cause of the mistake and avoid making a similar mistake again

【类同】lèitóng 大致相同 roughly the same; alike; similar:样式～ similar in style

【类推】lèituī 比照某一事物的道理推出跟它同类的其他事物的道理 analogize; reason by analogy:照此～ on the analogy of this | 其余～ reason out the rest by analogy

【类新星变星】lèixīnxīng biànxīng 类似新星的变星。类新星变星的亮度是突然变亮的,光谱性质和新星在某一变化时期的光谱一样。nova-like variable; variable that suddenly increases its brightness, with the same spectrum as that of a nova over a certain period

【类型】lèixíng 具有共同特征的事物所形成的种类 type; category

累 lèi ❶ 疲劳 tired; weary; fatigued:越干越有劲儿,一点儿也不觉得～。The more I work, the more energetic I am. I feel not at all tired. ❷ 使疲劳;使劳累 tire; wear out; strain:眼睛刚好,别～着它。The eyes have just recovered. Don't strain them. | 这件事别人做不了,还得～你。Since no one else can do it, I have to bother you. ❸ 操劳 work hard; toil:～了一天,该休息了。After working hard all day, you need a rest.

☞ léi on p.1166 and lěi on p.1168

酹 lèi 〈书 *fml.*〉把酒浇在地上,表示祭奠 offer libation to; ritual of pouring out wine upon the ground as a sacrifice to (a god or an ancestor)

擂 lèi 擂台 platform for martial contests; arena:打～ accept an challenge to join in a contest for supremacy in martial arts

☞ léi on p.1168

【擂台】lèitái 原指为比武所搭的台子。'摆擂台'指搭了台欢迎人来比武，'打擂台'是上擂台参加比武。现比赛中多用'摆擂台'比喻向人挑战，用'打擂台'比喻应战。platform for martial contests; ring; arena: 摆擂台 bǎi lèitái means putting up a platform and challenging anyone to join in a contest; 打擂台 dǎ lèitái means accepting the challenge to join in the contest. In the modern sense, 摆擂台 means giving a challenge, and 打擂台 means accepting a challenge.

颣 lèi 〈书 *fml.*〉缺点；毛病 shortcomings; defects; faults; mistakes; errors: 疵～ defects and faults

·lei（·ㄌㄟ）

嘞 ·lei 〈助词 *aux.*〉用法跟'喽'②相似，语气更轻快些 used in the same way as 喽·lou ②, but with a little more airy effect: 好～，我就去。All right, I'm going. | 雨不下了，走～！It has stopped raining. Let's go!
☞ lē on p. 1164

lēng（ㄌㄥ）

棱 lēng ☞ 红不棱登 hóng·bulēngdēng on p. 802，花不棱登 huā·bulēngdēng on p. 826 and 扑棱 pū·leng (pūlēng) on p. 1497
☞ léng on p. 1171 and líng on p. 1231

愣 lēng 〈拟声词 *onom.*〉形容纺车等转动的声音 sound of turning a spinning frame: 纺车～～转得欢。The spinning frame is working cheerfully.

léng（ㄌㄥˊ）

崚 léng [崚嶒] (léngcéng) 〈书 *fml.*〉形容山高 highness of a mountain

塄 léng 〈方 *dial.*〉田地边上的坡儿 slope of an edge of a field

【塄坎】léngkǎn 〈方 *dial.*〉田地边上的坡儿和田埂子 slopes of edges and ridges of fields

棱（稜） léng（～儿 léngr）❶ 物体上不同方向的两个平面连接的部分 arris; edge; edge made by two straight or curved surfaces coming together at an angle: 见～见角 angular | 桌子～儿 edges of a table ❷ 物体上条状的突起部分 ridges on an object: 瓦～ rows of tiles on a roof; corrugated | 搓板的～儿 ridges of a washboard
☞ lēng on p. 1171 and líng on p. 1231

【棱角】léngjiǎo ❶ 棱和角 edges and corners: 河沟里的石头多半没有～。Most of the stones in the river have no edges. ❷ 〈比喻 *fig.*〉显露出来的锋芒 pointedness: 他很有心计，但表面不露～。He is very good at scheming, but he keeps a low profile superficially.

【棱镜】léngjìng 用透明材料做成的多面体光学器件，在光学仪器中用来把复合光分解成光谱或用来改变光线的方向。常见的是三棱镜。prism; polyhedral optical instrument made of transparent material, usu. a triangular prism, which is used to disperse the compound light (white light) into a rainbow of colours, called a spectrum, or to change the direction of the light

【棱坎】léngkǎn 〈方 *dial.*〉same as 塄坎 léngkǎn

【棱台】léngtái 棱锥的底面和平行于底面的一个截面间的部分，叫做棱台 frustum of a pyramid; part of a pyramid between the base and a section parallel to the base

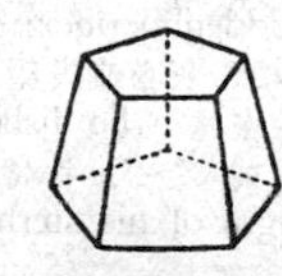
棱台 Frustum of a Pyramid

【棱柱】léngzhù 两个底面是平行的全等多边形，侧面都是平行四边形的多面体 prism; polyhedron with its two bases being equal congruent polygons, and all its sides being parallelograms

【棱锥】léngzhuī 一个多边形和若干个同一顶点的三角形所围成的多面体 pyramid; polyhedron having a polygonal base, the sides of which form the bases of triangular surfaces meeting at a common vertex

【棱子】léng·zi 〈方 *dial.*〉same as 棱 léng ①: 木头～ wood angle

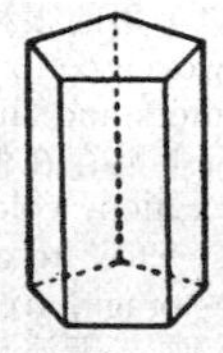
棱柱 Prism

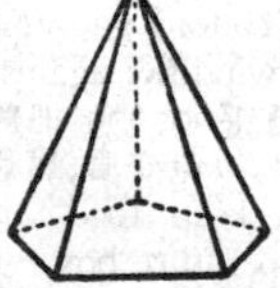
棱锥 Pyamid

楞 léng same as 棱(léng)

薐 léng ☞ 菠薐菜 (bōléngcài) on p. 147

lěng（ㄌㄥˇ）

冷 lěng ❶ 温度低；感觉温度低（跟'热'相对 as opposed to 'hot'）cold: ～水 cold water | 现在还不算～，雪后才～呢。It's not cold yet. It will be cold after it snows. | 你～不～？Do you feel cold? ❷ 〈方 *dial.*〉使冷（多指食物）cool (oft. of food): 太烫了，～一下再吃。It's too hot. Let it cool off before you take it. ❸ 不热情；不温和 cold in manner; frosty: ～言～语 sarcastic comments; ironical remarks | ～～地说了声'好吧'。He said coldly, 'All right.' ❹ 寂静；不热闹 unfrequented; deserted; out-of-the-way: ～落 unfrequented; deserted; cold-shoulder someone; treat someone coldly|～清清 desolate; deserted and quiet ❺ 生僻;少见的 strange; rare:～僻 out-of-the-way; secluded ❻ 不受欢迎的;没人过问的 receiving little attention; unwelcome:～货 goods in little demand|～门 unexpected winner; pull an upset; goods in not much demand ❼ 乘人不备的;暗中的;突然的 shot from hiding; unexpected:～箭 unexpected arrow shot; arrow shot from hiding|～枪 gun shot from hiding; sniper's shot|～不防 suddenly; unexpectedly; by surprise ❽〈比喻 *fig.*〉灰心或失望 disheartened; disappointed:心灰意～ be disheartened|看到他严厉的目光,我的心～了半截。I felt disheartened at the sight of his stern eyes. ❾(Lěng)姓 a surname

【冷板凳】lěngbǎndèng ☞ 坐冷板凳 zuò lěngbǎndèng on p.2577

【冷冰冰】lěngbīngbīng (～的 lěngbīngbīng·de) ❶ 形容不热情或不温和 cold in manner; frosty:～的脸色 cold expression; frosty looks ❷ 形容物体很冷 (of objects) ice-cold; icy:～的石凳 icy stone bench

【冷不丁】lěng·budīng〈方 *dial.*〉same as 冷不防 lěng·bufáng:～吓了一跳 be started unexpectedly

【冷不防】lěng·bufáng 没有预料到;突然 suddenly; unexpectedly; without warning; by surprise:～摔了一跤 fall suddenly

【冷布】lěngbù 防蚊蝇、糊窗户等用的很稀疏的布 (cotton) gauze; loosely woven cotton cloth for windows against mosquitoes and flies

【冷藏】lěngcáng 把食物、药品等贮存在低温设备里,以免变质、腐烂 refrigeration; cold storage; keep food, medicines, etc. in a low-temperature box:～库 cold storage; freezer

【冷场】lěng//chǎng ❶ 戏剧、曲艺等演出时因演员迟到或忘记台词造成的场面 awkward silence on the stage when an actor enters late or forgets his lines ❷ 开会时没有人发言的局面 awkward silence at a meeting

【冷嘲热讽】lěng cháo rè fěng 尖刻的嘲笑和讥讽 with freezing irony and burning satire; with biting sarcasm

【冷处理】lěngchǔlǐ ❶ 工件淬火后立即放进低温空气(0—80℃)中,叫做冷处理。工件经过冷处理以后,其机械性能较高,规格比较稳定。cold treatment; put a work-piece immediately into low-temperature (0-80℃) air after quenching so that its mechanical property is better and more stable ❷〈比喻 *fig.*〉事情发生后暂时搁置起来,等适当机会再作处理 shelve sth. that has happened for later treatment at a proper time

【冷床】lěngchuáng 农业上指避风、向阳、保温而不进行人工加温的苗床。适用于不太寒冷的地区。cold bed; cold frame; unheated seedling bed used in warmer areas

L

【冷淡】lěngdàn ❶ 不热闹;不兴盛 not brisk; slack; desolate:生意～。The trade is slack. ❷ 不热情;不亲热;不关心 cold; indifferent:态度～ indifferent attitude ❸ 使受到冷淡的待遇 treat coldly; cold-shoulder; slight:他强打着精神说话,怕～了朋友。He forced himself to perk up and keep the conversation going for fear that his friend would feel he'd been cold-shouldered.

【冷碟儿】lěngdiér〈方 *dial.*〉凉碟儿 cold dish; hors d'oeuvres

【冷丁】lěngdīng〈方 *dial.*〉same as 冷不防 lěng·bufáng:～地从草丛里跳出一只兔子来。Suddenly, a rabbit jumped out of the grass.

【冷冻】lěngdòng 降低温度使肉、鱼等所含的水分凝固 freeze:～设备 freezing equipment|把鲜菜～起来 freeze the fresh vegetables

【冷风】lěngfēng〈比喻 *fig.*〉背地里散布的消极言论 cold wind-rumour; gossip:吹～ spread rumour (or gossip)|刮～ spread rumour

【冷锋】lěngfēng 冷气团插入暖气团的底部,并推着暖气团向前移动,在这种情况下,冷、暖气团接触的地带叫做冷锋 cold front; forward edge of a cold air mass advancing under a warmer air mass

【冷敷】lěngfū 用冰袋或冷水浸湿的毛巾放在身体的局部以降低温度、减轻疼痛或炎症 cold compress; put an ice bag or a cold wet towel on a certain part of the body to reduce the temperature and alleviate pain or inflammation

【冷宫】lěnggōng 戏曲、旧小说中指君主安置失宠的后妃的地方,现在比喻存放不用的东西的地方 (in Chinese operas and old novels) cold palace — place to which disfavoured queens and concubines were banished; limbo; place where the idle goods are deposited:打入～ put sth. in the limbo; put sth. on the back shelf

【冷光】lěngguāng ❶ 指荧光和磷光,因为这种光线所含的热量极少,所以叫冷光 cold light; light not accompanied by the heat of combustion or incandescence, as fluorescent light and phosphorescent light ❷ 指冷酷严峻的目光 cold and stern look:眼里闪烁着逼人的～。His eyes glistened with a threatening look.

【冷柜】lěngguì 冰柜 freezer

【冷害】lěnghài 由于气温降低,使某些植物体遭受的破坏或死亡 damage to plants caused by a sudden drop in temperature

【冷汗】lěnghàn 由惊恐或休克等原因而出的汗,出汗时手足发冷,所以叫冷汗 cold sweat; sweat caused by fear or shock, accompanied by cold limbs

【冷荤】lěnghūn 荤的凉菜 cold meat; cold buffet

【冷货】lěnghuò 不容易卖出去的货物 unmarketable goods; goods in little demand; also 冷门货 lěngménhuò

【冷寂】lěngjì 清冷而寂静 cold and still:～的秋夜 cold and still autumn night

【冷加工】lěngjiāgōng 指对在常温下的金属进行加工 cold working (of metal in normal temperature)

【冷箭】lěngjiàn 乘人不备暗中射出的箭。也用来比喻暗地里害人的手段。arrow shot from hiding; sniper's shot; (fig.) hidden means of hurting sb.

【冷噤】lěngjìn 冷战;寒噤 shiver:打了个～ shiver with cold

【冷静】lěngjìng ❶ 人少而静;不热闹 (of a place) quiet:夜深了,街上显得很～。It's late in the night, and the street was evidently very quiet. ❷ 沉着而不感情用事 keep one's cool; sober; calm:头脑～ sober-minded; cool-headed; level-headed|～下来,好好儿想想。Calm down and think it over.

【冷峻】lěngjùn 冷酷严峻;沉着而严肃 grave and stern:神色～ grave and stern expression|～的目光 grave and stern look

【冷库】lěngkù 冷藏食物或药品的仓库 cold storage; storage for keeping frozen foods or medicines; also 冷藏库 lěngcángkù

【冷酷】lěngkù (待人)冷淡苛刻 unfeeling; callous; grim:～无情 unfeeling; cold-blooded

【冷厉】lěnglì 冷峻严厉 grave and stern:～的目光 grave and stern look

【冷脸子】lěngliǎn·zi 冷淡的脸色;不温和的脸色 cold face; severe expression

【冷落】lěngluò ❶ 不热闹 unfrequented; desolate:门庭～ unfrequented house|过去这里很～,现在变得很热闹了。It was very desolate here in the past. Now it has become very busy. ❷ 使受到冷淡的待遇 treat coldly; cold-shoulder; leave out in the cold:别～了他。Don't give him a cold shoulder.|受到～ be cold-shouldered

【冷门】lěngmén (～儿 lěngménr)原指赌博时很少有人下注的一门。现比喻很少有人从事的、不时兴的工作、事业等。(of gambling) stake to which few people choose to place a bet; (fig.) profession, trade or branch of learning that receives little attention; rarefied undertaking, programme, etc.:过去地质学是～儿。In the past, geology was a branch of learning that received little attention.

【冷漠】lěngmò (对人或事物)冷淡,不关心 cold and detached; unconcerned; indifferent:神情～ indifferent expression; indifferent look|～的态度 indifferent attitude

【冷凝】lěngníng 气体或液体遇冷而凝结,如水蒸气遇冷变成水,水遇冷变成冰 condensation; change of a gas or a liquid after becoming cold, e. g. steam changes to water or water changes to ice after it becomes cold

【冷暖】lěngnuǎn 寒冷和温暖。泛指人的生活起居。cold and warm; day-to-day life:关心群众的～ be concerned with the livelihood of the masses

【冷盘】lěngpán (～儿 lěngpánr)盛在盘子里的凉菜(多作下酒用 oft. served with wine) cold dish; hors d'oeuvres

【冷僻】lěngpì ❶ 冷落偏僻 deserted; out-of-the-way:地段～ deserted section of an area|～的山乡 out-of-the-way mountain village ❷ 不常见的(字、名称、典故、书籍等)(words, names, allusions, books, etc.) rare; unfamiliar:～字 rarely used word

【冷气】lěngqì ❶ 利用制冷设备,把空气冷却,通入建筑物、交通工具等内部,以降低其温度。所通的冷却的空气叫做冷气。air conditioning; method of cooling the air by means of cooling equipment to keep its humidity and temperature at desired levels in buildings, cars, etc. ❷ 通常也指上述设备 usually also such equipment

【冷气团】lěngqìtuán 一种移动的气团,本身的温度比到达区域的地面温度低,多在极地和西伯利亚大陆上形成 cold air mass; moving air mass with its temperature lower than the ground temperature in an area it reaches, mostly formed at the polar regions and the Siberian continent

【冷枪】lěngqiāng 乘人不备暗中射出的枪弹 sniper's shot:打～ fire a sniper's shot; snipe; stab in one's back

【冷峭】lěngqiào ❶ 形容冷气逼人 biting cold:北风～。The northern wind is biting. ❷ 形容态度严峻,话语尖刻 scathing remarks

【冷清】lěng·qing 冷静而凄凉 cold and cheerless; desolate; lonely; deserted:冷冷清清 very quiet|～的深夜 be quiet late at night|后山游人少,显得很～。The backside of the hill is less visited and looks very quiet.

【冷清清】lěngqīngqīng (～的 lěngqīngqīng·de)形容冷落、幽静、凄凉、寂寞 deserted; quiet; desolate; solitary; lonely:～的小巷 deserted lane; quiet lane|～的月色 quiet moonlight|通跨院儿的月亮门～地开着。The moon gate to the courtyard is quietly open.

【冷泉】lěngquán 温度在当地年平均气温以下的泉水 cold spring; spring, the water of which is colder than the annual average temperature in the local area

【冷却】lěngquè 物体的温度降低或使物体的温度降低 cool; become cool; make cool

【冷热病】lěngrèbìng ❶〈方 *dial.*〉same as 疟疾 nüè·ji ❷〈比喻 *fig.*〉情绪忽高忽低 blow cold and hot; capricious changes in mood

【冷若冰霜】lěng ruò bīng shuāng 形容人不热情、不温和。也形容态度严肃,使人不易接近。be as cold as ice; have a cold (icy or chilly)

manner

【冷色】lěngsè 给人以凉爽的感觉的颜色,如白、绿、蓝 cool colours, as white, green, blue; colour that gives someone a feeling of coolness

【冷森森】lěngsēnsēn (～的 lěngsēnsēn·de)形容寒气逼人 cold; chilly; chilling:山洞里～的。It's very cold (or chilly) inside the cave.

【冷杉】lěngshān 常绿乔木,茎高大,树皮灰色,小枝红褐色,有光泽,叶子条形,果实椭圆形,暗紫色。木材可制器具。fir (*Abies*); evergreen tree with a tall trunk, grey bark, lustrous red-brown twigs, flattened single needles and dark purple oval fruits; also 枞 cōng

【冷食】lěngshí 凉的食品,大多是甜的,如冰棍儿、冰淇淋等 cold snacks, mostly sweet, such as popsicle, ice-cream, etc.:病人忌～。Patients should avoid cold snacks.

【冷水】lěngshuǐ ❶ 凉水 cold water:泼～ pour cold water on; dampen the enthusiasm of|～浇头(比喻受到意外的打击或希望突然破灭) cold water pouring on one's head; splashing the head with cold water; (fig.) rude shock or a bitter disappointment ❷ 生水 unboiled water:喝～容易得病。If you drink unboiled water, you're likely to get sick.

【冷丝丝】lěngsīsī (～的 lěngsīsī·de)形容有点儿冷 a bit chilly; also 冷丝儿丝儿的 lěngsīrsīr·de

【冷飕飕】lěngsōusōu (～的 lěngsōusōu·de)形容很冷(of wind) cold; chilling; chilly

【冷烫】lěngtàng 烫发的一种方法,用药水而不用热能,所以叫冷烫 cold perm; (of hair style) permanent wave produced by applying chemical preparations

【冷笑】lěngxiào 含有讽刺、不满意、无可奈何、不屑于、不以为然等意味或怒意的笑 sneer; laugh grimly; grin with dissatisfaction, helplessness, bitterness, anger, etc.:嘴角挂着一丝～。There was a sneer in the corner of his mouth.

【冷血动物】lěngxuè dòngwù ❶ 变温动物的俗称 cold-blooded animal; poikilothermal animal ❷〈比喻 *fig.*〉没有感情的人 unfeeling person; coldhearted person

【冷言冷语】lěng yán lěng yǔ 含有讥讽意味的冷冰冰的话 sarcastic comments; ironical remarks

【冷眼】lěngyǎn ❶ 冷静客观的态度 with a calm and objective attitude; (with) a cold eye; (with) cool detachment:他坐在墙角里,～观察来客的言谈举止。He sat in a corner, watching with a cold eye how the guests were conducting themselves. ❷ 冷淡的待遇 cold shoulder:～相待 give someone the cold shoulder

【冷眼旁观】lěng yǎn páng guān 用冷静或冷淡的态度从旁观看(多指可以参加而不愿意参加)(unwilling to take part in sth. while one should) look on with a cold eye

【冷饮】lěngyǐn 凉的饮料,大多是甜的,如汽水、酸梅汤等 cold drinks, mostly sweet, as soda water, sweet-sour plum juice, etc.

【冷语冰人】lěng yǔ bīng rén 用尖酸刻薄的话伤害人 hurt sb. with sarcastic remarks

【冷遇】lěngyù 冷淡的待遇 letdown; cold shoulder:遭到～ be given the cold shoulder; be left out in the cold

【冷战】lěngzhàn 指国际间进行的战争形式之外的敌对行动 cold war; international hostile activities other than an actual war

【冷战】lěng·zhan 因寒冷或害怕浑身突然发抖 shiver:打了一个～ shiver with cold; also 冷颤 lěng·zhan

【冷字】lěngzì 冷僻的字 rarely used word; unfamiliar word

lèng(ㄌㄥˋ)

堎 lèng 长头堎(Chángtóulèng),地名,在江西 Changtouleng, geographical name of a place in Jiangxi Province

愣 lèng ❶ 失神;呆 dumbfounded; stupefied; dazed:发～ be in a trance; be in a daze; stare blankly|他～了半天没说话。He remained in a daze for a long time, without saying a word. ❷ 说话做事不考虑效果;鲁莽 rash; blunt; brusque:～小子 brusque young guy ❸〈方 *dial.*〉偏偏;偏要 insist on:明知不对,他～那么做。He knew it was wrong, but he insisted on doing it.

【愣神儿】lèng//shénr〈方 *dial.*〉发呆;发愣 stare blankly; be in a daze

【愣头愣脑】lèng tóu lèng nǎo 形容鲁莽冒失的样子 rash; impetuous; reckless

【愣头儿青】lèngtóurqīng〈方 *dial.*〉指鲁莽的人 brusque guy; rash fellow; hothead

【愣怔】lèng·zheng same as 睖睁 lèng·zheng

睖 lèng〈方 *dial.*〉睁大眼睛注视,表示不满意 stare blankly:她狠狠地～了他一眼。She stared hard at him.

【睖睁】lèng·zheng ❶ 发呆地直视 stare blankly:～着眼睛 look steadily and intently with eyes wide open ❷ 发愣 be in a trance; be in a daze; stare blankly ‖ also 愣怔 lèng·zheng

lī(ㄌㄧ)

哩 lī ☞ below

☞ lǐ on p. 1180, ·li on p. 1193 and yīnglǐ on p. 2298

【哩哩啦啦】lī·lilālā 零零散散或断断续续的样子 scattered; sporadic:他不会挑水,～洒了一地。He couldn't carry water with a shoulder pole, and splashed it all over the ground.|雨很大,客人～的直到中午还没到齐。It rained heavily. The guests came in dribs and drabs; not until after twelve were they all present.

【哩哩啰啰】lī·liluōluō 形容说话啰唆不清楚 verbose and unclear in speech; rambling and indistinct

【哩溜歪斜】līliùwāixié (～的 līliùwāixiéde)〈方 *dial*.〉❶ 歪歪扭扭;不正 crooked; askew; twisted:他的字写得～的。He has poor handwriting. *or* He writes a poor hand. ❷(走路)左右摇摆 stagger:这个醉汉～的走过来。The drunkard came along, staggering.

lí(ㄌㄧˊ)

杝 lí〈书 *fml*.〉same as 篱[2] lí
☞ 杝 duò on p.502

丽(麗) lí ❶ 丽水(Líshuǐ),地名,在浙江 Lishui, geographical name of a place in Zhejiang Province ❷ 高丽(Gāolí),朝鲜历史上的王朝,我国过去沿用指朝鲜 Korea; Koryo Dynasty in the history of Korea
☞ lì on p.1189

厘(釐) lí ❶(某些计量单位的)百分之一 (of measuring units) centi-:～米 centimetre; cm.|～升 centilitre ❷ 计量单位名称 *li*, a measuring unit a)长度,10 毫等于 1 厘,10 厘等于 1 分 length, with 10 *hao* equal to 1 *li*, with 10 *li* equal to 1 *fen* b)重量,10 毫等于 1 厘,10 厘等于 1 分 weight, with 10 *hao* equal to 1 *li*, 10 *li* equal to 1 *fen* c)地积,10 厘等于 1 分 area, with 10 *li* equal to 1 *fen* d)利率,年利率 1 厘是每年百分之一,月利率 1 厘是每月千分之一 interest rate, in annual rate with 1 *li* equal to 1 per cent per annum, and in monthly rate with 1 *li* equal to 0.1 per cent per month ❸〈书 *fml*.〉整理;治理 put in good order; rectify; regulate; collate
釐 lí ☞ 禧 xǐ on p.2055

【厘定】lídìng〈书 *fml*.〉整理规定 collate and stipulate (rules and regulations, etc.):重新～规章制度 reformulate rules and regulations

【厘金】líjīn〈旧时 *old*〉在内地交通要道对过往货物征收的税,清咸丰年间为镇压太平天国革命运动筹措军费而设,民国二十年改定税制时撤消 taxes levied on goods transported from one place to another in inland China. The taxes were imposed during the reign of Emperor Xianfeng of the Qing Dynasty as a way to raise military funds for cracking down on the Taiping Revolution (1851-1864) and abolished in the tax reform in 1930; also 厘捐 líjuān or 厘金税 líjīnshuì

【厘正】lízhèng〈书 *fml*.〉订正 correct; revise:～遗文 make corrections to a will

狸 lí ☞ below

【狸猫】límāo same as 豹猫 bàomāo

【狸子】lí·zi same as 豹猫 bàomāo

离[1](離) lí ❶ 分离;离开 leave; part from; be away from:～别 part|悲欢～合 joys and sorrows, partings and reunions; vicissitudes|貌合神～ be seemingly united but actually divided at heart; be superficially in harmony but actually at variance|他～家已经两年了。He's been away from home for two years. ❷ same as 距离 jùlí ①:我们村～车站很近。Our village is very close to the railway station.|～国庆节只有十天了。It's only ten days away from National Day. ❸ 缺少 short of; without:发展工业～不了钢铁。Industry cannot develop without steel. ❹(Lí)姓 a surname

离[2](離) lí 八卦之一,卦形是'☲',代表火 one of the Eight Diagrams, its form being '☲', representing fire; ☞ 八卦 bāguà on p.22

【离别】líbié 比较长久地跟熟悉的人或地方分开 part with a familiar person or from a familiar place for a longish period; leave; bid farewell:三天之后咱们就要～了。We'll part with each other in three days.|～母校已经两年了。It's two years since I left my old school.

【离愁】líchóu 离别的愁苦 sorrow of parting; pain of separation:～别绪(离别的愁苦心情) sorrows of parting

【离岛】lídǎo 指大岛屿周围的小岛 islets surrounding an island

【离队】lí//duì 脱离队伍;离开岗位 leave the ranks; leave one's post:不得擅自～。Don't leave your post without permission.

【离格儿】lí//gér(讲话或做事)不合公认的准则 go beyond what is proper; be out of place:你办的这事儿也太～了。What you've done is quite out of place.

【离宫】lígōng 帝王在都城之外的宫殿,也泛指皇帝出巡时的住所 temporary abode for an emperor on progresses (official tours)

【离合】líhé 分离和聚会 separation and reunion:～无常 unpredictable seperation and reunion|悲欢～ joys and sorrows, partings and reunions

【离合器】líhéqì 汽车、拖拉机以及其他机器上的一种装置。用离合器连接的两个轴或两个零件通过操纵系统可以结合或分开。clutch; device fitted on an automobile, tractor or other machines for controlling the driving shaft

【离婚】lí//hūn 依照法定手续解除婚姻关系 divorce; legal and formal dissolution of a marriage

【离间】líjiàn 从中挑拨使不团结、不和睦 sow discord; drive a wedge between; set one party against another:挑拨～ sow discord

【离解】líjiě 在可逆反应中,分子分解为离子、原子、原子团或较简单的分子。如醋酸分解成氢离子和醋酸根离子,碳酸钙分解成氧化钙和二氧化碳。dissociation; in a reversible reaction, a molecule is dissociated into ions, atoms, atomic groups or simpler molecules. For example, acetic acid is dissociated into hydrogen ion and acetate ion, and calcium carbonate is dissociated into calcium oxide and carbon dioxide

【离经叛道】lí jīng pàn dào 原指不遵循经书所说的道理,背离儒家的道统。现多比喻背离占主导地位的思想或传统。disobey the creeds laid down in the classics and eschew the Confucian tradition; depart from the classics and rebel against orthodoxy; rebel against orthodox teachings

【离开】lí//kāi 跟人、物或地方分开 leave; depart from; deviate from: 离得开 can go away from; can do without | 离不开 can't go away from; can't do without | 鱼～了水就不能活。Fish cannot live without water. | 他已经～北京了。He has left Beijing.

【离乱】líluàn 乱离 separation and war: 八年～eight years of separation and war | ～中更觉友情的可贵。One finds friendship even more valuable when in separation and turmoil.

【离叛】lípàn 叛离 rebel

【离谱】lí//pǔ (～儿 lí//pǔr) same as 离格儿 lí//gér: 说话～ speak off the beam

【离奇】líqí 不平常;出人意料 strange; odd; fantastic; bizarre: 情节～ bizarre plot | ～古怪 bizarre and strange | ～的故事 fantastic story

【离弃】líqì 离开,抛弃(工作、地点、人等) abandon; desert; forsake

【离情】líqíng 离别的情怀 sad feelings at parting: ～别绪 sorrows of parting

【离群索居】lí qún suǒ jū 离开同伴而过孤独的生活 live in solitude; live all alone

【离散】lísàn 分散不能团聚(多指亲属) be separated from one another; be dispersed, be scattered about: 家人～ The family were separated and scattered about.

【离索】lísuǒ〈书 *fml.*〉因分居而孤独;离散 desolate and lonely: ～之感 feelings of separation

【离题】lí//tí (文章或议论的内容)离开主题 digress from the subject; stray from the point: ～万里 far from the topic | 他说着说着就离了题。He departed from the subject as he spoke.

【离析】líxī〈书 *fml.*〉❶ 分离;离散 disintegrate: 分崩～ fall to pieces; come apart; disintegrate ❷ 分析;辨析 analyze

【离弦走板儿】lí xián zǒu bǎnr〈比喻 *fig.*〉说话或做事偏离公认的准则 off the standard; off the beam

【离乡背井】lí xiāng bèi jǐng 背井离乡 leave one's homeland; leave one's native place

【离心】líxīn ❶ 跟集体或领导不是一条心 be at odds with the community or the leadership: ～离德 disunity ❷ 离开中心 centrifugal: ～力 centrifugal force | ～作用 centrifugal effects

【离心离德】lí xīn lí dé 集体中的人不是一条心,不团结 torn by dissension and discord; (of a collective) each going his own way; lack of unity; disunity

【离心力】líxīnlì 物体沿曲线运动或作圆周运动时所产生的离开中心的力 (phys.) centrifugal force

【离休】líxiū 具有一定资历、符合规定条件的老年干部离职休养 (of veteran cadres who joined the Chinese revolution before October 1, 1949) retire: ～老干部 retired veteran cadres | 干部～制度 retirement system for veteran cadres who joined the Chinese revolution before October 1, 1949

【离异】líyì same as 离婚 lí//hūn

【离辙】lí//zhé〈比喻 *fig.*〉离开了正确的道路或正题 off the track; off the beam; off the point; depart from the subject

【离职】lí//zhí ❶ 暂时离开职位 leave one's job temporarily: ～学习 leave one's job and attend a study course ❷ 离开工作岗位,不再回来 leave one's job forever

【离子】lízǐ 原子或原子团失去或得到电子后叫做离子。失去电子的带正电荷,叫正离子(或阳离子);得到电子的带负电荷,叫负离子(或阴离子)。ion; electrically charged atom or group of atoms, the electrical charge of which results when a neutral atom or group of atoms loses or gains one or more electrons during chemical reactions, by the action of certain forms of radiant energy, etc.; the loss of electrons results in a positively charged ion (cation), the gain of electrons results in a negatively charged ion (anion)

【离子键】lízǐjiàn 正离子和负离子之间通过静电作用形成的化学键,如氯化钠(NaCl)分子中钠离子(Na^+)和氯离子(Cl^-)之间的键 ionic bond; electrovalent bond; chemical bond between two oppositely charged ions formed when one atom transfers electrons to another atom, as the bond between the sodium ion and (Na^+) chloride ion (Cl^-) in the formation of sodium chloride (NaCl); also 电价键 diànjiàjiàn

骊(驪) lí〈书 *fml.*〉纯黑色的马 black horse

【骊歌】lígē〈书 *fml.*〉告别的歌 farewell song

缅(纚) lí ☞ [绯缅] (línlí) on p. 1223 ☞ xǐ on p. 2054

梩 lí〈书 *fml.*〉锹一类的器具 tool like a spade

梨(棃) lí ❶ 梨树,落叶乔木或灌木,叶子卵形,花一般白色。果实是普通水果。品种很多。pear (*Pyrus spp.*); deciduous tree or shrub with ovate leaves, white blossoms and common fruits found in a great variety ❷ 这种植物的果实。有的地区也叫梨子。fruit of such plant; also called 梨子 lí·zi in some areas

【梨膏】lígāo 用梨汁和蜜制成的膏,有止咳作用 pear syrup (for the relief of coughs)

【梨园】Líyuán 据说唐玄宗曾教乐工、宫女在'梨园'演习音乐舞蹈。后来沿用梨园为戏院或戏曲界的别称。Pear Garden; theatre. It is said that Emperor Xuanzong of the Tang Dynasty (618-907) asked musicians and maids to rehearse music and dance in the Pear Garden and later it became a reference to the theatre or the theatre world:～界 the theatre

【梨园戏】líyuánxì 福建地方戏曲剧种之一,流行于该省南部地区 Pear Garden Opera; local opera popular in the southern part of Fujian Province

【梨园子弟】líyuán zǐdì 旧称戏曲演员 (old) opera actors; students of the Pear Garden; also 梨园弟子 líyuán dìzǐ

犁(犂) lí ❶ 翻土用的农具,有许多种,用畜力或机器(如拖拉机)牵引 plough:一张～ a plough ❷ 用犁耕地 work with a plough; plough:～田 plough fields

【犁铧】líhuá 安装在犁的下端,用来翻土的铁器,略呈三角形 ploughshare; share; triangular piece of iron fitted at the lower end as part of a plough that cuts the soil; also 铧 huá

【犁镜】líjìng 犁上的零件,是用铸铁或钢制成的一块弯板。安在犁铧上方,并向一侧倾斜,表面光滑,作用是把犁起的上翻在一边。mouldboard; curved plate of iron attached to a ploughshare for turning over soil

【犁牛】líniú 〈方 *dial.*〉耕牛 farm cattle

【犁杖】lí·zhang 〈方 *dial.*〉犁 plough

鹂(鸝) lí ☞ 黄鹂 huánglí on p. 852

喱 lí ☞ [咖喱] (gālí) on p. 618

剺 lí〈书 *fml.*〉用刀划 cut with a knife

蓠(蘺) lí ☞ 江蓠 jiānglí on p. 959

蜊 lí ☞ [蛤蜊] (gé·lí) on p. 654

鸳 lí same as 鹂 lí

漓¹ lí ☞ 淋漓 línlí on p. 1223

漓²(灕) Lí 漓江,水名,在广西 Lijiang River in Guangxi

缡(褵) lí〈古时 *arch.*〉妇女的佩巾 veil used by women: 结～ bridal veil (〈古时 *arch.*〉指女子出嫁 marry off)

璃(瓈) lí ☞ 玻璃 bō·lí on p. 146, 琉璃 (liú·lí) on p. 1244

嫠 lí〈书 *fml.*〉寡妇 widow

【嫠妇】lífù〈书 *fml.*〉same as 寡妇 guǎfù

犛 lí 牦牛 yak

蒺 lí ☞ [蒺藜] (jí·lí) same as 蒺藜 jí·lí

黎 lí ❶〈书 *fml.*〉众 multitude:～民 the masses ❷〈书 *fml.*〉黑 black; dark:～黑 black; dark ❸ (Lí) 姓 a surname

【黎黑】líhēi same as 黧黑 líhēi

【黎锦】líjǐn 黎族人民织的一种锦,上面有人物花鸟等图案 brocade woven by the people of the Li nationality

【黎民】límín〈书 *fml.*〉百姓;民众 common people; multitude

【黎明】límíng 天快要亮或刚亮的时候 dawn; daybreak:～即起 rise at dawn; get up at dawn|～时分 at dawn

【黎庶】líshù〈书 *fml.*〉百姓;民众 common people; masses

【黎族】Lízú 我国少数民族之一,主要分布在海南 Lis, minority ethnic people inhabiting Hainan Province

鲡(鱺) lí ☞ 鳗鲡 (mánlí) on p. 1298

罹 lí〈书 *fml.*〉遭遇;遭受(灾祸或疾病) suffer from; meet with:～祸 suffer misfortune|～病 fall ill; suffer from a disease

【罹难】línàn〈书 *fml.*〉遇灾、遇险而死;被害 get killed in a disaster or an accident; murdered: 不幸～ get unfortunately killed; die unfortunately

篱¹ lí ☞ [笊篱] (zhào·lí) on p. 2425

篱²(籬) lí 篱笆 hedge; fence: 樊～ fence|竹～茅舍 bamboo hedge and thatched hut

【篱笆】lí·ba 用竹子、芦苇、树枝等编成的遮拦的东西,一般环绕在房屋、场地等的周围 bamboo, reed or twig fence surrounding a house or a threshing ground

【篱落】líluò〈书 *fml.*〉same as 篱笆 lí·ba

【篱栅】lízhà 用竹子、树枝等做成的栅栏 paling of bamboo or twigs

醨 lí〈书 *fml.*〉薄酒 light wine; thin wine

藜 lí 一年生草本植物,茎直立,叶子互生,略呈三角形,花黄绿色。嫩叶可以吃。全草入药。lamb's-quarters (*Chenopodium album*); annual weed of the goosefoot family, with a vertical stem, deltoid leaves and yellowish-green flowers; tender leaves are edible and the whole weed is used for Chinese traditional medicine; also 灰菜 huīcài

【藜藿】líhuò〈书 *fml.*〉藜和藿,指粗劣的饭菜 coarse food; food made of weeds

黧 lí〈书 *fml.*〉黑;色黑而黄 black; dark and yellowish

【黧黑】líhēi〈书 *fml.*〉(脸色)黑 black; dark: 面目～ dark face; also 黎黑 líhēi

蠡 lí 〈书 *fml*.〉❶ 瓢 calabash shell serving as a dipper; dipper ❷ 贝壳 seashell

☞ lǐ on p.1183

【蠡测】lícè 〈书 *fml*.〉'以蠡测海'的略语,比喻以浅见揣度 abbr. for 以蠡测海 yǐ lí cè hǎi; (fig.) make an appraisal in one's superficial view; be shallow in understanding: 管窥～ look at the sky through a bamboo tube and measure the sea with a calabash — restricted in vision and shallow in understanding

劙 lí 〈书 *fml*.〉刺破;割破 pierce; cut

lǐ (ㄌㄧˇ)

礼(禮) lǐ ❶ 社会生活中由于风俗习惯而形成的为大家共同遵守的仪式 propriety; rite: 婚～ wedding | 丧～ funeral service ❷ 表示尊敬的言语或动作 decorum: ～节 courtesy; etiquette; manners | 敬～ salute ❸ 礼物 gift; present: 送～ give a gift | 献～ present a gift | 千里送鹅毛,～轻情意重。A gift sent from afar may be as light in itself as a goose feather, but it conveys a deep feeling. ❹ 〈书 *fml*.〉以礼相待 treat someone with due respect: ～贤下士 be courteous to the wise and condescending to the scholarly; (of a ruler or a high-ranking minister) treat worthy men with courtesy

【礼拜】lǐbài ❶ 宗教徒向所信奉的神行礼 religious service: ～堂 church | 做～ go to church ❷ 星期 week: 下～ next week | 开学已经三个～了。It's already three weeks since the new term began. ❸ 跟'天(或日)、一、二、三、四、五、六'连用,表示一星期中间的某一天[used together with 天 tiān (or 日 rì)、一 yī、二 èr、三 sān、四 sì、五 wǔ、六 liù' to indicate one of the days in the week]: ～三 Wednesday | ～六 Saturday ❹ 礼拜天的简称 abbr. for 礼拜天 lǐbàitiān

【礼拜寺】lǐbàisì 清真寺 mosque; Muslim temple

【礼拜堂】lǐbàitáng 基督教(新教)教徒举行宗教仪式的场所 church; building in which christians (of the Protestant denomination) hold relgious ceremonies

【礼拜天】lǐbàitiān 星期日(因基督教徒在这一天做礼拜) Sunday; day when Christians go to church; also 礼拜日 lǐbàirì

【礼宾】lǐbīn 按一定的礼仪接待宾客(多用在外交场合) protocol: ～服 ceremonial dress | ～司 Department of Protocol; Protocol Department

【礼成】lǐchéng 仪式结束 ceremony is over (said by the master of ceremonies)

【礼单】lǐdān 送礼时开列礼物名称和数目的单子 list of presents; also 礼帖 lǐtiě

【礼法】lǐfǎ 社会上通行的法纪和礼仪 rules of etiquette; proprieties

【礼佛】lǐ//fó 拜佛 worship the Buddha: 烧香～ burn joss sticks to worship the Buddha

【礼服】lǐfú 在庄重的场合或举行仪式时穿的服装 ceremonial robe or dress; full dress; formal attire

【礼服呢】lǐfúní 毛织直贡呢的别称 another name for 毛织直贡呢 máozhī zhígòngní

【礼花】lǐhuā 举行庆祝典礼时放的烟火 fireworks display held at celebrations

【礼教】lǐjiào 旧传统中束缚人的思想行动的礼节和道德 Confucian or feudal ethical code; etiquette and ethics that fettered the thoughts and actions in the old tradition

【礼节】lǐjié 表示尊敬、祝颂、哀悼之类的各种惯用形式,如鞠躬、握手、献花圈、献哈达、鸣礼炮等 courtesy; etiquette; protocol; ceremony; customary forms of etiquette showing respect, congratulation, condolence, as bowing, shaking hands, laying a wreath, presenting a hata and firing a gun salute, etc.

【礼金】lǐjīn 做礼物的现金 gift of money

【礼帽】lǐmào 跟礼服相配的帽子 hat that goes with a formal dress

【礼貌】lǐmào 言语动作谦虚恭敬的表现 courtesy; politeness; manners: 有～ be courteous; be polite; have good manners | 讲～ show courtesy; practise good manners | ～待人 be polite to others

【礼炮】lǐpào 表示敬礼或举行庆祝典礼时放的炮 salvo; (gun) salute

【礼品】lǐpǐn same as 礼物 lǐwù

【礼券】lǐquàn 由商店发行的一种代替礼物的凭证,持券人可到发券商店选购与券面指明的或与券面标出的金额等价的物品 coupon; certificate or ticket issued by a shop, which entitles the holder to a specified right, as redemption for cash or gifts, reduced purchase price, etc.

【礼让】lǐràng 表示礼貌的谦让 give priority to a person out of courtesy or consideration: 互相～ give each other the right of way politely | 在人行横道处,机动车应～行人。Motor vehicles are advised to make way for pedestrians at the crossings.

【礼尚往来】lǐ shàng wǎng lái 在礼节上讲究有来有往。现在也指你对我怎么样,我也对你怎么样。reciprocal courtesy; pay a person back in the same coin; deal with a man as he deals with you; give as good as one gets

【礼数】lǐshù ❶ 〈书 *fml*.〉礼仪的等级 different grades of courtesy; etiquette ❷ 礼貌;礼节 courtesy; etiquette; protocol; manners: 不懂～ have no manners

【礼俗】lǐsú 泛称婚丧祭祀交往等的礼节 etiquette and customs for wedding, funeral service, sacrificial rites: 不拘～ not stand on ceremony; not stick to formalities

【礼堂】lǐtáng 供开会或举行典礼用的大厅 assembly hall; auditorium

【礼物】lǐwù 为了表示尊敬或庆贺而赠送的物品,泛指赠送的物品 gift; present; sth. given to show respect or congratulation

【礼贤下士】lǐ xián xià shì 封建时代指帝王或大臣降低自己的身份敬重和结交一般有才德的人,使为自己效劳 (of feudal times) be courteous to the wise and condescending to the scholarly; (of a ruler or a high-ranking minister) treat worthy men with courtesy

【礼仪】lǐyí 礼节和仪式 ceremony and propriety; protocol: ~周到 well-thought-of ceremonies|外交~ diplomatic protocol

【礼义廉耻】lǐ yì lián chǐ 指崇礼、行义、廉洁、知耻。是管仲协助齐桓公推行政令时所依循的准则。propriety, righteousness, honesty, and a sense of shame; rule followed by Guan Zhong, Prime Minister, when he assisted Duke Huan of the State of Qi in the Warring States Period (770 B.C.-256 B.C.) in carrying out administrative orders

【礼遇】lǐyù 尊敬有礼的待遇 courteous reception: 受到隆重的~ be accorded a grand courteous reception

【礼赞】lǐzàn 怀着敬意地赞扬 praise in esteem: 这种为人类谋利益的高贵品质,是值得人民~的。The lofty character of seeking benefits for mankind deserves praises from the people.

李 lǐ ❶ 李子树,落叶小乔木,叶子倒卵形,花白色,果实球形,黄色或紫红色,是普通的水果 plum tree (*Prunus salicina*); small deciduous tree having obovate leaves, white flowers, yellow or purplish red fruits ❷ 这种植物的果实 plum, fruit of this plant ❸ (Lǐ)姓 a surname

【李逵】Lǐ Kuí《水浒传》中梁山泊好汉之一,绰号'黑旋风',具有农民的纯朴、粗豪的品质,反抗性很强,对正义事业和朋友很忠诚,但性情急躁。是刚直、勇猛而又鲁莽的人物典型,元代以来民间有许多关于他的故事。one of the Mount Liang heroes in the classical Chinese novel *Outlaws of the Marsh*, nicknamed the 'Black Whirlwind', having the simple, rude and forthright character of a peasant, rebellious and faithful to the just cause and friends, but impetuous in temper, regarded as a typical straightforward, honest, ferocious and rough person. Folk tales about him since the Yuan Dynasty (1271-1368) are legion.

【李自成起义】Lǐ Zìchéng Qǐyì 明末李自成所领导的农民大起义。起义军提出'均田免粮'的政治主张,队伍发展到百万人,成为当时农民战争中的主力军。公元1644年起义军在西安建立'大顺'农民革命政权,不久,攻克北京,推翻了明王朝的统治。后明将吴三桂勾结满洲贵族共同镇压起义军,起义失败,但李自成余部仍继续长期坚持抗清斗争。Li Zicheng Uprising; peasant uprising led by Li Zicheng in the declining years of the Ming Dynasty. Under the political slogan of 'equal land rights and exemption from grain tax', the rebel army enlisted one million troops, forming the main force in the peasants' war of the time. In 1644, it established its revolutionary power in Xi'an under the name of 'Da Shun' (Great Success) and soon captured Beijing, thus overthrowing the rule of the Ming Dynasty. Later, Wu Sangui, a general of the Ming Dynasty, colluded with the Manchu aristocrats in suppressing the rebel troops. The rebellion failed, but the remaining troops of Li Zicheng's continued their struggle against the Qing Dynasty for many years.

【李子】lǐ·zi ❶ 李子树 plum tree ❷ 李子树的果实 fruit of plum tree

里[1](裏、裡) lǐ ❶ (~儿 lǐr)衣服被褥等东西不露在外面的那一层;纺织品的反面 lining; inside (of clothing); reverse surface of a fabric: 被~儿 underneath side of a quilt|衣服~儿 lining of a garment|这面是~儿,那面是面儿。This is the inside, and that is the outside. ❷ 里边;里边的(跟'外'相对 as opposed to 'outside') in; inside; inner: ~屋 inner room|~圈 inner circle

里[2] lǐ ❶ 街坊 neighbourhood: 邻~ neighbours; neighbourhood|~弄 lane ❷ 家乡 native place: 故~ native place; hometown; homeland ❸ 〈古代 *arch.*〉五家为邻,五邻为里 five households form a *lin*, and five *lin* form a *li*. ❹ (Lǐ)姓 a surname

里[3] lǐ 长度单位,1市里等于150丈,合500米 *li* (currently called *shili*), traditional unit of length: 1 *shili* equal to 150 *zhang* or 500 metres

里(裏、裡) ·li ❶ 里面;内部(跟'外'相对 as opposed to 'outside') in; inside: 手~ in one's hands|箱子~ in the box|话~有话。There is more to it than what one says. ❷ 附在'这、那、哪'等字后边表示地点 used after 这 zhè、那 nà、哪 nǎ to indicate a place: 这~ here|那~ there|头~ in front; ahead; in advance, beforehand

【里边】lǐ·bian (~儿 lǐ·bianr)一定的时间、空间或某种范围以内 (of a given period of time, a given space and a given scope) inside; in; within: 柜子~ in the cabinet|他一年~没有请过一次假。He has not once asked for leave during the whole year. |这件事~有问题。There is something wrong with this matter. *or* Something is wrong with this matter.

【里程】lǐchéng ❶ 路程 mileage: ~表 odometer|往返~ mileage of a round trip ❷ 指发展的过程 course of development; course: 革命的~

course of the revolution

【里程碑】lǐchéngbēi ❶ 设于道路旁边用以记载里数的标志 milestone ❷〈比喻 *fig.*〉在历史发展过程中可以作为标志的大事 milestone in the course of historical development

【里出外进】lǐ chū wài jìn 不平整;参差不齐 irregular; uneven:墙砌得~ an unevenly built wall|牙长得~的。The teeth are uneven.

【里带】lǐdài 内胎的通称 general term for 内胎 nèitāi

【里勾外联】lǐ gōu wài lián 内外勾结,串通一气 collude with forces within and without:他和社会上的不法分子~,投机倒把,牟取暴利。He colluded with lawless persons within and without in speculative activities to make huge profits. also 里勾外连 lǐ gōu wài lián

【里急后重】lǐ jí hòu zhòng 痢疾的症状,有急于排泄粪便的感觉,但排不出去或不能排净 tenesmus; symptom of dysentery; feeling of urgent need to defecate or urinate, with a straining but unsuccessful effort to do it

【里脊】lǐ·ji 牛、羊、猪脊椎骨内侧的条状嫩肉,做肉食时称为里脊 tenderloin; lean pork taken from under the spinal column of a hog, the tenderest part of a loin; ~丝 shredded lean pork|滑溜~ saute fillet with thick gravy|糖醋~ sweet and sour fillet

【里间】lǐjiān (~儿 lǐjiānr)相连的几间房子里不直接通到外边的房间 inner room; also 里间屋 lǐjiānwū

【里拉】lǐlā 意大利的旧本位货币 lira (Italian monetary unit)[意 Itlalian: lira]

【里弄】lǐlòng〈方 *dial.*〉❶ 巷;小胡同(总称 collect.) lanes and alleys; neighbourhood ❷ 关于里弄居民的 of a neighbourhood; of a community:~工作 work related to neighbourhood affairs

【里面】lǐmiàn same as 里边 lǐ·bian

【里手】[1] lǐshǒu (~儿 lǐshǒur)赶车或操纵器械时指车或器械的左边 left-hand side (of a running vehicle or machine):骑自行车的人大都是从~上车。Most of the cyclists get on the bikes from the left.

【里手】[2] lǐshǒu 内行;行家 expert; old hand:行家~ expert; old hand

【里通外国】lǐ tōng wàiguó 暗中与外国勾结,进行背叛祖国的活动 collude with a foreign country to carry out illicit activities against one's country; have (or maintain) illicit relations with a foreign country

【里头】lǐ·tou same as 里边 lǐ·bian:屋子~坐满了人。The room was filled to capacity.|炉子~的煤已经烧得很红了。The coal inside the stove is glowing red.

【里外里】lǐwàilǐ ❶ 两方面合计 adding the two sums; a)减少收入加上增加支出 reduced income plus increased expenditure; b)减少支出加上增加收入 reduced expenditure plus increased income; c)预料的收入加上意外的收入 expected income plus unexpected income; d)预料的支出加上意外的支出 expected expenditure plus unexpected expenditure:这个月省了五十块钱,爱人又多寄来五十块,~有一百块的富余。I've saved 50 yuan, my wife also sent me 50 yuan, so altogether I have 100 yuan. ❷ 表示不论怎么计算(结果还是一样) no matter how you figure it out; either way:三个人干五天跟五个人干三天,~是一样。Three people working five days or five people working three days — either way it's all the same.

【里屋】lǐwū same as 里间 lǐjiān

【里弦】lǐxián 胡琴上演奏时靠里的比较粗的那根弦 thicker inner string on the *huqin*, a Chinese fiddle

【里巷】lǐxiàng 小街小巷;小胡同 lanes and alleys:他所写的多半是~间的琐事。Most of what he wrote about was trifles happening among those inhabiting lanes and alleys.

【里应外合】lǐ yìng wài hé 外面攻打,里面接应 collaborate from within with forces from without; act from inside in coordination with forces attacking from outside

【里子】lǐ·zi same as 里[1] lǐ ①:棉袄~ lining of a cotton-padded jacket

俚 lǐ 俚俗 vulgar; rustic; unrefined:~语 slang|~歌 folk song

【俚歌】lǐgē 民间歌谣 country song; folk song; rustic song

【俚曲】lǐqǔ 通俗的歌曲 popular music; pop; also 俗曲 súqǔ

【俚俗】lǐsú 粗俗 vulgar; rustic; unrefined

【俚语】lǐyǔ 粗俗的或通行面极窄的方言词,如北京话里的'撒丫子'(放开步子跑)、'开瓢儿'(打破头) slang; vulgar or rustic dialect, as 撒丫子 sā yā·zi (running with big strides), and 开瓢儿 kāipiáor (break the head) in the Beijing dialect

逦(邐) lǐ ☞ 迤逦 yǐlǐ on p.2269

哩 lǐ 又 also yīnglǐ 英里旧也作哩 mile; old form for 英里 yīnglǐ

☞ lī on p.1174 and ·li on p.1193

浬 lǐ 又 also hǎilǐ 海里旧也作浬 nautical mile; old form for 海里 hǎilǐ

悝 lǐ〈书 *fml.*〉忧;悲 worry; grief; sorrow

☞ kuī on p.1128

娌 lǐ ☞[妯娌](zhóu·lǐ) on p.2497

理 lǐ ❶ 物质组织的条纹;纹理 texture; grain (in wood, skin, etc.):木~ grain of wood|肌~ skin texture ◇条~ well-arranged; well-organized; well presented; in good order; orderly ❷ 道理;事理 reason; logic; truth:合~ reasonable; rational; logical|~屈 unreasonable; illogical; irrational; be on the wrong side; unjustified | ～当如此。That's just as it should be. ❸ 自然科学,有时特指物理学 natural science (esp. physics):～科 science | 数～化 mathematics, physics and chemistry ❹ 管理;办理 manage; run: 处～ handle; deal with; dispose of; settle; manage | ～财 manage financial affairs; manage money matters; conduct financial transactions | 当家～事 manage family affairs ❺ 整理;使整齐 put in order; tidy up:～发 have a haircut | ～一～书籍 put the books in order ❻ 对别人的言语行动表示态度;表示意见(多用于否定 usu. used in the negative) pay attention to; make a gesture or speak to: 路上碰见了,谁也没～谁。(They) ignored each other when (they) met on the road. *or* (They) did not speak to each other when (they) met on the road. | 置之不～ turn a deaf ear to ❼ (Lǐ) 姓 a surname

【理财】lǐ//cái 管理财物或财务 manage financial affairs; manage money matters; conduct financial transactions: 当家～ be the master of a family and manage its financial affairs | ～之道 the way of managing financial affairs

【理睬】lǐcǎi same as 理 lǐ⑥: 不加～ close one's ears to; pay no attention to; ignore; turn a deaf ear to | 大家都不～他。No one pays any attention to him.

【理茬儿】lǐ//chár 〈方 *dial.*〉对别人提到的事情或刚说完的话表示意见(多用于否定 oft. in the negative) respond to sth. sb. has mentioned or comment on what sb. has just said: 别理他的茬儿。Don't make any comment on what he says. | 人家跟你说话,你怎么不～? They are talking to you. Why don't you say something?

【理当】lǐdāng 应当;理所当然 ought to; should: ～如此。That's just as it should be.

【理短】lǐduǎn same as 理亏 lǐkuī

【理发】lǐ//fà 剪短并修整头发 have a haircut: ～员 hair dresser; barber | 我去理个发。I'm going to have a haircut. *or* I'm going to the hairdresser's.

【理该】lǐgāi 照理应该;理当 that's just as it should be: 您年纪这么大,我们～照顾您。You are getting old, and we should take care of you.

【理合】lǐhé 按理应当(旧时公文用语 used in old official documents) ought to; should: ～备文呈报 ought to prepare a document and submit it to; ought to submit a document to

【理化】lǐhuà 物理学和化学的合称 combined term for physics and chemistry

【理会】lǐhuì ❶ 懂得;领会 understand; comprehend: 这段话的意思不难～。This paragraph is not difficult to understand. ❷ 注意(多用于否定 oft. in the negative) pay attention to; take notice: 人家说了半天,他也没有～。They have talked for a long time, but he didn't pay any attention to them. ❸ 理睬;过问(多用于否定 oft. in the negative) care for; show interest in; pay attention to: 他在旁边站了半天,谁也没～他。He stood by for a long time, but no one cared for him. ❹ same as 理论 lǐlùn②;交涉(多见于早期白话 oft. in early vernacular) argue; debate ❺ 照料;处理(多见于早期白话 oft. in early vernacular) take care of; look after; handle; deal with

【理解】lǐjiě 懂;了解 understand; comprehend: 互相～ understand each other; mutual understanding | 加深～ deepen one's understanding; increase one's understanding; understand more deeply | 你的意思我完全～。I fully understand what you mean. *or* I understand you completely.

【理科】lǐkē 教学上对物理、化学、数学、生物等学科的统称 general term for the subjects of physics, chemistry, mathematics, biology, etc.

【理亏】lǐkuī 理由不足;(行为)不合道理 have no justification; be not justified; be in the wrong: 他自知～,慢慢地低下了头。Knowing that he was wrong, he lowered his head slowly.

【理疗】lǐliáo ❶ 物理疗法的简称 abbr. for 物理疗法 wùlǐ liáofǎ ❷ 用物理疗法治疗 give a physical therapy; treat a disease by physical means

【理路】lǐlù ❶ 思想或文章的条理 logical thinking; coherence; line of reasoning: ～不清的文章最难修改。It's most difficult to correct an article with poor logical thinking. ❷〈方 *dial.*〉道理 reason; sense: 他每句话都在～上,使人听了不能不心服。Everything he says is reasonable and convincing.

【理论】lǐlùn ❶ 人们由实践概括出来的关于自然界和社会的知识的有系统的结论 theory; principle; systematic conclusion about the knowledge of nature and society drawn through practice ❷ 辩论是非;争论; debate; argue; same as 讲理 jiǎnglǐ ①: 他正在气头上,我不想和他多～。He is in a fit of anger. I don't want to argue with him.

【理气】lǐqì 〈中医 *Chin.med.*〉指用药物来治疗气滞、气逆或气虚 regulating the flow of vital energy and removing obstruction to it

【理屈】lǐqū same as 理亏 lǐkuī: 他觉得自己有点～,没再说下去。Finding that he was somewhat on the wrong side, he said nothing more. *or* He felt he had a rather weak case, and said nothing more.

【理屈词穷】lǐ qū cí qióng 理由已被驳倒,无话可说 fall silent on finding oneself beaten in argument; have nothing more to say after finding all arguments refuted; be unable to advance any further arguments

【理事】lǐshì 处理事务;过问事情 handle affairs; manage affairs:他是个不当家不～的人。He does not manage family affairs.

【理事】lǐ·shì 代表团体行使职权并处理事情的人 council member; person who exercises power and manages affairs in the name of an organization or group:～会 council; board of directors|常务～ of the standing council member

【理所当然】lǐ suǒ dāng rán 从道理上说应当这样 as a matter of course; of course; naturally

【理想】lǐxiǎng ❶ 对未来事物的想像或希望(多指有根据的、合理的,跟空想、幻想不同 usu. founded and reasonable, and different from dream or illusion) ideal; imagination or hope for the future:当一名医生是我的～。It's my ideal to be a doctor. ❷ 符合希望的;使人满意的 be ideal:这件事办得很～。This matter was very well handled.|这项技术革新还不够～,要进一步钻研。This technical innovation has left something to be desired and should be further studied.

【理性】lǐxìng ❶ 指属于判断、推理等活动的(跟'感性'相对 as opposed to 'perceptual')(of reasoning by judgement, inference, etc.) rational:～认识 rational cognition ❷ 从理智上控制行为的能力 rational faculty; reason:失去～ lose one's reason

【理性认识】lǐxìng rèn·shi 认识的高级阶段。在感性认识的基础上,把所获得的感觉材料,经过思考、分析,加以去粗取精、去伪存真、由此及彼、由表及里的整理和改造,形成概念、判断、推理。理性认识是感性认识的飞跃,它反映事物的全体、本质和内部联系。rational cognition; rational knowledge; the higher stage of knowledge; on the basis of perceptual knowledge, arrange and reconstruct the data of sense perception obtained, through the exercise of thought and analysis, discarding the dross and selecting the essential, eliminating the false and retaining the true, proceeding from the one to the other and from the outside to the inside in order to form conception, judgement and inference. Rational knowledge is a leap from perceptual knowledge. It reflects the whole, essence and internal relations of things.

【理学】lǐxué 宋明时期的唯心主义哲学思想。包括以周敦颐、程颢、程颐、朱熹为代表的客观唯心主义和以陆九渊、王守仁为代表的主观唯心主义。前者认为'理'是永恒的、先于世界而存在的精神实体,世界万物只能由'理'派生。后者提出'心外无物,心外无理',认为主观意识是派生世界万物的本原。rationalistic Confucian philosophical school known to the West as Neo-Confucianism; idealist school of philosophical thought in the Song and Ming dynasties, including the objective idealists represented by Zhou Dunyi, Cheng Hao, Cheng Yi and Zhu Xi, who argued that 'rationalism' is eternal and is a spiritual substance prior to the world and that all things in the world were derived from 'rationalism', and the subjective idealists represented by Lu Jiuyuan and Wang Shouren, who proposed that 'there is nothing outside the mind and no rationalism (or reason) outside the mind' and that subjective consciousness is the origin of all things in the world; also 道学 dàoxué or 宋学 sòngxué

【理应】lǐyīng 照理应该 ought to; should:灾区有困难,我们～帮助。The disaster-affected areas are in difficulties, and we ought to help them.

【理由】lǐyóu 事情为什么这样做或那样做的道理 reason; ground; rationale:～充足 have every reason|毫无～ have neither rhyme nor reason

【理喻】lǐyù 用道理来解说,使当事人明白 explain by reasoning; reason with someone:不可～ be impervious to reason; won't listen to reason|可以～ can reason with|难以～ it's difficult to reason with

【理直气壮】lǐ zhí qì zhuàng 理由充分,因而说话有气势 speaking boldly or confidently with the knowledge that one is on the right side; having justice on one's side, one is bold and assured; with absolute assurance; justly and forcefully

【理智】lǐzhì 辨别是非、利害关系以及控制自己行为的能力 reason; intellect; ability to tell right from wrong, tell interest from disinterest and control one's behaviour:丧失～ lose one's reason; lose one's senses

锂 lǐ 金属元素,符号 Li (lithium)。银白色,在空气中易氧化而变暗,质软,是金属中最轻的,化学性质活泼。用于原子能工业和冶金工业,也用来制特种合金、特种玻璃等。lithium (Li); the lightest of all metallic chemical elements, silver-white and soft, apt to oxidize and darken, with reactive chemical properties; used in the atomic energy industry and metallurgical industry, and also for making special alloys and glasses

鲤 lǐ 鲤鱼,身体侧扁,背部苍黑色,腹部黄白色,嘴边有须一对。是我国重要的淡水鱼类之一。carp (*Cyprinus carpio*); flat fish with a black back and yellowish-white belly and a pair of feelers by the mouth, one of China's important freshwater fishes

澧 Lǐ 澧水,水名,在湖南。Lishui, name of a river in Hunan Province

醴 lǐ 〈书 *fml.*〉❶ 甜酒 sweet wine ❷ 甘甜的泉水 sweet water

鳢 lǐ 鱼类的一科,身体圆筒形,头扁,背鳍和臀鳍很长,尾鳍圆形,头部和躯干都有鳞片。最常见的是乌鳢。murrel（*Channa argus*）；snakehead；flat-headed fish having a round body，long dorsal and anal fins，and round tail fin，and scales on head and trunk；The most common species is the black murrel.

蠡 lǐ ❶ 用于人名，范蠡春秋时人 Li，used in personal names，as in 范蠡 Fan Li of the Spring and Autumn Period（475-221 B. C.）❷（Lǐ）蠡县，地名，在河北 Lixian，geographical name of a county in Hebei Province

☞ lí on p. 1178

lì（ㄌㄧˋ）

力 lì ❶ 物体之间的相互作用，是使物体获得加速度和发生形变的外因。力有三个要素，即力的大小、方向和作用点。force；interaction between or among things that is the external cause for the acceleration and deformation of a body. The three elements of force are：magnitude，direction and the point to which the force is applied. ❷ 力量；能力 power；strength；ability：人～ manpower｜物～ material power｜目～ sight；vision｜脑～ brains；mental capability｜药～ efficacy of a drug｜理解～ faculty of understanding｜说服～ convincing｜战斗～ fighting power ❸ 特指体力 physical power；physical strength：大～士 man of great physical strength｜四肢无～ feel weak in the limbs｜用～推车 push a cart forcefully ❹ 尽力；努力 exert one's efforts；do one's best；make every effort：～争上游 aim high；strive for the best｜维护甚～ safeguard or uphold effectively ❺（Lì）姓 a surname

【力巴】lì·ba〈方 *dial.*〉❶ 外行；不熟练 not adept；awkward；clumsy：～话 lay language｜做庄稼活，他可不～。He is not a layman in farm work. ❷ 外行人 layman；also 力巴头（lì·batóu）

【力避】lìbì 尽力避免 do what one can avoid or avert：～被动 try hard to avoid being passive｜～事故发生 try hard to avoid accident

【力不从心】lì bù cóng xīn 心里想做，可是能力够不上 ability falling short of one's wishes；unable to do as much as one wishes to

【力持】lìchí 努力坚持 insist on；uphold：～异议 insist on one's dissenting views｜～正义 uphold justice

【力畜】lìchù 用来耕地、运输等的家畜，如牛、马、骡子、驴、骆驼等 draught animal；beast of burden；domestic animals for ploughing land or transporting goods，including cattle，horse，mule，donkey，camel；also 役畜 yìchù

【力促】lìcù 尽力促使 make every effort to promote：～此事成功 try hard to make it a success

【力挫】lìcuò 奋力击败 try one's best to defeat：～对手 try one's best to beat his opponent｜～上届足球冠军 defeat the defending football champion with all their might

【力道】lìdào〈方 *dial.*〉❶ 力气；力量 strength；power：～大 powerful；strong｜有～ have strength ❷ 效力；作用 effect：化肥比粪肥～来得快。Chemical fertilizers are more effective than manure.

【力度】lìdù ❶ 力量大小的程序；力量的强度 intensity of force：风的～足以吹折这棵小树。The wind is strong enough to break this small tree. ❷ 指曲谱或音乐表演中音响的强度。从弱到强可分为最弱、更弱、弱、中弱、中强、强、更强、最强等。dynamics；effect of varying degrees of loudness or softness in the performance of music：pianissimo，diminuendo，piano，mezzopiano，mezzoforte，forte，crescendo，fortissimo ❸ 功力的深度；内涵的深度 depth of intension：这是一部有激情、有～的好作品。This is a good piece of work with passion and efficacy.

【力荐】lìjiàn 竭力推荐 recommend strongly：～贤能 strongly recommend the wise and able people｜～有真才实学的人担任此职 strongly recommend a person with genuine learning for this post

【力竭声嘶】lì jié shēng sī same as 声嘶力竭 shēng sī lì jié

【力戒】lìjiè 极力防止 strictly avoid；do everything possible to avoid；guard against：～骄傲 guard against arrogance｜～急躁 guard against impetuosity

【力矩】lìjǔ 表示力对物体产生转动效应的物理量，数值上等于力和力臂的乘积 moment of force；moment；torque；physical quantity of the rotation caused by a force to a body，with its numerical value equal to the product of the force and the arm of force

【力量】lì·liang ❶ same as 力气 lì·qi：人多～大。The more people，the greater strength.｜别看他个子小，～可不小。He is short，but he has great strength. ❷ 能力 power；force；ability：尽一切～完成任务。Do everything in one's power to fulfil the mission. ❸ 作用；效力 potency；efficacy；strength：这种农药的～大。This pesticide is strong.

【力偶】lì'ǒu 作用于物体上的大小相等、方向相反而且不在一直线上的两个力。力偶能使物体转动或改变转动状态。couple；two equal forces producing rotation by moving in parallel but opposite directions. It can produce rotation or change rotation.

【力气】lì·qi 筋肉的效能；气力 physical strength；effort：他的～大，一个人就搬起了这块大石头。He has great strength，and can lift this large stone alone.

【力气活】lì·qihuó（～儿 lì·qìhuór）费力的体力劳动 heavy work; strenuous work：打坯是个～儿。Making unfired bricks is strenuous work.

【力钱】lì·qian〈方 *dial.*〉脚钱 payment to a porter

【力求】lìqiú 极力追求；尽力谋求 make every effort to; do one's best to; strive to：～事成 strive to make sth. a success｜～提高单位面积产量 strive to raise the per-hectare (per-unit-area) yield

【力所能及】lì suǒ néng jí 自己的能力所能办到的 within one's ability; in one's power：让学生参加一些～的劳动。Let the students do the kind of physical work that they are capable of.

【力透纸背】lì tòu zhǐ bèi ❶ 形容书法遒劲有力 (of handwriting or calligraphy) powerful; forceful; (of calligraphy) of such a dynamic style that the strokes seem to penetrate the paper. ❷ 形容文章深刻有力 (of a piece of writing) powerful; penetrating

【力图】lìtú 极力谋求；竭力打算 try hard to; strive to：～实现自己的抱负 try hard to fulfil one's ambition

【力挽狂澜】lì wǎn kuáng lán〈比喻 *fig.*〉尽力挽回险恶的局势 do one's utmost to stem a raging tide; make vigorous efforts to turn the tables; try one's best to save a desperate situation

【力行】lìxíng 努力实践 be diligent in action; practise with earnestness：身体～ practise personally as one says

【力学】[1] lìxué 研究物体机械运动规律及其应用的学科 mechanics; branch of physics which deals with the law of the motion of the material bodies and its application

【力学】[2] lìxué〈书 *fml.*〉努力学习 study hard：～不倦 be tireless in studying

【力战】lìzhàn 努力奋战 fight with all one's might

【力争】lìzhēng ❶ 极力争取 strive for; strive to; work hard for; do all one can to：～上游 strive for the best｜～超额完成生产任务 do all one can to fulfil the production plan ❷ 极力争辩 argue strongly; contend vigorously：据理～ persistently reason things out

【力争上游】lìzhēng shàngyóu 努力奋斗，争取先进 aim high; strive for the best or for the first place

【力证】lìzhèng 有力的证据 strong evidence; convincing proof

【力主】lìzhǔ 极力主张 advocate strongly：～和谈 advocate peace; stand strongly for peace talks｜因为天气要变，他～提前出发。As the weather is going to change, he strongly advocates that they start off earlier.

【力作】lìzuò 精心完成的工力深厚的作品 masterpiece：这个剧本是他晚年的～。This script was a masterpiece in his late years.

历[1]（歷）lì ❶ 经历；经过 go through; undergo; experience：来～ origin; source｜～程 course｜～时半年 last for six months; it takes six months to｜身～其境 have personal experience in; be personally on the scene ❷ 统指过去的各个或各次 previous (occasions, sessions, etc.)：～年 the previous years｜～代 the dynasties｜～次 previous occasions｜～届 previous sessions ❸ 遍；一个一个地 covering all; one by one：～访各校 visited all schools, visited schools one by one｜～试诸方，均无成效。All prescriptions have been used, but they prove ineffective. ❹ (Lì) 姓 a surname

历[2]（厤、曆、歴）lì ❶ 推算年月日和节气的方法；历法 calendar; system of determining the beginning, length and divisions of a year and for arranging the year into days, weeks and months：阳～ solar calendar｜阴～ lunar calendar｜农～ traditional Chinese calendar; lunar calendar ❷ 记录年月日节气的书、表等 calendar; table, chart or book that shows such an arrangement, usually for a single year：日～ calendar｜挂～ wall calendar｜天文～ astronomical almanac

【历本】lìběn〈方 *dial.*〉same as 历书 lìshū

【历朝】lìcháo ❶ same as 历代 lìdài：～官制 systems of the civil service in all dynasties ❷ 指同一朝代各个君主的统治时期 successive reigns of a dynasty：明代营建北京宫城，永乐十八年基本建成，以后～续建，到正统六年才全部完成。Construction of the Forbidden City in Beijing in the Ming Dynasty was completed in the main in the 18th year of the Yongle Reign (1421), continued in the subsequent reigns, and was not totally completed until the 16th year of the Zhengtong Reign (1442)

【历陈】lìchén 一条一条地陈述 make presentations one by one

【历程】lìchéng 经历的过程 course; process：光辉的～ brilliant course

【历次】lìcì 过去的各次 all previous (occasions, etc.)：在～竞赛中他都表现得很突出。He did well in all past contests.

【历代】lìdài ❶ 过去的各个朝代 dynasties; successive dynasties; past dynasties：～名画 famous paintings through the ages ❷ 过去的许多世代 past generations：～务农 do farming for generations ❸ 经历各个时期 all past periods：这里的珍珠养殖业～不衰。The pearl farming here has kept flourishing through the ages.

【历法】lìfǎ 用年、月、日计算时间的方法。主要分为阳历、阴历和阴阳历三类。具体的历法还包括纪年的方法。calendric system of determining the beginning, length and divisions of a year and for arranging the year into days, weeks and month. There are mainly three kinds: the solar calendar, the lunar calendar and the lunisolar calendar. Specific methods also include annals, chronicles, etc.

【历届】lìjiè 过去各届 all previous (sessions, governments, etc.):～毕业生 graduates of all previous years|～人民代表大会 all the previous people's congresses

【历尽】lìjìn 多次经历或遭受 have gone through a lot of:～沧桑 have experienced various vicissitudes of life|～磨难 experience hardships and sufferings|～千辛万苦 have weathered all kinds of hardships and difficulties

【历经】lìjīng 经历;多次经过 have experienced; undergone or encountered many times:～劫难 have encountered many calamities|小庙～百余年的风雨剥蚀,已残破不堪。The small temple is dilapidated, having been ravaged by the elements for more than 100 years.

【历久】lìjiǔ 经过很长的时间 for a long time:～不衰 long lasting

【历来】lìlái 从来;一向 always; constantly; all through the ages:～如此。This has always been the case.|老校长～重视思想教育。The old school master has always attached great importance to the ideological education.|我国人民～就有勤劳勇敢的优良传统。The people of our country have cherished the fine tradition of hard work and bravery through the ages.

【历历】lìlì (物体或景象)一个一个清清楚楚的 (of objects or scenery) distinct; clear:～可数 can be seen clearly or distinctly; can be counted one by one|～在目 come clearly into view; leap up before the eyes

【历练】lìliàn ❶ 经历世事;锻炼 experience and training:孩子大了,要到外边～～。The child has grown up, and it is high time he went out to gain some experiences. ❷ 阅历多而有经验 be experienced:他～老成,办事稳重。He is very experienced and handles matters steadily and calmly.

【历年】lìnián 过去的很多年;以往各年 over the years; calendar year:～的积蓄 savings over the years|比照～,今年的收成算中上。The harvest is above the average this year as compared with the previous years. *or* The harvest is fairly good this year as compared with the previous years.

【历任】lìrèn 多次担任;先后担任 have successively held the posts of; have served successively as:～要职 have successively held important posts|参军后,～排长、连长等职 have held the posts of platoon leader and company commander after joining the army

【历时】lìshí (事情)经过时日 last (a period of time); take (a period of time):这一战役,～六十五天。The battle lasted 65 days.

【历史】lìshǐ ❶ 自然界和人类社会的发展过程,也指某种事物的发展过程和个人的经历 history; personal records; process of the development of Nature and the human society; or the experiences of the individuals in the course of the development of a certain event:地球的～ history of the earth|人类的～ history of mankind ❷ 过去的事实 past history:这件事早已成为～。That's past history already. ❸ 过去事实的记载 records of past facts ❹ 指历史学 history (a branch of study)

【历史观】lìshǐguān 人们对社会历史的总的看法,属于世界观的一部分。唯物史观和唯心史观是两种对立的历史观。outlook of history; general view on the history of society: materialistic outlook of history and idealist outlook of history are two antagonistic outlooks of history

【历史剧】lìshǐjù 指以历史故事为题材的戏剧 historical play

【历史唯物主义】lìshǐ wéiwù zhǔyì 马克思、恩格斯所创立的关于人类社会发展最一般规律的科学,是马克思主义哲学的重要组成部分,是无产阶级的世界观。历史唯物主义认为:社会历史发展具有自身固有的客观规律;社会存在决定社会意识,社会意识又反作用于社会存在;生产力和生产关系之间的矛盾,经济基础和上层建筑之间的矛盾是推动社会发展的基本矛盾。historical materialism; science founded by Karl Marx and Friedrich Engels that deals with the general law of development of human society and that is an important component part of the Marxist philosophy and the proletariat world outlook. Historical materialism holds that the historical development of society has its own inherent objective law, that social being determines social consciousness and social consciousness reacts on social being, and that the contradiction between the productive forces and the relations of production and the contradiction between the economic base and the superstructure are the fundamental contradictions that push the development of society. also 唯物史观 wéiwùshǐguān

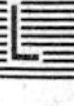

【历史唯心主义】lìshǐ wéixīn zhǔyì 关于人类社会发展的非科学的历史观。历史唯心主义认为社会意识决定社会存在,人们的思想动机是社会发展的根本原因,否认社会发展的客观规律。historical idealism; unscientific view of history on the development of human society; Historical idealism holds that social consciousness determines social being and that the ideological motives of people are the fundamental cause of social development. It negates the objective law of social development. also 唯心史观 wéixīn-shǐguān

【历世】lìshì same as 历代 lìdài

【历书】lìshū 按照一定历法排列年、月、日、节气、纪念日等供查考的书 almanac; usu. annual directory containing statistical and other information on years, months and dates, seasonal divisions, festivals, etc., arranged according to a certain calendar

【历数】lìshǔ 一个一个地举出来 count one by one; enumerate:～敌人的罪行 enumerate the crimes of the enemy|当面～对方违反协定的事实 enumerate the facts of violating the agreement on the part of the opposite party face to face

【历险】lìxiǎn 经历危险 experience dangers or adventures:山中～记 story of adventures in the Mountain

厉(厲) lì ❶ 严格 strict; rigorous:～行 practise; strictly enforce; vigorously enforce ❷ 严肃;猛烈 serious; vehement:严～ strict|～色 angry look; stern expression|雷～风行 do something quickly and determinedly; vigorously and speedily; resolutely|声色俱～ in a harsh voice and with a stern look ❸ (Lì)姓 a surname

〈古 *arch.*〉same as 砺 lì; also same as 癞 lài

【厉兵秣马】lì bīng mò mǎ ☞ 秣马厉兵 mò mǎ lì bīng on p.1368

【厉鬼】lìguǐ 恶鬼;鬼怪 evil spirit; ghost

【厉害】lì·hai 难以对付或忍受;剧烈;凶猛 difficult to deal with or endure; violent; radical; ferocious:心跳得～。The heart beats very fast.|天热得～。It is terribly hot. *or* The weather is terribly hot.|这着棋十分～。This move is very formidable.|这人可真～。This man is really aggressive. also 利害 lì·hai

【厉色】lìsè 严厉的面色;愤怒的表情 stern look; angry look; stern expression:正言～ speak in all seriousness

【厉声】lìshēng (说话)声音严厉 in a stern voice:～斥责 reprimand in a stern voice

【厉行】lìxíng 严格实行 strictly enforce; rigorously enforce:～节约 practise strict economy

立 lì ❶ same as 站[1] zhàn:～正 stand at attention|坐～不安 be on pins and needles; feel uneasy; be on tenterhooks; be fidgety ❷ 使竖立;使物件的上端向上 erect; set sth. up; put up:～竿见影 the shadow is seen as soon as a pole is put up; get instant results; get quick results|把梯子～起来。Set up the ladder. *or* Put up the ladder. ❸ 直立的 upright; vertical; erect:～柜 bookcase; wardrobe; closet; cupboard|～轴 vertical shaft; vertical scroll of painting or calligraphy ❹ 建立;树立 establish; found; set up:～功 make a contribution|～志 resolve; be determined to ❺ 制定;订立 draw up; conclude:～法 make laws; legislate; formulate laws and regulations|～约 conclude an agreement; contract|～个字据 make a written pledge; sign a written pledge ❻ 指君主即位 ascend the throne ❼ 指确定继承地位;确立 appoint; designate:～嗣 appoint one's successor; adopt an heir|～皇太子 designate a crown prince ❽ 存在;生存 exist; live:自～ earn one's own living; support oneself; stand on one's own feet|独～ independence ❾ 立刻 immediately; instantaneously:～奏奇效 produce immediate results; feel the effect immediately|～候回音。Your immediate reply is requested. ❿ (Lì)姓 a surname

【立案】lì//àn ❶ 在主管机关注册登记;备案 register; put on record:办厂须向主管机关～。To set up a factory, one should have it registered with the competent authorities. ❷ 设立专案 place a special case on file:～侦查 place a special case on file for investigation and prosecution

【立标】lìbiāo 航标的一种,外形像柱子或呈梯形,没有灯光设备 navigation mark shaped like a column or in a trapezium without any lighting device

【立场】lìchǎng ❶ 认识和处理问题时所处的地位和所抱的态度 position; stand; standpoint ❷ 特指阶级立场 class stand:～坚定 be steadfast in one's stand; take a firm stand

【立春】lì//chūn 交立春节气;春季开始 Beginning of Spring — the 1st of the 24 solar terms:明天～。Spring begins tomorrow.|立了春,天气就要转暖了。It is going to get warmer after the Beginning of Spring.

【立春】lìchūn 二十四节气之一,在2月3、4或5日。我国以立春为春季的开始。one of the 24 solar terms; day marking the beginning of the 1st solar term (Feb. 3, 4, or 5). The day is regarded as the beginning of spring in China.

☞ 节气 jié·qi on p.989 and 二十四节气 èrshísì jiéqì on p.516

【立此存照】lì cǐ cún zhào 立下这个(契约、字据),保存起来以备查考核对(旧时契约等文书中的习惯用语 jargon to be used in an old-fashioned contract or other document) This contract (or an agreement, etc.) is hereby concluded and to be filed for future reference.

【立等】lìděng ❶ 稍等一会儿 wait a moment:～可取 instant service ❷ 立刻等着(办) wait for an immediate action; wait for sth. to be done immediately:～回信 wait for an immediate reply

【立地】[1] lìdì ❶ 立在地上 stand on the ground:顶天～ of gigantic stature; of indomitable spirit; with one's head supporting the sky and feet planted on the ground｜～书橱（比喻学识渊博的人）bookcase；(fig.)man of great learning ❷ 指树木生长的地方 place where trees grow：～不同，树木的生长就有差异。As the places differ, the trees grow differently.

【立地】² lìdì same as 立刻 lìkè：放下屠刀，～成佛。Lay down your cleaver and you'll become a Buddha at once.

【立定】lìdìng ❶ 军事或体操口令，命令正在行进的队伍（也可以是一个人）停下并立正（word of command for use in an army or physical exercises, directed at a team or a person in a marching procession）Halt! ❷ 站稳 stand firmly：～脚跟 stand firmly on one's heels ❸ 牢固地确定 firmly established：～主意 resolute idea｜～志向 resolute aspiration；firm ambition

【立冬】lì//dōng 交立冬节气；冬季开始 Beginning of Winter：今天～。Winter begins today.｜立了冬，天气就冷了。It gets cold after winter begins.

【立冬】lìdōng 二十四节气之一，在11月7日或8日。我国以立冬为冬季的开始。one of the 24 solar terms；day marking the Beginning of Winter falls on November 7 or 8, regarded as the beginning of winter in China

☞ 节气 jié·qi on p. 989 and 二十四节气 èrshísì jiéqì on p. 516

【立法】lì//fǎ 国家权力机关按照一定程序制定或修改法律 make (or enact) laws；legislate：～机关 legislative body；legislature｜～程序 legislative procedure

【立方】lìfāng ❶ 指数是3的乘方，如 $a^3(a \times a \times a)$，$4^3(4 \times 4 \times 4)$ power with 3 as its radical exponent, as $a^3(a \times a \times a)$，$4^3(4 \times 4 \times 4)$ ❷ 立方体的简称 abbr. for 立方体 lìfāngtǐ ❸ 指立方米 square metre

【立方根】lìfānggēn 根指数是3的方根，如8的立方根是2 cube root；cube root with 3 as its radical exponent, e.g. the cube root of 8 is 2

【立方体】lìfāngtǐ 六个面积相等的正方形所围成的立体 cube；solid with six equal, square sides；also 正方体 zhèngfāngtǐ；简称 abbr. 立方 lìfāng

【立竿见影】lì gān jiàn yǐng〈比喻 *fig.*〉立见功效 shadow is seen as soon as a pole is put up；set up a pole and you see its shadow；get instant results；get quick results

【立功】lì//gōng 建立功绩 render meritorious service；do a deed of merit；make contributions；perform a feat：～受奖 render meritorious service and receive an award｜一人～，全家光荣。When one member renders meritorious service, he brings honour to the whole family.｜在救灾中他可立了大功。He rendered an outstanding service in helping people tide over the natural disaster.

【立功赎罪】lì gōng shú zuì 建立功劳以抵消所犯的罪过 do good deeds to atone for one's crimes；also 立功自赎 lì gōng zì shú

【立柜】lìguì 一种直立的较高的柜子，前面开门，有的装有隔板或若干抽屉，多用来存放衣物等 wardrobe；hanging cupboard；tall, upright piece of furniture with a door in the front, partitioned into cubicles and having several drawers for putting away clothes and other belongings

【立国】lìguó 建立或建设国家 found a state；build up a nation：农业工业为～之本。Agriculture and industry are the base on which the nation is built up.

【立候】lìhòu ❶ 站着等候 stand and wait：～多时 stand and wait for a long time ❷ same as 立等 lìděng ②：～回音。An immediate reply is requested. *or* A prompt reply is appreciated.

【立户】lì//hù ❶ 组织家庭；立户口 register for a household residence card；register for permanent residence ❷ 在银行存款时建立户头 open an account with the bank

【立即】lìjí same as 立刻 lìkè：接到命令，～出发。When you receive orders, set out immediately.

【立交】lìjiāo 立体交叉的简称 abbr. for 立体交叉 lìtǐ jiāochā：～桥 overpass；flyover；motorway interchange｜～工程 construction project for an overpass

【立交桥】lìjiāoqiáo 使道路形成立体交叉的桥梁，不同去向的车辆等可以同时通行 overpass；flyover；bridge or other passageway over a road or railway

【立脚】lì//jiǎo same as 立足 lìzú：～点 foothold；footing｜～不稳 unstable footing｜地方太小，立不住脚。The place is a bit too high for a foothold.

【立脚点】lìjiǎodiǎn ❶ 观察或判断事物时所处的地位 position from which one observes or judges an affair；standpoint；stand：为消费者着想，是产品设计的～。It's the standpoint in designing a product to take consumers needs in consideration. ❷ 生存或占有的地方 base：先巩固～，再求发展。First consolidate the base and then seek further development. ‖ also 立足点 lìzúdiǎn

【立井】lìjǐng 竖井 shaft mine

【立决】lìjué〈书 *fml.*〉立即处决（死刑犯）(of a criminal receiving death sentence) immediate execution；summary execution

【立克次氏体】lìkècìshìtǐ 介于细菌和病毒之间的微生物，比细菌小，在普通显微镜下看得见。种类很多，多以虱、蚤、壁虱等节肢动物为传播媒介。只有少数能引起人类疾病，如斑疹伤寒、恙虫病等。由美国病理学家立克次（Howard Taylor Ricketts）发现而得名。rickettsia；any of several families of gram-negative bacteria, observable under microscropes, that are the causative agents of certain diseases, such as typhus, Rocky Mountain spotted fever. They are transmitted to animals and humans by the bite of certain lice, ticks, etc, in whose bodies they live as parasites. It was discovered by Howard Taylor Ricketts, an American pathologist, hence its name.

【立刻】lìkè〈副词 *adv.*〉表示紧接着某个时候；马上 immediately; at once; right away：请大家～到会议室去。Please go to the meeting room right away, everybody. | 同学们听到这句话，～鼓起掌来。The students immediately burst into applause when they heard the word.

【立睖】lì·leng〈方 *dial.*〉❶ 用力睁大（眼睛）；外眼角向上挑 open the eyes as wide as possible, with the outside corners slanted upward：～着眼 stare with eyes slanted upward ❷ 竖起 erect：他想起这件事，后怕得头发根子都～起来。The memory of what happened struck such terror into him that his hair stood erect.

【立领】lìlǐng（～儿 lìlǐngr）衣服领子的一种样式，衣领不翻转（区别于'翻领' as opposed to 'turndown'）straight collar; style of collar：～衬衫 shirt with a straight collar

【立论】lìlùn 对某个问题提出自己的看法，表示自己的意见 air one's own views; present one's arguments：～精当 well-presented arguments

【立马】lìmǎ〈方 *dial.*〉（～儿 lìmǎr）same as 立刻 lìkè：事情打听清楚了，～给我个回话。Give me a call immediately after you get a clear picture of the matter.

【立秋】lì//qiū 交立秋节气；秋季开始 Beginning of Autumn：立了秋，把扇丢。The fans are put aside after autumn begins.

【立秋】lìqiū 二十四节气之一，在8月7、8或9日。我国以立秋为秋季的开始。one of the 24 solar terms; day marking the beginning of autumn falls on August 7, 8 or 9 and is regarded as the beginning of autumn season in China; ☞ 节气 jié·qi on p. 989 and 二十四节气 èrshísì jiéqì on p. 516

【立绒】lìróng 以蚕丝或化学纤维长丝织成底布，用人造丝作起绒经丝织成的丝织品，表面有丝绒，质地柔软坚固，一般用来做服装 cut velvet; rich fabric of silk or chemical filament with a soft thick pile, usually used for making clothes

【立射】lìshè 射击训练和比赛的一种姿势，站着射击 shoot from a standing position

【立身处世】lì shēn chǔ shì 指在社会上待人接物的种种活动 way one conducts oneself in society; establish oneself and get along with people in the world; also 立身行事 lì shēn xíng shì

【立时】lìshí same as 立刻 lìkè：他～省悟过来。He immediately became aware. | 剧团一到，～就来了许多的人。Many people came as soon as the art troupe arrived.

【立时三刻】lìshísānkè〈方 *dial.*〉立刻；马上 at once; right away; immediately：他一收到电报，～就动身回家。He immediately left for home when he received the telegraph.

【立誓】lì//shì 发誓 take an oath; vow

【立嗣】lìsì〈书 *fml.*〉没有儿子的人以别人的儿子承继；立继承人 adopt an heir

【立体】lìtǐ ❶ 具有长、宽、厚的（物体）three-dimensional; stereoscopic：～图形 solid figure ❷ 几何体 solid ❸ 上下多层次的；包括各方面的 multi-level; multi-layer; embracing all aspects：～交叉 grade separation | ～气候 solid climate | ～战争 three-dimensional warfare ❹ 具有立体感的 three-dimensional; stereoscopic：～电影 stereoscopic film

【立体电影】lìtǐ diànyǐng 使观众对画面有立体感觉的电影 stereoscopic film; three-dimensional (3-d) film; cinerama

【立体几何】lìtǐ jǐhé 研究立体图形的性质（形状、大小、位置等）的学科 solid geometry; branch of mathematics that deals with solid figures (shape, size and location)

【立体交叉】lìtǐ jiāochā 利用跨线桥、地道等使相交的道路在不同的平面上交叉 grade separation; 简称 abbr. 立交 lìjiāo

【立体角】lìtǐjiǎo 一个锥面所围成的空间部分 solid angle; angle formed by three or more planes meeting in a common point or formed at the vertex of a cone

【立体声】lìtǐshēng 使人感到声源分布在空间的声音。适当组合和安排传声器、放大系统和扬声器，能产生立体声效果。宽银幕电影、环幕电影或某些电视机、音响设备等多采用立体声。stereophony; stereo; sound reproduction as in films, records, tapes or broadcasting, using two or more channels to carry and reproduce through separate speakers a blend of sounds from separate sources

【立体图】lìtǐtú 利用透视原理，对物体的形状绘出的图形 hologram; three-dimensional picture of an object, drawn in perspective

【立夏】lì//xià 交立夏节气；夏季开始 Beginning of Summer：立了夏，把扇架。People begin to use fans to cool themselves after summer begins. | ～了，天气一天一天地热起来。It's going to get hot with each passing day after summer begins.

【立夏】lìxià 二十四节气之一，在5月5、6或7日。我国以立夏为夏季的开始。one of the 24 solar terms; day marking the beginning of the 7th solar term falls on May 5, 6, or 7, and it is regard as the beginning of summer in China ☞ 节气 jié·qi on p. 989 and 二十四节气 èrshísì jiéqì on p. 516

【立宪】lìxiàn 君主国家制定宪法，实行议会制度 constitutionalism：君主～ constitutional monarchy

【立项】lìxiàng 某项工程经有关部门批准立为建设项目 approval given by the competent authorities to a project for construction：这个车间当年～，当年施工，当年投产。This workshop was approved for construction, built and put into operation in the same year.

【立言】lìyán 〈书 *fml*.〉指著书立说 expound one's ideas in writing; achieve glory by writing; leave worthy writings to posterity

【立业】lì//yè ❶ 建立事业 establish a career：建功～ make contribution and establish a career ❷ 设置产业 establish a business; start a business：成家～ get married and start a business

【立意】lìyì ❶ 打定主意 be determined; make one's decision; make up one's mind：他～要出外闯一闯。He has made up his mind to make a living (or do business) away from home. ❷ 命意 conception; approach：这幅画～新颖。This painting shows an interesting new approach.

【立约】lì//yuē 订立契约或公约 conclude a contract, agreement or convention：～签字 conclude a contract and sign it｜租房先得立个约。A contract must be signed for the renting of a house.

【立账】lì//zhàng 建立账簿，记载货币、货物等进出事项 open an account; set up an accounting book to keep record of the entry and withdrawal of money, goods, etc.

【立正】lìzhèng 军事或体操口令，命令队伍（也可以是一个人）在原地站好 stand at attention

【立志】lì//zhì 立定志愿 resolve; be determined：～做一名教师 be determined or make up one's mind to be a teacher

【立轴】lìzhóu 长条形的字画，高而窄，尺寸比中堂小 vertical scroll of painting or calligraphy; wall scroll：一幅～ a wall scroll

【立锥之地】lì zhuī zhī dì 形容极小的一块地方（多用于"无立锥之地" oft. used in 无立锥之地 wú lì zhuī zhī dì) space small enough just for the point of an awl：贫无～ be so poor as to have no space even for the point of an awl; utterly destitute

【立字】lì//zì（～儿 lì//zìr）写下字据 sign an agreement, a contract, a receipt, a written statement, etc.：借钱得立个字。A written statement must be signed if you want to borrow money.｜空口无凭，～为据。A verbal statement is no guarantee; a written piece must be given as evidence.

【立足】lìzú ❶ 站得住脚，能住下去或生存下去 find home in; have a foothold somewhere：～未稳 unstable footing｜～之地 foothold; footing ❷ 处于某种立场 standpoint; stand：～基层，面向群众 have one's feet firmly planted at the grass roots and keep in view the broad masses of the people

【立足点】lìzúdiǎn same as 立脚点 lìjiǎodiǎn

吏 lì ❶〈旧时 *old*〉没有品级的小公务人员 government clerk：胥～ petty official ❷〈旧时 *old*〉泛指官吏（in a broad sense) official; mandarin：大～ high-ranking official｜酷～ cruel official

【吏胥】lìxū 〈书 *fml*.〉胥吏 petty official

【吏治】lìzhì 地方官吏的作风和政绩 administration of local officials：澄清～ bring order to the local administration｜～严明 strict and fair local administration

坜（壢） lì 中坜（Zhōnglì），地名，在台湾省 Zhongli, geographical name of a place in Taiwan Province

苈（藶） lì ☞［葶苈］(tínglì) on p. 1913

丽[1]（麗） lì 好看；美丽 beautiful; pretty; fine-looking：壮～ magnificent; imposing; majestic｜秀～ beautiful; pretty; handsome｜风和日～ gentle breeze and warm sunshine

丽[2]（麗） lì 〈书 *fml*.〉附着 depend on; attach oneself to：附～ adhere to; submit to

☞ lí on p. 1175

【丽人】lìrén 〈书 *fml*.〉美貌的女子 beautiful woman; beauty

【丽日】lìrì 〈书 *fml*.〉明亮的太阳 bright sun

【丽质】lìzhì（妇女）美好的品貌 beauty (of a woman)：天生～ natural beauty

励（勵） lì ❶ 劝勉 encourage：勉～ encourage; urge｜鼓～ encourage; urge｜奖～ award ❷（Lì）姓 a surname

【励精图治】lì jīng tú zhì 振作精神，想办法把国家治理好 exert oneself to make the country prosperous

【励志】lìzhì 〈书 *fml*.〉奋发志气，把精力集中在某方面 be determined to fulfil one's aspirations：～读书 study hard with determination｜～图强 be determined to make the country strong

呖（嚦） lì［呖呖］〈书 *fml*.〉〈拟声词 *onom*.〉形容鸟类清脆的叫声 warble of birds：莺声～ The orioles are warbling.

利 lì ❶ 锋利；锐利（跟'钝'相对 as opposed to 'blunt') sharp：～刃 sharp knife; sharp sword｜～爪 sharp claws ❷ 顺利；便利 smooth; favourable; advantage：不～ unfavourable; disadvantage｜成败～钝 successes or failures, advantages and disadvantages ❸ 利益（跟'害'或'弊'相对 as opposed to 'harm' or 'disadvantage') benefits; interests：～弊 advantages and disadvantages; plusses and minuses｜有～ be advantageous to; be favourable to｜兴～除害 promote what is useful and abolish what is harmful ❹ 利润或利息

profit; interest:暴～ sudden huge profit|薄～多销 small profits but quick turnover|本～两清 both the capital and interest have been cleared up ❺ 使有利 benefit:毫不～己，专门～人 bring benefit (or do good) to other people without any thought of oneself ❻ (Lì)姓 a surname

【利弊】lìbì 好处和害处 advantages and disadvantages; pros and cons:权衡～ weigh the advantages and disadvantages|两种方法各有～。There are both advantages and disadvantages about the two methods.

【利导】lìdǎo ☞ 因势利导 yīn shì lì dǎo on p. 2282

【利钝】lìdùn ❶ 锋利或不锋利 sharp or blunt:刀剑有～。The swords are either sharp or blunt. ❷ 顺利或不顺利 smooth going or rough; smoothness and ruggedness; fortune and misfortune:成败～ successes and failures, advantages and disadvantages

【利滚利】lì gǔn lì 高利贷的一种，利息变作本金再生利息，利上加利，越滚越多 at compound interest; a kind of usurious loan in which interest is tuned into capital for added interest like a snowball; also 利上滚利 lì shàng gǔn lì

【利害】lìhài 利益和损害 advantages and disadvantages; gains and losses:不计～ regardless of gains or losses|～得失 gains and losses|～攸关(利害所关，指有密切的利害关系) concern someone's vital interests

【利害】lì·hai same as 厉害 lì·hai

【利己主义】lìjǐ zhǔyì 只顾自己利益而不顾别人利益和集体利益的思想 egoism; tendency to consider only oneself and one's own interests without any thought of others and others' interests and the collective interests

【利金】lìjīn 〈方 *dial.*〉 same as 利息 lìxī

【利口】lìkǒu ❶ 能说会道的嘴 glib tongue:一张～ a glib tongue; also 利嘴 lìzuǐ ❷ 〈方 *dial.*〉爽口 tasty and refreshing:这几道凉菜，吃起来真～。These cold dishes are quite tasty and refreshing.

【利令智昏】lì lìng zhì hūn 贪图私利使头脑发昏，忘掉一切 be blinded by lust for gain

【利禄】lìlù 〈书 *fml.*〉(官吏的)钱财和爵禄 rank and wealth:功名～ high official positions and riches|～小人 villain bent on positions and riches

【利率】lìlǜ 利息和本金的比率 interest rate, which is the ration between interest and capital in a bank account

【利落】lì·luo ❶ (言语、动作)灵活敏捷，不拖泥带水 agile; nimble; dexterous:说话～ speak clearly|动作挺～ very agile movements ❷ 整齐有条理 neat; orderly:身上穿得干净～ neatly dressed ❸ 完毕 be over; finish; be settled:事情已经办～了。The matter is all settled.|病还没有好～ not yet recovered completely from illness

【利尿】lìniào 促进排尿 diuresis:吃西瓜～。Eating watermelon helps to promote diuresis.

【利器】lìqì ❶ 锋利的兵器 sharp weapon:精兵～ good troops and sharp weapons ❷ 有效的工具 good tool:计算机是统计工作的～。Computers are good tools for the systematic work.

【利钱】lì·qian same as 利息 lìxī

【利权】lìquán 经济上的权益(多指国家的) (oft. of countries) economic rights:～外溢 lose economic rights to foreigners|挽回～ recover economic rights

【利刃】lìrèn ❶ 锋利的刀刃 sharp blade; sharp edge ❷ 指锋利的刀、剑 sharp sword:手持～ hold a sharp sword

【利润】lìrùn 经营工商业等赚的钱 profit

【利市】lìshì ❶ 〈书 *fml.*〉 same as 利润 lìrùn:～三倍 threefold profits ❷ 〈方 *dial.*〉买卖顺利的预兆 good business; good market:发个～ find a good market ❸ 〈方 *dial.*〉吉利 lucky:讨个～ seek good luck ❹ 〈方 *dial.*〉送给办事人的赏钱 tips

【利税】lìshuì 利润和税金 profits and taxes:造纸厂已向国家上缴～一千万元。The paper mill has paid ten million yuan to the state in the form of profits and taxes.

【利索】lì·suo same as 利落 lì·luo:手脚～ nimble limbs|把屋子收拾～了。The room (or house) has been tidied.

【利息】lìxī 因存款、放款而得到的本金以外的钱(区别于'本金' differentiated from 'principal' or 'capital') (on a deposit or loan) interest

【利益】lìyì 好处 interest; benefit; profit:物质～ material benefits|个人～服从集体～。Subordinate the personal interests to the collective interests.

【利用】lìyòng ❶ 使事物或人发挥效能 use; utilize; make use of:废物～ make use of the waste materials|～当地的有利条件发展畜牧业 make use of the favourable local conditions to develop husbandry ❷ 用手段使人或事物为自己服务 use others for one's own ends:互相～ each using the other for his own ends

【利诱】lìyòu 用利益引诱 lure by promise of gain:威逼～ coerce and lure; alternate intimidation and bribery; combine threats with inducements

【利于】lìyú 对某人或某事物有利 be of advantage to; benefit:忠言逆耳～行。Frank words offend the ear but are good for improving one's conduct.

【利欲熏心】lì yù xūn xīn 贪财图利的欲望迷住了心窍 be blinded by greed; be obsessed with the desire for gains; be overcome by covetousness

【利嘴】lìzuǐ same as 利口 lìkǒu ①：一张～ a glib tongue|～不饶人。A person with a glib tongue never gives way to others.

沥(瀝) lì ❶ 液体一滴一滴地落下 drip; trickle：～血 drip blood ❷ 一滴一滴落下的液体 drop：余～ heeltap; small share of benefit | 竹～ (Chinese medicine) liquid from fumigating bamboo for reducing fever

【沥涝】lìlào 沥水淹了庄稼 waterlogging：～成灾 Waterlogging has caused serious damage.

【沥沥】lìlì〈书 *fml.*〉〈拟声词 *onom.*〉多形容风声或水声 sound of wind or of flowing waters：泉声～。Water keeps gurgling from the spring. |风吹～有声。The wind is blowing.

【沥青】lìqīng 有机化合物的混合物，黑色或棕黑色，呈胶状，有天然产的，也有分馏石油或煤焦油得到的。用来铺路面，也用做防水材料、防腐材料等。pitch; asphalt; bitumen; black or dark brown, sticky mixture of organic chemical compounds, produced naturally or by distilling from petroleum or coal tar oil. It is used for surfacing roads or for making waterproof materials and corrosion-proof materials. 通称 generally known as 柏油 bǎiyóu

【沥水】lìshuǐ 降雨之后，留在地面上的积水 waterlogging caused by excessive rainfall：这里地势低洼，～常淹庄稼。This is low-lying land and waterlogging often floods crops.

枥(櫪) lì〈书 *fml.*〉❶ 马槽 manger：老骥伏～ an old steed in the stable ❷ same as 栎 (lì)

例 lì ❶ 用来帮助说明或证明某种情况或说法的事物 example; instance：举～ give an example; cite an instance; take an example (or instance)|～证 illustration; example; case in point ❷ 从前有过，后来可以仿效或依据的事情 precedent：援～ cite a precedent | 先～ precedent|史无前～ unprecedented in history ❸ 调查或统计时指合于某种条件的事例 case; instance：病～ case|十五～中，八～有显著进步，四～进步不明显，三～无变化。Of the 15 cases, eight have made marked progress, four have made insignificant progress and three have remained the same. ❹ 规则；体例 rule; regulation：条～regulations; rules|发凡起～ introduction; preface; write an introduction as an example ❺ 按条例规定的；照成规进行的 regular; routine：～会 regular meetings|～行公事 routine; mere formality

【例规】lìguī ❶ 沿袭下来一贯实行的规矩；惯例 convention; usual practice ❷〈旧时 *old*〉指按照惯例给的钱物 customary dues：交～ pay customary dues ❸ 法例规章 rules; regulations

【例会】lìhuì 按照规定定期举行的会 regular meeting

【例假】lìjià ❶ 依照规定放的假，如元旦、春节、五一、国庆等 official holiday; legal holiday, as New Year's Day, Spring Festival, May Day, National Day ❷〈婉辞 *euph.*〉指月经或月经期 menstrual period; period

【例禁】lìjìn〈书 *fml.*〉法规明令禁止的事情; decreed prohibitions; what is prohibited under laws and regulations：有干～ break or offend decreed prohibitions

【例句】lìjù 用来作为例子的句子 illustrative sentence; example sentence

【例如】lìrú 举例用语，放在所举的例子前面，表示下面就是例子 for instance; for example (e.g.); such as：田径运动的项目很多，～跳高、跳远、百米赛跑等。There are many track and field events, such as high jump, long (or broad) jump, 100-metre dash, etc.

【例题】lìtí 说明某一定理或定律时用来做例子的问题 example; problem designed to illustrate a principle or method

【例外】lìwài ❶ 在一般的规律、规定之外 be an exception：大家都得遵守规定，谁也不能～。Everyone must obey the rules. There are no exceptions. ❷ 在一般的规律、规定之外的情况 exception：一般讲，纬度越高，气温越低，但也有～。Generally speaking, the higher the latitude, the lower the temperature, but there are also exceptions.

【例行公事】lìxíng-gōngshì 按照惯例处理的公事。多借指只重形式，不讲实效的工作。routine; routine business; mere formality; oft. referring to work done for formality's sake, to the neglect of actual results

【例言】lìyán 书的正文前头说明体例等的文字；凡例 introductory remarks; notes on the use of a book

【例证】lìzhèng 用来证明一个事实或理论的例子 illustration; example; case in point

【例子】lì·zi same as 例 lì ①：举个～ cite an example; give an example

疠(癘) lì〈书 *fml.*〉❶ 瘟疫 pestilence; plague：～疫 plague; pestilence ❷ 恶疮 sore; ulcer

【疠疫】lìyì〈书 *fml.*〉瘟疫 plague; pestilence

沴 lì〈书 *fml.*〉❶ 指灾气 miasma; poisonous air or vapour ❷ 伤害 harm; injure; hurt

【沴孽】lìniè〈书 *fml.*〉妖孽 evildoer; person or a thing associated with bad luck, evil or misfortune

戾 lì〈书 *fml.*〉❶ 罪过 crime; sin：罪～ crime ❷ 乖张 perverse; unreasonable：暴～ ruthless; tyrannic|乖～ perverse

隶(隸、隷) lì ❶ 附属 be subordinate to; be under：～属 be subordinate to; be under ❷ 旧社会里地位低下被奴役的人 person in servitude：奴～ slave|仆～ servant ❸ 衙役 runners：皂～ messenger; runner|～卒 government servants ❹ 汉字形体的一种 official script, one of the calligraphic styles of Chinese characters：～书 official script | 汉～ ancient style of calligraphy current in the Han Dynasty (206 B. C. -A. D. 220), simplified from *xiaozhuan* (小篆 xiǎozhuàn)

【隶书】lìshū 汉字字体,由篆书简化演变而成,汉朝的隶书笔画比较简单,是汉朝通行的字体 official script, relatively simple style of calligraphy dating back to the Han Dynasty (206 B. C. - A. D. 220), simplified from *xiaozhuan* (小篆 xiǎozhuàn), or lesser seal script

【隶属】lìshǔ (区域、机构等)受管辖;从属 be subordinate to; be under the jurisdiction or command of: 直辖市直接～国务院。A province-level municipality is under the direct control of the State Council.

【隶字】lìzì same as 隶书 lìshū

【隶卒】lìzú 衙门里的差役 government servants

珠(瓅) lì ☞ [玓珠] (dìlì) on p. 427

荔 lì 指荔枝 litchi; lichee: 鲜～ fresh litchi (or lichee) | ～肉 litchi pulp

【荔枝】lìzhī ❶ 常绿乔木,羽状复叶,小叶长椭圆形,花绿白色,果实球形或卵形,外皮有瘤状突起,熟时紫红色,果肉白色,多汁,味道很甜,是我国的特产 litchi (*Litchi chinensis*); lichee; evergreen tree of the soapberry family, with small long olive-shaped bipinnate leaves, greenish white blossoms, and spheric or oval fruit that consists of a single seed surrounded by a sweet, edible, juicy pulp, enclosed in a rough, brown or purlish-red, papery shell. ❷ 这种植物的果实 fruit of the tree

栎(櫟) lì 落叶乔木,叶子长椭圆形,花黄褐色,雄花是柔荑花序,坚果球形。叶子可饲柞蚕,木材可以做枕木、制家具,树皮含有鞣酸,可以做染料。oak (*Quercus*); deciduous tree with long, olive-shaped leaves, yellowish brown flowers (male flowers are borne in catkin inflorescence) and spheric nuts, leaves that feed tussah, wood used for railway sleepers and furniture, and bark containing tannic acid for dyestuffs; also 麻栎 málì or 橡 xiàng,通称 commonly called 柞树 zuòshù

☞ yuè on p. 2372

郦(酈) Lì 姓 a surname

轹(轢) lì〈书 *fml*.〉❶ 车轮碾轧 (of a cart) run over ❷ 欺压 bully; oppress: 陵～ run roughshod over somebody

俪(儷) lì ❶ 成对的;双的 paired; parallel: 骈～ parallelism | ～句 parallel sentences ❷ 指夫妇 married couple: ～影 photograph of a couple

俐 lì ☞ 伶俐 (líng·lì) on p. 1226

疬(癧) lì ☞ [瘰疬] (luǒlì) on p. 1280

莉 lì ☞ [茉莉] (mò·lì) on p. 1367

莅(蒞、涖) lì〈书 *fml*.〉到 arrive: ～临 arrive; be present | ～会 be present at a meeting | ～任 arrive at one's post; assume an official post

【莅会】lìhuì 到会;参加会议 be present at the meeting: ～讲话 be present and speak at the meeting

【莅临】lìlín〈书 *fml*.〉来到;来临 (多用于贵宾 oft. of distinguished guests) arrive; be present: 敬请～指导。Your presence and guidance are requested.

【莅任】lìrèn〈书 *fml*.〉(官吏)到职 (of an official) arrive at the post

鬲(鬴、曆) lì〈古代 *arch*.〉炊具,样子像鼎,足部中空 ancient cooking tripod with hollow legs

☞ gé on p. 654

栗[1] lì ❶ 栗子树,落叶乔木,叶子长圆形,背面有白色绒毛,花黄白色。果实为坚果,包在多刺的壳斗内,成熟时壳斗裂开而散出。果实可以吃,树皮和壳斗供鞣皮和染色用。chestnut (*Castanea mollissima*); deciduous tree having olive-shaped leaves with white hair on their backs, yellowish white flowers and edible nuts that come loose when the thorny burs ripen and crack open, and both burs and barks being useful for tanning and dyeing ❷ 这种植物的果实 fruit of the plant ❸ (Lì) 姓 a surname

栗[2] **(慄)** lì 发抖;哆嗦 tremble; shudder: 战～ tremble; shiver; shudder | 不寒而～ tremble with fear

【栗暴】lìbào 把手指弯曲起来打人头顶叫凿栗暴或打栗暴 knock on the head with the knuckles: 头上挨了几个～ be knocked on the head several times with one's knuckles; also 栗凿 lìzáo

【栗钙土】lìgàitǔ 栗色的土壤。在我国主要分布于西北地区和内蒙古自治区。腐殖质含量比黑土少,是比较肥沃的土壤。chestnut soil; fertile soil with less humus than black soil, mostly in northwest China and Inner Mongolia

【栗然】lìrán〈书 *fml*.〉战栗的样子 trembling; shuddering

【栗色】lìsè 像栗子皮那样的颜色 chestnut colour; maroon

【栗子】lì·zi ❶ 栗子树 chestnut tree ❷ 栗子树的果实 chestnut

砺(礪) lì〈书 *fml*.〉❶ 磨刀石 whetstone ❷ 磨(刀) whet; sharpen: 砥～ temper | 磨～ steel oneself; harden oneself

【砺石】lìshí〈书 *fml*.〉❶ 磨刀石 whetstone ❷ 粗石 gravel; debris

砾(礫) lì 小石块;碎石 gravel; shingle: 砂～ gravel; grit | 瓦～ debris; rubble | ～石 gravel | ～岩 conglomerate

【砾石】lìshí 经水流冲击磨去棱角的岩石碎块 gravel; loose mixture of pebbles and rock fragments

猁 lì ☞ [猞猁](shēlì) on p. 1692

莅 lì [莅草](lìcǎo)狼尾草 Chinese pennisetum (*Pennisetum alopecuroides*)

樆(欐) lì 〈书 *fml*.〉正梁;栋 ridge pole

蛎(蠣) lì 指牡蛎 oyster: ～黄(牡蛎的肉) oyster meat

唳 lì 〈书 *fml*.〉(鹤、鸿雁等)鸣叫 cry of a crane, wild goose, etc.: 风声鹤～ wailing of the wind and cranes

笠 lì 用竹或草编成的帽子,可以遮雨、遮阳光 large bamboo or straw hat with conical crown and broad brim: 斗～ a large hat with a conical crown and broad brim | 竹～ bamboo hat | 草～ straw hat

粝(糲、糲) lì 〈书 *fml*.〉糙米 unpolished rice; brown rice: 粗～ unpolished rice

粒 lì ❶ (～儿 lìr)小圆珠形或小碎块形的东西 grain; granule; pellet: 豆～儿 beans | 米～儿 a grain of rice | 盐～儿 grains of salt ❷〈量词 *classifier*〉用于粒状的东西 of grainlike things: 一～米 a grain of rice | 三～子弹 three bullets

【粒肥】 lìféi 颗粒肥料的简称 abbr. for 颗粒肥料 kēlì féiliào

【粒子】 lìzǐ 基本粒子 elementary particle

【粒子】 lì•zi same as 粒 lì ①: 豆～ beans | 盐～ grains of salt

綟 lì [綟木](lìmù)落叶灌木或小乔木,叶子卵状椭圆形,总状花序,花冠白色 Tibet lyonia (*Lyonia ovalifolia*); deciduous shrub or small deciduous tree with ellipticle ovate leaves, raceme flowers and a white crown

雳(靂) lì ☞ 霹雳 (pīlì) on p. 1464

跞(躒) lì 〈书 *fml*.〉走动 walk about: 骐骥一～,不能千里。 When a fine horse walks about, it can't cover 1,000 *li* in a day.

☞ luò on p. 1283

詈 lì 〈书 *fml*.〉骂 scold; curse, revile; berate; upbraid: ～骂 scold; abuse; curse | ～辞(骂人的话) abusive language; curses

傈 lì [傈傈族](Lìsùzú)我国少数民族之一,分布在云南和四川 Lisus; a minority ethnic people in Yunnan and Sichuan provinces

凓 lì 〈书 *fml*.〉寒冷 cold: ～冽(非常寒冷) very cold

痢 lì 痢疾 dysentery: 赤～ dysentery characterized by bloody feces | 白～ dysentery characterized by white mucous feces

【痢疾】 lì•ji 传染病,按病原体的不同,主要分为细菌性痢疾和阿米巴痢疾两种 dysentery; infectious disease characterized by intestinal inflammations, abdominal pain and frequent and intense diarrhea with bloody, mucous feces; classified on the basis of pathogens as bacterial dysentery and amoebic dysentery

☞ 细菌性痢疾 xìjūnxìng lì•ji on p. 2059

溧 lì 溧水 (Lìshuǐ),溧阳 (Lìyáng),地名,都在江苏 Lishui and Liyang, geographical names of places in Jiangsu Province

篥 lì ☞ [觱篥] (bìlì) on p. 109

鬁 lì ☞ [鬎鬁] (là•lì) on p. 1140

盭 lì 〈书 *fml*.〉凶狠;乖戾 ferocious; fierce and malicious; perverse; cantankerous

•li (•ㄌㄧ)

哩 •li 〈方 *dial*.〉〈助词 *aux*.〉❶ 跟普通话的'呢'相同,但只用于非疑问句 [same as 呢 •ne, but its use is restricted to declarative sentences]: 山上的雪还没有化～。 The snow on the mountain has not yet thawed. ❷ 用于列举,跟普通话的'啦'相同 [same as 啦•la, used in enumerating items]: 碗～,筷子～,都已经摆好了。 The dinner table has been set.

☞ lī on p. 1174, lǐ on p. 1180 and yīnglǐ on p. 2298

liǎ (ㄌㄧㄚˇ)

俩(倆) liǎ ❶ 两个 two: 咱～ we two; both of us; the two of us | 你们～ you two; the two of you, both of you | 一共五个,我吃了～,他吃了仨。 There are five in all. I ate two and he ate three. ❷ 不多;几个 some; several; a few: 就是有～钱儿,也不能乱花呀。 Even if you have some money, you can by no means squander it. | 一共只有这么～人,恐怕还不够。 There are only a few people. I'm afraid this is not enough. 注意 **NOTE**: '俩'后面不再接'个'字或其他量词 No 个 gè or other classifier is added after 俩.

☞ liǎng on p. 1208

lián (ㄌㄧㄢˊ)

奁(奩、匳、匲、籢) lián 〈古代 *arch*.〉妇女梳妆用的镜匣 toilet case used by women; wooden case with a looking glass and other toilet articles: 妆～(嫁妆) dowry

连[1] lián ❶ 连接 link; join; connect: 心～心 heart linked to heart | 骨肉相～ as closely linked as flesh and blood | 天～水,水～天。 The sky and the water seem to be linked to each other. | 藕断丝～。 The lotus root is cut to pieces, but their fibres remain connected. | 这两句话～不起来。 The two sentences are not connected. ❷ 连续;接续 continuously; in succession; one after another: ～阴天。It has been overcast for days on end. | ～年丰收。Bumper (or good) harvests have been reaped for years in a row. | ～打几枪 fire a succession of shots ❸ 包括在内 including: ～我三个人 three people including me | ～皮三十斤。It weighs 30 *jin*, including the packing | ～根拔 uproot ❹ 军队的编制单位，由若干排组成 company; military unit composed of several platoons ❺ (Lián)姓 a surname

连[2] lián 表示强调某一词或某一词组(下文多有'也、都'等跟它呼应)，含有'甚而至于'的意思 even [used correlatively with 也 yě, 都 dōu, etc.]: ～爷爷都笑了。Even grandpa laughed. | 她臊得～脖子都红了。She was flushed with shyness. | 你怎么～他也不认识? How come you don't even know him?

【连比】liánbǐ 三个或三个以上的数连续相比，这样的比叫做连比。如 3,5,7 的连比是 3:5:7。continued proportion; three or more numbers are arranged in continued proportion, e. g. the continued proportion for 3, 5, 7 is 3: 5: 7

【连鬓胡子】liánbìn-hú·zi 络腮胡子 whiskers; full beard

【连播】liánbō 广播电台或电视台把一个内容较长的节目分若干次连续播出 serial; radio or television programme aired in a continued series: 长篇评书～ continued broadcast of a lengthy story in episodes by a professional storyteller

【连词】liáncí 连接词、词组或句子的词，如'和、与、而且、但是、因为、如果' conjunction [used to connect words, phrases, clauses or sentences, such as 和 hé, 与 yǔ, 而且 érqiě, 但是 dànshì, 因为 yīnwèi and 如果 rúguǒ]

【连带】liándài ❶ 互相关联 interrelated: 人的作风与思想感情是有～关系的。The work style or the way of life of a person is related to his or her thoughts and feelings. ❷ 牵连 involve; implicate: 不但大人遭殃，还～孩子受罪。Not only the adults suffered, their children had a hard time too. ❸ 附带；捎带 by the way; in passing; incidentally: 修房顶的时候，～把门窗也修一修。When the roof is repaired, have the door and windows fixed by the way.

【连…带…】lián…dài… ❶ 表示前后两项包括在一起 indicating the inclusion of two items: ～本～利 principal and interest | ～车～牲口都借来了。Both the cart and animal have been borrowed. | ～老～小一共去了二十三个。Altogether, 23 people went there, old and young. ❷ 表示两种动作紧接着，差不多同时发生 indicating two actions almost taking place at the same time: ～说～唱 talking and singing | ～滚～爬 rolling and climbing | ～蹦～跳 hopping and skipping

【连裆裤】liándāngkù ❶ 裆里不开口的裤子(对'开裆裤'而言 as opposed to the child's pants with a slit in the seat) child's pants with no slit in the seat ❷ 互相勾结、包庇叫穿连裆裤 collude with each other; gang up with each other; band up with each other

【连队】liánduì 军队中对连以及相当于连的单位的习惯称呼 company; military term for a company or any unit at the company level

【连根拔】liángēnbá 〈比喻 *fig.*〉彻底铲除或消灭 tear up by the roots; uproot; eradicate

【连亘】liángèn 接连不断(多指山脉等) continuous (mountains): 山岭～ undulating chain of mountains and ridges | 长城～万里。The Great Wall stretches over 10,000 *li*.

【连拱坝】liángǒngbà 由许多拱形坝面和坝垛构成的坝，用钢筋混凝土筑成。拱形坝面迎着水，把水的压力传到坝垛上。multiple-arch dam or multi-arch dam; dam with many arched surfaces and buttresses built with reinforced concrete, with the arched surfaces receiving the water and transmitting the pressure of the water to the buttresses

【连贯】liánguàn 连接贯通 coherent: 上下句意思要～。The context should be coherent. *or* The two consecutive sentences must hang together. | 长江大桥把南北交通～起来了。The Yangtze River bridge links up the communication lines between north and south. also 联贯 liánguàn

【连锅端】liánguōduān 〈比喻 *fig.*〉全部除掉或移走 move sth. or do away with lock, stock and barrel: 据点的敌人，已经被我们～了。We have destroyed the enemy stronghold lock, stock and barrel. | 整个单位～，迁到外地去了。The entire organization has moved to another place.

【连环】liánhuán 一个套着一个的一串环 chain of rings, 〈比喻 *fig.*〉一个接着一个互相关联的 chain of events, etc.: ～计 a set of interlocking stratagems | ～画 picture-story book | ～锁 interlock | ～保 chain of responsibility | ～债 debt chain

【连环保】liánhuánbǎo 〈旧时 *old*〉官府统治人民的一种手段，把住在一起的几个人或几户人家组织起来，强迫他们相互监督，如果一人或一家出事，其余各人或各家都得连带负责 chain of responsibility; means used by the government in old China to exercise its rule over the people, by which people or households in a neighbourhood were organized and compelled to keep a watch on each other: if one person or one household offended the law, all other people or households were held jointly responsible for the offence.

【连环画】liánhuánhuà 按故事情节连续排列的许多幅画。一般每幅画都有文字说明。book (usu. for children) with a story told in pictures; picture-story book

【连枷】liánjiā 农具,由一个长柄和一组平排的竹条或木条构成,用来拍打谷物,使子粒掉下来 flail; farm tool consisting of a free-swinging flail made by tying a group of parallel bamboo or wooden sticks to the end of a long handle, used to thresh grain; also 梿枷 liánjiā

【连脚裤】liánjiǎokù 婴儿穿的一种裤子,裤脚不开口,包住脚底 infant's pants with bootees attached

【连接】liánjiē ❶(事物)互相衔接 join; link:山岭～ chain of mountains ❷ 使连接 connect; link:～线路 connect lines ‖ also 联接 liánjiē

【连接号】liánjiēhào 标点符号(—),表示把意义密切相关的词语连成一个整体 hyphen (—), used to connect two or three part of a compound word into a complete whole

【连结】liánjié same as 联结 liánjié

【连襟】liánjīn (～儿 liánjīnr)姐姐的丈夫和妹妹的丈夫之间的亲戚关系 husbands of sisters:他是我的～。He is the husband of my wife's sister.|他们是同事又是～。They are both colleagues and brothers-in-law.

【连累】lián·lěi 因事牵连别人,使别人也受到损害 implicate; involve; get someone into trouble:一家失火,～了邻居。One house caught fire, and the neighbours were involved.|一人做事一人当,决不～大家。I will be responsible for what I do, and will never involve others.

【连理】liánlǐ〈书 *fml.*〉❶ 不同根的草木枝干连生在一起,古人认为是吉祥的征兆 intertwining of the branches of different trees, a sign of good luck in the minds of ancients:～枝 interlocked trees|嘉禾～ an ear full of grains and branches of different trees interlocked ❷〈比喻 *fig.*〉恩爱夫妻 loving couple:结为～ get married

【连理枝】liánlǐzhī 枝干合生在一处的两棵树,多比喻恩爱夫妻 two trees with branches interlocked; (fig.)a loving couple

【连连】liánlián 连续不断 repeatedly; again and again:～称赞 praise somebody or something profusely|爷爷～点头。My grandfather nodded again and again.

【连忙】liánmáng 赶快;急忙 hastily; hurriedly; promptly:老大娘一上车,乘客就～让座。Seeing an old lady get on the bus, passengers made haste to offer her a seat.

【连袂】liánmèi same as 联袂 liánmèi

【连绵】liánmián (山脉、河流、雨雪等)接连不断 continuous; unbroken; uninterrupted:～起伏 continuous; rolling; unbroken|阴雨～。There was an unbroken spell of wet weather.|～不断的思绪 endless stream of thought; also 联绵 liánmián

【连年】liánnián 接连许多年 in successive years; in consecutive years; for years running; for years on end:～大丰收 reap exceptionally good harvests for years running

【连篇】liánpiān ❶(文字)一篇接一篇 throughout a piece of writing; page after page:～累牍 lengthy and tedious; one article after another ❷ 充满整个篇幅 pages and pages of empty verbiage:白字～ pages and pages of wrongly written characters

【连篇累牍】lián piān lěi dú 表示用过多篇幅叙述 lengthy and tedious; at great length

【连翩】liánpiān same as 联翩 liánpiān

【连任】liánrèn 连续担任同一职务(多指由选举而任职)be reappointed or reelected consecutively; renew one's term of office:连选～ be reelected consecutively|～两届工会主席 elected as chairman of the trade union twice

【连日】liánrì 接连几天 for days on end; day after day:～赶路 continue one's journey for days on end|～大雨,河水暴涨。The downpour, which went on uninterruptedly for days, caused the water surface of the river to surge drastically.|这个车间～超产。The workshop kept overfulfilling its production quotas for days on end.

【连声】liánshēng 一声紧接一声 say repeatedly; say again and again:～称赞 be praised again and again (or repeatedly); be profuse in one's praise|～答应 repeat one's answer time and again

【连史纸】liánshǐzhǐ 江西出产的一种纸,用竹子做原料,细密、洁白。本称连四,后讹称连史。*lianshi* paper; fine, pure white paper made from bamboo produced in Jiangxi Province. It was originally called 连四 liánsì, but was later erroneously called 连史 liánshǐ.

【连锁】liánsuǒ 一环扣一环,像锁链似的,形容连续不断 linked together like chain:～反应 chain reaction

【连锁店】liánsuǒdiàn 一个公司或集团开设的经营业务相关、方式相同的若干个商店 chain shops; chain of shops opened by a company or group and selling the same goods or doing the same business

【连锁反应】liánsuǒ fǎnyìng〈比喻 *fig.*〉若干个相关的事物,只要一个发生变化,其他都跟着发生变化 chain reaction; any sequence of events, each of which results in, or has an effect on the other:商品市场扩大了,就会引起工业生产的～。An expanding commodity market will give rise to a chain reaction in the industrial production.

【连台本戏】liántái běnxì 分好多次演出的很长的本戏,每次只演一两本 serialized theatrical performances

【连天】liántiān ❶ 接连几天 for several days in a row; for days on end:～阴雨。It was cloudy and drizzly for days on end.|～赶路 continue one's journey for days on end ❷ 连

续不间断 continuously; incessantly:叫苦～ make complaints one after another ❸ 形容远望山水、光焰等与天空相接（of a mountain, the horizon, flames, etc.）touch the sky:湖水～。The lake water and the sky seem to merge.|芳草～。A huge carpet of fragrant-smelling grass extends to the sky.|炮火～。Gunfire raged continuously for days.

【连通】liántōng 接连而又相通 be connected; be interlinked:大海和大洋是～的。The sea and the ocean are connected.|住宅区四周有道路～。The residential area is linked by roads in all directions; also 联通 liántōng

【连通器】liántōngqì 底部彼此连通的容器,同一种液体在连通器里液面永远保持相同的高度 connecting vessel; communicating vessel

【连同】liántóng 连;和 together with; along with:货物～清单一并送去。Send the goods along with the inventory list.|今年～去年下半年,他家共养猪一百五十多头。His family raised more than 150 pigs altogether this year and in the second half of last year.

【连写】liánxiě 指汉字用拼音字母注音时把每一个复音词的几个音节连起来写,如'rénmín（人民）、tuōlājī（拖拉机）'（in Chinese phonetic transcription）write the two or more syllables of a word together, e. g. rénmín for 人民, tuōlājī for 拖拉机

【连续】liánxù 一个接一个 continuously; successively; in a row; one after another:～不断 continuous; uninterrupted; continual|这个车间～创造了三次新记录。This workshop has set three new records in a row.

【连续剧】liánxùjù 分为若干集,在电台或电视台连续播放的情节连贯的戏剧 serial radio or television play:广播～ radio serial|电视～ TV serial

【连夜】liányè ❶ 当天夜里（就做）the same night; that very night; all through the night:乡长接到通知,～赶进城。The township head rushed to the city the night he received the notice. ❷ 接连几夜 for nights on end:连天～ days and nights

【连衣裙】liányīqún 上衣和裙子连在一起的女装 woman's dress; dress

【连阴天】liányīntiān 接连多日阴雨的天气 cloudy weather for several days running

【连阴雨】liányīnyǔ 很多天连续不断的雨 unbroken spell of wet weather

【连用】liányòng 连起来使用 use consecutively; use together:俩（liǎ）和个这两个字不能～。The two words, 俩 liǎ and 个 gè, do not go together.

【连载】liánzǎi 一个篇幅较长的作品在同一报纸或刊物上分若干次连续刊载 publish in instalments; serialize:小说～ novel carried in segments

【连中三元】lián zhòng sān yuán ❶〈旧时 *old*〉指在乡试、会试、殿试中接连考取解元、会元、状元 one who scores top marks consecutively in civil examinations at the provincial, national and palace levels ❷〈比喻 *fig.*〉在三次考试或比赛中连续得胜,或在一项比赛中连续三次取得成功 win the first place in examinations or sports contests three times in a row; win three gold medals in one sports contest

【连种】liánzhòng same as 连作 liánzuò

【连轴转】liánzhóuzhuàn〈比喻 *fig.*〉夜以继日地劳动 work day and night; work round the clock:工作一忙,我们几个人就得～。Whenever there is too much work, the few of us have to work 24/7.

【连珠】liánzhū 连接成串的珠子 string of beads;〈比喻 *fig.*〉连续不断的声音等 like a string of beads; in rapid succession:～炮 continuous gunfire; drumfire|妙语～ sparkling talk or discourse|～似的机枪声 a continuous rattle of machine-gun fire|捷报～似地传来。One piece of good news came after another.

【连属】liánzhǔ〈书 *fml.*〉连接;联结 join; link:两地～ link the two places|～成篇 combined into one article; also 联属 liánzhǔ

【连缀】liánzhuì 联结 link together; join together; put together:孤立地看,每一个情节都很平淡,～在一起,就有趣了。When taken separately, each of the episodes looks rather dull, but when put together, they're very interesting; also 联缀 liánzhuì

【连作】liánzuò 在一块田地上连续栽种同一种作物 continuous cropping on a plot; also 连种 liánzhòng, 连茬 liánchá or 重茬 chóngchá

【连坐】liánzuò 一个人犯法,他的家属、亲族、邻居等连带受处罚（in former times）be punished for being related to or friendly with someone who has committed an offence

怜（憐） lián ❶ 怜悯 empathize with; pity; have pity on; sympathize with:可～ pity; pitiful|～惜 empathy|同病相～。Fellow sufferers sympathize with each other. ❷ 爱 affection; love:～爱 tender love|爱～ show tender affection for

【怜爱】lián'ài 疼爱 love tenderly; have tender affection for:这孩子胖胖的、大眼睛,真叫人～。The plump child with big eyes is so lovable.

【怜悯】liánmǐn 对遭遇不幸的人表示同情 pity; take pity on; express sympathy for; have compassion for:～之心 sympathy; compassion; pity|我不需要别人的～,只希望得到大家的理解。I don't want any body's sympathy, but I want everybody's understanding.

【怜惜】liánxī 同情爱护 take pity on; have pity for:决不～恶人。Never take pity on evil people.

【怜恤】liánxù same as 怜悯 liánmǐn:孤寡老人得到四邻的～和多方面的照顾。The orphaned, widowed and aged people have received sympathy and care in many respects from their neighbours.

帘(❷簾) lián (～儿 liánr) ❶ 用布做成的望子 sign printed on a curtain, flag, etc.:酒～ wineshop sign ❷ 用布、竹子、苇子等做的有遮蔽作用的器物 screen or curtain made from cloth, bamboo or reeds:竹～ bamboo curtain|窗～儿 window curtain|门～儿 door curtain

【帘布】liánbù 轮胎里面所衬的布,作用是保护橡胶,抵抗张力 cord fabric (in tyres); fabric used in tyres to protect the rubber and resist tension; also 帘子布 lián·zibù

【帘子】lián·zi same as 帘 lián ②:竹～ bamboo screen or curtain|窗～ window curtain

莲 lián ❶ 多年生草本植物,生在浅水中,地下茎肥大而长,有节,叶子圆形,高出水面,花大,淡红色或白色,有香味。地下茎叫藕,种子叫莲子,都可以吃。lotus (*Nelumbo nucifera*); perennial herbal plant growing in shallow water, having fattened and knotted root, and orbicular leaves above water, pink or white fragrant flowers, both the root and seeds being edible; also 荷 hé,芙蓉 fúróng,芙蕖 fúqú, etc. ❷ 指莲子 lotus seeds:建～(福建产的莲子) Fujian lotus seeds (produced in Fujian)|湘～(湖南产的莲子) Hunan lotus seeds (produced in Hunan)

【莲菜】liáncài 〈方 *dial.*〉用做蔬菜的藕 lotus root used as a vegetable

【莲房】liánfáng 〈书 *fml.*〉 ❶ same as 莲蓬 lián·peng ❷ 指僧人的居室 monk's bedroom

【莲花】liánhuā ❶ 莲的花 lotus flower ❷ 指莲 lotus:养了几盆～ cultivated some pots of lotus flowers

【莲花白】liánhuābái 〈方 *dial.*〉结球甘蓝 cabbage

【莲花落】liánhuālào 曲艺的一种,用竹板打节拍,每段常以'莲花落,落莲花'一类的句子做衬腔或尾声 genre of ballad sung to the accompaniment of bamboo clappers, each paragraph using 莲花落 liánhuālào, 落莲花 làoliánhuā as its foil and coda

【莲蓬】lián·peng 莲花开过后的花托,倒圆锥形,里面有莲子 lotus seedpod; receptacle after the fading of the flower containing seeds

【莲蓬头】lián·pengtóu 〈方 *dial.*〉same as 喷头 pēntóu

【莲台】liántái same as 莲座 liánzuò ②

【莲心】liánxīn ❶ 莲子中的胚芽,绿色,有苦味,中医入药 bitter-tasting green plumule of a lotus seed, used for Chinese traditional medicine ❷ 〈方 *dial.*〉same as 莲子 liánzǐ

【莲子】liánzǐ 莲的种子,椭圆形,当中有绿色的莲心,肉呈乳白色,可以吃,也可入药 lotus seed; seed of lotus, oval-shaped, with green plumule and white edible flesh

【莲宗】liánzōng 即净土宗,因创始人慧远于庐山东林寺建白莲社而得名 Lotus Sect of Buddhism, or the Pure-land Sect of Buddhism, whose chief tenet is salvation by faith in Amitabha; Its founder Huiyuan set up the White Lotus Sect in the Donglin Temple at Mount Lushan. Hence the name.

【莲座】liánzuò ❶ 莲花的底部,呈倒圆锥形 lotus seat; receptacle of the lotus flower in the shape of an inverted cone ❷ 佛像的底座,由于多作莲花形而得名 Buddha's seat in the form of a lotus flower; lotus throne

涟 lián 〈书 *fml.*〉 ❶ 风吹水面所形成的波纹 ripples:～漪 ripples ❷ 泪流不断的样子 continuous flow (of tears); stream of tears:～洏 weeping|泣涕～～ tears streaming down one's face; tears flowing continuously

【涟洏】lián'ér 〈书 *fml.*〉形容涕泪交流 weeping copiously

【涟漪】liányī 〈书 *fml.*〉细小的波纹 ripples:微风吹过,湖面上泛起层层～。The lake rippled at the faintest touch of a gentle breeze.

梿 lián [梿枷](liánjiā) same as 连枷 liánjiā

联(聯) lián ❶ 联结;联合 unite; ally oneself with; join:～盟 union; alliance|～系 contact; ties; connection; relation|～络 liaison|～欢 get-together; party; social gathering|～名 jointly; jointly signed|三～单 triplicate form ❷ 对联 antithetical couplet (written on scrolls):春～ Spring Festival couplets or Spring Festival scrolls|挽～ elegiac couplet

【联邦】liánbāng 由若干具有国家性质的行政区域(有国、邦、州等不同名称)联合而成的统一国家,各行政区域有自己的宪法、立法机关和政府,联邦也有统一的宪法、立法机关和政府。国际交往以联邦政府为主体。federation; union; commonwealth; union of administrative regions with the power of a state, each administrative region having its own constitution, legislative body and government, but the union also having its central constitution, legislative body and government. International contacts are made mainly with the federal government.

【联播】liánbō 若干广播电台或电视台同时转播(某电台或电视台播送的节目) network radio or television broadcast:新闻～ network news programme

【联唱】liánchàng 两个以上的人连接着演唱或一个人、一个合唱队连着演唱两个以上的歌、曲牌等 two or more people sing one after another; person or chorus singing two or more songs continuously

【联电】liándiàn 联合通电(联名拍发宣布政治上

某种主张的电报）joint circular telegram stating some important political views

【联防】liánfáng ❶ 若干组织联合起来，共同防御、防范 joint defence; joint command of defence forces：军民～ joint defence by army and militia; army-civilian defence | 群众～ joint defence by the masses | 治安～ public security and joint defence ❷ 球赛中的联合防守（of ball games）zone defence

【联贯】liánguàn same as 连贯 liánguàn

【联合】liánhé ❶ 联系使不分散；结合 unite; ally：全世界无产者，～起来！Workers of all countries, unite! ❷ 结合在一起的；共同 joint; combined：～收割机 combine harvester | ～声明 joint statement | ～招生 joint enrolment ❸ 两块以上的骨头长在一起或固定在一起，叫做联合，如耻骨联合、下颌骨联合等 symphysis; growing together of bones originally separate, as of the two halves of the lower jaw or the two pubic bones, such as symphysis pubis, and symphysis mandible

【联合国】Liánhéguó 第二次世界大战结束后于1945年成立的国际组织，总部设在美国纽约。主要机构有联合国大会、安全理事会、经济和社会理事会、秘书处等。联合国宪章规定，其主要宗旨是维护国际和平与安全，发展国际友好关系，促进经济文化等方面的国际合作。United Nations (U. N.), an international organization set up in 1945 after the conclusion of World War II, with its headquarters in New York City, the United States. Its major departments are the U. N. General Assembly, Security Council, Economics and Social Council and the Secretariat, etc. According to the U. N. Charter, its main aim is to safeguard international peace and security, develop international friendly relations and promote international cooperation in economic, cultural and other fields.

【联合机】liánhéjī 两种以上的机器同时进行操作的联合装置，可以同时进行多种工作，完成各种作业。如联合收割机和联合采煤机。combine; combined device consisting of two or more machines working at the same time, such as the combine harvester and coal cutter-loader; also 康拜因 kāngbàiyīn

【联合收割机】liánhé shōugējī 收割农作物的联合机，能同时完成多种工作，如谷物联合收割机能将谷物割下、自动脱粒、把谷粒和作物的茎分开等 combine; harvester capable of doing several jobs at the same time, cutting, threshing, and separating grain from stalks; also 康拜因 kāngbàiyīn

【联合战线】liánhé zhànxiàn same as 统一战线 tǒngyī zhànxiàn

【联合政府】liánhé zhèngfǔ 两个或两个以上党派联合组成的政府 coalition government

【联合制】liánhézhì same as 康平纳 kāngpíngnà

【联欢】liánhuān（一个集体的成员或两个以上的集体）为了庆祝或加强团结，在一起欢聚 have a social gathering; have a get-together：～会 get-together; party | 军民～ get-together of soldiers and civilians

【联接】liánjiē same as 连接 liánjiē

【联结】liánjié 结合（在一起）join; connect; link; bind：画一条直线把这两点～起来。Draw a line to join the two points. | 锦州是～东北和华北的战略要点。Jinzhou is a place of strategic importance, connecting northeast and north China. also 连结 liánjié

【联句】liánjù〈旧时 *old*〉做诗的一种方式，两人或多人各做一句或两句，相联成篇（多用于宴席及朋友间酬应）connecting verses; literary game in which two or more persons each chant one or two lines of poetry until the lines in sequence make up an entire poem (most popular among friends at a banquet)：～赋诗 chant connecting lines for a poem | 即景～ improvise connecting lines for a poem with the scenery one is looking at as the theme

【联军】liánjūn 由两支或两支以上的武装组织联合而成的军队 allied forces; united army：东北抗日～ Northeast China anti-Japanese United Army

【联络】liánluò 彼此交接；接上关系 contact; keep in contact; communicate with; make liaison with：～员 contact person; liaison man | ～站 liaison station | 失掉～ lose contact | ～感情 start or keep up friendship or friendly relations; strengthen the ties of friendship | 他～了一些人办了一个读书会。He set up a study group together with some other people.

【联袂】liánmèi〈书 *fml.*〉手拉着手，比喻一同（来、去等）(fig.) go, come, etc. hand in hand：～而往 go together | ～而至 arrive together | ～登台献艺 perform together; also 连袂 liánmèi

【联盟】liánméng ❶ 两个或两个以上的国家为了共同行动而订立盟约所结成的集团 alliance; coalition; league; union; bloc formed by two or more countries to take joint action after concluding a treaty：反法西斯～ anti-fascist alliance ❷ 指个人、集体或阶级的联合 union of individuals, organizations or classes：工农～ worker-peasant alliance

【联绵】liánmián same as 连绵 liánmián

【联绵字】liánmiánzì〈旧时 *old*〉指双音的单纯词 binome; compound word consisting of two characters; 包括 including: a) 双声的，如仿佛、伶俐 alliterative compound or binome, e. g. 仿佛 fǎngfú, 伶俐 líng·lì; b) 叠韵的，如阑干、逍遥 rhyming compound or binome, e. g. 阑干 lángān, 逍遥 xiāoyáo; c) 非双声非叠韵的，如妯娌、玛瑙 neither alliterative compound nor rhyming compound, e. g. 妯娌 zhóu·lǐ, 玛瑙 mǎnǎo

【联名】liánmíng 由若干人或若干团体共同具名 round-robin (letter, message, etc.) jointly signed; jointly:～发起 jointly initiate; jointly sponsor|～写信 write a joint letter

【联翩】liánpiān 鸟飞的样子。形容连续不断。in close succession; together:浮想～ thoughts racing in one's mind|～而至 come in close succession; arrive one after another; also 连翩 liánpiān

【联赛】liánsài (在篮球、排球、足球等比赛中)三个以上同等级的球队之间的比赛 (basketball, volleyball, football) league series:全国足球甲级～ National Football Division A League

【联手】liánshǒu 联合;共同 jointly:十多位科学家～进行实地调查。More than ten scientists jointly conducted a field investigation.|这部电视剧由两家电视台～摄制。This TV play was co-produced by two TV stations.

【联网】liánwǎng 供电网络、电信网络、计算机网络等互相连接,形成更大的网络 interconnect of power transmission networks, telecommunication networks and computer networks to form a larger network:～发电 power supply from a grid (consisting of power plants and transmission lines located in different areas)

【联席会议】liánxí huìyì 不同的单位、团体为了解决彼此有关的问题而联合举行的会议 joint conference; joint meeting held by a number of organizations to solve problems between themselves

【联系】liánxì 彼此接上关系 contact; touch; connection; relation:保持～ stay connected|理论～实际 integrate theory with practice|密切～群众 maintain close ties with the masses|以后多写信,不要失掉～。Keep correspondence. *or* Don't lose contact.

【联想】liánxiǎng 由于某人或某事物而想起其他相关的人或事物;由于某概念而引起其他相关的概念 connect with mentally; associate with:～丰富 plenty of associations|看到他,使我～起许多往事。The sight of him brings me many associations of the past.

【联谊】liányì 联络友谊 keep up friendship; strengthen the bonds of friendship:～会 get-together; party|～活动 activities for promoting friendship

【联姻】liányīn 两家由婚姻关系结成亲戚 (of two families) be related by marriage; unite two families by marriage

【联营】liányíng 联合经营 operate a business with joint investment:～企业 joint venture|这个煤矿由三个县～。This coal mine is jointly run by three counties.

【联运】liányùn 不同的交通部门或分段的交通路线之间建立联系,连续运输,旅客或托运者只要买一次票或办一次手续,如水陆联运、国际联运等 through transport service; transport service jointly run by different transport departments or by different sections of a transport line, enabling a passenger or a consignor to get to his destination with a single ticket, such as land-and-sea through transport service, international through transport service, etc.

【联展】liánzhǎn 联合展览或展销 joint exhibition or joint sales fair:书画～ joint books and paintings sales fair|老年用品～ joint sales fair on old people's goods

【联属】liánzhǔ same as 连属 liánzhǔ

【联缀】liánzhuì same as 连缀 liánzhuì

裢 lián ☞ 褡裢 (dā•lián) on p. 344

廉(亷) lián ❶ 廉洁 incorrupt; honest and clean:清～ incorrupt; clean and honest|～耻 integrity and a sense of honour ❷ (价钱)低;便宜 cheap; inexpensive; low-priced:低～ cheap; of low price|价～物美 cheap and good; cheap price and good quality ❸ (Lián) 姓 a surname

【廉耻】liánchǐ 廉洁的操守和羞耻的感觉 integrity and sense of shame:不顾～ have no sense of shame; be shameless

【廉价】liánjià 价钱比一般低 cheap; inexpensive; low-priced:～书 cheap books

【廉洁】liánjié 不损公肥私;不贪污 honest and clean; incorruptible:～奉公 incorrupt and honest in performing one's official duties|刚正～ upright and incorruptible

【廉明】liánmíng 廉洁而清明 (of officials) upright and incorruptible:为官～ incorruptible official|～公正 incorruptible and impartial

【廉正】liánzhèng 廉洁正直 upright and honest:～无私 upright, honest and selfless

【廉政】liánzhèng 使政治廉洁 honest and clean government:～措施 measures to keep the government clean and honest|搞好～建设 build an honest and clean government

【廉直】liánzhí same as 廉正 liánzhèng:～之士 upright and honest person

磏 lián 〈书 *fml*.〉一种磨刀石 whetstone
☞ on p. 1532 qiān

鲢 lián 鲢鱼,身体侧扁,鳞细,背部青黑色,腹部白色,是我国重要的淡水鱼类之一 silver carp (*Hypophthalmichtys molitrix*); flat fish with small scales, green-black back and white belly; one of the important freshwater fishes in China; also 鲊 xù

濂 Lián ❶ 濂江,水名,在江西 Lianjiang, name of a river in Jiangxi Province ❷ 姓, a surname

臁 lián 小腿的两侧 two sides of the shank:～骨 shank bones (shin bone and splint bone)|～疮 ulcer on the shank

镰(鎌) lián 镰刀 sickle:钐～|开～ start to harvest

【镰刀】liándāo 收割庄稼和割草的农具,由刀片

和木把构成,有的刀片上带小锯齿 sickle

蠊 lián ☞ 蜚蠊 (fěilián) on p.562

鬑 lián 〈书 *fml*.〉形容须发长 long hair and beard

liǎn (ㄌㄧㄢˇ)

琏 liǎn 〈古代 *arch*.〉宗庙盛黍稷的器具 *lian*, a vessel used to hold grain at the imperial sacrifice

敛(斂) liǎn ❶〈书 *fml*.〉收起;收住 hold back; restrain:~容 assume a serious expression|~足 check one's steps; hold back from going ❷〈书 *fml*.〉约束 keep within bounds; restrain:~迹 temporarily desist from one's evil ways; lie low ❸ 收集;征收 collect:~钱 collect money illegally|横征暴~ extort heavy taxes and levies|把工具~起来。Collect the tools.

【敛步】liǎnbù 〈书 *fml*.〉收住脚步,不往前走 check one's steps; hold back one's steps

【敛财】liǎncái 搜刮钱财 accumulate wealth by unfair means

【敛迹】liǎnjì 〈书 *fml*.〉❶ 隐蔽起来,不敢再出头露面 temporarily desist from one's evil ways; lie low:盗匪~。The bandits have desisted temporarily from their evil ways.|~潜踪 lie low ❷ 约束自己的言行 restrain one's words and actions:屏气~ keep silence ❸ 退隐 retreat:~山林 retreat to a mountain forest; live in seclusion|~避贤 retire to make room for the virtuous

【敛钱】liǎn//qián 向大家收取费用或捐款 collect money; raise money:~办学 raise funds to run a school

【敛衽】liǎnrèn 〈书 *fml*.〉❶ 整整衣襟,表示恭敬 straighten one's lapels to show respect:~而拜 straighten one's lapels to salute ❷ 指妇女行礼 (of women) salute; also 裣衽 liǎnrèn

【敛容】liǎnróng 〈书 *fml*.〉收起笑容;脸色变得严肃 assume a serious expression:~正色 look serious

【敛足】liǎnzú 〈书 *fml*.〉收住脚步,不往前走 check one's steps; hold back from going

脸(臉) liǎn ❶ 头的前部,从额到下巴 face:圆~ round face|洗~ wash one's face ❷ (~儿 liǎnr)某些物体的前部 front part of sth.:门~儿 shop front; facade of a shop|鞋~儿 front top of a shoe ❸ 情面;面子 face:丢~ lose face|不要~ not spare one's feelings; have no consideration for one's feelings ❹ (~儿 liǎnr)脸上的表情 facial expression:笑~儿 smiling face|把~一变 change one's expression

【脸蛋儿】liǎndànr 脸的两旁部分,也泛指脸(多用于年幼的人 usu. children's) cheeks; face:小姑娘的~红得像苹果。The little girl's face is as red as an apple. also 脸蛋子 liǎndàn·zi

【脸红】liǎn hóng 指害臊 blush (with shame or embarrassment):说这话也不~? Don't you blush for what you've said?

【脸红脖子粗】liǎn hóng bó·zi cū 形容发急、发怒或激动时面部颈部红涨 get red in the face from anger, excitement or agitation:一点儿小事,何必争得~的。Why should you get so worked up in the heat of the argument over a trifle?

【脸颊】liǎnjiá 脸的两旁部分 cheeks; face:红润的~ ruddy cheeks|汗珠子顺着~直往下淌。Beads of sweat streamed down her cheeks.

【脸面】liǎnmiàn ❶ same as 脸 liǎn ①:~消瘦 thin face ❷ 情面;面子 face; someone's feelings:看我的~,不要生他的气了。For my sake, don't get angry with him.

【脸盘儿】liǎnpánr 指脸的形状、轮廓 shape of a face:圆~ round face|大~ big face; also 脸盘子 liǎnpán·zi

【脸庞】liǎnpáng same as 脸盘儿 liǎnpánr:鸭蛋形~ oval face

【脸皮】liǎnpí ❶ 脸上的皮肤 skin of a face:白净~ face with fair complexion|黑黄的~ sallow-looking swarthy face ❷ 指情面 face; self-pride:撕不破~ not have the heart to ignore sb.'s sensitivities ❸ 指羞耻的心理,容易害羞叫脸皮薄,不容易害羞叫脸皮厚 sense of shame; apt to be bashful or feel shy is called 'thin-skinned'; not apt to be bashful or feel shy is called 'thick-skinned'.

【脸谱】liǎnpǔ 戏曲中某些角色(多为净角)脸上画的各种图案,用来表现人物的性格和特征 types of facial makeup indicating personalities and characters in Chinese opera

【脸色】liǎnsè ❶ 脸的颜色 complexion; look:~微红 rosy complexion|~灰白 pale (or ashen) complexion ❷ 脸上表现出来的健康情况;气色 look; complexion:经过几个月调养,他的~比过去好多了。After a few months of nursing and special care, he looks much better than before. ❸ 脸上的表情 facial expression:~温和 mild look|~阴沉 sullen look|一看他的~,我就知道准是有什么好消息。I can see from the expression on his face that there is some good news.

【脸膛儿】liǎntángr 〈方 *dial*.〉same as 脸 liǎn ①:四方~ square face|~晒得黑黑的 suntanned face; sunburned face

【脸形】liǎnxíng 脸的形状 shape of one's face; facial features:~端正 have regular features|长方~ long face; also 脸型 liǎnxíng

【脸子】liǎn·zi 〈方 *dial*.〉❶ 容貌(多指美貌,用于不庄重的口气 in a frivolous tone) pretty face ❷ 不愉快的脸色 unpleasant look:他不会给你~看的。He won't chew you out for that. ❸ 情面；面子 face；one's feelings：他是要～的人，不能当着大伙儿丢这个丑。He is a man of honour who can't stand being disgraced in the face of everybody.

裣(襝) liǎn [裣衽](liǎnrèn) same as 敛衽 liǎnrèn ②

蔹(蘞) liǎn ☞ 白蔹 báiliǎn on p.35

liàn (ㄌㄧㄢˋ)

练(練) liàn ❶ 白绢 white silk：江平如～。The river runs as smoothly as silk. ❷〈书 *fml.*〉把生丝煮熟，使它柔软洁白 softening and whitening raw silk by boiling and scouring ❸ 练习；训练 practise；train；drill：～兵 military training；drill；troop training｜～功夫 practise one's skill；do exercises in gymnastics｜～毛笔字 practise calligraphy ❹ 经验多；纯熟 experienced；veteran；skilled：老～ experienced；seasoned；old hand｜干～ capable and experienced｜熟～ skilled；proficient；adept ❺ (Liàn) 姓 a surname

【练笔】liàn//bǐ ❶ 练习写作 practise writing ❷ 练习写字 practise calligraphy

【练兵】liàn//bīng ❶ 训练军队 train soldiers；drill soldiers ❷ 泛指训练各种人员 professional training：乒乓球队正抓紧赛前～。The table tennis team is busy with its practice sessions prior to the competition.

【练达】liàndá〈书 *fml.*〉阅历多而通达人情世故 experienced and worldly-wise：～老成 experienced

【练队】liàn//duì 参加游行或检阅之前练习队形、步伐等 drill in formation；drill for a parade

【练功】liàn//gōng 训练技能；练习功夫，有时特指练气功或武功 do exercises in gymnastics, *wushu*, acrobatics, etc.；practise one's skill：～房 training hall｜演员坚持～。The actors and actresses persist in honing their skills｜练过几年功，有两下子。Having practiced *wushu* for a few years, he's really good at it.

【练手】liàn//shǒu (～儿 liàn//shǒur)练习做活儿技能 try one's hand (at some skill)；practise one's skill：初学裁缝，先做点儿小孩儿衣服练练手。Having just started to learn tailoring, I'll try my hand at some children's clothes.

【练武】liànwǔ ❶ 学习或练习武艺 learn or practise martial arts：～强身 practise martial for physical fitness ❷ 学习或练习军事技术 learn or practise military skills：民兵利用生产空隙～。The militia learned military skills during breaks in production. ❸ 泛指学习或练习各项技术 learn or practise various skills：各行各业都在开展技术～。Those working in all industries and trades have started improving professional skills.

【练习】liànxí ❶ 反复学习，以求熟练 practise：～心算 practise mental arithmetic｜～写文章 practise writing ❷ 为巩固学习效果而安排的作业等 exercises：～题 problems for exercise；exercises｜～本 exercise book｜做～ do exercises｜交～ hand in exercises

炼(煉、鍊) liàn ❶ 用加热等办法使物质纯净或坚韧 smelting；refining；making；melting；heat sth. to purify or solidify it：～铁 iron smelting｜～钢 steel making｜～乳 condensed milk｜猪油～过了。The lard has been melted. ❷ 烧 burn；temper with fire：～山 set fire on a mountain；burn a mountain｜真金不怕火～。Genuine gold fears no fire. ❸ 用心琢磨，使词句简洁优美 weigh one's word；seek the right phrase：～字 think hard to choose the right word；cudgel one's brains for the right word｜～句 polish and repolish a sentence

【炼丹】liàn//dān 指道教徒用朱砂炼药 (of a Taoist practice) make pills of immortality

【炼话】liànhuà〈方 *dial.*〉指方言土语中意味深长、富于表现力的话 pithy expressions；piquant expressions；significant expressions in local dialects

【炼焦】liàn//jiāo 在隔绝空气的条件下，经高温加热，使煤分解，得到焦炭 make coke；coke；coal from which most of the gases have been removed by heating

【炼句】liànjù 写作时斟酌语句，使简洁优美 try to find the best turn of phrase；polish and repolish a sentence：要写好文章，还须炼字～。To write a good piece, one has to think hard of how to choose the right word and find the best turn of phrase.

【炼乳】liànrǔ 用鲜牛奶或羊奶经消毒浓缩加糖制成的饮料，可贮存较长时间 condensed milk；drink prepared from fresh milk by sterilization, condensation and adding sugar

【炼山】liàn//shān 为了造林或使森林更新，把山上的杂草、灌木或采伐剩余物用火烧掉 in order to afforest or reafforest a mountain, get rid of all grasses, bushes or stumps by burning

【炼油】liàn//yóu ❶ 分馏石油 oil refining ❷ 用加热的方法从含油的物质中把油分离出来 extract oil by heating ❸ 把动物油或植物油加热使适于食用 heat edible oil

【炼狱】liànyù ❶ 天主教指人生前罪恶没有赎尽，死后灵魂暂时受罚的地方 (Catholicism) purgatory, where the soul of the deceased is put through temporary suffering before entering heaven ❷〈比喻 *fig.*〉人经受磨练的艰苦环境 difficult circumstances in which people are tempered

【炼字】liànzì 写作时推敲用字 think hard over one's choice of words；cudgel one's brains for the right word; try to find the exact word

恋(戀) liàn ❶ 恋爱 love：初～ virgin love; first love｜失～ reject or cast off a previously accepted lover; be jilted; lose one's love; get a 'Dear John' letter; be disappointed in a love affair; disappointed love｜～人 lover; sweetheart ❷ 想念不忘；不忍分离 long for; feel attached to：留～ be reluctant (or unwilling) to leave; be reluctant (or unwilling) to part with｜～家 reluctant (or unwilling) to be away from home; be tied to home｜～～不舍 be reluctant (or unwilling) to part with; be reluctant (or unwilling) to leave

【恋爱】liàn'ài ❶ 男女互相爱慕 mutual love between man and woman：自由～ freedom of love; free love between man and woman ❷ 男女互相爱慕的行动表现 be in love; courtship：谈～ be in love; have a love affair

【恋歌】liàngē 表达爱情的歌曲 love song

【恋家】liàn//jiā 舍不得离开家 be unwilling or reluctant to be away from home：这孩子～，不愿意到外地去。This child is reluctant to leave home for somewhere else.

【恋恋不舍】liànliàn bù shě 形容舍不得离开 be reluctant to part from; hate to see sb. go：孩子们～，抱住他不放他走。The children were reluctant to part with him. They held him tightly, unwilling to let go of him.

【恋慕】liànmù 眷恋；爱慕 have a tender feeling towards; have affection for; adore：～之情 tender feelings

【恋念】liànniàn 眷恋思念 long for; yearn for：～的心情 longing or longings; yearning or yearnings｜侨胞们～着祖国。The overseas Chinese have longings for the motherland.

【恋情】liànqíng ❶ 依恋的感情 tender feeling or feelings：他对母校的房屋、树木、水塘有了故乡一样的～。He has the same tender feelings towards the buildings, trees and the pond of his old school as towards his home town. ❷ 爱恋的感情；爱情 romantic love; fling with (a boyfriend or girlfriend)：两个人的～已到如胶似漆的程度。The two of them stick to each other just like glue and lacquer; they are deeply in love.

【恋群】liànqún ❶ 依恋常在一起的人 feel attached to people with whom someone is often together：他从小～，出门在外，时常怀念家乡的亲友。Having attached himself to people living together since childhood, he always thinks of his relatives and friends in his home town when he is away. ❷ 动物依恋和自己生活在一块的群体 animals love their groups that live together with them：猕猴～。Monkeys are gregarious.

【恋人】liànrén 恋爱中男女的一方 sweetheart; loved one; girlfriend or boyfriend：一对～ a couple in love

【恋栈】liànzhàn 马舍不得离开马棚，讥讽做官的人舍不得离开自己的职位 (of an official) be loath to give up his post; a horse is loath to leave its stable

【恋战】liànzhàn 贪图获得战果，舍不得退出战斗(多用于否定式 oft. used in the negative) be over-zealous in fighting

殓(殮) liàn 把死人装进棺材 put a body into a coffin; encoffin：入～ put a corpse in a coffin｜成～ encoffin｜装～ dress up a corpse and put into in a coffin｜～葬 shroud and bury

链(鏈) liàn ❶ (～儿 liànr)链子 chain：锁～ chains; fetters; shackles｜铁～儿 iron chain; shackles｜表～儿 watchband ❷ 计量海洋上距离的长度单位。1 链等于 1/10 海里，合 185.2 米。cable length; 1/10 of a nautical mile or 185.2 metres

【链轨】liànguǐ same as 履带 lǚdài

【链球】liànqiú ❶ 田径运动田赛项目之一，运动员两手握着链球的把手，人和球同时旋转，最后加力使球脱手而出 hammer, metal ball attached to a short length of wire for throwing in an athletic contest, in which a competitor grasps the handle of the wire with both hands and spins his body and all for a few rounds before letting go of the metal ball with a sudden burst of energy ❷ 链球运动使用的投掷器械，球体用铁或铜制成，上面安有链子和把手 hammer, a metal ball weighing 16 pounds, hung from a wire handle thrown for distance in a track-and-field competition

【链条】liàntiáo ❶ 机械上传动用的链子 chain as used for mechanical transmission ❷ 〈方 *dial.*〉same as 链子 liàn·zi ①

【链子】liàn·zi ❶ 用金属的小环连起来制成的像绳子的东西 chain; a series of joined links, usu. of metal：铁～ iron chain ❷ 自行车、摩托车等的链条 roller chain of a bicycle, a motorcycle, etc.; chain

楝 liàn 落叶乔木，叶子互生，羽状复叶，小叶卵形或披针形，花小，淡紫色，果实椭圆形，褐色。木材可以制器具，种子、树皮、根皮都可入药。chinaberry (*Melia azedarach*); deciduous tree with small ovate bipinnate leaves or lanceolate leaves, small pale purple flowers, and brown oval fruits, its timber used for making implements, and its seeds, bark and root bark can be used as medicine.

潋(瀲) liàn [潋滟] (liànyàn) 〈书 *fml.*〉 ❶ 形容水满或满而溢出 overflowing; inundating：金樽～。The gold wine vessel is filled to overflowing. ❷ 形容水波流动 billowing; rippling：湖光～。There are glistening ripples on the lake.

鲢 liàn 鲱(fēi) Pacific herring (*Clupae harengus pallasi Cuvier et Valenciennes*)

liáng (ㄌㄧㄤˊ)

良 liáng ❶ 好 good; fine: 优～ fine; good | ～好 good; well | 善～ kind-hearted; good | ～药苦口。Effective medicine tastes bitter. | 消化不～ indigestion ❷ 善良的人 kind-hearted people: 除暴安～ get rid of lawless elements and protect the good ❸〈书 *fml.*〉很 very: ～久 for a very long time | 用心～苦 give much thought to something | 获益～多 benefit a great deal from ❹ (Liáng) 姓 a surname

【良策】liángcè 高明的计策;好的办法 good plan; sound strategy: 别无～。There is no other good plan.

【良辰】liángchén ❶ 美好的日子 happy day; happy moment; happy moments; happy time: ～吉日 happy and auspicious day ❷ 美好的时光 beautiful time: ～美景 fine moment and a beautiful scene

【良好】liánghǎo 令人满意;好 good; well: 手术经过～。The operation came off well. | 养成讲卫生的～习惯 foster the good habit of paying attention to hygiene

【良机】liángjī 好机会 good (or golden) opportunity: 莫失～。Don't let this good opportunity slip through your fingers.

【良家】liángjiā 指清白人家 respectable family: ～妇女 woman from a respectable family; respectable woman | ～子弟 children from a respectable family

【良久】liángjiǔ〈书 *fml.*〉很久 a good while; a long time: 沉思～ ponder for a long time; be lost in thoughts for a long time

【良民】liángmín ❶〈旧时 *old*〉指一般的平民(区别于'贱民' as opposed to 'social outcast') good citizen ❷〈旧时 *old*〉指安分守己的百姓 law-abiding people

【良人】liángrén ❶〈古代 *arch.*〉女子称丈夫 my goodman; my husband ❷〈古代 *arch.*〉指普通百姓(区别于奴、婢 as compared with 'servants' and 'maids') common people

【良师益友】liáng shī yì yǒu 使人得到教益和帮助的好老师、好朋友 good teacher and helpful friend

【良田】liángtián 肥沃的田地 fertile farmland: ～千顷 1,000 *qing* (1 *qing* = 6.6667 hectares) of fertile farmland | 荒漠变成～。Wilderness has become fertile farmland.

【良宵】liángxiāo〈书 *fml.*〉美好的夜晚 enjoyable night; happy moments of the night; jolly time of the evening: 大家欢聚一堂,共度～。Everybody was present at the party and had a most enjoyable night.

【良心】liángxīn 指对是非的内心的正确认识,特别是跟自己的行为有关的 conscience; feelings that one has about whether sth. having to do with one's own behaviour is right or wrong: 有～ have a conscience | 说～话 to be fair in all fairness | ～发现。The conscience is moved.

【良性】liángxìng ❶ 能产生好的结果的 with satisfactory result: ～循环 virtuous cycle ❷ 不至于产生严重后果的 benign: ～肿瘤 benign tumour

【良性肿瘤】liángxìng zhǒngliú 肿瘤的一种,周围有包膜,生长缓慢,细胞的形状和大小比较规则,肿瘤组织与正常组织之间的界限明显,在体内不会转移 benign tumour; one of the tumours covered by a membrane, growing slowly with the tissue independent of the surrounding normal tissues, without spreading to other parts of the body, and having regular size and shape.

【良言】liángyán 有益的话;好话 good advice: ～相劝 exhort someone by good advice | 金玉～ good advice; good counsel

【良药】liángyào 好的药(多用于比喻 usu. fig.) good medicine: 对症～ the right remedy | ～苦口利于病。Bitter but good medicine cures sickness.

【良莠不齐】liáng yǒu bù qí 指好人坏人都有(莠 *you*: 狗尾草,比喻品质坏的人 green bristle grass, here used as a metaphor for 'bad people') the good and the bad are intermingled

【良缘】liángyuán 美好的姻缘 good match; happy match: 喜结～ make a good match

【良知良能】liángzhī liángnéng 我国古代唯心主义哲学家指人类不学而知的、不学而能的、先天具有的判断是非善恶的本能 intuitive (or innate) knowledge and ability to tell right from wrong and good from evil without the need to learn, a view held by ancient Chinese idealistic philosophers

【良种】liángzhǒng 家畜或作物中经济价值较高的品种 fine breed; improved strain

俍 liáng〈书 *fml.*〉完美;良好 perfect; good

莨 liáng 指薯莨 dye yam (*Dioscorea cirrhosa*): ～绸 ☞ below

☞ làng on p. 1151

【莨绸】liángchóu same as 黑胶绸 hēijiāochóu

凉(涼) liáng ❶ 温度低;冷(指天气时,比'冷'的程度浅 lesser in degree than 'cold' when referring to weather) cool; cold: 阴～ shady and cool | ～水 cool water | 过了秋分天就～了。It gets cool after autumnal equinox. ❷〈比喻 *fig.*〉灰心或失望 disheartened or disappointed; lose heart; discouraged: 听到这消息,他心里就～了。His heart sank at the news. | 爹这么一说,我就～了半截儿。He was disappointed at what his father had said.

☞ liàng on p. 1210

【凉白开】liángbáikāi 放凉了的白开水 cold boiled water

【凉拌】liángbàn 把凉的食品加调料拌和 (of food) cold and dressed with sauce: ~菜 cold dish | ~粉皮 cold sheet jelly with dressings | 黄瓜可以~着吃。Cucumber can be eaten when it is cold and dressed with sauce.

【凉菜】liángcài 凉着吃的菜 cold dish

【凉碟】liángdié (~儿 liángdiér) 盛在碟子或小盘子里的凉菜 cold dish

【凉粉】liángfěn (~儿 liángfěnr) 一种食品,用绿豆粉等制成,多用作料凉拌着吃 bean-starch noodles

【凉快】liáng·kuai ❶ 清凉爽快 nice and cool; pleasantly cool: 下了一阵雨,天气~多了。It's much cooler after the rain. ❷ 使身体清凉爽快 cool oneself; cool off: 坐下~~再接着干。Let's sit down and cool off a bit before we start working again. | 到树阴下~一下。Let's sit in the shade and cool off a bit.

【凉帽】liángmào 夏天戴的遮挡阳光的帽子 summer hat; sun hat; straw hat

【凉棚】liángpéng 夏天搭起来遮蔽太阳的棚 mat awning; mat shed ◇手搭~(把手掌平放在额前)往前看 put one's hand before one's forehead and look ahead

【凉薯】liángshǔ 〈方 *dial.*〉豆薯 yam bean

【凉爽】liángshuǎng 清凉爽快 delightfully cool; pleasantly cool: 晚风习习,十分~。It's cool and soothing in the evening breeze.

【凉爽呢】liángshuǎngní 一种平纹的花呢,织后经热定型处理,具有坚固耐穿、挺括、光滑等优点,多用来做男女服装 plain fancy suiting, which is heat set after it is woven, durable, glossy and smooth, and used for making men's and women's suits; 俗称 popularly known as 毛的确良 máodíquèliáng

【凉水】liángshuǐ ❶ 温度低的水 cold water ❷ 生水 unboiled water

【凉丝丝】liángsīsī (~的 liángsīsī·de) 形容稍微有点儿凉 coolish; rather cool; a bit cool: 清晨的空气~的,沁人心肺。The cool air in the early morning is most refreshing.

【凉飕飕】liángsōusōu (~的 liángsōusōu·de) 形容有些凉 chilly; chill: 早立秋,~;晚立秋,热死牛。If autumn begins early in the morning, it will be cool in the weeks to come; if autumn begins late in the afternoon, it will stifle even the cattle to death.

【凉台】liángtái 可供乘凉的阳台或晒台 balcony; veranda

【凉亭】liángtíng 供休息或避雨的亭子 wayside pavilion; summer house; kiosk

【凉席】liángxí 夏天坐卧时铺的席,多用竹篾、草等编成 summer sleeping mat (of woven split bamboo, straw, etc.)

【凉鞋】liángxié 夏天穿的鞋帮通风的鞋 sandals; slippers

【凉药】liángyào 一般指败火、解热的中药,如黄连、大黄、黄芩等 Chinese traditional medicine of a cold nature for reducing fever or inflammation, such as the rhizome of Chinese goldthread (*Coptis chinensis*), rhubarb, the root of large-flowered skullcap (*Scutellaria baicalensis*); antipyretic

【凉意】liángyì 凉的感觉 slight chill in the air: 立秋过后,早晚有些~了。After the Beginning of Autumn there is a slight chill in the air in the mornings and evenings.

梁[1](樑) liáng ❶ 水平方向的长条形承重构件。木结构屋架中专指顺着前后方向架在柱子上的长木。roof beam; long, thick piece of wood used as a horizontal support for a roof in the wood frame of a house; (图见 ☞ figure for 房子 fáng·zi on p. 550) ❷ 通常也指檩 purlin: 正~ ridge purlin; ridge pole | 二~ secondary purlin | 无~殿 hall without a ridge pole ❸ 桥 bridge: 桥~ bridge | 津~ bridge ❹ 物体中间隆起成长条的部分 ridge: 鼻~ bridge of the nose | 山~ mountain ridge; ridge of a mountain

梁2 Liáng ❶ 战国时魏国迁都大梁(今河南开封)后,改称梁 a state during the Warring States Period, originally named Wei and renamed Liang after its capital was moved to Daliang, present-day Kaifeng of Henan Province ❷ 南朝之一,公元502—557年,萧衍所建 Liang Dynasty (502-557), founded by Xiao Yan, one of the Southern Dynasties; ☞ 南北朝 Nán-Běi Cháo on p. 1388 ❸ 后梁 Later Liang Dynasty (907-923), one of the Five Dynasties ❹ 姓 a surname

【梁上君子】liáng shàng jūnzǐ 汉朝陈寔的家里,夜间来了一个窃贼,躲在屋梁上,陈寔把他叫做梁上君子(见于《后汉书·陈寔传》),后来就用'梁上君子'做窃贼的代称 According to *History of Late Han · Biography of Chen Shi*, when a thief broke into the house of Chen Shi one night and hid himself on the beam, Chen Shi, showing a great sense of humour, called him a 'gentleman on the beam'. Thus the phrase 'gentleman on the beam' becomes a synonym to 'thief'.

【梁子】[1] liáng·zi 〈方 *dial.*〉山脊 ridge of a mountain

【梁子】[2] liáng·zi 评书、大鼓等曲艺中曲目的故事提纲 outline of a story in the traditional storytelling

椋 liáng [椋鸟] (liángniǎo) 鸟类的一科,性喜群飞,食种子和昆虫,有的善于模仿别的鸟叫。如八哥、欧椋鸟等。starling (*Sturnus*); any one kind of birds such as myna that are fond of flying in flocks, feeding on seeds and insects, and some of them good at imitating the cries of other birds

辌 liáng ☞ [辒辌] (wēnliáng) on p. 2004

量 liáng ❶ 用尺、容器或其他作为标准的东西来确定事物的长短、大小、多少或其他性质 measure; determine the length, size and quantity or other properties of a thing by means of a ruler, vessel or other standard measuring tool: ～地 measure land; measure a piece of ground | ～体温 take someone's temperature | 用尺～布 measure cloth with a ruler | 用斗～米 measure rice with a *dou* measure (1 *dou* = 1 decalitre) ❷ 估量 estimate; appraise; assess: 端～ look someone up and down | 酌～ weigh; consider; use one's judgement | 思～ think over; consider
☞ liàng on p. 1201

【量杯】liángbēi 量液体体积的器具,形状像杯,口比底大,多用玻璃制成,杯上有刻度 measuring glass; graduate; graduated glass for measuring liquid

【量程】liángchéng 测量仪表或仪器所能测试各种参数的范围 range of measuring various parameters by means of measuring metres or instruments

【量度】liángdù 长度、重量、容量以及功、能等各种量的测定 (of length, weight, capacity, work, energy, etc.) measurement

【量规】liángguī 界限量规 gauge

【量角器】liángjiǎoqì 量角度或画角用的器具,普通是半圆形,在圆周上刻着 0 到 180 的度数 protractor; instrument in the form of a graduated semicircle that is graded from 0 to 180 for plotting and measuring angles

【量具】liángjù 计量和检验用的器具,如尺、天平、块规、卡钳、量角器等 measuring tool, such as ruler, balance, slip gauge, callipers, protractor, etc.

【量块】liángkuài 块规 slip gauge

【量筒】liángtǒng 量液体体积的器具,呈直筒形,多用玻璃制成,上面有刻度 graduated, volumetric and measuring cylinder; graduate

粮(糧) liáng ❶ 粮食 grain; food; provisions: 杂～ food grains other than rice and wheat | 口～ grain ration | ～仓 granary ❷ 作为农业税的粮食 grains in the form of an agricultural tax: 钱～ grain tax; revenue | 公～ agricultural tax paid in the form of grains; grains delivered to the state | 完～ pay the grain tax

【粮仓】liángcāng ❶ 储存粮食的仓库 granary; barn ❷ 〈比喻 *fig.*〉盛产粮食的地方 grain-producing area

【粮草】liángcǎo 军用的粮食和草料 army provisions; rations and forage (or fodder): 兵马未动,～先行。Provisions should go before troops and horses; good preparations should be made before doing anything.

【粮荒】liánghuāng 指粮食严重缺乏 grain shortage; food scarcity: 闹～ suffer from grain shortage (or famine)

【粮秣】liángmò same as 粮草 liángcǎo: 成群结队的大车装着军火、～去支援前线。Large numbers of carts loaded with ammunition and provisions creaked and lumbered as they were headed for the front.

【粮农】liángnóng 以种植粮食作物为主的农民 food grain growers; peasants who grow food grains

【粮食】liáng·shi 供食用的谷物、豆类和薯类的统称 grain; cereals; general term for grain, beans and potatoes used as food

【粮食作物】liáng·shi zuòwù 稻、小麦和杂粮作物的统称 cereal crops; grain crops

【粮饷】liángxiǎng 〈旧时 *old*〉指军队中发给官、兵的口粮和钱 provisions and funds given to troops

【粮栈】liángzhàn 〈旧时 *old*〉经营批发业务的粮店;存放粮食的货栈 wholesale grain store; grain depot

【粮站】liángzhàn 调拨、管理粮食的机关 grain distribution station; grain supply centre

粱 liáng 〈书 *fml.*〉❶ 谷子的优良品种的统称 (general term for) fine strain of millet ❷ 精美的主食 fine grain; choice food: 膏～ fat meat and fine grain; rich food | ～肉 fine food

【粱肉】liángròu 〈书 *fml.*〉指精美的饭食 choice food

墚 liáng 我国西北地区称条状的黄土山岗 ridgelike loess hillocks in northwest China

踉 liáng ☞ 跳踉 tiàoliáng on p. 1905
☞ liàng on p. 1211

liǎng (ㄌㄧㄤˇ)

两[1](兩) liǎng ❶ 〈数目 *numeral*〉一个加一个是两个。'两'字一般用于量词和'半、千、万、亿'前 [usu. used before measure words and before 半 bàn, 千 qiān, 万 wàn, and 亿 yì] two; one plus one equals two: ～扇门 two doors | ～本书 two books | ～匹马 two horses | ～个半月 two and a half months | ～半儿 two halves | ～千块钱 two thousand yuan 注意 **NOTE:** 两和二用法不全同。读数目字只用二不用两,如一、二、三、四。小数和分数只用二不用两,如零点二(0.2)、三分之二。序数也只用二,如第二、二哥。在一般量词前,用两不用二。在传统的度量衡单位前,两和二一般都可用,用二为多(二两不能说两两)。新的度量衡单位前一般用两,如两吨、两公里。在多位数中,百、十、个位用二不用两,如二百二十二。千、万、亿的前面,两和二一般都可用,但如三万二千、两亿二千万,千在万、亿后,以用二为常。The uses of 两 liǎng and 二 èr are not entirely the same. When you read the numbers, you

L

use only 二, not 两, as 一,二,三,四. In decimals and fractions, use only 二, not 两, as 零点二(0.2),三分之二. In array, also use 二, as 第二,二哥. Before the common measure words, use 两, not 二. Before the traditional measuring units, usually both 两 and 二 can be used, but 二 is used more often (as 二两 cannot be replaced by 两两). Before the new measuring units, usually use 两, as 两吨, 两公里. In the multi-digit numbers, use 二, not 两 for 百 (hundreds place), 十 (tens place), 个位(unit place), as 二百二十二. Before 千,万,亿, usually both 两 and 二 can be used, but as in 三万二千,两亿二千万, when 千 is after 万,亿, 二 is more frequently used. ❷ 双方 both sides; either side: ～便 convenient to both sides; make it easy for both | ～可 both will do; either will do | ～全其美 satisfactory to both sides; meet the needs of both sides; meet rival claims | ～相情愿。Both sides are willing. ❸ 表示不定的数目,和'几'差不多 (more or less the same as '几') a few; some: 过～天再说。Leave it for a couple of days. | 他真有～下子。He is really clever and capable. *or* He really is smart. | 我跟你说～句话。I'll speak a few words to you.

两²**(兩)** liǎng 重量单位。10 钱等于 1 两,旧制 16 两等于 1 斤,市制 10 市两等于 1 市斤 *liang*, traditional unit of weight; 10 *qian* equal to 1 *liang*; in the old system, 16 *liang* equal to 1 *jin*; in the current system, 10 *shiliang* equal to 1 *shijin*

【两岸】liǎng'àn ❶ 江河,海峡等两边的地方 on the two sides of a river or strait ❷ 特指台湾海峡两岸,即我国的大陆和台湾省 especially designated to the both sides of the Taiwan Straits, namely, the mainland and the Taiwan Province of China

【两败俱伤】liǎng bài jù shāng 争斗的双方都受到损失 both sides suffer; neither side gains

【两边】liǎngbiān ❶ 物体的两个边儿 edges of an object: 这张纸～长短不齐。The two edges of this piece of paper aren't even in length. ❷ 两个方向或地方 two directions; two places: 这间屋子～有窗户,光线很好。This room has windows on both sides and has very good light. | 老大娘常常～走动,看望两个外孙女儿。Grandma is always going back and forth, visiting her two granddaughters. ❸ 双方;两方面 both parties; both sides: ～都说好了,明儿下午赛球。The two teams have agreed to play the match tomorrow afternoon.

【两边倒】liǎngbiāndǎo 形容动摇不定,缺乏坚定的立场和主张 trim one's sails to the wind; lean now to one side, then to the other; waver (said of one's stand or view)

【两便】liǎngbiàn ❶ 彼此方便(多用做套语 oft. as a set expression) be convenient to both; make things easy for both: 您甭等我了,咱们～。Please don't wait for me. That might be more convenient for both of us. ❷ 对双方或两件事都有好处 benefit both sides or two things; good for both: ～之法 method to the benefit of both sides | 公私～ benefit both the public and the private

【两不找】liǎng bù zhǎo 买货时货价与所付货款相当或交换货物时价值相当,彼此不用找补 that's just right (the exact amount in payment for sth. bought)

【两重性】liǎngchóngxìng same as 二重性 èrchóngxìng

【两党制】liǎngdǎngzhì 某些国家两个主要政党交替执政的制度。通常由在议会中,特别是下议院中占有多数议席或在总统选举中获胜的一个政党作为执政党,组织内阁,行使统治权。two-party system; bipartisan system; system by which two major political parties hold power alternately. Usually, the party which has the majority of seats in the parliament, esp. in the lower house, or wins the presidential election, becomes the party in power and forms the cabinet.

【两抵】liǎngdǐ 两相抵消 average out; balance or cancel each other: 收支～。Income and expenditure balance each other. *or* The account balances out.

【两点论】liǎngdiǎnlùn 指辩证法的全面观点,即全面地看问题,分清主次,不但看到事物的正面,也要看到它的反面;不但看到事物的现状,也要看到矛盾的双方经过斗争在一定条件下可以互相转化 dialectical method of observing and analysing problems in an overall way: distinguishing what is principal and what is secondary, not only seeing the positive aspect of a thing, but also its negative aspect; not only seeing the current state of a thing, but also the mutual transformation of the two aspects of a contradiction through struggle under certain conditions

【两公婆】liǎnggōngpó 〈方 *dial.*〉指夫妻俩 husband and wife; married couple

【两广】Liǎng Guǎng 广东和广西的合称 Two Guangs — Guangdong Province and Guangxi Zhuang Autonomous Region

【两汉】Liǎng Hàn 西汉和东汉的合称 Two Hans — the Western and the Eastern Han Dynasties

【两湖】Liǎng Hú 湖北和湖南的合称 Two Hus — Hubei and Hunan provinces

【两回事】liǎng huí shì 指彼此无关的两种事物 two entirely different things; two different matters: 善意的批评跟恶意的攻击完全是～。Well-meaning criticism and malicious attack are two entirely different things. also 两码事 liǎng mǎ shì

【两极】liǎngjí ❶ 地球的南极和北极 North and South Poles of the earth ❷ 电极的阴极和阳极；磁极的南极和北极 two poles of a magnet or an electric cell ❸〈比喻 *fig.*〉两个极端或两个对立面 two extremes or two opposites：～分化 polarization

【两江】Liǎng Jiāng 清初江南省和江西省合称'两江'，康熙后江南省分为江苏、安徽两省，三省地区仍沿称两江 Two Jiangs — Jiangnan and Jiangxi provinces in the early years of the Qing Dynasty; Jiangnan Province was divided into Jiangsu and Anhui Provinces after the reign of Emperor Kangxi, but the three provinces are still called the 'Two Jiangs'

【两脚规】liǎngjiǎoguī 绘图仪器，有两个可以开合的脚，上端固定在一个轴上，有分线规和圆规两种 compasses; dividers

【两晋】Liǎng Jìn 西晋和东晋的合称 Two Jins — the Western and the Eastern Jin Dynasties

【两可】liǎngkě ❶ 可以这样，也可以那样；两者都可以 both will do; either will do; could go either way：模棱～ ambiguous; equivocal｜这种会议参加不参加～。It's all right whether you attend this meeting or not ❷ 可能这样，也可能那样；两者都可能 either this or that; both are possible：行不行还在～哪！Whether it will do or not — either is possible.

【两口儿】liǎngkǒur same as 两口子 liǎngkǒu•zi：小～ young couple｜老～ old couple

【两口子】liǎngkǒu•zi 指夫妻俩 husband and wife; married couple：～和和美美地过日子。The husband and his wife are leading an amiable life.

【两立】liǎnglì 两个方面同时并存 coexist：势不～ irreconcilable; mutually exclusive; unable to coexist; unable to live together peacefully

【两利】liǎnglì 两方面都得到便利或利益 benefit both sides; convenient to both sides：劳资～ benefit both labour and capital; be beneficial both to labour and capital

【两码事】liǎng mǎ shì same as 两回事 liǎng huí shì

【两面】liǎngmiàn ❶ 正面和反面 obverse side and reverse side：这张纸～都写满了字。Both sides of the paper are covered with writing. ❷ same as 两边 liǎngbiān ②：～夹攻 attack from both sides; make a pincer attack｜左右～都是高山。There are high mountains to the right and to the left. ❸ 事物相对的两方面 two aspects; two opposites：～性 dual character｜～讨好 please both sides; curry favour with both sides; fawn on both sides｜问题的～我们都要看到。We should see the two aspects of the problem.

【两面光】liǎngmiànguāng〈比喻 *fig.*〉两方面讨好 please both parties：他说～的话是怕得罪人。He said something to please both sides for fear of offending people.

【两面派】liǎngmiànpài ❶ 指耍两面手法的人，也指对斗争的双方都敷衍的人 double-dealer ❷ 指两面手法 double-dealings; be two-faced：耍～ resort to double-dealing; be double-faced

【两面三刀】liǎng miàn sān dāo 指耍两面手法 double-dealing; double-cross：嘴甜心毒，～。talk sweetly with a vicious mind and resort to double-dealing

【两面性】liǎngmiànxìng 一个人或一个事物同时存在的两种互相矛盾的性质或倾向 duality; dual nature; duplicity; ambivalence

【两难】liǎngnán 这样或那样都有困难 face a difficult choice; be in a dilemma：进退～ be in a dilemma｜去也不好，不去也不好，真是～。I'm in a dilemma as to whether to go or not.

【两旁】liǎngpáng 左右两边 both sides; either side：卫队站在门口～。Guards stand on both sides of the gate.｜马路～种着整齐的梧桐树。The road is lined with neat Chinese parasol trees on both sides.

【两栖】liǎngqī ❶ 可以在水中生活，也可以在陆地上生活 amphibious：～动物 amphibious animals｜水陆～ amphibious ◇～作战 amphibious warfare; amphibious operations ❷〈比喻 *fig.*〉工作或活动在两种领域 work in two fields：影视～明星 amphibious film-TV stars

【两栖动物】liǎngqī dòngwù 脊椎动物的一纲，通常没有鳞或甲，皮肤没有毛，四肢有趾，没有爪，体温随着气温的高低而改变，卵生。幼时生活在水中，用鳃呼吸，长大时可以生活在陆地上，用肺和皮肤呼吸，如青蛙、蟾蜍、蝾螈等。amphibious animal; amphibian; a class of oviparous vertebrates, usu. having no scales, no shells and no hair on the skin, the limbs having toes but no claws, their body temperature changing with the rise and fall of the temperature. When they are young, they live in water and breathe with gills. After growing up, they live either in water or on land and breathe with lung and skin, such as frog, toad, salamander, etc.

【两栖植物】liǎngqī zhíwù 既能在陆地上生长又可以在水中生长的高等植物，如水蓼、蕹菜、池杉等 amphibious plants; amphibian; higher plants that can grow both on land and in water, such as water pepper (*Polygonum hydropiper*), water spinach (*Ipomoea aquatica*), pond cypress, etc.

【两歧】liǎngqí〈书 *fml.*〉(两种意见、方法)不统一 (of two opinions or methods) not tally; be inconsistent：办法应该划一，不能～。The methods should be standardized, not inconsistent.

【两讫】liǎngqì 商业用语，指卖方已将货付清，买方已将款付清，交易手续已了 (business Chinese) the goods are delivered and the bill is cleared：货款～。Both the payment for and the delivery of the goods purchased have been cleared. *or* Both payment and delivery have been cleared.

【两清】liǎngqīng 借贷或买卖双方账目已经结清 the accounts have been settled：谁也不欠谁，咱们～了。Neither of us owes to the other, and everything is settled.

【两全】liǎngquán 顾全两个方面 be satisfactory to both parties; have regard for both sides：～其美 please both sides｜想个～的办法 find a measure satisfactory to both sides

【两全其美】liǎng quán qí měi 做一件事顾全两个方面，使两方面都很好 satisfy both sides; satisfy rival claims

【两手】liǎngshǒu ❶（～儿 liǎngshǒur）指本领或技能 skill：有～儿 have some tricks｜留～儿 hold back some of his tricks｜给大家露～ show some of his tricks ❷ 指相对的两个方面的手段、办法等 dual tactics：领导工作得～抓 pay attention to both aspects of one's work as a leader; give equal stress to both aspects of one's work as a leader｜为防不测做～准备 prepare oneself for eventualities

【两头】liǎngtóu（～儿 liǎngtóur）❶ 这一头和那一头；事物相对的两端 both ends; either end：梭的形状是中间粗，～儿尖。A shuttle is big in the middle and pointed at both ends.｜抓～儿，带中间。Grasp the two ends to bring along the middle; sustain the advanced and help the backward so as to encourage the vast majority to move along. ❷ 双方；两方面 both sides; both aspects：这件事～都满意。This matter is satisfactory to both sides. ❸ 两个地方 two places：家里地里～儿照顾不过来 unable to take care of both household chores and the fields

【两下里】liǎngxià·li ❶ 双方；两方面 both parties; both sides：这办法对国家对农民～都有好处。This practice is good to both the state and the peasants.｜第三连、第五连都来了，～一共二百多人。Both the third and fifth companies have arrived, totalling more than 200 people. ❷ 两个地方 two places：一家人分在～住。Members of the family live in two places. ‖ also 两下 liǎngxià

【两下子】liǎngxià·zi ❶（动作）几次 a few times：轻轻搔了～ scratch a few times ❷ 指本领或技能 a few tricks of the trade; skill：别看他眼睛不好，干活儿可真有～ In spite of his eye trouble, he really is a smart worker.｜他就会这～，别的本事没有。He has nothing more than these few tricks of the trade.

【两相情愿】liǎng xiāng qíngyuàn 双方都愿意 both parties being willing; by mutual consent; also 两厢情愿 liǎng xiāng qíng yuàn

【两厢】liǎngxiāng ❶ 两边的厢房 wing rooms on either side of a one-storey house ❷ same as 两旁 liǎngpáng：站立～ stand on either side

【两小无猜】liǎng xiǎo wú cāi 男女小的时候在一起玩耍，天真烂漫，没有猜疑（of a little boy and a little girl) be innocent playmates

【两性】liǎngxìng ❶ 雄性和雌性；男性和女性 both sexes：～生殖 bisexual reproduction ❷ 两种性质 amphiprotic; amphoteric：～化合物 amphoteric compound｜氨基酸既有酸性也有碱性，它是～的。Amino acid is amphiprotic, both acid and basic.

【两性人】liǎngxìngrén 由于胚胎的畸形发育而形成的具有男性和女性两种生殖器官的人 bisexual person; hermaphrodite; person with both male and female organs as a result of abnormal development of the embryo; 通称 popularly known as 二性子 èrxìng·zi

【两性生殖】liǎngxìng shēngzhí 有性生殖 bisexual reproduction; sexual reproduction

【两袖清风】liǎng xiù qīng fēng〈比喻 *fig.*〉做官廉洁（of an official) have clean hands; remain uncorrupted

【两样】liǎngyàng 不一样 different：一样的客人，不能～待遇。Guests of the like should not be treated in different ways.

【两翼】liǎngyì ❶ 两个翅膀 both wings：鸟的～ both wings of a bird｜飞机的～ both wings of an airplane ❷ 军队作战时，在正面部队两侧的部队 both wings; both flanks：敌人的正面和～都遭到了猛烈的攻击。The front and both flanks of the enemy were fiercely attacked. *or* The enemy was fiercely attacked in the front and the two flanks.

【两院制】liǎngyuànzhì 某些国家议会分设两院的制度。两院议员一般都由选举产生并定期改选，两院都有立法和监督行政的权力，但名称各有不同，如英国叫上议院和下议院，美国、日本叫参议院和众议院，法国叫参议院和国民议会。two-chamber system; bicameral system; bicameralism, a political system in some countries. All the members of the two chambers are usu. elected and re-elected regularly and both chambers have the power to make laws and exercise supervision over the administration, but their names differ from country to country, such as the Upper and Lower houses in Britain, the Senate and the House of Representatives in the United States and Japan, and the Senate and National Assembly in France.

【两造】liǎngzào 指诉讼的双方 both parties to a lawsuit; both plaintiff and defendant：～具结完案。Both parties have signed the document to bring an end to the suit.

俩(倆) liǎng ☞ 伎俩 jìliǎng on p. 915 ☞ liǎ on p. 1193

唡(啢) liǎng 又 also yīngliǎng 英两旧也作 formerly as 唡 liǎng

緉(緉) liǎng 〈书 *fml*.〉〈量词 *classifier*〉双,用于鞋袜 a pair of (shoes or socks):一~丝履 a pair of silk shoes|绫袜一~ a pair of silk socks

裲(裲) liǎng [裲裆](liǎngdāng)〈古代 *arch*.〉指背心 vest or a sleeveless garment

蜽(蜽) liǎng ☞ [蝄蜽](wǎngliǎng) on p. 1983

魉(魎) liǎng ☞ [魍魉](wǎngliǎng) on p. 1983

liàng (ㄌㄧㄤˋ)

亮 liàng ❶ 光线强 bright; light: 明~ bright; brightly-lit; well-lit|豁~ spacious and bright|这盏灯不~。This lamp is not alight. ❷ 发光 shine; emit light: 天~了。It's dawn; it's daybreak; it's light already.|手电筒~了一下。The torch flashed for a second.|屋子里~着灯光。There is light in the room. ❸ (声音)强;响亮 loud and clear: 洪~ a resonant voice|她的歌声脆而~。She sings clearly and melodiously. ❹ 使声音响亮 make one's voice loud and clear: ~起嗓子 raise one's voice; lift one's voice ❺ (心胸、思想等)开朗;清楚 enlightened: 心明眼~ see and think clearly; sharp-eyed and clear-minded; having sharp eyes and a clear mind ❻ 显露;显示 reveal; show: ~相 pose for the audience on the stage before exit or after entrance (as in Beijing opera, dancing, etc.); state one's views; declare one's position|把底儿~出来 show one's cards on the table; reveal one's story; disclose one's stand or views|这种热带的蝙蝠,一~翅膀足有脸盆大。The wings of this kind of tropical bat are as large as a washbasin when they are spread.

【亮底】 liàng//dǐ ❶ 把底细公开出来 lay one's cards on the table; reveal frankly one's intentions, schemes, resources, etc.; reveal the whole story: 别让大家瞎猜了,你就~吧。Don't let the others make a wild guess. Lay your cards on the table ❷ 显示出结局 reveal the final result: 这场围棋赛还没~呢。The final result of the go match is not yet available.

【亮度】 liàngdù 发光体或反光体使人眼睛感到的明亮程度。亮度和所看到的物体的大小、发光或反光的强度及距离有关。brightness; brilliance; degree of brightness of the luminous body or the reflector felt by human eyes. The brightness is related to the size of the object seen, the intensity of the light emitted or reflected, and its distance.

【亮分】 liàng//fēn (~儿 liàng//fēnr) 进行某些比赛时,评分的人亮出所评的分数 marks given and shown by the panel of judges in the competitions of some sports: 请评委~儿。Judges, please show the marks you give.|裁判们亮出各人打的分儿。The judges signal the marks given to the competitors.

【亮光】 liàngguāng (~儿 liàngguāngr) ❶ 黑暗中的一点或一道光 light; beam of light; gleam of light; shaft of light: 夜已经很深了,他家的窗户上还有~。It is very late in the night, but there is still light on the window of his house. ❷ 物体表面反射的光 light reflected by the surface of an object: 这种布有~儿。The cloth is lustrous.

【亮光光】 liàngguāngguāng (~的 liàngguāngguāng·de) 形容物体光亮 shining: 一把~的镰刀 a shining sickle

【亮话】 liànghuà 明白而不加掩饰的话 to be frank: 打开天窗说~ frankly speaking|说~吧,我不能帮你这个忙。To be frank, I can't give you the help.

【亮晶晶】 liàngjīngjīng (~的 liàngjīngjīng·de) 形容物体明亮闪烁发光 glittering; sparkling; glistening: ~的露珠 glistening dewdrops|小星星,~。Little stars glitter.

【亮牌子】 liàng pái·zi 亮出牌子 lay the cards on the table; 〈比喻 *fig*.〉说出名字、表明身份等 reveal one's name and identity

【亮儿】 liàngr ❶ 灯火 light (of a lamp, candle, etc.): 拿个~来。Bring a light. ❷ 亮光 light: 远远看见有一点~。There is a light in the distance.

【亮闪闪】 liàngshǎnshǎn (~的 liàngshǎnshǎn·de) 形容闪亮发光 sparkling; glittering: ~的眼睛 sparkling eyes|~的启明星 glittering morning star; glittering Venus

【亮堂堂】 liàngtāngtāng (~的 liàngtāngtāng·de) 形容很亮 brightly lit; well lit; brilliant: 灯火通明,照得礼堂里~的。The auditorium was well lit with blazing lights. *or* Blazing lights lit up in the auditorium.

【亮堂】 liàng·tang ❶ 敞亮;明朗 light; bright: 新盖的商场又高大,又~。The newly-built shopping centre is large and light. ❷ (胸怀、思想等)开朗;清楚 clear; enlightened: 经过学习,心里更~了。After study, we had a much better understanding of what it's all about. ❸ (声音)响亮 (of voice) loud and clear: 嗓门~ clear and resonant voice|清清嗓子,唱~点儿。Clear your voice and sing louder.

【亮相】 liàng//xiàng ❶ 戏曲演员上下场时或表演舞蹈时由动的身段变为短时的静止的姿势,目的是突出角色情绪,加强戏剧气氛(in traditional opera) strike a pose on the stage after entrance and before exit ❷ 〈比喻 *fig*.〉公开露面或表演 debut; appear before the public and give performance: 刚刚结束冬训的国家女

排,今晚在福建省体育馆首次～。The national women's volleyball team made its first appearance in the Fujian Provincial Indoor Stadium this evening after finishing their winter training. ❸〈比喻 *fig.*〉公开表示态度,亮明观点 declare one's position; state one's views

【亮眼人】liàngyǎnrén 盲人称眼睛看得见的人 people with normal sight; bright-eyed ones (blind people's term for those who can see)

【亮锃锃】liàngzēngzēng (～的 liàngzēngzēng·de)形容闪光耀眼 shining; gleaming:～的铡刀 shining fodder chopper|新买的钢精锅,～的。The newly-bought aluminium pot is gleaming.

【亮铮铮】liàngzhēngzhēng (～的 liàngzhēngzhēng·de)形容闪光耀眼 shining; gleaming:一把～的利剑 a gleaming sharp sword

倞 liàng〈书 *fml.*〉索取 claim; ask for; request;same as 求 qiú ③

☞ jìng on p. 1031

凉(涼) liàng 把热的东西放一会儿,使温度降低 cool:粥太烫,～一～再喝。The porridge is too hot. I'll have it after it is less hot.

☞ liáng on p. 1204

悢 liàng〈书 *fml.*〉悲伤 sorrow; grief; sorrowful; sad:～然 sorrowful; sad

【悢悢】liàngliàng〈书 *fml.*〉❶悲伤;怅惘 sad; depressed; listless ❷眷念 think fondly of; feel nostalgic about

谅¹ liàng 原谅 forgive:～解 understand|体～ be considerate of; show sympathy for

谅² liàng 料想 I think; I suppose; I expect:～不见怪。I believe (am sure) that you will not blame me.|～他不能来。I don't think he will come.

【谅察】liàngchá (请人)体察原谅(多用于书信 oft. used in letters) ask for your understanding and forgiveness:不当之处,尚希～。If there is anything improper, your understanding and forgiveness are requested.

【谅解】liàngjiě 了解实情后原谅或消除意见 understand; make allowance for:他很～你的苦衷。He understands your difficulties.|大家应当互相～,搞好关系。All of us should try to understand each other and be on good terms.

辆(輛) liàng〈量词 *classifier*〉用于车(for vehicles):一～汽车 a car; an automobile; a motor vehicle|一～三轮 a tricycle

靓 liàng〈方 *dial.*〉漂亮;好看 beautiful; pretty; handsome:～仔 handsome young man|～女 pretty girl

☞ jìng on p. 1032

【靓女】liàngnǚ〈方 *dial.*〉漂亮的女子(多指年轻的) pretty girl

【靓仔】liàngzǎi〈方 *dial.*〉漂亮的小伙子 handsome young man

量 liàng ❶〈古代 *arch.*〉指测量东西多少的器物,如斗、升等 ancient Chinese measures or measuring containers, such as *dou* (a container as well as a unit of dry measure for grain equivalent to one decalitre), *sheng* (a container as well as a unit of dry measure for grain equivalent to one litre), etc. ❷能容纳或禁受的限度 capacity of tolerance or for taking food or drink:饭～ quantity of food taken by one person for a meal; appetite|气～ tolerance|胆～ courage|力～ strength; physical power ❸数量;数目 quantity; amount; volume:流～ flow|降雨～ rainfall; precipitation|饱和～ saturation|质～并重(质量和数量并重) equal stress on quality and quantity ❹估计;衡量 estimate; measure:～力 estimate one's strength, ability or resources|～入为出 keep expenditures within one's means; regulate one's expenditures according to one's income|～才录用 employ a person according to his ability

☞ liáng on p. 1205

【量变】liàngbiàn 事物在数量上、程度上的变化。是一种逐渐的不显著的变化,是质变的准备。quantitative change; change in quantity or degree, a gradual, indistinct change and a preparation for the qualitative change; ☞ 质变 zhìbiàn on p. 2473

【量词】liàngcí 表示人、事物或动作的单位的词。如'尺、寸、斗、升、斤、两、个、只(zhī)、支、匹、件、条、根、块、种、双、对、副、打(dá)、队、群、次、回、遍、趟(tàng)、阵、顿'等。量词经常跟数词一起用。measure word; classifier; word indicating a unit for person, thing or action, such as 尺 chǐ,寸 cùn,斗 dǒu,升 shēng,斤 jīn,两 liǎng,个 gè,只 zhī,支 zhī,匹 pǐ,件 jiàn,条 tiáo,根 gēn,块 kuài,种 zhǒng,双 shuāng,对 duì,副 fù,打 dá,队 duì,群 qún,次 cì,回 huí,遍 biàn,趟 tàng,阵 zhèn,顿 dùn. A measure word is usu. used together with a numeral.

【量力】liànglì 衡量自己的力量 estimate one's own strength or ability:度德～ act with due consideration of one's abilities|～而行 act according to one's capability; do what one can|你这是鸡蛋碰石头,太不～了。You act just like an egg striking a rock. You've overrated your own strength.

【量入为出】liàng rù wéi chū 根据收入的多少来定支出的限度 adjust one's expense according to one's income; make both ends meet; keep expenditure below income; live within one's means; cut one's coat according to one's cloth

【量体裁衣】liàng tǐ cái yī 按照身材剪裁衣裳 cut the garment according to the figure; cut out the dress to fit the body;〈比喻 *fig.*〉根据实际情况办事 act in accordance to actual circumstances or conditions

【量刑】liàngxíng 法院根据犯罪者所犯罪行的性质、情节,对社会危害的程度,以及认罪的表现,依法判处一定的刑罚 determination of punishment; mete out punishment; (of court) sentence criminal in accordance with the kind of crime, circumstances and degree of harm to society as well as criminal's degree of remorse

【量子】liàngzǐ 在微观领域中,某些物理量的变化是以最小的单位跳跃式进行的,而不是连续的,这个最小的单位叫做量子 quantum; in subatomic physics, the smallest unit of energy change in atoms, which occurs in discrete quantities and not in a continuous manner

晾 liàng ❶ 把东西放在通风或阴凉的地方,使干燥 dry in the air; air; air-dry; dry in a ventilated, shady and cool place: ～干菜 dry vegetables ❷ 晒(东西) sun; dry sth. in the sun: ～衣服 hang clothes out to dry | 海滩上～着渔网。Fishnets are drying on the beach. ❸ 撇在一边不理睬;冷落 ignore; slight; cold-shoulder: 他俩说个没完,把我～在一边。They talked endlessly to each other, letting me cool my heels. ❹ same as 凉 liàng

【晾晒】liàngshài 把东西摊开让日光晒 sun; air; spread out to air: ～粮食 dry grain in the sun | 被褥要经常～。Bedding needs frequent airing.

【晾台】liàngtái 楼顶上晾晒衣物的平台 (on the top of a building) terrace or veranda for sunning clothes

喨 liàng ☞ 嘹喨 liáoliàng on p. 1212

踉 liàng ☞ below
☞ liáng on p. 1205

【踉跄】liàngqiàng 走路不稳 stagger; walk unsteadily: 一个～,险些跌倒。He staggered and almost fell down. also 踉蹡 liàngqiàng

【踉蹡】liàngqiàng same as 踉跄 liàngqiàng

liāo (ㄌㄧㄠ)

撩 liāo ❶ 把东西垂下的部分掀起来 raise or lift sth. hanging down: ～裙子 lift a skirt | ～起帘子 lift (or raise) a curtain | 把头发～上去 brush back one's hair ❷ 用手舀水由下往上甩出去 scoop out water and sprinkle (with hands): 先～些水然后再扫地 sprinkle some water on the floor before sweeping
☞ liáo on p. 1212 and 撂 liào on p. 1215

蹽 liāo 〈方 *dial.*〉 ❶ 放开脚步走;跑 stride; run; rush; speed: 一气～了二十多里路 walk over 20 *li* at a stretch ❷ 偷偷地走开 slip away; sneak off; leave stealthily: 他一看形势不妙就～了。Sensing danger, he took to his heels.

liáo (ㄌㄧㄠˊ)

辽[1](遼) liáo 远 distant; remote; faraway: ～远 distant; remote; faraway | ～阔 vast; extensive

辽[2](遼) Liáo 朝代,公元 907—1125,契丹人耶律阿保机所建,在我国北部,初名契丹,938 年(一说 947 年)改称辽 Liao Dynasty (907 - 1125), established by Apoki of the Khitan people in North China, first called Khitan, and later changed to Liao in 938 (or 947)

【辽东】Liáodōng 辽河以东的地区,就是辽宁的东部和南部 area east of the Liaohe River, i. e. eastern and southern part of Liaoning Province

【辽阔】liáokuò 辽远广阔;宽广空旷 vast; extensive: ～的土地 vast territory; vast expanse of land | ～的海洋 boundless sea; vast ocean | 幅员～ vast territory

【辽西】Liáoxī 辽河以西的地区,就是辽宁的西部 area west of the Liaohe River, i. e. western part of Liaoning Province

【辽远】liáoyuǎn 遥远 distant; remote; faraway: ～的边疆 remote frontiers | ～的天空 distant sky | ～的未来 remote future

疗(療) liáo 医治 treat; cure: 医～ medical treatment; therapy | 治～ treat; cure; heal | 诊～ make a diagnosis and give treatment | 理～ physiotherapy | 电～ electrotherapy | ～养 recuperate; convalesce; rest up

【疗程】liáochéng 医疗上对某些疾病所规定的连续治疗的一段时间叫做一个疗程 course of continuous treatment for certain diseases; series of treatments: 理疗了两个～,腿疼就好了。My leg feels no pain after two courses of physiotherapy.

【疗饥】liáojī 〈书 *fml.*〉 解除饥饿;充饥 allay (or appease) the pang of hunger

【疗效】liáoxiào 药物或医疗方法治疗疾病的效果 curative effect; effect of medicinal or medical treatment: 青霉素对肺炎有显著的～。Penicillin is particularly effective against pneumonia.

【疗养】liáoyǎng 患有慢性病或身体衰弱的人,在特设的医疗机构进行以休养为主的治疗 recuperate; convalesce; rest up; (of one suffering from chronic disease or poor health) receive mostly recuperative treatment and rest in a specialized medical institution: ～院 sanatorium; rest home; convalescent hospital (or home) | 他在海滨～了半年。He went to the seaside to recuperate for half a year.

【疗养院】liáoyǎngyuàn 专用于疗养的医疗机构,多设在风景区或环境幽雅的地方 sanatorium; rest home; convalescent hospital (or home); specialized medical institution for recuperation, usually established in a scenic place or quiet environment

【疗治】liáozhì 治疗 treat; cure: ～烧伤 treat burns

膋(膋) liáo 古书上指肠子上的脂肪 fat on the intestines (in ancient books)

聊[1] liáo ❶ 姑且 merely; just; barely: ～以自慰 just to find relief; just to comfort oneself at the thought of...; just to console oneself | ～备一格 may serve as a specimen (or stopgap); stand in for the time being ❷ 略微 a little; slightly; somewhat: ～表寸心 as a small token of my feelings; just to show my gratitude ❸ (Liáo)姓 a surname

聊[2] liáo 〈书 *fml.*〉依赖;凭借 rely; depend: ～赖 sth. to rely upon; sth. to live for; sth. to occupy one's mind | 民不～生。The people have no means of livelihood.

聊[3] liáo 闲谈 chat: 闲～ chat; gossip | ～天儿 chat | 有空儿咱们～～。Let's have a chat when you are free.

【聊备一格】liáo bèi yī gé 姑且当作一种规格,表示暂且用来充数 may serve as a specimen (or stopgap); stand in for the time being

【聊赖】liáolài 精神上或生活上的寄托、凭借等(多用于否定式 usu. used in the negative) sth. to rely upon; sth. to live for; sth. to occupy one's mind: 无～ without anything to live on | 百无～ with nothing whatever to do; bored to death; overcome with boredom

【聊且】liáoqiě 姑且 tentatively; for the moment; merely

【聊胜于无】liáo shèng yú wú 比完全没有好一点 better than nothing; a little is better than none

【聊天儿】liáo//tiānr 谈天 chat; gossip: 俩人聊了一会儿天儿。The two of them chatted for a while. | 他一边喝茶,一边和战士们～。He chatted with the soldiers over a cup of tea.

【聊以自慰】liáo yǐ zì wèi 姑且用来安慰自己 merely to find relief in sth.; just comfort oneself at the thought that...; just to console oneself

【聊以卒岁】liáo yǐ zú suì 〈书 *fml.*〉勉强度过一年 just to tide over the year; barely make ends meet at the end of the year; barely eke out a living during the year

僚 liáo ❶ 官吏 official: 官～ official; bureaucrat ❷ 同一官署的官吏 associate in office: 同～ colleague; companion | ～属 subordinates; staff; officials under sb.'s authority

【僚机】liáojī 编队飞行中跟随长(zhǎng)机的飞机 wing plane; plane that follows the lead aircraft in a formation

【僚属】liáoshǔ 〈旧时 *old*〉指下属的官吏 subordinates; staff; officials under sb.'s authority

【僚友】liáoyǒu 〈旧时 *old*〉指在同一个官署任职的官吏 colleague; associate in office

【僚佐】liáozuǒ 〈旧时 *old*〉官署中的助理人员 assistant in a government office; aide

漻 liáo 〈书 *fml.*〉水清而深 (of water) clear and deep

寥 liáo ❶ 稀少 few; scarce; scanty: ～落 sparse; scattered; deserted; few and far between | ～若晨星 scattered; few and far between; as sparse (or few) as the morning stars ❷ 静寂 silent; quiet; deserted: 寂～ deserted and lonely ❸ 〈书 *fml.*〉空虚;空旷 vast; broad and empty: ～廓 boundless; vast; infinite | ～无人烟 empty and uninhabited; no trace of human habitation in sight

【寥廓】liáokuò 〈书 *fml.*〉高远空旷 boundless; vast; infinite: 视野～ a broad vision | ～的天空 boundless sky

【寥寥】liáoliáo 非常少 very few; sparse; scanty: ～可数 very few; just a sprinkling of | ～无几 very few; hardly any; sparse; scanty | ～数语,就点出了问题的实质 succinctly point out the essence of a problem

【寥落】liáoluò ❶ 稀少 sparse; scattered; few and far between: 疏星～。Only a few solitary stars were twinkling in the sky. ❷ 冷落;冷清 deserted; desolate; isolated: 荒园～ desolate wilderness | ～的小巷 deserted lane

【寥若晨星】liáo ruò chén xīng 稀少得好像早晨的星星 few and far between; scattered; as sparse (or few) as the morning stars

撩 liáo 撩拨 provoke; tease; stir up; excite (emotions): ～逗 tease; annoy; provoke | 春色～人。The beautiful spring season stirs the emotions.

☞ liāo on p.1211 and 撂 liào on p.1215

【撩拨】liáobō 挑逗;招惹 provoke; tease; incite: 任你百般～,他就是不动声色。In the face of every kind of provocation, he stayed calm and collected.

【撩动】liáodòng 拨动;拂动 provoke; stir up; pluck; excite: ～心弦 pluck one's heartstrings; be heart-stirring | 微风～着垂柳的枝条。The light breeze stirred the willow branches.

【撩逗】liáodòu 挑逗;招惹 tease; annoy; provoke: 他生气了,别再～他了。He is angry, so don't provoke him any more.

【撩乱】liáoluàn same as 缭乱 liáoluàn

【撩惹】liáorě 挑逗;招惹 tease; provoke: 他脾气暴,千万不能～他。He has a hot temper, so don't provoke him.

嘹 liáo ☞ below

【嘹亮】liáoliàng (声音)清晰响亮 (of sound) loud and clear; resonant: 歌声～loud singing | 阵地上吹起了～的冲锋号。The bugle sounded the charge loud and clear on the battle field. also 嘹喨 liáoliàng

【嘹喨】liáoliàng same as 嘹亮 liáoliàng

獠 liáo ［獠牙］(liáoyá) 露在嘴外的长牙 fang; buck-tooth; long, projecting tooth: 青面～ dark-face and protruding teeth (形容面貌凶恶 of evil and fiendish features)

潦 liáo ☞ below
☞ lǎo on p. 1163

【潦草】liáocǎo ❶ (字)不工整 (of handwriting) hasty and careless; illegible: 字迹～ careless handwriting; scrawl ❷ (做事)不仔细,不认真 sloppy; slovenly: 浮皮～ superficial and careless; casual; cursory; perfunctory

【潦倒】liáodǎo 颓丧;失意 dejected; frustrated: 穷困～ poverty-stricken and downtrodden; penniless and frustrated; down and out

寮 liáo 〈方 *dial.*〉小屋 hut; small house: 茅～ hut | 竹～ bamboo hut | 茶～酒肆 teahouses and wineshops

【寮房】liáofáng ❶ 寺院里僧人的住房 monk's cell or hut (in temple) ❷ 〈方 *dial.*〉简陋的住房 shed; hut; shabby house

嫽 liáo 〈书 *fml.*〉美好 fine; lovely; charming; glorious

缭 liáo ❶ 缠绕 entangled; twine: ～乱 confused; in a tangle; in a turmoil | ～绕 wind around; curl up; coil up ❷ 用针斜着缝 sew with slanting stitches: ～缝儿 stitch up a seam; seam | 把贴边～上 stitch a hem

【缭乱】liáoluàn 纷乱 confused; in a tangle; in a turmoil: 眼花～dazzled; dazzling | 心绪～ in a confused state of mind; bewildered; mind in a whirl; also 撩乱 liáoluàn

【缭绕】liáorào 回环旋转 wind around; curl up; coil up: 白云～ veiled in clouds | 炊烟～。Smoke curls from kitchen chimneys. | 歌声～。The song lingered in the air.

燎 liáo 延烧;烧 (of fire) spread; burn: 星星之火,可以～原。A single spark can start a prairie fire.
☞ liǎo on p. 1214

【燎泡】liáopào 由于火伤或烫伤,在皮肤或黏膜的表面形成的水泡 blister; blister on the skin or mucosa raised by a burn or scald; also 燎浆泡 liáojiāngpào

【燎原】liáoyuán (大火)延烧原野 (of big fire) set the prairie ablaze: ～烈火 wildland fire | 星火～。A single spark can start a prairie fire.

鹩 liáo ☞ ［鹪鹩］(jiāoliáo) on p. 973

簝 liáo 〈古代 *arch.*〉祭祀时盛肉的竹器 sacrificial bamboo utensil to hold meat

髎 liáo 〈中医 *Chin. med.*〉指骨节间的空隙,多用于穴位名 seam; space between two joints, usu. used in names of acupoints

liǎo (ㄌㄧㄠˇ)

了[1] liǎo ❶ 完毕;结束 finish; end; complete; settle; dispose of: ～结 finish; end; settle; wind up; bring to an end | ～账 bring to an end; settle or square accounts | 没完没～ endless; ceaseless; without stop; nonstop | 一～百～。All troubles end when the main trouble ends. | 不～～之 unresolved; leave unsettled; end up by doing nothing; end up with nothing definite | 这事儿已经～啦! This matter has been settled. ❷ 放在动词后,跟'得、不'连用,表示可能或不可能［used in conjunction with 得 dé and 不 bù after a verb to express possibility］: 办得～ can be done | 做得～ can be made | 来不～unable to come | 受不～ cannot stand or bear ❸ 〈书 *fml.*〉完全(不);一点(也没有) entirely (not); not a bit: ～不相涉 totally (or completely) unrelated (or irrelevant) | ～无惧色 show no trace of fear; show no fear at all; look completely undaunted | ～无进展 make little progress

了[2] **(瞭)** liǎo 明白;懂得 understand; know; realize: ～然 understand; be clear | ～解 understand; know; comprehend | 明～ understand; know clearly | ～如指掌 familiar with; know sth. like the palm or back of one's hand; as plain as pointing to one's hand; be thoroughly familiar (with sth.)
☞ ·le on p. 1166 and 瞭 liào on p. 1216

【了不得】liǎo·bu·dé ❶ 大大超过寻常;很突出 extraordinary; extreme; terrific: 高兴得～ extremely happy | 多得～ innumerable | 山沟里通了火车,在当地是一件～的大事。The opening of the railway in the valley was a momentous event. ❷ 表示情况严重,没法收拾 terrible; awful; dreadful; (of situation) too serious to manage: 可～,他昏过去了! Oh dear, he has fainted.

【了不起】liǎo·buqǐ ❶ 不平凡;(优点)突出 extraordinary; amazing; terrific; remarkable; and a half: 他的本事真～。He is really remarkable. | 一位～的发明家 really an inventor and a half ❷ 重大;严重 serious; grave: 没有什么～的困难。No difficulty is insurmountable.

【了当】liǎodàng ❶ 爽快 frank; outright; straightforward: 他说话脆快～。He does not mince his words; he is very forthright. ❷ 停当;完毕 completed; ready; settled; in order: 安排～ properly arranged | 收拾～ put things in order ❸ 处理;了结(多见于早期白话 oft. in early vernacular) handle; manage; deal with: 自能～得来 can handle (or manage) it by oneself | 费了许多手脚,才得～ expend much effort before getting sth. done

【了得】liǎo·de ❶ 用在惊讶、反诘或责备等语气的句子末尾,表示情况严重,没法收拾(多跟在'还'的后面 mostly followed by 还 hái) ［used at the end of a sentence expressing surprise, disagreement or reproach, to indicate seriousness]:哎呀！这还～！Goodness, how outrageous!|如果一跤跌下去，那还～！Falling down would be horrible! ❷ 不平常；很突出(多见于早期白话 oft. in early vernacular) extraordinary; outstanding; exceptional:这个人武艺十分～。His *wushu* skills are outstanding.

【了断】liǎoduàn same as 了结 liǎojié

【了结】liǎojié 解决；结束(事情) finish; settle; end; wind up; bring to an end:案子已经～。The case has been settled.|～了一桩心愿 fulfil one's wish

【了解】liǎojiě ❶ 知道得清楚 understand; know; comprehend:只有眼睛向下，才能真正～群众的愿望和要求。Only by contact with the people can we really understand their aspirations and needs. ❷ 打听；调查 look into; find out; acquaint oneself with:先去～情况 first find out what's going on|这究竟是怎么回事？你去～一下。Please find out what all this is about.

【了局】liǎojú ❶ 结束；了结 end; ending; outcome:后来呢，你猜怎样～？Can you guess the final outcome?|事情弄得没法～。The matter cannot be wrapped up.|不知何日～。No one knows when this will end. ❷ 解决办法；长久之计 settlement; solution; way out:你这病应该赶快治，拖下去不是个～。You should treat your illness as soon as possible. Putting things off is no solution.|在那儿住下去，终久不是～。Living there solves nothing.

【了了】liǎoliǎo 〈书 *fml.*〉明白；懂得 understand clearly:心中～ be well aware of sth.|不甚～ know little about; be unclear about

【了却】liǎoquè same as 了结 liǎojié:～一桩心事 relieve one's mind; take a load off one's mind

【了然】liǎorán 明白；清楚 understand; be clear:一目～clear at a glance|真相如何，我也不大～。I am not really clear about the truth.

【了如指掌】liǎo rú zhǐ zhǎng 形容对情况非常清楚，好像指着自己的手掌给人看 be in the know; familiar with; know sth. like the palm or back of one's hand; as plain as pointing to one's hand:他对这一带的地形～。He knows the terrain of this locality like the back of his hand.

【了事】liǎo//shì 使事情得到平息或结束(多指不彻底或不得已 usu. not thoroughly or reluctantly) end; finish; dispose of a matter; get sth. over; get through with sth.:含糊～ muddle through sth.; handle sth. in an unsatisfactory way|草草～ rush through something; get through sth. in a careless or perfunctory way|应付～ get through (or deal with) sth. in a careless or perfunctory way|他想尽快了了(·le)这件事。He wanted to complete this business as soon as possible.

【了手】liǎoshǒu 〈方 *dial.*〉(事情)办完；了结 dispose of a matter; finish (or end) the work on hand:只要这件事一～，我就立刻动身。I will leave as soon as I have disposed of this matter.

【了无】liǎowú 一点也没有 not at all; not the least; not the slightest:～睡意 not at all sleepy; not sleepy at all|～痕迹 without a trace (or vestige)|洁如冰雪，～纤尘 spotlessly clean; as clean as ice without a grain of dust

【了悟】liǎowù 〈书 *fml.*〉领悟；明白 understand; realize; comprehend; grasp:其中奥妙，尚未～。I have not grasped the intricacies of the situation yet.

【了账】liǎo//zhàng 结清账目 settle or square accounts;〈比喻 *fig.*〉事情结束 settle, end:就此～。It is all settled.

钌 liǎo 金属元素，符号 Ru (ruthenium)。银灰色，质硬而脆，存在于铂矿中，含量极少，用来制耐磨硬质合金等。ruthenium (Ru); hard, brittle, silver grey metallic element, present in small quantities in platinum (Pt) ore, used to produce hard, durable alloys, etc.

☞ liào on p.1215

蓼 liǎo 一年生草本植物，叶子披针形，花淡绿色或淡红色，果实卵形，扁平。茎叶有辣味。全草入药。knotweed (*Polygonum*); annual plant with lanceolar leaves, light green or red flowers, and flat oval fruits, stems and leaves having a peppery-taste, and the whole plant being useful as medicine; also 水蓼 shuǐliǎo

☞ lù on p.1263

【蓼蓝】liǎolán 一年生草本植物，茎红紫色，叶子长椭圆形，干时暗蓝色，花淡红色，穗状花序，结瘦果，黑褐色。叶子含蓝汁，可以做蓝色染料。indigo plant (*Polygonum tinctorium*); annual plant having reddish purple stem, long oval leaves which turn dark blue when dried, and light red flowers growing in a spike, and bearing blackish brown achenes, the blue juice from the leaves being used as a dye; also 蓝 lán

憭 liǎo 〈书 *fml.*〉明白；明了 understand; comprehend

燎 liǎo 挨近了火而烧焦(多用于毛发 usu. of hair) singe; charred by fire:火苗一蹿，～了眉毛。The flames darted up, singling his eyebrows.

☞ liáo on p.1213

liào (ㄌㄧㄠˋ)

尥 liào [尥蹶子](liào juě·zi)骡马等跳起来用后腿向后踢 (of mules, horses, etc.)

hind kick; kick with the hind legs: 这马好(hào)～,小心别让它踢着。Beware of this horse. It might kick you.

钌 liào [钌铞儿](liàodiàor)扣住门窗等的铁片,一端钉在门窗上,另一端有钩子钩在屈戌儿里,或者有眼儿套在屈戌儿上 hasp and staple; iron clasp used to fasten a door, a window, etc., with one end nailed to the door or window, and the other end having a hook or an opening that hooks onto or passes over a staple

☞ liǎo on p. 1214

料[1] liào ❶ 预料;料想 suppose; expect; anticipate: ～事如神 foresee with divine precision; foretell with miraculous accuracy; predict like a prophet; have a prophetic eye | 不出所～ as expected | ～不到他会来。We didn't expect him to come. ❷ 照看;管理 take care of; manage: 照～ look after; take care of | ～理 manage; arrange; attend to; take care of

料[2] liào ❶ (～儿 liàor)材料;原料 material; stuff: 木～ timber; lumber | 燃～ fuel | 布～ cotton fabric; cotton cloth | 加～ add raw material | 备～ ready materials (for production or construction) | 资～ material; information; data | 他就是这么块～。That is all he is capable of. ❷ 喂牲口用的谷物 (grain) feed (for animals); forage; fodder: 草～ fodder; forage | ～豆儿 soya beans or black beans used as livestock feed | 多给牲口加点～ increase the animal fodder ❸〈量词 *classifier*〉用于中医配制丸药,处方规定剂量的全份为一料 prescription for pills; prescribed dosage for making pills: 配一～药 make up a prescription ❹〈量词 *classifier*〉过去计算木材的单位,两端截面是一平方尺,长足七尺的木材叫一料 *liao*, old unit of measurement for timber equal to 7 *chi* by 1 square *chi*

【料定】liàodìng 预料并断定 be certain; know for sure: 我～他会来的。I'm sure he will come.

【料斗】liàodǒu 装牲口饲料的器具,多用柳条编成,形状像斗 dipper-shaped forage utensil, usu. made of wicker; also 料斗子 liàodǒu·zi

【料豆儿】liàodòur 喂牲口的黑豆、黄豆等,一般煮熟或炒熟 fried soya beans or black beans used as livestock feed, usu. boiled or toasted; also 料豆子 liàodòu·zi

【料及】liàojí〈书 *fml*.〉料想到 expect; anticipate: 中途大雨,原未～。We didn't expect such heavy rain on the way.

【料酒】liàojiǔ 烹调时当作料用的黄酒 cooking wine; yellow rice wine used as seasoning in cooking

【料理】liàolǐ 办理;处理 arrange; manage; attend to; take care of: ～家务 manage household affairs | ～后事 make funeral arrangements | 事情还没～好,我怎么能走。How can I leave without attending to these matters?

【料器】liàoqì 用玻璃的原料加颜料制成的手工艺品 glassware; coloured glass artifacts

【料峭】liàoqiào〈书 *fml*.〉形容微寒(多指春寒 usu. in early spring) chilly: 春寒～ early spring chill in the air

【料想】liàoxiǎng 猜测(未来的事);预料 think; expect; anticipate; presume: ～不到 who would have thought that...; unexpectedly | 他～事情定能成功。He expected things to be successful.

【料子】liào·zi ❶ 衣料 cloth for clothes; dress length: 一块衣裳～ a dress length ❷〈方 *dial*.〉特指毛料 woollen fabric: 穿着一身～中山装 dressed in woollen Sun Yat sen-style jacket and trousers ❸〈比喻 *fig*.〉适于做某种事情的人才 qualities; makings; stuff; person suited for some undertaking: 不是搞科研的～ not have the makings of a researcher | 他是个下棋的～。He is a good chess player.

撂(撩) liào ❶ 放;搁 put down; drop; shelve; leave behind: 他～下饭碗,又上工地去了。He put down his bowl, and immediately returned to the building site. | 事儿～下半个月了。The matter has been shelved for a fortnight. ❷ 弄倒 knock down; throw down; shoot down: 他脚下使了个绊儿,一下子把对手～在地上。He stuck out his foot and tripped his opponent. ❸ 抛弃;抛 abandon; discard; leave behind; cast aside: 他出门在外,把家全～给妻子了。He is away from home, and has left his wife to take care of everything.

☞ 撩 liāo on p. 1211 and liáo on p. 1215

【撂地】liàodì (～儿 liàodìr)指艺人在庙会、集市、街头空地上演出 (of folk artists) perform at a temple fair, market or on a street: ～卖艺 make a living as a street performer; also 撂地摊 liàodìtān

【撂荒】liào//huāng〈方 *dial*.〉不继续耕种土地,任它荒芜 leave land uncultivated; let the land lie idle: 减少～面积 reduce uncultivated areas

【撂跤】liào//jiāo〈方 *dial*.〉same as 摔跤 shuāi//jiāo ②

【撂手】liào//shǒu 不继续做下去;丢开 discontinue; put aside; wash one's hands of sth.; cease to be involved: ～不管 wash one's hands of sth. | 事情没有完,哪能就～? With matters still unsettled, how can you just walk away?

【撂挑子】liào tiāo·zi 放下挑子 put down a load on a carrying pole;〈比喻 *fig*.〉丢下应担负的工作,甩手不干 throw off one's responsibilities and stop working: 有意见归有意见,决不能～。It's alright to complaint, but one cannot shirk one's responsibilities.

廖 Liào 姓 a surname

瞭 liǎo 瞭望 watch from a height or a distance:在高处～着点儿 keep a lookout from up high
☞ 了[2] liǎo on p.1213

【瞭哨】liàoshào 放哨 go on sentry; stand guard; stand sentry or sentinel:巡营～ patrol and sentry the barracks

【瞭望】liàowàng ❶ 登高远望 look far out from a height:极目～,海天茫茫。As far as the eye can see, ocean and the sky stretch into the distance. ❷ 特指从高处或远处监视敌情 (esp.) observe the enemy from a height or distance; keep a lookout on the enemy:～哨 watchtower; observation post | 海防战士～着广阔的海面。Soldiers of the coastal defense are keeping a lookout over the wide ocean spaces.

【瞭望哨】liàowàngshào same as 观察哨 guānchásào

镣 liào 脚镣 fetters; shackles:～铐 shackles; chains; irons; fetters and handcuffs | 铁～ irons

【镣铐】liàokào 脚镣和手铐 fetters and handcuffs; shackles; irons; chains

liē(ㄌㄧㄝ)

咧 liē ☞ below
☞ liě on p.1216 and ·lie on p.1219

【咧咧】liēliē ☞大大咧咧 dà·daliēliē on p.355, 骂骂咧咧 mà·maliēliē on p.1292 and 笑咧咧 xiàoliēliē on p.2116

【咧咧】liē·lie〈方 dial.〉❶ 乱说;乱讲 gossip; make irresponsible remarks; speak carelessly:瞎～什么? What are you gossiping about? ❷ 小儿哭 (of children) blubber; cry; sob:别在这儿～了,快走吧! Stop that blubbering and go quickly!

liě(ㄌㄧㄝˇ)

咧 liě ❶ 嘴角向两边伸展 grin; stretch the corners of the mouth in both directions:～着嘴笑 grin from ear to ear | 把嘴一～ grimace; part the lips ❷〈方 dial.〉说(含贬义 derog.) talk:胡～ talk nonsense | 胡诌八～ fabricate wild tales; cook up stories
☞ liē on p.1216 and ·lie on p.1219

【咧嘴】liě//zuǐ 向两边延伸嘴角 grimace; grin; part the lips; stretch the corners of the mouth:龇牙～ snarl; show one's teeth; look ferocious | 咧开嘴笑起来 grin from ear to ear; one's mouth widen in a smile; beam

裂 liě〈方 dial.〉东西的两部分向两旁分开 split or break open; sever; split and part down the middle:衣服没扣好,～着怀。His shirt was unbuttoned, exposing his chest.
☞ liè on p.1218

liè(ㄌㄧㄝˋ)

列 liè ❶ 排列 arrange; line up; put in order:罗～ set out; list; enumerate | ～队 line up | 按清单上～的一项一项地清点 check the listed items one by one ❷ 安排到某类事物之中 list; enter in a list; rank:～入议程 place on the agenda | 把发展教育事业～为重要任务之一 rank education as one of our priorities ❸ 行列 rank; row; file:出～ step out of the ranks | 站在最前～ stand in the front row (or in the forefront) ❹〈量词 *classifier*〉用于成行列的事物 [used for a series or row of things]:一～火车 a train ❺ 类 sort; kind; category:不在此～ not in this category ❻ 各;众 various; each and every:～国 various countries | ～位观众 dear audience ❼ (Liè) 姓 a surname

【列兵】lièbīng 军衔,兵的最低一级 private; lowest enlisted rank in the military

【列车】lièchē 配有机车、工作人员和规定信号的连挂成列的火车 train; connected group of railroad cars pulled by a locomotive, serviced by a train crew and stipulated signals:国际～ international train | 旅客～ passenger train | 15次～train No. 15

【列车员】lièchēyuán 在客运列车上服务的人员 carriage attendant; train attendant; train crew; those working on a passenger train

【列当】lièdāng 一年生草本植物,多寄生在菊科植物的根上。茎肉质,叶子鳞片状,黄褐色,花紫色。全草入药。broomrape (*Orobanche Coerulescens*); brown annual parastic plant living on the roots of plants of the composite family, with a fleshy stem, scale-shaped leaves, and purple flowers, the whole plant used as medicine; also 草苁蓉 cǎocóngróng

【列岛】lièdǎo 群岛的一种,一般指排列成线形或弧形的,如我国的澎湖列岛、嵊泗列岛等 archipelago; island chain; chain of islands; group of islands strung out in a line or over an arc, e.g. the Penghu and Shengsi islands of China

【列队】lièduì 排列成队伍 line up; form into lines:～游行 line up for a parade | 群众～欢迎贵宾。The well wishers lined up to welcome the honoured guest.

【列国】lièguó 某一时期内并存的各国 number of states or countries coexisting during a certain period:～相争 states vying for supremacy | 周游～travel to many countries

【列举】lièjǔ 一个一个地举出来 list; enumerate: ～事实 cite facts | 指示中～了各种具体办法。Specific measures are laid out in the instructions.

【列宁主义】Lièníng zhǔyì 帝国主义和无产阶级革命时代的马克思主义。列宁(Владимир Ильич Ленин)在领导俄国革命的实践中,在同第二国际修正主义的斗争中,继承、捍卫了马克思主义,并在关于帝国主义的理论,关于社会主义可能首先在一国取得胜利,关于建立无产阶级新型政党,关于无产阶级革命和无产阶级专政等问题上,发展了马克思主义。Leninism; Marxism belonging to the age of imperialism and the proletarian revolution. During the course of leading the Russian Revolution and in the struggle against revisionist theories of the Second International (1889-1914), Lenin carried forward and defended Marxism, and he expanded it with his theories on imperialism, on the possible establishment of socialism in one country first, on the formation of a new kind of political party of the proletariat, and on the revolution and dictatorship of the proletariat.

【列强】lièqiáng 〈旧时 *old*〉指世界上同一时期内的各个资本主义强国 powers; big powers; strong capitalist countries of a certain historical period

【列位】lièwèi same as 诸位 zhūwèi: ～请坐。Everyone, be seated, please.

【列席】liè//xí 参加会议,有发言权而没有表决权 attend (a meeting) with the right to speak but not to vote

【列传】lièzhuàn 纪传体史书中一般人物的传记,如《史记·廉颇蔺相如列传》biography; biographical account (of common people in Chinese historiography, e. g. *Records of the Historian · Biographies of Lian Po and Lin Xiangru*

劣 liè ❶ 坏;不好(跟'优'相对 as opposed to 'good, excellent') bad; inferior; of low quality: ～等 poor; low-grade; of inferior quality | ～势 unfavourable or disadvantageous situation; inferior strength or position; weak | 恶～ mean; base; abominable; disgusting; despicable | 低～ inferior; low-grade | 优～ superior or inferior ❷ 小于一定标准的 minor; smaller than some standard: ～弧 minor arch

【劣等】lièděng 低等;下等 poor; low-grade; of inferior quality: ～货 low-grade (or inferior) goods

【劣根性】liègēnxìng 长期养成的、根深蒂固的不良习性 bad habit; deep-rooted or ingrained bad habit

【劣弧】lièhú 小于半圆的弧 minor arc; arc smaller than a semicircle

【劣迹】lièjì 恶劣的事迹(指损害人民的 harmful to the public) evil; misdeed; evildoing: ～昭彰 flagrant evildoing, notorious record | 他的～已被人告发。His misdeed has been reported to the authorities.

【劣马】lièmǎ ❶ 不好的马 inferior horse; nag ❷ 性情暴躁不容易驾驭的马 fiery steed; vicious horse; wild horse: 制伏～ tame a wild horse; break in a wild horse

【劣绅】lièshēn 品行恶劣的绅士 evil gentry: 土豪～ local tyrants and evil gentry

【劣势】lièshì 情况或条件比较差的形势 weakness; unfavourable or disadvantageous situation; inferior strength or position: 处于～ be in an unfavourable position; be weaker; inferior | 变～为优势 turn a weakness into a strength

【劣质】lièzhì 质量低劣 low or poor quality; inferior: ～煤 dross | ～烟酒 inferior tobacco and alcohol

冽 liè 〈书 *fml*.〉冷 cold; chilly; icy: 凛～ piercingly cold | 山高风～。Cold winds blow in the high mountains.

洌 liè 〈书 *fml*.〉(水、酒)清 (of water or alcoholic drink) crystal clear; limpid: 泉香而酒～ fragrant wine made from clear spring water

埒 liè 〈书 *fml*.〉❶ 同等;(相)等 equal; on a par with: 富～皇室 on a par with the imperial family in wealth; as wealthy as the royal family | 二人才力相～。They are equally talented. ❷ 指矮墙、田埂、堤防等 low wall, ridge; dyke, embankment, etc.: 河～ river embankment

烈 liè ❶ 强烈;猛烈 strong; intense; fierce; violent: ～火 fierce fire; raging flames | ～日 scorching sun; burning sun | ～酒 spirits; strong or stiff drink; hard liquor | 性子～ violent temper | 轰轰～～ vigorous; dynamic; on a grand and spectacular scale; with vim and vigour | 兴高采～ in high spirits; with great joy; jubilant ❷ 刚直;严正 stern; upright; staunch: 刚～ upright and unyielding; fiery and forthright ❸ 为正义而死难的 die for a just cause; sacrifice oneself for a just cause: ～士 martyr | 先～martyr of an older generation ❹ 〈书 *fml*.〉功业 exploits; achievements: 功～(功绩) contributions; merits and achievements

【烈度】lièdù 地震烈度的简称 abbr. for 地震烈度 dìzhèn lièdù

【烈风】lièfēng ❶ 气象学上指 9 级风(meteorol.) force 9 wind; strong gale ❷ 泛指强劲的风 general term for high wind

【烈火】lièhuǒ 猛烈的火 intense flames; fierce fire; raging flames: 熊熊的～ raging fire; blazing flames◇斗争的～ fiery struggle; intense struggle

【烈火见真金】lièhuǒ jiàn zhēnjīn 只有在烈火中烧炼才能辨别金子的真假 true gold stands the test of fire; pure gold proves its worth in a blazing fire;〈比喻 *fig.*〉关键时刻才能考验出人的品质 a crisis shows the true character of sb.

【烈女】liènǚ ❶ 刚正有节操的女子 chaste and pure woman ❷ 拼死保全贞节的女子 woman who dies defending her chastity

【烈日】lièrì 炎热的太阳 burning sun; scorching sun:~当空。The scorching sun blazed in the sky.

【烈士】lièshì ❶ 为正义事业而牺牲的人 martyr; person who dies for a just cause:革命~ revolutionary martyr | ~陵园 cemetery of revolutionary martyrs ❷〈书 *fml.*〉有志于建立功业的人 person of high endeavour; man of heroic ambitions:~暮年,壮心不已。A man of ambition retains his high aspirations even in old age. *or* The heart of an aging hero is as stout as ever.

【烈属】lièshǔ 烈士家属 family members of a revolutionary martyr

【烈性】lièxìng ❶ 性格刚烈 spirited; fiery; upright and unyielding:~汉子 man of character ❷ 性质猛烈 strong; intense; violent:~酒 hard liquor; strong drink; spirits | ~炸药 high explosive

【烈焰】lièyàn 猛烈的火焰 roaring flames; raging blaze:~腾空 towering flames

䴕 liè 啄木鸟 woodpecker (*Picus*)

捩 liè 扭转 turn; twist:~转 turn round | 转~点 turning point

猎(獵) liè ❶ 捕捉禽兽;打猎 hunt; catch birds and beasts:狩~ hunt | 渔~ fishing and hunting ❷ 打猎的 hunting:~人 hunter; huntsman | ~户 hunting family; hunter; huntsman | ~狗 hound; hunting dog | ~枪 shotgun; hunting rifle; fowling piece

【猎场】lièchǎng 划定范围供人打猎的山林或草原 hunting field; hunting ground; mountain, forest or grassland reserved for hunting

【猎狗】liègǒu 受过训练,能帮助打猎的狗 hound; hunting dog; dog trained as a helper for hunting; also 猎犬 lièquǎn

【猎户】lièhù ❶ 以打猎为业的人家 hunting family; family that lives by hunting ❷ 打猎的人 hunter; huntsman

【猎户座】lièhùzuò 星座,位置在天球赤道上。其中有两个一等星,五个二等星和其他更暗的星。猎户座即我国古代所说的参宿。Orion; Hunter; constellation lying on the celestial equator, containing two first-rate stars, five two-rate stars and other dimmer stars; equivalent to 参宿 cānsù in ancient Chinese astronomy

【猎猎】lièliè〈书 *fml.*〉〈拟声词 *onom.*〉形容风声及旗帜等被风吹动的声音 (of wind) whistling; flapping of a flag in the wind:北风~。The north wind is howling. | 红旗~,歌声嘹亮。The red flags flapped in the wind, and the singing was loud and clear.

【猎奇】lièqí 搜寻奇异的事情(多含贬义 usu. derog.) seek out novelty; look for the exotic and strange

【猎潜艇】lièqiántǐng 搜索、消灭敌潜艇的小型舰艇。装备有声纳、雷达等搜索器材和深水炸弹、小口径火炮等武器。submarine chaser; small naval vessel which searches for and destroys enemy submarines, equipped with search devices like sonar and radar, and armed with depth charges and small-calibre guns

【猎枪】lièqiāng 打猎用的枪 shotgun; hunting rifle; fowling piece:双筒~ double-barrel shotgun

【猎取】lièqǔ ❶ 通过打猎取得 hunt; obtain by hunting:原始社会的人用粗糙的石器~野兽。Primitive man hunted wild animals with crude stone implements. ❷ 夺取(名利 of fame and wealth) seek; pursue; strive for:~功名 seek scholarly honour or official rank; obtain a degree in the civil examinations | ~高额利润 pursue large profits

【猎犬】lièquǎn same as 猎狗 liègǒu

【猎人】lièrén 以打猎为业的人 hunter; huntsman; man who makes a living by hunting

【猎手】lièshǒu 打猎的人(多指技术熟练的 usu. skillful) hunter

【猎物】lièwù 猎取到的或作为猎取对象的鸟兽 prey; game; quarry:东北虎保护区只让老虎和它们的~生活。Only Manchurian tigers and their prey are allowed in the natural tiger reserves.

裂 liè ❶ 破而分开;破成两部分或几部分 split; crack; rend; break open; break up into two or more parts:分~ split; divide; break up | 破~ break; crack; burst; split; rupture | 决~ break with; rupture | ~纹 crack; crackle (on pottery, porcelain, etc.) | ~开 split open; rend; breach | 四分五~ disintegrate; split up; fall apart; rent by disunity | 手冻~了。(His) hands were chapped by the cold. ❷ 叶子或花冠的边缘上较大较深的缺口 gap; large, deep breach on the edge of a leaf or corolla

☞ liě on p. 1216

【裂变】lièbiàn ❶ 原子核分裂成两个(或更多个)其他元素的原子核,并放出电子 fission; process of splitting an atomic nucleus into two (or more) atomic nuclei of other elements, and releasing electrons in the process ❷ 泛指分裂变化 split; change through division:现代人追求小家庭,大家庭不断~。Modern people desire smaller families so the extended family is breaking up.

【裂缝】liè//fèng (~儿 liè//fèngr)裂成狭长的缝

儿 crack; rip; rift; tear or split into long narrow cracks:做门的木料没有干透,风一吹都～了。The door timber had not dried completely, and cracked when the wind blew.|墙裂了一道缝。There is a crack in the wall.

【裂缝】lièfèng (～儿 lièfèngr)裂开的缝儿 crack; crevice; rip; rift; fissure; come loose at the seams:墙上有一条～。There is a crevice in the wall.

【裂果】lièguǒ 干果的一类,果实成熟后果皮裂开,如蓇葖、荚果、蒴果、角果等 dehiscent fruit; fruits which split open when mature and dry, e. g. folliculus, legumes, capsules, bicarpel seeds, etc.

【裂痕】lièhén 器物破裂的痕迹 crack; fissure; rift; crack marks on an object:玻璃中间有一道～。There is a crack in the glass.◇两人之间一度有过～。At one point, there was a rift (or breach) in their relationship.

【裂化】lièhuà 在一定条件下,分子量较大的烷烃分解成分子量较小的烷烃和烯烃。是石油加工的重要方法,可分为热裂化(400－700℃)、催化裂化和加氢裂化。cracking; process of breaking down alkanes of greater molecular weight into alkane and alkene of smaller molecular weights under specific conditions, an important part of distillation of petroleum that can be thermal cracking (400－700℃), catalytic cracking and hydrocracking

【裂解】lièjiě 在比热裂化更高的温度(700℃以上)下进行的深度裂化 splitting decomposition; splitting; depth cracking undergone at a temperature higher than thermal cracking (above 700℃)

【裂口】liè//kǒu (～儿 liè//kǒur)裂成口儿 crack; split:手冻得～了。(His) hands were chapped by cold.|西瓜裂了口儿。The watermelon has split open.

【裂口】lièkǒu (～儿 lièkǒur)裂开的口儿 rip; breach; crack; split

【裂片】lièpiàn 边缘有裂的叶子或花冠由裂分成的小片叫做裂片 lobe (of leaf); leaf with divisions, or the small separate projections of a floral corolla

【裂纹】lièwén ❶ same as 裂璺 lièwèn ❷ 瓷器在烧制时有意做成的像裂璺的花纹 crackle (on pottery, porcelain, etc.); (of porcelain) pattern of cracks deliberate made during firing

【裂璺】liè//wèn 器物有裂开的痕迹 crack line; (of a utensil) split mark:～的破锅 cracked pot|水缸裂了一道璺。There is a crack in the water vat.

【裂璺】lièwèn 器物将要裂开的痕迹 crack; (of a utensil) mark to be splitted:茶碗有一道～。There is a crack in the tea cup.

【裂隙】lièxì 裂开的缝儿 crack; crevice; fracture; fissure:桌面上有一道～。There is a fissure on the table top.◇弥合双方感情上的～ smooth over the rift in a couple's relationship

趔 liè [趔趄](liè·qie)身体歪斜,脚步不稳 stagger; reel; lurch walk unsteadily with a swaying gait:他～着走进屋来。He staggered into the room.|打了个～,摔倒了 stagger and fall to the ground|口袋很重,他～了几下,没扛起来。He lurched under the heavy bag, but was unable to hoist it on to his shoulder.

躐 liè〈书 *fml.*〉❶ 超越 go beyond; overstep; skip over:～等 not follow the proper order|～级 (of student) skip a grade ❷ 践踏 trample

【躐等】lièděng〈书 *fml.*〉超越等级;不按次序 not follow the proper order

鱲 liè 鱼,体长4寸左右,侧扁,背部灰暗,两侧银白色,雄鱼带红色,有黑色斑纹,生殖季节色泽鲜艳。生活在淡水中。minnow (*Zacco platypus*); slim, fresh water fish, approximately 4 *cun* long with dark back and silvery sides, the male having reddish colouring with black stripes, which brighten during the mating season; also 桃花鱼 táohuāyú

鬣 liè 某些兽类(如马、狮子等)颈上的长毛 mane; long hair on the neck of certain animals (such as horses, lions, etc.)

【鬣狗】liègǒu 哺乳动物,外形略像狗,头比狗的头短而圆,额部宽,尾巴短,前腿长,后腿短,毛棕黄色或棕褐色,有许多不规则的黑褐色斑点。多生长在热带或亚热带地区,吃兽类尸体腐烂的肉。(striped) hyena (*Hyaena hyaenu*); mammal that lives mostly in tropical and sub-tropical zones, feeds on carrion, resembles the dog, but has a shorter and rounder head, broad forehead and short tail, its hind legs shorter than its forelegs, and having brownish or tawny fur and irregular black brown markings

·lie (·ㄌ丨ㄝ)

咧 ·lie〈方 *dial.*〉〈助词 *aux.*〉用法跟'了'、'啦'、'哩'相同[used like 了 ·le, 啦 ·la or 哩 ·li]:好～。Ok.|来～。Here it comes.|他愿意～!He is willing!

☞ liē on p.1216 and liě on p.1216

līn (ㄌ丨ㄣ)

拎 līn 用手提 carry; lift; hold:～着饭盒上班 carry a lunch box to work|他～了个木桶到河边去打水。He carried a wooden bucket to the river to fetch water.

【拎包】līnbāo〈方 *dial.*〉same as 提包 tíbāo

lín（ㄌㄧㄣˊ）

邻(鄰、隣) lín ❶ 住处接近的人家 neighbour; those who live close by: 四～(surrounding) neighbours|东～ neighbour living on the eastern side|～人 neighbour|远亲不如近～。A faraway relative cannot compare to a close neighbour. ❷ 邻接的;邻近的 neighbouring; adjacent; close; near: ～国 neighbouring country|～县 neighbouring county|～家 neighbour|～座 adjacent seat ❸〈古代 *arch.*〉五家为邻 administrative unit composed of five households

【邻邦】línbāng 接壤的国家 neighbouring country: 友好～ friendly neighbouring countries; (of countries) good neighbours

【邻角】línjiǎo 平面上两个角有公共顶点和一条公共边,它们的另一条边分别在公共边的两旁,这两个角就互为邻角 adjacent angles; two angles on a plane having the same vertex and a common side between them

【邻接】línjiē (地区)接连 (of areas) adjoin; next to; border on; be contiguous to: 河北省西边～山西省。Hebei Province borders on Shanxi Province in the west.

【邻近】línjìn ❶ 位置接近 near; close to; adjacent to: ～边界 close to the border|我国东部跟朝鲜接壤,跟日本～。To the east, China has a border with Korea and is also adjacent to Japan. ❷ 附近 nearby; vicinity; in the neighbourhood: 学校～有文化馆。There is a cultural centre close by the school.|～的一家姓赵的搬走了。The Zhao family in the neighbourhood has moved away.

【邻近色】línjìnsè 色相接近的颜色。如红与橙、橙与黄、黄与绿、绿与青、青与紫、紫与红。similar colours; close colours, e.g. red and orange, orange and yellow, yellow and green, green and blue, blue and purple, and purple and red

【邻居】línjū 住家接近的人或人家 neighbour; person or household living close by

【邻里】línlǐ ❶ 指家庭所在的乡里。也指市镇上互相邻接的一些街道。neighbourhood; village or small town where one has lived a long time; adjoining streets: ～服务站 neighbourhood service centre ❷ 同一乡里的人 neighbours; people of the same neighbourhood: ～纷纷前来祝贺。The neighbours all came to express their congratulations.

【邻舍】línshè same as 邻居 línjū: 街坊～neighbours|左右～ surrounding neighbours

林 lín ❶ 成片的树木或竹子 woods; forest; grove; expanse of trees or bamboo: 树～ woods; grove|竹～ bamboo grove|山～ mountain forest; wooded moun tain|防风～ windbreak ❷ 聚集在一起的同类的人或事物 circles; group of similar objects or persons: 儒～ scholarly circles|艺～ art circles|碑～ forest of steles; collection of stone inscriptions ❸ 林业 forestry: 农～牧副渔 farming, forestry, animal husbandry, sideline occupations and fishery ❹ (Lín) 姓 a surname

【林产】línchǎn 林业产物,包括木材,森林植物的根、茎、叶、皮、花、果实、种子、树脂、菌类以及森林中的动物等 timberland; forest farm products (including timer, roots, stems, leaves, bark, flowers, fruits, seeds, resin and fungi, as well as wild animals, etc.)

【林场】línchǎng ❶ 从事培育、管理、采伐森林等工作的单位 forestry (including tree nursery, lumber camp, etc.); unit that engages in forest planting, managing and logging ❷ 培育或采伐森林的地方 tree farm; plantation forestry farm; place where trees are cultivated or logged

【林丛】líncóng 树林子;树木丛生的地方 woods; woodland grove; place where trees grow thickly: 两岸的～,一望无边。The river banks are covered by thick trees as far as the eye can see.

【林带】líndài 为了防风、防沙等而培植的带状的树林 forest belt; belt of trees cultivated to block the wind and fix the shifting sand: 防护～ shelter belt|防风～ windbreak belt|防沙～ sand-break belt

【林地】líndì 生长着成片树木的土地 woodland; forest land; timberland; wooded field

【林分】línfēn 林业上指树种组成、林木年龄、疏密程度、森林起源等特征大致相同的大片森林地段 standing forest; stand; large tract of forest where the trees are of similar species, age, spacing, and origin, etc.

【林冠】línguān 森林中互相连接在一起的树冠的总体 crown cover; forest canopy; cover formed by contiguous crowns of trees in a forest

【林海】línhǎi 形容像海洋一样一望无际的森林 woods, immense forest; sea of trees

【林垦】línkěn 开垦荒山,植树造林 forestry and land reclamation; bring barren hills under cultivation and afforestation: ～事业 forestry and land reclamation undertakings

【林立】línlì 像树林一样密集地竖立着。形容很多 stand in great numbers (like trees in a forest): 高楼～。A jungle of tall buildings.|帆樯～。A forest of masts.|效区工厂～。There are many factories in the suburbs.

【林林总总】línlínzǒngzǒng 形容繁多 numerous; in great abundance; manifold: 展销会上的商品～,不下数万种。There are a great many products on display at the commodities fair, numbering in the thousands at least.

【林龄】línlíng 整个林分的平均年龄 age of

stand; average age of an entire standing forest

【林莽】línmǎng 茂密的林木和草丛 thick jungle, overgrown with thick trees and bushes: ～地带 thick jungle region

【林木】línmù ❶ same as 树林 shùlín ❷ 生长在森林中的树木(区别于'孤立木' as compared with 'lone tree') forest tree

【林农】línnóng 从事森林的培育、管理、保护等工作的农民 forest farmer; forester; one who engages in the cultivation, management and protection of a forest

【林檎】línqín 花红(植物)Chinese pear-leaf crab apple (*Malus asiatica* var. *rinki*) a plant

【林泉】línquán〈书 *fml.*〉❶ 林木山泉 woods and streams; forest spring: ～幽静 quiet woods and streams ❷ 借指隐居的地方 refers to a place of seclusion; hermitage: 退隐～ live in seclusion; live the life of a hermit

【林薮】línsǒu〈书 *fml.*〉❶ 指山林水泽,草木丛生的地方 forest and marsh; place thick with vegetation ❷〈比喻 *fig.*〉事物聚集的处所 collection; assemblage: 古小说～ collection of classical novels

【林涛】líntāo 森林被风吹动发出的像波涛一样的声音 soughing of the wind in a forest; roaring of the wind in the trees: ～呼啸 howling of the wind in the forest

【林网】línwǎng 指纵横交错,像网一样的林带 forest grid; intersecting tracts of woodland

【林下】línxià〈书 *fml.*〉山林田野,借指退隐的地方 mountain forests and fields; refers to retirement from official life: 优游～ live a leisurely and carefree life after retirement | 退隐～ retire to a country hermitage; retire from public life and live quietly in the countryside

【林相】línxiàng ❶ 由于林冠层次和林木组成结构的不同而表现出的森林外貌;森林的外形 appearance or configuration of a forest, caused by irregular canopy, different tree species and shapes: ～整齐 uniform forest ❷ 指森林的林木品质和生长情况 (of forest) quality (of trees, and growth): ～优良 high-grade forest

【林型】línxíng 林业上根据森林综合自然性状而划分的森林分类单位,如杜鹃林型、苔藓林型等 (forestry) forest type; classification of forests based on overall natural features, e.g. azalea forest type, bryophyte forest type, etc.

【林业】línyè 培育和保护森林以取得木材和其他林产品的生产事业 forestry (as an industry); productive undertakings of cultivating and protecting forests to obtain woods and other forest products

【林独】línyì 猞猁(shēlì) lynx (*Lynx Kerr*)

【林阴道】línyīndào 两旁有茂密树木的道路(一般比较宽) avenue; boulevard; mall; wide road lined with thick trees; also 林阴路 línyīnlù

【林苑】línyuàn〈古代 *arch.*〉专供统治者打猎玩乐的园林 imperial hunting ground; special park grounds reserved for members of the ruling class for hunting

【林政】línzhèng 有关森林的保护、培植、采伐等的管理事务 forest administration; forest service; all matters dealing with the protection, cultivation, logging, etc. of a forest

【林子】lín·zi 树林 forest; woods; grove

临(臨) lín ❶ 靠近;对着 face; overlook; confront; be close to: ～街 be close to the street; overlook or face the street | ～河 face the river; overlook the river | 背山～水 with the mountain behind and the water in front | 居高～下 occupy a commanding position (or height) | 如～大敌 brace; heavily guarded; well prepared; as if faced with a formidable foe ❷ 来到;到达 arrive; be present: 光～ presence (of a guest, etc.) | 莅～ arrive; be present | 身～其境 be personally on the scene | 双喜～门。A double blessing has descended upon the house. ❸ 将要;快要 about to; going to; on the point of; just before: ～别 at parting; just before parting | ～睡 before going to bed; just before sleeping | ～产 about to give birth; parturient | 这是我～离开北京的时候买的。I bought this just before leaving Beijing. ❹ 照着字画模仿 copy (calligraphy or painting): ～摹 copy (calligraphy or painting) | ～帖 practise calligraphy following a model | ～画 copy a painting ❺ (Lín)姓 a surname

【临别】línbié 将要分别 at parting; just before parting: ～赠言 parting advice; words of advice at parting | ～纪念 parting souvenir; something to remember someone by

【临产】línchǎn (孕妇)快要生小孩ㄦ (of pregnant woman) about to give birth; parturient; about to deliver

【临场】línchǎng ❶ 在考场参加考试;在竞赛场地参加竞赛 sit an examination (in specific location); enter a competition (in a competition venue): 缺乏～经验 lack real test experience | ～要沉着镇静。It's important to remain calm and cool-headed during a competition (or an examination). ❷ 亲自到现场 be personally present: ～指导 render on-the-spot guidance

【临池】línchí〈书 *fml.*〉相传汉朝有名的书法家张芝,在水池旁边练习写字,经常用池水洗砚台,使一池子的水都变黑了。后人因此称练习书法为临池。practise calligraphy; learn to write a good hand. Legend has it that Zhang Zhi, a famous calligrapher of the Han Dynasty, liked to practise calligraphy by a pond, and often washed his inkslab in the

pond, turning it black. The term has since come to mean 'practise calligraphy'.

【临床】línchuáng 医学上称医生给病人诊断和治疗疾病 (med.) clinical; diagnose and treat diseases:～经验 clinical experience|～教学 clinic; clinical instruction

【临到】líndào ❶ 接近到(某件事情) just before; on the point of; about to:～开会,我才准备好。I finished my preparations just as the meeting was about to begin. ❷ (事情)落到(身上) befall; happen to:这事～他的头上,他会有办法。Should this happen to him, he will find a solution.

【临风】línfēng 〈书 *fml.*〉当风;迎风 facing or against the wind:旌旗～招展。Banners and flags are streaming in the wind.

【临机】línjī 掌握时机(行动 take action) as the occasion requires; on the spur of the moment:～应变 resourceful; ingenious; act according to circumstances; adapt to changing circumstances; suit one's actions to changing conditions; cope with any contingency|～立断 make a quick (or prompt) decision at the right moment|～制胜 defeat one's opponent in timely fashion

【临街】línjiē 对着街道;靠着街道 face or overlook the street; be close to the street:～的窗口 window overlooking (or facing) the street|这三间平房～。These three single-storey houses face the street.|～有三棵柳树。There are three willow trees along the street.

【临界】línjiè 由一种状态或物理量转变为另一种状态或物理量的 critical; crisis; point at which a state or physical mass changes:～点 critical point; breakthrough point; point of transition|～角 critical angle

【临近】línjìn (时间、地区)靠近;接近 (of time or region) close to; close on; proximity:春节～了。The Spring Festival is drawing near.|他住在～太湖的一所疗养院里。He lives in a sanatorium close to the Taihu Lake.

【临渴掘井】lín kě jué jǐng 感到渴了才掘井 dig a well only when one is thirsty;〈比喻 *fig.*〉平时没有准备,事到临头才想办法 be unprepared; wait until the last moment; start acting too late

【临了】línliǎo (～儿 línliǎor)到最后;到末了 finally; at last; in the end:～还是决定由老王执笔。In the end, Lao Wang was asked to write it down. also 临末了儿 línmòliǎor

【临门】línmén ❶ 来到家门 arrive at the door; on the doorstep:贵客～。The distinguished guest has arrived.|双喜～。A double blessing has descended upon the house. ❷ 到达球门前 at the goal:～一脚 shot on goal

【临摹】línmó 模仿书画 copy (calligraphy or painting):～碑帖 copy a rubbing from a stone inscription

【临盆】línpén same as 临产 línchǎn

【临蓐】línrù same as 临产 línchǎn

【临深履薄】lín shēn lǚ bó《诗经·小雅·小旻》:'战战兢兢,如临深渊,如履薄冰'。后用'临深履薄'比喻谨慎戒惧。*The Book of Songs · Odes · Angry Heaven*: On the brink of a vale;/ I tremble twice or thrice/As if treading on thin ice;(fig.)with great caution and care

【临时】línshí ❶ 临到事情发生的时候 moment when sth. happens:～抱佛脚 embrace the Buddha's feet in one's hour of need—seek help at the last moment (or the eleventh hour); make a frantic last-minute effort|事先准备好,省得～着急。Advance preparation helps avoid any last-minute rush. ❷ 暂时;短期 temporary; provisional; interim; for a short time:～工 temporary worker; casual labourer; odd jobber; fill-in|～政府 provisional (or interim) government|～借用一下,明天就还。Let me borrow it awhile, and return it tomorrow.

【临时代办】línshí dàibàn 临时代理大使职务的外交官员 *chargé d'affaires ad interim*; diplomat temporarily acting for the ambassador

【临帖】lín//tiè 照着字帖练习写字(多指毛笔字 usu. brush calligraphy) practise calligraphy by following a model

【临头】líntóu (为难或不幸的事情)落到身上 (of embarrassment or misfortune) befall; happen; be imminent:大祸～faced with imminent disaster|事到～,要沉住气。Now the crisis is impending; one must keep calm.

【临危】línwēi ❶ (人)病重将死 critical condition; dying (of serious illness):这是他～时留下的话。These are his dying words. ❷ 面临生命的危险 facing death or deadly peril; in the hour of danger:～不惧 face danger fearlessly; courage in the face of danger; betray no fear in an hour of danger

【临危受命】lín wēi shòu mìng 在危难之时接受任命 be entrusted with a mission at a critical juncture; take on a mission in time of danger

【临危授命】lín wēi shòu mìng 在危亡关头勇于献出生命 lay down one's life at a critical moment; sacrifice oneself for the greater good:～,视死如归。Face death without flinching, and lay down one's life at a crucial juncture.

【临刑】línxíng 将要受死刑 just before execution

【临渊羡鱼】lín yuān xiàn yú《汉书·董仲舒传》:'临渊羡鱼,不如退而结网'。后用'临渊羡鱼'比喻只有愿望,不去实干,就无济于事。*History of Han · Biography of Dong Zhongshu*: 'Better to return home and make a net than to stand by the pond longing for fish.' (fig.) It is useless to dream without taking action.

【临月】línyuè (～儿 línyuèr)妇女怀孕足月,到了产期 date when baby is due; month when baby is due after full term pregnancy

【临战】línzhàn 临近或到了战斗、比赛的时候 on the eve of battle or competition; just before battle or competition:～的气氛十分浓厚。There was great anticipation on the eve of the contest.|进入防汛～状态 be in a state of readiness to prevent and combat flooding|运动员以～的姿态投入赛前训练。The athletes took part in pre-competition training in a state of excitement and anticipation.

【临阵】línzhèn ❶ 临近阵地;临近战斗的时候 on the battlefield; on the eve of battle; at a critical moment:～脱逃 desert on the eve of battle; turn tail in the face of danger; sneak away at a critical juncture|～磨枪 sharpen one's spear just before going into battle; last-minute preparation; take hurried action ❷ 指实地参加战斗 join in actual fighting; fight in the field:～指挥 field command|他有多年的～经验。He has many years of actual battle experience.

【临阵磨枪】lín zhèn mó qiāng 到了阵前才磨枪 sharpen one's spear just before going into battle;〈比喻 *fig*.〉事到临头才做准备 start preparations at the last moment; take action in great haste

【临阵脱逃】lín zhèn tuō táo 军人临作战时逃跑。也比喻事到临头而退缩逃避 desert on the eve of battle; (fig) turn tail in the face of danger; sneak away at a critical juncture; leave in the lurch

【临终】línzhōng 人将要死(指时间) on one's deathbed; just before death; last moments:～遗言 last words; dying will; last dying words

啉 lín ☞ [喹啉] (kuílín) on p. 1129

淋 lín ❶ 水或别的液体落在物体上 pour; sprinkle; drench; (of water or liquids) fall on an object:日晒雨～ sun-scorched and rain-drenched; exposed to the elements|衣服都～湿了。The clothes were soaked through. ❷ 使水或别的液体落在物体上 spray; sprinkle; drizzle; splash:在凉拌菜上～上点儿香油。Drizzle a little sesame oil over the cold dish.
☞ lìn on p. 1226

【淋巴】línbā 充满动物体内各组织间的无色透明液体,内含淋巴细胞,是由组织液渗入淋巴管中形成的。淋巴管是构造跟静脉相似的管子,分布在全身各部。淋巴在淋巴管内循环,最后流入静脉,是组织液流入血液的媒介。lymph; colourless, clear liquid which circulates throughout the animal body in ducts resembling blood veins; lymph contains lymphocytes, and is formed by tissue fluid seeping into the ducts; lymph eventually flows into the veins, and acts as an intermediary for tissue fluid to enter the blood [拉 latin: lympha]; also 淋巴液 línbāyè

【淋巴结】línbājié 由网状结缔组织构成的豆状体,分布在淋巴管的径路中,颈部、腋窝部和腹股沟部最多,能产生淋巴细胞并有过滤的作用,阻止和消灭侵入体内的有害微生物 lymph node (or gland); lymphonodus; lymphaden; nodes composed of reticular connective tissue distributed along the lymphatic ducts, concentrated mostly in the neck, armpit and groin areas; produce lymphocytes which act as filters to obstruct and wipe out harmful micro-organisms that invade the body; 旧称 formerly called 淋巴腺 línbāxiàn

【淋巴细胞】línbā xìbāo 白细胞的一种,产生于脾脏、淋巴结等器官,有产生和储存抗体的作用 leucocyte; lymphocyte; type of white blood cell produced in the spleen and lymph node (or gland); can make and store antibodies

【淋漓】línlí ❶ 形容湿淋淋往下滴 dripping; pouring; streaming:大汗～ dripping with sweat; sweating all over|墨迹～ full of ink marks|鲜血～ dripping with blood ❷ 形容畅快 free from inhibition; unrestrained:痛快～ impassioned and free|～尽致 (most) incisive and vivid; fully; thoroughly

【淋漓尽致】línlí jìn zhì 形容文章或谈话详尽透彻。也指暴露得很彻底。(most) incisive and vivid; fully; thoroughly; (of writing or speech) detailed and thorough; reveal fully; expose thoroughly

【淋漓柯】línlíkē 常绿乔木,叶子披针形,壳斗单生,坚果宽卵形 pasania (*Pasania cuspidula*); evergreen tree with lanceolar leaves, single cupules and hard, wide oval fruits; also 椤仔 sīzǐ

【淋淋】línlín 形容水、汗等向下流的样子 (of water, sweat, etc.) dripping; pouring; streaming:汗～ dripping with sweat|湿～ soaking wet; dripping wet; drenched|秋雨～ drizzling autumn rain

【淋浴】línyù 一种洗澡方式,让水从上面喷下来,人在下面冲洗 shower; shower bath; form of bathing in which water is sprinkled from above over the bather

绑 lín [绑缅] (línlí)〈书 *fml*.〉盛装的样子 richly dressed; also 绑缡 línlí
☞ chēn on p. 235

琳 lín〈书 *fml*.〉美玉 beautiful jade

【琳琅】línláng 美玉 beautiful jade;〈比喻 *fig*.〉优美珍贵的东西 sth. beautiful and valuable:～满目 superb collection of beautiful objects; feast for the eyes; dazzling display

【琳琅满目】línláng mǎn mù〈比喻 *fig*.〉各种美好的东西很多(多指书籍或工艺品 usu. books or handicrafts) superb collection of wonderful objects; feast for the eyes; dazzling display:在这次展览会上,真是～,美不胜收。The great variety of beautiful articles at the exhibition are a real feast for the eyes.

粼 lín [粼粼]〈书 *fml.*〉形容水、石等明净 (of water, stone, etc.) clear; crystalline; limpid: ～碧波 clear blue waves | 白石～ clear white stones

嶙 lín ☞ below

【嶙嶙】línlín〈书 *fml.*〉嶙峋 (of rocks, cliffs, etc.) rugged; jagged; craggy: 礁石～ jagged (or rugged) rocks; crags

【嶙峋】línxún〈书 *fml.*〉❶ 形容山石等突兀、重叠 (of mountain, cliffs, etc.) jagged; rugged; craggy; sharp and overlapping: 怪石～ jagged rocks in grotesque shapes | ～的山峦 rugged hills ❷ 形容人消瘦露骨 (of person) bony; thin: 瘦骨～ bony; bag of bones; all skin and bone; as thin as a latch ❸ 形容人刚正有骨气 upright; unyielding: 气节～ of unyielding integrity | 傲骨～ proud and unyielding; with innate pride

遴 lín 谨慎选择 choose (or select) carefully: ～选 recruit; select for a post | ～派 select and send | ～聘教师 recruit teachers
〈古 *arch.*〉same as 吝 lìn

【遴选】línxuǎn ❶ 选拔(人才) select (talent) for a post: ～德才兼备的人担任领导干部 select people of both ability and integrity as leading cadres ❷ 泛指挑选 choose; select: 该厂生产的彩电被～为展览样品。The colour TVs produced by this factory have been selected as exhibits.

潾 lín [潾潾] 形容水清 (of water) clear; limpid: ～的水波 clear ripples | 春水～ limpid river in spring

璘 lín〈书 *fml.*〉玉的光彩 lusture of jade

霖 lín same as 霖雨 línyǔ: 秋～ continuous heavy autumn rain | 甘～ timely rain; good soaking rain

【霖雨】línyǔ 连下几天的大雨 continuous heavy rain over several days

辚 lín [辚辚]〈书 *fml.*〉〈拟声词 *onom.*〉形容车行走时的声音 rattle; sound of a moving cart: 车～,马萧萧 chariots rattling and horses neighing

L **磷(燐)** lín 非金属元素,符号 P (phosphorum)。同素异形体有白磷、红磷和黑磷。磷酸盐是重要的肥料之一,磷的化合物可以治疗佝偻病、软骨病等。phosphorus (P); nonmetallic element existing in three allotropic forms — white, red and black phosphorus. Phosphate is an important fertilizer, and phosphorus compounds are used to treat rickets, and osteomalacia, etc.

【磷肥】línféi 以含磷为主的肥料,能促使作物的子粒饱满,提早成熟。如骨粉、过磷酸钙、磷矿粉等。phosphate fertilizer; fertilizer that contains mainly phosphorus, e. g. bone dust, potassium calcium, ground phosphate rock, etc., which make for full grains, and early ripening

【磷光】línguāng 某些物质受摩擦、振动或光、热、电波的作用所发的光,如金刚石经日光照射后,在暗处发出的青绿色光。方解石、萤石、石英、重晶石以及钙、钡、锶等的硫化物都能发出磷光。phosphorescence; light emitted by certain substances under the effects of friction, vibration, light, heat or electric waves, e. g. the green glow of diamonds in the dark after being radiated by sunlight. Calcite, fluorite, quartz barite, and the sulphide compounds of calcium, barium and strontium are all phosphorescent.

【磷火】línhuǒ 磷化氢燃烧时的火焰。人和动物的尸体腐烂时分解出磷化氢,并自动燃烧。夜间在野地里有时看到的白色带蓝绿色火焰就是磷火。phosphorescent light; will-o'-the-wisp; spontaneous burning of phosphine which emanates from decaying human and animal bodies, and sometimes appears as a bluish white flame in the wilderness at night; 俗称 commonly known as 鬼火 guǐhuǒ

【磷脂】línzhī 含有磷和氮的油脂,存在于动植物的细胞中。有营养价值,是很好的乳化剂。用来做糕点、糖果等,也用于化妆品、肥皂、橡胶、皮革等工业。phosphatide; phospholipid; animal and plant lipid containing phosphorus (P) and nitrogen (N); has nutritive value, is an excellent emulsifying agent, and is used in cakes, and sweets, etc., and also as an ingredient in production of cosmetics, soap, rubber, leather, etc.

瞵 lín〈书 *fml.*〉瞪着眼睛看 stare; gaze; watch with wide open eyes: 鹰～鹗视 eye vigilantly; look fiercely (at sth.)

鳞 lín ❶ 鱼类、爬行动物和少数哺乳动物身体表面具有保护作用的薄片状组织,由角质、骨质等构成 scale (of fish, etc.); thin, flat plates forming a protective surface on fish, reptiles and a few mammals, composed of cutin, sclerotin, etc. ❷ 像鱼鳞的 like the scales of a fish: ～茎 bulb | ～波 ripples | 遍体～伤 covered with bruises and injuries

【鳞波】línbō 像鱼鳞一样的波纹 scale-like ripples

【鳞次栉比】lín cì zhì bǐ 像鱼鳞和梳子的齿一样,一个挨着一个地排列着,多用来形容房屋等密集 cheek by jowl; in perfect order, like the teeth of a comb or overlapping fish scales; arranged in close formation; row upon row (of houses, etc.): 路旁各种建筑～。The street is lined with row upon row of diverse buildings. also 栉比鳞次 zhì bǐ líncì

【鳞介】línjiè〈书 *fml.*〉水中动物的统称 aquatic animals; animals that live in water

【鳞茎】línjīng 地下茎的一种,形状像圆盘,下部有不定根,上部有许多变态的叶子,内含营养物质,肥厚多肉,从鳞茎的中心生出地上茎。如洋葱、水仙等的地下茎。bulb; disk-shaped subterranean stem, characterized by fleshy metamorphosis leaves that contain nutritional substances, as in the onion and narcissus, and adventitious roots. Aerial stems grow from the centre of the bulb.

【鳞片】línpiàn ❶ 鱼身上一片一片的鳞 scale (of fish) ❷ 覆盖在昆虫翅膀或躯体上的壳质小片,带有颜色,或能折光,因而使昆虫具有鲜艳的光彩 squama; small chitin shell that covers the wings or body of an insect, either colourful or refractive, giving the insect a bright lustre ❸ 覆盖在芽的外面像鱼鳞的薄片,主要作用是保护嫩芽。春季植物发芽时,鳞片即脱落。bud scale; palea; thin, scale-like protective layer over a plant shoot that is shed when it sprouts

【鳞伤】línshāng 形容伤痕像鱼鳞一样多 have as many wounds as a fish has scales; be covered with wounds: 遍体~ covered with cuts and bruises; be a mass of bruises; be black and blue

【鳞爪】línzhǎo 〈书 *fml.*〉鳞和爪 scales and nails; 〈比喻 *fig.*〉事情的片断 (of a thing) bits; fragments; odd scraps: 这篇小文写的是往事回忆的~。This article is a fragmentary recollection of past events.

麟(麐) lín 〈书 *fml.*〉麒麟 kylin; (Chinese) unicorn: 凤毛~角 (precious and rare as) phoenix feathers and unicorn horns — rarity of rarities

【麟凤龟龙】lín fèng guī lóng 〈古代 *arch.*〉称麟凤龟龙为四灵,用来比喻品德高尚的人 (Chinese) unicorn, phoenix, turtle and dragon, known as the 'four divinities'; (fig.) man of moral integrity

lǐn (ㄌㄧㄣˇ)

菻 lǐn 拂菻 (Fúlǐn),我国古代称东罗马帝国 Fulin, ancient Chinese name for the Eastern Roman Empire; Byzantium

凛(凜) lǐn ❶ 寒冷 cold; frigid: ~冽 bitingly cold; bitter cold; piercingly cold ❷ 严肃;严厉 rigorous; strict; severe; stern: ~遵(严肃地遵照) strictly follow | ~然 severe; awe-inspiring | ~若冰霜 (of manners) as cold as ice; look severe (or stern); of a forbidding manner ❸ 〈书 *fml.*〉畏惧;害怕 afraid; fearful; apprehensive: ~于夜行 be afraid of (or dread) going on a journey by night

【凛冽】lǐnliè 刺骨地寒冷 bone-chilly; bitingly cold; bitter cold; piercingly cold: 北风~。The bitterly cold north wind.

【凛凛】lǐnlǐn ❶ 寒冷 cold; frigid: 寒风~ piercing wind ❷ 严肃;可敬畏的样子 stern; awe-inspiring: ~正气 awe-inspiring integrity | 威风~ majestic-looking; of an awe-inspiring demeanor; of a dignified bearing

【凛然】lǐnrán 严肃;可敬畏的样子 stern; awe-inspiring: 大义~ inspire awe by upholding justice | 态度~ stern in manner; with a severe manner | ~不可侵犯 stern and inviolable; of a stern and forbidding countenance

廪(廩) lǐn 〈书 *fml.*〉❶ 粮仓 granary: 仓~ granary ❷ 指粮食 grain

【廪生】lǐnshēng 明清两代称由府、州、县按时发给银子和粮食补助生活的生员 scholar of the Ming and Qing dynasties who lives on regular silver and grain allowances from prefecture, sub-prefecture or county anthorities; also 廪膳生 lǐnshànshēng or 廪膳生员 lǐnshànshēngyuán

懔(懍) lǐn same as 凛 lǐn ②③

檩(檁) lǐn 架在屋架或山墙上面用来支持椽子或屋面板的长条形构件 purlin; horizontal length of timber, placed on the frame or gables of the house and supporting the rafters or part of the roof; also 桁 héng or 檩条 lǐntiáo; (图见 ☞ figure for 房子 fáng·zi on p. 550)

【檩条】lǐn tiáo (~儿 lǐn tiáor) same as 檩 lǐn: 一根~ one purlin

【檩子】lǐn·zi 〈方 *dial.*〉same as 檩 lǐn

lìn (ㄌㄧㄣˋ)

吝 lìn ❶ 吝啬 stingy; miserly; mean; tight-fisted: ~惜 grudge; spare; stint | 悭~ stingy; miserly; close-fisted | 尚请不~赐教(书信用语 (term for correspondence) please do not stint on any comments you may have; please do not be sparing of any advice you have to give ❷ (Lìn)姓 a surname

【吝色】lìnsè 舍不得的神色 expression denoting unwillingness to spare; reluctance to give: 倾囊相助,毫无~ give away one's money without the slightest reluctance

【吝啬】lìnsè 过分爱惜自己的财物,当用不用 stingy; miserly; mean; niggardly: 大方些,别那么~。Be a little more generous and a lot less stingy.

【吝惜】lìnxī 过分爱惜,舍不得拿出(自己的东西或力量) grudging; parsimonious; be penurious (of possessions or effort) to the extent of extreme unwillingness to give up anything: ~钱 be a money pincher | 他干活儿,不会~自身的力气。He spared (or stinted) no effort in getting on with the work.

赁 lìn 租用 rent; lease; hire: 租~ rent; lease; hire | 出~ rent (or let) out | ~了一

辆车 rent (or hire) a car|这房子是早先～的。This house was let (or rented) out earlier.

淋 lìn 滤 filter; strain:过～ filter|～盐 strain salt|把这药用纱布～一下 strain the herbal medicine through a piece of gauze ☞ lín on p.1223

【淋病】lìnbìng 性病的一种,病原体是淋病双球菌,主要发生在尿道和生殖系统。患者尿道发炎,排尿疼痛,尿中带有脓血。gonorrhoea; venereal disease caused by diplococcus gonorrhoea that occurs mainly in the urethra and reproductive system. The patient suffers symptoms of urethritis, urodynia and urosepsis.

蔺 lìn ❶ ☞ 马蔺 mǎlìn on p.1289 ❷ (Lìn) 姓 a surname

膦 lìn 有机化合物的一类,由磷化氢的氢原子部分或全部被烃基取代而成的衍生物 phosphine; a kind of organic chemical compound derived from the hydrocarbon radical partially or completely replacing the hydrogen in phosphine

躏 lìn ☞ 蹂躏 (róulìn) on p.1633

líng (ㄌㄧㄥˊ)

〇 líng 数的空位(同'零'),多用于数字中 (usu. used in numbers) zero sign; nought (same as 零 líng):三～六号 No. 306|一九九～年 the year nineteen ninety

令 líng [令狐](Línghú) ❶ 古地名,在今山西临猗一带 Linghu, a place name in ancient China in the present-day Linyi, Shanxi Province ❷ (Línghú) 姓 a double-character surname
☞ lǐng on p.1232 and lìng on p.1235

伶 líng 〈旧时 *old*〉指戏曲演员 actor or actress (in traditional opera):～人 actor or actress|名～ famous (or popular) actor or actress|坤～actress(in traditional opera)|老～工(年老有经验的演员)old and skilled actor or actress

【伶仃】língdīng ❶ 孤独;没有依靠 lonely; solitary; left alone to fend for oneself:孤苦～ alone and abandoned; friendless and wretched; orphaned and helpless ❷ 瘦弱 thin and weak:瘦骨～ mere skeleton; all skin and bones ‖ also 零丁 língdīng

【伶俐】líng·lì 聪明;灵活 clever; bright; smart; quick-witted:口齿～ speak intelligently and eloquently; have the gift of the gab; be smart and fluent|这孩子真～。What a clever child!

【伶俜】língpīng 〈书 *fml.*〉孤独;孤单 lonely; solitary; all alone:～独居 live alone (or in seclusion)

【伶牙俐齿】líng yā lì chǐ 形容口齿伶俐,能说会道 eloquent; sharp-tongued; have the gift of the gab; have a glib (or ready) tongue

灵(靈、霛) líng ❶ 灵活;灵巧 quick; clever; bright; flexible; nimble:～敏 acute; agile; keen; sensitive|～机 sudden inspiration; brainwave|～便 agile; nimble; quick|心～手巧 quick-witted and nimble-fingered; clever and deft|机件失～。The components stopped working.|资金周转不～ difficulties in cash flow ❷ 精神;灵魂 mind; intelligence; spirit; soul:心～ mind; soul|英～ spirit of the brave departed; spirit of a martyr ❸ 神仙或关于神仙的 fairy; elf; sprite; deity:神～ gods; deities; divinities|～怪 elf; goblin; sprite ❹ 灵验 effective; efficacious; work:～药 miracle drug; elixir of life|这个法子很～。This method works well. ❺ 灵柩或关于死人的 bier; hearse; coffin containing a corpse; of the deceased:守～ stand guard at the bier; keep vigil beside the coffin|移～ move the hearse|停～ place in which to keep the coffin before burial|～位 temporary memorial tablet (of a deceased person)|～前摆满了花圈。Wreaths and floral tributes placed before the bier.

【灵便】líng·bian ❶(四肢、五官)灵活;灵敏 (of the four limbs and five sense organs — ears, eyes, mouth, nose and body) nimble; agile; quick:手脚～ be nimble|我耳朵不～,你说话大声点。I am hard of hearing. Please speak louder. ❷ (工具等)轻巧,使用方便 (of tools, etc.) easy to handle; handy:这把钳子使着真～。These pliers are very useful.

【灵车】língchē 运送灵柩或骨灰盒的车 hearse; car used to carry a bier or cinerary casket

【灵榇】língchèn 〈书 *fml.*〉same as 灵柩 língjiù

【灵床】língchuáng ❶ 停放尸体的床铺 bier; bed on which a corpse is laid ❷ 为死者虚设的床铺 bed made ready for the dead

【灵丹妙药】líng dān miào yào 灵验有效的奇药。迷信的人认为这种药能治百病。elixir; wonder drug; miraculous cure; panacea; drug of seemingly magical properties that the superstitious and gullible believed capable of curing all diseases;〈比喻 *fig.*〉能解决一切问题的办法 remedy for all problems; also 灵丹圣药 líng dān shèng yào

【灵幡】língfān (～儿 língfānr)旧俗出殡时孝子打的幡儿 (old custom) funeral streamer; long narrow white flag carried by a filial or dutiful son at a funeral procession

【灵符】língfú 神灵的符箓(迷信) magic figures drawn by Taoist priests to invoke or exorcise spirits and bring good or ill fortune

【灵府】língfǔ 〈书 *fml.*〉指思维器官 brain; organ of thinking

【灵感】línggǎn 在文学、艺术、科学、技术等活动中,由于艰苦学习,长期实践,不断积累经验和知识而突然产生的富有创造性的思路 inspiration; sudden creative revelation, of literary, artistic, scientific or technological nature, attributed to assiduous study, long-term practice, and consistent accumulation of knowledge and experience

【灵怪】língguài ❶ 传说中的神灵和妖怪 legendary deity; demon; monster; goblin:～故事 stories of fairies and demons ❷〈书 *fml*.〉神奇怪异 bizarre; miraculous and monstrous

【灵光】língguāng ❶〈旧时 *old*〉指神异的光辉 miraculous brightness; unearthly light or luminance ❷ 指画在神像头部四周的光辉 halo; aura; bright light around the head of a portrayed god or Buddha ❸〈方 *dial*.〉好;效果好 effective; excellent; wonderful

【灵慧】línghuì 灵敏聪慧 bright; clever; intelligent:赋性～ inherently intelligent; bright and clever

【灵魂】línghún ❶ 迷信的人认为附在人的躯体上作为主宰的一种非物质的东西,灵魂离开躯体后人即死亡 soul; believed by the superstitious to be an immaterial spiritual entity distinguished from but coexistent with the physical body of a person and a dominant spiritual force, and which leaves upon the person's death ❷ 心灵;思想 soul; spirit:纯洁的～ pure and honest soul|～深处 in the depth of one's soul (or heart) ❸ 人格;良心 conscience; soul:出卖～ sell one's soul (to the enemy, etc.) ❹〈比喻 *fig*.〉起指导和决定作用的因素 soul; guiding and decisive factor

【灵活】línghuó ❶ 敏捷;不呆板 nimble; agile; quick; supple:手脚～dexterous and nimble|脑筋～ be quick-witted; have a supple mind ❷ 善于随机应变;不拘泥 flexible; elastic; capable of acting appropriately according to circumstances, rather than form etc.:～性 flexibility; elasticity; mobility; adaptability|～运用 utilize flexibly|～调配人力物力 deploy manpower and material resources flexibly

【灵机】língjī 灵巧的心思 sudden inspiration; brainwave; dexterous mind:～一动,想出个主意来。On having a brainwave, a solution was found.

【灵境】língjìng〈书 *fml*.〉仙境 paradise; fairyland; wonderland:仙山～ elf mountain and fairyland|～缥缈 mysterious, ethereal fairyland

【灵柩】língjiù 死者已经入殓的棺材 coffin containing the remains of the deceased

【灵猫】língmāo 哺乳动物,嘴尖,耳朵窄,毛灰黄色,有黑褐色斑纹。肛门下部有分泌腺,能发香味。吃野果和小动物。产在我国浙江、福建、广东等省及东南亚各国。civet cat (*Viverridae*) catlike mammal with a gray-and-yellow coat dotted with blackish brown stripes, having anal scent glands that emit a musky odour, living on wild fruits and small animals, found in Zhejiang, Fujian and Guangdong provinces of China, and in Africa and Southeast Asia

【灵妙】língmiào 神妙;巧妙 clever; wonderful; ingenious:壁画中人物形象的勾勒自然～,独具一格。Figures in the mural are ingeniously and naturally portrayed.

【灵敏】língmǐn 反应快;能对极其微弱的刺激迅速反应 sensitive; keen; agile; acute; react promptly to the slightest stimulation:动作～ be agile in one's movements; quick of foot|军犬的嗅觉特别～。Military dogs have an extraordinarily acute sense of smell.

【灵敏度】língmǐndù ❶ 无线电接收机接收信号的能力,是测定接收机质量的一个标准 sensitivity; radio receiver's degree of sensitivity to signals that acts as a yardstick as to its quality ❷ 某些仪表的精确程度,例如极微弱的电流要用灵敏度高的电流计才能量出 accuracy; precision; indicator of precision in some meters, e.g. a low electric current may only be measured by a highly sensitive galvanometer

【灵牌】língpái same as 灵位 língwèi

【灵气】língqì ❶ 机灵劲儿;悟性 intelligence; power of understanding:两眼透着～ eyes expressive of a native intelligence|她很有～,一定能成为出色的服装设计师。She is a woman of intelligence, and will without doubt become an outstanding fashion designer. ❷ 神话传说中的超自然的力量;神奇的能力 supernatural power or force in fairy tales; miraculous power or force

【灵巧】língqiǎo 灵活而巧妙 dexterous; nimble; skilful; ingenious; agile:心思～agile mind|他的手挺～,能做各种精致的小玩意儿。With his skilful hands, he can make all kinds of exquisite miniature toys.

【灵寝】língqǐn 停放灵柩的地方 seat of a bier; place where a coffin is laid to perform burial rituals

【灵台】língtái ❶ 停灵柩、放骨灰盒或设置死者遗像、灵位的台 catafalque; seat of a bier; platform on which a bier, cinerary casket, photograph of the deceased or his temporary memorial tablet are placed:～左右排列着花圈。The catafalque is embanked with floral wreaths. ❷〈书 *fml*.〉心灵 heart; spirit; soul

【灵堂】língtáng 停灵柩、放骨灰盒或设置死者遗像、灵位供人吊唁的屋子(一般是正房)或大厅 mourning hall; room (usu. principal or main room) or main hall where the bier and cinerary casket of the deceased are placed, along with his photograph or temporary memorial tablet, to which the bereaved and others pay their last respects

【灵通】língtōng ❶(消息)来得快;来源广 having ready access to information; well-informed:他消息特别~。He is very well-informed. ❷〈方 *dial.*〉行;顶用 useful; effective:这玩意儿真~。The small gadget works really well. ❸〈方 *dial.*〉same as 灵活 línghuó:心眼儿~ be quick-witted

【灵童】língtóng 藏传佛教活佛圆寂后,寺院上层通过占卜等仪式,从活佛圆寂时出生的若干婴儿中选定的活佛的继承人 soul boy; successor to the Living Buddha selected from babies born on the Parinirvana of the Tibetan Living Buddha, by divination ceremonies conducted by the temple upper strata

【灵透】líng·tou〈方 *dial.*〉聪明;机敏 clever; bright; intelligent; smart:心眼儿~ be really smart|好一个~孩子。What a bright child.

【灵位】língwèi 人死后暂时设的木牌,上面写着死者的名字,用做供奉对象 spirit tablet; temporary memorial wooden tablet on which is written the name of the deceased person to whom last respects are to be paid

【灵犀】língxī〈古代 *arch.*〉传说,犀牛角有白纹,感应灵敏,所以称犀牛角为'灵犀'。现在用唐代李商隐诗句'心有灵犀一点通',比喻心领神会,感情共鸣。magic rhinoceros horn; (fig.) heartbeat in unison. According to legend, rhinoceros horn with its thread-like white core had high sensibility, and was thus termed. The line 'Hearts linked in a common beat understand each other without words', from a poem by the Tang-dynasty poet Li Shangyin, is used figuratively to mean tacit understanding (or comprehension or emotional empathetic response).

【灵性】língxìng ❶ 智慧;聪明才智 wisdom; intelligence; sagacity:他具有当导演的~。He has great sagacity as a director. ❷ 指动物经过人的驯养、训练而具有的智慧 (of animals) intelligence; aptitude of animals raised and trained in captivity:那匹马很有~,知道主人受了伤,就驮着他往回跑。The horse was very intelligent, and realizing that its master was wounded, bore him back to safety.

【灵秀】língxiù 灵巧秀丽 intelligent and beautiful; pretty and bright:聪慧~ intelligent and beautiful; pretty and bright|模样~的姑娘 girl of great beauty

【灵验】língyàn ❶ (办法、药物等)有奇效 (of a method, medicine, etc.) efficacious; effective:药到病除,非常~。As the medicine rapidly took effect, the symptoms abated. ❷ (预言)能够应验 (of a prediction) accurate; right; true:气象台的天气预报果然~,今天是个大晴天。The weather forecast turns out to be accurate, as it is, indeed, a fine day.

【灵异】língyì ❶ 指神怪 deities and spirits; fairies and elves ❷ 神奇;奇异 magical; miraculous; mystical:~的岩洞 mysterious cave|山水~ divine mountains and waters

【灵长目】língzhǎngmù 哺乳动物的一目,猴、类人猿属于这一目,是最高等的哺乳动物,大脑较发达,面部短,锁骨发育良好,四肢都有五趾,便于握物 primate; highest mammals comprising monkeys and apes, characterized by developed brains, short faces, well-developed collarbone and limbs ending in five digits which enable them to pick things up with ease

【灵芝】língzhī 蕈的一种,菌盖肾脏形,赤褐色或暗紫色,有环纹,并有光泽。可入药,有滋补作用。我国古代用来象征祥瑞。glossy ganoderma (*Ganoderma lucidum*); reddish brown or dark purple kidney-shaped fungus, with ring-like lustrous patterns, used to make medicine, and a symbol of auspiciousness in ancient China

苓 líng ☞ [茯苓](fúlíng) on p.597

囹 líng ☞ below

【囹圄】língyǔ 〈书 *fml.*〉监狱 prison; jail; gaol:身陷~ be jailed; be thrown into prison; also 囹圉 língyǔ

【囹圉】língyǔ same as 囹圄 língyǔ

泠 líng ❶〈书 *fml.*〉清凉 cool and fresh:~风 cool, fresh breeze ❷ (Líng)姓 a surname

【泠泠】línglíng〈书 *fml.*〉❶ 形容清凉 cool; chilly ❷ 形容声音清越 (of sound) clear and melodious:泉水激石,~作响。A stone fell into the spring with a clear, clean splash.

【泠然】língrán〈书 *fml.*〉形容声音清越 (of sound) clear and far-reaching; clear and melodious:钟磬~。The bells resounded loud and clear.

玲 líng ☞ below

【玲玲】línglíng〈书 *fml.*〉〈拟声词 *onom.*〉形容玉碰击的声音 tinkling of jade pieces:~盈耳 one's ears are filled with the tinkling of jade pieces

【玲珑】línglóng ❶ (东西)精巧细致 exquisite; beautiful; (of things) ingeniously and delicately made:小巧~ small and exquisite; delicate ❷ (人)灵活敏捷 (of people) nimble and clever:娇小~ petite and dainty|八面~ charming and able to win favour on all sides

【玲珑剔透】línglóng tītòu ❶ 形容器物细致,孔穴明晰,结构奇巧(多指镂空的手工艺品和供玩赏的太湖石等 oft. referring to describe fretwork handicrafts and Taihu stones for decoration) exquisitely made; delicately shaped; skillfully worked ❷ 形容人聪明伶俐 (of people) bright and clever; smart

柃 líng [柃木](língmù) 常绿灌木或小乔木,叶椭圆形或披针形,花小,白色,浆果球形。茎、叶、果实均入药。eurya plant (*Eurya ja-*

ponica); evergreen bush or small tree with oval or lanceolate leaves, small white flowers, and spherical berries, whose stem, leaves and fruits can be used as medicine

瓴 líng 〈书 *fml.*〉盛水的瓶子 water jar; ☞ 高屋建瓴 gāo wū jiàn líng on p.645

铃 líng ❶ (~儿 língr)用金属制成的响器,最常见的是球形而下开一条口,里面放金属丸;也有钟形而里面悬着金属小锤的,振动时相击发声。此外有电铃、车铃等,形式不一。bell; metal, usu. cup-shaped object with a flared mouth and a suspended ball or hammer inside, that makes a sound on being struck or tilted; electric and bicycle bells, etc. ❷ 形状像铃的东西 bell-shaped thing:哑~ dumb-bell|杠~ barbell|棉~ cotton boll ❸ 蕾铃 boll; bud:落~ shedding (or premature falling) of cotton bolls|结~ growth of cotton bolls

【铃铛】líng·dang 指晃荡而发声的铃,球形或扁圆形而下部或中部开一条口,里面放金属丸或小石子,式样大小不一,有骡马带的、儿童玩的或做服饰的 small bell; spherical or oval bell that produces a sound on being shaken, with an opening at its mouth, containing a metal ball or small stone; of various shapes and sizes, attached to livery bridles, used as toys, and to decorate garments.

【铃铎】língduó 挂在宫殿、楼阁等檐下的铃 bell hanging from the eaves of a palace or pavilion

聆 líng 〈书 *fml.*〉白色 white

鸰 líng ☞ [鹡鸰] (jílíng) on p.910

凌[1] (凌) líng ❶ 侵犯;欺侮 bully; insult:欺~ bully and humiliate|~辱 insult; humiliate; maltreat; treat insolently|盛气~人 domineering; arrogant; of an overweening manner ❷ 逼近 approach; draw close:~晨 before dawn; in the small hours ❸ 升高;在空中 rise high; tower (or soar) aloft:~空 soar high into the sky; be high up in the sky|~云 reach the clouds; soar to the sky|~霄 reach the clouds; soar to the sky ❹ (Líng)姓 a surname

凌[2] líng 〈方 *dial.*〉冰(多指块状或锥状的 usu. shaped like cubes or cones) ice:冰~ icicle|~锥 icicle

【凌晨】língchén 天快亮的时候 before dawn; in the small hours

【凌迟】língchí 古代的一种残酷死刑,先分割犯人的肢体,然后割断咽喉 put to death by dismembering the body, and ultimately cutting the throat (a cruel ancient form of capital punishment); also 陵迟 língchí

【凌泽】língduó 〈方 *dial.*〉 same as 冰锥 bīngzhuī

【凌驾】língjià 高出(别人);压倒(别的事物) place oneself above; override:不能把自己~于群众之上。One should not lord it over the masses.|救人的念头~一切,他转身向大火冲去。His logic overridden by his desire to save the people, he turned round and rushed into the blaze.

【凌空】língkōng 高高地在天空中或高升到天空中 soar high into the sky; be high in the sky; soar or tower aloft:高阁~ towering pavilion|雪花~飞舞。Snowflakes whirled down from the sky.|飞机~而过。The plane zoomed through the sky.

【凌厉】línglì 形容迅速而气势猛烈 swift and fierce; quick and powerful:朔风~ fierce north wind|~的攻势 rapid and fierce attacks

【凌轹】línglì 〈书 *fml.*〉❶ 欺压 bully and oppress ❷ 排挤 push out; squeeze out; exclude:~同人 squeeze out (or exclude) one's colleague ‖ also 陵轹 línglì

【凌乱】língluàn 不整齐;没有秩序 in disorder; in a mess; in confusion:~不堪 in a state of utter confusion; in a fearful mess|楼上传来~的脚步声。A flurry of footsteps was heard upstairs. also 零乱 língluàn

【凌虐】língnüè 〈书 *fml.*〉欺侮;虐待 maltreat; tyrannize; treat cruelly:~百姓 tyrannize the masses|备受~ suffer all kinds of maltreatment

【凌辱】língrǔ 欺侮;侮辱 bully; insult; humiliate:~弱小 ride roughshod over the small and weak|受尽~ suffer all kinds of humiliation

【凌侮】língwǔ 欺侮;侮辱 bully; insult; humiliate

【凌霄花】língxiāohuā 落叶藤本植物,攀援茎,羽状复叶,小叶卵形,边缘有锯齿,花鲜红色,花冠漏斗形,结蒴果。花、茎、叶都可入药。Chinese trumpet creeper (*Campsis grandiflora*); deciduous liana with a climbing stem, feather-like compound leaves, oval, saw-tooth edged leaflets, bright red flowers, funnel-shaped corollas, and capsules, whose flowers, stem and leaves can be used as medicine; also 鬼目 guǐmù and 紫葳 zǐwēi

【凌汛】língxùn 江河上游冰雪融化,下游还没有解冻而造成的洪水 ice run; flood caused when snow and ice has thawed on the upper, but not the lower, reaches of a river

【凌夷】língyí 〈书 *fml.*〉衰败;走下坡路 decline; deteriorate:风俗~。The customs are dying out (or in decline).|国势~。The state is declining (or in decline). also 陵夷 língyí

【凌云】língyún 直上云霄 reach the clouds; soar to the skies:高耸~ reach for the clouds|~壮志 high aspirations

【凌杂】língzá 错杂凌乱 in disorder; in a mess

【凌锥】língzhuī〈方 *dial.*〉same as 冰锥 bīngzhuī：屋檐上挂着一尺来长的～。Long icicles hung more than a foot long from the eaves.

陵 líng ❶ 丘陵 hill；mound：～谷变迁（比喻世事发生极大的变迁）mountains and valleys can change；cataclysmic changes occur；(fig.) great change in worldly affairs ❷ 陵墓 imperial tomb；mausoleum：中山～ Sun Yat-sen Mausoleum | 十三～ Tombs of the 13 Ming Emperors；Ming Tombs | 谒～ pay homage at sb.'s mausoleum ❸〈书 *fml.*〉欺侮；侵犯 bully；oppress；violate：～压 bully and oppress；ride roughshod over

【陵迟】língchí ❶〈书 *fml.*〉衰落 decline ❷ same as 凌迟 língchí

【陵轹】línglì same as 凌轹 línglì

【陵墓】língmù 领袖或革命烈士的坟墓；帝王或诸侯的坟墓 tomb (of a leader or revolutionary martyr)；mausoleum (of an emperor, a king, duke or prince)

【陵寝】língqǐn〈书 *fml.*〉帝王的坟墓及墓地的宫殿建筑 emperor's or king's resting place；mausoleum；palatial tomb of an emperor or king

【陵替】língtì〈书 *fml.*〉❶ 纲纪废弛 breakdown of law and order ❷ 衰落 decline：家道～ declines in a family's fortunes

【陵夷】língyí same as 凌夷 língyí

【陵园】língyuán 以陵墓为主的园林 cemetery；graveyard；tombs surrounded by a park：烈士～ cemetery of revolutionary martyrs

聆 líng〈书 *fml.*〉听 listen；hear：～听 listen (respectively) | ～教（听取教诲）listen to sb.'s wise advice；listen to sb.'s instruction；hear sb.'s words of wisdom

【聆取】língqǔ〈书 *fml.*〉听取 listen to：～各方意见 listen attentively to the criticisms of various parties

【聆听】língtīng〈书 *fml.*〉听 listen (respectively)：凝神～ listen attentively | ～教诲 listen to the instructions

菱 líng ❶ 一年生草本植物，生在池沼中，根生在泥里，叶子浮在水面，略呈三角形，边缘略有锯齿，花白色。果实的硬壳有角，绿色或褐色，果肉可以吃。water chestnut (*Trapa*)；annual herb found in lakes or ponds, its roots growing from mud on the lake or pond bed, having triangular saw-toothed leaves and white flowers that float on the water surface, and bearing green or brown fruits with hard pronged shells containing edible flesh ❷ 这种植物的果实 ling；water caltrop；fruit of such plant ‖ 通称 general term for 菱角 líng·jiao

【菱角】líng·jiao 菱的通称 general term for 菱 líng

【菱形】língxíng 邻边相等的平行四边形 diamond；rhombus；lozenge；parallelogram with equal adjacent sides

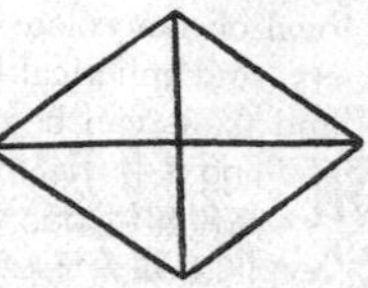

菱形 Rhombus

棂（欞、櫺） líng 旧式窗户的窗格子 (window) lattice；latticework；lattice of an old-style window：窗～ window lattice

蛉 líng ☞ 白蛉 báilíng on p. 35 and 螟蛉 mínglíng on p. 1359

笭 líng［笭箵］(língxīng)〈书 *fml.*〉打鱼时用的竹子编的盛器 bamboo basket (used for holding fish while angling)；creel

舲 líng〈书 *fml.*〉❶ 有窗户的船 boat with windows：～船 boat with windows ❷ 小船 small boat

翎 líng ❶（～儿 língr）鸟的翅膀或尾巴上的长而硬的羽毛，有的颜色很美丽，可以做装饰品 plume；quill；long and hard tail or wing feather of a bird. Plumes of beautiful colours can be used for decoration：雁～ wild goose feather | 鸡～儿 cock feather | 孔雀～ peacock feathers；peacock plumes | 鹅～扇 goose feather fan ❷ same as 翎子 líng·zi ①：花～ peacock feather (on a mandarin's hat)

【翎毛】língmáo ❶ 羽毛 plume；feather ❷ 指以鸟类为题材的中国画 type of Chinese painting featuring birds

【翎子】líng·zi ❶ 清代官吏礼帽上装饰的表示品级的翎毛 peacock feather worn at the back of a Qing Dynasty official's hat ❷ 戏曲中武将帽子上所插的雉尾 long pheasant tail feathers worn on a warrior's helmet in traditional Chinese opera

羚 líng ❶ 羚羊 antelope；gazelle ❷ 指羚羊角 antelope's horn

【羚牛】língniú 哺乳动物，像水牛，雌雄都有黑色的短角，肩部比臀部高，尾巴短，毛棕黄色或褐色。生活在高山上，吃青草、树枝、竹笋等。takin (*Budorcas taxicotor*)；herbivore mammal related to the musk ox and mountain goat, whose shoulders are higher than its rump, and that has a short tail and yellow or brown hair；both male and female have short black horns；living on high mountains and feeding on grass, tree twigs, bamboo shoots, etc.；also 扭角羚 niǔjiǎolíng and 牛羚 niúlíng

【羚羊】língyáng 哺乳动物的一类，形状和山羊相似，一般指新疆出产的赛加羚羊，雌雄都有角，毛灰黄色，面部有棕灰色条纹，四肢细长，跑得快，耐干渴。角白色或黄白色，略呈弓形，下段中空，可入药。antelope (*Antilope*)；gazelle；usu. refers to the *Saiga tatarica* of the Xinjiang Uygur Autonomous Region. Antelopes can run swiftly and live for long periods without water. They are characterized by yellowish grey hair, a reddish grey-striped face, long slender limbs. Both male and female have white or yellowish white arced horns that are hollow at the lower part and that are used as medicine. also 羚 líng

绫 líng 绫子 damask silk; silk fabric resembling satin but finer: 红～ red damask silk|～罗绸缎 silks and satins

【绫子】líng·zi 像缎子而比缎子薄的丝织品 damask silk; silk fabric resembling satin but finer

棱(稜) líng 穆棱(Mùlíng),地名,在黑龙江 Muling, a place in Heilongjiang Province

☞ lēng on p. 1171 and léng on p. 1171

祾 líng 〈书 *fml.*〉福 luck; blessing; happiness; good fortune

零1 líng ❶零碎;小数目的(跟'整'相对 as opposed to 'whole' or 'entire') fractional; fragmentary; part: ～用 defray incidental expenses|～售 retail; sell retail|化整为～ break up the whole into parts ❷(～儿 língr)零头;零数 extra; fraction; odd lot: 挂～儿 odd|年纪已经八十有～ 80-odd years old ❸放在两个数量中间,表示单位较高的量之下附有单位较低的量 placed between two numbers to indicate a small number or amount following a larger one: 一年～三天 a year and three days|八元～二分 eight yuan and two *fen* ❹数的空位,在数码中多作'〇' zero sign (0); nought: 三～一号 No. 301|二～～～年 the year 2000 ❺表示没有数量 zero; nought; nil: 一减一等于～。One minus one leaves nought (or zero).◇这种药的效力等于～。The medicine had no effect. ❻温度计上的零度 zero (on a thermometer): ～上五度 5℃ above zero|～下十度 10℃ below zero ❼(Líng)姓 a surname

零2 líng ❶(草木花叶)枯萎而落下(of grass, trees, flowers, or leaves) wither and fall: ～落 wither and fall|凋～ wither; decline ❷〈书 *fml.*〉(雨、泪等)落下(of rain, tears, etc.) fall: 涕～ shed tears

【零打碎敲】líng dǎ suì qiāo same as 零敲碎打 líng qiāo suì dǎ

【零担】língdàn 托运的货物不需要一辆货车运送的叫零担 odd cargo; (of consignment) amount less than a carload: ～货物 less than carload (LCL)|～运输 a less-than-carload lot

【零蛋】língdàn 表示没有数量,由于阿拉伯数字的'0'略呈蛋形,所以叫零蛋(含诙谐意 humor.) zero (0); nothing; Arabic numeral '0' (零 líng) looks slightly like an egg (蛋 dàn), therefore, zero is called 零蛋: 考试得了个～ get a zero mark in an examination; lay an egg in an exam

【零点】língdiǎn 夜里十二点钟 zero hour; midnight; twelve o'clock at night: ～十分 twelve ten at night

【零丁】língdīng same as 伶仃 língdīng

【零工】línggōng ❶短工 odd job; short-term hired labour: 打～ do odd jobs; odd job ❷做零工的人 odd-job man; casual labourer: 雇～ hire casual labourers

【零花】línghuā ❶零碎地花(钱) pay incidental expenses; spend on minor items: 这点儿钱,你留着～吧! Keep this money for incidental expenses. ❷(～儿 línghuār)零碎用的钱 pocket money: 妈妈给他五块钱做～儿。Mother gave him five yuan pocket money.

【零活儿】línghuór 零碎的工作或家务事 odd jobs; chores: 重活儿他干不了,做点～还行。He is unsuited to heavy work, but able to do odd jobs.

【零件】língjiàn 可以用来装配成机器、工具等的单个制件 part; spare part; spare; work appliance that can be fitted to a machine, tool, etc.

【零乱】língluàn same as 凌乱 língluàn

【零落】língluò ❶(花叶)脱落(of flowers and leaves) wither and fall: 草木～ bare trees and withered grass ❷(事物)衰败(of things) decay; decline: 家境～declining family finances|一片凄凉～的景象 a desolate look ❸稀疏不集中 scattered; sporadic: ～的枪声此起彼伏 sporadic gunfire (or shooting) broke out periodically.|村庄零零落落地散布在河边。Villages are scattered along the banks of the river.

【零七八碎】língqībāsuì ❶(～的 língqībāsuì·de)零碎而杂乱 scattered and disorderly: ～的东西放满了一屋子。The room is cluttered with all kinds of things.|被～的事儿缠住了,走不开。Bogged down by trivial matters, be unable to get away. ❷(～儿 língqībàsuìr)零散没系统的事情或没有大用的东西 odds and ends; miscellaneous trifles: 整天忙些个～儿 fuss over trifles throughout the day; be busy with trivia all day long|桌上放着好些他喜欢的～儿。Many of his favorite odds and ends are on the table.

【零钱】língqián ❶币值小的钱,如角、分 small change; change; money of small denominations, such as *jiao* and *fen* ❷零花的钱 pocket money: 我不抽烟,也不喝酒,一个月花不了多少～。Being neither a smoker nor a drinker, I spend very little of my monthly allowance. ❸仆人、茶房等正式工资以外的零碎收入 tips; gratuities; earnings of servants, waiters, etc., over and above their formal wages

【零敲碎打】líng qiāo suì dǎ 指以零零碎碎、断断续续的方式进行或处理 do sth. bit by bit, off and on; adopt a piecemeal approach; also 零打碎敲 líng dǎ suì qiāo

【零散】líng·sǎn 分散;不集中 scattered; dispersed: 把～的材料归并在一起 piece together

scraps of fabric | 桌子上～地放着几本书。Several books have been placed haphazardly on the table. | 二十多户人家零零散散地分布在几个山沟里。There are twenty households or more scattered over a few gullies.

【零声母】língshēngmǔ 指以 ɑ、e、o、i、u、ü 等元音起头的字音的声母,如'爱'(ài)、'鹅'(é)、'藕'(ǒu)、'烟'(iān)、'弯'(uān)、'渊'(üān)等 zero initial consonant (of a Chinese syllable) beginning with a vowel like ɑ, e, o, I, u and ü, e.g. 爱(ài),鹅(é),藕(ǒu),烟(iān),弯(uān) and 渊(üān); ☞声母 shēngmǔ on p.1720

【零食】língshí 正常饭食以外的零星食品 snacks; between-meal nibbles: 不吃～是好习惯。Not eating between meals is a good habit.

【零售】língshòu 把商品不成批地卖给消费者 retail; sell retail: ～店 retail shop | ～价格 retail price | 本店只～,不批发。This shop sells at retail prices only, and not wholesale.

【零数】língshù (～儿 língshùr) 以某位数为标准,不足整数的尾数,比如一千八百三十,以百位数为标准,三十是零数 fractional amount or number; remainder (beyond a round number); e.g. the number 1,830, has 30 as its remainder, when reckoning in units of one hundred

【零碎】língsuì ❶ 细碎;琐碎 trivial; trifling; fragmentary; scrappy: ～活儿 odd jobs | ～东西 fragmentary (or trivial) things | 这些材料零零碎碎的,用处不大。These fragmentary materials are of little use. ❷ (～儿 língsuìr) 零碎的事物 odds and ends; bits and pieces; oddments: 他正在拾掇～儿。He is tidying up the odds and ends.

【零头】língtóu (～儿 língtóur) ❶ 不够一定单位(如计算单位、包装单位等)的零碎数量 odd; fractional amount (less than a specific unit, such as computing and packing units, etc.): 整五元,没有～儿。That's five yuan exactly. | 装了六盒,还剩下这点儿～儿。There are a few bits and pieces left after packing up six boxes of materials. ❷ 材料使用后剩下的零碎部分 odds and ends; oddments; bits and pieces; remnants after use of materials: 没有整料,都是～儿。There is not a single whole length left, only bits and pieces.

【零星】língxīng ❶ 零碎的;少量的(不用做谓语 not used as a predicate) odd; fragmentary; spotty; piecemeal: ～材料 fragmentary material | ～土地 odd pieces of land | 我零零星星地听到一些消息。I heard some odd scraps of news. ❷ 零散(不用做谓语 not used as a predicate) scattered; sporadic: ～的枪声 sporadic gunfire | 下着零零星星的小雨。It is splattering. | 草丛间零零星星地点缀着一些小花。Small flowers are scattered throughout the dense grass.

【零讯】língxùn 零星的消息(多用做报刊专栏的名称 oft. used as the title of a column of brief news items) scraps of news

【零用】língyòng ❶ 零碎地花(钱);零碎地使用 defray incidental expenses: 一百块钱交伙食费,五十块钱～。An amount of 100 yuan was given out for accommodation and eating expenses, and 50 yuan for minor purchases. ❷ 零碎用的钱 pocket money: 如果缺～,就来我这里拿吧。If you are short of ready money, you can get some from me.

【零嘴】língzuǐ 〈方 *dial.*〉(～儿 língzuǐr) same as 零食 língshí: 吃～ nibble (or have snacks) between meals

龄 líng ❶ 岁数 age; years: 年～ age | 学～ school-age | 高～ advanced age; advanced in years ❷ 泛指年数 duration; length of time or service: 工～ length of service; years of service | 党～ party standing | 军～ length of military service | 舰～ ship's length of service | 炉～ furnace life ❸ 某些生物体发育过程中不同的阶段。如昆虫的幼虫第一次蜕皮前叫一龄虫;水稻长到七个叶叫七叶龄。instar; stadium; various stages of the development process of some organisms, e.g. the larva of an insect before its first exuviation is called the first-instar insect; and the rice produced after having leafed seven times is called seventh instar rice

鲮 líng 鱼,体侧扁,头短,口小,背部青灰色,腹部银白色。生活在淡水中,不耐低温,是珠江流域等地区的重要经济鱼类。dace (*Cirrhina molitorella*); laterally flat fish with a short head, small mouth, lime greenish back, and a silvery white stomach, important for fish farming in areas such as the Pearl River Valley, that lives in freshwater, and cannot endure low temperatures; also 土鲮鱼 tǔlíngyú

酃 Líng 酃县,地名,在湖南 Lingxian County (place in Hunan Province); 今改称 now called 炎陵县 yánlíngxiàn

醽 líng [醽醁](línglù)〈书 *fml.*〉美酒名 *linglu*, name of a good wine

lǐng (ㄌㄧㄥˇ)

令 lǐng 〈量词 *classifier*〉原张的纸五百张为一令 ream; 500 sheets of paper: 五～白报纸 five reams of newsprint

☞ líng on p.1226 and lìng on p. 1235

岭(嶺) lǐng ❶ 顶上有路可通行的山 mountain; ridge of a mountain; mountain with roads accessible to the top: 一道～ a ridge | 崇山峻～ lofty (or towering) mountain ridges | 翻山越～ cross hill and dale; climb mountain after mountain ❷ 高大

的山脉 mountain range; high (or lofty) mountains:南～ Nanling Mountains | 秦～ Qinling Mountains | 大兴安～ the Great Xing'an Mountain ❸ 专指大庾岭等五岭 Five Ridges including the Dayu Ridge:～南 south of the Five Ridges; area covering Guangdong and Guangxi

【岭南】Lǐngnán 指五岭以南的地区,就是广东、广西一带 south of the Five Ridges; area covering Guangdong and Guangxi

领 lǐng ❶ 颈;脖子 neck:～巾 scarf; neckerchief | 引～而望 crane one's neck to see; eagerly look forward to ❷ (～儿 lǐngr)领子 collar:衣～ collar | 翻～儿 turn down collar ❸ (～儿 lǐngr) same as 领口 lǐngkǒu ①:圆～儿 round neck | 尖～儿 V-neck | 和尚～儿 collar of a monk's robe ❹ 大纲;要点 outline; main points:要～ main points; essentials | 提纲挈～ bring out the essence; concentrate on the main points; give the gist (of sth.) ❺ 〈量词 *classifier*〉 a)〈书 *fml.*〉长袍或上衣一件叫一领 [used as classifier for gown or coat] b)席一张叫一领 [used for a length of matting] ❻ 带;引 lead; take; usher; head:率～ head; lead | ～导 lead; exercise leadership | ～队 lead a group | 把客人～到餐厅去 usher a guest into the dining hall ❼ 领有;领有的 possess; own; occupy:占～ occupy | ～土 territory | ～海 territorial sea; territorial waters | ～空 territorial air space; territorial sky or air ❽ 领取 receive; draw; take:招～ announce recovery of an item of lost property | ～工资 get (or draw) one's salary (or wages) | ～材料 draw materials ❾ 接受 accept; take:～教 ask advice; consult | ～情 appreciate the kindness; feel grateful to sb. | 心～ appreciate kindness ❿ 了解(意思) understand; comprehend; grasp:～略 experience; appreciate; realize; have a taste of | ～会 understand; comprehend; grasp | ～悟 comprehend; grasp; realize; understand

【领班】lǐngbān ❶ 厂矿企业里领导一班人工作 (of industrial enterprises) leader or head of a work team or group ❷ 领班的人 foreman; gaffer; supervisor; person holding such a post

【领唱】lǐngchàng ❶ 合唱时,由一个或几个人带头唱(有时由几个人轮流独唱) chorus led by one or a few people, or a solo sung by several persons in turn ❷ 领唱的人 leading singer (of a chorus)

【领带】lǐngdài 穿西服时,系(jì)在衬衫领子上而悬在胸前的带子 tie; necktie; band that fastens around the collar of a shirt and hangs down its front, usu. worn with a suit

【领导】lǐngdǎo ❶ 率领并引导朝一定方向前进 lead; exercise leadership; act as head and guide sb. in specific direction:集体～ collective leadership | ～人民由一个胜利走向另一个胜利 lead the masses from victory to victory ❷ 担任领导的人;领导者 leader; leadership; person holding such a post:～和群众相结合 identify a leader with the masses

【领道】lǐng//dào (～儿 lǐng//dàor)带路 lead the way:你给我们领个道儿吧。Please show us the way. | 路不熟,找个人～儿。As we are not familiar with the route, please find a guide to show us the way.

【领地】lǐngdì ❶ 奴隶社会、封建社会中领主所占有的土地 fief; manor (of a feudal lord); land occupied by a feudal lord in the slave or feudal society ❷ same as 领土 lǐngtǔ

【领队】lǐngduì ❶ 率领队伍 lead a group:老张～参加比赛。Lao Zhang led the group's participation in the contest. | ～的一架敌机首先被击中。The enemy plane leading the squadron was the first to be shot down. ❷ 率领队伍的人 leader of a group, sports team, etc.; captain; person who leads a group

【领港】lǐnggǎng ❶ 引导船舶进出港口 pilot a ship into or out of a harbour ❷ 担任领港工作的人 harbour pilot ‖ also 引港 yǐngǎng

【领钩】lǐnggōu (～儿 lǐnggōur)扣住衣领的金属钩,包括钩儿和环两部分,分别钉在领口上 hook and a eye on a collar; metal hook that secures a collar, comprising a hook and an eye fastened to the collar-band, respectively:一副～ a hook and eye set for a collar

【领海】lǐnghǎi 距离一国海岸线一定宽度的海域,是该国领土的组成部分 territorial waters; territorial sea; area of sea waters near the coastline of a country that forms a part of its territory

【领航】lǐngháng ❶ 引导船舶或飞机航行 navigate; pilot; direct the course of a ship or plane ❷ 担任领航工作的人 navigator; pilot; person doing such a job; also 领航员 lǐnghángyuán

【领花】lǐnghuā ❶ same as 领结 lǐngjié ❷ 军人、警察等戴在制服领子上表示军种、专业等的标志 collar insignia; symbol on the collar of uniform worn by soldiers, policemen, etc., denoting their particular service, function, etc.

【领会】lǐnghuì 领略事物而有所体会 understand; comprehend; grasp:认真～文件的精神 carefully study and grasp the essence of a document | 你把他的意思～错了。You misunderstood him.

【领江】lǐngjiāng ❶ 在江河上引导船舶航行 navigate a ship along a river ❷ 担任领江工作的人 river pilot; person doing such a job

【领教】lǐngjiào ❶ 接受人的教益或欣赏人的表演时说的客气话 used to express one's appreciation or thanks for advice, instruction or performance:老先生说得很对,～～! You, my venerable teacher, are quite right. Thank you for your advice! | 请你弹一个曲子,让我们~一下。Could you oblige us by playing a tune? ❷ 请教 ask advice; consult:有点儿小事向您~。I wish to consult you on a minor matter.

【领结】lǐngjié 穿西服时,系(jì)在衬衫领子前的横结 (bow) tie; length of tailored fabric tied in a horizontal knot at the collar of a shirt, usu. when wearing a suit

【领巾】lǐngjīn 系(jì)在脖子上的三角形的纺织品 scarf; neckerchief; triangular piece of textile fastened at the neck:红~ red scarf (as worn by a Young Pioneer)

【领空】lǐngkōng 一个国家的陆地、领水和领海上的整个空间,是该国领土的组成部分 territorial sky (or air); territorial air space; entire space above the land area, and territorial waters pertaining to one country

【领口】lǐngkǒu ❶ 衣服上两肩之间套住脖子的孔及其边缘 collar band; neckband; hole between the shoulders in a garment that slips over the neck:这件毛衣~太小。The neck of this sweater is too small. ❷ 领子两头相合的地方 place where the two ends of a collar meet:~上别着一个宝石别针。A jewelled brooch is pinned to the collar.

【领陆】lǐnglù 构成领土的陆地,包括边界以内的大陆部分和岛屿的陆地 territorial land; land domain; land that constitutes territory, including the mainland and island(s) within its territorial waters

【领路】lǐng//lù 带路 lead the way:他在前面~。He is leading the way ahead. | 这地方你熟悉吗?别领错了路。Are you familiar with this place? Don't lead us astray.

【领略】lǐnglüè 了解事物的情况,进而认识它的意义,或者辨别它的滋味 experience; appreciate; have a taste of; understand a matter and realize its significance, or discern its flavour:~江南风味 enjoy the local flavour in the area south of the Yangtze River

【领情】lǐng//qíng 接受礼物或好意而心怀感激 appreciate a kindness; feel grateful to sb. (when accepting a present or kindness):同志们的好意,我十分~。I am very grateful to the comrades for their kindness. | 我领这个情,但东西不能收。I appreciate your kindness, but cannot accept your gift.

【领取】lǐngqǔ 取发给的东西 draw; receive (sth. that is given out):~工资 draw a salary

【领事】lǐngshì 由一国政府派驻外国某一城市或地区的外交官员,主要任务是保护本国和它的侨民在该领事区内的法律权利和经济利益,管理侨民事务等 consul; diplomat appointed by the government of one country to a foreign city or area, whose major task is to protect that country, and its citizens' legal rights and economic benefits, and to administer affairs related to its citizens in that area

【领事馆】lǐngshìguǎn 一国政府驻在他国城市或某地区的领事代表机关 consulate; consular representative government post in a foreign city or area

【领事裁判权】lǐngshì cáipànquán 帝国主义国家通过不平等条约,在半殖民地或附属国攫取的一种特权,即它的侨民在当地的民刑事诉讼,所在国法庭无权审理,而由它派驻当地的领事依照本国法律审判 consular jurisdiction; privilege seized by an imperialist country in a semi-colonial or dependent state that has been established through unequal treaties, that deprives a local court of the right to handle civil and criminal cases against its citizens in the location, who are instead tried by the appointed consul to the locality, according to local national law

【领受】lǐngshòu 接受(多指接受好意 usu. kindness) accept; receive:~任务 accept a task | 这些礼物,我不能~。I cannot accept these gifts. | 他怀着激动的心情~了同志们的慰问。Filled with excitement, he accepted his comrades' good wishes.

【领属】lǐngshǔ 彼此之间一方领有或具有而另一方隶属或从属 leader and subordinate; (of two parties) one party possesses or has authority to which the other party is subordinate:~关系 subordination; leadership between a superior and a subordinate

【领水】lǐngshuǐ ❶ 分布在一个国家领土内的河流、湖泊、运河、港口、海湾等 inland waters; rivers, lakes, canals, harbours, gulfs, etc., within the territory of a country ❷ same as 领海 lǐnghǎi ❸〈方 *dial.*〉担任引航工作的人 (harbour) pilot; person in charge of pilotage

【领头】lǐng//tóu (~儿 lǐng//tóur)带头 take the lead; be the first (to do sth.):他~干了起来。He led the work. | 我领个头儿,大家跟着一起唱。I'll take the lead, and you all join me in singing.

【领土】lǐngtǔ 在一国主权管辖下的区域,包括领陆、领水、领海和领空 territory; region under the jurisdiction of the sovereignty of a state, covering territorial land, waters, sea and air space

【领舞】lǐngwǔ ❶ 群舞的时候,由一个或几个人领头舞蹈 lead a dance (by one or several persons) ❷ 担任领舞的人 leading dancer; person who leads a dance

【领悟】lǐngwù 领会;理解 comprehend; grasp; realize:我说的那些话,他好像还未~过来。He appeared not to grasp what I was driving at.

【领洗】lǐng//xǐ 领受洗礼,成为基督教徒 be baptized; receive baptism and become a Christian

【领先】lǐng//xiān ❶ 共同前进时走在最前面

lead; be in the lead; take the lead; take the foremost position in an advance:他迈开大步,～登上了山顶。Marching forward in great strides, he was the first to reach the top of the mountain. ❷〈比喻 *fig.*〉水平、成绩等处于最前列 lead; be in the lead; take the lead; (of a level, an achievement, etc.) be at the forefront:这个县的粮食产量处于全国～地位。This county leads the nation in grain output. |上半场二比一,北京足球队～。At the end of the first half the Beijing football team was leading 2:1.

【领衔】lǐngxián 在共同署名的文件上署名在最前面 head the list of names (on a document); be the first on a list ◇这部影片由一位新星～主演。A newcomer was given star billing in this film.

【领袖】lǐngxiù 国家、政治团体、群众组织等的领导人 leader (of a country, political group, mass organization, etc.)

【领养】lǐngyǎng 把别人家的孩子领来抚养,当做自己的子女 adopt (a child); take a child born into another family and raise it as one's own

【领有】lǐngyǒu 拥有(人口)或占有(土地) (of population or land) possess; own

【领域】lǐngyù ❶ 一个国家行使主权的区域 territory; domain; realm; area in which a state exercises its sovereignty ❷ 学术思想或社会活动的范围 field; sphere; realm; domain; range of academic thinking or social activity:思想～ ideological sphere|生活～ field in life|在自然科学～内,数学是最重要的基础。Mathematics is at the foundation of the natural sciences.

【领章】lǐngzhāng 军人或某些部门的工作人员佩带在制服的领子上的标志 collar badge; collar insignia; (of a soldier, or worker in a certain department) insignia worn on the collar of the uniform

【领主】lǐngzhǔ 奴隶社会和封建社会中受封在一个区域里掌握权力的人。在经济上是土地所有者,在政治上是统治者。feudal lord; suzerain; person assigned to wield power within a slave or feudal society. A feudal lord is, from an economic point of view, a landowner, and from a political point of view, a dictator.

【领子】lǐng·zi 衣服上围绕脖子的部分 collar; part of a garment that fits around the neck

【领奏】lǐngzòu ❶ 合奏的时候,由一个或几个人领头演奏 lead an instrumental ensemble performed by one or several musicians:～乐器 instrument leading an ensemble|～一曲 lead a tune ❷ 担任领奏的人 leading player in concert or band

【领罪】lǐngzuì 承认自己的罪过 admit one's guilt; plead guilty; confess a crime:甘愿～ be willing to admit one's guilt

lìng (ㄌㄧㄥˋ)

另 lìng 另外 other; another; separate:～选 choose (or select) another |～议 discuss separately; negotiate as a separate case|～有任务 have other tasks|～一回事 another matter|～纸抄寄 copy on to another piece of paper and post separately|走了～一条路 take a different road (or way)

【另案】lìng'àn 另外的案件 separate case:同案犯已作～处理。The accomplices have been handled as a separate case.

【另册】lìngcè〈旧时 *old*〉户口册的一种,统治者把盗匪、坏人的户口登记在上面 other register; other census book for listing criminals, bandits and other disreputable persons, as opposed to the 'regular register'

【另起炉灶】lìng qǐ lú zào ❶〈比喻 *fig.*〉重新做起 set up a new kitchen; make a fresh start; start all over again:这次试验失败了,咱们～。We have failed in this experiment; let's start again. ❷〈比喻 *fig.*〉另立门户或另搞一套 set up one's own kitchen; live in a separate house; get one's own way:这个分厂计划脱离总厂,～。This branch plans to break away from the general plant and carry on business independently.

【另外】lìngwài 在说过的之外;此外 in addition; besides; moreover; other:我还要跟你谈～一件事情。There is another matter I want to talk over with you.|他家新买了一台拖拉机,～还买了脱粒机。In addition to a tractor, his family has also bought a thresher.

【另行】lìngxíng 另外进行(某种活动) separately; engage in (some other activity):～通知 be notified later; wait till further notice|～规定 stipulate separately

【另眼相看】lìng yǎn xiāng kàn 用另一种眼光看待,多指看待某个人(或某种人)不同于一般 regard sb. with special respect; pay special regard to; look at sb. (or some kind of person) with different eyes

令¹ lìng ❶ same as 命令 mìnglìng ①:～各校切实执行 order all the schools conscientiously to implement certain measures ❷ same as 命令 mìnglìng ②:法～ laws and decrees|指～ written instructions or directives|军～ military order |口～ word of command; password ❸ 使 make; cause:～人兴奋 exciting|～人肃然起敬 be held in profound respect ❹ 酒令 drinking game:猜拳行～ play a finger-guessing drinking game ❺〈古代 *arch.*〉官名 official title:县～ county magistrate|太史～ official historian

令² lìng 时节 season:时～ season|夏～ summer-weather; summertime|冬～ winter;

climate in winter | 当～ in season

令[3] lìng ❶〈书 *fml.*〉美好 good; excellent: ～德 excellent virtue | ～名 good name or reputation | ～闻 good name or reputation ❷〈敬辞 *pol.*〉用于对方的亲属或有关系的人 [used for a relative or related person of the other party] your: ～尊 your father | ～兄 your brother | ～侄 your nephew | ～亲 your relation or relative; kinsman

令[4] lìng 小令(多用于词调、曲调名 usu. used in the name of a tonal pattern and rhyming scheme of *ci* poetry or tune of a song) short lyric; brief song-poem: 如梦～ short poem (or lyric) set to the tune of 'Rumeng Ling' | 叨叨～ short poem (or lyric) set to the tune of 'Daodao (Chattering) Ling'

☞ líng on p. 1226 and lǐng on p. 1232

【令爱】lìng'ài〈敬辞 *pol.*〉称对方的女儿 your daughter; also 令嫒 lìng'ài

【令嫒】lìng'ài same as 令爱 lìng'ài

【令出法随】lìng chū fǎ suí 法令发布了就要执行,违犯了法令就要依法惩处 rigorous enforcement of the law and decrees; punishment for violations according to law

【令箭】lìngjiàn〈古代 *arch.*〉军队中发布命令时用做凭据的东西,形状像箭 arrow-shaped token of authority used in the army in ancient China

【令郎】lìngláng〈敬辞 *pol.*〉称对方的儿子 your son

【令名】lìngmíng〈书 *fml.*〉美名;好名声 good name; good reputation

【令亲】lìngqīn〈敬辞 *pol.*〉称对方的亲戚 your relation or relative; kinsman

【令堂】lìngtáng〈敬辞 *pol.*〉称对方的母亲 your mother

【令闻】lìngwén〈书 *fml.*〉美好的名声 good name; good reputation

【令行禁止】lìng xíng jìn zhǐ 有令必行,有禁必止,形容严格执行法令 see to it that every order is executed without fail; strict enforcement of orders and prohibitions

【令尊】lìngzūn〈敬辞 *pol.*〉称对方的父亲 your father

呤 lìng ☞嘌呤 (piàolìng) on p. 1477

liū (ㄌㄧㄡ)

溜[1] liū ❶ 滑行;(往下)滑 slide; glide: ～冰 skating | 从山坡上～下来 slide down a slope ❷ 偷偷地走开 slip away; sneak off: 一说打牌,他就～了。He sneaked off when someone suggested a game of cards. ❸ 光滑;平滑 smooth; glossy: ～光 very smooth; glossy; sleek | 滑～ slippery ❹〈方 *dial.*〉看 glance; take a look: ～一眼心里就有了数 know what it is at a glance ❺ 顺着;沿 along: ～边 keep to the edge (of a road, river, etc.) | ～墙根儿走 walk along the foot of a wall ❻〈方 *dial.*〉很;非常 very; extremely: ～直 very straight; straight as a ramrod | ～薄 very thin | ～齐 very evenly | ～净 extremely clean

溜[2] liū same as 熘 liū

☞ liù on p. 1248

【溜边】liūbiān (～儿 liūbiānr) ❶ 靠着边 keep to the edge (of a road, river, etc.) ❷〈比喻 *fig.*〉遇事躲在一旁,不参与 avoid; dodge; adopt a furtive attitude when confronted with a problem: 他一向怕事,碰到矛盾就～了。Always chicken-hearted and overcautious, he avoids conflict whenever it arises.

【溜冰】liū//bīng ❶ 滑冰 skating ❷〈方 *dial.*〉穿着带四个小轮子的鞋在光滑坚硬的地面上溜;滑旱冰 roller-skating; glide along even, hard ground on a pair of four-wheeled skates

【溜槽】liūcáo 从高处向低处运送东西用的槽,多用竹木制成,也有在陡坡上挖成的。槽的内表面光滑,东西放在槽中会自己往下溜。chute; trough usually made of bamboo or wood, or dug out of a steep slope, that has a smooth inner surface, allowing things to slide from a higher to a lower place

【溜达】liū·da 散步;闲走 stroll; saunter; go for a walk: 吃过晚饭,到街上～～。Let's go for a walk through the streets after dinner. also 蹓跶 liū·da

【溜光】liūguāng〈方 *dial.*〉❶ 很光滑 very smooth; sleek; glossy: 头发梳得～ comb one's hair till it is smooth (or sleek) | ～的鹅卵石 glossy cobblestone ❷ 一点儿不剩 leave nothing; finish: 山上的树砍得～。The trees on the mountain side have all been felled.

【溜号】liū//hào〈方 *dial.*〉(～儿 liū//hàor) 溜走 sneak away; slink off: 会没散,他就～了。He stole away before the meeting was over. ◇人在课堂上,思想却～了 allow one's mind to wander when attending a lecture

【溜肩膀】liūjiānbǎng (～儿 liūjiānbǎngr) ❶ 双肩下垂叫溜肩膀 sloping shoulders ❷〈方 *dial.*〉〈比喻 *fig.*〉不负责任 irresponsible; lacking a proper sense of responsibility; devoid of any sense of responsibility

【溜溜儿】liūliūr〈方 *dial.*〉(～的 liūliūr·de) 整整 full; whole: ～等了一天,始终没见动静。He waited the whole day, but nothing happened from beginning to end.

【溜溜转】liūliūzhuàn 形容圆的东西不停地转动 (of a round object) spin continuously

【溜门】liūmén (～儿 liūménr) 乘人不备进入住宅(行窃) break into (a house) to steal; housebreak; burglarize: ～贼 burglar | ～撬锁 burglary and lock-picking; break-ins

【溜平】liūpíng 〈方 *dial.*〉很平 very smooth:～的路面 smooth road surface | 菜地整得～。The vegetable plot was cultivated smoothly and evenly.

【溜须拍马】liū xū pāi mǎ 〈比喻 *fig.*〉谄媚奉承 fawn; toady; shamelessly flatter; suck up to sb.

【溜之大吉】liū zhī dà jí do a guy; 偷偷地走开;一走了事(含诙谐意 humor.) do a guy; sneak away; slink off; seek safety in flight; make oneself scarce:他一看势头不对,转身就从后门～。Sensing possible danger, he did a guy at the back door.

【溜之乎也】liū zhī hū yě 偷偷地走开(含诙谐意 humor.) make oneself scarce; steal away; slink off:大家干得正欢,他却～。He made himself scarce while others were working feverishly.

【溜桌】liū//zhuō 因饮酒过量而滑到酒席桌下 slide under the table after over imbibing; get drunk:酒已经喝多了,再喝我非～不可。I have drunk too much already, any more and I'll be under the table (or be dead drunk).

熘(溜) liū 烹饪方法,炸或焯后,作料中加淀粉汁 sauté (with thick gravy); quick-fry; method of cooking whereby food is coated with flour or starch and seasonings after frying or scalding:～肝尖 liver sauté | 醋～白菜 quick-fry cabbage with vinegar | 滑～里脊 sauté fillet with thick gravy

瞜 liū 〈方 *dial.*〉看;斜视 look; look sideways at; look askance; cast sidelong glances:那人正斜着眼向这边～。That person is looking sideways in this direction.

蹓 liū 偷偷地走开 slip away; sneak off:他说着,一转身就想～。This said, he turned and sidled off.

☞ liù on p.1248

【蹓跶】liū·da same as 溜达 liū·da

liú (ㄌㄧㄡˊ)

刘(劉) Liú 姓 a surname

【刘海儿】Liú Hǎir 传说中的仙童,前额垂着短发,骑在蟾上,手里舞着一串钱 Liu Hair, legendary child fairy with short hair cut in bangs across his forehead, who rode a toad, while playing with a string of money

【刘海儿】liúhǎir 妇女或儿童垂在前额的整齐的短发 bang; fringe; (of women or children) well-groomed short hair cut straight across the forehead

浏(瀏) liú 〈书 *fml.*〉形容水流清澈 (of water) clear; limpid

【浏览】liúlǎn 大略地看 scan; glance over; skim through; browse:～市容 have a look around the city | 这本书我只～了一遍,还没仔细看。I have only scanned (or glanced through) the book, and have not yet started reading it.

留(畱) liú ❶ 停止在某一个处所或地位上不动;不离去 remain; stay on in a place:～校 stay at school during the vacation | ～任 retain a post; remain or continue in office | 他～在农村工作了。He stayed on working in the countryside. ❷ 留学 study abroad:～洋 study abroad | ～英 study in Britain ❸ 使留;不使离去 ask sb. to stay; keep sb. where he or she is; detain:挽～ persuade somebody to stay on | 拘～ detain; hold in custody | ～客人吃饭 ask a guest to stay for dinner ❹ 注意力放在某方面 concentrate on sth.:～心 be careful; take care | ～神 be careful; take care ❺ 保留 keep; reserve; save; retain:自～地 family plot; private plot; plot of land for personal needs | ～底稿 keep the draft (or manuscript) | ～胡子 grow a beard (or moustache) | 鸡犬不～ even fowls and dogs are not to be spared — ruthless mass slaughter ❻ 接受;收下 accept; take; keep:礼物先～下来。I accept this gift. | 书店送来的碑帖我～了三本。I kept three of the collections of rubbings of stone inscriptions sent over by the bookstore. ❼ 遗留 leave behind:旅客～言簿 book of suggestions or comments left by passengers | 祖先～给了我们丰富的文化遗产。Our ancestors have left us a rich cultural heritage. ❽ (Liú) 姓 a surname

【留班】liú//bān same as 留级 liú//jí

【留别】liúbié 〈书 *fml.*〉离开某地时赠送礼品或做诗词给留在那里的亲友 give a farewell gift or write a poem to a relative or friend when leaving a place

【留步】liúbù 〈客套话 *pol.*〉用于主人送客时客人请主人不要送出去 (said by a guest to his host or hostess on leaving) don't bother to see me out; don't bother to come any further

【留成】liú//chéng (～儿 liú//chéngr) 从钱财的总数中按一定成数留下来 retain a portion or percentage of the total money:利润～ retain a percentage of the profits

【留传】liúchuán 遗留下来传给后代 pass on to later generations; hand down (to descendants); leave sth. to posterity:祖辈～下来的秘方 secret recipe inherited from one's ancestors

【留存】liúcún ❶ 保存;存放 keep; preserve:这份文件～备查 keep this document for future reference ❷ 事物持续存在,没有消失 remain; be extant:湖边的古碑一直～到今天。This ancient tablet has been preserved right through to the present day. | 他的光辉业绩将永远～在人们的心中。His magnificent achievements will live in the hearts of the

people forever.

【留待】liúdài 搁置下来等待(处理) leave sth. till a later date; wait till later: 这些问题～下次会议讨论。These problems will be set by for further discussion at the next meeting.

【留得青山在,不怕没柴烧】liú dé qīng shān zài, bù pà méi chái shāo 〈比喻 *fig.*〉只要把人或实力保存下来,将来还会得到恢复和发展 as long as the mountain is still standing, we shan't lack fuel; while green mountains exist, there is no need to worry about firewood; where there is life, there is hope; as long as there is humanity, or strength, there can be achievement and success

【留地步】liú dì·bu same as 留余地 liú yúdì

【留都】liúdū 迁都之后,称原来的都城为留都。如明代迁都北京后称南京为留都。defunct capital; former capital on the establishment of a new one; one-time capital (e.g. Nanjing became the former capital after the Ming Dynasty made its capital in Beijing)

【留后路】liú hòulù (～儿 liú hòulùr)办事时防备万一不成而预先留下退路 leave open a line of retreat; prepare for contingencies

【留后手】liú hòushǒu (～儿 liú hòushǒur)为避免将来发生困难而采取留有余地的措施 leave room for maneuver (so as to avoid any difficulties that may occur)

【留级】liú//jí 学生学年成绩不及格,不能升级,留在原来的年级重新学习 (of pupils) fail to move up to the next grade (or year); repeat the year's work; stay another year in the same grade; repetition of a year; (of pupils who fail the year-end examination) re-take the year's course

【留连】liúlián same as 流连 liúlián

【留恋】liúliàn 不忍舍弃或离开 be reluctant to leave (a place); be loath to part (from sb. or with sth.): ～故土 be unwilling to tear oneself from one's hometown | 就要离开学校了,大家十分～。We were all reluctant to leave our old school.

【留门】liú//mén 夜里等人回来而不插门或不锁门 leave a door unlocked or unbolted at night in anticipation of sb.'s return: 他估计半夜才能回家,交代家里给他～。Thinking that he would not return until midnight, he asked his family to leave the door unlocked for him.

【留难】liúnàn 无理阻止,故意刁难 make things difficult for sb.; put obstacles in sb.'s way: 手续齐备的,都要及时办理,不得～。Those who have completed the formalities should be served in good time. No one is allowed to make things diffcult for them.

【留念】liúniàn 留做纪念(多用于临别馈赠 usu. of a parting gift) accept or keep as a memento: 合影～ have a group picture taken as a memento | 离京时送她一支钢笔～ give her a pen as a memento when she leaves Beijing

【留鸟】liúniǎo 终年生活在一个地区,不到远方去的鸟,如麻雀、画眉、喜鹊等 non-migratory (bird); bird that stays in its native habitat throughout the year such as the sparrow, *Garrulax canorus*, and magpie, rather than migrating in winter

【留情】liú//qíng 由于照顾情面而宽恕或原谅 show mercy or forgiveness (to spare sb's sensibilities); be lenient; be forbearing: 手下～ show compassion; be lenient | 毫不～ pitiless; show no mercy to sb.; ruthless

【留任】liúrèn (官员)留下来继续任职 (of officials) retain a post; remain (or continue) in office: 降级～ demote and retain in office | 新内阁已经组成,原外长～。A new cabinet was established, and the former foreign minister was retained in office.

【留神】liú//shén 注意;小心(多指防备危险或错误 usu. a warning to take precautions against danger or error) be careful; take care; look out for: 留点儿神,可别上当。Watch out and don't let yourself be cheated. | 车辆很多,过马路要～。Be careful when you cross a busy street.

【留声机】liúshēngjī 把录在唱片上的声音放出来的机器。有的地区叫话匣子。gramophone; phonograph; machine that plays recorded words or music; also 话匣子 huàxiá·zi in some areas

【留守】liúshǒu ❶ 皇帝离开京城,命大臣驻守,叫做留守。平时在陪都也有大臣留守。emperor's order to a minister to act on his behalf during his absence from the capital. A secondary capital also had a rear minister for this purpose. ❷ 部队、机关、团体等离开原驻地时留下少数人在原驻地担任守卫、联系等工作 (of a small number of people of troops, organs, organizations, etc.) remain for garrison or liaison duty after the emperor and his entourage have left the originally stationed place: ～处 rear office

【留宿】liúsù ❶ 留客人住宿 put up a guest for the night: 不得～闲人。You must not put up unauthorized personnel overnight. ❷ 停留下来住宿 stay overnight; put up for the night: 今晚在同学家～ stay at the home of a classmate tonight

【留题】liútí ❶ 在参观或游览的地方写下(意见、感想等) write down one's comments, impressions, etc., of a visit to a place of scenic or historical interest: ～簿 visitors' book ❷ 〈书 *fml.*〉游览名胜时因有所感而题写的诗句 poem written when one is touched or moved (by scenery or an event) during a visit to a resort

【留尾巴】liú wěi·ba 〈比喻 *fig.*〉事情做得不彻

底，还留有问题 leave sth. unfinished; with problems unresolved：工程要按期搞完，不能～。The project must be completed on schedule with no matters outstanding.

【留心】liú//xīn 注意 be careful; take care：～听讲 listen attentively to a lecture|参观的时候他很～，不放过每一件展品。During his visit he looked at every exhibit very carefully.

【留学】liú//xué 留居外国学习或研究 study abroad：～生 student studying abroad; returned student|～美国 study in the United States|早年他到欧洲留过学。He studied in Europe many years ago.

【留言】liúyán 离开某地时用书面形式留下要说的话 words written on departure; leave one's comments; leave a message：～牌 notice board|～簿 visitors' book|旅客～ messages left by passengers

【留洋】liú//yáng〈旧时 *old*〉指留学 study abroad

【留一手】liú yī shǒu（～儿 liú yī shǒur）不把本事全部拿出来 hold back a trick or two (when teaching a trade or skill)：老师傅把全部技艺传给徒工，再不像从前那样～了。No longer holding back on the odd trick of the trade like before, the old master taught all his skills to the apprentice.

【留意】liú//yì 注意；小心 be careful; take care; look out; keep one's eyes open：路面很滑，一不～，就会摔跤。The road surface is very slippery and without due care one could easily fall.

【留影】liú//yǐng 指以当前景物为背景，照相以留纪念 take a photograph as a memento; have a picture taken in a place, usu. against the background of one of its distinctive features, as a souvenir：在天安门前留个影 have a picture taken before Tian'anmen

【留影】liúyǐng 为留做纪念而照的相 photographic memento; picture taken as a souvenir：这是我们的毕业～。This is the photo taken at our graduation.

【留用】liúyòng ❶（人员）留下来继续任用 (of personnel) continue to be employed; keep on：～察看 be kept in office on a probationary basis|～人员 personnel (of a former regime or organization) who are retained (in the new one)|降职～ be demoted but kept in office ❷（物品）留下来继续使用 (of articles) keep for use：把要～的衣物挑出来，其他的就处理了。Pick out articles that have future use, and dispose of the rest.

【留余地】liú yúdì（说话、办事）不走极端，留下回旋的地步 allow for unforeseen circumstances; allow for some leeway; leave some elbowroom; leave room for maneuver and not go to extremes (when talking, or handling affairs)

【留针】liúzhēn 指针刺时把针留在穴位内一定时间，以增强针刺的效应 let acupuncture needle remain inserted in an acupoint for a fixed amount of time, for greater effect

【留职】liúzhí 保留职务 remain in office; retain one's post; remain on the roster：～察看 retain post on probationary basis (as disciplinary measure)|～停薪 take long leave of absence without pay; retain post on a suspended salary

【留驻】liúzhù 留下来驻扎 (of troops) be stationed; stay behind to garrison (a place)

流[1] liú ❶ 液体移动；流动 (of liquid) flow：～汗 perspire; sweat; perspire profusely|～血 bleed; shed blood|～鼻涕 have a running nose|水往低处～。Water flows downwards to a lower place. ❷ 移动不定 drift; move; wander; migrate：～转 roam; wander about; be on the move|～通 (of air, money, commodities, etc.) flow; circulate|～沙 drift sand; shifting sand; quicksand; running sand|～星 meteor; shooting star ❸ 流传；传播 spread; circulate; propagate：～芳 leave a good name; leave a reputation|～言 gossip; rumour ❹ 向坏的方面转变 degenerate; change for the worse：～于形式 become a mere formality; become formalistic|放任自～ let things drift ❺ 旧时的刑罚，把犯人送到边远地区去 banish; send into exile; send a criminal to a remote area as a punishment (a practice in old times)：～放 banish; send into exile ❻ 指江河的流水 stream; stream of water; current; torrent：河～ river|洪～ mighty torrent; powerful current|急～ rapid stream|中～ midstream◇开源节～ open up the source and regulate the flow ❼ 像水流的东西 sth. resembling a stream of water; current：气～ air current|暖～ warm current|寒～ cold current; cold wave|电～ electric current ❽ 品类；等级 class; rate; grade：名～ well-known people|女～ women; weaker sex|第一～ first class (or grade)|不入～ unqualified|三教九～ people in various trades; people of all walks

流[2] liú 流明的简称 abbr. for 流明 liúmíng

【流弊】liúbì 滋生的或相沿而成的弊端 malpractice; corrupt practices; abuses that have become common through sustained usage：革除～ get rid of (or do away with) malpractice

【流别】liúbié ❶ 江河的支流 branch of a river; affluent; tributary ❷（文章或学术）源流和派别 (of writing or learning) source; sect; school

【流播】liúbō〈书 *fml.*〉❶ 流传；传播 spread; circulate; hand down：惠泽～ be of benefit to people far and wide|～世间 spread throughout the world ❷ 流徙；播迁 move; wander; migrate：～异域 migrate to a foreign country

【流布】liúbù 传布 spread; circulate; disseminate; extend：广为～ spread widely; widely circulate or disseminate|～四海 spread (or circulate) all over the world

【流产】liú//chǎn ❶ 怀孕后，胎儿未满 28 周就产出。多由内分泌异常、剧烈运动等引起。产出的胎儿一般不能成活。abortion; miscarriage; birth of a foetus within 28 weeks of its conception, usu. caused by abnormal endocrine, excessive movement, a fall, etc.；通称 generally called 小产 xiǎochǎn or 小月 xiǎoyuè；☞人工流产 réngōng liúchǎn on p. 1616 ❷〈比喻 *fig*.〉事情在酝酿或进行中遭到挫折而不能实现 (of a task or mission etc.) miscarry; abort; fall through; fail to be realized during deliberations：撰写计划因人员变动而～。The plan for writing the book has been aborted owing to personnel changes.

【流畅】liúchàng 流利；通畅 easy and smooth; fluent：文字～ write with ease and grace|线条～ graceful lines|动作协调～ harmonious and graceful movements

【流程】liúchéng ❶ 水流的路程 flow path; distance travelled by a flow of water：水流湍急，个把小时，就能越过百里～。The stream flows so swiftly that it covers more than 100 *li* within a couple of hours. ◇生命的～ life span ❷ 工业品生产中，从原料到制成成品各项工序安排的程序 technological process; work flow; industrial production procedure, from treating raw materials right through to emergence of the finished product; also 工艺流程 gōngyì liúchéng

【流传】liúchuán 传下来或传播开 spread; circulate; hand down：大禹治水的故事，一直～到今天。The story of the great King Yu leading his people to try to control floods has been handed down to this very day.|消息很快就～开了。The news has rapidly circulated.

【流窜】liúcuàn 到处流动转徙；乱逃(多指盗匪或敌人 usu. of bandits or enemies) flee; abscond; be on the run：～作案 zigzag about the country committing crimes|追歼～的残匪 pursue and wipe out the remaining wandering bandits

【流弹】liúdàn 乱飞的或无端飞来的子弹 stray bullet; bullet shot at random：为～所伤 hurt by a stray bullet|中(zhòng)～牺牲 be hit and killed by a stray bullet

【流荡】liúdàng ❶ 流动；飘荡 flow; float; move：天空中～着朵朵白云。White clouds float through the sky. ❷ 流浪；飘泊 wander; rove; loaf about; roam about：在外～ wander from place to place

【流动】liúdòng ❶（液体或气体）移动 (of liquid or gas) flow; run; circulate; move：溪水缓缓地～。The stream has a sluggish flow.|空气～就形成风。Circulating air produces wind. ❷ 经常变换位置(跟'固定'相对 as opposed to 'fixed') going from place to place; mobile; on the move：～哨 patrol; person or soldier on patrol duty|～红旗 mobile red banner (awarded to a team, group, etc., for outstanding performance and retained by them until won by another)|～售货车 shop-on-wheels; mobile sales cart|电影放映队常年在农村～。The mobile film projection team goes from place to place giving shows to local farmers all the year round.

【流动资产】liúdòng zīchǎn 在企业的生产经营过程中，经常改变其存在状态的那些资产，例如原料、燃料、在制品、半成品、成品、现金和银行存款等（跟'固定资产'相对 as opposed to 'fixed assets'）current assets; liquid assets; revolving assets; circulating or floating assets; assets that change form within the production and management processes of an enterprise, such as raw materials, fuel, unfinished, semi-finished and finished products, cash, bank deposits, etc.

【流动资金】liúdòng zījīn 企业用以购买原材料、支付工资等的资金(跟'固定资金'相对 as opposed to 'fixed capital') circulating funds (or capital); operating funds; enterprise funds used to purchase raw materials, pay salaries, etc.

【流毒】liúdú ❶ 毒害流传 spread of a pernicious (or baneful) influence：～四方 pernicious influence spreading far and wide; exert a widespread pernicious affect|～无穷 ruthlessly spread an insidious influence ❷ 流传的毒害 pernicious influence; baneful influence; harmful affect：肃清～ root out this pernicious influence|封建礼教的～，千百年来不知戕害了多少青年男女。For thousands of years, countless young men and women fell prey to the baneful influence of the feudal ethical code.

【流芳】liúfāng〈书 *fml*.〉流传美名 leave a good name; leave a reputation：～百世 leave a good name for a hundred generations; leave a good name for posterity; leave a lasting reputation; win immortal fame

【流放】[1] liúfàng 把犯人放逐到边远地方 banish; exile; send (a criminal) into exile (to a remote place)

【流放】[2] liúfàng 把原木放在江河中顺流运输 float (logs) downstream

【流风】liúfēng〈书 *fml*.〉前代流传下来的风尚；遗风 customs handed down from past generations：～遗俗 customs handed down from past generations dating back to ancient times|～余韵 lasting (or remaining) influence of old customs; lingering customs and life styles of past generations

【流光】liúguāng 〈书 *fml.*〉❶ 光阴;岁月 time:～如箭。Time flies (like an arrow).|～易逝。Time flies. *or* Time passes away quickly. ❷ 闪烁流动的光,特指月光 twinkling light, esp. moonlight

【流会】liúhuì 指会议由于不足法定人数而不能举行 (of a meeting) failure to convene for want of a quorum

【流火】liúhuǒ ❶〈方 *dial.*〉丝虫病 filariasis ❷〈中医 *Chin. med.*〉指发病部位在小腿的丹毒 erysipelas of the leg

【流金铄石】liú jīn shuò shí 能使金石熔化 heat that could melt stone and metal;〈比喻 *fig.*〉天气极热(见于《楚辞·招魂》) (of weather) extremely hot (see *The Elegies of Chu · Summons of the Soul*); also 铄石流金 shuò shí liú jīn

【流寇】liúkòu 流窜不定的土匪 roving bandits; roving rebel bands

【流浪】liúlàng 生活没有着落,到处转移,随地谋生 wander; roam about; lead a vagrant's life; be a drifter; move from place to place, living on no assured source of income:～者 tramp; fugitive; vagrant; vagabond|～街头 rove (or roam) the streets

【流离】liúlí 〈书 *fml.*〉由于灾荒战乱而流转离散 become homeless and wander from place to place; live the life of a vagrant (because of famine or war):颠沛～ become homeless and wander from place to place; drift; lead the life of a vagrant|～转徙 drift from place to place as a refugee; wander about and be scattered everywhere

【流离失所】liúlí shī suǒ 到处流浪,没有安身的地方 be forced to leave home and live a vagrant's life; become destitute and homeless

【流丽】liúlì (诗文、书法等)流畅而华美 (of poetry, calligraphy, etc.) smooth and beautiful:文笔～ write smoothly and beautifully|～的音乐 smooth and beautiful music

【流利】liúlì ❶ 话说得快而清楚;文章读起来通畅 speak fluently or glibly; smooth writing style of an article:文章写得～。The article is written in a smooth, eloquent style.|他的英语说得很～。He speaks English fluently. ❷ 灵活;不凝滞 smooth; sleek; fluent:钢笔尖在纸上～地滑动着。The pen glided smoothly over the paper.

【流连】liúlián 留恋不止,舍不得离去 linger on; be reluctant to leave; feel unable to tear oneself away:～忘返 linger on; enjoy oneself so much as to forget to go home; overlook returning; stay on with no thought of leaving; also 留连 liúlián

【流量】liúliàng ❶ 单位时间内,通过河、渠或管道某处断面的流体的量。通常用立方米/秒或公斤/秒来表示。rate of flow; flow; discharge; volume of fluid passing through a section of a river, canal or pipeline within a unit of time, usu. indicated by cubic metre/second or kg./second ❷ 单位时间内,通过一定道路的人员、车辆等的数量 flow of traffic; number of people, vehicles, etc., traveling along a road within a unit of time:旅客～ flow of passengers|交通～ flow of traffic

【流露】liúlù (意思、感情)不自觉地表现出来 (of intent or feeling) reveal; betray; show unintentionally:～出真情 reveal one's true feelings|他的每一首诗,字里行间都～出对祖国的热爱。His love of the motherland is revealed between the lines of each of his poems.

【流落】liúluò 穷困潦倒,漂泊外地 wander about destitute (or homeless); lead a life of wandering poverty:～街头 wander homeless through the streets|～他乡 lead a wretched life far from home; be stranded in a strange land; wander destitute far from home|～江湖 wander from place to place leading a vagabond's life

【流氓】liúmáng ❶ 原指无业游民,后来指不务正业、为非作歹的人 rogue; hooligan; hoodlum; ruffian; rascal; originally referred to a jobless riff-raff, later to a ne'er-do-well with bad intent ❷ 指放刁、撒赖、施展下流手段等恶劣行为 immoral or indecent behaviour; hooliganism; indecency; odious behaviour manifest in delinquency and resorting to base acts:耍～ act indecently; behave like a hooligan; take liberties with women; sexually harass

【流氓无产者】liúmáng wúchǎnzhě 〈旧社会 *pre-1949*〉没有固定职业的一部分人或集团,大都是破产农民和失业的手工业者 lumpen proletariat; certain people or groups that had no regular occupations, mostly comprising bankrupt farmers and jobless artisans; also 游民无产者 yóumín wúchǎnzhě

【流民】liúmín 因遭遇灾害而流亡外地,生活没有着落的人 refugee; exiled person; displaced person; person who has no assured source of living because of a disaster or an exile

【流明】liúmíng 光通量单位,1 国际烛光照射在距离为 1 厘米、面积为 1 平方厘米的平面上的光通量,就是 1 流明 lumen; unit of luminous flux of one international unit of candlepower illuminating a surface distance of one cm. and an area of one sq. cm.; 简称 abbr. 流 liú

【流年】liúnián ❶〈书 *fml.*〉指光阴 fleeting time:似水～ time passing as swiftly as a flow of water ❷ 迷信的人称一年的运道 prediction of a person's luck in a given year:～不利 unlucky year

【流派】liúpài 指学术思想或文艺创作方面的派别 school; sect (of academic thinking or artistic or literary creations)

【流盼】liúpàn 转动目光看 lingering look; sidelong glance: 左右～ cast flirtatious glances here and there

【流气】liú·qì ❶ 轻浮油滑,不正派 rascally; behave in a frivolous, wily and indecent manner: 举止～ rascally behaviour | 歪戴着帽子,耸着肩膀,满脸～ one who looks rakish, wearing his hat askew, and shrugging his shoulders ❷ 流氓习气 rascally behaviour; hooliganism

【流散】liúsàn 流转散失;流落分散 wander about; roam and scatter: 有的文物～国外。Certain cultural relics are scattered throughout various foreign countries. | 当年～在外的灾民陆续返回了家乡。The people scattered and drifting through foreign lands, obliged to wander in poverty, have successfully returned to their homeland.

【流沙】liúshā ❶ 沙漠地区中不固定的、常常随风流动转移的沙 shifting sand; drift sand; quicksand; sand that moves and shifts with the wind in a desert area ❷ 堆积在河底、河口的松散、不稳定的沙 river silt; loose sand at the bottom or mouth of a river ❸ 随地下水流动转移的夹在地层中的沙土 quicksand; mud and sand between layers that moves or shifts with underground water

【流觞】liúshāng 古人每逢农历三月上巳日于弯曲的水渠旁集会,在上游放置酒杯,杯随水流,流到谁面前,谁就取杯把酒喝下,叫做流觞 ancient drinking game in which participants gathered at a winding canal on a specific day of the 3rd lunar month, and placed a full wine cup on the surface of the water of the canal's upper reaches. The gamer before whom the cup stopped after floating along the water should take it up and quaff the wine.

【流失】liúshī ❶ 指自然界的矿石、土壤自己散失或被水、风力带走,也指河水等白白地流掉 run off; be washed away; be eroded; (of minerals, and natural soil) be washed or blown away by water or wind; rivers, etc. flow away in a wasteful manner: 水土～ loss of water and soil erosion | 建造水库蓄积汛期的河水,以免～。At times of heavy rainfall river water is stored up in reservoirs to prevent its loss. ❷ 泛指有用的东西流散失去 loss (of useful things); drain; leaching: 肥效～ leaching of fertility | 抢救～的文物 salvage lost cultural relics ❸〈比喻 *fig.*〉人员离开本地或本单位 (of personnel) leave the locality or unit: 人才～ brain drain

【流失生】liúshīshēng 指中途辍学的没有完成义务教育学业的学生 drop-out; student who leaves school without finishing compulsory education

【流食】liúshí 液体食物,如牛奶、米汤、果汁等 liquid diet (such as milk, thin rice or millet gruel, fruit juice, etc.)

【流矢】liúshǐ 乱飞的或无端飞来的箭 flying or stray arrow: 身中(zhòng)～ be wounded (or hit) by a flying arrow

【流势】liúshì 指水流的快慢和强弱 speed and force (of a water current): 河水～很急。The river flows rapidly. | 洪水经过闸门,～稳定。The flood gushed through the sluice gate.

【流逝】liúshì 像流水一样迅速消逝 (of time) pass; elapse (as rapidly as running water): 时光～ the passage of time | 岁月～。Time passes like running water.

【流水】liúshuǐ ❶ 流动的水,比喻接连不断 running water; (fig.) (continuous) stream: ～作业 flow process; streamlined production; conveyer system; assembly line ❷ 指商店的销货额 turnover (in business of a shop): 本月做了十五万元的～。The shop had a turnover of 150,000 yuan this month.

【流水不腐,户枢不蠹】liúshuǐ bù fǔ, hùshū bù dù 流动的水不会腐臭,经常转动的门轴不会被虫蛀 running water is never stale and a moving door-hinge never gets rusty;〈比喻 *fig.*〉经常运动的东西不易受侵蚀 thing in use does not easily erode

【流水席】liúshuǐxí 客人陆续来到,随到随吃随走的宴客方式 continuous feast — one at which food is individually served to guests as they arrive

【流水线】liúshuǐxiàn 指按流水作业特点所组成的生产程序 assembly line; assembly line production process

【流水账】liúshuǐzhàng ❶ 每天记载金钱或货物出入的、不分类别的账目,也指记流水账的账簿 day-to-day account of transactions, including income and expenditure of cash or incoming and outgoing goods; current account; daybook ❷〈比喻 *fig.*〉不加分析罗列现象的叙述或记载 journal account; account or record of transactions without analysis

【流水作业】liúshuǐ zuòyè 一种生产组织方式,把整个的加工过程分成若干不同的工序,按照顺序像流水似地不断进行 flow process; streamlined operation; assembly line method; conveyer system; organizational method of production whereby the whole manufacturing procedure is divided into different stages that operate in a streamlined fashion

【流苏】liúsū 装在车马、楼台、帐幕等上面的穗状饰物 tassels; fringe; item of decoration seen on carriages, horse bridles, furnishings etc.

【流俗】liúsú 一般的风俗习惯(含贬义 derog.) latest trend; current fad

【流速】liúsù 流体在单位时间内流过的距离,一般用米/秒表示 current speed; current velocity; velocity of flow; flow rate; distance of flow (of liquid) within a unit of time, usu. expressed as metre/second

【流淌】liútǎng 液体流动 (of liquids) flow; run:热血～hot blood running|山泉在石涧中～。The mountain spring flows through the ravine.

【流体】liútǐ 液体和气体的统称,因它们都没有一定的形状,容易流动 fluid; general term for amorphous matter, such as liquids and gases

【流通】liútōng ❶ 流转通行;不停滞 (of air, money, commodities, etc.) circulate; flow: 空气～ air circulation ❷ 指商品、货币流转 circulation (of commodities or currencies)

【流亡】liúwáng 因灾害或政治原因而被迫离开家乡或祖国 be forced to leave one's hometown or native land (owing to a natural disaster or for political reasons); go into exile: ～海外 go into (or live in) exile abroad|～政府 government-in-exile

【流网】liúwǎng 渔网的一种,由许多片网连接成长带形放在水中直立呈墙状,随水流飘移,把游动的鱼挂住或缠住,用来捕捞各种水层的鱼类 drift net; flow net; a kind of fishing net shaped like a long belt with many segments, that stands erect in the water like a wall, moving with the water currents, and is used to catch fish swimming in different depths water

【流徙】liúxǐ ❶ 到处流动转徙,没有安定的生活 wander about; float about; drift about; lead an unstable life, moving from place to place ❷〈书 *fml.*〉same as 流放 liúfàng:～边远 be exiled to a remote frontier region

【流线型】liúxiànxíng 前圆后尖,表面光滑,略像水滴的形状。具有这种形状的物体在流体中运动时所受阻力最小,所以汽车、火车、飞机机身、潜水艇等的外形常做成流线型。streamlined; line of flow; shape that resembles a drop of water, being round at the front and pointed at the back, with a smooth surface; objects of this shape meet with the least resistance when moving through fluid, so cars, trains, plane fuselages, submarines, etc., are generally streamlined

【流向】liúxiàng ❶ 水流的方向 (of water) direction of current: 地下水也有一定的～。Underground water also flows in a specific direction. ❷ 指人员、货物等的流动去向 (of people, cargo, etc.) flow: 掌握旅客的～ascertain the direction of passenger flow|重视人才的～问题 pay attention to orientation of talents|确定商品的合理～ define the rational flow of commodities

【流泻】liúxiè (液体、光线等)迅速地流出、射出、跑过 (of liquid, light, etc.) pour out; gush out; emit: 泉水从山涧里～出来。Spring water flows from a mountain brook.|一缕阳光～进来。A gleam of sunshine poured into the room.

【流星】[1] liúxīng 分布在星际空间的细小物体和尘粒,叫做流星体。它们飞入地球大气层,跟大气摩擦发生热和光,这种现象叫流星。通常所说的流星指这种短时间发光的流星体。meteor; shooting star; luminous phenomenon observed when any of the many small bodies and dust particles travelling through the outer space, or a meteoroid emitting heat and light from friction with earth's atmosphere. The meteor usually seen is the meteoric shower. 俗称 popularly known as 贼星 zéixīng

【流星】[2] liúxīng ❶ 古代兵器,在铁链的两端各系一个铁锤 ancient weapon, composed of two iron hammers fixed on an iron chain ❷ 杂技的一种,在长绳的两端拴上盛着水的碗或火球,用手摆动绳子,使水碗或火球在空中飞舞 (in acrobatics) juggling with meteors; bowls of water or fireballs tied at both ends of a long string and look like meteors when an acrobat swings the string to set bowls or balls flying in the air

【流星赶月】liúxīng gǎn yuè 形容非常迅速,好像流星追赶月亮一样 meteoric; quickly; moving as quickly as a meteor running closely after the moon: 他～似地奔向渡口。He ran to the ferry like a meteor running after the moon.

【流星雨】liúxīngyǔ 短时间内出现许多流星的现象 meteor (or meteoric) shower; luminous phenomenon when a group of meteoroids, possibly the debris left by the passage of a comet, enter the earth's atmosphere in a short period of time

【流刑】liúxíng〈古代 *arch.*〉把犯人押送到边远地方服劳役的刑罚 punishment of banishment to remote areas

【流行】liúxíng 广泛传布;盛行 popular; prevalent; fashionable; in vogue; be about: ～性感冒 influenza; flu|这首民歌在我们家乡很～。This folk song is very popular in our home town.

【流行病】liúxíngbìng ❶ 能在较短的时间内广泛蔓延的传染病,如流行性感冒、脑膜炎、霍乱等 epidemic disease; disease that spreads quickly among people, as influenza, meningitis, cholera, etc. ❷〈比喻 *fig.*〉广泛流传的社会弊病 widely spread social malpractice

【流行歌曲】liúxíng gēqǔ ❶ 在一定时期内受到普遍欢迎,广泛传唱的歌曲 song that becomes very popular in a given period ❷ 指通俗歌曲 pop song; pop music; pop

【流行色】liúxíngsè 在一定时期内被人们普遍喜爱的颜色(多指服装 oft. of clothing) fashionable colour

【流血】liúxuè 特指牺牲生命或负伤 die a heroic death or get wounded; lose blood; shed blood; bleed: ～惨案 bloodshed massacre | ～斗争 sanguinary struggle | ～牺牲 shed blood and lay down one's life for a just cause

【流言】liúyán 没有根据的话(多指背后议论、诬蔑或挑拨的话 oft. referring to remarks made behind sb.'s back, or scandalous or provocative words) rumour; gossip: ～飞语 rumour and slander | ～惑众 fabricate rumours to mislead people | 散布～ spread rumours

【流溢】liúyì 充满而流出来;漫溢 overflowing: 泉水～ overflowing spring water | 园中百花竞艳,芳香～。The flowers are in full bloom, spreading fragrance all over the garden.

【流萤】liúyíng 指飞行不定的萤火虫 flying firefly: 几点～,上下飞舞。Some fireflies are dancing up and down.

【流域】liúyù 一个水系的干流和支流所流过的整个地区,如长江流域、黄河流域、珠江流域 river valley; river basin; drainage area; all the land drained by a river and its tributaries, as the Yangtze River basin, the Yellow River basin and the Pearl River basin

【流质】liúzhì 医疗上指食物是属于液体的,也指液体的食物 liquid diet for patients; liquid food

【流转】liúzhuǎn ❶ 流动转移,不固定在一个地方 wander about; roam; be on the move: 岁月～。How time flies! | ～四方 wander all over the country | ～的眼波 eyes as bright as the ripples on the lake ❷ 指商品或资金在流通过程中的周转 (of goods or capital) circulate ❸〈书 *fml.*〉指诗文等流畅而圆浑 (of writings, poems, etc.) smooth; flowing; fluent: 诗笔～ fluent style of poem writing | 声调和谐～ mellow and harmonious tone

琉(瑠)

liú ☞ below

【琉璃】liú·li 用铝和钠的硅酸化合物烧制成的釉料,常见的有绿色和金黄色两种,多加在黏土的外层,烧制成缸、盆、砖瓦等 coloured glaze; glaze made from aluminium silicate or sodium silicate, green or golden, used to coat the outer surface of an earthen ware, as jar, basin, tile, brick, etc.

【琉璃球】liú·liqiú (～儿 liú·liqiúr) ❶ 儿童玩具,琉璃质的小球 small glass ball used as a children's toy; small glazed ball ❷〈比喻 *fig.*〉人聪明伶俐 clever; quick-witted ❸〈比喻 *fig.*〉油滑、奸诈的人 sly person; crafty person; foxy person ❹〈比喻 *fig.*〉吝啬的人 mean person; miserly person; miser; niggard; skinflint: 那人是个～,一毛不拔。He is a miser and would even skin a flint.

【琉璃瓦】liú·liwǎ 内层用较好的黏土,表面用琉璃烧制成的瓦。形状和普通瓦相似而略长,外部多呈绿色或金黄色,鲜艳发光,多用来修盖宫殿或庙宇等 glazed tile; tile made from good clay and coated by glaze, green or golden, bright and glossy, looking like an ordinary tile but slightly longer; used mainly for roofs of palaces and temples

硫

liú 非金属元素,符号 S (sulphur)。有多种同素异形体,黄色,能与氧、氢、卤素(除碘外)和大多数金属化合。用来制造硫酸、火药、火柴、硫化橡胶、杀虫剂等,也用来治疗皮肤病。sulphur (S); pale-yellow, nonmetallic chemical element with many allotropes, which can be compounded with oxygen, hydrogen, halogens (with the exception of iodine) and most of the metals, and is used in making sulphuric acid, fire powder, matches, vulcanized rubber, and insecticides and in the treatment of skin diseases; 通称 commonly called 硫磺 liúhuáng

【硫化】liúhuà 把生橡胶、硫磺和炭黑等填料放在容器里,通入高压蒸气加热,使变成硫化橡胶 vulcanize; process of treating crude rubber with sulphur, carbon black or its compounds and subjecting it to high pressure steam heat in order to make it nonplastic and increase its strength and elasticity

【硫化橡胶】liúhuà xiàngjiāo 经过硫化的橡胶,弹性较好,耐热,不易折断,橡胶制品大都用这种橡胶制成 vulcanized rubber; vulcanized rubber has a better elasticity and is resistant tc heat and not apt to break. Most rubber products are made of vulcanized rubber. also 熟橡胶 shúxiàngjiāo; 通称 commonly called 橡皮 xiàngpí or 胶皮 jiāopí

【硫磺】liúhuáng 硫的通称 common name for 硫 liú

【硫酸】liúsuān 无机化合物,化学式 H_2SO_4。无色油状液体,含杂质时为黄色或棕色,是一种强酸,用来制造肥料、染料、炸药、医药品等,也用于石油工业和冶金工业。sulphuric acid (H_2SO_4), an inorganic compound in the form of a colourless oily liquid that turns yellow or brown when it contains foreign matters, used as a strong acid in making fertilizers, dyestuffs, explosive, drugs, etc. as well as in the petroleum and metallurgical industries.

遛

liú ☞ 逗遛 (dòuliú) on p. 475

☞ liù on p. 1247

馏

liú 蒸馏 distil

☞ liù on p. 1248

【馏分】liúfèn 分馏石油、煤焦油等液体时,在一定温度范围内蒸馏出来的成分。分馏石油,温度在 50－200℃ 之间的馏分是汽油,温度在 200—310℃ 之间的馏分是煤油。fraction, a part separated when petroleum, coal tar or other liquid is distilled within a given range of temperature: gasoline at the temperature of 50-200℃ and kerosene at the temperature of 200-300℃

旒 liú ❶〈书 *fml.*〉旗子上的飘带 streamer; ribbon on a flag ❷〈古代 *arch.*〉帝王礼帽前后的玉串 jade pendants on a crown: 冕～ emperor's ceremonial crown with tassels hanging on its front

骝 liú 古书上指黑鬣黑尾巴的红马 red horse with black hair on its neck and a black tail as described in ancient books

榴 liú 石榴 pomegranate

【榴弹】liúdàn ❶ 一种依靠炸药爆炸后产生的碎片、冲击波来杀伤或摧毁目标的炮弹 high explosive shell; shell that wounds or kills people or destroys an object with the fragments and blast wave after explosion; 旧称 formerly called 开花弹 kāihuādàn ❷ 泛指手榴弹、花榴弹和用炮发射的榴弹 general term for hand grenade, fragmentation shell and shells fired by cannons

【榴弹炮】liúdànpào 炮身较短、初速小、弹道弯曲的火炮,可用来射击各种地形上不同性质的目标 howitzer; short cannon firing shells at a small initial velocity and in a high trajectory, used to attack objects of different nature in all terrains

【榴火】liúhuǒ〈书 *fml.*〉石榴花的火红的颜色 fiery red; colour of pomegranate blossoms

【榴霰弹】liúxiàndàn 炮弹的一种,弹壁薄,内装黑色炸药和小钢球、钢柱、钢箭等,弹头装有定时的引信,能在预定的目标上空及其附近爆炸,杀伤敌方的密集人马 shrapnel; canister (shot); case shot; artillery shell filled with an explosive charge and many small steel balls, steel columns and steel arrows. It can explode in the air over the target or in its vicinity to destroy densely deployed enemy troops. also 霰弹 xiàndàn, 子母弹 zǐmǔdàn and 群子弹 qúnzǐdàn

飗 liú [飗飗]〈书 *fml.*〉微风吹动的样子 blowing of a gentle breeze

镏 liú [镏金](liújīn)把溶解在水银里的金子用刷子涂在器物表面,用来装饰器物 plating of tableware with gold dissolved in mercury

☞ liù on p. 1248

鹠 liú ☞ [鸺鹠](xiūliú) on p. 2159

瘤 liú 瘤子 tumour: 毒～ malignant tumour; cancer | 肉～ sarcoma

【瘤胃】liúwèi 反刍动物的胃的第一部分,内壁有很多瘤状突起。食物先在瘤胃里消化,再入蜂巢胃。rumen first stomach of a ruminant, with many tumour-like swellings on the inner wall. Food is first digested in the rumen before entering into the reticulum or honeycomb stomach.

【瘤子】liú·zi 肿瘤 tumour

镠 liú〈书 *fml.*〉成色好的金子 gold of fine quality

鎏 liú〈书 *fml.*〉❶ 成色好的金子 gold of fine quality ❷ same as 镏 liú

liǔ (ㄌㄧㄡˇ)

柳 liǔ ❶ 柳树,落叶乔木或灌木,叶子狭长,柔荑花序,种类很多,有垂柳、旱柳等 willow (*Salix*); deciduous tree or shrub, having narrow leaves, single, slipper-shaped bud scales, and staminate and pistillate catkins, in many strains, such as weeping willow (*Salix babylonica*), dry land willow (*Salix matsudana*), etc. ❷ 二十八宿之一 one of the 28 lunar mansions ❸ (Liǔ)姓 a surname

【柳暗花明】liǔ àn huā míng 形容柳树成阴,繁花耀眼的美景。宋代陆游有'山重水复疑无路,柳暗花明又一村'的诗句,后多用来比喻在困境中看到希望。beautiful scene of shady willows and blooming flowers; 'When surrounded by mountain ranges and girdled by winding river, I doubt of any road ahead; but after seeing the shady willows and blooming flowers, I come to another village.' — lines from a poem by Lu You of the Song Dynasty, now quoted to indicate hope when one is in difficulties.

【柳编】liǔbiān 用柳条编制的工艺品,如果篮、提篮、食品筐等 wickerwork, as fruit basket, food basket, etc.

【柳罐】liǔguàn 用柳条编成的斗状的汲水器具 wicker bucket

【柳眉】liǔméi 指女子细长秀美的眉毛 arched eyebrows (of a woman): ～杏眼 willow leaf-like eyebrows and apricot-like eyes; graceful eyebrows and large eyes | ～倒竖(形容女子发怒时耸眉的样子)(of a woman) raise eyebrows in anger; look angry; also 柳叶眉 liǔyèméi

【柳绵】liǔmián same as 柳絮 liǔxù; also 柳棉 liǔmián

【柳腔】liǔqiāng 山东地方戏曲剧种之一,流行于青岛及附近地区 local opera popular in Qingdao and its neighbouring areas in Shandong Province

【柳琴】liǔqín 弦乐器,外形像琵琶,比琵琶小,有四根弦 *liuqin*; plucked four-stringed instrument that looks like a *pipa* of a smaller size

【柳丝】liǔsī 指垂柳细长的枝条 drooping willow twigs

【柳体】Liǔ tǐ 唐代柳公权所写的字体,笔画遒劲,较颜体为瘦 Liu style (a calligraphic style created by Liu Gongquan of the Tang Dynasty) characterized by forceful strokes, thinner than the Yan style

【柳条】liǔtiáo (～儿 liǔtiáor)柳树的枝条,特指杞柳的枝条,可以编筐、篮子等 willow twig;

osier; wicker; it is used in weaving baskets

【柳条帽】liǔtiáomào 用柳条编成的安全帽,轻而结实 wicker safety helmet, which is light and sturdy

【柳絮】liǔxù 柳树种子上面像棉絮的白色绒毛,随风飞散 willow catkins; cotton-like white down, easy to be carried about by the wind

【柳腰】liǔyāo 指女子柔软的细腰 (of a woman) willowy (or slender) waist

【柳子】[1] liǔ·zi 指杞柳 Japanese pussy willow (*Salix multinervis*):一墩～ a clump of willow trees

【柳子】[2] liǔ·zi 柳子戏的主要曲牌 *liuzi*, a major tune in the *liuzi* opera

【柳子戏】liǔ·zixì 山东地方戏曲剧种之一,流行于山东西部和江苏北部、河南东部一带 local opera popular in western Shandong, northern Jiangsu and eastern Henan; also 弦子戏 xuánzixì

绺 liǔ ❶(～儿 liǔr)〈量词 *classifier*〉线、麻、头发、胡须等许多根顺着聚在一起叫一绺 tuft; skein; lock; wisp (of thread, hemp, hair, beard, etc.):一～丝线 a skein of silk thread|三～儿头发 three locks of hair ❷〈方 *dial*.〉绺窃 steal; steal from pockets:路上不小心,钱包让人～去了。The purse was stolen on the road due to my carelessness.

【绺窃】liǔqiè〈方 *dial*.〉从别人身上偷窃财物 steal from sb.'s pocket

【绺子】[1] liǔ·zi 绺儿 tuft:一～头发 a lock of hair

【绺子】[2] liǔ·zi〈方 *dial*.〉土匪帮伙 bandits; gansters

锍 liǔ 有色金属硫化物的互熔体,是铜、镍等冶炼过程中的中间产品。锍中含有贵重金属。matte; impure mixture of sulphides and an intermediate product from smelting the sulphide ores of copper, nickel, etc.

罶(罞) liǔ〈书 *fml*.〉捕鱼的竹篓子,鱼进去就出不来 fishing basket or cage which allows fish to swim in but not out

liù(ㄌㄧㄡˋ)

六[1] liù〈数目 *numeral*〉五加一后所得 six; sum of five plus one; ☞ 数字 shùzì on p.1791

六[2] liù 我国民族音乐音阶上的一级,乐谱上用做记音符号,相当于简谱的'5' note of the musical scale in the traditional Chinese music, corresponding to 5 in the numbered musical notation; ☞ 工尺 gōngchě on p.664

☞ lù on p.1259

【六部】liùbù 从隋唐开始,中国封建王朝的中央行政机构一般分为吏、户、礼、兵、刑、工各部,统称六部 Six Ministries, which formed the central government in the feudal dynasties since the Sui and Tang dynasties, arranged in order of importance: 吏部 Lìbù Ministry of Personnel, 户部 Hùbù Board of Revenues *or* Ministry of Finance 礼部 Lǐbù Ministry of Rites, 兵部 Bīngbù Ministry of War, 刑部 Xíngbù Ministry of Justice, and 工部 Gōngbù Ministry of Works

【六朝】Liù Cháo ❶ 吴、东晋、宋、齐、梁、陈,先后建都于建康(吴称建业,今南京),合称六朝 Six Dynasties; the Wu, Eastern Jin, Song, Qi, Liang and Chen between the downfall of the Han Dynasty in 220 and the reunification of China in 589, which all had their capital city in Jiankang (Nanjing of today) ❷ 泛指南北朝时期 the Northern and Southern Dynasties (420-589):～文 literary style of the Six Dynasties; rhythmical prose style with special emphasis on the art of parallelism|～书法 calligraphy of the Six Dynasties; ☞ 南北朝 Nán-Běi Cháo on p.1388

【六畜】liùchù 指猪、牛、羊、马、鸡、狗,也泛指各种家畜、家禽 six domestic animals (pig, ox, goat, horse, poultry and dog); all domestic animals and poultry:五谷丰登,～兴旺。An abundant harvest of all food crops accompanies the thriving of all domestic animals.

【六腑】liùfǔ〈中医 *Chin. med*.〉称胃、胆、三焦、膀胱、大肠、小肠为六腑 six hollow organs of stomach, gall bladder, *sanjiao*, bladder, large intestines and small intestines

【六根】liùgēn〈佛教 *Budd*.〉指眼、耳、鼻、舌、身、意,认为这六者是罪孽的根源 six root sources of sins — eyes, ears, nose, tongue, body and mind as regarded in Buddhism:～清净 be free from human desires and passions

【六合】liùhé〈书 *fml*.〉指上下和东西南北四方,泛指天下或宇宙 six directions — north, south, east, west, the above and the below; world; universe

【六甲】liùjiǎ ❶〈古代 *arch*.〉用甲、乙、丙、丁、戊、己、庚、辛、壬、癸十干和子、丑、寅、卯、辰、巳、午、未、申、酉、戌、亥十二支依次相配成六十组干支,其中起头是'甲'字的有六组,故称六甲。因笔画比较简单,多为儿童练字之用。six *jia*-headed Stem-Branch pairs; 60 Stem-Branch pairs formed alternately by the 10 Heavenly Stems of *jia*, *yi*, *bing*, *ding*, *wu*, *ji*, *geng*, *xin*, *ren*, *gui* and the 12 Earthly Branches of *zi*, *chou*, *yin*, *mao*, *chen*, *si*, *wu*, *wei*, *shen*, *you*, *xu*, *hai*. There are six pairs each beginning with *jia*, hence the six *jia*-headed Stem-Branch pairs. As these characters have fewer strokes, it is easier for children to practise calligraphy:学～ learn calligraphy ❷〈旧时 *old*〉妇女怀孕称身怀六甲 (a woman) be pregnant

【六路】liùlù 指上、下、前、后、左、右。泛指周围、各个方面 above, below, front, rear, left and right; around; all aspects:眼观～,耳听八方 have sharp eyes and keen ears; be observant and watchful

【六轮】liùlún 转轮手枪的一种,转轮上有六个装子弹的孔 revolver with six cartridges

【六亲】liùqīn 六种亲属,究竟指哪些亲属说法不一,较早的一种说法是指父、母、兄、弟、妻、子。泛指亲属 six relations; opinions are divided on which are the six relations, but one of the earliest versions are father, mother, elder brothers, younger brothers, wife, children; one's kin:～不认 unsympathetic; impersonal

【六亲不认】liùqīn bù rèn 形容人没有情义或不讲情面 refuse to recognize one's closest relatives and friends; refuse to have anything to do with all one's relatives and friends; disown all one's relatives and friends; be unfeeling, cold or arrogant

【六壬】liùrén 〈旧时 *old*〉一种占卜方法,用阴阳五行来推算吉凶祸福(六十组干支中,起头是'壬'字的有六组,故称六壬) six *ren*-headed Stem-Branch pairs; a kind of divination by which *yin* and *yang* and the five elements of metal, wood, water, fire and earth are used to tell one's good luck, ill luck, misfortune and fortune. (Among the 60 pairs of Heavenly Stems and Earthly Branches, there are six pairs beginning with *ren*, hence the 'six *ren*-headed Stem-Branch pairs'.) It refers to divination:精于～ good at practising divination

【六神】liùshén 古人指主宰心、肺、肝、肾、脾、胆六脏之神,泛指心神 gods believed by ancient Chinese to govern the six internal organs of heart, lungs, liver, kidneys, spleen and gallbladder; mind; state of mind:～不安 have no peace of mind; be distracted|～无主 have no peace of mind; be distracted

【六神无主】liù shén wú zhǔ 形容惊慌或着急而没有主意 distracted; be frightened out of one's wits; be at a loss what to do

【六书】liùshū 古人分析汉字而归纳出来的六种条例,即指事、象形、形声、会意、转注、假借 six categories of Chinese characters summarized by ancient Chinese: self-explanatory, pictographic, pictographic-phonetic, ideographic, mutually explanatory, phonetic loan

【六弦琴】liùxiánqín 弦乐器,有六根弦。一手按弦,一手拨弦。 guitar; six-stringed musical instrument plucked or strummed with the fingers or a plectrum; also 吉他 jítā

【六一儿童节】Liù-Yī Értóng Jié 全世界儿童的节日。国际民主妇女联合会为保障全世界儿童的权利,反对帝国主义者对儿童的虐杀和毒害,于1949年在莫斯科举行的会议上,决定以6月1日为国际儿童节。International Children's Day (June 1); the day of the children throughout the world. In order to safeguard the rights of the children throughout the world and oppose the killing and poisoning of children by imperialists, the International Democratic Women's Federation made a decision at a meeting held in Moscow in 1949, in which June 1 was adopted as the International Children's Day; also 六一国际儿童节 Liù-Yī-Guójì Értóng Jié, 国际儿童节 Guójì Értóng Jié or 儿童节 Értóng Jié

【六艺】liùyì ❶〈古代 *arch.*〉指礼(礼仪)、乐(音乐)、射(射箭)、御(驾车)、书(识字)、数(计算)等六种科目 six arts: rites, music, archery, charioteering, reading and writing, and arithmetic ❷〈古代 *arch.*〉指《诗》、《书》、《礼》、《乐》、《易》、《春秋》六种儒家经书 six classics: *The Book of Songs*, *Classic of Documents*, *The Book of Rites*, *The Book of Music*, *The Book of Changes*, and *The Spring and Autumn Annals*

【六欲】liùyù 〈佛教 *Budd.*〉指色欲、形貌欲等六种欲望,泛指人的各种欲望 six desires originating from six senses — eyes, ears, nose, tongue, body and mind; six attractions arising from colour, form, carriage, voice, softness and features:七情～ the seven human emotions of joy, anger, sorrow, fear, love, hate and desire and the six desires of colour, form, carriage, voice, softness and features

【六指儿】liùzhǐr ❶ 长了六个指头的手或脚 six-fingered hand or six-toed foot ❷ 有六指儿的人 person with a six-fingered hand

陆(陸) liù '六'的大写 six (complicated written form of the numeral 六 liù to be used when writing out cheques, receipts, etc. to avoid mistakes or alterations);
☞ 数字 shùzì on p.1791
☞ lù on p.1259

碌 liù [碌碡](liù·zhóu)农具,用石头做成,圆柱形,用来轧谷物,平场地 stone roller; farm implement made of stone in the form of a cylinder used for threshing grains or levelling a threshing ground; also 石磙 shígǔn
☞ lù on p.1261

遛 liù ❶ 慢慢走;散步 saunter; stroll:～大街 stroll around the streets; go window-shopping|闷得慌,出去～～。I feel bored, so let's go for a walk.|下午到市场～了一趟。I walked around in the market in the afternoon. ❷ 牵着牲畜或带着鸟慢慢走 walk an animal or bird:～鸟 take a walk with one's pet bird|～狗 walk a dog|～一～马 walk a horse
☞ liú on p.1244

【遛马】liù//mǎ 牵着马慢慢走,使马解除疲劳或减轻病势 walk a horse to relieve it from fatigue or alleviate its physical conditions

【遛鸟】liù//niǎo 带着鸟到幽静的地方去溜达 take a walk with pet birds in a park or a quiet places

【遛食】liù//shí 〈方 *dial.*〉(～儿 liù//shír)饭后散步,帮助消化 take a walk after a meal to aid digestion

【遛弯儿】liù//wānr 散步 take a walk; go for a stroll: 您到哪儿～去啦? Where did you go for a walk? | 晚饭后到公园遛了个弯儿。I went for a stroll in the park after supper. also 蹓弯儿 liù//wānr

【遛早儿】liùzǎor 早晨散步 take a morning stroll; also 蹓早儿 liùzǎor

馏 liù 把凉了的熟食蒸热 steam cooked food that has turned cold: ～馒头 heat up the steamed buns | 把剩菜～一～再吃 eat the leftovers after heating them

☞ liú on p. 1244

溜[1] (❸❹ 霤) liù ❶ 迅速的水流 swift current: 大～ strong current | 河里～很大。The river has a strong current. ❷〈方 *dial.*〉迅速;敏捷 swift; fast; quick: 眼尖手～ sharp-eyed and quick-limbed | 走得很～ walk very fast (or quickly) ❸ 房顶上流下来的雨水 rainwater from the roof: 檐～ eaves gutter | 承～ a gutter; a spout to take rainwater ❹ 檐沟 eaves gutter: 水～ rainwater pipe; pipe for guiding rainwater down from the eaves ❺ (～儿 liùr)排;条 line; column; row: 一～三间房 a row of three-room houses ❻ (～儿 liùr)某一地点附近的地方 surroundings; neighbourhood: 这～的果木树很多。There are plenty of fruit trees in this neighbourhood. ❼〈方 *dial.*〉练 practise: ～嗓子 train one's voice; exercise one's voice; practise singing

溜[2] liù〈方 *dial.*〉用石灰、水泥等抹(墙缝);堵、糊(缝隙) point; fill or refill the joints of a brick wall; fill (a crevice, fissure, etc.) with lime, cement, etc.: 墙砌好了,就剩下～缝了。The wall has been built and the remaining work is to point up. | 天冷了,拿纸条把窗户缝～上。It's cold now. Seal up the window crevices with paper slips.

☞ liū on p. 1236

【溜子】[1] liù·zi 矿井中的槽形传送工具 scraper-trough conveyer

【溜子】[2] liù·zi〈方 *dial.*〉土匪帮伙 bandits; gansters

【溜子】[3] liù·zi〈方 *dial.*〉迅速的水流 swift flow

镏 liù [镏子](liù·zi)〈方 *dial.*〉戒指 finger ring: 金～ gold ring

☞ liú on p. 1245

磟 liù [磟碡](liù·zhóu) same as 碌碡 liù·zhóu

鹨 liù 鸟类的一属,身体较小,嘴细长,尾巴长,常见的有田鹨 pipit (*Anthus*); small bird with a long, slender bill and a long tail. A common breed is the field pipit.

蹓 liù 慢慢走;散步 saunter; stroll: ～大街 stroll around the streets; go window-shopping | 到公园去～一～。Go for a stroll in the park.

☞ liū on p. 1237

【蹓弯儿】liù//wānr same as 遛弯儿 liù//wānr

【蹓早儿】liùzǎor same as 遛早儿 liùzǎor

·lo (·ㄌㄛ)

咯 ·lo〈助词 *auxu.*〉用法如'了'(·le)②,语气较重 of the same usage as 了②, but in a more emphatic tone: 当然～。Of course.

☞ gē on p. 649, kǎ on p. 1069 and luò on p. 1280

lōng (ㄌㄨㄥ)

隆 lōng ☞ 黑咕隆咚 hēi·gulōngdōng on p. 773

☞ lóng on p. 1251

lóng (ㄌㄨㄥˊ)

龙(龍) lóng ❶ 我国古代传说中的神异动物,身体长,有鳞,有角,有脚,能走,能飞,能游泳,能兴云降雨 dragon; mythological animal with a long body, scales, horns, wings and feet, which could walk, fly, swim and gather clouds to pour down rain ❷ 封建时代用龙作为帝王的象征,也把龙字用在帝王使用的东西上 The dragon was a symbol of the emperor in feudal China. The character was also affixed to things used by the emperor: ～颜 the face of the emperor; the look of the emperor | ～廷 imperial court | ～袍 imperial robe | ～床 the emperor's bed ❸ 形状像龙的或装有龙的图案的 shaped like a dragon; with the design of a dragon: ～舟 dragon boat | ～灯 dragon lantern; dragon-shaped lantern | ～车 imperial chariot | ～旗 imperial banner ❹ 古生物学上指古代某些爬行动物,如恐龙、翼手龙等 (of palaeontology) ancient reptiles such as dinosaur, pterodactyl, etc. ❺ (Lóng)姓 a surname

【龙齿】lóngchǐ 指古代某些哺乳动物牙齿的化石,中医入药 fossils of the teeth of some mammals in ancient times, now used in the Chinese traditional medicine

【龙船】lóngchuán 装饰成龙形的船,有的地区端午节用来举行划船竞赛 dragon boat; dragon-shaped racing boat; racing boat decorated in the shape of a dragon for boat races on the fifth day of the fifth month of the lunar calendar in some regions

【龙灯】lóngdēng 民间舞蹈用具,用布或纸做成的龙形的灯,灯架由许多环节构成,每节下面有一根棍子。表演时每人举着一节,同时舞动,用锣鼓伴奏 dragon lantern; long chain of lanterns made of cloth or paper, the first decorated in the shape of the dragon's head and the last in the shape of the dragon's tail. The frame of the Chain consists of many connected segments. Each lantern has a stick underneath and is held and waved by a person during the performance to the accompaniment of gongs and drums: 耍～ dragon dance

【龙洞】lóngdòng 天然的山洞,是石灰岩被含有碳酸气的水溶解而部分消失后形成的 dragon's cave; limestone cave; natural cave formed out of limestone due to erosion caused by water containing carbon dioxide

【龙飞凤舞】lóng fēi fèng wǔ 形容山势蜿蜒雄壮,也形容书法笔势舒展活泼 (of mountains or calligraphy) like dragons flying and phoenixes dancing; lively and vigorous flourishes in calligraphy; flamboyant style of calligraphy

【龙宫】lónggōng 神话传说中龙王的宫殿 legendary palace of the Dragon King

【龙骨】lónggǔ ❶ 鸟类的胸骨,善于飞翔的鸟类这块骨头形成较高的突起 bird's sternum, protruding high in birds particularly strong at flying ❷ 指古代某些哺乳动物骨骼的化石,如象、犀牛等。可入药。fossil fragments of the bones of some ancient mammals, such as elephant, rhinoceros, etc., of medicinal value ❸ 船只、飞机、建筑物等的像脊椎和肋骨那样的支撑和承重结构 keel; anything resembling a keel; spine-like or ridge-like supporting structure of a ship, airplane, a building, etc.

【龙骨车】lónggǔchē 一种木制的水车,带水的木板用木榫连接成环带以戽水,多用人力或畜力转动 dragon-bone water lift; square-pallet chain-pump pedalled or pulled by one or two persons

【龙井】lóngjǐng 绿茶的一种。形状扁平而直,色泽翠绿,产于浙江杭州龙井一带。*longjing* tea; Dragon Well tea, a famous green tea produced around the Dragon Well in Hangzhou, Zhejiang Province

【龙江剧】lóngjiāngjù 黑龙江地方戏曲剧种,在曲艺二人转的基础上吸收当地民间音乐发展而成 Longjiang opera, local opera in Heilongjiang Province; local opera developed on the basis of a song-and-dance duet popular in northeast China and absorbing local folk music

【龙卷风】lóngjuǎnfēng 风力极强而范围不大的旋风,形状像一个大漏斗,风速往往达到每秒一百多米,破坏力极大。在陆地上,能把大树连根拔起,毁坏各种建筑物和农作物;在海洋上,能把海水吸到空中,形成水柱。tornado; violently whirling column of air, with wind speeds of more than 100 metres per second, almost always seen as a rapidly rotating, slender, funnel-shaped cloud that usually uproots large trees and destroys everything on the land, and sucks sea water to form a water pillar in the air along its narrow path

【龙马精神】lóngmǎ jīngshén 唐代李郢《上裴晋公》诗:'四朝忧国鬓如丝,龙马精神海鹤姿。'后用来比喻健旺的精神。'Hoary as he is after serving four emperors, / He still looks like a dragon horse and stands like a crane.' The lines are quoted from the poem *To Duke Pei of Jin State* by Li Ying of the Tang Dynasty. The phrase refers to vigorous spirit.

【龙门刨】lóngménbào 刨床的一种,机床的立柱和横梁结构形状像门,用来加工较大的平面。加工时工件固定在工作台上做往复运动,刨刀做相应的间歇运动切削。double housing planer; planing machine with its beam-column structure shaped like a gate, used to process large planes. The workpiece is fixed on the working table and made to move backward and forward while the planer does intermittent cutting.

【龙门吊】lóngméndiào 一种大型起重机,横梁和立柱的结构成'门'字形,可以在轨道上移动,具有较大的起重量 gantry crane; crane with its beam-column structured shaped like a gate, which travels on rails and lifts heavy weights

【龙门阵】lóngménzhèn ☞ 摆龙门阵 bǎi lóngménzhèn on p. 43

【龙盘虎踞】lóng pán hǔ jù ☞ 虎踞龙盘 hǔ jù lóng pán on p. 821

【龙山文化】Lóngshān wénhuà 我国新石器时代晚期的一种文化,晚于仰韶文化,因最早发现于山东济南附近龙山镇而得名。遗物中常有黑而亮的陶器,所以也曾称为黑陶文化。Longshan Culture; Black-Pottery Culture; late Neolithic culture which was later than the Yangshao culture and is characterized by a burnished black pottery; named after Longshan, Shandong Province, where remains were first found in 1928

【龙生九子】lóng shēng jiǔ zǐ 古代传说,一龙所生的九条小龙,形状性格都不相同 according to an ancient legend, the dragon had nine sons and each of them was different from the others in form and character; 〈比喻 *fig.*〉同胞弟兄志趣各有差别,并不一样 brothers born of the same parents differ from each other; also 龙生九种 lóng shēngjiǔ zhǒng

【龙潭虎穴】lóng tán hǔ xué 〈比喻 *fig.*〉危险的境地 dragon's pool and tiger's den; danger spot; also 虎穴龙潭 hǔ xué lóng tán

【龙套】lóngtào ❶ 传统戏曲中成队的随从或兵卒所穿的戏装,因绣有龙纹而得名 costume with dragon designs, worn by groups of soldiers or attendants in traditional opera ❷ 穿龙套的演员,也指这样的角色 actor wearing such costume or playing a walk-on part in traditional opera

【龙腾虎跃】lóng téng hǔ yuè 形容威武雄壮,非常活跃 full of power and grandeur like dragons rising and tigers leaping; scene of bustling activity: 工地上～,热火朝天。There are bustling activities on the construction site; also 虎跃龙腾 hǔ yuè lóng téng

【龙头】[1] lóngtóu ❶ 自来水管的放水活门,有旋转装置可以打开或关上。龙头也用在其他液体容器上。water tap; faucet; device with a hand-operated valve for regulating the flow of a liquid from a pipe, barrel, etc; cock ❷〈方 *dial.*〉自行车的把(bǎ) handlebar of a bicycle

【龙头】[2] lóngtóu ❶〈比喻 *fig.*〉带头的、起主导作用的事物 leader; playing a leading role:～企业 leader enterprise; leading enterprise; key enterprise ❷〈方 *dial.*〉江湖上称帮会的头领 leader of a secret society (or an underworld gang)

【龙王】Lóngwáng 神话传说中在水里统领水族的王,掌管兴云降雨。迷信的人向龙王求雨。Dragon King (the God of Rain in Chinese mythology), in charge of gathering clouds to pour down rain; superstitious people always pray to the God for rainfall

【龙须面】lóngxūmiàn 一种非常细的面条儿 dragon whiskers noodles — long, thin noodles

【龙眼】lóngyǎn ❶ 常绿乔木,羽状复叶,小叶椭圆形。花黄白色,圆锥花序。果实球形,外皮黄褐色,果肉白色,可以吃,味甜,也可入药。产于福建、广东等地。longan (*Euphoria longan*); evergreen tree with pinnate compound and oblong leaflets, yellowish white flowers borne in panicles and ball-shaped fruit, which also has medicinal value, consisting of a single seed surrounded by a sweet, edible, white pulp, enclosed in a yellowish brown shell, growing in Fujian and Guangdong provinces, and some sther regions ❷ 这种植物的果实 fruit of this tree ‖ also 桂圆 guìyuán

【龙争虎斗】lóng zhēng hǔ dòu〈比喻 *fig.*〉双方势均力敌,斗争激烈 fighting between a tiger and a dragon; fight as closely as if between a tiger and a dragon; fierce struggle between well-matched opponents; contest between giants

【龙钟】lóngzhōng〈书 *fml.*〉身体衰老、行动不灵便的样子 decrepit; senile:老态～ senile; decrepit; doddering

【龙舟】lóngzhōu same as 龙船 lóngchuán:～竞渡 dragon-boat regatta; dragon-boat race。

茏(蘢) lóng ☞ 茏葱 lóngcōng and 葱茏 cōnglóng on p. 323

【茏葱】lóngcōng (草木)青翠茂盛 luxuriant growth of trees and grasses; verdant; luxuriantly green

咙(嚨) lóng ☞ 喉咙 hóu·lóng on p. 808

泷(瀧) lóng〈方 *dial.*〉急流的水(多用于地名) rapids; the character is often used as part of a geographical name:七里～(在浙江) Qililong, a place in Zhejiang Province

☞ shuāng on p. 1797

珑(瓏) lóng ☞ below

【珑璁】lóngcōng〈书 *fml.*〉❶ 金属、玉石等撞击的声音 tinkling sound of metal striking against metal or of jade striking against jade ❷ same as 茏葱 lóngcōng

【珑玲】lónglíng〈书 *fml.*〉❶ 金属、玉石等撞击的声音 tinkling sound of metal striking against metal or of jade striking against jade ❷ same as 光辉 guānghuī ②;明亮 bright; shining

栊(櫳、龒) lóng〈书 *fml.*〉❶ 窗户 window:房～ house window|帘～(带帘子的窗户) curtained window ❷ 养兽的栅栏 cage for beasts

昽(曨) lóng ☞[曚昽](rnénglóng) on p. 1325

胧(朧) lóng ☞[朦胧](rnénglóng) on p. 1325

砻(礱) lóng ❶ 去掉稻壳的工具,形状略像磨,多用木料制成 rice huller; wooden implement for hulling rice ❷ 用砻去掉稻壳 hull rice:～了两担稻子。Two *dan* (1 *dan* = 50 kg.) of rice were hulled.

【砻糠】lóngkāng 稻谷砻过后脱下的外壳 rice chaff

眬(矓) lóng ☞ 蒙眬 (rnénglóng) on p. 1325

聋(聾) lóng 耳朵听不见声音。通常把听觉迟钝也叫聋 deaf; hard of hearing:～哑 deaf and dumb; deaf-mute|耳～眼花 hard of hearing and dim-sighted

【聋子】lóng·zi 耳聋的人 deaf person

笼(籠) lóng ❶ 笼子 cage; coop:竹～ bamboo cage|兔～ rabbit cage|鸡从～里跑出来了。The chickens came out of the coop. ❷〈旧时 *old*〉囚禁犯人的刑具 instrument for confining a prisoner:囚～ prisoner's cage ❸ 蒸笼 steamer:小～包子 small steamed buns with meat stuffing|馒头刚上～。The buns have just been put into the steamer. ❹〈方 *dial.*〉把手放在袖筒里 put one's hands in the sleeves:～着手 put each hand in the opposite sleeve (for warmth)

☞ lǒng on p. 1252

【笼火】lóng//huǒ 用柴引火使煤炭燃烧;生火 make a fire; raise a fire:今天不冷,甭～了。It's not cold. There is no need to make a fire.

【笼屉】lóngtì 竹、木、铁皮等制成的器具,用来蒸食物 steamer; bamboo, metal or wooden utensil for steaming food (composed of several tiers); food steamer

【笼头】lóng·tou 套在骡马等头上的东西,用皮条或绳子做成,用来系缰绳,有的并挂嚼子 headstall; part of a halter or bridle that fits round the head of a horse or a mule, etc., made of leather or rope

【笼中鸟】lóngzhōngniǎo〈比喻 *fig.*〉受困而丧失自由的人 bird in a cage; person without freedom

【笼子】lóng·zi 用竹篾、木条、树枝或铁丝等制成的器具,用来养虫鸟或装东西 cage made of bamboo, wood, twig or iron wire for keeping birds, insects or holding things
☞ lǒng·zi on p.1252

【笼嘴】lóng·zui 使用牲口时,套在牲口嘴上,使它不能吃东西的器物,用铁丝、树条、竹篾等做成 muzzle made of iron wire, twigs or bamboo slips, put over the mouth of a draught animal to prevent it from eating while at work

舼(龓) lóng〈书 *fml.*〉有篷的小船 small boat with an awning

隆 lóng ❶ 盛大 grand; magnificent:～重 grand; ceremonious ❷ 兴盛 prosperous; thriving:兴～ prosperous; thriving; flourishing; brisk | ～盛 booming; thriving; abundant; flourishing ❸ 深厚;程度深 profound; intense; deep:～冬 midwinter; depth of winter | ～恩 great kindness; favour or grace | ～情 profound feelings; profound friendship; great kindness ❹ 凸出 swell; bulge:～起 a swelling ❺ (Lóng)姓 a surname
☞ lōng on p.1248

【隆冬】lóngdōng 冬天最冷的一段时期;严冬 midwinter; severely cold winter; winter at its coldest; depth of winter:～季节 cold winter season

【隆隆】lónglóng〈拟声词 *onom.*〉形容剧烈震动的声音 roar; rumble; boom:雷声～。The thunder rumbled. | 炮声～。The guns roared.

【隆情】lóngqíng 深厚的感情 profound feelings:～厚谊 profound feelings and great friendship

【隆庆】Lóngqìng 明穆宗(朱载垕)年号(公元1567-1572) Longqing, title of the reign (1567-1572) of Emperor Muzong (Zhu Zaihou) of the Ming Dynasty

【隆盛】lóngshèng〈书 *fml.*〉❶ 昌盛;兴盛 abundant; flourishing; prosperous:国势～。The country is prosperous. ❷ 盛大 grand; magnificent

【隆重】lóngzhòng 盛大庄重 grand; solemn; ceremonious:～的典礼 grand ceremony

【隆准】lóngzhǔn〈书 *fml.*〉高鼻梁儿 prominent nose

癃 lóng ❶〈书 *fml.*〉衰弱多病 senile and weak; infirmity:疲～ bent with age; hunchbacked ❷ 癃闭 retention of urine; difficulty in urination

【癃闭】lóngbì〈中医 *Chin. med.*〉指小便不通的病 retention of urine; difficulty in urination

窿 lóng〈书 *fml.*〉煤矿坑道 gallery in a coal mine:～工 coal miners | 清理废～ clear the discarded galleries | 把煤桶堆在～门口 pile the coal tubs by the gallery entrance

lǒng(ㄌㄨㄥˇ)

优(儱) lǒng [优侗](lǒngtǒng)〈书 *fml.*〉same as 笼统 lǒngtǒng

陇(隴) Lǒng ❶ 陇山,山名,在陕西、甘肃交界的地方 Longshan mountain, bordering Shaanxi and Gansu provinces ❷ 甘肃的别称 another name for Gansu Province

【陇剧】lǒngjù 甘肃地方戏曲剧种之一,由甘肃东部的皮影戏陇东道情发展而成 Gansu Opera; one of the local operas in Gansu, developed from leather-silhouette show and the chanting of folk tales, popular in the eastern part of Gansu

垄(壟、壠) lǒng ❶ 在耕地上培成的一行一行的土埂,在上面种植农作物 ridge (in a field) on which crops are planted:～沟 furrow; field ditch ❷ 田地分界的稍稍高起的小路;田埂 raised path between fields ❸ 形状像'垄'①的东西 sth. resembling a ridge:瓦～ corrugated tile

【垄断】lǒngduàn《孟子·公孙丑》:'必求垄断而登之,以左右望而罔市利。'原指站在市集的高地上操纵贸易,后泛指把持和独占。*Mencius·Gongsun Qiu*:'It is imperative to mount a vantage point that enables one to look left and right and know what is going on in a market place in order to monopolize it. The phrase has been simplified to mean monopolize or monopoly:～市场 monopolize (or corner) the market | ～集团 monopoly group

【垄沟】lǒnggōu 垄和垄之间的沟,用来灌溉、排水或施肥 field ditch; furrow; ditch for irrigation, drainage and applying fertilizer

【垄作】lǒngzuò 把农作物种在垄上,或把行间的土逐渐培在作物的根部形成垄,如甘薯就是用垄作的方法种植的 ridge culture; plant a crop on the ridges in a field or cover the roots of the crop in each row with the soil between two rows, such as in the cultivation of sweet potatoes

拢(攏) lǒng ❶ 合上 close:他笑得嘴都合不～了。He grinned from ear to ear. ❷ 靠近;到达 approach; reach:～岸 approach the shore; come alongside the shore | 靠～ sit or stand closer | 快～工地了。We've almost got to the worksite. ❸ 总合 add up; sum up:～共 altogether; all told; in all | ～总 altogether; all told; in all | 把账～一～ sum up the accounts ❹ 使不松散或不离开;收拢 bring together:～音 (of acoustic effect) concentrate the sound | 归～ put together | 用绳子把柴火～住 tie the firewood together with a

string|把孩子～在怀里 hold one's baby in one's arms|～住他的心 hold back one's heart ❺ 梳(头发) comb (hair): 她用梳子～了～头发。She arranged her hair with a comb.

【拢岸】lǒng//àn (船只)靠岸 (of a ship) come alongside the shore

【拢共】lǒnggòng 共计;总计 altogether; all told; in all: 镇上～不过三百户人家。There are altogether 300 households in the town.

【拢音】lǒng//yīn 使声波在一定范围内不分散,听起来声音更清晰 (of a building) quality of sound gathering and amplication, so that sound wave will not diffuse and will sound clearer within a given scope: 在露天剧场唱不～。The open-air theatre does not carry sound well. *or* The acounstics of the open-air theatre are not good.

【拢子】lǒng·zi 齿小而密的梳子 fine-toothed comb

【拢总】lǒngzǒng 共计;总计 altogether; all told; in all: 站上职工～五十个人。There are altogether 50 workers at the station.

笼(籠) lǒng ❶ 笼罩 envelop; cover: 暮色～住了大地。The land is enveloped in the gathering dusk. |整个山村～在烟雨之中。The whole village is enveloped in a misty rain. ❷ 笼子 (lǒng·zi) large box or chest; trunk: 箱～ trunks

☞ lóng on p. 1250

【笼络】lǒngluò 用手段拉拢人 win someone over by some means; draw over; rope in: ～人心 cultivate people's good will by...; buy people's support

【笼统】lǒngtǒng 缺乏具体分析,不明确;含混 general; sweeping; unclear: 他的话说得非常～。He spoke in very general terms. |他只是笼笼统统地解释一下。He only tried to explain in generalities.

【笼罩】lǒngzhào 像笼子(lóng·zi)似地罩在上面 envelop; shroud: 晨雾～在湖面上。The lake is shrouded in morning mist. |朦胧的月光～着原野。The land is bathed in the dim moonlight.

【笼子】lǒng·zi 〈方 *dial.*〉比较大的箱子 large box or chest; trunk

☞ lóng·zi on p. 1251

笓 lǒng 〈方 *dial.*〉 same as 笼(lǒng) ②。织笓(Zhīlǒng),地名,在广东。Zhilong, geographical name of a place in Guangdong Province

lòng (ㄌㄨㄥˋ)

弄 lòng 〈方 *dial.*〉小巷;胡同 (多用于巷名 oft. used in names of lanes) lane; alley; alleyway: 里～ lane|～堂 lane

☞ nòng on p. 1425

【弄堂】lòngtáng 〈方 *dial.*〉巷;弄 lane; alley; alleyway: ～口 the ends of a lane; entrances of a lane|～门 lane door|～房子 lane houses|三条～ three lanes

哢 lòng 〈书 *fml.*〉鸟叫 cries to a bird; chirping of a bird

崀 lòng 石山间的小片平地 small piece of flat land in a rocky mountain [壮 a word used by the ethnic Zhuang people]

lōu (ㄌㄡ)

搂(摟) lōu ❶ 用手或工具把东西聚集到自己面前 gather up; rake together: ～柴火 rake up twigs, dead leaves, etc. |～点儿干草烧 rake up some hay to raise a fire. ❷ 用手拢着提起来(指衣服) hold up; tuck up: ～起袖子 tuck up one's sleeves|他～着衣裳,迈着大步向前走。With a coat in hand, he swaggered down the road in giant strides. ❸ 搜刮(财物);尽力赚(钱) squeeze (money); extort: ～钱 extort money ❹ 〈方 *dial.*〉向自己的方向拨;扳 pull: ～扳机 pull a trigger ❺ 〈方 *dial.*〉核算 business accounting: ～算 business accounting|把账～一～ settle accounts

☞ lǒu on p. 1253

【搂头】lōutóu 〈方 *dial.*〉照着脑袋;迎头 head-on; directly: ～就是一拳 deal a head-on blow with one's fist

【搂头盖脸】lōu tóu gài liǎn 正对着头和脸 right in the face: 她抄起个碗对着那个人～扔过去。She picked up a bowl and threw it to the man right in his face. also 搂头盖顶 lōu tóu gài dǐng

䁖(瞜) lōu 〈方 *dial.*〉看(口气不庄重 in a casual manner) look: 这是你新买的吗?我～～。Is this the new one you've bought? Let me have a look. |这玩意儿不错,让我～一眼。This gadget is very nice. Let me have a look.

lóu (ㄌㄡˊ)

剅(剅) lóu 〈方 *dial.*〉堤坝下面排水、灌水的口子;横穿河堤的水道 opening under a dam or dyke for irrigation and drainage; water course through a dyke: ～口 mouth of a water course under a dyke|～嘴 mouth of a water course under a dyke

娄(婁) lóu ❶ 〈方 *dial.*〉(身体)虚弱 physically weak: 他动不动就病,身子骨儿可～啦。He's very weak and falls ill easily. ❷ 〈方 *dial.*〉(某些瓜类)过熟而变质 overripe and unfit to eat: ～瓜 overripe melon|西瓜～了保换。Replacement is guaranteed if the watermelon is overripe and unfit to eat. ❸ 二十八宿之一 the sixteenth of the twenty-eight constellations ❹ (Lóu)姓 a surname

【娄子】lóu·zi 乱子;纠纷;祸事 trouble; blunder:惹～ stir up trouble|捅～ make a mistake; make a blunder; make a nice mess of something; get into trouble|出～ get into trouble; go wrong

偻(僂) lóu ❶ ☞ 佝偻病 gōulóubìng on p. 681 ❷ [偻㑩](lóu·luó) same as 喽啰 lóu·luó
☞ lǚ on p. 1265

蒌(蔞) lóu ☞ below

【蒌蒿】lóuhāo 多年生草本植物,叶子互生,有柄,羽状分裂,背面密生灰白色细毛,花冠筒状,淡黄色。叶子可以做艾的代用品。beach wormwood (*Artemisia vulgaris*); perennial herbal plant having pinnately lobed leaves with greyish-white hair on the back, growing alternately, and yellowish tubular corolla. The leaves are used as a substitute for moxa.

【蒌叶】lóuyè 常绿木本植物,茎蔓生,叶子椭圆形,花绿色。果实有辣味,可以用来制酱。betel; betel pepper (*Piper betle*); evergreen woody plant having a trailing stem, oval leaves with stalks, green flowers and pungent fruits that are used in making sauce; also 蒟酱 jǔjiàng

喽(嘍) lóu [喽啰](lóu·luó)〈旧时 *old*〉称强盗头目的部下,现多比喻追随恶人的人 rank and file of a band of outlaws; (fig.) underling; lackey; also 喽罗 lóu·luó and 偻㑩 lóu·luó
☞ ·lou on p. 1256

溇(漊) Lóu 溇水,水名,在湖南 Loushui, name of a river in Hunan Province

楼(樓) lóu ❶ 楼房 storeyed building; tower:一座～ a building|大～ tall building|教室～ classroom building|高～大厦 tower ❷ 楼房的一层 floor; level; storey:一～(平地的一层) ground floor|一口气爬上十～ climb to the ninth floor at a stretch ❸ (～儿 lóur)房屋或其他建筑物上加盖的一层房子 superstructure:城～ gate tower|箭～ battlements ❹ 用于某些店铺的名称 [used in shop names]:茶～ tea house|酒～ restaurant|银～ jeweller's shop ❺ (Lóu)姓 a surname

【楼板】lóubǎn 楼房中上下两层之间的木板或水泥板 floor; floor slab, either wooden or cerement

【楼层】lóucéng 指楼房的一层 storey; floor; level:每个～都设有消火栓。On every floor there is a fire hydrant.

【楼道】lóudào 楼房内部的走道 corridor; passageway within a storeyed building:～里不要堆放杂物。Don't leave odds and ends in the corridor.

【楼房】lóufáng 两层或两层以上的房子 building of two or more storeys

【楼阁】lóugé 楼和阁,泛指楼房 building and attic (loft); house; building

【楼台】lóutái ❶〈方 *dial.*〉凉台 balcony ❷ 泛指楼 (多用于诗词戏曲 oft. in poetry and theatre) high building; tower:近水～ waterfront pavilion

【楼梯】lóutī 架设在楼房的两层之间供人上下的设备,形状像台阶 stairs; staircase; stairway

耧(耬) lóu 播种用的农具,由牲畜牵引,后面有人扶着,可以同时完成开沟和下种两项工作。有的地区叫耩子。drill barrow; drill; animal-drawn sowing plough held by a person behind, which can make furrow and sow seeds at the same time; known as 耩子 jiǎng·zi in some places

【耧播】lóubō 耩 (jiǎng) sow with a drill

【耧车】lóuchē〈古代 *arch.*〉称耧 plough

蝼(螻) lóu 蝼蛄 mole cricket:～蚁 mole ants

【蝼蛄】lóugū 昆虫,背部茶褐色,腹面灰黄色。前足发达,呈铲状,适于掘土,有尾须。生活在泥土中,昼伏夜出,吃农作物嫩茎。mole cricket (*Gryllotalpa africana*); nocturnal insect with a dark brown back and greyish-yellow belly, well-developed forelimbs in the shape of a spade used for digging earth; it lives in the earth, feeding on the young stems of crops; 通称 commonly called 蝲蝲蛄 làlàgǔ; 有的地区叫土狗子 known as 土狗子 tǔgǒu·zi in some places

【蝼蚁】lóuyǐ 蝼蛄和蚂蚁,用来代表微小的生物 mole crickets and ants; microbes,〈比喻 *fig.*〉力量薄弱或地位低微的人 weak person; person in a low position

【蝼螲】lóuzhì 古书上指蝼蛄 mole cricket (in ancient books)

髅(髏) lóu ☞ [髑髅](dúlóu) on p. 480 and [骷髅](kūlóu) on p. 1114

lǒu (ㄌㄡˇ)

搂(摟) lǒu ❶ 搂抱 hold in one's arms; hug; embrace:妈妈把孩子～在怀里。The mother held the child in her arms. ❷〈量词 *classifier*〉:两～粗的大树 a tree two arm-spans
☞ lōu on p. 1252

【搂抱】lǒubào 两臂合抱;用胳膊拢着 hug; embrace; cuddle:小姑娘亲热地～着小猫。The little girl cuddled her pet cat.

嵝(嶁) lǒu 岣嵝 (Gǒulǒu),山名,就是衡山,在湖南 Goulou, name of a mountain in Hunan Province; Mount Hengshan

篓(簍) lǒu (～儿 lǒur) 篓子 basket: 竹～ bamboo basket | 背～ basket carried on one's back | 油～ small-mouthed and big-bellied basket made of wicker chips or bamboo chips and lined with oil paper used to contain oil | 字纸～儿 wastepaper basket

【篓子】lǒu·zi 用竹子、荆条、苇篾儿等编成的盛东西的器具,从口到底比较深 basket; container made from bamboo, chaste tree twigs or reeds

lòu (ㄌㄡˋ)

陋 lòu ❶ 不好看;丑 plain; ugly: 丑～ ugly ❷ 粗劣;不精致 coarse: 粗～ coarse; crude | 因～就简 do things in a simple way; make do ❸ (住的地方)狭小,不华美 humble; mean: ～室 humble room | ～巷 mean alley ❹ 不文明;不合理 vulgar; corrupt; undesirable: ～俗 corrupt custom; undesirable custom | ～习 bad habit ❺ (见闻)少 (of knowledge) scanty; limited; shallow: 浅～ shallow | 孤～寡闻 limited in knowledge

【陋规】lòuguī 不好的惯例。旧时多指官吏索贿受贿 objectionable practices; demanding and accepting bribes by officials in old times: 革除～ get rid of the objectionable practices

【陋室】lòushì 简陋的房屋 humble room: 身居～ live in a humble room

【陋俗】lòusú 不好的风俗 corrupt customs; undesirable customs

【陋习】lòuxí 不好的习惯 corrupt customs; bad habits: 陈规～ outdated practices and undesirable customs

镂(鏤) lòu 雕刻 engrave; carve: 雕～ carve | ～刻 engrave | ～花 ornamental engraving | ～空 pierced work

【镂骨铭心】lòu gǔ míng xīn same as 刻骨铭心 kè gǔ míng xīn

【镂刻】lòukè ❶ 雕刻 carve; engrave: ～花纹 engraved designs ◇岁月在他的额头～下深深的皱纹。Deep lines have been carved on his forehead by age. ❷ 深深地记在心里;铭记 impress deeply (on the mind); engrave: 动人的话语～在她的心中。The touching words have been engraved on her memory.

【镂空】lòukōng 在物体上雕刻出穿透物体的花纹或文字 pierced work; reticulated work; openwork; fretwork: ～的象牙球 pierced ivory ball

瘘(瘻、瘺) lòu ❶ 瘘管 fistula: 痔～ piles and fistulas | 肛～ anal fistula ❷ 〈书 *fml*.〉瘰疬 scrofula

【瘘管】lòuguǎn 人或动物体内发生脓肿时生成的管子,管子的开口或在皮肤表面或与其他内脏相通,病灶内的分泌物可以由瘘管流出来。生理学实验上也指安在动物器官上的人工瘘管。fistula; abnormal passage from an abscess in a human or animal organ to the skin or to another internal organ, from which the secretion in the abscess flows out; artificial tube inserted into an animal organ

漏 lòu ❶ 东西从孔或缝中滴下、透出或掉出 leak; (of sth.) drip, seep or fall out of a hole or crevice: 壶里的水～光了。The water in the kettle has leaked out. ❷ 物体有孔或缝,东西能滴下、透出或掉出 sth. with holes or cracks from which water or oil leaks: ～勺 strainer; colander | 锅～了。The pan is leaking. | 那间房子～雨。That room is leaking. ❸ 漏壶的简称,借指时刻 abbr. for 漏壶 lòuhú, referring to a point of time: ～尽更深。The night is waning. ❹ 泄漏 divulge; leak: 走～风声 leak information; divulge a secret ❺ 遗漏 be missing; leave out by mistake: 挂一～万 list one point while missing ten thousand others in compiling a book | 这一行～了两个字。Two words are missing in this line. | 点名的时候,把他的名字给～了。His name was left out at roll-call.

【漏窗】lòuchuāng 园林建筑中不糊纸或不安玻璃的窗户 garden windows without glass or paper

【漏电】lòu//diàn 跑电 leak electricity

【漏洞】lòudòng ❶ 能让东西漏过去的不应有的缝隙或小孔儿 leaks or cracks in places where there should not be any ❷ (说话、做事、办法等)不周密的地方;破绽 (of speech, act, method, etc.) flaw; hole; loophole: 堵塞工作的～ plug up all loopholes in the work | 他的话里～百出。What he says is full of holes.

【漏兜】lòu//dōu 〈方 *dial*.〉不自觉把隐藏的事情泄漏出来 spill the beans; let the cat out of the bag: 这一手要得不够巧妙,～啦! You are not smart enough in doing this. You've revealed your secret! | 把事说漏了兜 reveal the actual situation by a slip of the tongue

【漏斗】lòudǒu 把液体或颗粒、粉末灌到小口的容器里用的器具,一般是由一个锥形的斗和一个管子构成 funnel; instrument consisting of an inverted cone with a hole at the small end, or a tapering or cylindrical tube with a wide, cone-shaped mouth, for pouring liquids, grains or powders into containers that have small openings

【漏风】lòu//fēng ❶ 器物有空隙,风能出入 leak air; not be airtight: 这个风箱～。This bellows is not airtight. | 窗户有缝儿,到冬天～。There are crevices in the windows which let in cold air in winter. ❷ 因为牙齿脱落,说话时拢不住气 speak indistinctly with one or more front teeth missing: 安上了假牙以后,他说话不再～了。Wearing false teeth, he speaks quite distinctly. ❸ 走漏风声 (of information, secrets) leak out: 这件事先别漏出风去。Don't leak out any information on this matter.

【漏光】lòu//guāng 感光材料（如胶片、感光纸等）由于封闭不严密而感光（of light-sensitive material such as film, sensitive paper） leak light

【漏壶】lòuhú〈古代 *arch*.〉计时的器具，用铜制成，分播水壶、受水壶两部。播水壶分二至四层，均有小孔，可以滴水，最后流入受水壶，受水壶里有立箭，箭上划分一百刻，箭随蓄水逐渐上升，露出刻数，用以表示时间。也有不用水而用沙的。water-clock; clepsydra; hourglass; device for measuring time by the fall or flow of water; ancient time-piece made of bronze consisting of two pots, the pot above with two to four levels, each having a small opening through which the water trickles from above to the lower level and finally to the other pot below in which a vertical, graduated arrow marked with 100 degrees rises bit by bit with the water to show the graduation indicating the time. In some cases, sand was used in place of water. also 漏刻 lòukè；简称 abbr. 漏 lòu

【漏勺】lòusháo 炊事用具，有许多小孔的金属勺子 strainer; colander; skimmer; skimming ladle

【漏失】lòushī ❶ 漏出而失掉 leak and lose：水分～ leaking and loss of water content ❷ 疏漏；失误 careless omission; oversight; slip; careless mistake; error：这一工作不能有半点～。There should be no careless mistakes in this work.

【漏税】lòu//shuì（纳税者）由于疏忽大意或者不了解税收法令而没有缴纳应缴的税款，通常指有意违反税收法令逃避应该缴纳的税款 evade payment of a tax; evade taxation; taxpayer failing to pay tax due to carelessness or ignorance of tax regulations; usu. evade tax payments intentionally in violation of relevant regulations

【漏脱】lòutuō 遗漏；遗失 missing; omission

【漏网】lòu//wǎng（罪犯、敌人等）没有被逮捕或歼灭（of a criminal, an enemy, etc.） slip through the net; escape unpunished：无一～ not a single criminal escapes｜～之鱼 fish that has slipped through the net;〈比喻 *fig*.〉侥幸脱逃的罪犯、敌人等 fugitive; runaway; criminal, enemy, etc., who has escaped by sheer luck

【漏泄】lòuxiè ❶（水、光线等）流出或透出（of water, light, etc.） leak; filter：汽缸～。The cylinder leaks.｜阳光从枝叶的缝隙中～下来。Sunbeams filtered through the foliage. ❷ 泄露；走漏 let out; leak; divulge; give away：～试题 leakage of the content of an exam paper｜～天机 give away a secret; leak out a secret

【漏夜】lòuyè 深夜 in the dead of night

【漏卮】lòuzhī〈书 *fml*.〉有漏洞的盛酒器 leaky wine cup;〈比喻 *fig*.〉国家利益外溢的漏洞 loophole causing loss of a nation's economic rights to foreigners

【漏子】lòu·zi ❶ same as 漏斗 lòudǒu ❷ same as 漏洞 lòudòng：这戏法儿变得让人看不出～来。He juggled so well that no one could find a flaw in it.

【漏嘴】lòu//zuǐ 说话不留神把不该说或不想说的话说了出来 let slip a remark; make a slip of the tongue

露 lòu 义同'露²'（lù），用于下列各条 same as 露² lù, limited to the following usages ☞ lù on p. 1263

【露白】lòu//bái 指在人前露出自己带的财物 show money or valuables one carries unintentionally

【露丑】lòu//chǒu 出丑；丢丑 make a fool of oneself in public：出乖～ make a show of oneself; make an exhibition of oneself

【露底】lòu//dǐ 泄漏底细 let a secret out：这事一定要保密，千万不能露了底。Keep it confidential and be sure not to let it out.

【露风】lòu//fēng 走漏风声 divulge a secret; leak out information

【露富】lòu//fù 显出有钱 show one's wealth

【露脸】lòu//liǎn ❶ 指因获得荣誉或受到赞扬，脸上有光彩 earn respect by doing sth. good; become known（by doing sth.）; be successful; shine：干出点儿名堂来，也露露脸 get into the limelight for doing sth. special ❷〈方 *dial*.〉（～儿 lòuliǎnr） same as 露面 lòu//miàn：他有好几天没在村里～了。He hasn't appeared in the village for a few days.

【露马脚】lòu mǎjiǎo〈比喻 *fig*.〉隐蔽的事实真相泄漏出来 give oneself away; let the cat out of the bag：说谎早晚总要～。Lies are bound to be exposed sooner or later

【露面】lòu//miàn（～儿 lòu//miànr）出现在一定的场合（多指人出来交际应酬） make an appearance（usu. to socialize or meet friends）; show up：公开～ make public appearances; appear or reappear on public occasions

【露苗】lòu//miáo 种子萌发后，幼苗露出地表面（of sprouts） come out; also 出苗 chū//miáo

【露怯】lòu//qiè〈方 *dial*.〉因为缺乏知识，言谈举止发生可笑的错误 display one's ignorance in speech or behaviour; make a fool of oneself：从小长在城市里，乍到农村难免～。As a city-bred person since childhood, it's only natural（for him） to make blunders in his first days in the countryside.

【露头】lòu//tóu ❶（～儿 lòu//tóur）露出头部 show one's head：他从洞里爬出来，刚一～儿就被我们发现了。He crawled out of the cave and was discovered as soon as he showed his head. ❷〈比喻 *fig*.〉刚出现；显出迹象 show a sign：旱象已经～。The dry spell has showed its sign.

☞ lùtóu on p. 1264

【露馅儿】lòu//xiànr 〈比喻 *fig.*〉不愿意让人知道的事暴露出来 let the cat out of the bag; give the game away; spill the beans：这本来是捏造的，一对证，就～了。As this was fabricated, it gave away as soon as it was checked.

【露相】lòu//xiàng 〈方 *dial.*〉(～儿 lòu//xiàngr)露出本来面目 show one's true colours

【露一手】lòu yī shǒu (在某一方面或某件事上)显示本领 make an exhibition of one's abilities or skills (in a certain aspect or in doing sth.); show off：他唱歌真不错，每次联欢总要～。He is really a good singer and shows off at every get-together.

•lou (•ㄌㄡ)

喽(嘍) •lou 〈助词 *aux.*〉❶ 用法如'了'(•le)①，用于预期的或假设的动作 [used as 了 •le ① after a verb to indicate the completion of an envisaged or supposed action]：吃～饭就走。I'll go as soon as I have my meal.｜他要知道～一定很高兴。I'm sure he'll be glad to hear it. ❷ 用法如'了'(•le)②，带有提醒注意的语气 [used as 了• le ② at the end of a sentence to call attention to a new situation]：水开～。The water is boiling.｜起来～。Get up!

☞ lóu on p. 1253

lū (ㄌㄨ)

撸 lū 〈方 *dial.*〉❶ 捋(luō) rub one's palm along：挽着裤脚，～起袖子 roll up the bottoms of the trousers and the sleeves｜把树枝上的叶子～下来 strip a twig of its leaves by running the palm of one's hand along it ❷ 撤消(职务) dismiss a person from his post：他因犯了错误，职务也给～了。He was dismissed from his post for his mistake. ❸ 训斥；斥责 scold; dress down：挨了一顿～ get a scolding; get a dressing down

【撸子】lū•zi 〈方 *dial.*〉小手枪 small pistol

噜 lū [噜苏](lū•sū)〈方 *dial.*〉啰唆 wordy; long-winded; over-elaborate; troublesome; speaking or writing at great, tiresome length

lú (ㄌㄨˊ)

卢(盧) Lú 姓 a surname

【卢比】lúbǐ 印度、巴基斯坦、孟加拉、尼泊尔、斯里兰卡等国的本位货币。rupee, name of the legal currencies of India, Pakistan, Bangladesh, Nepal, and Sri Lanka

【卢布】Lúbù 俄罗斯等国的本位货币 rouble; basic monetary unit of Russia and some other countries [俄 Russian：рубль]

【卢沟桥事变】Lúgōuqiáo Shìbiàn same as 七七事变 Qī-Qī Shìbiàn

芦(蘆) lú ❶芦苇 reed：～花 reed catkins｜～根 reed rhizome｜～席 reed mat ❷ (Lú)姓 a surname

☞ lǔ on p. 1258

【芦荡】lúdàng 苇荡 reed marshes

【芦篚】lúfěi 〈方 *dial.*〉same as 芦席 lúxí

【芦花】lúhuā 芦苇花轴上密生的白毛 reed catkins

【芦笙】lúshēng 苗、侗等少数民族的管乐器，用若干根芦竹管和一根吹气管装在木制的座子上制成 reed-pipe wind instrument used by such minority ethnic peoples as the Miaos, Yaos and Dongs consisting of a mouthpiece and a series of reed pipes fixed on a wooden base

【芦苇】lúwěi 多年生草本植物，多生在水边，叶子披针形，茎中空，光滑，花紫色，花的下面有很多丝状的毛。茎可以编席，也可以造纸。地下茎可入药。reed (*Phragmites communis*); perennial herbal plant growing by the watersides, having lanceolate leaves, purple flowers with many silky hairs underneath, slippery hollow stem that is used in weaving mats and making paper, and rhizome that is a medicinal herb; also 苇 wěi or 苇子 wěi•zi

【芦席】lúxí 用苇篾编成的席子 reed mat

庐[1](廬) lú 简陋的房屋 simple house; hut：茅～ thatched hut｜～舍 house; farmhouse

庐[2](廬) Lú ❶ 指庐州(旧府名，府治在今安徽合肥) Luzhou, old name of the seat of a prefecture in present-day Hefei in Anhui Province：～剧 Luju opera ❷ (Lú)姓 a surname

【庐山真面】Lú Shān zhēn miàn 苏轼诗《题西林壁》：'横看成岭侧成峰，远近高低各不同，不识庐山真面目，只缘身在此山中。'后来用'庐山真面'比喻事物的真相或人的本来面目。*Inscription on Xilin Cliff* by Su Shi of the Song Dynasty: 'This side a range of hills and there a peak./ From different vantage points, a different mountain./ To me it is not given to know the true face of Lushan/ Because I am upon it.' 'The true face of Lushan' is used figuratively to mean truth about a person or matter. also 庐山真面目 Lú Shān zhēn miàn mù

【庐舍】lúshè 〈书 *fml.*〉房屋；田舍 house; farmhouse

垆[1](壚) lú 黑色的土壤 black soil; black earth：～土 black soil; black earth

垆[2](壚、鑪) lú 酒店里安放酒瓮的土台子，借指酒店 earthen

stand for wine jars; wine shop: 酒～ wine shop | 当～(卖酒) sell wine

【垆坶】lúmǔ 壤土旧称垆坶 loam; old name for 壤土 rǎngtǔ

【垆埴】lúzhí〈书 *fml.*〉黑色的黏土 black clay

炉(爐、鑪) lú 炉子 stove: 火～ fireplace; fire stove | 锅～ boiler | 电～ electric oven; electric furnace | 高～ blast furnace | 围～取暖 sit around a stove for warmth

【炉箅子】lúbì·zi 炉膛和炉底之间承煤漏灰的铁屉子 fire grate; metal frame confining coal in a stove

【炉衬】lúchèn 用耐火材料砌成的冶炼炉的内壁 furnace lining (built of refractory bricks)

【炉火纯青】lú huǒ chún qīng 相传道家炼丹,到炉子里的火发出纯青色的火焰的时候,就算成功了 Legend has it that the Taoists made pills of immortality and claimed success only when the stove fire begins to glow a pure blue.〈比喻 *fig.*〉学问、技术或办事达到了纯熟完美的地步 attain the highest degree of perfection in learning, skills, or in doing sth.

【炉料】lúliào 矿石和其他原料按一定比例配成的混合物,冶炼时把它们装到炉里 furnace charge; furnace burden; mixture of ores and other materials blended in fixed proportions, which is charged into a furnace for smelting

【炉龄】lúlíng 工业上指炉衬的使用期限,一般根据两次大修之间冶炼的次数和时数来计算 furnace life; time limit for the use of a furnace lining, usu. calculated on the basis of the number of times the molten iron or steel is tapped and the number of hours between two major overhauls of a furnace

【炉桥】lúqiáo〈方 *dial.*〉same as 炉箅子 lúbì·zi

【炉台】lútái (～儿 lútáir)炉子上头可以放东西的平面部分 stove top; level part around the stove on which sth. can be placed: 把饭放在～上,免得凉了。Put your food on the stove top to keep it warm.

【炉膛】lútáng (～儿 lútángr)炉子里面烧火的地方 chamber of a stove or furnace: 把～改小一点,就能省煤。Make the stove chamber a bit smaller to save coal.

【炉条】lútiáo 炉膛与炉底之间承燃料的铁条,作用与炉箅子相同 fire bars between the furnace and the bottom of a stove for retaining coal, similar to fire grate

【炉瓦】lúwǎ 用耐火材料做成的瓦状物,砌在炉内做为内衬 stove tiles made of refractory materials for lining

【炉灶】lúzào 炉子和灶的统称 kitchen range; cooking range: 修理～ repair a kitchen range ◇另起～ start sth. anew

【炉渣】lúzhā ❶ 冶炼时杂质经氧化与金属分离形成的渣滓。有些炉渣可用来制炉渣水泥、炉渣砖、炉渣玻璃等 slag; cinder; refuse formed of impurities in an ore when they are separated from the metal through oxidization during the smelting process. Some of the slags are used in making cement, bricks, glass, etc. ❷ 煤燃烧后结成的焦渣 coke slag formed after the coal is burned ‖ also 熔渣 róngzhā

【炉子】lú·zi 供做饭、烧水、取暖、冶炼等用的器具或装置 stove; oven; furnace; utensil or equipment for cooking, heating warer, supplying heat, smelting, etc.

泸(瀘) Lú ❶ 泸水,就是今金沙江在四川宜宾以上、云南四川交界处的一段 Lushui River, a section of the Jinsha River between Yibin in Sichuan and the area bordering Yunnan and Sichuan provinces ❷ 泸水,就是今怒江 Lushui River; Nujiang River of today

【泸州大曲】Lúzhōu dàqū 四川泸州出产的白酒,酒味醇美 Luzhou Liquor, a liquor produced in Luzhou, Sichuan Province, famous for its mellowness

纑(纑) lú ❶〈书 *fml.*〉织细麻布的线坯子 semi-finished flaxen thread ❷ 古书上指苎麻一类的植物 ramie or any other similar fibrous plant in ancient books

栌(櫨) lú ☞ [欂栌](bólú) on p.152 and 黄栌 huánglú on p.852

轳(轤) lú ☞ 辘轳 lù·lú on p.1263

胪(臚) lú〈书 *fml.*〉陈列 set out; display; exhibit: ～列 enumerate; list | ～陈 narrate in detail; state

【胪陈】lúchén〈书 *fml.*〉一一陈述(多用于旧式公文或书信 used in old-style documents or letters) narrate in detail; state: 谨将经过实情,～如左。The following is a detailed account of the course of events.

【胪列】lúliè〈书 *fml.*〉❶ 列举 enumerate; list: ～三种方案,以供采择。Three plans are prepared for choice. ❷ 陈列 display: 珍馐～ delicacies on display

胪(矑) lú〈书 *fml.*〉瞳人 pupil of the eye

鸬(鸕) lú [鸬鹚](lúcí)水鸟,羽毛黑色,有绿色光泽,嘴扁而长,暗黑色,上嘴的尖端有钩。能游泳,善于捕鱼,喉下的皮肤扩大成囊状,捕得鱼就放在囊内。我国南方多饲养来帮助捕鱼。cormorant (*Phalacrocorax carbo sinensis*); water fowl good at swimming and diving and catching fish having black feathers with green lustre, a long, dark, flat bill with a hook on the upper jaw, and the skin under the throat forming a bag in which caught fish are kept, bred in the southern Chinese provinces for catching fish; 通称 generally known as 鱼鹰 yúyīng; 有的地区叫

墨鸦 known as 墨鸦 mòyā in some regions

颅(顱) lú 头的上部,包括头骨和脑。也指头。cranium; skull; also the head; (图见 ☞ figure for 骨骼 gǔgé on p.693)

【颅骨】lúgǔ ☞ 头骨 tóugǔ on p.1930

【颅腔】lúqiāng 颅内的空腔,顶部略呈半球形,底部高低不平。颅腔内有脑子。cranial cavity; cavity in the skull: its top is semi-spheric and its bottom is rough and the brain is in the cavity

舻(艫) lú 〈书 *fml.*〉船头,也指船 stern or bow (of a ship): 舳~ a convoy of ships linked stem to stern with one another

鲈(鱸) lú 鲈鱼,身体上部青灰色,下部灰白色,身体两侧和背鳍有黑斑。生活在近海,秋末到河口产卵。perch (*Lateolabrax japonicus*); fish with a greenish-grey back and greyish belly, and black spots on both sides of the body and the dorsal fin, living in offshore waters and spawning at river estuaries

lǔ (ㄌㄨˇ)

芦(蘆) lǔ ☞ 油葫芦 yóu·hulǔ on p.2320

☞ lú on p.1256

卤(鹵、滷) lǔ ❶ 盐卤 bittern ❷ 卤素 halogen ❸ 用盐水加五香或用酱油煮 stew chickens, ducks, meat, etc., with salt and five kinds of spices or in soya sauce: ~味 pot-stewed meats | ~鸡 pot-stewed chicken | ~鸭 pot-stewed duck | ~口条(卤煮猪舌) pot-stewed pig's tongue ❹ 用肉类、鸡蛋等做汤加淀粉而成的浓汁,用来浇在面条等食物上 thick gravy of meat, egg and starch used as a sauce dressing for noodles, etc.: 打~面 noodles with thick gravy ❺ (~儿 lǔr)饮料的浓汁 thick infusion: 茶~儿 strong tea (to be diluted before drinking)

【卤菜】lǔcài 卤制的荤菜 pot-stewed meat or fowl

【卤化】lǔhuà 通常指有机化合物分子中引入卤素原子的反应,包括氟化、氯化、溴化和碘化 halogenate; processes such as chlorination, bromination, and iodination, to induce chemical reaction by introducing a halogen into an organic compound

【卤莽】lǔmǎng same as 鲁莽 lǔmǎng

【卤水】lǔshuǐ ❶ 盐卤 bittern ❷ 从盐井里取出供熬制井盐的液体 brine; liquid drawn from a salt well, from which to extract salt

【卤素】lǔsù 卤族元素,包括氟、氯、溴、碘、砹五种元素 halogens, including fluorine, chlorine, bromine, iodine and astatine

【卤味】lǔwèi 卤制的冷菜,如卤鸡、卤肉等 pot-stewed fowl, meat, etc. served cold

【卤虾】lǔxiā 食品,把虾磨成糊状,加盐制成 salted shrimp gravy

【卤虾油】lǔxiāyóu 卤虾的清汁 shrimp sauce

【卤制】lǔzhì 用卤的方法制作 stew chickens, ducks, meat, etc. in soya sauce; same as 卤 lǔ ③

【卤质】lǔzhì 土壤中所含的碱质 alkali found in soils

虏(虜) lǔ ❶ same as 俘虏 fúlǔ ① ❷ same as 俘虏 fúlǔ ② ❸〈古代 *arch.*〉指奴隶 slave ❹〈书 *fml.*〉对敌方的蔑称 (derog.) enemy: 敌~ enemy | 强~ strong enemy

【虏获】lǔhuò 俘虏敌人,缴获武器 capture (men and arms)

掳(擄) lǔ 把人抢走 take people away by force; carry off; capture: ~掠 plunder; pillage; loot | ~人勒赎 kidnap and blackmail

【掳掠】lǔlüè 抢劫人和财物 take a person and his property by force; plunder; pillage; loot: 奸淫~ rape and pillage

鲁[1] lǔ ❶ 迟钝;笨 stupid; dull: 愚~ slow-witted; stupid | ~钝 slow-witted; stupid ❷ 莽撞;粗野 rash; rough; rude: 粗~ rough; rude | ~莽 rash; rude

鲁[2] Lǔ ❶ 周朝国名,在今山东曲阜一带 state of Lu; one of the warring states into which China was divided during the Eastern Zhou period (770-256 B.C.), in the Qufu area of modern Shandong Province ❷ 山东的别称 another name for Shandong Province: ~菜 Shandong cuisine ❸ (Lǔ) 姓 a surname

【鲁班尺】lǔbānchǐ 木工所用的曲尺 carpenter's square

【鲁钝】lǔdùn 愚笨;不敏锐 slow-witted; obtuse; stupid: 赋性~ stupid

【鲁莽】lǔmǎng 说话做事不经过考虑;轻率 crude and rash; rash: 说话~ speak rashly | ~从事 act rashly; act without thought; also 卤莽 lǔmǎng

【鲁鱼亥豕】lǔ yú hài shǐ 把'鲁'字写成'鱼'字,把'亥'字写成'豕'字。指文字传写刊刻错误。confusion of 鲁 lǔ with 鱼 yú and of 亥 hài with 豕 shǐ; clerical or typographical errors made by confusing similar characters

【鲁直】lǔzhí 鲁莽而直率 be frank in an impetuous way

橹[1](艪、艣、艪) lǔ 使船前进的工具,比桨长而大,安在船梢或船旁,用人摇 scull; sweep; tool for propelling a boat, larger and longer than an oar, placed over the stern or by the side, operated manually

橹[2] lǔ 〈书 *fml.*〉大盾牌 big shield

镥 lǔ 金属元素，符号 Lu (lutetium)。是一种稀土金属。银白色，质软。用于原子能工业。lutecium (Lu); rare earth metallic metal, silver white and soft; used in the atomic energy industry

lù (ㄌㄨˋ)

六 lù ❶ 六安 (Lù'ān)，山名，又地名，都在安徽 Lu'an, name of both a mountain and a place in Anhui Province ❷ 六合 (Lùhé)，地名，在江苏 Luhe, name of a place in Jiangsu Province

☞ liù on p. 1246

甪 lù ❶ 甪直 (Lùzhí)，地名，在江苏 Luzhi, name of a place in Jiangsu Province ❷ 甪堰 (Lùyàn)，地名，在浙江 Luyan, name of a place in Zhejiang Province

【甪里】Lùlǐ ❶ 古地名，在今江苏吴县西南 name of an ancient place southwest of Wuxian County in Jiangsu Province ❷ (Lùlǐ) 姓 a double-character surname

陆(陸) lù ❶ 陆地 land: 大～ continent | 登～ land | ～路 land route; by land | 水～交通 land and water transport ❷ (Lù) 姓 a surname

☞ liù on p. 1247

【陆沉】lùchén 陆地下沉或沉没 sinking of land; 〈比喻 *fig.*〉国土沦丧 loss of land to a foreign country

【陆稻】lùdào 旱稻 dryland rice; upland rice; dry rice

【陆地】lùdì 地球表面除去海洋（有时也除去江河湖泊）的部分 dry land; land; parts of the earth's surface excluding the seas (sometimes excluding the rivers and lakes as well)

【陆风】lùfēng 气象学上指沿海地带夜间从大陆吹向海洋的风 terral; land breeze; meterological term referring to wind blowing from coastal areas to the sea at night

【陆架】lùjià same as 大陆架 dàlùjià

【陆军】lùjūn 陆地作战的军队。现代陆军通常由步兵、炮兵、装甲兵、工程兵等兵种和各专业部队组成。ground force; land force; army; combination of infantry, artillery, armoured force, engineering corps and professional units

【陆离】lùlí 形容色彩繁杂 varicoloured: 光怪～ grotesque in shape and gaudy in colour

【陆路】lùlù 旱路 land route: ～交通 overland communication; land communication

【陆棚】lùpéng same as 大陆架 dàlùjià

【陆坡】lùpō ☞ 大陆架 dàlùjià on p. 359

【陆桥】lùqiáo ❶ 连接两块大陆的陆地，如地质史上的连接亚洲和北美洲的陆地，和现在连接北美洲和南美洲的巴拿马地峡。陆桥往往用于说明生物和古人类的迁移路线。land bridge; land connecting two continents, such as the land connecting Asia and North America in the geological history and the Isthmus of Panama connecting North American and South America. The land bridge is often used to indicate the migrating routes of living things and primitive mammals. ❷ 海运的货物到达港口后，改为陆运，到另一港口再改为海运，两个港口之间的这一段陆地叫陆桥 after goods transported by sea arrive at a port, they are transported by land to another port for shipping, the land between the two ports being called land bridge

【陆禽】lùqín 鸟的一类，翅膀短圆，不能远飞，善于在陆地上行走，如原鸽、原鸡、鹌鹑等 a class of birds with short, round wings that cannot fly but walk on land, as wild pigeon (dove), jungle fowl (cock or hen), quail, etc.

【陆续】lùxù 〈副词 *adv.*〉表示先先后后，时断时续 one after another; in succession: 来宾～地到了。The guests arrived one after another. | 一到三月，桃花、李花和海棠陆陆续续都开了。The peach, plum and crabapple trees blossom one after another from January to March.

【陆运】lùyùn 陆路（铁路、公路等）上的运输 land transportation; transportation by railway and road

录(録) lù ❶ 记载；抄写 record; write down; copy: 记～ take notes | 登～ register | 抄～ make a copy of | 摘～ take passages; make extracts; extract; excerpts | 过～ copy from one notebook or account to another | 有闻必～ record whatever one hears ❷ 录制 record: ～音 record song, music, speeches, etc. | ～像 videotape; video | ～放 record and play back; recorded broadcast ❸ 原指为备用而登记，后转指采取或任用 choose; employ; hire: 收～ employ; include; enter; enroll; recruit; record | ～用 employ ❹ 用做记载物的名称 list of items: 目～ table of contents; catalogue; list; contents | 语～ quotations | 同学～ schoolmates' address book | 回忆～ memoirs; reminiscences; recollections

【录放】lùfàng 录音或录像并放出所录的声音或图像 record and play back; recorded broadcast

【录供】lùgòng 法律上指讯问时记录当事人说的话 take down a confession or testimony during an interrogation

【录取】lùqǔ 选定（考试合格的人）enroll; recruit; admit (those who are qualified in an exam): 择优～ enroll only those who excel in an exam | ～新生三百名 enroll 300 students

【录像】lù//xiàng 用光学、电磁等方法把图像和伴音信号记录下来 videotape; video; record images and accompanying sounds by optical and electromagnetic means: ～机 video recorder | ～设备 videotaping equipment | 当时的场面都录了像。The scene of that time was videotaped.

【录像】lùxiàng 用录像机、摄像机记录下来的图像 video; images recorded by a video recorder or camera: 放～ video showing | 看～ see a video showing

【录像带】lùxiàngdài ❶ 录像用的磁带 videotape; video cassette ❷ 利用机器记录下影像和声音并可以重新放出的磁带 videotape; tape onto which images and sounds have been recorded through a video recorder or camera and which can be replayed

【录像机】lùxiàngjī 用来记录图像和声音,并能重新放出的机器。有不同类型,通常指磁带录像机。video recorder; machine for recording images and sounds and for replaying what has been recorded; of different varieties, usu. referring to videotape recorder

【录像片儿】lùxiàngpiānr same as 录像片 lùxiàngpiàn

【录像片】lùxiàngpiàn 用放录像的方式映出的影片、电视片(一般单独发行,不在电视台播映 usu. distributed independently, not for broadcasting on TV) video film or TV play

【录音】lù//yīn 用机械、光学或电磁等方法把声音记录下来 record; tape; record sounds by mechanical, optical or electromagnetic means: ～机 tape recorder | ～棚 recording studio

【录音】lùyīn 用录音机记录下来的声音 sound recording; sounds recorded by a tape recorder: 放～ play back the recording | 听～ listen to the recording

【录音带】lùyīndài ❶ 录音用的磁带 magnetic tape; tape ❷ 经过录音可以重新播出的磁带 recorded tape of sounds for replaying

【录音电话】lùyīn diànhuà 装有录音设备的电话,能自动录下通话内容 telephone set with a recorder

【录音机】lùyīnjī 把声音记录下来并能重新放出的机器。有不同的类型,通常指磁带录音机。recorder; cassette recorder; machine for recording sounds and for replaying what has been recorded; of different varieties, usu. referring to tape recorder

【录影】lù//yǐng〈方 *dial.*〉same as 录像 lù//xiàng

【录影】lùyǐng〈方 *dial.*〉same as 录像 lùxiàng

【录用】lùyòng 收录(人员);任用 employ; take sb. on the staff: 量材～ give a person a job commensurate with his abilities | 择优～ choose the best candidate for a job

【录制】lùzhì 用录音机或录像机把声音或形象记录下来,加工制成某种作品 record sounds or images by means of a tape recorder or videotape recorder to make a work: ～唱片 record a disc | ～电视剧 record a TV film

辂 lù ❶〈古代 *arch.*〉车辕上用来挽车的横木 horizontal front bar on a cart or carriage ❷ 古代的一种大车 large carriage in ancient times

赂 lù〈书 *fml.*〉❶ 赠送财物;贿赂 give costly presents; bribe ❷ 财物,特指赠送的财物 bribe; presents given to someone as a bribe

菉 lù 梅菉 (Méilù),地名,在广东 Meilu, name of a place in Guangdong Province

☞ lǜ on p. 1267

崇 lù 土山间的小片平地 small piece of flat land between two earth hills [壮 Zhuàng]

鹿 lù ❶ 哺乳动物反刍类的一科,种类很多,四肢细长,尾巴短,一般雄兽头上有角,个别种类雌的也有角,毛多是褐色,有的有花斑或条纹,听觉和嗅觉都很灵敏 deer (*Cervus*); ruminant mammal with long, slender limbs, a short tail, brown hair and antlers for the male and also for the female of some species, some with spots or stripes on the body, having sharp hearing and smelling senses ❷ (Lù) 姓 a surname

【鹿角】lùjiǎo ❶ 鹿的角。特指雄鹿的角,中医入药 deer horn; antler, esp. that of a stag, used as a traditional Chinese medicine: ～胶 deer-horn glue ❷ 鹿砦 abatis

【鹿茸】lùróng 雄鹿的嫩角没有长成硬骨时,带茸毛,含血液,叫做鹿茸。是一种贵重的中药。pilose antler of a young stag, before it ossifies, downy and containing blood, a precious Chinese medicine

【鹿死谁手】lù sǐ shéi shǒu 以追逐野鹿比喻争夺天下,'不知鹿死谁手'表示不知道谁能获胜,现多用于比赛 chasing of a deer to see who's the winner; (fig.) struggle for supremacy. The phrase 'at whose hand will the deer die' means that one is uncertain which rivaling side will be the winner, and it is mostly used of sports competitions.

【鹿砦】lùzhài 军用的一种障碍物,把树木的枝干交叉放置,用来阻止敌人的步兵或坦克。因形状像鹿角而得名。abatis; barricade of felled trees, with branches pointed toward the enemy, oft. reinforced with barbed wire to stop an enemy's infantry or tanks, so called because it resembles deer horns; also 鹿寨 lùzhài

【鹿寨】lùzhài same as 鹿砦 lùzhài

渌 Lù 渌水,发源于江西,流入湖南 Lushui River, originating in Jiangxi Province and flowing into Hunan Province; also 渌江 Lùjiāng

逯 Lù 姓 a surname

绿 lù 义同'绿'(lǜ),用于'绿林,绿营'等 same as 绿 (lǜ) in meaning, used in 绿林 lùlín, 绿营 lùyíng, etc.

☞ lǜ on p. 1267

【绿林】lùlín 西汉末年王匡、王凤等领导农民起义,聚集在绿林山(今湖北大洪山一带)。后来用'绿林'泛指聚集山林反抗官府或抢劫财物的

集团。in the declining years of the Western Han Dynasty, Wang Kuang and Wang Feng led a peasants' uprising and gathered their forces in the Lulin Mountains (around the Dahong Mountain in Hubei Province today). Hence the term 'greenwood hero,' referring to people who gather in mountain forests to fight against the government or plunder valuables: ～好汉 greenwood hero-brigand; outlaw | 称雄～ rule the roost in the greenworld

【绿林起义】Lùlín Qǐyì 西汉末年的农民大起义。公元 17 年,王匡、王凤在绿林山(今湖北大洪山一带)组织饥民起义,称绿林军,反对王莽政权。公元 23 年,起义军建立更始政权。同年在昆阳大败王莽军,乘胜西进,攻占长安,推翻了王莽政权。Lulin Uprising (17); great peasants' uprising in the declining years of the Western Han Dynasty. In 17, Wang Kuang and Wang Feng organized famine refugees in an uprising in the Lulin Mountain area (around the Dahong Mountain in Hubei Province today), and called themselves Lulin (Green Forests) Army to oppose Wang Mang's regime. In 23, the uprising troops established the Gengshi regime, defeated Wang Mang's troops in Kunyang, and, advancing westward, captured Chang'an and overthrew the Wang Mang regime.

【绿营】lùyíng 清代由汉人编成的分驻在地方的武装力量,用绿旗做标志 Green Camps; armed forces composed of Chinese troops stationed in different localities, using green banners as a symbol in the Qing Dynasty

騄 lù [騄駬] (lù'ěr) 〈古代 *arch.*〉骏马名 name of a fine horse; also 騄耳 lù'ěr

琭 lù [琭琭]〈书 *fml.*〉形容稀少 rare; scanty: ～如玉 as rare as jade

禄 lù ❶ 〈古代 *arch.*〉称官吏的俸给 official's salary in feudal China; emolument: 俸～ official's salary | 高官厚～ high position and handsome salary | 无功受～ get a reward without real contribution ❷ (Lù) 姓 a surname

【禄蠹】lùdù 〈书 *fml.*〉指追求功名利禄的人 sinecurist

【禄位】lùwèi 〈书 *fml.*〉俸禄和官职 official rank and salary

碌 lù ❶ 平凡(指人 referring to a person) commonplace; mediocre: 庸～ mediocre ❷ 事务繁杂 busy: 忙～ busy; fully occupied | 劳～ work hard; toil; drudge

☞ liù on p. 1247

【碌碌】lùlù ❶ 平庸,没有特殊能力 mediocre; commonplace: 庸庸～ mediocre and unambitious | ～无为 lead a vain and humdrum life ❷ 形容事务繁杂、辛辛苦苦的样子 busy with miscellaneous work: ～半生 plod away for half a lifetime

睩 lù 〈书 *fml.*〉眼珠转动 turning of the eyeballs

路 lù ❶ 道路 road; path; way: 陆～ land route | 水～ water route; waterway | 大～ main road | 同～ on the same way; go the same way ❷ 路程 journey; distance: 八千里～ a distance of 8,000 *li*; a journey over 8,000 *li* | ～遥知马力 a horse's strength is to be known only after covering a long distance; distance tests a horse's stamina ❸ (～儿 lùr) 途径;门路 way; means: 生～ means of livelihood; way out | 活～儿 means of livelihood; means of subsistence; way out ❹ 条理 logic; line; sequence: 理～ logical thinking | 思～ train of thought; thinking | 笔～ style or technique of calligraphy, writing, poetry or painting ❺ 地区;方面 region; district: 南～货 goods from the south | 外～人 outsiders | 各～英雄 heroes from different fields or different parts of the country ❻ 路线 route: 三～进军 advance along three routes | 七～公共汽车 bus No. 7 ❼ 种类;等次 sort; grade; class: 这一～人 this sort of people | 哪一～病? What kind of disease is this? | 头～货 top class goods | 纸有好几～。There are several kinds of paper. | 二三～角色 second- or third-class role ❽ (Lù) 姓 a surname

【路标】lùbiāo ❶ 交通标志 road sign ❷ 队伍行动时沿路所做的联络标志 route marking; route sign made by a marching troop

【路不拾遗】lù bù shí yí 东西掉在路上没有人捡走据为己有。形容社会风气很好。no one picks up and pockets anything left on the road — good social mores; also 道不拾遗 dào bù shí yí

【路程】lùchéng ❶ 运动的物体从起点到终点经过路线的总长度 total distance from start to finish covered by an object in motion ❷ 泛指道路的远近 distance travelled; journey: 五百里～ a distance of 500 *li* | 三天～ three days' journey | 打听前面的～ ask about the distance ahcad ◇革命的～ the course of the revolution

【路倒儿】lùdǎor 〈方 *dial.*〉因贫病冻饿而倒毙在路上的人 body of a person who has dropped dead by the roadside, victim of poverty, illness, cold or hunger

【路道】lùdào 〈方 *dial.*〉❶ 途径;门路 way; approach: ～熟 beaten track | ～粗(形容门路广) have wide connections ❷ 人的行径(多用于贬义 oft. derog.) behaviour: 来人～不正。The person's behaviour is questionable.

【路灯】lùdēng 装在道路上照明用的灯 street lamp; road lamp

【路堤】lùdī 在低地上修筑的高于原地面的路基 embankment; roadbed built on low land

【路段】lùduàn 指道路的一段 section of a highway or railway: 有的～,推土机、压道机一齐

上，修得很快。One section of the highway is done quickly because bulldozers and steamrollers are used.

【路费】lùfèi 旅程中所用的钱，包括交通、伙食、住宿等方面的费用 travelling expenses; covering transportation, food and accommodation

【路风】lùfēng 指铁路部门的工作作风和风气 work style of the railway workers; quality of the railway service

【路规】lùguī 铁路上指有关火车运行的规章制度 regulations for train operation and rail services

【路轨】lùguǐ ❶ 铺设火车道或电车道用的长条钢材 rail; one of two parallel lines of continuous steel bars forming railway or tram tracks ❷ 轨道 track

【路过】lùguò 途中经过（某地） pass by or through (a place)：从北京到上海，～济南 pass through Jinan en route from Beijing to Shanghai

【路徽】lùhuī 铁路系统使用的标志。我国铁路路徽仝为机车正面轮廓，由'人'字和钢轨横断面的形状构成图案，象征人民铁道的意思 railway emblem; the emblem of the Chinese railways is an outline of the front of the steam engine, which happens to be a combination of the Chinese character 人 rén with the cross-section of a rail, meaning that the railways belong to the people

【路基】lùjī 铁路和公路的基础，一般分为路堤和路堑 roadbed, either embarkment or cutting for railway or highway

【路祭】lùjì 旧俗出殡时亲友在灵柩经过后路旁祭奠（old custom) offer sacrifices by the roadside as a funeral procession passes

【路劫】lùjié （盗匪）拦路抢劫 (of bandits) rob on the highway

【路警】lùjǐng 铁路上维持秩序、保护交通安全的警察 railway police, responsible for guaranteeing order and safety along the railway

【路径】lùjìng ❶ 道路（指如何到达目的地说） route; way (to reach a certain destination)：～不熟 not know one's way around | 迷失～ lose one's way ❷ 门路 method; ways and means：经过多次试验，找到了成功的～ find the road to success after many trials and errors

【路局】lùjú 指铁路或公路的管理机构 railway or highway bureau

【路考】lùkǎo 让司机在指定的道路上驾驶汽车，以考查其技术是否合格。是汽车驾驶员资格考试的项目之一。road driving test; driver is required to drive a car on a designated section of a road to show whether he is qualified for road driving

【路口】lùkǒu （～儿 lùkǒur）道路会合的地方 crossroads; street crossing; street intersection; entrance to a road or street：三岔～ road fork; junction where three roads meet | 十字～ crossroads | 丁字～ T-shaped road junction | 把住～ control the road junction

【路况】lùkuàng 道路的情况（指路面、交通流量等） road conditions (road surface, road traffic flow, etc.)

【路面】lùmiàn 道路的表层，用土、小石块、混凝土或沥青等铺成 road surface; pavement made of earth, small stones, concrete or bitumen, etc.：～平整 level road surface

【路牌】lùpái 标明交通路线或地名的牌子 street sign, indicating traffic lanes and name of the street

【路签】lùqiān 火车站上准许列车通行的凭证，列车到站后，如果不发给路签就不能通行 train-staff; pass that allows a train to pass through a station. A train is not allowed to pass through without the pass after arriving at a station.

【路堑】lùqiàn 在高地上挖的低于原地面的路基 cutting; roadbed cut into a high land

【路人】lùrén 行路的人 passer-by; wayfarer; 〈比喻 *fig.*〉不相干的人 stranger：～皆知 be known to all; known by every passer-by | 视若～ treat someone as a stranger

【路上】lù·shang ❶ 道路上面 on the road：～停着一辆车。There is a car parked on the road. ❷ 在路途中 on the way; en route：～要注意饮食。Be careful with your food and drink on your journey.

【路数】lùshù ❶ same as 路子 lù·zi ❷ 着数 (zhāoshù) (of martial arts) act; movement：学两手散打的～ learn some routines in martial arts ❸ 底细 exact details; inside story：摸不清来人的～ can't find the exact details about the visitor

【路条】lùtiáo 一种简便的通行凭证 travel permit; pass

【路途】lùtú ❶ 道路 road; way：他经常到那里去，熟识～。He is a frequent visitor there and knows the roads very well. ❷ same as 路程 lùchéng：～遥远 a long way to go; far away

【路线】lùxiàn ❶ 从一地到另一地所经过的道路（多指规定或选定的 oft. designated or selected) route; itinerary ❷ 思想上、政治上或工作上所遵循的根本途径或基本准则 line; guideline for ideology, politics or work：坚持群众～ persist in the mass line

【路障】lùzhàng 设置在道路上的障碍物 roadblock; barricade：清除～ remove (or clear) roadblocks (or barricades)

【路政】lùzhèng 公路、铁路的管理工作 road administration

【路子】lù·zi 途径；门路 way; approach; means; connections; pull：～广 have many social connections; have a wide range of choices; have many resources to draw upon | 走～ make use of one's social connections to achieve personal purpose; get sth. through pull ◇她演唱的～宽。She has a broad approach to her singing.

僇 lù〈书 *fml*.〉❶ 侮辱 insult; humiliation ❷ same as 戮 lù

蓼 lù〈书 *fml*.〉形容植物高大(of a plant) tall

☞ liǎo on p.1214

箓(籙) lù ☞ 符箓 fúlù on p.600

漉 lù 液体往下渗;滤 seep through; filter:～网 vat-net|～酒 filter wine

【漉网】lùwǎng 造纸时滤去纸浆里水分的网,用金属丝、竹丝或人造纤维等制成 vat-net, made of metal wires, thin bamboo strips or artificial fibres, used in papermaking to filter water out of the pulp

醁 lù ☞ [醽醁] (línglù) on p.1232

辘 lù ☞ below

【辘轳】lù·lú 利用轮轴原理制成的一种起重工具,通常安在井上汲水。机械上的绞盘有的也叫辘轳。well-pulley; windlass; winch; instrument for lifting water from a well; mechanical winch is also called 辘轳 lù·lú

【辘辘】lù·lù〈拟声词 *onom*.〉形容车轮等的声音 rumbling of cart wheels:风车～而动。The windmill rumbles.|牛车发出笨重的～声。The ox cart rumbled down the road. ◇饥肠～ rumbling of an empty stomach

戮[1] lù 杀 kill; slay:杀～ kill; slay|屠～ slaughter

戮[2](勠) lù〈书 *fml*.〉并;合 join; combine; unite:～力 join forces; join hands

【戮力同心】lù lì tóng xīn 齐心合力,团结一致 unite in a concerted effort; make concerted efforts

菉 lù〈古时 *arch*.〉指荩草 licorice (*Glycyrrhiza*)

罶 lù〈书 *fml*.〉小渔网 small fishnet

【罶簌】lùsù same as 簏簌 lùsù

𫚙 lù 鱼类的一属,身体侧扁,眼和嘴都大,鳞呈栉状。生活在近海岩石间。*Sebastichthys elegans*; laterally flat fish with big eyes, a big mouth and comb-like scales, living among rocks in the offshore seas

潞 Lù ❶ 潞水,就是今山西的浊漳河 Lushui, the Shuozhang River of today in Shanxi Province ❷ 潞江,就是怒江 Lujiang River or Nujiang River

璐 lù〈书 *fml*.〉美玉 fine jade

簏 lù ❶〈书 *fml*.〉竹箱 bamboo trunk:书～ a learned yet useless person ❷〈方 *dail*.〉竹篾、柳条等编成的圆筒形器具,多用于盛零碎东西;篓儿 bamboo basket or basket woven from willow twigs:字纸～ waste-paper basket

【簏簌】lùsù〈书 *fml*.〉形容下垂 hanging down; drooping. also 罶簌 lùsù

鹭 lù 鸟类的一科,嘴直而尖,颈长,飞翔时缩着颈。白鹭、苍鹭较为常见。heron (*Ardeola*); bird with a straight and pointed beak, and a long neck, which flies with a shrunk neck, its common breeds being white egret and heron

【鹭鸶】lùsī 白鹭 little egret (*Egretta garzetta*)

麓 lù〈书 *fml*.〉山脚 foot or a mountain or a hill:山～ foot of a mountain or a hill|泰山南～ at the southern foot of Mount Taishan

露[1] lù ❶ 凝结在地面或靠近地面的物体表面上的水珠。是接近地面的空气温度逐渐下降(仍高于0℃)时,使所含水汽达到饱和后形成的。dew; small drops of water condensed on the ground surface or on the surfaces of bodies close to the ground surface when the warm air cools gradually, but remains above 0℃ after the vapour is suturated; 通称 generally known as 露水 lù·shui ❷ 用花、叶、果子等蒸馏,或在蒸馏液中加入果汁等制成的饮料 syrup; beverage distilled from flowers, fruit or leaves; drink made from distilled water mixed with fruit juice:荷叶～ lotus leaf syrup|果子～ fruit syrup|玫瑰～ rose syrup

露[2] lù ❶ 在房屋、帐篷等的外面,没有遮盖 outside a house, a tent, having no covering above:～天 open air; outdoor|～营 camp; encamp|～宿 sleep in the open ❷ 显露;表现 show; reveal; betray:揭～ expose; reveal|暴～ expose; reveal; lay bare|吐～ confess; disclose|披～ disclose; reveal|藏头～尾 hide the head and show the tail; show part of the truth but not all of it|脸上～出了笑容。A smile appeared on her face.

☞ lòu on p.1255

【露布】lùbù ❶〈书 *fml*.〉檄文 war proclamation ❷〈书 *fml*.〉军中捷报 announcement of victory ❸〈古代 *arch*.〉不封口的诏书或奏章 unsealed imperial edict or memorial to the throne ❹〈方 *dial*.〉指布告、海报等 notice; bulletin; playbill

【露点】lùdiǎn 空气在气压不变的条件下冷却,使所含的水汽达到饱和状态的温度 dew point; temperature at which water vapour in the air is saturated while the air cools under the constant atmospheric pressure

【露骨】lùgǔ 用意十分显露,毫不含蓄 thinly veiled; undisguised; barefaced:你说得这样～,我不相信他没听懂。You spoke in such nonequivocal terms that I don't think he was not aware of it.

【露酒】lùjiǔ 含有果汁或花香味的酒 alcoholic drink mixed with fruit juice

【露水】lù·shui ❶ 露[1]①的通称 general term for 露 lù ① ❷〈比喻 *fig*.〉短暂的、易于消失的 ephemeral:～姻缘 short-lived marriage|～夫妻 man and woman living together without being married

【露宿】lùsù 在室外或野外住宿 sleep in the open:～街头 sleep in the street|风餐～ eat in the wind and sleep in the open; experience hardships on a long journey or in fieldwork

【露台】lùtái〈方 *dial*.〉晒台 flat roof (for drying clothes, etc.)

【露天】lùtiān ❶ 指在房屋外 in the open (air); outdoors:～电影 open-air cinema; film shown in the open air|把金鱼缸放在～里 put the gold fish bowl in the open air ❷ 上面没有遮盖物的 without covering above:～剧场 open-air theatre|～煤矿 open-cut coal mine

【露头】lùtóu 岩石和矿床露出地面的部分。矿床的露头是矿床存在的直接标记。outcrop, part of rock or vein that protrudes from the ground and serves as a sign of the presence of ore deposits; outcropping; also 矿苗 kuàngmiáo

☞ lòu// tóu on p. 1255

【露头角】lù tóujiǎo〈比喻 *fig*.〉初次显露才能 (of a young person) beginning to show ability or talent; budding

【露营】lù//yíng ❶ 军队在房舍外宿营 (of an army) camp (out); encamp; bivouac ❷ 以军队组织形式到野外过夜,晚间有行军、营火会等活动 camp like an army unit, including march and camp fire at night

【露珠】lùzhū 指凝聚像珠子的露水 dewdrop; also 露水珠儿 lù·shuizhūr

·lu (·ㄌㄨ)

氇 ·lu ☞ [氆氇](pǔ·lu) on p. 1502

lú (ㄌㄩˊ)

驴(驢) lú 哺乳动物,比马小,耳朵长,胸部稍窄,毛多为灰褐色,尾端有毛。多用做力畜。ass (*Equus asinus*); donkey; mammal with long ears, slightly narrower chest, greyish-brown hair and hairy tail tip, smaller than a horse, usu. serving as a draught animal

【驴唇不对马嘴】lú chún bù duì mǎ zuǐ〈比喻 *fig*.〉答非所问或事物两下不相合 donkeys' lips don't match horses' jaws; incongruous; irrelevant:这个比方打得不妥当,有点～。The analogy is rather far-fetched. also 牛头不对马嘴 niú tóu bù duì mǎ zuǐ

【驴打滚】lúdǎgǔn (～儿 lúdǎgǔnr) ❶ 高利贷的一种。放债时规定,到期不还,利息加倍。利上加利,越滚越多,如驴翻身打滚,所以叫驴打滚。snowballing usury; a kind of usury in which a borrower has to pay interest on interest if he is unable to pay back the debt due, with the amount growing just like snowballing or the donkey rolling its body ❷ 一种食品。用黄米面夹糖做成,蒸熟后,滚上黄豆面。a kind of food made of glutinous millet flour and sugar and covered with soya bean flour after it is steamed

【驴肝肺】lúgānfèi〈比喻 *fig*.〉极坏的心肠 donkey's internal organs; ill intent:好心当作～ take someone's good will for ill intent

【驴骡】lúluó 公马和母驴交配所生的杂种,身体较马骡小,耳朵较大,尾部的毛较少 hinny; offspring of a male horse and a female donkey, with a smaller body than mule, large ears, and little hair on the tail; also 驮骎 juétí

【驴年马月】lú nián mǎ yuè 指不可知的年月(就事情遥遥无期,不能实现说) year of the donkey and month of the horse — time that will never come (as there is no such year or month in the Chinese calendar):照你这么磨磨蹭蹭,～也干不成。If you go on dawdling like this, you will achieve nothing no matter how long you do it. also 猴年马月 hóu nián mǎ yuè

【驴皮胶】lúpíjiāo 阿胶(ējiāo) donkey-hide gelatin

【驴皮影】lúpíyǐng〈方 *dial*.〉皮影戏,因剧中人物剪影用驴皮做成而得名 leather-silhouette show; shadow play; so called because the figures for casting shadows are made of donkey hide

【驴子】lú·zi〈方 *dial*.〉驴 donkey; ass

闾 lú ❶〈书 *fml*.〉里巷的门 gate of (or entrance to) an alley:倚～而望 waiting at the entrance to an alley (for the return of a loved one) ❷〈书 *fml*.〉里巷;邻里 alleys and lanes; neighbourhood:乡～ village|～里 native village; home town|～巷 alley; lane; alleyway ❸〈古代 *arch*.〉二十五家为一闾 neighbourhood of 25 families in ancient China ❹ (Lú) 姓 a surname

【闾里】lúlǐ〈书 *fml*.〉乡里 one's neighbours; one's neighbourhood; one's native village; one's home town

【闾巷】lúxiàng〈书 *fml*.〉小的街道,借指民间 alley; lane; alleyway

【闾阎】lúyán〈书 *fml*.〉❶ 平民居住的地区,借指民间 neighbourhood of commoners:～繁富,库藏充足。The people are well-off, and the storehouses are full. ❷ 指平民 common people

【闾左】lúzuǒ〈书 *fml*.〉贫苦人民居住的地区,借指贫苦人民 poor neighbourhood; poor people:陈胜、吴广起于～。Chen Sheng and Wu Guang rose from squalid poverty.

榈 lú ☞ 棕榈 zōnglú on p. 2555

lǚ（ㄌㄩˇ）

吕 lǚ ❶ ☞ 律吕 lǜlǚ on p. 1267 ❷（Lǚ）姓 a surname

【吕剧】lǚjù 山东地方戏曲剧种之一，腔调由山东琴书发展而成 Lü opera, one of the local operas in Shandong Province developed on the basis of a local form of storytelling to the accompaniment of a dulcimer

【吕宋烟】lǚsòngyān 雪茄烟，因菲律宾吕宋岛所产的质量好而得名 Luzon cigar; cigar produced in Luzon of the Philippines for its fine quality

侣 lǚ 同伴 companion; associate：伴～ companion; mate; partner | 旧～ old friends | 情～ lovers

【侣伴】lǚbàn 伴侣 companion; mate; partner

捋 lǚ 用手指顺着抹过去，使物体顺溜或干净 smooth out or clean sth. with the fingers; stroke：～胡子 stroke one's beard | ～麻绳 smoothen the hemp rope

☞ luō on p. 1276

旅[1] lǚ ❶ 在外地做客；旅行 travel; stay away from home：～客 tourist | ～途 journey | 行～ luggage; baggage | 商～ travelling traders | ～日侨胞 overseas Chinese residing in Japan | ～京同学会 Union of Students in Beijing ❷〈书 *fml.*〉same as 稆 lǚ

旅[2] lǚ ❶ 军队的编制单位，隶属于师，下辖若干团或营 brigade; army unit below the division and in charge of several regiments or battalions ❷ 指军队 army; troops; forces：劲～ strong army | 军～之事 military affairs ❸〈书 *fml.*〉共同 joint; together：～进～退 advance and retreat together with somebody — have no views of one's own; always follow somebody else's steps forward or backward — have no views of one's own

【旅伴】lǚbàn 旅途中的同伴 travelling companion; fellow traveller

【旅程】lǚchéng 旅行的路程 route; itinerary; journey：万里～ a journey of over 10,000 *li* | 踏上～ start one's journey

【旅次】lǚcì〈书 *fml.*〉旅途中暂居的地方 stopping place on one's journey

【旅店】lǚdiàn same as 旅馆 lǚguǎn

【旅费】lǚfèi 路费 travelling expenses

【旅馆】lǚguǎn 营业性的供旅客住宿的地方 inn; hotel

【旅进旅退】lǚ jìn lǚ tuì 跟大家同进同退。形容自己没有什么主张，跟着别人走。advance and retreat together with others — having no views of one's own; always follow the steps of others, forward or backward — have no views of one's own

【旅居】lǚjū 在外地或外国居住 live away from one's native place; sojourn：～巴黎 reside in Paris | 这几张照片是我～成都时照的。These pictures were taken during my stay in Chengdu.

【旅客】lǚkè 旅行的人 hotel guest; traveller; passenger

【旅鸟】lǚniǎo 候鸟在迁徙途中有规律地从某地经过而不在那里繁殖或越冬，这种鸟叫做该地区的旅鸟 passing migrant; migratory bird that passes a certain area without stopping for reproduction or winter

【旅社】lǚshè 旅馆（多用做旅馆的名称 oft. used in hotel names) hotel

【旅舍】lǚshè〈书 *fml.*〉same as 旅馆 lǚguǎn

【旅途】lǚtú 旅行途中 on a journey; during a trip：～风光 scenery seen during a trip | ～见闻 what one sees and hears during a trip; traveller's notes | ～劳顿 fatigued by a journey; travel-worn | 踏上～ start one's journey

【旅行】lǚxíng 为了办事或游览从一个地方去到另一个地方（多指路程较远的 oft. over a long distance) travel; journey; tour; go from one place to another on business or for sightseeing：～团 tour group; travelling group; touring party | ～结婚 get married on a trip | 春季～ spring tour; spring travel | 到海南岛去～ a tour or a trip to the Hainan Island

【旅行社】lǚxíngshè 专门办理各种旅行业务的服务机构，给旅行的人安排食宿、交通工具等 travel service; travel agency; agency that makes travel arrangements for tourists or other travellers, such as transportation, hotels, and itineraries

【旅游】lǚyóu 旅行游览 tour; tourism：～胜地 places of tourist interest | ～旺季 tourist season | 放假后我们将到青岛～。We are going to have a tour to Qingdao during the vacation.

铝 lǚ 金属元素，符号 Al(aluminum)。银色，质轻，化学性质活泼，延展性强，导电、导热性能好。是工业的重要原料，用途广泛。aluminium (Al); silvery, lightweight, easily worked metallic chemical element that is reactive and has a strong extensibility and electric and heat conductivity, widely used as an important raw material in industry

稆(穭) lǚ 谷物等不种自生的 self-sown：～生 self-sown。

偻[1]**(僂)** lǚ〈书 *fml.*〉弯曲（指身体）hunchbacked; bent：伛（yǔ）～ with one's back bent

偻[2]**(僂)** lǚ〈书〉迅速；立刻 instantly; directly; at once：不能～指（不能立刻指出来）unable to point out right away

☞ lóu on p. 1253

屡(屢) lǚ 屡次 time and again; repeatedly：～见不鲜 not uncommon; nothing new | ～教不改 persist in doing wrong against repeated advice; refuse to mend one's ways despite repeated admonitions | ～战～胜

win every battle fought; won every match played; fought many battles and won every one of them; score one victory after another

【屡次】lǚcì 一次又一次 time and again; repeatedly:～三番 again and again; time and again; over and over again; one after another|他们～创造新记录。They chalked up one record after another.

【屡次三番】lǚ cì sān fān 形容次数很多 many times; again and again; over and over again.

【屡见不鲜】lǚ jiàn bù xiān 数(shuò)见不鲜 common occurrence; nothing new

【屡教不改】lǚ jiào bù gǎi 多次教育，仍不改正 refuse to mend one's ways despite repeated disciplinary actions; also 累教不改 lěi jiào bù gǎi

【屡屡】lǚlǚ same as 屡次 lǚcì:他写这篇回忆录的时候，～搁笔沉思。While writing his reminiscences, he laid down his pen and fell into meditation again and again.

【屡试不爽】lǚ shì bù shuǎng 屡次试验都没有差错 put to repeated tests and proved right

缕(縷) lǚ ❶ 线 thread:细针密～ delicate and fine needlework|千丝万～ have close ties with; have a thousand and one links with|不绝如～ critical situation; very precarious; hung by a thread ❷ 一条一条，详详细细 detailed; in detail:～述 give a detailed account of|条分～析 detailed analysis ❸〈量词 *classifier*〉用于细的东西 wisp; lock; strand:一～麻 a strand of hemp|一～头发 a lock of hair|一～炊烟 a curl of smoke; a wisp of smoke

【缕陈】lǚchén〈书 *fml.*〉缕述(多指下级向上级陈述意见 esp. when reporting to a superior) state in detail :具函～ state in detail by letter

【缕缕】lǚlǚ 形容一条一条，连续不断 continuously; endlessly:丝丝～ endlessly|村中炊烟～上升。Curls of smoke rose continuously from the village chimneys.

【缕述】lǚshù 详细叙述 state in detail; give all the details; go into details (or particulars):人所共知的事实，这里不拟～。No details shall be given here about the facts known to everybody.

【缕析】lǚxī 详细地分析 make a detailed analysis:条分～ make a careful and detailed analysis

膂 lǚ〈书 *fml.*〉脊骨 backbone

【膂力】lǚlì 体力 muscular strength; physical strength; brawn:～过人 possessing extraordinary muscular strength

褛(褸) lǚ ☞［褴褛］(lánlǚ) on p. 1147

履 lǚ ❶ 鞋 shoe:衣～ clothes and footwear|革～ leather shoes|削足适～ cut the feet to fit the shoes ❷ 踩；走 tread on; walk on:～险如夷 go over a dangerous situation as if walking on level ground — cope with a crisis without difficulty|如～薄冰 as if walking on thin ice ❸ 脚步 footstep:步～ walk ❹ 履行 carry out; honour; fulfil:～约 honour a contract

【履带】lǚdài 围绕在拖拉机、坦克等车轮上的钢质链带。装上履带可以减少对地面的压强，并能增加牵引能力。caterpillar tread; track; continuous steel chain roller belt over the cogged wheels on each side of a tractor or tank, used to reduce the pressure on the ground and increase the drawing capacity; also 链轨 liànguǐ

【履历】lǚlì ❶ 个人的经历 personal record (of education, work experience, and attainments); antecedents:～表 (British) curriculum vitae (cv); (American) résumé|他的～很简单。He has a very simple résumé. ❷ 记载履历的文件 curriculum vitae; résumé:请填一份～。Please fill in the form of vitae.

【履任】lǚrèn〈书 *fml.*〉指官员上任 assume office; take an official post

【履险如夷】lǚ xiǎn rú yí 行走在险峻的地方像走在平地上一样 go over a dangerous pass as if walking on level ground;〈比喻 *fig.*〉处于险境而毫不畏惧，也比喻经历危险，但很平安 cope with a crisis without difficulty; emerge unscathed from a crisis

【履行】lǚxíng 实践(自己答应做的或应该做的事) honour (what one has promised to or should do):～诺言 keep one's word; fulfil (or carry out) one's promise|～合同 honour a contract|～手续 go through formalities; go through a procedure

【履约】lǚyuē〈书 *fml.*〉实践约定的事；践约 keep a promise, pledge, agreement, appointment, etc.

lǜ (ㄌㄩˋ)

律 lǜ ❶ 法律；规则 law; statute; rule:定～ law|规～ law|纪～ discipline ❷ 我国古代审定乐音高低的标准，把乐音分为六律和六吕，合称十二律 (of classical Chinese music) pitch; tone; 12 pitch-pipes used to determine the temperament of a number ❸ 旧诗的一种体裁 ancient style of poetry:五～ an eight-line poem with five characters to each line and a strict tonal pattern and rhyme scheme|七～ an eight-line poem with seven characters to each line and a strict tonal pattern and rhyme scheme|排～ a verse form, made up of an indefinite number of rhymed couplets with five or seven characters in each line; ☞律诗 lǜshī ❹〈书 *fml.*〉约束 restrain; keep under control:～己 be strict with oneself|～

人 be strict with others | 自～ exercise strict self-discipline ❺ (Lǜ)姓 a surname

【律己】lǜjǐ 约束自己 restrain oneself：严于～ be strict with oneself; discipline oneself

【律令】lǜlìng 法律条令；法令 laws and decrees; laws and statutes

【律吕】lǜlǚ〈古代 *arch.*〉用竹管制成的校正乐律的器具，以管的长短(各管的管径相等)来确定音的不同高度。从低音管算起，成奇数的六个管叫做'律'；成偶数的六个管叫做'吕'。后来用'律吕'作为音律的统称。12 bamboo pipes of the same calibre used to correct the temperament of music, using their different lengths to determine different pitches of the sounds. Counting from the pipe of the lowest pitch, the odd-numbered pitch-pipes are called *lü* (律) and the even-numbered ones *lü* (吕). *Lü* and *Lü* are used as the general term for temperament of music.

【律师】lǜshī 受当事人委托或法院指定，依法协助当事人进行诉讼，出庭辩护，以及处理有关法律事务的专业人员 lawyer; (British) barrister; (British) solicitor; (American) attorney; professional person entrusted by a party to a lawsuit or by a court to assist the party in the lawsuit and handle other legal matters

【律诗】lǜshī 旧诗体裁之一，形成于唐初。格律较严，每首八句，二、四、六、八句要押韵，三四两句、五六两句要对偶，字的平仄有定规。每句五个字的叫五言律诗，七个字的叫七言律诗。verse; poem of eight lines, each having five or seven characters set down in accordance with a strict tonal pattern and rhyme scheme. The 2nd, 4th, 6th and 8th lines must rhyme; the 3rd and 4th lines, the 5th and 6th lines must form a pair of couplets respectively; the rise or fall of the tone of each character must follow a certain pattern. A poem composed in this pattern with five characters in each line is called 五言律诗 wǔyǎn lǜshī; one with seven characters in each line 七言律诗 qīyǎn lǜshī.

【律条】lǜtiáo ❶ 法律条文 articles or clauses of a law：触犯～ violate a law ❷ 泛指准则 code; rules：做人的～ the code of conduct

【律宗】lǜzōng 我国佛教宗派之一，唐代道宣所创，以注重戒律著称 Legalistic School, one of the eight Buddhist schools in China founded by Daoxuan in the Tang Dynasty, known for its strict enforcement of commandments

俥 lǜ ☞ [猢俥] (hulǜ) on p. 817

虑(慮) lǜ ❶ 思考 consider; ponder; think over：考～ consider; think over | 深谋远～ think deeply and plan carefully; be circumspect and farsighted; foresight | 千～一得 even a fool occasionally hits on a good idea ❷ 担忧；发愁 concern; be anxious; worry：忧～ be anxious; be worried | 疑～ misgivings; doubt | 顾～ misgivings; apprehension; worry | 过～ be over-anxious; worry overmuch | 不足为～ give no cause for anxiety

菉 lǜ [菉豆] (lǜdòu) ☞ 绿豆 lǜdòu on p. 1267 ☞ lù on p. 1260

率 lǜ 两个相关的数在一定条件下的比值 (of two related numbers under certain condition) rate; proportion; ratio：效～ efficiency | 速～ speed; rate | 税～ tax rate; tariff rate | 圆周～ ratio of the circumference of a circle to its diameter | 废品～ rate of rejects | 出勤～ rate of attendance

☞ shuài on p. 1794

绿 lǜ 像草和树叶茂盛时的颜色，蓝颜料和黄颜料混合即呈现这种颜色 green; colour of the grass and tree leaves when they are luxuriant; mixture of blue and yellow pigments：嫩～ light green | 浓～ dark green | 桃红柳～。The peach blossoms are pink and the willow trees are green. | 青山～水 green mountains and blue water

☞ lù on p. 1260

【绿茶】lǜchá 茶叶的一大类，是用高温破坏鲜茶叶中的酶，制止发酵制成的，沏出来的茶保持鲜茶叶原有的绿色。种类很多，如龙井、大方等。green tea; tea made by heating fresh tea leaves in high temperatures to destroy the enzyme contained in them and prevent fermentation so that, when brewed, the leaves can retain their greenness. There are many kinds of green tea, such as the *longjing* and the *dafang* teas.

【绿灯】lǜdēng 安装在交叉路口，指示可以通行的绿色信号灯 green light (a traffic signal); green signal lights installed at the crossroads for the passing of the traffic：开～ switch on the green lights

【绿地】lǜdì 指城镇中经过绿化的空地 greenery patches; greens (in a town or city)

【绿豆】(菉豆) lǜdòu 一年生草本植物，叶子由三片小叶组成，花小，金黄色或绿黄色，荚果内有绿色的种子。种子供食用，又可酿酒。mung bean (*Phaseolus aureus*); green gram; annual herbal plant with each leaf consisting of three leaflets and small, golden or greenish yellow flowers, and edible, green seeds in the pods that are used for food and also for making wine

【绿豆糕】lǜdòugāo 一种糕点，用绿豆粉、白糖等制成 pastry made of mung bean flour and sugar, etc.

【绿豆蝇】lǜdòuyíng 苍蝇的一种，身体较家蝇大，黄绿色而带亮光，喜欢吃腥臭腐败的肉类，能传染疾病 green fly; fly with a shining yellow-green body bigger than a common fly, which likes to eat rotten meats and infects diseases

【绿肥】lǜféi 把植物的嫩茎叶翻压在地里，经过发酵分解而成的肥料 green manure; manure made from the tender stems and leaves of plants left in the fields for fermentation and decomposition

【绿化】lǜhuà 种植树木花草，使环境优美卫生，防止水土流失 make (a place) green by planting trees, flowers, etc. to beautify the environments, improve hygiene and prevent the loss of water and soil; afforest: ～山区 afforest the mountain areas | 城市的～ plant trees in and around a city

【绿卡】lǜkǎ 某些国家发给外国侨民的长期居留证 green card, issued by certain countries to foreigners for permanent residence

【绿篱】lǜlí 用木本或草本植物密植而成的围墙 hedgerow; hedge; fence formed by a row of closely planted shrubs, bushes or trees

【绿帽子】lǜmào·zi same as 绿头巾 lǜtóujīn

【绿内障】lǜnèizhàng 青光眼 glaucoma

【绿茸茸】lǜrōngrōng (～的 lǜrōngrōng·de)形容碧绿而稠密 lush green: ～的稻田 a lush green paddy | ～的羊胡子草像绒毯子一样铺在地上。The ground is covered with green cotton grass like a velvet.

【绿色植物】lǜsè zhíwù 含有叶绿素的植物，除少数细菌、真菌、一部分藻类和若干寄生的高等植物以外，常见的植物都是绿色植物 green plants; plants containing chlorophyll; most plants we usu. see being green plants, with the exception of a small number of germs and fungi, some algae, and certain parasitic higher plants

【绿生生】lǜshēngshēng (～的 lǜshēngshēng·de)形容碧绿而鲜嫩 fresh and green: ～的菠菜 fresh green spinach | 田野披上了～的春装。The fields are covered with the greenery of the spring.

【绿头巾】lǜtóujīn 元明两代规定娼家男子戴绿头巾。后来称人妻子有外遇为戴绿头巾 green scarf; scarf worn by a man whose wife was prostitutes as stipulated in the Yuan and Ming dynasties; (now) cuckold; husband whose wife has sexual intercourses with another man. also 绿帽子 lǜmào·zi

【绿阴】lǜyīn 指树阴 green shade of trees: ～蔽日。The rich foliage of trees has shut out the sun.

【绿茵】lǜyīn 绿草地 carpet of green grass; greensward: ～场(指足球场) football field

【绿莹莹】lǜyíngyíng (～的 lǜyíngyíng·de)形容晶莹碧绿 glittering green: ～的宝石 glittering green stone | 秧苗在雨中显得～的。In the rain rice seedlings were glistening green.

【绿油油】lǜyōuyōu (～的 lǜyōuyōu·de)形容浓绿而润泽 fresh green: ～的麦苗 fresh green wheat seedlings | 鹦鹉一身～的羽毛，真叫人喜欢。The fresh green feathers of the parrot are really lovely.

【绿洲】lǜzhōu 沙漠中有水、草的地方 oasis; area in a desert where there are water and grass

葎 lǜ [葎草](lǜcǎo)一年生或多年生草本植物，密生短刺，叶子对生，掌状分裂，花淡绿色，果穗略作球形。果实可入药。scandent hop (*Humulus scandens*); annual or perennial herbal plant having palmate leaves growing in pairs, pale green flowers and spheric fruits; and fruit used for the Chinese traditional medicine

氯 lǜ 气体元素，符号 Cl(chlorum)。黄绿色，有毒，有强烈的刺激性臭味，容易液化。用来漂白、杀菌或制造漂白粉、染料、颜料、农药、塑料等。chlorine (Cl); greenish yellow, poisonous, gaseous chemical element with a disagreeable odour, apt to be liquidized, used as a bleaching agent, in disinfection, and in making bleaching powder, dyestuffs, paint, insecticides and plastics; 通称 commonly called 氯气 lǜqì

【氯纶】lǜlún 用聚氯乙烯树脂制成的纤维，能耐强酸强碱，遇火不燃烧，用来做工厂的滤布、工作服和电缆的绝缘材料。氯纶的保暖性能好，也用来编织衣物和絮衣被等。polyvinyl chloride fibre; fibre made from polyvinyl chloride, resistant to acid, alkaline and fire, used in making filtering cloth, work overalls and insulating materials for cables. Good for keeping warm, the material is used to weave knitwear and padding clothes and quilts

【氯气】lǜqì 氯的通称 general term for 氯 lǜ

滤(濾) lǜ 使液体通过纱布、木炭或沙子等，除去杂质，变为纯净(间或用于气体) strain; filter; purify a liquid and remove the impurities by passing it through gauze, charcoal or sand (occasionally for gases): 过～ filter | ～器 filter | ～纸 filter paper

【滤波】lǜbō 用一定的装置把不同频率的电磁振荡分离开，只让所需要的频率通过 wave filter; use a certain device that passes electromagnetic vibrations of certain frequencies or frequency ranges while preventing the passage of others

【滤尘】lǜchén 用滤器过滤，使所含的尘土微粒分离出去 dust filter; use of a porous device to remove dust particles from air

【滤器】lǜqì 过滤用的装置，用多孔性材料、松散的固体颗粒、织品等装在管子或容器中构成。滤器只让液体和气体通过，把其中所含的固体微粒分离出去。filter; strainer; device consisting of porous material, loose solid grains and fabric, and a tube or a vessel, which passes only a liquid or gas and prevents the passage of solid particles

【滤色镜】lǜsèjìng 有色透明镜片。只能透过某种色光，而吸收掉其他色光。在摄影中利用它吸收一部分色光，改变拍摄所得影像的色调。最常用的是黄色和黄绿色的，多用玻璃或塑料制成。(colour) filter; transparent lense that passes only a certain colour light and absorbs the others. In photography, a filter is used to absorb part of the colour light and change the tone of the image obtained. The common types of filters are yellow and yellow-green in colour and made of glass or plastic.

【滤液】lǜyè 过滤后得到的澄清液体 filtrate; filtered liquid

【滤渣】lǜzhā 过滤时分离出来的固体颗粒 residue left from a filtering process

【滤纸】lǜzhǐ 用纯洁纤维制成的质地疏松的纸，一般裁成圆形，用时卷成锥形放在漏斗中，可以过滤溶液 filter paper; soft, porous paper made of pure fibre, usu. round in shape, and rolled into a cone and placed in a funnel when used for the filtering of a liquid

镳(鑢) lǜ〈书 *fml*.〉❶ 打磨铜、铁、骨、角等的工具 implement for burnishing bronze, iron, bone, horn, etc. ❷ 打磨 burnish; sand; polish; shine

luán (ㄌㄨㄢˊ)

峦(巒) luán〈书 *fml*.〉山(多指连绵的) hill; mountains in a range: 山～ hill; mountain | 冈～ hill; hillock; ridge | 峰～ ridges and peaks | 重～叠嶂 mountain ranges; range upon range of mountains

【峦嶂】luánzhàng 直立像屏障的山峦 screen-like mountain peak

娈(孌) luán〈书 *fml*.〉相貌美 beautiful; pretty; handsome

孪(孿) luán〈书 *fml*.〉孪生 twin: ～子 twin boys

【孪生】luánshēng (两人)同一胎出生 twins: ～子 twin boys | ～兄弟 twin brothers; 通称 commonly called 双生 shuāngshēng

栾(欒) luán ❶ 栾树，落叶乔木，羽状复叶，小叶卵形，花淡黄色，圆锥花序，结蒴果，长椭圆形。种子圆形，黑色。叶子含鞣质，可制栲胶。花可做黄色染料。golden-rain tree (*Koelreuteria paniculata*); deciduous tree with pinnatifid compound leaves, oval leaflets, yellowish flowers borne in panicles, oblong capsules, and black round seeds; its leaves containing tannin are used for making tannin extracts and its flowers for making yellow dyes ❷ (Luán)姓 a surname

挛(攣) luán 蜷曲不能伸直 contraction: ～缩 contracture | 拘～ contraction | 痉～ spasm; convulsion

【挛缩】luánsuō 蜷曲收缩 contracture: 局部软组织～，血液循环不良。Contracture of local soft tissues causes poor blood circulation.

鸾(鸞) luán 传说中凤凰一类的鸟 fabulous bird related to the phoenix

【鸾俦】luánchóu〈书 *fml*.〉〈比喻 *fig*.〉夫妻 married couple: 永结～ be a married couple for life | ～凤侣 a happy couple

【鸾凤】luánfèng〈比喻 *fig*.〉夫妻 married couple: ～和鸣(夫妻和美) be blessed with conjugal felicity; be a happy couple | ～分飞(夫妻离散) separation of a married couple

脔(臠) luán〈书 *fml*.〉切成小片的肉 small slice of meat: ～割 cut meat into small slices; slice up; carve up; cut up | 尝鼎一～ taste a small slice of the meat in the pot to know the whole of it

【脔割】luángē〈书 *fml*.〉分割; 切碎 slice up; carve up; cut up

圞(圝、圞) luán〈方 *dial*.〉❶ 圆 round: 皮球溜～。The ball is round. ❷ 整个的 whole: 清蒸～鸡 steamed whole chicken

滦(灤) Luán 滦河，水名，在河北 Luanhe, name of a river in Hebei Province

銮(鑾) luán ❶ 铃铛 small tinkling bell: ～铃 small tinkling bell ❷ 皇帝车驾上有銮铃，借指皇帝的车驾 imperial carriage: 迎～ greet the emperor

【銮驾】luánjià same as 銮舆 luányú

【銮铃】luánlíng〈旧时 *old*〉车马上系的铃铛 tinkling bells on a carriage

【銮舆】luányú 皇帝的车驾 imperial carriage

luǎn (ㄌㄨㄢˇ)

卵 luǎn ❶ 动植物的雌性生殖细胞，与精子结合后产生第二代 ovum; egg; spawn; female reproductive cell of an animal or a plant that produces offspring once it is conceived with sperm ❷ 昆虫学上特指受精的卵，是昆虫生活周期的第一个发育阶段 fertilized egg of an insect, the first stage of the development of the life cycle of an insect ❸〈方 *dial*.〉称睾丸或阴茎(多指人的 oft. of a man) testis; testicle; penis; genitals

【卵白】luǎnbái same as 蛋白 dànbái ①

【卵巢】luǎncháo 女子和雌性动物的生殖腺。除产生卵子外，还分泌激素促进子宫、阴道、乳腺等的发育。人的卵巢在腹腔的下部骨盆内，扁椭圆形，左右各一，分列在子宫的两侧。ovary; gonad of a woman or a female animal. Apart from producing eggs, it also secretes hormone to promote the development of the uterus, vagina and mammary gland. A woman has two oval-shaped ovaries in the pelvis in the lower part of the abdominal cavity, one on either side of the womb.

【卵黄】luǎnhuáng 蛋黄 yolk; yellow substance of an egg

【卵块】luǎnkuài 某些卵生动物的卵产生后粘在

一起，形成块状，叫做卵块 egg cluster; eggs produced by some oviparous animals stuck together to form a cluster

【卵泡】luǎnpāo 卵巢内的囊泡，由卵细胞及其周围的细胞所组成 follicle; sac in the ovary consisting of an egg cell (ovum) and the cells surrounding it

【卵生】luǎnshēng 动物由脱离母体的卵孵化出来，叫做卵生 oviparity; oviparous; producing eggs which hatch after leaving the body of the female

【卵石】luǎnshí 岩石经自然风化、水流冲击和摩擦所形成的卵形或接近卵形的石块，表面光滑，直径 5—150 毫米，是天然建筑材料，用于铺路、制混凝土等 cobble; pebble; rock weathered and worn smooth and round into the shape of an egg with the diameter of from 5-150 millimetres, used as a natural building material for surfacing roads and making concrete

【卵胎生】luǎntāishēng 某些卵生的动物如鲨等，卵在母体内孵化，母体不产卵而产出幼小的动物。这种生殖的方式叫做卵胎生。ovoviviparity; ovoviviparous; designating certain oviparous animals, as sharks, which produce eggs with enclosing membranes, that are hatched within the body of the female so that the female body does not lay eggs but gives birth to the young

【卵细胞】luǎnxìbāo same as 卵 luǎn ①

【卵翼】luǎnyì 鸟用翼护卵，孵出小鸟(of a bird) cover with wings in brooding; 〈比喻 *fig.*〉养育或庇护(多含贬义 oft. derog.) shield like a bird protecting eggs under its wings: ～之下 under the aegis of; be shielded by

【卵用鸡】luǎnyòngjī 主要为产蛋而饲养的鸡种，如来亨鸡 chicken raised for egg production (e.g. the Leghorn chicken); layer

【卵子】luǎnzǐ same as 卵 luǎn ①

【卵子】luǎn·zi 〈方 *dial.*〉 same as 卵 luǎn ③

luàn (ㄌㄨㄢ)

乱(亂) luàn ❶ 没有秩序；没有条理 having no order; in disorder; in a mess; in confusion: 一团～麻 a mass of tangled flax | ～七八糟 a nice mess | 人声马声～成一片 din and traffic; cacophony of voices and the neighing of horses | 这篇稿子改得太～了，要重抄一下。The manuscript is too messy. You have to copy it out. ❷ 战争；武装骚扰 war; armed riot: 变～ turmoil; upheaval; unrest | 叛～ rebellion; revolt; insurrection | 兵～ mutiny; the scourge of war | 避～ take refugee ❸ 使混乱；使紊乱 throw into disorder; confuse; mix up: 扰～ disturb; disrupt; harrass; confuse | 惑～ confuse | 以假～真 mix the false with the true ❹ (心绪)不宁 in a confused state of mind; in turmoil: 心烦意～ be fretful and confused; be vexed and confused; be terribly upset | 他的心里～得一点主意也没有。He is so confused that he doesn't know what to do. ❺ 任意；随便 indiscriminate; random; arbitrary: ～吃 eat indiscriminately | ～跑 run all over the place; dash about | ～出主意 give offhand advice; give offhand ideas ❻ 不正当的男女关系 illicit sexual relations: 淫～ illicit sexual relations; promiscuous

【乱兵】luànbīng 叛乱或溃散的兵 rebellious soldiers; mutinous soldiers; defeated and dispersed soldiers

【乱臣】luànchén 作乱的臣子 treacherous (or rebellious) minister or subject: ～贼子 traitors and usurpers

【乱纷纷】luànfēnfēn (～的 luànfēnfēn·de) 形容杂乱纷扰 in disorder; disorderly; confused; chaotic: ～的人群 a tumultuous crowd | 他心里～的，怎么也安静不下来。He's rather disturbed and can hardly calm down.

【乱坟岗】luànféngǎng same as 乱葬岗子 luànzàng-gǎng·zi

【乱哄哄】luànhōnghōng (～的 luànhōnghōng·de) 形容声音嘈杂 in noisy disorder; in a hubbub; tumultuous; in an uproar: ～地嚷成一片。There was an uproar.

【乱乎】luàn·hu 〈方 *dial.*〉混乱 in confusion; in chaos; also 乱糊 luàn·hu

【乱离】luànlí 因遭战乱而流离失所 be separated by war; be rendered homeless by war

【乱伦】luànlún 指在法律或风俗习惯不允许的情况下近亲属之间发生性行为 commit incest; have sex with sb. one is closely related and not permitted either by law or by customs to marry

【乱民】luànmín 〈旧时 *old*〉统治者指造反作乱的百姓 common people in revolt; rebellious people; rebels, as described by the rulers

【乱蓬蓬】luànpēngpēng (～的 luànpēngpēng·de) 形容须发或草木凌乱 dishevelled; tangled; jumbled: 衣冠不整，头发也～的 be sloppily dressed and have dishevelled hair | ～的茅草 a jumbled mass of reeds

【乱七八糟】luànqībāzāo 形容混乱；乱糟糟的 at sixes and sevens; a nice mess; be messy: 稿子涂改得～，很多字都看不清楚。The script was altered in an aweful mess, and many characters are hardly recognizable. | 他越想越没主意，心里～的。The more he thought, the less he knew what to do. He was wholly perturbed.

【乱世】luànshì 混乱动荡的时代 troubled times; turbulent days

【乱弹】luàntán 清代乾隆(1736—1795)、嘉庆(1796—1820)年间对昆腔、弋阳腔以外的戏曲腔调的统称。以皮黄为主的京剧是从乱弹发展出来的。*luantan* tones; general term for opera styles other than the *Kun* and *Yiyang* operas during the Qianlong and Jiaqing reigns of the Qing Dynasty. The Peking Opera, which was characterized by the *Xipi* and *erhuang* tones, was developed on the basis of the *luantan* tones.

【乱弹琴】luàntánqín〈比喻 *fig*.〉胡闹或胡扯 act or talk like a fool; talk nonsense:在这关键时刻,人都走了,真是~! The people have all left at this critical moment. It's sheer nonsense.

【乱套】luàn//tào 乱了次序或秩序 out of order; muddle things up; turn things upside down:各行其是,非~不可。If everyone acts as he pleases, everything will be in a muddle.|会场上吵成一片,乱了套了。They argued vehemently at the meeting. It was a terrible mess.

【乱腾腾】luànténgténg (~的 luànténgténg·de)形容混乱或骚动 confused; upset:心里~的,不知怎么办才好。Feeling much disturbed, I was at a loss what to do.

【乱腾】luàn·teng 混乱;不安静,没有秩序 confused; disorderly; restless:刚说到这里,会场上就~起来了。Just as he came to this point in his speech, the meeting was out of order.

【乱营】luàn//yíng〈方 *dial*.〉〈比喻 *fig*.〉秩序混乱 disorder:枪声一响,敌人~了。The firing of guns threw the enemy into disorder.|老师刚走开,教室里就乱了营了。Right after the teacher left, the classroom turned into a beehive.

【乱杂】luànzá 杂乱 chaotic; untidy; jumble; jumble up; be in a jumble:事情~,没有头绪。Everything is in a jumble. I've no idea what to start with.

【乱葬岗子】luànzàng-gǎng·zi 无人管理任人埋葬尸首的土岗子 disorderly graves; unattended burial mounds; also 乱坟岗 luànféngǎng

【乱糟糟】luànzāozāo (~的 luànzāozāo·de)形容事物杂乱无章或心里烦乱 chaotic; untidy; in a mess:桌子上~的,得清理一下。The table is a mess. We have to tidy it up.|坐也不是,站也不是,心里~的 feel very perturbed as if on pins and needles

【乱真】luànzhēn 模仿得很像,使人不辨真伪(多指古玩、书画 oft. referring to antiques and paintings) look genuine due to close imitation:以假~ mix the false with the real; mix the spurious with the genuine|复制精细,几可~。The fine copy can almost pass for the genuine one.

【乱子】luàn·zi 祸事;纠纷 disturbance; trouble; disorder:闹~ make trouble; create disturbance|出~ create disturbance; run into trouble

lüě(ㄌㄩㄝˇ)

掠 lüě〈方 *dial*.〉顺手拿;抄 pick up:~起一根棍子就打 pick up a stick and beat someone|晾在门口的衣裳不知让谁给~去了。It's hard to tell who has taken away the clothes being dried in front of the door.
☞ lüè on p.1271

lüè(ㄌㄩㄝˋ)

掠 lüè ❶ 掠夺(多指财物) plunder; pillage; sack:抢~ take by force; loot; rob; plunder|~取 seize; grab; plunder|奸淫掳~ rape and loot ❷ 轻轻擦过或拂过 scud; skim over; sweep past; brush past; graze:凉风~面。A cool breeze brushed my face.|燕子~过水面。The swallows skimmed over the water.|炮弹~过夜空。The shells flashed through the night sky.|他用手~一下额前的头发。He brushed the hair in front of his forehead with his hand.◇嘴角上~过一丝微笑。A faint smile flickered across her lips. ❸〈书 *fml*.〉用棍子或鞭子打 beat with a stick or whip:拷~ torture during interrogation
☞ lüě on p.1271

【掠夺】lüèduó 抢劫;夺取: plunder; rob; pillage:~财物 rob someone of one's property|经济~ economic plunder

【掠夺婚】lüèduóhūn 原始社会的一种婚姻习俗,男子用抢劫女子的方式成亲,是对偶婚向一夫一妻制过渡的重要标志。这种习俗在某些地区曾长期留存。marriage by capture; marriage custom in the primitive society, by which a man took a woman by force as his wife — important sign for the transfer from pairing marriage to monogamous marriage. The custom remained for a long time in some regions. also 抢婚 qiǎnghūn

【掠美】lüèměi 掠取别人的美名 claim credit due to sb. else:这是名家的手笔,我不敢~。This comes from the hand of a master. I can't claim credit for it.

【掠取】lüèqǔ 夺取;抢夺 seize; grab; plunder:~财物 rob a person of his goods|~资源 plunder resources

【掠视】lüèshì 目光迅速地掠过;扫视 sweeping glance:站在房门口向室内~一周 stand at the door and take a sweeping glance over the room

【掠影】lüèyǐng 一掠而过的影像,指某些场面的大致的情况(多用于标题 oft. used in titles) glimpse; brief description of an occasion:浮光~ skimming over the surface; superficial|《自然博物馆~》*A Glimpse of the Natural Museum*

略[1]（畧）lüè ❶ 简单，略微（跟'详'相对 as opposed to 'detailed'）brief; sketchy：大～ general outline; broad outline; general idea | 粗～ rough; sketchy | ～图 sketch; sketch map | ～读 read a little | ～知一二 know a little | ～有所闻 have heard a little | 这个提纲写得太～了。The outline is too brief. ❷ 简单扼要的叙述 brief account：史～ historical outline; outline history | 事～ biographical sketch | 节～ excerpts; extracts | 要～ summary; outline ❸ 省去；简化 omit; delete; leave out：从～ be omitted | 省～ omit; leave out; delete | 中间的部分～去不说。The middle part is left out. *or* No mention is made of the middle part.

略[2]（畧）lüè 计划；计谋 plan; scheme; strategy：方～ plan; scheme; programme | 策～ strategy | 谋～ plan; scheme; strategy; astuteness and resourcefulness | 战～ strategy | 雄才大～ of great capability and bold vision

略[3]（畧）lüè 夺取（多指土地 usu. of land）capture; seize：侵～ aggression | 攻城～地 take cities and seize territories

【略称】lüèchēng 简称 abbreviation; shortened form

【略略】lüèlüè 稍微 slightly; briefly：微风吹来，湖面上～漾起波纹。The lake rippled gently in the breeze. | 我～说了几句，他就明白了。I said only a few words, and he saw my point.

【略识之无】lüè shí zhī wú 指识字不多（'之'和'无'是古汉语常用的字 之 zhī and 无 wú being frequently used characters in ancient Chinese）know only a few simple characters

【略图】lüètú 简略的图形；简单的图画 sketch map; sketch

【略微】lüèwēi 稍微 slightly; a little; somewhat：～歇一会儿。I had a little rest. | 擦破了皮，～流了点血。I got a scratch and it bled a little.

【略为】lüèwéi 稍微 slightly; a little; somewhat：～增加 a slight increase; increase slightly (a little) | 他～定了定神。He calmed down a little.

【略语】lüèyǔ 由词组紧缩而成的合成词，如：土改（土地改革）、扫盲（扫除文盲）、脱产（脱离生产）、节育（节制生育）、沧桑（沧海桑田）abbreviation; shortening, e.g. 土改 tǔgǎi for 土地改革 tǔdì gǎigé，扫盲 sǎo//máng for 扫除文盲 sǎochú wénmáng，脱产 tuō//chǎn for 脱离生产 tuōlí shēngchǎn，节育 jiéyù for 节制生育 jiézhì shēngyù，沧桑 cāngsāng for 沧海桑田 cānghǎi sāngtián

锊 lüè〈古代 *arch.*〉重量单位，约合六两 ancient unit of weight, equivalent to six taels

啮（囵）lüè ☞［啰啮］(kūlüè) on p.1114

lūn（ㄌㄨㄣ）

抡（掄）lūn ❶ 用力挥动 brandish; swing：～拳 shake a fist | ～刀 brandish a sword | ～起铁锤打炮眼 swing a sledge hammer ❷ 挥动胳膊抛出去；扔 throw：把菜～了一地。Vegetables were thrown all over the ground.

☞ lún on p.1273

lún（ㄌㄨㄣˊ）

仑（侖）lún〈书 *fml.*〉条理；伦次 system; turn

伦（倫）lún ❶ 人伦 human relations, esp. as conceived by feudal ethics：～常 feudal order of importance or seniority in human relationships | ～理 ethics; moral principles | 五～ five cardinal relationships in traditional ethics — between monarch and subject, father and son, husband and wife, among brothers and among friends | 天～ natural bonds and ethical relationships between members of a family ❷ 条理；次序 logic; order：～次 logical sequence; coherence ❸ 同类；同等 peer; match：不～不类 neither fish nor fowl; nondescript; grotesque | 比拟不～ incomparable; beyond comparison | 英勇绝～ matchlessly brave ❹（Lún）姓 a surname

【伦巴】lúnbā 交际舞的一种，原是古巴的黑人舞，4/4拍 rumba (dance); modern dance of Cuban origin and complex rhythm［西 Spanish: rumba］

【伦比】lúnbǐ〈书 *fml.*〉同等；匹敌 match; equal：史无～ unrivalled (*or* peerless, unequalled) in history | 无与～ unmatched; unparalleled

【伦常】lúncháng 我国封建社会的伦理道德。封建时代称君臣、父子、夫妇、兄弟、朋友五种关系为五伦，认为这种尊卑、长幼的关系是不可改变的常道，称为伦常。feudal order of importance or seniority in human relationships; feudal ethics in China; the relationships between monarch and subject, father and son, husband and wife, among brothers and among friends were called the five cardinal relationships in traditional ethics in the feudal times. They were the normal and constant ethics that must remain unchanged.

【伦次】lúncì 语言、文章的条理次序 coherence; logical sequence：语无～ speak incoherently or illogically | 文笔错杂，毫无～。The writing is tangled, utterly lacking in coherence.

【伦理】lúnlǐ 指人与人相处的各种道德准则 ethics; moral principles for dealing with people

【伦理学】lúnlǐxué 关于道德的起源、发展,人的行为准则和人与人之间的义务的学说 ethics; study of the origin and development of the morals, the standards of conduct and the obligations among humans

【伦琴】lúnqín 射线强度单位,1伦琴约等于1居里的放射线在1小时内所放出的射线量。这个单位名称是为纪念德国物理学家伦琴(Wilhelm Konrad Röntgen)而定的。roentgen; unit of measuring the intensity of rays, named after the German physicist Wilhelm Konrad Röntgen, with 1 roentgen approximately equal to the quantity of rays emitted by the radioactive rays of 1 curie in one hour

论(論) Lún 论语(古书名,内容主要是记录孔子及其门徒的言行) *Analects*, book which mainly recorded the words and deeds of Confucius and his disciples:上~ *Analects Part One*|下~ *Analects Part Two*

☞ lùn on p.1275

抡(掄) lún 〈书 *fml.*〉挑选,选拔 choose; select:~材 select men of ability

☞ lūn on p.1272

岺(崙) lún 崑岺(Kūnlún),山名,在新疆、西藏和青海。今作昆仑。Kunlun Mountains, bordering Xinjiang, Tibet and Qinghai, now written as 昆仑 kūnlún

囵(圇) lún ☞ 囫囵 húlún on p.817

沦(淪) lún ❶ 沉没 sink:沉~ sink; sink into|~于海底 sink to the bottom of the sea ❷ 没落;陷入(不利的境地) decline; fall; be reduced to:~落 become a vagabond; be homeless; fall; decline |~陷 fall into the hands of|~为奴隶 be reduced to slavery

【沦肌浃髓】lún jī jiā suǐ 浸透肌肉,深入骨髓 penetrate to the marrow;〈比喻 *fig.*〉感受或受影响深 be deeply impressed; be greatly affected

【沦落】lúnluò ❶ 流落 wander:~街头 wander in the street; be driven into the streets (to become a tramp, beggar, vagabond, etc.); be reduced to beggary, vagrancy, etc. ❷〈书 *fml.*〉没落;衰落 fall low; come down in the world; decline:道德~ morally depraved; moral depravity|家境~ be reduced to poverty ❸ 沉沦 sink; sink into:~风尘 sink into prostitution|半壁江山~敌手。Half of the country was occupied by the enemy. *or* Half of the country fell into the enemy hands.

【沦没】lúnmò 〈书 *fml.*〉❶ 沉没;湮没 sink; submerge ❷ (人)死亡 (of a person) die; also 沦殁 lúnmò

【沦丧】lúnsàng 消亡;丧失 be lost; be ruined:国土~。The territory was lost.

【沦亡】lúnwáng ❶ (国土)失陷;(国家)灭亡 lose the territory; (the territory) fall into the enemy hands; perish; fall; downfall; be destroyed; be annexed ❷ 沦落;丧失 lose; fall; be reduced to; decline:道德~ morally depraved; moral depravity

【沦陷】lúnxiàn ❶ (领土)为敌人占领;失陷 (of territory, etc.) be occupied by the enemy; fall into enemy hands:~区 area occupied by the enemy; enemy-occupied area ❷〈书 *fml.*〉淹没 submerge; inundate; flood; drown

纶(綸) lún ❶〈书〉青丝带子 black silk ribbon ❷〈书 *fml.*〉钓鱼用的丝线 fishing line:垂~ fishing ❸ 指某些合成纤维 synthetic fibres:锦~ polyamide fibre|涤~ polyvinyl chloride fibre|腈~ acrylic fibres|丙~ polypropylene fibre

☞ guān on p.713

轮(輪) lún ❶ (~儿 lúnr)轮子 wheel:车~ wheel|齿~儿 gear|三~摩托车 three-wheeled motorcycle ◇历史的巨~ the wheel of history ❷ 形状像轮子的东西 sth. resembling a wheel; disc; ring:日~ sun disk|月~ full moon|年~ annual ring; growth ring|耳~ helix ❸ 轮船 steamboat; steamer; ship:江~ river steamer|油~ oil tanker|~渡 ferry|~埠 port; wharf; harbour ❹ 依照次序一个接替一个(做事) take turns; by turn:~换 take turns; rotate|~班 in shifts; by turns; in rotation|~值 be on duty|~训 training in rotation|一个人~一天 each person on duty by turns for a day|你快准备好,马上~到你了。Get ready quickly. It will soon be your turn. ❺〈量词 *classifier*〉a) 多用于红日、明月等 [oft. used for the sun, the moon, etc.]:一~红日 red sun|一~明月 bright moon b)(~儿 lúnr)用于循环的事物或动作 round; sth. or movement that goes in a cycle:头~影院 top-class cinema (which has the priority to show new films)|我大哥也属马,比我大一~(即大十二岁)。My elder brother was born also in the Year of Horse and 12 years older than I.|篮球冠军赛已经打了一~儿。The basketball championships have finished its first round. *or* The first round has been finished at the basketball championships.

【轮班】lún//bān (~儿 lún//bānr)分班轮流 (work) in shifts; in rotation; take turns:~替换 work in shifts|民兵轮着班放哨。The militiamen took turns standing guard

【轮埠】lúnbù 轮船码头 wharf; port; dock; pier; quay

【轮唱】lúnchàng 演唱者分成两个或两个以上的组,按一定时距先后错综演唱同一旋律的歌曲 round; canon; troll; musical composition in which two or more rhythmical voices enter at different times at the union

【轮船】lúnchuán 利用机器推动的船,船身一般用钢铁制成 steamer; ship; steamboat; boat made of iron and propelled by an engine

【轮次】lúncì ❶ 按次序轮流 in turn; by turns: ～入内 enter in turn | ～上场 enter the field one after another | ～陪住 take turns to stay with and look after sb. ❷ 轮流的次数,轮换一遍叫一个轮次 number of turns or rounds; times: 每日由一人值班,十个人轮流,一个月也就三个～。One person needs to be on duty each day, so if ten people take turns, it's only three rounds per month.

【轮带】lúndài same as 轮胎 lúntāi

【轮渡】lúndù 运载行人、车辆等渡过河流、湖泊、海峡的轮船以及其他设备 ferry; boat and other equipment devices that carry passengers and vehicles across rivers, lakes and straits

【轮番】lúnfān 轮流(做某件事) take turns (to do sth.): ～上阵 go into battle one after another; takes turns to pitch in; take turns to play in a game

【轮辐】lúnfú 车轮上连接轮辋和轮毂的部分 spoke; rod connecting the hub and rim of a wheel

【轮毂】lúngǔ 车轮的中心装轴的部分 (wheel) hub; (wheel) boss; nave

【轮换】lúnhuàn 轮流替换 rotate; take turns: ～休息 take a rest in turn; take turns to rest | 剧目～演出 put on stage performances by using different programmes in turns | 干部～着去参加学习。The cadres took turns to study.

【轮回】lúnhuí ❶〈佛教 *Budd.*〉指有生命的东西永远像车轮运转一样在天堂、地狱、人间等六个范围内循环转化 samsara; metempsychosis; reincarnation; (of a life) transmigrate eternally within six realms, including paradise, hell and the human world, like an ever-turning wheel ❷ 循环 circle; circulate: 四季～。The four seasons succeed one another.

【轮机】lúnjī ❶ 涡轮机的简称 abbr. for 涡轮机 wōlúnjī ❷ 轮船上的动力机 motor; engine in a ship

【轮奸】lúnjiān 两个或两个以上男子轮流强奸同一女子 gang rape; rape of a woman by two or more men

【轮空】lúnkōng 在分几轮的比赛中,某队或某人在某一轮(多为第一、二轮)没有安排对手而直接进入下一轮比赛,叫做轮空 bye; situation in a round (oft. the 1st and 2nd rounds) of a sports competition in which a player or a team does not have an opponent to play against and advances straight to the next round of the competition

【轮廓】lúnkuò ❶ 构成图形或物体的外缘的线条 contour; rough sketch; profile; silhouette; outline of a figure or an object: 他画了一个人体的～。He drew an outline of a human figure. | 城楼在月光下面显出朦胧的～。The gate tower stood in vague silhouette against the moonlight. ❷(事情的)概况 survey; general situation: 我只知道个～,详情并不清楚。I've only got a rough idea of the whole situation.

【轮流】lúnliú 依照次序一个接替一个,周而复始 take turns; do sth. in turn: ～值日 work on shifts in turn | ～坐庄 take turns to be the resident buyer of a business firm; take turns to be a banker or a dealer in a gambling game

【轮牧】lúnmù 把一定范围的草原划为几个区,轮流牧放。这样可以使牧草有轮流生长的时间,使牲畜经常吃到好草。rotation grazing; herding in different parts of a pasture in turn so as to leave enough time for the grass to grow enough to feed the animals

【轮生】lúnshēng 叶序的一种,茎的每个节上长三个或更多的叶子,环列在节的周围,如夹竹桃、黑藻等的叶子都是轮生叶 verticillate; leaf arrangement or phyllotaxy, with three or more leaves growing around each node of a stem, such as the leaves of the oleander and black algae: ～叶 verticillate leaf; whorled leaf

【轮胎】lúntāi 汽车、拖拉机、自行车等的轮子外围安装的环形橡胶制品,一般分内胎、外胎两层。内胎较薄,可以充气;外胎较厚,耐磨,可以保护内胎。轮胎充气后,能够减弱沿地面行驶时产生的震动。tyre; circular rubber product (usu. in two parts: the inner tube and the exterior tyre) installed on the rim of wheels of an automobile, a tractor, a bicycle, etc. The inner tube is thin and air can be pumped into it, while the thick and durable exterior tyre protects the interior one, and after air is pumped in, tyres can reduce shocks on a vehicle; 通称 generally called 车胎 chētāi or 轮带 lúndāi

【轮辋】lúnwǎng 车轮周围边缘的部分 rim of a wheel

【轮系】lúnxì 机器上互相啮合以传递轴的运动的齿轮传动系统 assembly of joggled gears and associated parts for transmitting the motion or power of an axle

【轮休】lúnxiū ❶ 某一个耕种时期不种植农作物,让土地空闲起来,以恢复地力 (of land) lie fallow in rotation; rotation farming; way to restore soil fertility and increase per-unit yield by planting no crops in the soil for a period of time ❷ (职工)轮流休息 (of workers) take holidays by turns; rotate days off; stagger holidays

【轮训】lúnxùn (人员)轮流训练 (of staff workers) training in rotation: 干部～ training cadres in rotation | 脱产～ out-service training in rotation

【轮养】lúnyǎng 渔业上指一个养鱼塘里,轮换着饲养不同种类的鱼 raise various species of fishes in rotation in the same pond

【轮椅】lúnyǐ 装有轮子的椅子,通常供行走困难的人使用 wheelchair; chair with wheels used by people who cannot walk

【轮值】lúnzhí 轮流值班 rotating duty：清洁卫生工作由大家～。The cleaning work will be taken care of by everyone in turns.

【轮轴】lúnzhóu 简单机械，由一个轮子和同心轴组成，实质是可以连续旋转的杠杆。轮子半径是轴半径的几倍，作用在轮上的动力就是作用在轴上阻力的几分之一。轮和轴的半径相差越大就越省力。辘轳、纺车等就属于这一类。wheel and axle; wheel shaft; simple mechanism consisting of a wheel and a concentric axle that acts a continuously rotating lever. Since the radius of the wheel is several times longer than that of the axle, the force needed to move the wheel is several times less than the resisting friction on the axle. The greater the difference between the radius of the wheel and the axle, the more energy-saving it becomes; a theory according to which the windlass, spinning wheel, etc., are manufactured.

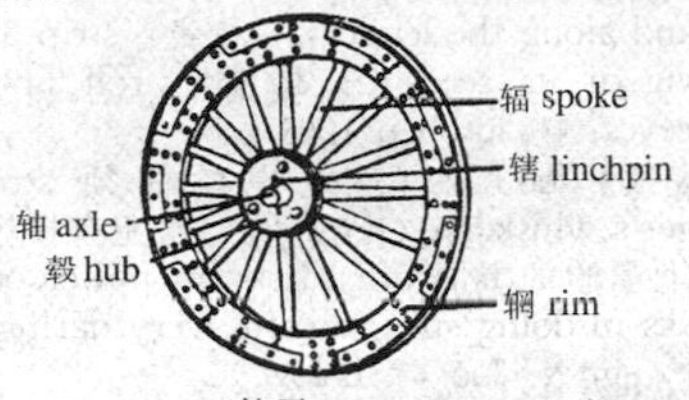

轮子 Wheel
（旧式的 Old-fashioned）

【轮转】lúnzhuàn ❶ 旋转；循环 rotate：四时～。The four seasons rotate. ❷〈方 *dial.*〉same as 轮流 lúnliú：～着值夜班 take turns on night shifts

【轮子】lún·zi 车辆或机械上能够旋转的圆形部件 wheel; round parts that move on vehicles or machinery

【轮作】lúnzuò 在一块田地上依次轮换栽种几种作物。轮作可以改善土壤肥力，减少病害。crop rotation; practice of regularly changing the crops planted on a piece of land in order to preserve the quality of the soil and prevent plant diseases and insect pests; also 轮栽 lúnzāi，轮种 lúnzhòng，倒茬 dǎochá or 调茬 diàochá

lǔn（ㄌㄨㄣˇ）

坨（埨）lǔn〈方 *dial.*〉田地中的土垄 ridge in a field; raised path in a field

lùn（ㄌㄨㄣˋ）

论（論）lùn ❶ 分析和说明事理 analyse and explain：议～ talk about; comment｜讨～ discuss｜辩～ argue; debate｜就事～事 consider or judge sth. as it is; deal with a matter on its merits ❷ 分析和说明事理的话或文章 words or articles that analyse and explain sth.：舆～ public opinion｜立～ put forward one's view｜社～ editorial ❸ 学说 theory; doctrine：唯物～ materialism｜进化～ evolutionism｜相对～ theory of relativity; relativity ❹ 说；看待 speak of; mention; treat：相提并～ mention in the same breath; group together; place on a par｜不能一概而～ cannot be treated all alike; not to be lumped together ❺ 衡量；评定 decide on; determine; appraise; evaluate：～罪 bring sb. to justice｜～功行赏 dispense rewards and honours according to merit; reward people according to their contributions｜请假超过一学期三分之一，以休学～。Taking off more than one third of the days in a semester is regarded as being suspended from school. ❻ 按照某种单位或类别说 by; in terms of：～天 by day｜～件 by piece｜买鸡蛋是～斤还是～个儿？Are the eggs sold by the *jin* or by piece?｜～庄稼活儿，他是把好手。He is a good hand as far as farm work is concerned. ❼（Lùn）姓 a surname
☞ Lún on p. 1273

【论辩】lùnbiàn 辩论 argue, debate，～有力。It's a strong argument.｜针锋相对地进行～ argue in a tit-for-tat way

【论处】lùnchǔ 判定处分 decide on sb.'s punishment; punish：依法～ punish according to law｜按违法的行为～ be punished for breaking law

【论敌】lùndí 指政治、学术等方面的争论的对手 adversary; one's rival in a political or academic debate

【论点】lùndiǎn 议论中的确定意见以及论证这一意见的理由 argument; thesis：这篇文章～突出，条理分明。The argument set forth in the article is clear-cut and the reasoning is systematic.

【论调】lùndiào 议论的倾向；意见（常含贬义 oft. derog.）viewpoint; argument：悲观的～ a tragic tone｜这种～貌似公允，很容易迷惑人。This kind of seemingly fair argument easily confuses people.

【论断】lùnduàn 推论判断 inference; judgment; thesis：科学～ scientific judgment

【论据】lùnjù ❶ 逻辑学指用来证明论题的判断 reasoning using logic ❷ 立论的根据（多指事实 oft. factual）grounds of argument; argument：充足的～ substantive argument; sufficient grounds of argument

【论理】lùn//lǐ 讲道理 reason (with sb.)：当面～ reason with sb. face to face｜他为什么那样说？把他找来论论理。Why did he say that? Go and bring him here so we can argue it out.

【论理】lùnlǐ ❶ 按理说 normally; as things should be: ～我早该回家去探望一下,只是工作实在放不下。Normally I would go home early, but it's not possible today because of my work. ❷ 逻辑 logic: 合乎～ be logical; stand to reason

【论理学】lùnlǐxué 逻辑学的旧称 old name for 逻辑学 luó·jixué

【论难】lùnnàn 针对对方的论点进行辩论 debate; challenge in debate; argue against the opponent's viewpoint: 两个学派各执一说,互相～。Sticking to their respective arguments, the two schools of thought challenged each other's viewpoints.

【论述】lùnshù 叙述和分析 analyse; expound: 本文准备就以下三个问题分别加以～。This article will analyse the following three questions one by one.

【论说】[1] lùnshuō 议论(多指书面的 oft. in written form) discuss; talk about: ～文 argumentation|～体 in an argumentative style

【论说】[2] lùnshuō 按理说 normally; as things should be: ～这个会他应该参加,不知道为什么没有来。Normally, he should have attended the meeting. I don't know why he didn't come.

【论坛】lùntán 对公众发表议论的地方,指报刊、座谈会等 forum; tribune; place to express oneself in public, e. g. newspaper, periodical or symposium, etc. : 工人～ workers' tribune|这是最近～上引起激烈争论的问题。This question has caused heated debate in the public forum recently.

【论题】lùntí 真实性需要证明的命题 proposition whose authenticity needs proving

【论文】lùnwén 讨论或研究某种问题的文章 thesis; dissertation; treatise; paper or essay on a certain problem: 学术～ research paper; scientific paper; academic thesis|毕业～ undergraduate thesis; graduate dissertation

【论战】lùnzhàn 指在政治、学术等问题上因意见不同互相争论 polemics; argue or debate between different viewpoints on political, academic or other issues

【论争】lùnzhēng same as 论战 lùnzhàn: 这次～的焦点是文艺的提高和普及的问题。This controversy focuses on artistic improvement and popularization.

【论证】lùnzhèng ❶ 逻辑学指引用论据来证明论题的真实性的论述过程,是由论据推出论题时所使用的推理形式(of logic) process of deduction that proves the truth of a proposition on the basis of evidence ❷ 论述并证明 expound and prove: ～会 meeting to assess the feasibility of a project|经过调查～,综合研究,确定具体措施 work out specific measures after investigation and comprehensive analysis ❸ 立论的根据 grounds of argument; evidence

【论著】lùnzhù 带有研究性的著作 research work; treatise; work; book

【论资排辈】lùn zī pái bèi 指按资历辈分决定级别、待遇的高低 go by seniority; decide rank and treatment according to seniority; give top priority to seniority in promotion: 在用人上,要打破～的旧观念。It is necessary to break the outdated concept of promotion by seniority.

【论罪】lùn//zuì 判定罪行 decide on the nature of the guilt; find sb. guilty of a crime: 依法～ punish according to the law|按贪污～ find sb. guilty of embezzlement

luō(ㄌㄨㄛ)

捋 luō 用手握住条状物向一端滑动 rub one's palm along sth. long; strip sth. long by closing the palm around it and running one's hand along the length: ～榆钱儿 strip an elm twig of its seeds|～起袖子 roll up one's sleeves; ☞ lǚ on p. 1265

【捋虎须】luō hǔxū 捋老虎的胡须 stroke a tiger's whiskers; 〈比喻 *fig*.〉触犯有权势的人或做冒险的事情 offend sb. in power or take risks in doing sth. ; do sth. very daring

啰(囉) luō ☞ below
☞ luó on p. 1278 and ·luo on p. 1284

【啰唆】luō·suō ❶ (言语)繁复 (of words) long-winded; loquacious; garrulous; wordy; repetitive: 老太太嘴碎,爱～。The old lady is garrulous. |他啰啰唆唆说了半天,还是没把问题说清楚。He kept talking for a long time but failed to get his ideas across. ❷ (事情)琐碎;麻烦 (of a thing) trivial; petty; troublesome; fussy: 事情倒不难做,就是～。Though it is not difficult to do, it is quite troublesome. |手续办起来才知道挺～。I didn't know how troublesome these formalities were until I tried to go through them. ‖ also 啰嗦 luō·suō

【啰嗦】luō·suō same as 啰唆 luō·suō

落 luō ☞ 大大落落 dà·daluōluō on p. 355 ☞ là on p. 1139, lào on p. 1163 and luò on p. 1281

luó(ㄌㄨㄛˊ)

罗[1](羅) luó ❶ 捕鸟的网 net for catching birds: ～网 net; trap ◇天～地网 nets above and snares below; tight encirclement ❷ 张网捕(鸟) catch (birds) with a net: 门可～雀。You can even catch birds on their doorstep (meaning that visitors are so few and far between). ❸ 招请;搜集 collect; gather; recruit: ～致 enlist the services of; recruit | 网～ enlist; employ | 搜～ collect; gather ❹ 陈列 display; set out; spread out: ～列 spread out; set out | 星～棋布 spread out like stars in the sky or pieces on the chessboard ❺ 一种器具,在木框或竹框上张网状物,用来使细的粉末或流质漏下去,留下粗的粉末或渣滓 sieve; strainer; sifter; screen; utensil made of wood- or bamboo-framed mesh, used to strain fine particles or liquids through the mesh and retain the coarse particles or residue on the mesh: 绢～ silk sieve | 铜丝～ copper-wired sifter | 把面过一次～ sift the flour ❻ 过罗 sieve; sift: ～面 sift flour | 把面再～一过儿 sift the flour over again ❼ 质地稀疏的丝织品 silk gauze; sparsely woven silk fabric: ～衣 gauze clothes | ～扇 gauze fan | 轻～ light gauze | 绫～绸缎 silks and satins ❽ (Luó)姓 a surname

罗[2]**(羅)** luó〈量词 *classifier*〉商业用,十二打(144 件)为一罗 measurement in commerce; 12 dozen (144 pieces); gross

【罗布】luóbù 罗列;分布 spread out; lay out; distribute: 营地上账篷～。Tents are spread throughout the campsite.

【罗锅】luóguō ❶ (～儿 luóguōr)驼背 humpbacked; hunchbacked: 他有点～儿。He's a bit hunchbacked. ❷ (～儿 luóguōr)指驼背的人 hunchback; humpback: 这人是个～儿。The man is a hunchback. also 罗锅子 luóguō·zi ❸ 拱形 arched: ～桥 arch bridge

【罗锅】luó·guo 弯(腰) bend (the back); arch; flex: ～着腰坐在炕上 sit hunched up on a *kang*

【罗汉】luóhàn〈佛教 *Budd.*〉称断绝了一切嗜欲,解脱了烦恼的僧人 arhat; monk who has given up all desires and is free from earthly concerns [阿罗汉之省,梵 abbreviation of 阿罗汉 āluóhàn, Sanskrit: arhat]

【罗汉病】luóhànbìng〈方 *dial.*〉血吸虫的成虫寄生在肝脏和肠内引起的病 snail fever; schistosomiasis; disease caused by imagoes of schistosome living in one's liver and intestines

【罗汉豆】luóhàndòu〈方 *dial.*〉蚕豆 broad bean

【罗汉果】luóhànguǒ ❶ 多年生藤本植物。叶卵形或长卵形,花淡黄色。果实近圆形,烘干后可入药。(*Momordica grosvenori*); mangosteen; perennial liane having oval leaves, pale yellow flowers and almost round fruit that can be used in medicine after being dried ❷ 这种植物的果实 fruit of this plant

【罗睺】luóhóu 占星的人所说的星名,认为它能支配人间的吉凶祸福 name of a constellation that astrologers believe can dominate the fate of humans

【罗经】luójīng same as 罗盘 luópán

【罗掘】luójué〈书 *fml.*〉原指城被围困,粮食断绝,只得罗雀(张网捉麻雀)掘鼠(挖洞捕老鼠)来充饥的困窘情况(见于《新唐书·张巡传》)。后用来比喻尽力筹措或搜索财物 catch birds with nets and rats by digging holes, in order to allay one's hunger in a besieged city that has run out of food (*New History of Tang · Biography of Zhang Xun*); (fig.) try one's utmost to scrape up money; try hard to survive in dire straits: 多方～ try all sorts of ways to scrape up money | ～俱穷 all sources of money and goods exhausted | ～一空 use up everything

【罗口】luókǒu 针织衣物的袖口、袜口等能够伸缩的部分 rib cuffs; rib top of sockets

【罗拉】luólā ❶ 辊(gǔn) roller ❷ 纺织机上用来拉紧纱线的机件 roller; mechanical part to pull tight yarn on a loom

【罗勒】luólè 一年生草本植物,叶子卵圆形,略带紫色,花白色或略带紫色。茎和叶有香气,可做香料,又可入药。sweet basil (*Ocimum basilicum*); aromatic annual herbal plant having purplish oval leaves, and white flowers sometimes with a purple hue, both its aromatic stems and leaves used as a spice and medicine; 通称 generally known as 矮糠 ǎi·kāng; also 萝芳 luólè

【罗列】luóliè ❶ 分布;陈列 distribute; set out; exhibit; display: 亭台楼阁,～山上。Towers and pavilions are laid out on the mountain. ❷ 列举 enumerate: ～现象 enumerate phenomena | 仅仅～事实是不够的,必须加以分析。It's not enough just to enumerate the facts; it's necessary to analyse them.

【罗马公教】Luómǎ gōngjiào 天主教 Catholic Church

【罗马数字】Luómǎ shùzì 古代罗马人记数用的符号。数字有 I,V,X,L,C,D,M 七个,依次表示下列数值:1,5,10,50,100,500,1000。记数的方法如下 Roman numerals, including I,V,X,L,C,D,M, respectively meaning 1,5,10,50,100,500,1000. The counting rules are as follows: a)相同的数字并列,表示相加,如 III = 3, XX = 20 same numerals juxtaposed meaning addition, e.g III = 3, XX = 20; b)不同的数字并列,右边的小于左边的,表示相加,如 VIII 是 5 + 3 = 8 different numerals juxtaposed, with the right one smaller than the left one, meaning addition, e.g. VIII means 5 + 3 = 8; c)不同的数字并列,左边的小于右边的,表示右边的减去左边的,如 IX 是 10 - 1 = 9 different numerals juxtaposed, with the left one smaller than the right one, meaning subtraction, e.g. IX means 10 - 1 = 9; d)数字上加一条横线,表示一千倍,如 $\overline{X}$ 是 10×1,000 = 10,000 adding a line above a numeral to express 1,000 times that number, e.g. $\overline{X}$ is 10 ×1,000 = 10,000;这几个方法结合起来,就可

以表示所有的数，如 XIV 是 10+(5-1)=14。The above methods combined can express all numbers, e.g. XIV means 10+(5-1)=14.

【罗曼蒂克】luómàndìkè 浪漫的 romantic

【罗曼司】luómànsī 富有浪漫色彩的恋爱故事或惊险故事 romance; romantic love story or adventurous story

【罗盘】luópán 测定方向的仪器，由有方位刻度的圆盘和装在中间的指南针构成 compass; device used to determine geographic direction, usu. consisting of a disc marked with the directions and a magnetic needle fixed at the centre

【罗圈】luóquān (～儿 luóquānr) 罗[1]⑤的圆形框子 round frame

【罗圈儿揖】luóquānryī 指旋转身体向周围的人作的揖 bows made (with hands clasped) to people on all sides

【罗圈腿】luóquāntuǐ 向外弯曲成弧形的两条腿，这种畸形多由佝偻病引起 bowlegged; bandy-legged; condition where the legs have an outward curvature in the region of the knee, usu. caused by rachitis

【罗网】luówǎng 捕鸟的罗和捕鱼的网 net used to catch birds; fishing net ◇自投～ hurl oneself willingly into the net | 冲决世俗的～ break free from worldly conventions

【罗纹】luówén same as 螺纹 luówén ①

【罗唣】luózào same as 啰唣 luózào

【罗织】luózhī 〈书 *fml.*〉虚构罪状，陷害无辜的人 frame sb.; set sb. up: ～诬陷 frame a case against sb. | ～罪名 cook up charges; frame a case against sb.

【罗致】luózhì 延聘；搜罗(人才) enlist the services of competent people; secure sb. in one's employment; collect; gather together

觌(覼) luó [觌缕](luólǚ)〈书 *fml.*〉详细叙述 relate in detail; go into particulars: 不烦～ not be tired of going into detail | 非片言所能～。It's impossible to make it clear in a few words.

㑩(儸) luó ☞ [偻㑩] (lóu·luó) on p. 1253

萝(蘿) luó 通常指某些能爬蔓的植物 climbing plant; vine: 藤～ Chinese wisteria | 茑～ cypress vine | 女～ usnea | 松～ usnea

【萝卜】(蘿蔔) luó·bo ❶ 二年生草本植物，叶子羽状分裂，花白色或淡紫色。主根肥大，圆柱形或球形，皮的颜色因品种不同而异，是普通蔬菜之一。radish (*Raphanus Sativus*); turnip; biennial herbal plant having feather-like, white or purplish leaves, and round or cylindrical roots that differ in colour among different strains, used as a common vegetable ❷ 这种植物的主根 root of this plant ‖ also 莱菔 láifú

【萝卜花】luó·bohuā 眼球角膜发生溃疡，好转后，在角膜上遗留下的白色瘢痕 white dots left on the cornea after one is cured of keratitis; 俗称 popularly known as 萝卜花 luó·bohuā

【萝艻】luólè same as 罗勒 luólè

【萝藦】luómó 多年生草本植物，叶子心脏形，花白色带淡紫色斑纹，果实纺锤形，种子扁卵形。全草入药。asclepiad (*Metaplexis japonica*); perennial herbal plant having heart-shaped leaves, white flowers with light purple stripes, spindle-shaped fruit, and egg-shaped flat seeds, used wholly in Chinese medicine

啰(囉) luó [啰唣](luózào) 吵闹寻事(多见于早期白话 oft. in early vernacular) stir up trouble

☞ luō on p. 1276 and ·luo on p. 1284

逻(邏) luó 巡察 patrol; make one's rounds: 巡～ patrol | ～骑 patrolling mounted police | ～卒 patrolling soldier; patrolman

【逻辑】luó·ji ❶ 思维的规律 logic; order of thinking: 这几句话不合～。This statement is illogical. ❷ 客观的规律性 objective law; logic: 生活的～ logic of life | 事物发展的～ law of development ❸ same as 逻辑学 luó·jixué

【逻辑思维】luó·ji sīwéi 指人在认识过程中借助于概念、判断、推理反映现实的思维方式。它以抽象性为特征，撇开具体形象，揭示事物的本质属性。logical thinking; abstract thinking; way of thinking that uses concepts, judgment and deductive reasoning to analyse reality during the process of human beings acquiring knowledge; logical thinking is abstract and excludes specific images, and discloses the intrinsic nature of a thing or an object; also 抽象思维 chōu xiàng sī wéi

【逻辑学】luó·jixué 研究思维的形式和规律的科学 logic; science that studies the form and order of thinking; 旧称 formerly called 名学 míngxué, 辩学 biànxué and 论理学 lùnlǐxué

脶(腡) luó 手指纹 fingerprint

猡(玀) luó ☞ 猪猡 (zhūluó) on p. 2500

㑩(饠) luó ☞ [饽㑩] (bìluó) on p. 107

㑩(玀) luó ☞ 珂㑩版 (kēluóbǎn) on p. 1088

椤(欏) luó ☞ [桫椤] (suōluó) on p. 1842

锣(鑼) luó 打击乐器，用铜制成，形状像盘子，用锣槌敲打 gong; percussion instrument made of copper in the shape of a disk and beaten with a wooden hammer: 敲～打鼓 beat drums and gongs | 鸣～开道 strike gongs to clear the way

【锣鼓】luógǔ 锣和鼓，泛指各种打击乐器 gong and drum; general term for all sorts of percussion instruments: ～喧天。A deafening sound of drums and gongs fills the air.

箩(籮) luó 用竹子编的器具,大多方底圆口,制作比较细致,用来盛粮食或淘米等 square-bottomed bamboo basket, of fine craftsmanship, for storing grain or for washing rice: 稻~ bamboo basket for storing rice | 淘~ bamboo basket for washing rice

【箩筐】luókuāng 用竹子或柳条等编成的器具,或圆或方,或方底圆口,用来盛粮食、蔬菜等 large bamboo or wicker basket, round or square, or square-bottomed, round-mouthed, used to store grain, vegetables, etc.

骡(贏) luó ☞ below

【骡子】luó·zi 哺乳动物,驴和马交配所生的杂种,比驴大,毛多为黑褐色。寿命长,体力大,我国北方多用做力畜。一般不能生殖。mule; generally sterile hybrid offspring of a donkey and a horse, larger than a donkey, with long ears, a short mane and dark brown hair, has a long lifespan, and oft. used as a draught animal for its strength and tenacity; ☞ 驴骡 lǘluó on p. 1264 and 马骡 mǎluó on p. 1290

螺 luó ❶ 软体动物,体外包有锥形、纺锤形或扁椭圆形的硬壳,上有旋纹,如田螺、海螺 spiral shell (*Cipangopaludina* or *Bellamya*); trumpet snail; mollusc with a conical, spindle-shaped or flat-oval shell marked with spiral lines ❷ 螺旋形的指纹 whorl in a fingerprint

【螺钿】luódiàn 一种手工艺品,用螺蛳壳或贝壳镶嵌在漆器、硬木家具或雕镂器物的表面,做成有天然彩色光泽的花纹、图形 mother-of-pearl inlay; lacquerware; hardwood furniture or pieces of carving inlaid with snail or conch shells to form patterns of natural colour and sheen; also 螺甸 luódiàn

【螺钉】luódīng 圆柱形或圆锥形金属杆上带螺纹的零件 screw; cylindrical or conical metal rod with incised spirals; also 螺丝钉 luósīdīng or 螺丝 luósī

【螺号】luóhào 用大的海螺壳做成的号角 conch; shell trumpet; trumpet made from a big conch

【螺距】luójù 螺纹上两个相邻的牙之间的距离 screw pitch; thread pitch; distance between two adjacent gear teeth

【螺母】luómǔ 组成螺栓的配件。中心有圆孔,孔内有螺纹,跟螺钉的螺纹相啮合,用来使两个零件固定在一起。screw nut; fitting with a central threaded hole that is designed to fit around and secure a bolt or screw; used to fasten two parts; also 螺帽 luómào, 螺丝母 luósīmǔ or 螺丝帽 luósīmào

【螺栓】luóshuān 有螺纹的圆杆和螺母组合成的零件,用来连接并紧固,可以拆卸 bolt; fastener consisting of a threaded pin or rod and a matching nut, designed to connect and fasten two parts, and to be disassembled

【螺丝】luósī same as 螺钉 luódīng

【螺丝刀】luósīdāo 改锥 screwdriver

【螺丝钉】luósīdīng same as 螺钉 luódīng

【螺丝攻】luósīgōng 丝锥 screw tap

【螺丝扣】luósīkòu same as 螺纹 luówén ②

【螺丝帽】luósīmào same as 螺母 luómǔ

【螺丝母】luósīmǔ same as 螺母 luómǔ

【螺丝起子】luósīqǐ·zi 改锥 screwdriver

【螺蛳】luó·sī 淡水螺的通称,一般较小 general term for freshwater snails, usu. small

【螺纹】luówén ❶ 手指上的纹理,也指脚趾上的纹理 whorl in fingerprint or toe print ❷ 机件的外表面或内孔表面上制成的螺旋线形的凸棱 screw thread; projected spiral thread on a workpiece's outer surface or hole's interior surface; also 螺丝扣 luósīkòu

【螺旋】luóxuán ❶ 像螺蛳壳纹理的曲线形 spiral; helix; curves akin to the veins of a spiral shell: ~体 spiral form or structure | ~桨 screw propeller ❷ 简单机械,圆柱体表面有像螺蛳壳上的螺纹的叫阳螺旋,在物体孔眼里的螺纹叫阴螺旋。阴阳螺旋配合,旋转其中一个就可以使两者沿螺旋移动,螺纹越密,螺旋直径越大越省力。螺钉、螺栓、压榨机、千斤顶等都是螺旋的利用。screw; spiral; simple mechanism, where the spiral line on the exterior surface of a cylinder is called the positive spiral and the one inside the bore of an object is called the negative spiral, and when the two spirals fit, turning one of them will move both following the helix; The denser the screw thread or the wider its diameter, the more energy-saving it becomes. Screws, bolts, mills, jacks, etc., are examples of the spiral in use.

【螺旋桨】luóxuánjiǎng 产生动力使飞机或船只航行的一种装置,由螺旋形的桨叶构成,旋转时桨叶的斜面拨动流体靠反作用而产生动力 screw propeller; rotary propelling device consisting of spiral-shaped blades that produce power to cause a plane or a ship to move. The inclining blade of a propeller produces a counteractive force by stirring the air as it revolves.

【螺旋体】luóxuántǐ 介于细菌和原生动物之间的一类微生物,弯曲呈螺旋状,不产生芽孢,没有细胞膜,有伸缩能力。梅毒、回归热等都是这类微生物引起的。leptospira; spirochete; spiral-shaped micro-organism in between bacteria and protozoa, having no spores or cell membrane yet is flexible. Diseases such as syphilis and recurring fever, etc., are caused by such sort of micro-organisms.

luǒ (ㄌㄨㄛˇ)

倮 luǒ 〈书 *fml.*〉 same as 裸 luǒ

蓏 luǒ 古书上指瓜类植物的果实 referring to melon in ancient books

裸(躶、羸) luǒ 露出;没有遮盖 bare; naked; exposed: ～露 uncovered; exposed|～体 naked|赤～～ naked without a stitch on; be stark naked; be undisguised

【裸露】luǒlù 没有东西遮盖 uncovered; exposed:岩石～ exposed rock|～在地面上的煤层 exposed coal seam

【裸麦】luǒmài 青稞 barley; highland barley

【裸视】luǒshì ❶ 用裸眼看 see with the naked eye:～视力 sight with the naked eye ❷ 裸眼的视力 sight of the naked eye: ～达到 1.0 的才能报考。Those whose naked eyesight is 1.0 or above are allowed to apply for the entrance examination.

【裸体】luǒtǐ 光着身子 naked; nude: ～画 painting of a nude|赤身～ be stark naked; not wearing a stitch

【裸线】luǒxiàn 没有绝缘材料包裹的金属导线,如电车的架空线 bare metal wire without exterior insulation, e. g. trolley wire of a trolley bus

【裸眼】luǒyǎn 指不戴眼镜进行目力测试的眼睛 naked eye, as a term used when testing eyesight:～视力 sight of the naked eye

【裸子植物】luǒzǐ-zhíwù 种子植物的一大类,胚珠和种子都是裸露的,胚珠外面没有子房,种子外面没有果皮包着,松、杉、银杏等都属于裸子植物(区别于'被子植物' as compared with 'angiosperm') gymnosperm; species of spermatophyte whose ovule and seeds are exposed instead of being enclosed within an ovary or wrapped in a pericarp. Pine, fir, gingko, etc., belong to this species

瘰 luǒ [瘰疬](luǒlì)病,多发生在颈部,有时也发生在腋窝部,是由于结核杆菌侵入颈部或腋窝部的淋巴结而引起的,症状是局部发生硬块,溃烂后经常流脓,不易愈合 scrofula; struma; disease of tuberculosis affecting the lymph nodes, especially in the neck and sometimes the armpit, with symptoms of local hardening, ulceration and constant suppuration, not easily healed

蠃 luǒ ☞ [蜾蠃](guǒluǒ) on p. 746

luò(ㄌㄨㄛˋ)

泺(濼) Luò 泺水,水名,在山东 Luoshui, name of a river in Shandong Province

☞ 泊 pō on p. 1491

荦(犖) luò〈书 *fml.*〉明显 conspicuous; apparent; obvious: 卓～ prominent; outstanding

【荦荦】luòluò〈书 *fml.*〉(事理)明显 (of reason) conspicuous; apparent; obvious: ～大端(明显的要点或主要的项目) major items; salient points

咯 luò ☞ 吡咯 (bǐluò) on p. 100

☞ gē on p. 649, kǎ on p. 1069 and ·lo on p. 1248

洛 Luò ❶ 洛河,水名,在陕西 Luohe River, in Shaanxi Province ❷ 洛河,水名,发源于陕西,流入河南。古时作'雒'。Luohe River, originating in Shaanxi Province and flowing into Henan Province; 洛 written as 雒 luò in ancient times ❸ (Luò)姓 a surname

【洛阳纸贵】Luòyáng zhǐ guì 晋代左思《三都赋》写成以后,抄写的人非常多,洛阳的纸都因此涨价了(见于《晋书·文苑传》) when Zuo Si of the Jin Dynasty had finished writing his *Three Capital Rhapsody*, so many people copied it that the price of paper in Luoyang city rose (*History of Jin · Biographies of Scholars*); 〈比喻 *fig.*〉著作广泛流传,风行一时 (of a work) popular and widely distributed

骆 luò ❶ 古书上指黑鬃的白马 white horse with a black mane in ancient books ❷ (Luò)姓 a surname

【骆驼】luò·tuo 哺乳动物,身体高大,背上有驼峰,蹄扁平,蹄底有肉质的垫,适于在沙漠中行走。有双重眼睑,不怕风沙。能反刍,有高度耐饥渴的能力。嗅觉灵敏,能嗅出远处的水源,又能预感大风的到来。供骑乘或运货,是沙漠地区主要的力畜。camel (*Camelus*); humped, long-necked, tall ruminant mammal with fleshy, flat hooves, suited for travelling in the desert. Double eyelids make it able to withstand sandstorms. The camel is highly capable of enduring thirst and hunger, and its sensitive nose can smell a water source from afar and sense an impending wind storm. In desert regions, it is the main means of transport and beast of burden.

【骆驼绒】luò·tuoróng 呢绒的一种,背面用棉纱织成,正面用粗纺毛纱织成一层细密而蓬松的毛绒,多用来做衣帽的里子 camel-hair cloth; woollen cloth with the outside woven with cotton thread, and the inside of coarse slub woven into a layer of fine and fluffy fuzz, often used for the lining of clothes and hats; also 驼绒 tuóróng

络 luò ❶ 网状的东西 sth. like a net: 橘～ tangerine pith|丝瓜～ towel-gourd sponge ❷〈中医 *Chin. med.*〉指人体内气血运行通路的旁支或小支 collateral channels in the human body through which vital energy, blood and nutriment circulate: 经～ main and collateral channels ❸ 用网状物兜住 hold sth. in place with a net: 头上～着一个发网 keep one's hair in place with a hairnet ❹ 缠绕 twine; wind; entwine: ～纱 winding yarn; spooling|～丝 winding silk|～线 winding thread

☞ lào on p.1163

【络腮胡子】luòsāi-hú·zi 连着鬓角的胡子 whiskers; 络 also written as 落 luò

【络纱】luòshā 纺织生产中的一种操作,将纱线卷绕在筒管上,加长纱线的长度,使有适当的卷装形式和较大的容积,同时除掉纱线上的杂质或疵点 winding yarn; spooling; doff; spinning skill, of winding yarn on a bobbin in order to lengthen the yarn and shape it into a proper, big reel and at the same time remove impurities and defects; also 落纱 luòshā

【络绎】luòyì〈书 *fml.*〉(人、马、车、船等)前后相接,连续不断 (of people, horses, vehicles, boats, etc.) follow one after another: ~不绝 in an endless stream; continuous flow of something

珞 luò ☞ 珞巴族 Luòbāzú; 赛璐珞 sàilùluò on p.1649 and 璎珞 yīngluò on p.2300

【珞巴族】Luòbāzú 我国少数民族之一,分布在西藏 Lhoba (Lopa) people, on of China's minority peoples in the Tibet Autonomous Region

烙 luò ☞ 炮烙 (páoluò) on p.1448

☞ lào on p.1163

硌 luò〈书 *fml.*〉山上的大石 big stone on a mountain

☞ gè on p.657

落 luò ❶ 物体因失去支持而下来 (of an object) drop; fall: ~泪 shed tears | 花瓣~了。The petals of the flowers fell. ❷ 下降 go down; set: ~潮 ebb | 太阳~山了。The sun has set. | 飞机从天空中~下来。The airplane fell from the sky. ❸ 使下降 lower: ~幕 lower the curtains | 把帘子~下来。Let down the blinds. ❹ 衰败;飘零 decline; come down: 衰~ decline | 破~ dilapidated | 没~ decline; decay | 零~ decayed; scattered; sporadic; straggly | 沦~ degenerate; come down in the world; be reduced to poverty ❺ 遗留在后面 lag behind; fall behind: ~选 be defeated in an election | ~后 lag behind | ~伍 drop behind the ranks; become outdated | 名~孙山 flunk; fail in a competition ❻ 停留;留下 sojourn; stay: ~脚 stay for a time; put up | ~户 settle down | 不~痕迹 leave no trace ❼ 停留的地方 place to stay: 下~ whereabouts | 着~ whereabouts ❽ 聚居的地方 settlement; place to gather together: 村~ village | 聚~ settlement ❾ 归属 fall into; belong to: 政权~在人民手里了。Political power has fallen into the hands of the people. | 经过争取,这个光荣任务才~到咱们组里。It was only through our struggle that this glorious task fell on our group. ❿ 得到 get; have; win: ~空 have free time | ~埋怨 get nothing but blame ⓫ 用笔写 write; put to paper: ~款 sign one's name | ~账 make an entry in an account book; enter sth. in an account

☞ là on p.1139, lào on p.1163 and luō on p.1276

【落榜】luò//bǎng 指考试没有被录取 fail in an entrance examination: 高考落了榜 fail in the college entrance examination

【落笔】luòbǐ 下笔 put pen to paper; start to write or draw: 他的画是在先有了生活体验而后才~的。He started to paint only after he had experienced life.

【落标】luò//biāo 指在招标中没有中标。泛指在竞争中失败 failure in a bid; generally referring to failure in a competition: 在选举中有几位候选人~了。Several candidates have met with failure in the election.

【落膘】luò//biāo (~儿 luò//biāor)(牲畜)变瘦 (of livestock) become thin; become emaciated: 由于饲养不经心,牛羊都落了膘。Due to the lack of conscientiousness in rearing, cattle and sheep become thin.

【落泊】luòbó〈书 *fml.*〉❶ 潦倒失意 be down and out: 家贫~ be penniless and down and out; be in dire straits ❷ 豪迈,不拘束 casual; unconstrained; unconventional ‖ also 落魄 luòbó

【落魄】luòbó〈书 *fml.*〉same as 落泊 luòbó

☞ luòpò

【落槽】luò//cáo ❶ 河流水位降低,归入河槽 (of river water) become lower and tamed ❷〈方 *dial.*〉家道衰落 (of family fortune) decline ❸ (~儿 luò//cáor) 榫头放入卯眼安好 rabbet placed well in mortise ❹〈方 *dial.*〉指心里平静;熨帖 calm; at ease: 事情没办好,心里总是不~。As long as the matter remains unsettled, I won't be able to put my mind at rest.

【落草】[1] luòcǎo 到山林当强盗(多见于早期白话 oft. in early vernacular) take to the woods; become an outlaw: ~为寇 take to the woods to become a bandit

【落草】[2] luòcǎo〈方 *dial.*〉(~儿 luòcǎor) 指婴儿出生 (of an infant) be born

【落差】luòchā ❶ 由于河床高度的变化所产生的水位的差数,如甲地水面海拔为 20 米,乙地为 18 米,这一段的落差就是 2 米 drop; fall in the changing elevation of riverbed, e.g. if Point A is 20 metres above sea level and Point B is 18 metres above sea level, the drop between them is 2 metres ❷〈比喻 *fig.*〉对比中的差距或差异 relative gap or differencc: 调整心理上的~ adjust one's mentality | 两种工资之间的~较大。There's a wide gap between the two salary groups.

【落潮】luò//cháo 退潮 ebb tide; low tide

【落尘】luòchén 降尘 dust

【落成】luòchéng (建筑物)完工 (of a building) be completed: ~典礼 inauguration ceremony | 大桥已经~,日内即可正式通车。The bridge has been completed and will be open to traffic in a few days.

【落得】luò·de 落到(很坏的境遇) end up (in a very bad situation): 倒行逆施,～身败名裂的可耻下场。He ended up a man of notoriety because of his perverse acts.

【落地】luò//dì ❶(物体)落在地上(of an object) fall to the ground: 花轿～。The bridal sedan chair landed safely on the ground. ◇心里一块石头落了地。A rock has been lifted from my heart. ❷指婴儿刚生下来 (of an infant) be born: 呱呱～ come into this world with a loud cry; be born

【落地窗】luòdìchuāng 下端直到地面或楼板的高而长的窗子 French window; high and long window whose bottom reaches the ground or floor

【落地灯】luòdìdēng 放在室内地上的有立柱和底座的电灯 floor lamp; standard lamp; tall electrical lamp with a column and a base, placed on the floor

【落第】luò//dì 科举考试(乡试以上)没考中 fail in imperial examinations at and above the township level

【落发】luò//fà 剃掉头发(出家做僧尼) tonsure; take the tonsure (to become a Buddhist monk or nun): ～为僧 take the tonsure and become a Buddhist monk

【落谷】luògǔ〈方 *dial.*〉在秧田中播种稻种 sow rice seeds in the field

【落黑】luòhēi〈方 *dial.*〉天色变黑,进入夜间;天黑 get dark; become dark: 天还没～,他就到了。He arrived before darkness fell.

【落后】luò//hòu ❶在行进中落在别人后面 lag behind; fall behind: 我们的船先过了桥洞,他们的船稍微～一点。Our boat took the lead in passing through the arch of the bridge, while theirs fell a bit behind. ❷工作进度迟缓,落在原定计划的后面 (of work) proceed slowly and lag behind schedule ❸停留在较低的发展水平,落在客观形势要求的后面 remain at a undeveloped stage; lag behind what the objective situation requires; be out of date: ～的生产工具 outmoded production tools | 虚心使人进步,骄傲使人～。Modesty helps one move forward, whereas conceit makes one lag behind.

【落户】luò//hù ❶在他乡安家长期居住 settle down in a place other than one's home town: 我祖父那一辈就在北京落了户。My grandfather's generation settled down in Beijing. ❷登记户籍;报户口 register; apply for a resident's permit: 新生婴儿应及时～。Parents should apply on time for a resident's permit for their newborn.

【落花流水】luò huā liú shuǐ 原来形容春景衰败,现在比喻惨败 (orig.) blighted spring scenery; (fig.) be utterly defeated; be in a sorry plight

【落花生】luò·huashēng ❶一年生草本植物,叶子互生,有长柄,小叶倒卵形或卵形,花黄色,子房下的柄伸入地下才结果。果仁可以榨油,也可以吃。是重要的油料作物之一。peanut; annual herbal plant having long-stemmed, inter-grown, egg-shaped leaves and yellow flowers, and yielding edible fruit when the stems under the ovary extend into the soil; important oil-bearing plant ❷这种植物的果实 peanut; fruit of this plant ‖ also 花生 huāshēng,有的地区叫仁果、长生果 known as 仁果 rénguǒ and 长生果 chángshēngguǒ in some areas

【落荒】luòhuāng 离开大路,向荒野逃去(多见于早期白话 oft. in early vernacular) take to the wilds; take to flight: ～而逃 be defeated and flee

【落脚】luò//jiǎo (～儿 luò//jiǎor)指临时停留或暂住 stay (for a time); stop over; put up: ～点 temporary lodging | 城里旅馆大多客满,差点儿找不到～的地方。Most of the hotels in the city are full, and we almost didn't find a place to stay.

【落井下石】luò jǐng xià shí〈比喻 *fig.*〉乘人危急的时候加以陷害 hit a person when he's down; also 投井下石 tóu jǐng xià shí

【落空】luò//kōng 没有达到目的或目标;没有着落 come to nothing; fail; fall through: 希望～ fail to attain one's wish | 两头～ come to naught both ways

【落款】luò//kuǎn (～儿 luò//kuǎnr)在书画、书信、礼品等上面题上款和下款 write the names of the sender and the recipient on a painting, calligraphic work, book, letter, gift, etc.

【落款】luòkuǎn (～儿 kuòkuǎnr)在书画、书信、礼品等上面题的上款和下款 names of the sender and recipient written on a painting, calligraphic work, book, letter, gift, etc.

【落雷】luòléi 霹雳 thunder

【落落】luòluò ❶形容举止潇洒自然 (of demeanour) natural and at ease: ～大方 natural and at ease ❷形容跟别人合不来 unsociable: ～寡合 stand-offish; unsociable; aloof

【落马】luò//mǎ 骑马驰骋时,从马上掉下来。也比喻打败仗或竞赛失利 fall off a horse when riding; (fig.) suffer a defeat in a battle or a failure in competition: 中弹～ be hit by a bullet and fall off the horse | 半决赛中,上届冠亚军双双～。In the semi-finals, both the former champion and the former runner-up lost the game.

【落寞】luòmò 寂寞;冷落 lonely; desolate; also 落漠 luòmò and 落莫 luòmò

【落墨】luòmò same as 落笔 luòbǐ: 思绪万千,无从～ cannot put pen to paper as too many feelings well up in the heart | 写意画贵在大处

～,得其神似。The beauty of freehand painting lies in its overall brushwork and spiritual likeness.

【落幕】luòmù 闭幕 curtain falls; lower the curtain; bring down the curtain

【落难】luò//nàn 遭遇灾难,陷入困境 meet with misfortune; be in distress

【落魄】luòpò (又读 also pronounced luòtuò) 〈书 *fml.*〉❶ 潦倒失意 be in dire straits; be down and out: ～江湖 be down and out in life ❷ 豪迈,不拘束 unconstrained; unconventional; untrammelled by formality and convention
☞ luòbó

【落日】luòrì 夕阳 setting sun: ～的余晖 lingering glow of the setting sun

【落腮胡子】luòsāi-hú·zi same as 络腮胡子 luòsāi-hú·zi

【落纱】luòshā same as 络纱 luòshā

【落生】luòshēng 〈方 *dial.*〉(婴儿)出生 (of a baby) be born

【落实】luòshí ❶ (计划、措施等)通过周密的研究,达到具体明确、切实可行 (of a plan, measure, etc.) practicable; achievable; workable towards definite objectives after thorough research: 生产计划要订得～。The production plan should be practicable. ❷ 使落实 carry out; make sure; ascertain: ～政策 implement a policy | 要～计划,～措施,并层层～责任。It is imperative to carry out the plan, decide on the measures to be taken, and ascertain the responsibilities of each level. ❸ 〈方 *dial.*〉(心情)安稳;塌实 feel at ease: 事情没有把握,心里总是不～。I just cannot set my mind at ease, since the matter is still unsettled.

【落市】luòshì 〈方 *dial.*〉❶ 果品、蔬菜等过了时令 (of fruit, vegetables, etc.) be out of season ❷ (市场等)停止贸易 (of markets, etc.) close

【落水】luò//shuǐ 掉在水里 fall into water; 〈比喻 *fig.*〉堕落 degenerate; sink low; backslide; corrupt

【落水狗】luòshuǐgǒu 〈比喻 *fig.*〉失势的坏人 bad person who is down

【落水管】luòshuǐguǎn 水落管 downspout; downpipe

【落汤鸡】luòtāngjī 形容浑身湿透,像掉在热水里的鸡一样 (of a person) like a drenched chicken; like a drowned rat; be soaked through; drenched and bedraggled

【落套】luòtào 指文艺作品的内容、形式、手法等陷入老一套,没有创新 (of the content, form, etc., of a literary work) conform to a conventional pattern without originality; fall into a rut: 创作一定要有新意,要有新的东西,才能不～。Only with originality can artistic creation avoid the fate of falling into a rut.

【落体】luòtǐ 因受重力作用由空中落下的物体 falling body; object that drops or comes down freely under the influence of gravity: 自由～运动 movement of a freely falling body

【落托】luòtuō same as 落拓 luòtuò

【落拓】luòtuò 〈书 *fml.*〉❶ 潦倒失意 in dire straits; down and out: 自嗟～ sigh over one's own fate ❷ 豪迈,不拘束 untrammelled by convention; casual; unconventional; unconstrained: ～不羁 untrammelled by formality and convention; unconventional and uninhibited

【落网】luò//wǎng 指犯罪分子被捕 (of a criminal) fall into the net; be captured; be arrested: 三名贩毒分子先后～。Three drug-traffickers were collared one after another.

【落伍】luò//wǔ ❶ 掉队 fall behind the ranks; straggle; drop behind; drop out: 他不愿～,一脚高一脚低地紧跟着走。Not wanting to be left back, he staggered along closely behind. ❷ 〈比喻 *fig.*〉人或事物跟不上时代 (of a person or a thing) out of date; behind the times; backward: 产品设计～。The design of the product is out of date.

【落乡】luòxiāng 〈方 *dial.*〉(地点)离城市稍远 (of a place) a bit far away from town

【落选】luò//xuǎn 没有被选上 fail to be chosen or elected; lose an election

【落叶归根】luò yè guī gēn 叶落归根 leaves fall to return to their roots; return (esp. from overseas) and settle down in one's native place when one gets old

【落叶树】luòyèshù 到冬季树叶枯黄凋落的树,如柳树、槐树等 deciduous tree, whose leaves wither, become yellow and fall in winter, e. g. willow, pagoda tree, etc.

【落音】luò//yīn (～儿 luò//yīnr)(说话、歌唱的声音)停止 (of talking or singing) stop: 他的话刚～,你就进来了。You came in just as he stopped talking.

【落英】luòyīng 〈书 *fml.*〉❶ 落花 fallen or falling flowers: ～缤纷 petals falling in riotous profusion ❷ 初开的花 newly opened flowers; new blooms

【落账】luò//zhàng 登上账簿 make an entry in an account book; enter sth. in an account: 这笔款还没～。This sum of money hasn't been entered in the account.

【落照】luòzhào 落日的光辉 glow of the setting sun

【落座】luò//zuò 坐到座位上 take a seat: 先是互致问候,然后各自落了座。Each took his seat after greeting each other. | 各位观众请～,表演就要开始了。Be seated, ladies and gentlemen — the performance is going to start.

跞(躒) luò ☞ 卓跞 (zhuóluò) on p. 2533
☞ lì on p. 1193

雒 Luò ❶ same as 洛 luò ② ❷ 姓 a surname

摞 Luò ❶ 把东西重叠地往上放 pile up; stack up: 补丁～补丁 patch over a patch | 把箱子～起来。Stack up the trunks. ❷〈量词 *classifier*〉用于重叠放置的东西 pile; stack: 一～碗 a stack of bowls | 一～书 a stack of books | 一～竹筐 a stack of bamboo baskets

漯 luò 漯河（Luòhé），地名，在河南 Luohe, name of a place in Henan Province

☞ Tà on p. 1849

·luo（·ㄌㄨㄛ）

啰（囉） ·luo〈助词 *aux*.〉用在句末，表示肯定语气 [used at the end of a sentence to indicate an affirmative tone]: 你放心好～。You may just as well set your mind at rest. | 照章纳税，自然是对的～! It is of course right to pay taxes according to the regulations.

☞ luō on p. 1276 and luó on p. 1278

M

m̄ (ㄇ)

姆 m̄ [姆妈](m̄mā)〈方 *dial.*〉❶ 母亲 mom; mummy; mother ❷〈尊称 *honor.*〉年长的已婚妇女 [when addressing a married elderly woman] aunt; auntie: 张家～ Auntie Zhang
☞ mǔ on p. 1373

ḿ (ㄇ́)

呒(嘸) ḿ〈方 *dial.*〉没有 not have; be without: ～办法。No way.

【呒啥】ḿshá〈方 *dial.*〉没有什么 nothing: ～关系。Doesn't matter. | ～听头。There's little worth listening.

呣 ḿ〈叹词 *interj.*〉表示疑问 [in an interrogative sentence]: ～什么? Parden? *or* What did you say?
☞ m̀ on p. 1285

m̀ (ㄇ̀)

呣 m̀〈叹词 *interj.*〉表示应诺 [by way of response]: ～,我知道了。Uh-huh, I see.
☞ ḿ on p. 1285

mā (ㄇㄚ)

妈 mā ❶ 母亲 ma; mum; mummy; mother ❷ 称长一辈或年长的已婚妇女 [form of address for a married woman of an older generation]: 姑～(paternal) aunt | 姨～(maternal) aunt | 大～elder aunt ❸〈旧时 *old*〉连着姓称中年或老年的女仆 [form of address for middle-aged or old maid servant, oft. followed by a surname] nanny: 王～ Nanny Wang | 鲁～Nanny Lu

【妈妈】mā·ma ❶ 母亲 ma; mum; mummy; mother ❷〈方 *dial.*〉对上年纪的妇女的尊称 [form of address for an elderly woman]

【妈祖】māzǔ 我国东南沿海地区传说中的海上女神 Mazu, or Goddess of the Sea, worshipped by fishermen in China's southeast coastal areas

孖 mā〈方 *dial.*〉成对;双 pair; twin: ～髻山(山名,在广东) Maji Mountain; Twin-chignon Mountain, in Guangdong Province | ～仔 twin boys

【孖仔】māzǎi〈方 *dial.*〉双生子 twin boys; boy twins

抹(❷摗) mā ❶ 擦 wipe; mop up: ～桌子 wipe a table clean with a piece of rag ❷ 用手按着并向下移动 slip sth. off; take sth. down: 把帽子～下来 take one's hat down
☞ mǒ on p. 1365 and mò on p. 1367

【抹布】mābù 擦器物用的布块等 dishcloth; rag

【抹搭】mā·da〈方 *dial.*〉(眼皮)向下而不合拢 (of eyelids) half close; droop: ～着眼皮 with one's eyes half closed

【抹脸】mā//liǎn 突然改变脸色,多指由和气变得严厉 pull a long face suddenly: 抹不下脸来(碍于情面,不能严厉对待) cannot face up to somebody (for fear of hurting feelings); cannot bring oneself to confront somebody squarely

【抹澡】mā//zǎo〈方 *dial.*〉擦澡 rub oneself down with a wet towel; take a sponge bath

蚂 mā [蚂螂](mā·lang)〈方 *dial.*〉蜻蜓 dragonfly
☞ mǎ on p. 1292 页 and mà on p. 1292

麻 ma ☞ below
☞ má on p. 1286

【麻麻黑】mā·mahēi〈方 *dial.*〉(天)快黑或刚黑 nightfall; twilight; dusk: 天～了,村头一带灰色的砖墙逐渐模糊起来。As dusk fell, the greyish brick walls at the entrance to the village gradually faded into darkness.

【麻麻亮】mā·maliàng〈方 *dial.*〉(天)刚有些亮 dawning; on the verge of daybreak: 天刚～他就起床了。He got up at the crack of dawn.

摩 mā ☞ below
☞ mó on p. 1362

【摩挲】mā·sā 用手轻轻按着并一下一下地移动 caress; stroke; smooth sth. out with one's hand: ～衣裳 smooth one's clothes out with a hand
☞ mósuō on p. 1363

má (ㄇㄚ́)

吗 má〈方 *dial.*〉什么 what: 干～? What for? | ～事? What's up? | 你说～? What did you say? | 要～有～。You'll have everything you want here.
☞ mǎ on p. 1291 and ·ma on p. 1292

麻[1]（蔴）má ❶ 大麻、亚麻、苎麻、黄麻、剑麻、蕉麻等植物的统称 hemp (*Cannabis sativa*); any plants resembling the hemp, such as flax, ramie, jute, sisal hemp, abaca, etc. ❷ 麻类植物的纤维，是纺织等工业的重要原料 fibre of hemp, a major textile material ❸ 芝麻 sesame: ～酱 sesame paste | ～油 sesame oil

麻[2] má ❶ 表面不平，不光滑 rough; coarse-grained: 这种纸一面光，一面～。This kind of paper is smooth on one side and coarse on the other. ❷ same as 麻子 má·zi ①: ～脸 pockmarked face ❸ 带细碎斑点的 flecked; speckled: ～蝇 flesh fly | ～雀 sparrow ❹(Má) 姓 a surname

麻[3] má 感觉轻微的麻木 feeling slight prickles, stings or tremors; tingling; numb: 腿～了 felt pins and needles in the legs | 吃了花椒，舌头有点儿发～。My tongue felt slight prickles and tremors after I had eaten some Chinese prickly ash.

☞ mā on p. 1285

【麻包】mábāo same as 麻袋 mádài

【麻痹】mábì ❶ 神经系统的病变引起的身体某一部分知觉能力的丧失和运动机能的障碍 paralysis; loss or impairment of sensation or function in certain part of the human body, caused by disease of the nerves ❷ 失去警惕性；疏忽 be remiss of; oversight: ～大意 carelessness; off one's guard ‖ also 麻痹 mábì

【麻布】mábù 用麻织成的布，多用来做衬布或包装物品。细麻布叫夏布，可以做衣料。flax; hemp fabrics, oft. used for lining or packaging; linen, material for making clothes

【麻袋】mádài 用粗麻布做的袋子 gunnybag; gunnysack; burlap sack

【麻刀】má·dao 跟石灰和在一起抹墙用的碎麻 shredded hemp fibre, mixed with lime to make wall plaster

【麻捣】mádǎo 〈书 *fml*.〉 same as 麻刀 má·dao

【麻豆腐】mádòu·fu 做团粉等剩下的渣子，可以做菜吃 cooking starch residue, a material for making dishes

【麻烦】má·fan ❶ 烦琐；费事 knotty; troublesome: ～得很 too much trouble | 这个问题很～。This is a knotty problem. | 服务周到，不怕～。Be considerate to our clients, and go to all lengths to serve them. ❷ 使人费事或增加负担 put sb. to trouble; trouble sb.; bother: ～您啦！I'm afraid I put you to too much trouble. | 自己能做的事，决不～别人。One should never bother others to do things one can manage by oneself.

【麻纺】máfǎng 用麻的纤维纺成纱 spin jute, hemp or flax fibres into yarn

【麻风】máfēng 慢性传染病，病原体是麻风杆菌。症状是皮肤麻木，变厚，颜色变深，表面形成结节，毛发脱落，手指脚趾变形等。leprosy; chronic contagious disease caused by *Mycobacterium leprae* that thickens and darkens the skin and impairs its sensation and causes tubercles on it, causes body hair to fall off, and deforms fingers and toes; also 癞 lài, 大麻风 dàmáfēng or 痳风 máfēng

【麻花】[1] máhuā (～儿 máhuār) 食品，把两三股条状的面拧在一起，用油炸熟 fried dough twist; food made by deep-frying two or three dough sticks that are twisted together

【麻花】[2] máhuā 〈方 *dial*.〉(～儿 máhuār) 形容衣服因穿久了磨损成要破没破的样子 (of clothes) threadbare; worn thin; worn out: 两只袖子都～了。The sleeves have become threadbare from too much wear and tear.

【麻将】májiàng 牌类娱乐用具，用竹子、骨头或塑料制成，上面刻有花纹或字样，共 136 张 mahjong tiles, made of bamboo, bone or plastics, with patterns or characters engraved on them, each mahjong set consisting of 136 tiles; also 麻雀 máquè

【麻酱】májiàng 芝麻酱 sesame paste

【麻秸】má·jie 剥掉皮的麻秆 peeled flax stalk; husked hemp stalk

【麻经儿】májīngr 缕状的生麻，捆扎小物件用 raw flax string; fine flax fibre for binding small objects

【麻雷子】máléi·zi 一种爆竹，放起来响声很大 firecracker that emits a deafening noise when being exploded

【麻利】má·li ❶ 敏捷 nimble; deft; dexterous: 手脚～ nimble-limbed | 他干活儿很～。He is quick and neat in doing his work. ❷〈方 *dial*.〉迅速；赶快 quick; fast: 单位开会，叫你～回去。You've been asked to return to the office as soon as possible — there is a meeting waiting for you.

【麻脸】máliǎn 有麻子的脸 pockmarked face

【麻木】mámù ❶ 身体某部发生像蚂蚁爬那样不舒服的感觉或感觉完全丧失 numb; prickly feeling, or complete loss of sensation in a body part: 浑身～。A numbness electrified itself through the entire body. | 手脚～。Both one's hands and feet have gone numb. ❷〈比喻 *fig*.〉思想不敏锐，反应迟钝 apathetic; insensitive; lifeless: 思想～ wooden mind

【麻木不仁】mámù bù rén 肢体麻痹，没有感觉 dead to all feelings; 〈比喻 *fig*.〉对外界的事物反应迟钝或漠不关心 be petrified apathetic; slow and stupid in handling sth.

【麻雀】máquè ❶ 鸟，头圆，尾短，嘴呈圆锥状，头顶和颈部是栗褐色，背面褐色，杂有黑褐色斑点，尾羽暗褐色，翅膀短小，不能远飞，善于跳跃，啄食谷粒和昆虫。有的地区叫家雀儿或老家贼。sparrow (*Fringillidae*); small bird with round head, short tail with dark brown feathers, tapered beak, chestnut-brown crest and neck, brown back with brownish dark speckles, short and small wings that keep it from long-distance flying, adept at leaping, and feeding on grain and insects; also known in some regions as 家雀 jiāquè or 老家贼 lǎojiāzéi ❷ 麻将 májiàng

【麻纱】máshā ❶ 用麻的细纤维纺成的纱 yarn of ramie, flax, etc. ❷ 用细棉纱或棉麻混纺织成的平纹布。常有纵向的突起条纹。多用来做夏季的衣服。cambric; hair cords; fine linen or cotton fabric, usu. with embossed warps, oft. used for making summer clothing

【麻石】máshí 凿成的石块,用于建筑或铺路 chiselled stone slab or block for building houses or paving roads: ～板 chiselled stone slab | ～栏杆 stone railing

【麻酥酥】másūsū (～的 másūsū·de)形容轻微的麻木 slightly numb; tingling: 天气越来越冷了,脚放到水里去,冻得～的。It's getting colder and colder, and when (I) put my feet in the cold water, it gives me a tingling feeling.

【麻线】máxiàn (～儿 máxiànr)麻制的线 flaxen thread; linen thread

【麻药】máyào 麻醉剂 anaesthetic

【麻衣】máyī 麻布做成的衣服,旧俗用做孝服 gunny clothes; old-fashioned mourning garment made of hemp

【麻油】máyóu 芝麻油 sesame oil

【麻渣】mázhā 亚麻、芝麻等种子榨油后留下的渣滓 ramie or sesame dregs from extraction of oil

【麻疹】mázhěn 急性传染病,病原体是麻疹病毒。儿童最易感染,发病时先发高烧,上呼吸道和结膜发炎,两三天后全身起红色丘疹。能并发肺炎、中耳炎、百日咳、腮腺炎等疾病。通称疹子,有的地区叫痧子。measles; acute contagious disease caused by measles virus, with children the most susceptible to it, with high fever and infection of the upper respiratory tract and conjunctivitis at the onset, followed two or three days later by the outbreak of read papulae all over the body, and likely to cause such complications as pneumonia, tympanitis, whooping cough, and parotitis; 通称 generally known as 疹子 zhěn·zi or 痧子 shā·zi in some regions; also 麻疹 mázhěn

【麻织品】mázhīpǐn 用麻做原料织成的物品,如夏布、工业用的亚麻帆布、包装用的麻袋等 linen fabrics, such as linen, flax canvas for industrial use, and gunny sack for packaging

【麻子】má·zi ❶ 人出天花后留下的疤痕 pockmarks: 他脸上有几点～。He's got a few pockmarks on his face. ❷ 脸上有麻子的人 person with a pockmarked face

【麻醉】mázuì ❶ 用药物或针刺等方法使整个有机体或有机体的某一部分暂时失去知觉,多在施行外科手术时采用,分为全身麻醉、局部麻醉和脊髓麻醉三种 anaesthesia; use of medication or acupuncture to induce temporary insensitivity to pain to facilitate surgery, in three categories: general, local, and spinal anaesthesia ❷〈比喻 *fig*〉用某种手段使人认识模糊、意志消沉 corrupt; poison sb's mind (by a certain means)

【麻醉剂】mázuìjì 能引起麻醉现象的药物。全身麻醉时多用乙醚、氯仿等,局部麻醉时多用可卡因、普鲁卡因等,此外如吗啡、鸦片等都可用做麻醉剂。anaesthetic; medicine that induces temporary insensitivity to pain; aether, chloroform, etc. are used for general anaesthesia; and cocaine and procaine are used for local anaesthesia; other anaesthetics include heroin and opium; also 麻药; 通称 generally known as 蒙药 méngyào

痳 má [痳痹](mábì)、[痳风](máfēng)、[痳疹](mázhěn); ☞ 麻痹 mábì, 麻风 máfēng on p. 1286 and 麻疹 mázhěn on p. 1287

蟆(蟇) má ☞蛤蟆 há·má on p. 753

mǎ (ㄇㄚˇ)

马(馬) mǎ ❶ 哺乳动物,头小,面部长,耳壳直立,颈部有鬣,四肢强健,每肢各有一蹄,善跑,尾生有长毛。是重要的力畜之一,可供拉车、耕地、乘骑等用。皮可制革。horse (*Equus caballus*); large, solid-hoofed herbivorous quadruped with a mane on its nape, good at galloping, with long hair growing on its tail; major draught animal for pulling carts, ploughing, and mounting, its hide a material for leather ❷ 大 big; large: ～蜂 hornet | ～勺 ladle ❸(Mǎ) 姓 a surname

【马鞍】mǎ'ān 马鞍子,也用来形容或比喻两头高起中间低落的事物 saddle; sth. resembling a saddle in shape

【马鞍子】mǎ'ān·zi 放在骡马背上供骑坐的器具,两头高,中间低 saddle; seat with two upturned ends for a rider on the back of a horse or a mule

【马帮】mǎbāng 驮运货物的马队 caravan

【马瓟儿】mǎbáor 一年生蔓草,茎细,叶三角形或扁心脏形,花小,白色,果实圆形,种子灰白色,扁平 *Melothria indica*; annual creeping plant with slender stalks, triangular or heart-shaped leaves, tiny white flowers, round capsules that contain flat, greyish white seeds

【马鞭】mǎbiān 驱使坐骑用的鞭子,泛指赶牲口的鞭子 horsewhip; also 马鞭子 mǎbiān·zi

【马弁】mǎbiàn〈旧时 *old*〉军官的护兵 bodyguard of an army officer

【马表】mǎbiǎo 体育运动比赛用的表,通常只有分针和秒针,按动转钮可以随时使它走或停,能测出 1/5 秒或 1/10 秒的时间。最初用于赛马计时,因而得名。stopwatch; watch with only a minute hand and a second hand that can be stopped or started at any instant, capable of marking one fifth or one tenth of a second, known in early days as horse racing clock for it was used for that purpose; also 停表 tíngbiǎo or 跑表 pǎobiǎo

【马不停蹄】mǎ bù tíng tí 〈比喻 *fig.*〉一刻也不停留，一直前进 make a hurried journey without a stop; keep going without a single halt

【马车】mǎchē ❶ 马拉的载人的车，有的轿式，有的敞篷式，有的双轮，有的四轮 horse-drawn carriage; berlin; waggonette; brougham ❷ 骡马拉的大车 mule- or horse-drawn cart

【马齿徒增】mǎ chǐ tú zēng 《谷梁传》僖公二年：'璧则犹是也，而马齿加长矣。'后用'马齿徒增'谦称自己虚度年华，没有成就。have grown old yet accomplished nothing. *The Guliang Commentary・Duke Xi 2nd Year*: 'While the jade sceptre remains the same, the horse's teeth keep growing in number and size.' A phrase of self-depreciation that means 'outgrow one's usefulness.'

【马刺】mǎcì 马靴后跟上镶的钉形金属物，骑马时用来踢马的腹部，使马快跑 spur; device with a small spike or a spiked wheel worn on a rider's heel for urging a horse forward by kicking at its belly

【马褡子】mǎdā・zi 挂在马身上的大型褡裢 flap; fender; a pair of bags worn across a horseback

【马达】mǎdá 电动机的通称 popular term for 电动机 diàndòngjī

【马大哈】mǎdàhā ❶ 粗心大意 heedless; unmindful: 保管文件，可不能～。One must not be careless when taking care of documents. ❷ 指粗心大意的人 scatterbrain; careless and forgetful person: 他是个～，做事总是丢三落四的。He is so forgetful that he does nothing without leaving some loose ends.

【马刀】mǎdāo 一种供劈刺用的长刀，刀身微弯，长约 1 米，是骑兵冲锋时的武器 sabre; slightly curved sword about one metre in length used by cavalry; also 战刀 zhàndāo

【马到成功】mǎ dào chénggōng 战马一到就取胜，形容人一到马上取得成果 win instant success; gain an immediate victory

【马道】mǎdào 〈旧时 *old*〉校场或城墙上跑马的路 horse track in a drill ground or on the top of a city wall

【马灯】mǎdēng 一种手提的能防风雨的煤油灯，骑马夜行时能挂在马身上 barn lantern; lantern; kerosene-fueled hand-held lantern resistant to wind and rain, that can be hung on a horse during a night trip

【马镫】mǎdèng 挂在马鞍子两旁供骑马人踏脚的东西 stirrup; flat-based loop or ring hung from either side of a horse's saddle to support the rider's foot in mounting or riding

【马店】mǎdiàn 主要供马帮客人投宿的客店 caravansary; caravanserai; inn with a large courtyard to cater to caravan merchants

【马队】mǎduì ❶ 成队的马，多用于运输货物 caravan; team of horses carrying goods ❷ 骑兵队伍 cavalry; contingent of mounted troops

【马翻人仰】mǎ fān rén yǎng ☞ 人仰马翻 rén yǎng mǎ fān on p. 1621

【马粪纸】mǎfènzhǐ 黄纸板的俗称 popular term for 黄纸板 huángzhǐbǎn

【马蜂】mǎfēng hornet; common term for 胡蜂 húfēng; also 蚂蜂 mǎfēng

【马蜂窝】mǎfēngwō 马蜂的窝 hornet's nest; 〈比喻 *fig.*〉难于对付的人或能引起麻烦和纠纷的事 sb. or sth. difficult to deal with or likely to cause trouble: 她这个～谁也惹不起。She's a terror, and nobody can afford to offend her.

【马夫】mǎfū 〈旧时 *old*〉称饲养马的人 groom; sb. taking care of horses or a stable

【马竿】mǎgān (～儿 mǎgānr) 盲人探路用的竿儿 blindman's stick; white stick

【马革裹尸】mǎ gé guǒ shī 用马皮把尸体包裹起来，指军人战死于战场 be wrapped in horsehide after laying down one's life in the battlefield; lay down one's life on the battlefield; die in the last ditch

【马褂】mǎguà (～儿 mǎguàr)〈旧时 *old*〉男子穿在长袍外面的对襟的短褂，以黑色的为最普通。原来是满族人骑马时所穿的服装。mandarin jacket (worn over a gown); originally a garment worn by horseback-riding Manchus

【马倌】mǎguān (～儿 mǎguānr) 专职养马的人 groom; stableman

【马锅头】mǎguōtóu 〈方 *dial.*〉率领马帮的人 leader of a caravan

【马海毛】mǎhǎimáo 安哥拉山羊的毛，弹性好，耐压，有特殊光泽，是制造长毛绒织物的优良原料 mohair; shiny, resilient, and silky long hair of the Angora goat, a fine material for making plush fabrics

【马号】[1] mǎhào 公家养马的地方 public stable

【马号】[2] mǎhào 骑兵用的较细长的军号 long-tubed bugle (used by cavalry)

【马赫】mǎhè 飞机、火箭等在空气中移动的速度与音速的比。由奥地利物理学家马赫(Ernst Mach)得名。Mach number; ratio of the speed of an aircraft or rocket in the air to the speed of sound, named after the Austrian physicist Ernst Mach (1838-1916)

【马后炮】mǎhòupào 象棋术语，借来比喻不及时的举动 belated action or advice; belated effort, a Chinese chess term used figuratively: 事情都做完了，你才说要帮忙，这不是～吗? You come and offer to help when it's all done. Isn't that a bit late?

【马虎】mǎ・hu 草率；敷衍；疏忽大意；不细心 careless; casual: 这人太～。He's a rather careless fellow.|做事要认真,～可不行! Take whatever you do seriously — carelessness brings you nowhere. also 马糊 mǎ·hu

【马糊】mǎ·hu same as 马虎 mǎ·hu

【马甲】mǎjiǎ 〈方 *dial*.〉背心 vest; sleeveless garment

【马架】mǎjià 〈方 *dial*.〉❶ 小窝棚 small shack; shed ❷ 用来背东西的三角形的木架 triangular wooden rack for carrying things on one's back ‖ also 马架子 mǎjià·zi

【马脚】mǎjiǎo 〈比喻 *fig*.〉破绽 sth. that gives the game away:露出～ give away; let slip

【马厩】mǎjiù 饲养马的房子 stable

【马驹子】mǎjū·zi 小马 foal; colt; filly

【马克】mǎkè 德国的旧本位货币 mark; former monetary unit of Germany [德 German: Mark]

【马克思列宁主义】Mǎkèsī-Lièníng zhǔyì 马克思主义和列宁主义的合称 Marxism-Leninism; 简称 abbr. 马列主义 Mǎ-Liè zhǔyì; ☞马克思主义 Mǎkèsī zhǔyì; 列宁主义 Lièníng zhǔyì on p.1217

【马克思主义】Mǎkèsī zhǔyì 马克思(Karl Marx)和恩格斯(Friedrich Engels)所创立的无产阶级思想体系。它的基本组成部分是马克思主义哲学即辩证唯物主义和历史唯物主义、政治经济学和科学社会主义。三者构成有机的统一体。马克思主义科学地阐明了自然界、人类社会和思维发展的一般规律,揭露了资本主义的剥削本质,指明资本主义必然灭亡,社会主义必然胜利。它是无产阶级和劳动人民进行革命的科学,是无产阶级政党指导思想的理论基础。Marxism; proletarian ideological system initiated by Karl Marx (1818-1883) and Friedrich Engels (1820-1895) and predicated on Marxist philosophy, in which dialectical materialism and historical materialism, political economics and scientific socialism form an organic whole. In a scientific way, Marxism expounds the general laws governing the development of nature, human society and thought, exposes capitalism's nature of exploitation, and points out that capitalism is doomed and socialism will win. It is the science by which the proletariat and the labouring people wage revolution; it is also the theoretical basis for the guideline of the proletarian party.

【马口铁】mǎkǒutiě 镀锡铁 tinplate; galvanized iron

【马裤】mǎkù 特为骑马方便而做的一种裤子,膝部以上肥大,以下极瘦 riding breeches; calf-length trousers flaring at the sides of the thighs and fitting snugly below the knees.

【马裤呢】mǎkùní 用精梳毛线织成的呢子,表面有明显斜纹,质地厚实,因最初多用做马裤而得名。也适于做外套、大衣等。whipcord; thick and durable worsted woollen fabric with a steep, diagonally ribbed surface, known as 'breeches fabric' because it was mostly used for the making of such trousers in the early days, also suitable for the making of coats and overcoats

【马快】mǎkuài 〈旧时 *old*〉官署里从事侦查逮捕罪犯的差役 mounted couriers; policemen in charge of investigating criminal cases and arresting suspects

【马拉松】mǎlāsōng ❶ 指马拉松赛跑 marathon ❷〈比喻 *fig*.〉时间持续得很久的(多含贬义 oft. derog.) tedious; long-winded: ～会议 marathon meeting|～演说 marathon speech

【马拉松赛跑】mǎlāsōng sàipǎo 一种超长距离赛跑,比赛距离为42,195米。古代希腊人在马拉松镇击败入侵的波斯军队,希腊士兵斐迪辟从马拉松一气跑到雅典(全程42,195米)报捷后即死去。为了纪念这一事迹,1896年在雅典举行的近代第一届奥林匹克运动会中,用这个距离作为一个竞赛项目,定名为马拉松赛跑。marathon; long-distance running race of 42,195 metres, first instituted in the first modern Olympic games held in Athens in 1896, in commemoration of the Greek soldier who died after running nonstop for the above-mentioned distance from Marathon to Athens with news of Greek's victory over the invading Persian army

【马兰】mǎlán ❶ 多年生草本植物,叶互生,披针形,边缘有粗锯齿,花紫色,形状跟菊花相似 *Kalimeris indica*; perennial herb with alternate sawteeth-edged lanceolar leaves and purple flowers akin to chrysanthemums ❷ same as 马蔺 mǎlìn

【马蓝】mǎlán 常绿草本植物,呈灌木状,叶子对生,有柄,椭圆形,边缘有锯齿,暗绿色,有光泽,花紫色。茎叶可制蓝靛。acanthaceous indigo (*Strobilanthes cusia*); evergreen bush-like herb with purple flowers and opposite oval leaves that have sawteeth edges, and are the colour of a shiny dark green, both its leaves and stalks used as materials for the making of indigo

【马力】mǎlì 功率单位,1马力等于每秒钟把75千克重的物体提高1米所作的功。合0.735千瓦。horsepower (h.p.); unit of power equal to 0.735 kw or the power needed to lift a 75-kg. weight by one metre per second

【马利亚】Mǎlìyà 《圣经》中耶稣的母亲。据《福音书》记载,她是童贞女,由圣灵感孕而生耶稣。Mary; Virgin Mary; mother of Jesus. According to *The New Testament · Luke*, Mary was a virgin who conceived Jesus by communion with the Holy Spirit. 马 also put as 玛 mǎ

【马列主义】Mǎ-Liè zhǔyì 马克思列宁主义的简称 abbr. for 马克思列宁主义 Mǎkèsī-Lièníng zhǔyì

【马蔺】mǎlìn 多年生草本植物,根茎粗,叶子条形，花蓝紫色。叶子富于韧性，可以用来捆东西，又可以造纸，根可制刷子。Chinese small iris (*Iris lactea* var. *chinensis*); perennial plant having a thick rootstalk that can be used to make brushes, bluish purple flowers, and strip-like leaves resilient enough to be used to bundle things or make paper; also 马莲 mǎlián or 马兰 mǎlán

【马铃薯】mǎlíngshǔ ❶ 多年生草本植物，羽状复叶，小叶有柄，卵圆形，花白色或蓝紫色。地下块茎肥大，供食用。potato (*Solanum tuberosum*); perennial plant with pinnately compound small leaves of oval shape and with leaf-stalks, flowers either white or bluish purple in colour, and edible large tubers ❷ 这种植物的块茎 potato, the edible tubers of the plant of the same name ‖ 在不同的地区有洋芋、土豆儿、山药蛋等名称 known by various names in different regions, such as 洋芋 yángyù, 土豆儿 tǔdòur, 山药蛋 shānyàodàn, etc.

【马陆】mǎlù 节肢动物，身体圆长，由很多环节构成，除第一、第二、第三、第四和末节外，每节有脚两对，头部有短触须一对，背面有黄黑色相间的环纹。生活在阴湿的地方，有臭腺。昼伏夜出，吃草根或腐败的植物。julid (*Orthomorpha pekuensis*); nocturnal arthropod with foetid glands, a pair of short tentacles on its head, and a cylindrical body that consists of many segments each with two pairs of legs with the exception of the 1st, 2nd, 3rd, 4th and last segments and that has yellow-and-black loopy patterns on its back, living in damp places and feeding on grass roots and rotten plants

【马路】mǎlù ❶ 城市或近郊的供车马行走的宽阔平坦的道路 road; street; avenue ❷ 泛指公路 (in a broad sense) highways

【马路消息】mǎlù xiāoxi same as 马路新闻 mǎlù xīnwén

【马路新闻】mǎlù xīnwén 指道听途说的消息 grapevine news; hearsay; rumour: ～，不要轻信。Don't give easy credulity to news from the grapevine. also 马路消息 mǎlù xiāoxi

【马骡】mǎluó 公驴和母马交配所生的杂种，身体较大，耳朵较小，尾部的毛蓬松 mule; offspring of a male donkey and a female horse, with a large body, small ears, and a fluffy hairy tail

【马马虎虎】mǎ·mǎhūhū ❶ 马虎；随随便便 palter with sth.; do things in a slipshod way; make a hash of sth.: 终身大事要慎重，怎么能～？Marriage, with its lifetime significance, should be taken seriously, and it is not something to be paltered with? ❷ 勉强；凑合 so so; passable; not so bad: 近来身体还～。I feel all right lately. | 日子～过得去。Life has been passable these days.

M

【马趴】mǎpā 身体向前跌倒的姿势 fall flat on one's face: 摔了个大～ fall flat on one's face

【马匹】mǎpǐ 马(总称) (collect.) horse

【马屁精】mǎpìjīng 指善于拍马屁的人 sycophant; flatterer

【马前卒】mǎqiánzú 〈旧指 *old*〉在车前头供奔走役使的人，现用来比喻为别人效力的人(多含贬义 oft. derog.) pawn; cat's paw; servant waiting by a carriage to be called upon to run errands; (now referring to) people who serve others

【马枪】mǎqiāng 骑兵使用的一种枪，构造跟步枪相似，但枪身较短而轻便，射程较步枪近 carbine; cavalry gun similar to a rifle in structure but shorter and more handy than it, with a shorter firing range; also 骑枪 qíqiāng

【马赛克】mǎsàikè ❶ 一种小型瓷砖，方形或六角形，有各种颜色，可以砌成花纹和图案，多用来铺室内地面 mosaic; tiny multi-coloured square or hexagonal porcelain pieces used as a flooring material that can be arranged in different pictures or patterns ❷ 用马赛克做成的图案 mosaic; patterns and pictures arranged with such pieces

【马上】mǎshàng 立刻 at once; immediately; straight away; right away: 快进去吧，电影～就要开演了。Hurry up and come on in. The movie is soon to begin.

【马勺】mǎsháo 盛粥或盛饭用的大勺，多用木头制成 ladle; kitchen utensil, usu. made of wood, for dispensing porridge or rice when a meal is being served

【马失前蹄】mǎ shī qián tí 〈比喻 *fig.*〉偶然发生差错而受挫 horse stumbles; horse trips and falls on its knees; make a mistake by accident; suffer an accidental setback

【马首是瞻】mǎ shǒu shì zhān 古代作战时士兵看着主将的马头决定进退 (of soldiers in ancient times) take the cue for advance or withdrawal from the position of the head of the commander's mount; 〈比喻 *fig.*〉跟随别人行动或听从别人指挥 dance to sb's tune; follow on the heels of sb.

【马术】mǎshù 骑马的技术 horsemanship: ～表演 equestrian show

【马蹄】mǎtí ❶ 马的蹄子 horse's hoof ❷ 〈方 *dial.*〉荸荠 water chestnut

【马蹄表】mǎtíbiǎo 圆形或马蹄形的小钟，多为闹钟 round or hoof-shaped desk clock, usu. an alarm clock

【马蹄铁】mǎtítiě ❶ 钉在马、驴、骡子的蹄子底下的 U 字形的铁，作用是使蹄子耐磨 horseshoe; U-shaped steel nailed into the hoofs of a horse, donkey, mule, etc. so that the hoofs become more resistant to wear and tear; 通称 generally known as 马掌 mǎzhǎng ❷ U 字形的磁铁 U-shaped magnet; horseshoe magnet

【马蹄形】mǎtíxíng ❶ 三面构成 U 字形而一面

是直线的形状 hoof-like shape ❷ U 字形 U-shaped

【马蹄袖】mǎtíxiù 清代男子礼服的袖口,马蹄形 horsehoof-shaped cuff on a Manchu man's jacket or gown during the Qing Dynasty

【马铁】mǎtiě 可锻铸铁 malleable cast iron

【马桶】mǎtǒng 大小便用的有盖的桶,多用木头或搪瓷制成。有的地区也叫马子。nightstool; closestool; commode; chamber pot; lidded wooden or enamel receptacle used in a bedroom as a toilet; known in some regions as 马子 mǎ·zi

【马头琴】mǎtóuqín 蒙古族弦乐器,有两根弦,琴身呈梯形,琴柄顶端刻有马头做装饰 Mongolian bowed stringed instrument with a trapezoidal body and a scroll carved in the image of a horse's head

【马戏】mǎxì 原来指人骑在马上所做的各种表演,现在指节目中有经过训练的动物,如狗熊、马、猴子、小狗等参加的杂技表演 circus; originally referring to the performances of actors and actresses on horseback; now referring to a show of acrobats and performing bears, horses, monkeys, dogs and other animals: ~团 circus troupe

【马靴】mǎxuē 骑马人穿的长筒靴子,也指一般的长筒靴子 cowboy boots; riding boots

【马仰人翻】mǎ yǎng rén fān ☞ 人仰马翻 rén yǎng mǎ fān on p. 1621

【马贼】mǎzéi 〈旧时 *old*〉称成群骑马抢劫的盗匪 pack of mounted bandits

【马扎】mǎzhá (~儿 mǎzhár)一种小型的坐具,腿交叉,上面绷帆布或麻绳等,可以合拢,便于携带 campstool; folding stool topped with canvas or woven hemp ropes; also 马劄 mǎzhá

【马劄】mǎzhá same as 马扎 mǎzhá

【马掌】mǎzhǎng ❶ 马蹄下面的角质皮 cutin skin of a horse's hoof ❷ 马蹄铁①的通称 general term for 马蹄铁 mǎtítiě ①

【马子】mǎ·zi 〈方 *dial.*〉❶ same as 马桶 mǎtǒng ❷ 土匪 bandit; brigand

【马鬃】mǎzōng 马颈上的长毛 horse's mane

【马醉木】mǎzuìmù 常绿灌木,叶子长卵形,花小,白色,花冠呈壶状,向下垂,供观赏。叶有剧毒,可做杀虫药,牛马误食后会发生醉态。Japanese pieris (*Pieris japonica*); evergreen bush having drooping tiny white flowers with kettle-shaped corollas, and highly poisonous long-oval leaves that are material for making insecticides and that induce a state of drunkenness in cattle or horses which had eaten them by mistake; also 梫木 qǐnmù

吗 mǎ [吗啡](mǎfēi)药名,有机化合物,化学式 $C_{17}H_{19}O_3N \cdot H_2O$,白色结晶性粉末,味苦,有毒,是由鸦片制成的。用做镇痛剂,连续使用容易成瘾。morphine; organic compound (formula $C_{17}H_{19}O_3N \cdot N_2O$) in the form of a white crystalline powder extracted from opium, with a bitter taste, toxic, used as a pain-killer that is highly addictive if used repeatedly

☞ má on p. 1285 and ·ma on p. 1292

犸 mǎ ☞ 猛犸 měngmǎ on p. 1326

玛 mǎ ☞ below

【玛钢】mǎgāng 可锻铸铁 malleable cast iron

【玛瑙】mǎnǎo 矿物,主要成分是二氧化硅,有各种颜色,多呈层状或环状,质地坚硬耐磨,可用做磨具、仪表轴承等,也可做贵重的装饰品 agate; chalcedony composed mainly of silicon dioxide, with multi-layered or curved bands of different hues, of a hard texture that makes it an ideal material for grinder, bearings for meters and apparatuses, and precious jewellery

码1 mǎ ❶ (~儿 mǎr)表示数目的符号 sign or thing indicating number: 数~ numerical code | 号~ number | 页~ page number | 价~ listed price ❷ 表示数目的用具 instrument used to indicate number: 筹~ chip; counter | 砝~(of a balance) weight ❸ 〈量词 *classifier*〉用于事情[indicating the same thing or the same kind]: 这是两~事。These are two different things. | 你说的跟他说的是一~事。The two of you were talking about the same thing.

码2 mǎ 堆叠 pile up; put things in good order: 把这些砖头~齐了。Stack the bricks neatly, please.

码3 mǎ 英美制长度单位,1 码等于 3 英尺,合 0.9144 米 yard (yd.); (Brit. and Amer. metric unit): 1 yard = 3 feet, or 0.9144 metre

【码放】mǎfàng 有次序地摆放;按一定位置堆放 pile up; place in a stack; stack: ~整齐 place sth. in neat stacks | 各种器材~得井井有条。Various equipment has been piled up in orderly stacks.

【码头】mǎ·tou ❶ 在江河沿岸及港湾内,供停船时装卸货物和乘客上下的建筑 wharf; dock; quay; pier; facility built parallel to the shoreline for loading and unloading freight and passengers ❷ 〈方 *dial.*〉指交通便利的商业城市 port city; commercial and transportation hub: 水陆~ port city with a well-developed land and water transport network

【码洋】mǎyáng 图书出版发行部门指全部图书定价的总额 total price volume; total volume of books based on prices marked on books to be published or distributed: 这次图书联展共投入图书品种 500 多个,约 150 多万~。This joint book exhibition features more than 500 titles, with a total price of approximately 1.5 million yuan.

【码子】mǎ·zi ❶ 表示数目的符号 numeral

code：苏州～ numeral code of Suzhou ❷ 圆形的筹码 counter; chip ❸ 解放前金融界称自己能调度的现款(in pre-liberation banking) cash at one's own disposal

蚂 mǎ ☞ below
☞ mā on p. 1285 and mà on p. 1292

【蚂蜂】mǎfēng same as 马蜂 mǎfēng

【蚂蟥】mǎhuáng 蛭纲动物，我国常见的是宽体蚂蟥，身体略呈纺锤形，扁平而较肥壮，背面通常暗绿色，前吸盘小。生活在水田、湖沼中，能刺伤皮肤，但不吸血。leech (*Hirudinea*); a common type of which in China has a flat and fat spindle-like body with a greenish dark back and a tiny acetabulum, lives in paddy fields, marshes and lakes, can pierce and hurt the skin, but does not suck blood

【蚂蟥钉】mǎhuángdīng 有两条腿的钉子，一般呈冂形 staple; U-shaped nail with two legs

【蚂蚁】mǎyǐ 昆虫，体小，长形，黑色或褐色，头大，有一对复眼，触角长，腹部卵形。雌蚁和雄蚁有翅膀，工蚁没有。在地下筑巢，成群穴居。ant (*Monorium minimum*); hymenopterous insect with a tiny elongated body, black or ochre in colour, egg-shaped abdomen, and long antennas and compound eyes on a big head, living in some degree of social organization in underground nests. Female and male ants have wings, but ergates don't have them.

【蚂蚁搬泰山】mǎyǐ bān Tàishān 〈比喻 *fig*.〉群众力量大，齐心协力，就可以完成巨大的任务 ants can move Mount Taishan; united efforts of the masses can accomplish mighty tasks

【蚂蚁啃骨头】mǎyǐ kěn gǔ·tou 指利用小型设备或小的力量一点一点地苦干来完成一项巨大的任务 ants gnawing at a bone — concentrating small equipment on a big job; plod away at a big job bit by bit

mà (ㄇㄚˋ)

杩 mà [杩头](mà·tou)床两头或门扇上下两端的横木 wooden rail; top and bottom rails of a bed, door, or window

祃 mà 古代在军队驻扎的地方举行的祭礼(of ancient times) sacrificial ceremonies held at an army garrison

蚂 mà [蚂蚱](mà·zha)〈方 *dial*.〉蝗虫 locust
☞ mā on p. 1285 and mǎ on p. 1292

骂(罵) mà ❶ 用粗野或恶意的话侮辱人 verbally abuse; curse; swear; call names：～街 shout abuse in public | 张嘴就～ let loose a barrage of abuse ❷ 斥责 condemn; rebuke; reprove; scold：他爹～他不长进。His father scolded him for not working hard to make progress.

【骂大街】mà dàjiē same as 骂街 mà//jiē

【骂架】mà//jià 吵架；相骂 kick up a row

【骂街】mà//jiē 不指明对象当众漫骂 shout abuse in public; call people names in public：泼妇～(as provocative as) a termagant shouting abuse in the street

【骂骂咧咧】mà·maliēliē 指在说话中夹杂着骂人的话 foul-mouthed; grumbling and swearing：有话好好说，不要～的。Cut out your foul-mouthed abuse — if you have a reason, say it properly.

【骂名】màmíng 挨骂的名声 bad name; notoriety：蒙受～get a bad reputation | 留下千古～ earn oneself eternal infamy

【骂娘】màniáng 骂人时恶毒地侮辱别人的母亲，泛指漫骂 abuse sb. by calling his mother names; (in a broad sense) curse; swear

【骂山门】mà shānmén 〈方 *dial*.〉漫骂；骂 curse roundly; call names

【骂阵】mà//zhèn ❶ 在阵前叫骂，激怒敌方应战(多见于旧小说 oft. in old fiction) shout abuse to infuriate an enemy so as to challenge him to a showdown ❷〈方 *dial*.〉same as 骂街 mà//jiē

·ma (·ㄇㄚ)

吗(么) ·ma 〈助词 *aux*.〉❶ 用在句末表示疑问[used at the end of a question]：明天他来～？Is he coming tomorrow? | 你找我有事～？Is there something you want to see me about? ❷ 用在句中停顿处，点出话题[used to form a pause in a sentence before introducing the theme of what one is going to say]：这件事～，其实也不能怪他。This, actually, is not his fault. | 钱～，能省点就省点。Talking about money, well, save it wherever you can.
☞ má on p. 1285 and mǎ on p. 1291
☞么·me on p. 1312 and 幺 yāo on p. 2225

嘛(么) ·ma 〈助词 *aux*.〉❶ 表示道理显而易见[indicating that sth. speaks for itself]：有意见就提～。Air your complaints if you have any. | 这也不能怪他，头一回做～。He's not to blame. After all, it was the first time he'd done it. | 他自己要去～，我有什么办法？He insisted on going there — what could I do about it? ❷ 表示期望、劝阻[expressing hope or giving advice]：你不要走得那么快～！Don't you walk so fast. | 不让你去，就别去～。Don't go if you are not asked to. ❸ 用在句中停顿处，唤起听话人对于下文的注意[indicating a pause in a sentence to call attention to what one is going to say]：科学～，就得讲究实事求是。Where science is concerned, we should be really practical. | 其实～，责任在领导，不能怪群众。As a matter of fact, the blame is on the leadership, instead of the masses. 注意 **NOTE**: 表示疑问语气用'吗',不用'嘛'。In an interrogative sentence 吗 ·ma is used instead of 嘛.

☞ 么 ·me on p. 1312 and 幺 yāo on p. 2225

mái (ㄇㄞˊ)

埋 mái ❶(用土、沙、雪、落叶等)盖住 cover up (with earth, sand, snow, fallen leaves, etc.); bury: 掩～ bury | ～地雷 lay a mine | 道路被大雪～住。The road was buried in snow. ❷ 藏;隐没 hide; conceal: ～伏 ambush | 隐姓～名 live in anonymity; conceal one's identity

☞ mán on p. 1297

【埋藏】máicáng ❶ 藏在土中 lie hidden in the earth; bury: 山下～着丰富的煤和铁。There are rich coal and iron ore deposits under the mountain. ❷ 隐藏 conceal: 他是个直爽人,从来不把自己想说的话～在心里。He's a straightforward person who always speaks his mind whenever he has something to say. ❸ 把某种制剂放在人或动物的皮下组织内。对于人是为了医疗,对于家畜大多是为了催肥。implant; imbed; practice of implanting a certain preparation in the subcutaneous tissue of a human body for medical purposes, or a domestic animal oft. for fattening purposes

【埋伏】mái·fú ❶ 在估计敌人要经过的地方秘密布置兵力,伺机出击 lie in ambush; ambush: 中～ be trapped in an ambush | 四面～ soldiers lying in ambush in all directions | 把人马分做三路,两路～,一路出击。The troops were divided into three groups, with two of them concealed in an ambush, and one launching an attack. ❷ 潜伏 hide; lie low: 这是一支～在敌占区的别动队。This was a special detachment hidden in the enemy-occupied area.

【埋名】máimíng 隐瞒真实名字,不让人家知道 conceal one's identity; keep one's identity hidden; live incognito: 隐姓～ live in anonymity

【埋没】máimò ❶ 掩埋;埋起来 cover up (with earth, snow, etc.); bury: 耕地被流沙～。The farmland has been obliterated by drifting sand. ❷ 使显不出来;使不发挥作用 sweep sb. under the carpet; neglect; stifle: ～人才 stifle talent

【埋设】máishè 挖开土安设并埋好 fit sth. underground: ～地雷 plant a mine | ～管道 lay a pipeline

【埋汰】mái·tai 〈方 *dial.*〉❶ 脏;不干净 filthy; dirty: 这条被子太～了。This quilt is filthy. ❷ 用尖刻的话挖苦人 insult; ridicule: 别拿话～人。Don't try to make a fool of other people.

【埋头】mái//tóu 专心,下工夫 immerse oneself in; be engrossed in: ～工作 bury oneself in one's work | ～苦干 quietly immerse oneself in hard work; quietly put one's shoulder to the wheel

【埋葬】máizàng ❶ 掩埋尸体 bury (a dead person): 他死后,～在公墓里。After he died, his remains were buried in a cemetery. ❷ 〈比喻 *fig.*〉消灭;消除 eliminate; wipe out: ～旧世界。Bury the old world.

霾 mái 空气中因悬浮着大量的烟、尘等微粒而形成的混浊现象 haze; obscuration of the sky by a wide dispersion of smoke or dust particles in the air; 通称 generally known as 阴霾 yīnmái

mǎi (ㄇㄞˇ)

买(買) mǎi ❶ 拿钱换东西(跟'卖'相对 as opposed to 'sell') buy; purchase: ～票 buy a ticket | ～布 buy a piece of cloth | 卖出粮食,～进化肥。Sell the grain and buy the chemical fertilizers. ❷ (Mǎi) 姓 a surname

【买办】mǎibàn 殖民地、半殖民地国家里替外国资本家在本国市场上经营企业、推销商品的代理人 comprador; (of a colonial or semi-colonial country) native agent running factories or selling commodities in the local market for foreign capitalists

【买办资本】mǎibàn zīběn 殖民地、半殖民地中买办资产阶级所拥有的资本 comprador capital; capital owned by the comprador bourgeoisie in a colonial or semi-colonial country

【买办资产阶级】mǎibàn zīchǎn jiējí 殖民地、半殖民地国家里,勾结帝国主义并为帝国主义侵略政策服务的大资产阶级。买办资产阶级依靠帝国主义,跟本国的封建势力也有极密切的联系。在旧中国,买办资产阶级掌握政权,发展成为官僚资产阶级。comprador bourgeoisie; (of a colonial or semi-colonial country) the big bourgeoisie working hand in glove with imperialism and serving the imperialist policy of aggression, relying on capitalism while maintaining an intimate relationship with the domestic feudal forces; in old China the comprador bourgeoisie took control of the political power and degenerated into the bureaucratic bourgeoisie; also 买办阶级 mǎibàn jiējí

【买椟还珠】mǎi dú huán zhū 楚国人到郑国去卖珍珠,把珍珠装在匣子里,匣子装饰得很华贵。郑国人就买下匣子,把珍珠退还了(见于《韩非子·外储说左上》)。*Hanfeizi · Outer Repository of Persuasions* (*Upper Left*): When a merchant of the state of Chu went to the state of Zheng to sell a pearl contained in an glamorous box, a local man bought the box and returned the pearl to the merchant. 〈比喻 *fig.*〉没有眼光,取舍不当 keep the glittering casket and give back the pearls — show lack of judgement; make the wrong choice; attend to the superficial and neglect the essential

【买关节】mǎi guānjié 用财物买通别人;行贿赂 grease the hand of sb.; pay off; bypass law, rules, etc. by bribery

【买好】mǎi//hǎo(～儿 mǎi//hǎor)(言语行动上)故意讨人喜欢(in speech or behaviour) try to win sb.'s favour; ingratiate oneself with; play up to:献媚～ resort to coquetry

【买空卖空】mǎi kōng mài kōng ❶ 一种商业投机行为,投机的对象多为股票、公债、外币、黄金等,或者预料价格要涨而买进后再卖出,或者预料价格要跌而卖出后再买进,买时并不付款取货,卖时也并不交货收款,只是就一进一出间的差价结算盈余或亏损 speculate on the rise and fall of the prices of stocks, treasury bonds, foreign currency, gold, etc., buying in anticipation of a price rise for the purpose of reselling, or selling in anticipation of a price fall for the purpose of buying again, with transactions done without goods or money changing hands but by calculating the gains or losses on the basis of the differences between purchase and sale ❷〈比喻 *fig.*〉招摇撞骗,搞投机活动 swindle; profiteer

【买路钱】mǎilùqián ❶〈旧时 *old*〉指行人被强盗拦住被迫交出的钱物 money extorted by highwaymen from travellers ❷〈比喻 *fig.*〉车辆在公路上向关卡交付的费用(含诙谐意 humor.) highway toll

【买卖】mǎi·mai ❶ 生意 buying and selling; business; deal; transaction:～兴隆。Business is brisk.|做了一笔～have struck a deal; have concluded a transaction ❷ 指商店(private) shop:他在城里开了家小～。He opened a small store in town.

【买卖人】mǎi·mairén 指商人 businessman; trader; merchant

【买面子】mǎi miàn·zi 看对方的情面表示可以通融 make an exception on account of sb.'s clout; defer to sb.:不是我不买你的面子,实在这事不好办。I'd be happy to defer to your wishes, but there's really nothing I can do about it.

【买通】mǎitōng 用金钱等收买人以便达到自己的目的 bribe; buy over; buy off:～官府(of old days) bribe local authorities

【买账】mǎi//zhàng 承认对方的长处或力量而表示佩服或服从(多用于否定式 usu. in the negative) acknowledge the superiority or seniority of; show respect for:不买他的账。(People) just won't buy it.

M

【买主】mǎizhǔ 货物或房产等的购买者 buyer; customer:这批货有了～了。This batch of goods have found a buyer.

【买醉】mǎizuì 买酒痛饮,多指借酒行乐或消愁 buy liquor and imbibe it to seek pleasure or dispel melancholy

荬(蕒) mǎi ☞[苣荬菜](qǔ·mǎicài) on p.1591

mài(ㄇㄞˋ)

劢(勱) mài〈书 *fml.*〉勉力;努力 diligence; effort

迈[1](邁) mài 提脚向前走;跨 step; stride:～步 take a step; make a step; step forward|～进 enter; come into|～过门坎 step over the threshold

迈[2](邁) mài 老 advanced in years; old:老～senile|年～aged

迈[3](邁) mài 英里(用于机动车行车速度 for calculating the speed of an automobile) mile:一个钟头走三十～30 miles per hour|司机把速度开到八十～。The driver raised the speed to 80 miles.

【迈步】mài//bù 提脚向前走;迈出步子 step; pace; tread:向前～make a step forward|不敢～dare not make a move|迈一大步 walk in big strides

【迈方步】mài fāngbù(～儿 mài fāngbùr)很稳很慢地走路(多用来形容旧时书生、官吏的文绉绉的动作)(oft. of a scholar or official of old times) walk with measured steps; stride leisurely forward; also 迈四方步 mài sìfāngbù

【迈进】màijìn 大踏步地前进 stride forward; forge ahead

麦[1](麥) mài ❶ 一年生或二年生草本植物,子实用来磨面粉,也可以用来制糖或酿酒,是我国北方重要的粮食作物。有小麦、大麦、黑麦、燕麦等多种 wheat (*Triticum*); annual or biannual cereal grass that is a major crop in north China, bearing a kind of grain to be ground into flour or used to make sugar or brew alcoholic beverages, including wheat, barley, rye, oat, etc. ❷ 专指小麦 exclusive term for wheat ‖ 通称麦子 general term for wheat ❸ (Mài)姓 a surname

麦[2](麥) mài 麦克斯韦的简称 abbr. for 麦克斯韦 màikèsīwéi

【麦草】màicǎo〈方 *dial.*〉麦秸 wheat stalks

【麦茬】màichá ❶ 麦子收割后,遗留在地里的根和茎的基部 wheat stubble ❷ 指麦子收割以后准备种植或已经种植的(土地或作物) field of wheat stubble that is either ready for growing other crops or already sown:～地 stubbly farmland|～白薯 sweet potatoes cultivated after wheat harvest

【麦季】màijì 收割麦子的季节 wheat harvesting season:～里农活最紧。Farmers are the busiest during the wheat-harvesting season.|今年～收成好。The wheat harvest this year was rather good.

【麦秸】màijiē 脱粒后的麦秆 wheat straw

【麦酒】màijiǔ 啤酒 beer

【麦糠】màikāng 紧贴在麦粒外面的皮儿，脱下后叫麦糠 wheat husks

【麦克风】màikèfēng 微音器的通称 general term for 微音器 wēiyīnqì

【麦克斯韦】màikèsīwéi 磁通量单位，磁场的磁感应强度为1高斯时，垂直于磁力线方向的平面上每平方厘米通过的磁通量就是1麦克斯韦。这个单位名称是为纪念英国物理学家麦克斯韦(James Clerk Maxwell)而定的 maxwell; cm.-gramme-second unit of magnetic flux named after the British physicist James Clerk Maxwell (1831-1879), equal to a magnetic flux going through a one square centimetre surface positioned vertical to the magnetic line of force to a magnetic field of one gauss; 简称 abbr. 麦 mài

【麦客】màikè〈方 *dial.*〉麦收季节受雇为人收麦或干其他活儿的短工 farmhand hired to gather in wheat or do other farm chores during the wheat-harvesting season

【麦口】màikǒu〈方 *dial.*〉(～儿 màikǒur) 麦子将熟未熟的时候 ripening stage of a wheat crop; also 麦口期 màikǒuqī or 麦口上 màikǒushàng

【麦浪】màilàng 指田地里大片麦子被风吹得起伏像波浪的样子 rippling wheat; billowing wheat fields：～滚滚。The wheat was rippling in the wind.

【麦粒肿】màilìzhǒng 眼病，由葡萄球菌侵入眼睑的皮脂腺引起。症状是眼睑疼痛，眼睑的边缘靠近睫毛处出现粒状的小疙瘩，局部红肿。stye; sty; partial inflammatory swelling on the edge of the eyelid, with tiny boils flaring near the eyelash, caused by the intrusion of staphylococcus into the eyelid's sebaceous gland; 通称 popularly known as 针眼 zhēnyǎn

【麦芒】màimáng (～儿 màimángr) 麦穗上的芒 awn of wheat

【麦苗】màimiáo 小麦、大麦、黑麦、燕麦等作物的幼苗 wheat seedling; seedling of barley, rye, oat, etc.

【麦片】màipiàn 食品，是用燕麦或大麦粒压成的小片 oatmeal; meal made from ground or flattened oats or barley grain

【麦淇淋】màiqílín 用氢化植物油(有时混以猪油)和脱脂牛奶、食盐、卵磷脂、色素等配制成的固体，黄白色，是黄油的代用品 margarine; yellowish white butter substitute made from vegetable oils (sometimes mixed with pork fat) with skimmed milk, salt, lecithin, pigment, etc.

【麦秋】màiqiū 收割麦子的时候。收割的日期各地不同，一般是在夏季 wheat harvest season, which may fall on different dates in summer in different places：～快到了，农民忙着做准备工作。The wheat harvest season is setting in, and farmers are busy preparing for it.

【麦收】màishōu 收割麦子 wheat harvest：～季节 wheat harvesting season

【麦莛】màitíng (～儿 màitíngr) 麦秆上连着穗儿的那一段 section of a wheat stalk that is linked with the wheat ear

【麦芽糖】màiyátáng 糖的一种，化学式 $C_{12}H_{22}O_{11}\cdot H_2O$。白色晶体，不如蔗糖甜，能分解成单糖，是饴糖的主要成分。用来制糖果或药品。malt sugar (formula $C_{12}H_{22}O_{11}\cdot H_2O$), a white crystalline substance not as sweet as sugar, capable of disintegrating into monose, and constituting the major ingredient in maltose, and used in confectionary and pharmaceutical industries

【麦子】mài·zi ☞ 麦[1] mài ① ②

卖(賣) mài ❶ 拿东西换钱(跟'买'相对 as opposed to 'buy') sell; fetch：～房子 put one's house up for sale | 把余粮～给国家 sell surplus grain to the state ❷ 为了自己的利益出卖祖国或亲友 betray (one's country or friends)：～国 treason; betray one's nation | ～友求荣 betray one's friends for personal gain ❸ 尽量用出来；不吝惜 do the best one can; do one's utmost; to the best of one's ability：～劲儿 exert oneself in doing sth. | ～力气 spare no effort ❹ 故意表现在外面，让人看见 flaunt; parade：～功 boast about one's merit | ～弄 show off; swagger | ～俏 coquet; philander; make eyes at ❺〈量词 *classifier*〉〈旧时 *old*〉饭馆中称一个菜为一卖 (in a restaurant) dish：一～炒腰花 a dish of stir-fried pork kidneys

【卖唱】mài//chàng 在街头或公共场所歌唱挣钱 sing for a living; make a living singing in the street or any other public place

【卖春】màichūn 指卖淫 engage in sexual intercourse for money; prostitution

【卖大号】mài dàhào 指零售店把紧俏商品大量地卖给某人或单位 (oft. of a shop) profiteer by selling goods in short supply to a single person or place in batches; also 卖大户 mài dàhù

【卖呆】mài//dāi〈方 *dial.*〉(～儿 mài//dāir) ❶ 在大门外呆呆地看(多用于妇女 oft. a woman) stand idly at the gate and stare blankly ❷ 发愣 daze; stare blankly：别～了，快走吧！Stop standing there doing nothing. Hurry up and go. ❸ 看热闹 watch the fun：许多人围在那里～。A crowd gathered there to watch what was going on.

【卖底】mài//dǐ〈方 *dial.*〉故意泄露底细 let in on; let out a secret on purpose

【卖功】mài//gōng 在人前夸耀自己的功劳 brag; boast of one's contribution：～邀赏 attempt to get something by boasting

【卖狗皮膏药】mài gǒupí gāo·yao〈比喻 *fig.*〉说得好听，实际上是骗人 sell quack remedies; practise quackery; sell oneself by boasting：不要～了，谁不知道你那两下子？Cut out all the quackery, since everybody knows what you are capable of.

【卖乖】mài//guāi 自鸣乖巧 show off cleverness：得了便宜还～act nonchalantly after gaining sth. unwarranted; swagger and brag after having gained some advantages

【卖关节】mài guānjié 指暗中接受贿赂，给人好处 take bribe and do sb. a favour

【卖关子】mài guān·zi ❶ 说书人说长篇故事，在说到重要关节处停止，借以吸引听众接着往下听，叫卖关子（of a storyteller）stop by the time a story arrives at a cliffhanger to keep the audience in suspense ❷〈比喻 *fig.*〉说话、做事在紧要的时候，故弄玄虚，使对方着急而答应自己的要求 keep people guessing：有话快说，别～了！Come on! Don't keep us guessing.

【卖官鬻爵】mài guān yù jué〈旧时 *old*〉指当权者出卖官职、爵位，聚敛财富 accept bribery and confer official titles for money

【卖国】mài//guó 为了私利投靠敌人，出卖祖国和人民利益 turn traitor to one's motherland：～贼 traitor to one's country｜～求荣 seek power and wealth by betraying one's country; turn traitor for selfish purposes

【卖国贼】màiguózéi 出卖祖国的叛徒 traitor to one's motherland

【卖好】mài//hǎo（～儿 mài//hǎor）用手段向别人讨好 curry favour with; ingratiate oneself with; play up to; fawn on

【卖劲】mài//jìn（～儿 mài//jìnr）把劲头使出来 exert all one's strength; spare no effort; same as 卖力气 mài lì·qi ①：很～work hard｜多卖点劲。Please work a little harder.

【卖老】mài//lǎo 摆老资格 pride oneself on being a veteran; self-importance of the aged：倚老～flaunt one's seniority and experience｜我不敢在你跟前～。Who am I to flaunt my seniority and experience?

【卖力】màilì same as 卖力气 mài lì·qi ①

【卖力气】mài lì·qi ❶ 尽量使出自己的力量 do one's very best; exert oneself to the utmost：他做事很～。He does whatever he does with utmost effort. also 卖力 màilì ❷ 指靠出卖劳动力（主要是体力劳动）来维持生活 live by the sweat of one's brow; make a living by physical labour

【卖命】mài//mìng ❶ 指为某人、某集团所利用或为生活所迫而拼命干活儿 exert oneself for sb. or some organization, or for survival; slave for ❷ 下最大力气做工作 work oneself to the bone：悠着点儿干，不要太～了。Take it easy; don't overwork yourself.

【卖弄】mài·nong 有意显示，炫耀（自己的本领）show off; brandish; make a show of oneself：～小聪明 show off one's smartness｜别再在大伙儿跟前～。Stop showing off in front of everybody.

【卖俏】mài//qiào 装出娇媚的姿态诱惑人 play the coquette; coquette; flirt：倚门～lean against the door and flirt with whoever passes by

【卖人情】mài rénqíng 故意给人好处，使人感激自己 do sb. a favour for selfish consideration

【卖身】mài//shēn ❶ 把自己或妻子儿女等卖给别人（多为生活所迫 of sb. trying desperately to eke out a living）sell oneself or a family member：～契 indenture by which one sells oneself or a member of one's family｜～投靠 sell one's soul to an enemy; seek favour by putting oneself at sb's beck and call ❷ 指卖淫 sell one's body; prostitute

【卖身投靠】màishēn tóukào 出卖自己，投靠有财有势的人 barter away one's honour for sb.'s patronage;〈比喻 *fig.*〉丧失人格，充当坏人的工具 willingly serve as sb's cat's paw

【卖笑】màixiào 指娼妓或歌女为生活所迫，用声色供人取乐（of a prostitute or sing-song girl）show a smiling face and flirt：～生涯 make a living as a prostitute or sing-song girl

【卖解】màixiè〈旧时 *old*〉指以表演各种杂技挣钱谋生 eking out a living by performing acrobatics：～班子 acrobatic troupe｜跑马～acrobatic horsemanship show

【卖艺】mài//yì 指在街头或娱乐场所表演杂技、武术、曲艺等挣钱 make a living as a performer：街头～be a street-performer

【卖淫】mài//yín 妇女出卖肉体 prostitute oneself

【卖友】mài//yǒu 出卖朋友 betray one's friend：～求荣 betray one's friend for power and position

【卖主】màizhǔ 货物或房产等的出售者 seller; bargainer：跟～当面议价 negotiate a price with a seller

【卖嘴】mài//zuǐ 用说话来显示自己本领高或心肠好 boast; brag about one's skill or goodwill; indulge in clever talk：他只会～，一动真的就不行了。He brags a lot. Ask him to go for real and he'll just freak out.

【卖座】mài//zuò（～儿 mài//zuòr）指戏院、饭馆、茶馆等顾客上座的情况（of a theatre, etc.）draw large audiences;（of a restaurant, teahouse, etc.）attract a constant stream of patrons：这出戏不～。This play is a turkey.

脉（脈、衇）mài ❶ 动脉和静脉的统称 arteries and veins ❷ 脉搏的简称 abbr. for 脉搏 màibó ❸ 植物叶子、昆虫翅膀上像血管的组织（of a leaf, an insect's wing, etc.）vein：叶～vein in a leaf ❹ 像血管一样连贯而成系统的东西 range; vein; sth. linking up to form a blood-vessel-like network：山～mountain range｜矿～mineral vein ☞ mò on p. 1367

【脉案】mài'àn〈中医 *Chin. med.*〉对病症的断语，一般写在处方上 diagnosis usu. written on a prescription

【脉搏】màibó 心脏收缩时，由于输出血液的冲击引起的动脉的跳动。医生可根据脉搏来诊断疾病。pulse; sphygmus; regular throbbing or pulsation of the arteries, caused by the successive contractions of the heart; 简称 abbr. 脉 mài; also 脉息 màixī

【脉冲】màichōng ❶ 指电流或电压的短暂的起伏变化。各种高频脉冲广泛用在无线电技术中。pulse; momentary sudden fluctuation in electrical voltage or current ❷ 指变化规律类似电脉冲的现象，如脉冲激光器 device that pulsates, such as the pulsed laser

【脉动】màidòng 像脉搏那样地周期性运动或变化 pulsation

【脉金】[1] màijīn〈中医 *Chin. med.*〉consultation fee

【脉金】[2] màijīn 石英脉中含的粒状金子 gold grains in quartzite; also 山金 shānjīn

【脉理】màilǐ ❶〈书 *fml.*〉脉络条理 run; alignment: 山川～run of mountains and rivers ❷ 指中医医理 principles of traditional Chinese medicine: 精通～well-versed in traditional Chinese medicine

【脉络】màiluò ❶〈中医 *Chin. med.*〉对动脉和静脉的统称 arteries and veins ❷〈比喻 *fig.*〉条理或头绪 train of thought; sequence of ideas: ～分明 clear and logical presentation of ideas | 这篇文章的～很清楚。This article is closely knit and presents its ideas in a clear, logical way.

【脉络膜】màiluòmó 眼球里的一层薄膜，由纤维组织、小血管和毛细血管组成，棕红色，在巩膜和视网膜之间 chorioid; choroid coat; delicate, highly vascular layer of the eye that is continuous with the iris and lies between the sclera and the retina; (图见 ☞ figure for 眼 yǎn on p. 2210)

【脉石】màishí 矿石中与有用矿物伴生的无用物质 gangue; veinstone

【脉息】màixī same as 脉搏 màibó

【脉象】màixiàng〈中医 *Chin. med.*〉指脉搏所表现的快慢、强弱、深浅等情况 pulse condition; type of pulse

【脉枕】màizhěn〈中医 *Chin. med.*〉诊脉时，垫在患者手腕下的小枕头 wrist-cushion, on which a patient rests his or her wrist for the doctor to feel the pulse

唛 mài〈方 *dial.*〉商标 trademark

【唛头】màitóu〈方 *dial.*〉货物包装外面所做的标记 mark on package of goods; also 商标 shāngbiāo

霡(霢) mài [霡霂](màimù)〈书 *fml.*〉小雨 drizzle

mān (ㄇㄢ)

嫚 mān〈方 *dial.*〉(～儿 mānr) 女孩子 gal; also 嫚子 mān·zi

☞ màn on p. 1302

颟(顢) mān [颟顸](mān· hān) 糊涂而又马虎 muddle-headed and careless: 颟颟顸顸 floppy and absent-minded | 那人太～，什么事都做不好。That man is so muddle-headed. He can't do anything right.

mán (ㄇㄢˊ)

埋 mán [埋怨](mányuàn) 因为事情不如意而对自己认为原因所在的人或事物表示不满 complain; grumble: 互相～blame each other | 落～be blamed | 只能怪你自己没有处理好，不能～别人。You are to blame for mishandling the situation, and you can't shift the blame on to others.

☞ mái on p. 1293

蛮(蠻) mán ❶ 粗野，不通情理 churlish; brusque: 野～barbarous | ～横 arrogant and unreasonable | ～不讲理 be impervious to reason; wilful; obstinate ❷ 鲁莽；强悍 crude; reckless; intrepid: ～干 act recklessly | ～劲 by sheer muscle ❸ 我国古代称南方的民族 ancient name for ethnic peoples in the south ❹〈方 *dial.*〉很；挺 quite; pretty: ～好 pretty good | ～大 so big | 你装得倒～像！You acted as if it were real.

【蛮缠】mánchán 不讲道理地纠缠 nag at sb.: 胡搅～harass sb. persistently | 怕他～个没完，只好答应了。I gave in for fear of his endless harassment.

【蛮干】mángàn 不顾客观规律或实际情况去硬干 act rashly; act recklessly; be foolhardy: 要实干巧干，不能～。(We) should work hard and intelligently, not blindly.

【蛮横】mánhèng (态度) 粗暴而不讲理 (of attitude) fierce and petulant; rude and unreasonable; arbitrary; peremptory: 态度～unreasonable attitude | ～无理 rude and unreasonable; peremptory

【蛮荒】mánhuāng ❶ 野蛮荒凉 barbarous: ～时代 age of savagery ❷〈书 *fml.*〉指文化落后的偏远地方 remote and underdeveloped place: 历险阻，入～go through formidable hardship and danger and into the land of barbarity

【蛮劲】mánjìn 猛而死的力气 sheer masculine strength; sheer muscle: 小伙子有股子～。The young man really has muscle. | 干活不能光靠～，要会找窍门。Sheer muscle is not enough — we've got to find the ropes.

【蛮子】mán·zi〈旧时 *old*〉北方人称口音跟自己

语音不同的南方人 barbarian; northerners' contemptuous term for southerners: 南～barbarian from the south

谩 mán 欺骗;蒙蔽 deceive; hoodwink ☞ màn on p.1300

蔓 mán [蔓菁](mán·jing) ☞ 芜菁 wújīng on p.2027
☞ màn on p.1300 and wàn on p.1979

馒 mán ☞ below

【馒首】mánshǒu 〈方 *dial.*〉馒头 steamed bun; steamed bread

【馒头】mán·tou ❶ 一种用发酵的面粉蒸成的食品,一般上圆而下平,没有馅儿 steamed bread usu. in a conical shape ❷ 〈方 *dial.*〉包子 stuffed bun: 肉～meat-stuffed bun

瞒(瞞) mán 把真实情况隐藏起来,不让别人知道;隐瞒 hide the truth from: 欺～deceive; dupe | ～上不～下。You may cheat the high-ups but you cannot cheat those below you. | 这事～不过人。There is no way to keep people in the dark about it for ever.

【瞒哄】mánhǒng 欺骗;哄骗 deceive; pull the wool over sb.'s eyes: 你这话只能～小孩儿。What you said could only deceive a child.

【瞒上欺下】mán shàng qī xià 瞒哄上级,欺压下属和群众 deceive those above and bully those below

【瞒天过海】mán tiān guò hǎi 〈比喻 *fig.*〉用欺骗的手段,暗中行动 cross the sea under camouflage — practise deception; pull the wool over sb.'s eyes

鞔 mán ❶ 把皮革固定在鼓框的周围,做成鼓面 mount hide on a drum: 蛇皮可以～鼓。Snakeskin can be used to mount a drum. ❷ 把布蒙在鞋帮上 fix the vamp on a last: ～鞋 making shoes

鳗 mán 鳗鲡的简称 abbr. for 鳗鲡 mánlí

【鳗鲡】mánlí 鱼,身体长形,表面多黏液,上部灰黑色,下部白色,前部近圆筒形,后部侧扁,鳞小,埋在皮肤下面。头尖,背鳍、臀鳍和尾鳍连在一起,无腹鳍。生活在淡水中,成熟后到海洋中产卵。捕食小动物。eel (*Angulillarostrata*); fish whose elongated body is slippery, has dark grey back and white belly, and is cylindrical in its upper part and flat in its lower part, with a tiny head, tiny scales buried underneath the skin, linked dorsal, anal and caudal fins but no ventral fin, living on small animals in freshwater but laying eggs in the sea; also 白鳝 báishàn or 白鳗 báimán; 简称 abbr. 鳗 mán

鬘 mán 〈书 *fml.*〉形容头发美(of hair) beautiful

mǎn (ㄇㄢˇ)

满[1](滿) mǎn ❶ 全部充实;达到容量的极点 full; filled; packed: 会场里人都～了。The assembly hall is filled to capacity. | 装～了一车。The truck has got a full load. ❷ 使满 fill: ～上这一杯吧! Fill the glass, please. ❸ 达到一定期限 expire; reach the limit: 假期已～。The holiday is over. | 不～一年 less than one year ❹ 全 completely; entirely; perfectly: ～身油泥 smeared all over with grease | ～口答应 consent readily | ～不在乎 not care a damn; care nothing ❺ 满足 satisfy; contented: ～意 satisfaction | 心～意足 perfectly satisfied ❻ 骄傲 complacent; conceited: 自～conceited | ～招损,谦受益。One loses by pride and gains by modesty. *or* Complacency spells loss while modesty brings benefit.

满[2](滿) Mǎn ❶ 满族 Manchus, a minority ethnic people in China: ～人 Manchus ❷ 姓 a surname

【满不在乎】mǎn bù zài·hu 完全不放在心上 do not give a damn for; shrug it off; do not mind at all; make nothing of; not worry at all; not care in the least; give (or take) no heed: 别人都在替他着急,他却～。Everybody was concerned about him, but he wasn't worried at all.

【满城风雨】mǎn chéng fēng yǔ 形容事情传遍各处,到处都在议论着(多指坏事)(of a scandal, etc.) cause a big uproar; (become) the talk of the town

【满打满算】mǎn dǎ mǎn suàn 全部算在内 reckoning in every item (of income or expenditure); at the very most: ～也只有半天时间,怎么也赶不到了。There being only half a day's time at the most, there is no way we can reach there on time.

【满当当】mǎndāngdāng (～的 mǎndāngdāng·de)很满的样子 ample; full: 家具、电器把屋里摆得～的。The house is packed with furniture and electrical appliances. | 大厅里人坐得～的。The hall was filled to capacity.

【满登登】mǎndēngdēng (～的 mǎndēngdēng·de)很满的样子 full to the brim; very full: 今年收成好,仓库里装得～的。The harvest this year was so good that the granary has been filled to overflowing.

【满点】mǎndiǎn 达到规定的钟点 full work hours: 出满勤,干～full attendance and full work hours | 这个商店坚持～营业。The store adheres to full working hours.

【满额】mǎn//é 名额已满 meet a quota: 报名已经～。The enrolment quota has already been fulfilled.

【满分】mǎnfēn (～儿 mǎnfēnr)指规定的最高的分数 full marks：打～give full marks | 得～get full marks

【满服】mǎn//fú 满孝 be at the expiration of a mourning period

【满腹】mǎnfù 充满肚皮；充满心中(of stomach or mind) preoccupied with; filled with：～心事 consumed by anxieties | ～疑云 feel very suspicious | ～文章 well versed in writing | 牢骚～with pent-up grievances; full of resentment; full of grumbles

【满腹经纶】mǎn fù jīnglún 〈比喻 *fig.*〉人很有政治才能，也比喻很有才学 profoundly learned; be possessed of learning and ability

【满共】mǎngòng 〈方 *dial.*〉总共；一共：in all; altogether：三个班级～是九十八个学生。There are 98 students altogether in the three classes.

【满怀】[1] mǎnhuái ❶ 心中充满 have one's heart filled with; be imbued with：～信心 with full confidence in | 豪情～imbued with pride ❷ 指整个前胸部分 referring to one's chest：跟他撞了一个～bump into sb.

【满怀】[2] mǎnhuái 指所饲养的适龄的母畜全部怀孕 (of sheep, cattle, etc.) bear a full litter; be all pregnant

【满坑满谷】mǎn kēng mǎn gǔ 形容到处都是，多得很 in every valley and ravine — in large numbers; in great abundance; in plenty

【满口】mǎnkǒu ❶ 整个口腔 mouthful：～假牙 a mouthful of artificial teeth; whole set of artificial teeth ❷ 纯一(指说话的口音、内容)(of accent or content of a speech) pure：～普通话 speak with standard Chinese | ～谎言 unreserved promise | ～之乎者也 talk with a lot of literary words and phrases ❸ 表示口气肯定，没有保留 unreservedly：～答应 readily agree

【满满当当】mǎnmǎndāngdāng (～的 mǎnmǎndāngdāng·de)很满 full to the brim：挑着～的两桶水 carry two brimming buckets of water | 过往的车子，都～地载着建筑材料。The passing vehicles were without exception loaded full with building materials.

【满满登登】mǎnmǎndēngdēng (～的 mǎnmǎndēngdēng·de)很满 full; ample：工作日程排得～的 action-packed agenda

【满门】mǎnmén 全家 whole family：～抄斩(in feudal China) execution of the entire family | 祸及～。The entire family was implicated in the case.

【满面】mǎnmiàn 整个面部 have one's face covered with：笑容～grinning from ear to ear; be all smiles | ～春风 beaming with joy; radiant with happiness

【满面春风】mǎnmiàn chūnfēng 形容愉快和蔼的面容 beam with satisfaction; radiant with happiness; also 春风满面 chūnfēng mǎnmiàn

【满目】mǎnmù same as 满眼 mǎnyǎn ②：琳琅～ feast for the eyes | ～凄凉。A scene of desolation met the eye everywhere.

【满拧】mǎnnǐng 〈方 *dial.*〉完全相反；根本不一致 contradict; in total discrepancy

【满腔】mǎnqiāng 充满心中 have one's bosom filled with：～热情 full of enthusiasm | ～的热血已经沸腾。Our blood is seething.

【满勤】mǎnqín 全勤 be present at work every day; full attendance：出～perfect attendance record | 他每月都是～。His attendance at work is full every month.

【满山遍野】mǎn shān biàn yě 遍布山野，形容很多 abundant; over hills and dales

【满师】mǎn//shī 学徒学习期满；出师 serve out one's apprenticeship：学徒三年～。The apprenticeship requires three years of service.

【满世界】mǎn shì·jie 〈方 *dial.*〉到处 everywhere：你这孩子在家干点儿什么不好，～瞎跑什么？Why run around everywhere, you naughty boy! Why not stay home and find something meaningful to do?

【满堂】mǎntáng ❶ 全场，也指全场的人 whole audience：～掌声。The entire audience burst with warm applause. ❷〈方 *dial.*〉满座 sell-out; capacity audience; full house：近来剧院天天～，票不好买。The theatre is full every day, and tickets are hard to come by. ❸ 充满厅堂(of a house) jammed; filled：金玉～house replete with wealth

【满堂彩】mǎntángcǎi (演出时)全场喝彩 win great applause; bring the house down：他唱的一句倒板就得了个～。He brought the house down at the first line of opening singing.

【满堂灌】mǎntángguàn 指上课完全由教师讲授的一种教学方式 cram teaching; intensive teaching

【满堂红】mǎntánghóng 形容全面胜利或到处兴旺 resounding victory; success on all fronts

【满天飞】mǎntiānfēi 形容到处乱跑 always on the go; rush here, there and everywhere：钦差大臣～。Imperial envoys were sent everywhere. | 他这人～，让我到哪儿去找？Where can I find the guy, who is running about all day long?

【满孝】mǎn//xiào 指为尊长服丧期满 serve a prescribed period of mourning from beginning to end

【满心】mǎnxīn 心中充满(某种情绪)；整个心里 from the bottom of one's heart：～欢喜 genuinely elated | ～愿意 wholehearted willingness

【满眼】mǎnyǎn ❶ 充满眼睛 eyeful：他一连两夜没有睡，～都是红丝。His eyes were bloodshot because he hadn't had a good sleep the last two days. ❷ 充满视野 get an eyeful of：走到山腰，看见～的山花。Half way up the hill he saw mountain flowers in bloom everywhere.

【满意】mǎnyì 满足自己的愿望；符合自己的心意

to one's satisfaction：他非常～这个工作。He was pleased with this job.｜顾客对他的热诚服务感到很～。His clients were satisfied with his warm service.

【满员】mǎn//yuán（部队、人员、火车乘客等）达到规定名额（of an army）at full strength；（of an office staff）full；no vacancy；（of train passengers）full

【满月】mǎn//yuè（婴儿）出生后满一个月（of an infant）one month old

【满月】mǎnyuè ☞ 望月 wàngyuè on p.1985

【满载】mǎnzài ❶ 运输工具装满了东西或装足了规定的吨数 laden；loaded to capacity；fully loaded；laden with ❷ 指机器、设备等在工作时达到额定的负载（of machine，equipment，etc.）run at full capacity

【满载而归】mǎnzài ér guī 装满了东西回来，形容收获极丰富 come back with fruitful results；return from a highly rewarding experience

【满洲】Mǎnzhōu ❶ 满族的旧称 old name for 满族 Mǎnzú ❷〈旧指 *old*〉我国东北一带 Manchuria；northeast China

【满足】mǎnzú ❶ 感到已经足够了 satisfied；contented：只要能不亏本，我就～了。I'll be very happy if I don't lose money in the deal.｜他从不～于已有的成绩。He never rest on his laurels. ❷ 使满足 satisfy；meet the demand of sb.：提高生产，～人民的需要。Increase production to meet the demand of the people.

【满族】Mǎnzú 我国少数民族之一，主要分布在辽宁、黑龙江、吉林、河北、北京和内蒙古 Manchus，a minority ethnic people mainly inhabiting Liaoning，Heilongjiang，Jilin，Hebei，Beijing and Inner Mongolia

【满嘴】mǎnzuǐ 满口 mouthful：～起疱 lips infested all over with boils｜～喷粪（指所说的话全是胡说八道或尽是脏字）let loose a barrage of invective；talk trash

【满座】mǎn//zuò（～儿 mǎn//zuòr）（剧场等公共场所）座位坐满或按座位出售的票卖完（of theatre or other public venues）sellout；all seats booked：这部影片很受欢迎，场场～。The movie was a sellout each time it was shown.

螨（蟎）mǎn 节肢动物的一类。有一对或几对单眼，也有无眼的，雄的一般比雌的小，大多数是圆形或椭圆形。有的寄居在人或动物体上，吸血液，能传染疾病。疥虫就是螨类动物。mite（*Acarina*）；arthropod with or without one or several pairs of simple eyes，with a round or olive-shaped body and the male smaller than the female，free living or parasitic on humans or animals by sucking their blood，and capable of spreading diseases；sarcoptic mite being one of the arthropods

màn（ㄇㄢˋ）

曼 màn ❶ 柔美；细腻 graceful；charming in a delicate way：～舞 graceful dance；dancing elegantly ❷ 长；远 prolonged；long-drawn-out：～延 extend；spread｜～声 lingering voice or sound

【曼德琳】màndélín 弦乐器，有四对金属弦 mandolin；musical instrument with a pear-shaped wooden body and four pairs of metal strings

【曼妙】mànmiào〈书 *fml.*〉（音乐、舞姿等）柔美（of music）melodious；（of dance）lithe and graceful：姿态～graceful posture｜～的琴声 melodious notes of a violin，fiddle，etc.

【曼声】mànshēng 声音拉得很长 drawl；lengthen one's voice：～吟哦 recite in a slow and measured tone｜～歌唱 sing with a drawl

【曼陀铃】màntuólíng same as 曼德琳 màndélín

【曼延】mànyán 连绵不断 meander；winding：～曲折的羊肠小道 zigzagging narrow mountain path

谩 màn 轻慢，没有礼貌 rude；disrespectful：～骂 hurl invectives；mud slinging

☞ mán on p.1298

【谩骂】mànmà 用轻慢、嘲笑的态度骂 vituperate；snap

墁 màn ❶ 用砖、石等铺地面 pave；surface a floor with brick，stone，etc.：花砖～地 floor paved with ornamental tiles ❷〈方 *dial.*〉用灰土抹墙 plaster a wall：墙壁～得溜平 plaster a wall and give it a polished surface

蔓 màn 义同'蔓'（wàn），多用于合成词 same as 蔓 màn［oft. used in compound words］

☞ mán on p.1298 and wàn on p.1979

【蔓草】màncǎo 爬蔓的草 tendril；vine

【蔓生植物】mànshēng-zhíwù 具有攀援茎或缠绕茎的植物 trailing plant；bindweed；rambler

【蔓延】mànyán 形容像蔓草一样不断向周围扩展 creep；extend：～滋长 develop｜火势～。The fire is spreading.

幔 màn 为遮挡而悬挂起来的布、绸子、丝绒等 curtain；screen：布～cotton curtain｜窗～window curtain

【幔帐】mànzhàng same as 幔 màn

【幔子】màn·zi〈方 *dial.*〉same as 幔 màn

漫 màn ❶ 水过满，向外流 overflow；brim over：水～出来了。Water was overflowing. ❷ 到处都是；遍 all over a place；everywhere：～山遍野 over hills and dales｜黄沙～天 sky smothered by a sandstorm｜～天大雾 thick pall of fog；thickening fog ❸ 广阔；长 extensive；long：～长 long｜长夜～～ long night *or* The night dragged on and on. ❹ 不受约束；随便 unbridled；casual：散～ill-disciplined｜～谈 random talk；random notes｜～无限制 unrestricted｜～无目的 aimless ❺ 莫；不

要 let alone:～道 not to mention|～说是你,他来也不行。Even if he is here I don't think he can do it, not to mention you and you alone.

【漫笔】mànbǐ 随手写来没有一定形式的文章(多用于文章的题目 oft. of the title of an article) sketch; random thoughts; random notes:灯下～notes by the lamp

【漫不经心】màn bù jīngxīn 随随便便,不放在心上 absent-minded; also 漫不经意 màn bù jīngyì

【漫步】mànbù 没有目的而悠闲地走 saunter; ramble:～江岸 take a stroll by the river|独自在田间小道上～ramble along an idyllic path in solitude ◇艺苑～ sketches on the arts

【漫长】màncháng 长得看不见尽头的(时间、道路等)(of time or road etc.) extend endlessly; long:～的岁月 during the long years|～的河流 long river

【漫道】màndào same as 慢道 màndào

【漫灌】mànguàn ❶ 一种粗放的灌溉方法,不平整土地,也不筑畦,让水顺着坡往地里流 flood irrigation ❷ (洪水)流入;漫进(某地区)(of flood) overflow:大水～,城郊街道都被淹了。The excessive water inundated the streets in the suburbs.

【漫画】mànhuà 用简单而夸张的手法来描绘生活或时事的图画。一般运用变形、比拟、象征的方法,构成幽默、诙谐的画面,以取得讽刺或歌颂的效果。caricature; cartoon; humorous sketch or drawing that depicts life or current affairs by exaggeration, analogue, or symbolism

【漫话】mànhuà 不拘形式地随意谈论 casual talk; rambling chat:～家常 chitchat; small talk

【漫漶】mànhuàn 文字、图画等因磨损或浸水受潮而模糊不清 blurred; illegible:字迹～。The words have become illegible.

【漫卷】mànjuǎn (旗帜)随风翻卷 (of flags) flutter; wave:彩旗～。Colourful streamers fluttered in the wind.

【漫流】mànliú ❶ 指降水经过植物截留、渗入地表和填充洼地后,多余的水成片流动或成为时分时合的水流(of rainwater) run off; (of water having been intercepted by plants, penetrated earth's surface, and filled up depressions) flow in small patches or trickles that now come together, now separate ❷ 泛指水过满,向外流 (in a broad sense) overflow; brim over:沿湖筑堤,不让湖水～。A dyke was built round the lake to prevent it from overflowing.

【漫骂】mànmà 乱骂 inveigh; obloquy

【漫漫】mànmàn (时间、地方)长而无边的样子(of time) long and slow; (of place) boundless:～长夜 long night|路途～ road that knows no end|四野都是一眼望不到头的～白雪。A vast stretch of snow extends in all directions as far as the eye could see.

【漫儿】mànr 指金属钱币没有字的一面 obverse side of a coin; side of a copper coin that bears the principal design

【漫山遍野】màn shān biàn yě 遍布山野,形容很多 over hills and dales:羊群～,到处都是。Sheep herds were seen grazing all over the meadowland.

【漫说】mànshuō same as 慢说 mànshuō

【漫谈】màntán 不拘形式地就某问题谈自己的体会或意见 random talk:～形势 free discussion on the world situation

【漫天】màntiān ❶ 布满了天空 all over the sky:～大雪 whirling snow|尘土～sky obliterated by a dust storm ❷ 形容没边儿的;没限度的 monstrous:～大谎 monstrous lie|～要价 demand an extortionate price

【漫无边际】màn wú biānjì ❶ 非常广阔,一眼望不到边 infinite; vast:大青山下是～的草原。A boundless grassland lies at the foot of the Daqing Mountain. ❷ 指谈话、写文章等没有中心,离题很远(of talk, writing, etc.) far-fetched:～地谈些与问题无关的话 make a long-winded speech that drifts far from the subject

【漫延】mànyán 曼延 pervade; stretch:沙漠一直～到遥远的天边。The desert stretches to the distant horizon.

【漫溢】mànyì 水过满,向外流 overflow; spill:洪流～。The mighty river overflowed its banks.

【漫游】mànyóu 随意游玩 ramble; wander:～西湖 roam about the West Lake|～世界 trot the world; go trotting the globe

【漫游生物】mànyóu shēngwù 生活在海洋或河流中,活动范围比较广的动物,如鲸、乌贼、鳗鲡等 nomadic marine animal, such as whale, cuttle fish, eel, etc.

【漫语】mànyǔ ❶ 泛泛的话;不着边际的话 random remarks; wild flights of imagination; long-windedness:～空言 lone-winded empty talk ❷ 漫话 random notes (多用作书名、文章标题 oft. used in the title of a book or article) random notes:《青春～》*Random Remarks on Youth*

慢1 màn ❶ 速度低;走路、做事等费的时间长(跟'快'相对 as opposed to 'quick') slow; time-consuming:～车 slow train|～走 wait a minute; just a second|～手～脚 slow in doing things|你走～一点儿,等着他。Slow down a little bit and wait until he catches up. ❷ 从缓 hold on; slow down:且～。Hold on a moment.|～点儿告诉他,等两天再说。Wait for a couple of days before let him in on it. ❸ 莫;不要 no; not:～道 say nothing of|～说 let alone

慢2 màn 态度冷淡,没有礼貌 supercilious; rude:傲～cocky; arrogant|怠～haughty;

overbearing

【慢车】mànchē 中途停站较多，全程行车时间较长的火车或汽车（多用于客运）way train, passenger train that stops at every station along a route

【慢词】màncí 长的、节奏缓慢的词叫慢词，如《木兰花慢》、《沁园春》long *ci* poem of unhurried rhythm, such as *Mulan Huaman* and *Qin Yuan Chun*

【慢待】màndài ❶（对人）冷淡 give sb. the cold shoulder：不能～了朋友。On no account should we cold-shoulder a friend. ❷〈客套话 *pol.*〉指招待不周 do poorly in treating a guest：今天太～了，请多包涵。Forgive us for our inconsiderateness today.

【慢道】màndào 慢说；别说 say nothing of; let alone：～群众有意见，连我们自己也感到不满。Don't say the masses are complaining; we ourselves are not happy either. also 漫道 màndào

【慢火】mànhuǒ 文火；微火 slow fire：～炖肉 keep meat simmering over a gentle fire

【慢件】mànjiàn ☞ 快件 kuàijiàn ① on p. 1120

【慢慢腾腾】màn·mantēngtēng（～的 màn·mantēngtēng·de）慢腾腾 maddeningly slow; at snail's pace; also 慢慢吞吞 màn·mantūntūn

【慢慢悠悠】màn·manyōuyōu（～的 màn·manyōuyōu·de）慢悠悠 leisurely

【慢坡】mànpō 斜度很小的坡 gentle slope

【慢说】mànshuō〈连词 *conj.*〉别说 let alone; say nothing of：这种动物，～国内少有，全世界也不多。This kind of animal is few and far between in the entire world, let alone in China. also 漫说 mànshuō

【慢腾腾】màntēngtēng（～的 màntēngtēng·de）形容缓慢 unhurriedly; with measured slowness：这样～地走，什么时候才能走到呢？When shall we arrive there if we keep on at this pace? | 他低下头，拖长了声音，一字一句～地念着。He lowered his head and began reading slowly, word by word, and sentence by sentence. also 慢吞吞 màntūntūn

【慢条斯理】màntiáo-sīlǐ 形容动作缓慢，不慌不忙 with deliberate slowness：他说话做事总是～的。He is slow no matter what he says or does.

【慢性】mànxìng ❶ 发作得缓慢的；时间拖得长久的 slow; chronic：～病 chronic disease | ～中毒 slow poisoning | ～痢疾 chronic dysentery ❷（～儿 mànxìngr）慢性子 slow-tempered

【慢性病】mànxìngbìng 病理变化缓慢或不能在短时期内治好的病症，如结核病、心脏病等 chronic disease, such as tuberculosis and heart trouble, that develop slowly and cannot be cured within a short period of time

【慢性子】mànxìng·zi ❶ 做事迟缓的性情 phlegmatic temperament：～人 slowpoke ❷ 指慢性子的人 slowcoach; slowpoke：她是个～，家里失了火也不会着急。She is a slowcoach and never gets flurried even if her house has caught fire.

【慢悠悠】mànyōuyōu（～的 mànyōuyōu·de）形容缓慢 slow; unhurried：他做事说话总是～的。Whatever he says or does, he is a kind of slow. | 她～地向我们走来。She walked towards us in measured steps. also 慢慢悠悠 màn·manyōuyōu

嫚 màn〈书 *fml.*〉轻视；侮辱 scorn; insult ☞ mān on p. 1297

【嫚骂】mànmà〈书 *fml.*〉谩骂 rail

缦 màn〈书 *fml.*〉没有花纹的丝织品 plain silk fabrics

熳 màn ☞ 烂熳 lànmàn on p. 1149

镘（槾） màn〈书 *fml.*〉抹墙用的抹子（mǒ·zi）trowel

māng（ㄇㄤ）

牤（牻） māng ☞ below

【牤牛】māngniú〈方 *dial.*〉公牛 bull; ox

【牤子】māng·zi〈方 *dial.*〉公牛 ox; bull

máng（ㄇㄤˊ）

邙 máng 北邙（Běimáng），山名，在河南洛阳 Beimang, name of a mountain in Luoyang, Henan Province

芒 máng ❶ 多年生草本植物，生在山地和田野间，叶子条形，秋天茎顶生穗，黄褐色，果实多毛 Chinese silvergrass (*Miscanthus sinensis*); perennial herb in mountains and the fields, growing linear leaves, and bearing ochre-coloured ears and hairy fruit in autumn ❷ 某些禾本科植物子实的外壳上长的针状物 awn; beard; slender, bristle-like appendage found on the spikelets of certain grasses

【芒草】mángcǎo same as 芒 máng ①

【芒刺在背】máng cì zài bèi 形容坐立不安，像芒和刺扎在背上一样 feel uneasy as if having a thorn in one's side

【芒果】mángguǒ same as 杧果 mángguǒ

【芒硝】mángxiāo mirabilite; same as 硭硝 mángxiāo

【芒种】mángzhòng 二十四节气之一，在6月5、6或7日 Grain in Ear, one of the 24 seasonal division points that falls on June 5, 6 or 7; ☞ 节气 jié·qi on p. 989 and 二十四节气 èrshísì jiéqì on p. 516

忙 máng ❶ 事情多，不得空（跟'闲'相对 as opposed to 'idle'）busy; occupied：繁～ extremely busy | 这几天很～。I have been busy these days. | ～里偷闲 snatch a bit of leisure from an action-packed schedule ❷ 急

迫不停地、加紧地做 hurry; rush; make haste: 你近来～些什么? What are you busy with lately? | 他一个人～不过来。He was too busy to finish it all by himself.

【忙不迭】mángbùdié 急忙;连忙 hurriedly; hastily: ～地跑了过来 come over in a hurry | ～地赔不是 make haste to apologize

【忙叨】máng·dao 〈方 *dial.*〉匆忙;忙碌 busy: 啥事儿这样～? What keeps you so busy? | 忙忙叨叨地披上衣服就走了。He draped a coat over his shoulders and went away in a hurry. also 忙叨叨 mángdāodāo

【忙乎】máng·hu 忙碌 hard at work; bustle about: 他～了一天,但一点儿也不觉得累。He bustled about the entire day, yet didn't feel tired at all.

【忙活】máng//huó (～儿 máng//huór)急着做活 busy working: 这几天正～。I have been busy working the last few days. | 你忙什么活? What are you bustling about?

【忙活】mánghuó (～儿 mánghuór)需要赶快做的活 rush work; emergency task: 这是件～,要先做。This is an urgent job that has to be tackled first.

【忙活】máng·huo same as 忙碌 mánglù: 他们俩已经～了一早上了。The two of them have been hard at work for the entire morning.

【忙里偷闲】mánglǐ tōuxián 在忙碌中抽出一点空闲时间 snatch a little of leisure from a busy life

【忙碌】mánglù 忙着做各种事情 engrossed in work; busy: 忙忙碌碌 as busy as a bee | 为了大家的事情,他从早到晚～着。He bustles around from morning till night for the good of the public.

【忙乱】mángluàn 事情繁忙而没有条理 busy and flurried; hectic: 工作～ feel flurried in one's work | 克服～现象 stop working in a rush and a muddle

【忙音】mángyīn 电话机拨号后由于对方占线而发出的连续而短促的嘟嘟声,表示不能接通(of a telephone) busy tone

【忙于】mángyú 忙着做(某方面的事情) busy with: ～收集资料 busy with collecting data | 整天～家务 busy with family chores all day long

【忙月】mángyuè ❶ 指农事繁忙的月份 busy farming season: 一到～,全家都搞农活儿。The entire family go to work in the fields when the busy season sets in. ❷〈方 *dial.*〉〈旧 *old*〉指农忙、过年过节等时期的帮工 seasonal worker; labourer hired during a busy farming season or festival

杧 máng [杧果](mángguǒ) ❶ 常绿乔木,叶子互生,长椭圆形,质厚。花黄色。果实略呈肾脏形,熟时黄色,核大,果肉黄色,可以吃。产于亚热带地区。mango (*Mangifera indica*); subtropical evergreen tree bearing thick and long oval leaves in alternate phyllotaxy, yellow flowers, and kidney-shaped fruit with edible yellow flesh ❷ 这种植物的果实 mango ‖ also 芒果 mángguǒ

尨 máng 〈书 *fml.*〉 ❶ 长毛的狗 long-haired dog ❷ 杂色 parti-coloured: ～服 dress in a motley of colours

☞ méng on p. 1324

盲 máng ❶ 看不见东西;瞎 blind: ～人 the blind | 夜～ nyctalopia; night blindness ❷〈比喻 *fig.*〉对某种事物不能辨别或分辨不清 ignorant; illiterate: 文～ illiteracy | 色～ achromatopsia; colour blindness | 法～ one who knows little or nothing about law ❸ 盲目地 impetuous; rash: ～动 rashness in one's action | ～从 blind obedience

【盲肠】mángcháng 大肠的一段,上接回肠,下连结肠,下端有阑尾 blind gut; caecum; part of the large intestine with its upper end attached to the ileum and its lower end to the colon, and with the appendix on its lower end; (图见 ☞ figure for 消化系统 xiāohuà xìtǒng on p. 2100)

【盲肠炎】mángchángyán ❶ 病,多由阑尾炎引起。阑尾部发炎后蔓延到整个盲肠,就成为盲肠炎。typhlitis; disease caused when appendicitis spread to the entire caecum ❷ 阑尾炎的俗称 popular term for 阑尾炎 lánwěiyán

【盲从】mángcóng 不问是非地附和别人;盲目随从 follow sb. or sth. blindly; blind submission: 遇事要多动动脑子,不能～。Use your brain when something happens. Don't ever follow it blindly.

【盲点】mángdiǎn 眼球后部视网膜上的一点,和黄斑相邻,没有感光细胞,不能接受光的刺激,物体的影像落在这一点上不能引起视觉,所以叫盲点 scotoma; blind spot; point next to the yellow spot on the retina in the rear of the eyeball that does not react to the stimulation of light due to the absence of light-sensitive cells, causing the loss of vision on this point; (图见 ☞ figure for 眼 yǎn on p. 2210)

【盲动】mángdòng 没有经过慎重考虑,没有明确的目的就行动 act blindly; rash in one's action: 遇事要冷静,不可浮躁～。Stay cool when something happens, and guard against flippancy and rashness.

【盲干】mánggàn 不顾主客观条件或目的不明确地去干 plunge into action without knowing what one is doing; do sth. regardless of whether it is possible or not; do sth. aimlessly: 只凭热情～是不行的。Enthusiasm gets nowhere in the absence of purpose.

【盲谷】mánggǔ 一端被峭壁堵塞的谷地。峭壁下有洞,是地面河流流入地下的地方。多见于石灰岩地区。blind valley; valley with one end cut short by a cliff, usu. in a limestone area, where a river begins flowing underground

【盲流】mángliú ❶ 盲目流入到某地(多指从农村流入城市) unplanned flow of usu. rural population to an urban area: ～人口 those from the countryside or small towns who enters a large city at their own choice ❷ 指盲目流入的人 person who enters a large city at his or her own choice

【盲目】mángmù 眼睛看不见东西 blind; 〈比喻 *fig.*〉认识不清 do sth. without knowing what one's doing: ～行动 blind action | ～崇拜 blind worship | ～乐观 unrealistically optimistic

【盲棋】mángqí 眼睛不看棋盘而下的棋,多为中国象棋。下盲棋的人用话说出每一步棋的下法。blind chess, oft. referring to Chinese chess game in which one of the two players or both dictate their moves without looking at the chessboard

【盲区】mángqū 指雷达、探照灯、胃镜等探测或照射不到的地方 blind area; area inaccessible to the beams of radar, searchlight or gastroscope: 雷达～radar's blind area | 胃镜～gastroscopic blind area

【盲人】mángrén 失去视力的人 blind person; the blind

【盲人摸象】mángrén mō xiàng 传说几个瞎子摸一只大象,摸到腿的说大象像一根柱子,摸到身躯的说大象像一堵墙,摸到尾巴的说大象像一条蛇,各执己见,争论不休 blind men trying to size up the elephant. Legend has it that several blind men were sizing up an elephant, and were locked in an endless squabble about what the animal looked like, as each mistook the part within his reach for the whole — he who touched a leg said the elephant looked like a pillar, he who touched the body argued that it resembled a wall, and he who grabbed the tail believed it looked like a snake, and so on and so forth. 〈比喻 *fig.*〉对事物了解不全面,固执一点,乱加揣测 take a part for the whole like the blind men trying to size up the elephant

【盲人瞎马】mángrén xiāmǎ《世说新语·排调》:'盲人骑瞎马,夜半临深池' *A New Account of Tales of the World·Humour*: A blind man was travelling by riding a horse that was also blind, and danger was imminent when he unknowingly arrived at a deep pool at midnight. 〈比喻 *fig.*〉境况极端危险 in a perilous situation; in for a disaster

【盲蛇】mángshé 一种无毒蛇,形状像蚯蚓,尾极短,鳞片圆形,体暗绿色,长约十几厘米,是我国蛇类中最小的一种。吃昆虫等。blind snake (*Typhlopidac*); benign earthworm-like snake that feeds on insects, has an extremely short tail and a dark green body covered with round scales, and at a dozen centimetres in length is the smallest of its kind in China

【盲文】mángwén ❶ same as 盲字 mángzì ❷ 用盲字刻写或印刷的文字 braille publication

【盲信】mángxìn ☞ 瞎信 xiāxìn on p. 2061

【盲字】mángzì 专供盲人使用的拼音文字,字母由不同排列的凸出的点子组成 braille, a system of lettering for use by the blind, in which each character is a combination of raised dots that are read by touch

氓 máng ☞ 流氓 liúmáng on p. 1241
☞ méng on p. 1324

茫 máng ❶ 形容水或其他事物没有边际、看不清楚 boundless and indistinct: 渺～distant and indistinct | ～无头绪 lose track of the sequence of events; confused and without a clue ❷ 无所知 ignorant; in the dark: ～然 at a loss

【茫茫】mángmáng 没有边际看不清楚(多形容水) (of water) vast and indistinct: ～大海 vast sea | 前途～bleak prospects | ～一片白雾 a world lost in a thick pall of fog

【茫昧】mángmèi 〈书 *fml.*〉模糊不清 dim; blurred: 往事多已～。Past events have mostly become fading memories.

【茫然】mángrán ❶ 完全不知道的样子 oblivious; in the dark about sth.: 事情发生的原因和经过我都～。I'm really in the dark about the cause and process of what happened. ❷ 失意的样子 disheartened; embittered: ～自失 feel lost; be lost in a reverie

【茫无头绪】máng wú tóuxù 一点头绪也没有;事情摸不着边儿 not make head nor tail of sth.; be at sea

硭 máng [硭硝](mángxiāo)无机化合物,是含有10个分子结晶水的硫酸钠($Na_2SO_4 \cdot 10H_2O$),白色或无色,是化学工业、玻璃工业、造纸工业的原料,医药上用做泻药 mirabilite; Glauber's salt ($Na_2SO_4 \cdot 10H_2O$), sodium sulphate containing 10-molecular crystal water, white in colour or transparent, used as a laxative, and a chemical, glass-making, and paper-making raw material; also known as 芒硝 mángxiāo

铓 máng ☞ 锋铓 fēngmáng on p. 587

【铓锣】mángluó 云南少数民族的打击乐器,用铜制成,有大中小多种。有时将多面大小不同的锣挂在木架上,交错敲击。*mangluo*, copper gong chimes; percussion instrument of the minority ethnic peoples of Yunnan Province, consisting of a set of gongs of different sizes hanging on a wooden stand to be struck at alternately

牻 máng 〈书 *fml.*〉毛色黑白相间的牛 black-and-white cattle

mǎng (ㄇㄤˇ)

莽[1] mǎng ❶ 密生的草 thick weeds; rank undergrowth: 丛～ thickets | 草～ thick growth of grass ❷〈书 *fml*.〉大 huge; big ❸ (Mǎng)姓 a surname

莽[2] mǎng 鲁莽 impertinent: ～撞 impetuous | ～汉 clodpole; churl

【莽苍】mǎngcāng (原野)景色迷茫。也指原野。(wilderness) indistinct; hazy; also referring to 原野 yuányě

【莽汉】mǎnghàn 粗鲁冒失的男子 boorish fellow

【莽莽】mǎngmǎng ❶ 形容草木茂盛(of trees and plants) luxurious: 杂草～thick clusters of weeds ❷ 形容原野辽阔,无边无际(of countryside) vast; unbounded: ～群山 a topographical turmoil of mountains

【莽原】mǎngyuán 草长得很茂盛的原野 meadowland; prairie; steppcs: 无垠的～boundless grassland

【莽撞】mǎngzhuàng 鲁莽冒失 rude and impetuous: 行动～rashness of action | 恕我～。Forgive me for my bluntness.

漭 mǎng [漭漭]〈书 *fml*.〉形容广阔无边 wide; spread from horizon to horizon

蟒 mǎng ❶ 蟒蛇 boa; python ❷ 蟒袍的简称 abbr. for 蟒袍 mǎngpáo

【蟒袍】mǎngpáo 明清时大臣所穿的礼服,上面绣有金黄色的蟒 ceremonial robe with golden designs of pythons, worn by ministers during the Ming and Qing dynasties

【蟒蛇】mǎngshé 无毒的大蛇,体长可达 6 米,头部长,口大,舌的尖端有分叉,背部黑褐色,有暗色斑点,腹部白色,多生活在热带近水的森林里,捕食小禽兽 python (*Pythons*); boa constrictor; big nonvenomous snake with a long head, large mouth, forked tongue and a body six metres in maximum length, with dark-spotted deep brown back and white belly, usu. living close to waters in tropical forests, and feeding on small birds and animals; also 蚺蛇 ránshé

māo (ㄇㄠ)

猫(貓) māo ❶ 哺乳动物,面部略圆,躯干长,耳壳短小,眼大,瞳孔随光线强弱而缩小放大,四肢较短,掌部有肉质的垫,行动敏捷,善跳跃,能捕鼠,毛柔软,有黑、白、黄、灰褐等色 cat (*Felis catus*); mammal agile in action, adept at leaping, and capable of catching rats, with a round face, small ears, large eyes whose pupils enlarge or contract according to the intensity of light, short limbs, fleshy paws, and a long body with soft fur that may be black, white, yellow or greyish brown in colour ❷〈方 *dial*.〉躲藏 hide: ～在家里不敢出来 hide at home and dare not go out

☞ máo on p. 1309

【猫睛石】māojīngshí 矿物,主要成分是氧、铅和铍,黄绿色,质脆,有玻璃光泽。是一种宝石。做装饰品时多磨成圆球形,看起来很像猫的眼睛。cat's eye (a gem); cymophane; yellowish green mineral consisting mainly of oxygen, lead and beryllium, oft. fashioned into gems in the shape of a ball that looks like a cat's eye; 通称 popularly known as 猫儿眼 māoryǎn

【猫哭老鼠】māo kū lǎoshǔ〈比喻 *fig*.〉假慈悲;假装同情 cat weeping over the dead mouse — shed crocodile tears; also 猫哭耗子 māo kū hào·zi

【猫儿腻】māornì〈方 *dial*.〉指隐秘的或暧昧的事;花招 hanky-panky; goings-on: 他们之间的～,我早就看出来了。I have long seen through the hanky-panky between the two of them.

【猫儿食】māorshí〈比喻 *fig*.〉很小的饭量 small appetite

【猫儿眼】māoryǎn 猫睛石的通称 popular term for 猫睛石 māojīngshí

【猫头鹰】māotóuyīng 鸟,身体淡褐色,多黑斑,头部有角状的羽毛,眼睛大而圆,昼伏夜出,吃鼠、麻雀等小动物,对人类有益。常在深夜发出凄厉的叫声,迷信的人认为是一种不吉祥的鸟。也叫鸱鸺(chīxiu),有的地区叫夜猫子。owl (*Strigiformes*); nocturnal bird of prey having a light brown body with black spots, disks of modified feathers on its head, and large and round eyes, feeding on small animals such as rats and sparrows, and regarded by superstitious people as an inauspicious bird for its mournful and shrill midnight hooting; also 鸱鸺 chīxiū, known in some areas as 夜猫子 yèmāo·zi

【猫熊】māoxióng 哺乳动物,体长 4—5 尺,形状像熊,尾短,通常头、胸、腹、背、臀白色,四肢、两耳、眼圈黑褐色,毛粗而厚,性耐寒。生活在我国西南地区高山中,吃竹叶、竹笋。是我国特产的一种珍贵动物。panda (*Ailuropoda melanoleuca*); giant panda; bear-like mammal and endangered species having a body 1.3-1.65 metres in length and covered with thick and close-set hair that protects it from subfreezing temperatures, white head, chest, abdomen, back and hips, dark brown legs, ears and eye sockets, living on bamboo leaves and shoots in high mountains in southwest China; also 熊猫 xióngmāo, 大熊猫 dàxióngmāo and 大猫熊 dàmāoxióng

【猫眼】māoyǎn 门镜的俗称 popular term for 门镜 ménjìng

【猫眼道钉】māoyǎndàodīng 道钉②的俗称 popular term for 道钉 dàodīng ②

【猫鱼】māoyú (～儿 māoyúr)用来喂猫的小鱼 small fish, esp. for feeding cats

máo (ㄇㄠ)

毛[1] máo ❶ 动植物的皮上所生的丝状物;鸟类的羽毛 hair; feather: 羽～feathers | 羊～

wool|枇杷树叶子上有许多细～。Loquat tree leaves are covered with down. ❷ 东西上长的霉 mildew：馒头放久了就要长～。Steamed bread becomes mildewed if it is kept for too long. ❸ 粗糙；还没有加工的 semi-finished：～坯 semi-finished product|～铁 pig iron ❹ 不纯净的 gross：～利 gross profit|～重 gross weight ❺ 小 little；small：～孩子 little child|～贼（小偷儿）petty thief；pilferer ❻指货币贬值（of money）devalue；depreciate：钱～了。Money has gone down in value. ❼（Máo）姓 a surname

毛[2] máo ❶ 做事粗心，不细致 sloppy；clumsy：～手～脚 clumsy and brash|～头～脑 foolish ❷ 惊慌 frightened；flurried：心里直发～ feel scared|这下可把他吓～了。This scared him out of his wits. ❸〈方 *dial.*〉发怒；发火 be enraged；be offended：把他惹～了，你要吃大亏。You are in for big trouble if you make him see red.

毛[3] máo 一圆的十分之一；角 *mao*，fractional Renminbi unit that equals *jiao* or 0.1 yuan or 10 *fen*

【毛笔】máobǐ 用羊毛、鼬毛等制成的笔，供写字、画画等用 brush made from wool，weasel hair，etc.，for writing or painting

【毛边】máobiān ❶ 经裁剪而没有锁边的布边儿；书籍装订后未经裁切的边缘 selvage；raw edge：～书 uncut book ❷ 毛边纸的简称 abbr. for 毛边纸 máobiānzhǐ

【毛边纸】máobiānzhǐ 用竹纤维制成的纸，淡黄色，适合用毛笔书写，也用来印书 light yellow paper made from bamboo pulp for Chinese calligraphy or book printing；简称 abbr. 毛边 máobiān

【毛病】máo·bìng ❶ 指器物发生的损伤或故障 mishap；breakdown；blunder；〈比喻 *fig*〉工作上的失误 error ❷ 缺点；坏习惯 weakness；bad habit：这孩子上课时有做小动作的～。This child often gets fidgety in class. ❸〈方 *dial.*〉病 disease；poor health：孩子有～，不要让他受凉了。The kid is in poor health，so don't let him catch cold.

【毛玻璃】máobō·lí 用金刚砂等磨过或用氢氟酸浸蚀过而表面粗糙的玻璃。半透明，多用在建筑物的门窗上。frosted glass；glass abraded with emery or eroded with hydrofluoric acid so as to look translucent under a roughened or speckled decorative surface，oft. for use on doors and windows；also 磨砂玻璃 móshā bō·lí

【毛布】máobù 用较粗的棉纱织成的布 coarse cotton cloth；coarse calico

【毛糙】máo·cao 粗糙；不细致 crude；perfunctory：这活儿干得太～。The work done was cursory at best.

【毛茶】máochá 供制红茶或绿茶的原料茶 raw tea leaves；tea leaves supplied for the making of green or dark tea；also known as 毛条 máotiáo

【毛虫】máochóng 某些鳞翅目昆虫的幼虫，每环节的疣状突起上丛生着毛 caterpillar；worm-like，hairy or spiny larva of a lepidopteran；also 毛毛虫 máo·maochóng

【毛刺】máocì（～儿 máocìr）金属工件的边缘或较光滑的平面上因某种原因而产生的不光、不平的部分。通常应加工去掉毛刺。burr；protruding，ragged metal edge or irregular protuberance on the smooth surface of a metal object that have to be smoothed

【毛豆】máodòu 大豆的嫩荚，外皮多毛，种子青色，可做蔬菜 fresh downy soya bean pod with the seeds green and tender to be used as vegetable

【毛发】máofà 人体上的毛和头发 hair on the human body：～直立（形容极度惊恐 in a state of extreme fear）one's hair stand on end；hair-raising

【毛纺】máofǎng 用动物纤维（主要是羊毛）为原料纺成纱 woollen textile；spinning of wool or other animal fibres into yarn：～织品 woollen textiles

【毛茛】máogèn 多年生草本植物，茎叶有茸毛，单叶，掌状分裂，花黄色，有光泽，果穗作球状。植株有毒，可入药。buttercup（*Ranunculus*）；perennial plant that is poisonous and of medicinal value，having downy stalk and palmately simple leaves，yellow and shiny flowers，and bearing ball-shaped ears

【毛估】máogū 粗略地估计 make a rough estimate：～一下，这片早稻亩产不会低于八百斤。By a rough estimation the early rice in this paddy field will yield no less than 800 *jin* per *mu*.

【毛咕】máo·gu〈方 *dial.*〉有所疑惧而惊慌 foreboding；apprehensive；running scared：走进荒滩，心里直～。A sense of foreboding descended on my heart when I set foot in the desolate land.

【毛骨悚然】máo gǔ sǒngrán 形容很害怕的样子 hair-raising；send shivers down through one's spine

【毛孩】máohái（～儿 máoháir）指生下来在面部和身上长有较长的毛的孩子 hairy child；one born with face and body covered with an abundance of hair

【毛孩子】máohái·zi 小孩儿，也指年轻无知的人 little child；suckling：十年前你还是一个不懂事的～呢！Ten years ago you were still an ignorant suckling.

【毛烘烘】máohōnghōng（～的 máohōnghōng·de）形容毛很多的样子 fleecy；furry

【毛乎乎】máohūhū（～的 máohūhū·de）形容毛密而多 hairy；shaggy

【毛尖】máojiān 绿茶的一种，用精细挑选的幼嫩芽叶加工而成，如信阳毛尖（产于河南）、都匀毛尖（产于贵州）*maojian*，a kind of green tea made from carefully picked tender leaves, the best of which is found in Xinyang of Henan Province, and Duyun of Guizhou Province

【毛巾】máojīn 擦脸和擦身体用的针织品,织成后经纱拳曲,露在表面,质地松软而不光滑 towel; knitware used for wiping or drying the face or body, with curled warps that make it soft and absorbent

【毛巾被】máojīnbèi 质地跟毛巾相同的毯子 towelling coverlet; also 毛巾毯 máojīntǎn

【毛举细故】máo jǔ xì gù 烦琐地列举细小的事情 enumerate trivial matters; obsessed with minute detail; also 毛举细务 máo jǔ xì wù

【毛孔】máokǒng 汗孔 pore

【毛裤】máokù 用毛线织成的裤子 woollen pants

【毛拉】máolā ❶ 对伊斯兰教学者的尊称 maula; Maulana; Maulana; mullah, title for an Islamic scholar ❷ 我国新疆地区某些穆斯林对阿訇的称呼 maula, Maulana; mullah, a term of address for an ahung among Muslims in certain areas of Xinjiang, China [阿拉伯 Arabic: mawla]

【毛蓝】máolán 比深蓝色稍浅的蓝色 darkish blue: ～布 blue cloth

【毛利】máolì 企业总收入中只除去成本而没有除去其他费用时的利润(区别于'净利' as compared with 'net profit') gross profit; profit in which no costs have been deducted other than production cost

【毛料】máoliào 用兽毛纤维或人造毛等纺织成的料子 woollen fabric or artificial fabric

【毛驴】máolǘ (～儿 máolǘr)驴,多指身体矮小的驴 donkey, esp. one of small stature

【毛毛】máo·mao 〈方 *dial.*〉对婴儿的爱称 baby, a term of endearment for an infant

【毛毛虫】 máo·maochóng same as 毛虫 máochóng

【毛毛雨】máo·maoyǔ ❶ 指形成雨的水滴极细小、下降时随气流在空中飘动、不能形成雨丝的雨。通常指很小的雨。mizzle; drizzle; rain gently in fine, mistlike drops that, instead of falling in streaks, drift with the air current ❷ 事前有意放出风声、信息让人有所准备叫做下毛毛雨 tip off; let sb. in on information before making it public

【毛南族】Máonánzú 我国少数民族之一,分布在广西 Maonans; Maonan ethnic people who live in the Guangxi Zhuang Autonomous Region

【毛囊】máonáng 包裹在毛发根部的囊 hair follicle; (图见 ☞ figure for 皮肤 pífū on p. 1464)

【毛坯】máopī ❶ 已具有所要求的形体,还需要加工的制造品;半成品 semi-finished product ❷ 机器制造中,材料经过初步加工,需要进一步加工才能制成零件的半成品,多指铸件或锻件 unfinished machine part that is prepared for eventual finishing, oft. referring to castings and forgings ‖ also known as 坯料 pīliào

【毛皮】máopí 带毛的兽皮,可用来制衣、帽、褥子等 fur; pelt; skin of an animal with the hair or fur still on it, for the making of clothing, hats, beddings, etc.

【毛片】máopiān ❶ 指拍摄后未经加工的影片 takes; unedited film footage ❷ 指极为暴露的色情影片或电视片 hard-core pornographic movie or television play

【毛票】 máopiào (～儿 máopiàor) 角票 Renminbi banknote with domination of one, two or five *jiao*

【毛渠】máoqú 从斗渠引水送到每一块田地里的小渠道 branch ditch; lateral ditch; ditch that divert water from a trunk ditch to the fields

【毛茸茸】máoróngróng (～的 máoróngróng·de) 形容动植物细毛丛生的样子 fluffy; fleecy: ～的小白兔 fluffy white rabbit

【毛瑟枪】máosèqiāng 〈旧时 *old*〉对德国毛瑟(Mauser)工厂制造的各种枪的统称。通常多指该厂制造的步枪。Mauser; rifles or pistols made in the Mauser Factory in Germany, usu. referring to a Mauser rifle

【毛手毛脚】máo shǒu máo jiǎo 做事粗心大意,不沉着 unkempt; slovenly

【毛遂自荐】Máo Suì zì jiàn 毛遂是战国时代赵国平原君的门客。秦兵攻打赵国,平原君奉命到楚国求救,毛遂自动请求跟着去。到了楚国,平原君跟楚王谈了一上午没有结果。毛遂挺身而出,陈述利害,楚王才答应派春申君带兵去救赵国。后来用'毛遂自荐'比喻自己推荐自己。Mao Sui was a hanger-on of Marquis Pingyuan of Zhao during the Warring States Period. When the state of Qin was attacking the state of Zhao, the marquis was dispatched as a convoy to the state of Chu to ask for help, and Mao Sui went on the mission on his own volition. The negotiation between the marquis and the duke of Chu went on for an entire morning but fell through. It was Mao Sui who stepped forward bravely, explained the seriousness of the situation to the duke, and talked him into dispatching Marquis Chunshen to the rescue of the state of Zhao. From this proverb is derived the phrase '毛遂自荐 Máo Suì zì jiàn', meaning 'volunteer to do something.' or 'recommend oneself for a position or task'.

【毛太纸】máotàizhǐ 类似毛边纸而稍薄的纸,略带黑色,多产于福建 *maotai* paper; writing paper tinner and darker than *maobian* paper, usu. produced in Fujian Province

【毛毯】máotǎn 用兽毛纤维、化学纤维等织成的毯子 woollen blanket; blanket, woven of woollen or chemical fibres

【毛桃】máotáo ❶ 毛桃树,野生的桃树 wild peach tree ❷ 毛桃树的果实 wild peach

【毛条】máotiáo same as 毛茶 máochá

【毛头纸】máotóuzhǐ 一种纤维较粗、质地松软的白纸,多用于糊窗户或包装 *maotou* paper;

white paper of coarse fibre and loose and soft texture, oft. used for wrapping or papering windows; also 东昌纸 dōngchāngzhǐ

【毛窝】máowō 〈方 *dial*.〉棉鞋 cotton padded shoes

【毛细管】máoxìguǎn ❶ 连接在小动脉和小静脉之间的最细小的血管,血液中的氧与细胞组织内的二氧化碳在毛细管里进行交换 capillary; minute blood vessel which connects arteries and veins and in which oxygen in the blood replaces carbon dioxide in the cellular tissue; also 毛细血管 máoxì xuèguǎn or 微血管 wēixuèguǎn ❷ 直径特别细小的管子 tube having a small internal diameter; ☞毛细现象 máoxì xiànxiàng

【毛细现象】máoxì xiànxiàng 毛细管插入浸润液体中,管内液面上升,高于管外,毛细管插入不浸润液体中,管内液面下降,低于管外的现象。毛巾吸水,地下水沿土壤上升都是毛细现象。capillarity; a phenomenon in which when a tiny tube is inserted into an absorbent liquid, the surface of the liquid inside the tube rises above that of the liquid outside it, and vice versa if the liquid is unabsorbent; examples including a towel absorbing water, and subterranean water rising in soil

【毛线】máoxiàn 通常指羊毛纺成的线,也指羊毛和人造毛混合纺成的线或人造毛纺成的线 knitting wool; woollen yarn; yarn of blend fabric of wool and synthetic fibre

【毛丫头】máoyā·tou 指年幼无知的女孩子 pert girl; chit; little girl

【毛样】máoyàng 还没有按照版面的形式拼版的校样 galley proof

【毛腰】máo//yāo 〈方 *dial*.〉弯腰 crouch; stoop; bend low: 一～钻进山洞 climb into a mountain cave by crouching one's body; also 猫腰 máoyāo

【毛衣】máoyī 用毛线织成的上衣 woollen sweater; sweater; woolly

【毛蚴】máoyòu 长着毛的幼虫的总称 (collect.) miracidium; hairy larva

【毛躁】máo·zao ❶ (性情)急躁 irascible; testy; touchy: 脾气～of a short-tempered disposition ❷ 不沉着;不细心 impatient; careless: 他做事有些～。He is kind of impatient in getting things done.|毛毛躁躁是办不好事的。Being impatient and careless gets nowhere.

【毛泽东思想】Máo Zédōng sīxiǎng 马克思列宁主义的普遍真理和中国革命具体实践相结合而形成的思想体系,是以毛泽东为主要代表的中国共产党,在马克思列宁主义指导下,在半个多世纪中领导中国人民进行民主革命和社会主义革命、社会主义建设的实践经验的结晶 Mao Zedong Thought; ideological system that combines the universal truth of Marxism-Leninism with the concrete practice of the Chinese revolution, and a crystallization of the more-than-a-half-century experience of the Communist Party of China with Mao Zedong as the chief representative in leading the Chinese people in the democratic revolution and the socialist revolution and construction under the guidance of Marxism-Leninism

【毛织品】máozhīpǐn ❶ 用兽毛纤维或人造毛等纺织成的料子 woollen textiles; woollen fabrics, woven of woollen or artificial fibres ❷ 用毛线编织的衣物 woollen knitwear

【毛痣】máozhì 医学上指高出皮肤表面并且长有毛的痣 (med.) hairy nevus; hairy mole

【毛重】máozhòng 货物连同包装的东西或牲畜家禽等连同皮毛在内的重量(区别于'净重' as compared with 'net weight') gross weight; combined weight of goods and packaging; weight of undressed meat

【毛猪】máozhū 活猪(多用于商业 oft. used in commerce) living pig

【毛装】máozhuāng (书籍)不切边的装订(of book) binding with the pages untrimmed

【毛子】máo·zi ❶〈旧时 *old*〉称西洋人(含贬义 derog.) Westerners; foreigner ❷〈方 *dial*.〉〈旧时 *old*〉指土匪 highwayman; bandit ❸〈方 *dial*.〉细碎的毛或线 tuft of hair or yarn; bits and ends of hair or yarn: 没做什么针线活儿,倒沾了一身布～。I haven't done much needlework yet I've got cotton crumbs all over me.

矛 máo 古代兵器,在长杆的一端装有青铜或铁制成的枪头 lance; pike; ancient weapon with a bronze or iron head fixed on a long pole: 长～spear|～盾 spear and shield

【矛盾】máodùn ❶ 矛和盾是古代两种作用不同的武器。古代故事传说,有一个人卖矛和盾,夸他的盾最坚固,什么东西也戳不破;又夸他的矛最锐利,什么东西都能刺进去。旁人问他,'拿你的矛来刺你的盾怎么样?'那人没法回答了(见于《韩非子·难一》)。后来'矛盾'连举,比喻言语行为自相抵触 Spear and shield were weapons of ancient times that played different roles. According to *Hanfeizi·Rebuttals*: A man peddling spears and shields was praising his wares, saying that his shields were utterly impregnable and that his spears could pierce anything in the world. He was, however, speechless when someone asked him what would happen if he pitted one of his spears against one of his shields. The word has since been used figuratively to mean contradiction or contradictory: ～百出 riddled with contradictions|自相～self-contradictory ❷ 辩证法上指客观事物和人类思维内部各个对立面之间的互相依赖而又互相排斥的关系 (in dialects) contradiction; interdependent and mutually repelling relationship between the opposites in any objective matter or thought ❸ 形式逻辑中指两个概念互相排斥或两个判断不能同时是真也不能同时是假的关系 (in formal logic) the contradiction between two opposing concepts, or the relationship between two judgements that cannot be both true or both false ❹ 泛指对立的事物互相排斥 conflict between two opposing things:他俩的意见有～。They held conflicting views.

【矛盾律】máodùnlǜ 形式逻辑的基本规律之一,要求在同一思维过程中,对同一对象不能同时作出两个矛盾的判断,即不能既肯定它,又否定它。如不能说'水是物质',同时又说'水不是物质',这两个判断中必有一个是假的。矛盾律要求思想前后一贯,不能自相矛盾。公式是:'甲不是非甲'或'甲不能既是乙又不是乙'。law of contradiction; one of the basic norms of formal logic, which demands that one should not pass two contradictory judgements on the same subject of a thought, that is to say, one cannot affirm and negate it at the same time. For instance, one cannot say that water is a matter while insisting that it is not, because either one or the other of the judgements must be false. The law of contradiction calls for consistency of thought from beginning to the end, and allows no self-contradiction. The formula: A isn't non-A./A cannot be both B and non-B.

【矛头】máotóu 矛的尖端(多用于比喻 usu. fig.) spearhead:把讽刺的～指向坏人坏事。Let's target satire at bad people and bad deeds.

茆 máo ❶ 同 same as 茅 máo ① ❷(Máo) 姓 a surname

茅 máo ❶ 白茅 cogon (*Imperata cylindrical* var. *major*) ❷ (Máo) 姓 a surname

【茅草】máocǎo 白茅一类的植物 cogon; grass of the genus *imperata*

【茅房】máofáng 厕所 lavatory; urinal

【茅坑】máokēng ❶ 厕所里的粪坑 latrine pit ❷ 〈方 *dial.*〉厕所(多指简陋的)(simple and crude) latrine; outhouse

【茅庐】máolú 草屋 thatched hut

【茅棚】máopéng 用茅草等搭的棚子 thatched shack

【茅塞顿开】máo sè dùn kāi 原来心里好像有茅草堵塞着,现在忽然被打开了。形容忽然理解、领会。realization hit upon one; see the light all of a sudden; be enlightened in no time

【茅舍】máoshè 〈书 *fml.*〉茅屋 thatched cottage:竹篱～ thatched cottage with a bamboo-fenced courtyard

【茅厕】máo·si 〈方 *dial.*〉厕所(cèsuǒ) toilet

【茅台酒】máotáijiǔ 贵州仁怀县茅台镇出产的白酒,酒味香美 *mautai*, a famous Chinese liquor with an exceptional fragrance and strong taste, produced in Maotai Town in Guizhou Province's Renhuai County; 简称 abbr. 茅台 máotái

【茅屋】máowū 屋顶用茅草、稻草等盖的房子,大多简陋矮小 thatched hut; crude and low dwelling with its roof thatched with cogon-grass or straw

牦(氂) máo [牦牛](máoniú) 牛的一种,全身有长毛,黑褐色、棕色或白色,腿短。是我国青藏高原地区的主要力畜。yak (*Bos grunniens*); short-limbed bovine mammal covered with long hair dark brown, brown or white in colour, used as a major draught animal in Qinghai-Tibet Plateau

旄 máo 〈古代 *arch.*〉在旗杆头上用牦牛尾做装饰的旗子 flag hoisted up on poles topped with a tassel made of a yak's tail 〈古 *arch.*〉same as 耄 mào

酕 máo [酕醄](máotáo)〈书 *fml.*〉大醉的样子 dead drunk:～大醉 as drunk as a fiddle

猫(貓) máo [猫腰](máoyāo) same as 毛腰 máoyāo

☞ māo on p.1305

锚 máo 船停泊时所用的器具,用铁制成。一端有两个或两个以上带倒钩的爪儿,另一端用铁链连在船上,抛到水底或岸边,用来稳定船舶。anchor; heavy iron object with two or more barbed flukes, attached to a vessel by a steel chain, and cast overboard to keep the vessel in place by gripping the bottom or shore of a river or ocean

【锚泊】máobó (船舶等)借助于锚而停留在水面某处 anchor; berth a vessel by an anchor

【锚地】máodì 水域中专供船舶抛锚停泊及船队编组的地点 anchorage; place for the anchoring of vessels or marshalling a shipping fleet

【锚固】máogù 在钢筋混凝土结构中,为使钢筋可靠地固定在混凝土里,对钢筋进行处理,叫做锚固,如把钢筋的端部做成弯钩或增加钢筋长度等 anchor; anchorage; practice of bending one end of a reinforcing steel bar into a hook or lengthening it so that it can be more securely fixed in a structure of reinforced concrete

【锚位】máowèi 船舶抛锚处的地理位置 anchorage, where a ship is anchored

髦 máo 〈古代 *arch.*〉称幼儿垂在前额的短头发 child's bangs; fringe of hair cut short and straight across the forehead of a child

髳 Máo 周朝国名,在今山西南部 Mao, name of a state during the Zhou Dynasty, in the southwest of present-day Shanxi Province

蝥 máo ☞ 斑蝥 bānmáo on p.48

蟊 máo 吃苗根的害虫 insect that feeds on the roots of saplings

【蟊贼】máozéi 危害人民或国家的人 vermin; person jeopardizing the interests of the people or a country

mǎo (ㄇㄠˇ)

冇 mǎo 〈方 *dial.*〉没有 not have; there is not; be without

卯[1] mǎo 地支的第四位 *mao*；the fourth of the 12 Earthly Branches；☞ 干支 gānzhī on p. 627

卯[2] mǎo same as 卯眼 mǎoyǎn

【卯时】mǎoshí 旧式计时法指早晨五点钟到七点钟的时间 period of the day from 5 a. m. to 7 a. m.，according to a time system in China before the introduction of clock

【卯榫】mǎosǔn 卯眼和榫头 mortise and tenon

【卯眼】mǎoyǎn 器物的零件或部件利用凹凸方式相连接的地方的凹进部分 mortise；cavity in a component part for receiving a tenon：凿个～儿 cut a mortise

峁 mǎo 我国西北地区称顶部浑圆、斜坡较陡的黄土丘陵 loess hill with relatively steep slopes and round crest in northwest China

泖 mǎo〈书 *fml.*〉水面平静的小湖 small lake with an unruffled water surface

昴 mǎo 二十八宿之一 Mao；the 18th of the 28 constellations in ancient Chinese astronomy

铆 mǎo ❶ same as 铆接 mǎojiē ❷ 指铆接时锤打铆钉的操作 riveting

【铆钉】mǎodīng 铆接用的金属元件，圆柱形，一头有帽 rivet；metal bolt or pin having a head on one end

【铆钉枪】mǎodīngqiāng 敲打铆钉用的风动工具，形状略像枪 riveting gun，gun-shaped pneumatic tool for riveting purposes

【铆工】mǎogōng ❶ 金属铆接工作 riveting ❷ 做铆接工作的工人 riveter

【铆接】mǎojiē 连接金属板或其他器件的一种方法，把要连接的器件打眼，用铆钉穿在一起，在没有帽的一端锤打出一个帽，使器件固定在一起 fasten with a rivet；put rivets through the hole bored into two or more objects and fasten them by hammering the headless end of the rivets into a head

【铆劲儿】mǎo//jìnr 集中力气，一下子使出来 use every ounce of one's energy；go all out；redouble one's effort：几个人一～，就把大石头抬走了。These people removed the boulder with just one concerted heave.｜铆着劲儿干 exert oneself on a job

mào（ㄇㄠˋ）

芼 mào〈书 *fml.*〉拔取（菜、草）pick；pull up (grass，vegetable)

皃 mào same as 貌 mào

茂 mào ❶ 茂盛 luxuriant；dense：～密 rank；lush｜根深叶～（of a tree）having deep roots and thick foliage ❷ 丰富精美 rich and fine：图文并茂（of a book）well-written text graced with thoughtful illustrations

【茂密】màomì （草木）茂盛而繁密（of vegetation）luxuriant：树木～dense woods｜～的竹林 lush green bamboo grove

【茂年】màonián〈书 *fml.*〉壮年；壮年时期 in the prime of one's life

【茂盛】màoshèng ❶（植物）生长得多而茁壮（of plants）luxuriant：庄稼长得很～。The crops are doing real fine. ❷〈比喻 *fig.*〉经济等兴旺 booming：财源～ plentiful financial resources

眊 mào〈书 *fml.*〉眼睛昏花 blurred eyesight；dim-sighted

冒 mào ❶ 向外透；往上升 belch；emit；evaporate：～烟 belch smoke｜～泡 bubbling｜～汗 sweating｜热气直往外～。The steam kept evaporating.｜墙头～出一个人头来。The head of a person emerged from behind the wall. ❷ 不顾（危险、恶劣环境等）risk；brave （danger，harsh condition，etc.）：～险 run the risk｜～雨 brave the rain｜～天下之大不韪 fly in the face of the will of the public；risk public condemnation ❸ 冒失；冒昧 prematurely；recklessly；venture to do sth.：～进 premature development；impatience for success｜看见那人好像是他，我～喊一声。I thought it was him but I was not sure，so I ventured to give him a yell. ❹ 冒充 falsify one's identity；pass for：～领 claim one's ownership of something that belongs to somebody else｜～认 accept somebody. as being something he or she is not｜谨防假～。Beware of fakes. ❹（Mào）姓 a surname

☞ mò on p. 1367

【冒场】mào//chǎng 戏剧演出时，演员没到该上场时而上场（of a performer during a theatrical show）go onstage before one's cue

【冒充】màochōng 假的充当真的 pass for：～内行 pass oneself for an expert｜用党参～人参 pass off dangshen（*Codonopsis pilosola*）as ginseng

【冒顶】mào//dǐng 地下采矿时，矿井中的顶板塌下来 cave-in；roof off；collapse of a mining pit's ceiling

【冒渎】màodú〈书 *fml.*〉冒犯亵渎 blaspheme；desecrate：～神灵 blaspheme the deities

【冒犯】màofàn 言语或行为没有礼貌，冲撞了对方 displease sb. because of improper word or deed；tread on sb's toes：～尊严 affront somebody's self-esteem｜孩子不懂事，对您多有～，请原谅。The child doesn't behave well. Please forgive him for offending you.

【冒功】mào//gōng 把别人的功劳说成自己的功劳 claim someone else's credit for oneself：～请赏 ask for a reward by claiming someone else's credit for oneself

【冒号】màohào 标点符号（：），主要用在提示性话语之后，用来提示下文［punctuation mark mainly used after a word to introduce what is to follow in a text] colon (:)

【冒火】mào//huǒ (～儿 mào//huǒr) 生气；发怒 flare up; become angry: 他气得直～。The man was besides himself with anger. | 有话好好说，冒什么火！If you have anything to say, just say it — what's the point of getting yourself worked up like that?

【冒尖】mào//jiān (～儿 mào//jiānr) ❶ 装满而且稍高出容器 packed; piled high with sth.; near overflowing: 筐里的菜已经～了。The basket has been packed near overflowing with vegetables. ❷ 稍稍超过一定的数量 a little more than: 弟弟十岁刚～。The younger brother is a little over 10. ❸ 突出 top-notch; preeminent; outstanding: 他在班上学习～。He is a top student in the class. ❹ 露出苗头 occur; come to light: 问题一～，就要及时加以解决。Problems should be solved as soon as they occur.

【冒进】màojìn 超过具体条件和实际情况的可能，工作开始得过早，进行得过快 rash advance; premature step; jump the gun; start doing sth. too soon or when and where conditions do not permit

【冒昧】màomèi (言行)不顾地位、能力、场合是否适宜(多用做谦辞 usu. hum.) venture; make bold; take the liberty: 不揣～May I take the liberty to ... | ～陈辞 make bold to present one's opinion

【冒名】mào//míng 假冒别人的名义 assume someone else's name: ～顶替 assume the identity of another person; take someone else's place by counterfeiting

【冒牌】mào//pái (～儿 mào//páir) (货物)冒充名牌 bogus; counterfeit: ～货 counterfeit; fake

【冒失】mào·shi 鲁莽；轻率 indiscreet; harebrained: ～鬼 madcap | 说话不要太～。Don't be too blunt whenever you say something.

【冒失鬼】mào·shiguǐ 做事莽撞的人 hotspur; rantipole: 这个～差点儿把我撞倒。This daring villain almost knocked me down.

【冒天下之大不韪】 mào tiānxià zhī dà bù wěi 不顾天下的反对，公然做罪恶极大的事 risk public condemnation and do sth. outrageous; fly in the face of public opinion

【冒头】mào//tóu ❶ 露出苗头(sign or symptom of sth.) show up; emergence of the tip of an iceberg: 骄傲情绪已经～了。Signs of conceitedness have become obvious. ❷ same as 出头 chū//tóu ④: 看上去他的年纪有三十～。He looks to be on the wrong side of 30.

【冒险】mào//xiǎn 不顾危险地进行某种活动 risk; take a chance on: ～家 adventurist | ～行为 risky behaviour | ～突围 break through enemy encirclement at great risk

贸 mào 交易；贸易 transaction; trade

【贸然】màorán 轻率地；不加考虑地 rashly; headlong: ～从事 act rashly | 这样～下结论，不好。It won't do to jump at conclusions.

【贸易】màoyì 进行商业活动 commercial activity: 对外～foreign trade | ～公司 trading company

【贸易风】màoyìfēng 信风，因古代通商，在海上航行时主要借助信风而得名 trade wind; consistent wind blowing northeasterly in the Northern Hemisphere and southeasterly in the Southern Hemisphere, named so because in old times oceangoing commercial vessels relied mainly on it for a smooth journey

耄 mào 指八九十岁的年纪，泛指老年 octogenarian: 老～ real old | ～耋之年 advanced in age

鄮 Mào 古县名，在今浙江宁波市一带 Maoxian; name of an ancient county in present-day Ningbo, Zhejiang Province

袤 mào〈书 *fml.*〉长度，也指南北的长度 length; north-to-south length: 延～万余里 extend for more than 10,000 *li*

鄚 mào (旧读 formerly pronounced mò) 鄚州(Màozhōu)，地名，在河北 Maozhou, name of a place in Hebei Province

萩 mào [萩蕿](màosǎo) 多年生草本植物，生在水中，根状茎横生，叶三棱状条形，上部伸出水面，伞形花序，花淡红色。叶子可编织凉帽，根状茎可食用。flowering rush (*Butomus umbellatus*); perennial hydrophilous herb with its upper section protruding above the water level, having an edible amphitropous rhizome, triangular linear leaves that make an ideal material for weaving sun hats, and umbrella-shaped flowers in pink colour

帽 mào ❶ 帽子 hat; cap: 呢～woollen hat | 草～straw hat ❷ (～儿 màor) 罩或套在器物上头，作用或形状像帽子的东西 cap; cover: 笔～儿 cap of a pen | 螺丝～儿 screw nut | 笼屉～儿 lid of a food steamer

【帽翅】màochì (～儿 màochìr) 纱帽后面伸向左右像翅膀的部分 wing-like flaps protruding from the back of a gauze cap worn by officials in Chinese dynastic periods

【帽耳】mào'ěr 帽子两旁护耳朵的部分 (of a cap) earflaps

【帽花】màohuā (～儿 màohuār) same as 帽徽 màohuī

【帽徽】màohuī 安在制服帽子前面正中的徽章 cap badge; cap insignia

【帽盔儿】màokuīr 没有帽檐帽舌的硬壳帽子，帽顶上一般缀有硬疙瘩 skullcap; close-fitting brimless and peakless cap usu. with a knob on the top

【帽舌】màoshé 帽子前面的檐，形状像舌头，用来遮挡阳光。有的地区叫帽舌头。peak (of a cap); visor; also known as 帽舌头 màoshé·tou in some regions

【帽檐】màoyán（～儿 màoyánr）帽子前面或四周突出的部分 brim of a hat

【帽子】mào·zi ❶ 戴在头上保暖、防雨、遮日光等或做装饰的用品 cap; hat; snug-fitting covering to protect the head from cold, rain or sunlight, or as an ornament：一顶～a cap ❷〈比喻 *fig.*〉罪名或坏名义 accusation; charge; label：批评应该切合实际，有内容，不要光扣大～。Be practical and substantial whenever you criticize someone — on no account should you call unwarranted names.

媢 mào〈书 *fml.*〉嫉妒 envy：～嫉 be green-eyed

瑁 mào ☞ 玳瑁 dàimào on p. 370

毷 mào［毷氉］(màosào)〈书 *fml.*〉烦恼 vexation

貌 mào ❶ 相貌 looks; appearance：面～outlook｜容～looks ❷ 外表的形象；样子 view; picture：全～complete view; whole picture｜～合神离 appearing like-minded but being contrary-minded in reality

【貌合神离】mào hé shén lí 表面上关系很密切而实际上怀着两条心(of two persons or parties) appear united but divided at heart

【貌似】màosì 表面上很像 seem to be; look like：～公允 be seemingly fair and square｜～强大 appear to be all-powerful

【貌相】màoxiàng ❶ 相貌 looks; facial features ❷ 看相貌；看外表 judge by the way sb. looks：人不可～，海水不可斗量。You can't judge people by appearance, and measure the ocean by the decalitre.

瞀 mào〈书 *fml.*〉❶ 目眩 dizzy; dazzled ❷ 心绪纷乱 nonplussed; at sixes and sevens ❸ 愚昧 ignorant

懋 mào ❶〈书 *fml.*〉劝勉；勉励 inspire; encourage：～赏 hand out incentives ❷〈书 *fml.*〉盛大 grand; splendid：～典 grand ceremony｜～勋 brilliant merit ❸ same as 茂 mào

·me（·ㄇㄜ）

么(麽、❶末) ·me ❶ 后缀 suffix：这～in this case｜那～in that case｜怎～how come｜多～how ❷ 歌词中的衬字 inserted in a line for balance or euphony：五月的花儿红呀～红似火。Red as fire are the flowers in May!
☞ 嘛 ·ma and 吗·ma on p. 1292，幺 yāo on p. 2225，麽 mó on p. 1362 and 末 mò on p. 1365

M **嚜** ·me〈助词 *aux.*〉跟'嘛'的用法相同 same as 嘛 ·ma in usage

méi（ㄇㄟˊ）

没[1] méi same as 没有[1] méiyǒu

没[2] méi same as 没有[2] méiyǒu
☞ mò on p. 1366

【没边儿】méibiānr〈方 *dial.*〉❶ 没有根据 far-fetched; unjustified：别说这～的话。Cut out all the falsehood. ❷ 没有边际 go too far：吹牛吹得～了 go too far in boasting about something.｜这孩子淘气淘得～。The child is hopelessly mischievous.

【没词儿】méi//cír 没话可说 be caught tongue-tied; get stuck

【没关系】méi guān·xi 不要紧；不用顾虑 doesn't matter; don't worry

【没劲】méijìn ❶（～儿 méijìnr）没有力气 weak：浑身～feel completely spent ❷ 没有趣味 boring; dull：这电影真～。This movie was boring.

【没精打采】méi jīng dǎ cǎi 形容不高兴，不振作 have the blues; out of humour; out of sorts：他～地坐在地下，低着头，不吱声。He sat there in low spirits and speechless, his head hanging low. also 无精打采 wú jīng dǎ cǎi

【没来由】méiláiyóu 无缘无故；无端 for no reason at all; unaccountably

【没落子】méi lào·zi〈方 *dial.*〉生活没有着落；穷困 poor; cannot make ends meet; also 没落儿 méilàor

【没脸】méi//liǎn 没有脸面 feel ashamed; be crestfallen：～见人 cannot look people straight in the eye｜～出门 too ashamed to appear in public

【没…没…】méi…méi… ❶ 用在两个同义的名词、动词或形容词前面，强调没有[used before two synonyms to emphasize the sense of 'without']：～皮～脸 know neither shame nor propriety｜～羞～臊 have no sense of shame｜～着～落 be uncertain; do not know where to get started｜～完～了 drag on and on; endless ❷ 用在两个反义的形容词前面，多表示应区别而未区别(有不以为然的意思)[used before two antonyms to indicate that distinction should but is not made]：～大～小 treat an elder or senior flippantly because of familiarity｜～深～浅 impudent and thoughtless｜～老～少 lose sight of somebody's seniority and thus behave improperly because of familiarity

【没门儿】méi//ménr〈方 *dial.*〉❶ 没有门路；没有办法 do not know how; incapable of doing sth.：让我去办这样的事，我可～。I really don't know how to handle matters like this. ❷ 表示不可能 impossible：凭你这成绩想考大学，～。With an academic record like that you have no way of passing the college entrance exams. ❸ 表示不同意 no way; nothing doing：他想一个人独占，～！He wants to hog all of it? No way!

【没命】méimìng ❶ 指死亡 die; meet one's demise：不是他及时把我送到医院，我早～了。I would have died had he not sent me to the hospital in time. ❷ 拼命；不顾一切 desperately; for all one's worth：受了伤的小鹿～地奔跑。The wounded deer galloped for all its worth. | 这些生长在河边的孩子一见了水就玩得～啦！These boys who grew up by the river played like mad the moment they came across the pool. ❸ 指没有福气 have no luck

【没跑儿】méipǎor 表示必定如此；无疑 doubtless：这次你算输定了，～！You'll lose the game this time — that's for sure.

【没谱儿】méi//pǔr 心中无数；没有一定的计划 feel uncertain; undecided：这事怎么办，我还没个谱儿。I have no idea what to do with it.

【没趣】méiqù（～儿 méiqùr）没有面子；难堪 feel snubbed：自讨～ invite ridicule; bring contempt upon oneself | 给他一个～。Give him the cold shoulder. | 他觉得～，只好走开了。Feeling snubbed, he had no choice but to go away.

【没商量】méi shāng·liáng 没有讨论的可能；没有回旋的余地 no room for bargaining; non-negotiable：你一点儿不让步，这事儿就～了。The deal is dead if you don't make any concessions.

【没什么】méi shén·me 没关系 do not matter：碰破了一点儿皮，～。Just a little scrape, nothing serious. | ～，请进来吧！Never mind, come on in.

【没事】méi//shì ❶ 没有事情做，指有空闲时间 have nothing to do; be free：～在家看书，别到外边瞎跑。Stay home and read if you don't have anything particular to do — don't go away and fool around. ❷ 没有职业 jobless; out of work：他近来～，在家闲着。He's been home doing nothing, having lost his job lately. ❸ 没有事故或意外 nothing serious：经过医生抢救，他～了，大家可以放心。(I) can assure everybody here that he is all right now after emergency treatment. ❹ 没有干系或责任 bear no responsibility：你只要把问题说清楚就～了。You'll be clean if you tell all the truth.

【没事人】méishìrén（～儿 méishìrénr）与某事无关的人；对某种情况毫不在乎的人 persons look unconcerned about sth. wrong; persons not give a damn：他捅了那么大的娄子，却像个～似的。He caused such big trouble, but he looked as if nothing had happened.

【没说的】méishuō·de ❶ 指没有可以指责的缺点 perfect; flawless：这小伙子既能干又积极，真是～。The young man is both able and earnest — you couldn't find a better one. ❷ 指没有商量或分辩的余地 no question about it; no doubt：这车你们使了三天了，今天该我们使了，～！You've been using the car for three days. Today it's our turn, and there's no question about it. ❸ 指不成问题，没有申说的必要 needless to say; naturally; of course：咱们哥儿俩，这点小事儿还不好办，～。I'm your buddy, and it goes without saying. I'll lend you a hand in a small matter like this. ‖ also 没有说的 méiyǒu shuō·de or 没的说 méi·deshuō

【没挑儿】méitiāor 没有可指摘的毛病 flawless：这筐橘子真～。You couldn't find better oranges anywhere. | 她的服务态度那是～了。Her service couldn't be better.

【没完】méi//wán（事情）没有了结 (in a quarrel) have not finished with sb.; not through：～没结。We are not through yet. | 他欺负人，我跟他～。He's such a bully, I won't let him off lightly.

【没戏】méi//xì〈方 *dial.*〉没指望；没希望 beyond hope; hopeless

【没羞】méixiū 脸皮厚；不害羞 be brazen; blatant; also 没羞没臊 méixiū méisào

【没样儿】méiyàngr 没规矩 wilful; wayward; have no manners：这孩子给大人宠得真～了。This kid has really been spoiled by the grown-ups.

【没意思】méi yì·si ❶ 无聊 bored：一个人待在家里实在～。I'm bored stiff staying at home alone. ❷ 没有趣味 dull; boring：这个电影平淡无奇，真～！This movie doesn't say anything interesting — it's boring.

【没影儿】méiyǐngr ❶ 没有踪影 without a trace; disappear：等我追出门，他早跑得～了。He was nowhere to be seen when I ran out of the door. ❷ 没有根据 groundless：你说他去过，这是～的事。You said he had been there, but it was not true.

【没有】[1] méi·yǒu ❶ 表示'领有、具有'等的否定 [negative form of 'have' or 'possess'] do not have; be without：～票 no ticket available | ～理由 no excuse ❷ 表示存在的否定 [negative form of 'existence'] there is no ...：屋里～人。There's nobody home. ❸ 用在'谁、哪个'等前面，表示'全都不' [precede 谁 shéi or 哪个 nǎ·ge to mean 'nobody']：～谁会同意这样做。No one will ever agree to do so. | ～哪个说过这样的话。Nobody has ever said anything like this. ❹ 不如；不及 be not so ...：你～他高。You are not so tall as him. | 谁都～他会说话。Nobody has a better gift of the gab than he. ❺ 不够；不到 less than; no more than：来了～三天就走了。He left after staying here for barely three days.

【没有】[2] méi·yǒu〈副词 *adv.*〉❶ 表示'已然'的否定 [negative form of 'have done' or 'have happened'] have not; not yet：他还～回来。He hasn't come home yet. | 天还～黑呢。It hasn't turned dark yet. ❷ 表示'曾经'的否定 [negative form of 'did'] did not：老张上个星

期～回来过。Old Zhang did not come back last week. | 银行昨天～开门。The bank did not open yesterday.

【没缘】méiyuán 没有缘分；无缘 have no luck with sb. or sth.

【没辙】méi//zhé 没有办法 at one's wit's end; not know what to do：他不肯去，我也～。He refused to go, and there is nothing I can do about it. | 这下子可没了辙了。Now I'm at a loss what to do next.

【没治】méizhì〈方 *dial.*〉❶ 情况坏得无法挽救 beyond repair; incurable ❷ 无可奈何 nothing can be done; at one's wit's end：我真拿他～。I'm at my wit's end how to deal with a man like him. ❸（人或事）好得不得了（of person or matter）couldn't be better; super：这么精致的牙雕简直～了。This piece of ivory carving looks so exquisite, it's unbelievable.

【没准儿】méi//zhǔnr 不一定；说不定 who knows; probably：这事～能成。Perhaps it will work. | 去不去还没个准儿呢。There's no telling if we'll be allowed to go.

玫 méi〈书 *fml.*〉一种玉石 a kind of jade

【玫瑰】méi·gui ❶ 落叶灌木，茎干直立，刺很密，叶子互生，奇数羽状复叶，小叶椭圆形，花多为紫红色，也有白色的，有香气，果实扁圆形。是栽培较广的观赏植物。花瓣可用来熏茶、做香料、制蜜饯等。rose (*Rosa rugosa*); deciduous shrub with thorns, alternate, compound leaves, oval leaflets, purplish red or white fragrant flowers, and oval fruit; a widely cultivated ornamental plant, whose petals are used for perfume, to scent tea leaves, and in the making of candied fruit ❷ 这种植物的花 flower of the plant

【玫瑰紫】méi·guizǐ 像紫红色玫瑰花一样的颜色 rose-red in colour; also 玫瑰红 méi·guihóng

枚 méi ❶〈量词 *classifier*〉跟'个'相近，多用于形体小的东西 similar to 个 gè (piece), for small items：三～奖章 three souvenir badges | 不胜～举 too many to recount ❷ (Méi)姓 a surname

眉 méi ❶ 眉毛 eyebrow; brow：浓～ heavy eyebrows | ～开眼笑 look cheerful ❷ 指书页上方空白的地方 top margin of a page：书～ top margin | ～批 notes and commentary at the top of a page

【眉端】méiduān ❶ 两眉之间 space between the eyebrows：愁上～ wear a worried frown; have a worried look ❷ 指书页的上端 top of a page

【眉飞色舞】méi fēi sè wǔ 形容喜悦或得意 enraptured; exultant：说到得意的地方，他不禁～。He could not help but exult when talking about a matter of personal pride.

【眉峰】méifēng 指眉毛；眉头 brows：～紧皱 knit one's brows

【眉高眼低】méi gāo yǎn dī 指脸上的表情、神色 facial expression：他就是不愿看人～来行事。He is nobody's yes man.

【眉睫】méijié 眉毛和眼睫毛 eyebrows and eyelashes;〈比喻 *fig.*〉近在眼前 urgent; imminent：失之～（在眼前错过）miss somebody. or something in plain sight | 事情迫于～（时间紧迫）matter of extreme urgency

【眉开眼笑】méi kāi yǎn xiào 形容高兴愉快的样子 be all smiles; beam with joy

【眉来眼去】méi lái yǎn qù 形容以眉眼传情。也用来形容暗中勾结。flirt with each other; exchange amorous glances; make undercover deals with sb.; collude

【眉棱】méiléng 生长眉毛的略略鼓出的部位 part of forehead that juts out slightly just above the eyebrows：～骨 superciliary ridge

【眉毛】méi·mao 生在眼眶上缘的毛 eyebrow

【眉毛胡子一把抓】méi·mao hú·zi yī bǎ zhuā〈比喻 *fig.*〉做事不分主次轻重缓急，一齐下手 try to deal with important and trivial matters simultaneously

【眉目】méimù ❶ 眉毛和眼睛，泛指容貌 brows and eyes; (in a broad sense) features：～清秀 have delicate features ❷（文章、文字的）纲要；条理 logic (of writing); sequence of ideas：～不清（of writing）not well organized | 在重要的字句下面划上红道，以清～。Underscore in red important words and sentences in order to be clear and well organized.

【眉目】méi·mu 事情的头绪 prospect of a solution; sign of a positive outcome：把事情弄出点～再走。Don't leave until matters begin to take shape.

【眉批】méipī 在书眉或文稿上方空白处所写的批注 notes and commentary at the top of a page

【眉清目秀】méi qīng mù xiù 形容容貌俊秀 have delicate features; have finely chiselled features

【眉梢】méishāo 眉毛的末尾部分 tip of the brow：喜上～ look very happy | ～间显露出忧郁的神色 melancholy cast between the brows

【眉题】méití 报刊等排在正式标题上方的提示性标题。字号比正式标题略小。(in newspaper or periodical) header; running head; overline; title, oft. underlined, placed above a headline but in a smaller typeface

【眉头】méitóu 两眉附近的地方 brows：皱～ knit one's brows | ～紧锁 frown severely | ～一皱，计上心来 knit one's brows and a plan (or stratagem) comes to mind

【眉心】méixīn 两眉之间的地方 space between the eyebrows

【眉眼】méiyǎn 眉毛和眼睛，泛指容貌、神情 brows and eyes; (in a broad sense) appearance; looks：小姑娘～长得很俊。The little girl is very pretty.

【眉宇】méiyǔ 两眉上面的地方，泛指容貌 forehead；(in a broad sense) appearance；looks：～不凡 extraordinary appearance

莓(苺) méi 指某些果实很小、聚生在球形花托上的植物 certain kinds of berries：草～ strawberry｜蛇～ Indian strawberry

娒 méi 人名用字 used in personal names

梅(楳、槑) méi ❶ 落叶乔木，品种很多，性耐寒，叶子卵形，早春开花，花瓣五片，有粉红、白、红等颜色，味香。果实球形，青色，成熟的黄色，都可以吃，味酸。Chinese plum (*Prunus mume*)；deciduous tree from a wide variety, cold-resistant, with oval leaves, pink, white and red fragrant five-petal flowers that bloom in early spring, bearing green round berries that ripen into yellow fruit, both of which are edible, and have a tart flavour. ❷ 这种植物的花 flower of the plant ❸ 这种植物的果实 fruit of the plant ❹ (Méi)姓 a surname

【梅毒】méidú 性病的一种，病原体是梅毒螺旋体。症状是：初期出现硬性下疳，发生淋巴结肿胀；第二期，出现各种皮疹，个别内脏器官发生病变；第三期，皮肤、黏膜形成梅毒瘤，循环系统或中枢神经系统发生病变。有的地区叫杨梅。syphilis；venereal disease engendered by the micro-organism treponema pallidum, whose symptoms are hard chancre and adenophyma in the initial stage, various types of rashes and pathological changes in certain internal organs in the second stage, and the formation of syphilomas in the skin and mucous membrane, and pathological changes in the circulation or central nervous system in the third stage；called 杨梅 yángméi in some places

【梅花】méihuā ❶ 梅树的花 plum blossom ❷ 〈方 *dial.*〉腊梅 winter sweet

【梅花鹿】méihuālù 鹿的一种，夏季毛栗红色，背部有白斑，冬季毛变成棕黄色，白斑变得不明显。四肢细而强壮，善跑。皮可制革。雄鹿有角，初生的角叫鹿茸，可入药。sika (*Cervus nippon*)；deer whose hide is reddish and white spotted in summer and turns a lighter shade of brown in winter and can be used for the making of leather, having slender, supple legs that enable it to run swiftly, the males having antlers, which, when newly grown and covered in a velvety pilose layer, are used to make medicine

【梅花针】méihuāzhēn 皮肤针的一种，因针柄的一端装五枚小针，状如梅花，故名 pyonex；a kind of cutaneous acupuncture, the shape of its five-needle percussopunctator resembling a Chinese plum blossom；☞ 皮肤针 pífūzhēn on p.1464

【梅雨】méiyǔ same as 黄梅雨 huángméiyǔ；also 霉雨 méiyǔ

【梅子】méi·zi ❶ 梅树 Chinese plum tree ❷ 梅树的果实 fruit of the Chinese plum tree；plum

脢(脄) méi 背脊肉 tenderloin：～子肉(里脊) tenderloin

郿 méi 郿县，在陕西。今作眉县。Méixiàn, name of a county that is now put as 眉县 Méixiàn, in Shaanxi Province

嵋 méi 峨嵋(Éméi)，山名，在四川 Emei, name of a mountain in Sichuan Province；also 峨眉 Éméi

猸 méi [猸子](méi·zi)]即山獾，哺乳动物，像猫而小，生活在树林中 crab-eating mongoose (*Helictis moschata*)；mammal similar to a cat but smaller, living in forests

湄 méi 〈书 *fml.*〉水边；岸旁 river bank

媒 méi ❶ 媒人 matchmaker；go-between：做～ be a matchmaker｜～妁之言 words of a matchmaker ❷ 媒介 intermediary：～质 media｜触～ catalytic

【媒介】méijiè 使双方(人或事物)发生关系的人或事物 intermediary；medium；vehicle：苍蝇是传染疾病的～。The fly is vehicle for disease.

【媒婆】méipó (～儿 méipór)以做媒为职业的妇女 woman matchmaker

【媒人】méi·ren 男女婚事的撮合者；婚姻介绍人 matchmaker；go-between

【媒妁】méishuò 〈书 *fml.*〉媒人 matchmaker：父母之命，～之言 match arranged at the parents' order and on the advice of a matchmaker

【媒体】méitǐ 指交流、传播信息的工具，如报刊、广播、广告等 media, including newspapers, magazines, radio and TV broadcasts and advertising：新闻～ news media

【媒怨】méiyuàn 〈书 *fml.*〉招致怨恨 cause ill will；incur hard feelings

【媒质】méizhì 介质 medium

【媒子】méi·zi 用来诱骗同类上当的(人或动物)(human or animal) decoy, used to trick others of the same species：鸟～ decoy bird｜他是个冒充顾客诱人购买假货的～。He is the decoy that tricks customers into buying fake goods.

楣 méi 门框上边的横木 lintel of a door：门～ lintel of a door

煤 méi 矿物，黑色固体，主要成分是碳、氢、氧和氮。是古代植物体在不透空气或空气不足的情况下受到地下高温高压而形成的。按形成阶段和炭化程度的不同，可分为泥煤、褐煤、烟煤和无烟煤。主要用做燃料和化工原料。coal；black solid mineral mainly consisting of carbon, hydrogen, oxygen and nitrogen, formed by ancient carbonized plant-life that has been compressed over centuries by high, subterranean temperature and pressure, subdivided into peat, brown coal, soft coal and anthracite, according to different forming levels and degrees of carbonization, mainly used as fuel and chemical material; also 煤炭 méitàn

【煤层】méicéng 地下上下两个岩层之间分布着煤炭的一层 coal seam; coal bed

【煤耗】méihào 用煤做燃料的机器装置,作出单位数量的功或生产出单位数量的产品所消耗的煤量 coal consumption; amount of coal consumed by coal-fuelled equipment when working out units of consumption per unit of production

【煤核儿】méihúr 没烧透的煤块或煤球 partly-burnt briquette; coal cinder

【煤化】méihuà 炭化 carbonization

【煤斤】méijīn 煤(总称) coal (collect.)

【煤精】méijīng 煤的一种,质地致密坚硬,色黑。多用来雕刻工艺品。graphite; black amber; jet; a kind of coal, dense and solid in quality, used for carving handicrafts

【煤末】méimò (～儿 méimòr)细碎成面儿的煤 culm; also 煤末子 méimò·zi

【煤气】méiqì ❶ 干馏煤炭等所得的气体,主要成分是氢、甲烷、乙烯、一氧化碳,并有少量的氮、二氧化碳等。无色无味无臭,有毒。用做燃料或化工原料。gas; gas obtained from dry distillation of coal, mainly consisting of hydrogen, methane, ethene, carbon monoxide and small amounts of nitrogen and carbon dioxide, colourless, tasteless and odourless, but poisonous, used for fuel or chemical material ❷ 煤不完全燃烧时产生的气体,主要成分是一氧化碳,无色无臭,有毒,被人和动物吸入后与血液中的血红蛋白结合能引起中毒 gas, obtained from incompletely burned coal, mainly consisting of carbon monoxide, colourless, odourless, but poisonous if absorbed by humans or animals owing to its combination with haemoglobin in the blood; also 煤毒 méidú ❸ 液化石油气的俗称 popular term for liquefied petroleum gas

【煤气灯】méiqìdēng 本生灯的通称 common term for 本生灯 běnshēngdēng

【煤气机】méiqìjī 用煤气、天然气、沼气等做燃料的内燃机 internal-combustion engine powered by gas, natural gas, methane, etc.

【煤球】méiqiú (～儿 méiqiúr)煤末加水和黄土制成的小圆球,是做饭取暖等的燃料 (egg-shaped) briquette, made of culm, water and loess, used for cooking and heating

【煤炭】méitàn same as 煤 méi

【煤田】méitián 可以开采的大面积的煤层分布地带 coal field

M

【煤烟子】méiyān·zi 物体燃烧时,冒出的烟聚积成的黑灰,是制墨的主要原料 soot; black dust; powder in the smoke of coal, oil, wood or other fuels; basic material for ink-making

【煤窑】méiyáo 用手工开采的小型煤矿 coal pit

【煤油】méiyóu 轻质石油产品的一类,从石油中经分馏或裂化而得。无色液体,挥发性比汽油低,比柴油高,用做燃料。有的地区叫火油、洋油。kerosene; paraffin; mixture of liquid hydrocarbons obtained by distilling petroleum, colourless, with a volatility higher than that of diesel oil but lower than that of gasoline, and widely used as a fuel, cleaning solvent, etc.; in some places called 火油 huǒyóu or 洋油 yángyóu

【煤渣】méizhā 煤燃烧后剩下的东西 coal cinder

【煤砟子】méizhǎ·zi 小块的煤 small piece of coal

【煤砖】méizhuān 煤末加水制成的砖形的煤块。用做燃料。(brick-shaped) briquette; coal dust mixed with water and pressed into a block for burning in a fireplace

禖 méi 〈古代 *arch.*〉求子的祭祀 prayers and sacrifices for progeny offered to gods

酶 méi 生物体的细胞产生的有机胶状物质,由蛋白质组成,作用是加速有机体内进行的化学变化,如促进体内的氧化作用、消化作用、发酵等。一种酶只能对某一类或某一个化学变化起催化作用。enzyme; ferment; any of various proteins, such as pepsin, originating in living cells and capable of producing certain chemical changes in organic substances through catalytic action, as in oxygenization, digestion and fermentation in the body. One kind of enzyme only can play the role of catalysis within any particular category of substance or chemical change.

镅 méi 金属元素,符号 Am (americium)。银白色,有放射性,由人工核反应获得。americium (Am); silver white, radioactive metal element, obtained through artificial nuclear reaction

鹛 méi 鸟类的一属,羽毛多为棕褐色,嘴尖,尾巴长。栖息在丛林中,叫的声音婉转好听。babbler (*Muscicapidae*); bird with brown plumage, a sharp beak, and a long tail that sings in loud chattering notes, and lives in the jungle

霉(❶黴) méi ❶ 霉菌 mould; mildew ❷ 东西因霉菌的作用而变质 become mildewy; go mouldy: ～烂 mildew and rot | 发～ become mildewy | ～豆腐 mouldy bean curd

【霉菌】méijūn 真菌的一类,用孢子繁殖,种类很多,如天气湿热时衣物上长的黑霉,制造青霉素用的青霉,手癣、脚癣等皮肤病的病原体 mould; a kind of eumycete bred through sporulation, such as the black mould that forms on clothes in damp weather, the green mould used for making penicillin, and pathogens of skin diseases like ringworm on the hands and feet

【霉烂】méilàn 发霉腐烂 mildew and rot

【霉气】méi·qì ❶ 霉烂的气味 damp: 破烂衣裳

散发着～。Worn-out clothes smell of mildew. ❷〈方 *dial.*〉不吉利；倒霉 bad luck：刚出门就下雨，真～。What bad luck! Just as (we) went out it started to rain.

【霉天】méitiān 黄梅天 early summer rains

【霉头】méitóu ☞ 触霉头 chù méitóu on p. 295

【霉雨】méiyǔ same as 黄梅雨 huángméiyǔ; also 梅雨 méiyǔ

糜(穈、穈) méi 糜子 broom corn millet：～黍 broom corn millet ☞ mí on p. 1330

【糜子】méi·zi 稷子(jì·zi) broom corn millet (*Panicum miliaceum*)

měi (ㄇㄟˇ)

每 měi ❶ 指全体中的任何一个或一组(偏重个体之间的共性) every; each (with an emphasis on the common characteristic of individuals)：把节省下来的～一分钱都用在生产上 spend every saved penny on production｜～两个星期开一次小组会 hold a team meeting every two weeks｜～人做自己能做的事。Each does what he can. ❷ 表示反复的动作中的任何一次或一组 on each occasion：这个月刊～逢十五日出版。The monthly magazine is published on the 15th day of each month.｜最简单的秧歌舞是～跨三步退一步。The simplest *yangge* dance consists of one step backward after every three steps forward. ❸ 每每 often：春秋佳日，～作郊游。On fine days in spring and autumn (we) often go outing in the countryside.

【每常】měicháng ❶ 往常 habitually in the past ❷ 常常 often

【每况愈下】měi kuàng yù xià 指情况越来越坏。本作'每下愈况'(见于《庄子·知北游》,原义是愈下愈甚。steadily deteriorate; go from bad to worse; originally put as '每下愈况 měi xià yù kuàng'. see *Zhuang Zi · Knowledge Rambling in the North*) (况 *kuang*：甚 even)

【每每】měiměi 〈副词 *adv.*〉表示同样的事情不只发生一次，跟'往往'相同(一般用于过去的或经常性的事情) often; same as 往往 wǎngwǎng：他们常在一起，～一谈就是半天。They often got together, and when they did they would chat for hours.

【每年】měinián ❶ 年年 every year：村里～元宵节都闹花灯。The village displays festive lanterns during the Lantern Festival every year. ❷〈方 *dial.*〉往年 in the past：～从没见过这么大的洪水。There has never been such a heavy flood in the past.

美[1] měi ❶ 美丽；好看(跟'丑'相对 as opposed to 'ugly') beautiful; pretty：这小姑娘长得真～。The little girl is really beautiful.｜这里的风景多～呀！What beautiful scenery here! ❷ 使美丽 beautify：～容 beauty treatment｜～发 (of men) get a haircut; (of women) go to the hairdresser's ❸ 令人满意的；好 very satisfactory; good：～酒 good wine｜价廉物～ be cheap and at the same time very good｜日子过得挺～ live quite happily ❹ 美好的事物；好事 beautiful things：～不胜收。There are more beautiful things than the eye can take in.｜成人之～ help somebody. attain his goals; lend countenance to somebody.; bring a romance to a happy ending ❺〈方 *dial.*〉得意 be pleased with oneself：老师夸了他几句，他就～得了不得。After just a few words of praise from the teacher he felt enormously pleased with himself.

美[2] Měi ❶ 指美洲 America：南～ South America｜北～ North America ❷ 指美国 United States of America：～圆 US dollar｜～籍华人 Chinese American citizen

【美不胜收】měi bù shèng shōu 美好的东西太多，一时接受不完(看不过来) too many beautiful things for the eye to behold：展览会上的工艺品，琳琅满目，～。We were dazzled by the endless array of beautiful handiwork exhibits, which were more than the eye could behold.

【美餐】měicān ❶ 可口的饭食 tasty food：～佳肴 delicious food ❷ 痛快地吃 eat one's fill：～一顿 have an excellent dinner

【美差】měichāi 指肥缺，泛指好差事(就个人好处多说 in terms of personal benefit) cushy job; pleasant task：出差桂林可是件～。What a pleasant assignment you have, going to Guilin on business!

【美称】měichēng 赞美的称呼 good name：四川向有天府之国的～。Sichuan has always enjoyed the reputation of being 'Nature's Storehouse'.

【美德】měidé 美好的品德 virtue; goodness; moral excellence：勤奋节俭是我国人民的传统～。Diligence and frugality are our traditional virtues.

【美发】měifà 梳理修饰头发，使美观 (of men) get a haircut; (of women) go to the hairdresser's：～师 hair dresser｜～厅 barber's

【美感】měigǎn 对于美的感受或体会 aesthetic feeling; aesthetic perception：她的舞姿富有～。Her dancing posture and movements are full of aesthetic perception.

【美工】měigōng ❶ 电影等的美术工作，包括布景的设计，道具、服装的设计和选择等(of film, etc.) art design, including set design, choice and design of props, costumes, etc. ❷ 担任电影等的美术工作的人 (of film, etc.) artistic designer

【美观】měiguān (形式)好看；漂亮 (of appearance) pleasing to the eye; beautiful：房屋布置

得很～。The room is artistically decorated.｜～大方 artistic and in good taste

【美好】měihǎo 好(多用于生活、前途、愿望等抽象事物)(of life, future, and aspirations) fine; glorious:～的愿望 fine wish｜～的未来 glorious future

【美化】měihuà 加以装饰或点缀使美观或美好 beautify; embellish:～校园 beautify campus｜～市容 beautify the appearance of a city

【美金】měijīn same as 美圆 měiyuán

【美景】měijǐng 美好的景色 beautiful scenery or landscape:良辰～ a pleasant day and a fine landscape

【美酒】měijiǔ 味道醇美的酒;好酒 good wine:～佳肴 mellow wine and delicious food

【美丽】měilì 使人看了发生快感的;好看 beautiful:～的花朵 beautiful flowers｜祖国的山河是多么庄严～! How solemn and beautiful are the motherland's mountains and rivers!

【美满】měimǎn 美好圆满 happy; perfectly satisfactory:～姻缘 happy marriage｜～的生活 happy life｜小两口儿日子过得美美满满。The young couple live a happy life.

【美貌】měimào ❶ 美丽的容貌 good looks:天生～ born beauty ❷ 容貌美丽 pretty; beautiful:她长得十分～。She is very pretty.｜～的年轻女子 beautiful young lady

【美美】měiměi (～的 měiměi·de)尽兴地;尽情地;痛快地 to one's heart's content:～地吃一顿 eat one's fill｜～地睡上一觉 have a sound sleep

【美梦】měimèng〈比喻 *fig.*〉不切实际的美好幻想 impractical but fond illusion; dream:～破灭。A fond illusion was shattered.

【美妙】měimiào 美好,奇妙 beautiful; splendid; wonderful:～的歌喉 beautiful singing voice｜～的诗句 beautiful verse of poetry

【美名】měimíng 美好的名誉或名称 good name; good reputation:英雄～,流芳百世。A hero's good name will remain for ever a sweet remembrance.

【美女】měinǚ 美貌的年轻女子 beautiful young woman

【美气】měiqì〈方 *dial.*〉舒服;安逸 comfortable; easy:日子过得挺～。We lead a very comfortable life.

【美人】měirén (～儿 měirénr)美貌的女子 beautiful woman

【美人蕉】měirénjiāo 多年生草本植物,叶片大,互生,长椭圆形,有羽状叶脉。总状花序,花红色或黄色。供观赏。canna (*Cannaceae*); perennial grass plant, with large, oval, alternate leaves with feathery veins and a raceme, with red or yellow showy flowers

【美容】měiróng 使容貌美丽 have a facial; beautify appearance:～院 beauty salon｜～手术 cosmetic surgery

【美声】měishēng 一种产生于意大利的歌唱发声方法,特点是花腔装饰乐句流利灵活,音与音的连接平滑匀净 bel canto; smooth, cantabile style of singing originating in Italy, characterized by florid ornamentation and a smooth, even continuity between notes:～唱法 bel canto

【美食】měishí 精美的饮食 choice food:讲究～ be fastidious about one's food｜～街 food selling street

【美食家】měishíjiā 精于品尝菜肴的人 gourmet

【美事】měishì 好事;美好的事情 good luck:没想到这样的～会轮到我! Little did I imagine that I should be blessed with such a good fortune.

【美术】měishù ❶ 造型艺术 fine arts ❷ 专指绘画 painting

【美术片儿】měishùpiānr same as 美术片 měishùpiàn

【美术片】měishùpiàn 利用各种美术创作手段拍摄的影片,如动画片、木偶片、剪纸片等 animated cartoons, puppetry, etc.

【美术字】měishùzì 有图案意味或装饰意味的字体 artistic calligraphy; artistic lettering

【美谈】měitán 使人称颂的故事 story passed on with approval:千古～ salutary tale over a thousand years｜廉颇负荆请罪,至今传为～。The story of Lian Po bearing a bramble rod which he asked to be used for his own punishment is still circulated as an example worthy of emulation.

【美味】měiwèi 味道鲜美的食品 delicious food:～佳肴 delicious food｜珍馐～ delicacies and delicious food

【美学】měixué 研究自然界、社会和艺术领域中美的一般规律与原则的科学。主要探讨美的本质,艺术和现实的关系,艺术创作的一般规律等。aesthetics; the study of the general laws and principles governing the sense of beauty in nature, society and art, with emphasis on the nature of beauty, the relationship between art and reality, and the general norms for creative work

【美言】měiyán ❶ 代人说好话 tell sb. about the good quality of a person in order to get an advantage for him or her:～几句 speak favourably on somebody's behalf｜～一番 put in a word for somebody. ❷〈书 *fml.*〉美好的言辞 nice or fine words

【美意】měiyì 好心意 good intentions; kindness:谢谢您的～。Thank you for your kindness.

【美育】měiyù 以培养审美的能力、美的情操和对艺术的兴趣为主要任务的教育。音乐和美术是美育的重要内容。aesthetic education; education focusing on developing the ability to appreciate beauty; sense of beauty and love for art. Music and art are important aspects of aesthetic education.

【美誉】měiyù 美好的名誉 good reputation：教师享有辛勤的园丁的～。Teachers enjoy the good reputation of being diligent gardeners.

【美元】měiyuán same as 美圆 měiyuán

【美圆】měiyuán 美国的本位货币 US dollar, monetary unit of the United States; also 美金 měijīn or 美元 měiyuán

【美展】měizhǎn 美术作品展览 art exhibition

【美制】měizhì 单位制的一种，以英尺为长度的主单位，磅为质量的主单位，秒为时间的主单位。美制的某些单位在实际数值上与英制的相应单位略有差别。American system of weights and measures, with the foot as the unit of length, the pound as the unit of mass, and the second as the unit of time, different in some cases from their British counterparts in actual numbers

【美中不足】měi zhōng bù zú 虽然很好，但还有缺陷 blemish on an otherwise perfect thing; blemish on a thing of beauty：登泰山而没能看到日出，总觉得～。The trip stopped short of perfection when (we) failed to see the sun rise on climbing to the summit of Mount Taishan.

【美洲鸵】měizhōutuó 鸟，体形和鸵鸟相似而较小，足有三趾，善走。产于美洲草原地带。rhea (*Rhea americana*); bird similar to ostrich but smaller, with three toes, a good walker, native to the grasslands of America; also 鹈鹕 lái'ǎo

【美滋滋】měizīzī（～的 měizīzī·de）形容很高兴或很得意的样子 very pleased with oneself：他听到老师的赞扬，心里～的。He was very pleased with himself when the teacher praised him.｜看着茂盛的庄稼，他～地咧着嘴笑了。Looking at his luxuriant crops, he grinned with satisfaction.

浼 měi〈书 *fml.*〉❶ 污染 contaminate ❷ 请托 entrust a person to do sth.：央～ go and ask somebody a favour

渼 měi〈书 *fml.*〉波纹 ripples

镁 měi 金属元素，符号 Mg (magnesium)。银白色，质轻，燃烧时发出眩目的白色光。用来制闪光粉、烟火等，镁铝合金用于航空器材方面。magnesium (Mg); silver white and light metal element that gives off a glittering dazzling white light when ignited, used for making flashlight powder, smoke powder etc., or as a raw material for making magnadure, an aircraft material

【镁光】měiguāng 镁粉燃烧所发的强光 magnesium light：～灯 magnesium lamp

mèi (ㄇㄟˋ)

沬 Mèi 商朝的都城，又称朝歌(Zhāogē)，在今河南汤阴南 capital city of the Shang Dynasty, also called Zhaoge, south of present-day Tangyin, Henan Province

妹 mèi ❶ 妹妹 younger sister：姐～ sisters｜兄～ elder brother and younger sister ❷ 同辈而年纪比自己小的女子 younger female of the same generation：表～ younger female cousin｜师～ junior female apprentice ❸〈方 *dial.*〉年轻女子；女孩子 young girl：外来～ young women from a different locality｜农家～ young peasant women

【妹夫】mèi·fu 妹妹的丈夫 younger sister's husband; brother-in-law

【妹妹】mèi·mei ❶ 同父母（或只同父、只同母）而年纪比自己小的女子 younger sister of the same parentage; consanguineous younger sister ❷ 同族同辈而年纪比自己小的女子 younger female of the same generation：叔伯～ younger female cousins｜远房～ younger female distant cousins

【妹婿】mèixù〈书 *fml.*〉same as 妹夫 mèi·fu

【妹子】mèi·zi〈方 *dial.*〉❶ 妹妹 younger sister ❷ 女孩子 young girl

昧 mèi ❶ 糊涂；不明白 have hazy notions about; be ignorant of：蒙～ uncultured｜愚～ ignorant｜素～平生（一向不认识）not previously had the pleasure of making somebody's acquaintance ❷ 隐藏 hide：拾金不～ desist from pocketing money one has picked up ◇～良心 betray one's conscience ❸〈书 *fml.*〉昏暗 dark; gloomy：幽～ dim ❹〈书 *fml.*〉冒犯；冒昧 venture; risk：～死 risk one's life

【昧良心】mèi liángxīn 违背良心（做坏事）do evil deeds that go against the dictates of one's conscience：可不能～赚黑钱！Never make money in a way that conflicts with one's conscience!

【昧死】mèisǐ〈书 *fml.*〉冒死罪（多用于臣下向君主上书时 oft. used when a minister submits a written statement to the monarch) risk one's life：～上言 state one's views at the risk of one's life｜～以闻 risk one's life to let others hear one's views

【昧心】mèixīn 昧良心 do evil deeds that conflict with one's conscience：不说～话 do not say things that go against one's conscience

袂 mèi〈书 *fml.*〉袖子 sleeve：分～ part (from each other)｜联～而往 arrive one after another

谜 mèi [谜儿](mèir)〈方 *dial.*〉谜语 riddle
☞ 猜谜儿 cāi//mèir on p.176 and 破谜儿 pò//mèir on p.1495
☞ mí on p.1319

痗 mèi〈书 *fml.*〉忧思成病 illness caused by anxiety

寐 mèi 睡 sleep：假～ drowse; catnap｜喜而不～ too happy and excited to sleep｜梦～

以求 long for something day and night

媚 mèi ❶ 有意讨人喜欢；巴结 fawn on; curry favour with; flatter; toady to: 谄～ flatter | 献～ curry favour with ❷ 美好；可爱 charming; fascinating; enchanting: 妩～ charming | 春光明～ bright spring days

【媚骨】mèigǔ ☞ 奴颜媚骨 nú yán mèigǔ on p. 1426

【媚世】mèishì 讨好世俗 try to please the public: ～之作 works that play to the gallery

【媚俗】mèisú 媚世 try to please the public: 趋时～ follow the fashion and pander to the public

【媚态】mèitài ❶ 讨好别人的姿态 obsequiousness: 种种～，一副奴才相。All these fawning expressions are merely the servile habits of a flunkey. ❷ 妩媚的姿态 feminine charms

【媚外】mèiwài 对外国奉承巴结 fawn on (or toady to) foreign powers: 崇洋～ be enamoured of things foreign and obsequious to foreigners

【媚悦】mèiyuè 有意讨人喜欢 curry favour with: ～流俗 cater to the current fashion

魅 mèi 传说中的鬼怪 evil spirit; demon: 鬼～ ghosts and goblins | 魑～ evil spirits

【魅惑】mèihuò 诱惑 captivate; bedevil: ～力 charm

【魅力】mèilì 很能吸引人的力量 charm; enchantment; fascination: 富有～ full of charm | 艺术～ artistic charm

【魅人】mèirén 使人陶醉；吸引人 charming; attractive: 景色～ charming scenery

mēn (ㄇㄣ)

闷 mēn ❶ 气压低或空气不流通而引起的不舒畅的感觉 stuffy; stifling: ～热 hot and stuffy | 打开窗户吧，房里太～了。Open the windows, it's so stuffy in here. ❷ 使不透气 cover tightly: 茶刚泡上，～一会儿再喝。I have just made the tea, but it needs to draw for a while. ❸ 不吭声；不声张 speechless; silent: ～头儿 quietly | ～声不响 keep silent ❹ 〈方 *dial.*〉声音不响亮 (of voice or sound) muffled: 他说话～声～气的。He speaks in muffled tones. ❺ 在屋里呆着，不到外面去 shut oneself or sb. indoors: 他整天～在家里看书。He shuts himself indoors and reads all day.

☞ mèn on p. 1323

【闷沉沉】mēnchénchén (～的 mēnchénchén·de) ❶ 形容因气压低或空气不流通而感觉不舒畅 stuffy: ～的房间 stuffy room ❷ 形容声音低沉 (of voice) muffled: 雷在远处～地响。There came the muffled sound of distant thunder.

☞ mènchénchén on p. 1323

【闷锄】mēnchú 在种子发芽之前把表层的土锄松并除去杂草，以便于种子发芽出土 weed and loosen topsoil so that the seeds can germinate

【闷气】mēnqì same as 闷 mēn①: 这间地下室久不用了，又～又潮湿。The basement is stuffy and damp as it has not been used for a long time.

☞ mènqì on p. 1323

【闷热】mēnrè 天气很热，气压低，湿度大，使人感到呼吸不畅快 hot and stifling; sultry; muggy: 今天这样～，怕是要下雨了。Today is so sultry; it seems likely to rain.

【闷声闷气】mēn shēng mēn qì (～的 mēn shēng mēn qì·de) 形容声音低沉，不响亮 (of sb.'s voice) low: 他感冒了，说话有些～的。He has a cold. That's why when he talks he sounds congested.

【闷头儿】mēn//tóur 暗中(努力)，不声张 (work hard) quietly or silently: ～干 work doggedly in silence | ～写作 write with quiet resolve

mén (ㄇㄣˊ)

门(門) mén ❶ 房屋、车船或用围墙、篱笆围起来的地方的出入口 (of house, bus, ship or places enclosed by wall or fence) door; gate: 前～ front gate | 屋～ room door | 送货上～ deliver goods to the customer's door; (图见 ☞ figure for 房子 fáng·zi on p. 550) ❷ 装置在上述出入口，能开关的障碍物，多用木料或金属材料做成 door (usu. made of wood or metal): 铁～ iron door | 栅栏～儿 fence gate | 两扇红漆大～ red painted double-leaf gate ❸ (～儿 ménr) 器物可以开关的部分 any opening: 柜～儿 cupboard door | 炉～儿 stove door ❹ 形状或作用像门的 valve; switch: 电～ switch | 水～ water valve | 气～ air valve | 闸～ floodgate | 球～ goal ❺ (～儿 ménr) 门径 way to do sth.: 窍～ key to a problem | 炼钢的活儿我也摸着点～儿了。I've got the hang of steelmaking. ❻ 〈旧时 *old*〉指封建家族或家族的一支，现在指一般的家庭 branch of a family or clan, referring to a family: 张～王氏 Mrs. Zhang, née Wang; Mrs. Zhang whose maiden name is Wang | 长～长子 eldest son of the eldest branch of a clan | 满～ whole family | 双喜临～ double blessing has descended upon the house ❼ 宗教、学术思想上的派别 (religious) sect; school (of thought): 儒～ Confucianism | 佛～ Buddhism | 左道旁～ heretical sect ❽ 传统指称跟师傅有关的 tradional term relating to the master or teacher: 拜～ take sb. as one's teacher | 同～ learn from the same teacher or master | ～徒 follower ❾ 一般事物的分类 class; category: 分～别类 put into different categories | 五花八～ multifarious; of all sorts ❿ 生物学中把具有最基本最显著的共同特征

的生物分为若干群，每一群叫一门，如原生动物门、裸子植物门等。门以下为纲。phylum; biological term denoting a major primary subdivision in the animal kingdom, consisting of one or more related classes, such as protozoa, gymnosperm, etc. Below the phylum is class. ⓫ 压宝时下赌注的位置名称，也用来表示赌博者的位置，有'天门'、'青龙'等名目。position in a gambling game where stakes are laid; position opposite where stakes are laid, known as 'heavenly gate', 'green dragon', etc. ⓬〈量词 *classifier*〉a) 用于炮［of artillery］：一～大炮 a cannon; b) 用于功课、技术等［of field of study or technical training］：三～功课 three courses of study | 两～技术 two skills ⓭（Mén）姓 a surname

【门巴】ménbā 医生 doctor［藏 Tibetan language］

【门巴族】Ménbāzú 我国少数民族之一，分布在西藏 Monba, one of China's minority ethnic groups that lives in Tibet

【门板】ménbǎn ❶ 房屋的比较简陋的木板门（多指取下来做别的用处的）（can usu. be removed for other uses）door plank ❷ 店铺临街的一面作用像门的木板，早晨卸下，晚上装上 shutters（wooden boards placed in the windows of shops facing the street, that are taken down in the morning when business commences, and replaced in the evening when the shop closes）

【门匾】ménbiǎn 安置在门额上的匾 horizontal inscribed board placed on the lintel of a gate or door

【门鼻儿】ménbír 钉在门上的铜制或铁制半圆形物，可以跟钌铞儿、铁棍等配合把门扣住或加锁 bolt staple, U-shaped piece of wire or metal with pointed ends for securing a bolt or padlock

【门钹】ménbó 旧式大门上所安的像钹的东西，上边有环，叫门时用环敲门钹发出声音 gate cymbal with ring-shaped knocker（fixed to old-style gates）

【门插关儿】ménchā·guanr 安在门上的短横闩，关门时插上，开门时拔出来 door bolt that latches when the door is closed and withdraws when opened; movable bar or rod that slides into a socket and secures a door or gate

【门齿】ménchǐ 上下颌前方中央部位的牙齿。人的上下颌各有四枚，齿冠呈凿形，便于切断食物。通称门牙，有的地区叫板牙。front tooth; incisor; chisel-shaped crowns of the four front teeth used to bite off food; generally called 门牙 ményá; in some places called 板牙 bǎnyá;（图见 ☞ figure for 齿 chǐ on p. 263）

【门当户对】mén dāng hù duì 指男女双方家庭的社会地位和经济状况相当，结亲很合适 be well-matched in social and economic status（for purposes of marriage）

【门道】méndào same as 门洞儿 méndòngr

【门道】mén·dao same as 门路 mén·lu ①：农业增产的～很多。There is no lack of ways and means of increasing agricultural production. | 外行看热闹，内行看～。While laymen watch only the fanfare, professionals are keen to spot the tricks of the trade.

【门第】méndì 指整个家庭的社会地位和家庭成员的文化程度等 family status：书香～ intellectual background | ～相当 well-matched family status

【门丁】méndīng〈旧时 *old*〉给官府或大户人家看门的人 doorman; gatekeeper

【门钉】méndīng（～儿 méndīngr）宫殿、庙宇等大门上成排成列的圆头装饰物 disc-shaped decoration on the gate of a palace, temple, etc.

【门洞儿】méndòngr ❶ 大门里面有顶的较长的过道 gateway; doorway：～风大，别着凉了。There is a strong wind in the doorway — don't catch cold. ❷ 泛指住家的大门（in a broad sense）door of a residence：他家就是东边第三个～。His house is the third door to the east.

【门斗】méndǒu 在屋门外设置的小间，有挡风、防寒作用 small vestibule outside the door of a house that keeps out the cold, wind, etc.

【门对】ménduì（～儿 ménduìr）门上的对联 antithetical couplet affixed to a door jamb

【门墩】méndūn（～儿 méndūnr）托住门扇转轴的墩子，用木头或石头做成 wooden or stone block that supports the pivot of a door

【门额】mén'é 门楣上边的部分 upper part of the lintel of a door

【门阀】ménfá 旧时在社会上有权有势的家庭、家族 family of power and influence（in feudal China）

【门房】ménfáng（～儿 ménfángr）❶ 大门口看门用的房子 gate house ❷ 看门的人 gatekeeper; doorman

【门扉】ménfēi 门扇 door leaf：半掩着～ half open door ◇打开心灵的～ open the door to the heart

【门风】ménfēng 指一家或一族世代相传的道德准则和处世方法 ethics and moral standards to which a family or a clan keeps：败坏～ discredit the family's moral standards

【门岗】méngǎng 大门口所设的岗哨 gate sentry

【门馆】ménguǎn ❶ 家塾 old-style private family school：～先生 resident private tutor ❷ 家塾教师 resident private tutor ❸ 官僚、贵族供门客住的房屋 living quarters for hangers-on（of aristocrats, bureaucrats, etc.）

【门户】ménhù ❶ 门（总称）（collect.）door：～紧闭 doors tightly shut | 小心～。Watch the door and beware of intruders. ❷〈比喻 *fig.*〉出入必经的要地 important passageway：塘沽新港是北京东通海洋的～。The new Tanggu port is Beijing's eastern gateway to the sea.

❸ 指家① family：兄弟分居，自立～。The brothers have each set up their own homes. ❹ 派别 faction；sect：～之见 parochial prejudice ❺ 门第 family status：～相当 families well-matched in social status

【门户之见】ménhù zhī jiàn 学术、艺术等领域中由宗派情绪产生的偏见（of study or art）sectarian bias；sectarianism

【门环】ménhuán 装在门上的铜环或铁环 knocker；also 门环子 ménhuán•zi

【门禁】ménjìn 机关团体、富贵人家等门口的戒备防范（of institutions or rich families）entrance guard：～森严 heavily guarded entrance

【门警】ménjǐng 守门的警卫 police guard at an entrance

【门径】ménjìng same as 门路 mén•lu ①：他深入群众，虚心学习，找到了解决问题的～。He at last found the key to the problem through maintaining close ties with the masses and open-mindedly studying.

【门静脉】ménjìngmài 由胃、肠、脾、胰腺、胆囊等的静脉汇流而成的较大的静脉。门静脉流入肝脏又分成很多小静脉。portal vein, the large vein conveying blood to the liver from the veins of the stomach, intestines, spleen, pancreas, gall, etc. subdividing into many smaller veins after flowing into liver

【门镜】ménjìng 一种安装在房门上的透明小圆镜，屋里人可通过它看清门外的来人。peephole in a door；俗称 popularly called 猫眼 māoyǎn

【门坎】ménkǎn same as 门槛 ménkǎn

【门槛】ménkǎn ❶（～儿 ménkǎnr）门框下部挨着地面的横木（也有用石头的）threshold (sometimes stones)；（图见 ☞ figure for 房子 fáng•zi on p. 550）❷〈方 *dial*.〉窍门，也指找窍门或占便宜的本领 trick；know-how：你不懂～。You don't know the knack.｜他～精，不会上当。He is too smart to be taken in.‖also 门坎 ménkǎn

【门可罗雀】mén kě luó què 大门前面可以张网捕雀；形容宾客稀少，十分冷落 you can catch sparrows on the doorstep；(fig.) visitors are few and far between

【门客】ménkè 封建官僚贵族家里养的帮闲或帮忙的人 aristocrat's hanger-on

【门口】ménkǒu（～儿 ménkǒur）门跟前 entrance；doorway：学校～ school entrance

【门框】ménkuàng 门扇四周固定在墙上的框子 door frame；（图见 ☞ figure for 房子 fáng•zi on p. 550）

【门廊】ménláng ❶ 连接院门和屋门的廊子 porch ❷ 屋门前的廊子 portico

【门类】ménlèi 依照事物的特性把相同的集中在一起而分成的类 class；kind；category；department：～繁多 numerous categories｜～齐全 complete with all the necessary departments

【门里出身】mén•li chūshēn〈方 *dial*.〉出身于具有某种专业或技术传统的家庭或行业 born of a family with a certain traditional skill or trade：说到变戏法，他是～。Talking of conjurers, he comes from a family of professionals.

【门帘】ménlián（～儿 ménliánr）门上挂的帘子 door curtain；also 门帘子 ménlián•zi

【门联】ménlián（～儿 ménliánr）门上的对联 scrolls pasted on either side of a door forming a couplet；door jamb couplet

【门脸儿】ménliǎnr〈方 *dial*.〉❶ 城门附近的地方 vicinity of a city gate ❷ 商店的门面 facade of a shop

【门铃】ménlíng（～儿 ménlíngr）安装在门里边的铃铛或电铃，门外的人可在门上拉铃或按电钮唤人开门 doorbell

【门楼】ménlóu（～儿 ménlóur）大门上边牌楼式的顶 arch over a gateway

【门路】mén•lu ❶ 做事的诀窍；解决问题的途径 way to do sth.：广开生产～ tap new sources of production ❷ 特指能达到个人目的的途径 social connection by which one can get what he wants；pull：走～solicit help from potential backers｜钻～ jockey for advantage

【门楣】ménméi ❶ 门框上端的横木 lintel of a door；（图见 ☞ figure for 房子 fáng•zi on p. 550）❷ 指门第 family status：光耀～ bring honour to one's family

【门面】mén•mian 商店房屋沿街的部分 facade of a shop；〈比喻 *fig*.〉外表 appearance：装修～ decorate the facade of a shop｜支撑～keep up appearances；put on a front

【门面话】mén•mianhuà 应酬的或冠冕堂皇而不解决问题的话 formal and insincere remarks；lip service

【门牌】ménpái 钉在大门外的牌子，上面标明地区或街道名称和房子号码等 house number plate, showing district, street name and house number

【门票】ménpiào 公园、博物馆等的入场券（of park, museum, etc.）entrance ticket

【门儿清】ménrqīng〈方 *dial*.〉了解得非常清楚；很懂行 know very well；know inside out

【门人】ménrén ❶ same as 学生 xuéshēng ② ❷ same as 门客 ménkè

【门扇】ménshàn same as 门 mén ②：～上贴着春联。There are Spring Festival couplets on the door leaves.

【门神】mén•shén 旧俗门上贴的神像，用来驱逐鬼怪（迷信）(superstition) door-god whose picture was oft. pasted on the front door of a house in old China, as a talisman

【门生】ménshēng ❶ same as 学生 xuéshēng ②：得意～ one's brilliant student ❷ 科举考试及第的人对主考官的自称 me；I；your student (term used by a successful candidate in an imperial examination to refer to himself before the chief examiner)

【门市】ménshì 商店零售货物或某些服务性行业的业务 retail sales:～部 retail department|今天是星期天,所以～很好。Today is Sunday, so retail sales are brisk.

【门闩】ménshuān 门关上后,插在门内使门推不开的木棍或铁棍 door bolt (wood or iron); also 门栓 ménshuān

【门厅】méntīng 大门内的厅堂 entrance hall

【门庭】méntíng ❶ 门口和庭院 courtyard:洒扫～ clean the courtyard|～若市。The courtyard is alive with activity. ❷ 指家庭或门第 family status:改换～change one's family status|光耀～ bring honour to one's family

【门庭若市】méntíng ruò shì 门口和庭院里热闹得像市场一样,形容交际来往的人很多 the doorway to the chamber looks like a marketplace; courtyard is as crowded as a marketplace — a much visited house or a shop whose business is booming

【门徒】méntú same as 学生 xuéshēng ②;弟子 disciple; follower; adherent

【门外汉】ménwàihàn 外行人 layman:他在体育方面完全是个～。He is a layman in sports.

【门卫】ménwèi 守卫在门口的人 entrance guard

【门下】ménxià ❶ 门客 aristocrat's hanger-on ❷ same as 学生 xuéshēng ② ❸ 指可以传授知识或技艺的人的跟前 study under sb. with a special skill:我想投在您老的～。I want to study under you.|许多青年作家都出于他的～。Many young writer has studied under him.

【门限】ménxiàn 〈书 *fml.*〉 same as 门槛 ménkǎn ①

【门牙】ményá 门齿的通称 popularly known as 门齿 ménchǐ

【门诊】ménzhěn 医生在医院或诊所里给不住院的病人看病 outpatient service

【门子】mén·zi ❶ 指衙门里或贵族、达官家里看门管传达的人 gatekeeper or doorman at a yamen or at the house of a senior official ❷ same as 门路 mén·lu ②:找～ solicit social connections ❸〈方 *dial.*〉〈量词 *classifier*〉相当于'件'(equal to) piece; item:这～亲事老两口很称心。The elderly couple is satisfied with this marriage contract.

扪 mén 〈书 *fml.*〉按;摸 touch; feel:～心 search one's heart

【扪心】ménxīn 〈书 *fml.*〉摸摸胸口,表示反省 self-search; search one's heart:～自问 examine or search one's conscience|清夜～search one's heart in the depth of night

钔 mén 金属元素,符号 Md (mendelevium)。有放射性,由人工核反应获得。mendelevium (Md); radioactive metal element obtained from artificial nuclear reaction

璊(璊) mén 〈书 *fml.*〉赤色的玉 red jade

亹 mén 亹源(Ményuán),地名,在青海。今作门源。Menyuan, name of a place in Qinghai Province, present-day 门源 Ményuán

☞ wěi on p. 1997

mèn (ㄇㄣˋ)

闷 mèn ❶ 心情不舒畅;心烦 bored; depressed; in low spirits:愁～feel gloomy|～～不乐 depressed ❷ 密闭;不透气 tightly closed; sealed:窒～ stuffy|～子车 boxcar

☞ mēn on p. 1320

【闷沉沉】mènchénchén (～的 mènchénchén·de)形容心情郁闷 depressed; gloomy:整天呆在家里,心里～的。I feel depressed staying at home all day long.

☞ mēnchénchén on p. 1320

【闷罐车】mènguànchē 〈方 *dial.*〉闷子车 boxcar

【闷棍】mèngùn 乘人不备时狠狠打的一棍 staggering blow (with a cudgel);〈比喻 *fig.*〉突如其来的沉重打击 unexpected blow:打～rob a victim after beating him unconscious with a club|歹徒从背后给他一个～。A thug struck him a blow from behind.|为了这事我吃了他一～。Owing to this matter, I was greeted with the sharp end of his tongue.

【闷葫芦】mènhú·lu ❶〈比喻 *fig.*〉极难猜透而令人纳闷的话或事情 enigma; puzzle; riddle:这几句没头没脑的话真是个～。Those abrupt remarks were a puzzle to everyone. ❷〈比喻 *fig.*〉不爱说话的人 man of few words:她是个～,一天到晚难得张口。Reticent by nature, she speaks hardly a word the whole day.

【闷葫芦罐儿】mènhú·luguànr 扑满 earthenware money box; piggy bank

【闷倦】mènjuàn 烦闷厌倦,无精打采 bored and listless:无所事事,～难耐 feel bored to distraction at having nothing to do

【闷雷】mènléi 声音低沉的雷 muffled thunder;〈比喻 *fig.*〉精神上突然受到的打击 unpleasant shock

【闷闷不乐】mèn mèn bù lè 因有不如意的事而心里不快活 depressed; in low spirits:他这几天～,不知出了什么事儿。He is in low spirits these days and no one knows why.

【闷气】mènqì 郁结在心里没有发泄的怨恨或愤怒 sulks:有意见就提,别生～! Speak, if you have an opinion to express, don't just sulk.

☞ mēnqì on p. 1320

【闷子车】mèn·zichē 铁路上指带有铁棚的货车(就没有窗户不通气而言)。有的地区也叫闷罐车。railway boxcar, windowless freight train with an iron ceiling; also 闷罐车 mènguànchē in some places

焖 mèn 紧盖锅盖,用微火把食物煮熟或炖熟 boil in a covered pot over a low heat; braise:～饭 cook rice over a low heat|油～笋 braised bamboo shoots with vegetable oil|～

一锅肉 stew a pot of pork

懑(懣) mèn 〈书 *fml*.〉 ❶ 烦闷 feel vexed ❷ 愤慨;生气 angry; indignant:愤～ feel indignant

·men (·ㄇㄣ)

们 ·men 用在代词或指人的名词后面,表示复数 [used after a personal pronoun or a noun referring to a person to form a plural]: 我～ we|你～ you|乡亲～ folks|同志～ comrades 注意 **NOTE**:名词前有数量词时,后面不加'们',例如不说'三个孩子～'。们 is not to be used after a noun that has a numeral modifier, as in 三个孩子(three children), instead of 三个孩子们.

mēng (ㄇㄥ)

蒙[1](矇) mēng ❶ 欺骗 cheat; deceive:欺上～下 hoodwink those above and delude those below|别～人,谁不知道你的用意! Stop kidding! Everyone knows your intentions. ❷ 胡乱猜测 make a wild guess:想好了再回答,别瞎～。No wild guesses! Answer after thinking it over.

蒙[2] mēng 昏迷;神志不清 unconscious; senseless:头发～ feel one's head swim

☞ méng on p.1324, Měng on p.1326 and 矇 méng on p.1326

【蒙蒙亮】mēngmēngliàng 天刚有些亮 daybreak

【蒙骗】mēngpiàn 欺骗 cheat; deceive:～顾客 cheat customers

【蒙事】mēngshì 〈方 *dial*.〉做假骗人 hoodwink; deceive

【蒙松雨】mēng·songyǔ 〈方 *dial*.〉(～儿 mēng·songyǔr)很细的雨 fine drizzle

【蒙头转向】mēng tóu zhuàn xiàng 形容头脑昏乱,辨不清方向 lose one's bearings; be utterly confused

méng (ㄇㄥˊ)

尨 méng [尨茸](méngróng)〈书 *fml*.〉蓬松 fluffy;

☞ máng on p.1303

氓(甿) méng 〈古代 *arch*.〉称百姓(多指外来的 usu. person from another place) common people; also 萌 méng

☞ máng on p.1304

虻(蝱) méng 昆虫的一科,体长椭圆形,头阔,触角短,复眼大,黑绿色,口吻粗,腹部长大。生活在田野杂草中,雄的吸植物的汁液或花蜜,雌的吸人和动物的血液。幼虫生活在泥土、池沼、稻田中,吃昆虫、草根等。horsefly (*Tabanidae*); gadfly; any of various flies of oval body, wide head, short feelers, large, black and green compound eyes, that lives on insects and grass roots in grassland, the male feeding on nectar, the female on human or animal blood, the young living in soil, pools and fields

萌[1] méng 萌芽;萌生 sprout; bud ◇故态复～ relapse into one's old bad habits

萌[2] méng 〈古 *arch*.〉 same as 氓 méng

【萌动】méngdòng ❶ (植物)开始发芽(of plants) sprout; shoot forth; germinate; bud: 草木～。The plants are coming into leaf. ❷ (事物)开始发动 (of sth.) start:春意～。Spring is stirring.

【萌发】méngfā ❶ 种子或孢子发芽 sprout; shoot forth; bud; germinate:雨后杂草～。Weeds began to sprout after the rain. ❷〈比喻 *fig*.〉事物发生 emerge; come forth:～一种强烈的求知欲望 be seized with a thirst for knowledge

【萌生】méngshēng 开始发生;产生(多用于抽象事物 oft. referring to sth. abstract) come into being; arise:～邪念 conceive an evil idea|～一线希望 arouse a glimmer of hope

【萌芽】méngyá ❶ 植物生芽 sprout; bud; germinate;〈比喻 *fig*.〉事物刚发生 originate:～状态 embryonic stage ❷〈比喻 *fig*.〉新生的未长成的事物 rudiment; shoot; seed; germ: 新型生产关系的～ budding of a new pattern of production relationships

蒙 méng ❶ 遮盖 cover:～头盖脑 cover head|用手～住眼 cover somebody's eyes with hands|～上一张纸 cover a piece of paper ❷ 受 suffer:～难 fall into imminent danger|～你照料,非常感谢。Thank you very much for your kind care. ❸ 蒙昧 ignorance:启～ enlighten ❹ (Méng)姓 a surname

☞ mēng on p.1324 and Měng on p.1326

【蒙蔽】méngbì 隐瞒真相,使人上当 hoodwink; deceive; hide the truth from:花言巧语～不了人。Honeyed words do not fool any one.

【蒙尘】méngchén 〈书 *fml*.〉蒙受风尘(指君主因战乱逃亡在外)(of the emperor fleeing the capital because of the turmoil of war) be exposed to wind and dust:天子～。The emperor fled the capital.

【蒙馆】méngguǎn 〈旧时 *old*〉指对儿童进行启蒙教育的私塾 private school

【蒙汗药】ménghànyào 戏曲小说中指能使人暂时失去知觉的药(in operas and classic novels) narcotic that causes loss of consciousness

【蒙哄】ménghǒng 哄骗 deceive; hoodwink; swindle; cheat:～顾客 cheat customers

【蒙混】ménghùn 用欺骗的手段使人相信虚假的事物 deceive or mislead:～过关 get by under false pretences

【蒙眬】ménglóng 快要睡着或刚醒时，两眼半开半闭，看东西模糊的样子 half asleep; drowsy; somnolent：睡眼～eyes heavy with sleep; also 矇眬 ménglóng

【蒙昧】méngmèi ❶ 未开化；没有文化 barbaric; uncivilized; uncultured：～时代 age of barbarism ❷ 不懂事理；愚昧 ignorant; benighted; unenlightened：～无知 unenlightened; benighted; childishly ignorant

【蒙昧主义】méngmèi zhǔyì 一种认为人类社会的种种罪恶都是文明和科学发展的结果，主张回复到原始的蒙昧状态的思想 obscurantism, opposition to the increase and spread of knowledge, considering all evil in human society to be the result of civilization and scientific development, advocating a return to primitive and uncivilized times

【蒙蒙】méngméng ❶ 雨点很细小 drizzly：～细雨 fine drizzle; also 濛濛 méngméng ❷ 模糊不清的样子 misty：云雾～ misty

【蒙难】méng//nàn（有名、有地位的人）遭受到灾祸（of a famous or influential person) be confronted with danger; fall into the clutches of an enemy

【蒙师】méngshī〈旧时 *old*〉指对学童进行启蒙教育的老师。后泛指启蒙老师。private school teacher who teaches pupils to read and write; referring to teacher who initiates students into a specific field of study

【蒙受】méngshòu 受到；遭受 suffer; sustain：～耻辱 be subjected to humiliation｜～恩惠 be bestowed with a favour｜～不白之冤 suffer an injustice

【蒙太奇】méngtàiqí 电影用语，有剪辑和组合的意思。它是电影导演的重要表现方法之一，为表现影片的主题思想，把许多镜头组织起来，使构成一部前后连贯、首尾完整的电影片。montage, technique of combining in a single composition pictorial elements from various sources, as parts of different photographs or fragments of printing, either to give the impression that the elements belonged together originally, or to allow each element to retain its separate identity as a means of adding interest or meaning to the composition ［法 French: montage］

【蒙童】méngtóng〈旧时 *old*〉称刚刚读书识字的儿童 child who has just started to learn to read and write

【蒙学】méngxué same as 蒙馆 méngguǎn

【蒙药】méngyào 麻醉剂的通称 common name for 麻醉剂 mázuìjì

【蒙冤】méng//yuān 蒙受冤枉 be wronged; suffer an injustice：亲人～ relatives suffer injustice

盟[1] méng ❶〈旧时 *old*〉指宣誓缔约，现在指团体和团体、阶级和阶级或国和国的联合 originally referring to taking an oath and making a treaty, now indicating alliance between groups, classes or states：工农联～ worker-peasant alliance｜同～国 allied country ❷ 结拜的（弟兄）sworn (brothers)：～兄 sworn elder brother｜～弟 sworn younger brother ❸ 内蒙古自治区的行政区域，包括若干旗、县、市 league (administrative division of the Inner Mongolian Autonomous Region, including prefectures, counties and cities)

盟[2] méng（旧读 formerly pronounced míng）发（誓）take an oath

【盟邦】méngbāng 结成同盟的国家 allied country; ally

【盟国】méngguó same as 盟邦 méngbāng

【盟誓】méng//shì 发誓；宣誓 take an oath：盟个誓 take an oath｜对天～ swear by Heaven; also 明誓 míng//shì

【盟誓】méngshì〈书 *fml.*〉盟约 treaty of alliance

【盟兄弟】méngxiōngdì 把兄弟 sworn brothers

【盟友】méngyǒu ❶ 结成同盟的朋友 sworn friends; ally ❷ 指盟国 allied countries

【盟约】méngyuē 缔结同盟时所订立的誓约或条约 oath of alliance; treaty of alliance

【盟主】méngzhǔ〈古代 *arch.*〉诸侯同盟中的领袖。后代用来称一些集体活动的首领或倡导者。leader (or chief) of an alliance; overlord

甍 méng〈书 *fml.*〉屋脊 ridge of a roof：雕～ carved ridge of a roof

瞢 méng〈书 *fml.*〉目不明 (of eyes) blurred; dim：目光～然 have dim eyesight

幪 méng ☞［帡幪］(píngméng) on p. 1490

濛 méng〈书 *fml.*〉形容细雨 drizzle：细雨其～ drizzling rain

【濛濛】méngméng same as 蒙蒙 méngméng ①

檬 méng ☞［柠檬］(níngméng) on p. 1417

曚 méng［曚昽］(ménglóng)〈书 *fml.*〉日光不明 (of daylight) dim

朦 méng［朦胧］(ménglóng) ❶ 月光不明 (of moonlight) dim ❷ 不清楚；模糊 obscure; hazy：暮色～ evening haze｜烟雾～ misty

鹲 méng 鸟类的一属，身体大，灰色或白色，嘴大而直，尾部有长羽毛。生活在热带海洋上，吃鱼类。tropicbird (*Phaethontidae*); tropical marine bird with a large grey or white body, long straight beak, and long tail feathers, that lives on tropical oceans, and feeds on fish

礞 méng［礞石］(méngshí) 岩石，有青礞石和金礞石两种。青礞石呈不规则的块状，青灰色或灰绿色。金礞石呈不规则的块状或粒状，棕黄色。可入药。chlorite schist, any of a class of crystalline metamorphic rocks, dividing into green chlorite schist and golden chlorite schist, the former appearing as irregular lumps, dark green or grey green in colour, the latter, as irregular lumps or grains, yellowish brown in colour, used for medicine

矇 méng 〈书 *fml*.〉眼睛失明 blind;
☞ 蒙 mēng on p.1324

【矇眬】ménglóng same as 蒙眬 ménglóng

艨 méng [艨艟](méngchōng)〈古代 *arch*.〉战船 warship; also 蒙冲 méngchōng

měng (ㄇㄥˇ)

勐[1] měng 〈书 *fml*.〉勇敢 brave

勐[2] měng 云南西双版纳傣族地区旧时的行政区划单位 *meng*; former administrative district in Xishuangbanna, Yunnan Province

猛 měng ❶ 猛烈 fierce; violent:勇～ valiant|突飞～进 advance by leaps and bounds|炮火很～。There was heavy gunfire. ❷ 忽然:突然 suddenly:他听到枪声,～地从屋里跳出来。Hearing gunfire, he leapt to his feet and dashed out of the room. ❸ 把力气集中地使出来 vigorously; with sudden force:～着劲儿干 work with vim and vigour

【猛不丁】měng·budīng 〈方 *dial*.〉猛然;突然 suddenly; unexpectedly:他～地大喊了一声。He suddenly gave out a yell.

【猛不防】měng·bufáng 突然而来不及防备 by surprise; unexpectedly; unawares:他正说得起劲,～背后有人推了他一把。As he was talking, and warming to his theme, someone unexpectedly pushed him from behind.

【猛孤丁】měnggūdīng 〈方 *dial*.〉猛然;突然 suddenly; abruptly

【猛将】měngjiàng 勇猛的将领 valiant general; 〈比喻 *fig*.〉不顾艰险而勇往直前的人 valiant person who takes hardships in his stride

【猛进】měngjìn 不怕困难,勇敢前进;很快地前进 push ahead vigorously; advance in long and rapid strides:高歌～ stride forward singing songs of triumph|突飞～advance by leaps and bounds

【猛劲儿】měngjìnr ❶ 集中用力气 spurt of energy:一～,就超过了前边的人。Summoning a spurt of energy, (I) overtook the others. ❷ 集中起来一下子使出来的力气 great force:搬重东西要用～。(You) have to exert great effort when moving heavy articles. ❸ 勇猛的力量 great vigour:这小伙子干活有股子～。This young chap works with vim and vigour.

【猛可】měngkě (～的 měngkě·de)突然(多见于早期白话 oft. in the earlier vernacular) suddenly

【猛烈】měngliè ❶ 气势大,力量大 fierce; vigorous; violent:～的炮火 heavy shellfire|这里气候寒冷,风势～。The weather here is bitterly cold with violent gusts of wind. ❷ 急剧 furious:心脏～地跳动着。The heart is beating furiously.

【猛犸】měngmǎ 古哺乳动物,形状和大小都跟现代的象相似,全身有长毛,门齿向上弯曲,生活在寒冷地带,是第四纪的动物,已经绝种 mammoth (*Mammuthus primigenius*); large, elephantine mammal of the extinct genus *Mammuthus*, from the Pleistocene Epoch, with hairy skin and ridged molar teeth, that lived in frigid zones; also 毛象 máoxiàng

【猛禽】měngqín 凶猛的鸟类,如鹫、鹰、枭等。嘴短而尖锐,上嘴尖有钩,翼大,龙骨很发达,善飞行,脚短而健壮,趾有钩状的爪,视力敏锐,吃其他鸟类和小动物。bird of prey; any of numerous predacious, flesh-eating birds, such as the eagle, hawk, kite, vulture, falcon, or owl, with a sharp, downwardly curving beak, broad wingspan, a robust sternum, capable of soaring flight, with short, strong legs, hooked talons, sharp eyesight; lives on other birds and small animals

【猛然】měngrán 忽然;骤然 suddenly; abruptly:～回头 hastily turn one's head|～一惊 be shocked suddenly

【猛士】měngshì 勇敢有力的人;勇士 brave and strong man; brave warrior

【猛兽】měngshòu 指哺乳动物中体大而性情凶猛的食肉类,如虎、狮、豹等。这类动物捕食其他动物,有的危害人类。beast of prey; flesh-eating predatory mammal, such as the tiger, lion, leopard, etc. that lives on other animals, and sometimes assaults humans

【猛省】měngxǐng same as 猛醒 měngxǐng

【猛醒】měngxǐng 猛然觉悟;忽然明白过来 suddenly realize or wake up; also 猛省 měngxǐng

【猛鸷】měngzhì 指鹰 eagle

【猛子】měng·zi 下水游泳时头朝下钻入水中的动作 dive deep into the water:扎～ make a dive|他身子一纵,一个～就不见了。He dived into the water and disappeared.

蒙 Měng 蒙古族 Mongol ethnic group
☞ mēng on p.1324 and méng on p.1324

【蒙古包】měnggǔbāo 蒙古族牧民居住的圆顶帐篷,用毡子做成 yurt, circular, movable dwelling used by Mongolian people, made of felt

【蒙古人种】Měnggǔ rénzhǒng 世界三大人种之一,体质特征是皮肤黄色,头发黑而直,脸平,主要分布在亚洲东部和东南部 Mongoloid race, one of the three major races in the world, characterized by yellow skin, black, straight hair, and prominent cheekbones, mainly living in East and Southeast Asia; also 黄种 Huángzhǒng

【蒙古族】Měnggǔzú ❶ 我国少数民族之一,分布在内蒙古、吉林、黑龙江、辽宁、宁夏、新疆、甘肃、青海、河北、河南 Mongolian minority ethnic group, distributed throughout the Inner Mongolia, Jilin, Heilongjiang, Liaoning, Ningxia, Xinjiang, Gansu, Qinghai, Hebei and Henan ❷ 蒙古国人数最多的民族 Mongolians or Mongols, the largest ethnic group in the state of Mongolia

【蒙族】Měngzú 蒙古族的简称 abbr. for 蒙古族 Měnggǔzú

锰 měng 金属元素,符号 Mn (manganese)。银白色,质硬而脆。主要用来制造锰钢等合金。manganese (Mn); silver white, hard and brittle metal element, mainly used for making manganese steel, etc.

蜢 měng ☞ 蚱蜢 zhàměng on p. 2406

艋 měng ☞ [舴艋] (zéměng) on p. 2399

獴 měng 哺乳动物的一属,身体长,脚短,口吻尖,耳朵小。捕食蛇、蛙、鼠、鱼、蟹等动物。蟹獴就是獴属的动物。mongoose (*Herpestes*), mammal with a long body, short legs, sharp muzzle, small ears, that feeds on snakes, frogs, rats, fish, crabs, etc. The crab-eating mongoose is of the same genus.

懵(懞) měng 懵懂 muddled; ignorant: ~然无知 be totally ignorant

【懵懂】měngdǒng 糊涂;不明事理 muddled; ignorant: 懵懵懂懂 muddled-headed | 聪明一世,~一时 smart all one's life but foolish just once

蠓 měng 昆虫的一科,成虫体很小,褐色或黑色,触角细长,翅短而宽。幼虫长圆柱状,灰白色或带黄白色,表面光滑。蛹长椭圆形,褐色。卵长纺锤形,黄白色。某些雌蠓吸食人畜的血液。有些蠓能传染疾病。biting midge (*Ceratopogonidae*); any of the minute biting gnats. Adults have a small brown or black body with long, fine feelers and short, wide wings while its larvae have a long, round, greyish white or yellowish white body and smooth skin. Its pupa has an oval, brown body, and its eggs are spindle-like, and yellowish white. Some female midges suck the blood of human beings or animals. Some midges may spread disease.

【蠓虫儿】měngchóngr 蠓科的昆虫 biting midge

mèng (ㄇㄥˋ)

孟 mèng ❶ 指农历一季的第一个月 first month of a lunar season; ☞ 仲 zhòng on p. 2491 and 季 jì on p. 918 ❷〈旧时 *old*〉在兄弟排行的次序里代表最大的 eldest among brothers ❸ (Mèng) 姓 a surname

【孟春】mèngchūn 春季的第一个月,即农历正月 first month of spring; first lunar month

【孟冬】mèngdōng 冬季的第一个月,即农历十月 1st month of winter, 10th lunar month

【孟浪】mènglàng〈书 *fml.*〉鲁莽;冒失 rash; impetuous: ~从事 act rashly | 话语~ rash words; wild words

【孟秋】mèngqiū 秋季的第一个月,即农历七月 first month of autumn; seventh lunar month

【孟什维克】mèngshíwéikè 俄国社会民主工党的一个机会主义派别。1903 年俄国社会民主工党召开第二次代表大会,在讨论党纲及组织原则问题上分成两派,反对列宁主张的机会主义分子在选举党的领导机构时获得少数选票,所以有这称号。后来堕落为资产阶级反革命派,1912 年被驱逐出党。Menshevik (Russian word meaning 'minority', as opposed to 'Bolshevik', meaning 'majority'), an anti-Leninist opportunist fraction of the Russian Social-Democratic Workers' Party that won a minority number of votes during election for the leadership at the Party's Second National Congress in 1903 because of its opposition to Lenin's ideas during discussions on the Party Constitution and organizational principles. The Mensheviks later degenerated and became a counter-revolutionary bourgeois fraction and was expelled from the Party in 1912. [俄 Russian: меньшевик,少数派 minority]

【孟夏】mèngxià 夏季的第一个月,即农历四月 first month of summer; fourth lunar month

梦(夢) mèng ❶ 睡眠时局部大脑皮层还没有完全停止活动而引起的脑中的表象活动 dream, a succession of images, thoughts, or emotions passing through the mind during sleep when part of the cerebral cortex is still in action ❷ 做梦 dream: ~见 dream of ❸〈比喻 *fig.*〉幻想 fancy: ~想 fancy

【梦话】mènghuà ❶ 睡梦中说的话。睡眠时抑制作用没有扩散到大脑皮层的全部,语言中枢有时还能活动,这时就会有说梦话的现象。talking while asleep; somniloquy; sleep-talking; words uttered in one's sleep, resulting from the working of the language centre, as inhibition of function during sleep does not spread through the whole cerebral cortex; also 梦呓 mèngyì or 呓语 yìyǔ ❷〈比喻 *fig.*〉不切实际,不能实现的话 nonsense; daydream

【梦幻】mènghuàn 梦境 dream: 离奇的遭遇犹如~ dream-like bizarre experience | 从~中醒来 wake up from a dream

【梦幻泡影】mènghuàn pàoyǐng 原是佛经的话,说世界上的事物都像梦境、幻术、水泡和影子一样空虚。今比喻空虚而容易破灭的幻想 pipe dream, originally a Buddhist term meaning that all things on earth are as empty and illusory as dreamland, magic, bubbles and shadow; (fig.) empty and easily shattered fantasy

【梦境】mèngjìng 梦中经历的情境,多用来比喻美妙的境界(usu. fig.) dreamland; dream world: 乍到这山水如画的胜地,如入~一般。On arriving at the famous scenic spot, (I) felt as if I were in a dreamland.

【梦寐】mèngmèi 睡梦 dream; sleep: ~难忘 be

unable to forget sth. even in one's dreams|～以求 long for something. day and night

【梦寐以求】mèngmèi yǐ qiú 睡梦中都想着寻找,形容迫切地希望着 crave sth. to the extent that one even dreams about it; long (or yearn) for sth. day and night

【梦乡】mèngxiāng 指睡熟时候的境界 dreamland:他实在太疲倦了,一躺下便进入了～。He was so tired that as soon as his head hit the pillow, he entered dreamland.

【梦想】mèngxiǎng ❶ 幻想;妄想 dream; illusion; fancy; fanciful vision; vain hope; wishful thinking:他对未来充满～。He is full of fancy for the future. ❷ 渴望 dream of; cherish an earnest desire; want so much to:他小时候～着当一名飞行员。He dreamed of being a pilot in his childhood.

【梦魇】mèngyǎn 睡眠中做一种感到压抑而呼吸困难的梦,多由疲劳过度,消化不良或大脑皮层过度紧张引起 nightmare; oppressive and suffocating dream in sleep, mostly caused by fatigue, indigestion or excessive tension of the cerebral cortex

【梦遗】mèngyí 梦中遗精 wet dream; involuntary emission of semen during sleep; nocturnal emission

【梦呓】mèngyì same as 梦话 mènghuà

mī (ㄇㄧ)

咪 mī [咪咪]〈拟声词 *onom.*〉形容猫叫的声音 mew; miaow; meow; vocal sound made by a cat:小猫～叫。A cat mews.

眯(瞇) mī ❶ 眼皮微微合上 narrow one's eyes:～缝 narrow one's eyes|～着眼睛笑 narrow one's eyes into a smile ❷〈方 *dial.*〉小睡 nap:～一会儿 take a nap

☞ mí on p.1330

【眯瞪】mī·deng〈方 *dial.*〉小睡 nap:困了,就先～一会儿。Take a nap if you are sleepy.

【眯盹儿】mī//dǔnr〈方 *dial.*〉打盹儿 doze off; take a nap:困极了先眯个盹儿。Take a nap first if (you) feel too sleepy.

【眯缝】mī·feng 眼皮合拢而不全闭 narrow one's eyes:他不说话,只是～着眼睛笑。He didn't say a word, but smiled with narrow eyes.

mí (ㄇㄧˊ)

M

弥(彌) mí ❶ 遍;满 full; overflowing:～漫 inundate; be covered with; be filled with; be permeated by; fill the air; spread all over; permeate|～天大谎 monstrous lie; outrageous lie ❷ 填满;遮掩 cover; fill:～补 cover; make up for; remedy; make good|～缝 cover up; gloss over ❸ 更加 more; still more; even more:欲盖～彰 try to cover up a fault (mistake, crime, etc.) only to make it more conspicuous|～足珍贵 more precious; more valuable ❹ (Mí)姓 a surname

【弥补】míbǔ 把不够的部分填足 make up for; remedy; make up; make good; cover a deficit; cover a loss:～缺陷 remedy a defect|不可～的损失 irreparable loss

【弥封】mífēng 把试卷上填写姓名的地方折角或盖纸糊住,目的是防止舞弊 fold a corner to cover or seal the examinee's name on an exam paper so as to prevent fraudulence

【弥缝】míféng 设法遮掩或补救缺点、错误,不使别人发觉 (of faults, mistakes, blunders, crimes, etc.) cover up; gloss over; plug up holes

【弥合】míhé 使愈合 heal; close; bridge:～伤口 heal a wound ◇～感情上的裂痕 close a rift

【弥勒】Mílè 佛教菩萨之一,佛寺中常有他的塑像,胸腹袒露,满面笑容 Maitreya; Bodhisattva as represented by a very stout monk with a broad smile and naked breast and exposed paunch [梵 Sanskrit: Maitreya]

【弥留】míliú〈书 *fml.*〉病重快要死了 be seriously ill and dying:～之际 on one's deathbed

【弥漫】mímàn (烟尘、雾气、水等)充满;布满 (of smoke, mist, water, etc.) be about inundate; be covered with; be filled with; be permeated by; fill the air; spread all over; permeate:烟雾～ be filled with smoke|乌云～了天空。The sky is covered up with dark clouds. also 瀰漫 mímàn

【弥蒙】míméng 形容烟雾等茫茫一片看不分明 misty; foggy:云雾～ enveloped or veiled in a thick mist|硝烟～ filled with the smoke of gunpowder; also 瀰濛 míméng

【弥撒】mí·sa 天主教的一种宗教仪式,用面饼和葡萄酒表示耶稣的身体和血来祭祀天主 Mass; Catholic rite consisting of prayers and consecration of bread and wine as the body and blood (sacrifice) of Christ to God: [拉 Latin: missa]

【弥散】mísàn (光线、气体、声音等)向四外扩散 (of light, air, sound, etc.) spread or diffuse in all directions

【弥天】mítiān 满天,形容极大 monstrous; huge:～大祸 great misfortune; great trouble; disaster; calamity|～大罪 great crime; heinous crime

【弥天大谎】mí tiān dà huǎng 极大的谎话 whopper; monstrous lie; outrageous lie

【弥陀】Mítuó 阿弥陀佛的略称 short term for 阿弥陀佛 Ēmítuófó; also 弥陀佛 Mítuófó

【弥望】míwàng〈书 *fml.*〉充满视野;满眼 as far as one's vision extends:春色～。It is spring everywhere.

【弥月】míyuè〈书 *fml.*〉❶ (初生婴儿)满月 completion of the first month after the birth of a baby ❷ 满一个月；整月 a full month：新婚～。It's one month after the wedding.

迷 mí ❶ 分辨不清，失去判断能力 be unable to tell this from that; lose one's sense of judgement; be lost; be confused：～了路 get lost; lose one's way｜～了方向 lose one's bearings; get lost ❷ 因对某人或某一事物发生特殊爱好而沉醉 indulge in; be fascinated by; be crazy about：～恋 indulge in; be addicted to｜看电影入了～ be addicted to films ❸ 沉醉于某一事物的人 devotee (of sth.); fan; enthusiast：球～ ball fan｜戏～ theatre-goers ❹ 使看不清；使迷惑；使陶醉 confuse; perplex; fascinate; enchant; enthral：财～心窍 be obsessed by lust for money｜景色～人 captivating scenery; enchanting scenery

【迷彩】mícǎi 指能起迷惑作用使人不易分辨的色彩 colours that confuse or mislead people：～服 camouflage clothes; fatigue clothes (or clothing)

【迷瞪】mí·deng 〈方 *dial.*〉心里迷惑；糊涂 muddle; confuse; get muddled; get confused

【迷宫】mígōng 门户道路复杂难辨，人进去不容易出来的建筑物 labyrinth; maze; building with an intricate network of winding passages hard to follow without losing one's way

【迷航】míháng (飞机、轮船等)迷失航行方向 (of a plane, ship, etc.) drift off course; lose one's course; get lost

【迷糊】mí·hu (神志或眼睛)模糊不清 misted; blurred; dimmed; be unconscious; be muddle-headed：病人有时清楚，有时～。The patient is sometimes in his right mind and is sometimes unconscious.

【迷魂汤】míhúntāng 迷信所说地狱中使灵魂迷失本性的汤药 (superstition) a magic potion used in the hell to take the innate nature from the soul; 〈比喻 *fig.*〉迷惑人的语言或行为 words or acts that confuse or mislead people; also 迷魂药 míhúnyào

【迷魂阵】míhúnzhèn 〈比喻 *fig.*〉能使人迷惑的圈套、计谋 trick, trap or scheme that confuse or mislead people

【迷惑】mí·huò ❶ 辨不清是非；摸不着头脑 puzzle; confuse; perplex; baffle：～不解 feel puzzled; feel perplexed ❷ 使迷惑 confuse; mislead：花言巧语～不了人。No honeyed words can mislead people.

【迷津】míjīn 〈书 *fml.*〉使人迷惑的错误道路(津原指渡河的地方，后来多指处世的方向) misleading ferry; wrong road that misleads people (津 *jin* originally meant ferry, and has later been used to indicate the way one behaves)：指破～(点破错误的方向) show the misleading ferry (point out where a person has gone astray)

【迷离】mílí 模糊而难以分辨清楚 blurred; misted：～恍惚 completely confounded｜睡眼～ eyes dimmed with sleep

【迷恋】míliàn 对某一事物过度爱好而难以舍弃 be dead gone on sb. or sth.; be infatuated with; madly cling to：～酒色 be addicted to alcoholic drinking and women｜～家乡的特产 strong liking for the special products from one's native place

【迷路】mí//lù ❶ 迷失道路 lose one's way; get lost：山林中容易～。It's easy to get lost in mountain forests.｜走到半道上迷了路 get lost on one's way ❷ 〈比喻 *fig.*〉失去了正确的方向 lose one's right direction; go astray

【迷路】mílù ☞ 内耳 nèi'ěr on p.1398

【迷漫】mímàn 漫天遍野，茫茫一片，看不分明 boundless and indistinct; vast and hazy：烟雾～ be enveloped in mist; be covered in thick mist｜风雪～ be engulfed in a snowstorm

【迷茫】mímáng ❶ 广阔而看不清的样子 vast and hazy：大雪铺天盖地，原野一片～。The vast plain was obscured by the falling flakes of snow. ❷ (神情)迷离恍惚 completely confounded; confused; perplexed; dazed：神色～ look confounded; look confused; confused look on one's face｜小姑娘用～的眼光打量着陌生的来客。The little girl sized up the strange visitor with a confounded look.

【迷蒙】míméng ❶ 昏暗看不分明 vast and hazy; same as 迷茫 mímáng ①：烟雨～ enveloped in rain and mist｜夜雾～ under the thick pall of a night fog｜暮色～ be enshrouded in the deepening dusk; also 迷濛 míméng ❷ (神志)模糊不清 be unconscious：他从～中醒了过来。He regained consciousness from a state of delirium.

【迷梦】mímèng 沉迷不悟的梦想 pipe dream; fond illusion：他终于从～中觉醒过来。He finally aroused from a fond dream.

【迷你】mínǐ 指同类物品中较小的；小型的 mini：～裙(超短裙) mini-skirt｜～计算机(微型计算机) mini-computer

【迷人】mírén 使人陶醉；使人迷恋 enchanting; captivating; attractive：景色～ enchanting scenery

【迷失】míshī 弄不清(方向)；走错(道路) lose (one's way, etc.); take a wrong road

【迷途】mítú ❶ 迷失道路 lose one's way：～的羔羊 stray sheep ❷ 错误的道路 wrong path：误入～ go astray

【迷惘】míwǎng 由于分辨不清而困惑，不知怎么办 be perplexed; be at a loss：精神～ be listless; be absent-minded; look perplexed

【迷雾】míwù ❶ 浓厚的雾 dense fog：在～中看不清航道。It is hard to see a course clearly in heavy fog. ❷ 〈比喻 *fig.*〉使人迷失方向，脱离实际的事物 anything that misleads people

【迷信】míxìn ❶ 信仰神仙鬼怪等 superstition;

superstitious belief; blind faith; blind worship; belief in deities, immortals, ghosts, etc. ❷ 泛指盲目的信仰崇拜 (in a broad sense) have blind faith in; make a fetish of: 破除～,解放思想。Do away with blind faith and emancipate the mind.

【迷走神经】mízǒu-shénjīng 第十对脑神经,由延髓发出,分布在头、颈、胸、腹等部,有调节内脏、血管、腺体等机能的作用 vagus; vagus nerve; 10th pair of cranial nerves arising in the medulla oblongata, providing parasympathetic innervation to the head, neck, lungs, and most of the abdominal organs and adjusting the functions of the internal organs, blood vessels, glands, etc.

【迷醉】mízuì 迷恋,陶醉;沉迷 intoxicate; enchant; revel; go high: 采茶姑娘的歌声此起彼落,令人～。The hill reverberated with the sweet, modulating singing of the girls picking tea. | ～于过去,就会妨碍更好地前进。Resting on one's laurels will hinder further progress.

祢(禰) Mí 姓 a surname

眯(瞇) mí 尘埃等杂物进入眼中,使一时不能睁开看东西(of dust, etc.) get into one's eye: 沙子～了眼。The dust has got into (my) eye.

☞ mī on p.1328

猕(獼) mí ☞ below

【猕猴】míhóu 猴的一种,上身皮毛灰褐色,腰部以下橙黄色,有光泽,面部微红色,两颊有颊囊,臀部的皮特别厚,不生毛,尾短。以野果、野菜等为食物。macaque (*Macaca mulatta*); macacus monkey; rhesus monkey; monkey having a lustrous, greyish-brown fur on the upper part of its body and an orange fur on the lower part, a pink face, cheek pouches, thick-skinned, hairless buttocks and a short tail, feeding on wild fruits and wild vegetables

【猕猴桃】míhóutáo ❶ 落叶藤本植物,叶子互生,圆形或卵形,花黄色,浆果球形。果实可以吃,又可入药,茎皮纤维可以做纸,花可以提制香料。kiwi fruit (*Actinidia chinensis*); deciduous vine having alternate, orbicular or ovate leaves, yellow flowers and an edible, egg-sized pulpy fruit. The fruit is also used for the Chinese medicine, the skin fibres of its stem is used in making paper and its flowers in extracting essence. ❷ 这种植物的果实 fruit of the vine ‖ 有的地区叫羊桃或杨桃 also 羊桃 yángtáo or 杨桃 yángtáo in some areas

谜 mí ❶ 谜语 riddle; conundrum: 灯～ lantern riddles; riddles written on lanterns | 哑～ enigma; puzzle ❷〈比喻 *fig*.〉还没有弄明白的或难以理解的事物 enigma; mystery; puzzle; sth. that is not clear or difficult to understand: 这个问题到现在还是一个～,谁也猜不透。This problem remains a mystery to this day, and no one can figure it out.

☞ mèi on p.1330

【谜底】mídǐ ❶ 谜语的答案 answer to a riddle ❷〈比喻 *fig*.〉事情的真相 truth of a matter: 揭开～,真相大白。Everything fell into place after the truth was found out.

【谜面】mímiàn 指猜谜语时说出来或写出来供人做猜测线索的话 clue to a riddle; words said or written as clues for people guessing riddles

【谜团】mítuán〈比喻 *fig*.〉一连串捉摸不定的事物;疑团 enigma; mystery; a series of elusive matters

【谜语】míyǔ 暗射事物或文字等供人猜测的隐语。如'麻屋子,红帐子,里头住着白胖子'射'花生';'齿在口外'射'呀'字 riddle; conundrum; insinuation for sth. or character for people to guess. For example: 'In a crude hut (麻屋子 máwū・zi) with a red mosquito-net (红帐子 hóngzhàng・zi) lives (住着 zhù・zhe) a white fatty (白胖子 báipàng・zi)' suggests 'peanut (花生 huāshēng)'; 'the teeth (齿 chǐ) are outside the mouth (在口外 zài kǒuwài)' suggests the character for '呀 (yā or ・ya)'.

【谜子】mí・zi〈方 *dial*.〉谜语 riddle: 猜～ guess a riddle

篾(籋) mí (～儿 mír) 竹篾、苇篾等 bamboo strip; reed stalk: 席～儿 thin strips of the skin of bamboo; also 蔑子 mí・zi

醚 mí 有机化合物的一类,是一个氧原子连接两个烃基而成的化合物。如甲醚、乙醚等。ether; organic chemical compound which combines one oxygen atom and two hydrocarbons, as methyl ether, ether, etc.

糜 mí ❶ 粥 gruel; porridge; paste: 肉～ minced meat ❷ 烂 rotten: ～烂 rotten; dissipated ❸ 浪费 waste: ～费 waste | 奢～ extravagant ❹ (Mí) 姓 a surname

☞ méi on p.1317

【糜费】mífèi same as 靡费 mífèi

【糜烂】mílàn 烂到不可收拾 rotten to the core; dissipated; debauched: 伤口～。The wound is rotting. | ～不堪 rotten to the core ◇生活～ lead a dissipated (or fast) life

縻 mí〈书 *fml*.〉系住 fasten; tie; do up: 羁～ win a person over by hook or by crook; draw over

麋 mí 麋鹿 elk; David's deer

【麋鹿】mílù 哺乳动物,毛淡褐色,雄的有角,角像鹿,尾像驴,蹄像牛,颈像骆驼,但从整个来看哪一种动物都不像。性温顺,吃植物。原产我国,是一种稀有的珍贵兽类。elk (*Alces machlis*); David's deer; moose; meek mammal and endangered species originating in China, covered with brownish hair, having deer's antler (male only), donkey's tail, ox's hoofs and camel's neck, but looking like none of these four animals on the whole, feeding on plants; also 四不像 sìbùxiàng

靡 mí 浪费 spend extravagantly; waste: ～费 waste; spend extravagantly | 奢～ extravagant

☞ mǐ on p. 1332

【靡费】míféi 浪费 waste: 节约开支,防止～ economize on expenditure and prevent waste; also 糜费 míféi

蘼 mí ☞ 荼蘼 túmí on p. 1940

濔 mí ☞ below

【濔漫】mímàn same as 弥漫 mímàn

【濔濛】míméng same as 弥蒙 míméng

蘼 mí [蘼芜] (míwú) 古书上指芎䓖 (xiōngqióng)的苗 seedling of rhizome of *chuanxiong* (*Liguoticum wallichii*), as mentioned in ancient books

醾(醿、醾) mí ☞ 酴醾 túmí on p. 1941

mǐ (ㄇㄧˇ)

米[1] mǐ ❶稻米;大米 (husked) rice: 机～ non-glutinous rice | 糯～ glutinous rice ❷ 泛指去掉壳或皮后的种子,多指可以吃的 (in a broad sense) shelled or husked seed: 小～ husked millet | 高粱～ husked sorghum | 花生～ peanut kernel; shelled peanut | 菱角～ ling; water caltrop ❸ 小粒像米的东西 small grain: 海～ dried sea shrimp | ～兰 chu-lan tree (*Aglaia odorata*) ❹ (Mǐ) 姓 a surname

米[2] mǐ 长度单位。在国际单位制中,1 米是光在真空中于 1/299792458 秒时间间隔内所经过的路程;在公制中,是通过巴黎子午线全长的四千万分之一。1 米等于 10 分米,合 3 市尺。metre; basic metric unit of linear measure; equal to 10 decimetres or three Chinese *chi*, officially equal to the distance light travels in a vacuum in 1/299792458 of a second; in the metric system, equal to 1/40,000,000 of the meridian passing through Paris; ☞ 国际单位制 guójì dānwèizhì on p. 740 and 国际公制 guójì gōngzhì on p. 740

【米醋】mǐcù 以大米等为原料酿制的食醋 rice vinegar; table vinegar made of rice as its raw material

【米豆腐】mǐdòu·fu〈方 *dial*.〉一种食品,用大米磨成的浆制成,形状像豆腐 food made of rice pulp in the shape of bean curd

【米饭】mǐfàn 用大米或小米做成的饭。特指用大米做成的饭。cooked rice or cooked millet; more said of cooked rice

【米粉】mǐfěn ❶大米磨成的粉 ground rice; rice flour: ～肉 steamed rice flour pork ❷大米加水磨成浆,过滤后弄成团,然后制成的细条食品,可煮食 rice-flour noodles; rice with water added is ground into pulp which is filtered and made into a dough and then into fine strips; also 米面 mǐmiàn ③

【米粉肉】mǐfěnròu 把肉切成片,加米粉、作料,蒸熟,叫米粉肉。也叫粉蒸肉。有的地区叫鲊(zhǎ)肉。steamed rice flour pork; cut pork into thick slices, add rice flour and dressings, and then steam it until it is eatable; also 粉蒸肉 fěnzhēngròu and called 鲊肉 zhǎròu in some areas

【米泔水】mǐgānshuǐ 淘过米的水 water in which rice has been washed

【米黄】mǐhuáng same as 米色 mǐsè

【米酒】mǐjiǔ 用糯米、黄米等酿成的酒 rice wine; wine made of glutinous rice or glutinous millet

【米糠】mǐkāng 紧贴在稻子、谷子的米粒外面的皮,脱下后叫米糠 rice bran; broken outer coat of rice, millet separated from the flour after grinding, as by sifting

【米粒】mǐlì (～儿 mǐlìr)米的颗粒 grain of rice

【米粮川】mǐliángchuān 盛产粮食的大片平地 rich and large rice-producing area: 荒滩变成～。The barren beach has become a granary.

【米面】mǐmiàn ❶ 大米和面 rice and wheat flour ❷ (～儿 mǐmiànr) same as 米粉 mǐfěn ① ❸〈方 *dial*.〉一种食品,把大米加水磨成的浆,用'旋子' ① 做成像粉皮的薄片,再切成细条而成 rice-flour noodles, a kind of food made by grinding rice with water into pulp, using a copper plate to make it into thin sheet jelly and cutting it into small, slender strips

【米色】mǐsè 白而微黄的颜色 cream colour

【米汤】mǐ·tāng ❶ 煮米饭时取出的汤 water in which rice has been cooked ❷ 用少量的大米或小米等熬成的稀饭 thin rice or millet gruel

【米突】mǐtū 米(长度单位)的旧称 old name for metre [法 French: mètre]

【米线】mǐxiàn〈方 *dial*.〉same as 米粉 mǐfěn ②: 过桥～ cross-the-bridge rice-flour noodles; rice-flour noodles from Yunnan; rice-flour noodles in piping hot sauce

【米制】mǐzhì 国际公制 metric system

【米珠薪桂】mǐ zhū xīn guì 米像珍珠,柴像桂木,形容物价昂贵,生活困难 exorbitantly high cost of living; rice is as precious as pearls and firewood as expensive as cassia

【米猪】mǐzhū 体内有囊虫寄生的猪。因囊虫为黄豆大小的囊泡,内有白色米粒状头节,所以叫米猪。pig having parasitic cysticercus (or bladder-worm), a worm in the form of a vesica the size of a soya bean, inside which its white rice-shaped head and neck are partly enclosed in a bladder-like cyst, hence the name, which literally means 'pig with rice grains'

【米蛀虫】mǐzhùchóng 蛀米的虫子 rice worm; 〈比喻 *fig.*〉投机倒把、发昧心财的粮商 rice profiteer

芈 mǐ ❶ 羊叫 (of a sheep) baa; bleat; cry of a sheep or goat ❷ (Mǐ) 姓 a surname

浰(瀰) mǐ 〈书 *fml.*〉水满 overflowing with water

【浰迤】mǐyǐ 〈书 *fml.*〉形容平坦 flat: ～平原 flat (or level) plain

洣 Mǐ 洣水,水名,在湖南 Mishui, name of a river in Hunan Province

弭 mǐ ❶ 〈书 *fml.*〉平息;消灭 quell; crash down on: 消～ put an end to; prevent; stop | ～患 remove a source of trouble | ～战 quell a rebellion; stop a civil war ❷ (Mǐ) 姓 a surname

【弭谤】mǐbàng 〈书 *fml.*〉止息诽谤 stop a slander

【弭兵】mǐbīng 〈书 *fml.*〉平息战争 stop a war; have a truce

【弭除】mǐchú 〈书 *fml.*〉消除 eliminate; dispel; remove; clear up: ～成见 dispel (or remove, eradicate) prejudices

【弭患】mǐhuàn 〈书 *fml.*〉消除祸患 remove a source of trouble

【弭乱】mǐluàn 〈书 *fml.*〉平息战乱 put down a rebellion; stop a civil war

脒 mǐ 有机化合物的一类,是含有 $CNHNH_2$ 原子团的化合物,如磺胺脒 amidine; organic chemical compound containing the $CNHNH_2$ atomic group, as sulphaguanidine

敉 mǐ 〈书 *fml.*〉安抚;安定 soothe; pacify: ～平 crack down; put down; suppress

【敉平】mǐpíng 〈书 *fml.*〉平定 put down (a rebellion); quell; suppress: ～叛乱 put down a rebellion

靡¹ mǐ 〈书 *fml.*〉 ❶ 顺风倒下 be blown down by the wind: 风～ be in vogue; be fashionable | 披～ blown about and bent by the wind; be routed; be defeated and dispersed ❷ 美好 fine; excellent; splendid: ～丽 splendid; extravagant; magnificent

靡² mǐ 〈书 *fml.*〉无;没有 not have; there is not; be without: ～日不思 not a day passes without one's thinking of somebody or something

☞ mí on p. 1331

【靡丽】mǐlì 〈书 *fml.*〉华丽;奢华 splendid; magnificent; resplendent; luxurious; extravagant

【靡靡】mǐmǐ 颓废淫荡;低级趣味的(乐曲) (of music) decadent; vulgar; obscene: ～之音 decadent music

【靡然】mǐrán 一边倒的样子 universally: 天下～从之 win universal support; whole country supports a person (a leader); enjoy support from the whole population

mì (ㄇㄧˋ)

汨 mì 汨罗江(Mìluó Jiāng),发源于江西,流入湖南洞庭湖 Miluo River, originating in Jiangxi Province and flowing into Lake Dongting in Hunan Province

觅(覔) mì 寻找 look for; hunt for; seek: 寻～ look for; hunt for | ～食 look for food

【觅求】mìqiú 寻找;寻求 look for; hunt for; seek: 四处～ look about for something or somebody | ～乐趣 seek pleasure

【觅取】mìqǔ 寻求取得 look for; hunt for; seek: 到深山老林～珍贵的木材 look for valuable timber in the mountain forests

泌 mì 分泌 secrete: ～乳量 lactation | ～尿器 urinary organs

☞ bì on p. 107

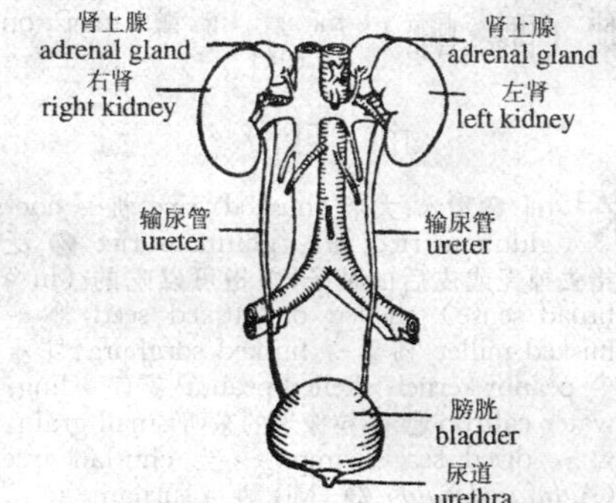

人的泌尿器
Human Urinary Organ

【泌尿器】mìniàoqì 分泌尿和排泄尿的器官,是肾脏、输尿管、膀胱、尿道等的统称 urinary organs, including the organs both in the secretion and discharge of the urine, such as the kidney, ureter, urinary bladder, urethra, etc.

宓 mì ❶ 〈书 *fml.*〉安静 tranquil; quiet ❷ (Mì) 姓 a surname

秘(祕) mì ❶ 秘密 secret; mystery: ～诀 secret | ～室 private room | ～事 private matter or affair ❷ 保守秘密 keep sth. secret; hold sth. back: ～而不宣 conceal something; keep sth. secret | ～不示人 hide something from others ❸ 罕见;稀有 rare: ～宝 rare treasure | ～籍 rare book

☞ bì on p. 107

【秘宝】mìbǎo 罕见的珍宝 rare treasure

【秘本】mìběn 珍藏的罕见的图书或版本 treasured copy of a rare book

【秘而不宣】mì ér bù xuān 守住秘密,不肯宣布 keep sth. secret; not let anyone know a secret

【秘方】mìfāng 不公开的有显著医疗效果的药方 secret recipe; recipe with good medical effect, which is kept from public knowledge: 祖传～ secret recipe handed down from one's ancestors

【秘府】mìfǔ 宫廷中收藏图书秘籍的地方 place in the palace where rare and valuable books are kept

【秘籍】mìjí 珍贵罕见的书籍 valuable and rare books: 孤本～ only existing copy of a rare book

【秘诀】mìjué 能解决问题的不公开的巧妙办法 secret (of success); concealed ingenious solution to a problem: 成功的～ secret of (or key to) one's success

【秘密】mìmì ❶ 有所隐蔽,不让人知道的(跟'公开'相对 as opposed to 'public') secret; concealed; kept from public knowledge: ～文件 secret papers; confidential document|～来往 secret contacts ❷ 秘密的事情 sth. secret: 保守～ keep it a secret|军事～ military secret

【秘史】mìshǐ 指统治阶级内部没有公开的历史,也指关于私人生活琐事(多是腐朽生活作风)的记载 secret history (as of a feudal ruler); inside story (mostly about a decadent life style): 宫廷～ secret history of the imperial court

【秘书】mìshū ❶ 掌管文书并协助机关或部门负责人处理日常工作的人员 secretary; person who keeps documents and assists his superior in handling day-to-day affairs: ～长 secretary-general|部长～ minister's secretary ❷ 秘书职务 job and post: ～处 secretariat|担任～工作 work as a secretary

【秘闻】mìwén 罕为人知的传闻(多指有关私人生活的)unknown information (oft. concerning sb.'s private life): ～轶事 secrets and anecdotes|官闱～ palace secrets|披露～ disclose unknown information

密 mì ❶ 事物之间距离近;事物的部分之间空隙小(跟'稀'、'疏'相对 as opposed to 'thin', 'sparse') (of space between two things) small; close; dense; thick: ～植 close planting|稠～ thick; dense|紧～ close; tight|严～ tight; close; compact; well-knit|这一带的树长得太～了。The trees in this area are planted too close together. ❷ 关系近;感情好 intimate; close: ～友 intimate friends; close friends 亲～ close; intimate ❸ 精致;细致 fine; meticulous: 细～ meticulous care|精～ fine; exquisite; delicate ❹ 秘密 secret; confidential: ～电 confidential message|～谈 secret talk|～约 secret agreement|机～ secret; confidential information|保～ keep a secret; keep something confidential ❺ (Mì)姓 a surname

【密报】mìbào ❶ 秘密地报告 secretly report; inform against a person: 是谁～了这件事? Who has secretly reported this matter? ❷ 秘密的报告 secret report: 得到～ receive (get, obtain) a secret report

【密闭】mìbì ❶ 严密封闭 tightly closed: 门窗～。The doors and windows are tightly closed. ❷ 严密封闭的 airtight; hermetic: ～容器 airtight container

【密布】mìbù 分布得很稠密 be densely covered; be densely distributed: 繁星～。Myriads of stars are densely distributed over the sky.|阴云～。The sky was overcast. *or* Dark clouds were gathering.

【密电】mìdiàn ❶ 密码电报;秘密的电报 coded telegram; cipher telegram ❷ 指拍发密电 send a secret telegraph

【密度】mìdù ❶ 疏密的程度 density; thickness: 人口～ population density; density of the population|果树的～不宜太大。Fruit trees should not be planted too close together. ❷ 物质的质量跟它的体积的比值,即物质单位体积的质量 density; ratio of the mass of an object to its volume, that is, the mass of the volume of an object per unit

【密封】mìfēng ❶ 严密封闭 seal up: 用白蜡～瓶口,以防药物受潮或挥发 seal up the mouth of the bottle with white wax to keep the medicine from moisture and evaporation ❷ 严密封闭的 tightly sealed: ～舱 sealed cabin; airtight cabin|一听～的果汁 an airtight tin of fruit juice

【密告】mìgào 密报 secretly report; inform against a person

【密会】mìhuì ❶ 秘密会见 meet secretly or in secret ❷ 秘密会议 secret meeting

【密级】mìjí 指国家事务秘密程度的等级,一般分为绝密、机密、秘密三级 classification of confidential government documents and state affairs; usu. there are three classes: top secret or most confidential, secret or confidential, and restricted

【密集】mìjí 数量很多地聚集在一处 concentrated; crowded together: 人口～ densely populated; thickly populated|～防守 close defence

【密件】mìjiàn 需要保密的信件或文件 confidential paper or letter; classified matter; classified material

【密林】mìlín 茂密的树林(多指大片的) thick or dense forest; thick wood: ～深处 in the depth of a dense forest

【密令】mìlìng ❶ 秘密命令、指令 secret order or instructions ❷ 秘密下达的命令、指令 secret order or instruction

【密码】mìmǎ 在约定的人中间使用的特别编定的秘密电码或号码(区别于'明码'as compared

M

with 'plain code') cipher; cipher code; secret code; secret code specially prepared for use among appointed people: 破译～ break a secret code|～锁 coded lock

【密密层层】mì·micéngcéng (～的 mì·micéngcéng·de)形容很密很多 thick; packed closely; layer upon layer (or ring upon ring); dense: 山坡上有～的酸枣树,很难走上去。Access to the hill is denied by wild jujube thickets on the slopes.

【密密丛丛】mì·micóngcóng (～的 mì·micóngcóng·de)形容茂密 dense; thick: ～的杨树林 dense poplar forest

【密密麻麻】mì·mimámá (～的 mì·mimámá·de)又多又密(多指小的东西 oft. of small things) close and numerous; thickly dotted: 纸上写着～的小字。The paper was filled with small, closely-written characters.

【密密匝匝】mì·mizāzā (～的 mì·mizāzā·de)很稠密的样子 packed; thick: 车厢里的人挤得～的。The rail coaches are packed with passengers. also 密匝匝 mìzāzā

【密谋】mìmóu 秘密计划(多指坏的 oft. sth. bad) conspire; plot; scheme: ～叛变 conspire to defect

【密切】mìqiè ❶ 关系近 close; intimate: 两人关系很～。The two of them are very close to each other. *or* They two are on intimate terms. ❷ 使关系近 build, foster or establish close links (between two parties): 进一步～干部与群众的关系 build closer relations between the cadres and the masses ❸ (对问题等)重视,照顾得周到 careful; intent; close: ～注意 follow or watch closely; pay close attention to|～配合 cooperate closely

【密商】mìshāng 秘密商议 hold private counsel; hold secret talks: ～对策 hold secret talks on countermeasures

【密使】mìshǐ 秘密派遣的使者;负有秘密使命的使者 secret emissary; secret envoy; envoy carrying a secret mission

【密室】mìshì 四面严密关闭的房间;秘密的房间(指不让外人知道的地方 place not known to outsiders) room used for secret purposes; tightly closed room: 策划于～ plot behind closed doors

【密实】mì·shi 细密;紧密 closely knit; dense; thick: 这批棉衣针脚做得真～。These cotton-padded clothes are tightly sewed with small stitches.

【密司脱】mìsītuō 先生(多见于早期翻译作品 oft. in early translations) mister: ～王(王先生) Mr. Wang

【密斯】mìsī 小姐(多见于早期翻译作品 oft. in early translations) miss: ～王(王小姐) Miss Wang

【密谈】mìtán 秘密交谈 have a secret or confidential talk; talk behind closed doors: 附耳～talk in whispers|两个人～了一阵。The two of them had a secret talk for a while.

【密探】mìtàn 做秘密侦探工作的人(多用来称对方的 oft. used for the opposing party) secret agent; spy

【密友】mìyǒu 友谊特别深的朋友 close or fast friend; bosom friend: 至亲～ close relatives and good friends

【密语】mìyǔ ❶ 秘密的通信用语。为了保密,通常用数字、字母、单词等代替真实的通信内容 coded language; numerals, letters and words usu. used to replace true communications in order to keep it confidential; also 暗语 ànyǔ ❷ 秘密交谈 talk in private: 他俩正在低头～。The two of them are talking in whispers, their heads hanging low.

【密约】mìyuē ❶ 秘密约定 secret agreement; secret treaty: ～幽会 rendezvous; (of lovers) tryst ❷ 秘密签订的条约 secret treaty: 签订～ sign a secret treaty

【密云不雨】mì yún bù yǔ 满天浓云而不下雨 dense clouds but no rain; 〈比喻 *fig.*〉事情正在酝酿,尚未发作 sth. in the offing

【密召】mìzhào 秘密召唤 call back secretly: ～回京 call a person back to Beijing secretly

【密诏】mìzhào 秘密的诏书 secret edict

【密植】mìzhí 在单位面积土地上适当缩小作物行距和株距,增加播种量,增加株数 close planting; properly reduce the space between two rows or two plants within a unit area so as to increase the amount of seeds sown or the number of seedling planted

【密旨】mìzhǐ 秘密的谕旨 secret edict

【密致】mìzhì (物质)结构紧密;致密(matter) of compact structure: 质地～ compactness; compact

幂(冪) mì ❶〈书 *fml.*〉覆盖东西的巾 cloth cover ❷〈书 *fml.*〉覆盖;罩 cover ❸ 表示一个数自乘若干次的形式叫幂,如 t 自乘 n 次的幂为 t^n power; product of the multiplication of a quantity by itself, for example, t^n is the nth power of t; ☞ 乘方 chéngfāng on p.252

谧 mì 〈书 *fml.*〉安宁,平静 quiet; still; tranquil: 安～quiet; still; tranquil|静～ quiet; still; tranquil|恬～ quiet; still; tranquil

蓂 mì ☞ 菥蓂 xīmì on p.2046
☞ míng on p.1359

幎 mì 〈书 *fml.*〉same as 幂 mì

嘧 mì [嘧啶](mìdìng)有机化合物,化学式 $C_4H_4N_2$。无色液体或结晶物质,有刺激性气味。用来制化学药品。pyrimidine ($C_4H_4N_2$), organic chemical compound in the form of a colourless liquid or crystal with an irritant odour, used in making chemicals.

M

蜜 mì ❶ 蜂蜜 honey：酿～ make honey｜割～ cut off the honeycomb to get honey ❷ 像蜂蜜的东西 sth. like honey：糖～ molasses ❸ 甜美 honeyed; sweet：甜～ sweet｜甜言～语 honey-coated words; sweet words

【蜜蜂】mìfēng 昆虫，身体表面有很密的绒毛，前翅比后翅大，雄的触角较长，母蜂和工蜂有毒刺，能蜇人。成群居住。工蜂能采花粉酿蜜，帮助某些植物传粉。蜂蜜、蜂蜡、王浆有很大的经济价值。honeybee (*Apis mellifera*; *Apis cerana*); bee; four-winged, hairy hymenopteran insect, with the forewings larger than the hind wings. The male has longer feelers, and both the queen and the worker have poisonous, biting stings. The bees often live in organized colonies, with the workers gathering pollen and nectar, and helping some plants to transfer the pollen from a stamen to the upper tip of the pistil of a flower. Honey, beeswax and royal jelly all have high economic values.

【蜜饯】mìjiàn ❶ 用浓糖浆浸渍果品等 candied fruit; preserved fruit：～海棠 candied crabapple ❷ 蜜饯的果品等 candied fruits

【蜜色】mìsè 像蜂蜜那样的颜色；淡黄色 light yellow; honey colour

【蜜丸子】mìwán·zi 用蜂蜜调和药面儿制成的丸药 a bolus made of powdered Chinese medicine and honey

【蜜腺】mìxiàn 某些植物的花上分泌糖汁的腺。有的植物蜜腺长在雄蕊或雌蕊的基部，如白菜；有的植物蜜腺长在花冠上，如萝卜。nectary; organ of a flower of certain plants that secretes nectar, growing at the base part of the male pistil or female pistil of such plants as cabbage, or on the corolla of such plants as turnip

【蜜源】mìyuán 指能大量供蜜蜂采蜜的植物 nectar source; plants that produce ample nectar for bees to gather

【蜜月】mìyuè 新婚第一个月 honeymoon：～旅行 honeymoon trip｜度～ honeymoon; spend or be on one's honeymoon

【蜜枣】mìzǎo（～儿 mìzǎor）蜜饯的枣儿 candied date or jujube

mián（ㄇㄧㄢˊ）

眠 mián ❶ 睡眠 sleep：失～ insomnia｜安～ sleep in peace; sleep peacefully; have a sound sleep｜长～（指死亡）eternal sleep (death) ❷ 某些动物的一种生理现象，在一个较长时间内不动不吃 dormancy：冬～ hibernation; hibernate｜蚕三～了。The silkworms have become inactive for the third time.

绵（緜） mián ❶ 丝绵 silk floss ❷ 绵延 continuous：～亘 continuous; unending｜～长 very long｜连～ unbroken; uninterrupted; continuous ❸ 薄弱；柔软 soft：～薄 feeble strength; humble effort｜～软 soft; weak ❹〈方 *dial.*〉（性情）温和 mild-tempered; gentle; meek：你别瞧他不声不响，性子挺～，心可大啦。He may be quiet and mild-tempered, but he has great ambitions.

【绵白糖】miánbáitáng 颗粒很小，略呈粉末状的白糖 fine white sugar

【绵薄】miánbó〈谦辞 *hum.*〉指自己薄弱的能力 (my) meagre strength; humble effort：愿在文化工作方面，稍尽～。(I)'ll do what little I can in cultural work.

【绵长】miáncháng 延续很长（of time）very long：～岁月 long period of years｜福寿～（对老年人的祝辞）。(to an elderly person) (I) wish you a happy and long life.

【绵绸】miánchóu 用碎丝、废丝等为原料纺成丝后织成的丝织品，表面不平整，不光滑 fabric made from waste silk, with its surface neither smooth nor glossy

【绵亘】miángèn 接连不断（多指山脉等 of mountains, etc.）undulate; stretch in an unbroken chain：大别山～在河南、安徽和湖北三省的边界上。The Dabie Mountains stretch along the borders of Henan, Anhui and Hubei provinces.

【绵和】miánhé〈方 *dial.*〉柔和；温和 soft; mild：酒性～ mild wine｜他脾气挺～的。He is mild-tempered.

【绵里藏针】mián lǐ cáng zhēn ❶ 形容柔中有刚 needle hidden in silk floss; an iron hand in a velvet glove ❷〈比喻 *fig.*〉外貌柔和，内心刻毒 ruthless character behind a gentle appearance

【绵力】miánlì〈书 *fml.*〉微薄的力量 meagre strength; humble effort：略尽～。(I)'ll do what little I can.

【绵连】miánlián 连绵 unbroken; uninterrupted; continuous; also 绵联 miánlián

【绵密】miánmì（言行、思虑）细密周到（of speech, behaviour or thinking）meticulous; detailed; circumspect：文思～（of writing）thoroughly thought out

【绵绵】miánmián 连续不断的样子 continuous; unbroken：秋雨～。The autumn rain goes on and on.

【绵软】miánruǎn ❶ 柔软（多用于毛发、衣被、纸张等 hair, clothes, paper, etc.）soft：～的羊毛 soft wool ❷ 形容身体无力 weak：他觉得浑身～，脑袋昏沉沉。He feels weak all over and befuddled.

【绵糖】miántáng same as 绵白糖 miánbáitáng

【绵甜】miántián（味道）柔和而甘甜（多指酒类 oft. referring to wine）(of taste) mild and mellow

【绵延】miányán 延续不断 continuous; unbroken：～千里的山脉 mountains extending

M

(or stretching) a thousand *li*

【绵羊】miányáng 羊的一种，公羊多有螺旋状大角，母羊角细小或无角，口吻长，四肢短，趾有蹄，尾肥大，毛白色，长而卷曲。性温顺。变种很多，有灰黑等颜色。毛是纺织品的重要原料，皮可制革。sheep (*Ovis aries*); male sheep having big, spiral horns and female sheep having small or no horns, long lips, short limbs, hoofed toes, a big and fat tail and long, curled, white wool. It is meek and has many variant species, including grey and black ones. Its wool is an important raw material for the textile industry.

【绵纸】miánzhǐ 用树木的韧皮纤维制的纸，色白，柔软而有韧性，纤维细长如绵，所以叫绵纸。多用做皮衣衬垫、鞭炮捻子、电池包装等。tissue paper; white, soft and tensile paper made of bast fibre from trees. Its fibre is as fine and long as silk floss (绵), hence the name. It is used in lining leather jackets, making the spill in a firecracker, packaging electric cells, etc.

【绵子】mián·zi〈方 *dial.*〉丝绵 silk floss; silk wadding

棉 mián ❶ 草棉和木棉的统称，通常多指草棉 general name for cotton and kapok ❷ same as 棉花 mián·hua ②：～纺 cotton spinning｜～布 cotton cloth ❸ 像棉花的絮状物 cotton-like floss：石～ asbestos｜腈纶～ acrylic fibres｜膨松～ bulk fibre

【棉饼】miánbǐng 棉子榨油后剩下的压成饼状的渣滓。可做饲料或肥料。cottonseed cake; cottonseed meal ground up in the shape of cakes after the oil has been removed for fodder or fertilizer

【棉布】miánbù 用棉纱织成的布 coton; cotton cloth

【棉的确良】miándíquèliáng 涤棉布的俗称 cotton dacron; fabric mixture of cotton and synthetic polyester, popular name for 涤棉布 dímiánbù

【棉纺】miánfǎng 用棉花纺成纱 cotton spinning：～厂 cotton mill

【棉猴儿】miánhóur 风帽连着衣领的棉大衣 (knee-length) parka; anorak; hooded cotton-padded coat

【棉花】mián·hua ❶ 草棉的通称 (general term for) cotton ❷ 棉桃中的纤维，用来纺纱、絮衣服被褥等 fibre in the cotton boll used for spinning yarn or making cotton wadding (for clothes, quilts, etc.)

【棉花胎】mián·huatāi〈方 *dial.*〉same as 棉絮 miánxù ②

【棉花套子】mián·hua tào·zi〈方 *dial.*〉same as 棉絮 miánxù ②

【棉铃】miánlíng 棉花的果实，初长时形状像铃叫棉铃，长成后像桃叫棉桃。一般不加分别，通称棉桃。cotton boll; rounded seed pod of cotton known as cotton bell when it is young and looks like a bell and boll when it grows up and looks like a boll, but usu. not differentiated from each other, known generally the cotton boll

【棉毛】miánmáo 指一种比较厚的棉针织品 thick cotton knitwear：～衫 cotton (interlock) jersey (worn as underwear)｜～裤 cotton (interlock) trousers (worn as underwear)

【棉农】miánnóng 以种植棉花为主的农民 cotton grower

【棉皮鞋】miánpíxié 衬有绒、毡等材料的皮鞋 leather shoes lined with velvet or felt

【棉签】miánqiān (～儿 miánqiānr) 一端裹有少许棉花的小细棍，用于医疗上皮肤局部消毒或处理伤口等 cotton swab; very small stick, one end of which is wrapped with a tiny amount of cotton, used for sterilizing skin or cleaning wounds

【棉纱】miánshā 用棉花纺成的纱 cotton yarn

【棉桃】miántáo 棉花的果实，特指长成后形状像桃的 cotton boll; fruit of the cotton, esp. after it grows up; ☞ 棉铃 miánlíng

【棉套】miántào 絮了棉花的套子，套在茶壶、饭桶等外面起保暖作用 cotton-padded covering for a tea pot, cooked rice container, etc. to keep tea, rice or other food warm

【棉田】miántián 种植棉花的田地 cotton field

【棉线】miánxiàn 用棉纱制成的线 cotton; cotton thread

【棉絮】miánxù ❶ 棉花的纤维 cotton fibre：这种棉花的～长。The fibre of this cotton is longer. ❷ 用棉花纤维做成的可以絮被褥等的胎 cotton wadding (for a quilt, bedding, etc.)

【棉织品】miánzhīpǐn 用棉纱或棉线织成的布和衣物 cotton goods; cotton textiles; cotton fabrics

【棉子】miánzǐ 棉花的种子，可以榨油 cottonseeds; also 棉籽 miánzǐ

【棉籽】miánzǐ same as 棉子 miánzǐ

miǎn (ㄇㄧㄢˇ)

丏 miǎn〈书 *fml.*〉遮蔽；看不见 sheltered; covered; out of sight

免 miǎn ❶ 去掉；除掉 exempt; dispense with; excuse sb. from sth.：～税 tax free; exempt someone from tax｜～费 free; free of charge｜任～名单 namelist of appointments and removals｜俗礼都～了。(We)'ll dispense with all unnecessary formalities. ❷ 避免 avoid; avert; escape：～疫性 immunity｜事前做好准备，以～临时忙乱。Get things ready in advance so as to avoid confusion and rush at the last moment. ❸ 不可；不要 be not allowed：闲人～进。No admittance except on business.｜～开尊口 keep quiet; keep one's mouth shut

【免不得】miǎn ·bu·de 免不了 be unavoidable; be bound to be: 在这个问题上他们的看法分歧很大,～有一场争论。They differ greatly on this question, so a dispute is unavoidable.

【免不了】miǎn ·bu liǎo 不可避免;难免 be unavoidable; be bound to be: 在前进的道路上,困难是～的。There are bound to be difficulties in the course of our advance.|刚会走的孩子～要摔跤。A baby who has just started learning to walk is liable to fall or trip.

【免除】miǎnchú 免去;除掉 prevent; avoid: 兴修水利,～水旱灾害 build irrigation works to prevent droughts and floods

【免得】miǎn·de 以免 so as not to; so as to avoid: 多问几句,～走错路。Make some more enquiries so as not to go the wrong way.|我再说明一下,～引起误会。Let me explain once again to avoid misunderstanding.

【免费】miǎn//fèi 免缴费用;不收费 free; gratis; free of charge: ～医疗 free medical service|展览会～参观。Admission to the exhibition is free.

【免冠】miǎnguān ❶ 脱帽,古时表示谢罪,后来表示敬意 take one's hat off (in salutation) ❷ 不戴帽子 bareheaded; without a hat on: 交一寸半身～相片两张。Two half-length, bareheaded, full-faced photos required.

【免检】miǎnjiǎn 免除检查 exempt from inspection or examination: ～物品 goods (or articles) exempt from inspection (or examination)

【免考】miǎnkǎo same as 免试 miǎnshì ①

【免票】miǎnpiào ❶ 不收费的票 free pass; free ticket: 每人发一张火车～。Everyone is given a free train ticket. ❷ (入场、乘车等)不要票 free of charge: 儿童身高不满一米的坐公共汽车～。Children under one metre in height take a bus free of charge.

【免试】miǎnshì ❶ 允许不经过考试(升学或晋职等) be allowed not to take an examination (for entrance or promotion); also 免考 miǎnkǎo ❷ 免除测试 be exempted from a test

【免税】miǎn//shuì 免缴税款 exempt from taxation: 海关～放行。The customs office grants free-duty clearance for something.

【免俗】miǎnsú 言行不拘于世俗常情(多用于否定式 oft. used in the negative) words and acts not confined to common practice: 未能～ be unable to break away from convention

【免刑】miǎnxíng 经法院审判决定,免予刑事处分 be exempt from punishment upon a court decision

【免修】miǎnxiū 允许不学习(某种课程) be exempt from (a course): ～外语 be excused from the foreign language course

【免验】miǎnyàn 免除检验 exempt from customs examination: ～产品 goods exempt from examination

【免役】miǎnyì 免除某种规定的服役,如兵役、劳役 exempt from compulsory services, such as military service and corvée

【免疫】miǎnyì 由于具有抵抗力而不患某种传染病,有先天性免疫和获得性免疫两种 immunity (from disease); congenital immunity or acquired immunity from certain infections disease

【免战牌】miǎnzhànpái 向对方表示不应战的牌子(多见于旧小说、戏曲 oft. in old novels, operas, etc.) sign used to show refusal to accept a challenge

【免职】miǎn//zhí 免去职务 remove from office; relieve sb. of his post: 由于贪污而被～ be removed from office due to corruption|他被免了职后做别的工作去了。He took another job after he was removed from office.

【免罪】miǎn//zuì 不给予法律处分 exempt from punishment: ～释放 be exempted from punishment and released

沔 Miǎn 沔水,汉水的上游,在陕西,古代也指整个汉水 Mianshui, the upper reaches of the Han River in Shaanxi Province; also referring to the whole Han River in ancient times

黾(黽) miǎn 〈书 *fml.*〉 same as 渑 miǎn ☞ mǐn on p. 1349

眄 miǎn '眄' miàn 的又音 variant pronunciation for 眄 miàn

俛 miǎn ☞ [僶俛] (mǐnmiǎn) on p. 1349 ☞ fǔ on p. 602

勉 miǎn ❶ 努力 strive; exert oneself: 奋～ exert oneself; make great efforts ❷ 勉励 encourage; urge; exhort: 自～ spur oneself on|互～ encourage one another|有则改之,无则加～。Correct mistakes if you've made any and guard against them if not. ❸ 力量不够而尽力做 strive to do what is beyond one's power: ～强 reluctant; unwilling|～为其难 undertake a difficult task beyond one's ability or power; be obliged to do a difficult job

【勉力】miǎnlì 努力;尽力 exert oneself; try hard; make great efforts: ～为之 exert oneself to the utmost; do one's best

【勉励】miǎnlì 劝人努力;鼓励 encourage; urge: 互相～ encourage each other|老师～同学继续努力。The teacher urged his students to keep working hard.

【勉强】miǎnqiǎng ❶ 能力不够,还尽力做 manage with an effort; do sth. with difficulty: 这项工作我还能～坚持下来。I can manage to go on with this work. ❷ 不是甘心情愿的 reluctant; grudging: 碍着面子,～答应下来了。For the sake of his face, (he) agreed reluctantly. ❸ 使人做他自己不愿意做的事 force a person to do sth.: 他不去算了,不要～他了。

Don't force him to if he is not going. ❹ 牵强;理由不充足 unconvincing; strained; far-fetched:这种说法很~,怕站不住脚。The argument is very unconvincing. I'm afraid that it will be untenable. ❺ 将就;凑合 barely enough:这点儿草料~够牲口吃一天。The cattle fodder is barely enough for a single day.

【勉为其难】miǎn wéi qí nán 勉强做能力所不及的事 undertake a difficult task beyond one's ability or power; be obliged to take on a difficult job

娩(挽) miǎn 分娩 childbirth; delivery; parturition; give birth

☞ wǎn on p.1975

【娩出】miǎnchū 胎儿、胎盘和胎膜等从母体内产出来 coming out of the foetus from its mother's body with its placenta and foetal membrane

勔 miǎn〈书 *fml.*〉勤勉 diligent; hardworking; industrious

冕 miǎn 天子、诸侯、卿、大夫所戴的礼帽,后来专指帝王的礼帽 crown or coronet (worn by an emperor, prince, duke, etc., later referring esp. to an emperor's crown):加~礼 coronation

【冕旒】miǎnliú 天子的礼帽和礼帽前后的玉串 jade ornaments hanging on the front and back of an emperor's ceremonial hat

偭 miǎn〈书 *fml.*〉❶ 向;面向 towards; face sb. or sth. ❷ 违背 violate:~规越矩(违背正常的法度) violate the law

渑(澠) miǎn 渑池(Miǎnchí),地名,在河南 Mianchi, name of a place in Henan Province

☞ Shéng on p.1721

湎 miǎn ☞ 沉湎 chénmiǎn on p.237

愐 miǎn〈书 *fml.*〉❶ 思;想 think; ponder; consider ❷ 勤勉 diligent; industrious; hardworking

缅[1] miǎn 遥远 remote; far back:~怀 recall; cherish the memory of | ~想 recollect; look back on (past events)

缅[2] miǎn〈方 *dial.*〉卷(juǎn) roll up:~上袖子 roll up a sleeve | 把边儿~过去 roll the edge of something

【缅怀】miǎnhuái 追想(已往的事迹)(of past events) recall; cherish the memory of:~先烈创业的艰难 recall the hardships the martyrs went through in starting the revolutionary cause

【缅邈】miǎnmiǎo〈书 *fml.*〉遥远 remote; far back

【缅想】miǎnxiǎng 缅怀 recall; think of (past events)

靦 miǎn [靦覥](miǎn·tiǎn) same as 腼腆 miǎn·tiǎn

☞ tiǎn on p.1899

M

腼 miǎn [腼腆](miǎn·tiǎn)因怕生或害羞而神情不自然 bashful; feel shy; not at ease with other people:小孩儿见了生人有点~。The child was a bit shy with strangers. also 靦覥 miǎn·tiǎn

鮸 miǎn 鱼,身体长,侧扁,棕褐色,口大而微斜,尾鳍呈楔形。生活在海中。slate cod croaker (*Sciaena albiflora*); long, flat brown marine fish with a big, slightly inclined mouth and a wedge-shaped tail fin; 通称 commonly known as 鳘鱼 mǐnyú

miàn (ㄇㄧㄢˋ)

面[1](靣) miàn ❶ 头的前部;脸 face; front part of the head:~孔 face | 笑容满~ smile all over one's face; smiling face ❷ 向着;朝着 face; toward:背山~水 with a mountain behind and a river (or lake) in front | 这所房子~南坐北。The house faces south. ❸ (~儿 miànr)物体的表面,有时特指某些物体的上部的一层 surface; top; face:水~ water surface; surface of a river, lake, sea, etc. | 地~ ground surface | 路~ road surface | 圆桌~儿 top of a round table | ~儿磨得很光。The surface is well polished. *or* The surface is polished until it shines. ❹ 当面 face to face; personally; directly:~谈 have a face-to-face talk | ~洽 discuss directly with a person | ~交 hand-deliver ❺ (~儿 miànr)东西露在外面的那一层或纺织品的正面 outside; right side of a fabric:鞋~儿 front uppers of a shoe | 这块布做里儿,那块布做~儿。Use this piece of cloth for the lining and that piece for the outside. ❻ 几何学上指一条线移动所构成的图形,有长有宽,没有厚 surface; figure formed by moving a line, having length and breadth, but no thickness ❼ 部位或方面 part; side; aspect:正~ front; obverse side; right side | 反~ reverse side; wrong side; back side | 片~ one-sided; unilateral | 全~ overall; all-round; general | 多~手 all-rounder; versatile person | ~~俱到 attend to each and every aspect of a matter ❽ 方位词后缀 [suffix to words indicating the bearings]:上~ above | 前~ front | 外~ outside | 左~ on the left | 西~ west ❾〈量词 *classifier*〉a)用于扁平的物件 [for flat objects]:一~镜子 a mirror | 两~旗子 two flags; b)用于会见的次数 [for the number of times two people meet each other]:见过一~ have met once

面[2](麵、麪) miàn ❶ 粮食磨成的粉,特指小麦磨成的粉 flour, especially wheat flour:白~ fine wheat flour | 豆~ bean flour | 小米~ millet flour | 玉米~ corn flour | 高粱~ sorghum flour ❷ (~儿 miànr)粉末 powder:药~儿 medicinal powder

|胡椒～儿 powdered pepper; ground pepper ❸ 面条 noodles: 挂～ dried noodles|切～ cut noodles|汤～ noodles in soup|一碗～ a bowl of noodles ❹〈方 *dial.*〉指某些食物纤维少而柔软 soft and floury food with fewer fibres: ～倭瓜 soft and floury pumpkin|煮的红薯很～。The cooked sweet potato is very soft and floury.|这个瓜是脆的,那个瓜是～的。This melon is crisp, and that melon is soft and floury.

【面案】miàn'àn 炊事分工上指煮饭、烙饼、蒸馒头之类的工作;白案 aspect of Chinese cooking including cooking rice, baking cakes and steaming buns; also 白案 bái'àn

【面包】miànbāo 食品,把面粉加水等调匀,发酵后烤制而成 bread; food baked from a leavened, kneaded dough

【面包车】miànbāochē 旅行车的俗称,因外形略像长方形面包 minibus; van; popular name for a tourist bus in the shape of a loaf of bread

【面包圈】miànbāoquān (～儿 miànbāoquānr)炸成的或烤成的环形面包 doughnut; fried bread ring

【面壁】miànbì ❶ 脸对着墙,指对事情不介意或无所用心 facing the wall; be unconcerned or indifferent ❷〈佛教 *Budd.*〉指脸对着墙静坐默念。南北朝时印度僧达摩来华,据传在嵩山少林寺面壁而坐九年,潜心修道。后来用'面壁'指专心于学业。sit in silence and read silently, facing the wall. It is said that when Bodhidharma, a Mahayana Buddhist monk from India, came to China in the Southern and Northern Dynasties (the sixth century), he sat facing a wall in the Shaolin Temple at Mount Songshan and devoted himself to self-cultivation for nine years. Hence the phrase 'facing the wall', meaning 'utter devotion to study'. ❸〈旧时 *old*〉一种体罚,脸对着墙站着 a kind of physical punishment for students, by which a student is ordered to stand facing a wall

【面茶】miànchá 食品,糜子面等加水煮成糊状,吃时加麻酱、椒盐等 seasoned millet mush; thick porridge made by boiling millet flour and water and adding sesame paste and spiced salt

【面点】miàndiǎn 以面粉、米粉为主要原料制作的点心 pastry; snacks made from wheat or rice flour

【面对面】miàn duì miàn 脸对着脸,当面 facing each other; face-to-face; vis-à-vis: 两个人～坐着。The two of them sat face to face.|～地提意见 make comments and criticisms in the face of sb.

【面额】miàn'é 票面的数额 denomination: 大～ big denominations|各种～的人民币 Renminbi notes of different denominations

【面坊】miànfáng 磨面粉的作坊 flour mill

【面肥】miànféi 发面时用来引起发酵的面块,内含大量酵母。有的地区叫老面、面头。leaven; leavening dough; small piece of fermenting dough put aside to be used for inducing fermentation in a fresh batch of dough; also 老面 lǎomiàn or 面头 miàntóu in some areas

【面粉】miànfěn 小麦磨成的粉 flour; wheat flour

【面馆】miànguǎn (～儿 miànguǎnr)出售面条、馄饨等面食的馆子 restaurant serving noodles, dumplings and other Chinese food made from wheat flour

【面红耳赤】miàn hóng ěr chì 形容因急躁、害羞等脸上发红的样子 blush; become red in the face from hot temper, shyness, etc.: 两个人为些小事争得～。The two of them argued heatedly until both became red in the face. *or* They had a heated argument.

【面糊】miànhù ❶ 用面粉加水调匀而成的糊状物 paste; well-blended mixture of wheat flour and water ❷〈方 *dial.*〉糨糊 mixture of starch and water used as an adhesive for paper or other light materials

【面糊】miàn·hu〈方 *dial.*〉食物纤维少而柔软 soft and floury: 白薯蒸熟了,很～。The sweet potatoes are cooked soft and floury.

【面黄肌瘦】miàn huáng jī shòu 脸色发黄、肌肤消瘦,形容营养不良或有病的样子 sallow and emaciated; lean and haggard; description for malnutrition or sickness

【面积】miànjī 平面或物体表面的大小 area: 土地～ land area|建筑～ floor space

【面颊】miànjiá 脸蛋儿 cheek: ～红润 red cheeks; rosy cheeks

【面巾】miànjīn〈方 *dial.*〉洗脸的布;毛巾 towel

【面筋】miàn·jin 食品,用面粉加水拌和,洗去其中所含的淀粉,剩下的混合蛋白质就是面筋 gluten; mixture of proteins left from wheat flour mixed with water by removing the starch

【面具】miànjù ❶ 戴在面部起遮挡保护作用的东西 mask; covering for the face to conceal or protect it: 防毒～ gas mask ❷ 假面具 mask

【面孔】miànkǒng 脸 face: 和蔼的～ kind face|板着～ put on a stern expression ◇这些产品样式陈旧,一副老～。These products are old-fashioned in their old looks.

【面料】miànliào ❶ 做衣服鞋帽等的面儿用的料子 surface fabric; material for making the outside (of a garment, shoes, hats, etc.): 大衣～ surface fabric for an overcoat ❷ 用来贴在物件表层的材料 surface material; material for the surface layer of an object: 家具～ surface material for furniture

【面临】miànlín 面前遇到;面对(问题、形势等) be faced with (an issue, a situation, etc.); be confronted with; be up against: 我们～着

极其艰巨而又十分光荣的任务。We are confronted with an extremely arduous but very glorious task.

【面码儿】miànmǎr 吃面条时用来拌面的蔬菜 fresh vegetables served with noodles

【面貌】miànmào ❶ 脸的形状；相貌 face；features ❷〈比喻 *fig.*〉事物所呈现的景象、状态 appearance of things：社会～ social mores｜精神～ mentality

【面面观】miàn miàn guān 从各个方面进行的观察（多用作文章标题 oft. used in composition titles）overview：婚恋问题～ A General Survey of Marriage and Love

【面面俱到】miàn miàn jù dào 各方面都照顾到，没有遗漏 attend to each and every aspect of a matter：写文章要突出重点，不必～。Give prominence to the main points. Don't write everything.

【面面相觑】miàn miàn xiāng qù 你看我，我看你，形容大家因惊惧或无可奈何而互相望着，都不说话 look at each other in dismay；gaze at each other in speechless despair

【面目】miànmù ❶ same as 面貌 miàomào ①：～狰狞 grotesque look｜～可憎 abominable or disgusting in appearance ❷ same as 面貌 miànmào ②：政治～ political outlook｜不见庐山真～ not see the true features of the Lushan Mountain｜～全非 totally different；be changed beyond recognition；complete change ❸ 面子；脸面 face；honour；self-respect；sense of shame：要是任务完不成，我有何～回去见首长和同志们。If I fail to fulfil the task, what face do I have to see my leaders and comrades?

【面目全非】miànmù quán fēi 事物的样子改变得很厉害（多含贬义 oft. derog.）be changed beyond recognition；completely changed；totally different

【面目一新】miànmù yī xīn 样子完全变新（指变好）take on an entirely new look；present a completely new appearance：这个工厂经过改建，已经～了。The factory has taken on an entirely new look after being reconstructed.

【面庞】miànpáng 脸的轮廓 face；contours of the face：小孩儿圆圆的～，水汪汪的大眼睛，真惹人喜欢。The baby is really lovely with a round face and bright eyes.

【面盆】[1] miànpén〈方 *dial.*〉洗脸用的盆 washbasin；washbowl

【面盆】[2] miànpén 和(huó)面用的盆 bowl for kneading dough

【面坯儿】miànpīr 已煮好而未加作料的面条 cooked noodles without dressings

【面皮】[1] miànpí〈方 *dial.*〉脸皮 face；cheek

【面皮】[2] miànpí〈方 *dial.*〉(～儿 miànpír) 包子、饺子、馄饨等的皮儿 wrapper (of dumpling, etc.)

【面洽】miànqià 当面接洽 discuss with a person face to face；take up a matter with a person personally：～公事 discuss business matters in person｜详情请和来人～。For particulars, please see the caller.

【面前】miànqián 面对着的地方 before；in (the) face of；in front of：～是一条大河。In front of (us) is a big river.｜艰巨的任务摆在我们～。A difficult task is laid before us.

【面人儿】miànrénr 用染色的糯米面捏成的人物像 dough figurine；figurines made from dough of dyed glutinous rice flour

【面容】miànróng 面貌；容貌 face；facial features：～枯槁 emaciated；look haggard｜～和蔼 look amiable

【面如土色】miàn rú tǔ sè 脸色跟土一样，没有血色。形容极端惊恐。look ashen；look pale；look extremely terrified：吓得～ turn pale with fright

【面色】miànsè 脸上的气色 complexion：他～红润，身体很健康。He has rosy cheeks and is in very good health.

【面纱】miànshā ❶ 妇女蒙在脸上的纱 veil ❷〈比喻 *fig.*〉掩盖真实面目的东西 sth. like a veil that conceals the truth：揭开宫廷的神秘～ unveil the mysteries of the palace

【面善】miànshàn ❶ 面熟 look familiar：这人好～，就是一下子想不起名字。The man looks familiar to me, but (I) can't remember his name at once. ❷ 面容和蔼 look amiable：～心恶 be affable of mien and evil of heart｜碰见一位～的老人 meet an affable old man

【面神经】miànshénjīng 第七对脑神经，分布在面部的两侧，主管面部肌肉的动作、泪腺和唾液腺的分泌 facial nerves；seventh pair of cranial nerves distributed over the two sides of the face that supply motor fibres especially to the muscles of the face and connect the secretion of the tear gland and the salivary gland with the brain

【面生】miànshēng 面貌生疏；不熟识 look unfamiliar：当着～的人，他显得十分拘谨。He looked very ill at ease in face of strangers.

【面食】miànshí 用面粉做的食品的统称（general term for）pastry；wheaten food

【面世】miànshì 指作品、产品与世人见面；问世 be published；come out：诗人两本新作～。Two new books of the poet have been published.｜更新换代产品即将～。A new line of products will come out soon.

【面试】miànshì 对应试者进行当面考查测试 interview；meeting of people face to face to evaluate and question applicants：通过～，破格录取 be admitted as an exception after an interview

【面首】miànshǒu〈书 *fml.*〉指供贵妇人玩弄的美男子 kept man of noblewoman；noblewoman's gigolo；handsome man who is kept by a noblewomen to play with（面 *mian*：指脸

face；首 *shou*：指头发 hair）

【面授】miànshòu ❶当面传授 teach in sb.'s presence：～机宜 personally instruct a person on the line of action to pursue；give a confidential briefing；brief a person on how to act ❷当面讲授的教学方式（区别于'函授'as compared with 'teach by correspondence'）teach face to face

【面熟】miànshú 面貌熟悉（但说不出是谁）look familiar（but can't tell who he or she is）：这人看着～，像在哪儿见过。That person looks familiar but I simply can't place him.

【面塑】miànsù 民间工艺，用加彩色的糯米面捏成各种人物形象 dough modelling；folk art of making figurines from dough made of coloured glutinous rice flour

【面谈】miàntán 当面商谈；当面交谈 talk face to face；take up a matter with sb. personally：改日～ have a face-to-face talk postponed｜～招考问题 talk about matters concerning enrolment

【面汤】[1] miàntāng〈方 *dial.*〉洗脸的热水 hot water for washing face

【面汤】[2] miàntāng 煮过面条的水 water in which noodles have been boiled

【面汤】miàn·tang〈方 *dial.*〉汤面 noodles in soup

【面条】miàntiáo（～儿 miàntiáor）用面粉做的细条状的食品 noodles；long narrow strips of dough

【面团】miàntuán（～儿 miàntuánr）和（huó）好了的成块的面 dough；soft，kneaded mass of flour mixed with water

【面团团】miàntuántuán 形容脸肥胖 plump；chubby：～若富家翁 look plump like a rich man

【面无人色】miàn wú rén sè 脸上没有血色，形容极端恐惧 look ghastly pale；have no colour in the cheeks；be extremely terrified

【面相】miànxiàng 相貌；样子 facial features；looks；appearance：因为天黑，没有看清他是什么～。I didn't see clearly what he looked like in the darkness.

【面叙】miànxù 当面叙谈 talk face to face：就此搁笔，余容～。So much for my letter today — please let me tell you the rest directly when we meet.

【面议】miànyì 当面商议 negotiate face to face；take up a matter with sb. personally：价格～。The price will be negotiated face to face.

【面罩】miànzhào 挡在或戴在面部起遮蔽或保护作用的罩子 mask；face guard；face covering to conceal or protect the face

【面值】miànzhí 票据等上面标明的金额 denomination；par value；face value；nominal value

【面砖】miànzhuān 陶土烧制的砖，有装饰性花纹，用来砌在墙的表面 tile；brick with decorative designs to surface a wall

【面子】[1] miàn·zi ❶物体的表面 outside；face；outer part：被～ quilt cover｜这件袍子的～很好看。The outside of the robe looks very nice. ❷体面；表面的虚荣 reputation；prestige；face：爱～ be anxious to save face；be very sensitive｜要～ be anxious to save one's face；be concerned about face-saving｜你这话伤了他的～。What you've said has hurt his self-respect. ❸情面 feelings；sensibilities：给～ show due respect for a person's feelings｜碍于～，只好答应了。Out of consideration for his feelings，I have to agree.

【面子】[2] miàn·zi 粉末 powder：药～ medicinal powder

眄 miàn 又 also miǎn〈书 *fml.*〉眄视 give a sidelong glance

【眄视】miànshì〈书 *fml.*〉斜着眼看 give a sidelong glance

miāo（ㄇㄧㄠ）

喵 miāo〈拟声词 *onom.*〉形容猫叫的声音 mew；miaow；sound made by a cat

miáo（ㄇㄧㄠˊ）

苗 miáo ❶（～儿 miáor）初生的种子植物，有时专指某些蔬菜的嫩茎或嫩叶 seedling；young plant；tender stem and leaves of certain vegetables：幼～ seedling｜青～ young plant｜麦～儿 wheat seedling｜豆～儿 pea seedling｜蒜～ garlic shoot｜韭菜～ chive seedling｜间～ thin out seedling｜补～ fill the gaps with seedlings ❷后代 offspring：～裔 offspring；descendants｜他们家就这一根～儿。Their family has only this descendant. ❸某些初生的饲养的动物 young of some animals：鱼～ fry｜猪～ piglet；pigling ❹疫苗 vaccine：牛痘～ bovine vaccine｜卡介～ BCG（Bacille Calmette-Guérin）vaccine ❺（～儿 miáor）形状像苗的 sth. like a young plant：火～儿 flame；tongue of flame ❻（Miáo）姓 a surname

【苗床】miáochuáng 培育作物幼苗的场所，有温床、冷床、露地苗床等 seedbed；hotbed；cold bed；open seedbed；bed of soil in which seedlings are grown for transplanting

【苗而不秀】miáo ér bù xiù《论语·子罕》：'苗而不秀者有矣夫！'只长了苗而没有秀穗 *The Analects·Zihan*：'There are young plants that fail to produce blossoms！'〈比喻 *fig.*〉资质虽好，但是没有成就。也比喻虚有其表 people who are gifted but have no achievements and look impressive but have no real worth

【苗剧】miáojù 苗族戏曲剧种，流行于湘西苗族聚居的地区 local opera of the Miao nationality，which is popular in the areas inhabited by Miao people in western Hunan Province

【苗木】miáomù 培育的树木幼株。一般种植在苗圃里,可以用种子繁殖,也可以用嫁接、插枝等方法取得。forestry nursery stock; saplings grown in the nursery, either by seed sowing or by grafting and transplanting cuttings

【苗圃】miáopǔ 培育树木幼株或某些农作物幼苗的园地 nursery (of young plants)

【苗儿】miáor〈方 *dial.*〉苗头 symptom of a trend; suggestion of a new development:这事情有点～了。The matter has begun to take form.|猪瘟刚露～就被控制住了。The hog cholera was controlled as soon as the first symptom was shown.

【苗条】miáo·tiao (妇女身材)细长柔美 (of a woman's body shape) slender; slim

【苗头】miáo·tou 略微显露的发展的趋势或情况 traces of a trend; suggestion of a new development:注意抓事故～。Watch out for the tell-tale signs of accidents.

【苗绣】miáoxiù 苗族妇女制作的刺绣 embroidery made by women of the Miao nationality

【苗裔】miáoyì〈书 *fml.*〉后代 progeny; descendants; offspring

【苗猪】miáozhū 仔猪(zǐzhū) pigling; piglet

【苗子】miáo·zi ❶〈方 *dial.*〉same as 苗 miáo ① ❷〈比喻 *fig.*〉继承某种事业的年轻人 young successor to a certain cause:他是个好～,有培养前途。He is a good young successor, and has great potential for development. ❸〈方 *dial.*〉苗头 symptom of a trend; suggestion of a new development

【苗族】Miáozú 我国少数民族之一,分布在贵州和湖南、云南、广西、四川、广东、湖北 Miaos; minority ethnic people inhabiting Guizhou, Hunan, Yunnan, Sichuan, Guangdong and Hubei provinces, and the Guangxi Zhuang Autonomous Region

描 miáo ❶ 照底样画(多指用薄纸蒙在底样上画 by placing a thin piece of paper on the original design or pattern) trace; copy:～花 trace a flower|～图 trace designs; copy designs|～张花样子 copy or trace a flower pattern ❷ 在原来颜色淡或需要改正的地方重复地涂抹 retouch; touch up:～红 trace in black ink over characters printed in red (in learning to write with a brush)|～眉打鬓 pencil (or paint) one's eyebrows and trim one's sideboards|写毛笔字,一笔是一笔,不要～。In practising Chinese calligraphy, write with a sure hand and don't retouch.

【描红】miáohóng ❶ 儿童用毛笔蘸墨在红模子上描着写字 trace in black ink over characters printed in red (in learning to write with a brush):先～,后临帖。First trace in black ink over characters printed in red and then practise calligraphy after a model ❷ 红模子 characters printed in red:写一张～ trace in black ink over a sheet of characters printed in red

【描画】miáohuà 画;描写 paint; draw; depict, describe:～治山改水的蓝图 draw a blueprint of reforesting mountains and taming rivers

【描绘】miáohuì 描画 depict; describe; portray:这些作品生动地～了我国农村的新气象。These works vividly depict the new look of the rural areas in our country.

【描记】miáojì 某些仪器中作用像笔的装置根据光电信号等描出线状图形,作为所监测对象情况的记录 records of line graphs traced on the photoelectric signals for what is monitored by a device like a pen in certain instruments

【描金】miáojīn 用金银粉在器物或墙、柱图案上勾勒描画,作为装饰 outline designs in gold on vessels, walls or pillars

【描摹】miáomó ❶ 照着底样写和画 trace; copy ❷ 用语言文字表现人或事物的形象、情状、特性等 (by spoken and written language) depict; portray; delineate:小说和戏剧常常用对话～一个人的性格。Novels and plays often portray the character of a person in the form of dialogues.

【描述】miáoshù 形象地叙述;描写叙述 describe:他生动地～了那件事的经过。He gave a vivid account of what happened.|作品朴实地～了农民的生活。The work gave a simple and factual description of peasant life.

【描图】miáo//tú 在原图上覆盖透明或半透明的纸,用绘图仪器照图样描绘墨线 tracing; copy of a drawing, made by tracing the lines on a superimposed, transparent or translucent sheet of paper

【描写】miáoxiě 用语言文字等把事物的形象表现出来 depict; portray; describe sth. in language:～风景 portray a landscape|～人物的内心活动 describe the inner feelings of a character

鹋 miáo ☞ 鸸鹋 érmiáo on p. 511

瞄 miáo 把视力集中在一点上;注视 fix one's gaze on; take aim:枪～得准 take good aim; aim accurately

【瞄准】miáo//zhǔn (～儿 miáo//zhǔnr) ❶ 射击时为使子弹、炮弹打中一定目标,调整枪口、炮口的方位和高低 lay; sight; take aim; aim; train on; adjust the sight of a gun or cannon in order to hit a target accurately:～靶子 aim at the target|把枪口～侵略者 aim a gun at an aggressor ❷ 泛指对准 (in a broad sense) aim at; direct to:这个工厂～市场的需求,生产出多种规格的产品。Catering to the market demand, the factory has produced a good variety of products.

miǎo (ㄇㄧㄠˇ)

杪 miǎo ❶ 树梢 tip of a twig ❷ 指年月或四季的末尾 end (of a year, month or season)：岁～ year end|月～ end of a month|秋～ end of autumn

胁 miǎo〈中医 *Chin. med.*〉指腹部两侧，第十二肋软骨下方、髂骨上方的软组织部分 flanks; soft tissues below the twelfth ribs and above the ilium on both sides of the belly

眇 miǎo〈书 *fml.*〉❶ 原指一只眼睛瞎，后来也指两只眼睛瞎 (orig.) sightlessness of one eye; blindness in both eyes ❷ 渺小；微小 tiny; insignificant; very small

秒 miǎo 计量单位名称 unit of measure a)时间，60 秒等于 1 分 a fraction of time; second = 1/60 of a minute; b)弧或角，60 秒等于 1 分 arc or angle; second = 1/60 of a minute; c)经度或纬度，60 秒等于 1 分 latitude or longitude, second = 1/60 of a minute

【秒表】miǎobiǎo 体育运动、科学研究等常用的一种计时表，测量的最小数值可达 1/5 秒、1/10 秒、1/50 秒不等 stopwatch; timepiece used in sports competition or training, and scientific research, the least or minimum value of measure being 1/5 of a second, 1/10 of a second, 1/50 of a second, etc.

【秒针】miǎozhēn 钟表上指示秒数的指针 (of a clock or watch) second hand

淼 miǎo〈书 *fml.*〉形容水大 (of an expanse of water) vast：～茫 (of an expanse of water) stretch as far as the eye can see|浩～ vast expanse of water|碧波～～ vast stretch of blue water

【淼茫】miǎománg 渺茫 (of an expanse of water) stretch as far as the eye can see

渺 miǎo ❶ 渺茫 (of an expanse of water) vast; vague; distant and indistinct：～若烟云 as vague as mist|～无人迹 remote and uninhabited|～无声息 quiet; still; silent; noiseless|音信～然 have not heard from a person; be never heard from again ❷ 渺小 tiny; insignificant：～不足道 insignificant; negligible; not worth mentioning

【渺茫】miǎománg ❶ 因遥远而模糊不清 vague; distant and indistinct：音信～ haven't heard from him; be never heard of again; there has been no news about a person; never been heard of ever since ❷ 因没有把握而难以预期 uncertain：前途～ have an uncertain future

【渺然】miǎorán 渺茫，不见踪影 vague; distant and indistinct; out of sight：音信～ be never heard of again|踪迹～ out of sight; lose sight of

【渺无人烟】miǎo wú rén yān 迷茫一片，没有人家，形容十分荒凉 desert; uninhabited; without a trace of human habitation; bleak and desolate：原野茫茫，～ vast expanse of uninhabited wilderness

【渺小】miǎoxiǎo same as 藐小 miǎoxiǎo

【渺远】miǎoyuǎn same as 邈远 miǎoyuǎn

缈 miǎo ☞ [缥缈] (piāomiǎo) on p.1475

藐 miǎo ❶ 小 small; petty：～小 insignificant; tiny; negligible ❷ 轻视；小看 slight; despise; look down upon：言者谆谆，听者～～(教诲的言辞恳切，而听的人却不以为然)。The speaker talked earnestly, but the listeners paid no attention. *or* Earnest words fall on deaf ears.

【藐视】miǎoshì 轻视；小看 despise; look down upon：在战略上要～敌人，在战术上要重视敌人。Strategically we should despise the enemies, but tactically we should take them seriously.

【藐小】miǎoxiǎo 微小 tiny; negligible; insignificant; paltry：集体的力量是伟大的，个人的力量是～的。The strength of a collective is great, whereas that of an individual is tiny.

邈 miǎo〈书 *fml.*〉遥远 faraway; remote; distant

【邈远】miǎoyuǎn 遥远 faraway; distant; remote：～的古代 remote antiquity; ancient times|～的蓝天 distant blue sky; also 渺远 miǎoyuǎn

miào (ㄇㄧㄠˋ)

妙 miào ❶ 好；美妙 wonderful; excellent; fine：～品 fine-quality goods; excellent goods; fine work of art; exquisite work|～境 wonderland; dreamland|～不可言 wonderful beyond description; too good for description|这个办法真～。That's an excellent way (or approach). ❷ 神奇；巧妙；奥妙 ingenious; clever; subtle：～计 excellent idea; clever idea; brilliant idea; good idea|～策 brilliant idea; good plan; wonderful scheme|～用 wonderful effect; good effect; magic effect|～算 clever idea; wonderful scheme; excellent plan|～诀 knack; secret formula; clever way of doing something|～手回春 magic cure; effective cure brings the dying back to life; effect a miraculous cure and bring the dying back to life|莫名其～ baffling; mysterious; for no apparent reason

【妙笔】miàobǐ 神妙的笔法或文笔 excellent writing; magic writing：～生花 wonderful writing with vivid description

【妙计】miàojì 巧妙的计策 excellent plan; brilliant scheme; good idea：锦囊～ clever scheme kept in an embroidered bag; clever scheme to be revealed|想了个～ hit upon an excellent idea

【妙诀】miàojué 高妙的诀窍 clever way; ingenious method：农业增产的～在于科学种田。The clever way of increasing farm production is scientific farming.

【妙龄】miàolíng 指女子的青春时期 youthfulness (of a girl)：～女郎 young lady

【妙趣】miàoqù 美妙的意趣 wit and interest：～天成 natural wit and humour｜～无穷 full of wit and humour

【妙趣横生】miàoqù héngshēng 洋溢着美妙意趣(多指语言、文章或美术品 oft. of words, article or work of art) full of wit and humour; very witty

【妙手】miàoshǒu 技艺高超的人 highly skilled person; master：绝代～ unrivalled master｜～回春 magic cure; effective cure brings the dying back to life; effect a miraculous cure and bring the dying back to life

【妙手回春】miào shǒu huí chūn ☞ 着手成春 zhuó shǒu chéng chūn on p. 2535

【妙药】miàoyào 灵验的药 efficacious medicine; wonder drug：灵丹～ cure-all; panacea; magic pills and wonder drugs; miraculous cure

【妙用】miàoyòng 奇妙的作用 wonderful effect; magical effect：～无穷 work infinite wonders

【妙语】miàoyǔ 有意味或动听的言语 witticism; witty remark：～双关 clever pun｜～惊人 unsurpassed beauty of expression

【妙招】miàozhāo (～儿 miàozhāor)奇妙高超的着数 clever trick; ingenious device; clever move; also 妙着 miàozhāo

【妙着】miàozhāo same as 妙招 miàozhāo

庙(廟) miào ❶〈旧时 *old*〉供祖宗神位的处所 temple; shrine：宗～ ancestral temple｜家～ family shrine ❷ 供神佛或历史上有名人物的处所 temple：寺～ temple; monastery｜土地～ temple of the village god｜文～ Confucian temple｜岳～ temple of Yue Fei (a patriotic general in the Southern Song Dynasty)｜山顶上有一座～。There is a temple atop the mountain. ❸〈书 *fml*.〉指朝廷 imperial court：～堂 imperial hall｜廊～ imperial court ❹〈书 *fml*.〉已死皇帝的代称 late emperor：～号(of a deceased emperor) posthumous title of honour｜～讳 name of a deceased emperor, high official, etc. ❺ 庙会 temple fair：赶～ go to the temple fair

【庙号】miàohào 我国封建时代，皇帝死后，在太庙立室奉祀时特起的名号，如高祖、太宗等 temple title; title, usu. with a 祖 'founder' or 宗 'ancestor', given to an emperor posthumously when his spirit tablet was established in the imperial ancestral temple, e. g. Emperor Gaozu and Emperor Taizong

【庙会】miàohuì 设在寺庙里边或附近的集市，在节日或规定的日子举行 fair; temple fair

【庙堂】miàotáng ❶ 庙宇 imperial ancestral temple ❷〈书 *fml*.〉指朝廷 imperial court

【庙宇】miàoyǔ same as 庙 miào ②

【庙主】miàozhǔ ❶ 主持庙中事务的和尚或道士 abbot; Buddhist monk or Taoist priest in charge of a temple ❷〈书 *fml*.〉指宗庙里的牌位 memorial tablet in an ancestral temple

【庙祝】miàozhù 寺庙中管香火的人 acolyte; temple attendant in charge of incense and religious service

玅 miào〈书 *fml*.〉same as 妙 miào

缪 Miào 姓 a surname
☞ miù on p. 1361 and móu on p. 1371

miē (ㄇㄧㄝ)

乜 miē〈方 *dial*.〉same as 乜斜 miē·xie ①
☞ Niè on p. 1416

【乜斜】miē·xie ❶ 眼睛略眯而斜着看(多表示瞧不起或不满意 oft. an expression of contempt or dissatisfaction) squint; look askance at：他～着眼睛，眼角挂着讥诮的笑意。He squinted with a sneering look in the corner of his eye. ❷ 眼睛因困倦眯成一条缝 eyes partly closed due to sleepiness or fatigue：～的睡眼 half-closed eyes heavy with sleep

咩(哶) miē〈拟声词 *onom*.〉形容羊叫的声音 baa; bleat

miè (ㄇㄧㄝˋ)

灭(滅) miè ❶ 熄灭 (of a light, fire, etc.) go out：火～了。The fire has gone out.｜灯～了。The light went out. ❷ 使熄灭 extinguish; put out; turn off：～灯 turn off the light｜沙土可以～火。Sand can put out a fire. ❸ 淹没 submerge; drown：～顶 get drowned ❹ 消灭；灭亡 perish; die out; become extinct; wither away：自生自～ emerge and perish of itself｜物质不～ conservation of matter ❺ 使不存在；使消灭 destroy; exterminate; wipe out：～蝇 kill flies｜长自己的志气，～敌人的威风 boost one's own morale and deflate the arrogance of the enemy

【灭茬】miè//chá (～儿 miè//chár)收割后把农作物留在地里的茎和根除掉 clean the stubble (fields); get rid of short stumps of grain left standing after harvesting

【灭此朝食】miè cǐ zhāo shí 消灭了敌人以后再吃早饭('此'指敌人)，形容痛恨敌人，希望立刻加以消灭(语本《左传》成公二年：'余姑翦灭此而朝食') wipe out the enemy before having breakfast; hate the enemy and be anxious to finish off the enemy quickly (see *The Zuo Commentary·Duke Cheng 2nd Year*: 'I'll wipe out all the enemies before having breakfast.')

【灭顶】miè//dǐng 水漫过头顶，指淹死 be drowned; water rising above one's head：～之灾(指致命的灾祸) fatal disaster

【灭火】miè//huǒ 把火弄灭 put out a fire; extinguish a fire; cut out an engine：～沙 sand for extinguishing a fire｜～器 fire extinguisher

【灭火器】mièhuǒqì 消防用具，通常是在圆铁筒里面装着可以产生灭火气体、泡沫等的化学物质，用时喷射在火焰上 fire extinguisher; portable device, usu. a metal cylinder containing chemicals that can produce gas or foam and can be sprayed on a fire to put it out

【灭迹】miè//jì 消灭做坏事时留下的痕迹 destroy the evidence of one's evildoing：毁尸～ get rid of a corpse to destroy evidence of murder｜销赃～ destroy the evidence of one's wrongdoing by disposing of the spoils

【灭绝】mièjué ❶ 完全消灭 become extinct; stamp out：使苍蝇蚊子死净～ wipe out all mosquitoes and flies ❷ 完全丧失 completely lose：～人性 inhuman; savage; cannibalistic

【灭口】miè//kǒu 害怕泄漏秘密而害死知道内情的人 do away with a witness or accomplice：杀人～ silence a witness by killing him; kill a person to prevent him from disclosing a secret

【灭门】mièmén 一家人都被杀害；一家人全死光 exterminate an entire family; kill all members of a family：～绝户 exterminate a whole family; kill all members of a family｜～之祸 disaster of execution of a whole family

【灭亡】mièwáng（国家、种族等）不再存在或使不存在（of a country, a race, etc.）peril; be destroyed; become extinct; die out：自取～ court destruction; bring ruin upon oneself

【灭种】mièzhǒng ❶ 消灭种族 exterminate a race; commit genocide：亡国～ destroy a country and exterminate a race ❷ 绝种 become extinct：这种动物已濒临～。This species of animal is on the verge of extinction.

【灭族】mièzú〈古代 *arch.*〉残酷刑罚，一人犯罪，他的父母兄弟妻子等亲属都一齐被杀 extermination of an entire family; brutal punishment imposed when one member of a family committed a crime and his parents, brothers, wife and children were killed together with him

蔑[1] miè〈书 *fml.*〉❶ 小；轻 little; light：～视 despise; disdain; slight; look down upon ❷ 无；没有 no; not; none; nothing：～以复加 in the extreme; cannot be surpassed; reach the limit

蔑[2]（衊） miè ☞ 诬蔑 wūmiè on p. 2018 and 污蔑 wūmiè on p. 2017

【蔑称】mièchēng ❶ 轻蔑地称呼 call a person in contempt; call a person contemptuously ❷ 轻蔑的称呼 contemptuous name

【蔑视】mièshì 轻视；小看 scorn; show contempt for：～困难 scorn difficulties｜脸上流露出～的神情 reveal a contemptuous expression on one's face

篾 miè 竹子劈成的薄片，也泛指苇子或高粱秆上劈下的皮 thin bamboo strip; rind of reed or sorghum：～席 bamboo mat｜～匠 basketry craftsman

【篾白】mièbái〈方 *dial.*〉篾黄 inner skin of a bamboo stem

【篾黄】mièhuáng 竹子的篾青以里的部分，质地较脆。有的地区叫篾白。inner skin of a bamboo stem; inner layer of a bamboo stem, more frangible than the outer layer; also 篾白 mièbái in some places

【篾匠】mièjiàng 用竹篾制造器物的小手工业者 craftsman who makes articles from bamboo strips

【篾片】mièpiàn ❶ 竹子劈成的薄片 thin bamboo strip ❷〈旧时 *old*〉称在豪富人家帮闲凑趣的人 hanger-on; sycophant

【篾青】mièqīng 竹子的外皮，质地较韧 outer cuticle of a bamboo stem with pliability

【篾条】miètiáo 条状的篾，用来编制器物 bamboo strip for weaving baskets, etc.

【篾子】miè·zi 篾条；篾片 bamboo strip：竹～ bamboo strip

蠛 miè［蠛蠓］(mièměng) 古书上指蠓 midge recorded in the ancient books

mín（ㄇㄧㄣˊ）

民 mín ❶ 人民 the people：国泰～安 country prospering and its people living in peace｜为～除害 get rid of a scourge for the people ❷ 指某种人 person of a certain occupation：藏～ Tibetan｜回～ Hui; Moslem｜农～ peasant｜渔～ fisherman｜牧～herdsman｜居～ resident｜侨～ resident living abroad ❸ 民间的 folk; of the people：～歌 folk song｜～谣 folklore ❹ 非军人；非军事的 civilian：军～团结 unity between the army and the civilian people｜拥政爱～ support the government and cherish the people｜～航公司 civil aviation corporation｜～用机场 civil airport

【民办】mínbàn 群众集体创办；私人创办 be run by the community or privately run：～小学 primary school run by the community or a private primary school｜～企业 private enterprise

【民变】mínbiàn〈旧时 *old*〉指人民群众对统治者的反抗运动 mass uprising; popular revolt：～蜂起 popular revolts broke out all over the country｜激起～ incite rebellion among the people; drive the people into rebellion

【民兵】mínbīng 不脱离生产的、群众性的人民武装组织，也称这种组织的成员 militia; people's armed organization not divorced from production; also members of the organization

【民不聊生】mín bù liáo shēng 人民没办法生活 people have no means of livelihood; masses live in dire poverty; people are destitute：军阀混战，～。Incessant fighting among the warlords made life impossible for the people.

【民船】mínchuán 载客和运货的船;民用船只 junk or small boat carrying passengers and freight; junk or small boat for civilian use

【民法】mínfǎ 规定公民和法人的财产关系(如债权、继承权等)以及跟它相联系的人身非财产关系(如劳动、婚姻、家庭等)的各种法律 civil law; laws concerning the property relations of the citizens and legal persons (e.g. creditor's rights, right of succession, etc.) and personal non-property relations (e.g. labour, marriage, family, etc.); ☞ 法律 fǎlǜ on p. 527

【民房】mínfáng 属于私人所有的住房;民用住房 house owned by a citizen; private house

【民愤】mínfèn 人民大众对有罪恶的人的愤恨 popular indignation; people's anger at the guilty people: 不杀不足以平～ have to be executed to assuage the people's anger

【民风】mínfēng 社会上的风气;民间风尚 folkways; local traits: ～淳朴。The people are simple and honest. | ～强悍。The people are fierce and doughty.

【民夫】mínfū 〈旧时 *old*〉称为官府、军队服劳役的人 conscripted labourer; people who do corvée labour for the government and army; also 民伕 mínfū

【民歌】míngē 民间口头流传的诗歌或歌曲,多不知作者姓名 folk song; song of anonymous authorship made and handed down among the people

【民工】míngōng ❶ 在政府动员或号召下参加修筑公路、堤坝或帮助军队运输等工作的人 labourer working on a road or dam construction project, or helping the army with transportation in response to a government call ❷ 指到城市打工的农民 peasant hired for a temporary job in the city

【民国】Mínguó 指中华民国 Republic of China (1912-1949)

【民航】mínháng 民用航空的简称 abbr. for 民用航空 mínyòng hángkōng: ～班机 civil aircraft; civil airplane

【民间】mínjiān ❶ 人民中间 popular; folk; among the people: ～文学 folk literature | ～音乐 folk music | 这个故事多少年来一直在～流传。For many years the story has circulated among the people. ❷ 非官方的 non-governmental; people-to-people: ～贸易 non-governmental trade | ～往来 non-governmental contact; people-to-people exchange

【民间文学】mínjiān wénxué 在人民中间广泛流传的文学,主要是口头文学,包括神话、传说、民间故事、民间戏曲、民间曲艺、歌谣等 folk literature; literature circulating widely among the people, mainly oral literature, including mythology, legends, folk tales, folk operas, folk ballads, folk rhymes, etc.

【民间艺术】mínjiān yìshù 劳动人民直接创造的或在劳动群众中广泛流传的艺术,包括音乐、舞蹈、造型艺术、工艺美术等 folk arts; arts created by the working people and widely circulating among the people, including folk music, folk dance, plastic arts, arts and crafts, etc.

【民警】mínjǐng 人民警察 people's police; people's policeman

【民居】mínjū 民房 dwelling; private house: 江南～ houses in areas south of the Yangtze River

【民力】mínlì 人民的财力 financial resources of the people: 珍惜～ cherish the financial resources of the people

【民命】mínmìng 人民的生命 lives of the people: 国脉～ national lifeline and the people's livelihood

【民瘼】mínmò 〈书 *fml.*〉人民的疾苦 hardships or miseries of the people

【民女】mínnǚ 百姓家的女子 woman from an ordinary family

【民品】mínpǐn 民用物品(区别于'军品' as compared with 'military products') civilian products

【民气】mínqì 人民对关系国家、民族安危存亡的重大局势所表现的意志 people's morale; popular morale: ～旺盛 high morale of the people; people's morale being high

【民情】mínqíng ❶ 人民的生产活动、风俗习惯等情况 conditions of the people; production, life, customs and habits of the people: 熟悉～ be familiar with the conditions of the people ❷ 指人民的心情、愿望等 public feelings; feelings and aspirations of the people: 体恤～ understand the feelings and aspirations of the people

【民权】mínquán 指人民在政治上的民主权利 civil rights; democratic political rights of the people

【民权主义】mínquán zhǔyì 三民主义的一个组成部分 Principle of Democracy, one of the Three People's Principles (Nationalism, Democracy and the People's Livelihood) put forward by Dr. Sun Yat-sen; ☞ 三民主义 sānmín zhǔyì on p. 1653

【民生】mínshēng 人民的生计 people's livelihood: 国计～ national economy and people's livelihood | ～凋敝 people living in destitution

【民生主义】mínshēng zhǔyì 三民主义的一个组成部分 Principle of the People's Livelihood, one of the Three People's Principles; ☞ 三民主义 sānmín zhǔyì on p. 1653

【民事】mínshì 有关民法的 civil; relating to civil law: ～权利 civil rights | ～诉讼 civil lawsuits; ☞ 民法 mínfǎ

【民事法庭】mínshì fǎtíng 负责审理民事案件的法庭 civil court; court hearing civil lawsuits;

简称 abbr. 民庭 míntíng

【民事权利】mínshì quánlì 民法上所规定的权利 civil rights as stipulated in the civil law

【民事诉讼】mínshì sùsòng 关于民事案件的诉讼 civil action, process, or lawsuit

【民俗】mínsú 民间的风俗习惯 folkways; folk custom: 考察～ study and investigate folk customs

【民俗学】mínsúxué 以民间风俗、传说、口头文学等为研究对象的学科 folklore; study and scientific investigation of the unwritten traditional beliefs, legends, sayings, customs, etc. of a culture

【民庭】míntíng 民事法庭的简称 abbr. for 民事法庭 mínshì fǎtíng

【民团】míntuán 〈旧时 *old*〉地主豪绅组织的地方武装 civil corps; local armed forces organized by a landlord

【民校】mínxiào ❶ 成年人利用闲暇时间学习文化的学校 spare-time school for adults ❷ 民间开办的学校 school run by local people

【民心】mínxīn 人民共同的心意 popular feelings; common aspiration of the people: ～所向 what conforms to the common aspirations of the people; trend of public feeling

【民信局】mínxìnjú 〈旧时 *old*〉私营的以递送信件、包裹以及办理汇兑等为主的机构，同时兼办运货、兑换货币等业务 private institution where letters, parcels and remittances are handled along with freight transport and money exchange services

【民选】mínxuǎn 由人民群众选举 elected by the people: ～代表 representatives or deputies elected by the people

【民谚】mínyàn 民间谚语，如：'人不可貌相，海水不可斗量'，'路遥知马力，日久见人心' common proverbs, e. g. 'A man cannot be known by his looks, nor can the sea be measured with a dipper.' 'As distance tests a horse's strength, so time reveals a person's heart.'

【民谣】mínyáo 民间歌谣，多指与时事政治有关的 folk rhyme (esp. of the topical and political type)

【民意】mínyì 人民共同的意见和愿望 will of the people; popular will: ～测验 poll; public opinion poll | ～不可侮。The will of the people must not be slighted.

【民营】mínyíng 人民群众投资经营；私人经营 private; with private investment: ～企业 private enterprise

【民用】mínyòng 人民生活所使用的 civil; for civil use: ～航空 civil aviation | ～建筑 civil building | ～五金器材 hard ware for civilian use

【民怨】mínyuàn 人民群众对反动统治者的怨恨 popular resentment: ～沸腾(形容人民群众对反动统治者的怨恨达到极点)。The people are boiling with resentment.

【民乐】mínyuè 民间器乐 folk music, played with traditional instruments: ～队 orchestra of traditional instruments; traditional instruments orchestra | ～合奏 ensemble of traditional instruments

【民运】mínyùn ❶ 有关人民生活物资的运输工作 transportation of goods for the livelihood of the people ❷〈旧时 *old*〉私营的运输业 private transport industry ❸ 指民众运动 mass movement; mass campaign: ～工作 mass movement work | ～干事 clerks doing mass movement work

【民贼】mínzéi 对国家和人民犯了严重罪行的人 people who committed serious crimes against the state and the people: 独夫～ dictator; tyrant and enemy of the people

【民宅】mínzhái 民居；民房 private house

【民政】mínzhèng 国内行政事务的一部分，在我国，民政包括选举、行政区划、地政、户政、国籍、民工动员、婚姻登记、社团登记、优抚、救济等 civil administration; civil affairs, including election, administrative division, land administration, residence administration, nationality, mobilization of temporary labourers, marriage registration, registration of public organizations, special care and relief of disabled servicemen and family members of revolutionary martyrs and servicemen, relief, etc.

【民脂民膏】mín zhī mín gāo 〈比喻 *fig.*〉人民用血汗换来的财富 wealth of the people created with their blood and sweat; flesh and blood of the people

【民智】mínzhì 指一个国家的人民所具有的文化知识 education of the people in a country: 开发～ develop education of the people | ～渐开 gradually educate the people

【民众】mínzhòng 人民大众 masses; common people; populace: 唤起～ arouse the masses; awaken the masses

【民主】mínzhǔ ❶ 指人民有参与国事或对国事有自由发表意见的权利 democracy; democratic rights; right of the people to participate in the state affairs and to air their views freely on the state affairs ❷ 合于民主原则 democratic: 作风～ democratic work-style | ～办厂 run a factory on a democratic basis

【民主党派】mínzhǔ dǎngpài 接受中国共产党的领导、参加人民民主统一战线的其他政党的统称。有中国国民党革命委员会、中国民主同盟、中国民主建国会、中国民主促进会、中国农工民主党、中国致公党、台湾民主自治同盟和九三学社等。democratic parties; political parties that accept the leadership of the Chinese Communist Party and join the people's democratic united front, including the Revolutionary Committee of the Chinese Kuomintang, the Chinese Democratic League, the China

Democratic National Construction Association, the China Association for Promoting Democracy, the Chinese Peasants and Workers Democratic Party, the China Zhi Gong Party (Public Interest Party), the Taiwan Democratic Self-Government League and the Jiu San (September 3) Society

【民主改革】mínzhǔ gǎigé 废除封建制度、建立民主制度的各项社会改革,包括土地制度的改革,婚姻制度的改革,企业经营管理的民主化,以及某些少数民族地区的农奴解放、奴隶解放等 democratic reform; social reform to abolish feudal systems and establish democratic systems, include land reform, reform of the marriage system, democratization of enterprise management, and emancipation of serfs and slaves in regions inhabited by minority peoples

【民主革命】mínzhǔ gémìng 以反封建为目的的资产阶级性质的革命,如法国大革命和我国的新民主主义革命 democratic revolution; revolution of a bourgeois character against feudalism, such as the French Revolution and the New Democratic Revolution in China

【民主国】mínzhǔguó 共和国 republic; democratic state

【民主集中制】mínzhǔ-jízhōngzhì 在民主基础上的集中和在集中指导下的民主相结合的制度。民主集中制是马克思列宁主义政党、社会主义国家机关和人民团体的组织原则。democratic centralism; system of combining centralism on the basis of democracy and democracy under centralized guidance. It is the organizational principle of a Marxist-Leninist party, the state organs of a socialist country and a people's organization.

【民族】mínzú ❶ 指历史上形成的、处于不同社会发展阶段的各种人的共同体 nation; nationality; ethnic group; historically developed community of people living in a given stage of social development ❷ 特指具有共同语言、共同地域、共同经济生活以及表现于共同文化上的共同心理素质的人的共同体 community of people with a common language, a common territory, a common economic life and common psychological quality manifested in a common culture

【民族共同语】mínzú gòngtóngyǔ 一个民族共同使用的语言。现在我国汉民族的共同语就是普通话。common national language; common language for the people of the Han ethnic background in China being the standard Chinese language

【民族区域自治】mínzú qūyù zìzhì 中国共产党运用马克思列宁主义关于民族问题的理论,结合我国具体情况而制定的解决民族问题的基本政策。根据这个政策,各少数民族以自己的聚居区域的大小不同而建立自治区、自治州和自治县等自治机关,在国务院统一领导下,除行使一般地方国家机关职权外,可以依照法律规定的权限行使自治权。regional autonomy of minority ethnic people; regional ethnic autonomy; fundamental policy made by the Communist Party of China by applying the Marxist-Leninist theory on ethnic issues in the light of the concrete conditions in China to deal with ethnic affairs. In accordance with this policy, the minority peoples establish organs of self-government of regions, prefectures and counties according to different sizes of the areas they inhabit, and exercise the right to autonomy within the limits of power provided by law apart from exercising the general power of local state organs under the unified leadership of the State Council.

【民族形式】mínzú xíngshì 一个民族所独有,为本民族人民大众所习惯、所爱好的表现形式 national style; national form; form of expression peculiar to a nation and favoured by the people of the nation

【民族学】mínzúxué 以氏族、部落、部族、民族等人们的共同体为研究对象的学科 ethnology; branch of learning that studies the cultures of the communities, such as clans, tribes, ethnic peoples, nationaltiy, etc.

【民族英雄】mínzú yīngxióng 捍卫本民族的独立、自由和利益,在抗击外来侵略的斗争中表现无比英勇的人 national hero; man of extraordinary courage displayed in the struggle for national independence, freedom and interests against foreign aggression

【民族运动】mínzú yùndòng 为反对民族压迫,争取民族平等和民族独立而进行的斗争 national movement; patriotic movement; movement or struggle against national oppression and for national equality and national independence

【民族主义】mínzú zhǔyì ❶ 资产阶级对于民族的看法及其处理民族问题的纲领和政策。在资本主义上升时期的民族运动中,在殖民地、半殖民地国家争取国家独立和民族解放的运动中,民族主义具有一定的进步性。nationalism; view of the bourgeoisie on nation and its programme and policy for handling problems related to different nationalities. Nationalism showed certain progressive character in the movement for national equality and national independence at the rise of capitalism, and in the movement for national independence and national liberation in colonial and semi-colonial countries. ❷ 三民主义的一个组成部分 Principle of Nationalism, one of the Three People's Principles; ☞ 三民主义 sānmín zhǔyì on p. 1653

【民族资本】mínzú zīběn 殖民地、半殖民地或民族独立国家中民族资产阶级所拥有的资本 capital of the national bourgeoisie in a colonial or semi-colonial country or one which has won national independence

【民族资产阶级】mínzú zīchǎn jiējí 殖民地、半殖民地国家和某些新独立国家里的中等资产阶级 national bourgeoisie; middle bourgeoisie in a colonial, semi-colonial, or newly independent country

【民族自决】mínzú zìjué 指每一个民族有权按照自己的愿望来处理自己的事情,不容别人强加干涉。民族自决是被压迫民族、殖民地和半殖民地人民所争取的基本权利。national self-determination; fundamental right fought for by the oppressed nations and the people in the colonies and semi-colonies, which means that every nation has the right to handle its own affairs according to its own wishes and brooks no interference from others

苠 mín 庄稼生长期较长,成熟期较晚 crop that grows longer and ripens late:～高粱 late sorghum | 黄谷子比白谷子～。The yellow millet grows longer than the white millet.

忞 mín 〈书 *fml.*〉勉力 exert oneself; make efforts; work hard; try one's best

旻 mín 〈书 *fml.*〉❶ 秋天 autumn ❷ 天空 sky:苍～ blue sky

【旻天】míntiān 〈书 *fml.*〉❶ 秋天 autumn ❷ 泛指天 (in a broad sense) sky

岷 Mín ❶ 岷山,山名,在四川、甘肃交界的地方 Minshan, name of a mountain bordering Sichuan and Gansu provinces ❷ 岷江,水名,在四川 Minjiang, name of a river in Sichuan Province

珉(瑉、碣) mín 〈书 *fml.*〉像玉的石头 jade-like stone

缗(緡) mín 〈书 *fml.*〉❶ 穿铜钱用的绳子 string for putting cash together in ancient times ❷ 〈量词 *classifier*〉用于成串的铜钱,每串一千文 *min*; a string of bronze coins; one *min* or string equals 1,000 coins or cents:钱三百～ 300 *min* (or strings)

mǐn (ㄇㄧㄣˇ)

皿 mǐn ☞ 器皿 qìmǐn on p. 1526

闵 mǐn ❶ same as 悯 mǐn ❷ (Mǐn) 姓 a surname

抿1 mǐn 用小刷子蘸水或油抹(头发等) smooth one's hair with a small brush dipped in water or oil:～了～头发 brush one's hair with water or oil

抿2 mǐn ❶ (嘴、耳朵、翅膀等)稍稍合拢;收敛 tuck; furl; (of lips, ears, wings, etc.) close slightly:～着嘴笑 smile with closed lips | 小兔子跑着跑着,忽然两耳向后一～,站住了。The rabbit was running when it stopped suddenly with its ears furled backward. | 水鸟儿一～翅膀,钻入水中。A water bird tucked its wings and dived into the water. ❷ 嘴唇轻轻地沾一下碗或杯子,略微喝一点 sip; touch the bowl or glass with one's lips and drink a little:～了一口酒 take a sip of wine

【抿子】mǐn·zi 妇女梳头时抹油等用的小刷子 small hairbrush used by a woman with oil; also 筤子 mǐn·zi

黾(黽) mǐn [黾勉](mǐnmiǎn)〈书 *fml.*〉努力;勉力 strive; exert oneself; try hard:～从事 exert oneself to the utmost; do one's best; also 僶俛 mǐnmiǎn

☞ miǎn on p. 1337

泯 mǐn 消灭;丧失 vanish; lose; die out:～灭 vanish; die out | ～没 vanish; sink into oblivion; become lost | 良心未～ still have some conscience

【泯灭】mǐnmiè (形迹、印象等)消灭 disappear; vanish; (of traces, impressions, etc.) die out:这几部影片给人留下了难以～的印象。These films have left an indelible impression on the people.

【泯没】mǐnmò (形迹、功绩等)消灭;消失 (of traces, impressions, etc.) vanish; sink into oblivion; become lost:烈士的功绩是不会～的。The contributions of the revolutionary martyrs will never be forgotten.

闽 Mǐn ❶ 闽江,水名,在福建 Minjiang, name of a river in Fujian Province ❷ 福建的别称 Min, another name for 福建 Fújiàn

【闽菜】mǐncài 福建风味的菜肴 Fujian cuisine

【闽剧】mǐnjù 福建地方戏曲剧种之一,流行于该省东北部 Min Opera, local opera popular in northeast Fujian Province; also 福州戏 fúzhōuxì

僶(僶) mǐn [僶俛](mǐnmiǎn) same as 黾勉 mǐnmiǎn

悯 mǐn ❶ 怜悯 commiserate; pity; sympathy:其情可～。His case deserves sympathy. ❷ 〈书 *fml.*〉忧愁 sorrow; sadness; worry:～然涕下 weep sadly; shed sad tears

【悯惜】mǐnxī 怜惜 take pity on; have pity for (on); feel pity for

【悯恤】mǐnxù 怜悯 feel compassion for; have pity on; have (or show) sympathy for:～孤儿 have sympathy for the orphans

筤 mǐn 竹篾 thin bamboo strip

【筤子】mǐn·zi same as 抿子 mǐn·zi

敏 mǐn ❶ 疾速;敏捷 quick; nimble; agile:～感 sensitive | 灵～ quick-witted ❷ 聪明;机警 quick; alert; quick-witted:聪～ clever | 机～ quick-witted ❸ (Mǐn)姓 a surname

【敏感】mǐngǎn 生理上或心理上对外界事物反应很快 sensitive; quick physiological or psychological response to what happens in the outside world:有些动物对天气的变化非常～。Some animals are very sensitive to the changes in the weather. | 他是一个～的人，接受新事物很快。He is a sensitive man and accepts new things very quickly. ◇宗教问题向来是个～的问题。Religion has always been a sensitive issue.

【敏慧】mǐnhuì 聪明，有智慧 bright; intelligent: ～的姑娘 bright girl

【敏捷】mǐnjié（动作等）迅速而灵敏（of movements, etc.）quick; nimble; agile: 思维～ be quick in thinking; quick-witted | 行动～ nimble-limbed

【敏锐】mǐnruì（感觉）灵敏；（眼光）尖锐 sharp (eyes); acute (senses); keen: 思想～ have acute mind; have a penetrating mind | 目光～ have sharp eyes; be keen-sighted | ～的洞察力 have keen insight

湣 mǐn〈古代 *arch.*〉谥号用字，如《史记》有鲁湣公（《春秋》作鲁闵公）the late (followed by a title or a name); a Chinese character used in a posthumous title, such as 'the late Duke Min of Lu' as mentioned in the *Records of the Historian*. In the *Spring and Autumn Annals*, a different Chinese character is used which has the same pronunciation and function.

暋(敃) mǐn〈书 *fml.*〉强横 arrogant; despotic; brutal

愍(惽) mǐn〈书 *fml.*〉same as 悯 mǐn

慜 mǐn〈书 *fml.*〉聪明敏捷 smart and quick

鳘 mǐn 鳘鱼，鮸（miǎn）鱼的通称 slate-cod croaker (*Nibea diacanthus*); common name for 鮸鱼 miǎnyú

míng（ㄇㄧㄥˊ）

名 míng ❶（～儿 míngr）名字；名称 name: 人～ name of a person | 书～ title of a book | 命～ name after; give a name to | 报～ enter one's name (in a competition, entrance examination, etc.) | 给他起个～儿 give him a name ❷ 名字叫做 given name: 这位女英雄姓刘～胡兰。The family name of this heroine is Liu and her given name is Hulan. ❸ 名义 in the name of: 你不该以出差为～，到处游山玩水。You should not take a pleasure trip in the guise of a business trip. ❹ 名声；名誉 fame; reputation; renown: 出～ make one's name known; make a big name; become famous | 有～ famous; well-known | 世界闻～ world-famous; world-renowned; world-known ❺ 出名的；有名声的 celebrated; well-known; noted: ～医 noted doctor | ～著 masterpiece; classic | ～画 masterpiece; famous painting | ～山大川 famous mountains and great rivers ❻〈书 *fml.*〉说出 describe; express: 莫～其妙 baffling; mysterious; be unable to make head or the tail of something | 不可～状 indescribable; beyond description ❼〈书 *fml.*〉占有 take; possess: 一文不～ not have a single cent in one's pocket; | 不～一钱 without a cent under one's name ❽〈量词 *classifier*〉用于人 [indicating number of people]: 三百多～工作人员 more than 300 staff members | 录取新生四十～ enrol 40 new students ❾（Míng）姓 a surname

【名不副实】míng bù fù shí 名称或名声与实际不相符；有名无实 name falls short of the reality; be sth. more in name than in reality; be unworthy of the name or title; also 名不符实 míng bù fú shí

【名不虚传】míng bù xū chuán 确实很好，不是空有虚名 have a well-deserved reputation; deserve the reputation one enjoys; live up to one's reputation

【名册】míngcè 登记姓名的簿子 register; roll: 花～ roll; register; muster roll

【名产】míngchǎn 著名的产品 famous product: 织锦是我国杭州的～。Brocade is a famous product of Hangzhou.

【名称】míngchēng 事物的名字（也用于人的集体）name of a thing (also of an organization)

【名垂千古】míng chuí qiāngǔ 好的名声永远流传 go down in history; also 名垂千秋 míng chuí qiānqiū

【名垂青史】míng chuí qīngshǐ 好的名声和事迹载入史籍永远流传 go down in history; be crowned with eternal glory

【名词】míngcí ❶ 表示人或事物名称的词，如'人、牛、水、友谊、团体、今天、中间、北京、孔子' noun; substantive; any of a class of words naming or denoting a person, thing, etc. Example: person, ox, water, friendship, organization, today, middle, Beijing, Confucius ❷（～儿 míngcír）术语或近似术语的字眼（不限于语法上的名词）(not limited to the category of nouns in grammar) technical term; terminology: 化学～ chemical term | 新～儿 new term; new expression ❸ 表达三段论法结构中的概念的词 name; word expressing a concept in syllogism

【名次】míngcì 依照一定标准排列的姓名或名称的次序 standing; list of names showing their rank and order, as in achievement: 比赛中他成绩较好，所以～也靠前。As he performed better in the competition, he was ranked among those on top.

【名刺】míngcì〈书 *fml.*〉名片 visiting card; calling card; name card

【名存实亡】míng cún shí wáng 名义上还有，实际上已经不存在 cease to exist except in name; exist in name only

【名单】míngdān（～儿 míngdānr）记录人名的单子 name list: 开列～ make a list of names | 受奖人～ list of award winners

【名额】míng'é 人员的数额 number of people

assigned or allowed; quota of people: ～有限，报名从速。Since the number of people allowed is limited, enter your name as soon as possible.

【名分】míngfèn 〈书 *fml.*〉指人的名义、身份和地位 (of a person) capacity, status or position: 正～ assign a right job to suit one's status or position

【名副其实】míng fù qí shí 名称或名声与实际相符合 name matches the reality; be sth. in reality as well as in name; be worthy of the name; also 名符其实 míng fú qí shí

【名贵】míngguì 著名而且珍贵 rare; famous and precious: ～的字画 priceless scrolls of calligraphy and painting | 鹿茸、麝香等都是～的药材。Pilose antler and musk are rare medicinal herbs.

【名号】mínghào 名字和别号 person's name and alias

【名讳】mínghuì 〈旧时 *old*〉指尊长或所尊敬的人的名字 name of one's elder and better or of a respected person

【名迹】míngjì ❶ 著名的古迹 famous place of historical interest ❷ 名家的手迹 master's original calligraphic work ❸〈书 *fml.*〉声誉功业 reputation and achievement

【名家】Míngjiā 先秦时期以辩论名实问题为中心的一个思想派别，以惠施、公孙龙为代表。名家的特点是用比较严格的推理形式来辩论问题，但有时流于诡辩。它对我国古代逻辑学的发展有一定贡献。School of Logicians (in the Spring and Autumn and Warring States Periods that contributed to the development of logic in ancient China); school of thought represented by Hui Shi and Gongsun Long, which centred on the debate on the concept and reality by using strict reasoning, which, however, sometimes was reduced to sophistry

【名家】míngjiā 在某种学术或技能方面有特殊贡献的著名人物 master; famous expert; person of academic or artistic distinction

【名缰利锁】míng jiāng lì suǒ 名和利像缰绳和锁链，会把人束缚住 fetters of fame and wealth; fame and wealth that fetter a person like reins and chains

【名教】míngjiào 以儒家所定的名分和儒家的教训为准则的道德观念，曾在思想上起过维护封建统治的作用 Confucian ethical code; ethical code based on the Confucian statuses and teachings, which played an ideological role in safeguarding the feudal rule

【名节】míngjié 名誉和节操 reputation and moral integrity: 保全～ preserve one's reputation and moral integrity

【名句】míngjù 著名的句子或短语 well-known phrase; much quoted line: 千古传诵的～ well-known phrase that has been on everybody's lips from generation to generation

【名款】míngkuǎn 书画上题的作者姓名 colophon; name inscribed on a painting or a piece of calligraphy: 这幅古画没有～，需请专家考证。No name of the painter is inscribed on this painting, so an expert should be invited to ascertain it.

【名利】mínglì 指个人的名位和利益 fame and gain; fame and wealth: 不求～ not seek fame and gain | ～双收 achieve both fame and gain | 清除～思想 get rid of the desire for fame and gain

【名利场】mínglìchǎng 指世人争名逐利的场所 vanity fair; place where people pursue fame and gain

【名列前茅】míng liè qiánmáo 指名次列在前面 rank among the best; take one of the first places; stand at the top; be among the best of successful candidates (前茅 *qianmao*: 春秋时代楚国行军，有人拿着茅当旗子走在队伍的前面 used as the sign of the front runner, derived from the practice of the troops of the state of Chu during the Spring and Autumn Period, with the soldier walking in the lead of a march always holding a cogon grass in his hand as the banner.)

【名伶】mínglíng 〈旧时 *old*〉称著名的戏剧演员 famous actors or actresses: 一代～ famous actors or actresses of the times

【名流】míngliú 著名的人士 (多指学术界、政治界的) celebrities (of the academic and political circles); distinguished personages: 社会～ celebrities from all walks of life | 学界～ noted figures of the academic circles

【名录】mínglù 登记人名或其他事物名称的簿子；名册 directory; roster; roll

【名落孙山】míng luò Sūn Shān 宋朝孙山考中了末一名回家，有人向他打听自己的儿子考中了没有，孙山说：'解名尽处是孙山，贤郎更在孙山外'(见于宋范公偁《过庭录》)。后用来婉言应考不中。fall behind Sun Shan — fail in an exam or a competition. According to *Records of Ancestor's Teachings* by Fan Gongcheng of the Song Dynasty, when a man by the name of Sun Shan in the Song Dynasty returned home after finishing last in an imperial examination, a neighbour asked him whether his son had passed the exam or not. Sun Shan replied: 'At the end of the list of the successful candidates is Sun Shan, after whom is your son.'

【名门】míngmén 指有声望的人家 eminent family; old and well-known family; distinguished family; illustrious family: ～贵族 eminent families and the nobility | ～闺秀 daughter of an eminent family

【名目】míngmù 事物的名称 items; names of things: 巧立～ invent all kinds of names | ～繁

多 a multitude of items; names or items of every description

【名牌】míngpái ❶（～儿 míngpáir）出名的牌子 famous brand:～货 goods of best brands|～商品 famous-brand commodities|～大学 prestigious university ❷ 写着人名的牌子；标明物品名称等的牌子 nameplate; name tag:席位摆放着代表们的～。The nameplates of the delegates are placed at their seats.

【名片】míngpiàn（～儿 míngpiànr）交际时所用的向人介绍自己的长方形硬纸片，上面印着自己的姓名、职务、地址等 visiting card; calling card; name card; card with one's name, title or position, address, etc. printed

【名气】míng·qi 名声 reputation; fame; name:小有～ enjoy some reputation|他是一位很有～的医生。He is a reputed (or famous) doctor.

【名人】míngrén 著名的人物 celebrity; notable; famous person; eminent person:文化～ celebrities in cultural circles|～墨迹 original work by a famous calligrapher or painter

【名山】míngshān 著名的大山 famous mountain:～大川 famous mountains and great rivers

【名山事业】míngshān shìyè《史记·太史公自序》:'藏之名山，副在京师，俟后世圣人君子。'后来称著书立说为'名山事业'。devoted to writing; take up writing as one's lifetime career. *Records of the Historian·Author's Preface*: 'Hidden in the famous mountains, and holding office in the capital city, I await to be a sage in the later age.' From this line is derived the phrase, 'a career in the mountains', alluding to writing.

【名声】míngshēng 在社会上流传的评价 reputation; estimation in which a person or a thing is commonly held:好～ good reputation|～很坏 have an unsavoury reputation; be infamous|～在外 be well-known

【名胜】míngshèng 有古迹或优美风景的著名的地方 place famous for its scenery or historical relics; scenic spot:游览～ visit well-known scenic spots|～古迹 places of historic interest and scenic beauty; scenic spots and historical sites

【名师】míngshī 有名的教师或师傅 noted teacher or master:～出高徒 great teacher produces a brilliant student

【名士】míngshì ❶〈旧时 *old*〉指以诗文等著称的人 person with a literary reputation ❷〈旧时 *old*〉指名望很高而不做官的人 celebrity with no official post

【名士派】míng·shìpài〈旧时 *old*〉指知识分子中不拘小节、狂放不羁的一流人，也指这种人的作风 unconventional and untrammelled intellectual; style of an unconventional person

【名氏】míngshì 姓名 name

【名手】míngshǒu 因文笔、技艺等高超而著名的人 famous artist, player, etc.:国术～ famous Chinese Wushu master

【名数】míngshù 带有单位名称的数，如 3 斤、5 本、4 尺 2 寸等 concrete number; numeral-classifier compound, such as three *jin*, five copies, four *chi* and two *cun*

【名宿】míngsù 出名的老前辈 well-known veterans:武林～ well-known martial arts masters|教育界的～ well-known scholars in the educational circles

【名堂】míng·tang ❶ 花样；名目 variety; item; trick:联欢会上～真多，又有舞蹈，又有杂耍。It's a great variety show at the party with so much to see — dances, juggling, etc. ❷ 成就；结果 achievement; result:依靠群众一定会搞出～来的。Depending on the masses, you will surely achieve something.|跟他讨论了半天，也没讨论出个～来。I discussed with him for a long time but couldn't get anything out of him. ❸ 道理；内容 reason; why; for what; there is sth. in or behind:真不简单，这里面还有～呢。It's not a simple matter. There is something behind it.

【名帖】míngtiě 名片 visiting card:客人递上～。The visitor handed in his name card.

【名望】míngwàng 好的名声；声望 renown; fame and prestige; good reputation:～高 high reputation|张大夫医术高明，在这一带很有～。Doctor Zhang has fine medical skill and enjoys a good reputation in this area.

【名位】míngwèi 名声和地位 fame and position:埋头苦干，不计～ bend over one's work without thinking of fame and position; work hard and take no account of one's fame and position

【名物】míngwù 事物及其名称 thing and its name

【名下】míngxià 某人名义之下，指属于某人或跟某人有关 under someone's name; belong to someone; have sth. to do with sb.:今儿下午的活儿是小李替我干的，工作量不能记在我的～。Xiao Li did the work for me this afternoon, thus the amount of work should not be registered under my name.|这事怎么搞到我～来了? How could I be blamed for it? *or* How could it have anything to do with me?

【名衔】míngxián 头衔 title

【名学】míngxué 逻辑学的旧称 old name for 逻辑学 luójìxué

【名言】míngyán 著名的话 well-known saying; celebrated dictum; famous remark:至理～ wise dictum; golden saying

【名义】míngyì ❶ 做某事时用来作为依据的名称或称号 name; name or title by which sth. is being done:我以个人的～保证，一定提前完成任务。I pledge in my own name to fulfil the task ahead of time. ❷ 表面上；形式上（后面

多带'上'字 usu. followed by 上 shàng)nominal; titular; in name:她～上是总管,实际上却什么都不管。In name, she is in full charge, but in fact, she takes care of nothing.

【名义工资】míngyì gōngzī 工人付出劳动力时所得到的以货币表现出来的工资。名义工资不能确切反映出工资的实际水平,因为名义工资不变,实际工资可以因物价的涨跌而降低或上升。nominal wages; wages stated in terms of money paid for the labour done. The nominal wages cannot exactly reflect the actual level of the wages, because the nominal wages do not change, the real wages fall or rise with the rise or fall of the prices. ☞ 实际工资 shíjì gōngzī on p.1742

【名优】[1] míngyōu 名伶 famous actor or actress: 一代～ famous actor or actress of the times

【名优】[2] míngyōu 有名的,高质量的(商品) famous or high-quality (commodity)

【名誉】míngyù ❶ 名声 fame; reputation:爱惜～ treasure one's reputation ❷ 名义上的(多指赠给的名义,含尊重意 usu. given as an honour and showing respect) honorary:～会员 honorary member|～主席 honorary chairman; honorary president

【名媛】míngyuàn 〈书 *fml.*〉有名的女子 famous lady

【名章】míngzhāng 刻着人名的图章 seal inscribed with a name

【名正言顺】míng zhèng yán shùn 名义正当,道理也讲得通 fitting and proper; name is correct and what is said accords with reason — perfectly justifiable

【名著】míngzhù 有价值的出名著作 masterpiece; classic; valuable, famous book; famous work:文学～literary classic; famous literary work; literary masterpiece|世界～ world classic

【名状】míngzhuàng 说出事物的状态(多用在否定词后面 usu. used in the negative) give the right name for sth.; describe:难以～的奇花异卉 exotic flowers and rare plants that words fail to describe|兴奋之情,不可～。The excitement is indescribable.

【名字】míng·zi ❶ 一个或几个字,跟姓合在一起,用来代表一个人,区别于别的人 name or given name; one or more than one character combined with a family name to represent a person and distinguish him or her from another:他现在的～是上学时老师给起的。His current name was given by his teacher when he went to school. ❷ 一个或几个字,用来代表一种事物,区别于别种事物 one or more than one characters representing a thing different from another:这村子的～叫张各庄。The name of this village is Zhanggezhuang.

明[1] míng ❶ 明亮(跟'暗'相对 as opposed to 'dim') bright; brilliant; light:～月 bright moon|天～ daybreak|灯火通～。The place is brightly lit. ❷ 明白;清楚 clear; distinct:问～ ask|说～ explain; make one's points clear|黑白分～ black and white clearly distinguished; right and wrong clearly distinguished; sharp contrast between black and white|去向不～ not know one's whereabouts; not know where one has gone ❸ 公开;显露在外;不隐蔽(跟'暗'相对 as opposed to 'hidden')open:～沟 open ditch|有话～说 speak one's mind plainly; put (or lay) one's cards on the table|～令公布 make public by official order|～枪易躲,暗箭难防。It's easy to dodge an open spear thrust, but it's difficult to guard against an arrow shot from behind. ❹ 眼力好;眼光正确;对事物现象看得清 sharp-eyed; clear-sighted:聪～ clever; bright; intelligent|英～wise; brilliant|精～强干 intelligent and capable|耳聪目～ sharp-eyed and sharp-eared; have good sight and hearing; can see and hear well|眼～手快 sharp-eyed and quick-moving; be sharp of sight and quick of hand ❺ 光明 bright:弃暗投～ forsake darkness for light; renounce a bad cause and come over to the just side|～人不做暗事。An honest man will never engage in underhand dealings. *or* An honest man will never do anything underhand. ❻ 视觉 sight:双目失～ lose the sight of both eyes; go blind in both eyes ❼ 懂得;了解 understand:深～大义 know what is right and proper|不～利害 do not know the advantages and disadvantages; be unaware of the serious consequences ❽ 〈书 *fml.*〉表明;显示 show; reveal; make known:开宗～义 make clear the purpose and main theme from the very beginning|赋诗～志 write a poem to state one's ambition ❾ 〈副词 *adv.*〉明明 obviously; evidently; doubtlessly:～知故问 ask while knowing the answer already; know the answer but ask purposely

明[2] míng 次于今年、今天的 immediately following this year, this day:～天 tomorrow|～晨 tomorrow morning|～年 next year|～春 next spring

明[3] Míng ❶ 朝代,公元1368—1644,朱元璋所建。先定都南京,永乐年间迁都北京。Ming Dynasty (1368-1644) founded by Zhu Yuanzhang with its capital city established in Nanjing and moved to Beijing during the reign of Yongle (1403-1425) ❷ 姓 a surname

【明白】míng·bai ❶ 内容、意思等使人容易了解;清楚;明确 clear; obvious; plain:他讲得十分～。He spoke very clearly. ❷ 公开的;不含糊的 open; unequivocal; explicit:有意见就～提出来。If you have your own opinions, state them openly. ❸ 聪明;懂道理 sensible;

reasonable：他是个～人，不用多说就知道。He is a sensible man, and knows it before you say too much. ❹ 知道；了解 know; understand：～其中的奥妙 know what is behind sth.｜他是怎么想的，我心里全～。I know all what he is thinking of.

【明摆着】míngbǎi·zhe 明显地摆在眼前，容易看得清楚 obvious; clear; plain：～有困难，他还是硬把这活儿揽下来了。Though he knew the difficulties perfectly, he insisted on taking on the job.

【明辨是非】míng biàn shì fēi 把是非分清楚 make a clear distinction between right and wrong

【明察】míngchá 清楚地看到 see clearly：～秋毫 be sharp-eyed enough to perceive even the minutest detail｜～其奸 see through sb's treachery

【明察暗访】míng chá àn fǎng 明里观察，暗里询问了解（情况等）observe publicly and investigate privately

【明察秋毫】míng chá qiū háo〈比喻 *fig.*〉为人非常精明，任何小问题都看得很清楚 intelligent; sharp-eyed enough to perceive the minutest detail（秋毫 *qiu hao*：秋天鸟兽身上新长的细毛，比喻极细小的东西 fine feather or hair birds or animals grow in autumn;（fig.）extremely tiny things）

【明畅】míngchàng（语言、文字等）明白流畅（of language, words, etc.）clear and lucid; lucid and smooth：行文～，寓意深远。The writing is clear and lucid, and has profound implications.

【明澈】míngchè 明亮而清澈；transparent; bright and limpid：一双～的眼睛 a pair of bright and limpid eyes｜池水～如镜。The pool is as clear as a mirror.

【明处】míngchù ❶ 明亮的地方；有光亮的地方 where there is light：拿到～一看，才知道是张地图。Only when（we）looked at it in the light did we know it was a map. ❷ 公开的场合 in public; in the open：有话说在～。If you've got anything to say, say it openly.

【明达】míngdá 对事理有明确透彻的认识；通达 sensible; understanding：～公正 sensible and fair-minded

【明灯】míngdēng〈比喻 *fig.*〉指引群众朝光明正确方向前进的人或事物 beacon; bright lamp; person or thing guiding the masses forward in a bright and correct direction：指路～ beacon showing the way

【明断】míngduàn 明确地辨别案件或纠纷的是非，做出公正的判决或判断 pass fair judgement; clearly tell the right from the wrong in a lawsuit or dispute, and pass a fair judgement

【明矾】míngfán 无机化合物，含有结晶水的硫酸钾和硫酸铝复盐，化学式 $KAl(SO_4)_2 \cdot 12H_2O$。无色晶体，水溶液有涩味。用来制皮革、造纸等。也可做媒染剂和净水剂，医药上用做收敛剂。alum（$KAl(SO_4)_2 \cdot 12H_2O$）; inorganic chemical compound containing crystallized potassium sulphate and aluminium sulphate, used as astringent, mordant, and water-purifying agent and in the manufacture of baking powder, dyes, leather and paper; also 明石 míngshí; 通称 commonly called 白矾 báifán

【明沟】mínggōu 露天的下水道 open drain

【明后天】mínghòutiān 明天或后天 tomorrow or the day after tomorrow：他～来。He is coming tomorrow or the day after tomorrow.

【明晃晃】mínghuānghuāng（～的 mínghuānghuāng·de）光亮闪烁 gleaming; shining：～的马刀 gleaming sabre｜他的胸前～地挂满了奖章。Shining badges and medals hung across his chest.

【明黄】mínghuáng 纯正鲜亮的黄色 pure and bright yellow

【明慧】mínghuì〈书 *fml.*〉聪明；聪慧 intelligent; bright; clever

【明火】mínghuǒ ❶〈古代 *arch.*〉用铜镜等映日聚光所取的火 fire taken from the sunlight reflected on a bronze mirror ❷ 有焰的火（区别于'暗火' as compared with 'smouldering fire'）flame ❸ 指点着火把（抢劫）（robbery）carry torches：～抢劫 open robbery

【明火执仗】míng huǒ zhí zhàng 点着火把，拿着武器，公开活动（多指抢劫 oft. in a robbery）carry torches and weapons — do evil openly

【明间儿】míngjiānr 直接跟外面相通的房间 room with a door that opens to the courtyard or to a street

【明鉴】míngjiàn ❶ 明镜 bright mirror; clear mirror ❷ 指可为借鉴的明显的前例 clear precedence that can be used for reference ❸ 明察，旧时常用来称颂人见识高明（old term of praise for sb.'s opinion）brilliant idea; penetrating judgement

【明教】míngjiào〈敬辞 *pol.*〉高明的指教（多用于书信 usu. used in a letter）your brilliant idea; your advice：敬聆～。Your brilliant advices are requested.

【明旌】míngjīng same as 铭旌 míngjīng

【明净】míngjìng 明亮而洁净 bright and clean; clear and bright：～的橱窗 clear and bright show-window｜湖水～ clear lake｜北京秋天的天空分外～。The autumn sky in Beijing is especially clear and bright.

【明镜】míngjìng 明亮的镜子 bright mirror; clear mirror：湖水清澈，犹如～。The lake is as clear and bright as a mirror.

【明镜高悬】míngjìng gāo xuán 传说秦始皇有一面镜子，能照见人心的善恶（见于《西京杂记》），后来用'明镜高悬'比喻法官判案的公正严明 According to *Miscellaneous Records of the Western Capital*, Qin Shihuang, the first emperor of the Qin Dynasty (221 B.C.-209 B.C.), had a mirror which could show the good or evil of a person. This gave rise to the phrase 'clear mirror hung on high' to mean impartiality and strictness of a judge in trialing cases. also 秦镜高悬 qínjìng gāo xuán

【明快】míngkuài ❶（语言、文字等）明白通畅；不晦涩不呆板 sprightly; (of speaking and writing) lucid and lively：笔法～ lucid and lively style of writing ❷ 性格开朗直爽；办事有决断 forthright; straightforward：她为人～达观，工作起来雷厉风行。She takes a philosophical attitude towards others, but handles her work vigorously and resolutely.

【明来暗往】míng lái àn wǎng 公开或暗地里来往，形容关系密切，来往频繁（多含贬义 oft. derog.）have overt and covert contacts with a person; have close contacts with a person

【明朗】mínglǎng ❶ 光线充足（多指室外 oft. outdoors）bright and clear：那天晚上的月色格外～。The moonlight was especially bright and clear that evening.｜初秋的天气是这样～清新。The weather in early autumn is so clear and fresh. ❷ 明显；清晰 clear; obvious：态度～ clear-cut position; unequivocal attitude｜听了报告，他的心里～了。Hearing the speech, he was able to get things in perspective. ❸ 光明磊落；开朗 ②；爽快 forthright; bright and cheerful：性格～ forthright and cheerful｜这些作品都具有～的风格。These works are all forthright and cheerful.

【明理】mínglǐ ❶ 明白道理 sensible; reasonable：读书～ be educated and reasonable｜他是个～的人。He is a sensible person. ❷（～儿 mínglǐr）明显的道理 obvious truth or fact：～不用细讲。You don't have to give details on an obvious truth.

【明丽】mínglì（景物）明净美丽（of scenery）bright and beautiful：山川～ bright and beautiful mountains and rivers｜阳光～ bright and beautiful sunshine

【明亮】míngliàng ❶ 光线充足 well-lit; bright：灯光～ ablaze with light; brightly lit｜打开窗户，屋子就会～些。The room will be brighter when the windows are opened. ❷ 发亮的 shining; shiny; bright：小姑娘有一双～的眼睛。The little girl has shining (or bright) eyes. ❸ 明白 become clear：听了这番解释，老张心里～了。Hearing the explanation, Lao Zhang became enlightened. ❹ 清晰响亮 clear and loud：歌声～。The singing is clear and loud.

【明了】míngliǎo ❶ 清楚地知道或懂得 understand; be clear about：你的意思我～，就这样办吧！I understand what you mean. Do it as you've said.｜不～实际情况就不能做出正确的判断。Without a clear understanding of the actual situation, one can't make correct judgement. ❷ 清晰；明白 clear; plain：简单～ simple and clear; concise and explicit

【明令】mínglìng 明文宣布的命令 explicit order; formal decree; public proclamation：～禁止 be prohibited by decree｜～实施 implementation of a formal decree

【明码】míngmǎ ❶ 公开通用的电码（区别于'密码'as compared with 'cipher code'）plain code：～电报 plain code telegram ❷ 商业上指标明价格 list prices; clearly marked prices：～标价 list prices; clearly marked prices｜～售货 sell goods at market prices

【明媒正娶】míng méi zhèng qǔ〈旧时 *old*〉指有媒人说合，按传统结婚仪式迎娶的婚姻 be legally and formally married; marriage arranged by a matchmaker and instituted with a traditional wedding

【明媚】míngmèi ❶（景物）鲜明可爱（of scenery）lovely; bright and beautiful; radiant and enchanting：春光～ bright and beautiful spring sunshine; radiant and enchanting spring sunshine｜河山～ land of enchanting beauty ❷（眼睛）明亮动人（of eyes）bright and charming

【明面】míngmiàn（～儿 míngmiànr）表面；明处 apparently; on the surface：他～上是说儿子，其实是说给别人听的。On the surface, he was reproaching his son; in fact, he means his remarks for others.｜把问题摆到～上倒好解决些。It's easier to solve the questions by putting them on the table.

【明灭】míngmiè 时隐时现；忽明忽暗 now in view, now hidden; appearing and vanishing：星光～ stars twinkle

【明明】míngmíng〈副词 *adv.*〉表示显然如此或确实（下文意思往往转折）obviously; plainly; undoubtedly (followed by a turn in meaning in the latter part of the context)：这话～是他说的，怎么转眼就不认账了？This is obviously his remark, how could he have denied it in an instant?

【明眸】míngmóu 明亮的眼睛 bright eyes：～皓齿（形容女子的美貌）(of a beautiful lady) bright eyes and white teeth

【明目张胆】míng mù zhāng dǎn 形容公开地大胆地做坏事 brazenly; flagrantly; do evil things openly and boldly

【明年】míngnián 今年的下一年 next year

【明盘】míngpán（～儿 míngpánr）〈商业用语 *com.*〉指买卖双方在市场上公开议定的价格 price negotiated between the seller and the buyer

【明器】míngqì〈古代 *arch.*〉陪葬的器物。最初的明器是死者生前用的器物，后来是用陶土、木头等仿制的模型。burial objects. At the beginning, the burial objects were those used by the dead during his lifetime; later, imitation earthen and wood vessels were used. also 冥器 míngqì

【明前】míngqián 绿茶的一种，用清明前采摘的细嫩芽尖制成 *mingqian* tea; green tea processed from the fresh leaves picked before Pure Brightness, a day which falls on April 4 or 5

【明枪暗箭】míng qiāng àn jiàn 〈比喻 *fig.*〉公开的和隐蔽的攻击 both overt and covert attacks; spear thrusts in the open and arrows shot from hiding

【明抢】míngqiǎng 公然抢劫 daylight robbery: ～暗偷 rob in broad daylight and steal in dark corners | ～明夺 rob and seize in the daylight

【明情理儿】míngqínglǐr 〈方 *dial.*〉明显而用不着争辩的道理 obvious and indisputable reason

【明渠】míngqú 露在地面上的渠道 open ditch

【明确】míngquè ❶ 清晰明白而确定不移 clear-cut; explicit; unequivocal; clear and definite: 目的～ clear aim | ～表示态度 take a clear-cut stand | 大家～分工，各有专责。There is a clear division of labour among us, each having his or her responsibility. ❷ 使清晰明白而确定不移 clarify; make clear; make definite: 这次会议～了我们的方针任务。The meeting clarified our policy and task.

【明儿】míngr ❶ same as 明天 míngtiān ①: ～见。See you tomorrow. | 他～一早就动身。He'll start off very early tomorrow morning. also 明儿个 míngrgè ❷ same as 明天 míngtiān ②: ～你长大了，也学开飞机。How about learning how to pilot a plane when you grow up?

【明人】míngrén ❶ 眼睛能看见的人（区别于'盲人' as compared with 'the blind'）seeing person; good-sighted person ❷ 指心地光明的人 honest person; forthright person; sensible person: ～不做暗事 honest person does not engage in underhand dealings; forthright person does not do anything underhand; honest man does nothing underhand

【明日】míngrì same as 明天 míngtiān

【明日黄花】míngrì huánghuā 苏轼诗《九日次韵王巩》:'相逢不用忙归去，明日黄花蝶也愁。'原指重阳节过后，菊花即将枯萎，便再没有什么好玩赏的了。后来用'明日黄花'比喻已失去新闻价值的报道或已失去应时作用的事物。'There is no hurry about going home now that we've met;/Even the butterflies worry the flowers will wither tomorrow.' The two lines, quoted from *A Poem in Response to Wang Gong on Double-Ninth Day* by Su Shi, described chrysanthemums after the Double-Ninth Festival, meaning that they would soon shrivel and be of no interest to visitors any longer. The phrase, derived from the poem, refers to a news report that has lost its news value or to sth. that has turned stale and is no longer of interest.

【明锐】míngruì ❶ 明亮而锐利 bright and sharp: 目光～ bright and keen eyes | ～的刀锋 shining and sharp blade ❷〈书 *fml.*〉聪明机敏 clever and quick: 性～，有决断。He is quick and resolute.

【明闪闪】míngshǎnshǎn（～的 míngshǎnshǎn·de）形容闪烁发光 shining; glistening; glittering: ～的灯光 glittering lights | 她长着一双～的大眼睛。She has a pair of large bright eyes.

【明示】míngshì 明确地指示；明白地表示 instruct in no uncertain terms; clearly indicate: ～后学。As a junior scholar, I await your enlightening instructions. | 伫候～ look forward to hearing your instruction

【明誓】míng//shì ☞ 盟誓 méng//shì on p. 1325

【明说】míngshuō 明白说出 speak frankly; speak openly: 这事不便于～。We'd better not state it so explicitly. | 话里虽没～，心里却有想法。He didn't say anything definitely, although he had ideas of his own.

【明堂】míngtáng〈方 *dial.*〉❶ 打晒粮食的场地 threshing ground ❷ 院子 courtyard; yard; compound ‖ also 明唐 míngtáng

【明唐】míngtáng same as 明堂 míngtáng

【明天】míngtiān ❶ 今天的下一天 tomorrow ❷ 不远的将来 near future: 展望美好的～ look forward to the bright future

【明文】míngwén 见于文字的（指法令、规章等）(of laws, regulations, etc.) proclaimed in writing: ～规定 stipulate in explicit terms; expressly provide

【明晰】míngxī 清楚；不模糊 distinct; clear: 雾散了，远处的村庄越来越～了。The fog has dispersed, and the village in the distance is becoming more and more distinct. | 现在他对全部操作过程有了一个～的印象。Now he has a clear impression on the whole process of the operation.

【明细】míngxì 明确而详细 clear and detailed: 分工～ clear and minute division of labour

【明显】míngxiǎn 清楚地显露出来，容易让人看出或感觉到 clear; obvious; evident; distinct: 字迹～ clear handwriting | 目标～。The target is quite clear.

【明线】míngxiàn 文学作品中人物活动或事件发展所直接呈现出来的线索 thread shown directly as a result of the development of a person's activity or an event in a literary work

【明晓】míngxiǎo 明白；通晓 understand; be familiar with; be versed in: ～音律 be well versed in music

【明效大验】míng xiào dà yàn 很显著的效验 clear (or clinching) proof of effectiveness; telling (or marked) effects

【明信片】míngxìnpiàn 专供写信用的硬纸片，邮寄时不用信封。也指用明信片写成的信。postcard; card sold by the post office for sending short messages by mail, without an envelope; also a letter written on a postcard

【明星】míngxīng ❶ 古书上指金星 Venus as described in ancient books ❷ 称有名的演员、运动员等 famous performer or athlete：电影～ film star｜足球～ football star｜交际～ social butterfly

【明修栈道，暗度陈仓】míng xiū zhàndào, àn dù Chéncāng 楚汉相争中，刘邦在进军南郑途中烧掉栈道，表示不再返回关中，用以打消项羽的疑虑；随后率兵偷度陈仓，打败楚将，又回到咸阳。后来用'明修栈道，暗度陈仓'比喻用假象迷惑对方以达到某种目的。pretend to prepare to advance along one path while following another secretly; do one thing under cover of another. In the fight between the states of Chu and Han, Liu Bang burned the plank road built on the face of a cliff on his way to Nanzheng to show that he would not return to Guanzhong in order to rid Xiang Yu of his doubts. Later, Liu led his army to cross the river at Chencang and returned to Xianyang after defeating the Chu general and his troops. Since then, 'pretend to prepare to advance along one path while following another secretly' has been used to liken the use of pretence or cover to confuse the opposing party to achieve a certain purpose.

【明秀】míngxiù 明媚秀丽 bright and beautiful：～的江南景色 beautiful scenery south of the lower reaches of the Yangtze River

【明眼人】míngyǎnrén 对事物观察得很清楚的人；有见识的人 person with a discerning eye; person of good sense：～都知道，他这一套是蒙人的。Anybody with sharp eyes could see he played these tricks to deceive people.

【明艳】míngyàn 鲜明艳丽；明丽 bright-coloured and beautiful：风光～ bright and beautiful scenery｜服饰～ gorgeous dress｜～的石榴花 bright-coloured pomegranate blossoms

【明油】míngyóu 在烹调好的菜肴上浇的油叫明油 oil poured on a cooked dish

【明喻】míngyù 比喻的一种，明显地用另外的事物来比拟某事物，表示两者之间的相似关系。常用'如'、'像'、'似'、'好像'、'像…似的'、'如同'、'好比'等比喻词，如'此时心情，正像这无水的枯井'。simile; figure of speech in which one thing is likened to another different similar thing by the use of 如 rú, 像 xiàng, 似 sì, 好像 hǎoxiàng, 像…似的 xiàng…sì·de, 如同 rútóng, 好比 hǎobǐ, to express certain similarity between the two. Example: 'My feeling now is just like this dry well.'

【明早】míngzǎo ❶ 明天早上 tomorrow morning ❷〈方 *dial.*〉same as 明天 míngtiān

【明杖】míngzhàng（～儿 míngzhàngr）指盲人用来探路的手杖 stick used by a blind person in walking

【明朝】míngzhāo〈方 *dial.*〉same as 明天 míngtiān

【明哲保身】míng zhé bǎo shēn 原指明智的人不参与可能给自己带来危险的事，现在指因怕犯错误或有损自己利益而对原则性问题不置可否的处世态度 use one's wits to protect himself from possible danger; be worldly-wise and play safe; originally meaning a sensible person refuses to take part in an affair that will possibly bring him danger; worldly attitude of wavering on issues of principle for fear of making a mistake or harming one's own interests

【明争暗斗】míng zhēng àn dòu 明里暗里都在进行争斗 both open strife and veiled struggle; overt contention and covert struggle

【明正典刑】míng zhèng diǎn xíng 依照法律，处以极刑 carry out a death sentence according to the law

【明证】míngzhèng 明显的证据 clear proof

【明知】míngzhī 明明知道 know perfectly well; be fully aware：～故问 ask while already knowing the answer｜～故犯 knowingly commit a crime (a mistake, etc.) or break (rules, the law, etc.)｜你～他不愿意参加，为什么又去约他？You know quite well that he did not want to join you, but why did you make the appointment with him?

【明志】míngzhì 表明志向 show one's aspirations：淡泊～ show one's lofty aspirations by simple living｜这首诗是借菊花～。In this poem, the poet gives expression to his lofty aspirations by alluding to chrysanthemums.

【明智】míngzhì 懂事理；有远见；想得周到 sensible; sagacious; wise：决策～ make a wise decision｜～的举动 sensible measure

【明珠】míngzhū〈比喻 *fig.*〉珍爱的人或美好的事物 crown jewel; bright pearl; beloved person; lovely thing：掌上～ bright pearl in the palm; beloved daughter

【明珠暗投】míngzhū àn tóu〈比喻 *fig.*〉怀才不遇或好人失足参加坏集团，也泛指珍贵的东西得不到赏识 bright pearl cast into darkness; person of talent or thing of value unrecognized; good person fallen among a bad company

【明子】míng·zi 松明 pine torch

鸣 míng ❶（鸟兽或昆虫）叫（of bird, animal or insect）chirp; cry：鸟～ bird chirps｜蝉～ cicada chirps｜虫～ insects chirp ❷ 发出声音；使发出声音 ring; make a sound：耳～ ringing in the ears｜雷～ thunder roars｜自～钟 clock｜孤掌难～ impossible to clap with one hand｜礼炮齐～ fire a gun salute in unison｜～鼓 beat a drum｜～锣开道 beat gongs to clear the way ❸ 表达；发表（情感、意

见、主张）(feeling, complaint, opinion) air; express: ～谢 express one's thanks | ～冤 voice one's grievances | ～不平 complain about wrongdoings | 百家争～ a hundred schools of thought contend

【鸣鞭】míngbiān ❶ 挥动鞭子使发出响声 crack a whip: ～走马 whip a horse; crack the whip to spur the horse on ❷〈古代 *arch.*〉皇帝仪仗中的一种，鞭形，挥动发出响声，使人肃静 a kind of whip used by an imperial guard of honour, which made a cracking sound when waved as a signal for silence; also 静鞭 jìngbiān

【鸣镝】míngdí〈古代 *arch.*〉一种射出时带响的箭 whistling arrow used in ancient times

【鸣鼓而攻之】míng gǔ ér gōng zhī 指公开宣布罪状，加以声讨（见于《论语·先进》）make an open indictment and denounce (see *Analects · Former Visit*)

【鸣叫】míngjiào（鸟、昆虫等）叫 (of bird, insect, etc.) chirp: 蟋蟀～ cricket chirps ◇汽笛～。The siren wails.

【鸣金】míngjīn 敲锣，古代作战时作为收兵的信号 beat gongs as a signal for recalling the troops in the ancient times: ～收兵 beat the gongs to recall the troops

【鸣锣开道】míng luó kāi dào 封建官吏出行时，前面有人敲锣要行人让路。现比喻为某事物的出现制造舆论。beat gongs to clear the way for officials in feudal times; prepare the public for a coming event; pave the way for sth.

【鸣禽】míngqín 鸟的一类，叫声悦耳，如伯劳、画眉、黄鹂等 songbird; singing bird, such as shrike, hwa-mei, oriole, etc.

【鸣谢】míngxiè 表示谢意（多指公开表示 oft. publicly) express one's thanks: ～启事 notice expressing one's thanks to benefactors | 登报～ have a notice of thanks printed in the newspaper

【鸣冤】míngyuān 喊叫冤屈 voice grievances; complain of unfairness: 击鼓～ beat the drum to call for redress | ～叫屈 voice grievances; complain and call for redress

【鸣啭】míngzhuàn（鸟）婉转地鸣叫 (of birds) twitter; sing; warble: 黄莺～。The oriole twitters. | 云雀～着冲向天空。The skylark sang and soared upward in the sky.

茗 míng 原指某种茶叶，今泛指喝的茶 (ori.) a certain tea; (in a broad sense) tea: 香～ scented tea | 品～ drink tea or sip tea for judgement of its quality

M

洺 Míng 洺河，水名，在河北 Minghe, name of a river in Hebei Province

冥 míng ❶ 昏暗 dark; obscure: 幽～ dark; obscure | 晦～ dark and gloomy ❷ 深奥；深沉 deep; profound: ～思 be deep in thought | ～想 reverie; deep thought ❸ 糊涂；愚昧 dull; stupid: ～昧 stupidity | ～顽 thickheaded; dull and stubborn ❹ 迷信的人称人死后进入的世界；阴间 underworld; nether world: ～府 underworld; nether world

【冥暗】míng'àn 昏暗 dark; dim; dusky: 日落西山，天渐～。The day turns dim as the sun sets in the west.

【冥钞】míngchāo 迷信的人给死人烧的假钞票 paper made to resemble bank notes and burned for the dead

【冥府】míngfǔ 迷信的人指人死后鬼魂所在的地方 underworld; nether world

【冥茫】míngmáng〈书 *fml.*〉苍茫；迷茫 indistinct; dusky; vast and hazy: 夜色～。The dusk is gathering. also 溟茫 míngmáng

【冥蒙】míngméng same as 溟濛 míngméng

【冥器】míngqì same as 明器 míngqì

【冥寿】míngshòu 指已经死去的人的寿辰 birthday anniversary of the dead

【冥思苦索】míng sī kǔ suǒ 深沉地思索 think hard; deep thought; rack one's brain; also 冥思苦想 míng sī kǔ xiǎng

【冥顽】míngwán〈书 *fml.*〉昏庸顽钝 thickheaded; stupid: ～不灵 dull and stupid; impenetrably thickheaded

【冥王星】míngwángxīng 太阳系九大行星之一，按离太阳由近而远的次序计为第九颗，公转周期约为 248 年，自转周期约 6.4 天。是九大行星中最小的行星。Pluto; one of the nine planets of the solar system; the smallest and the ninth in average distance from the sun, its period of revolution, c. 248 earth years; period of rotation, 6.4 earth days; (图见 ☞ figure on 太阳系 tàiyángxì on p. 1855)

【冥想】míngxiǎng 深沉的思索和想像 meditation; reverie; deep thought: 歌声把我们带到对蒙古大草原的美丽的～中去了。On hearing the song, I fell into a reverie about the Mongolian grasslands.

【冥衣】míngyī 迷信的人给死人烧的纸衣 clothes made of paper and burned for the dead

铭 míng ❶ 在器物、碑碣等上面记述事实、功德等的文字（大多铸成或刻成）；鞭策、勉励自己的文字（写出或刻出）inscription; sth. (one's achievement, contribution, etc.) inscribed, cast or engraved, as on an object or monument; short note for self-encouragement (written or inscribed): 墓志～ epitaph; inscription on the memorial tablet in front of a tomb | 砚～ inscription on an inkslab | 座右～ motto; maxim ❷ 在器物上刻字，表示纪念；比喻深刻记住 sth. inscribed on an object for memento; keep sth. in heart: ～功 inscribed one's exploits | ～心 engraved on one's heart | ～肌镂骨（比喻感恩极深）be engraved on one's flesh and bone; (fig) be deeply grateful | ～诸肺腑（比喻永记不忘）be deeply engraved in one's mind; (fig.) be remembered for ever

【铭感】mínggǎn〈书 *fml.*〉深刻地记在心中，感激不忘 be deeply grateful：大家对我如此关切和照顾，使我终身～。I'll feel profoundly grateful for the rest of my life for the care and consideration you've given me.

【铭记】míngjì ❶ 深深地记在心里 bear firmly in mind; always remember：～教诲 always remember one's instructions; one's instructions (or teachings) will be borne in mind; bear one's teachings firmly in mind ❷ 铭文 inscription; epigraph

【铭旌】míngjīng〈旧时 *old*〉竖在灵柩前标志死者官衔和姓名的长幡 long streamer inscribed with the deceased's official title and name posted in front of the coffin; also 明旌 míngjīng

【铭刻】míngkè ❶ 铸在器物上面或刻在器物、碑碣等上面的记述事实、功德等的文字 inscription; sth. (facts, achievements, contributions, etc.) inscribed or cast on an object or a tablet：古代～ ancient inscription ❷ same as 铭记 míngjì ①：沉痛的教训～在心中 bear the bitter lesson firmly in mind

【铭牌】míngpái 装在机器、仪表、机动车等上面的金属牌子，上面标有名称、型号、性能、规格及出厂日期、制造者等字样 nameplate; data plate; metal plate inscribed with the name, type number, property, specification, date of manufacture, and fixed on a machine, instrument, motor vehicle, etc.

【铭文】míngwén 器物、碑碣等上面的文字(大多铸成或刻成) inscription; epigraph：铜器～ inscription on a bronzeware

【铭心】míngxīn〈比喻 *fig.*〉感念不忘 be engraved on one's heart; be remembered with gratitude：刻骨～ deeply engraved in one's heart

蓂 míng [蓂荚](míngjiá)〈古代 *arch.*〉传说中一种象征祥瑞的草 a kind of grass symbolic of good luck

☞ mì on p. 1334

溟 míng〈书 *fml.*〉海 sea：东～ east sea | 北～ north sea

【溟茫】míngmáng same as 冥茫 míngmáng

【溟濛】míngméng〈书 *fml.*〉形容烟雾弥漫，景色模糊 misty; indistinct; drizzly; also 冥蒙 míngméng

榠 míng [榠楂](míngzhā) 榅桲(wēn·po) quince (*Cydonia oblonga*)

暝 míng〈书 *fml.*〉❶ 日落；天黑 (of the sun) set; (of the sky) grow dark：日将～。The sun is setting. | 天已～。Dusk has fallen. ❷ 黄昏 dusk; evening twilight

瞑 míng ❶ 闭眼 close one's eyes：～目 close one's eyes when one dies ❷ 眼花 dim-sighted：耳聋目～ be hard of hearing and dim-sighted

【瞑目】míngmù 闭上眼睛(多指人死时心中没有牵挂) close one's eyes in death; die content：死不～ would not close one's eyes when one dies; would not rest easy when one dies

螟 míng same as 螟虫 míngchóng

【螟虫】míngchóng 昆虫，种类很多，主要侵害水稻，也侵害高粱、玉米、甘蔗等，是我国南方主要害虫之一 snout moth's larva (*Aphomia gularis* or *Plodia interpunctella*); one of the major destructive insects in the south of China that destroys rice as well as sorghum, corn, sugarcane, etc.

【螟蛉】mínglíng《诗经·小雅·小宛》：'螟蛉有子，蜾蠃负之。'螟蛉是一种绿色小虫，蜾蠃是一种寄生蜂。蜾蠃常捕捉螟蛉存放在窝里，产卵在它们身体里，卵孵化后就拿螟蛉作食物。古人误认为蜾蠃不产子，喂养螟蛉为子，因此用'螟蛉'比喻义子。corn earworm (*Heliothis zea*); adopted son. *The Book of Songs·Odes·Cooing Dove*: 'Corn earworms have young larvae, wasps carry them away to their hives.' Wasp is a parasitic bee that catches corn earworms, a kind of small green insects, and keep them in its hive so as to lay eggs in their bodies; when the eggs are hatched, they feed on the corn earworms. In ancient times this phenomenon was misinterpreted and thus it was wrongly believed that wasps did not breed offspring but instead fed corn earworms as their offspring. Hence the allusion of corn earworm to an adopted son.

mǐng (ㄇㄧㄥˇ)

酩 mǐng [酩酊](mǐngdǐng) 形容大醉 be dead drunk：～大醉 be dead drunk

mìng (ㄇㄧㄥˋ)

命[1] mìng ❶ 生命；性命 life：一条～ a life | 救～ save one's life | 丧了～ lose one's life; get killed ❷ 寿命 life-span：短～ die young; be short-lived | 长～百岁 long life; may you live to be one hundred ❸ same as 命运 mìnyùn ①：～苦 ill fate; be doomed to a life of misfortunes or poverty | 认～ resign oneself to fate | 算～ fortune-telling | 宿～论 fatalism

命[2] mìng ❶ same as 命令 mìnglìng ①；指派 order; command：～驾 order one's carriage; set out ❷ same as 命令 mìnglìng ②；指示 instruct; order; command：奉～ be ordered to; be instructed to; receive an order or instruction | 待～ await instruction ❸ 给与(名称等) assign (a name, title, etc.)：～名 name; name after | ～题 assign a topic (or subject); set a question

【命案】mìng'àn 杀人的案件 case concerning

the death of a person：一桩～ a case of murder；homicide case

【命笔】mìngbǐ〈书 *fml.*〉执笔作诗文或书画 take up one's pen to write or to paint；set pen to paper：欣然～ gladly set pen to paper；be happy to write

【命大】mìngdà 命运好；幸运 good luck；lucky：～福大 good luck and good fortune｜他从六楼跌下来没摔死，真是～。He was lucky to survive a fall from the sixth floor.

【命定】mìngdìng 命中注定（迷信）（superstition）be determined by fate；be predestined

【命妇】mìngfù 封建时代被赐予封号的妇女，一般为官员的母亲、妻子 woman with a title conferred by the emperor，usu. the mother or wife of an official

【命根】mìnggēn〈比喻 *fig.*〉最受某人重视的晚辈，也比喻最重要或最受重视的事物 lifeblood；one's very life；member of the younger generation most treasured by someone；most important or most treasured thing；also 命根子 mìnggēn·zi

【命官】mìngguān 封建时代由朝廷任命的官员 official appointed by the imperial court

【命驾】mìngjià〈书 *fml.*〉吩咐人驾车，也指乘车出发 order a carriage；set out：敬希早日～来京。It is earnestly hoped that you will come to Beijing at an early date.

【命令】mìnglìng ❶ 上级对下级有所指示（superior to inferior）order；command：连长～一排担任警戒。The company commander ordered the first platoon to keep watch. ❷ 上级给下级的指示（superior to inferior）order；command：司令部昨天先后来了两道～。The command gave us two orders yesterday.

【命令句】mìnglìngjù 祈使句 imperative sentence

【命令主义】mìnglìng zhǔyì 脱离实际、脱离群众，只凭强迫命令的办法来推动工作的领导作风。是官僚主义的一种表现。commandism；style of work on the part of leaders that is divorced from reality and the masses and gets work done by coercion；manifestation of bureaucraticism

【命脉】mìngmài 生命和血脉，比喻关系重大的事物 lifeblood；lifeline；thing of vital importance：经济～ economic lifelines｜水利是农业的～。Irrigation is the lifeblood of agriculture.

【命名】mìng//míng 授予名称 name（sb. or sth.）：～典礼 naming ceremony

【命数】mìngshù same as 命运 mìngyùn ①

【命题】mìng//tí 出题目 assign a topic or a subject：～作文 set a topic for composition；assign a subject for composition

【命题】mìngtí 逻辑学指表达判断的语言形式，由系词把主词和宾词联系而成。例如：'北京是中国的首都'，这个句子就是一个命题。（logic）proposition；language form of expression and judgement，consisting of a copulative verb that links a subject with an object. Example：the statement 'Beijing is the capital of China' is a proposition.

【命途】mìngtú〈书 *fml.*〉指平生的遭遇、经历 one's life or experiences：～坎坷 life full of frustrations｜～多舛（chuǎn）suffer many setbacks during one's life

【命相】mìngxiàng〈旧时 *old*〉指生辰八字、生肖等。迷信的人认为根据人的生辰八字可以推算出一个人命运的好坏，根据男女双方的生肖可以推测成为配偶是否相宜。person's birthday in eight Chinese characters（including the year，month，day and hour of his or her birth）and the animal symbol of the year he was born in. Superstitious people believe that on the basis of the eight characters and the animal symbols of the birth years，a fortune-teller could foretell what would happen in a person's life and whether a man and a woman in love would match for a happy couple.

【命意】mìngyì ❶（作文、绘画等）确定主题 set a theme for a composition or a motif for a drawing ❷ 含意 implication：大家不了解他这句话的～所在。No one understood the implication of what he said.

【命运】mìngyùn ❶ 指生死、贫富和一切遭遇（迷信的人认为是生来注定的）destiny；fate；lot（superstitious people believe life and everything else are predestined）：悲惨的～ tragic lot｜～不济 ill luck；bad luck ❷〈比喻 *fig.*〉发展变化的趋向 trend of development and change：关心国家的前途和～ be concerned with the future and destiny of the country

【命中】mìngzhòng 射中；打中（目标） hit the target（or mark）；score a hit：～目标 hit the target（or mark）｜～率 percentage of hits

miù（ㄇㄧㄡˋ）

谬 miù 错误；差错 wrong；false；erroneous；mistaken：荒～ absurd；ridiculous；preposterous～论 fallacy；absurd theory；wrong argument｜大～不然 be entirely wrong；totally incorrect｜差之毫厘，～以千里。An error of the breadth of a hair may lead you a thousand *li* astray. *or* A slight error in the beginning may result in a big mistake in the end.

【谬错】miùcuò same as 谬误 miùwù

【谬奖】miùjiǎng〈书 *fml.*〉过奖 lavish compliments：多承～，实不敢当。（I）wish I could deserve your compliments.

【谬论】miùlùn 荒谬的言论 fallacy；falsehood；false（or absurd）theory：批驳～ refute a fallacy

【谬说】miùshuō 谬论;妄说 fallacy; absurd theory:无知～ ignorance and fallacy

【谬误】miùwù 错误;差错 error; mistake:真理总是在同～的斗争中发展的。Truth always develops through its struggle against falsehood.

【谬种】miùzhǒng ❶ 指荒谬错误的言论、学术流派等 fallacy; absurd or erroneous opinion, school, etc.:～流传 dissemination of error ❷ 坏东西;坏蛋(骂人的话 curse) scoundrel; bad egg; bad actor; bad hat; bad apple; bad lot

缪 miù ☞ 纰缪 pīmiù on p.1461
☞ Miào on p.1344 and móu on p.1371

mō(ㄇㄛ)

摸 mō ❶ 用手接触一下(物体)或接触后轻轻移动 feel; stroke; touch:我～了～他的脸,觉得有点儿发烧。I stroked his face and found he had a slight fever. ❷ 用手探取 feel for; grope for; fumble:～鱼 catch fish with both hands (in a pond)|他在口袋里～了半天,～出一张纸条来。He felt in his pocket for a while and finally took out a slip of paper. ❸ 试着了解;试着做 try to find out; feel out; sound out:～底 know or get to know the actual situation|逐渐～出一套种水稻的经验来 gradually gain good experience in growing rice ❹ 在黑暗中行动;在认不清的道路上行走 grope in the dark; walk on a road one is unfamiliar with:～到床边开亮了灯 grope one's way to the bedside and turn on the light|～了半夜才到家 feel one's way till midnight before getting home

【摸底】mō//dǐ 了解底细 know the real situation:～测验 test to learn the real situation of the students|几个人的技术水平,他都～。He knows the technical level of these few people.

【摸黑儿】mō//hēir 在黑夜中摸索着(行动) grope one's way on a dark night:～赶路 hurry on in the dark night

【摸门儿】mō//ménr 〈比喻 *fig.*〉初步找到做某件事情的方法 get the hang of sth.; have the knack of:摸着点儿门儿 learn a bit of the knack|不～ know nothing

【摸哨】mō//shào 暗中袭击敌方的岗哨 sneak up on an enemy sentinel

【摸索】mō·suǒ ❶ 试探着(行进) grope; fumble; feel about:他们在暴风雨的黑夜里～着前进。They nosed their way forward in a snowstorm at night. ❷ 寻找(方向、方法、经验等)(of direction, method, experience, etc.) find out; search for:在工作中初步～出一些经验 gain some experience in the work

【摸头】mō//tóu (～儿 mō//tóur)由于接触客观事物而有所了解(多用于否定 usu. in a negative) get to know sth.; begin to understand:我刚来,对这件事一点不～。I don't know anything about this matter because I'm a newcomer.

【摸营】mō//yíng 暗中袭击敌人的兵营 steal up to an enemy barrack and wipe out the enemy troops

mó(ㄇㄛˊ)

无(無) mó ☞ 南无 nāmó on p.1381
☞ wú on p.2018

谟 mó 〈书 *fml.*〉same as 计划 jìhuà ①;策略 plan:宏～ grand plan

馍(饝、麽) mó 〈方 *dial.*〉馒头 steamed bun; steamed bread:蒸～ steamed bun; steamed bread|白面～ steamed bread made of wheat flour; also 馍馍 mó·mo

嫫 mó 用于人名,嫫母,传说中的丑妇[used in the name of a person] Momu, an ugly woman in Chinese mythology

摹 mó 照着样子写或画,特指用薄纸蒙在原字或原画上写或画 copy; trace; copy a drawing or a calligraphy by following its lines on a superimposed, transparent sheet:描～ depict; portray; delineate|临～ copy (a model of painting or calligraphy)|～写 copy; intimate|～本 copy book

【摹本】móběn 临摹或翻刻的书画本 album of artistic or calligraphic reproductions

【摹仿】mófǎng same as 模仿 mófǎng

【摹绘】móhuì 〈书 *fml.*〉依原样绘制;描画 draw; paint; depict; describe:～宫殿图样 reproduce the blueprint of a palace

【摹刻】mókè ❶ 摹写书画等并雕刻 carve a reproduction of an inscription or painting ❷ 摹刻的成品 carved reproduction of an inscription or painting

【摹拟】mónǐ same as 模拟 mónǐ

【摹效】móxiào 模仿;仿效 imitate, copy; also 模效 móxiào

【摹写】móxiě ❶ 照着样子写 copy; imitate ❷ 泛指描写(in a broad sense) describe; depict:～人物情状 depict characters in various situations‖also 模写 móxiě

【摹印】móyìn ❶〈古代 *arch.*〉用于印玺的一种字体 style of characters or lettering on ancient imperial seals ❷ 摹写书画等并印刷 copy and print

【摹状】mózhuàng 描摹 depict; portray; delineate

模 mó ❶ 法式;规范;标准 pattern; standard:～型 model|～式 pattern; model|楷～ model; example ❷ 仿效 imitate:～仿 imitate|～拟 imitate; simulate ❸ 指模范 model:劳～ model worker|评～ elect model workers
☞ mú on p.1372

【模本】móběn 供临摹用的底本 calligraphy or painting model

【模范】mófàn ❶ 可以作为榜样的；值得学习的 model; fine example; exemplary person or thing：～事迹 exemplary deeds｜～人物 model ❷ 值得学习的、作为榜样的人 model：劳动～ model worker｜选～ elect a model worker

【模仿】mófǎng 照某种现成的样子学着做 imitate; copy; model oneself on：用口哨～布谷鸟叫 whistle the cries of a cuckoo｜小孩子总喜欢～大人的动作。Children always like to ape the movements of adults. also 摹仿 mófǎng

【模胡】mó·hu same as 模糊 mó·hu

【模糊】mó·hu ❶ 不分明；不清楚 blurred; indistinct; dim; vague：字迹～ blurred writing *or* The writing was blurred.｜神志～ be unconscious｜认识～ have confused ideas｜～概念 confused concept｜睡梦中模模糊糊觉得有人敲门。I found indistinctly someone knocking the door in the dream. ❷ 混淆 confuse; blur：不要～了是非界限。Don't obscure the distinction between right and wrong. ‖ also 模胡 mó·hu

【模棱】móléng（态度、意见等）含糊；不明确（of attitude, opinion, etc.）equivocal; ambiguous：～两可 equivocal; ambiguous

【模拟】mónǐ 模仿 imitate; simulate：～动作 simulation movement｜～考试 mock test; also 摹拟 mónǐ

【模式】móshì 某种事物的标准形式或使人可以照着做的标准样式 pattern; model：～图 ideograph｜～化 patterning

【模特儿】mótèr ❶ 艺术家用来写生、雕塑的描写对象或参考对象，如人体、实物、模型等。也指文学家借以塑造人物形象的原型。model; mannequin; person who poses for an artist or photographer; any person or thing serving as a subject for an artist or writer ❷ 用来展示新样式服装的人或人体模型 person or mannequin employed to display clothes by wearing them：时装～ fashion model［法 French：modèle］

【模效】móxiào same as 摹效 móxiào

【模写】móxiě same as 摹写 móxiě

【模型】móxíng ❶ 依照实物的形状和结构按比例制成的物品，多用来展览或实验 model; small copy or imitation of an existing object made to scale for exhibition or experiment：十大建筑～ models of the ten key buildings ❷ 铸造中制砂型用的工具，大小、形状和要制造的铸件相同，常用木料制成 mould; matrix; pattern; tool for making sand moulds in casting with its size and shape identical to the desired casting ❸ 用压制或浇灌的方法使材料成为一定形状的工具 matrix; die; tool for working the material into a desired shape by pressing and moulding; also 模子 mú·zi

【模压】móyā 橡胶等可塑性材料的一种加工方法，一般是把模型加热，把粉状或片状的材料放在模型内，压成各种制品 mould pressing; method of processing plastic materials like rubber, by which the matrix is heated and the powdered or sliced material is put in the mould and pressed into different kinds of products

膜 mó（～儿 mór）❶ 人或动植物体内像薄皮的组织 membrane：耳～ eardrun; tympanum｜肋～pleura｜横膈～ diaphragm｜脑～炎 meningitis｜苇～儿 membrane of reed ❷ 像膜的薄皮 film; thin coating：橡皮～ rubber sheet｜纸浆表面结成薄～。A thin film formed on the surface of the pulp.

【膜拜】móbài 跪在地上举两手虔诚地行礼 prostrate：顶礼～ pay homage to; make a fetish of; prostrate oneself in worship

麽 mó ☞ 幺麽 yāomó on p. 2226
☞ 么 ·me on p. 1312

摩[1] mó ❶ 摩擦；接触 rub; scrape; touch：～拳擦掌 rub one's fists and palms｜～肩擦背 jostling against each other ◇ ～天岭 mountain ridge towering into the sky｜～天楼 skyscraper ❷ 抚摩 stroke：按～ massage｜母亲～着孩子的脸。The mother is stroking the face of her child. ❸ 研究切磋 mull over; study：观～ view and emulate｜揣～ try to fathom; try to figure out

摩[2] mó 摩尔的简称 abbr. for 摩尔 mó'ěr
☞ mā on p. 1285

【摩擦】mócā ❶ 物体和物体紧密接触，来回移动 rub; move two objects with friction over each other in a back-and-forth motion ❷ 两个相互接触的物体，当有相对运动或有相对运动趋势时，在接触面上产生的阻碍运动的作用。摩擦可分为滑动摩擦和滚动摩擦两种。friction, resistance to motion of two moving objects or surfaces over each other; there are two kinds of friction, i.e. sliding friction and rolling friction ❸（个人或党派团体间）因彼此利害矛盾而引起的冲突 friction; clash (between two political parties or groups) arising from interest or contradiction ‖ also 磨擦 mócā

【摩擦力】mócālì 两个相互接触的物体，当有相对运动或有相对运动趋势时，在接触面上产生的阻碍运动的作用力。摩擦力可分为静摩擦力和滑动摩擦力两种。frictional force; friction, the force which makes it difficult for one object to slide along the surface of another when the two come into contact and move or have a tendency to move in oposite directions, categorized into static friction and sliding friction

【摩擦音】mócāyīn 擦音 fricative

【摩登】módēng 指合乎时兴的式样；时髦 modern; fashionable：～家具 fashionable furniture｜～女郎 fashionable girl

【摩电灯】módiàndēng 安在自行车上面的一种照明装置,通常由灯头和小型发电机两部分构成 dynamo-powered lamp (on a bicycle, etc.), a lighting device fitted on a bicycle, usu. consisting of a lamp and a small power generator; also 磨电灯 módiàndēng

【摩尔】mó'ěr 物质的量的单位,当分子、原子或其他粒子等的个数约为 6.02×10^{23} 时,就是1摩尔 mole; unit of measurement for the quantity of matter, with one mole of a substance containing 6.02×10^{23} molecules, atoms or any other particles; 简称 abbr. 摩 mó

【摩肩击毂】mó jiān jī gǔ ☞ 肩摩毂击 jiān mó gǔ jī on p.941

【摩肩接踵】mó jiān jiē zhǒng 肩碰肩,脚碰脚。形容人很多,很拥挤。very crowded; jostle each other in a crowd with shoulder against shoulder, foot against foot; also 肩摩踵接 jiān mó zhǒng jiē

【摩羯座】mójiézuò 黄道十二星座之一 Capricorn; Capricornus; one of the 12 zodiacal constellations; ☞ 黄道十二宫 huángdào shí'èrgōng on p.851

【摩拳擦掌】mó quán cā zhǎng 形容战斗或劳动前精神振奋的样子 rub one's fists and palms — be eager for action; be itching to have a go

【摩氏硬度表】Móshì yìngdùbiǎo 德国矿物学家摩氏(Friedrich Mohs)制定的鉴定矿物硬度的标准。取十种常见的矿物,按软硬程度排列:1.滑石;2.石膏;3.方解石;4.萤石;5.磷灰石;6.长石;7.石英;8.黄玉;9.刚石;10.金刚石。其他矿物可以依次和这些矿物比较,以决定其硬度。'摩氏'现译作莫氏。Mohs' scale (named after Friedrich Mohs, a German mineralogist); arbitrary scale used to indicate relative hardness of minerals, arranged in 10 ascending degrees: 1. talc; 2. gypsum; 3. calcite; 4. fluorite; 5. apatite; 6. orthoclase; 7. quartz; 8. topaz; 9. corundum; and 10. diamond. The hardness of other minerals can be determined by comparison with these minerals. 摩氏 is now also translated as 莫氏 mòshì

【摩挲】mósuō 用手抚摩 stroke; caress ☞ mā·sā on p.1285

【摩天】mótiān 跟天接触,形容很高 towering into the sky; very high: ~岭 towering mountain ridge; cloud-capped mountain | ~大楼 skyscraper

【摩托】mótuō 内燃机 motor; internal combustion engine

【摩托车】mótuōchē 装有内燃发动机的两轮车或三轮车。有的地区叫机器脚踏车。motorcycle; motor bicycle; motorbike; two-wheeled or three-wheeled vehicle propelled by an internal combustion engine; also 机器脚踏车 jīqì jiǎotàchē in some places

【摩托艇】mótuōtǐng 汽艇 motorboat

【摩崖】móyá 在山崖上刻的文字、佛像等 inscription or Buddhist image engraved on a cliff: ~石刻 stone carvings on a cliff

磨 mó ❶ 摩擦 rub; wear: 脚上~了几个大泡 get some big blisters on one's feet from the rubbing. ◇我劝了他半天,嘴唇都快~破了。I talked till my jaws ached as I tried to bring him around. ❷ 用磨料磨物体使光滑、锋利或达到其他目的 grind; polish; sharpen; shape, smooth by friction: ~刀 sharpen a knife by grinding | ~墨 rub an inkstick on an inkslab | ~玻璃 polish glass | 铁杵~成针。An iron pestle is ground into a needle. ❸ 折磨 wear down; wear out: 他被这场病~得改了样子了。The illness has worn him down to a mere shadow. ❹ 纠缠;磨烦(mò·fan) trouble; pester; worry: 这孩子可真~人。What an annoying child he is. ❺ 消灭;磨灭 obliterate; die out: 百世不~ will endure for centuries ❻ 消耗时间;拖延 waste time; dawdle: ~洋工 dawdle on one's work; waste time on a job | ~工夫 time-consuming; take time ☞ mò on p.1370

【磨擦】mócā same as 摩擦 mócā

【磨蹭】mó·ceng ❶ (轻微)摩擦 rub (lightly); stroke (gently): 右脚轻轻地在地上~着 scrape his right foot lightly on the floor ❷ 缓慢地向前行进,比喻做事动作迟缓 dawdle; loiter; move slowly: 他的腿病已有好转,拄着棍儿可以往前~了。His leg is getting better and he can slowly move forward with the support of a stick. | 你们磨磨蹭蹭的,事情什么时候能做完? If you go on dawdling like this, when will you ever be able to finish? ❸ 纠缠 pester; nag: 我跟爸爸~了半天,他才答应明天带咱们到动物园玩去。I kept on nagging my father until he promised to take us to the zoo tomorrow.

【磨穿铁砚】mó chuān tiě yàn 〈比喻 *fig.*〉用功读书,持久不懈 study assiduously; wear out an iron inkslab

【磨床】móchuáng 金属切削机床,用来加工工件表面,使光洁,提高精确度。加工时,砂轮高速旋转,打磨工件。grinder; grinding machine; metal machine tool fixed with a high-speed sand wheel for polishing the surface of a work-piece or improving its precision

【磨刀不误砍柴工】mó dāo bù wù kǎn chái gōng 〈比喻 *fig.*〉花时间做好准备工作,不会耽误工作的进度 sharpening an axe won't delay the cutting of firewood; making preparations won't delay the progress in the work

【磨电灯】módiàndēng same as 摩电灯 módiàndēng

【磨工夫】mó gōng·fu 耗费时间 consume time: 跟他商量事真~。It takes too much time to discuss things with him.

【磨耗】móhào same as 磨损 mósǔn wear and

tear

【磨合】móhé 新组装的机器，通过一定时期的使用，把摩擦面上的加工痕迹磨光而变得更加密合 break in; grind in; wear in; new machine must go through a period of breaking in; also 走合 zǒuhé

【磨砺】mólì 摩擦使锐利，比喻磨练 go through the mill; steel oneself; harden oneself; discipline oneself: 他知道只有时时刻刻～自己，才能战胜更大的困难。He knows that only when he steels himself from time to time can he overcome still greater difficulties.

【磨炼】móliàn（在艰难困苦的环境中）锻炼 put oneself through the mill; temper oneself; steel oneself: ～才干 increase your ability through training | ～意志 temper one's willpower; also 磨练 móliàn

【磨料】móliào 工业上用的研磨材料，硬度大，机械强度高。金刚石、石英、刚玉等是天然磨料，人造刚玉、碳化硅等是人造磨料。abrasive; abradant; industrial material with great hardness and high mechanical strength for grinding and polishing. Diamond, quartz, corundum, etc. are natural abrasives while man-made corundum, silicon carbide, etc. are artificial abrasives.

【磨轮】mólún（～儿 mólúnr）砂轮 grinding wheel; abrasive wheel

【磨灭】mómiè（痕迹、印象、功绩、事实、道理等）经过相当时期逐渐消失 efface; obliterate (trace, impression, achievement, fact, reason, etc.); wear away: 不可～的功绩 indelible achievement | 年深月久，碑文已经～。The inscription on the tablet has worn away with the passage of time.

【磨难】mónàn 在困苦的境遇中遭受的折磨 tribulation; hardship; suffering: 童年的～铸就了他那刚强的性格。The sufferings in his childhood tempered his unyielding character. also 魔难 mónàn

【磨砂玻璃】móshā-bō·li 毛玻璃 ground glass, frosted glass

【磨蚀】móshí ❶ 流水、波浪、冰川、风等所携带的沙石等磨损地表。也指这些被携带的沙石之间相互摩擦而破坏。abrasion; wearing sth. away by rubbing or scraping, as of the ground surface by flowing water, waves, glaciers, wind, etc.; destruction caused by friction between sand or gravel carried in flowing water, wind, etc. ❷ 使逐渐消失 erode; blunt; wear off: 岁月流逝～了他年轻时的锐气。His dashing spirit in youth has been blunted with the passing of time.

M

【磨损】mósǔn 机件或其他物体由于摩擦和使用而造成损耗 (of machine parts or other bodies) wear and tear; loss and damage; resulting from friction and use

【磨牙】mó//yá〈方 *dial.*〉多费口舌；无意义地争辩 argue pointlessly

【磨牙】móyá 医学上指臼齿 (med.) molar

【磨洋工】mó yánggōng 工作时拖延时间，也泛指工作懒散拖沓 dawdle over one's work; (in a broad sense) loaf on the job; lie down on the job

【磨折】mózhé same as 折磨 zhémó

【磨嘴】mó//zuǐ〈方 *dial.*〉same as 磨牙 mó//yá; also 磨嘴皮子 mó zuǐpí·zi

嬷 mó（旧读 formerly pronounced mā）［嬷嬷］(mó·mo)〈方 *dial.*〉❶ 称呼年老的妇女 form of address for an elderly woman ❷ 奶妈 wet nurse

蓙 mó ☞ 萝蓙 luómó on p. 1278

蘑 mó 蘑菇 mushroom: 口～ edible mushroom with lush white umbrella | 鲜～ fresh mushroom | 白～ white mushroom; edible mushroom

【蘑菇】[1] mó·gu 指供食用的蕈类，特指口蘑 edible mushroom, esp. one with lush white umbrella

【蘑菇】[2] mó·gu ❶ 故意纠缠 worry; pester; keep on at: 你别跟我～，我还有要紧事儿。Don't pester me. I've got something urgent to attend to. ❷ 行动迟缓，拖延时间 dawdle; dilly-dally: 你再这么～下去，非误了火车不可！If you go on dawdling like this, you'll miss the train.

【蘑菇云】mó·guyún 由于原子弹、氢弹爆炸而产生的蘑菇形的云状物，其中含有大量烟尘。火山爆发及星体碰撞等也能形成蘑菇云。mushroom cloud (esp. from nuclear explosion); dust and smoke produced in the shape of mushrooms after the explosion of an atomic bomb or hydrogen bomb; such cloud produced during a volcanic eruption or the collision of heavenly bodies

魔 mó ❶ 魔鬼 demon; devil; monster; evil spirit: 恶～ evil spirit | 妖～ demon | 病～ illness | 旱～ drought ❷ 神秘；奇异 magic; mystic: ～力 magic power | ～术 magic［魔罗之省，梵 abbreviation of 魔罗 móluó, Sanskrit: māra］

【魔法】mófǎ 妖魔的法术；妖术 sorcery; witchcraft

【魔方】mófāng 一种智力玩具，是一个可以变换拼装的正方体，由若干块小正方体组成，六个平面色彩不同。游戏时使六面颜色混杂，经过转换，以恢复原状。Rubic's cube; toy consisting of 27 small cubes, each cube with six equal, square sides of different colours, which can be worked into different designs and returned to the original by changing the sides when played in a game

【魔怪】móguài 妖魔鬼怪 fiends; demons and monsters;〈比喻 *fig.*〉邪恶的人或势力 evil person or force

【魔鬼】móguǐ 宗教或神话传说里指迷惑人、害人性命的鬼怪 devil; demon; 〈比喻 *fig*.〉邪恶的人或势力 monster; evil person or force

【魔窟】mókū 魔怪的巢穴 den of monsters; 〈比喻 *fig*.〉邪恶势力盘踞的地方 place occupied by an evil force

【魔力】mólì 使人爱好、沉迷的吸引力 magical power; magic; charm: 这个故事有一种~抓住我的心。This story has the magical power that seizes my heart.

【魔难】mónàn same as 磨难 mónàn

【魔术】móshù 杂技的一种,以迅速敏捷的技巧或特殊装置把实在的动作掩盖起来,使观众感觉到物体忽有忽无,变化不测 magic; conjuring; sleight of hand; a kind of acrobatics or a performing skill of producing baffling effects or illusions by sleight of hand, concealed apparatus, etc.; also 幻术 huànshù or 戏法 xìfǎ

【魔王】mówáng ❶〈佛教用语 *Budd*.〉指专做破坏活动的恶鬼 mara; prince of the devil ❷〈比喻 *fig*.〉非常凶暴的恶人 tyrant; despot; fiend: 混世~ monster; devil incarnate; fiend in human shape | 杀人~ butcher; murderer

【魔芋】móyù ❶ 多年生草本植物,掌状复叶,小叶羽状分裂,花紫褐色,花轴上部棒形,地下茎球形,可以吃,又可制淀粉 giantarum (*Amorphophallus*); perennial herb with palmate compound leaves and pinnately lobed leaflets, purplish-brown flowers, a vertical stem at the upper part of the floral axis and a tuber at the base that is edible and used to make starch ❷ 这种植物的地下茎 underground stem of this plant ‖ also 蒟蒻 jǔruò

【魔掌】mózhǎng 〈比喻 *fig*.〉凶恶势力的控制 devil's clutches; evil hands; control of a vicious force: 逃出~ escape from the clutches of the devil

【魔杖】mózhàng 魔术师所用的棍儿 magic wand; wand used by a magician

【魔障】mózhàng 〈佛教用语 *Budd*.〉恶魔所设的障碍 barrier set up by a monster

【魔爪】mózhǎo 〈比喻 *fig*.〉凶恶的势力 claws; tentacles; devil's talons; vicious force: 斩断侵略者的~ cut off the tentacles of the aggressors

【魔怔】mó·zheng 举动异常,像有精神病一样 devil's craze; abnormal act done as if by a person suffering from a mental disease

劘 mó 〈书 *fml*.〉削;切 cutting; cut

mǒ (ㄇㄛˇ)

抹 mǒ ❶ 涂抹 apply; smear; plaster; put on: ~粉 apply face powder | ~上点药膏 apply some ointment | ~一层糨糊 put on a layer of paste ◇月光在淡灰色的墙上~了一层银色。The moonlight has covered the light grey wall with a layer of silver. ❷ 擦 wipe: 他吃完饭把嘴一~就走了。He wiped his mouth with the back of the hand and left after having his meal. ❸ 勾掉;除去;不计在内 cross (or strike, blot) out; erase: ~杀 cancel; erase; obliterate; blot out | ~零 cross out the fraction | 把这行字~了。Cross out this line. ❹〈量词 *classifier*〉用于云霞等[used of cloud, etc.]: 一~彩霞 a wisp of rosy cloud ☞ mā on p.1285 and mò on p.1367

【抹脖子】mǒ bó·zi 拿刀割脖子,多指自杀 commit suicide; cut one's own throat

【抹彩】mǒ//cǎi 指戏曲演员老生、小生、武生等行当面部化装 facial make-up for actors in Chinese operas

【抹黑】mǒ//hēi 涂抹黑色,比喻丑化 discredit; paint black; throw mud at; bring shame on; blacken sb.'s name: 干吗要往自己脸上~? Why should you discredit yourself? | 他决不会给集体~的。He would never bring shame on our collective.

【抹零】mǒ//líng (~儿 mǒ//língr)付钱时不计算整数之外的尾数 cross out the fraction; not count the small change (in a payment)

【抹杀】mǒshā 一概不计;完全勾销 obliterate; blot out; write off: 一笔~ be totally blotted out; write off at one stroke | 这个事实谁也~不了。No one can deny this fact. also 抹煞 mǒshā

【抹煞】mǒshā same as 抹杀 mǒshā

【抹稀泥】mǒ xīní 〈方 *dial*.〉和(huò)稀泥 paper over the cracks; gloss things over

【抹一鼻子灰】mǒ yī bí·zi huī 想讨好而结果落得没趣 try to please someone but get a snub; have one's nose rubbed in the dust

【抹子】mǒ·zi 瓦工用来抹灰泥的器具 trowel; tool with a thin, flat, pointed blade used by a bricklayer or plasterer for applying and shaping mortar; also 抹刀 mǒdāo

mò (ㄇㄛˋ)

万 mò [万俟](Mòqí)姓 a surname ☞ wàn on p.1977

末[1] mò ❶ 东西的梢;尽头 tip; end: ~梢 tip; end | 秋毫之~ end of an animal's autumn hair — minute title ❷ 不是根本的、主要的事物(跟'本'相对 as opposed to 'essential') nonessential; minor details: 本~倒置 put trifles before essentials | 舍本逐~ attend to the trifles to the neglect of essentials ❸ 最后;终了;末尾 end; last stage: 春~ end of spring | ~班车 last bus; last chance or turn | 明~农民大起义 peasant uprisings towards the end of the Ming Dynasty ❹ (~儿 mòr)末子 powder; dust: 锯~ saw dust | 茶叶~儿 broken tea leaves; tea dust | 把药研成~儿 pestle medicinal

herbs into powder

末2 mò 戏曲角色行当，扮演中年男子，京剧归入老生一类 role of a middle-aged man in traditional operas; old man in Peking Opera

☞ 么 ·me on p.1312

【末班车】mòbānchē ❶ 按班次行驶的最后一班车 last bus; also 末车 ❷〈比喻 *fig.*〉最后的一次机会 last chance; last turn

【末代】mòdài 指一个朝代的最后一代；末世 last reign of a dynasty: ～皇帝 last emperor of a dynasty | ～子孙 last generation

【末伏】mòfú ❶ 立秋后的第一个庚日，是最后的一伏 first *gen* day (on which the Heavenly Stem — *gen* — comes across an Earthly Branch) immediately after the Beginning of Autumn sets in, which marks the beginning of the last or third *fu* (hottest 10-day period) of the year ❷ 通常也指从立秋后第一个庚日起到第二个庚日前一天(共十天)的一段时间 10-day period that starts from the first *gen* day immediately following the Beginning of Autumn and ends prior to the second *gen* day ‖ also 终伏 zhōngfú or 三伏 sānfú

【末后】mòhòu 最后 last; finally; in the end: ～，主席宣布散会。In the end, the chairman declared the meeting over.

【末节】mòjié 小节 nonessentials; minor details: 细枝～minor details; nonessentials

【末了】mòliǎo (～儿 mòliǎor) 最后 last; finally; in the end: 第五行～的那个字我不认识。I don't know the last word of the fifth line. | 大家猜了半天，～还是小伍猜中了。Everyone guessed for a while, but in the end, Xiao Wu made the right guess. also 末末了儿 mòmòliǎor

【末流】mòliú ❶ 已经衰落并失去原有的精神实质的学术、文艺等流派 late and decadent stage of a school of thought, literature, etc. ❷ 等级或质量低的 shoddy; inferior; low-grade; of the lowest quality: ～演员 minor actor or actress; poor actor or actress | ～水平 lowest level

【末路】mòlù 路途的终点，比喻没落衰亡的境地 impasse; dead end: 穷途～ impasse; dead end

【末年】mònián (历史上一个朝代或一个君主在位时期)最后的一段时期 last years of a dynasty or reign: 明朝～ last years of the Ming Dynasty | 道光～ last years of the reign of Emperor Daoguang

【末期】mòqī 最后的一段时期 last phase; final phase; last stage: 唐代～ last period of the Tang Dynasty | 新石器时代～ final phase of the Neolithic Age

【末日】mòrì〈基督教 *Christ.*〉指世界的最后一天，一般泛指死亡或灭亡的日子(用于憎恶的人或事物 of an abominable person or thing) doomsday; Day of Judgement; Judgement Day; the end: ～来临 approach of the doomsday

【末梢】mòshāo 末尾 tip; end: 五月～ end of May | 她在辫子的～打了一个花结。She tied a ribbon bowknot at the tip end of her plait.

【末梢神经】mòshāo shénjīng 神经从神经中枢发出后分布到各组织的部分，作用是感受外来的刺激并把这些刺激传达到神经中枢，又把神经中枢的命令传达到各部组织 nerve end; end part of a nerve coming from the nerve centre and stretches to a tissue, its function being to sense the external stimulation and transmit the stimulation to the nerve centre and transmit the commands from the nerve centre to the tissues

【末世】mòshì 一个历史阶段的末尾的时期 last phase (of an age): 封建～ last years of feudalism

【末尾】mòwěi 最后的部分 end; last part: 排在～ stand at the end of a queue | 文章～还需斟酌。The end of the article needs more deliberation.

【末叶】mòyè (一个世纪或一个朝代)最后一段时期 last years (of a century or dynasty): 18世纪～ end of the 18th century | 清朝～ last years of the Qing Dynasty

【末子】mò·zi 细碎的或成面儿的东西 powder; dust: 煤～ coal dust

【末座】mòzuò 座位分尊卑时，最卑的座位叫末座 end seat; seat at the end of a table or row, when the seats are arranged for the eminent and the inferior, the seat for the inferior is called the end seat

没1 mò ❶ (人或物)沉下或沉没 sink; submerge: ～入水中 submerge | 太阳将～未～的时候，水面泛起了一片红光。There was a red glow on the lake when the sun was setting. ❷ 漫过或高过(人或物) overflow; rise beyond: 雪深～膝。The snow was knee-deep. | 河水～了马背。The river water overflowed the horseback. ❸ 隐藏；隐没 disappear; hide: 出～ haunt; appear and disappear ❹ 没收 confiscate: 抄～ search and confiscate ❺ 一直到完了；尽；终 till the end: ～世 all one's life; life long | ～齿 all one's life (齿 *chi*: 年齿 age) ❻ same as 殁 mò

没2 mò ☞ 没奈何 mònàihé

☞ méi on p.1312

【没齿不忘】mò chǐ bù wàng 终身不能忘记 will never forget to the end of one's days; remember for the rest of one's life; also 没世不忘 mò shì bù wàng

【没落】mòluò 衰败；趋向灭亡 decline; wane: ～贵族 declining aristocrat | 家道～ declining family financial situation | 腐朽～ decadent and declining

【没奈何】mònàihé 实在没有办法；无可奈何 be utterly helpless; have no way out; have no

M

alternative：小黄等了很久不见他来，～只好一个人去了。Xiao Huang waited for a long time, but he didn't show up, so he had to go alone.

【没世】mòshì 指终身；一辈子 lifelong; all one's life：～不忘 will never forget to the end of one's days; remember for the rest of one's life

【没收】mòshōu 把犯罪的个人或集团的财产强制地收归公有，也指把违反禁令或规定的东西收去归公 confiscate; expropriate; confiscate the property of a criminal individual or group; also meaning to confiscate contraband

茉 mò［茉莉］(mò·lì) ❶ 常绿灌木，叶子卵形或椭圆形，有光泽，花白色，香味浓厚。供观赏，花可用来熏制茶叶。jasmine (*Jasminum sambac*); evergreen shrub with lustrous, ovate or elliptical leaves and fragrant white flowers, used for ornament or in making jasmine tea ❷ 这种植物的花 flower of the plant

抹 mò ❶ 把和好了的泥或灰等涂上后再用抹(mǒ)子弄平 daub; plaster：～墙 plaster a wall; daub plaster on a wall ❷ 紧挨着绕过 skirt; bypass：转弯～角 beat about the bush; talk in a roundabout way; full of twists and turns

☞ mā on p.1285 and mǒ on p.1365

【抹不开】mò·bu kāi same as 磨不开 mò·bu kāi

【抹得开】mò·de kāi same as 磨得开 mò·de kāi

【抹面】mòmiàn 在建筑物的表面抹上泥、石灰、水泥等材料，有时再刷上灰浆或做出各种花纹 face the surfaces of a building with mud, limestone, cement, etc., sometimes also whitewash them or add decorative designs

殁 mò〈书 *fml.*〉死 die：病～ die of illness; also 没 mò

沫 mò ❶（～儿 mòr）沫子 foam; froth：唾～ saliva｜肥皂～儿 soapsuds; lather｜马跑得满身是汗，口里流着白～。The horse was wet with sweat after running, foam flowing down from its mouth. ❷〈书 *fml.*〉唾液 saliva：相濡以～ help each other in adversity

【沫子】mò·zi 液体形成的许多小泡；泡沫 foam; froth

陌 mò 田间东西方向的道路，泛指道路 road; path between fields (running east and west)：阡～ paths in the fields｜～头杨柳 roadside willows｜巷～ streets and lanes｜～路 stranger

【陌路】mòlù〈书 *fml.*〉指路上碰到的不相识的人 stranger (whom one passes in the street)：视同～ treat like a stranger; cut someone dead; also 陌路人 mòlùrén

【陌生】mòshēng 生疏；不熟悉 strange; unfamiliar：～人 stranger｜我们虽然是第一次见面，并不感到～。Although this was only our first meeting, we didn't feel like strangers.

妹 mò 用于人名，妺喜，传说中夏王桀的妃子 character used in names, as in Moxi, a concubine of King Jie, the last monarch of the Xia Dynasty

冒 mò 冒顿(Mòdú)，汉初匈奴族一个单于(chányú)的名字 Modu, name of a chieftain of Xiongnu or the Huns in the early Han Dynasty

☞ mào on p.1310

脉(脈) mò［脉脉］默默地用眼神或行动表达情意 affectionate; loving; amorous; express one's affection silently with eyes or actions：～含情 full of tenderness and love｜她～地注视着远去的孩子们。She followed with loving eyes the departing figures of the children.

☞ mài on p.1296

莫 mò ❶〈书 *fml.*〉表示'没有谁'或'没有哪一种东西' no one; nothing; none：～不欣喜。Everyone was happy.｜～名其妙。No one can understand why it is good. *or* No one can explain why it is good. ❷ 不 no; not：～如 not as good as; would be better｜一筹～展 be at the end of one's wits｜爱～能助 be desirous but unable to help; be willing but powerless to help｜～衷一是 unable to agree or decide which is right ❸ 不要 don't：～哭。Don't cry.｜我不懂这里的规矩，请～见怪。I don't know the rules here. Please take no offence. ❹ 表示揣测或反问［indicating guessing or questioning］：～非 Is it possible that ...?｜～不是 It's possible that ... ❺ (Mò)姓 a surname

〈古 *arch.*〉also same as 暮 mù

【莫不】mòbù 没有一个不 there's no one who doesn't or isn't：铁路通车以后，这里的各族人民～欢欣鼓舞。People of all ethnic backgrounds here were jubilant after the railway was opened to traffic.

【莫不是】mòbùshì 莫非 can it be that; is it possible that

【莫测高深】mò cè gāoshēn 没法揣测究竟高深到什么程度，多指言行使人难以了解或理解 unfathomable; enigmatic

【莫大】mòdà 没有比这个再大；极大 greatest; utmost：～的光荣 greatest honour｜～的幸福 greatest happiness

【莫非】mòfēi〈副词 *adv.*〉表示揣测或反问，常跟'不成'呼应［indicating guessing or questioning, oft. in response to 'not'］can it be that; is it possible that：他将信将疑地说，～我听错了？He said with doubt: Did I hear wrongly?｜今天她没来，～又生了病不成？She is absent today. Can she be ill again?

【莫可指数】mò kě zhǐ shǔ 掰着指头也数不过来，形容数量很多 countless; innumerable; beyond counting on one's fingers

【莫名其妙】mò míng qí miào 没有人能说明它的奥妙(道理),表示事情很奇怪,使人不明白。'名' 也作明。no one can explain it—indicating sth. is so strange that no one can understand it; be unable to make head or tail of sth.; be baffled; 名 also 明 míng

【莫逆】mònì 彼此情投意合,非常相好 intimate; very friendly:～之交 bosom friends|在中学时代,他们二人最称～。The two of them were examples of what bosom friends were when they were in middle school.

【莫如】mòrú 不如(用于对事物的不同处理方法的比较选择 compare for a better choice in handling things) would be better; might as well:他想,既然来到了门口,～跟着进去看看。Now that he'd come to the entrance, he thought he might as well go in with the others to have a look.|与其你去,～他来。It would be better for him to come than for you to go. 注意 **NOTE**:'不如'除了比较得失之外,还可以比较高下,如'这个办法不如那个好','莫如'没有这一种用法。'不如' can also be used to compare between the high and the low, for example:'这个办法不如那个好 (This method is not so good as that one.)', but '莫如' cannot be used like that.

【莫若】mòruò same as 莫如 mòrú:休息的时候,与其坐在家里发闷,～出去走走。It would be better to go out for a walk than sit in low spirits at home when you take a rest.

【莫须有】mòxūyǒu 宋朝奸臣秦桧诬陷岳飞谋反,韩世忠不平,去质问他有没有证据,秦桧回答说'莫须有',意思是'也许有吧'。后来用来表示凭空捏造 Qin Hui (1090-1155), the treacherous Prime Minister of the Southern Song Dynasty, falsely accused Yue Fei, a patriotic general, of plotting a rebellion. When Han Shizhong, another patriotic general, indignantly questioned him whether he had any evidence, Qin Hui replied: '莫须有', meaning 'maybe there is'. Since then, the three characters have been used to mean unwarranted; groundless; fabricated; trumped-up:～的罪名 fabricated charge; unwarranted charge

【莫邪】mòyé same as 镆铘 mòyé

【莫衷一是】mò zhōng yī shì 不能得出一致的结论 unable to agree or decide which is right:对于这个问题,大家意见纷纷,～。Opinions are quite divided on this question.

眛 mò〈书 *fml.*〉❶ 目不明;目不正 poor eye sight; squint eyes ❷ 不顾(危险、恶劣环境等);冒 disregard (dangers, risks, poor environment, etc.):～险搜奇 search for wonders despite dangers

秣 mò ❶ 牲口的饲料 fodder:粮～ grain and fodder ❷ 喂牲口 feed animals:～马厉兵 feed the horses and sharpen the weapons; make preparations for war; prepare for battle

【秣马厉兵】mò mǎ lì bīng 喂饱马,磨快兵器,指准备作战 feed the horses and sharpen the weapons in preparation for battle (厉 same as 砺); also 厉兵秣马 lì bīng mò mǎ

脈 mò [脈脈] same as 脉脉 mòmò

蓦 mò 突然 suddenly; unexpectedly; abruptly; all of a sudden:～地 suddenly; unexpectedly; abruptly; all of a sudden|～然 suddenly; unexpectedly; abruptly; all of a sudden

【蓦地】mòdì 出乎意料地;突然 suddenly; unexpectedly; abruptly; all of a sudden:～大叫一声 shout abruptly or suddenly

【蓦然】mòrán 不经心地;猛然 suddenly; abruptly:～醒悟 wake up suddenly|～看去,这石头像一头卧牛。At first sight, the stone looks like a lying ox.

貊(貉) Mò 我国古代称东北方的民族 *mo*, an ancient Chinese term for the ethnic peoples of the northeast

☞ 貉 háo on p.773 and hé on p.791

漠 mò ❶ 沙漠 desert:大～ vast expanse of desert|～北 north of the Gobi Desert ❷ 冷淡地;不经心地 indifferent; unconcerned:～视 treat with indifference|～不关心 indifferent; unconcerned

【漠不关心】mò bù guān xīn 形容对人或事物冷淡,一点也不关心 indifferent; unconcerned

【漠漠】mòmò ❶ 云烟密布的样子 misty; foggy:湖面升起一层～的烟雾。A thick mist rose over the lake. ❷ 广漠而沉寂 vast and lonely:远处是～的平原。In the distance is a vast and lonely plain.

【漠然】mòrán 不关心不在意的样子 indifferent; apathetic; unconcerned:～置之 remain indifferent towards sth.; look on with unconcern|处之～ be indifferent to|～无动于衷(毫不动心) remain indifferent; be unmoved

【漠视】mòshì 冷淡地对待;不在意 ignore; overlook; treat with indifference; pay no attention to:不能～群众的根本利益。The masses' fundamental interests must not be treated with indifference.

寞 mò 安静;冷落 lonely; deserted:寂～ lonely|落～ lonely, desolate

靺 mò [靺鞨](Mòhé)我国古代东北方的民族 Mohe, an ethnic group living in northeast China in ancient times

嘿 mò same as 默 mò

☞ hēi on p.795

墨[1] mò ❶ 写字绘画的用品,是用煤烟或松烟等制成的黑色块状物,间或有用其他材料制成别种颜色的,也指用墨和水研出来的汁 China (or Chinese) ink; ink stick; black stick made of coal soot or burned pine soot for writing, painting, etc., occasionally of other materials for different colours：一块～ an ink stick｜一锭～ an ink stick｜研～ rub the inkstick on an inkslab｜笔～纸砚 writing brush, inkstick, paper and inkslab｜～太稠了。The ink is too thick. ❷ 泛指写字、绘画或印刷用的某种颜料（in a broad sense）pigment; ink：～水 ink (liquid)｜油～ printing ink ❸ 借指写的字和画的画 handwriting or painting：～宝 treasured scrolls of calligraphy or painting｜遗～ letters, manuscripts, paintings, calligraphy left behind by a deceased ❹〈比喻 *fig.*〉学问或读书识字的能力 learning or the ability to read：胸无点～ uneducated; unlearned; unlettered; completely illiterate ❺ 木工打直线用的墨线，借指规矩、准则 carpenter's line marker; rules and regulations：绳～ carpenter's line marker or ink marker｜矩～ carpenter's ink square ❻ 黑 black; pitch-dark：～菊 dark chrysanthemum｜～镜 sunglasses; dark glasses ❼〈书 *fml.*〉贪污 corruption; graft; embezzlement：贪～ embezzlement｜～吏 corrupt official ❽ 古代的一种刑罚，刺面或额，染上黑色，作为标记 tattooing the face and painting it black (a punishment in ancient China); also 黥 qíng ❾（Mò）指墨家 Mohist school ❿（Mò）姓 a surname

墨2 Mò 指墨西哥 Mexico：～洋（墨西哥银元）Mexican silver dollar

【墨宝】mòbǎo 指可宝贵的字画，也用来尊称别人写的字或画的画 treasured scroll of calligraphy or painting; your beautiful handwriting; your beautiful painting：请赐～。May I have one of your treasured scrolls of calligraphy or painting?

【墨斗】mòdǒu 木工用来打直线的工具。从墨斗中拉出黑线，放到木材上，绷紧，提起墨线后松手，趁着弹力打上黑线。carpenter's ink marker; tool used by a carpenter to mark straight lines. Pull an ink thread out of a U-shaped ink bowl, put it on the timber, stretch it tight, lift it up and let it go, thus marking the desired line by means of the elasticity.

【墨斗鱼】mòdǒuyú 乌贼的俗称 popular name for 乌贼 wūzéi

【墨海】mòhǎi 盆状的大砚台 big basin-like inkstone

【墨盒】mòhé（～儿 mòhér）文具，多用铜制，方形或圆形，像小盒子，内放丝绵，灌上墨汁，供毛笔蘸用 ink box (for Chinese calligraphy or painting); small, round or square bronze case with silk floss and black ink in it for a writing brush to dip before writing; also 墨盒子 mòhé·zi

【墨黑】mòhēi 非常黑；很暗 pitch-dark; inky black：天阴得～，恐怕要下大雨。It is very dark. I'm afraid a downpour is imminent. ◇两眼～（比喻对事物一无所知）be in the dark; (fig.) be completely ignorant of a matter

【墨迹】mòjì ❶ 墨的痕迹 ink marks; ink stains：～未干 before the ink is dry ❷ 某人亲手写的字或画的画 person's handwriting or painting

【墨家】Mòjiā 先秦时期的一个政治思想派别，以墨子（名翟 dí）为创始人。主张人与人平等相爱（兼爱），反对侵略战争（非攻）。墨家同时也是有组织的团体，在战争中扶助弱小抵抗强暴。但是相信有鬼（明鬼），相信天的意志（天志）。墨家后期发展了墨翟思想的积极部分，对朴素唯物主义、古代逻辑学的发展都有一定的贡献。Mohist School, a political and ideological school of thought founded by Mo Di in the Spring and Autumn and Warring States Periods, advocating equality and love among people and opposition to aggressive war. The Mohist School was also an organized group that helped the weak to resist brutal force. However, they believed in ghosts and heavenly will. The Mohists developed the positive part of Mo Di's thought and made contributions to the development of naive materialism and ancient logic.

【墨晶】mòjīng 水晶的一种，深棕色，略近黑色。可做眼镜片。smoky quartz; a kind of crystal, dark brown and slightly close to black, and used in making glasses

【墨镜】mòjìng 用墨晶制成的眼镜，泛指用黑色或墨绿色等镜片做的眼镜，有养目和避免强烈光线刺眼的作用 sunglasses; glasses made of smoky quartz; glasses made of black or blackish green lenses, used to protect the eyesight and avoid strong light

【墨客】mòkè〈书 *fml.*〉指文人 literary men; men of letters：骚人～ literary men; men of letters

【墨吏】mòlì〈书 *fml.*〉贪污的官吏 corrupt officials

【墨绿】mòlǜ 深绿色 blackish green

【墨守成规】Mò shǒu chéngguī 战国时墨子善于守城，后来用'墨守成规'形容因循守旧，不肯改进 stick to rules; stay in a rut. During the Warring States Period, Mo Di was very good at defending the city, and later 'Mo Di sticking to rules' has been used to implicate sticking to old ways and refusing to make improvements.

【墨水】mòshuǐ（～儿 mòshuǐr）❶ 墨汁 prepared Chinese ink ❷ 写钢笔字用的各种颜色的水 ink of different colours for writing with a pen：蓝～ blue ink｜红～ red ink ❸〈比喻 *fig.*〉学问或读书识字的能力 learning or the ability to read：他肚子里还有点儿～。He's something of a scholar.

【墨线】mòxiàn ❶ 木工用来打直线的装在墨斗上的线绳 line in a carpenter's ink marker ❷ 用墨线打出来的直线 line made with a

carpenter's ink marker

【墨刑】mòxíng 古代的刑罚，在罪犯脸上刺字并涂墨 tattooing the face and painting it black (a punishment in ancient China)

【墨鸦】mòyā ❶〈书 *fml.*〉形容书法拙劣 scribbling; poor handwriting ❷〈方 *dial.*〉鸬鹚 cormorant

【墨鱼】mòyú 乌贼的俗称 popular name for 乌贼

【墨汁】mòzhī (～儿 mòzhīr)用墨加水研成的汁，也指用黑色颜料加水和少量胶质制成的液体 prepared Chinese ink; liquid made from black dyestuff, water and glue

镆 mò [镆铘](mòyé)古代宝剑名 Moye, name of an ancient double-edged treasured sword; also 莫邪 mòyé

瘼 mò〈书 *fml.*〉病；疾苦 illness; disease; sufferings; hardships: 民～ sufferings of the people

默 mò ❶ 不说话；不出声 silent; tacit; quiet: ～读 read silently | ～认 tacit consent | 沉～ silent | ～不作声 keep silent ❷ 默写 write from memory: ～生字 write new characters or words from memory ❸ (Mò) 姓 a surname

【默哀】mò'āi 为表示悼念，低下头默默地肃立着 stand in silent tribute

【默祷】mòdǎo 不出声地祈祷；心中祷告 pray in silence; say a silent prayer

【默读】mòdú 不出声地读书，是语文教学上训练阅读能力的一种方法 read silently; method of training the reading ability in language teaching: ～课文 read a text silently

【默剧】mòjù 哑剧 pantomime; mime

【默默】mòmò 不说话；不出声 quiet; silent: ～无言 silently; without saying a word

【默默无闻】mò mò wú wén 不出名；不为人知道 unknown to the public; without attracting public attention: 他经常～地为大伙儿做好事。He always does good deeds for others without attracting public attention.

【默念】mòniàn ❶ 默读 read silently: ～一首古诗 read an classical poem silently ❷ 心里思想 recollect; recall; think back: ～当年情景，如在昨日。As I called those years to mind, I felt as if they were yesterday.

【默片】mòpiàn 无声片 mute film; silent film

【默契】mòqì ❶ 双方的意思没有明白说出而彼此有一致的了解 tacit agreement; tacit understanding: 配合～ play in perfect unison; act in perfect unison; cooperate perfectly well ❷ 秘密的条约或口头协定 secret treaty or oral agreement

M

【默然】mòrán 沉默无言的样子 silent; speechless: 二人～相对。The two of them sat face to face in silence.

【默认】mòrèn 心里承认，但不表示出来 give tacit consent to; tacitly approve; acquiesce in: 你不申辩，不就等于～了吗？If you don't speak in defence, does that mean your tacit consent?

【默诵】mòsòng ❶ 不出声地背诵 read silently ❷ 默读 read silently to oneself from memory

【默算】mòsuàn ❶ 心中暗自盘算 calculate; figure; plan ❷ 心算 do mental arithmetic; do sums in one's heart

【默写】mòxiě 凭着记忆把读过的文字写出来 write what has been read from memory

【默许】mòxǔ 没有明白表示同意，但是暗示已经许可 tacitly consent to; acquiesce in: 他不说话，就是～了。His silence means tacit consent.

磨 mò ❶ 把粮食弄碎的工具，通常是两个圆石盘做成的 mill; millstones; a pair of large, flat, round stones between which grains are ground: 一盘～ a pair of millstones | 电～ electric mill | 推～ work a pair of millstones ❷ 用磨把粮食弄碎 grind; mill: ～面 grind wheat or rice into flour | ～豆腐 grind soya beans to make bean curd | ～麦子 grind wheat ❸ 掉转；转变 turn round: 把汽车～过来 turn a car round ◇我几次三番劝他，他还是～不过来。I had talked to him again and again, but he simply wouldn't come round.

☞ mó on p. 1363

【磨不开】mò·bu kāi ❶ 脸上下不来 feel embarrassed; be put out: 本想当面说他两句，又怕他脸上～。I hesitated to criticize him for fear of making him uncomfortable. ❷ 不好意思 feel embarrassed (for fear of impairing personal relations, losing face, offending someone, etc.): 他有错误，就该批评他，有什么～的？If he's made a mistake, you should criticize him. Why should you hesitate and feel embarrassed? ❸〈方 *dial.*〉想不通；行不通 be unable to straighten out one's thinking; be unable to come round: 我有了～的事，就找他去商量。When I have something I can't straighten out, I would talk to him for help. ‖ also 抹不开 mò·bu kāi

【磨叨】mò·dao ❶ 翻来覆去地说 keep talking; talk on and on; chatter away: 说两句就行了，别再～啦。Just a few words, and stop your talking. ❷〈方 *dial.*〉谈论 gossip; talk: 你们刚才又在～啥？What are you talking about?

【磨得开】mò·de kāi ❶ 脸上下得来 not feel embarrassed; be at ease: 你当面挖苦人，人家脸上～吗？Would he be embarrassed if you speak ironically in his face? ❷ 好意思 have the nerve, face or cheek: 她请客你不去，你～吗？Do you have the nerve to turn down her invitation? ❸〈方 *dial.*〉想得通；行得通 be convinced; come round: 这个理我～，您就放心吧。Don't worry. I can see your reason. ‖ also 抹得开 mò·de kāi

【磨烦】mò·fan ❶ 没完没了地纠缠(多指向人要

求什么) trouble; pester; nag (always requesting sb. to do sth.):这孩子常常~姐姐给他讲故事。The child often pestered his sister to tell him stories. ❷ 动作迟缓拖延 delay; loiter; dawdle:不必~了,说办就办吧。Don't delay any more. Get it started right away.

【磨坊】mòfáng 磨面粉等的作坊 mill; also 磨房 mòfáng

【磨盘】mòpán ❶ 托着磨的圆形底盘 nether (or lower) millstone ❷〈方 *dial.*〉same as 磨 mò ①

【磨扇】mòshàn 磨的上下两片石盘 upper and lower millstones

貘(貊) mò 哺乳动物,尾短,鼻子突出很长,能自由伸缩,皮厚毛少,前肢四趾,后肢三趾。产于热带地区。tapir (*Tapirus*); tropical mammal with a short tail, a long, protruding nose which can stretch out and draw back freely, thick skin with little hair, the forelimbs having four toes and the hind limbs having three toes living in tropical regions

缪 mò〈书 *fml.*〉绳索 rope

礳 mò 礳石渠(Mòshíqú),地名,在山西 Moshiqu, name of a place in Shanxi Province

耱 mò same as 耢 lào ①

mōu (ㄇㄡ)

哞 mōu〈拟声词 *onom.*〉形容牛叫的声音 moo; low; bellow; sound made by an ox

móu (ㄇㄡˊ)

牟 móu ❶ 牟取 obtain; seek; try to gain:~利 seek private (or selfish) interests; seek personal gain ❷ (Móu) 姓 a surname
☞ mù on p. 1378

【牟利】móu//lì 谋取私利 seek private (or selfish) interests; seek personal gain:非法~ seek private interests by illegal means

【牟取】móuqǔ 谋取(名利) seek; obtain (fame and money); try to gain:~暴利 seek exorbitant profits; reap staggering (or colossal) profits

侔 móu〈书 *fml.*〉相等;齐 equal; match:相~ match each other

眸 móu 眸子 pupil (of the eye); eye:凝~ gaze | 明~皓齿 bright eyes and white teeth

【眸子】móuzǐ 本指瞳人,泛指眼睛 pupil (of the eye); (in a broad sense) eye

谋 móu ❶ 主意;计谋;计策 stratagem; plan; scheme:阴~ plot; scheme; conspiracy | 足智多~ wise and resourceful; shrewd and full of stratagems ❷ 图谋;谋求 seek; work for:~生 earn a living; seek a livelihood | ~害 murder | 为人类~福利 work for the interests of humanity ❸ 商议 consult:不~而合 agree without prior consultation

【谋臣】móuchén 参与谋划或善于出谋划策的臣子 emperor's counsellor:~猛将 wise counsellors and brave generals

【谋反】móufǎn 暗中谋划反叛(国家) conspire against the state; plot a rebellion:蓄意~ premeditated plot; plot a rebellion deliberately

【谋害】móuhài 谋划杀害或陷害 plot to murder:~忠良 plot a frame-up against a loyal and virtuous person

【谋和】móuhé 谋求和平或和解 sue for peace

【谋划】móuhuà 筹划;想办法 plan; scheme; try to find a solution:仔细~ plan carefully | ~赈灾义演 plan a performance to relieve the people in the calamity-stricken areas

【谋虑】móulǜ 谋划;考虑 contemplate; deliberate; consider carefully:~深远 think deeply

【谋略】móulüè 计谋策略 strategy; astuteness and resourcefulness:运用~ use astuteness and resourcefulness | ~深远 well-planned strategy

【谋面】móumiàn〈书 *fml.*〉彼此见面,相识 meet each other or be acquainted with each other:素未~ have never met each other before

【谋求】móuqiú 设法寻求 seek; strive for; be in quest of:~解决办法 try to find a solution

【谋取】móuqǔ 设法取得 seek; obtain; try to gain:~利益 seek gains

【谋杀】móushā 谋划杀害 murder:惨遭~ be murdered | 一桩~案 a murder case

【谋生】móushēng 设法寻求维持生活的门路 earn a living; seek a livelihood:出外~ leave home to seek a livelihood

【谋士】móushì 出谋献计的人 adviser; counsellor

【谋事】móushì ❶ 计划事情 plan matters:~在人。The soundness of a plan depends on the man who makes it. ❷ 指找职业 look for a job:设法~ try to find a job

【谋私】móusī 谋取私利 seek private gains:以权~ use one's power to seek private gains

【谋陷】móuxiàn 设法陷害 frame up; set sb. up:~忠良 frame against a loyal and honest man | 遭人~ be set up

【谋职】móuzhí 谋取职业或职位 plan; scheme:出外~ go job-hunting | 四处~ look for a job everywhere

蛑 móu ☞ [蝤蛑] (yóumóu) on p. 2325

麰 móu〈古代 *arch.*〉称大麦 barley

缪 móu ☞ 绸缪 chóumóu on p. 277
☞ Miào on p. 1344 and miù on p. 1361

M

鍪 móu ☞ 兜鍪 dōumóu on p. 471

mǒu (ㄇㄡˇ)

某 mǒu〈指示代词 *pron.*〉❶ 指一定的人或事物(知道名称而不说出)[know sb. or sth. without naming it] certain; some: 张～ Mr. Zhang|解放军～部 a certain unit of the PLA ❷ 指不定的人或事物 indefinite person or thing: ～人 a certain person|～地 a certain place|～种线索 a certain clue ❸ 用来代替自己或自己的名字,如'某,张飞是也。'又如姓张的自称'张某'或'张某人'。(referring to oneself): 'Oh, this is Zhang Fei.' For another example, a person named Zhang may call himself 'Zhang' or 'this Zhang'. ❹ 用来代替别人的名字(常含不客气意 oft. impolitely) [used to replace the name of another person]: 请转告刘～,做事不要太过分。Please tell Mr. Liu not to overdo himself. ‖ 注意 **NOTE**: 有时叠用 Sometimes the character 某 is used in reiterative locution: ～～人 that person; so and so|～～学校 that school

mú (ㄇㄨˊ)

毪 mú 毪子 woollen fabric made in Tibet

【毪子】mú·zi 西藏产的一种氆氇 woollen fabric made in Tibet

模 mú (～儿 múr) 模子 mould; matrix; pattern: 铅～ lead mould|铜～儿 copper mould

☞ mó on p. 1361

【模板】múbǎn 浇灌混凝土工程用的模型板,一般用木料或钢材制成 shuttering; formwork, usu. made of wood or steel for pouring concrete work

【模具】mújù 生产上使用的各种模型 mould; matrix; pattern; die

【模样】múyàng (～儿 múyàngr) ❶ 人的长相或装束打扮的样子 appearance; look: 这孩子的～像他爸爸。The child takes after his father. *or* The child looks like his father.|看你打扮成这～,我几乎认不出来了。You are beyond recognition the way you've been dressed up. ❷ 表示约略的情况(只用于时间、年岁) indicating a rough estimate of time or age: 等了大概有半个小时～ have waited for about half an hour|这个人有三十岁～。The man is around thirty. ❸ 形势;趋势;情况 situation; trend: 不像要留客人吃饭的～。It's not likely to ask the guests to stay for the dinner.|看～,这家饭馆像是快要关张了。Judging from its appearance, the restaurant is about to close down.

【模子】mú·zi same as 模型 móxíng ③: 铜～ copper mould|石膏～ gypsum mould|糕饼～ bread mould

mǔ (ㄇㄨˇ)

母 mǔ ❶ 母亲 mother; Alma Mater ～女 mother and daughter|老～ one's old mother ◇～校 Alma Mater ❷ 家族或亲戚中的长辈女子 one's female elders: 祖～ grandmother|伯～ aunt; wife of father's elder brother|姑～ aunt; father's sister|姨～ aunt; mother's sister|舅～ wife of mother's brother ❸ (禽兽)雌性的(跟'公'相对 as opposed to 'male')(of animals) female: ～鸡 hen|～牛 cow|这头驴是～的。This donkey is a female (or a jenny). ❹ (～儿 mǔr)指一凸一凹配套的两件东西里的凹的一件 nut, a metal block with a threaded hole through its centre, for a screw: 这套螺丝的～儿毛了。The nut for this screw has become unusable. ❺ 有产生出其他事物的能力或作用的 origin; parent: 工作～机 machine tool|失败乃成功之～。Failure is the mother of success. ❻ (Mǔ) 姓 a surname

【母爱】mǔ'ài 母亲对于儿女的爱 mother love; maternal love: 无私的～ unselfish mother love|从小失去～ devoid of maternal love since childhood

【母本】mǔběn 接受花粉、结成子实或采用压条等方法进行繁殖的植株 female parent; plant reproduced by receiving pollen and bearing fruits or by layering; also 母株 mǔzhū

【母畜】mǔchù 雌性牲畜。畜牧业上通常指能生小牲畜的雌性牲畜。mother of a domestic animal; female animal; dam; (in animal husbandry) female animal which can produce young animals

【母法】mǔfǎ ❶ 指根本法,即宪法 fundamental law; constitution ❷ 一国的立法如果源于或模仿外国的法律,则称该外国的法律为母法 If the law made by one country originates in or imitates one of a foreign country, the law of that country is the fundamental law.

【母蜂】mǔfēng 蜜蜂中能产卵的雌蜂,身体在蜂群中最大,腹部很长,翅短小,足比工蜂长,后足上没有花粉篮。在正常情况下,每一个蜂巢只有一只母蜂。queen bee; bee that produces eggs, with a biggest body than other bees, a long belly, short wings, longer feet than the worker, and no pollen baskets on the hind feet; also 蜂王 fēngwáng

【母机】mǔjī 工作母机的简称 abbr. for 工作母机 gōngzuò mǔjī

【母金】mǔjīn 本金 principal; capital

【母老虎】mǔlǎohǔ〈比喻 *fig.*〉凶悍的妇女 tigress; vixen; malicious woman

【母亲】mǔ·qīn 有子女的女子,是子女的母亲 mother; woman having a child or children;

mother of the children ◇ 祖国，我的～! Homeland, my mother!

【母权制】mǔquánzhì 原始公社初期形成的女子在经济上和社会关系上占支配地位的制度。由于经营农业、饲养家畜和管理家务，都以妇女为主，又由于群婚，子女只能确认生母，这样就形成了以女子为中心的母系氏族公社。后来被父权制所代替。matriarchy; form of social organization in the early period of the primitive commune, in which the mother was recognized as the head of the family or tribe in handling economic and social relations. As the women were in charge of farm production, animal breeding and house keeping and also because of group marriage, the children could only recognize their own mothers. Matriarchic communes were thus formed with women as their centres, until they were later superseded by patriarchy.

【母乳】mǔrǔ 母亲的奶汁 breast milk; mother's milk

【母树】mǔshù 采伐迹地上保留的采种用的树木，也泛指专供采集种子或枝条用的树 mother tree; seed tree; maternal tree: ～林 maternal wood

【母体】mǔtǐ 指孕育幼体的人或雌性动物的身体 mother's body; (female) parent

【母系】mǔxì ❶ 在血统上属于母亲方面的 maternal: ～亲属 maternal relatives ❷ 母女相承的 matrilineal; matriarchal: ～家族制度 matriarchy

【母线】mǔxiàn ❶ 电站或变电站输送电能用的总导线。通过它，把发电机、变压器或整流器输出的电能输送给各个用户或其他变电所。bus; bus bar; conductor or group of conductors serving as a common connection in a power station or substation, through which the power coming from the generators, transformers or rectifiers is transmitted to the users or other substations ❷ 数学上指依一定条件运动而产生面的直线（math.）generatrix; generator; straight line that moves under given conditions to form a plane

【母校】mǔxiào 称本人曾经在那里毕业或学习过的学校 Alma Mater; one's old school; school where a person once studied or where one completed one's education

【母性】mǔxìng 母亲爱护子女的本能 maternal instinct; instinct by which a mother takes care of her children

【母液】mǔyè 化学沉淀或结晶过程中分离出沉淀或晶体后剩下的饱和溶液 mother liquor; mother solution; saturated solution left after the sediment or crystal is separated in the process of chemical sedimentation or crystallization

【母音】mǔyīn 元音 vowel

【母语】mǔyǔ ❶ 一个人最初学会的一种语言，在一般情况下是本民族的标准语或某一种方言 mother tongue; first language one learns to speak, usu. the standard language of one's own nationality or a certain dialect ❷ 有些语言是从一个语言演变出来的，那个共同的来源，就是这些语言的母语 parent language; linguistic parent; language from which other languages evolved

【母质】mǔzhì 某种物质由另一种物质生成，后者就是前者的母质，如成土母质、生油母质 parent material; a material produced by another material, the latter being the parent material of the former, such as parent material and oil-bearing material

【母钟】mǔzhōng master clock; ☞ 子母钟 zǐmǔzhōng on p. 2540

牡 mǔ 雄性的（跟'牝'相对 as opposed to 'female'）male: ～牛 bull

【牡丹】mǔ·dan ❶ 落叶灌木，叶子有柄，羽状复叶，小叶卵形或长椭圆形，花大，单生，通常深红、粉红或白色，是著名的观赏植物。根皮入药时叫丹皮。peony (*Paeonia*); tree peony; ornament of deciduous shrub having pinnatifid, compound leaves with stalks, ovate or oblong leaflets, and big, red, pink or white solitary flowers, its root and bark used for traditional Chinese medicine ❷ 这种植物的花 peony, the flower of the plant

【牡蛎】mǔlì 软体动物，有两个贝壳，一个小而平，另一个大而隆起，壳的表面凹凸不平。肉供食用，又能提制蚝油。肉、壳、油都可入药。oyster (*Ostreidae*); soft-shelled animal with two coarse shells, one small and flat, and the other big and bulging, with its meat used for food and making oyster oil. Oyster meat, shell and oil are used as traditional Chinese medicine; also 蚝 háo or 海蛎子 hǎilì·zi

亩（畝） mǔ 地积单位，10 分等于 1 亩，100 亩等于 1 顷。现用市亩，1 市亩等于 60 平方丈，合 666.7 平方米 *mu*, unit of land measure; 10 *fen* equal 1 *mu*; 100 *mu* equal 1 *qing*; currently called *shimu*, 1 *shimu* equals 60 square *zhang* or 666.7 square metres

坶 mǔ ☞ 垆坶 lúmǔ on p. 1257

拇 mǔ same as 拇指 mǔzhǐ

【拇战】mǔzhàn 指划拳 finger-guessing game; drinking game

【拇指】mǔzhǐ 手和脚的第一个指头 thumb; big toe; also 大拇指 dà·mǔzhǐ

峬 mǔ 峬矶角（Mǔjī Jiǎo），岬角名，在山东 Mujijiao, name of a promontory in Shandong Province

姆 mǔ ☞ 保姆 bǎomǔ on p. 67
☞ m̄ on p. 1285

姥 mǔ 〈书 *fml.*〉年老的妇人 old woman
☞ lǎo on p. 1162

铒 mǔ ☞ 钴铒 gǔmǔ on p. 695

啲 mǔ 又 also yīngmǔ 英亩旧也作啲 former name for 英亩 yīngmǔ

木[1] mù ❶ 树木 tree：伐～ fell a tree | 果～ fruit tree | 独～不成林。A single tree won't make up a wood. ❷ 木头 timber；wood：枣～ date wood | 榆～ elm wood | 檀香～ sandal wood ❸ 棺材 coffin：棺～ coffin | 行将就～ have one foot in the grave ❹ (Mù)姓 a surname

木[2] mù ❶ 质朴 simple；plain：～讷 inarticulate ❷ 麻木 numb；wooden：两脚冻～了。Both my feet were numb with cold. | 舌头～了，什么味道也尝不出来。My tongue has lost all its sense of taste.

【木版】mùbǎn 上面刻出文字或图画的木制印刷板 block；wood block engraved with an inscription or a design：～水印 watercolour block printing；also 木板 mùbǎn

【木版画】mùbǎnhuà 木刻 woodcut；wood engraving

【木本】mùběn 有木质茎的 xylophytic；woody

【木本水源】mù běn shuǐ yuán 〈比喻 *fig.*〉事物的根本 root of a tree and the source of a stream — the root of a matter

【木本植物】mùběn zhíwù 具有木质茎的植物，如杨、柳等乔木和玫瑰、丁香等灌木 xylophyte；woody plant，including trees (such as popular，willow，popular，etc.) and shrubs (such as rose，etc.)

【木菠萝】mùbōluó ❶ 常绿乔木，高达 10 米，叶子卵圆形，花小，聚合成椭圆形。果实可以吃。原产印度。jackfruit (*Artocarpus integrifolia*)；Indian evergreen tree，10 metres tall，having ovate leaves and small flowers clustered in oval shapes，and edible fruits ❷ 这种植物的果实 jackfruit，the fruit of the tree ‖ also 菠萝蜜 bōluómì

【木材】mùcái 树木采伐后经过初步加工的材料 wood；timber；lumber

【木柴】mùchái 作燃料或引火用的小块木头 firewood；small pieces of wood for fire

【木船】mùchuán 木制的船，通常用橹、桨等行驶 wooden boat propelled by a scull or an oar

【木呆呆】mùdāidāi (～的 mùdāidāi·de)形容发呆的样子 in a daze；in a trance：他像失去了知觉似的，～地站在窗前。He stood before the window staring blankly as if he had lost consciousness.

【木雕】mùdiāo 在木头上雕刻形象、花纹的艺术。也指用木头雕刻成的作品。woodcarving；art of carving images，designs，etc.，on a piece of wood；also woodcarving or wood sculpture：大型～ large woodcarving | ～艺人 a wood sculptor

【木雕泥塑】mù diāo ní sù 用木头雕刻或泥土塑造的偶像，形容人呆板或静止不动 idol carved in wood or moulded in clay；as wooden as a dummy；also 泥塑木雕 ní sù mù diāo

【木耳】mù'ěr 菌的一种，生长在腐朽的树干上，形状如人耳，黑褐色，胶质，外面密生柔软的短毛。可供食用。edible fungus (*Auricularia auricula*)；blackish-brown edible fungus growing on decaying tree trunks，shaped like a human ear，gelatinous，and having short hair on the surfaces

【木筏】mùfá 用长木材结成的筏子 raft；flat，buoyant structure of long logs fastened together；also 木筏子 mùfá·zi

【木芙蓉】mùfúróng ❶ 落叶灌木或小乔木，叶子阔卵形，花白色、粉红色或红色，单瓣或重瓣，结蒴果，扁球形，有毛 cotton rose (*Hibiscus mutabilis*)；deciduous shrub or tree having broad ovate leaves，white，pink or red solitary or multiple flowers and hairy，flat，spherical capsules ❷ 这种植物的花 cotton rose，the flower of this plant ‖ also 芙蓉 fúróng or 木莲 mùlián

【木工】mùgōng ❶ 制造或修理木器、制造和安装房屋的木制构件的工作 woodwork；carpentry；building and repairing of wooden things，esp. the wooden parts of buildings，etc.：～活 woodwork ❷ 做这种工作的工人 woodworker；carpenter：请～来修理 ask a carpenter to make repairs

【木屐】mùjī 木板拖鞋 clogs

【木简】mùjiǎn 〈古代 *arch.*〉用来写字的木片 wooden slips for writing

【木匠】mù·jiang 制造或修理木器、制造和安装房屋的木制构件的工人 carpenter；worker who builds or repairs wooden things，esp. the woodwork of a building

【木强】mùjiàng 〈书 *fml.*〉质朴刚强 honest and staunch：为人～敦厚 be upright and unyielding

【木槿】mùjǐn 落叶灌木或小乔木，叶子卵形，互生，掌状分裂，花钟形，单生，通常有白、红、紫等颜色，茎的韧皮可抽纤维，做造纸原料，花和种子可入药 rose of Sharon (*Hibiscus syriacus*)；deciduous shrub or small tree，with alternate ovate leaves，palmate lobed，single，bell-like flowers of white，red and purple colours，the fibres from its bark used in making paper，and both its flowers and seeds being medically useful

【木刻】mùkè 版画的一种，在木板上刻成图形，再印在纸上 woodcut；wood engraving；also 木版画 mùbǎnhuà

【木刻水印】mùkè shuǐyìn 一种彩色套印技术，用于复制美术品，根据画稿着色浓淡、阴阳向背的不同，分别刻成许多块版，依照色调进行套印或叠印 watercolour block printing；printing of paintings，drawings，etc.，from engraved blocks coated with ink or dyes based on the originals；colour printing technique used for reproduction of paintings；旧称 formely also called 饾版 dòubǎn

【木料】mùliào 初步加工后具有一定形状的木材 timber; lumber

【木马】mùmǎ ❶ 木头制成的马 wooden horse ❷ 木制的运动器械，略像马，背上安双环的叫鞍马，没有环的叫跳马 vaulting horse; pommel horse; wooden sports apparatus in the shape of a horse ❸ 形状像马的儿童游戏器械，可以坐在上面前后摇动 (children's) hobby-horse; rocking horse

【木马计】mùmǎjì 传说古代希腊人攻打特洛伊城九年不下，后来用了一个计策，把一批勇士藏在一只特制的木马中，佯装撤退，扔下木马。特洛伊人把木马当作战利品运进城内。夜里木马中的勇士出来打开城门，与攻城军队里应外合，占领了特洛伊城。后来用特洛伊木马指潜伏在内部的敌人，把潜伏到敌方内部进行破坏和颠覆活动的办法叫木马计。stratagem of the Trojan horse; Trojan horse. Legend has it that the ancient Greeks, having attacked Troy for nine years without being able to conquer it, used a huge, hollow wooden horse with brave soldiers hidden inside, pretended to retreat and left it at the gate of Troy. When the Trojans brought it into the city as a spoil of war, the soldiers hidden in it crept out at night and opened the gates to let in the Greek army, which finally captured the city. Later, a Trojan horse refers to any person, group, or thing that seeks to subvert a nation, organization, etc, from within; the sending of people into the territory of the enemy or into its organization for subversion from within is called the stratagem of the Trojan horse.

【木棉】mùmián ❶ 落叶乔木，叶子掌状分裂，花红色，结蒴果，卵圆形。种子的表皮长有白色纤维，质柔软，可用来装枕头、垫褥等。kapok (*Gossampinus malabaricus*); silk cotton; deciduous tree with palmately lobed leaves, red flowers and ovate capsules, and seeds which are covered by a soft, white fibre that is used to fill pillows, cushions, mattresses, etc.; also 红棉 hóngmián and 攀枝花 pānzhīhuā ❷ 木棉种子表皮上的纤维 silky fibres around the seeds of the plant

【木乃伊】mùnǎiyī ❶ 长久保存下来的干燥的尸体，特指古代埃及人用特殊的防腐药品和埋葬方法保存下来的没有腐烂的尸体 mummy; dried dead body that has been long preserved, esp. one by ancient Egyptians with the use of special antiseptics and burial methods ❷〈比喻 *fig.*〉僵化的事物 sth. rigid or ossified

【木讷】mùnè〈书 *fml.*〉朴实迟钝，不善于说话 inarticulate; simple and slow (of speech): ～寡言 honest and reticent

【木牛流马】mù niú liú mǎ 三国时诸葛亮所创造的运输工具。相传就是人推的木制小车。wooden ox and gliding horse; army service wheelbarrows invented by Zhuge Liang, a statesman and military strategist in the Three Kingdoms Period

【木偶】mù'ǒu 木头做的人像，常用来形容痴呆的神情 puppet; marionette; wooden image; carved figures, oft. used to describe an idiotic expression: 这时他像一个～似的靠在墙上出神。At this time he was seen leaning against the wall in a trance like a carved figure.

【木偶片儿】mù'ǒupiānr same as 木偶片 mù'ǒupiàn

【木偶片】mù'ǒupiàn 美术片的一种，用摄影机连续拍摄木偶表演的各种动作而成 puppet film; animated film made on the basis of a puppet show

【木偶戏】mù'ǒuxì 用木偶来表演故事的戏剧。表演时，演员在幕后一边操纵木偶，一边演唱，并配以音乐。由于木偶形体和操纵技术的不同，有布袋木偶、提线木偶、杖头木偶等。puppet show; puppet play; play in which puppets are used to portray a story. In a performance, an actor or actress, while singing to the accompaniment of music while, manipulates puppets that are worked by strings or sticks or in the form of cloth bags. also 傀儡戏 kuǐlěixì

【木排】mùpái 放在江河里的成排地结起来的木材。为了从林场外运的方便，有水道的地方常把木材结成木排，使顺流而下。raft; stack of logs, boards, etc., fastened together into a sort of platform to be floated on water, as a means of conveying the component logs, boards, etc., wherever a forest farm is linked by a waterway

【木器】mùqì 用木材制造的家具 wooden furniture; wooden articles

【木琴】mùqín 打击乐器，由若干长短不同的短木条组成，按音高顺序排列架上，多排成两排，用两根小木槌敲打，声音清脆 xylophone; percussion instrument consisting of short wooden bars graduated in length, mostly in two rows, to produce the notes of the scale when struck with mallets

【木然】mùrán 一时痴呆不知所措的样子 stupefied: ～地望着远方 look stupefied into the distance

【木炭】mùtàn 木材在隔绝空气的条件下加热得到的无定形碳，黑色，质硬，有很多细孔。用做燃料，也用来过滤液体和气体，还可做黑色火药。charcoal; porous, amorphous form of carbon, black and hard, produced by heating logs with the air cut off, and used as fuel or in filters for gas and liquid; 通称 commonly called 炭 tàn

【木炭画】mùtànhuà 用木炭条绘成的画 charcoal drawing; drawing made with a charcoal pencil

【木头】mù·tou 木材和木料的统称 wood; log;

timber：一块～ a piece of wood｜一根～ a piece of wood｜～桌子 wooden table

【木头人儿】mù·tourénr〈比喻 *fig.*〉愚笨或不灵活的人 woodenhead; blockhead; slow coach

【木犀】mù·xi ❶ 常绿小乔木或灌木，叶子椭圆形，花小，白色或暗黄色，有特殊的香气，结核果，卵圆形。花供观赏，又可做香料。sweet-scented osmanthus (*Osmanthus fragrans*); evergreen tree or shrub with oblong leaves, small, white or yellowish flowers, a special sweet scent, ovate drupels, and flowers that are used for ornament or making perfumes and spices; 通称 commonly called 桂花 guìhuā ❷ 这种植物的花 flower of the plant; 通称 commonly called 桂花 guìhuā ❸ 指经过烹调的打碎的鸡蛋（多用于菜名、汤名 oft. used in dish or soup names）cooked, scrambled eggs：～肉 meat stir-fried with scrambled eggs｜～汤 eggdrop soup｜～饭 fried rice with scrambled eggs ‖ also 木樨 mù·xi

【木樨】mù·xi same as 木犀 mù·xi

【木锨】mùxiān 扬场时用来铲粮食的木制农具，形状跟铁锹相似 wooden spade; wooden farm implement shaped like an iron spade for shovelling grains in winnowing

【木星】mùxīng 太阳系九大行星之一，按离太阳由近而远的次序计为第五颗，绕太阳公转周期约 11.86 年，自转周期约 9 小时 50 分。是九大行星中体积最大的一个。Jupiter; one of the nine major planets in the solar system, the largest and the fifth in distance from the sun, about 11.86 earth years in a period of revolution, and about 9 hours 50 minutes in a period of rotation; (图见 ☞ figure for 太阳系 tàiyángxì on p. 1855)

【木已成舟】mù yǐ chéng zhōu〈比喻 *fig.*〉事情已成定局，不能改变 The wood is already made into a boat. What is done cannot be undone.

【木鱼】mùyú（～儿 mùyúr）打击乐器，也是僧尼念经、化缘时敲打的响器，用木头做成，中间镂空 wooden fish; percussion instrument made of a hollow wooden block, originally used by Buddhist monks to beat rhythm when chanting scriptures or begging alms

【木枕】mùzhěn 枕木 (of rail tracks) sleeper

【木质部】mùzhìbù 茎的最坚硬的部分，由长形的木质细胞构成。木质部很发达的茎就是通常使用的木材。xylem; woody vascular tissue of a plant, the hardest part of the stem, composed of long woody cells. The well-developed stem of the xylem is the commonly used timber.

【木质茎】mùzhìjīng 木质部发达、质地比较坚硬的茎，如松、杉、槐的茎 developed stem of hard texture of the xylem, as the stem of pine, cypress, scholartree, etc.

目 mù ❶ 眼睛 eye：有～共睹 be obvious to all｜历历在～ appear vividly before one's eyes ❷ 网眼；孔 mesh; eye; hole：八十～筛 80-mesh sieve or screen｜一方寸的网上，竟有百～之多。There are as many as 100 meshes per square *cun* in the net ❸〈书 *fml.*〉看 look; regard：～为奇迹 regard as a miracle ❹ 大项中再分的小项 item：项～ item｜细～ detailed catalogue; detailed items ❺ 生物学中把同一纲的生物按照彼此相似的特征分为几个群叫做目，如鸟纲中有雁形目、鸡形目、鹤形目等，松柏纲中有银杏目、松柏目等。目以下为科。order; classification of a group of related plants or animals ranking above a family and below a class, such as the wild goose order, the chicken order and the crane order, etc., in the bird class, and the ginkgo order and pine order in the pine and cypress class ❻ 目录 contents; catalogue; table of contents; list of things：书～ booklist; title catalogue｜药～ medicine catalogue｜剧～ programme of performance; list of plays or operas ❼ 名称 title：题～ topic; subject; title｜巧立名～ create all sorts of names; make various pretexts ❽ 计算围棋输赢的单位 eye; unit of moves in *weiqi* or go：中方棋手仅以一～半之优获胜。The Chinese player won by one and a half eyes.

【目标】mùbiāo ❶ 射击、攻击或寻求的对象 objective; target (of shooting, attack, etc.)：看清～ see the target clearly｜发现～ sight a target ❷ 想要达到的境地或标准 goal; aim; objective：奋斗～ objective of a struggle

【目不见睫】mù bù jiàn jié 眼睛看不见自己的睫毛，比喻没有自知之明 eye can't see its lashes; (fig.) have no idea about one's own weaknesses

【目不交睫】mù bù jiāo jié 形容夜间不睡觉或睡不着觉 not sleep a wink at night

【目不窥园】mù bù kuī yuán 汉董仲舒专心读书，'三年目不窥园'（见于《汉书·董仲舒传》）。后世用来形容埋头读书。Dong Zhongshu in the Han Dynasty buried himself in his studies and 'never took a peep into the garden for three years' (See *History of Han · Biography of Dong Zhongshu*). The expression has been used to indicate 'bury oneself in one's studies'.

【目不忍睹】mù bù rěn dǔ 形容景象十分凄惨，使人不忍心看 cannot bear to look at; sight is too dreadful to be seen; also 目不忍视 mù bù rěn shì

【目不识丁】mù bù shí dīng《旧唐书·张弘靖传》：'今天下无事，汝辈挽得两石力弓，不如识一丁字。'据说'丁'应写作'个'，因为字形相近而误。后来形容人不识字说'不识一丁'或'目不识丁'。*Old History of Tang · Biography of Zhang Hongjing*: 'It's all quiet over the land. You'd better start to learn the simple character 丁 dīng than to draw hard bows.' It is said that the character 丁 should be 个 gè, and the mistake was made because they are similar in form. People of later generations have used the phrase 'not know a 丁 dīng' to describe illiteracy.

【目不暇接】mù bù xiá jiē 东西太多,眼睛看不过来 too many things for the eye to take in: 春节期间,文艺节目多得令人~。There are too many theatrical performances to see during the Spring Festival. also 目不暇给 mù bù xiá jǐ

【目不转睛】mù bù zhuǎn jīng 不转眼珠地(看),形容注意力集中 look with fixed gaze; regard with rapt attention

【目测】mùcè 不用仪器仅用肉眼测量 estimate range by eye; visual range estimation

【目次】mùcì same as 目录 mùlù ②

【目瞪口呆】mù dèng kǒu dāi 形容受惊而愣住的样子 stupefaction; gaping; dumbstruck; stupefied; be struck dumb with surprise

【目的】mùdì 想要达到的地点或境地;想要得到的结果 purpose; aim; goal; objective; intention; end; place or realm to be reached: ~地 destination | ~是想探索问题的由来。The purpose is to probe the cause of the issue.

【目睹】mùdǔ 亲眼看到 eye witness; see with one's own eyes: 耳闻~ what one sees and hears

【目光】mùguāng ❶ 指视线 sight; vision; view: 大家的~都投向发言者。Everyone cast his eyes on the speaker. ❷ 眼睛的神采 expression in one's eyes: ~炯炯 bright eyes; flashing eyes; penetrating eyes ❸ 眼光;见识 vision; sight: ~如豆 vision as narrow as a bean — of narrow vision; short-sighted | ~远大 far-sighted; far-seeing

【目光短浅】mùguāng duǎnqiǎn 形容缺乏远见 short-sighted

【目光如豆】mùguāng rú dòu 形容眼光短浅 short-sighted; vision as narrow as a bean — of narrow vision

【目光如炬】mùguāng rú jù 眼光像火炬那样亮,形容见识远大 far-sighted; eyes blazing like torches; looking ahead with wisdom

【目击】mùjī 亲眼看到 witness; see with one's own eyes: ~者 eyewitness; witness | ~其事 witness the event

【目见】mùjiàn 亲眼看到 see for oneself: 耳闻不如~。Seeing for oneself is better than hearing from others. *or* Seeing is believing.

【目今】mùjīn 现今 nowadays; these days

【目镜】mùjìng 显微镜、望远镜等光学仪器上对着眼睛的一端所装的透镜 eyepiece; ocular; lens or lenses nearest the viewer's eye or eyes in a telescope, microscope or other optical instruments; also 接目镜 jiēmùjìng

【目空一切】mù kōng yīqiè 形容骄傲自大,什么都看不起 consider everybody and everything beneath one's notice; be supercilious and arrogant

【目力】mùlì 视力 sight; vision

【目录】mùlù ❶ 按一定次序开列出来以供查考的事物名目 catalogue; list: 图书~ library catalogue | 财产~ inventory of one's property ❷ 书刊上列出的篇章名目(多放在正文前 mostly before the text of a book) table of contents; contents

【目论】mùlùn 〈书 *fml.*〉〈比喻 *fig.*〉没有自知之明或浅陋狭隘的见解 have no self-knowledge or have a superficial and narrow-minded view

【目迷五色】mù mí wǔ sè 形容颜色又杂又多,因而看不清楚,比喻事物错综复杂,分辨不清 dazzled by a riot of colour; bewildered by a complicated situation

【目前】mùqián 指说话的时候 for now; at present; at the moment: ~形势 present (or current) situation | 到~为止 till now; so far; to date; up till the present moment

【目送】mùsòng 眼睛注视着离去的人或载人的车、船等 follow a person or a car, boat carrying the person with one's eyes; watch a person go; gaze after: ~亲人远去 gaze affectionately after the receding figure of one's loved one

【目无全牛】mù wú quán niú 一个杀牛的人最初杀牛,眼睛看见的是整个的牛(全牛),三年以后,技术纯熟了,动刀时只看到皮骨间隙,而看不到全牛(见于《庄子·养生主》)。用来形容技艺已达到十分纯熟的地步。(of an experienced butcher) see an ox not as whole but only as parts to be cut — be supremely skilled. According to *Zhuangzi · Nourishment of the Soul*, a butcher sees the whole ox when he first learns to kill an ox, but after three years, he becomes highly skilled and sees only the space between the bone and skin of an ox when he begins to kill it and cannot see the whole of it. The expression is used to indicate perfect skill.

【目无余子】mù wú yú zǐ 眼睛里没有旁人,形容骄傲自大 supercilious; arrogant; as if there were no other people in one's eyes

【目下】mùxià 目前;眼下 at present; right now: ~较忙,过几天再来看你。(I) am quite busy right now, but will come and see you in a few days.

【目眩】mùxuàn 眼花 dizzy; dazzled: 灯光强烈,令人~。The light is too dazzling.

【目语】mùyǔ 〈书 *fml.*〉用眼睛传达意思 communicate with the eyes

【目中无人】mù zhōng wú rén 形容骄傲自大,看不起人 look down upon; be supercilious; be overweening; consider everyone beneath one's notice; consider nobody worth notice

仫 mù [仫佬族](Mùlǎozú)我国少数民族之一,分布在广西 Mulaos; one of the ethnic groups in China inhabiting the Guangxi Zhuang Autonomous Region

牟 mù 地名用字 character used in names of places:～平(在山东) Muping in Shandong Province|中～(在河南) Zhongmu in Henan Province

☞ móu on p.1371

沐 mù ❶ 洗头发,也泛指洗涤 wash one's hair; (in a broad sense) wash:～浴 bathe; take a bath|栉风～雨 combed by the wind and washed by the rain; brave wind and rain ❷〈书 *fml.*〉借指蒙受 receive or be given:～恩 receive one's kindness ❸(Mù)姓 a surname

【沐恩】mù'ēn〈书 *fml.*〉蒙受恩惠 receive one's favour or kindness

【沐猴而冠】mùhóu ér guàn 沐猴(猕猴)戴帽子,装成人的样子 monkey wearing a hat — worthless person in imposing attire;〈比喻 *fig.*〉装扮得像个人物,而实际并不像 dress up as an important man, but actually is not

【沐浴】mùyù ❶ 洗澡 have (or take) a bath ❷〈比喻 *fig.*〉受润泽 be bathed in:每朵花,每棵树,每根草都～在阳光里。Every flower, every tree and every weed are bathed in the sunshine. ❸〈比喻 *fig.*〉沉浸在某种环境中 immersed in certain circumstances:他们～在青春的欢乐里。They revelled in the joy of youth.

苜 mù [苜蓿](mù·xu)多年生草本植物,叶子互生,复叶由三片小叶构成,小叶长圆形。开蝶形花,紫色,结荚果。是一种重要的牧草和绿肥作物。alfalfa (*Medicago sativa*); lucerne; perennial herbal plant with alternate compound leaves each consisting of three oblong leaflets, and purple papilionaceous flowers and capsules, used as fodder and green manure; also 紫花苜蓿 zǐhuā mù·xu

牧 mù 牧放 tend (sheep, cattle, etc.); herd:畜～ animal husbandry; livestock breeding|游～ nomadic life; rove about as a nomad; move about from pasture to pasture|～区 pastureland; pasture|～羊 tend sheep

【牧草】mùcǎo 野生或人工栽培的可供牲畜牧放时吃的草 herbage; forage grass; grass growing wildly or artificially cultivated for domestic animals

【牧场】mùchǎng ❶ 牧放牲畜的草地 pastureland; pasture; grazing land; also 牧地 mùdì ❷ 牧养牲畜的企业单位 livestock farm; ranch; animal breeding enterprise

【牧放】mùfàng 把牲畜放到草地里吃草和活动 herd; tend; put out to pasture; also 放牧 fàngmù

【牧歌】mùgē 牧人、牧童放牧时唱的歌谣,泛指以农村生活情趣为题材的诗歌和乐曲 pastoral; madrigal; pastoral song; song sung by a herdsman; song, poem and music with the rural life and interests as their themes

【牧工】mùgōng 受雇放牧的人;牧场工人 hired herdsman; hired labourer on a ranch

【牧民】mùmín 牧区中以畜牧为生的人 herdsman; people who live on stock breeding

【牧区】mùqū ❶ 放牧的地方 pastureland; pasture ❷ 以畜牧为主的地区 pastoral area

【牧犬】mùquǎn 经过训练能帮助人牧放的狗 shepherd dog; sheepdog; dog trained to keep watch on the sheep

【牧人】mùrén 放牧牲畜的人 herdsman

【牧师】mù·shi 新教的一种神职人员,负责教徒宗教生活和管理教堂事务 pastor; minister; clergyman; Protestant clergy who takes care of the religious life of Christians and church affairs

【牧童】mùtóng 放牛放羊的孩子(多见于诗词和早期白话 oft. seen in poems and early vernacular) shepherd boy; buffalo boy

【牧畜】mùxù 畜牧 stockbreeding:当地居民大都以～为生。Most of the local people live on stockbreeding.

【牧主】mùzhǔ 牧区中占有牧场、牲畜,雇用牧工的人 herd owner (who owns livestock and pastures and hires herdsmen)

钼 mù 金属元素,符号 Mo (molybdenum)。银白色,用来制特种钢,也用于电器生产中。molybdenum (Mo), a silvery white metallic chemical element used in making special alloy steels and electrical appliances

募 mù 募集(财物或兵员等)(of money, soldiers, etc.) raise; collect; enlist; recruit:～捐 collect donations; solicit contributions|～款 raise money (or fund)|招～ recruit

【募兵】mù//bīng 招募兵员 recruit soldiers:～制 mercenary system

【募兵制】mùbīngzhì 以雇佣形式招募兵员的制度 mercenary system

【募股】mù//gǔ 募集股金 raise capital by issuing shares

【募化】mùhuà (和尚、道士等)求人施舍财物(of Buddhist monks or Taoist priests) collect alms; beg alms:四方～ beg alms from place to place

【募集】mùjí 广泛征集 raise; collect:～经费 raise a fund

【募捐】mù//juān 募集捐款或物品 solicit contributions; collect donations:为残疾人～ collect donations for the disabled|～赈灾 solicit contributions to relieve the people in calamity-stricken areas

墓 mù 坟墓 grave; tomb; mausoleum:公～ cemetery|烈士～ martyrs' cemetery

【墓碑】mùbēi 立在坟墓前面或后面的石碑,上面刻有关于死者姓名、事迹等的文字 tombstone;

gravestone; stone in front of or behind a grave, inscribed with the name and a short life story of the deceased

【墓表】mùbiǎo 墓碑,也指碑上刻的关于死者生平事迹的文字 tombstone; inscription of a short life story of the deceased

【墓道】mùdào 坟墓前面的甬道,也指墓室前面的甬道 path leading to a grave; tomb passage aisle leading to the coffin chamber of an ancient tomb

【墓地】mùdì 埋葬死人的地方;坟地 cemetery; graveyard; burial ground

【墓祭】mùjì 在坟墓前祭奠;扫墓 pay respects to a deceased person at his or her grave

【墓室】mùshì 坟墓中放棺椁的处所 coffin chamber

【墓穴】mùxué 埋棺材或骨灰的坑 coffin pit; open grave; pit for burying a coffin or ashes

【墓茔】mùyíng 坟茔 grave; tomb; graveyard; cemetery

【墓葬】mùzàng 考古学上指坟墓 grave:～群 graves

【墓志】mùzhì 放在墓里刻有死者生平事迹的石刻。也指墓志上的文字。有的有韵语结尾的铭。stone tablet inscribed with a life story of the deceased within a tomb; inscription on the memorial tablet, some inscriptions having rhymed endings; also 墓志铭 mùzhìmíng

幕 mù ❶ 覆盖在上面的大块的布、绸、毡子等;帐篷 canopy; tent; a large piece of cloth, silk, felt, etc. stretched over poles:帐～ tent ◇夜～ veil of night ❷ 挂着的大块的布、绸、丝绒等(演戏或放映电影所用的) curtain; a large piece of hanging cloth, silk, velvet, etc. (used in performances or film showing):开～ opening; open; rise of a curtain | 闭～ closing; close; fall of a curtain | 银～ screen ❸〈古代 *arch.*〉战争时将帅办公的地方 office of a commanding officer during a war:～府 office of a commanding officer | ～僚 aide to a commanding officer or general ❹ 戏剧较完整的段落,每幕可以分若干场 (of a play) act, which is divided into scenes:第二～第一场 first scene of the second act; Scene 1, Act 2 ◇看了这幅画,我不禁回忆起儿时生活的一～来。The sight of this painting brought me back to a scene of my childhood life.

【幕宾】mùbīn 幕僚或幕友 aide or private assistant:聘为～ be appointed as an aide to a commanding general

【幕布】mùbù same as 幕 mù ②

【幕府】mùfǔ ❶〈古代 *arch.*〉将帅办公的地方 office of a commanding general ❷ 日本明治以前执掌全国政权的军阀 shogunate; shogun; warlord who ruled Japan before the Meiji Reform

【幕后】mùhòu 舞台帐幕的后面,多用于比喻(贬义 derog.) behind the scenes; backstage (usu. used in figurative way):～策动 plot behind the scenes | ～交易 behind-the-scenes deal

【幕僚】mùliáo〈古代 *arch.*〉称将帅幕府中参谋、书记等为幕僚,后泛指文武官署中佐助人员(一般指有官职的) aides and staff in the office of a commanding general; aide to a ranking official or general

【幕友】mùyǒu 明清地方官署中无官职的佐助人员,分管刑名、钱谷、文案等事务,由长官私人聘请 private adviser; private assistant without an official position, attending to legal, fiscal or secretarial duties in a local yamen (government house); popularly known as 师爷 shī·ye

睦 mù ❶ 和睦 peaceful; harmonious:～邻 good neighbourliness | 婆媳不～ old lady and her daughter-in-law do not get along well ❷ (Mù) 姓 a surname

【睦邻】mùlín 跟邻居或相邻的国家和睦相处 good-neighbourliness:～政策 good-neighbour policy

慕 mù ❶ 羡慕;仰慕 admire; yearn for:景～ respect; admire; esteem; revere | ～名 admire a person's reputation; admiration for a famous person ❷ 依恋;思念 miss; long for:爱～ adore; admire | 思～ miss ❸ (Mù) 姓 a surname

【慕名】mù//míng 仰慕别人的名气 admire a person's reputation; out of admiration for a famous person:～而来 be attracted to a place by its reputation as a scenic spot; see a stranger because of his or her reputation

【慕尼黑】Mùníhēi 德国南部城市。1938 年英、法、德、意四国首脑在这里举行会议,签订了慕尼黑协定,英法以出卖捷克斯洛伐克向德国求得妥协。后来用'慕尼黑'指外交上牺牲别国利益而与对方妥协的阴谋。Munich, a city in southern Germany, where the heads of state of Britain, France, Germany and Italy met and signed the Munich Pact in 1938, under which Britain and France ceded Czechoslovakia to Nazi Germany. Since then, 'Munich' has been used to refer to a diplomatic scheme to compromise at the sacrifice of the interests of another country. [德 German: München]

【慕容】Mùróng 姓 a surname

暮 mù ❶ 傍晚 dusk; evening; sunset:～色 dusk; twilight | 朝三～四 blow hot and cold; play fast and loose; chop and change ❷ (时间)将尽;晚 towards the end; late:～春 late spring | ～年 evening of one's life; old age; declining years | 天寒岁～。It gets cold as the year draws to an end.

【暮霭】mù'ǎi 傍晚的云雾 evening mist:～沉沉。The evening mist became heavier. | 森林被～笼罩着,黄昏降临了。The forest was enveloped in the evening haze as dusk fell.

【暮春】mùchūn 春季的末期；农历的三月 late spring (the third month of the lunar year)

【暮鼓晨钟】mù gǔ chén zhōng 佛教规矩，寺庙中晚上打鼓，早晨敲钟(ritual of a monastery) beat the drum in the evening and toll the bell in the morning；〈比喻 *fig*.〉可以使人警觉醒悟的话 words that alert and awaken people; also 晨钟暮鼓 chén zhōng mù gǔ

【暮景】mùjǐng ❶ 傍晚的景色 twilight; sunset scene ❷ 老年时的景况 life in old age; evening of one's life：桑榆～ in the evening of one's life

【暮年】mùnián 晚年 declining years; old age; evening of one's life：烈士～，壮心不已。A heroic man still has lofty aspirations in his declining years. *or* A heroic man, though declining in years, still has lofty aspirations.

【暮气】mùqì 不振作的精神和疲疲塌塌不求进取的作风(跟'朝气'相对 as opposed to 'high spirit and vigour') low spirit and lethargy; lethargy; apathy：～沉沉 lethargic; apathetic; lifeless

【暮秋】mùqiū 秋季的末期；农历的九月 late autumn (the ninth month of the lunar year)

【暮色】mùsè 傍晚昏暗的天色 dusk; twilight; gloaming：～苍茫 gathering dusk; thickening shades of dusk

【暮生儿】mù·shēngr〈方 *dial*.〉父亲死后才出生的子女；遗腹子 posthumous child; child born after his father dies

【暮岁】mùsuì ❶ 一年将尽的时候 towards the end of the year ❷ 晚年 old age; one's later years

穆 mù ❶ 恭敬；严肃 solemn; reverent：静～ quiet and solemn | 肃～ grave; solemn and quiet ❷ (Mù)姓 a surname

【穆斯林】mùsīlín 伊斯兰教信徒 Moslem; Muslim [阿拉伯 Arab: muslim]

霂 mù ☞ [霡霂](màimù) on p. 1297

N

ń(ㄋˊ)

嗯(唔) ń '嗯'ńg 的又音 different pronunciation of 嗯 ńg

☞ 唔 wú on p.2028

ň(ㄋˇ)

嗯(呒) ň '嗯'ňg 的又音 different pronunciation of 嗯 ňg

ǹ(ㄋˋ)

嗯(呃) ǹ '嗯'ǹg 的又音 different pronunciation of 嗯 ǹg

nā(ㄋㄚ)

那 Nā 姓 a surname

☞ 哪 nǎ on p.1382 and nà on p.1383

南 nā [南无](nāmó)〈佛教用语 *Budd.*〉表示对佛尊敬或皈依 Namah; Namo; Buddhist term of reverence for, or devotion to, the Buddha, Triratna, or Amitabha [梵 Sanskrit: namas]

☞ nán on p.1388

ná(ㄋㄚˊ)

拿(拏) ná ❶ 用手或用其他方式抓住、搬动(东西) take; hold; bring: 他手里~着一把扇子。He had a fan in his hand. | 把这些东西~走。Take these things away. ❷ 用强力取;捉 catch; capture; seize: ~下敌人的碉堡 seize an enemy pillbox | ~住三个匪徒。(The police) nabbed three bandits. ◇凭他多年的教学经验,这门课他~得下来。With many years' teaching experience behind him he has no problem with this course. ❸ 掌握 control; grasp: ~权 in power | ~事 have the final say | 这事儿你~得稳吗? Are you sure you have the final say on this? ❹ 刁难;要挟 bluff; blackmail: 这件事谁都干得了,你~不住人。I don't think you can bluff me, as everybody can handle things like this. ❺ 装出;故意做出 act; make believe: ~架子 put on airs | ~腔作势 put on an act; behave in an affected way ❻ 领取;得到 get; obtain: ~工资 receive a wage or salary; get one's pay | ~一等奖 win a first-class award ❼ 强烈的作用使物体变坏 cause sth. to go bad by a strong force of one kind or another: 这块木头让药水~白了。The chemical solution has turned this piece of wood white. | 碱搁得太多,把馒头~黄了。The steamed bread was browned by too much soda. ❽〈介词 *prep.*〉引进所凭借的工具、材料、方法等,意思跟'用'相同 [used to introduce the tool, material, method, etc., for doing sth., similar to the function of 用 yòng] with; by: ~尺量 measure sth. with a ruler | ~眼睛看 size sth. or sb. up with one's eyes | ~事实证明。Let facts speak for themselves. ❾〈介词 *prep.*〉引进所处置的对象 [used to introduce the object]: 别~我开玩笑。Don't make fun of me. | 简直~他没有办法。I simply don't know how to deal with the guy.

【拿办】nábàn 把犯罪的人捉住法办 apprehend; bring sb. to justice: 革职~dismiss sb. from office for prosecution

【拿大】ná//dà〈方 *dial.*〉自以为比别人强,看不起人;摆架子 wax arrogant; act high and mighty; be arrogant: 他待人谦和,从不~。He's a self-effacing guy who never puts on airs. | 人家虚心求助,他倒拿起大来了。He waxed snobbish when people came to learn from him.

【拿顶】ná//dǐng 用手撑在地上或物体上,头朝下而两脚腾空 handstand; act of balancing on hands, with one's feet in the air; also 拿大顶 ná dàdǐng

【拿获】náhuò 捉住(犯罪的人) apprehend; collar; nab (a criminal): 将罪犯~归案 seize a criminal and bring him to justice

【拿架子】ná jià•zi same as 摆架子 bǎi jià•zi

【拿摩温】námówēn ☞ 那摩温 nàmówēn on p. 1384

【拿捏】ná•nie〈方 *dial.*〉❶ 扭捏 hem and haw; vacillate: 有话快说,~个什么劲儿! Stop wobbling and be straight out! ❷ 刁难;要挟 make things difficult for sb; coerce: 你别~人。Don't make things difficult for people.

【拿腔拿调】ná qiāng ná diào 指说话时故意用某种声音、语气(多含厌恶意 oft. derog.) speak with a deliberate tone; also 拿腔捏调 ná qiāng niē diào or 拿腔作调 ná qiāng zuò diào

N

【拿腔作势】ná qiāng zuò shì 装腔作势 same as 装腔作势 zhuāng qiāng zuò shì

【拿乔】ná//qiáo 装模作样或故意表示为难，以抬高自己的身价 try to impress people by acting affectedly or feigning hesitation

【拿权】ná//quán 掌握权柄 in control; in the saddle

【拿人】ná//rén 〈方 *dial*.〉❶ 刁难人；要挟人 be difficult with sb.; create difficulties for sb.：别～人，没有你，我们也能干。Stop being difficult. Don't think we cannot manage without you. ❷ 指吸引人 fascinate：他说评书特别～。He tells engrossing stories.

【拿事】ná//shì 负责主持事务 in charge; be the decision-maker：偏巧父母都出门了，家里连个～的人也没有。The parents happened to be away, leaving nobody to make a decision for the family.

【拿手】náshǒu ❶（对某种技术）擅长 be at one's best in doing sth.; be good at：～好戏 one's forte｜～节目 reserved number or programme｜画山水画儿他很～。He's at his best in landscape painting. ❷ 成功的信心；把握 be positive about doing sth.：有～be positive about sth.｜没～not so sure about sth.

【拿手好戏】ná shǒu hǎo xì ❶ 指某演员特别擅长的戏 performance that shows an actor at his best ❷〈比喻 *fig*.〉某人特别擅长的本领 forte; special skill or expertise ‖ also 拿手戏 náshǒuxì

【拿糖】ná//táng 〈方 *dial*.〉拿乔 put on airs and graces; appeas affected and stagy

【拿问】náwèn 逮捕审问 apprehend sb. for interrogation：革职～be removed from one's post and prosecuted

【拿印把儿】ná yìnbàr 指做官；掌权 come in power; be put in control; also 拿印把子 ná yìnbà·zi

【拿主意】ná zhǔ·yi 决定处理事情的方法或对策 make a decision：究竟去不去，你自己～吧。I'd rather let you decide whether to go or not.

挐 ná 〈书 *fml*.〉牵引；纷乱 tow; drag; chaos

镎 ná 金属元素，符号 Np (neptunium)。银白色，有放射性。neptunium (Np); silvery radioactive metallic element

nǎ (ㄋㄚˇ)

乸 nǎ 〈方 *dial*.〉雌；母的 female：鸡～(母鸡) hen

哪[1]（那）nǎ 〈疑问代词 *interrog. pron*.〉a)后面跟量词或数词加量词，表示要求在几个人或事物中确定一个[followed by a classifier or numeral-classifier combination] which：我们这里有两位张师傅，您要见的是～位？We've got two Mr. Zhangs here. Which one do you want to see?｜这些诗里头～两首是你写的？Which two poems in the collection did you write? b)单用，跟'什么'相同，常和'什么'交互着用[used singularly] what; [oft. used alternatively with 什么 shén·me] what ... what：什么叫吃亏，～叫上算，全都谈不到。What's worth it, what's not — neither is relevant here. 注意 **NOTE**: '哪'后面跟量词或数词加量词的时候，在口语里常常说 něi 或 nǎi，单用的'哪'在口语里只说 nǎ。以下哪个①、哪会儿、哪门子、哪些、哪样各条在口语里常常说 něi- 或 nǎi-。In oral Chinese, 哪 nǎ is oft. pronounced něi or nǎi when followed by a classifier or a numeral-classifier combination, 哪 nǎ when used independently, and oft. něi- or nǎi- in 哪个 nǎi·ge ①, 哪会儿 nǎihuìr, 哪门子 nǎimén·zi, 哪些 nǎixiē, and 哪样 nǎiyàng.

哪[2]（那）nǎ 表示反问[in rhetorical question] how can; how could：没有革命前辈的流血牺牲，～有今天的幸福生活？How could the happy life be possible today without members of the older revolutionary generation shedding their blood and laying down their lives?

☞ ·na on p. 1385, né on p. 1397, 那 Nā on p. 1381 and nà on p. 1383

【哪个】nǎ·ge ❶ 哪一个 which one：你们是～学校的？Which school are you from? ❷〈方 *dial*.〉谁 who：～敲门？Who's knocking at the door?

【哪会儿】nǎhuìr ❶ 问过去或将来的时间 when：你是～从广州回来的？When did you return from Guangzhou?｜这篇文章～才能脱稿？When shall this article be ready? ❷ 泛指不确定的时间 whenever：赶紧把粮食晒干入仓，说不定～天气要变。Dry the grain and put it into the granary as fast as you can — there's no telling when the weather frowns.｜你要～来就～来。Come here whenever you feel like to. ‖ also 哪会子 nǎhuì·zi

【哪里】nǎ·li ❶ 问什么处所 where：你住在～？Where do you live?｜这话你是从～听来的？Where did you hear it from? ❷ 泛指任何处所 wherever：农村和城市，无论～，都是一片欣欣向荣的新气象。Whether in villages or cities, a thriving scene prevails.｜她走到～，就把好事做到～。She performs good deeds wherever she finds herself. ❸ 用于反问句，表示意在否定[used in the negative in rhetorical questions]：这样美好的生活，～是解放前能想到的？Who would ever have imagined such a happy life before liberation? (＝不是… it is not ...)｜～知道刚走出七八里地，天就下起雨来了？Who would have known that it began to rain when we were merely seven or eight *li* into the journey? (=不料… did not expect that ...) ❹〈谦辞 *hum*.〉用来婉转地推辞对自己的褒奖[used when responding politely to a compliment]:'你这篇文章写得真好!''～,～!' 'Your article was well written!' 'Oh, by no means. I feel flattered.'

【哪门子】nǎmén·zi〈方 *dial*.〉什么,用于反问的语气,表示没有来由[emphasizing in a rhetorical question] what on earth ...; how could ...:好好儿的,你哭～? Good heavens, what on earth are you crying for? |你们说的是～事呀! What on earth are you talking about?

【哪怕】nǎpà〈连词 *conj*.〉表示姑且承认某种事实[expression of an assumption] even though; no matter what; even if:～他是三头六臂,一个人也顶不了事。He wouldn't handle it all by himself even if he had three heads and six arms. |衣服只要干净就行,～有几个补丁。(I)'ll be happy to have clean clothing to wear even if it has patches on it.

【哪儿】nǎr 哪里 where:你上～去? Where are you going? |～有困难,他就出现在～。He is seen wherever there are difficulties. |当初～会想到这些山地也能长出这么好的庄稼? How could we know in the beginning that the mountainsides would produce such good crops?

【哪些】nǎxiē 哪一些 which; who; what:这次会议都有～人参加? Who will be present at the meeting? |你们讨论～问题? Which topics are you discussing?

【哪样】nǎyàng (～儿 nǎyàngr)〈疑问代词 *interrog. pron*.〉❶ 问性质、状态等 what kind; what:你要～儿颜色的毛线? What colour do you want your woolen yarn to be? ❷ 泛指性质、状态 whatever; any kind:这儿的毛线颜色齐全,你要～的就有～的。The woolen yarn here comes in all colours, and you can get whatever colour you want.

nà(ㄋㄚˋ)

那[1] nà〈指示代词 *demons. pron*.〉指示比较远的人或事物[demonstrating sb. or sth. farther away from the speaker] that; those a)后面跟量词、数词加量词,或直接跟名词[followed by a classifier, a numeral-classifier combination or a noun]:～老头儿 that old man|～棵树 that tree|～两棵树 those two trees|～地方 that place|～时候 at that time b)单用[used alone]:～是谁? Who is that person over there? |～是本校的。That belongs to our school. |～是1937年。That was the year of 1937.

注意 **NOTE**: a)单用的'那'限于在动词前,在动词后面用'那个',只有跟'这'对举的时候可以用'那'。那 nà is used alone when it precedes a verb, takes the form of 那个 nàgè when it follows a verb, and can be used only as an opposite to 这 zhè; for example:说这道～的 talk about this and that|看看这,看看～,真有说不出的高兴。We were immensely happy seeing the place this way and that. b)在口语里,'那'单用或者后面直接跟名词,说 nà 或 nè;'那'后面跟量词或数词加量词常常说 nèi 或 nè。以下那程子,那个,那会儿,那些,那样各条在口语里都常常说 nèi-或 nè-。那么,那么点儿,那么些,那么着各条在口语里都常常说 nè。In oral Chinese, 那 nà is pronounced nà or nè whether it is used independently or followed directly by a verb; nèi or nè when followed by a classifier or a numeral-classifier combination. In spoken Chinese, 那 in the entries of 那程子 nèichéng·zi, 那个 nèi·ge, 那会儿 nèihuìr, 那些 nèixiē, 那样 nèiyàng is usu. pronounced nèi or nè; and oft. nè in 那么 nè·me, 那么点儿 nè·mediǎnr, 那么些 nè·mexiē and 那么着 nè·me·zhe.

那[2] nà〈连词 *conj*.〉same as 那么③:～就好好儿干吧! Then let's do it well. |你不拿走,～你不要啦? You are not taking it — does that mean you don't want it?

☞ Nā on p. 1381 and 哪 nǎ on p. 1382

【那程子】nàchéng·zi〈方 *dial*.〉那些日子(指过去的时间) those days; at that time:～我很忙,没有工夫来看你。I was busy those days. That's why I could not find time to see you.

【那达慕】nàdámù 内蒙古地区蒙古族人民传统的群众性集会,过去多在祭敖包时举行,内容有摔跤、赛马、射箭、舞蹈等。解放后,还在会上进行物资交流、交流生产经验等活动。Nadam; traditional festival of the Mongols in the Inner Mongolia Autonomous Region, which in old days took place when libations and sacrifices were offered to *aobao* (sand, stone or earth mound believed to be the abode of certain holy spirit), and was celebrated with such events as wrestling, horse races, archery, and dancing. In post-1949 years, bartering and the swap of experience in production are added to the festival.

【那个】nà·ge ❶ 那一个 that:～院子里花草很多。There are lots of flowers and grass in that courtyard. |～比这个结实点儿。This one is sturdier than that one. ❷ 那东西;那事情 that thing; that matter:那是画画儿用的,你要～干什么? That is used for painting. What do you want it for? |你别为～担心,不会出事儿。Don't worry about that. Nothing will go wrong. ❸ 用在动词、形容词之前,表示夸张[precede a verb or an adjective to indicate a certain degree of exaggeration]:他干得～欢哪,就甭提了! He went at the job so vigorously that I just don't know how to describe it. ❹ 代替不便直说的话(含有婉转或诙谐的意味 [used in place of certain words for euphemism or humour]:你刚才的脾气也太~了。A moment ago you got carried away by anger just a little too far. (=不好。So bad you got angry like that.)|他这人做事,真有点~。The way he does things is ... well, I don't know what's the word for it. (=不应当。He shouldn't do things the way he did it.)

【那会儿】nàhuìr 指示过去或将来的时候 at that time; by that time:记得~他还是个小孩子。I remember he was still a kid at the time.|要是到~农业全部机械化了,那才美呢! It will be wonderful if agriculture can be completely mechanized by that time. also 那会子 nàhuì·zi

【那里】nà·li 指示比较远的处所 there; that place:~出产香蕉和荔枝。That place produces bananas and litchis.|我刚从~回来。I've just returned from there.|他们~气候怎么样? What's the weather like in their place?

【那么】nà·me ❶ 指示性质、状态、方式、程度等 [indicating property, state of affairs, method, degree, etc.] so; as... as...; in that way; to the extent that:我不好意思~说。I find it embarrassing to put it that way.|像油菜花~黄。It is as yellow as the rape flower.|来了~多的人。So many people came. ❷ 放在数量词前,表示估计 [precede a number to indicate a rough count]:借~二三十个麻袋就够了。It will be enough to borrow 20 to 30 sacks. ❸ 表示顺着上文的语意,申说应有的结果(上文可以是对方的话,也可以是自己提出的问题或假设) [indicating a presumable result from what is entailed in the preceding sentence uttered by oneself or someone else] then; in that case:这样做既然不行,~你打算怎么办呢? What will you do now that this isn't right? |如果你认为可以这么办,~咱们就赶紧去办吧! If that's the way you want, let's do it quickly.|also 那末 nà·me

【那么点儿】nà·mediǎnr 指示数量小 so little; so few:~东西,一个箱子就装下了。A suitcase is large enough for these few things.|~事儿,一天就办完了,哪儿要三天? That bit of work can be done in a single day —three days are not needed.

【那么些】nà·mexiē 指示数量大 so much; so many:~书,一个星期哪看得完? How can one read so many books in a week's time?

【那么着】nà·me·zhe 指示行动或方式(behave or do sth.) in a certain way; that way:你再~,我可要恼了! I'll get angry if you do it again.|你帮病人翻个身,~他也许舒服点儿。Can you help the patient turn over, so that he may feel a bit better.

【那末】nà·me same as 那么 nà·me

【那摩温】nàmówēn 解放前上海用来称工头。也译作拿摩温。transliteration of 'number one', which refers to a foreman, forewoman, overseer in pre-1949 Shanghai

【那儿】nàr ❶ 那里 there:~的天气很热。The weather is rather hot over there. ❷ 那时候(用在'打、从、由'后面 used after 打 dǎ, 从 cóng, or 由 yóu) that time:打~起,他就每天早晨用半小时来锻炼身体。Since then he has been doing morning exercises for thirty minutes a day.

【那些】nàxiē 指示两个以上的人或事物 [referring to more than two persons or things] those:奶奶爱把~事儿讲给孩子们听。Grandma is fond of telling children those stories.

【那样】nàyàng (~儿 nàyàngr) 指示性质、状态、方式、程度等 [indicating property, state, method, degree, etc.] like that; such; so; that way:~儿也好,先试试再说。All right, let's try it out.|他不像你~拘谨。He's not as self-conscious as you.|这个消息还没有证实,你怎么就急得~儿了! The news hasn't been proved yet. How come you are worried like that? |别这样~的了,你还是去一趟的好。Don't hesitate. Better go and see to it yourself. 注意 **NOTE**: '那(么)样'可以做定语或状语,也可以做补语。'那么'不做补语。比如'急得那样儿',不能说成'急得那么'。那(么)样 nà(·me)yàng can be used as an attribute or a complement, but 那么 nà·me cannot be used as a complement. For example, 急得那样儿 jí·de nàyàngr cannot be put as 急得那么 jí·de nà·me.

【那阵儿】nàzhènr 已经过去的那一段时间 in those days; at that time:刚才~,好大的雨呀! What a downpour just a moment ago! |昨天吃晚饭~,你上哪儿了? Where were you during suppertime yesterday? also 那阵子 nàzhèn·zi

郍(**那**) Nà 周朝国名,在今湖北荆门东南 Na, name of a state during the Zhou Dynasty, to the southeast of present-day Jingmen, Hubei Province

呐 nà [呐喊](nàhǎn)大声喊叫助威 shout; yell:摇旗~ wave banners and shout at the top of one's voice

☞ 哪·na on p.1385, nè on p.1397 and 呢·ne on p.1397

纳[1] nà ❶ 收进来;放进来 accommodate:出~ cashier|闭门不~shut sb. out; deny sb. admittance ❷ 接受 accept:~降 accept an enemy's offer of surrender|采~accept ❸ 享受 enjoy:~凉 enjoy the cool (of the shade or night) ❹ 放进去 bring into:~入正轨 set sth. on the right track ❺ 交付(捐税、公粮等) pay

(tax); hand in (tax grain):～税 pay tax|交～公粮 hand in grain to the state ❻ (Nà) 姓 a surname

纳[2] nà 缝纫方法,在鞋底、袜底等上面密密地缝,使它结实耐磨(of sewing) sew close stitches over the sole of a shoe or sock:～鞋底子 stitch the sole of a cloth shoe

【纳彩】nàcǎi 〈古代 *arch.*〉定亲时男方送给女方聘礼叫做纳彩(of a bridegroom-to-be's family in old days) present gifts to a bride's family at the time of betrothal

【纳粹】Nàcuì 第一次世界大战后兴起的德国民族社会主义工人党,是以希特勒为头子的最反动的法西斯主义政党 Nazi; National Socialist German Workers' Party, formed after the First World War, the most reactionary fascist party with Adolf Hitler as the ringleader [德 German: Nazi, short form of Nationalsozialistische (Partei)]

【纳福】nàfú 享福(多指安闲地在家居住,旧时也用做问安的客套话 oft. a carefree family life, (in old days) a polite term of greeting) enjoy life

【纳罕】nàhǎn 诧异;惊奇 puzzled; wondering: 他一看家里一个人也没有,心里很～。He wondered why no one was home.

【纳贿】nàhuì ❶ 受贿 take a bribe ❷ 行贿 offer a bribe

【纳凉】nàliáng same as 乘凉 chéng//liáng: 在树下～enjoy the cool under a tree

【纳粮】nà//liáng 〈旧 *old*〉指交纳钱粮 deliver grain as a tax in kind

【纳闷】nà//mèn ❶ (～儿 nà//mènr)因为疑惑而发闷 bewildered; puzzled: 他听说有上海来的长途电话找他,一时想不出是谁,心里有些～。When told that someone in Shanghai had made a long-distance call to him, he was somewhat puzzled about who it could be. ❷ 烦闷(多见于早期白话 oft. in early vernacular) in the doldrums; downcast

【纳聘】nà//pìn 旧俗定婚时男方给女方聘礼 (old custom) bridegroom's family delivering betrothal gifts to the bride's family

【纳入】nàrù 放进;归入(多用于抽象事物 oft. for abstract things) subsume; bring into:～正轨 set something on the right track|～计划 subsume something into a plan

【纳税】nà//shuì 交纳税款 pay tax

【纳西族】Nàxīzú 我国少数民族之一,分布在云南、四川 Naxis, a Chinese minority ethnic people inhabiting Yunnan and Sichuan provinces

【纳降】nàxiáng 接受敌人的投降 accept an enemy's offer of surrender

肭 nà ☞腽肭 wànà on p.1966

衲 nà ❶ 补缀 patch up: 百～衣 clothes clustered with patches|百～本 book of selected works ❷ 和尚穿的衣服,和尚用做自称 *kasaya*, monk's patchwork vestment; monk's first-person term of address: 老～(老和尚指自己) I; this old monk

钠 nà 金属元素,符号 Na (natrium)。银白色,质软,有延展性,化学性质极活泼,容易氧化,燃烧时发出黄色光。在工业上用途很广。natrium (Na); silvery-white metal element that is soft and malleable, and easily oxidized because of its volatile chemical property, emitting a yellow light when burning, used extensively in industry

【钠灯】nàdēng 把钠填充在真空的玻璃泡中制成的灯,通电时发出强烈的黄色光。用于矿井或街道照明。sodium lamp; electrical vacuum lamp bulb filled with natrium so that it emanates an intense yellowish light, for use in mines or as street lamps

娜 nà 人名用字 na, used in personal names ☞ nuó on p.1430

捺 nà ❶ 按;摁 press:～手印 put one's finger-print on paper ❷ 忍耐;抑制 restrain; hold back:～着性子 hold back one's temper|勉强～住心头的怒火 contain one's anger ❸ (～儿 nàr)汉字的笔画,向右斜下,近末端微有波折,形状是'㇏'(in a Chinese character) right-falling stroke that starts with the stroke '㇏', slants downward to the lower right corner, and ends with a slight bend

·na (·ㄋㄚ)

哪(呐) ·na 〈助词 *aux.*〉前一字韵尾是-n,'啊(·a)'变成'哪(·na)'[When the terminal consonant of the word before 啊 a is -n, 哪·na is to be used instead of 啊·a]: 谢谢您～。Thanks a lot.|我没留神～! I didn't notice it.|同志们加油干～! Comrades, come on! ☞啊·a on p.2

☞ nǎ on p.1382, né on p.1397, 呐 nà on p.1384, nè on p.1397 and 呢 ·ne on p.1397

nǎi (ㄋㄞˇ)

乃(迺、廼) nǎi 〈书 *fml.*〉❶ 是;就是;实在是 be:《红楼梦》～一代奇书。*A Dream of Red Mansions* is an extraordinary classic for its time.|失败～成功之母。Failure is the mother of success. ❷ 于是 that is why...; hence; thus: 因山势高峻,～在山腰休息片时。The mountain being high and steep, we took a break midway up the slope. ❸ 才 unless: 惟虚心～能进步。You cannot make progress unless you remain modest. ❹ 你;你的 your:～父 your father|～兄 your elder brother

【乃尔】nǎi'ěr 〈书 *fml.*〉如此;像这样 so much;

like this：何其相似～！What a striking similarity！

【乃至】nǎizhì same as 甚至 shènzhì：他的逝世，引起了全市～全国人民的哀悼。His death struck grief into the hearts of the people of the entire city and even the entire country. also 乃至于 nǎizhìyú

艿 nǎi ☞芋艿 yùnǎi on p.2348

奶(嬭) nǎi ❶ 乳房 breast ❷ 乳汁的通称 milk：牛～（cow）milk｜羊～goat milk｜给孩子吃～feed an infant with milk ❸ 用自己的乳汁喂孩子 breastfeed：～孩子 suckle a baby

【奶茶】nǎichá 搀和着牛奶或羊奶的茶 milk tea；tea mixed with cow or goat milk

【奶疮】nǎichuāng 乳腺炎的通称 mastitis；popular term for 乳腺炎 rǔxiànyán

【奶粉】nǎifěn 牛奶、羊奶除去水分制成的粉末，易于保存，食用时用开水冲成液体 dehydrated cow or goat milk；milk powder；powdered milk，easy to store and to be diluted with boiling water when being served

【奶积】nǎijī〈中医 *Chin. med.*〉指小儿因哺乳不当而引起的消化不良的病。症状是面色青黄，全身发热，吐奶，多睡，消瘦。indigestion of a baby caused by improper breastfeeding，with such symptoms as ashen and sallow complexion，fever all over the body，vomiting when being breastfed，drowsiness，and loss of weight

【奶酒】nǎijiǔ 用牛奶等为原料制成的发酵饮料 alcoholic beverage made from fermented milk；also 奶子酒 nǎi·zijiǔ

【奶酪】nǎilào 用动物的奶汁做成的半凝固食品 cheese；semi-solid food made from animal milk

【奶妈】nǎimā 受雇给人家奶孩子的妇女 wet nurse；woman employed to suckle another woman's baby

【奶毛】nǎimáo（～儿 nǎimáor）婴儿出生后尚未剃过的头发 foetal hair；hair of a newborn baby

【奶名】nǎimíng（～儿 nǎimíngr）童年时期的名字；小名 infant name；pet name

【奶奶】nǎi·nai ❶ 祖母 paternal grandmother；grandma ❷ 称跟祖母辈分相同或年纪相仿的妇女 respectful term of address for an elderly woman about the age of one's grandmother ❸〈方 *dial.*〉same as 少奶奶 shàonǎi·nai

【奶娘】nǎiniáng〈方 *dial.*〉same as 奶妈 nǎimā

【奶牛】nǎiniú same as 乳牛 rǔniú

【奶皮】nǎipí（～儿 nǎipír）牛奶、羊奶等煮过后表面上凝结的含脂肪的薄皮 milk skin；thin layer of soft，fatty material that solidifies on the surface of boiled cow or goat milk

【奶水】nǎishuǐ same as 乳汁 rǔzhī：～足 have enough milk for breastfeeding

【奶头】nǎitóu（～儿 nǎitóur）❶ same as 乳头 rǔtóu ❷ 奶嘴 nipple of a feeding bottle

【奶牙】nǎiyá 乳齿的通称 milk tooth；popular term for 乳齿 rǔchǐ

【奶羊】nǎiyáng 专门用来产奶的羊 milch goat

【奶油】nǎiyóu 从牛奶中提出的半固体物质，白色，微黄，脂肪含量较黄油为低。通常用做制糕点和糖果的原料。cream；yellowish white semi-solid substance from unhomogenized milk，with a lower fat content than butter，a material for pastry and confectionery

【奶罩】nǎizhào same as 乳罩 rǔzhào

【奶子】nǎi·zi ❶ 统称牛奶、羊奶等供食用的动物的乳汁 milk of cow，goat，or other animals ❷〈方 *dial.*〉same as 乳房 rǔfáng ❸〈方 *dial*〉same as 奶妈 nǎimā

【奶嘴】nǎizuǐ（～儿 nǎizuǐr）装在奶瓶口上的像奶头的东西，用橡皮制成 rubber nipple of a feeding bottle

氖 nǎi 气体元素，符号 Ne（neon）。无色无臭无味，大气中含量极少，化学性质不活泼。放电时发出红色光，用来制霓虹灯等。neon（Ne）；colourless，no smell，tasteless and chemically inert gaseous element occurring in small amounts in the earth's atmosphere，emitting a reddish light when discharge electricity，and used therefore as a material for the making of neon lamps；通称 popularly known as 氖气 nǎiqì

【氖灯】nǎidēng 把氖气填充在真空管里制成的灯，通电时发出红色光，亮度随电压大小而变，光线能透过烟雾，多用做信号灯 neon light；neon lamp；neon-filled tubular electrical lamp that gives off reddish light that changes its luminosity with voltage and penetrates smoke or fog，oft. used as signal lamp

【氖气】nǎiqì 氖的通称 popular term for 氖 nǎi

迺 nǎi ❶ same as 乃 nǎi ❷（Nǎi）姓 a surname

哪(那) nǎi '哪'（nǎ）的口语音 pronunciation of '哪 nǎ' in oral Chinese；☞哪[1] nǎ 注意 NOTE on p.1382

倷 nǎi〈方 *dial.*〉你 you

nài（ㄋㄞˋ）

奈 nài ❶ 奈何 helpless；powerless：无～cannot but；have no choice｜怎～only to ... because ... ❷〈书 *fml.*〉怎奈；无奈 cannot but

【奈何】nài//hé ❶ 用反问的方式表示没有办法，意思跟'怎么办'相似 [similar in meaning to 怎么办 'what's to be done' when used in a rhetorical question]：徒唤～ in helplessness keep asking oneself what is to be done｜无可

～have no choice but to reconcile oneself to sth. |～不得 can do nothing about ... ❷〈书 *fml.*〉用反问的方式表示如何 [meaning 'what can you do about this' in a rhetorical question]：民不畏死，～以死惧之？The people fear not death. Why threaten them with it? ❸ 中间加代词，表示'拿他怎么办'[meaning 'what you can do with him' when used rhetorically with a pronoun in between 奈 nài and 何 hé]：凭你怎么说，他就是不答应，你又奈他何！He wouldn't budge an inch no matter what the persuasion. What can you do with him?

佴 Nài 姓 a surname

☞ èr on p.517

柰 nài 柰子 crab apple

【柰子】nài·zi 苹果的一种 crab apple (*Malus asiatica*)

耐 nài 受得住；禁得起 stand；resistant：～烦 patient |～用 durable；stand wear and tear |～火砖 refractory brick |吃苦～劳 industrial and hardworking |锦纶袜子～穿。Socks made of polyamide fibre are rather durable.

【耐烦】nàifán 不急躁；不怕麻烦；不厌烦 patient；composed：见你迟迟不来，他已经等得不～了。He was getting impatient when you were so slow in coming.

【耐火材料】nàihuǒ cáiliào 熔点一般在1,580℃以上的材料，用于锅炉、冶金炉、坩埚、玻璃窑等。常用的耐火材料有耐火黏土、石英石、白云石、石墨、菱镁矿等。refractory material；fireproof material with a melting point of above 1,580 degrees Celsius, to be used in boilers, blast furnaces, crucibles and glass furnaces. Among common refractory materials are refractory clay, quartzite, dolomite, graphite, magnesite, etc.

【耐久】nàijiǔ 能够经久 durable；long-lasting：坚固～stout and durable

【耐看】nàikàn （景物、艺术作品等）禁得起反复的观看、欣赏（of scenery, works of art, etc.）have lasting appeal：书中的插图精美～。The illustrations in the book are finely drawn and can stand careful scrutiny.

【耐劳】nài//láo 禁得起劳累 industrious：吃苦～ able to stand hardship

【耐力】nàilì 耐久的能力 stamina：长跑能锻炼～。Long-distance running helps increase people's stamina.

【耐人寻味】nài rén xún wèi 意味深长，值得仔细体会琢磨 thought-provoking；meaningful；provide much food for thought

【耐心】nàixīn 心里不急躁，不厌烦 patient：～说服 persuade sb. with patience |只要～地学，什么技术都能学会。You can learn any skill so long as you can study patiently.

【耐性】nàixìng 能忍耐、不急躁的性格 patient character；endurance：越是复杂艰巨的工作，越需要～。The more difficult and complex the work, the more enduring you should become.

【耐用】nàiyòng 可以长久使用；不容易用坏 durable；stand wear and tear：搪瓷器具比玻璃器具经久～。Enamelware stands wear and tear better than glassware.

萘 nài 有机化合物，化学式 $C_{10}H_8$。白色晶体，有特殊气味，容易挥发和升华。用来制染料、树脂、香料、药品等。naphthalene ($C_{10}H_8$)；white odd-odour volatile crystalline hydrocarbon that is used for the making of dyes, resin, perfume, pharmaceuticals, etc.

鼐 nài〈书 *fml.*〉大鼎 big tripod；large caldron

褦 nài [褦襶](nàidài)〈书 *fml.*〉不晓事；不懂事 insensible；unreasonable：～子（不晓事的人）blockhead

nān (ㄋㄢ)

囡(囝) nān〈方 *dial.*〉❶ 小孩儿 child：小～little child |男小～boy |女小～girl ❷ 女儿 daughter：她有一个儿子一个～。She has a son and a daughter.

☞ 囝 jiǎn on p.944

【囡囡】nānnān〈方 *dial.*〉对小孩儿的亲热称呼 [term of endearment for a child] little darling

nán (ㄋㄢˊ)

男[1] nán ❶ 男性（跟'女'相对 as opposed to 'female'）male：～学生 male student |一～一女 a man and a woman ❷ 儿子 son：长～ eldest son

男[2] nán 封建五等爵位的第五等 the lowest of five ranks of aristocracy in feudal years：～爵 baron

【男盗女娼】nán dào nǚ chāng 男的偷盗，女的卖淫。指男女都做坏事或思想行为极其卑鄙恶劣。the men being robbers and the women harlots；being nothing but pillage and licentiousness；behave like thieves and prostitutes

【男儿】nán'ér 男子汉 real man：好～man of honour |～志在四方。A real man goes wherever his ambition takes him.

【男方】nánfāng 男的一方面（多用于有关婚事的场合 usu. of a marriage）husband's side

【男家】nánjiā 婚姻关系中男方的家（of a marriage）husband's family

【男科】nánkē 医院中专门医治男性生殖系统疾病的一科（of a hospital）andrologic department

【男男女女】nánnánnǚnǚ 指有男有女的一群人

group of men and women：大街上，～个个都衣着整齐。All the people in the streets，men and women alike，were impeccably attired.

【男女】nánnǚ ❶ 男性和女性 man and woman：青年～young men and woman｜～青年 youngsters｜～平等 equality between men and women｜～老少 men and women，old and young ❷〈方 *dial.*〉儿女 sons and daughters ❸ 骂人的话（多见于早期白话 oft. in early vernacular）（term of abuse）man and woman：狗～ a bitch and a bastard｜贼～female crooks and male muggers

【男人】nánrén 男性的成年人 man

【男人】nán·ren same as 丈夫 zhàng·fu

【男生】nánshēng 男学生 male student；man student；men students；boy student

【男声】nánshēng 声乐中的男子声部，一般分男高音、男中音、男低音 male voice，including tenor，baritone，and bass in a chorus

【男士】nánshì 对成年男子的尊称（honor.）gentleman

【男性】nánxìng 人类两性之一，能在体内产生精细胞（of humans）male sex；one of two genders that has organs to produce spermatozoa for fertilizing ova

【男子】nánzǐ 男性的人 man；male

【男子汉】nánzǐhàn 男人（nánrén，强调男性的健壮或刚强）man esp. one who is masculine and steadfast；true man：有的妇女干起活儿来，赛过～。There are women who work better than men.

南 nán ❶ 四个主要方向之一，早晨面对太阳时右手的一边 south（one of the four directions）；direction to the right of sunrise：～边儿 to the south｜～头儿 on the southern side｜～方 the south｜～风（从南来的风）southerly wind｜山～south of the mountain｜坐北朝～facing south ❷ 南部地区，在我国指长江流域及其以南的地区 the south；（of China）regions south of the Yangtze River：～味 southern flavour；southern school of cooking｜～货 native produce from south China ❸（Nán）姓 a surname

☞ nā on p.1381

【南半球】nánbànqiú 地球赤道以南的部分 Southern Hemisphere

【南梆子】nánbāng·zi 京剧中西皮唱腔的一种 *nanbangzi* tune；singing style that falls into the category of the *xipi* tune in Peking Opera

【南北】nán-běi ❶ 南边和北边 north and south ❷ 从南到北（指距离 of distance）from north to south：这个水库～足有五里。The reservoir extends five *li* from north to south.

【南北朝】Nán-Běi Cháo 4 世纪末叶至 6 世纪末叶，宋、齐（南齐）、梁、陈四朝先后在我国南方建立政权，叫南朝（公元 420—589），北魏（后分裂为东魏和西魏）、北齐、北周先后在我国北方建立政权，叫北朝（公元 386—581），合称为南北朝 Northern and Southern Dynasties（late 4th century to late 6th century），referring to the Southern Dynasties（420-589）that included the Song，（Southern）Qi，Liang，and Chen in south China，and the Northern Dynasties（386-581）that included the Northern Wei（which later split into the Eastern Wei and Western Wei），Northern Qi，and Northern Zhou in north China

【南边】nán·bian ❶（～儿 nán·bianr）same as 南 nán ① ❷ same as 南 nán ②

【南昌起义】Nánchāng Qǐyì the Nanchang Uprising；☞八一南昌起义 Bā-Yī Nánchāng Qǐyì on p.23

【南朝】Nán Cháo 宋、齐、梁、陈四朝的合称 Southern Dynasties（420-589），namely，the Song（420-479），Qi（479-502），Liang（502-557）and Chen（557-589）dynasties；☞南北朝 Nán-Běi Cháo

【南斗】nándǒu 斗（dǒu）⑥的通称，由六颗星组成（general term for）Southern Dipper，a constellation consisting of six stars

【南豆腐】nándòu·fu 食品，豆浆煮开后加入石膏使凝结成块而成了。有的地区叫嫩豆腐。southern-style beancurd；tofu；soft food made from puréed soya beans known in some regions as 嫩豆腐 nèndòu·fu

【南方】nánfāng ❶ same as 南 nán ① ❷ same as 南 nán ②

【南宫】Nángōng 姓 a surname

【南瓜】nánguā ❶ 一年生草本植物，能爬蔓，茎的横断面呈五角形。叶子心脏形。花黄色，果实一般扁圆形或梨形，嫩时绿色，成熟时赤褐色。果实可做蔬菜，种子可以吃。pumpkin（*Cucurbita pepo*）；cushaw；annual trailing vine having stalks with a pentagon-shaped cross-section，heart-shaped leaves and yellow flowers，bearing edible oblate or pear-shaped fruit that is green when tender and deep brown when ripe and that contains edible seeds ❷ 这种植物的果实 pumpkin；large pulpy round fruit of the pumpkin‖在不同地区有倭瓜、老倭瓜、北瓜、番瓜等名称 known variously as 倭瓜 wōguā，老倭瓜 lǎowōguā，北瓜 běiguā，or 番瓜 fānguā in different regions

【南国】nánguó〈书 *fml.*〉指我国的南部 south China

【南胡】nánhú 二胡，因原先流行在南方得名 *erhu*，a two-stringed Chinese fiddle that is also called 'southern fiddle' because it originated in the south

【南货】nánhuò 南方所产的食品，如笋干、火腿等 preserved farm produce from south China，such as dried bamboo shoots and ham

【南极】nánjí ❶ 地轴的南端，南半球的顶点 the South Pole；Antarctica ❷ 南磁极，用 S 来表示 the South Magnetic Pole（S）

【南柯一梦】Nánkē yī mèng 淳于棼做梦到大槐

安国做南柯太守，享尽富贵荣华，醒来才知道是一场大梦，原来大槐安国就是住宅南边大槐树下的蚁穴（见于唐李公佐《南柯太守传》）。后来用'南柯一梦'泛指一场梦，或比喻一场空欢喜。According to *The Governor of the Southern Tributary* by Li Gongzuo of the Tang Dynasty, a drunk man by the name of Chunyu Fen dreamed of becoming the Governor of the Southern Tributary or the 'Great and Peaceful Kingdom of the Scholartree' and enjoying all the comforts of luxury and pomp — only to wake up and realize that the so-called 'Great and Peaceful Kingdom of the Scholartree' was none other than an ants' nest under the big Chinese scholartree south of his house. From the proverb is derived the phrase, 'the dream of the southern tributary', meaning a fond dream or wishful thinking.

【南面】[1] nánmiàn 面朝南。古代以面朝南为尊位，君主临朝南面而坐，因此把为君叫做'南面为王'、'南面称孤'等。facing south. In ancient China the southern direction was regarded as the direction of dignity, and a monarch always sat facing south whenever he held a court session. Thus a man who took the throne would claim himself emperor while facing south or face south and proclaim, 'I, the Lonely One'.

【南面】[2] nánmiàn（～儿 nánmiànr）南边儿 the south

【南明】Nán Míng 明亡后，明皇室后裔先后在我国南方建立的政权，史称南明 Southern Ming, the political power established in south China after the downfall of the Ming Dynasty by descendants of the imperial family and the adherents to them

【南欧】Nán Ōu 欧洲南部，包括希腊、罗马尼亚、前南斯拉夫地区、阿尔巴尼亚、保加利亚、意大利、圣马力诺、马耳他、西班牙、安道尔和葡萄牙等国 Southern Europe, a region that encompasses Greece, Romania, the former Yugoslavia, Albania, Bulgaria, Italy, San Marino, Malta, Spain, Andorra, and Portuguese

【南齐】Nán Qí 南朝之一，公元 479—502，萧道成所建 South Qi (479-502), one of the Southern Dynasties founded by Xiao Daocheng; ☞ 南北朝 Nán-Běi Cháo

【南腔北调】nán qiāng běi diào 形容口音不纯，掺杂方音 speak with the accent of a dialect

【南曲】nánqǔ ❶ 宋元明时流行于南方的各种曲调的统称，调子柔和婉转，用管乐器伴奏 southern tunes, a general term for the tunes and melodies popular in south China during the Song, Yuan and Ming dynasties, known for their soft and graceful notes, and sung to the accompaniment of wind instruments ❷ 指用南曲演唱的戏曲 *nanqu*; opera sung in southern tunes

【南式】nánshì 北京一带指某些手工业品、食品的南方的式样或制法 southern style; (a reference among people in and around Beijing to the flavour of food and handicraft works done in the style of south China: ～盆桶 southern-style basins and tubs | ～糕点 southern-style cakes and pastries

【南宋】Nán Sòng 朝代，公元 1127—1279，自高宗（赵构）建炎元年起到帝昺（赵昺）祥兴二年宋朝灭亡止。建都临安（今浙江杭州）。Southern Song Dynasty (1127-1279), which rose in the 1st year of the Jianyan reign of Emperor Gaozong (Zhao Gou) and fell in the 2nd year of the Xiangxing reign of Emperor Dibing (Zhao Bing), with Lin'an (present-day Hangzhou, Zhejiang Province) as its capital

【南糖】nántáng 南式糖果；南方生产的糖食 confectionary produced in south China; southern Chinese confectionary

【南味】nánwèi（～儿 nánwèir）南方风味的 southern flavour: ～糕点 cakes and pastries with a southern flavour

【南戏】nánxì 古典地方戏的一种，南宋初年形成于浙江温州一带，用南曲演唱。到明朝演变为传奇。*nanxi*; classical local opera sung to the *nanqu* tune, which emerged in the early years of the Southern Song Dynasty in what is today's Wenzhou, Zhejiang Province, and was evolved into the *chuanqi* drama by the Ming Dynasty; also 戏文 xìwén

【南亚】Nán Yà 亚洲南部，包括巴基斯坦、印度、孟加拉、尼泊尔、锡金、不丹和斯里兰卡等国 South Asia, including such countries as Pakistan, India, Bangladesh, Nepal, Sikkim, Bhutan, and Sri Lanka, etc.

【南洋】Nányáng ❶ 清末指江苏、浙江、福建、广东沿海地区。特设南洋通商大臣，由两江总督兼任，管理对外贸易、交涉事务。Nanyang, name of a region towards the end of the Qing Dynasty, which encompassed the coastal provinces of Jiangsu, Zhejiang, Fujian and Guangdong, where foreign trade and affairs were under the administration of the Grand Minister for the Southern Seas, a post concurrently assumed by the Viceroy of Jiangnan and Jiangxi ❷ 南洋群岛 old name for areas south beyond the South China Sea, including Malay Archipelago, Malay Peninsula and Indonesia

【南音】nányīn ❶ 曲艺的一种，流行于珠江三角洲，唱词基本为七字句，格律严谨，用扬琴、椰胡、三弦、洞箫、琵琶等伴奏 *nanyin*, ballad singing popular in the Pearl River Delta, with lyrics consisting of seven-character lines that follow strict tonal pattern and rhyme scheme, and are sung to the accompaniment of *yangqin* (dulcimer), *yehu* (two-stringed bowed fiddle), *sanxian* (three-stringed plucked instrument), *dongxiao* (vertical

N

bamboo flute), and *pipa* (ballon guitar) ❷ 流行于福建的古典音乐,格调高雅,旋律优美 nanyin; classical Chinese music popular in Fujian Province, marked for its graceful artistic aura and melodious tone; also 南管 nánguǎn or 南乐 nányuè

【南辕北辙】nán yuán běi zhé 心里想往南去,却驾车往北走。try to go south by driving the chariot to the north;〈比喻 *fig.*〉行动和目的相反 act in opposite to one's goal

【南针】nánzhēn 就是指南针 compass;〈比喻 *fig.*〉辨别正确方向的依据 guideline

难(難) nán ❶ 做起来费事的(跟'易'相对 as opposed to 'easy') hard; difficult:~办 hard to do|笔画多的字很~写。It is difficult to write Chinese characters with many strokes.|这条路~走。This road is hard for travellers. ❷ 使感到困难 make things difficult for sb.:这一下子可把我~住了。This question really baffled me. ❸ 不容易;不大可能 not easy; impossible:~免 unavoidable|~保 be not sure; cannot say for sure ❹ 不好 disagreeable; displeasing:~听 sound terrible|~看 ugly

〈古 *arch.*〉same as 傩 nuó

☞ nàn on p.1392

【难熬】nán'áo 难以忍受(疼痛或艰苦的生活等)(of pain or hardship) have a tough row to hoe; unbearable:饥饿~ can hardly bear the pang of hunger

【难保】nánbǎo 不敢保证;保不住 there is no guarantee that...; cannot say for sure; hard to say:今天~不下雨。Nobody can say for sure that it won't rain today.

【难产】nánchǎn ❶ 分娩时胎儿不易产出。难产的原因主要是产妇的骨盆狭小,胎儿过大或位置不正常等(区别于'顺产' as compared with 'natural labour') difficult labour; dystocia, caused by the pelvis being too narrow, the baby being too big or in an abnormal position ❷〈比喻 *fig.*〉著作、计划等不易完成(of a book, plan, etc.) slow in coming; overdue

【难处】nánchǔ 不容易相处 difficult to get along with:他只是脾气暴躁些,并不算~。He is just a bit quick-tempered, but not difficult to get along with.

【难处】nán·chu same as 困难 kùn·nan:各有各的~。Every man has his own troubles.|这工作没有什么~。This job is not really too difficult.

【难当】nándāng ❶ 难以担当或充当 hard to handle:~重任 find it hard to take an important task|好人~。It's not easy to be a good guy. ❷ 难以禁受 unbearable:羞愧~ feel mortally ashamed

【难道】nándào〈副词 *adv.*〉加强反问的语气 [used to reiterate a rhetorical question]:河水~会倒流吗? Rivers never flow backward, don't they?|他们做得到,~我们就做不到吗? If they can do it, why can't we? also 难道说 nándàoshuō [注意] **NOTE**:句末可以用'不成'呼应 The word 难道 nándào may be echoed at the end of a sentence with the rhetorical word 不成 bùchéng; 如 for example:~他病了不成? He isn't ill, is he?|~就罢了不成! We should not leave the matter alone, should we?

【难得】nándé ❶ 不容易得到或办到(有可贵意) hard or not possible to come by (for being precious):人才~。Great talents are hard to come by.|灵芝是非常~的药草。Glossy ganoderma is a rare medicinal herb.|他在一年之内两次打破世界纪录,这是十分~的。It was no mean feat for him to chalk up the world record twice in a year's time. ❷ 表示不常常(发生) seldom; rarely:这样大的雨是很~遇到的。This kind of downpour is extremely rare.

【难点】nándiǎn 问题不容易解决的地方 knot; hitch; stumbling block:突破~ overcome a knotty problem

【难度】nándù 工作或技术等方面困难的程度 degree of difficulty:~大 of great difficulty

【难分难解】nán fēn nán jiě ❶ 双方相持不下(多指竞争或争吵、打斗),难以开交 inextricably attached; (of two parties) be neck and neck in a competition, a dispute or fight ❷ 形容双方关系异常亲密,难于分离 sentimentally attached to each other|also 难解难分 nán jiě nán fēn

【难怪】nánguài ❶ 怪不得 no wonder; small wonder:~他今天这么高兴,原来新机器试验成功了。No wonder he was so happy today. It turned out that the trial run of the new machine was a success. ❷ 不应当责怪(含有谅解的意思) understandable; can be hardly blamed:这也~,一个七十多岁的人,怎能看得清这么小的字呢! He was really not to be blamed — how can you count on a man in his seventies to see such small letters clearly?

【难关】nánguān 难通过的的关口 knotty problem; barrier;〈比喻 *fig.*〉不易克服的困难 hard nut to crack:突破~solve a key problem|攻克一道道~。Surmount one barrier after another.

【难过】nánguò ❶ 不容易过活 be hard off; have a hard time:那时家里人口多,收入少,日子真~。At the time the going was tough for our family, as we had a small income but many mouths to feed. ❷ same as 难受 nánshòu:肚子里~得很。He felt very uncomfortable in his stomach.|他听到老师逝世的消息,心里非常~。He was terribly sad over the news about his teacher's death.

【难堪】nánkān ❶ 难以忍受 intolerable; unbearable：～的话 annoying remarks|天气闷热～。It was terribly hot and sultry. ❷ 难为情 embarrassed; abashed：予人～out to embarrass sb.|他感到有点～，微微涨红了脸。His face went faintly red with embarrassment.

【难看】nánkàn ❶ 丑陋；不好看 of unpleasant or unsightly appearance; ghastly; unsightly：这匹马毛都快掉光了，实在～。The horse looks ugly as it has lost nearly all its hair. ❷ 不光荣；不体面 embarrassing; shameful：小伙子干活儿要是比不上老年人，那就太～了。It's a shame if a young man doesn't work as well as an old one. ❸（神情、气色等）不和悦；不正常（of mood, expression, etc.）displeasing; sullen; abnormal：他的脸色很～，像是在生气。He looks gloomy, as if he was angry.

【难免】nánmiǎn 不容易避免 unavoidable; bound to happen：没有经验，就～要走弯路。Mistakes are unavoidable for someone who is inexperienced.|搞新工作，困难是～的。You are bound to come across difficulties whenever you take on a new job.

【难能可贵】nán néng kě guì 难做的事居然能做到，值得宝贵 commendable for making the impossible possible; worthy of esteem for attaining sth. difficult：过去草都不长的盐碱地，今天能收这么多粮食，的确～。It is admirable of them to have got such a good harvest of grain from a saline-alkali land where even grass could not survive in the past.

【难人】nánrén ❶ 使人为难 sticky; tough; thorny：这种～的事，不好办。There's little I can do about this kind of sticky business. ❷ 担当为难的事情的人 person left alone with a delicate matter in hand：有麻烦我们帮助你，决不叫你做～。We'll stand by you if you are in trouble; we won't leave you in the lurch.

【难色】nánsè 为难的表情 look uncomfortable or uneasy：面有～with a look of disinclination; look reluctant to do sth.

【难事】nánshì 困难的事情 sth. hard to do; difficult job or task：天下无～，只怕有心人。Where there is a will, there is a way.

【难受】nánshòu ❶ 身体不舒服 feel queasy; feel uncomfortable：浑身疼得～suffer a splitting ache all over one's body ❷ 伤心；不痛快 smart from; feel sad; feel bad：他知道事情做错了，心里很～。He felt terribly sorry upon learning that he had messed it up.

【难说】nánshuō ❶ 不容易说；不好说；难于确切地说 not sure; hard to say; you can never tell：在这场纠纷里，很～谁对谁不对。It's hard to say who's right and who's wrong in this dispute.|他什么时候回来还很～。I'm not sure when he'll be back. ❷ 难于说出口 find it hard to say：你就照着事实说，没有什么～的。It won't be so difficult if you just tell the truth.

【难题】nántí 不容易解决或解答的问题 problem; knotty point; tough one; hot potato：出～pose a difficult question|算术～arithmetic brain-teaser|再大的～也难不倒咱们。Nothing can baffle us no matter what the difficulty is.

【难听】nántīng ❶（声音）听着不舒服；不悦耳（of sound）awful; unpleasant：这个曲子怪声怪调的，真～。This song sounds weird — it is just sickening. ❷（言语）粗俗刺耳（of an uttering）repulsive; strident; vulgar：开口骂人，多～！How awful, cursing people like that! ❸（事情）不体面（of sth.）disgraceful; outrageous：这种事情说出去多～！What a disgrace if this sort of thing is made known to all.

【难为】nán·wei ❶ 使人为难 bring pressure on sb; make things difficult for sb.：她不会唱歌，就别再～她了。She cannot sing, so don't force her to. ❷ 多亏（指做了不容易做的事）（accomplish sth. difficult）thanks to; by the grace of：一个人带好十多个孩子，真～了她。It would be impossible to look after more than a dozen children without her. ❸〈客套话 *pol.*〉用于感谢别人代自己做事［expression of one's gratitude to sb.］thank you for ...：～你给我提一桶水来。It's so kind of you to fetch me a pail of water.|车票也替我买好了，真～你呀。I'm grateful to you for booking the train ticket for me.

【难为情】nánwéiqíng ❶ 脸上下不来；不好意思 discomfited; shamefaced：别人都学会了，就是我没有学会，多～啊！Everybody has learned the ropes and I'm the only person who hasn't. What an embarrassment! ❷ 情面上过不去 discomfiture; embarrassment：答应吧，办不到；不答应吧，又有点～。If we accept it we can't really get it done, but it's embarrassing to turn it down.

【难兄难弟】nánxiōng-nándì 东汉陈元方的儿子和陈季方的儿子是堂兄弟，都夸耀自己父亲的功德，争个不休，就去问祖父陈寔。陈寔说：'元方难为弟，季方难为兄'（见于《世说新语·德行篇》）。意思是元方好得做他弟弟难，季方好得做他哥哥难。后来用"难兄难弟"形容兄弟都非常好。今多反用，讥讽两人同样坏。Chen Yuanfang and Chen Jifang were two brothers during the Eastern Han Dynasty, and their sons were locked in a heated debate on whose father had performed the greater merits for the country. The debate being inconclusive, they asked their grandfather, Chen Shi, for judgment. The old man said, 'Yuanfang has done so well that it is hard for anyone to be his younger brother, while Jifang has do so well that it is hard for anyone to be his elder brother.'（See *A New Account of Tales of the*

N

World • Virtue) From this proverb is derived the phrase to mean 'good brothers', but it is oft. used to refer derogatively to persons who are both bad, meaning 'birds of a feather'.

☞ nànxiōng-nàndì on p. 1392

【难言之隐】nán yán zhī yǐn 难于说出口的藏在内心深处的事情 sth. on one's mind that is embarrassing to tell, usu. an ailment one does not want to talk about

【难以】nányǐ 难于 hard to; difficult to: ～形容 indescribable; beyond description | ～置信 unbelievable

【难于】nányú 不容易;不易于 hard to; difficult to: ～收效 hard to get a result; not likely to produce satisfactory results

喃 nán [喃喃]〈拟声词 *onom*.〉连续不断地小声说话的声音 mutter; murmur: ～自语 murmuring to oneself

楠(柟) nán [楠木](nánmù) ❶ 常绿大乔木,叶子椭圆形或长披针形,表面光滑,背面有软毛,花小,绿色,结浆果,蓝黑色。木材是贵重的建筑材料,也可供造船用。产于云南、四川等地。*nanmu* (*Phoebe nanmu*); evergreen giant tree having smooth oval or long lanceolate leaves with soft down on their backs and tiny green flowers, bearing bluish dark berries, producing timber that is a precious material for construction, shipbuilding and other purposes, found in Yunnan and Sichuan provinces ❷ 这种植物的木材 *nanmu* wood

nǎn (ㄋㄢˇ)

赧(赦) nǎn 因羞愧而脸红 shamefaced; blush for shame: ～颜 look embarrassed

【赧然】nǎnrán〈书 *fml*.〉形容难为情的样子 look abashed: ～一笑 smile in one's shyness

【赧颜】nǎnyán〈书 *fml*.〉因害羞而脸红 blush for shyness; be shamefaced: ～苟活 eke out an inglorious existence | ～汗下 sweating with shame

腩 nǎn ☞牛腩 niúnǎn on p. 1420

蝻 nǎn 蝗蝻 nymph of a locust

nàn (ㄋㄢˋ)

难(難) nàn ❶ 不幸的遭遇;灾难 tragedy; trouble; catastrophe: 遭～ be caught in a disaster | 遇～ perish unexpectedly in a disaster | 空～ air crash | 大～临头 in imminent danger; calamity close at hand | 多～兴邦。A nation was reborn of a disaster. ❷ 质问 take sb. to task: 非～ condemn | 责～ blame | 问～ test sb. with difficult questions

☞ nán on p. 1390

【难胞】nànbāo 称本国的难民(多指在国外遭受迫害的侨胞) compatriot in distress (oft. persecution by a foreign government)

【难民】nànmín 由于战火、自然灾害等原因而流离失所、生活困难的人 refugee; victim of war, natural adversity, etc.: 救济～ come to the relief of refugees

【难兄难弟】nànxiōng-nàndì 彼此曾共患难的人;彼此处于同样困难境地的人 fellow sufferers; people in the same boat

☞ nánxiōng-nándì on p. 1391

【难友】nànyǒu 一同蒙难的人 fellow sufferer; fellow inmate

nāng (ㄋㄤ)

囊 nāng ☞ below

☞ náng on p. 1392

【囊揣】nāngchuài ❶ 虚弱;懦弱(多见于早期白话 oft. in early vernacular) cowardly; feeble ❷ same as 囊膪 nāngchuài

【囊膪】nāngchuài 猪胸腹部的肥而松的肉 fatty, floppy meat from the abdomen of a pig

囔 nāng [囔囔](nāng·nang) 小声说话 mutter; murmur; speak in a low voice

náng (ㄋㄤˊ)

囊 náng ❶ 口袋 pocket; bag: 药～ medicine pouch | 琴～ bag containing a fiddle, etc. | 皮～ leather bag | 探～取物 as easy as picking one's own pocket ❷ 像口袋的东西 bag-shaped thing: 肾～ scrotum | 胆～ gall bladder ❸〈书 *fml*.〉用袋子装 to pocket sth.; put sth. into a bag: ～括 encompass; sweep

☞ nāng on p. 1392

【囊空如洗】náng kōng rú xǐ 口袋里空得像洗过了一样。形容一个钱都没有。one's purse as empty as if washed clean; be penniless; without a penny in one's purse; broke

【囊括】nángkuò 把全部包罗在内 encompass; sweep: ～四海(指封建君主统一全国 of a feudal monarch) bring an entire country under imperial rule | 这个队～了田赛的全部冠军。The team swept all the field events.

【囊生】nángshēng 西藏农奴主家的奴隶(in Tibet in former times) *nangzan*; household slave; also 朗生 lǎngshēng

【囊中物】nángzhōngwù〈比喻 *fig*.〉不用费多大力气就可以得到的东西 that which is already in the bag; sth. certain of attainment

【囊肿】nángzhǒng 良性肿瘤的一种,多呈球形,有包膜,内有液体或半固体的物质。肺、卵巢、皮脂腺等器官内都能发生。cyst, a kind of benign tumour with a membrane, usu. in the shape of a ball, and containing liquid or semi-solid substance, which may occur in lungs, ovary, sebaceous gland, etc.

馕 náng 一种烤制成的面饼,维吾尔、哈萨克等民族当做主食 *nang*; crusty pancake, a staple food of the Uygurs and Kazaks

☞ nǎng on p. 1393

nǎng(ㄋㄤˇ)

曩 nǎng〈书 *fml*.〉以往;从前;过去的 bygone; past; old: ～日 bygone days | ～年 earlier years | ～时 of yore | ～者(从前) in the past; formerly

攮 nǎng (用刀)刺 stab (with a knife)

【攮子】nǎng·zi 短而尖的刀,是一种旧式的武器 dagger; old-style weapon with short, pointed blade。

馕 nǎng 拼命地往嘴里塞食物 wolf down; gobble; devour

☞ náng on p. 1393

nàng(ㄋㄤˋ)

齉 nàng 鼻子不通气,发音不清 snuffle, as when the nose is partially blocked: 受了凉,鼻子发～snuffle with a cold

【齉鼻儿】nàngbír ❶(语音)发齉 snuffle: 他感冒了,说话有点～。He had a cold, and that's why he snuffled when he spoke. ❷ 指说话时鼻音特别重的人 speak with a heavy twang

nāo(ㄋㄠ)

孬 nāo〈方 *dial*.〉❶ 坏;不好 inferior; bad: 这个牌子的电器最～。The electrical appliances under this brand are of the worst quality. ❷ 怯懦;没有勇气 timid; cowardly: ～种 coward; chicken-hearted person

【孬种】nāozhǒng〈方 *dial*.〉怯懦无能的人;坏家伙(骂人的话 curse.) caitiff; craven

náo(ㄋㄠˊ)

呶 náo〈书 *fml*.〉叫嚷 talk noisily: 喧～ clamour

☞ 努 nǔ on p. 1426

【呶呶】náonáo〈书 *fml*.〉形容说起话来没完没了使人讨厌 chatter, prattle: ～不休 babble on

诶(譊) náo〈书 *fml*.〉喧闹;争辩 make big noise; wrangle

【诶诶】náonáo〈书 *fml*.〉形容争辩的声音 noise of argument

挠(撓) náo ❶(用手指)轻轻地抓 scratch (using one's hand): ～痒痒 scratch an itch | 抓耳～腮 tweak one's ears and scratch one's cheeks — a sign of anxiety or delight ❷ 使别人的事情不能顺利进行;阻止 thwart; get in the way of sb.'s business; obstruct: 阻～ obstruction ❸ 弯曲 bend;〈比喻 *fig*.〉屈服 give in; flinch: 不屈不～indomitable; unyielding | 百折不～unswerving

【挠度】náodù 表示构件(如梁、柱、板等)受到外力时发生弯曲变形的程度,以构件弯曲后各横截面的中心至原轴线的距离来度量 deflection; the process of a structure (e. g. girder, column, board, etc.) being bent or deformed under stress. The degree of deflection is indicated by the distance from the centre of the cross-section of the bent structure to its original axial line.

【挠钩】náogōu 顶端是大铁钩的带长柄的工具 iron hook with a long handle

【挠头】náotóu 用手抓头,形容事情麻烦复杂,使人难以处理 set sb. to scratch his head; troublesome; knotty: 遇到了～的事。Just came across a knotty problem. | 这种事情真叫人～。Things like this are rather troublesome.

【挠秧】náoyāng 除净稻田中的杂草,使根部泥土变松。挠秧可以促进秧苗根系的发育,并能促进分蘖。weed rice fields and loosen the soil around a seedling to facilitate root growth and tiller

侬(憹) náo ☞ 懊侬 àonáo on p. 20

猫(嶩) Náo 古山名,在今山东临淄一带 Naoshan, ancient name of a mountain in present-day Linzi, Shandong Province

硇(碙、砌) náo ☞ below

【硇砂】náoshā 天然产的氯化铵,可入药 natural ammoniac, which can be used as a medicine

【硇洲】Náozhōu 岛名,在广东 Naozhou, name of an island in Guangdong Province

注意 **NOTE**: 硇字有的书中误作'硇',误读 gāng。In some books 硇 náo is misspelled as 碙 and thus mispronounced as gāng.

铙(鐃) náo ❶ 打击乐器,像钹,中间突起部分比钹的小 *nao* (cymbal), one of a pair of concave brass plates struck together as percussion instruments, with a knob smaller than that of a *bo* ❷ 古代军中乐器,像铃铛,中间没有舌 cymbals; ancient military musical instrument that resembles an inverted bell minus its tongue ❸ (Náo) 姓 a surname

【铙钹】náobó 大型的钹 large cymbals

蛲(蟯) náo [蛲虫](náochóng) 寄生虫,身体很小,白色,像线头。寄生在人体的小肠下部和大肠里,雌虫常从肛门爬出来产卵。患者常觉肛门奇痒,并有消瘦、食欲不振等症状。pinworm (*Enterobius vermicularis*); tiny white parasitic nematode worm that infests the human intestines and rectum, with the female oft. wriggling out of the anus to lay eggs, causing an intense itch and loss of weight and appetite

猱 náo 古书上说的一种猴(in ancient books) monkey

夒 náo〈书 *fml*.〉same as 猱 náo

嶩 náo〈书 *fml*.〉same as 猱 náo；元代书法家嶩嶩(Náonáo)，字子山。Nao Nao, whose style name was Zishan, was a calligrapher of the Yuan Dynasty.

nǎo (ㄋㄠˇ)

垴(堖) nǎo〈方 *dial*.〉山岗、丘陵较平的顶部(多用于地名 oft. used in the name of a place) flat mountaintop or hilltop：削～填沟 remove hilltops to fill up gullies | 南～(地名，在山西) Nannao(name of a place in Shanxi Province) | 沙洲～(地名，在湖南) Shazhounao(name of a place in Hunan Province)

恼(惱) nǎo ❶ 生气 displeased; incensed; furious：～恨 hate; resent | 把他惹～了。He was offended. | 你别～我！Leave me alone! ❷ 烦闷；心里不痛快 vexed; upset：烦～fed up | 苦～feel miserable | 懊～regretful

【恼恨】nǎohèn 生气和怨恨 begrudge; feel bitter about：我说了你不愿意听的话，心里可别～我！Don't be angry with me if I said something you didn't want to listen.

【恼火】nǎohuǒ 生气 be fuming at; irritated：大为～be very upset

【恼怒】nǎonù ❶ 生气；发怒 resentful; see red：这些恶毒的攻击，使他十分～。He was greatly enraged by the vicious attacks. ❷ 使恼怒；触怒 enrage：一句话～了他，于是再也不和我说话了。Enraged by just one of my remarks, he refused to speak to me any more.

【恼人】nǎorén 令人感觉焦急烦恼 irritating; annoying

【恼羞成怒】nǎo xiū chéng nù 由于羞愧和恼恨而发怒 exacerbated; feel humiliated and angry

脑(腦) nǎo ❶ 人体中管全身知觉、运动和思维、记忆等活动的器官，是神经系统的主要部分，由前脑、中脑和后脑构成。高等动物的脑只有管全身感觉、运动的作用。brain; human organ that is a major part of the nerve system, functions as the coordinating centre of sensation, movement and of intellectual and nervous activity, and consists of the forebrain, midbrain, and afterbrain; by contrast, the brain of a higher animal functions as the center of sensation and movement only ❷ 指头(tóu)① head：～袋 head | 探头探～crane one's neck to peer; act stealthily ❸ 脑筋 mind：人人动～，个个动手，大挖生产潜力。Let's work with our minds and hands to tap the potentials in production. ❹ 指从物体中提炼出的精华部分 essence：樟～camphor | 薄荷～peppermint camphor; methol ❺ 事物剩下的零碎部分；田地的边角地方 remnant of sth.; corners of a field：针头线～needles and threads | 田头地～the edges and corners of a farm plot; tiny bits of land

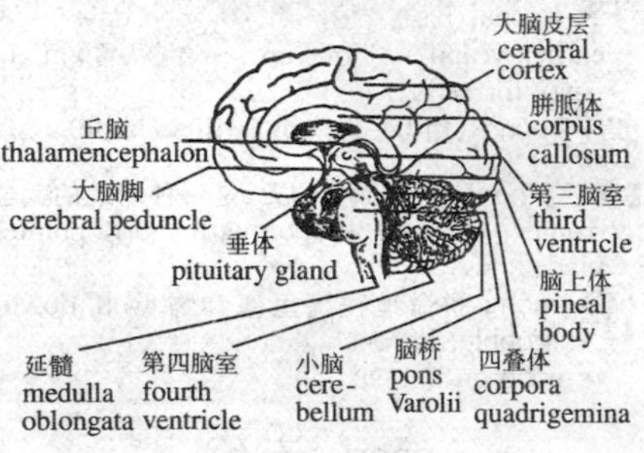

人的脑 Human Brain

【脑充血】nǎochōngxuè 脑部血管血液增多的病症，发病时有颜面发红、眼花、耳鸣、头痛等症状 encephalemia, a disease caused by an increase of blood in cerebral blood vessels, with such symptoms as flush, giddiness, tinnitus, and headache

【脑袋】nǎo·dai ❶ 头(tóu)① head; skull：秃～bald head | 耷拉着～hang one's head; one's head hanging low ❷ 脑筋 memory; brain：你的～真的好使，几十年前的事还能记得。You can even remember things that happened decades ago. You really have a good memory.

【脑袋瓜】nǎo·daiguā 脑袋 head; also 脑袋瓜子 nǎo·daiguā·zi

【脑瓜儿】nǎoguār 脑袋 head; also 脑瓜子 nǎoguā·zi

【脑海】nǎohǎi 指脑子(就思想、记忆的器官说 as the organ for thinking and remembering) mind; brain：十五年前的旧事，重又浮上他的～。Memories of what happened 15 years ago came flashing across his mind. | 烈士英勇的形象涌现在我的～。The heroic images of the martyrs came to my mind.

【脑脊液】nǎojǐyè 无色透明液体，充满于脑室、脊髓中央管和蛛网膜(脑膜的中层)下腔中，并在这些地方循环活动。有保护中枢神经系统和运走中枢神经系统代谢产物的作用。cerebrospinal fluid (CSF), colourless transparent liquid that fills and flows in a cycle in the ventricles, spinal cord and the lower cavity of the arachnoid (the middle meninx), protects the central nerve system and removes metabolic substances from it

【脑际】nǎojì 脑海（就记忆、印象说）(with respect to memory and impression) mind

【脑浆】nǎojiāng 头骨破裂时流出来的脑髓 brains, referring to cerebellum and medulla oblongata when they are exposed after the skull is crushed

【脑筋】nǎojīn ❶ 指思考、记忆等能力 brains; mind; capacities of thinking, memory, etc.：动～rack one's brains｜他～好，多少年前的事还记得很清楚。He has a good memory, remembering what happened many years ago clearly. ❷ 指意识 ideas; concepts：旧～old concepts｜老～ossified ways of thinking｜新～new ideas｜～开通 open-minded

【脑壳】nǎoké〈方 *dial.*〉☞头 tóu ①

【脑力】nǎolì 人的记忆、理解、想像等的能力 mental power; intelligence, such as memory, understanding, imagination, etc.

【脑力劳动】nǎolì láodòng 以消耗脑力为主的劳动，如管理国家事务，组织生产，以及从事政治、文化和科学研究等活动 mental labour, referring to such work as managing state affairs, organizing production, and conducting political or cultural activity or scientific research

【脑颅】nǎolú 指头的上部，包括头骨和脑 upper part of the head, including the skull and the brain

【脑满肠肥】nǎo mǎn cháng féi 形容不劳而食的人吃得很饱，养得很胖 the idle rich; (of a person) heavy-jowled and potbellied; well-fed and doing nothing

【脑门儿】nǎoménr 前额 forehead; also 脑门子 nǎomén·zi

【脑膜】nǎomó 脑表面的结缔组织，有三层，最外层是硬脑膜，中间是蛛网膜，里层是软脑膜。脑膜和脊膜相连，中间有脑脊液。脑膜有保护脑的作用。meninges; three membranes, i.e. dura mater(outer layer), arachnoid (middle layer), and pia mater (inner layer), that line the skull, linked with the spinal membranes and enclosing cerebrospinal fluid, having a role in protection the brain

【脑贫血】nǎopínxuè 脑部血管血液过少的病症，有面色苍白、四肢无力、恶心、头痛、耳鸣等症状 cerebral anaemia, a deficiency of blood in cerebral blood vessels, causing pale complexion, weakness in hands and feet, nausea, headache, a drumming in the ears, etc.

【脑桥】nǎoqiáo 后脑的一部分，与小脑相连，上接中脑，下接延髓。它和延髓能传导感觉器官的感觉给大脑皮层，并传导大脑皮层的兴奋到脊髓以外的其他部分。pons Varolii; band of nerve fibres that belongs to the tritocerebrum, connects the mesencephalon and the medulla oblongata below the cerebellum, works with the medulla oblongata to transmit senses to the pallium and the excitation of the pallium to body parts beyond the spinal cord；(图见 ☞ figure for 脑 nǎo on p.1394)

【脑儿】nǎor 供食用的动物脑髓或像脑髓的食品 animal brains used as food; jellied food：猪～pig's brains｜羊～goat's brains｜豆腐～jellied beancurd

【脑上体】nǎoshàngtǐ 内分泌腺之一，在第三脑室的后上部，形状像松树的果实。7岁以下小儿的脑上体比较发达，所分泌的激素有抑制性腺成熟的作用。pineal body; pineal gland; one of the endocrine glands in the upper rear part of the third ventricle, the pineal body is a pine nut-shaped conical mass of tissue which is relatively more developed in a child less than seven years old, and the hormone it secretes plays a role in restraining the maturity of the sex gland; also 松果腺 sōngguǒxiàn or 松果体 sōngguǒtǐ；(图见 ☞ figure for 脑 nǎo on p.1394)

【脑勺】nǎosháo〈方 *dial.*〉头的后部 back of the head：后～back of the head; also 脑勺子 nǎosháo·zi

【脑神经】nǎoshénjīng 在人体脑颅的底部，由延髓、脑桥、中脑、间脑等发出的神经，共有十二对。除迷走神经支配心脏和胃肠的活动外，其余都管颈部以上的知觉和运动。cranial nerves; the 12 pairs of nerves at the bottom of the human skull that are stemmed from the medulla oblongata, the pons, the mesocerebrum (midbrain) and the diencephalon (interbrain). With the exception of the pneumogastric nerves that control the heart, stomach and the intestines, the cranial nerves control the senses and movements of the organs above the neck.

【脑室】nǎoshì 脑的空腔，共分四个，四个脑室上下相通，内部充满脑脊液 brain ventricles; the four interconnected cavities in the brain that are filled with cerebrospinal fluid；(图见 ☞ figure for 脑 nǎo on p.1394)

【脑髓】nǎosuǐ 指脑 nǎo ① brains

【脑溢血】nǎoyìxuè 病，脑血管发生病变，血液流出管壁，使脑机能遭受破坏。血管硬化、血压突然上升等都能引起脑溢血。发病前有头痛、头晕、麻木、抽搐等症状。cerebral haemorrhage; pathological change oft. heralded by headache, dizziness, numbness, twitches, etc., and precipitated by vascular sclerosis or the sudden rise of blood pressure, causing blood to penetrate the walls of the cerebral blood vessels and thus damaging the functions of the brains

【脑汁】nǎozhī 费脑筋叫'绞脑汁' brains; oft. in the phrase: rack one's brais

【脑子】nǎo·zi ❶ 脑 nǎo ① ❷ 脑筋 brains; mind：他～好，又用功，学习成绩很好。He has a good brain and works hard — that's why he does so well in his studies.｜这个人太没～了，才几天的事儿就忘了。The man has such a

N

bad memory, he has forgot what happened only a few days ago.

瑙 nǎo ☞玛瑙 mǎnǎo on p. 1291

nào (ㄋㄠˋ)

闹(鬧) nào ❶ 喧哗;不安静 boisterous; cacophonous: 热～ be bustling with activity|～哄哄 chaotic|这里～得很,没法儿看书。It's so noisy here that I cannot concentrate on my reading. ❷ 吵;扰乱 make a noise; disturb: 又哭又～ make a tearful scene|两个人又～翻了。The two of them fell out once again. |孙悟空大～天宫 The Monkey King wreaks havoc in the Heavenly Palace. ❸ 发泄(感情)vent: ～情绪 throw a tantrum|～脾气 vent one's spleen ❹ 害(病);发生(灾害或不好的事) fall (ill); (sth. bad) happen: ～肚子 have loose bowels; suffer stomachache|～水灾(of a place) stricken by floods|～矛盾(between two persons) fall out|～笑话 make a laughing stock of oneself ❺ 干;弄;搞 be engaged in sth. : ～革命 carry out revolution; launch a revolution|～生产 go in for production|把问题～清楚 find out the truth about sth. ; get to the bottom of sth. ❻ 开玩笑;逗 tease; joke: 打～ frolic; rollick|～洞房 charivari in the bridal chamber

【闹别扭】nào biè·niu 彼此有意见而合不来;因不满意对方而故意为难 be difficult with sb. ; be at odds with sb. : 两个人常～。The couple are being difficult with each other again. |这不是成心跟我～吗? Isn't he making things difficult for me?

【闹场】nàochǎng 〈旧时 *old*〉指单纯用锣鼓演奏的音乐。过去农村演戏,在开演前用以吸引观众或在演出结束后用以送客。fanfare of gongs and drums heralding a theatrical performance in the country or seeing the audience off after it; also 开台锣鼓 kāi tái luó gǔ

【闹洞房】nào dòngfáng same as闹房 nàofáng

【闹肚子】nào dù·zi popular term of 腹泻 fùxiè

【闹房】nào//fáng 新婚的晚上,亲友们在新房里跟新婚夫妇说笑逗乐 (of well-wishers on a wedding night) charivari in the bridal chamber; also 闹新房 nào xīnfáng or 闹洞房 nào dòngfáng

【闹鬼】nào//guǐ ❶ 发生鬼怪作祟的事情 (迷信) (superstition) haunting of ghosts ❷〈比喻 *fig.*〉背地里做坏事;捣鬼 play tricks; hanky-panky

【闹哄】nào·hong 〈方 *dial.*〉 ❶ 吵闹;喧闹 clamour; raise a hullabaloo about sth. : 有意见你就提,～什么! Cut all the noise and speak up! |一下子,村前村后～开了。In no time the village was set abuzz. ❷ 许多人在一起忙着办事(of many people) bustle about: 大家～了好一阵子,才算把那堆土给平了。The crowd hustled and bustled for a while before they finally levelled off the earth mound.

【闹哄哄】nàohōnghōng (～的 nàohōnghōng·de)形容人声杂乱 tumultuous: 逢集的日子,大街上总是～的。The main street is always in a clamour whenever a rural fair is on.

【闹荒】nào//huāng 旧社会里农民遇到荒年时进行抗租、吃大户等活动(of peasants in old lean years) mount a riot in which they reject taxes and raid the rich and the powerful

【闹饥荒】nào jī·huang ❶ 指遭遇荒年 struck by famine: 从前我们那里三年两头～。Crop failures used to be commonplace in my home village. ❷〈方 *dial.*〉〈比喻 *fig.*〉经济困难 have trouble making ends meet; run short of money

【闹架】nào//jià 〈方 *dial.*〉吵嘴打架 kick up a row; brawl; altercation

【闹剧】nàojù ❶ 喜剧的一种,通过滑稽情节和热闹场面,来揭示剧中人物行为的矛盾,比一般喜剧更夸张 farce; genre of comedy; light humorous play dramatizing conflicts in human behaviour by means of hyperbole that is more intensified than in an ordinary comedy; also 趣剧 qùjù or 笑剧 xiàojù ❷〈比喻 *fig.*〉滑稽、荒谬的事情 sth. ludicrous; absurdity

【闹乱子】nào luàn·zi 惹祸;惹出麻烦 cause tumult; in for trouble: 骑快车容易～。You are in for trouble if you ride your bicycle too fast.

【闹脾气】nào pí·qi 发脾气;生气 flare up; throw a tantrum

【闹气】nào//qì 〈方 *dial.*〉(～儿 nào//qìr)跟人生气吵架 fall out with sb.

【闹情绪】nào qíngxù 因工作、学习等不合意而情绪不安定,表示不满 be unhappy; be discontented; in low spirits

【闹嚷嚷】nàorāngrāng (～的 nàorāngrāng·de)形容喧哗 noisy: 窗外～的,发生了什么事情? It's so noisy outside the window — what's it all about?

【闹热】nàorè 〈方 *dial.*〉same as 热闹 rè·nao

【闹市】nàoshì 繁华热闹的街市 busy, noisy street

【闹事】nào//shì 聚众捣乱,破坏社会秩序 instigate a mass riot; make trouble to disturb social order

【闹腾】nào·teng ❶ 吵闹;扰乱 kick up a racket: 又哭又喊,～了好一阵子。Crying and yelling, he went on like this for a while. ❷ 说笑打闹 make merry noisily: 屋里嘻嘻哈哈的～得挺欢。The roomful of people were having a good time talking and laughing. ❸ 搞 launch; put together; kick off: 这些副业是群众自发～起来的。These sideline occupations were launched by the folks spontaneously.

【闹天儿】nào// tiānr〈方 *dial.*〉天气不好(多指下雨或下雪) have too much rain or snow; come across a foul weather: 一连好几天都～, 好容易才遇见这么一个晴天儿。The sky cleared at long last, after so many days of rain.

【闹戏】nàoxì (～儿 nàoxìr)〈旧时 *old*〉称以丑角表演为主的戏曲, 通过引人发笑的人物和情节来讽刺社会的阴暗面 comic opera starring a clown and poking fun into the seamy side of society with amusing characters and plots

【闹笑话】nào xiào·hua (～儿 nào xiào·huar) 因粗心大意或缺乏知识经验而发生可笑的错误 make a laughing stock of oneself, due to carelessness, lack of experience or knowledge: 我刚到广州的时候, 因为不懂广州话, 常常～。People were laughing when I first arrived in Guangzhou, because I did not understand Cantonese.

【闹新房】nào xīnfáng same as 闹房 nàofáng

【闹玄虚】nào xuánxū 玩弄手段迷惑人 pull the wool over sb.'s eyes; to sound deliberately mysterious about sth.

【闹意见】nào yìjiàn 因意见不合而彼此不满 rift; breach in a friendly relationship caused by disagreement

【闹意气】nào yìqì 由于偏激情绪而闹矛盾; 意气用事 overreact to sth. not to one's liking: 开展批评和自我批评是为了增进团结, 不能～, 泄私愤。Carrying out criticism and self-criticism is meant to strengthen solidarity. Thus one must not overreact to criticism or vent personal grudge.

【闹灾】nàozāi 发生灾害 victimized by a disaster

【闹着玩儿】nào·zhe wánr ❶ 做游戏 frolic; play games ❷ 用言语或行动戏弄人 tease; make fun of sb. ❸ 用轻率的态度来对待人或事情 regard sth. important as being trifling; treat sb. or sth. in a frivolous manner: 你要是不会游泳, 就别到深的地方去游, 这可不是～的。Don't go to where the water is deep if you don't know how to swim, for this is no laughing matter.

【闹钟】nàozhōng 能够在预定时间发生铃声的钟 alarm clock

淖 nào〈书 *fml.*〉烂泥; 泥坑 mire: 泥～quagmire

【淖尔】nào'ěr 湖泊, 多用于地名 nur, meaning 'lake', used as part of a place name: 罗布～(罗布泊, 在新疆) Lop Nur, a lake in Xinjiang; also 罗布泊 luóbùpō | 达里～(达里泊, 在内蒙古) Dalai Nur, a lake in Inner Mongolia; also 达里泊 dálǐpō [蒙 Mongolian]

臑 nào ❶ 中医学指自肩至肘前侧靠近腋部的隆起的肌肉 biceps ❷ 古书上指牲畜的前肢 (in ancient books) forelimbs of a domestic animal

né (ㄋㄜˊ)

哪 né 哪吒(Né·zhā), 神话里神的名字 Nezha, a god in Chinese mythology

☞ nǎ on p. 1382 and ·na on p. 1385

nè (ㄋㄜˋ)

讷 nè〈书 *fml.*〉(说话)迟钝(of speech) slow: 木～falter (in saying sth.) | 口～stammer

【讷讷】nènè〈书 *fml.*〉形容说话迟钝 speak hesitantly: ～不出于口 speak under one's breath

那 nè '那'(nà)的口语音 variant pronunciation of 那 nà in oral Chinese

☞ 那[1] nà 注意 NOTE on p. 1383

呐 nè same as 讷

☞ nà on p. 1384, 哪·na on p. 1385 and 呢·ne on p. 1397

·ne (·ㄋㄜ)

呢(呐) ·ne〈助词 *aux.*〉❶ 用在疑问句(特指问、选择问、正反问)的末尾, 表示疑问的语气 [used at the end of a special, alternative, or rhetorical question to indicate a question]: 这个道理在哪儿～? What's the reason for all this? | 你学提琴～, 还是学钢琴～? Which do you want to learn, the violin or the piano? | 你们劳动力够不够～? Do you have enough labour force? | 人～? 都到哪儿去了? Where on earth is everybody? | 他们都有任务了, 我～? They have all got their assignments, where's mine? ❷ 用在陈述句的末尾, 表示确认事实, 使对方信服(含有指示而兼夸张的语气) [used at the end of a declarative sentence to reinforce the assertion or play up the effect of exaggeration]: 收获不小～。The harvest is not bad, is it? | 晚场电影八点才开～。The night show of the movie won't start until eight. | 远得很, 有两三千里地～。It's a long way to go, for the two places are about two or three thousand *li* apart. | 这个药灵得很～, 敷上就不疼。This ointment is rather effective — you'll not feel the pain any more once you have applied it. ❸ 用在陈述句的末尾, 表示动作或情况正在继续 [used at the end of a declarative sentence to indicate the continuation of an action or situation]: 她在井边打水～。She's fetching water from the well. | 别走了, 外面下着雨～。Don't go. It's still raining out there. | 老张, 门外有人找你～。Old Zhang, someone wants to see you. ❹ 用在句中表示停顿(多对举) [used to mark a pause in the middle of a sentence

(oft. meaning ‘one way or another’)]：如今～，可比往年强多了。The situation today is, well, a lot better than previous years. | 喜欢～，就买下；不喜欢～，就别买。If you like it, buy it; if you don’t, then don’t buy it.
☞ ní on p. 1404，呐 nà on p. 1384，哪·na on p. 1385 and nè on p. 1397

něi（ㄋㄟˇ）

哪(那) něi ‘哪’(nǎ)的口语音 a variant pronunciation of 哪 nǎ in oral Chinese；☞哪[1] nǎ 注意 NOTE on p. 1382

馁 něi〈书 *fml.*〉❶ 饥饿 hungry：冻～cold and hungry ❷ 失掉勇气 disheartened：气～crestfallen | 自～self-defeat ❸〈书 *fml.*〉(鱼)腐烂(of fish) putrid：鱼～肉败。Both fish and meat have gone bad.

nèi（ㄋㄟˋ）

内 nèi ❶ 里头；里头的(跟‘外’相对 as opposed to ‘out’)in；inside：～衣 underwear | ～部 interior | 室～indoors | 国～at home | 年～before the year-end ❷ 指妻或妻的亲属[referring to wife or wife’s relative]：～人 wife | ～侄 nephew；son of wife’s sister | ～弟(a husband’s) younger brother-in-law ❸ 指内心或内脏 heart；internal organ：～省 introspection | ～疚 twinge of guilt；compunction | 五～俱焚 stricken with grief and mortification ❹〈书 *fml.*〉指皇宫 imperial palace：大～residential quarters of the imperial palace
〈古 *arch.*〉same as 纳 nà

【内部】nèibù 某一范围以内 within：～联系 internal relations | ～消息 confidential information；inside story

【内场】nèichǎng 戏曲舞台桌子后面的区域(跟‘外场’相对 as opposed to ‘outer stage’)(in a theatre) inner stage；space behind a table onstage：～椅(设在舞台桌子后面的坐椅)chair behind a table onstage

【内臣】nèichén ❶ 宫廷的近臣 chamberlain ❷ 指宦官 eunuch

【内出血】nèichūxuè 出血的一种，流出血管的血液停留在身体内部而不排至体外，如脑出血、肾上腺出血、胰出血等 internal haemorrhage；bleeding inside the body，such as cerebral haemorrhage，adrenal haemorrhage，pancreas bleeding，etc.

【内地】nèidì 距离边疆(或沿海)较远的地区 hinterland；inland；area far from a country’s frontier (or coast)

【内弟】nèidì 妻子的弟弟 (husband’s) brother-in-law；wife’s younger brother

【内定】nèidìng 在内部决定(多指人事安排)decision (oft. regarding personnel arrangement) by authorities before public announcement：出场队员已经～。The starting lineup for the game has been decided prior to the game.

【内耳】nèi’ěr 耳朵最里面的一部分，是由复杂的管状物构成的，分为半规管、前庭和耳蜗三部分，主管听觉和身体的平衡 internal ear；inner ear；the portion of the ear including the semicircular canals，vestibule，and cochlea，and functioning to keep hearing and body in balance；also 迷路 mílù；☞半规管 bànguīguǎn on p. 53，前庭 qiántíng on p. 1535 and 耳蜗 ěrwō on p. 514 (图见 ☞ figure for 耳朵 ěr·duo on p. 512)

【内分泌】nèifēnmì 人或高等动物体内有些腺或器官能分泌激素，不通过导管，由血液带到全身，从而调节有机体的生长、发育和生理机能，这种分泌叫做内分泌 endocrine；internal secretion；hormones secreted by some organs and glands of humans and other higher animals，being transmitted directly，not via any ducts，to the entire body by blood to regulate the growth，maturity and physiological functions of the body

【内封】nèifēng same as 扉页 fēiyè

【内服】nèifú 把药吃下去(区别于‘外敷’as compared with ‘external administration’) oral administration；to be taken orally

【内阁】nèigé ❶ 某些国家中的最高行政机关，由内阁总理(或首相)和若干阁员(部长、总长、大臣或相)组成 cabinet，the supreme executive organ in some countries，consisting of a prime minister (or premier) and a number of cabinet members (ministers) ❷ 明清两代的中央政务机构 Grand Secretariat，central administrative organ during the Ming and Qing dynasties

【内功】nèigōng 锻炼身体内部器官的武术或气功(区别于‘外功’as compared with ‘external kung fu’) internal kung fu；exercises to benefit the internal organs in *wushu* or *qigong*

【内骨骼】nèigǔgé 人或高等动物体内的支架，是由许多块骨头和软骨组成的 endoskeleton；internal supporting skeleton in a human being or a higher animal，consisting of a number of bones and cartilages；(图见☞骨骼 figure for gǔgé on p. 693)

【内顾之忧】nèigù zhī yōu 在外对家事或国事的忧虑 internal distresses or troubles；trouble on the home front；family trouble：无～free from domestic worries

【内海】nèihǎi ❶ 除了有狭窄水道跟外海或大洋相通外，全部为陆地所包围的海，如地中海、波罗的海等 continental sea；sea surrounded by land and with or without a narrow river to link with an outer sea or ocean，such as the Mediterranean and the Baltic Sea；also 内陆海 nèilùhǎi ❷ 沿岸全属于一个国家因而本身也属于该国家的海，如渤海是我国的内海 inland sea; sea with its shoreline belonging entirely to a nation, such as the Bohai Sea of China

【内涵】nèihán ❶ 一个概念所反映的事物的本质属性的总和,也就是概念的内容。例如'人'这个概念的内涵是能制造工具并使用工具进行劳动的动物。intension; connotation; sum total of the essential properties of matter as reflected by a definition; content of a definition; For example, the connotation of the definition of 'man' is 'animal that can make and use tools to engage in physical labour'. ☞外延 wàiyán on p.1971 ❷ 内在的涵养 self-cultivation:他是个~很深厚的青年。He's a profoundly self-cultivated young man. *or* He is a typical case of smooth waters running deep.

【内行】nèiháng ❶ 对某种事情或工作有丰富的知识和经验 know the ropes; be knowledgeable about or experienced in an issue or certain work:他对养蜂养蚕都很~。He knows the ropes of apiculture and silkworm breeding. ❷ 内行的人 old hand; master; maestro:向~请教。Learn from the experts.

【内耗】nèihào ❶ 机器或其他装置本身所消耗的没有对外做功的能量 internal friction; energy wasted by the friction inside a machine or installation ❷〈比喻 *fig.*〉社会或部门内部因不协调、闹矛盾等造成的人力物力的无谓消耗 infight; waste of human or material resources due to disunity in an organization or a society

【内河】nèihé 处于一个国家之中的河流叫做该国家的内河 inland river; river situated within the territory of a country

【内讧】nèihòng 集团内部由于争权夺利等原因而发生冲突或战争 internecine strife; internal conflict or war precipitated by the scramble for power or interest; also 内哄 nèihòng

【内画】nèihuà 在以玛瑙、玻璃、水晶等为原料的透明或半透明器皿内壁绘制的图画。是我国独有的一门艺术。inside painting; unique Chinese art of painting on the insides of a transparent or translucent container made of agate, glass, crystal, etc.

【内踝】nèihuái 踝部内侧的突起部分,是由胫骨下端构成的 internal malleolus; medial malleolus, protrusion inboard the ankle, consisting of the lower end of the tibia

【内婚制】nèihūnzhì 原始社会的一种婚姻形式,部落内若干氏族互相通婚 (of the primitive society) intermarriage system; system whereby members of different clans in the same tribe are allowed to marry each other; also 族内婚 zúnèihūn

【内急】nèijí 指急着要解手 can't wait to go to the toilet

【内寄生】nèijìshēng 一种生物寄生在另一种生物的体内,叫做内寄生。如蛔虫寄生在人的肠子里。endoparasitism, the biological phenomenon of an organism living parasitically within another organism, such as the bellyworm living in a human body's guts

【内奸】nèijiān 暗藏在内部做破坏活动的敌对分子 mole; secret enemy agent:铲除~ferret out enemy agents

【内艰】nèijiān〈书 *fml.*〉母亲的丧事 mother's funeral:丁~during one's mother's funeral

【内景】nèijǐng 戏剧方面指舞台上的室内布景,电影、电视方面指摄影棚内的布景 indoor setting; indoor scene; stage setting of the interior of a house; interior setting of a film or TV studio

【内疚】nèijiù 内心感觉惭愧不安 feel the stab of conscience; remorse:~于心 have a guilty conscience

【内聚力】nèijùlì 同种物质内部相邻各部分间的吸引力 cohesion; mutual attraction to hold neighbouring elements within a matter together

【内眷】nèijuàn 指女眷 female family member

【内科】nèikē 医院中主要用药物而不用手术来治疗内脏疾病的一科 internal medicine; department of a hospital where ailing internal organs are treated mostly with medication rather than surgery

【内裤】nèikù 贴身穿的单裤 briefs; panties; underpants

【内涝】nèilào 由于雨量过多,地势低洼,积水不能及时排除而造成的涝灾 waterlogging; disaster caused by failure to divert excessive rainfall from a low lying place

【内里】nèilǐ〈方 *dial.*〉内部;内中 interior:这件事儿~还有不少曲折。There are still quite a few complications in this matter.

【内力】nèilì 指一个体系内各部分间的相互作用力。把宇宙看做一个体系,星体间的相互作用力就是内力;把原子看做一个体系,电子与原子核的相互作用力就是内力。internal force; reciprocal force between different parts in a system. For instance, interplanetary forces are regarded as the internal forces of the universe, and the mutual force between the electron and the nucleus may be seen as the internal force of the atom.

【内流河】nèiliúhé 不流入海洋而注入内陆湖或消失在沙漠里的河流,如我国的塔里木河 continental river; river that empties itself into an inland lake or disappears in a desert, such as the Tarim River of China; also 内陆河 nèilùhé

【内陆国】nèilùguó 周围与邻国土地毗连,没有海岸线的国家,如亚洲的蒙古,非洲的乌干达等国就是内陆国 landlocked country; country without a coastline, such as Mongolia of Asia and Uganda of Africa

【内陆湖】nèilùhú 在大陆内部不通海洋的湖,湖水含盐分和矿物质较多,如我国的青海湖 inland lake; lake that has no outlet to the sea and whose water has a high content of salt and minerals, such as the Qinghai Lake of China

【内乱】nèiluàn 指国内的叛乱或统治阶级内部的战争 civil strife; internecine disorder of the ruling class: 发生～be caught in a civil strife| 平定～quell an internecine war

【内幕】nèimù 外界不知道的内部情况(多指不好的 oft. scandalous) inside story: 揭开～uncover an inside story; let the cat out of the bag

【内难】nèinàn 国内的灾难或变乱 domestic turmoil or calamity

【内能】nèinéng 物体内部分子无规则运动产生的动能和分子间相对位置所决定的势能的总称 potential energy determined by the kinetic energy engendered in the irregular movement of molecules in an object and by the relative positions between the molecules

【内胚层】nèipēicéng 胚胎的内层。肠、胃、消化腺、肺等是由内胚层形成的。endoderm; the innermost layer of an embryo, where intestines, stomach, digestive gland, and lungs are formed; also 内胚叶 nèipēiyè; (图见 ☞ figure for 胚层 pēicéng on p.1452)

【内皮】nèipí 医学上指覆盖在血管、淋巴管、心脏等内部表面的上皮组织 endothelium; thin layer of epidermis tissue that lines blood vessel, lymphatic, heart, etc.

【内亲】nèiqīn 和妻子有亲属关系的亲戚的统称,如内兄、连襟等 in-laws of a man; wife's relatives

【内勤】nèiqín ❶ 部队以及有外勤工作的机关、企业称在内部进行的工作 (of the army, an organization or an enterprise) office work (as opposed to 'field work'): ～人员 office staff ❷ 从事内勤工作的人 office staff

【内倾】nèiqīng 指人性格沉静,说话含蓄,做事谨慎,不喜欢社交活动,比较关心内心世界 introvert; tendency to be quiet of character, reserved of words, and prudent of deeds, dislike socializing and direct one's thoughts and interests mostly toward oneself

【内情】nèiqíng 内部情况 inside story: 熟悉～be in the know; be an insider

【内燃机】nèiránjī 热机的一种,燃料在汽缸里燃烧,产生膨胀气体,推动活塞,由活塞带动连杆转动机轴。内燃机用汽油、柴油或煤气做燃料。internal-combustion engine; engine in which fuel petrol, diesel or gas is burned within the cylinder to produce compressed gas that propels the piston to move the crankshaft through a connecting rod

【内热】nèirè ❶〈书 *fml.*〉内心焦灼 internal heat ❷〈中医 *Chin. med.*〉指由阴虚或阳盛而导致的病理现象,患者有心烦、口渴、便秘、口舌生疮等症候 physiological disorder caused by insufficiency of body fluid or excessive vital energy, characterized by irritability, thirst, constipation; mouth ulceration, etc.

【内人】nèi·rén 对人称自己的妻子 my wife

【内容】nèiróng 事物内部所含的实质或存在的情况 content; essence; what is contained in sth.: 这次谈话的～牵涉的面很广。The conversation covered a wide range of topics. | 这个刊物～丰富。The magazine has got lots of stuff in it.

【内伤】nèishāng ❶〈中医 *Chin. med.*〉由饮食不适、过度劳累、忧虑或悲伤等原因引起的病症 physiological disorder caused by improper diet, fatigue, worry or sorrow ❷ 泛指由跌、碰、挤、压、踢、打等原因引起的气、血、脏腑、经络的损伤 internal injury; fracture or injury inflicted on vital energy, blood, viscera, arteries or veins by fall, concussion, crushing, pressure, kicking, strike, etc.

【内室】nèishì 里间,多指卧室 inner room; oft. bedroom

【内水】nèishuǐ 一个国家领陆范围以内的河流、湖泊和领海基线向陆一面的内海、海港、海湾、海峡内的水域 territorial waters; rivers, lakes on the territorial land of a country as well as the water surfaces of inland seas, harbours, bays and straits at the continental side of the baseline of the territorial seas

【内胎】nèitāi 轮胎的一部分,用薄橡胶制成,装在外胎里边,充气后产生弹性 inner tube, made of thin rubber, fixed inside a tyre, and inflated to acquire a springiness; 通称 popularly known as 里带 lǐdài

【内廷】nèitíng 帝王的住所 imperial residence

【内外】nèiwài ❶ 内部和外部;里面和外面 inside and out: ～有别 distinguish what's for domestic information from what's for publicity | 长城～north and south of the Great Wall; regions on both sides of the Great Wall ❷ 表示概数 approximately; about; around: 一个月～about a month's time| 五十岁～around 50 years old

【内外交困】nèi wài jiāo kùn 国内的政治经济等方面和对外关系方面都处于十分困难的地步 in dire straits at home and abroad; beset with internal political and economic troubles and difficult foreign relations

【内务】nèiwù ❶ 指国内事务(多指民政 oft. civil affairs) internal affairs: ～部 Ministry of Internal Affairs ❷ 集体生活室内的日常事务,如整理床铺、按规定放置衣物、做清洁卫生等 routine work, such as making bed and putting things in their proper places, to keep a dormitory, barracks, etc., clean and tidy

【内线】nèixiàn ❶ 安置在对方内部探听消息或进行其他活动的人,也指这种工作 undercover agent; sb. planted among the ranks of an enemy or adversary to spy or carry out other activities; spying of this nature ❷ 处在敌方包围形势下的作战线 interior front; front within an enemy-controlled area: ～作战 fight in the heart of an enemy-occupied area ❸ 一

个单位内的电话总机所控制的、只供内部用的线路 intercom; telephone lines controlled by the switchboard of an organization and for internal use only ❹ 指内部的关系或门路 clout; connection: 走~get sth. done through one's connection

【内详】nèixiáng 在信封上写'内详'或'名内详',代替发信人的姓名地址[in lieu of sender's name and address on an envelop] 'see inside'; 'name and address of sender enclosed'

【内向】nèixiàng ❶ 面向国内 home-oriented: ~型经济 domestic-oriented economy ❷(性格、思想感情等)深沉、不外露(of temperament) introverted; withdrawn: 小王性格~。Xiao Wang is somewhat introverted. | 他是~人,不轻易发表意见。He's a kind of withdrawn, and seldom speaks his mind.

【内销】nèixiāo 本国或本地区生产的商品在国内或本地区市场上销售(对'外销'而言 as opposed to 'export')(of commodities) domestic sale; for sale on the local market: ~商品 commodities for the home market | 出口转~sale export goods on the home market

【内斜视】nèixiéshì 病,一眼或两眼的瞳孔经常向中间倾斜 strabismus; cross-eye; disease that causes one or both eyes to turn inwards towards the nose; popularly known as 对眼 duìyǎn or 斗眼 dòuyǎn; ☞斜视 xiéshì on p. 2121

【内心】nèixīn ❶ 心里头 bottom of the heart; innermost world; soul: ~深处 in one's heart of hearts | 发自~的笑 a heartfelt smile ❷ 三角形三个内角的平分线相交于一点,这个点叫做三角形的内心。内心也是三角形内切圆的圆心。incentre; intersection of bisectors of the three internal angles of a triangle; also the center of the inscribed circle in a triangle

【内省】nèixǐng 在心里进行反省 introspect; self-search

【内兄】nèixiōng 妻子的哥哥 wife's elder brother; husband's elder brother-in-law

【内秀】nèixiù 外表似乎粗鲁或笨拙但实际上聪明而细心 great wisdom or aptitude camouflaged by clumsiness or crudity

【内衣】nèiyī 指衬衣、衬裤等贴身穿的衣服 underwear; undergarment

【内因】nèiyīn 事物发展变化的内部原因,即事物内部的矛盾性。内因是事物发展的根本原因。internal cause; cause for the development of something or the change in it; contradictory nature of things; Internal causes are the basic reason for the development of things.

【内应】nèiyìng ❶ 隐藏在对方内部做策应工作 collaborate from within the opponant's side with sb. from without: ~外合 strike from within and without ❷ 指做内应的人 planted agent; plant

【内忧】nèiyōu ❶ 内部的忧患,多指国家内部的不安定 domestic unrest: ~外患 domestic unrest and foreign invasion ❷〈书 *fml.*〉内心忧虑 anxiety ❸〈书 *fml.*〉指母丧 loss of one's mother in death

【内在】nèizài ❶ 事物本身所固有的(跟'外在'相对 as opposed to 'extrinsic') inherent; intrinsic: ~规律 inherent law | ~因素 intrinsic factor ❷ 存于内心,不表露在外面 innermost; inner: 感情~be introverted

【内脏】nèizàng 人或动物胸腔和腹腔内器官的统称。内脏包括心、肺、胃、肝、脾、肾、肠等。viscera; internal organs of a human being or an animal, such as the heart, lungs, stomach, liver, spleen, kidney, intestines, etc.

【内宅】nèizhái 指住宅内女眷的住处 inner chamber; house for female members of a family

【内债】nèizhài 国家向本国公民借的债 internal debt; domestic loan

【内掌柜】nèizhǎngguì 指'掌柜'的妻子 wife of a shopkeeper; also 内掌柜的 nèizhǎngguì·de

【内障】nèizhàng 主要发生在瞳孔和眼内的疾病,如白内障、青光眼等 diseases that affect the pupil and the eye, such as cataract, glaucoma, etc.

【内争】nèizhēng 内部斗争 infight

【内政】nèizhèng 国家内部的政治事务 internal affairs: 不干涉别国~non-interference in each other's internal affairs; refrain from interfering in the internal affairs of a foreign country

【内侄】nèizhí 妻子的弟兄的儿子 son of wife's brother; nephew

【内侄女】nèizhínǚ 妻子的弟兄的女儿 daughter of wife's brother

【内痔】nèizhì 肛门内部黏膜上长的痔疮 piles; internal haemorrhoids

【内中】nèizhōng 里头 inside; interior: ~情形非常复杂。The situation there is very complicated. | 你不晓得~的事。You know nothing about the inside story.

【内助】nèizhù〈书 *fml.*〉指妻子 wife: 贤~virtuous wife; one's better half

【内传】nèizhuàn ❶ 一种传记小说,以记载人物的遗闻逸事为主 biography based on the life and anecdotes of a person ❷〈古代 *arch.*〉指专门解释经义的书 ancient books on exegesis of classics

【内子】nèizǐ〈书 *fml.*〉内人 my wife

那 nèi '那'(nǎ)的口语音 another pronunciation of 那 nà in oral Chinese; ☞那[1] nà 注意 NOTE on p.1383

nèn(ㄋㄣˋ)

恁 nèn〈方 *dial.*〉❶ 那么;那样 so; such: ~大胆! How dare you! | ~有劲儿! So energetic! | 要不了～些（那么多）。Don't need so much. ❷ 那 that：～时 in those days | ～时节 at that time ❸ 这么；这样 this；like this：这几棵牡丹，正不知费了多少工夫，方培植得～茂盛。For these few peonies to flourish like this, who would tell how much work has been put into it.

☞ nín on p. 1417

【恁地】nèndì 〈方 *dial.*〉 ❶ 这么；那么 like that；in that way：不要～说。Don't put it that way. ❷ 怎么；如何 how；why：这人看着面熟，～想不起来？The man looks so familiar, but how come I can't remember who he is?

嫩 ❶ 初生而柔弱；娇嫩（跟'老'相对 as opposed to 'tough'）delicate；tender：～叶 tender leaves | ～芽 bud | 小孩儿肉皮儿～。Young kids have delicate skin. ◇小姑娘脸皮～，不肯表演。The young girl is too shy to give a performance. ❷ 指某些食物烹调时间短，容易咀嚼（跟'老'相对 as opposed to 'well done'）（of cooked food）rare；tender；underdone：这肉片炒得很～。The sauted sliced pork is very tender. ❸（某些颜色）浅（of colour）light；pale：～黄 light yellow | ～绿 pale green ❹ 阅历浅，不老练 callow；green；immature：他担任总指挥还嫌～了点儿。He is too inexperienced to be the general director.

【嫩红】nènhóng 像初开杏花那样的浅红色 apricot pink；colour of newly blooming apricot flowers

【嫩黄】nènhuáng 像韭黄那样的浅黄色 light yellow；colour of hotbed chives

【嫩绿】nènlǜ 像刚长出来的树叶那样的浅绿色 soft green；light green；colour of newly growing tree leaves

【嫩生】nèn·sheng 〈方 *dial.*〉 ❶ 嫩 very tender；very delicate：这韭菜真～，包饺子最好。The leek is so tender and fresh, it makes good stuffing for dumplings. ❷ 不成熟；不老练 unseasoned；unskilled：我侄子还～，您多照顾点儿。My nephew is still a greenhorn. Please be so kind as to take care of him for me.

néng（ㄋㄥˊ）

能 néng ❶ 能力；才干 gift；faculty；talent：技～know-how；skill | ～耐 ability | 无～之辈 featherbrains；ninnyhammer ❷ 度量物质运动的一种物理量，一般解释为物质做功的能力。能的基本类型有：势能、动能、热能、电能、磁能、光能、化学能和原子能等。一种能也可以转化成另一种能。能的单位和功的单位相同。energy；physical quantity for measuring movement of matter；capacity of matter or radiation to do work, in the following inter-convertible categories：potential energy, kinetic energy, heat energy, electric energy, magnetic energy, light energy, chemical energy, atomic energy, etc., all of which are measured with the same physical quantity as work；also 能量 néngliàng ❸ 有能力的 capable：～人 talent | ～手 crackajack | ～者多劳。Able person should do more. ❹ 能够 can；be able to：蜜蜂～酿蜜。Bees can make honey. | 咱们一定～完成任务。We can certainly fulfill the task. | 这本书什么时候～出版？When can this book be published? 注意 **NOTE**：

a）'能'表示具备某种能力或达到某种效率，'会'表示学得某种本领。初次学会某种动作用'会'，恢复某种能力用'能'。The word 能 néng is used to indicate possession of certain ability or capacity, whereas the word 会 huì is used to mean a skill that has just been learned. 会 huì is used for ability that has just been learned, while 能 néng is used for an ability that has just been recovered. 如 for instance：小弟弟会走路了。Your younger brother has just learned how to walk. | 他病好了，能下床了。Having just recovered from illness, he is up and about once again. 具备某种技能可以用'能'，也可以用'会'。Either 能 néng or 会 huì can be used for the possession of certain skill or ability. 如 for instance：能写会算 capable of writing and counting. 达到某种效率，用'能'，不用'会'。The word 能 néng is used instead of 会 huì for the attainment of efficiency in certain field. 如 for instance：她一分钟能打一百五十字。She's capable of typing 150 Chinese characters a minute. b）名词前面文言可以用'能'，白话只用'会'。In classical Chinese, a noun can be preceded by 能 néng；in vernacular, a noun can be preceded only by 会 huì. 如 for instance：能诗善画 well versed in both poetry and painting | 会英语 know how to read and write in English | 会象棋 know how to play Chinese chess c）跟'不…不'组成双重否定，'不能不'表示必须，'不会不'表示一定 used between 不…不 bù…bù to express negation of negation, such as 不能不 bùnéngbù, which indicates obligation, and 不会不 bùhuìbù, which indicates certainty or great probability. 如 for instance：你不能不来啊！On no account should you decline to come. | 他不会不来的。It's impossible he will not come. 在疑问或揣测的句子里都表示可能。Both 不能不 bùnéngbù and 不会不 bùhuìbù express possibility in a question. 如 for instance：他不能（会）不答应吧？He won't turn down the offer, will he? d）对于尚未实现的自然现象的推测，用'能（够）'，不用'可（以）'。The word 能（够）néng（gòu）is used instead of 可（以）when speculating on a natural phenomenon. 如 for instance: 这雨能下长么? Can it rain for a long time? e)用在跟某些动词结合表示被动的可能性时,用'可',不用'能'。The word 可 kě instead of 能 néng is used to combine with certain verbs to mean a passive possibility. 如 for instance: 我们是不可战胜的。We are invincible.

〈古 *arch.*〉 same as 耐 nài

【能动】néngdòng 自觉努力、积极活动的 self-motivated; active: 主观～性 self-motivation | ～地争取胜利 strive for victory by taking the initiative into one's own hands

【能干】nénggàn 有才能,会办事 gifted; talented: 她精明～,算得个女中豪杰。Smart and with great ability, she can be counted as an outstanding woman.

【能工巧匠】néng gōng qiǎo jiàng 工艺技术高明的人 skilled workers and talented artisans

【能够】nénggòu ❶ 表示具备某种能力,或达到某种程度 can; be able to: 人类～创造工具。Man can make tools. | 他～独立工作了。He has become capable of working on his own. ❷ 表示有条件或情理上许可 possible; probable: 下游～行驶轮船。The lower reaches are navigable for steamers. | 明天的晚会家属也～参加。Family members are welcome to tomorrow's party.

【能级】néngjí 原子、分子、原子核等在不同状态下运动所具有的能量值。这种数值是不连续的,好像台阶一样,所以叫能级。energy level, the inconsecutive, stair-like quantized energy of movement of atom, molecule and atomic nucleus under different circumstances

【能见度】néngjiàndù 物体能被正常目力看到的最大距离,也指物体在一定距离时被正常目力看到的清晰程度。能见度好坏通常是由空气中悬浮着的细微水珠、尘埃等的多少决定的。visibility, the maximum distance, or degree of clearness, in which objects are perceptible to the normal eyesight, depending on the quantity of particles of water, dust, etc. suspended in the air

【能力】nénglì 能胜任某项任务的主观条件 faculty; ability: ～强 have great ability | 他经验丰富,有～担当这项工作。He is experienced and has the ability to take on the job.

【能量】néngliàng ❶ 能 néng ② ❷〈比喻 *fig.*〉人显示出来的活动能力 ability; capacity: 别看人不多,～可不小。Despite their small number, they can really get a lot of things done.

【能耐】néng·nai 技能;本领 aptitude; ability: 他的～真不小,一个人能管这么多机器。He's great, attending to so many machines all by himself.

【能掐会算】néng qiā huì suàn 迷信的人指会掐诀算卦,泛指能推测事物的发展,预知未来(of superstition) be able to tell people's fortunes; be able to predict the course of events and the future

【能屈能伸】néng qū néng shēn 能弯曲也能伸展,指人在不得志的时候能忍耐,在得志的时候能施展才干、抱负 able to take failure or adversity when in straits and put one's talent to good use when in success; know when to eat humble pie and when to hold one's head high

【能人】néngrén 指在某方面有才能的人 talented person; man of ability: ～辈出。People of great ability come to the fore en masse.

【能事】néngshì 擅长的本领(常跟'尽'字配合 oft. used with 尽 jìn) knack; skill one is good at: ～已尽 having done all one can | 在会演中,各剧种百花齐放,极尽推陈出新之～。The variety show turned out to be a flourish of all opera genres, with no effort spared to weed through the old to bring forth the new.

【能手】néngshǒu 具有某种技能对某项工作、运动特别熟练的人 dab; crackajack: 织布～ skilled weaver | 射箭～ sharpshooting archer

【能说会道】néng shuō huì dào 指善于言辞,很会说话 have the gift of the gab; have a glib tongue

【能源】néngyuán 能产生能量的物质,如燃料、水力、风力等 energy resources, referring to fuel, hydraulic power, wind power, etc. that can produce energy

ńg(兀́)

嗯(唔) ńg 又 also ń〈叹词 *interj.*〉表示疑问[indicating questioning]: ～? 你说什么? Eh, what did you say? | ～? 这是什么字? What, what does this word mean?

☞ 唔 wú on p. 2028

ňg(兀ˇ)

嗯(呒) ňg 又 also ň〈叹词 *interj.*〉表示出乎意外或不以为然[indicating surprise or disapproval]: ～! 钢笔怎么又不出水啦? Oh no, why doesn't my fountain pen work once again? | ～! 你怎么还没去? Hey, haven't you gone yet?

ǹg(兀̀)

嗯(叽) ǹg 又 also ǹ〈叹词 *interj.*〉表示答应[indicating a reply] yea: 他～了一声,就走了。He muttered an 'Uh-huh', and disappeared in no time.

nī(ㄋ丨)

妮 nī [妮子](nī·zi)〈方 *dial.*〉女孩儿 girlie; also 妮儿 nīr

N

ní（ㄋㄧˊ）

尼 ní 尼姑 nun：～庵 nunnery｜僧～Buddhist nun

【尼格罗—澳大利亚人种】Nígéluó-Àodàlìyà rénzhǒng 世界三大人种之一，体质特征是皮肤黑，嘴唇厚，鼻子扁宽，头发鬈曲，主要分布在非洲、大洋洲、印度南部、斯里兰卡等地 semi-transliteration of Negroid-Australian, one of three major races of humanity, characterized by black pigmentation, thick lips, broad, flat noses and curly hair, inhabiting mainly Africa, the Oceania, south India and Sri Lanka; also 黑种 hēizhǒng

【尼姑】nígū 出家修行的女佛教徒 nun, esp. Buddhist nun, woman under vows of cultivating oneself according to Buddhist doctrines

【尼古丁】nígǔdīng 烟碱 nicotine

【尼龙】nílóng 分子中含有酰胺键的树脂，也指由这种树脂做成的塑料，种类很多。耐磨、耐油性强、不易吸收水分。可制轴承、齿轮、滑轮、输油管等机件，也可做日用品。这种树脂制成的纤维旧称尼龙，现在叫做锦纶。nylon, resin containing acylamino in its molecules; any variety of plastic made of it that stands tear and wear, is highly resistant to oil, has little absorbency and makes an ideal material for the making of bearings, gear wheels, chain wheels, oil pipelines, as well as articles for daily use. The fibre made of this material was known as 尼龙 nílóng before, but it is known today as 锦纶 jǐnlún.

坭 ní ❶ 同'泥'，用于'红毛坭' same as 泥, as in the term 红毛坭 hóngmáoní ❷ 地名用字，如白坭（在广东）*ni*, a Chinese character for use in place names, such as Baini, a place in Guangdong Province

呢 ní 呢子 woollen fabric：毛～woollen fabrics｜厚～大衣 heavy woolen overcoat｜～绒哔叽 serge; beige

☞ ·ne on p. 1398

【呢喃】nínán ❶ 形容燕子的叫声（of swallows）tweet; chirp ❷〈书 *fml.*〉形容小声说话 mumble：～细语 speak in a soft voice

【呢绒】níróng 毛织品的统称。泛指用兽毛或人造毛等原料织成的各种织物。woollen fabrics; textile goods made from wool or synthetic fibre

【呢子】ní·zi 一种较厚较密的毛织品，多用来做制服、大衣等 thick, closely-woven woollen fabric, oft. used to make uniforms or overcoats, etc.

兒[1]（郳）Ní 周朝国名，在今山东滕州东南 Ni, name of a state during the Zhou Dynasty to the southeast of present-day Tengzhou, Shandong Province

兒[2] Ní 姓 a surname; same as 倪 ní

☞ 儿 ér on p. 509

泥 ní ❶ 含水的半固体状的土 semi-solid mud; wet, soft earth：～坑 quagmire; muddy pit｜烂～sodden mud ❷ 半固体状的像泥的东西 sth. that looks like semi-solid mud：印～ink paste｜枣～jujube jam｜蒜～mashed garlics

☞ nì on p. 1406

【泥巴】níbā〈方 *dial.*〉泥 clay; dirt

【泥肥】níféi 用做肥料的淤泥，肥效持久，可以做基肥 sludge, a manure with lasting fertility that may be used as base fertilizer

【泥工】nígōng〈方 *dial.*〉same as 瓦工 wǎgōng

【泥垢】nígòu 泥和污垢 dirt; grime：满脸～dirty face; grime-smeared face

【泥浆】níjiāng 黏土和水混合成的半流体，通常指泥土和水混合成的半流体 slurry; mud, a semi-fluid mixture of clay and water

【泥金】níjīn 一种用金属粉末制成的颜料，用来涂饰笺纸，或调和在油漆里涂饰器物 powdered golden metal that serves as a paint for stationery; powdered golden metal mixed in lacquer to be used as a coating material

【泥坑】níkēng 烂泥淤积的低洼地。也用于比喻。mud pit; quagmire;（fig.）predicament

【泥淖】nínào 烂泥；泥坑（也用于比喻 also used figuratively）morass; mire

【泥泞】nínìng ❶ 因有烂泥而不好走 muddy：雨后道路～。After the rain the road became muddy and slippery. ❷ 淤积的烂泥 mire; mud：陷入～get stuck in the mire; be quagmired

【泥牛入海】ní niú rù hǎi〈比喻 *fig.*〉一去不复返 like a clay oxen entering the sea — never to be heard from; gone forever

【泥鳅】ní·qiū 鱼，身体圆柱形，尾端侧扁，鳞小，有黏液，背部黑色，有斑点，腹面白色或灰色。头小而尖，嘴有须5对。常生活在河湖、池沼、水田等处，潜伏泥中。loach（*Misgurnus anguillicaudatus*）; small edible fish having slippery cylindrical body, flat tail, tiny scales, black and flecked back and white or gray belly, pointed small head, and five pairs of feelers on the mouth, inhabiting in the mire of rivers, lakes, ponds, paddy fields, etc.

【泥人】nírén（～儿 nírénr）用黏土捏成的人的形象 clay figurine

【泥沙俱下】ní shā jù xià 泥土和沙子都跟着流下来 sand and mud being washed down together;〈比喻 *fig.*〉好坏不同的人或事物混杂在一起 mingling of good and bad; people of all descriptions

【泥石流】níshíliú 山坡上大量泥沙、石块等经山洪冲击而形成的短暂的急流。泥石流对建筑物、公路、铁路、农田等有很大破坏作用。landslide; mud-rock flow; brief, rapid flow of mud, sand and rocks caused by mountain flood, which is highly destructive to buildings, roads, railways, and farmland

【泥水匠】níshuǐjiàng 泥瓦匠 bricklayer; tiler; plasterer

【泥塑】nísù 民间工艺,用黏土捏成各种人物形象 clay sculpture, usu. in the image of human beings, a form of folk art

【泥塑木雕】ní sù mù diāo ☞木雕泥塑 mù diāo ní sù on p. 1374

【泥胎】nítāi 尚未用金粉(或金箔)、颜料装饰过的泥塑的偶像 clay figurine, usu. the statue of an idol, before being decorated with gold powder (or gold foil) and pigments

【泥胎儿】nítāir 没有经过烧制的陶器坯子 unfired earthenware

【泥潭】nítán same as 泥坑 níkēng

【泥炭】nítàn 煤的一种,炭化程度最低,像泥土,黑色、褐色或棕色,是古代埋藏在地下、未完全腐烂分解的植物体。农业上可做有机肥料,工业上用来制煤气、水煤气、甲醇等,也可用做燃料。peat; clay-like sort of coal with the lowest degree of carbonization, black, ochre or brown in colour, resulting from partially decomposed plants buried underground since remote antiquity, used in farming as an organic fertilizer, and in industry for the making of coal gas, water gas, methanol, or as a fuel; also 泥煤 níméi

【泥塘】nítáng 烂泥淤积的洼地 bog; morass

【泥土】nítǔ ❶ same as 土壤 tǔrǎng ❷ same as 黏土 niántǔ

【泥腿】nítuǐ 〈旧时 *old*〉对农民的轻蔑称呼。也说泥腿子。country bumpkin; hillbilly; also 泥腿子 nítuǐ·zi

【泥瓦匠】níwǎjiàng 做砌砖、盖瓦等工作的建筑工人 bricklayer; tiler; also 泥水匠 níshuǐjiàng

【泥岩】níyán 一种黏土岩,厚而不分层,较黏土结实 mudstone; clay rock, thick and without laminations, sturdier than clay

【泥雨】níyǔ 水滴中含有大量尘土微粒的雨 dusty rain; rain that carries a large quantity of dust

【泥沼】nízhǎo 烂泥坑(也用于比喻)swamp; slough (also for figurative use)

【泥足巨人】nízú jùrén 〈比喻 *fig.*〉实际非常虚弱的庞然大物 colossus with feet of clay; sth. that is mammoth and frightening in size but weak in essence

怩 ní ☞忸怩 niǔní on p. 1422

铌 ní 金属元素,符号 Nb (niobium)。灰白色,质硬,有超导性,用来制耐高温合金、电子管等。niobium (Nb); greyish white hard metal element with superconducting property, employed as a material for the making of high temperature-resisting alloys, electronic tubes, etc.

倪 ní ❶ ☞端倪 duānní on p. 484 ❷ (Ní) 姓 a surname

猊 ní ☞狻猊 suānní on p. 1834

婗 ní ☞婴婗 yīní on p. 2260

輗 ní 〈古代 *arch.*〉大车辕端与横木相接的关键 joint of the axle with the crossbar of a carriage

蜺 ní 〈书 *fml.*〉❶ 寒蝉 cicada in cold weather ❷ same as 霓 ní

霓(蜺) ní 大气中有时跟虹同时出现的一种光的现象。形成的原因和虹相同,只是光线在水珠中的反射比形成虹时多了一次,彩带排列的顺序和虹相反,红色在内,紫色在外。颜色比虹淡。secondary rainbow, a phenomenon of light that occurs simultaneously with, and for the same reason as, a primary rainbow, but different from the latter in that sunlight is reflected on water drops for one more time, that the colour sequence is reversed, with red on the inside and violet on the outside, and that it is considerably less intense; also 副虹 fùhóng; ☞虹 hóng on p. 806

【霓虹灯】níhóngdēng 灯的一种,在真空玻璃管里充入氖或氩等惰性气体,两端安装电极,通电后发出红、蓝等颜色的光。多用做广告灯或信号灯。neon; neon light, electrical lamp in the form of a vacuum glass tube filled with such inert gas as neon and argon and fixed with an electrode on either end so that it emits light red, blue or in other colours when electricity is switched on, used mostly for advertisement and signaling

齯 ní 〈书 *fml.*〉老年人牙齿落尽后重生的细齿,古时作为长寿的象征 tiny tooth newly grown in a toothless old person, considered in old times as a sign of longevity

鲵 ní 大鲵、小鲵的统称 salamander (*Megalobatrachus davidianus*) or (*Hynobius chinensis*)

麑 ní 古书上指小鹿(in ancient books) young deer

nǐ (ㄋㄧˇ)

拟(擬) nǐ ❶ 设计;起草 drift: ～了一个计划草案 draft a plan ❷ 打算;想要 plan; be going to: ～于明天起程 has planed to start the journey tomorrow ❸ 模仿 imitate: ～态 simulation | 模～ mock ❹ 相比 collate: 比～ draw a parallel | ～于不伦 draw an ill-fitted parallel ❺ 猜测;假设 surmise; infer: 虚～ hypothetical; unreal

【拟订】nǐdìng same as 草拟 cǎonǐ: ～计划 map out a draft plan | ～方案 work out the ways and means for

N

【拟定】nǐdìng ❶ 起草制定 formulate：～远景规划 formulate a long-term plan ❷ 揣测断定 assume; surmise

【拟稿】nǐ//gǎo（～儿 nǐ//gǎor）起草稿子（多指公文 oft. a document）draft：校长亲自～呈报上级。The principal personally drafted the document and submitted it to the higherup.｜秘书拟了一个稿儿。The secretary made a draft.

【拟古】nǐgǔ 模仿古代的风格、艺术形式 imitate an ancient style or ancient forms of art：～之作 imitation of classical work

【拟人】nǐrén 修辞方式，把事物人格化。例如童话里的动物能说话。personify; a figure of speech to endow inanimate objects with human qualities, such as animals in a fairy tale that can talk

【拟态】nǐtài 某些动物的形态、斑纹，颜色等跟另外一种动物、植物或周围自然界的物体相似，借以保护自身，免受侵害的现象。在昆虫中拟态最多，如木叶蝶的外形像枯叶，竹节虫的身体像竹节。mimicry, the resemblance in form, colour or skin pattern of an animal to another animal or plant or the natural environment it finds itself in, as an aid in concealment or self-protection, a phenomenon most common among insects, such as the *Kallima chinensis* assuming the appearance of a withered leaf and a stick insect looking like a bamboo stalk

【拟议】nǐyì ❶ 事先的考虑 consideration before doing sth.：事实证明了他的～是完全正确的。Facts indicate that his proposal is a correct one. ❷ same as 草拟 cǎonǐ：小组一致通过了他所～的学习计划。The group unanimously endorsed the study plan he had drafted.

【拟音】nǐyīn 影视片制作、戏曲表演中模拟自然界和社会生活中的各种音响效果，如雷声、马蹄声等（of cinematography, theatrical performance, etc.）sound effect; acoustic result in imitating sounds in nature or life, such as thunder and the sound of horse hoofs

【拟于不伦】nǐ yú bù lún 拿不能相比的人或事物来比方 draw inapt parallels

【拟作】nǐzuò 模仿别人的风格或假托别人的口吻而写的作品 piece of writing patterned after a certain author or in imitation of sb. else's style

你 nǐ〈代词 *pron.*〉❶ 称对方（一个人）you; singular 注意 **NOTE**：有时也用来指称'你们' also used plurally sometimes, such as：～校 your school｜～局 your bureau｜～军 your army ❷ 泛指任何人 everyone; anyone（有时实际上指我 sometimes referring to the spearker）：他的才学叫～不得不佩服。You cannot but admire him for his talent and scholarship.｜这孩子要我给他买手风琴，一天三番五次地老跟～在这个问题上兜圈子。The child wants me to buy him an accordion, and he keeps pestering me about it on a daily basis. 注意 **NOTE**：'你'跟'我'或'他'配合，表示'这个…'和'那个…'的意思。When used correlatively with 我 wǒ or 他 tā, the pair thus formed means 'each other', 'one another', or 'one after another.'：三个人～看看我，我看看～，谁也没说话。The three of them kept looking at each other without saying a word.｜～一条，他一条，一共提出了五六十条建议。With everybody making his or her contributions, they put together a total of fifty or sixty proposals.

【你们】nǐ·men〈代词 *pron.*〉称不止一个人的对方或包括对方在内的若干人［second person plural］you：～歇一会儿，让我们接着干。Why don't you take a break and let us keep on with the job?｜～几个谁年龄大？Who of you is the oldest?

【你死我活】nǐ sǐ wǒ huó 形容斗争非常激烈（of a fight）life-and-death; fierce

旎 nǐ［旖旎］（yǐnǐ）on p. 2270

儗 nǐ〈书 *fml.*〉same as 拟 nǐ

薿 nǐ［薿薿］〈书 *fml.*〉形容茂盛 dense; exuberant：黍稷～lush green crops

nì（ㄋㄧˋ）

伲 nì〈方 *dial.*〉我；我们 I; we

泥 nì ❶ 用土、灰等涂抹墙壁或器物 plaster (a wall, object, etc.)：～墙 cover the wall with stucco｜把炉子～一～ fix a stove with mortar｜窗户玻璃的四周都用油灰～上 seal up the seams of the glass panes of a window with putty ❷ 固执 obdurate; mulish：拘～be dogmatic｜～古 stick to old tradition
☞ní on p. 1404

【泥古】nìgǔ 拘泥古代的制度或说法，不知结合具体情况加以变通 be bigoted to old ways; inflexible：～不化 be ossified in one's way of thinking

【泥子】nì·zi 油漆木器或铁器时为了使表面平整而涂抹的泥状物，通常用桐油、石膏、松香等制成 putty; dough-like cement made by mixing tung oil with gypsum, rosin, etc., to be used as a finishing coat on woodwork or iron objects; also 腻子 nì·zi

昵（暱） nì 亲热 intimate：亲～be intimate with sb.

【昵称】nìchēng 表示亲昵的称呼 term of endearment; pet name

逆 nì ❶ 向着相反的方向（跟'顺'相对 as opposed to 'for'）against; contrary; inverse：～风 in the teeth of the wind｜～流

counter-current | ～定理 converse theorem | 倒行～施 go against the historical trend; try to turn the clock back ❷ 抵触;不顺从 disobey; defy: 忤～unfilial | ～耳(of a remark) jar on the ear; unpleasant to the ear | 顺者昌,～者亡。Those who submit prosper, and those who resist are doomed. ❸ 不顺当 adverse: ～境 in the face of adversity ❹ 背叛者 rebel: 叛～turn traitor | ～产 breech delivery ❺ 〈书 *fml*.〉迎接 greet; meet: ～旅 hotel; inn | ～战 rise to the challenge of an adversary. ❻ 事先 in advance: ～料 prognosticate | ～知 know sth. before it happens

【逆差】nìchā 对外贸易上输入超过输出的贸易差额(跟'顺差'相对 as opposed to 'surplus') (in foreign trade) deficit; unfavourable balance in payment

【逆产】[1] nìchǎn 背叛国家民族的人的财产 national traitor's property: 抄没～confiscate the property of a traitor

【逆产】[2] nìchǎn (妇女)生产时胎儿的脚先出来 breech delivery; delivery of a fetus with the feet appearing first; also 倒产 dàochǎn

【逆定理】nìdìnglǐ 将某一定理的条件和结论互换所得的定理就是原来定理的逆定理。如:'在一个三角形中,如果两条边相等,它们所对的角也相等',它的逆定理是'在一个三角形中,如果两个角相等,则它们所对的边也相等'。converse theorem; the theorem derived by crossing over the condition and conclusion of a certain theorem, for instance, the converse theorem of the theorem that 'if a triangle has two sides of equal length, the angles opposite them are equal too' is that 'if a triangle has two angles that are equal, then the sides opposite them are of equal length as well'

【逆耳】nì'ěr (某些尖锐中肯的话)听起来使人感到不舒服(of a poignant but to-the-point remark) unpleasant to the ear; grate on the ear: 忠言～good advice jars on the ear | ～之言 advice unpleasant to hear

【逆反】nìfǎn 一种心理现象,对事情所作的反应跟当事人的意愿或多数人的反应完全相反。如有的人的逆反心理表现为别人都反对的事,他偏要赞成;越是不希望他做的事,他越是要做。rebellious behaviour; a psychological phenomenon in which one's reaction to what has happened goes against the will of the party involved or the reaction of the majority of people. One manifestation of the rebellious behaviour is to support sth. that everybody else is opposed to, or do sth. everybody else does not want him or her to do.

【逆反应】nìfǎnyìng 通常指向反应物方向进行的化学反应 counter-reaction; chemical reaction that occurs in the direction of the reactant

【逆风】nì//fēng 迎面对着风 go against the wind: 扬场时不要站在～的位置。When winnowing make sure you do not stand against the wind.

【逆风】nìfēng 跟行进方向相反的风 head wind; contrary wind: 遇上了～,船就走不快了。We are caught in the head wind — that's why the boat isn't moving fast.

【逆光】nìguāng 摄影时利用光线的一种方法。光线从被摄物体的背后(即对着摄影机镜头)而来,运用逆光对勾画物体轮廓和表现透明的或毛茸茸的物体,效果较好。(of photography) backlight; backlighting; use of illumination from behind the object (i.e. going direct against the) camera lens to set off its contours or its quality of transparency or downiness

【逆境】nìjìng 不顺利的境遇 adverse circumstances; adversity: 身处～be caught in adversity

【逆来顺受】nì lái shùn shòu 对恶劣的环境或无理的待遇采取忍受的态度 resign oneself to adversity or unreasonable treatment; take a humiliation lying down

【逆料】nìliào same as 预料 yùliào: 事态的发展不难～。The course of event is foreseeable.

【逆流】nìliú ❶ 逆着水流方向 go against the current: ～而上 sail upstream ❷ 跟主流方向相反的水流 countercurrent; 〈比喻 *fig*.〉反动的潮流 reactionary trend; do sth. that flies in the face of public will

【逆旅】nìlǚ 〈书 *fml*.〉旅馆 inn; hotel

【逆水】nì//shuǐ (行进的方向)跟水流方向相反(跟'顺水'相对 as opposed to 'sail downstream') go against the current; sail upstream

【逆水行舟】nì shuǐ xíng zhōu 谚语:'逆水行舟,不进则退。'As the old Chinese proverb goes, 'A boat sailing up the river must forge ahead or it will be driven back.' 〈比喻 *fig*.〉学习或做事就好像逆水行船,不努力就要退步 either you study hard or work hard, or you allow yourself to lag behind

【逆向】nìxiàng 反着原来的或规定的方向 opposite direction: ～行驶 drive in the opposite direction; drive in a direction not allowed by traffic rules

【逆行】nìxíng (车辆等)反着规定的方向走(of vehicles, etc.) go in the wrong direction: 单行线,车辆不得～。One-way lane. No reverse traffic.

【逆序】nìxù 排列的次序跟通常的相反 backward sequence: ～编排 inverted layout | ～词典 reverse dictionary; also 倒序 dàoxù

【逆运算】nìyùnsuàn 在一个等式中,用相反的运算方法,从得数求出原式中某一个数的方法。如在 2+4=6 的等式中,可以用减号由得数 6 求出该式中的加数 2 或加数 4。inversion operation; reciprocal operation; the use of an inverted method in an equation to derive a certain number from the solution. For example, in the equation 2+4=6, a

N

subtraction sign may be employed to derive the addend 2 or 4 from the solution 6.

【逆转】nìzhuǎn 向相反的方向或坏的方面转变；倒转 reverse; go from bad to worse; worsen：局势～deterioration in the situation|自然规律不可～。The law of nature can never be reversed.

【逆子】nìzǐ 忤逆不孝的儿子 unfilial son

匿 nì 隐藏；不让人知道 take cover; conceal：隐～ hole up; lie low|～名 incognito; anonymous|～居深山 live a hermit's life in the mountains|～影藏形 conceal one's identity

【匿藏】nìcáng 隐藏；藏匿 hide; go into hiding：～逃犯 shield a fugitive|～枪支弹药 illegal possession of arms and ammunition

【匿迹】nìjì 躲藏起来，不露形迹 disappear; go into hiding：销声～disappear into nowhere; hide from the scene|～海外 go into hiding in a foreign country

【匿名】nìmíng 不具名或不写真实姓名 anonymous：～信 anonymous letter

【匿名信】nìmíngxìn 不具名或不写真实姓名的信，多是为了达到攻讦、恐吓、欺骗等目的而写的 anonymous letter; letter that is signed with an unreal name or not signed at all, oft. for such purposes as attacking, intimidating and cheating

【匿影藏形】nì yǐng cáng xíng 隐藏形迹，不露真相 lie low; conceal one's identity; also 匿影潜形 nì yǐng qián xíng

埿 nì［坤埿］(pìnì) on p. 1469

惄 nì〈书 *fml*.〉忧思 be ill at ease; perturbed

睨 nì〈书 *fml*.〉斜着眼睛看 look askance：睥～cast a sidelong glance at|～视 look out of the corner of one's eye

腻 nì ❶ 食品中油脂过多，使人不想吃 so greasy or fatty as to spoil one's appetite：油～oily|炖肉有点～。The stew is a bit too greasy.|肥肉～人。Fatty meat makes one sick. ❷ 腻烦；厌烦 be bored with; loathe：～得慌 be bored to death|他那些话我都听～了。I'm really tired of listening to his rehashed remarks. ❸ 细致 fastidious：细～ be meticulous or particular to the minute detail; fine and smooth ❹ 黏 grimy：油振布沾手很～。A begrimed dish towel feels sticky to the touch. ◇～友 close friend ❺ 污垢 filth; grime：尘～dirt|垢～accumulated dust

【腻烦】nì·fan ❶ 因次数过多或时间过长而感觉厌烦 be fed up with：老哼这个小曲儿你不觉得～吗？Aren't you tired of always humming that tune?|等了半天还不见人来，他心里有点儿～了。He got impatient after waiting for him in vain for so long. ❷ 厌恶 repugnant; loathesome：他那身打扮，真叫人～。His attire looks disgusting.

【腻歪】nì·wai〈方 *dial*.〉same as 腻烦 nì·fan

【腻味】nì·wei〈方 *dial*.〉same as 腻烦 nì·fan

【腻友】nìyǒu〈书 *fml*.〉亲密的朋友 bosom friend

【腻子】nì·zi same as 泥子 nì·zi

溺 nì ❶ 淹没在水里 drowned; inundated：～死 die from drowning; drowned ❷ 沉迷不悟，过分 obsessed; unduly：～信 be obsessed with; be possessed by|～爱 undue love

☞ niào on p. 1415

【溺爱】nì'ài 过分宠爱（自己的孩子）pamper; dote; spoil (one's children)

【溺水】nìshuǐ 淹没在水里 drowning：～身亡 die from drowning; be drowned

【溺婴】nìyīng 把刚生下来的婴儿淹死叫溺婴 infanticide by drowning

榐 nì［榐木］(nìmù) 八角枫 alangium tree (*Alangium chinense*)

蠠（䘌） nì〈中医 *Chin. med*.〉指虫咬的病 disease caused by insect bite; ☞阴蠠 yīnnì on p. 2284

niān（ㄋㄧㄢ）

拈 niān 用两三个手指头夹取（东西）；捏 nip; grasp sth. with two or three fingers; pinch：～阄儿 draw lots|～弓搭箭 draw one's bow and set an arrow on its string|从罐子里～出一块糖 take a piece of candy from the jar ◇～轻怕重 be picky about one's job; prefer the light to the heavy

【拈花惹草】niān huā rě cǎo 指男子乱搞男女关系或狎妓 womanize; fool around with women; frequent brothels; also 惹草拈花 rě cǎo niān huā

【拈阄儿】niān//jiūr same as 抓阄儿 zhuā//jiūr

【拈轻怕重】niān qīng pà zhòng 接受工作时挑拣轻易的，害怕繁重的 be picky about one's job; favour the light over the heavy

【拈香】niānxiāng 信神佛的人到庙里烧香 worship the Buddha by burning incense sticks in a temple

蔫 niān ❶ 花木、水果等因失去所含的水分而萎缩 (of flowers, plants, fruits, etc.) wilt; wizen; desiccate：常浇水，别让花儿～了。You've got to water the flowers from time to time to prevent them from withering.|苹果搁～了，皱皱巴巴的。See all the wrinkles — the apples have shriveled up. ❷ 精神不振 depressed; in low spirit：孩子有些～，像是生病了。The boy hasn't been himself today. Perhaps he's ill. ❸〈方 *dial*.〉(性子)慢；不爽利 (of one's disposition) slow; dawdling：～性子 of an unhurried temperament|别看他人～，却很有主见。He is a man of ideas despite his sluggish ways.

【蔫不唧】niān·bujī〈方 *dial*.〉（～儿的 niān·

bujīr·de) ❶ 形容人情绪低落、精神不振的样子(of a person) lackadaisical; sluggish; droopy:他这两天老那么～的，是不是哪儿不舒服了？He's been so droopy the last couple of days. Is he not feeling well? ❷ 不声不响；悄悄 dumb; quiet:我还想跟他说话，没想到他～地走了。I had got something to say to him, but he left without so much as saying goodbye to me.

【蔫呼呼】niānhūhū (～的 niānhūhū·de)形容人性子慢，做事不干脆利索(of temperament) slow and hesitant

【蔫儿坏】niānrhuài 指人惯于暗中使坏(of a person) sneaky; crafty; secretive:这个人～，你要留神。The guy is a kind of sneaky, so you've got to be careful.

【蔫头耷脑】niān tóu dā nǎo (～的 niān tóu dā nǎo·de)形容耷拉着脑袋，没精打采的样子 downcast; miserable; droopy:他干了一天的活，累得～的，连句话也不愿意说。He was so exhausted from the day's work that he did not even want to say a word.◇地里的茄秧被晒得～的。The eggplant seedlings have shriveled up under the sun.

nián (ㄋㄧㄢˊ)

年(秊) nián ❶ 时间的单位，公历1年是地球绕太阳一周的时间，平年365日，闰年366日，每4年有1个闰年 year (according to the Gregorian calendar, a year equals the time the earth takes to move a full cycle around the sun, and there are 365 days in a common year and 366 days in a leap year, which occurs once in every four years:今～ this year|去～last year|三～五载 in a few years' time 注意 **NOTE**:前边直接加数词，不用量词。A numeral is added directly before the character 年 nián and a classifier is not necessary. ❷ 每年的 yearly; annual:～会 annual meeting|～鉴 almanac|～产量 annual output ❸ 岁数 age:～纪 age|～龄 age|忘～交 close friends who are very different in age; friendship between old and young persons|益寿延～prolong one's life ❹ 一生中按年龄划分的阶段 age; stage in one's life:童～childhood|幼～infancy|少～teenage|青～youth|中～middle age|老～old age ❺ 时期；时代 age; times:近～recent years|明朝末～towards the end of the Ming Dynasty|光绪～间 during the reign of Emperor Guangxu of the Qing Dynasty ❻ 一年中庄稼的收成 harvest of the year:～成 the harvest of the year|～景 the financial situation of the year|丰～rich harvest|歉～lean year ❼ 年节 festival; New Year:新～New Year; Spring Festival|过～celebrate Spring Festival|给大家拜～extend New Year's greetings to everyone ❽ 有关年节的(用品)(of articles) associated with Spring Festival:～糕 New Year's cake|～货 commodities and food purchased for New Year's celebrations|～画 New Year's painting ❾ 科举时代同年登科的关系 relationship between those who passed the imperial examinations in the same year:～兄 form of address among successful candidates of imperial exams of the same year|～谊 friendship between successful candidates of imperial exams|同～ fellow imperial examinee ❿ (Nián) 姓 a surname

【年辈】niánbèi 年龄和辈分 age and generation on the genealogical chart of a family or clan:～相当(of two or more persons) compatible in age and seniority; of about the same age and generation

【年表】niánbiǎo 将重大历史事件按年月编排的表格 chronological table (of important historical events)

【年菜】niáncài 过农历年时做的比平日丰盛的蔬菜鱼肉等食品 meat and vegetable dishes prepared more lavishly than usual for the traditional lunar New Year's dinner

【年成】nián·cheng 一年的收成 year's harvest:～不坏 fairly good year|今年是个好～。The harvest of this year is going to be a good one.

【年齿】niánchǐ 〈书 *fml.*〉年纪 age:～渐长(zhǎng) get in on age

【年初】niánchū 一年的开头几天 beginning of the year

【年代】niándài ❶ 时代；时期；时间(多指过去较远的)age; time long past:～久远 age-old; of remote antiquity|黑暗～dark age|这件古董恐怕有～了。I'm afraid this antique goes back to many, many years ago. ❷ 每一世纪中从'…十'到'…九'的十年，如1990—1999是二十世纪九十年代 decade, such as the 1990s, which denotes the 1990-1999 period

【年底】niándǐ 一年的最后几天 year-end; the last few days of a year

【年度】niándù 根据业务性质和需要而有一定起讫日期的十二个月 year; any 12-month period prescribed for a purpose:会计～accounting year|财政～fiscal year|～计划 annual plan|～预算 annual budget

【年饭】niánfàn 农历除夕全家人团聚在一起吃的饭(during Spring Festival) dinner on New Year's Eve, a customary occasion for family reunion

【年份】niánfèn ❶ 指某一年 a given year:这两笔开支不在一个～。These two expenses were not incurred in the same year. ❷ 经历年代的长短 age:这件瓷器的～比那件久。This piece of porcelain is older than that one.

【年富力强】nián fù lì qiáng 年纪轻，精力旺盛 in one's prime (富 *fu*:指未来的年岁多 have

N

many years to live)

【年高德劭】nián gāo dé shào 年纪大，品德好 (of an old person) venerated age and high morality

【年糕】niángāo 用黏性大的米或米粉蒸成的糕，是农历年的应时食品 New Year's cake, made of steamed glutinous rice or rice flour

【年根】niángēn (～儿 niángēnr) same as 年底 niándǐ

【年庚】niángēng 指一个人出生的年月日时 birthday, esp. the year, month, day and hour of one's birth

【年关】niánguān 年底。旧例在农历年底结账，欠租、负债的人觉得过年像过关一样难，所以称为年关。year-end; (old) end of the lunar year, when those in debt were on tenterhooks because by Chinese custom it was the time for all accounts to be settled

【年光】niánguāng ❶ 年华；时光 time; years: ～易逝。How time flies! ❷ 年成；年景 the year's harvest: 今年～不好。The harvest this year wasn't good. ❸ 〈方 *dial.*〉年头儿 years: 那～，不得不靠借债过日子。During those years we had to make ends meet by borrowing money.

【年号】niánhào 纪年的名称，多指帝王用的，如'贞观'是唐太宗(李世民)的年号，现在也指公元纪年 reign title; usu. of a monarch such as the 'Zhenguan' reign of Emperor Taizong (Li Shimin) of the Tang Dynasty; Gregorian calendar (A.D.)

【年华】niánhuá 时光；年岁 years in one's lifetime: 虚度～idle away one's time | ～方富(年轻有望)in the prime of one's life

【年画】niánhuà 民间过农历年时，张贴的表现欢乐吉庆气象的图画 New Year's painting; any one of the auspicious paintings to be pasted up for the celebration of the Chinese lunar New Year

【年会】niánhuì (社会团体等)一年一度举行的集会 (of a social organization, etc.) annual meeting

【年货】niánhuò 过农历年时的应时物品，如糕点、年画、花炮等 commodities prepared for Spring Festival celebrations, including pastries, New Year's paintings, firecrackers, etc.

【年级】niánjí 学校中依据学生修业年限分成的班级，如规定小学修业年限为几年，学校中就编为几个年级 grade; classes classified according to a prescribed number of school terms, thus a six-year primary school has six grades

【年纪】niánjì (人的)年龄；岁数(of a person) age: ～轻 young age | 小小～，懂得什么！Do you really know a thing or two as a young kid?

【年假】niánjià ❶ same as 寒假 hánjià ❷ 过年期间放的假 Spring Festival holidays; New Year holidays

【年间】niánjiān 指在某个时期、某个年代内 historical period: 唐宋～Tang-Song periods | 明朝洪武～Hongwu reign of the Ming Dynasty

【年鉴】niánjiàn 汇集截至出版年为止(着重最近一年)的各方面或某一方面的情况、统计等资料的参考书，如世界年鉴、经济年鉴 almanac; yearbook; reference book carrying reports and statistics on various fields or a particular field of endeavour by the year of its publication, such as the World Yearbook and the Economics Yearbook

【年节】niánjié 农历新年；春节 the lunar New Year; Spring Festival

【年谨】niánjǐn 〈方 *dial.*〉 same as 荒年 huāngnián

【年景】niánjǐng ❶ same as 年成nián·cheng: 好～year of good harvest | 正常～normal harvest year ❷ 过年的景象 lunar New Year's festive atmosphere: 一派热闹的～。A scene of jubilee met the eye everywhere during Spring Festival.

【年来】niánlái 一年以来；近年以来 since the beginning of the year; over the last few years: ～这里的旅游业有很大的发展。Tourism has come a long way here over the last few years.

【年历】niánlì 印有一年的月份、星期、日期、节气等的印刷品 single-page calendar; calendar with all the months, weeks, dates and solar terms printed on the same page: ～卡片 single-page calendar

【年利】niánlì 按年计算的利息 annual interest

【年龄】niánlíng 人或动植物已经生存的年数 age; number of years a person, animal or plant has lived: 入学～school age | 退休～retiring age | 根据年轮可以知道树木的～。You can tell a tree's age from counting its growth rings.

【年轮】niánlún 木本植物的主干由于季节变化生长快慢不同，在木质部的断面显出的环形纹理。年轮的总数大体相当于树的年龄。annual ring; growth ring; concentric rings seen in the cross-section of the trunk of a woody plant, formed as a result of different growth speeds in different seasons; number of growth rings approximately representing the age of a tree

【年迈】niánmài 年纪老 old and tired; old; aged; elderly; in an advanced age: ～力衰 senile; old and infirm

【年貌】niánmào 年岁和相貌 age and appearance: ～相当 well matched in age and appearance

【年谱】niánpǔ 用编年体裁记载某个人生平事迹的著作 chronological life; annalist-style record of a person's life

【年青】niánqīng 处在青少年时期 young; juvenile; youthful: ～的一代 a young generation;

the younger (or rising) generation|你正～,应把精力用到学习上去。As a youngster, you should concentrate your efforts on your studies.

【年轻】niánqīng 年纪不大 young (多指十几岁至二十几岁 usu. referring to sb. in his teens until twenties): ～人 young people; youth|～力壮 young and vigorous (or strong)

【年少】niánshào ❶ same as 年轻 niánqīng: 青春～ be quite young; be in one's very first youth; be in one's tender years|～有为 young and promising; young and able ❷ 青少年(多指男子 usu. referring to men) youth; youngster; young man: 翩翩～ young spark; beau; elegant young man|英俊～ handsome young man

【年深日久】nián shēn rì jiǔ 指时间久远 age-old; after a long lapse (or period) of time: 这已经是～的事情了。It happened long, long ago. also 年深月久 nián shēn yuè jiǔ; 年深岁久 nián shēn suì jiǔ

【年时】niánshí ❶〈方 *dial.*〉same as 年头儿 niántóur ② ❷〈书 *fml.*〉same as 往年 wǎngnián

【年时】nián·shi 〈方 *dial.*〉same as 去年 qùnián: 他们是～才结婚的。They got married only last year.

【年事】niánshì〈书 *fml.*〉same as 年纪 niánjì: ～已高 be advanced in years

【年岁】niánsuì ❶ 年纪 niánjì: 他虽然上了～,干起活来可不服老。Despite his advanced age, he works as if he were a young man. ❷ 年代;年头儿 year; age: 从前遇到荒旱～,就得出外逃荒。In lean years in the past people had to flee from famine.|因为～久远,大家把这件事情忘了。Since it happened so many years ago, everyone has forgotten it. ❸〈方 *dial.*〉same as 年成 nián·cheng: 他问了我家乡的～如何。He asked me about this year's harvest in my native place.

【年头儿】niántóur ❶ same as 年份 niánfèn: 我到北京已经三个～了(前年到北京,前年、去年、今年是三个年头儿)。It's the third year since I came to Beijing (counting from the year before last). ❷ 多年的时间 years; years on end; a long time; a long while; ages: 他干这一行,有～了。He's been in this trade for years. ❸ same as 时代 shídài; times: 这～可不兴那一套了。Nowadays that sort of thing is no longer in fashion. ❹ same as 年成 nián·cheng: 今年～好,麦子比去年多收两三成。The harvest is good this year, the yield of wheat being 20 or 30 per cent more than that of last year.

【年尾】niánwěi 年末;年终 the end of the year

【年息】niánxī same as 年利 niánlì

【年下】nián·xia 过农历年的时候(多指年底和年初一段时间 usu. the days around the turn of the year) lunar New Year's Eve and New Year

【年限】niánxiàn 规定的或作为一般标准的年数 term; fixed or standard number of years: 修业～number of years set for a course of study|延长农具的使用～ prolong the service life of a farm implement

【年薪】niánxīn 按年计算的工资 annual salary; yearly pay

【年夜】niányè 农历一年最后一天的夜晚 lunar New Year's Eve: ～饭 family reunion dinner on the lunar New Year's Eve

【年月】nián·yue ❶ 时代;年头儿 times; age: 战争～ wartime ❷ 日子;岁月 days; years: 漫长的～ long years; aeons

【年终】niánzhōng 一年的末了 end of the year; year-end: ～结账 year-end settlement of accounts|～鉴定 year-end appraisal

【年资】niánzī 年龄和资历 seniority; age and years of service: 她是本医院～较高的医生。She is one of the senior doctors at our hospital.

【年尊】niánzūn 年纪大 older in age; advanced in age: ～辈长 be of an older age and generation

粘 nián ❶ same as 黏 nián ❷ (Nián) 姓 a surname

☞ zhān on p. 2409

鲇(鯰) nián 鲇鱼,身体表面多黏液,无鳞,背部苍黑色,腹面白色,头扁口阔,上下颌有4根须,尾圆而短,不分叉,背鳍小,臀鳍与尾鳍相连。生活在河湖池沼等处,白昼潜伏水底泥中,夜晚出来活动,吃小鱼、贝类、蛙等。catfish (*Siluriformes*); a kind of fish with a scale-free body covered with mucus, a black back and white belly, a flat head, a wide mouth, two pairs of barbels on its upper and lower jaws, a short round tail without a fork, a small dorsal fin, and fused anal and tail fins. Living in rivers, lakes and ponds, this nocturnal fish, hiding in riverbed mud during daytime, feeds on small fish, shellfish, frogs, etc.

黏 nián 像糨糊或胶水等所具有的、能使一个物体附着在另一物体上的性质 sticky; glutinous; adhesive: ～液 glutinous liquid|～米 sticky rice; glutinous rice|胶水很～。The glue is very sticky.

【黏度】niándù 液体或半流体流动难易的程度,越难流动的物质黏度越大,胶水、凡士林等都是黏度较大的物质 viscosity; extent to which a fluid or semi-fluid resists the force tending to cause it to flow, where the stronger the resistance, the higher the viscosity; glue, vaseline, etc., are substances with a relatively high viscosity

【黏附】niánfù 黏性的东西附着在其他物体上 (of sth. sticky) adhere to; stick to; cleave to;

cling to (sth. else)

【黏合】niánhé 黏性的东西使两个或几个物体粘(zhān)在一起 bind; bond; adhere; hold two or more objects together with a sticky substance: ～剂 binder; adhesive; bonding agent

【黏糊】nián·hu ❶ 形容东西黏 sticky; glutinous: 大米粥里头加点儿白薯又～又好吃。The rice porridge will be sticky and tasty with some sweet potatoes added.|他刚糊完窗户,弄了黏黏糊糊的一手糨子。He has just finished papering the windows, and his hands are sticky with paste. ❷ 形容人行动缓慢,精神不振作 (of a person) languid; slow-moving: 别看他平时很～,有事的时候比谁都利索。He looks languid, but is more efficient than anyone when things come up. | also 黏糊糊 niánhūhū; 黏糊糊儿的 niánhūhūr·de

【黏结】niánjié 黏合在一起 cohere; bond; adhere: ～力 cohesion; cohesive force; adhesiveness|互相～ cohere to each other

【黏菌】niánjūn 介于动物和植物之间的微生物,形态各异,无叶绿素,多为腐生,少为寄生,是研究生物化学、遗传学等的重要材料 slime mould; slime fungus; organism in various shapes considered to be sth. between plant or animal, with no chlorophyll, most species being saprophytic, some parasitic, used as important material for biochemical and genetic research

【黏米】niánmǐ〈方 *dial.*〉same as 黍子 shǔ·zi

【黏膜】niánmó 口腔、气管、胃、肠、尿道等器官里面的一层薄膜,内有血管和神经,能分泌黏液 mucous membrane; mucosa; lubricating membrane lining an internal surface of an organ (e.g. mouth, trachea, stomach, intestines, urethra, etc.), which contains blood vessels and nerves, and secretes mucus

【黏儿】niánr〈方 *dial.*〉像糨糊或胶的半流体 gum; resin; viscid semi-fluid-like paste or glue: 枣～ date tree resin|松树出～了。Resin is seeping out of the pine trees.

【黏土】niántǔ 含沙粒很少,有黏性的土壤,养分较丰富,能保水、保肥,但通气透水性差,耕种时需要改良 clay soil; fine-grained, rich cohesive soil that retains water and fertilizers, but needs improvement for tilling because of its poor permeability

【黏涎】nián·xian〈方 *dial.*〉(说话、动作、表演等)不爽快;冗长而无味 (of speech, movement, performance, etc.) tedious; dull; boring

【黏涎子】niánxián·zi〈方 *dial.*〉人嘴里的黏液 saliva; drool

【黏液】niányè 人和动植物体内分泌出来的黏稠液体 mucus; the viscous, slippery substance that is secreted inside human and animal bodies, and plants

【黏着】niánzhuó 用胶质把物体固定在一起 stick together; adhere; fix objects together with a sticky substance

【黏着力】niánzhuólì 附着力 adhesion; cohesion

【黏着语】niánzhuóyǔ 词的语法意义主要由加在词根上的词缀来表示的语言,如土耳其语、日语等 agglutinative language; language where the grammatical meaning of a word is expressed by the affix, e.g. Turkish, Japanese, etc.

niǎn (ㄋㄧㄢˇ)

涊 niǎn〈书 *fml.*〉形容出汗 sweating; perspiring

捻(撚) niǎn ❶ 用手指搓 twist with fingers: ～线 twist a thread|～条绳子 twist up a rope ❷ (～儿 niǎnr)捻子 thing made by twisting: 纸～儿 paper spill|灯～儿 lampwick ❸〈方 *dial.*〉蔫 dredge up: ～河泥 dredge up sludge from a river

【捻度】niǎndù 在单位长度的纱中,纤维所捻成的回旋数。纱的强度主要由捻度决定,一般捻度大强度也大。twist; number of turns (or twists) of a fibre of yarn in a unit length; strength of yarn is determined by its twist; the higher the twist, the greater the strength

【捻捻转儿】niǎn·nianzhuànr 儿童玩具,用木头或塑料等制成,扁圆形,中间有轴,一头尖,玩时用手捻轴使旋转 humming-top; children's toy made of wood or plastic, oval-shaped and with an axis in the middle and a pointed end, set spinning by hand

【捻子】niǎn·zi 用纸搓成的条状物或用线织成的带状物 spill; wick; twisted cord of paper or woven tape of cotton threads: 药～ medicated thread; medicated wick|纸～ paper spill

辇 niǎn〈古代 *arch.*〉用人拉的车,后来多指皇帝、皇后坐的车 human-drawn carriage; (later oft. referring to) imperial carriage: 龙车凤～ carriages for the emperor and empress

碾(辗) niǎn ❶ 碾子 millstone; roller: 石～ millstone; stone roller ❷ 滚动碾磙子等使谷物去皮、破碎,或使其他物体破碎、变平 grind or husk grain or sth. else with a millstone; roll out: ～米 husk rice|把盐粒～碎 grind grains of salt ❸〈书 *fml.*〉磨制;雕琢玉石 grind and polish; polish (jade)

【碾场】niǎn//cháng〈方 *dial.*〉在场上轧谷物;打场 thresh or husk grain on a threshing ground

【碾坊】niǎnfáng 把谷物碾成米或面的作坊 grain mill; workshop where grain is husked or ground into flour; also 碾房 niǎnfáng

【碾磙子】niǎngǔn·zi 碾子①的主要部分,是一个圆柱形的石头,可以轧碎粮食或去掉粮食的皮 stone roller; major part of a millstone in a cylindrical shape which grinds or husks grains; also 碾砣 niǎntuó

【碾盘】niǎnpán 承受碾磙子的石头底盘 bedstone; lower millstone; millstone upon which a stone roller is used

【碾砣】niǎntuó same as 碾磙子 niǎngǔn·zi

【碾子】niǎn·zi ❶ 轧碎谷物或去掉谷物皮的石制工具，由碾磙子和碾盘组成 millstone; stone tool used to grind or husk grains, consisting of a roller and a bedstone ❷ 泛指碾轧东西的工具 roller; any tool for grinding or crushing things: 汽～ steamroller | 药～ mortar and pestle for grinding herbal medicines

撵 niǎn ❶ 驱逐；赶走 drive out; oust: 把他～出去。Drive him out. ❷〈方 *dial.*〉追赶 catch up with: 他走得快，我～不上他。He walked too fast and I couldn't catch up with him.

蹍 niǎn〈方 *dial.*〉踩 trample; step on; tread

niàn (ㄋ丨ㄢ)

廿 niàn 二十 twenty

念1 niàn ❶ 想念 miss; think of: 惦～ think of; miss | 怀～ cherish the memory of; think of | 你回来得正好，娘正～着你呢！You're back just in time! Mother has been missing you. ❷ 念头 thought; idea: 杂～ distracting thoughts | 一～之差 wrong thought in passing; wrong decision made in a moment of weakness ❸ (Niàn) 姓 a surname

念2 (唸) niàn ❶ 读① read aloud: ～信 read a letter aloud | ～口诀 read a pithy formula | 他把上级的指示～给大家听。He read out the directive from the higher authorities. ❷ 读③ attend school: 他～过中学。He has been to middle school.

念3 niàn '廿'的大写 capital form of 廿 niàn

【念白】niànbái same as 道白 dàobái

【念叨】niàn·dao ❶ 因惦记或想念而在谈话中提到 remember through talking; talk about again and again in recollection or anticipation; be always talking about: 这位就是我们常～的老校长。This is the old principal we're always talking about. ❷〈方 *dial.*〉说；谈论 talk about; speak about; say; talk over; discuss: 我有个事儿跟大家～～。I've got something to talk to you about. also 念道 niàn·dao

【念佛】niànfó 信佛的人念'阿弥陀佛'或'南无(nāmó)阿弥陀佛' pray to the Buddha; (of Buddhists) chant 'Amitabha' or 'Namo Amitabha,' the name of the Buddha, while praying: 吃斋～ be a reverent Buddhist and practise vegetarianism | 诵经～ chant scriptures and the name of the Buddha

【念经】niàn//jīng 信仰宗教的人朗读或背诵经文 (of religious people) recite or chant scriptures

【念旧】niànjiù 不忘旧日的交情 keep old friendships in mind; remember (or retain) old friends: 要是他还～，应该出席这次聚会。He will come to the party if he still remembers his old friends.

【念念不忘】niànniàn bù wàng 牢记在心，时刻不忘 constantly bear in mind; always keep in mind; constantly think of: 他所～的是祖国的命运和民族的前途。What he constantly bears in mind is the fate of his motherland and the future of his nation.

【念念有词】niànniàn yǒu cí ❶〈旧时 *old*〉迷信的人小声念咒语或说祈祷的话 (of superstitious people) mutter incantations (i.e. curse or prayer) ❷ 指人不停地自言自语 mumble (to oneself); continuously speak softly to oneself

【念书】niàn//shū same as 读书 dú//shū

【念头】niàn·tou 心里的打算 thought; idea; intention: 转～ nurse an idea | 邪恶的～ an evil idea

【念物】niàn·wù same as 纪念品 jìniànpǐn: 这本画册送给你做个～吧。Keep this picture album as a souvenir.

【念心儿】niàn·xīnr same as〈方 *dial.*〉纪念品 jìniànpǐn

【念珠】niànzhū (～儿 niànzhūr) same as 数珠 shùzhū

埝 niàn 田里或浅水里用来挡水的土埂 baulk (balk); boundary ridge; low bank between fields or in a shallow pool, for blocking the flow of water: 堤～ dyke; embankment

niáng (ㄋ丨ㄤˊ)

娘 (孃) niáng ❶ 母亲 mother; mum; ma: 爹～ father and mother; parents | 亲～ one's own mother ❷ 称长一辈或年长的已婚妇女 (a form of address for a married woman who is elderly or of an older generation): 大～ aunt | 婶～ aunt; wife of one's father's younger brother ❸ 年轻妇女 a young woman: 渔～ a young fisherwoman | 新～ bride

【娘家】niáng·jia 已婚女子的自己父母的家(区别于'婆家' as compared with her 'parents-in-law's home') married woman's parents' home: 回～ (of a married woman) visit one's parental home

【娘舅】niángjiù〈方 *dial.*〉same as 舅父 jiùfù

【娘娘】niáng·niang ❶ 指皇后或贵妃 empress or imperial concubine: 正宫～ empress ❷ 信神的人称呼女神 (of superstition) term of address for a goddess: ～庙 Temple of the Goddess of Fertility

【娘儿】niángr 长辈妇女和男女晚辈合称，如母亲和子女、姑母和侄子侄女（后面必带数量词 followed by a numeral-classifier compound）term referring to a woman and member(s) of the generation younger than she, e.g. mother and her children, aunt and nephew or niece：～俩 the mother and her son (or daughter); the woman and her nephew (or niece)｜～三个合计了半天，才想出一个好主意来。The mother and her two children finally hit upon a good idea after a long discussion.

【娘儿们】niángr·men ❶ 长辈妇女和男女晚辈合称 term referring to a woman and member(s) of the younger generation ❷〈方 *dial.*〉称成年妇女（含轻蔑意，可以用于单数 derog., can be used in single form）woman; broad; hussy ❸〈方 *dial.*〉same as 妻子 qīzǐ

【娘胎】niángtāi 怀着胎儿的母体。人尚未出生，说'在娘胎里'；已经出生，说'出了娘胎'；生来就具有某种特征，说'从娘胎带来'的。mother's womb. 'In one's mother's womb' means before one is born; 'out of one's mother's womb' means one is born; and a characteristic coming 'from one's mother's womb' is innate.

【娘姨】niángyí〈方 *dial.*〉保姆；女佣人 maid-servant

【娘子】niáng·zǐ ❶〈方 *dial.*〉same as 妻子 qīzǐ ❷ 尊称青年或中年妇女（多见于早期白话 usu. in early vernacular）madam; ma'am; a polite form of address for a young or middle-aged woman

【娘子军】niáng·zǐjūn 隋末李渊的女儿统率的军队号称娘子军，后用来泛称由女子组成的队伍 women's detachment; any contingent entirely made up of women; a term derived from the name of a contingent led by Li Yuan's daughter towards the end of the Sui Dynasty

niàng（ㄋㄧㄤˋ）

酿（釀） niàng ❶ 酿造 make (wine); brew (beer)：～酒 make wine; brew beer ❷ 蜜蜂做蜜 (of bees) make (honey)：～蜜 make honey ❸ 逐渐形成 lead to; result in; form gradually：～成大祸 lead to a disaster ❹ 烹调方法，将肉、鱼、虾等剁碎做成的馅填或塞入掏空的柿子椒、冬瓜等，然后用油煎或蒸 (cooking method) fill hollowed bell peppers, wax gourds, etc., with minced meat, fish, shrimp, etc. and fry or steam them ❺ 酒 wine; liquor：佳～ good wine

【酿酶】niàngméi 酵母中引起酒精发酵的酶的总称 zymase; enzyme complex in a yeast that catalyzes the breakdown of sugar into alcohol

【酿母菌】niànmǔjūn same as 酵母 jiàomǔ

【酿热物】niàngrèwù 发酵时能产生热的有机物，如牛马粪、稻草、麦秸、玉米秸、草叶等。用来为温床加热。fermenting material; any organic matter that produces heat when leavened, e.g. cattle and horse manure, wheat and rice straw, maize stalk, grass, etc., used to heat a hotbed

【酿造】niàngzào 利用发酵作用制造（酒、醋、酱油等）make (wine, vinegar, soy sauce, etc.); brew (beer, etc.)

niǎo（ㄋㄧㄠˇ）

鸟（鳥） niǎo 脊椎动物的一纲，体温恒定，卵生，嘴内无齿，全身有羽毛，胸部有龙骨突起，前肢变成翼，后肢能行走。一般的鸟都会飞，也有的两翼退化，不能飞行。燕、鹰、鸡、鸭、鸵鸟等都属于鸟类。bird; oviparity and a family of the vertebrate, having invariable body temperature, no teeth, a body covered with feather, protruding keels in the chest, wings evolved from the forelimbs, and rear limbs that can walk. Usually a bird can fly, but some cannot because of degenerated wings. The swallow, eagle, chicken, duck and ostrich belong to this family.
☞ diǎo on p. 446

【鸟害】niǎohài 农作物或农产品由于鸟群啄食造成的损害 bird pest; damage to crops or farm caused by birds

【鸟尽弓藏】niǎo jìn gōng cáng〈比喻 *fig.*〉事情成功以后，把曾经出过力的人一脚踢开 cast sb. aside when he has served one's purpose; ☞兔死狗烹 tù sǐ gǒu pēng on p. 1945

【鸟瞰】niǎokàn ❶ 从高处往下看 get a bird's-eye view; get an aerial view：登上西山，可以～整个京城。From the top of the Western Hills, one can get a bird's-eye view of the whole city of Beijing. ❷ 事物的概括描写 general survey of a subject; bird's-eye view：世界大势～ general survey of the world situation

【鸟枪】niǎoqiāng ❶ 打鸟用的火枪 fowling piece ❷ same as 气枪 qìqiāng

【鸟枪换炮】niǎoqiāng huàn pào〈比喻 *fig.*〉情况有很大的好转或条件有很大的改善 conditions (or situations) have changed for the better or greatly improved

【鸟儿】niǎor 指较小的能飞行的鸟 small bird; birdie

【鸟兽散】niǎo shòu sàn〈比喻 *fig.*〉成群的人纷纷散去（含贬义）(derog.)(of a crowd) scatter; flee：如～ flee helter-skelter; flee in every direction; scatter like startled birds and animals｜作～ flee helter-skelter; flee in every direction; scatter like startled birds and animals

【鸟语花香】niǎo yǔ huā xiāng 鸟儿叫，花儿飘香，多形容春天媚人的景象 birds sing and

flowers exude fragrance (oft. used to describe a fine spring day): 桃红柳绿,～。The peach trees are in bloom and the willows are turning green; birds are singing and flowers exuding fragrance.

【鸟葬】niǎozàng same as 天葬 tiānzàng

茑 niǎo 落叶小乔木,茎略能爬蔓,叶子掌状分裂,略作心脏形,表面有柔毛,花带绿色,果实球形。生长在四川等地的深山中。cypress vine (*Quamoclit pennata*); small deciduous arbour with intertwining stems, roughly heart-shaped palmate leaves with hair on the surface, greenish flowers, and spherical fruit, growing in remote mountains in Sichuan and other areas

袅 niǎo〈书 *fml.*〉same as 袅 niǎo

袅(嫋、嬝) niǎo 细长柔弱 slender and delicate: ～娜 slender and graceful; willowy

【袅袅】niǎoniǎo ❶ 形容烟气缭绕上升 (of smoke) curl upward; ascend slowly; coil up: 炊烟～。Smoke is curling and uncurling upward from kitchen chimneys.|～腾腾的烟雾 smoke rising slowly in the air ❷ 形容细长柔软的东西随风摆动 (of slender, soft things) sway in the wind: 垂杨～。Drooping willows are dancing in the wind. ❸ 形容声音延长不绝 (of sound) linger: 余音～。The music lingered in the air.

【袅袅婷婷】niǎoniǎotíngtíng〈书 *fml.*〉形容女子走路体态轻盈 (of the figure of a woman as she walks) lithe; graceful; refined

【袅娜】niǎonuó (旧读 formerly pronounced: niǎonuǒ)〈书 *fml.*〉❶ 形容草木柔软细长 (of plants) soft and slender: 春风吹着～的柳丝。The slender willow twigs were swaying gently in the spring breeze. ❷ 形容女子姿态优美 (of the figure of a woman) delicate; graceful; willowy

【袅绕】niǎorào〈书 *fml.*〉缭绕不断 linger: 歌声～。The song lingers in the air.

嬲 niǎo〈书 *fml.*〉❶ same as 戏弄 xìnòng ❷ same as 纠缠 jiūchán

niào (ㄋㄧㄠˋ)

尿 niào ❶ 人或动物体内,由肾脏产生,从尿道排泄出来的液体 urine; liquid produced in the kidneys and discharged through the urethra in the bodies of humans or animals ❷ 撒尿 urinate; piss; pee: ～尿 urinate; piss; pee; make water

☞ suī on p.1836

【尿布】niàobù 包裹婴儿身体下部或铺在婴儿床上接尿用的布 diaper; napkin; nappy; cloth arranged around the lower part of a baby's body or spread on a baby's bed to absorb urine; also called 褯子 jiè·zi in some areas

【尿床】niào//chuáng 在床上遗尿 wet the bed; bed-wetting

【尿道】niàodào 把尿输出体外的管子,自膀胱通向体外,有括约肌控制开闭 urethra; canal through which urine is discharged from the bladder, its movements controlled by a sphincter muscle; (图见 ☞ figure for 泌尿器 mìniàoqì on p.1332)

【尿肥】niàoféi 用做肥料的尿,含氮较多 urine used as manure, which contains relatively high amount of nitrogen

【尿炕】niào//kàng 在炕上遗尿 wet the kang; wet the bed

【尿素】niàosù 有机化合物,化学式$CO(NH_2)_2$。无色晶体,溶于水,人尿中约含有2%。用做肥料、饲料等,也用于制造炸药、塑料。urea; carbamide; an organic compound, a soluble, colourless crystalline solid, which makes up 2% of human urine; used in making fertilizer, fodder, explosive, plastics, etc.; also 脲 niào

【尿血】niào//xiě 尿中带血或只排血液而没有尿 haematuria; presence of blood in the urine; urinate blood

脲 niào 尿素 urea; carbamide

溺 niào same as 尿 niào

☞ nì on p.1408

niē (ㄋㄧㄝ)

捏(揑) niē ❶ 用拇指和别的手指夹 hold between the finger and thumb; pinch: ～住这支笔 hold the pen between the finger and thumb|把米里的虫子～出来 pick worms out of the rice ◇命～在人家手里 have one's life at the mercy of sb. else ❷ 用手指把软东西弄成一定的形状 knead; press and stretch sth. soft into a desired shape with the fingers; mould: ～泥人儿 mould clay figurines|～饺子 make dumplings ❸ 使合在一起 put together; bring together: ～合 put together; bring together|两人性格不合,～不到一块儿去。Being incompatible in temperament, they do not get along. ❹ 故意把非事实说成是事实 fabricate; concoct; make up; deliberately tell a falsehood as the truth: ～造 fabricate; make up

【捏合】niēhé ❶ 使合在一起 put together; bring together ❷ 凭空虚造;捏造(多见于早期白话 oft. in early vernacular) fabricate; concoct; make up

【捏积】niējī〈中医 *Chin. med.*〉指用手捏小儿的脊柱两旁以治疗消化不良、腹泻等疾病 chiropractic; method of treating children's digestive disorders by massaging the muscles along the spine

N

【捏弄】niē·nong ❶ 用手来回捏 fiddle with; play with: 说话时,她下意识地~着胸前的纽扣。As she talked, she subconsciously fiddled with the buttons on the front of her clothes. ❷ 摆布;耍弄 order about; manipulate: 我们得自己拿主意,不能由着他们~。We should make decisions on our own, instead of allowing ourselves to be ordered about. ❸ 私下里商量 discuss in private: 这事他俩一~,就那么办了。The two of them put their together in private — that's how they got it done. ❹ 编造;捏造 fabricate; concoct; make up

【捏一把汗】niē yī bǎ hàn 因担心而手心出汗,形容心情极度紧张 with sweat wetting one's palms — be breathless with anxiety; be extremely nervous; be keyed up; be on edge: 杂技演员表演走钢丝,观众都替他~。We were breathless as we watched the acrobats walking along the tightrope. also 捏把汗 niē bǎ hàn

【捏造】niēzào 假造事实 fabricate; concoct; fake; trump up: ~罪名 trump up charges

nié(ㄋㄧㄝˊ)

苶 nié 疲倦;精神不振 tired; listless; lethargic; fatigued; jaded: 发~ look listless | 疲~ be tired; be fatigued | 他今天有点~。He looks kind of listless today.

niè(ㄋㄧㄝˋ)

乜 Niè 姓 a surname
☞ miē on p. 1344

隉(陧) niè ☞ 杌隉 wùniè on p. 2037

聂(聶) Niè 姓 a surname

臬 niè〈书 *fml*.〉❶ 射箭的目标;靶子 target; mark set up for archery practice ❷〈古代 *arch*.〉测日影的标杆 gnomon; column on a sundial that casts a shadow indicating the time of day ❸ 法度;标准 criterion; standard

【臬兀】nièwù same as 臲卼 nièwù

涅 niè〈书 *fml*.〉❶ 可做黑色染料的矾石 alunite that can be used as a black dye ❷ 染黑 dye sth. black

【涅而不缁】niè ér bù zī 用涅染也染不黑 remain unstained even in black dye;〈比喻 *fig*.〉品格高尚,不受外界污染(语出《论语·阳货》) upright; incorruptible (originally from *Analects·Yang Huo*)

【涅槃】nièpán〈佛教用语 *Budd*.〉指所幻想的超脱生死的境界,也用做'死'(指佛或僧人)的代称 nirvana; imagined state where one goes beyond life and death; also used to refer to (a Buddha's or monk's) death [梵 Sanskrit: nirvāna]

惗 niè ☞ 地惗 dìniè on p. 422

啮(齧、囓) niè〈书 *fml*.〉(鼠、兔等动物)用牙啃或咬 (of animals such as rats and rabbits) gnaw; nibble

【啮合】nièhé 上下牙齿咬紧;像上下牙齿那样咬紧 clench the teeth; fit closely together like teeth; mesh; engage; interlock: 两个齿轮~在一起。The two cogwheels meshed.

【啮噬】nièshì 咬 gnaw;〈比喻 *fig*.〉折磨 torment; harass: 失子的悲痛,~着母亲的心。The mother's heart was tormented by the loss of her son.

茶(籋) niè〈书 *fml*.〉same as 镊 niè

嗫(囁) niè [嗫嚅](nièrú)〈书 *fml*.〉形容想说话而又吞吞吐吐不敢说出来的样子 speak haltingly; mutter and mumble

嵲 niè ☞ 嵽嵲 diéniè on p. 451

槷 niè〈书 *fml*.〉❶ 箭靶子的中心 bull's eye; centre of a target ❷〈古代 *arch*.〉测日影的标杆 gnomon; column that projects a shadow, used as an indicator of the position of the sun

镊(鑷) niè ❶ 镊子 tweezers ❷(用镊子)夹 pick up sth. with tweezers: 把瓶子里的酒精棉球~出来。Use tweezers to pick up the alcohol-soaked cotton balls from the bottle.

【镊子】niè·zi 拔除毛或夹取细小东西的用具,一般用金属制成 tweezers; small implement, generally made of metal, used for plucking hairs or picking up small objects

镍 niè 金属元素,符号 Ni(niccolum)。银白色,质坚韧,延展性强,有磁性,在常温中不跟空气中的氧起作用,用来制特种钢和其他合金、催化剂等,也用于电镀。nickel (Ni); silvery, hard, ductile, ferromagnetic metallic element that does not combine with oxygen in the air at normal temperatures, used in special steel and other alloys, catalytic agents, etc., and for electroplating

【镍币】nièbì 镍质的货币 nickel coin; nickel

颞(顳) niè ☞ below

【颞骨】niègǔ 颞颥部的骨头,位于顶骨的下方,形状扁平 temporal bone; flat bone at the temple below the parietal bone

【颞颥】nièrú 头部的两侧靠近耳朵上方的部位 temple; the region on either side of the head over the ears

臲 niè [臲卼](nièwù)〈书 *fml*.〉不安定 unsettled; restless; unpeaceful; also 臬兀 nièwù

蹑(躡) niè ❶ 放轻(脚步) walk on tiptoe; slink; sneak; creep: 他轻轻地站起来,~着脚走过去。He stood up quietly and sneaked over. ❷ 追随；跟踪 follow; be after：～踪 follow the trail of; track ❸〈书 *fml.*〉踩 tread; step on; trample：～足 tiptoe

【蹑手蹑脚】niè shǒu niè jiǎo（～的 niè shǒu niè jiǎo·de）形容走路时脚步放得很轻 walk gingerly; walk on tiptoe; sneak; slink：他～地走进了卧室。He slunk into the bedroom.

【蹑踪】nièzōng〈书 *fml.*〉追踪 follow the trail of; track; trace; trail

【蹑足】niè zú ❶ 放轻脚步 tiptoe; walk with light steps; creep：他～走到门口。He tiptoed to the door. ❷〈书 *fml.*〉插足；参加 participate in; join; take part in：～其间（参加进去）participate; partake; be a party to

孽（孼） niè ❶ 邪恶 evil; vicious; malicious; wicked：妖～ evildoer; devil; fiend ❷ 罪恶 sin; crime; devilry：造～ commit a sin｜罪～ sin; crime ❸〈书 *fml.*〉不忠或不孝 treacherous; faithlcss; perfidious; impious：～臣 disloyal official (in feudal times)｜～子 incorrigible son

【孽根】niègēn 罪恶的根源；祸根 root of evil; bane; ruin：～未除。The root of the evil has not been eliminated.

【孽海】nièhǎi same as 业海 yèhǎi

【孽障】nièzhàng same as 业障 yèzhàng

【孽种】nièzhǒng ❶ same as 祸根 huògēn ❷〈旧时 *old*〉长辈骂不肖子弟为孽种 (said of sb.'s descendant) vile spawn; bastard

蘖 niè 树枝砍去后又长出来的新芽。泛指植物由茎的基部长出的分枝。tiller; shoot growing from where a branch is cut off; twig growing from the base of the stem of a plant

【蘖枝】niè zhī 植物分蘖时长出来的分枝 twig; branch stem

糵（糱） niè〈书 *fml.*〉酿酒的曲 distiller's yeast

nín（ㄋㄧㄣˊ）

恁 nín same as 您 nín（多见于早期白话 oft. in early vernacular）

☞ nèn on p. 1402

您 nín〈人称代词 *personal pron.*〉你（含敬意）(said with respect) you：老师，～早！Good morning, Sir (or Ma'am)!｜～二位想吃点儿什么？What would the two of you like to eat?

níng（ㄋㄧㄥˊ）

宁（寧、甯） níng ❶ 安宁 peaceful; tranquil; quiet：～静 peaceful; tranquil; quiet｜坐卧不～ be unable to sit down or sleep at ease; be fidgety; be on tenterhooks ❷〈书 *fml.*〉使安宁 pacify; appease; mollify; placate：～边（使边境不受侵扰）guard the border (against invasion)｜息事～人 pacify people and settle the matter ❸〈书 *fml.*〉省视；探望（父母）visit (one's parents)：～亲 pay a visit to one's parents｜归～ (of a married woman) visit one's parents ❹（Níng）南京的别称 Ning, another name for Nanjing：沪～铁路 the Shanghai-Nanjing railway

☞ nìng on p. 1419

【宁靖】níngjìng〈书 *fml.*〉（地方秩序）安定 (of local order) stable; peaceful

【宁静】níngjìng（环境、心情）安静 (of environment or mind) peaceful; tranquil; quiet; calm：游人散后，湖边十分～。The tourists having left, all becomes quiet by the lake.｜心里渐渐～下来 (of mind) calm down gradually

【宁亲】níngqīn〈书 *fml.*〉same as 省亲 xǐngqīn

【宁日】níngrì 安宁的日子 peaceful days; peace：国贼不除，永无～。There can be no peace until the traitors are done away with.

【宁帖】níngtiē（心境）宁静；安稳 (of state of mind) tranquil; peaceful; calm：夜间咳嗽，睡不～ cough at night and have a restless sleep

【宁馨儿】níngxīn'ér〈书 *fml.*〉原意是'这么样的孩子'，后来用做赞美孩子的话 lovely child; term originally means 'such a child', later used to praise a child

苧（薴） níng 有机化合物，化学式$C_{10}H_{16}$。无色液体，有香味，存在于柑橘类的果皮中。用来制香料等。limonene ($C_{10}H_{16}$); organic compound and colourless liquid with a fragrance, found in the peel of citrus fruits, used in producing perfume, flavouring, etc.

☞ 苎 zhù on p. 2508

拧（擰） níng ❶ 用两只手握住物体的两端分别向相反的方向用力 twist; wring; hold the two ends of something with two hands and turn them in opposite directions：～手巾 wring a towel｜把麻～成绳子 twist hemp into a rope ❷ 用两三个手指扭住皮肉使劲转动 tweak; hold the flesh of sb. with two or three fingers and twist with force：～了他一把 give him a tweak

☞ nǐng on p. 1419 and nìng on p. 1419

咛（嚀） níng ☞ 叮咛 dīngníng on p. 453

狞（獰） níng（面目）凶恶 (of facial expression) ferocious; hideous：～恶 fierce; ferocious｜～笑 grin hideously; smile grimly

【狞笑】níngxiào 凶恶地笑 grin hideously; smile grimly：发出一阵～ give a grim laugh

柠（檸） níng［柠檬］(níngméng) ❶ 柠檬树，常绿小乔木，叶子长椭圆形，质厚，花单生，外面粉红色，里面白色。果实长椭圆形或卵形，两端尖，果肉味极酸，可制饮料，果皮黄色，可提取柠檬油。lemon (*Citrus limon*); evergreen tree with thick elongated oval leaves, and sour, elongated oval or egg-shaped yellow fruit with pointed ends, which can be used to produce juice, and whose flowers, in simple inflorescence, are pink on the outside and white on the inside ❷ 这种植物的果实 lemon; the fruit of the plant

聍(聹) níng ☞［耵聍］(dīngníng) on p. 454

鬡(鬡) níng ☞［鬇鬡］(zhēngníng) on p. 2444

凝 níng ❶ 凝结 congeal; coagulate; curdle; condense: ～固 solidify | ～冻 freeze | 冷～ condensate; condensation ❷ 注意力集中 with fixed attention: ～思 think hard; contemplate | ～视 gaze; fix one's eyes on

【凝冻】níngdòng 凝结；冻结 freeze: 河水～。The river is frozen.

【凝固】nínggù ❶ 由液体变成固体 solidify; turn from liquid into solid: 蛋白质遇热会～。Protein becomes solid when heated. ❷〈比喻 *fig*.〉固定不变；停滞 stiff; fixed; stubborn; inflexible: 思想～ stubborn thought | ～的目光 fixed eyes

【凝固点】nínggùdiǎn 晶体物质凝固时的温度，也就是这种物质液态和固态可以平衡共存的温度 solidifying point; temperature at which a crystal matter solidifies, or the temperature at which both the liquid and solid states coexist in such a matter

【凝固汽油弹】nínggù qìyóudàn 一种爆炸时能发出高温火焰的炸弹，内装用汽油和其他化学药品制成的胶状物，爆炸时向四周溅射，发出1,000℃左右的高温，并能粘在其他物体上长时间燃烧 napalm bomb; bomb that emits high-temperature flames upon explosion, containing a gelatinous substance made of gas and other chemicals, which sprays when the bomb explodes, releasing heat of around 1,000℃, and which can adhere to other matters and burn for a long time

【凝固热】nínggùrè 单位质量的某种物质在熔点时，从液态变成固态所放出的热量，叫做这种物质的凝固热 heat of solidification; heat released by a unit mass of a certain matter on solidification

【凝合】nínghé 凝结，聚合 coagulate; congeal; solidify

【凝华】nínghuá 物质由气态不经液态直接变为固态 sublimate; transform directly from a gaseous state to a solid without becoming a liquid

【凝集】níngjí 凝结在一起；聚集 agglomerate; agglutinate: 心中疑云～。Suspicion grows in one's heart. | 诗篇～着诗人对祖国的真挚感情。The poem embodies the poet's genuine feelings towards his motherland.

【凝结】níngjié 由气体变成液体或由液体变成固体 coagulate; (of gas) transform into liquid; (of a liquid) transform into a solid: 池面上～了薄薄的一层冰。The pond is covered with a thin layer of ice. ◇鲜血～成的战斗友谊 friendship between comrades-in-arms baptized by blood

【凝聚】níngjù ❶ 气体由稀变浓或变成液体 (of vapour or gas) condense; become denser or change into liquid: 荷叶上～着晶莹的露珠。Glistening dewdrops have formed on the lotus leaves. ❷ 聚集；积聚 accumulate; concentrate: 这部作品～着他一生的心血。This work is a crystallization of his life-long efforts.

【凝聚力】níngjùlì ❶ 内聚力 cohesive force; cohesion ❷ 泛指使人或物聚集到一起的力量 cohesion; force that gathers people or things together: 加强社会和民族的～ increase the cohesion of the society and the nation

【凝练】níngliàn (文字)紧凑简练 (of language) condensed; concise; compact; laconic; terse: 文笔～ write in a laconic style; also 凝炼 níngliàn

【凝眸】níngmóu〈书 *fml*.〉凝目 fix one's eyes on; focus one's eyes upon: ～远望 gaze into the distance

【凝目】níngmù 目不转睛地(看) fix one's eyes on; focus one's eyes upon: ～注视 stare at; gaze with fixed eyes

【凝神】níngshén 聚精会神 with fixed (concentrated; rapt) attention; attentively: ～思索 be deep in contemplation | ～端详 scrutinize (examine) attentively

【凝视】níngshì 聚精会神地看 gaze fixedly; stare; be all eyes: ～谛听 watch and listen with rapt attention

【凝思】níngsī 集中精神思考 meditate; be lost in thought; be in deep thought; brood: ～默虑 mull over; contemplate; ponder

【凝望】níngwàng 目不转睛地看；注目远望 gaze at; stare at; look with fixed eyes; be all eyes

【凝想】níngxiǎng 凝思 meditate; ponder; contemplate: 他时而奋笔疾书，时而又搁笔～。He now wrote quickly and energetically, now put down the pen and fell deep into a reverie.

【凝脂】níngzhī〈书 *fml*.〉凝固了的油脂 congealed fat;〈比喻 *fig*.〉洁白细嫩的皮肤 fair, soft and glossy skin: 肤如～ have fair, soft and glossy skin

【凝滞】níngzhì ❶ 停止流动；不灵活 stagnant; static; immobile; unmoving: 两颗～的眼珠出神地望着窗外 look out of the window with dull (or vacant) eyes ❷〈书 *fml*.〉凝聚 condense; cohere; thicken

【凝重】níngzhòng ❶ 端庄;庄重 dignified; noble: 雍容～ have a dignified bearing | 神态～ look dignified ❷ (声音)浑厚 (of sound or voice) resonant; deep and powerful: ～深沉的乐曲 deep, solemn music | 声音～有力 deep, powerful voice ❸ 浓重 heavy; dense; thick: ～的乌云 heavy dark clouds

nǐng (ㄋㄧㄥˇ)

拧(擰) nǐng ❶ 控制住物体向里转或向外转 twist; screw; hold an object and turn it inward or outward: ～螺丝 turn a screw | 墨水瓶盖儿太紧,～不开了。The lid of the ink bottle is too tight to unscrew. ❷ 颠倒;错 mistaken; wrong: 他想说'狗嘴里长不出象牙',说～了,说成'象嘴里长不出狗牙',引得大家哄堂大笑。He meant to say 'no elephant tusks will come out of a dog's mouth', but screwed it up by saying, 'no dog's tusks will come out of an elephant's mouth', which set the whole room roaring. ❸ 别扭;抵触 differ; disagree; be at cross-purposes; discord: 两个人越说越～。The more they talked, the more they disagreed.

☞ níng on p. 1417 and nìng on p. 1419

nìng (ㄋㄧㄥˋ)

宁[1](寧、甯) nìng ❶ 宁可 would rather; better: ～死不屈 would rather die than yield | ～为玉碎,不为瓦全(比喻宁愿壮烈地死去,不愿苟且偷生) rather be a broken piece of jade than an unbroken piece of pottery; (fig.) better to die in glory than live in dishonour ❷〈书 *fml.*〉岂;难道 could there be; how is it possible: 山之险峻,～有逾此? Could there be a mountain more precipitous than this?

宁[2](甯) Nìng 姓 a surname

☞ níng on p. 1417

【宁可】nìngkě 表示比较两方面的利害得失后选取的一面(往往跟上文的'与其'或下文的'也不'相呼应 oft. preceded by 与其 yǔqí or followed by 也不 yěbù) would rather; expressing the choice preferred after comparing the advantages and disadvantages of two choices: 与其在这儿等车,～走着去 would rather walk there than wait for the bus here | 他～自己吃点亏,也不叫亏了人。He would rather stand to lose than make other people lose. 注意 **NOTE**: 如果舍弃的一面不明显或无须说出,可以单说选取的一面(常常加'的好·dehǎo',意思等于'最好是…') The speaker can state the preferred choice without mentioning the choice given up, which is not obvious or does not have to be mentioned, oft. followed by 的好·dehǎo, meaning 'it would be best' 如 e.g.: 我们～警惕一点的好。We'd better be more vigilant.

【宁肯】nìngkěn same as 宁可 nìngkě

【宁缺毋滥】nìng quē wú làn 宁可缺少一些,不要不顾质量一味求多 rather go without than make do with a substandard substitute; rather go without than have sth. shoddy — put quality before quantity

【宁死不屈】nìng sǐ bù qū 宁可死去,也不屈服 rather die than submit (or surrender)

【宁愿】nìngyuàn same as 宁可 nìngkě: ～牺牲,也不退却。Better to die than retreat.

佞 nìng ❶ 惯于用花言巧语谄媚人 given to flattery; smarmy; unctuous: 谄～ flatter; fawn on; adulate; curry favour with | 奸～ beguiling | ～人 toady; sycophant | ～臣 a sycophantic official or courtier ❷〈书 *fml.*〉有才智 talented; intelligent; wise: 不～(谦称自己 being modest about oneself) unintelligent

【佞笑】nìngxiào 奸笑;谄笑 sinister smile; ingratiating smile; sycophantic smile

【佞幸】nìngxìng〈书 *fml.*〉❶ 以谄媚而得到宠幸 win favour with flattery ❷ 以谄媚得到君主宠幸的人 toady; sycophant; people who win the favour of a king or an emperor with flattery: 任用～ assign sycophants to office

拧(擰) nìng〈方 *dial.*〉倔强 pigheaded; stubborn; obstinate; unyielding; pertinacious: 这孩子脾气真～,不叫他去他偏要去。The pigheaded child insisted on going though he was told not to.

☞ níng on p. 1417 and nǐng on p. 1419

泞(濘) nìng〈书 *fml.*〉烂泥 mud; marsh; bog: 泥～ muddy; miry | 路～难行。It is hard to travel on the muddy roads.

niū (ㄋㄧㄡ)

妞 niū (～儿 niūr) 女孩子 girl: 大～ big girl | 他家有两个～儿。He has two daughters.

【妞妞】niūniū〈方 *dial.*〉小女孩儿 little girl

【妞子】niū·zi〈方 *dial.*〉小女孩儿 little girl

niú (ㄋㄧㄡˊ)

牛[1] niú ❶ 哺乳动物,身体大,趾端有蹄,头上长有一对角,尾巴尖端有长毛。是反刍类动物,力气大,供役使、乳用或乳肉两用,皮、毛、骨等都有用处。我国常见的有黄牛、水牛、牦牛等几种。cattle; ox; cow; large, strong, ruminant mammal with hooves, a pair of horns on its head and long hair at the end of its tail, raised for draught purposes or for its meat and/or milk products, with its skin, hair, bones and other parts also useful. Breeds usually seen in China include ox, water buffalo and yak. ❷〈比喻 *fig.*〉固执或骄傲 stubborn or arrogant: ～气 arrogant; overbearing | ～脾气 stubborn; obstinate; pertinacious ❸ 二十八宿之一 one of the 28 constellations ❹ (Niú) 姓 a surname

牛[2] niú 牛顿的简称 abbr. for 牛顿 Niúdùn

【牛蒡】niúbàng 二年生草本植物，叶子互生，心脏形，有长柄，背面有毛，花管状，淡紫色，根多肉。根和嫩叶可做蔬菜，种子和根可入药。great burdock (*Arctium lappa*); biannual herbaceous plant having heart-shaped, alternate leaves with long stalk and hair on the back, pale purple tubular flowers and a succulent root, its root and tender leaves edible, and its seeds and root used in medicine

【牛鼻子】niúbí·zi〈比喻 *fig.*〉事物的关键或要害 crux; critical point of a matter: 弄清词义古今异同的情况，就牵住了学习古代汉语的～。Once you have a clear idea of the similarities and dissimilarities of a written character's ancient and modern meanings, you've got the crux of learning ancient Chinese.

【牛脖子】niúbó·zi〈方 *dial.*〉same as 牛脾气 niúpí·qi: 犯～ get stubborn

【牛刀小试】niú dāo xiǎo shì〈比喻 *fig.*〉有很大的本领，先在小事情上施展一下 a master hand's first small display; show some of one's ability; ☞ 割鸡焉用牛刀 gē jī yān yòng niúdāo on p. 651

【牛痘】niúdòu ❶ 牛的一种急性传染病，病原体和症状与天花极相近 cowpox; acute contagious disease of cattle, having pathogens and symptoms similar to those of smallpox ❷ 痘苗 smallpox pustule; vaccine pustule: 种～ give a smallpox vaccination; get a smallpox vaccination

【牛犊】niúdú 小牛 calf; also 牛犊子 niúdú·zi

【牛顿】niúdùn 力的单位，使质量 1 千克的物体产生 1 米/秒^2 的加速度所需的力就是 1 牛顿。1 牛顿等于 10^5 达因。这个单位名称是为纪念英国科学家牛顿(Sir Isaac Newton)而定的。newton; unit of force required to accelerate a mass of 1 kg. 1 metre per second per second, equal to 100,000 dynes, named after the British scientist Sir Isaac Newton; abbr. 牛 niú

【牛耳】niú'ěr ☞ 执牛耳 zhí niú'ěr on p. 2459

【牛鬼蛇神】niúguǐ-shéshén 奇形怪状的鬼神 monsters and demons;〈比喻 *fig.*〉社会上的丑恶事物和形形色色的坏人 forces of evil in the society; evil people of all descriptions

【牛黄】niúhuáng〈中药 *Chin. med.*〉指病牛的胆汁凝结成的黄色粒状物或块状物。是珍贵的药材。bezoar; yellow granular substance or mass of material formed from the bile of diseased cattle; valuable medicinal ingredient

【牛角尖】niújiǎojiān (～儿 niújiǎojiānr)〈比喻 *fig.*〉无法解决的问题或不值得研究的小问题 insoluble or insignificant problem: 钻～ take unnecessary pains over insignificant matters; split hairs

【牛劲】niújìn (～儿 niújìnr) ❶ 大力气 great strength; tremendous effort: 费了～ exert all one's strength ❷ same as 牛脾气 niúpí·qi: 犯～ get stubborn

【牛郎星】niúlángxīng 牵牛星的通称 common name for 牵牛星 qiānniúxīng

【牛郎织女】niúláng zhīnǚ ❶ 指牛郎星和织女星 the stars Altair and Vega ❷ 古代神话中人物。织女是天帝的孙女，与牛郎结合后，不再给天帝织云锦，天帝用天河将他们隔开，只准每年农历七月七日相会一次。相会时喜鹊在银河上给他们搭桥，称为鹊桥。现在用'牛郎织女'比喻长期分居两地的夫妻。Cowherd and Weaving-girl, two characters in ancient mythology. The Weaving girl stops weaving clouds for her grandfather, the God of Heaven, after marrying the cowherd, so the God of Heaven separates them with the River of Heaven (the Milky way), permitting them to meet only once a year, on the 7th day of the 7th lunar month, when magpies build a bridge for them over the river — the Magpie Bridge. Today the term is used to refer to husband and wife living in different parts of the country.

【牛马】niúmǎ〈比喻 *fig.*〉为生活所迫供人驱使从事艰苦劳动的人 slave; workhorse; one who has to work very hard for others to scrape a living

【牛毛】niúmáo〈比喻 *fig.*〉很多、很密或很细 great in number or density; very fine: ～细雨 drizzle; mizzle | 苛捐杂税，多如～ innumerable heavy taxes and levies

【牛虻】niúméng 昆虫，虻的一种，身体长椭圆形，有灰、黑、黄褐等色，胸部和腹部有花纹。雄的吸食植物的汁液和花蜜，雌的吸食牛、马等家畜的血液。gadfly (*Tabanus bovinus*); insect of the family Tabanidae, which has a grey, black or yellowish-brown elongated oval body, and bears patterns on its thorax and belly, the male sucking plant juice and nectar, while the female sucking the blood of livestock such as cattle and horses

【牛腩】niúnǎn〈方 *dial.*〉牛肚子上和近肋骨处的松软肌肉，也指用这种肉做成的菜肴 sirloin; tenderloin; tender loin of cattle at the stomach and near the ribs; dish made of beef from those parts

【牛排】niúpái 大而厚的牛肉片，也指用大而厚的牛肉片做成的菜肴 beefsteak; large, thick slice of beef, or a dish made of it

【牛皮】niúpí ❶ 牛的皮(多指已经鞣制的 oft. tanned) cowhide ❷〈比喻 *fig.*〉柔韧或坚韧 tensile; pliable; flexible; tough: ～糖 sticky candy|～纸 kraft paper ❸ 说大话叫吹牛皮 [when preceded by the verb 吹 chuī] blowing one's horn; brag

【牛皮癣】niúpíxuǎn 慢性皮肤病,症状是先出现丘疹,以后有容易脱落的薄鳞片,多生在肘部、膝部,局部发痒,不传染 psoriasis; chronic, non-infectious skin disease characterized by appearance of papulae, which are later covered with thin, loose scales, often seen at the elbows and knees, causing itching

【牛皮纸】niúpízhǐ 质地坚韧、拉力强的纸,黄褐色,用硫酸盐木浆制成,多用于包装 kraft (paper); tough brown paper with great tensile strength, made from wood pulp treated with a solution of sodium sulfate, used chiefly for wrapping paper

【牛脾气】niúpí·qi 倔强执拗的脾气 stubbornness; obstinacy; bullheadedness; wilfulness

【牛气】niú·qi〈方 *dial.*〉形容自高自大的骄傲神气 arrogant; overbearing; haughty; proud

【牛溲马勃】niúsōu mǎbó 牛溲是牛尿(一说车前草),马勃是一种菌类,都可做药用 cattle urine (or ribgrass according to another theory) and puffball (a fungus), both used as medicines;〈比喻 *fig.*〉虽然微贱但是有用的东西 sth. cheap but useful

【牛头刨】niútóubào 刨床的一种,机床刀架部分形状像牛头,用来加工较小的平面。加工时工件固定在工作台上,刨刀做往复运动切削。shaping machine; hacksaw; planer with a blade adapter in the shape of a bull's head, used for shaping smaller surfaces, the blade moving back and forth cutting the work piece fixed on the work stand

【牛头不对马嘴】niú tóu bù duì mǎ zuǐ ☞ 驴唇不对马嘴 lǘ chún bù duì mǎ zuǐ on p. 1264

【牛头马面】Niútóu Mǎmiàn 迷信传说阎王手下的两个鬼卒,一个头像牛,一个头像马 Ox Head and Horse Face; two demon attendants of the King of Hell in mythology;〈比喻 *fig.*〉各种阴险丑恶的人 insidious people; treacherous people; sinister people; wicked people

【牛性】niúxìng same as 牛脾气 niúpí·qi

【牛鞅】niúyàng 牛拉东西时架在脖子上的器具 yoke; tool set on the neck of an ox when pulling things; also 牛鞅子 niúyàng·zi

【牛饮】niúyǐn 形容大口地喝 gulp; drink gallons

【牛仔裤】niúzǎikù 紧腰身、浅裆、裤腿很瘦的裤子,多用较厚实的布制成 jeans; pants tight at the waist and legs, with a low crotch, oft. made of thick and durable cloth; 仔 also put as 崽 zǎi

niǔ (ㄋㄧㄡˇ)

扭 niǔ ❶ 掉转;转动 turn round: ～过头来向后看 look around ❷ 拧 (nǐng) twist; wrench; wrest; wring: 把树枝子～断 twist a twig to break it ❸ 拧伤(筋骨) sprain; wrench: ～了腰 sprain one's back ❹ 身体左右摇动(多指走路时)(as one walks)(of one's body) roll; swing: ～秧歌 do the *yangko* dance|～了两步 make two steps in a swaying gait ❺ 揪住 seize; grapple with: ～打 wrestle; grapple|两人～在一起。The two were grappling with each other. ❻ 不正 crooked; skew; slant: 七～八歪 twist around; crooked|歪歪～～ crooked; askew; shapeless and twisted

【扭摆】niǔbǎi (身体)扭动摇摆 (of the body) sway: 推手车的人左右～着身子。The man pushing the cart is twisting his body left and right.|她～着腰慢步走来。She walked over, her hips swaying.

【扭打】niǔdǎ 互相揪住对打 wrestle; grapple: 他俩～在一起,拉也拉不开。The two of them were grappling with each other, and couldn't be pulled apart.

【扭搭】niǔ·da 走路时肩膀随着腰一前一后地扭动 swing one's shoulders as one walks; walk with a swing; walk with a swaying gait: 那女人～～地走了。The woman walked away with a swaying gait.

【扭股儿糖】niǔgǔrtáng 用麦芽糖制成的两股或三股扭在一起的食品,多用来形容扭动或缠绕的形状 Chinese maltose candy, with two or three strands twisted together, oft. used to describe a twisted or winding shape

【扭结】niǔjié 纠缠;缠绕在一起 twist together; tangle up; entangle; entwine: 在织布以前要将棉纱弄湿,才不会～。The cotton yarn should be wetted before weaving so that it won't get entangled.|几件事～在一起,一时想不出解决的办法。Several of these problems are so tangled up that there's no solution at present.

【扭力】niǔlì 使物体发生扭转形变的力 twisting (or torsion) force

【扭力天平】niǔlì tiānpíng 测量重力场变化的仪器。由钨丝悬挂一根两端有小球的金属杆构成。重力场变化时,金属杆发生偏转。多用于探矿。torsion balance; instrument for measuring changes in the field of gravity, consisting of a metal rod with a small ball at each end hanging from a tungsten wire, where the metal rod turns when the field of gravity changes; the instrument is used for prospecting

【扭捏】niǔ·nie 本指走路时身体故意左右摇动,今多形容举止言谈不大方(ori.) walk with an

N

affected swing; behave and talk unnaturally and diffidently; be affectedly bashful; hem and haw: 她～了大半天，才说出一句话来。After much affected embarrassment, she finally said something.|有话直截了当地说，别扭扭捏捏的。Stop hemming and hawing; if you have something to say, out with it.

【扭曲】niǔqū ❶ 扭转变形 distort; twist; contort: 地震发生后，房屋倒塌，铁轨～。After the earthquake, buildings collapsed and railroads were twisted out of shape. ❷〈比喻 *fig.*〉歪曲；颠倒（事实、形象等）distort; falsify; misrepresent (facts, images, etc.): 被～的历史恢复了本来面目。Distorted history has been restored to its true colours.

【扭送】niǔsòng 揪住违法犯罪分子送交司法机关 seize (an offender or a criminal) and deliver him to the police

【扭头】niǔ//tóu（～儿 niǔ//tóur）❶（人）转动头 turn one's head away; turn away: ～不顾 turn away and ignore|他扭过头去，不理人家。He turned away and cut the others dead. ❷ 转身 turn round: 大妈二话没说，～就走。The old woman turned and walked off, without saying a word.

【扭秧歌】niǔ yāng•ge 跳秧歌舞 do the *yangko* dance

【扭转】niǔzhuǎn ❶ 掉转 turn; swing: 他～身子，向车间走去。He turned round and headed for the workshop. ❷ 纠正或改变事物的发展方向或目前的状况 turn back; reverse; remedy; correct or change the developing direction of things or the current state: ～局面 turn the tide; change the situation|～乾坤 reverse the course of events|必须～理论脱离实际的现象。The discrepancy between theory and practice should be corrected.

狃 niǔ 因袭；拘泥 be bound by; be constrained by: ～于习俗 be bound by custom|～于成见 be bound by prejudice

忸 niǔ［忸怩］(niǔní) 形容不好意思或不大方的样子 blushing; bashful; shy; uneasy; constrained: ～的神情 bashful expression|别忸忸怩怩的，大方一些。Stop being bashful; take it easy.

纽 niǔ ❶ 器物上可以抓住而提起来的部分 handle; knob; a part of an apparatus designed to be held and lifted with the hand: 秤～ the lifting cord of a steelyard|印～ the knob of a seal ❷ 丝扣 silk button: ～襻 button loop|衣～ button ❸ 枢纽 bond; tie; link: ～带 link; tie ❹（～儿 niǔr）瓜果等刚结的果实 immature fruit: 南瓜～ young pumpkin fruit

【纽带】niǔdài 指能够起联系作用的人或事物 link; tie; bond; sb. or sth. that acts as a link: 批评和自我批评是团结的～，是进步的保证。Criticism and self-criticism are the bonds of unity and guarantees of progress.

【纽扣】niǔkòu（～儿 niǔkòur）可以把衣服等扣起来的小形球状物或片状物 button; small ball-shaped or disk-shaped fastener used to join two parts of a garment

【纽襻】niǔpàn（～儿 niǔpànr）扣住纽扣的套儿 button loop

【纽子】niǔ•zi same as 纽扣 niǔkòu

杻 niǔ 古书上说的一种树 a kind of tree recorded in ancient books

☞ chǒu on p. 279

钮 niǔ ❶ same as 纽 niǔ ❷ ☞ 电钮 diànniǔ on p. 439 ❸（Niǔ）姓 a surname

niù（ㄋㄧㄡˋ）

拗（抝）niù 固执；不随和；不驯顺 stubborn; obstinate; headstrong: 执～ stubborn; obstinate; headstrong|脾气很～ have an obstinate temper

☞ ǎo on p. 19 and ào on p. 19

【拗不过】niù•bu guò 无法改变（别人的坚决的意见）be unable to dissuade; fail to talk sb. out of doing sth.: 他～老大娘，只好答应了。Unable to dissuade the old woman, he had to comply.

nóng（ㄋㄨㄥˊ）

农（農、辳）nóng ❶ 农业 agriculture; farming: 务～ be engaged in agriculture|～具 farm tools|～田水利 irrigation and water conservancy|～林牧副渔 farming, forestry, animal husbandry, sideline production and fishery ❷ 农民 peasant; farmer: 老～ old peasant|茶～ tea grower|菜～ vegetable grower ❹（Nóng）姓 a surname

【农产品】nóngchǎnpǐn 农业中生产的物品，如稻子、小麦、高粱、棉花、烟叶、甘蔗等 agricultural products; farm produce, e. g. rice, wheat, sorghum, cotton, tobacco, sugarcane, etc.

【农场】nóngchǎng 使用机器、大规模进行农业生产的企业单位 farm; enterprise engaged in large-scale mechanized agricultural production

【农村】nóngcūn 以从事农业生产为主的人聚居的地方 rural area; countryside; country; place where people engaged in agricultural production live

【农夫】nóngfū〈旧时 *old*〉称从事农业生产的男子 farmer; peasant; ploughman

【农妇】nóngfù 农家妇女 peasant woman; farm woman

【农耕】nónggēng 农业耕种；农作 farming; husbandry: 不事～ neglect farm work|～劳作 do farm work

【农工】nónggōng ❶ 农民和工人 peasants and workers: 扶助～ support the peasants and workers ❷ 农业工人的简称 abbr. for 农业工人 nóngyè gōngrén; farm worker; farm labourer

【农户】nónghù 从事农业生产的人家 peasant household

【农活】nónghuó (～儿 nónghuór) 农业生产中的工作,如耕地、播种、施肥、收割等 farm work; farm chores; work in agricultural production, e.g. tilling, sowing, fertilizing, reaping, etc.

【农机】nóngjī 农业机械 agricultural machinery; farm machinery: ～部门 department of agricultural machinery|～工业 agricultural machinery industry

【农家】nóngjiā 从事农业生产的人家 peasant family: ～生活 rural life|～子弟 children from peasant families

【农家】Nóngjiā 先秦时期反映农业生产和农民思想的学术派别。著作目录见于《汉书·艺文志》,多已失传。school of Agriculturists; pre-Qin academic school which reflects agricultural production and peasant ideology. The subjects of this school are listed in *History of Han·Records of Art and Literature*, most of which have been lost.

【农家肥料】nóngjiā féiliào 农家自己生产的肥料,如粪肥、绿肥等(区别于作为商品的化学肥料 as compared with 'chemical fertilizer' as a commodity) manure; farmyard manure; homemade fertilizer, e.g. muck, green manure, etc.

【农具】nóngjù 进行农业生产所使用的工具,如犁、耙、耧等 farm implements; farm tools, e.g. plough, rake, drill, etc.

【农垦】nóngkěn 农业垦殖 land reclamation and cultivation: ～事业 the cause of land reclamation and cultivation

【农历】nónglì ❶ 阴阳历的一种,是我国的传统历法,平年 12 个月,大月 30 天,小月 29 天,全年 354 天或 355 天(一年中哪一月大,哪一月小,年年不同)。由于平均每年的天数比太阳年约差 11 天,所以在 19 年里设置 7 个闰月,有闰月的年份全年 383 天或 384 天。又根据太阳的位置,把一个太阳年分成 24 个节气,便于农事。纪年用天干地支搭配,60 年周而复始。这种历法相传创始于夏代,所以又称夏历。lunar calendar; traditional Chinese calendar, according to which a common year has 354 or 355 days in total, 12 months of 30 days or 29 days (the number of days in a month varies in different years). As the average number of days in a lunar year is 11 days shorter than a solar year, seven leap months are added every 19 years, so a leap year has 383 or 384 days. According to changes in the position of the sun, a solar year is divided into 24 seasonal division points to facilitate farming. The years are designated by pairing items from the Heavenly Stems and Earthly Branches respectively so that 60 years form a cycle. It is said that the lunar calendar was created during the Xia Dynasty. Hence the term, *xiali*, or Xia calendar. also 旧历 jiùlì; generally called 阴历 yīnlì ❷ 农业上使用的历书 farmers' almanac; almanac for agricultural production

【农忙】nóngmáng 指春、夏、秋三季农事繁忙(时节) farming season; busy season (in farming) in spring, summer and autumn

【农贸市场】nóngmào shìchǎng 以农副业产品贸易为主的个体摊贩市场 market of farm produce; market where individual traders sell farm and sideline products; commonly called 自由市场 zìyóu shìchǎng

【农民】nóngmín 在农村从事农业生产的劳动者 farmer; peasant; peasantry; one who is engaged in agricultural production in rural areas

【农民起义】nóngmín qǐyì 农民为了反抗地主阶级的政治压迫和经济剥削而进行的武装斗争 peasant uprising; peasant revolt; armed struggle of peasants against political oppression and the economic exploitation of the landlord class

【农民战争】nóngmín zhànzhēn 封建社会农民为反对地主阶级的反动统治而进行的革命战争。一般有鲜明的战斗口号,活动范围较大,例如清代的太平天国革命。peasant war; revolutionary war of peasants against the reactionary rule of the landlord class during feudalism, generally having distinct rallying slogans and spreading to a large area, e.g. the Taiping Heavenly Kingdom Rebellion

【农奴】nóngnú 封建社会中隶属于农奴主或封建主的农业生产劳动者。在经济上受剥削,没有人身自由和任何政治权利。serf; agricultural labourer owned by a lord in feudal society, who was deprived of personal freedom and political rights and suffered economic exploitation

【农奴主】nóngnúzhǔ 占有农奴和生产资料的人 serf owner; one who owns serfs and the means of production

【农人】nóngrén same as 农民 nóngmín

【农舍】nóngshè 农民住的房屋 farmhouse; cottage; the dwelling of a farmer

【农时】nóngshí 农业生产中,配合季节气候,每种作物都有一定的耕作时间,称为农时 farming season; the time of the year in which a certain farm crop has to be sown or planted according to changes in the climate of a given region: 不误～sow or grow a farm crop in the proper season

【农事】nóngshì 农业生产中的各项工作 farm work; farming: ～繁忙 busy with farm work

【农田】nóngtián 耕种的田地 farmland; cultivated land; cropland: ～水利 irrigation and water conservancy

N

【农闲】nóngxián 指冬季农事较少(时节) slack season in farming

【农械】nóngxiè 喷农药用的器械,如喷雾器、喷粉机等 apparatus for spraying pesticides, e.g. sprayer, duster, etc. e.g.

【农学】nóngxué 研究农业生产的科学,内容包括作物栽培、育种、土壤、气象、肥料、农业病虫害等 agronomy; agriculture; science of agricultural production, including the planting and breeding of crops, soil, meteorology, fertilizers, plant diseases and pests, etc.

【农谚】nóngyàn 有关农业生产的谚语,是农民从长期生产实践中总结出来的经验,对于农业生产有一定的指导作用。如'谷雨前后,种瓜点豆','头伏萝卜二伏菜'。farmers' saying; peasants' proverb; saying about agricultural production and from experience farmers have gathered through long years of productive practice, serving as useful guide for agricultural production, e. g. 'Around Grain Rain, grow melons and peas,' and 'Grow turnips in the first period of the hot season, and cabbages in the second'

【农药】nóngyào 农业上用来杀虫、杀菌、除草,毒杀害鸟、害兽以及促进作物生长的药物的统称 agricultural chemicals; pesticide; farming chemicals; general name for chemicals used to kill pests, germs and harmful birds and animals, and for weeding, and promoting crop growth

【农业】nóngyè 栽培农作物和饲养牲畜的生产事业。在国民经济中的农业,还包括林业、渔业和农村副业等项生产在内。agriculture; farming; enterprise of growing crops and raising livestock; As a part of the national economy, it also includes forestry, fishery, and rural sideline occupations.

【农业工人】nóngyè gōngrén 在农场从事农业生产的工人 agricultural labourer; farm labourer; farm worker; 简称 abbr. 农工 nónggōng

【农业国】nóngyèguó 工业不发达、国民经济收入中以农业收入为主要部分的国家 agricultural country; country with an undeveloped industrial base, where agricultural income constitutes the major part of the national revenue

【农业合作化】nóngyè hézuòhuà 用合作社的组织形式,把个体的、分散的农业经济改变成比较大规模的、集体的社会主义农业经济 cooperative transformation of agriculture; agricultural cooperative movement; transforming an individual, scattered agricultural economy into a larger-scale, collective socialist agricultural economy by organizing cooperatives; also 农业集体化 nóngyè jítǐhuà

【农业税】nóngyèshuì 国家对从事农业生产、有农业收入的单位或个人所征收的税 agricultural tax; tax levied by the state from units or individuals engaged in agricultural production and having agricultural incomes

【农艺】nóngyì 指作物的栽培、选种等技术 agriculture; technology of crop growing, seed selection, etc.

【农用】nóngyòng 指为农业或农民所使用 farm-oriented; agricultural; used in agriculture or by farmers: ~物资 farm-oriented commodities

【农作物】nóngzuòwù 农业上栽种的各种植物,包括粮食作物、油料作物、蔬菜、果树和做工业原料用的棉花、烟草等 crop; cultivated plants or agricultural produce, e.g. grain, oil plants, vegetables, fruit, and industrial crops, e.g. cotton, tobacco, etc.; abbr. 作物 zuòwù

侬(儂) nóng ❶〈方 *dial.*〉你 you ❷ 我 I(多见于旧诗文 oft. in old poems) ❸(Nóng) 姓 a surname

【侬人】Nóngrén 指居住在广西和云南交界地区的壮族 the Zhuangs inhabiting the area bordering the Guangxi and Zhuang Autonomous Region in Yunnan Province

哝(噥) nóng [哝哝](nóng•nong) 小声说话 murmur; whisper; speak in undertones; say in a low indistinct voice; utter indistinctly: 她在姐姐的耳边~了好半天。She whispered in her elder sister's ear for a long time.

浓(濃) nóng ❶ 液体或气体中所含的某种成份多;稠密(跟'淡'相对 as opposed to 'light') dense; thick; (of liquid or gas) containing much of a certain component: ~墨 thick, dark ink|~云 heavy cloud|~茶 strong tea ◇~眉 heavy eyebrows; thick eyebrows ❷ 程度深 (of degree or extent) great; strong: 兴趣很~ take a great interest in sth. |睡意正~ be in a deep sleep

【浓淡】nóngdàn (颜色)深浅 (of colour) shade; hue; tint: ~适宜 just the right shade of colour

【浓度】nóngdù 一定量溶液中所含溶质的量,通常用所含溶质质量占全部溶液质量的百分比来表示 density; thickness; concentration; quantity of solute in a certain measure of solution, usually represented by the percentage of the mass of the solute in the total mass of the solution

【浓厚】nónghòu ❶(烟雾、云层等)很浓 (of smoke, fog, clouds, etc.) dense; thick; heavy: ~的黑烟 thick dark smoke ❷(色彩、意识、气氛)重 (of colour, mentality, atmosphere) strong; pronounced: ~的地方色彩 pronounced (or marked) local colour|~的封建意识 strong feudal mentality ❸(兴趣)大 (of interest) great; strong; acute; intense; lively; keen: 孩子们对打乒乓球兴趣都很~。The children take a lively interest in the table tennis.

【浓烈】nóngliè 浓重强烈 strong; thick; heavy:

香气～heavy scent|～的色彩 rich, strong colours|～的乡土气息 marked local flavour

【浓眉】nóngméi 黑而密的眉毛 dark and thick eyebrow:～大眼 thick eyebrows and big eyes

【浓密】nóngmì 稠密(多指枝叶、烟雾、须发等 oft. of foliage, smoke, fog, hair, etc.) dense; thick

【浓墨重彩】nóng mò zhòng cǎi 指叙述或描写着墨多 narration or description with attention to detail and in colourful language

【浓缩】nóngsuō ❶ 用加热等方法使溶液中的溶剂蒸发而溶液的浓度增高 concentrate; condense; increase the density of a solution by evaporating the solvent using various methods such as heating, etc. ❷ 泛指用一定的方法使物体中不需要的部分减少,从而使需要部分的相对含量增加 enrich; increase the proportion of required parts in a substance by decreasing unnecessary parts through using certain methods:～铀 enriched uranium|～食物 enriched food ◇这个建筑～了中国数千年来的装饰艺术。This building is a crystallization of several millennia of Chinese art of decoration.

【浓艳】nóngyàn (色彩)浓重而艳丽 (of colour) rich and gaudy

【浓郁】[1] nóngyù (花草等的香气)浓重(of fragrance of flowers, grass, etc.) rich; strong; powerful:～的花香迎面扑来。A strong fragrance of flowers greeted the nostrils.

【浓郁】[2] nóngyù ❶ 繁密 dense; thick:～的松林 dense pine forest ❷ (色彩、情感、气氛等)重 (of colour, feeling, atmosphere, etc.) exuberant; strong; rich:春意～ luxuriant spring|色调～ rich hue|感情～ strong feeling|～的生活气息 rich taste of life|这个歌曲抒情气氛十分～。The song is rich in emotion. ❸ (兴趣)大 (of interest) great; strong; keen:兴致～ be in high spirits|～的兴趣 keen interest

【浓重】nóngzhòng (烟雾、气味、色彩等)很浓很重 (of smoke, fog, scent, colour, etc.) dense; thick; strong:山谷中的雾越发～了。The fog in the valley was thickening.|桂花发出～的香味 strong fragrance sent forth by the osmanthus|他说话带有～的乡音。He speaks with a strong accent.|这位老人画的花卉,设色十分～。This elderly man's paintings of flowers are distinguished by exuberant colouration.

【浓妆艳抹】nóng zhuāng yàn mǒ 形容女子妆饰艳丽 (of a woman) richly attired and heavily made-up

脓(膿) nóng 某些炎症病变所形成的黄绿色汁液,含大量白细胞、细菌、蛋白质、脂肪以及组织分解的产物 pus; yellowish-white fluid formed in infected tissue, consisting of white blood cells, germs, protein, fat and debris of tissue

【脓包】nóngbāo ❶ 身体某部组织化脓时因脓液积聚而形成的隆起 pustule; small inflamed elevation of the skin that is filled with pus, caused by the festering of certain tissues in the body ❷〈比喻 *fig.*〉无用的人 jerk; good-for-nothing; ne'er-do-well; worthless fellow

【脓肿】nóngzhǒng 一种病理现象,发炎的组织一部分坏死、液化并形成脓液而积聚在组织中 abscess; pathological phenomenon where the tissue contains a collection of pus formed by necrosis and disintegration of inflamed tissue

秾(穠) nóng〈书 *fml.*〉草木茂盛 luxuriant; lush:夭桃～李 beautiful peach and plum blossoms

醲(醲) nóng〈书 *fml.*〉酒味厚 (of wine) rich-flavoured; mellow

nòng (ㄋㄨㄥˋ)

弄 nòng ❶ 手拿着、摆弄着或逗引着玩儿 toy with; fiddle with; fool with:他又～鸽子去了。He's gone to play with the pigeons again.|小孩儿爱～沙土。Children like to play in the sand. ❷ 做;干;办;搞 do; manage; handle; deal with; operate:～饭 prepare a meal|这活儿我做不好,请你帮我～～。I can't do this work properly. Will you please help me with it?|把书～坏了 ruined the book|这件事总得～出个结果来才成。We've got to reach some resolution of this matter. ❸ 设法取得 manage to obtain; get; fetch:～点水来 fetch some water ❹ 耍;玩弄 play; manipulate; manoeuvre:～手段 play tricks|舞文～墨 play on word; show off one's literary skill ☞ lòng on p. 1252

【弄潮儿】nòngcháo'ér ❶ 在潮水中搏击、嬉戏的年青人,也指驾驶木船的人 young person swimming or playing in tidewater; beach swimmer; rowing man ❷〈比喻 *fig.*〉敢于在风险中拼搏的人 adventurer; person who dares to take risks; dare devil

【弄鬼】nòng//guǐ〈方 *dial.*〉捣鬼 play tricks; hatch a plot; do mischief; play the devil

【弄假成真】nòng jiǎ chéng zhēn 本来是假装的,结果却变成真事。What was make-believe has become reality.

【弄巧成拙】nòng qiǎo chéng zhuō 想要巧妙的手段,结果反而坏了事 outsmart oneself; try to be clever only to end up with a blunder; suffer from being too smart

【弄权】nòng//quán 把持权柄,滥用权力 manipulate power for personal ends; abuse power:奸臣～。Treacherous court officials abuse their powers.

【弄瓦】nòngwǎ〈书 *fml.*〉指生下女孩子 have a newborn daughter; (古人把瓦给女孩子玩 in ancient times baby girls were given a curved tile, used as a spindle, to play with; 瓦 *wa*: 原始的纺锤 primitive spindle)

【弄虚作假】nòng xū zuò jiǎ 耍花招,欺骗人 practise fraud; employ trickery; resort to deception; play tricks

【弄璋】nòngzhāng 〈书 *fml*.〉指生下男孩子 have a newborn son (古人把璋给男孩子玩 in ancient times baby boys were given a jade tablet to play with; 璋 *zhang*: 一种玉器 a kind of jadewares)

nòu (ㄋㄡˋ)

耨(鎒) nòu 〈书 *fml*.〉❶ 锄草的农具 weeding hoe ❷ 锄草 weed: 深耕细～ deep ploughing and meticulous weeding

nú (ㄋㄨˊ)

伮 nú 人名用字 *nu*, used in a person's name

奴 nú ❶ 旧社会中受压迫、剥削、役使而没有人身自由等政治权利的人(跟'主'相对 as opposed to 'master') (in pre-1949 China) bondservant; serf; one bound in servitude, suffering from oppression and exploitation, and without personal freedom and other political rights: ～隶 slave|农～ serf ❷ 青年女子自称(多见于早期白话 oft. in early vernacular) [term of self-address for young women] I; me ❸ 像对待奴隶一样地蹂躏、使用 enslave; subjugate; oppress and make to work like a slave: ～役 enslave; subjugate

【奴婢】núbì 男女奴仆。太监对皇帝、后妃等也自称奴婢。servant; slave; maidservant; term of self-address used by a eunuch before an emperor, empress, etc.

【奴才】nú·cai ❶ 家奴;奴仆(明清两代宦官和清代满人、武臣对皇帝自称;清代满人家庭奴仆对主人自称) serf; (term of self-address used by eunuchs in the Ming and Qing dynasties, and Manchurians and military officials in the Qing Dynasty before an emperor; term of self-address used by servants in Qing-dynasty Manchurian households before their masters) your servant ❷ 指甘心供人驱使,帮助作恶的人 lackey; flunky; person of slavish or unquestioning obedience

【奴化】núhuà (侵略者及其帮凶)用各种方法使被侵略的民族甘心受奴役 (of invaders and their accomplices) enslave; subject the people to enslavement by various measures: ～教育 education aimed at enslavement|～思想 slave ideology

【奴家】nújiā 青年女子自称(多见于早期白话 oft. in early vernacular) [term of self-address for a young woman] I; me

【奴隶】núlì 为奴隶主劳动而没有人身自由的人,常常被奴隶主任意买卖或杀害 slave; one who works for a slave owner and has no personal freedom, often bought, sold or killed by slave-owners at will

【奴隶社会】núlì shèhuì 一种社会形态,以奴隶主占有奴隶和生产资料为基础。奴隶社会的生产力比原始公社有所提高,手工业、农业和畜牧业,脑力劳动和体力劳动都有了分工,奴隶主和奴隶形成两个对立阶级,奴隶主为了镇压奴隶的反抗建立了奴隶主专政的国家。slave society; society based on slave-owners' possession of slaves and means of production. In a slave society productivity is higher than in a primitive commune, and divisions of labour has been effected between handicraft industry, agriculture and animal husbandry, as well as between mental and manual labour, and slaves and slave-owners form two opposing classes, with the latter establishing a dictatorial government to suppress the former.

【奴隶主】núlìzhǔ 占有奴隶和生产资料的人,是奴隶社会里的统治阶级 slave-owner; slaveholder; member of the ruling class of a slave society in the possession of slaves and means of production

【奴仆】núpú 〈旧时 *old*〉在主人家里从事杂役的人(总称) servant; lackey

【奴性】núxìng 甘心受人奴役的品性 servility; slavishness: ～十足的汉奸 an extremely servile traitor to China

【奴颜婢膝】nú yán bì xī 形容卑躬屈膝奉承巴结的样子 subservient; servile

【奴颜媚骨】nú yán mèi gǔ 形容卑躬屈膝谄媚讨好的样子 bowing and scraping; sycophancy and obsequiousness

【奴役】núyì 把人当做奴隶使用 enslave; keep in bondage

孥 nú 〈书 *fml*.〉❶ 儿女 children; sons and daughters: 妻～ wife and children ❷ 妻子和儿女 wife and children

驽 nú 〈书 *fml*.〉❶ 驽马 inferior horse; jade ❷ 〈比喻 *fig*.〉人没有能力 incompetent; incapable; unfit; unqualified: ～钝 dull; stupid|～才 incompetent

【驽钝】núdùn 〈书 *fml*.〉愚笨;迟钝 dull; stupid

【驽马】númǎ 〈书 *fml*.〉跑不快的马 inferior horse; jade

nǔ (ㄋㄨˇ)

努(❷拗、呶、㕯) nǔ ❶ 使出(力气) exert (one's efforts); put forth (one's strength): ～力 make efforts; try hard; exert oneself|～劲儿 put forth all one's strength ❷ 凸出 bulge; protrude: ～着眼睛 with bulging eyes|～着嘴 purse one's lips ❸ 〈方 *dial*.〉用力太过,身体

内部受伤 injure oneself by overexertion
☞ 呶 náo on p. 1393

【努力】nǔ//lì 把力量尽量使出来 make efforts; try hard; exert oneself: ~工作 work hard | ~学习 put great effort into one's studies | 大家再努一把力。Let's all make still greater efforts.

【努责】nǔzé 医学上指大便或分娩时腹部用力 (med.) use the force of the abdomen muscles while defecating or in labour

【努嘴】nǔ//zuǐ (~儿 nǔ//zuǐr) 向人撅嘴示意 purse one's lips as a signal: 奶奶直~儿,让他别再往下说。Grandma pursed her lips at him, hinting that he should stop talking.

弩 nǔ 弩弓 crossbow: 万~齐发 all the crossbows shot at once | 剑拔~张 be at loggerheads; ready to jump at each other's throat

【弩弓】nǔgōng 〈古代 *arch.*〉兵器,一种利用机械力量射箭的弓 crossbow; weapon that shoots arrows using mechanical force

【弩箭】nǔjiàn 用弩弓发射的箭 arrow shot from a crossbow; crossbow arrow

砮 nǔ 〈书 *fml.*〉可做箭镞的石头 stone arrowhead

胬 nǔ [胬肉](nǔròu)〈中医 *Chin. med.*〉指眼球结膜增生而突起的肉状物。未遮蔽住角膜的称'胬肉',遮蔽住角膜的称'胬肉攀睛'。pterygium; abnormal mass of tissue arising from the conjunctiva of the eye, which may or may not grow over the cornea

nù (ㄋㄨˋ)

怒 nù ❶ 愤怒 anger; rage; fury: 恼~ angry; irritated; pissed | 发~ get angry; get cross; get mad | ~容满面 look full of rage; flush with anger | 老羞成~ get angry as a result of embarrassment ❷ 形容气势很盛 forceful; vigorous; dynamic; vehement: ~涛 furious (or raging) billows | 狂风~号 howling, vehement wind | 百花~放 flowers blooming in profusion

【怒潮】nùcháo 汹涌澎湃的浪潮 raging tide; tidal bore;〈比喻 *fig.*〉声势浩大的反抗运动 large-scale resistance movement

【怒叱】nùchì 愤怒地责骂 angrily rebuke; indignantly denounce; berate

【怒斥】nùchì 愤怒地斥责 angrily rebuke; indignantly reprimand; berate; inveigh against: ~叛徒 berate a traitor

【怒冲冲】nùchōngchōng (~的 nùchōngchōng·de)形容非常生气的样子 in a rage; in a huff; furiously; beside oneself with rage

【怒发冲冠】nù fà chōng guān 头发直竖,把帽子都顶起来了。形容非常愤怒。standing hair pushing up one's hat — bristle with anger; be in a towering rage; be infuriated; burst with indignation

【怒放】nùfàng (花)盛开 (of flowers) in full bloom; run riot: 春天,桃花、杏花争相~。In spring, peaches and apricots bloom in a riot of colour. ◇心花~ be brimming with joy

【怒号】nùháo 大声叫唤(多用来形容大风) (oft. of wind) howl; roar: 狂风~。A violent wind is howling.

【怒吼】nùhǒu 猛兽发威吼叫(of beasts of prey) roar; howl; roar; howl;〈比喻 *fig.*〉发出雄壮的声音 emit loud, resonant sounds: 狂风大作,海水~。The wind howled and the sea roared.

【怒火】nùhuǒ 形容极大的愤怒 fury; indignation: 压不住心头的~ be unable to restrain one's fury | ~中烧 be ablaze with anger; be burning with anger (or wrath)

【怒目】nùmù ❶ 发怒时瞪着两眼 glare; glower; look daggers; scowl: 横眉~ look daggers at | ~而视 glare at; glower at; stare angrily ❷ 发怒时瞪着的眼睛 glaring eyes; a fierce stare: ~圆睁 glaring eyes

【怒气】nùqì 愤怒的情绪 anger; rage; fury: ~冲冲 in a great rage; be boiling with rage

【怒容】nùróng same as 怒色 nùsè: ~满面 a face contorted with anger

【怒色】nùsè 愤怒的表情 angry look: 面带~ wear an angry scowl

【怒视】nùshì 愤怒地注视 glare at; glower at; look daggers at; scowl at: ~着凶残的敌人 glower at the cruel enemy

【怒涛】nùtāo 汹涌起伏的波涛 furious (or raging) billows; precipitous sea: ~澎湃 billows raging with great fury

【怒族】Nùzú 我国少数民族之一,分布在云南 the Nu people, or the Nus, one of China's minority ethnic peoples living in Yunnan Province

傉 nù 用于人名,秃发傉檀,东晋时南凉国君 *nu*, used in a person's name, e.g. Nutan the Bald, king of Southern Liang in the Eastern Jin Dynasty

nǚ (ㄋㄩˇ)

女 nǚ ❶ 女性(跟'男'相对 as opposed to 'male') female; woman: ~工 woman worker | ~学生 woman (girl) student | 少~ young girl; maiden | 男~平等 equality of men and women ❷ 女儿 daughter; girl: 长~ the eldest daughter | 生儿育~ bear and bring up children ❸ 二十八宿之一 one of the 28 constellations into which the celestial sphere is divided in ancient Chinese astronomy
〈古 *arch.*〉same as 汝 rǔ

【女儿】nǚ'ér 女孩子(对父母而言) daughter

N

【女方】nǚfāng 女的方面（多用于有关婚事的场合 oft. used on marriage-related occasions）bride's side; wife's side

【女工】[1] nǚgōng ❶ 女性的工人 woman worker ❷〈旧时 *old*〉指女佣人 woman servant; maid

【女工】[2] nǚgōng〈旧时 *old*〉指女子所做的纺织、缝纫、刺绣等工作和这些工作的成品 needlework; work of weaving, sewing, embroidery, etc. that a woman does, and its products; also 女红 nǚgōng

【女公子】nǚgōngzǐ 对别人的女儿的尊称 respectful term used to refer to sb. else's daughter

【女红】nǚgōng〈书 *fml.*〉same as 女工[2] nǚgōng

【女皇】nǚhuáng 女性皇帝 empress

【女家】nǚjiā 婚姻关系中女方的家；女方 bride's side; bride's family; wife's family

【女眷】nǚjuàn 指女性眷属 womenfolk of a family

【女郎】nǚláng 称年轻的女子 young woman; maiden; girl: 妙龄～ young woman | 摩登～ fashionable woman

【女伶】nǚlíng same as 女优 nǚyōu

【女流】nǚliú 妇女（含轻蔑意 derog.）weaker sex: ～之辈 the weaker sex

【女气】nǚ·qi 形容男子的举止神态像女子（of a man）effeminate; womanish

【女墙】nǚqiáng 城墙上面呈凹凸形的短墙 parapet wall; parapet; low wall with uneven surface; also 女儿墙 nǚ'érqiáng

【女权】nǚquán 妇女在社会上应享的权利 women's rights; rights due to women in a society: 尊重～ respect women's rights

【女人】nǚrén 女性的成年人 woman; women; womenfolk

【女人】nǚ·ren 妻子 wife

【女色】nǚsè 女子的美色 women's beauty; feminine charms: 贪恋～ hanker after women

【女神】nǚshén 神话传说中的女性神 goddess; mythical female being of supernatural powers or attributes

【女生】nǚshēng 女学生 woman student; girl student; schoolgirl: ～宿舍 women students' dorm

【女声】nǚshēng 声乐中的女子声部，一般分女高音、女中音、女低音 female voices in vocal music, including soprano, mezzo-soprano and alto

【女史】nǚshǐ 本为古代女官的名称。旧时借用为对妇女知识分子的尊称。（in ancient times）woman scribe;（old-time respectful form of address）woman scholar

【女士】nǚshì 对妇女的尊称 lady; madam; ladies（polite form of address for women）

【女王】nǚwáng 女性国王 queen; woman sovereign

【女巫】nǚwū 以装神弄鬼、搞迷信活动为业的女人 sorceress; witch; woman who makes a living by practising sorcery; also 巫婆 wūpó

【女性】nǚxìng ❶ 人类两性之一，能在体内产生卵细胞 the female sex or gender, able to produce ova ❷ same as 妇女 fùnǚ: 新～ modern women; emancipated women

【女婿】nǚ·xu ❶ 女儿的丈夫 son-in-law ❷〈方 *dial.*〉same as 丈夫 zhàng·fu

【女优】nǚyōu〈旧时 *old*〉称戏曲女演员 actress of traditional opera

【女招待】nǚzhāodài〈旧时 *old*〉饮食店、娱乐场所等雇佣来招待顾客的青年妇女 waitress; young woman who serves customers in a restaurant or a public place of entertainment

【女真】Nǚzhēn 我国古代民族，满族的祖先，居住在今吉林和黑龙江一带，公元 1115 年建立金国 Nuchen, an ethnic people in ancient China who were ancestors of the Manchus, who inhabited what is today's Jilin and Heilongjiang provinces, and founded the Jin Dyansty in 1115; ☞ 金[2] jīn on p. 1003

【女主人】nǚzhǔ·ren 客人对家庭主妇的尊称 [respectful form of address for the female head of a household] hostess; mistress

【女子】nǚzǐ 女性的人 woman; female

钕 nǚ 金属元素，符号 Nd（neodymium）。是一种稀土金属。淡黄色，在空气中容易氧化，用来制合金和光学玻璃等，也用于激光材料。neodymium（Nd）; yellow rare-earth metal element that becomes easily oxidized in the air, used to produce alloys and optical glass, or as a laser material

籹 nǚ ☞［粔籹］（jùnǚ）on p. 1051

nǜ（ㄋㄩˋ）

恧 nǜ〈书 *fml.*〉惭愧 be ashamed: 惭～ feel ashamed

衄（衂、鼻丑） nǜ〈书 *fml.*〉❶ 鼻孔出血，泛指出血 nosebleed; bleeding: 鼻～ nosebleed | 齿～ bleeding gums ❷ 战败 be defeated in battle: 败～ be defeated

朒 nǜ〈书 *fml.*〉❶ 指农历月初月亮出现在东方，也指那时的月光 the moon appearing in the east in the early days of a lunar month; moonlight at such a time ❷ 欠缺；不足 deficient; inadequate; insufficient

nuǎn（ㄋㄨㄢˇ）

暖（煖、煗、暝） nuǎn ❶ 暖和 warm: 风和日～ gentle wind and warm sun | 春～花开。In the warmth of spring all flowers bloom. | 天～了，不用生炉子了。It's warm now, so we don't

need to light a stove. ❷ 使变温暖 warm; warm up: ～酒 heat wine｜～一～手 warm one's hands

☞ 煖 xuān on p. 2171

【暖房】nuǎn//fáng ❶ 旧俗在亲友结婚的前一天前往新房贺喜 old custom where people go to the bridal chamber on the eve of a wedding to offer congratulations ❷ same as 温居 wēn//jū

【暖房】nuǎnfáng same as 温室 wēnshì

【暖锋】nuǎnfēng 暖气团沿着冷气团慢慢上升,并推着冷气团向前移动,在这种情况下,冷、暖气团接触的地带叫做暖锋 warm front, where a mass of warm air and a mass of cold air meet, the former rising over the latter and pushing the latter forward

【暖阁】nuǎngé 〈旧时 *old*〉为了设炉取暖在大屋子里隔出来的小房间 partitioned-off section of a large room with a stove to provide heating

【暖烘烘】nuǎnhōnghōng (～的 nuǎnhōnghōng·de)形容温暖宜人 nice and warm; genially warm

【暖呼呼】nuǎnhūhū (～的 nuǎnhūhū·de)形容暖和 warm; warm and cozy ◇听了老师这番话,孩子们心里～的。The teacher's words warmed the children's hearts.

【暖壶】nuǎnhú ❶ same as 暖水瓶 nuǎnshuǐpíng ❷ 有棉套等保暖的水壶 pot with a padded cover, etc., to keep it warm ❸ same as 汤壶 tānghú

【暖和】nuǎn·huo ❶ (气候、环境等)不冷也不太热 (of weather, environment, etc.) warm; comfortably warm; nice and warm: 北京一过三月,天气就～了。In Beijing, it turns warm immediately after March.｜这屋子向阳,很～。The south-facing room is very warm. ❷ 使暖和 warm; warm up: 屋里有火,快进来～～吧! There is a fire in the room. Come in and get warm.

【暖帘】nuǎnlián 冬天用的棉门帘,能挡风保暖 quilted door curtain used in winter to block the cold wind and keep warm

【暖流】nuǎnliú 从低纬度流向高纬度的洋流。暖流的水温比它所到区域的水温高。warm current; ocean current flowing from lower latitudes to higher latitudes, of which the temperature is higher than that of the areas it passes ◇一股～涌上心头。Warmth welled up in one's heart.

【暖瓶】nuǎnpíng same as 暖水瓶 nuǎnshuǐpíng

【暖气】nuǎnqì ❶ 利用锅炉烧出蒸汽或热水,通过管道输送到建筑物内的散热器(俗称暖气片)中,散出热量,使室温增高。管道中的蒸汽或热水叫做暖气。central heating; warm up rooms in a building by conveying steam or hot water produced by a boiler through pipes into the radiators of the building; also referring to hot steam or water in the pipes ❷ 指上述的设备 (central) heating equipment ❸ 暖和的气体 warm gas; warm air

【暖气团】nuǎnqìtuán 一种移动的气团,本身的温度比到达区域的地面温度高,多在热带大陆或海洋上形成 warm air mass; moving mass of air, the temperature of which is higher than the surface temperature of the area it passes, oft. forming over a tropical continent or the ocean

【暖融融】nuǎnróngróng (～的 nuǎnróngróng·de) same as 暖烘烘 nuǎnhōnghōng: 炭火驱走了寒气,整个房间～的。The charcoal fire drove away the cold, warming up the entire room.

【暖色】nuǎnsè 给人以温暖的感觉的颜色,如红、橙、黄 warm colour, e.g. red, orange and yellow

【暖寿】nuǎnshòu 旧俗在过生日的前一天,家里的人和关系较近的亲友来祝寿 old custom of celebration on the eve of one's birthday, together with one's family and close relatives

【暖水瓶】nuǎnshuǐpíng 保温瓶的一种,瓶口较小,通常用来保存热水。也叫暖壶或暖瓶,有的地区叫热水瓶。thermos flask; thermos bottle; a kind of vacuum flask with a small mouth, usu. used to contain hot water; also called 暖壶 nuǎnhú, 暖瓶 nuǎnpíng or 热水瓶 rèshuǐpíng in some areas

【暖袖】nuǎnxiù 为了御寒缝在棉袄袖口里面增加袖长的一截棉袖子 lengthened section of the sleeves of a padded coat to keep warm in winter

【暖洋洋】nuǎnyángyáng (～的 nuǎyángyáng·de)形容温暖 warm: ～的春风 warm spring breeze ◇几句话说得我心里～的。The words warmed my heart.

nüè (ㄋㄩㄝˋ)

疟(瘧) nüè same as 疟疾 nüè·ji

☞ yào on p. 2231

【疟疾】nüè·ji 急性传染病,病原体是疟原虫,传染媒介是蚊子,周期性发作。由于疟原虫的不同,或隔一日发作,或隔二日发作,也有的不定期发作。症状是发冷发热,热后大量出汗,头痛,口渴,全身无力。通称疟子(yào·zi),有的地区叫脾寒。malaria; ague; paludine swamp fever; acute infectious disease characterized by cycles of chills, fever, sweating, headache, thirst and weakness, caused by the parasitic infection of red blood cells by a protozoan of the genus *Plasmodium* and transmitted by masquitoes, attacking every other day, every three days, or irregularly; commonly known as 疟子 yào·zi; also called 脾寒 píhán in some areas

虐 nüè ❶ 残暴狠毒 cruel; tyrannical; brutal; ruthless: 暴～ atrocious｜酷～ ex-

N

tremely cruel | ～待 maltreat; abuse; ill-use | ～政 tyrannical government; tyranny ❷〈书 *fml.*〉灾害 disaster: 乱～并生。Rebellions and disasters do not come singly.

【虐待】nüèdài 用残暴狠毒的手段待人 ill-treat; maltreat; ill-use: ～狂 sadism | 受～ suffer maltreatment | ～病人 ill-treat patients

【虐杀】nüèshā 虐待人而致死 torture sb. to death; cause sb.'s death by maltreatment

【虐政】nüèzhèng 暴虐的政策法令 tyrannical government; tyranny

nún (ㄋㄨㄣˊ)

磨 nún〈书 *fml.*〉香气 fragrance; aroma; sweet smell: 温～(温暖芳香) warm and fragrant

nuó (ㄋㄨㄛˊ)

挪 nuó 挪动；转移 move; shift: ～用 divert (funds) | 把桌子～一下。Move the table a little.

【挪动】nuó·dong 移动位置 move; shift: 往前～了几步 move a few steps forward | 把墙边儿的东西～一下，腾出地方放书架。Move the things next to the wall to make room for the book shelves.

【挪借】nuójiè 暂时借用(别人的钱) get a short-term loan; borrow money for a short time

【挪窝儿】nuó//wōr〈方 *dial.*〉离开原来所在的地方；搬家 move; move to somewhere else

【挪移】nuóyí〈方 *dial.*〉❶ same as 挪借 nuójiè: ～款项 loan a sum of money for a short time ❷ 挪动；移动 move; shift: 向前～了几步 move a few steps forward

【挪用】nuóyòng ❶ 把原定用于某方面的钱移到别的方面来用 divert (funds); appropriate (funds); use money for a purpose other than what it was originally intended for: 专款专用，不得～。The special fund shall not be diverted for any other purpose. ❷ 私自用(公家的钱) embezzle; appropriate; line one's pocket with public funds: ～公款 embezzle public funds; misappropriation of public funds

娜 nuó (旧读 formerly pronounced as nuǒ) ☞ [婀娜] (ēnuó) on p.503 and [袅娜] (niǎonuó) on p.1415

☞ nà on p.1385

傩(儺) nuó〈旧时 *old*〉迎神赛会，驱逐疫鬼 ritual to exorcize ghosts that bring diseases

【傩神】nuóshén 驱除瘟疫的神 god that drives away pestilence

nuò (ㄋㄨㄛˋ)

诺 nuò ❶ 答应；允许 promise: ～言 promise; pledge | 许～ make a promise ❷ 答应的声音(表示同意 show agreement) yes; aye; yea: 唯唯～～ be a yes-man; assent meekly | ～～连声 keep on saying 'yes'

【诺尔】nuò'ěr same as 淖尔 nào'ěr，多用于地名 [often used as part of a place name] nur: 什里～(在青海) Shili Nur (in Qinghai Province) | 烧锅～(在吉林) Shaoguo Nur (in Jilin Province)

【诺言】nuòyán 应允别人的话 promise; pledge; word: 信守～ keep one's word

喏[1] nuò〈方 *dial.*〉〈叹词 *interj.*〉表示让人注意自己所指示的事物 [used to call attention to sth.] look; see; there: ～，这不就是你的那把雨伞? There! Isn't that your umbrella? | ～，～，要这样挖才挖得快。See? It's faster digging this way.

喏[2] nuò〈书 *fml.*〉same as 诺 nuò

☞ rě on p.1611

搦 nuò〈书 *fml.*〉❶ 持；握；拿着 hold (in one's hand): ～管 hold a writing brush; take up the pen ❷ 挑；惹 provoke; challenge: ～战 challenge to a fight

【搦管】nuòguǎn〈书 *fml.*〉执笔，也指写诗文 take up the pen; write poetry and prose

【搦战】nuòzhàn 挑战(多见于早期白话 oft. in early vernacular) provoke sb. into a fight; challenge sb. to a fight

锘 nuò 金属元素，符号 No (nobelium)。有放射性，由人工核反应获得。nobelium (No), radioactive metal element obtained from artificial nuclear reactions

懦 nuò same as 懦弱 nuòruò: 怯～ timid; timorous

【懦夫】nuòfū 软弱无能的人 coward; craven; weakling

【懦弱】nuòruò 软弱，不坚强 cowardly; weak; spineless: ～无能 be weak and incompetent

糯(稬、稬) nuò 黏性的(米谷) glutinous (cereal): ～米 polished glutinous rice | ～高粱 glutinous sorghum

【糯稻】nuòdào 米粒富于黏性的稻子 glutinous rice

【糯米】nuòmǐ 糯稻碾出的米，可以做糕点，也可以酿酒 polished glutinous rice, which can be used to make pastry and also wine; also 江米 jiāngmǐ

【糯米纸】nuòmǐzhǐ 用淀粉加工制成的像纸的薄膜，可以吃，用做糖果、糕点等的内层包装 wafer; rice-paper; edible, paper-thin film made of starch, used to wrap sweets, cookies, etc.

O

ō(ㄛ)

噢 ō〈叹词 *interj.*〉表示了解[expressing understanding]:~,原来是他! Oh, it's him!

ó(ㄛˊ)

哦 ó〈叹词 *interj.*〉表示将信将疑[expressing doubt]:~,他也要来参加我们的会? So, he's coming to our meeting too?
☞ é on p.504 and ò on p.1431

ǒ(ㄛˇ)

嚄 ǒ〈叹词 *interj.*〉表示惊讶[expressing surprise]:~,你们也去呀! What? Are you going too?
☞ huō on p.875 and huò on p.886

ò(ㄛˋ)

哦 ò〈叹词 *interj.*〉表示领会、醒悟[expressing realization and understanding]:~,我懂了。Oh! I see. *or* Oh! Now I understand. |~,我想起来了。Ah, I remember.
☞ é on p.504 and ó on p.1431

ōu(ㄡ)

区(區) Ōu 姓 a surname
☞ qū on p.1586

讴(謳) ōu ❶ 歌唱 sing:~歌 sing the praises of; eulogize ❷ 民歌 folk song; ballad:吴~ folk songs from the state of Wu|越~ folk songs from the state of Yue

【讴歌】ōugē〈书 *fml.*〉歌颂 sing the praises of; eulogize; pay tribute to

【讴吟】ōuyín〈书 *fml.*〉歌吟;歌唱 sing; chant:时而低声细语,时而高声~ sometimes whisper, sometimes sing out

沤(漚) ōu 水泡 bubble; froth:浮~ bubbles on the water surface; foam
☞ òu on p.1433

瓯¹(甌) ōu〈方 *dial.*〉瓯子 bowl; cup:茶~ tea cup|酒~ wine cup

瓯²(甌) Ōu 浙江温州的别称 Ou, another name for Wenzhou, a city in Zhejiang Province

【瓯绣】ōuxiù 浙江温州出产的刺绣 embroidery produced in Wenzhou, Zhejiang Province

【瓯子】ōu·zi〈方 *dial.*〉same as 盅 zhōng

欧¹(歐) Ōu 姓 a surname

欧²(歐) Ōu 指欧洲 Europe:西~ Western Europe|~化 Europeanize; westernize

欧³(歐) ōu 欧姆的简称 abbr. for 欧姆 ōumǔ

【欧化】ōuhuà 指模仿欧洲的风俗习惯、语言文字等 Europeanize; westernize; imitate European customs and languages

【欧椋鸟】ōuliángniǎo 鸟,羽毛蓝色,有光泽,带乳白色斑点,嘴小带黄色,眼靠近嘴根,性好温暖,常群居,吃植物的果实或种子 starling (*Sturnidae*); shepherd bird; bird that has shiny blue feathers with milky white dots, small, yellowish beak and eyes placed close to the beak, like mild climates, lives in flocks and feeds on fruits and seeds

【欧罗巴人种】Ōuluóbā rénzhǒng 世界三大人种之一,体质特征是肤色较淡,头发柔软而呈波形,鼻子较高,分布在欧洲、美洲、亚洲西部和南部 Europa; white race; one of the three main human races, characterized by fair complexion, soft, wavy hair and high nose bridge, mainly distributed throughout Europe, America, Western and South Asia; also 白种 báizhǒng [拉 Latin: 欧罗巴 Europa]

【欧姆】ōumǔ 电阻单位,导体上的电压是1伏特,通过的电流是1安培时,电阻就是1欧姆。这个单位名称是为纪念德国物理学家欧姆(Georg Simon Ohm)而定的。ohm; abbr. O; unit of electrical resistance equal to that of a conductor in which a current of one ampere is produced by a potential of one volt across it, named after the German physicist Georg Simon Ohm; 简称 abbr. 欧 ōu

【欧体】Ōu tǐ 唐代欧阳询及其子欧阳通所写的字体,笔画刚劲,结构谨严 Ouyang style; calligraphic style created by Ouyang Xun and his son Ouyang Tong of the Tang Dynasty, characterized by vigorous brushstrokes and compact structures

【欧西】Ōuxī〈旧时 *old*〉指欧洲 Europe:~各国 European countries

【欧阳】Ōuyáng 姓 a two-character surname

殴(毆) ōu 打(人) beat; hit:斗~ fist fight; have fisticuffs|~伤 beat and injure

【殴打】ōudǎ 打(人) beat; hit 互相～exchange blows|被人～ be beaten

鸥(鷗) ōu 鸟类的一科,多生活在海边,主要捕食鱼类,头大,嘴扁平,前趾有蹼,翼长而尖,羽毛多为白色,如海鸥 gull (*Latidae*); family of aquatic birds, e.g. the seagull, with large head, flat beak, webbed toes, long, pointed wings, and usually white plumage, feeding mainly on fish

噢(噢) ōu ❶〈叹词 *interj*.〉表示醒悟、惊异或赞叹 expressing understanding, surprise or admiration:～,我想起来了。Oh, I remember. |～,你们俩倒挺对脾气。Well, you two are certainly getting along well.|累坏了身体也不行～! You really must not tire yourself out! ❷〈拟声词 *onom*.〉sound of crying:他急得～～地哭。He wept with frustration.

ǒu (又)

呕(嘔) ǒu 吐(tù) vomit; throw up:～血 spit blood

【呕吐】ǒutù 膈肌、腹部肌肉突然收缩,胃内食物被压迫经食管、口腔而排出体外 vomit; throw up; puke; ejection of the stomach contents through the oesophagus and mouth caused by pressure on the stomach as muscles in the midriff and abodmen suddenly constrict

【呕心】ǒuxīn 形容费尽心思 exert one's utmost effort(多用于文艺创作 oft. in creative work):～之作 work embodying great effort

【呕心沥血】ǒu xīn lì xuè 形容费尽心思 exert one's utmost effort; work one's heart out; take painstaking effort:为教育事业～ spare no effort for the cause of education

【呕血】ǒu//xuè 食管、胃、肠等消化器官出血经口腔排出。呕出的血液呈暗红色,常混有食物的渣滓。haematemesis; spit blood from haemorrhage in oesophagus, stomach or intestines. The blood is dark red and usually mixed with food remains.

怄(慪) ǒu ❶烧火时柴草等没有充分燃烧而产生大量的烟 heavy smoke from poorly burning firewood orgrass:～了一屋子烟。The room is filled with heavy smoke. ❷冒烟、不起火苗地烧 smoulder; burn with smoke and no flame:把这堆柴火～了。Burn off this pile of firewood. ❸用燃烧艾草等的烟驱蚊蝇 expel flies and mosquitoes with the smoke from burning wormwood:～蚊子 smoke out mosquitoes

偶1 ǒu 用木头、泥土等制成的人像 idol; human figure sculpted from wood, clay and the like:木～ wooden human figure|～像 idol

偶2 ǒu ❶双数;成对的(跟'奇(jī)'相对 as opposed to 'odd') even; in pairs:～数 even number|～蹄类 artiodactyl|无独有～not unique and has a match; never come singly but in pairs ❷配偶 spouse; mate:佳～ a happily married couple

偶3 ǒu 偶然;偶尔 by accident; by chance; haphazard; once in a while; now and then:中途～遇 come across on the way; run into sb. on the way|～一为之 do sth. once in a while

【偶尔】ǒu'ěr ❶间或;有时候 now and then; sometimes; at long intervals:他经常写小说,～也写诗。Most of the time he writes stories, but he also composes poems now and then. ❷偶然发生的 happen by chance; accidental:～的事 accident; chance event

【偶发】ǒufā 偶然发生的 accidental; chance; fortuitous:～事件 chance occurrence; freak accident

【偶合】ǒuhé 无意中恰巧相合 coincident:我们两人的见解一致这完全是～,事先并没有商量过。It is sheer coincidence that we have the same opinion. We did not discuss it beforehand.

【偶或】ǒuhuò 偶尔;间或;有时候 occasionally; now and then; sometimes; once in a while:～迟到一次,就感到内心不安 feel upset for being late once in a while

【偶然】ǒurán ❶事理上不一定要发生而发生的;超出一般规律的 accidental; fortuitous; unexpected; unusual:～事故 accident|～因素 fortuitous element|在公园里～遇见一个老同学 run into an old classmate in the park; come across an old classmate in the park ❷偶尔;有时候 now and then; once in a while; sometimes:闹市里～也能听到几声鸟鸣。Occasionally birds can be heard in the downtown area.

【偶然性】ǒuránxìng 指事物发展、变化中可能出现也可能不出现,可以这样发生也可以那样发生的情况。偶然性和事物发展过程的本质没有直接关系,但它的后面常常隐藏着必然性。科学的任务就是要透过复杂的偶然现象来揭露事物发展的客观规律,即必然性(跟'必然性'相对 as opposed to 'certain', 'inevitable')。random; contingent; fortuitous; unforeseen; possibility that, in the course of development and change an event may or may not occur, may take this form or that. What happens fortuitously is not directly related to the essence of its development, but is often backed by the inevitable. The task of scientific research is to uncover the objective laws of development — the inevitable — behind complex random phenomena.

【偶人】ǒurén 用土木等制成的人形物 clay or wooden human figure

【偶数】ǒushù 能够被2整除的整数,如2,4,6,-8。正的偶数也叫双数。even number; whole

number that can be divided exactly by two, such as 2, 4, 6 and －8. A positive, even number is also called 双数 shuāngshù.

【偶像】ǒuxiàng 用木头、泥土等雕塑的供迷信的人敬奉的人像 idol; clay or wooden human figure used in worship by the superstitious; 〈比喻 *fig.*〉盲目崇拜的对象 object of idolatry or blind worship

耦 ǒu ❶〈书 *fml.*〉两人并耕 (of two persons) plough side by side ❷ same as 偶[2] ǒu

【耦合】ǒuhé〈物理学 *phys.*〉指两个或两个以上的体系或两种运动形式间通过相互作用而彼此影响以至联合起来的现象。如放大器级与级之间信号的逐级放大量通过阻容耦合或变压器耦合;两个线圈之间的互感是通过磁场的耦合。coupling; phenomenon of two or more systems or motional forms interacting, influencing each other and even combining; For example, gradual amplification of signals at different levels in an amplifier is achieved through resistance-capacitance coupling, or transformer coupling; and mutual inductance of two circuits is effected through magnetic field coupling.

藕(蕅) ǒu 莲的地下茎,长形,肥大有节,白色,中间有许多管状的孔,折断后有丝。可以吃。lotus root; edible long white, and thick jointed underground lotus stem with tubular cavities. When the root snaps, its fibres stay joined.

【藕断丝连】ǒu duàn sī lián〈比喻 *fig.*〉表面上好像已断了关系,实际上仍然挂牵着(多指爱情上的) (usu. of lovers) still cherish love for each other though seemingly separated

【藕粉】ǒufěn 用藕制成的粉 lotus root starch

【藕荷】ǒuhé 浅紫而微红的颜色 pale lavender pink; also 藕合 ǒuhé

【藕灰】ǒuhuī same as 藕色 ǒusè

【藕色】ǒusè 浅灰而微红的颜色 pale pinkish grey

òu (ㄡˋ)

沤(漚) òu 长时间地浸泡,使起变化 soak sth. in a liquid for a long time to achieve desired change of the material; macerate: ～麻 ret flax or hemp; retting; rotting | ～粪 make compost

☞ ōu on p. 1431

【沤肥】òuféi ❶ 将垃圾、青草、树叶、厩肥、人粪尿、河泥等放在坑内,加水浸泡,经分解发酵制成肥料 make compost; pile garbage, grass, leaves, barnyard manure, human manure and riverbed mud into a pit and add water so it all decomposes and ferments into fertilizer ❷ 指用这种方法制成的肥料。有的地区叫窖肥。compost; waterlogged compost; also known as 窖肥 jiàoféi in some areas

怄(慪) òu〈方 *dial.*〉❶ 怄气 sulk; have the sulks ❷ 使怄气;使不愉快 annoy; upset; irritate: 你别故意～我。Don't try to annoy me.

【怄气】òu//qì 闹别扭,生闷气 be at odds with sb.; be difficult and sulky; be in a fit of sulks; be annoyed: 不要～。Don't be annoyed. | 怄了一肚子气 have a bellyful of grievances

P

pā（ㄆㄚ）

粑 pā〈方 *dial.*〉❶（食物等）烂糊；软和（of food) soft；succulent；mushy；pappy：老牛筋炖不～。It's hard to stew beef tendons to succulence.｜饭煮～了。The rice was cooked kind of watery. ❷ 软；软弱 soften；moderate；assuage：经劝解，他的口气～多了。He softened his tone after much coax.

趴 pā ❶ 胸腹朝下卧倒 prostrate；lie facing down；lie prone：～在地上射击 lie on one's stomach and shoot ❷ 身体向前靠在物体上；伏 bend over；lean on：～在桌子上画图。He was bending over the desk and drawing.

派 pā［派司］（pā·si）❶ 指厚纸印成的或订成本儿的出入证、通行证等 pass；permit；card or tiny booklet allowing entry to and exit from a place ❷ 指通过；准予通过（检查、关卡、考试等）pass a checkup，an examination，etc.；grant permission to enter a place
☞ pài on p.1440

啪 pā〈拟声词 *onom.*〉形容放枪、拍掌或东西撞击等声音［indicating the sound of gunshot；clapping，or slapping］thwack；crackle；bang：鞭子甩得～～地响。The whip crackled sharply when it was flicked.

葩 pā〈书 *fml.*〉花 flower：奇～异草 fabulous flowers and strange grass

pá（ㄆㄚˊ）

扒 pá ❶ 用手或用耙子一类的工具使东西聚拢或散开 scrape together；rake up：～草 rake up hey ❷〈方 *dial.*〉用手搔；抓；挠 scratch；scrape：～痒 scratch an itch ❸ 扒窃 be a pickpocket：钱包被小偷～走了。The wallet was stolen. ❹ 一种煨烂的烹调法 stew；braise：～羊肉 stewed mutton｜～白菜 braised Chine cabbage
☞ bā on p.25

【扒糕】págāo 用荞麦面制成的凉拌食物 buckwheat pudding served as a cold dish

【扒灰】pá//huī same as 爬灰 pá//huī

【扒拉】pá·la〈方 *dial.*〉用筷子把饭拨到嘴里 scrape rice into one's mouth with chopsticks：他～了两口饭就跑出去了。He ran out after barely finishing his meal.
☞ bā·la on p.25

【扒犁】pá·li same as 爬犁 pá·li

【扒窃】páqiè 从别人身上偷窃（财物）pilfer；pick sb.'s pocket；steal

【扒手】páshǒu 从别人身上偷窃财物的小偷 pickpocket；thief ◇政治～political swindler；political trickster；also 掱手 páshǒu

杷 pá ☞［枇杷］（pí·pá）on p.1466

爬 pá ❶ 昆虫、爬行动物等行动或人用手和脚一起着地向前移动（of insects，reptiles or human beings）crawl；go on all fours；worm one's way（into）：蝎子～进了墙缝。A scorpion crawled into a crack in the wall.｜这孩子会～了。The baby has learned how to crawl now. ❷ 抓着东西往上去；攀登 climb：～树 climb up a tree｜～绳 climb a rope｜～山 climb a mountain；mountaineer ◇墙上～满了藤蔓。The wall is covered all over with ivy. ❸ 由倒卧而坐起或站起（多指起床）get up；sit up；stand up：为了赶火车，他五点就～了起来。He got up at five in order to catch the train.｜他病得已经～不起来了。He's so ill that he has become bedridden. ◇在哪里跌倒，就在哪里～起来。Get up wherever you fall.

【爬虫】páchóng 爬行动物的旧称 old term for 爬行动物 páxíng dòngwù

【爬灰】pá//huī 俗指公公跟儿媳妇儿通奸 commit adultery with one's daughter-in-law；also 扒灰 pá//huī

【爬犁】pá·li〈方 *dial.*〉雪橇（qiāo）sledge；sleigh；also 扒犁 pá·li

【爬墙虎】páqiánghǔ ❶ 爬藤榕 Boston ivy（*Parthenocissus tricuspidata*）❷ 红葡萄藤 red grapevine（*Ampelopsis tricuspidata*）

【爬山虎】páshānhǔ ❶ 落叶藤本植物，叶子互生，叶柄细长，花浅绿色。结浆果，球形。茎上有卷须。能附着在岩石或墙壁上。ivy（*Parthenocissus tricuspidata*）；defoliating trailing liana having phyllotaxy lobed leaves with long，slender footstalks，pale green flowers，berrylike fruit，and curling claspers that enable it to attach itself to rocks or walls ❷〈方 *dial.*〉山轿 mountain litter；sedan chair to carry its passenger up a mountain

【爬升】páshēng ❶（飞机、火箭等）向高处飞行（aircraft，rocket，etc.）fly up；soar；gain height ❷〈比喻 *fig.*〉逐步提高 inch up；increase gradually：商品销售额～。The volume of commodity sales is rising steadily.

【爬藤榕】páténgróng 常绿灌木,攀缘茎,叶子椭圆形或椭圆状披针形,绿色,背面灰白色。攀缘在树干或墙壁上。Boston ivy (*Parthenocissus tricuspidata*); Japanese ivy; evergreen shrub climbing on tree trunks or walls, and having green leaves with a grayish white back, and oval or lanceolat-eoval in shape; also 爬墙虎 páqiánghǔ

【爬梯】pátī ❶ 坡度较陡,人上下时需双手扶梯的楼梯 stairway; staircase, usu. with banisters and installed at a steep gradient ❷ 铁链或绳索做成的直上直下的梯子 ladder; chain or rope ladder

【爬行】páxíng ❶ 爬 creep; crawl: ~动物 reptile ❷ 〈比喻 *fig.*〉墨守陈规,慢腾腾地干 move or work at a snail's pace: ~思想 mentality of getting things done slowly

【爬行动物】páxíng dòngwù 脊椎动物的一纲,身体表面有鳞或甲,体温随着气温的高低而改变,用肺呼吸,卵生或卵胎生,无变态,如蛇、蜥蜴、龟、鳖、玳瑁等 reptile; oviparous or ovoviviparous scaly vertebrate breathing with lungs, with body temperature changing with that of the air; such as snakes, lizards, turtles, tortoises, etc.; 旧称 formerly called 爬虫 páchóng

【爬泳】páyǒng 游泳的一种姿势,身体俯卧在水面,两腿打水,两臂交替划水。用这种姿势游泳,速度最快。crawl stroke; swimming with one's body lying face downward and propelled with alternate overarm movements and rapid straight-legged kicks, believed to be the fastest of all swimming strokes

耙(钯) pá ❶ 耙子 rake; harrow: 钉~ iron-toothed rake | 粪~ night-soil rake ❷ 用耙子平整土地或聚拢、散开柴草、谷物等 rake; manipulate a rake to loosen or smooth soil, or gather or scatter hey, faggot or grain: 地已~好了。The fields have been raked over. | 把麦子~开晒晒 use a rake to scatter wheat stalks for sunning

☞ bà on p. 29 and 钯 bǎ on p. 29

【耙子】pá·zi 聚拢和散开柴草、谷物或平整土地的农具,有长柄,一端有铁齿、木齿或竹齿 rake; long-handled farm implement with iron, wood or bamboo teeth for gathering or scattering hey, faggot or grain or smoothing farmland

琶 pá ☞琵琶 pí·pá on p. 1466

搿 pá [搿手](páshǒu) pickpocket; same as 扒手 páshǒu

筢 pá [筢子](pá·zi) 搂(lōu)柴草的器具,多用竹子、铁丝等制成 faggot rake, oft. made from bamboo or iron wire

潖 pá 潖江口(Pájiāngkǒu),地名,在广东 Pajiangkou, name of a place in Guangdong

pà(ㄆㄚˋ)

帊 pà 〈书 *fml.*〉same as 帕[1] pà

帕[1] pà 用来擦手擦脸的纺织品,多为方形 handkerchief; kerchief (oft. of a square shape): 手~ handkerchief

帕[2] pà 帕斯卡的简称 abbr. for 帕斯卡 pàsīkǎ

【帕斯卡】pàsīkǎ 压强单位,物体每平方米的面积上受到的压力为 1 牛顿时,压强就是 1 帕斯卡。这个单位名称是为纪念法国科学家帕斯卡(Blaise Pascal)而定的。pascal; unit of pressure equal to one newton per square metre, named after the French scientist Blaise Pascal; 简称 abbr. 帕 pà

怕 pà ❶ 害怕;畏惧 be afraid of; have a horror of: 老鼠~猫。Rats are afraid of cats. | 任何困难都不~ fear no difficulties whatsoever ❷ 恐怕 anxious; apprehensive a) 表示担心 for fear; be worried: ~他太累,所以叫人去帮忙。I asked people to help him out lest he get too tired. b) 表示估计;也许 surmise: 这个瓜~有十几斤吧。I surmise the melon weighs several kilograms.

【怕人】pàrén ❶ 见人害怕 be afraid of people ❷ 使人害怕;可怕 spooky; eerie: 洞里黑得~。It is eerily black in the cave.

【怕生】pàshēng (小孩儿)怕见生人;认生 (of a young child) be shy with strangers: 孩子小,~。The child is still too young not to be afraid of people.

【怕事】pà//shì 怕惹是非 be afraid of getting into trouble: 胆小~ cowardly and overcautious

【怕羞】pà//xiū 怕难为情;害臊 sheepish; timorous; timid: 小姑娘~,躲到姑姑身后去了。The young girl ducked behind her aunt in a moment of abashment.

pāi(ㄆㄞ)

拍 pāi ❶ 用手掌打 pat; tap with a palm: ~球 bounce a ball | ~手 clap one's hands | ~掉身上的土 pat the dust off one's clothes ◇惊涛~岸。Surging waves kept pounding the shore. ❷ (~儿 pāir) same as 拍子 pāi·zi ①: 蝇~儿 flyswatter ❸ same as 拍子 pāi·zi ②: 合~ rhythmic; in sync with | 二分之一~ one-half time ❹ 用摄影机把人、物的形象照在底片上 take; shoot (a photograph, movie; etc.): ~电影 shoot a movie | ~照片 take a photograph; take a snapshot ❺ 发(电报等) send (a telegraph): ~电报 send telegraph ❻ 拍马屁 lick sb's boots; fawn; toady: 吹吹~~ stoop to boasting and flattery

【拍案】pāi'àn 拍桌子(表示强烈的愤怒、惊异、赞赏等感情)smite or pound the table (in indignation; surprise or admiration):～而起(形容十分愤怒)smite the table and jump to one's feet (in a moment of rage)|～叫绝(形容非常赞赏)thump the table and shout 'bravo'(to show great appreciation)

【拍巴掌】pāi bā·zhang 拍手 clap one's hands; applaud

【拍板】pāi//bǎn ❶ 打拍板 strike a pair of clappers to mark the rhythm:你唱,我来～。You'll sing and I'll beat time for you. ❷ 商行拍卖货物,为表示成交而拍打木板 rap the gavel to clinch a business deal ❸〈比喻 *fig*.〉主事人做出决定 make a decision:～定案 deliver a verdict on a case|这件事得由厂长～。The final say on this matter rests with the factory director.

【拍板】pāibǎn 打击乐器,用来打拍子。一般用三块硬质木板做成,互相打击能发出清脆的声音。clappers; two or three pieces of hardwood held between the fingers and struck against each other rhythmically in a sharp and clear sound

【拍打】pāi·da ❶ 轻轻地打 pat sth. gently:～身上的雪 pat snow off one's coat ❷ 扇动(翅膀)flail:小鸟～着翅膀。The tiny bird flailed its wings.

【拍档】pāidàng〈方 *dial*.〉❶ 协作;合作 team up with; collaborate:两位名演员在这部影片中～饰演男女主角。Two big stars will collaborate as protagonists in this movie. ❷ 协作或合作的人 partner; collaborator:最佳～ best collaborator

【拍发】pāifā 发出(电报)send (a telegram); cable (a news dispatch)

【拍花】pāihuā 指用能使人迷糊的药诱拐小孩 use a knockout drug to abduct a child

【拍马】pāimǎ 拍马屁 fawn:逢迎～go out of one's way to curry favour with sb.|溜须～ ingratiate oneself into sb.'s favour

【拍马屁】pāi mǎpì 指谄媚奉承 lick sb.'s boots

【拍卖】pāimài ❶ 以委托寄售为业的商行当众出卖寄售的货物,由许多顾客出价争购,到没有人再出更高一些的价时,就拍板,表示成交 auction; public sale in which property or items of merchandise are sold to the highest bidder ❷ 称减价抛售;甩卖 mark-down sales; sale:大～ clearance sales

【拍摄】pāishè same as 拍 pāi④:～电影 shoot a movie

【拍手】pāi//shǒu 两手相拍,表示欢迎、赞成、感谢等;鼓掌 clap one's hands as a gesture of welcome, approval and gratitude; applaud:～欢迎 greet a guest by applause|～称快(拍着手喊痛快,多指仇恨得到消除)clap one's hands with joy (oft. on being avenged)

【拍拖】pāituō〈方 *dial*.〉指谈恋爱 in courtship; go steady

【拍胸脯】pāi xiōngpú 表示没有问题,可以担保 slap one's chest to guarantee or promise sth.:你敢～,我就放心了。You really set my mind at ease by slapping your chest like that.

【拍照】pāi//zhào 照相 photography:～留念 have a picture taken and keep it as a memento

【拍纸簿】pāizhǐbù 纸的一边用胶粘住、便于一页一页撕下来的本子 pad; a stack of paper sheets glued together at one edge, to be torn down one page at a time to take note on it

【拍子】pāi·zi ❶ 拍打东西的用具 racket; swatter:苍蝇～flyswatter|网球～tennis racket ❷ 音乐中,计算乐音历时长短的单位(of music) rhythm:打～(按照乐曲的节奏挥手或敲打) beat rhythm (using either hands or clappers)

pái(ㄆㄞˊ)

俳 pái ❶〈古代 *arch*.〉指滑稽戏 comedy ❷〈书 *fml*.〉诙谐;滑稽 comical; funny:～谐 humorous

【俳句】páijù 日本的一种短诗,以十七个音为一首,首句五个音,中句七个音,末句五个音 *haiku*; form of Japanese verse containing three lines in a total of 17 syllables — five in the first line, seven in the second line, and five in the third line

【俳谐】páixié〈书 *fml*.〉诙谐 humorous:～文(古代指隐喻、调笑、讥讽的文章) writing that is metaphorical, funny, or sarcastic

【俳优】páiyōu〈古代 *arch*.〉指演滑稽戏的艺人 comedian

排1 pái ❶ 一个挨一个地按着次序摆 line up; align:～队 line up|～字 typesetting|把椅子～成一行。Arrange the chairs in a line. ❷ 排成的行列 row; line:他坐在后～。He sat in the last row. ❸ 军队的编制单位,连的下一级,班的上一级 platoon; army unit below the company and above the squared ❹〈量词 *classifier*〉用于成行列的东西 row; line:一～子弹 a clip of cartridges|一～椅子 a row of chairs|上下两～牙齿 upper and lower rows of teeth ❺ 排演 rehearse :～戏 rehearse a play|彩～dress rehearsal|这是一出新～的京剧。This is a newly rehearsed Peking Opera.

排2 pái ❶ 一种水上交通工具,用竹子或木头平排地连在一起做成 raft; buoyant platform made by binding parallel bamboo poles or logs together and used as a vessel ❷ 指扎(zā)成排的竹子或木头,便于放在水里运走 raft made of bamboo poles or logs so that they can be conveyed down a river

排3 pái ❶ 用力除去 remove; dislodge:～除 get rid of|～挤 discriminate against; exclude|～涝 drain excessive water from a waterlogged place|～灌 irrigation and drainage|把水～出去 drain water from a place ❷ 推；推开 push; push away：～闼(tà)直入 push the door open and enter the room unceremoniously|～门而出 open the door and go straight out

排[4]pái 一种西式点心，用面粉做成浅盘子形状的底，在上面加糊状的奶油、果酱或巧克力等而制成 pie; Western-style filling in a pastry-lined dish and covered with a soupy crust made from cream, jam or chocolate：苹果～ apple pie

☞ pǎi on p. 1440

【排奡】pái'ào 〈书 *fml.*〉(文笔)矫健 (of writing) dynamic：其文纵横～。His writing is untrammeled and dynamic.

【排版】pái//bǎn 依照稿本把文字、图版等排在一起，拼成版面 composing; putting text and illustrations together to form a page

【排比】páibǐ 修辞方式，用一连串内容相关、结构类似的句子成分或句子来表示强调和一层层的深入。如：'我们说，长征是历史纪录上的第一次，长征是宣言书，长征是宣传队，长征是播种机。''因此，没有满腔的热忱，没有眼睛向下的决心，没有求知的渴望，没有放下臭架子、甘当小学生的精神，是一定不能做，也一定做不好的'。parallelism; use of parallel sentences of relevant meanings and similar structures to emphasize or render depth to the narration. For example, 'We answer that the Long March is the first of its kind in the annals of history, that it is a manifesto, a propaganda force, a seeding machine.' 'Therefore one certainly cannot make an investigation, or do it well, without zeal, a determination to direct one's eyes downward and a thirst for knowledge, and without shedding the ugly mantle of pretentiousness and becoming a willing pupil.'

【排笔】páibǐ 油漆、粉刷或画家染色用的一种笔，由平列的一排笔毛或几枝笔连成一排做成 broad brush made of a row of pen-shaped brushes for use in painting, colouring or finishing

【排叉儿】páichàr 食品，长方形的薄面片(多为两层)，中间划三条口子，把面片的一头从口子中掏出来，用油炸熟 deep-fried crunchy thin and oblong pieces of dough curled at one end and with three knife cuts on it; also 排杈儿 páichár

【排杈儿】páichàr ❶ 室内较矮而窄的隔断 low and narrow partition in a room ❷ same as 排叉儿 páichàr

【排场】pái·chǎng ❶ 表现在外面的铺张奢侈的形式或局面 grand style; ostentation; extravagance：～大 of a grand scale|讲～ be given to doing things in a grandiose way ❷ 铺张而奢侈 extravagant ❸〈方 *dial.*〉体面；光彩 dignified; respectable：集体婚礼又～，又省钱。A group wedding is dignified and saves money.

【排斥】páichì 使别的人或事物离开自己这方面 ostracize; repulse：～异己 exclude outsiders; reject those who dare to differ|带同种电荷的物体相～。Two like electric charges repel each other.|现实主义的创作方法并不～艺术上的夸张。Realism in creative writing is not necessarily at odds with artistic exaggeration.

【排除】páichú 除掉；消除 eliminate; get rid of; abate：～积水 drain the excessive water|～险情 avert a dangerous situation|～万难，奋勇直前 surmount every difficulty, conquer all obstacles, and forge ahead courageously

【排挡】páidǎng 汽车、拖拉机等用来改变牵引力的装置，用于改变行车速度或倒车 gear; clutch; device in an automobile or tractor to change speed or direction; 简称 abbr. 挡 dǎng

【排档】páidàng 〈方 *dial.*〉设在路旁、广场上的售货处 row of market stalls：服装～garment-selling stalls|个体～individual business stalls

【排队】pái//duì 一个挨一个顺次排列成行 queue up; line up：～上车 queue up for a bus ◇把问题排排队，依次解决 size up the problems in hand so as to solve them one by one

【排筏】páifá 杉木、毛竹等编成的筏子 timber raft; bamboo raft

【排放】páifàng ❶ 排出(废气、废水、废渣)discharge (waste gas, liquid, residue, etc.)：～污水 discharge sewage|～瓦斯 discharge inflammable gas from a mine ❷ 动物排精或排卵(of male animals) ejaculate; (of female animals) ovulate

【排风扇】páifēngshàn 换气扇 ventilating fan

【排骨】páigǔ 供食用的猪、牛、羊等的肋骨、脊椎骨(of pork, mutton, and beef) spareribs

【排灌】páiguàn 排水和灌溉 drainage and irrigation：机械～ mechanized irrigation and drainage|～设备 irrigation and drainage installations

【排行】páiháng (兄弟姐妹)依长幼排列次序 seniority among siblings：他～第二。He's the second child in his family.

【排击】páijī 排斥攻击 ostracize and attack

【排挤】páijǐ 利用势力或手段使不利于自己的人失去地位或利益 elbow sb. out; oust a recusant by power or by using underhand tricks

【排检】páijiǎn (图书、资料等)排列和检索(of books, data, etc.) arrange a way to facilitate retrieval：～法 data programming and retrieval methodology|汉字～知识 knowledge about alignment and retrieval of the Chinese characters

【排解】páijiě ❶ 调解(纠纷) mediate; reconcile：经过～，一场冲突才算平息。The conflict was finally resolved through mediation. ❷ 排遣 divert oneself from a bad mood, etc.：～愁闷 allay the anxiety of

【排涝】pái//lào 排除田地里过多的积水，使农作物免受涝害 drain excessive water from a plot of farmland to protect farm crops from waterlogging

【排雷】pái//léi 排除地雷或水雷 removal of mines or torpedoes; mine clearance

【排练】páiliàn 排演练习 rehearse：～文艺节目 prepare and rehearse for variety show

【排列】páiliè ❶ 顺次序放 align; make an ordered arrangement：按字母次序～set in an alphabetical order｜依姓氏笔画多少～(of names on a list) arranged according to the number of strokes in the surnames ❷ 由 m 个不同的元素中取出 n($n \leqslant m$)个，按一定的顺序排成一列，叫做由 m 中取 n 的排列。排列数记作A_m^n，公式是 $A_m^n = m(m-1)(m-2)\cdots(m-n+1)$ permutation; practice of choosing a set of n ($n \leqslant m$) from m numbers of elements and arranging them in an ordered set, known as 'permutation of n from m'. Permutations are recorded as A, n and m, the formula being $A_m^n = m(m-1)(m-2)\cdots(m-n+1)$

【排律】páilǜ 长篇的律诗。一般是五言。(in Chinese literature) lengthy poem with each line usu. containing five Chinese characters

【排卵】pái//luǎn 发育成熟的卵子从卵巢排出。人的排卵期通常在下次月经开始前的第 14 天左右。ovulate; discharge an egg from the ovary; A woman begins her period of ovulation around 14 days before the beginning of her next menstruation period.

【排名】pái//míng 排列名次 ranking：他的成绩在比赛中～第五。He ranked fifth in the competition.

【排难解纷】pái nàn jiě fēn 调解纠纷 settle a dispute; pour oil on troubled waters

【排偶】pái'ǒu (文句)排比对偶(of literature) antithetic parallelism

【排炮】páipào ❶ 许多门炮同时向同一方向、目标进行射击的炮火(artillery) barrage of cannon fire; concerted artillery bombardment ❷ 劈山造田、开矿掘巷道等工程中，连接许多炮眼同时进行的爆破 chain explosion; engineering method for leveling off mountains, land reclamation, mining, and tunneling

【排遣】páiqiǎn 借某种事消除(寂寞和烦闷) assuage (loneliness, boredom, anxiety, etc.) by doing sth.：心中的郁闷难以～。He was heavy with melancholy within him, yet he knew no way of how to cheer himself up.

【排枪】páiqiāng 许多支枪同时向同一方向、目标进行射击的火力 volley of rifle shots in the same direction and on the same target

【排球】páiqiú ❶ 球类运动项目之一，球场长方形，中间隔有高网，比赛双方(每方六人)各占球场的一方，用手把球从网上空打来打去 volleyball; ballgame played on a rectangular court on which two competing 6-member teams are separated in the middle by a high net and hit the ball over the net with the hands or arms so that it hits the ground on the opponent's side ❷ 排球运动使用的球，用羊皮或人造革做壳，橡胶做胆，大小和足球相似 volleyball; ball about the size of a soccer ball, made of sheepskin or synthetic leather and with a rubber bladder in it

【排山倒海】pái shān dǎo hǎi 〈比喻 *fig.*〉力量强，声势大 with earth-shaking momentum; with a momentum forceful enough to topple the mountains and overturn the seas

【排水量】páishuǐliàng ❶ 船舶在水中所排开的水的重量，分为空船排水量和满载排水量。满载排水量用来表示船只的大小，通常以吨为单位。displacement; bareboat displacement; full-load displacement, which indicates the capacity of boat; amount of water displaced by a boat in a river, lake, ocean, etc, usu. measured by the ton ❷ 河道或渠道在单位时间内排出水的量，通常以立方米/秒为单位 discharge capacity of a river or spillway per unit time, that is, cubic metres per second

【排他性】páitāxìng 一事物不容许另一事物与自己在同一范围内并存的性质 exclusiveness; property of one thing excluding the coexistence of another in the same environment

【排头】páitóu 队伍的最前面，也指站在队伍最前面的人 person at the head of a procession; file leader：站在～standing at the head of a row｜向～看齐 keep level with your file leader｜～是小队长。The man standing at the head of the line is the team leader.

【排头兵】páitóubīng 站在队伍最前面的兵 soldier at the head of a formation; 〈比喻 *fig.*〉带头的人 pacesetter; vanguard

【排外】páiwài 排斥外国、外地或本党派、本集团以外的人 xenophobia; mentality of excluding people from another country, region, party or clique

【排尾】páiwěi 队伍的最后面，也指站在队伍最后面的人 person at the end of a row：站在～standing at the end of a row｜～是副队长。The one standing at the end of the row is the deputy team leader.

【排戏】pái//xì 排演戏剧 rehearse a drama

【排险】pái//xiǎn 排除险情 remove a danger

【排泄】páixiè ❶ 使雨水、污水等流走 drain off rainwater, sewage, etc. ❷ 生物把体内新陈代谢产生的废物排出体外。如动物排尿、排汗、呼出二氧化碳。又如植物把多余的水分和矿物质排出体外。defecate; discharge; excrete; (of an organism) discharging waste matter, produced through metabolisms, out of the body; (of animals) excrete urine, breathe out carbon dioxide, etc.; (of plants) discharge excessive water and minerals

【排揎】pái·xuan 〈方 *dial.*〉数说责备；训斥 berate; chide; give sb. a dressing-down:他已经认错了,你别再～他了。Why don't you stop chiding him now that he has acknowledged his mistake.

【排演】páiyǎn 戏剧等上演前,演员在导演的指导下,逐段练习 rehearse; (of performers) practice a play episode by episode under the guidance of the director for later public performance

【排椅】páiyǐ 相连成排的椅子,多用于影剧院、俱乐部、礼堂等 seats in a row, oft. in a theatre, club, auditorium, etc.

【排印】páiyìn 排版和印刷 typesetting and printing:～书稿 typesetting the manuscript of a book and get it ready for printing|文稿已交付～。The manuscripts are ready for the press.

【排忧解难】pái yōu jiě nàn 排除忧虑,解除危难 relieve sb. of anxieties by helping him solve problems

【排中律】páizhōnglǜ 形式逻辑基本规律之一,在同一时间和同一条件下,对同一对象所作的两个矛盾判断不能同时都假,必有一真。如一个是假的,另一个一定是真的,不能有中间情况。公式是:'甲或非甲'或'甲是乙或甲不是乙'。law of excluded middle; basic rule of formal logic, whereby the two contradictory judgment passed on the same subject at the same time and under the same conditions cannot be both false, that is, one judgment must be true, or if one judgment is false, the other is bound to be true, and there is no middle way in between. The formula: 'A or not A' or 'A is B or A is not B'.

【排字】pái//zì 印刷以前按一定的格式排出印刷物的文字 typesetting; setting a text according to a certain format to get ready for printing

徘 pái [徘徊](páihuái) ❶ 在一个地方来回地走 loiter; walk up and down; pace back and forth:他独自在江边～。He walked up and down by the river, alone. ❷〈比喻 *fig*.〉犹疑不决 dither; vacillate; waver:～歧路 hesitate at the crossroads; linger in the wrong path ❸〈比喻 *fig*.〉事物在某个范围内来回浮动、起伏 ebb and flow; rise and fall; oscillate; hover:这个厂的产值一直在三百万元左右～。The output value of this factory has all along hovered around 3 million yuan.

棑 pái same as 排² pái

牌 pái ❶(～儿 páir) same as 牌子 pái·zi ①:广告～billboard|标语～placard ❷(～儿 páir) same as 牌子 pái·zi ②:门～ door plate|自行车～儿 bicycle license plate ❸(～儿 páir) same as 牌子 pái·zi③:冒～儿 fake|英雄～金笔'Hero'-brand gold pen ❹一种娱乐用品(也用为赌具)cards; dominoes:纸～cards|扑克～playing cards|打～playing cards; playing mahjong ❺ same as 牌子 pái·zi ④:词～ title of a *ci* poem|曲～title of a ballad-singing tune

【牌匾】páibiǎn 挂在门楣上或墙上,题着字的木板 tablet; plaque; inscribed horizontal or vertical board hanging on the wall or the lintel of a door

【牌坊】páifāng 形状像牌楼的建筑物,旧时多用来表彰忠孝节义的人物,如功德牌坊、贞节牌坊 archway; (of old days) memorial building erected in honour of society's role models, such as archways in honour of officials, generals or scholars who had performed meritorious deeds or excelled in imperial exams, as well as archways memorizing chaste women

【牌号】páihào (～儿 páihàor) ❶ 商店的字号 logo of a store; name of a shop:这家餐馆换了～。The restaurant has changed its name. ❷ 商标 trademark; brand; same as 牌子 pái·zi ③:货架上陈列着各种～的电视机。On display on the shelves are television sets of different brands.|这种～的香水是上等货。This brand of perfume is a top-notch product.

【牌价】páijià 规定的价格(多用牌子公布)list price; posted price:零售～retail sales price|批发～wholesale price

【牌九】páijiǔ 骨牌 *paijiu*; a kind of Chinese dominoes

【牌楼】pái·lou 做装饰用的建筑物,多建于街市要冲或名胜之处,由两个或四个并列的柱子构成,上面有檐。为庆祝用的牌楼是临时用竹、木等扎彩搭成的。ornamental archway; ceremonial gateway; oft. built in the streets, scenic spots or places of cultural interest, consisting of two or four pillars under an elaborately constructed and lacquered rooftop, oft. with flying eaves; makeshift archways are often erected to mark certain events by putting bamboo poles or logs together

【牌示】páishì 张贴在布告牌上的文告 bulletin; public notice

【牌位】páiwèi 指神主、灵位或其他题着名字作为祭祀对象的木牌 memorial tablet; wooden tablet inscribed with the name of a god, ancestor, or deceased family member, as a ritual object to be used in a sacrificial ceremony

【牌照】páizhào 政府发给的行车的凭证,也指发给某些特种营业的执照 license plate for an automobile; business license certificate

【牌子】pái·zi ❶ 张贴文告、广告、标语等的板状物 billboard for public notices, advertisements or slogans:球场四周竖立着各种广告～。An assortment of advertising billboards have been erected around the stadium. ❷ 用木板或其他材料做的标志,上边多有文字 plate; sign; tablet:菜～ vegetable price tab|水～ small wooden or cardboard chip serving as a token for buying tap water ❸ 企业单位为自

己的产品起的专用的名称 brand; brand name: 老～old brand; established brand | 闯～open up the market for a certain brand of products ❹ 调曲的调子 title of a *ci* poem; title of a ballad-singing tune

【牌子曲】pái·ziqǔ 指把若干民族小调和若干曲艺曲牌连串起来演唱一段故事的一类曲 a kind of ballad to be sung in a combination of different ballad and folksong tunes

箄 pái same as 簰 pái
☞ bēi on p. 79

簰(簿) pái same as 排² pái

pǎi (ㄆㄞˇ)

迫(廹) pǎi [迫击炮](pǎijīpào)从炮口装弹,以曲射为主的火炮,炮身短,射程较近,轻便灵活,能射击遮蔽物后方的目标 mortar; flexible short large-bore cannon with projectiles loaded from the muzzle and for firing at high angles to hit targets hidden behind camouflages
☞ pò on p. 1493

排 pǎi 〈方 *dial.*〉用楦子填紧或撑大新鞋的中空部分使合于某种形状 stretch a new pair of shoes with lasts to adjust them into desired shape: 把这双鞋～一～。Stretch this pair of shoes with lasts.
☞ pái on p. 1437

【排子车】pǎi·zichē 用人力拉的一种车,没有车厢,多用于运货或搬运器物 flat-bedded large cart pulled by manpower, oft. for hauling goods; also 大板车 dàbǎnchē

pài (ㄆㄞˋ)

哌 pài [哌嗪](pàiqín) 药名,有机化合物,化学式 $NHC_2H_4NHC_2H_4$。白色结晶,有驱除蛔虫和蛲虫等作用。piperazine; paiperazine ($NHC_2H_4NHC_2H_4$), a crystalline white organic compound used medically as an anthelmintic for bellyworms and pinworms

派 pài ❶ 指立场、见解或作风、习气相同的一些人 group of people with the same political stand, viewpoints, work style or lifestyle: 党～political party | 学～discipline of learning | 宗～faction | 乐观～optimists ❷ 作风或风度 mien; manner; style: 气～bearing | ～头 manner ❸ 〈方 *dial.*〉有派头儿;有风度 chic; stylish: 小王穿上这身衣服真够～的。Xiao Wang looks rather stylish in this suit. ❹ 〈量词 *classifier*〉 a)用于派别 school; faction: 两～学者对这个问题有两种不同的看法。Scholars of the two different schools of thought are worlds apart on this issue. b)用于景色、气象、声音、语言等(前面用'一'字)[used with the numeral 一 yī to indicate scene, atmosphere, sound, remark, etc.]: 好一～北国风光。What beautiful northern landscape! | 一～新气象。What a thriving atmosphere! | 一～胡言 a pack of lies ❺ 〈书 *fml.*〉江河的支流 tributary ❻ 分配;派遣;委派;安排 distribute; dispatch; appoint; arrange: 分～distribution | 调(diào)～allocate; assign | ～人送去 have sth. sent to sb. | ～用场 put sth. to use ❼ 摊派 apportion; assign: ～粮～款 levy grain and money ❽ 指摘(别人过失) castigate; blame: ～不是 take sb. to task; put the blame on sb. ☞ pā on p. 1434

【派别】pàibié 学术、宗教、政党等内部因主张不同而形成的分支或小团体 school; sect; faction; small organised dissentient group within a larger one, esp. in politics, academics and religion

【派不是】pài bù·shi 指摘别人的过失 put the blame on sb.: 自己不认错,还派别人的不是。Instead of acknowledging his mistake, he shifted the blame onto someone else.

【派出所】pàichūsuǒ 我国公安部门的基层机构,管理户口和基层治安等工作 police substation; the lowest public security organ in charge of residence administration and public security work at the grass-roots level in China

【派力司】pàilìsī 用羊毛织成的平纹毛织品,表面现出纵横交错的隐约的线条,适宜于做夏季服装 palace; tabby woolen fabric with subtle crisscrossing lines, suitable for the marking of summer garments

【派遣】pàiqiǎn (政府、机关、团体等)命人到某处做某项工作 (government, organization, group, etc.) dispatch to a place to do certain work: ～代表团出国访问 dispatch a delegation to visit a foreign country

【派生】pàishēng 从一个主要事物的发展中分化出来 derive: ～词 derivative

【派生词】pàishēngcí ☞ 合成词 héchéngcí on p. 781

【派头】pàitóu (～儿 pàitóur)气派 style; manner: ～十足 supercilious; overweening; swashbuckling | 很有～quite stylish

【派系】pàixì 指某些政党或集团内部的派别 fractions in a political party or clique

【派性】pàixìng 指维护派系私利的表现 factionalism: 闹～engage in factionalist activities | 消除～overcome factionalism

【派驻】pàizhù 受到派遣驻在某地(执行任务)be commissioned to station or post at a place: ～国外 be posted abroad | 有些单位已经撤消了～地方的机构。Some central government departments have abolished their local offices.

蒎 pài 有机化合物,化学式 $C_{10}H_{18}$。化学性质稳定,不易被无机酸和氧化剂分解。pinane ($C_{10}H_{18}$); organic compound with such stable chemical property that it is not easily disintegrated by inorganic acids and oxidants

湃 pài ☞ 滂湃 pāngpài on p. 1445 and 澎湃 péngpài on p. 1459

pān (ㄆㄢ)

扳 pān same as 攀 pān
☞ bān on p. 46

番 pān 番禺(Pānyú), 地名, 在广东 Panyu, name of a place in Guangdong
☞ fān on p. 529

潘 Pān 姓 a surname

攀 pān ❶ 抓住东西向上爬 climb; clamber: ～登 climbing|～树 climb up a tree|～着绳子往上爬 climb up a rope hand over hand ❷ 用手拉; 抓住 grab; hold onto; cling to: ～折 pull down a twig, etc. and break it off|～缘 climb; clamber ❸ 指跟地位高的人结亲戚或拉关系 seek connection in high places: 高～ try to associate with sb. of importance|～亲 claim kinship with sb. |～龙附凤 play up to people of power and influence ❹ 设法接触; 牵扯 involve; implicate: ～谈 strike up a conversation|～扯 implicate sb. in a crime|～供 implicate sb. in one's confession; make wild charges

【攀比】pānbǐ 援引事例比附 compare unrealistically with sb. better than oneself: 互相～ make unrealistic comparison with each other

【攀扯】pānchě 牵连拉扯 implicate (sb. in a crime): 这件事跟他没关系, 你别～他。Don't implicate him because this has nothing to do with him.

【攀登】pāndēng 抓住东西爬上去 clamber; scale ◇～科学高峰 scale new heights of science

【攀附】pānfù ❶ 附着东西往上爬(of a plant) climbing; trailing: 藤蔓～树木。Vines climb all over the trees. ❷〈比喻 *fig.*〉投靠有权势的人, 以求高升 cotton up to sb. in power in search of a promotion: ～权贵 seek affiliation with the rich and powerful

【攀高枝儿】pān gāozhīr 指跟社会地位比自己高的人交朋友或结成亲戚。有的地区说巴高枝儿。make friends or claim kinship with sb. of a higher social status; put as 巴高枝儿 bā gāozhīr in some regions

【攀供】pāngòng 指招供的时候凭空牵扯别人(of a confessing suspect) fabricate charges to implicate sb. in a crime

【攀交】pānjiāo 跟地位高的人结交 befriend people in high places

【攀龙附凤】pān lóng fù fèng 巴结或投靠有权势的人 climber over the dragon and follow the phoenix; curry favour with the rich and powerful; play up to people of power and influence; also 附凤攀龙 fù fèng pān lóng

【攀亲】pān//qīn ❶ 拉亲戚关系 claim kinship: ～道故 claim ties of blood or friendship ❷ 议婚; 订婚 arrange a marriage: 给儿子攀了一门亲 arrange marriage for a son

【攀禽】pānqín 鸟的一类, 脚短而健壮, 善于攀树, 嘴坚硬, 有的有锋利的钩, 常捕食害虫, 如啄木鸟、杜鹃等 scansorial birds; a kind of strong birds such as woodpeckers and cuckoos that are adept at climbing trees and have short legs, rigid beaks, and oft. sharp claws allowing them to prey on pest insects

【攀谈】pāntán 拉扯闲谈 strike up a chat; engage in a chit-chat; chat up sb.: 两人～起来很相投。The two of them had a most congenial conversation.

【攀诬】pānwū 牵连; 诬陷 frame sb. up: ～好人 implicate an innocent person

【攀援】pānyuán same as 攀缘 pānyuán

【攀缘】pānyuán ❶ 抓着东西往上爬 climb; scale ❷〈比喻 *fig.*〉投靠有钱有势的人往上爬 cotton up to the rich and power in order to climb up the social ladder; also 攀援 pānyuán

【攀缘茎】pānyuánjīng 不能直立, 靠卷须或吸盘状的器官附着在别的东西上生长的茎, 如葡萄、黄瓜、常春藤等的茎 climbing vine; scandent plant such as grapevine; cucumber and ivy, that cannot stand on its own and has to cling to other things with its claspers or cupules

【攀折】pānzhé 拉下来折断(花木) pull a twig or flower down and break it off: 爱护花木, 请勿～。Protect the flowers and trees. No pickings allowed.

【攀枝花】pānzhīhuā 木棉树 bombax

pán (ㄆㄢˊ)

爿 pán〈方 *dial.*〉❶ 劈成片的竹木等 slit bamboo or chopped wood: 柴～ chopped wood|竹～slit bamboo ❷〈量词 *classifier*〉田地一片叫一爿 piece of land ❸〈量词 *classifier*〉商店、工厂等一家叫一爿 number of shops, factories, etc.

胖 pán〈书 *fml.*〉安泰舒适 peaceful and comfortable: 心广体～when the mind is at ease, the body becomes healthy; carefree mind and well-nourished body
☞ pàng on p. 1447

般 pán〈书 *fml.*〉欢乐 bliss; elation
☞ bān on p. 47 and bō on p. 146

盘(盤) pán ❶〈古代 *arch.*〉盥洗用具的一种 washbasin ❷ (～儿 pánr) same as 盘子 pán·zi ①: 茶～儿 tea tray|托～ tray ❸ (～儿 pánr) 形状或功用像盘子①的东西 sth. in the shape, or with the function, of a plate: 磨～ millstone|算～abacus|字～(upper or lower) case|棋～chessboard ◇地～domain; sphere of influence ❹ (～儿 pánr)指商品行情 market situation: 开～opening quotation on stock exchange|收～ closing quotation on stock exchange | 平～ balanced stock exchange quotation ❺ 回旋地绕 wind; coil: ～旋 circling; winding|～杠子 work out on the horizontal bars | ～马弯弓 bestride the horse and bend the bow — ready to fight ❻ 垒、砌、搭(炕、灶) construct a brick *kang* or stove: 南屋的炕拆了还没～。The *kang* in the southern room hasn't been built after it was torn down the other day. ❼ 仔细查问或清点 examine; look into: ～问 make an inquiry|～根究底 try to get to the bottom of sth. |～货 make an inventory of a warehouse|一年～一次账 check the accounts once a year ❽ 指转让(工商企业) transfer (the ownership of firm): 出～sell (a factory, company, etc.)|招～put a business up for sale|受～take over a company ❾ 搬运 move: ～运 transport; ship|由仓库朝外头～东西 move things out of a warehouse ❿〈量词 *classifier*〉: 一～机器 a machine|一～磨 a set of millstone|乒乓球赛进行了两～单打和一～双打。The table tennis championship has gone through two singles games and one doubles game. ⓫ (Pán)姓 a surname

【盘剥】pánbō 指利上加利地剥削 exploit; practise usury: 重利～lend money at a usurious rate

【盘查】pánchá 盘问检查 interrogate and check: ～过路行人 stop pedestrians for interrogation

【盘缠】pán•chan 路费 travel allowance; money needed to cover expenses on a journey

【盘秤】pánchèng 杆秤的一种,秤杆的一端系着一个盘子,把要称的东西放在盘子里 steelyard with a pan on it; a kind of balance with a pan hanging on its short arm to take the item to be weighed, and a long graduated arm along which a eight is moved until it balances

【盘川】pánchuān 〈方 *dial.*〉路费 travel expenses

【盘存】páncún 用清点、过秤、对账等方法检查现有资产的数量和情况 take an inventory; take an inventory of assets on hand by checking the amount, weighing the merchandise, and checking the accounts

【盘错】páncuò〈书 *fml.*〉(树根或树枝)盘绕交错,也用来比喻事情错综复杂 (of tree roots or branches) intertwining; intricate: 枝桠～(of a tree) intertwining and gnarling branches|问题～,一时难以解决。The problems are so mixed up that a quick solution is out of the question.

【盘道】pándào 弯曲的路,多在山地 zigzagging mountain road

【盘点】pándiǎn 清点(存货)make an inventory of: ～库存 take stock

【盘店】pándiàn 指把店铺全部的货物器具等转让给人 transfer a business; transfer the ownership of a shop, merchandize and all, to sb. else

【盘费】pán•fei 路费 money needed on a journey

【盘杠子】pán gàng•zi 在单杠上做各种翻腾的动作 do gymnastic movements on the horizontal bar

【盘根错节】pán gēn cuò jié 树根盘绕,木节交错(of a tree) twisted roots and gnarled branches;〈比喻 *fig.*〉事情复杂,不易解决(of problems, etc.) too complicated to be solved quickly

【盘根问底】pán gēn wèn dǐ 盘问事情的根由底细 making inquires in order to get to the bottom of sth. that has happened; also 盘根究底 pán gēn jiū dǐ

【盘亘】pángèn〈书 *fml.*〉(山)互相连接(of mountains) undulating: 山岭～交错 topographical turmoil of mountains

【盘古】Pángǔ 我国神话中的开天辟地的人物(in Chinese mythology) Pan Gu, creator of the universe

【盘桓】pánhuán ❶〈书 *fml.*〉逗留 linger; stay; same as 徘徊 páihuái ①: ～终日 wander about all day long|在杭州～了几天,游览了各处名胜。We spent a few days sightseeing in Hangzhou. ❷ 曲折;盘曲 zigzag; spiral: ～髻 wear one's hair into a bun ❸ 回环旋绕 linger: 这个想法一直～脑际。The idea has seized upon him for some time.

【盘货】pán//huò 商店等清点和检查实存货物 make an inventory of stock on hand: 今日～,暂停营业。Inventory Day — Business Closed

【盘缴】pánjiǎo〈方 *dial.*〉❶ 日常开支 daily expenses: 他家人口多,～大。His family spend a lot because there are so many mouths to be taken care of ❷ 路费 travel expenses

【盘诘】pánjié 仔细追问(可疑的人)cross-question; interrogate (sb. suspicious-looking): 戒严期间,对进城的人严加～。During the martial law period, all those entering the city were subjected to strict questioning.

【盘结】pánjié 旋绕 coiling: 森林里古木参天,粗藤～。Ancient trees in the forest heap up rich piles of foliage in the sky, with vines coiling around their trunks.

【盘究】pánjiū 盘问追究 cross-examine and investigate

【盘踞】pánjù 非法占据;霸占(地方)take illegal possession of a place: 一股海匪～小岛。A pack of pirates are entrenched on the isle. also 盘据 pánjù

【盘库】pán//kù 查点仓库物品 make an inventory of goods in a warehouse

【盘马弯弓】pán mǎ wān gōng 韩愈诗《雉带箭》:'将军欲以巧伏人,盘马弯弓惜不发。' *Arrowhead with a Pheasant Feather Tail* by Han Yu, 'To subdue the enemy with ingenuity,/ Rather than by sheer force,/The general manoeuvred his mount in a circular trot./ The bow was pulled in all seriousness,/Yet the arrow is not shot'.〈比喻 *fig*.〉先做出惊人的姿势,不立刻行动 make a show of intimidation without springing into action at once; (盘马 *pan ma*:骑着马绕圈子 run in circles on horseback;弯弓 *wan gong*:张了弓要射箭 draw the bow for shooting the arrow)

【盘尼西林】pánníxīlín 青霉素的旧称 formerly called 青霉素 qīngméisù

【盘弄】pánnòng 来回抚摸;拨弄 toy with:随手摘了一根野草,在手上～pick a wild grass absent-mindedly and toy with it in the hand

【盘曲】pánqū〈书 *fml*.〉曲折环绕 spiraling:古树枝干～twisted trunk and knurled branches of an ancient tree|山路～而上。The footpath winds its way up the mountain. also 蟠曲 pánqū

【盘儿菜】pánrcài 切好并适当搭配,放在盘子中出售的生菜肴 ready-to-cook dish; assortment of meats and vegetables, etc. for sale in a food market, prepared according to a recipe and made ready for the stove

【盘绕】pánrào 围绕在别的东西上面 encircling; coil:长长的藤葛～在树身上。Long vines coiled around the trunk of the tree.

【盘山】pánshān 环绕在山上的 wind up a mountain:～道 zigzagging mountain trail|～公路 winding mountain highway|～水渠 canal winding around a mountain

【盘跚】pánshān same as 蹒跚 pánshān

【盘石】pánshí same as 磐石 pánshí

【盘算】pán·suan 心里算计或筹划 calculate; figure; plan:这笔钱添些什么东西,老汉～了好几天。It took the old man quite a few days to figure out what to buy with this money.

【盘梯】pántī 一种扶梯,中间竖立一根圆柱,柱旁辐射式地安装若干折扇形的梯形,盘旋而上,多用于瞭望台或塔中 spiral staircase; staircase with the steps spread out like a fan and rising in a spiral round a central axis, oft. installed on an observation deck or inside a pagoda

【盘腿】pán//tuǐ 坐时两腿变曲交叉地平放着 (sit) cross-legged

【盘陁】pántuó same as 盘陀 pántuó

【盘陀】pántuó〈书 *fml*.〉❶ 形容石头不平 jagged; rocky ❷ 曲折回旋 tortuous; winding:～路 zigzagging road; also 盘陁 pántuó

【盘问】pánwèn 仔细查问 cross-question:再三～,他才说出实情。He told the truth as a result of an unrelenting interrogation.

【盘膝】pánxī same as 盘腿 pán//tuǐ:～而坐 sit cross-legged

【盘香】pánxiāng 绕成螺旋形的线香 incense coil

【盘旋】pánxuán ❶ 环绕着飞或走 loop; circle; whirl:飞机在天空～。An aircraft was circling in the sky.|山路曲折,游人～而上。Travellers trudged up the mountain along a looping path.◇这件事在我脑子里～了好久。I've been mulling over this for a long time. ❷ 徘徊;逗留 hang on; dawdle; linger:他在花房里～了半天才离开。He had dawdled in the greenhouse for a long time before he left.

【盘运】pányùn 搬运 carry; transport

【盘账】pán//zhàng 查核账目 check accounts; audit

【盘子】pán·zi ❶ 盛放物品的浅底的器具,比碟子大,多为圆形 tray; plate; shallow circular vessel that is larger than a saucer ❷ 指商品行情 market situation; market prices

槃 pán〈书 *fml*.〉same as 盘 pán ①②⑤

磐 pán〈书 *fml*.〉大石头 monolith; boulder:～石 huge rock

【磐石】pánshí 厚而大的石头 rock of a massive size:安如～be rock-firm; also 盘石 pánshí

磻 pán 磻溪(Pánxī),地名,在浙江 Panxi, name of a place in Zhejiang Province

蹒(蹣) pán [蹒跚](pánshān)腿脚不灵便,走路缓慢、摇摆的样子 dodder; stagger; shuffle:步履～walk in unsteady steps; shuffle along; also 盘跚 pánshān

蟠 pán 蟠曲 coil; curl:龙～虎踞 where the dragon is coiled and the tiger crouches — place of strategic importance

【蟠曲】pánqū same as 盘曲 pánqū

【蟠桃】[1]pántáo ❶ 桃的一种,果实扁圆形,汁不多。核仁也可以吃。flat peach (*Prunus persica* var. *compressa*); a kind of peach tree bearing fruit that is flat in shape and not very juicy, with an edible kernel ❷ 这种植物的果实 flat peach‖有的地区叫扁桃 known in some areas as 扁桃 biǎntáo

【蟠桃】[2]pántáo 神话中的仙桃 (in Chinese mythology) peach of immortality

鞶(❷鞶) pán〈书 *fml*.〉❶ 大带子 belt; ribbon ❷ 小囊 small bag

pàn(ㄆㄢˋ)

判 pàn ❶ 分开;分辨 tell apart; tell the difference:～别 differentiate|～断 judge; pass a judgment|～明 issue a verdict ❷ 明显(有区别)(differ) apparently; evidently:新旧社会～然不同。The new society is worlds' apart from the old one.|前后～若两人 become a totally different person; no longer one's old self ❸ 评定 judge; decide:裁～referee; umpire|评～pass judgment on sth. or sb.｜～卷子 mark exam papers ❹ 判决 pass a verdict：审～put sb. on trial｜～案 pass a verdict on a legal case｜公～announce the verdicton a case in public

【判别】pànbié 辨别(不同之处) differentiate：～是非 tell right from wrong｜提高～能力 enhance one's sense of judgment

【判处】pànchǔ 判决处以某种刑罚 condemn sb. to a certain penalty：～有期徒刑一年 sentenced to one year's imprisonment

P

【判词】pàncí ❶ 判决书的旧称 old term for 判决书 pànjuéshū ❷ 断语；结论 judgment；conclusion

【判定】pàndìng 分辨断定 determine；judge：～去向 determine the whereabouts of sb.｜从一句话里很难～他的看法。It's hard to tell from just a single remark what stand he takes.

【判读】pàndú 利用已知的视觉信息符号来判断新获得的视觉信息的含义 interpret；read and make a judgment；make use of visual data in hand to determine the implication of visual data that have been newly acquired：卫星照片～ interpretation of satellite photos｜通过图像分析，把断层的活动性质～出来 interpret the nature of a fault movement through graphical analyses

【判断】pànduàn ❶ 思维的基本形式之一，就是肯定或否定某种事物的存在，或指明它是否具有某种属性的思维过程。在形式逻辑上用一个命题表达出来。judge；basic form of thinking，i.e.，the process of thinking to confirm or negate the existence of sth. or determine if it possesses certain property，expressed as a proposition in formal logic ❷ 断定 judgment：你～得很正确。You've made a sound judgment.｜正确的～sound judgment ❸〈书 *fml.*〉判决(案件) pass a verdict on a legal case

【判罚】pànfá 根据有关规定加以处罚 penalize：违反交通规则的司机将被～。Drivers who have violated traffic rules will be penalized.｜运动员在禁区犯规，～点球。One of the football players committed a foul in the penalty area，and a penalty kick was awarded to the opposing team.

【判分】pàn//fēn (～儿 pàn//fēnr)对试卷或参加比赛人员的表演、动作等判定分数 mark (exam papers)；give scores to an athlete according to his or her performance and execution：～严 (of a judge or referee) be strict in meting out points｜～标准 standards for scoring

【判官】pànguān 唐宋时期辅助地方长官处理公事的人员，迷信传说中用来指阎王手下管生死簿的官 (in Tang and Song dynasties) magistrate's assistant in trying handling government affairs and trying legal cases；(of superstition or mythology) judge in Hades

【判决】pànjué ❶ 法院对审理结束的案件做出决定 (of the court) pass judgment on a case：～书 court verdict；court decision；court ruling ❷ 判断，决定 judgment；decision：比赛中队员要服从裁判的～。In sports competition the athletes should obey the referee's decisions.

【判决书】pànjuéshū 法院根据判决写成的文书 court verdict；written judgment

【判例】pànlì 已经生效的判决，法院在判决类似案件时可以援用为先例，这种被援用的先例叫做判例。判例有时具有与法律同等的效力。legal precedence；judicial precedent；concluded case to be cited as an example — oft. as legally binding as law — in deciding a similar case

【判明】pànmíng 分辨清楚；弄清楚 verify；ascertain：～是非 make a clear distinction between right and wrong｜～真相 verify the facts

【判若鸿沟】pàn ruò Hónggōu 形容界线很清楚，区别很明显 (of a boundary or distinction) clearly cut；(of difference) conspicuous；as different as poles apart；☞ 鸿沟 Hónggōu on p. 807

【判若云泥】pàn ruò yún ní 高低差别好像天上的云彩和地下的泥土的距离那样远 be as far apart as the clouds in the sky are from the land on earth；be worlds' apart；also put as 判若天渊 pàn ruò tiān yuān

【判刑】pàn//xíng 判处刑罚 pass a sentence on (a convict)；sentence (a convict) to (death，imprisonment，etc.)

【判罪】pàn//zuì 法院根据法律给犯罪的人定罪 (of a court judge) declare sb. guilty

拚 pàn 舍弃不顾 go all out in doing sth.：～弃 ditch；cast aside｜～命 defy death；do sth. for all one's worth
☞ 拼 pīn on p. 1478

【拚命】pàn//mìng〈方 *dial.*〉拼命 defy death；do sth. by risking one's life；do sth. for all one's worth

泮 pàn ❶〈书 *fml.*〉融解 dissolve；unfreeze ❷ 指泮宫。清代称考中秀才为'入泮'。semi-circular pool within the precincts of a former provincial college；chief college of an ancient state. During the Qing Dynasty，passing the imperial exam at the county level is known as 'enrolling in the provincial college'. ❸ (Pàn) 姓 a surname

【泮宫】pàngōng 古代的学校 college in ancient China

盼 pàn ❶ 盼望 yearn for；expect：切～expect on tiptoe｜～星星～月亮，才～到亲人归来。They have waited day in and day out，and lo and behold，their loved ones were home at last. ❷ 看 look：左顾右～look this way and that；look around

【盼头】pàn·tou 指可能实现的良好愿望 sth. to look forward to；hope：这年月呀，越活越有～啦！Life these days is getting increasingly hopeful.

【盼望】pànwàng 殷切地期望 yearn for; look forward to:他～早日与亲人团聚。He looked forward to rejoining his loved ones.

叛 pàn 背叛 be disloyal to; walk out on; jilt:～贼 treacherous traitor|～匪 rebels|众～亲离 be deserted by family and friends alike; with one's followers in revolt and one's close associates deserting

【叛变】pànbiàn 背叛自己的一方,采取敌对行动或投向敌对的一方 turn traitor; turn renegade:～投敌 turn traitor and cross over to the enemy

【叛国】pàn//guó 背叛祖国 commit treason:～罪 high treason|～分子 sb. guilty of treason

【叛离】pànlí 背叛 defection:～祖国 turn one's back on one's motherland; betray and desert one's own country

【叛乱】pànluàn 武装叛变 insurgence; mutiny:发动～mount an insurrection|武装～armed rebellion|～分子 rebel

【叛卖】pànmài 背叛并出卖(祖国、革命)betray one's motherland or revolution:～民族利益 betray the national interest of one's own country

【叛逆】pànnì ❶ 背叛 revolt:～行为 act of rebellion ❷ 有背叛行为的人 rebel; defiant person

【叛逃】pàntáo 背叛逃亡 defect

【叛徒】pàntú 有背叛行为的人 apostate; deserter; defector

畔 pàn ❶(江、湖、道路等)旁边;附近 side; border of a river, lake, road, etc.:湖～lakeside|路～roadside|桥～by a bridge|枕～pillow (talk, intimacy, etc.) ❷ 田地的边界 border of a field
〈古 *arch.*〉same as 叛 pàn

袢 pàn ❶ same as 襻 pàn ❷ ☞[袷袢] qiāpàn on p. 1526

鋬 pàn 器物上用手提的部分(of a utensil) handle:壶～kettle handle|桶～pail handle

襻 pàn ❶(～儿 pànr)用布做的扣住纽扣的套 button loop; buttonhole:纽～儿 buttonhole ❷(～儿 pànr)形状或功用像襻的东西 anything in the shape, or with the function, of a button loop:车～cart strap|鞋～儿 shoe strap|篮子～儿 basket handle ❸ 用绳子、线等绕住,使分开的东西连在一起 tie; fasten with a rope, string, etc.:～上几针 put in a few stitches|用绳子～住 bundle sth. with rope

pāng(ㄆㄤ)

乓 pāng〈拟声词 *onom.*〉形容枪声、关门声、东西砸破声等 bang; pop, slam; crash:～的一声枪响。The rifle went off with a bang.|乒乒～～响成一片。There was a great rattle out there.

雱(霶、雾) pāng〈书 *fml.*〉❶ 雪下得很大 heavy snow ❷ same as 滂 pāng

滂 pāng〈书 *fml.*〉❶ 水势浩大的样子(of water) torrential; tumbling ❷ 形容水涌出 (of water) roaring and rushing

【滂湃】pāngpài 水势浩大 (of water) in spate; torrential

【滂沱】pāngtuó 形容雨下得很大 torrential:大雨～downpour; raining cats and dog ◇涕泗～(形容哭得很厉害,眼泪、鼻涕流得很多) let loose a flood of tears; tears and snivel running abundantly down one's face

膀(胮) pāng (大片的皮肉)浮肿 swell:～肿 swollen; bloated|他的心脏病不轻,脸都～了。With a bloated face like that, his is indeed a serious case of heart disease.
☞ bǎng on p. 58, bàng on p. 59 and páng on p. 1446

páng(ㄆㄤˊ)

彷(徬) páng [彷徨](pánghuáng)走来走去,犹疑不决,不知往哪个方向去 dither; vacillate; pace up and down in indecision:～歧途 vacillate at a crossroads|～失措 at one's wit's end; also 旁皇 pánghuáng
☞ fǎng on p. 551

庞[1](龐、❶❷厐) páng ❶ 庞大 massive; mammoth:～然大物 behemoth ❷ 多而杂乱 hodgepodge; mishmash:～杂 in a jumbled mess ❸ (Páng) 姓 a surname

庞[2](龐) páng (～儿 pángr)脸盘 face:面～face

【庞大】pángdà 很大(常含过大或大而无当的意思,指形体、组织或数量等)(oft. over-sized, or large but inappropriate, referring to size, organization, number, etc.) enormous:体积～of enormous proportions|开支～enormous expenditure|机构～cumbersome organization

【庞然大物】pángrán dà wù 外表上庞大的东西 huge monster; colossus; juggernaut

【庞杂】pángzá 多而杂乱 jumbled:机构～jumbled and often overlapped organization|内容～(of a book, report, etc.) mind-boggling content|文字～long-winded and wordy text

逄 Páng 姓 a surname

旁 páng ❶ 旁边 side; edge:路～roadside|～观 look on with folded arms|～门 side door|～若无人 be overweening; act as if no one were around|目不～视 not let one's eyes wander — absolute concentration ❷ 其他;另外 other; else:～人 someone else|他有～的事

先走了。He left early because he had something else to attend to. ❸（～儿 pángr）汉字的偏旁（of Chinese characters）lateral radical：竖心～儿 radical written as 忄|立人～儿 radical written as 亻❹ 广泛 comprehensive；capacious；far-flung：～征博引 support one's view by copious quotations

〈古 *arch.*〉same as 傍 bàng

【旁白】pángbái 戏剧角色背着台上其他剧中人对观众说的话 aside；words spoken in a play for the audience to hear，but supposed not to be heard by the other characters

【旁边】pángbiān（～儿 pángbiānr）左右两边；靠近的地方 beside；by：马路～停着许多小汽车。Many cars are parked by the road.

【旁出】pángchū（支脉、枝杈等）从旁边分出去（of a tributary，branch，etc.）branch out from the side

【旁顾】pánggù 顾及其他事物 attend to other matters：无暇～have no time to attend to other matters；having one's hands full dealing with sth.

【旁观】pángguān 置身局外，在一边看 look on；be an onlooker：冷眼～stand aloof；look on in callousness|袖手～look on with folded arms

【旁观者清】páng guān zhě qīng 旁观的人看得清楚 spectator sees most clearly；onlooker sees the game best；☞ 当局者迷 dāng jú zhě mí on p.384

【旁皇】pánghuáng same as 彷徨 pánghuáng

【旁及】pángjí 连带涉及 involve；implicate

【旁落】pángluò（应有的权力）落到别人手中（of decision-making power）fall into someone else's hands：大权～。Power has fallen into some other people's hands.

【旁门】pángmén（～儿 pángménr）正门旁边的或整个建筑物侧面的门 side door

【旁门左道】páng mén zuǒ dào ☞ 左道旁门 zuǒ dào páng mén on p.2572

【旁敲侧击】páng qiāo cè jī〈比喻 *fig.*〉说话或写文章不从正面直接说明，而从侧面曲折表达（of speech，article，etc.）attack by innuendo；make oblique references and sly injurious remarks

【旁人】pángrén 其他的人；另外的人 someone else；other people：这件事由我负责，跟～不相干。I am accountable for this，which has nothing to do with anyone else.

【旁若无人】páng ruò wú rén 好像旁边没有人，形容态度自然或高傲 act as if there were no one else present — be self-assured or supercilious

【旁听】pángtīng ❶ 参加会议而没有发言权和表决权 attending a meeting as a visitor with no right to speak and vote ❷ 非正式地随班听课 attending a class as an auditor：～生 auditor|他在北京大学～过课。He had attended Peking University as an auditor.

【旁骛】pángwù〈书 *fml.*〉在正业以外有所追求；不专心 pursue sth. other than one's principle occupation or responsibility；show lack of devotion to one's career：驰心～be infatuated with unwarranted pursuits

【旁系亲属】pángxì qīnshǔ 直系亲属以外在血统上和自己同出一源的人及其配偶，如兄、弟、姐、妹、伯父、叔父、伯母、婶母等 collateral relatives；relatives descended from the same stock but by a different blood line，such as brother，sister，uncle and aunt on both paternal and maternal sides，etc.

【旁征博引】páng zhēng bó yǐn 为了表示论证充足而广泛地引用材料（to bear out a thesis，etc.）collate extensively；extensive collation

【旁证】pángzhèng 主要证据以外的证据；间接的证据 circumstantial evidence；collateral evidence

【旁支】pángzhī 家族、集团等系统中不属于嫡系的支派 collateral branch of a family or clan

蒡 páng［蒡葧］（pángbó）古书上指茼蒿（in ancient books）crowndaisy；Chrysanthemum coronarium

☞ bàng on p.59

膀 páng［膀胱］（pángguāng）人或高等动物体内储存尿的器官，囊状，位于盆腔内。是由平滑肌构成的，有很大的伸缩性。尿由肾脏顺着输尿管进入膀胱。有的地区叫尿脬。urinary bladder，membranous sac containing urine in the pelvic cavity of a human being or a higher animal，consisting of smooth muscles and being thus very elastic；known in some regions as 尿脬 suī·pāo；（图见 ☞ figure for 泌尿器 mìniàoqì on p.1332）

☞ bǎng on p.58，bàng on p.59 and pāng on p.1445

磅 páng［磅礴］（pángbó）❶（气势）盛大（of momentum，manner，scale，etc.）monumental；imposing：气势～of a great momentum ❷（气势）充满 fill；permeate：～宇内（of the force of justice）permeate the entire world

☞ bàng on p.59

螃 páng［螃蟹］（pángxiè）节肢动物，全身有甲壳，眼有柄，足有五对，前面一对长成钳状，叫螯，横着爬。种类很多，通常生长在淡水里的叫河蟹，生长在海里的叫海蟹。crab（*Cancer pagurus*）；arthropod with a carapace，moving sideways with five pairs of legs，the first pair of which are modified as pincers，in two categories — freshwater crabs and sea crabs；简称 abbr. 蟹 xiè

鳑 páng［鳑鲏］（pángpí）鱼，体形和鲫鱼相似，比鲫鱼小。眼有彩色光泽，背面淡绿色，略带蓝色的闪光，腹面银白色。生活在淡水中，吃水生植物，卵产在蚌壳里。bitterling（*Rhodeus sericeus*）；fish similar to the crucian but smaller in size，having eyes in multiple hues，pale green back with a bluish gleam，and silvery white abdomen，feeding on hydrophytes in freshwater, and laying eggs in clam shells

pǎng（ㄆㄤˇ）

嗙 pǎng〈方 *dial.*〉自夸；吹牛 brag; blow one's own trumpet：开～ start crowing about oneself｜胡吹乱～shoot one's mouth off

耪 pǎng 用锄翻松土地 hoe; loosen soil with a hoe：～地 hoe the fields｜～谷子 weed a millet field

髈 pǎng〈方 *dial.*〉大腿 thigh
☞ bǎng on p. 58

pàng（ㄆㄤˋ）

胖（胖） pàng（人体）脂肪多，肉多（跟'瘦'相对 as opposed to 'thin'）(of human body) fat; fleshy：肥～ obese｜这孩子真～。What a chubby child.
☞ pán on p. 1441

【胖墩墩】pàngdūndūn（～的 pàngdūndūn·de）形容人矮胖而结实（of a person）thickset; short and thickset

【胖墩儿】pàngdūnr 称矮而胖的人（多指儿童 oft. child）roly-poly; fatty person

【胖乎乎】pànghūhū（～的 pànghūhū·de）形容人肥胖 plump; chubby

【胖头鱼】pàngtóuyú 鳙（yōng）carp; bighead

【胖子】pàng·zi 肥胖的人 fatty; fat person

pāo（ㄆㄠ）

抛（拋） pāo ❶ 扔；投掷 pitch; fling; hurl：～球 toss a ball｜～物线 parabola｜～砖引玉 cast a brick to attract jade — offer a commonplace lead to solicit valuable council ❷ 丢下 jilt; desert; ditch：～妻别子 desert one's wife and leave one's son behind｜跑到第三圈，他已经把别人远远地～在后面了。By the time he reached his third lap he had already left all the other competitors behind. ❸ 暴露 expose; show：～头露面 expose oneself in public; steal the limelight ❹ 抛售 dump; sell in large quantities：～出股票 dump one's stock shares

【抛费】pāofèi〈方 *dial.*〉糟蹋；浪费（东西）fritter away; squander

【抛光】pāoguāng 对工件等表面加工，使高度光洁。通常用附有磨料的布、皮革等制的抛光轮来进行，还有电解抛光、化学抛光等。polish; buffing; technique to polish metal objects by using a ragwheel, electroanalysis, or chemicals

【抛荒】pāo//huāng ❶ 土地不继续耕种，任它荒芜（of cultivated land）left uncultivated ❷（学业、业务）荒废（of one's studies, work）get rusty through disuse

【抛脸】pāo//liǎn〈方 *dial.*〉丢脸 lose face

【抛锚】pāo//máo ❶ 把锚投入水中，使船停稳。汽车等中途发生故障而停止行驶。(of boats, ships, etc.) drop anchor; (of automobiles) break down ❷〈方 *dial.*〉〈比喻 *fig.*〉进行中的事情因故中止（of things）stop midway; stoppage

【抛弃】pāoqì 扔掉不要 desert; abandon; cast off; leave in the lurch：～家园 desert one's home and property｜～旧观念 eschew outdated concepts

【抛却】pāoquè 抛掉；抛弃 throw over; quit：～不切实际的幻想 quit unrealistic ideas

【抛射】pāoshè 利用弹力或推力送出 project; catapult; launch

【抛售】pāoshòu 预料价格将跌或为压低价格而大量卖出商品 sell commodities in large quantities in anticipation of, or in order to bring about, a fall in price

【抛头露面】pāo tóu lù miàn〈旧时 *old*〉指妇女出现在大庭广众之中（封建道德认为是丢脸的事）。现在指某人公开露面（多含贬义 oft. derog.）(of women) appear in public — behaviour that flies in the face of feudal morality; show oneself in public in order to steal the limelight

【抛物面】pāowùmiàn 抛物线以它的对称轴为轴旋转一周所成的曲面。分为椭圆抛物面和双曲抛物面。paraboloid or hyperbolic paraboloid; curved surface that comes about by turning a parabola around its symmetrical axis

【抛物面镜】pāowùmiànjìng 反射面为抛物面的镜子。光源在焦点上时，光线经镜面反射后变成平行光束。汽车灯、探照灯中装有抛物面镜。parabolic mirror; mirror whose reflector takes the shape of a paraboloid, so that when the source of light coincides with its focus the reflected light becomes parallel. Parabolic mirror is fixed in automobile headlights and searchlight.

【抛物线】pāowùxiàn 平面上到定点 O 和定直线 l 距离相等的动点 P 的轨迹。定点 O 叫做抛物线的焦点。将一物体向上斜抛出去所经的路线就是抛物线。parabola; plane curve formed by the intersection of a right circular cone with a plane parallel to a generator of the cone; trail described by the point P when it moves on a plane to the fixed-point O at an equal distance to the fixed straight line L, with O

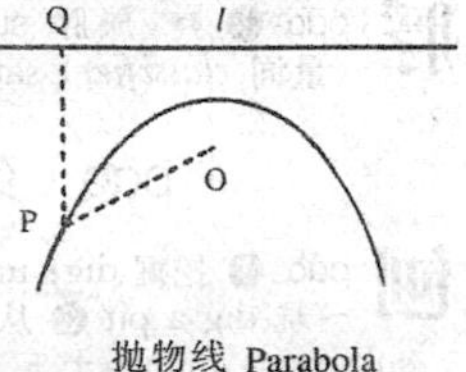

抛物线 Parabola

serving as the parabola's focus. The arc described by an object when it is thrown from one spot to another is also a parabola.

【抛掷】pāozhì 扔;丢弃 throw; cast; toss:～雪球 throw snow balls at one another|莫把年华轻～。Don't ever waste the precious time of your life.

【抛砖引玉】pāo zhuān yǐn yù〈谦辞 *hum.*〉〈比喻 *fig.*〉用粗浅的、不成熟的意见引出别人高明的、成熟的意见 cast a brick to attract jade — offer a few somewhat immature remarks to solicit other people's wise and mature opinions

P

泡1 pāo ❶(～儿 pāor)鼓起而松软的东西 sth. puffy and soft:豆～儿 beancurd puff|眼～(swollen) upper eyelid ❷〈方 *dial.*〉虚而松软;不坚硬 spongy; porous:～枣 spongy jujube|～线 bulked yean|这块木料发～。This piece of wood is kind of porous.

泡2 pāo〈方 *dial.*〉小湖,多用于地名 small lake; used as part of a place name:月亮～(在吉林) Yueliangpao, a place in Jilin Province|莲花～(在黑龙江) Lianhuapao, a place in Heilongjiang Province

泡3 pāo〈量词 *classifier*〉用于屎和尿[indicating number of excretions]
☞ pào on p.1450

【泡货】pāohuò〈方 *dial.*〉体积大而分量小的物品 light but bulk goods

【泡桐】pāotóng 落叶乔木,叶子大,卵形或心脏形,表面光滑,背面有茸毛,圆锥花序,花冠紫色,结蒴果,长圆形。木材质地疏松,可制乐器、模型等。paulownia (*Paulownia*); empress tree; princess tree; defoliating tree having large egg- or heart-shaped leaves with a smooth face and a downy back, loose branching clusters of flowers with purple corollas, elongated round capsules, and a kind of soft wood that is used for the making of musical instruments and models; also 桐 tóng

【泡子】pāo·zi〈方 *dial.*〉小湖,多用于地名 tiny lake; oft. used in a place name:～沿(在辽宁) Paoziyan, a place in Liaoning|干～(在内蒙古) Ganpaozi, a place in Inner Mongolia
☞ pào·zi on p.1451

脬 pāo ❶ ☞ 尿脬 suī·pào on p.1836 ❷〈量词 *classifier*〉same as 泡3 pāo

páo(ㄆㄠˊ)

刨 páo ❶挖掘 dig; unearth:～土 dig earth|～坑 dig a pit ❷从原有事物中除去;减去 substract; minus:十五天～去五天,只剩下十天了。Fifteen minus five — there are only ten days left.
☞ bào on p.72

【刨除】páochú 从原有的事物中除去;减去 leave out; exclude; minus

【刨根儿】páo//gēnr〈比喻 *fig.*〉追究底细 get to the bottom of things; look deeply into:这件事带出了另一件事,可非刨刨根儿不可。Something else emerged from what happened, and we need to get to the bottom of it.

【刨根问底儿】páo gēn wèn dǐr 追究底细;寻根究底 get into the whys and wherefores of things

咆 páo〈书 *fml.*〉(猛兽)怒吼;嗥(of animals) howl; bellow; yell:～哮 roar

【咆哮】páoxiào ❶(猛兽)怒吼(of an animal of prey) roar ❷形容水流的奔腾轰鸣,也形容人的暴怒喊叫(of water) roar on; tumble; (of people) bellow; yell in a fury:黄河～。The Yellow River rumbles on.|～如雷 in a thundering rage

狍(麅) páo same as 狍子 páo·zi

【狍子】páo·zi 鹿的一种,耳朵和眼都大,颈长,尾很短,后肢略比前肢长,冬季毛棕褐色,夏季毛栗红色,臀部灰白色,雄的有角。吃青草、野果和野菌等。roe deer (*Capreolus capreolus*); roe; a kind of deer having large ears and eyes, long neck, short tail, forelimbs slightly shorter than hindlimbs, grayish white hips, fur turning dark brown in winter and chestnut red in summer, the males sporting a pair of three-pointed antlers, feeding on grass, wild fruit and mushrooms

庖 páo〈书 *fml.*〉❶厨房 kitchen:～厨 kitchenette ❷厨师 cook:名～(有名的厨师) renowned chef

【庖厨】páochú〈书 *fml.*〉❶厨房 kitchen; kitchenette ❷厨师 cook; chef

【庖代】páodài〈书 *fml.*〉替别人做他分内的事 take sb. else's work into one's hand; ☞ 越俎代庖 yuè zǔ dài páo on p.2374

炮 páo ❶炮制中药的一种方法,把生药放在热铁锅里炒,使它焦黄爆裂,如用这种方法炮制的姜叫炮姜 bake; prepare Chinese medicine by roasting it in a hot iron pan until it turns yellow and cracks, such as baked ginger ❷〈书 *fml.*〉烧;烤(食物) bake; roast
☞ bāo on p.63 and pào on p.1451

【炮格】páogé 古代的一种酷刑 hot bronze pillar, ancient instrument of cruel torture

【炮炼】páoliàn 用加热的方法把中药原料里的水分和杂质除去 heat a medicinal herb to remove moisture and impurity

【炮烙】páoluò(旧读 formerly pronounced páogé)就是'炮格',古代的一种酷刑 same as 炮格 páogé; ancient instrument of cruel torture

【炮制】páozhì ❶用中草药原料制成药物的过程。方法是烘、炮、炒、洗、泡、漂、蒸、煮等。concoct; preparing Chinese herbal medicine by drying by the fire, roasting, stir frying, washing, soaking in water, bleaching, steaming, boiling, etc. ❷ 泛指编造;制订(贬义 derog.) (in a broad sense) fabricate; contrive; hatch

袍 páo (～儿 páor) 中式的长衣服 gown; robe:皮～ fur overcoat | 棉～儿 cotton-padded gown | 长～ gown; robe | 旗～儿 cheongsam, a body-hutting women's dress; also 袍子 páo·zi

【袍哥】páogē 〈旧时 *old*〉西南各省的一种帮会的成员。也指这种帮会组织。member of a gang in southwestern provinces in China; Paoge, name of the gang

【袍笏登场】páo hù dēng chǎng 身穿官服,手执笏板,登台演剧 go onstage dressed up in an official robe and holding a scepter in hand; 〈比喻 *fig.*〉上台做官(含讽刺意 derog.) take office

【袍泽】páozé 〈书 *fml.*〉《诗经·秦风·无衣》:'岂曰无衣?与子同袍。王于兴师,修我戈矛,与子同仇。岂曰无衣?与子同泽。王于兴师,修我矛戟,与子偕作。'这首诗讲兵士出征的故事。'袍'和'泽'都是古代的衣服名称,后来称军队中的同事叫袍泽 *The Book of Songs · Folksongs of Qin · Having No Clothes*: 'How can you say you have no clothes? /With you I'll share my padded robe. /The king's decreed to dispatch troops, /Let's ready our dagger-axes and spears. /With you I'll go to fight our common foe. /How can you say you have no clothes? /With you I shall share my underwear. /The king's decreed to dispatch troops, /Let's ready our lances and halberds. /Together with you I'll go into action.' In these lines about soldiers on the eve of an expedition, 袍 páo and 泽 zé mean 'padded robe' and 'underwear' respectively in ancient times; the phrase 袍泽 later acquired a new meaning — 'comrades-in-arms':～之谊 the camaraderie between comrades-in-arms | ～故旧 friends who are both veteran soldiers

【袍罩儿】páozhàor 套在袍子外面的大褂;罩袍 overall; dust-gown

【袍子】páo·zi 袍 gown; robe

匏 páo [匏瓜](páoguā) ❶ 一年生草本植物,叶子掌状分裂,茎上有卷须。果实比葫芦大,对半剖开可做水瓢。gourd (*Lagenaria siceraria* var. *depressaw*); annual herb having palmately compound leaves and curling tendrils growing from its stem, bearing a fruit which is larger than a calabash and can be split in two to serve as ladles ❷ 这种植物的果实 fruit of gourd

跑 páo 走兽用脚刨地(of animals) dig the ground with paws or hoofs:～槽(牲口刨槽根)(of draft animal) dig a trough | 虎～泉(在杭州)Tiger-dug Spring, a scenic spot in Hangzhou

☞ pǎo on p. 1449

pǎo(ㄆㄠˇ)

跑 pǎo ❶ 两只脚或四条腿迅速前进 run; gallop:赛～race | ～了一圈儿 finish a lap during a race, jogging, etc. | 鹿～得很快。Deer can run real fast. ◇火车在飞～。The train is running at a high speed. ❷ 逃走 run away; escape:别让兔子～了。Don't let the rabbit run away. | ～了和尚～不了庙。The monk may run away, but not his temple. ❸ 〈方 *dial.*〉走 walk; loiter:～路 go to a place by foot ❹ 为某种事务而奔走 go about doing sth; run an errand:～码头 make a living as a vagrant merchant | ～材料 go about getting the materials needed | ～买卖 go about soliciting clients ❺ 物体离开了应该在的位置 be off a place; leak:～电 electricity leakage | ～油 oil leakage | ～气 gas leakage | 信纸叫风给刮～了。The letter paper has been blown away by the wind. ❻ 液体因挥发而损耗 (of a liquid) evaporate:瓶子没盖严,汽油都～了。The cap having not been tightly fixed, all the gasoline in the bottle has evaporated.

☞ páo on p. 1449

【跑表】pǎobiǎo 马表 stopwatch

【跑步】pǎo//bù 按照规定姿势往前跑 run; jog

【跑车】pǎo//chē ❶ 指矿山斜井中绞车提升时钢丝绳突然折断或因其他原因致使车溜坡的事故 slide of a mining trolley; accident in an inclined mine pit, caused by a snapped steel cable or other reasons ❷ 列车员随车工作(of a conductor, stewardess, etc.) on duty on a train

【跑车】pǎochē ❶ 赛车 racing car ❷ 林区运木材用的一种车 timber carriage

【跑单帮】pǎo dānbāng 指个人往来各地贩卖货物牟取利润 one-man team traveling around selling goods

【跑刀】pǎodāo 冰刀的一种,装在速度滑冰冰鞋的底下,刀口较窄而平直 race skates; skate with a narrow and straight blade for speed skating

【跑道】pǎodào ❶ 供飞机起飞和降落时滑行用的路 runway; airstrip; paved strip on which planes land and take off ❷ 运动场中赛跑用的路,也指速度滑冰比赛用的路 racing track; skating rink

【跑电】pǎo//diàn 由于绝缘部分损坏,电流逸出电线或电器的外部 electricity leakage; leakage of electricity caused by damaged insulation; also 漏电 lòu//diàn

【跑调儿】pǎo//diàor 走调儿(of singing) go out of tune

【跑肚】pǎo//dù 泻肚 have loose bowels

【跑反】pǎo//fǎn〈旧时 *old*〉指为躲避兵乱或匪患而逃往外地 flee from war or banditry; also 逃反 táofǎn

【跑光】pǎo//guāng 感光材料(如胶片、感光纸)因封闭不严而感光(of light-sensitive materials) be exposed to light accidentally

【跑旱船】pǎo hànchuán 一种民间舞蹈，扮演女子的人站在用竹片等和布扎成的无底船中间，船舷系在身上。另一人扮演艄公，手持木桨，作划船状。艄公与船上的人合舞，或边舞边唱，如船漂浮在水面之上。有的地区也叫采莲船。boat-sailing on land; folk dance with a man who rolls an oar in hand while dancing and singing a ditty and a woman performing with a bottomless model boat (made from a cloth-covered bamboo framework) suspended on her body; also known in some areas as 采莲船 cǎiliánchuán

【跑江湖】pǎo jiānghú 指以卖艺、算卦、相面等为职业，来往各地谋求生活 making a vagrant life as a street acrobat, fortune-teller, hysiognomist, etc.

【跑街】pǎojiē〈方 *dial.*〉❶ 跑外 act as a traveling agent or salesman ❷ 担任跑外工作的人 traveling agent or salesman

【跑龙套】pǎo lóngtào ❶ 在戏曲中扮演随从或兵卒 play a walk-on part on stage ❷〈比喻 *fig.*〉在人手下做无关紧要的事 be an also-run; play a bit role

【跑马】pǎo//mǎ ❶ 骑着马跑 ride a horse ❷ 指赛马 horseracing: ～场 racecourse; racing course ❸〈方 *dial.*〉遗精 seminal emission

【跑马卖解】pǎo mǎ mài xiè〈旧时 *old*〉指骑马表演各种技艺，以此赚钱谋生 make a living by performing acrobatics on horseback; also 跑马解 pǎo mǎ xiè or 跑解马 pǎo xiè mǎ

【跑码头】pǎo mǎ·tou 指在沿海沿江河的大城市往来做买卖 go on business trips between coastal cities; be a vagrant merchant

【跑买卖】pǎo mǎi·mai 来往各地做生意 be a traveling businessman

【跑跑颠颠】pǎopǎodiāndiān (～的 pǎopǎodiāndiān·de)形容奔走忙碌 bustle around: 她一天到晚～，热心为群众服务。She bustles about every day helping neighbours out.

【跑跑跳跳】pǎopǎotiàotiào (～的 pǎopǎotiàotiào·de)形容连跑带跳，很活泼的样子 skip; run about; (of youngsters) run and jump in a vivacious way

【跑片儿】pǎo//piānr 几个影院用同一个拷贝放映影片时，来回迅速运送拷贝叫跑片儿 pass copies around among cinemas showing the same film at the same time; also 跑片子 pǎo//piān·zi

【跑墒】pǎo//shāng 失墒的通称(in farming) loss of moisture in soil

【跑生意】pǎoshēng·yi same as 跑买卖 pǎo-mǎi·mai

【跑堂儿】pǎotángr 指饭馆中做端菜送饭工作 work as a waitor (or waitress) in a restaurant

【跑题】pǎo//tí 走题(of talk, writing, etc.) irrelevant; beside the point: 这段话～了，应该删去。This passage is irrelevant and should be deleted.

【跑腿儿】pǎo//tuǐr 为人奔走做杂事 run errands; do legwork

【跑外】pǎowài (商店或作坊等的工作人员)专门在外面办货、收账或兜揽生意(of a shop clerk, office worker, etc.) do fieldwork, such as procuring supplies, collecting payments, or soliciting business: ～的 serving as a field-worker

【跑鞋】pǎoxié 参加赛跑时穿的轻便皮鞋，鞋底窄而薄，前掌和后跟装有钉子。是钉鞋的一种。track shoes; light leather shoes with narrow and thin soles and with spikes on tab soles and heels; a kind of spiked shoes

【跑圆场】pǎo yuánchǎng 戏曲演员表演长途行走时，围着舞台中心快步绕圈子(of a theatrical performer) run around the center of a stage to indicate that the character is on a journey

【跑辙】pǎo//zhé〈方 *dial.*〉离开车辙，多比喻说话离题 run off the track; (fig.) stray from the point; beat about the bushes: 他不说正题老～。Instead of hitting the nail on its head, he keeps straying from the point.

pào (ㄆㄠˋ)

奅 pào〈书 *fml.*〉大 large; big

泡 pào ❶ (～儿 pàor)气体在液体内使液体鼓起来造成的球状或半球状体 (of a liquid giving off bubbles of gas) effervesce; fizz; bubble and hiss: 水～ bubbles | 肥皂～儿 soap bubbles ❷ (～儿 pàor)像泡一样的东西 bubble; blister; air ball; sth. in the shape of a bubble: 灯～儿 bulb | 手上起了～ get blisters on one's hand ❸ 较长时间地放在液体中 soak; brew; infuse: 两手在水里～得发白 one's hands turn pale after being soaked in water ❹ 故意消磨(时间) dally; dilly-dally; hang about: 在茶馆～了俩钟头 hang about in a teahouse for two hours

☞ pāo on p.1448

【泡病号】pào bìnghào (～儿 pào bìnghàor)指借故称病不上班，或小病大养 malinger; pretend or exaggerate illness to shun work

【泡菜】pàocài 把洋白菜、萝卜等放在加了盐、酒、花椒等的凉开水里泡制成的一种带酸味的菜 pickles; pickled vegetables; cabbage, radish, etc., preserved in brine spiced with salt, wine, prickly ash

【泡饭】pàofàn 加水重煮的或用开水泡的比较稀的米饭 gruel from recooked rice; cook cooked rice in boiling water

【泡蘑菇】pào mó·gu 故意纠缠，拖延时间

hedge; play for time; prevaricate：别～了，快点干活儿吧。Cut all the dillydallying! Do what you are supposed to do —and quick.

【泡沫】pàomò 聚在一起的许多小泡 suds; bubbles; lathers

【泡沫塑料】pàomò sùliào 海绵状有很多小气孔的塑料，用树脂经机械搅拌发泡或加入起泡剂制成。质轻，能隔热、隔音、减震、耐湿、耐腐蚀。如聚氯乙烯泡沫塑料、聚苯乙烯泡沫塑料。plastic sponge; foamed plastics; foamy plastics made of PVC, polystyrene, etc. (oft. with foaming agent added), that is light, insulates heat and sound, absorbs shock, and resists moisture and erosion

【泡泡纱】pào·paoshā 一种棉织品，布面呈凹凸状的皱纹 seersucker; plainwoven cotton fabric with crinkled surface

【泡泡糖】pào·paotáng 口香糖的一种，咀嚼后可以吹出泡泡儿 chewing gum; bubble gum; a kind of candy that can be blown into large bubbles through the lips

【泡汤】pào//tāng 〈方 *dial.*〉落空 come to naught; fizzle out; miscarriage：这笔买卖～了。The deal ended up in a miscarriage.

【泡漩】pàoxuán 波浪翻滚并有漩涡的水流 whirlpool

【泡影】pàoyǐng 〈比喻 *fig.*〉落空的事情或希望 vanish like soap bubbles; come to naught：梦幻～fizzle out like a dream｜满腔热望，化为～。All the ardent hopes finally vanished like bubbles.

【泡子】pào·zi 〈方 *dial.*〉灯泡 electric bulb; light bulb

☞ pāo·zi on p.1448

炮(砲、礮) pào ❶ 口径在2厘米以上，能发射炮弹的重型射击武器，火力强，射程远。种类很多，有迫击炮、榴弹炮、加农炮、高射炮等。也叫火炮。我国古代的炮最早是用机械发射石头的。火药发明后，改为用火药发射铁弹丸。cannon; artillery piece; any heavy-duty firearm more than 2 cm in calibre and extensive in fire range, including mortar, howitzer, cannon and anti-aircraft artillery. The earliest artillery pieces invented in ancient China were a kind of mechanism designed to shoot rocks, and it was not until the invention of powder that they were used to shell iron pills ❷ 爆竹 firecracker：鞭～firecracker string ❸ 爆破土石等在凿眼里装上炸药后叫作炮 load of explosives in earth, rock, etc., for demolition purposes

☞ bāo on p.63 and páo on p.1448

【炮兵】pàobīng 以火炮为基本装备，用火力进行战斗的兵种。也称这种兵种的士兵。artillery; troops specializing in using artillery pieces; artilleryman

【炮铳】pào·chong 〈方 *dial.*〉爆竹 firecracker

【炮弹】pàodàn 用火炮发射的弹药，通常由弹头、药筒、引信、发射药、底火等部分构成，弹头能爆炸。按用途分为穿甲弹、爆破弹、燃烧弹、烟幕弹等。有时专指弹头。shell; explosive projectile for use in a big gun or mortar — such as armour-piercing bullet, blasting cartridge, incendiary bullet and smoke shell — that consists of warhead, cylinder, fuse, propellant, and ignition cartridge; sometimes referring to 'bullet'

【炮灰】pàohuī 〈比喻 *fig.*〉参加非正义战争去送命的士兵 cannon fodder; army conscripts for an unjust war

【炮火】pàohuǒ 指战场上发射的炮弹与炮弹爆炸后发出的火焰 artillery fire; gunfire：～连天。Gunfire raged across the sky.

【炮击】pàojī 用炮火轰击 bombard; shell：停止～stop the bombardment

【炮舰】pàojiàn 以火炮为主要装备的轻型军舰，主要用来保护沿海地区和近海交通线，轰击敌人海岸目标，掩护部队登陆等 gunboat; light-duty warship equipped mainly with artillery pieces, used to protect coastal areas and off-shore transportation lines, bombard enemy targets along a seacoast, cover the landing of troops, etc.

【炮舰外交】pàojiàn wàijiāo 指为达到侵略、扩张的目的而推行的以武力作后盾的外交政策 gunboat diplomacy; aggressive or expansionist diplomatic policy backed with force; also 炮舰政策 pàojiàn zhèngcè

【炮楼】pàolóu 高的碉堡，四周有枪眼，可以瞭望、射击 blockhouse; tall stronghold with embrasures on all sides for observation and shooting

【炮钎】pàoqiān 钎子 rock drill; chisel

【炮手】pàoshǒu 操作火炮的战士 gunner; artilleryman

【炮塔】pàotǎ 火炮上的装甲防护体。坦克、自行火炮、军舰上的主炮等，一般都采用炮塔装置，有旋转式和固定式两种。gun turret; turret that provides protection for artillery piece; installation that is either fixed or rotary for the main artillery piece of a tank, self-propelled artillery, or warship

【炮台】pàotái 〈旧时 *old*〉在江海口岸和其他要塞上构筑的供发射火炮的永久性工事 fort; battery; permanent defense works built in old times at seaports and other places of strategic importance

【炮膛】pàotáng 炮筒里放置炮弹和射击时炮弹穿过的圆筒状空腔(of an artillery piece) bore

【炮艇】pàotǐng 以火炮为主要装备的小型舰艇，主要在沿海或内河巡逻，轰击敌人的沿岸目标，掩护部队登陆，布雷和用深水炸弹攻击敌人潜艇等 gunboat; small boat equipped with artillery pieces for patrolling coastal waters or inland rivers, bombarding enemy targets, shielding the landing of troops, planting mines, or ambushing enemy submarines with depth charges; also 护卫艇 hùwèitǐng

【炮筒子】pàotǒng·zi ❶ 火炮射击时炮弹穿过的圆筒状装置 bore of an artillery piece ❷〈比喻 *fig.*〉性情急躁、心直口快、好发议论的人 person who shoots off his mouth

【炮眼】pàoyǎn ❶ 掩蔽工事的火炮射击口 porthole; embrasure ❷ 爆破前在岩石等上面凿的孔,用来装炸药 blasthole; dynamite, hole bored into the surface of a rock to be loaded with demolishing powder

【炮衣】pàoyī 套在炮外面的布套 gun cover

【炮仗】pào·zhang 爆竹 firecracker

疱(皰) pào 皮肤上长的像水泡的小疙瘩 pimple; ulcer; abscess; boil

pēi (ㄆㄟ)

呸 pēi〈叹词 *interj.*〉表示唾弃或斥责 [indicating disdain, annoyance or disapproval] pah; bah; pooh:～! 你怎么干那种损人利己的事! Bah! How could you rip off people like that!

胚(肧) pēi 初期发育的生物体,由精细胞和卵细胞结合发展而成 embryo; rudimentary organism resulting from the combination of spermatid and ovum

【胚层】pēicéng 人或高等动物的胚胎,由于细胞的迅速分裂,胚胎体内的细胞不断增加,于是分裂为三层,即外胚层、中胚层和内胚层,总称胚层 germinal layers; referring to ectoderm, mesoderm and entoderm, the three cell layers resulting from the rapid breakup of cells and the constant increase in the number of cells within the human or higher-animal embryo; also 胚叶 pēiyè

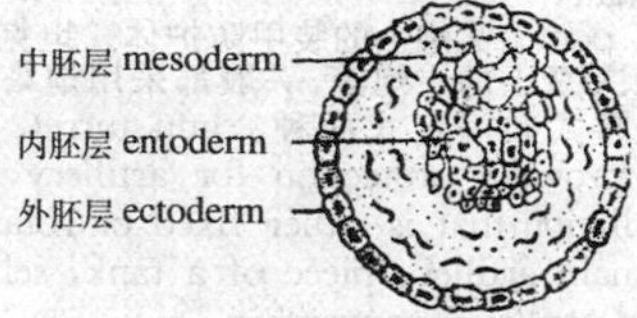

胚层 Germinal Layers

【胚胎】pēitāi ❶ 在母体内初期发育的动物体,由卵受精后发育而成。人的胚胎借脐带与胎盘相连,通过胎盘从母体吸取营养。embryo; organism developed from a fertilized egg in its primary stage of growth inside the mother's body; human embryo draws nutrition from the mother's body through the placenta, which is linked to the embryo by the umbilical cord ❷ 泛指事物的萌芽 (in a broad sense) beginning or rudimentary stage of sth.

【胚芽】pēiyá ❶ 植物胚的组成部分之一。胚芽突破种子的皮后发育成叶和茎。plumule; component part of a botanic embryo that breaks through the skin of a seed and grows into leaves and stalk ❷〈比喻 *fig.*〉刚萌生的事物 sth. nascent; bud:矛盾的～contradiction in the bud

衃 pēi〈书 *fml.*〉凝聚的血 coagulated, congealed and curdled blood

痞 pēi 又 also pèi〈中医 *Chin. med.*〉指疮 sore

【痞瘟】pēilěi〈中医 *Chin. med.*〉指荨麻疹 urticaria; hives

醅 pēi〈书 *fml.*〉没过滤的酒 unfiltered wine

péi (ㄆㄟˊ)

陪 péi ❶ 陪伴 keep sb. company; accompany:失～。Excuse me, but I must be leaving now. |～客人 show one's guest around a place; keep one's visitor company ❷ 从旁协助 assist:～审 serve on a jury

【陪伴】péibàn 随同做伴 keep sb. company:她住院期间,丈夫一直在身边～。She had the company of her husband all the time during her stay in the hospital.

【陪绑】péibǎng 处决犯人时,为了逼出口供或迫使投降,把不够死刑的犯人、暂缓执行死刑的犯人和即将处决的犯人一起绑赴刑场(of criminals not up to the death penalty or those who have been sentenced to death with a reprieve) be taken to the executioner's ground and put together with those to be executed so as to intimidate them into making a confession or surrender

【陪衬】péichèn ❶ 附加其他事物使主要事物更突出;衬托 set off; enhance:雕梁画栋～着壁画,使大殿显得格外华丽。The main hall looks exceptionally resplendent, with its murals set in sharp relief against carved rafters and lacquered pillars. ❷ 陪衬的事物 foil; setoff; complement

【陪床】péichuáng 指病人家属等留在病房照料住院的病人 stay in a hospital ward to look after a patient

【陪吊】péidiào〈旧时 *old*〉丧家开吊时设专人招待来客叫陪吊 person invited during a funeral to help greet those who come to offer condolences

【陪都】péidū〈旧时 *old*〉在首都以外另设的一个首都 provisional capital; alternate capital

【陪房】péi·fang〈旧时 *old*〉指随嫁的女仆 maid that moves over with a bride to her husband's family as personal servant

【陪祭】péijì 祭礼中陪同主祭人主持仪式 person who helps preside over a sacrificial ceremony

【陪嫁】péijià same as 嫁妆 jià·zhuang

【陪客】péi·ke 主人邀来陪伴客人的人 sb. invited to a dinner party to help entertain a guest

【陪奁】péilián〈方 *dial.*〉嫁妆 dowry

【陪审】péishěn 非职业审判人员到法院参加案件审判工作 act as an assessor in a law case; serve on a jury

【陪侍】péishì 陪伴服侍 wait upon (an elderly): 老人病重期间一直有儿女～。During the time the old man was very ill he always had his children waiting upon him.

【陪送】péi·song ❶ 旧俗结婚时娘家送给新娘(嫁妆)(old custom) parents' gifts for their soon-to-get-married daughter ❷ 嫁妆 dowry: 她结婚时什么～也不要。She declined the offer of a dowry when she was married.

【陪同】péitóng 陪伴着一同(进行某一活动) accompany: ～前往参观 accompany sb. on a visit

【陪夜】péiyè 指夜里照料病人 sleep over to wait upon a patient

【陪音】péiyīn 泛音 harmonic; overtone

【陪葬】péizàng ❶ 殉葬 be buried alive with the deceased ❷ 〈古代 *arch.*〉指臣子或妻妾的灵柩葬在皇帝或丈夫的灵柩或坟墓的近旁(of a coffin containing the remains of a court minister, the empress or an imperial concubine) be buried by the side of the grave or coffin of an emperor; (of a wife's remains) be buried beside the remains of her husband

培 péi ❶ 为了保护植物或墙、堤等,在根基部分堆上土 bank up with earth (to protect the roots of a plant, to strengthen the base of a wall, dyke, etc.): 玉米根部要多～点儿土。More earth should be banked up around the roots of the corn. | 将堤坝加高～厚 reinforce a dyke by heightening and thickening it with earth ❷ 培养(人) train; cultivate (personnel): ～训 training

【培土】péi//tǔ 在作物生长期中,把行间或株间的土培在作物茎的基部周围,有防止植株倒伏,便利排水灌溉,以及促进作物根部发育等作用 mound; earth up; cover the lower part of a plant with soil to prevent lodging and facilitate drainage and irrigation and the growth of the root; also 壅土 yōngtǔ

【培训】péixùn 培养和训练(技术工人、专业干部等) train (workers, professionals, government functionaries, etc.): ～班 training class | ～业务骨干 train core members of a profession

【培养】péiyǎng ❶ 以适宜的条件使繁殖 cultivate; culture; develop; prepare conditions for sth. to grow or reproduce: ～细菌 culturing of bacteria ❷ 按照一定的目的长期地教育和训练;使成长 train; groom; prepare sb. for a particular task, occupation, etc. through long-term training and education: ～人才 cultivate new talents | ～接班人 groom sb. as a successor

【培育】péiyù 培养幼小的生物,使它发育成长 cultivate; nurture; breed: ～树苗 bred tree saplings | 选择优良品种,进行～ select fine strains of plants, or fine breeds of animals, for breeding ◇～一代新人 bring up a new generation of successors

【培植】péizhí ❶ 栽种并细心管理(植物) cultivate (plants): 许多野生草药已开始用人工～。Quite a few wild medicinal herbs have been brought under cultivation. ❷ 培养(人才); 扶植(势力)使壮大 train; foster: ～新生力量 nurture new blood for a cause | ～亲信 build up the circle of one's confidants

赔 péi ❶ 赔偿 compensate: ～款 indemnity | 这块玻璃是我碰破的,由我来～。I broke this piece of glass. Let me pay for it. ❷ 向受损害或受伤害的人道歉或认错 apologize: ～礼 make a formal apology | ～罪 apologize for offending sb. | ～不是 express regret ❸ 做买卖损失本钱(跟'赚'相对 as opposed to 'make a profit') make a loss in business: ～本 sustain a loss in a deal | ～钱 lose money | 年终结账,算算是～是赚。Let's see if we have made some money or not when we settle the accounts by the end of the year.

【赔本】péi//běn 本钱、资金亏损 lose money: ～生意 business a loss | 做买卖赔了本 lose money in doing business

【赔不是】péi bù·shi same as 赔罪 péi//zuì: 给他赔个不是。Tell him you are sorry.

【赔偿】péicháng 因自己的行动使他人或集体受到损失而给予补偿 make up for a loss; compensate: 照价～ compensate according to a price | ～损失 pay for a financial loss

【赔垫】péidiàn 因垫付而使自己的钱财暂受损失 make a compensation for sb.: 钱数太大,我可～不起。This is too much for me to pay for you.

【赔话】péi//huà 说道歉的话 offer an apology: 你得罪了人家,总得赔个话才是。Now that you have offended him, you'd better go out of your way to apologize to him.

【赔款】péi//kuǎn ❶ 损坏、遗失别人或集体的东西用钱来补偿 pay compensation for damaging or losing sb.'s property ❷ 战败国向战胜国赔偿损失和作战费用 indemnify; (of a defeated nation) pay for the losses and war costs inflicted on a victorious nation

【赔款】péikuǎn ❶ 赔偿别人或集体受损失的钱 payment as a compensation for a financial loss caused to sb. ❷ 战败国向战胜国赔偿损失和作战费用的钱 indemnity; money a defeated nation pays to a victorious nation for the latter's losses and war costs

【赔了夫人又折兵】 péi·le fū·ren yòu zhé bīng 《三国演义》里说,周瑜出谋划策,把孙权的妹妹许配刘备,让刘备到东吴成婚,想乘机扣留,夺还荆州。结果刘备成婚后带着夫人逃出吴国。周瑜带兵追赶,又被诸葛亮的伏兵打败。人们讥笑周瑜'赔了夫人又折兵'。后用来比喻想占便宜,没有占到便宜,反而遭受损失。According to an episode in the classical Chinese novel *Romance of Three Kingdoms*, Zhou Yu hatched a plot to lure Liu Bei to the kingdom of Wu by marrying Sun Quan's younger sister to Liu Bei so that he could detain the king of the kingdom of Shu and regain control of the important city of Jingzhou. Liu Bei, however, not only attended the wedding but also fled with his bride. An exacerbated Zhou Yu led his troops in a hot pursuit of the bridegroom, only to be routed in an ambush laid by Liu Bei's prime minister, Zhuge Liang. Hence the saying, 'give one's enemy a wife and lose one's soldiers as well — pay a double penalty for attempting to gain an unwarranted advantage'.

【赔礼】péi//lǐ 向人施礼认错 admit one's mistake and ask for forgiveness:我错怪了人,应该向人～。I owe him an apology because I blamed him for something he didn't do.|向他赔了个礼。He said he was wrong and asked for his forgiveness.

【赔钱】péi//qián ❶ same as 赔本 péi//běn:～的买卖 losing business ❷ 损坏或遗失别人的东西用钱来补偿 make up for losing or damaging sb.'s property with payment:碰坏了人家的东西要～。When you break somebody's property you've got to pay.

【赔情】péi//qíng〈方 *dial.*〉same as 赔罪 péi//zuì:你既然错怪了他,那就赶快给他赔个情吧! Now that you have blamed him for no reason at all, make haste and beg for his pardon.

【赔小心】péi xiǎo·xīn 以谨慎、迁就的态度对人,博得人的好感或使息怒 act humbly towards sb.; do all one can to accommodate or appease sb.

【赔笑】péi//xiào 以笑脸对人,使人息怒或愉快 smile an apologetic or obsequious smile; also 赔笑脸 péi xiàoliǎn

【赔账】péi//zhàng ❶ 因经手财物时出了差错而赔偿损失 pay for the loss of money or property entrusted to one ❷〈方 *dial.*〉赔本儿 lose money in a transaction

【赔罪】péi//zuì 得罪了人,向人道歉 apologize for a fault

毰 péi [毰毸](péisāi)〈书 *fml.*〉形容羽毛披散(of feathers) dishevelled; tousled

锫 péi 金属元素,符号 Bk (berkelium)。有放射性,由人工方法获得。berkelium (Bk); radioactive metallic element that is obtained synthetically

裴 Péi 姓 a surname

pèi(ㄆㄟˋ)

沛 pèi〈书 *fml.*〉盛大;旺盛 exuberant; abundant:～然 bounteous|充～ bountiful; profuse

帔 pèi〈古代 *arch.*〉披在肩背上的服饰。妇女用的帔绣着各种花纹。cape; women's embroidered shawl wrapped around the shoulders:凤冠霞～ phoenix coronet and colourful cape

佩(❷珮) pèi ❶ 佩带 wear; sport:～刀 wear a sword at the waist|腰～盒子枪 carry a Mauser pistol at the waist ❷〈古时 *arch.*〉系在衣带上的装饰品 pendant hanging on one's coat belt:玉～jade pendant ❸ 佩服 admire:钦～admiration|这种精神可敬可～。This spirit is highly adorable.

【佩带】pèidài ❶(把手枪、刀、剑等)插在或挂在腰部 wear (a pistol, sword, sabre, etc.) at the waist:～武器 carry a weapon ❷ same as 佩戴 pèidài

【佩戴】pèidài (把徽章、符号等)挂在胸前、臂上、肩上等部位 wear (a badge, insignia, etc.) on the chest, arm, or shoulder:学生出入校门必须～校徽。Students should wear school badges when they enter or leave the school. also 佩带 pèidài

【佩服】pèi·fú 感到可敬可爱;钦佩 think highly of; revere:这姑娘真能干,我不禁暗暗地～她。The girl is a crackajack, and I cannot help secretly admiring her.

【佩兰】pèilán 多年生草本植物,茎直立,叶子披针形,边缘有锯齿,花紫红色。全株有香气,可制芳香油,又可入药。fragrant thoroughwort (*Eupatorium fortunei*); perennial herb having upright stalks, lanceolate leaves with sawtooth edges, and purplish red flowers, the whole body useful for medical use or for the extraction of perfume; also 兰草 láncǎo

配 pèi ❶ 两性结合 join in wedlock; make a couple:～偶 spouse|婚～marriage|英雄～模范,真是美满姻缘。A war hero marries a model worker — what a nice matchup. ❷ 配偶,多指妻子 spouse (usu. referring to a wife):择～choose a spouse|元～first wife ❸ 使(动物)交配(of animals) mate:～马 mate horses|～种 breed animals or plants ❹ 按适当的标准或比例加以调和或凑在一起 mingle; mix things according to standard or ratio:～颜色 blend colours|～药 make up a prescription|搭～collocate; arrange in pairs or groups ❺ 有计划地分派 allot; apportion:～售 sell goods by rationing|支～control|分～distribute ❻ 把缺少的一定规格的物品补足 replenish:～零件 find a component part to replace the one that has broken down|～钥匙 have a key made to fit a lock|～套 supplement ❼ 衬托;陪衬 set off; match:～角 supporting role|红花～绿叶 red flowers set off beautifully against green leaves|这段二黄用唢呐来～。This segment of *erhuang* melody shall be sung to the accompaniment of the *suona* horn. ❽ 够得上；符合；相当 measure up to; be worthy of：只有这样的人，才～称为先进工作者。Only a man like that deserves to be a model worker.｜他的穿着和他的年龄很不相～。The way he dresses himself doesn't match his age at all. ❾ 充军 exile; banish：发～banish sb. to an out-of-the-way place as a punishment｜～军 be deported to a remote place for penal servitude

【配备】pèibèi ❶ 根据需要分配（人力或物力）distribute (manpower, resources) according to need：～骨干力量 staff an organization with people who can handle knotty problems｜～三辆吉普车 equip (a factory, etc.) with three jeeps ❷ 布置（兵力）deploy (troops)：按地形～火力 deploy firearms according to the terrain of a place ❸ 成套的设备、装备等 complete set of equipment：现代化的～complete set of modern equipment

【配餐】pèicān ❶ 按照一定标准把各种食品搭配在一起 prepare a meal according to a menu：根据病人的不同需要进行～。Dietal arrangements vary with the needs of the patients. ❷ 搭配在一起的各种食品，如合装在一起的面包片、香肠、火腿等 foods that have been assorted and put together, such as bread with sausage, ham, etc.：方便～convenient snack｜营养～nutritious snack

【配搭】pèidā ❶ 跟主要的事物合在一起做陪衬 supplement：这出戏，配角儿～得不错。The bit roles in this play are well casted. ❷ 搭配 collocate

【配搭儿】pèi·dar 帮助或陪衬主要事物的人或物 be a sidekick; complement：我唱不了主角，给你当个～还行。I can not sing the leading character — all I can do is to be a sidekick for you.

【配电盘】pèidiànpán 分配电量的设备，安装在发电站、变电站以及用电量较大的电力用户中，上面装着各种控制开关、监视仪表及保护装置 electricity distributor; (in a power plant, transformer substation, or a major electricity consumer) installation fixed with switches, monitoring metres and apparatuses, and protection devices for distributing electricity

【配殿】pèidiàn 宫殿或庙宇中正殿两旁的殿 flank hall; flanks of the main hall of a palace or temple

【配对】[1] pèi//duì (～儿 pèi//duìr) 配合成双 pair; match：这两名选手～参加双打比赛。The two players were paired to take part in the doubles event.

【配对】[2] pèi//duì (～儿 pèi//duìr)（动物）交尾 (of animals) mate

【配方】[1] pèi//fāng 把不完全平方式变为完全平方式叫做配方。如把 x^2+6x 加上 $(\frac{6}{2})^2$，得 x^2+6x+9，即 $(x+3)^2$。(in mathematics) change an incomplete square form into a complete one, for example, x^2+6x plus $(\frac{6}{2})^2$ equals x^2+6x+9, or $(x+3)^2$

【配方】[2] pèi//fāng 根据处方配制药品 prescription; prescribe a medicine

【配方】pèifāng 指化学制品、冶金产品等的配制方法 formula for compounding a chemical or metallurgical product; 通称 generally called 方子fāng·zi

【配房】pèifáng 厢房 wing-suite

【配合】pèihé ❶ 各方面分工合作来完成共同的任务 coordinate; cooperate：他两人的双打～得很好。The two of them showed superb teamwork in the doubles event. ❷ 机械或仪器上关系密切的零件结合在一起，如轴与轴瓦等 (of component parts of a machine or apparatus, e.g. axis and step brass) mesh; synchronize

【配合】pèi·he 合在一起显得合适，相称 compatible：绿油油的枝叶衬托着红艳艳的花朵，那么～，那么美丽。What harmony, and what a graceful scene the red flowers have conjured up in the rich verdure of the leaves!

【配火】pèi//huǒ same as 回火 huí//huǒ ①

【配给】pèijǐ same as 配售 pèishòu

【配件】pèijiàn ❶ 指装配机器的零件或部件 spare parts; accessories ❷ (～儿 pèijiànr) 损坏后重新安装上的零件或部件 fittings; replacement for a broken part or accessory

【配角】pèi//jué (～儿 pèi//juér) 合演一出戏，都扮主要角色 be co-stars in a play; co-star：他们俩常在一起～，合演过《将相和》、《群英会》等。The two of them often performed together, having co-starred such major stage productions as *The Union of a General and a Grand Councillor* and *The Meeting of Heroes*.

【配角】pèijué (～儿 pèijuér) ❶ 戏剧、电影等艺术表演中的次要角色 supporting role in a drama, film and other forms of the performing art ❷〈比喻 *fig.*〉做辅助工作或次要工作的人 one who plays second fiddle to sb.

【配军】pèijūn 被发配充军的罪犯（多见于早期白话 oft. in early vernacular) convict being banished to a remote place for servitude

【配料】pèi//liào 生产过程中，把某些原料按一定比例混合在一起 charge mixture; batching; prepare for production by mixing different raw materials according to a recipe：～车间 batching workshop

【配偶】pèi'ǒu 指丈夫或妻子（多用于法律文件 oft. used in legal documents) spouse; husband or wife

【配平】pèipíng 通过计算，给化学方程式的两边各项各自配上不同的系数，使反应前后各种原子的个数分别相等 balancing; supplement a different modulus to either side of a chemical equation to strike equilibrium in the numbers of atoms before and after a chemical reaction

【配器】pèiqì 根据乐谱安排一种或多种相互配合的乐器(演奏) orchestrate; arrange an ensemble of musical instruments according to a music score for a concert performance

【配色】pèisè 把各种颜色按照适当的标准调配 blend colours according to certain standards

【配售】pèishòu 某些产品,特别是生活必需品在不能充分供应的情况下,按限定的数量和价格售给消费者 ration; fix the official allowance of a product in short supply among consumers

【配套】pèi//tào 把若干相关的事物组合成一整套 form a complete set:~工程 projects that come in a complete package|大中小厂,~成龙,分工协作,提高生产水平。Factories of all sizes are streamlined in a division of labour in order to raise productivity.

【配伍】pèiwǔ 把两种或两种以上的药物配合起来同时使用 compatibility of medicines when administered together

【配戏】pèi//xì 把配合主角演戏 play a supporting role on stage

【配享】pèixiǎng〈古时 *arch.*〉指死去的功臣随着死去的帝王一起受到祭祀。孔子的门人或在经学上有成就的人死后随孔子一起受到祭祀也叫配享。(of a deceased court minister who had performed meritorious deeds during his lifetime) be honoured at a sacrificial ceremony together with a deceased emperor; (of a disciple of Confucius, or one who excelled in the study of Confucian classics during his lifetime) be worshiped along with Confucius

【配药】pèi//yào 根据处方配制药物 make up a prescription; prepare a prescription

【配音】pèi//yīn 译制影片或电视剧时,用某种语言录音代替原片或原剧上的录音。摄制影片或电视剧时,演员的话音和歌声用别人的代替,也叫配音。replace the soundtrack of a film or a television in an alternative language; do dialogue or singing in replacement of the actors and actresses in a film or television play

【配乐】pèi//yuè 诗朗诵、话剧等按照情节的需要配上音乐,以增强艺术效果 accompany a poetry recital or drama with background music to enhance the artistic ambience:~诗歌朗诵 poem recitals with musical accompaniment

【配制】pèizhì ❶ 把两种以上的原料按一定的比例和方法合在一起制造 make up sth. by mixing different raw materials methodically according to a recipe:~药剂 compound medicine|~鸡尾酒 blend a cocktail ❷ 为配合主体而制作(陪衬事物) companion objects:书内~了多幅精美插图。The book is graced with quite a few exquisite illustrations.

【配置】pèizhì 配备布置 deploy; allocate:~兵力 deploy troops

【配种】pèi//zhǒng 使雌雄两性动物的生殖细胞结合以繁殖后代,分为天然交配和人工授精两种 breeding; natural breeding; artificial insemination

【配子】pèizǐ 生物体进行有性生殖时所产生的性细胞。雌雄两性的配子融合后形成合子。gamete; mature germ cell able to unite with another in sexual reproduction. A zygote is produced when a male gamete integrates with a female gamete.

【配子体】pèizǐtǐ 植物世代交替中产生配子或具有单倍数染色体的植物体 gametophyte; gamete-producing form of a plant that has alternation of generations between this and the asexual form, or one that has an odd duplicating number of chromosomes

旆(斾) pèi ❶〈古时 *arch.*〉末端形状像燕尾的旗 swallow-tailed flag ❷〈书 *fml.*〉泛指旌旗 (in a broad sense) banners and flags

辔 pèi 驾驭牲口用的嚼子和缰绳 bit of a bridle and rein:鞍~saddle and bridle|按~徐行 keep a grip on the bridle and amble along

【辔头】pèitóu 辔 bridle

霈 pèi〈书 *fml.*〉❶ 大雨 heavy rain:甘~rain that comes at the right time; well-timed rain ❷ 雨多的样子 rainy

pēn(ㄆㄣ)

喷 pēn (液体、气体、粉末等)受压力而射出(of liquid, gas, powder) spew; spurt; spout; gush:~泻 spurt|~泉 fountain|火山~火 fire-spewing volcano|~气式飞机 jet plane
☞ pèn on p.1458

【喷薄】pēnbó 形容水涌起或太阳上升的样子(of water) gush out; (of the sun) rise brilliantly:~欲出的一轮红日 emerging morning sun in all its splendour

【喷灯】pēndēng 能喷射火焰的工具,多用于烧灼和焊接。常用煤油、煤气、酒精、乙炔等做燃料。blowtorch; blowlamp; portable lamp fueled with kerosene, gas, alcohol, acetylene, etc. for burning and welding

【喷发】pēnfā 喷出来。特指火山口喷出熔岩。erupt; esp. eruption of lava from a volcano

【喷饭】pēnfàn 吃饭时看到或听到可笑的事,突然发笑,把嘴里的饭喷出来,所以形容事情可笑说'令人喷饭' (while having a meal) laugh so hard as to spew one's food; split one's sides with laughter

【喷粪】pēn//fèn〈比喻 *fig.*〉说脏话或说没有根据、没有道理的话(骂人的话 curse) utter foul-mouthed abuse:满嘴~ shout obscenity

【喷灌】pēnguàn 灌溉的一种方法,利用压力把水通过喷头喷到空中,形成细小的水滴,再落到地面或植物体上 sprinkling irrigation; spray irrigation; a method of irrigation whereby sprinklers are used to spray drops of water on plauts, soil or grass

【喷壶】pēnhú 盛水浇花的壶,喷水的部分像莲蓬。有的地区叫喷桶。watering can; sprinkling can, with a lotus-shaped spout; known in some regions as 喷桶 pēntǒng

【喷火器】pēnhuǒqì 一种喷射火焰的近战武器。主要用来消灭敌人和烧毁敌方武器、装备器材等。flamethrower; firearm used mainly to destroy an enemy's troops, weapons and equipment at a close range; also 火焰喷射器 huǒyàn pēnshèqì

【喷口】pēnkǒu 戏曲演出中指道白或演唱时对字音作有力的喷发,作用是使字音刚劲有力,送得远 speak or sing with stress; method of speaking or singing in traditional opera so that the words come out with force and reach far

【喷漆】pēn//qī 用压缩空气将涂料喷成雾状涂在木器或铁器上 spray paint on a wooden or metal utensil by means of a paint spray gun

【喷漆】pēnqī 人造漆的一种,用硝酸纤维素、树脂、颜料、溶剂等制成。通常用喷枪均匀地喷在物体表面,耐水,耐机油,干得快,用于漆汽车、飞机、木器、皮革等。spray paint; spray lacquer; material made from pyroxylin, resin, dyestuff, and solvent that resists water and oil and dries fast, to be sprayed evenly on the surface of an automobile, airplane, wooden utensil, leather, etc.

【喷气发动机】pēnqì fādòngjī 使燃料燃烧时产生的气体高速喷射而产生动力的发动机。高速飞机和火箭都使用这种发动机。jet engine; engine which produces thrust by burning a combination of fuel and air which releases a powerful stream of hot gases, for use on jet planes and rockets

【喷气式飞机】pēnqìshì fēijī 用喷气发动机做动力装置的飞机。速度很高,超音速飞机都是这种类型的飞机。jet plane; plane propelled by a jet engine fixed in it to fly at a high speed; supersonic airplane

【喷泉】pēnquán 向外喷水的泉 fountain

【喷洒】pēnsǎ 喷射散落 spray; sprinkle: ～农药 spray insecticide

【喷射】pēnshè 利用压力把液体、气体或固体颗粒喷出去 spew; squirt; gushing out of liquid, gas, or particles under high pressure

【喷水池】pēnshuǐchí 为了点缀风景装有人造喷泉的水池 artificial fountain; fountain built for landscaping purposes

【喷嚏】pēntì 由于鼻黏膜受刺激,急剧吸气,然后很快地由鼻孔喷出并发出声音,这种现象叫打喷嚏 sneeze; sudden involuntary and noisy expulsion of air from the nose caused by irrigation of the nostrils; also 嚏喷 tì·pen

【喷桶】pēntǒng 〈方 *dial.*〉 same as 喷壶 pēnhú

【喷头】pēntóu 喷壶、淋浴设备、喷洒设备等出水口上的一种装置,形状像莲蓬,有许多细孔。有的地区叫莲蓬头。shower nozzle; sprinkling spout; lotus-shaped device with lots of tiny holes in it, fixed on a watering can, bathing shower or sprinkling installation; known in some regions as 莲蓬头 liánpéngtóu

【喷涂】pēntú 喷(漆)spray paint

【喷吐】pēntǔ 喷出(光、火、气等)(light, fire, gas, etc.) spurt; spill: 炉口～着鲜红的火苗。Red tongues of fire keep curling and uncurling at the mouth of the furnace.

【喷雾器】pēnwùqì 利用空吸作用将药水或其他液体变成雾状,均匀地喷射到其他物体上的器具,由压缩空气的装置和细管、喷嘴等组成 sprayer; atomizer; device consisting of an air-compressor, a nozzle, and a tiny tube, that makes use of the suctioning role of compressed air to atomize a liquid and spray it onto the surface of an object

【喷涌】pēnyǒng (液体)迅速地往外冒(of a liquid) gush; spout: 山泉～。Spring water gushes out in the mountains. | 黑褐色的原油从钻井台上～出来。Dark crude oil spurted from the drilling derricks. ◇激情～。A tide of passion surged through the heart.

【喷子】pēn·zi 喷射液体的器具 sprayer

【喷嘴】pēnzuǐ (～儿 pēnzuǐr)喷射流体物质用的零件,一般呈管状,出口的一端管孔较小 spray nozzle; component of a sprayer in the shape of tube with a nozzle small in diameter

pén (ㄆㄣˊ)

盆 pén ❶ (～儿 pénr)盛东西或洗东西用的器具,口大,底小,多为圆形 basin; round utensil with a large opening and small bottom for use as a receptacle or for washing: 花～儿 flower pot | 脸～basin | 澡～bath tub ❷ 形状略像盆的东西 sth. akin to a basin: 骨～pelvis | ～地(geological term) basin

【盆地】péndì 被山或高地围绕的平地 basin; plain area skirted by mountains or highland

【盆花】pénhuā (～儿 pénhuār)栽种在花盆里供观赏的花草 potted flower

【盆景】pénjǐng (～儿 pénjǐngr)一种陈设品,盆中栽小巧的花草,配以小树和小山等,像真的风景一样 miniature landscape; potted tree and rockery of small sizes that combine with flower or grass to resemble a scaled-down landscape

【盆腔】pénqiāng 骨盆内部的空腔。膀胱和尿道等泌尿器官都在盆腔内。女子的子宫、卵巢等也在盆腔内。pelvic cavity; cavity inside the pelvis that contains bladder, urethra and other urinary organs, as well as womb and ovary in a woman's case

【盆汤】péntāng 澡堂中设有澡盆的部分(区别于'池汤'as compared with 'bath pool') of a public bath; bathtub cubicle; also 盆塘 péntáng

【盆浴】pényù 一种洗澡方式,把水放入澡盆内洗

tub bath; bath in a tub

【盆栽】pénzāi ❶ 在花盆里栽种 grow flowers or plants in a pot:～花卉 potted flower|～葡萄 potted grapevine ❷ 指盆里栽种的花木 potted flower or tree:案头摆着常绿的～。An evergreen potted plant is one of the fixtures on the desk.

【盆子】pén•zi 盆 tub

湓 pén〈书 *fml.*〉水往上涌(of water)spurt; spout:～涌 gushing out|～溢(水涨满泛滥)overflow

pèn(ㄆㄣˋ)

喷 pèn〈方 *dial.*〉(～儿 pènr) ❶ 果品、蔬菜、鱼虾等大量上市的时期(fruit, vegetable, sea food, etc.) come in season:对虾～儿 prawns in season|西瓜正在～儿上。Watermelons have just come in season now. ❷〈量词 *classifier*〉开花结实的次数;成熟收割的次数 number of times of flowering, fruit bearing, or harvesting:头～棉花 first cotton crop of the year|绿豆结二～角了。The mung beans are putting out the second round of pods of the year.

☞ pēn on p. 1456

【喷香】pènxiāng 香气浓厚 aromatic:～扑鼻。A fragrance, heady but rather sweet, saluted my nostrils.|～的小米饭 delicious cooked millet; also 喷喷香 pènpènxiāng

pēng(ㄆㄥ)

匉 pēng〈书 *fml.*〉same as 砰 pēng

抨 pēng〈书 *fml.*〉弹劾(tánhé) impeach

【抨击】pēngjī 用评论来攻击(某人或某种言论、行动)censure; animadvert upon sb.'s word or deed:～时弊 lash out at a social ailment

【抨弹】pēngtán〈书 *fml.*〉❶ same as 抨击 pēngjī ❷ 弹劾 impeach

怦 pēng〈拟声词 *onom.*〉形容心跳[indicating heartthrobs]:～然心动(of one's heart) miss a beat|吓得心里～～直跳。A dart of fear set his heart pounding.

砰 pēng〈拟声词 *onom.*〉形容撞击或重物落地的声音[indicating the sound of sth. falling heavily or being struck by sth. else]:～的一声,木板倒了。The plank fell with a bang.

烹 pēng ❶ 煮(菜、茶) cook(food); brew (tea):～饪 cuisine|～调 cook ❷ 烹饪方法,先用热油略炒,然后加酱油等作料搅拌,随即盛出 quick-fry in hot oil and stir in sauce:～对虾 quick-fried prawns

【烹茶】pēng//chá 煮茶或沏茶 make tea

【烹饪】pēngrèn 做饭做菜 cuisine; culinary art:～法 culinary art|擅长～ be good at cooking

【烹调】pēngtiáo 烹炒调制(菜肴)cook dishes:～五味 the five flavours of cooking|～能手 expert cook

嘭 pēng〈拟声词 *onom.*〉bang:一阵～～～的敲门声。There arose an incessant thumping of the door.

澎 pēng〈方 *dial.*〉溅 splash:～了一身水 be splashed all over with water

☞ péng on p. 1459

péng(ㄆㄥˊ)

芃 péng [芃芃]〈书 *fml.*〉形容植物茂盛(of plants) exuberant

朋 péng ❶ 朋友 pal; buddy; chum:良～ true friend|宾～满座 a roomful of guests ❷〈书 *fml.*〉结党 gang up:～比为奸 gang up with sb. for evil ends ❸〈书 *fml.*〉伦比 rival; equal:硕大无～of an unparalleled size

【朋比为奸】péng bǐ wéi jiān 互相勾结干坏事 act in collusion; conspire

【朋党】péngdǎng 指为争权夺利、排斥异己而结合起来的集团 cabal; clique; small group of people who are involved in a bid for power and do not allow others to join them:～之争 factional strife

【朋友】péng•you ❶ 彼此有交情的人 friend ❷ 指恋爱的对象 boyfriend; girlfriend:姑娘多大了,有～了没有? How old is she and has she got a boyfriend?

堋 péng 我国战国时代科学家李冰在修建都江堰时所创造的分水堤,作用是减杀水势 watershed dyke; dyke built by Li Bing, a scientist of the Warring States Period, at the Dujiang Weir to mitigate the velocity of water flow

弸 péng〈书 *fml.*〉充满 be full of

彭 Péng 姓 a surname

棚 péng ❶ 遮蔽太阳或风雨的设备,用竹木等搭架子,上面覆盖草席等 awning; canopy; usu. made from bamboo or timber with a straw mat roof:天～overhead canopy|凉～ mat-awning|在园子里搭一个～rig up an awning in a garden ❷ 简陋的房屋 shack; makeshift shelter:牲口～animal shed|工～ work shed|碾～millstone shack ❸ 天花板 ceiling:顶～ceiling|糊～paper ceiling

【棚车】péngchē same as 篷车 péngchē

【棚户】pénghù 住在简陋房屋里的人家 slum; shack dwelling household

【棚圈】péngjuàn 有棚子的圈 animal pen with a roof atop it

【棚子】péng·zi same as 棚 péng②：草～straw-thatched shack|马～horse shed

蓬 péng ❶ same as 飞蓬 fēipéng① ❷ 蓬松 downy; tousled：～着头 with one's hair uncombed ❸〈量词 *classifier*〉用于枝叶茂盛的花草(of flowers, plants, etc.) clump; cluster：一～凤尾竹 a cluster of fernleaf hedge bamboo

【蓬荜增辉】péng bì zēng huī〈谦辞 *hum.*〉表示由于别人到自己家里来或张挂别人给自己题赠的字画等而使自己非常光荣 'This humble abode of mine has been honoured by your presence (*or* by your gift of a scroll of painting or calligraphy)'(蓬荜 *peng bi*：蓬门荜户的省略 short for 蓬门荜户 péng mén bì hù); also 蓬荜生辉 péng bì shēng huī

【蓬勃】péngbó 繁荣；旺盛 burgeoning; going strong：～发展 robust growth|朝气～full of youth and vitality|一片蓬蓬勃勃的气象。A scene of prosperity meets the eye everywhere.

【蓬蒿】pénghāo ❶〈方 *dial.*〉茼蒿 crowndaisy chrysanthemum (*Chrysanthemum coronarium*) ❷ 飞蓬和蒿子，借指草野 bitter fleabane and wormwood; (fig.) weed-infested wasteland

【蓬户瓮牖】péng hù wèng yǒu 用蓬草编成的门，破瓮做的窗户。形容穷苦人家的简陋房屋。ramshackle house with wicker door and makeshift window fashioned out of a broken jar; (fig.) house of an impoverished family

【蓬莱】Pénglái 神话中渤海里仙人居住的山 Penglai Island on the Bohai Sea; fabled abode of immortals

【蓬乱】péngluàn 草、头发等松散杂乱(of grass, hair, etc.) dishevelled; unkempt：头发～tousled hair

【蓬门荜户】péng mén bì hù 用草、树枝等做成的门户。形容穷苦人家所住的简陋的房屋。rundown abode built of straw and tree branches; (fig.) dilapidated house of the poor

【蓬茸】péngróng〈书 *fml.*〉形容草生长得很多很盛(of grass) luxuriant：绿草～lush green grass|蓬蓬茸茸的杂草 overgrowing weeds

【蓬松】péngsōng 形容草、叶子、头发、绒毛等松散开(of grass, leaves, hair, floss, etc.) fluffy; puffy

【蓬头垢面】péng tóu gòu miàn 形容头发很乱，脸上很脏的样子 with disheveled hair and dirty face

硼 péng 非金属元素，符号 B (borum)。无定形硼为粉末状，暗棕色；晶体硼灰色，有光泽，硬度和金刚石相似。用来制合金、火箭燃料等，在医药、农业和玻璃等工业中应用广泛。borum (B); glossy non-metal element that is dark brown when being amorphous and gray when being crystalline, having a hardness akin to that of diamond, used as a material for the making of alloys or as a fuel for rockets, but more widely employed in pharmaceutical and glassmaking industries and agriculture

搒(榜) péng〈书 *fml.*〉用棍子或竹板子打 spank sb. with a stick or bamboo board

☞ bàng on p.59 and 榜 bǎng on p.57

鹏 péng 传说中最大的鸟 roc; mythological bird of the largest size

【鹏程万里】péng chéng wàn lǐ〈比喻 *fig.*〉前程远大 may the roc fly for 10,000 *li*; having a promising future

澎 péng 澎湖列岛(Pénghú Lièdǎo)，我国群岛名，在台湾海峡中 Penghu Archipelago in the Taiwan Straits, China

☞ pēng on p.1458

【澎湃】péngpài ❶ 形容波浪互相撞击(of waves) swell and swirl; billow：波涛汹涌～billowing waves ❷〈比喻 *fig.*〉声势浩大，大势雄伟 imposing; majestic; august：激情～的诗篇 passionate poem

篷 péng ❶(～儿 péngr)遮蔽日光、风、雨的设备，用竹木、苇席或帆布等制成(多指车船上用的)(on a vehicle, boat, etc.) awning (with a wooden or bamboo framework and covered with reed mat or canvas)：船～awning of a boat|～窗(帆船窗户)(on a sailboat) porthole|敞～儿汽车 open car|把～撑起来 rig up a tent ❷ 船帆 sail：扯起～来 hoist a sail

【篷车】péngchē ❶ 有顶的货车 covered truck; box wagon ❷〈旧时 *old*〉带篷的马车 horse-drawn cart with an awning ‖ also 棚车 péngchē

【篷子】péng·zi same as 篷 péng ①

膨 péng 胀大 swell：～胀 inflate; swell; puff out

【膨大】péngdà 体积增大 inflate; expand

【膨脝】pénghēng ❶〈书 *fml.*〉肚子胀的样子 potbellied：～大腹 potbelly; paunch ❷〈方 *dial.*〉物体庞大，不灵便 cumbersome; unwieldy

【膨化】pénghuà (谷物等)由于在加热、加压的情况下突然减压而膨胀(of graim, etc.) popped; heat pop rice, etc., under pressure until it pops：～米 pop rice|～食品 pop-heated food

【膨体纱】péngtǐshā 用腈纶纺成的类似毛线的东西。将腈纶纤维加热拉伸，再将其中一部分加热使松驰，两种纤维混纺成线，经过蒸气处理，就成为膨体纱。膨体纱的特点是蓬松、柔软。bulked yarn; yarn made from heat-extended and cohered acrylic fibre, and steamed and extended so that it looks thicker and feels fluffy

【膨胀】péngzhàng ❶ 由于温度升高或其他因素，物体的长度增加或体积增大 extend in length or swell in size due to high temperature or other causes ❷ 借指某些事物扩大或增长 expand; increase：通货～(monetary) infla-

tion
【膨胀系数】péngzhàng xìshù 物体在温度上升1℃时所增大的体积和原来体积的比或所增加的长度和原来长度的比 coefficient of expansion; ratio between the additional cubage or length caused by 1℃-increase of temperature and the original cubage or length

鬅 péng 头发松散(of hair) fluffy:～松 fluffy

【鬅鬙】péngsēng〈书 *fml*.〉头发散乱的样子(of hair) dishevelled

【鬅松】péngsōng 头发蓬松(of hair) ruffled; tousled

蟛 péng [蟛蜞](péngqí)螃蟹的一种,体小,生长在水边 amphibious crab(*Sesarma intermedia*); brackish-water crab

pěng (ㄆㄥˇ)

捧 pěng ❶ 用双手托 clasp; hold in both hands:～着花生米 cup a quantity of groundnuts in one's hands|双手～住孩子的脸 cup the face of a child in one's hands ❷〈量词 *classifier*〉用于能捧的东西 double-handful of:一～枣儿 a double-handful of jujubes|捧了两～米 scoop up two double-handfuls of rice ❸ 奉承人或代人吹嘘 flatter; laud:～场 sing the praise of sb.

【捧杯】pěng//bēi 获得奖杯,特指在竞赛中夺得冠军(of sports competition) win the cup; win a championship

【捧场】pěng//chǎng 原指特意到剧场去赞赏戏曲演员表演,今泛指故意替别人的某种活动或局面吹嘘 patronize an actor's stage performance; show support to sb. with one's presence on an occasion or in an activity

【捧腹】pěngfù 捧着肚子。形容大笑 guffaw; double up with laughter:令人～make people laugh heartily|～大笑 double up with laughter

【捧哏】pěng//gén 相声的配角用话或表情来配合主角逗人发笑(of a sidekick to a comic dialogue) play the fool to help amuse the audience

【捧角】pěng//jué(～儿 pěng//juér)给某个戏曲演员捧场 give publicity to an actor or actress

pèng (ㄆㄥˋ)

椪 pèng [椪柑](pènggān) ❶ 常绿小乔木,叶片小,椭圆形,花白色,果实大,皮橙黄色,汁多味甜 Chinese honey (*Citrus poonensis*); perennial tree having small oval leaves, white flowers and large and yellow fruit that is juicy and sweet ❷ 这种植物的果实 orange

碰(掽、踫) pèng ❶ 运动着的物体跟别的物体突然接触 touch; bump:～杯 clink glasses in a toast|不小心腿在门上～了一下 accidentally bang one's leg against a door ❷ 碰见;遇到 come across sb.; bump into sb.:～面 meet with sb.|在路上～到一位熟人 bump into an acquaintance in the street ❸ 试探 take one's chance:～～机会 take a chance; take a gamble|我去～一下看,说不定他在家。Let me take a chance — perhaps he is home now.

【碰杯】pèng//bēi 饮酒前举杯轻轻相碰,表示祝贺 clink glasses in a toast

【碰壁】pèng//bì〈比喻 *fig*.〉遇到严重阻碍或受到拒绝,事情行不通 run up against a stone wall; be rebuffed:到处～run into snags everywhere

【碰钉子】pèng dīng•zi〈比喻 *fig*.〉遭到拒绝或受到斥责 be rebuffed; hit a snag

【碰见】pèng//•jiàn 事先没有约定而见到 meet unexpectedly; run into:昨天我在街上～他。I bumped into him in the street yesterday.

【碰劲儿】pèng//jìnr〈方 *dial*.〉same as 碰巧 pèngqiǎo:～打中了一枪。I hit the target by sheer luck. also 碰巧劲儿 pèng qiǎo jìnr

【碰面】pèng//miàn 会面;会见 see each other; meet:我同他约定今天在这里～。I made an appointment to meet him here today.

【碰碰车】pèng•pengchē 一种供儿童游乐用的电动车,在特定的场地上开动,以车与车互相碰撞取乐 bumper car; power-driven vehicles to be driven in a secluded place by children to amuse themselves by bumping into one another

【碰碰船】pèng•pengchuán 一种供儿童游乐用的电动船,在特定的水池中开动,以船与船互相碰撞取乐 bumper boat; electricity-powered boats to be driven on a cordoned-off part of a lake by children to amuse themselves by bumping into one another

【碰巧】pèngqiǎo 凑巧;恰巧 by chance; unexpectedly; inadvertently:我正想找你,～你来了。What a coincidence! I was looking for you when you came.

【碰锁】pèngsuǒ 撞锁 spring lock; also 碰簧锁 pènghuángsuǒ

【碰头】pèng//tóu ❶ 会面;会见 go into a huddle; hold an impromptu conference:请他带去吧,他们天天都～。You'd better bring him along, as they have brief meetings on a daily basis. ❷〈方 *dial*.〉磕头 kowtow:～求饶 beg for mercy by kowtowing

【碰头会】pèngtóuhuì 以交换情况为主要内容的会,一般时间很短 briefing; brief meeting for the swap of information

【碰一鼻子灰】pèng yī bí•zi huī 遭到拒绝或斥责,落得没趣 be snubbed; be slighted

【碰撞】pèngzhuàng ❶ 物体相碰或相撞;撞击 crash; clash; clash head-on into:搬运瓷器要避免～。Clashes should be avoided when moving porcelainware. ❷ 冲犯 drive sb. up the wall:不要拿话去～他。Don't drive him up the wall whenever you talk to him.

pī(ㄆㄧ)

丕 pī〈书 *fml.*〉大 big; great:～业 great cause|～变 tremendous change

邳 Pī ❶ 邳州,地名,在江苏 Pizhou, name of a place in Jiangsu Province ❷ (Pī)姓 a surname

批1 pī ❶〈书 *fml.*〉用手掌打 slap:～颊 box sb.'s face ❷〈书 *fml.*〉刮;削 scrape; peel; skin ❸ 对下级文件表示意见或对文章予以批评(多指写在原件上) write a comment or instruction on a report submitted for deliberation:～示 written instruction (on a report submitted for advice)|～改 correct; revise; go over|～公事 write an instruction on a government issue ❹ 批判;批评 criticize; carp:挨了一通～be given a dressing down

批2 pī ❶ 大量(买卖货物)(of buying and selling) batch; bulk:～发 wholesale|～购 buy goods wholesale ❷〈量词 *classifier*〉用于大宗的货物或多数的人 batch; shipment; group:一～纸张 one shipment of paper|今年第一～到边疆去的同学已经出发。The first group of school graduates assigned to work in border regions has set off.

批3 pī (～儿 pīr)棉麻等未捻成线、绳时的细缕 cotton or flax fibre:线～儿 cotton fibre|麻～儿 flax fibre

【批驳】pībó 批评或否决别人的意见、要求 repulse; veto; say no to:～错误论调 refute an erroneous theory

【批点】pīdiǎn ❶ 在书刊、文章上加评语和圈点 make marks of dots or circles and write comments on a book, journal, composition, etc. ❷〈方 *dial.*〉褒贬;指摘 comment; criticize

【批发】pīfā 成批地出售商品 wholesale:～部 wholesale department|～价格 wholesale price

【批复】pīfù 对下级的书面报告批注意见答复 formal instruction written on a submitted report

【批改】pīgǎi 修改文章、作业等并加批语 mark; correct an article or homework

【批件】pījiàn 经上级批示过的文件 document with a leader's instruction written on it

【批量】pīliàng ❶ 成批地(制造) batched (production):这种仪器已开始～生产。This type of instrument has gone into batched production. ❷ 产品成批生产的数量 batch:大～large batches|～小 small batches

【批零】pīlíng 批发和零售 wholesale and retail sale:～兼营 wholesale and retail business|～差价 difference between wholesale and retail prices

【批判】pīpàn ❶ 对错误的思想、言论或行为做系统的分析,加以否定 criticize; repudiate:～虚无主义 critique of nihilism ❷ 批评 criticism:自我～self-criticism ❸ (～地 pīpàn·di) 分清正确的和错误的或有用的和无用的(去分别对待) (critically) discriminate between the right and the wrong, between the useful and the useless (so as to treat them differently):～地继承文学艺术遗产 be critically inherite literary and art legacies

【批评】pīpíng ❶ 指出优点和缺点;评论好坏 criticize; comment:文艺～criticism of literature and art ❷ 专指对缺点和错误提出意见 be critical of sb. or sth.; denounce; repudiate; upbraid:～她对顾客的傲慢态度。She was criticized for her arrogant attitude towards customers.

【批示】pīshì ❶ (上级对下级的公文)用书面表示意见 (of a superior) write instructions on a document submitted (by a subordinate):计划已经呈报上级了,等～下来就动手。The plan has been submitted to the leaders for approval and will be carried out once it is approved. ❷ 批示的文字 written instructions:这个材料上有张局长的～。This document bears the instructions by Bureau Director Zhang.

【批条子】pī tiáo·zi 领导或主管人员在条子上批示,表示同意某种要求 write out a short note of approval or disapproval of a certain demand

【批文】pīwén (上级或有关部门)批复的文字或文件 document bearing a formal instruction from a leading department

【批语】pīyǔ ❶ 对文章、作业等的评语 comments written on the margins of an article or composition ❷ 批示公文的话 comments or instructions written on an official document

【批阅】pīyuè 阅读并加以批示或批改 read while making corrections or writing comments:～文件 read and comment on a document

【批注】pīzhù ❶ 加批语和注解 annotate and comment ❷ 指批评和注解的文字 marginalia; annotations and commentaries:书眉有小字～。There are annotations and comments in small typefaces in the top margins of the pages in this book.

【批准】pī//zhǔn 上级对下级的意见、建议或请求表示同意 approve, endorse; ratify:～他休假一个月。His request for a one-month absence of leave has been granted.

伾 pī [伾伾]〈书 *fml.*〉有力气的样子 strong; muscular

纰 pī 布帛丝缕等破坏,披散 (of cloth; thread, etc.) come undone; come apart:线～了。The thread has come untwisted.

【纰漏】pīlòu 因粗心而产生的差错;小事故或漏洞 blunder; oversight:出～make a slip

【纰缪】pīmiù〈书 *fml.*〉错误 mistake; oversight; slip

坯(坏) pī ❶ 砖瓦、陶瓷、景泰蓝等制造过程中,用原料做成器物的形状,还没有放在窑里或炉里烧的,叫做坯 bricks, pieces of pottery or cloisonne, etc., already in desired shapes but not yet fired in the kiln: 砖～ unfired brick; adobe ❷ 特指土坯 abode: 打～ build a rammed-earth wall | 脱～ mould adobe bricks ❸ 〈方 *dial.*〉(～儿 pīr) 指半成品 semi-finished products: 面～(煮熟而未加作料的面条) cooked noodles without seasoning | 酱～儿 fermented soya paste before adding seasoning | 钢～ steel ingot | ～布 raw cloth; grey

☞ 坏 huài on p. 842

【坯布】pībù 织成后还没有经过印染加工的布 unbleached and undyed cloth; grey

【坯料】pīliào 毛坯 semi-finished products; blank

【坯胎】pītāi 某些器物的坯 base; blank: 搪瓷的金属～ metal base of enamelware

【坯子】pī·zi ❶ same as 坯 pī ①: 砖～ unfired brick; adobe ❷ same as 坯 pī ③: 酱～ fermented soya paste before adding seasoning | 线～ semi-finished coffon garn ❸ 指未来可能成为做某事的人(多指青少年) up-and-coming young people; person who can amount to something in the future

披 pī ❶ 覆盖或搭在肩背上 drape over one's shoulders; wrap around: ～着斗篷 have a cloak wrapped around one's shoulders ◇～星戴月 get up by starlight, and do not knock off work till the moon rises ❷ 打开; 散开 open; unfurl: ～卷 open a book ❸ (竹木等)裂开 (of bamboo, wood, etc.) split: 这根竹竿～了。The bamboo pole has got cracks in it.

【披发左衽】pī fà zuǒ rèn 〈古代 *arch.*〉指东方、北方少数民族的装束 (of minority ethnic people in east and north China in ancient times) wear one's hair down and fold one's clothes to the left (左衽 *zuo ren*: 大襟开在左边儿 folding one's clothes to the left)

【披风】pīfēng same as 斗篷 dǒu·peng ①

【披拂】pīfú 〈书 *fml.*〉飘动; (微风)吹动 swing; sway; (of breeze) blow gently: 枝叶～。The leaves and branches swayed gently in the breeze. | 春风～。A spring breeze rustled softly.

【披肝沥胆】pī gān lì dǎn 〈比喻 *fig.*〉开诚相见,也比喻极尽忠诚 split one's liver and gall with exertion; lay open one's heart; be utterly devoted

【披挂】pīguà ❶ 〈旧指 *old*〉穿戴盔甲,后也泛指穿戴衣装 put on a suit of armour; (in a broad sense) put on clothes: 猎人们～整齐,准备上路。The hunters dressed and got ready to set out. ◇几员足坛老将再次～上阵。Several veteran footballers will be playing again. ❷ 指穿戴的盔甲(多见于早期白话 oft. seen in early vernacular) suit of armour

【披红】pīhóng 把红绸披在人的身上或物体上,表示喜庆或光荣 drape a band of red silk over an object or sb.'s shoulders on a festive occasion, or as a token of honour: ～戴花 have red silk draped over one's shoulders and a big red paper flower pinned to one's chest

【披怀】pīhuái 〈书 *fml.*〉敞开胸怀,指开诚相见 be completely open; be frank and honest

【披甲】pījiǎ 穿上铠甲 put on a suit of armour

【披坚执锐】pī jiān zhí ruì 穿上坚固的铠甲,拿起锋利的武器。多指将领亲赴战场打仗。buckle on one's armour and take up weapons — go forth to battle

【披肩】pījiān ❶ 披在肩上的服饰 tippet; decorative garment draped over the shoulders ❷ 妇女披在上身的一种无袖短外衣 cape; shawl; women's sleeveless outer garment

【披荆斩棘】pī jīng zhǎn jí ❶ 〈比喻 *fig.*〉扫除前进中的困难和障碍 clear away all difficulties and obstacles to one's progress ❷ 形容克服创业中的种种艰难 overcome any hardships that may occur in the course of one's career

【披卷】pījuàn 翻阅书籍 browse through books

【披览】pīlǎn 〈书 *fml.*〉翻阅 browse; look through: ～群书 read extensively

【披沥】pīlì 〈书 *fml.*〉'披肝沥胆'的略语 short term for 披肝沥胆 pī gān lì dǎn

【披露】pīlù ❶ 发表; 公布 publish; announce: 全文～ article published in full text | ～会谈内容 make public the content of the talks ❷ 表露 reveal; disclose: ～肝胆 be openhearted

【披麻带孝】pī má dài xiào 旧俗子女为父母居丧,要服重孝,如身穿粗麻布孝服,腰系麻绳等,叫披麻带孝 (old custom) wear hemp garments, with a hemp rope tied at the waist to signify mourning at the death of a parent; 带 also put as 戴 dài

【披靡】pīmǐ ❶ (草木)随风散乱地倒下 (of trees and grasses) be randomly uprooted and swept away in the wind ❷ (军队)溃散 (of army) flee: 望风～ flee at the mere sight of the oncoming force | 所向～ sweep away all obstacles

【披散】pī·san (毛发、枝条等)散着下垂 (of hair, tree branch, etc.) hang loose

【披沙拣金】pī shā jiǎn jīn 〈比喻 *fig.*〉从大量的事物中选择精华 panning gold from sand; select the essence from a mass of dross

【披头散发】pī tóu sàn fà 形容头发长而散乱 long, unkempt hair; hair in disarray

【披屋】pīwū 同正房两侧或后面相连的小屋,多用来堆放杂物 hovel; small room linked to a main room on either side, or at the rear wall, often used for storing odds and ends

【披星戴月】pī xīng dài yuè 形容早出晚归,辛勤劳动,或昼夜赶路,旅途劳顿 go to work before dawn, not to return till after dark; or travel on a journey right through the night

【披阅】pīyuè 披览;阅读 read; peruse:～文稿 peruse the manuscript

狉 pī ☞ below

【狉狉】pīpī〈书 *fml*.〉形容野兽蠢动 (of a place wild animals) move about:鹿豕～ alive with deer and boar

【狉獉】pīzhēn〈书 *fml*.〉草木丛杂,野兽出没 rank grass, and wild animals roaming from place to place; also 獉狉 zhēnpī

砒 pī ❶ 砷的旧称 old name for arsenic ❷ 砒霜 arsenic:红～ red arsenic | 白～ white arsenic

【砒霜】pīshuāng 无机化合物,是不纯的三氧化二砷。白色粉末,有时略带黄色或红色,有剧毒。用来制杀虫药或杀鼠药。arsenic; inorganic compound of impure arsenic trioxide that is usu. white, yellowish, or red powder of high toxicity, used in the making of pesticides; also 白砒 báipī, 红砒 hóngpī or 信石 xìnshí;有的地区叫红矾 known in some areas as 红矾 hóngfán

纰(鈚) pī〈书 *fml*.〉纰箭,箭头较薄而阔,箭杆较长 arrow with a fine, broad head mounted on a long shaft

铍 pī〈书 *fml*.〉❶ 针砭用的长针 long needle used in acupuncture ❷ 长矛 long lance
☞ pí on p.1466

性 pī〈书 *fml*.〉谬误 falsehood

辟(闢) pī [辟头](pītóu) same as 劈头 pītóu ②
☞ bì on p.108 and pì on p.1469

锟 pī〈书 *fml*.〉箭簇 metal arrowhead
☞ bī on p.96

劈 pī ❶ 用刀斧等砍或由纵面破开 slit; chop; cleave (with a sword or an ax):～木柴 chop wood | ～成两半 cleave sth. in two ◇～风斩浪 plough the wind and the waves ❷ (木头等)裂开 (of wood) crack:板子～了。The wooden board has cracked. | 钢笔尖写～了。The pen nib has split. ❸〈方 *dial*.〉(嗓音)嘶哑 (of voice) hoarse:他喊了半天,声音都快～了。He shouted until he was hoarse. ❹ 正对着;冲着(人的头、脸、胸部) right against (one's face, head, chest, etc.):～头 straight on one's head | ～脸 right against one's face ❺ 雷电毁坏或击毙 be destroyed or struck by lightning:老树让雷～了。The old tree was struck by lightning. ❻ 简单机械,由两个斜面合成,纵剖面呈三角形,如楔子和刀、斧等的刃儿就属于这一类 wedge; simple device consisting of two inclined planes that take the shape of a triangle in vertical section, e.g. chock, sword blade, ax blade, etc.
☞ pǐ on p.1468

【劈波斩浪】pī bō zhǎn làng 船只行进时冲开波浪 (of ships) cleave through the waves;〈比喻 *fig*.〉排除前进中的困难和障碍 clear away difficulties and overcome obstacles

【劈刺】pīcì 军事上劈刀和刺杀的统称 (military) saber or bayonet fighting

【劈刀】[1] pīdāo 刀背较厚的刀,用来劈竹子、木头等 ax; axe; tool with a bladed head mounted on a handle, usu. used for splitting bamboo or wood

【劈刀】[2] pīdāo 用军刀劈杀的技术 saber fighting

【劈里啪啦】pī·lipālā〈拟声词 *onom*.〉形容连续不断的爆裂、拍打等的声音 continuous sounds of crackling, slapping, etc.:窗外传来～的鞭炮声。The firecrackers crackled and spat outside the window. | 掌声～地响起来。Continuous applause ensued. also 噼里啪啦 pī·lipālā

【劈脸】pīliǎn 正冲着脸;迎面 right against the face:～就是一个大嘴巴 slap sb. across the face

【劈面】pīmiàn same as 劈脸 pīliǎn

【劈啪】pīpā〈拟声词 *onom*.〉形容拍打或爆裂的声音 sound of crackling, slapping, etc.:～的枪声 crackling of gunfire | 孩子们劈劈啪啪地鼓起掌来。The children began clapping their hands. also 噼啪 pīpā

【劈杀】pīshā 用刀砍杀(多指军人骑在马上用军刀杀敌 usu. of a soldier on horseback) slash at sb. with a sable

【劈山】pīshān 用人力或爆破等方式开山 level off hilltops; blast cliffs; cut into a mountain using human labour or explosives:～引水 cut through a mountain to let in water | ～造田 level off hilltops and turn the land into farmlands | ～筑路 blast cliffs to build highways or railways

【劈手】pīshǒu 形容手的动作迅速,使人来不及防备 (of one's hand) make a sudden snatch by taking sb. unawares:～一巴掌 slash out at sb. | ～夺过球拍 snatch a racket (from sb.)

【劈头】pītóu ❶ 正冲着头;迎头 straight on the head; right in the face:走到门口～碰见老王从里边出来。As he arrived at the entrance he bumped straight into Lao Wang, who was on his way out. ❷ 开头;起首 at the very beginning:他进来～第一句话就问试验成功了没有。The moment he came in he asked whether or not the experiment had been successful. also 辟头 pītóu

【劈头盖脸】pī tóu gài liǎn 正对着头和脸盖下来,形容来势凶猛 directly to sb.'s head and face (oft. used to describe a ferocious oncoming force):瓢泼似的大雨～地浇下来。The rain poured down. also 劈头盖脑 pī tóu gài nǎo or 劈头盖顶 pī tóu gài dǐng

【劈胸】pīxiōng 对准胸前 right against the chest:～一把抓住 grasp sb. by the front of his coat

噼 pī ☞ below

【噼里啪啦】 pī·lipālā same as 劈里啪啦 pī·lipālā

【噼啪】 pīpā same as 劈啪 pīpā

霹 pī ☞ below

【霹雷】 pīléi same as 霹雳 pīlì

【霹雳】 pīlì 云和地面之间发生的一种强烈雷电现象。响声很大,能对人畜、植物、建筑物等造成很大的危害。thunderbolt; thunderclap; heavy discharge of lightning accompanying thunder, often causing damage to humans, animals, plants, and buildings; also 落雷 luòléi

【霹雳舞】 pīlìwǔ 产生于美国贫民区黑人中间的一种舞蹈,舞姿有翻转、旋转、摆动、摹拟表演以及飘浮、滑动等动作 break dancing; dance originating from black Americans living in urban slum districts, featuring a series of gymnastic movements, such as acrobats, spins, swinging, mimicry, hovering, and gliding

pí (ㄆ丨ˊ)

皮 pí ❶ 人或生物体表面的一层组织 skin; rind; peel; surface tissue of humans and organisms:牛～ cowhide|荞麦～ buckwheat husk|碰掉了一块～ scrape off a piece of skin ❷ 皮子 leather; hide; fur:～箱 leather case|～鞋 leather shoes|～袄 fur coat ❸ (～儿 pír) 包在或围在外面的一层东西 cover; wrapper:包袱～儿 cloth cover ❹ (～儿 pír)表面 surface:地～ the earth's surface|水～儿 water surface ❺ (～儿 pír)某些薄片状的东西 thin sheet:铅～ lead plate|粉～儿 sheet jelly made from vegetable starch|豆腐～儿 bean-curd sheet; tofu sheet ❻ 有韧性的 soggy; hard, tenacious:～糖 hard candy ❼ 酥脆的东西受潮后变韧 (of crisp food) become soggy from the affect of dampness:花生放～了,吃起来不香了。The peanuts have gone soft and don't taste as good as before. ❽ 顽皮 naughty:调～ naughty|这孩子真～。What a naughty child! ❾ 由于受申斥或责罚次数过多而感觉无所谓 case-hardened; could not care less; no longer care after being repeatedly scolded or punished ❿ 指橡胶 rubber:橡～ rubber|～筋 rubber band ⓫ (Pí)姓 a surname

【皮板儿】 píbǎnr 指皮桶子毛下面的皮 fur lining (of jacket or overcoat)

【皮包】 píbāo 用皮革制成的手提包 leather handbag

【皮包公司】 píbāo gōngsī 指没有固定资产、没有固定经营地点及定额人员,只提着皮包,从事社会经济活动的人或集体,多挂有公司的名义 briefcase company; paper company; individual or collective committed to social and economic activity, with a briefcase full of documents, but no fixed assets, fixed business location, or regular staff; also 皮包商 píbāoshāng

【皮包骨】 pí bāo gǔ 形容极端消瘦 skinny; bag of bones; also 皮包骨头 píbāo gǔtóu

【皮层】 pícéng ❶ 人或生物体组织表面的一层 cortex; outer layer of the structure of a human body or organism:肾脏～ kidney cortex|植物茎的～ plant-stem cortex ❷ 大脑皮层的简称 abbr. for 大脑皮层 dànǎo pícéng

【皮尺】 píchǐ 用漆布等做的卷尺 tape measure, made of wax cloth

【皮带】 pídài 用皮革制成的带子,特指用皮革制成的腰带 leather belt

【皮带轮】 pídàilún 机器上的安装传动带的轮子 (belt) pulley; wheel installed on a machine, used to transmit power by means of a band or belt passing over its rim

【皮蛋】 pídàn 松花 preserved egg

【皮肤】 pífū ❶ 身体表面包在肌肉外部的组织,人和高等动物的皮肤由表皮、真皮和皮下组织三层组成,有保护身体、调节体温、排泄废物等作用 skin; integument of an animal separated from its body; skin of human and higher animals, composed of epidermis, dermis, and subcutaneous tissue, its function being to protect the body, adjust the body temperature, and sweat out impurities ❷ 〈书 *fml.*〉〈比喻 *fig.*〉肤浅 superficial:～之见 superficial views

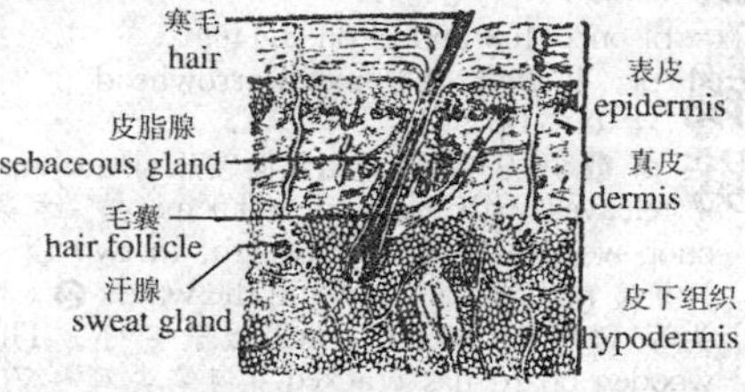

人的皮肤 Humam Skin

【皮肤针】 pífūzhēn ❶ 一种针刺用的针,由数枚小针固定在细柄上构成,装五枚的叫梅花针,装七枚的叫七星针。治疗时,手持细柄,用针尖在一定部位的皮肤上扣打。needles used in cutaneous acupuncture; therapy in which five needles (known as plum-blossom needles) or seven needles (known as seven-star needles) are fixed vertically to the end of a stick and tapped lightly on the skin surface of a certain area ❷ 用这种针进行治疗的方法 cutaneous acupuncture

【皮傅】 pífù 〈书 *fml.*〉凭肤浅的认识牵强附会 give a strained, superficial interpretation

【皮革】 pígé 用牛、羊、猪等的皮去毛后制成的熟皮,可以做鞋、箱及其他用品 leather; hide; dehaired skin of an ox, sheep, pig, or other animals, usu. used to make shoes, suitcases, and other articles

【皮辊花】pígǔnhuā 粗纱进行细纺时,由于纱线断头而卷绕在皮辊或绒辊上的棉纤维。皮辊花可以重新加工使用。lap waste; roller lap; recyclable cotton fiber entwined on leather or plush rollers in the process of fine spinning due to the breaks in yarn; also 白花 báihuā

【皮猴儿】píhóur 风帽连着衣领的皮大衣或这种式样的人造毛、呢绒做衬里的大衣 hooded fur overcoat; leather parka; leather coat with a funnel cap linked to the collar or coat of this style, with fur on the outside, and a woolen or synthetic lining

【皮花】píhuā same as 皮棉 pímián

【皮黄】píhuáng 戏曲声腔,西皮和二黄的合称 short for 西皮 xīpí and 二黄 èrhuáng, two main types of music in traditional opera; also 皮簧 píhuáng

【皮货】píhuò 毛皮货物的总称 furs; peltry; fur goods:～商 fur dealer

【皮夹子】píjiā·zi 用薄而软的皮革等做成的扁平小袋,带在身边装钱或其他小的用品 wallet; pocketbook; small, flat purse made of fine soft leather, usu. for containing money or other small articles; also 皮夹儿 píjiār

【皮匠】pí·jiang ❶ 修补旧鞋或制鞋的小手工业者 cobbler; shoe maker or polisher ❷ 制造皮革的小手工业者 tanner; small handicraftsman specializing in leather goods

【皮筋儿】píjīnr 橡皮筋 rubber band:跳～ rubber skipping band; jumping a rubber band; also 猴皮筋儿 hóupíjīnr

【皮开肉绽】pí kāi ròu zhàn 指人因被毒打,皮肉开裂 torn skin and gaping flesh (after being beaten or flogged)

【皮库】píkù 医院中保存皮肤组织供移植用的设备 (in hospital) installations for storing skin tissue reserved for transplants

【皮里阳秋】pí lǐ Yángqiū 指藏在心里不说出来的评论。'阳秋'即'春秋',晋简文帝(司马昱)母郑后名阿春,避讳'春'字改称。这里用来代表'批评',因为相传孔子修《春秋》,意含褒贬。well-disguised or implicit remarks. 阳秋 refers to 春秋 chūnqiū (spring and autumn), the title of a historical book, i. e. *Spring and Autumn Annals*. The book was renamed 阳秋 in the reign of Emperot Jianwen (Sima Yu) of the Jin Dynasty for the deferential taboo of the character 春 chūn, which was part of the emperor dowager's given name 阿春 (Achun). The phrase refers to implicit criticism, as Confucius both praised and disparaged past dynasties when he revised the *Spring and Autumn Annals*, or *Chunqiu* in Chinese.

【皮脸】píliǎn 〈方 *dial.*〉 ❶ 顽皮 naughty ❷ 形容不知羞耻 shameless

【皮脸儿】píliǎnr 布鞋鞋脸儿正中用窄皮条沿起的圆梗 round thong at the centre of the vamp of a cloth shoe

【皮毛】pímáo ❶ 带毛的兽皮的总称 fur; hide with hair:貂皮、狐皮都是很贵重的～。Marten and fox are both expensive furs. ❷〈比喻 *fig.*〉表面的知识 smattering; superficial knowledge:略知～ have only a superficial knowledge (of a subject)

【皮棉】pímián 棉花轧去种子后的纤维,是纺织工业的原料 ginned cotton; lint (cotton); fiber of deseeded cotton, usu. used as raw material in the textile industry

【皮囊】pínáng 皮制的口袋 leather bag;〈比喻 *fig.*〉人的躯体(贬义 derog.) human body:臭～ this mortal flesh | 空有～ have a body of no value

【皮球】píqiú 游戏用具,是一种有弹性的空心球,多用橡胶制成 rubber ball; flexible hollow ball, often made of rubber, used in ball games

【皮肉】píròu 皮和肉,指肉体 skin and flesh; body:我不过伤了点～,没什么。I sustained a minor abrasion; there was no serious injury. | ～之苦 suffering of the flesh | ～生涯(指女子卖淫的生活) (of women) career of prostitution

【皮实】pí·shi ❶ 身体结实,不易得病 (of body) sturdy; seldom falling ill:这孩子真～,从来没闹过病。What a sturdy child! He has never been ill. ❷(器物)耐用而不易破损 (of utensils) durable; not easily broken

【皮糖】pítáng 用糖加适量的淀粉熬制成的糖果,韧性很强 chewy candy, made from sugar and starch

【皮桶子】pítǒng·zi 做皮衣用的成件的毛皮 fur lining (for a leather overcoat); also 皮桶儿 pítǒngr

【皮下组织】píxià zǔzhī 皮肤下面的结缔组织,含脂肪较多,质地疏松,其中有血管、淋巴管、神经等。可以保持体温、缓和机械压力等。subcutaneous tissue; connective tissue beneath the skin, rich in fat and loose in texture, containing blood vessels, lymphatic vessels, and nerves, that helps maintain body temperature and ease mechanical pressure; (图见 ☞ figure for 皮肤 pífū)

【皮相】píxiàng 指只从表面看;不深入 skin-deep; superficial:～之谈 superficial talk

【皮硝】píxiāo 朴硝的通称 common name for 朴硝 pòxiāo

【皮笑肉不笑】pí xiào ròu bù xiào 形容虚伪地笑、阴险地笑或不自然地笑 put on a false smile; smile hypocritically

【皮衣】píyī 用毛皮或皮革制成的衣服 fur clothing; leather clothing

【皮影戏】píyǐngxì 用兽皮或纸板做成的人物剪

影来表演故事的戏曲，民间流行很广。表演时，用灯光把剪影照射在幕上，艺人在幕后一边操纵剪影，一边演唱，并配以音乐。shadow play; shadow puppet; popular folk opera in which performers use leather or cardboard silhouettes to enact plays. A light is shone on to a screen, behind which performers operate the silhouettes while singing to the accompaniment of music; also 影戏 yǐngxì; 有的地区叫驴皮影 known in some areas as 驴皮影 lǘpíyǐng

P

【皮张】pízhāng 做制革原料用的兽皮 hide; pelt; animal fur used for making leather

【皮掌儿】pízhǎngr 钉在鞋底前后的皮子 outsole; outside sole of a shoe

【皮疹】pízhěn 皮肤表面出现的各种小疙瘩，常成片出现 skin rash; tetter; eruption; occurrence of small lumps, often large in number, on the skin

【皮之不存，毛将焉附】 pí zhī bù cún máo jiāng yān fù 皮都没有了，毛还长在哪儿？（见于《左传》僖公十四年。'焉附'原作'安傅'。）With the skin gone, what can the hair adhere to? (*The Zuo Commentary · Duke Xi 14th Year*, 焉附 yānfù was orig. put as 安傅 ānfù); 〈比喻 *fig.*〉事物没有基础，就不能存在 thing cannot exist without its basis

【皮脂】pízhī 指人或动物的皮肤分泌出来的油脂 sebum; fatty lubricant matter secreted by the sebaceous glands of human or animal skin

【皮脂腺】pízhīxiàn 人或动物体上分泌油脂的腺，在真皮中，很小，多为囊状，开口在毛囊中 sebaceous glands; very small and mostly capsular glands in the dermis of the human or animal body that secrete fatty matter and open at the hair follicles; (图见 ☞ figure for 皮肤 pífū)

【皮纸】pízhǐ 用桑树皮、楮树皮或笋壳等制成的一种坚韧的纸，供制造雨伞等用 coarse paper made from the bast fiber of the mulberry, paper mulberry, or peels of bamboo shoots, usu. used for making umbrellas

【皮质】pízhì ❶ 某些内脏器官的表层组织 cortex; outer tissue layer of certain internal organs ❷ 大脑皮层的简称 abbr. for 大脑皮层 dànǎo pícéng

【皮重】pízhòng 货物包装材料的重量，也指称东西时用的盛器的重量 tare; weight of the packing for goods, or weight of the container of articles to be weighed

【皮子】pí·zi 皮革或毛皮 leather or fur

芘 pí [芘芣](pífú)古书上指锦葵 (in ancient writings) Chinese mallow

陂 pí 黄陂(Huángpí)，地名，在湖北 Huangpi, name of a place in Hubei Province
☞ bēi on p. 76 and pō on p. 1491

枇 pí [枇杷](pí·pá) ❶ 常绿乔木，叶子长椭圆形，花小，白色，圆锥花序。果实淡黄色或橙黄色，外皮上有细毛。生长在较温暖的地区，果实可以吃，叶子和核可入药。loquat (*Eriobotrya japonica*); evergreen tree that grows in warm regions, with oval leaves and white, small flowers in panicles. Its edible fruit is light, or orange in colour, and its skin is downy. Its leaves and pits can be used for medicine. ❷ 这种植物的果实 fruit of this tree

狓 pí ☞ [獾狮狓](huòjiāpí) on p. 887

毗(毘) pí 〈书 *fml.*〉❶ 毗连 adjoin; be adjacent to: ～邻 be adjacent to ❷ 辅助 assist

【毗连】pílián 连接 adjoin; border on; be connected with: 樯桅～。Masts and ships tied together. | 江苏省北部跟山东省～。The northern part of Jiangsu Province borders on Shandong Province.

【毗邻】pílín （地方）毗连（of places) adjoin; border on

蚍 pí ☞ below

【蚍蜉】pí fú 〈书 *fml.*〉大蚂蚁 large ant

【蚍蜉撼大树】pífú hàn dà shù 〈比喻 *fig.*〉力量很小而想动摇强大的事物，不自量力 attempt to move heavy things with inferior strength; ridiculously overrate oneself

铍 pí 金属元素，符号 Be (beryllium)。灰白色，质硬而轻。用于原子能工业中，铍铝合金用来制飞机、火箭等。beryllium (Be); off-white metallic element that is hard and light and oft. used in the atomic-energy industry. The beryllium-aluminum alloy is used for making aircraft and space rockets.
☞ pī on p. 1463

郫 Pí 郫县，在四川 Pixian County, in Sichuan Province

疲 pí ❶ 疲乏；劳累 tired; weary; exhausted: 精～力尽 be worn out | ～于奔命 be weighed down with sth. ❷ same as 疲软 píruǎn ②: 及时更新换代，使产品畅销不～ timely upgrading of products so as to avoid a slow-down in their marketability

【疲惫】píbèi ❶ 非常疲乏 weary; exhausted; tired out: ～不堪 be in a state of utter exhaustion ❷ 使非常疲乏 tire sb. out: ～敌军 tire out the enemy

【疲敝】píbì 人力、物力受到消耗，不充足 (of manpower, material resources, etc.) be running low; become inadequate

【疲顿】pídùn 〈书 *fml.*〉非常疲乏 be tired out: ～不堪 be extremely tired

【疲乏】pífá same as 疲劳 píláo ①②

【疲倦】píjuàn 疲乏；困倦 tired and sleepy; be spent

【疲困】píkùn ❶ 疲乏 tired: 他日夜操劳，不顾～。He works tirelessly day and night. ❷

(经济状况等)疲软 (of economic situation, etc.) weaken:～不振 sluggish

【疲劳】píláo ❶ 因体力或脑力消耗过多而需要休息 tired; requiring rest after being drained of physical strength and energy ❷ 因运动过度或刺激过强,细胞、组织或器官的机能或反应能力减弱 fatigue; temporary failure of power to respond on the part of the functions of a cell, tissue, or organ, brought on by overwork or excessive stimulation:听觉～ hearing fatigue|肌肉～ muscular fatigue ❸ 因外力过强或作用时间过久而不能继续起正常的反应 failure to maintain normal reactions under tremendous or sustained stress:弹性～ elastic fatigue|磁性～ magnetic fatigue

【疲软】píruǎn ❶ 疲乏无力 fatigued and weak:身子～ feel weak ❷ 指行情价格低落、货物销售不畅或货币汇率呈下降趋势 slump; inactive and slow; economic situation in which market prices go down, commodities sell poorly, and the currency exchange rate shows a downward trend:价格～ price slumps|市场～ sluggish market

【疲弱】píruò 疲乏无力;衰弱 tired and weak; frail and fatigued:身体～ feel weak|他拖着～的双腿继续前进。He dragged his tired legs and trudged on.

【疲塌】pí·ta 松懈拖沓 slack; negligent:工作～ be slack at one's work|作风疲疲塌塌 in a slack manner; also 疲沓 pí·ta

【疲于奔命】pí yú bēn mìng 原指不断受到命令或逼迫而奔走疲劳,后来也指事情繁多忙不过来 be worn out by much running around, being ordered around and under pressure; be weighed down with work; have one's hands full

陴 pí〈书 *fml.*〉女墙 parapet wall

埤 pí〈书 *fml.*〉增加 increase
☞ pì on p.1469

啤 pí ☞ below

【啤酒】píjiǔ 以大麦和啤酒花为主要原料发酵制成的酒,有泡沫和特殊的香味,味道微苦,含酒精量较低 beer; alcoholic beverage usu. made from barley, flavoured with hops, and brewed by slow fermentation, low in alcohol content, effervescent, with a slightly bitter flavour; also 麦酒 màijiǔ

【啤酒花】píjiǔhuā ❶ 多年生草本植物,蔓生,茎和叶柄上有刺,叶子卵形,雌雄异株。果穗呈球果状,用来使啤酒具有苦味和香味,又可入药。hops (*Humulus lupulus*); perennial creeping dioecious herb with oval leaves, and spinose stems and leafstalks. Its cone-shaped catkins are usu. used to add a slightly bitter flavour and aroma to beer, or for medicine ❷ 这种植物的果穗 catkins of a hop ‖ also 忽布 hūbù, 蛇麻 shémá or 酒花 jiǔhuā

舭 pí 越南地名用字,如丐舭 (Gàipí) part of certain place names in Viet Nam e.g. 丐舭 Gàipí

琵 pí ☞ below

【琵琶】pí·pá 弦乐器,用木料制成,有四根弦,下部为瓜子形的盘,上部为长柄,柄端弯曲 pipa; plucked, four stringed instrument made of wood, with a fingerboard shaped like a melon-seed, and a long bending neck

【琵琶骨】pí·pagǔ〈方 *dial.*〉肩胛骨 bladebone

椑 pí〈古时 *arch.*〉一种椭圆形的酒器 elliptic drinking vessel
☞ bēi on p.78

脾 pí 人或高等动物的内脏之一,椭圆形,赤褐色,质柔软,在胃的左侧。脾的作用是制造新的血细胞与破坏衰老的血细胞,产生淋巴球与抗体,贮藏铁质,调节脂肪、蛋白质的新陈代谢等。spleen; elliptic, russet-coloured, soft organ to the left of the stomach in human and higher animals, whose function is the final destruction of aged blood cells, the making new blood cells, production of lymphocytes and antibodies, storage of iron, and adjustment of the metabolism to fat and protein; also 脾脏 pízàng

【脾寒】pí·han〈方 *dial.*〉疟疾 malaria; ague: 打～(发疟疾) suffer from malaria

【脾气】pí·qi ❶ 性情 temperament; disposition:她的～很好,从来不急躁。She has a good temper and never gets angry. ❷ 容易发怒的性情;急躁的情绪 bad temper; irritable disposition:发～ flare up; lose one's temper; flare up|～大 hot-tempered

【脾胃】píwèi〈比喻 *fig.*〉对事物爱好、憎恶的习性 taste; propensity for liking or disliking sth.:两人～相投。The two people share similar tastes.|这事不合他的～。This goes against his propensity.

【脾性】píxìng〈方 *dial.*〉性格;习性 temperament; disposition; nature:一个人有一个人的～。People differ in temperament. ◇摸清了秧苗的～ find out the nature and characteristics of the rice seedlings

【脾脏】pízàng 脾 spleen

鲏 pí ☞ [鳑鲏] (pángpí) on p.1446

裨 pí〈书 *fml.*〉辅佐的;副 secondary; assistant; minor:偏～ assistant|～将 subordinate or lower-ranking general
☞ bì on p.108

【裨将】píjiàng〈古代 *arch.*〉指副将 subordinate or lower-ranking general

蜱 pí 节肢动物,身体椭圆形,头胸部和腹部合在一起,有四对脚。种类很多,有的吸植物的汁,对农作物害处很大;有的吸人、畜的血,能传染脑炎、回归热、恙虫病等。tick (*Ixodoidea*); arachnid with an elliptic body, four pairs of feet, and an overlapping head, thorax, and abdomen. There are many species: some suck the sap from plants, and are harmful to crops, while others suck the blood of humans or animals, and spread infectious diseases such as cephalitis, relapsing fever, and acariasis; also 壁虱 bìshī

罴(羆) pí 棕熊 brown bear

膍 pí〈古代 *arch.*〉指牛的百叶 beef tripe

【膍胵】píchī〈方 *dial.*〉鸟类的胃 stomach of birds:鸡～ chicken's stomach

貔 pí 古书上说的一种野兽 (in ancient writings) mythical wild animal

【貔虎】píhǔ〈比喻 *fig.*〉勇猛的军队 brave troops

【貔貅】píxiū ❶ 古书上说的一种猛兽 (in ancient writing) a kind of wild animal ❷〈比喻 *fig.*〉勇猛的军队 brave troops

【貔子】pí·zi〈方 *dial.*〉黄鼠狼 yellow weasel

鼙 pí [鼙鼓](pígǔ)〈古代 *arch.*〉军队中用的小鼓 small drum used in the army:～喧天 deafening sound of beating military drums

pǐ (ㄆㄧˇ)

匹[1] pǐ ❶ 比得上;相当;相配 be equal to; be a match for:～配 match|难与为～ hard to match ❷ 单独 single; alone:～夫 ordinary person

匹[2](❷疋) pǐ〈量词 *classifier*〉❶ 用于马、骡等 [for horse, mules, etc.]:两～骡子 two mules|三～马 three horses ❷ 用于整卷的绸或布(五十尺、一百尺不等)(of silk or cloth 50 or 100 *chi* in length) bolt; bale:一～绸子 a bolt of silk|两～布 two bolts of cloth ❸〈方 *dial.*〉用于山 [for mountains]:一～山 a mountain|翻过那～山就到了。After climbing that mountain we will arrive at our destination.

☞ 疋 yǎ on p. 2196

【匹敌】pǐdí 对等;相称 be well matched; be equal to each other:两方势力～。The two sides are of equal force.

【匹夫】pǐfū ❶ 一个人,泛指平常人 ordinary man:国家兴亡,～有责。Every common man should feel responsible for the wellbeing of his motherland. ❷ 指无学识、无智谋的人(多见于早期白话 oft. in early vernacular) ignorant or unintelligent person:～之辈 ignorant person

【匹夫之勇】pǐ fū zhī yǒng 指不用智谋,只凭个人刚烈的勇气 foolhardiness; recklessly adventurous and bold; undisciplined courage lacking wisdom and intelligence

【匹马单枪】pǐ mǎ dān qiāng ☞ 单枪匹马 dān qiāng pǐ mǎ on p. 376

【匹配】pǐpèi ❶〈书 *fml.*〉结成婚姻;婚配 mate; marry:～良缘 get married ❷ (元器件等)配合 (of components, parts, etc.) matching:功率～ of matching power|阻抗～ matching impedance

【匹头】pǐ·tou〈方 *dial.*〉❶ 指布或绸缎等剪好的成件或成套的衣料 tailored garment or suit in cloth or silk ❷ 布匹 piece goods; fabrics

庀 pǐ〈书 *fml.*〉❶ 具备 possess; be provided with ❷ 治理 control and treatment

圮 pǐ〈书 *fml.*〉毁坏;倒塌 fall apart; be destroyed:倾～ collapse

仳 pǐ [仳离](pǐlí)〈书 *fml.*〉夫妻分离,特指妻子被遗弃(of husband and wife) be separated, esp. a forsaken wife

否 pǐ ❶ 坏;恶 bad; wicked; evil:～极泰来 out of the depths of misfortune comes bliss ❷ 贬斥 censure; denounce:臧～人物(评论人物的优劣) remark on sb.'s strong and weak points

☞ fǒu on p. 591

【否极泰来】pǐ jí tài lái 坏的到了尽头,好的就来了 Extreme adversity is the beginning of prosperity.(否,泰 *pi*, *tai*:六十四卦中的卦名,否是坏的卦,泰是好的卦 Divinatory symbols within the Sixty-Four Diagrams. *pi* symbolizes misfortune while *tai* symbolizes bliss.)

吡 pǐ〈书 *fml.*〉诋毁;斥责 defame; scold; blame

☞ bǐ on p. 100

痞 pǐ ❶ 痞块 lump in the abdomen ❷ 恶棍;流氓 ruffian; riffraff:～子 ruffian|地～流氓 local bullies and loafers

【痞块】pǐkuài〈中医 *Chin. med.*〉指腹腔内可以摸得到的硬块 hard, discernible lump in the abdomen; also 痞积 pǐjī

【痞子】pǐ·zi 恶棍;流氓 ruffian; riffraff

劈 pǐ ❶ 分开;分 divide; split:～成三股 split sth. into three strands ❷ 分裂;使离开原物体 break sth sth off sth. else sth. else; strip off:～莴苣叶 strip off the outer leaves of a lettuce ❸ 腿或手指等过分叉开 spread legs or fingers out widely

☞ pī on p. 1463

【劈叉】pǐchà 体操、武术等的一种动作,两腿向相反方向分开,臀部着地 exercise in gymnastics or martial arts that entails doing the splits

【劈柴】pǐ·chái 木头劈成的木块或小木条,供烧火做饭、取暖用,小块的多用来引火 firewood; narrow strips or small blocks of wood, usu. used as fuel for cooking or heating, while the smaller pieces are generally for kindling

【劈账】pǐ//zhàng 拆账 share out proceeds at a

certain ratio：三七～ profits shared in a three-seven split

擗 pǐ ❶ 用力使离开原物体 break sth. off sth. else：～棒子(玉米) pick corn ❷〈书 *fml.*〉用手拍胸 beat one's chest：～踊 beat one's chest and stamp one's feet

【擗踊】pǐyǒng〈书 *fml.*〉悲痛时捶胸顿足 beat one's chest and stamp one's feet (in sorrow)

癖 pǐ 癖好；嗜好 addiction；hobby：烟～ cigarette addiction｜洁～ cleanliness｜嗜酒成～，于健康不利。Alcohol addiction is harmful to health.

【癖好】pǐhào 对某种事物的特别爱好 favorite hobby；special fondness for sth.：他对于书画有很深的～。He is especially fond of painting and calligraphy.

【癖习】pǐxí 个人所特有的嗜好和习惯 (of an individual) distinctive hobby or habit

【癖性】pǐxìng 个人特有的癖好和习性 natural inclination；proclivity；propensity

嚭(噽) pǐ〈书 *fml.*〉大 big

pì (ㄆㄧˋ)

屁 pì ❶ 由肛门排出的臭气 fart；pungent intestinal gas discharged through the anus：放～ fart；break wind；expel intestinal gas ❷〈比喻 *fig.*〉没用的或不足道的事物 useless or negligible things：～话 nonsense；rubbish｜～大点事也值得大惊小怪。A trifling matter like this does not merit such a fuss. ❸ 泛指任何事物，相当于'什么'，多用于否定或斥责 anything；nothing (usu. used for negation or blame)：你懂个～。You know nothing! ｜别翻了，包里～都没有。Stop looking through that bag；there's nothing in there that you want.

【屁股】pì·gu ❶ 臀部 buttocks (of humans)；bottom；behind；backside ❷ 泛指动物身体后端靠近肛门的部分 rump；hindquarters；part surrounding the anus at the hindquarters of an animal：胡蜂的～上有刺。The wasp's sting is in its rump. ❸ 借指某些事物末尾的部分 end；butt：香烟～ cigarette butt｜汽车～冒烟了。The car is emitting fumes from its rear.｜紧紧咬住敌人～不放 closely follow the enemy's trail

【屁股蛋儿】pì·gudànr〈方 *dial.*〉臀部 buttocks；bottom；backside；also 屁股蛋子 pì·gudàn·zi

【屁股蹲儿】pì·gudūnr〈方 *dial.*〉身体失去平衡但未倒下而屁股着地的姿势 fall on one's hips；point at which the posterior touches the ground when sb. has lost his balance：摔了个～ fall on one's bottom

【屁股帘儿】pì·guliánr〈方 *dial.*〉系在穿开裆裤的小孩儿的腰上，遮住屁股的布帘儿、棉帘儿，有保暖作用 diaper-type swaddling for infants；cotton cloth wrapped around a child's bottom when it is wearing split pants, so as to cover and keep it warm；also 屁股帘子 pì·gulián·zi or 屁帘儿 pìliánr

【屁滚尿流】pì gǔn niào liú 形容非常惊恐或十分狼狈的样子 (used to describe sb. in extreme terror or discomposure) terror-stricken：吓得～ be frightened out of one's wits；be scared shitless

【屁话】pìhuà 指毫无价值或随意乱说的话(含厌恶意 derog.) nonsense；rubbish；meaningless or fanciful words

钚(鈚) pì〈书 *fml.*〉裁截；割裂 cut apart；divide

埤 pì [埤垸](pìnì)〈书 *fml.*〉城上矮墙 parapet wall

☞ pí on p. 1467

淠 Pì 淠河，水名，在安徽 Pihe River, in Anhui Province

睥 pì [睥睨](pìnì)〈书 *fml.*〉眼睛斜着看，形容高傲的样子 look sideways (in an arrogant manner)

辟[1](闢) pì ❶ 开辟 open up；break：各家自～园地，培育树苗。Every household has opened up a garden plot of its own for cultivating tree seedlings.｜这一带将～为新的旅游区。This area is to be developed into a new tourist area. ❷ 透彻 penetrating；incisive：精～ pointed｜透～ profound；incisive ❸ 驳斥或排除(不正确的言论或谣言)(incorrect opinions or rumours) refute or obviate：～谣 deny a rumour｜～邪说 refute heretical ideas

辟[2] pì〈书 *fml.*〉法律；法 law：大～(古代指死刑) capital punishment (in ancient times)

☞ bì on p. 108 and pī on p. 1463

【辟谣】pì//yáo 说明真相，驳反谣言 refute a rumour；deny a rumour and state the truth

媲 pì 匹敌；比得上 be equal to；be a match for

【媲美】pìměi 美(好)的程度差不多；比美 of comparable beauty；equal to (sth.) in advantage：该产品可与世界名牌货～。This product is the equal of any world famous brand.

僻 pì ❶ 偏僻 out-of-the-way；secluded：～巷 side lane｜～处一隅 live in a remote corner ❷ 性情古怪，跟一般人合不来 eccentric；one that does not get along well with others：怪～ strange and eccentric｜孤～ unsociable and eccentric ❸ 不常见的(多指文字 oft. of words) rare；not often seen：生～ uncommon｜冷～ unfamiliar

【僻静】pìjìng 背静 secluded

【僻陋】pìlòu (地区)偏僻而荒凉 (of an area) remote and desolate

【僻壤】pìrǎng 偏僻的地方 out-of-the-way place：穷乡～ impoverished and out-of-the-way village｜荒山～ barren and remote hills

澼 pì ☞［洴澼］(píngpì) on p.1490

甓 pì〈书 *fml*.〉砖 brick

鸊 pì［鸊鷉］(pìtī)水鸟，形状略像鸭，比鸭小，翼短小，不善飞，羽毛暗黄褐色，两翼灰褐色，颈和前胸浅赤褐色，腹部白色。通常浮在水面，有时潜入水中，捕食小鱼、昆虫等。grebe (*Podicipedidae*); aquatic diving bird, similar to a duck but smaller, and with a shorter wing span, of mostly dark brown plumage, with taupe coloured wings, light russet on its neck and breast, and white on the belly, and sometimes diving into the water to feed on small fish and insects

譬 pì 比喻；比方 analogy; metaphor; instance：～喻 metaphor｜～如 for example｜设～ assume an example

【譬方】pìfāng 比方 analogy

【譬如】pìrú 比如 for example; for instance; such as

【譬喻】pìyù 比喻 metaphor; simile; analogy; figure of speech

piān（ㄆㄧㄢ）

片 piān ☞ below
☞ piàn on p.1473

【片儿】piānr same as 片 piàn ①，用于'相片儿、画片儿、唱片儿'等词 as in 相片儿 xiàngpiānr，唱片儿 chàngpiānr，etc.

【片子】piān·zi ❶ 电影胶片，泛指影片 film; (in a broad sense) movie：换～ change film｜送～ send film ❷ 爱克斯光照相的底片 negative of a roentgenogram：拍～ take a negative ❸ 留声机的唱片 gramophone record; disc
☞ piàn·zi on p.1474

扁 piān［扁舟］(piānzhōu)小船 small boat; skiff：一叶～ a small boat
☞ biǎn on p.116

偏[1] piān ❶ 不正；倾斜（跟'正'相对 as opposed to 'upright'）not straight; inclined to one side; leaning：～锋 by-stroke (technique in calligraphy)｜太阳～西了。The sun is to the west now. ❷ 单独注重一方面或对人对事不公正 partial; prejudiced; emphasize one side or unfairly treat sb. or sth.：～重 lay particular stress on｜～爱 have partiality for sb. or sth.｜兼听则明，～信则暗 listening to both sides brings enlightenment; heeding only one side brings benightedness｜～于基础理论的研究 pay special attention to the study of foundation theories ❸ 辅助的；不占主要地位的 assistant; not occupying a leading position：～将 assistant general｜～师 auxiliary force ❹ 与某个标准相比有差距 differ from a certain standard; inequality or disparity：体温～高 temperature on the high side｜工资～低 relatively low salary ❺〈客套话 *pol*.〉表示先用或已用过茶饭等（多接用'了'字 oft. followed by 了·le）[used to indicate one has already eaten]：我～过了，您请吃吧。I have eaten already. You go ahead, please.

偏[2] piān 偏偏 wilfully; insistently; persistently; only; just：不让我去我～去。I was not allowed to go, but I insisted.｜庄稼正需要雨水的时候，可天～不下雨。The crops are in dire need of a rainfall, but unfortunately there is no sign of it.

【偏爱】piān'ài 在几个人或几件事物中特别喜爱其中的一个或一件 favour; have partiality for sth.; especially favour sb. or sth. among a group of persons or things：在国画中，他～写意画。In traditional Chinese painting, he is especially fond of freehand brushwork.

【偏安】piān'ān 指封建王朝失去中原而苟安于仅存的部分领土(of a feudal regime) be content to retain sovereignty over just a part of the country while the Central Plain is lost：～一隅 be content to exercise sovereignty over only part of the country

【偏差】piānchā ❶ 运动的物体离开确定方向的角度 deviation; angle formed by the departure of a moving object from an established direction：第一发炮弹打歪了，修正了～后，第二发便击中了目标。The first cannonball was misfired, but after the deviation had been rectified, the second attempt was successful. ❷ 工作上产生的过分或不及的差错 (of work, job, etc.) aberration; error

【偏饭】piānfàn ☞ 吃偏饭 chī piānfàn on p.257

【偏方】piānfāng（～儿 piānfāngr）民间流传不见于古典医学著作的中药方 folk remedy or prescription, not to be found in classical works on medicine

【偏房】piānfáng ❶ 指四合院中东西两厢的房子 wing-room; wing house; houses located on the east and west side of a traditional housing compound ❷ same as 妾 qiè ①

【偏废】piānfèi 重视几件事情中的某件或某些事而忽视其他 do one thing and neglect another; pay attention to one thing at the expense of another：工作与学习，二者不可～。Neither work nor study can be neglected.

【偏锋】piānfēng ❶ 书法上指用毛笔写字时笔锋斜出的笔势 slanting strokes in calligraphy：他的楷书常用～，别具一格。He has distinguished himself through his use of slanting strokes in regular script. ❷ 泛指写文章、说话等从侧面着手的方法 (in a broad sense) indirect approach to a subject (of speech, writing, etc.)

【偏好】piānhǎo〈方 *dial*.〉same as 偏巧

piānqiǎo ①:我正去他家找他,～在街上碰见了。I was on the way to his home, and happened to meet him in the street.

【偏好】piānhào 对某种事物特别爱好 have a special fondness for sth.:在曲艺中他～京韵大鼓。Amongst all Chinese folk art forms, he has a special fondness for story-telling in the Beijing dialect, accompanied by a drum.|防止凭个人的～处理问题 curb the practice of dealing with issues on the criterion of personal partiality

【偏护】piānhù 偏私袒护 be partial to and side with; be biased and shield:一味～孩子,不利于他们健康成长。It is not good for the healthy growth of children to take their part blindly, without question.

【偏激】piānjī (意见、主张等)过火 (of opinion, proposition, etc.) extreme:言词～ extreme words|～情绪 extreme mood

【偏见】piānjiàn 偏于一方面的见解;成见 prejudice; bias:消除～ eliminate bias

【偏枯】piānkū ❶〈中医 *Chin. med.*〉指半身不遂的病 hemiplegia ❷〈比喻 *fig.*〉偏于一方面,发展不平衡 lopsided; unbalanced development

【偏劳】piānláo〈客套话 *pol.*〉用于请人帮忙或谢人代自己做事 [used when asking sb. for help or thanking sb. for his help]:请你～吧,我实在脱不开身。Can I trouble you to do this? I really cannot stop what I am doing at the moment.|谢谢你,多～了。Thanks for all your trouble.

【偏离】piānlí 指因出现偏差而离开确定的轨道、方向等 deviate; diverge; depart from the established track or direction:炮弹～了射击目标。The cannonball went off course on the path to its intended target.|飞机～了航线。The aircraft deviated from its flight path.

【偏盲】piānmáng 指一只眼失明 lose the sight of one eye; be blind in one eye

【偏旁】piānpáng (～儿 piānpángr)在汉字形体中常常出现的某些组成部分,如'位、住、俭、停'中的'亻','国、固、圈、围'中的'囗','偏、翩、篇、匾'中的'扁','拎、伶、翎、零'中的'令',都是偏旁 character components or basic structural parts of Chinese characters, for example, 亻 as in 位 wèi,住 zhù,俭 jiǎn,停 tíng; 囗 as in 国 guó,固 gù,圈 quān,围 wéi; 扁 biǎn as in 偏 piān,翩 piān,篇 piān,匾 biǎn; and 令 lìng as in 拎 līn,伶 líng,翎 líng,零 líng

【偏僻】piānpì 离城市或中心区远,交通不便 remote; out-of-the-way:～的山区 remote mountainous area|地点～ at an out-of-the-way location

【偏偏】piānpiān〈副词 *adv.*〉❶ 表示故意跟客观要求或客观情况相反 insistently; persistently; purposely do sth. in direct opposition to the objective requirement or situation:经过大家讨论,问题都解决了,他～还要钻牛角尖。The problem was solved after discussion, but he nevertheless went to the unnecessary trouble of looking further into it. ❷ 表示事实跟所希望或期待的恰恰相反 contrary to expectations:星期天他来找我,～我不在家。He called on me last Sunday, but I happened to be out. ❸ 表示范围,跟'单单'略同 only; alone:别的小组都完成了定额,为什么～咱们没完成? All the other groups have achieved their production quota, why have we yet to finish?

【偏颇】piānpō〈书 *fml.*〉偏于一方面;不公平 biased; partial; unfair:这篇文章的立论失之～。The line of reasoning in this article is biased.

【偏巧】piānqiǎo ❶ 恰巧 it so happened that:我们正在找他,～他来了。He showed up just as we were looking for him. ❷ same as 偏偏 piānpiān ②:我找他两次,～都不在家。I have been to his house twice, but he happened to be out both times.

【偏衫】piānshān 僧尼的一种服装,斜披在左肩上 Buddhist vestment worn draped over the left shoulder

【偏生】piānshēng〈方 *dial.*〉same as 偏偏 piānpiān ①②

【偏师】piānshī〈书 *fml.*〉指在主力军翼侧协助作战的部队 auxiliary force; back-up troops fighting on the flank or wing of the main force

【偏食】[1] piānshí 日偏食和月偏食的统称 common name for partial solar eclipse and partial lunar eclipse

☞ 日食 rìshí on p. 1627 and 月食 yuèshí on p. 2371

【偏食】[2] piānshí 只喜欢吃某几种食物,如只喜欢吃鱼、肉,而不喜欢吃蔬菜 partiality for certain foods e.g. liking for fish and meat but not vegetables; limited diet

【偏手儿】piānshǒur ☞ 拉偏手儿 lā piānshǒur on p. 1138

【偏私】piānsī 照顾私情 favouritism; partiality; bias

【偏瘫】piāntān 身体一侧发生瘫痪,多由脑内出血而引起 hemiplegia; paralysis of one lateral half or part of the body as a result of a brain hemmorrhage; also 半身不遂 bàn shēn bù suí

【偏袒】piāntǎn 袒护双方中的一方 be partial to and side with; give unprincipled protection to one of two parties; ☞ 左袒 zuǒtǎn on p. 2573

【偏疼】piānténg 对晚辈中某个人或某些人特别疼爱 favour one or some (of one's juniors) more than others

【偏题】piāntí 冷僻的考题 catch (or trick) question (in an examination):出～ set a trick question

【偏析】piānxī 合金在凝固过程中形成的化学成

分不均匀的现象 segregation; disproportion of the chemical components of an alloy during meiosis

【偏向】piānxiàng ❶ 不正确的倾向(多指掌握政策过左或过右,或在几项工作中只注重某一项) erroneous tendency; Leftist or Rightist deviation in the implementation of a policy; stress laid on sth. to the neglect of sth. else):发现~,要及时纠正。As soon as we discover any deviation, it must be rectified. ❷ 偏于赞成(某一方面) prefer; incline:今年春游我~于去香山。I feel inclined to go to the Fragrant Hills for this year's spring outing. ❸(对某一方)无原则的支持或袒护;不公正 be partial to; give unprincipled support or protection to (one side)

【偏心】piānxīn 偏向一方面;不公正 partiality; bias:说~话 biased talk|对待学生不能~。One must not treat students with partiality.

【偏心轮】piānxīnlún 一种轴孔偏向一边的轮形零件。装在轴上,轴旋转时,轮的外缘推动另一机件,产生往复运动。多用来带动机械的开关、活门等。eccentric wheel; eccentric; wheel-shaped mechanical device consisting of a disk through which a shaft is keyed eccentrically, and a circular strap which works freely around the rim of the disk to communicate its motion to one end of a rod whose other end is constrained to move in a straight line so as to produce reciprocating motion; usu. used to drive the switch and valve of a machine

【偏心眼儿】piānxīnyǎnr 指偏向一方的心地 intentionally partial:我爷爷有~,让哥哥去,就是不让我去。My grandpa is biased; he let my brother go there but would not allow me. also 偏心眼子 piānxīnyǎn•zi

【偏远】piānyuǎn 偏僻而遥远 remote; faraway:~地区 remote area

【偏振】piānzhèn 横波的振动矢量(垂直于波的传播方向)偏于某些方向的现象。纵波只沿着波的方向振动,所以没有偏振。polarization; action of the vibration vector of transverse waves (perpendicular to the radiate direction of waves) deviating from an established direction. Longitudinal waves vibrate parallel to the direction of waves only, and thus have no polarization.

【偏执】piānzhí 偏激而固执 stubbornly biased:~的见解 stubbornly biased view

【偏重】piānzhòng 着重一方面 stress one thing (at the expense of another):学习只~记忆而忽略理解是不行的。When studying one should not stress memorization at the expense of comprehension.

【偏转】piānzhuǎn 射线、磁针、仪表指针等因受力而改变方向或位置 deflection; (rays, magnetic needles, indicators, etc.) turn from a fixed direction or position as a result of stress

犏 piān [犏牛](piānniú)公黄牛和母牦牛交配所生的第一代杂种牛,比牦牛驯顺,比黄牛力气大。母犏牛产乳量高,公犏牛没有生殖能力,母犏牛可以和黄牛或牦牛交配繁殖后代。产于我国西南地区。first-generation hybrid of ox and female yak that is more docile than a yak and stronger than an ox; breed developed in southwestern China, the female having a high yield of milk, and the male having no reproductive capability while the female can propagate by mating with an ox or yak

篇 piān ❶ 首尾完整的文章 full article:~章段落 paragraphs of an article|《荀子·劝学~》*Xunzi • Exhortation on Learning* ❷(~儿 piānr)写着或印着文字的单张纸 a sheet of paper, usu. written or printed with words:歌~儿 song sheet|单~儿讲义 lecture sheet ❸(~儿 piānr)〈量词 *classifier*〉用于文章、纸张、书页(一篇是两页)等 sheet; leaf; piece, usu. in two pages (for paper, articles, book leaves, etc.):一~论文 an essay|三~儿纸 three sheets of paper|这本书缺了一~儿。A leaf is missing from this book.

【篇幅】piān•fu ❶ 文章的长短 length (of a piece of writing):这篇评论的~只有一千来字。This comment only comprises a thousand characters. ❷ 书籍报刊等篇页的数量(of books, newspapers, magazines, etc.) number of pages an article takes up:用整版~刊登这篇文章 publish this article in full page

【篇目】piānmù ❶ 书籍中篇章的标题 chapter title of a book ❷ 书籍中篇章标题的目录 table of contents; list of articles

【篇页】piānyè 篇和页,泛指篇章 leaves and pages; chapter:这个问题在全书的不少~中都有论述。Several chapters of this book discuss and elaborate on this issue.

【篇章】piānzhāng 篇和章,泛指文章 sections and chapters; (in a broad sense) writings:~结构 structure of an article ◇历史~ chapters in history

【篇子】piān•zi same as 篇 piān ②

翩 piān 〈书 *fml.*〉很快地飞,形容动作轻快 fly swiftly:~然 lightly|~若惊鸿 be slim and graceful

【翩翩】piānpiān ❶ 形容轻快地跳舞,也形容动物飞舞 dance lightly; (of animals) flutter:~起舞 flutter|~飞鸟 fluttering birds ❷〈书 *fml.*〉形容举止洒脱(多指青年男子 oft. referring to young men) elegant; light-hearted:~少年 elegant young man|风度~ in an elegant manner

【翩然】piānrán 〈书 *fml.*〉形容动作轻快的样子 lightly; trippingly; swiftly:~飞舞 fly swiftly|~而至 come tripping down

【翩跹】piānxiān 〈书 *fml.*〉形容轻快地跳舞 dance lightly:~起舞 dance with quick, light steps; dance trippingly

pián (ㄆㄧㄢˊ)

便 pián ☞ below
☞ biàn on p.121

【便便】piánpián 形容肥胖 bulging; swelling; fat:大腹～ potbellied

【便宜】pián·yi ❶ 价钱低 cheap; at a bargain price ❷ 不应得的利益 unearned gains; unmerited advantages:占～ gain extra advantage by unfair means ❸ 使得到便宜 let sb. off lightly; give sb. unmerited advantages:～了你。You have been let off lightly.
☞ biànyí on p.122

骈 pián 并列的;对偶的 parallel; antithetical:～句 parallel sentences|～肩(肩挨着肩,形容人多) shoulder to shoulder (of a crowd)

【骈俪】piánlì 文章的对偶句法 (of writing) art of parallelism

【骈拇枝指】pián mǔ zhī zhǐ 骈拇指脚的大拇指跟二拇指相连,枝指指手的大拇指或小拇指旁边多长出来的一个手指。骈拇枝指比喻多余的或不必要的事物。double toe or finger; 骈拇 refers to the big toe being webbed to the adjacent toe and 枝指 refers to an additional finger next to the thumb or little finger;(fig.) superfluous; matters redundant or unnecessary

【骈体】piántǐ 要求词句整齐对偶的文体,重视声韵的和谐和词藻的华丽,盛行于六朝 (区别于'散体' as compared with '*santi*', a prose style free from parallelism') parallel style; peculiarly artificial prose style much cultivated during the Six Dynasties, characterized by parallel construction of pairs of sentences and counterbalancing of tonal patterns without the use of rhyme

【骈阗】piántián 〈书 *fml.*〉聚集;罗列;众多 close together; side by side; numerous:士女～。Men and women are everywhere, side by side. also 骈填 piántián or 骈田 piántián

【骈文】piánwén 用骈体形式写的文章 parallel prose; prose written in the parallel style

【骈枝】piánzhī 〈书 *fml.*〉骈拇枝指的略语 short for 骈拇枝指 piǎn mǔ zhī zhǐ:～机构 superfluous institution

胼 pián ☞ below

【胼胝】piánzhī 趼子(jiǎn·zi) callosity; callus; also 跰趾 piánzhī

【胼胝体】piánzhītǐ 大脑两半球的底部联合大脑两半球的神经纤维组织 callosum; wide arched band of commissural fibers connecting the two cerebral hemispheres of the brain at the base of the longitudinal fissure;(图见 ☞ figure for 脑 nǎo on p.1394)

缏 pián 〈方 *dial.*〉用针缝 stitch; sew with needle;
☞ biàn on p.123

楩 pián 古书上说的一种树 a tree genus as described in ancient writings

跰 pián [跰跹] (piánzhī) same as 胼胝 piánzhī

蹁 pián 〈书 *fml.*〉形容走路脚不正 lame; walk with a limp

【蹁跹】piánxiān 〈书 *fml.*〉形容旋转舞动 whirl about (when dancing)

piǎn (ㄆㄧㄢˇ)

谝 piǎn 〈方 *dial.*〉夸耀;显示 show off:～能 show off one's abilities, skills, etc.

piàn (ㄆㄧㄢˋ)

片 piàn ❶ (～儿 piànr)平而薄的东西,一般不很大 flat, thin, small piece of sth.; slice; flake:布～儿 small pieces of cloth|玻璃～儿 fragments of glass|纸～儿 scraps of paper|明信～儿 post cards ❷ 指电影片、电视剧等 film; TV play:～约 film contract|～酬 pay for making a film ❸ (～儿 piànr)指较大地区内划分的较小地区 part of a place:分～传达 pass on (news, instructions, etc.) district by district ❹ 用刀横割成薄片(多指肉) (of meat) carve into slices:～肉片儿 slice meat; cut a piece of meat into slices ❺ 不全的;零星的;简短的 incomplete; brief; partial:～面 one-sided|～刻 a short while|～言 brief words|～纸只字 a few characters on a small piece of paper ❻ 〈量词 *classifier*〉a)用于成片的东西 [for slices, tablets, etc.]:两～儿药 two tablets b)用于地面和水面等 [for a piece of land, a stretch of water etc.]:一～草地 a tract of meadow|一～汪洋 a vast expanse of water c)用于景色、气象、声音、语言、心意等(前面用'一'字 used with the numeral 一 yī) [for a scenario, kind of atmosphere, sound, language, feeling, etc.]:一～新气象 a new look|一～欢腾 a scene of great rejoicing|一～脚步声 a patter of footsteps|一～胡言 all nonsense|一～真心 in all sincerity
☞ piān on p.1470

【片酬】piànchóu 付给参加拍摄电影片或电视剧的演员的报酬 remuneration for an actor or actress playing a role in a film or a TV play

【片段】piànduàn 整体当中的一段(多指文章、小说、戏剧、生活、经历等 oft. of an article, novel, drama, life, experience, etc.) part of an entirety; extract; fragment; also 片断 piànduàn

【片断】piànduàn ❶ same as 片段 piànduàn ❷ 零碎;不完整 fragmentary; incomplete:～经验 fragments of one's experiences|～的社会现象

slices of social phenomena

【片甲不存】piàn jiǎ bù cún 形容全军被消灭 the army has been completely wiped out; also 片甲不留 piàn jiǎ bù liú

【片警】piànjǐng 负责某一片地区社会治安工作的警察 the police responsible for social security in a certain area; also 片儿警 piànrjǐng

【片刻】piànkè 极短的时间;一会儿 a short while; an instant:～不离 not leave even for an instant|稍等～ wait a moment

【片面】piànmiàn ❶ 单方面的 unilateral:～之词 an account given by one party only ❷ 偏于一面的(跟'全面'相对 as opposed to 'comprehensive') one-sided:～性 one-sidedness|～观点 a lopsided view|～地看问题 take a one-sided approach to problems

【片面性】piànmiànxìng 形而上学思想方法的一种表现。在认识事物时,不是全面地去分析具体事物的矛盾,抹煞事物所固有的共性与个性、绝对与相对的辩证关系。one-sidedness; metaphysical way of thinking where the contradictions of a specific matter are not comprehensively analyzed, and the dialectical relationships between the matter's inherent commonness and individuality, and absoluteness and relativity, are disregarded

【片儿会】piànrhuì 按地区临时分组召开的会 neighborhood meeting; temporary group meeting

【片儿汤】piànrtāng 一种面食,用和好了的面擀成薄片,弄成小块,煮熟连汤吃 soup containing thin slices of dough

【片时】piànshí same as 片刻 piànkè

【片头】piàntóu 电影片、电视片主要内容前面的部分,一般有片名、制片厂名、演职员名等 credits; preamble to a film or a TV play, usu. including the title, the name of the producer and the cast

【片瓦无存】piàn wǎ wú cún 一块整瓦也没有了,形容房屋全被毁坏(of house) not a single tile remaining — completely destroyed

【片言】piànyán 简短的几句话 a few words; brief words:～只字 (in) only a few words|～可决 can be settled in a few words

【片言只字】piàn yán zhī zì ☞ 片纸只字 piàn zhǐ zhī zì

【片艳纸】piànyànzhǐ 一种一面光的纸,韧性较强 machine-glazed, resilient quality of paper (glossy on one side)

【片约】piànyuē 约请演员参加拍摄某部电影片或电视剧所签订的协议 invitation to an actor or actress to play a part in a certain film or a TV play

【片纸只字】piàn zhǐ zhī zì 指零碎的文字材料 fragments of writing; also 片言只字 piàn yán zhī zì

【片子】piàn·zi ❶ same as 片 piàn①:铁～ small pieces of sheet iron ❷ 名片 name card ☞ piān·zi on p.1470

【片子地】piàn·zidì 〈方 *dial.*〉小块荒地 small plot of wasteland

骗[1] piàn ❶ 用谎言或诡计使人上当;欺骗 deceive; fool; hoodwink sb. with lies or tricks:～人 deceive sb.|受～ be taken in ❷ 用欺骗的手段取得 cheat; swindle; obtain by deceitful means:～钱 cheat sb. out of his money

骗[2](騗) piàn ☞ 骗马 piànmǎ and 骗腿儿 piàntuǐr

【骗局】piànjú 骗人的圈套 fraud; hoax; confidence trick:设下～ set a fraud

【骗马】piànmǎ 骗腿儿上马 swing (or leap) into the saddle; mount a horse

【骗取】piànqǔ 用欺骗的手段取得 gain sth. by cheating; cheat (or trick, swindle) sb. out of sth.:～钱财 defraud sb. of his money|～爱情 steal away sb.'s love|～上级的信任 worm one's way into a superior's trust

【骗术】piànshù 骗人的伎俩 deceitful trick; ruse; hoax

【骗腿儿】piàntuǐr 侧身抬起一条腿 swing one's leg sideways:他一～跳上自行车就走了。He swung onto the saddle of his bike and rode off.

【骗子】piàn·zi 骗取财物的人 swindler; imposter; cheat; trickster:江湖～ mountebank ◇政治～ political swindler

piāo(ㄆㄧㄠ)

剽 piāo ❶ 抢劫;掠夺 rob; hijack; plunder:～掠 plunder|～窃 plagiarize ❷ 动作敏捷 (of movement, action, etc.) nimble; swift:～悍 quick and fierce

【剽悍】piāohàn 敏捷而勇猛 agile and brave; quick and fierce; also 慓悍 piāohàn

【剽窃】piāoqiè 抄袭窃取(别人的著作) plagiarize (works by other people):～行为 plagiarism; plagiary

【剽取】piāoqǔ same as 剽窃 piāoqiè plagiarize

【剽袭】piāoxí 剽窃;抄袭 plagiarize

漂 piāo ❶ 停留在液体表面不下沉 float; drift; stay on the surface of liquid:树叶在水面上～着。Leaves floated on the water. ❷ 顺着风向、液体流动的方向移动 move downstream or in the direction of the wind:远远～过来一只小船。A small boat drifted in from far away.

☞ piǎo on p.1476 and piào on p.1477

【漂泊】piāobó ❶ 随波浮动或停泊 drift or berth (in the direction of the waves):游艇～在附近的海面上。A yacht drifted in the sea nearby. ❷〈比喻 *fig.*〉职业生活不固定,东奔西走 wander about; have no steady profession or lifestyle:～异乡 wander aimlessly in a strange land‖also 飘浮 piāofú

【漂浮】piāofú ❶ 漂 float：水上～着几只小船。A few boats are floating on the water. ◇离开了幼儿园，孩子们的笑容总是～在我的脑海里。After I left the kindergarten, the children's smiles still hovered in my mind. ❷〈比喻 *fig.*〉工作不塌实，不深入（of style of work）superficial；on an unsteady footing：作风～ showy style of work ‖ also 飘泊 piāobó

【漂流】piāoliú ❶ 漂在水面随水浮动 be carried along on the water；drift about：沿江～进行科学考察 be carried along by the river current on a scientific investigation ❷ 漂泊；流浪 wander；roam about：～四海 wander around the world ‖ also 飘流 piāoliú

【漂儿】piāor〈方 *dial.*〉鱼漂 fishing float

【漂移】piāoyí ❶ 漂浮的物体朝某个方向移动 drift；floating object moving in a certain direction：冰块随着海流～。The block of ice drifted along on the sea current. ❷ 电子器件受环境温度、电压变化等的影响，使电子线路的工作频率、电压等不能稳定在某一点的现象 drift；（of electronic units） failure of the working frequency and pressure of electronic circuits to be fixed at a certain point as a result of changes in the pressure or temperature of the external environment：频率～ frequency drift｜零点～ zero drift

【漂游】piāoyóu ❶ 轻缓地浮动 move slowly；drift：～的云 moving clouds｜顺水～ drift downstream ❷ same as 漂泊 piāobó②：四处～ wander about

慓 piāo〈书 *fml.*〉same as 剽 piāo ②

【慓悍】piāohàn same as 剽悍 piāohàn

缥 piāo［缥缈］(piāomiǎo)形容隐隐约约，若有若无 dimly discernible；misty；faint：虚无～ visionary；ethereal｜云雾～ misty；also 飘渺 piāomiǎo

☞ piǎo on p. 1476

飘(飃) piāo ❶ 随风摇动或飞扬 wave or flutter (in the wind)：～摇 sway｜红旗～～。The Red Flag flutters.｜外面～着雪花。Snowflakes are drifting outdoors. ❷ 形容腿部发软，走路不稳 walk unsteadily due to a weakness in the legs：两腿发～weak, unsteady legs ❸ 轻浮；不塌实 giddy；anxious：作风有点～ a little bit giddy (in lifestyle, approach to study or work, etc.)

【飘泊】piāobó same as 漂泊 piāobó

【飘尘】piāochén 颗粒较小能够长时间在空中飘浮的粉尘，可以随气流飘到很远的地方，造成大面积污染 airborne dust；small-grain dust that floats in the air for a long time and that can follow air currents for a long distance, polluting large areas

【飘带】piāo·dài (～儿piāo·dàir)旗帜、衣帽等上面做装饰的带子，下端多为剑头形，可随风飘动 ribbon；streamer；decorative band on a flag, item of clothing, or cap, usu. arrow-shaped at one end, that flutters in the wind

【飘荡】piāodàng ❶ 随风飘动或随波浮动 move in the wind or with the tide；drift；float；flutter：红旗迎风～。The red flag flapped in the wind.｜小船在水中～。The boat drifted on the water.｜校园里～着欢乐的歌声。Joyous singing wafted through the campus. ❷ same as 漂泊 piāobó②：弃家避难，四处～run away from home and wander about seeking refuge

【飘动】piāodòng （随着风、波浪等）摆动；飘 float (in the air or upon the waves)；flutter；drift：彩旗迎风～。Colourful flags flapped in the wind.｜小船在水面上～。A small boat drifted on the water.

【飘拂】piāofú 轻轻飘动 float slowly：白云～ floating white clouds

【飘浮】piāofú same as 漂浮 piāofú

【飘忽】piāohū ❶（风、云等）轻快地移动（of wind, cloud, etc.）move swiftly；fleet：烟雾～ foggy ❷ 摇摆；浮动 swing；sway；rock：情绪～不定 in uncertain mood

【飘零】piāolíng ❶（花、叶等）坠落；飘落（of flowers, leaves, etc.）fade and fall；whirl and scatter：黄叶～。Brown leaves came whirling down.｜雪花～。Snowflakes came falling down. ❷〈比喻 *fig.*〉失去依靠，生活不安定 adrift；dispossessed；live in uncertainty：四处～ wander about｜～半世 wander for half one's life

【飘流】piāoliú same as 漂流 piāoliú

【飘落】piāoluò 飘着降下来 drift and fall slowly；descend slowly and lightly：黄叶～。Brown leaves drifted slowly down.｜伞兵徐徐～。The paratroopers descended slowly through the air.

【飘渺】piāomiǎo same as 缥缈 piāomiǎo

【飘飘然】piāopiāorán ❶ 轻飘飘的，好像浮在空中 feel high；feeling of floating in the air：喝了几杯酒，脚下不觉有些～。After having drunk several glasses of wine, he felt light on his feet. ❷ 形容很得意 self-satisfied；complacent；smug：听了几句奉承话，他不由得～起来。Having been flattered on a few occasions, he could not help but feel complacent.

【飘然】piāorán ❶ 形容飘摇的样子 float in the air：浮云～而过。Fleecy clouds floated by. ❷ 形容轻捷或迅速的样子 swiftly；nimbly：他骑上白马～而去。He mounted a horse and left swiftly. ❸ 形容轻松愉快的样子 happy and relaxed：～自在 easy and comfortable

【飘洒】piāosǎ 飘舞着落下来 drift with the wind；swirl down；fall：细雨～。There was a fine drizzle in the air.｜天空～着雪花。Snowflakes danced in the air.

P

【飘洒】piāo·sa (姿态)自然;不呆板 (of posture) natural; free and easy; unconstrained: 他写的字很～。He writes characters in natural, unconstrained strokes. | 仪态～ natural deportment

【飘散】piāosàn (烟雾、气体等)飘扬散开;飞散 (of smoke, mist, gas, etc.) drift away; disperse:炊烟随着晚风袅袅～。Smoke from the kitchen chimneys curled upwards in the evening breeze. | 微风里～着一股清香。A fragrance floated on the breeze.

【飘逝】piāoshì ❶ 飘动流散 float and disperse: 白云～。White clouds floated by. ❷ 消逝 pass by; wear away; disappear: 岁月～。Time passed by.

【飘舞】piāowǔ 随风飞舞或摇摆 rock or sway in the wind:雪花漫天～。A flurry of snowflakes filled the sky. | 柳条迎风～。The willow branches swayed in the breeze.

【飘扬】piāoyáng 在空中随风摆动 wave in the wind; flutter; fly:彩旗迎风～。Colourful flags fluttered in the wind. also 飘飏 piāoyáng

【飘摇】piāoyáo 在空中随风摇动 sway in the wind:烟云缭绕,～上升。Mist and clouds drifted up. also 飘飖 piāoyáo

【飘飖】piāoyáo same as 飘摇 piāoyáo

【飘曳】piāoyè 随同摆动;摇曳 sway:柔软的柳枝在晨风中～。Willow branches swayed in the morning breeze.

【飘移】piāoyí 飘流移动 drift:帆船向岸边～过来。Sailboats drifted towards the bank. | 降落伞向着目标方向～。Parachutes drifted towards their target.

【飘逸】piāoyì ❶〈书 *fml*.〉洒脱,自然,与众不同 possessing natural grace; free and easy; be different from others:神采～ have an elegant bearing | 字体凝重而～ in thick and free stroke ❸ 飘浮;飘散 float;scatter:白云～white clouds floating about | 院子里～着花香。The courtyard is permeated with the fragrance of flowers.

【飘溢】piāoyì 飘荡洋溢 drift about:公园里～着兰花的阵阵清香。The fragrance of orchids drifted through the park.

【飘游】piāoyóu 漫无目的地游荡 wander aimlessly:四处～ wander about

【飘悠】piāo·you 在空中或水面上轻缓地浮动 drift leisurely (through the air or on the water):小船在水里慢慢地～着。A small boat drifted slowly and leisurely through the water. | 几片树叶飘飘悠悠地落下来。A few leaves whirled to the ground.

螵 piāo [螵蛸](piāoxiāo)螳螂的卵块,干燥后可入药 egg capsule of a mantis, usu. used for medicine when dried

piáo (ㄆㄧㄠˊ)

朴 Piáo 姓 a surname
☞ pō on p. 1491, pò on p. 1493 and pǔ on p. 1500

嫖(闞) piáo 男子玩弄妓女 (of men) visit prostitutes; go whoring: ～妓 visit prostitutes | ～娼 whoring

【嫖客】piáokè 指玩弄妓女的男子 brothel (or whorehouse) whoremonger; whoremaster; frequenter

瓢 piáo (～儿 piáor) 用来舀(yǎo)水或撮取面粉等的器具,多用对半剖开的匏瓜做成,也有用木头挖成的 gourd ladle; wooden dipper; utensil for bailing out water or gathering up flour, usu. made from a split gourd or wood

【瓢泼】piáopō 形容雨大 heavy rain: ～大雨 torrential rain; downpour

【瓢子】piáo·zi〈方 *dial*.〉❶ 瓢 gourd ladle ❷ 匙子 spoon

薸 piáo〈方 *dial*.〉浮萍 duckweed (*Lemna*)

piǎo (ㄆㄧㄠˇ)

莩 piǎo same as 殍 piǎo
☞ fú on p. 597

殍 piǎo ☞ 饿殍 èpiǎo on p. 507

漂 piǎo ❶ 漂白 bleach: ～过的布特别白。Cloth becomes much whiter after being bleached. ❷ 用水冲去杂质 rinse; clear away impurities with water: ～朱砂 rinse vermilion
☞ piāo on p. 1474 and piào on p. 1477

【漂白】piǎobái 使本色或带颜色的纤维、织品等变成白色,通常使用过氧化氢、次氯酸钠、漂白粉和二氧化硫等 bleach; make fibers or fabrics whiter through the use of hydrogen peroxide, sodium hypochlorite, bleaching powder, or sulfur dioxide

【漂白粉】piǎobáifěn 无机化合物,化学式 $Ca(ClO)_2$。白色粉末,有氯气的臭味,是常用的消毒剂和漂白剂。bleaching powder; inorganic compound, chemical formula $Ca(ClO)_2$, in white powder form with the odour of chlorite, widely used as sanitizing agent or bleach

【漂染】piǎorǎn 对纺织品进行漂白和染色 (of textiles) bleaching and dyeing

【漂洗】piǎoxǐ 用水冲洗 rinse: ～衣裳 rinse clothes

缥 piǎo〈书 *fml*.〉❶ 青白色 pale green ❷ 青白色丝织品 pale-green silk
☞ piāo on p. 1475

瞟 piǎo 斜着眼睛看 look askance at; glance sideways at:他一面说话,一面用眼～老李。While he was speaking, he cast a sidelong glance at Lao Li.

piào(ㄆㄧㄠˋ)

票 piào ❶ 作为凭证的纸片 ticket; a slip of paper used as a certificate:车~ bus ticket|戏~ theater ticket|投~ cast a vote ❷(~儿 piàor)钞票 bank note; bill:大~ notes of high face-value|零~儿 notes of small denominations ❸(~儿 piàor)〈旧时 *old*〉强盗称抢来做抵押的人 hostage; person held for ransom by kidnappers:绑~儿 kidnap|赎~儿 ransom a kidnapped person ❹〈方 *dial.*〉〈量词 *classifier*〉:一~货 a shipment of goods|一~生意 a deal|一~买卖 a business transaction ❺ 指非职业性的戏曲表演 non-professional performance (of opera, etc.):玩儿~ perform as an amateur|~友儿 amateur performer

【票车】piàochē〈方 *dial.*〉指运载旅客的列车 passenger train

【票额】piào'é 票面数额 sum stated on a check or bill; denomination; face value

【票房】[1] piàofáng (~儿 piàofángr)戏院、火车站、轮船码头等处的售票处 ticket office (at a railway station, airport, etc.); box office (at a theatre, stadium, etc.)

【票房】[2] piàofáng (~儿 piàofángr)〈旧时 *old*〉指票友聚会练习的处所 club for amateur performers (of Beijing opera, etc.)

【票房价值】piàofáng jiàzhí 指上演电影、戏剧等因卖票而获得的经济效益 box-office value; profits gained from selling tickets (for films, plays, etc.)

【票根】piàogēn 票根的存根 counterfoil; stub

【票号】piàohào〈旧时 *old*〉指山西商人所经营的以汇兑为主要业务的钱庄。在清末曾操纵全国的金融,是当时最大的商业资本。draft bank (banking institution established by Shanxi merchants during the late Qing Dynasty which dealt in drafts, or bills of exchange, and served as the largest source of commercial capital, having all financial dealings under its control); also 票庄 piàozhuāng

【票汇】piàohuì 凭邮局或银行签发的汇款票据领取汇款的汇兑 draft remittance; remittance by draft endorsed by a post office or bank

【票据】piàojù ❶ 按照法律规定形式制成的写明有支付一定货币金额义务的证件 bill; note; legal certification of obligation to pay a certain sum of money ❷ 出纳或运送货物的凭证 voucher; receipt; certificate verifying the receipt and payment of money or the transportation of goods

【票面】piàomiàn 钞票和某些票据上所标明的金额 face value; nominal value; the sum of money stated on banknote and other bills

【票选】piàoxuǎn 用投票的方式选举 elect (or vote) by ballot

【票友】piàoyǒu 称业余的戏曲演员 amateur performer of a traditional opera

【票证】piàozhèng 由有关部门发的购买某些物品等的凭证,如粮票、油票、布票等 coupons; tickets or certificates issued by certain government departments for purchasing rationed articles, e.g. grain coupons; oil coupons; clothing coupons

【票庄】piàozhuāng same as 票号 piàohào

【票子】piào·zi 钞票 banknote; paper money; bill

僄 piào〈书 *fml.*〉❶ 轻便敏捷 swift and nimble:~悍(轻捷勇猛) agile and brave ❷ 轻薄 frivolous

嘌 piào〈书 *fml.*〉疾速 fast; speedy

【嘌呤】piàolìng 有机化合物,化学式 $C_5H_4N_4$。无色晶体,在人体内嘌呤氧化而变成尿酸。purine; organic compound, chemical formula $C_5H_4N_4$, colourless crystal that oxidizes into uric acid in the human body

漂 piào〈方 *dial.*〉(事情、账目等)落空 (of a matter, account, etc.) come to nothing; fall through; draw a blank; be in vain:那事没有什么指望,~了。That matter is hopeless; it has come to nothing.

☞ piāo on p.1474 and piǎo on p.1476

【漂亮】piào·liang ❶ 好看;美观 sassy; nice-looking; pretty; beautiful:她长得~。She is pretty.|衣服~ beautiful clothes|节日里,孩子们打扮得漂漂亮亮的。Children dress smartly at festivals. ❷ 出色 remarkable; brilliant; outstanding; beautiful:事情办得~。A nice job indeed.|打了一个~仗 win a brilliant victory in a battle|普通话说得很~ speak beautiful Mandarin Chinese

【漂亮话】piào·lianghuà 说得好听而不兑现的话 fine words; high-sounding words of no actual value:说~没有用,做出来才算。It is not high-sounding words but actual deeds that really count.

骠 piào〈书 *fml.*〉❶ 形容马快跑 (of horses) galloping; running fast ❷ 勇猛 brave; valiant:~勇 brave

☞ biāo on p.128

piē(ㄆㄧㄝ)

氕 piē 氢的同位素之一,符号 ^1H (protium)。原子核中有一个质子,是氢的主要成分,普通的氢中含有 99.98% 的氕。protium(^1H); proton within atomic nucleus, making up 99.98 per cent of what is contained in hydrogen

撇[1] piē 弃置不顾;抛弃 cast aside; throw away; abandon:~开 leave aside|把老一套都~了 reject stereotypes

撇[2] piē 从液体表面上轻轻地舀 skim; carefully scoop off the surface of liquid: ～油 skim off the grease | ～沫儿 skim off the scum ☞ piě on p. 1478

【撇开】piē//·kāi 放在一边;丢开不管 leave aside; lay away: 撇得开 be able to set sth. aside | 撇不开 unable to set sth. aside | 先～次要问题不谈,只谈主要的两点 leave aside the questions of minor importance and focus on discussing the two main points

【撇弃】piēqì 抛弃;丢开 cast away; abandon; discard: ～不顾 cast aside and abandon

【撇脱】piētuō 〈方 *dial*.〉❶ 简便;容易 simple; easy; convenient: 说得～,你来试试! It's easy to say; give it a try yourself! ❷ 洒脱;干脆利落 frank; straightforward

瞥 piē 很快地看一下 shoot a glance at; glare at; snatch a glimpse: 一～ a glimpse | 弟弟要插嘴,哥哥～了他一眼。He was about to butt in when his elder brother darted him a look of disapproval.

【瞥见】piējiàn 一眼看见 catch a glimpse of; catch sight of: 在街上,无意间～了多年不见的老朋友。While on the street I caught sight of an old friend whom I had not seen for years.

【瞥视】piēshì 很快地看一下 cast a quick glance at: 他和蔼地～了一下每个听讲学生。He gave each of the students attending the lecture a brief, amiable glance.

piě (ㄆㄧㄝˇ)

苤 piě [苤蓝](piě·lan) ❶ 甘蓝的一种,叶子卵形或长圆形,有长柄,叶片有波状缺刻或裂片,花黄白色。茎部发达,扁圆形,肉质,是普通蔬菜。kohlrabi (*Brassica oleracea* var. *gongylodes*); a kind of cabbage with leaves that are oval with corrugated notches or lobes, yellow-white flowers, and an enlarged, fleshy, turnip-shaped edible stem ❷ 这种植物的茎 stem of this plant ‖ also 球茎甘蓝 qiújīng gānlán

撇 piě ❶ 平着扔出去 throw sideward; fling; cast: ～砖头 throw a brick | ～手榴弹 throw hand grenades ◇把早晨说的事～到脑后去了。(He) forget the matter discussed in the morning. ❷ 用撇嘴的动作表示轻视、不以为然或不高兴等 curl one's lip (in contempt, disbelief or disappointment): 她嘴一～,什么也没说,走开了。She curled her lips and left without saying a single word. ❸ (～儿 piěr)汉字的笔画,向左斜下,形状是'丿'left-falling stroke (in Chinese calligraphy) ❹ 〈量词 *classifier*〉用于像撇儿的东西 [for things resembling the left-falling stroke]: 他留着两～儿胡子。His moustache is in two wings. ☞ piē on p. 1478

【撇嘴】piě//zuǐ 下唇向前伸,嘴角向下,表示轻视、不以为然或不高兴 twist lips (in contempt, disbelief or disappointment); jut out underlip, making corners of the mouth turn down: ～摇头 twist lips and shake the head | 小孩儿～要哭。The child's mouth contorted as she wavered on the brink of tears.

镦 piě 〈方 *dail*.〉烧盐用的敞口锅,用于地名,表示是烧盐的地方 pot for making salt, usu. used as part of a place name to denote that it is a salt producer: 潘家～(在江苏) Panjiapie, a place in Jiangsu Province

piè (ㄆㄧㄝˋ)

嫳 piè [嫳屑](pièxiè)〈书 *fml*.〉形容衣服飘动 (of clothes) fluttering

pīn (ㄆㄧㄣ)

拼[1](拚) pīn 合在一起;连合 piece together; join together: ～音 spelling | ～版 making up | 把两块木板～起来 join the two wooden boards together

拼[2](拚) pīn 不顾一切地干;豁出去 do sth. adventurously; do one's utmost: ～命 be ready to risk one's life ☞ pàn on p. 1444

【拼版】pīn//bǎn 按书刊要求的大小和式样,把排好顺序的文字、图版等拼成版面 (print) makeup; format making; piecing together of text and pictures according to the required size and layout

【拼搏】pīnbó 使出全部力量搏斗或争取 struggle hard; exert one's strength to the utmost; go all out: 顽强～ struggle hard | ～精神 the spirit of hard struggle | 日夜奋战,与洪水～ battle against floods day and night

【拼刺】pīncì ❶ 军事训练时拿着木枪两人对刺 (in military drills) bayonet practice between two soldiers ❷ 步兵打仗时短距离接触,用枪刺格斗 (in battlefields) bayonet fight; combat at bayonets points between infantrymen

【拼凑】pīncòu 把零碎的或分散的合在一起 piece together; put together fragments or pieces: 她把零碎的花布～起来做了个靠垫。She pieced together remnants of coloured cloth and made a cushion.

【拼合】pīnhé 合在一起;组合 join together; fit together; assemble: 把七巧板重新～起来 reassemble the tangram

【拼接】pīnjiē 拼合连接 piece together; join together: 把几块木板～在一起 join several wooden boards together

【拼命】pīn//mìng ❶ 把性命豁出去;以性命相拼 risk one's life; go all out regardless of personal danger: 跟歹徒～ struggle with a villain at the risk of one's life ❷〈比喻 *fig.*〉尽最大的力量；极度地 exert one's strength to the utmost; with all one's might; desperately：～地工作 work with all one's might｜～往山顶爬 climb indomitably to the summit

【拼盘】pīnpán（～儿 pīnpánr）用两种以上的凉菜（多为卤肉、海蜇、松花等冷荤）摆在一个菜盘里拼成的菜 assorted cold dish; course made up of two cold dishes or more such as stewed meat, jellyfish, and preserved eggs

【拼死】pīnsǐ same as 拼命 pīn//mìng

【拼死拼活】pīnsǐ-pīnhuó ❶ 不顾一切地斗争；拼个死活 put up a life-and-death struggle ❷ 用尽全部精力 exert one's utmost; for all one is worth：他整天～地干。He works desperately hard all day long.

【拼写】pīnxiě 用拼音字母按照拼音规则书写 spell; write using the phonetic alphabet according to phonetic rules

【拼音】pīnyīn 把两个或两个以上的音素结合起来成为一个复合的音，如 b 和 iāo 拼成 biāo（标）combine two phonemes or more into a compound syllable, i. e. 标 biāo is a combination of b and iāo

【拼音文字】pīnyīn wénzì 用符号（字母）来表示语音的文字。现代世界各国所用的文字多数是拼音文字，我国的藏文、蒙文、维吾尔文等也都是拼音文字。alphabetic (system of) writing used widely around the world. In China, alphabetic letters are used to write in the Tibetan, Mongolian, and Uygur languages. ☞ 音素文字 yīnsù wénzì on p. 2287 and 音节文字 yīnjié wénzì on p. 2286

【拼音字母】pīnyīn zìmǔ ❶ 拼音文字所用的字母 letters of the phonetic alphabet ❷ 指汉语拼音方案采用的为汉字注音的二十六个拉丁字母 phonetic letters; 26 Latin letters of the alphabet adopted in the Chinese phonetic system for phonetic notation of Chinese characters

【拼缀】pīnzhuì 连接；组合 join together：图案由许多大小不等的三角形～而成。The patterns were joined together by a number of triangles in various sizes.

姘 pīn 非夫妻关系而发生性行为 have illicit sexual relations with：～夫 adulterer｜～妇 adulteress

【姘居】pīnjū 非夫妻关系而同居 live illicitly as husband and wife; cohabit

【姘头】pīn·tou 非夫妻关系而发生性行为的男女，也指有这种关系的男方或女方 paramour; mistress; a man and a woman who have an illicit relationship

pín（ㄆㄧㄣˊ）

玭（蠙）pín〈书 *fml.*〉蚌珠 pearls and freshwater mussels

贫1 pín ❶ 穷（跟'富'相对 as opposed to 'rich'）poor; impoverished：～农 poor farmers｜～民 pauper｜～苦 poverty-stricken ❷ 缺少；不足 inadequate; deficient：～血 anaemia ❸〈旧时 *old*〉僧道自称的谦辞 humble term of self-address for a monk：～僧 me (as a Buddhist monk)｜～道 me (as a Taoist monk)

贫2 pín〈方 *dial.*〉絮叨可厌 garrulous; loquacious：这个人嘴真～。This man really is garrulous.｜你老说那些话，听着怪～的。You are so loquacious, constantly repeating yourself like that.

【贫乏】pínfá ❶ 贫穷 poor; impoverished：家境～ poor family ❷ 缺少，不丰富 lacking; deficient：内容～ deficient in content｜知识～ poor in knowledge｜生活经验～ lack life experience

【贫骨头】[1] píngǔ·tou〈方 *dial.*〉指爱贪小便宜的人或小气的人 person keen on petty gain or a stingy person

【贫骨头】[2] píngǔ·tou〈方 *dial.*〉说话多而使人讨厌的人 idle chatterer; windbag

【贫寒】pínhán 穷苦 poverty-stricken：家境～ (of a family) in financial difficultty｜～人家 impoverished family

【贫瘠】pínjí（土地）薄；不肥沃 (of soil) barren; infertile; impoverished

【贫贱】pínjiàn 指贫穷而社会地位低下 poor and of low social status：～不移（不因贫贱而改变志向）not give up one's ambition because of straitened and humble circumstances

【贫窭】pínjù〈书 *fml.*〉same as 贫穷 pínqióng

【贫苦】pínkǔ 贫困穷苦；生活资料不足 poor; badly off; lacking living materials：～出身 be born into a poor family｜家境～(of a family) in financial difficulty

【贫矿】pínkuàng 品位较低的矿石或矿床 lean ore; low-grade ore or mineral deposit

【贫困】pínkùn 生活困难；贫穷 impoverished; in straitened living conditions：～潦倒 be down and out｜～的山区改变了面貌。The previously impoverished mountain area has taken on a new look.

【贫民】pínmín 职业不固定而生活穷苦的人 poor people; people without regular work who live in poverty

【贫民窟】pínmínkū 指城市中贫苦人聚居的地方 slum; urban area densely populated by poor people

【贫农】pínnóng 完全没有土地或只占有极少的土地和一些小农具的人，一般依靠租种土地生活，也出卖一部分劳动力 poor farmers; peasants who have little or no land at all and possess few farming tools, usu. living by renting land from landlords and selling their labour

【贫气】[1] pín·qi 行动态度不大方；小气 (of actions, attitudes, etc.) stingy; niggardly

【贫气】[2] pín·qi 絮叨可厌 annoyingly garrulous：一句话说了又说，真～。You have already said that on countless occasions; you really are garrulous.

【贫穷】pínqióng 生产资料和生活资料缺乏 poor; impoverished; lacking a means of production or material possessions necessary for life

【贫弱】pínruò 贫穷衰弱（多指国家、民族 oft. of a country or a nation）poor and weak

P

【贫血】pínxuè 人体的血液中红细胞的数量或血红蛋白的含量低于正常的数值时叫做贫血。通常局部血量减少也叫贫血，如脑贫血。anaemia; condition in which the amount of red blood cells or the content of hemoglobin in the blood is lower than normal; deficiency in total volume of blood, e.g. cerebral anaemia

【贫油】pínyóu 指缺乏石油资源 oil-poor; lacking petroleum resources

【贫嘴】pínzuǐ 爱多说废话或开玩笑的话 garrulous; loquacious; tendency to talk too much and tell jokes：耍～ love of gossip

【贫嘴薄舌】pín zuǐ bó shé 指话多而尖酸刻薄，使人讨厌 be annoyingly garrulous and sharp-tongued; also 贫嘴贱舌 pín zuǐ jiàn shé

频 pín 屡次；连续几次 frequently; repeatedly：～繁 frequent｜～仍 repeatedly｜～～点头 frequently nod head

【频传】pínchuán 接连不断地传来（多指好的消息 oft. of good news）keep pouring in：捷报～。Good tidings on the victory keep snowing in.｜喜讯～。Good news kept pouring in.

【频次】píncì 指某事物在一定时间、一定范围内重复出现的次数 frequency; (of a matter) rate of recurrence over a certain period or within a certain scope

【频带】píndài 介于两个特定频率之间的所有频率的连续范围 frequency band; waveband; sequent range of all frequencies between two established frequencies

【频道】píndào 在电视广播中，高频影像信号和伴音信号占有的一定宽度的频带（of radio or television）channel; frequency band in which high-frequency picture signals and sound signals occupy a defined space

【频段】pínduàn 把无线电波按频率不同而分成的段，有低频、中频、高频、超高频等 frequency range; radio-wave ranges classified according to frequency, i.e. low-frequency; medium-frequency; high-frequency; super-high-frequency

【频繁】pínfán （次数）多 frequently; often; many times：交往～ frequent contacts｜活动～ occur frequently

【频率】pínlǜ ❶ 物体每秒振动的次数，单位是赫兹。人能听到的声音的频率是20—20,000赫兹，一般交流电的频率是50赫兹。frequency; (of objects) number of vibrations per second, marked units of hertz. The frequency of sounds discernible to the human ear range from 20HZ to 20,000HZ. The frequency of alternate currents is usu. 50HZ. also 周率 zhōulǜ ❷ 在单位时间内某种事情发生的次数 number of occurrences of sth. per unit of time

【频频】pínpín 连续不断地 repeatedly; again and again：～举杯 propose toasts repeatedly｜～得手 succeed time and again

【频谱】pínpǔ 复杂振荡分解为振幅不同和频率不同的谐振荡，这些谐振荡的幅值按频率排列的图形叫做频谱。广泛应用在声学、光学和无线电技术等方面。frequency spectrum; images formed when a complex oscillation disperses to harmonic oscillations of varying swings and frequencies and the amplitudes of the harmonic oscillations are arranged in the order of frequency, frequently applied in acoustic, optical and radio technologies

【频仍】pínréng〈书 *fml.*〉连续不断；屡次（多用于坏的方面 usu. in negative sense）frequent; repeated：灾害～stricken by repeated disasters

【频数】pínshuò〈书 *fml.*〉次数多而接连 frequent and continuous：病人腹泻～。The patient suffered from frequent, continuous bowel movements.

嫔（嬪） pín〈书 *fml.*〉皇帝的妾；皇宫中的女官 concubine of an emperor; woman attendant at imperial court：妃～ concubines

蘋 pín 蕨类植物，生在浅水中，茎横生在泥中，质柔软，有分枝，叶有长柄，四片小叶生在叶柄顶端，到夏秋时候，叶柄的下部生出小枝，枝上生子囊，里面有孢子 clover fern (*Marsilea quadrifolia*), grows horizontally in the mud of shallow water, has long, soft stems with four small leaves at the top, and branches, with slim ascus bearing twigs grow from the lower part of the stems in summer and autumn; also 田字草 tiánzìcǎo

☞ 苹 píng on p.1489

嚬 pín〈书 *fml.*〉same as 颦 pín

颦 pín〈书 *fml.*〉皱眉 knit the brows：～眉 knit one's brows｜一～一笑 every frown and every smile; each facial expression

【颦蹙】píncù〈书 *fml.*〉皱着眉头，形容忧愁 knit the brows; be worried：双眉～ knit one's brows

pǐn（ㄆㄧㄣˇ）

品 pǐn ❶ 物品 article：商～ commodity｜产～ product｜战利～ spoils of victory or of war ❷ 等级 grade; class：上～ superior grade｜下～ inferior grade｜精～ elaborate work｜极～

super grade ❸ 封建时代官吏的级别，共分九品 the nine ranks of officials in feudal times ❹ 种类 kind：～种 variety | ～类 category ❺ 品质 quality；character：人～ moral quality | ～德 moral character ❻ 辨别好坏；品评 decide with discrimination；taste；sample：～茶 savour tea | 这人究竟怎么样，你慢慢就～出来了。In time you will figure out what sort of person he really is. ❼ 吹（管乐器，多指箫）play (wind instrument，esp. a vertical bamboo flute)：～箫 blow a bamboo flute | ～竹弹丝 blow a bamboo flute and play a stringed instrument ❽ (Pǐn) 姓 a surname

【品尝】pǐncháng 仔细地辨别；尝试(滋味) taste；sample；savour：～鲜桃 taste a fresh peach | ～名酒 sample liquor of famous brand

【品德】pǐndé 品质道德 moral character：～高尚 lofty moral character

【品第】pǐndì 〈书 *fml.*〉❶ 评定高低，分列等次 appraise；rate；grade ❷ 指等级、地位 grade；rank；position；status

【品格】pǐngé ❶ 品性；品行 moral character：～高尚 lofty moral character ❷ 指文学、艺术作品的质量和风格 (of literary or artistic works) quality and style：他近期和早期的绘画～迥异。His recent paintings differ greatly from his earlier works.

【品红】pǐnhóng 比大红略浅的红色 fuchsine；magenta；shade of red slightly lighter than scarlet

【品级】pǐnjí ❶〈古代 *arch.*〉官吏的等级 official rank in feudal times ❷ 各种产品、商品的等级 grade (of products，commodities，etc.)

【品节】pǐnjié 品行节操 moral integrity：～卓异 eminent in moral integrity

【品蓝】pǐnlán 略带红的蓝色 reddish blue

【品类】pǐnlèi 种类 category；class：～繁多 a great number of categories

【品绿】pǐnlǜ 像青竹的绿色 bamboo green

【品貌】pǐnmào ❶ 相貌 look；appearance：～俊俏 pretty and charming ❷ 人品和相貌 character and look；personality and appearance：～兼优 of pleasing looks and a good character

【品名】pǐnmíng 物品的名称 name of an article

【品目】pǐnmù 物品的名目 names and descriptions of items：～繁多 a wide variety

【品评】pǐnpíng 评论高下 appraise；comment on：～产品质量 appraise the quality of products | 他看了牲口的牙齿，～着毛色腿脚。He remarked on the state of health of the livestock after examining and appraising their teeth.

【品题】pǐntí 〈书 *fml.*〉评论(人物、作品等) appraise (a person，a piece of work，etc.)

【品头论足】pǐn tóu lùn zú ☞ 评头论足 píng tóu lùn zú on p. 1489

【品脱】pǐntuō 英美制容量单位，1 品脱等于1/2 夸脱。英制 1 品脱合 0.5683 升，美制 1 品脱合 0.4732 升。pint；British and American unit of capacity. One pint equals 0.5 quart. According to British capacity measurement，one pint equals 0.5683 liters；and in American capacity measurement one pint equals 0.4732 liters.

【品位】pǐnwèi ❶〈书 *fml.*〉指官吏的品级；官阶 rank of an official in feudal times ❷ 矿石中有用元素或它的化合物含量的百分率，含量的百分率愈大，品位愈高 grade；percentage of a useful element or its compounds in an ore (the larger the percentage，the higher the grade) ❸ 指物品质量；文艺作品所达到的水平 quality of an article；(of literary and artistic works) level：高～的蚕丝 high-quality silk | 节目的艺术～较高。The program has a high level of artistry.

【品味】pǐnwèi ❶ 尝试滋味；品尝 taste；sample；savour：经专家～，认为酒质优良。This wine is designated as of fine quality，after being sampled by experts. ❷ 仔细体会；玩味 savour；ponder；deliberate：他经过细细～，才明白了那句话的含义。He finally understood the meaning of that sentence after careful deliberation. ❸ (物品的)品质和风味 (of articles) quality and flavour：由于吸收了异味，茶叶～大受影响。Owing to the tea having absorbed a peculiar odour，its flavour and quality have deteriorated.

【品系】pǐnxì 指来源于同一祖先，性状表现大致相同的一群个体 strain；a group of presumed common ancestry with roughly the same quality and characteristics

【品行】pǐnxíng 有关道德的行为 moral conduct：～端正 be well behaved

【品性】pǐnxìng 品质性格 character and disposition：～敦厚 of honest and sincere character

【品议】pǐnyì same as 品评 pǐnpíng

【品月】pǐnyuè 浅蓝色 pale blue

【品藻】pǐnzǎo 〈书 *fml.*〉评论(人物) make a critical appraisal of (a person)

【品质】pǐnzhì ❶ 行为、作风上所表现的思想、认识、品性等的本质 character；intrinsic quality；essence of one's thinking，cognition，and character reflected in actions and manner：道德～ moral character ❷ 物品的质量 quality (of commodities，etc.)：江西瓷～优良。Chinaware made in Jiangxi is of the best quality.

【品种】pǐnzhǒng ❶ 经过人工选择和培育、具有一定经济价值和共同遗传特点的一群生物体（通常指栽培植物、牲畜、家禽等）breed；strain；group of organisms that are artificially selected and cultivated，have common inherited characteristics and are of commercial value，i. e. cultivated plants，livestock，and poultry ❷ 泛指产品的种类 (of products) variety；assortment：增加花色～ increase the variety (of products) | ～齐全 have a complete assortment (of goods)

【品族】pǐnzú 指来源于同一母畜的畜群,它们具有与同族祖先相类似的特征和特性,遗传性稳定 strain; breed of common ancestry, with inherited characteristics and features

榀 pǐn〈量词 *classifier*〉一个屋架叫一榀 measurement unit used for a roof truss is a *pin*

pìn(ㄆㄧㄣˋ)

牝 pìn 雌性的(指鸟兽,跟'牡'相对 of some birds and animals, as opposed to 'male') female:~牛 cow|~鸡 hen

聘 pìn ❶ 聘请 engage:~任 appoint to a position|~用 engage ❷〈书 *fml.*〉聘问 visit:报~ pay a visit|~使往来 exchange of state visits ❸ 定亲 betroth:~礼 betrothal gift ❹ 女子出嫁 (of women) get married:出~ get married|~姑娘 marry one's daughter off

【聘金】pìnjīn ❶ 旧俗订婚时,男方送给女方的钱财 (old custom) betrothal money presented by a bridegroom to the family of the bride; bride price ❷ 聘请人做事所付给的钱 money paid to the person engaged for specific work

【聘礼】pìnlǐ ❶ 聘请时表示敬意的礼物 gifts in honour of sb.'s engagement ❷ 订婚时,男家向女家下的定礼 betrothal gifts (from the bridegroom's to the bride's family)

【聘请】pìnqǐng 请人担任职务 engage; invite:~教师 hire a teacher|~专家指导 invite experts for instruction

【聘任】pìnrèn 聘请人担任(职务) engage sb. as; appoint sb. to a position:~制 engagement system|工厂~他为总工程师。The factory engaged him as chief engineer.

【聘书】pìnshū 聘请人的文书 letter of appointment

【聘问】pìnwèn〈古代 *arch.*〉指代表本国政府访问友邦 visit a state as an envoy on behalf of one's native government

【聘用】pìnyòng 聘请任用;聘任 employ; engage; appoint to a position:~贤能 employ able persons|~技术人员 engage technicians

pīng(ㄆㄧㄥ)

乒 pīng ❶〈拟声词 *onom.*〉:~的一声枪响 crack of a gun ❷ 指乒乓球 table tennis:~赛(乒乓球比赛) table-tennis match|~坛(乒乓球界) table tennis circles

【乒乓】pīngpāng ❶〈拟声词 *onom.*〉rattling sound:雹子打在屋顶上~乱响。Hailstones came rattling down on the roof. ❷ same as 乒乓球 pīngpāngqiú ①:打~ play table tennis

【乒乓球】pīngpāngqiú ❶ 球类运动项目之一,在球台中央支着球网,双方分站在球台两端用球拍把球打来打去。有单打和双打两种。table tennis; ping-pong; singles or doubles ball game event played on a tabletop divided in the middle by a net, using small paddles and a small celluloid hollow ball ❷ 乒乓球运动使用的球,用赛璐珞制成,直径约 4 厘米 table tennis ball; ball used for the table-tennis game, usu. made of celluloid, about four centimetres in diameter

俜 pīng ☞ 伶俜 língpīng on p. 1226

娉 pīng [娉婷](pīngtíng)〈书 *fml.*〉形容女子的姿态美 (of a woman) has a graceful demeanour:体态~a graceful posture|举止~ with a graceful demeanour

píng(ㄆㄧㄥˊ)

平 píng ❶ 表面没有高低凹凸,不倾斜 flat; even; smooth; surface neither rough nor inclined:~坦 flat|马路很~。The road is smooth and level.|把纸铺~了 smooth out the paper ❷ 使平 level out or up; make level or even:~了三亩地 level up three *mu* of land|把沟~了种庄稼 level the gully to plant crops ❸ 两相比较没有高低、先后;不相上下 be on the same level; equal:~辈 of the same generation|~槽 slots on the same level|~列 place side by side|~局 draw|~起~坐 on an equal footing|~了世界纪录 equal a world record ❹ 平均;公平 fair; impartial; egalitarian:~分 divide equally|持~之论 stick to impartial views ❺ 安定 calm; peaceful; quiet:风~浪静 calm water and a gentle breeze|心~气和 be even-tempered ❻ 用武力镇压;平定 quell; suppress by armed force; put down:~叛 put down a rebellion|~乱 calm chaos ❼ 抑止(怒气) restrain one's anger:你先把气~下去再说。You'd better not speak until you have suppressed your anger. ❽ 经常的;普通的 common; ordinary:~时 at ordinary times|~淡 flat; ordinary ❾ 平声 level tone:~仄 level and oblique tones|~上去入 the four tones in classical Chinese ❿ (Píng) 姓 a surname

【平安】píng'ān 没有事故,没有危险;平稳安全 safe and sound; without accident or danger:~无事。All is well.|一路~! Have a good trip!|平平安安地到达目的地 arrive at a destination safely

【平白】píngbái ❶ 无缘无故 for no reason; gratuitously:~无故 for no reason ❷ (文辞等)浅显通俗 (of writing, language, etc.) easy to read and understand:诗句~如话。The poem is as plain as ordinary speech.

【平板】píngbǎn ❶ 平淡死板,没有曲折变化 mundane and rigid; dull and stereotyped; without variation:样式~ in a flat style|他一

句一句～地说下去。He spoke sentence after sentence in a monotone. ❷ 钳工刮研用的工具,用很厚的铸铁板制成,一面很平 flat sheet; flatbed; tool made of a thick cast-iron slab, with one side smooth, usu. used by a locksmith for scraping

【平板车】píngbǎnchē ❶ 运货的三轮车,载货的部分是平板 flatbed tricycle; tricycle towing a flat sheet for carrying goods; also 平板三轮 píngbǎn sānlún ❷ 没有车帮的大型运货卡车 flatbed; large truck for carrying goods, without sides

【平板仪】píngbǎnyí 测量地形用的仪器,可以测量高度和距离,由水准仪、图板和三脚架等组成 surveying panel; device for surveying height and distance in topography, usu. comprising spirit level, plan table, and tripod

【平版】píngbǎn 版面空白部分和印刷部分都没有凹凸纹的印刷版,如石版、金属平版等 planographic plate; completely smooth printing plate for printing as lithography or offset i.e. stone plate; metal plate;

【平辈】píngbèi 相同的辈分 of the same generation

【平步青云】píng bù qīng yún〈比喻 *fig.*〉一下子达到很高的地位 rapidly reach a very high status; have a meteoric rise

【平槽】píng//cáo 江河的水面高达河岸 (of rivers) be level with the banks:雨下得平了槽。It rained so heavily that the river surged almost to overflowing.

【平产】píngchǎn 与相比较的产量大体相当 output being about the same as that of the previous period, season and year:今年全县粮食增产的乡占百分之九十五,～的占百分之五。This year 95 per cent of the county's townships increased their grain production, while the remainder showed no increase.

【平常】píngcháng ❶ 普通;不特别 ordinary; common; not special:话虽～,意义却很深刻。Although these were plain words, they were nevertheless of great significance. ❷ 平时 usually; at ordinary times:他虽然身体不好,但～很少请假。Although he is not in the best of health, he seldom asks for leave.

【平车】píngchē ❶ 铁路货车的一种,没有车顶和车壁,用来装运大型建筑材料、压延钢材或各种机器等 railway flatcar; platform wagon; railway wagon without top and sides, usu. for loading and carrying bulky building material, rolled steel, or machinery ❷ 没有车帮的兽力车或人力车 flatbed cart; animal-drawn vehicle or hand cart without sides

【平畴】píngchóu〈书 *fml.*〉平坦的田地 level farmland:千里～ vast expanse of level farmland|～沃野 well-cultivated fertile land

【平川】píngchuān 地势平坦的地方 level land; plain:～广野 flat, open wilderness|一马～ wide expanse of flat land

【平旦】píngdàn〈书 *fml.*〉天亮的时候 dawn; daybreak

【平淡】píngdàn (事物、文章等)平常;没有曲折 (of things, articles, etc.) flat; insipid; without variation:～无奇 commonplace; prosaic|～无味 dull|语调～ in pedestrian tones

【平等】píngděng ❶ 指人们在社会、政治、经济、法律等方面享有相等待遇 (of people) enjoy equality in social status, politics, economy, and law, etc. ❷ 泛指地位相等 (in a broad sense) equality; equal in status:～互利 equality and mutual benefit|男女～ equality of the sexes

【平籴】píngdí〈旧时 *old*〉指官府在丰收时用平价买进谷物,以待荒年卖出 (of local authorities) buy grain at standard prices in years of bumper harvest so as to sell it at a fair price in times of famine

【平地】píng//dì 把土地整平 level the land; rake the soil smooth:播种前要翻地、～。You should turn over and smooth out the soil before sowing.

【平地】píngdì 平坦的土地 level land; flat ground:找一块～修操场 find a piece of flat land for a playground

【平地风波】píngdì fēngbō〈比喻 *fig.*〉突然发生的事故或纠纷 sudden, unexpected accident, or trouble

【平地楼台】píngdì lóutái〈比喻 *fig.*〉原来没有基础而白手建立起来的事业 undertaking that starts from scratch

【平地一声雷】píngdì yī shēng léi〈比喻 *fig.*〉名声地位突然升高。也比喻突然发生一件可喜的大事 sudden rise in fame and position; unexpected happy event

【平定】píngdìng ❶ 平稳安定 stability and peace; calm down:局势～stable situation|他的情绪逐渐～下来。He gradually calmed down. ❷ 平息(叛乱等) quell; put down (a rebellion, etc.)

【平动】píngdòng 物体运动时,物体内任何两点连成的直线始终保持它的方向不变,这种运动叫作平动 translation(of an object); translational motion; remove or change from one place to another while keeping the straight line between any two points in the object moving in the same direction; nonrational displacement; also 平移 píngyí

【平凡】píngfán 平常;不稀奇 ordinary; common; not rare:他们在～的工作中做出了不～的成绩。They have made extraordinary achievements in ordinary work.

【平反】píngfǎn 把判错的案件或做错的政治结论改正过来 redress (a misjudged case or a mistaken political conclusion); rehabilitate:～昭雪 exonerate|～冤案 rehabilitate a misjudged case

【平方】píngfāng ❶ 指数是 2 的乘方，如 a^2（a×a），3^2（3×3）second power (of a quantity); square, i.e. a^2（a×a），3^2（3×3）❷ 指平方米 square metre (sq. m.)

【平房】píngfáng ❶ 只有一层的房子（区别于'楼房' as compared with 'multi-story building'）single-story house ❷〈方 *dial.*〉用灰土做顶的平顶房屋 house with a plastered flat roof

【平分】píngfēn 平均分配 divide equally; share alike

P

【平分秋色】píngfēn qiūsè〈比喻 *fig.*〉双方各占一半（of two parties）share sth. on a fifty-fifty basis

【平服】píngfú ❶ 安定 stabilize; calm down: 心情难以～ find it hard to keep one's composure ❷ 服气 be convinced: 拿出真本事，才能叫人心里～。People will be convinced only when they see your genuine ability.

【平复】píng·fù ❶ 恢复平静 calm down; be pacified: 风浪渐渐～。The storm gradually subsided. | 等他情绪～后再说。I won't talk about it until he calms down. ❷（疾病或创伤）痊愈复原（of diseases or wounds）be cured; be healed: 病体日渐～。The patient gradually recovered with each passing day.

【平光】píngguāng 屈光度为零的（眼镜），如太阳镜和防护眼镜都是平光的 anastigmatic; with zero diopter; plain glass, e.g. sunglasses or goggles

【平和】pínghé ❶（性情或言行）温和（of temperament, words, or deeds）gentle; mild; moderate: 语气～ in a placid tone | 态度～ moderate attitude ❷（药物）作用温和；不剧烈（of medicines）mild; not acute ❸ 平静；安宁 peaceful; quiet: 气氛～ peaceful atmosphere ❹〈方 *dial.*〉（纷扰）停息（of troubles）subside; quiet down: 这场争端终于～下来。The dispute has finally quieted down.

【平衡】pínghéng ❶ 对立的各方面在数量或质量上相等或相抵 balance; equilibrium; (of antithetic sides) be equal or offset in quantity or quality: 产销～ balance between production and sales | 收支～ balance between income and expenditure ❷ 几个力同时作用在一个物体上，各个力互相抵消，物体保持相对静止状态、匀速直线运动状态或绕轴匀速转动状态 balance; object operated by several forces that counteract one another so that the object maintains a state of stillness, uniform-speed rectilinear motion, or uniform-speed winding movement

【平衡觉】pínghéngjué 因身体所处位置的变化而引起的感觉。内耳中的半规管和前庭是平衡觉的器官。sense of equilibrium; sense induced by the change of a body's location. The semicircular canal and vestibule in the inner ear are organs related to the sense of equilibrium.

【平衡木】pínghéngmù ❶ 女子体操器械的一种，是一根长而窄的方木头，两端支起并固定在支架上 balance beam; long, narrow wooden beam supported in a horizontal position at two ends and fixed on brackets; part of the equipment used in women's gymnastics ❷ 女子竞技体操项目之一，运动员在平衡木上做各种动作 balance beam; women's gymnastics event in which athletes perform a set of movements on a balance beam

【平滑】pínghuá 平而光滑 level and smooth: 冰面～如镜。The frozen water is as smooth as a mirror.

【平滑肌】pínghuájī 由长纺锤形细胞组成的肌肉，平滑，没有横纹。是构成胃、肠、膀胱等内脏的肌肉，它的运动不受人的意志支配。smooth muscle; involuntary muscle; smooth muscle tissue made up of elongated spindle-shaped cells without cross striations, found in vertebrate visceral structures (such as the stomach, intestines, and bladder), its functions not subject to conscious mental control; also 不随意肌 bùsuíyìjī

【平话】pínghuà 我国古代民间流行的口头文学形式，有说有唱，宋代盛行，由韵体散体相间发展为单纯散体，例如以散文为主的《三国志平话》、《五代史平话》popular story; ancient Chinese literary style of singing and storytelling that came in vogue during the Song Dynasty (960-1279). It was originally in a style free from parallelism or rhyme and then developed into a simple prose style. Examples are *Popular Stories of Three Kingdom* and *The Story of the Five Dynasties*, both in prose style; also 评话 pínghuà

【平缓】pínghuǎn ❶（地势）平坦，倾斜度小（of terrain）flat; gentle; with low obliquity: 黄河中下游地势～。The terrain in the middle and lower reaches of the Yellow River is flat and smooth. ❷ 平稳；缓慢 slow and placid: 气温变化～ low variations in temperature | 水流～。The water flows gently. ❸（心情、声音等）缓和；平和（of mood, voice, etc.）mild; placid; gentle: 语调～ mild tone

【平毁】pínghuǐ 铲平或填平，使毁坏或失去原来的作用 demolish; raze in order to destroy the original function of sth.: ～工事 destroy a piece of work

【平价】píngjià ❶ 平抑上涨的物价 bring down rising prices ❷ 平抑了的货物价格 stabilized prices (for goods): ～米 rice sold at government-controlled prices | ～收购 purchase at government-set prices ❸ 普通的价格；公平的价格 fair price; normal price ❹ 指一国本位货币规定的含金量。也指两个金本位（或银本位）国家间本位货币法定含金量（或含银量）的比值。par; parity; established gold content of the monetary unit of one country, or ratio between the legal gold content (or silver content) of the standard currencies of two countries practicing the gold standard (or silver standard)

【平角】píngjiǎo 一条射线以端点为定点在平面上旋转半周所成的角。角的一边是另一边的反向延长线。平角为180°。straight angle; angle whose sides lie in opposite directions from the vertex in the same straight line and which equals two right angles. A straight angle is 180°.

【平金】píngjīn 一种刺绣,在缎面上用金银色线盘成各种花纹 embroidery done in gold or silver thread coiled evenly into various designs on satin

【平靖】píngjìng ❶ 用武力镇压叛乱,使趋于安定 quell; suppress (a rebellion) by force; stabilize:~内乱 put down civil strife ❷(社会秩序)稳定安静 (of social orders) stable; peaceful:时局~stable current situation

【平静】píngjìng (心情、环境等)没有不安或动荡 (of mood, environment, etc.) calm; quiet; tranquil; without turbulence:激动的心情久久不能~。He was very excited, and it was a long time before he calmed down.|风浪已经~下去了。The storm has calmed.|他说话的声音仍然很~。He continued to speak calmly.

【平局】píngjú same as 和局 héjú

【平均】píngjūn ❶ 把总数按份儿均匀计算 average; mean; quotient obtained by dividing the sum total of a set of figures by the number of figures:二十筐梨重一千八百斤,~每筐重九十斤。The 20 baskets of pears weighed 900 kilograms in total, each basket weighing an average of 45 kilograms. ❷ 没有轻重或多少的分别 equally; no difference in weight, number, etc.:~发展 balanced development|~分摊 share out equally

【平均主义】píngjūn zhǔyì 主张人们在工资、劳动、勤务各方面享受一律的待遇的思想,认为只有绝对平均才算是平等,是个体手工业和小农经济的产物 equalitarianism; egalitarianism; social philosophy which is an outcome of individual handicraft industry and small-scale peasant economy, advocating equality esp. with respect to salary, labour, and service, and believing that only absolute equipartition can be counted as real equality

【平空】píngkōng same as 凭空 píngkōng

【平列】píngliè 平着排列;平等列举 place side by side; enumerate on an equal footing:不能把客观原因与主观原因~起来分析。We should not place subjective reasons on a par with objective reasons in our analysis.

【平流】píngliú 空气水平方向的运动。使气温上升的叫暖平流,使气温下降的叫冷平流。advection; horizontal movement of a mass of air that causes changes in temperature. The movement that causes the temperature to rise is warm advection, and that which makes the temperature drop is cool advection.

【平炉】pínglú 炼钢炉的一种,放原料的炉底像浅盆,炉体用耐火材料砌成,燃烧用的煤气和热空气由两侧的开口通入 open-hearth furnace; open hearth; Martin furnace; steel-making furnace that features a shallow-basin-shaped bottom for containing materials, a hearth built of fireproof materials, and openings at both sides to let in coal gas and hot air; also 马丁炉 mǎdīnglú

【平米】píngmǐ 平方米的简称 abbr. for 平方米 píngfāngmǐ

【平面】píngmiàn 最简单的面。在一个面内任取两点连成直线,如直线上所有的点都在这个面上,这个面就是平面。plane; simplest surface of such a nature that a straight line joining any two of its points lies wholly on the surface

【平面波】píngmiànbō 波从一点发散出去形成球面,如果这种波从无限远处传来,所形成的球面就可以看作是一个平面,所以叫做平面波。光波中,光线和波面垂直,所以平面波的光线可以看作是平行的。plane wave; wave diverging from one point usually forms a spherical surface, and if the wave comes from an infinite distance, the spherical surface can be viewed as a plane surface. Hence the term, plane wave. In light waves, the rays are vertical to the wave surface, so the rays of plane waves can be considered parallel.

【平面几何】píngmiàn jǐhé 研究平面图形的性质(形状、大小、位置等)的学科 plane geometry; science that studies the property of plane graphs (as shape, size, location, etc.)

【平面交叉】píngmiàn jiāochā 两条或两条以上相交的道路在同一平面上交叉,常见的有十字形交叉、丁字形交叉、环形交叉等 level crossing; grade crossing; crossing of two or more lines or circles on the same level; 简称 abbr. 平交 píngjiāo

【平面镜】píngmiànjìng 反射面是平面的镜子,日常所用的镜子就属于这一种。镜前的物体在镜中形成虚像,像和物体的大小相同,跟镜面的距离相等,左右方向相反。plane mirror; mirror whose reflection surface is flat. A mirror for everyday use is a plane mirror. The object in front of the mirror forms a virtual image in it, and the image is of the same size and of the same distance from the mirror's surface, but its right and left sides are reversed.

【平面图】píngmiàntú ❶ 在平面上所示的图形 plan; plane figure; figure shown on a plane ❷ 构成物体形状的所有线段垂直投影于平面上所示的图形 ichnography; figure shown on a plane by vertical projection of all the line segments that compose the shape of an object

【平民】píngmín 泛指普通的人（区别于贵族或特权阶级 as compared with 'aristocracy or privileged classes'）commoners; the populace; ordinary people: ～百姓 common people

【平明】píngmíng 〈书 *fml.*〉天亮的时候 daybreak; dawn

【平年】píngnián ❶ 阳历没有闰日或农历没有闰月的年份。阳历平年 365 天，农历平年 354 天或 355 天。non-leap year; common year; year with no leap day on the solar calendar or no leap month on the lunar calendar. The common year has 365 days on the solar calendar, and 354 or 355 days on the lunar calendar. ❷ 农作物收成平常的年头儿 average year (in crop yield)

【平平】píngpíng 不好不坏；寻常 average; neither good nor bad: 程度～ to a mediocre extent | 成绩～ not brilliant scores

【平平当当】píngpíngdāngdāng 形容做事顺利 get sth. done without a hitch

【平铺直叙】píng pū zhí xù 说话或写文章时不讲求修辞，只把意思简单而直接地叙述出来 speak or write in a simple, straightforward way without being elaborate rhetorically

【平起平坐】píng qǐ píng zuò 〈比喻 *fig.*〉地位或权力平等 be equal in position or power

【平权】píngquán 权利平等，没有大小之分 (enjoy) equal rights: 男女～。Men and women enjoy equal rights.

【平日】píngrì 一般的日子(区别于特定的日子，如节假日或特指的某一天 as compared with 'special days that are holidays, or days of particular reference') on ordinary days

【平绒】píngróng 织物表面有平整而短密的绒毛的棉织品 velveteen; clothing fabric usu. of cotton, in twill or plain weave, made with a short close weft pile in imitation of velvet

【平射炮】píngshèpào 初速大，弹道低伸的一类火炮，如加农炮、反坦克炮等 flat fire gun; flat trajectory gun; fire gun with a low-projected trajectory and fast initial velocity, such as cannon and anti-tank gun

【平身】píngshēn 〈旧时 *old*〉指行跪拜礼后立起身子（多见于旧小说、戏曲 oft. in old novels and traditional opera) stand up after kowtowing

【平生】píngshēng ❶ 终身；一生 all one's life: 他～第一次看到大海。He saw the sea for the first time in his life. ❷ 从来；平素 usually: 素昧～never have the opportunity to make sb.'s acquaintance | 他～是很艰苦朴素的。He generally lives frugally and works hard.

【平声】píngshēng 古汉语四声之一。古汉语的平声字在普通话里分成阴平和阳平两类。level tone; (first of the four tones in classical Chinese pronunciation, which has evolved into the high and level tone 阴平 yīnpíng and the rising tone 阳平 yángpíng in modern standard pronunciation; ☞ 四声 sìshēng on p.1821

【平时】píngshí ❶ 一般的、通常的时候（区别于特定的或特指的时候 as compared with 'esp.') ordinarily; normally; usually ❷ 指平常时期（区别于非常时期，如战时、戒严时 as compared with 'times of stress, e. g. war time or under martial law; periods of enforced martial law, etc.') peacetime

【平实】píngshí 平易朴实 simple and unadorned: 待人～ treat others amiably and simply | 文笔～ writing in natural style

【平视】píngshì 两眼平着向前看 look straight ahead: 立正时两眼要～。Keep your eyes straight ahead when standing at attention.

【平手】píngshǒu（～儿 píngshǒur）不分高下的比赛结果 draw; tie; come out even in a contest: 甲乙两队打了个～儿。The game between Teams A and B ended with a tie.

【平水期】píngshuǐqī 河流处于正常水位的时期 period when a river is at its normal level; also 中水期 zhōngshuǐqī

【平顺】píngshùn 平稳顺畅；没有波折 smooth sailing; plain sailing; without twists and turns: 发展～ develop smoothly | 呼吸～ smooth, even respiration | 生活～如常。My life is going as smoothly as ever.

【平素】píngsù 平时；素来 usually: 他这个人～不好说话。He is a man of few words. | 张师傅～对自己要求很严。Master Zhang generally makes strict demands of himself.

【平台】píngtái ❶ 晒台 terrace; flat roof ❷ same as 平房 píngfáng ② ❸ 生产和施工过程中，为操作方便而设置的工作台，有的能移动和升降 platform designed to facilitate production or construction, sometimes movable horizontally or vertically, or both

【平坦】píngtǎn 没有高低凹凸（多指地势）(of land, etc.) level; even; smooth: 宽阔～的马路 broad and smooth road

【平添】píngtiān 自然而然地增添 add or give to sth. as an effect or a result: 新建的街心公园给周围居民～了许多乐趣。The newly built street park has added delight to the lives of the neighborhood residents.

【平粜】píngtiào 〈旧时 *old*〉遇到荒年，官府把仓库里的粮食按平价卖出 (of local authorities) sell the grain stored in granaries at fair prices in years of famine

【平头】píngtóu ❶ 男子发式，顶上头发剪平，从脑后到两鬓的头发全部推光 crew cut; men's hairstyle where the hair on the crown is cut short and even and that on the temples and on the back of the head is close cropped ❷ 指普通；平常（人）ordinary or common (people): ～百姓 common people ❸ 〈方 *dial.*〉用在数字前面，表示整数 full; round; complete (usu. used before numbers): ～甲子（六十岁）on reaching sixty years of age

【平头数】píngtóushù〈方 *dial.*〉十、百、千、万等不带零头的整数 round figure (numbers given in tens, hundreds, thousands, etc.)

【平头正脸】píng tóu zhèng liǎn (～儿的 píng tóu zhèng liǎnr·de)形容相貌端正 have regular facial features

【平妥】píngtuǒ 平稳妥帖 smooth, plain, and appropriate:文章措辞～。This article is simply and appropriately worded.

【平纹】píngwén 单根经纱和单根纬纱交织成的简单纹路 plain weave; simple lines interwoven by a single warp and a single weft

【平稳】píngwěn ❶ 平安稳定,没有波动或危险 stable; safe and steady, without fluctuation or danger:局势～ stable situation|物价～。Prices are stable.|病情～。The patient's condition is stable.|今年汛期,海河的水情一直～。During this year's floods the Haihe River remained stable. ❷(物体)稳定,不摇晃 (of objects) stable; not swaying or rocking:把桌子放～了。Steady the table.

【平西】píngxī 太阳在西方将要落 (of the sun) be about to set in the west:太阳已经～了,还是这么热。The sun has almost set, but it still feels hot.

【平昔】píngxī 往常 in the past:我～对语法很少研究,现在开始感到一点兴趣了。I used to study hardly any grammar, but am now beginning to take an interest in it.

【平息】píngxī ❶(风势、纷乱等)平静或停止 (of wind, whirlpool, etc.) calm down; quieten; stop:一场风波～了。The trouble is over.|枪声渐渐～下来。The gunfire has gradually subsided. ❷ 用武力平定 quell; put down (a rebellion, etc.); suppress:～骚乱 put down a riot|～叛乱 suppress a rebellion

【平心而论】píng xīn ér lùn 平心静气地评论 comment in all fairness

【平心静气】píng xīn jìng qì 心情平和,态度冷静 calm; dispassionate in attitude

【平信】píngxìn 不挂号的一般信件 ordinary mail; mail that is not registered

【平行】píngxíng ❶ 等级相同,没有隶属关系的 (of two or more organizations) at the same level, without one being subordinate to the other:～机关 government departments of equal rank ❷ 两个平面或一个平面内的两条直线或一条直线与一个平面始终不能相交,叫做平行 parallel; two straight lines on two planes, or on the same plane, or on a straight line with a plane, that are equidistant and hence will never cross each other ❸ 同时进行的 simultaneous; concurrent:～作业 simultaneous operation|～发展 simultaneous development

【平行四边形】píngxíng sìbiānxíng 两组对边分别平行的四边形。矩形、菱形、正方形都是平行四边形的特殊形式。parallelogram; quadrilateral with opposite sides parallel and equal. The rectangle, diamond, and square are forms of parallelogram.

【平行线】píngxíngxiàn 在同一平面内不相交的两条直线 parallel lines; two straight lines that never meet on the same plane

【平行作业】píngxíng zuòyè 在同一施工场所,使尽可能多的工种在相互配合、相互制约的条件下同时作业 simultaneous operations on the same construction site; different types of work, as many as possible, simultaneously under way under conditions of mutual cooperation and mutual conditioning

【平衍】píngyǎn〈书 *fml.*〉平展 open and flat; plain and broad:土地～,一望无际 a vast, flat land stretching as far as the eye can see

【平野】píngyě 城市以外的广阔平地 vast, flat land in the countryside

【平一】píngyī〈书 *fml.*〉平定统一 put down rebellions and unify the land:～宇内 put down rebellions and unify the nation as a whole

【平移】píngyí same as 平动 píngdòng

【平议】píngyì ❶ 公平地论定是非曲直 pass a fair judgment on ❷〈书 *fml.*〉评论;评议 appraise and make comment on through discussion

【平抑】píngyì 抑制使稳定 control and stabilize:～物价 stabilize prices|他尽力使自己的怒火～下来。He tried his best to contain his anger.

【平易】píngyì ❶(性情或态度)谦逊和蔼 (of temperament or attitude) unassuming and amiable:～近人 amiable and easy to approach|～可亲 amiable and easy-going ❷(文章)浅近易懂 (of writing) plain and easy to understand:语言简洁～。The article was written in a pithy language.

【平易近人】píng yì jìn rén ❶ 态度谦逊和蔼,使人容易接近 (of attitude) amiable and easy in approach ❷(文字)浅显,容易了解 (of writing) easy to read and understand

【平庸】píngyōng 寻常而不突出;平凡 mediocre; ordinary; commonplace; not outstanding:才能～ of limited ability|相貌～ ordinary facial features|～的一生 a mediocre life

【平鱼】píngyú 鲳鱼 butterfish (*Stromateidae*)

【平原】píngyuán 起伏极小,海拔较低的广大平地 plain; extensive level area at low altitude with few falls and rises

【平月】píngyuè 阳历平年的二月叫平月,有28天 February of a non-leap year, having 28 days

【平允】píngyǔn 公平适当 fair and just; equitable:分配得很～ be distributed in an equitable manner|话说得很～,令人心服。Talks were equitable and convincing.

【平仄】píngzè 平声和仄声,泛指由平仄构成的诗文的韵律 level and oblique tones, esp. used for rules of rhyming in Chinese poetry

【平展】píngzhǎn ❶（地势）平坦而宽敞（of land, etc.）open and flat:地势～ extensive, flat land|～的场院 open backyard ❷ 平而舒展 unruffled; unwrinkled; pressed:他穿一身～可体的新军装。He is wearing a new, freshly pressed army uniform that fits him well.

【平展展】píngzhǎnzhǎn（～的 píngzhǎnzhǎn·de）形容平坦或平整 level or smooth:～的大马路 broad, even road

【平整】píngzhěng ❶ 填挖土方使土地平坦整齐 level off; excavate and fill with earth to make the land level:～土地 level up the land ❷ 平正整齐;（土地）平坦整齐（of land）smooth; level:马路又宽又～。The street is broad and even.

【平正】píng·zheng ❶ 没有皱褶 unruffled:这张纸很～。This piece of paper is clean and smooth. ❷ 不歪斜 straight and even:墁的砖又～又密合。The bricks were laid close and even.

【平装】píngzhuāng（书籍）用单层的纸做封面,书脊不成弧形的装订（区别于'精装' as compared with 'a clothbound book'）（of books, etc.）paperbound; paperback; book-binding in which a single sheet of paper is used as a cover and the spine of the book is not curved:～本 paperback（book）; paperbound edition

【平足】píngzú same as 扁平足 biǎnpíngzú

【平作】píngzuò 把农作物种在耕耙平整、没有畦或垄的田地里。平作适用于降雨较多而均匀的平原地区。flat culture; method of cultivation where crops are grown in fields that have been levelled off, rather than separated by ridges. This mode of farming is appropriate for plain areas where there is abundant rainfall.

冯 píng ❶ ☞ 暴虎冯河 bào hǔ píng hé on p.74 ❷〈古 *arch.*〉same as 凴（凭）píng ☞ Féng on p.588

评 píng ❶ 评论;批评 comment; criticize; review:短～ brief comment|书～ book review|获得好～ receive favourable comments ❷ 评判 judge; appraise; assess:～分儿 give a mark|～选模范 choose models

【评比】píngbǐ 通过比较,评定高低 appraise through comparison; compare and assess:～生产成绩 compare and appraise the results of production

【评点】píngdiǎn 批评并圈点（诗文）criticize and assess（a literary work）

【评定】píngdìng 经过评判或审核来决定 pass judgment through appriasals or evaluations:～职称 determine professional titles|考试成绩已经～完毕。The assessment of grades in the examination is complete.

【评断】píngduàn 评论判断 judge; arbitrate:～是非 judge between right and wrong

【评分】píng//fēn（～儿 píng//fēnr）根据成绩评定分数（用于生产、教育、体育等）score; give a mark according to one's performance（usu. used in production, education, sports, etc.）

【评分】píngfēn 评定的分数 mark given:他以最高的～,获得本届大赛的第一名。He had the top marks of all competitors during the competition and so won first place.

【评改】pínggǎi 批改 correct:～作文 correct a composition

【评功】píng//gōng 评定功绩 appraise sb.'s merits:～授奖 appraise merits and issue awards|给他评了三等功。He was honoured with a third-class merit citation.

【评估】pínggū 评议估计;评价 assess; evaluate:对入股资金的经济效益进行～ assess the economic benefits of the shareholders' capital|定期对学校的办学水平进行～ make regular assessments of the educational level of the school

【评话】pínghuà ❶ same as 平话 pínghuà ❷ 曲艺的一种,由一个人用当地方言讲说,如苏州评话 *pinghua*; folk storytelling art form in which the performer tells a story in a local dialect, e.g. the Suzhou dialect

【评级】píng//jí 评定干部、职工在工资、待遇等方面的等级 grade（government functionaries, workers, etc.）in such aspects as salary and benefits

【评价】píngjià ❶ 评定价值高低 appraise; evaluate; determine or fix the value of:～文学作品 appraise a literary work ❷ 评定的价值 assessed value:观众给予这部电影很高的～。The audience spoke highly of this film.

【评奖】píng//jiǎng 通过评比对优秀的给以奖励 grant awards through comparison and appraisal:年终～ grant awards at the end of the year

【评介】píngjiè 评论介绍 review and introduction:新书～ review of a new book

【评剧】píngjù 流行于华北、东北等地的地方戏曲剧种,最早产生于河北东部滦县一带,吸收了河北梆子、京剧等艺术成就。早期叫蹦蹦儿戏,也叫落子（lào·zi）。*pingju*; traditional opera popular in north and northeast China, which came into being in Luanxian County in eastern Hebei Province and later absorbed the artistic styles of Peking Opera and the Hebei Opera; also called 蹦蹦儿戏 bèngbèngrxì（in earlier times）or 落子 lào·zi

【评理】píng//lǐ 评断是非 judge between right and wrong:谁是谁非,由大家～。Let the masses judge who is right and who is wrong.

【评论】pínglùn ❶ 批评或议论 comment on; criticize or talk about:～好坏 comment on the good and the bad ❷ 批评或议论的文章 comment; commentary; review; article for comment and discussion: 发表～ publish a commentary

【评判】píngpàn 判定是非、胜负或优劣 pass judgment on; judge; decide (between right and wrong, winner and loser; superior and inferior): ～员 judge|～公允 make an equitable judgment

【评审】píngshěn 评议审查 examine and appraise: ～员 appraiser|～验收 check and appraise before acceptance|～文艺作品 make a critical examination and appraisal of a literary work

【评书】píngshū 曲艺的一种,多讲说长篇故事,用折扇、手帕、醒木等做道具 storytelling; folk art form in which the performer tells a long story using a folding fan, a handkerchief, and a gavel as props

【评述】píngshù 评论和叙述 commentary; comment and depiction

【评说】píngshuō 评论;评价 comment on; appraise; evaluate: ～古人 comment on the ancients|任人～ let others evaluate|是非功过,自有～。The right and wrong and the merits and demerits will be equitably evaluated.

【评弹】píngtán ❶ 曲艺的一种,流行于江苏、浙江一带,有说有唱,由评话和弹词结合而成 *pingtan*; folk art form combining storytelling and ballad singing, popular in Jiangsu and Zhejiang provinces ❷ 评话和弹词的合称 collective term for storytelling and ballad singing

【评头论足】píng tóu lùn zú 指无聊的人随便谈论妇女的容貌,也比喻 在小节上多方挑剔 (of silly people) make frivolous remarks about a woman's appearance; (fig.) find fault in small matters; be overcritical; also 评头品足 píng tóu pǐn zú or 品头论足 pǐn tóu lùn zú

【评析】píngxī 评论分析 comment and analyze: ～剧中主要角色 comment on the leading roles in a play|对比赛结果进行全面～ have an overall review and analysis on the result of the competition

【评薪】píng//xīn 评定工资 discuss and determine sb.'s salary

【评选】píngxuǎn 评比并推选 choose and appraise through comparison: ～先进工作者 choose advanced workers

【评议】píngyì 经过商讨而评定 appraise through discussion: 根据每个厂生产的实际情况进行～,确定等级 appraise and grade according to each factory's performance in production

【评语】píngyǔ 评论的话 comment; remark: 操行～ remarks on one's conduct

【评阅】píngyuè 阅览并评定(试卷或作品) read and appraise (an examination paper or a work): ～作文 read and appraise one's composition|考卷已经～完毕。The test papers have all been graded.

【评骘】píngzhì 〈书 *fml*.〉 same as 评定 píngdìng: ～书画 pass judgment on paintings and calligraphic works

【评注】píngzhù 评论并注解 make commentary and annotation: ～《聊斋志异》make commentaries and annotations on *Strange Stories from a Chinese Studio*

【评传】píngzhuàn 带有评论的传记 critical biography

坪 píng ❶ 平地(原指山区或黄土高原上的,多用于地名 orig. used to refer to mountainous area or the Loess Plateau and now oft. used as part of a place name) level ground: 草～ lawn|停机～ aircraft depot|杨家～(在陕西) Yangjiaping, name of a place in Shaanxi Province ❷ 〈方 *dial*.〉土地或房屋面积单位,1坪约合3.3平方米 *ping*, unit of measurement for an area of land or of a house. One *ping* equals 3.3 square metres.

【坪坝】píngbà 〈方 *dial*.〉平坦的场地 level, open space

苹(蘋) píng ☞ below
☞ 蘋 pín on p.1480

【苹果】píngguǒ ❶ 落叶乔木,叶子椭圆形,花白色带有红晕。果实圆形,味甜或略酸,是普通水果。apple tree; deciduous tree that has oval leaves and white flowers with a pink flush and that bears round, edible fruit, generally with a sweet or slightly tart taste ❷ 这种植物的果实 apple (*Malas pumila*), fruit of this plant

【苹果绿】píngguǒlǜ 浅绿 apple green

凭[1](憑、凴) píng ❶ (身子)靠着 (of body) lean on; lean against: ～几 lean on a small table ❷ 倚靠;倚仗 depend on; rely on: 劳动人民～着智慧和双手创造世界。The working people create the world with their intelligence and labour. ❸ 证据 evidence; proof: ～据 evidence|文～ diploma|口说不足为～。Oral expressions cannot be taken as evidence. ❹ 根据 base on; take as the basis: ～票付款 payable to bearer

凭[2](憑、凴) píng 〈连词 *conj*.〉无论 no matter: ～你跑多快,我也赶得上。I'll catch up with you no matter how fast you run.

【凭单】píngdān 做凭证的单据 bill or document of warrant

【凭吊】píngdiào 对着遗迹、坟墓等怀念(古人或旧事) visit a historical site, a tomb, etc., and think of (persons who have passed away or past events): ～烈士墓 pay a visit to a martyr's tomb|到杭州西湖去的人,总要到岳王坟前～一番。A visit to the Tomb of Yue Fei is a must for visitors to the West Lake in Hangzhou.

【凭借】píngjiè 依靠 rely on; depend on:人类的思维是～语言来进行的。Humankind thinks in words.

【凭据】píngjù 作为凭证的事物 evidence; proof; sth. used as testimonial

P

【凭空】píngkōng 没有依据地 without foundation; out of the void:～捏造 make something out of nothing; fabricate|～想像 imagine without foundation; also 平空 píngkōng

【凭栏】pínglán 靠着栏杆 lean on a railing:～远眺 lean on a railing and gaze into the distance

【凭陵】pínglíng〈书 *fml.*〉❶ 仗势侵犯;欺凌 encroach on; ride roughshod over ❷ 凭借 rely on; depend on

【凭恃】píngshì 倚仗;仗恃 rely on; depend on:～天险 rely on natural barriers for defense

【凭眺】píngtiào 在高处向远处看(多指欣赏风景 usu. for enjoyment of a distant view from a height) gaze from a high place into the distance:依栏～ lean on a railing and enjoy a view in the distance

【凭险】píngxiǎn 依靠险要的地势 rely on a place strategically located and of difficult access:～抵抗 make use of a strategic place to fight back|～据守 hold fast to natural barriers as defenses

【凭信】píngxìn 信赖;相信 trust; believe:不足～ not trustworthy

【凭依】píngyī 根据;倚靠 base oneself on; rely on:无所～ have nothing to go by

【凭仗】píngzhàng 倚仗 rely on; depend on:～着顽强不屈的精神克服了重重困难 overcome all kinds of difficulties with an indomitable spirit

【凭照】píngzhào 证件或执照 certificate or license:领取～ be granted with a license

【凭证】píngzhèng 证据 proof; evidence; certificate

枰 píng 棋盘 chessboard:棋～ chessboard

帡 píng [帡幪](píngméng) ❶〈古代 *arch.*〉称帐幕之类覆盖用的东西。在旁的叫帡,在上的叫幪。covering; that covering the sides of sth. is known as *ping*, and that covering the top of sth. is a *meng* ❷〈书 *fml.*〉庇护 protect; shield; shelter

洴 píng [洴澼](píngpì)〈书 *fml.*〉漂洗(丝绵) rinse (silk wadding)

屏 píng ❶ 屏风 screen:画～ painted screen ◇孔雀开～ peacock spreading its tail (to display its fine feathers) ❷ (～儿 píngr)屏条 a set of vertically hung scrolls:四扇～儿 a set of four scrolls ❸ 遮挡 shield sb. or sth.:～蔽 screen; shield

☞ bīng on p.139 and bǐng on p.140

【屏蔽】píngbì ❶ 像屏风似的遮挡着 screen; shield; give shelter to with, or as if with, a screen:～一方 screen an area ❷ 屏障 protective screen:东海岛是雷州湾的～。The Donghai Island provides a protective screen for Leizhou Bay.

【屏藩】píngfān〈书 *fml.*〉❶ 屏风和藩篱 screen and hedge;〈比喻 *fig.*〉周围的疆土 surrounding territories ❷ 保护捍卫 protect; shield ‖ also 藩屏 fānpíng

【屏风】píngfēng 放在室内用来挡风或隔断视线的用具,有的单扇,有的多扇相连,可以折叠 screen; indoor device for sheltering from wind or blocking the view. Some screens consist of a single leaf, and some link together and fold.

【屏门】píngmén 隔断里院和外院或隔断正院和跨院的门,最少的四扇 screen door; door between the outer and inner courtyards, or between the main and side courtyards, usu. composed of four or more narrow doors linked together

【屏幕】píngmù 显像管壳的一个组成部分。用玻璃制成,屏的里层涂有荧光粉,当电子撞击屏幕时就发出光点,可显示出波形或图像。screen; glass plate as a component part of a kinescope set, pasted with fluorescent dye on the inside, displaying waves or pictures formed of light spots when hit by electrons

【屏条】píngtiáo (～儿 píngtiáor)成组的条幅,通常四幅合成一组 a set of vertically hung scrolls (usu. four in a row) of painting or calligraphy

【屏障】píngzhàng ❶ 像屏风那样遮挡着的东西(多指山岭、岛屿等) barrier; protective screen; thing that gives screen-like shelter and protection (such as mountains, islands, etc.):燕山山地和西山山地是北京天然的～。The Yanshan and Xishan mountains provide natural barriers for Beijing. ❷〈书 *fml.*〉遮挡着 provide a protective screen for:～中原 provide a protective screen for central China

瓶(**缾**) píng (～儿 píngr)瓶子 bottle; vase; jar:～胆 liner (of a thermos flask)|花～儿 flower vase

【瓶胆】píngdǎn 保温瓶中间装水或其他东西的部分 liner (of a thermos flask); inner container for water etc.; ☞ 保温瓶 bǎowēnpíng on p.67

【瓶颈】píngjǐng ❶ 瓶子的上部较细的部分 bottleneck; narrow section near the mouth of a bottle ❷〈比喻 *fig.*〉事情进行中容易发生阻碍的关键环节 bottle neck; key link prone to mishaps in the process of sth.:扭转～现象

change the bottle-neck phenomenon; solve the bottle-neck problem

【瓶装】píngzhuāng (饮料等)用瓶子包装的 bottled; (of drinks) packed in bottles

【瓶子】píng·zi 容器,一般口较小,颈细肚大,多用瓷或玻璃制成 bottle; vase; jar; flask; container typically of glass or porcelain having a comparatively small mouth, a narrow neck, and a full body

萍(蓱) píng 浮萍 duckweed

【萍水相逢】píng shuǐ xiāng féng 〈比喻 *fig.*〉向来不认识的人偶然相遇(of strangers) chance encounter

【萍踪】píngzōng 〈书 *fml.*〉形容踪迹漂泊不定,像浮萍一般 wander like drifting duckweed along uncertain tracks

㻂 píng same as 屏 píng

鲆 píng 鱼类的一种,身体侧扁,呈片状,长椭圆形,有细鳞,左侧灰褐色,有黑色斑点,右侧白色,两眼在左侧。生活在浅海中,右侧向下卧在沙底,以小动物为食物。left-eyed flounder (*Bothidae*); bastard halibut; fish with an oblong, oval, laterally compressed body with small scales, having both eyes on its left side. Its left side is taupe and black-dotted, and its right side is white. It lives in shallow sea and lies on the sand with its right side down, feeding on small organisms.

pō (ㄆㄛ)

朴 pō [朴刀](pōdāo)一种旧式兵器,刀身狭长,刀柄略长,双手使用 old-type sword with a long blade and a short hilt, wielded with both hands

☞ Piáo on p.1476, pò on p.1493 and pǔ on p.1500

钋 pō 金属元素,符号 Po (polonium)。银白色,有放射性,钋和铍混合可制备中子源。polonium (Po); silvery-white, radioactive metallic element that can be made a neutron source by mixing with beryllium

陂 pō [陂陀](pōtuó)〈书 *fml.*〉不平坦 not level

☞ bēi on p.76 and pí on p.1466

坡 pō ❶ (~儿 pōr)地形倾斜的地方 slope; ground that forms an incline: 山~ mountain slope | 高~ high slope ❷ 倾斜 sloping; slanting: ~度 degree of slant | 板子~着放 put the board on a slant

【坡地】pōdì 山坡上倾斜的田地 sloping field; field on the mountain slope

【坡度】pōdù 斜坡起止点的高度差与水平距离的比值。如起止点的高度差为 12 米,水平距离为 1,000 米,坡度是 0.012。degree of an incline; gradient; slope; ratio of the altitude difference to the horizontal distance between the starting and ending points of a slope. For example, if the altitude difference between the starting and ending points is 12 metres, and the horizontal distance between the two points is 1,000 metres, the degree of the slope is 0.012.

【坡田】pōtián same as 坡地 pōdì

泊(泺) pō 湖 (多用于湖名 oft. used in lake names) lake: 湖~ lakes | 梁山~(在今山东) Liangshan Lake, in today's Shandong Province | 罗布~(在新疆) Lop Nur, in the Xinjiang Uygur Autonomous Region ◇血~ pool of blood

☞ bó on p.149 and 泺 luò on p.1280

泼[1] (潑) pō 用力把液体向外倒或向外洒,使散开 sprinkle; splash; spill; forcibly pour or scatter liquid: 扫地时,~一点水,免得尘土飞扬。Sprinkle some water on the floor before sweeping it so as to avoid dust flying about.

泼[2] (潑) pō ❶ 蛮横不讲理 rude and unreasonable: 撒~ be unreasonable and make a scene ❷ 〈方 *dial.*〉有魄力;有生气;有活力 bold and vigorous: 他做事很~。He is bold and resolute in his work. | 大伙儿干得真~。Everybody was working vigorously.

【泼妇】pōfù 指凶悍不讲理的妇女 shrew; virago; rude and unreasonable woman

【泼剌】pōlà 〈拟声词 *onom.*〉形容鱼在水里跳跃的声音 splash; sound made by fish jumping in the water; also 泼剌剌 pōlà·la

【泼辣】pō·la ❶ 凶悍而不讲理 rude and unreasonable; shrewish ❷ 有魄力;勇猛 daring and resolute: 大胆~ bold and resolute | 干活很~ be bold and vigorous in one's work

【泼冷水】pō lěngshuǐ 〈比喻 *fig.*〉打击人的热情 dampen one's enthusiasm for

【泼墨】pōmò 国画的一种画法,用笔蘸墨汁大片地洒在纸上或绢上,画出物体形象,像把墨汁泼上去一样 splash-ink; technique of traditional Chinese painting in which the painter dips the brush in ink and paints images of objects on paper or silk in bold and unrestrained strokes so that the painting looks as if it had been splashed with ink: ~山水 splashed-ink landscape

【泼醅】pōpēi 〈书 *fml.*〉same as 酦醅 pōpēi

【泼皮】pōpí 流氓;无赖 knave; gangster; blackguard

【泼洒】pōsǎ 泼下(液体等);洒 spill (liquid); splash: 他手一抖,杯子里的茶水~出来。As his hand quivered momentarily, tea spilled out of the cup. ◇月光如水,~在静谧的原野上。The moonlight looked like water splashed over the peace and quiet of the field.

【泼水节】Pōshuǐ Jié 我国傣族和中南半岛某些民族的传统节日，在公历四月中。节日期间，人们穿着盛装，互相泼水祝福，并进行拜佛、赛龙舟、文艺会演、物资交流等活动。Water-Splashing Festival; traditional festival in April of Solar Calendar celebrated by the Dais and some ethnic peoples in Indo-China Peninsular during which folks are dressed in their holiday's best, exchange goodwill by sprinkling water on each other, worship Buddha, hold dragon boat races and variety shows, and buy and sell goods

【泼天】pōtiān 形容极大、极多(多见于早期白话 oft. used in early vernacular) extremely great in size, extent or degree; enormous: ～大祸 catastrophe | ～家业 large family property | ～本事 considerable ability

钹(鏺) pō〈方 *dial.*〉❶ 用镰刀、钐(shàn)刀等抡开来割(草、谷物等) cut (grass or grain) with sickle or chopper ❷ 一种镰刀 sickle

颇1 pō〈书 *fml.*〉偏；不正 inclined to one side; oblique: 偏～ biased; partial

颇2 pō〈书 *fml.*〉很；相当地 quite; rather; considerably; well; significantly: ～佳 quite good | ～为费解 rather difficult to understand | ～感兴趣 be greatly interested in | ～不以为然 highly disapprove of sth.

酦(醱) pō〈书 *fml.*〉酿(酒) make wine ☞ fā on p.524

【酦醅】pōpēi〈书 *fml.*〉酿酒 make wine; also 泼醅 pōpēi

pó(ㄆㄛˊ)

婆 pó ❶ 年老的妇女 old woman: 老太～ old woman ❷ (～儿 pór)〈旧时 *old*〉指某些职业妇女 woman in a certain occupation: 媒～儿 woman matchmaker | 收生～ midwife ❸ 丈夫的母亲 husband's mother; mother-in-law: 公～ husband's parents; parents-in-law | ～媳 mother-in-law and daughter-in-law

【婆家】pó·jia 丈夫的家(区别于'娘家' as compared with 'wife's family') husband's family; also 婆婆家 pó·pojiā

【婆罗门教】Póluóménjiào 印度古代的宗教，崇拜梵天(最高的神)，后来经过改革，称为印度教 Brahmanism; Brahma-worshiping religion of ancient India that was later reformed and called Hinduism; [婆罗门，梵 Sanskrit: brāhmana]

【婆娘】póniáng〈方 *dial.*〉❶ 泛指已婚的妇女 (in a broad sense) married woman ❷ 妻 wife

【婆婆】pó·po ❶ 丈夫的母亲 husband's mother; mother-in-law ◇基层单位上面的～太多，层层审批，难以办事。It's difficult for the units at the grass-roots level to get things done for they have to get the go-ahead from too many higher-ups. ❷〈方 *dial.*〉祖母；外祖母 grandmother; grandma

【婆婆妈妈】pó·pomāmā (～的 pó·pomāmā·de) 形容人行动缓慢、言语啰唆或感情脆弱 (of a person) moving slowly and talking too much of unimportant things or be easily upset; like an old woman; old-womanish; garrulous; loquacious; talkative: 你快一点吧，别这么～的了。Hurry up! Don't fuss like an old woman. | 他就是这么～的，动不动就掉眼泪。He's such a sissy. He easily breaks down and cries.

【婆婆嘴】pó·pozuǐ 形容嘴碎，说话絮叨。也指说话絮叨的人。nagging tongue; also refers to a garrulous person

【婆娑】pósuō 盘旋(多指舞蹈) whirling; dancing: ～起舞 start dancing; stroll about and start dancing ◇树影～。The trees sway gently in the breeze.

【婆姨】póyí〈方 *dial.*〉❶ 泛指已婚妇女 (in a broad sense) married woman ❷ 妻 wife

鄱 pó 鄱阳(Póyáng)，湖名，在江西 Poyang Lake (in Jiangxi Province)

繁 Pó 姓 a surname
☞ fán on p.534

皤 pó〈书 *fml.*〉❶ 白色 white: 白发～然 white-haired ❷ 大(腹) (of belly) big: ～其腹 be potbellied; with a protruding abdomen

pǒ(ㄆㄛˇ)

叵 pǒ〈书 *fml.*〉❶ 不可 impossible ❷ 便；就 just; then

【叵测】pǒcè 不可推测(贬义 derog.) unfathomable; unpredictable: 居心～ harbour dark designs; nurse evil intentions; with hidden intent | 心怀～ with a heart hard to fathom; with ulterior motives

【叵耐】pǒnài ❶ 不可容忍；可恨(多见于早期白话 oft. used in early vernacular) intolerable; can not tolerate; can not put up with ❷ 无奈 can not help but; have no alternative ‖ also 叵奈 pǒnài

钷 pǒ 金属元素，符号 Pm (promethium)。是一种稀土元素。有放射性，由人工获得。银白色，用来制荧光粉等。promethium (Pm); metallic chemical element of the rare-earth group, with radioactivity and can be obtained artificially, silver in colour, can be used to make phosphor powder

笸 pǒ ☞ below

【笸篮】pǒlán 用柳条或篾条等编成的篮子 basket made of wicker or thin bamboo strips

【笸箩】pǒ· luo 用柳条或篾条编成的器物，帮较浅，有圆形的，也有略呈长方形的 shallow

round or quadrate utensil made of wicker or thin bamboo strips：针线～ sewing basket

pò（ㄆㄛˋ）

朴 pò 朴树，落叶乔木，叶子卵形或长椭圆形，花小，淡黄色，果实圆形，黑色，有核，木材可制器具 Chinese hackberry（*Celtis sinensis*）；deciduous tree with oval-shaped leaves and small，pale-yellow blossom，bearing round dark fruits with stones inside，the wood of which can be used to make utensils

☞ Piáo on p.1476，pō on p.1491 and pǔ on p.1500

【朴硝】pòxiāo 含有食盐、硝酸钾和其他杂质的硫酸钠，是海水或盐湖水熬过之后沉淀出来的结晶体。可用来硝皮革，医药上用做泻药或利尿药。mirabilite；Glauber's salt；sodium sulfate containing salt，niter and other impurities，extracted from sea water or saltlake water，used to taw leather or as cathartic or diuretic；通称 generally known as 皮硝 píxiāo

迫（廹）pò ❶ 逼迫；强迫 compel；force；press；coerce；constrain；oblige：压～ oppress｜～害 persecute｜饥寒交～ suffer hunger and cold｜被～出走 be compelled to leave ❷ 急促 urgent；pressing：急～ pressing；imperative｜窘～ poverty-stricken；hard pressed｜～不及待 be utterly impatient；cannot wait｜从容不～ calmly；leisurely ❸ 接近 approach；go towards（or near）：～近 get close to；draw near

☞ pǎi on p.1440

【迫不得已】pò bù dé yǐ 迫于无奈，不由得不那样（做）have no alternative（but to）；be forced（or driven，compelled）to；（do sth.）against one's will；compelled by circumstances；under the pressure of circumstances

【迫不及待】pò bù jí dài 急迫得不能再等待 unable to hold oneself back；brook no delay；too impatient to wait；in haste；jump to do sth.

【迫害】pòhài 压迫使受害（多指政治性的 esp. because of political reasons）treat sb. cruelly；persecute；oppress cruelly：遭受～ suffer persecution；be subjected to persecution｜～致死 hound sb. to death

【迫降】pòjiàng ❶ 飞机因迷航、燃料用尽或发生故障等不能继续飞行而被迫降落 forced landing；crash-landing；emergency landing that an aircraft has to make due to disorientation，fuel exhaustion or malfunction ❷ 强迫擅自越境或严重违犯飞行纪律的飞机在指定的机场降落 compel an aircraft that crosses the border illegally or seriously violates flight rules to land in a designated airport

☞ pòxiáng

【迫近】pòjìn 逼近 approach；get close to；draw near；imminent：～年关。The end of the year is approaching（when accounts must be settled）.｜～胜利 be nearing victory；come in sight of victory

【迫临】pòlín 逼近 come near to；come in sight of；be impending；get close to：～考期。The examination is impending（or is imminent）.

【迫切】pòqiè 需要到难以等待的程度；十分急切 needing immediate attention or action；urgent；pressing；imperative：工人们～要求提高技术水平。The workers badly need to improve their technological level.｜农民对机械化的要求越来越～了。The farmers have an increasingly urgent demand for mechanization.

【迫使】pòshǐ 用强力或压力使（做某事）make sb. do sth. with pressure；force；press；compel；oblige；coerce：～对方让步 force one's opponent to make concessions｜时间～我们不得不改变计划。We had to change our plan due to the lack of time.

【迫降】pòxiáng 逼迫敌人投降 force the enemy to surrender

☞ pòjiàng

【迫在眉睫】pò zài méi jié〈比喻 *fig.*〉事情临近眼前，十分紧迫 extremely urgent；imminent；pressing；overriding；constraining

珀 pò ☞［琥珀］（hǔpò）on p.822

破 pò ❶ 完整的东西受到损伤变得不完整 split or cracked into pieces；broken；damaged；torn；worn-out：～烂 tattered；ragged；worn-out｜手～了 cut one's hand｜纸戳～了 poke a hole in the paper ❷ 使损坏 break；damage：～釜沉舟 break the caldrons and sink the boats ❸ 使分裂；劈开 split；cleave；cut：势如～竹 as forceful as splitting bamboo；with a crushing force｜～开西瓜 cut up the watermelon ❹ 整的换成零的 change（money）：一元的票子～成两张五角的。Change a one-yuan note into two 5-*jiao* notes. ❺ 突破；破除（规定、习惯、思想等）break；do away with（rules and regulations，habits，ideas，etc.）：～格 make an exception｜～例 make an exception ❻ 打败（敌人）；打下（据点）defeat（the enemy）；capture（a city）：攻～城池 capture a city｜大～敌军 inflict a crushing defeat on an enemy ❼ 花费 spend：～钞 spend money｜～费 go to some expense｜～工夫 spend time ❽ 使真相露出；揭穿 expose the truth of；lay bare：～案 solve a case｜说～ puncture a fallacy｜一语道～ get to the heart of the matter in a few words ❾ 讥讽东西或人不好（含厌恶意 derog.）（of sb. or sth.）lousy；shabby：谁看那～戏！Who wants to see that poor show!

【破案】pò//àn 查出刑事案件的真相 find out

the truth of a criminal case; bust a case; crack a criminal case:限期～ solve a case to a deadline

【破败】pòbài ❶ 残破 ruined; dilapidated; run-down:山上的小庙已经～不堪。The small temple on the mountain is utterly dilapidated. ❷ 衰败 decline; wane; be at the wane:～的家庭 family on the decline

【破冰船】pòbīngchuán 一种特制的轮船,能用尖而硬的船头冲破较薄的冰层,或使船身左右摇摆,压破较厚的冰层。主要用于开辟冰区航路。ice-breaker; ship specially built to break thin ice layers with its sharp and hard bow or crush thick ice layers by rocking its body, so as to break a passage through ice

【破财】pòcái 破费钱财,多指遭遇意外的损失,如失窃等 suffer unexpected personal financial loss, such as theft; lose money:～免灾 lose money just to avoid misfortune|这事情又叫你劳神～了。This matter taxed your mind and money again.

【破产】pò//chǎn ❶ 债务人不能偿还债务时,法院根据本人或债权人的申请,做出裁定,把债务人的财产变价依法归还各债主,其不足之数不再偿付 bankruptcy; judging of a court on the application of a person or his creditors when he is not able to repay his debt, according to which the debtor's properties are sold at current prices to repay the creditors and the rest of debt will not be repaid ❷ 丧失全部财产 go bankrupt; go broke; lose all of one's properties:一场大火使村上的许多农家破了产。Many farmers went bankrupt due to the big fire. ❸〈比喻 *fig.*〉事情失败(多含贬义 usu. derog.)(of a matter) fall through; come to nothing; come to naught; be bankrupt:计划～。The plan fell through.|阴谋～。The plot has fallen through.

【破钞】pòchāo 为请客、送礼、资助、捐献等而破费钱(大多在感谢别人因为自己而花钱时用做客气话 usu. used to show one's gratefulness for others) spend money on feast, presents, financial aid or contribution; spend money; go to some expense

【破除】pòchú 除去(原来被人尊重或信仰的事物) do away with (sth. respected or believed in); get rid of; eradicate; break with:～情面 not spare anybody's feelings|～迷信 do away with superstitions or blind faith; topple old idols

【破读】pòdú 同一个字形因意义不同而有两个以上读音的时候,把习惯上认为最通常的读音之外的读音,叫做破读,如'喜好'的'好'读去声(区别于'美好'的'好'读上声)split reading — the way in which a character is pronounced when it has a meaning or function other than its usual one (e.g. 好 hào in 喜好 xǐhào is a 'split reading' of 好 hǎo, which is pronounced hǎo in 美好 měihǎo)

☞ 如字 rúzì on p. 1636 and 读破 dúpò on p. 479

【破读字】pòdúzì 指读破的字 character of split reading; ☞ 读破 dúpò on p. 479

【破费】pòfèi 花费(金钱或时间) spend (money or time); go to some expense:不要多～,吃顿便饭就行了。Don't go to any expense. A simple meal will do.|要完成这项工程,还得～工夫。We have to spend more time to complete this project.

【破釜沉舟】pò fǔ chén zhōu 项羽跟秦兵打仗,过河后把锅都打破,船都弄沉,表示不再回来(见于《史记·项羽本纪》)。比喻下决心,不顾一切干到底。cut off all means of retreat; burn one's boats. In a war against the state of Qin, Xiang Yu had the cauldrons broken and the boats sunk (after crossing), to show his determination in a 'make or break it' situation (*Records of the Historian · Official Records of Xiang Yu*)

【破格】pògé 打破既定规格的约束 break the restriction of prescribed rules; break a rule; make an exception:～提升 break a rule to promote sb.|～录用 break a rule to engage sb.

【破罐破摔】pò guàn pò shuāi〈比喻 *fig.*〉有了缺点、错误,不加改正,任其自流,或反而有意朝更坏的方向发展 smash a pot to pieces just because it's cracked — write off one's situation as hopeless and act recklessly

【破坏】pòhuài ❶ 使建筑物等损坏 destroy; wreck (buildings, etc.):～桥梁 destroy a bridge|～文物 cultural vandalism; damage cultural relics ❷ 使事物受到损害 do great damage to; damage; disrupt:～生产 sabotage production|～名誉 damage sb.'s reputation ❸ 变革(社会制度、风俗习惯等)(social systems, custom, etc.) change completely or violently ❹ 违反(规章、条约等)(regulation, agreement, etc.) violate; break:～协定 violate an agreement|～规矩 break the rules ❺ (物体的组织或结构)损坏 decompose; destroy (the composition of a substance):维生素C因受热而～。Vitamin C is destroyed when heated.

【破获】pòhuò ❶ 破案并捕获罪犯 crack a case and capture the criminal ❷ 识破并获得秘密 unearth; uncover (a secrecy)

【破戒】pò//jiè ❶ 信教或受过戒的人违反宗教戒律 (of a religious person) break the religious commandments ❷ 戒烟、戒酒以后重新吸烟、喝酒 break one's vow of abstinence from smoking or drinking

【破镜重圆】pò jìng chóng yuán 南朝陈代将要灭亡的时候,驸马徐德言把一个铜镜破开,跟妻子乐昌公主各藏一半,预备失散后当做信物,以后果然由这个线索而夫妻团聚(见唐代孟棨《本事诗》)。后来用'破镜重圆'比喻夫妻失散或决裂后重又团圆。broken mirror joined together — reunion of husband and wife after an imposed separation or rupture. According to the poem *Original Incidents of Poems* by Meng Qi of the Tang Dynasty, towards the end of the Chen Dynasty of the Southern Dynasties, the emperor's son-in-law Xu Deyan broke a mirror in halves, keeping a half himself and leaving the other to his wife Princess Yuechang, as a keepsake for reunion in case they were separated. Later the mirror helped the couple reunite.

【破旧】pòjiù 又破又旧 old and shabby; worn-out; dilapidated:～衣服 worn-out clothes|院墙和屋子都很～。Both the house and the courtyard walls are old and crumbling of age.

【破旧立新】pò jiù lì xīn 破除旧的,建立新的 destroy the old and establish the new; eradicate the old and foster the new:～,移风易俗。Destroy old customs and habits and establish new ones.

【破句】pòjù 指在不是一句的地方读断或点断 pause or mark pauses in reading at the wrong place

【破口大骂】pò kǒu dà mà 指用恶语大声地骂 shout abuse; let loose a torrent of abuse; hurl all kinds of abuse

【破烂】pòlàn ❶ 因时间久或使用久而残破 tattered; ragged; worn-out (due to age or long-time use):～不堪 torn and tattered|衣衫～ dressed in rags ❷ (～儿 pòlànr)破烂的东西;废品 junk; scrap:捡～ scavenge for odds and ends from a garbage heap|收～ collect waste for recycling|一堆～儿 a heap of junk

【破浪】pòlàng (船只)冲过波浪(of ships) cleave the waves; brave the waves:乘风～ ride the waves and winds|在急流中～前进 cleave (or cut, plough) through the rapids

【破例】pò//lì 打破常例 break a rule; make an exception:～放行 break a rule to let sb. pass|制度要严格遵守,不能～。The regulations should be followed to the letter and no exceptions shall be made.

【破脸】pò//liǎn 不顾情面,当面争吵 turn against; fall out; quarrelling with sb. without any consideration of personal feelings

【破裂】pòliè ❶ (完整的东西)出现裂缝;开裂 (of an intact subject) break; split; rupture; crack; fracture; burst:棉桃成熟时,果皮～。The skin of cotton bolls cracks when they get ripe. ❷ 双方的感情、关系等遭破坏而分裂(affections or relations) break; sever; disrupt:谈判～。The negotiation broke down.

【破裂摩擦音】pòliè mócāyīn 塞擦音的旧称 old term for 塞擦音 sāicāyīn

【破裂音】pòlièyīn 塞音的旧称 old term for 塞音 sāiyīn

【破陋】pòlòu 破旧简陋 shabby and crude:房屋～。The house is shabby and crude.

【破落】pòluò ❶ (家境)由盛而衰(of family wealth and position) decline; fall into reduced circumstances; be reduced to poverty:～户 impoverished family; family that has gone down in the world|家业～ declined family property ❷ 破败 ruined; dilapidated:～的茅屋 rundown cottage

【破落户】pòluòhù 指先前有钱有势而后来败落的人家 impoverished family; family used to be rich and powerful but went down in the world

【破谜儿】pò//mèir ❶ 猜谜儿 solve a riddle ❷ 〈方 *dial.*〉出谜儿给人猜 ask a riddle

【破门】pòmén ❶ 砸开门 burst (or force) open the door:～而入 break into; force open a door ❷ 足球、冰球、手球等运动指将球攻进球门(in football, handball, ice hockey, etc.) score a goal:～得分 score a goal ❸ 开除出教会 excommunicate sb. (from the church)

【破灭】pòmiè (幻想或希望)落空(of hopes or illusions) fall through; be shattered; evaporate into thin air

【破墨】pòmò 国画的一种画法。为使墨色浓淡相互渗透,使画面滋润鲜明,用浓墨破淡墨,或用淡墨破浓墨。broken-ink; method of Chinese painting characterized by the infiltration of thick and thin ink that makes the configuration full and distinctive

【破碎】pòsuì ❶ 破成碎块 broken into pieces; tattered:这纸年代太久,一翻就～了。The paper is of an old age and becomes tattered at the slightest touch. ◇山河～ disintegrated country ❷ 使破成碎块 smash (or break) sth. to pieces; crush:这个破碎机每小时可以～多少吨矿石? How many tons of ore can this machine crush in an hour?

【破损】pòsǔn 残破损坏 damaged; worn; torn:托运的木箱有些～。The wooden box for consignment is somewhat damaged.

【破题】pòtí 八股文的第一股,用一两句话,说破题目的要义 first two sentences giving the theme (originally said of an old stereotyped eight-legged essay); ☞ 八股 bāgǔ on p.21

【破题儿第一遭】pò tí·er dì yī zāo 〈比喻 *fig.*〉第一次做某件事 first time one ever does sth.; first time ever:登台演戏我还是～。This is the first time that I have acted on the stage.

【破体字】pòtǐzì 〈旧指 *old*〉不合正体的俗字 Chinese characters which are not of standardized scripts

【破涕】pòtì 停止哭 stop crying:～为笑 smile through tears; melt into smiles; turn tears into smiles

【破天荒】pòtiānhuāng 唐朝时荆州每年送举人去考进士都考不中,当时称天荒(天荒:从未开垦过的土地),后来刘蜕考中了,称为破天荒(见于孙光宪《北梦琐言》卷四)。比喻事情第一次出现。occur for the first time; be unprecedented. During the Tang Dynasty, the provincial graduates from Jingzhou always failed in the highest imperial examination, which was thus dubbed 'uncharted territory'. Later, when Liu Rui succeeded in the exam, he was hailed as the first man to break this 'uncharted territory', according to Volume Four of *Trifling Words of Northern Dream* by Sun Guangxian

P

【破土】pòtǔ ❶ 指建筑开始时或埋葬时挖地动工 break ground (to start a building project or bury a coffin) ❷ 指春天土地解冻后翻松泥土,开始耕种 start spring ploughing (when the soil thaws) ❸ 指种子发芽后幼苗钻出地面 (of a seedling) break through the soil

【破五】pòwǔ (～儿 pòwǔr)旧俗指农历正月初五。过去一般商店多在破五以后才开始营业。(old custom) the 5th day of the 1st lunar month (after which the shops are reopened and business is resumed)

【破相】pò//xiàng 指由于脸部受伤或其他原因而失去原来的相貌 (of facial features) be marred by a scar, etc.

【破晓】pòxiǎo (天)刚亮 dawn; daybreak:天色～。Day is breaking.

【破鞋】pòxié 指乱搞男女关系的女人 loose woman; promiscuous woman; sexually immoral woman

【破颜】pòyán 转为笑容 break into a smile:～一笑 break one's stern countenance and smile; crack a smile

【破译】pòyì 识破并译出获得的未知信息,如密码、古代曲谱或文字等 decode; decipher; translate (an unknown message such as code, ancient music score or characters) into easy-to-understand language

【破约】pò//yuē 不遵守共同订立的条文或预先的约定 break one's promise; break a jointly-established clause or agreement

【破绽】pò·zhàn 衣物的裂口 burst seam;〈比喻 *fig*.〉说话做事时露出的漏洞 flaw; weak point; leak in one's remarks or deeds:～百出 be riddled with holes

【破折号】pòzhéhào 标点符号(—),表示话题的转换,或者表示底下有个注释性的部分 dash; punctuation mark representing a change of topics or explanation

粕 pò〈书 *fml*.〉渣滓 dregs (of rice):糟～ waste matter; dregs; dross|豆～ dregs of bean

魄 pò ❶ 迷信的人指依附于人的身体而存在的精神 soul; spiritual matter believed by religious people as dependent on human's body:魂～ soul ❷ 魄力或精力 vigour; spirit:气～ boldness of vision|体～ physique

☞ bó on p. 151 and tuò on p. 1963

【魄力】pò·lì 指处置事情所具有的胆识和果断的作风 daring and resolution; boldness; courage and decisiveness in handling matters

·po (·ㄆㄛ)

桲 ·po ☞ [榅桲] (wēn·po) on p. 2004

pōu (ㄆㄡ)

剖 pōu ❶ 破开 cut open; rip open:解～ dissect; anatomy|～腹 lay open the bowel; disembowel|横～面 cross section ❷ 分辨;分析 analyse; examine; dissect:～析 analyse; dissect|～明事理 explain the reason

【剖白】pōubái 分辩表白 explain oneself; vindicate oneself:～心迹 lay one's heart bare|总想找个机会向他～几句。I am trying to find an opportunity to explain myself to him.

【剖腹】pōufù 破开腹腔 lay open the bowel; disembowel:～自尽 lay open the bowel and commit suicide; hara-kiri|～手术 Caesarean section (or operation)

【剖腹藏珠】pōu fù cáng zhū 剖开肚子来藏珍珠 rip (or cut) open the stomach to hide a pearl;〈比喻 *fig*.〉为物伤身,轻重倒置 hold onto sth. trivial for dear life

【剖解】pōujiě 分析(道理等) analyse (reasons, etc.):～细密 make a minute analysis

【剖面】pōumiàn 物体切断后呈现出的表面,如球体的剖面是个圆形 section; plane surface exposed by cutting, e.g. the section of a ball is circular; also 截面 jiémiàn,切面 qiēmiàn or 断面 duànmiàn

【剖视】pōushì 剖析观察(多用于抽象事物 usu. sth. abstract) analyse and look into:～人物的精神境界 analyse and look into a person's inner world

【剖视图】pōushìtú 用一假想平面剖切物体的适当部分,然后把观察者与剖开平面之间的部分移开,余下部分的视图叫剖视图 cut-open view; cutaway view; view of the section of an object being cut through by an imagined surface

【剖析】pōuxī 分析 analyse; dissect:这篇文章～事理十分透彻。This article made a thorough analysis of the way things are.

póu (ㄆㄡˊ)

抔 póu〈书 *fml*.〉用手捧东西 hold sth. with cupped hands:一～土 a handful of earth

掊 póu〈书 *fml*.〉❶ 聚敛;搜括 amass wealth by heavy taxation; exact ❷ 挖掘 dig; excavate

☞ pǒu on p. 1497

裒 póu〈书 *fml*.〉❶ 聚 gather; collect:～辑 compile; collect|～然成集 be collected into a volume ❷ 取出 draw out; take out:～多益寡(取有余,补不足) take from what is in excess to make good what is deficient; cut off from the long to add to the short; take from those who have too much and give to those who have too little

【裒辑】póují〈书 *fml*.〉辑录 collect; compile:此书系从类书中～而成。This book is a collection of selected reference books.

pǒu (ㄆㄡˇ)

掊 pǒu〈书 *fml*.〉❶ 击 hit; attack:～击 give blows; attack; blast; lash out at ❷ 破开 cut open; break

☞ póu on p.1496

pū (ㄆㄨ)

仆 pū 向前跌倒 fall forward; fall prostrate:前～后继 advance and fill the breach left by fallen comrades; advance wave upon wave

☞ pú on p.1499

扑(撲) pū ❶ 用力向前冲,使全身突然伏在物体上 throw oneself on or at sth.; pounce on:孩子高兴得一下～到我怀里来。The child threw himself joyfully into my arms. ◇和风～面。A pleasant breeze caresses the face.|香气～鼻。A fragrance greeted the nostrils. ❷ 把全部心力用到(工作、事业等上面) dedicate all one's energies to a cause; devote:他一心～在教育事业上。He devotes himself heart and soul to the cause of education. ❸ 扑打;拍打 flap; flutter:～蝶 catch a butterfly|～蝇 flap at a fly|海鸥～着翅膀,直冲海空。The seagull fluttered its wings and soared high into the sky.|小孩的身上～了一层痱子粉。The child was dabbed all over with talcum. ❹〈方 *dial*.〉伏 bend over:～在桌上看地图 bend over a map on the desk

【扑鼻】pūbí 形容气味浓烈(of strong scent) assail the nostrils:香气～。A sweet smell greeted us.|玫瑰发出～的芳香。The roses gave off sweet scent.

【扑哧】pūchī〈拟声词 *onom*.〉形容笑声或水、气挤出的声音[sound of snorting or fizzing]:～一笑 snort with laughter|～一声,皮球撒了气。The ball went soft with a fizz. also 噗嗤 pūchī

【扑打】pūdǎ 用扁平的东西猛然朝下打 swat; hit (sb. or sth.) hard with a flat object:～蝗虫 swat locusts

【扑打】pū•da 轻轻地拍 pat; beat; tap gently:～身上的雪花 pat snow off the clothes

【扑跌】pūdiē ❶ 武术中的相扑或摔跤 sumo; wrestling ❷ 向前跌倒 fall forward:他脚下一绊,～在地上。He stumbled and fell.

【扑粉】pūfěn ❶ 化妆用的香粉 face powder ❷ 爽身粉 talcum powder

【扑虎儿】pūhǔr〈方 *dial*.〉向前扑跌两手着地的动作 fall forward:摔了个～ fall forward

【扑救】pūjiù 扑灭火灾,抢救人和财物 put out a fire to save life and property

【扑克】pūkè 一种纸牌,共52张,分黑桃、红桃、方块、梅花四种花色,每种有A,K,Q,J,10,9,8,7,6,5,4,3,2各一张,现在一般都另增大王、小王各一张,玩法很多 poker; playing cards; a kind of card-game that can be played in many ways, including 52 cards with four patterns — black heart, red heart, diamond and plum flower — with each pattern consisting of 13 cards marked A, K, Q, J, 10, 9, 8, 7, 6, 5, 4, 3 and 2, but a modern set is added with two clowns

【扑空】pū//kōng 没有在目的地找到要找的对象 fail to get or achieve what one wants; fail to find a person where he is supposed to be; come away empty-handed:我到他家里去找他,扑了一个空。I went to his home to see him but he wasn't in.

【扑棱】pūlēng〈拟声词 *onom*.〉形容翅膀抖动的声音 sound of flapping of wings:～一声,飞起一只小鸟。There was a flutter of wings and up flew a bird.

【扑棱】pū•leng 抖动或张开 flutter or spread open:翅膀一～,飞走了。With a flap of wings, (it) flew away.|穗子～开像一把小伞。The tassel spread open like a small umbrella.

【扑脸】pūliǎn (～儿 pūliǎnr)扑面 blow on (or against)one's face:热气～。The hot air blew on the face.

【扑满】pūmǎn 用来存钱的瓦器,像没口的小酒坛,上面有一个细长的孔。钱币放进去之后,要打破扑满才能取出来。piggy bank; money-box; crockery for collecting money shaped like a wine-jar with a slot for putting in coins. The money can be retrieved only by breaking the crockery.

【扑面】pūmiàn 迎着脸来 blow on (or against) one's face:清风～。A gentle breeze caressed our faces.

【扑灭】pū//miè 扑打消灭 stamp out; put out; extinguish; wipe out; mop up:～蚊蝇 wipe out mosquitoes and flies|～大火 put out a fire

【扑闪】pū•shan 眨;闪动 blink; wink:他～着一双大眼睛。His big eyes blinked.

【扑扇】pū•shan〈方 *dial*.〉扑棱(pū•leng) flap; flutter:～翅膀 flutter wings

【扑朔迷离】pūshuò mílí《木兰辞》:'雄兔脚扑朔,雌兔眼迷离,两兔傍地走,安能辨我是雄雌。'雄兔脚乱动,雌兔眼半闭着,但是跑起来的时候就很难辨别哪是雄的,哪是雌的。unable to distinguish whether one is a male or a female. *The Ballad of Mulan*: 'The male rabbit kicks its fluffy feet as it scampers,/ The eyes of the female rabbit are blurred by fluffy tufts of hair,/ But when they run side by side in the field,/ You can hardly tell the doe from the buck.'〈比喻 *fig*.〉事物错综复杂,难于辨别 bewildering; confusing

P

【扑簌】pūsù 形容眼泪向下掉的样子(of tears) trickling down:～～掉下眼泪 tears trickle down; also 扑簌簌 pūsùsù

【扑腾】pūtēng〈拟声词 *onom*.〉形容重物落地的声音 sound of a heavy fall; flop; thump; thud:小王～一声,从墙上跳下来。Xiao Wang fell down from the wall with a thud.

【扑腾】pū·teng ❶ 游泳时用脚打水 move one's legs up and down in the water; flop; also 打扑腾 dǎ pū·teng ❷ 跳动 throb; palpitate:他吓得心里直～。His heart was throbbing with fear.|鱼卡在冰窟窿口直～。The fish flopped helplessly in the ice hole. ❸〈方 *dial*.〉活动 hustle; bustle; keep the ball rolling:这个人挺能～。He is quite a go-getter. ❹ 挥霍;浪费 spend freely; squander:钱全～完了 squander all the money

【扑通】pūtōng〈拟声词 *onom*.〉形容重物落地或落水的声音 sound of sth. heavily dropping into the water or to the ground; flop; thump; splash; pit-a-pat:～一声,跳进水里 fall into the water with a splash; also 噗通 pūtōng

铺 pū ❶ 把东西展开或摊平 spread; extend; unfold; open or spread out sth.:～床 make the bed|～轨 lay a railway track|～被褥 spread the bedding|～平道路 pave the way ◇平～直叙 tell in a simple, straightforward way ❷〈方 *dial*.〉〈量词 *classifier*〉用于炕[for bed]:一～炕 a brick bed

☞ pù on p. 1502

【铺陈】[1] pūchén ❶〈方 *dial*.〉摆设;布置 spread out; arrange; decorate:～酒器 lay out the drinking vessels ❷ 铺叙 narrate in detail; describe at great length; elaborate:～经过 describe a process in detail

【铺陈】[2] pūchén〈方 *dial*.〉指被褥和枕头等床上用品 bedclothes; bedding (including pillows, quilts; mattress, etc.)

【铺衬】pū·chen 碎的布头或旧布,做补钉或袼褙用 small pieces of cloth used for patches

【铺床】pū//chuáng 把被褥铺在床上 make the bed

【铺垫】pūdiàn ❶ 铺;垫 cushion:床上～了厚厚的褥子。The bed was laid with a thick mattress. ❷ (～儿 pūdiànr)铺在床上的卧具 bedding ❸ 陪衬;衬托 foreshadowing:由于作者对情节的发展事先作了～,因而后来发生的故事并不使读者感到突然。Because of the foreshadowing on the development of the story, the readers were not surprised at what happened later.

【铺盖】pūgài 平铺着盖 spread (evenly) over:把草木灰～在苗床上。Spread plant ash evenly over a seedbed.

【铺盖】pū·gai 褥子和被子 bedding; bedclothes

【铺盖卷儿】pū·gaijuǎnr 搬运时卷成卷儿的被褥 bedding roll; bedroll; luggage roll; a portable roll of bedding; also 行李卷儿 xíng·lijuǎnr

【铺轨】pū//guǐ 铺设铁轨 lay a railway track

【铺路】pū//lù ❶ 铺设道路 paving; pave a road:～石 flagstone|修桥～ build bridges and pave roads ❷〈比喻 *fig*.〉为做某件事创造条件 pave the way; create conditions for doing sth.

【铺排】pūpái ❶ 布置;安排 put in order; arrange:大小事都～得停停当当。Everything was well arranged. ❷ 铺张 be extravagant:～太过 extravagant and wasteful

【铺砌】pūqì 用砖、石等覆盖地面或建筑物的表面,使平整 pave; cover the surface of the ground or buildings with brick or flat stones:广场用方砖～。The square was paved with square bricks.

【铺设】pūshè ❶ 铺(铁轨、管线);修(铁路)lay; build (a road, railway, etc.) ❷ 布置;安排 put in order; arrange:卧室～得很素雅。The bedroom is elegantly furnished.

【铺天盖地】pū tiān gài dì 形容声势大,来势猛,到处都是 overspread; blot out the sky and cover up the earth; be swarming with sth.

【铺叙】pūxù (文章)详细地叙述 (of an article) narrate in detail; elaborate:～事实 elaborate on the facts

【铺展】pūzhǎn 铺开并向四外伸展 spread out; sprawl:蔚蓝的天空～着一片片的白云。Fleecy clouds spread over the blue sky.

【铺张】pūzhāng ❶ 追求形式上好看,过分讲究排场 extravagant; using or spending too much for the sake of formality:反对～浪费 be against extravagance and waste ❷ 夸张 exaggerate; overstate:描写过于～,让人看了生疑。The depiction was so overstated as to be unbelievable.

【铺张扬厉】pūzhāng yánglì 形容极其铺张 indulge in extravagance and ostentation; be extremely wasteful

噗 pū〈拟声词 *onom*.〉puff:～,一口气吹灭了灯 blow out a candle with one puff|子弹把尘土打得～～直冒烟。Bullets whipped up clouds of dust.

【噗嗤】pūchī same as 扑哧 pūchī

【噗噜噜】pūlūlū〈拟声词 *onom*.〉形容泪珠等一个劲儿地往下掉[used to describe a flood of tears rolling down the cheek] trickle:一阵心

酸，眼泪～地往下掉。Tears trickled down with a gush of grief. also 噗碌碌 pūlūlū

【噗通】pūtōng same as 扑通 pūtōng

潽 pū 液体沸腾溢出（of liquid）boil and spill over

pú（ㄆㄨˊ）

仆(僕) pú ❶ 仆人（跟'主'相对 as opposite to 'master'）servant：男～ manservant | 女～ maidservant ❷〈古时 *arch*.〉男子谦称自己 man's self-deprecating term for himself

☞ pū on p. 1497

【仆从】púcóng〈旧时 *old*〉指跟随在身旁的仆人，现比喻跟随别人，自己不能做主的人或集体 footman; retainer; henchman; used to refer to a servant who followed his master all the time, and now referring to a person or a group of people that do not have their own mind：～国家 vassal country

【仆妇】púfù〈旧时 *old*〉指年龄较大的女仆 older female servant

【仆仆】púpú 形容旅途劳累 travel-stained; travel-worn and weary：风尘～ endure the hardship of travel

【仆人】púrén 指被雇到家庭中做杂事、供役使的人 servant; person employed to perform services or run errands, esp. household duties for another

【仆役】púyì same as 仆人 púrén

匍 pú ☞ below

【匍匐】púfú ❶ 爬行 crawl; creep：～前进 crawl forward | ～奔丧（形容匆忙奔丧）hasten home for the funeral ❷ 趴 lie prostrate; lie prone：孩子们～在炕上画画儿。Children lay prostrate on the brick bed drawing pictures. | 有些植物的茎～在地面上。Some plants have trailing (or creeping) stems.

【匍匐茎】púfújīng 不能直立向上生长、平铺在地面上的茎。这种茎的节上长叶和根，如甘薯、草莓等的茎。stolon; creeping stem that lies on or above the soil surface and bears foliage leaves, as in the sweet potato or strawberry

莆 Pú ❶ 指福建莆田市 short for Putian, a city in Fujian Province ❷ 姓 a surname

【莆仙戏】púxiānxì 福建地方戏曲剧种之一，流行于莆田、仙游一带 Puxian opera; local opera of Fujian Province, popular in the areas of Putian and Xianyou; also 兴化戏 xīnghuàxì

菩 pú ☞ below

【菩萨】púsà ❶〈佛教 *Budd*.〉指修行到了一定程度、地位仅次于佛的人 Bodhisattra; person who has achieved great moral and spiritual wisdom and is a potential Buddha［菩提萨埵之省，梵 abbreviation of 菩提萨埵 pútísàduǒ, Sanskrit：bodhi-sattva］❷ 泛指佛和某些神（in a broad sense）Buddha; deity; god ❸〈比喻 *fig*.〉心肠慈善的人 kindhearted person

【菩提】pútí〈佛教用语 *Budd*.〉指觉悟的境界 bodhi; supreme wisdom or enlightenment, necessary to the attainment of Buddha hood［梵 Sanskrit：bodhi］

脯 pú 指胸脯 chest; breast

☞ fǔ on p. 604

【脯子】pú·zi 鸡、鸭等胸部的肉 breast meat（of chicken, duck, etc.）：鸡～ chicken breast

葡 pú ☞ below

【葡萄】pú·táo ❶ 落叶藤木植物，叶子掌状分裂，圆锥花序，开黄绿色小花。果实圆形或椭圆形，成熟时紫色或黄绿色，味酸甜，多汁，是常见的水果，也是酿酒的原料。grape（*Vitis*）; deciduous vine with palm-like leaves and cone-shaped cluster of green-yellow blossoms, bearing round, sweet, juicy berries, generally purple or green-yellow, that can be eaten raw or used to make wine ❷ 这种植物的果实 fruit of this plant

【葡萄干】pú·táogān（～儿 pú·táogānr）晒干的葡萄 raisin; dried grapes

【葡萄灰】pú·táohuī 浅灰而微红的颜色 grey-red

【葡萄酒】pú·táojiǔ 用经过发酵的葡萄制成的酒，含酒精量较低 wine; a kind of alcoholic beverage made from fermented juice of grapes, low in alcohol content

【葡萄胎】pú·táotāi 病，妇女受孕后胚胎发育异常，在子宫内形成许多成串的葡萄状小囊，囊内含有液体。能引起子宫穿孔或严重贫血。hydatidiform mole; vesicular mole; abnormal development of an embryo in the form of a cluster of hydatids with liquid inside, may cause perforation of womb and serious anemia

【葡萄糖】pú·táotáng 有机化合物，化学式 $C_6H_{12}O_6$。无色或白色结晶粉末，有甜味，是一种最普通的单糖。广泛存在于生物体中，特别是葡萄中含量多，是人和动物能量的主要来源。医药上用做滋补剂，也用来制糖果等。glucose; grape sugar; dextrose; crystalline, sweet monosaccharide occurring in an organism, especially in grapes, being a major source of energy for human beings and animals, used as tonic or to make candy（$C_6H_{12}O_6$）; also 右旋糖 yòuxuántáng

【葡萄紫】pú·táozǐ 深紫中带灰的颜色 grey, dark purple

蒱 pú ☞［摴蒱］chūpú on p. 290

蒲1 pú ❶ 指香蒲 reed mace（*Typha*）; cattail; club grass：～棒 the spike of cattail | ～草 cattail ❷ 指菖蒲 calamus（*Acorus cala-*

mus)：～剑 calamus leaves

蒲2 Pú ❶ 指蒲州(旧府名，府治在今山西永济西) referring to Puzhou, a former prefecture, with its seat of administration to the east of present-day Yongji, Shanxi Province ❷ 姓 a surname

【蒲棒】púbàng (～儿 púbàngr)香蒲的花穗，黄褐色，形状像棒子 brownish clublike flower spike of cattail (or reed mace, club grass)

【蒲包】púbāo (～儿 púbāor) ❶ 用香蒲叶编成的装东西的用具 utensil made of cattail leaves ❷〈旧时 *old*〉指用蒲包儿装着水果或点心的礼品 gift of fruit or pastries (packed in a cattail bag)：点心～ a cattail bag of refreshments

【蒲草】púcǎo ❶ 香蒲的茎叶，可供编织用 stem or leaf of cattail ❷〈方 *dial.*〉沿阶草 dwarf lilyturf

【蒲墩】púdūn (～儿 púdūnr)用香蒲叶、麦秸等编成的厚而圆的垫子，农村中用做坐具 cattail hassock used as a stool; thick firm rush cushion

【蒲公英】púgōngyīng ❶ 多年生草本植物，全株含白色乳状汁液，叶子倒披针形，羽状分裂，花黄色，头状花序，结瘦果，褐色，有白色软毛。根茎入药。dandelion (*Taraxacum officinale*); perennial herb containing milky fluid, and having jagged leaves, yellow flowers, brown akene fruits covered with white fur, the root of which is used for medicine ❷ 这种植物的花 flower of dandelion ‖ also 黄花地丁 huánghuā dìdīng

【蒲节】Pú Jié 端午节(因旧时风俗端午节在门上挂菖蒲叶避邪而得名) Calamus Festival; Dragon Boat Festival (5th day of the 5th lunar month, on which calamus leaves used to be hung at the door to ward off evil spirits)

【蒲剧】pújù 山西地方戏曲剧种之一，流行于该省南部地区 local opera popular in the southern parts of Shanxi Province; also 蒲州梆子 púzhōu bāng·zi

【蒲葵】púkuí 常绿乔木，叶子大，大部分掌状分裂，裂片长披针形，圆椎花序，生在叶腋间，花小，果实椭圆形，成熟时黑色。生长在热带和亚热带地区，叶子可以做扇子。Chinese fan palm (*Livistona chinensis*); evergreen tree with mostly divided leaves in a palmate fashion, the leaflets being linear. The panicles of small flowers grow in axils. The ripe fruit is ovil-shaped and black. The plant grows in tropical and sub-tropical areas, and its leaves can be used to make fans.

【蒲柳】púliǔ 水杨，是秋天很早就凋零的树木；旧时用来谦称自己体质衰弱或地位低下 big catkin willow (*Salix gracilistyla*); tree that defoliates in early autumn; (in old times) modest expression formerly meaning oneself is weak or low in status：～之姿 weak in nature｜～庸材 mediocre; lacking ability

【蒲绒】púróng 香蒲的雌花穗上长的白绒毛，可以用来絮枕头 cattail wool; fine hair growing on the female flowers of cattails, used for stuffing pillows; also 蒲茸 púróng

【蒲扇】púshàn (～儿 púshànr)用香蒲叶做成的扇子 cattail leaf fan; fan made of a cattail leaf

【蒲式耳】púshì'ěr 英美制容量单位(计量干散颗粒用)，1 蒲式耳等于 8 加仑。英制 1 蒲式耳合 36.37升，美制 1 蒲式耳合 35.24 升。bushel; unit of dry measure containing eight gallons, equivalent in Britain to 36.37 litres (imperial bushel), and in the United States to 35.27 litres (Winchester bushel); 旧称 also called 斛 hú in old times

【蒲团】pútuán 用香蒲草、麦秸等编成的圆形的垫子 cattail hassock; rush cushion; round-shaped cushion woven with cattail leaves, wheat straw, etc.

酺 pú〈书 *fml.*〉聚会饮酒 drink party; drink feast

璞 pú 含玉的石头，也指没有琢磨的玉 stone containing jade, or uncut jade

【璞玉浑金】pú yù hún jīn 没有经过琢磨的玉，没有经过提炼的金 uncut jade and unrefined gold;〈比喻 *fig.*〉天然美质，未加修饰 unadorned beauty; also 浑金璞玉 hún jīn pú yù

镤 pú 金属元素，符号 Pa (protactinium)。灰白色，有放射性。protactinium (Pa); greyish-white, radioactive metal

濮 Pú ❶ 濮阳，地名，在河南 Puyang, name of a place in Henan Province ❷ 姓 a surname

pǔ (ㄆㄨˇ)

朴(樸) pǔ 朴实；朴质 simple; plain：俭～ thrifty and simple; economical｜诚～ honest and unaffected｜～素 simple; plain ☞ Piáo on p.1476, pō on p.1491 and pò on p.1493

【朴厚】pǔhòu 朴实厚道 honest and kind; virtuous and unaffected：心地～ have an honest and kind heart

【朴陋】pǔlòu 朴素简陋 simple and crude：陈设～ furnished in a simple and crude way

【朴茂】pǔmào〈书 *fml.*〉朴厚 simple and honest; simple and loyal

【朴实】pǔshí ❶ 朴素 simple; plain：他穿得很～。He was plainly dressed.｜客厅布置得～而雅致。The sitting room is decorated in a simple and elegant manner. ❷ 质朴诚实 sincere and honest; guileless：言行～ sincere and honest in words and deeds｜性格～ have a guileless disposition ❸ 塌实；不浮夸 earnest; down-to-earth：演唱风格～ sing in an earnest style｜作品～地描写了山区人民的生活。It made a down-to-earth depiction of life in the mountain area.

【朴素】pǔsù ❶（颜色、式样等）不浓艳，不华丽（of colour, style, etc.）simple; plain：她穿得～大方。She was plainly but gracefully dressed. ◇他的诗～而感情真挚。His poems are simple in style and exuberant in genuine feelings. ❷（生活）节约，不奢侈（of lifestyle）frugal; thrifty; plain and modest：艰苦～hardworking and plain-living｜生活～ plain living ❸ 朴实，不浮夸；不虚假 simple; naive; unaffected：～的感情 simple feelings｜～的语言 unaffected language ❹ 萌芽状态的；未发展的 embryonic; undeveloped：古代～的唯物主义哲学 naive materialism in the ancient time

【朴学】pǔxué 朴实的学问，后来特指清代的考据学 down-to-earth learning; textology in the Qing Dynasty

【朴直】pǔzhí 朴实直率 honest and straightforward：语言～ speak in an honest and straightforward way｜文笔～ simple and straightforward writing

【朴质】pǔzhì 纯真朴实；不矫饰；质朴 simple and unadorned; natural：语言～ unaffected language｜为人～ be simple and honest

埔 pǔ 地名用字 used in place names：黄～（在广东）Huangpu (in Guangdong Province)

☞ bù on p. 173

圃 pǔ 种菜蔬、花草的园子或园地 garden; a piece of ground for growing vegetables, flowers, ornamental shrubs, etc.：菜～ vegetable plot｜苗～ seed plot; seedling nursery｜花～ flower nursery

浦 pǔ ❶水边或河流入海的地方（多用于地名 oft. used in place names）riverside; river mouth：乍～（在浙江）Zhapu (in Zhejiang Province)｜～口（在江苏）Pukou (in Jiangsu Province) ❷（Pǔ）姓 a surname

普 pǔ ❶ 普遍；全面 general; universal：～选 general election｜～查 general investigation; general survey｜～照 illuminate all things｜～天同庆 the whole nation joins in jubilation ❷（Pǔ）姓 a surname

【普遍】pǔbiàn 存在的面很广泛；具有共同性的 universal; general; widespread; common; existing or occurring extensively：～化 generalize｜～性 universality｜～真理 universal truth｜～现象 universal phenomenon｜～流行 universally popular｜～提高人民的科学文化水平 generally improve the scientific and cultural level of the people｜乒乓球运动在我国十分～。Table tennis is very popular in China.

【普查】pǔchá 普遍调查 general investigation (or survey)：人口～ census｜地质～ reconnaissance survey

【普度】pǔdù〈佛教用语 *Budd.*〉指广施法力，使众生得到解脱 deliver all living creatures from torment：～众生 deliver the multitude of people from misery

【普洱茶】pǔ'ěrchá 云南西南部出产的一种黑茶，多压制成块。因产地的部分地区在清代属于普洱府而得名。Pu'er tea; a kind of dark tea, usually made into the form of cakes, produced in southwestern Yunan, a part of which belongs to Pu'er Prefecture, hence the name

【普法】pǔfǎ 普及法律知识 popularize law：～教育 popularizing-law education｜～工作 law popularization

【普及】pǔjí ❶ 普遍地传到（地区、范围等）(in certain areas or within certain scopes, etc.) spread extensively：这本书已～全国。This book has reached every part of the country. ❷ 普遍推广，使大众化 popularize; disseminate; spread among the people：～卫生常识 spread the elementary knowledge of health and medicine｜在～的基础上提高 raise standards on the basis of popularization

【普及本】pǔjíběn 大量销行的书籍，在原有版本外，发行的用纸较次、开本较小、装订从简、定价较低的版本 popular edition; books published in large amount, with second-rate paper, in smaller size, simpler binding and lower price than the original edition

【普罗】pǔluó 普罗列塔利亚的简称 abbr. for 普罗列塔利亚 pǔluó liètǎ lìyà：～作家 proletarian writer｜～文学 proletarian literature

【普罗列塔利亚】pǔluóliètàlìyà 无产阶级的音译 transliteration of proletariat; 简称 abbr. 普罗 pǔluó［法 French: prolétariat］

【普米族】Pǔmǐzú 我国少数民族之一，分布在云南、四川 Pumi people; Pumis, living in Yunnan and Sichuan Provinces

【普天同庆】pǔ tiān tóng qìng 天下的人一同庆祝 whole nation joins in the jubilation

【普通】pǔtōng 平常的；一般的 common; general; ordinary; plain; average：～人 average person; the man in the street｜～劳动者 ordinary labourer

【普通话】pǔtōnghuà 现代汉语的标准语，以北京语音为标准音，以北方话为基础方言，以典范的现代白话文著作为语法规范 putonghua; common speech (of the Chinese language); standard Chinese pronunciation; standard Chinese taking Beijing dialect as the basic pronunciation, the Northern dialects as the basis and the modern Chinese vernacular writings as grammar standards

【普通教育】pǔtōng jiàoyù 指实施一般文化科学知识的教育。我国实施普通教育的机构主要为中小学。regular education; education on the general scientific and cultural education that is mainly conducted by primary and middle schools in China

【普通邮票】pǔtōng yóupiào 邮政部门根据日常邮政需要而发行的一般性邮票（跟'纪念邮票'

相对 as opposed to 'commemorative stamp') regular stamp; ordinary stamp issued by the postal authorities according to general postal requirements

【普选】pǔxuǎn 一种选举方式，有选举权的公民普遍地参加国家权力机关代表的选举 general election; election gen. participated by citizens with election rights for representatives of organs of state power

【普照】pǔzhào 普遍地照耀 illuminate all things: 阳光～大地。The sun illuminates every corner of the land.

溥 pǔ ❶〈书 *fml.*〉广大 broad ❷〈书 *fml.*〉普遍 common; universal ❸(Pǔ) 姓 a surname

谱 pǔ ❶ 按照对象的类别或系统，采取表格或其他比较整齐的形式，编辑起来供参考的书 register or record for easy reference (in the form of charts, tables, lists, etc.) according to the category or system of the object: 年～ chronicle of sb.'s life | 食～ cookbook; menu ❷ 可以用来指导练习的格式或图形 manual; guidebook; instructions or diagrams guiding practice: 画～ picture copybook | 棋～ chess manual ❸ 曲谱 music score; music: 歌～ music of a song | 乐～ music score; music | 根据这首歌的～另外配了一段词。New lyrics have been composed to the music of this song. ❹ 就歌词配曲 set to music; compose (music): 把这首诗～成歌曲。Set this poem to music. ❺(～儿 pǔr)大致的标准；把握 sth. to count on; a fair amount of confidence: 他做事有～儿。He knows what he is doing. *or* He does things with confidence. | 心里没个～ have nothing definite in mind ❻(～儿 pǔr)显示出来的派头、排场等 wealth or splendour displayed: 摆～ try to appear rich and elegant; try to impress

【谱表】pǔbiǎo 乐谱中用来记载音符的五根平行横线 stave; staff; set of five horizontal parallel lines on which music is written

【谱牒】pǔdié〈书 *fml.*〉家谱 genealogy; family tree; genealogical tree

【谱号】pǔhào 确定五线谱上音高位置的符号 clef; symbol at the beginning of a stave showing the pitch of the notes

【谱系】pǔxì ❶ 家谱上的系统 pedigree; family tree; table or list of a person's ancestors ❷ 泛指事物发展变化的系统 (in a broad sense) system of the development of things

【谱写】pǔxiě 写作(乐曲等) compose (music): 这支曲子是他～的。This tune was composed by him. ◇革命先烈抛头颅，洒热血，～下可歌可泣的壮丽诗篇。The revolutionary martyrs wrote one touching poem after another by shedding their blood and laying down their lives for their people and country.

【谱子】pǔ·zi 曲谱 music score; music

氆 pǔ [氆氇](pǔ·lu)藏族地区出产的一种羊毛织品，可做床毯、衣服等 woolen fabric procued in Tibet for making blankets, garments, etc.

镨 pǔ 金属元素，符号 Pr (praseodymium)。是一种稀土金属。浅黄色。用来制有色玻璃、陶瓷、搪瓷，也用作催化剂。praseodymium (Pr); pale-yellow, malleable chemical element of the rare-earth group, which is used to colour glasses, earth-wear and enamels or as catalytic

蹼 pǔ 某些两栖动物、爬行动物、鸟类和哺乳动物脚趾中间的薄膜，在水中用来拨水。青蛙、龟、鸭、水獭等都有。web; piece of skin joining together the toes of some amphibians, reptiles, birds or mammals that swim, eg. frogs; turtles, ducks and otters

pù (ㄆㄨˋ)

铺[1](舖) pù (～儿 pùr) 铺子；商店 shop; store: 肉～ meat shop; butcher's | 杂货～儿 grocery

铺[2](舖) pù 用板子搭的床 plank bed: 床～ bed

铺[3](舖) pù 旧时的驿站，现多用于地名，如五里铺、十里铺 courier (in old times); oft. used in place names, as in 五里铺 Wǔlǐpù and 十里铺 Shílǐpù

☞ pū on p.1498

【铺板】pùbǎn 搭铺用的木板 bed board; bed plank

【铺保】pùbǎo〈旧时 *old*〉称以商店名义所做的保证，在保单上盖有商店的图章 shop guarantor; guarantee for a person given by a shopkeeper with a seal of the shop

【铺底】pùdǐ ❶〈旧时 *old*〉商店、作坊等营业上应用的家具、杂物的总称 shop fixtures; furniture and odds and ends of a shop or workshop ❷〈旧时 *old*〉指商店、作坊等房屋的租赁权；转租商店、作坊等房屋时，在租金之外付给原承租人的费用 lease right of shops or workshops; charge paid to the original lease-holder in addition to rent when subletting a shop or workshop

【铺户】pùhù same as 商店 shāngdiàn

【铺家】pù·jia〈方 *dial.*〉same as 商店 shāngdiàn

【铺面】pùmiàn ❶ 商店的门面 shop front; storefront: 沿街～装修一新。The shop fronts along the street were refurnished anew. ❷ 指商店内接待顾客的地方 places in a shop receiving customers: 文化用品柜台设在一楼～。The counter for articles of cultural use is on the first floor.

【铺面房】pùmiànfáng 临街有门面，可以开设商店的房屋 shop building; buildings with fronts facing the street that can be used as shops

【铺位】pùwèi 设有床铺的位置(多指轮船、火车、旅馆等为旅客安排的)bunk; berth; sleeping place on a ship, train or in a hotel

【铺子】pù·zi 设有门面出售商品的处所 places where goods are sold; shop; store

堡 pù 多用于地名。五里铺、十里铺等的'铺'字,有的地区写作'堡'。*pu*, a word used in place names, e.g. 铺 pù in 五里铺 Wǔlǐpù or 十里铺 Shílǐpù can be replaced by 堡 pù

☞ bǎo on p. 69 and bǔ on p. 155

瀑 pù 瀑布 waterfall: 飞~ waterfall

☞ Bào on p. 75

【瀑布】pùbù 从山壁上或河身突然降落的地方流下的水,远看好像挂着的白布 waterfall; falls; cataract; sault; spout; linn; stream or river that falls from a height such as cliff, looking like a piece of white cloth from afar

曝(暴) pù 〈书 *fml.*〉晒 expose to the scorching sun: 一~十寒 expose something to sun-heat for one day and to cold for ten days

☞ bào on p. 74 and 暴 bào on p. 74

【曝露】pùlù 〈书 *fml.*〉露在外头 expose to the open air: ~于原野之中 be exposed to the open air in the field

【曝晒】pùshài 晒 expose to the scorching sun: 经过夏季烈日~,他的脸变得黑红黑红的。His face was deeply tanned by the smouldering sun of summer.

Q

qī (ㄑㄧ)

七 qī ❶〈数目 *numeral*〉六加一后所得 seven; or six plus one; ☞数字 shùzì on p. 1791 ❷〈旧时 *old*〉人死后每隔七天祭奠一次,直到第四十九天为止,共分七个'七' seventh-day mourning period; Chinese custom to hold a memorial service on every seventh day following a person's death until the 49th day; 注意 **NOTE**: '七'字单用或在一词一句末尾或在阴平、阳平、上声字前念阴平,如'十七、五七、一七得七、七夕、七年、七两';在去声字前念阳平,如'七月、七位'。本词典为简便起见,条目中的'七'字,都注阴平。The character 七 is pronounced in the high and level tone when it is used independently or at the end of a phrase or sentence, such as in 十七 shíqī, 五七 wǔqī, 一七得七 yīqīdéqī, 七夕 qīxī, 七年 qīnián, 七两 qīliǎng; and it is pronounced in the rising tone when it precedes a character that is pronounced in the falling tone, such as in 七月 qīyuè and 七位 qīwèi; For convenience's sake, the 七 in all entries is marked with a level tone.

【七…八…】qī…bā… 嵌用名词或动词(包括词素),表示多或多而杂乱 [nouns or verbs are inserted in this combination to indicate a large amount or a mess]: ～手～脚 with everybody lending a hand | ～嘴～舌 with everybody talking and nobody listening; with ev erybody trying to put in a word or two | ～拼～凑 knock together; scissors-and-paste | ～颠～倒 at sixes and sevens; topsy-turvy | ～零～落 scattered here and there; in disarray | ～上～下 on tenterhooks; on pins and needles | ～扭～歪 be twisted this way and that; crooked | ～折～扣(折扣很大) one deduction after another

【七步之才】qī bù zhī cái 指敏捷的文才 seven-step talent; literary genius; ☞煮豆燃萁 zhǔ dòu rán qí on p. 2507

【七古】qīgǔ 每句七字的古体诗 classical style of poetry with seven characters to each line; ☞古体诗 gǔtǐshī on p. 691

【七绝】qījué 绝句的一种。一首四句,每句七个字。four-line poem with seven characters to a line and a strict tonal pattern and rhyme scheme; septasyllabic (or seven-syllable) quatrain; ☞绝句 juéjù on p. 1060

【七老八十】qīlǎobāshí 指年纪很老,七八十岁 in late seventies and early eighties; very old: 别看他～的,身体硬朗着呢。He looks hale and hearty despite his old age.

【七律】qīlǜ 律诗的一种。一首八句,每句七个字。eight-line poem with seven characters to each line and a strict tonal pattern and rhyme scheme; septasyllabic (or seven-syllable) regulated verse; ☞律诗 lǜshī on p. 1267

【七七】qīqī 旧俗人死后每七天祭奠一次,最后一次是第四十九天,叫七七(old custom) 'Double Seven' service; 7th memorial service that falls on the last day of the seven-period, 49-day memorial for a deceased; also 尽七 jìnqī; 满七 mǎnqī; 断七 duànqī

【七七事变】 Qī-Qī Shìbiàn 1937 年7月7日,日本侵略军突然向我国北平(今北京)西南卢沟桥驻军进攻,驻军奋起抗击,抗日战争从此开始。这次事变叫做七七事变。July 7th Incident of 1937; on July 7, 1937, the Japanese invaders raided the Chinese garrison at the Lugou Bridge to the southwest of present-day Beijing, known in the West as Marco Polo Bridge, and the Chinese army rose in a counterattack, thus unveiling the War of Resistance against Japan; also 卢沟桥事变 Lúgōuqiáo Shìbiàn

【七巧板】qīqiǎobǎn 一种玩具,用正方形薄板或厚纸裁成形状不同的七小块,可以拼成各种图形 tangram; Chinese puzzle square cut into seven pieces to be combined into a variety of patterns

【七窍】qīqiào 指两眼、两耳、两鼻孔和口 seven orifices in the human head, referring to eyes, ears, nostrils and mouth: ～流血 bleed from every orifice

【七窍生烟】qīqiào shēng yān 形容气愤之极,好像耳目口鼻都冒火 livid; as if one's ears, eyes, mouth and nose are spitting rage

【七色板】qīsèbǎn 光学仪器,是一块涂着红、橙、黄、绿、蓝、靛、紫七种颜色的圆板,固定在横轴上,如果急速旋转,就呈现白色,可以用它证明由七种色光合成白光的原理 Newton's disk; seven-colour disk; optical apparatus in the form of a disk fixed on a horizontal axis and painted red, orange, yellow, green, blue, indigo, and violet, which blend into the colour white when the disk is set to turn around rapidly, thereby justifying the principle that light is the compound of the seven colours

【七十二行】qīshí'èr háng 泛指工、农、商等各行各业 all professions and trades; all walks of life:～,行行出状元。You can excel no matter what job you do.

【七夕】qīxī 农历七月初七的晚上。神话传说,天上的牛郎织女每年在这天晚上相会。seventh evening of the seventh lunar month, when the legendary Herd-boy joins the Weaving-girl for their annual tryst

【七弦琴】qīxiánqín same as 古琴 gǔqín

【七言诗】qīyánshī 每句七字的旧诗,有七言古诗、七言律诗和七言绝句 poem with seven characters to a line, including the seven-syllable poem, the eight-line poem with seven characters to each line, and the four-line poem with seven characters to each line, with the latter two governed by a strict tonal pattern and a rhyme scheme

【七一】Qī-Yī 中国共产党建党纪念日。1921 年 7 月下旬中国共产党召开第一次全国代表大会, 1941 年党中央决定以召开这次大会的 7 月份的第一天,即 7 月 1 日,为党的生日。July 1st Party Day; anniversary of the founding of the Communist Party of China in late July 1921, which is celebrated on the first day of July according to a 1941 Party decision

沏 qī (用开水)冲;泡 brew with boiling water:～茶 make tea|用开水把糖～开 melt sugar in boiling water

妻 qī 妻子(qī·zi) wife:夫～ husband and wife|未婚～ fiancée|～离子散 tear a family apart|～儿老小 one's parents, wife and children

☞ qì on p.1525

【妻儿老小】qī ér lǎo xiǎo 指全体家属(就家中有父母妻子等的人而言) married man's family; man's parents, wife and children

【妻舅】qījiù 妻子的弟兄 wife's brother; brother-in-law

【妻小】qīxiǎo 妻子和儿女,也指妻子 wife and children; reference to one's wife

【妻子】qīzǐ 妻子和儿女 wife and children

【妻子】qī·zi 男女两人结婚后,女子是男子的妻子 wife; married woman in relation to her husband

柒 qī ❶'七'的大写 seven; the upper case of seven to be used when writing out cheques, invoices, etc. to forestall errors and alterations; ☞数字 shùzì on p. 1791 ❷(Qī) 姓 a surname

栖(棲) qī 本指鸟停在树上,泛指居住或停留(orig. of a bird) perch; (of all living things) dwell; stay:～息 dwell; rest|两～amphibious

☞ xī on p. 2045

【栖身】qīshēn 居住(多指暂时的 oft. temporary) lodge; reside; sojourn:无处～have no place to stay|～之所 habitat; home

【栖息】qīxī 停留;休息(多指鸟类 oft. of birds) tarry; rest; inhabit

【栖止】qīzhǐ〈书 *fml.*〉栖身 lodge; reside; dwell

桤(榿) qī 指桤木 alder:～林 alder forest

【桤木】qīmù 落叶乔木,叶子长倒卵形,果穗椭圆形。木材质较软。alder (*Alnus glutinosa*); tree bearing toothed obovate leaves, olive-shaped ears, and softwood

郪 Qī 郪江,水名,在四川 Qijiang, a river in Sichuan Province

凄(❶❷凄、❸悽) qī ❶寒冷 icy; frigid; chilly:风雨～～chilly wind and endless rain ❷形容冷落萧条 disheartening; somber; grim; dismal:～凉 desolate|～清 bloomy ❸形容悲伤难过 lamentable; heartbroken; woebegone:～然 mournful; sad|～切 melancholy

【凄惨】qīcǎn 凄凉悲惨 plaintive; dreary:歌声～ mournful tone of a song|晚境～spend one's remaining years in poverty and melancholy

【凄恻】qīcè〈书 *fml.*〉哀伤;悲痛 heartbroken; sorrowful

【凄楚】qīchǔ〈书 *fml.*〉凄惨痛苦 wretched; miserable

【凄怆】qīchuàng〈书 *fml.*〉凄惨;悲伤 piteous; painful; lugubrious

【凄风苦雨】qī fēng kǔ yǔ 形容天气恶劣 moaning wind and pattering rain;〈比喻 *fig.*〉境遇悲惨凄凉 in wretched circumstances; distress; also 凄风冷雨 qī fēng lěng yǔ

【凄厉】qīlì (声音)凄凉而尖锐 (of voice) sad and shrill:～的喊叫声 heartrending wail|风声～。The wind moaned dismally over the fields.

【凄凉】qīliáng ❶寂寞冷落(多用来形容环境或景物 oft. used to describe environment or scenery) desolate; dreary:残垣断壁,一片～。There was something utterly dreary about these crumbling walls. ❷凄惨 sad; miserable:身世～ life experience steeped in misery|～的岁月 years of poverty and misery

【凄迷】qīmí〈书 *fml.*〉❶(景物)凄凉而模糊(of scenes and sights) fuzzy and dreary:月色～the moon donning a dreary cue and a fuzzy image ❷悲伤;怅惘 grief-stricken:神情～woebegone looks

【凄切】qīqiè 凄凉而悲哀,多形容声音 afflicting; grievous:寒蝉～。Cicadas were wailing woefully over the chill of the day.

【凄清】qīqīng ❶形容清冷 sombre; cheerless:～的月光 cheerless moonlight|秋景～ dreary autumn scene ❷凄凉 sad; lamentable:琴声

～ plaintive tune of a zither

【凄然】qīrán 〈书 *fml.*〉形容悲伤 distressing：～泪下。Tears of sorrow roll down the cheeks.

【凄婉】qīwǎn ❶ 哀伤 doleful：流露出不胜～之情 pitiful outpouring of sorrowful feelings ❷（声音）悲哀而婉转（of sound）plaintively melodious：～的笛声 heartrending notes of a flute

【凄惘】qīwǎng 悲伤失意；怅惘 distracted；listless：～之情 feeling of frustration and sadness

萋 qī［萋萋］形容草长得茂盛的样子 exuberant：芳草～green grass wafting a delicate fragrance in the air

桼 qī 〈书 *fml.*〉same as 漆 qī

戚[1] qī ❶ 亲戚 relative：～谊（亲戚关系）relatives｜～友（亲戚朋友）family members and friends ❷（Qī）姓 a surname

戚[2]（感）qī 忧愁；悲哀 grief；woe；sadness：哀～ mournful；plaintive｜休～相关 go together through thick and thin；share weal and woe together

戚[3]（鏚）qī 〈古代 *arch.*〉兵器，像斧 axe-like weapon

期 qī ❶ 预定的时日；日期 prescribed length of time；date：定～at regular intervals｜限～deadline；time limit｜到～fall due；expire｜过～作废 become null and void upon expiration ❷ 一段时间 term；stage：学～ school term；semester｜假～holiday；vacation｜潜伏～latency｜三个月为一～。Each period lasts three months. ❸〈量词 *classifier*〉用于分期的事物 period；term：训练班先后办了三～。The training class was run three times.｜这个刊物已经出版了十几～。This magazine has published a dozen or so issues. ❹ 约定时日 appoint；schedule：不～而遇 come across each other by chance ❺ 等候所约的人，泛指等待或盼望 expect；anticipate：～待 anticipation｜～望 expectation

☞ jī on p.898

【期待】qīdài 期望；等待 await；look forward to：～着你早日学成归来。We look forward to your finishing your studies with flying colours and returning home at an early date.｜决不辜负您的～。I will not let you down.

【期货】qīhuò 约定期限交付的货物（跟'现货'相对 as opposed to 'merchandise on hand'）futures

【期间】qījiān 某个时期里面 period；course：农忙～during the busy farming season｜春节～during Spring Festival｜抗战～during the War of Resistance against Japan

【期刊】qīkān 定期出版的刊物，如周刊、月刊、季刊等 periodical, such as weekly, monthly and quarterly

【期考】qīkǎo 学校在学期结束前举行的考试 final exam；term exam

【期票】qīpiào 定期支付商品、货币的票据 promissory note

【期期艾艾】qīqī àì'ài 汉代周昌口吃，有一次跟汉高祖争论一件事，说：'臣口不能言，然臣期期知其不可'（见《史记·张丞相列传》）。又三国魏邓艾也口吃，说到自己的时候连说'艾艾'（见《世说新语·言语》）。后来用'期期艾艾'形容口吃。According to *Records of the Historian · Biography of Prime Minister Zhang*, Zhou Chang, a stuttering court official of the Han Dynasty, was arguing with Emperor Gaozu when he said, 'Though I cannot express it adequately, I, I definitely know that this cannot be done.' Another case of stuttering is found in the person of Deng Ai, a general of the kingdom of Wei of the Three Kingdoms Period who, according to *A New Account of Tales of the World · Diction*, was given to stammering whenever he pronounced his own name. Hence the Chinese phrase which means 'stammer' or 'stutter'.

【期求】qīqiú 希望得到 hanker after：无所～ have nothing to hanker after

【期望】qīwàng 对未来的事物或人的前途有所希望和等待 expect on tiptoe：～这条铁路早日建成通车。It is our ardent hope that this railway will be completed and open to traffic at an early date.｜决不辜负大家的～。I will never let all of you down.

【期限】qīxiàn 限定的一段时间，也指所限时间的最后界线 deadline；time limit：～很短。The time limit is rather short.｜～三个月。The term is three months.｜限你五天～。(I)'ll give you five days to get the job done｜～快到了。The deadline is drawing near.

【期许】qīxǔ 〈书 *fml.*〉期望（多用于对晚辈 usu. to one's juniors）ardent expectation：有负师长～。I'm afraid I have let you down.

【期颐】qīyí 〈书 *fml.*〉指人百岁的年纪 100 years old；centenarian：寿登～ live long enough to celebrate the 100th birthday

【期于】qīyú 希望达到；目的在于 be purported to

欺 qī ❶ 欺骗 bamboozle；beguile：自～～人 try to deceive others only to end up in deceiving oneself｜童叟无～。Nobody'll get cheated, old and young. ❷ 欺负 bully；hoodwink：仗势～人 act as a bully by taking advantage of sb. else's influence or power｜～人太甚 go too far in insulting sb.

【欺负】qī·fu 用蛮横无理的手段侵犯、压迫或侮辱 bluster；coerce：～人 bully｜受尽～ have one's fill of humiliation

【欺行霸市】qī háng bà shì 欺负同行，称霸市场。形容蛮横经商。cow others in the same trade and monopolize the market；run business in a domineering way

【欺哄】qīhǒng 说假话骗人 hoodwink; fool:这话只能～三岁小孩。Only a three-year-old will believe such a lie.

【欺凌】qīlíng 欺负;凌辱 bully and insult:～百姓 run roughshod over the people

【欺瞒】qīmán 欺骗蒙混 dupe; pull the wool over sb.'s eyes

【欺蒙】qīméng 隐瞒事物真相来骗人 conceal the truth in an attempt to cheat sb.

【欺骗】qīpiàn 用虚假的言语或行动来掩盖事实真相,使人上当 deceive; trick; try to gain unfair advantage by falsifying word or deed

【欺辱】qīrǔ 欺负;凌辱 humiliate; insult:受尽～have one's fill of insult

【欺软怕硬】qī ruǎn pà yìng 欺负软弱的,害怕强硬的 bully the weak and be scared of the tough

【欺生】qīshēng ❶ 欺负或欺骗新来的生人 humbug a stranger or newcomer ❷ 驴马等对不常使用它的人不驯服(of draught animals) refuse to behave towards a stranger:这马～,我使唤不了。This horse is unfriendly towards strangers. I don't think I can control it.

【欺世盗名】qī shì dào míng 欺骗世人,窃取名誉 win popularity by dishonest means; win undeserved prestige by cheating the public

【欺侮】qīwǔ same as 欺负 qī•fu

【欺压】qīyā 欺负压迫 run roughshod over:～百姓 oppress the people|受尽～has one's fill of oppression

【欺诈】qīzhà 用狡猾奸诈的手段骗人 fraudulence; swindling

攲 qī〈书 *fml.*〉倾斜;歪 be aslant; be wry; be oblique:～侧 lean to one side

【攲侧】qīcè〈书 *fml.*〉倾斜 lean to one side; aslant

欹 qī same as 攲 qī
☞ yī on p.2260

蛣 qī [蛣蜣](qīqiāng)古书指蜣螂 dung beetle in ancient books

缉 qī 缝纫方法,用相连的针脚密密地缝 sew in close and linked stitches:～边儿 sew the hem with close stitches|～鞋口 sew a shoe welt with close stitches
☞ jī on p.898

頬(魌) qī ❶〈古代 *arch.*〉驱疫时扮神的人所蒙的面具,形状很丑恶 grotesque mask worn by a god impersonator to exorcize pestilence ❷〈书 *fml.*〉丑陋 ugly

嘁 qī ☞ below

【嘁哩喀喳】qī•likāchā 形容说话做事干脆、利索(of speech and action) snappy and clear-cut; quick-witted and nimble-limbed; 喳 chā also 嚓 chā

【嘁嘁喳喳】qīqīchāchā〈拟声词 *onom.*〉形容细碎的说话声音 sound of chattering; also 嘁嘁嚓嚓 qīqīchāchā

漆 qī ❶ 用漆树皮里的黏汁或其他树脂制成的涂料。涂在器物上,可以防止腐坏,增加光泽。lacquer; sap of the lacquer tree or other resin used to varnish wooden utensils to help resist wear and tear ❷ 把漆涂在器物上 paint; lacquer; cover sth. with lacquer:把大门～成红色的 paint the front door red ❸(Qī) 姓 a surname

【漆包线】qībāoxiàn 表面涂着一层薄绝缘漆的金属导线,多用于制造电机和电讯装置中的线圈 enamel-insulated wire; thinly lacquered wire to be used for the making of coils in electric machinery

【漆布】qībù 用漆或其他涂料涂过的布,可用来铺桌面或做书皮等 varnished cloth, a material for tablecloth or book covers

【漆雕】qīdiāo ❶ 雕漆 lacquerware ❷(Qīdiāo) 姓 a surname

【漆工】qīgōng ❶ 油漆门窗、器物的工作 lacquering; painting ❷ 做上述工作的工人 painter; lacquer man

【漆黑】qīhēi 非常黑;很暗 jet-black; pitch-dark:～的头发 jet-black hair|～的夜 in the pitch dark of the night|洞内一片～。It's pitch-dark inside the cave.

【漆黑一团】qīhēi yī tuán ❶ 形容非常黑暗,没有一点光明 utterly dark; as black as night ❷ 形容一无所知 in a fog; totally in the dark about sth. ‖ also 一团漆黑 yī tuán qīhēi

【漆匠】qī•jiang 称制作油漆器物的小手工业者 lacquerware worker

【漆皮】qīpí (～儿 qīpír)器具表面涂漆的一层 shellac; coating of lacquer

【漆片】qīpiàn 一种涂料,用时以酒精等溶解,涂在器具上能很快地干燥 raw lacquer, which is dissolved in alcohol before being put to use and dries fast when it is painted on furniture or utensils

【漆器】qīqì 一种手工艺品,表面上有一层漆。也泛指表面上涂有漆的器物。lacquerware, a kind of handicraft; lacquerwork

【漆树】qīshù 落叶乔木,叶子互生,羽状复叶,小叶卵形或椭圆形,圆锥花序,花小,黄绿色,果实扁圆。树的液汁与空气接触后呈暗褐色,叫做生漆,可用做涂料,液汁干后可入药。lacquer tree (*Rhus verniciflua*); defoliating tree bearing alternate pinnately compound leaves that are either oval or olive-shaped, panicles of yellowish green tiny flowers, and oblate fruit, and producing a sap that turns dark ocher upon contact with air and is used as a paint, or medicine when dried

蹊 qī [蹊跷](qīqiāo)奇怪;跷蹊 weird, fishy:这件事来得有点～。There is something mysterious about all this.
☞ xī on p.2050

蜮 qī 不同科、属的一群软体动物的统称。这类动物的背壳隆起,略呈圆锥形,没有螺旋纹。生活在海边礁石上，吃浮游生物和藻类。general term for mollusk; invertebrate having a soft body protected by a hard shell that looks somewhat like a taper and does not have a spiral pattern, inhabiting offshore reefs and feeding on planktons and algae

㫓 qī ❶ 东西湿了之后将要干，未全干 drying; almost dry：雨过了，太阳一晒，路上就渐渐～了。The sun came out after the rain and the road gradually dried up. ❷ 用沙土等吸收水分 soak up water with sand or earth：地上有水，铺上点儿沙子～一～。Soak up puddles of rainwater on the road by spreading sand over them.

Q

qí（ㄑㄧˊ）

七 qí ☞七 qī on p.1504

亓 Qí 姓 a surname

齐[1]（齊）qí ❶ 整齐 neat; even; uniform：队伍排得很～。People were lined up in neat rows. ❷ 达到同样的高度 be level with：水涨得～了岸。The water has surged to the brink of the banks.｜向日葵都～了房檐了。The sunflowers have grown so tall that they are level with the eaves of houses. ❸ 同样；一致 identical; same：～名 be as well-known as｜人心～，泰山移。When people think with one mind, even Mount Tai can be removed. ❹ 一块儿；同时 at the same time; simultaneously：百花～放 a hundred flowers blossoming｜并驾～驱 run neck and neck｜男女老幼～动手。Everybody pitched in, men and women, old and young. ❺ 完备；全 ready; in order：东西预备～了。All the things are ready.｜人还没有来～。Some of the people are yet to show up.｜钱都凑～了。(We) have pooled the amount of money we need. ❻ 跟某一点或某一直线取齐 cut close to; even out：～着根儿剪断 cut the plants close to their roots｜～着边儿画一道线 draw a line close to the edge of sth. ❼（旧读 formerly pronounced jì）指合金 alloy：锰镍铜～alloy of manganese, nickel and copper

〈古 *arch.*〉same as 斋 zhāi in the phrase 斋戒 zhāijiè

齐[2]（齊）Qí ❶ 周朝国名，在今山东北部和河北东南部 Qi, name of a state during the Zhou Dynasty, in what is present-day north Shandong and southeast Hebei ❷ 指南齐 Southern Qi Dynasty (479-502) ❸ 指北齐 Northern Qi Dynasty (550-577) ❹ 唐末农民起义军领袖黄巢所建国号 Qi, reign title of a kingdom founded by Huang Chao, a peasant uprising leader towards the end of the Tang Dynasty ❺ 姓 a surname

☞ jì on p.915

【齐备】qíbèi 齐全（多指物品 oft. of things）complete; all ready：货色～ commodities of complete specifications｜行装～，马上出发。The travelers went on a journey after getting everything ready.

【齐步走】qíbù zǒu 军事口令，令队伍保持整齐的行列，以整齐的步伐前进（term of command）Quick time, march!

【齐唱】qíchàng 两个以上的歌唱者，按同一旋律同时演唱 chorus; group singing; sing in unison

【齐齿呼】qíchǐhū ☞四呼 sìhū on p.1821

【齐楚】qíchǔ 整齐（多指服装 oft. attirement）neat and smart：衣冠～be impeccably attired

【齐东野语】Qídōng yěyǔ《孟子·万章上》：'此非君子之言，齐东野人之语也。'后用'齐东野语'比喻道听途说、不足为凭的话。*Mencius · Wanzhang (I)*：'This is not the uttering of a gentleman, but hearsay of the barbarians of east Qi.' Hence the phrase 'hearsay of east Qi'.

【齐集】qíjí 聚集；集拢 congregate; assemble; gather：各国朋友～北京。Friends from various countries gathered in Beijing.

【齐眉穗儿】qíméisuìr 妇女或儿童垂在前额与眉相齐的短发 bang; fringe of hair cut straight across the forehead

【齐名】qímíng 有同样的名望 equally well-known; enjoy the same popularity：唐代诗人中，李白与杜甫～。Among all the Tang poets, Li Bai and Du Fu enjoyed equal fame.

【齐全】qíquán 应有尽有（多指物品 oft. of things）have everything that one expects; well-stocked：百货公司已经把冬季用品准备～。The department store has been well-stocked with all the necessities for the winter.

【齐头并进】qí tóu bìng jìn 不分先后地一齐前进或同时进行 advance side by side; do several things at once

【齐心】qíxīn 思想认识一致 of one mind：～合力 act in an concerted effort｜只要大家～了，事情就好办了。We can easily get things done if we work as one.

【齐整】qízhěng 整齐 neat; well arranged：公路两旁的杨树长得很～。The poplar trees that flank both sides of the highway have grown to almost the same height.

【齐奏】qízòu 两个以上的演奏者，同时演奏同一曲调 play musical instruments in unison

祁 Qí ❶ 指安徽祁门 Qimen, a place in Anhui Province：～红（祁门出的红茶）*qihong*, a black tea produced in Qimen ❷ 指湖南祁阳 Qiyang, a place in Hunan Province：～剧 *Qiju*, a local opera of Hunan Province ❸ 姓 a surname

圻 qí〈书 *fml.*〉边界 boundary

☞ yín on p.2289

芪 qí ☞[黄芪] huángqí on p.853

岐 qí ❶ 岐山(Qíshān)地名,在陕西 Qishan, name of a place in Shaanxi Province ❷ same as 歧 qí ❸(Qí) 姓 a surname

【岐黄】qíhuáng 黄帝和岐伯。我国古代著名的医书《黄帝内经·素问》,多用黄帝和岐伯问答的形式写成。后来把'岐黄'作中医学术的代称。*qihuang*, combination of two surnames that is synonymous to 'traditional Chinese medicine,' derived from the fact that *The Yellow Emperor's Canon of Internal Medicine* was written in the form of a dialogue between Qi Bo and Huang Di, the Yellow Emperor:~之术 science of traditional Chinese medicine

其1 qí ❶ 他(她、它)的;他(她、它)们的 his; her; its; their:各得~所 to the satisfaction of one and all; each is properly provided for; each is in his proper place|自圆~说 give a good explanation of what one has said or done; make out a good case ❷ 他(她、它);他(她、它)们 he; she; it; they:促~早日实现 bring sth. to fruition at an early date|不能任~自流。On no account should we let matters go along its natural course. ❸ 那个;那样 that; such:查无~事。Investigation indicates that nothing of the sort has happened.|不厌~烦 go to great lengths; take great pains; be very patient ❹ 虚指[used as a functional word]:忘~所以 forget oneself; get swell-headed

其2 qí 〈书 *fml.*〉〈助词 *aux.*〉❶ 表示揣测、反诘[indicating conjecture or retort]:岂~然乎? Is this really the case? |~奈我何? What can they do about me? ❷ 表示命令[indicating an instruction]:子~勉之! Work to the best of your ability please!

其3 qí 〈词尾 *suffix*〉:极~extremely|尤~in particular|如~if; in case|大概~。That's about it.

☞ jī on p.894

【其次】qícì ❶ 次第较后;第二(用于列举事项 when enumerating items, events, etc.) next; then; on the other hand:他第一个发言,~就轮到了我。He's the first to speak, and I am the next.|你这次下去,首先要做好社会调查工作,~要参加一些劳动。During your stay at the grass-roots level this time, first, do a good job in social investigation, and second, take part in some physical labour. ❷ 次要的地位 secondary:内容是主要的,形式还在~。Content is more important than anything else, and form is secondary.

【其间】qíjiān ❶ 那中间;其中 between; among; amidst; in the midst of:厕身~find one self among...|~定有缘故。There must be a reason to this. ❷ 指某一段时间 during this or that period; in the intervening years:离开学校已经好几年了,这~,他的科学研究工作成绩显著。During the years since he left school he has distinguished himself in research work.

【其貌不扬】qí mào bù yáng 指人的容貌平常或丑陋 be unimpressive in looks; look homely

【其实】qíshí 〈副词 *adv.*〉表示所说的是实际情况(承上文而含转折)in fact; as a matter of fact; actually:这个问题从表面上看似乎很难,~并不难。This problem looks like a hard nut to crack, but actually it is not really so difficult.

【其它】qítā same as 其他 qítā (用于事物 referring to things rather than people)

【其他】qítā 别的 other than; apart from:今天的文娱晚会,除了京剧、曲艺以外,还有~精彩节目。The variety show today has got a lot of good stuff apart from Peking Opera, ballad singing and comic dialogues.

【其余】qíyú 剩下的 other (persons or things); rest; remainder:除了有两人请假,~的人都到了。Everybody is here except two who have called in sick.

【其中】qízhōng 那里面 among; in; of:果园里一共有五万棵果树,~梨树占30%。Pears account for 30 per cent of the 50,000 fruit trees in the orchard.

奇 qí ❶ 罕见的;特殊的;非常的 rare; special; very:~事 rare phenomenon|~闻 sth. unheard-of|~志 noble aspiration|~勋 outstanding meritorious deed|~耻大辱 huge humiliation|商品~缺 commodity in great demand|山势~险 stupendous mountain cliffs ❷ 出人意料的;令人难测的 unexpected; unpredictable:~兵 ingenious manoeuvre of troops|~袭 surprise attack|出~制胜 subdue an enemy by catching it unawares ❸ 惊异 extraordinary; out of the ordinary:惊~ amazing|不足为~nothing out of the ordinary ❹(Qí) 姓 a surname

☞ jī on p.894

【奇拔】qíbá 奇特挺拔 statuesque:山峰~statuesque mountain peak

【奇兵】qíbīng 出乎敌人意料而突然袭击的军队 manoeuvring of troops that catches an enemy unawares:出~取胜 defeat an enemy by mounting a surprise attack

【奇才】qícái ❶ 杰出的才能 wizard; genius:这一战显出他的指挥~。The battle showed him at his best as a gifted commander. ❷ 具有杰出才能的人 person of unusual talent

【奇耻大辱】qí chǐ dà rǔ 极大的耻辱 galling shame and deep insult

【奇峰】qífēng 奇特的山峰 vagarious mountain peak:~突起。A mountain soared into the clouds in a spectacular form.

【奇怪】qíguài ❶ 跟平常的不一样 strange;

odd; weird: 海里有不少～的动植物。The sea teams with strange animals and plants. ❷ 出乎意料，难以理解 surprising; incomprehensive: 真～，为什么这时候他还不来呢？I wonder why he did not show up now.

【奇观】qíguān 指雄伟美丽而又罕见的景象或出奇少见的事情 wonder; spectacle:《今古～》*Wonders Present and Past*, a book by Baowen Laoren | 钱塘江的潮汐是一大～。The tidal bore of the Qiantang River is one of the wonders of nature.

【奇幻】qíhuàn ❶ 奇异而虚幻 fantastic; visionary: ～的遐想 fantastic imagination ❷ 奇异变幻 dreamlike; kaleidoscopic: 景色～。There is something dreamlike about the scene.

Q

【奇货可居】qí huò kě jū 指商人把难得的货物囤积起来，等待高价出售 rare commodity worth hoarding for a higher price; rare merchandise worth buying; 〈比喻 *fig.*〉人有某种独特的技能或成就，拿它作为要求名利地位的本钱 appear to have a hit on one's hands; regard one's special skill or achievement as a bargaining chip for gain and fame

【奇迹】qíjì 想像不到的不平凡的事情 miracle; marvel: 创造～perform a miracle | 她的病居然～般地好起来了。Her recovery from illness was nothing short of a miracle.

【奇崛】qíjué 〈书 *fml.*〉奇特突出 exceptional; phenomenal: 文笔～exceptional style of writing

【奇妙】qímiào 稀奇巧妙（多用来形容令人感兴趣的新奇事物 oft. used to describe novel things）wonderful; intriguing: 构思～one-of-a-kind conception | ～世界 the wonderful world

【奇葩】qípā 奇特而美丽的花朵 exotic flower: ～异草 exotic flowers and precious herbs | ～斗妍（of flowers）wreaked up a riot of colour ◇这篇小说是近来文坛上出现的一朵～。This short story is hailed as a phenomenon in its own right to have emerged on the literary scene lately.

【奇巧】qíqiǎo 奇特巧妙；新奇精巧 ingenious; exquisite: ～的玉雕 ingenious piece of jade carving | 园内假山造型～。The artificial rockery in the garden is marked for the ingenuity of its design.

【奇谈】qítán 令人觉得奇怪的言论或见解 strange theory or argument: 海外～ strange tales from overseas | ～怪论 ridiculous theory

【奇特】qítè 跟寻常的不一样；奇怪而特别 peculiar; one of a kind: 装束～ be attired in a strange way | 在沙漠地区常常可以看到一些～的景象。Strange mirages are not uncommon in the desert.

【奇伟】qíwěi 奇特雄伟 singularly magnificent: 建筑～architecture of a unique style

【奇文共赏】qí wén gòng shǎng 新奇的文章共同欣赏（语见晋陶潜《移居》诗：'奇文共欣赏，疑义相与析'）现多指把荒谬、错误的文章发表出来供大家识别和批判 'A remarkable work should be shared and its subtleties discussed,' a line from the poem *Migration* by Tao Qian of the Jin Dynasty; publish an article with an erroneous viewpoint usu. to solicit public criticism

【奇闻】qíwén 奇特动听的事情 sth. inconceivable; unbelievable story: ～趣事 strange stories and amazing anecdotes

【奇袭】qíxí 出其不意地打击敌人（多指军事上 oft. military）surprise attack; raid

【奇效】qíxiào 预想不到的效果或效力 unusual efficacy: 这种药对治疗风湿病有～。This drug is a miraculous cure for rheumatism.

【奇形怪状】qí xíng guài zhuàng 不正常的，奇奇怪怪的形状 strange sight: 在石灰岩洞里，到处是～的钟乳石。Stalactites in shapes ranging from the spectacular to the grotesque are everywhere in this limestone cave.

【奇勋】qíxūn 特殊的功勋 extraordinarily meritorious exploit: 屡建～have quite a few unusual meritorious exploits under one's belt

【奇异】qíyì ❶ same as 奇怪 qíguài ①: 海底是一个～的世界。The seabed is a world of wonders. ❷ 惊异 surprised; astounded: 路上的人都用～的眼光看着这些来自远方的客人。Surprise was palpable in the eyes of the passersby as they looked at the guests from afar.

【奇遇】qíyù 意外的、奇特的相逢或遇合（多指好的事 oft. positive）fortuitous meeting; happy encounter: 深山～ happen encounter in the mountains | 他俩多年失去联系，想不到在会上见面，真是～！Who would have imagined that the two of them could come across each other at the meeting after a departure of so many years.

【奇装异服】qí zhuāng yì fú 与当时社会上一般人衣着式样不同的服装（多含贬义 oft. derog.）bizarre dress; outlandish outfit

歧 qí ❶ 岔（道）；大路分出的（路）（of roads）fork; branch: ～途 wrong way ❷ 不相同；不一致 be at variance with; different from: ～义 ambiguity; different meaning | ～视 discriminate against

【歧出】qíchū 一本书、一篇文章之内文字前后不符（多指术语等 of the use of words, esp. technical terms in a book, article, etc.）inconsistency; discrepancy

【歧化】qíhuà 指在化学反应中，同一种元素的一部分原子（或离子）被氧化，另一部分原子（或离子）被还原（in chemical reaction）disproportionate; referring to the phenomenon in a chemical reaction that some of the atoms or ions in an element are oxidized while the others are deoxidized

【歧路】qílù 从大路上分出来的小路 branch

road; forked road

【歧路亡羊】qílù wáng yáng 杨子的邻居把羊丢了,没有找着。杨子问:'为什么没找着?'邻人说:'岔路很多,岔路上又有岔路,不知道往哪儿去了'(见于《列子·说符》)。According to *Lie Zi·On Incantations*, when a neighbour had lost his lamb, Yang Zi asked him why he couldn't retrieve it. The neighbour answered, 'The road has so many branches, and each branch has so many sub-branches that I really had no idea in which way my lamb had gone.'〈比喻 *fig.*〉因情况复杂多变而迷失方向,误入歧途 go astray under complicated circumstances

【歧视】qíshì 不平等地看待 discriminate against:种族～racial discrimination; racism

【歧途】qítú same as 歧路 qílù;〈比喻 *fig.*〉错误的道路 wrong way:受人蒙骗,误入～be misled and go astray

【歧义】qíyì (语言文字)两歧或多歧的意义,有两种或几种可能的解释(of a wording) leave room for different interpretations; ambiguity

【歧异】qíyì 分歧差异;不相同 difference; discrepancy

祈 qí ❶ 祈祷 pray:～福 pray for blessings ❷ 请求;希望 ask for; entreat; request:～求 plead for|～望 wish|敬～指导。Your advice is respectfully requested. ❸(Qí) 姓 a surname

【祈祷】qídǎo 一种宗教仪式,信仰宗教的人向神默告自己的愿望(of a religious follower) say one's prayers; do one's devotional

【祈求】qíqiú 恳切地希望或请求 pray; entreat for; plead for:～来年有个好收成 pray for a good harvest in the new year|脸上流露出～的神情。There was a beseeching look on his face.

【祈使句】qíshǐjù 要求或者希望别人做什么事或者不做什么事时用的句子,如:'你过来。''把书递给我。''大家别闹了!'在书面上,句末用句号或感叹号。imperative sentence; sentence structure ended with a full stop or exclamatory mark, to be used when requesting or hoping sb. to do, or refrain from doing, sth.; for example: 'Come over!' 'Pass the book over to me.' 'Cut all the noise!'

祇 qí〈书 *fml.*〉地神 God of the Earth; ☞ 神祇 shénqí on p.1707

☞ 只 zhǐ on p.2465

荠(薺) qí ☞[荸荠] bí·qí on p.96

☞ jì on p.919

俟 qí ☞[万俟] mòqí on p.1365

☞ sì on p.1823

疷 qí〈书 *fml.*〉病 ailment

耆 qí 六十岁以上的(人)(of a person) over sixty years of age:～老 old man|～年 old age

〈古 *arch.*〉same as 嗜 shì

【耆老】qílǎo〈书 *fml.*〉老年人。特指德行高尚受尊敬的老人。old man, esp. one with high moral value and held in high esteem

【耆宿】qísù〈书 *fml.*〉指在社会上有名望的老年人 venerable elderly man

颀 qí〈书 *fml.*〉(身体)修长高大(of stature) tall:～长 tall in build

【颀长】qícháng (身量)高(of stature) tall

【颀伟】qíwěi (身材)高大魁梧 tower of a man; strong

脐(臍) qí ❶ 肚脐 navel:～带 umbilical cord ❷ 螃蟹肚子下面的甲壳 abdomen of a crab:尖～pointed belly flap (in a male crab)|团～round belly flap (in a female crab)

【脐带】qídài 连接胚胎与胎盘的带状物,由两条动脉和一条静脉构成。胚胎依靠脐带与母体联系,是胚胎吸取养料和排出废料的通道。umbilical cord, consisting of two arteries and one vein, connecting the fetus with the placenta of the mother and transmitting nourishment from the mother and discharging wastes from the fetus

旂 qí ❶〈古代 *arch.*〉一种旗子 a kind of flag ❷ same as 旗 qí ①

埼(碕) qí〈书 *fml.*〉弯曲的岸 winding shore

萁 qí〈方 *dial.*〉豆秸 beanstalk:豆～beanstalk

畦 qí 有土埂围着的一块块排列整齐的田地,一般是长方形的 farm plot; rectangular piece of land separated by ridges:～田 embanked farm plot|菜～vegetable bed|种了一～韭菜 grow one plot of leek

【畦灌】qíguàn 灌溉的一种方法,把灌溉的土地分成面积较小的畦,灌溉时,每个畦依次灌水。适用于小麦、谷子等作物。plot-by-plot irrigation; divide a wheat or millet field with ridges and irrigate them one by one

【畦田】qítián 周围筑埂可以灌溉和蓄水的田 ridged field; field surrounded by ridges to facilitate irrigation and water storage

跂 qí〈书 *fml.*〉❶ 多出的脚趾 extra toe ❷ 形容虫子爬行(of an insect) crawl

☞ qì on p.1525

崎 qí〈书 *fml.*〉倾斜;不平坦 sloping; rugged:～径 rugged path

【崎岖】qíqū 形容山路不平;(of a mountain path) rugged〈比喻 *fig.*〉处境艰难 straitened circumstances:山路～ tortuous mountain road|～坎坷的一生 a lifetime full of twists and turns

淇 Qí 淇河,水名,在河南 Qihe, name of a river in Henan Province

骐 qí〈书 *fml.*〉青黑色的马 black horse:～骥(骏马) steed

骑 qí ❶ 两腿跨坐(在牲口或自行车等上面) ride (an animal or bicycle): ～马 on horseback; in the saddle; horseback riding|～自行车 ride a bicycle ❷ 兼跨两边 straddle: ～缝 seal across two sheets of paper ❸ 骑的马,泛指人乘坐的动物 mount; horse or other animal one rides: 坐～one's mount ❹ 骑兵,也泛指骑马的人 cavalrymen; horseback rider: 轻～light cavalry; hussar|铁～fine war horse|车～horse and carriage

【骑兵】qíbīng 骑马作战的兵种,也指这个兵种的士兵 cavalry; cavalryman

【骑缝】qífèng 两张纸的交接处(多指单据和存根连接的地方)joint of the edges of two sheets of paper: 在三联单的～上盖印 affix a seal across the perforation between the two halves of a voucher

【骑虎难下】qí hǔ nán xià 〈比喻 *fig.*〉事情中途遇到困难,为形势所迫,又难以中止 he who rides a tiger is afraid to dismount—irrevocably but unwillingly committed; unable to extricate oneself from a difficult situation

【骑楼】qílóu 〈方 *dial.*〉楼房向外伸出在人行道上的部分。骑楼下的人行道叫骑楼底。arcade house with a covered passageway beneath it; the passage way is called 骑楼底 qílóudǐ

【骑马找马】qí mǎ zhǎo mǎ 〈比喻 *fig.*〉东西就在自己这里,还到处去找。也比喻一面占着现在的位置,一面另找更称心的工作。sit on the very horse one is looking for — look for sth. that's right under one's nose; hold on to one job while seeking for a better one

【骑墙】qíqiáng 〈比喻 *fig.*〉立场不明确,站在斗争双方的中间,哪一方面也不得罪 straddle the fence: ～派 fencesitter; weathercock|～观望 ride the fence

【骑手】qíshǒu 擅长骑马的人 good rider; horseman

琪 qí 〈书 *fml.*〉美玉 fine jade

琦 qí 〈书 *fml.*〉 ❶ 美玉 fine jade ❷ 不凡的;美好的 outstanding; distinguished: ～行(美好的品德)consummate morale conduct

棋(**棊、碁**) qí ❶ 文娱项目的一类,一副棋包括若干颗棋子和一个棋盘,下棋的人按一定的规则摆上或移动棋子来比输赢,有象棋、围棋、军棋、跳棋等。象棋、围棋也是体育运动项目。chess, game of strategic skill for two players, played on a chequered board, on which pieces are moved and capture opposing pieces according to prescribed rules; board game, such as Chinese chess, the game of go, kriegspiel, halma, etc., of which Chinese chess and the game of go are also sports events ❷ 指棋子儿 chessman; piece: 落～无悔 no backstepping

【棋布】qíbù 像棋子似地分布着。形容多而密集 scattered like pieces on a chessboard: 星罗～as numerous as stars and pieces on a chessboard; be studded with

【棋逢对手】qí féng duì shǒu 〈比喻 *fig.*〉双方本领不相上下 be well-matched; also 棋逢敌手 qí féng dí shǒu

【棋局】qíjú ❶ 指下棋过程中双方对阵的形势 development in a game of chess ❷ 〈旧 *old*〉指棋盘 chessboard

【棋迷】qímí 下棋或看下棋而入迷的人 chess fan; chess enthusiast

【棋盘】qípán 下棋时摆棋子用的盘,上面画着一定形式的格子 chessboard; chequered board for a board game

【棋谱】qípǔ 用图和文字说明下棋的基本技术或解释棋局的书 chess manual

【棋艺】qíyì 下棋的技艺 skill in playing chess: 钻研～study the techniques of playing chess

【棋子】qízǐ (～儿 qízǐr)用木头或其他材料制成的下棋用的小块。通常用颜色分为数目相等的两部分或几部分,下棋的人各使用一部分。piece (of a board game); chessman; pieces made of wood or other materials, divided equally between two or more players in a chess game

蛴(**蠐**) qí [蛴螬](qícáo)金龟子的幼虫,白色,圆柱状,向腹面弯曲。生活在土里,吃农作物的根和茎,是害虫。在不同的地区有地蚕,土蚕,核桃虫的名称。grub; larva of scarab white in colour and cylindrical in shape that slightly bends towards its belly, living in soil and feeding on the roots and stalks of farm crops, therefore regarded as an insect pest; known variously in different regions as 地蚕 dìcán, 土蚕 tǔcán and 核桃虫 hétáochóng

祺 qí 〈书 *fml.*〉吉祥 propitious; felicitous

锜 qí ❶ 〈古代 *arch.*〉烹煮器皿,底下有三足 *qi*, a cooking vessel in the design of a tripod ❷ 〈古代 *arch.*〉一种凿子 chisel

綦 qí ❶ 〈书 *fml.*〉极;很 absolutely; very: 言之～详 explain sth. to the minute detail ❷(Qí) 姓 a surname

【綦切】qíqiè 〈书 *fml.*〉迫切;殷切 avid; earnest: 念子～heartfelt yearning for one's son|希望～ardent hope

蜞 qí ☞[蟛蜞] péngqí on p. 1460

旗(❶**旂**) qí ❶ 旗子 flag: 国～national flag|红～red flag|挂～hoist a flag ❷ 指八旗 Eight Banners, Mongol military and administrative organizations: 汉军～Banner of Han Troops ❸ 属于八旗的,特指属于满族的 of the Eight Banners, esp. of the Manchu people: ～人 Manchus|～袍 cheongsam ❹ 八旗兵驻屯的地方,现在地名沿用 garrisons of the Eight Banners, which have become place names: 正黄～Xulun Xar Banner ❺ 内蒙古自治区的行政区划单位,相当于县

banner, a county-level administrative division in the Inner Mongolia Autonomous Region

【旗杆】qígān 悬挂旗子用的杆子 flag pole; flag post

【旗鼓相当】qí gǔ xiāngdāng 〈比喻 *fig.*〉双方力量不相上下 well-matched in strength; a Roland for an Oliver:这两个足球队~,一定有一场精彩的比赛。As these two soccer teams are about equal, the game between them is bound to be a hot one.

【旗号】qíhào 〈旧时 *old*〉标明军队名称或将领姓氏的旗子 banner that bears the name of an army or the surname of the commander; 现比喻某种名义(多指借来做坏事) (fig.) pretext (oft. for doing sth. bad); excuse

【旗舰】qíjiàn 某些国家的海军舰队司令、编队司令所在的军舰,因舰上挂有司令旗(夜间加挂司令灯),所以叫旗舰。中国人民解放军叫指挥舰。flagship; ship that carries a fleet or squadron commander and bears his flag (and lantern at night), known in the Chinese People's Liberation Army as 'commanding ship'

【旗开得胜】qí kāi dé shèng 军队的战旗刚一展开就打了胜仗 emerge victorious as soon as one army's standard is hoisted; win the first battle; 〈比喻 *fig.*〉事情一开始就取得好成绩 succeed at the first try

【旗袍】qípáo (~儿 qípáor)妇女穿的一种长袍,原为满族妇女所穿 cheongsam, mandarin gown; body-hugging woman's dress originating from the Manchus

【旗人】Qírén 〈旧称 *old*〉清代隶属八旗的人,特指满族 banner people; member of one of the Eight Banners during the Qing Dynasty, esp. a Manchu person

【旗手】qíshǒu 在行列前打旗子的人〈比喻 *fig.*〉领导人或先行者 standard-bearer; leader; vanguard:鲁迅先生是新文化运动的~。Lu Xun was a great standard-bearer of the New Culture Movement.

【旗语】qíyǔ 航海上或军事上,在距离较远,说话不能听见的场合,用旗子来通讯的方法。单手执旗或双手各执一旗,以不同的挥旗动作表达通讯内容。flag signal; means of communication in navigation or war at distances that are out of earshot, brandishing a flag single-handed or in each hand in different postures to get different messages across

【旗帜】qízhì ❶ 旗子 flag; banner; streamer:节日的首都到处飘扬着五彩缤纷的~。Colourful flags are fluttering everywhere in the capital city on the festive day. ❷ 〈比喻 *fig.*〉榜样或模范 role model:培养典型,树立~。Cultivate pace setters and foster role models. ❸ 〈比喻 *fig.*〉有代表性或号召力的某种思想、学说或政治力量等 idea, theory or political force that is representative of certain people or has a certain rallying force

【旗帜鲜明】qízhì xiānmíng 〈比喻 *fig.*〉观点、立场非常明确 hold an unequivocal stand; never mince one's words on matters of consequence

【旗子】qí·zi 用绸、布、纸等做成的方形、长方形或三角形的标志,大多挂在杆子上或墙壁上 flag; pennant made of silk, cloth, or paper, and square, oblong or triangular in design, mostly hoisted on a pole or posted on a wall

蕲[1](**蘄**) qí 〈书 *fml.*〉求 beseech; plead; petition

蕲[2](**蘄**) Qí ❶ 指蕲州(旧州名,州治在今湖北蕲春南)Qizhou, old name of a prefecture seated south of present-day Qichun, Hubei Province ❷ (Qí)姓 a surname

【蕲艾】qí'ài ☞艾[1] ài on p. 5

【蕲求】qíqiú 〈书 *fml.*〉祈求 crave; pray for

鲯 qí [鲯鳅](qíqiū)鱼,身体长而侧扁,黑褐色,头高而大,眼小,背鳍很长,尾鳍分叉深。生活在海洋中。dorado (*Coryphaena hippurus*); dolphinfish; sea fish having a long brownish dark body with a flat side, big and crested head, tiny eyes, long dorsal fins, and a deeply bifurcated tail fin

鳍 qí 鱼类的运动器官,由刺状的硬骨或软骨支撑薄膜构成。按它所在的部位,可分为胸鳍、腹鳍、背鳍、臀鳍和尾鳍。fin; flattened appendage consisting of spinous bones or cartilages that form the framework for a membrane cover, attached to various parts of a fish, including pectoral fin, pelvic fin, dorsal fin, anal fin and tail fin

1. 背鳍 dorsal fin　2. 尾鳍 tail fin
3. 胸鳍 pectoral fin　4. 腹鳍 pelvic fin
5. 臀鳍 anal fin

鳍 Fins

麒 qí ❶ ☞麒麟 qílín ❷(Qí) 姓 a surname

【麒麟】qílín 〈古代 *arch.*〉传说中的一种动物,形状像鹿,头上有角,全身有鳞甲,有尾。古人拿它象征祥瑞。kylin; Chinese unicorn; Chinese mythological animal akin to the deer, sporting antlers on the head and a tail, covered all over with scales, regarded by ancients as a mascot; 简称 abbr. 麟 lín

鬐 qí 〈书 *fml.*〉马鬃 horse mane

qǐ (ㄑㄧˇ)

乞 qǐ ❶ 向人讨；乞求 beg；panhandle；supplicate：～怜 beg for pity；bet for mercy｜～食 beg for alms；beg for food｜～援 plead for reinforcement ❷(Qǐ) 姓 a surname

【乞哀告怜】qǐ āi gào lián 乞求别人哀怜和帮助 beg for mercy；piteously beg for help

【乞丐】qǐgài 生活没有着落而专靠向人要饭要钱过活的人 beggar；panhandler

【乞怜】qǐlián 显出可怜相，希望得到别人的同情 beg for pity：摇尾～seek pity like a dog wagging its tail；fawn obsequiously

【乞灵】qǐlíng 〈书 *fml*.〉向神佛求助（迷信）(superstition) invoke help from a god；〈比喻 *fig*.〉乞求不可靠的帮助 beg for help that is unreliable

【乞巧】qǐqiǎo 农历七月初七的晚上，妇女在院子里陈设瓜果，向织女星祈祷，请求帮助她们提高刺绣缝纫的技巧。是旧时的一种民间风俗。begging for cleverness ceremony；old Chinese custom whereby melons and fruit are laid out in a courtyard on the seventh evening of the seventh month to be offered as sacrifices by young women to the Star of the Weaving-Girl

【乞求】qǐqiú 请求给予 plead for；implore：～施舍 beg for alms｜～宽恕 plead for forgiveness

【乞食】qǐshí 〈书 *fml*.〉要饭 beg for food；go panhandling

【乞讨】qǐtǎo 向人要钱要饭等 go begging：沿街～go door-to-door begging

【乞降】qǐxiáng 请求对方接受投降 beg to surrender

【乞援】qǐyuán 请求援助 ask for aid：四处～seek high and low for assistance

芑 qǐ 古书上说的一种植物 glutinous rehmannia (in ancient books)

屺 qǐ 〈书 *fml*.〉没有草木的山 barren mountain

岂(豈) qǐ 〈书 *fml*.〉〈副词 *adv*.〉表示反问[indicating a rhetorical question]：～有此理 What nonsense!｜如此而已，～有他哉？That's all there is to it!

〈古 *arch*.〉same as 恺 kǎi or 凯 kǎi

【岂但】qǐdàn 用反问的语气表示'不但'[conjunction indicated in a rhetorical tone] not only：～你不知道，连我自己也不清楚呢。Not only you are in the dark, even I myself am not clear about all this.

【岂非】qǐfēi 用反问的语气表示'难道不是'[used in a rhetorical tone] would it not be；isn't it：～怪事？It is strange, isn't it?｜这样解释～自相矛盾？Wouldn't this kind of explanation be self-contradictory?

【岂敢】qǐgǎn 怎么敢；哪里敢（多用做客套话 oft. pol.）how dare I...；I don't deserve such honour：我～单独行动 How dare I do it alone?｜～～，些许小事，何足挂齿？I wish I deserved your compliment —this modest effort on my part is not worth mentioning.

【岂可】qǐkě 用反问的语气表示'不可以'[used in a rhetorical tone] on no account should；how could：～言而无信 How could you go back on your word?｜～坐以待毙？How could we sit still waiting for our doom?

【岂有此理】qǐ yǒu cǐ lǐ 哪有这样的道理（对不合情理的事表示气愤 indicating anger at sth. unreasonable）who ever heard of such absurdity；outrageous：做错了事，还要怪别人，真是～！You made the mistake but you shift the blame onto others. How outrageous!

【岂止】qǐzhǐ 用反问的语气表示'不止'[used in a rhetorical tone] let alone；not to mention：为难的事还多呢，～这一件？There are so many hard nuts to crack, let alone this one.

企 qǐ 抬起脚后跟站着，今用为盼望的意思 stand on tiptoe；expect on tiptoe；look forward to：～盼 yearn for｜～望 ardent hope

【企鹅】qǐ'é 水鸟，体长约1米，嘴很坚硬，头和背部黑色，腹部白色，足短，尾巴短，翅膀小，不能飞，善于潜水游泳，在陆地上直立时像有所企望的样子，多群居在南极洲及附近岛屿上 penguin (*Spheniscidae*)；its Chinese name means 'expectant bird'；water fowl having a body approximately one metre long, with black upper parts and white underparts, short limbs and tail, and wings developed into scaly flippers that make it impossible to fly but are good for swimming underwater, always looking like expecting something when standing on its legs, living gregariously mostly in Antarctica and nearby islands in the Southern Hemisphere

【企及】qǐjí 盼望达到；希望赶上 hope to attain：难以～unattainable

【企口板】qǐkǒubǎn 一侧有凹槽，另一侧有凸榫的木板，拼接后结合紧密，不易翘起。多用做地板等。matched board；wood board featuring a groove on one side and tenon on the other side, to be tightly fitted with one another to prevent from warping, oft. used as flooring material

【企慕】qǐmù 仰慕 admire

【企盼】qǐpàn 盼望 hope for；yearn for：～未来 look forward to the future｜～合家欢聚 yearn for a happy family reunion

【企求】qǐqiú 希望得到 hanker after：他一心只想把工作搞好，从不～什么。All he wanted was nothing but to do a good job.

【企图】qǐtú 图谋；打算 seek to；attempt；intention：敌军逃跑的～没有得逞 The enemy troops made a vain attempt at escaping.｜在这篇作品中，作者～表现的主题并不突出。

This piece of creative writing failed to bring into focus the theme the author intended to portray.

【企望】qǐwàng 希望 look forward to：翘首～ expect on tiptoe

【企业】qǐyè 从事生产、运输、贸易等经济活动的部门，如工厂、矿山、铁路、公司等 enterprise; business; entities engaged in production, transport, trade or other economic activity, such as factory, mine, railway, trading company, etc.

【企业化】qǐyèhuà ❶ 工业、商业、运输等单位按照经济核算的原则，独立计算盈亏(of industrial, commercial, transport and other entities) run on a commercial basis, that is, to calculate profits and losses on the basis of accounting ❷ 使事业单位能有正常收入，不需要国家开支经费，并能自行进行经济核算 set a non-profiting entity on a business basis so that it can make money just like an enterprise does

【企足而待】qǐ zú ér dài 抬起脚后跟来等着 wait on tiptoe;〈比喻 *fig.*〉不久的将来就能实现 (of sth. long expected) soon to come true

玘 qǐ〈书 *fml.*〉一种玉 a kind of jade

杞 Qǐ ❶ 周朝国名，在今河南杞县 Qi, name of a state during the Zhou Dynasty, in present-day Qixian, Henan Province ❷ 姓 a surname

【杞人忧天】Qǐ rén yōu tiān 传说杞国有个人怕天塌下来，吃饭睡觉都感到不安(见于《列子·天瑞》) according to *Lie Zi·Heaven's Gift*, legend has it that a man was on tenterhooks for fear of a collapse of the sky;〈比喻 *fig.*〉不必要的忧虑 be haunted by an imaginary fear; also 杞人之忧 Qǐ rén zhī yōu

启(啟、啓) qǐ ❶ 打开 open：～封 open an envelope|～门 open the door|某某～(信封上用语，表示由某人拆信 written right after the name of the receiver of a letter on the envelope) to be opened personally by ❷ 开导 enlighten; guidance：～蒙 teach a beginner|～发 inspire ❸ 开始 commence; begin：～行 begin a journey|～用 put in use ❹ 陈述 state; inform：敬～者(〈旧时 *old*〉用于书信的开端 a set phrase to begin a letter) I bet to state|某某～(用于书信末署名处 a set phrase that concludes a letter) Respectfully yours ❺〈旧时 *old*〉文体之一，较简短的书信 missive：小～ short missive|谢～ thank-you note ❻(Qǐ) 姓 a surname

【启程】qǐchéng 起程；上路 set out; begin a journey

【启齿】qǐchǐ 开口(多指向别人有所请求) bring up a matter; start to say sth. (oft. a request)：难以～ find it hard to say what one wants to say|不便～feel embarrassed to bring a matter up

【启迪】qǐdí 开导；启发 inspire; enlighten：～后人 for the enlightenment of posterity

【启碇】qǐ//dìng 起锚 weigh anchor and set sail

【启动】qǐdòng (机器、仪表、电气设备等)开始工作(of a machine, an apparatus, an electrical device, etc.) rev up; switch on：～电流 switch on the electricity|～继电器 start a relay|车轮～set wheels in motion

【启发】qǐfā 阐明事例，引起对方联想而有所领悟 enlighten; cite examples to elicit response and help sb. see the point：～性报告 inspirational report|～群众的积极性 arouse the enthusiasm of the masses

【启封】qǐ//fēng 打开封条，也指拆开封着的信件等 unseal; open an envelope or wrapper

【启蒙】qǐméng ❶ 使初学的人得到基本的、入门的知识 initiate a beginner in a discipline of learning：～老师 first teacher; teacher who initiates a student into a field of learning|～读物 primer ❷ 普及新知识，使摆脱愚昧和迷信 popularize new knowledge to deliver people from fatuity and superstition：～运动 Enlightenment Movement

【启蒙运动】qǐméng yùndòng ❶ 17—18 世纪欧洲资产阶级的民主文化运动。启发人们反对封建传统思想和宗教的束缚，提倡思想自由、个性发展等。Enlightenment; 18th-century European democratic cultural movement that was opposed to traditional feudal and religious fetters on people's mind, and advocated freedom of thinking and development of individuality ❷ 泛指通过宣传教育使社会接受新事物而得到进步的运动 (in a broad sense) campaign designed to promote social progress by giving publicity to and education in nascent things

【启明】qǐmíng 我国古代指日出以前，出现在东方天空的金星 Qiming Star, classical Chinese name for Venus, which emerged in the east prior to sunrise ☞ 金星 jīnxīng on p. 1006

【启示】qǐshì 启发指示，使有所领悟 inspiration; revelation：这本书～我们应该怎样度过自己的一生。The book provides some revelations on how to spend our lives in this world.

【启事】qǐshì 为了说明某事而登在报刊上或贴在墙壁上的文字 notice; announcement：征稿～ notice inviting contributions to a publication

【启衅】qǐxìn 挑起争端 provoke a dispute：两次世界大战都是德国军国主义者首先～的。Both World Wars were instigated by German militarists.

【启用】qǐyòng 开始使用 invoke; put to use; unveil：～印章 start using a new official seal|～新秀 to start rookies in an undertaking, game, etc.|铁路已建成～。The railway has been completed and opened to traffic.

【启运】qǐyùn 起运 start shipment of cargo

起[1] qǐ ❶ 由坐卧爬伏而站立或由躺而坐 stand up; get up; rise: ～来 get up|～立 stand up|～床 get up|早睡早～retire early and get up early ❷ 离开原来的位置 remove: ～身 set out|飞机～飞 takeoff |你～开点儿。Could you please set aside? ❸ 物体由下往上升 go up; rise: 皮球不～了。The rubber ball won't bounce. ❹ 长出(疱、疙瘩、痱子)appear; outgrow (bleb, lump, heat rash, etc.): 夏天小孩儿身上爱～痱子。Children are prone to prickly heat in summer. ❺ 把收藏或嵌入的东西弄出来 remove; take down: ～货 get goods from a warehouse|～钉子 remove a nail ❻ 发生 rise; take place: ～风了。The wind rose. |～疑心 become suspicious|～作用 take effect ❼ 发动;兴起 launch; initiate: ～兵 rise in an armed uprising|～事 start an armed rebellion ❽ 拟写 draft: ～稿子 work out a draft|～草 draft a document ❾ 建立 establish: ～伙 set up a mess|～会 set up an association|白手～家 start from scratch|平地～高楼 tall buildings mushroomed from an open field ❿ 领取(凭证)draw; obtain: ～行李票 get one's luggage tag |～护照 get one's passport ⓫ (从、由…)开始 preceded by; from: ～止 beginning and end|～讫 from the beginning to the end|由这儿～就只有小路了。Starting from here only narrow paths are available. ⓬用在动词后,表示(从、由…)开始[used after a verb to indicate beginning or starting point]: 从二号算～ be calculated beginning from the second day of the month|从头学～ start to learn something all over again; start from the very beginning|从何说～! Don't know where to begin. ⓭〈方 *dial*.〉〈介词 *prep*.〉放在时间或处所词的前边,表示始点[used before nouns of time and place to indicate the point of departure]: 您～哪儿来? Where did you come from? |～这儿往北 go north from here ⓮〈方 *dial*.〉〈介词 *prep*.〉放在处所词前面,表示经过的地点[used before nouns of place to indicate movement]: 看见一个人～窗户外面走过去。I saw someone passing by the window.

起[2] qǐ 〈量词 *classifier*〉❶ 件;次 case; instance: 这样的案子每年总有几～。Cases like this occur several times a year. |防止了一～事故。An accident has been thus forestalled. ❷ 群;批 batch; group: 外面进来一～人。In came a group of people. |他们分六～往地里送肥料。They delivered manure to the fields in six batches.

起 //·qǐ ❶ 用在动词后,表示向上[used after a verb] upwards; up: 抬～箱子往外走 lift a box to go out ❷ 用在动词后,表示力量够得上或够不上[used after a verb to indicate if it is within or beyond one's power to do sth.]: 经得～考验 be able to withstand the test|太贵了,买不～。It's too expensive and I can't afford it. 注意 **NOTE**: 动词和'起'之间常有'得'字或'不'字。In this use, the word 得 ·de or 不 bù is inserted between the verb and 起。❸ 用在动词后,表示事物随动作出现[used after a verb to indicate sth. happening right after the action]: 乐队奏～迎宾曲。The band struck up a tune of welcome. |会场响～热烈掌声。The assembly hall was resounded with warm applauses. ❹ 用在动词后,表示动作涉及人或事[used after a verb to indicate sb. or sth. involved in the action]: 他多次问～过你。He enquired about you on several occasions. |想～一件事。Something occurred to my mind.

【起岸】qǐ'àn 把货物从船上搬运到岸上 unload a boat: 缩短货物～时间 shorten the time needed for unloading the boats

【起霸】qǐ//bà 戏曲演员表演武将上阵前所做的整盔、束甲等一套程序动作(in traditional opera) stylized movements that launch a military character into action

【起爆】qǐbào 点燃引信或按动电钮使爆炸物爆炸 detonate: ～药 primer; detonating agent|准时～detonate on time

【起笔】qǐbǐ ❶ 书法上指每一笔的开始 first stroke of a Chinese character: ～的时候要顿一顿。A pause is needed before you start writing a Chinese character. ❷ 检字法上指一个字的第一笔 first stroke of a Chinese character in a radical index

【起兵】qǐbīng 出动军队;发动武装斗争 dispatch troops; launch an armed struggle: ～抗敌 rise in resistance against an enemy|～造反 rise in a revolt

【起步】qǐbù ❶ 开始走 start: 车子～了。The car began to move. ❷〈比喻 *fig*.〉事情开始进行 make a beginning: 我国女子举重虽然～晚,但已具有相当高的水平。Despite being a latecomer in women's weightlifting, China has come a long way in this sports event.

【起草】qǐ//cǎo 打草稿 draw up; draft: ～文件 draft a document|这个报告是谁起的草? Who drafted this report?

【起承转合】qǐ chéng zhuǎn hé 〈旧时 *old*〉写文章常用的行文的顺序,'起'是开始,'承'是承接上文,'转'是转折,'合'是全文的结束。泛指文章做法。four steps in writing an essay: introduction, elucidation of the theme, transition to another viewpoint, and summary

【起程】qǐchéng 上路;行程开始 set out; start on a journey: 连夜～。They set out that very night.

【起初】qǐchū 最初;起先 at first; in the beginning; to begin with: ～我不同意他这种做法,

后来才觉得他这样做是有道理的。At first I disapproved of his method, but later I came to realise that he was right. |～他一个字不识,现在已经能看报写信了。At first he could not read and write, but now he can even read newspapers and write letters.

【起床】qǐ//chuáng 睡醒后下床(多指早晨 oft. in the morning) get up:他每天总是天刚亮就～。He gets up at dawn everyday.

【起点】qǐdiǎn ❶ 开始的地方或时间 starting point:～站 starting station|任何伟大的成就都只是继续前进的新的～。A great achievement is, if anything, the starting point for something new. ◇拆整卖零,降低零售～。Whole packages of commodities are unpacked for sale on a piecemeal basis in order to bring down the starting point for the retail sale price. ❷ 专指径赛中起跑的地点 starting mark for a track race

【起电盘】qǐdiànpán 利用感应生电现象取得少量静电的装置,由一个绝缘物质做的圆盘和一个有绝缘柄的金属圆盘组成 electrophorus; apparatus for generating static electricity through induction, consisting of an insulated disk that is given a negative charge by friction and a metal plate that is given a net positive charge by induction when brought in contact with the disk by operating the plate's insulated handle

【起吊】qǐdiào 用起重机吊起重物 lift by crane

【起碇】qǐ//dìng same as 起锚 qǐ//máo

【起飞】qǐfēi ❶(飞机、火箭等)开始飞行(of aircraft; rocket; etc.) take off ❷〈比喻 *fig.*〉事业开始上升、发展(of an undertaking) get off to a good start; take off:经济～ economic takeoff |这个厂所以能～,主要靠科学管理。This factory was able to get off to a good start mainly by sound management.

【起伏】qǐfú ❶ 一起一落 undulate; rise and fall:麦浪～a field of wheat swaying in a wind|这一带全是连绵～的群山。The place is a vast stretch of rolling mountains. ❷〈比喻 *fig.*〉感情、关系等起落变化(of feelings, relationship, etc.) ups and downs; tumult:思绪～ mind constricted with conflicting emotions |病情～不定(a patient's) fluctuating condition|两国关系出现了一些～。There have been ups and downs in the bilateral relations between the two nations.

【起复】qǐfù ❶〈古代 *arch.*〉官吏遭父母丧,守制未满期而应召任职。明清两代专指服父母丧期满后重新出来做官。(of an official) be summoned to resume office before the mourning period for one's parent is over; (during the Ming and Qing dynasties) resume office upon finishing mourning for one's deceased parent ❷ 指官吏革职后重新被起用(of an official) be reappointed after removal from office

【起稿】qǐ//gǎo 打草稿 make a draft

【起根】qǐgēn〈方 *dial.*〉❶(～儿 qǐgēnr)从来;一向 as always; all along:他～儿就没有这个打算。This was not his idea from the very beginning. ❷ 从根本上;从头 begin with:这事还得～说起。The whole matter has to be traced back to day one.

【起更】qǐ//gēng〈旧 *old*〉夜间第一次打更 begin to sound the night watches

【起旱】qǐhàn 不走水路,走陆路(多指步行或乘坐旧式交通工具) travel by land (on foot or by old means of transport)

【起航】qǐháng (轮船、飞机等)开始航行(of a boat) set sail; (of an aircraft) take off:天气恶劣,不能～。The weather being foul, no take-off is scheduled.

【起哄】qǐ//hòng ❶(许多人在一起)胡闹;捣乱(of a crowd of people) create a disturbance:不得聚众～。No Brawling! ❷ 许多人向一两个人开玩笑(of a crowd of people) jeer; boo and hoot; tease clamorously:人家拿我开心,你也～。Everyone was making fun of me, yet you got a piece of action too.

【起火】qǐ//huǒ ❶ 生火做饭 raise a fire to cook:星期天你家～不～? Does your family prepare meals on Sunday? |在食堂吃饭比自己～方便。It's more convenient eating in the cafeteria than preparing your own meals. ❷ 发生火灾 catch fire:仓库～了。The warehouse has caught fire. ❸ 着急发脾气 get angry; act up:你别～,听我慢慢儿对你说。Don't fly off the handle. Be patient and let me explain.

【起火】qǐ·huo 带着苇子秆的花炮,点着后能升得很高 a kind of firecracker fixed with a reed stalk that can fly high into the sky

【起获】qǐhuò 从窝藏的地方搜查出(赃物、违禁品等) track down and recover (stolen goods, contrabands, etc.):～一批黄色书刊 have seized a batch of pornographic books and magazines

【起急】qǐjí〈方 *dial.*〉心中焦急或以急躁态度对人 get impatient; lose one's patience:你先别～,好好听我说。Patient and listen to me carefully.

【起家】qǐ//jiā 创立事业 start (a business, undertaking):白手～start from scratch

【起见】qǐjiàn '为(wèi)…起见',表示为达到某种目的[used in the phrase] in order to; for the sake of:为安全～,必须系上保险带。You've got to wear a safety belt for your safety.

【起劲】qǐ jìn (～儿 qǐ jìnr)(工作、游戏等)情绪高,劲头大 energetic; enthusiastic (in work, games, etc.):大家干得很～。Everybody worked energetically. |同学们又说又笑,玩得

很～。The classmates had a good time laughing and chattering.

【起居】qǐjū 指日常生活 daily life：孩子在托儿所饮食～都有规律。Children are able to live a well-orchestrated daily life in the nursery.

【起圈】qǐ//juàn 把猪圈、羊圈、牛栏等里面的粪便和所垫的草、土弄出来，用做肥料。有的地区叫清栏或出圈。remove manure from a pigsty, sheepfold, cowshed, etc; known in some regions as 清栏 qīng//lán or 出圈 chū//juàn

【起开】qǐ·kai 〈方 *dial.*〉走开；让开 step aside; stand aside：请你～点，让我过去。Please budge a few inches and let me pass.

【起课】qǐ//kè 一种占卜法，摇铜钱看正反面或掐指头算干支，推断吉凶 start a session of divination by tossing coins, pinching one's fingers, etc.

Q

【起来】qǐ//·lái ❶ 由躺而坐，由坐而站 rise; stand up：你～，让老太太坐下。Stand up and let this old lady sit down. ❷ 起床 get up：刚～就忙着下地干活儿。As soon as he got up he began to get ready for farm chores in the field. ❸ 泛指兴起、奋起、升起等 rise; take off：群众～了 The ardour of masses has been aroused.｜飞机～了。The airplane is up and high in the sky now.

【起来】//·qǐ//·lái ❶ 用在动词后，表示向上 [used after a verb to indicate an upward movement]：中国人民站～了。The Chinese people have stood up. ❷ 用在动词或形容词后，表示动作或情况开始并且继续 [used after a verb or adjective to indicate the beginning or continuation of an action]：一句话把屋子里的人都引得笑～。The remark set everyone in the room laughing.｜唱起歌来 begin to sing｜天气渐渐暖和～。It began to become warmer. ❸ 用在动词后，表示动作完成或达到目的 [used after a verb to indicate the completion of an action or attainment of a goal]：我们组是前年组织～的。Our group was put together the year before last year.｜想～了，这是鲁迅的话。I've got it — it's a line from Lu Xun. ❹ 用在动词后，表示估计或着眼于某一方面 [used after a verb to indicate estimation or venture an opinion]：看～，他不会来了。By the look of it he won't come.

【起立】qǐlì 站起来（多用做口令 oft. used as an instruction) On your feet!：～，敬礼 Stand up and salute!｜全体～。On your feet, everybody!

【起落】qǐluò 升起和降落 take-off and touchdown：飞机～take-offs and touchdowns at an airport｜价格～price fluctuation｜船身随浪～。The boat rocked with the rise and fall of the waves. ◇心潮～ one's heart pounding with a tumult of emotions

【起码】qǐmǎ 最低限度 say the least; minimum：～的条件 fundamental requirement｜我这次出差，～要一个月才能回来。It takes a month, to say the least, for me to return from this business trip.

【起锚】qǐ//máo 把锚拔起，船开始航行（of a boat) weigh anchor and set

【起名儿】qǐ//míngr 取名字；给予名称：name; give a name to：给孩子起个名儿 give the child a name

【起跑】qǐpǎo 赛跑时按比赛规则在起点做好预备姿势后开始跑（of runners in a race) get ready and start; on your marks

【起跑线】qǐpǎoxiàn 赛跑时起点的标志线 starting line ◇在同一～上展开平等竞争。Carry out competition on an equal footing.

【起讫】qǐqì 开始和终结 beginning and end：写明～日期 clarify dates of the beginning and end of an event in writing

【起色】qǐsè 好转的样子(多指做得不好的工作或沉重的疾病 oft. sth. done badly or serious ailment) show improvement; turn for the better; pick up：她的病已有～。Her condition has begun to improve.｜经过整顿，生产大有～。Production picked up markedly thanks to rectification efforts.

【起身】qǐ//shēn ❶ 动身 set out：我明天～去上海。I'll set out for Shanghai tomorrow. ❷ 起床 get out of bed; get up：他每天～后，就清扫院子。He sweeps the courtyard after he gets up everyday. ❸ 身子由坐、卧状态站立起来 stand up：～回礼 stand up to return a courtesy

【起事】qǐshì 发动武装斗争 start an armed struggle

【起誓】qǐ//shì 发誓；宣誓 vow：对天～swear by God

【起首】qǐshǒu 起先；开头 originally; in the beginning：～我并不会下棋，是他教我的。I didn't know how to play chess until he taught me.

【起死回生】qǐ sǐ huí shēng 使死人或死东西复活。多形容医术或技术高明。(oft. in praise of the skill of a good doctor) snatch a patient from the jaws of death; make the dead come back to life

【起死人，肉白骨】qǐ sǐrén, ròu báigǔ 使死人复活，使白骨长肉 revive the dead and flesh up the bones;〈比喻 *fig.*〉给人以极大的恩德 do sb. a great service

【起诉】qǐsù 向法院提起诉讼 sue; prosecute：～状 indictment; bill of complaint

【起跳】qǐtiào 跳高、跳远、跳水等开始跳跃时的动作(in high jump, long jump, diving, etc.) take off

【起头】qǐ//tóu（～儿 qǐ//tóur)开始；开头(kāi//tóu) take the lead; make a beginning：先从我这儿～。Start from me first.｜你先给大家起个头儿吧。Why don't you give us a lead please?｜这事情是谁起的头儿？Who started all this?

【起头】qǐtóu (～儿 qǐtóur) ❶ 开始的时候 at first; in the beginning:～他答应来的,后来因为有别的事不能来了。In the beginning he promised to come, but he failed to show up because something else cropped up. ❷ 开始的地方 start; beginning:你刚才说的话我没听清楚,你从～儿再说一遍。I didn't quite catch you. Please repeat it from the beginning.

【起先】qǐxiān 最初;开始 at the outset; in the beginning:这样做,～我有些想不通,后来才想通了。In the beginning I was puzzled by the way the matter was handled, and I didn't get over it until some time afterwards.|蒙眬中听见外面树叶哗哗响,～还以为是下雨,仔细一听,才知道是刮风。In my drowsiness I heard the rustle of tree leaves out there, and I thought it was raining; only after I listened carefully did I realise it was the wind.

【起小儿】qǐxiǎor 从幼年时候起;从小 since childhood:他～身体就很结实。He's been strong since childhood.

【起衅】qǐxìn same as 启衅 qǐxìn

【起行】qǐxíng 起程;动身 start on a journey:他今天下午三点钟就要～。He'll set out at three in the afternoon.

【起眼儿】qǐyǎnr 看起来醒目,惹人重视(多用于否定式 usu. in the negative) be striking; eye-catching:别看这些东西不怎么～,日常生活却离不了它们。You may seldom notice these things, but you cannot do without them in daily life.

【起夜】qǐyè 夜间起来小便 get up in the night to urinate

【起疑】qǐ//yí 发生怀疑;产生疑心 smell fishy; become questionable:他举动反常,让人～。There is something fishy about his strange behaviour.

【起义】qǐyì ❶ 为了反抗反动统治而发动武装革命 rise in an uprising:农民～peasant uprising|南昌～Nanchang Uprising of August 1, 1927 ❷ 背叛所属的集团,投到正义方面 revolt and cross over:阵前～(of an army) launch an uprising and cross over on the battlefield

【起意】qǐ//yì 产生某种念头(多指坏的 usu. evil) hit upon an idea:见财～hit upon an idea at the sight of money

【起因】qǐyīn (事件)发生的原因 cause (of an event):事故的～正在调查。The cause of the accident was under investigation.

【起用】qǐyòng ❶ 重新任用已退职或免职的官员 reinstate (an official who has retired or been removed) ❷ 提拔使用 promote; appoint sb. to a post:～新人 entrust rookies with important tasks|大胆～年轻干部。Be bold in promoting young and up-and-coming functionaries.

【起源】qǐyuán ❶ 开始发生 originate; stem from:秦腔～于陕西。The *Qinqiang* opera has its roots in Shaanxi.|世界上一切知识无不～于劳动。All the knowledge in the world originated without exception from labour. ❷ 事物发生的根源 origin:生命的～ origin of life

【起运】qǐyùn (货物)开始运出(多指运往外地 oft. transporting to other places) (of goods) start shipment:办理～手续 go through formalities to start shipment of goods|救灾物资正在～。Disaster-relief goods are being shipped out.

【起赃】qǐ//zāng 从窝藏处把赃款、赃物搜出来 track down and recover stolen money and goods

【起早贪黑】qǐ zǎo tān hēi 起得早,睡得晚。形容人辛勤劳动(of a diligent person) start work early and knock off late; work from dawn to dusk;贪黑 also put as 搭黑 dāhēi or 摸黑 mōhēi

【起止】qǐzhǐ 开头和结尾;开始和结束 beginning and end:～日期 dates of beginning and end

【起重船】qǐzhòngchuán 浮吊 crane ship

【起重机】qǐzhòngjī 提起或移动重物用的机器,种类很多,广泛用于仓库、码头、车站、矿山、建筑工地等 hoist; crane; derrick; equipment that comes in a good variety for hoisting or move heavy things, widely used in warehouses, harbours, workshops, mines and construction sites; generally known as 吊车 diàochē

【起子】[1] qǐ·zi ❶ 开瓶盖的工具,前端是椭圆形的环,后面有柄,多用金属制成 bottle opener; device with an oval ring at one end and a handle at the other, usu. made of metal, and used for opening bottles ❷ 〈方 *dial.*〉改锥 screw driver ❸ 〈方 *dial.*〉焙(bèi)粉 baking powder

【起子】[2] qǐ·zi ❶ 〈量词 *classifier*〉群;批 group; batch:一～客人 a group of guests

【起坐间】qǐzuòjiān 〈方 *dial.*〉专供闲坐谈天或接待客人等的房间 living room; sitting room; room where people sit together to chat or receiving a guest

绮 qǐ ❶ 有花纹或图案的丝织品 figured woven silk fabrics; damask:～罗 fabulous silk fabrics ❷ 美丽;美妙 fabulous; gorgeous:～丽 beautiful

【绮丽】qǐlì 鲜艳美丽(多用来形容风景 usu. of scenery) beautiful; fabulous:～的景色 fabulous scenery|风和日暖,西湖显得更加～。The West Lake become more bewitching on a day of gentle breeze and warm sunshine.

棨 qǐ 〈古代 *arch.*〉官吏出行时用来证明身份的东西,用木制成,形状像戟 halberd-like wooden object to certify an official's identity on an inspection tour

胷 qǐ 古书上指腓肠肌 gastrocnemius in ancient books

綮 qǐ same as 棨 qǐ
☞ qìng on p.1578

稽 qǐ [稽首](qǐshǒu)古时的一种礼节,跪下,拱手至地,头也至地(arch.) kowtow; Chinese custom of kneeling and touching the ground with hands and the forehead in worship or submission
☞ jī on p.898

qì (ㄑㄧˋ)

气(氣) qì ❶ 气体 gas:毒~poison gas|煤~coal gas|沼~marsh gas; methane ❷ 特指空气 air:~压 atmospheric pressure|打开窗子透一透~。Open the window to let in fresh air. ❸(~儿 qìr) same as 气息 qìxī ①:没~儿了 stop breathing|上~不接下~ run short of breath; breathless ❹ 指自然界冷热阴晴等现象 weather:天~weather|~候 climate|~象 meteorology|秋高~爽 clear sky and crisp air of an invigorating autumn ❺ same as 气味 qìwèi ①:香~fragrance|臭~foul odour|泥土~ smell of earth ❻ 人的精神状态 morale; spirits:勇~courage|朝~勃勃 full of vigour ❼ 气势 momentum; impetus; imposing manner; avalanche:~吞山河 filled with heroic spirit that shakes mountains and rivers; full of daring ❽ 人的作风习气 manner; bearing:官~bureaucratic airs|娇~finicky|孩子~childish ❾ 生气;发怒 angry; enraged:他~得直哆嗦。He trembled with anger. ❿ 使人生气 enrage:故意~他一下 get him angry on purpose|你别~我了! Stop annoying me. ⓫ 欺负;欺压 insult; bully:挨打受~be bullied and insulted|再也不受他的~了。I want no more of his insults. ⓬〈中医 *Chin. med.*〉指人体内能使各器官正常地发挥机能的原动力 vital energy; energy of life:元~vital energy|~虚 deficiency of vital energy ⓭〈中医 *Chin. med.*〉指某种病象 certain symptoms:湿~ eczema|痰~ apoplexy

【气昂昂】qì'áng'áng (~的 qì'áng'áng·de)形容人精神振作、气势威武 full of dash:雄赳赳,~valiantly and spiritedly

【气泵】qìbèng 风泵 air pump

【气不忿儿】qì bù fènr〈方 *dial.*〉看到不平的事,心中不服气 be jealous; take other people's success badly

【气冲冲】qìchōngchōng (~的 qìchōngchōng-de)形容非常生气的样子 furious; beside oneself with rage

【气冲牛斗】qì chōng niú dǒu 形容气势或怒气很盛 anger shooting up to the skies — in a towering rage; furious; (牛斗 *niudou*:二十八宿的牛宿和斗宿,泛指天空 two of the 28 constellations, generally used to refer to the sky); also 气冲斗牛 qì chōng dǒu niú

【气冲霄汉】qì chōng xiāohàn 形容大无畏的精神和气概 dauntless; fearless

【气喘】qìchuǎn 每分钟呼吸次数增多或深度增加,并伴有吸气费力的症状 asthma, a respiratory disease marked by an increase in the number of breaths per minute or the depth of breathing and accompanied by paroxysms of difficult breathing; also known as 哮喘 xiàochuǎn; abbr. 喘 chuǎn

【气窗】qìchuāng 主要用来通风透气的窗子,一般开在房屋的顶部 transom window; fanlight; window opened on a rooftop for ventilation purposes

【气锤】qìchuí 空气锤 air hammer; pneumatic hammer

【气粗】qìcū ❶ 脾气暴躁 hot-tempered:我这个人~,大家多担待着点。I am kind of hot-tempered and hope you can bear with it. ❷ 气势很盛 insolent; haughty; domineering:~胆壮。Haughtiness feeds hardihood.|财大~。A moneybag can afford to be high and mighty.

【气垫】qìdiàn ❶ 一种可以注入空气的橡皮垫子,多用来放在长期卧床病人的受压部位下,缓解局部压力 air cushion; inflatable rubber cushion to be placed under a bed-ridden patient's body to alleviate pressure ❷ 从气垫船底喷出的高压空气 high-pressure jetting from underneath a hovercraft

【气垫船】qìdiànchuán 利用高压空气的支承力而离开水面航行的船。高压空气从船底喷向水面,把船身托起,减少航行阻力,一般用螺旋桨或喷气推进。hovercraft; vehicle that travels over water on a cushion of air provided by a downward blast to minimize the friction, and is usu. propelled by a screw propeller or jetting water

【气度】qìdù 气魄和度量;气概 deportment; spirit:~不凡 of unusual verve

【气短】qìduǎn ❶ 因疲劳、空气稀薄等原因而呼吸短促 gasp for air (because of fatigue, rarified air, etc); wheeze:爬到半山,感到有点~。I found myself gasping for air when I climbed midway up the mountain. ❷ 志气沮丧或情绪低落 crestfallen; dismayed; dispirited:试验失败并没有使他~。He didn't lose heart when his experiment fell through.

【气氛】qìfēn 一定环境中给人某种强烈感觉的精神表现或景象 ambience; atmophere:会场上充满了团结友好的~。An atmosphere of unity and friendship prevailed over the meeting.

【气愤】qìfèn 生气;愤恨 exasperated; fuming; disgruntled:他听了这种不三不四的话非常~。He was exasperated by such dubious remarks.

【气概】qìgài 在对待重大问题上表现的态度、举动或气势(专指正直、豪迈的) lofty quality; mettle:中国人民有战胜一切困难的英雄~。The Chinese people have the courage to pit their mettles against all odds.

【气割】qìgē 用氧炔吹管或氢氧吹管的火焰切割金属材料 gas cutting; cutting of metals with an oxyacetylene or oxyhydrogen blowpipe

【气根】qìgēn 由植物茎或叶的部分所生出的不定根,部分或全部露出地上,常带绿色,能吸大气中的水分和养分。玉蜀黍、榕树等有气根。aerial root; adventitious root; (of such plants as maize and banyan tree) root attached to the stalk or leaves and exposed entirely or partially to draw water and nutrition from the air, often green in colour

【气功】qìgōng 我国特有的一种健身术。基本分两类,一类是静立、静坐或静卧,使精神集中,并且用特殊的方式进行呼吸,促进循环、消化等系统的机能。另一类是用柔和的运动操、按摩等方法,坚持经常锻炼,以增强体质。*qigong*; deep breathing exercise practiced on a regular basis to keep fit, in two categories: one requiring the practitioner to stand, sit or lie still, concentrate his or her mind, and breathe in a special way to promote circulation and digesting in the body, and the other calling for the use of mild physical exercises or massage

【气管】qìguǎn 呼吸器官的一部分,管状,是由半环状软骨构成的,有弹性,上部接喉头,下部分成两支,通入左右两肺。有的地区叫气嗓。windpipe; trachea; part of the respiratory organ in the form of a thin-walled tube of cartilaginous and membranous tissue, with its upper end attached to the larynx and its lower end branching into two ducts to carry air to the lungs: tracheotomy; known in some regions as 气嗓 qìsǎng (图见☞figure for 肺 fèi on p.563)

【气贯长虹】qì guàn cháng hóng 形容正气磅礴,像是要贯通天空的长虹一样 as lofty as the rainbow spanning the sky; imbued with sublime heroism

【气锅】qìguō 一种沙锅,中央有通到锅底而不伸出锅盖的管儿,烹调时在管儿周围放食物,连沙锅放在锅里蒸,水蒸气从管儿进入沙锅,食物蒸熟并得浓汁 steampot; casserole; a kind of terrine with a duct running through the bottom but stopping short of the lid so that when it is placed in a steamer, vapour can enter through the duct to heat the food stacked around it, resulting in a well-cooked dish soaked in a thick gravy: ~鸡 chicken casserole

【气焊】qìhàn 用氧炔吹管或氢氧吹管的火焰焊接金属材料 gas welding; welding metal materials by means of an oxyacetylene or oxyhydrogen blowpipe

【气候】qìhòu ❶ 一定地区里经过多年观察所得到的概括性的气象情况。它与气流、纬度、海拔高度、地形等有关。climate; meteorological conditions of a particular region, having to do with air currents, latitude, altitude and topography, defined on the basis of many years of careful observation ❷〈比喻 *fig.*〉动向或情势 situation; trend:政治~political climate ❸〈比喻 *fig.*〉结果或成就 result; achievement:几个人瞎闹腾,成不了~。Judging from the way they mess about things they can never get anywhere. ☞成气候 chéng qìhòu on p.246

【气呼呼】qìhūhū(~的 qìhūhū·de)形容生气时呼吸急促的样子 livid; in a huff

【气急】qìjí 呼吸急促,上气不接下气,多由缺氧、情绪紧张等引起 gasp for breath; out of breath as a result of oxygen deficiency or nervousness

【气急败坏】qìjí bàihuài 上气不接下气,狼狈不堪。形容十分慌张或恼怒。flustered and exasperated; utterly discomfited

【气节】qìjié 坚持正义,在敌人或压力面前不屈服的品质 moral integrity; unyielding quality in the face of an enemy or pressure:民族~moral integrity of a patriot|革命~moral integrity of a revolutionary

【气井】qìjǐng 为开采天然气用钻机从地面打到气层的井 gas well; well drilled into the depth of earth for the tapping of natural gas

【气孔】qìkǒng ❶ 植物体表皮细胞之间的小孔,是植物体和外界交换气体的出入口。主要分布在叶子的背面,用显微镜才能看见。stomate; stoma, one of the minute pores mainly in the epidermis of a leaf through which air and water vapour pass, visible only when observed through a microscope ❷ same as 气门 qìmén ① ❸ 铸件内部的孔洞,是铸造过程中产生的或进入的空气造成的。气孔是铸件的一种缺陷。gas hole; pores in a piece of casting resulting from air let in or produced in the process of casting, considered as a flaw; also 气眼 qìyǎn ❹ 建筑物或其他物体上用来使空气或其他气体通过的孔 air hole; holes in a building or object for ventilation; also 气眼 qìyǎn

【气口】qìkǒu 指戏曲、曲艺演员在行腔过程中换气吸气的地方(of a theatrical performer) way to catch a breath while vocalizing

【气力】qìlì 力气 strength:用尽~exert oneself to the utmost; with all one's strength|年纪大了,~不如以前了。I'm getting old, and so much weaker than when I was younger.

【气量】qìliàng ❶ 指才识和品德的高低 moral character ❷ 指能容纳不同意见的度量 degree of magnanimity:这个人很有~,从不计较别人说他些什么。He has a big heart, and what people say about him never bothers him. ❸ 指容忍谦让的限度 tolerance:~大的人对这点儿小事是不会介意的。Broad-minded people are never bothered about such trifles.

【气流】qìliú ❶ 流动的空气 air current; airstream ❷ 由肺的膨胀或收缩而吸入或呼出的气,是发音的动力 breath; air inhaled and exhaled in respiration that makes pronunciation possible

【气楼】qìlóu 房屋顶上突起来的部分,两侧有窗,用来通风或透光 small ventilation tower on the top of a roof, with windows on both sides for ventilation or to let in sunlight

【气轮机】qìlúnjī steam turbine; air-turbine; abbr. for 燃气轮机 ránqì lúnjī

【气脉】qìmài ❶ 血气和脉息 vigour and pulse: ～调和 sap and pulse in perfect condition ❷ 指诗文中贯穿前后的思路、脉络(of literary composition) line of thought; sequence of ideas

【气脉儿】qì·mair 指人的精力、气力等 vigour; energy

【气煤】qìméi 烟煤的一种,隔绝空气加热可产生大量煤气,有的气煤还可用来炼油和提取化工原料。单独用这种煤炼的焦强度低,块小,所以多用来和其他烟煤配合炼焦。gas coal; a type of bituminous coal that produces large amount of gas when heated airtight and that can also be used to refine oil or extract chemical materials, oft. used together with other types of bituminous coal for coking because if it used alone for this purpose the coke produced tends to be of a low intensity and in small lumps

【气门】qìmén ❶ 昆虫等陆栖的节肢动物呼吸器官的一部分,在身体的表面,是空气的出入口 spiracle; stigma; any of several tracheal openings in the exoskeleton of an insect or any other triphibian arthropod, as part of the respiratory organ; also 气孔 qìkǒng ❷ 轮胎等充气的活门,主要由气门心和金属圈构成。空气由气门压入后不易逸出(of a tyre) valve, which consists of a rubber tube and a metal eyelet to prevent air from leaking ❸ 某些机器上进出气体的装置 air valve, device in a machine for the passage of air

【气门心】qìménxīn ❶ 充气轮胎等的气门上用弹簧或橡皮管做成的活门,空气压入不易逸出(of a tyre) valve, which is made of a spring or rubber tube to prevent air from leaking ❷ 做气门心用的橡皮管 rubber tube in an air valve

【气囊】qìnáng ❶ 鸟类呼吸器官的一部分,是由薄膜构成的许多小囊,分布在体腔内各个器官的空隙中,有些气囊在皮下或骨的内部(of a bird) air sac; part of the respiratory organ of a bird, in the form of many bag-like cavities enclosed by membranes in the spaces of various organs of a bird, some of which are beneath the skin or inside bone cavities ❷ 用涂有橡胶的布做成的囊,里面充满比空气轻的气体,多用来做高空气球或带动飞艇上升 gasbag; expansible bag made of rubberized fabric for holding a gas that is lighter than air and used as ballon or to propel an airship into the sky

【气恼】qìnǎo 生气;恼怒 angry; incensed; irate

【气馁】qìněi 失掉勇气 lose heart; disheartened; crestfallen: 胜利了不要骄傲,失败了不要～。Don't sit on your laurels, and don't take defeat lying down either.

【气派】qìpài ❶ 指人的态度作风或某些事物所表现的气势 air; manner: 大国～largess of a big country ❷ 神气;有精神 style; polish; grace: 他穿上这身服装,多～! How smart he looks in this suit.

【气泡】qìpào 气体在固体、液体的内部或表面形成的球状或半球状体 bubble; thin, spherical or hemispherical film of liquid filled with air or gas in a liquid or solid matter

【气魄】qìpò ❶ 魄力 verve; daring: 他办事很有～。He has guts and verve whatever he does. ❷ same as 气势 qìshì: 天安门城楼的～十分雄伟。The rostrum atop the Tian'anmen Gate is a structure of imposing grandeur.

【气枪】qìqiāng 利用压缩空气发射铅弹的器械,多用来打鸟 airgun; gun that discharges lead pellets by compressed air

【气球】qìqiú 在薄橡皮、涂有橡胶的布、塑料等制成的囊中灌入氢、氦、空气等气体所制成的球。气球充入比空气轻的气体时,可以上升。种类很多。有的用做玩具,有的用做运载工具。Balloon, balloon; flexible, nonporous bag made of thin rubber or rubberized fabric and inflated with air that can rise and float if it is filled with a gas, like oxygen and helium, that is lighter than the surrounding air. There are different kinds of balloons. Some are used as toys, and others can be used as means of delivery.

【气色】qìsè 人的精神和面色 complexion: 近来他的～很好,满面红光。He looks fine lately with a rosy complexion.

【气势】qìshì (人和事物)表现出的某种力量和形势(of people and things)momentum: ～磅礴 of great momentum|人民大会堂～雄伟。The Great Hall of the People in Beijing is marked for its imposing grandeur.

【气势汹汹】qìshì xiōngxiōng (～的 qìshì xiōngxiōng·de)形容盛怒时很凶的样子 fierce; truculent; overbearing

【气数】qì·shu 指人生存或事物存在的期限;命运(用于大事情,含有迷信色彩)(divination on matters of consequence) destiny; fate: ～将尽(of a dynasty or regime) be nearing its fated end

【气态】qìtài 物质的气体状态,是物质存在的一种形态 gaseous state, a form of matter in existence

【气体】qìtǐ 没有一定形状,没有一定体积,可以流动的物体。在常温下,空气、氧气、沼气等都是气体。gas; state of matter without form and shape and with ability to diffuse readily; under normal temperature, air, oxygen, methane, etc. are gases

【气田】qìtián 可以开采的蕴藏大量天然气的地带 gas field; area yielding natural gas in great amount

【气筒】qìtǒng 产生压缩空气的工具,由圆形金属筒、活塞等构成,多用来给轮胎和球胆打气 inflator; air pump; instrument to inflate tyres or the rubber bladder of a ball, consisting of a piston in a metal tube

【气头上】qìtóu·shang 发怒的时候 in a tantrum:他正在～,别人的话听不进去 He is throwing a tantrum now, and won't listen to anyone.

【气团】qìtuán 在水平方向上温度、湿度等比较均匀的空气团。高可达数公里,宽可达数千里。在冷、暖气团相接触的地带,常有显著的天气变化。air mass; large body of air with only small horizontal variations of temperature, pressure, and moisture, of such a large size several kilometres in height and several thousand kilometres in width; striking changes in the weather are caused when a cold air mass comes into contact with a warm air mass

【气吞山河】qì tūn shānhé 形容气魄很大 full of power and grandeur; sublime and heroic; magnificent

【气味】qìwèi ❶ 鼻子可以闻到的味ㄦ smell; flavour; odour:～芬芳 sweet and pleasant smell|丁香花的～很好闻。The lilac flower smells good. ❷〈比喻 *fig.*〉性格和志趣(多含贬义 oft. derog.) taste; reek; smack:～相投 congenial to each other; be two of a kind

【气温】qìwēn 空气的温度 temperature; atmospheric temperature:～下降 a drop in the temperature

【气息】qìxī ❶ 呼吸时出入的气 breath:～奄奄 at one's last gasp; dying ❷ 气味 smell:一阵芬芳的～从花丛中吹过来。A sweet scent wafted from a cluster of flowers. ◇生活～ smack of everyday life|时代～ ethos of the times

【气象】qìxiàng ❶ 大气的状态和现象,例如刮风、闪电、打雷、结霜、下雪等 meteorological phenomena, such as wind, lightning, thunder, frost, snow, etc. ❷ same as 气象学 qìxiàngxué ❸ 情景;情况 ambience; scene:一片新～take on a new outlook ❹ 气派;气势 appearance:～宏伟 magnificent appearance

【气象台】qìxiàngtái 对大气进行观测、研究并预报天气的机构。规模较小的还有气象站、气象哨等。meteorological observatory; observatory; (of small scales) weather station; institution designed and equipped for making observations and forecasts of astronomical, meteorological, or other natural phenomena

【气象万千】qìxiàng wànqiān 形容景色和事物多种多样,非常壮观。spectacular; majestic; all-encapsulating scene of sublimity

【气象学】qìxiàngxué 研究天气现象和变化规律等的学科 meteorology; science that deals with the phenomena of the atmosphere, especially weather and weather conditions

【气性】qì·xing ❶ 脾气;性格 temperament; disposition:～温顺 of a docile disposition ❷ 指容易生气或生气后一时不易消除的性格 irritable disposition; bad temper:这孩子～大。The child is hot-tempered.

【气咻咻】qìxiūxiū (～的 qìxiūxiū·de) same as 气吁吁 qìxūxū

【气吁吁】qìxūxū (～的 qìxūxū·de)形容大声喘气的样子 run short of breath; gasp for breath

【气虚】qìxū〈中医 *Chin. med.*〉指面色苍白,呼吸短促,四肢无力,常出虚汗的症状 general debility; deficiency of vital energy, with such symptoms as pale complexion, short breaths, fatigue, and abnormal sweating

【气旋】qìxuán 直径达数百公里的空气旋涡。旋涡的中心是低气压区,风从四周向中心刮。气旋在北半球以逆时针方向旋转,在南半球以顺时针方向旋转。气旋过境时往往阴雨连绵或降雪。cyclone; atmospheric system characterized by the rapid, inward circulation of air masses about a low-pressure centre, usually accompanied by stormy, often destructive, weather. Cyclones circulate counterclockwise in the Northern Hemisphere and clockwise in the Southern Hemisphere, and occur when it is overcast and rainy or snowing.

【气压】qìyā 气体的压强,通常指大气的压强 atmospheric pressure; barometric pressure

【气眼】qìyǎn same as 气孔 qìkǒng ③④

【气焰】qìyàn〈比喻 *fig.*〉人的威风气势(多含贬义 oft. derog.) arrogance; bluster :～万丈 swollen with arrogance|～嚣张 behave with unbearable insolence

【气宇】qìyǔ 气度;气概 carriage; manner:～不凡 man of no common looks|～轩昂(man) of an impressive and dignified carriage

【气韵】qìyùn 文章或书法绘画的意境或韵味(of writing, painting or calligraphy) character; style:～生动 spirit-resonance|画面简洁,～无穷。Despite of its unadorned simplicity, the painting is marked by an immeasurable spiritual resonance.

【气质】qìzhì ❶ 指人的相当稳定的个性特点,如活泼、直爽、沉静、浮躁等。是高级神经活动在人的行动上的表现。temperament; disposition, such as vivacity, straightforwardness, calmness, agitation, etc., which are manifestations of the high nerve system in a human being's activity ❷ 风格;气度 quality;

makings：革命者的～ makings of a revolutionary

【气壮山河】qì zhuàng shān hé 形容气概像高山大河那样雄伟豪迈 as magnificent as high mountains and mighty rivers; full of power and grandeur; magnificent

讫 qì ❶（事情）完结（of things）settled; completed：收～cash received｜付～paid｜验～examined ❷ 截止 end：起～beginning and end

迄 qì ❶到 up to：～今 up to now ❷始终；一直（用于'未'或'无'前 used before 未 wèi or 无 wú）from beginning to end; throughout：～未见效。No effect has ever been achieved

Q

【迄今】qìjīn 到现在 up to now; till now：自古～since remote antiquity｜～为止 up to this day; by now

汔 qì〈书 *fml*.〉庶几 so that; so as to

弃(棄) qì 放弃；扔掉 abandon; discard：抛～desert｜舍～give up｜遗～abandon｜～权 abstain｜～之可惜 loath to throw sth. away

【弃暗投明】qì àn tóu míng 离开黑暗，投向光明 forsake darkness for light；〈比喻 *fig*.〉与黑暗势力断绝关系走向光明的道路 abandon the evil and cross over to the good

【弃儿】qì'ér 被父母遗弃的小孩儿 abandoned child; foundling

【弃妇】qìfù〈书 *fml*.〉被丈夫遗弃的妇女 abandoned wife

【弃旧图新】qì jiù tú xīn 抛弃旧的，谋求新的。多指由坏的转向好的，由邪路走上正路。turn over a new leaf; mend one's ways：翻然改悔，～repent of one's wickedness and start afresh

【弃权】qì//quán 放弃权利（用于选举、表决、比赛等）abstain from one's right in election or voting; waive one's right in a competition

【弃学】qìxué 中途放弃学业 drop out of school; become a school dropout：～经商 abandon school to start a business

【弃养】qìyǎng〈书 *fml*.〉〈婉辞 *euph*.〉指父母死亡 lose one's parents

【弃置】qìzhì 扔在一旁 discard; dump：～不顾 abandon｜～不用 put sth. aside

汽 qì ❶ 液体或某些固体受热而变成的气体，例如水变成的水蒸气 vapour; steam; such as the vapour phase of water ❷ 特指水蒸气 steam：～机 steam engine｜～船 steamboat

【汽车】qìchē 用内燃机做动力，主要在公路上或马路上行驶的交通工具，通常有四个或四个以上的橡胶轮胎。用来运载人或货物。automobile; means of passenger or cargo transportation by land, powered by an internal-combustion engine, and fixed on at least four rubber wheels

【汽船】qìchuán ❶ 用蒸汽机发动的船，多指小型的 steamboat; small vessel propelled by one or more steam-driven propellers or paddles ❷ same as 汽艇 qìtǐng

【汽锤】qìchuí 蒸汽锤 steam hammer

【汽灯】qìdēng 白热照明灯具的一种。点着以后，利用本身的热量把煤油变成蒸气，喷射在炽热的纱罩上，发出白色的亮光。gas lamp; gaslight; lamp that jets burning gas onto a heated mantle to provide light

【汽笛】qìdí 轮船、火车等装置的发声器，使气体由气孔中喷出，发出大的音响 steam whistle; horn;（of boat, train, etc.）device for making whistling sounds by means of forced air or steam

【汽缸】qìgāng 内燃机或蒸汽机中装有活塞的部分，呈圆筒形 cylinder; piston chamber in a internal-combustion engine or steam engine

【汽化】qìhuà 液体变为气体 vaporize; ☞沸腾 fèiténg on p. 565 and 蒸发 zhēngfā on p. 2444

【汽化器】qìhuàqì 汽油机上的部件，作用是把汽油变成雾状，按一定比例和空气混合，形成供汽缸燃烧的混合气 carburettor; apparatus for carburation of petrol and air in an internal-combustion engine; also 化油器 huàyóuqì

【汽化热】qìhuàrè 单位质量的物质在温度不变的情况下，从液态变成气态时所吸收的热量，叫做这种物质的汽化热 heat of vaporization; quantity of heat needed per unit to turn a liquid into vapour under a constant temperature

【汽机】qìjī ❶ 蒸汽机的简称 abbr. for 蒸汽机 zhēngqìjī ❷ 汽轮机的简称 abbr. for 汽轮机 qìlúnjī

【汽酒】qìjiǔ 含有二氧化碳的酒，用某些水果酿成，有葡萄汽酒、菠萝汽酒等 light sparkling wine; any of various effervescent wines produced by a process involving fermentation of certain fruit, such as grapes and pineapples, in the bottle

【汽轮机】qìlúnjī 涡轮机的一种，利用高压蒸汽推动叶轮转动，产生动力。转速高、功率大，较为经济。steam turbine; high-spinning, powerful and cost-effective turbine operated by highly pressurized steam directed against vanes on a rotor; 简称 abbr. 汽机 qìjī

【汽碾】qìniǎn 压路机的一种，用蒸汽发动机做动力机 steamroller; a kind of road roller powered by a steam engine; also 汽碾子 qìniǎn·zi

【汽暖】qìnuǎn 蒸汽通过暖气设备散发热量而使室温增高的供暖方式 steam heating; heating system in which steam is generated in a boiler and piped to radiators to increase room temperature

【汽水】qìshuǐ（～儿 qìshuǐr）加一定压力，使二氧化碳溶于水中，加糖、果汁、香料等制成的冷饮料 aerated water; soft drink; soda water; effervescent water, usually containing sugar, juice, spice, etc., charged under pressure with carbon dioxide

【汽艇】qìtǐng 用内燃机发动的小型船舶，速度高 motorboat; small boat propelled by an internal-combustion engine; also 快艇 kuàitǐng or 摩托艇 mótuōtǐng

【汽油】qìyóu 轻质石油产品的一类，从石油中经分馏而得。易挥发，容易燃烧，用做内燃机燃料、溶剂等。gasoline; gas; volatile mixture of flammable liquid hydrocarbons derived chiefly from crude petroleum and used principally as a fuel for internal-combustion engines and as a solvent

【汽油机】qìyóujī 用汽油做燃料的内燃机。在汽车上应用最广。petrol engine; internal-combustion engine using petrol as fuel, most extensively used in automobiles

妻 qì 〈书 *fml.*〉把女子嫁给(某人) marry a woman to a man
☞ qī on p. 1505

炁 qì same as 气 qì, such as in 坎炁 kǎnqì, 中药上指脐带 referring to umbilical cord in traditional Chinese medicine

泣 qì ❶ 小声哭 snivel; sob: 暗~cry to oneself | 哭~in tears | ~不成声 choke with sobs ❷ 眼泪 tears: 饮~swallow one's own tears | ~下如雨 tears stream down one's cheeks

【泣不成声】qì bù chéng shēng 哭得喉咙哽住，出不来声音。形容极度悲伤。choke with sobs; feel extremely sad

【泣诉】qìsù 哭着诉说 give a tearful account: 鸣咽~tell what has happened between sobs

亟 qì 〈书 *fml.*〉屡次 repeatedly; time and again: ~来问讯 come repeatedly to ask for information
☞ jí on p. 904

契(契) qì ❶〈书 *fml.*〉用刀雕刻 engrave; carve ❷〈书 *fml.*〉刻的文字 carved inscription: 书~carved characters | 殷~late Shang-Dynasty bone inscriptions ❸ 买卖房地产等的文字，也是所有权的凭证 deeds; contract; legal document that proves sale or purchase or ownership of real estate: 地~title deed for land | 房~title deed for a house ❹ 投合 agree; get alone: ~友 bosom friend | 默~tacit agreement | 投~hit it off
☞ Xiè on p. 2124

【契丹】Qìdān 我国古代民族，是东胡的一支，在今辽河上游西剌木伦河一带，过着游牧生活。10世纪初耶律阿保机统一各族，建立契丹国。Qidan; Khitan; an ethnic people in ancient China who were a branch of the Eastern Hus inhabiting the valley of the Xar Murun River in the upper reaches of the Liaohe River. In the 10th century, Yelü Abaoji (or Ye-lü Apao-chi) unified all the Khitan tribes and established the kingdom of Khitan. ☞ 辽 Liáo on p. 1211

【契合】qìhé ❶ 符合 tally with: 扮演屈原的那个演员，无论是表情还是服装都很~屈原的身份。The actor who played the role of Qu Yuan was compatible to the identity of the ancient poet whether in deportment or attire. ❷ 合得来；意气相投 get along; share the same interest: 他俩说话投机，感情~。The two of them hit it off nicely.

【契机】qìjī 指事物转化的关键 turning point; juncture: 抓住~，扭转局面 seize the opportunity and turn the situation around

【契据】qìjù 契约、借据、收据等的总称 deeds; contract; receipt

【契友】qìyǒu 情意相投的朋友 close friend

【契约】qìyuē 证明出卖、抵押、租赁等关系的文书 contract; deed; charter

砌 qì ❶ 用和好的灰泥把砖、石等一层层地垒起 lay bricks or stones with mortar: 堆~(of writing) laboured and ornate | ~墙 build a wall | ~灶 build a stove | ~烟囱 erect a chimney ❷ 台阶 step: 雕栏玉~carved balustrades and marvel steps
☞ qiè on p. 1555

跂 qì 〈书 *fml.*〉抬起脚后跟站着 stand on tiptoe: ~望 yearn for
☞ qí on p. 1511

葺 qì 〈书 *fml.*〉用茅草覆盖房顶，今指修理房屋 thatch; cover a roof with straw; repair a house: 修~refurbish (a house)

愒 qì 〈书 *fml.*〉same as 憩 qì: 小~take a nap
☞ hè on p. 792 and kài on p. 1079

碛 qì ❶ 沙石积成的浅滩 moraine ❷ 沙漠 desert

碶 qì 〈方 *dial.*〉用石头砌的水闸 stone dam: ~闸 stone dam | 截江筑~sever the flow of a river by building a dam across it

槭 qì 槭树，落叶小乔木，枝干光滑，叶子掌状分裂，秋季变成红色或黄色。花黄绿色，结翅果。木材坚韧，可以制造器具。maple (*Acer saccharinum*); defoliating tree having smooth trunk and branches, palmate leaves that turn red or yellow in autumn, yellowish green flowers and samara, and producing hardwood for the making of furniture

磜 qì 小磜(Xiǎoqì)，地名，在江西。磜头(Qìtóu)，地名，在福建 Xiaoqi, name of a place in Jiangxi Province; Qitou, name of a place in Fujian Province

器(噐) qì ❶ 器具 ware; utensil: 瓷~porcelain ware | 木~wooden implement | 铁~iron tool | ~物 utensils ❷ 器官 organ: 消化~digestive organ | 生殖~reproductive organ ❸ 度量 capacity: ~量 tolerance; magnanimity ❹ 才能；人才 talent; ability: 大~晚成 great vessels are long in reaching completion — talent mature slowly ❺〈书 *fml.*〉器重 think highly of

【器材】qìcái 器具和材料 equipment and material：照相～photographic kit｜无线电～radio equipment｜铁路～railway gear

【器官】qìguān 构成生物体的一部分，由数种细胞组织构成，能担任某种独立的生理机能，例如由上皮组织、结缔组织等构成的，有泌尿机能的肾脏 organ，consisting of several kinds of cell tissues and capable of performing a certain physiological function independently，such as kidney，an urinary organ which consists of epithelial and connective tissues

【器件】qìjiàn 仪器、器械上的主要零件。电子仪器中特指晶体管、电子管。parts of an apparatus or appliance，such as transistor and vacuum tube in an electronic apparatus

Q

【器具】qìjù 用具；工具 appliance；utensil

【器量】qìliàng 气量；度量 capacity of mind；tolerance：～大 open-minded；magnanimous

【器皿】qìmǐn 某些盛东西的日常用具的统称，如缸、盆、碗、碟等 household utensils，including jars，basins，bowls，plates，etc.

【器物】qìwù 各种用具的统称 implements；utensils

【器械】qìxiè ❶ 有专门用途的或构造较精密的器具 apparatus usu. with an intricate structure：体育～sports apparatuses｜医疗～medical apparatuses ❷ 武器 weapon

【器械体操】qìxiè tǐcāo 凭借体育器械（如单杠、鞍马、平衡木等）做的体操 gymnastics on or with apparatus，such as horizontal bar，pommel horse，balance beam，etc.

【器宇】qìyǔ〈书 *fml.*〉人的外表；风度 poise；deportment：～不凡 unusual poise｜～轩昂 carry oneself with unusually poise

【器乐】qìyuè 用乐器演奏的音乐（区别于'声乐' as compared with 'vocal music'）instrumental music

【器重】qìzhòng （长辈对晚辈，上级对下级）看重；重视 think highly of（one's junior）：他的工作能力强，对自己要求严，领导上很～他。He is capable and strict with himself，and his leaders regard him highly.

憩（憇） qì〈书 *fml.*〉休息 rest；take a rest：小～take a short rest｜同作同～work and rest together with sb.

【憩室】qìshì 心脏、胃、肠、气管、喉头等器官上因发育异常而形成的囊状或带状物 diverticulum；abnormal pouch or sac branching out from a hollow organ or structure，such as heart，stomach，intestine，trachea and larynx

蟿 qì［蟿螽］（qìzhōng）古书指蚱蜢 grasshopper in ancient books

qiā（ㄑㄧㄚ）

掐 qiā ❶ 用指甲按；用拇指和另一个指头使劲捏或截断 shrivel；pinch；nip；squeeze or break sth. between the thumb and a finger：～两下也可以止痒。The itch can be stopped by a pinch or two.｜不要～公园里的花儿。Don't pick flowers in a park.｜把豆芽菜的须子～一～cut tassels from bean sprouts with fingers ❷ 用手的虎口紧紧按住 press；squeeze with part of the hand between the thumb and the index finger：一把～住 grip sth. with one's hand ❸〈方 *dial.*〉（～儿 qiār）〈量词 *classifier*〉拇指和另一手指尖相对握着的数量［amount of sth. held between thumb and finger］pinch；handful：一～儿韭菜 a pinch of leeks

【掐诀】qiājué 和尚、道士念咒时用拇指掐其他指头的关节（when chanting mantras）calculate on one's fingers：～念咒 pinch the knuckles of the fingers with the thumb while reciting incantations

【掐算】qiāsuàn 用拇指掐着别的指头来计算 count sth. on one's fingers

【掐头去尾】qiā tóu qù wěi 除去前头后头两部分，也比喻除去无用的或不重要的部分 break off both ends of sth.；（fig.）get rid of sth. useless or unimportant

袷 qiā［袷袢］（qiāpàn）维吾尔、塔吉克等民族所穿的对襟长袍 Uygur or Tajik rob buttoning down the front

☞ 夹 jiá on p. 931

葜 qiā ☞［菝葜］báqiā on p. 27

鹘 qiā 咬 bite

☞ 嗑 kè on p. 1099

qiá（ㄑㄧㄚˊ）

拤 qiá 用两手掐住 clutch sth. in both hands

qiǎ（ㄑㄧㄚˇ）

卡 qiǎ ❶ 夹在中间，不能活动 jam；cram；lodge：鱼刺～在嗓子里。A fish bone got stuck in（his）throat. ❷ 把人或财物留住（不肯调拨或发给）；阻挡 withhold；hold back：会计对不必要的开支～得很紧。The accountant kept a tight grip on unnecessary expenses.｜～住敌人的退路。Cut off the enemy's retreat. ❸ 用手的虎口紧紧按住 hold sth. in place with part of the hand between the thumb and the index finger：～脖子 seize sb. by the throat ❹ same as 卡子 qiǎ·zi ①：发～hair pin ❺ same as 卡子 qiǎ·zi ②：税～tax checkpost｜关～customs office

☞ kǎ on p. 1068

【卡脖子】qiǎ bó·zi 用双手掐住别人的脖子，比喻抓住要害，置对方于死地 scrag；seize sb. by the throat；（oft. fig.）expose sb. to mortal danger；kill sb.：～旱（农作物秀穗时遭受的干旱）strangler drought，one that occurs when crops are earing

【卡具】qiǎjù 夹具 clamping apparatus; fixture

【卡壳】qiǎ//ké ❶ 枪膛、炮膛里的弹壳退不出来(of cartridge, shell case, etc.) jam ❷〈比喻 *fig.*〉办事等遇到困难而暂时停顿。比喻人说话中断,说不出来。get stuck; be held up; get stuck in the middle of a speech:他说着说着就~了。He stammered all of a sudden in the middle of a speech.

【卡子】qiǎ·zi ❶ 夹东西的器具 clip; fastener: 头发~hairpin ❷ 为收税或警备而设置的检查站或岗哨 checkpost for taxation or security; sentry

qià(ㄑㄧㄚˋ)

洽 qià ❶ 和睦;相互协调一致 in harmony; agree:融~on friendly terms|意见不~fail to see eye to eye ❷ 商量;接洽 consult; arrange with:~借 explore the possibility of getting a loan|~妥 reach agreement during a consultation|面~ take up a matter with somebody personally; discuss with somebody face to face ❸ 广博;周遍 extensive; wide:博识~闻 well-read; erudite

【洽商】qiàshāng 接洽商谈 negotiate; consult: ~有关事宜 negotiate on certain matters

【洽谈】qiàtán same as 洽商 qiàshāng:~生意 negotiate on a transaction

恰 qià ❶ 恰当 proper; appropriate:措辞不~inappropriate choice of word ❷ 恰恰;正 exactly; precisely:~到好处 just right|~合时宜 appropriate to the occasion|~如其分 just right; proper

【恰当】qiàdàng 合适;妥当 suitable; proper:这篇文章里有些字眼儿用得不~。Some of the words are misused in this article.|事情处理得很~。The issue was handled just right.

【恰好】qiàhǎo 正好 happen to; just right:你来得~,我正要找你去呢 You came at the right moment — I was about to look for you.|你要看的那本书~我这里有。I happen to have the book you are looking for.

【恰恰】qiàqià 正好;正 exactly; precisely:~相反 on the contrary|我跑到那里~十二点。I got there at 12 sharp.

【恰巧】qiàqiǎo 凑巧 by chance:他正愁没人帮他卸车,~这时候老张来了。He was looking for someone to help unload the car when Old Zhang showed up.

【恰如】qiàrú 正好像 just like:晚霞~一幅图画。The evening glow is just like a painting.

【恰如其分】qià rú qí fèn 办事或说话正合分寸 appropriate; just right:~的批评 make an appropriate criticism|措辞~weigh one's wording properly

【恰似】qiàsì same as 恰如 qiàrú:这消息~晴天霹雳,令人十分震惊。The information came like a thunderbolt out of the blue.

葖 qià [葖草](qiàcǎo)多年生草本植物,秆直立,簇生,叶片狭窄,灰绿色,圆锥花序。生长在温暖地区和热带山麓,是良好的牧草。prairie junegrass(*Koeleria cristata*); perennial grass growing in clusters, having narrow and pale-green leaves and panicle flowers, growing in temperate areas and tropical mountains, used as a quality forage grass

髂 qià [髂骨](qiàgǔ)腰部下面腹部两侧的骨,左右各一,略呈长方形,上缘略呈弓形,下缘与耻骨和坐骨相连而形成髋骨 ilium; bone growing on either side of the abdomen beneath the waist, slightly oblong in shape, with its upper edge slightly curved, and its lower edge linked with the pubis and the hucklebone to form the hipbone; also 肠骨 chánggǔ;(图见☞figure for 骨骼 gǔgé on p. 693)

qiān(ㄑㄧㄢ)

千 qiān ❶〈数目 *numeral*〉十个百 ten hundred:小麦亩产突破~斤。Per-*mu* wheat yield topped the 1,000 *jin* mark. ❷〈比喻 *fig.*〉很多 countless; innumerable:~方百计 in a thousand and one ways; by every possible means; by hook or by crook|~军万马 thousands upon thousands of horses and soldiers ❸(Qiān)姓 a surname

【千锤百炼】qiān chuí bǎi liàn ❶〈比喻 *fig.*〉多次的斗争和考验 thoroughly steeled; finely honed ❷〈比喻 *fig.*〉对诗文等做多次的精细修改(of literary works) polish time and again; revise repeatedly

【千儿八百】qiān·er-bābǎi 一千或比一千略少 thousand or slightly less:~人 more than eight hundred; less than one thousand|~块钱 less than a thousand yuan

【千方百计】qiān fāng bǎi jì 形容想尽或用尽种种方法 by hook or by crook; by every possible means

【千分表】qiānfēnbiǎo 一种精度很高的量具 dial gauge; graduated surface or face on which a measurement, such as speed, is indicated by a moving needle or pointer; ☞百分表 bǎifēnbiǎo on p.40

【千分尺】qiānfēnchǐ 百分尺 micrometer

【千分数】qiānfēnshù 分母是1000的分数,通常用千分号来表示,如$\frac{19}{1000}$写作19‰ one-thousandth, usu. indicated with the sign ‰, for instance, 19/1000 is written as 19‰

【千夫】qiānfū〈书 *fml.*〉指众多的人 numerous people:~所指(为众人所指责)face a thousand accusing fingers; be universally condemned

【千古】qiāngǔ ❶ 长远的年代 through the ages; since remote antiquity:~奇闻 unheard-of strange tail | ～绝唱 all-time masterpiece; unparalleled masterpiece; acme of perfection ❷〈婉辞 *euph.*〉哀悼死者，表示永别(多用于挽联、花圈等的上款 used in an elegiac couplet or on wreaths dedicated to the dead) eternal peace to; Eternal peace to Mr. So-and-so!

【千斤】 qiānjīn 指责任重［indicating the weightiness of a task, responsibility, etc.］a thousand *jin*; weighty: ～重担 (zhòngdàn) weighty responsibility

【千斤】 qiān·jin ❶ 千斤顶的简称 abbr. for 千斤顶 qiānjīndǐng ❷ 机器中防止齿轮倒转的装置，由安置在轴上的有齿零件和弹簧等组成 pawl; hinged or pivoted device adapted to fit into a notch of a ratchet wheel to prevent backward motion

Q

【千斤顶】 qiānjīndǐng 一种顶起重物的工具，常用的有液压式和螺旋式两种 hoisting jack; jack; usu. portable device for raising heavy objects by means of force applied with a screw or hydraulic press; 简称 abbr. 千斤 qiānjīn

【千金】 qiānjīn ❶ 指很多的钱 a thousand pieces of gold; a lot of money: ～难买 not to be had even for a thousand pieces of gold; sth. money cannot buy ❷〈比喻 *fig.*〉贵重；珍贵 precious; valuable: 一字～。A single word is worth a thousand pieces of gold. | ～之躯。A thousand pieces of gold are easier to come by than a person of exceptional talent, beauty, etc. ❸〈敬辞 *honor.*〉称别人的女儿 Your (His) Excellency's daughter

【千钧一发】 qiān jūn yī fà 千钧的重量系在一根头发上 a hundred weight hanging by a hair; 〈比喻 *fig.*〉极其危险 in imminent danger; in an extremely precarious situation; (钧 *jun*: 古代重量单位，等于三十斤 unit of weight in ancient times, equivalent to 30 *jin*); also 一发千钧 yī fà qiān jūn

【千卡】 qiānkǎ 大卡 kilocalorie (kcal; cal)

【千克】 qiānkè 质量或重量的单位，1 千克是国际千克原器的质量，等于 1,000 克，合 2 市斤。也叫公斤。kilogram; equivalent to 1,000 grams or 2 *jin*; also 公斤 gōngjīn; ☞ 国际单位制 guójì dānwèizhì on p. 740 and 国际公制 guójì gōngzhì on p. 740

【千里鹅毛】 qiān lǐ émáo 谚语：'千里送鹅毛，礼轻情意重。'从很远的地方带来极轻微的礼物，表示礼轻情意重。As the proverb goes, 'a goose feather sent from a thousand *li* away may be insignificant, but the feeling it conveys is very deep.' A small gift with great meaning; The present is trifling but the feeling is profound.

【千里马】 qiānlǐmǎ 指骏马 horse that covers a thousand *li* a day; winged steed; 〈比喻 *fig.*〉有才干的人才 person of great ability

【千里眼】 qiānlǐyǎn ❶ 形容眼光敏锐，看得远 foresight; farsighted ❷〈旧时 *old*〉称望远镜 telescope; field glasses

【千里之堤，溃于蚁穴】 qiān lǐ zhī dī, kuì yú yǐxué 千里长的大堤，由于小小的一个蚂蚁洞而溃决 One ant-hole may cause the collapse of a thousand-*li* dyke. 〈比喻 *fig.*〉小事不注意，就会出大问题 Slight negligence may lead to great disaster.

【千里之行，始于足下】 qiān lǐ zhī xíng, shǐ yú zú xià 一千里的路程是从迈第一步开始的。比喻事情的成功都是由小到大逐渐积累的(见于《老子》六十四章)。'A journey of a thousand *li* begins under one's feet,' according to Chapter 64 of *Laozi*. Success is built on the accumulation of many trials and errors in figurative sense.

【千粒重】 qiān lì zhòng 1,000 粒种子的重量。表示种子的饱满程度。千粒重高，说明子粒大而饱满。用来鉴定某些农作物的品质，估计某些农作物的产量。thousand-grain weight; indication of the plumpness of seeds or the quality of a farm crop — the larger the thousand-grain weight, the more plump the seeds or the larger the crop yield

【千虑一得】 qiān lǜ yī dé《史记·淮阴侯传》：'智者千虑，必有一失；愚者千虑，必有一得。''千虑一得'指平凡的人的考虑也会有可取的地方。也用为发表意见时自谦的话。*Records of the Historian · Biography of Marquis of Huaiyin*: 'A wise man is bound to make a mistake out of a thousand thoughts, whereas a foolish man is bound to gain a grain of truth out of a thousand considerations. [self-deprecating term to be used when presenting one's opinions] My observations may contain a grain of truth.

【千虑一失】 qiān lǜ yī shī 指聪明人的考虑也会有疏漏的地方。Even a wise man makes mistakes. ☞ 千虑一得 qiān lǜ yī dé

【千篇一律】 qiān piān yī lǜ 指诗文公式化，泛指事物只有一种形式，毫无变化(of the writing of articles, documents, etc.) stereotyped; (of things) nothing new; monotonous

【千奇百怪】 qiān qí bǎi guài 形容事物奇异而多样 a cornucopia of strange things

【千秋】 qiānqiū ❶ 泛指很长久的时间 thousand years; ages: ～万代 from generation to generation | ～功过 merits and demerits of sb. to be judged by posterity ❷〈敬辞 *honor.*〉称人寿辰 your birthday

【千岁】 qiānsuì 尊称王公(多用于戏曲中 usu. in traditional opera) prince: ～爷 Your Royal Highness

【千瓦】 qiānwǎ 电的功率实用单位，1 千瓦就是 1,000 瓦特 kilowatt (kw.), a unit of power equal to 1,000 watts 〈旧作 *old*〉瓩 qiānwǎ

【千万】 qiānwàn 务必(表示恳切叮咛 of an admonition) must; make sure to: ～不可大意。On no account should we take this lightly. |

这件事你～记着。Do keep this in mind.

【千…万…】qiān…wàn… ❶ 形容非常多 countless; numerous:～山～水(形容道路遥远而险阻 describing a long and arduous journey) countless mountains and valleys | ～军～马(形容雄壮的队伍和浩大的声势 describing the mightiness of an army) vast host of infantry and cavalry; hordes of troops; millions of troops | ～秋～岁 the ages to come; from generation to generation | ～头～绪 a thousand and one things to attend to; complexities of a situation; too complicated to unravel | ～丝～缕(形容关系非常密切 of a close relationship) linked in a hundred and one ways to sb. | ～言～语 no amount of words suffice to | ～呼～唤 call sb. a great many times; invite sb. time and again | ～变～化 kaleidoscopic change; epoch-making change; ever-changing | ～辛～苦 go through untold hardships; innumerable trials and tribulations | ～差～别 be worlds' apart; be poles' apart ❷ 表示强调 [indicating emphasis] absolutely:～真～确 absolutely true | ～难～难 extremely difficult

【千载难逢】qiān zǎi nán féng 一千年也难得遇到。形容机会难得。golden opportunity; once-in-a-lifetime opportunity

【千载一时】qiān zǎi yī shí 一千年才有这么一个时机。形容机会难得。chance that comes once in a thousand years; chance of a lifetime

【千张】qiān·zhang 食品,是一种薄的豆腐干片 dried beancurd sheet

【千姿百态】qiān zī bǎi tài 形容姿态多种多样,各不相同 in different poses and different expressions

仟 qiān '千'的大写 thousand; upper case of 千

阡 qiān 〈书 *fml.*〉❶ 田地中间南北方向的小路 north-south footpath in the fields:～陌 network of paths that cover a field ❷ 通往坟墓的道路 path conducting to a tomb

【阡陌】qiānmò 〈书 *fml.*〉田地中间纵横交错的小路 crisscross footpaths between fields:～纵横 place crisscrossed by roads | ～交通 connected footpaths

芊 qiān ☞below

【芊眠】qiānmián same as 芊绵 qiānmián

【芊绵】qiānmián 〈书 *fml.*〉草木茂密繁盛(of grass or trees) luxuriant; thick; also 芊眠 qiānmián

【芊芊】qiānqiān 〈书 *fml.*〉草木茂盛(of grass and trees) exuberant; profuse

扦 qiān ❶ (～儿 qiānr) same as 扦子 qiān·zi ①:蜡～儿 candlestick ❷ same as 扦子 qiān·zi ②:～手 customs inspector ❸ 〈方 *dial.*〉插 insert:～门 bolt a door | 把花～在瓶里 put flowers in a vase ❹ 〈方 *dial.*〉修(脚);削 pedicure; peel:～脚 pedicure | ～苹果 peel an apple

【扦插】qiānchā 截取植物的根、茎、叶等的一段插在土壤里,使长成新的植株 make a cuttage; cut a piece from a root, stem, or leaf and plant it in the soil for propagation

【扦手】qiānshǒu 〈旧时 *old*〉关卡上的检查员 customs inspector; also 扦子手 qiān·zishǒu

【扦子】qiān·zi ❶ 金属、竹子等制成的针状物或主要部分是针状的器物 slender, pointed piece of metal, bamboo, etc.:铁～iron poker | 竹～bamboo spike ❷ 插进装着粉末状或颗粒状货物的麻袋等从里面取出样品的金属器具,形状像中空的山羊角 sharp-pointed metal tube, in the shape of a goat's hollow horn, used to extract samples of grains, powder, etc. from sacks

迁(遷) qiān ❶ 迁移 move:～居 take up residence somewhere else | ～葬 remove a coffin from one grave to another | 拆～evacuate a house for demolition ❷ 转变 change:变～vicissitudes | 事过境～。This is a thing of the past, and the situation has changed. ❸ 〈书 *fml.*〉调动官职 tansfer of official post:左～be demoted

【迁都】qiān//dū 迁移国都 move the capital to another place

【迁就】qiānjiù 将就别人 concede; give in:坚持原则,不能～。We should never concede to anybody on matters of principle. | 你越～他,他越贪得无厌。The more you try to give in, the greedier he becomes.

【迁居】qiānjū 搬家 move house:～处地 take up residence in another place

【迁流】qiānliú 〈书 *fml.*〉(时间等)迁移流动(of time, etc.) flow past:岁月～。Time flows past.

【迁怒】qiānnù 把对甲的怒气发到乙身上,或自己不如意时跟别人生气 take it out on sb.; vent one's spleen on sb. who's not to blame:～于人 shift the blame onto sb. else

【迁徙】qiānxǐ same as 迁移 qiānyí:人口～resettlement of population

【迁延】qiānyán 拖延 procrastinate; delay:～时日 cause a long delay; become long drawn-out

【迁移】qiānyí 离开原来的所在地而另换地点 move; migrate:～户口 transfer one's household registration from one place to another | 工厂由城内～到郊区。The factory has been moved from downtown to the suburbs. ◇随着时间的～,这件事逐渐被淡忘了。The passage of time has gradually consigned what happened to the remotest corner of the mind.

瓩 qiānwǎ 千瓦旧也作瓩 old Chinese version of 千瓦 qiānwǎ

岍 Qiān 岍山,山名,在陕西 Qianshan, name of a mountain in Shaanxi Province

佥[1]（僉）qiān〈书 *fml.*〉全；都 unanimous；together：～同（一致赞成）consensus

佥[2]（僉）qiān same as 签 qiān

汧 qiān 汧阳（Qiānyáng），地名，在陕西。今作千阳。Qianyang，name of a place in Shaanxi Province；present-day Qianyang

钎 qiān same as 钎子 qiān·zi：钢～steel chisel

【钎子】qiān·zi 在岩石上凿孔的工具，用六角、八角或圆形的钢棍制成，有的头上有刃，用压缩空气旋转的钎子当中是空的 bit；rock drill；implement fashioned out of hexagonal，octagonal or round steel rod，with cutting edges and a pointed end for boring holes in rock by repeated blows，and hollowed for rotation-abrasion operation by compressed air；also 炮钎 pàoqiān

牵（牽）qiān ❶ 拉着使行走或移动 lead along：～引 pull；draw｜～着一头牛往地里走 lead a bull to the fields by the nose ❷ 牵涉 involve：～连 implicate｜～制 contain；check

【牵缠】qiānchán 牵扯；纠缠 involve sb.；get sb. entangled：家事～bogged down by family affairs｜这件事～了许多人。This incident involved quite a few people.

【牵肠挂肚】qiān cháng guà dù 形容非常挂念，很不放心 feel deep anxiety；be very worried

【牵扯】qiānchě 牵连；有联系 involve；implicate：别把他～进去。Don't drag him in.｜这两件事～不到一块儿去。These two things have absolutely nothing to do with each other.

【牵掣】qiānchè ❶ 因牵连而受影响或阻碍 hold up；impede：互相～hold each other up｜抓住主要问题，不要被枝节问题～住。Let's focus on the main issue rather than waste too much time on minor matters. ❷ same as 牵制 qiānzhì

【牵动】qiāndòng ❶ 因一部分的变动而使其他部分跟着变动 produce a change in sb. or sth.；affect；influence：～全局 have an impact on the overall situation ❷ 触动 touch；move：一谈到上海，就～了他的乡思。The mere mention of Shanghai struck a nostalgic chord in his heart.

【牵挂】qiānguà 挂念 worry；think about：爸爸妈妈嘱咐他在外边要好好工作，家里的事不用～。His parents told him to do a good job away from home without worrying too much about family.

【牵记】qiānjì 牵挂；惦念 keep thinking about；be anxious about；miss

【牵就】qiānjiù same as 迁就 qiānjiù

【牵累】qiānlěi ❶ 因牵制而使受累 weigh down；tie down：家务～be weighed down by family chores ❷ 因牵连而受累；连累 implicate；involved：～无辜 implicate the innocent

【牵连】qiānlián ❶ 因某个人或某件事产生的影响而使别的人或别的事不利 adversely involve；implicate：清朝的几次文字狱都～了很多人。Many people were implicated during each of the crackdowns on the literati that happened during the Qing Dynasty. ❷ 联系在一起 be related：这两件事是互相～的，一定要妥善处理。These two things are related and should therefore be properly handled.

【牵念】qiānniàn same as 挂念 guàniàn

【牵牛星】qiānniúxīng 天鹰座中最亮的一颗星，是一等星，隔银河与织女星相对 Herd-boy star；Altair，the brightest star of the Aquila that is opposite the Vega across the Milky Way；generally known as 牛郎星 niúlángxīng

【牵强】qiānqiǎng 勉强把两件没有关系或关系很远的事物拉在一起 farfetched；not readily believable because of improbable elements：～附会 stretch the meaning｜这条理由有些～。These reasons are a bit farfetched.

【牵涉】qiānshè 一件事情关联到其他的事情或人 involve；concern；drag in：这案件～到很多人。Quite a few people were involved in this case.

【牵头】qiān//tóu 出面临时负责某事；领头 take the lead；be the first to do sth.：由研究所～，十几个科研单位参加，召开了有关人才流动的讨论会。With the research institute taking the lead and a dozen or so research offices participating，a discussion meeting was held on the transfer of staff members.｜这件事请你牵个头吧。I would like you to take the lead to get it done.

【牵线】qiān//xiàn ❶ 耍木偶牵引提线 pull the wire；〈比喻 *fig.*〉在背后操纵 control from behind the scenes：～人 wire-puller ❷ 撮合；介绍①act as go-between；be a matchmaker：他们俩谈恋爱是我牵的线。I was the matchmaker who brought them together in courtship.

【牵线搭桥】qiān xiàn dā qiáo〈比喻 *fig.*〉从中撮合 act as go-between

【牵一发而动全身】qiān yī fà ér dòng quán shēn〈比喻 *fig.*〉动一个极小的部分就影响全局 pull one hair and you move the whole body — slight move in one part may affect the whole situation

【牵引】qiānyǐn（机器或牲畜）拉（车辆、农具等）(of machine or draught animal) drag (vehicle，farm implement，etc.)；draw：机车～列车前进。The train，drawn by a locomotive，sped forward along the railway.｜在甘肃河西走廊，可以见到骆驼～的大车。Camel-drawn carts can be seen in the Hexi Corridor of Gansu Province.

【牵引力】qiānyǐnlì 机车、拖拉机、船只等的发动机所产生的拖动能力 pulling force; traction force (of the engine of a rolling stock, tractor, boat, etc.)

【牵制】qiānzhì 拖住使不能自由活动(多用于军事 oft. used in military affairs) pin down; hold in check: 我军用两个团的兵力~了敌人的右翼。Our army deployed two regiments and pinned down the enemy's right wing.

铅 qiān ❶ 金属元素,符号 Pb (plumbum)。银灰色,质软而重,延性弱,展性强,容易氧化。用来制合金、蓄电池、电缆的外皮等。plumbum (Pb), a soft, heavy, and silvery metal element more malleable than ductile and easily oxidized, used as a material for the making of alloys and batteries and sheathing cables ❷ 铅笔心 lead, the thin rod of graphite in a pencil

☞ yán on p. 2207

【铅版】qiānbǎn 把铅合金熔化后灌入纸型压成的印刷版 stereotype; lead-alloy printing plate cast from a matrix molded from a raised printing surface, such as type

【铅笔】qiānbǐ 用石墨或加颜料的黏土做笔心的笔 pencil; cylindrical implement for writing, drawing, or marking, consisting of a thin rod of graphite, coloured clay encased in wood

【铅笔画】qiānbǐhuà 用铅笔绘成的图画。描绘方法和木炭画类似,但较木炭画光暗层次更分明,笔法更细致。pencil drawing; art of representing objects or forms on a surface chiefly by means of a pencil, similar to charcoal drawing but with more depth and being more meticulous

【铅垂线】qiānchuíxiàn 把铅锤或其他重锤悬挂于细线上,使它自由下垂,沿下垂方向的直线叫做铅垂线。铅垂线与水平面相垂直。plumb line; thin line from which a plum or any other weight is suspended to determine verticality

【铅灰】qiānhuī 像铅一样的浅灰颜色 leaden; lead gray: ~的天空飘着雪花。Snowflakes kept drifting from a leaden sky.

【铅球】qiānqiú ❶ 田径运动项目之一,运动员用手托住铅球,然后用力推出去 shot; shot put; athletic event in which contestants attempt to put a heavy metal ball as far as possible ❷ 田径运动使用的投掷器械之一,球形,用铁或铜做外壳,中心灌铅 shot; lead-filled iron or copper ball that is put for distance in the shot put

【铅丝】qiānsī 镀锌的铁丝,不易生锈。颜色像铅,所以叫铅丝。galvanized wire; lead wire (so called because of its leaden colour)

【铅条】qiāntiáo ❶ 排版印刷时夹在各行铅字间的条状物,用铅、锑、锡的合金制成 slug; lead; thin strip of alloy of lead, antimony and tin, used to separate lines of type ❷ 自动铅笔的笔心 lead in an automatic pencil

【铅印】qiānyìn 用铅字排版印刷,大量印刷时,排版后制成纸型,再浇制铅版 letterpress, relief and typographic printing; process of printing from a lead stereotype with impressions from a paper-matrix

【铅直】qiānzhí 与水平面垂直的 vertical; plumb; ☞铅垂线 qiānchuíxiàn

【铅字】qiānzì 用铅、锑、锡合金铸成的印刷或打字用的活字 type; small block of lead-antimony-tin alloy bearing a raised letter or character on the upper end for printing or typing

悭(慳) qiān ❶ 吝啬 stingy; miserly ❷ 缺欠 lack; shortage: 缘~一面(缺少一面之缘) have had no chance of making sh.'s acquaintance

【悭吝】qiānlìn 吝啬;小气 stingy; miserly; ~鬼 miser; niggard; skinflint

谦 qiān 谦虚 modest: ~恭 humble; modest | ~让 decline politely | 自~self-depreciating | 满招损,~受益。Complacency spells loss, while modesty brings benefit.

【谦卑】qiānbēi 谦虚,不自高自大(多用于晚辈对长辈 towards a senior) humble; modest

【谦辞】qiāncí ❶ 表示谦虚的言辞,如'过奖、不敢当'等 depreciatory expression, such as 'I feel flattered' and 'I wish I could deserve your compliment' ❷ 谦让推辞 decline an offer politely: 大家诚意推举你,你就别~了。We meant it when we recommended you, so don't decline it any more.

【谦恭】qiāngōng 谦虚而有礼貌 modest and courteous

【谦和】qiānhé 谦虚和蔼 modest and amiable: 为人~ be amiable towards people

【谦谦君子】qiānqiān jūnzǐ 原指谦虚、能严格要求自己的人。现多指故作谦虚而实际虚伪的人。(orig.) modest gentleman who is strict with himself; hypocrite

【谦让】qiānràng 谦虚地不肯担任,不肯接受或不肯占先 modestly decline: 您当发起人最合适,不必~了。You are just the right person to sponsor the event. Don't be so modest as to decline the offer. | 客人互相~了一下,然后落了座。The guests politcly offered their seats to each other before settling down in them.

【谦顺】qiānshùn 谦虚恭顺 modest and deferential: 态度~take a modest and deferential attitude

【谦虚】qiānxū ❶ 虚心,不自满,肯接受批评 modest; self-cffacing: ~谨慎 modest and prudent ❷ 说谦虚的话 make modest remarks: 他~了一番,终于答应了我的请求。After making a few modest remarks he accepted my re quest.

【谦逊】qiānxùn 谦虚恭谨 modest and unassuming

签[1]（签）qiān ❶ 为了表示负责而在文件、单据上亲自写上姓名或画上记号 sign; autograph:～发 sign to endorse a document to be issued|～押 sign one's name|请你～个字。Please sign your name on it. ❷ 用比较简单的文字提出要点或意见 write down brief comments on a document:～呈 submit a document to one's superior|～注意见 sign one's name and write down one's opinions on a document

签[2]（签、籤）qiān ❶（～儿 qiānr）上面刻着文字符号用于占卜或赌博、比赛等的细长小竹片或小细棍 bamboo slip or tiny stick engraved with signs or characters for divination, gambling or competition:抽～儿 draw lots|求～(迷信 superstition) seek divination by drawing lots ❷（～儿 qiānr）作为标志作的小条儿 tag; label:标～儿 sticker|书～儿 bookmark|在书套上贴一个浮～儿 put a sticker on a book cover ❸（～儿 qiānr）竹子或木材削成的有尖儿的小细棍 bamboo slip or pointed stick:牙～儿 tooth pick ❹ 粗粗地缝合 tack; fasten cloth or a seam with a loose basting stitch

【签到】qiān//dào 参加会议或上班时在簿子上写上名字或在印就的名字下面写个'到'字,表示已经到了 register one's attendance at a meeting or work:～簿 attendance book

【签订】qiāndìng 订立条约或合同并签字 ink (an agreement, treaty, etc.); conclude or sign a treaty or contract:两国～了贸易议定书和支付协定。The two nations concluded a trade protocol and a payment agreement.

【签发】qiānfā 由主管人审核同意后,签名正式发出(公文、证件)sign and issue (a document, certificate, etc.):施工单位～工程任务单。The construction team issues engineering dispatch forms.|～护照 issue a passport

【签名】qiān//míng 写上自己的名字 sign one's name; put down one's signature

【签收】qiānshōu 收到公文信件等后,在送信人指定的单据上签字,表示已经收到 sign after receiving sth.:挂号信须由收件人～。A receipt for a registered letter is to be signed by the recipient.

【签署】qiānshǔ 在重要文件上正式签字 sign officially:～联合公报 officially sign a joint communiqué

【签筒】qiāntǒng ❶ 一种竹筒,装占卜或赌博用的签子 tub-like holder of lot-stocks ❷ same as 扦子 qiān·zi ②

【签押】qiānyā〈旧时 *old*〉在文书上签名或画记号,表示负责 put one's signature or seal on an official document to indicate responsibility

【签约】qiān//yuē 签订合约或条约 sign a treaty or agreement

【签证】qiānzhèng ❶ 指一国主管机关在本国或外国公民所持的护照或其他旅行证件上签注、盖印,表示准其出入本国国境 visa; official authorization appended to the passport of a citizen or alien, permitting entry into or exit from a particular country ❷ 指经过上述手续的护照或证件 passport with a visa appended

【签注】qiānzhù ❶ 在文稿或书籍中贴上或夹上纸条,写出可供参考的材料。今多指在送首长批阅的文件上,由经办人注出拟如何处理的初步意见（orig.）attach a slip of paper to a manuscript or book with reference materials; (now) write one's own opinions on a document before submitting it to a superior for examination and approval ❷ 在证件表册上批注意见或有关事项 write comments or points for attention on a certificate, document, or table

【签子】qiān·zi ☞签[2] qiān ①③

【签字】qiān//zì 在文件上写上自己的名字,表示负责 sign; affix one's signature to indicate responsibility

愆 qiān〈书 *fml.*〉❶ 罪过;过失 fault; transgression:～尤 error; fault; sin ❷ 错过(时期) miss the deadline; pass the time limit

【愆期】qiānqī〈书 *fml.*〉延误日期 pass the appointed time; delay

【愆尤】qiānyóu〈书 *fml.*〉过失;罪过 fault; sin

鹐 qiān 尖嘴的鸟啄食(of a bird with a sharp beak) peck at:别让鸡～了地里的麦穗。Don't let the chickens peck at the wheat ears.

骞 qiān〈书 *fml.*〉❶ 高举 hold high ❷ same as 搴 qiān

搴 qiān〈书 *fml.*〉❶ 拔 pull:斩将～旗 behead an enemy general and pull down his flag ❷ same as 骞 qiān

磏 qiān 大磏(Dàqiān),地名,在贵州 name of a place in Guizhou Province

☞ lián on p. 1199

岍 qiān〈书 *fml.*〉same as 愆 qiān

褰 qiān〈书 *fml.*〉撩起;揭起(衣服、帐子等) lift (skirt, bed-curtain, etc.)

韆 qiān ☞ 鞦韆 qiūqiān on p. 1582

qián（ㄑㄧㄢˊ）

荨（蕁、薚）qián [荨麻](qiánmá) ❶ 多年生草本植物,叶子对生,卵形,开穗状小花,茎和叶子都有细毛,皮肤接触时能引起刺痛。茎皮纤维可以做纺织原料。nettle *Urtica*; perennial plant having opposite toothed leaves, apetalous flowers, and stinging hairs on both its stalk and leaves that cause skin irritation on contact, the skin of the stalk being a textile raw material ❷ 这种植物的茎皮纤维 nettle fibre

☞ xún on p. 2187

钤 qián ❶ 图章 seal; chop ❷ 盖(图章) affix a seal to: ～印 print of a seal ❸ 〈书 *fml.*〉 锁 lock; 〈比喻 *fig.*〉 管束 restrict: ～束 keep under control

【钤记】 qián jì 〈旧时 *old*〉 机关团体使用的图章，多为长形，不及染或关防郑重(of a government organisation) seal; stamp (oft. oblong in shape, not as important as signet 印 yìn or army seal 关防 guānfáng)

前 qián ❶ 在正面的(指空间，跟'后'相对 referring to space, as opposed to 'behind') front: ～门 front door | 村～村后 around the village ❷ 往前走 straight ahead: 勇往直～ forge ahead | 畏缩不～ hang back in fear; recoil from (danger, a heavy task, etc.) ❸ 次序靠近头里的(跟'后'相对 as opposed to 'behind') first; front: ～排 front row | ～三名 the top three ❹ 过去的；较早的(指时间，跟'后'相对 of time; as opposed to 'later') ago; before: ～天 the day before yesterday | 从～ in the past | ～功尽弃。What's done has come undone. | ～所未有 unprecedented | ～无古人，后无来者 unparalleled in the past nor to be matched in the future; unique ❺ 从前的(指现在改变了名称的机构等 of an institution having changed its name now) former; formerly: ～政务院 former State Administrative Council ❻ 指某事物产生之前 earlier; prior to: ～科学(科学产生之前) pre-science | ～资本主义(资本主义产生之前) pre-capitalism ❼ 未来的(用于展望) future; prospect: ～程 future | ～景 prospects | 往～看，不要往后看。Look forward, rather than look backward. ❽ 前线；前方 front; forefront: 支～ support the forefront

【前半晌】 qiánbànshǎng 〈方 *dial.*〉 (～儿 qiánbànshǎngr) 上午 before noon; in the morning

【前半天】 qiánbàntiān (～儿 qiánbàntiānr) 上午 before noon; in the morning; also 上半天 shàngbàntiān

【前半夜】 qiánbànyè 从天黑到半夜的一段时间 first half of the night (from nightfall to midnight); also 上半夜 shàngbànyè

【前辈】 qiánbèi 年长的，资历深的人 member of the older generation; elder; senior

【前臂】 qiānbì 胳膊上由肘至腕的部分 forearm; the part of the arm between the wrist and the elbow; (图见 ☞ figure for 身体 shēntǐ on p. 1701)

【前边】 qián·bian (～儿 qián·bianr) same as 前面 qián·mian

【前车之鉴】 qián chē zhī jiàn 《汉书·贾谊传》: '前车覆，后车诫' *History of Han · Biography of Jia Yi*: 'The overturned of the cart ahead is a warning to the cart behind'; 〈比喻 *fig.*〉 当做鉴戒的前人的失败教训 lesson drawn from sb. else's mistake

【前尘】 qiánchén 〈书 *fml.*〉 指从前的或从前经历的事 what happened in the past: 回首～look back on the past

【前程】 qiánchéng ❶ same as 前途 qiántú: 锦绣～bright future | ～远大 promising future ❷ 〈旧时 *old*〉 指读书人或官员企求的功名职位 desired career or rank sought after by an intellectual or official

【前导】 qiándǎo ❶ 在前面引路 lead the way ❷ 在前面引路的人 guide; person who leads the way

【前敌】 qiándí 前方面对敌人的地方 front line: 身临～come personally to the front

【前额】 qián'é 额，因额在头的前部，所以叫前额 forehead; the part of the face between the eyebrows, the normal hairline, and the temples

【前方】 qiánfāng ❶ same as 前面 qián·mian ①: 左～ahead to the left | 右～ahead to the right | 他的目光注视着～。He fixed his eyes straight ahead of him. ❷ 接近战线的地区(跟'后方'相对 as opposed to 'rear area') front: 支援～support those fighting in the front | 开赴～march towards the forefront

【前房】 qiánfáng 称死去的妻子(区别于现在的妻子 as compared with 'present wife') ex-wife; reference to one's deceased wife

【前锋】 qiánfēng ❶ 先头部队 vanguard: 红军的～渡过了大渡河。The vanguard of the Red Army had crossed the Dadu River. ❷ 篮球、足球等球类比赛中主要担任进攻的队员(in basketball, soccer, etc.) forward; player whose task is to attack or score

【前夫】 qiánfū 死去的或离了婚的丈夫(区别于现在的丈夫 as compared with 'present husband') ex-husband

【前赴后继】 qián fù hòu jì 前面的人上去，后面的人就跟上去。形容踊跃前进，连续不断。advance wave upon wave; fight unremittingly

【前功尽弃】 qián gōng jìn qì 以前的成绩全部废弃 one's past merits will count for nothing; all one's labour has been in vain

【前汉】 Qián Hàn 西汉 Western Han Dynasty

【前后】 qiánhòu ❶ 比某一特定时间稍早或稍晚的一段时间。around; about: 国庆节～around the National Day ❷ (时间)从开始到末了(of time) from beginning to end; altogether: 这项工程从动工到完成～仅用了半年时间。It took six months altogether to bring this project to completion. ❸ 在某一种东西的前面和后面 in front and behind: 村子的～各有一条公路。There is a highway running in front of it and another one behind it.

【前…后…】 qián…hòu… ❶ 表示两种事物或行为在空间或时间上一先一后 one after another: ～街～巷 street with an alleyway behind it | ～因～果 cause and effect | ～思～想 mull over something time and again | ～呼～拥

with a large retainers swarming around|～倨～恭(形容对人态度前后截然不同 indicating a change in attitude; 倨 *ju*: 傲慢 arrogance) let one's arrogance give way to humility; revert from arrogance to humility ❷ 表示动作的向前向后 backward and forward: ～俯～仰 bowing forward and leaning backward|～仰～合 double over with (laughter); stagger forward and back

【前后脚儿】qiánhòujiǎor 指两个人或几个人离去或到来的时间很接近 almost at the same time; one close behind another: 我们俩～进的门。The two of us stepped in the door at almost the same time.

【前脚】qiánjiǎo (～儿 qiánjiǎor) ❶ 迈步时在前面的一只脚 the forward foot in a step: ～一滑,后脚也站不稳。When I slipped on my front foot, I lost my balance on the other foot. ❷ 与后脚连说时表示在别人前面(时间上很接近)(used along with 后脚 hòujiǎo) no sooner ... than: 我～进大门,他后脚就赶到了。No sooner had I stepped into the door than he arrived.

【前襟】qiánjīn 上衣、袍子等前面的部分 front part of a robe or jacket

【前进】qiánjìn 向前行动或发展 advance; go forward; march on; forge ahead; move forward; develop

【前景】[1] qiánjǐng 图画、舞台、银幕、屏幕上看上去离观者最近的景物 foreground; closest aspects to the viewer of a picture, stage or screen

【前景】[2] qiánjǐng 将要出现的景象 prospect; vista; perspective; future: 大丰收的～令人欣喜。The prospect of a great harvest filled people with joy.

【前臼齿】qiánjiùchǐ 位置在犬齿的后面、臼齿的前面的牙齿,人类的前臼齿上下颌各四个,齿冠的咀嚼面上有两个或三个突起,适于磨碎食物 premolar teeth; teeth behind the canine teeth and before the molars; humans have four such teeth on the upper and lower jaws, respectively, with two or three protuberances on the mastication surface of its corona, which are suitable for grinding food; (图见 ☞ figure for 齿 chǐ on p. 263)

【前科】qiánkē 曾被判处有期徒刑刑罚并已执行完毕的人又犯新罪,其前罪的处刑事实叫做前科 criminal past; criminal record; facts of previous term(s) of imprisonment imposed on a criminal who has committed a new offence

【前例】qiánlì 可以供后人援用或参考的事例 precedent; case that can be cited or referred to by later generations: 史无～ unprecedented in history; without any parallel in history|这件事情有～可援。This case has a precedent to go by.

【前列】qiánliè 最前面的一列 forefront; front row or rank; 〈比喻 *fig.*〉带头的地位 in the van of; vanguard; leading position: 站在斗争的最～ be in the van of the struggle

【前列腺】qiánlièxiàn 男子或雄性哺乳动物生殖器官的一个腺体,人体在膀胱的下面,大小和形状跟栗子相似,所分泌的液体是精液的一部分 prostate (gland); gland of the reproductive organs of a man or male mammal, which is under the bladder of the human body, resembling a chestnut both in size and shape, whose secretions are a part of semen

【前面】qián·mian(～儿 qián·mianr) ❶ 空间或位置靠前的部分 in front; at the head; ahead; forward: 亭子～有一棵松树。There is a pine tree in front of the pavilion.|～陈列的都是新式农具。The exhibits ahead are all new-style farm implements. ❷ 次序靠前的部分;文章或讲话中先于现在所叙述的部分 above; proceeding; afore-mentioned; forepart: 这个道理,～已经讲得很详细了。The reason has already been stated exhaustively above.

【前脑】qiánnǎo 脑的一部分,由大脑两半球和间脑构成 forebrain; part of the brain composed of its two hemispheres and the diencephalon

【前年】qiánnián 去年的前一年 year before last

【前怕狼后怕虎】qián pà láng hòu pà hǔ 形容顾虑重重,畏缩不前 fear wolves ahead and tigers behind — be full of fear; be overcautious; be plagued by all sorts of fears; be so full of apprehension that one recoils in fear; also 前怕龙后怕虎 qián pà lóng hòu pà hǔ

【前仆后继】qián pū hòu jì 前面的人倒下,后面的人继续跟上去。形容英勇奋斗,不怕牺牲。take up the positions of the fallen and rise to fight one after another; as one falls, others step into the breach; advance fearlessly; struggle bravely, ready to lay down one's life

【前妻】qiánqī 死去的或离了婚的妻子(区别于现在的妻子 as compared with 'present wife') former wife; ex-wife; wife who has died or divorced

【前期】qiánqī 某一时期的前一阶段 early stage; early days; former stage of some period: ～工程 front-end engineering

【前愆】qiánqiān 〈书 *fml.*〉以前的过失 past faults; past wrongdoings

【前驱】qiánqū 在前面起引导作用的人或事物 forerunner; precursor; pioneer; progenitor: 革命～ revolutionary forerunner (or predecessor)

【前儿】qiánr 〈方 *dial.*〉same as 前天 qiántiān; also 前儿个 qiánr·ge

【前人】qiánrén 古人;以前的人 forebears; forefathers; predecessors: ～种树,后人乘凉。When earlier generations plant trees, posterity shall enjoy the cool under the shade — enjoy the fruits of the labour of one's ancestors or predecessors; profit by the labour of one's forefathers; toil for the benefit of one's descendants|我们现在进行的伟大事业,是～所不能想像的。The great undertakings in which we are engaged today were beyond our forefathers' imaginations.

【前任】qiánrèn 在现在担任某项职务的人之前担任这个职务的 predecessor; person who held a post before the incumbent one:～部长 former minister|他是工会的～主席。He was the ex-president of the trade union.

【前日】qiánrì same as 前天 qiántiān

【前晌】qiánshǎng〈方 *dial.*〉上午 forenoon; morning

【前哨】qiánshào 向敌军所在方向派出的警戒小分队 outpost; advance guard; security detachment dispatched in the direction where enemy troops are stationed

【前身】qiánshēn ❶ 本为佛教用语,指前世的身体,今指事物演变中原来的组织形态或名称等 predecessor; body of the previous life (a term of Buddhism); original organizational form, name, etc. of sth. during the process of its development:人民解放军的～是工农红军。The People's Liberation Army grew out of the Workers' and Peasants' Red Army. ❷ (～儿 qiánshēnr)上衣、袍上等前面的部分;前襟 front part of a Chinese robe, jacket, etc.

【前生】qiánshēng same as 前世 qiānshì

【前世】qiánshì 迷信指人生的前一辈子 (superstition) previous existence; previous life

【前事不忘,后事之师】qián shì bù wàng, hòu shì zhī shī《战国策·赵策一》:'前事之不忘,后事之师。'指记住过去的经验教训,可以作为以后的借鉴 'Past experience, if not forgotten, is a guide for the future' — lessons learned from the past can serve as a guide for the future (*Intrigues of the Warring States · Intrigues of Zhao I*).

【前所未有】qián suǒ wèi yǒu 历史上从来没有过 hitherto unknown; unprecedented; never existed in history:～的规模 unprecedented scale

【前台】qiántái ❶ 剧场中在舞台之前的部分。借指演出的事务工作。proscenium; part in front of a theatre stage; routine work of performance ❷ 舞台面对观众的部分,是演员表演的地方 stage; downstage; part of a stage that faces the audience ❸〈比喻 *fig.*〉公开的地方(含贬义 derog.)onstage; in public:他只是在～表演,背后还有人指挥。He was acting onstage, while others were pulling the strings behind the scenes.

【前提】qiántí ❶ 在推理上可以推出另一个判断来的判断,如三段论中的大前提、小前提 premise; condusion that can draw other inferences, e.g. the major and minor premises in syllogism ❷ 事物发生或发展的先决条件 prerequisite; presupposition; predicate; precondition of the occurrence and development of sth.

【前天】qiántiān 昨天的前一天 day before yesterday

【前庭】qiántíng 内耳的一部分,在半规管和耳蜗之间,外侧和下侧都有孔,内部有两个囊状物,囊内有听神经。可维持身体平衡。vestibule; part of the inner ear between the semicircular canal and cochlea, with holes on the outer and lower sides, and two cystidiums inside, in which there is the auditory or acoustic nerve, that maintains balance in the body

【前头】qián·tou same as 前面 qiān·mian

【前途】qiántú 原指前面的路程 journey ahead;〈比喻 *fig.*〉将来的光景 future prospect:光明的～ bright future|～远大 (have a) bright future; (person of) great promise

【前往】qiánwǎng 前去;去 go to; leave for; proceed to:启程～ leave for|陪同～ escort somebody to (somewhere)

【前卫】qiánwèi ❶ 军队行军时在前方担任警戒的部队 advance guard; vanguard; outpost troops on march at the front ❷ 足球、手球等球类比赛中担任助攻与助守的队员,位置在前锋与后卫之间 halfback; player who assists in attack or defense in ball games such as football and handball, and plays between the vanguard and fullback

【前无古人】qián wú gǔrén 前人从来没有做过的;空前 unprecedented in history; have no parallel in history:他们创造了～的奇迹。The miracle they created had no parallel in history.

【前夕】qiánxī ❶ 前一天的晚上 eve; evening of the previous day:国庆节的～ on the eve of National Day ❷〈比喻 *fig.*〉事情即将发生的时刻 eve; moment before sth. is going to happen:大决战的～ on the eve of a great decisive battle

【前贤】qiánxián〈书 *fml.*〉有才德的前辈 sages; wise and virtuous elders

【前嫌】qiánxián 以前的嫌隙 old grudges; past grievances; previous feeling of animosity:～冰释。The old grievance has melted like ice.|捐弃～ discard past enmity

【前线】qiánxiàn 作战时双方军队接近的地带(跟'后方'相对 as opposed to 'rear') front; frontline; battlefront; region where the troops of the two parties are close to each other in a fight ◇企业的领导身临～,跟工人群众打成一片。The leaders of the enterprise went to the workshops in person, identifying themselves with the workers and masses.

【前言】qiányán ❶ 写在书前或文章前面类似序言或导言的短文;引言 preface; foreword; introduction; short piece written at the front of a book or an article similar to a preface or foreword ❷ 前面说过的话 words said earlier;

previous statements：～不搭后语 speak incoherently; utter words that do not hang together; talk disjointedly; babble in disconnected phrases

【前沿】qiányán 防御阵地最前面的边沿 forward position; front edge; foremost edge of a defensive position：～阵地 forward position ◇～科学 frontier science

【前仰后合】qián yǎng hòu hé 形容身体前后晃动(多指大笑时 usu. when laughing) rock forwards and backwards; sway to and fro; also 前俯后合 qián fǔ hòu hé and 前俯后仰 qián fǔ hòu yǎng

【前夜】qiányè same as 前夕 qiánxī：激战～ on the eve of fierce fighting

Q

【前因后果】qiányīn hòuguǒ 事情的起因和其后的结果，指事情的全过程 cause and effect; entire process

【前站】qiánzhàn 行军或集体出行时将要停留的地点或将要到达的地点 next point at which a travelling party is to stop; next stop on a march; ☞ 打前站 dǎ qiánzhàn on p. 350

【前兆】qiánzhào 某些事物在将要暴露或发作之前的一些征兆 omen; forewarning; foreshadow; premonition; augury; signs of what will be revealed later or is to come：由于地球内部地质结构千差万别，各地出现的地震～也不尽相同。Because the inner geological structures of the earth vary greatly, earthquake warning signs in different places are not exactly the same.

【前肢】qiánzhī 昆虫或有四肢的脊椎动物身体前面靠近头部的两条腿 foreleg; forelimb; two front legs close to the head of an insect or a vertebrate with four limbs

【前缀】qiánzhuì 加在词根前面的构词成分，如'老鼠、老虎'里的'老'、'阿姨'里的'阿' prefix; word-formation element added before the root, such as 老 lǎo in 老鼠 lǎo·shǔ and 老虎 lǎohǔ, and 阿 ā in 阿姨 āyí; also 词头 cítóu

【前奏】qiánzòu ❶ same as 前奏曲 qiánzòuqǔ ❷〈比喻 *fig.*〉事情的先声 prelude; preliminary preparations; harbinger of sth.

【前奏曲】qiánzòuqǔ 大型器乐曲的序曲，是为大型器乐创造气氛的短小器乐曲，一般跟整部乐曲有统一的情调 prelude; overture for a grand instrumental composition; short instrumental composition creating the atmosphere for the grand one, usu. sharing a unified atmosphere with the entire composition

虔 qián 恭敬 pious; sincere; devout：～诚 devout; sincere; pious; reverent | ～心 sincere; devout; pious

【虔诚】qiánchéng 恭敬而有诚意(多指宗教信仰 usu. of religious belief) devout; sincere; pious; reverent：～的信徒 devout believer or follower

【虔敬】qiánjìng 恭敬 reverent; devotional; highly respectful

【虔心】qiánxīn ❶ 虔诚的心 pious; sincere; devout：一片～ a pious heart ❷ 虔诚 devout; sincere; pious; reverent：～忏悔 repent sincerely

钱[1]**(錢)** qián ❶ 铜钱 copper coin; cash：一个～ a copper coin | ～串儿 strings of coins ❷ 货币 money：银～ silver money | 一块～ one *yuan* ❸ 款子 fund; sum：一笔～ a sum of money | 饭～ money for a restaurant bill | 车～ fare | 买书的～ money for buying books ❹ 钱财 wealth; riches：有～有势 both rich and influential ❺ (～儿 qiánr)形状像铜钱的东西 anything that resembles a copper coin in shape：纸～ paper made in the form of coins and burned as an offering to the dead | 榆～儿 elm tree seeds ❻(Qián) 姓 a surname

钱[2]**(錢)** qián 重量单位。10 分等于 1 钱，10 钱等于 1 两。*qian*, unit of weight; 10 *fen* equals to one *qian*, and 10 *qian* equals one *liang*

【钱包】qiánbāo (～儿 qiánbāor)装钱用的小包儿。多用皮革、塑料等制成。wallet; purse; small bag to hold money, usu. made of leather, plastic, etc.

【钱币】qiánbì 钱(多指金属的货币 usu. money made of metal) coin

【钱财】qiáncái 金钱 wealth; money

【钱串子】qiánchuàn·zi ❶ 穿铜钱的绳子 string running through the holes of copper coins; string of cash;〈比喻 *fig.*〉过分看重金钱的 money-minded; miserly; pay too much attention to money：～脑袋 money-minded fellow; money-grubber; person who puts money above everything else ❷ 节肢动物，体长 1－2 寸，由许多环节构成，每个环节有一对细长的脚，触角很长。生活在墙角、石缝等潮湿的地方，吃小虫。arthropod; millipede; 1-2 inch arthropod composed of many segments, each of which has a pair of long and thin feet, and long feelers, inhabiting the foot of a wall, stone crevices and other damp places, and feeding on insects; also 钱龙 qiánlóng

【钱谷】qiángǔ ❶ 货币和谷物 money and grain; levies in kind and cash ❷ 清代主管财政的(幕僚) (during the Qing Dynasty) revenue clerk; magistrate's assistant responsible for public finance or the collection of taxes; revenue clerk：～师爷 (in the Qing Dynasty) magistrate's assistant responsible for the collection of taxes

【钱粮】qiánliáng ❶〈旧时 *old*〉指田赋 land tax; taxes on farm lands：完～ pay land tax ❷ same as 钱谷 qiǎngǔ ②：～师爷 (during the Qing Dynasty) magistrate's assistant responsible for the collection of taxes; revenue clerk

【钱票】qiánpiào（～儿 qiánpiàor）纸币；钞票 paper money or currency; banknote

【钱眼】qiányǎn（～儿 qiányǎnr）铜钱当中的方孔 square hole in the centre of a copper coin: 钻～儿（形容人贪财好利）be a real money grabber

【钱庄】qiánzhuāng〈旧时 *old*〉由私人经营的以存款、放款、汇兑为主要业务的金融业商店 old-style Chinese private bank; old-style banking house; private monetary shops mainly engaged in the business of deposits, credits and remittance

钳（箝、❷拑）qián ❶ same as 钳子 qián·zi ①：老虎～ pincers; pliers|～形攻势 pincer movement; two-pronged offensive ❷ 用钳子夹 hold or grip with pincers: 钉子太小，～不住。The nail is too small to grip with pincers. ❸ 限制；约束 clamp; restrain: ～制 clamp down on; pin down; suppress|～口 keep one's mouth shut; muzzle sb. by threat or manipulation

【钳床】qiánchuáng 钳工用的工作台，台边装有老虎钳 plier lathe; operating platform of a fitter equipped with pincer pliers on the edge

【钳工】qiángōng ❶ 以锉、钻、铰刀、老虎钳等手工工具为主进行机器装配和零部件修整的工种 benchwork; work of assembling machines and trimming parts, mainly with hand tools such as a file, drill, reamer, and pincer pliers ❷ 做这种工作的技术工人 fitter; worker doing such a job

【钳击】qiánjī 夹击 pincer movement; two-pronged surprise attack or offensive

【钳口结舌】qián kǒu jié shé 形容不敢说话 keep one's mouth shut; keep mum; tongue-tied; be too scared to speak

【钳制】qiánzhì 用强力限制，使不能自由行动 clamp down on; pin down; suppress; restrain with force from acting freely: ～言论 muzzle or gag opinions on public affairs|～住敌人的兵力 pin down the enemy's armed forces

【钳子】qián·zi ❶ 用来夹住或夹断东西的器具 pliers; pincers; forceps; tool used to hold or cut things ❷〈方 *dial.*〉耳环 earrings

乾 qián ❶ 八卦之一，卦形是'☰'，代表天 *qian*, one of the Eight Trigrams in the form of '☰', representing heaven; ☞ 八卦 bāguà on p. 22 ❷〈旧时 *old*〉称男性的 male: ～造 bridegroom; (fortune-telling) a man's horoscope|～宅 bridegroom's family

☞ 干[5] gān on p. 624

【乾坤】qiánkūn 象征天地、阴阳等 heaven and earth; Yin and Yang; universe; etc.: 扭转～（根本改变已成的局面）bring about or effect a radical change in the existing state of affairs; reverse the course of events; completely change the situation

【乾隆】Qiánlóng 清高宗（爱新觉罗弘历）年号（公元 1736-1795）Qianlong; title of the reign of Qing Gaozong (Aisin Giroro Hongli) (1736-1795)

【乾造】qiánzào ❶〈旧时 *old*〉指婚姻中的男方 bridegroom; man to be married ❷〈旧时 *old*〉指男子的生辰八字（fortune-telling）a man's horoscope

【乾宅】qiánzhái〈旧时 *old*〉称婚姻中的男家 bridegroom's family; family of a man to be married

掮 qián〈方 *dial.*〉用肩扛（东西）carry on the shoulder: ～着行李到车站去 carry luggage or traveller's bags to the station

【掮客】qiánkè 指替人介绍买卖，从中赚取佣金的人 broker; person who introduces business to others to earn brokerage ◇政治～ political broker

靬 qián 骊靬（Líqián），汉朝县名 Liqian, a county in the Han Dynasty

犍 qián 犍为（Qiánwéi），地名，在四川 Qianwei, a place in Sichuan Province

☞ jiān on p. 943

墘 qián 车路墘（Chēlùqián），地名，在台湾省 Cheluqian, a place in Taiwan Province

潜（潛）qián ❶ 隐在水下 hide under water; submerge; dive: ～泳 underwater swimming; underwater dive|～入海底 dive to the bottom of the sea ❷ 隐藏；不露在表面 hide; lurk; be latent: ～伏 hide; lurk; be latent; lie low|～流 undercurrent; underflow|～移默化 influence unconsciously; exert a subtle influence (on somebody's thinking, character, etc.); influence imperceptibly; act on subtly ❸ 秘密地 secretly; stealthily; on the sly: ～逃 abscond; desert ❹ 指潜力 potential: 革新挖～ tap the potential to make innovations ❺（Qián）姓 a surname

【潜藏】qiáncáng 隐藏 hide; be hidden, be latent: ～在心里的痛苦 pain hidden in one's heart|把～的坏人清除出去 clear out hidden bad persons

【潜伏】qiánfú 隐藏；埋伏 hide; lurk; lie low; be latent: ～着危险 latent or hidden danger

【潜伏期】qiánfúqī 病毒或细菌侵入人体后，要经过一定的时期才发病，这段时期，医学上叫做潜伏期（med.）incubation period; latent period; period before a disease comes on after a virus or bacterium has infected one's body

【潜航】qiánháng 在水下航行（of a submarine）submerge: 潜艇连续～了二十天。The submarine had submerged for 20 days in succession.

【潜居】qiánjū 隐居 live in seclusion; live in solitude; be a hermit: ～乡间 live in seclusion in the countryside

【潜力】qiánlì 潜在的力量 latent capacity; potential; potentiality: 挖掘～ tap potential; exploit potentialities

【潜流】qiánliú 潜藏在地底下的水流。也比喻潜藏在内心深处的感情。undercurrent; underflow; water current hidden underground; (fig.) feelings hidden deep in one's heart

【潜热】qiánrè 单位质量的物质在温度不变的情况下从一个相转变到另一个相(如从固体变为液体)所放出或吸收的热 latent heat; heat emitted or absorbed when a substance of a certain quality changes from one phase into another (e.g. from solid into liquid) without a change in temperature

【潜入】qiánrù ❶ 偷偷地进入 sneak; steal; infiltrate:～国境 slip into the country ❷ 钻进(水中) dive into; submerge; go under (water):～海底 dive to the bottom of the sea

【潜水】qiánshuǐ 在水面以下活动 dive; go underwater:～衣 diving suit|～艇 submarine; U-boat|～员 diver; frogman

【潜水艇】qiánshuǐtǐng ☞ 潜艇 qiántǐng

【潜水衣】qiánshuǐyī 潜水员在水面以下工作时穿的服装,包括衣服、鞋、帽三部分,不漏水,一般附有贮藏氧气的装置 diving suit; uniform of a diver underwater, including clothes, cap and a pair of shoes, which are waterproof, usu. attached to a oxygen container

【潜水员】qiánshuǐyuán 穿着潜水衣在水面以下工作的人员 diver; frogman; person who works underwater, wearing a diving suit

【潜台词】qiántáicí ❶ 指台词中所包含的或未能由台词完全表达出来的言外之意 unspoken words in a play left to the understanding of the audience; what is implied, or not fully expressed, by an actor's lines ❷〈比喻 *fig.*〉不明说的言外之意 what is actually meant; implication that is not spoken openly

【潜逃】qiántáo 偷偷地逃跑(多指罪犯 usu. of criminals) abscond; flee secretly:～在外 abscond|防止罪犯～ prevent the criminals from absconding

【潜艇】qiántǐng 主要在水面下进行战斗活动的军舰。以鱼雷或导弹等袭击敌人舰船和岸上目标,并担任战役侦察。submarine; warship that mainly fights underwater, attacking enemy ships and targets on land using torpedoes or guided missiles, as well as in charge of reconnaissance in a battle; also 潜水艇 qiánshuǐtǐng

【潜望镜】qiánwàngjìng 在潜水艇或地下掩蔽工事里观察水面或地面以上敌情所用的光学仪器,用一系列的折光镜做成 periscope; optical instrument used to observe the enemy's situation on water or land from a submarine or underground covered fortification, that is made of a series of enoscopes

【潜心】qiánxīn 用心专而深 devote oneself; work with great concentration:～研究 devote oneself to studying; concentrate on studies|～于典籍四十年 has applied oneself to the study of historical records for 40 years

【潜行】qiánxíng ❶ 在水面以下行动 move underwater:潜水艇可以在海底～。Submarines can move about under the sea. ❷ 秘密行走 slink; move stealthily

【潜血】qiánxuè same as 隐血 yǐnxuè

【潜移默化】qián yí mò huà 指人的思想或性格受其他方面的感染而不知不觉地起了变化 influence unconsciously; exert a subtle influence (on sb.'s thinking, character, etc.); influence imperceptibly; act on subtly

【潜意识】qiányìshí 下意识 subconsciousness; the subconscious

【潜泳】qiányǒng 指游泳时身体在水面下游动 underwater swimming; move one's body underwater when swimming

【潜在】qiánzài 存在于事物内部不容易发现或发觉的 latent; hidden; potential; existing in sth., but cannot be found or discovered easily:～意识 subconsciousness; the subconscious|～力量 latent force|～危险 hidden danger|～威胁 hidden threat

【潜踪】qiánzōng 隐藏踪迹(多含贬义 usu. derog.) conceal one's whereabouts; go into hiding

黔1 qián〈书 *fml.*〉黑色 black

黔2 Qián 贵州的别称 another name for Guizhou Province

【黔剧】qiánjù 贵州地方戏曲剧种,由曲艺文琴(一种用扬琴伴奏的说唱形式)发展而成,原来叫文琴戏 Qian opera, local opera of Guizhou Province developed from *quyi wenqin* (a form of popular entertainment that consists mainly of talking and singing accompanied by the dulcimer; formerly called Wenqin opera

【黔驴技穷】Qián lǘ jì qióng〈比喻 *fig.*〉仅有的一点伎俩也用完了 'The Guizhou donkey has exhausted its tricks'; at one's wit's end; be at the end of one's resources; ☞ 黔驴之技 Qián lǘ zhī jì

【黔驴之技】Qián lǘ zhī jì 唐朝柳宗元的《三戒·黔之驴》说,黔(现在贵州一带)这个地方没有驴,有人从外地带来一头,因为用不着,放在山下。老虎看见驴个子很大,又听见它的叫声很响,起初很害怕,老远就躲开。后来逐渐接近它,驴只踢了老虎一脚。老虎看见驴的技能只不过如此,就把它吃了。后来就用'黔驴之技'比喻虚有其表,本领有限。tricks of the Guizhou donkey; cheap tricks; According to the *Three Cautionary Tales · The Donkey of Guizhou* by Liu Zongyuan of the Tang Dynasty, there were no donkeys in the Guizhou region until someone brought one from somewhere else and abandoned it at the foot of a mountain, for he did not need it. At first, frighten by its large size and loud cry, a local tiger kept far away from it; but when the tiger approached gradually, all the donkey could do was to give the intruder a kick. Realizing that was the limit of the donkey's skill, the tiger ate it up; (fig.) look impressive but lack real worth; be striking only in appearance but with only limited skill

【黔首】qiánshǒu 〈古代 *arch.*〉称老百姓 common people

灊 qián 〈古 *arch.*〉地名,在今安徽霍山东北 Qian, a place in northeast of present-day Huoshan Mountains in Anhui Province

qiǎn (ㄑㄧㄢˇ)

肷(膁) qiǎn 身体两旁肋骨和胯骨之间的部分(多指兽类的 usu. of animals) part between the ribs and the hips on both sides of the body; ☞狐肷 húqiǎn on p. 818

浅(淺) qiǎn ❶ 从上到下或从外到里的距离小(跟'深'相对,②③④⑤同 as opposed to 'deep', same as ②③④⑤) shallow; of little depth; possessing a short distance from the top to the bottom or from the outside to the inside: ～滩 shallow; shoal | 水～ shallow water | 屋子的进深～。There is little room from the entrance of the house to its rear. ❷ 浅显 simple; easy; not difficult: ～易 simple; easy | 这些读物内容～,容易懂。These readings are easy to understand. ❸ 浅薄 superficial: 功夫～ not well trained ❹ (感情) 不深厚 not close; not intimate; not chummy: 交情～ not on familiar terms; of nodding acquaintance ❺ (颜色) 淡 (of colour) light: ～红 light red | ～绿 thin green ❻ (时间) 短 not long (in time); for a short while: 年代～ the recent past | 相处的日子还～ have been together for a short time
☞ jiān on p. 940

【浅薄】qiǎnbó ❶ 缺乏学识或修养 shallow; superficial; scant; meagre; lacking in knowledge or accomplishment: 知识～ meagre knowledge; superficial knowledge ❷ (感情等) 不深; 微薄 (of feelings, etc.) shallow; lacking depth: 缘分～ shallow predestined affinity | 情意～ little affection ❸ 轻浮; 不淳朴 flighty; frivolous: 时俗～ prevalent frivolous custom of the time

【浅尝】qiǎncháng 不往深处研究(知识、问题等) dubble in or at; only make a superficial study (of knowledge, problems, etc.): ～辄止(刚入门就不再钻研) stop striving after obtaining a little knowledge about sth.; be satisfied with a smattering of knowledge

【浅海】qiǎnhǎi 水深在 200 米以内的海域 shallow sea; epeiric sea; epicontinental sea; sea less than 200 metres deep

【浅见】qiǎnjiàn 肤浅的见解 superficial view; humble opinion: ～寡闻 superficial views and meagre knowledge

【浅近】qiǎnjìn same as 浅显 qiǎnxiǎn: ～易懂 simple and easy to understand; plain and easily comprehensible

【浅陋】qiǎnlòu 见识贫乏; 见闻不广 shallow; meagre; mean; deficient in knowledge; narrow-minded

【浅露】qiǎnlù (措词) 不委婉, 不含蓄 (of wording) blunt; explicit; neither moderate nor implicit: 词意～ explicit phrase

【浅明】qiǎnmíng same as 浅显 qiǎnxiǎn: ～的道理 simple reason

【浅说】qiǎnshuō 浅显易懂的解说(多用做书名或文章的题目 usu. used in the title of a book or article) elementary introduction: 《无线电～》 *An Elementary Introduction to Radio*

【浅滩】qiǎntān 海、湖、河中水浅的地方 shoal; shallow; place of shallow water in a sea, river or lake

【浅显】qiǎnxiǎn (字句、内容) 简明易懂 (of words and expressions or content) plain; obvious; easy to read and understand: ～而有趣的通俗科学读物 simple and interesting popular scientific literature

【浅学】qiǎnxué 学识浅薄 superficial knowledge; little or shallow learning

【浅易】qiǎnyì same as 浅显 qiǎnxiǎn

【浅子】qiǎn·zi 一种盛东西的用具, 一般是圆形, 周围的边儿较浅 shallow container; usu. round container with shallow edges; also 浅儿 qiǎnr

遣 qiǎn ❶ 派遣; 打发 send; dispatch; transmit: ～送 send back; repatriate | 调兵～将 move troops; deploy forces ❷ 消除; 发泄 dispel; expel; drive away: 消～ diversion; pastime | ～闷 dispel or relieve boredom; seek relief from boredom; do sth. as a diversion

【遣词】qiǎncí (说话、写文章) 运用词语 wording; (of speech or writing) use of words: ～造句 wording and phrasing; diction; choice of words and construction of sentences; also 遣辞 qiǎncí

【遣返】qiǎnfǎn 遣送回到原来的地方 repatriate; send back to the original place: ～战俘 repatriate prisoners of war

【遣散】qiǎnsàn ❶ 〈旧时 *old*〉机关、团体、军队等改组或解散时, 将人员解职或使退伍 disband; dismiss; send away; dismiss or demobilize personnel at the reorganization or disbandment of an organization, army, etc.; ～费 severance pay; release pay; compensation for disbandment ❷ 解散并遣送所俘获的敌方军队、机关等人员 disband and repatriate captured enemy troops, staff members of enemy government organizations, etc.; 全部伪军立即缴械～。All the puppet troops were disarmed and repatriated.

【遣送】qiǎnsòng 把不合居留条件的人送走 send back; repatriate; send away sb. who is not qualified to reside:～出境 deport|～回原籍 send back to one's native town or ancestral home

嗛 qiǎn 猴子的颊囊 ape's jaws
〈古 *old*〉same as 谦 qiān and 歉 qiàn

谴 qiǎn ❶ 责备;申斥 condemn; censure; reproach; reprimand:～责 denounce; condemn; censure; reproach|自～己过 self-reproach of one's own errors ❷〈书 *fml.*〉官员获罪降职 (of an official) be demoted on account of wrongdoing:～谪 (of an official) be demoted (because of offens es, mistakes, etc.)

Q

【谴责】qiǎnzé 责备;严正申斥 condemn; denounce; censure; reproach:世界进步舆论都～这一侵略行径。Progressive public opinion across the world all strongly condemned the act of aggression.

【谴谪】qiǎnzhé〈书 *fml.*〉官吏因犯罪而遭贬谪 (of officials) be demoted (because of offenses, mistakes, etc.)

缱 qiǎn [缱绻](qiǎnquǎn)〈书 *fml.*〉形容情投意合,难舍难分;缠绵 lingering; abiding; (of love between a couple) deeply attached to each other; (of two persons) be in such complete agreement so as to be unable to bear parting from each other

qiàn (ㄑㄧㄢˋ)

欠[1] qiàn ❶ 困倦时张口出气 yawn; open the mouth to breathe when one feels tired:～伸 stretch oneself and yawn ❷ 身体一部分稍微向上移动 raise slightly (a part of one's body):～脚儿 stand on tiptoe|～了～身子 rise slightly; rise halfway from one's seat

欠[2] qiàn ❶ 借别人的财物等没有还或应当给人的事物还没有给 owe; be in debt; be behind with; have not returned belongings, etc., borrowed from others; have not given sth. to others that should be given:赊～ buy or sell on credit; give or get credit|～账 bills due; outstanding account|～债 be in debt; run into debt; owe a debt|～情 owe somebody a favour; owe somebody a debt of gratitude; have yet to return a favour done to somebody|～着一笔钱没还 owe (somebody) a sum of money ❷ 不够;缺乏 not enough; insufficient; lacking; wanting:～佳 not good enough; not up to the mark; below average|～妥 not proper; improper; far from correct or appropriate|～火 be undercooked|～考虑 without due consideration|万事俱备,只～东风。Everything is ready, all that is needed is a fair wind — all is on hand except the crucial piece.

【欠安】qiàn'ān〈婉辞 *euph.*〉称人生病 not feel well; be slightly indisposed

【欠产】qiàn//chǎn 产量未达到规定的指标 shortfall in output or production

【欠火】qiàn//huǒ 指饭、菜等的火候不够 be undercooked; (of rice, dishes, etc.) insufficient duration and degree of cooking:这屉馒头还欠点儿火。These buns haven't been steamed long enough.

【欠情】qiàn// qíng (～儿 qiànqíngr)得到别人的好处还没有酬谢 owe sb. a favour; owe sb. a debt of gratitude; have yet to return a favour to sb.; have not rewarded sb. for his or her kindness:人家热情接待,我还没有道谢,觉得有点～。Having not thanked them for their warm reception, I feel a bit indebted to them.|咱俩谁也不欠谁的情。Now neither of us owes the other a favour; we are even.

【欠缺】qiànquē ❶ 缺乏;不够 be short of; be lacking in; be deficient in; be inadequate:经验还～,但是热情很高 be very enthusiastic in spite of inexperience ❷ 不够的地方 shortcoming; deficiency; inadequacy:事情办得很圆满,没有什么～。It has been handled perfectly, almost flawlessly.

【欠伸】qiànshēn 打呵欠,伸懒腰 stretch oneself and yawn

【欠身】qiàn// shēn 稍微起身向前,表示对人恭敬 rise slightly; rise halfway from one's seat (to show one's respect):他欠了欠身,和客人打招呼。He rose slightly to greet the guests.

【欠条】qiàntiáo (～儿 qiàntiáor)欠别人财物所立的字据;借条 receipt for a loan; written pledge for borrowing sth. or money; piece of paper signed in acknowledgement of debt; IOU

【欠资】qiànzī 指寄邮件时未付或未付足邮资。这种欠资邮件,邮局要向收件人补收邮资,或退给寄件人补足邮资。postage due; fail to pay enough postage when mailing a letter; the post office requests the receiver, or return a mail to the sender, to make up for the deficiency of postage

纤(縴) qiàn 拉船用的绳子 rope for towing a boat; tow-rope:～绳 rope for towing a boat; tow-rope
☞ xiān on p. 2072

【纤夫】qiànfū 指以背纤拉船为生的人 boat tracker; person who earns a living by pulling the tow line of boats on the shoulder

【纤绳】qiànshéng 拉船用的绳子 rope for towing a boat; tow-rope

【纤手】qiànshǒu 给人介绍买卖的人(多指介绍房地产交易的人 usu. of real-estate business) estate agent; real estate broker; person who introduces business to others; also 拉纤的 lāqiàn·de

芡 qiàn ❶ 一年生草本植物,生在水池中,全株有刺,叶子圆形,像荷叶,浮在水面。花单生，花瓣紫色，花托形状像鸡头，种子供食用。Gorgon euryale (*Euryale ferox*); annual herb found in ponds, covered all over with prickles, having round leaves resembling those of a lotus floating on the water, solitary flowers with purple petals and chicken-head-shaped receptacles, and edible seeds; also 鸡头 jītóu and 老鸡头 lǎojītóu ❷ 做菜时用芡粉调成的汁 starch used in cooking; sauce made of the seed powder of Gorgon euryale: 勾～ add some starch

【芡粉】qiànfěn 用芡实做的粉，勾芡用。一般用其他淀粉代替芡粉。seed powder of Gorgon euryale (usu. replaced by other starch)

【芡实】qiànshí 芡的种子，供食用，又可制淀粉 Gorgon fruit; Semen Euryales; Gorgon euryale seed, which is edible, and can be used to make starch; also 鸡头米 jītóumǐ

茜(蒨) qiàn ❶ 茜草 madder ❷ 红色 alizarin red; crimson: ～纱 red gauze

☞ xī on p. 2045

【茜草】qiàncǎo 多年生草本植物，根圆锥形，黄赤色，茎有倒生刺，叶子轮生，心脏形或长卵形，花冠黄色，果实球形，红色或黑色。根可做红色染料，也可入药。madder (*Rubia*); perennial herb that has yellowish-red conical roots, a stem covered with anatropous prickles, verticillate heart-shaped or long oval leaves, yellow corollas, spherical red or black fruit, and roots that can be used to make red dye and medicine

倩[1] qiàn 〈书 *fml.*〉美丽 beautiful; pretty; attractive; handsome: ～装 beautiful attire or costume; handsome dress | ～影 beautiful figure; well-proportioned form or photo (of a beautiful woman)

倩[2] qiàn 请人代替自己做 ask sb. to do sth. in one's name: ～人执笔 employ a person to write an article in one's name

【倩影】qiànyǐng 美丽的身影（多指女子）(usu. of a woman) beautiful figure; well-proportioned form

堑 qiàn 隔断交通的沟 moat; ditch; chasm; trench that cuts off a road: ～壕 trench; entrenchment | 长江天～ natural chasm of the Yangtze River; with the Yangtze River providing a natural barrier against attack ◇吃一～，长一智。With every pitfall comes greater knowledge.

【堑壕】qiànháo 在阵地前方挖掘的、修有射击掩体的壕沟，多为曲线形或折线形 trench; entrenchment; usu. curved or broken-line-shaped ditch with shooting emplacements in front of a battlefield

绮 qiàn 〈书 *fml.*〉青赤色丝织品。用于人名。*qian*, dark-red silk; often used in people's names

椠 qiàn 〈书 *fml.*〉❶〈古代 *arch.*〉记事用的木板 wood-block used in ancient China to record events ❷ 书的刻本 engraved edition of books: 宋～ Song Dynasty wood-block edition | 元～ Yuan Dynasty wood-block edition

嵌 qiàn 把较小的东西卡进较大东西上面的凹处（多指美术品的装饰 usu. of decorative art) inlay; embed; set; insert sth. small into a concave setting in a bigger object: ～石 inlaid stones | ～银 set with silver pieces | 桌面上～着象牙雕成的花。The tabletop is inlaid with flowers carved out of ivory.

☞ kàn on p. 1082

慊 qiàn 〈书 *fml.*〉憾；恨 regret; sorrow; hate

☞ qiè on p. 1556

歉 qiàn ❶ 收成不好 poor (harvest); crop failure: ～年 lean year; year of poor harvest | 以丰补～ make up for a crop failure with a bumper harvest; store up in bumper years to make up for lean years ❷ 对不住人的心情 apology; regret; feel sorry: 抱～ be sorry; apologize | 道～ apologize; offer or make an apology | 深致～意 extend sincere apologies; express profound regret

【歉疚】qiànjiù 觉得对不住别人，对自己的过失感到不安 feel guilty; be remorseful; feel sorry for sb.; be uneasy over one's mistake: ～心情 be in a remorseful mood | 深感～ feel deep guilty; be deeply remorseful

【歉然】qiànrán 形容歉疚的样子 regret; feel apologetic: ～不语 feel apologetic and remain silent

【歉收】qiànshōu 收成不好（跟'丰收'相对 as opposed to 'bumper harvest') poor harvest; crop failure: 粮食～ poor grain harvest

【歉岁】qiànsuì 收成不好的年份 lean year; year of poor harvest

【歉意】qiànyì 抱歉的意思 apology; regret: 表示～ offer an apology; express one's regrets

qiāng (ㄑㄧㄤ)

抢(搶) qiāng ❶〈书 *fml.*〉触；撞 touch; knock: 呼天～地 cry out to heaven and knock one's head on the ground — utter cries of anguish ❷ same as 戗 qiāng ①

☞ qiǎng on p. 1546

呛(嗆) qiāng 因水或食物进入气管引起咳嗽，又突然喷出 choke; cough and suddenly spit up water or food that has entered one's windpipe: 吃饭吃～了 choke over one's food | 喝得太猛，～着了 take a big gulp and almost choke

☞ qiàng on p. 1547

羌 Qiāng ❶ 我国古代民族，原住在以今青海为中心，南至四川，北接新疆的一带地区，东汉时移居今甘肃一带，东晋时建立后秦政权（公

元 384-417) Qiang, an ethnic people ancient in China that originally inhabited a region centring on present-day Qinghai Province, extending to Sichuan Province to the south, and the Xinjiang Autonomous Region to the north, then moving to the region around present-day Gansu Province during the Eastern Han Dynasty, and establishing the Later Qin regime during the Eastern Jin Dynasty (384-417) ❷ 指羌族 Qiang living in Sichuan Province: ～笛 Qiang flute | ～语 Qiang language

【羌笛】qiāngdí 羌族管乐器,双管并在一起,每管各有六个音孔,上端装有竹簧口哨,竖着吹 Qiang flute; wind instrument of the Qiang people with two tubes side by side, each of which has six sound holes, equipped with a bamboo reed whistle at the top, and played vertically

【羌族】Qiāngzú 我国少数民族之一,分布在四川 Qiang, one of China's minority peoples living in Sichuan Province

玱(瑲) qiāng 〈书 *fml*.〉〈拟声词 *onom*.〉形容玉器相撞的声音 jingling sound of jade

枪[1](槍、鎗) qiāng ❶ 旧式兵器,在长柄的一端装有尖锐的金属头,如红缨枪、标枪 spear; old-style weapon with a sharp metal point at one end of the long handle, such as the red-tasselled spear and the javelin ❷ 口径在2厘米以下,发射枪弹的武器,如手枪、步枪、机关枪等 rifle; gun; firearm; weapon that fires bullets with a bore less than 2 cm., such as a pistol, rifle, and machine-gun ❸ 性能或形状像枪的器械,如发射电子的电子枪,气焊用的焊枪 equipment that functions or is shaped like a gun, such as electron gun for transmitting electrons, and a welding torch for gas welding

枪[2](槍) qiāng 枪替 sit in for sb. at an examination: 打～ sit for an exam in place of another person | ～手 substitute for another at an examination

【枪毙】qiāngbì 用枪打死(多用于执行死刑 usu. of executing a death sentence) execute by shooting

【枪刺】qiāngcì 安在步枪、冲锋枪枪头上的钢刀或钢锥,用于刺杀 bayonet; steel knife or awl affixed to the top of a rifle or sub-machine gun for bayonet charges

【枪打出头鸟】qiāng dǎ chū tóu niǎo 〈比喻 *fig*.〉首先打击或惩办带头的人 shoot the bird that takes the lead — first strike, or punish the person who takes the lead

【枪弹】qiāngdàn 用枪发射的弹药,由药筒、底火、发射药、弹头构成。有时专指弹头。cartridge; ammunition fired by a gun, composed of a shell casing, primer, propellant powder and bullet; sometimes with special reference to a bullet; 通称 general term for 子弹 zǐdàn

【枪法】qiāngfǎ ❶ 用枪射击的技术 marksmanship; skill of gun-shooting: 他～高明,百发百中。He is an excellent marksman, a crack shot. ❷ 使用长枪(古代兵器)的技术 skill to wield a spear (an ancient weapon): ～纯熟 skilled spearman

【枪杆】qiānggǎn (～儿 qiāngǎnr) 枪身,泛指武器或武装力量 gun; stock of a gun; generally refer to weapons or armed forces; also 枪杆子 qiānggǎn·zi

【枪击】qiāngjī 用枪射击 shoot with a gun: 遭～身亡 be shot dead | 双方展开～。The two parties started shooting at each other.

【枪决】qiāngjué same as 枪毙 qiāngbì: 就地～ execute by shooting on the spot

【枪林弹雨】qiāng lín dàn yǔ 枪支如林,子弹如雨。形容激战的战场 hail or rain of bullets ('pikes as dense as trees in a forest, and bullets showering down like rain'); refer to battlefield of a fierce battle: 他是个老战士,在～中多次立功。He is a veteran soldier who has performed much meritorious deeds on the raging battlefield.

【枪榴弹】qiāngliúdàn 利用步枪、马枪枪口部分的发射器和特制空包弹发射的小型炸弹 rifle grenade; grenade launcher; small explosive fired by an ejector and a special blank cartridge on the muzzle of a rifle or carbine

【枪杀】qiāngshā 用枪打死 shoot dead; kill by firearm; gun fatality: 惨遭～ be gunned down in cold blood

【枪手】qiāngshǒu ❶〈旧时 *old*〉指持枪(古代兵器)的兵 spearman; soldier who held a spear (an ancient weapon) ❷ 射击手 marksman; gunner; gunman

【枪手】qiāng·shou 枪替的人 one who sits in an exam for sb. else

【枪替】qiāngtì 指考试作弊,冒名替别人做文章或和答题 sit for sb. in an examination; cheat in an examination by writing essays or answering questions in sb. else's name; also 打枪 dǎqiāng

【枪乌贼】qiāngwūzéi 软体动物,形状略似乌贼,但稍长,体苍白色,有淡褐色的斑点,尾端呈菱形,触角短,有吸盘。生活在海洋里。squid (*Loligo*); calamari; marine mollusk that slightly resembles cuttlefish in shape, but is a little longer, with a pale white body covered with light brown spots, a diamond-shaped tail, short feelers, and a sucker; 通称 general term for 鱿鱼 yóuyú

【枪械】qiāngxiè 枪(总称 general term for) firearms; armaments

【枪眼】qiāngyǎn ❶ 碉堡或墙壁上开的供向外开枪射击的小孔 embrasure; small hole on a pillbox or wall for shooting at targets outside

❷（～儿 qiāngyǎnr）枪弹打的洞 bullet hole

【枪战】qiāngzhàn 互相用枪射击的战斗 gun battle; shoot-out; (of two parties) fight by shooting each other with guns: 激烈的～ fierce shoot-out

【枪支】qiāngzhī 枪（总称）(general term for) gun; firearms: ～弹药 arms and ammunition

【枪子儿】qiāngzǐr same as 枪弹 qiāngdàn

戗（戧） qiāng ❶ 方向相对；逆 towards the opposite direction: ～风 against the wind｜～辙儿走（逆着规定的交通方向走）go against the prescribed traffic direction; go in the wrong direction ❷（言语）冲突 verbal clash: 两人说～了，吵了起来。Their views clashed, and this eventually led to a quarrel.

☞ qiàng on p. 1547

【戗风】qiāngfēng 逆风；顶风 against the wind: 回来的路上～，车骑得慢。On our way back we were cycling slowly against the wind.

戕 qiāng 〈书 *fml.*〉杀害；残害 kill: 自～（自杀）kill oneself; commit suicide; take one's own life

【戕害】qiānghài 伤害 damage; ruin; injure: ～健康 ruin one's health｜～心灵 injure the mind

【戕贼】qiāngzéi 伤害；损害 harm; injure; undermine: ～身体 undermine or ruin one's health

斨 qiāng 古代的一种斧子 ancient axe

将（將） qiāng 〈书 *fml.*〉愿；请 please; wish; ask; appeal for: ～进酒。Please have a drink.

☞ jiāng on p. 959 and jiàng on p. 964

酤（醑） qiāng 藏族用青稞酿成的一种酒 Tibetan liquor made from highland barley

跄（蹌） qiāng ［跄跄］ qiāngqiāng 〈书 *fml.*〉形容行走合乎礼节 walk in a correct, formal manner; also 跄跄 qiāngqiāng

☞ qiàng on p. 1548

腔 qiāng ❶（～儿 qiāngr）动物身体内部空的部分 cavity; hollow part of the body of an animal: 口～ oral cavity｜鼻～ nasal cavity｜胸～ thoracic cavity｜腹～ abdominal cavity｜满～热血 full of indignation◇炉～儿 furnace cavity ❷（～儿 qiāngr）话 talk; speech: 开～ start talking｜答～ answer; respond ❸（～儿 qiāngr）乐曲的调子 tune: 高～ high-pitched tune｜花～ coloratura｜昆～ melodies that originated in Kunshan, Jiangsu Province, in the Yuan Dynasty, and became popular during the ensuing Ming and Qing dynasties｜唱～儿 sing tunes｜唱走了～儿 sing out of tune ❹（～儿 qiāngr）说话的腔调 tone; accent: 京～ pure Beijing dialect｜山东～ Shandong accent｜学生～ schoolboy talk; classroom tone of a schoolboy ❺〈量词 *classifier*〉用于宰杀过的羊（多见于早期白话 oft. in early vernacular）slaughtered sheep: 一～羊 a mutton carcass

【腔肠动物】qiāngcháng-dòngwù 无脊椎动物的一门，体壁由内外两胚层构成，两层之间为胶质，身体中间有一个空腔，既是消化器官，又是体腔。体形有两种，一为钟形或伞形，如水母，一为圆筒形，如水螅和珊瑚。多生活在海洋中。coelenterate (*Coelenterata*); invertebrate, usu. living in the ocean, whose body wall is composed of an endoderm and ectoderm, with gel in between, and having a cavity in the middle of the body that serves as a digestive organ and a coelom, resembling either a clock or umbrella in shape, as in a jellyfish, or a circular cylinder, as in hydra and coral

【腔调】qiāngdiào ❶ 戏曲中成系统的曲调，如西皮、二黄等 tune; systematic tune of operas, such as *xipi* and *erhuang* ❷ 调子 tone ❷ 指说话的声音、语气等 accent; intonation: 听他说话的～是山东人。Judging by his accent, he is from Shandong.

【腔子】qiāng·zi ❶ 胸腔 chest; bosom ❷ 动物割去头后的躯干 headless carcasses of animals

蜣 qiāng ［蜣螂］(qiāngláng) 昆虫，全身黑色，胸部和脚有黑褐色的长毛，吃动物的尸体和粪尿等，常把粪滚成球形。有些地区叫屎壳郎。dung beetle (*Scarabaeidae*); insect that is black all over its body, covered with black-and-brown long hairs, feeds on animal corpses, dung, urine, etc., and often rolls the dung into a ball; also called 屎壳郎 shǐ·kelàng in some areas

锖 qiāng ［锖色］(qiāngsè) 某些矿物表面因氧化作用而形成的薄膜所呈现的色彩，常常不同于矿物固有的颜色 tarnish; colour of the thin film on the surface of some minerals due to oxidation, often different from their inherent colour

锵（鏘） qiāng 〈拟声词 *onom.*〉形容金属或玉石撞击的声音 clang; gong; jingling sound of metal or jade: 锣声～～ continuous clanging of gongs

跄（蹡） qiāng ［跄跄］ same as 跄跄 qiāngqiāng

☞ qiàng on p. 1548

镪 qiāng ［镪水］(qiāngshuǐ) 强酸的俗称 commonly known as strong acid

☞ qiǎng on p. 1547

qiáng（ㄑㄧㄤˊ）

强（強、彊） qiáng ❶ 力量大（跟'弱'相对 as opposed to 'weak'）strong; powerful; mighty; of great power or force: ～国 powerful nation; strong country; power｜富～ rich and powerful｜身～体壮

strong and healthy|工作能力～ very capable in work ❷ 感情或意志所要求达到的程度高；坚强 excel；be demanding；be resolute；of a high degree demanded by one's feelings or will：要～ be eager to excel；be anxious to outdo others|责任心～，工作就做得好。Only with a strong sense of responsibility can one do a good job. ❸ 使用强力；强迫 by force；forcibly：～制 force；compel；coerce；impel|～渡 force or fight one's way across a river|～占 seize；forcibly take；occupy by force of arms|～索财物 take possession of other people's property by forcible means ❹ 使强大或强壮 strengthen；enhance：富国～兵 enrich the country and strengthen national defence；make the country prosperous and the army strong|～身之道 way to keep fit (by physical exercises and/or by taking tonics) ❺ 优越；好(多用于比较 usu. used for comparison) better；stronger：今年的庄稼比去年更～。The crops are doing better this year than last year. ❻ 用在分数或小数后面，表示略多于此数(跟'弱'相对 as opposed to 'a little less than') slightly more than；a little over；plus；used after fractions or decimals to indicate a number a little more than the original number：实际产量超过原定计划 12%～。The actual output has exceeded a little over 12 per cent of the original plan. ❼ (Qiáng) 姓 a surname

☞ jiàng on p. 964 and qiǎng on p. 1547

【强暴】qiángbào ❶ 强横凶暴 violent；brutal；ferocious：～的行为 act of violence ❷ 强暴的势力 ferocious adversary；brute force；despotic strength：不畏～ defy brute force|铲除～ root out tyranny；eradicate or wipe out a ferocious adversary

【强大】qiángdà (力量)坚强雄厚 powerful；big and powerful；formidable；mighty：～的国家 powerful country or nation|阵容～ have a strong lineup|国力日益～。National power is getting stronger day by day.

【强盗】qiángdào 用暴力抢夺别人财物的人 robber；bandit；person who seizes others' property by force ◇法西斯～ fascist bandits

【强调】qiángdiào 特别着重或着重提出 stress；emphasize；underline；lay stress on：我们～自力更生。We stress self-reliance.|不要～客观原因。Don't overstress objective factors.

【强度】qiángdù ❶ 作用力的大小及声、光、电、磁等的强弱 intensity；degree of acting force and amount of sound, light, electricity, magnetism, etc.：音响～ sound or acoustic intensity|磁场～ intensity of a magnetic field ◇劳动～ intensity of labour；labour-intensive ❷ 物体抵抗外力作用的能力 strength；ability of a substance to resist the action of outside forces：抗震～ shock strength；anti-seismic strength

【强渡】qiángdù 用炮火掩护强行渡过敌人防守的江河 push across a river；force or fight one's way across a river under fire cover

【强风】qiángfēng 气象学上指 6 级风 (meterol.) strong breeze；force 6 wind；☞ 风级 fēngjí on p. 579

【强丐化】qiánggàohuà 〈方 *dail.*〉指用强硬手段索取食物、金钱等的乞丐 beggar who forces people to give him food, money, etc.

【强攻】qiánggōng 用强力攻击；强行进攻 storm；attack violently and force one's way into：～敌营 storm the enemy camp|～篮下，投进一球 (of basketball) score by slam-dunking

【强固】qiánggù 坚固 strong；solid；impregnable：～的工事 strong fortifications|为国家工业化打下～的基础 lay a solid foundation for national industrialization

【强国】qiángguó ❶ 国力强大的国家 powerful nation；strong country；power；country of great national power or strength ❷ 使国家强大 make a nation powerful：～之本在于发展经济。Economic development is fundamental to make a nation powerful.|Economic development is the foundation for making a nation powerful.

【强横】qiánghèng 强硬蛮横不讲理 brutal and unreasonable；tyrannical；overbearing；despotic：～无理 overbearing and unreasonable；unruly|态度～ despotic in attitude；rude and unreasonable

【强化】qiánghuà 加强；使坚强巩固 strengthen；enhance；consolidate；intensify：～记忆 improve one's memory|～训练 accentuated training

【强击机】qiángjījī 用来从低空、超低空对敌方目标强行攻击的飞机 attack plane；plane used to attack low-altitude or minimum-altitude enemy targets；〈旧称 *old*〉冲击机 chōngjījī and 攻击机 gōngjījī

【强加】qiángjiā 强迫人家接受某种意见或作法 impose；force people to accept (a certain view or way of doing things)：～于人 impose (one's views, will, etc.) on others

【强奸】qiángjiān 男子使用暴力与女子性交 rape；violate；defile；(of a male) have forced sex with a female using violence ◇～民意(指统治者把自己的意见强加于人民，硬说成是人民的意见) outrage public opinion；(of rulers) impose their views on the people, asserting them as the people's ideas

【强健】qiángjiàn (身体)强壮 strong and healthy；sturdy：筋骨～ be physically strong|～的体魄 be physically strong；have a strong constitution

【强劲】qiángjìng 强有力的 powerful；forceful；

vigorous：～的对手 powerful opponent｜～的海风 strong wind blowing from the sea

【强力】qiánglì ❶ 强大的力量 great force：～夺取 seize by great force｜～压下自己的感情 suppress one's feelings with a strong will ❷ 物体抵抗外力作用的能力 power of resistance; strength; ability of a substance to resist the action of an outside force：由于纱支改细，纱的～随之下降。As the yarn became thinner, its strength reduced accordingly.

【强梁】qiángliáng 强横；强暴 brutal; violent; ferocious：不畏～ defy brute force; stand in no fear of bullies

【强烈】qiángliè ❶ 极强的；力量很大的 strong; powerful; violent; intense：～的求知欲 yearning for knowledge｜太阳光十分～。The sunlight is very intense. ❷ 鲜明的；程度很高的 striking; intense; keen; sharp：～的对比 sharp or striking contrast｜～的民族感情 keen sense of national feeling ❸ 强硬激烈 strong and vehement：～反对 fiercely or strongly oppose｜～的要求 forceful request

【强弩之末】qiáng nǔ zhī mò《汉书·韩安国传》：'强弩之末，力不能入鲁缟。'强弩射出的箭，到最后力量弱了，连鲁缟(薄绸子)都穿不透。*History of Han · Biography of Han Anguo*: 'An arrow at the end of its flight becomes so weak that it cannot pass through a thin silk fabric.'〈比喻 *fig.*〉很强的力量已经微弱 strong force that has been exhausted

【强权】qiángquán 指对别的国家进行欺压、侵略所凭借的军事、政治、经济的优势地位 power; might; dominant in the military, political and economic power on which a country relies when bullying and oppressing another country：～政治 power politics

【强人】qiángrén ❶ 强有力的人；坚强能干的人 strong man; person who is powerful, strong and capable：经理是一个女～，几年工夫，把企业搞得十分红火。Being a woman of strong character, the manager turned the enterprise into a going concern in a few years. ❷ 强盗(多见于早期白话 oft. in early vernacular) bandit; robber

【强身】qiángshēn 通过体育锻炼或服用药物等使身体强壮 keep fit by physical exercise or taking tonics：～术 way to keep fit｜习武～ keep fit by practising wushu

【强盛】qiángshèng 强大而昌盛(多指国家 oft. of a country) powerful and prosperous

【强手】qiángshǒu 水平高、能力强的人 person of ability and talent

【强似】qiángsì 较胜于；超过 better than; superior to：今年的收成又～去年。The harvest this year is better than last year. also 强如 qiángrú

【强酸】qiángsuān 酸性反应很强烈的酸，腐蚀性很强，在水溶液中能产生大量的氢离子，如硫酸、硝酸、盐酸等。俗称镪水。strong acid; very corrosive acid of strong acidic reaction, which can produce a great deal of hydrogen ions in an aqueous solution, e. g. sulphuric acid, hydrogen nitrate, hydrochloric acid, etc.; popularly known as 镪水 qiāngshuǐ

【强项】[1] qiángxiàng 指实力较强的竞争项目(多指体育运动 usu. of sports) competitive item in which one is strong; game or event in which one is strong

【强项】[2] qiángxiàng〈书 *fml.*〉不肯低头，形容刚强正直不屈服 strong; unyielding; resolute; inflexible

【强心剂】qiángxīnjì 能使心脏肌肉收缩力量增加和心脏搏动次数减慢，从而改进血液循环的药物，如蟾酥、洋地黄等 cardiac stimulant; cardiotonic; medicine that can improve blood circulation by strengthening muscle systolic force and the beats of the heart, e. g. dried venom of toad, digitalis, etc.

【强行】qiángxíng 用强制的方式进行 force; do sth. using coercive methods：～通过 force through｜～登陆 forced landing

【强行军】qiángxíngjūn 部队执行紧急任务时进行的高速行军 forced march; rapid march of troops when carrying out urgent tasks

【强压】qiángyā 用强力压制 suppress; hold down by great force：～怒火 hold back one's anger

【强硬】qiángyìng 强有力的；不肯退让的 strong; tough; unyielding：～的对手 tough opponent｜态度～ unyielding attitude, intransigent attitude; hard-nosed approach

【强占】qiángzhàn ❶ 用暴力侵占 seize; forcibly take; occupy by violence：～地盘 forcibly occupy turf ❷ 用武力攻占 occupy by force of arms：～有利地形 occupy favourable terrain by force of arms

【强直】qiángzhí ❶ 肌肉、关节等由于病变不能活动 rigidity; tetany; (of muscle, joints, etc.) cannot move because of pathologies ❷〈书 *fml.*〉刚强正直 strong-willed and upright

【强制】qiángzhì 用政治或经济力量强迫 force; compel; impel; coerce; force by political or economic strength：～执行 execute by force

【强壮】qiángzhuàng ❶ (身体)结实，有力气 (of a body) strong, robust; sturdy; powerful：～的体魄 of strong build; of robust construction ❷ 使强壮 strengthen; build up：～剂 tonic; roborant｜这药能～病人体质。This medicine can improve patients' health.

墙(墻、牆)

qiáng ❶ 砖、石或土等筑成的屏障或外围 wall; protective screen or periphery built of bricks, stones, earth, etc.：一堵～ a wall｜砖～ brick wall｜土～ earthen wall; wall made of earth｜院～ courtyard wall; wall surrounding a house｜城～ city wall ◇人～ wall of people (as in football games during a free kick); wall;（图见☞ figure for 房子 fáng·zi on p. 550）❷ 器物上像墙或起隔断作用的部分 anything that looks like a wall or serves the purpose of partitioning

【墙报】qiángbào 壁报 wall newspaper

【墙壁】qiángbì same as 墙 qiáng ①

【墙倒众人推】qiáng dǎo zhòng rén tuī〈比喻 *fig.*〉在失势或倒霉时，备受欺负 be browbeaten and bullied in every way when one is out of power or has bad luck

【墙根】qiánggēn（～儿 qiánggēnr）墙的下段跟地面接近的部分 foot of a wall; lower part of a wall that is close to the ground

【墙角】qiángjiǎo 两堵墙相接而形成的角（指角本身，也指它里外附近的地方）corner; corner formed by two walls (including the corner and the surrounding area)

【墙脚】qiángjiǎo ❶ same as 墙根 qiánggēn ❷〈比喻 *fig.*〉基础 foundation; base

【墙裙】qiángqún 加在室内墙壁下半部起装饰和保护作用的表面层，用水泥、瓷砖、木板等材料做成 dado; decorative and protective layer on the surface of the lower part of an indoor wall, made of cement, ceramic tile, boards, etc.; also 护壁 hùbì

【墙头】qiángtóu ❶（～儿 qiángtóur）墙的上部或顶端 top of a wall ❷ 矮而短的围墙 low and short enclosure ❸〈方 *dial.*〉same as 墙 qiáng ①

【墙纸】qiángzhǐ 粘贴在墙壁上起装饰和保护作用的纸 wallpaper; decorative and protective paper pasted on walls; also 壁纸 bìzhǐ

蔷（薔）qiáng［蔷薇］(qiángwēi) ❶ 落叶灌木，茎细长，蔓长，枝上密生小刺，羽状复叶，小叶倒卵形或长圆形，花白色或淡红色，有芳香。果实可入药。rose (*Rosaceae*); deciduous bush with a long, thin stem, long tendrilled vine, small thorns closely covering the branches, pinnately compound leaves, small, inverted oval or oval leaves, and usu. white or light red fragrant flowers, whose fruit can be used as medicine ❷ 这种植物的花 flower of such plant ‖ also 野蔷薇 yěqiángwēi

嫱（嬙）qiáng 古代宫廷里的女官 lady-in-waiting; woman attendant in the courts of ancient China

樯（檣、艢）qiáng〈书 *fml.*〉桅杆 mast: 帆～如林 forest of masts

qiǎng（ㄑㄧㄤˇ）

抢¹（搶）qiǎng ❶ 抢夺；争夺 grab; rob; loot; snatch: ～劫 rob; loot; plunder｜～球 snatch the ball from somebody's hands｜他把书～走了。He snatched the book and made away with it. ❷ 抢先；争先 vie for; compete for; scramble for: ～步上前 rush over｜～着说了几句 vie for a few words｜大家都～着参加义务劳动。All of us vied with each other to take part in voluntary labour. ❸ 赶紧；突击 hurry; rush: ～修 rush to repair; rush-repair; do rush repairs｜～收～种 rush-harvest and rush-plant; harvest and plant in a rush

抢²（搶）qiǎng 刮掉或擦掉物体表面的一层 scrape or scratch the surface layer off an object: 磨剪子～菜刀 sharpen scissors and kitchen knives｜锅底有锅巴，～一～再洗。As the bottom of the pot is covered with rice crust, scrape it before washing.｜摔了一跤，膝盖上～去了一块皮 fall and scrape the skin off one's knees

☞ qiāng on p. 1541

【抢白】qiǎngbái 当面责备或讽刺 tell off; reproach or ridicule sb. to their face

【抢答】qiǎngdá 抢先回答（问题）hurry to answer a question before others; race to be the first to answer a question: 百科知识～比赛 competition to be first to answer questions in all fields

【抢夺】qiǎngduó 用强力把别人的东西夺过来 snatch; wrest; seize; grab. from others by force: ～财物 seize property

【抢购】qiǎnggòu 抢着购买 panic buying; rush to purchase; run on the shops

【抢劫】qiǎngjié 用暴力把别人的东西夺过来，据为己有 rob; loot; plunder; seize others' belongs by violence: ～财物 plunder valuable things｜拦路～ waylay and rob; mug

【抢救】qiǎngjiù 在紧急危险的情况下迅速救护 rescue; save; salvage; rapidly relieve a sick or injured person in a desperate and dangerous situation: ～伤员 rescue a wounded soldier; give first-aid to a wounded soldier｜～危险的堤防 salvage a dangerous dyke

【抢掠】qiǎnglüè 强力夺取（多指财物 usu. of property）loot; sack; plunder; grab; seize by force; take a woman by force and take her for wife

【抢亲】qiǎng//qīn 一种婚姻风俗，男方通过抢劫女子的方式来成亲。也指抢劫妇女成亲。traditional wedding custom by which a man takes a woman for marriage by force; take a woman by force and take her for wife

【抢墒】qiǎngshāng 趁着土壤湿润时赶快播种 lose no time in sowing while the earth is still moist

【抢收】qiǎngshōu 庄稼成熟时，为了避免遭受损害而赶紧突击收割 rush in the harvest; get in the (matured) crops quickly (to avoid harm)

【抢手】qiǎngshǒu（货物等）很受欢迎，人们争先购买 sell like hot cakes; enjoy good sale; (of goods, etc.) be so popular as to be snatched up:～货 goods in short supply; commodities that consumers rush to buy|球赛门票十分～。Tickets for the ball game were going quickly.

【抢先】qiǎng// xiān (～儿 qiǎng// xiānr)赶在别人前头;争先 act before others; forestall; beat; try to be the first to do sth.:～发言 begin to speak before anyone else; try to be the first on the floor|～一步 beat sb. to it|青年人热情高,干什么活儿都爱～儿。Filled with enthusiasm, young people hate to fall behind others in whatever they do.

【抢险】qiǎngxiǎn 发生险情时迅速抢救,以避免或减少损失 rush to deal with an emergency (to avoid or reduce losses):抗洪～ combat a flood and rush to deal with an emergency

【抢修】qiǎngxiū 建筑物、道路、机械等遭到损坏时立即突击修理 rush to repair; rush-repair; do rush repairs; do a crash job of repairing damaged buildings, roads, machines, etc.:～线路 rush to repair the line

【抢占】qiǎngzhàn ❶ 抢先占领 race to seize or occupy:～高地 race to control a highland ❷ 非法占有 occupy illegally; take illegal possession of; squat:～集体财产 illegally take possession of collective property

【抢种】qiǎngzhòng 抓紧时机,突击播种 rush-planting; make the best of the opportunity to rush to sow

【抢嘴】qiǎngzuǐ ❶〈方 *dial.*〉抢先说话 try to get the first chance to speak:按次序发言,谁也别～。Let's take turns speaking instead of trying to talk all at once. ❷ 抢着吃 scramble for food

羟(羥) qiǎng 羟基 hydroxyl (group)

【羟基】qiǎngjī 由氢和氧两种原子组成的一价原子团(—OH) hydroxyl (group); univalent atomic group composed of hydrogen (H) and oxgyen (O) atoms; also 氢氧基 qīngyǎngjī and 氢氧根 qīngyǎnggēn

强(強、彊) qiǎng 勉强 make an effort; strive; try hard; force: ～笑 force a smile; give a forced smile |～辩 try to make a case through false arguments; defend oneself by sophistry|～不知以为知 pretend to know what one does not know

☞ jiàng on p. 964 and qiáng on p. 1543

【强逼】qiǎngbī 强迫 compel; force; coerce:自愿参加,不～ volunteer for an undertaking without any coercion

【强辩】qiǎngbiàn 把没有理的事硬说成有理 try to make a case through false arguments; defend oneself by sophistry; stubbornly asserting sth. unreasonable as reasonable

【强词夺理】qiǎng cí duó lǐ 本来没有理,硬说成有理 use lame arguments; resort to sophistry; reason fallaciously; stubbornly assert sth. unreasonable as reasonable

【强迫】qiǎngpò 施加压力使服从 compel; force; coerce; exert pressure on sb. to make them obey:～命令 command and compel; coercion and commandism; make sb. do sth. by coercion|个人意见不要～别人接受。Don't compel others to accept your personal opinions.

【强求】qiǎngqiú 硬要求 impose; force; insist on:写文章可以有各种风格,不必～一律。Articles can be written in various styles, and it is not necessary to insist on uniformity.

【强人所难】qiǎng rén suǒ nán 勉强别人做为难的事 make sb. do what is difficult for them; try to make sb. do what they won't or can't:他不会唱戏,你偏要他唱,这不是～吗? He does not sing in an opera, yet you insisted on asking him to sing. Aren't you trying to make him do what he can't?

【强使】qiǎngshǐ 施加压力使做某事 compel; force; exert pressure on sb. to make them do sth.:～服从 force or compel sb. to obey

【强颜】qiǎngyán〈书 *fml.*〉勉强做出(笑容) force a smile; put on an air of cheerfulness:～欢笑 try to look cheerful; force a smile on one's face when not in a good mood

镪 qiǎng〈古代 *arch.*〉称成串的钱 string of copper coins

☞ qiāng on p. 1543

襁(繦) qiǎng〈书 *fml.*〉背小孩子用的宽带子 broad belt to carry a baby on the back with

【襁褓】qiǎngbǎo 包裹婴儿的被子和带子 swaddling clothes; quilt and belt to wrap up a baby:母亲历尽辛苦,把他从～中抚育成人。Experiencing all kinds of hardships, his mother brought him up from infancy.

qiàng (ㄑㄧㄤˋ)

呛(嗆) qiàng 有刺激性的气体进入呼吸器官而感觉难受 irritate (respiratory organs); discomfort when an irritating gas enters the respiratory organs:油烟～人。The oil smoke irritated people.|炒辣椒的味儿～得人直咳嗽。The smell of red pepper being fried is so irritating that it makes people cough continuously

☞ qiāng on p. 1541

戗(戧) qiàng ❶ 斜对着墙角的屋架 prop; roof truss obliquely opposite a corner ❷ 支撑柱子或墙壁使免于倾倒的木头 wooden support; piece of wood that supports a pillar or wall to prevent it from falling over ❸ 支撑 prop up; shore up; buttress:用两根木头来～住这堵墙。Buttress the wall with two

logs.
☞ qiāng on p. 1543

【戗面】qiàngmiàn (～儿 qiàngmiànr) ❶ 揉面时,一面揉一面加进干面粉 add dry flour while kneading dough ❷ 揉进了干面粉的发面 leavened dough mixed with flour:～馒头 steamed bread made of leavened dough mixed with flour|～大饼 steamed pancake made of leavened dough mixed with flour

炝(熗) qiàng ❶ 一种烹饪方法,将菜肴放在沸水中略煮,取出后再用酱油、醋等作料来拌 way to cook by boiling meat or vegetables for a while, then dressing with soy sauce, vinegar, etc.:～蛤蜊 boiled and dressed clams|～芹菜 boiled and dressed celery ❷ 一种烹饪方法,先把肉、葱花等用热油略炒,再加作料和水煮 way to cook by frying meat and chopped spring onions quickly in hot oil, and then cooking it with sauce and water:～锅肉丝面 fry meat strips and noodles in hot oil|用葱花儿～～锅 fry chopped spring onions in hot oil (to flavour a dish)

跄(蹌) qiàng [跄踉](qiàngliàng)〈书 *fml.*〉走路不稳 stagger; walk unsteadily; also 踉跄 liàngqiàng and 蹡踉 qiàngliàng
☞ qiāng on p. 1543

蹡(蹡) qiàng [蹡踉] same as 跄踉 qiàngliàng
☞ qiāng on p. 1543

qiāo(ㄑㄧㄠ)

悄 qiāo ☞ below
☞ qiǎo on p. 1551

【悄悄】qiāoqiāo (～儿地 qiānqiāor·di) 没有声音或声音很低;(行动)不让人知道 quietly; on the quiet; secretly; with little or no noise; (of one's movements) without being noticed: 我生怕惊醒了他,～儿地走了出去。I walked out quietly so as not to awaken him.|部队在深夜里～地出了村。The army quietly slipped out of the village at midnight.

【悄悄话】qiāo·qiaohuà 低声说的不让局外人知道的话;私下说的梯己话 whisper in private; words only for one's ears; confidential talk

硗(磽、墝) qiāo ☞ below

【硗薄】qiāobó (土地)坚硬不肥沃;瘠薄 (of land) hard and infertile; barren; unproductive: 田地～ barren field

【硗确】qiāoquè same as 硗薄 qiāobó

雀 qiāo [雀子](qiāo·zi) 雀斑(quèbān) freckles
☞ qiǎo on p. 1551 and què on p. 1602

跷(蹺) qiāo ❶ 抬起(腿);竖起(指头) lift up (a leg); hold up (a finger): 把腿～起来 lift up a leg; with one's legs crossed|～着大拇指 hold up one's thumb ❷ 脚后跟抬起,脚尖着地 on tiptoes; raise one's heels to stand on the toes:～起脚看墙上的布告 stand on tiptoes to read the bulletin on the wall ❸ 高跷 stilts: 登在二尺多高的～上扭秧歌 do a *yangge* dance on stilts over two feet high ❹〈方 *dial.*〉跛(bǒ);瘸 limp; hobble

【跷蹊】qiāo·qi 奇怪;可疑 fishy; suspicious; dubious: 我觉得他说的话有些～。There's something fishy in what he said. also 蹊跷 qīqiāo

【跷跷板】qiāoqiāobǎn 儿童游戏用具,在狭长而厚的木板中间装上轴,再装在支柱上,两端坐人,一起一落游戏 seesaw; children's plaything made of a long, narrow and thick board equipped with a pivot and balaure on a pillar in the middle, allowing a child to sit at either end and play by one end going up while the other goes down

跻(蹻) qiāo same as 跷 qiāo
☞ 屩 juē on p. 1057

锹(鍫) qiāo 铁锹 spade; shovel

劁 qiāo 阉割 geld; castrate:～猪 castrate a pig

敲 qiāo ❶ 在物体上面打,使发出声音 knock; beat; strike; rap:～门 knock at the door|～锣打鼓 beat drums and gongs (in celebration of sth.) ❷ 敲竹杠;敲诈 overcharge; fleece; swindle money out of sb.; force sb. to pay through the nose: 有的商人一听顾客是外乡口音,往往就要～一下子。Some businessmen overcharge customers on discovering that they spoke in different accent.

【敲边鼓】qiāo biāngǔ〈比喻 *fig.*〉从旁帮腔;从旁助势 speak in support of sb.; speak or act to back sb. up; try to assist sb. from the sidelines: 这件事你出马,我给你～。You take care of the matter, while I try to assist you from the sidelines. also 打边鼓 dǎ biāngǔ

【敲打】qiāo·dǎ ❶ same as 敲 qiāo ①: 锣鼓～得很热闹。Drums and gongs were struck boisterously. ❷〈方 *dial.*〉指用言语刺激或批评别人 say sth. to irritate sb.; keep sb. in their place with criticisms: 冷言冷语～人 irritate people with sarcastic comments|我这人缺点很多,往后还得请您常～着点儿。I have many shortcomings, so please criticize me frequently from now on.

【敲定】qiāodìng 确定下来;决定 settle; decide finally; make a final decision: 方案有待最后～。The plan must be finally settled.|这事还得他当场～。This matter has to be decided by him on the spot.

【敲骨吸髓】qiāo gǔ xī suǐ〈比喻 *fig.*〉残酷剥削 cruel, bloodsucking exploitation

【敲门砖】qiāoménzhuān〈比喻 *fig.*〉借以求得名利的初步手段 preliminary ways or means to seek fame and wealth:封建时代的文人常把读书当成～,一旦功名到手,书籍也就被束之高阁了。In feudal times, scholars used to regard study as a stepping stone to officialdom, and would put their books on high shelves upon obtaining official positions.

【敲诈】qiāozhà 依仗势力或用威胁、欺骗手段,索取财物 extort; blackmail; racketeer; shake down; extort others' property by relying on one's power or by threat or fraud

【敲竹杠】qiāo zhúgàng 利用别人的弱点或借某种口实抬高价格或索取财物 fleece; overcharge; make sb. pay through the nose; put the lug on; take advantage of sb.'s weak points or use sth. as a pretext to raise the price or extort other's property

橇 qiāo ❶ 在冰雪上滑行的交通工具,如雪橇 sled; sleigh; sledge; means of transport that slides on ice or snow, e.g. snow sledge ❷〈古时 *arch.*〉在泥路上行走的用具 equipment for walking on a muddy road

幧 qiāo [幧头](qiāotóu)〈古代 *arch.*〉男子束发的头巾 head-covering for men in ancient China to tie their hair up; also 帩头 qiàotóu

缲(幓) qiāo 缝纫方法,做衣服边儿或带子时把布边儿往里头卷进去,然后藏着针脚缝 hem with invisible stitches; method of hemming the edges of clothes or belts by rolling in the edges of cloth to hide the stitches:～边儿 hem the edges

☞ 缫 sāo on p.1658

qiáo (ㄑㄧㄠˊ)

乔¹(喬) qiáo ❶ 高 tall:～木 arbour; tree ❷(Qiáo) 姓 a surname

乔²(喬) qiáo 假(扮) disguise; pretend to be:～装 disguise; simulate; dress up

【乔木】qiáomù 树干高大,主干和分枝有明显的区别的木本植物,如松、柏、杨、白桦等 arbor; tree; woody plant with a tall trunk that is obviously different from its branches, e.g. pine, cypress, poplar, white birch, etc.

【乔其纱】qiáoqíshā 一种有细微均匀皱纹的丝织品,薄而透明,多用来做窗帘、舞裙、夏季妇女衣服等 georgette; silk fabric with fine and even wrinkles, thin and transparent, usu. used to make curtains, dance skirts, summer clothes for women, etc. [法 French: crêpegeorgette]

【乔迁】qiáoqiān《诗经·小雅·伐木》:'出自幽谷,迁于乔木。'〈比喻 *fig.*〉人搬到好的地方去住或官职高升(多用于祝贺) according to *The Book of Songs·Odes·Lumbering*: '(of chirping birds) Flying from the depth of a vale,/ And moving to tall trees.' (usu. term of congratulations) move to a better place; get a promotion; be transferred to a higher post:～之喜 housewarming celebration; joy of moving into a new residence

【乔装】qiáozhuāng 改换服装以隐瞒自己的身份 disguise; simulate; dress up; change one's clothes to conceal one's true identity:～打扮 disguise; dress up; masquerade; deck oneself out as sb.

侨(僑) qiáo ❶ 侨居 live abroad; reside in a foreign country:～民 national of a particular country residing abroad|～胞 countrymen or nationals living abroad ❷ 侨民 person living abroad; national residing in a foreign country:华～ Chinese nationals living abroad; overseas Chinese|外～ foreign residents; aliens; expatriates

【侨胞】qiáobāo 侨居国外的同胞 countrymen or nationals living abroad

【侨汇】qiáohuì 侨民汇回国内的款项 overseas remittance; remittance from nationals living abroad

【侨居】qiáojū 在外国居住,古代也指在外乡居住 live abroad; (in ancient China) reside in a strange land:～海外 reside abroad; sojourn in a foreign land

【侨眷】qiáojuàn 指侨民在国内的家眷 relatives of nationals living abroad who remain in the homeland

【侨民】qiáomín 住在外国而保留本国国籍的居民 national of a particular country residing abroad

【侨务】qiáowù 有关侨民的事务 affairs concerning nationals living abroad:～工作 work on affairs concerning nationals living abroad

荞(蕎) qiáo [荞麦](qiáomài) ❶ 一年生草本植物,茎略带红色,叶互生,三角状心脏形,有长柄,总状花序,花白色或淡粉红色,瘦果三角形,有棱,子实磨成粉供食用 buckwheat (*Fagopyrum* spp.); annual herb with a slightly red stem, triangular heart-shaped and long-stemmed alternate leaves, raceme, white or light pink flowers, triangular edged achenes, and seeds that are edible when ground into flour ❷ 这种植物的子实 seed of such plant

荍 qiáo ❶ 古书上指锦葵 high mallow in ancient books ❷ same as 荞 qiáo

峤(嶠) qiáo 〈书 *fml.*〉山尖而高 (of mountains) high and pointed

☞ jiào on p.980

桥(橋) qiáo ❶ same as 桥梁 qiáoliáng ① bridge:一座～ a bridge|木～ wooden or plank bridge|石～ stone bridge|铁～ iron bridge ❷(Qiáo) 姓 a surname

【桥洞】qiáodòng (～儿 qiáodòngr) same as 桥孔 qiáokǒng

【桥墩】qiáodūn 桥梁下面的墩子,用石头或混凝土等做成（bridge）pier；block under a bridge，made of stones，concrete，etc.

【桥涵】qiáohán 桥梁和涵洞的合称 bridges and culverts

【桥孔】qiáokǒng 桥梁下面的孔 bridge opening；archway in a bridge；opening under a bridge

【桥梁】qiáoliáng ❶ 架在水面上或空中以便行人、车辆等通行的建筑物 bridge；structure built across water or in the air to provide passage for pedestrians，vehicles，etc. ❷〈比喻 *fig.*〉能起沟通作用的人或事物 bridge；person or thing that serves as a link：～作用 play the role of a bridge；serve as a link

Q

【桥牌】qiáopái 一种扑克牌游戏。四个人分两组对抗，按规则叫牌、出牌，以得分多的一方为胜。这种牌戏，英语称为 bridge，语源不明，拼法跟作'桥'讲的 bridge 相同，汉译误解为'桥'。bridge；card game for four players who play in pairs，bidding or playing according to the rules，in which the party scoring more points is victorious；called 'bridge' in English，etymology unknown，though its spelling is the same as 'bridge'. Hence the mistranslation in Chinese，*qiao*，meaning 'bridge'.

【桥头】qiáotóu 桥两头和岸接连的地方 either end of a bridge（connected with the banks）

【桥头堡】qiáotóubǎo ❶ 为控制重要桥梁、渡口而设立的碉堡、地堡或据点 bridgehead；pillbox，bunker and strongpoint to control an important bridge or ferry ❷ 设在大桥桥头的像碉堡的装饰建筑物 bridge tower；decorative structure built on either end of a bridge that resembles a pillbox ❸ 泛指作为进攻的据点（gen.）strongpoint for attacks

【桥堍】qiáotù 桥头 either end of a bridge

硚（礄） qiáo 地名用字 used in place names：～头（在四川）e. g. Qiaotou，in Sichuan Province｜～口（在汉口）Qiaokou，in Hankou，a district of Wuhan

盉（盉） qiáo〈古代 *arch.*〉碗一类的器皿 container similar to a bowl

翘（翹） qiáo ❶ 抬起（头）raise or lift up（one's head）：～首 raise or lift up one's head and look；crane one's neck ❷（木、纸等）平的东西因由湿变干而不平（of wood，paper，etc.）become warped or bent（when drying）

☞ qiào on p. 1552

【翘楚】qiáochǔ〈书 *fml.*〉〈比喻 *fig.*〉杰出的人才 outstanding（or talented）person；person of outstanding ability

【翘棱】qiáo·leng〈方 *dial.*〉same as 翘 qiáo②

【翘企】qiáoqǐ〈书 *fml.*〉翘首企足，形容盼望殷切 raise one's head and stand on tiptoes — eagerly look forward to：不胜～ look forward to sth. with eager anticipation

【翘首】qiáoshǒu〈书 *fml.*〉抬起头来望 raise or lift up one's head and look；crane one's neck：～瞻仰 look up at sth. reverentially｜～星空 look up at the starry sky｜～故国 look up at the sky in the direction of one's native land

【翘望】qiáowàng ❶ 抬起头来望 raise or lift up one's head to look at sth. ❷ 殷切盼望 look forward to sth. eagerly；expect：观众～已久的电影周下月初在北京开幕。The long-anticipated film week will start in Beijing at the beginning of next month.

谯 qiáo ❶ 谯楼 watchtower；drum tower ❷（Qiáo）姓 a surname

☞ 诮 qiào on p. 1552

【谯楼】qiáolóu〈书 *fml.*〉❶ 城门上的瞭望楼 watchtower（on a city gate）❷ 鼓楼 drum tower

鞒（鞽） qiáo 马鞍上拱起的部分 pommel and cantle of a saddle；saddle bow；arched part of a saddle

蕉 qiáo［蕉萃］（qiáocuì）same as 憔悴 qiáocuì

☞ jiāo on p. 973

憔 qiáo［憔悴］（qiáocuì）形容人瘦弱，面色不好看 haggard；pining away；wan and sallow；thin and pallid：她病了一场，显得～多了。She looked much more haggard after falling ill. also 顦顇 qiáocuì

樵 qiáo ❶ 柴 firewood：砍～ cut firewood ❷〈书 *fml.*〉打柴 gather firewood：～夫 woodman；woodcutter｜渔～ fishing and cutting wood

瞧 qiáo 看 look；see；watch：～见 see；notice；catch sight of｜～书 read a book｜～病（of a patient）see or consult a doctor｜～热闹 watch the fun；be an onlooker in a dispute，quarrel，fight，etc.；look on with folded arms｜～一～ take a look｜他～亲戚去了。He went to visit his relative.

【瞧不起】qiáo·bu qǐ 看不起 look down upon；despise；turn up one's nose at；have no regard for；hold in contempt

【瞧得起】qiáo·de qǐ 看得起 think much or highly of；look up to；have high regard for；see much in

【瞧见】qiáo//·jiàn 看见 see；notice；catch sight of：瞧得见 visible；noticeable；tangible｜瞧不见 invisible；unnoticeable；intangible｜他～光荣榜上有自己的名字。He saw his name on the honour roll.

顦 qiáo［顦顇］（qiáocuì）same as 憔悴 qiáocuì

qiǎo（ㄑㄧㄠˇ）

巧 qiǎo ❶ 心思灵敏，技术高明 skilful；ingenious；clever：～干 work ingeniously；do sth. cleverly | 能工～匠 skilful craftsman; skilful worker and ingenious artisan | 他的手艺很～。His workmanship is excellent. ❷ (手、口)灵巧 (of sb.'s hand or tongue) clever; deft; glib: 心灵手～ be clever and deft; have a lively mind and a quick hand | 他嘴～,学谁像谁。With his glib tongue, he could imitate anyone. ❸ 恰好;正遇在某种机会上 accidentally; luckily; opportunely; coincidentally: 恰～ by chance; as chance would have it | 偏～ it so happens; as luck would have it | 凑～ luckily; fortunately; as luck would have it | ～遇 run into sb. by accident; encounter by chance | 来得真～ arrive at a most opportune moment | 我一出大门就碰到他,真～极了。As luck would have it, I ran into him just as I walked out of the gate. ❹ 虚浮不实的(话)(of words) cunning; sly; artful; deceitful; fine-sounding: 花言～语 fine words; fine-sounding words; honeyed words

【巧夺天工】qiǎo duó tiān gōng 精巧的人工胜过天然,形容技艺极其精巧 superb or wonderful workmanship surpassing nature; so wonderful in workmanship as to surpass nature; superb craftsmanship: 象牙雕刻的人物花鸟,生动活泼,～。The ivory carvings of figures, flowers and birds are crafted as if by the invisible hands of god.

【巧妇难为无米之炊】qiǎo fù nán wéi wú mǐ zhī chuī 没有米,再能干的妇女也做不出饭 'the cleverest housewife can't cook a meal without rice';〈比喻 *fig*.〉缺少必要的条件,再能干的人也很难做成事 even the most capable person can hardly fulfill sth. without the necessary conditions

【巧合】qiǎohé (事情)凑巧相合或相同 coincidence; by chance or coincidence: 他们俩同年,生日又是同一天,真是～。It is sheer coincidence that they were both born on the same day of the same year.

【巧计】qiǎojì 巧妙的计策 clever device; artful scheme; smart trick; artifice

【巧匠】qiǎojiàng 工艺技术高明的人 fine craftsman; skilled worker; person of high workmanship: 能工～ skilful craftsman; skilful worker and ingenious artisan

【巧劲儿】qiǎngjìnr〈方 *dial*.〉❶ 巧妙的手法 clever method; trick: 常常练习,慢慢就找着～了。You'll learn the trick through frequent practice. ❷ 凑巧的事 coincidence: 我正找他,他就来了,真是～。What a coincidence! He showed up just when I was looking for him.

【巧克力】qiǎokèlì 以可可粉为主要原料,再加上白糖、香料制成的食品 chocolate; food made of cocoa (the major raw ingredient), sugar and flavouring

【巧立名目】qiǎo lì míngmù 定出许多名目,以达到某种不正当的目的 invent all sorts of names — concoct various excuses; devise a variety of titles to achieve some unjustifiable purpose

【巧妙】qiǎomiào (方法或技术等)灵巧高明,超过寻常的 (of methods or skills, etc.) ingenious; clever; smart: 构思～ ingeniously conceived | ～的计策 smart scheme; crafty strategy | ～地运用比喻,可以使语言生动活泼。Language can be enlivened by the ingenious use of metaphors.

【巧取豪夺】qiǎo qǔ háo duó 用欺诈的手段取得或凭强力夺取(财物、权利) (of property and rights) obtain by cheating or by force; obtain by trickery or seize by force

【巧言令色】qiǎo yán lìng sè 指用花言巧语和假装和善来讨好别人 clever talk and ingratiating manner; pleasing words and smooth manners; be hypocritical; try to please others with sweet words in a false kind and gentle manner (令 *ling*: 美好 pleasant)

【巧遇】qiǎoyù 凑巧遇到 encounter by chance; run into sb. by accident: 抵达云南的当天,～泼水节。It happened to be the time of the Water-Sprinkling Festival when we arrived at Yunnan Province.

悄 qiǎo ❶ 没有声音或声音很低 quiet; silent; with little or no noise: ～声 quietly; softly; whisper ❷〈书 *fml*.〉忧愁 sad; worried; grieved

☞ qiāo on p. 1548

【悄寂】qiǎojì 寂静无声 quiet; silent; noiseless: 山野～ tranquil mountain scene

【悄然】qiǎorán ❶ 形容忧愁的样子 sad; worried; sorrowful; grieved: ～落泪 shed tears sadly; shed tears in sorrow ❷ 形容寂静无声 quietly; softly; noiselessly

【悄声】qiǎoshēng 没有声音或声音很低 quietly; softly; in a low voice; with little or no noise: ～细语 speak gently; speak in a soft, low voice | 他蹑手蹑脚,～走进房间。Walking gingerly, he entered the room quietly.

雀 qiǎo 义同'雀'què,用于'家雀儿、雀盲眼' sparrow; word that has a similar meaning to 雀 què, used in terms such as 家雀儿 jiāqiǎor and 雀盲眼 qiǎo·mangyǎn

☞ qiāo on p. 1548 and què on p. 1602

【雀盲眼】qiǎo·mangyǎn〈方 *dial*.〉夜盲 night blindness; nyctalopia

愀 qiǎo [愀然](qiǎorán)〈书 *fml*.〉形容神色严肃或不愉快 look stern or grieved: ～作色 turn stern | ～不悦 look displeased

qiào (ㄑㄧㄠˋ)

壳(殼) qiào 坚硬的外皮 shell; crust; hard outer covering of sth.: 甲～

crust|地～ earth's crust|金蝉脱～ cicada sloughs off its skin — make a strategic escape; escape by cunning manoeuvres
☞ ké on p.1091

【壳菜】qiàocài 贻贝(生活在浅海岩石上的带壳软体动物)。通常指贻贝的肉。mussel(*Mytilidae*); mollusk with a shell that lives on rocks by a shallow sea; usu. refers to the meat of such a creature

【壳斗】qiàodǒu 某些植物果实特有的一种外壳,如包在栗子外面的有刺硬壳 cupule; special shell that some plants have, e.g. the hard, prickled shell of chestnut

俏 qiào ❶ 俊俏;样子好看;动作灵活 pretty; handsome; good-looking; smart; dexterous and quick to act: 打扮得真～ be smartly dressed|走着～步儿 have a mincing gait ❷ 指货物的销路好 sell like hot cakes; sell well; be saleable; be in great demand: ～货 goods that sell well; commodities in great demand|行情看～。The market is going strong. ❸〈方 *dial.*〉烹调时加上(俏头) seasoning; season a dish when cooking: ～点儿韭菜 season a dish with leeks

【俏货】qiàohuò 畅销的商品 goods that sell well; commodities in great demand

【俏丽】qiàolì 俊俏美丽 handsome; pretty; charming: 容貌～ look pretty or handsome

【俏皮】qiào·pi ❶ 容貌或装饰好看 (of sb.'s features or decorations) beautiful; handsome; stylish; smart ❷ 举止活泼或谈话有风趣 lively (manners); witty (talk): ～话 witty remark; witticism; wisecrack

【俏皮话】qiào·pihuà (～儿 qiào·pihuàr) ❶ 含讽刺口吻的或开玩笑的话 wisecrack; sarcastic or ironical remark; joking words ❷ 歇后语 two-part allegorical saying, with the first part describing the situation and the second part (oft. implied) carrying the message

【俏式】qiào·shi〈方 *dial.*〉俊俏 pretty; handsome; charming

【俏头】qiào·tou ❶ 烹调时为增加滋味或色泽而附加的东西,如香菜、青蒜、木耳、辣椒等 seasoning; things added when cooking dishes to improve their tastes or colour and lustre, e.g. coriander, garlic shoots, edible black fungus, hot pepper ❷ 戏曲、评书中引人喜爱的身段、道白或穿插 tidbits (e.g. crowd-pleasing postures, spoken parts or interludes in operas and storytelling)

诮(譙) qiào〈书 *fml.*〉❶ 责备 blame; reproach; censure: ～呵 rebuke; reproach; reprove ❷ 讥讽 sneer at; deride: 讥～ criticize sarcastically; jeer at sb.
☞ 谯 qiáo on p.1550

【诮呵】qiàohē〈书 *fml.*〉责备;呵斥 rebuke; reproach; reprove: ～之词 reproachful remarks

峭(陗) qiào ❶ 山势又高又陡 (of mountains) high and steep; precipitous; abrupt: ～立 rise steeply|陡～ sheer; precipitous ❷〈比喻 *fig.*〉严厉 severe; stern; harsh: ～直 strict; stern; severe

【峭拔】qiàobá ❶ (山)高而陡 (of mountains) high and steep; precipitous: 山势～ high and precipitous mountains ❷ 形容文笔雄健 (of writing style) vigorous; robust: 笔锋～刚劲 write in a forceful and vigorous style

【峭壁】qiàobì 陡直的山崖 cliff; steep; precipice; sheer cliff: 悬崖～ sheer precipices and overhanging rocks; cliffs and precipices

【峭立】qiàolì 陡立 rise steeply: ～的山峰 steep peak|岩石～。Rocks jut out steeply.

【峭直】qiàozhí〈书 *fml.*〉严峻刚直 stern; strict; severe; upright and outspoken: 秉性～ be stern or severe by nature

帩 qiào [帩头](qiàotóu)〈古代 *arch.*〉男子束发的头巾 head-covering of men to tie up their hair; also 幧头 qiāotóu

窍(竅) qiào ❶ 窟窿 aperture; orifice: 七～ seven orfices (of the head, i.e., the eyes, ears, nostrils, and mouth) ❷〈比喻 *fig.*〉事情的关键 key to sth.; knack: 诀～ knack; trick|～门儿 key (to a problem); knack; trick|一～不通 be utterly ignorant of something

【窍门】qiàomén (～儿 qiàoménr) 能解决困难问题的好方法 key (to a problem); knack; trick; good method to solve a difficult problem: 开动脑筋找～ use one's brains or head to try to find the key to a problem (or try to get the knack of doing something)

偢 qiào〈方 *dial.*〉傻 stupid; foolish
☞ chǒu on p.279

翘(翹、蹺) qiào 一头儿向上仰起 hold up; stick out; curl up; (of one end) turn or bend upwards: 板凳没放稳,这头儿一压,那头儿就往上一～。The bench is unsteady, so one end turn upwards when the other is pressed.
☞ qiáo on p.1550

【翘辫子】qiào biàn·zi 死 (含讥笑或诙谐意 sarcastic or humor.) die; drop dead: 袁世凯做皇帝没几天就～了。Yuan Shikai had just taken the throne when he kicked the bucket.

【翘尾巴】qiào wěi·ba〈比喻 *fig.*〉骄傲自大 cocky; haughty and snooty

撬 qiào 把棍棒或刀、锥等的一头插入缝中或孔中,用力扳(或压)另一头 prize; pry; jimmy; insert one end of a stick, knife or an awl, etc., into a seam or hole, while pulling (or pressing) the other end with strength: ～石头 pry up a stone|～起箱子盖 prize or pry open the cover of a case|钥匙丢了,只好把门～开。As the key was lost, we had to prize the door open.

【撬杠】qiàogàng 一端锻成扁平状的铁棍,用来撬起或移动重物 crowbar; pinch bar; ripping bar; iron bar forged into a flat shape, used to pry up or move heavy things

鞘 qiào 装刀剑的套子 sheath; scabbard; cover of a knife or sword: 剑～ sword sheath|刀出～ unsheathe a knife;
☞ shāo on p.1689

【鞘翅】qiàochì 叩头虫、金龟子等昆虫的前翅,质地坚硬,静止时,覆盖在膜质的后翅上,好像鞘一样 elytrum; hard fore-wing of a click beetle, scarab, etc., that covers a membranous hindwing resembling a sheath when it is still; also 翅鞘 chìqiào

撽 qiào 〈书 *fml.*〉从旁边敲打 beat from the sides

躈 qiào 〈书 *fml.*〉牲畜的肛门 anus of an animal

qiē (ㄑ丨ㄝ)

切 qiē ❶ 用刀把物品分成若干部分 cut; slice; chop; divide a thing into several parts with a knife: 把瓜～开 slice up a melon |把肉～成肉丝儿 shred meat◇～断敌军退路 cut off the enemy's retreat ❷ 直线、圆或面等与圆、弧或球只有一个交点时叫做切 tangency; single point of intersection of a straight line, circle or plane, etc., with a circle, arc or sphere
☞ qiè on p.1554

【切除】qiēchú 用外科手术把身体上发生病变的部分切掉 remove; resect; excise; cut off a pathological part of one's body through a surgical operation: ～肿瘤 remove a tumour| 他最近做了一次外科～手术。He recently had a surgical appendectomy.

【切磋】qiēcuō 切磋琢磨 carve and polish — learn from each other by exchanging views; compare notes: ～学问 compare notes when studying

【切磋琢磨】qiē cuō zhuó mó 〈古代 *arch.*〉把骨头加工成器物叫'切',把象牙加工成器物叫'磋',把玉加工成器物叫'琢',把石头加工成器物叫'磨' processing bones into a utensil was called 切 qiē; 磋 cuō, processing ivory; 琢 zhuó, processing jade; and 磨 mó, processing stone; 〈比喻 *fig.*〉互相商量研究,学习长处,纠正缺点 learn from each other by comparing notes in order to redress one's shortcomings

【切点】qiēdiǎn 直线与圆、直线与球、圆与圆、平面与球或球与球相切的交点 point of tangency; point of contact; point of intersection of a straight line and a circle or sphere, two circles, a plane and a sphere, or two spheres

【切割】qiēgē ❶ 用刀等把物品截断 cut; carve up; cut off sth. using a knife ❷ 利用机床切断或利用火焰、电弧烧断金属材料 cut; cut through metal objects using a machine tool, flame or electric torch; also 割切 gēqiē

【切花】qiēhuā 从植株上剪下供瓶养或装饰等用的花枝 cut flowers off a plant for cultivation in a bottle or as decoration, etc.: 鲜～ freshly cut flowers|一束～ a bouquet of cut flowers

【切汇】qiēhuì 指在外汇黑市交易中,买进外汇的人用手法骗过卖主,暗中扣下一部分应付的钱 (of a person who deals in foreign exchange) secretly deduct a sum of money payable by deceit and fraud in black market deals involving foreign exchange

【切口】qiēkǒu 书页裁切一边的空白处 margin; blank spot on the cut side of a book page
☞ qièkǒu on p.1554

【切面】[1] qiēmiàn 切成的面条 cut noodles; machine-made noodles

【切面】[2] qiēmiàn ❶ 剖面 section ❷ 和球面只有一个交点的平面叫做球的切面;只包含圆柱、圆锥的一条母线的平面叫做圆柱或圆锥的切面 tangent plane; plane that has a single point of intersection with a spherical surface; plane that contains a single generatrix of a cylinder or circular cone

【切片】qiē//piàn 把物体切成薄片 slice; cut sth. into slices

【切片】qiēpiàn 用特制的刀具把生物体的组织或矿物切成的薄片。切片用来在显微镜下进行观察和研究。section; slice of a tissue of an organism or mineral cut with a special cutting tool, used for observation and study under a microscope

【切线】qiēxiàn 平面内和圆只有一个交点的直线叫做圆的切线;和球面只有一个交点的直线叫做球的切线 tangent (line); straight line that has a single point of intersection with a circle on a plane or a spherical surface

【切削】qiēxiāo 利用机床的刀具或砂轮等削去作件的一部分,使作件具有一定形状、尺寸和表面光洁度 cut; cutting; cut a part of sth. with the cutting tool, grinding wheel, etc., of a machine tool to make a regular shape and size and a smooth finish

qié (ㄑ丨ㄝˊ)

伽 qié ☞ below
☞ gā on p.618 and jiā on p.926

【伽蓝】qiélán 佛寺 Buddhist temple [僧伽蓝摩之省,梵 Sanskrit: saṃghārāma]

【伽南香】qiénánxiāng 沉香 agalloch eaglewood (*Aquilaria agallocha*)

茄 qié 茄子 eggplant (*Solanum melongena*); aubergine: 拌～泥 mashed eggplant (a cold dish)

☞ jiā on p. 926

【茄子】qié·zi ❶ 一年生草本植物,叶椭圆形,花紫色。果实球形或长圆形,紫色,有的白色或浅绿色,表面有光泽,是普通蔬菜 eggplant (*Solanum melongena*); aubergine; annual herb that has oval leaves, purple flowers, spherical or oval fruit that are purple, white or light green, with a surface lustre, used as a common vegetable ❷ 这种植物的果实 fruit of such a plant

qiě (ㄑㄧㄝˇ)

且[1] qiě ❶ 暂且;姑且 just; for the time being; for a while: ～慢 wait a minute; hold it; not go or do so soon | 你～等一下。Just a minute. ❷〈方 *dial.*〉表示经久 for a long time; for quite some time: 买枝钢笔～使呢。Buy a pen that will last you quite some time. | 他要一说话,～完不了呢。Once he starts talking, it will be quite a while before he stops. ❸(Qiě) 姓 a surname

且[2] qiě〈书 *fml.*〉〈连词 *conj.*〉❶ 尚且 even: 死～不怕,困难又算什么? Since even death holds no fear for us, hardship is nothing. | 君～如此,况他人乎? If even you are in this frame of mind, how can I expect more of others? ❷ 并且;而且 and; also; both ... and ...: 既高～大 both tall and big

☞ jū on p. 1043

【且慢】qiěmàn 暂时慢着(含阻止意 implying prevention) wait a minute; hold on; don't go (or do) so soon: ～,听我把话说完。Wait a minute, let me finish what I have to say. *or* Wait a minute, please hear me out.

【且…且…】qiě…qiě… 分别用在两个动词前面,表示两个动作同时进行[used before two verbs respectively to indicate two simultaneous actions] while; as: ～谈～走 talk while walking | ～战～退 carry on fighting while retreating

【且说】qiěshuō〈旧 *old.*〉小说中的发语词 [used in old Chinese novels] let's begin with

qiè (ㄑㄧㄝˋ)

切 qiè ❶ 合;符合 correspond to; conform to or with; accord with: 文章～题。The article keeps to the point. | 说话不～实际 unrealistic or impractical speech; one's talk does not correspond to reality ❷ 贴近;亲近 close to; warm: ～身 of immediate concern or interest to oneself | 亲～ warm; kind; affectionate ❸ 急切;殷切 eager; keen; anxious: 迫～ urgent; pressing; imperative; compelling | 恳～ sincere and earnest | 回国心～ eager to be home; anxious to return to one's native land ❹ 切实;务必: must; have to: ～记 be sure to remember | ～忌 avoid by all means | ～不可骄傲。One must not be conceited. ❺ 用在反切后头,表示前两字是注音用的反切。如'塑,桑故切'。used after 反切 fǎnqiè, a Chinese way of pronunciation in which two preceding characters indicate the pronunciation of a given character (e.g. the pronunciation of 塑 sù is indicated as 桑故切 sānggùqiè, i.e., the combination of the consonant s in 桑 sāng and the vowel u in 故 gù); ☞ 反切 fǎnqiè on p. 538

☞ qiē on p. 1553

【切齿】qièchǐ 咬紧牙齿,形容非常愤恨 grind one's teeth; gnash one's teeth; hate bitterly: ～痛恨 grind one's teeth in hatred; nurture a bitter hatred

【切当】qièdàng 恰当 suitable; proper; appropriate; to the point: 用词～ use a proper word; use the right word in the right place; be properly worded

【切肤之痛】qiè fū zhī tòng 切身感受到的痛苦 keenly felt pain; agony; acute pain

【切骨之仇】qiè gǔ zhī chóu 形容极深的仇恨 bitter enmity; strongly felt hatred; profound animosity

【切合】qièhé 十分符合 suit; fit in with; correspond to; accord with: ～实际 fit in with the reality; be practical; suit the actual condition of

【切记】qièjì 牢牢记住 keep firmly in mind; be sure to remember; must always remember: 遇事～要冷静。When something unexpected happens, you must always remember not to panic.

【切忌】qièjì 切实避免或防止 must guard against; avoid by all means; must not do in any circumstance: ～滋长骄傲情绪。Be careful to avoid becoming conceited.

【切近】qièjìn ❶ 贴近;靠近 near; nearby: 远大的事业要从～处做起。A great cause must begin with what is ordinary and close by. *or* A grand undertaking always has a humble beginning. ❷ (情况)相近;接近 similar; close to: 这样注解比较～原作之意。The explanatory note seems to be closer to the meaning of the original work.

【切口】qièkǒu 帮会或某些行业中的暗语 jargon; cant; password; secret language of underground gangs or some trades

☞ qiēkǒu on p. 1553

【切脉】qièmài〈中医 *Chin. med.*〉指诊脉 feel the pulse

【切末】qiè·mo 戏曲舞台上所用的简单布景和大小道具。名称起于元曲,原作砌末。simple stage property; simple settings and props of various sizes used on opera stages, originating from 砌末 qiè·mo in Yuan opera

【切切】qièqiè ❶ 千万;务必(多用于书信中 used mostly in letters) be sure to; must (do):～不可忘记 be sure not to forget ❷ 用于布告、条令等末尾,表示叮咛 used at the end of a public notice, regulation, etc., to express exhortation or warning:～此布。This notice is to be regarded in all seriousness. ❸ 恳切;迫切 eagerly; earnestly; imperatively:～请求 request earnestly ❹ same as 窃窃 qièqiè ①

【切身】qièshēn ❶ 跟自己有密切关系的 of immediate concern or interest to oneself:～利益 one's immediate or vital interests|这事跟我有～关系。This matter is of immediate concern to me. ❷ 亲身 personal:～体验 one's own or personal experience|他说的是个人～的体会。He talked about his intimate knowledge.

【切实】qièshí 切合实际;实实在在 down-to-earth; practical; realistic; in earnest:～可行 feasible; workable; realistic or practical|～改正 correct (one's mistakes) in real earnest|切切实实地做好工作 do one's job in a down-to-earth way

【切题】qiètí 切合题目,没有离题 keep to the point; be relevant to the subject; stick to the topic; be related to the topic under discussion

【切要】qièyào 十分必要;紧要 vital; essential; indispensable:～的知识 essential knowledge|眼前～解决的是原材料问题。For the time being raw materials are a problem that cries for a solution.

【切音】qièyīn 用两字拼成另一个字的音 use two Chinese characters to represent the pronunciation of a third character; ☞ 反切 fǎnqiè on p. 538

【切中】qièzhòng (言论或办法)正好击中(某种弊病) hit (the mark); (of an opinion or a method) happen to hit (some vulnerable point):～要害 strike home; hit the nail on the head; hit the mark|～时弊 strike hard at current social evils; criticize the ills of society sharply

郄 Qiè 姓 a surname
〈古 *arch.*〉same as 郤 xì

妾 qiè ❶〈旧时 *old*〉男子在妻子以外娶的女子 concubine; woman married to a man after his first wife ❷〈古时 *arch.*〉女子谦称自己 used by women in humble reference to themselves

怯 qiè ❶ 胆小;害怕 timid; cowardly; nervous; chicken-hearted:胆～timid; cowardly|～场 have stage fright ❷(贬称)北京人贬称外地方音(指北方各省)(derog.) used by people in Beijing to refer to all other northern dialects:他说话有点儿～。He speaks with a northern accent. ❸〈方 *dial.*〉不大方,不合时;俗气 inelegant; outmoded; vulgar:这两种颜色配起来显得～。The two colours look gaudy when mixed together. ❹〈方 *dial.*〉缺乏知识;浅薄 lacking in knowledge; shallow; superficial:露～ reveal one's inadequacies; cut a poor figure

【怯场】qiè//chǎng 在人多的场面上发言、表演等,因紧张害怕而神态举动不自然 have stage fright; fail to look or act naturally due to nervousness or fright when giving a speech or performance, etc., in front of many people

【怯懦】qiènuò 胆小怕事 timid and overcautious; weak and cowardly:生性～ timid and overcautious by nature

【怯弱】qièruò 胆小软弱 timid and weak-willed; chicken-hearted:～女子 chicken-hearted woman

【怯生】qièshēng〈方 *dial.*〉见到不熟识的人有些害怕和不自然;怕生 shy with strangers; timid and diffident in the presence of strangers:孩子～,客人一抱他就哭。Shy with strangers, the baby cries the moment it finds itself in the arms of a stranger.

【怯生生】qièshēngshēng (～的 qièshēngshēng·de)形容胆怯畏缩的样子 shy and timid; nervous

【怯声怯气】qiè shēng qiè qì 形容说话时带有胆小和不自然的语气 lumpish; talk timidly and nervously; (speak) in a timid and unnatural tone:他说话～的。He speaks nervously.

【怯阵】qiè//zhèn 临阵胆怯,也借指怯场 feel nervous right before going into battle; be battle-shy; have stage fright:初次出战,有点～。Seeing action for the first time, he was a bit battle-shy.

砌 qiè [砌末] (qiè·mo) ☞ 切末 qiè·mo on p. 1554
☞ qì on p. 1525

窃(竊) qiè ❶ 偷 steal; pilfer; pinch:行～ steal; practice theft|～案 burglary; case of theft ◇～国大盗 arch-usurper of state power ❷ 偷偷地 secretly; stealthily; surreptitiously; furtively:～笑 laugh secretly; laugh up one's sleeve|～听 eavesdrop; bug; wiretap ❸〈书 *fml.*〉〈谦 *hum.*〉指自己(意见) used to refer to oneself (or one's own opinion):～谓 I would like to say|～以为不可。In my humble opinion, this won't work.

【窃案】qiè'àn 偷窃的案件 burglary; case of theft

【窃夺】qièduó 用非法手段夺取;窃取 usurp; grab; steal; seize by illegal means

【窃国】qièguó 篡夺国家政权 usurp state power; seize supreme power by force or wiles

【窃据】qièjù 用不正当手段占据(土地、职位) usurp; seize; unjustly or illegally occupy (land or posts)：～高位 occupy a high position|～要津 unjustly occupy a high post; usurp an important post

【窃密】qiè//mì 盗窃机密 steal secret information

【窃窃】qièqiè ❶ 形容声音细小 in a soft voice; whispering：～私语 whisper; talk privately or secretly; speak in a subdued voice; also 切切 qièqiè ❷ 暗地里 in secret; stealthily：内心～自喜 feel secretly delighted

【窃取】qièqǔ 偷窃（多做比喻用 usu. fig.）usurp; seize; steal; grab：～职位 usurp an official position|～胜利果实 grab the fruits of victory

【窃听】qiètīng 暗中偷听，通常指利用电子设备偷听别人的谈话 eavesdrop; wiretap; tap; bug; listen in on others' talk stealthily with electronic equipment

【窃贼】qièzéi 小偷儿 thief; burglar; pilferer

挈 qiè ❶ 举；提 lift; raise; take up：提纲～领 concentrate on the main points; take up the highlights ❷ 挈带；带领 take along：～眷 take one's family along|扶老～幼 bring along the old and the young

【挈带】qièdài 携带；带领。借指提拔 take along; lead-promote

惬(愜、悏) qiè〈书 *fml.*〉(心里)满足 satisfied; gratified：～意 pleased; satisfied

【惬当】qièdàng〈书 *fml.*〉恰如其分；适当 proper; appropriate

【惬怀】qièhuái〈书 *fml.*〉心中满足 pleased; satisfied

【惬意】qièyì 满意；称心；舒服 pleased; satisfied：～的微笑 (give) a happy smile|树阴下凉风习习，十分～。A cool breeze was blowing pleasantly in the shade.

趄 qiè 倾斜 slanting; inclined：～坡儿 slope|～着身子 (of a person) lean sideways
☞ jū on p. 1045

慊 qiè〈书 *fml.*〉满足；满意 satisfied; contented; pleased; gratified：意犹未～ have not given full expression to one's satisfaction
☞ qiàn on p. 1541

朅 qiè〈书 *fml.*〉❶ 去 go; leave ❷ 勇武 brave; courageous; valiant

锲 qiè〈书 *fml.*〉雕刻 carve; engrave; chisel：～而不舍 keep on chiselling or chipping away — work with perseverance; stick to sth. with perseverance; make steady or unflagging efforts

【锲而不舍】qiè ér bù shě 雕刻一件东西，一直刻下去不放手 keep on chiselling or chipping away;〈比喻 *fig.*〉有恒心，有毅力 work with perseverance; stick to sth. with perseverance; make steady or unflagging efforts：学习要有～的精神。Study requires perseverance.

箧(篋) qiè〈书 *fml.*〉小箱子 small suitcase; small box：书～ small rattan box for books|藤～ wicker suitcase|行～ travelling case

qīn（ㄑㄧㄣ）

钦 qīn ❶ 敬重 admire; adore; respect：～佩 admire; esteem; respect; hold in high regard|～仰 revere; respect; esteem; venerate ❷ 指皇帝亲自(做) by the emperor himself：～定 (of writings) authorized by the sovereign himself|～赐 granted or bestowed by the emperor ❸(Qīn) 姓 a surname

【钦差】qīnchāi 由皇帝派遣，代表皇帝出外办理重大事件的官员 imperial envoy; imperial commissioner; official dispatched by the emperor to handle important affairs on his behalf

【钦差大臣】qīnchāi dàchén 钦差。现多指上级机关派来的、握有大权的工作人员(多含讥讽意 oft. satirical) imperial commissioner; imperial envoy; (now) dispatched staff invested by higher authorities with full powers

【钦迟】qīnchí 敬仰(旧时书函用语 used in old-style letters) admire; revere; venerate

【钦定】qīndìng 经君主亲自裁定的(多指著述 usu. of writing) authorized by the sovereign himself

【钦敬】qīnjìng 钦佩尊敬 admire and respect：受人～ be admired and respected

【钦慕】qīnmù 敬慕 admire and respect; hold in esteem：～之情，溢于言表 one's feeling of reverence mixed with admiration comes through in overtones

【钦佩】qīnpèi 敬重佩服 respect; admire; esteem; hold in high regard：～的目光 admiring look; (look at somebody) with admiration|他这种舍己为人的精神，使人十分～。His altruistic spirit commanded our great admiration.

【钦羡】qīnxiàn 钦佩羡慕 admire and respect：～的目光 admiring look; (look at somebody) with admiration

【钦仰】qīnyǎng〈书 *fml.*〉钦佩景仰 revere; venerate; esteem; respect

侵 qīn ❶ 侵入 invade; intrude into; infringe upon; encroach on：～害 invade; encroach on; make inroads on|入～ invade; make inroads into ❷ 接近(天明) approaching (daybreak)：～晓 approaching daybreak|～晨 towards daybreak; at the approach of dawn

【侵晨】qīnchén 天快亮的时候 towards daybreak; at the approach of dawn

【侵夺】qīnduó 凭势力夺取别人财产 violate; encroach upon; take away; seize another's property by force

【侵犯】qīnfàn ❶ 非法干涉别人，损害其权利

encroach on; infringe upon; violate; interfere with others illegally to infringe upon their rights:～版权 infringe copyright; piracy|～农民利益 infringe upon peasants' interests ❷ 侵入别国领域 invade the territory of another country; make inroads; encroach or infringe on:～领空 violate a country's territorial skies or airspace

【侵害】qīnhài ❶ 侵入而损害 invade; encroach on; make inroads on:防止害虫～农作物 prevent pests from harming farm crops ❷ 用暴力或非法手段损害 harm or damage by force or by illegal means:不得～人民群众利益。The interests of the people must not be harmed.

【侵凌】qīnlíng 侵犯欺负 encroach; infringe; bully and humiliate; browbeat and insult

【侵略】qīnlüè 指一个国家(或几个国家联合起来)侵犯别国的领土、主权,掠夺并奴役别国的人民。侵略的主要形式是武装入侵,有时也采用政治干涉、经济和文化渗透等方式。aggression; invasion; (of one nation or several allied nations) act of invading the territory, infringing upon the sovereignity, and plundering and enslaving the people of another country by resorting to the use of force in the main and at times by such means as political interference, and economic and cultural infiltration:～战争 war of aggression; invasive war|文化～ cultural invasions

【侵权】qīnquán 侵犯、损害他人的合法权益 tort; violate or infringe upon others' lawful rights or interests

【侵扰】qīnrǎo 侵犯骚扰 invade and harass:～边境 harass a country's border frontiers; make border raids

【侵入】qīnrù ❶ 用武力强行进入境内 invade; intrude into; make incursions into; make inroads into; cross the border by force:～边境 intrude into the border frontiers ❷(外来的或有害的事物)进入内部 (of extraneous or harmful things) invade the interior:由于冷空气～,气温急剧下降。The temperature dropped drastically owing to the intrusion of a cold front.

【侵蚀】qīnshí ❶ 逐渐侵害使变坏 corrode; erode; eat into:病菌～人体 germs corrode the human body ❷ 暗中一点一点地侵占(财物) misappropriate or embezzle (property) bit by bit:～公款 misappropriate or embezzle public property funds bit by bit

【侵吞】qīntūn ❶ 暗中非法占有(别人的东西或公共的财物、土地等) embezzle; misappropriate (others' belongings or public property land, etc.):～公款 embezzle public funds ❷ 用武力吞并别国或占有其部分领土 swallow up; annex; forcibly seize another country's territory or occupy territory in part

【侵袭】qīnxí 侵入并袭击 make inroads into; make incursions into; invade and attack; hit; assault:～领空 invade (sb. else's) airspace ◇沿海一带常遭台风～。The coastal areas are often hit by typhoons.

【侵越】qīnyuè 侵犯(权限) encroach; trespass; exceed or overstep one's power or authority; go beyond one's brief; *ultra vires*

【侵早】qīnzǎo same as 侵晨 qīnchén

【侵占】qīnzhàn ❶ 非法占有别人的财产 seize or take illegal possession of another's property; occupy by force ❷ 用侵略手段占有别国的领土 invade and occupy another country's territory

亲(親) qīn ❶ 父母 parents:父～ father|母～ mother|双～ parents ❷ 亲生的 one's own (flesh and blood):～女儿 one's own daughter ❸ 血统最接近的 related by blood; next of kin:～弟兄(同父母的弟兄) blood brother|～叔叔(父亲的亲弟弟) first uncle (younger brother of one's father) ❹ 有血统或婚姻关系的 relative; kin:～属 relatives; kinsfolk|～戚 relative|～人 family members; parents; spouse, children, etc.; kith and kin|～友 relatives and friends; kith and kin|姑表～ cousinship|沾～带故 have ties of kinship or friendship; be related somehow or other ❺ 婚姻 marriage; match:结～ marry; get married|定～ be engaged; be betrothed to|～事 marriage ❻ 指新妇 bride:娶～(of a man) get married|送～ her family escorting the bride by to the bridegroom's home or the wedding party|迎～(of the bridegroom's family) send a party to escort the bride to the bridegroom's home or the wedding party ❼ 关系近;感情好(跟'疏'相对 as opposed to 'distant') close; intimate; dear:～近 be close to; be on intimate terms with; be friendly with|～密 close; intimate; dear|～爱 dear; beloved; cherished|～热 loving; affectionate; intimate; warmhearted|不分～疏 regardless of close or distant relationship; make no distinction between one's relatives or friends and others ❽ 亲自 in person; personally:～身 personal; firsthand; done or made by oneself|～手 personally; oneself; with one's own hands|～口 (say or speak) personally|～眼所见 see with one's own eyes; eyewitness ❾ 跟人亲近(多指国家 usu. of countries) in favour of; supporting:～华 pro-Chinese|～美 pro-American ❿ 用嘴唇接触(人或东西),表示亲热 kiss; touch (sb. or sth.) with the lips as a form of endearment:～嘴 kiss|他～了～孩子。He kissed the baby.

☞ qìng on p. 1579

【亲爱】qīn'ài 关系密切,感情深厚 dear; beloved; cherished; of close relations and deep emotion:~的祖国 one's beloved country or homeland|~的同志 dear comrade|~的母亲 dear mother

【亲本】qīnběn 杂交时所选用的父本或母本 parent; selected male or female parent for crossbreeding

【亲笔】qīnbǐ ❶ 亲自动笔(写) write in one's own hand; autograph:~信 letter in one's own handwriting; handwritten letter|这是他~写的。It is in his own writing. ❷ 指亲自写的字 one's own handwriting; autograph:这几个字是鲁迅先生的~。These words are in Lu Xun's handwriting.

Q

【亲传】qīnchuán 亲身传授 impart (knowledge) or teach personally:~弟子 one's own disciple; disciple whom one has taught personally

【亲代】qīndài 产生后一代生物的生物,对后一代生物来说是亲代,所产生的后一代叫子代 parental generation; organism that produces the later (or filial) generation

【亲等】qīnděng 计算亲属关系亲疏远近的单位,如父母和子女为一亲等,祖父母和孙子女为二亲等 degree of kinship; unit of counting close and distant kinship, e.g. the relationship between parents and children is the first-degree of kinship, and that of grandparents and grandchildren, second-degree of kinship

【亲故】qīngù 亲戚故旧 relatives and old friends:遍访~ visit all the relatives and old friends

【亲和力】qīnhélì 两种或两种以上的物质结合成化合物时互相作用的力 affinity; force that acts mutually between two or more substances synthesizing chemical compounds

【亲近】qīnjìn 亲密而接近 be close to; be friendly with; be on intimate terms with:这两个小同学很~。The two little classmates are on intimate terms.|他热情诚恳,大家都愿意~他。As he is warmhearted and sincere, everyone wants to be friends with him.

【亲眷】qīnjuàn ❶ same as 亲戚 qīn·qi ❷ 眷属 family members, esp. wife and children

【亲口】qīnkǒu (话)出于本人的嘴 say (or speak) personally:这是他~告诉我的。He told me this himself.

【亲历】qīnlì 亲身经历 experience personally; be personally on the scene; be involved directly:~其境 experience personally; be personally on the scene|这是我~的事,所以印象极深。I personally experienced it, so the matter has left a deep impression on me.

【亲临】qīnlín 亲自到(某处) make a personal appearance (at a place); come or go to (a place) in person:~其境 make a personal appearance (at a place); come or go to (a place) in person|~现场 make a personal appearance at the scene|~指导 be present to give guidance|~抗洪前线 come to the frontier to fight the floods in person

【亲密】qīnmì 感情好,关系密切 close; dear; intimate; of deep emotion and close relations:他俩非常~。The two of them are on intimate terms.|~战友 close comrade-in-arms

【亲昵】qīnnì 十分亲密 intimate; affectionate; attached:他~地依偎在母亲怀里。He nestled in his mother's arms affectionately.

【亲朋】qīnpéng 亲戚朋友 relatives and friends; relatives and acquaintances:~好友 relatives and friends

【亲戚】qīn·qi 跟自己家庭有婚姻关系或血统关系的家庭或它的成员 relative; family, or a member connected to one's family by marriage or blood relations:一门~ a group of relatives (usu. from the same family or clan)|我们两家是~。Our two families are related.|他在北京的~不多,只有一个表姐。He has no relative in Beijing except for an older female cousin.

【亲切】qīnqiè ❶ 亲近;亲密 warm; close; affectionate:他想起延安,像想起家乡一样~。Warm feelings surged in him when he recalled Yan'an, the place that felt like home to him. ❷ 形容热情而关心 kind; hearty; cordial; enthusiastic and caring:老师的~教导 teacher's kind guidance

【亲情】qīnqíng 亲人的情义 emotional attachment among family members:父女~ affection between father and daughter|不念~ regardless of the emotional attachment among family members|祖国处处有~。The warm feeling among the people, like the emotional attachment among family members, may be found everywhere in our motherland.

【亲热】qīnrè 亲密而热情 affectionate; intimate; warmhearted; loving:大伙儿就像久别重逢的亲人一样,~极了。Our faces all beamed with joy and warmth like loved ones meeting again after a long separation.|乡亲们围着子弟兵,亲亲热热地问长问短。The villagers mobbed the people's army, making warmhearted inquiries.

【亲人】qīnrén ❶ 直系亲属或配偶 kinsfolk; relative; directly related members of one's family or spouse's family; one's family members; one's parents, spouse, children, etc.; one's kith and kin:他家里除母亲以外,没有别的~。Besides his mother, he has no other relatives at home. ❷〈比喻 *fig.*〉关系亲密、感情深厚的人 dear ones; those dear to one

【亲善】qīnshàn 亲近而友好 (as between countries) friendship and goodwill:两国~。The two countries have maintained friendly relations.

【亲身】qīnshēn same as 亲自 qīnzì:～经历 personal experience; firsthand experience

【亲生】qīnshēng ❶ 自己生育 one's own child:小明是她～的。Xiao Ming is her own child. ❷ 自己生育的或生育自己的 one's own (children or parents):～子女 one's own children|～父母 one's own parents

【亲事】qīn·shi 婚事 marriage:操办～ arrange one's marriage

【亲手】qīnshǒu 用自己的手(做) (done) with one's own hands; in person; personally; oneself:你～种的两棵枣树,现在长得可大啦。The two jujube trees that you planted with your own hands have grown very tall.

【亲疏】qīnshū (关系)亲近和疏远 (of relationships) close and distant:不分～,一视同仁。We regard all as equals, making no distinction between friends and non-friends.

【亲属】qīnshǔ 跟自己有血统关系或婚姻关系的人 kinsfolk; relatives; person related to oneself by blood or marriage:直系～ lineal relatives|旁系～ collateral relatives

【亲体】qīntǐ 产生后一代生物的雌性个体或雄性个体 parent; male or female individual organism that produces the subsequent generation

【亲痛仇快】qīn tòng chóu kuài 亲人痛心,仇人高兴 sadden one's own people and gladden the enemy; bring grief to one's own people and joy to the enemy:决不能做～的事。We must not do anything to sadden our friends and delight our enemies. also 亲者痛,仇者快 qīnzhětòng, chóuzhěkuài

【亲王】qīnwáng 皇帝或国王的亲属中封王的人 prince; relative of an emperor or a king who is granted the title of prince

【亲吻】qīnwěn 用嘴唇接触(人或物),表示亲热、喜爱 kiss; touch (people or things) with the lips to express one's affection or love

【亲信】qīnxìn ❶ 亲近而信任 be close with and trust:～小人 be close with and trust villains ❷ 亲近而信任的人(多含贬义 usu. derog.) trusted follower; confidant; person with whom one is close to and trusts:培植～ cultivate trusted followers

【亲眼】qīnyǎn 用自己的眼睛(看) (see) with one's own eyes; (witness) personally:～所见 see with one's own eyes|参观的人～看到了这几年农民生活的巨大变化。The visitors have seen for themselves the tremendous changes in peasants' lives over the past few years.

【亲友】qīnyǒu 亲戚朋友 relatives and friends; kith and kin

【亲鱼】qīnyú 指发育到性成熟阶段,有繁殖能力的雄鱼或雌鱼 parent fish; male or female fish that has developed into sexual maturity with reproductive capacity; also 种鱼 zhǒngyú

【亲缘】qīnyuán 指血缘关系;亲代遗传关系 affinity; blood relations; consanguinity

【亲征】qīnzhēng 指帝王亲自出征 (of an emperor) take command of an expedition in person

【亲政】qīnzhèng 幼年继位的帝王成年后亲自处理政事(of a young sovereign who succeeded to the throne in childhood) assume the reins of government upon coming of age; personally manage or attend to government affairs upon coming of age

【亲知】qīnzhī 亲身知道 know at firsthand:真正～的是具有实践经验的人。Those who are in possession of real knowledge have acquired it through practice.

【亲炙】qīnzhì〈书 *fml*.〉直接受到教诲或传授 study under sb.'s direct guidance; be directly under sb.'s tutorship

【亲子】qīnzǐ 人或其他动物的上一代跟下一代 (of human or other animals) parents and children — two immediate generations; the former and later generations:～关系 parent-offspring relationship

【亲自】qīnzì 自己(做) personally; in person; (do sth. by) oneself:你～去一趟,和他当面谈谈。Please go there yourself to have a face-to-face talk with him.|库房的门总是由他～开关,别人从来不经手。He always opens and closes the door of the storeroom himself, never allowing others to handle it.

【亲族】qīnzú 家属和同族;家族 members of the same clan

【亲嘴】qīn//zuǐ (～儿 qīn//zuǐr)两个人以嘴唇相接触,表示亲爱 kiss; (of two persons) touch with the lips to express love or affection

衾 qīn ❶ 被子 quilt:～枕 quilt and pillow ❷ 尸体入殓时盖尸体的东西 pall; material that covers an encoffined corpse:衣～棺椁 pall and coffin

骎 qīn [骎骎]〈书 *fml*.〉形容马跑得很快的样子 (of horses) gallop; advance rapidly;〈比喻 *fig*.〉事业进展得很快 (of a cause) make progress at seven-league strides; develop apace:祖国建设～日上。Our motherland is going apace in its economic development.

嵚 qīn [嵚崟](qīnyín)〈书 *fml*.〉形容山高 (of a mountain) high; towering

qín (ㄑㄧㄣˊ)

芹 qín 芹菜 celery;药～ medicinal celery

【芹菜】qíncài 一年或二年生草本植物,羽状复叶,小叶卵形,叶柄肥大,绿色或黄白色,花绿白色,果实扁圆形。是普通蔬菜。celery (*Apium graveolens*); annual or biennial green or yellowish white herb with feather-shaped compound leaves, oval leaflets, plump petioles and oval fruits, which serves as a common vegetable

【芹献】qínxiàn〈书 *fml*.〉〈谦称 *hum*.〉赠人的礼品或对人的建议 my humble gift or suggestion; ☞ 献芹 xiànqín on p.2084

芩 qín 古书上指芦苇一类的植物 reeds in ancient books

矜(獾) qín〈古代 *arch*.〉指矛柄 handle of a spear

☞ guān on p.715 and jīn on p.1007

秦 Qín ❶ 周朝国名,在今陕西中部、甘肃东部。公元前 221 年统一中国,建立秦朝。state of Qin (897-221 B.C.); state of the Zhou Dynasty, centred around present-day Shaanxi Province and eastern Gansu Province, which unified China and established the Qin Dynasty in 221 B.C. ❷ 朝代,公元前221—公元前206 年,秦始皇嬴政所建,建都咸阳(在今陕西咸阳市东) Qin Dynasty (221-206 B.C.); dynasty established by Ying Zheng or Qinshihuang (First Emperor of the Qin Dynasty) with its capital in Xianyang (east of present-day Xianyang in Shaanxi Province) ❸ 指陕西和甘肃,特指陕西 Qin; another name for Shaanxi and Gansu provinces (esp. Shaanxi Province) ❹ (Qín) 姓 a surname

【秦吉了】qínjíliǎo 文学作品中所说的一种鸟,样子和八哥儿相似,能模仿人说话的声音。据说产于陕西,所以叫秦吉了。parrot from Shaanxi; a kind of parrot-like bird often mentioned in literary works, which can imitate the human voice, and is said to be found in Shaanxi Province, hence its name

【秦艽】qínjiāo 草本植物,根土黄色,互相缠在一起,长一尺多,叶子和茎相连,都是青色,花紫色。根可入药。large-leaved gentian (*Gentiana macrophylla*); herb with tangled yellowish brown roots more than 33 cm in length, a series of blue leaves and stems connected with each other, and purple flowers; its roots can be used as medicine

【秦晋】Qín Jìn 春秋时秦、晋两国国君几代都互相通婚,后用'秦晋'指两姓联姻 (during the Spring and Autumn Period the princes of the states of Qin and Jin were related by marriage through several generations) alliance between two families by marriage; matrimonial ties between two families: 愿偕～ wish to forge a good relationship by marriage | 结～之好 (of two families, etc.) be allied through marriage

【秦镜高悬】Qín jìng gāo xuán ☞ 明镜高悬 míng jìng gāo xuán on p.1354

【秦楼楚馆】qínlóu-chǔguǎn〈旧时 *old*〉指歌舞场所,也指妓院 places for song and dance; quarters of pleasure; brothels

【秦腔】qínqiāng ❶ 流行于西北各省的地方戏曲剧种,由陕西、甘肃一带的民歌发展而成,是梆子腔的一种 Shaanxi opera; local opera popular in China's northwestern provinces, developed from the folk songs of Shaanxi and Gansu provinces and the surrounding areas; a kind of *bangzi*; also 陕西梆子 Shaanxi *bangzi* ❷ 北方梆子的统称 general term for northern *bangzi*

【秦篆】qínzhuàn 小篆 form of script of the Qin Dynasty (oft. used on seals)

揿 qín〈书 *fml*.〉same as 擒 qín

棄 qín〈书 *fml*.〉same as 琴 qín

琴 qín ❶ 古琴 *qin*, seven-stringed plucked instrument in some ways similar to the zither ❷ 某些乐器的统称,如风琴、钢琴、提琴、口琴、胡琴等 general name for certain musical instruments, e.g. 风琴 fēngqín, 钢琴 gāngqín, 提琴 tíqín, 口琴 kǒuqín, and 胡琴 húqín ❸ (Qín) 姓 a surname

【琴键】qínjiàn 风琴、钢琴等上装置的白色和黑色的键 (white and black) keys (on musical instruments such as organs and pianos, etc.)

【琴瑟】qínsè 琴和瑟两种乐器一起合奏,声音和谐,用来比喻融洽的感情(多用于夫妇) *qin* and *se*, two-stringed musical instruments which play in great harmony; (fig.) (usu. between husband and wife) harmonious emotion: ～甚笃 (of husband and wife) be in great harmony

【琴师】qínshī 戏曲乐队中操琴伴奏的人 fiddler; performer who plays a stringed instrument as an accompanist in an orchestra for traditional Chinese opera

【琴书】qínshū 曲艺的一种,说唱故事,用扬琴伴奏,有山东琴书、徐州琴书等 story-telling, mainly in song, with musical accompaniment of the dulcimer; a kind of folk art form with rich local flavour, esp. in parts of Shandong and Xuzhou

覃 Qín 姓 a surname

☞ tán on p.1860

禽 qín ❶ 鸟类 birds; fowl: 飞～ flying birds | 鸣～ songbirds | 家～ domestic fowl; poultry ❷〈书 *fml*.〉鸟兽的总称 general term for birds and animals

〈古 *arch*.〉same as 擒 qín

【禽兽】qínshòu 鸟兽 birds and beasts;〈比喻 *fig*.〉行为卑鄙恶劣的人 person of mean and odious behaviour: 衣冠～ beast in human clothing or shape; brute | ～行为 brutish acts; bestial acts

勤 qín ❶ 尽力多做或不断地做(跟'懒'或'惰'相对 as opposed to 'lazy') diligent; industrious; assiduous; hardworking; try one's best to do more or keep doing sth.: 手～ diligent | ～学苦练 study diligently and train hard|人～地不懒。Where the tiller is tireless the land is fertile. ❷ 次数多；经常 often; frequent:～洗澡 take baths regularly|夏季雨水～。It rains often (or frequently) in summer. |他来得最～，差不多天天来。He is the most frequent visitor, coming almost every day. ❸ 勤务 work; duty; service:内～ office work |外～ field work ❹ 在规定时间内准时到班的工作或劳动 (office, school, etc.) attendance; work or labour that requires the working staff to be in their places within the prescribed times:出～ attend class; be in the workplace|缺～ absent from work or the workplace|考～ check on attendance|执～ be on duty|空～ air duty|地～ ground service or duty ❺ (Qín)姓 a surname

【勤奋】qínfèn 不懈地努力(工作或学习) diligent; assiduous; industrious; make untiring efforts (in one's work or studies)

【勤工俭学】qín gōng jiǎn xué ❶ 利用学习以外的时间参加劳动，把劳动所得作为学习、生活费用 part-work and part-study program; system of allowing students to engage in labour in their spare time, and use the earnings to pay for their studies and cover their living expenses ❷ 我国某些学校采取的办学的一种方式，学生在学习期间从事一定的劳动，学校以学生劳动的收入作为办学资金 work-study programme; method of operation adopted by certain schools in the country, in which students engage in some labour during their studies, and the schools use these earnings as funds for running the school

【勤俭】qínjiǎn 勤劳而节俭 hardworking and thrifty:～建国 build up the country through hard work and frugality|～过日子 live industriously and frugally; lead an industrious and thrifty life

【勤谨】qín·jin 〈方 *dial.*〉勤劳；勤快 industrious; hardworking:工作～ work industriously or diligently

【勤恳】qínkěn 勤劳而塌实 diligent and conscientious; earnest and assiduous:～地劳动 work diligently or industrially|勤勤恳恳地工作 work industrially and conscientiously

【勤苦】qínkǔ 勤劳刻苦 diligent; hardworking; assiduous:～练习 practice hard|～的生活 hard work and plain living

【勤快】qín·kuai 手脚勤，爱劳动 diligent; hardworking; industrious:手脚～ quick and industrious|他们很～，天一亮，就下地干活。They were very diligent and started work in the fields at daybreak.

【勤劳】qínláo 努力劳动，不怕辛苦 diligent; industrious; assiduous; hardworking:～勇敢的人民 diligent and courageous people; industrious and valiant people

【勤勉】qínmiǎn same as 勤奋 qínfèn:工作～ work diligently or industriously|～学习 study hard or diligently

【勤勤】qínqín 〈书 *fml.*〉形容诚恳或殷勤 attentive; solicitous; considerate; sincere:雅意～ your kind consideration

【勤王】qíngwáng 〈书 *fml.*〉❶ 君主的统治地位受到内乱或外患的威胁而动摇时，臣子发兵援救 (of feudal officials) send troops to rescue the emperor when his dominance is undermined due to the threat of internal disorder or foreign aggression:～之师 troops to the rescue of the emperor ❷ 为王朝尽力 serve the royal house

【勤务】qínwù ❶ 公家分派的公共事务 duty; service; public service assigned by an organization ❷ 军队中专门做杂务工作的人 orderly; person who does odd jobs in an army

【勤务兵】qínwùbīng 〈旧时 *old*〉军队中给军官办理杂务的士兵 orderly; soldier who does odd jobs for officers in an army

【勤务员】qínwùyuán 部队或机关里担任杂务工作的人员 one who does odd jobs in the armed forces or government organizations ◇做人民的～ be a servant to the people

【勤杂人员】qínzá rényuán 勤务员的总称 orderly; subsidiary staff doing odd jobs

嗪 qín 译音用字，如吖嗪、哒嗪、哌嗪 transliterated word, such as 吖嗪 yāqín, 哒嗪 dáqín and 哌嗪 pàiqín

溱 qín 溱潼(Qíntóng)，地名，在江苏 Qintong, a place in Jiangsu Province

☞ zhēn on p. 2437

廑 qín 〈书 *fml.*〉same as 勤 qín

☞ jǐn on p. 1010

擒 qín 抓；捉拿 capture; catch; seize; take: 欲～故纵 leave sb. at large so as to better apprehend him; give sb. enough line or rope; play cat and mouse with sb.|～贼先～王 to catch a gang of brigands, first catch their chieftain; capture a ringleader first in order to capture all his underlings

【擒获】qínhuò 捉住；抓获 catch; capture; arrest:～歹徒 capture a scoundrel

【擒拿】qínná ❶ 拳术中一种针对人的各部关节和穴位，用各种方法使对方无法反抗的技法 martial arts for incapacitating an opponent by manipulating his joints and acupoints ❷ 泛指捉拿 arrest; capture; catch:～罪犯 capture a criminal

噙 qín (嘴或眼里)含 hold in the mouth or the eyes:～着烟袋 hold a pipe between one's lips|～着眼泪 eyes brimming with tears; hold back tears; tears filled one's eyes

檎 qín ☞ 林檎 línqín on p. 1221

螓 qín 古书上指一种像蝉的昆虫 a kind of cicada-like insect in ancient books

懃 qín ☞ 慇懃 yīnqín on p. 2289

qǐn (ㄑㄧㄣˇ)

梫 qǐn ❶ 古书上指肉桂 (in ancient books) cinnamon tree; Chinese cinnamon tree; cassia-bark tree ❷ same as 梫木 qǐnmù

【梫木】 qǐnmù 马醉木 Japanese andromeda (*Pieris polita*)

锓 qǐn 〈书 *fml.*〉雕刻 carve; engrave; etch: ～版 carved block (for printing)

寝(寢) qǐn ❶ 睡 sleep: 废～忘食 (so absorbed or occupied as to) forget about eating and sleeping; (so engrossed or absorbed as to) forget food and rest ❷ 卧室 bedroom: 入～ go to sleep | 就～ retire for the night; go to bed; turn in | 寿终正～ pass away ❸ 帝王的坟墓 coffin chamber; tomb (of an emperor): 陵～ mausoleum; imperial burial place ❹ 〈书 *fml.*〉停止; 平息 stop; end; cease: 其议遂～。(那种议论于是平息) The discussion then came to an end.

【寝车】 qǐnchē 火车的卧铺车厢 sleeping car or carriage; sleeper; also 卧车 wòchē

【寝宫】 qǐngōng ❶ 帝、后等居住的宫殿 palace where the royal couple, etc., sleep ❷ 帝王的陵墓中的墓室 chamber in a mausoleum

【寝食】 qǐnshí 睡觉和吃饭，泛指日常生活 sleeping and eating; food and rest — one's daily life: ～不安 unable to sleep and eat peacefully; feel uneasy even when eating and sleeping; be worried waking or sleeping

【寝室】 qǐnshì 卧室，多指集体宿舍中的 (usu. dormitory) bedroom

qìn (ㄑㄧㄣˋ)

吣(吢、唚) qìn ❶ 猫、狗呕吐 (of cats or dogs) vomit ❷ 谩骂 abuse; rail; yelp; spit out hogwash: 满嘴胡～ talk hogwash; be foul-mouthed; let out a stream of abuse

沁 qìn ❶ (香气、液体等)渗入或透出 (of fragrance, liquid, etc.) ooze; seep; exude: ～人心脾 seep into the heart; refreshing; invigorating | 额上～出了汗珠。Beads of sweat stood on (his) forehead. ❷ 〈方 *dial.*〉头向下垂 lower or droop one's head: ～着头 bend one's head ❸ 〈方 *fml.*〉往水里放 put in water

【沁人心脾】 qìn rén xīn pí 指呼吸到新鲜空气或喝了清凉饮料使人感到舒适。现也用以形容欣赏了美好的诗文、乐曲等给人以清新、爽朗的感觉。seep into the heart; refreshing; invigorating; feel comfortable when breathing fresh air or having a cold drink; feel refreshed and cheerful when appreciating a beautiful poem, article, musical composition, etc.

揿(搇) qìn 〈方 *dial.*〉按 press; push: ～电铃 ring a bell

qīng (ㄑㄧㄥ)

青 qīng ❶ 蓝色或绿色 blue or green: ～天 blue sky | ～山绿水 green hills and blue waters — beautiful scenery; beautiful country scene; scenic spot | ～苔 moss ❷ 黑色 black: ～布 black cloth ❸ 青草或没有成熟的庄稼 green grass; young crop: 踏～ walk on the green grass — go for an outing in early spring | 看(kān)～ keep watch on the ripening crops ❹ 〈比喻 *fig.*〉年轻 young: ～年 youth; young people ❺ 指青年 youth; young people: ～工(青年工人) young worker | 知～ educated youth (usu. refers to secondary school graduates unable to pursue their studies in institutions of higher learning during the Cultural Revolution) ❻ (Qīng)姓 a surname

【青帮】 Qīng Bāng 帮会的一种，最初参加的人多半以漕运为职业，在长江南北的大中城市里活动。后来由于组成分子复杂，为首的人勾结官府，变成反动统治阶级的爪牙。*Qingbang*; Green Gang; secret society whose earliest participants mostly engaged in the smuggling by water of grain to large or medium-sized cities in the southern and northern areas of the Yangtze River, later to become a flunkey of the reactionary ruling class due to its complex network and the collusion of its chieftain with the local authorities

【青菜】 qīngcài ❶ 跟白菜相近的一种植物，叶子直立，勺形或圆形，绿色。是普通蔬菜。plant similar to Chinese cabbage, with green spoon-shaped or circular erect leaves; also 小白菜 xiǎobáicài ❷ 蔬菜的统称 general term for green vegetables; greens

【青草】 qīngcǎo 绿色的草(区别于'干草' as compared with 'hay') green grass

【青出于蓝】 qīng chū yú lán《荀子·劝学》:'青，取之于蓝，而青于蓝。'蓝色从蓼蓝提炼而成，但是颜色比蓼蓝更深。后来用'青出于蓝'比喻学生胜过老师，后人胜过前人。According to *Xunzi·Exhortation on Learning*, blue comes from the indigo plant but is bluer than the plant itself; (fig.) disciple outdoes the master; later generation excels the former one

【青春】 qīngchūn ❶ 青年时期 youth; youthfulness: 把～献给祖国。Dedicate our youth to the motherland. ◇老厂恢复了～。The old factory regained its former vigour. ❷ 指青年人的年龄 (多见于早期白话 oft. in early vernacular) age of young people: ～几何? How old is that youth?

【青春期】qīngchūnqī 男女生殖器官发育成熟的时期。通常男子的青春期是十四岁到十六岁，女子的青春期是十三岁到十四岁。puberty; adolescence; period during which the reproductive organs of the male or female become mature, which for the male generally ranges from 14 to 16 years old, and for the female, 13 to 14

【青瓷】qīngcí 不绘画只涂上淡青色釉的瓷器 celadon (ware); porcelain decorated without paint but only a light blue glaze

【青葱】qīngcōng 形容植物浓绿 verdant; fresh green; lush; (of plants) deep green: ～的草地 fresh green grassland | 窗外长着几棵竹子，～可爱。The bamboo trees outside the window are lush and lovely.

【青翠】qīngcuì 鲜绿 verdant; fresh green; luxuriant green: ～的西山 luxuriant green Western Hills | 雨后，垂柳显得格外～。The weeping willows looked fresher and greener after the rain.

【青蚨】qīngfú 传说中的虫名 a kind of insect mentioned in ancient literature; 〈古代 *arch.*〉借指铜钱 copper cash

【青冈】qīnggāng 槲栎(húlì) large-leafed oak (*Quercus dentata*); also 青㭎 qīnggāng

【青㭎】qīnggāng same as 青冈 qīnggāng

【青光眼】qīngguāngyǎn 眼内的压力增高引起的眼病，症状是瞳孔放大，角膜水肿，呈灰绿色，剧烈头痛，呕吐，视力急剧减退 glaucoma; eye disease caused by the increase of pressure in the eye, marked by symptoms such as mydriasis, greyish green dropsy corneas, severe headaches, vomiting, and a sharp decline in eyesight; also 绿内障 lǜnèizhàng

【青果】qīngguǒ 〈方 *dial.*〉same as 橄榄 gǎnlǎn ②

【青红皂白】qīng hóng zào bái 〈比喻 *fig.*〉是非、情由等 right and wrong; truth and falsehood; hows and whys of a matter: 不分～ make no distinction between right and wrong | 不问～ be undiscriminating; do sth. rashly without first asking what the matter is about

【青黄不接】qīng huáng bù jiē 指庄稼还没有成熟，陈粮已经吃完 surplus grains of the preceding year(s) are almost eaten up, but the new crops are not yet ripe; 〈比喻 *fig.*〉人力或物力等暂时的缺乏 temporary shortage of human or material resources, etc.

【青灰】qīnghuī 一种含有杂质的石墨，青黑色，常用来刷外墙面或搪炉子，也可做颜料 greenish lime; a kind of livid graphite that contains impurities, often used to paint the surface of an outer wall or line a stove, or used as a pigment

【青衿】qīngjīn 〈旧时 *old*〉读书人穿的一种衣服。借指读书人。scholars' garment; scholars; young intellectuals

【青筋】qīngjīn 指皮肤下可以看见的静脉血管 blue veins; visible venous blood vessel under the skin

【青稞】qīngkē ❶ 大麦的一种，粒大，皮薄。主要产在西藏、青海等地，可做糌粑，又可酿酒。*qingke* barley (*Hordeum vulgare* var. *nudem*); highland barley; a kind of barley with large grains and thin rind, mainly produced in Tibet, Qinghai, etc., which can be used to make *zanba* (roasted barley flour which is a staple good for Tibetans), or wine ❷ 这种植物的子实 seeds of such a plant ‖ also 青稞麦 qīngkēmài，元麦 yuánmài，稞麦 kēmài or 裸麦 luǒmài

【青睐】qīnglài 〈书 *fml.*〉same as 青眼 qīngyǎn

【青莲色】qīngliánsè 浅紫色 pale purple; heliotrope

【青龙】qīnglóng ❶ same as 苍龙 cānglóng ① ❷ 道教所信奉的东方的神 oriental god worshipped in Taoism

【青楼】qīnglóu 〈书 *fml.*〉妓院 brothel

【青绿】qīnglǜ 深绿 dark green: ～的松林 dark green pine forest

【青梅】qīngméi 青色的梅子 green plum

【青梅竹马】qīngméi zhúmǎ 李白《长干行》:'郎骑竹马来，绕床弄青梅。同居长干里，两小无嫌猜。'后来用'青梅竹马'形容男女小的时候天真无邪，在一起玩耍 According to *A Trip to Changgan* by Li Bai, 'The boy rides on a bamboo stick for a horse, playing with the girl around the bed. The two little kids living in Changgan play innocently together.' This phrase refers to males and females playing innocently together during childhood (竹马 *zhuma*: 儿童放在胯下当马骑的竹竿 bamboo stick a child rides for a horse).

【青霉素】qīngméisù 抗生素的一种，是从青霉菌培养液中提制的药物。常用的是青霉素的钙盐、钾盐或钠盐。对葡萄球菌、链球菌、淋球菌、肺炎双球菌等有抑制作用。penicillin; a kind of antibiotic extracted from the culture solution of penicillic bacteria, of which the varieties in common use include calcium, sylvite or sodium salt, which can restrain staphylococcus, streptococcus, double pneumococcus, etc. 旧称 formerly called 盘尼西林 pánníxīlín

【青面獠牙】qīng miàn liáo yá 形容面貌狰狞凶恶 frightening or terrifying in appearance

【青苗】qīngmiáo 没有成熟的庄稼(多指粮食作物) (usu. of grain crops) young crop; green shoots of grains; crop that has not become mature yet

【青年】qīngnián ❶ 指人十五六岁到三十岁左右的阶段 youthful; young; (of humans) age ranging from 15 or 16 to approximately 30 years old: ～人 youth; young people | ～时代 one's youth ❷ 指上述年龄的人 youth; young people; person of the above mentioned age:

新～ new youth | 好～ worthy or excellent young person

【青年节】Qīngnián Jié ☞ 五四青年节 Wǔ-Sì Qīngnián Jié on p. 2031

【青皮】[1] qīngpí 〈方 *dial.*〉无赖 scoundrel; hooligan: ～流氓 impertinent rascal

【青皮】[2] qīngpí 中药上指未成熟的橘子的果皮或幼果 peel, or young fruit of unripe orange in traditional Chinese medicine

【青纱帐】qīngshāzhàng 指长得高而密的大面积高粱、玉米等 large area of tall and thick Chinese sorghum, corn, etc.

【青史】qīngshǐ 史书 annals of history; history; historical record: ～留名 fill history with one's renown; go down in the annals of history; have a niche in history; be crowned with eternal glory | 永垂～ go down in the annals of history with one's deeds and renown

【青丝】[1] qīngsī 〈书 *fml.*〉黑发,多指女子的头发 (usu. of a woman) black hair: 一缕～ a lock of black hair | 三尺～ flowing long hair

【青丝】[2] qīngsī 青梅等切成的细丝,放在糕点馅内,或放在糕点面上做点缀 finely cut green plums, etc., used as fillings in cakes or part of the icing on cakes

【青饲料】qīngsìliào 绿色的饲料,如新鲜的野草、野菜、绿树叶等 greenfeed; green fodder, such as fresh weeds, edible wild herbs and green leaves

【青蒜】qīngsuàn 嫩的蒜梗和蒜叶,做菜用 garlic shoots; tender garlic stalks and leaves used as vegetables

【青苔】qīngtái 指阴湿的地方生长的绿色的苔藓植物 moss (*Musci*); green bryophyte grows in dark and damp places

【青天】qīngtiān ❶ 蓝色的天空 blue sky ❷〈比喻 *fig.*〉清官 just judge; upright magistrate: 老百姓管包公叫包～。Bao Zheng was called Just-minded Magistrate Bao by the common people.

【青天白日】qīng tiān bái rì 白天(含强调意) (for emphasis) bright daylight; broad daylight: ～的,竟敢拦路抢劫。They even dared mug people in broad daylight.

【青天霹雳】qīngtiān pīlì 晴天霹雳 bolt from the blue; thunderbolt from an unclouded sky

【青田石】qīngtiánshí 一种以叶蜡石为主要成分的石料,多为青色,产于浙江青田的方山,是制印章的名贵材料 blue stone quarried in Qingtian County, Zhejiang Province; precious stone for making seals, mainly composed of pyrophyllite, usually blue in colour, found in the Fangshan Mountain in Qingtian County, Zhejiang Province

【青铜】qīngtóng 铜、锡等的合金,青灰色或灰黄色,硬度大,耐磨,抗蚀性好,多用来做铸件和制造零件 bronze; alloy of copper, tin, etc., greenish lime or greyish yellow, characterized by great hardness, and strong resistance to wear and corrosion, usually used to make casts and parts

【青铜器时代】qīngtóngqì shídài ☞ 铜器时代 tóngqì shídài on p. 1924

【青蛙】qīngwā 两栖动物,头部扁而宽,口阔,眼大,皮肤光滑,颜色因环境而不同,通常为绿色,有灰色斑纹,趾间有薄膜相连。生活在水中或靠近水的地方,善跳跃,会游泳,多在夜间活动。雄的有发声器官,叫声响亮。吃田间的害虫,对农业有益。幼体叫蝌蚪。frog (*Rana*); amphibious and oft. nocturnal animal that has a flat and broad head, wide mouth, big eyes, smooth skin, and membrane connecting the toes, whose colour varies with its environment, but is usually green and dotted with grey stripes; living in or near water, good at jumping and swimming, the male having vocal organs to cry loudly and clearly, feeding on pests in fields and therefore beneficial to agriculture, and the young called tadpoles; generally called 田鸡 tiánjī

【青葙】qīngxiāng 一年生草本植物,高二三尺,叶子互生,卵形至披针形,花淡红色,供观赏。种子叫青葙子(qīngxiāngzǐ),中医入药。feather cockscomb (*Celosia argentea*); annual herb 2 or 3-*chi* tall, with alternate oval or lanceolar leaves, light red flowers used ornamentally, whose seeds, called 青葙子 qīngxiāngzi, are used in traditional Chinese medicine

【青眼】qīngyǎn 指人高兴时眼睛正着看,黑色的眼珠在中间;比喻对人的喜爱或重视(跟'白眼'相对 as opposed to 'supercilious or scornful look') look squarely at sb. or sth. when one feels happy, with black eyes ball in the middle of the sockets; (fig.) favour; good graces; like or think highly of sb.

【青猺】qīngyáo 花面狸 masked civet (*Viverridae*)

【青衣】qīngyī ❶ 黑色的衣服 black clothes: ～小帽 casual clothes; plain informal dress ❷〈古代 *arch.*〉指婢女 maid; housemaid ❸ 戏曲中旦角的一种,扮演中年或青年妇女,因穿青衫而得名 female role; actress in traditional Chinese opera who plays the part of a young or middle-aged woman, so named because she wears a black dress

【青鼬】qīngyòu 哺乳动物,身体大小像家猫,头的背面和侧面、四肢和尾巴都呈棕黑色,肩部黄色,腹部黄灰色。吃松鼠、蜜蜂等。毛皮可用来制衣服。yellow-throated marten (*Charronia flavigula*); mammal the size of a domestic cat, with all-black back and sides of the head, limbs and tail, all black, with yellow shoulders, and a yellowish grey stomach, which feeds on squirrels, bees, etc., its fur used to make clothes; also 黄猺 huángyáo

【青鱼】qīngyú 鱼,外形像草鱼,但较细而圆,青黑色,腹部色较浅。是我国重要的淡水鱼类之一。black carp (*Mylopharyngodon piceus*); livid fish that resembles grass carp in appearance, but is thinner and rounder, and a lighter-coloured stomach; also 黑鲩 hēihuàn

【青云】qīngyún 〈比喻 *fig.*〉高的地位 high official position:平步～ rise rapidly in the (official) world; experience a meteoric rise

【青云直上】qīngyún zhí shàng 〈比喻 *fig.*〉官职升得很快很高 be promoted quickly and to a high position in an official career; be promoted to higher and higher posts quickly; get rapid promotions

【青贮】qīngzhù 把青饲料埋起来发酵。青贮的饲料与空气隔绝,产生有机酸,经久不坏,并可减少养分的损失。ensile; store in silos; bury green fodder to ferment, cut off from air, to produce organic acid, which is very durable, and can reduce the loss of nutrients

【青紫】qīngzǐ ❶〈书 *fml.*〉〈古代 *arch.*〉高官印绶、服饰的颜色 高官显爵 colour of the seal, silk tassel and dress of a senior official in ancient China; 〈比喻 *fig.*〉high official titles ❷ ☞ 发绀 fāgàn on p. 520

轻(輕) qīng ❶ 重量小;比重小(跟'重'相对 as opposed to 'heavy') light; of little weight:身～如燕 as light as a swallow|油比水～,所以油浮在水面上。Oil is lighter than water, and floats on its surface. ❷ 负载小;装备简单 light; easy to carry; with light load or simple equipment:～装 light; with light packs; light military equipment|～骑兵 light cavalry|～车简从 travel with light luggage and few attendants; travel light with a small entourage ❸ 数量少;程度浅 small in number, degree, etc.:年纪～ be young|工作很～ light work load|～伤 minor wound; slight injury ❹ 轻松 relaxed; carefree; light-hearted:～音乐 light music|无病一身～。To be healthy is a blessing. *or* Good health is a blessing. ❺ 不重要 unimportant; not important; of no significance:责任～ carry a light responsibility|关系不～ have an important bearing on; be quite important ❻ 用力不猛 gently; softly; lightly:～抬～放 handle gently; handle with care|～～推了他一下 push him gently; give him a gentle push ❼ 轻率 rashly; impetuously:～信 credulous; gullible; readily believe|～举妄动 act rashly and blindly; act impetuously; make some rash move; take reckless actions ❽ 不庄重;不严肃 flighty; frivolous; not serious:～佻 frivolous; skittish; coquettish; flirtatious|～薄 frivolous; flirtatious ❾ 轻视 belittle; make light of; regard sb. or sth. as of no importance:～慢 treat sb. rudely; slight sb.|～敌 take the enemy lightly; underestimate the strength of the enemy|～财重义 prize righteousness and benevolence above wealth; treasure friendship more than wealth; be big-hearted

【轻便】qīngbiàn ❶ 重量较小,建造较易,或使用方便 light; portable; handy; of little weight, easily built or easy to use:～铁路 light railway; field railway|～自行车 light-bodied bicycle ❷ 轻松;容易 convenient; easy:贪图～,反而误事 spoil sth. by seeking convenience

【轻薄】qīngbó 言语举动带有轻佻和玩弄意味(多指对女性 usu. toward a woman) frivolous; flirtatious:态度～ frivolous attitude

【轻车简从】qīng chē jiǎn cóng 指有地位的人出门时,行装简单,跟随的人不多 (of a person of high position) travel with light luggage and few attendants; travel light with a small entourage; also 轻装简从 qīng zhuāng jiǎn cóng

【轻车熟路】qīng chē shú lù 驾着轻便的车在熟路上走 drive in a light carriage on a familiar road; 〈比喻 *fig.*〉对情况熟悉做起来容易 (do) sth. one knows well enough and can manage with ease

【轻敌】qīngdí 轻视敌人,不加警惕 take the enemy lightly; underestimate the strength of the enemy:麻痹～ be off guard and take the enemy lightly|～思想 thought of underestimating the enemy

【轻而易举】qīng ér yì jǔ 形容事情很容易做 be easy to do; be a piece of cake for sb.; come easy (to sb.)

【轻浮】qīngfú 言语举动随便,不严肃不庄重 frivolous; flighty; light; light-headed; be casual in speech or behaviour; not serious:举止～ be frivolous in behaviour

【轻歌曼舞】qīng gē màn wǔ 轻松愉快的音乐和柔和优美的舞蹈 light, pleasant music and graceful dance

【轻工业】qīnggōngyè 以生产生活资料为主的工业,包括纺织工业、食品工业、制药工业等 light industry; industry that mainly produces the means of livelihood, e.g. textile, food and pharmaceutical industries

【轻忽】qīnghū 不重视;不注意;轻率疏忽 neglect; overlook; pay little attention to; attach no importance to; act rashly:～职守 neglect one's duties; dereliction of duty|事关重大,不容～。The matter is of such great importance that we can't afford to make light of it.

【轻活】qīnghuó (～儿 qīnghuór)不大费力气的活儿 light work; soft job; easy job; jobs that require or need no great effort

【轻机关枪】qīngjīguānqiāng 机关枪的一种。重量较轻,可由单人携带和使用。light machine gun; a kind of machine gun, which is lightweight, and can be carried and used by a single person

【轻贱】qīngjiàn ❶（人）下贱（of a person）mean and worthless; inferior; lowly ❷ 看不起；小看 despise; belittle; look down upon：受人～ be despised or belittled; be looked down upon

【轻健】qīngjiàn 轻快而矫健 nimble; brisk; spry and light：步履～ walk at a brisk pace; walk in brisk or springy steps

【轻捷】qīngjié 轻快敏捷 spry and light; nimble; springy; agile：～的脚步 brisk steps｜～地跳下马来 dismount agilely（from horseback）

【轻金属】qīngjīnshǔ 通常指比重小于 5 的金属，如钠、钾、镁、钙、铝、钛等 light metal; usu. metal with a specific gravity less than five, e. g. sodium, potassium, magnesium, calcium, aluminum, and titanium

【轻举妄动】qīng jǔ wàng dòng 不经慎重考虑，盲目行动 act rashly; act impetuously; take reckless action; act blindly without careful consideration

【轻口薄舌】qīng kǒu bó shé 形容说话刻薄 make caustic comments; speak sarcastically; also 轻嘴薄舌 qīng zuǐ bó shé

【轻快】qīngkuài ❶（动作）不费力（of sb.'s movement）brisk; spry; light：脚步～ brisk steps ❷ 轻松愉快 relaxed; lively; light：～的曲调 lively tune｜洗完澡，身上～多了 feel more relaxed after taking a bath

【轻狂】qīngkuáng 非常轻浮 extremely frivolous：举止～ extremely frivolous in behaviour

【轻慢】qīngmàn 对人不敬重，态度傲慢 treat sb. without proper respect; slight：～失礼 act impolitely by slighting sb.｜不可～客人 should not slight any guest

【轻描淡写】qīng miáo dàn xiě 着力不多地描写或叙述；谈问题时把重要问题轻轻带过 touch on lightly; mention casually; play down; slur over; not make much of an effort in describing or recounting sth.; touch on important issues lightly in discussion

【轻蔑】qīngmiè 轻视；不放在眼里 scornful; contemptuous; disdainful; despising：～的眼光 disdainful look

【轻诺寡信】qīng nuò guǎ xìn 随便答应人，很少能守信用 make promises easily but seldom keep them; be liberal with promises that one does not mean to keep

【轻飘】qīngpiāo ❶ same as 轻飘飘 qīngpiāopiāo：～的柳絮 fluffy willow catkins ❷ 轻浮不踏实 flighty and impractical：作风～ be flighty and impractical

【轻飘飘】qīngpiāopiāo（～的 qīngpiāopiāo·de）❶ 形容轻得像要飘起来的样子 light; buoyant; as light as if floating：垂柳～地摆动。The branches of the drooping willows were swaying lightly. ❷（动作）轻快灵活；（心情）轻松、自在（of sb.'s movement）nimble; agile;（of sb.'s mood）buoyant; light-hearted; relaxed; carefree：他高兴地走着，脚底下～的。She tripped along joyfully as if treading on air.

【轻骑】qīngqí ❶ 轻装的骑兵 light cavalry ❷ 指轻便的两轮摩托车 moped; light-bodied two-wheel motorbike

【轻巧】qīng·qiǎo ❶ 重量小而灵巧 light and ingenious; handy：这小车真～。This car is really light.｜他身子很～。He is very light. ❷ 轻松灵巧 nimble; agile：动作～ nimble in movement｜他操纵机器，就像船夫划小船一样～。He operated the machine as dexterously as a boatman rowing a small boat. ❸ 简单容易 simple; easy：说得倒～。It's easy to talk.

【轻取】qīngqǔ 轻而易举地战胜对手 romp; rout; win without difficulty; win hands down; beat one's opponent easily：这场比赛北京队以 5：0～客队。The Beijing team easily routed the guest team by 5 to 0 in the match.

【轻柔】qīngróu 轻而柔和 soft; gentle; pliable：衣料质地～ of soft texture｜～的枝条 pliable twigs｜声音～ gentle voice

【轻生】qīngshēng 不爱惜自己的生命（多指自杀）make light of one's life; not treasure one's own life（usu. to refer to sb. committing suicide on taking one's own life）

【轻声】qīngshēng 说话的时候有些字音很轻很短，叫做'轻声'。如普通话中的'了、着、的'等虚词和做后缀的'子、头'等字都念轻声。有些双音词的第二字也念轻声，如'萝卜'的'卜'，'地方'的'方'。（of Chinese pronunciation）light tone（e. g. particles in *putonghua* like 了 le，着 zhe and 的 de，suffixes like 子 zi and 头 tou，and the second character of some disyllables like 卜 bo in 萝卜 luó·bo，and 方 fang in 地方 dì·fang

【轻省】qīng·sheng〈方 *dail.*〉❶ 轻松 easy; relaxed：如今添了个助手，你可以稍微～点儿。Now you have an assistant, you will find your job easier. ❷ 重量小；轻便 light：这个箱子挺～。This case is very easy to carry.

【轻视】qīngshì 不重视；不认真对待 belittle; despise; scorn; look down on; take sth. lightly; attach no importance to; treat sb. or sth. not seriously：～劳动 look down on manual labour｜受人～ be looked down upon; be slighted

【轻率】qīngshuài（说话做事）随随便便，没有经过慎重考虑 rash; hasty; indiscreet; thoughtless;（speak or act）without careful consideration：举止～ rash in behaviour｜～从事 act rashly; do sth. rash; make light of a task｜结论过于～leap to a conclusion

【轻水】qīngshuǐ 普通水（H_2O）经过净化，用做反应堆的冷却剂和中子的慢化剂，叫做轻水 light water; purified ordinary water（H_2O）used as a cooler in a reactor and a moderator of neutrons

【轻松】qīngsōng 不感到有负担；不紧张 light; relaxed; carefree; without burden; not feel nervous：～活儿 light work; soft job; cushy job|～愉快 feel at ease

【轻佻】qīngtiāo 言语举动不庄重，不严肃 frivolous; flirtatious; giddy; skittish：举止～ skittish behaviour

【轻微】qīngwēi 不重的；程度浅的 light; slight; trifling; negligible; to a small extent：～劳动 light work|～脑震荡 slight cerebral concussion|他睡着了，发出～的鼾声。He fell asleep, snoring slightly.

【轻武器】qīngwǔqì 射程较近，便于携带的武器。如步枪、冲锋枪、机关枪、反坦克火箭筒等。light weapon; light arms; small arms; arms with short ranges, that are easy to carry, e.g. rifles, submachine guns, machine guns, anti-tank rocket launchers

【轻侮】qīngwǔ 轻蔑侮辱 scorn and insult; trifle with; treat with disrespect; slight and insult：国家的尊严岂容～！The dignity of a nation admits of no disrespect.

【轻闲】qīngxián 轻松安闲；（活儿）不重 relaxed; (of one's job) light; at leisure

【轻信】qīngxìn 轻易相信 credulous; gullible; be credulous; readily place trust in; readily believe：～谣言 give ready credence to rumours

【轻型】qīngxíng（机器、武器等）在重量、体积、功效或威力上比较小的 light-duty; light; (of machines, arms, etc.) small in weight, volume, efficiency or power：～电影摄影机 lightweight movie camera|～坦克 light tank

【轻扬】qīngyáng same as 轻飏 qíngyáng

【轻飏】qīngyáng 轻轻飘扬 sway; float; flutter; wave or fly gently：柳絮～。The willow catkins are swaying gently. also 轻扬 qīngyáng

【轻易】qīng·yì ❶ 简单容易 easily; simply：胜利不是～得到的。One cannot achieve a victory easily. ❷ 随随便便 rashly; lightly; offhanded：他不～发表意见。He never voices his opinion rashly.

【轻音乐】qīngyīnyuè 指轻快活泼、以抒情为主、结构简单的乐曲，包括器乐曲、舞曲等 light music; simple-structured lively tunes that mainly express or convey feelings, e.g. instrumental compositions, dance music, etc.

【轻盈】qīngyíng ❶ 形容女子身体苗条，动作轻快 (of a woman) slender and graceful; nimble; lithe; light-footed; lightsome：体态～ have a slender and graceful figure; with lithe and graceful posture|～的舞步 light-footed steps (in dancing) ❷ 轻松 lighthearted; breezy; relaxed：～的笑语 breezy laugh and talk

【轻悠悠】qīngyōuyōu ❶ 形容轻飘飘的样子 leisurely; gently; quietly; ethereally：只见蝴蝶在花丛中～地飞来飞去。The butterflies are fluttering gently among flowers. ❷ 形容声音轻柔 (of sound or music) cantabile; melodious; smooth and flowing：～的琴声由远处传来。Gentle and melodious strumming could be heard in the distance.

【轻于鸿毛】qīng yú hóng máo〈比喻 *fig.*〉死得不值得：lighter than a goose feather; die an insignificant death（鸿毛 *hongmao*：大雁的毛 feather from a wild goose）：死有重于泰山，有～。Some deaths are weightier than Mount Tai, while some are lighter than a feather.

【轻元素】qīngyuánsù 原子量较小的元素，如氢、氦等 light elements, e.g. hydrogen, helium, etc.

【轻重】qīngzhòng ❶ 重量的大小；用力的大小 weight ❷ 程度的深浅；事情的主次 degree; relative importance：大夫根据病情～来决定病人要不要住院。A doctor decides to hospitalize his patient based on the severity of the case.|工作要分～缓急，不能一把抓。We should distinguish between major and minor work and prioritize. ❸（说话做事的）适当限度 (in speech or behaviour) propriety; proper limits; seemliness; suitability：小孩子说话不知～。Small kids don't know the proper way to talk.

【轻重倒置】qīng zhòng dào zhì 把重要的和不重要的弄颠倒了 put the trivial above the important; reverse the order of importance; take the branch for the root

【轻重缓急】qīng zhòng huǎn jí 指事情有次要的、主要的、缓办的、急办的区别 relative importance or urgency; proper handling：做工作要注意～。Work should be handled in priority.

【轻舟】qīngzhōu〈书 *fml.*〉小船 small boat; skiff; cog; sampan; cockleshell; dinghy

【轻装】qīngzhuāng ❶ 轻便的行装 light packs：～就道 travel light ❷ 轻便的装备 light equipment：～部队 lightly equipped army

【轻装简从】qīng zhuāng jiǎn cóng ☞ 轻车简从 qīng chē jiǎn cóng

氢(氫)

qīng 气体元素，符号 H (hydrogenium)。无色无臭无味，是元素中最轻的。氢的同位素有氕、氘、氚三种。在工业上用途很广。hydrogen (H); gaseous element, colourless, tasteless and odourless, the lightest of all elements, having three isotopes: protium, deuterium, and tritium, which are widely used in industry; generally called 氢气 qīngqì

【氢弹】qīngdàn 核武器的一种，用氢的同位素氘和氚为原料，用特制的原子弹作为引起爆炸的装置，当原子弹爆炸时，所产生的高温使氘和氚发生聚合反应形成氦核子而产生大量的能并引起猛烈爆炸。氢弹的威力比原子弹大得多。hydrogen bomb; H bomb; fusion bomb; nuclear weapon made from a hydrogen isotope-deuterium, detonated by a specially made atomic bomb, which upon explosion causes high temperatures, in turn leading to the polyreaction of deuterium and tritium in the formation of helium nuclei, releasing enormous atomic energy and a destructive explosion; hydrogen bombs are far more powerful than atomic bombs; also 热核武器 rè héwǔqì

【氢离子浓度指数】qīnglízǐ nóngdù zhǐshù 表示溶液酸性或碱性程度的数值,即所含氢离子浓度的常用对数的负值。如某溶液所含氢离子的浓度为每升 10^{-5}克,它的氢离子浓度指数就是5。氢离子浓度指数一般在0到14之间,当它为7时,溶液呈中性;小于7时呈酸性,值愈小,酸性愈强;大于7时呈碱性,值愈大,碱性愈强。通称pH值。hydrogen ion concentration index, generally expressed as pH; numerical value indicating the acidity or alkalinity degree of a solution, i.e., the negative value of the common logarithm of ionized hydrogen concentration, e.g. if the hydrogen ion concentration in a solution is 10^{-5} g. per litre, then its pH is 5, with pH generally between 0 and 14, where a solution is neutral at 7, acids are below 7, and alkalis above 7; the smaller the reading, the more acid a solution; the larger the reading, the more alkaline a solution

【氢气】qīngqì 氢的通称 general term for hydrogen

【氢氧根】qīngyǎnggēn same as 羟基 qiǎngjī

倾 qīng ❶ 歪;斜 slant; incline; bend; be askew: ~斜 incline; slant; lean; tilt; fall away | 身子向前~着 lean forward; bend forward ❷ 倾向 tendency; trend; inclination; proclivity; propensity; preference; proneness; liability: 左~ left deviation | 右~ right deviation ❸ 倒塌 collapse; topple; fall down; break down; founder; tumble: ~覆 collapse; overturn | 大厦将~。The building is about to crumble. ❹ 使器物反转或歪斜,尽数倒出里面的东西 overturn and pour out; dump; empty: ~箱倒箧 search in all trunks; empty out all one's boxes and suitcases | ~盆大雨 downpour; torrential rain; cloudburst; drencher; soaker ❺ 用尽(力量) use up (one's energy): ~听 be all ears; listen attentively to; lend an attentive ear to | ~诉 pour out | ~全力把工作做好 make every effort to do a good job; do all one can for the job; exert oneself to the utmost to do a good job ❻〈书 *fml.*〉压倒 overwhelm; overbear; overpower: 权~朝野 hold sway the whole nation

【倾侧】qīngcè same as 倾斜 qīngxié: 塔身~。The tower is tilted. | 身子稍一~就倒在地上。He bent slightly and fell to the ground.

【倾巢】qīngcháo 出动全部力量(多含贬义 oft. derog.) turn out in full force: ~来犯。The whole nest poured out to attack. | ~出动 turn out in full force or strength

【倾城倾国】qīng chéng qīng guó 形容女子容貌很美。语本《汉书·外戚传》:'一顾倾人城,再顾倾人国'。(of a woman) have breath-taking beauty; be a stunning beauty; be of unmatched beauty. *History of Han·Biographies of Emperors' Mothers and Wives*: 'At first sight (of the woman) the city crumbled, and at the second, the entire country fell.'

【倾倒】qīngdǎo ❶ 由歪斜而倒下 topple over; tumble; collapse ❷ 十分佩服或爱慕 greatly admire; adore; prostrate oneself: 他的演技,令全场观众为之~。All the audience are overwhelmed by his acting.

【倾倒】qīngdào 倒转或倾斜容器使里面的东西全部出来 tip; dump; empty; pour out: 他猛一使劲儿就把一车土都~到沟里了。With a heave he emptied a wheelbarrow of earth into the ditch. ◇在诉苦会上她把那一肚子的苦水都~出来了。She poured out all her bitterness at the grievance meeting.

【倾动】qīngdòng 使人佩服感动 win admiration and create a sensation: ~一时 cause a great sensation; create a furore; have convulsive effect on one's mind

【倾覆】qīngfù ❶(物体)倒下 (of object) collapse; fall; come down plump; tip; capsize ❷ 使失败;颠覆 overthrow; overturn; topple; subvert; topple over; capsize; keel over; tip over; upset: ~国家 overthrow or topple a state

【倾家荡产】qīng jiā dàng chǎn 把全部家产丧失净尽 lose all one's property; run through one's fortune; be reduced to poverty and ruin; become bankrupt and homeless; exhaust one's wealth

【倾角】qīngjiǎo 直线或平面与水平线或水平面所成的角,或一直线与其在平面上的射影所成的角。inclination; dip; angle formed between a beeline and a plane, or between a horizontal line and a level, or between a beeline and its projection on a plane; also 倾斜角 qīngxiéjiǎo

【倾慕】qīngmù 倾心爱慕 adore; greatly admire; hold in high esteem: 彼此~ adore each other; have a strong admiration for each other | ~的心情 great admiration; adoration

【倾盆】qīngpén 形容雨极大 (of rain) pour (down hard): ~大雨 downpour; pouring rain; torrential rain; cloudburst; drencher; soaker; rain cats and dogs; pour; rain hard

【倾诉】qīngsù 完全说出(心里的话) pour out; give full vent to (what's in one's mind): ~衷情 pour out one's feelings | 尽情~ give full vent to one's innermost feelings

【倾塌】qīngtā 倒塌 collapse; fall down: 房舍

～。The house turnbled down.

【倾谈】qīngtán 尽情地交谈 have a heart-to-heart talk; pour one's heart to (out to) each other: 促膝～ sit knee to knee for a heart-to-heart talk

【倾听】qīngtīng 细心地听取(多用于上对下) heed; (of a superior) listen attentively to; lend an attentive ear; be all ears for; give audience to; give ear to; hearken (to): ～群众的意见 heed public opinion

【倾吐】qīngtǔ same as 倾诉 qīngsù: ～衷肠 pour oneself out; speak one's heart freely; share one's innermost feelings; confide in sb.; get sth. of one's chest; unburden oneself

【倾箱倒箧】qīng xiāng dào qiè 把箱子里的东西都倒出来 turn out all one's boxes and suitcases; 〈比喻 *fig.*〉尽其所有 give all one has

【倾向】qīngxiàng ❶ 偏于赞成(对立的事物中的一方) prefer; be inclined to; be in favour of; lean towards (one party of a contradiction): 两种意见我比较～于前一种。Between the two opinions I prefer the former. ❷ 发展的方向; 趋势 tendency; trend; inclination; proclivity; propensity; preference; proneness; liability; direction: 纠正不良～ stop unhealthy trend

【倾销】qīngxiāo 在市场上用低于市场价格的价格,大量抛售商品。目的在击败竞争对手,夺取市场。dump; launch a cut-throat sale; place goods on the market in large quantities and at a low price in order to defeat competitors and grab the market

【倾斜】qīngxié ❶ 歪斜 incline; slant; lean; tilt; slope; fall away; lurch; tip: ～度 inclination; gradient; lean | 屋子年久失修,有些～。The house is in disrepair, with pieces fallen away. ❷〈比喻 *fig.*〉偏向于某一方 be in favour of; give preferential treatment to; lean to (one side)

【倾泻】qīngxiè (大量的水)很快地从高处流下 pour; come down in torrents: 大雨之后,山水～下来,汇成了奔腾的急流。After the downpour, the flood rushed down the mountain and converged into rapid torrents.

【倾心】qīngxīn ❶ 一心向往; 爱慕 yearn toward; adore; set one's affections on; be enamoured of; admire wholeheartedly: 一见～ fall in love at first sight ❷ 拿出真诚的心 wholehearted; heart-to-heart: ～交谈,互相勉励 talk heart to heart and uplift each other

【倾轧】qīngyà 在同一组织中排挤打击不同派系的人 engage in factional strife; jostle against each other; discord; conflict with: 勾心斗角,互相～ intrigue against each other; plot against each other

【倾注】qīngzhù ❶ 由上而下地流入 pour into; pour down; transfuse; shower: 一股泉水～到深潭里。A mountain stream pours down into the pool. ❷ (感情、力量等)集中到一个目标上 (of feelings, effort, etc.) concentrate on; transfuse; devote; throw into: 母亲的爱～在儿女身上。The mother showered all her affection on her children. | 毕生精力～于教育事业 devote one's life (all one's energy) to the cause of education

卿 qīng ❶〈古时 *arch.*〉高级官名 senior official: ～相 high court official and chief minister ❷〈古时 *arch.*〉君称臣 (form of address for a court official by an emperor) you ❸〈古时 *arch.*〉夫妻或好朋友之间表示亲爱的称呼 term of endearment used between husband and wife, or among close friends ❹ (Qīng) 姓 a surname

【卿卿我我】qīng qīng wǒ wǒ 形容男女间非常亲昵 (used to describe intimacy between a man and woman) bill and coo

圊 qīng〈书 *fml.*〉厕所 latrine: ～土 human excrement | ～粪 manure from latrines

【圊肥】qīngféi〈方 *dial.*〉厩(jiù)肥 barnyard manure

清1 qīng ❶ (液体或气体)纯净没有混杂的东西(跟'浊'相对 as opposed to 'turbid') (of gases or liquids) pure; clear; unmixed: 水～见底。The water is so limpid that the bottom can be seen. | 天朗气～ clear skies ❷ 寂静 quiet; silent; still: ～静 quiet; tranquil; serene; peaceful | 冷～ lacking excitement; cheerless; desolate; quiet and empty; deserted ❸ 公正廉洁 impartial; honest; upright; disinterested: ～官 honest officials; clean-handed officials | ～廉 honest and clean; clean-handed; incorruptible ❹ 清楚 clear; lucid: 说不～ talk confusingly | 问～底细 find out the truth by through inquiry ❺ 单纯 simple; plain: ～唱 sing opera arias without make-up | ～茶 green tea; tea served without refreshments ❻ 一点不留 completely: 把账还～了 pay off a debt ❼ 清除不纯的成分;使组织纯洁 clear away or off; clear... of sth.; purify; clean up: ～党 purge a political party; carry out a purge ❽ (账目)还清;结清 (of accounts) be settled: ～欠 pay off arrears | 账已经～了。The accounts have been paid off. ❾ 点验 count; check: ～一～行李的件数。Check the luggage.

清2 Qīng ❶ 朝代,公元 1616-1911,满族人爱新觉罗·努尔哈赤所建,初名后金,1636年改为清。1644 年入关,定都北京。Qing Dynasty (1616-1911), founded by Aisin Gioro Nurhachi, originally known as the Late Jin Dynasty, and changed to Qing in 1636. In 1644 the Qing forced its way across the Great Wall and made Beijing the capital ❷ 姓 a surname

【清白】qīngbái ❶ 纯洁;没有污点 pure; clean;

unblemished; unsullied; innocent; sinless; clean-handed; blameless: 历史～ have a stainless past; have a clean personal record ❷〈方 *dial.*〉清楚;明白 clear; lucid: 他说了半天也没把问题说～。He didn't make himself clear, even after repeated explanations.

【清册】qīngcè 详细登记有关项目的册子 detailed and itemized list; inventory: 材料～ detailed list of materials | 固定财产～ inventory of fixed assets

【清茶】qīngchá ❶ 用绿茶泡成的茶水 green tea ❷ 指只有茶水而没有糖果点心 tea served without refreshments

【清查】qīngchá 彻底检查 check; examine: ～仓库 make an inventory of a warehouse

【清偿】qīngcháng 全部偿还(债务) pay off; clear (off); acquit; discharge (debts)

【清场】qīng//chǎng 清理公共场所 clear a public place of visitors: 散戏后,再～打扫。Clear and clean the theatre after the opera is over.

【清唱】qīngchàng 不化装的戏曲演唱形式,一般只唱某出戏中的一段或数段 sing opera arias without make-up

【清彻】qīngchè same as 清澈 qīngchè

【清澈】qīngchè 清而透明 limpid; crystal-clear; lucid: 湖水～见底。The lake water is so clear that you can see the bottom. also 清彻 qīngchè

【清晨】qīngchén 日出前后的一段时间 early morning; cockcrow

【清除】qīngchú 扫除净尽;全部去掉 clear away; remove; eliminate; clean out; purge; rid; weed out; get rid of; scavenge; debride: ～积雪 remove the snow on the road | ～积弊 eliminate long-standing drawbacks | ～内奸 purge agent provocateurs (from a political party); get rid of agent provocateurs

【清楚】qīng·chu ❶ 事物容易让人了解、辨认 clear; distinct; explicit: 字迹～ written in clear hand | 话说得不～ speak unclearly | 把工作交代～ make everything clear upon the handing over of work ❷ 对事物了解很透彻 be keenly aware: 头脑～ of sound mind; sane ❸ 了解 know; be aware: 这件事的经过他很～。He is clear about what has happened. | 这个问题你～不～? Do you understand this question or not?

【清纯】qīngchún ❶ 清秀纯洁 pretty and pure: ～秀丽 pretty and innocent | 她～得像一朵玉兰。She is as pure and fresh as a magnolia. ❷ 清新纯净 fresh and pure: 泉水～ fresh spring water | 雨后空气～。The air is pure and clear after rain.

【清醇】qīngchún (气味、滋味)清而纯正 mellow and pure (in taste and smell): 酒味～可口。The wine is pure and mellow.

【清脆】qīngcuì ❶ (声音)清楚悦耳(of sound) clear and melodious; ringing: ～的鸟语声 clear chirping of birds | ～的歌声 clear and melodious singing ❷ (食物)脆而清香 crisp and fresh: 鲜黄瓜～可口。Fresh cucumber is crisp and savoury.

【清单】qīngdān 详细登记有关项目的单子 list of items; checklist; stock list; bill; databook; muster: 开～ make an inventory | 物资～ inventory | 列一个～ make a detailed list

【清淡】qīngdàn ❶ (颜色、气味)清而淡;不浓 (of colour, smell) light; weak; delicate: 一杯～的龙井茶 a cup of light Longjing tea | ～的荷花香气 delicate scent of lotus ❷ (食物)含油脂少 (of food) light; not greasy or rich: 我这两天感冒了,想吃点～的菜。I've had a cold these days and want to eat something light. ❸ 清新淡雅 fresh, simple and elegant: ～的艺术风格 simple and elegant style of art ❹ 营业数额少 (of business) dull; slack: 农忙时进城的人不多,生意比较～。When the season is busy few farmers go to town, and business is rather slack.

【清道】qīngdào ❶ 打扫街道;清除路上的障碍 sweep the streets; clear the road of barricades ❷〈古代 *arch.*〉帝王或官吏外出时在前引路,驱散行人 clear the way for the carriage of an emperor or a high official

【清点】qīngdiǎn 清理查点 make an inventory; sort through and check: ～物资 make an inventory of materials

【清炖】qīngdùn 烹调法,汤中不放酱油慢慢炖(肉类) cook by boiling slowly without any soy sauce; stew; simmer: ～鸡 stewed chicken without soy sauce

【清风】qīngfēng 凉爽的风 slight refreshing wind; breeze; cool breeze; soothing wind; gentle wind; air; zephyr: ～徐来。A cool breeze is blowing gently.

【清福】qīngfú 指清闲安适的生活 life of leisure and ease: 享～ enjoy a life of leisure and ease

【清高】qīnggāo 指人品纯洁高尚,不同流合污 of noble and chaste character; aloof from petty politics and material pursuits; morally lofty and upright

【清稿】qīnggǎo 誊清了的稿子 clean copy; fair copy

【清供】qīnggòng ❶ 清雅的供品,如松、竹、梅、鲜花、香火和素的食物等 elegant offerings such as pine, bamboo, plums, flowers or vegetarian foods ❷ 指古器物、盆景等供玩赏的东西 ornaments such as curios, potted landscapes, etc.: 案头～ desk ornaments

【清官】qīngguān 称廉洁公正的官吏 honest and upright officials; clean-handed officials; incorruptible officials

【清规】qīngguī 佛教规定的僧尼必须遵守的规则 monastic rules or commandments for monks and nuns

【清规戒律】qīngguī jièlǜ ❶ 僧尼、道士必须遵守的规则和戒律 regulations, taboos and commandments for Buddhists and Taoists ❷ 泛指规章制度,多指束缚人的死板的规章制度 rigid rules and conventions; dos and don'ts; taboos; fetters

【清寒】qīnghán ❶ same as 清贫 qīngpín: 家境～ come from a humble or impoverished family ❷ 清朗而有寒意 clear and cold: 月色～。The moon is clear and cold.

【清还】qīnghuán 清理归还;清偿 clean up and pay off; discharge (a debt): ～图书 sort through library books and return the due ones

【清寂】qīngjì 冷清寂静 cold and quiet: ～的月夜 chilly and quiet moonlit night

【清减】qīngjiǎn 〈婉辞 *euph*.〉指人消瘦 thin, emaciated

【清剿】qīngjiǎo 全部消灭;肃清 suppress and wipe out; eliminate; sweep: ～土匪 suppress bandits; wipe out bandits

【清洁】qīngjié 没有尘土、油垢等 clean; dust-free; spotless; sanitary: ～剂 detergent | 屋子里很～。The room is very clean. | 注意～卫生。Pay attention to environmental sanitation and personal hygiene.

【清劲风】qīngjìngfēng 气象学上指5级风 (meteorol.) wind of force 5; ☞ 风级 fēngjí on p. 579

【清净】qīngjìng ❶ 没有事物打扰 free from disturbance and noise; peace and quiet: 耳根～ have peace for one's ears; far from the madding crowd ❷ 清澈 clear; limpid; lucid: 湖水～见底。The lake is so clear that you can see to the bottom of it.

【清静】qīngjìng (环境)安静;不嘈杂 (of surroundings) quiet; peaceful; tranquil: 我们找个～的地方谈谈。Let's go to a quiet place and talk.

【清君侧】qīngjūncè《公羊传》定公十三年:'晋赵鞅取晋阳之甲,以逐荀寅与士吉射。荀寅与士吉射者曷为者也? 君侧之恶人也。此逐君侧之恶人,曷为以叛言之? 无君命也。'唐李商隐《有感》诗:'古有清君侧,今非乏老成。''清君侧'指清除君主身边的奸佞。rid the king's court of evil officials; purge the king's court. According to *The Gongyang Commentary*, in the 13th Year of Duke Ding, 'Zhao Yang of the state of Jin offered the armour of Jin Yang as a reward to encourage Xun Yin and Shi Ji in a shoot-out. Who were Xun Yin and Shi Ji? They were both evil court officials who happened to be right-hand men of the King of Jin. Zhao Yang took this measure to rid the duke of evil people, but why was he accused of being disloyal to the duke? Because he did this without the king's orders.' Tang-dynasty poet Li Shangyin said in *Afterthoughts*: 'In ancient times there was someone who rose to purge the king's court; today there is no lack of mature and cool-headed people.'

【清客】qīngkè 〈旧 *old*〉指在官僚地主家里帮闲的门客 hangers-on of high-ranking officials or landlords: 豪门～ hangers-on of influential families

【清口】qīngkǒu 爽口 tasty and refreshing: 拌黄瓜吃着～。Cucumber salad is tasty and refreshing.

【清苦】qīngkǔ 贫苦(旧时多形容读书人 of intellectuals in old times) poor; underprivileged; poverty-stricken; pinched; ill-provided: 生活～ live a spartan life; live in privation

【清栏】qīng//lán 〈方 *dial*.〉起圈(juàn) remove manure from a pigsty, sheepfold, stable, etc.

【清朗】qīnglǎng ❶ 凉爽晴朗 cool and clear; crisp and bright; cloudless; unclouded; fair; fine; sunny: ～的月夜 serene moonlit night | 天气～。It's a fair day. or The weather is fine. ❷ 清净明亮 clear and bright: 眉目～ shapely eyebrows and bright eyes | 一双大眼～有神 with big bright eyes ❸ 清楚响亮 clear and sonorous: ～的声音 loud voice; ringing sound ❹ 清新明快 (of writings) refreshingly clear and lively: 笔调～ write in a refreshing and lively style

【清冷】qīnglěng ❶ 凉爽而略带寒意 chilly: ～的秋夜 chilly autumn night ❷ 冷清 deserted; empty: 旅客们都走了,站台上十分～。The passengers were all gone and the platform was quite deserted.

【清理】qīnglǐ 彻底整理或处理 sort out; clean up; clear up; tidy up; straighten up; put in order: ～仓库 take stock; make an inventory of warehouse stocks | ～账目 clear up debts | ～积案 clear up the unsolved cases | ～古代文献 put in order ancient documents

【清丽】qīnglì 清雅秀丽 (of handwriting or articles) lucid and elegant; (of a scene, etc.) fresh and pleasant: 文章～ article of elegant writing | 气质～ of fresh and nice temperament | ～的景色 quiet and exquisite scenery

【清廉】qīnglián 清白廉洁 (of officials) honest and clean; clean-handed; incorruptible; fair and disinterested: 为政～ be an incorruptible official

【清凉】qīngliáng 凉而使人感觉爽快 cool and refreshing; cool and pleasant; cooling; refrigerant: ～汽水 cold soda pop | ～的薄荷味儿 refreshing mint smell

【清凉油】qīngliángyóu 用薄荷油、樟脑、桂皮油、桉叶油等加石蜡制成的膏状药物。应用范围很广,对头痛、轻微烫伤等有一定疗效,但不能根治。cooling ointment; essential balm; tiger balm; ointment made from menthol, camphor, cassia oil, eucalyptus oil, etc., with paraffin; widely used, esp. for effective treatment of headache, minor burns, etc.; 〈旧称 *old*〉万金油 wànjīnyóu

【清亮】qīngliàng 清脆响亮 clear and sonorous; resonant; ringing: 嗓音～ have a resonant voice|～的歌声 clear and loud singing

【清亮】qīng·liang ❶ same as 清澈 qīngchè ❷ 明白 clear in one's mind; of sound awareness: 心里一下子～了。At once I was all clear about it. ❸〈方 *dial.*〉清楚; 清晰 clearly seen; sharp to the eye: 石碑上的字迹看不～。The inscription on the monument cannot be clearly read.

Q

【清冽】qīngliè same as 清冷 qīnglěng ①; 清凉 qīngliáng: 溪水～。The water in the brook feels chilly.

【清凌凌】qīnglīnglīng (～的 qīnglīnglīng·de)形容水清澈而有波纹 (of water) clear and rippling; also 清泠泠 qīnglīnglīng

【清明】[1] qīngmíng ❶ (政治)有法度,有条理 (of politics) characterized by good government, healthy justice, and systematic rule: ～之治 good governance ❷ (头脑)清楚;清醒 (of mind) clear; sober: 神志～ have a conscious mind; as cool as a cucumber ❸ 清澈而明朗 clear and bright: 月色～。The moonlight is bright.

【清明】[2] qīngmíng 二十四节气之一,在 4 月 4, 5 或 6 日。民间习惯在这天扫墓。Pure Brightness; one of the 24 solar periods, occurring on April 4, 5 or 6, when traditionally people visit their ancestral tombs; ☞节气 jiéqì on p. 989 and 二十四节气 èrshísì jiéqì on p. 516

【清贫】qīngpín 贫穷(旧时多形容读书人 of intellectuals in old times) poor; impoverished; penniless; underprivileged; ill-provided: 家道～ come from an impoverished family|～自守 live in reduced circumstances but maintain integrity

【清平】qīngpíng 太平 peaceful; tranquil: ～世界 peaceful world|海内～ tranquility within the four seas

【清漆】qīngqī 人造漆的一种,用树脂、亚麻油或松节油等制成,不含颜料,涂在木器表面形成一层透明薄膜,现出木材原有的纹。也用来制造磁漆等。varnish; synthetic colourless paint made from resin, linolein, turpentine, etc., which provides a glossy transparent coating on the surface of woodwork, so that the original grain of wood can be clearly seen, also used to make lacquer, enamel, etc.

【清讫】qīngqì 收付了结(多指款项 usu. payment) received; fully paid

【清切】qīngqiè ❶ 清晰真切 clear and distinct: 她说话的声音太低,听不～。He spoke in such low voice that I simply couldn't catch it.|泪眼模糊,看不～。With eyes blurred by tears, I couldn't see clearly. ❷ 凄切 sad; plangent; plaintive: 不时传来孤雁～的哀鸣。Plangent cries of a lone wild goose could be heard from time to time.

【清秋】qīngqiū 秋季,特指深秋 autumn, esp. late autumn: ～天气,西山红叶正艳。It was late autumn, and the maple leaves were aflame on the Western Mountains.

【清癯】qīngqú 〈书 *fml.*〉 same as 清瘦 qīngshòu: 面容～ thin face

【清热】qīng//rè〈中医 *Chin. med.*〉指用药物清除内热 relieve internal heat: ～解毒 relieve internal heat; detoxify|～化痰 relieve internal heat and reduce phlegm

【清扫】qīngsǎo 彻底扫除 clean up; give a through cleaning; sweep; scavenge: ～街道 clean up the street

【清瘦】qīngshòu〈婉辞 *euph.*〉指人瘦 thin; slim; slender

【清爽】qīngshuǎng ❶ 清洁凉爽 clean, cool and fresh; refreshing: 雨后空气～。The air is refreshing after the rain. ❷ 轻松爽快 relaxed and relieved: 任务完成了,心里很～。He felt greatly relieved after fulfilling his mission. ❸〈方 *dial.*〉整洁;干净 neat and clean; tidy ❹〈方 *dial.*〉清楚;明白 clear; aware: 神志～ conscious|把话讲～ make sense in speech ❺〈方 *dial.*〉清淡爽口 light and tasty: 滋味～ taste fresh

【清水衙门】qīngshuǐ yá·men〈旧 *old*〉指不经手钱财,不能从中捞取油水的官府,现多用来比喻经费少、福利少的事业单位。government office that does not handle money matters and therefore has little chance for personal gain; (usu. fig.) organization with limited funds and resources

【清算】qīngsuàn ❶ 彻底地计算 carefully calculate and check; settle; clear; square; pay off; liquidate: ～账目 settle accounts; balance accounts ❷ 列举全部罪恶或错误并做出相应的处理 expose all evil-doings or mistakes, and inflict punishment accordingly; call or bring to account: ～恶霸的罪恶 expose and condemn the crimes of a local tyrant

【清谈】qīngtán 本指魏晋间一些士大夫不务实际,空谈哲理,后世泛指一般不切实际的谈论 philosophical prate among impractical scholar-bureaucrats during the Wei-Jin period; generally refers to empty talk; idle talk; phrase-mongering; windbaggery; prate; prittle-prattle; bunk; chin-music; burble; gab: ～误国。Empty talk will ruin the country.

【清汤】qīngtāng 没有菜的汤(有时搁点儿葱花或豌豆苗等 cooked with a little chopped shallots, pea sprouts, etc.) clear soup; light soup; consomme

【清通】qīngtōng（文章）层次清楚，文句通顺（of writings）well-organised and fluent; smooth: 文章要写得～，必须下一番苦功。If you want to write a clear and smooth essay, you have some work cut out for you.

【清玩】qīngwán ❶ 供赏玩的雅致的东西，如盆景、金石、书画等 elegant objects for keepsake and enjoyment, e.g. miniature gardens, metals and stones, paintings and calligraphy works, etc. ❷ 赏玩 appreciate the beauty of; admire; enjoy; delight in

【清婉】qīngwǎn 清越婉转（of voice）clear and sweet: 歌声～。The singing is clear and sweet sounding.

【清晰】qīngxī same as 清楚 qīngchu: 发音～ clear pronunciation|～可辨 clearly seen; discernible; distinguishable

【清洗】qīngxǐ ❶ 洗干净 clean; wash; launder; rinse: 炊具要经常～消毒。Cooking utensils should always be cleaned and sanitized. ❷ 清除（不能容留于内部的分子）purge; ferret out; eliminate; get rid of: ～内奸 ferret out agent provocateurs

【清闲】qīngxián 清静闲暇 carefree and idle; at leisure; at ease: ～自在 enjoy leisure; feel at ease; live a leisurely life|他一时还过不惯～的退休生活。He finds it hard to adjust himself to a leisurely life of retirement.

【清香】qīngxiāng 清淡的香味 delicate fragrance; faint scent; pleasant and refreshing smell: ～可口 tasty and refreshing|晨风吹来野花的～。The morning breeze wafted over the scent of wild flowers.

【清心】qīngxīn ❶ 心境恬静，没有挂虑 with peace of mind; carefree; undisturbed: 摆脱家务就可以～了。One can be carefree without household chores to attend to. ❷ 使清心 free sb. from worry; set one's mind at ease; purify the heart: ～寡欲 have a pure heart and few desires; purge one's mind of desires and ambitions ❸〈中医 *Chin. med.*〉指清除心火 relieve internal heat: ～明目 relieve internal heat and improve eyesight

【清新】qīngxīn ❶ 清爽而新鲜 fresh and clean: 刚下过雨，空气～。It has just rained and the air is fresh and clean. ❷ 新颖不俗气 original; fresh and refined: 色调～ original hue|画报的版面～活泼。The layout of the pictorial is fresh and lively.

【清馨】qīngxīn〈书 *fml.*〉清香 delicate fragrance; faint scent: 满园～。The garden is permeated with refreshing and delicate fragrances.

【清醒】qīngxǐng ❶（头脑）清楚；明白 clear-headed; sober; keep a level head: 早晨起来，头脑特别～。Your mind is particularly fresh in the morning after getting up. ❷（神志）由昏迷而恢复正常 regain consciousness; come to: 病人已经～过来。The patient has come to.

【清秀】qīngxiù 美丽而不俗气 pretty and graceful: 面貌～ have fine and delicate features|妹妹比姐姐长得要～一些。The younger sister looks prettier than the older one.

【清雅】qīngyǎ ❶ 清新高雅 fresh and elegant; refined: 风格～ in an elegant style|言辞～ in refined language ❷ 清秀文雅 delicate and comely: 仪容～ graceful appearance

【清样】qīngyàng 从最后校改的印刷版上打下来的校样，有时也指最后一次校定的校样。final proof; foundry proof

【清夜】qīngyè 寂静的深夜 in the still of night: ～自思 be lost in reflection in the depths of night; be deep in thought in the still of night

【清一色】qīngyīsè ❶ 指打麻将牌时某一家由一种花色组成的一副牌（of mah-jong）all of one suit ❷〈比喻 *fig.*〉全部由一种成分构成或全部一个样子 uniform; undiversified; homogeneous: 到会的人穿的都是～的中山装。All present at the meeting were wearing Sun Yat-sen uniforms without exception.

【清议】qīngyì〈旧时 *old*〉指名流对当代政治或政治人物的议论 political remarks by prestigious people

【清逸】qīngyì 清新脱俗 fresh and refined: 笔调～ write in a fresh and elegant style|琴声～悦耳。The music from the piano is refreshing and sweet.

【清音】[1] qīngyīn ❶ 曲艺的一种，流行于四川，用琵琶、二胡等伴奏 *qingyin*; ballad-singing popular in Sichuan Province, accompanied by lute, *erhu* (two-stringed Chinese fiddle), etc. ❷〈旧时 *old*〉婚丧中所用的吹奏乐 wind music played at weddings or funerals

【清音】[2] qīngyīn 发音时声带不振动的音 *sotto voce*; voiceless sound; ☞带音 dàiyīn on p.372

【清莹】qīngyíng 清澈而明亮 limpid and bright: ～的泪珠 glistening tears|～的湖水 limpid and sparkling lake

【清幽】qīngyōu（风景）秀丽而幽静（of landscapes）quiet and beautiful; enchanting and secluded: 月色～ quiet moonlit charm

【清油】qīngyóu〈方 *dial.*〉❶ 菜油 rapeseed oil; canola oil ❷ 茶油 tea oil ❸ 素油 edible vegetable oil: ～大饼 pancake cooked in vegetable oil

【清越】qīngyuè（声音）清脆悠扬（of sound）clear and melodious: ～的歌声 clear and melodious song

【清早】qīngzǎo same as 清晨 qīngchén: 明日～出发。We will set off early the next morning.

【清湛】qīngzhàn〈书 *fml*.〉same as 清澈 qīngchè：池水～。The pond is crystal clear.

【清丈】qīngzhàng 详细地丈量土地 measure (a piece of land)

【清账】qīng//zhàng 结清账目 settle accounts; square or clear an account

【清账】qīngzhàng 经过整理的详细账目 cleared accounts：开一篇～ open a clean account

【清真】qīngzhēn ❶〈书 *fml*.〉纯洁质朴 simple and unadorned; plain：诗贵～，更要有寄托。The value of a poem lies in its simplicity, but more so in its spiritual value. ❷ 伊斯兰教的 Islamic; Muslim：～寺 mosque|～食堂 Muslim canteen|～点心 halal cakes (made without pork fat)

【清真教】Qīngzhēnjiào ☞伊斯兰教 Yīsīlánjiào on p. 2257

【清真寺】qīngzhēnsì 伊斯兰教的寺院 mosque; also 礼拜寺 lǐbàisì

【清蒸】qīngzhēng 烹调法，不放酱油带汤蒸（鸡、鱼、肉等）steam; cooking method (for chicken, fish, meat, etc.) in clear soup (usu. without soy sauce)：～鲥鱼 steamed hilsa herring

【清正】qīngzhèng 清廉公正 honest and upright：为官～ be an honest and upright official

蜻 qīng ☞ below

【蜻蜓】qīngtíng 昆虫，身体细长，胸部的背面有两对膜状的翅，生活在水边，捕食蚊子等小飞虫，能高飞。雌的用尾点水而产卵于水中。幼虫叫水虿，生活在水中。是益虫。dragonfly (*Polycanthagyna melanictera*); mosquito hawk; darning needle; water nymph; beneficial aquatic insect with a long slender body and two pairs of reticulated or net-veined wings on its back, living by water and feeding on small winged insects such as mosquitoes, etc., and capable of flying high, the female laying eggs in water with a slight dip of the cauda, with its larvae called 水虿 shuǐchà (dobson)

【蜻蜓点水】qīngtíng diǎn shuǐ〈比喻 fig.〉做事肤浅不深入 like a dragonfly skimming the water surface; a light touch; merely scratching the surface of a problem without going deep into the substance

鲭 qīng 鱼类的一科，身体呈梭形而侧扁，鳞圆而细小，头尖，口大。鲐鱼就属于鲭科。Atlantic mackerel (*Scomber scombrus Linnaeus*); family of fish characterized by a shuttle-shaped and laterally flat body, tiny head, and big mouth; chub marckerel, one of the fish in this family

☞ zhēng on p. 2444

qíng（ㄑㄧㄥˊ）

勍 qíng〈书 *fml*.〉强 powerful; strong：～敌 powerful foe

情 qíng ❶ 感情 feeling; emotion; affection; sensation; heart; sentiment; reins; susceptibility：热～ enthusiastic; passionate; warm; passion; enthusiasm; ardour; ebullience; fervour; flame; zest|无～ unkind; heartless; ruthless; pitiless; stone-hearted; relentless; inhuman; ruthlessness; callousness; implacability; inexorability|温～ warmth; warm feelings ❷ 情面 feelings; kindness; favour：人～ human feelings; human relationship; favour|讲～ plead for sb.|托～ ask sb. to intercede|求～ plead; beg for leniency ❸ 爱情 love; passion; affection：～书 love letter|～话 lovers' prattle; sweet talk; (whisper) sweet nothings|谈～ have a romance with sb.; be on a date with sb. ❹ 情欲；性欲 sexual desire; libido; lust：春～ lust; love|催～ stimulate the oestrus of a female animal by artificial means|发～期 oestrum; the rut; heat ❺ 情形；情况 situation; state; condition; circumstance：病～ condition (of an illness)|军～ military situation|实～ truth|灾～ disaster conditions ❻ 情理；道理 reason; sense：合～合理 reasonable and fair; it stands to reason that...; it figures; in reason; within reason|不～之请 my presumptuous request

【情爱】qíng'ài ❶ 爱情 (esp. between a man and woman) love; affection ❷ 指人与人互相爱护的感情 caring love

【情报】qíngbào 关于某种情况的消息和报告，多带机密性质 intelligence; information; tip-off; witting; gen：～员 intelligence agent; intelligencer|军事～ military intelligence|科学技术～ scientific and technological information or intelligence

【情不自禁】qíng bù zì jìn 抑制不住自己的感情 cannot contain oneself (for certain feelings); let oneself go; cannot refrain from; cannot help oneself; cannot help (doing sth.); (do sth.) in spite of oneself

【情操】qíngcāo 由感情和思想综合起来的，不轻易改变的心理状态 moral integrity; character：高尚的～ noble character

【情场】qíngchǎng 指有关谈情说爱的事 arena of love; love affair; love relationship：～风波 storms of love|～失意 be frustrated in love; be a failure in love

【情敌】qíngdí 因追求同一异性而彼此发生矛盾的人 rival in a love triangle

【情调】qíngdiào 思想感情所表现出来的格调；事物所具有的能引起人的各种不同感情的性质 sentiment; taste; mood; emotional appeal; ambiance; atmosphere：～健康 healthy sentiments|异国～ exotic atmosphere

【情窦初开】qíngdòu chū kāi 指刚懂得爱情(多指少女 esp. of a young woman) first awakening or stirrings of love; be open to love for the first time

【情分】qíng·fèn 人与人相处的情感;情义 mutual affection; emotional ties (of friendship, etc.):朋友～ friendship|兄弟～ brotherly love; brotherhood; fraternity|两家做了几辈子邻居,素来～好。The two families have been neighbours for generations and have always been on good terms.

【情夫】qíngfū 男女两人,一方或双方已有配偶,他们之间发生性爱的违法行为,男方是女方的情夫 illicit male lover of a married woman; fancy man; paramour

【情妇】qíngfù 男女两人,一方或双方已有配偶,他们之间发生性爱的违法行为,女方是男方的情妇 illicit female lover of a married man; mistress; fancy woman; ladylove; paramour

【情感】qínggǎn ❶ 对外界刺激肯定或否定的心理反应,如喜欢、愤怒、悲伤、恐惧、爱慕、厌恶等 emotion; feeling; positive or negative mental state that responds to outside stimulation or disturbance, e. g. joy, anger, sorrow, fear, love, abhor, etc. ❷ 感情 affection; attachment:两人～很深。They are strongly attached to each other.

【情歌】qínggē 表现男女爱情的歌曲 love song; ballad; madrigal

【情话】qínghuà ❶ 男女间表示爱情的话 lovers' prattle; whispered sweet talk ❷〈书 *fml.*〉知心话 heart-to-heart talk

【情怀】qínggē 含有某种感情的心境 emotions; sentiments; feelings:抒发～ express one's feelings and thoughts

【情急】qíngjí 因为希望马上避免或获得某种事物而心中着急 moment of desperation (to seize or avoid sth.):～智生(心中着急而突然想出聪明的办法) hit upon a good idea in a moment of desperation; good ideas come at times of crisis|一时～,做出失礼的事来。He did something disrespectful in a moment of despair.

【情节】qíngjié 事情的变化和经过 plot; scenario; case; circumstances:故事～ plot; story|～生动 a lively plot|根据～轻重分别处理。Each will be dealt with according to the seriousness of the case.

【情结】qíngjié 心中的感情纠葛;深藏心底的感情 complex; love knot:化解不开的～ inextricably complex|浓重的思乡～ strong nostalgia

【情景】qíngjǐng (具体场合的)情形;景象 scene; sight; spectacle; circumstances:比起广州来,北京的冬天另是一番～。Compared with Guangzhou, winter in Beijing presents quite a different sight.

【情境】qíngjìng 情景;境地 circumstances; condition; situation

【情况】qíngkuàng ❶ same as 情形 qíng·xing:思想～ state of mind; thinking|工作～ how one works; work experience|～特殊。The case is special. ❷ 指军事上的变化 military situation or developments:这两天前线没有什么～。Nothing has happened at the front the last couple of days.

【情郎】qíngláng 相恋的青年男女中的男子 woman's lover; spark; beau; inamorato

【情理】qínglǐ 人的常情和事情的一般道理 reason; sense:不近～ unreasonable; irrational|～难容 beyond all reason; contrary to reason|话很合乎～。What he said is reasonable.

【情侣】qínglǚ 相恋的男女或其中的一方 lovers (or either of a pair of lovers); sweethearts

【情面】qíng·miàn 私人间的情分和面子 favour; feelings:顾～ with consideration for sb.'s feelings|留～ spare one's feelings|不讲～ no place for sentiment|打破～ offend sb.'s feelings

【情趣】qíngqù ❶ 性情志趣 temperament and interests; disposition and inclination:二人～相投。The two of them are temperamentally compatible. ❷ 情调趣味 emotional appeal; interest:～正浓 greatly appealing or palatable|这首诗写得很有～。This poem is very sentimentally appealing.

【情人】qíngrén 相爱中的男女的一方 lover; sweetheart; sweetie

【情杀】qíngshā 因爱情纠纷而引起的凶杀 murder for love:～案 case of murder for love

【情诗】qíngshī 男女间表示爱情的诗 love poem

【情势】qíngshì 事情的状况和发展的趋势;形势② trend of events; situation:～紧迫。The situation is urgent.|洞察敌我～ perceive the situation on our side as well as on the enemy's

【情事】qíngshì 情况;现象 case; phenomenon:详细询问家乡的～ ask in detail about things in one's hometown

【情书】qíngshū 男女间表示爱情的信 love letter

【情丝】qíngsī 指缠绵的情意 affection; tender feelings:～万缕 a wealth of tender love

【情思】qíngsī ❶ 情意;情感 emotion; sentiment; tender regards; affection; ties of love ❷ 情绪;心思 thoughts and feelings

【情死】qíngsǐ 指相爱的男女因婚姻不遂而死 (of lovers) commit suicide after not being able to marry; die for love

【情素】qíngsù same as 情愫 qíngsù

【情愫】qíngsù〈书 *fml.*〉❶ 感情 feelings; attachment:朝夕相处,增加了他们之间的～。Staying together for quite a while, they have developed stronger feelings toward each other. ❷ 本心;真情实意 innermost feelings; true feelings:互倾～ pour out their feelings for each other ‖ also 情素 qíngsù

【情随事迁】qíng suí shì qiān 思想感情随着情况的变迁而发生变化 feelings change with circumstances

【情态】qíngtài 神态 bearing; expression; manner; mien: 塑像~逼真。The bearing of the statue is quite realistic.

【情投意合】qíng tóu yì hé 形容双方思想感情融洽,心意相合 (of a couple) be congenial; share much in common

【情网】qíngwǎng 指不能摆脱的爱情 snares of love; net of love; web of love: 坠入~ fall in love; be caught in the snares of love

【情味】qíngwèi 情调;意味 sentiment; taste; overtone; flavour: 这幅画充满了田园~。The painting is imbued with pastoral sentiments.

Q

【情形】qíng·xing 事物呈现出来的样子 situation; condition; state of affairs; case; circumstances; way: 生活~ living conditions | 村里的~ situation in the village | 如何办理,到时候看~再说。As to how to deal with it, we shall have to wait and see.

【情绪】qíng·xù ❶ 人从事某种活动时产生的兴奋心理状态 emotion; feeling; frame of mind; mood; humour; sentiment; spirits; vein; morale: 生产~ enthusiasm for production | 战斗~ fighting morale | 急躁~ anxiety; impatience | ~高涨 in high spirits ❷ 指不愉快的情感 moodiness; depression; sullenness: 闹~ sulk; grizzle; pout; brood | 他有点儿~。He is in a bit of a sulk.

【情义】qíngyì 亲属、同志、朋友相互间应有的感情 ties of kinship, friendship, comradeship, etc.; emotional attachment: 姐姐待他很有~。His elder sister shows affection towards him.

【情谊】qíngyì 人与人相互关切、爱护的感情 friendly feelings: 深厚的~ deep friendship

【情意】qíngyì 对人的感情 friendly regards; affection; goodwill: ~绵绵 deep and continuous feelings; long-lasting love

【情由】qíngyóu 事情的内容和原因 how and why; reason: 问清~,再作处理。Find out the cause of it before you make a decision.

【情欲】qíngyù 对异性的欲望 sensual or carnal desire; lust; passion

【情缘】qíngyuán 男女相爱的缘分 predestined love between a man and woman: ~已断。Their love is over. | ~未了。Their love knows no end.

【情愿】qíngyuàn ❶ 心里愿意 willingly; of one's own accord; of one's free will; ungrudgingly: 甘心~ willing; without protest | 两相~。Both are willing. ❷ 宁愿;宁可 would rather; prefer: ~死,也不屈服 would rather die than surrender

【情知】qíngzhī 明明知道 be in full knowledge of sth.; know for certain; be fully aware

【情致】qíngzhì 情趣;兴致 interest; taste: ~各异 have different tastes | 别有~ of special appeal

【情种】qíngzhǒng 感情特别丰富的人;特别钟情的人 Casanova; lady-killer; person of a sentimental type, esp. one who easily falls in love

【情状】qíngzhuàng 情形;状况 circumstances; situation; condition: 其中~,难以言述。It's hard to describe the situation there.

晴 qíng 天空无云或云很少 sunny; clear; cloudless; fine: ~天 fine day | 天~了。It's clearing up.

【晴好】qínghǎo same as 晴朗 qínglǎng: 天气~。The weather is fine.

【晴和】qínghé 晴朗暖和 clear and warm: 天气~。It's a clear, warm day.

【晴空】qíngkōng 晴朗的天空 clear sky; cloudless sky: ~万里 stretches of blue sky; not a speck of cloud in the sky; clear and boundless sky

【晴朗】qínglǎng 没有云雾,日光充足 clear; sunny: 天气~。It's a sunny day.

【晴天霹雳】qíngtiān pīlì 〈比喻 *fig.*〉突然发生的意外事件 bolt from the blue; (of sth. that happens) out of a clear or blue sky; also 青天霹雳 qīngtiān pīlì

赜 qíng 承受 receive; bear: ~受财产 inherit a fortune | 别净~现成的。Don't always expect to have something on tap.

【赜等】qíngděng 〈方 *dial.*〉 ❶ 坐等(责备、惩罚) sit back and wait for (censure, punishment, etc.) ❷ 坐享(现成的) just enjoy what is available without making any effort

【赜受】qíngshòu 承受;继承 receive; inherit

氰 qíng 碳和氮的化合物,化学式$(CN)_2$。无色气体,有刺激性臭味,剧毒,燃烧时发桃红色火焰。cyanogen $(CN)_2$; dicyanogen; chemical compound of nitrogen and carbon in the form of colourless and highly poisonous gas with a pungent odour, producing peach-coloured flames when burning

檠(檠) qíng 〈书 *fml.*〉 ❶ 灯台;蜡台 lamp stand; candlestick ❷ 矫正弓弩的器具 device for holding a crossbow in position

擎 qíng 往上托;举 raise; hold up; lift up: 众~易举。Many hands make light work.

黥(剠) qíng 〈书 *fml.*〉 ❶ 在脸上刺上记号或文字并涂上墨,古代用做刑罚,后来也施于士兵,以防逃跑 (ancient punishment for a criminal, or later to prevent desertion) brand a person's face by a process of pricking and tattooing with an indelible pigment ❷ 在人体上刺上带颜色的文字、花纹和图形 tattoo; mark a person's body with a tattoo

qǐng(ㄑㄧㄥˇ)

苘(檾、莔) qǐng 苘麻 Indian mallow; piemarker; *Abutilon theophrasti*

【苘麻】qǐngmá ❶ 一年生草本植物,茎皮多纤维,叶子大,心脏形,密生柔毛。花单生,黄色。是重要的纤维植物之一,供制绳索用,种子供药用。piemarker (*Abutilon theophrasti*); annual herb having a fibrous stem covering, heart-shaped, fluffy broad leaves and single yellow flowers, that is an important fibrous plant used for making ropes, its seeds used to make medicine ❷ 这种植物的茎皮纤维 fibres from such a plant ‖ popular known as 青麻 qīngmá

顷[1] qǐng地积单位。100 亩等于 1 顷。现用市顷,1 市顷合 6.6667 公顷 (currently called 市顷 shìqǐng) unit of area, equal to 100 *mu* or 6.6667 hectares: 两～地 two *qing* of land|碧波万～ boundless expanse of blue waves

顷[2] qǐng〈书 *fml.*〉❶ 顷刻 (in) a split second; (in) a short while; instantly: 少～ in a little while|有～ for a while|俄～ soon ❷ 不久以前;刚才 just now; just: ～闻 on hearing|～接来信 have just received your letter ❸ 左右(指时间)(of time) about: 光绪二十年～ about the 20th year of Emperor Guangxu's reign (1895)
〈古 *old*〉same as 倾 qīng

【顷刻】qǐngkè 极短的时间 (in) a split second; transience; (in) a short while; (in) a brace of shakes; (in) half a shake; (in) two shakes; (in) two shakes of a lamb's tail; instantly; in an instant; in no time: 一阵狂风吹来,江面上～间掀起了巨浪。A gale blew in, and instantly the surging river swelled up.

请 qǐng ❶ 请求 request; ask; beg; pray; solicit; petition; desire: ～教 consult; seek advice|～假 ask for leave|～人帮忙 ask for help|你可以～老师给你开个书目。Why don't you ask your teacher for a list of books? ❷ 邀请;聘请 invite; engage; send for; retain: 催～ hasten; hurry sb. up|～客 play the host; treat sb. (to a meal, etc.); stand treat; entertain; fete|～医生 send for a doctor|～人做报告 ask sb. to give a speech or talk ❸〈敬辞 *pol.*〉用于希望对方做某事 (term of respect) please; if you please: 您～坐。Sit down please.|～准时出席。Present yourself on time please. ❹〈旧时 *old*〉指买香烛、纸马、佛龛等 buy (incense, joss sticks, paper horses, Buddhist shrine, etc.)

【请安】qǐng//ān ❶ 问安 wish sb. good health; pay respects to sb. (usu. elders) ❷〈方 *dial.*〉打千儿 salute by bending one's left knee and drooping one's right hand

【请便】qǐngbiàn 请对方自便 (ask the other person to go ahead with an action one doesn't want to get involved in) do as you wish; as you please; please yourself: 我不愿意去,你要是想去,那就～吧。Well, I don't want to go; but if you do, just go ahead.

【请春客】qǐng chūnkè〈旧时 *old*〉民间的一种习俗,过春节后,宴请亲友邻居 (traditional custom) invite relatives or friends to dinner shortly after the Spring Festival

【请调】qǐngdiào 请求调动(工作) ask for a transfer (to another job): ～报告 application for a transfer

【请功】qǐnggōng 请求上级给有功人员记功 ask a superior to record a merit for sb.; recommend that sb. be rewarded for his or her meritorious service: 全连干部战士为炊事班～。All the soldiers and officers in the company recommended the cooking squad for an honourable citation.

【请假】qǐng//jià 因病或因事请求准许在一定时期内不做工作或不学习 ask for leave: 因病～一天 call in sick for a day; ask for a day's sick leave|他请了十天假回家探亲。He asked for ten day's leave to go home to visit his family.

【请柬】qǐngjiǎn same as 请帖 qǐngtiě

【请教】qǐngjiào 请求指教 seek advice from sb.; ask for sb.'s advice; ask sb. for advice; consult: 虚心向别人～ learn from others|我想～您一件事。I'd like to consult you on a matter.

【请君入瓮】qǐng jūn rù wèng 武则天命令来俊臣审问周兴,周兴还不知道。来俊臣假意问周兴:'犯人不肯认罪怎么办?'周兴说:'拿个大瓮,周围用炭火烤,把犯人装进去,什么事他会不承认呢?'来俊臣叫人搬来一个大瓮,四面加火,对周兴说:'奉令审问老兄,请老兄入瓮!'周兴吓得连忙磕头认罪(见于《资治通鉴·唐纪》二十)。*Comprehensive Mirror for Aid in Government·Chronicles of Tang* (Vol. 20): Empress Wu Zetian sent order for Lai Junchen to interrogate Zhou Xing. Lai asked Zhou with false nonchalance, 'What's to be done if a criminal refuses to plead guilty?' Zhou, who was in the dark about the empress' arrangement, replied: 'Just bring in a large vat, burn charcoal around it, put the criminal into it, and then let's see if he would still deny anything.' Lai Junchen did as told, lighting a fire under a big vat that was brought in, and then said to Zhou: 'I have an order to interrogate Your Excellency. Please kindly step into this vat yourself!' Zhou Xing was so frightened that he kowtowed repeatedly and confessed his crimes; 〈比喻 *fig.*〉拿某人整治别人的法子来整治他

自己 pay sb. back in his own coin; serve sb. with the same sauce

【请客】qǐng//kè 请人吃饭、看戏等 play the host; stand treat; treat sb. (to dinner, a performance etc.); entertain guests

【请命】qǐngmìng ❶ 代人请求保全生命或解除困苦 plead on sb.'s behalf: 为民～ plead for the people; speak for the people ❷〈旧时 *old*〉下级向上司请示 ask (one's superior) for instructions

【请求】qǐngqiú ❶ 说明要求,希望得到满足 ask; request; beg; pray; petition; solicit: ～援助 ask for assistance | 他～上级给他最艰巨的任务。He asked his higher-ups to assign him the toughest job. ❷ 所提出的要求 request; appeal: 领导上接受了他的～。The leaders granted his request.

Q

【请赏】qǐng//shǎng 请求给予奖赏 ask a superior to bestow a reward on sb. for merit: 邀功～ claim credit and seek reward for another's achievements

【请示】qǐngshì (向上级)请求指示 ask for or request instructions: 这件事须～上级后才能决定。This matter is subject to further instructions from higher authorities.

【请帖】qǐngtiě 邀请客人时送去的通知 (written) invitation

【请托】qǐngtuō 请求和托付(别人办事) request and entrust (sb. to do sth.)

【请问】qǐngwèn〈敬辞 *pol.*〉用于请求对方回答问题 excuse me; please: ～这个字怎么读? Excuse me, but could you tell me how to say this word?

【请降】qǐng//xiáng 向对方请求投降 beg to surrender

【请缨】qǐngyīng《汉书·终军传》:'南越(粤)与汉和亲,乃遣[终]军使南越说其王,欲令入朝,比内诸侯。军自请,愿受长缨,必羁南越王而致之阙下。'后用来指请求杀敌或请求给予任务。*History of Han · Biography of Zhong Jun*: 'After the Han Dynasty pacified the kingdom of Southern Yue through marriage, Zhong Jun was dispatched as an envoy to summon the king of Southern Yue to the court as a warning to the various dukes. Zhong Jun requested a long rope from the emperor and pledged that he would use the rope to catch the king of Southern Yue and bring him to His Majesty.' From this story is derived the saying *qingying* (缨 *ying*: 带子 rope or belt), meaning to volunteer for battle or a mission

【请愿】qǐng//yuàn 采取集体行动要求政府或主管当局满足某些愿望,或改变某种政策措施 action taken by a large number of people wanting the government or sb. in a position of authority to meet a certain demand or change a certain policy or course of action; present a petition; petition; entreat; sue

【请战】qǐng//zhàn 请求上级准予参加战斗 ask for a battle assignment: ～书 written request for a battle assignment

【请罪】qǐng//zuì 自己犯了错误,主动请求处分;道歉 admit one's error and ask for punishment; apologize: 负荆～ bear bramble twigs upon one's back and beg for punishment

庼(廎) qǐng〈书 *fml.*〉小厅堂 small hall

綮 qǐng ☞肯綮 kěnqǐng on p. 1100
☞ qǐ on p. 1520

謦 qǐng [謦欬] qǐngkài〈书 *fml.*〉❶ 咳嗽 cough ❷ 借指谈笑 talk and laugh: 亲承～ listen with reverence to sb. (oft. an elderly scholar)

qìng (ㄑㄧㄥˋ)

庆(慶) qìng ❶ 庆祝;庆贺 celebrate; felicitate; congratulate; jubilate; rejoice; whoop it up: ～寿 celebrate a birthday (usu. of an elderly person) | ～丰收 celebrate a harvest | ～功大会 meeting to celebrate a victory; celebration ❷ 值得庆祝的周年纪念日 anniversary; occasion for grand celebration: 国～ National Day | 校～ school anniversary; anniversary of the founding of a school ❸(Qìng) 姓 a surname

【庆典】qìngdiǎn 隆重的庆祝典礼 celebration; festive ceremony; pageant: 十周年～ 10th-anniversary celebration | 大桥落成～ celebration for the completion of a bridge

【庆父不死,鲁难未已】Qìngfǔ bù sǐ, Lǔ nàn wèi yǐ《左传》闵公元年:'不去庆父,鲁难未已。'庆父是鲁国公子,曾一再制造内乱,先后杀死两个国君。后来用'庆父不死,鲁难未已'比喻不除掉制造内乱的罪魁祸首,国家就不得安宁。according to *The Zuo's Commentaries on the Spring and Autumn Annals* in the 1st Year of Reign of Duke Min: 'The disaster of Lu would know no end if Qingfu had not died.' Qingfu was a prince of the state of Lu in the Spring and Autumn Period who launched a series of civil struggles, and in the course of it killed two dukes of the state; (fig.) there will be no peace for a nation without getting rid of those bent on creating internal unrest

【庆贺】qìnghè 为共同的喜事表示庆祝或向有喜事的人道喜 celebrate (a grand occasion); congratulate sb. on sth.; felicitate sb. on sth.: ～丰收 celebrate a harvest | ～胜利 celebrate a victory

【庆历】Qìnglì 宋仁宗(赵祯)年号(公元 1041—1048) Qingli (1041-1048), title of the reign of Zhao Zhen, Emperor Song Renzong

【庆幸】qìngxìng 为事情意外地得到好的结局而感到高兴 felicitate oneself on (an unexpected favourable outcome); rejoice; congratulate oneself (on)

【庆祝】qìngzhù 为共同的喜事进行一些活动表示高兴或纪念 celebrate; felicitate; rejoice; jubilate; whoop it up: ～国庆 celebrate National Day|～元旦 celebrate New Year's Day

亲(親) qìng ☞ below
☞ qīn on p.1557

【亲家】qìng·jia ❶ 两家儿女相婚配的亲戚关系 relatives by marriage: 儿女～ relatives by the marriage of one's children ❷ 称儿子的丈人、丈母或女儿的公公、婆婆 parents of one's daughter-in-law or son-in-law; parents-in-law of one's son or daughter

【亲家公】qìng·jiagōng 称儿子的丈人或女儿的公公 father-in-law of son or daughter; father of daughter-in-law or son-in-law

【亲家母】qìng·jiamǔ 称儿子的丈母或女儿的婆婆 mother-in-law of one's son or daughter; mother of one's daughter-in-law or son-in-law

凊 qìng〈书 *fml.*〉凉 cool

箐 qìng〈方 *dial.*〉山间的大竹林,泛指树木丛生的山谷。多用于地名,如梅子箐(在云南),杉木箐(在贵州)。big bamboo graves in mountain valleys; also generally refers to a wooded valley; mostly used in place names, e.g. 梅子箐 méizǐqìng (in Yunnan Province), 杉木箐 shānmùqìng (in Guizhou Province)

磬 qìng ❶〈古代 *arch.*〉打击乐器,形状像曲尺,用玉或石制成 *qing*, ancient percussion instrument made from jade or stone ❷ 佛教的打击乐器,形状像钵,用铜制成 Buddhist percussion instrument shaped like an alms bowl and made of bronze

罄 qìng〈书 *fml.*〉尽;空 exhaust; consume; use up: 告～ run out|～其所有 empty one's purse; offer all one has

【罄尽】qìngjìn 没有剩余 with nothing left; exhausted: 家资～。The family's resources have been exhausted.

【罄竹难书】qìng zhú nán shū 把竹子用完了都写不完 too numerous to inscribe on all bamboo strips;〈比喻 *fig.*〉事实(多指罪恶)很多,难以说完(古人写字用竹简,竹子是制竹简的材料 in ancient times bamboo strips were used to write on)(oft. of crimes) too numerous to cover

qióng (ㄑㄩㄥˊ)

邛 qióng 邛崃 (Qiónglái),山名,在四川 Qionglai Mountain, in Sichuan Province

穷(窮) qióng ❶ 缺乏生产资料和生活资料;没有钱(跟'富'相对 as opposed to 'rich') lacking means of production and livelihood; with little or no money; poor: 贫～ poor; impoverished; needy; penniless; starving; impecunious|改变一～二白的面貌 lift (sb.) from a state of poverty and ignorance ❷ 穷尽 end; limit: 无～无尽 endless; boundless; without end; unlimited; eternal; interminable; ceaseless; incessant|理屈辞～ not have a leg to stand on|日暮途～ come to the end of one's rope; be on one's last legs; head for doom ❸ 用尽;费尽 exhaust; use up: ～兵黩武 use all one's armed might to wage war; wantonly engage in military ventures|～目远望 look as far as one's eyes can see ❹ 彻底(追究) thoroughly (investigate or look into): ～究 make a thorough study of sth.; probe deeply into sth.; thoroughly inquire into|～追猛打 run down (enemy troops) ❺ 极端 extremely; in the extreme; to the utmost; abominably: ～凶极恶 extremely vicious; diabolic; nefarious; felonious|～奢极侈 live in the lap of luxury; live in extreme extravagance; wallow in luxury

【穷兵黩武】qióng bīng dú wǔ 使用全部武力,任意发动侵略战争 use all one's armed might to wage war; wantonly engage in military ventures

【穷愁】qiógchóu 穷困愁苦 poverty-stricken and full of worries: ～潦倒 impoverished and dejected

【穷措大】qióngcuòdà 穷困的读书人(含轻蔑意 derog.) impoverished intellectual; also 穷醋大 qióngcùdà

【穷乏】qióngfá 贫穷,没有积蓄 have few blessings in life; living in poverty; living in want; living in reduced circumstances; have a lean purse; impoverished; destitute; indigent

【穷光蛋】qióngguāngdàn 穷苦人(含轻蔑意 derog.) pauper; poor wretch; penniless vagrant

【穷极无聊】qióng jí wúliáo 指困窘到极点,无所依托;无事可做,非常无聊 wretched; helpless; have nothing to do; be extremely bored

【穷竭】qióngjié〈书 *fml.*〉费尽;用尽 use up; exhaust; consume: ～心计 rack one's brains

【穷尽】qióngjìn 尽头 end; limit: 群众的智慧是没有～的。The masses have unlimited sources of intelligence.

【穷寇】qióngkòu 穷途末路的贼寇,泛指残敌 cornered enemy; (gen.) hard-pressed enemy

【穷苦】qióngkǔ 贫穷困苦 impoverished; poverty-stricken; miserable

【穷匮】qióngkuì〈书 *fml.*〉贫穷匮乏 live in need; cannot make ends meet; be short of money

【穷困】qióngkùn 生活贫穷,经济困难 suffer from financial problems; poverty-stricken; destitute; be straitened for money; be in straitened circumstances; indigent; needful: ～潦倒 be down and out; fall into want; be as poor as a church-mouse; be reduced to destitution

【穷忙】qióngmáng ❶〈旧 *old*〉指为了生计而忙碌奔走 busy trying to make ends meet; run around to eke out a living; live a hectic life ❷ 事情繁杂,非常忙碌 have a hectic schedule; be awfully busy

【穷年累月】qióng nián lěi yuè 指接连不断,时间长久 year in, year out; for years on end; year after year; for many years; for a long time:从前农民们～地辛苦劳动,但生活仍旧很苦。In the old days farmers toiled in the fields year in, year out, yet they were barely able to keep heart and soul together.

【穷人】qióngrén 穷苦的人 the poor; have-nots; paupers; the destitute

【穷山恶水】qióng shān è shuǐ 形容自然条件很差,物产不丰富的地方 barren hills and unhealthy rivers; land lacking natural resources and productivity:把～改造成了米粮川 turn barren land into a granary

【穷奢极侈】qióng shē jí chǐ 极端奢侈,尽量享受 debauchery and dissipation; extremely extravagant; go to the extremes of extravagance; indulge oneself in luxuries; wallow in luxury; also 穷奢极欲 qióng shē jí yù

【穷酸】qióngsuān 贫穷寒酸;穷而迂腐(旧时用来讥讽文人 speaking sarcastically of an old-time scholar) poor and pedantic; poor and humble; miserable

【穷途】qióngtú 路的尽头 dead end;〈比喻 *fig.*〉穷困的境况 straitened circumstances; destitution:～末路 be at the end of one's rope

【穷途潦倒】qióngtú liáodǎo 形容无路可走,非常失意 be down and out; fall into hopeless straits; have no way of making a living; be at the end of one's tether; be penniless and frustrated

【穷途末路】qióngtú mòlù 形容无路可走 be at the end of one's rope; come to a dead end

【穷乡僻壤】qióng xiāng pì rǎng 荒凉贫穷而偏僻的地方 backwater; remote and backward place; out-of-the-way place

【穷形尽相】qióng xíng jìn xiàng 原指描写刻画十分细致生动,现在也用来指丑态毕露 (orig.) give a lively and detailed account; be exposed in all one's ugliness

【穷凶极恶】qióng xiōng jí è 形容极端残暴恶毒 extremely vicious; diabolic; nefarious; felonious; flagitious

【穷原竟委】qióng yuán jìng wěi 深入探求事物的始末 get to the bottom of sth.; make a thorough inquiry into sth.; track down; follow home

【穷源溯流】qióng yuán sù liú 追究事物的根源并探寻其发展的经过 explore the origin of sth. and follow its development; trace back

茕(㷀、惸) qióng〈书 *fml.*〉❶ 孤单;孤独 solitary; lonely ❷ 忧愁 worried; woebegone

【茕茕】qióngqióng〈书 *fml.*〉形容孤孤单单,无依无靠 all alone; solitary and helpless:～孑立 stand alone in desolation

穹 qióng〈书 *fml.*〉穹隆,借指天空 vault; dome; sky:苍～ blue dome of the sky; empyrean; firmament; ether

【穹苍】qióngcāng〈书 *fml.*〉天空 vault of the heavens; blue dome of the sky; empyrean; firmament; ether

【穹隆】qiónglóng〈书 *fml.*〉指天空中间高四周下垂的样子,也泛指高起成拱形的 (of heaven) vault; dome; arched roof

【穹庐】qiónglú〈书 *fml.*〉游牧民族居住的圆顶帐篷,用毡子做成 yurt; felt tent with a vaulted roof, a dwelling of nomadic tribes

藭(藭) qióng ☞[芎䓖] xiōngqióng on p. 2153

筇 qióng [筇竹] (qióngzhú) 竹子的一种,可以做手杖 a kind of bamboo used to make walking sticks

琼(瓊) qióng ❶〈书 *fml.*〉美玉,泛指精美的东西 jasper; fine jade; sth. exquisite:～楼玉宇(华丽的房屋) jasper palaces and jade pavilions; magnificent palace; mansion of fabulous architecture | 玉液～浆 top-quality wine ❷ (Qióng) 指琼崖(海南岛)或琼州(旧府名,在海南岛上,府治在今海南琼山) abbr. for Qiongya or Qiongzhou, old name of a prefecture on Hainan Island, with its seat in Qiongshan

【琼浆】qióngjiāng 指美酒 good wine:～玉液 top-quality wine

【琼剧】qióngjù 海南的地方戏曲剧种。由潮剧、闽南梨园戏吸收当地人民的歌谣曲调发展而成。Hainan opera; local opera of Hainan Province, developed from the *chaoju* and *liyuan* operas of southern Fujian Province and by drawing on local ballads; also 海南戏 hǎinánxì

【琼脂】qióngzhī 植物胶的一种,用海产的石花菜类制成,无色、无固定形状的固体,溶于热水。可制冷食、微生物的培养基等。agar; gelatin derived from sea agar, a colourless and shapeless solid that is soluble in hot water and used to make cold foods, as a medium for bacterial culture, etc.; also 石花胶 shíhuājiāo; generally known as 洋菜 yángcài or 洋粉 yángfěn

蛩 qióng 古书上指蟋蟀 (in ancient books) cricket

跫 qióng [跫然] (qióngrán)〈书 *fml.*〉形容脚步声 sound of the shift of footsteps; footfalls:足音～ clop-clop of footsteps; pattering feet

銎 qióng〈书 *fml.*〉斧子上安柄的孔 hole of an axe where a handle is fixed

蒉 qióng［蒉茅］(qióngmáo) 古书上说的一种草 *qiongmao*, kind of grass as described in in ancient books

qiū (ㄑㄧㄡ)

丘(❸坵) qiū ❶ 小土山；土堆 mound; hillock; knoll; hummock; rideau：荒～ barren or desolate hillock｜沙～ dune; sand dune; dene; sandbank; sand hill｜坟～子 grave mound ❷ 浮厝 cover with earth, or bricks and stones, prior to burial：先把棺材～起来。Cover the coffin with earth. ❸〈量词 *classifier*〉水田分隔成大小不同的块,一块叫一丘 plot (of paddy field bordered by ridges)：一～田 a plot of paddy field ❹ (Qiū) 姓 a surname

【丘八】qiūbā〈旧时 *old*〉称兵('丘'字加'八'字成为'兵'字,含贬义)(derog.) soldier (whose Chinese character, 兵 bīng is composed of 丘 and 八, hence the term *qiuba*)

【丘陵】qiūlíng 连绵成片的小山 hills：～起伏 a range of undulating hills｜～地带 hilly land; hilly country

【丘墓】qiūmù〈书 *fml.*〉坟墓 grave; tomb; sepulchre; last home; tumuli

【丘脑】qiūnǎo 间脑的一部分,椭圆形,左右各一,围成第三脑室。直接与大脑皮层相连,除嗅觉处,人体各部所感受的冲动都经过它传递给大脑皮层。thalamencephalon; thalamus; oval-shaped segment of the midbrain, on either side of the third ventricle of the brain, which directly joins the cerebral cortex and relays sensory impulses (except for smell) to the cerebral cortex (图见 ☞ figure for 脑 nǎo on p. 1394)

【丘疹】qiūzhěn 皮肤表面由于某些疾病而起的小疙瘩,半球形,多为红色 papule; pimple; small inflamed elevation of the skin, usually in the shape of a small half-ball, caused by certain ailments

邱 qiū ❶ same as 丘 qiū ❷ (Qiū) 姓 a surname

龟(龜) qiū 龟兹 (Qiūcí),古代西域国名,在今新疆库车一带 Kuqa, ancient kingdom in the Western Regions, in present-day Kuqa County, the Xinjiang Uygur Autonomous Region

☞ guī on p. 729 and jūn on p. 1066

秋(烁) qiū ❶ 秋季 autumn; fall：深～ late autumn｜～风 autumn wind｜～雨 autumn rain｜～高气爽 clear and crisp autumn day; fine autumn day ❷ 庄稼成熟或成熟时节 harvest; harvest time：麦～ wheat harvest｜大～ autumn harvest ❸ 指一年的时间 year：千～万岁 for thousands of years; for ever｜一日不见,如隔三～。One day's departure away from you is like three years. ❹ 指某个时期(多指不好的 usu. troubled) period of time：多事之～ eventful period of time; troubled times｜危急存亡之～ critical time ❺ (Qiū) 姓 a surname

【秋波】qiūbō〈比喻 *fig.*〉美女的眼睛或眼神 bright and clear eyes of a beautiful woman：暗送～ send silent and endearing messages with bewitching eyes; give sb. the eye; make eyes at sb.; make secret and amorous overtures to sb.; cast amorous or flirtatious glances at sb.

【秋分】qiūfēn 二十四节气之一,在9月22,23或24日。这一天南北半球昼夜都一样长。Autumn Equinox; one of the 24 solar terms, occurring on Sept. 22, 23, or 24, on which day both hemispheres share days and nights of the same length; ☞ 节气 jiéqì on p. 989 and 二十四节气 èrshísì jiéqì on p. 516

【秋分点】qiūfēndiǎn 赤道平面和黄道的两个相交点的一个,夏至以后,太阳从北向南移动,在秋分那一天通过这一点 autumnal equinoctial point; autumnal equinox; one of the two intersecting points of the celestial equator and the ecliptic, through which point the sun moves from the north to the south on the exact day of Autumn Equinox

【秋风】qiūfēng ❶ 秋天的风 autumn wind ❷ ☞打秋风 dǎ qiūfēng on p. 350

【秋风扫落叶】qiūfēng sǎo luòyè〈比喻 *fig.*〉强大的力量扫荡衰败的势力(of powerful forces) make a clean sweep of forces that are decayed

【秋高气爽】qiū gāo qì shuǎng 形容秋天天空晴朗明净,气候凉爽宜人 clear and crisp autumn day; fine autumn day; clear and cool autumn day

【秋毫】qiūháo 鸟兽在秋天新长的细毛 newly grown down on an animal or bird in autumn;〈比喻 *fig.*〉微小的事物 miniscule things; minute detail：～无犯 not cause the slightest trouble to people｜明察～ be extremely discerning; having a highly discerning eye

【秋毫无犯】qiūháo wú fàn 形容军队纪律严明,丝毫不侵犯群众的利益 (of highly disciplined troops) not commit the slightest offence against people's interests; not cause the slightest trouble to the people

【秋后算账】qiū hòu suàn zhàng〈比喻 *fig.*〉等事情发展到最后阶段再判断谁是谁非,也比喻事后等待时机进行报复 wait until the dust settles to reckon with sb.; bide one's time to settle old scores

【秋季】qiūjì 一年的第三季,我国习惯指立秋到立冬的三个月时间,也指农历七、八、九三个月

autumn; fall; 3rd season of the year, referring in China to the three months from the Beginning of Autumn to the Beginning of Winter, and also July, August and September on the Chinese lunar calendar; ☞四季 sìjì on p.1821

【秋景】qiūjǐng ❶ 秋天的景色 autumn scenery; autumnal scenes ❷ 秋天的收成 autumn harvest: 今年～好于去年。The harvest this autumn is better than last year.

【秋老虎】qiūlǎohǔ 指立秋以后仍然十分炎热的天气 autumn heat wave; spell of hot weather after the Beginning of Autumn; Indian summer

Q

【秋凉】qiūliáng 指秋季凉爽的时候 cool autumn days: 等～再去吧。We'll go again when the autumn days start to get cool.

【秋粮】qiūliáng 秋季收获的粮食 crops harvested in autumn; autumn crops

【秋令】qiūlìng ❶same as 秋季 qiūjì ❷ 秋季的气候 autumn weather: 冬行～(冬天的气候像秋天)。We are having a mild winter.

【秋千】(鞦韆) qiūqiān 运动和游戏用具,在木架或铁架上系两根长绳,下面拴上一块板子。人在板上利用脚蹬板的力量在空中前后摆动。swing; sport or play apparatus, made of a seat (e.g. a plank) suspended from a horizontal log or iron bar by two long ropes, on which one can ride back and forth through the air

【秋色】qiūsè 秋天的景色 autumn scenery: ～宜人。The autumn scenery is enchanting.

【秋试】qiūshì 明清两代科举制度,乡试在秋季举行,叫做秋试 (in the Ming and Qing dynasties) imperial examinations which were held in autumn at the provincial level; autumn imperial examinations

【秋收】qiūshōu ❶ 秋季收获农作物 autumn harvest: 人们都在忙着～。People are all busy getting in the autumn harvest. ❷ 秋季收获的农作物 harvested autumn crops: 今年～比去年强。The harvest this autumn is better than last year.

【秋收起义】Qiūshōu Qǐyì 1927 年 9 月毛泽东发动和领导湖南东部和江西西部一带工农举行的武装起义。这次起义成立了工农革命军第一军第一师,在井冈山创立了第一个农村革命根据地。Autumn Harvest Uprising; armed uprising of workers and peasants led by Mao Zedong in September 1927, in eastern Hunan and western Jiangxi, giving birth to the First Division of the First Army of the Workers' and Peasants' Revolutionary Army of China and the creation of the first rural revolutionary base area in the Jinggang Mountains

【秋水】qiūshuǐ〈比喻 *fig.*〉人的眼睛(多指女子的) limpid eyes (oft. of a woman): 望穿～ gaze with eager expectation

【秋天】qiūtiān same as 秋季 qiūjì

【秋闱】qiūwéi〈书 *fml.*〉same as 秋试 qiūshì

【秋汛】qiūxùn 从立秋到霜降的一段时间内发生的河水暴涨 flood occurring during the period from the Beginning of the Autumn to the Descent of Frost

【秋游】qiūyóu 秋天出去游玩(多指集体组织的) (oft. organized by a collective) autumn outing

蚯 qiū [蚯蚓] qiūyǐn 环节动物,身体柔软,圆而长,环节上有刚毛,生活在土壤中,能使土壤疏松,它的粪便能使土壤肥沃,是益虫 earthworm (*Pheretima*); angleworm; fishworm; red worm; dew worm; annelid with a long soft cylindrical body, with bristles on the segments, which burrows into and helps aerate soil, a beneficial creature whose dejecta can enrich soil; also generally known as 曲蟮 qūshàn

萩 qiū 古书上说的一种蒿类植物(as recorded in ancient books) wormwood

穐(龝) qiū〈书 *fml.*〉same as 秋 qiū

湫 qiū 水池 pond; pool: 大龙～(瀑布名,在浙江雁荡山) Dalong (Great Dragon) Pool (waterfall, located in the Yandang Mountains, Zhejiang Province)
☞ jiǎo on p.978

楸 qiū 楸树,落叶乔木,叶子三角状卵形或长椭圆形,花冠白色,有紫色斑点。木材供建筑用。Chinese catalpa (*Catalpa bungei*); defoliate arbor having triangular or oval-shaped leaves, a white coronal spotted with purple, and wood that is used as a building material

鹙 qiū 古书上说的一种水鸟,头和颈上都没有毛 (as recorded in ancient books) bald crane; water bird with a bald head and neck

鳅(鰌) qiū ☞泥鳅 níqiū on p.1404; [䲡鳅] qíqiū on p.1513

鞦 qiū ❶ same as 鞧 qiū ❷ ☞鞦韆 qiūqiān

【鞦韆】qiūqiān same as 秋千 qiūqiān

鞧(鞦) qiū ❶ ☞ 后鞧 hòuqiū on p.811 ❷〈方 *dial.*〉收缩 contract; shrink: ～着眉毛 wrinkle or knit one's brows; frown | 大辕马～着屁股向后退。The big shaft-horse reared and retreated.

qiú (ㄑㄧㄡˊ)

仇 Qiú 姓 a surname
☞ chóu on p.276

囚 qiú ❶ 关押;囚禁 put sb. behind the bars; imprison; jail; put in jail; enjail; lock up; jug; embar; encage; chain; gaol; quod: 被～ be in jail ❷ 囚犯 prisoner; convict; captive; jailbird; prison bird: 罪～ convict | 死～ criminal waiting for execution

【囚车】qiúchē 解送犯人用的车 prison van; prisoners' van

【囚犯】qiúfàn 关在监狱里的犯人 prisoner; convict; captive; jailbird; prison bird; lag

【囚禁】qiújìn 把人关在监狱里 imprison; enjail; put in jail; lock up; jug; embar; encage; chain; gaol; quod; hold in captivity: 他被单独～在一间小牢房里。He was locked up in solitary confinement in a small cell.

【囚首垢面】qiú shǒu gòu miàn 形容久未梳头和洗脸,像囚犯的样子 appear like a prisoner, with dishevelled hair and unwashed face

【囚徒】qiútú same as 囚犯 qiúfàn

【囚衣】qiúyī 供囚犯穿的特制衣服 prison garb; prison uniform

犰 qiú [犰狳](qiúyú)哺乳动物,身体分前、中、后三段,头顶、背部、尾部和四肢有角质鳞片,中段的鳞片有筋肉相连接,可以伸缩,腹部多毛,趾有锐利的爪,善于掘土。昼伏夜出,吃昆虫、蚁和鸟卵等。产于南美等地。armadillo (*Dasypus*); nocturnul mammal with a three-segmented (front, middle and rear) body, covered with bony plates on the head and back, and around the tail and limbs, with the plates on the back (middle segment) being joined with flesh and thus flexible and retractable, characterized by a hairy abdomen and pointed clawed toes, burrowing into the earth, feeding on insects, ants, bird eggs, etc., and native to South America and some other regions

求 qiú ❶ 请求 ask; beg; request; solicit; entreat: ～救 seek help; ask for help; send out rescue signals|～教 ask sb. for advice; seek advice from sb.; consult sb.|～您帮我做一件事。Would you please do me a favour? ❷ 要求 aim at; make efforts for; strive for: 力～改进 strive for improvement|精益～精 refine; always endeavour to do even better; keep improving (one's work, etc.)|生物都有～生存的本能。All living creatures have an instinct for survival. ❸ 追求;探求;寻求 seek; pursue; look after; search for; hanker after; quest for; aspire after; hunt for: ～学问 in pursuit of knowledge|实事～是 come down to earth; keep one's feet on the ground; seek truth from facts; be realistic and truthful|刻舟～剑 cut a mark on a moving boat in order to find where one's sword dropped into the river; stupid ways of doing things without considering changes in the circumstances|不～名利 without consideration for fame or gain; seek neither fame nor fortune ❹ 需求;需要 demand; need: 供～关系 relation between supply and demand|供过于～ supply exceeds demand ❺ (Qiú) 姓 a surname

【求爱】qiú'ài 向异性提出请求,希望得到对方的爱情 propose to sb.; pay court to; court; woo

【求告】qiúgào 央告(别人帮助或宽恕自己) implore; entreat; beg; supplicate; beseech (sb. for help or forgiveness): 四处～ seek help everywhere; beg around for help|～无门 have nowhere to turn to for help

【求婚】qiú//hūn 男女的一方请求对方跟自己结婚 make a proposal (to); propose (to); pop the question (to)

【求见】qiújiàn 请求进见(多指下对上 oft. a subordinate to a superior) ask to see; inquire for; request an interview with; seek or request an audience with

【求教】qiújiào 请教 ask sb. for advice; seek advice from sb.; consult sb.: 登门～ call on sb. for counsel|不懂的事要向别人～。Ask for advice about things you do not understand.

【求解】qiújiě 数学上指从已知条件出发,根据定律、定理等寻求未知问题的答案 find a solution to a mathematical problem (by working from given postulates, laws and theorems)

【求借】qiújiè 请求别人借给(钱或物) ask sb. for a loan; ask sb. to lend sth.

【求救】qiújiù 请求援救(多用于遇到灾难和危险时 oft. during a disaster or in danger) ask for help; seek help; ask sb. to come to the rescue: 发出～信号 signal SOS/GMDSS; send a signal for help

【求靠】qiúkào 请求别人同意自己投靠他(多指负担生活 oft. bearing one's living expenses) turn to sb. for support; seek refuge with sb.: ～亲友 seek refuge with relatives or friends

【求偶】qiú'ǒu 追求异性;寻求配偶 seek a spouse; look for a life partner

【求乞】qiúqǐ 请求人家救济;讨饭 beg (for food, money, etc.)

【求签】qiú//qiān 迷信的人在神佛面前抽签来占吉凶 (of a superstitious person) draw lots at a temple for soothsaying

【求亲】qiú//qīn 男女一方的家庭向对方的家庭请求结亲 (of a family) make an offer of marriage to another family on behalf of their son or daughter; seek a marriage alliance (with another family)

【求情】qiú//qíng 请求对方答应或宽恕 (for approval or mercy) implore; plead with sb.; beg sb. for; beg for (mercy on sb.); put in a good word for sb.; intercede with sb. for (sth. or another person): ～告饶 beg for pardon or leniency

【求全】qiúquán ❶ 要求完美无缺(多含贬义 oft. derog.) aim at perfection; ask for perfection: ～思想 perfectionist ideal ❷ 希望事情成全 try to round sth. off; try to achieve sth. through compromise: 委曲～ stoop to compromise; compromise for the general interest

【求全责备】qiú quán zé bèi 苛责别人,要求完美无缺 demand perfection of sb.; nit-pick at sb.; take sb. to task for perfection: 对人不～。Don't expect anybody to be perfect.

【求饶】qiú//ráo 请求饶恕 beg for mercy, pardon and leniency

【求人】qiú//rén 请求别人帮助 ask for help: 要靠自己努力,不能事事～。Depend on yourself, since you cannot ask for help for everything.

【求生】qiúshēng 谋求活路;设法活下去 seek survival; keep oneself alive; struggle for survival

【求实】qiúshí 讲求实际 be realistic; be practical-minded; be pragmatic: 提倡～精神 call for a down-to-earth approach; take a matter-of-fact attitude

Q

【求索】qiúsuǒ 寻求探索 explore; seek; grope for; search for; quest after: ～新的路子 explore a new path

【求同存异】qiú tóng cún yì 找出共同点,保留不同点 seek common ground while maintaining differences

【求学】qiúxué ❶ 在学校学习 be at school; attend school; pursue one's studies ❷ 探求学问 seek knowledge; (do sth.) in pursuit of knowledge

【求援】qiúyuán 请求援助 ask for help or assistance; request reinforcements: 向友军～ request reinforcements from friendly troops

【求战】qiúzhàn ❶ 寻求战斗;寻找对方与之作战 seek battle: 敌军进入山口,～不得,只得退却。The enemy troops entered the mountain pass but, failing to provoke a battle, retreated. ❷ 要求参加战斗 ask to go into battle: 战士～心切。The soldiers are itching for battle.

【求证】qiúzhèng 寻找证据或求得证实 seek proof, confirmation and verification; search for evidence

【求之不得】qiú zhī bù dé 想找都找不到(多用于意外地得到时 oft. of sth. unexpected) more than one could wish for; most welcome; rare: 这真是～的好事啊! This is really a rare occasion!

【求知】qiúzhī 探求知识 seek knowledge: ～欲 thirst for knowledge|～精神 desire for knowledge; spirit of learning

【求职】qiúzhí 谋求职业;寻求工作 look for a job; apply for a job; seek a position; hunt for a job

【求治】qiúzhì 请求给以治疗 seek medical treatment; ask a doctor for help

【求助】qiúzhù 请求援助 turn to sb. for help; seek help (from sb.); ask sb. for help; resort to (sth.): 向人～ ask people for help

虬(虯) qiú ❶ same as 虬龙 qiúlóng ❷ 〈书 *fml.*〉拳曲 coiled; curled: ～须 curly beard or moustache

【虬龙】qiúlóng 〈古代 *arch.*〉传说中的有角的小龙 small dragon with horns in Chinese mythology

【虬髯】qiúrán 〈书 *fml.*〉拳曲的胡子,特指两腮上的 curly whiskers

【虬须】qiúxū 〈书 *fml.*〉拳曲的胡子 curly beard or moustache

泅 qiú 浮水 float on water; swim: ～渡 swim across|～水而过 swim across the water; swim over

【泅渡】qiúdù 游泳而过(江、河、湖、海) swim across (a river, lake or the sea): 武装～ swim across a river with one's weapons; swim across in battle gear

俅1 Qiú 俅人,我国少数民族'独龙族'的旧称 old name for Dulong people, one of China's minority ethnic peoples

俅2 qiú [俅俅] qiúqiú 〈书 *fml.*〉恭顺的样子 deferentially; in a respectful and submissive manner

馗 qiú 〈书 *fml.*〉逼迫 force; compel; coerce

酋 qiú ❶ 酋长 chief of a tribe ❷ (盗匪、侵略者的)首领 chieftain (of bandits, aggressors): 匪～ bandit chief|贼～ chieftain of a gang of thieves|敌～ enemy chieftain

【酋长】qiúzhǎng 部落的首领 chief of a tribe; emir; sheikh

【酋长国】qiúzhǎngguó 以部落首领为最高统治者的国家。封建关系占统治地位,有的还保留氏族制度的残余。emirate; sheikhdom; nation or territory ruled by an emir, in which feudalism dominates and there are vestiges of clanship

逑 qiú 〈书 *fml.*〉配偶 spouse; life mate; consort; helpmate; marrow

尿 qiú 〈方 *dial.*〉男性生殖器 penis; cock

球(❸毬) qiú ❶ 以半圆的直径为轴,使半圆旋转一周而成的立体;由中心到表面各点距离都相等的立体 sphere; globe; orb; figure formed by circumrotation of a semi-circle on its diameter, all points of which are equidistant from a fixed point (centre): ～体 sphere; spheroid|～面 spherical surface|～心 central point or centre of a sphere ❷ (～儿 qiúr)球形或接近球形的物体 spherical object or anything of similar shape; ball: 煤～儿 balls of coal|棉～儿 tampon; cotton ball ❸ 指某些体育用品 ball, etc. (used in games): 篮～ basketball|乒乓～儿 ping-pong ball|冰～ puck ❹ 指球类运动 ballgame: ～技 skill in playing a ballgame|～迷 (football, etc.) fan|看～去 go to watch a (football, etc.) match or game ❺ 特指地球 globe; earth; world: 全～ entire globe; whole world; global|寰～ entire globe; whole world|北半～ Northern Hemisphere

【球场】qiúchǎng 球类运动用的场地，如篮球场、足球场、网球场等。其形式大小根据各种球类的要求而定。ground for ballgames, such as (basketball, tennis, badminton, volleyball, etc.) court, (football, baseball, etc.) field, (baseball) park, (ice hockey) rink, etc., the size of which depends on the regulations of different ballgames

【球胆】qiúdǎn 篮球、排球或足球等内层的空气囊，用薄橡皮制成，打足空气后，球就富于弹性 bladder; sac-like receptacle of air inside a basketball, volleyball, football, etc., made of thin rubber: Only when the bladder is inflated with air is the ball able to bounce.

【球果】qiúguǒ 穗状花序的一种，球形或圆锥形，由许多覆瓦状的木质鳞片组成，长成之后，很像果实，如松柏的雌花穗 cone; strobilus; spherical or cone-shaped reproductive structure in certain plants, consisting of overlapping woody scales, and looking like fruit when fully mature, e.g. female cone of pine or cypress

【球技】qiújì 球类运动的技巧；球艺 skill in playing a ballgame

【球茎】qiújīng 地下茎的一种，球状，多肉质，如荸荠的地下茎 corm; rhizome, spherical and fleshy, as in chufa

【球菌】qiújūn 细菌的一类，圆球形、卵圆形或肾脏形，种类很多，如双球菌、链球菌、葡萄球菌等 coccus; microorganism of a spherical, oval or kidney-like shape, of many kinds, e.g. diplococcus, streptococcus, staphylococcus, etc.

【球路】qiúlù 打球、踢球等的路数 tactics in playing a ballgame: ～刁钻 play with tricky strokes (as in tennis); tricky footwork (as in soccer)|不了解对方的～，连连失误 make repeated errors because of lack of knowledge of the tactics of the opponent

【球门】qiúmén 足球、冰球等运动中在球场两端设置的像门框的架子，是射球的目标。架子后面有网，球射进球门后落在网里。goal; net; goalposts (football, etc.); frame-like structure set on either end of a football field, hockey rink, etc., through which players try to send a ball or puck to score, which is connected to a net behind it for the ball or puck to be caught inside

【球迷】qiúmí 喜欢打球或看球赛而入迷的人 (football, etc.) fan

【球面】qiúmiàn 半圆以直径为轴旋转而形成的曲面；球的表面 spherical surface; surface formed by turning a semicircle around its diameter

【球面度】qiúmiàndù 立体角的单位，当立体角的顶点位于球心，它在球面上所截取的面积等于以球半径为边长的正方形面积时，该角就是一球面度 steradian; SI unit of solid angle, equal to the solid angle subtended at the centre of a sphere by an area on the surface of the sphere that is equal to the radius squared

【球面角】qiúmiànjiǎo 球面上两个大圆相交所成的角 spherical angle; angle formed at the intersection of the arcs of two great circles

【球面镜】qiúmiànjìng 反射面是球面的镜子，根据反射面凹凸的不同，分为凹面镜和凸面镜 spherical mirror in two types: concave mirror and convex mirror

【球磨机】qiúmójī 磨碎或加工各种材料的机器。一般是由绕水平轴回转的圆筒或锥形筒构成的，内装铁球和砾石等。利用铁球的冲击和研磨作用将材料打碎和磨细，广泛用于磨矿石。ball mill; grinding or processing machine, generally consisting of a cylinder or cone filled with steel balls or gravel, etc., revolving around a level axis, which serves to crush and grind through the pressure of the steel balls, etc.

【球墨铸铁】qiúmò-zhùtiě 含有球状石墨的铸铁，机械强度高，有韧性和延性。主要用来代替钢铸造重型机械和机械零件。nodular cast iron; ductile iron; cast iron containing spherical graphite, being tough and ductile, and having high mechanically strength, used an alternative to iron in making heavy machines and machine parts

【球拍】qiúpāi 用来打乒乓球、羽毛球、网球等的拍子 (tennis, badminton, ping-pong, etc.) racket; bat; (ping-pong) paddle; also 球拍子 qiúpāi•zi

【球儿】qiúr ❶ 小的球 small ball ❷ 特指小孩儿玩的小玻璃球(也有用石头做的)(for children to play with) marble; glass ball

【球赛】qiúsài 球类比赛 ballgame; match

【球台】qiútái ❶ 球体被两个平行平面所截而夹在两平面中间的部分 part of a sphere intersected by two parallel planes ❷ 打台球、乒乓球等用的像桌子的东西 (billiard, ping-pong, etc.) table

【球体】qiútǐ 球面所包围的立体 sphere; spheroid;

【球鞋】qiúxié 一种帆布帮儿、橡胶底的鞋 gym shoes; tennis shoes; sneakers; running shoes

【球心】qiúxīn 与球面各点距离相等的一点；球的中心 centre of a sphere

【球艺】qiúyì 球类运动的技巧 skill in playing a ballgame: 切磋～ compare notes on ball-playing techniques

赇 qiú〈书 *fml.*〉贿赂 bribe: 受～ take or accept bribes

銶 qiú〈古代 *arch.*〉一种凿子 chisel

遒 qiú〈书 *fml.*〉强健；有力 vigorous; forceful; powerful: ～劲 vigorous; powerful

【遒劲】qiújìng〈书 *fml.*〉雄健有力 imposingly vigorous; powerful: 笔力～ bold strokes of the brush|风骨～ vigorous or bold style|苍老～的古松 sturdy old pine tree

巯(巰) qiú same as 巯基 qiú jī

【巯基】qiú jī 由氢和硫两种原子组成的一价原子团(—SH) sulphydryl; univalent radical composed of hydrogen and sulfur atoms; also 氢硫基 qīngliújī

裘 qiú ❶〈书 *fml.*〉毛皮的衣服 fur coat: 狐～ fox coat | 集腋成～。The finest bits of fox fur are used to make a fur coat. *or* Many a little makes a mickle. ❷ 姓 (Qiú) a surname

【裘皮】qiúpí 毛皮 fur: ～服装 fur coats | ～制品 fur products

璆 qiú〈书 *fml.*〉美玉 fine jade

蝤 qiú [蝤蛴](qiúqí) 古书上指天牛的幼虫,白色 (as recorded in ancient books) longicorn's larva, white

☞ yóu on p. 2325

鼽 qiú〈书 *fml.*〉鼻子堵塞不通 suffer from nasal congestion

qiǔ (ㄑㄧㄡˇ)

糗 qiǔ ❶〈古代 *arch.*〉指干粮 solid food ❷〈方 *dial.*〉饭或面食成块状或糊状 (of rice or noodles) be sticky or caked together: 面条儿都～了。The noodles are stuck together.

qū (ㄑㄩ)

区(區) qū ❶ 区别;划分 distinguish; differentiate; discriminate: ～分 distinguish; differentiate; discriminate ❷ 地区;区域 area; region; zone; district: 山～ mountainous area | 解放～ liberated area | 工业～ industrial zone | 住宅～ residential quarters | 风景～ scenic area; parkland; tourist resort ❸ 行政区划单位,如自治区、市辖区、县辖区等 (as an administrative division) autonomous region; district under the jurisdiction of a city; district of a county

☞ Ōu on p. 1431

【区别】qūbié ❶ 把两上以上的对象加以比较,认识它们不同的地方;分别 distinguish; differentiate; discriminate; set apart; tell the difference between; make a distinction between: ～好坏 distinguish between good and bad; tell good from evil | ～对待 discriminate (between); differentiate (between) ❷ 彼此不同的地方 difference; distinction: 我看不出这两个词在意义上有什么～。I can't see any difference in meaning between the two words.

【区分】qūfēn same as 区别 qūbié ①: ～优劣 distinguish between superior and inferior; differentiate superior from inferior | 严格～不同性质的矛盾 make a strict distinction between contradictions of different nature; strictly distinguish between different kinds of contradictions

【区划】qūhuà 地区的划分 divide into districts: 行政～ administrative divisions

【区间】qūjiān 交通运输、通讯联络上指全程线路中的一段 part of the regular routes or connections for transportation or communication: ～车(某条交通线上只行驶于某一地段的车) shuttle bus; bus travelling only between two points on a certain transportation route

【区区】qūqū ❶ (数量)少;(人或事物)不重要 (of number, amount or sum) petty; (of a person) unimportant; of minor importance; (of sth.) trivial; trifling: ～之数,不必计较。You don't have to care about such a pittance. | ～小事,何足挂齿! Such a trivial matter is hardly worth mentioning! ❷〈旧时 *old*〉〈谦辞 *hum.*〉我(语气不庄重 politely but insincerely) me; my humble self: 此人非他,就是～。It's none other than my humble self.

【区域】qūyù 地区范围 within a region or area; pertaining to a region or area: ～性 regional | ～自治 regional autonomy

曲[1] qū ❶ 弯曲 (跟'直'相对 as opposed to 'straight') bent; curved; crooked; winding; zigzag: ～线 curve | ～尺 trisquare | 弯腰～背 hunchbacked; with one's back bent | 山回水～ zigzagging river through a mountain range | ～径通幽 winding path leading to a secluded spot ❷ 使弯曲 bend; flex; inflect; curve; crook; incurvate; warp: ～肱而枕 sleep with one's head resting on a bent arm (肱 *gong*: 胳膊 arm) | ～突徙薪 take precautions before it's too late ❸ 弯曲的地方 bend; crook: 河～ river bend ❹ 不公正;无理 injustice; unreasonableness: 是非～直 right and wrong, straight and crooked; between right and wrong ❺(Qū)姓 a surname

曲[2](麴、粬) qū 用曲霉和它的培养基(多为麦子、麸皮、大豆的混合物)制成的块状物,用来酿酒或制酱 leaven; yeast; cake made from aspergillus and its culture base (usu. a mixture of wheat, bran and soybean), used in the making of wine or soy sauce

☞ qǔ on p. 1591

【曲笔】qūbǐ ❶〈古时 *arch.*〉指史官不据事直书,有意掩盖真相的记载 (of an ancient official historian) distort facts to hide the truth ❷ 写文章时故意离开本题,而不直书其事的笔法 writing style characterized by deliberate digression: 故作～ deliberately digress in writing

【曲别针】qūbiézhēn 用金属丝来回折弯做成的夹纸片的东西 (for fastening papers) clip; paper clip; also 回形针 huíxíngzhēn

【曲柄】qūbǐng 曲轴的弯曲部分，作用是通过它和连杆把活塞的往复运动变成曲轴的旋转运动，或把曲轴的旋转运动变成活塞的往复运动 crank; bent handle of a shaft, which operates (together with the shaft attached perpendicularly) to convert reciprocal motion into circular motion, or circular motion into reciprocal motion

【曲尺】qūchǐ 木工用来求直角的尺，用木或金属制成，像直角三角形的勾股二边 trisquare; carpenter's square, made of wood or metal, with two legs at a right angle; also 矩尺 jǔchǐ or 角尺 jiǎochǐ

【曲棍球】qūgùnqiú ❶ 球类运动项目之一，用下端弯曲的棍子把球击入对方球门，射入对方球门多的为胜 field hockey; hockey; ballgame in which players carrying sticks curved at the end attempt to drive a small ball into the opposing team's goal, with the team who scores more goals being the winner ❷ 曲棍球运动使用的球，圆形，体小而硬 hockey ball (small and hard)

【曲解】qūjiě 错误地解释客观事实或别人的原意（多指故意地 usu. deliberately) misinterpret; twist; distort; wrench; contort; misconstrue; misrepresent; colour

【曲颈甑】qūjǐngzèng 蒸馏物质或使物质分解用的一种器皿，多用玻璃制成，形状略像梨，颈部弯向一侧 retort; laboratory vessel made of glass and slightly pear-shaped, with a recurved neck, mostly used for distillation

【曲里拐弯】qū·liguǎiwān（～儿的 qū·lǐguǎiwānr·de）弯弯曲曲 winding; tortuous; zigzag; snaky; sinuous; sinuate; wiggly: 树林里的小路～儿的。The path zigzags through the woods.

【曲率】qūlǜ 表明曲线在其上某一点的弯曲程度的数值。曲率越大，表示曲线的弯曲程度越大。curvature; numerical value measuring the degree of a curve at a given point, where the greater the degree, the greater the deviation of the curve from a straight line

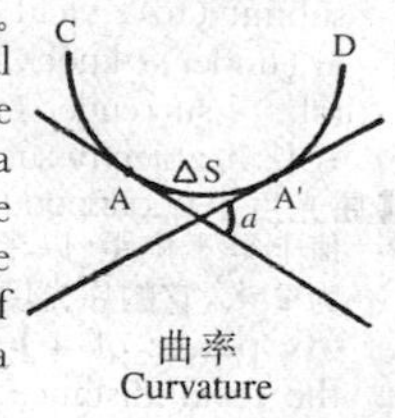

曲率
Curvature

【曲霉】qūméi 真菌的一类，菌体由许多丝状细胞组成，有些分枝的顶端为球形，上面生有许多孢子。是常见的霉菌，能引起水果、食物等霉烂，可用来酿酒、制酱油和酱等。aspergillus; genus of fungus, the solid form of which consists of a lot of thread-like cells, and some branching tissues topped with spores and shaped like balls. A common mold causing fruit or food spoilage, it is used for the making of wine, soy sauce, etc.

【曲面】qūmiàn 曲线按一定条件运动的轨迹，如球面、圆柱面 curved surface; arched surface; camber; curve; surface generated by a curve rotating on certain conditions, such as spherical surface, cylindrical surface

【曲曲弯弯】qūqūwanwān（～的 qūqūwānwān·de）形容弯曲很多 winding; meandering: 山坳里尽是～的羊肠小道。There are a lot of narrow meandering footpaths in the valley.｜黄河～地流过河套。The Yellow River meanders its way through the Hetao region (at the Great Bend of the Yellow River).

【曲蟮】qū·shàn 蚯蚓的通称 general term for 蚯蚓 qiūyǐn; also 蛐蟮 qū·shàn

【曲射炮】qūshèpào 初速小、弹道弯曲的一类火炮，如迫击炮、榴弹炮等 high-angle-firing gun (e.g. mortar, howitzer, etc.)

【曲突徙薪】qū tū xǐ xīn 有一家的烟囱很直，旁边堆着许多柴火，有人劝主人改建弯曲的烟囱，把柴火搬开，不然有着火的危险，主人不听，不久果然发生了火灾（见于《汉书·霍光传》）*History of Han · Biography of Huo Guang*: There was once a house with a straight chimney on the roof and a big pile of firewood by it. The owner was advised to rebuild the straight chimney into a bent one and remove the firewood to avoid the risk of fire, but he just turned a deaf ear to it. Shortly afterwards a fire broke out;〈比喻 *fig.*〉事先采取措施，防止危险发生 take precautions before it's too late; better safe than sorry

【曲线】qūxiàn ❶ 按一定条件运动的动点的轨迹，如圆、螺旋线 curve such as circle and conchoid; line drawn by a continously moving point under certain conditions ❷ 在平面上表示的物理、化学、统计学过程等随参数变化的线 (on a physical, chemical or statistical graph) line deviating from being straight with the change of a certain parameter

【曲意逢迎】qū yì féng yíng 违反自己的本心去迎合别人的意思 go out of one's way to curry favour with sb.

【曲折】qūzhé ❶ 弯曲 tortuous; winding; meandering: 沿着池塘有一条～的小路。There is a winding path along the pond. ❷ 复杂的、不顺当的情节 complicated circumstances; intricate plot: ～变化 sharp turns; dramatic changes｜这件事情里面还有不少～。There are many complications in it.

【曲直】qūzhí 无理和有理 right and wrong: 分清是非～ distinguish between right and wrong; tell right from wrong; make a distinction between right and wrong

【曲轴】qūzhóu 把机械的往复运动变为回转运动，或把回转运动变为往复运动的轴。轴的中部有一个或几个曲柄，是柴油机、汽油机等的重要部件。crankshaft; bent axle; crank; shaft of a machine that converts circular motion into reciprocal motion, or vice versa, with one or several bent handles attached; vital part of diesel engines, gas engines, etc.

岖(嶇) qū ☞崎岖 qíqū on p.1511

佉 qū 〈书 *fml.*〉驱逐 expel; drive out; banish

诎 qū ❶〈书 *fml.*〉缩短 curtail; shorten ❷〈书 *fml.*〉言语迟钝 slow of speech ❸ same as 屈 qū ❹(Qū)姓 a surname

驱(驅、敺) qū ❶ 赶(牲口) drive (a domestic animal); spur; goad (on): ～马前进 spur a horse on ❷ 快跑 gallop at top speed: 长～直入 drive straight in; drive deep into an area (or country)|并驾齐～ (run) neck and neck (with); keep abreast of or with; be on a par with; keep pace with; 〈*adj.*〉nip and tuck ❸ 赶走 expel; drive out; drive away; cast out; fight off; chase away; chuck: ～逐 banish; drive out; expel; rout out|～除 get rid of; eliminate|～虫剂 anthelmintic; parasiticide; vermicide; insectifuge

【驱策】qūcè 用鞭子赶;驱使 whip on; drive; spur; goad (on)

【驱车】qūchē 驾驶或乘坐车辆(多指汽车) drive; ride (oft. in a car): ～前往经济开发区参观访问 travel in a car (or drive) to visit an economic development zone

【驱除】qūchú 赶走;除掉 drive away; get rid of; eliminate: ～蚊蝇 repel mosquitoes and flies|～恐惧 get rid of one's fear

【驱赶】qūgǎn ❶ same as 赶 gǎn④: ～马车 drive a cart ❷ 赶走 drive away; expel: ～苍蝇 whisk away flies

【驱迫】qūpò 驱使;逼迫 force; compel; impel; drive; goad on: 为良心所～ driven by one's conscience

【驱遣】qūqiǎn ❶ same as 驱使 qūshǐ ①: 任人～ be pushed around ❷〈书 *fml.*〉赶走 drive out; expel ❸ 消除;排除(情绪) get rid of; banish; remove; dispel (unpleasant emotions): ～烦闷 banish one's anguish

【驱散】qūsàn ❶ 赶走,使散开 scatter; disperse; dispel; dissipate; break up: ～围观的人 disperse the crowd of onlookers|大风～了乌云。A gale dispelled the dark clouds. ❷ 消除;排除 get rid of; banish; dispel; drive away; dissipate: 习习的晚风～了一天的闷热。The gentle evening breeze dispelled the suffocating heat of the day.

【驱使】qūshǐ ❶ 强迫人按照自己的意志行动 order about; push around ❷ 推动 prompt; impel; drive; propel; goad on: 被好奇心所～ driven by curiosity

【驱邪】qūxié (用符咒等)驱逐邪祟(迷信 superstition) expel an evil spirit by incantations, etc.; exorcise (evil spirits); cast out (devils)

【驱逐】qūzhú 赶走 drive out; expel; banish; rout out; eject: ～出境 deport; expel; banish; renvoi|～入侵者 drive out invaders

【驱逐舰】qūzhújiàn 以火炮和反潜武器为主要装备的中型军舰,主要用于护航、警戒和反潜。装备有导弹的驱逐舰叫导弹驱逐舰。destroyer; mid-size warship armed with guns and anti-submarine weapons in the main, used for convoy, guard and anti-submarine purposes. Those armed with missiles are known as guided missile destroyers.

屈 qū ❶ 弯曲;使弯曲 bend; bow; crouch; crook: ～指 bend one's fingers|～膝 go down on one's knees; kneel; genuflect|猫～着后腿,竖着尾巴。The cat bent its hind legs and put its tail straight up. ❷ 屈服;使屈服 submit (to); yield (to); succumb (to); subdue: 宁死不～ would rather die than surrender|威武不能～ not to be subdued by force; be unyielding in the face of a mighty power ❸ 理亏 in the wrong: ～心 have a weak case|理～词穷 have nothing to say to justify oneself ❹ 委屈;冤枉 wrong; treat unfairly or unjustly: 受～ be wronged; be put in the wrong|叫～ complain about being wronged; protest against an injustice done to oneself; cry out one's grievance ❺(Qū)姓 a surname

【屈才】qū//cái 大才小用,指人的才能不能充分发挥 work at a job unworthy of one's talents; waste one's talents

【屈从】qūcóng 对外来压力不敢反抗,勉强服从 submit (to); yield (to); succumb (to): 决不～于恶势力 never yield to an evil force

【屈打成招】qū dǎ chéng zhāo 清白无罪的人冤枉受刑,被迫招认 confess to false charges under torture; subject a person to torture in order to force a confession

【屈服】qūfú 对外来的压力妥协让步,放弃斗争 submit (to); yield (to); succumb (to); buckle (under); knock under to; knuckle under to (sb.); surrender (to); bend (to); bow (to): ～投降 abjectly surrender (to); also 屈伏 qūfú

【屈光度】qūguāngdù 透镜的折光强度单位,数值上等于焦距(以米表示)除 1。如透镜的焦距为 2 米,它的屈光度就是 1/2。diopter; refractive power of a lens, equal to 1 divided by the focal distance (in metres) of the lens, e.g. if the focal distance of a glass is 2 metres, its refractive power will be 1/2

【屈驾】qūjià 〈敬辞 *honor.*〉委屈大驾(多用于邀请人 oft. used when extending an invitation) condescend to make the journey; be kind enough to honour us with your presence: 明日请～来舍一叙。Would you be kind enough to pay me a visit tomorrow?

【屈节】qūjié 〈书 *fml.*〉❶ 失去气节 forfeit one's honour or dignity: ～事仇 forfeit one's dignity in serving the enemy|～辱命 forfeit one's honour and fail in one's mission ❷ 降

低身份 stoop; humble oneself: 卑躬～ bow and scrape; abase oneself; act with servility; be submissive and subservient; cringe

【屈就】qūjiù 〈客套话 *pol.*〉用于请人担任职务 condescend to take a post offered: 要是您肯～,那就太好了。It would be very kind of you to condescend to take this post.

【屈居】qūjū 委屈地处于(较低的地位) be reconciled to a lower position than one deserves: ～亚军 have to settle for being a runner-up

【屈戌儿】qū·qur 铜制或铁制的带两个脚的小环儿,钉在门窗边上或箱、柜正面,用来挂上钌铞或锁,或者成对地钉在抽屉正面或箱子侧面,用来固定 U 字形的环儿 metal fastening; copper or iron ringlet with two latches fixed to a door, window, or the front of a trunk for hitching a hasp or padlock; U-shaped fastenings, fixed in pairs to the front of drawers or the side of trunks

【屈辱】qūrǔ 受到的压迫和侮辱 indignity; humiliation; mortification; abasement

【屈枉】qū·wang 冤枉 treat unjustly; wrong; put sb. in the wrong: 别～了好人。Don't put good people in the wrong.

【屈膝】qūxī 下跪 go down on one's knees; bend one's knees; kneel; 〈比喻 *fig.*〉屈服 submit: ～投降 abjectly surrender (to); kiss the ground; knuckle under (to)| 卑躬～ grovel; abase oneself; bow and scrape

【屈戌】qūxū 〈书 *fml.*〉 same as 屈戌儿 qū·qur

【屈折语】qūzhéyǔ 词的语法作用主要由词的形式变化来表示的语言,如俄语、德语 inflectional language; language in which a change in the form of a word indicates a change in its grammatical function, e.g. Russian, German

【屈指】qūzhǐ 弯着手指头计算数目 count on one's fingers: ～可数(形容数目很少) can be counted on one's fingers; (of things or people) rare| ～一算,离家已经十五年了。You can count — I've been away from home for 15 years.

【屈尊】qūzūn 〈客套话 *pol.*〉降低身份俯就 condescend; stoop: ～求教 condescend to learn from others; consult with others; seek advice from others

胠 qū 〈书 *fml.*〉 ❶ 腋下腰上的部位 part of the human body between the armpit and waist; flank ❷ 从旁边打开 open from the side: ～箧(指偷窃) pry open a trunk (to steal)

祛 qū 祛除 dispel; drive away: ～痰 expel phlegm| ～暑 ward off summer heat| ～疑 remove suspicion or doubt

【祛除】qūchú 除去(疾病、疑惧或迷信人所谓邪祟等) (of disease, fear, evil spirits, etc.) dispel; get rid of; drive out; relieve; exorcise: ～风寒 dispel a chill| ～紧张心理 relieve tension

【祛疑】qūyí 〈书 *fml.*〉消除别人的疑惑 remove suspicion or doubt

【祛淤】qūyū 〈中医 *Chin. med.*〉指祛除淤血 remove gore (coagulated blood); also 化淤 huàyū

袪 qū 〈书 *fml.*〉 ❶ 袖口 sleeve cuff ❷ same as 祛 qū

蛆 qū 苍蝇的幼虫,体柔软,有环节,白色,前端尖,尾端钝,或有长尾。多生在粪便、动物尸体和不洁净的地方。maggot; larva of a fly; white, soft-bodied annelid with a pointed front and blunt rear or a long tail; often found in excrement, decaying dead animals or unclean places

【蛆虫】qūchóng 蛆, maggot; 〈比喻 *fig.*〉专干坏事的卑鄙可耻的人 shameless scoundrel

躯(軀) qū 身体 human body: 身～ body; stature| 七尺之～ stature of seven *chi* (usu. a fully grown man)| 为国捐～ dedicate one's life to one's country

【躯干】qūgàn 人体除去头部、四肢所余下的部分叫躯干 trunk; torso; also 胴 dòng

【躯壳】qūqiào 肉体 (对'精神'而言 as opposed to 'soul') body; outer form

【躯体】qūtǐ 身躯;身体 body; soma; human body; physical body; material body: ～魁梧 full-bodied; (man) of a sturdy muscular physique; strapping; beefy; have a tall burly frame

焌 qū ❶ 把燃烧物放入水中使熄灭 immerse a burning thing into water to extinguish the fire: 把香火儿～了。Douse the joss sticks. ❷ 烹调方法,烧热油锅,先放作料,再放蔬菜迅速地炒熟 stir-fry; cooking method where condiments and vegetables are immediately added to heated oil, and stir-fried until ready: ～豆牙 stir-fried bean-sprouts

☞ jùn on p. 1067

【焌油】qūyóu 〈方 *dial.*〉烹调方法,把油加热后浇在菜肴上 cooking method where heated oil is sprayed over a half-cooked dish

趋(趨) qū ❶ 快走 hasten; rush; hurry: ～前 hurry ahead| 疾～而过 hurry past ❷ 趋向;归向 tend toward; tend to become; go in the direction of; head for: 大势所～ as is the general trend; general trends| 日～繁荣 advance toward prosperity day by day| 意见～于一致。We've come to an agreement. *or* We've reached an agreement. ❸ 鹅或蛇伸头咬人 (of a goose or snake) pop its head out and bite a person; strike at; snap at 〈古 *arch.*〉 same as 促 cù

【趋避】qūbì 快走躲开;规避 avoid (danger) by shifting quickly aside; dodge: ～不及 have no time to dodge| 见车飞驰而来,赶紧～一旁 dodge aside at the sight of a oncoming speeding car

【趋奉】qūfèng 趋附奉承 toady (to sb.); fawn (on sb.); curry favour (with sb.): 阿谀～ cringe; blarney; adulate (sb.); flatter (sb.); suck up (to sb.); smarm (over sb.)

【趋附】qūfù 迎合依附 ingratiate oneself with; curry favour with: ～权贵 attach oneself to bigwigs

【趋光性】qūguāngxìng 某些昆虫或鱼类常常奔向有光的地方,这种特性叫做趋光性 phototaxis; inclination of some insects or fish toward a source of light; also 慕光性 mùguāngxìng

【趋时】qūshí 赶时髦 follow the fashion; go with the times; follow the trend; be in the swim: 穿戴～ dress fashionably

【趋势】qūshì 事物发展的动向 trend; current; tendency; direction; tide; uptrend; stream; wind: 历史发展的必然～ inevitable trend in the development of history

【趋向】qūxiàng ❶ 朝着某个方向发展 tend to; be inclined to; go in the direction of: 病情～好转 (of a patient) be better day by day; begin to recover | 这个工厂由小到大,由简陋～完善。The factory is going from small to big, from crude to perfect. ❷ same as 趋势 qūshì: 总～ general trend

【趋炎附势】qū yán fù shì 奉承依附有权有势的人 serve the hour; serve the time; be a flunky; be a time-server; be time-serving

【趋之若鹜】qū zhī ruò wù 像鸭子一样,成群地跑过去。多比喻许多人争着去追逐不好的事物 go after in a flock like ducks; scramble for sth. oft. disapproving

蛐 qū ☞ below

【蛐蛐儿】qū·qur 〈方 *dial.*〉 蟋蟀 cricket (*Gryllus chinensis*)

【蛐蟮】qū·shàn same as 曲蟮 (qū·shàn)

麹 qū ❶ same as 曲[2] qū ❷ (Qū) 姓 a surname

觑(覷、覰) qū 把眼睛合成一条细缝(注意地看) look (attentively) with eyes partly closed; squint: 偷偷儿地～了他一眼 cast him a secret glance | 他微微低着头,～着细眼。He slightly lowered his head, his eyes narrowed. | ～起眼睛,看看地面上有没有痕迹 squint to check for traces on the ground

☞ qù on p. 1594

【觑觑眼】qūqūyǎn 〈方 *dial.*〉指近视眼 short-sighted; near-sighted

黢 qū 黑 black; dark: ～黑 completely dark; pitch-black; pitch-dark | 黑～～ pitch-black; pitch dark

【黢黑】qūhēi 很黑;很暗 completely dark; pitch-black; pitch-dark: 两手尽是墨,～的 both hands black with ink | 山洞里～,什么也看不见。The cave is quite dark, with nothing at all visible.

嚁 qū 〈拟声词 *onom.*〉形容吹哨子的声音或蟋蟀叫的声音 sound of whistling; chirping of a cricket

qú (ㄑㄩˊ)

劬 qú 〈书 *fml.*〉劳苦;勤劳 toil; hard work: ～劳 fatigue; overwork

【劬劳】qúláo 〈书 *fml.*〉 劳累 fatigue; overwork: 不辞～ make light of overwork

朐 qú 临朐 (Línqú), 地名,在山东 name of a place in Shandong

鸲 qú 鸟类的一属,身体小,尾巴长,羽毛美丽,嘴短而尖 crested myna (*Acrido theres cristatellus*) genus of birds, characterized by a small body, long tail, beautiful plumage, and short needle-like beak

【鸲鹆】qúyù ☞八哥 bā·ge on p. 21

渠[1] qú ❶ 人工开凿的水道 (artificial) water course; channel; canal; aqueduct; trench; penstock: 沟～ trench; canal; conduit; ditch | 河～ channel | 水到～成。(fig.) Success will come when conditions are ripe. | 这条～的最深处是一丈五。The channel is one and half *zhang* at its deepest. ❷ 〈书 *fml.*〉 大 big; great: ～帅 commander in chief ❸ (Qú) 姓 a surname

渠[2] **(佢)** qú 〈方 *dial.*〉他 he; him

【渠道】qúdào ❶ 在河湖或水库等的周围开挖的水道,用来引水排灌 (dug near a river, lake or reservoir for the purpose of irrigation) ditch; channel; trench ❷ 途径;门路 channel; way; means: 扩大商品流通～ extend the outlets for commodities; enlarge commodity circulation

蕖 qú ☞芙蕖 fúqú on p. 594

磲 qú ☞ [砗磲] chēqú on p. 233

璩 qú ❶ 〈书 *fml.*〉 玉环 jade bracelet or jade earrings ❷ (Qū) 姓 a surname

瞿 Qú 姓 a surname

☞ jù on p. 1054

鼩 qú [鼩鼱] qújīng 哺乳动物,身体小,形状像老鼠,但吻部细而尖,头部和背部棕褐色,腹部棕灰色或灰白色。多生活在山林中,捕食昆虫、蜗牛、蚯蚓等小动物,也吃植物种子和谷物。shrew (*Sorex Linnaeus*); shrewmouse; small mouse-like mammal with a narrow and pointed snout, a brown head and back, and grey belly, mostly living in mountain forests, feeding on insects, snails, earthworms, etc., as well as seeds and grain

蘧 qú ❶ [蘧然] (qúrán) 〈书 *fml.*〉惊喜的样子 pleasantly surprised ❷ (Qú) 姓 a surname

欋 qú 〈古代 *arch.*〉 指四齿的耙子 rake or fork with four prongs

氍(氈) qú [氍毹](qúshū)毛织的地毯，演戏多用来铺在地上，因此用'氍毹'或'红氍毹'借指舞台 wool carpet (oft. used to cover the ground for staging an opera); (fig.) stage; arena; also 红氍毹 hóngqúshū

籧 qú [籧篨](qúchú)〈古代 *arch.*〉指用竹或苇编的粗席 rough mat of bamboo or reed

臞 qú〈书 *fml.*〉same as 癯 qú

鸜 qú [鸜鹆](qúyù) same as 鸲鹆 qúyù

癯 qú〈书 *fml.*〉瘦 thin; emaciated: 清～ thin

蠷 qú [蠷螋](qúsōu)昆虫，体扁平狭长，黑褐色，前翅短而硬，后翅大，折在前翅下，有些种类无翅，尾端有角质的尾铗，多生活在潮湿的地方 earwig (*Labidura japonica*); insect having a flat, elongated dark brown body, short hard fore-wings, large under-wings folded under the fore-wings (some varieties having no wings), with pincer-like appendages protruding from the rear of the abdomen, and often living in wet places; also 蠼螋 qúsōu

衢 qú〈书 *fml.*〉大路 thoroughfare; highway: 通～ thoroughfare

蠼 qú [蠼螋](qúsōu) same as 蠷螋 qúsōu

qǔ (ㄑㄩˇ)

曲 qǔ ❶ 一种韵文形式，出现于南宋和金代，盛行于元代，是受民间歌曲的影响而形成的，句法较词更为灵活，多用口语，用韵也更接近口语。一支曲可以单唱，几支曲可以合成一套，也可以用几套曲子写戏曲。*Qu*; lyric; genre of verse to be sung, originating in the Southern Song and Jin Dynasties, and becoming popular in the Yuan Dynasty; derived from folk ballads, but more flexible in syntax than wording, and with more colloquialisms and spoken rhymes. A lyric can be performed alone or several verses can merge into a set. Several sets can be adapted as a traditional opera. ❷ (～儿 qǔr)歌曲 song; tune; melody: ～调 tune; melody; music | 戏～ traditional opera | 小～儿 ditty; ballad | 高歌一～ sing a song loud and clear ❸ 歌谱 music of a song:《义勇军进行曲》是聂耳作的～。*March of the Volunteers* is composed by Nie Er.

☞ qū on p. 1586

【曲调】qǔdiào 戏曲或歌曲的调子 music; tune; melody; strain; descant: ～优美 beautiful melody

【曲高和寡】qǔ gāo hè guǎ 曲调高深，能跟着唱的人很少。旧指知音难得。现比喻言论或艺术作品不通俗，能理解或欣赏的人很少。(of a song) too highbrow to be popular; (formerly of a bosom friend or soul mate) be one in a thousand; (of a statement or work of art) so highbrow that few can understand or enjoy

【曲剧】qǔjù ❶ 泛指解放后由曲艺发展而成的新型戏曲。有北京曲剧、河南曲剧、安徽曲子戏等 *quju*; (generally refers to) new genre of Chinese opera derived from storytelling and ballad-singing after Liberation, e.g. Beijing *quju*, Henan *quju*, Anhui *quzixi*, etc.; also 曲艺剧 qǔyìjù ❷ 特指北京曲剧，以单弦为主，吸收其他曲种发展而成 (esp.) Beijing *quju*, mainly composed of *danxian* (traditional storytelling ballads), and developed from a mixture of other types of operas

【曲目】qǔmù 歌曲、乐曲或戏曲的名目 number; items of song or performance; repertoire: 这次演唱会演出的～有三十多个。There are more than 30 numbers to be performed in the concert. | 评弹《真情假意》是个中篇～。The *pingtan* (storytelling ballad in Suzhou dialect) *Genuine Affection and False Pretence* is a medium-length number.

【曲牌】qǔpái 曲的调子的名称，如'滚绣球'、'一枝花'等 name of the tunes to which a lyric is composed, e.g. *gunxiuqiu*, *yizhihua*, etc.

【曲谱】qǔpǔ ❶ 辑录并分析各种曲调格式供人作曲时参考的书，如清人王奕清等所编的《曲谱》book of collected lyrics, e.g. *A Collection of Lyrics* compiled by Wangyiqing from the Qing Dynasty ❷ 戏曲或歌曲等不包括词的部分；乐谱 musical score of a Chinese opera or song; music book; (sheet) music

【曲艺】qǔyì 富有地方色彩的各种说唱艺术，如弹词、大鼓、相声、快板儿等 various forms of folk performing art rich in local flavour, including ballads sung in dialect, musical storytelling, comic dialogues, clapper-talk, etc.

【曲子】qǔ·zi same as 曲 qǔ ①②: 这支～好听。It is a nice song. *or* It's a pleasant melody.

苣 qǔ [苣荬菜](qǔ·mǎicài)多年生草本植物，野生，叶子互生，广披针形，边缘有不整齐的锯齿，花黄色。茎叶嫩时可以吃。witloof; endive (*Cichorium endivia*); perennial wild herb, having alternating pointed leaves irregularly serrated on the edges, bearing yellow flowers, the tender stems and leaves being edible

☞ jù on p. 1050

取 qǔ ❶ 拿到手里 get; fetch; take; draw; collect; pick up: ～款 withdraw money (from one's bank account) | ～行李 collect or get one's luggage | 把电灯泡～下来。Remove the electric bulb. ❷ 得到；招致 gain; seek; aim at: ～乐 amuse oneself; make merry; find or take delight in; do sth. for fun; get one's jollies | ～暖 warm oneself (by a fire, etc.); keep warm|～信于人 be trusted; gain trust; win the confidence of others|自～灭亡 court one's own ruin; cut one's own throat; sign one's own doom ❸ 采取;选取 adopt; assume; choose; select: ～道 by way of; through|录～ enroll; recruit; admit; matriculate|可～ advisable; acceptable|给孩子～个名儿 choose a name for a baby

【取保】qǔ//bǎo 找保人(多用于司法上 oft. legal) get sb. to bail one out; be bailed out: ～释放 be released on bail; be bailed out; be out on bail

【取材】qǔcái 选取材料 draw on; get certain sources (for a book, film, etc.): 就地～ draw on local resources|这本小说～于炼钢工人的生活。The novel is based on the life of steelworkers.

【取长补短】qǔ cháng bǔ duǎn 吸取长处来弥补短处 learn from other's strengths and offset one's own weaknesses; learn from others to improve oneself

【取代】qǔdài ❶ 排除别人或别的事物而占有其位置 replace; substitute; supersede; take over; take the place of; supplant: 用机器～手工生产 machines taking over manual work ❷ 化学上指有机物分子里的某些原子或原子团通过化学反应被其他原子或原子团所代替 displacement; substitution; chemical reaction in which certain atoms or radicals are replaced by other atoms or radicals

【取道】qǔdào 指选取由某地经过的路线 by way of; through; via: ～武汉,前往广州 go to Zhuangzhou by way of Wuhan; head for Zhuangzhou through Wuhan

【取得】qǔdé 得到 get; achieve; gain; obtain; acquire; procure: ～联系 get in touch with sb.|～经验 gain experience; become experienced

【取灯儿】qǔdēngr 〈方 *dial.*〉火柴 match (narrow stick of wood that ignites)

【取缔】qǔdì 明令取消或禁止 prohibit; ban; suppress; clamp down; put the lid on: ～无照商贩 clamp down on unlicensed vendors

【取而代之】qǔ ér dài zhī 排除别人或别的事物而代替其位置 replace sb. or sth.; supercede sb. or sth.

【取法】qǔfǎ 效法 follow the example of; emulate; model oneself on: ～乎上,仅得其中。Even if you model yourself on the best, the best you could achieve is mediocracy.

【取给】qǔjǐ 取得供给(后面多跟有'于'字 usu. followed by 于 yú) draw supplies: 建设资金主要～于内部积累。The capital for construction was mainly drawn from internal accumulation.

【取经】qǔ//jīng 本指佛教徒到印度去求取佛经,今比喻向先进人物、单位或地区吸取经验 (of a Buddhist) go on a pilgrimage to India for Buddhist scriptures; (fig.) learn from the experience of sb. or some place

【取精用弘】qǔ jīng yòng hóng 从大量的材料里提取精华 extract the best from plentiful resources; 弘 is also put as 宏 hóng

【取景】qǔ//jǐng 摄影或写生时选取景物做对象 (in photography or painting) find a view

【取决】qǔjué 由某方面或某种情况决定(后面多跟有'于'字 usu. followed by 于 yú) be decided by; be determined by; depend on; hinge on; rest with: 成绩的大小～于努力的程度。What you achieve depends on what efforts you make.

【取乐】qǔlè (～儿 qǔlèr)寻求快乐 make merry; seek pleasure; take delight in; do sth. for fun; get one's jollies: 说笑话～ amuse oneself by telling jokes|你别拿我～儿。Don't make fun of me.

【取闹】qǔnào ❶ (跟人)吵闹;捣乱 kick up a row; make trouble; create a fuss; rock the boat: 无理～ kick up a row ❷ 对人开玩笑;取乐 make fun of sb.; play a prank on sb.: 不该拿有残疾的同学～。You shouldn't make fun of students with physical handicaps.

【取暖】qǔnuǎn 利用热能使身体暖和 warm oneself (by a fire or heater); keep warm: ～设备 heating facilities|生火～ make a fire to keep warm

【取齐】qǔqí ❶ 使数量、长度或高度相等 make even; even up (numbers, length, height): 衣服的长短可照老样～。Make the coat's measurements even with the old sample. ❷ 聚齐;集合 assemble; gather; meet: 上午九时在大门口～,一块儿出发。Assemble at the gate at 9:00 in the morning and let's leave in a group.

【取巧】qǔ//qiǎo 用巧妙的手段谋取不正当利益或躲避困难 resort to trickery for avoiding difficulties; resort to crafty means for personal gain: 投机～ seek personal gain through speculation|～图便 take advantage of every opportunity for personal gain

【取舍】qǔshě 要或不要;选择 accept or reject; choose; opt: ～得宜 make the right choice|对文化遗产,应该有批判地加以～。We should approach cultural heritage critically.

【取胜】qǔshèng 取得胜利 post a victory over sb.; win a victory; achieve success; win; succeed

【取消】qǔxiāo 使原有的制度、规章、资格、权利等失去效力 (of rules and regulations, qualifications, rights, etc.) abolish; nullify; cancel; annul; call off: ～资格 be deprived of one's credentials|～不合理的规章制度 abolish unreasonable rules and regulations; also 取销 qǔxiāo

【取销】qǔxiāo same as 取消 qǔxiāo

【取笑】qǔxiào 开玩笑;嘲笑 laugh at; make fun

of; poke fun at; play a joke on; make game of; make sport of; ridicule; tease; jest with: 被别人～ be ridiculed|他说话有点口吃,你别～他。He stutters. Don't laugh at him.

【取信】qǔxìn 取得别人的信任 win trust; gain trust: ～于人 be trusted; win the confidence of others

【取样】qǔyàng 从大量物品或材料中抽取少数做样品 take a sample: ～检验 make a sample test; also 抽样 chōuyàng

【取悦】qǔyuè 取得别人的喜欢;讨好 try to please; curry favour with; cater to the tastes of; ingratiate oneself with (sb.): ～于人 try to please|～上司 curry favour with one's superior; play up to one's superior

【取证】qǔzhèng 取得证据 gather or collect evidence: 广泛～ gather evidence on a broad basis|调查～ investigate and collect evidence

【取之不尽,用之不竭】qǔ zhī bù jìn, yòng zhī bù jié 形容很丰富,用不完 (of resources) inexhaustible

娶 qǔ 把女子接过来成亲(跟'嫁'相对 as opposed to 'be married to') marry (a woman): 嫁～ marriage|～妻 take a wife|～媳妇儿 take a wife

【娶亲】qǔ//qīn 男子结婚,也指男子到女家迎娶 (of a man) get married; (of a man) go to pick up his bride at her house, part of traditional Chinese wedding rituals

龋 qǔ 牙齿有病而残缺 tooth decay; caries

【龋齿】qǔchǐ ❶ 病,由于口腔不清洁,食物残渣在牙缝中发酵,产生酸类,破坏牙齿的釉质,形成空洞,有牙疼、齿龈肿胀等症状 tooth decay; caries; dental caries; process of decay of a tooth by acid from fermenting food residues between teeth which are not thoroughly cleaned, spoiling the glaze of the tooth and leaving a cavity, causing toothaches, gumboils, etc. ❷ 患这种病的牙 decayed tooth ‖ also 蛀齿 zhùchǐ, and commonly known as 虫牙 chóngyá, 虫吃牙 chóngchīyá

qù (ㄑㄩˋ)

去[1] qù ❶ 从所在地到别的地方(跟'来'①相对 as opposed to 'come') go (from here to there): ～路 way of advancing; the way to|～向 whereabouts|从成都～重庆 from Chengdu to Chongqing|他～了三天,还没回来。He has been away for three days, and has not come back yet. ❷ 离开 leave; depart; be off: ～国 leave one's country|～世 pass away; depart from this world|～职 no longer hold one's post; quit one's job; resign from office|～留两便。Go or stay, do as you like. ❸ 失去;失掉 lose; be out of; be bereft of: 大势已～ The situation is beyond salvation. *or* It's a lost cause. *or* The game is as good as lost. ❹ 除去;除掉 get rid of; remove; relieve: ～病 prevent or cure a disease|～火 relieve internal heat; relieve inflammation|～皮 remove the peel or skin|这句话～几个字就简洁了。Delete one or two words, and the sentence reads more concise. ❺ 距离 be away from: 两地相～四十里。The two places are 40 *li* apart.|～今五十年。It was 50 years ago. ❻ 过去的(时间,多指过去的一年) past (oft. referring to the year just past): ～年 last year|～秋(去年秋天) last autumn|～冬今春 last winter and this spring ❼〈婉辞 *euph.*〉指人死 (meaning 'die') pass away; depart; be gone; depart from this world; go to a better place: 他不到四十岁就先～了。He passed away before he was 40. ❽ 用在另一动词前表示要做某事 [used before another verb to indicate a future action] be about to; be going to: 你们～考虑考虑。You may go and think about it.|自己～想办法。Go and figure out a way for yourself. 注意 **NOTE**: 表示离开说话人所在地自行做某件事时用'去',表示到说话人所在地参与某件事时用'来'。when indicating an action of leaving the speaker, use 去 qù; while for an action coming toward the speaker, use 来 lái ❾ 用在动词或动词结构后面表示去做某件事 [used after a verb or verbal structure to indicate an action that has started] have gone to do sth.: 游泳～了 have gone for a swim|他听报告～了。He has gone to listen to a report.|回家吃饭～了 have gone home for dinner 注意 **NOTE**: ⑧⑨的'去'可以一前一后同时用,表示去了要做某件事,如:他～听报告～了。去 qù in ⑧⑨ can be used simultaneously before or after a verb or verb-object structure to indicate 'have gone to do sth.,' e.g. He has gone to listen to a report. ❿ 用在动词结构(或介词结构)与动词(或动词结构)之间,表示前者是后者的方法、方向或态度,后者是前者的目的 [used between a verbal structure or prepositional structure and a verb or verbal structure to indicate the former is the way, direction or attitude of the latter, while the latter is the purpose of the former] to; in order to; through; by; from: 提了一桶水～浇花 take a bucket of water to water the flowers|要从主要方面～检查 conduct an inspection from the principal aspect|用辩证唯物主义的观点～观察事物 look at things from a dialectical-materialist point of view ⓫〈方 *dial.*〉用在'大、多、远'等形容词后,表示'非常…','…极了'的意思(后面加'了') [used after an adjective such as 大 dà, 多 duō, 远 yuǎn, etc. and ending with 了 ·le to indicate degree] very; extremely: 这座楼可

大了～了！What an enormous building！|他到过的地方多了～了！He has travelled to countless places！⑫ 去声 falling tone：平上～入 level tone，rising tone，falling tone and entering tone

去[2] qù 扮演（戏曲里的角色）play a role；act a part in（a local opera）：在《断桥》中，他～白娘子。He played the role of Lady White in *The Broken Bridge*.

去 //·qù ❶ 用在动词后，表示人或事物随动作离开原来的地方［used after a verb to suggest the movement away of the speaker in the middle of an action］away：拿～ take it away|捎～ take it（away）with you ❷ 用在动词后，表示动作的继续等［used after a verb to indicate a continued action］on：信步走～（＝过去）take a leisurely walk toward or up to|让他说～。（＝下去）Let him talk on.|一眼看～（＝上去）look far ahead；look across

【去处】qùchù ❶ 去的地方 whereabouts：我知道他的～。I know where he is. ❷ 场所；地方 place；spot；site：那里林木幽深，风景秀丽，是一个避暑的好～。It's an ideal summer resort with the peace and quiet of woods and the beauty of landscape.

【去火】qù//huǒ〈中医 *Chin. med.*〉指消除身体里的火气 relieve internal heat：消痰 ～ reduce phlegm and relieve internal heat|喝绿豆汤，可～。Mung-bean soup can help relieve internal heat.

【去就】qùjiù 担任或不担任职务 leave or remain in one's post：～未定。It's not certain whether he will leave or remain in his post.

【去路】qùlù 前进的道路；去某处的道路 way of advancing；the way to；outlet：挡住他的～。His way forward was blocked.

【去年】qùnián 今年的前一年 year before the present year；last year；yesteryear

【去任】qù//rèn（官吏）去职 no longer hold the official post；resign from office；relinquish one's official post

【去日】qùrì〈书 *fml.*〉已过去的岁月 bygone days；past；past times；（of）yore：～苦多。Many are the days that have gone by.

【去声】qùshēng ❶〈古代 *arch.*〉汉语四声的第三声 falling tone；one of the four tones in classical Chinese ❷ 普通话字调中的第四声 the fourth tone in modern standard Chinese pronunciation；☞四声 sìshēng on p.1821

【去世】qùshì（成年人）死去；逝世（of an adult）die；pass away；depart from this world；go to a better place；depart；be gone

【去暑】qù//shǔ 驱除暑气 get rid of summer heat：～降温 relieve heat and bring in coolness

【去岁】qùsuì same as 去年 qùnián

【去向】qùxiàng 去的方向 direction in which sb. has gone；whereabouts：不知～（of the one spoken of）have no idea where sb. has gone；（of the speaker）I am lost

【去雄】qùxióng 果树或玉蜀黍等进行品种间的杂交时，把所选母株的雄蕊去掉 emasculate；castrate；removal of the stamens of a maternal plant in the cross breeding of different strains of fruit，maize，etc.

【去职】qù//zhí 不再担任原来的职务 no longer hold the official post

阒 qù〈书 *fml.*〉形容没有声音 quiet；still；silent：～寂 stillness；dead silence|～然 absolutely quiet|～无一人 quiet and empty

【阒然】qùrán〈书 *fml.*〉形容寂静无声的样子 absolutely quiet；utterly still；deadly silent；soundless：四野～。All was quiet across the vast expanse of country.

趣 qù ❶（～儿 qùr）趣味；兴味 interest；palate；delight：活泼有～ lively and interesting|自讨没～儿 spoil the scene|桃红柳绿，相映成～。The peach and willow trees are a delightful contrast to each other. ❷ 有趣味的 interesting；amusing；diverting；sapid；intriguing；arresting；funny：～事 amusement；fun；joke；funny thing|～闻 joke；anecdote；funny story ❸ 志趣 interest；inclination：异～（志趣不同）of different tastes

〈古 *old*〉same as 促 cù

【趣剧】qùjù 闹剧 slapstick；farce

【趣事】qùshì 有趣的事 amusement；fun；joke；funny thing：逸闻～ anecdotes；episodes；jokes|说起学生时代的一些～，大家都笑了。All laughed when they talked about those funny things that had happened in their school years.

【趣味】qùwèi 使人愉快、使人感到有意思、有吸引力的特性 interest；palate；delight：很～ arresting；amusing|～无穷 full of fun；fascinating

【趣闻】qùwén 有趣的传闻 joke；funny story；anecdote：轶事～ anecdote

觑（覻、覷） qù〈书 *fml.*〉看；瞧 look；stare；gaze：～视 gaze；look|～伺 watch|小～ glance|面面相～ look at each other dumbly|冷眼相～ cast a cold eye at sb.；treat sb. coldly

☞ qū on p.1590

·qu（·ㄑㄩ）

戌 ·qu ☞［屈戌儿］qū·qur on p.1589

☞ xū on p.2161

quān（ㄑㄩㄢ）

卷 quān〈书 *fml.*〉弩弓 crossbow

悛 quān 〈书 *fml*.〉悔改 repent; be contrite; be penitent: 怙恶不～(坚持作恶,不肯悔改) persist in evil and refuse to repent

圈 quān ❶ (～儿 quānr) same as 圈子 quān•zi ①: 铁～儿 iron ring|项～ neck ring|画了一个～儿 draw a circle|桌子周围挤着一～儿人。The table is surrounded by a ring of people.|跑了三～儿 run three laps ❷ same as 圈子 quān•zi ②: ～内 within the circle; inside|～外 outside (the circle)|包围～ ring of siege; ring of encirclement ❸ 在四周加上限制(多指地方); 围 (usu. with a fence) enclose; encircle: ～地 fence off a field|用篱笆把菜地～起来 enclose the vegetable field with a fence ❹ 画圈做记号 mark with a circle: ～选 select or choose by drawing a circle around the name of a candidate or item|数目字都用笔～出来 circle all numbers (with a pen)|把这个错字～了 circle the incorrect words

☞ juān on p. 1054 and juàn on p. 1056

【圈点】quāndiǎn 在书或文稿上加圆圈或点,作为句读的记号,或用来标出认为值得注意的语句 highlight (a book or text) with small circles or dots, to mark out noteworthy statements or words

【圈定】quāndìng 用画圈的方式确定(人选、范围等) approve (a candidate, range, etc.) by drawing a circle on it

【圈拢】quān•long 〈方 *dial*.〉❶ 团结;使不分散 hold together; unite: ～志趣相投的一块儿干 get people of the same mind together to make a joint effort ❷ 拉拢 hook in; rope in: 他受坏人～,被拉下了水。He was hooked in and sunk to corruption.

【圈套】quāntào 使人上当受骗的计策 snare; trap; mesh; toil; web; springe; put-up job; frame-up story: 设下～ set a trap; lay a snare|落入～ be caught in a trap; fall into a trap; play into sb.'s hands

【圈椅】quānyǐ 靠背和扶手接连成半圆形的椅子 round-backed armchair

【圈阅】quānyuè 领导人审阅文件后,在自己的名字处画圈,表示已经看过 (of leader) circle one's name on a document to confirm it has been checked or approved

【圈子】quān•zi ❶ 圆而中空的平面形;环形;环形的东西 circle; ring: 大家在操场上围成一个～。All of them formed a circle in the playground. ◇到公园去兜个～ go for a round in the park|说话不要绕～。Don't beat around the bush. ❷ 集体的范围或活动的范围 circle; clique: 小～ clique|生活～ living world; circle of life|他陷在敌人～里了。He was encircled by the enemy.

棬 quān 〈书 *fml*.〉曲木制成的饮器 drinking vessel made of bended wood

鄯 quān 地名用字,如柳树鄯、毕家鄯(在河北),蒙鄯(在天津) *quan*, used in names of places, e.g. Liushuquan and Bijiaquan in Hebei Province, and Mengquan in Tianjin

quán (ㄑㄩㄢˊ)

权(權) quán ❶ 〈书 *fml*.〉秤锤 sliding weight of a steelyard or Roman balance; counterpoise ❷ 〈书 *fml*.〉权衡 weigh (A against B); consider; balance: ～其轻重 strike a balance; have sth. weighed ❸ 权力 power; authority; might; influence; potency: 当～ be in power; wield power|有职有～ hold office and have power|掌握大～ wield the sceptre|生杀予夺之～ power over life and death ❹ 权利 right; entitlement; title; droit: 人～ human rights|公民～ civil rights; franchise|选举～ right to vote; franchise|发言～ right to speech; voice; say; say-so ❺ 有利的形势 advantageous or favourable position: 主动～ initiative|制空～ control of airspace; air domination; air supremacy ❻ 权变;权宜 adaptability to self-interest; expediency; advisability: ～诈 trickery; duplicity; falseheartedness|～谋 political choice; diplomacy|通～达变 adaptable to changing circumstances; not be bound by rules; be flexible ❼ 权且;姑且 (take a stopgap measure) for the time being; for the moment: ～充 be taken temporarily as|死马～当活马医 treat a dead horse as if it were alive; (fig.) try something as last resort to save a helpless situation ❽ (Quán) 姓 a surname

〈旧 *old*〉same as 颧 quán

【权变】quánbiàn 随机应变 be adaptable to a changing situation; trim the sails; play it by ear

【权标】quánbiāo 中间插着一把斧头的一捆木棍,古代罗马把它作为权力的象征。'权标'的译音是'法西斯'。意大利独裁者墨索里尼的法西斯党名称由此而来。fasces; bundle of rods bound together around an axe with the blade projecting, seen in ancient Roman as an emblem of authority. 'Fasces' is transliterated as 'fascist,' as used by the Fascist Party led by the Italian dictator Mussolini.

【权柄】quánbǐng 所掌握的权力 power (in hand); authority

【权臣】quánchén 掌握大权而专横的大臣 influential (usu. domineering) minister: ～用事。The influential ministers wield power.|～祸国。The powerful court officials were bringing disaster to the country.

【权贵】quánguì 居高位、掌大权的人 influential official; man of weight; bigwig

【权衡】quánhéng 秤锤和秤杆 sliding weight

and weighing arm of a steelyard;〈比喻 *fig*.〉衡量、考虑 balance; calculate; weigh: ～轻重 weigh A against B; judge the comparative importance | ～利弊 weigh advantages against disadvantages | ～得失 try to strike a balance; weigh gains against losses

【权力】quánlì ❶ 政治上的强制力量 power; authority: 国家～ state power | 全国人民代表大会是最高国家～机关。The National People's Congress is the supreme organ of power in China. ❷ 职责范围内的支配力量 scope of one's official power; jurisdiction: 行使大会主席的～ function as chairperson of a conference; exercise the functions of chair of a conference

Q

【权利】quánlì 公民或法人依法行使的权力和享受的利益（跟'义务'相对 as opposed to 'obligation'）right to be performed by a citizen or juristic person and the interest he enjoys

【权利能力】quánlì nénglì 指依法能够享有一定权利和承担一定义务的资格。是行为能力的前提。ability to exercise one's rights and honour one's obligations, which is a precondition of ability; ☞ 行为能力 xíngwéi nénglì on p. 2145

【权略】quánlüè 随机应变的谋略；权谋 political choice; diplomacy

【权门】quánmén 权贵人家 dignitary family; influential family: 依附～ attach oneself to a dignitary

【权谋】quánmóu 随机应变的计谋 diplomacy

【权能】quánnéng 权力和职能 power and functions

【权且】quánqiě 暂且；姑且（take a stopgap measure) tentatively; for the time being; for the moment: ～如此。It's as such for the moment. | 吃几片饼干～充饥。Have some cookies for now as refreshment.

【权时】quánshí ❶ 暂时 temporarily; for the time being ❷〈书 *fml*.〉权衡时势 size up the situation: ～度势 take stock of the current situation

【权势】quánshì 权柄和势力 power and influence; ascendancy; ascendance: 依仗～ throw one's weight about

【权术】quánshù 权谋；手段（多含贬义 oft. derog.）art of politics; political trickery：玩弄～ play politics

【权数】quánshù〈书 *fml*.〉指应变的机智 tact; wit; resource

【权威】quánwēi ❶ 使人信服的力量和威望 authority; authoritativeness: ～著作 authoritative book | ～的动物学家 authority on zoology; authoritative zoologist ❷ 在某种范围里最有威望、地位的人或事物 person or thing of authority; authority: 他是医学～。He is a medical authority. | 这部著作是物理学界的～。The book is authoritative in the field of physics.

【权位】quánwèi 权力和地位 power and status: 不谋～ without angling for any power or status; seek no power or status

【权限】quánxiàn 职权范围 scope of one's power and functions; jurisdiction: 管理～ limits of managerial authority | 超越～ exceed one's authority; go beyond one's authority; overstep one's authority

【权宜】quányí 暂时适宜；变通 expedience; expediency: ～之计 expedient; makeshift; stopgap; expedience

【权益】quányì 应该享受的不容侵犯的权利 rights and interests: 合法～ legal rights

【权舆】quányú〈书 *fml*.〉❶ same as 萌芽 méngyá ①: 百草～。All kinds of plants are beginning to germinate. ❷（事物）开始（of things) begin; start; commence

【权诈】quánzhà 奸诈 duplicity; trickery; false-heartedness

全 quán ❶ 完备；齐全 all ready; complete: 这部书不～。This book is not complete. | 东西预备～了。Everything is ready at hand. | 棉花苗已出～。All the cottonseeds have sprouted. ❷ 保全；使完整不缺 save sth. from damage; keep sth. intact or complete: 两～其美 make the best of both worlds; have it both ways ❸ 整个 whole; entire; all: ～神贯注 concentrate on sth.; be preoccupied with; be deeply absorbed in sth. | ～家光荣 glory of the whole family | ～书十五卷。The whole book comes in 15 volumes. ❹ 完全；都 completely; entirely; wholly: 他讲的话我～记下来了。I took down all he said. | 一声巨响，大家～被吓住了。All of us were shocked by the blaring sound. ❺ (Quán) 姓 a surname

【全般】quánbān 整个；全面 whole; entire; all; complete; full: ～工作 entire work

【全豹】quánbào〈比喻 *fig*.〉事物的全部 whole picture; panorama; the all in one; overall situation; ☞ 管中窥豹 guǎn zhōng kuī bào on p. 717

【全本】quánběn ❶（～儿 quánběnr）指演出时间较长、故事情节完整的（戏曲）complete version of a full-length opera: ～《西游记》complete version of *Journey to the West* ❷ 足本 unexpurgated version (of a book, etc.)

【全部】quánbù 各个部分的总和；整个 all; entire; whole; complete; total; full; a whole lot of; the all in one: ～力量 every bit of one's strength | 工程已～竣工。The project has been entirely completed. | 问题～解决。All the problems have been resolved.

【全才】quáncái 在一定范围内各方面都擅长的人才 versatile person who is expert at many things; all-rounder: 文武～ be versatile in both civil and military service. | 在文娱体育活动方面他是个～。He is an all-rounder in both entertainment and sports.

【全称】quánchēng 名称未简化前的完整形式 full name; unabbreviated form: 少先队的～是少年先锋队。The full name of Young Pioneers is Communist Young Pioneers.

【全程】quánchéng 全部路程 entire journey; whole distance: 运动员都坚持跑完～。All the runners stuck it out to the whole distance.

【全等形】quánděngxíng 各部分能够完全重合的两个或几个几何图形叫做全等形 congruent figures

【全都】quándōu 全;都 all; every; without exception: 人～到齐了。All have come. | 去年种的树～活了。All the trees planted last year have survived.

【全方位】quánfāngwèi 指四面八方;各个方向或位置 omnidirectional; all-round: ～外交 all-round diplomacy | ～出击 hit out in all directions | ～经济协作 all-round economic cooperation

【全份】quánfèn (～儿 quānfènr)完整的一份儿 complete set: ～茶点 whole set of refreshments | ～表册 complete set of lists and forms

【全副】quánfù 整套;全部(多用于精神、力量或成套的物件 usu. of energy, strength, or set of sth.) complete; full: ～精力 full energy | ～武装 be fully armed; be in full battle gear

【全乎】quán·hu (～儿 quán·hur)齐全 complete; all ready: 这家商店虽小,货物倒是很～。Small as it is, the shop has a full range of goods in stock.

【全会】quánhuì (政党、团体)全体会议的简称 plenary session; plenum (of a political party or group): 中央～ the Plenary Session of the Central Committee (of the CPC) | ～公报 bulletin of a plenary session

【全集】quánjí 一个作者(有时是两个或几个关系密切的作者)的全部著作编在一起的书(多用做书名 usu. used in titles of books) complete works; complete edition; collected works; collected edition: 《列宁～》*Collected Works of Lenin* | 《鲁迅～》*Collected Works of Lu Xun* | 《马克思恩格斯～》*Complete Works of Marx and Engels*

【全家福】quánjiāfú ❶ 一家大小合拍的相片儿 photo of the whole family ❷ 荤的杂烩 hotchpotch (Chinese dinner delicacy for family gatherings)

【全局】quánjú 整个的局面 general or overall situation; situation as a whole: ～观念 overall point of view | 胸怀～ with the whole picture in mind

【全开】quánkāi 印刷上指整张的纸 (of printing) standard-sized sheet of paper: ～宣传画 full-size poster

【全劳动力】quánláodònglì 指体力强能从事轻重体力劳动的人(多就农业劳动而言 esp. farm worker) able-bodied person; also 全劳力 quánláolì

【全力】quánlì 全部力量或精力 full energy or strength: 用尽～ exert all one's strength; spare no effort | ～支持 all-out support; do all one can to support | ～以赴 go all out; spare no effort; put one's best leg forward; make an all-out effort; pull out all stops; put one's back into sth.; to the best of one's ability or power

【全貌】quánmào 事物的全部情况;全部面貌 complete picture; panorama; full view: 先弄清楚问题的～,再决定处理办法。Get the complete picture of the problem before you decide on a solution. | 仅据一点,难以推想～。You cannot conjure up a complete picture merely by seeing one bit of it.

【全面】quánmiàn 各个方面的总和(跟'片面'相对 as opposed to 'partial') overall; general; all-sided; full-scale; comprehensive; all-round; whole; total; complete; entire: ～性 comprehensiveness | 照顾～ take everything into consideration | ～情况 overall picture | ～发展 all-round or full-scale development

【全民】quánmín 一个国家内的全体人民 all the people (within a country); whole people; entire people: ～公决 general referendum | ～动员 mobilization of a whole nation

【全民所有制】quánmín suǒyǒuzhì 生产资料和产品归全体人民所有的制度,是社会主义所有制的高级形式 ownership by the whole people; social system according to which all means of production and its products are owned by the people as a whole

【全能】quánnéng 在一定范围内样样都擅长 all-round; versatile: ～冠军 versatile champion | 十项～运动员 decathlete

【全能运动】quánnéng yùndòng 某些运动项目(如田径、体操、游泳)中的综合性比赛项目,要求运动员在一天或两天内把几个比赛项目按照规定的顺序比赛完毕,按各项成绩所得分数的总和判定名次 composite athletic contest, e.g. track events, gymnastics, swimming, etc., in which each contestant participates in all the required events in a prescribed sequence within one or two days, and the overall winner is judged by adding up all scores from these events

【全盘】quánpán 全部;全面(多用于抽象事物 oft. of abstract things) whole; all; overall; total: ～计划 overall plan | ～考虑 give total consideration

【全票】quánpiào ❶ 全价的车票、门票等 full-price ticket ❷ 指选举中的全部选票 all the votes in an election: 他以～当选为职工代表。He was unanimously elected deputy to the workers' congress.

Q

【全勤】quánqín 指在一定时期内不缺勤 full attendance during a certain period：出～ have recorded full attendance|他这个月～。He had perfect attendance this month.

【全球】quánqiú 整个地球；全世界 whole world; entire globe

【全权】quánquán （处理事情的）全部的权力 full power; full authority; plenary power：～大使 plenipotentiary|～代表 plenipotentiary (deputy)

【全权代表】quánquán dàibiǎo 对某件事有全权处理和决定的代表。外交上的全权代表须持有国家元首的全权证书。plenipotentiary (deputy); representative fully authorized to handle an issue or make a decision. A diplomatic plenipotentiary must have authorized certification by the head of his country.

Q

【全然】quánrán 完全地 completely; utterly：他一切为了集体，～不考虑个人的得失。He does everything for the collective, utterly disregarding personal gain and loss.

【全色片】quánsèpiàn 对全部可见光都能感受的胶片 panchromatic film

【全身】quánshēn 整个身体 all over (the body); from head to foot; from tip to toe：用尽了～的力气 exert all one's strength

【全神贯注】quán shén guàn zhù 全副精神高度集中 concentrate on sth.; be absorbed in sth.; be preoccupied with sth.

【全盛】quánshèng 极其兴盛或强盛（多指时期）florescence; prime; heyday：唐朝是律诗的～时期。The *lushi* poetry was in its prime during the Tang Dynasty.

【全食】quánshí abbr. for 日全食或月全食的简称 abbr. for 日全食 rìquánshí or 月全食 yuèquánshí ☞日食 rìshí on p. 1627 and 月食 yuèshí on p. 2371

【全始全终】quán shǐ quán zhōng （做事）从头到尾都很完美一致 stick to a duty or undertaking till the end; see sth. through; start well and end well

【全数】quánshù 全部（可以计数的东西）total amount or number; whole sum：借款～归还。The loan is totally paid back.

【全速】quánsù 所能达到的最高速度 full speed; maximum speed; full split; full tilt：～航行！Steer at full throttle! *or* Full speed ahead! *or* Full steam ahead! |部队～前进。The troops are advancing at full speed.

【全体】quántǐ ❶ 各部分的总和；各个个体的总和（多指人 oft. of people）all; wholeness; total number：～会员 all the members|～出席。All are present.|看问题不但要看到部分，而且要看到～。When approaching a problem, one should see the whole as well as the parts. ❷ 全身 all over (the body)：被雨淋得～透湿 be wet all over; be soaked through; be soaked to the skin

【全天候】quántiānhòu 不受天气限制的，在任何气候条件下都能使用或工作的 usable or operative in all kinds of weather; all-weather：～公路 all-weather road|～飞机 all-weather aircraft

【全托】quántuō 把幼儿交给托儿所或幼儿园昼夜照管，只在节假日接回家，叫全托（区别于'日托' as compared with 'daycare'）boarding nursery (in which babies are taken home during holidays); total childcare

【全文】quánwén 指文章、文件的全部文字 full text：～转载 be reprinted in full

【全武行】quánwǔháng ❶ 戏曲中指规模较大的武打 full-scale acrobatic fight in traditional opera：排演一出～好戏 rehearse a wonderful opera of acrobatic fighting ❷ 指打群架，泛指进行暴力行动 gang war; punch-up; (in a broad sense) violence; hooliganism

【全息】quánxī 反映物体在空间存在时的整个情况的全部信息 holographical information; information that records the complete situation of an object's existence

【全息照相】quánxī zhàoxiàng 记录被物体反射或透射的波的全部信息的技术。全息照相有光学、声学、X 射线、微波等多种。用这种技术照的相富有立体感。在某些检验技术和信息存储、立体电影等方面有广泛的用途。holography; technique of making a three-dimensional image of an object by recording the interference patterns formed by a split laser beam, which is applied in optics, acoustics, x-rays, microwave, etc.; holograms produced by this technique are three-dimensional and are widely used in certain fields of inspection, data storage, vectorgraph, etc.

【全线】quánxiàn ❶ 全部战线 all along the frontline (of a war)：～反攻 launch a counter-attack on all fronts|～出击 launch an attack on all fronts ❷ 整条路线 whole line; entire length：这条铁路已～通车。The whole railway line has been opened to traffic.|～工程，克期完成。The whole length of the project has been completed within the deadline.

【全心全意】quán xīn quán yì 用全部的精力 wholeheartedly; heart and soul：～为人民服务。Serve the people wholeheartedly.

【全休】quánxiū 指职工因病在一定时期内不工作 (of an employee) take full sick leave：医嘱～两周。The doctor prescribed complete rest of two weeks.

【全音】quányīn 包括两个半音的音程叫全音 musical interval of two semitones; whole tone; tone; step; whole step; ☞半音 bànyīn on p. 54

【全知全能】quán zhī quán néng 无所不知，无所不能 omniscient and omnipotent

佺 quán 偓佺（Wòquán）〈古代 *arch.*〉传说中的仙人 mythical fairy

诠 quán〈书 *fml.*〉❶ 诠释 expound; annotate: ～解 interpret ❷ 事理;真理 reason; truth: 真～ truth

【诠次】quáncì〈书 *fml.*〉❶ 编次;排列 arrange sth. in order; put in order ❷ same as 层次 céngcì ①;伦次 lúncì: 辞无～ incoherent speech (or writing)

【诠释】quánshì〈书 *fml.*〉说明;解释 expound; annotate; gloss

【诠注】quánzhù 注解说明 note; annotation; comment

荃 quán 古书上说的一种香草 aromatic plant recorded in ancient books

泉 quán ❶ 泉水 spring: 温～ hot spring | 矿～ mineral spring; spa | 清～ clear spring | 甘～ sweet spring water ❷ 泉眼 mouth of a spring ❸ 钱币的名称 name for ancient coin: ～币 ancient coin ❹ (Quán) 姓 a surname

【泉流】quánliú 泉水形成的水流 stream of spring water

【泉水】quánshuǐ 从地下流出来的水 water flowing naturally from underground; spring water

【泉下】quánxià 黄泉之下,指阴间 after world; the nether world; ☞黄泉 huángquán on p. 853

【泉眼】quányǎn 流出泉水的窟窿 mouth of a spring

【泉涌】quányǒng 像泉水一样不断涌出来 gush out; stream: 泪如～ with tears streaming down | 文思～ streams of consciousness (writing)

【泉源】quányuán ❶ 水源 fountainhead; riverhead; wellhead; water-head; wellspring; fountain; fount; spring-head ❷〈比喻 *fig.*〉力量、知识、感情等的来源或产生的原因 source (of strength, information, emotion, etc.): 生命的～ source of life | 智慧的～ source of wisdom | 力量的～ source of strength

辁 quán〈书 *fml.*〉❶ 没有辐的车轮 spokeless wheel ❷ 浅薄 shallow; superficial: ～才(浅薄的才气或才能) superficial talent or ability

拳 quán ❶ 拳头 fist: 双手握～ clench one's fists; make a fist | ～打脚踢 cuff and kick; beat up ❷ 拳术 Chinese boxing: 打～ do shadowboxing | 练～ practise shadowboxing | 一套～ a set of shadowboxing | 几手好～ a few smart punches in boxing | 太极～ shadowboxing ❸ 拳曲 bend; curl up; huddle (up): 老大娘～着腿坐在炕上。The old lady sat on the *kang* with her legs curled up.

【拳棒】quánbàng 指武术 martial arts; kung fu

【拳击】quánjī 体育运动项目之一。比赛时两个人戴着特制的皮手套互相击打,以击倒对方或击中对方有效部位次数多为胜。boxing; sport in which two opponents, wearing boxing gloves, fight with fists, where the winner is the one who delivers a knockout or more legal blows

【拳脚】quánjiǎo ❶ 拳头和脚 fists and feet: ～相加 come to blows ❷ 指拳术 Chinese boxing: 会几手～ can perform a few sets of Chinese boxing

【拳曲】quánqū (物体)弯曲 (of things) curl up; bend: ～的头发 curly hair

【拳拳】quánquán〈书 *fml.*〉形容恳切 earnestly; sincerely: 情意～ sincere feelings | ～之忱 sincerity; sincere affection; also 惓惓 quánquán

【拳师】quánshī 以教授或表演拳术为职业的人 boxing coach; boxing master; pugilist

【拳手】quánshǒu 拳击运动员 boxer: 业余～ amateur boxer

【拳术】quánshù 徒手的武术 Chinese boxing

【拳头】quán·tóu 手指向内弯曲合拢的手 fist; a bunch of fives; mauley; dukes: 把～握得紧紧的 clench one's fist; with clenched fist | 举起～喊口号 raise one's fist and shout slogans

【拳头产品】quán·tóu chǎnpǐn 指优异的、有市场竞争能力的产品 knockout products; highly competitive products; products of excellent quality

铨 quán〈书 *fml.*〉❶ 选拔 choose; select: ～叙 examine one's official credentials (so as to make a decision for rank or position) ❷ 衡量轻重 weigh (advantages against disadvantages)

【铨叙】quánxù〈旧时 *old*〉政府审查官员的资历,确定级别、职位 examine an official's credentials so as to make a decision concerning rank or position

痊 quán 病愈 recover from an illness: ～愈 be fully recovered (from an illness)

【痊愈】quányù 病好了 be fully recovered (from an illness)

惓 quán [惓惓] quánquán same as 拳拳 quánquán

筌 quán〈书 *fml.*〉捕鱼的竹器 bamboo trap for fishing: 得鱼忘～ forget the trap after catching the fish; forget the means by which one attains a goal; forget those who help one achieve success

蜷(踡) quán 蜷曲 coil; curl (up); twist: ～缩 crouch; huddle (up) | 花猫～作一团睡觉。The kitten was sleeping curled up on the sofa.

【蜷伏】quánfú 弯着身体卧倒 curl up; huddle (up): 他喜欢～着睡觉。He likes to curl up when sleeping.

【蜷局】quánjú〈书 *fml.*〉蜷曲 coil; curl; twist

【蜷曲】quánqū 弯曲(多形容人或动物的肢体 oft. used for the body of a person or animal) coil; curl; twist: 两腿～起来 with legs bent | 草丛里有一条～着的赤练蛇。There is a dinodom rufozonatum (a kind of poisonous snake) coiled in the grass.

【蜷缩】quánsuō 蜷曲而收缩 crouch; huddle (up); gather up; scrunch: 小虫子～成一个小球儿。The little insect rolls itself into a ball.

醛 quán 有机化合物的一类，是醛基和烃基(或氢原子)连接而成的化合物，如甲醛、乙醛等 aldehyde; organic chemical compound from aldehyde radicle and alkyl radicle, e.g. aldehyde, ethylal, etc.

鳈 quán 鱼类的一属，体长5—6寸，身体深棕色，有斑纹，口小。为我国东部平原地区特产的小鱼。fat minnow (*Sarcocheilichthys lacustris*); a kind of fish, 5 or 6 *cun* long, having a dark-brown striped body, small mouth; local specialty from the eastern plains of China

鬈 quán ❶ (头发)弯曲 (of hair) curly; wavy; crimped: ～发 wavy hair ❷ 形容头发美 (of hair) beautiful

颧 quán [颧骨] (quán·gǔ) 眼睛下边两腮上面突出的颜面骨 cheekbone

quǎn (ㄑㄩㄢˇ)

犬 quǎn 狗 dog: 警～ police dog | 猎～ hunting dog | 牧～ shepherd dog; sheepdog | 军用～ military dog | 丧家之～ stray dog | 鸡鸣～吠 cocks crowing and dogs barking; (fig.) (of an inhabited area) enjoying a peaceful life

【犬齿】quǎnchǐ 齿的一种，上下颌各有两枚，在门齿的两侧，齿冠锐利，便于撕裂食物 canine tooth; a kind of tooth, situated in pairs in the upper jaw and lower jaw on each side of the fore-tooth; sharp, good for ripping into food; also 犬牙 quǎnyá; (图见 ☞ figure for 齿 chǐ on p. 263)

【犬马】quǎnmǎ 〈古时 *arch.*〉臣下对君主自比为犬马，表示愿供驱使 (of a liegeman) form of self-address in front of a sovereign to indicate willingness to do the latter's bidding: 效～之劳 willing to serve Your Majesty faithfully (just like a horse)

【犬儒】quǎnrú 原指古希腊抱有玩世不恭思想的一派哲学家，后来泛指玩世不恭的人 cynic (for merly referred to a group of ancient Greek philosophers who looked at the world scornfully and negatively; later used for all people thinking this way)

【犬牙】quǎnyá ❶ same as 犬齿 quǎnchǐ ❷ 狗牙 fang (of a dog)

【犬牙交错】quǎnyá jiāocuò 形容交界处参差不齐，像狗牙一样。泛指局面错综复杂。(of a common boundary) jigsaw-like; jagged; interlocking; (gen. of the pattern of an event) full of twists and turns; anfractuous; tortuous

【犬子】quǎnzǐ 〈谦辞 *hum.*〉对人称自己的儿子 my son

甽 quǎn 〈书 *fml.*〉田间小沟 ditch in a crop field

【甽亩】quǎnmǔ 〈书 *fml.*〉田间；田地 field; plough-land; farm

绻 quǎn ☞[缱绻](qiǎnquǎn) on p. 1540

quàn (ㄑㄩㄢˋ)

劝(勸) quàn ❶ 拿道理说服人，使人听从 persuade; advise; urge: 规～ remonstrate; expostulate; advise | ～导 persuade; advise; exhort | ～解 appease; propitiate; mediate | 他身体不好，你应该～他休息休息。He is weak in health, so you should talk him into taking a rest. ❷ 勉励 encourage: ～勉 admonish and encourage

【劝导】quàndǎo 规劝开导 persuade; advise; exhort: 听从～ take sb.'s advice; defer to sb.'s advice; follow sb.'s recommendations | 耐心～ exhort with patience

【劝告】quàngào ❶ 拿道理说服人，使人改正错误或接受意见 advise; urge; exhort; admonish: 再三～ repeatedly admonish ❷ 希望人改正错误或接受意见而说的话 advice; warning; exhortation; recommendation; tip: 你要多听听大家的～。You had better listen to everyone's advice.

【劝和】quànhé 劝人和解 mediate; make peace

【劝化】quànhuà ❶ 〈佛教 *Budd.*〉指劝人为善，泛指劝勉感化 (of a Buddhist) urge people to do good; (gen.) advise and influence; encourage and reform ❷ 募化 solicit donations for a Buddhist temple; collect alms

【劝驾】quàn//jià 劝人出去担任职务或做客 urge sb. to accept a post or an invitation

【劝架】quàn//jià 劝人停止争吵、打架 try to stop a quarrel or fight; conciliate; mediate

【劝解】quànjiě ❶ 劝导宽解 mollify; appease; propitiate; soothe: 经过大家～，他想通了。He became convinced after so much persuasion from everybody. ❷ same as 劝架 quàn//jià: 从旁～ go and appease somebody

【劝诫】quànjiè 劝告人改正缺点错误，警惕未来 dissuade; admonish; exhort; expostulate: 他把我当成亲兄弟一样，时时～我，帮助我。He treats me as his own brother and often gives me warnings and help.

【劝进】quànjìn 劝说实际上已经掌握政权而有意做皇帝的人做皇帝 make a formal appeal to a minister or general who holds real power and covets the throne to declare himself king or emperor

【劝酒】quàn//jiǔ (酒席上)劝人喝酒 (at a banquet) urge sb. to drink: 主人举杯频频～。Glass in hand, the host toasted everyone around.

【劝勉】quànmiǎn 劝导并勉励 admonish and encourage：互相～ encourage each other

【劝募】quànmù 用劝说的方式募捐 solicit contributions：多方～，集资百万。After many persuasive efforts, they have raised a million yuan.

【劝说】quànshuō 劝人做某种事情或使对某种事情表示同意 persuade; advise; talk sb. around to doing sth.; talk sb. into doing sth.; reason with sb.; prevail on sb. to do sth.：反复～ make repeated efforts to persuade｜不听～ turn a deaf ear to sb.'s advice

【劝慰】quànwèi 劝解安慰 comfort; console; soothe：他多次来信～我，嘱咐我不要泄气。He wrote me many times to give me comfort and ask me not to lose heart.

【劝降】quàn//xiáng 劝人投降 induce (the enemy) to capitulate

【劝诱】quànyòu 劝说诱导 induce; prevail on; bring around

【劝止】quànzhǐ same as 劝阻 quànzǔ

【劝阻】quànzǔ 劝人不要做某事或进行某种活动 dissuade sb. from; disadvise sb. against; talk sb. out of (doing) sth.：好言～ kindly advise sb. not to do sth.｜极力～ try every means to dissuade sb. from doing sth.

券[1] quàn 票据或作为凭证的纸片 certificate; ticket; bill; note; warrant; voucher; credence：公债～ government bond｜入场～ admission ticket

券[2] quàn alternate pronunciation for 券 xuàn ☞券 xuàn on p. 2175

quē（ㄑㄩㄝ）

炔 quē 炔烃 alkyne ☞ Guì on p. 734

【炔烃】quētīng 不饱和烃的一类，分子中含有叁键结构的开链烃，如乙炔(HC≡CH)等 unsaturated hydrocarbon, contained in molecules of open chain hydrocarbons with a triple bond, e. g. acetylene (HC≡CH, etc.)

缺 quē ❶ 缺乏；短少 be short of; lack; be devoid of; be empty of; be scant in; be wanting in; run short of; be shy of; (of sth.) be absent; be deficient：～人 be short of hands; be shorthanded｜～材料。The material is scarce. *or* be short of material｜庄稼～肥～水就长不好。Crops won't grow well lacking fertilizer and water. ❷ 残破；残缺；broken; incomplete; imperfect：～口 gap; breach; nick; jag; indentation｜完满无～ complete (with not a single part missing); full; perfect｜这本书～了两页。Two pages are missing from this book. ❸ 该到而未到 be absent (from); absent oneself (from)：～勤 be absent from duty or work｜～课 be absent from class; miss a class｜～席 be absent; absent oneself; be among the missing; (legal) default ❹〈旧时 *old*〉指官职的空额，也泛指一般职务的空额 (of an official position) unfilled; (generally of a post or work position) vacant; open：出～ (of a high post) fall vacant｜肥～ lucrative job｜补一个～ fill a vacancy

【缺德】quē//dé 缺乏好的品德。指人做坏事，恶作剧，开玩笑，使人为难等等 wicked; villainous; virtueless; mean; vicious; mischievous; rotten：～话 wicked words; vicious remarks｜～事 offence; rotten thing; mean trick｜真～！What a rotten thing! *or* How dirty!

【缺点】quēdiǎn 欠缺或不完善的地方（跟'优点'相对 as opposed to 'strength' or 'virtue'）shortcoming; defect; weakness; flaw; demerit; drawback; blemish; disadvantage; weak point：克服～ overcome one's shortcomings; get over one's weaknesses｜这种浅色花布很好看，～是不禁脏。The light-printed cloth looks nice, but the drawback is that it dirties easily.

【缺额】quē'é 现有人员少于规定人员的数额；空额 vacancy：还有五十名～。We are still 50 people short.

【缺乏】quēfá（所需要的、想要的或一般应有的事物）没有或不够（of things that one needs, wants or should have）be short of; lack; be without enough; be in want of：材料～。The materials are lacking.｜～经验 lack experience｜～锻炼 be in want of exercise

【缺憾】quēhàn 不够完美，令人感到遗憾的地方 imperfection; disappointment; regret：因故未能赶上参加开幕式，实在是个～。What a pity he missed the opening ceremony for some reason.

【缺刻】quēkè 指叶子边缘上的凹陷 notch at the edge of a leaf; incision

【缺口】quēkǒu ❶（～儿 quēkǒur）物体上缺掉一块而形成的空隙 gap; breach; nick; indentation; jag：围墙上有个～。There is a gap in the boundary wall.｜碗边儿上碰了个～儿。The bowl has a chipped edge. ❷ 指（经费、物资等）短缺的部分（of funds, materials, etc.）gap; shortfall：原材料～很大。There is a still major shortfall in the supply of raw materials.

【缺漏】quēlòu 欠缺遗漏 gaps and omissions：弥缝～ fill in gaps and supply omissions

【缺略】quēlüè 欠缺；不完整 incomplete; imperfect; deficient：释文～。Something is missing in the transcription of the text.

【缺门】quēmén（～儿 quēménr）空白的门类 gap or vacancy (in a branch of learning, etc.)：～产品 product gap｜填补～ fill in a gap

【缺欠】quēqiàn ❶ same as 缺点 quēdiǎn ❷

same as 缺少 quēshǎo：～科技人才 be in want of technological talent｜由于资金～，计划只得暂停。The plan is suspended for lack of funds.

【缺勤】quē//qín 在规定时间内没有上班工作 be absent from duty or work：～率 absence；absence rate｜因病～ be absent on account of illness；be on a sick leave

【缺少】quēshǎo 缺乏(多指人或物数量不够 oft. things or people not enough) be short of；lack；be in want of：～零件 be short of spare parts｜～雨水 suffer from lack of rain｜～人手 be short of hands；be shorthanded

【缺损】quēsǔn ❶ 破损 damage：如有～，照价赔偿。If there is any damage，full compensation will be paid. ❷ 医学上指身体的某个部分或器官缺少或发育不完全 malformation or any development defect in a human body

【缺席】quē//xí 开会或上课时没有到 be absent from (a meeting，class，etc.)；absent oneself from：因事～ be absent on account of an engagement｜他这学期没有缺过席。He has never missed a single class this term.

【缺陷】quēxiàn 欠缺或不够完备的地方 downside；defect；flaw；fault；blemish；limitation；deficiency；bug：生理～ physical defect

【缺嘴】quēzuǐ〈方 *dial.*〉❶（～儿 quēzuǐr)唇裂 harelip ❷ 指在吃的方面没有得到满足 with one's appetite for food unsatisfied；be underfed：这孩子不～，可总也胖不起来。The child is well-fed，but always looks thin.

阙 quē〈书 *fml.*〉❶ 过失 fault；error ❷ same as 缺 quē ❸（Quē）姓 a surname

☞ què on p. 1604

【阙如】quērú〈书 *fml.*〉欠缺；空缺 be deficient：竟告～ be found wanting

【阙疑】quēyí 把疑难问题留着，不下判断 leave a difficult problem untackled：暂作～ leave it open

qué（ㄑㄩㄝˊ）

瘸 qué 行走时身体不稳；跛(bǒ) limp；be lame；be gammy；be crippled：～腿 lame leg｜～着走 limp；walk with a limp；gimp｜摔～了腿 be crippled by a fall

【瘸子】qué·zi 瘸腿的人；跛子 cripple；lame person；gimp

què（ㄑㄩㄝˋ）

却[1]（卻）què ❶ 后退 back off；fall back；step back；retreat；recoil；stand back；drop back；retrocede：退～ retreat；make a retreat；draw back；fall back；haul off；retire；recoil｜～步 step back；take a step back；hang back ❷ 使退却 drive back；repulse：～敌 drive the enemy back ❸ 推辞；拒绝 refuse；decline；reject；turn down：推～ refusal；decline｜～之不恭。It would be impolite to decline.｜盛情难～。It's too kind an offer to say 'no' to. ❹ 去；掉 get rid of；lose：冷～ cool down；cool off｜忘～ forget；efface；be oblivious of｜失～信心 lose heart；lose confidence

却[2]（卻）què〈副词 *adv.*〉表示转折，比'倒、可'的语气略轻(weaker than 倒 dào or 可 kě) but；yet；however：我有许多话要说，一时～说不出来。I have a lot to say，but am at a loss for words.｜文章虽短～很有力。The article is short yet forceful.

【却病】quèbìng〈书 *fml.*〉避免生病；消除疾病 prevent or cure a disease：～延年 prevent disease and prolong life

【却步】quèbù 因畏惧或厌恶而向后退(from fear or disgust) step back；hang back：望而～ step back when confronted with a tough job or in danger；shrink from (something unpleasant，difficult，dangerous，etc.)｜～不前 step back；shrink｜不因困难而～。Don't shrink before difficulties.

【却说】quèshuō 旧小说的发语词，'却说'后头往往重提上文说过的事(used in an old style of storytelling to introduce the next part，oft. followed by a review of the last part) the story goes that ...

【却之不恭】què zhī bù gōng 对于别人的馈赠、邀请等，如果拒绝，就显得不恭敬 it would be impolite to refuse (gift，invitation，etc.)：～，受之有愧。It would be disrespectful to decline，but embarrassing to accept.

埆 què〈书 *fml.*〉土地不肥沃(of land or soil) infertile

悫（慤、愨）què〈书 *fml.*〉诚实 honesty；sincerity；faithfulness

雀 què 鸟类的一科，体形较小，发声器官较发达，有的叫声很好听，嘴呈圆锥状，翼长，雌雄羽毛的颜色多不相同，雄鸟的颜色常随气候改变，吃植物的果实或种子，也吃昆虫。燕雀、锡嘴都属于这一科。sparrow (*Passeriformes*)；finch；bird family，small，with well-developed vocal organs，good at singing，having a taper-like beak and long wings，the colour of the male oft. changing with the climate and differing from that of the female，feeding on fruit，seeds，and insects as well. Both brambling and hawfinch belong to this family.

☞ qiāo on p. 1548 and qiǎo on p. 1551

【雀斑】quèbān 皮肤病，患者多为女性。症状是面部出现黄褐色或黑褐色的小斑点，不疼不痒。freckle；fleck；lentigo；sunspot；skin ailment，mostly afflicting women，with symptoms of brownish or dark spots on the facial skin, but not accompanied by pain or itching

【雀鹰】quèyīng 猛禽的一种,比鹰小,羽毛灰褐色,腹部白色,有赤褐色横斑,脚黄色。雌的比雄的稍大。捕食小鸟。饲养的雌鸟可以帮助打猎。sparrow hawk (*Accipiter nisus*); bird of prey, smaller than a hawk, having brownish grey plumage, a white abdomen, with a single reddish brown band along the sides, and yellow feet, preying on small birds, the female slightly bigger than the male. A tamed female hawk can assist in hunting. also 鹞 yào; 通称 commonly known as 鹞子 yào·zi or 鹞鹰 yàoyīng

【雀跃】quèyuè 高兴得像雀儿一样地跳跃 jump for joy; jump with joy: 欢欣～ jump for or with joy|～欢呼 jump and cheer

确[1](碻、塙、硞) què ❶ 符合事实的;真实的: true; actual; authentic; genuine; real; unfeigned: 的～ really; indeed|正～ correct; right; proper; errorless; accurate; (leg.) valid|～证 prove convincingly; corroborate|～有其事。There is indeed such a thing. *or* It's true. ❷ 坚固;坚定 firm; solid; steadfast: ～立 establish; set up; fix|～信 be assured; be sure; be certain; be convinced; be confident|～守 uphold firmly; abide by faithfully

确[2] què 〈书 *fml.*〉 same as 埆 què

【确保】quèbǎo 确实地保持或保证 make certain; ensure; guarantee; insure; assure: ～安全 ensure safety|～交通畅通 guarantee smooth flow of traffic|加强田间管理,～粮食丰收 enhance field management to guarantee a harvest of crops

【确当】quèdàng 正确恰当;适当 proper; appropriate; suitable: 立论～ make the right point|措词十分～。The wording is appropriate.

【确定】quèdìng ❶ 明确而肯定 definite; certain; firm: ～的答复 definite reply|～的胜利 sure victory ❷ 明确地定下 make certain; make sure; determine; decide on; fix; ascertain; set the seal on: ～了工作之后就上班。I will start working after the job is landed.|还没有～候选人名单。The list of candidates is not yet fixed.

【确乎】quèhū 的确 really; indeed: 经过试验,这办法～有效。This method has proven really effective through experimentation.|屋子又宽绰又豁亮,～不坏。The house is indeed a nice one, spacious and full of light.

【确立】quèlì 稳固地建立或树立 set up; establish; fix; build up: ～制度 establish a system|～信念 form a belief; build up confidence

【确切】quèqiè ❶ 准确;恰当 true; appropriate; exact; precise: ～不移 definite and firm|用字～ proper or precise use of words ❷ same as 确实 quèshí: 消息～。The news is reliable.|～的保证 sure guarantee

【确认】quèrèn 明确承认(事实、原则等) confirm; affirm; notarize; validate; acknowledge: 参加会议的各国～了这些原则。The participating countries affirmed these principles.

【确实】quèshí ❶ 真实可靠 true; exact; authentic; reliable; trustworthy; credible: ～性 authenticity; trustworthiness; credibility|～的消息 reliable news|这件事他亲眼看到,说得确确实实。He witnessed the accident and gave an accurate account of all details. ❷ 〈副词 *adv.*〉对客观情况的真实性表示肯定 truly; really; indeed; for sure: 他最近～有些进步。He's really made some progress recently.|这件事～不是他干的。He didn't really do it.

【确守】quèshǒu 确实地遵守 faithfully abide by; uphold firmly; observe determinedly; doubtlessly comply with: ～合同 abide by the contract faithfully|～信义 act in strict good faith

【确信】quèxìn ❶ 确实地相信;坚信 hold the firm belief (that); firmly believe (that); be confident (that); be sure of or that; be certain of or that; be convinced of or that: 我们～这一崇高理想一定能实现。We are confident that the great ideal will be realised. ❷ 确实的信息 true, definite news; firm response: 不管事成与否,请尽速给个～。Whether successful or not, just send definite news.

【确凿】quèzáo (也有读 also pronounced quèzuò 的)非常确实 authentic; irrefutable; undeniable; conclusive; beyond dispute: ～不移 undeniable or irrefutable|～的事实 indisputable fact|证据～。The evidence is conclusive.

【确诊】quèzhěn 诊断确定 diagnose; make a diagnosis: 经过检查,～为肺炎。He was diagnosed as having pneumonia after a checkup.

【确证】quèzhèng ❶ 确切地证实 prove convincingly or conclusively; corroborate: 我们可以～他的论断是错误的。We can prove conclusively that his assertion is wrong. ❷ 确切的证据或证明 conclusive evidence; definite proof; corroboration: 在～面前他不得不承认自己的罪行。In the face of the conclusive evidence, he could not but plead guilty.

阕 què ❶ 〈书 *fml.*〉终了 end; cease: 乐～。The music come to an end. ❷ 〈量词 *classifier*〉 a) 歌曲或词一首叫一阕 a song or a stanza of *ci* poem: 弹琴一～ play a song (on a musical instrument)|填一～词 write a *ci* poem; b) 一首词的一段叫一阕 A stanza of a *ci* poem is known as *que*.

鹊 què 喜鹊 magpie; pie

【鹊巢鸠占】què cháo jiū zhàn〈比喻 *fig.*〉强占别人的房屋、土地、产业等 grab a house, land, property, etc., that doesn't belong to one

【鹊起】quèqǐ〈比喻 *fig.*〉名声兴起、传扬 (of fame) spread; rise: 声誉～ rise to fame | 文名～ rise to literary fame

【鹊桥】quèqiáo 民间传说天上的织女七夕渡银河与牛郎相会,喜鹊来搭成桥,叫做鹊桥 Magpie Bridge. Legend has it that on the 7th day of the 7th lunar month on the bridge formed by numerous magpies fly over to form a bridge with their bodies to help the Weaving-girl cross the Milky Way for an annual tryst with her lover, the Cowherd: ～相会(比喻夫妻或情人久别后团聚) (of husband and wife, or lovers) reunite after a long separation | 搭～(比喻为未婚男女撮合) (fig.) make a match (bring about a marriage)

碏 què 用于人名,石碏,春秋时卫国大夫 *que*, used in given names; Shique, senior official in the State of Wei during the Spring and Autumn Period

阙 què ❶〈古代 *arch.*〉皇宫大门前两边供瞭望的楼,泛指帝王的住所 watchtower on either side of a palace gate; (gen.) imperial palace: 官～ imperial palace | 伏～(跪在宫门前) kneel down before a palace gate ❷ 神庙、陵墓前竖立的石雕 stone carving erected in front of a temple or tomb;

☞ quē on p. 1602

榷[1] què〈书 *fml.*〉专卖 monopoly: ～茶 monopoly on tea | ～税(专卖业的税) tax on monopolies

榷[2](搉) què 商讨 discuss: 商～ consult; confer

qūn (ㄑㄩㄣ)

囷 qūn〈古代 *arch.*〉一种圆形的谷仓 a type of circular granary or barn

逡 qūn〈书 *fml.*〉退让;退 give way; concede; move back; recede

【逡巡】qūnxún〈书 *fml.*〉有所顾虑而徘徊或不敢前进 hesitate to move forward; hang back; shrink back: ～不前 hesitate to move ahead

qún (ㄑㄩㄣˊ)

宭 qún〈书 *fml.*〉群居 living in groups or herds; gregarious; social

裙(帬) qún ❶ 裙子 skirt: 布～ cloth skirt | 短～ short skirt | 连衣～ (woman's) dress | 百褶～ pleated skirt ❷ 形状或作用像裙子的东西 sth. that looks or serves as a skirt: 围～ apron | 墙～ dado

【裙钗】qúnchāi〈旧时 *old*〉妇女的服饰,借指妇女 petticoats and hairpins; women

【裙带】qúndài〈比喻 *fig.*〉跟妻女姊妹等有关的(含讽刺意 ironical) connected through a female family member: ～官(因妻女姊妹的关系而得到的官职) official whose position is granted by favouritism shown to a female member of his family rather than by his merit | ～关系(被利用来相互勾结攀援的姻亲关系) nepotism (using relations for secret collusion and social advancement) | ～风(搞裙带关系的风气) prevailing nepotism; nepotistic practices

【裙子】qún·zi 一种围在腰部以下的服装 skirt; petticoat

群(羣) qún ❶ 聚在一起的人或物 (composed of people, things, animals, etc.): crowd; group; throng; cluster; knot: 人～ crowd of people; crowd | 鸡～ flock of chickens | 建筑～ cluster of buildings | 成～结队 in large numbers; in groups ❷ 众多的人 large numbers of people: 超～ above the average; be outstanding; unusual | ～言堂 where everybody has his say | ～策～力 pool the wisdom and efforts of many people; make joint efforts; pull together ❸ 成群的 in groups; in large numbers: ～峰 chain of mountain peaks | ～居 living in groups or herds; gregarious | ～集 gather up; assemble; throng; troop together; swarm; huddle together ❹〈量词 *classifier*〉用于成群的人或东西 group; herd; swarm; flock, etc: 一～孩子 a group of children | 一～马 a herd of horses

【群策群力】qún cè qún lì 大家共同出主意,出力量 pool the wisdom and efforts of many people; make joint efforts; pull together

【群唱】qúnchàng 曲艺的一种表演形式,三个或三个以上的人交替着唱 form of folk art in which three or more performers sing alternately

【群岛】qúndǎo 海洋中彼此相距很近的一群岛屿,如我国的舟山群岛、西沙群岛等 archipelago; group of scattered islands, e. g. Zhoushan Archipelago and Xisha Archipelago in China

【群芳】qúnfāng 各种美丽芳香的花草 beautiful and fragrant flowers;〈比喻 *fig.*〉众多的女子 charming women: ～谱 catalogue of flowers | ～竞艳 beautiful women vying for attention | 技压～ show outstanding skill

【群婚】qúnhūn 原始社会的一种婚姻形式,几个女子共同跟别的氏族的几个男子结婚。同一氏族内的人禁止通婚。communal marriage; form of marriage in primitive society in which a group of women together marry a group of men from a different clan, but men and women within the same clan are forbidden to marry

【群集】qúnjí 成群地聚集 get together; assemble; mass; congregate; throng; troop together; swarm: 人们～在广场上。People are assembling in the square.

【群居】qúnjū ❶ 成群聚居 living in groups, herds, etc.; gregarious; social: ～穴处 living in groups in caves ❷〈书 *fml.*〉很多人聚在一起 (of many people) stay together: ～终日 stay together all day long

【群龙无首】qún lóng wú shǒu〈比喻 *fig.*〉一群人中没有领头的人 a group of people without a leader

【群落】qúnluò ❶ 生存在一起并与一定的生存条件相适应的动植物的总体 (composed of people, animals or plants) community; colony ❷ 同类事物聚集起来形成的群体 group (of buildings, etc.): 风景～ scattered scenic spots | 古建筑～ cluster of ancient buildings

【群氓】qúnméng〈书 *fml.*〉统治者对人民群众的蔑称 (derog.) (used by a ruler to refer to the people) common herd

【群魔乱舞】qún mó luàn wǔ 形容一群坏人猖狂活动 (of a gang of villains) act fiercely or savagely; run amok

【群起】qúnqǐ 很多人一同起来(做某事)(of people) rise in a mass (to do sth.): ～响应。All rise up to respond. | ～而攻之 (of people) rise or turn against sb.; rise together to attack sb.

【群轻折轴】qún qīng zhé zhóu 许多不重的东西也能压断车轴。比喻小的坏事如果任其发展下去,也能造成严重后果(见《战国策·魏策一》:'臣闻积羽沉舟,群轻折轴,众口铄金')。many a little weight loaded on a cart can break its wheel shaft; (fig.) A minor bad deed, if left unchecked, can have grave consequences. *Intrigues of the Warring States Period · Intrigues of Wei I*: 'This humble minister has learned that a load of feathers if heavy enough can sink a boat, many a little weight loaded on a cart can break its wheel shaft, and public clamour can melt metal.'

【群情】qúnqíng 群众的情绪 public sentiment; popular feelings; feelings of the masses: ～欢洽 prevailing joy and harmony | ～激奋。The public is aroused and excited. | ～鼎沸。Public excitement rose to a boiling point.

【群体】qúntǐ ❶ 由许多在生理上发生联系的同种生物个体组成的整体,如动物中的海绵、珊瑚和植物中的某些藻类 colony; group of the same biologically related kinds of animals or plants together, e. g. sponge, coral, some algae ❷ 泛指本质上有共同点的个体组成的整体 group; generally referring to a collective whose members have sth. in common in essence: 英雄～ group of heroes | 企业～ group of enterprises | 建筑～ cluster of buildings

【群威群胆】qún wēi qún dǎn 群众团结一致所表现的力量和勇敢精神 mass power and courage

【群雄】qúnxióng〈旧时 *old*〉称在时局混乱中称王称霸的一些人 warlords; lords or tyrants involved in separatist wars during political chaos: ～割据。The country was fragmented by rival warlords.

【群言堂】qúnyántáng 指领导干部贯彻群众路线,充分发扬民主,广泛听取意见,并能集中正确意见的工作作风(跟'一言堂'相对 as opposed to 'where one person alone has the say') (of a leader's working style) follow the mass line; carry democracy forward and listen to public opinions; pooling public wisdom; let everyone have their say; (of a leader) rule by the voice of the majority

【群英】qúnyīng 指许多有才干的人,也指许多英雄人物 galaxy of talents or heroes: ～会 gathering of talents, heroes and model workers, etc.; meeting of outstanding people | ～欢聚 splendid gathering of accomplished people

【群英会】qúnyīnghuì 赤壁之战的前夕,在东吴文官武将的一次宴会上,周瑜说:'今日此会可名群英会。'(见《三国演义》第四十五回)现在借指先进人物的集会。gathering of heroes; *Romance of Three Kingdoms · Chapter 45*: At a banquet of officials and generals of the kingdom of Wu, Zhou Yu said, 'Today's get-together may be called a "gathering of heroes."' (fig.) meeting of model workers or outstanding people

【群众】qúnzhòng ❶ 泛指人民大众 (in a broad sense) the masses; people: ～大会 mass rally | 深入～ go among the masses | 听取～的意见 listen to public opinion ❷ 指没有加入共产党、共青团组织的人 person who is not a member of the Chinese Communist Party or the Chinese Communist Youth League ❸ 指不担任领导职务的人 rank and file; grass-roots

【群众关系】qúnzhòng guān·xi 指个人和他周围的人们相处的情况 one's relations or ties with other people; popularity

【群众路线】qúnzhòng lùxiàn 中国共产党的一切工作的根本路线。一方面要求在一切工作或斗争中,必须相信群众、依靠群众并组织群众用自己的力量去解决自己的问题。另一方面要求领导贯彻'从群众中来到群众中去'的原则,即在集中群众意见的基础上制定方针、政策,交给群众讨论、执行,并在讨论、执行过程中,不断根据群众意见进行修改,使之逐渐完善。mass line; the basic line for all the work of the Chinese Communist Party. On the one hand, it requires that when working or struggling, leaders should trust and rely on the masses and motivate them to solve their problems on their own; on the other, leaders should carry out the principle of 'coming from the masses and going back among the masses', which is to shape principles and policies on the basis of pooling the opinions of the masses, and presented these principles and policies to the masses for discussion and implementation while continuously rectifying and perfecting them according to feedbacks from the masses.

【群众运动】qúnzhòng yùnxiàn 有广大人民参加的政治运动或社会运动 mass movement; mass campaign

【群众组织】qúnzhòng zǔzhī 有广大群众参加的非国家政权性质的团体,如工会、妇联、共青团、学生会等 mass organization; non-government organization (e.g. Trade Unions, Women's Federation, Communist Youth League, Student Unions, etc.)

麇(麕) qún 〈书 *fml*.〉成群 in large numbers; in groups: ~集 get together; assemble; swarm | ~至 come in large numbers

☞ jūn on p. 1066

【麇集】qúnjí 〈书 *fml*.〉聚集;群集 get together; assemble; swarm

Q

R

rán（ㄖㄢˊ）

蚺（蚦） rán［蚺蛇］(ránshé) same as 蟒蛇 mǎngshé

然 rán ❶ 对；不错 true；right；correct：不以为～do not think so；disagree ❷ 如此；这样；那样 like that；so：不尽～not like that｜知其～，不知其所以～clear about the hows but not the whys ❸〈书 *fml.*〉然而 but；however；nonetheless：此事虽小，～亦不可忽视。This is a minor matter，but that doesn't mean it should be ignored. ❹ 副词或形容词后缀［adverb or adjective suffix］：忽～suddenly｜突～all of a sudden｜显～obviously｜欣～gladly｜飘飘～ wax complacent；be carried away with

〈古 *arch.*〉also same as 燃 rán

【然而】rán'ér〈连词 *conj.*〉用在句子的开头，表示转折［used at the beginning of a sentence to indicate transition of meaning］but；yet：他虽然失败了很多次，～并不灰心。He has failed repeatedly，yet he remains undeterred.

【然后】ránhòu〈连词 *conj.*〉表示接着某种动作或情况之后［indicating an act that happens after a certain act or under a certain condition］afterwards；then：学～知不足。The more you learn，the more inadequate you feel.｜先研究一下，～再决定。Let's think it over and then make a decision.

【然诺】ránnuò〈书 *fml.*〉允诺 assure；make a promise；vow；same as 答应 dā·ying ②：重～(不轻易答应别人，答应了就一定履行)be serious about making and keeping a commitment

【然则】ránzé〈书 *fml.*〉〈连词 *conj.*〉用在句子的开头，表示'既然这样，那么…'［used at the beginning of a sentence］in that case；then：～如之何而可？(那么怎么办才好？) Then，what is to be done?

髯（髥） rán 两腮的胡子，也泛指胡子 whiskers；general term for beard：美～well-trimmed beard｜虬～curly whiskers｜白发苍～silver-haired；grey-haired

【髯口】rán·kou 戏曲演员演出时所戴的假胡子 artificial beard or whiskers worn by an actor in traditional opera

燃 rán ❶ 燃烧 burn；light：自～spontaneous combustion｜～料 fuel ❷ 引火点着 ignite：～灯 light a lamp｜～香 burn incense

【燃点】[1] rándiǎn 加热使燃烧；点着 ignite；inflame：～灯火 light a lamp

【燃点】[2] rándiǎn 某种物质着火燃烧所需要的最低温度叫做这种物质的燃点 ignition point；minimum temperature needed for a material to burn；also 着火点 zháohuǒdiǎn

【燃放】ránfàng 点着爆竹等使爆发 set off (fireworks，etc.)：～鞭炮 set off firecrackers｜～烟火 set off fireworks

【燃料】ránliào 能产生热能或动力的可燃物质，主要是含碳物质或碳氢化合物。按形态可分为固体燃料(如煤、炭、木材)、液体燃料(如汽油、煤油)和气体燃料(如煤气、沼气)。也指能产生核能的物质，如铀、钚等。fuel；inflammable material such as carbon and hydrocarbon that can be consumed to produce heat or energy，in three categories：solid fuel，such as coal，coke and wood；liquid fuel，such as gasoline and kerosene；and gaseous fuel，such as coal gas and methane；also fissionable material used to produce nuclear energy，such as uranium and plutonium

【燃眉之急】rán méi zhī jí 像火烧眉毛那样的紧急 as pressing as a fire singeing one's eyebrows；〈比喻 *fig.*〉非常紧迫的情况 emergency；urgent situation

【燃气轮机】ránqìlúnjī 涡轮机的一种，利用高压的燃烧气体推动叶轮转动，产生动力。体积小，重量轻，功率大，效率高。gas turbine；a kind of turbines that provides power by propelling a turbine wheel with a burning gas under high pressure，marked for its small size，light weight，high power and efficiency；简称 abbr. 气轮机 qìlúnjī

【燃烧】ránshāo ❶ 物质剧烈氧化而发光、发热。可燃物质和空气中的氧剧烈化合是最常见的燃烧现象。burn；cause to undergo combustion，the most common form of burning being the drastic chemical combination of a combustible material with oxygen in the air ❷〈比喻 *fig.*〉某种感情、欲望高涨 be consumed with strong emotion，desire，etc.：怒火在胸中～burning with anger

【燃烧弹】ránshāodàn 一种能使目标燃烧的枪弹或炸弹，一般用黄磷、凝固汽油等作为燃烧剂 incendiary bomb；bullet or bomb generally containing phosphor or napalm and designed to set a target on fire；also 烧夷弹 shāoyídàn

【燃烧瓶】ránshāopíng 装有液体燃烧剂的玻璃

瓶，投掷后玻璃瓶破碎而燃烧 Molotov cocktail; bomb made of flammable liquid contained in a bottle that breaks and sets a target on fire

rǎn（ㄖㄢˇ）

冉(冄) Rǎn 姓 a surname

【冉冉】rǎnrǎn〈书 *fml.*〉❶（毛、枝条等）柔软下垂（of hair, tree branch, etc.）droop softly ❷ 慢慢地 steadily; slowly: ～而来 come unhurriedly | 月亮～上升。The moon rose slowly.

苒(苒) rǎn ☞ 荏苒 rěnrǎn on p.1623

染 rǎn ❶ 用染料着色 dye: 印～dyeing | ～布 dye cloth ◇夕阳～红了天空。The setting sun dyed the sky a crimson red. ❷ 感染；沾染 come down with; contract: 传～contagious | ～病 contagious disease | 熏～exert a gradual impact on | 一尘不～not soiled with a single particle of dust; spotless; pure-hearted

【染病】rǎn//bìng 得病；患病 fall ill; come down with a disease: ～在床 be bed-ridden

【染坊】rǎn·fang 染绸、布、衣服等的作坊 dyehouse; dye-works (for silk, cloth, clothing, etc.)

【染缸】rǎngāng 染东西的大缸 dye vat; dyejigger;〈比喻 *fig.*〉对人的思想产生坏影响的地方或环境 place or environment apt to poison people's mind

【染料】rǎnliào 直接或经媒染剂作用而能附着在纤维和其他材料上的有色物质，有的可以跟被染物质化合。种类很多，以有机化合物为主。dyestuff; dye; a variety of substances, mainly organic compounds, used to colour a fibre or other material by attaching to it directly or through an intermediary or chemical combination

【染色】rǎnsè ❶ 用染料使纤维等材料着色。有时需要用媒染剂。dye; colour; use a dyestuff to colour a fabre or other material, sometimes with an intermediary ❷ 为了便于观察细菌，把细菌体染成蓝、红、紫等颜色 practice of dying cells blue, red, purple, etc. for observation purposes

【染色体】rǎnsètǐ 存在于细胞核中能被碱性染料染色的丝状或棒状体，细胞分裂时可以观察到，由核酸和蛋白质组成，是遗传的主要物质基础。各种生物的染色体有一定的大小、形态和数目。chromosome; thread- or stick-like linear strand of nucleic acid and proteins in the nucleus of animal and plant cells that can be observed during a cell division, constitutes the major material basis for genetic heredity, and varies in size, form and number in different animals and plants

【染指】rǎnzhǐ 春秋时，郑灵公请大臣们吃甲鱼，故意不给子公吃，子公很生气，就伸指向盛甲鱼的鼎里蘸上点汤，尝尝滋味走了（见于《左传》宣公四年）。后世用'染指'比喻分取非分的利益。get a finger on sth., according to *The Zuo Commentary · Duke Xuan 4th Year*, during the Spring and Autumn Period, when Duke Ling of Zheng was feasting his major ministers with stewed turtle, he deliberately declined to offer Zi Gong a share of it. The latter was so incensed that he dipped his finger into the tripod that contained the stew, tasted it, and went away. Later generations coined the phrase 'get a finger on sth.' to mean 'impinge upon' or 'violate'.

rāng（ㄖㄤ）

嚷 rāng 义同'嚷'(rǎng)，只用于'嚷嚷' with the same meaning as 嚷 rǎng, limited to the phrase 嚷嚷 rāng·rang
☞ rǎng on p.1609

【嚷嚷】rāng·rang ❶ 喧哗；吵闹 yak; shout; yell; make an uproar: 别～，人家还在休息。Cut the noise. People are taking a rest. ❷ 声张 make widely known: 这事～出去，对谁都不好。It does either of us no good if this is let out.

ráng（ㄖㄤˊ）

儴 ráng ☞ [俇儴] (kuāngráng) on p.1123

勷 ráng ☞ [劻勷] (kuāngráng) on p.1123

蘘 ráng [蘘荷] (ránghé) 多年生草本植物，根茎圆柱形，淡黄色，叶子互生，椭圆状披针形，花大，白色或淡黄色，蒴果卵形。花穗和嫩芽可以吃，根入中药。mioga ginger (*Zingiber mioga*); perennial herb having pale yellow cylindrical rhizomes used as a traditional Chinese medicine, alternate lanceolately elliptic leaves, large white or light yellow flowers and egg-shaped capsules, its flowers and tender leaves being edible

瀼 Ráng 瀼河，水名，在河南 Ranghe, name of a river in Henan Province
☞ ràng on p.1610

【瀼瀼】rángráng〈书 *fml.*〉形容露水多 dewy

禳 ráng same as 禳解 rángjiě: ～灾 ward off a calamity by prayers, etc.

【禳解】rángjiě〈书 *fml.*〉迷信的人向鬼神祈祷消除灾殃 (of superstition) pleading with ghosts and gods to ward off disasters or misfortune

穰 ráng (～儿 rángr) ❶〈方 *dial.*〉稻、麦等的秆子 rice or wheat stalk: ～草 straw ❷ same as 瓤 ráng

【穰穰】rángráng〈书 *fml.*〉五谷丰饶 abundance of grain:～满家 good harvest that has filled granaries to overflowing

瓤 ráng ❶（～儿 rángr）瓤子 pulp; flesh; pith:橘子～儿 pulp of an orange|黑子红～儿的西瓜 watermelon with black seeds and red flesh ❷（～儿 rángr）泛指某些皮或壳里包着的东西 sth. contained in a hull or shell:秫秸～pith of a sorghum stalk|信～儿 letter inside an envelope ❸〈方 *dial.*〉不好;软弱 not good; feeble:你赶车的技术真不～。You're not bad at driving a cart.|病后身体～feel weak in the aftermath of an illness

【瓤子】ráng·zi ❶瓜果皮里包着种子的肉或瓣儿(of fruit and melon) pulp; flesh ❷ same as 瓤 ráng ②:表～mechanism of a watch|秫秸～ pith of a sorghum stalk

禳 ráng 脏（见于旧小说 in old novels）dirty:衣服～了。The clothing has got dirty.

rǎng（ㄖㄤˇ）

壤 rǎng ❶土壤 soil:沃～fertile soil ❷地 earth:天～之别 worlds' apart|霄～heaven and earth ❸地区 area:接～border on; be bordered by|穷乡僻～ remote, backward place; backwaters

【壤土】rǎngtǔ ❶细砂和黏土含量比较接近的土壤。土粒粗大而疏松,能保水、保肥,适于种植各种植物。loam; soil composed of about the same amount of sand and clay, with large and loose granules that facilitate water and fertilization conservation and the growth of a variety of farm crops; also 二性土 èrxìngtǔ ❷〈书 *fml.*〉土地;国土 land; national territory

攘(❸纕) rǎng〈书 *fml.*〉❶排斥 keep at bay; reject:～除 uproot; get rid of|～外(抵御外患)resist foreign invaders ❷抢 grab; seize:～夺 snatch; seize ❸捋起(袖子)roll up (sleeve):～臂 roll up one's sleeves and flail one's arms

【攘臂】rǎngbì〈书 *fml.*〉激奋时捋起袖子,伸出胳膊 push up one's sleeves and bare one's arms in excitement or agitation:～高呼 raise one's arms and shout at the top of one's voice|～瞋目(捋袖伸臂,瞪着眼睛,形容发怒)roll up one's sleeves, raise one's arms, and stare with wide open eyes

【攘除】rǎngchú〈书 *fml.*〉same as 排除 páichú:～奸邪 ferret out evil elements

【攘夺】rǎngduó〈书 *fml.*〉夺取 grab:～政权 seize state power

【攘攘】rǎngrǎng〈书 *fml.*〉形容纷乱 tumultuous; chaotic

嚷 rǎng ❶喊叫 howl; bawl; holler:别～了,人家都睡觉了。Stop yelling! People are sleeping. ❷吵闹 kick up a hullabaloo; raise a pandemonium:～也没用,还是另想别的办法吧。There is no use making all the noise. Let's think about the way out. ❸〈方 *dial.*〉责备;训斥 rebuke; castigate; berate:这事让妈妈知道了又该～我了。Mum will get after me if she finds out.

☞ rāng on p.1608

ràng（ㄖㄤˋ）

让(讓) ràng ❶把方便或好处给别人 give up sth. for the benefit of sb. else:退～decline (a favour) politely and modestly|～步 give in; concede|弟弟小,哥哥～着他点儿。As the elder brother, you should give in a little to your younger brother.|见困难就上,见荣誉就～step forward wherever there are difficulties and retreat from credit ❷请人接受招待 invite; offer:～茶 offer a cup of tea|把大家～进屋里 usher everybody into the room ❸索取一定的代价,把财物的所有权转移给别人 trade in; sell (property ownership):出～sell|转～transfer the possession of sth. ❹表示指使、容许或听任 instigate; allow; let:谁～你来的? Who let you come?|～我仔细想想。Let me think it over.|要是～事态发展下去,后果会不堪设想。If things are allowed to run unchecked the consequence will be disastrous. ❺避开;躲闪 make way; make room:～路 make way|请～开点儿。Stay out of the way, please. ❻ same as 被[3] bèi ①:行李～雨给淋了。The luggage got wet in the rain. 注意 **NOTE**:'被'字后面的施事有时可以省略,但'让'字后面的施事不能省略,如可说'行李被淋了',不说'行李让淋了'。The agent of an action behind the character 被 bèi can oft. be deleted, as in 行李被淋了, but not so behind 让 ràng, such as in 行李让淋了, in which 雨 yǔ is incorrectly omitted.

【让步】ràng//bù 在争执中部分地或全部地放弃自己的意见或利益 concede; give in; yield; give up one's own opinion or interest partially or entirely in an argument:相互～make mutual concessions|在原则问题上决不～。Never make concessions on matters of principle.

【让利】ràng//lì 把部分利益或利润让给别人 transfer part of interest or profit to sb.:～销售 cut-price sale

【让路】ràng//lù 给对方让开道路 make way for; give sb. the right of way

【让位】ràng//wèi ❶让出统治地位或领导职位 abdicate; step down (from a ruling or leading position):老干部主动～,退居二线。Veteran cadres willingly step down and play second fiddle to younger leaders. ❷让出座位 offer one's seat to sb.:在公共汽车上,他主动

给老人～。On the bus he always offer his seat to old people.

【让贤】ràng//xián 把职位让给有才干的人 relinquish one's post in favour of sb. better qualified：退位～step down to make room for sb. better qualified

【让座】ràng//zuò（～儿 ráng//zuòr）❶ 把座位让给别人 offer one's seat to sb.：电车上青年人都给老年人～。On the trolley bus it is not uncommon to see young people offering their seats to the elderly. ❷ 请客人入座 invite sb. to be seated：主人～又让茶，十分热情。The host warmly invited his guests to be seated and offered them tea.

瀼 ràng 瀼渡河（Ràngdù Hé），水名，在重庆 Rangdu River, name of a river in Chongqing

☞ ráng on p. 1608

ráo（ㄖㄠˊ）

荛（蕘）ráo〈书 *fml*.〉柴火 faggot; firewood：刍～ collect firewood and mow grass

饶（饒）ráo ❶ 丰富；多 rich; abundant; exuberant：富～ fertile | 丰～ rich and fertile | ～有风趣 humorous; full of wit and humour ❷ 另外添 throw in; make an extra offer：～头 give gratis; throw in sth. | 有两人去就行了，不要把他也～在里头。Two persons will do, and don't drag him in. ❸ 饶恕；宽容 forgive; spare：～他这一回。Spare him this time. ❹〈方 *dial*.〉〈连词 *conj*.〉表示让步，跟'虽然，尽管'意思相近 [indicating a concession] although; despite：～这么让着他，他还不满意。He wasn't satisfied no matter how many concessions I made. ❺（Ráo）姓 a surname

【饶命】ráo//mìng 免予处死；给予活命 spare one's life

【饶舌】ráoshé 唠叨；多嘴 chatty; prattling; voluble：对这个问题我不想多～。I don't want to talk too much about this.

【饶恕】ráoshù 免于责罚 forgive; pardon; spare sb. punishment

【饶头】ráo·tou 多给的少量东西（多用于买卖场合 oft. in market transaction）sth. extra given free：这个小的是个～。This little one is an extra.

娆（嬈）ráo ☞ 娇娆 jiāoráo on p. 970 and 妖娆 yāoráo on p. 2226

☞ rǎo on p. 1610

桡（橈）ráo〈书 *fml*.〉划船的桨 oar

【桡骨】ráogǔ 前臂靠大指一侧的骨头，与尺骨并排，上端与尺骨、肱骨构成肘关节，下端与腕骨构成腕关节。radius; long, slightly curved one of the two bones that is closer to the side of the thumb and parallel to the ulna, with its upper end linked with the ulna and the shoulder bone to form the elbow joint and its lower end combined with the carpal to form the wrist;（图见 figure for 骨骼 gǔgé on p. 693）

rǎo（ㄖㄠˇ）

扰（擾）rǎo ❶ 扰乱；搅扰 harass; disturb：干～ interfere in | 打～ disturb ❷〈书 *fml*.〉混乱；紊乱 turmoil; chaos：纷～ disturbance | ～攘 hustle and bustle; confusion ❸〈客套话 *pol*.〉因受人款待而表示客气 give sb. a good deal of bother：叨～ many thanks for your hospitality | 我～了他一顿饭。He was so kind as to take me to dinner.

【扰动】rǎodòng ❶ 动荡；骚动 in chaos; be turbulent：明朝末年，农民纷纷起义，～及于全国。Towards the end of the Ming Dynasty peasant uprisings broke out one after another, engulfing the entire country in chaos. ❷ 干扰；搅动 excite; disturb：地面温度升高，～气流迅速增强。A rise in the surface temperature caused a rapid increase in the velocity of air currents.

【扰乱】rǎoluàn 搅扰，使混乱或不安 harass; cause chaos; upset：～治安 cause public disturbance | ～思路 interrupt one's train of thought | ～睡眠 disturb sb.'s sleep

【扰攘】rǎorǎng〈书 *fml*.〉骚乱；纷乱 hustle and bustle; traffic and din：干戈～ war and turmoil

【扰扰】rǎorǎo〈书 *fml*.〉形容纷乱 chaotic; confused; in disorder

娆（嬈）rǎo〈书 *fml*.〉烦扰；扰乱 harass; disturb

☞ ráo on p. 1610

rào（ㄖㄠˋ）

绕（繞、❷❸遶）rào ❶ 缠绕 coil; wind：～线 wind thread ❷ 围着转动 move round; revolve：运动员～场一周。The athletes went running around the arena. ❸ 不从正面通过，从侧面或后面迂回过去 make a detour; bypass：～行 make a detour | ～远儿 go the wrong way round | 把握船舵，～过暗礁。Take a firm control of the rudder and negotiate the boat around a submerged reef. ❹（问题、事情）纠缠（of a question or issue）baffle; befuddle：一些问题～在他的脑子里。Some questions are still confusing him. | 我一时～住了，账目没算对。I got baffled as I didn't get the accounts right.

【绕脖子】rào bó·zi〈方 *dial*.〉❶ 形容说话办

事曲折，不直截了当 beat about the bush：你简单地说吧，别净～。Just put it simply and stop beating about the bush. ❷ 形容言语、事情曲折费思索 (of language or an issue) knotty; tricky：这道题真～。This is indeed a baffling question. | 他尽说些～的话。He is given to beating about the bush.

【绕道】rào//dào (～儿 rào//dàor) 不走最直接的路，改由较远的路过去 make a detour; go by a roundabout route：～而行 make a detour

【绕口令】ràokǒulìng (～儿 ràokǒulìngr) 一种语言游戏，用声、韵、调极易混同的字交叉重叠编成句子，要求一口气急速念出，说快了读音容易发生错误。也叫拗口令，有的地区叫急口令。tongue twister; practice of reciting sentences consisting of a succession of words of similar consonantal sounds, rhymes and tones that are easily confused when being articulated rapidly; also 拗口令 àokǒulìng; known in some regions as 急口令 jíkǒulìng

【绕圈子】rào quān·zi ❶ 走迂回曲折的路 circle; take a circuitous route：人地生疏，难免～走冤枉路。Strangers to the place are apt to make unnecessary detours. ❷〈比喻 *fig.*〉不照直说话 beat about the bush：他绕了个圈子又往回说。He had hardly finished his presentation when he began beating about the bush once again.

【绕弯儿】rào//wānr ❶〈方 *dial.*〉same as 散步 sàn//bù：他刚吃完饭，在院子里～。He's just had his supper and is taking a walk in the courtyard. | 我出去绕个弯儿就回来。I'll go for a walk and be back soon. ❷ same as 绕弯子 rào wān·zi

【绕弯子】rào wān·zi〈比喻 *fig.*〉不照直说话 beat about the bush：有意见，就直截了当地说出来，不要～。If you have anything to say, say it. Don't beat about the bush.

【绕远儿】rào//yuǎnr ❶ (路线) 迂回曲折而较远 make an unnecessary detour：这条路很好走，可就是～。The road is smooth, but makes quite a detour. ❷ 走迂回曲折而较远的路 make a detour and go the long way round：我宁可绕点远儿也不翻山。I would rather go the long way round than climb over the mountain.

【绕组】ràozǔ 电机或电器中用漆包线等绕成的许多线圈的组合 winding; combinations of electrically conducting coils of enamelled wire in an electric motor or appliance

【绕嘴】ràozuǐ 不顺口 tongue-twisting：这话说起来～。This sentence is a kind of tongue twisting.

rě (ㄖㄜˇ)

若 rě ☞[般若] (bōrě) on p.146 and 兰若 lánrě on p.146

☞ ruò on p.1645

喏 rě ☞唱喏 chàngrě on p.224

☞ nuò on p.1430

惹 rě ❶ 招引；引起 (不好的事情) court or invite (sth. bad)：～事 cause trouble | ～祸 court disaster | ～麻烦 got into trouble ❷ (言语、行动) 触动对方 offend or provoke sb. (with words or behaviour)：不要把他～翻了。Don't ruffle his feathers. | 这人脾气大，不好～。The chap has a fiery temper and is not to be provoked. ❸ (人或事物的特点) 引起爱憎等的反应 (of a person or thing) cause (liking or disliking etc.)：～人注意 draw attention | ～人讨厌 make a nuisance of oneself | 一句话把大家～得哈哈大笑。A single remark set everybody rocking with laughter.

【惹火烧身】rě huǒ shāo shēn〈比喻 *fig.*〉自讨苦吃或自取毁灭 ask for trouble; stir up a fire only to burn oneself — court disaster; also 引火烧身 yǐn huǒ shāo shēn

【惹祸】rě//huò 引起祸事 court trouble; make trouble：～招灾 make trouble and court disaster | 他惹了祸，吓得躲起来了。He made trouble and was so scared that he went into hiding.

【惹乱子】rě luàn·zi 闯祸；惹祸 court disaster; stir up trouble

【惹气】rě//qì 引起恼怒 get angry：犯不上为这点儿事情～。It's senseless getting upset over such a trifle. | 没想到因一句话惹了一肚子气。Little had he thought that a single remark could lead to such displeasure.

【惹事】rě//shì 引起麻烦或祸害 make trouble：他在外惹了不少事。He caused a lot of trouble out there.

【惹是非】rě shì·fēi 引起麻烦或争端 provoke a controversy; stir up trouble

【惹是生非】rě shì shēng fēi same as 惹是非 rě shì·fēi

【惹眼】rěyǎn 显眼；引人注意 conspicuous; showy

rè (ㄖㄜˋ)

热(熱) rè ❶ 物体内部分子不规则运动放出的一种能。物质燃烧都能产生热。heat; a form of energy released by irregular motion of atoms or molecules in a matter; the kind of energy released by any combustible material ❷ 温度高；感觉温度高 (跟'冷'相对 as opposed to 'cold') warm; high temperature：～水 hot water | 趁～打铁 strike while the iron is hot | 三伏天很～。It can get real hot during the dog days. ❸ 使热；加热 (多指食物 oft. food) heat; warm：～一～饭 heat up a meal | 把菜汤～一下 heat a soup ❹ 生病引起的高体温 fever; high body temperature caused by illness：发～run a temperature｜退～bring down a fever ❺ 情意深厚 endearing；chummy：亲～intimate｜～爱 love｜～心肠儿 warm-hearted ❻ 形容非常羡慕或急切想得到 craze for；covet；envy：眼～envious｜～中 hanker after；be given to ❼ 受很多人欢迎的 popular；in great demand：～货 commodity in great demand；goods that sell like hot cakes｜～门儿 in great demand；popular ❽ 加在名词、动词或词组后，表示形成的某种热潮［used behind a noun，verb or phrase］craze；fad；fever：足球～soccer craze｜旅游～travel craze｜自学～self-study craze ❾ 放射性强 strongly radioactive；thermal：～原子 thermal atom

【热爱】rè'ài 热烈地爱 love deeply；like sth. with gusto：～工作 devote heart and soul to one's work｜～祖国 have deep love for one's motherland

【热币】rèbì same as 游资 yóuzī ②

【热肠】rècháng 热心；热情 warm-hearted：～人 affectionate person｜古道～ considerate and warm-hearted

【热潮】rècháo 形容蓬勃发展、热火朝天的形势 upsurge；mass enthusiasm：掀起植树造林～。Launch an afforestation campaign.

【热忱】rèchén 热情 enthusiasm and devotion；warm-heartedness：满腔～ unstinting warm-heartedness｜爱国～patriotic sentiment

【热诚】rèchéng 热心而诚恳 cordial；warm and sincere：～的爱戴 treat sb. with adoration；adore｜待人十分～be warm and sincere

【热处理】rèchǔlǐ 使材料内部结构发生变化而取得某种性能的一种工艺，一般是把材料加热到一定温度，然后进行不同程度的冷却。主要用于金属材料。heat or thermal treatment；technological process to impart a certain property in a material — usu. metal — by raising it to a certain temperature and cooling it a certain level

【热传导】rèchuándǎo 热能从物体温度较高的部分沿着物体传到温度较低的部分，是固体传热的主要方式 heat conduction；major mode of conducting heat from the part of a solid matter with a higher temperature to the part with a lower temperature；also 导热 dǎorè

【热带】rèdài 赤道两侧南北回归线之间的地带。热带受到太阳的热量最多，冬季夏季的昼夜长短相差不多，全年气温变化不大，降雨多而均匀。torrid zone；tropics；central latitude zone of the earth，between the Tropic of Cancer and the Tropic of Capricorn，where the solar energy is the most intense，the yearly temperature and the lengths of day and night in winter and summer show little difference，and precipitation is abundant and even；also 回归带 huíguīdài

【热带鱼】rèdàiyú 产于热带或亚热带海中的鱼类，一般指其中可供观赏的鱼。这些鱼体小，活泼，形状奇异，颜色美丽。tropical fish；any of various small，brightly coloured fishes native to tropical or subtropical waters that are small，vivacious，colourful，and in exotic shapes，and oft. kept in home aquariums for ornamental purposes

【热点】rèdiǎn ❶ 指某时期引人注目的地方或问题 hot spot（in a certain time period）；centre of attention：古都西安成为旅游的～。The ancient capital city of Xi'an has emerged as a popular tourist attraction. ❷ 物理学上指温度高于周围环境的局部区域（physics）hot-spot；area with a higher temperature than in the surroundings

【热电厂】rèdiànchǎng 在供电的同时，还利用汽轮机所排出的蒸汽供热的火力发电厂 thermal power plant；plant that provides electricity as well as heat by utilizing the steam emitted from steam turbines；also 电热厂 diànrèchǎng

【热度】rèdù ❶ 冷热的程度 degree of heat：物体燃烧需要一定的～。An object requires a certain degree of heat to burn. ❷ 指高于正常的体温 fever；temperature：打了一针，～已经退了。An injection has brought the fever down. ❸ 指热情 ardour；enthusiasm：搞实验，要持之以恒，不能只有五分钟的～。To conduct an experiment calls for perseverance，and sudden whims get nowhere.

【热风】rèfēng 干燥的热空气流动形成的风 hot wind；hot air；wind resulting from the motion of arid and hot air

【热敷】rèfū 用热的湿毛巾、热砂或热水袋等放在身体的局部来治疗疾病。热敷能促进局部血液循环，加速炎症过程的变化，并使炎症逐渐消退。hot compress；treat a disease by applying a hot and wet towel，heated sand or hot-water bag on part of the body to promote blood circulation and speed up inflammation until it gradually subsides；also 热罨 rèyǎn

【热狗】règǒu 中间夹有热香肠、酸菜、芥末油等的面包。是英语 hot dog 的意译。hot dog；transliteration of the English word hot dog；heated sausage served in a long bread roll seasoned with pickles and mustard

【热固性】règùxìng 某些塑料、树脂等加热软化成形，冷凝后再加热也不再软化，这种性质叫热固性。酚醛塑料等有这种性质。thermofixability；property of resins，bakelite，etc.，to be permanently hardened and solidified on being heated

【热管】règuǎn 一种用做传热元件的金属管，两端密封，管壁附有多孔材料，管内充有一定量液体。用于宇航、冶金、电子、轻工业等部门。heat pipe；metal tube lined with a porous material，with both ends sealed，and containing certain amount of liquid，used as a thermal component in astronautical，metallurgical，electronic，and manufacturing industries

【热合】rèhé 指塑料、橡胶等材料加热后黏合在一起 heatseal; thermofix; bind plastic, rubber, etc. by heating

【热核反应】rèhé-fǎnyìng 在极高温度下,轻元素的原子核产生极大的热运动而互相碰撞,聚变为另一种原子核 thermonuclear reaction; fusion of atomic nuclei in a light element at high temperatures; also 聚变 jùbiàn

【热核武器】rèhé-wǔqì same as 氢弹 qīngdàn

【热烘烘】rèhōnghōng (～的 rèhōnghōng·de)形容很热 hot; very warm: 炉火很旺,屋子里～的。With the brazier burning cheerfully it was rather warm in the room.

【热乎】rè·hu same as 热和 rè·huo; also 热呼 rè·hu

【热呼】rè·hu same as 热乎 rè·hu

【热乎乎】rèhūhū (～的 rèhūhū·de)形容热和 warm; heart-warming; also 热呼呼 rèhūhū

【热呼呼】rèhūhū same as 热乎乎 rèhūhū

【热化】rèhuà ❶ 联合生产电能和热能的一种方式。火力发电厂除供应电能,还利用蒸汽机已经作过功的蒸汽或燃气轮机排出的废气供应蒸汽或热水。thermalize; method of joint generation of electricity and heat, such as in a thermal power plant which not only generates electricity but also supplies steam or hot water by utilizing the exhaust steam from steam engines or gas turbines ❷ 使受热熔化 melt with heat

【热火】rè·huo ❶ same as 热烈 rèliè: 广场上锣鼓喧天,场面可～啦。A fanfare of gongs and drums converted the plaza into a most exhilarating scene. ❷ 热和 nice and warm: 两个人谈得很～。The two of them had a most agreeable chat.

【热火朝天】rè huǒ cháo tiān 形容场面、情绪或气氛热烈高涨(of a place) bustling with activity; (of mood or atmosphere) high spirited

【热货】rèhuò 受人欢迎而畅销的货物 goods in great demand; also 热门货 rèménhuò

【热和】rè·huo ❶ 热(多表示满意) nice and warm (expression of satisfaction): 锅里的粥还挺～。The porridge in the pot is rather warm. ❷ same as 亲热 qīnrè: 同志们一见面就这么～。The comrades took to each other immediately after they met.

【热机】rèjī 各种变热能为机械能的机器的统称,如蒸汽机、内燃机、汽轮机等 heat engine; general term for steam engine, internal-combustion engine, steam turbine, etc., that turns heat into mechanical power

【热加工】rèjiāgōng 指对在高温状态下的金属进行加工。一般有铸造、热轧、热处理、锻造等工艺,有时也包括焊接。hot-working; hot work; work a metal product under a high temperature through such technological processes as casting, hot rolling, heat treating, forging, and, sometimes, welding

【热辣辣】rèlālā (～的 rèlālā·de)形容热得像被火烫着一样 burning hot; scorching: 太阳晒得人～的。The sun is a real scorcher on the face. | 他听了大家的批评,脸上～的。He felt his cheeks burning after hearing everybody's criticism.

【热浪】rèlàng ❶ 猛烈的热气 heat wave; hot wave ❷ 〈比喻 *fig.*〉热烈的场面、气氛等 craze; fervent occasion, atmosphere, etc.: 商品生产的～越来越高。There rose an upsurge of commodity production. ❸ 指热的辐射 heat radiation

【热泪】rèlèi 因非常高兴、感激或悲伤而流的眼泪 tears of joy, gratitude or sadness: ～盈眶 tears well up in one's eyes | 两眼含着～ eyes brimming with tears

【热力】rèlì 由热能产生的作功的力 heating power

【热力学温标】rèlìxué wēnbiāo thermodynamic scale; same as 开氏温标 Kāishì wēnbiāo

【热力学温度】rèlìxué wēndù 热力学温标的标度,用符号 T 表示 thermodynamic temperature, as represented with the letter 'T'

【热恋】rèliàn 热烈地恋爱 be passionately in love; be head over heels in love

【热量】rèliàng 温度高的物体把能量传递到温度低的物体上,所传递的能量叫做热量。通常指热能的多少,单位是焦耳,通常也用卡。quantity of heat; amount of heat transmitted from a high-temperature object to a low-temperature object, measured by the joule or the calorie in general

【热烈】rèliè 兴奋激动 animated; vivacious: 气氛～ ebullient atmosphere | ～响应 warm response | ～的掌声 warm applause | 小组会上发言很～。There was an animated discussion during the panel meeting.

【热流】rèliú ❶ 指激动振奋的感受 warmth; heart-warming feelings: 读了由各地寄来的慰问信,不由得一股～传遍全身。A warmth coursed through my body when I read sympathetic letters from all over the country. ❷ same as 热潮 rècháo: 改革的～ upsurge of reform

【热门】rèmén (～儿 rèménr)吸引许多人的事物 cause of popular interest: ～货 commodity in short demand | ～学科 popular discipline of learning | ～话题 subject of great topical interest

【热敏性】rèmǐnxìng 半导体的导电能力随外界温度升高而增加,随外界温度降低而减小的性质 thermosensitivity; property of a semi-conductor whose electricity-conducting capacity goes up or down with the rise or fall of environmental temperature

【热闹】rè·nao ❶ (景象)繁盛活跃(of a scene) bustling with activity; lively: ～的大街 busy street | 广场上人山人海,十分～。The square was crowded with people and bustling with activity. ❷ 使场面活跃,精神愉快 enliven; liven up:我们准备组织文娱活动,来～一下。We'll organize a party to liven things up.|到了节日大家～～吧! Let's have a jolly time during the festival. ❸ (～儿 rè·naor)热闹的景象 scene of bustle and excitement:他只顾着瞧～,忘了回家了。He was so amazed by what was going on that he forgot to go home.

【热能】rènéng 物质燃烧或物体内部分子不规则地运动时放出的能量。通常也指热量。thermal energy; heat energy; energy released by a burning material or the irregular motion of molecules inside an object; usu. also referring to quantity of heat

【热膨胀】rèpéngzhàng 物体在温度变化时体积发生变化的现象 thermal expansion; heat expansion; expansion of the volume of an object in a higher temperature

【热平衡】rèpínghéng ❶ 指与外界接触的物体,它的内部温度各处均匀并与外界温度相等 thermal equilibrium; equilibrium of temperature within and without an object upon contact with an environment ❷ 指物体在同一时间内释放的热量和吸收的热量相等而相互抵消 mutual cancellation between the heat an object releases with the heat it absorbs at the same time

【热气】rèqì 热的空气 hot air;〈比喻 *fig.*〉热烈的情绪或气氛 warm atmosphere; vivacious mood:～腾腾 seething with activity|人多议论多,～高,干劲大。More people mean more discussion, more enthusiasm and more energy.

【热切】rèqiè 热烈恳切 ardent; earnest:～的愿望 earnest wish; fervent hope|～期待你早日回来。We look forward to your return at an early date.

【热情】rèqíng ❶ 热烈的感情 zeal; enthusiasm:爱国～patriotic zeal|工作～devotion to work|满腔～brimming with warm feeling|～洋溢 glowing with enthusiasm|～奔放 bubbling with enthusiasm ❷ 有热情 enthusiastic; warm-hearted:～服务 warm-hearted service|待人～be warm-hearted towards people|农民对前来参观的外宾非常～。The farmers were warm-hearted towards the foreigners who came to visit.

【热容量】rèróngliàng 物体温度升高1℃所需要吸收的热量,叫做该物体的热容量。数值上等于该物体的比热和它的质量的乘积。thermal capacity; heat capacity; calorific capacity; amount of heat needed for increase the temperature in an object by one degree Celsius, equal in numerical value to the product of its specific heat and mass; 简称 abbr. 热容 rèróng

【热身】rèshēn 正式比赛前进行训练、比赛,使适应正式比赛并达到最佳竞技状态 warm up; train or take part in competition(s) to prepare athletes to reach the best state prior to a formal competition:～赛 warm-up match|～训练 warm-up training|这场比赛只是以练兵、～为目的。The game is for training and warming up.

【热水袋】rèshuǐdài 盛热水的橡胶袋,用于热敷或取暖 hot-water bottle or bag for hot compression or warmth

【热水瓶】rèshuǐpíng same as 暖水瓶 nuǎnshuǐpíng

【热水器】rèshuǐqì 利用可燃气体或电使水加热的器具,用于淋浴 hot water heater; geyser; bathroom fixture using gas or electricity to heat water

【热塑性】rèsùxìng 某些塑料、树脂等可反复进行加热、软化、冷却、凝固,这种性质叫热塑性。聚氯乙烯、聚苯乙烯等有这种性质。thermoplasticity; property of certain resins and plastics, such as PVC and polystyrene, to be repeatedly heated, intenerated, cooled and solidified

【热腾腾】rètēngtēng (～的 rètēngtēng·de)形容热气蒸发的样子 piping hot:一笼～的包子 a steamer of piping hot stuffed buns|太阳落了山,地上还是～的。Even after the sun had set, the ground remained hot.

【热天】rètiān 炎热的天气 sweltering weather; summer:一到～,他这病就好了。His ailment is gone when it gets hot.

【热土】rètǔ 指长期居住过的或有深厚感情的地方 home town; native place; place where one has lived for a long time or which one is emotionally attached:～难离 hard to tear leave one's beloved land|不忘家乡一片～。Don't forget the place you call home.

【热望】rèwàng ❶ 热烈盼望 yearn for; look forward on tiptoe:～的目光 expectant eyes ❷ 热切的希望 warm hope; strong expectation:满怀～fill the heart with warm hope|不负您的一片～。I hope I'll not let you down.

【热线】[1] rèxiàn same as 红外线 hóngwàixiàn

【热线】[2] rèxiàn ❶ 为了便于马上联系而经常准备着的直接连通的电话或电报线路 hot line; direct telephone or telegraph line established for instant contact, information, counselling, etc.:～点播 order a radio or television programme by hot line|～联系 hot-line contact|～服务 hot-line service ❷ 通向热点的路线 busy route:旅游～busy tourist route

【热孝】rèxiào 祖父母、父母或丈夫去世不久身穿孝服,叫热孝在身(of a woman) wearing mourning for one's recently deceased grandparent, parent or husband

【热效率】rèxiàolǜ 发动机中转变为机械功的热量与所消耗的热量的比值 heat efficiency; thermal efficiency; ratio between the heat energy that has been converted into mechanical energy in an engine and the heat energy thus consumed

【热效应】rèxiàoyìng 指物质系统在物理的或化学的等温过程中只做膨胀功时所吸收或放出的热量。根据反应性质的不同，分为燃烧热、生成热、中和热、溶解热等。calorific effect; fuel factor; heat energy absorbed or released by a material system when performing expansion work only during a physical or chemical isothermal process, which falls into such categories as heat of combustion, heat of formation, heat of neutralization, and heat of dissolution according to the nature of the reaction

【热心】rèxīn 有热情，有兴趣，肯尽力 enthusiastic; warm-hearted：～人 person with a warm heart|～给大家办事 run errands warm-heartedly for everyone|他对工会工作很～。He's enthusiastic in trade union work.

【热心肠】rèxīncháng（～儿 rèxīnchángr）待人热情、做事积极的性情 warm heart; warm-heartedness

【热学】rèxué 物理学的一个分支。研究热的性质、热的传播、热效应、物体受热后的变化、温度的测定等。heat, a branch of physics in the study of the characteristics of heat, its diffusion, thermal efficiency, changes caused in heated objects, and the determination of temperature

【热血】rèxuè〈比喻 *fig.*〉为正义事业而献身的热情 warm blood; devotion to a just cause：满腔～full of zeal; filled with enthusiasm|～男儿 red-blooded man|～沸腾 seethe with righteous indignation

【热血动物】rèxuè dòngwù same as 恒温动物 héngwēn dòngwù

【热血沸腾】rèxuè fèiténg〈比喻 *fig.*〉情绪高涨、激动 seething with excitement; one's blood boils

【热饮】rèyǐn 饮食业中指热的饮料，如热茶、热咖啡等 hot drink, such as tea, coffee, etc.

【热源】rèyuán 发出热量的物体，如燃烧的木柴、煤炭等 source of heat, such as burning wood, coal, etc.

【热战】rèzhàn 指使用武器的实际战争（对'冷战'而言 as opposed to 'cold war'）hot war; war fought with real weapons

【热障】rèzhàng 飞机、火箭等在空中超音速飞行时，其表面气流的温度很高，使金属外层强度降低，甚至熔化或烧毁，这种现象叫做热障 heat barrier; phenomenon in which the temperature of the air current on the surface of an aircraft or rocket on a supersonic flight rises so high that it reduces the intensity of its metal cover or even melts or burns it down

【热中】rèzhōng ❶ 急切盼望得到个人的地位或利益 crave for; hanker after (personal position or interests)：～名利 run after personal fame and gain ❷ 十分爱好某种活动 be keen on; be fond of (doing sth.)：～于滑冰 be keen on skating ‖ also 热衷 rèzhōng

rén（ㄖㄣˊ）

人 rén ❶ 能制造工具并使用工具进行劳动的高等动物 humanity; higher animal that can make tools and use them in labour：男～ man|女～woman|～们 people|～类 human being ❷ 每人；一般人 everyone：～手一册 a copy to everyone|～所共知 be known to all ❸ 指成年人 adult man or woman：长大成～ grown-up ❹ 指某种人 certain category of people：工～worker|军～serviceman|主～host|介绍～matchmaker ❺ 别人 peoples; other people：～云亦云 parrot; echo|待～诚恳 be sincere to people ❻ 指人的品质、性格或名誉 personality; character; morality：丢～be disgraced; lose face|这个同志～很好。The comrade is a good person.|他～老实。He is an honest man. ❼ 指人的身体或意识 one's state of health or mind：这两天～不大舒服 not feel well the last couple of days|送到医院～已经昏迷过去了 lose consciousness upon being rushed to the hospital ❽ 指人手、人才 hand; manpower：～浮于事 be overstaffed|我们这里正缺～。We are short of hands here.

【人才】réncái ❶ 德才兼备的人；有某种特长的人 person of ability and integrity; talent：～难得。Real talent is hard to come by.|～辈出。People of talent come forth in large numbers. ❷ 指美丽端正的相貌 handsome; pretty：一表～man of remarkable looks|有几分～rather good-looking ‖ also 人材 réncái

【人材】réncái same as 人才 réncái

【人潮】réncháo 像潮水般的人群 constant stream of people：～如涌。People come in a constant stream.

【人称】rénchēng 某些语言中动词跟名词或代词相应的语法范畴。代词所指的是说话的人叫第一人称，如'我、我们'；所指的是听话的人叫第二人称，如'你、你们'；所指的是其他的人或事物叫第三人称，如'他、她、它、他们'。名词一般是第三人称。有人称范畴的语言，动词的形式跟着主语的人称变化，有的语言还跟着宾语的人称变化。person; any of three groups of pronoun forms with corresponding verb inflections that distinguish the speaker (first person, such as 'I' and 'we'), the individual addressed (second person, such as 'you'), and the individual or thing spoken of (third person, such as 'he,' 'she,' 'it,' 'they'). Nouns are generally in third person, while the person of a verb follows that of the subject or, as is the case with some languages, that of the object.

【人次】réncì〈复合量词 *compound classifier*〉表

示若干次人数的总和。如以参观为例，第一次三百人，第二次五百人，第三次七百人，总共是一千五百人次。person-time; sum total of persons and times. Take, for example, admission to an exhibition. If 300 persons visited it the first time, 500 the second time, and 700 the third time, then the total admission would be 1,500 person-times.

【人大】réndà 人民代表大会的简称 abbr. for 人民代表大会 rénmín dàibiǎo dàhuì：～代表 deputy to the National People's Congress｜省～ Provincial People's Congress

【人道】[1] réndào ❶ 指爱护人的生命、关怀人的幸福、尊重人的人格和权利的道德 humanity; morality of valuing other people's life, caring for other people's happiness, respecting personal dignity and rights ❷〈古代 *arch.*〉指封建礼教所规定的人伦 human relations based on feudal ethics ❸〈书 *fml.*〉泛指人事或为人之道 general reference to moral standards or moral principles

【人道】[2] réndào 指人性交（就能力说，多用于否定式 oft. in the negative）sexual competence

【人道主义】réndào zhǔyì 起源于欧洲文艺复兴时期的一种思想体系。提倡关怀人、尊重人、以人为中心的世界观。法国资产阶级革命时期，把它具体化为'自由'、'平等'、'博爱'等口号。它在资产阶级革命时期起过反封建的积极作用。humanitarianism; ideological system originating in the European Renaissance that advocates the world outlook of being concerned wholly with the welfare of the human race, respecting people, and always giving centre stage to humanity, a doctrine that boiled down to 'liberty, equality and fraternity' during the French Bourgeois Revolution, and played a positive anti-feudal role during the bourgeois revolution as a whole

【人地生疏】rén dì shēngshū 指初到一个地方，对地方情况和当地的人都不熟悉 be unfamiliar with a place and the people there

【人丁】réndīng ❶〈旧时 *old*〉指成年人 grown-up person ❷ same as 人口 rénkǒu

【人定胜天】rén dìng shèng tiān 指人力能够战胜自然 Man is able to conquer nature.

【人犯】rénfàn〈旧时 *old*〉泛指某一案件中的被告或牵连在内的人 the accused and those implicated in a crime：一干～defendants and the implicated

【人贩子】rénfàn·zi 贩卖人口的人 human trafficker

【人份】rénfèn〈复合量词 *compound classifier*〉以一个人需要的量为一人份 person-portion; portion：麻疹疫苗三十万～measles vaccines for 300,000 persons; 300,000 measles inoculations

【人夫】rénfū〈旧时 *old*〉指受雇用或被征发服差役的人 workhand; corvée labourer; servant; also 人伕 rénfū

【人浮于事】rén fú yú shì 工作人员的数目超过工作的需要；事少人多 more hands than needed; overstaffed

【人格】réngé ❶ 人的性格、气质、能力等特征的总和 integration of a person's personality, temperament and ability ❷ 个人的道德品质 moral character：～高尚 noble character ❸ 人的能作为权利、义务的主体的资格 person, as an entity with rights and obligations：不得侵犯公民的～。A citizen's person brooks no violation.

【人格化】réngéhuà 童话、寓言等文艺作品中常用的一种创作手法，对动物、植物以及非生物赋予人的特征，使它们具有人的思想、感情和行为 personify; personification; method of creative writing in fairy tales, fables, etc. to represent an animal, plant, or inanimate object as having personality or the thoughts, feelings and behaviour of a human being

【人格权】réngéquán 人身权的一种，指公民本身固有的权利，包括生命健康权、姓名权、肖像权、名誉权等 rights to human dignity; category of the rights of person, a citizen's rights that include the rights of life, health, name, portrait, reputation, etc.; ☞ 人身权 rénshēnquán

【人工】réngōng ❶ 人为的（区别于'自然'或'天然' as compared with 'natural'）man-made; artificial：～呼吸 artificial respiration｜～降雨 artificial rainfall ❷ 人力；人力做的工 manpower; manual labour：～操作 manual operation｜抽水机坏了，暂时用～车水。The pump had broken down and we had to draw water by pedalling the waterwheel. ❸ 工作量的计算单位，指一个人做工一天 man-day; work done by one person in one day：修建这条水渠需用很多～。Digging this canal calls for a lot of manpower.

【人工呼吸】réngōng hūxī 用人工帮助呼吸的急救法。一般中毒、触电、溺水、休克等患者，在呼吸停止而心脏还在跳动时可以用人工呼吸的方法来急救。artificial respiration; restore or maintain respiration in a person who has stopped breathing as a result of poisoning, electric shock, drowning or shock by using mechanical, manual or mouth-to-mouth means to force air into and out of the lungs while the heart is still beating

【人工降雨】réngōng jiàngyǔ 用人工使还没有达到降雨阶段的云变成雨降下 artificial rainfall; procedure to induce rain from clouds not yet condensing into rain drops

【人工流产】réngōng liúchǎn 在胚胎发育的早期，利用药物、物理性刺激或手术使胎儿脱离母体的方法 abortion; induced termination of pregnancy and expulsion of an early embryo or fetus by medication, physical means or surgery; also 堕胎 duòtāi；通称 popularly known as 打胎 dǎtāi；简称 abbr. 人流 rénliú

【人工授精】réngōng shòujīng 用人工方法采取雄性动物的精液，输入雌性动物的子宫里，使卵子受精 artificial insemination; procedure to extract semen from a male animal by artificial means and introduce it into the uterus of a female animal to induce pregnancy

【人工智能】réngōng zhìnéng 利用电子计算机模拟人类智力活动的学科 artificial intelligence; branch of computer science concerned with development of machines with the capacity to simulate intelligent human behaviour

【人公里】réngōnglǐ〈复合量词 *compound classifier*〉运输企业计算客运工作量的单位，把一个旅客运送一公里为一人公里 passenger-km.; unit for counting the number of passengers transported over a distance, with one passenger-km. equal to transporting one passenger over one km.

【人海】rénhǎi ❶ 像汪洋大海一样的人群 ocean of faces; huge crowd of people：人山～ sea of people ❷〈书 *fml.*〉〈比喻 *fig.*〉社会 society：～沧桑 vicissitudes of human society

【人和】rénhé 指人心归向，上下团结 unity of public will; social stability：～百事兴。Social stability is the key to prosperity in all walks of life.｜天时不如地利，地利不如～。Heaven's favourable weather is less important than Earth's advantageous terrain; and Earth's advantageous terrain is less important than human unity.

【人寰】rénhuán〈书 *fml.*〉same as 人间 rénjiān：惨绝～ most inhuman; be tragic beyond comparison in this world

【人祸】rénhuò 人为的祸害 man-made disaster; bane：天灾～ natural adversities and man-made disasters

【人际】rénjì 指人与人之间 interpersonal：～关系 human relations｜～交往 human communications

【人迹】rénjì 人的足迹 traces of human visitation; human footprints：～罕至 (of a place) rarely visited by a soul; uncharted (territory)

【人家】rénjiā（～儿 rénjiār）❶ same as 住户 zhùhù：这个村子有百十户～。The village has about a hundred households. ❷ same as 家庭 jiātíng：勤俭～ thrifty family ❸ 指女子未来的丈夫家 family of one's husband-to-be：她已经有了～儿了。She's already betrothed.

【人家】rén·jia〈代词 *pron.*〉❶ 指自己或某人以外的人；别人 [excluding oneself or a certain person] another person; other persons：～都不怕，就你怕。Nobody is afraid, except you.｜～是人，我也是人，我就学不会？They are human, and so am I. Why can't I learn it? ❷ 指某个人或某些人，意思跟'他'或'他们'相近 [referring to a certain person or certain persons] he, she, or they：你把东西快给～送回去吧。Hurry up and send it back to him. ❸ 指'我'（有亲热或俏皮的意味 in an endearing or mischievous context）I：原来是你呀，差点没把～吓死！It's you — you nearly scared me to death!

【人尖子】rénjiān·zi 出类拔萃的人；特殊的人 outstanding person：要论庄稼活，在村里他是个～。He's the top farmer of the village. also 人尖儿 rénjiānr

【人间】rénjiān 人类社会；世间 world; human world：～乐园 paradise on earth｜春满～ world bathed in the warmth of spring｜～地狱 hell on earth; human inferno

【人杰】rénjié〈书 *fml.*〉杰出的人 outstanding personality

【人杰地灵】rén jié dì líng 指杰出的人物出生或到过的地方成为名胜之区 place renowned for being the birthplace of persons of great merits; place made famous by those who have filled the land with their outstanding deeds

【人精】rénjīng ❶ 老于世故的人 worldly-wise person ❷ 特别聪明伶俐的小孩儿 child prodigy

【人均】rénjūn 按每人平均计算 per capita：～收入 per-capita income｜全村栽了四万多株树，～一百株。The village planted more than 40,000 trees, averaging 100 per person.

【人口】rénkǒu ❶ 居住在一定地区内的人的总数 population; total number of residents in an area：～普查 census; population census｜这个区的～有一百三十多万。There is a population of more than 1.3 million in this district. ❷ 一户人家的人的总数 number of mouths to be fed in a family; number of family members：他们家～不多。There are not many people in their family. ❸ 泛指人 person; mouth to be fed：添～ have a newborn baby｜拐带～ abduction; human trafficking ❹ 人的嘴 mouth：脍炙～ much vaunted

【人口学】rénkǒuxué 以人口现象、人口发展条件和发展规律为研究对象的学科 demography; study of population-associated phenomena, the conditions for population growth and the norms for it

【人困马乏】rén kùn mǎ fá 形容体力疲劳不堪（不一定有马）men getting weary and their steeds being spent; (of people) spent; tired; exhausted

【人来疯】rénláifēng 指小孩在有客人来时撒娇、胡闹 (of a child) run more wild and prankish than usual in the presence of family guests

【人老珠黄】rén lǎo zhū huáng〈比喻 *fig.*〉妇女老了被轻视，像珍珠年代久了变黄就不值钱一样 (of women) no longer be held in esteem in old age, like a pearl whose lustre has faded over time

【人类】rénlèi 人的总称 humanity：～社会 human society; society|造福～work for the benefit of humanity

【人类学】rénlèixué 研究人类起源、进化和人种分类等的学科 anthropology; study of the characteristics of humanity such as its origin, evolution, and races

【人力】rénlì 人的劳力；人的力量 manpower：爱惜～物力 treasure human and material resources|用机械代替～mechanize physical labour|非～所及 humanly impossible; beyond the ability of human beings

【人力车】rénlìchē ❶ 由人推或拉的车（区别于'兽力车'和'机动车'as compared with 'animal-drawn cart' and 'power-driven vehicle'）cart drawn or pushed by a man ❷〈旧时 *old*〉一种用人拉的车，有两个橡胶车轮，车身前有两根长柄，柄端有横木相连，主要用来载人 rickshaw; light passenger vehicle with two rubber wheels and two long handles joined with a crossbar and pulled by one person

R

【人流】[1] rénliú 像河流似的连续不断的人群 stream of people：不尽的～涌向广场。A constant stream of people flocked to the square.

【人流】[2] rénliú 人工流产的简称 abbr. for 人工流产 réngōng liúchǎn

【人伦】rénlún 封建礼教所规定的人与人之间的关系，特指尊卑长幼之间的关系，如君臣、父子、夫妇、兄弟、朋友的关系 interpersonal relations, esp. those between superior and inferior, and old and young, in feudal ethics, such as the relationship between monarch and court minister, father and son, husband and wife, between brothers and between friends

【人马】rénmǎ ❶ 指军队 forces; troops：全部～安然渡过了长江。All the troops crossed the Yangtze River in safety. ❷ 泛指某个集体的人员 general term for members of a collective：原班～original team; old cast|我们编辑部的～比较整齐。Our editorial department is well-staffed.

【人马座】rénmǎzuò 黄道十二星座之一 Sagittarius; one of the 12 constellations of the zodiac; ☞黄道十二宫 huángdào shí'èrgōng on p.851

【人们】rén•men 泛称许多人 people; public：草原上的～people of the grasslands|天冷了，～都穿上了冬装。It's getting cold and people are putting on their winter clothes.

【人面兽心】rén miàn shòu xīn 面貌虽然是人，但心肠像野兽一样凶恶残暴 face of a man but the heart of a fierce beast — beast in human form

【人民】rénmín 以劳动群众为主体的社会基本成员 the people; basic members of society consisting mainly of the labouring masses

【人民币】rénmínbì 我国法定货币。以圆为单位。Renminbi (RMB); Chinese currency with yuan as the unit

【人民代表大会】rénmín dàibiǎo dàhuì 我国人民行使国家权力的机关。全国人民代表大会和地方各级人民代表大会代表由民主协商选举产生。people's congress; people's state apparatus of China, with delegates elected to the National People's Congress and the people's congresses at various local levels through democratic consultations; 简称 abbr. 人大 réndà

【人民法院】rénmín fǎyuàn 我国行使审判权的国家机关，分最高人民法院、地方各级人民法院和专门人民法院 people's court; judiciary organ of China consisting of the Supreme People's Court, people's courts at various local levels, and specialized people's courts

【人民检察院】rénmín jiǎncháyuàn 我国行使检察权的国家机关，分最高人民检察院、地方各级人民检察院和专门人民检察院 people's procuratorate; state procuratorial apparatus of China consisting of the Supreme People's Procuratorate, people's procuratorates at various local levels, and specialized people's procuratorates

【人民警察】rénmín jǐngchá 我国的公安人员，是武装性质的治安行政力量 people's police; armed public security administrative force of China; 简称 abbr. 民警 mínjǐng

【人民民主专政】rénmín mínzhǔ zhuānzhèng 工人阶级（经过共产党）领导的、以工农联盟为基础的人民民主政权 people's democratic dictatorship; people's democratic political power led by the working class (through the Communist Party) and based on the Worker-Peasant Alliance

【人民内部矛盾】rénmín nèibù máodùn 指在人民利益根本一致的基础上的矛盾，是非对抗性的 contradictions among the people; non-antagonistic contradictions based on the fundamental unity of interests of the people

【人民陪审员】rénmín péishěnyuán 我国司法机关从人民群众中吸收的参加审判的人员。由人民选举产生，在人民法院执行职务期间，同审判员有同等权力。people's assessor; representative elected from among citizens to participate in court trials with equal power as a court judge; 简称 abbr. 陪审员 péishěnyuán

【人民团体】rénmín tuántǐ 民间的群众性组织，如红十字会、中华医学会、中国人民外交学会等 non-government organization; people's organization, such as the Red Cross Society, China Medical Association, the Chinese People's Diplomatic Society, etc.

【人民武装】rénmín wǔzhuāng 属于人民的武装力量。在我国，指人民解放军和民兵等武装组织，特指民兵等群众性武装组织。people's armed forces; referring in China to the People's Liberation Army, the militia and other mass military organizations; special reference to the militia and other mass armed forces

【人民性】rénmínxìng 指文艺作品中对人民大众的生活、思想、情感、愿望等的反映(in works of literature and art) affinity to the people; popular feeling; affinity to the people's life, thoughts, feelings and wishes

【人民战争】rénmín zhànzhēng 以人民军队为骨干、有广大人民群众参加的革命战争 people's war; revolutionary war involving the broad masses of the people and with the people's army as the backbone

【人民政府】rénmín zhèngfǔ 我国各级人民代表大会的执行机关和国家行政机关 people's government; executive department of the people's congress at various levels and the state administrative organ of China

【人命】rénmìng 人的生命(多用于受到伤害时 oft. used when life is in jeopardy) human life:一条～a death|～关天 with human life at stake

【人莫予毒】rén mò yú dú 目空一切,认为没有人能伤害我 who dare harm me — a typical case of biggety(毒 *du*:伤害 do harm)

【人品】rénpǐn ❶ 人的品质 moral character:～高尚 of noble character ❷ 人的仪表 looks:～出众 of outstanding looks

【人情】rénqíng ❶ 人的感情;人之常情 human feelings; common sense:不近～not amenable to reason ❷ same as 情面 qíng·miàn:托～seek sb.'s favour|不讲～lose sight of the human side of things ❸ 恩惠;情谊 favour:做个～do sb. a favour|空头～empty promise ❹ 指礼节应酬等习俗 etiquette; custom:行～follow an established practice|尽～observe social etiquette ❺ same as 礼物 lǐwù:送～present a gift

【人情世故】rénqíng shìgù 为人处世的道理 ways of the world; worldly wisdom:不懂～be not worldly-wise

【人情味】rénqíngwèi (～儿 rénqíngwèir) 指人通常具有的情感 normal human feelings; empathy:他的话富于～。It is really considerate of him to say these words.

【人权】rénquán 指人享有的人身自由和各种民主权利 human rights, referring to a citizen's right of person and freedom and democratic rights:侵犯～violation of human rights|保障～guarantee human rights

【人群】rénqún 成群的人 throng; crowd:他在～里挤来挤去。He elbowed this way and that through the crowd.

【人儿】rénr ❶ 小的人形 figurine:捏了一个泥～have molded a clay figurine with hand ❷ 〈方 *dial.*〉指人的行为仪表 behaviour and bearing:他～很不错。He's a nice man.

【人人】rénrén 所有的人;每人 everybody; everyone:我为～,～为我。One for all, and all for one.|～都有一双手,别人能干的活儿我也能干。As everybody has two hands, I can do whatever others are capable of doing.

【人日】rénrì 〈旧称 *old*〉正月初七 7th day of the 1st lunar month

【人山人海】rén shān rén hǎi 形容聚集的人极多 ocean of people; huge gathering of people:体育场上,观众～。The stadium was packed to overflowing.

【人身】rénshēn 指个人的生命、健康、行动、名誉等(着眼于保护或损害)(when referring to the protection or harm of the person) person; as an entity of life, health, behaviour, reputation, etc.:～自由 freedom of the person|～攻击 personal abuse

【人身权】rénshēnquán 与公民人身不能分离而又不直接与经济利益相联系的民事权利,分为人格权和身份权两类 right of the person; civil right inseparable from a citizen's person but not directly related to his or her economic interests, in two categories, i. e. the right of person and the right of identity

【人身事故】rénshēn shìgù 生产劳动中发生的伤亡事件 accident involving casualties; death or injury caused in productive labour

【人身自由】rénshēn zìyóu 指公民的身体不受侵犯的自由。如不得非法逮捕、搜查和拘留等。freedom of person; personal freedom that protects a citizen from illegal arrest, searching, detention, etc.

【人参】rénshēn 多年生草本植物,主根肥大,肉质,黄白色,掌状复叶,小叶卵形,花小,淡黄绿色,果实扁圆形。根和叶都可入药,有滋补作用。ginseng (*Panax quinquefolius*); perennial plant, having large and fleshy roots yellowish white in colour, palmately compound leaves small in size and oval in shape, small, light yellowish green flowers, and flat and round fruit, with both roots and leaves used as tonics

【人生】rénshēng 人的生存和生活 human existence and life:～观 outlook on life|～大事 highlights in a person's life; matter of consequence in a person's life|～两件宝,双手与大脑。Hands and brains are the two treasures in a person's life.

【人生观】rénshēngguān 对人生的看法,也就是对于人类生存的目的、价值和意义的看法。人生观是由世界观决定的。outlook on life; person's opinions on life, including the purpose, value and significance of the existence of humanity in the world. A person's outlook on life is decided by his or her outlook on the world. ☞ 世界观 shìjièguān on p. 1753

【人声】rénshēng 人发出的声音 human voice:～鼎沸 babel of voices; din|～嘈杂 hubbub of voices

【人士】rénshì 有一定社会影响的人物 personage; person with certain social influence:民主～democratic personage|各界～people of all walks of life|党外～non-Party personage|爱国～patriotic personage

【人氏】rénshì 人（指籍贯说，多见于早期白话 referring to a person's native place, oft. in early vernacular）native：当地～local；native person|你姓什么？哪里～？What's your family name, and where do you come from?

【人世】rénshì 人间；世间 human world；this world；also 人世间 rénshìjiān

【人事】rénshì ❶ 人的离合、境遇、存亡等情况 occurrences in a person's life, such as departures and reunions, circumstances, subsistence and death ❷ 关于工作人员的录用、培养、调配、奖惩等工作 personnel matters, including employment, training, deployment, reward and penalty, etc.：～科 personnel department|～材料 personnel data|～安排 personnel arrangement ❸ 指人与人之间的关系 interpersonal relation：～纠纷 interpersonal dispute|～磨擦 interpersonal friction ❹ 事理人情 ways of the world：不懂～have no idea of the ways of the world ❺ 人力能做到的事 what is humanly possible：尽～do what one can do ❻ 人的意识的对象 consciousness：他昏迷过去，～不知。He has lost consciousness. ❼〈方 *dial.*〉礼物 gift；present：这次回去得给老大娘送点～，表表我的心意。When I visit my family this time, I'll give the old lady some gifts as a token of my heart.

【人手】rénshǒu 做事的人 worker；hand：～不足 short of hands

【人寿年丰】rén shòu nián fēng 人健康，年成好，形容生活安乐美好 harvest is good and the people healthy；scene of prosperity and contentment

【人梯】réntī ❶ 一个人接一个人踩着肩膀向高处攀登叫搭人梯 human ladder, built by one person standing atop the shoulders of another ❷ 指为别人的成功而作自我牺牲的人 person who willingly makes self-sacrifices for the success of sb. else：甘当～willing to serve as a human ladder

【人体】réntǐ 人的身体 human body：～模型 manikin|～生理学 human physiology

【人同此心，心同此理】rén tóng cǐ xīn, xīn tóng cǐ lǐ 指对某些事情，大多数人的感受和想法大致相同 people feel and think alike on certain matter

【人头】réntóu ❶ 人的头（of a person）head ❷ 指人 people：按～分 distribute according to the number of people|～税（旧时以人口为课税对象所征收的税）poll tax；（in old days）capitation（tax）❸（～儿 réntóur）指跟人的关系 relationship with people：～熟 know a lot of people ❹〈方 *dial.*〉（～儿 réntóur）指人的品质 morality；character：～儿次（人品差）mean person

【人望】rénwàng 声望；威望 popularity；prestige：素有～be prestigious

【人微言轻】rén wēi yán qīng 指地位低，言论主张不受人重视 words of the lowly carry little weight

【人为】rénwéi ❶〈书 *fml.*〉人去做 human effort：事在～。It counts on human effort to accomplish something. ❷ 人造成的（用于不如意的事 refer to sth. undesirable）man-made：～的障碍 man-made barrier|～的困难 difficulty caused by sb. on purpose

【人为刀俎，我为鱼肉】rén wéi dāo zǔ, wǒ wéi yú ròu〈比喻 *fig.*〉人家掌握生杀大权，自己处在被宰割的地位 meat on sb.'s chopping block — be at sb.'s mercy

【人文】rénwén 指人类社会的各种文化现象 cultural activities in human society：～科学 humanities|～景观 scenes and sights of cultural interest

【人文科学】rénwén kēxué same as 社会科学 shèhuì kēxué

【人文主义】rénwén zhǔyì 欧洲文艺复兴时期的主要思潮，反对宗教教义和中古时期的经院哲学，提倡学术研究，主张思想自由和个性解放，肯定人是世界的中心。是资本主义萌芽时期的先进思想，但缺乏广泛的民主基础，有很大的局限性。humanism；major trend of thought of the Renaissance that is opposed to religious doctrines and scholasticism of the mediaeval times, advocates academic studies, freedom of thought and the emancipation of individuality, and asserts that human beings are the centre of the world；advanced trend of thought that occurred during the infancy of capitalism but rather limited for lack of a broad popular basis；☞文艺复兴 wényì fùxīng on p. 2008

【人物】rénwù ❶ 在某方面有代表性或具有突出特点的人 personage；person of distinction：英雄～heroic figure；hero；heroine|风流～ man of the times ❷ 文学和艺术作品中所描写的人（in works of literature and art）character ❸ 以人物为题材的中国画（of traditional Chinese painting）figure painting

【人像】rénxiàng 刻画人体或相貌的绘画、雕塑等艺术品 work of art（painting, sculpture, etc.）portraying the body or looks of a human being

【人心】rénxīn ❶ 指众人的感情、愿望等 popular feeling：振奋～heartening|大快～to the immense satisfaction of the people|～所向 accord with public will|～惶惶 public disquiet ❷ 指人的心地，特指善良的心地 heart, esp. kind-heartedness：～不古 degeneration of social mores|他并不是没有～的人。He isn't a heartless man.

【人行道】rénxíngdào 马路两旁供人步行的便道 pavement；sidewalk

【人行横道】rénxíng-héngdào 大城市马路上划出的供行人横穿马路的一段道，一般画有斑马线的标志 zebra crossing; pedestrian crosswalk marked with white stripes

【人性】rénxìng 在一定的社会制度和一定的历史条件下形成的人的本性 human nature; sum of qualities and traits shared by all human beings under a given social system and historical conditions

【人性】rén·xing 人所具有的正常的感情和理性 human feelings; reason:不通～unfeeling and unreasonable|灭绝～inhuman

【人性论】rénxìnglùn 一种主张人具有天生的、固定不变的共同本性的观点 theory of human nature; theory that human beings share the same inherent and changeless nature

【人选】rénxuǎn 为一定目的挑选出来的人 candidate; person chosen for a certain purpose:适当～suitable candidate|决定秘书长的～decide who will be secretary-general

【人烟】rényān 指人家,住户 people and cooking smoke; signs of human habitation (烟 *yan*:炊烟 cooking smoke):～稠密 densely populated|荒无～desolate and uninhabited

【人仰马翻】rén yǎng mǎ fān 形容混乱或忙乱得不可收拾的样子 men and horses thrown off their feet — badly battered; thrown into confusion; also 马翻人仰 mǎ fān rén yǎng and 马仰人翻 mǎ yǎng rén fān

【人样】rényàng (～儿 rényàngr) ❶ 人的形状;人应具有的仪表、礼貌等 proper human appearance; proper looks, etiquette, etc.:身上脏得不像个～person who is awfully dirty|把孩子惯得一点～都没有。The child is terribly spoiled. ❷ 指有出息的人 person of substance; successful person:不混出个～来,不要回来见我。Don't come back and see me until you have amounted to something.

【人意】rényì 人的心愿、意志 wish; expectation:尽如～to the satisfaction of sb.

【人影儿】rényǐngr ❶ 人的影子 shadow of a human being:窗帘上有个～。The form of a person was silhouetted against the window curtain. ❷ 人的形象或踪影 trace of a person's presence:天黑得对面看不见～。It was so dark that you couldn't even see someone standing right in front of you.|他一出去,连～也不见了。Once he went out he simply disappeared into nowhere.

【人鱼】rényú 儒艮的俗称 popular term for 儒艮 rúgèn

【人员】rényuán 担任某种职务的人 personnel; staff:机关工作～office worker|值班～staff member on duty|～配备 deployment of personnel

【人缘儿】rényuánr 跟人相处的关系(有时指良好的关系) relations with other people; popularity:没～unpopular|有～popular|～不错 have a good reputation

【人猿】rényuán same as 类人猿 lèirényuán

【人云亦云】rén yún yì yún 人家说什么自己也跟着说什么,形容没有主见 parrot; have no views of one's own

【人造】rénzào 人工制造的,非天然的 man-made; artificial:～纤维 synthetic fibre|～地球卫星 man-made ground satellite

【人造磁铁】rénzào cítiě 以钢或磁合金为原料,经人工磁化而成的磁铁 man-made magnetic steel; artificially magnetized or magnet steel alloy

【人造地球卫星】rénzào dìqiú wèixīng 用火箭发射到天空,按一定轨道绕地球运行的物体 man-made earth satellite; satellite launched onto earth's orbit with a rocket

【人造革】rénzàogé 类似皮革的塑料制品,通常将熔化的树脂加配料涂在纺织品上,经加热处理而成。也有用加配料的树脂经滚筒压制而成的,有的有衬布。imitation or artificial leather; leatherette; leather-like plastics fashioned by coating a fabric with molten resin and heat treatment, or made by rolling a resin preparation into a sheet, sometimes with lining cloth

【人造石油】rénzào shíyóu 从油页岩或煤中提炼的或化工合成的类似天然石油的液体 synthetic oil; oil refined from oil shale or coal or artificially synthesized that resembles crude oil

【人造卫星】rénzào wèixīng 用火箭发射到天空,按一定轨道绕地球或其他行星运行的物体 man-made satellite or other object launched into the orbit of earth or other planets with a rocket

【人造纤维】rénzào xiānwéi 用人工方法制成的纤维,是用天然的高分子化合物为原料制成的,竹子、木材、甘蔗渣、棉子绒等都是制造人造纤维的原料。根据人造纤维的形状和用途,分为人造丝、人造棉和人造毛三种。synthetic fibre; fibre artificially made from natural macromolecular compound such as bamboo, wood, bagasse and silk floss. There are three categories of synthetic fibre: rayon, artificial cotton and artificial wool, differentiated by their respective shapes and applications.

【人造行星】rénzào xíngxīng 用火箭发射到星际空间,摆脱地球的引力,按一定轨道绕太阳运行的物体 man-made planet, rocketed into interplanetary space, where, beyond the earth's gravity, it rotates around the sun along a certain orbit

【人证】rénzhèng 由证人提供的有关案件事实的证据(区别于'物证'as compared with 'material evidence') testimony of an eye witness

【人质】rénzhì 一方拘留的对方的人,用来迫使对方履行诺言或接受某些条件 hostage; person held by one party as security that the opposing party will meet specified terms

【人治】rénzhì 先秦时期儒家的政治思想,主张君主依靠贤能来治理国家 rule by men; pre-Qin Confucian idea that advocates the rule of the country by a monarch relying on men of virtue and talent

【人中】rénzhōng 人的上唇正中凹下的部分 philtrum; vertical groove on the median line of the upper lip

【人种】rénzhǒng 具有共同起源和共同遗传特征的人群。世界上的人种主要有尼格罗—澳大利亚人种(即黑种),蒙古人种(即黄种),欧罗巴人种(即白种)。human race; population distinguished by the same origin and genetically transmitted common physical characteristics, there being three major human races in the world — Negroid-Australian, Mongoloid and Caucasoid

壬 rén ❶ 天干的第九位 *ren*, 9th of the 10 Heavenly Stems; ☞干支 gānzhī on p. 627 ❷ (Rén)姓 a surname

仁1 rén ❶ 仁爱 benevolence:～心 kind-heartedness|～政 benevolence government|～至义尽 with the utmost decency and kindness ❷〈敬辞 *honor.*〉用于对对方的尊称 your excellency:～兄 my respected elder brother|～弟 my respected younger brother|～伯 your honourable father ❸ (Rén)姓 a surname

仁2 rén (～儿 rénr)果核或果壳最里头较柔软的部分,大多可以吃 kernel; seed of a fruit stone or nut that is usu. edible:杏～儿 apricot stone; almond|核桃～儿 walnut meat|花生～儿 shelled peanut ◇虾～儿 shrimp meat

【仁爱】rén'ài 同情、爱护和帮助人的思想感情 benevolence; humanity

【仁慈】réncí 仁爱慈善 benevolent; kind:～的老人 a kind old man

【仁弟】réndì 对比自己年轻的朋友的敬称,老师对学生也用(多用于书信等 usu. used in a letter to a younger male friend or former male student) my dear friend

【仁果】rénguǒ ❶ 果实的一种,果肉大部分由花托发育而成,如苹果、梨等 pulp fruit; a kind of fruit with a soft, moist meat that grows out of the thalamus, such as apple and pear ❷〈方 *dial.*〉same as 落花生 luò·huashēng

【仁厚】rénhòu 仁爱宽厚 kind-hearted and tolerant:～待人 treat people with generosity

【仁人君子】rénrén jūnzǐ 能热心助人的人,也指心地纯正、道德高尚的人 gentlemen; kindly folk; people who are ready to help others; people with the purity of heart and nobility of morality

【仁人志士】rénrén zhìshì 仁爱而有节操的人 benevolent and righteous person

【仁兄】rénxiōng 对朋友的敬称(多用于书信等 polite term in letter writing) my dear friend

【仁义】rényì 仁爱和正义 benevolence and righteousness:～道德 virtue and morality

【仁义】rén·yi〈方 *dial.*〉性情和顺善良 amiable; kind

【仁者见仁,智者见智】rén zhě jiàn rén, zhì zhě jiàn zhì《易经·系辞》:'仁者见之谓之仁,智者见之谓之智。'指对同一个问题,各人观察的角度不同,见解也不相同。the saying 'the benevolent see benevolence and the wise see wisdom' quoted from *The Book of Changes·Great Treatise* means that different people have different opinions on the same issue because of different points of view

【仁政】rénzhèng 仁慈的政治措施 benevolent government:施行～carry out a policy of benevolence

【仁至义尽】rén zhì yì jìn 形容对人的善意和帮助已经做到最大的限度 do everything called for by humanity and duty; do what is humanly possible to help; be magnanimous

任 rén ❶ 任县(Rén Xiàn)、任丘(Rénqiū),地名,都在河北 Renxian and Renqiu, names of places in Heibei Province ❷ (Rén) 姓 a surname

☞ rèn on p. 1624

rěn (ㄖㄣˇ)

忍 rěn ❶ 忍耐;忍受 endure; tolerate:容～forbearance|～痛 endure pain|～让 exercise reconciliation|是可～,孰不可～? If this can be tolerated, then what can be called intolerable? ❷ 忍心 bring oneself to (do sth.); have the heart to:残～cruel|于心不～ have not the heart to (do sth.)

【忍俊不禁】rěn jùn bù jīn 忍不住笑 cannot help laughing

【忍耐】rěnnài 把痛苦的感觉或某种情绪抑制住不使表现出来 show restraint; control or repression of pain or other feelings

【忍气吞声】rěn qì tūn shēng 形容受了气而强自忍耐,不说什么话 swallow an insult

【忍让】rěnràng 容忍退让 exercise forbearance; be forbearing and conciliatory:互相～be mutually accommodating|一再～show restraint time and again

【忍辱负重】rěn rǔ fù zhòng 为了完成艰巨的任务,忍受屈辱,承担重任 endure humiliation in order to carry out an important mission

【忍辱含垢】rěn rǔ hán gòu 忍受耻辱 bite the dust; eat humble pie

【忍受】rěnshòu 把痛苦、困难、不幸的遭遇等勉强承受下来 bear; tolerate; put up with (pain, difficulty, misfortune, etc.):无法～beyond one's endurance|～苦难 endure hardships

【忍痛】rěntòng 忍受痛苦(多形容不情愿 oft. unwillingly) suffer pain:～不言 bear pain in silence|～割爱 give up sth. no matter how painful it is|～离去 reluctantly part from sb.

【忍无可忍】rěn wú kě rěn 要忍受也没法儿忍受 be driven beyond forbearance; come to the end of one's patience

【忍心】rěn//xīn 能硬着心肠(做不忍做的事 do

sth. one is reluctant to) have the heart to; be hard-hearted enough to

荏¹ rěn ☞白苏 báisū on p.37

荏² rěn 〈书 *fml*.〉软弱 weak; weak-kneed: 色厉内～fierce of mien but faint of heart

【荏苒】rěnrǎn 〈书 *fml*.〉(时间)渐渐过去(of time) slip by: 光阴～,转瞬已是三年。Time ticktocked away, and three years were soon over.

【荏弱】rěnruò 〈书 *fml*.〉same as 软弱 ruǎnruò

稔 rěn 〈书 *fml*.〉❶ 庄稼成熟(of farm crop) ripe: 丰～good harvest ❷ 年;一年 year: 不及三～而衰(of an undertaking) start going downhill in less than three years ❸ 熟悉(多指对人 oft. a person) be familiar with: 素～have known sb. for a long time|～知 be familiar with

【稔知】rěnzhī 〈书 *fml*.〉熟知 know well: ～其为人 know sb. well

rèn (ㄖㄣˋ)

刃(刄) rèn ❶ (～儿 rènr)刀剪等的锋利部分;刀口 blade: 刀～blade of a knife|这把斧子锩了～了。This axe has become blunted. ❷ 刀 knife: 利～sharp knife|白～战 bayonet fighting ❸ 〈书 *fml*.〉用刀杀 kill with a knife or sword: 自～kill oneself with a knife|手～奸贼 kill a traitor with one's own hand

【刃具】rènjù same as 刀具 dāojù

认(認) rèn ❶ 认识;分辨 recognize; identify: ～字 be able to read; be literate|～清是非 distinguish between right and wrong|自己的东西,自己来～。Come over and make out what belongs to you. ❷ 跟本来没有关系的人建立某种关系 enter into a relationship with sb.: ～了一门亲 establish relationship through marriage; acknowledge relationship with a relative|～老师 accept sb. as one's teacher ❸ 表示同意;承认 admit; own: 公～established (fact)|否～deny|～可 accept; approve of|～输 admit defeat|～错儿 admit a mistake; apologize ❹ 认吃亏(后面要带'了' followed by 了·le) accept a loss, or the consequence of sth. unpleasant: 你不用管,这事我～了。Leave it to me, and I'll just accept the consequence, whatever it is.

【认不是】rèn bù·shi same as 认错 rèn//cuò

【认错】rèn//cuò (～儿 rèn//cuòr)承认错误 admit that one's wrong: 他既然～了,就原谅他这一次吧。Since he has apologized, forgive him just this once.

【认得】rèn·de same as 认识 rèn·shi ①: 我不～这种花。I don't know anything about this flower.|我～这位先生。I know this gentleman.

【认定】rèndìng ❶ 确定地认为 believe; maintain: 我们～一切事物都是在矛盾中不断向前发展的。It is our belief that all things develop constantly in the midst of contradictions. ❷ 明确承认;确定 affirm; endorse: 审核～技术合同 examine and endorse a technical contract|犯罪事实清楚,证据确定、充分,足以～。The crime can be established now that the facts have been clarified and the evidence is full and conclusive.

【认罚】rèn//fá 同意受罚 ready to receive a penalty: 情愿～be willing to be penalized|说错了,我～。I said something wrong, and I'm willing to accept the penalty.

【认购】rèngòu 应承购买(公债等)(public bonds, etc.) buy; subscribe: 自愿～make one's own decision in buying sth.|～债券 offer to buy treasure bonds

【认脚】rènjiǎo 〈方 *dial*.〉鞋左右两只不能换着穿 put the right shoe on the right foot

【认可】rènkě 许可;承认 approve of; endorse: 点头～nod one's approval|这个方案被双方～。Both parties accepted the plan.

【认领】rènlǐng ❶ 辨认并领取 claim: 拾得金笔一支,希望失主前来～。Someone has found a gold pen. Whoever owns it may come and claim it. ❷ 把别人的孩子当做自己的领来抚养 adopt; take into one's family through legal means and raise as one's own child

【认命】rèn//mìng 承认不幸的遭遇是命中注定的(迷信)(superstition) accept fate; resign oneself to fate

【认生】rènshēng (小孩子)怕见生人(of a child) be shy with strangers

【认识】rèn·shi ❶ 能够确定某一人或事物是这个人或事物而不是别的 recognize; know: 我～他。I know him.|他不～这种草药。He doesn't know anything about this herbal medicine. ❷ 指人的头脑对客观世界的反映(of human mind) understanding or knowledge (of the objective world): 感性～perceptual knowledge|理性～rational knowledge

【认识论】rèn·shilùn 关于人类认识的来源、发展过程,以及认识与实践的关系的学说。由于对思维和存在何者为第一性的不同回答,分成唯心主义认识论和唯物主义认识论。theory of knowledge; epistemology; branch of philosophy that studies the origin and development of human knowledge, and the relationship between knowledge and practice, which falls into two categories — idealist theory of knowledge and materialist theory of knowledge — due to differences on whether thought or being is primary

【认输】rèn//shū 承认失败 throw in the towel; admit defeat: 他没认过输。He never takes defeat lying down.

【认死理】rèn sǐlǐ（～儿 rèn sǐlǐr）坚持某种道理或理由，不知变通 stubborn; bull-headed; inflexible：这个人就是有点～，心还是好的。He's a kind of stubborn, but he has his heart in the right place.

【认同】rèntóng ❶ 认为跟自己有共同之处而感到亲切 identify oneself with：民族～感 sense of national identity ❷ 承认；认可 approve of; recognize：这种研究方法已经得到学术界的～。This research approach has been recognized in the academic circles.

【认头】rèn//tóu 不情愿而勉强承受；认吃亏 resign oneself to a loss：明知受骗也只好～。He had to accept the deal even though he knew he was being double-crossed.

【认为】rènwéi 对人或事物确定某种看法，做出某种判断 maintain; believe：我～他可以担任这项工作。I believe he is up to the job.

【认贼作父】rèn zéi zuò fù〈比喻 *fig.*〉把敌人当亲人 take the foe for one's father — befriend an enemy

【认账】rèn//zhàng 承认所欠的账 acknowledge a debt;〈比喻 *fig.*〉承认自己说过的话或做过的事（多用于否定式 usu. in the negative）admit what one has said or done：不肯～deny what one has said or done｜隔了那么久，他能认这个账？It's been a long time since it happened. Would he admit it?

【认真】rèn//zhēn 信以为真；当真 take seriously; take to heart：人家说着玩儿，你怎么就认起真来了？I was joking. Why take it seriously?

【认真】rènzhēn 严肃对待，不马虎 conscientious; earnest; serious：～学习 study hard｜工作～work hard

【认证】rènzhèng 公证机关对当事人提出的文件审查属实后给予证明 attest; notarize; practice of a notary public to witness and certify a document provided

【认罪】rèn//zuì 承认自己的罪行 plead guilty：低头～hang one's head and plead guilty｜～悔过 own up to one's crime and repent

仞 rèn〈古时 *arch.*〉八尺或七尺叫做一仞 *ren*, measure of length, equal to 7 or 8 *chi*：万～高山 mountain that is immeasurably high｜为山九～，功亏一篑。The lack of one basketful of earth spoils the entire effort to build a nine-*ren* mountain. *or* A failure is a failure even though it has come so close to success.

讱 rèn〈书 *fml.*〉（言语）迟钝 slow of speech; inarticulate

任1 rèn ❶ 任用 appoint; assign to a post：委～appointment to a post｜被～为厂长 be appointed director of a factory ❷ 担任 take office; assume a post：～职 take up a post｜连选连～elected to a consecutive term of office ❸ 担当；承受 bear; endure：～劳～怨 be hardworking and never complain ❹ 职务 official post：就～take office｜担负重～be assigned to an important post ❺〈量词 *classifier*〉用于担任官职的次数 number of terms served on an official post

任2 rèn ❶ 任凭；听凭 let; allow; permit：放～give rein to｜～意 wilfully｜听之～之 let things run unchecked｜衣服的花色很多，～你挑选。There are a big variety of garments here, and you can choose any way you want. ❷ 不论；无论 no matter：东西放在这里，～什么也短不了。If you put your things here none of them will be lost no matter what happens.｜～谁也不准乱动这里的东西。Nobody is allowed to fiddle with what's stored here no matter who you are.

☞ rén on p. 1622

【任便】rèn//biàn 任凭方便；听便 as you see fit; as you like：你来不来～。You may come or not as you see fit.

【任从】rèncóng 任凭；听凭 give sb. a free hand to do sth.

【任何】rènhé 不论什么 any; whatever; whichever; whoever：～人都要遵纪守法。All people should without exception observe discipline and abide by law.｜我们能够战胜～困难。We can overcome difficulties no matter what they are.

【任教】rèn//jiào 担任教师工作 teach; be a teacher：他在大学～。He teaches in college.｜他在这所学校里任过教。He once taught in this school.

【任课】rèn//kè 担任讲课工作 be a lecturer; teach class：～教师 teacher of a class

【任劳任怨】rèn láo rèn yuàn 做事不辞劳苦，不怕别人埋怨 work hard regardless of criticism; willingly bear the burden of office

【任免】rènmiǎn 任命和免职 appointments and removals：～名单 list of appointments and removals

【任命】rènmìng 下命令任用 appoint：～他为处长。He was appointed department head.

【任凭】rènpíng ❶ 听凭 allow; let sb. do as he pleases：去还是不去，～你自己。You may go or stay as you please.｜～风浪起，稳坐钓鱼船。Sit tight in one's fishing boat despite the rising wind and waves — maintain one's composure in times of adversity. ❷ 无论；不管 no matter：～什么困难也阻挡不住我们。We are not to be daunted by whatever difficulty there is.

【任期】rènqī 担任职务的规定期限 term of office：～将满 one's term drawing to an end｜～三年 a three-year term of office

【任情】rènqíng ❶ same as 尽情 jìnqíng ❷〈书 *fml.*〉任性；放纵感情 headstrong; wilful：～率性 indulge in one's emotions

【任人唯亲】rèn rén wéi qīn 任用跟自己关系密切的人,而不管他德才如何 appoint sb. by favouritism, disregarding his or her moral character and talent

【任人唯贤】rèn rén wéi xián 任用德才兼备的人,而不管他跟自己的关系是否密切 appoint sb. on his or her merits only, disregarding his or her relationship with oneself

【任务】rèn·wu 指定担任的工作;指定担负的责任 task; assignment; quota:生产～output quota|超额完成～overfulfil one's work|本校今年的招生～是五百名。The enrolment quota for our school this year is 500.

【任性】rènxìng 放任自己的性子,不加约束 have no self-restraint; wayward; headstrong:～胡闹 be headstrong and wild|他有时不免孩子气,有点～。He is childish and impulsive sometimes.

【任意】rènyì ❶ 没有拘束,不加限制,爱怎么样就怎么样 arbitrary; wilful:～行动 act wantonly|～畅谈 have a nice and free chat ❷ 没有任何条件的 unconditional:～三角形 unconditional triangle

【任用】rènyòng 委派人员担任职务 assign sb. to a post; appoint:～贤能 appoint able persons to important posts|～得人 use the wise and employ the capable

【任职】rèn//zhí 担任职务 hold a post:～财政部 hold a post in the Ministry of Finance|他在交通部门任过职。He worked for a while in the transport department.

【任重道远】rèn zhòng dào yuǎn 担子很重,路程又长 burden is heavy and the road is long;〈比喻 *fig.*〉责任重大 be entrusted with a major mission, task, etc.

纫 rèn ❶ 引线穿过针鼻儿 thread a needle:老太太眼花了,～不上针。The old lady's vision had become so blurred, she couldn't thread the needle. ❷ 用针缝 stitch:缝～sew ❸〈书 *fml.*〉深深感激(多用于书信 oft. in letter and writing) thanks a lot:至～高谊。Thank you so much for your great kindness.

【纫佩】rènpèi〈书 *fml.*〉感激佩服 feel gratefulness and admiration towards sb.

韧(韌、靭) rèn 受外力作用时,虽然变形而不易折断;柔软而结实(跟'脆'相对 as opposed to 'fragile') (of an object or material) resilient; capable of changing its shape without breaking when under an outside force:坚～tenacious|柔～resilient|～度 tenacity|～性 tenacity; malleability

【韧带】rèndài 白色带状的结缔组织,质坚韧,有弹性,能把骨骼连接在一起,并能固定某些脏器如肝、脾、肾等的位置 ligament; white band of tough and elastic fibrous tissue connecting bones or cartilages at a joint or keeping liver, spleen, kidney and other organs in position

【韧劲】rènjìn (～儿 rènjìnr)顽强不屈的劲头 dauntlessness; tenacity:他做事有一股～。He is tenacious whatever he does.

【韧皮部】rènpíbù 植物学上指茎的组成部分之一,由筛管和韧皮纤维构成 phloem; food-conducting tissue of vascular plants, consisting of sieve tubes and bast fibre

【韧皮纤维】rènpí xiānwéi 韧皮部的组成部分之一,由两端尖的细长细胞构成,质柔韧,富于弹力,如苎麻等的纤维 bast; bast fibre; part of the phloem tissue, such as the fibre of ramie, that consists of thin and long cells with pointed ends and is strong, resilient and elastic

【韧性】rènxìng ❶ 物体受外力作用时,产生变形而不易折断的性质 resilience; toughness; tenacity; property of a material that changes its form but does not break under stress ❷ 指顽强持久的精神 persistence; tenacity:工作任务越艰巨越需要～。The more arduous the work becomes, the more tenacity is needed.

轫 rèn〈书 *fml.*〉支住车轮不使旋转的木头 log used to brake the wheels of a vehicle:发～lift the log to set a vehicle going

牣 rèn〈书 *fml.*〉充满 full of; brimming with:充～filled to overflowing

饪(飪) rèn 做饭做菜 cook:烹～cooking; culinary art

妊(姙) rèn 妊娠 be pregnant:～妇 woman in pregnancy

【妊妇】rènfù 孕妇 pregnant woman; expectant mother

【妊娠】rènshēn 人或动物母体内有胚胎发育成长;怀孕(of a woman or a female animal) pregnant; gestation:～期 period of gestation; gestational period

纴(紝) rèn〈书 *fml.*〉纺织 weave

衽(衽) rèn〈书 *fml.*〉❶ 衣襟 front of a garment ❷ 睡觉用的席子 sleeping mat:～席 straw mat

葚 rèn ☞ 桑葚儿 sāngrènr on p.1657 ☞ shèn on p.1711

rēng (ㄖㄥ)

扔 rēng ❶ 挥动手臂,使拿着的东西离开手 throw; propel through the air with a motion of the arm:～球 toss a ball|～手榴弹 throw a hand grenade ❷ 抛弃;丢 throw away:这条鱼臭了,把它～了吧。The fish is stinking. Let's throw it away.|这事他早就～在脖子后边了。He has long forgotten about it.

réng (ㄖㄥˊ)

仍 réng ❶ 依照 remain:一～其旧(完全照旧) remain the same; stay intact ❷〈书 *fml.*〉

频繁 frequently; often:频～frequent ❸〈书 *fml.*〉仍然 still:～须努力 need to redouble one's effort|病～不见好。His condition is yet to improve.

【仍旧】réngjiù ❶ 照旧 remain the same:修订版体例～。The revised edition has maintained the style of the previous edition. ❷ same as 仍然 réngrán:他虽然遇到许多困难,可是意志～那样坚强。He's had his fill of twists and turns, yet he remains as determined as ever.

【仍然】réngrán〈副词 *adv.*〉表示情况继续不变或恢复原状[indicating continuity or resumption of a situation] still; yet:他～保持着老红军艰苦奋斗的作风。He still maintains the hardworking style of a Red Army veteran.|他把信看完,～装在信封里。He put the letter back into the envelope after he'd read it.

礽 réng〈书 *fml.*〉same as 福 fú

rì (ㄖˋ)

日 rì ❶ 太阳 sun:～出 sunrise|～落 sunset ❷ (Rì) 指日本 Japan:～圆 Japanese yen|～语 Japanese ❸ 从天亮到天黑的一段时间;白天(跟'夜'相对 as opposed to 'night') day; daytime; interval from sunrise to sunset:～班 day shift|～场 daytime show|～～夜夜 days and nights|夜以继～(work) day and night ❹ 地球自转一周的时间;一昼夜;天 24-hour period during which the earth completes one rotation on its axis; day:今～today|明～tomorrow|多～不见。Haven't seen you for ages.|改～再谈。Let's talk about it again some other day. ❺ 每天;一天一天地 on a daily basis; everyday; daily:～记 diary|～新月异 take on a new look with each passing day|生产～有增加。Production is increasing on a daily basis.|经济～趋繁荣。The economy is growing steadily. ❻ 泛指一段时间 period of time:往～bygone days|来～in future|昔～in the past ❼ 特指某一天 particular day:假～holiday|生～birthday|国庆～National Day

【日班】rìbān 白天工作的班次 day shift

【日斑】rìbān same as 太阳黑子 tàiyáng hēizǐ

【日报】rìbào 每天早上出版的报纸 daily; newspaper published in the morning on a daily basis

【日薄西山】rì bó xī shān 太阳快要落山了 sun being about to set;〈比喻 *fig.*〉衰老的人或腐朽的事物临近死亡 on one's last legs; on the wane

【日不暇给】rì bù xiá jǐ 形容事务繁忙,没有空闲 be fully occupied every day; be pressed for time

【日常】rìcháng 属于平时的 everyday; day-to-day:～生活 everyday life|～工作 routine work|～用品 daily necessities

【日场】rìchǎng 戏剧、电影等在白天的演出(of a theatre or cinema) daytime show:～戏 matinée|～电影 daytime movie show

【日程】rìchéng 按日排定的行事程序 agenda; schedule:议事～agenda|工作～work schedule|此事已提到～上。The matter has been put on the agenda.

【日戳】rìchuō 刻有年月日的戳子 date stamp; datemark

【日耳曼人】Rì'ěrmànrén 约公元前 5 世纪起分布在欧洲斯堪的纳维亚半岛南部、日德兰半岛、波罗的海和北海南岸的一些部落 Teuton; Germanic people; tribes inhabiting south Scandinavian Peninsular, Jutland, the southern shore of the Baltic Sea and the North Sea beginning from the 5th century B.C.

【日珥】rì'ěr 太阳表面上红色火焰状的炽热气体,由氢、氦、钙等元素组成。日全食时肉眼能看见,平时要用分光镜才能看见。solar prominence; red flame-like incandescent gas on the surface of the sun, consisting of hydrogen, helium, calcium and other elements, observable during a total solar eclipse or with the help of a spectroscope

【日工】rìgōng ❶ 白天的活儿 daywork ❷ 按天数计算工资的临时工人,也指这种临时工作 day labourer; labourer hired and paid by the day; also this kind of labour

【日光】rìguāng ❶ 太阳发出的光 sunlight ❷ 时光(多见于早期白话 oft. in early vernacular) time; hour:～尚早。It's still early.

【日光灯】rìguāngdēng same as 荧光灯 yíngguāngdēng

【日光浴】rìguāngyù 光着身子让日光照射以促进新陈代谢,增强抵抗力,保持身体健康的方法 sunbath; expose one's body to sun in order to promote metabolism, enhance resistance against virus, and keep fit

【日晷】rìguǐ 利用太阳投射的影子来测定时刻的装置。一般是在有刻度的盘的中央装着一根与盘垂直的金属棍儿。sundial; instrument that indicates local apparent solar time by the shadow cast by a central pointer projecting vertically on a surrounding calibrated dial; also 日规 rìguī

【日后】rìhòu 将来;以后 in the days to come; in the future:这孩子～一定有出息。The child will amount to something in the future.|～出了问题,你可不要怪我。Don't blame me if something goes wrong later.

【日华】rìhuá 阳光通过云中的小水滴或冰粒时发生衍射,在太阳周围形成的彩色光环,内紫外红 solar halo; circular band of coloured light around the sun, purple inside and red on the outside, caused by the diffraction of sun light by water or ice particles suspended in the intervening clouds

【日积月累】rì jī yuè lěi 长时间地积累 accumulate on a daily and monthly basis：每天读几页书，～就读了很多书。Read a few pages every day, and in time you'll have finished reading a lot of books.

【日记】rìjì 每天所遇到的和所做的事情的记录，有的兼记对这些事情的感受 diary; daily record of events and experiences, and observations：～本 diary｜工作～work diary｜记～keep a diary

【日记账】rìjìzhàng 簿记中主要账簿的一种，按日期先后记载各项账目，不分类。根据日记账记载总账。journal; daybook; major category of account books in which items are recorded by the day and without classification, and which provide the basis for the record of the general ledger; also 序时账 xùshízhàng

【日间】rìjiān same as 白天 bái·tiān

【日见】rìjiàn 一天一天地显示 grow conspicuous on a daily basis; with each passing day：～好转 get better with each passing day

【日渐】rìjiàn 一天一天慢慢地 day by day (slowly)：～进步 make slow but steady progress

【日界线】rìjièxiàn 国际日期变更线 international dateline; dateline

【日久天长】rì jiǔ tiān cháng 时间长，日子久 in the course of time; year in, year out：～，养成习惯就不好了。It does you no good if you turn what you are doing into a habit in the course of time.

【日就月将】rì jiù yuè jiāng 每天有成就，每月有进步。形容积少成多 achieve sth. every day and make progress every month — many a little makes a mickle (就 *jiu*：成就 achievement; 将 *jiang*：前进 progress)

【日来】rìlái 近几天来 lately; over the last few days：～偶染小恙。I came down with a minor ailment lately.

【日理万机】rì lǐ wàn jī 形容政务繁忙（多指高级领导人 oft. of a ranking official) attend to numerous affairs of state every day; be occupied with state affairs

【日历】rìlì 记有年、月、日、星期、节气、纪念日等的本子，一年一本，每日一页，逐日揭去 calendar; a series of pages showing the months, days, weeks, solar terms, festivals, etc. of a particular year, to be torn away a page a day

【日冕】rìmiǎn 太阳大气的最外层，亮度约为光球的一百万分之一。日全食时，可以看到黑暗的太阳表面周围有一层淡黄色光芒。solar corona; corona; faintly yellow ring surrounding the outmost atmospheric layer of the sun with a luminosity one millionth of that of the photosphere, visible in the form of pale yellow light surrounding the dark surface of the sun during a total solar eclipse

【日暮途穷】rì mù tú qióng 天黑下去了，路走到头了 day is waning and the road is ending; 〈比喻 *fig.*〉到了末日 on one's last legs; at the end of one's rope

【日内】rìnèi 最近几天里 in a couple of days; in a day or two：大会将于～举行。The meeting will take place in a couple of days.

【日期】rìqī 发生某一事情的确定的日子或时期 date; particular day or period of time at which sth. happened or is expected to happen：发信的～date of a letter｜起程的～date for departure｜开会的～是6月21日到27日。The meeting will take place from June 21 to 27.

【日前】rìqián 几天前 a few days ago; other day：～他曾来过一次。He came the other day.

【日趋】rìqū 一天一天地走向 change with each passing day; day by day：～繁荣 become prosperous on a daily basis｜～没落 do downhill with each passing day

【日色】rìsè 太阳的光，指时间的早晚 time of the day judging by the luminosity of the sun：～不早了，快点赶路吧。It's getting dark, so let's hurry up on our journey.

【日上三竿】rì shàng sān gān 太阳升起来离地已有三根竹竿那么高。多用来形容人起床晚。The sun is three poles high — it's late in the morning (usu. referring to getting up late)

【日食】rìshí 月球运行到地球和太阳的中间时，太阳的光被月球挡住，不能射到地球上来，这种现象叫日食。太阳全部被月球挡住时叫日全食，部分被挡住时叫日偏食，中央部分被挡住时叫日环食。日食都发生在农历初一。solar eclipse; partial or complete obscuring of the sun by the moon when it moves right in between the earth and the sun, which takes place on the first day of a lunar month, known as total solar eclipse when the sun is entirely obscured, partial solar eclipse when it is partially obscured, and solar annular eclipse when the central part of it is obscured

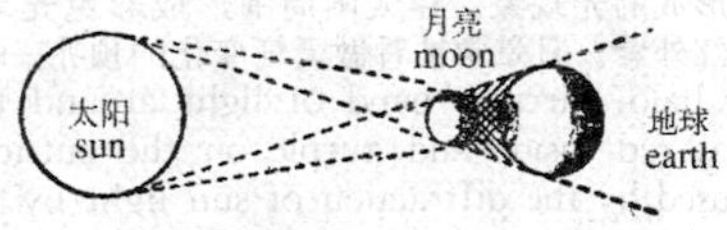

日食 Solar Eclipse

【日头】rìtóu ❶ same as 日子 rì·zi ①（多见于早期白话，下同 oft. in early vernacular, same below)：我也有盼着他的～。There were also days when I missed him. ❷ 指白天 daytime：半个～half a day

【日头】rì·tou same as 太阳 tàiyáng

【日托】rìtuō 白天把幼儿托付给托儿所或幼儿园，晚上接回家，叫日托（区别于'全托'as compared with 'full-time care') day care; nursery or kindergarten where children are sent during the day but go home at night

【日夕】rìxī〈书 *fml*.〉日夜；朝夕 day and night：～相处 be together day and night

【日心说】rìxīnshuō〈古时 *arch*.〉天文学上的一种学说，认为太阳处于宇宙的中心，地球和其他行星都围绕太阳运动 heliocentric theory；ancient astronomical theory that believes the sun is at the centre of universe，with the earth and other planet revolving around it

【日新月异】rì xīn yuè yì 每天每月都有新的变化，形容进步、发展很快 make progress with each passing day and each passing month；develop rapidly

【日夜】rìyè 白天黑夜 day and night；round the clock：～兼程 travel at double speed day and night|～三班轮流生产 keep production going round the clock on three shifts

R

【日以继夜】rì yǐ jì yè ☞ 夜以继日 yè yǐ jì rì on p.2241

【日益】rìyì 一天比一天更加 increasingly；day by day：生活～改善。Livelihood improved steadily.

【日用】rìyòng ❶ 日常生活应用的 daily use：～品 daily-use necessities ❷ 日常生活的费用 daily expenses：一部分钱做～，其余的都储蓄起来。Part of the money is spent on daily expenses，and the rest goes to the savings deposit.

【日用品】rìyòngpǐn 日常应用的物品，如毛巾、肥皂、暖水瓶等 daily-use necessities，such as towel，soap，thermos bottle，etc.

【日元】rìyuán same as 日圆 rìyuán

【日圆】rìyuán 日本的本位货币 yen，the currency of Japan；also 日元 rìyuán

【日月】rìyuè（～儿 rìyuèr）❶ same as 日子 rì·zi ③：战斗的～militant life|幸福的～happy life ❷ 时间；时光 time

【日月如梭】rì yuè rú suō 太阳和月亮像穿梭似地来去，形容时间过得很快 sun and the moon shuttle back and forth — how time flies

【日晕】rìyùn 日光通过云层中的冰晶时，经折射而形成的光现象。在太阳周围形成彩色光环，内红外紫。日晕常被看做天气变化的预兆。solar halo；circular band of light around the sun，red inside and purple on the outside，caused by the diffraction of sun light by ice particles suspended in the clouds，oft. regarded as a sign for weather change

【日照】rìzhào 一天中太阳光照射的时间。日照长短随纬度高低和季节而变化，并和云量、云的厚度以及地形有关。夏季我国北方日照长，南方日照短，冬季相反。sunshine；sunshine time；daily duration for a place to be exposed to direct rays from the sun，which varies with latitude and season and is also as related with the amount and thickness of clouds and topography. North China has more sunshine while south China has less sunshine in summer，and vice versa in winter.

【日臻】rìzhēn 一天一天地达到 approach（a goal or a state，etc.）day by day：～完善 be brought to perfection with each passing day|～成熟 mature steadily

【日志】rìzhì 日记（多指非个人的 oft. non-individual）journal；daily record：教室～classroom journal|工作～daily record of work

【日中】rìzhōng same as 正午 zhèngwǔ

【日子】rì·zi ❶ 日期 date：这个～好容易盼到了。The day we'd been awaiting came at last. ❷ 时间（指天数）number of days：他走了有些～了。He's gone for quite a few days. ❸ 指生活或生计 life；livelihood：～越过越美。Life is getting better steadily.

驲 rì〈古代 *arch*.〉驿站用的马车 post-chaise；carriage for a post station

róng（ㄖㄨㄥˊ）

戎[1] róng〈书 *fml*.〉❶ 兵器；武器 weapon；arms：兵～arms ❷ 军事；军队 military affairs；army：～马 steed；war-horse|～装 army uniform|投笔从～renounce the pen for the sword；give up writing for a military career

戎[2] Róng ❶ 我国古代称西方的民族 Rongs，ancient Chinese reference to the tribes-people in the West ❷ 姓 a surname

【戎行】rónghána〈书 *fml*.〉军旅；行伍 army：久历～have served in the army for a long time；be a veteran soldier

【戎机】róngjī〈书 *fml*.〉❶ 指战争；军事 war；battle：迅赴～rush to the battlefield|通晓～well-versed in military manoeuvres ❷ 指战机 opportunity for combat：贻误～lose a good opportunity in a battle

【戎马】róngmǎ〈书 *fml*.〉军马，借指从军、作战 army horse，referring to military career：～生涯 military life|～倥偬（形容军务繁忙）busy with military duties

【戎装】róngzhuāng〈书 *fml*.〉军装 army uniform

肜 róng 古代的一种祭祀 a kind of sacrificial offering in ancient times

茸 róng ❶ 草初生纤细柔软的样子（of newly-grown grass）downy；short；short soft and fine ❷ 指鹿茸 young pilose antler：参～（人参和鹿茸）ginseng and pilose antler

【茸毛】róngmáo 指人或动物的绒毛；植物体上的细毛（of human being or animal）fine hair；down；（of plants）fuzz

【茸茸】róngróng（草、毛发等）又短又软又密（of grass，hair，etc.）downy；short，soft and thick：～的绿草 carpet of green grass|这孩子长着一头～的黑发。Soft，thick hair covers the head of the boy.

荣(榮) róng ❶ 草木茂盛(of trees and plants) thrive; flourish:欣欣向~ full of life and vigour; thriving; prospering|本固枝~。When the root is firm, the branches flourish. ❷ 兴盛 prosperous:繁~ booming ❸ 光荣(跟'辱'相对 as opposed to 'disgrace')glory:~誉 honour|~耀 glory|虚~vanity|~获冠军 be honoured as champion ❹ (Róng) 姓 a surname

【荣光】róngguāng 荣耀;光荣 glorious:无上~ highest honour; feel immensely honoured

【荣归】róngguī 光荣地归来 return in honour:~故里 return home in glory|衣锦~ homecoming after winning high honours and social recognition

【荣华】rónghuá 〈书 *fml.*〉草木开花 (of plants) flower; bloom;〈比喻 *fig.*〉兴盛或显达 prosperity; high and influential official position:~富贵 high rank and great wealth

【荣获】rónghuò 光荣地获得 be honoured with:~冠军 win a championship

【荣军】róngjūn 荣誉军人的简称 abbr. for 荣誉军人 róngyù jūnrén

【荣任】róngrèn 指人担任要职(多用于称颂 oft. used in praise) be honoured with an important post

【荣辱】róngrǔ 光荣和耻辱 honour and disgrace:~与共 share weal and woe|将个人的~得失置之度外 have no regard for personal honour or disgrace

【荣幸】róngxìng 光荣而幸运 feel lucky; feel honoured:见到您感到十分~。I feel greatly honoured to see you.|躬逢盛会,不胜~之至。We shall be greatly honoured by your gracious presence at the grand occasion.

【荣耀】róngyào 光荣 honour; glory

【荣膺】róngyīng 〈书 *fml.*〉光荣地接受或承当 be honoured with a post or title:~战斗英雄的称号 be honoured with the title of combat hero

【荣誉】róngyù 光荣的名誉 honour; credit:~感 sense of honour|~称号 honourary title|爱护集体的~cherish the honour of the collective

【荣誉军人】róngyù jūnrén 对残废军人的尊称 respectful term for disabled soldier

绒(羢、毧) róng ❶ same as 绒毛 róngmáo①:鸭~eiderdown|驼~camel wool ❷ 上面有一层绒毛的纺织品 fabrics with soft nap or pile:棉~cotton velvet|丝~velvet|长毛~plush|灯心~corduroy ❸ (~儿 róngr)刺绣用的细丝 fine floss for embroidery:红绿~儿 red and green floss

【绒布】róngbù 有绒毛的棉布,柔软而保暖 flannelette; cotton flannel, a soft and warm fabric

【绒花】rónghuā (~儿 rónghuār)用丝绒制成的花、鸟等 velvet flowers, birds, etc.

【绒毛】róngmáo ❶ 人或动物身体表面和某些器官内壁长的短而柔软的毛 fine hair; down; villus; fine, hairlike epidermal outgrowth on human beings or animals or inside certain organs ❷ 织物上连成一片的纤细而柔软的短毛 nap; pile; soft or fuzzy surface of fabric

【绒线】róngxiàn ❶ 刺绣用的粗丝线 floss for embroidery ❷ 〈方 *dial.*〉毛线 knitting wool

容1 róng ❶ 容纳;包含 hold; contain:~量 capacity|无地自~so ashamed that one wants to sink through the ground|这个礼堂能~两千人。The auditorium is large enough to seat 2,000 people. ❷ 宽容;原谅 tolerate; forgive:~忍 tolerate|大度~人 be magnanimous and tolerable|情理难~ incompatible with the accepted code of human conduct ❸ 允许;让 allow; permit:~许 permission|不~分说 admit or allow no explanation to be offered; allow of no excuse ❹ 〈书 *fml.*〉或许;也许 maybe; probably:~或有之。This may have happened. ❺ (Róng)姓 a surname

容2 róng ❶ 脸上的神情和气色 facial expression:笑~smiling face|愁~worried look|怒~angry looks|~光 one's face glows in happiness, excitement, etc.|病~sickly appearance ❷ 相貌 looks; appearance:~貌 looks|~颜 looks|仪~bearing|整~ facelift ❸ 〈比喻 *fig.*〉事物所呈现的景象、状态 state of sth.; situation:军~ bearing of a soldier|市~appearance of a city|阵~battle formation; lineup

【容光】róngguāng 脸上的光彩 facial expression; bearing:~焕发 glowing with health

【容或】rónghuò 〈书 *fml.*〉或许;也许 maybe; perhaps; probably:这篇文章是根据本人回忆写的,与事实~有出入。This article is based on memory, so it's possibly not altogether accurate.

【容积】róngjī 容器或其他能容纳物质的物体的内部体积 volume; capacity; amount of space in a container or any other three-dimensional object

【容量】róngliàng ❶ 容积的大小叫做容量 capacity; amount of space in a container ❷ 容纳的数量 volume:电~electric capacity; capacitance|热~thermal capacity|通讯~telecommunications capacity

【容留】róngliú 容纳;收留 provide shelter to; take sb. in

【容貌】róngmào 相貌 facial features; looks:~端庄 look demure and graceful|~秀丽 sweet and charming looks

【容纳】róngnà 在固定的空间或范围内接受(人或事物)have a capacity for; accommodate:这个广场可以~十万人。The square is large enough to hold 100,000 people.|修建了一个

可以～上千床位的疗养院。They have built a sanatorium with more than 1,000 beds.

【容器】róngqì 盛物品的器具,如盒子、箩筐、搪瓷盆、玻璃杯等 container; vessel, such as box, basket, enamel basin, glass, etc.

【容情】róngqíng 加以宽容(多用于否定式 oft. in the negative) show mercy; tolerate:我们对坏人坏事是决不～的。We have no leniency for evildoers.

【容人】róng//rén 指宽厚待人 tolerant:～的雅量 magnanimity|心胸狭隘,容不得人 narrow-minded and intolerant

【容忍】róngrěn 宽容忍耐 condone; put up with; endure; abide:他的错误行为使人不能～。No one can tolerate his bad conduct.

【容身】róng//shēn same as 安身 ān//shēn:～之地 place to stay; roof over one's head

【容许】róngxǔ ❶ 许可 permit; allow:原则问题决不～让步。There should be no concessions whatsoever on matters of principle. ❷ 或许;也许 perhaps; probably:此类事件,十年前～有之。Such things might have happened a decade ago.

【容颜】róngyán 容貌;脸色 facial features; looks:～秀美 have graceful and sweet looks

【容易】róngyì ❶ 做起来不费事的 easy:说时～做时难 easier said than done|这篇文章写得很通俗,～看。This article reads well as it is written in an easy-to-understand language. ❷ 发生某种变化的可能性大 likely; apt to:～生病 be prone to illness|白衣服～脏。White clothes get dirty easily.|这种麦子不～倒伏。This strain of wheat does not get lodged easily.

【容止】róngzhǐ〈书 *fml.*〉仪容举止 demeanour:～俊雅 graceful demeanour

【容重】róngzhòng 单位体积物体的重量。内部没有空隙的物体的容重和它的比重相等。unit weight; unit weight of an object with no space inside it equals its specific gravity

嵘(嶸) róng ☞[峥嵘] zhēngróng on p. 2443

蓉 róng ❶ 用某些植物的果肉或种子制成的粉状物 flour made from mashed fruit or seeds:豆～fine bean jam|椰～mashed coconut kernel stuffing ❷ ☞ 芙蓉 fúróng on p. 594 and 苁蓉 cōngróng on p. 323 ❸(Róng) 四川成都的别称 Rong, another name for Chengdu, capital of Sichuan Province

溶 róng 溶化;溶解 dissolve:～液 solution|～剂 solvent|樟脑～于酒精而不～于水。Camphor dissolves in alcohol but not in water.

【溶洞】róngdòng 石灰岩被含有二氧化碳的流水所溶解而形成的天然洞穴 limestone cave; natural cave in a limestone area resulting from the wash of water containing carbon dioxide

【溶化】rónghuà ❶ (固体)溶解(of solid matter) dissolve:砂糖放在热水中就会～。Granulated sugar dissolves once it is put in hot water. ❷ same as 融化 rónghuà

【溶剂】róngjì 能溶解其他物质的物质,如能溶解糖、食盐等而形成溶液的水 solvent; substance, usu. a liquid, capable of dissolving another substance, such as water, which can dissolve sugar, salt, etc.; 旧称 formerly called 溶媒 róngméi

【溶胶】róngjiāo 直径在十万分之一到千万分之一厘米之间的质点分布于介质中所形成的物质。介质为气体的叫气溶胶,如烟;介质为液体的叫液溶胶,如墨汁;介质为固体的叫固溶胶,如泡沫玻璃。sol; colloidal substance resulting from the distribution of particles one 100,000th to one 10 millionth centimetre in diameter in a medium, including aerosol, such as smoke, which has a gas medium, liquid sol, such as prepared Chinese ink, which has a liquid medium, and solid sol, such as foam glass, which has a solid medium; also 胶体溶液 jiāotǐ róngyè

【溶解】róngjiě 一种物质均匀分布在另一种物质中成为溶液。如把一勺儿糖放进一杯水中,就成为糖水。melt; dissolve; mix a substance evenly in a liquid to make a solution, such as dissolving a spoonful of sugar to produce a cup of sweet water

【溶解度】róngjiědù 在一定温度和压力下,物质在一定量溶剂中溶解的最高量。通常以在100克溶剂中达到饱和时所溶解的克数来表示。solubility; maximum amount of matter to be dissolved in a certain amount of solvent under a given temperature and pressure, usu. indicated in terms of grammes at saturation level in 100 grammes of solvent

【溶解热】róngjiěrè 物质溶解过程中的热效应。溶解热的大小与温度、压力、溶质、溶剂种类、溶液浓度等有关。heat of solution; heat effect of matter while dissolving, having to do with temperature, pressure, solvend, type of solvent, the density of it, etc.

【溶溶】róngróng〈书 *fml.*〉(水)宽广的样子(of water) broad:～的江水 broad and gentle river ◇月色～flood of moonlight

【溶蚀】róngshí 水流溶解并搬运岩石中的可溶物质,这种作用在石灰岩地区最为明显 corrosion; (of water flow) dissolving and moving dissolvable matter in rocks, a phenomenon common in a limestone topography

【溶血】róngxuè 红细胞破裂,红细胞内的血红蛋白逸出 haemolysis; breaking down of the erythrocytes with liberation of hemoglobin

【溶液】róngyè 两种或两种以上的不同物质以分子、原子或离子形式组成的均匀、稳定的混合物。有固态的,如合金;有液态的,如糖水;有气态的,如空气。通常指液态溶液。solution; homogeneous and stable mixture of two or more substances in the form of molecules, atoms or ions, which may be solids (such as alloys), liquids (such as sweet water), or gases (such as air); generally referring to liquid solution; also 溶体 róngtǐ

【溶胀】róngzhàng 高分子化合物吸收液体而体积膨大的现象，如明胶在水中、橡胶在苯中都会发生溶胀 swelling; swelling of a macromolecular compound absorbing a certain liquid, such as gelatin in water or rubber in benzene

【溶质】róngzhì 溶解在溶剂中的物质，如溶解在水里的食盐 solute; solvend; substance dissolved in a solvent, such as salt in water

瑢 róng ☞ [玱瑢](cōngróng) on p. 323

榕 róng ❶ 榕树，常绿乔木，树干分枝多，有气根，树冠大，叶子互生，椭圆形或卵形，花黄色或淡红色，果实倒卵形，黄色或赤褐色。生长在热带地方。木料可制器具，叶、气根、树皮可入药。banyan (*Ficus benghalensis*); evergreen tropical tree characterized by a ramificated trunk, branches that send out air-roots to the ground, alternate oval leaves, yellow or pale red flowers, and yellow or russet obovate fruit, its wood used for making furniture, its leaves, air-roots and bark used for their medical value ❷ (Róng) 福建福州的别称 another name for Fuzhou, capital of Fujian Province

熔 róng 熔化 melt; fuse; smelt: ～点 melting point | ～焊 welding | ～炉 smelting furnace; melting pot

【熔点】róngdiǎn 晶体物质开始熔化为液体时的温度。非晶体物质（如玻璃、石蜡、塑料等）没有熔点可言。melting, fusing and fusion point; temperature at which a crystalline matter becomes a liquid at standard atmospheric pressure. Non-crystalline matters, such as glass, paraffin, plastics, etc., do not have a melting point to speak of.

【熔断】róngduàn ❶ 加热使金属片或金属丝断开 fuse; break sheet metal or wire by heating ❷ 金属片或金属丝受热断开 fusing; break of sheet metal or wire under the impact of heat

【熔合】rónghé 两种或两种以上固态金属熔化后合为一体 (of two or more solid metals) melt into one

【熔化】rónghuà 固体加热到一定温度变为液体，如铁加热至1,530℃以上就熔化成铁水。大多数物质熔化后体积膨胀。melt; change a material from a solid to a liquid state by application of heat. For instance, iron melts at 1,530 degrees Celsius. Most materials swell when they have been melted. also 熔解 róngjiě and 熔融 róngróng

【熔剂】róngjì 熔炼、焊接或锻接时，为促进原料、矿石或金属的熔化而加进的物质，如石灰石、二氧化硅等 flux; substances, such as limestone and silicon dioxide, that are added to accelerate the melting of raw materials, ores or metals being melted, welded, forged

【熔解】róngjiě same as 熔化 rónghuà: ～热 heat of fusion

【熔解热】róngjiěrè 单位质量的晶体物质在熔点时，从固态变成液态所吸收的热量，叫做这种物质的熔解热 heat of fusion; per-unit amount of heat absorbed by a crystalline substance when turning from a solid to a liquid state at its melting point

【熔炼】róngliàn ❶ 熔化炼制 smelt: 把矿石跟焦炭一起放在高炉里～ charge a furnace with ore and coke for smelting ❷〈比喻 *fig.*〉锻炼 temper; steel: 战火～了战士们的钢铁意志。The war has tempered the soldiers' will-power.

【熔炉】rónglú ❶ 熔炼金属的炉子 smelting furnace ❷〈比喻 *fig.*〉锻炼思想品质的环境 crucible; circumstance for steeling one's mind and character: 革命的～ crucible of revolution

【熔融】róngróng same as 熔化 rónghuà

【熔岩】róngyán 从火山或地面的裂缝中喷出来或溢出来的高温岩浆，冷却后凝固成岩石 lava; molten rock that reaches the earth's surface through a volcano or fissure; rock formed by the cooling and solidifying of molten rock

【熔冶】róngyě 熔化冶炼 smelt

【熔铸】róngzhù 熔化并铸造 melt and cast: ～生铁 cast pig iron ◇对生活素材加以概括和提炼，进而～成为有血有肉的艺术形象。Materials garnered from everyday life are summarized and refined, and further worked on to bring forth vivid artistic images.

蝾(蠑) róng [蝾螈](róngyuán) 两栖动物，形状像蜥蜴，头扁，表皮粗糙，背面黑色，腹面红黄色，四肢短，尾侧扁。生活在水中，卵生。幼体形状像蝌蚪。吃小动物。salamander (*Cynops orientalis*); newt; lizard-like oviparous amphibian with flat head, rough skin, black back and reddish yellow belly, short limbs, and laterally flat tail, living in water and feeding on small animals, with tadpole-like larva

镕 róng same as 熔 róng

融 róng ❶ 融化 melt; thaw: 消～ thaw | 春雪易～。Spring snow thaws easily. ❷ 融合；调和 blend; in harmony: ～洽 harmonious | 水乳交～ as congenial as water and milk ❸ 流通 circulate: 金～ finance

【融合】rónghé 几种不同的事物合成一体 fuse; merge; mix together; connect: 文化～ cultural ferment; also 融和 rónghé

【融和】rónghé ❶ 和暖 warm; genial: 天气～ The weather is soothingly warm. ❷ 融洽；和谐 be harmonious with; get along: 感情～ sentimental congeniality | 气氛～ pleasant atmosphere ❸ same as 融合 rónghé

【融化】rónghuà (冰、雪等) 变成水 (of ice and

snow) thaw; melt; also 溶化 rónghuà

【融会】rónghuì same as 融合 rónghé：～贯通 know sth. from A to Z｜把人物形象的温柔和刚毅很好地～在一起。The tenderness of heart and the fortitude of will-power are perfectly blended in the image of the protagonist.

【融会贯通】róng huì guàn tōng 参合多方面的道理而得到全面的透彻的领悟 know sth. from A to Z through comprehensive research

【融解】róngjiě same as 融化 rónghuà：春天来了，山顶的积雪～了。Spring has set in, and the snow on the mountaintop is thawing.

【融洽】róngqià 彼此感情好，没有抵触 on good terms：关系～ congenial relations｜～无间 on intimate terms

【融融】róngróng〈书 *fml.*〉❶ 形容和睦快乐的样子 state of rapprochement：大家欢聚一堂，其乐～。An cordial atmosphere prevailed over the happy get-together. ❷ 形容暖和 warm：春光～。Spring fills the air with warmth.

【融通】róngtōng ❶ 使（资金）流通 circulate (capital)：～资金 collect and circulate funds ❷ 融会贯通 know sth. form A to Z through comprehensive research：～古今 thorough knowledge of the past and the present ❸ 使融洽；相互沟通 harmonize; communicate：～感情 communicate with one another to achieve congeniality in feelings

【融资】róng//zī 通过借贷、租赁、集资等方式而使资金得以融合并流通 finance; pool funds or capital for circulation through loans, leases, fund-raising, etc.

【融资】róngzī 通过借贷、租赁、集资等方式而得以融合并流通的资金 funds or capital for circulation, pooled through loans, leases, fund-raising, etc.

rǒng（ㄖㄨㄥˇ）

冗(宂) rǒng ❶ 多余的 superfluous; redundant：～员 surplus staff members; surplus workers｜～词赘句 wordiness and long-winded sentences; verbosity ❷ 烦琐 overelaborate and tedious：～杂 superfluous and complicated ❸ 繁忙的事 busy schedule：希拨～出席。Please find time from your busy schedule and honour us with your presence.

【冗笔】rǒngbǐ 指文章或图画中多余无用的笔墨 superfluity in writing or painting; unnecessary touches or strokes

【冗长】rǒngcháng（文章、讲话等）废话多，拉得很长(of writing or speech) tedious; lengthy; long-winded

【冗繁】rǒngfán same as 冗杂 rǒngzá：他整天被～的琐事拖住了腿。He has his hands full dealing with a miscellany of fussy, trivial matters all day long.

【冗务】rǒngwù 繁杂的事务 heavy workload; fussy affairs：～缠身 weighed down by tons of trivia

【冗员】rǒngyuán 指机关中超过工作需要的人员 redundant personnel in an organization：裁减～ cut down on surplus personnel

【冗杂】rǒngzá（事务）繁杂(of things to be tackled) miscellaneous

毹(氄、毻) rǒng（毛）细而软(feathers or hair) fine and soft：～毛 soft hair｜羽毛发～fine and soft feathers

【毹毛】rǒngmáo 细而软的毛 downy hair：刚孵出来的小鸡长着一身～。Newly hatched chicks are covered with downy feathers.

róu（ㄖㄡˊ）

柔 róu ❶ 软 soft; supple：～软 soft｜～韧 pliant｜～枝嫩叶 soft twigs and tender leaves ❷ 使变软 soften：～麻 soak jute, hemp, etc. to soften it ❸ 柔和（跟'刚'相对 as opposed to 'stern'）gentle：～情 tender feelings｜～顺 meek｜温～ gentle and tender｜娇～ tender and charming ❹（Róu）姓 a surname

【柔肠】róucháng 温柔的心肠 tender heart;〈比喻 *fig.*〉缠绵的情意 tender feelings：～寸断 lovelorn; heartbroken｜～百结 broken-hearted

【柔道】róudào 体育运动项目之一，近似摔跤。两人徒手赤足搏击，以摔倒对方或使对方背着地30秒为胜。jujitsu; judo; a sport akin to wrestling involving two opponents manoeuvring bare-handed and bare-footed, with the one who flattens the opponent or keeps his back on the ground for 30 seconds being the winner

【柔和】róuhé ❶ 温和而不强烈 soft; gentle; mild：声音～ mellifluous voice｜光线～ soft light ❷ 柔软；软和 soft; gentle：线条～soft line｜手感～feel velvety

【柔滑】róuhuá 柔软而光滑 soft and smooth：～如脂 as soft and smooth as cream｜丝绸手感～。Silks feels soft and smooth to the touch.

【柔美】róuměi 柔和而优美 gentle; mellifluous：音色～mellifluous tone colour｜～的舞姿 mellow dance

【柔媚】róumèi ❶ 柔和可爱 gentle and lovely：～的晚霞 soft glow of sunset｜舞姿轻盈～lithe dance movement ❷ 温柔和顺，讨人喜欢 tender and charming：～谦恭 charming and courteous

【柔嫩】róunèn 软而嫩 tender; delicate：～的幼苗 tender seedling

【柔情】róuqíng 温柔的感情 gentle-heartedness; tender feelings：～蜜意 tender affection｜～似水 tender and soft as water; deeply attached

【柔韧】róurèn 柔软而有韧性 soft and pliant：枝条～resilient twig｜～的皮革 tough and pliable leather｜他从小就练体操，身体～性很好。He's been practising gymnastics since a child and developed a remarkable resiliency in his body.

【柔软】róuruǎn 软和；不坚硬 soft：～体操 lithe gymnastics｜～的毛皮 downy fur

【柔润】róurùn 柔和润泽 soft and smooth：皮肤～delicate skin｜～的嗓音 mellifluous voice

【柔弱】róuruò same as 软弱 ruǎnruò：生性～weak natural disposition｜～的幼芽 fragile sprout

【柔顺】róushùn 温柔和顺 meek：性情～of meek disposition

【柔婉】róuwǎn ❶ 柔和而婉转 dulcet；tuneful：唱腔～sweet-toned singing｜～的语调 melodious tone ❷ same as 柔顺 róushùn：性格～mild temperament

【柔细】róuxì 柔和而细 soft and fine：声音～soft voice｜～的柳枝 delicate willow twig

揉 róu ❶ 用手来回擦或搓 rub；caress：～眼睛 rub one's eyes｜把纸都～碎了。The paper was crumbled in the hand. ❷ 团弄 knead；roll：～面 knead dough｜把泥～成小球 roll clay into tiny balls ❸〈书 *fml.*〉使东西弯曲 cause sth. to bend：～木为耒。bend a piece of wood into the handle of an ancient farm tool

【揉搓】róu·cuo ❶ same as 揉 róu ① ❷〈方 *dial.*〉same as 折磨 zhé·mó

【揉磨】róu·mo〈方 *dial.*〉same as 折磨 zhé·mó

辋 róu〈书 *fml.*〉❶ 车轮的外框 rim of a wheel ❷ same as 揉 róu ③

煣 róu〈书 *fml.*〉用火烤木材使弯曲 bend a piece of wood on fire

糅 róu 混杂 mix；mingle：杂～mingle｜～合 mix；blend

【糅合】róuhé 搀和；混合（多指不适宜合在一起的）mix；blend（things that are oft. incompatible to each other）

【糅杂】róuzá 不同的事物混杂在一起（of different things）mix；make a hotchpotch

蹂 róu〈书 *fml.*〉踩；践踏 trample：～踏 trample｜～躏 trample on

【蹂躏】róulìn 践踏 trample；〈比喻 *fig.*〉用暴力欺压、侮辱、侵害 oppress by force；ride roughshod over；violate：～人权 violate human rights

鰇 róu 古书上指枪乌贼 squid，as mentioned in ancient books

鞣 róu 用鞣料使兽皮变柔软，制成皮革 tan；convert hide into leather，as by treating with tannin：～皮子 tan leather｜这皮子～得不够熟。The hide isn't properly tanned.

【鞣料】róuliào 能使兽皮柔软的物质，如铬盐、栲胶、鱼油等 tanning material；tannin，such as chromic salts，tannin extract，fish oil，etc.

【鞣制】róuzhì 用鞣料加工兽皮，制成皮革 leather tanning；process of converting hide into leather：把～皮子的手艺传给徒弟 pass leather-tanning skills onto a disciple

ròu（ㄖㄡˋ）

肉 ròu ❶ 人或动物体内接近皮的部分的柔韧的物质。某些动物的肉可以吃。flesh；soft tissue of a human or animal body below the skin；flesh of certain animals being edible and known as meat ❷ 某些瓜果里可以吃的部分 pulp；flesh of fruit，melon：枣～jujube pulp｜桂圆～longan meat｜冬瓜～厚。The wax gourd is rich in pulp. ❸〈方 *dial.*〉不脆；不酥 spongy；squashy：～瓤儿西瓜 squashy watermelon ❹〈方 *dial.*〉性子慢，动作迟缓 slow-tempered；sluggish：～脾气 phlegmatic temperament｜那个人太～，一点儿利索劲儿也没有。The man is lethargic and can never get things done crisply.

【肉搏】ròubó 徒手或用短兵器搏斗 fight hand to hand or with short weapons：～战 bayonet fight｜战士们用刺刀跟敌人～。The soldiers fought the enemy troops at bayonet points.

【肉搏战】ròubózhàn same as 白刃战 báirènzhàn

【肉畜】ròuchù 专供食用的牲畜 fat stock；flesher；beef cattle；livestock raised for meat

【肉苁蓉】ròucōngróng 一年生草本植物，根呈块状，肉质，茎圆柱形，叶片鳞状，叶和茎黄褐色，花紫褐色。可入药。saline cistanche（*Cistanche salsa*）；annual medicinal herb having fleshy root tubers，tan-coloured cylindrical stem，scale-like leaves and purplish brown flowers

【肉感】ròugǎn 性感（多指女性 oft. of women）sex appeal；sexiness

【肉冠】ròuguān 鸟类头顶上长的肉质突起，形状略像冠，红色或略带紫色 comb；crown-like fleshy crest or ridge that grows on the head of birds，red or slightly purplish

【肉桂】ròuguì 常绿乔木，叶子长椭圆形，有三条叶脉，开白色小花。树皮叫桂皮，可入药或做香料，叶、枝和树皮磨碎后，可以蒸制桂油。Cinnamon tree（*Cinnamomum cassia*）；evergreen tree having long oval leaves each with three veins，and tiny white flowers，whose bark，known as cassia or cinnamon，is a drug and a spice，and whose leaves，branches and bark can be ground to extract oil；also 桂 guì

【肉红】ròuhóng 像肌肉那样的浅红色 pale red；flesh-coloured

【肉鸡】ròujī 肉用鸡 table hen；broiler

【肉瘤】ròuliú 骨头、淋巴组织、造血组织等部位发生的恶性肿瘤，如骨肉瘤 sarcoma; malignant tumour arising between bones or from lymph or haemopoietic tissues, such as osteoma (bone tumour)

【肉麻】ròumá 由轻佻的或虚伪的言语、举动所引起的不舒服的感觉 fulsome; disgusting; sickening; uncomfortable feeling at flirtatious or insincere language or behaviour

【肉糜】ròumí 〈方 *dial.*〉细碎的肉 minced meat

【肉牛】ròuniú same as 菜牛 càiniú

【肉排】ròupái 牛排或猪排 steak; beef or pork steak

【肉皮】ròupí 通常指猪肉的皮 pork skin

【肉皮儿】ròupír 〈方 *dial.*〉人的皮肤 human skin; complexion

【肉票】ròupiào (～儿 ròupiàor)指被盗匪掳去当人质的人，盗匪借以向他的家属勒索钱财 hostage (held for ransom); person held by a bandit as security to extort money or property: 撕～(指杀死人质) kill a hostage

R

【肉鳍】ròuqí 乌贼、枪乌贼等软体动物体上的鳍状物，用来帮助游泳 fleshy fin, fin-like outgrowth on cuttlefish, calamari and other mollusks for swimming

【肉禽】ròuqín 专供食用的家禽 fowl; poultry raised for food

【肉色】ròusè 像皮肤那样浅黄带红的颜色 flesh colour; incarnadine; light brownish pink: ～丝袜 incarnadine pantyhose

【肉身】ròushēn 〈佛教用语 *Budd.*〉指肉体 mortal body

【肉食】ròushí 以肉类为食物；吃荤 carnivorous: ～动物 carnivorous animal; carnivore

【肉食】ròu·shi 肉类食物 meat; meat dish: 随着生活水平的提高，人们的～消费也不断增长。People's meat consumption rises steadily with improvement in the standard of living.

【肉松】ròusōng 用牛、猪等的瘦肉加工制成的绒状或碎末状的食品，干而松散 dried meat floss; lean beef or pork processed in the form of floss or fine particles

【肉体】ròutǐ 人的身体(区别于'精神'as compared with 'spirit') human body; flesh: 备受精神和～的苦痛 have had one's fill of mental and physical trauma

【肉痛】ròutòng 〈方 *dial.*〉心疼；舍不得 be reluctant to lose sth. or depart from sb.; feel distressed at sth. lost or wasted

【肉头】ròutóu 〈方 *dial.*〉❶ 软弱无能 effeminate; sissy ❷ 傻 fatuous; daft: 他净办这种～事！It's just like him, always acting foolish like this! ❸ same as 吝啬 lìnsè

【肉头】ròu·tou 〈方 *dial.*〉丰满而柔软；软和 fleshy; plump; soft: 这孩子的手多～！How chubby the kid's hands are! | 这种米做出来的饭挺～。This kind of rice is rather plump when cooked.

【肉刑】ròuxíng 摧残人的肉体的刑罚 corporal punishment

【肉眼】ròuyǎn ❶ 人的眼睛(表明不靠光学仪器的帮助) naked eyes (in the absence of optical instrument): ～看不见细菌。Bacteria cannot be observed with naked eyes. ❷〈比喻 *fig.*〉平庸的眼光 layman's eyes; mediocre sense of judgement: 凡夫～ mortals of the mundane world

【肉用鸡】ròuyòngjī 主要供食用而饲养的鸡品种，如九斤黄 broiler; table hen, such as *jiujinhuang*, a Chinese chicken breed

【肉欲】ròuyù 性欲(含贬义 derog.) carnal desire; sexual desire

【肉质】ròuzhì 生物学上指松软肥厚像肉一样的物质 fleshy; biological term referring to sth. consisting of, or resembling flesh: 仙人掌有～茎。Cacti have fleshy stems.

【肉中刺】ròuzhōngcì 〈比喻 *fig.*〉最痛恨而急于除掉的东西(常跟'眼中钉'连用 oft. used together with 眼中钉 yǎnzhōngdīng) thorn in one's flesh; sth. one hates most and is impatient to get rid of

【肉赘】ròuzhuì same as 疣 yóu

rú (ㄖㄨˊ)

如[1] rú ❶ 适合；依照 in keeping with; in accordance with: ～意 to one's liking | ～愿 have one's wish fulfilled | ～期完成 fulfil sth. on schedule | ～数还清 pay in full ❷ 如同 like; as if: 爱厂～家 love one's factory like family | 十年～一日 be consistent for a decade in doing sth. | ～临大敌 as if faced with a formidable foe ❸ 及；比得上(只用于否定，比较得失或高下 used in the negative only when making a comparison) as good as; stand comparison with: 我不～他。I am not as good as he. | 百闻不～一见。Seeing is believing. | 与其那样，不～这样。It was better doing it this way than doing it that way. ❹ 表示超过 surpass; exceed: 光景一年强～一年。The prospects are getting better with each passing year. ❺ 表示举例 for example; such as: 唐朝有很多大诗人，～李白、杜甫、白居易等。There were many celebrated poets during the Tang Dynasty, such as Li Bai, Du Fu, and Bai Juyi, etc. ❻〈书 *fml.*〉到；往 go to: ～厕 go to the bathroom ❼ (Rú) 姓 a surname

如[2] rú 如果 if; in the event of: ～不及早准备，恐临时措手不及。We'll be caught unawares if we do not get ready in time.

如[3] rú 古汉语形容词后缀，表示状态[adjective suffix in classical Chinese indicating a certain state]: 空空～也。Nothing whatsoever has been left there. | 侃侃～也 keep talking like that

【如臂使指】rú bì shǐ zhǐ《汉书·贾谊传》:'如身之使臂,臂之使指' according to *History of Han·Biography of Jia Yi*, 'It is just like a human body using its arms, and like the arms using the fingers.'〈比喻 *fig.*〉指挥如意 be in perfect command of sth.

【如常】rúcháng 跟平常一样;照常 as usual:平静~as quiet as usual|起居~be up and about as usual

【如出一辙】rú chū yī zhé 形容两件事情非常相像 be exactly the same; be no different from each other; be cut from the same cloth

【如初】rúchū 跟当初一样 as always; as of old; as before:消除嫌隙,两人和好~。The two of them returned to good terms as usual after ironing out all the misunderstandings.

【如此】rúcǐ 这样 be true of; like this:~勇敢 as brave as this|理当~rightly so|事已~,后悔也是枉然。It's no use crying over spilled milk.

【如次】rúcì same as 如下 rúxià:其理由~。The reasons are as follows.

【如弟】rúdì〈旧时 *old*〉称结拜的弟弟 sworn younger brother

【如法炮制】rú fǎ páozhì 依照成法炮制药剂,泛指照现成的方法办事 act ditto; prepare herbal medicine by the prescribed method — follow a set pattern; follow suit

【如故】rúgù ❶ 跟原来一样 as before:依然~remain intact; remain the same ❷ 如同老朋友一样 like old friends:一见~become friends at first sight

【如果】rúguǒ〈连词 *conj.*〉表示假设 if; in case:你~有困难,我可以帮助你。I can render a hand if you have difficulties.

【如何】rúhé 怎么;怎么样 how:近况~? How's everything lately?|此事~办理? How to go about this?|不知~是好。Don't know what to do.

【如虎添翼】rú hǔ tiān yì〈比喻 *fig.*〉强大的得到援助后更加强大,也比喻凶恶的得到援助后更加凶恶 like a tiger that has grown wings — strong force being redoubled; evil force becoming more atrocious with extra help

【如花似锦】rú huā sì jǐn 形容风景、前程等十分美好 like flowers and brocade; beautiful (scenery); bright (future)

【如火如荼】rú huǒ rú tú 像火那样红,像荼(茅草的白花)那样白。原比喻军容之盛(见于《国语·吴语》),现用来形容旺盛,热烈或激烈。as red as fire and as white as the flower of couch grass; phrase originating from *Discourse on the State·Discourse on Wu* to describe the mightiness of an army, used figuratively to indicate sth. prosperous, vigorous, or intense

【如饥似渴】rú jī sì kě 形容要求非常迫切 as if thirsting or hungering for sth.; with great eagerness; also 如饥如渴 rú jī rú kě

【如胶似漆】rú jiāo sì qī 形容感情深厚,难舍难分 stick to each other like glue or lacquer; be deeply attached to each other

【如今】rújīn same as 现在 xiànzài:事到~,只好不了了之。As things stand now we have no choice but to leave it alone.|~再用老眼光看问题可不行了。It won't do to see things in old ways nowadays. 注意 **NOTE:**'现在'可以指较长的一段时间,也可以指极短的时间,'如今'只能指较长的一段时间。现在 xiànzài may refer to a period of time long or short, whereas 如今 denotes a long period of time.

【如来】Rúlái 释迦牟尼的十种称号之一。意思是从如实之道而来,开创并揭示真理的人。Tathagata, one of the 10 titles of Sakyamuni that means 'one who has come by the path of the ultimate truth'

【如雷贯耳】rú léi guàn ěr 形容人的名声很大(of sb.'s name); strike one's ears like thunder; leave a deep impression:久闻大名,~。Your exalted name has long resounded in my ears.

【如鸟兽散】rú niǎo shòu sàn 像受惊的鸟兽一样四处逃散(含贬义 derog.) run about like frightened birds and animals; flee helter-skelter; be in a rout

【如期】rúqī 按照期限 on schedule; on time:~完成 fulfil a task according to schedule|~抵达目的地 arrive on time

【如其】rúqí same as 如果 rúguǒ

【如日中天】rú rì zhōng tiān〈比喻 *fig.*〉事物正发展到十分兴盛的阶段(of an undertaking) reach the apogee; at the acme

【如若】rúruò same as 如果 rúguǒ

【如丧考妣】rú sàng kǎo bǐ 像死了父母一样的伤心和着急(含贬义 derog.) look grieved or distressed like one had been bereaved of one's parents

【如上】rúshàng 如同上面所叙述或列举的 as mentioned in the foregoing; as aforementioned:~所述 as stated above|特将经过详情报告~。The above is a detailed account of what happened.

【如实】rúshí 按照实际情况 factually; truthfully; veraciously:~汇报 make a truthful account

【如释重负】rú shì zhòng fù 像放下重担子一样,形容心情紧张后的轻松愉快 feel a sense of relief; (feel) as if relieved of a burden

【如数家珍】rú shǔ jiā zhēn 像数自己家里的珍宝一样,形容对列举的事物或叙述的故事十分熟悉 know sth. at one's fingertips; cite examples or relate a story with great familiarity

【如数】rúshù 按照原来的或规定的数目 in full of the original or designated number:~归还 repay sth. in full|~交纳税款 pay tax in full

【如汤沃雪】rú tāng wò xuě 像热水浇在雪上 like hot water being poured over snow; 〈比喻 *fig.*〉事情极容易解决 (of matters) easily done

【如同】rútóng 好像 same as; like; as: 灯火通明,~白昼 as brightly lit as daytime | 工厂绿化得~花园一般。So many trees and plants have been planted in the factory that it looks like a garden.

【如下】rúxià 如同下面所叙述或列举的 as follows: 列举~ (facts, items; proposals, etc.) are as follows | 现将应注意的事情说明~。The following is an explanation of the things to be remembered.

【如兄】rúxiōng 〈旧时 *old*〉称结拜的哥哥 sworn elder brother

【如许】rúxǔ 〈书 *fml.*〉❶ 如此;这样 such; in this way: 泉水清~。The spring water is so clear. | ~非凡的才智 such unusual ability and wisdom ❷ 这么些;那么些 so much; so many: 枉费~工力。Such much labour has been wasted.

【如一】rúyī 没有变化;完全一致 identical; consistent: 始终~ remain the same from beginning to the end | 表里~be what one professes to be; true to one's word

【如蚁附膻】rú yǐ fù shān 像蚂蚁附着在有膻味的东西上 like ants clinging to sth. rank; 〈比喻 *fig.*〉许多臭味相投的人追求某种恶劣的事物,也比喻依附有钱有势的人 many people of similar foul inclinations swarming after sth. abominable; lick the boots of the rich and powerful

【如意】rú//yì 符合心意 be satisfied; as one wishes: 称心~be perfectly satisfied | 事事不如他的意。Nothing seems to be going the way he wanted.

【如意】rúyì 一种象征吉祥的器物,用玉、竹、骨等制成,头呈灵芝形或云形,柄微曲,供赏玩 *ruyi*; S-shaped ornamental sceptre made of jade, bamboo or bone, with a head in the shape of a glossy ganoderma or cloud, and a slightly curved stem

【如意算盘】rúyì suàn·pán 〈比喻 *fig.*〉只从好的一方面着想的打算 wishful thinking; smug calculations

【如影随形】rú yǐng suí xíng 好像影子老是跟着身体一样 like the shadow following the person; 〈比喻 *fig.*〉两个人常在一起,十分亲密 two people closely associated with each other

【如鱼得水】rú yú dé shuǐ 〈比喻 *fig.*〉得到跟自己很投合的人或对自己很适合的环境 like a stranded fish put back into water — (of a person) come by sb. of one's taste or be in an environment appropriate to oneself

【如愿】rú//yuàn 符合愿望 see one's dream come true: ~以偿(愿望实现) have one's wish fulfilled | 这回可如了老人的愿。For the old man it was a dream come true.

【如字】rúzì 一种注音法。同一个字形因意义不同而有两个或两个以上读法的时候,按照习惯上最通常的读法叫读如字,例如'美好'的'好'读上声(区别于'喜好'的'好'读去声)。method of phonetic notation to pronounce a Chinese character having several pronunciations as it is commonly enunciated. For instance, 好 hǎo in 美好 měihǎo is pronounced in the rising tone to distinguish it from the 好 hào in 喜好 xǐhào which is pronounced in the falling tone. ☞ 破读 pòdú on p. 1494

【如坐针毡】rú zuò zhēn zhān 形容心神不宁 be on tenterhooks; on pins and needles

茹 rú ❶ 〈书 *fml.*〉吃 eat: ~素 be a vegetarian | 含辛~苦 put up with all sorts of hardships ❷ (Rú) 姓 a surname

【茹苦含辛】rú kǔ hán xīn ☞ 含辛茹苦 hán xīn rù kǔ on p. 762

【茹毛饮血】rú máo yǐn xuè 原始人不会用火,连毛带血地生吃禽兽,叫做茹毛饮血 eat animal flesh raw and drink its blood — life of primitive people before the discovery of fire

铷 rú 金属元素,符号 Rb (rubidium)。银白色,质软,化学性质极活泼,在光的作用下易放出电子,遇水发生爆炸。用于制光电池和真空管等。rubidium (Rb); silver-white, soft element of an extremely active chemical property that releases electrons under the impact of light and explodes in water, used as a material for the making of photocells and vacuum tubes

儒 rú ❶ 指儒家 Confucianism: ~术 Confucian doctrines | ~生 Confucian scholar ❷ 〈旧时 *old*〉指读书人 scholar: 腐~stale and pedantic scholar | ~医 scholar-doctor | 老~old scholar

【儒艮】rúgèn 哺乳动物,全身灰褐色,腹部色淡,无毛,头圆,眼小,无耳壳,吻部有刚毛,前肢作鳍形,后肢退化,母兽有一对乳头。生活在海洋中,食海草。dugong (*Dugong dugon*); dust-coloured and hairless herbivorous marine mammal with its belly in a lighter colour, having a round head with small eyes and bristles on its muzzle but no earlaps, flipper-like forelimbs, and degenerated hindlimbs, and feeding on seaweeds, the female having a pair of teats; 俗称 popularly known as 人鱼 rényú

【儒家】Rújiā 先秦时期的一个思想流派,以孔子为代表,主张礼治,强调传统的伦常关系等 Confucian School; Confucianism; Confucianists; pre-Qin school of thought represented by Confucius who advocated the rule of rites and traditional ethics

【儒将】rújiàng 有读书人风度的将帅 general with a scholarly manner

【儒教】Rújiào 指儒家。从南北朝开始叫做儒教,跟佛教、道教并称。Confucianism, which,

beginning from the Northern and Southern Dynasties was regarded as a religion comparable to Buddhism and Taoism ☞ 儒家 Rújiā

【儒略历】rúlüèlì 公历的前身。一年365天,分为十二个月。单月每月31天,双月每月30天,二月份例外,只有29天。四年一闰,闰年二月份有30天,全年366天。因公元前46年古罗马统帅儒略·恺撒(Julius Caesar)开始采用而得名。Julian calendar; predecessor of the Grogorian calendar; calendar established by the Roman Emperor Julius Caesar in 46 B.C. One year consisted of 365 days divided into 12 months, with 31 days in each odd month and 30 days in each even month, with the exception of February, which had only 29 days. Every fourth year was a leap ycar, in which February had 30 days, adding up the total days of the year to 366.

【儒生】rúshēng 原指遵从儒家学说的读书人,后来泛指读书人 orig. referring to Confucian scholar, now a general reference to scholar or intellectual

【儒术】rúshù 儒家的学术 Confucian teachings

【儒学】rúxué ❶ 儒家的学说 Confucianism ❷ 元明清时代各州、府、县设立的供生员读书的学校 government-run Confucian school at province, prefecture or county level during the Yuan, Ming and Qing dynasties

【儒雅】rúyǎ 〈书 *fml.*〉❶ 学问深湛 well-educated; erudite ❷ 气度温文尔雅 scholarly and refined:风流~elegant in manners

【儒医】rúyī 〈旧时 *old*〉指读书人出身的中医 scholar-doctor in traditional Chinese medicine

薷 rú ☞ 香薷 xiāngrú on p.2091

嚅 rú ☞ below

【嚅动】rúdòng 想要说话而嘴唇微动(of lips) open and close one's lips slightly in an attempt to speak:她~着嘴唇,想要说什么。Her lips parted, as if she had something to say.

【嚅嗫】rúniè 〈书 *fml.*〉same as 嗫嚅 nièrú

濡 rú 〈书 *fml.*〉❶ 沾湿;沾上 soak; moisten:~笔 dip a writing brush in ink|~湿 become wet|耳~目染 learn something by hearing and seeing it done over time; pick up something ❷ 停留;迟滞 delay; linger:~滞 delay|~迹 stop over

【濡染】rúrǎn 〈书 *fml.*〉❶ same as 沾染 zhānrǎn ❷ same as 浸润 jìnrùn

【濡湿】rúshī 沾湿;潮湿 get wet; soak

孺 rú 小孩子 child:妇~women and children|~子 child

【孺人】rúrén 〈古代 *arch.*〉称大夫的妻子,明清七品官的母亲或妻子封孺人。也通用为妇人的尊称。wife of a senior official; title for the mother or wife of a 7th-rank court official in the Ming and Qing dynasties; also generally used as an honorific term of address for women

【孺子】rúzǐ 〈书 *fml.*〉小孩子 child:黄口~mere child

【孺子可教】rúzǐ kě jiào 指年轻人有出息,可以把本事传授给他 promising young man who is worth teaching

【孺子牛】rúzǐniú 春秋时,齐景公与儿子嬉戏,景公叼着绳子当牛,让儿子牵着走(见于《左传》哀公六年)。后来用'孺子牛'比喻甘愿为人民大众服务的人 herd boy's willing ox, alluding to the story in *The Zuo Commentaries · Duke Ai 6th Year* that during the Spring and Autumn Period, Duke Jing of the state of Qi once played a children's game by letting his son lead him by the rope held in his mouth like an ox. The phrase was thus become a reference to a person with utter devotion to the people:横眉冷对千夫指,俯首甘为~。Fierce-browed, I coolly defy a thousand pointing fingers; head bowed, like a willing ox I serve the children.

襦 rú 〈书 *fml.*〉短衣;短袄 short jacket

颥 rú ☞ 颞颥 (nièrú) on p.1416

蠕(蝡) rú (旧读 formerly pronounced ruǎn)蠕动 wriggle; squirm:~形动物 worm

【蠕动】rúdòng 像蚯蚓爬行那样动 wriggle like a worm:小肠是经常在~着的。The small intestine wriggles from time to time.

【蠕蠕】rúrú 形容慢慢移动的样子 wriggling; squirming:~而动 wriggle along

【蠕形动物】rúxíng dòngwù 无脊椎动物的一大类,构造比腔肠动物复杂,身体长形,左右对称,质柔软,没有骨骼,没有脚,如绦虫、蛔虫等 worm (*Vermes*); a category of feetless invertebrates, such as cestode and bellyworm, having a soft and symmetrical elongated body, and more complicated in structure than coelenterates

rǔ (ㄖㄨˇ)

汝 rǔ ❶ 〈书 *fml.*〉你 you:~曹 you people|~辈 you (plural) ❷ (Rǔ) 姓 a surname

乳 rǔ ❶ 生殖 breed; give birth to:孳~(of animals, etc.) reproduction ❷ 乳房 breast; mamma:~罩 bra|~腺 mammary gland ❸ 奶汁 milk:母~mother's milk|~牛 milch cow; dairy cattle|代~粉 ersatz milk powder|水~交融 get along with each other like water and milk ❹ 像奶汁的东西 milk-like substance:豆~ soya bean milk|~胶 emulsion; latex paint ❺ 初生的;幼小的 newborn:~燕 young swallow|~猪 suckling pig|

～牙 deciduous tooth

【乳白】rǔbái 像奶汁那样的颜色 milky white; cream-coloured:～的烟云 cottony mist and clouds

【乳钵】rǔbō 研药末等的器具,形状略像碗 mortar; bowl-like vessel in which substances are crushed or ground with a pestle

【乳齿】rǔchǐ same as 乳牙 rǔyá

【乳畜】rǔchù 专门养来产奶的家畜,如乳牛、乳用山羊等 dairy livestock, such as milch cow, goat, etc.

【乳儿】rǔ'ér 以乳汁为主要食物的小儿,通常指一周岁以下的婴儿 nursing infant; suckling; child less than one year old

【乳房】rǔfáng 人和哺乳动物乳腺集合的部分。发育成熟的女子和雌性哺乳动物的乳房比较膨大。breast, either of two mammary glands on the chest of a human being; udder, bag-like organ containing the mammary glands in an mammal. The breasts of a grown-up woman and the udders of female animals are relatively large in size.

R

【乳腐】rǔfǔ〈方 *dial.*〉same as 豆腐乳 dòu·furǔ

【乳化】rǔhuà 为使原来互不相混的两种液体混合起来,把其中一种液体变成微小颗粒分散在另一液体中,叫做乳化。如把肥皂水和油充分搅动,使油变成微小颗粒悬浮在肥皂水中。emulsify; make into an emulsion; put two liquids that not mix together and stir until small globules of one liquid suspend in the other, such as stirring a mixture of soapsuds and oil so that the latter suspends in the former in numerous tiny globules

【乳黄】rǔhuáng 像奶油那样的淡黄色 pale yellow; creamy:～的围墙 creamy wall

【乳剂】rǔjì 经过乳化的溶液。通常是水和油的混合液,有两种类型,一种是水分散在油中,一种是油分散在水中。emulsion; usu. emulation of oil in water, or water in oil

【乳胶】rǔjiāo 粘木板等用的一种胶,成分是聚醋酸乙烯树脂,乳白色液体,直接使用或加少量水调制,胶合强度较高 emulsion; latex; polyvinyl acetate emulsion, in milky-white liquid form, used with or without water as a high-intensity adhesive to glue wooden boards, etc.

【乳酪】rǔlào 酪 cheese

【乳糜】rǔmí 肠系膜淋巴管内的液体跟胰液、胆汁、肠液等混合而失去酸性所成的乳状液体。乳糜被吸收到血液中,是体内各种组织的营养物质。chyle; milky fluid from mesenteric gland that has lost its acidity after being mixed with pancreatic juice, bile, intestinal juice, etc. and is absorbed in blood as a nutrition for various organs

【乳名】rǔmíng 小名;奶名 infant name; pet name

【乳母】rǔmǔ same as 奶妈 nǎimā

【乳牛】rǔniú 专门养来产奶的牛,产奶量比一般的母牛高 milch cow; dairy cattle, which produces more milk than an ordinary cow; also 奶牛 nǎiniú

【乳头】rǔtóu ❶ 乳房上圆球形的突起,尖端有小孔,乳汁从小孔流出。nipple; teat; small projection near the centre of the mammary gland containing the outlets of the milk ducts through which young mammals obtain milk from the adult female; also 奶头 nǎitóu ❷ 像乳头的东西 nipple-like object:真皮～leather nipple|视神经～optic papilla

【乳腺】rǔxiàn 人或哺乳动物乳房内的腺体。发育成熟的女子和雌性哺乳动物的乳腺发达,能分泌乳汁。mammary gland; gland inside the breasts of a human being or animal, with those of a woman and female animal more developed and capable of secreting milk

【乳臭】rǔxiù 奶腥气(对年幼人表示轻蔑)(derogative term for a young person) smelling of milk — childish:～未干 wet behind the ears|～小儿 mere suckling; greenhorn

【乳牙】rǔyá 人和哺乳动物出生后不久长出来的牙齿。婴儿乳牙在出生后六七个月开始长出门齿,到两岁半长全,共二十个,六至八岁时乳牙开始脱落,换成恒牙。deciduous tooth; milk tooth; any of the temporary first teeth of a young child or mammal. An infant begins to grow fore-teeth six or seven months after birth, which are completed in number (20) at two and a half years of age, and which begin to fall off and be replaced by constant teeth from six to eight. also 乳齿 rǔchǐ or 奶牙 nǎiyá

【乳油】rǔyóu ❶ 指从乳汁中分离出来的脂肪含量较高的部分,是食品工业的重要原料 cream; fatty component of milk, used as a major raw material in foodstuff processing industry ❷ same as 乳剂 rǔjì

【乳罩】rǔzhào 妇女保护乳房使不下垂的用品 brassière; bra; woman's undergarment worn to protect and give contour to the breasts

【乳汁】rǔzhī 由乳腺分泌出来的白色液体,含有水、蛋白质、乳糖、盐类等营养物质 milk; whitish liquid containing water, proteins, lactose, salt, and other nutritions that is produced by the mammary glands of all mature female mammals;通称 generally known as 奶 nǎi

【乳脂】rǔzhī 从动物乳汁中提取的脂肪,有牛乳脂(黄油)、羊乳脂等,可供食用或制糕点、糖果 butterfat; substance drawn from milk, including cattle butter and goat butter, used as food or for the making of pastry and confection

【乳浊液】rǔzhuóyè 一种液体的小滴分散在另一种液体中形成的混合物。乳浊液是浑浊的,静置相当时间后,它的组成部分会按比重不同分为上下两层,如牛奶。emulsion; mixture of two liquids that do not mix, with one suspending in the other in tiny droplets. Such a mixture looks turbid and will become separated in two layers according to specific gravity after being left undisturbed for a period of time, such as milk; also 乳状液 rǔzhuàngyè

辱 rǔ ❶ 耻辱(跟'荣'相对 as opposed to 'honour') disgrace; dishonour: 羞～insult | 屈～humiliation | 奇耻大～galling shame and humiliation ❷ 使受耻辱;侮辱 insult; humiliate: 折～humiliate | ～骂 hurl insults on | 丧权～国 humiliate the nation and forfeit its sovereignty; surrender a country's sovereign rights under humiliating terms ❸ 玷辱 bring disgrace to: ～没 sully; tarnish | ～命 fail a mission ❹〈书 *fml.*〉〈谦辞 *hum.*〉表示承蒙 feel honoured; be grateful: ～临 feel honoured by sb.'s presence at a function | ～承指教。Thank you for your advice.

【辱骂】rǔmà 污辱谩骂 call sb. names; hurl insults

【辱命】rǔmìng〈书 *fml.*〉没有完成上级的命令或朋友的嘱咐 fail to carry out an order by one's superior or a request by one's friend: 幸不～。(I) trust you will accomplish your mission.

【辱没】rǔmò 玷污;使不光彩 bring disgrace to; be unworthy of: 我们一定完成任务,决不～先进集体的光荣称号。We are determined to fulfil the task and never bring disgrace to our honourary title as an advanced collective.

鄏 rǔ 郏鄏(Jiárǔ),古山名,在今河南洛阳西北 Jiaru, ancient name of a mountain to the northwest of Luoyang, Henan Province

擩 rǔ〈方 *dial.*〉插;塞 put in; fill in; tuck: 一只脚～到泥里了。One foot happened to step in the mud. | 那本小说不知～到哪里了。The novel was tucked into who knows where.

rù (ㄖㄨˋ)

入 rù ❶ 进来或进去(跟'出'相对 as opposed to 'go out') come into; enter: 投～input | ～冬 winter has set in | 由浅～深 from the easy to the difficult | 纳～正轨 set sth. on the right track ❷ 参加到某种组织中,成为它的成员 enrol; become member of an organization: ～学 enrol in a school | ～团 be admitted into the Communist Youth League | ～伍 be conscripted ❸ 收入 income: 岁～state revenue in a fiscal year | ～不敷出 spend more than one earns | 量～为出 live within one's means ❹ 合乎 agree with; conform to: ～时 stylish | ～情～理 fair and just ❺ 入声 entering tone: 平上去～ high and level entering tone

【入不敷出】rù bù fū chū 收入不够开支 having difficulty making end meet; falling short of expenditure

【入超】rùchāo 在一定时期(一般为一年)内,对外贸易中进口货物的总值超过出口货物的总值(跟'出超'相对 as opposed to 'favourable balance of trade') unfavourable balance of trade within a period of time (usu. a year); import surplus

【入定】rùdìng 佛教徒的一种修行方法,闭着眼睛静坐,控制身心各种活动(of Buddhists) sit in meditation as a form of mental cultivation

【入耳】rù'ěr 中听 pleasant to the ear: 不堪～offensive to the ear | 这句话十分～。The remark was rather pleasant to the ear.

【入伏】rù//fú 进入伏天;伏天开始 beginning of the hottest days of the year.

【入港】rùgǎng (交谈)投机(多见于早期白话 oft. in early vernacular) (talk or chat) in full agreement: 二人说得～。The two of them were immersed in a congenial conversation.

【入彀】rùgòu〈书 *fml.*〉❶ 唐太宗在端门看见新进士鱼贯而出,高兴地说,'天下英雄入吾彀中矣'(见于《唐摭言·述进士》)'彀'是使劲张弓,'彀中'指箭能射及的范围。后来用'入彀'比喻受人牢笼,由他操纵。range of an arrow shot; (fig.) under one's thumb. According to *Collected Phrases of Tang · Accounts of Metropolitan Graduates*, on seeing successful candidates in the highest imperial examinations coming out of the Gate of Correct Demeanor one after another, Emperor Taizong of the Tang Dynasty said in delight, 'All the heroes under heaven are now under my thumb.' ❷〈比喻 *fig.*〉合乎一般程式或要求 conform to general formalities and requirements ❸ 投合;入神 absorbed: 听得～be absorbed in what one's hearing | 两人谈得～。The two of them were absorbed in a congenial conversation.

【入股】rù//gǔ 加入股份 become a shareholder: 踊跃～vying with one another to buy a share

【入骨】rùgǔ 形容达到极点 to the marrow: 恨之～hate sb. or sth. to the marrow

【入国问禁】rù guó wèn jìn 进入别的国家,先问清他们的禁令 entering a country, enquire about its prohibitions; ☞入境问俗 rù jìng wèn sú

【入画】rùhuà 画入画图,多用来形容景物优美 suitable for a painting; picturesque: 桂林山水,处处可以～。Every bit of the landscape of Guilin is worthy of a painter's brush.

【入伙】[1] rù//huǒ 加入某个集体或集团 join a gang; join in partnership

【入伙】[2] rù//huǒ 加入集体伙食 have one's meals at a cafeteria

【入寂】rùjì〈佛教用语 *Budd.*〉称僧尼死亡(of monks or nuns) pass away; die; nirvana

【入境】rù//jìng 进入国境 enter a country: ～签

证 entry visa | 办理～手续 go through entry formalities

【入境问俗】rù jìng wèn sú《礼记·曲礼》:'入竟(境)而问禁,入国而问俗。'进入别国的境界,先问清他们的禁令;进入别国的都城,先问清他们的风俗。现在说成'入国问禁'和'入境问俗'。*The Book of Rites · Rites of Discretion*: On crossing the boarder into another country, make sure to enquire about the local taboos; when entering its capital, make sure to ask about the local customs and habits. Put separately as 入国问禁 rù guó wèn jìn and 入境问俗 in contemporary use.

【入口】rù//kǒu ❶ 进入嘴中 enter the mouth ❷ 外国的货物运进来,有时也指外地的货物运进本地区 import; (of goods from a foreign country or somewhere else) transported into

【入口】rùkǒu 进入建筑物或场地所经过的门或口儿 entrance to a building or site: ～处 entrance | 车站～entrance to a railway or bus station

R

【入寇】rùkòu 〈书 *fml.*〉 same as 入侵 rùqīn: ～边关 invade a frontier pass

【入殓】rù//liàn 把死者放进棺材里 put a corpse in a coffin; encoffin

【入列】rùliè 出列的或迟到的人进入队伍行列 (of sb. who is late or who has come out of the line) take one's place in a line; line up; fall in

【入流】rùliú ❶ 封建王朝把官员分成九品(九个等级),九品以外的官员进入九品内叫入流(of feudal government hierarchy) make the high officialdom; enter into one of nine ranks of officialdom ❷ 泛指进入某个等级 be qualified: 他演技拙劣,是个不～的演员。Judging from his lamentable performance he is not a qualified actor.

【入垄】rùlǒng 〈方 *dial.*〉(交谈)投机(of conversation) congenial; agreeable

【入梅】rù//méi 进入黄梅季 rainy season begins; ☞ 黄梅季 huángméijì on p. 853

【入寐】rùmèi 入睡 fall asleep: 思绪万千,辗转不能～。It was all so mixed up in her mind that he tossed and turned in bed.

【入门】rù//mén (～儿 rù//ménr)得到门径;初步学会 learn the basics of sth.: ～既不难,深造也是办得到的。Rudimentary knowledge is easy to obtain, and complete mastery of it is manageable as well.

【入门】rùmén 指初级读物(多用做书名 oft. used as part of a book title) ABC; learner's; beginner's; primer:《摄影～》*A Learner's Book on Photography* |《国际象棋～》*An Introduction to Chess*

【入梦】rùmèng 进入梦境,指睡着(zháo),有时也指别人出现在自己的梦中 fall asleep; (of a person) appear in one's dream

【入迷】rù//mí 喜欢某种事物到了沉迷的程度 be enamoured; be enraptured: 老爷爷讲故事,孩子们听得入了迷。The children listened to grandpa's story with rapt attention.

【入眠】rùmián ❶ 入睡 fall asleep: 由于过度兴奋,久久不能～。He was so excited that sleep eluded him. ❷ 蚕在每次蜕皮的时候不动不吃叫入眠(of an exuviating silkworm) neither eat nor move

【入魔】rù//mó 迷恋某种事物到了失去理智的地步 be hypnotized; be infatuated with sth.

【入木三分】rù mù sān fēn 相传晋代书法家王羲之在木板上写字,刻字的人发现墨汁透入木板有三分深(见于唐代张怀瓘《书断》)。后用来形容书法有力,也用来比喻议论深刻。According to *Appraisal of Calligraphy* by Zhang Huaiguan of the Tang Dynasty, when an engraver was working on a piece of calligraphy written by the celebrated Jin-dynasty calligrapher Wang Xizhi on a piece of wood, he found that the strokes were so forceful that the ink had penetrated the wood board by 3 *fen*. Hence the phrase, 'penetrating the board by three *fen*', referring to forceful handwriting, or the profundity of a viewpoint or an observation.

【入侵】rùqīn (敌军)侵入国境 invade; intrude: 全歼～之敌 annihilate the invaders lock, stock and barrel

【入情入理】rù qíng rù lǐ 合乎情理 fair and reasonable: 他说得～,大家听得心服口服。Everybody was sincerely convinced by his fair and reasonable explanations.

【入神】rù//shén ❶ 对眼前的事物发生浓厚的兴趣而注意力高度集中 with rapt attention (to what is happening or going on): 他越说越起劲,大家越听越～。As he talked with more and more gusto, we came more and more under his spell. ❷ 达到精妙的境地 enthralling; enchanting: 这幅画画得很～。The painting is enthralling in its presentation.

【入声】rùshēng 古汉语四声之一。普通话没有入声,古入声字分别读成阴平(如'屋、出')、阳平(如'国、直')、上声(如'铁、北')、去声(如'客、绿')。有些方言有入声,入声字一般比较短促,有时还带辅音韵尾。entering tone, one of the four tones in classical Chinese pronunciation extinct in standard Chinese but retained in some local dialects. The entering tone is brief and sometimes carries a terminal nasal consonant, and falls into four tones — the high and level tone (as in 屋 wū and 出 chū), the rising tone that is equivalent to that in modern standard Chinese (as in 国 guó and 直 zhí), the falling-rising tone (as in 铁 tiě and 北 běi), and the falling tone (as in 客 kè and 绿 lǜ).

【入时】rùshí 合乎时尚(多指装束 oft. dressing) hip; trendy; stylish: 打扮～fashionably attired|穿着～look modish in one's attire

【入世】rùshì 投身到社会里 become a member of society:～不深 be inexperienced in society

【入手】rùshǒu 着手;开始做 start with; proceed from:从调查研究～start with investigation and study|音乐教育应当从儿童时代～。Education in music should begin with the children.

【入睡】rùshuì 睡着(zháo)fall asleep

【入土】rù//tǔ 埋到坟墓里 be entombed:～为安 bury the remains and bring peace to the deceased|老人说自己是个半截儿～的人了。The old man said that he was having one foot in the grave already.

【入托】rùtuō (小孩儿)送入托儿所 (of small children) start going to a nursery

【入微】rùwēi 达到十分细致或深刻的地步 in minute detail; in every possible way:体贴～take care of sb. the best one could|演员的表情细腻～。The actor performed through the nuance of his facial expressions.

【入闱】rùwéi 科举时代应考的或监考的人进入考场(of examinees or invigilators before an imperial exam) enter the examination hall

【入味】rùwèi (～儿 rùwèir) ❶ 有滋味 delectable; toothsome; yummy:菜做得很～。The dish is pleasing to the palate. ❷ 有趣味 interesting:这出戏我们越看越～。As we watched the drama we became increasingly enraptured by it.

【入伍】rùwǔ 参加部队 enlist in the armed forces; join up:应征～be conscripted

【入席】rù//xí 举行宴会或仪式时各就位次(at a banquet, ceremony, etc.) take one's seat:来宾～。Time for the distinguished guests to be seated.|依次～be seated one after another

【入乡随乡】rù xiāng suí xiāng ☞ 随乡入乡 suí xiāng rù xiāng on p.1838

【入绪】rùxù 有了头绪 take shape:这项工作刚刚～。The project has just taken shape.

【入选】rùxuǎn same as 中选 zhòng//xuǎn

【入学】rù//xué ❶ 开始进某个学校学习 enrol in a school:～考试 entrance exam|明天检查体格,后天就～。Physical checkup is scheduled for tomorrow, and school begins the day after tomorrow. ❷ 开始进小学学习(of a child) start school:～年龄 school age

【入眼】rùyǎn 中看 pleasing to the eye:看得～pleasing to the eye|看不～not to one's liking|其他裙子都不怎么样,只有这条还～。None of the skirts look good — only this one is somewhat pleasing to the eye.

【入药】rùyào 用做药物 be used as medicine:龟甲中医～。Tortoise shell is used for medication in traditional Chinese medicine.

【入夜】rùyè 到了晚上 as night falls; at nightfall:～时分 at nightfall|～灯火通明。The place is ablaze with light when night falls.

【入院】rù//yuàn (需要住在医院里治疗的人)进入医院 (of a patient who needs to stay in a hospieal for treatment) be hospitalized:办理～手续 go through the formalities for admittance to a hospital

【入账】rù//zhàng 记入账簿中 enter into an account book:货款已经～。The money for buying goods has been entered into the account book.|昨天送来的礼物尚未～。The gifts received yesterday are yet to be entered into the account book.

【入主出奴】rù zhǔ chū nú 韩愈《原道》:'入于彼,必出于此;入者主之,出者奴之;入者附之,出者污之。'意思是说崇信了一种说法,就必然会排斥另一种说法;把前者奉做主人,把后者当做奴仆;附和前者,污蔑后者。后来用'入主出奴'比喻在学术上持门户之见。*On the Origin of the Way* by Han Yu: Once one has adopted one idea he is bound to reject another one, regard the former as the master and the latter as the slave, and chime in with the former and sling mud at the latter. Hence the Chinese phrase, 'espouse one idea to the expulsion of another', which refers to academic sectarianism.

【入赘】rùzhuì 男子到女家结婚并成为女家的家庭成员(of a man) marry into the bride's family

【入坐】rù//zuò same as 入座 rù//zuò

【入座】rù//zuò 就位 be seated; take one's seat:宾主～。Both the host and his guests have taken their seats.|对号～take one's seat according to the number on the ticket. also 入坐 rù//zuò

洳 rù ☞ [沮洳](jùrù) on p.1051

蓐 rù 〈书 *fml.*〉草席;草垫子(多指产妇的床铺 oft. bed of a woman in maternity) straw mat; straw mattress:坐～(坐月子) confinement in childbirth

溽 rù 〈书 *fml.*〉湿润 damp; humid:～热 damp and close; suffocatingly hot|～暑 sweltering summer

【溽热】rùrè 潮湿而闷热 muggy; sweltering

【溽暑】rùshǔ 夏天潮湿而闷热的气候 hot and humid summer

缛 rù 〈书 *fml.*〉繁琐;繁重 cumbrous; onerous:～礼 elaborate rules of etiquette|繁文～节 cumbersome formalities; red tape

褥 rù 褥子 bedding:被～ quilt and bedding|～单 bedcover

【褥疮】rùchuāng 由于局部组织长期受压迫,血液循环发生障碍而引起的皮肤和肌肉等组织的坏死和溃烂。长期卧床不能自己移动的病人,骶部和髋部都容易发生褥疮。decubitus ulcer; bedsore; pressure-induced ulceration of the skin and putrescence of muscle and other tissues, caused by obstructed blood circulation and occurring mostly in the sacrum and hips of a patient confined to bed for a long time

【褥单】rùdān（～儿 rùdānr）蒙在褥子上的布 bed sheet; also 褥单子 rùdān·zi

【褥套】rùtào ❶ 出门时装被褥等的布套，反面中间开口，两头各有一个兜儿，步行时搭在肩上，骑牲口时搭在牲口背上 bed tick; bedding sack (having a slit in the centre of the undercover and a pocket on either end, to be carried over the shoulder or the back of pack animal) ❷ 做褥子用的棉花胎 cotton wadding of a bed tick

【褥子】rù·zi 睡觉时垫在身体下面的东西，用棉花做成，也有用兽皮等制成的 mattress; pad of heavy cloth or leather filled with soft material and used as or on a bed

ruá（ㄖㄨㄚˊ）

挼 ruá〈方 *dial.*〉❶（纸、布等）皱（of paper, cloth, etc.）wrinkle; crease：这张纸～了。This sheet of paper is crumpled. ❷（布）快要磨破（of cloth）be threadbare; wear thin：衬衫穿～了。The shirt has become threadbare.

☞ ruó on p. 1645

ruán（ㄖㄨㄢˊ）

堧（壖）ruán〈书 *fml.*〉城郭旁、宫殿庙宇外或河边的空地 open space outside a city wall, palace, temple, etc.; open riverbank

ruǎn（ㄖㄨㄢˇ）

阮 ruǎn ❶阮咸（乐器）的简称 abbr. for 阮咸（乐器）ruǎnxián（plucked musical instrument）：大～ large *ruanxian* | 中～ medium-size *ruanxian* ❷（Ruǎn）姓 a surname

【阮咸】ruǎnxián 弦乐器，形状略像月琴，柄长而直，有四根弦，现在也有三根弦的。相传因西晋阮咸善弹这种乐器而得名。*ruanxian*, a four- or three-stringed plucked musical instrument named after Ruan Xian, a musician of the Western Jin Dynasty, looking roughly like the *yueqin*；简称 abbr. 阮 ruǎn

软（輭）ruǎn ❶ 物体内部的组织疏松，受外力作用后，容易改变形状（跟'硬'相对 as opposed to 'hard'）（of an object or material）soft; loose-textured and easy to change shape under an outside force：柔～soft |～木 softwood| 柳条很～。Willow twigs are rather pliant. ❷ 柔和 gentle：～风 gentle breeze|～语 soft voice| 话说得很～speak in a soft voice ❸ 软弱 weak：两腿发～。The two legs threatened to buckle. |欺～怕硬 bully the weak and fear the strong ❹ 能力弱；质量差 poor in ability, quality, etc.：功夫～ half-baked skill|货色～shabby goods ❺ 容易被感动或动摇 soft-hearted; easy to change one's mind：心～tender-hearted|耳朵～credulous ❻（Ruǎn）姓 a surname

【软包装】ruǎnbāozhuāng ❶ 用塑料袋、铝箔等质地较软的包装材料密封包装 soft package; package using plastic bag, aluminium foil or other soft materials：～饮料 soft-packaged drink|～烧鸡 soft-packaged baked chicken ❷ 指用来密封包装商品的质地较软的材料，如塑料袋、铝箔袋等 soft packaging material, including plastic bags and aluminium foil

【软磁盘】ruǎncípán 以聚脂塑料膜片为基底的磁盘。不固定在电子计算机内，存取方便。floppy disc; plastic disc coated with magnetic material and covered by a protective jacket, easy to fit in and be taken out of a computer; 简称 abbr. 软盘 ruǎnpán

【软刀子】ruǎndāo·zi〈比喻 *fig.*〉使人在不知不觉中受到折磨或腐蚀的手段 soft knife; imperceptibly ways or means of harming people：～杀人 harm people with a soft knife

【软缎】ruǎnduàn 一种丝织品，质地柔软，光泽很强，多用来做刺绣用料和装饰品等 silk fabric in satin weave, soft and shiny and oft. used as embroidery material

【软腭】ruǎn'è 腭的后部，是由结缔组织和肌肉构成的 soft palate; movable fold consisting of connective tissues and muscle and suspended from the rear of the hard palate;（图见 ☞ figure for 人的喉 rén·dehóu on p. 808）

【软耳朵】ruǎn'ěr·duo 指没有主见容易听信别人的话的人 soft ear; credulous person

【软风】ruǎnfēng ❶ 微风；和风 gentle breeze：～拂面。A gentle breeze caressed people's faces. ❷ 气象学上指 1 级风（meteor.）light air; wind with a speed of from 2 to 5 kilometres per hour, according to the Beaufort scale; ☞风级 fēngjí on p. 579

【软膏】ruǎngāo 用油脂或凡士林等和药物混合制成的半固体的外用药物，如硫碘软膏、青霉素软膏等 salve; ointment; viscous or semisolid substance made by mixing grease or vaseline with certain medicament for external medication, such as sulphide-iodide or penicillin ointment

【软骨】ruǎngǔ 人或脊椎动物体内的一种结缔组织。在胚胎时期，人的大部分骨骼是由软骨组成的。成年人的身体上只有个别的部分还存在着软骨。cartilage; tough, elastic, fibrous connective tissue found in various parts of a human or vertebrate body. The bones of a human fetus consist mostly of cartilages, which is converted largely to bones with maturation, so that few cartilages remain in an adult person's body.

【软骨头】ruǎngǔ·tou〈比喻 *fig.*〉没有气节的人

spineless person; weak-kneed person

【软骨鱼】ruǎngǔyú 鱼的一类,骨骼全由软骨构成,鳞片多为粒状,或全体无鳞。多生活在海洋中。鲨鱼、鳐等都属于软骨鱼类。cartilaginous fish; marine fish such as shark and skate, whose skeleton consists entirely of cartilage and whose body is scaleless or covered with granular scales

【软化】ruǎnhuà ❶ 由硬变软 intenerate; soften: 骨质～症 malacopathia ❷ 由坚定变成动摇;由倔强变成顺从 change from steadfast to wavering; from being stiff to being compliant: 态度逐渐～softening attitude ❸ 使软化 soften:～血管 soften the blood vessels

【软化栽培】ruǎnhuà zāipéi 蔬菜栽培的一种方法,使蔬菜茎叶在不见阳光的条件下生长。这样栽培的蔬菜呈浅黄色,细嫩,纤维少,如韭黄、蒜黄等。blanching culture; method of cultivating a vegetable without exposing it to sunshine so that it acquires a pale yellow colour and becomes tender and less fibrous, such as chives and blanched garlic leaves

【软话】ruǎnhuà 温和的话,多指表示歉意、告饶或抚慰的话 soft words; words or remarks designed to apologize, plead or comfort: 你就说几句～让老太太消消气吧。Say something nice to the old lady please to calm her anger.

【软和】ruǎn·huo 柔软;柔和 soft; fluffy:～的羊毛 fluffy wool|～话儿 soothing words|木棉枕头很～。Pillows padded with kapok feels soft.

【软件】ruǎnjiàn ❶ 计算机系统的组成部分,是指挥计算机进行计算、判断、处理信息的程序系统或设备。包括汇编程序、操作系统、编译程序、诊断程序、控制程序、数据管理系统等。computer software; software; programme or device for such procedures as compilation, operation, word-processing, diagnosis, control, data management, etc., that directs a computer in making calculations or judgements or data processing ❷ 借指生产、科研、经营等过程中的人员素质、管理水平、服务质量等 software, referring to personnel credentials, managerial level, service quality in production, scientific research, business operation, etc.

【软禁】ruǎnjìn 不关进牢狱但是不许自由行动 house arrest; confinement to one's quarters, rather than prison, by judicial order

【软绵绵】ruǎnmiānmiān (～的 ruǎnmiānmiān·de) ❶ 形容柔软 soft: 鞋底～的,穿着特别舒服。With such soft soles, the shoes are very comfortable to wear. ❷ 形容软弱无力 feeble; enfeebled: 病虽好了,身子还是～的。I'm well now but still feel weak.

【软磨】ruǎnmó 用和缓的手段纠缠 coax; cajole: ～硬抗 alternate cajole with coercion

【软木】ruǎnmù ☞ 栓皮 shuānpí on p. 1794

【软盘】ruǎnpán 软磁盘的简称 abbr. for 软磁盘 ruǎncípán

【软片】ruǎnpiàn 胶片(对'硬片'而言 as opposed to 'photographic plate') film

【软弱】ruǎnruò ❶ 缺乏力气 weak; feeble: 病后身体～be weak after an ailment ❷ 不坚强 effete; wishy-washy; prissy: ～无能 weak and incompetent

【软食】ruǎnshí 容易咀嚼和消化的食物 soft diet; pap

【软水】ruǎnshuǐ 不含或只含少量钙盐、镁盐类的水,如雨水 soft water; water containing little or no dissolved salts of calcium or magnesium, such as rain water

【软梯】ruǎntī same as 绳梯 shéngtī

【软体动物】ruǎntǐ-dòngwù 无脊椎动物的一门,体柔软,没有环节,两侧对称,足是肉质,多数具有钙质的硬壳,生活范围很广,水中和陆地上都有,如蚌、螺、蜗牛、乌贼等 mollusk; phylum of invertebrates such as clams, spiral shells, snails and cuttle fish, with a symmetrical soft body without segments, oft. in a calcareous shell, fleshy feet, and a wide range of habitat in water and on land

【软卧】ruǎnwò 火车卧车上的软席卧铺位(of a train) soft berth on a sleeper; soft sleeper

【软武器】ruǎnwǔqì 指用来破坏敌人无线电设备效能的电子干扰装备等 soft weapon; jammer; electronic jamming device

【软席】ruǎnxí 火车上比较舒适的、软的坐位或铺位 soft seat or berth; cushioned seat or berth in a railway carriage

【软饮料】ruǎnyǐnliào 不含酒精的饮料,如汽水、橘子水等 soft drink; nonalcoholic carbonated beverage, such as soda pop and orangeade, etc.

【软硬兼施】ruǎn yìng jiān shī 软的手段和硬的手段一齐用(含贬义 derog.) use both hard and soft tactics; couple threats with promises; use the stick and the carrot

【软着陆】ruǎnzhuólù 人造卫星、宇宙飞船等利用一定装置,改变运行轨道,逐渐减低降落速度,最后不受损坏地降落到地面或其他星体表面上 soft landing; (of satellite, spaceship, etc.) change orbit and reduce speed with the aid of certain devices so as to land on the earth or any other planet without damage

【软组织】ruǎnzǔzhī 医学上指肌肉、韧带等 soft tissue, such as muscle and ligament

朊 ruǎn ☞ 蛋白质 dànbáizhì on p. 382

耎 ruǎn 〈书 *fml.*〉 same as 软 ruǎn

ruí (ㄖㄨㄟˊ)

緌 ruí 〈书 *fml.*〉帽子上或旗杆顶上的缨子 tassel of a hat or flagpole

蕤 ruí ☞［葳蕤］(wēiruí) on p.1987

ruǐ (ㄖㄨㄟˇ)

桵 ruǐ 古书上指一种植物 a kind of plant, as mentioned in ancient books

蕊(蕋、蘂) ruǐ 花蕊 stamen; pistil: 雄～stamen|雌～pistil

橤(縈、蘂) ruǐ〈书 *fml.*〉形容下垂 droop; dangle; sag

ruì (ㄖㄨㄟˋ)

芮 Ruì 姓 a surname

汭 ruì〈书 *fml.*〉河流会合或弯曲的地方(of a river) bend; where two rivers converge

枘 ruì〈书 *fml.*〉榫子 tenon: 方～圆凿(形容格格不入) square peg in a round hole — incompatible

【枘凿】ruìzáo (也有读 also pronounced ruìzuò)〈书 *fml.*〉same as 凿枘 záoruì

蚋(蜹) ruì 昆虫,体长 2—3 毫米,黑色,头小,触角粗短,复眼明显,翅阔透明,吸食人畜的血液。幼虫头部方形,尾部稍膨大,生活在水中。buffalo gnat (*Simuliiae*); black fly; insect having a black body 2-3 mm. in length with a small head, short and thick antennas, eyes that are strikingly facetted, and wide and transparent wings, sucking human and animal blood, with its larva sporting a squarish head and large afterbody and living in water

锐 ruì ❶ 锐利(同'钝'相对 as opposed to 'blunt') sharp: 尖～sharp ◇敏～nimble-minded|～不可当 irresistible ❷ 锐气 drive; dash; morale: 养精蓄～conserve energy and build up strength ❸ 急剧 drastic: ～进 rapid advance|～减 sharp fall

【锐不可当】ruì bù kě dāng 形容来势凶猛,不可阻挡 overpowering; overwhelming: ～的攻势 irresistible attack

【锐角】ruìjiǎo 大于 0°而小于直角(90°)的角 acute angle; angle between 0 and 90 degrees

【锐利】ruìlì ❶ (刃锋等) 尖而快 (of blade, etc.) sharp-edged: ～的匕首 razor-sharp dagger ❷ (目光、言论、文笔等)尖锐(of eyesight, opinion, writing, etc.) shrewd; sagacious; perceptive; discerning: 眼光～penetrating eye |～的笔锋 sagacious style of writing

【锐敏】ruìmǐn (感觉)灵敏;(眼光)尖锐(of perception) discerning; shrewd; (of eyesight) keen; sharp

【锐气】ruìqì 勇往直前的气势 dash; drive; morale: 挫其～sap (an opponent's) morale

【锐意】ruìyì 意志坚决,勇往直前 determined; bent on; resolute: ～进取 be determined to make new progress|～兴革,励精图治。Be devoted to reform and brace oneself up to run one's country well

瑞 ruì ❶ 吉祥 propitious; opportune: 祥～auspicious|～雪 snow that bodes well for farmers ❷ (Ruì) 姓 a surname

【瑞签】ruìqiān 写着吉利话的纸条,多用红纸,在春节期间张贴 slip of red paper with auspicious words to be pasted up during Spring Festival

【瑞雪】ruìxuě 应时的好雪 timely snowfall: ～兆丰年。A timely snow bodes well for a year of abundance.|华北各省普降～。A timely snow fell over north Chinese provinces.

睿(叡) ruì〈书 *fml.*〉看得深远 farsighted: ～智 intelligent|～哲 wise and farsighted

【睿智】ruìzhì〈书 *fml.*〉英明有远见 intelligent and farsighted

rún (ㄖㄨㄣˊ)

瞤 rún〈书 *fml.*〉❶ 眼皮跳动(of eyelids) twitch ❷ 肌肉抽缩跳动 spasmodic muscular contraction

rùn (ㄖㄨㄣˋ)

闰 rùn 一回归年的时间为 365 天 5 时 48 分 46 秒。阳历把一年定为 365 天,所余的时间约每四年积累成一天,加在二月里;农历把一年定为 354 天或 355 天,所余的时间约每 3 年积累成一个月,加在一年里。这样的办法,在历法上叫做闰。intercalary; insert an extra day or month in the calendar. Because a tropical year lasts for 365 days, 5 hours, 48 minutes and 46 seconds, the Gregorian calendar sets the year at 365 days and adds an extra day that equals the total of the surplus time to February of every 4th year, whereas the Chinese lunar calendar sets the year at 354 or 355 days while the surplus time adds up to an extra month that is inserted in every 3rd year.

【闰年】rùnnián 阳历有闰日的一年叫闰年,这年有 366 天。农历有闰月的一年也叫闰年,这年有 13 个月,即 383 天或 384 天。intercalary year, which contains 366 days in the Gregorian calendar; leap year, which contains 383 or 384 days in 13 months, occurs in every third year in the Chinese lunar calendar

【闰日】rùnrì 阳历四年一闰,在二月末加一天,这一天叫做闰日 leap day; intercalary day; extra day that occurs in February once every four years in the Gregorian calendar

【闰月】rùnyuè 农历三年一闰,五年两闰,十九年七闰,每逢闰年所加的一个月叫闰月。闰月加在某月之后就称闰某月。(in Chinese lunar calendar) intercalary month; leap month. In Chinese lunar calendar, an intercalary month occurs once every three years, twice every five years, and seven times in every 19 years, with the extra months added to an intercalary year known as 'intercalary month'.

润 rùn ❶ 细腻光滑;滋润 moist; sleek: 光～ shiny and sleek | ～泽 sheen | 墨色很～ full-bodied ink | 珠圆玉～ round as a pearl and smooth as jade ❷ 加油或水,使不干燥 lubricate with oil or water; make slippery or smooth: 浸～ soak; infiltrate | ～肠 lubricate the intestines; ease constipation | ～嗓子 moisten one's throat ❸ 使有光彩(指修改文章) polish (piece of writing): ～色 touch up; spruce up | ～饰 touch up ❹ 利益;好处 profit; reward: 分～ distribute a profit | 利～ profit

【润笔】rùnbǐ 指给做诗文书画的人的报酬 money paid to a writer, painter or calligrapher

【润格】rùngé 指为人做诗文书画所定的报酬标准 pay rate for the service of a writer, painter or calligrapher

【润滑】rùnhuá 加油脂等以减少物体之间的摩擦,使物体便于运动 lubricate; apply lubricant to a mechanism to reduce friction and facilitate movement

【润滑油】rùnhuáyóu 涂在机器轴承等摩擦部分的油质,作用是润滑、冷却和用来密封等,一般是分馏石油的产物,也有从动植物油中提炼的 lubricating oil; lubricant; oil refinery product or animal or plant extraction to be applied to a machine in order to lubricate, keep temperature down or seal

【润例】rùnlì same as 润格 rùngé

【润色】rùnsè 修饰文字 polish a piece of writing; touch up: 这篇译稿太粗糙,你把它～一下。Please polish this piece of translation, which is very crude.

【润饰】rùnshì same as 润色 rùnsè: ～文稿 touch up a manuscript

【润泽】rùnzé ❶ 滋润;不干枯 moist; sleek: ～如玉 as sleek as jade | 雨后荷花显得更加～可爱了。The lotus flowers looked fresher and more lovely after the rain. ❷ 使滋润 moisten; lubricate: 用油～轮轴 lubricate wheels and axles with oil

【润资】rùnzī same as 润笔 rùnbǐ

ruó (ㄖㄨㄛˊ)

挼 ruó 〈书 *fml.*〉揉搓 crumble; rub: ～挲(摩挲;搓) caress; rub

☞ ruá on p. 1642

【挼搓】ruó·cuo same as 揉搓 róu·cuo: 别把鲜花～坏了。Don't touch the flowers — they'll be ruined.

ruò (ㄖㄨㄛˋ)

若[1] ruò 如;好像 as if; like: 安之～素 bear hardship with equanimity | 欣喜～狂 beside oneself with joy | ～隐～现 partly hidden and partly visible | 旁～无人 act as if no one was around; overweening | ～无其事 act as if nothing has happened

若[2] ruò 〈书 *fml.*〉如果 if: 人不犯我,我不犯人;人～犯我,我必犯人。We will not attack unless we are attacked; if we are attacked, we will certainly counterattack.

若[3] ruò 〈书 *fml.*〉你 you: ～辈 you people; you

☞ rě on p. 1611

【若虫】ruòchóng 蝗虫、椿象等不完全变态的昆虫,在卵孵化之后,翅膀还没有长成期间,外形跟成虫相似,但较小,生殖器官发育不全,这个阶段的昆虫叫做若虫,例如蝗蝻就是蝗虫的若虫 nymph; larval form of certain insects, such as grasshoppers and stink bugs, usu. resembling the adult form but smaller and lacking fully developed reproductive organs

【若非】ruòfēi 要不是 were it not for: ～亲身经历,岂知其中甘苦。You don't know the sweetness and bitterness of it unless you have personally experienced it.

【若夫】ruòfū 〈书 *fml.*〉〈助词 *aux.*〉用在句子的开头[used at the beginning of a sentence] a)表示发端[introduce a subject] as for b)表示转向另一方面[indicate a change of subject] with regard to

【若干】ruògān 多少(问数量或指不定量) how much; how many; a few; several: 价值～? What's the value? | 关于发展教育的～问题 on several issues about development of education

【若何】ruòhé 如何 how; what: 结果～,还不得而知。The result is still unknown.

【若即若离】ruò jí ruò lí 好像接近,又好像不接近 be neither close nor distant; maintain a lukewarm relationship

【若明若暗】ruò míng ruò àn 〈比喻 *fig.*〉对问题或情况有所认识却不很清楚,也指对某事态度不明朗 have a blurred picture of an issue or situation; take an evasive attitude towards sth.

【若是】ruòshì 如果;如果是 if; in case: 他～不来,咱们就找他去。If he does not show up, let's go and find him. | 我～他,决不会那么办。I wouldn't have done it that way if I were him.

【若无其事】ruò wú qí shì 好像没有那么回事似的,形容不动声色或漠不关心 as if nothing had happened; maintain calm and collected; indifferent

【若隐若现】ruò yǐn ruò xiàn 形容隐隐约约 half hidden, half visible：远望白云缭绕，峰峦～。The mountains in the distance shimmered ethereally in the clouds.

【若有所失】ruò yǒu suǒ shī 感觉好像丢掉了什么，形容心情怅惘 look distracted; feel as if sth. were missing

偌 ruò 这么；那么（多见于早期白话 oft. in early vernacular）such; so

【偌大】ruòdà 这么大；那么大（多见于早期白话 oft. in early vernacular）so big：～年纪 so old｜～的京城 such a large capital city

鄀 Ruò 春秋时楚国的都城，在今湖北宜城东南 Ruo, capital city of the state of Chu during the Spring and Autumn Period, situated to the southeast of present-day Yicheng, Hubei Province

弱 ruò ❶ 气力小；势力差（跟'强'相对 as opposed to 'strong'）weak; feeble：软～ weak｜衰～aged and frail｜他年纪虽老，干活并不～。Old as he is, he doesn't show any weakness in work. ❷ 年幼 young：老～old and young ❸ 差；不如 inferior; compare unfavourably with：他的本领不～于那些人。He's no less capable than those people. ❹〈书 *fml.*〉丧失（指人死）lose sb. in death：又～一个。One more man is gone. ❺ 用在数字后面，表示略少于此数（跟'强'相对 as opposed to 'a little more than'）(following a fraction or decimal) a little less than：三分之二～a little less than two thirds

【弱不禁风】ruò bù jīn fēng 形容身体虚弱，连风吹都禁不住 too fragile to stand a gust of wind; extremely delicate

【弱点】ruòdiǎn 不足的地方；力量薄弱的方面 shortcoming; weak point：他的～是爱听奉承话。He has a weakness for flattery.｜攻击性差是这个乒乓球队的～。Lack of offense is a weakness of this table tennis team.

【弱冠】ruòguàn〈古代 *arch.*〉男子二十岁行冠礼，表示已经成人，因为还没达到壮年，叫做弱冠，后来泛指男子二十左右的年纪 young man around 20 and thus eligible to wear a hat but not considered to be in his prime; young adult about 20 years old：年方～just around 20 years of age

【弱肉强食】ruò ròu qiáng shí 指动物中弱者被强者吃掉。借指弱者被强者欺凌、吞并。weak being at the mercy of the strong — the law of the jungle

【弱视】ruòshì 眼球无器质性病变而视觉减弱的症状 amblyopia; lazy eye; dimness of vision, especially when occurring in one eye without apparent physical defect or disease

【弱项】ruòxiàng 实力弱的项目（多指体育比赛项目 oft. referring to sports event）weak event; weak area

【弱小】ruòxiǎo 又弱又小 small and weak：～民族 small and weak nation｜～的婴儿 small and weak baby

【弱智】ruòzhì 指智力发育低于正常水平 mentally retarded：～儿童 retarded child

婼 ruò 婼羌（Ruòqiāng），地名，在新疆。今作若羌。name of a place in Xinjiang, also Qarkilik, written as 若羌 ruòqiāng in contemporary use

☞ chuò on p. 314

蒻 ruò 古书上指嫩的香蒲 young rush (*Typha japonica*) as mentioned in ancient books

箬（篛） ruò ❶ 箬竹 indocalamus ❷ 箬竹的叶子 indocalamus leaf

【箬帽】ruòmào 箬竹的篾或叶子制成的帽子，用来遮雨和遮阳光 broad-rimmed hat made of indocalamus strips or leaves and worn against rain and sunshine：蓑衣～ bamboo hat and palm leaf raincoat

【箬竹】ruòzhú 竹的一种，茎高三四尺，中空，节显著，叶子宽而大，秋季叶子的边缘变白色，叶可以编制器物或竹笠，还可以包粽子 indocalamus (*Indocalamus tessellates*); a variety of bamboo, a little more than one metre tall, with hollow stem and conspicuous joints, broad and large leaves whose edges turn white in autumn and which are used for basketry, making hats, or wrapping dumpling made of glutinous rice

爇（焫） ruò〈书 *fml.*〉点燃；焚烧 light up; burn：～烛 light a candle

S

sā (ㄙㄚ)

仨 sā 三个(后面不能再接'个'字或其他量词)[not to be followed by 个 gè or any other classifier] three:～人 three people|哥儿～the three of us pals|～瓜俩枣(比喻一星半点的小事、小东西) three melons and two jujubes; (fig.) minor matter; penny thing; something not worth bothering about

挲(抄) sā ☞摩挲 mā·sā on p.1285 ☞ shā on p.1666 and suō on p.1842

撒 sā ❶ 放开;张开 let go; unlash:～手 let go one's hold|～网 cast a fishing net|一～线,风筝就上去了。The kite soared skyward immediately after the string attached to it was reeled off. ❷ 尽量使出来或施展出来(贬义 derog.) let oneself go:～赖 kick up a row|～酒疯 act foolish while drunk
☞ sǎ on p.1648

【撒村】sā//cūn 〈方 *dial.*〉说粗鲁下流的话 speak vulgar language; act like a country bumpkin:～骂街 shout abuse in the street

【撒旦】sādàn 〈基督教用语 *Christ.*〉指魔鬼 Satan; Devil; evil adversary of God [希伯来 Hebrew: Sạṭạn]

【撒刁】sā//diāo 狡猾耍赖 act in a slick and shameless way:别～,没人吃你那一套。Stop being lubricious! Nobody wants to buy it.

【撒欢儿】sā//huānr 〈方 *dial.*〉因兴奋而连跑带跳(多指动物 oft. of animals) gambol; frisk

【撒谎】sā//huǎng same as 说谎 shuō//huǎng

【撒娇】sā//jiāo (～儿 sā//jiāor)仗着受人宠爱故意作态 act spoiled; act like a spoiled child:～使性 act as willfully as a pampered child|小女孩儿爱～。Girls love to act spoiled.

【撒酒疯】sā jiǔfēng (～儿 sā jiǔfēngr)喝酒过量后,借着酒劲任性胡闹 be drunk and act crazy; be roaring drunk; also 发酒疯 fā jiǔfēng

【撒拉族】Sālāzú 我国少数民族之一,主要分布在青海和甘肃 Sarlas (or Salas), an ethnic minority people mainly inhabiting Qinghai and Gansu provinces

【撒赖】sā//lài 蛮横胡闹;耍无赖 make a scene; raise hell:她又是哭,又是闹,躺在地上～。She made a scene lying on the ground, now crying, now whimpering.

【撒尿】sā//niào 排泄尿 piss; pee

【撒泼】sāpō 大哭大闹,不讲道理 be unreasonable and make a scene:～放刁 act in a rascally manner|～打滚 make a scene by rolling about the floor

【撒气】sā//qì ❶(球、车胎等 of a ball, tyre, etc.)空气放出或漏出 leak; go soft ❷ 拿旁人或借其他事物发泄怒气 vent one's spleen on sb. or sth.:你心里不痛快,也不能拿孩子～。Don't take it out on the children no matter how pissed off you are.

【撒手】sā//shǒu 放开手;松手 let go; let go one's hold:～不管 wash one's hands off sth.|你拿稳,我～了。Hold it tight. I'll let go.◇～人世(指死亡)(of people) kick the bucket; die

【撒手锏】sāshǒujiǎn 旧小说中指厮杀时出其不意地用锏投掷敌手的招数(a term used in old fiction) catch an enemy unawares by an unexpected thrust with the mace;〈比喻 *fig.*〉最关键的时刻使出的最拿手的本领 trump card

【撒腿】sā//tuǐ 放开脚步(跑) take to one's heels; beat it:他听说哥哥回来了,～就往家里跑。He made off to home upon learning that his elder brother was back.

【撒丫子】sā yā·zi 〈方 *dial.*〉放开脚步(跑);撒腿(多含诙谐意 oft. humor.) take to one's heels; beat it double-quick; also 撒鸭子 sā yā·zi

【撒野】sā//yě (对人)粗野、放肆;任意妄为,不讲情理 act wildly; behave atrociously

【撒呓挣】sā yì·zheng 熟睡时说话或动作 talk and act while asleep

sǎ (ㄙㄚˇ)

洒(灑) sǎ ❶ 使(水或其他东西)分散地落下 sprinkle; spray:扫地的时候先～些水。Sprinkle some water on the ground before sweeping it. ❷ 分散地落下 descend in scattered drops or particles:把～在地上的粮食捡起来。Pick up the grain scattered on the ground. ❸(Sǎ)姓 a surname
〈古 *arch.*〉洒 same as 洗 xǐ

【洒狗血】sǎ gǒuxiě (戏曲演员) 脱离情节而卖弄滑稽、武艺或做其他过火的表演(of theatrical actors) show off antics, acrobatics or other exaggerated performances that have nothing to do with the plot onstage

【洒家】sǎjiā 我(早期白话中用于男性自称 man's term of addressing himself in early vernacular) I; me

【洒泪】sǎlèi 掉泪;落泪 shed tears:~而别 bid a tearful farewell

【洒落】sǎluò ❶ 分散地落下 drip; trickle down:一串串汗珠~在地上。Sweat kept dripping down to the ground. ❷ 潇洒;洒脱 show pizazz; free and easy:谈笑~show pizazz in talk and writing|丰姿~be charming in a natural way

【洒洒】sǎsǎ 形容众多(多指文辞 oft. of diction) in great numbers:洋洋~prolific|~万言 amount to 10,000 words

【洒扫】sǎsǎo 洒水扫地 sprinkle water and sweep the floor; sweep:~庭除 sweep the courtyard

【洒脱】sǎ·tuo (言谈、举止、风格)自然;不拘束 (of speech, deportment, style, etc.) free and unaffected; unrestrained

靸 sǎ 〈方 *dial.*〉把鞋后帮踩在脚后跟下;穿(拖鞋) wear cloth shoes with the backs trodden down; slip on slippers:别~着鞋往外面跑。Don't shuffle out with the backs of your shoes trodden down.

S

【靸鞋】sǎxié ❶ 拖鞋 slippers ❷ 鞋帮纳得很密,前脸较深,上面缝着皮梁的布鞋 cloth shoes having closely stitched uppers and deep vamps with leather straps over them

撒 sǎ ❶ 把颗粒状的东西分散着扔出去;散布(东西) scatter (granules); sprinkle; spread:~种 sowing|年糕上~了一层白糖 sprinkle a layer of white sugar over glutinous rice cakes ❷ 散落;洒 spill; drop:把碗端平,别~了汤。Keep the bowl level, and don't spill the soup. ❸ (Sǎ)姓 a surname

☞ sā on p. 1647

【撒播】sǎbō 把作物的种子均匀地撒在田地里,必要时进行覆土 broadcast sowing; scatter crop seeds evenly over a large area and, where necessary, cover them with soil

潵 Sǎ 潵河,水名,在河北 Sahe, name of a river in Hebei Province

sà(ㄙㄚˋ)

卅 sà 三十 thirty:五~运动 May 30th Movement of 1925

挲(撒) sà 〈书 *fml.*〉侧手击 attack sideways; make a flank thrust

☞ shā on p. 1666

飒 sà ❶ 形容风声(of wind) sough; whish; whoosh ❷ 〈书 *fml.*〉凋零;衰老 flaccid; sag; shrivel

【飒然】sàrán 〈书 *fml.*〉形容风声(of wind) soughing; whooshing:有风~而至。There came the soughing of a rising wind.

【飒飒】sàsà 形容风、雨声(of wind or rain) whistle; rustle:秋风~rustling autumnal wind|白杨树迎风~地响。The poplar trees whistled in the wind.

【飒爽】sàshuǎng 〈书 *fml.*〉豪迈而矫健 valiant:~英姿 look bright and brave

脎 sà 有机化合物的一类,是含有相邻的两个羰基的化合物和两个分子苯肼缩水而成的衍生物 osazone; organic compound that is the dehydrated derivative of bimolecular phenylhydrazine and a compound with two neighbouring carbonyls

萨(薩) Sà 姓 a surname

【萨噶达娃节】Sàgádáwá Jié 藏族地区纪念释迦牟尼诞生的节日,在藏历四月十五日 Sa-ga Zla-ba, Tibetan festival to mark the anniversary of Sakyamuni's birthday, which falls on the 15th day of the 4th month according to the Tibetan calendar

【萨克管】sàkèguǎn 管乐器,有音键和嘴子,用于管弦乐队中,也可以用做独奏乐器。为比利时萨克斯(Adolphe Sax)所创造。saxophone, metal woodwind instrument having keys and a single-reed mouthpiece, used in orchestras or solos. The first saxophone was invented by Adolphe Sax of Belgium.

【萨满教】Sàmǎnjiào 一种原始宗教,流行于亚洲、欧洲的极北部等地区。萨满是跳神作法的巫师。shamanism, primitive religion popular in Asia, the northernmost part of Europe, and other regions, embracing a belief in powerful spirits who can be exorcized only by a shaman — person who works with the supernatural as a priest [萨满,满 Manchu: shaman]

【萨其马】sàqímǎ 一种糕点,把油炸的短面条用糖等黏合起来,切成方块儿 Manchu candied fritter cut in squares [满 Manchu]

sāi(ㄙㄞ)

思 sāi ☞于思 yúsāi on p. 2336

☞ sī on p. 1815

揌(㩙) sāi same as 塞 sāi ①

毸 sāi ☞[毰毸](péisāi) on p. 1454

腮(顋) sāi 两颊的下半部 cheek:双手托~ place one's cheeks in both hands

【腮帮子】sāibāng·zi 腮 cheek; also 腮帮 sāibāng

【腮颊】sāijiá 腮 cheek

【腮腺】sāixiàn 两耳下部的唾液腺,是唾液腺中最大的一对,所分泌的唾液含大量消化酶 parotid gland; largest pair of salivary glands situated at the base of each ear, excreting saliva that is rich in digestive enzyme; also 耳

下腺 ěrxiàxiàn; ☞ 唾液腺 tuòyèxiàn on p. 1962; (图见 ☞ figure for 消化系统 xiāohuà xìtǒng on p. 2100)

塞 sāi ❶ 把东西放进有空隙的地方;填入 fill in; stuff: 箱子里还可～几件衣服。There is room in the suitcase to fill in a few pieces of clothing. | 把窟窿～住。Stop the hole. ❷ (～儿 sāir) 塞子 stopple; plug: 软木～cork | 瓶～bottle stopper

☞ sài on p. 1649 and sè on p. 1661

【塞车】sāi//chē 堵车 traffic jam; traffic congestion

【塞尺】sāichǐ ☞ 厚薄规 hòubóguī on p. 813

【塞规】sāiguī 一种量具,用来测量孔眼和凹形工件 plug gauge; instrument for gauging holes and concave workpieces; ☞ 界限量规 jièxiàn liángguī on p. 1000

【塞子】sāi·zi 塞住容器口使内外隔绝的东西 stopper; plug; spigot; cork: 瓶～bottle stopper

噻 sāi ☞ below

【噻吩】sāifēn 有机化合物,化学式 C_4H_4S。无色液体,有特殊气味,溶于乙醇和乙醚,不溶于水。是制造染料、药物等的原料。thiophene (C_4H_4S), organic compound in the form of a colourless liquid with a peculiar odour that dissolves in ethanol and aether but not in water, used as a raw material for dyes and medicaments

【噻唑】sāizuò 有机化合物,化学式 C_3H_3NS。无色或淡黄色液体,容易挥发。用于合成药物、染料等。thiazole (C_3H_3NS), organic compound in the form of a colourless or pale yellow volatile liquid that is used as a material for synthesizing pharmaceuticals, dyes, etc.

鳃 sāi 某些水生动物的呼吸器官,多为羽毛状、板状或丝状,用来吸取溶解在水中的氧 gill; branchia; respiratory organ of certain aquatic animals, mostly feathery, tabular or filamentary, for inhaling dissolved oxygen from water

sài (ㄙㄞˋ)

塞 sài 可做屏障的险要地方 place serving as a strategic barrier; place of strategic importance: 边～frontier fortress | 要～fort; fortress; fortification

☞ sāi on p. 1649 and sè on p. 1661

【塞北】Sàiběi 塞外 region north of the Great Wall: ～江南 area north of the Great Wall as fertile as the region south of the Yangtze River

【塞外】Sàiwài 指长城以北的地区 region north of the Great Wall: ～风光 landscape north of the Great Wall

【塞翁失马】sài wēng shī mǎ 边塞上一个老头儿丢了一匹马,别人来安慰他,他说:'怎么知道这不是福呢?'后来这匹马竟带着一匹好马回来了(见于《淮南子·人间训》)。Just like the old frontiersman losing his horse, who knows but that this may be a blessing in disguise? According to the book *Huainanzi · Lessons of Human World*, an old man living in a border region was comforted by his friends after he had lost his horse. 'This may be a blessing in disguise, who knows?' one of them said. Indeed, the horse later returned to the man in the company of a better horse. 〈比喻 *fig.*〉坏事在一定条件下可以变为好事。A bad thing may become a good thing under certain conditions.

赛[1] sài ❶ 比赛 match; game; competition: ～跑 race | ～诗会 poetry recitation competition | 足球～soccer game ❷ 胜;比得上 put sb. to shame; better than; stand comparison: 这些姑娘干活～过小伙子。In work these young women can put young men to shame.

赛[2] sài 〈旧时 *old*〉祭祀酬报神恩(迷信) worship gods; offer sacrifices to holy spirits: 祭～offer sacrifices to gods | ～神 pay homage to gods

【赛场】sàichǎng 比赛的场所 sports arena; ring; court

【赛车】sài//chē 比赛自行车、摩托车或汽车 cycle racing; motorcycle race; auto race

【赛车】sàichē ❶ 专供比赛用的自行车 racing bicycle; also 跑车 pǎochē ❷ 泛指专供比赛用的车 racing car, etc.

【赛程】sàichéng ❶ 体育比赛途经的路程或距离 (of racing) distance: 自行车大赛～为 70 公里。A major cycle race covers a distance of 70 km. ❷ 比赛的程序或日程 agenda of a sports meet: ～过半 halfway through a sports meet | ～因故将重新排定。For some reason the agenda for competitions will be reshuffled.

【赛会】sàihuì 旧时的一种迷信活动,用仪仗和吹打演唱迎神像出庙,游行街巷或村庄间 ceremonial parade of religious statues from a temple through the streets or among villages to the accompaniment of a band in old times

【赛璐玢】sàilùfēn 玻璃纸的一种,无色,透明,有光泽,可以染成各种颜色,多用于包装 cellophane; thin, colourless, transparent and shiny cellulose material that can be dyed in different colours and used as wrapping

【赛璐珞】sàilùluò 塑料的一种,由胶棉(低氮含量的硝化纤维)和增塑剂(主要是樟脑)、润滑剂、染料等加工制成。透明,可以染成各种颜色,容易燃烧。用来制造玩具、文具等。celluloid; a kind of plastic made from collodion (nitrocellulose with a low nitrogen content), plasticizer (camphor in the main), lubricant

S

and dyestuff, being transparent and inflammable, and dyed in different colours for the making of toys and stationery; 旧称 known in old times as 假象牙 jiǎxiàngyá

【赛马】sài//mǎ 运动项目的一种,比赛骑马速度 horse racing

【赛跑】sàipǎo 比赛跑步速度的运动,有短距离、中距离、长距离和超长距离赛跑。另外还有跨栏、接力、障碍和越野赛跑等。race, including sprint, medium-, long- and extra-long-distance races, as well as hurdle, relay, steeplechase and cross-country races

【赛区】sàiqū 综合性的或大型的比赛划分的比赛地区(of a comprehensive or large sports meet) venue

【赛事】sàishì 比赛活动 sports competition; match; game:～频繁 action-packed competition schedule

sān (ㄙㄢ)

三 sān ❶ 数目,二加一后所得 three; two plus one; ☞数字 shùzì on p. 1791 ❷ 表示多数或多次 several times:～番五次 time and again |一而再,再而～again and again; repeatedly

【三八妇女节】Sān-Bā Fùnǚ Jié 国际妇女斗争的纪念日。1909年3月8日,美国芝加哥女工因要求男女平等权利而举行示威,次年8月在丹麦哥本哈根召开的国际第二次社会主义者妇女大会上决定,为了促进国际劳动妇女的团结和解放,以每年3月8日为妇女节。March 8th International Women's Day. On March 8, 1909, women workers in Chicago, the United States, took to the street in a demonstration for the equality of men and women and other rights. At the 2nd International Socialist Women's Conference held in Copenhagen, Denmark, in August the following year, a decision was reached to designate March 8 as the Women's Day in order to promote the unity and liberation of labouring women throughout the world. also 国际妇女节 Guójì Fùnǚ Jié

【三百六十行】sānbǎi liùshí háng 泛指各种行业 all trades and professions; all walks of life: ～,行行出状元。There may be 360 professions, but in each of them there are always people who excel.

【三板】sānbǎn ☞ 舢板 shānbǎn on p. 1672

【三宝】sānbǎo 〈佛教 *Budd.*〉指佛、法、僧。佛指大知大觉的人,法指佛所说的教义,僧指继承或宣扬教义的人。*triratna*, the triad of the Buddha (the Enlightened One), the *dharma* (universal truth), and the *sangha* (monks who have authoritatively studied, taught and preserved the teachings of the Buddha)

【三北】Sān Běi 指我国东北、西北、华北 general reference to northeast, northwest and north China:～防护林体系,被称为北方'绿色万里长城'。The network of forest belts encompassing northeast, northwest and north China is dubbed the 'Green 10,000-*Li* Great Wall'.

【三不管】sānbùguǎn 泛指没人管的(事情或地区)(of sth. or an area) under nobody's jurisdiction; be nobody's business:～地区 place under nobody's jurisdiction

【三不知】sānbùzhī 原指对事情的开头、中间和结尾一无所知,后泛指什么都不知道 know nothing about the beginning, middle and end of sth.; know nothing: 一问～say 'I don't know' to every question; not know a thing

【三叉神经】sānchā-shénjīng 第五对脑神经,从脑桥发出,每侧分三支,分布在眼、上颌、下颌等部位。主要管颜面、牙齿、角膜、鼻腔、口唇、大部分头皮和脑膜的感觉。trigeminus; trigeminal nerve; either of the 5th pair of cranial nerves that has three branches on either side that extend to the eyes and upper and lower jaws respectively, having sensory and motor functions in the face, teeth, corneas, nasal cavity, mouth, lips, and most part of the scalp and meninges

【三长两短】sān cháng liǎng duǎn 指意外的灾祸、事故,特指人的死亡 sth. untoward; unhappy event; sth. unfortunate, such as disaster, accident, and particularly death

【三从四德】sān cóng sì dé 封建礼教束缚、压迫妇女的道德标准之一。三从是'未嫁从父,既嫁从夫,夫死从子'。四德是'妇德、妇言、妇容、妇功'(妇女的品德、辞令、仪态、女工)。(for a woman according to Confucian ethics) three obediences — to father before marriage to husband after marriage and to son after husband's death — and four virtues — morality, proper speech, modest manner and diligent work

【三寸不烂之舌】sān cùn bù làn zhī shé 指能言善辩的口才 eloquence; have a silver tongue; also 三寸舌 sān cùn shé

【三大差别】sān dà chābié 指社会主义国家中存在的工农之间、城乡之间、脑力劳动和体力劳动之间的差别 (in a socialist country) three major distinctions (between town and country, industry and agriculture, and physical and mental labour)

【三点式】sāndiǎnshì ☞比基尼 bǐjīní on p. 98

【三段论】sānduànlùn 形式逻辑间接推理的基本形式之一,由大前提和小前提推出结论。如'凡金属都能导电'(大前提),'铜是金属'(小前提),'所以铜能导电'(结论)。syllogism; reasoning from the general to the specific; deduction; basic form of deducting a conclusion from a major premise and a minor premise, for instance, all metals are conductive (major premise), copper is a metal (minor premise), and therefore, copper is conductive (conclusion); also 三段论法 sānduànlùnfǎ or

三段论式 sānduànlùnshì

【三番五次】 sān fān wǔ cì 屡次 repeatedly; time and again; over and over again

【三废】 sānfèi 在工业生产中所产生的废气、废水、废渣的总称 (in industrial production) three wastes (i. e. waste gas, wastewater, and industrial residue)

【三伏】 sānfú ❶ 初伏、中伏、末伏的统称。夏至后第三个庚日是初伏第一天,第四个庚日是中伏第一天,立秋后第一个庚日是末伏第一天,初伏、末伏各十天,中伏十天或二十天。通常也指从初伏第一天到末伏第十天的一段时间。三伏天一般是一年中天气最热时期。three *fu*; periods of summer heat wave, each beginning with a day of *geng* (the day of the seventh Heavenly Stem crosses an Earthly Branch). The third day of *geng* following the Summer Solstice marks the beginning of the 10-day early *fu* (the first heat wave), and the fourth day of *geng* marks the beginning of the 10- or 20-day middle *fu* (the second heat wave), and the first day of *geng* after the Beginning of Autumn serves as the start of the third 10-day *fu* (the third heat wave). Three *fu* refers to the hottest period of the year. ❷ 特指末伏 third summer heat wave of the year

【三副】 sānfù 轮船上船员的职务名称,职位次于二副 (navigation) third mate; third officer, second in position to second officer; ☞大副 dàfù on p. 356

【三纲五常】 sāngāng wǔcháng 封建礼教所提倡的人与人之间的道德标准。三纲指父为子纲、君为臣纲、夫为妻纲。五常传说不一,通常指仁、义、礼、智、信。feudal ethical code; Three Cardinal Guides (ruler guides subject, father guides son, and husband guides wife) and Five Constant Virtues (benevolence, righteousness, propriety, wisdom and fidelity)

【三姑六婆】 sāngū liùpó 三姑指尼姑、道姑、卦姑(占卦的),六婆指牙婆(以介绍人口买卖为业的妇女)、媒婆、师婆(女巫)、虔婆(鸨母)、药婆(给人治病的妇女)、稳婆(接生婆)(见于元陶宗仪《辍耕录》卷十)。旧社会里三姑六婆往往借着这类身分干坏事。因此通常用'三姑六婆'比喻不务正业的妇女。three kinds of middle-aged women (nuns, female Taoists and women fortune-tellers) and six categories of elderly women (women traffickers in human beings, matchmakers, witches, procuresses, women quacks and midwives), according to *Talks in the Intervals of Ploughing · Vol. 10* by Tao Zongyi of the Yuan Dynasty; women of dubious character and making a living by dishonest means

【三顾茅庐】 sān gù máo lú 东汉末年,刘备请隐居在隆中(湖北襄阳附近)草舍的诸葛亮出来运筹划策,去了三次才见到。后用来泛指诚心诚意一再邀请。make three calls at the thatched cottage — repeatedly request sb. to take up a responsible post. Towards the end of the Eastern Han Dynasty, Liu Bei paid three consecutive visits to Zhuge Liang, a master strategist who lived in a thatched cottage near Xiangyang in present-day Hubei Province, to show his sincerity for Zhuge to end a life seclusion and become his strategic advisor.

【三国】 Sān Guó 魏、蜀、吴三国并立的时期(魏,公元 220—265;蜀,公元 221—263;吴,公元 222—280) Three Kingdoms (220-280) — Wei (220-265), Shu (221-263) and Wu (222-280); ☞魏 Wèi on p. 2002, 蜀 Shǔ on p. 1785 and 吴 Wú on p. 2027

【三合板】 sānhébǎn 用三层薄木胶合而成的板材。是最常见的一种胶合板。three-ply board, a most common plywood

【三合房】 sānhéfáng 一种旧式房子,三面是屋子,前面是墙,中间是院子 courtyard dwelling with houses on three sides with a screen wall in front of it; also 三合院儿 sānhéyuànr

【三合土】 sānhétǔ 石灰、砂和碎砖加水拌和后,经浇灌夯实而成的建筑材料,干燥后坚硬,可用来打地基或修筑道路 rammed earth; mixture of lime, clay and sand to which water is added, rammed solid in the construction of foundations or roads

【三花脸】 sānhuāliǎn (~儿 sānhuāliǎnr) 戏曲角色行当中的丑 three-flower face (another name for *chou* 丑, presumably from the outline of the white patch on the face)

【三皇五帝】 Sān Huáng Wǔ Dì 指古代传说中的帝王,说法不一,通常称伏羲、燧人、神农为三皇。或者称天皇、地皇、人皇为三皇。五帝通常指黄帝、颛顼(Zhuānxū)、帝喾(Dìkù)、唐尧、虞舜。Three Wise Kings and Five August Emperors; legendary Chinese rulers of remote antiquity. The three kings refer to Fuxi, Suiren, and Shennong according to one version of the legend, or the King of Heaven, the King of Earth, and the King of Man according to another. The five emperors refer to Yellow Emperor, Emperor Zhuanxu, Emperor Ku, Emperor Yao, and Emperor Shun.

【三极管】 sānjíguǎn 有三个电极的管子。电子管三极管由屏极、栅极、阴极组成,晶体管三极管由发射极、基极、集电极组成。radio triode; triode; vacuum electron tube containing an anode, a control grid, and a cathode; transistor triode containing an emitter, a base electrode and a collector electrode

【三级跳远】 sānjí tiàoyuǎn 田径运动项目之一,运动员经过快速助跑后连续跳三步,第一步用起跳的脚落地,第二步用另一只脚落地,第三步两脚落地(track event) triple jump; hop, step and jump

【三缄其口】 sān jiān qí kǒu 形容说话十分谨慎,

S

不肯或不敢开口(语出《说苑·敬慎》) with one's lips sealed; be cautious of what one says; reluctant to, or dare not, speak out (originating in *Congeries of Persuasions · Discretion Cherished*)

【三焦】sānjiāo 〈中医 *Chin. med.*〉指自舌的下部沿胸腔至腹腔的部分 part of the body from below the tongue through the thorax to the abdominal cavity; three visceral cavities with internal organs; ☞ 上焦 shàngjiāo on p. 1682, 中焦 zhōngjiāo on p. 2482 and 下焦 xiàjiāo on p. 2065

【三角】sānjiǎo ❶ 三角学的简称 abbr. for 三角学 sānjiǎoxué trigonometry ❷ 形状像三角形的东西 triangle: 糖～(食品) triangular steamed bread stuffed with brown sugar

【三角板】sānjiǎobǎn 绘图用具,是用木头或塑料等制成的三角形薄片。其中一角为直角,其他两角或各为45°,或一角为60°,另一角为30°。set square; flat wooden or plastic drawing instrument in the shape of a triangle with a right angle and two 45° angles or with one at 60° and the other 30°; also 三角尺 sānjiǎochǐ

【三角带】sānjiǎodài 一种断面为梯形的传动带,用在有槽的皮带轮上 V-belt; vee belt; transmission belt with a trapeziform cross-section, to be used on grooved wheels

【三角函数】sānjiǎo hánshù 在直角三角形中,各边长度两两之间的比值是锐角的函数。每个锐角有六个三角函数,记做正弦(sin)、余弦(cos)、正切(tg)、余切(ctg)、正割(sec)、余割(csc)。例如锐角∠A的三角函数, $\sin A=\frac{a}{c}$, $\cos A=\frac{b}{c}$, $\mathrm{tg}A=\frac{a}{b}$, $\mathrm{ctg}A=\frac{b}{a}$, $\sec A=\frac{c}{b}$, $\csc A=\frac{c}{a}$, 见图(一)。三角函数的概念可推广到任意角。对于任意角α,以角的顶点为原点,角的始边作X轴正方向,建立平面直角坐标系XOY,设P(x,y)为角α终边上任意一点,P点到原点距离为 $r=\sqrt{x^2+y^2}>0$。则 $\sin\alpha=\frac{y}{r}$, $\cos\alpha=\frac{x}{r}$, $\mathrm{tg}\alpha=\frac{y}{x}$, $\mathrm{ctg}\alpha=\frac{x}{y}$, $\sec\alpha=\frac{r}{x}$, $\csc\alpha=\frac{r}{y}$,见图(二)。circular function; trigonometric function; function expressed as the ratio of the sides of a right triangle, with each acute angle having six trigonometric functions — sine, cosine, tangent, cotangent, secant, and cosec. For example, the trigonometric function of the acute angle is ∠A: $\sin A=\frac{a}{c}$, $\cos A=\frac{b}{c}$, $\mathrm{tg}A=\frac{a}{b}$, $\mathrm{ctg}A=\frac{b}{a}$, $\sec A=\frac{c}{b}$, $\csc A=\frac{c}{a}$, ☞ figure I. The concept of trigonometric function can be extended to any angles. Take arbitrary angle α for example. Use the vertex of angle α as the origin, and its initial line as the positive direction of the axis X, and establish the plane right-angle coordinate system XOY. Suppose P(x, y) is an arbitrary point on the terminal line of α, and the distance from P to the origin is $r=\sqrt{x^2+y^2}>0$. *Then* $\sin\alpha=\frac{y}{r}$, $\cos\alpha=\frac{x}{r}$, $\mathrm{tg}\alpha=\frac{y}{x}$, $\mathrm{ctg}\alpha=\frac{x}{y}$, $\sec\alpha=\frac{r}{x}$, $\csc\alpha=\frac{r}{y}$, ☞ figure II

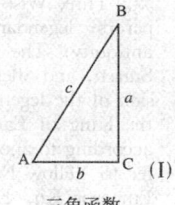

(I)
三角函数
Trigonometric Function

(II)
三角函数
Trigonometric Function

【三角恋爱】sānjiǎo liàn'ài 指两个男子和一个女子或两个女子和一个男子之间的恋爱 love triangle; eternal triangle; love of two men with a woman or two women with a man

【三角铁】sānjiǎotiě ❶ 角钢的俗称 popular term for 角钢 jiǎogāng ❷ 打击乐器,用于管弦乐队,是一根弯成三角形的细金属条,用金属槌敲打发音 triangle; musical percussion instrument that consists of a steel rod bent into triangular shape, open at one corner, and is struck with a small metal hammer

【三角形】sānjiǎoxíng 平面上三条直线或球面上三条弧线所围成的图形。三条直线所围成的图形叫平面三角形;三条弧线所围成的图形叫球面三角形。triangle; three-sided polygon; figure having three sides that are either three different straight lines (hence known as 'plane triangle') or the three arcs on a spherical surface (hence known as spherical triangle); also 三边形 sānbiānxíng

【三角学】sānjiǎoxué 数学的一个分支,主要研究三角函数和它的性质,以及三角函数在几何学上的应用 trigonometry; branch of mathematics devoted to the study of the trigonometric function and its properties, as well as its application in geometry; 简称 abbr. 三角 sānjiǎo

【三角债】sānjiǎozhài 一方是另一方的债务人或债权人,同时又是第三方的债权人或债务人,这三方之间的债务,叫三角债 inter-corporate triangular debt; debt chain; tripartite relationship of debt in which one party is the other two parties' debtor or creditor

【三角洲】sānjiǎozhōu 河口地区的冲积平原，大致成三角形，如我国的长江三角洲 delta; usu. triangular alluvial deposit at the mouth of a river or tidal inlet, such as the Yangtze River Delta of China

【三脚架】sānjiǎojià 安放照相机、测量仪器等用的有三个支柱的架子 tripod; adjustable three-legged stand, as for supporting a camera or a surveying apparatus

【三教九流】sān jiào jiǔ liú 三教指儒教、佛教、道教；九流指儒家、道家、阴阳家、法家、名家、墨家、纵横家、杂家、农家。泛指宗教、学术中各种流派或社会上各种行业。也用来泛称江湖上各种各样的人。three religions (Confucianism, Taoism and Buddhism) and nine schools of thought (the Confucians, the Taoists, the Yin-Yang, the Legalists, the Logicians, the Mohists, the Political Strategists, the Eclectics, and the Agriculturists); also a general term for various religious sects and academic schools, or people of various professions and trades; all sorts of people; also 九流三教 jiǔ liú sān jiào

【三节】sānjié 端午、中秋、春节合称三节 three festivals, i.e. the Dragon Boat Festival, the Mid-Autumn Festival and the Spring Festival

【三九】sānjiǔ 冬至后第十九天至第二十七天，是一年中最冷的时候 third of three nine-day periods, from the 19th day to the 27th day after the Winter Solstice; the coldest days of winter: ～天气 bitterly cold weather | ～严寒 inclement winter weather; also 三九天 sānjiǔtiān

【三军】sān-jūn ❶ 指陆军、海军、空军 three armed services, i.e., infantry, navy and air force ❷ 对军队的总称 general term for army

【三 K 党】Sānkèidǎng 美国的一个反动恐怖组织。提倡种族歧视，迫害黑人及一切进步人士，并从事其他破坏活动。Ku Klux Klan (KKK), reactionary terrorist organization in the United States that advocates racist discrimination, persecutes Blacks and progressive personages, and is engaged in sabotage

【三棱镜】sānléngjìng 截面呈三角形的棱镜 (triangular) prism

【三联单】sānliándān 一式三份合印一页的空白单据，在骑缝处编号盖章。三联单填写后，其中一联由本单位存查，其余两联分送有关方面。triplicate form; billhead in triplicate with serial number and seals stamped across the junction of two sheets. After a triplicate form is filled in, one copy of it is put on the file while the other two copies are sent to the parties concerned.

【三令五申】sān lìng wǔ shēn 再三地命令和告诫 instruct and warn repeatedly; enjoin repeatedly; repeated injunctions

【三六九等】sān liù jiǔ děng 许多等级，种种差别 strictly stratified hierarchy; hierarchical strictness

【三轮车】sānlúnchē 安装三个轮的脚踏车，装置车厢或平板，用来载人或装货 tricycle; pedicab; vehicle having three wheels, one at the front and two at the back, usu. propelled by pedals, and fixed with a carriage or a flatbed for carrying passengers or goods; also 三轮儿 sānlúnr

【三昧】sānmèi 〈佛教用语 *Budd.*〉意思是使心神平静，杂念止息，是佛教的重要修行方法之一。借指事物的诀要。*samadhi*; a major form of self-cultivation that requires profound and utterly absorptive contemplation undisturbed by desire or emotion; secret; key: 深得其中～ master the secrets of an art [梵 Sanskrit: samādhi]

【三民主义】sānmín zhǔyì 孙中山在他所领导的中国资产阶级民主革命中提出的政治纲领即民族主义、民权主义和民生主义。民族主义是推翻满族统治，恢复汉族政权；民权主义是建立民国；民生主义是平均地权。在十月革命的影响和中国共产党的帮助下，孙中山制定了联俄、联共、扶助农工三大政策，并于 1924 年重新解释了三民主义。民族主义是反对帝国主义，主张国内各民族一律平等；民权主义是建立为一般平民所共有、非少数人所得而私的民主政治；民生主义是平均地权，节制资本。Three Principles of the People, i.e. Nationalism (which means to overthrow the Manchu rule and restore the Han rule to China), Democracy (which means to establish a republic) and the People's Livelihood (which means to share out the land equally among the peasantry), which serve as the political programmes put forward by Dr. Sun Yat-sen for the Chinese bourgeois democratic revolution under his leadership. Under the influence of the October Revolution of Russia, with the help of the Chinese Communist Party, Dr. Sun formulated the three cardinal policies of allying with Soviet Russia, with the Chinese Communist Party and supporting the workers and peasants in 1923, and reinterpreted his Three People's Principles in 1924: Nationalism is to oppose imperialism and advocate equality between people of all ethnic backgrounds, Democracy is to establish democratic politics shared by all the common people rather than monopolized by a handful of people, and the People's Livelihood means to share out land equally and economize on capital

【三明治】sānmíngzhì 夹有肉、干酪等的面包 sandwich; two or more slices of bread with a filling such as meat or cheese placed between them

【三亲六故】sān qīn liù gù 泛指亲戚和故旧 (in a broad sense) relatives, friends and acquaintances

【三秋】sānqiū ❶ 秋收、秋耕和秋播的统称 three

S

autumn jobs of harvesting, ploughing and sowing ❷〈书 *fml.*〉指秋季的三个月 three autumn months; 也指秋季的第三个月,即农历九月 3rd autumn month, i. e. 9th lunar month ❸〈书 *fml.*〉指三个秋天;三年 three years: 一日不见,如隔~。A day away from a dear one is like three years; absence makes the heart grow fonder.

【三三两两】sānsānliǎngliǎng 三个一群两个一伙(多指人)(oft. of people) in twos and threes; in knots: 傍晚,人们~地在河边散步。At dusk people are seen strolling by the river in twos and threes.

【三色版】sānsèbǎn 铜制的照相凸版。将彩色原稿制成三块印版,用红、蓝、黄三种原色的油墨套印,能印出彩色的印刷品。three-colour halftone; three-colour block; coppery photo-engraving for colour prints, in which a coloured manuscript is prepared in three printing blocks for overprinting using the three primary colours of red, blue and yellow

【三牲】sānshēng 指用于祭祀的牛、羊、猪 three domestic animals, i. e. cattle, sheep and pigs, used as sacrificial offerings

S

【三思】sānsī 反复考虑 think thrice; think carefully: 事关重大,请你~。Please think carefully because it's a matter of great importance. | ~而后行 think thrice before you act; look before you leap

【三天打鱼,两天晒网】sān tiān dǎ yú, liǎng tiān shài wǎng 〈比喻 *fig.*〉学习或做事缺乏恒心,时常中断,不能坚持 go fishing for three days and dry the nets for two; work by fits and starts; lack perseverance

【三天两头儿】sān tiān liǎng tóur 指隔一天,或几乎每天 every other day; almost every day: 他~地来找你干什么? What's he up to, looking for you almost on a daily basis?

【三头对案】sān tóu duì àn 指与事情有关的双方及中间人(或见证人)在一起对质,弄清真相 confrontation of three parties, i.e. the plaintiff, the defendant and the witness, in court

【三头六臂】sān tóu liù bì〈比喻 *fig.*〉了不起的本领 (with) three heads and six arms; supernatural power: 离开群众,你就是有~也不顶用。You can get nowhere if you stay aloft of the people, even if you have three heads and six arms.

【三维空间】sānwéi kōngjiān 点的位置由三个坐标决定的空间。客观存在的现实空间就是三维空间,具有长、宽、高三种度量。数学、物理等学科中引进的多维空间的概念,是在三维空间基础上所做的科学抽象。three-dimensional space; space in which positions of points are determined by three coordinates; the space in objective reality is a three-dimensional space with three kinds of measurement of length, width and height; the concept of three-dimensional space introduced to such disciplines of learning as mathematics and physics is the result of scientific abstraction on the basis of three-dimensional space. also 三度空间 sāndù kòngjiān

【三位一体】sān wèi yī tǐ〈基督教 *Christ.*〉称耶和华为圣父,耶稣为圣子,圣父、圣子共有的神的性质为圣灵。虽然父子有别,而其神的性质融合为一,所以叫三位一体。一般用来比喻三个人、三件事或三个方面联成的一个整体。Trinity; Trine; union of three divine persons, the Father (Jehovah), Son (Jesus), and Holy Spirit, in one God; (generally in a figurative sense) three-in-one combination; trinity

【三…五…】sān…wǔ… ❶ 表示次数多[indicating many times]: ~番~次 time and again | ~令~申 repeated injunctions ❷ 表示不太大的大概数量[indicating quantity, number, etc. that is not very large]: ~年~载(几年) in a few years' time

【三下五除二】sān xià wǔ chú èr 珠算口诀之一。常用来形容做事及动作敏捷利索。[mnemonic rhyme for reckoning by the abacus] three-down-five-reject-two; rejecting two of the three to make a new five; neat and quick

【三夏】sānxià ❶ 夏收、夏种和夏管的统称 three summer jobs (of harvesting, planting, and field management) ❷〈书 *fml.*〉指夏季的三个月 the three summer months

【三弦】sānxián (~儿 sānxiánr) 弦乐器,木筒两面蒙蟒皮,上面有长柄,有三根弦。分大三弦和小三弦两种,大三弦又叫大鼓三弦,用做大鼓书的伴奏乐器;小三弦又叫曲弦,用做昆曲的伴奏乐器。*sanxian*; three-stringed plucked instrument having a three-stringed long stem attached to a wooden cylinder whose both ends are covered with boa skin. There are greater *sanxian*, used in accompaniment of *dagu* (musical and versified storytelling), and lesser *sanxian*, used as an accompanying instrument for Kunqu Opera. 通称 popularly known as 弦子 xián·zi

【三线】sānxiàn 我国国防上指后方,是支援前线的战略基地 third-line region, a national defence term that refers to the rear areas of the mainland in the early 1960s

【三心二意】sān xīn èr yì 形容犹豫不决或意志不坚定 be of two minds; shilly-shally; be half-hearted: 既然决定了,就不能~。There should be no more shilly-shallying once the decision was made.

【三星】sānxīng ❶ 猎户座中央三颗明亮的星,冬季天将黑时从东方升起,天将明时在西方落下,常根据它的位置估计时间 Orion's belt; three shiny stars in the centre of the constellation Orion, which rise in the east at dusk in winter and set in the west at dawn, thus making it possible to reckon time of the day by their positions ❷ 民间称福、禄、寿三神为三星 gods of happiness, wealth and longevity as known in folklore

【三言两语】sān yán liǎng yǔ 几句话。形容话很少。in a few words; in one word or two:这件事不是～说得完的。This can't be accounted for in a few words.

【三一三十一】sān yī sānshí yī 珠算口诀之一。常用来指按三份平均分配。[mnemonic rhyme for reckoning by the abacus] equally shared among three parties:所付的费用,大家～分摊。The expenses shall be equally shared among the three of us.

【三灾八难】sān zāi bā nàn〈佛教 *Budd.*〉指水灾、火灾、风灾为大三灾;刀兵、饥馑、疫疠为小三灾。八难指影响见佛求道的八种障碍如作恶多端、安逸享受、盲哑残疾、自恃聪明才智等。后泛指各种灾难、疾病。three disasters (three greater ones: flood, fire and windstorm; and three lesser ones: war, famine and pestilence) and eight impediments (including evil-doing, pleasure-seeking, physical handicaps such as blindness and muteness, and self-overconfidence in one's own intelligence); (general reference to) calamities and diseases

【三藏】Sān Zàng 佛教经典分为经、律、论三个部分,总称三藏。经,总说根本教义;律,述说戒律;论,阐发教义。(Budd.) tripitaka, referring to sutra-pitaka (scriptures), zinaya-pitaka (commandments) and abhidharma-pitaka (treatises)

【三朝】sānzhāo ❶ 指新婚后第三天,旧俗这一天新妇回娘家(old custom) 3rd day of marriage, a time for the bride to pay a visit to her parents ❷ 指婴儿初生后第三天,旧俗这一天为婴儿洗三 old custom of giving bath to a baby on the 3rd day of its birth

【三只手】sānzhīshǒu〈方 *dial.*〉指从别人身上偷东西的小偷;扒(pá)手 fleet-fingered thief; pickpocket; thief

【三足鼎立】sān zú dǐng lì 像鼎的三条腿那样站立着 standing like the three legs of a tripod;〈比喻 *fig*〉三方面的势力对峙 tripartite confrontation

【三座大山】sān zuò dà shān〈比喻 *fig.*〉我国新民主主义革命时期的三大敌人,即:帝国主义、封建主义和官僚资本主义 three big mountains, i.e. imperialism, feudalism and bureaucrat-capitalism, which weighed down on the backs of the Chinese people during the period of New Democratic Revolution

弎 sān same as 三 sān

叁 sān '三'的大写 upper case of the numeral '3'; ☞数字 shùzì on p. 1791

毵(毿) sān [毵毵](sānsān)〈书 *fml.*〉毛发、枝条等细长的样子(of hair, twigs, etc.) thin and long:～下垂(of hair or twig) hanging thin and long | 柳枝～slender and long willow twigs

sǎn (ㄙㄢˇ)

伞(傘、❶繖) sǎn ❶ 挡雨或遮太阳的用具,用油纸、布、塑料等制成,中间有柄,可以张合 umbrella; device for protection from rain or sun consisting of a collapsible, usu. circular canopy made of oiled paper, cloth, plastic, etc., mounted on a central rod:一把～an umbrella | 旱～parasol; sunshade | 雨～umbrella ❷ 像伞的东西 umbrella-like:降落～parachute ❸ (Sǎn) 姓 a surname

【伞兵】sǎnbīng 用降落伞着陆的空降兵 paratrooper; parachuter

散 sǎn ❶ 没有约束;松开;分散 come loose; fall apart:～漫 slovenly; slipshod | 松～loose; unorganized | 行李没打好,都～了。The luggage fell apart duc to improper packing. | 队伍别走～了。Don't let the procession break up. ❷ 零碎的;不集中的 fragmentary; scattered:～装 in bulk | ～居 live scattered ❸ 药末(多用做中药名 oft. used in traditional Chinese medicinal names) medicinal powder:健胃～digestive powder | 丸～膏丹 pills, powders, ointments and boluses

☞ sàn on p. 1656

【散兵游勇】sǎnbīng yóuyǒng 指失去统属的士兵。现也比喻没有组织到某项集体活动中而独自行动的人。stragglers and disbanded soldiers; (fig.) disorganized persons who act independent of a collective activity

【散工】sǎngōng 零工;短工 odd job; odd-job worker; temporary worker

☞ sàn//gōng on p. 1656

【散光】sǎnguāng 视力缺陷的一种,有散光眼的人看东西模糊不清,由角膜或晶状体表面的弯曲不规则,使进入眼球中的影像分散成许多部分引起 astigmatism; visual defect in which the irregular curvature of the cornca or the lens of the eye prevents light rays from focusing clearly at one point on the retina, resulting in blurred vision

【散记】sǎnjì 关于某一事物或活动的零碎记述(多用做文章标题或书名 oft. used in the title of an article or a book) random notes; sketches; sidelights:《旅美～》*American Sketches*

【散剂】sǎnjì 干燥而疏松的粉末状或颗粒状药物 powder medicine; pulvis

【散架】sǎn//jià 完整的东西散开 fall apart; fall to pieces;〈比喻 *fig.*〉散伙或垮台 collapse, disband; dissolve:木盆～了。The wooden bucket fell apart. | 浑身酸疼,骨头像散了架似的。I was aching all over, as if my limbs were falling apart. | 这个小组要不是你们几个撑着,早就～了。Without the support

S

of you guys this group would have broken up long ago.

【散居】sǎnjū 分散居住 live scattered:一家人～各地。Members of the family lived in different places.

【散漫】sǎnmàn ❶ 随随便便,不守纪律 undisciplined; lax in discipline; slack; careless and sloppy:自由～slackness in discipline ❷ 分散;不集中 unorganized; scattered:文章～零乱,层次不清。The article is disorganized and lacks unity and coherence.

【散曲】sǎnqǔ 盛行于元、明、清三代的没有宾白的曲子形式,内容以抒情为主,有小令和散套两种 non-dramatic song mainly expressing one's emotions, in vogue during the Yuan, Ming and Qing dynasties, in two categories — *xiaoling* (short tonal poem) and *santao* (sequence of *sanqu* songs of a certain musical mode)

【散射】sǎnshè ❶ 光线通过有尘埃的空气等媒质时,部分光线向多方面改变方向。超短波发射到电离层时也发生散射。scattering; dispersion; dispersal of part of a beam of radiation into a range of directions as a result of physical interactions with dusty air or other media. The same also happens to radiation of extra-short waves to the ionosphere. ❷ 两个基本粒子碰撞时,运动方向改变(of two elementary particles) change direction of movement upon collision ❸ 在某些情况下,声波投射到不平的分界面或媒质中的微粒上而向不同方向传播 diffusion; scattering of sound wave by reflection from a rough surface or specks in a medium; also 乱反射 luànfǎnshè

【散套】sǎntào 散曲的一种,由同一宫调的若干支曲子组成的组曲 *santao*; sequence of *sanqu* songs of the same musical mode

【散体】sǎntǐ 不要求词句齐整对偶的文体(区别于'骈体'as compared with 'rhythmical prose style, marked by parallelism and ornateness') prose style free from parallelism; simple, direct prose style

【散文】sǎnwén ❶ 指不讲究韵律的文章(区别于'韵文' as compared with 'literary composition in rhyme') prose; ordinary writing without metrical structure ❷ 指除诗歌、戏剧、小说外的文学作品,包括杂文、随笔、特写等 literary works including scribbles, essays, and sketches, as distinguished from poetry, drama and fiction

【散装】sǎnzhuāng 指原来整包整桶的商品,出售时临时分成小包小袋,或零星出售不加包装 unpackaged; loose packed; in bulk:～洗衣粉 bulk detergent|～白酒 liquor in bulk

【散座】sǎnzuò (～儿 sǎnzuòr) ❶〈旧指 *old*〉剧场中包厢以外的座位 seats in a theatre, not including the balcony and boxes ❷〈旧指 *old*〉人力车夫拉的不固定的主顾 random patron of a rickshaw puller ❸ 饭馆指为零散客人设的座位 restaurant seat for single diners

糁(糝) sǎn〈方 *dial.*〉米饭粒儿 cooked rice grain

☞ shēn on p.1704

馓 sǎn [馓子](sǎn·zi)油炸的面食,细条相连扭成花样 grid-like deep-fried dough twist

sàn(ㄙㄢˋ)

散 sàn ❶ 由聚集而分离 disperse; separate:～场(of a meeting) breakup|解～disband|烟消云～vanish like mist and smoke; turn to dust and ashes|会还没有～。The meeting is not over yet. ❷ 散布 distribute; disseminate:发～diffuse; diverge|公园里～满花香。The fragrance of flowers was diffused throughout the park.|～传单 distribute leaflets ❸ 排除 dispel:～闷 relief one's boredom|～心 refresh oneself; unwind oneself ❹〈方 *dial.*〉解雇 sack; unemploy:旧社会资本家随便～工人。In old times capitalists could sack their workers at will.

☞ sǎn on p.1655

【散播】sànbō 散布开 disseminate; spread:～种子 broadcast sowing|～谣言 spread rumours; go rumourmongering

【散布】sànbù 分散到各处 sow; spread; disseminate:～传单 distribute leaflets|羊群～在山坡上吃草。Flocks of sheep are grazing here and there on the hillocks.|～流言飞语 sow lies and slanders

【散步】sàn//bù 随便走走(作为一种休息方式) take a walk; go for a walk or stroll:休息时,到河边散散步。Take a stroll by the river during the break.

【散场】sàn//chǎng 戏剧、电影、比赛等一场结束,观众离开(of a theatrical performance, movie show, sports competition, etc.) be over:电影～了。The movie is over.

【散发】sànfā 发出;分发 lend; send out or forth; emit; waft:花儿～着阵阵的芳香。The flowers lent a sweet perfume in whiffs.|～文件 circulate a document

【散工】sàn//gōng 收工;放工 go off work; knock off:今天提前～。We finished work earlier today.

☞ sǎngōng on p.1655

【散会】sàn//huì 一次会议结束,参加的人离开会场(of a meeting) break up; come to an end

【散伙】sàn//huǒ (团体、组织等)解散(of a group, organization, etc.) disband; dissolve

【散落】sànluò ❶ 分散地往下落 fall scattered:花瓣～了一地。The ground was scattered with fallen petals. ❷ 分散;不集中 be scattered:草原上～着数不清的牛羊。The meadowland is strewn with countless grazing cattle and sheep. ❸ 因分散而失落或流落 disappear in different places; disperse:一家骨肉不知～何方。The family was torn apart, and the members were scattered where god knows.

【散闷】sàn//mèn 排遣烦闷 divert oneself from boredom:～消愁 seek diversion from one's worries|到公园散散闷。Go refresh yourself in the park.

【散失】sànshī ❶ 分散遗失 be missing; be lost:那部书稿在战乱中～了。The manuscripts of the work were lost in war and turmoil. ❷(水分等)消散失去(of moisture) dissipate; vaporise; be lost:水果、蔬菜贮藏在地窖里,水分不容易～。Fruit and vegetables do not lose their moisture easily if they are stored in a cellar.

【散水】sàn·shuǐ 在房屋等建筑物外墙的墙脚周围,用砖石、混凝土铺成的斜坡。宽度多在一米上下,作用是把雨水排离墙角,以保护地基。apron; slanting strip of brick, stone or cement, oft. one metre in width, paved at the foot of the outer wall of a building to drain rainwater from the corner of the wall and protect the foundation

【散摊子】sàn tān·zi 散伙 break up; disband; also 散摊儿 sàn tānr

【散戏】sàn//xì 戏剧演出结束,观众离开剧场(of a show, play, opera, etc.) be over

【散心】sàn//xīn 使心情舒畅;解闷 drive away one's cares; relieve boredom:出去走走,散散心。Let's take a walk and refresh ourselves.

sāng(ㄙㄤ)

丧(喪、丧) sāng 跟死了人有关的(事情) funeral; mourning:～事 funeral affairs|治～ make funeral arrangement

☞ sàng on p.1658

【丧服】sāngfú 为哀悼死者而穿的服装。我国旧时习俗用本色的粗布或麻布做成。mourning apparel. By an old Chinese custom, mourning apparels are made from coarse cloth or hemp fabrics in their original colours.

【丧家】sāngjiā 有丧事的人家 family of the deceased

【丧礼】sānglǐ 有关丧事的礼仪 obsequies; funeral

【丧乱】sāngluàn 〈书 *fml.*〉指死亡祸乱的事 disturbance and bloodshed; tragic disaster

【丧事】sāngshì 人死后处置遗体等事 funeral arrangements:办～ handle affairs associated with a funeral|～从简 simplify all the funeral arrangements

【丧葬】sāngzàng 办理丧事,埋葬死者 burial:～费 funeral expenses

【丧钟】sāngzhōng 西方风俗,教堂在宣告本区教徒死亡或为死者举行宗教仪式时敲钟叫做敲丧钟。因此用丧钟来比喻死亡或灭亡。knell; funeral bell; death knell. By the Western custom, a church rings its bells slowly and solemnly by way of announcing the death of a follower in the parish or when holding a religious service for the deceased. Hence the term, knell, meaning death or downfall.

桑 sāng ❶ 桑树,落叶乔木,树皮有浅裂,叶子卵形,花单性,花被黄绿色。叶子是蚕的饲料,嫩枝的韧皮纤维可造纸,果穗可以吃,嫩枝、根的白皮、叶和果实均可入药。mulberry (*Morus*); deciduous tree having shallow cracks in its bark, oval leaves that are used to feed silkworms, unisexual flowers in yellowish green perianths, and edible berries, the bark fibre of its tender branches being a paper-making material, and its tender branches, the white skin of its roots, leaves and fruits being of medical value ❷(Sāng)姓 a surname

【桑那浴】sāngnàyù 一种利用蒸汽排汗的沐浴方式。起源于芬兰。sauna bath; Finnish steam bath designed to accelerate perspiration [桑那 also transliterated as 桑拿 sāngná]

【桑皮纸】sāngpízhǐ 用桑树皮做的纸,质地坚韧 mulberry (bark) paper; paper made from mulberry bark, of a resilient texture

【桑葚儿】sāngrènr 桑葚(sāngshèn) mulberry (fruit)

【桑葚】sāngshèn 桑树的果穗,成熟时黑紫色或白色,味甜,可以吃 mulberry; sweet and edible fruit of the mulberry tree, turning dark purple or white when ripe; also 桑葚子 sāngshèn·zi

【桑榆暮景】sāng yú mù jǐng 落日的余辉照在桑榆树梢上 the last rays of the setting sun lingering on the top of a mulberry tree; 〈比喻 *fig.*〉老年的时光 evening of life; old age

【桑梓】sāngzǐ 〈书 *fml.*〉《诗经·小雅·小弁》:'维桑与梓,必恭敬止。'是说家乡的桑树和梓树是父母种的,对它要表示敬意。后人用来比喻故乡。mulberry and catalpa, referring to one's native place. *The Book of Songs·Odes·Happy Jackdaws*: 'The mulberry and catalpa raised by parents/ Must be looked up to with great esteem.

sǎng(ㄙㄤˇ)

搡 sǎng 〈方 *dial.*〉猛推 shove; thrust:推推～～shoves and thrusts|把他～了个跟头。He was shoved off his feet and fell to the ground.

嗓 sǎng ❶ same as 嗓子 sǎng·zi ①❷(～儿 sǎngr)嗓音 voice:小～儿 soft voice|哑～儿 hoarse voice

【嗓门儿】sǎngménr same as 嗓音 sǎngyīn:～大 have a loud voice

【嗓音】sǎngyīn 说话或歌唱的声音 voice：～洪亮 resonant voice

【嗓子】sǎng·zi ❶ 喉咙 throat；larynx：～疼 sore throat ❷ 嗓音 voice：放开～唱 sing at the top of one's voice

磉 sǎng 柱子底下的石礅 base of a pillar；pedestal

颡 sǎng 〈书 *fml.*〉额；脑门子 forehead

sàng（ㄙㄤˋ）

丧（喪、丧） sàng 丧失 lose；be bereaved：～尽天良 inhuman；utterly conscienceless｜～权辱国 humiliate the nation and forfeit its sovereignty；national betrayal

☞ sāng on p. 1657

【丧胆】sàng//dǎn 形容非常恐惧 terrified；terror-stricken：敌军闻风～。The enemy troops panicked at the news.

【丧魂落魄】sàng hún luò pò 形容非常恐惧的样子 be scared out of one's wits；shaken to the core；also 丧魂失魄 sàng hún shī pò

【丧家之犬】sàng jiā zhī quǎn 〈比喻 *fig.*〉失去靠山，到处乱窜，无处投奔的人（of a person）behave like a disowned dog；homeless dog；stray cur；also 丧家之狗 sàng jiā zhī gǒu

【丧命】sàng//mìng 死亡（多指凶死或死于暴病 usu. from violence or of the sudden attack of a severe illness）meet one's death；get killed

【丧偶】sàng'ǒu 〈书 *fml.*〉死了配偶 be bereaved of one's spouse：中年～lose one's wife or husband at middle age

【丧气】sàng//qì 因事情不顺利而情绪低落 downhearted；dejected；crestfallen：灰心～feel disheartened｜垂头～feel demoralized

【丧气】sàng·qi 倒霉；不吉利 be unlucky；be out of luck；have bad luck：～话 gloomy talk

【丧权辱国】sàng quán rǔ guó 丧失主权使国家蒙受耻辱 surrender a country's sovereign rights under humiliating terms

【丧生】sàng//shēng 丧命 meet one's death；lose one's life；be killed

【丧失】sàngshī 失去 lose；forfeit：～信心 lose confidence｜～工作能力 lose the ability to work

【丧亡】sàngwáng 死亡；灭亡 demise；death；downfall

【丧心病狂】sàng xīn bìng kuáng 丧失理智，像发了疯一样。形容言行昏乱而荒谬或残忍可恶到了极点。in a frenzy；in such violent mental agitation as to be extremely absurd or brutal

【丧志】sàngzhì 丧失志气；失去进取心 dispirited；demoralized；dejected：玩物～sap one's aspiration by seeking pleasure

sāo（ㄙㄠ）

搔 sāo 用指甲挠 scratch：～头皮 scratch one's head｜～到痒处 scratch where it itches（〈比喻〉说到点子上 hit the nail on the head）｜～首弄姿 stroke one's hair in coquetry；posture and preen oneself（形容卖弄姿容 be coquettish）

骚[1] sāo 扰乱；不安定 disturb；upset：～乱 commotion；tumult｜～扰 harass；harassment

骚[2] sāo ❶ 指屈原的《离骚》reference to Qu Yuan's poem *Encountering Sorrow*（*Li Shao*）：～体 *sao* style；verse style derived from Qu Yuan's *Li Shao* or *Encountering Sorrow* ❷〈书 *fml.*〉泛指诗文 poetry：～人 poet

骚[3] sāo ❶ 指举止轻佻，作风下流 flirtatious；loose；lascivious：风～skittish｜～货 tart；loose woman；lascivious woman ❷〈方 *dial.*〉雄性的（某些家畜）（of certain domestic animals）male：～马 stallion｜～驴 jackass ❸ same as 臊 sāo

【骚动】sāodòng ❶ 扰乱，使地方不安宁 disturbance；local unrest ❷ 秩序紊乱；动乱 disorder；disturbance：会场～。The audience in the meeting hall agitated.｜在人群里引起一阵～。This caused some disturbance in the crowd.

【骚客】sāokè〈书 *fml.*〉诗人 poet

【骚乱】sāoluàn 混乱不安 disturbance；riot

【骚扰】sāorǎo 使不安宁；扰乱 harass：外敌～边境。The foreign enemy kept harassing the border region.｜土匪～村寨。The villages are being harassed by bandits.

【骚人】sāorén〈书 *fml.*〉诗人 poet

【骚体】sāotǐ 古典文学体裁的一种，以模仿屈原的《离骚》的形式得名 *sao* style；verse style derived from Qu Yuan's poem *Li Shao*（*Encountering Sorrow*），characterized by the use of six-syllable couplets，the two lines of each couplet being connected by *xi* 兮，a modal particle

缫（缲） sāo 把蚕茧浸在热水里，抽出蚕丝 soak cocoons in hot water and reel silk from them；reel

☞ 缲 qiāo on p. 1549

臊 sāo 像尿或狐狸的气味 smell of urine or of the fox：～气 stench；stink；foul smell｜腥～smell of rotten fish

☞ sào on p. 1660

sǎo（ㄙㄠˇ）

扫（掃） sǎo ❶ 用笤帚、扫帚除去尘土、垃圾等 sweep away dust，garbage，etc. with a broom or whisk：～雪 sweep away the snow|把地～～～sweep the floor ❷ 除去；消灭 wipe out：～雷 mine sweeping|～盲 eliminate illiteracy ❸ 很快地左右移动 move right and left quickly；sweep across：～射 strafe|眼光向人群～～sweep one's eyes across a crowd ❹ 归拢在一起 put together：～数 total number；whole amount

☞ sào on p.1659

【扫除】sǎochú ❶ 清除肮脏的东西 clean up；clean：大～major housecleaning|室内室外要天天～。A cleanup both indoors and outdoors is needed every day. ❷ 除去有碍前进的事物 remove；wipe out：～障碍 remove an obstacle|～文盲 eliminate illiteracy

【扫荡】sǎodàng ❶ 用武力或其他手段肃清敌人 round up enemy troops by use of force or other means；mop up ❷ 泛指彻底清除 root out；do away with thoroughly：旧社会遗留下来的腐朽东西，都应当～。Vestiges of decadence of the old society should be rooted out.

【扫地】sǎo//dì ❶ 用笤帚、扫帚清除地上的脏东西 sweep the floor ❷〈比喻 *fig.*〉名誉、威风等完全丧失（of honour；credibility，etc.）be dragged in the dust；reach rock bottom：威信～be shorn of one's prestige|斯文～consign the literate to the dust；bring disgrace on civilization

【扫地出门】sǎo dì chū mén 没收全部财产，赶出家门 sweep the garbage out；confiscate one's property and drive him out of the family；be disowned

【扫黄】sǎo//huáng 扫除各种黄色书刊、音像制品等 anti-pornography campaign，in which pornographic books，magazines and audiovisual products are confiscated

【扫雷】sǎo//léi 排除敷设的地雷或水雷 mine sweeping or clearance

【扫盲】sǎo//máng 扫除文盲，对不识字或识字很少的成年人进行识字教育，使他们脱离文盲状态 wipe out illiteracy；effort to teach adults how to read and write and bring them out of illiteracy

【扫描】sǎomiáo ❶ 利用一定装置使电子束、无线电波等左右移动而描绘出画面、物体等图形 scan；use of a device to move electron beams or radio waves over a picture or object and draw the patterns accordingly ❷ 借指扫视 cast a quick glance

【扫墓】sǎo//mù 在墓地祭奠、培土和打扫。现也指在烈士碑墓前举行纪念活动 sweep a grave to pay respects to a dead person；memorial service taking place before the tomb of a revolutionary martyr：清明～pay respects to the deceased on the Pure Brightness Day

【扫平】sǎopíng 扫荡平定 quell；crack down on：～匪患 crack down on banditry

【扫射】sǎoshè ❶ 用机关枪、冲锋枪等左右移动连续射击 strafe；continuous sweeping attack with a machine gun or tommy gun ❷ 指目光或灯光向四周掠过 sweep；glance；run a searchlight over

【扫视】sǎoshì 目光迅速地向周围看（of cycs）glance：向台下～了一下。He tossed a glance at the audience.

【扫数】sǎoshù 尽数；全数 total；whole amount：～还清 all paid off|～入库 all put in storage

【扫榻】sǎotà〈书 *fml.*〉打扫床上灰尘，表示欢迎客人 clear away bed's dust；sweep the mat（in anticipation of a visitor）：～以待 get everything ready for sb.'s visit

【扫堂腿】sǎotángtuǐ 武术招数，用一只腿猛力横扫以绊倒对方 sweep one's leg violently to knock down the opponent－a martial arts manoeuver；also 扫腿 sǎotuǐ

【扫听】sǎo·ting〈方 *dial.*〉探询；从旁打听 make inquiries about

【扫尾】sǎo//wěi 结束最后部分的工作 wind up；round off

【扫兴】sǎo//xìng 正当高兴时遇到不愉快的事情而兴致低落 have one's spirits dampened；feel disappointed：别说～的话。Stop making disappointing remarks.|你要不去，岂不扫了大伙儿的兴。You'll disappoint everybody if you choose not to go.

嫂 sǎo ❶ 哥哥的妻子 elder brother's wife；sister-in-law：兄～elder sister-in-law|表～cousin's wife ❷ 泛称年纪不大的已婚妇女（form of address for a married woman about one's own age）sister：王～Sister Wang|大～Elder Sister

【嫂夫人】sǎofū·ren 对朋友尊称他的妻子（polite form of address for a friend's wife）your wife

【嫂嫂】sǎo·sao〈方 *dial.*〉嫂子 elder brother's wife；elder sister-in-law

【嫂子】sǎo·zi 哥哥的妻子 elder brother's wife；elder sister-in-law：二～second elder brother's wife|堂房～cousin's wife

溲 sǎo ☞［菽溲］（màosǎo）on p.1311

sào（ㄙㄠˋ）

扫（掃） sào 义同'扫'（sǎo），用于'扫帚'、'扫把'等 same in meaning as 扫（sweep），used in 扫帚 or 扫把，which both mean broom

☞ sǎo on p.1658

【扫把】sàobǎ〈方 *dial.*〉same as 扫帚 sào·zhou

【扫帚】sào·zhou 除去尘土、垃圾等的用具，多用竹枝扎成，比笤帚大 broom；bamboo twigs，straw，or bristles bound together and attached to a stick or handle，and used for sweeping

【扫帚星】sào·zhouxīng 彗星的通称 popular

term for comet:〈旧时 *old*〉迷信的人认为出现扫帚星就会发生灾难。因此扫帚星也用为骂人的话,如果认为发生的祸害是由某人带来的,就说某人是扫帚星。Superstitous people regard the occurrence of the comet as the harbinger of a disaster, and thus comet becomes a curse that is synonymous to jinx. For example, someone who has brought ill luck is oft. cursed as a 'comet'.

埽 sào ❶ 把树枝、秫秸、石头等捆紧做成的圆柱形的东西。治理黄河时用它保护堤岸防水冲刷。cylindrical bundle of tree twigs, sorghum stalks and stone, used to protect the dykes of the Yellow River from soil erosion ❷ 用许多埽做成的水工建筑物 water conservancy structure made of such bundles

梢 sào ❶ 像圆锥体的形状 conical shape ❷ ☞锥度 zhuīdù on p.2529

☞ shāo on p.1688

瘙 sào〈古代 *arch.*〉指疥疮 scabies

【瘙痒】sàoyǎng (皮肤)发痒(of skin) itch:～难忍 unbearable itch

氉 sào ☞ [毷氉] (màosào) on p.1312

臊 sào same as 羞① xiū:害～bashful; shy | ～得脸通红 blush scarlet

☞ sāo on p.1658

【臊气】sàoqì〈方 *dial.*〉倒霉 bad luck; out of luck; down on one's luck

【臊子】sào·zi〈方 *dial.*〉肉末或肉丁(多指烹调好加在别的食物中的) minced or diced meat, oft. cooked to be added to other food:羊肉～面 noodles topped with minced mutton

sè (ㄙㄜˋ)

色 sè ❶ 颜色 colour:红～red | 三～版 three-colour printing block | 五颜六～multi-coloured; colourful ❷ 脸上表现的神情;神色 countenance; look; expression:喜形于～light up with pleasure; look pleased | 面不改～ do not change colour; keep one's face bravely; preserve appearance | 和颜悦～ kind and pleasant countenance; amiable manner ❸ 种类 kind:货～goods | 各～各样 rich and varied ❹ 情景;景象 scene; scenery:景～scenery | 夜～nocturnal scene | 行～匆匆 hit the road in haste ❺ 物品的质量 quality:成～purity (of gold) | 足～100 percent pure ❻ 指妇女美貌 feminine charms:姿～good looks | ～艺双绝 be at once a stunning beauty and a consummate artist ❼ 指情欲 lust:～情 pornography | ～胆 unbridled lust

☞ shǎi on p.1668

【色彩】sècǎi ❶ 颜色 colour; hue:～鲜明 bright-coloured ❷〈比喻 *fig.*〉人的某种思想倾向或事物的某种情调 propensity; emotional appeal:思想～ideological appeal | 地方～local flavour

【色调】sèdiào ❶ 指画面上表现思想、情感的色彩及浓淡。各种红色或黄色构成的色调属于暖色调,用来表现兴奋、快乐等情感;各种蓝色或绿色构成的色调属于寒色调,用来表现忧郁、悲哀等情感。tone; hue; shade of colour; general effect of colour and shade in expressing an idea or emotion in painting, various shades of red or yellow are warm tones that give expression to excitement and happiness, while different shades of blue or green are cold tones that express melancholy, sadness, etc. ❷〈比喻 *fig.*〉文艺作品中思想感情的色彩(of works of literature and art) ideological or sentimental appeal:作品含有忧郁、悲凉的～。The work is tinged with a sombre and doleful appeal.

【色光】sèguāng 带颜色的光。白色的光通过棱镜分解成七种色光。chromatic light; coloured light; white light passing through a prism breaks up into seven chromatic lights

【色觉】sèjué 各种有色光反映到视网膜上所产生的感觉 colour vision; vision induced by reflection of various chromatic lights on the retina

【色拉】sèlā 西餐中的一种凉拌菜,一般是由熟土豆丁、香肠丁等加调味汁拌和而成 salad; cold dish of chopped boiled potato, sausage, or other food, prepared with a dressing such as mayonnaise; also transliterated as 沙拉 shālā

【色厉内荏】sè lì nèi rěn 外表强硬而内心怯懦 put on an appearance of stern firmness while being weak inwardly; fierce of mien but faint of heart; threatening in manner but cowardly at heart

【色盲】sèmáng 眼睛不能辨别颜色的病,常见的是红绿色盲,患者不能区别红绿两种颜色。也有只能区别明暗不能区别色彩的全色盲。色盲多为先天性的,患者多为男子。achromatopsia; colour blindness; defective colour perception; a common type of colour-blind patient cannot perceive red and green, but there are also those who are blind to all colours and who can only perceive light and shade; achromatopsia is usu. congenital, and most patients are male

【色目人】Sèmùrén 元代统治者对西域各族人及西夏人的总称 people of special category — one of the classes into which China's population was divided during the Yuan Dynasty, including Central Asian allies of the Mongols, mostly Uygurs and other Turks (placed next below the Mongols and above the Han Chinese)

【色情】sèqíng 男女情欲 sexual urge:～狂 sex mania; erotomania | ～小说 erotic fiction

【色弱】sèruò 程度较轻的色盲，辨别颜色的能力低 colour blindness of a lesser degree

【色散】sèsàn 复色光被分解成单色光而形成光谱的现象 chromatic dispersion; phenomenon of multihued light dispersing into single chromatic lights to form the spectrum

【色素】sèsù 使有机体具有各种不同颜色的物质，如红花具有的红色素，紫花具有的紫色素等。某些色素在生理过程中起很重要的作用，如血液中的血色素能输送氧气，植物体中的绿色素能进行光合作用。pigment; substance, such as haematochrome in red flowers and purpurin in purple flowers, that renders a characteristic colour in plant or animal tissue. Some pigments play a major role in the physiological process, such as hemachrome that can transmit oxygen in the blood, and chlorophyll that causes photosynthesis in a plant.

【色相】sèxiàng ❶ 色彩所呈现出来的质的面貌。如日光通过三棱镜分解出的红、橙、黄、绿、青、紫六种色相。colour of the spectrum, such as red, orange, yellow, green, blue and violet produced by sunlight through a prism ❷〈佛教 *Budd.*〉指一切物体的形状外貌。后来也指女子的容貌和体态 *rupa*; corporeality; feminine charms; female sexual appeal: 牺牲～(of a woman) offer sexual favour to gain sth. in return

【色欲】sèyù 性欲；情欲 sexual urge; lust

【色泽】sèzé 颜色和光泽 colour and lustre: ～鲜明 bright and lustrous

涩(澀、澁) sè ❶ 像明矾或不熟的柿子那样使舌头感到麻木干燥的味道 puckery; astringent; taste numbing to the tongue, as of alum or raw persimmon ❷ 摩擦时阻力大；不滑润 rasping; scraping; grating: 滞～hard-going | 轮轴发～，该上油了。The wheel shaft is a kind of rasping. It needs oiling. ❸（文句）难读；难懂 difficult to understand; unreadable: 晦～obscure | 艰～intricate and abstruse

【涩滞】sèzhì 呆滞；不流畅 stagnant; rough: 声音～grating sound | 文笔～obscure style of writing | 一双～失神的眼睛 a pair of dull and glazy eyes

啬(嗇) sè 吝啬 stingy; miserly

【啬刻】sè·ke〈方 *dial.*〉吝啬 stingy; miserly

铯 sè 金属元素，符号 Cs (caesium)。银白色，质软，化学性质极活泼，在光的作用下易放出电子，遇水发生爆炸。用于制光电池和真空管等。caesium (Cs); silvery, soft metal element that has an active chemical property, releases electrons under light, explodes with water, and is used as a material for the making of batteries and vacuum tubes

瑟 sè〈古代 *arch.*〉弦乐器，像琴。现在所用的瑟有两种，一种有二十五根弦，另一种有十六根弦。*se*; lute; zither-like plucked instrument having 50 strings in ancient times but the modern version has 25 or 16 strings

【瑟瑟】sèsè ❶ 形容轻微的声音(of the wind) rustling: 秋风～。The autumnal wind rustles. ❷ 形容颤抖(of a person) trembling: ～发抖 tremble with cold or fear

【瑟缩】sèsuō 身体因寒冷、受惊等而蜷缩或兼抖动 curl up and shiver with cold; cower

塞 sè 义同'塞'(sāi)，用于某些合成词中 [*same as* 塞 sāi in meaning, used in certain compound words]

☞ sāi on p. 1649 and sài on p. 1649

【塞擦音】sècāyīn 气流通路紧闭然后逐渐打开而摩擦发出的辅音，如普通话语音的 z、c、zh、ch、j、q。塞擦音的起头近似塞音，末了近似擦音，所以叫塞擦音 affricate; complex speech sound consisting of a stop consonant followed by a fricative, e. g. z, c, zh, ch, j, and q in the *pinyin* system of *putonghua*; known in the past as 破裂摩擦音 pòliè mócāyīn

【塞音】sèyīn 气流通路紧闭然后突然打开而发出的辅音，如普通话语音的 b、p、d、t、g、k plosive; stop; consonant produced by complete closure of the oral passage and subsequent release accompanied by a burst of air, as in the sound b, p, d, t, g and k in the *pinyin* system of *putonghua*; also 爆发音 bàofāyīn; known in the past as 破裂音 pòlièyīn

【塞责】sèzé 对自己应负的责任敷衍了事 palter; act perfunctorily: 敷衍～be perfunctory in performing one's duties

濇(濇) sè〈书 *fml.*〉same as 涩 sè

穑(穡) sè ☞ 稼穑 jiàsè on p. 937

sēn (ㄙㄣ)

森 sēn ❶ 形容树木多 heavy wooded: ～林 jungle; forest ❷〈书 *fml.*〉繁密；众多 dense; luxuriant; thick; multitudous: ～罗万象（纷然罗列的各种事物现象）myriads of things; everything under the sun ❸ 阴暗 glum; dreary; somber; moody: 阴～gruesome; ghastly

【森林】sēnlín 通常指大片生长的树木；林业上指在相当广阔的土地上生长的很多树木，连同在这块土地上的动物以及其他植物所构成的整体。森林是木材的主要来源，同时有保持水土，调节气候，防止水、旱、风、沙等灾害的作用。forest; dense growth of trees and underbrush covering a large area; wooded area with animals and other plants inhabiting in it. Forests are a major source of timber and play a major role in preserving water and soil, regulating the weather, and preventing floods, draught, windstorm, sandstorm and other natural calamities.

【森罗殿】sēnluódiàn 迷信传说指阎罗所居住的殿堂 Hall of Darkness, where Yama Raja (the King of Hell) lives

【森然】sēnrán ❶ 形容繁密直立(of tall trees) dense; thick:林木～dense cluster of towering trees ❷ 形容森严可畏 spine-chilling; awesome; eerie; ghostly:大殿幽暗～。There's sth. melancholy and spine-chilling about the main hall.

【森森】sēnsēn ❶ 形容树木茂盛繁密(of trees) dense; thick; luxuriant:松柏～dense pine and cypress trees ❷ 形容阴森岑寂 ghastly; eerie:阴～eeriness

【森严】sēnyán 整齐严肃;(防备)严密 stern; strict:壁垒～fortified bulwark|戒备～heavy security; carefully guarded

sēng (ㄙㄥ)

僧 sēng 出家修行的男性佛教徒;和尚 Buddhist monk; monk; man who has been tonsured, lives in a monastery and is devoted to Buddhism:～人 monk|～衣 monastic habit [僧伽之省,梵 Sanskrit: samgha (monastic order)]

【僧多粥少】sēng duō zhōu shǎo 〈比喻 *fig.*〉人多东西少,不够分配 there's little porridge but too many monks to feed; not enough to satisfy everyone

【僧侣】sēnglǚ 僧徒,也借来称某些别的宗教(如古印度婆罗门教、中世纪天主教)的修道人 monks and priests; (of Brahmanism of ancient India, mediaeval Catholicism, etc.) clergy

【僧尼】sēngní 和尚和尼姑 Buddhist monks and nuns

【僧俗】sēngsú 僧尼和一般人 clergy and laity; religious and lay

【僧徒】sēngtú 和尚的总称 Buddhist monks

鬙 sēng ☞ 鬅鬙 péngsēng on p.1460

shā (ㄕㄚ)

杀(殺) shā ❶ 使人或动物失去生命;弄死 slay; kill; put to death; slaughter; butcher:～虫 insecticide|～鸡 butcher a chicken|～敌 wipe out an enemy ❷ 战斗 fight:～出重围 fight one's way out of a heavy encirclement ❸ 削弱;减少;消除 weaken; reduce; abate:减～reduction|～价 price reduction|～暑气 reduce the effect of summer heat|风势稍～。The wind has subsided a little.|拿人～气 vent one's spleen on sb. ❹ same as 煞①:～笔 stop writing|～尾 bring sth. to an end ❺ 用在动词后,表示程度深 [used after a noun] extremely; exceedingly:气～drive sb. mad|恨～morbid hatred|笑～人 ridiculous to the extreme ❻ 〈方 *dial.*〉药物等刺激皮肤或黏膜使感觉疼痛 hurt; smart; (of medicine) cause a sharp, usu. superficial, stinging pain in the skin or mucous membrane:伤口用酒精消毒～得慌。It really hurts to disinfect the wound with alcohol.|肥皂水～眼睛。The suds made my eyes smart.

【杀风景】shā fēngjǐng 损坏美好的景色 be an eyesore; 〈比喻 *fig.*〉在兴高采烈的场合使人扫兴 spoil the fun; be a wet blanket; also 煞风景 shā fēngjǐng

【杀害】shāhài 杀死;害死(多指为了不正当目的) murder; do sb. in; kill for an unjustified reason:惨遭～be murdered in cold blood|～野生动物 kill wildlife

【杀机】shājī 杀人的念头 murderous intentions

【杀鸡取卵】shā jī qǔ luǎn 〈比喻 *fig.*〉只图眼前的好处而损害长远的利益 kill the hen to get the eggs; kill the goose that lays the golden eggs

【杀鸡吓猴】shā jī xià hóu 〈比喻 *fig.*〉惩罚一个人来吓唬另外的人 kill the chicken to frighten the monkey — punish someone as a warning to others; also 杀鸡给猴看 shā jī gěi hóu kàn

【杀价】shā//jià 压低价格。指买主利用卖主急于出售的机会,大幅度地压低价格。beat a seller down; (of a buyer) beat a seller down to an extremely low price by taking advantage of his eagerness to sell

【杀戒】shājiè 〈佛教 *Budd.*〉指禁止杀害生灵的戒律 taboo against taking life:大开～go on a killing rampage; kill by great numbers

【杀菌】shā//jūn 用日光、高温、氯气、石炭酸、酒精、抗生素等杀死病菌 disinfect; sterilize; cleanse so as to destroy or prevent the growth of disease-carrying microorganisms by using sunlight, heat, chlorine, carbolic acid, alcohol, antibiotics, etc.

【杀戮】shālù 杀害(多指大量地) massive killing; massacre; slaughter:～无辜 wonton killing of innocent people

【杀气】[1] shāqì 凶恶的气势 aura of death; murderous look:～腾腾 murderous-looking; ferocious

【杀气】[2] shāqì 发泄不愉快的情绪;出气 vent one's spleen:你有委屈就说出来,不该拿别人～。Get it off your chest if you feel you've been wronged. Don't take it out on others.

【杀青】shāqīng ❶ 古人著书写在竹简上,为了便于书写和防止虫蛀,先把青竹简用火烤干水分,叫做杀青。后来泛指写定著作。ancient practice to bake fresh bamboo slips on the fire until they were dry and ready for writing on; (in a broad sense) finalize a manuscript ❷ 绿茶加工制作的第一道工序,把摘下的嫩叶加

高温，破坏其中的酵素，抑制发酵，使茶叶保持固有的绿色，同时减少叶中水分，使叶片变软，便于进一步加工 preserve the greenness of tea leaves; 1st step in the making of green tea by heating tender tea leaves that have been freshly picked to destroy the ferment in them and prevent fermentation, preserve their greenness, reduce the moisture in them, and soften them for further processing

【杀人不见血】shā rén bù jiàn xiě 〈比喻 *fig.*〉害人的手段非常阴险毒辣，人受了害还一时察觉不出 kill without spilling blood; kill by subtle means

【杀人不眨眼】shā rén bù zhǎ yǎn 形容极其凶狠残忍，杀人成性 diabolical; kill without blinking

【杀人越货】shā rén yuè huò 杀害人的性命，抢夺人的财物（越：夺取）；指盗匪的行为（of banditry）kill a person and seize his goods; rob and kill（越 *yue* meaning 'seize'）

【杀伤】shāshāng 打死打伤 kill and wound; inflict casualties on：～力 antipersonnel capacity

【杀身】shāshēn 被杀害；丧身 be killed; lose one's life：～之祸 fatal disaster

【杀身成仁】shā shēn chéng rén 为正义或崇高的理想而牺牲生命 die to achieve virtue; die for a just cause or a noble ideal

【杀生】shāshēng 称宰杀牲畜、家禽等生物 take animal life

【杀手】shāshǒu 刺杀人的人 killer：职业～assassin; murderer

【杀手锏】shāshǒujiǎn ☞ 撒手锏 sāshǒujiǎn on p.1647

【杀一儆百】shā yī jǐng bǎi 杀一个人来警戒许多人 execute one as a warning to a hundred; 儆 also put as 警 jǐng

杉 shā 义同'杉'(shān)，用于'杉木、杉篙' same as 杉 shān in meaning, used in 杉木 shāmù and 杉篙 shāgāo

☞ shān on p.1671

【杉篙】shāgāo 杉(shān)树一类的树干砍去枝叶后制成的细而长的杆子，通常用来搭脚手架或撑船 fir pole, oft. used for building a scaffold or for punting a boat

【杉木】shāmù 杉(shān)树的木材 fir wood

沙[1] shā ❶ 细小的石粒 sand; grit：风～sandstorm | 防～林 anti-sandstorm forestbelt | 飞～走石 dust and stone fly as in storm; wind that carries sand and drives stones ❷ 像沙的东西 sand-like substance：豆～puree; sweetened bean paste ❸（Shā）姓 surname

沙[2] shā（嗓音）不清脆，不响亮（of voice）raucous; hoarse; husky：～哑 hoarse | ～音 raucous sound

沙[3] shā 沙皇 czar

☞ shà on p.1667

【沙包】shābāo ❶ 像小山一样的大沙堆 sand dune ❷ 沙袋 sandbag

【沙暴】shābào 尘暴 sandstorm; sandy-dust storm

【沙场】shāchǎng 广阔的沙地。多指战场 vast stretch of gravelly land;（oft.）battlefield; battleground：久经～be a seasoned soldier; be experienced

【沙船】shāchuán 一种遇沙不易搁浅的大型平底木帆船 large junk

【沙袋】shādài 装着沙子的袋子，打仗时堆积起来，用来掩护，也用于防洪、防火、体育锻炼等 sandbag

【沙俄】Shā'é 指沙皇统治下的俄国 czarist Russia; tsarist Russia

【沙发】shāfā 装有弹簧或厚泡沫塑料等的坐具，两边一般有扶手 sofa; settee; long seat stuffed with springs or thick plastic foams and upholstered, usu. with arms on both ends

【沙肝儿】shāgānr〈方 *dial.*〉牛、羊、猪的脾脏作为食品时叫沙肝儿 spleen of a pig, cow or sheep used as food

【沙锅】shāguō 用陶土和沙烧成的锅，不易与酸或碱起化学变化，大多用来做菜或熬药 casserole; earthen pot, which is not liable to chemical reaction to acid or alkali and used mostly for cooking or decoct medicine

【沙锅浅儿】shāguōqiǎnr 沙浅儿 shallow earthen pot

【沙荒】shāhuāng 由大风或洪水带来的大量沙土形成的不能耕种的沙地 sandy waste; sandy wasteland; infertile sedimentary land resulting from high wind or floods

【沙皇】shāhuáng 俄国和保加利亚过去皇帝的称号 tsar; czar; title of emperor in Russia and Bulgaria in bygone days［沙，俄 Russian：царь］

【沙浆】shājiāng same as 砂浆 shājiāng

【沙金】shājīn 自然界中混合在沙里的粒状金子 placer gold; alluvial gold

【沙拉】shālā 色拉 salad

【沙里淘金】shā lǐ táo jīn 从沙子里淘出黄金 wash grains of gold out of the sands;〈比喻 *fig.*〉费力大而成效少。也比喻从大量的材料中选取精华。extract the essential from a large mass of material; get small returns for great effort

【沙砾】shālì 沙和碎石块 grit; gravel

【沙龙】shālóng ❶ 17 世纪末叶和 18 世纪法国巴黎的文人和艺术家常接受贵族妇女的招待，在客厅集会，谈论文艺，后来因而把有闲阶级的文人雅士清谈的场所叫做沙龙 salon; large room, such as a drawing room, used for receiving and entertaining guests. Towards the end of the 17th century and during the 18th century, aristocratic ladies in Paris often entertained writers and artists in the parlors of their residences and discussed literature and art with them. Hence the term, 'salon', a place where the idle rich gather and engage in idle talk. ❷ 泛指文学、艺术等方面人士的小型聚会(in a broad sense) small gathering of men of letters, artists, and those of social or intellectual distinction：艺术～art salon | 摄影～photographers' salon [法 French：salon (drawing room)客厅]

【沙门】shāmén 出家的佛教徒的总称 *sramana*; ascetic Buddhist mendicant; monk [梵 sanskrit：śramaṇa]

【沙弥】shāmí 指初出家的年轻的和尚 *sramanera*; young Buddhist novice [梵 sanskrit：śrāmaṇera]

【沙漠】shāmò 地面完全为沙所覆盖，缺乏流水，气候干燥，植物稀少的地区 desert; sand-covered region of little rainfall, parching weather, and sparse vegetation

【沙鸥】shā'ōu 文学作品中指栖息于沙滩或沙洲上的鸥一类的鸟 sandpiper (*Scolopacidae*); small wading shorebird inhabiting sand beaches or sand bars

【沙盘】shāpán ❶ 盛着细沙的盘子，可在上面写字 sand table; table containing fine sand for writing ❷ 用沙土做成的地形模型，一般用木盘盛着 landform model made from sand and earth contained in a wooden trencher

【沙碛】shāqì 〈书 *fml*.〉沙漠 desert

【沙浅儿】shāqiǎnr 比较浅的沙锅 shallow earthen pot; also 沙锅浅儿 shāguōqiǎnr

【沙丘】shāqiū 沙漠、河岸、海滨等地由风吹而堆成的沙堆 sand dune; mound or ridge of wind-blown sand in a desert, or by a river or the sea

【沙瓤】shāráng (～儿 shārángr)某些种西瓜熟透时瓤变松散而呈细粒状，叫沙瓤儿 mushy watermelon pulp

【沙壤土】shārǎngtǔ 含沙粒较多，细土较少的土壤。土质松散，宜于耕作。land containing more sand than soil, and thus of a loose texture, suitable for cultivation

【沙沙】shāshā 〈拟声词 *onom*.〉形容踩着沙子、飞沙击物或风吹草木等的声音 rustle; soft fluttering or crackling sounds made by drifting sand clashing with objects or wind blowing through grass or trees：走在河滩上，脚下～地响。(They) mushed along through the river beach. | 风吹枯叶，～作响。Withered leaves rustled in the wind.

【沙滩】shātān 水中或水边由沙子淤积成的陆地 sand beach; alluvial sandy waterside land, or sandy land surrounded by water

【沙田】shātián 沙土田 farmland reclaimed from sand flats; sandy land

【沙土】shātǔ 由百分之八十以上的沙和百分之二十以下的黏土混合而成的土壤 soil containing over 80 per cent of sand and below 20 per cent of clay; 泛指含沙很多的土 sandy soil

【沙文主义】Shāwén zhǔyì 一种资产阶级民族主义，把自己民族利益看得高于一切，主张征服和奴役其他民族。因拿破仑手下的军人沙文(Nicolas Chauvin)狂热地拥护拿破仑用暴力向外扩张法国的势力，所以把这种思想叫做沙文主义。chauvinism; bourgeois nationalism that regards the interests of one's own nation above anything else and advocates conquering and enslaving other nations, an idea that is named after Nicolas Chauvin, who served in Napoleon's army, and frantically supported his use of violence to expand the sphere of influence of France

【沙哑】shāyǎ (嗓子)发音困难，声音低沉而不圆润 (of voice) rough and grating; hoarse; husky; raucous

【沙眼】shāyǎn 眼的慢性传染病，病原体是一种病毒，症状是结膜上形成灰白色颗粒，逐渐形成瘢痕，刺激角膜，使角膜发生溃疡 trachoma; chronic contagious eye disease caused by the gram-negative bacterium *Chlamydia trachomatis* and characterized by formation of granules on the conjunctiva, gradually resulting in scars that irritate cornea and cause ulcers in it

【沙鱼】shāyú same as 鲨鱼 shāyú

【沙灾】shāzāi 因大风或洪水带来大量沙土而造成的灾害 sandstorm; strong wind carrying clouds of sand and dust through the air; disaster caused by floods carrying large amounts of sand and silt

【沙洲】shāzhōu 江河里由泥沙淤积成的陆地 shoal; sandbank; land on a river caused by sedimentation

【沙柱】shāzhù 沙漠中被旋风卷起成柱子形状的飞沙 dust devil; sand column; small whirlwind, usu. of short duration, that swirls dust, debris and sand to great heights

【沙子】shā·zi ❶ 细小的石粒 sand; grit ❷ 像沙的东西 small grains; pellets：铁～iron pellets; shot

【沙嘴】shāzuǐ 由河流挟带的泥沙构成的一种海岸堆积地貌，形状像镰刀，基部与岸相连，前端伸入海中 sandspit; coastal accumulational landform formed by silt washed down a river, assuming the shape of a sickle with its 'handle' attached to the seashore and its 'tip' stretching into the sea

纱 shā ❶ 棉花、麻等纺成的较松的细丝，可以捻成线或织成布 yarn; continuous strand of loosely twisted threads of cotton, hemp, etc., used in twisting thicker threads or weaving：～厂 cotton mill | 棉～cotton yarn | 纺～textile | 60 支～60-count yarn ❷ 用纱织成的经纬线很稀的织品 sheer：窗～gauze for screening windows | ～布 gauze ❸ 像窗纱一样的制品 curtain-like fabrics：铁～wire gauze | 塑料～plastic gauze ❹ 某些纺织品的类名 textile product：乔其～georgette | 泡泡～seersucker

【纱包线】shābāoxiàn 用棉纱缠绕着做绝缘层的导线，多用于绕制电机和电讯装置中的线圈 cotton-covered wire, usu. for use in the making of coils for motors and telecommunications devices

【纱布】shābù 包扎伤口用的消过毒的经纬纱很稀疏的棉织品 gauze; thin, loosely woven surgical dressing made of cotton

【纱橱】shāchú 蒙有冷布或铁纱的储存食物的橱柜 screen cupboard; cupboard covered with cotton or wire gauze

【纱窗】shāchuāng 蒙有冷布或铁纱的窗户 screen window; window covered with cotton or wire gauze

【纱灯】shādēng 用薄纱糊成的灯笼 gauze lantern

【纱锭】shādìng 纺纱机上的主要部件，用来把纤维捻成纱并把纱绕在筒管上成一定形状。通常用纱锭的数目来表示纱厂规模的大小。spindle; rod on a spinning machine that bears the bobbins with which a fibre is spun into thread and on which the spun thread is wound; also 纺锭 fǎngdìng or 锭子 dìng·zi

【纱笼】shālóng 东南亚一带人穿的用长布裹住身体的服装 sarong; loose-fitting, skirtlike garment consisting of a long strip of cloth tucked round the waist or under the armpits, worn by men and women in southeast Asia [马来 Malay: saron]

【纱帽】shāmào 〈古代 *arch.*〉文官戴的一种帽子。后用做官职的代称。gauze hat worn by an official in old times; official post; also 乌纱帽 wūshāmào

【纱罩】shāzhào ❶ 罩食物的器具，用竹木等制成架子，蒙上铁纱或冷布，防止苍蝇落在食物上 gauze sheath; gauze or screen stretched over a bamboo or wooden sheath, used to cover over food and protect it from flies ❷ 煤气灯或挥发油灯上的罩，用亚麻等纤维编成网状再在硝酸钍、硝酸锶溶液中浸制而成，遇热即发强光 mantle (of a lamp); device in gas lamps consisting of a sheath of screen (made of flax or other fibres and dipped in thorium nitrate or strontium nitrate) that gives off brilliant illumination when heated by the flame

刹 shā 止住(车、机器等) stop (a vehicle); put on the brakes; turn off a machine: 把车～住 stop a car by applying the brakes◇～住不正之风 stem all unhealthy social trends ☞ chà on p. 206

【刹车】shā//chē ❶ 用闸等止住车的行进 stop a vehicle by applying the brakes; put on the brakes ❷ 停止动力来源，使机器停止运转 stop a machine by cutting off the power; turn off a machine ❸ 〈比喻 *fig.*〉停止或制止 check; stem: 浮夸风必须～。The tendency to boast and exaggerate one's achievements should be checked. also 煞车 shā//chē

【刹车】shāchē 使汽车、摩托车等停止前进的机件、装置 brake; device for slowing or stopping motion, as of a vehicle, especially by contact friction; also 煞车 shāchē

砂 shā same as 沙¹ shā ①

【砂布】shābù 粘有金刚砂的布，用来磨光金属器物的表面 emery cloth; abrasive cloth; cloth with carborundum glued to it, used for polishing the surface of a metal object

【砂浆】shājiāng 建筑上砌砖石用的黏结物质，由一定比例的沙子和胶结材料(水泥、石灰膏、黏土等)加水和成 mortar; material prepared by mixing cement, lime, sand, and water and hardened in place to bind together bricks or stones; also 灰浆 huījiāng or 沙浆 shājiāng

【砂礓】shājiāng 矿物，质地坚硬，不透水，大的块状，小的颗粒状。可用来代替砖石做建筑材料。conglomerate; hard and nonabsorbent mineral blocks or granules, used as a building material in substitution for brick and stone

【砂轮】shālún (～儿 shālúnr)磨刀具和零件用的工具，用磨料和胶结物质混合后，在高温下烧结制成，多作轮状 emery wheel; grinding wheel; abrasive wheel; tool for grinding cutting tools and machine parts, made by mixing and agglomerating emery and cementing materials under high temperature; also 磨轮 mólún

【砂囊】shānáng ❶ 指鸟类的胃，胃里贮有吞入的砂粒，用来磨碎食物 gizzard; bird stomach containing granules of sand with which to grind food eaten ❷ 指蚯蚓的胃 earthworm's stomach

【砂皮】shāpí 〈方 *dial.*〉same as 砂布 shābù

【砂糖】shātáng 结晶颗粒较大、像砂粒的糖。分赤砂糖和白砂糖两种，赤砂糖含少量的糖蜜，白砂糖纯度较高。brown or white granulated sugar, with the former containing a tiny amount of molasses, and the latter of a relatively high purity

【砂型】shāxíng 铸造中用潮湿型砂制成的模型。把铸件的模型用一定方法埋在砂子里，然后取出，模型就在砂中留下相同的空隙。mould for sand-casting; sand mould; mould made by burying the model of a casting into wet sand and then taking it out, leaving a cavity to be used for casting

【砂眼】shāyǎn 翻砂过程中，气体或杂质在铸件内部或表面形成的小孔，是铸件的一种缺陷 sand holes; blowholes; tiny holes left by gas bubbles or impurities on or in a casting during the process of sand-casting

【砂样】shāyàng 钻探时取出的供化验分析用的岩石样品 petroleum drilling mud cuttings; rock sample obtained by drilling into the depth of earth for laboratory analysis

【砂纸】shāzhǐ 粘有玻璃粉的纸，用来磨光竹木器物的表面 abrasive paper; sand paper; paper on which glassdust is glued for polishing bamboo or wooden utensils

挱(挲) shā 〈书 *fml*.〉杂糅 mix; blend ☞sà on p.1648

莎 shā 用于地名、人名。莎车(Shāchē),地名,在新疆。*sha*, used in place or personal names, i.e., Shache (Yarkant), name of a place in Xinjiang
☞ suō on p.1841

铩(鎩) shā ❶〈古代 *arch*.〉一种长矛 spear ❷〈书 *fml*.〉摧残;伤害 wound; injure:～羽 with wings clipped; frustrated

【铩羽】shāyǔ〈书 *fml*.〉翅膀被摧残 with one's wings clipped;〈比喻 *fig*.〉失意或失败 crestfallen; frustrated; defeated:～而归 come home feeling frustrated

挲(抄) shā ☞[挓挲](zhā·shā) on p. 2403
☞ sā on p.1647 and suō on p.1842

痧 shā〈中医 *Chin. med*.〉指霍乱、中暑等急性病 acute disease such as cholera and sunstroke:绞肠～dry cholera

【痧子】shā·zi〈方 *dial*.〉麻疹 measles

煞 shā ❶ 结束;收束 terminate; cut short; hold back:～账 close accounts | 锣鼓～住后,一个男孩儿领头唱起来。The fanfare of gongs and drums stopped abruptly, and a boy launched a chorus into action. ❷ 勒紧;扣紧 tauten; squeeze:～车 apply the brakes | ～一～腰带 tighten up one's belt ❸ same as 杀 shā ③⑤
☞ shà on p.1667

【煞笔】shā//bǐ 写文章、书信等结束时停笔 finish writing; write the final line of an article, letter, etc.

【煞笔】shābǐ 文章最后的结束语 concluding sentence; finishing touch:这篇散文的～很精彩。The conclusion of this piece of prose was brilliantly written.

【煞车】[1] shā//chē 把车上装载的东西用绳索紧勒在车身上 firmly fasten a load (on a vehicle); lash down

【煞车】[2] shā//chē same as 刹车 shā//chē

【煞车】shāchē same as 刹车 shāchē

【煞风景】shā fēngjǐng same as 杀风景 shā fēngjǐng

【煞尾】shāwěi ❶ 结束事情的最后一段;收尾 wrap up; finalize; conclude; bring to a close; put to an end:事情不多了,马上就可～。There being not much work left, we can wrap up at once. ❷ 北曲套数中最后的一支曲子 fine melody in a sequence of songs in the northern operas of the Yuan Dynasty ❸ 文章、事情等的最后一段(of an article, event, etc.) end; conclusion; final stage:～部分需要重写。The concluding part of the document needs rewriting.

裟 shā ☞[袈裟] jiāshā on p.930

鲨 shā [鲨鱼](shāyú)鱼,种类很多,身体纺锤形,稍扁,鳞为盾状,胸、腹鳍大,尾鳍发达。有的种类头上有一个喷水孔。生活在海洋中,性凶猛,行动敏捷,捕食其他鱼类。经济价值很高。shark (*Selachii*); any of numerous ferocious and agile fish-feeding marine fishes of the class *Chondrichthyes* (subclass *Elasmobranchii*), which have a streamlined, spindle-like body covered with shield-shaped scales, large pectoral and pelvic fins and well-developed caudal fins; some varieties have a spiracle on the head; sharks are of a high economic value; also 鲛 jiāo or 沙鱼 shāyú

shá (ㄕㄚˊ)

啥 shá〈方 *dial*.〉什么 what; why; how come:有～说～say what's on one's mind; speak one's mind | 到～地方去? Where are you going?

【啥子】shá·zi〈方 *dial*.〉什么;什么东西 what?; what's this?

shǎ (ㄕㄚˇ)

傻(儍) shǎ ❶ 头脑糊涂,不明事理 brainless; foolish; stolid:～头～脑 brainless; harebrained | 装疯卖～play the fool or idiot | 吓～了 be flabbergasted; be astounded ❷ 死心眼,不知变通 stubborn; inflexible:～干 peg away at sth. slavishly | ～等 wait for single-mindedly

【傻瓜】shǎguā 傻子(用于骂人或开玩笑 curse or humor.) fool; ass; jackass; moron

【傻瓜相机】shǎguā xiàngjī 自动或半自动照相机的俗称,一般不需调焦距和测算曝光时间 point-and-shoot camera; automatic or semiautomatic camera that saves focusing and setting time of exposure

【傻呵呵】shǎhēhē (～的 shǎhēhē·de)糊涂不懂事或老实的样子 simpleminded; silly; foolish:孩子听故事听得入了神,～地瞪大了两只眼睛。The child listened to the story with rapt attention, wide-eyed and dumb with wonder. | 别看他～的,心里可有数。Maybe he looks dumb, but he knows what's going on.

【傻乎乎】shǎhūhū (～的 shǎhūhū·de)傻呵呵 idiotic; daft; dollish

【傻劲儿】shǎjìnr ❶ 傻气 folly; asininity ❷ 形容人力气大或只知道凭力气干 sheer enthusiasm; doggedness:光靠～蛮干是不行的,得找窍门。Enthusiasm alone won't do. You've got to work skillfully.

【傻帽儿】shǎmàor〈方 *dial*.〉形容人傻,没见过世面 foolish; stupid;也指这样的人 jackass; idiot; sucker

【傻气】shǎqì 形容愚蠢、糊涂的样子 brainless; dumb; idiotic; fatuous

【傻笑】shǎxiào 无意义地一个劲儿地笑 laugh foolishly; smirk

【傻眼】shǎ//yǎn 因出现某种意外情况而目瞪口呆，不知所措 get a nasty shock; be flabbergasted; be nonplussed; be astounded

【傻子】shǎ·zi 智力低下，不明事理的人 fathead; simpleton; ass

shà（ㄕㄚˋ）

沙 shà〈方 *dial.*〉摇动，使东西里的杂物集中，以便清除 sift; sieve; put sth. through a sieve or other straining device in order to separate the fine from the coarse particles：把米里的沙子～一～。Sift the rice and sort out the sand.

☞ shā on p.1663

啑 shà ❶ same as 唼 shà ❷ same as 歃 shà

☞ dié on p.451

唼 shà［唼喋］(shàzhá)〈书 *fml.*〉形容成群的鱼、水鸟等吃东西的声音(of school of fish or flock of water birds) sound of feeding

厦(廈) shà ❶（高大的）房子 tall building：广～large house; huge building｜高楼大～high buildings and large mansions; high-rises ❷〈方 *dial.*〉房子里靠后墙的部分，在柁之外 Chinese-style portico; part of a house attached to the back wall and beyond the girder：前廊后～having a porch in front of a building and a portico behind it

☞ xià on p.2069

嗄 shà〈书 *fml.*〉嗓音嘶哑(of the voice) hoarse

☞ á on p.2

歃 shà〈书 *fml.*〉用嘴吸取 suck

【歃血】shàxuè〈古代 *arch.*〉举行盟会时，嘴唇涂上牲畜的血，表示诚意 smear the blood of a sacrifice on the mouth — a ritual of pledging an oath：～为盟 swear an oath of alliance by smearing the mouth with the blood of a sacrifice

煞[1] shà 迷信的人指凶神 bogey; ogre：凶神恶～devils and fiends

煞[2] shà 极；很 very：～费苦心 take great pains; cudgel one's brains

☞ shā on p.1666

【煞白】shàbái 由于恐惧、愤怒或某些疾病等原因，面色极白，没有血色 ghastly pale; deathly pale; pallid

【煞费苦心】shà fèi kǔxīn 形容费尽心思 rack one's brains

【煞气】shà//qì 器物因有小孔而慢慢漏气(of anything with air inside) leak; have a flat tyre：车带～了。My car has a flat tyre.

【煞气】shàqì ❶ 凶恶的神色 ferocious look ❷ 迷信的人指邪气 demon; evil emanations; perverse trend

【煞有介事】shà yǒu jiè shì ☞像煞有介事 xiàng shà yǒu jiè shì on p.2098

箑 shà〈书 *fml.*〉扇子 fan

霎 shà 短时间；一会儿 split second; short moment; instant：一～in a twinkling｜～时 instantly

【霎时】shàshí 霎时间 in a twinkling; in a split second; in a jiffy

【霎时间】shàshíjiān 极短时间 in a twinkling：一声巨响，～天空中出现了千万朵美丽的火花。With a deafening roar a myriad of beautiful fiery flowers burst forth in the sky. also 霎时 shàshí

shāi（ㄕㄞ）

筛[1]**(篩)** shāi ❶ 筛子 sieve; sifter：过～sieve; sift ❷ 把东西放在罗或筛子里，来回摇动，使细碎的漏下去，粗的留在上头 sift; separate or sift out coarse particles and retain the fine by means of a sieve or screen：～面 sift flour｜把糠～净 sift rice to remove the bran ❸〈比喻 *fig.*〉经挑选后淘汰 screen; (of a job applicant, etc.) be eliminated after being screened：他担心考不好给～下来。He was afraid of failing the test and thus being eliminated from the list.

筛[2]**(篩)** shāi ❶ 使酒热 warm up wine over a fire：把酒～一～再喝。Warm up the wine before drinking it. ❷ 斟(酒) pour (wine)

筛[3]**(篩)** shāi〈方 *dial.*〉敲(锣) beat (a gong)：～了三下锣。The gong was beaten three times.

【筛骨】shāigǔ 头骨之一，在颅腔底的前部，两个眼眶之间，鼻腔的顶部，是颅腔和鼻腔之间的分界骨 ethmoid; bone at the front of the base of the cranium, at the root of the nose and between the two eye sockets, serving as the boundary between the cranial cavity and the nasal cavity

【筛糠】shāi//kāng〈比喻 *fig.*〉因惊吓或受冻而身体发抖 shiver with fear or cold

【筛选】shāixuǎn ❶ 利用筛子进行选种、选矿等 use a sieve to select seeds, dress ore, etc. ❷ 泛指通过淘汰的方法挑选 select through elimination：经过多年的杂交试验，～出优质高产的西瓜新品种。After years of experimentation with hybridization, new strains of high-quality and high-yielding water melon have been selected

【筛子】shāi·zi 用竹条、铁丝等编成的有许多小孔的器具，可以把细碎的东西漏下去，较粗的成块的留在上头 sieve; sifter; screen; utensil of bamboo-strip or wire mesh or closely perforated metal, used straining, sifting, ricing, etc., in which the fine is separated from coarse granules

酾(釃) shāi '酾[1]'(shī)的又音 another pronunciation of 酾[1] shī

shǎi(ㄕㄞˇ)

色 shǎi(～儿 shǎir)颜色 colour; hue: 掉～(of colour) fade | 套～ chromatography; colour process | 不变～儿 not change colour; not change one's countenance

☞ sè on p. 1660

【色酒】shǎijiǔ〈方 *dial.*〉用葡萄或其他水果为原料制成的酒，一般带有颜色，酒精含量较低 wine brewed from grapes or other fruits, in different hues and of a low alcoholic content

【色子】shǎi·zi 一种游戏用具或赌具，用骨头、木头等制成的立体小方块，六面分刻一、二、三、四、五、六点 dice; small cube made from bone or wood, with one to six dots engraved on the six sides, used as a gambling tool; 有的地区叫骰子(tóu·zi) known in some regions as 骰子 tóu·zi

shài(ㄕㄞˋ)

晒(曬) shài ❶ 太阳把热照射到物体上(of the sun) shine upon: 烈日～得人头昏眼花。One feels dizzy under the scorching sun. ❷ 在阳光下吸收光和热 absorb light and heat of the sun; dry in the sun: ～粮食 dry grain in the sun | 让孩子们多～太阳。Let the kids bask in the sun more. *or* Give the kids more sunbath. ❸〈方 *dial.*〉〈比喻 *fig.*〉置之不理；慢待 slight; turn one's back on sb.

【晒垡】shàifá 使已经用犁翻起来的土在太阳光下晒。能改善土壤结构，提高土壤温度，有利于种子发芽和根系生长。sun the earth which has been ploughed up so that soil structure can be improved and soil temperature raised to facilitate the sprouting of seeds and the growth of the roots of crops

【晒暖儿】shàinuǎnr〈方 *dial.*〉在日光下取暖 bask in the sunshine: 靠在墙根～lean against the foot of a wall and enjoy the sun

【晒台】shàitái 在楼房屋顶设置的露天小平台，供晒衣物或乘凉用 balcony; flat roof of a building, or balustraded elevated platform projecting from the wall of a building, for drying laundries or enjoy the cool in summer

【晒图】shài//tú 把描在透明或半透明纸上的图和感光纸重叠在一起，利用日光或灯光照射，复制图纸 make a blueprint; blueprint; photographic reproduction made by exposing to sunlight or lamplight light-sensitive paper placed underneath drawings on transparent or translucent paper

【晒烟】shàiyān 晒干或晾干的烟叶，是旱烟、水烟和雪茄、烟丝的原料。也指制造晒烟的烟草。sun-cured tobacco; tobacco leaves dried in the sun or wind, to be shredded for smoking in long-stemmed Chinese pipes or water pipes, or serve as raw material for making cigars and cigarettes; tobacco leaves ready for sun-drying

shān(ㄕㄢ)

山 shān ❶ 地面形成的高耸的部分 hill; mountain: 一座～ a mountain | 高～ tall mountain ❷ 形状像山的东西 sth. mountain-like: 冰～ iceberg ❸ 蚕蔟 bunch of straw in which silkworms spin cocoons: 蚕上～了。The silkworms have gone into the straw bundles to spin their cocoons. ❹ 指山墙 gables: 房～ gables of a house ❺(Shān)姓 a surname

【山坳】shān'ào 山间的平地 col

【山包】shānbāo〈方 *dial.*〉小山 small hill

【山崩】shānbēng 山上大量的岩石和土壤塌下来 landslide; landslip; rockfall

【山茶】shānchá 常绿乔木或灌木，叶子卵形，有光泽，花红色或白色，蒴果球形，种子球形，黑色。山茶是一种名贵的观赏植物，花很美丽，通常叫茶花。种子可以榨油。camellia; evergreen tree or shrub of the genus *Camellia*, especially *C. japonica*, having shiny oval leaves, red or white flowers, ball-shaped capsules, and black, round seeds from which oil can be extracted, regarded as a precious ornamental plant for its showy flowers, popularly known as 茶花 cháhuā

【山城】shānchéng 山上的或靠山的城市 mountain city; city situated in or by mountains

【山川】shānchuān 山岳和河流 landscape; mountains and rivers: ～壮丽 spectacular landscape

【山村】shāncūn 山区的村庄 mountain village

【山地】shāndì ❶ 多山的地带 mountainous region; hilly area; rolling country: 开发～资源 tap mountain resources ❷ 在山上的农业用地 hillside field: 开垦～ reclaim land from mountain slopes

【山顶洞人】Shāndǐngdòngrén 古代人类的一种，生活在旧石器时代晚期，距今约一万八千年。化石在1933年发现于北京西南周口店龙骨山山顶洞中。Upper Cave Man; primitive man dating back to approximately 18,000 years ago and whose fossil remains were found in 1933 at Longguo Mountain at Zhoukoudian to the southwest of Beijing

【山东梆子】Shāndōng bāng·zi 山东地方戏曲剧种之一，流行于山东大部分地区和河北河南的部分地区 Shandong clapper opera; local opera popular in most part of Shandong Province and part of Hebei and Henan provinces

【山东快书】Shāndōng kuàishū 曲艺的一种，说词合辙押韵，表演者一面叙说，一面击铜板伴奏，节奏较快。流行于山东、华北、东北等地。Shandong clapper ballad-singing, in which the ballad-singer tells a story while tapping a pair of copper clappers in his hand in a rapid rhythm, popular in Shandong and north and northeast China

【山峰】shānfēng 山的突出的尖顶 mountain peak

【山旮旯儿】shāngālár 〈方 *dial.*〉偏僻的山区 place tucked away in the mountains; out-of-the-way place in the mountains; remote mountain area; also 山旮旯子 shāngālá·zi

【山冈】shāngāng 不高的山 knap; knoll; hillock

【山岗子】shāngǎng·zi 不高的山 tump; low hill; mound

【山高皇帝远】shān gāo huángdì yuǎn 指地处偏远，法律、制度管束不到 remote area where law enforcement is lax; also 天高皇帝远 tiān gāo huángdì yuǎn

【山高水低】shān gāo shuǐ dī 〈比喻 *fig.*〉意外发生的不幸事情（多指死亡）sth. unfortunate, esp. death; unexpected misfortune

【山歌】shāngē 形式短小、曲调爽朗质朴、节奏自由的民间歌曲，流行于南方农村或山区，多在山野劳动时歌唱 folk song sung during work in the fields or in mountain areas, popular in rural or mountain areas in south China

【山根】shāngēn（～儿 shāngēnr）same as 山脚 shānjiǎo

【山沟】shāngōu ❶ 山间的流水沟 gully ❷ 山谷 valley; ravine ❸ 指偏僻的山区 remote mountain area：过去的穷～，如今富裕起来了。The poor mountainous area of yesterday has become prosperous today.

【山谷】shāngǔ 两山之间低凹而狭窄的地方，中间多有溪流 mountain valley; ravine in which there is oft. a river

【山国】shānguó 指多山的国家或多山的地方 mountain-rimmed country; mountainous country; hilly region

【山河】shānhé 大山和大河，指国家或国家某一地区的土地 mountains and rivers; land of a country：大好～beautiful motherland | 锦绣～ beautiful land

【山洪】shānhóng 因下大雨或积雪融化，由山上突然流下来的大水 mountain torrents：～暴发。Torrents of water came rushing down the mountain.

【山货】shānhuò ❶ 山区的一般土产，如山查、榛子、栗子、胡桃等 mountain produce, such as haws, hazels, chestnuts and walnuts ❷ 指用竹子、木头、苘麻、粗陶瓷等制成的日用器物，如扫帚、簸箕、麻绳、沙锅、瓦盆等 daily utensils fashioned out of bamboo, wood, piemarker (*Abutilon theophrasti*), coarse ceramics, etc., including broom, dustpan, hemp rope, earthen pot, and pottery basin：～铺 mountain product store

【山积】shānjī 〈书 *fml.*〉东西极多，堆得像山一样 be piled mountain high：货物～。Merchandise is piled mountain high.

【山脊】shānjǐ 山的高处像兽类的脊梁骨似的高起部分 ridge (of a mountain or hill)

【山涧】shānjiàn 山间的水沟 mountain stream

【山脚】shānjiǎo 山的靠近平地的部分 foot of a mountain or hill

【山轿】shānjiào 用椅子捆在杠子上做成的乘坐用具，由人抬着走 litter; couch mounted on shafts and used to carry a single passenger

【山口】shānkǒu 连绵的山岭中间较低处，多为通道经过的地方 mountain pass; col; pass between two mountain peaks; gap in a ridge

【山岚】shānlán 〈书 *fml.*〉山间的云雾 mountain mists：～瘴气 mountain miasma

【山里红】shān·lihóng ❶ 山里红树，落叶乔木，叶子卵形，花白色。果实圆形，深红色，有白色斑点，味酸，可以吃，也可入药 large-fruited Chinese hawthorn (*Crataegus pinnatifida var. major*); deciduous tree having oval leaves, white flowers, and deep red, white-speckled rotund fruit that tastes sour and is edible and of medical value ❷ 这种植物的果实。有的地方叫红果儿。hawthorn; known in some regions as 红果儿 hóngguǒr

【山梁】shānliáng 山脊 ridge (of a mountain or hill)

【山林】shānlín 有山有树林的地方 mountain forest; wooded mountain

【山陵】shānlíng ❶〈书 *fml.*〉山岳 hills ❷〈旧时 *old*〉指帝王的坟墓 imperial mausoleum; tomb of an emperor

【山岭】shānlǐng 连绵的高山 chain of mountains; undulating mountains

【山路】shānlù 山间的道路 mountain path：～崎岖 rough and rugged mountain path

【山麓】shānlù 山脚 foot of a mountain; piedmont

【山峦】shānluán 连绵的山 mountain chain; multipeaked mountain：～起伏 undulating mountains; rolling hills

【山脉】shānmài 成行列的群山，山势起伏，向一定方向延展，好像脉络似的，所以叫做山脉 mountain range; mountain chain

【山毛榉】shānmáojǔ 落叶乔木，高可达二十多米，叶子卵形或长椭圆形，花萼有丝状的毛，结坚果。木材可做铁道枕木。beech; deciduous tree of the genus *Fagus*, more than 20 metres in maximum height, having oval or elongated oval leaves and calyces covered with filamentous down, bearing hard nuts, and producing timber that can be used as railroad crossties; also 水青冈

S

shuǐqīnggāng

【山门】shānmén ❶〈佛教 *Budd.*〉寺院的大门 gateway to a temple ❷ 指佛教 Buddhism

【山盟海誓】shān méng hǎi shì ☞ 海誓山盟 hǎi shì shān méng on p. 757

【山南海北】shān nán hǎi běi ❶ 指遥远的地方 faraway; far and wide: ~,到处都有勘探人员的足迹。The prospectors have left their footprints all over the land. ❷〈比喻 *fig.*〉说话漫无边际 prolix; rambling: 两人~地谈了半天。The two of them chitchatted for a long time. also 天南海北 tiān nán hǎi běi

【山炮】shānpào 一种适于山地作战的轻型榴弹炮,重量较轻,能迅速分解结合,便于搬运 mountain gun; light-duty howitzer; mountain artillery that can be quickly disassembled and assembled; 旧称 known in old times as 过山炮 guòshānpào

【山坡】shānpō 山顶与平地之间的倾斜面 mountainside; mountain slope; hillslope

【山墙】shānqiáng 人字形屋顶的房屋两侧的墙壁 gable; triangular section of wall at the end of a pitched roof, occupying the space between the two roof slopes; also 房山 fángshān;(图见 ☞ figure for 房子 fáng·zi on p. 550)

【山清水秀】shān qīng shuǐ xiù 形容山水风景优美 green hills and limpid waters; picture-perfect scenery; also 山明水秀 shān míng shuǐ xiù

【山穷水尽】shān qióng shuǐ jìn 山和水都到了尽头,前面再没有路可走了 where the hills and streams end;〈比喻 *fig.*〉陷入绝境 at the end of one's rope, tether or resources; in dire straits; at one's wit's end

【山区】shānqū 多山的地区 mountainous area: 支援~建设 aid development in mountainous areas

【山水】shānshuǐ ❶ 山上流下来的水 water running down a mountain ❷ 山和水。泛指有山有水的风景。mountains and waters; landscape; scenery with mountains and waters: 桂林~甲天下。The landscape of Guilin is matchless under heaven. ❸ 指山水画 landscape painting: 泼墨~ splash-ink landscape painting

【山水画】shānshuǐhuà 以山水等自然风景为题材的中国画 landscape painting; landscape

【山桐子】shāntóngzǐ 落叶乔木,叶子卵形,圆锥花序,花黄绿色,有香气,浆果球形,红色或红褐色。木材可以制器具。idesia (*Idesia polycarpa*); deciduous tree having oval leaves, fragrant, greenish yellow panicle flowers, red or reddish brown berries, and wood useful for the making of furniture; also 椅 yī

【山头】shāntóu ❶ 山的顶部;山峰 hilltop; mountaintop ❷ 设立山寨的山头 mountaintop with a hamlet perched on it; stronghold;〈比喻 *fig.*〉独霸一方的宗派 faction: 拉~ cultivate a faction

【山洼】shānwā 山中的洼地;山谷 valley; depression in the mountains

【山窝】shānwō 偏僻的山区 tucked-away mountain area; also 山窝窝 shānwō·wo

【山坞】shānwù 山间平地;山坳 glen; col

【山西梆子】Shānxī bāng·zi ☞ 晋剧 jìnjù on p. 1016

【山系】shānxì 同一造山运动形成,并沿一定走向规律分布的若干相邻山脉的总体,叫做山系 mountain system; several neighbouring mountain ranges resulting from the same orogenic movement and distributed in a certain direction

【山峡】shānxiá 两山夹水的地方;两山夹着的水道 gorge; strip of water sandwiched in between two mountain cliffs

【山险】shānxiǎn 山势险要的地方 perilous mountain terrain

【山响】shānxiǎng 响声极大 deafening; thunderous: 北风刮得门窗乒乓~。The doors and windows are rattling noisily in the north wind.

【山魈】shānxiāo ❶ 猕猴的一种,体长约达一米,尾巴很短,鼻子深红色,面部皮肤蓝色,有微紫的皱纹,吻部有白须,全身毛黑褐色,腹部灰白色,臀部鲜红色。产在非洲西部,多群居,吃小鸟、野鼠等。mandrill (*Mandrillus sphinx*); gregarious macaque having a body one metre in length and covered with dark brown hair, short tail, gray belly, dark red nose, blue facial skin with pale purple wrinkles, white beard on the muzzle, and bright red buttocks, and feeding on small birds, field mice, etc. ❷ 传说中山里的独脚鬼怪 mythological one-legged mountain ghost

【山崖】shānyá 山的陡立的侧面 cliff; perpendicular rock face of a mountain

【山羊】shānyáng ❶ 羊的一种,角的基部略作三角形,角尖向后,四肢强壮,善于跳跃,毛不弯曲,公羊有须,变种很多,有黑、灰等颜色。皮可以制革,毛皮可以制衣褥。goat (*Capra hircus*); ovine animal in many variant breeds and black, gray and other colours, having a pair of horns which protrude from a roughly triangular base and point backward, skin that can be used for leather making, and fur for making clothing and bedding, good at leaping on well-developed limbs, the male being bearded ❷ 一种体操器械,也叫跳跃器 buck; a gymnastics apparatus: 跳~ jump the buck; also 跳跃器 tiàoyuèqì

【山腰】shānyāo 山脚和山顶之间大约一半的地方 halfway up a mountain; also 半山腰 bàn shānyāo

【山药】shān·yao ❶ 薯蓣的通称 general term for 薯蓣 shǔyù ❷〈方 *dial.*〉甘薯 sweet potato

【山药蛋】shān·yaodàn〈方 *dial.*〉马铃薯 potato

【山野】shānyě ❶ 山和原野 mountains and plains; countryside: 小白花开遍～。The mountainsides are blanketed under a cover of tiny white flowers. ❷ 草野 rural area; countryside: ～小民 clodhopper; country bumpkin

【山雨欲来风满楼】shān yǔ yù lái fēng mǎn lóu 唐代许浑《咸阳城东楼》诗句，现多用来比喻冲突或战争爆发之前的紧张气氛 Rising wind forebodes a coming storm. Originating from *The East City Tower of Xianyang*, a poem by Xu Hun of the Tang Dynasty, the expression refers to tension before the outbreak of a conflict or war.

【山芋】shānyù〈方 *dial*.〉甘薯 sweet potato

【山岳】shānyuè 高大的山 lofty mountains

【山查】shānzhā same as 山楂 shānzhā

【山楂】shānzhā ❶ 落叶乔木，叶子近于卵形，有三至五裂片，花白色。果实球形，比山里红略小，深红色，有小斑点，味酸，可以吃，也可入药 Chinese hawthorn(*Crataegus pinnatifida*); deciduous tree having roughly oval leaves with three to five slivers and white flowers, its fruit, deep red, speckled, ball-shaped and slightly smaller than that of the large-fruited Chinese hawthorn (*Crataegus pinnatifida var. major*), being edible with a sour taste and of medical value ❷ 这种植物的果实 hawthorn; haw; also 山查 shānzhā

【山楂糕】shānzhāgāo 食品，用去核的山楂磨碎，加糖、淀粉等煮熟，凉后凝冻而成 haw jelly cake

【山寨】shānzhài ❶ 在山林中设有防守的栅栏的地方 mountain fastness; fortified mountain village ❷ 有寨子的山区村庄 fortified mountain village

【山珍海味】shān zhēn hǎi wèi 山野和海洋里的各种珍贵的食品。多指丰盛的菜肴。delicacies from land and sea; dainties of every kind; also 山珍海错 shān zhēn hǎi cuò

【山茱萸】shānzhūyú 落叶小乔木，叶子对生，长椭圆形，花黄色。果实为核果，长椭圆形，枣红色，可入药。fruit of medicinal cornel (*Cornus officinalis*); small deciduous tree having oblong opposite leaves, yellow flowers, and dark red oblong stone fruit (drupes) of medical value

【山庄】shānzhuāng ❶ 山村 mountain village ❷ 山中住所；别墅 mountain village; mountain villa: 避暑～mountain resort

【山子】shān·zi〈方 *dial*.〉假山 artificial mountain; rockery; also 山子石儿 shān·zishír

【山嘴】shānzuǐ (～儿 shānzuǐr)伸出去的山脚的尖端 spur; lateral ridge projecting from a mountain or mountain range

芟 shān ❶ 割(草) mow ❷ 除去 weed out; eliminate: ～除 delete; cross out

【芟除】shānchú ❶ 除去(草) weed out: ～杂草 weeding ❷ 删除 delete: 文辞繁冗，～未尽。The diction is too wordy, and no amount of deletion can solve its problem.

【芟秋】shānqiū 立秋以后在农作物地里锄草、松土，使农作物早熟、子实饱满，并防止杂草结子 weed the farmland and loose the soil after Beginning of Autumn (August 7 or 8) in order to quicken and improve the ripening process of a farm crop and prevent weeds from bearing seeds; also 删秋 shānqiū

【芟夷】shānyí〈书 *fml*.〉❶ 除(草) mow; weed ❷ 铲除或消灭(某种势力) eliminate; exterminate ‖ also 芟荑 shānyí

【芟荑】shānyí same as 芟夷 shānyí

杉 shān 常绿乔木，树冠的形状像塔，叶子长披针形，花单性，果实球形。木材白色，质轻，有香味，供建筑和制器具用。China fir (*Cunninghamia lanceolata*); evergreen tree having a pagoda-shaped crown, long lanceolate leaves, unisexual flowers, ball-like fruit, and white, light and fragrant wood useful in architecture or furniture making
☞ shā on p.1663

删(刪) shān 去掉(文辞中的某些字句) delete; strike out: ～繁就简 simplify by striking out the superfluous | 这一段可以～去。This paragraph may be deleted.

S

【删除】shānchú 删去 delete; strike, cut and cross out: ～多余的文字。Cut out the unnecessary words.

【删繁就简】shān fán jiù jiǎn 删去多余的文字或内容使简明扼要 simplify by cutting out the superfluous: 教材要～。A textbook should avoid the superfluous and adopt the succinct.

【删改】shāngǎi 删削并改动 delete and change; revise: ～原稿 revise and cut down on a manuscript

【删节】shānjié 删去文字中可有可无或比较次要的部分 expurgate; abridge: ～本 expurgated version; abridged version | 文章太长，发表时作了一些～。The article was too long and some deletion was made before it was published.

【删节号】shānjiéhào ☞ 省略号 shěnglüèhào on p.1722

【删略】shānlüè 删节省略 leave out; omit: 文章转载时作了～。The article was shortened when it was republished.

【删秋】shānqiū same as 芟秋 shānqiū

【删汰】shāntài 删削淘汰 blot out; cut down on; delete: 原文过繁，略加～。The original text was too elaborate, and slight deletion had to be made.

【删削】shānxuē 删改削减(文字) delete; cut out; strike out

苫 shān 用草做成的盖东西或垫东西的器物 mat; flat piece of woven straw material used as a cover or cushion: 草～子 straw mat
☞ shàn on p.1673

钐 shān 金属元素,符号 Sm (samarium)。是一种稀土金属。银白色,质硬。用做激光材料等,也用于原子能工业。samarium (Sm); silvery rare-earth element of a hard texture, used as a laser material and in nuclear industry

☞ shàn on p.1674

衫 shān (～儿 shānr) 单上衣 unlined upper garment:衬～shirt; blouse|汗～T-shirt|棉毛～cotton interlock jersey

姗(姍) shān [姗姗](shānshān)形容走路缓慢从容的姿态 slowly; leisurely:～来迟(形容来得很晚)be slow in coming; be late

珊(珊) shān ☞below

【珊瑚】shānhú 许多珊瑚虫的石灰质骨骼聚集而成的东西。形状像树枝,多为红色,也有白色或黑色的。可供玩赏,也用做装饰品。coral; calcareous skeleton in the shape of tree branches secreted by marine polyps, mostly red and occasionally white or black, used to make ornaments or jewelry

【珊瑚虫】shānhúchóng 腔肠动物,身体呈圆筒形,有8个或8个以上的触手,触手中央有口。多群居,结合成一个群体,形状像树枝。骨骼叫珊瑚。产在热带海中。actinozoan (*Anthozoa*); coral polyp; tropical marine coelenterate having a body in the shape of a cylinder, and eight or more tentacles each with an opening in the end, chiefly colonial and forming a colony in the shape of tree branches whose calcareous skeleton is known as coral

【珊瑚岛】shānhúdǎo 主要由珊瑚虫的骨骼堆积成的岛屿 coral island; island resulting from accumulations of calcareous skeletons secreted by coral polyps

【珊瑚礁】shānhújiāo 主要由珊瑚虫的骨骼堆积成的礁石,多见于热带海洋中 coral reef; reef consisting mainly of piles of calcareous coral skeletons

埏 shān〈书 *fml*.〉用水和(huó)土;和泥 blend or mix earth or clay with water

栅(柵) shān [栅极](shānjí)多极电子管中最靠近阴极的一个电极,具有细丝网或螺旋线的形状,有控制板极电流的强度,改变电子管的性能等作用 grid; electrode closest to the cathode (negative pole) of a multipolar electron tube, in the shape of a network or coil of fine wires, playing a role in regulating electricity over the grid and changing the function of the electron tube

☞ zhà on p.2405

舢 shān [舢板](shānbǎn)近海或江河上用桨划的小船,一般只能坐两三个人;海军用的较窄而长,一般可坐十人左右 sampan; flat-bottomed skiff usu. propelled by oars on coastal waters or rivers, large enough for two or three persons; naval sampan, having a long and narrow body and large enough for 10 persons; also 三板 sānbǎn or 舢舨 shānbǎn

痁 shān 古书上指疟疾(in ancient books) malaria; swamp fever

扇(❶❷搧) shān ❶ 摇动扇子或其他薄片,加速空气流动 fan; move or cause a current of air with a fan or sth. like it:～煤炉子 fan coal stove|～扇(shàn)子 wave a fan; fan oneself ❷ 用手掌打 box; hit with the palm of a hand:～了他一耳光。He received a box on the ears. ❸ same as 煽 shān②

☞ shàn on p.1674

【扇动】shāndòng ❶ 摇动(像扇子的东西)flap; fan:～翅膀 flap wings ❷ same as 煽动 shāndòng

跚 shān ☞[蹒跚](pánshān) on p.1443

煽 shān ❶ same as 扇 shān ① ❷ 鼓动(别人做不应该做的事)instigate; incite; stir up:～动 instigation|～惑 inflame; agitate by demagogy

【煽动】shāndòng 鼓动(别人去做坏事)instigate:～闹事 incite a riot|～暴乱 instigate a violent rebellion

【煽风点火】shān fēng diǎn huǒ〈比喻 *fig*.〉鼓动别人做某种事(多指坏的) fan the flames; inflame and agitate people; stir up trouble

【煽惑】shānhuò 鼓动诱惑(别人去做坏事) agitate people by demagogy

潸(潸) shān〈书 *fml*.〉形容流泪 in tears; tearful

【潸然】shānrán〈书 *fml*.〉流泪的样子 tearful; in tears:～泪下 tears trickling down one's cheeks

【潸潸】shānshān〈书 *fml*.〉形容流泪不止 in tears; tearful:热泪～tears streaming down one's cheeks|不禁～can't hold back one's tears

膻(羶) shān 像羊肉的气味 smell of mutton:～气 smell of mutton|～味 odour of mutton

羴 shān same as 膻 shān

shǎn (ㄕㄢˇ)

闪 shǎn ❶ 闪避 duck; dodge:～开 step aside|～过去 get out of the way|～在树后 duck behind a tree ❷ (身体)猛然晃动 be shaken:他脚下一滑,～了～,差点跌倒。He slipped, and was so shaken that he almost gave way. ❸ 因动作过猛,使一部分筋肉受伤而疼痛 sprain; pull one's muscle:～了腰 sprain one's waist ❹ 闪电 lightning:打～ discharge a flash of lightning ❺ 突然出现 appear suddenly：～念(of an idea) flash across one's mind| 山后～出一条小路来。A tiny footpath suddenly presented itself behind the mountain. ❻ 闪耀 spark; flash; emit：～金光 emit golden rays|电～雷鸣 the lightning flashes and the thunders roar|眼里～着泪花 tears glisten in one's eyes ❼〈方 *dial.*〉甩下；丢下 leave out; leave behind：出发时我们一定来叫你，不会把你～下。We'll give you a yell when we set out, and we won't leave you behind. ❽ (Shǎn)姓 a surname

【闪避】shǎnbì 迅速侧转身子向旁边躲避 duck; sidestep：～不及 too late to dodge

【闪电】shǎndiàn 云与云之间或云与地面之间所发生的放电现象，会发出很强的电光 lightning; abrupt, discontinuous natural discharge of electricity and flashes of light between clouds or between clouds and earth's surface

【闪电战】shǎndiànzhàn 闪击战 lightning war; blitzkrieg; blitz

【闪躲】shǎnduǒ 躲闪；躲避 dodge; evade：～不开 too late or slow to dodge|他有意～我的目光。His eyes deliberately dodged mine.

【闪光】shǎn//guāng 现出光亮；发光 glisten; glow：萤火虫在草丛中闪着光。Fireflies glowed among the grasses.

【闪光】shǎnguāng 突然一现或忽明忽暗的光亮 flash：流星变成一道～，划破黑夜的长空。The shooting stars turned themselves into a flash of light that slashed across the dark sky.

【闪光灯】shǎnguāngdēng ❶ 一种照明装置，能产生强度很大而持续时间很短的闪光，用于摄影 flashlight; photo flash; photographic device that discharges a strong beam of light in a short duration ❷ 灯标的主要部分，能发出定时瞬息明灭或轮换强弱和色彩的闪光，以电灯、汽油灯、煤气灯等为光源 flashlight; main component of a beacon, capable of discharging evanescent light or shifting the intensity and colour of the beams, with electric, gas or gasoline light as its source

【闪击】shǎnjī 集中兵力突然袭击 surprise attack

【闪击战】shǎnjīzhàn 利用大量快速部队和新式武器突然发动猛烈的进攻，企图迅速取得战争胜利的一种作战方法 lightning war; blitzkrieg; blitz; swift, sudden military offensive mounted by large fast-advancing troops and new weapons, aimed at a quick victory; also 闪电战 shǎndiànzhàn

【闪念】shǎnniàn 突然一现的念头 flash of thought

【闪闪】shǎnshǎn 光亮四射；闪烁不定 sparkling; glistening; glittering：电光～flashes of lightning|～发光 glowing

【闪射】shǎnshè 闪耀；放射(光芒) radiate; glitter; shine：远处有车灯～。In the distance the lamps of an automobile were glittering.|眼睛里～着幸福的光芒。Happiness glittered in his eyes.

【闪身】shǎn//shēn (～儿 shǎn//shēnr)侧着身子 move sideways; move on one's side：～挤进门去 squeeze through the door sideways

【闪失】shǎnshī 意外的损失；岔子 mishap; accident：万一有个～，后悔就晚了。It would be too late if sth. goes wrong.

【闪烁】shǎnshuò ❶ (光亮)动摇不定，忽明忽暗 glimmer; glisten; twinkle：江面上隐约～着夜航船的灯光。The lights of sailing boats glimmered faintly on the river. ❷ (说话)稍微露出一点想法，但不肯说明确；吞吞吐吐 hum and haw; prevaricate; equivocate：～其词(形容说话吞吞吐吐，躲躲闪闪)speak evasively|他闪闪烁烁，不做肯定答复。He hummed and hawed, and gave a noncommittal reply.

【闪现】shǎnxiàn 一瞬间出现；呈现 flash before one; flash：往事又～在眼前。Past events flashed before his eyes.

【闪耀】shǎnyào 闪烁①；光彩耀眼 glitter; shine：繁星～glittering stars|塔顶～着金光。The top of the pagoda glittered in gold luminosity.

陕(陝) Shǎn ❶ 指陕西 Shaanxi ❷ 姓 a surname

【陕西梆子】Shǎnxī bāng·zi Shaanxi clapper opera; same as 秦腔 qínqiāng ①

掺(摻) shǎn 〈书 *fml.*〉持；握 hold; grasp：～手 shake hands

☞ càn on p. 188 and chān on p. 209

睒(睒) shǎn 眨巴眼；睛睛很快地开闭 wink; blink; twinkle：那飞机飞得很快，一～眼就不见了。The airplane flew really fast, and vanished in the twinkling of an eye.

S

shàn(ㄕㄢˋ)

讪 shàn ❶ 讥讽 chaff; gibe; scoff：～笑 deride ❷ 难为情的样子 discomfited; red-faced; mortified：脸上发～ blush in embarrassment

【讪脸】shànliǎn〈方 *dial.*〉小孩子在大人面前嬉皮笑脸(of children in the presence of adults) grin mischievously; grin and grimace

【讪讪】shànshàn 形容不好意思、难为情的样子 embarrassed; diffident：他觉得没趣，只好～地走开了。Feeling he was not wanted, he walked away looking embarrassed.

【讪笑】shànxiào 讥笑 ridicule; gibe; scoff

汕 shàn 汕头(Shàntóu)，地名，在广东。Shantou, name of a place in Guangdong

苫 shàn 用席、布等遮盖 cover with a mat, tarpaulin, etc.：要下雨了，快把场里的麦子～上。Hurry up! Cover up the wheat on the threshing ground. It's going to rain.

☞ shān on p. 1671

【苫背】shàn//bèi 盖房子时,在草、席等上面抹上灰和泥土做成房顶底层 building the base of a roof by covering straw, matting, etc. with mortar

【苫布】shànbù 遮盖货物用的大雨布 tarpaulin; waterproofed canvas used to cover and protect things from moisture

钐(鐥、釤) shàn 〈方 *dial.*〉抡开镰刀或钐镰大片地割 cut with a sickle:～草 cut grass with a sickle

☞ shān on p. 1672

【钐镰】shànlián 一种把儿很长的大镰刀 scythe; implement consisting of a long, curved single-edged blade with a long handle, used for mowing or reaping; also 钐刀 shàndāo

疝 shàn 病,某一脏器通过周围组织较薄弱的地方而隆起。头、膈、腹股沟等部都能发生这种病。hernia; protrusion of an organ through surrounding tissues in the body, a disease that may occur in the head, the midriff and the groin

S 【疝气】shànqì 通常指腹股沟部的疝。症状是腹股沟凸起或阴囊肿大,时有剧痛。hernia; inguinal hernia, a disease characterized by protrusion of the midriff or the tumefaction of the scrotum; also 小肠串气 xiǎocháng chuànqì

单(單) Shàn ❶ 单县,在山东 Shanxian, name of a county in Shandong Province ❷ (Shàn) 姓 a surname

☞ chán on p. 209 and dān on p. 374

赸 shàn 〈书 *fml.*〉躲开;走开 go away; go into hiding

剡 Shàn 古县名,在今浙江嵊县 Shanxian, ancient county in present-day Shengxian County, Zhejiang Province

☞ yǎn on p. 2209

扇 shàn ❶ (～儿 shànr)扇子 fan:蒲～palm-leaf fan|电～electric fan|折～儿 folding fan ❷ 指板状或片状的东西 panel:门～door panel|隔～partition screen ❸ 〈量词 *classifier*〉用于门窗等 [for doors, windows, etc.]:一～门 a door|一～磨 a milling stone|两～窗子 two windows

☞ shān on p. 1672

【扇贝】shànbèi 软体动物,壳略作扇形,色彩多样,表面有很多纵沟,生活在海中。体内的闭壳肌制成干贝,是一种珍贵的食品。scallop (*Pecten*); fan shell; marine mollusk of the family *Pectinidae*, having multihued fan-shaped bivalve shells with a radiating fluted pattern, whose edible adductor muscle is dried and used as a precious food; also 海扇 hǎishàn

【扇车】shànchē 一种农械,由木箱和装有叶片的轴构成。转动叶片可以扇风,从而把谷类的壳和米粒分开。winnowing machine; winnower; farm instrument for separating chaff from grain by means of a current of air, consisting of a wooden box and a shaft fixed with radiating blades that revolve and move the air; also 风车 fēngchē

【扇骨】shàngǔ (～儿 shàngǔr)折扇的骨架,多用竹、木等制成 ribs or mount of a folding fan, usu. made of bamboo or wood; also 扇骨子 shàngǔ·zi

【扇面儿】shànmiànr 折扇或团扇的面儿,用纸、绢等做成 covering of a fan, fashioned out of paper or thin silk

【扇坠】shànzhuì (～儿 shànzhuìr)系在扇柄下端的装饰物,多用玉石等制成 fan pendant; object of ornamentation oft. made of jade

【扇子】shàn·zi 摇动生风的用具 fan; device for creating a current of air or a breeze:一把～a fan|扇(shān)～wave a fan in one's hand

墠(壇) shàn ❶〈古代 *arch.*〉祭祀用的平地 level ground for holding sacrificial rituals ❷ 北墠(Běishàn),地名,在山东 Beishan, name of a place in Shandong Province

掸(撣) Shàn ❶ 我国史书上对傣族的一种称呼 *Shan*, referring to the Dai ethnic group in Chinese history books ❷ 缅甸民族之一,大部分居住在掸邦(自治邦名) Shan people, a Burmese ethnic people mostly inhabiting the Shan State of Myanmar

☞ dǎn on p. 379

掞 shàn 〈书 *fml.*〉舒展;铺张 stretch out; extravagant

善 shàn ❶ 善良;慈善(跟'恶'相对 as opposed to 'evil') good; virtuous:～举 good deed|～事 virtuous deed|心怀不～mean ill; harbour evil or ill intentions ❷ 善行;善事(跟'恶'相对 as opposed to 'evil dealing') benevolence; charitable act; philanthropic deed:行～do good deeds|劝～规过 advise people to do good and refrain from evil ❸ 良好 wise; satisfactory; good:～策 wise policy; best policy|～本 best edition of a book ❹ 友好;和好 kind; friendly; amiable:友～friendly|相～be friendly to each other|亲～goodwill; fraternity ❺ 熟悉 familiar:面～look familiar ❻ 办好;弄好 do well; do a good job:～后 take care of remaining problems|～始～终 begin well and end well|工欲～其事,必先利其器。A labourer who wants to do a good job has to sharpen his tools before anything else. ❼ 擅长;长于 be good at; be well-versed in:勇猛～战 valiant and well-versed in the art of war|多谋～断 resourcefulness and good sense of judgement ❽ 好好地 properly:～自保重 take care; take good care of yourself|～为说辞 put in a good word or two for sb. ❾ 容易;易于 apt to; liable to:～变 be apt to change; be changeable|～忘 forgetful; have a bad memory ⑩ (Shàn) 姓 a surname

【善罢甘休】shàn bà gān xiū 好好地了结纠纷,不闹下去(多用于否定 usu. used in the negative) leave the matter at that; let it go at that: 决不能~ not take one's defeat lying down

【善本】shànběn 〈古代 *arch.*〉书籍在学术或艺术价值上比一般本子优异的刻本或写本 reliable text; good edition: ~书 rare book | ~目录 catalogue of rare books

【善处】shànchù 〈书 *fml.*〉妥善地处理 deal discreetly with; conduct oneself well

【善感】shàngǎn 容易引起感触 (of a person) sensitive: 多愁~ sentimental and susceptible

【善后】shànhòu 妥善地料理和解决事件发生以后遗留的问题 deal with problems arising from an accident, etc.: 处理~问题 deal with the aftermath of some problem

【善举】shànjǔ 〈书 *fml.*〉慈善的事情 philanthropic act: 共襄~ work together to make a charitable activity a success

【善类】shànlèi 〈书 *fml.*〉善良的人(多用于否定式 usu. used in the negative) good people: 此人行迹诡秘,定非~。He cannot possibly be a good man, judging from the surreptitious way he carries himself.

【善良】shànliáng 心地纯洁,没有恶意 good and honest; kind-hearted: 心地~ kind-hearted | ~的愿望 best of intentions

【善男信女】shànnán-xìnnǚ 〈佛教 *Budd.*〉指信仰佛教的人们 Buddhist believers; Buddhist devotees

【善始善终】shàn shǐ shàn zhōng 事情从开头到结束都做得很好 start well and end well; do well from start to finish; see sth. through

【善事】shànshì 慈善的事 charitable deeds; good deeds

【善心】shànxīn 好心肠 be kind-hearted; kindness; mercy; benevolence

【善意】shànyì 善良的心意;好意 goodwill; good intentions: ~的批评 well-meaning criticism

【善于】shànyú 在某方面具有特长 be good at; be adept in; be specialized in a certain field: ~辞令 have a ready tongue | ~团结群众 know well how to rally the masses

【善战】shànzhàn 善于打仗 be good at fighting; be skilful in battle: 英勇~ fight bravely and skillfully

【善终】shànzhōng ❶ 指人因衰老而死亡,不是死于意外的灾祸 die a natural death; die in one's bed ❷ 把事情的最后阶段工作做完做好 end well: 善始~ start well and end well

禅(禪) shàn 禅让 abdicate and hand over the crown to another person: 受~ ascend the throne abdicated by the emperor | ~位 abdicate the throne

☞ chán on p. 210

【禅让】shànràng 帝王把帝位让给别人 abdicate and hand over the crown to another person

骟 shàn 割掉牲畜的睾丸或卵巢 castrate (an animal); geld (a male animal); spay (a female animal): ~马 castrate a horse; castrated horse

鄯 shàn 鄯善 (Shànshàn), 地名, 在新疆 Shanshan (Pigan), name of a place in Xinjiang

墡 shàn 古书上指白色黏土 white clay as described in ancient books

缮 shàn ❶ 修补 repair; mend: 修~ repair ❷ 缮写 copy; write: 议定书用两种文字各~一份。The protocol is written in two languages and made available in two separate copies.

【缮发】shànfā 缮写后发出 copy and send out: ~公文 copy and send out the official document

【缮写】shànxiě 誊写;抄写 write out; copy: ~书稿 make a clean copy of a manuscript

擅 shàn ❶ 擅自 act (or do sth.) without authorization (or permission); do sth. on one's own authority: ~离职守 leave one's post without permission ❷ 长于;善于 be good at; be expert in: 不~辞令 be not good at speech; lack facility in polite or tactful speech

【擅长】shàncháng 在某方面有特长 be good at; be expert in; be skilled in: ~书法 be good at calligraphy

【擅场】shàngchǎng 〈书 *fml.*〉压倒全场;在某种专长方面超过一般人 dominate the scene; be the supreme arbiter: ~之作 unequalled work

【擅权】shànquán 独揽权力;专权 monopolize power; have sole power; arrogate all authority to oneself

【擅自】shànzì 对不在自己的职权范围以内的事情自作主张 do sth. without authorization: 不得~改变安全操作规程。No unauthorized changes shall be made in the rules of safe operation.

膳(饍) shàn 饭食 meals; board: 早~ breakfast | 午~ lunch | 晚~ supper; dinner | 用~ have a meal

【膳费】shànfèi 膳食所需的费用 board expenses

【膳食】shànshí 日常吃的饭和菜 meals; food

嬗 shàn 〈书 *fml.*〉❶ 更替;蜕变 transmute; transform ❷ same as 禅 shàn

【嬗变】shànbiàn 〈书 *fml.*〉演变 evolution

赡 shàn ❶ 赡养 support; provide for ❷ 〈书 *fml.*〉丰富;充足 sufficient; abundant: 宏~ extensive knowledge | 力不~(力不足) beyond one's ability

【赡养】shànyǎng 供给生活所需,特指子女对父母在物质上和生活上进行帮助 support; provide for; supply the necessities, esp. the material assistance and livelihood given by children to their parents：～费 payment for the support of one's parents；alimony｜～父母 support one's parents

蟮 shàn ☞ 曲蟮 qū·shàn on p. 1587

鳝(鱓) shàn 鳝鱼，通常指黄鳝 eel（*Anguillidae*）；finless eel；usu. the yellow eel

shāng（ㄕㄤ）

伤(傷) shāng ❶ 人体或其他物体受到的损害 wound；injury：内～ internal injury｜虫～ insect bites｜探～ flaw detection；defect detection；fault detection｜轻～不下火线 remain at the battlefront with minor wounds ❷ 伤害 injure；hurt：～了筋骨 injure the muscles and bones｜出口～人 make offensive remarks；speak offensively｜～感情 hurt one's feelings ❸ 悲伤 be distressed；be grieved：忧～ grief；sorrow｜哀～ grief；sorrow｜～感 sentimental；sick at heart ❹ 因过度而感到厌烦（多指饮食）get sick of sth.（food and drink）；develop an aversion to sth.：～食 be sick from overeating；suffer from indigestion｜吃糖吃～了 get sick from eating too many candies ❺ 妨碍 be harmful to；hinder：无～大雅 not offend anyone；not affect the major principles；not matter much｜有～风化 be harmful to the morals

【伤疤】shāngbā ❶ 伤口愈合后留下的痕迹 scar ❷〈比喻 *fig.*〉过去的错误、隐私、耻辱等 errors，privacy and humiliation of the past：揭～ reveal one's past mistakes，privacy or humiliation

【伤悼】shāngdào 怀念死者而感到悲伤 mourn sorrowfully（for somebody's death）：顷得噩耗，～不已。I'm greatly grieved to hear the sad news.

【伤风】shāng//fēng 感冒 catch cold；have a cold

【伤风败俗】shāng fēng bài sú 指败坏风俗（多用来谴责道德败坏 oft. used to denounce morally degeneration）offend public decency；corrupt public morals

【伤感】shānggǎn 因感触而悲伤 sentimental；sick at heart：对景思人，无限～。Feel extremely sorrowful to see the sight and think of one's people.

【伤害】shānghài 使身体组织或思想感情等受到损害 injure；harm；hurt：睡眠过少会～身体。Too little sleep is harmful to the health.｜～自尊心 injure（or hurt）one's pride

【伤寒】shānghán ❶ 急性肠道传染病，病原体是伤寒杆菌，症状是体温持续在 39—40℃，脉搏缓慢，脾脏肿大，白细胞减少，腹部出现玫瑰色疹 typhoid fever；typhoid；an acute infectious disease caused by a bacillus（*Salmonella typhi*）and acquired by ingesting food or water contaminated by excreta；characterized by a fever of 39-40°C，slow pulse，enlargement of the spleen，decrease of the white cells and the appearance of rosy rashes on the belly；also 肠伤寒 chángshānghán ❷〈中医 *Chin. med.*〉指外感发热的病，特指发热、恶寒无汗、头痛项僵的病 diseases caused by harmful cold factors；febrile diseases；fevers，esp. characterized by bad cold with no sweating，headache and stiff neck

【伤号】shānghào 受伤的人（多用于军队 usu. used among army personnel）the wounded

【伤耗】shāng·hao 损耗 damage

【伤痕】shānghén 伤疤。也指物体受损害后留下的痕迹。scar；bruise；mark left after a body is cut：～累累 many cuts and bruises

【伤口】shāngkǒu 皮肤、肌肉、黏膜等受伤破裂的地方 wound；cut；injury to a body in which the skin，muscle and mucous membrane are broken，cut，etc.

【伤脑筋】shāng nǎojīn 形容事情难办，费心思 knotty；troublesome；bothersome：这件事真让人～。This matter is really a headache.

【伤神】shāng//shén ❶ 过度耗费精神 overtax one's nerves；be nerve-racking：做这事真够～的。It is really nerve-racking to get this job done. ❷ 伤心 sad；grieved：黯然～ feel depressed（or dejected）

【伤生】shāng//shēng 伤害生命 be injurious（or harmful）to life

【伤势】shāngshì 受伤的情况 condition of an injury or wound：～严重 be seriously injured or wounded

【伤逝】shāngshì〈书 *fml.*〉悲伤地怀念去世的人 mourn the death of somebody

【伤天害理】shāng tiān hài lǐ 指做事残忍，灭绝人性 defy Heaven and reason；atrocious；outrageous；inhuman

【伤亡】shāngwáng 受伤和死亡；受伤和死亡的人 injuries and deaths；casualties：～惨重 suffer heavy casualties｜交战双方各有～。The two sides at war suffered casualties.

【伤心】shāng//xīn 由于遭受不幸或不如意的事而心里痛苦 sad；grieved；broken-hearted：～事 a heartbreaking affair；a painful memory；an old sore｜～落泪 shed sad tears；weep in grief

【伤心惨目】shāng xīn cǎn mù 非常悲惨，使人不忍心看 too ghastly to look at；tragic（scene）

【伤员】shāngyuán 受伤的人员（多用于军队 usu. used among army personnel）wounded personnel；the wounded

汤(湯) shāng [汤汤]（shāngshāng）〈书 *fml.*〉水流大而急 swift，violent stream of water；torrent：河水～。The river is in full spate.｜浩浩～ mighty and torrential

☞ tāng on p. 1864

殇(殤) shāng 〈书 *fml.*〉没有到成年就死去 die young

商[1] shāng ❶ 商量 discuss; consult: 协～ consultation | 面～ discuss face to face | 有要事相～。There is an important matter to be discussed. ❷ 商业 business; commerce: 经～ go into business; engage in business; become a businessman | 通～ have trade relations with; have commercial intercourse with ❸ 商人 businessman; tradesman; merchant; dealer; trader: 布～ cotton dealer | ～旅 travelling merchants ❹ 除法运算中,被除数除以除数所得的数。如 10÷2=5 中,5 是商。quotient; result obtained when one number is divided by another. Example: In the formula 10÷2=5,5 is the quotient. ❺ 用某数做商 use a number as a quotient: 八除以二～四。Four is the quotient when eight is divided by two.

商[2] shāng ❶ 〈古代 *arch.*〉五音之一,相当于简谱的'2' note of the ancient Chinese five-tone scale, corresponding to 2 in numbered musical notation; ☞ 五音 wǔyīn on p. 2032 ❷ 二十八宿中的心宿 Heart Constellation of the 28 constellations in ancient astronomy

商[3] Shāng ❶ 朝代,公元前 1600—公元前 1046,汤所建 Shang Dynasty (1600-1046 B.C.) founded by Tang ❷ 姓 a surname

【商标】shāngbiāo 一种商品表面或包装上的标志、记号(图画、图案形文字等),使这种商品和同类的其他商品有所区别 trademark; symbol or mark (drawing, design, word, letter, etc.) used on a product or its packing by a manufacturer or dealer to distinguish the product from those of competitors

【商埠】shāngbù 〈旧时 *old*〉与外国通商的城镇 trading port; town or city having trading relations with foreign countries

【商场】shāngchǎng ❶ 聚集在一个或相连的几个建筑物内的各种商店所组成的市场 emporium; mart consisting of different shops, assembled in one building or several adjoining buildings ❷ 面积较大、商品比较齐全的综合商店 large department store: 百货～ department store ❸ 指商界 commercial circle; business world

【商船】shāngchuán 运载货物和旅客的船 merchant ship; ship carrying freight and passengers

【商店】shāngdiàn 在室内出售商品的场所 shop; store; indoor place where commodities are sold: 百货～ department store | 零售～ retail shop

【商定】shāngdìng 商量决定 decide through consultation; agree: 这事如何处理还没有最后～。It has not yet been finally agreed on how this matter will be settled.

【商兑】shāngduì 〈书 *fml.*〉商量斟酌 consult and consider; discuss and deliberate

【商贩】shāngfàn 指现买现卖的小商人 small retailer; pedlar

【商贾】shānggǔ 〈书 *fml.*〉商人(总称) merchants (collect.)

【商行】shāngháng 商店(多指较大的) trading company; commercial firm

【商号】shānghào 商店 shop; store; business establishment

【商会】shānghuì 商人为了维护自己利益而组成的团体 chamber of commerce; organization of merchants to guard their interest

【商计】shāngjì 商量;计议 have discussions or consultations; discuss and consult: ～要事 discuss important matters

【商检】shāngjiǎn 商品检验 commodity inspection: ～部门 department of commodity inspection | ～工作 work of commodity inspection

【商界】shāngjiè 指商业界 business circles; commercial circles

【商籁体】shānglàitǐ ☞ 十四行诗 shísìhángshī on p. 1735; [商籁,法 French: sonnet]

【商量】shāng·liáng 交换意见 consult; discuss; talk over with sb.; exchange views: 遇事要多和群众～。Consult the masses when matters arise. | 这件事要跟他～一下。I have to discuss the matter with him.

【商旅】shānglǚ 指来往外地买卖货物的商人 travelling merchants

【商贸】shāngmào 商业和贸易 business and trade: ～系统 business and trading system | ～活动 business and trading activities

【商品】shāngpǐn ❶ 为交换而生产的劳动产品。具有使用价值和价值的两重性。商品在不同的社会制度中,体现着不同的生产关系。commodity; product of labour produced for exchange, having the dual character of use value and value, and embodying different relations of production under a different social system ❷ 泛指市场上买卖的物品 commodity; goods; merchandise; goods bought and sold in the market

【商品房】shāngpǐnfáng 指作为商品出售的房屋 commercial housing; housing on sale as a commodity

【商品经济】shānpǐn jīngjì 以交换为目的而进行生产的经济形式 commodity economy; a mode of economy conducted for exchange; ☞ 商品生产 shāngpǐn shēngchǎn

【商品粮】shāngpǐnliáng 指作为商品出售的粮食 commodity grain; marketable grain; grains on sale as a commodity

【商品流通】shāngpǐn liútōng 以货币为媒介的商品交换 commodity circulation; commodity exchange with money as its media

【商品生产】shāngpǐn shēngchǎn 以交换为目的

而进行的产品生产 commodity production; production of products conducted for exchange

【商洽】shāngqià 接洽商谈 arrange a discussion with sb.; take up (a matter) with sb.; discuss with:为落实双方合作事宜,请速派人前来～。In order to finalize the matters concerning cooperation between the two sides, send your man here for discussion as soon as possible.

【商情】shāngqíng 指市场上的商品价格和供销情况 market conditions; market prices and marketing:～调查 market survey|熟悉～ be familiar with the market conditions|～资料 market data

【商榷】shāngquè 商讨 discuss; deliberate:这个问题尚待～。This question is yet to be discussed.|他的论点还有值得～的地方。His argument is still open to discussion.

【商人】shāngrén 贩卖商品从中取利的人 businessman; merchant; trader; man who buys and sells commodities for profit

【商谈】shāngtán 口头商量 exchange views; confer; discuss; negotiate:～工作 discuss work|对这个问题双方进行了长时间的～。The two sides have discussed this issue for a long time.

S

【商讨】shāngtǎo 为了解决较大的、较复杂的问题而交换意见;商量讨论 discuss; deliberate over; exchange views on major and complicated issues:会议～了两国的经济合作问题。The meeting discussed the issue on the economic cooperation between the two countries.

【商务】shāngwù 商业上的事务 commercial affairs; business affairs:～往来 commercial intercourse; business contact

【商业】shāngyè 以买卖方式使商品流通的经济活动 commerce; trade; business; the economic activities to circulate commodities in the form of buying and selling

【商议】shāngyì 为了对某些问题取得一致意见而进行讨论 confer; discuss; have discussions on certain issues in order to get unanimous agreement:这个问题如何解决,还需好好～一下。How to settle this issue (or solve this problem) still requires serious discussion.

【商约】shāngyuē 国家之间缔结的通商条约 commercial treaty (concluded between two countries)

【商战】shāngzhàn 指商业上为商品销路而进行的激烈竞争 fierce competition to promote the sale of commodities

【商酌】shāngzhuó 商量斟酌 discuss and consider; deliberate over:此项工作有待进一步～。This work needs further discussion and consideration.

觞(觴) shāng 〈古代 *arch.*〉称酒杯 wine cup; drinking vessel:举～相庆 raise cups in congratulations; propose a toast to sb.

墒(䵮) shāng 土壤适合种子发芽和作物生长的湿度 moisture in the soil; moisture in the soil suitable for the germination of seeds and the growth of crops:抢～ seize time in sowing while there is sufficient moisture in the soil|保～ preserve the soil moisture|跑～ lose moisture in the soil

【墒情】shāngqíng 土壤湿度的情况 soil moisture content

熵 shāng ❶ 热力体系中,不能利用来做功的热能可以用热能的变化量除以温度所得的商来表示,这个商叫做熵 entropy; measure of the amount of energy unavailable for work in a thermodynamic system, derived by dividing the changing amount of thermal energy with the temperature ❷ 科学技术上泛指某些物质系统状态的一种量度或者某些物质系统状态可能出现的程度 entropy; measurement of the systematic state of certain substances or the degree of frequency for the possible occurrence of the systematic state of a certain substance

shǎng (ㄕㄤˇ)

上 shǎng 指上声,'上²'(shàng) ⑭的又音 variant pronunciation for 上² shàng

【上声】shǎngshēng 四声之一,上声(shàngshēng)的又音 variant pronunciation for 上声 shàngshēng; rising tone or falling-rising tone; second or third of the four pronunciations for a Chinese character

垧 shǎng 土地面积单位,各地不同,东北地区多数地方合十五亩,西北地区合三亩或五亩 *shang*; land measure equal to 15 *mu* in most parts of the Northeast and three or five *mu* in the Northwest

晌 shǎng ❶ (～儿 shǎngr)一天以内的一段时间 period of time of the day:工作了一～ have worked for the morning|前半～儿 morning|晚半～儿 afternoon ❷〈方 *dial.*〉晌午 noon:～觉 midday nap|歇～ take a midday nap or rest

【晌饭】shǎngfàn〈方 *dial.*〉❶ 午饭 midday meal; lunch; also 晌午饭 shǎng·wufàn ❷ 农忙时午前或午后增加的一顿(或两顿)饭 extra daytime meal during the busy farming season

【晌觉】shǎngjiào〈方 *dial.*〉午觉 afternoon nap:睡～ take an afternoon nap; also 晌午觉 shǎng·wujiào

【晌午】shǎng·wu 中午 midday; noon

赏¹ shǎng ❶ 赏赐;奖赏 grant (or bestow) a reward; award:有～有罚 mete out due rewards and punishments ❷ 赏赐或奖赏的东西 reward; award:悬～ post a reward|领～ receive an award ❸ (Shǎng)姓 a surname

赏[2] shǎng ❶ 欣赏;观赏 marvel at; feast one's eyes on:～月 enjoy the bright full moon (during the Mid-Autumn Festival)|～花 marvel at flowers|雅俗共～ appeal to both the refined and the vulgar ❷ 赏识 recognise; appreciate:赞～ appreciate; be appreciated; think highly of

【赏赐】shǎngcì ❶〈旧指 *old*〉地位高的人或长辈把财物送给地位低的人或晚辈 grant (or bestow) a reward; award; property or valuables granted by a man of high position to a man of low position, or by a senior to a junior ❷ 指赏赐的财物 reward; award

【赏罚】shǎngfá 奖赏有功的人,处罚有过失的人 rewards and punishments:～分明 be fair in meting out rewards and punishments; discriminating in one's rewards and punishments

【赏封】shǎngfēng〈旧时 *old*〉指装在红封套里的或者用红纸包起来的赏钱 gift money in a red packet (given to children or servants on festive occasions) in old times

【赏格】shǎnggé 悬赏所定的报酬数 reward offered

【赏光】shǎng//guāng〈客套话 *pol.*〉用于请对方接受自己的邀请 (used when requesting sb. to accept an invitation) May I have the pleasure of your presence...

【赏鉴】shǎngjiàn 欣赏鉴别(多指艺术品 work of art) appreciate and evaluate :～名画 appreciate and evaluate a famous painting

【赏赉】shǎnglài〈书 *fml.*〉赏赐 give a reward; bestow a favour

【赏脸】shǎng//liǎn〈客套话 *pol.*〉用于请对方接受自己的要求或赠品 honour me with your presence; request another person to accept one's gift, invitation, etc.

【赏钱】shǎng·qián 赏给人的钱 tip

【赏识】shǎngshí 认识到别人的才能或作品的价值而予以重视或赞扬 recognize the worth of; appreciate; recognize sb.'s talent or the value of sb.'s work, and speak highly of it

【赏玩】shǎngwán 欣赏玩味(景物、艺术品等) admire the beauty of sth.; delight in; enjoy; fondle:～山景 enjoy mountain scenery|～古董 fondle antiques

【赏析】shǎngxī 欣赏并分析(诗文等) make appreciative remarks on (poems, articles, etc.):唐诗～ appreciative remarks on Tang poetry|京剧艺术～ an appreciative analysis of the Peking Opera

【赏心悦目】shǎng xīn yuè mù 指因欣赏美好的情景而心情舒畅 find what one sees pleasing to both the eye and the mind

【赏阅】shǎngyuè 欣赏阅读(诗文等) read for pleasure, appreciation or enjoyment:～佳作 read an excellent piece of work for enjoyment

shàng(ㄕㄤˋ)

上[1] shàng ❶ 位置在高处的 up; upper; above:～部 upper part|～游 upper reaches|往～看 look up ❷ 等级或品质高的 high grade or high quality; top grade or top quality:～等 top-notch; high grade|～级 authorities above (or at a higher level)|～品 top quality ❸ 次序或时间在前的 preceding (in order or time):～卷 first volume; Volume I; first part; Part I|～次 last time|～半年 the first half of a year ❹〈旧时 *old*〉指皇帝 formerly, referring to the emperor:～谕 imperial edict; imperial decree ❺ 向上面 upward:～缴 turn over (revenues, tax, etc.) to the higher authorities|～升 rise; go up; increase|～进 make progress; go forward

上[2] shàng ❶ 由低处到高处 come or go up; ascend:～山 climb up a mountain|～楼 go upstairs; ascend the stairs|～车 get on a car (bus, etc.) ❷ 到;去(某个地方) go to; leave for:～街 go shopping|～工厂 go to the factory|他～哪儿去了? Where has he gone? *or* Where is he? ❸ 向上级呈递 submit sth. to a higher authority:～书 submit a written request (statement, paper, etc.) to a higher authority ❹ 向前进 forge ahead; go ahead:老张快～,投篮。Be quick! Lao Zhang. Shoot! |见困难就～,见荣誉就让。Advance where there are difficulties to overcome, and retreat where there is an honour in store. ❺ 出场 appear on stage; enter the court:这一场戏,你应该从左边的旁门～。In this scene, you should get on stage from the side door on the left.|这一场球,你们五个先～。The five of you will start the first game. ❻ 把饭菜等端上桌子 serve; lay dishes on the table:～饭 serve a meal|～菜 serve dishes|～茶 serve tea ❼ 添补;增加 fill; supply; replenish:～水 feed water to a steam engine|～货 replenish supplies for sale ❽ 把一件东西安装在另一件东西上;把一件东西的两部分安装在一起 fix; place sth. in position; fix one thing on another; fix two parts together:～刺刀 fix bayonets|～螺丝 tighten a screw; fix screws ❾ 涂;搽 apply; paint; smear:～颜色 apply colours|～药 apply medicine ❿ 登载 carry; print:～报 printed in a newspaper; reported in a newspaper|～账 make an entry in the account book; enter in the account book ⓫ 拧紧 wind, screw up; tighten:～弦 wind a watch (or clock)|表该～了。It's time to wind the watch. ⓬ 到规定时间开始工作或学习等 start work or study at a fixed time:～班 begin work|～课 begin a lesson ⓭ 达到;够

(一定数量或程度) up to; as many as:～百人 up to 100 people|～年纪 get on in age ⓮(又 shǎng)四声之一;上声 variant pronunciation for 上声 fall-rising tone; third of the four pronunciations for a Chinese character:平～去入 level tone, rising tone or fall-rising tone, falling tone and entering tone; four tones of classical Chinese pronunciation

上[3] shàng 我国民族音乐音阶上的一级,乐谱上用做记音符号,相当于简谱的'1' note of the scale in traditional Chinese music, corresponding to 1 in numbered musical notation; ☞ 工尺 gōngchě on p. 664

上 //·shàng 用在动词后 [used as a complement to a verb] ❶ 表示由低处向高处 up; upward:爬～山顶 climb up to the top of the mountain (or hill) ❷ 表示有了结果或达到目的 [indicating the attainment of an objective]:锁～门 lock the door; lock up|考～了大学 be admitted into a university|那时他家穷得连饭都吃不～。His family was too poor to have anything to eat in those years. ❸ 表示开始并继续 indicating that an action has started and in progress:爱～了农村 fall in love with the countryside

上 ·shang ❶ 用在名词后,表示在物体的表面 [used after a noun to indicate the surface of sth.] on:脸～ on one's face|墙～ on the wall|桌子～ on the table ❷ 用在名词后,表示在某种事物的范围以内 [used after a noun to indicate the limited scope of a thing] at; in:会～ at a meeting|书～ in the book|课堂～ in the classroom|报纸～ in the newspaper ❸ 用在名词后,表示某一方面 [used after a noun to indicate a certain aspect]:组织～ organizationally|事实～ in fact; as a matter of fact|思想～ ideologically; mentally

【上班】shàng//bān (～儿 shàng//bānr) 在规定的时间到工作地点工作 go to work; start work; be on duty

【上板儿】shàng//bǎnr 〈方 *dial.*〉商店停止营业时,门窗外面用木板挡上,叫做上板儿。泛指商店停止营业。(of a shop) put up the shutters for the night; close up

【上半晌】shàngbànshǎng 〈方 *dial.*〉(～儿 shàngbànshǎngr) same as 上午 shàngwǔ

【上半时】shàngbànshí 足球、篮球等球类比赛,全场比赛分作两段时间进行,前一段时间叫上半时 first half; in football and some other ball games, a match is divided into two halves, and the first part of the time is called first half; also 上半场 shàngbànchǎng

【上半天】shàngbàntiān (～儿 shàngbàntiānr) same as 上午 shàngwǔ

【上半夜】shàngbànyè 前半夜 before midnight

【上报】shàng//bào 刊登在报纸上 be printed in a newspaper:老张的模范事迹上了报了。Lao Zhang's exemplary deeds have been reported in the newspapers.

【上报】shàngbào 向上级报告 submit a report, etc. to a higher authority:年终决算要及时填表～。The annual accounts should be filled in the forms and delivered in time.

【上辈】shàngbèi (～儿 shàngbèir) ❶ same as 祖先 zǔxiān ① ❷ 家族中的上一代 elder generation of one's family; one's elders

【上辈子】shàngbèi·zi ❶ same as 上辈 shàngbèi ①:我们～在清朝初年就从山西迁到这个地方了。Our ancestors moved from Shanxi to this place in the early year of the Qing Dynasty. ❷ 前世(迷信 superstition) previous existence

【上臂】shàngbì 胳膊上由肩至肘的部分 upper arm; (图见 ☞ figure for 身体 shēntǐ on p. 1701)

【上边】shàng·bian (～儿 shàng·bianr) same as 上面 shàng·mian

【上膘】shàng//biāo (牲畜)长肉 (of animals) become fat; fatten:精心饲养,耕畜就容易～。Farm animals get easily fattened up if fed properly.

【上宾】shàngbīn 尊贵的客人 distinguished guest; guest of honour:待为～ be treated as a distinguished guest

【上苍】shàngcāng 苍天 Heaven; God

【上操】shàng//cāo 指出操 go out to drill; be drilling

【上策】shàngcè 高明的计策或办法 best plan; best way out; best thing to do

【上层】shàngcéng 上面的一层或几层(多指机构、组织、阶层) upper levels; upper strata:～领导 higher-up authorities|～人物 people in the upper echelons; personages of the upper levels

【上层建筑】shàngcéng jiànzhù 指建立在经济基础上的政治、法律、宗教、艺术、哲学等的观点,以及适合这些观点的政治、法律等制度。经济基础决定上层建筑,上层建筑反映经济基础。superstructure; views on politics, law, religion, arts, philosophy, etc. built on the economic base, and the systems, including policies, laws, etc. suited to these views. The economic base determines the superstructure, while the superstructure reflects the economic base.

【上场】shàng//chǎng 演员或运动员出场 appear onstage; enter the court

【上场门】shàngchǎngmén 戏曲工作者指舞台右首(就观众说是左首)的出入口,角色大多从这儿上场 (in the theatre) entrance (of a stage); the entrance and exit on the right of the stage (on the left to the audience), through which most of the actors and actresses get on to the stage

【上朝】shàng//cháo ❶ 臣子到朝廷上拜见君主

奏事议事 (of courtiers) go to court ❷ 君主到朝廷上处理政事 (of a sovereign) hold court

【上乘】shàngchéng 本佛教用语,就是'大乘'。一般借指文学艺术的高妙境界或上品。也泛指事物质量好或水平高。(orig.) a Buddhist term referring to Mahayana (Great Vehicle); (of literary and art works) be of superior quality; first-class; (of things in general) be of good or high quality:～之作 superb work|质量～ top quality

【上蔟】shàng//cù 蚕发育至一定时期,停止吃东西,爬到蔟上吐丝做茧,叫做上蔟 (of silkworms) be placed on small straw bundles to spin cocoons; silkworms stop eating and climb on small straw bundles to spin cocoon when they grow to a certain stage

【上蹿下跳】shàng cuān xià tiào ❶ (动物 of animals)到处蹿蹦 run and jump all over:小松鼠～,寻找食物。The squirrels ran around looking for food. ❷〈比喻 *fig.*〉人到处活动 run around on sinister errands (贬义 derog.):～,煽风点火 run round to stir up trouble; run round to whip up hostility

【上代】shàngdài 家族或民族的较早的一代或几代叫上代 previous generation; former generations

【上党梆子】Shàngdǎng bāng•zi 山西地方戏曲剧种之一,流行于该省东南部(古上党郡)地区 *Shandang bangzi*; local opera popular in the ancient Shangdang Prefecture in present-day southeast Shanxi Province

【上当】shàng//dàng 受骗吃亏 be taken in; be fooled; be duped

【上等】shàngděng 等级高的;质量高的 vintage; first-class; first-rate; top-class; superior:～货 first-class goods; top-class goods|～衣料 high-quality material

【上等兵】shàngděngbīng 军衔,高于列兵 (military rank) private first class; enlisted man ranking just above a private

【上帝】Shàngdì ❶ 我国古代指天上主宰万物的神 Lord on High, an ancient Chinese mythological deity who watches over human society and regulates the working of the universe ❷〈基督教 *Christ.*〉所崇奉的神,认为是宇宙万物的创造者和主宰者 God, the creator and ruler of the universe

【上吊】shàng//diào 用绳子吊在高处套着脖子自杀 hang oneself; commit suicide by tying a rope about the neck and suddenly suspending the body so as to cause strangulation

【上调】shàngdiào ❶ 调到上面工作 transfer sb. to a post at a higher level:他已经从车间～到厂部了。He has been transferred from the workshop to the factory headquarters. ❷ 上级调用(财物等) transfer goods, funds, etc. to a unit at a higher level:这是～的木材。This is the timber to be transferred to a unit at a higher level.

☞ shàngtiáo on p.1685

【上冻】shàng//dòng 结冰;因冷凝结 freeze:今年冬天不冷,快到冬至了还没～。It's not cold this winter. The Winter Solstice is drawing near, but it's not yet frozen.|地上了冻了。The ground is frozen.

【上颚】shàng'è ❶ 某些节肢动物的第一对摄取食物的器官,生在口两旁的上方,上面长着许多短毛 mandible (of certain arthropods); pair of hairy, biting jaws of an insect or other arthropod, growing on the upper sides of the mouth ❷ 脊椎动物的上颌 upper jaw or maxilla of vertebrates

【上方宝剑】shàngfāng bǎojiàn 皇帝用的宝剑。戏曲和近代小说中常说持有皇帝赏赐的上方宝剑的大臣,有先斩后奏的权力。imperial sword, it is oft. described in Chinese operas and modern novels that a minister carrying an imperial sword granted by an emperor had the power to execute a criminal before reporting the case to the emperor; also 尚 for 上 shàng

【上房】shàngfáng same as 正房 zhèngfáng ①

【上访】shàngfǎng 人民群众到上级机关反映问题并要求解决 request an audience with a higher authority to air one's grievances and seek help in solving the problems; apply for an audience with the higher authorities to lodge a complaint and appeal for help

【上坟】shàng//fén 到坟前祭奠死者 visit a grave to honour the memory of the dead

【上风】shàngfēng ❶ 风刮来的那一方 windward:烟气从～刮过来。The smoke came from windward. ❷〈比喻 *fig.*〉作战或比赛的一方所处的有利地位 gain advantage; have an edge over; be in a superior position; get the upperhand:这场球赛,上半场甲队占～。Team A got the upperhand in the first half of the match.

【上峰】shàngfēng〈旧时 *old*〉指上级长官 superior; boss

【上岗】shàng//gǎng 到执行守卫、警戒等任务的岗位 take up a post as a guard:～指挥交通 be on point duty to direct the traffic flow ◇只有达到服务标准的营业员才能～工作。Only those who are ready to observe the rules and the prescribed standards of service for a shop assistant can take up posts behind the counters.

【上告】shànggào ❶ 向上级机关或司法部门告状 complain to the higher authorities; appeal to a higher court ❷ 向上级报告 report to one's superior

【上工】shàng//gōng ❶ (工人、农民等)每天开始工作 (of workers, peasants, etc.) go to work; start work ❷ 指雇工第一天到雇主家干活 (of a hired person) begin work at the

S

employer's house on the first day

【上供】shàng//gòng ❶ 指摆上祭祀物品 offer up a sacrifice; lay offerings on the altar ❷〈比喻 *fig*.〉向有权势的人送礼,以求得照顾 give presents to higher-ups expecting favours in return

【上钩】shàng//gōu 鱼吃了鱼饵被钩住 rise to the bait; swallow the bait; get hooked;〈比喻 *fig*.〉人被引诱上当 fall into a trap

【上古】shànggǔ 较早的古代,在我国历史分期上多指商周秦汉这个时期 remote antiquity; remote ages; period of the Shang, Zhou, Qin and Han dynasties (1600 B.C. to A.D. 220) in the Chinese history

【上官】Shàngguān 姓 a surname

【上轨道】shàng guǐdào〈比喻 *fig*.〉事情开始正常而有秩序地进行 get on the right track; begin to work smoothly; things become normal and get on smoothly

【上好】shànghǎo 顶好;最好 first-class; best-quality:~的茶叶 quality tea

【上颌】shànghé 口腔的上部 upper jaw; maxilla; also 上颚 shàng'è; ☞ 颌 gé on p.654

S

【上呼吸道】shànghūxīdào 呼吸道的上部,包括鼻腔、咽、喉和气管,上呼吸道内壁有黏膜 upper respiratory tract, including the nasal cavity, pharynx, larynx and windpipe, and having mucous membrane on the inner wall

【上火】shàng//huǒ ❶〈中医 *Chin. med*.〉把大便干燥或鼻腔黏膜、口腔黏膜、结合膜等发炎的症状叫上火 suffer from excessive internal heat (with such symptoms as constipation, conjunctivitis and inflammation of the nasal and oral cavities):他~了,眼睛红红的。He suffered from excessive internal heat, and that's why he's got red eyes. ❷〈方 *dial*.〉(~儿 shàng//huǒr)发怒 get angry

【上级】shàngjí 同一组织系统中等级较高的组织或人员 higher level; higher authorities; one's superior:~机关 higher authorities; a higher body|~组织 organization at the higher level|~领导深入下层。Leaders at higher levels go down to the grass-roots levels to see how things stand there.|完成~交给的任务 fulfil an assignment entrusted by one's superior

【上家】shàngjiā (~儿 shàngjiār)几个人打牌、掷色子、行酒令等的时候,如轮流的次序是甲乙丙丁…,乙是甲的下家、丙的上家,丙是乙的下家、丁的上家 (in mahjong, card games, etc.) player whose turn comes just before the others; in these games, when the players play by turns in the order of A,B,C,D,..., B is the player whose turn comes just before C and after A, and C is the player whose turn comes just before D and after B

【上江】Shàngjiāng ❶ 长江上游地区 upper Yangtze River reaches ❷ 清代安徽、江苏两省称上下江,上江指安徽,下江指江苏 In the Qing Dynasty, Anhui and Jiangsu provinces were called the upper and lower Yangtze River regions, the upper region being Anhui and the lower region being Jiangsu.

【上浆】shàng//jiāng 用淀粉等加水制成的黏性液体浸润纱、布、衣服等物,使增加光滑耐磨的性能 sizing of yarn, fabrics, clothes, etc. so as to make them more slippery and wear-proof

【上将】shàngjiàng 军衔,将官的一级,高于中将 general, ranking above lieutenant general; (U.S. & Brit. Army, U.S. Air Force, U.S. & Brit. Marine Corps) general; (U.S. & Brit. Navy) admiral; (Brit. Air Force) air chief marshal

【上焦】shàngjiāo〈中医 *Chin. med*.〉指胃的上口到舌头的下部,包括心、肺、食管等,主要功能是呼吸、血液循环等 part of the body cavity above the diaphragm and below the tongue, including the heart, lungs, gullet, its main functions being breathing and blood circulation

【上缴】shàngjiǎo 把收入的财物、利润和节余等缴给上级 turn over (revenues, profits, surplus materials, etc.) to the higher authorities:~利润 turn over part of the profits to the state

【上界】shàngjiè 迷信的人指天上神仙居住的地方 (superstition) the world above; the abode of the gods

【上紧】shàngjǐn〈方 *dial*.〉赶快;加紧 lose no time (in doing sth.); make haste; speed up:麦子都熟了,得~割啦! The wheat is ripe. Let's make haste and get ready for the harvest.

【上进】shàngjìn 向上;进步 go forward; make progress:~心 the desire to do better; the urge for improvement|发愤~ work hard to improve oneself|不求~ not strive to make progress

【上劲】shàng//jìn (~儿 shàng//jìnr)精神振奋,劲头儿大;来劲 with gusto; with great vigour:越干越~儿 work with increasing vigour (or gusto)

【上课】shàng//kè 教师讲课或学生听课 attend class; go to class:学校里八点开始~。Classes begin at eight

【上空】shàngkōng 指一定地点上面的天空 in the sky; overhead:接受检阅的机群在天安门~飞过。The planes flew past over Tian'anmen Square for the review.

【上口】shàngkǒu ❶ 指诵读诗文等纯熟时,能顺口而出 be able to read aloud fluently:琅琅~ be easy to read out; read fluently and smoothly ❷ 诗文写得流利,读起来顺口 be suitable for reading aloud; make smooth reading

【上口字】shàngkǒuzì 京剧中指按照传统念法念的字，某些字跟北京音略有区别，如'尖、千、先'念 ziān、ciān、siān 不念 jiān、qiān、xiān；'脸'念 jiǎn，不念 liǎn；'哥、可、何'念 guō、kuǒ、huó，不念 gē、kě、hé words in Peking Opera pronounced in the traditional manner and slightly different from the Beijing dialect, such as '尖、千、先' pronounced ziān, ciān and siān instead of jiān, qiān and xiān; '脸' pronounced jiǎn, instead of liǎn; '哥、可、何' pronounced guō, kuǒ, huó, instead of gē, kě and hé

【上款】shàngkuǎn（～儿 shàngkuǎnr）书画家为人写字绘画、一般人写信或送人礼品时，在这些东西上面所题的对方的名字、称呼等 name of the recipient (as inscribed on a painting or a calligraphic scroll presented as a gift); name of the addressee (of a letter or package)

【上来】shànglái ❶ 开始；起头 begin; get started：一～就有劲 be energetic right from the start | ～先少说话。Don't talk too much at the beginning. ❷〈书 *fml.*〉总括以上叙述 to sum up the aforesaid; to sum up what has been said in the foregoing：～所言 to sum up what has been said above

【上来】shàng//·lái 由低处到高处来 come up：他在楼下看书，半天没～。He has been reading a book and hasn't come upstairs for a long time.

【上来】//·shàng//·lái ❶ 用在动词后，表示由低处到高处或由远处到近处来［used after a verb to indicate coming from a lower place to a higher place or from a distant place to a nearer place］：部队从两路增援～。Reinforcements arrived by two routes. | 端上饭来。Serve the meal. ❷ 用在动词后，表示成功(指说、唱、背诵等)［used after a verb to indicate success in speaking, singing, reciting, etc.］：那首诗他念了两遍就背～了。He recited the poem after reading it twice. | 这个问题你一定答得～。You can surely answer this question. ❸〈方 *dial.*〉用在形容词后面，表示程度的增加［used after an adjective to indicate an increase in degree］：天色黑～了。It is getting dark. | 中秋节后，天气慢慢凉～。The weather is getting cooler little by little after the Mid-Autumn Festival.

【上联】shànglián（～儿 shàngliánr）对联的上一半 the first line of a couplet

【上脸】shàng//liǎn〈方 *dial.*〉受人抬举，自以为得意而更加放肆 get impudent when complimented：这孩子不懂事，才夸他两句就～了。The child is rather silly; a little praise turns his head.

【上梁不正下梁歪】shàngliáng bù zhèng xiàliáng wāi〈比喻 *fig.*〉上面的人行为不正，下面的人也就跟着学坏。If the upper beam is not straight, the lower ones will go aslant. *or* If those above behave improperly, those below will do the same.

【上列】shàngliè 上面所开列的 listed above; aforementioned; above：～各项工作都要抓紧抓好。All aspects of work listed above must be done well and in good time.

【上流】shàngliú ❶ 上游 upper reaches (of a river)：长江～ upper reaches of the Yangtze River ❷〈旧时 *old*〉指社会地位高的 upper-class：～社会 high society; polite society

【上路】shàng//lù ❶ 走上路程；动身 set out on a journey; start off：你几时～？When will you start off? ❷ 上轨道 get on the right track; begin to work properly：工作还没有～ has not set to work properly; has not got the knack of one's job

【上马】shàng//mǎ〈比喻 *fig.*〉开始某项较大的工作或工程 start (a big project, etc.)：这项工程即将～。The project will start soon.

【上门】shàng//mén ❶ 到别人家里去；登门 come or go to see sb.; call; drop in; visit：送货～ deliver goods to the doorstep ❷ 上门闩 shut the door (or lock up) for the night; bolt the door ❸ 指商店停止营业 close down; stop doing business temporarily ❹ 指入赘 marry into and live with one's bride's family：～女婿 live-in son-in-law

【上面】shàng·mian（～儿 shàng·mianr）❶ 位置较高的地方 above; over; on top of; on the surface of：小河～跨着一座石桥。A stone bridge sits astride a stream. ❷ 次序靠前的部分；文章或讲话中前于现在所叙述的部分 above-mentioned; aforesaid; foregoing; preceding：～列举了各种实例。In the foregoing we cited various examples. ❸ 物体的表面 surface of a thing：墙～贴着标语。Slogans were pasted on the wall. ❹ 方面 aspect; respect; regard：他在品种改良～下了很多功夫。He took great pains in improving the breeds. ❺ 指上级 higher authorities; higher-ups：～派了两名干部到我们这儿帮助工作。Two cadres have been sent from above to help us with the work. ❻ 指家族中上一辈 elder generation of one's family; the elders

【上年】shàngnián 去年 last year：～我们俩见过一面。We met once last year.

【上年纪】shàng nián·ji 年老 be getting on in years; be stricken in years：上了年纪了，腿脚不那么灵便了。Stricken in years, he isn't so surefooted as before.

【上皮组织】shàngpí zǔzhī 由许多密集的细胞和少量的细胞间质(黏合细胞的物质)构成的一种组织，覆盖在身体的表面、体腔的内壁、体内的管和囊的内壁以及某些器官的游离面上 epithelial tissue; cellar tissue consisting of one or more layers of cells with little intercellular material (a substance that binds cells) and covering external body surfaces, hollow organs or vessels, and the epitomes of certain organs

【上品】shàngpǐn 上等品级 highest grade; best of all:龙井是绿茶中的～。The Longjing is the best of all green teas.

【上坡路】shàngpōlù ❶ 由低处通向高处的道路 an uphill road; upward slope ❷〈比喻 *fig.*〉向好的或繁荣的方向发展的道路 road to a good trend; road to prosperity

【上去】shàng//·qù 由低处到高处去 mount; go up:登着梯子～ mount a ladder

【上去】//·shàng//·qù 用在动词后,表示由低处向高处,或由近处向远处,或由主体向对象[used after a verb to indicate a movement from a lower place to a higher place, from a nearer place to a distant place, or from subject to object]:顺着山坡爬～ climb up the slope|大家连忙迎～。We all rushed up to meet him.|把所有的力量都使～了 exert oneself to the utmost

【上人】shàngrén〈旧时 *old*〉对和尚的尊称 respectful form of address for a monk

【上人】shàng·ren〈方 *dial.*〉指父母或祖父母 parents or grandparents

S 【上人儿】shàng//rénr〈方 *dial.*〉饭馆、剧场等指陆续有顾客、观众来(of a restaurant, theatre, etc.) receive patrons; be patronized

【上任】shàng//rèn 指官吏就职 take a post as an official:走马～ take up an official post; assume office

【上任】shàngrèn 称前一任的官吏 predecessor

【上色】shàngsè(货品)上等;高级 best-quality; top-grade:～绿茶 top-grade green tea|～材料 best-quality materials

【上色】shàng//shǎi(在图画、工艺美术品等上面)加颜色 colour or pigment (a picture, map, work of art, etc.):地图的轮廓已经画好,还没～。The map has been outlined, but not yet coloured.

【上山】shàng//shān ❶ 到山上去;到山区去 go up a hill or mountain:～砍柴 gather firewood in the mountains|～下乡(of urban school-leavers) settle in the countryside and mountain areas ❷〈方 *dial.*〉〈婉辞 *euph.*〉指人死亡,埋入坟地 die and be buried ❸〈方 *dial.*〉指蚕上蔟(of silkworms) be placed on small straw bundles to spin cocoons:再过一两天,蚕就要～了。The silkworms will be placed on the small straw bundles to spin cocoon in a couple of days.

【上上】shàngshàng ❶ 最好 highest; very best:～策 the best plan ❷ 指比前一时期再往前的(一个时期) before last:～星期 the week before last|～月 the month before last

【上身】shàng//shēn 新衣初次穿在身上 start wearing (a new dress):这件新褂子刚～就撕了个口子。The new jacket was torn shortly after I started wearing it.

【上身】shàngshēn ❶ 身体的上半部 torso:他～只穿一件衬衫。He is wearing only a shirt. ❷(～儿 shàngshēnr)上衣 upper outer garment; shirt; blouse; jacket:她穿着白～,花裙子。She is wearing a white blouse and a floral skirt.

【上升】shàngshēng ❶ 由低处往高处移动 move upward:一缕炊烟袅袅～。A wisp of smoke is curling up from the kitchen chimney. ❷(等级、程度、数量)升高;增加 rise (to a higher point, degree, rank, etc.); ascend:气温～。The temperature is going up.|产量大幅度～。Production has risen by a big margin.

【上声】shàngshēng,又 shǎngshēng ❶ 古汉语四声的第二声 rising tone (the second of the four tones in classical Chinese pronunciation) ❷ 普通话字调的第三声 falling-rising tone (the third of the four tones in modern standard Chinese pronunciation) ‖ ☞ 四声 sìshēng on p. 1821

【上士】shàngshì 军衔,军士的最高一级(military rank) sergeant first class; (U.S. Army) sergeant first class; (Brit. Army) staff sergeant; (U.S. Navy) petty officer first class; (Brit. Navy) chief petty officer; (U.S. Air Force) technical sergeant; (Brit. Air Force) flight sergeant; (U.S. Marine Corps) technical sergeant or staff sergeant; (Brit. Marine Corps) colour sergeant

【上市】shàng//shì ❶(货物)开始在市场出售 go (or appear) on the market:六月里西红柿大量～。There are plenty of tomatoes on the market in June.|这是刚～的苹果。These apples have just come in. ❷ 到市场上 go to market:～买菜去。I'm going grocery-shopping.

【上世】shàngshì same as 上代 shàngdài

【上手】[1] shàngshǒu ❶ 位置较尊的一侧 left-hand seat; seat of honour; also 上首 shàngshǒu ❷ 上家 player whose turn comes just before sb. else

【上手】[2] shàngshǒu ❶〈方 *dial.*〉动手(of work, etc.) commence; get started:这事我一个人干就行了,你们就不用～了。I alone can do the job; you don't have to join in. ❷ 开始 start; begin:今天这场球一～就打得很顺利。The ball game went smoothly from the very start.

【上书】[1] shàng//shū〈旧时 *old*〉指私塾先生给儿童讲授新课(of an old-style private tutor) teach a new lesson to children

【上书】[2] shàng//shū 给地位高的人写信(多陈述政治见解 usu. expounding one's political views) submit a written statement to a higher authority; send in a memorial:～中央 submit a written statement to the central authorities

【上述】shàngshù 上面所说的（多用于文章段落或条文等结尾 usu. used at the end of a paragraph or an article) mentioned above; above-mentioned; aforementioned; aforesaid：～各条，望切实执行。You are expected to carry out to the letter the regulations mentioned above.

【上水】shàngshuǐ ❶ 上游 upper reaches of a river ❷ 向上游航行 sail upstream：～船 an upstream boat; a boat sailing upstream

【上水】shàng·shui〈方 *dial.*〉食用的牲畜的心、肝、肺 haslet; the heart, liver and lungs of an animal for food

【上水道】shàngshuǐdào 供给生活、消防或工业生产上用的清洁水的管道 water-supply line; pipeline that supplies clean water for household consumption, fire extinguishing, industrial production, etc.

【上司】shàng·si 上级 superior; boss：顶头～ one's immediate superior

【上诉】shàngsù 诉讼当事人不服第一审的判决或裁定，按照法律规定的程序向上一级法院请求改判 appeal (to a higher court); law suit appeal to a higher court for the change of a verdict in the prescribed legal procedure if he or she refuses to obey the verdict made in the first instance.

【上溯】shàngsù ❶ 逆着水流往上游走 go upstream ❷ 从现在往上推（过去的年代）trace back (to the past centuries); date back to

【上算】shàngsuàn 合算 paying; worthwhile：不～ not worthwhile; not pay | 烧煤气比烧煤～。It's more economical to use gas than coal.

【上岁数】shàng suì·shu（～儿 shàng suì·shur）上年纪 be getting on in age

【上台】shàng//tái ❶ 到舞台或讲台上去 take the podium; appear onstage：～表演 perform on a stage; go up on to the stage and perform | ～讲话 take the floor ❷〈比喻 *fig.*〉出任官职或掌权（多含贬义 oft. derog.) take an official post or assume power; come (or rise) to power

【上堂】shàng//táng ❶ 到公堂 go to court：～受审 go to the court and stand trial; be on trial ❷〈方 *dial.*〉上课 attend class; go to class

【上膛】shàng//táng 把枪弹推进枪膛里或把炮弹推进炮膛里准备发射 load a gun with bullets or load a cannon with shells and get ready to shoot：子弹上了膛。The gun is loaded.

【上膛】shàngtáng 腭的通称 general term for 腭 è

【上体】shàngtǐ〈书 *fml.*〉same as 上身 (shàngshēn) ①

【上天】shàng//tiān ❶ 上升到天空 go up to the sky; fly sky-high：人造卫星～。Another of our satellites has gone up. ❷ 迷信的人指到神佛仙人所在的地方（superstition) go to heaven; 也用做婉辞指人死亡（euph.) die; pass away

【上天】shàngtiān 迷信的人指主宰自然和人类的天 Heaven; Providence; God：～保佑。God bless me.

【上调】shàngtiáo（价格等）向上调整；提高（价格等）adjust (prices) upward; raise (prices) ☞ shàngdiào on p. 1681

【上头】shàng//tóu〈旧时 *old*〉女子未出嫁时梳辫子，临出嫁才把头发拢上去结成发髻，叫做上头 (of a girl on her wedding day) start wearing her hair in a bun; a woman usu. wore her hair in plaits before she was married off and started wearing her hair in a bun on her wedding day

【上头】shàng·tou 上面 above; over; upper

【上尉】shàngwèi 军衔，尉官的一级，高于中尉 (military rank) captain, ranking above first lieutenant; (U. S. & Brit. Army, U. S. Air Force, U. S. & Brit. Marine Corps) captain; (U. S. & Brit. Navy) lieutenant; (Brit. Air Force) flight lieutenant

【上文】shàngwén 书中或文章中某一段或某一句以前的部分 foregoing paragraphs or chapters; preceding part of a text

【上午】shàngwǔ 指半夜十二点到正午十二点的一段时间，一般也指清晨到正午十二点的一段时间 morning; period of time from 00:00 to 12:00 noon; usu. the period from daybreak to noon

【上下】[1] shàngxià ❶ 在职位、辈分上较高的人和较低的人 high and low; old and young：机关里～都很忙。All people in the organization, from the leadership to the staff, are very busy. | 孩子考上大学，全家上上下下都很高兴。All members of the family, old and young, are very happy to have the child admitted to a college. ❷ 从上到下 from top to bottom; up and down：摩天岭～有十五里。The Motian Mountain Ridge is 15 *li* long from top to bottom. | 我～打量着这位客人。I look the visitor up and down. ❸（程度）高低；好坏；优劣 relative superiority or inferiority：不相～ be neck and neck; equally matched | 难分～ hard to tell who is stronger (or better) ❹ 用在数量词后面，表示大致是这个数量［used after round numbers］around; about：这里一亩地能有一千斤～的收成。The land here can yield about 1,000 *jin* per *mu*.

【上下】[2] shàngxià 从高处到低处或从低处到高处 go up or down：山上修了公路，汽车～很方便。With the highway built on the mountain, automobiles can go up and down easily.

【上下其手】shàng xià qí shǒu〈比喻 *fig.*〉玩弄手法，暗中作弊 practise fraud; manoeuvre for some evil end; get up to tricks

【上下文】shàngxiàwén 指文章或说话中与某一

S

词语或文句相连的上文和下文 context; parts of a sentence, paragraph, discourse, etc. immediately next to or surrounding a specified word or passage and determining its exact meaning:这个词的含义联系～不难理解。It's not difficult to understand the implication of this word from the context.

【上弦】shàngxián 月相的一种,农历每月初七或初八,太阳跟地球的连线和地球跟月亮的连线成直角时,在地球上看到月亮呈 D 形 first quarter (of the moon); appearance of the moon on the 7th or 8th day of every lunar month when the line between the sun and the earth and the line between the earth and the moon form a right angle and the moon viewed from the earth is in the D shape:～月 moon at the first quarter

【上限】shàngxiàn 时间最早或数量最大的限度 upper limit; maximum permissible or prescribed (跟'下限'相对 as opposed to 'lower limit')

【上相】shàngxiàng 指某人在相片上的面貌比本人好看 look nice in a photograph; be photogenic

S 【上校】shàngxiào 〈军衔 *military rank*〉校官的一级,高于中校 colonel, ranking above lieutenant colonel; (U. S. & Brit. Army, U. S. Air Force, U. S. & Brit. Marine Corps) colonel; (U. S. & Brit. Navy) captain; (Brit. Air Force) group captain

【上鞋】shàng//xié 把鞋帮鞋底缝在一起 sew the upper and the sole together; sole a shoe; stitch a sole to an upper; also 绱鞋 shàngxié

【上心】shàngxīn 对要办的事情留心;用心 set one's heart on sth.:这孩子读书不～。The child does not set his mind on his studies.

【上行】shàngxíng ❶ 我国铁路部门规定,列车在干线上朝着首都的方向行驶,在支线上朝着连接干线的车站行驶,叫做上行。上行列车编号用偶数,如 12 次,104 次等。(of trains) going to the capital from any part of the country; up; upgoing: up trains are given even numbers, such as Train No. 12, Train No. 104, etc. ❷ 船从下游向上游行驶 (of boats) going upstream; upriver ❸ 公文由下级送往上级 (of documents) sent to the upper levels

【上行下效】shàng xíng xià xiào 上面或上辈的人怎样做,下面的人就学着怎样做(多指不好的事 oft. of sth. bad) if a leader or a senior sets a bad example, his subordinates or children will follow suit; subordinates follow the example of their superiors or seniors; those below follow the example of those above

【上学】shàng//xué ❶ 到学校学习 go to school; attend school; be at school:我每天早晨七点钟～。I go to school at seven every morning. ❷ 开始到小学学习 begin primary school:这孩子～了没有? Is the child at school?

【上旬】shàngxún 每月一日到十日的十天 first 10 days of a month

【上演】shàngyǎn (戏剧、舞蹈等)演出 (of plays, dances, etc.) stage; perform:这个月～了三台新戏。Three new plays were staged (or performed, presented) this month.

【上夜】shàngyè 〈旧时 *old*〉指值班守夜 be on duty at night; on night duty

【上衣】shàngyī 上身穿的衣服 upper outer garment; jacket

【上议院】shàngyìyuàn 某些国家两院制议会的组成部分。上议院有权否决下议院所通过的法案,议员由间接选举产生或由国家元首指定,任期比下议院议员长,有的终身任职,也有世袭的。上议院名称各国叫法不一,如英国叫贵族院,美国、日本叫参议院等。upper house; part of a two-chamber parliament in some countries; the upper house has the power to veto a bill passed by the lower house, its members are elected by indirect ballot or appointed by the head of state and have longer terms of office than those of the lower house, and the position of some members may even be lifetime or hereditary. The names of the upper house differ from country to country: it is called the House of Lords in Britain, and Senate in the United States and Japan.

【上瘾】shàng//yǐn 爱好某种事物而成为癖好 be addicted to sth.; get into the habit of doing sth.:喝茶喝上了瘾,一天不喝就难受。He has got into the habit of drinking tea, and feels uncomfortable if he has no tea for one day.

【上映】shàngyìng (电影)放映 show (a film); screen:近来常有新片～。New films were shown very often recently.

【上游】shàngyóu ❶ 河流接近发源地的部分 upper reaches (of a river) ❷〈比喻 *fig.*〉先进 advanced:力争～ aim high

【上元节】Shàngyuán Jié 元宵节 Lantern Festival (the 15th of the 1st lunar month)

【上涨】shàngzhǎng (水位、商品价格等)上升 (of water level, price) rise; go up:河水～。The river has risen. | 物价～。The prices are going up.

【上账】shàng//zhàng 登上账簿 make an entry in an account book; enter sth. in an account:刚收到的款子已经～了。The sum of money just received has been entered in the account.

【上照】shàngzhào 〈方 *dial.*〉上相 photogenic; come out well in a picture

【上阵】shàng//zhèn 上战场打仗 go into battle; 〈比喻 *fig.*〉参加比赛、劳动等 take part in a match or pitch into the work

【上肢】shàngzhī 人体的主要部分之一,包括上臂、前臂、腕和手 upper limbs; one of the main parts of the human body, including the upper arms, forearms, wrists and hands

【上中农】shàngzhōngnóng 经济地位比较富裕，占有较多生产资料，有轻微剥削的中农 upper-middle peasant; well-off middle peasant possessing more means of production and having slight degree of cxploitation of local peasants; also 富裕中农 fùyù zhōngnóng

【上装】shàng//zhuāng 演员化装 make up (for a theatrical performance)

【上装】shàngzhuāng〈方 *dial.*〉上衣 top; upper outer garment; jacket

【上座】shàngzuò 坐位分尊卑时，最尊的坐位叫上座 seat of honour when the seats are divided to show due respect to sb.

【上座儿】shàng//zuòr 指戏院、饭馆等处有顾客到来 (of restaurants) draw customers; (of theatres, etc.) draw an audience; presence of customers: 戏园子里～已到八成。The theatre is already 80 per cent full. *or* Eighty percent of the seats in the theatre have been sold.

尚[1] shàng ❶ 尊崇；注重 esteem; value; set great store by: 崇～ uphold; champion; advocate | ～武 encourage a war-like or martial spirit; warmongering ❷ 风尚 prevailing custom: 时～ fashion; vogue of the day ❸ (Shàng) 姓 a surname

尚[2] shàng〈书 *fml.*〉❶ 还(hái) still; yet: 为时～早。It is still too early. *or* The time is not yet ripe. | ～待研究 pending further discussion ❷ 尚且[used in the negative, followed by a negative with even greater force of denial] (not) even ..., let alone ...

【尚方宝剑】shàngfāng bǎojiàn ☞ 上方宝剑 shàngfāng bǎojiàn on p. 1681

【尚且】shàngqiě〈连词 *conj.*〉提出程度更甚的事例作为衬托，下文常用'何况'等呼应，表示进一层的意思 [used in the negative, followed by a clause beginning with 何况 hékuàng, a negative with even greater force of denial] (not) even ...; let alone ...: 为了人民的事业，流血～不惜，再别说流这点儿汗了！For the people's cause, even blood shedding is not to be spared, to say nothing of sweating.

【尚书】shàngshū〈古代 *arch.*〉官名。明清两代是政府各部的最高长官。title of a high official; chief steward for writing (in the Qin and Han dynasties); imperial secretary (from Han Dynasty to Northern and Southern Dynasties); minister (in Ming and Qing dynasties)

【尚武】shàngwǔ 注重军事或武术 encourage a military or martial spirit; warmongering: ～精神 military or martial spirit

绱(鞝) shàng 把鞋帮、鞋底缝在一起 sole a shoe; stitch the sole to the upper: ～鞋 sole a shoe; stitch the sole to the upper

【绱鞋】shàngxié same as 上鞋 shàng//xié

·shang (·尸尢)

裳 ·shang ☞ 衣裳 yī·shang on p. 2257
☞ cháng on p. 221

shāo (尸幺)

捎 shāo 顺便带 take along sth. to or for sb.; bring to sb.: ～封信 bring a letter to sb. | ～件衣服 bring a dress | ～个口信 take a message to sb.
☞ shào on p. 1691

【捎带】shāodài 顺便；附带 incidentally; in passing: 你上街时～把信发了。When you go shopping, please post my letter for me.

【捎带脚儿】shāodàijiǎor〈方 *dial.*〉顺便 incidentally; in passing: 你要的东西我～就买来了。By the way, I've brought the stuff you want.

【捎脚】shāo//jiǎo (～儿 shāo//jiǎor) 运输中顺便载客或捎带货物 pick up passengers or goods on the way; give sb. a lift: 回去是空车，捎个脚儿吧！Since you take no one in your car on the way back, please give me a lift.

烧(燒) shāo ❶ 使东西着火 burn; set fire to: 燃～ burn | ～毁 burn down; destroy ❷ 加热或接触某些化学药品、放射性物质等使物体起变化 cook; heat up or use certain chemicals, radioactive substances to cause changes in a substance: ～水 heat up water | ～饭 cook rice | ～砖 bake (or fire) bricks | ～炭 make charcoal | 盐酸把衣服～坏了。Hydrochloric acid destroyed the suit. ❸ 烹调方法，先用油炸，再加汤汁来炒或炖，或先煮熟再用油炸 cooking; stew after frying or fry after stewing: ～茄子 stewed eggplant | 红～鲤鱼 carp stewed in brown sauce | ～羊肉 stewed mutton ❹ 烹调方法，就是烤 cooking; roast: 叉～ grilled meat | ～鸡 roast chicken ❺ 发烧 run a fever; have a high temperature: 他现在～得厉害。He is running a high fever. ❻ 比正常体温高的体温 fever: ～退了。The fever is down. | 退～了。The fever is going down. ❼ 过多的肥料使植物体枯萎或死亡 damage or injure by excessive or improper use of fertilizer ❽ 因财富多而忘乎所以 be carried away by riches: 有两个钱就～得不知怎么好了！A fat purse has turned his head. *or* He is forgetting himself with a fat purse.

【烧包】shaobāo〈方 *dial.*〉由于变得富有或得势而忘乎所以 get swollen-headed with one's new riches; forget oneself with new riches

【烧杯】shāobēi 实验室中配制溶液或加热液体用的玻璃杯，杯口上有便于倒出液体的嘴 beaker (used in a laboratory); jarlike container of glass or metal with a lip for pouring, used by chemists, druggists, etc., for blending solutions or heating liquids

【烧饼】shāo·bing 烤熟的小的发面饼,表面多有芝麻 sesame seed cake

【烧锅】shāoguō 一种涂有釉质的钢制炊具 a glazed steel cooker

【烧锅】shāo·guo 做烧酒的作坊 (liquor) distillery

【烧化】shāohuà 烧掉(尸首、祭品等) cremate; burn (paper, etc. as an offering to the dead)

【烧荒】shāo//huāng 开垦前烧掉荒地上的野草 burn the grass on waste land

【烧毁】shāohuǐ 焚烧毁灭;烧坏 destroy by fire; burn up

【烧火】shāo//huǒ 使柴、煤等燃烧(多指炊事) make a fire; light a fire; tend the kitchen fire: ～做饭 make a fire for cooking

【烧结】shāojié 把小块矿石或粉末状物质加热,使固结 sintering; agglomeration; agglutination; bonded mass of metal ores or powdered particles shaped and partially fused by pressure and heating below the melting point

【烧酒】shāojiǔ same as 白酒 báijiǔ

【烧烤】shāokǎo 烧制或烤制的肉食品的统称 barbecue; a general term for the meats barbecued or grilled

【烧料】shāoliào 用含有硅酸盐的岩石粉末与纯碱混合,并加上颜料,加热熔化,冷却后凝成的物质。跟玻璃相似,但熔点较低,透明度也较小(有的不透明)。用来制造器皿或手工艺品。imitation frosted glass (used to make lamps and handicrafts); material made by mixing powdered rock containing silicates, soda ash and dyestuffs, heating the mixture to a melting point and cooling it for coagulation

【烧卖】shāo·mai 食品,用很薄的烫面皮包馅儿,顶上捏成折儿,然后蒸熟。俗误作烧麦。steamed dumpling with the dough gathered at the top; popularly mistaken for 烧麦 shāomài

【烧瓶】shāopíng 实验室中加热或蒸馏液体用的玻璃瓶,常见的有圆底烧瓶、锥形烧瓶、蒸馏烧瓶等 flask (used in a laboratory); glass bottle-like containers used in laboratories to heat or distill liquids, including round-base flask, conical flask, distillery flask, etc.

【烧伤】shāoshāng 火焰的高温以及强酸、强碱、X射线、原子能射线等跟身体接触后使组织受到的损伤 burn (an injury); injury from burning of tissues on the body after contacting the high temperature of fire, strong acid, strong base, X-ray, atomic ray, etc.

【烧香】shāo//xiāng ❶ 信仰佛教、道教或有迷信思想的人拜神佛时把香点着插在香炉中,叫烧香 burn joss sticks (before an idol); (of Buddhist devotees, Taoists or superstitious people) burn joss sticks in tripods when paying homage to a deity ❷〈比喻 *fig.*〉给人送礼,请求关照 give presents to people, seeking favours

【烧心】shāoxīn ❶ 胃部烧灼的感觉,多由胃酸过多刺激胃黏膜引起 upset stomach; have heartburn; feeling of burning in the stomach, mostly caused by the stimulation of the mucous membrane of the stomach by excessive acidity in the gastric juice ❷〈方 *dial.*〉(～儿 shāoxīnr)(包心的蔬菜)菜心因发生病害而发黄 (of cabbages) turn yellow at the heart due to plant diseases

【烧心壶】shāoxīnhú〈方 *dial.*〉茶炊 tea-urn; samovar; tea kettle

【烧夷弹】shāoyídàn 燃烧弹 incendiary bomb

【烧纸】shāo//zhǐ 迷信的人烧纸钱等,认为可供死者在阴间使用 burn paper money for the dead

【烧纸】shāo·zhǐ 纸钱的一种,在较大的纸片上刻出或印上钱形 paper money with printed coins, to be burned as an offering to the dead

【烧灼】shāozhuó 烧、烫,使受伤 burn; scorch; singe; get burned

梢 shāo (～儿 shāor) 条状物的较细的一头 tip; thin end of a twig, etc.: 树～ top of a tree | 眉～ tip of the brow | 辫～ end of a plait

☞ sào on p.1660

【梢公】shāogōng same as 艄公 shāogōng

【梢头】shāotóu 树枝的顶端 tip of a branch: 月上柳～。The moon rose to the top of the willow tree.

稍 shāo 稍微 a little; a bit; slightly; a trifle: 衣服～长了一点。The coat is a bit too long. | 你～等一等。Please wait a moment. *or* Just a moment, please.

☞ shào on p.1691

【稍稍】shāoshāo 稍微 a little: ～休息一下。Take a brief rest; take a breather.

【稍微】shāowēi〈副词 *adv.*〉表示数量不多或程度不深 a little; a bit; slightly; a trifle: ～放点糖就好吃了。Put in a little sugar, and it tastes better. | ～大意一点就要出毛病。A little carelessness leads to a mistake. | 今天～有点冷。It's rather chilly today.

【稍为】shāowéi same as 稍微 shāowēi

【稍许】shāoxǔ 稍微 a little; a bit; slightly; a trifle: 接到他的电话,心里～安定了些。After receiving his call, I became a bit calmer.

蛸 shāo ☞ 蟏蛸 xiāoshāo on p.2104

☞ xiāo on p.2104

筲 shāo 水桶,多用竹子或木头制成 pail (usu. made of bamboo strips or wood); bucket

【筲箕】shāojī 淘米洗菜等用的竹器,形状像簸箕 bamboo pan for washing rice, vegetables, etc.

艄 shāo ❶ 船尾 stern: 船～ stern ❷ 舵 rudder; helm: 掌～ be at the helm | 撑～ punting a boat with a long bamboo pole

【艄公】shāogōng 船尾掌舵的人。也泛指撑船的

人。helmsman; boatman; also 梢公 shāogōng

鞘 shāo 鞭鞘,拴在鞭子头上的细皮条等 whiplash; the thin leather strip tied at the tip of a whip

☞ qiào on p. 1553

sháo (ㄕㄠˊ)

勺(❶杓) sháo ❶(～儿 sháor)舀东西的用具,略作半球形,有柄 spoon; ladle:一把～儿 a ladle; a dipper|马～ ladle|铁～ iron spoon ❷ 容量单位。10 撮等于1勺,10勺等于1合(gě)。unit of capacity: 10 *cuo* (10 millilitres) equals one *shao* (one centilitre); 10 *shao* equals one *ge* (one decilitre)

☞ 杓 biāo on p. 125

【勺口儿】sháo·kour〈方 *dial.*〉指厨师烹调的滋味 taste of dishes prepared by a cook:请尝尝这位师傅的～怎么样。Please have a taste of the dishes prepared by this chef.

【勺状软骨】sháozhuàng ruǎngǔ 喉部上方的三角形小软骨,左右各一,位置在环状软骨的后上部。声带附着在勺状软骨前部的突起部分上。cartilage spatulata; triangular cartilages above the larynx, one on each side of the rear upper part of the cricoid, with the vocal chords attached on their front tips

【勺子】sháo·zi 较大的勺儿 ladle; scoop

芍 sháo [芍药](sháo·yao)❶ 多年生草本植物,羽状复叶,小叶卵形或披针形,花大而美丽,有紫红、粉红、白等颜色,供观赏。根可入药。Chinese herbaceous peony (*Paeonia lactiflora*); perennial plant having pinnately compound leaves that are either lanceolate or oval leaflets, large and splendid flowers that are purple, pink, white, etc. and of a high ornamental value, and roots that are used for medicine ❷ 这种植物的花 peony flower

苕 sháo〈方 *dial.*〉甘薯 sweet potato; also 红苕 hóngsháo

☞ tiáo on p. 1901

韶 sháo〈书 *fml.*〉美 splendid; beautiful:～光 beautiful springtime; glorious youth

【韶光】sháoguāng〈书 *fml.*〉❶ 美丽的春光 beautiful springtime ❷〈比喻 *fig.*〉美好的青年时代 glorious youth

【韶华】sháohuá〈书 *fml.*〉same as 韶光 sháoguāng

【韶秀】sháoxiù〈书 *fml.*〉清秀 delicate and pretty:仪容～ pretty looking

shǎo (ㄕㄠˇ)

少 shǎo ❶ 数量小(跟'多'相对 as opposed to 'many, much, more')few; little; less:～量 a little; small quantity; small amount; little bit; scanty|～见多怪。The less a man sees, the more he is surprised at whatever he sees. ❷ 不够原有或应有的数目;缺少 be short of; insufficient; not enough; lack; less than needed (跟'多'相对 as opposcd to 'more'):账算错了,～一块钱。This account is wrong; we are one yuan short.|全体同学都来了,一个没～。All schoolmates have come, and no one is absent. ❸ 丢;遗失 missing:屋里～了东西。Something is missing in the room. ❹ 亏欠 owe:～人家的钱都还清了。All the money we owed to others have been repaid. ❺ 暂时;稍微 a little while; a moment:～候 wait a moment; wait a minute|～待 wait a moment; ☞ shào on p. 1690

【少安毋躁】shǎo ān wú zào 耐心等待一下,不要急躁 stay calm, don't get excited; be patient and wait a while

【少不得】shǎo·bu dé 少不了 cannot do without; be indispensable with:得到别人的帮助,～登门致谢。Since we have received help from others, we should at least visit them to express our thanks.

【少不了】shǎo·bu liǎo 短不了 cannot do without; cannot dispense with:办这个事儿,一定～你。We can't do this without you.

【少见】shǎojiàn ❶〈客套话 *pol.*〉表示很少见到对方 see little of sb.:～了,您近来好吗? I've seen very little of you. How have you been lately? ❷ 难得见到;罕见 seldom seen; infrequent; rare:这种情景一般很～。This scene is usu. very rare.

【少见多怪】shǎo jiàn duō guài 由于见闻少,遇见平常的事情也感到奇怪 the less a man sees, the more he is surprised at sth. ordinary; the less a man has seen, the more he has to wonder at sth. common; ignorant people are easily taken by surprise

【少刻】shǎokè 少(shǎo)时 after a little while; a moment later

【少礼】shǎolǐ〈客套话 *pol.*〉❶ 请人不必拘于礼节 please don't stand on ceremony:贤侄～。Do make yourself at home, dear nephew. ❷ 称自己礼貌不周到 lack of manners:恕我～。Excuse me for my flippancy.

【少量】shǎoliàng 比较少的数量和分量 a small amount; a little; a few

【少陪】shǎopéi〈客套话 *pol.*〉对人表示因事不能相陪(when apologizing for taking leave) excuse me but I have to go; I'm afraid I must be leaving now

【少时】shǎoshí 过了不大一会儿;不多时 after a little while; a moment later; before long:～雨过天晴,院子里又热闹起来了。Soon the rain stopped, the sun came out, and the courtyard became busy again.

【少数】shǎoshù 较小的数量 a small number; few; minority:～服从多数。The minority is subordinate to the majority.

【少数民族】shǎoshù mínzú 多民族国家中人数最多的民族以外的民族,在我国指汉族以外的兄弟民族,如蒙古、回、藏、维吾尔、哈萨克、苗、彝、壮、布依、朝鲜、满等民族 ethnic minority; those other than the majority ethnic people in a multi-ethnic country; in China, referring to the fraternal ethnic peoples other than the Hans, such as the Mongol, Hui, Tibetan, Uygur, Kazak, Miao, Yi, Zhuang, Bouyei, Korean, and Manchu peoples

【少许】shǎoxǔ 一点儿;少量 a little; a few; a modicum

shào(ㄕㄠˋ)

少 shào ❶ 年纪轻(跟'老'相对 as opposed to 'old') young:~年 early youth; juvenile; teenagers|~女 young girl|男女老~ men and women, old and young|青春年~ in the prime of youth; in the prime of life ❷ 少爷 son of a rich family; young master:恶~ wicked young man from a wealthy or influential family; young ruffian|阔~ young man from a rich or wealthy family; son of a rich man ❸ (Shào)姓 a surname

☞ shǎo on p.1689

【少白头】shàobáitóu ❶ 年纪不大而头发已经变白 turn prematurely grey ❷ 指年纪不大而头发已经变白的人 young person with greying hair

【少不更事】shào bù gēng shì 指人年纪轻,经历的事不多,缺少经验 young and inexperienced; green

【少东家】shàodōng·jia 〈旧时 *old*〉称东家的儿子(form of address used by an employee to his employer's son or by a tenant-peasant to his landlord's son) young master

【少儿】shào'ér 少年儿童 children:~读物 children's books

【少妇】shàofù 年轻的已婚女子 young married woman

【少将】shàojiàng 军衔,将官的一级,低于中将(military rank) major general, ranking below the lieutenant general; (U.S. & Brit. Army, U.S. Air Force, U.S. & Brit. Marine Corps) major general; (U.S. & Brit. Navy) rear admiral; (Brit. Air Force) air vice marshal

【少林拳】shàolínquán 拳术的一派,因唐初嵩山少林寺僧徒练习这种拳术而得名 the Shaolin school of boxing, named after the Shaolin Monastery on Mount Songshan where the monks practised it in the early years of the Tang Dynasty

【少奶奶】shàonǎi·nai ❶ 〈旧时 *old*〉仆人称少爷的妻子(a form of address used by servants) young mistress ❷ 〈旧时 *old*〉〈尊称 *honor.*〉别人的儿媳妇 sb. else's daughter-in-law

【少男】shàonán 年轻未婚的男子 unmarried young man:~少女 young men and young women

【少年】shàonián ❶ 人十岁左右到十五六岁的阶段 early youth (10 to 16 in age):~时代 early youth ❷ 指上述年龄的人 boy or girl in early teens; juvenile:~宫 children's palace|~之家 children's centre; children's club ❸ 〈书 *fml.*〉指青年男子 young man:翩翩~ handsome young man; dashing young man; lively young man

【少年犯】shàoniánfàn 在我国指年满十四岁不满十八岁因犯罪情节严重而被依法判处徒刑的犯人 juvenile delinquent; Chinese term for delinquent above 14 and below 18 in age having committed serious crimes

【少年宫】shàoniángōng 在学校以外对少年儿童进行教育和开展集体文化活动的机构 children's palace; institution where children receive education or take part in cultural activities after school

【少年老成】shàonián lǎochéng 原指人虽年轻,却很老练,举动谨慎,现在多指年轻人缺乏朝气 old head on young shoulders; young but mature; old young man; young person lacking in vigour and drive

【少年先锋队】shàonián xiānfēngduì 我国和某些国家的少年儿童的群众性组织 Young Pioneers; children's mass organization in China and some other countries; 简称 abbr. 少先队 shàoxiānduì

【少女】shàonǚ 年轻未婚的女子 young girl

【少尉】shàowèi 军衔,尉官的一级,低于中尉(military rank) second lieutenant, ranking below the first lieutenant; (U.S. & Brit. Army, U.S. Air Force, U.S. & Brit. Marine Corps) second lieutenant; (U.S. Navy) ensign; (Brit. Navy) acting sub-lieutenant; (Brit. Air Force) pilot officer

【少先队】shàoxiānduì 少年先锋队的简称 abbr. for 少年先锋队 shàonián xiānfēngduì

【少相】shào·xiang 相貌显得年轻 young-looking:她长得~,岁数儿可不小了。She looks much younger than her age.

【少校】shàoxiào 军衔,校官的一级,低于中校(military rank) major, ranking below lieutenant colonel; (U.S. & Brit. Army, U.S. Air Force, U.S. & Brit. Marine Corps) major; (U.S. & Brit. Navy) lieutenant commander; (Brit. Air Force) squadron leader

【少爷】shào·ye ❶ 〈旧时 *old*〉仆人称主人的儿子(form of address used by servants of a house) young master ❷ 〈旧时 *old*〉〈尊称 *honor.*〉别人的儿子 your son; sb. else's son

【少壮】shàozhuàng 年轻力壮 young and vigorous:～派 mavericks; up-and-coming|～不努力,老大徒伤悲。He who does not exert oneself in youth will regret it in old age. *or* Laziness in youth spells regret in old age.

召 Shào ❶ 周朝国名,在今陕西凤翔一带 Shao, name of a state in the Zhou Dynasty, located in and around Fengxiang in Shaanxi Province of today ❷ (Shào) 姓 a surname

☞ zhào on p. 2424

卲 shào same as 劭 shào ②

邵 Shào 姓 a surname

劭 shào 〈书 *fml.*〉 ❶ 劝勉 encourage; urge; exhort: 先帝～农 the late emperor encouraged farming ❷ 美好(多指道德品质 oft. referring to moral character) excellent; admirable: 年高德～ old and admirable

绍[1] shào 〈书 *fml.*〉继续;继承 carry on; continue

绍[2] Shào 指浙江绍兴 Shaoxing in Zhejiang Province: ～酒 Shaoxing rice wine

【绍介】shàojiè 介绍 introduce

【绍剧】shàojù 浙江地方戏曲剧种之一,原名绍兴乱弹,通称绍兴大班,流行于绍兴一带 Shaoxing Opera; a local opera popular in Shaoxing and around, Zhejiang Province, originally known as *Shaoxing Luantan*, generally called *Shaoxing Daban*

【绍兴酒】shàoxīngjiǔ 浙江绍兴出产的黄酒 Shaoxing rice wine; a rice wine produced in the Shaoxing area in Zhejiang Province; also 绍酒 shàojiǔ

捎 shào 稍微向后倒退(多指骡马等 of a mule, horse, etc.) draw back a few steps

☞ shāo on p. 1687

【捎马子】shàomǎ·zi 〈方 *dial.*〉马褡子 saddlebag

【捎色】shào//shǎi 退色 fade (in colour)

哨[1] shào ❶ 侦察;巡逻 reconnaissance; patrol: ～探 patrolman ❷ 为警戒、侦察等任务而设的岗位 sentry post; post: ～卡 frontier sentry post or strategic sentry post|岗～ sentry post|观察～ observation post|放～ stand on sentry duty ❸ 〈量词 *classifier*〉支;队(用于军队 of army troops) detachment; contingent: 一～人马 a detachment of troops

哨[2] shào ❶ (鸟)叫 (of birds) warble; chirp ❷ 〈方 *dial.*〉说话;闲谈(含贬义 derog.) idle talk; gossip: 神聊海～ shoot the bull (or breeze); talk and chat idly ❸ (～儿 shàor)哨子 whistle: 吹～儿 blow a whistle

【哨兵】shàobīng 执行警戒任务的士兵的统称 (general term for) sentry; guard

【哨卡】shàoqiǎ 设在边境或要道的哨所 frontier sentry post; strategic sentry post

【哨所】shàosuǒ 警戒分队或哨兵所在的处所 sentry post; post: 边防～ frontier guard post

【哨位】shàowèi 哨兵执行任务的岗位 sentry post; post

【哨子】shào·zi 用金属或塑料等制成的能吹响的器物,多在集合人员、操练或体育运动时使用 whistle; instrument made of metal or plastic for making whistling sounds to summon people, or in drills and sports competitions

睄 shào 〈方 *dial.*〉略看一眼 throw a glance at; cast a glance at

稍 shào [稍息](shàoxī)军事或体操口令,命令从立正姿势变为休息姿势 Stand at east!; At ease!; military command or an exercise command to change the posture of attention to the posture of at ease

☞ shāo on p. 1688

潲[1] shào ❶ 雨斜着落下来(of rain) slant in: 快关窗户,别让雨点～进来。Close the window quickly. Don't let the raindrops slant in. ❷ 〈方 *dial.*〉洒水 sprinkle: 打桶水～～院子。Fetch a bucket of water to sprinkle the yard.|往菜上～水 spray the vegetables with water

潲[2] shào 〈方 *dial.*〉用泔水、米糠、野菜等煮成的饲料 swill; slops: 猪～ hogwash; swill (or slops) for swine

【潲水】shàoshuǐ 〈方 *dial.*〉泔水 swill; slops; hogwash

shē (ㄕㄜ)

畲 Shē same as 畬 Shē

奢 shē ❶ 奢侈 luxurious; extravagant: 穷～极欲 indulge in wanton luxury and extravagance ❷ 过分的 excessive; inordinate; extravagant: ～望 extravagant hopes; wild wishes; wishful thinking

【奢侈】shēchǐ 花费大量钱财追求过分享受 luxurious; extravagant; wasteful; spend a lot of money on luxurious life: ～品 luxury goods; luxuries|生活～ live in luxury; live it up

【奢华】shēhuá 花费大量钱财摆门面 luxurious; sumptuous; extravagant: 陈设～ be luxuriously furnished

【奢靡】shēmí 奢侈浪费 extravagant and dissipated; also 奢糜 shēmí

【奢念】shēniàn 过高的想法;奢望 unrealistic hopes; wild wishes

【奢求】shēqiú 过高的要求 extravagant claims; excessive demands; unreasonable demands: 我只想有一个安静的工作环境,别无～。I have no unreasonable demands, but a quiet working environment.

【奢望】shēwàng 过高的希望 extravagant hopes; wild wishes: 心存～ harbour wild wishes

【奢想】shēxiǎng same as 奢望 shēwàng

赊 shē 赊欠 buy or sell on credit：～购 buy on credit|～销 sell on credit|前账未清，不能再～。No more credit before the old accounts are cleared up.

【赊购】shēgòu 用赊欠的方式购买 buy on credit

【赊欠】shēqiàn 买卖货物时买方延期交款，卖方延期收款 buy or sell on credit

【赊销】shēxiāo 用赊欠的方式销售 sell on credit

【赊账】shē//zhàng 把买卖的货款记在账上延期收付；赊欠 credit system; system of buying or selling on credit：现金买卖，概不～。Cash only and no credit. *or* Cash and carry.

猞 shē [猞猁]（shēlì）哺乳动物，外形像猫，但大得多。尾巴短，两耳的尖端有两撮长毛，两颊的毛也长。全身淡黄色，有灰褐色的斑点，尾端黑色。善于爬树，行动敏捷，性凶猛，皮毛厚而软。lynx (*Felis lynx*); mammal which looks like a cat, but is much bigger, having a short tail with a black end, two tufts of long hair at the tips of the ears, long hair on the cheeks, greyish-brown spots on the yellowish body; good at climbing trees, agile and ferocious, and known for its thick, soft, and valuable fur; also 林狸 línyì

S

畲 Shē 指畲族 She, a minority ethnic group

【畲族】Shēzú 我国少数民族之一，主要分布在福建、浙江、江西、广东、安徽 She people, an ethnic minority distributed over Fujian, Zhejiang, Jiangxi, Guangdong and Anhui provinces

畬 shē 〈书 *fml.*〉焚烧田地里的草木，用草木灰做肥料的耕作方法。这样耕种的田地叫畬田。slash-and-burn cultivation; method of farming, by burning the vegetation to clear the fields and using the ash as manure; the fields so cultivated are called 畬田 shētián

☞ yú on p. 2340

shé（ㄕㄜˊ）

舌 shé ❶ 舌头 tongue ❷ 像舌头的东西 sth. shaped like a tongue：帽～ peak of a cap|火～ tongues of flame ❸ 铃或铎中的锤 tongue of a bell; clapper

【舌敝唇焦】shé bì chún jiāo 形容话说得太多，费尽唇舌 keep talking till one's tongue and lips are parched; wear oneself out in pleading, expostulating, etc.

【舌根音】shégēnyīn 语音学上指舌面后部上升，靠着或接近软腭（或硬腭和软腭中间）发出的辅音，如普通话语音中的 g、k、h velar (e.g. g, k, h); sounds articulated with the back of the tongue touching or near the soft palate, such as g, k, and h in standard Chinese pronunciation; also 舌面后音 shémiànhòuyīn

【舌耕】shégēng 〈书 *fml.*〉指依靠教书谋生 make a living by teaching

【舌尖音】shéjiānyīn 语音学上指舌尖顶住或接近门齿、上齿龈、硬腭前部发出的辅音。普通话语音中的 z、c、s、d、t、n、l、zh、ch、sh、r 都是舌尖音。细分起来，z、c、s 是舌尖前音，d、t、n、l 是舌尖中音，zh、ch、sh、r 是舌尖后音。apical sounds; sounds articulated with the apex, or tip, of the tongue touching the front teeth, the upper gum, or the hard palate, such as z, c, s, d, t, n, l, zh, ch, sh, and r in standard Chinese pronunciation. To be specific, z, c, and s are the front apical sounds; d, t, n, and l are middle apical sounds; and zh, ch, sh, and r are rear apical sounds

【舌剑唇枪】shé jiàn chún qiāng ☞ 唇枪舌剑 chún qiāng shé jiàn on p. 313

【舌面后音】shémiànhòuyīn 舌根音 velar sounds

【舌面前音】shémiànqiányīn 语音学上指舌面前部上升，靠着或接近齿龈、前硬腭发出的辅音，如普通话语音中的 j、q、x dorsal (e.g. j, q, x); sounds articulated with the front of the tongue rising and touching or near the gum and the front hard palate, such as j, q, and x in standard Chinese pronunciation

【舌苔】shétāi 舌头表面上滑腻的物质。健康的人，舌苔薄白而润。医生常根据病人舌苔的情况来诊断病情。coating on the tongue; fur; fur-like or fuzzy coating; diseased matter on the tongue in illness. The fur of a healthy person is thin, white and smooth. A doctor often diagnoses a patient's conditions by observing the coating on his tongue.

【舌头】shé·tou ❶ 辨别滋味、帮助咀嚼和发音的器官，在口腔底部，根部固定在口腔底上 tongue; organ attached to the floor of the mouth, used in the ingestion of food, the perception of taste, and, in humans, the articulation of speech sounds ❷ 指为侦讯敌情而活捉来的敌人 enemy soldier captured for the purpose of extracting information：抓～ capture an enemy soldier for espionage purposes

【舌下神经】shéxià-shénjīng 第十二对脑神经，从延髓发出，分布在舌的肌肉中，管舌肌的运动 hypoglossal nerve; 12th pair of cranial nerves which connect the medulla oblongata with the muscles of the tongue

【舌下腺】shéxiàxiàn 口腔底部舌下方的唾液腺，左右各一 sublingual gland; saliva glands under the tongue at the floor of the mouth, one on each side; ☞ 唾液腺 tuòyèxiàn on p. 1962

【舌咽神经】shéyān-shénjīng 第九对脑神经，从延髓发出，分布在咽头和舌头等处，主要管咽头肌肉运动、唾腺分泌和味觉 glossopharyngeal nerve; 9th pair of cranial nerves which connect the medulla oblongata with the tongue and the larynx and control the muscular movement of the larynx, the secretion of the sublingual glands and sense of taste

【舌战】shézhàn 激烈辩论 have a verbal battle

with; argue heatedly with; hot dispute; verbal battle:一场～ heated dispute; battle royal |诸葛亮～群儒。Zhuge Liang had a verbal battle with a group of scholars.

折 shé ❶ 断(多用于长条形的东西 used of long articles) break; snap:树枝～了。A branch snapped.|桌子腿撞～了。A table leg was bumped and broken. ❷ 亏损 lose money in business:～本儿 lose money in one's business|～耗 damage; loss ❸(Shé)姓 a surname

☞ zhē on p.2427 and zhé on p.2428

【折本】shé//běn (～儿 shé//běnr)赔本 lose money in business:～生意 losing business; bad bargain|做买卖折了本儿。He lost money in his business.

【折秤】shé//chèng 货物重新过秤时因为已经损耗而分量减少,或货物大宗称进,零星称出而分量减少 damage and loss to goods (such as vegetables, fruits, etc.) in the course of re-weighing, or when goods are weighed in a large quantity and weighed out in small quantities

【折耗】shéhào 物品或商品在制造、运输、保管等过程中数量上的损失 damage and loss (to goods during manufacture, transportation, storage, etc.):用鲜菜腌成咸菜,～很大。There is a lot of weight loss when fresh vegetables are pickled.

佘 Shé 姓 a surname

蛇(虵) shé 爬行动物,身体圆而细长,有鳞,没有四肢。种类很多,有的有毒,有的无毒。吃青蛙等小动物,大蛇也能吞食大的兽类。snake (*Ophidia*); serpent; limbless reptiles with an elongated, round, scaly body, lidless eyes, and a tapering tail, feeding on small animals such as frogs. Big snakes also devour big beasts; and some species have a poisonous bite.

☞ yí on p.2262

【蛇胆】shédǎn〈中医 *Chin. med.*〉指蝮蛇的胆,有杀虫等作用 gall bladder of snake; gall bladder of pit viper, useful for killing insects or worms

【蛇毒】shédú 毒蛇体内所含的有毒物质。提炼后可入药。snake venom, a poisonous substance in the body of a poisonous snake, extracted and purified to be used as a Chinese medicine

【蛇蜕】shétuì〈中医 *Chin. med.*〉指蛇蜕下来的皮,用来治惊风、抽搐、癫痫等 snake slough; exuviation; skin cast off by a snake, to be used to treat infantile convulsion, twitch, epilepsy, etc.

【蛇蝎】shéxiē 蛇和蝎子 snakes and scorpions;〈比喻 *fig.*〉狠毒的人 sinister vicious people

【蛇行】shéxíng ❶ 全身伏在地上,爬着前进 move with the body on the ground; crawl ❷ 形容像蛇爬行时蜿蜒曲折的样子 move like a snake; meander:小溪～,绕林而过。The brook winds its way around the woods.

【蛇足】shézú〈比喻 *fig.*〉多余无用的事物 feet added to a snake by an ignorant artist; sth. superfluous; ☞ 画蛇添足 huà shé tiān zú on p.839

阇 shé [阇梨](shélí) 高僧,泛指僧 eminent monk; Buddhist monk; [阿阇梨之省,梵 Sanskrit: ācārya; abbr. for 'acarya']

☞ dū on p.476

揲 shé〈古代 *arch.*〉用蓍草占卦时,数蓍草的数目,把它分成几份儿 count the number of alpine yarrow plants and divide them into shares for the performance of divination

☞ dié on p.451

shě (ㄕㄜˇ)

舍(捨) shě ❶ 舍弃 give up; abandon:四～五入 round off; to the nearest whole number|～近求远 seek far and wide for what lies close at hand ❷ 施舍 give alms; dispense charity:～粥 dispense porridge|～药 dispense medicine

☞ shè on p.1696

【舍本逐末】shě běn zhú mò 舍弃事物的根本的、主要的部分,而去追求细枝末节。形容轻重倒置。attend to trifles and neglect essentials; put the trivial before the important

【舍不得】shě·bu·de 很爱惜,不忍放弃或离开,不愿意使用或处置 hate to use or part with; grudge; begrudge:妈妈～孩子出远门。The mother is reluctant to leave her child far away from home.|他从来～乱花一分钱。He has always hated to waste a single cent.

【舍得】shě·de 愿意割舍;不吝惜 be willing to part with; not grudge:你～把这本书送给他吗? Are you willing to give this book to him? |他学起技术来,真～下工夫。He has never begrudged time to learn skills.

【舍己为公】shě jǐ wèi gōng 为了公共的利益而牺牲个人的利益 sacrifice oneself for the public interest

【舍己为人】shě jǐ wèi rén 为了他人而牺牲自己的利益 sacrifice one's own interests for the sake of sb. else

【舍近求远】shě jìn qiú yuǎn 舍弃近的寻找远的。形容做事走弯路或追求不切实际的东西。seek from afar what lies close at hand; forgo what is close at hand and seek what is far afield; take a wrong road in doing sth. or seek sth. impractical; also 舍近图远 shě jìn tú yuǎn

【舍脸】shě//liǎn〈方 *dial.*〉不顾面子向人求助(多指出于不得已 oft. be obliged to) cast aside considerations of one's face

【舍命】shě//mìng 不顾性命；拼命 risk one's life; sacrifice oneself：～抢救国家财产 save state property at the risk of one's life

【舍弃】shěqì 丢开；抛弃；放弃 give up; abandon：～不顾 give up sth. regardless of oneself

【舍身】shěshēn 原指佛教徒牺牲肉体表示虔诚，后来泛指为祖国或为他人而牺牲自己 give one's life; sacrifice oneself; originally referring to a Buddhist who sacrifices his flesh to show piety, later to those who sacrifice themselves for their country or for sb. else：～为国 sacrifice oneself for one's motherland

【舍生取义】shě shēng qǔ yì 为正义而牺牲生命 lay down one's life for a just cause

【舍死忘生】shě sǐ wàng shēng 形容不顾性命危险 disregard one's own safety; risk one's life; also 舍生忘死 shě shēng wàng sǐ

shè（ㄕㄜˋ）

厍 shè ❶〈方 *dial.*〉村庄（多用于村庄名）*she*; village, used in the name of a place to indicate a village ❷（Shè）姓 a surname

设 shè ❶ 设立；布置 set up; establish; found：～防 set up defences; fortify; garrison｜～宴 give a dinner (or banquet); host a dinner｜总部～在北京。The headquarters were established in Beijing. ❷ 筹划 work out：～计 work out; design; plot｜想方～法 try by every means; do everything possible; try by hook or by crook ❸ 假设 given; suppose; if：～想 assume; imagine｜～$x=1$ given: $x=1$｜～长方形的宽是 x 米。Suppose the width of a rectangle is x metres. ❹〈书 *fml.*〉假如；倘若 if; in case：～有困难，当助一臂之力。You can count on me to help in case of difficulty.

【设备】shèbèi ❶ 设置以备应用 equip; provide equipment：新建的工人俱乐部～得很不错。The newly-built Workers' Club is well equipped. ❷ 进行某项工作或供应某种需要所必需的成套建筑或器物 equipment; installation; facilities：厂房～ premises and equipment; plant or workshop installations｜机器～ machines and other equipment｜自来水～ water plant equipment

【设法】shèfǎ 想办法 think of a way; try; do what one can：～解决 try to solve; try to find a solution｜～克服困难 try to overcome the difficulties

【设防】shèfáng 设置防卫力量 set up defences; fortify; garrison：步步～ set up defences at every step

【设伏】shèfú 布置伏兵 lay an ambush：～擒敌 lay an ambush to take enemy soldiers

【设或】shèhuò〈书 *fml.*〉假如 if; suppose

【设计】shèjì 在正式做某项工作之前，根据一定的目的要求，预先制定方法、图样等 design; plan; work out methods and drawings in line with the purpose and demands before a certain project is started：～师 designer｜～图纸 design blueprints; design drawings

【设立】shèlì 成立；建立（组织、机构等）establish; set up; found：～监察小组 set up a supervision group｜新住宅区～了学校、医院和商店。A school, a hospital and shops have been set up in the new residential area.

【设若】shèruò〈书 *fml.*〉假如 if; suppose; provided

【设色】shèsè（绘画）涂色；着色 fill in colours on a sketch; lay paint on (canvas); colour：这幅画布局新颖，～柔和。This painting is original in composition and quiet in colour

【设身处地】shè shēn chǔ dì 设想自己处在别人的地位或境遇中 put oneself in sb. else's shoes

【设施】shèshī 为进行某项工作或满足某种需要而建立起来的机构、系统、组织、建筑等 installation; facilities; setup, system, organization, buildings established for a certain aspect of work or to meet certain needs：生活～ service facilities｜服务～相当齐全。A complete array of service facilities are available.

【设使】shèshǐ 假如；如果 if; suppose; in case

【设想】shèxiǎng ❶ 想像；假想 imagine; envisage; conceive; assume：不堪～ unimaginable; too dreadful to contemplate｜他提出了关于技术改造的大胆～。He has come up with a bold tentative plan on technical transformation. ❷ 着想 have consideration for：应该处处替国家～。We should have consideration for the state in every respect.

【设置】shèzhì ❶ 设立 set up; establish：这座剧院是为儿童～的。This theatre has been set up for the children. ❷ 安放；安装 put up; install：～障碍 lay obstacles

社 shè ❶ 某些集体组织 organized body; agency; society：诗～ poetry society｜报～ press; newspaper office or organization｜通讯～ news agency｜合作～ cooperative｜集会结～ (the right of) assembly and association ❷ 某些服务性单位 certain services：茶～ teahouse｜旅～ inn; hotel｜旅行～ travel service ❸〈古代 *arch.*〉把土神和祭土神的地方、日子和祭礼都叫社 god of the land; day, altar, and ritual for offering sacrifices to the god of the land：春～ spring sacrifice｜秋～ autumn sacrifice｜～日 sacrifice day｜～稷 god of the land; god of the grain; state; country; the land

【社会】shèhuì ❶ 指由一定的经济基础和上层建筑构成的整体。也叫社会形态。原始共产主义社会、奴隶社会、封建社会、资本主义社会、共产主义社会是人类社会的五种基本形态。society; community; combination of the economic base and the superstructure; social formation; the primitive communist society, the slave society, the feudal society, the capitalist society and the communist society being the five basic formations of society. ❷ 泛指由于共同物质条件而互相联系起来的人群 group of people regarded as forming a single community on the basis of common material conditions; also 社会形态 shèhuì xíngtài

【社会必要劳动】shèhuì bìyào láodòng 指在现有社会正常的生产条件下，在社会平均劳动熟练程度和强度下，生产某种产品所需要的劳动。用劳动时间来衡量。socially necessary labour; labour necessary for the production of a certain product under normal social production conditions and with the average skill and intensity of social labour, measured by work time

【社会存在】shèhuì cúnzài 指社会物质生活条件的总和，主要指物质资料的生产方式。社会存在决定社会意识，社会意识又反作用于社会存在。social being; total of social material and living conditions, mainly referring to the mode of production of materials. Social being decides social consciousness while social consciousness reacts on social being.

【社会工作】shèhuì gōngzuò 本职工作之外没有报酬的为群众服务的工作 off-the-job work done without pay for the community; community work

【社会关系】shèhuì guān·xì ❶ 指个人的亲戚朋友关系 human relations in society; social relations; personal relations of one's relatives and friends ❷ 人们在共同活动的过程中彼此间结成的关系。一切社会关系中最主要的是生产关系，即经济关系，其他政治、法律等关系的性质都决定于生产关系。The relations formed among people in the course of common activities. The most primary of social relations are those of production, that is to say, all other relations, including the economic relations, political relations, legal relations, etc. are decided by the relations of production.

【社会活动】shèhuì huó·dòng 本职工作以外的集体活动，如党团活动、工会活动等 social activities; public activities; collective activities outside one's job, such as those of the Party, the Youth League and the trade unions

【社会教育】shèhuì jiàoyù 指学校以外的文化教育机关(如图书馆、博物馆、文化宫、展览会、俱乐部、少年宫等)对人民群众和少年儿童所进行的教育 social education; adult and child education conducted by cultural and educational institutions other than schools, such as libraries, museums, cultural palaces, exhibitions, clubs, and children's palaces

【社会科学】shèhuì kēxué 研究各种社会现象的科学，包括政治经济学、法律学、历史学、文艺学、美学、伦理学等 social sciences; sciences dealing with all kinds of social phenomena, including political economics, law, history, study of art and literature, aesthetics, and ethics

【社会青年】shèhuì qīngnián 指既不上学也未就业的青年 unemployed youth after leaving school

【社会形态】shèhuì xíngtài ☞ 社会 shèhuì①

【社会学】shèhuìxué 研究社会生活、社会制度、社会行为、社会变迁和发展及其他社会问题的学科 sociology; branch of study dealing with social life, social system, social conduct, social changes and development, and other social issues

【社会意识】shèhuì yìshí 指政治、法律、道德、艺术、哲学、宗教等观点 social consciousness; views on politics, law, ethics, art, philosophy, religion, etc.; ☞ 社会存在 shèhuì cúnzài

【社会制度】shèhuì zhìdù 社会的经济、政治等制度的总称 social system; general term for the economic, political and other systems of a society

【社会主义】shèhuì zhǔyì ❶ 指科学社会主义 socialism; scientific socialism ❷ 指社会主义制度，是共产主义的初级阶段。在社会主义社会里，无产阶级掌握了国家政权，所有制的形式主要有全民所有制和劳动群众集体所有制，分配原则是'各尽所能，按劳分配'。社会主义的本质，是解放生产力，发展生产力，消灭剥削，消除两极分化，最终达到共同富裕。socialist system, the primary stage of communism. In the socialist society, the proletariat has taken the political power, the forms of ownership are mainly the ownership of the whole people and the collective ownership of the working people, and the principle of distribution is 'from each according to his ability, to each according to his work'. The essence of socialism is to emancipate and develop the productive forces, exterminate exploitation, put an end to polarization and finally achieve common prosperity.

【社会主义革命】shèhuì zhǔyì gémìng 由无产阶级及其先锋队共产党领导的，以推翻资本主义制度，建立社会主义制度和实现共产主义为目的的革命 socialist revolution; revolution led by the proletariat and its vanguard the Communist Party, and aimed at overthrowing the capitalist system, establishing the socialist system and achieving communism

【社会主义所有制】shèhuì zhǔyì suǒyǒuzhì 生产资料和劳动产品归社会公有的制度，是社会主义生产关系的基础。我国目前主要有两种形式，即全民所有制和劳动群众集体所有制。socialist ownership, the system under which the means of production and the products of labour are publicly owned, and which is the foundation for the socialist relations of production. There are mainly two forms of socialist ownership in China at present, namely, the ownership of the whole people and the collective ownership of the working people.

【社火】shèhuǒ 民间在节日的集体游艺活动，如狮舞、龙灯等 traditional merry-making festivities in villages, including lion dance, dragon lantern dance, etc.：玩～ hold traditional merry-making activities

【社稷】shèjì '社'指土神，'稷'指谷神，古代君主都祭社稷，后来就用'社稷'代表国家 god of land and god of grains. It was a custom in ancient times for the monarch to offer sacrifices to the god of land and the god of grains. Their names combined have later come to refer to 'nation'.

【社交】shèjiāo 指社会上人与人的交际往来 social intercourse; social contact; social life：～活动 social activities｜～场合 social occasions

【社论】shèlùn 报社或杂志社在自己的报纸或刊物上，以本社名义发表的评论当前重大问题的文章 editorial; article giving the opinions of a newspaper or magazine on a major topical issue

S

【社评】shèpíng same as 社论 shèlùn

【社区】shèqū 社会上以某种特征划分的居住区 community; residential area with certain special characteristics：旧金山华人～ Chinese community in San Francisco

【社团】shètuán 各种群众性的组织的总称，如工会、妇女联合会、学生会等 mass organizations, such as trade union, women's federation, students' union, etc.

【社戏】shèxì 〈旧时 *old*〉农村中迎神赛会时演出的戏。一般在庙里戏台上演出，也有露天搭台演出的。village theatrical performance given on religious festivals, usu. held onstage in a temple, but also on a platform put up temporarily for the occasion

【社员】shèyuán 某些以社命名的组织的成员 member of a society, club, etc.

舍[1] shè ❶ 房屋 house; hut：宿～ dormitory｜校～ school buildings ❷ 舍间 my place：敝～ my place｜寒～ my humble place ❸ 养家畜的圈 shed：猪～ pigsty｜牛～ cow shed ❹〈谦辞 *hum.*〉用于对别人称自己的辈分低或年纪小的亲属 [referring to one's relatives younger than or junior to oneself] my：～侄 my nephew｜～弟 my younger brother ❺（Shè）姓 a surname

舍[2] shè 古代三十里为一舍 an ancient unit of distance equal to 30 *li*（里）：退避三～ retreat 90 *li*; keep a good distance from sb.

☞ shě on p. 1693

【舍间】shèjiān 〈谦称 *hum.*〉自己的家 my humble abode; my house; my place：请来～一叙。Would you please come to my humble house for a chat? also 舍下 shèxià

【舍利】shèlì 〈佛教 *Budd.*〉称释迦牟尼遗体焚烧之后结成珠状的东西，后来也指德行较高的和尚死后烧剩的骨头 sarira; relic; sth. like beads formed after the cremation of the body of Sakyamuni, founder of Buddhism; also the bones left after eminent monks died; also 舍利子 shèlìzǐ; [梵 Sanskrit：śarīra]

【舍亲】shèqīn 〈谦称 *hum.*〉自己的亲戚 my relative; a relative of mine

【舍下】shèxià 舍间 my humble abode; my house; my place

拾 shè 〈书 *fml.*〉轻步而上 walk up with light steps

☞ shí on p. 1744

【拾级】shèjí 〈书 *fml.*〉逐步登阶 climb the steps one by one：我们～而上，登上了顶峰。We climbed the hill step by step until we got to the top.

射 shè ❶ 用推力或弹力送出（箭、子弹、足球等）shoot (arrow, bullet, football, etc.)：发～ shoot; fire｜扫～ strafe; sweep｜～箭 shoot an arrow｜～出三发炮弹 fire three shells｜右锋乘机～入一球。The right forward took an opportunity to shoot and netted. ❷ 液体受到压力通过小孔迅速挤出 discharge liquid in a jet through small holes by means of pressure：喷～ jet; spout; spurt｜注～ inject｜管子坏了，～了他一身的水。The pipe was broken and shot water all over him. ❸ 放出（光、热、电波等）emit; send out (light, heat, etc.)：反～ reflect｜辐～ radiate｜～线 ray｜光芒四～ radiate brilliant light in all directions｜月光从树梢的空隙里～到地上。The moon shed its light over the ground through the trees. ❹ 有所指 allude to sth.：暗～ hint at; insinuate｜影～ insinuate

【射程】shèchéng 弹头等射出后所能达到的距离 range (of fire); distance covered by the bullet or warhead after it is shot

【射电望远镜】shèdiàn wàngyuǎnjìng 利用定向天线和灵敏度很高的微波接收装置来接收星体发出的无线电波以观测天体的设备。这种望远镜比光学望远镜的观测距离远得多，并且使用上不受时间和气候变化的影响。radio telescope; device using a directional antenna and a highly sensitive microwave receiver to receive radio waves from a celestial body for observational purposes. A radio telescope observes much farther than the optical telescope and its use is not affected by the time and weather conditions.

【射电源】shèdiànyuán 宇宙空间中发射较强烈无线电波的天体，如脉冲星、类星体等 radio source; any celestial source of radio-frequency radiation, such as pulsar, quasar, etc.

【射击】shèjī ❶ 用枪炮等火器向目标发射弹头

shoot; fire; use a gun or cannon to shoot bullets, shells or warheads at targets ❷〈体育 *sports*〉比赛的一种，按照比赛时所用枪支、射击距离、射击目标和射击姿势，分为不同项目 sharp shooting, a competition sport featuring a number of events differentiated on the basis of the guns used, shorting distances, targets and shooting positions

【射箭】shè//jiàn ❶ 用弓把箭射出去 shoot an arrow ❷ 体育运动项目之一，在一定的距离外用箭射靶 archery, a competition sport; shoot arrows at a target from a given distance

【射界】shèjiè 指火器射击时所能达到的范围 area (or field) of fire; firing range

【射猎】shèliè 打猎 hunting with bow and arrow or firearms

【射流】shèliú 喷射成束状的液体。如空气从气管中喷出，水从水枪中喷出等都能形成射流 efflux, such as air from an air pump, and water from a nozzle; liquid ejected in a beam

【射门】shè//mén 足球、手球等比赛时把球直接踢向或投向对方的球门 shoot (at the goal) in football, handball, etc.

【射频】shèpín 无线电波的频率，频率范围从 3—3000 千兆赫。这个频率范围内的电波，可以用天线辐射出去。radio frequency, ranging from 3000 to 3,000,000 MHz; radio waves within this range can be emitted through an antenna.

【射手】shèshǒu ❶ 指射箭或放枪炮的人（多指熟练的）sharp shooter; marksman; archer: 机枪～ machine gunner ❷ 指足球等比赛中射门技术熟练的运动员 goal scorer in football, etc.

【射线】shèxiàn ❶ 波长较短的电磁波，包括红外线、可见光、紫外线、X 射线、丙种射线等。速度高、能量大的粒子流也叫射线，如甲种射线、乙种射线和阴极射线等。ray; electromagnetic wave with a shorter wavelength, including infrared, visible light, ultraviolet ray, X-ray, gamma ray, etc.; The particle beam with high velocity and energy stimulation is also called ray, such as alpha ray, beta ray, cathode ray, etc. ❷ 数学上指从一个定点出发，沿着单一方向运动的点的轨迹；直线上某一点一旁的部分 (math.) line that extends from a given point along a given direction; path of a moving point along a given direction; part of a straight line next to a given point

【射影】shèyǐng ❶ 从一点向一条直线或一个平面作垂线，垂足叫做这点在这条直线或平面上的射影；一条线段的各点在一条直线或一个平面上射影的连线叫做这条线段在这条直线或平面上的射影 projection; when a perpendicular line is drawn from a point to a straight line or a plane, the intersection is the projection of the point on the straight line or the plane; when all the points on a section of a line are projected on a straight line or a plane, the line connecting all the projected points is called the projection of that section of a line on the straight line or the plane ❷ 古书上说水中有一种叫'蜮'的动物能含沙喷射人影使人致病 water demon; animal described in ancient books as being able to project a human figure by injecting sand from its mouth to cause diseases to humans; same as 蜮 yù; ☞ 含沙射影 hán shā shè yǐng on p. 762

涉 shè ❶ 徒步过水，泛指从水上经过；渡 wade; ford: 跋山～水 climb mountains and cross rivers | 远～重洋 travel across the seas ❷ 经历 go through; experience: ～险 go through perils ❸ 牵涉 involve: ～及 involve; relate to; touch upon; deal with | ～嫌 be suspected of being involved in a crime

【涉笔】shèbǐ 用笔写作；动笔 wet the brush; start writing or painting: ～成趣 (of a writer or painter) produce a good work as soon as the brush is set to paper

【涉及】shèjí 牵涉到；关联到 involve; relate to; touch upon: 案子～到好几个人。The case involves quite a few people. | 这个问题～面很广。This issue is related to a wide range of aspects.

【涉猎】shèliè 粗略地阅读 do desultory reading; read cursorily: 有的书必须精读，有的只要稍加～即可。Some books are for intensive study and some are for cursory reading.

【涉禽】shèqín 鸟的一类，属于这一类的鸟，颈、嘴、脚和趾都长，适于在浅水中涉行并捕食水中鱼虾等，如鹤、鹭等 wading bird; wader; a species of birds such as crane, egret, etc., with a long neck, a long bill, long feet and long toes, which wade in the shallow water and feed on fishes and shrimps

【涉世】shèshì 经历世事 gain life experience: ～未深 have scanty experience of life; have seen little of the world

【涉讼】shèsòng 牵涉到诉讼之中 be involved in a lawsuit

【涉外】shèwài 涉及与外国有关的 concerning foreign affairs or foreign nationals: ～工作 work involving foreign countries or nationals | ～问题 issue related to foreign countries or foreign nationals

【涉嫌】shèxián 有跟某件事情有关的嫌疑 be suspected of being involved in sth.; be a suspect: ～人犯 suspects in a crime

【涉足】shèzú〈书 *fml.*〉指进入某种环境或生活范围 set foot in: ～其间 set foot there | 后山较为荒僻，游人很少～。The backside of the hill is quite desolate. Few visitors set their feet there.

赦 shè 赦免 remit (a punishment); pardon: 大～ general pardon | 特～ special pardon | 十恶不～ guilty of unpardonable evil; unpardonably wicked

【赦免】shèmiǎn 依法定程序减轻或免除对罪犯的刑罚 remit (a punishment); pardon; ☞ 大赦 dàshè on p. 362 and 特赦 tèshè on p. 1876

摄[1]（攝）shè ❶ 吸取 absorb; assimilate: ～取 absorb; assimilate; take in | ～食 feed ❷ 摄影 take a photograph of; shoot: ～制 film; produce

摄[2]（攝）shè 〈书 *fml.*〉保养 conserve (one's health): ～生 conserve one's health; keep fit | ～护（调护）take good care of

摄[3]（攝）shè 代理 act for: ～政 act as regent

【摄理】shèlǐ 代理 hold office in an acting capacity: ～国政 act as a regent; regency

【摄取】shèqǔ ❶ 吸收（营养等）absorb; assimilate; take in: ～食物 take in food | ～氧气 inhale oxygen ❷ 拍摄（照片或电影、电视镜头）take a photograph of; shoot: ～几个镜头 take a few snapshots

【摄生】shèshēng 〈书 *fml.*〉保养身体 conserve one's health; keep fit: ～养性 keep fit and cultivate one's nature | ～之道 way to longevity

【摄食】shèshí 摄取食物（多指动物 of animals）feed

【摄氏度】Shèshìdù 摄氏温标的单位 Celsius; centigrade; ☞ 摄氏温标 Shèshì wēnbiāo

【摄氏温标】Shèshì wēnbiāo 温标的一种，规定在一个标准大气压下，纯水的冰点为 0 度，沸点为 100 度，0 度和 100 度之间均匀分成 100 份，每份表示 1 度。这种温标是瑞典天文学家摄尔修斯（Anders Celsius）制定的。Celsius or centigrade temperature scale; temperature scale invented by the Swedish astronomer Anders Celsius, under which the freezing point is zero degree for one standard atmospheric pressure, and the boiling point is 100 degrees, the space between them being divided evenly into 100 parts each indicating one degree

【摄氏温度】Shèshì wēndù 摄氏温标的标度，用符号'℃'表示 Celsius; centigrade, indicated by the symbol ℃

【摄卫】shèwèi 〈书 *fml.*〉保养身体 conserve one's health; keep fit

【摄像】shèxiàng 用摄像机拍摄实物影像 make a video recording (with a video camera or TV camera): ～师 video cameraman

【摄像机】shèxiàngjī 电视技术中用来摄取景物的装置。它可将图像分解并变成电信号，用来拍摄文体节目、集会及个人娱乐活动、婚礼等的实况。有黑白、彩色和立体摄像机几种。video camera or television camera; device to shoot sights and scene in television, which is capable of converting the images into electrical signals to film theatrical programmes, meetings, personal entertainment activities, weddings, etc. There are black-and-white camera, colour camera and three-dimensional camera.

【摄行】shèxíng 〈书 *fml.*〉代行职务 act in sb. else's capacity: ～政事 handle government affairs in an acting capacity

【摄影】shèyǐng ❶ 通过胶片的感光作用，用照相机拍下实物影像 photography; take a picture; also 照相 zhào // xiàng ❷ 拍电影 shoot a film; cinematography

【摄影机】shèyǐngjī ❶ 照相机 camera ❷ 电影摄影机的简称 motion-picture camera; cinecamera; cinematograph

【摄政】shèzhèng 代君主处理政务 act as regent

【摄制】shèzhì 拍摄并制作（电影片、电视片等）shoot and produce (movie films, TV plays, etc.)

滠（灄）shè 滠口（Shèkǒu），地名，在湖北 Shekou, name of a place in Hubei Province

慑（懾、慴）shè 〈书 *fml.*〉害怕；使害怕 fear; be awed: ～服 submit in fear; succumb; cow somebody into submission | 威～ deter

【慑服】shèfú ❶ 因恐惧而顺从 submit in fear; succumb ❷ 使恐惧而屈服 cow sb. into submission

歙 Shè 歙县，在安徽 Shexian County in Anhui Province
☞ xī on p. 2050

麝 shè ❶ 哺乳动物，形状像鹿而小，无角，前腿短，后腿长，善于跳跃，尾巴短，毛黑褐色或灰褐色。雄麝的犬齿很发达，肚脐和生殖器之间有腺囊，能分泌麝香。musk deer (*Moschus moschiferus*); mammal which looks like a deer but is smaller, hornless, having short forelegs, long hind legs, a short tail and blackish brown or greyish brown hair, good at jumping, the male having well-developed canine teeth and a sac (musk bag) between the navel and the reproductive organ that secretes musk; 通称 generally known as 香獐子 xiāng zhāng·zi ❷ 麝香的简称 abbr. for 麝香 shèxiāng

【麝香】shèxiāng 雄麝的肚脐和生殖器之间的腺囊的分泌物，干燥后呈颗粒状或块状，有特殊的香气，有苦味，可以制香料，也可入药 musk; substance with a strong, penetrating odour, obtained from a small sac (musk bag) under the skin of the abdomen between the navel and reproductive organ in the male musk deer, turned into particles or lumps after being dried, used as the basis of numerous perfumes and Chinese medicine; 简称 abbr. 麝 shè

shéi(ㄕㄟˊ)

谁 shéi 又 shuí 疑问代词[also pronounced shuí, interrogative pronoun] ❶ 问人 who:你找～? Whom are you looking for? |今天～值日? Who is on duty today? 注意 **NOTE**: '谁'可以指一个人或几个人,方言中有用'谁们'表示复数的'谁' may be one person or more than one person; in dialects, '谁们' is used in a plural sense ❷ 用在反问句里,表示没有一个人 used in rhetorical questions to indicate no one:～不说他好。Who wouldn't speak well of him? 注意 **NOTE**: 反问句中用'谁知道'有时候是'不料'的意思 in rhe-torical questions, '谁知道' sometimes means 'unexpectedly; to one's surprise':我本是跟他开玩笑,～知道他真急了。I had wanted to crack a joke, but he was really annoyed. ❸ 虚指,表示不知道的什么人或无须说出姓名和说不出姓名的人 used in a supposition to indicate someone; sb.:我的书不知道被～拿走了。Someone must have taken away my book. |今天没有～来过。No one has ever come here. ❹ 任指,表示任何人 anyone; anybody a)用在'也'或'都'前面,表示所说的范围之内没有例外[used before '也' or '都' to indicate no exception within a given scope]:这件事～也不知道。No one knows about this matter. |大家比着干,～都不肯落后。Everyone is working hard. No one wants to lag behind. b)主语和宾语都用'谁',指不同的人,表示彼此一样[used in both the subject and object to indicate two different people]:他们俩～也说不服～。Neither of them could convince the other. c)两个'谁'字前后照应,指相同的人[used to refer to the same person]:大家看～合适,就选～当代表。Whoever is deemed fit by everybody is elected a deputy.

【谁边】shéibiān 何处;哪里 where:知向～? Where are they gone?

【谁个】shéigè 〈方 *dial.*〉哪一个人;谁 who:～不服他。Everybody is convinced of him. |此事～不知,～不晓。This matter is known to all.

【谁人】shéirén 谁;什么人 who:这是～造的谣? Who started this rumour? |～不知,他是植棉的能手。Everybody knows that he is a good cotton grower.

【谁谁】shéishéi 叠用的疑问代词,用来表示无须说出的某些人的名字[dual interrogative pronoun to indicate people whose name or names need not be mentioned]:乡亲们传说着～立了大功,～当了英雄。Everyone was talking about who had rendered meritorious service and who had won the title of hero.

shēn(ㄕㄣ)

申[1] shēn 说明;申述 state; express; explain:～言 voice; declare|～说 state; explain|三令五～ repeated injunctions; issue orders one after another|重～前令 reiterate the previous orders

申[2] shēn 地支的第九位 9th of the 12 Earthly Branches; ☞ 干支 gānzhī on p.627

申[3] Shēn ❶ 上海的别称 Shen, another name for 上海 shànghǎi ❷ 姓 a surname

【申办】shēnbàn 申请办理或举办 bid for hosting sth.:～下届运动会 bid for the next sports meet

【申报】shēnbào 用书面向上级或有关部门报告 report to a higher authority or a department concerned:向税务部门如实～营业额 declare the business turnover as it is to the tax authorities

【申辩】shēnbiàn (对受人指责的事)申述理由,加以辩解 defend oneself; explain oneself; argue (or plead) one's case:允许受批评的人～ allow the criticized to defend himself

【申斥】shēnchì 斥责 rebuke (多用于对下属 usu. one's subordinates); reprimand:严厉～了他一顿 reprimand him severely

【申饬】shēnchì ❶〈书 *fml.*〉告诫 warn; admonish; also 申敕 shēnchì ❷ same as 申斥 shēnchì

【申敕】shēnchì same as 申饬 shēnchì ①

【申令】shēnlìng 下令;命令 issue an order:～全国 issue an order to all over the country

【申明】shēnmíng 郑重说明 declare; state; avow:～理由 give one's reason for doing sth.

【申请】shēnqǐng 向上级或有关部门说明理由,提出请求 apply for sth. by giving one's reasons to authorities or a department concerned; file an application:～书 application|～助学金 apply for a grant

【申时】shēnshí 旧式计时法指下午三点钟到五点钟的时间 old-fashioned method of timing the period of the day from 3 p.m. to 5 p.m.

【申述】shēnshù 详细说明 state; explain in detail:～理由 state one's reason|～来意 explain the purpose of one's visit

【申说】shēnshuō 说明(理由) state (reasons):反复～ state one's reason repeatedly

【申诉】shēnsù ❶ 国家机关工作人员和政党、团体成员等对所受处分不服时,向原机关或上级机关提出自己的意见 appeal; (of a government functionary or a member of a political party or organization) apply for a reconsideration of the disciplinary measure made against him ❷ 诉讼当事人或其他公民对已发

生效力的判决或裁定不服时，依法向法院提出重新处理的要求 appeal; a litigant or any other citizen refuses to obey the valid court decision or ruling, and requests the court to reconsider the decision

【申讨】shēntǎo 声讨 openly condemn; denounce

【申屠】Shēntú 姓 two-character surname

【申谢】shēnxiè 表示谢意 acknowledge one's indebtedness; express one's gratitude

【申雪】shēnxuě 表白或洗雪冤屈 appeal for redress of a wrong; redress a wrong; also 伸雪 shēnxuě

【申冤】shēn//yuān ❶ 洗雪冤屈 redress an injustice; right a wrong: ～吐气 have an injustice redressed and feel elated | 为民～ redress an injustice for the people; also 伸冤 shēn//yuān ❷ 自己申诉所受的冤屈，希望得到洗雪 appeal for the redress of a wrong

屾 shēn 〈书 *fml.*〉两山并立 twin peaks; two mountains standing side by side

伸 shēn （肢体或物体的一部分）展开（of the body or limbs, of part of sth.）stretch; extend: ～直 straighten | ～展 extend | 延～ extend; stretch

S

【伸懒腰】shēn lǎnyāo 人疲乏时伸展腰和上肢 stretch oneself; stretch one's limbs

【伸手】shēn//shǒu ❶ 伸出手 stretch (or hold) out one's hand; 〈比喻 *fig.*〉向别人或组织要（东西、荣誉等）beg for sth. or honour: 有困难我们自己解决，不向国家～。If there is any difficulty, we'll overcome it by ourselves. We'll not ask the government for help. ❷ 指插手（含贬义 derog.）have a hand in; meddle in; poke one's nose into

【伸缩】shēnsuō ❶ 引长和缩短；伸出和缩进 retract; draw and be drawn back: 有的照相机的镜头能够前后～。The lenses of some cameras are retractable. ❷〈比喻 *fig.*〉在数量或规模上作有限的或局部的变动 flexible; elastic; adjustable: ～性 elasticity or flexibility | 没有～的余地 leave no latitude; leave no room for manoeuvring

【伸腿】shēn//tuǐ ❶ 钻入；插足；占一份好处（含厌恶意 with a sense of disgust）step in to gain an advantage ❷（～儿 shēn//tuǐr）指人死亡（含诙谐意 humor.）kick the bucket; turn up one's toes

【伸雪】shēnxuě same as 申雪 shēnxuě

【伸延】shēnyán 延伸 extend; stretch: 公路一直～到山脚下。The road extends to the foot of the mountain.

【伸腰】shēn//yāo 挺直身体 straighten one's back; straighten oneself up; 〈比喻 *fig.*〉不再受人欺侮 not to be bullied

【伸冤】shēn//yuān same as 申冤 ① shēn//yuān

【伸展】shēnzhǎn 向一定方向延长或扩展 spread; extend; stretch: 金色的麦田一直～到远远的天边。The golden wheat fields stretch all the way to the horizon.

【伸张】shēnzhāng 扩大（多指抽象事物 oft. referring to sth. abstract）uphold; promote: ～正义 uphold justice

身 shēn ❶ 身体 body: ～上 on one's body | 转过～去 turn round; face about | ～高五尺 five *chi* tall | 翻了一个～ turn over one's body ❷ 指生命 life: 奋不顾～ regardless of one's personal safety ❸ 自己；本身 oneself; personally: 以～作则 set a good example with one's own conduct | ～先士卒 charge at the head of one's men | ～临其境 be personally the scene | ～为领导，当然应该走在群众的前面。As a leader, you ought to set an example for the masses. ❹ 人的品格和修养 one's moral character and conduct: 修～ cultivate one's moral character | 立～处世 conduct oneself in society ❺ 物体的中部或主要部分 main part of a structure; body: 车～ body of a vehicle | 河～ river bed | 船～ hull of a ship | 机～ fuselage ❻（～儿 shēnr）〈量词 *classifier*〉用于衣服（for clothes）suit: 换了～衣裳 change a suit | 做两～儿制服 make two suits of clothes

【身败名裂】shēn bài míng liè 地位丧失，名誉扫地 bring shame and ruin upon oneself; be utterly discredited

【身板】shēnbǎn （～儿 shēnbǎnr）身体；体格 body; bodily health: 他七十多了，～儿还挺结实。At the age of over 70, he still has a strong physique.

【身边】shēnbiān ❶ 身体的近旁 at (or by) one's side: 年老多病的人～需要有人照料。Old and sick people should have people by their side to take care of them. ❷ 指身上 (have sth.) on one; with one: 我～没有带钱，你给我先垫一下。I have no money on me. Please pay it for me.

【身材】shēncái 身体的高矮和胖瘦 stature; figure: ～高大 of a tall and big build | ～苗条 have a slender (or slim) figure

【身长】shēncháng ❶ 人体的高度 height (of a person) ❷ 衣服从肩到下摆的长度 length (of a garment from shoulder to hemline)

【身段】shēnduàn ❶ 女性的身材或身体的姿态 (woman's) figure: ～优美 graceful figure ❷ 戏曲演员在舞台上表演的各种舞蹈化的动作 (dancer's) posture

【身分】shēn·fen same as 身份 shēn·fen

【身份】shēn·fen ❶ 指自身所处的地位 status; capacity; identity: 他是什么～？What's his capacity? | 她以主人的～发出邀请。She has issued invitations in her capacity as the host. | 他以受害人家属的～要求法庭严惩被告。He demanded in the capacity as a family member of the victim that the court severely punish the accused. ❷ 指受人尊重的地位 honourable position; dignity: 有失～ be beneath one's dignity | 他是位有～的人。He is a man of dignity. ❸〈方 *dial.*〉(～儿 shēn·fenr) 物品的质量 quality of sth.: 这布～不坏。The quality of this cloth is not bad. ‖ also 身分 shēn·fen

【身高】shēngāo 人体的高度 height (of a person)

【身后】shēnhòu 指死后 after one's death

【身家】shēnjiā ❶ 本人和家庭 oneself and one's family: ～性命 one's personal safety and that of one's family ❷〈旧时 *old*〉指家庭出身 family background: ～清白 comes from a respectable family

【身价】shēnjià ❶〈旧时 *old*〉人身买卖的价格 buying and selling prices of a person ❷ 指一个人的社会地位 social status: ～百倍 steep rise in one's social status

【身教】shēnjiào 用自己的行动做榜样 teach others by one's own example: 言传～ teach by personal example and verbal instruction | ～重于言教 example is better than precept

【身历】shēnlì 亲身经历 experience personally: ～其境 personally go through (or experience) a situation

【身历声】shēnlìshēng〈方 *dial.*〉立体声 stereo

【身量】shēn·liang (～儿 shēn·liangr) 人的身材; 个子 height (of a person); stature: ～不高 not tall

【身躯】shēnqū 身体; 身材 body; stature: 健壮的～ a sound body | ～高大 tall of stature

【身上】shēn·shang ❶ 身体上 on one's body: ～穿一件灰色制服 wear a grey uniform | 你～不舒服, 早点去休息吧。You are not feeling well. Take a rest earlier. ◇希望寄托在青年人～。Our hopes are placed on the young people. ❷ 随身(携带) (have sth.) on one; with one: ～没带笔。Haven't got a pen with me.

【身世】shēnshì 指人生的经历、遭遇(多指不幸的 oft. unfortunate) life experience: ～凄凉 have had a sad life

【身手】shēnshǒu 本领 skill; talent: 好～ good skill | 大显～ give full play to one's skill, talent, etc.

【身受】shēnshòu 身亲受到 experience personally: 感同～ feel as if one experiences sth. personally | ～其害 personally experience the baneful influence (or evil effects) of sth.

【身体】shēntǐ 一个人或一个动物的生理组织的整体, 有时专指躯干和四肢 body; whole of the physiological tissues of a human or an animal, esp. the trunk and four limbs

【身体力行】shēn tǐ lì xíng 亲身体验, 努力实行 earnestly practise what one advocates; practise what one preaches

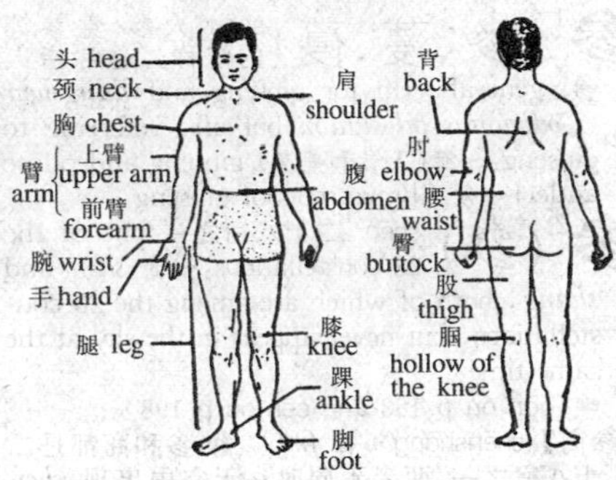

人的身体 Human Body

【身条儿】shēntiáor 身材; 个子 figure; height; stature: 瘦瘦的～ have a slim figure | ～匀称 of proportional build; of fine physical proportions

【身外之物】shēn wài zhī wù 个人身体以外的东西(指财产等, 表示无足轻重的意思) mere worldly possessions; possessions outside one's person (such as properties) that mean little

【身先士卒】shēn xiān shì zú 作战时将帅亲自带头, 冲在士兵前面。现多用来比喻领导带头走在群众前面。(of a commanding general) lead one's men in a charge; charge at the head of one's men; now it is used to liken leaders setting a fine example for the masses in doing everything

【身心】shēnxīn 身体和精神 body and mind: 大力开展文娱体育活动, 增进职工～健康。Organize cultural and sports activities in a big way to make the workers and staff physically and mentally healthy.

【身影】shēnyǐng 从远处看到的身体的模糊形象 person's silhouette; form; figure; dim image of a human body viewed in the distance

【身孕】shēnyùn 怀了胎儿的现象 pregnancy: 有了三个月的～ be three months pregnant

【身子】shēn·zi ❶ 身体 body: ～不大舒服 not feel well ❷ 身孕 pregnancy: 她已经有了六七个月的～。She is already six or seven months pregnant.

【身子骨儿】shēn·zigǔr〈方 *dial.*〉体格; 身体 one's health; physique: ～结实 very strong physically

呻 shēn〈书 *fml.*〉吟诵 recite

【呻吟】shēnyín 指人因痛苦而发出声音 groan; moan: 病人在床上～。The patient groaned in bed.

侁 shēn [侁侁]〈书 *fml.*〉形容众多 myriad; a great number of; many; multitude

诜 shēn [诜诜]〈书 *fml.*〉形容众多 myriad; a great number of; many; multitude

S

参[1]（參、蓡、蔘）shēn 人参、党参等的统称。通常指人参。general term for ginseng and *dangshen* (*Codonopsis pilosula*), but oft. referring to ginseng：～茸（人参和鹿茸）ginseng and pilose antler｜～须 fibrous roots of ginseng

参[2]（參）shēn 二十八宿之一 one of the 28 constellations：～商 *shen* and *shang*, both of which are among the 28 constellations, but never appear in the sky at the same time

☞ cān on p.183 and cēn on p.198

【参商】shēnshāng〈书 *fml.*〉❶ 参和商都是二十八宿之一，两者不同时在天空中出现 *shen* and *shang*, two of the 28 constellations that never appear in the sky at the same time；〈比喻 *fig.*〉亲友不能会面。Two friends or relatives are always separated and can never meet each other. ❷〈比喻 *fig.*〉感情不和睦 estranged and irreconcilable

绅 shēn ❶〈古代 *arch.*〉士大夫束在腰间的大带子 girdle (worn by ancient officials and literary men) ❷ 绅士 gentry：乡～ country gentleman；rural gentry｜土豪劣～ local tyrants and evil gentry

【绅耆】shēnqí 指旧时地方上的绅士和年老而有声望的人 local gentry and reputed elders

【绅士】shēnshì 指旧时地方上有势力、有功名的人，一般是地主或退职官僚 gentleman；gentry；usu. landlords or retired officials with local influence

【绅士协定】shēnshì xiédìng ☞ 君子协定 jūnzǐ xiédìng on p.1066

珅 shēn〈书 *fml.*〉一种玉 a kind of jade

诜 shēn [诜诜]（shēnshēn）〈书 *fml.*〉形容众多 numerous；myriad；a great many；a lot of；lots of；multitude

莘[1] shēn [莘莘]（shēnshēn）〈书 *fml.*〉形容众多 numerous；a great many；a lot of：～学子 students；large numbers of students

莘[2] Shēn ❶ 莘县，在山东 Shenxian, a county in Shandong Province ❷ 姓 a surname

☞ xīn on p.2133

砷 shēn 非金属元素，符号 As（arsenium）。有灰、黄、黑三种同素异形体，有毒。用于制硬质合金，砷的化合物用做杀菌剂和杀虫剂。arsenic (As)；nonmetallic chemical element with grey, yellow and black allotropic substances, and used in making hard alloys. Its chemical compounds are used as germicides and insecticides；旧称 also 砒 pī in old times

甡 shēn [甡甡]（shēnshen）〈书 *fml.*〉形容众多 a great many；lots of；a lot of；numerous；myriad；multitude

娠 shēn〈书 *fml.*〉怀孕 pregnancy：妊～ pregnancy

深 shēn ❶ 从上到下或从外到里的距离大（跟'浅'相对，③④⑤⑥同 as opposed to 'shallow'，③④⑤⑥ are the same）deep；long distance from above to below or from outside to inside：～耕 deep ploughing｜～山 remote mountains；untraversed mountain｜这院子很～。The courtyard is very deep. ❷ 深度 depth：这里的河水只有三尺～。The river is only three *chi* (one metre) deep.｜这间屋子宽一丈，～一丈四。The room is one *zhang* wide and 1.4 *zhang* deep. ❸ 深奥 profound；abstruse；difficult to understand：由浅入～ from the shallow to the deep；from the easy to the difficult｜这本书很～，初学的人不容易看懂。This book is very difficult for beginners. ❹ 深刻；深入 penetrating；profound；in-depth；incisive：～谈 have an in-depth conversation；have a deep or penetrating discussion｜影响很～ have a profound impact on；have great influence over ❺（感情）厚；（关系）密切 (of a relation) close；(of feelings) profound；intimate：～情厚谊 profound feelings and friendship｜两人的关系很～。The two of them have a very close relationship. ❻（颜色）浓 (of colour) dark；deep：～红 crimson；deep red｜～绿 dark green｜颜色太～。The colour is too dark. ❼ 距离开始的时间很久 a very long time from the beginning：～秋 late autumn｜夜已经很～了。It's very late in the night. *or* It is already in the dead of night. ❽ 很；十分 very；greatly；fully；deeply：～知 know very well；know fully｜～信 fully believe；be deeply convinced｜～恐 be very much afraid；be awfully afraid｜～表同情 show deep or profound sympathy｜～有此感 share a similar feeling

【深奥】shēn'ào（道理、含义）高深不易了解 (of reason, meaning) abstruse；profound；recondite：～的道理 a profound truth；abstruse philosophy

【深闭固拒】shēn bì gù jù〈比喻 *fig.*〉坚决不接受新事物或别人的意见 obstinately conservative；firmly refuse to accept new things or others' opinions

【深藏若虚】shēn cáng ruò xū 形容把宝贵的东西收藏起来，好像没有这东西似的（见于《史记·老庄申韩列传》）hide one's valuables and act as if one had nothing (see *Records of the Historian · Biographies of Laozi, Zhuangzi, Shen Buhai and Hanfeizi*)；〈比喻 *fig.*〉人有知识才能但不爱在人前表现 be extremely modest about one's talent or ability；never seek to boast or show off

【深层】shēncéng ❶ 较深的层次 depth；deeper layers ❷ 深入的；更进一步的 deep-going；thorough；incisive：～原因 deep-seated cause｜～意义 profound significance

【深长】shēncháng（意思）深刻而耐人寻味 profound (of meaning, intention, etc.)：意味～ profound meaning; profound implications｜用意～ profound intention

【深沉】shēnchén ❶ 形容程度深 deep：暮色～。Dusk is deepening.｜～的夜 deepening night｜～的哀悼 profound grief; profound condolence ❷（声音）低沉（of sound or voice) low-pitched; deep; dull：铁镐碰着冻硬的土地，发出～的声响。The spade produced low-pitched, dull sounds when it touched the hard frozen ground. ❸ 沉着持重；思想感情不外露 undemonstrative; reserved：～的微笑 knowing smile; significant smile｜这人很～，不容易捉摸。He's a deep and elusive person.

【深仇大恨】shēn chóu dà hèn 极深极大的仇恨 bitter and deep-seated hatred; profound hatred

【深度】shēndù ❶ 深浅的程度；向下或向里的距离 degree of depth; depth：测量河水的～ sound the depth of the river ❷（工作、认识）触及事物本质的程度 profundity; depth; thoroughness; (of work, understanding, etc.) degree of getting to the essence of things：对这个问题大家理解的～不一致。There is difference among us in the depth of understanding of this problem. ❸ 事物向更高阶段发展的程度 degree of development to a higher stage or level：向生产的～和广度进军 boost production both in depth and in breadth ❹ 程度很深的 extremely; greatly; deeply：～近视 extremely near-sighted

【深更半夜】shēngēng-bànyè 深夜 at a dead of night; in the small hours of night; in the middle of the night

【深沟高垒】shēn gōu gāo lěi 很深的壕沟和高大的营垒，指坚固的防御工事 deep trenches and high ramparts; fortified defence works

【深广】shēnguǎng 程度深，范围大 deep and broad：影响～ of wide and profound influence｜见识～ of wide experience and deep knowledge

【深闺】shēnguī〈旧时 *old*〉指富贵人家的女子所住的闺房（多在住宅的最里面 oft. built in the innermost part of a house) boudoir; chamber for a young, usu. unmarried, woman of a rich family

【深海】shēnhǎi 水深超过 200 米的海域 deep sea; sea exceeding 200 metres in depth

【深厚】shēnhòu ❶（感情）浓厚（of feelings) deep; profound：～的友谊 profound friendship｜～的感情 deep (or profound) feelings ❷（基础）坚实 solid; deep-seated：这一带是老根据地，群众基础非常～。There is a solid foundation among the masses in this old base area.

【深呼吸】shēnhūxī 尽力吸气然后尽力呼出 deep breathing

【深化】shēnhuà ❶ 向更深的阶段发展 go deeper; deepen：矛盾～ intensification of a contradiction｜认识不断～ deepening of the process of cognition ❷ 使向更深的阶段发展 go further; develop to a deeper stage：～改革 deepen the reform; further the reform

【深加工】shēnjiāgōng 对产品作进一步的、更精细的加工 intensive processing of products：逐步提高～产品出口的比重 gradually increase the proportion of the intensively-processed (high value-added) products for export

【深交】shēnjiāo ❶ 深厚的交情 deep friendship：我和他往日并无～。He and I are not very close friends. ❷ 密切地交往 close contact：你不愿和他～，也不要得罪他。You don't want to have close contact with him, neither should you offend him.

【深究】shēnjiū 认真追究 go into (a matter) seriously; get to the bottom of (a matter)：对这些小事不必～。You don't have to go into these small matters seriously.

【深居简出】shēn jū jiǎn chū 平日老在家里呆着，很少出门 live in the seclusion of one's own home

【深刻】shēnkè ❶ 达到事情或问题的本质的 get to the essence of a matter or problem; deep, profound, deep-going：～剖析 deep analysis; profound analysis｜这篇文章内容～，见解精辟。This article is profoundly written and contains incisive views. ❷ 内心感受程度很大的 deeply; greatly：印象～ deep impression｜～的体会 deep understanding; profound knowledge; deeply realise

【深谋远虑】shēn móu yuǎn lǜ 周密地计划，往长远里考虑 think deeply and plan carefully; be circumspect and far-sighted

【深浅】shēnqiǎn ❶ 深浅的程度 depth：你去打听一下这里河水的～，能不能蹚水过去。Go and find out how deep the river is and whether we can wade across it. ❷〈比喻 *fig.*〉分寸 proper limits (for speech or action); sense of propriety：说话没～ speak inappropriately

【深切】shēnqiè ❶ 深挚而亲切 heartfelt; deep; profound:：～的关怀 be deeply concerned about; show profound concern for｜～的怀念 cherish the memory of ❷ 深刻而切实 penetrating and realistic; deep; thorough：～地了解 understand thoroughly

【深情】shēnqíng ❶ 深厚的感情 deep feeling; deep love：无限～ boundless feelings｜满怀～ full of deep feelings｜～厚谊 profound sentiments of friendship; profound friendship ❷ 感情深厚 profound friendship; deep feeling：他站在高台上，～地望着家乡的土地。Standing on a high terrace, he looked with deep emotion at the land of his native place.

【深秋】shēnqiū 秋季的末期 late autumn

【深入】shēnrù ❶ 透过外部，达到事物内部或中心 go deep into; penetrate into: 孤军～ an isolated army penetrating enemy territory|～实际 go deep into the realities of life; be in close contact with social reality|～人心 strike root in the hearts of the people ❷ 深刻；透彻 thorough; deep-going: ～地分析 deep analysis; profound analysis|这个问题需要作～的调查研究。A thorough investigation will be made of this problem.

【深入浅出】shēn rù qiǎn chū 指文章或言论的内容很深刻，措辞却浅显易懂 explain the profound in simple terms

【深山】shēnshān 山里山外距离远、人不常到的山岭 remote mountains: ～老林常有野兽出没。Beasts often haunt the remote, heavily wooded mountains.

【深水炸弹】shēnshuǐ zhàdàn 一种到水下预定深度时爆炸的炸弹。由舰艇或飞机投放，主要用于炸毁在水下的敌方潜艇等。depth charge; depth bomb; powerful explosive charge that is dropped from a ship or airplane and explodes under water; used esp. against submarines

S

【深思】shēnsī 深刻地思考 think deeply about; ponder deeply over: 好学～ be fond of learning and thinking deeply

【深思熟虑】shēn sī shú lǜ 深入细致地考虑 careful consideration; think deeply and carefully

【深邃】shēnsuì ❶same as 深 shēn ①: ～的山谷 deep valley ❷ 深奥 profound; abstruse; recondite: 哲理～ abstruse philosophy

【深谈】shēntán 深入地交谈 discuss thoroughly; go deeply into: 我们见过面，但没有～。We met each other, but did not have a thorough discussion.

【深通】shēntōng 精通 have a thorough understanding of; be well versed in: ～傣语 have a thorough command of the ethnic Dai language

【深透】shēntòu 深刻而且透彻 deep and thorough: 分析～ make a deep and thorough analysis of

【深望】shēnwàng 深切地盼望 sincerely wish; earnestly hope: ～诸位通力合作 look forward to your full cooperation

【深文周纳】shēn wén zhōu nà 定罪名很苛刻，想尽方法把无罪的人定成有罪。泛指不根据事实而牵强附会地妄加罪名。apply the law with the utmost severity and try everything possible to make sb. appear guilty; (in a broad sense) accuse sb. of a crime he did not commit

【深恶痛绝】shēn wù tòng jué 厌恶、痛恨到极点 hate bitterly; abhor; detest

【深信】shēnxìn 非常相信 be deeply convinced; firmly believe: ～不疑 believe without a shadow of doubt

【深省】shēnxǐng 深刻地醒悟 wake up to a sharp awareness of the truth: 发人～ make one wide awake; make one wake up to reality or the truth; also 深醒 shēnxǐng

【深醒】shēnxǐng same as 深省 shēnxǐng

【深夜】shēnyè 指半夜以后 late at night; in the wee hours of the morning

【深意】shēnyì 深刻的含意 profound meaning: 话说得扼要而有～ (remarks) be short but mean a lot

【深渊】shēnyuān 很深的水 abyss: 万丈～ bottomless abyss

【深远】shēnyuǎn (影响、意义等)深刻而长远 (of influence, significance, etc.) profound and lasting; far-reaching

【深造】shēnzào 进一步学习以达到更高的程度 take a more advanced course of study or training; pursue advanced studies: 出国～ pursue advanced studies abroad

【深宅大院】shēn zhái dà yuàn 一家居住的房屋多而有围墙的大院子 imposing dwellings and spacious courtyards; compound of many mutually containing quadrangles, usu. occupied by one family

【深湛】shēnzhàn 精深 profound and thorough: ～的著作 profound work|学识～ profound learning|功夫～ consummate skill

【深挚】shēnzhì 深厚而真诚 deep and sincere: ～的友谊 deep and sincere friendship; intimate friendship

【深重】shēnzhòng (罪孽、灾难、危机、苦闷等)程度高 (of sin, calamity, suffering, crisis, distress, etc.) very grave; extremely serious: 罪孽～grave sins|～的灾难 grave disaster

莘 shēn [莘莘] (shēnshēn) 〈书 *fml.*〉形容繁盛茂密 luxuriant and lush

糁(糝、籸) shēn (～儿 shēnr)谷类磨成的碎粒 crushed grain: 玉米～儿 crushed maize

☞ sǎn on p. 1656

鲹(鰺) shēn 鱼类的一科，身体侧扁，侧面呈卵圆形，鳞细，胸鳍呈镰刀状，尾鳍分叉。生活在海中。scad or jack fish (*Decapterus*); flat, ovate marine fish with small scales, a sickle-like pectoral fin and a Y-shaped tail fin

燊 shēn 〈书 *fml.*〉炽盛 flaming ablaze; flourishing

shén (ㄕㄣˊ)

什(甚) shén ☞ below

☞ shí on p. 1735 and 甚 shèn on p. 1710

【什么】shén·me 〈疑问代词 *interrog. pron.*〉

❶ 表示疑问 [used in the interrogative] a)单用,问事物 [used separately to ask what]:这是~? What is this? |你找~? What are you looking for? |他说~? What did he say? |~叫押韵? What is rhyme? b)用在名词前面,问人或事物 [used before a noun to ask who or what]:~人? Who is he? |~事儿? What's the matter? |~颜色? What colour? |~地方? Where? ❷ 虚指,表示不确定的事物 [used to refer to anything indefinite]:他们仿佛在谈论~。It seems that they are talking about something|我饿了,想吃点儿~。I'm hungry. I want to have sth. to eat. ❸ 任指 [used to refer to things in general] a)用在'也'或'都'前面,表示所说的范围之内没有例外 [used before 也 or 都 to indicate that there is no exception within the limits mentioned]:他~也不怕。He is afraid of nothing; he fears nothing; he has nothing to be afraid of|只要认真学,~都能学会。Only if you learn earnestly, you can learn everything. b)两个'什么'前后照应,表示由前者决定后者 [used one 什么 after another 什么 to indicate that the first one determines the other]:想~说~。Feel free to say what's on your mind. *or* Say whatever you like to. |你~时候去,我也~时候去。Whenever you go, I'll go. ❹ 表示惊讶或不满 [used to express surprise or discontent]:~!九点了,车还没有开! What's happened! It's nine. The bus is not yet leaving! |这是~鞋!一只大一只小的! What damned shoes! One is big and the other is smaller. ❺ 表示责难 [used to express censure]:你笑~?(不应该笑。) What are you laughing at? (You should not have laughed.)|你说呀!装~哑巴?(不必装哑巴。) Speak up! Stop playing dumb. ❻ 表示不同意对方说的某一句话 [used to indicate disagreement with what has been said]:~晒一天?晒三天也晒不干。One Day? It won't be dried even in three days. ❼ 用在几个并列成分前面,表示列举不尽 [used before a number of coordinate phrases to indicate an incomplete list]:~送个信儿啊,跑个腿儿啊,他都干得了。He can do everything, sending a message and running errands.

【什么的】shén·me·de 用在一个成分或并列的几个成分之后,表示'…之类'的意思 [used after one phrase, a number of coordinate phrases or a number of items to indicate the meaning of 'what not' or 'things like that']:他就喜欢看文艺作品~。He likes to read literary works and things like that. |修修机器,画个图样~,他都能对付。He can manage repairing a machine, drawing a design, and things like that.

神 shén ❶ 宗教指天地万物的创造者和统治者,迷信的人指神仙或能力、德行高超的人物死后的精灵 god; deity; divine being; divinity; (in religion) the creator and ruler of the universe; (in superstition) the immortal; spirit of a person with lofty moral character or with supernatural power after his death:~位 memorial tablet; spirit tablet|财~ God of Wealth|无~论 atheism|多~教 polytheism ❷ 神话传说中的人物,有超人的能力 (in mythology) man with magic power; supernatural person:料事如~ predict like a prophet|用兵如~ direct military operations with super skills ❸ 特别高超或出奇,令人惊异的;神妙 supernatural; magical; miraculous; amazing:~速 amazingly fast; at lightning speed|~效 magical effect|这事真是越说越~了。The more it is talked about, the more incredible it becomes. ❹ 精神;精力 spirit; mind:凝~ with rapt attention|费~ take the trouble of; may I trouble you to|聚精会~ concentrate one's attention; with rapt attention|两目炯炯有~ bright and piercing eyes ❺ (~儿 shénr)神气 expression; look; air; manner:~色 expression; look; countenance|~情 expression; look; air|瞧他那个~儿,准是有什么心事。Look at his expression. He must have something weighing on his mind. ❻ 〈方 *dial.*〉聪明;机灵 smart; clever:瞧!这孩子真~。Look! What a smart child! ❼ (Shén)姓 a surname

【神奥】shén'ào 神秘;奥妙 mysterious; profound and subtle:日食和月食是一种自然现象,不像迷信的人所说的那么~。The solar eclipse and lunar eclipse are natural phenomena. They are not as mysterious as the superstitious people have indicated.

【神不守舍】shén bù shǒu shè 指神魂不定 be distracted (舍 *she*:这里指人的躯体 referring to the human body)

【神不知,鬼不觉】shén bù zhī, guǐ bù jué 形容做事极为隐秘,别人一点也不知道 unknown to god or ghost; without anybody knowing it; with great secrecy

【神采】shéncǎi 人面部的神气和光采 demeanour; mien; countenance:~飞扬 be in fine fettle|~奕奕(精神饱满的样子) brim with energy and vitality

【神差鬼使】shén chāi guǐ shǐ ☞ 鬼使神差 guǐ shǐ shén chāi on p. 733

【神驰】shíchí 心思飞向(某种境界) one's thoughts fly to; range in fancy:~心往 be carried away by|~故国 nostalgic thoughts about the ancient kingdom

【神出鬼没】shén chū guǐ mò 〈比喻 *fig.*〉变化巧妙迅速,或一会儿出现,一会儿隐没,不容易捉摸(多指用兵出奇制胜,让敌人摸不着头脑 oft. referring to military operations that take surprise attacks) come and go like a shadow;

appear and disappear mysteriously

【神道】[1] shéndào ❶ 迷信的人关于鬼神祸福的说法 superstitions about the ghosts, gods, fortune and misfortune ❷ same as 神 shén ①

【神道】[2] shéndào 墓道 Holy Way, passage way leading to a tomb; tomb passage: ～碑 stone tablet on a tomb passage on which are engraved the deeds of the deceased; inscription on such a stone tablet

【神道碑】shéndàobēi 墓道前记载死者事迹的石碑。也指这种碑上的文字。stone tablet on the Holy Way, inscribed with the deeds of the deceased; inscription on a Holy Way stele

【神甫】shén·fu 天主教、东正教的神职人员 Father (title of respect for a Roman Catholic priest); also 神父 shén·fu or 司铎 sīduó

【神工鬼斧】shén gōng guǐ fǔ ☞ 鬼斧神工 guǐ fǔ shén gōng on p.733

【神怪】shénguài 神仙和鬼怪 gods and spirits: ～小说 fiction about gods and ghosts

【神汉】shénhàn 男巫师 sorcerer

【神乎其神】shén hū qí shén 神秘奇妙到了极点 fantastic; wonderful; miraculous

S

【神化】shénhuà 把人当做神来看待 deify

【神话】shénhuà ❶ 关于神仙或神化的古代英雄的故事,是古代人民对自然现象和社会生活的一种天真的解释和美丽的向往 mythology; myth; fairy tale; stories about immortals or deified heroes, and reflecting ancient people's naive explanations of natural phenomena and social life as well as their beautiful longings ❷ 指荒诞的无稽之谈 preposterous nonsense

【神魂】shénhún 精神;神志(多用于不正常时 oft. abnormal) state of mind; mind: ～颠倒 be infatuated|～不定 be distracted; be deeply perturbed; have the jitters

【神机妙算】shén jī miào suàn 惊人的机智,巧妙的谋划。形容有预见性,善于估计客观情势,决定策略。resourcefulness and superb planning; showing miraculous foresight and accurate estimation of the situation when formulating a strategy

【神交】shénjiāo ❶ 指心意投合、相知很深的朋友 soul mate; friends with mutual understanding and admiration ❷ 彼此没有见过面,但精神相通,互相倾慕 friendship grown out of mutual admiration between persons who have never met: 二人～已久,今日才得相见。The two of them have long cherished admiration for each other, but they have never met until today.

【神经】shénjīng ❶ 把中枢神经系统的兴奋传递给各个器官,或把各个器官的兴奋传递给中枢神经系统的组织,是由许多神经纤维构成的 nerve; tissues that transmit the excitation of the central nervous system to the organs or transmit the excitation of the organs to the central nervous system consist of many nervous fibres; ☞ 脑神经 nǎoshénjīng on p.1395; 植物性神经 zhíwùxìng shénjīng on p.2464 ❷ 指精神失常 be out of mind: 犯～ have bats in the belfry; have lost one's marbles; be deranged

【神经病】shénjīngbìng ❶ 神经系统的组织发生病变或机能发生障碍的疾病,症状是麻木、瘫痪、抽搐、昏迷等 neuropathy; any disease of the nervous system with such symptoms as numbness, paralysis, tic, and coma ❷ 精神病的俗称 Popular term for 精神病 jīngshénbìng

【神经错乱】shénjīng cuòluàn 通常指犯精神病 mental disorder; suffer from mental disorder

【神经过敏】shénjīng guòmǐn ❶ 神经系统的感觉机能异常锐敏的症状,神经衰弱的患者多有这种症状 neuroticism; symptom for unusually sensitiveness of the sensory function of the nervous system ❷ 通常指多疑,好大惊小怪 neurotic; oversensitive; oversuspicious

【神经衰弱】shénjīng shuāiruò 一种神经活动机能失调的病。症状是头痛、耳鸣、健忘、失眠、容易兴奋激动并且容易疲劳等。neurasthenia; disease of functional imbalance of the nervous activities, including such symptoms as headache, tinnitus, amnesia, insomnia, irritability and fatigue

【神经系统】shénjīng xìtǒng 人或动物体内由神经原组成的系统,包括中枢神经系统和周围神经系统,主要作用是使机体内部各个器官成为统一体,并能使机体适应外界的环境 nervous system; system in a human or animal body, consisting of neurons and including the central nervous system and the peripheral nervous system, with its major role to combine various organs into a integral whole and adapt the body to the external circumstances

【神经质】shénjīngzhì 指人的神经过敏、胆小怯懦、情感容易冲动的性质 nervousness, with such symptoms as neuroticism, timidity and emotion

【神龛】shénkān 供神像或祖宗牌位的小阁子 shrine; tiny receptacle for idol or ancestral tablet

【神来之笔】shén lái zhī bǐ 指绝妙的文思或词句 inspired writing; stroke of genius

【神聊】shénliáo 漫无边际地闲聊 indulge in idle and empty talk: 他俩天南海北地～起来。The two of them chattered away about everything under the sun.

【神灵】shénlíng 神 ① 的总称 general term for shén ①

【神秘】shénmì 使人摸不透的;高深莫测的 mysterious; mystical: 科学技术并不是那么～,只要努力钻研,就可以掌握它。Science and technology are no mystery. As long as you study hard, you can master them.

【神妙】shénmiào 非常高明、巧妙 wonderful; marvellous; ingenious: ～莫测 wonderful;

marvellous|笔法～ wonderful style of writing; ingenious brushwork

【神明】[1] shénmíng 神①的总称 general term for 神 shén ①:奉若～ worship; make a fetish of

【神明】[2] shénmíng 指精神状态 mental state:内疚～ feel guilty|～不衰 remain full of spirits

【神农】Shénnóng 我国古代传说中的人物,相传他教人从事农业生产,又亲尝百草,发明医药 Shennong; the Holy Farmer; legendary figure in Chinese mythology, supposed to have taught people to engage in farm production and personally tasted a myriad of herbs before they were used as curative plants

【神女】shénnǚ ❶ 女神 goddess ❷〈旧时 *old*〉指妓女 prostitute

【神品】shénpǐn 绝妙的作品(多指书画 oft. said of a painting or a piece of calligraphy) a sublime work

【神婆】shénpó 女巫 sorceress; witch; also 神婆子 shēnpó·zi

【神奇】shénqí 非常奇妙 magical; mystical; miraculous:这一古代传说被人们渲染上一层～的色彩。Through the ages, this legend has acquired an element of mystery and wonder.

【神祇】shénqí〈书 *fml.*〉'神'指天神,'祇'指地神,'神祇'泛指神(*shen* refers to the God of Heaven, and *qi* refers to the God of Earth) gods, deities

【神气】shén·qì ❶ 神情 expression; air; manner:团长的～很严肃。The regiment commander had a very stern look on his face.|他说话的～特别认真。He speaks in a particularly serious manner. ❷ 精神饱满 impressive; spirited; vigorous:战士们穿上新军装,显得很～。The soldiers look very impressive in their new uniforms. ❸ 自以为优越而表现出得意或傲慢的样子 putting on airs; cocky; overweening:～活现 very cocky; at high and mighty

【神枪手】shénqiāngshǒu 用枪射击非常准确的人 crack shot; expert marksman; sharpshooter

【神情】shénqíng 人脸上所显露的内心活动 expression; look; air:～抑郁 look depressed|他脸上露出愉快的～。He looks happy. *or* He wears a happy expression.

【神权】shénquán ❶ 迷信的人认为鬼神所具有的支配人们命运的权力 divine authority; power possessed by gods and ghosts to manipulate the fate of the people in the minds of superstitious people ❷ 奴隶社会、封建社会的最高统治者宣扬他们的统治权力是神所赋予的,所以把这种统治权力叫做神权 rule with divine right; theocracy. The rulers in the slave and feudal societies claimed that their right to rule was granted by the deities.

【神人】shénrén ❶ 神仙;道家指得道的人 spiritual being; (Taoism) immortal ❷ 仪表不凡的人 man of striking appearance

【神色】shénsè 神情 expression; look:～匆忙 look in a hurry|～自若 be perfectly calm and collected; show composure and presence of mind

【神伤】shénshāng〈书 *fml.*〉心中伤感;精神颓丧 dejected; depressed; listless:黯然～ feel depressed; feel dejected

【神神道道】shén·shendāodāo 形容言谈举止失常的样子 talk strangely and act queerly; in a bizarre and eccentric manner:他成天～的,也不知道在干些什么。He is very weird all the time. No one could know what he is up to. also 神神叨叨 shén·shendāodāo

【神圣】shénshèng 极其崇高而庄严的;不可亵渎的 sacred; holy:～的使命 sacred mission|我国的～领土,不容侵犯。Our sacred territory tolerates no violation.

【神圣同盟】Shénshèng Tóngméng 1815年拿破仑一世的帝国崩溃后,俄国、普鲁士和奥地利三国君主在巴黎订约结成的反动同盟。它的目的是为了镇压欧洲各国人民的革命运动和民族解放运动。现也用来指反动势力之间的同盟或合作。Holy Alliance (1815-1830); reactionary alliance formed in 1815 by the rulers of Russia, Austria and Prussia in Paris after the collapse of Napoleon I Empire to suppress the popular revolutionary movement and the national liberation movement in Europe; reference to alliance or cooperation among reactionary forces

【神使鬼差】shén shǐ guǐ chāi ☞ 鬼使神差 guǐ shǐ shén chāi on p. 733

【神思】shénsī 精神;心绪 state of mind; mindset:～不定 be distracted

【神似】shénsì 精神实质上相似;极相似 be alike in spirit; be an excellent likeness:他画的虫鸟,栩栩如生,十分～。The insects and birds he paints are extremely lifelike.

【神速】shénsù 速度快得惊人 marvellously quick; amazing speed:收效～yield amazingly quick results|兵贵～。Speed is vital in war. *or* Speed is precious in war. *or* It's speed that counts in war.

【神算】shénsuàn ❶ 准确的推测 accurate prediction ❷ 神妙的计谋 miraculous scheme

【神态】shéntài 神情态度 expression; manner; bearing; mien:～自若 look (or appear) calm and at ease

【神通】shéntōng 原是佛教用语,指无所不能的力量,今指特别高明的本领(orig. Budd. term) magic power; remarkable ability:～广大 have omnipotent magic powers; possess unusual powers; be infinitely resourceful|大显～ display one's prowess; give full play to one's ability

【神童】shéntóng 指特别聪明的儿童 child prodigy

【神往】shénwǎng 心里向往 be carried away; be rapt; be charmed: 心驰～ yearn after as if one's mind were already there | 黄山云海,令人～。The sea of clouds over the Huangshan Mountain is fascinating

【神威】shénwēi 神奇的威力 martial prowess; invincible might: 大显～ display or show invincible might

【神位】shénwèi 宗庙、祠堂中或祭祀时设立的牌位 spirit tablet in an ancestral temple or ancestral hall or posted temporarily for a sacrificial rite

【神武】shénwǔ〈书 *fml.*〉英明威武(多用于称道帝王将相 oft. said of an emperor or a great general) divine and mighty: ～雄才 divine and mighty ability or talent

【神物】shénwù〈书 *fml.*〉❶ 神奇的东西 wonder; prodigy; phenomenon ❷ 指神仙 supernatural being; deity

【神悟】shénwù〈书 *fml.*〉敏捷的理解力 divine intelligence

【神仙】shén·xiān ❶ 神话传说中的人物,有超人的能力,可以超脱尘世,长生不老 supernatural being; celestial being; immortal ❷〈比喻 *fig.*〉能预料或猜透事情的人 person who has the power of clairvoyance ❸〈比喻 *fig.*〉逍遥自在、毫无拘束和牵挂的人 person free from worldly cares

【神像】shénxiàng ❶ 神佛的图像、塑像 picture or statue of a god or the Buddha ❷〈旧时 *old*〉指遗像 portrait or photo of the deceased

【神效】shénxiào 惊人的效验;神奇的功效 magical effect; miraculous effect

【神学】shénxué 援用唯心主义哲学来论证神的存在、本质和宗教教义的一种学说 theology; study of the presence and attributes of god and religious doctrines by means of idealist philosophy

【神医】shényī 指医术非常高明的医生 highly skilled doctor; miracle-working doctor

【神异】shényì ❶ 神怪 gods and spirits: ～小说 fiction about gods and spirits ❷ 神奇 magical; mystical; miraculous: ～景色 a miraculous sight

【神勇】shényǒng 形容人非常勇猛 extraordinarily brave; superhumanly brave: ～无敌 extraordinarily brave and invincible

【神游】shényóu〈书 *fml.*〉感觉中好像亲游某地 make a spiritual tour; range in fancy: 故国～ make a spiritual visit to an ancient kingdom | ～天外 wander to the outer space in a dream

【神宇】shényǔ〈书 *fml.*〉神情仪表 mien; bearing; air

【神韵】shényùn 精神韵致(多用于艺术作品 in literature and art) romantic charm: 他不过淡淡几笔,却把这幅山水点染得很有～。Just a few light strokes, and he painted the landscape with great charm.

【神职人员】shénzhí rényuán 天主教、东正教等教会中负责宗教事务的专职人员(of Catholicism, Eastern Orthodox church, etc.) clergy; clergymen

【神志】shénzhì 知觉和理智 consciousness; senses; mind: ～不清 be unconscious | ～模糊 be in a trance; be in a haze; be stoned

【神智】shénzhì 精神智慧 mind; intellect

【神州】Shénzhōu 战国时人驺衍称中国为'赤县神州'(见于《史记·孟子荀卿列传》),后世用'神州'做中国的代称 Divine Land, reference to China coined by a man living in the Warring States Period named Zou Yan (see *Records of the Historian · Biographies of Mencius and Xunzi*)

【神主】shénzhǔ 写着死人名字的狭长的小木牌,是供奉和祭祀的对象 small, long, slender wooden tablet inscribed with the name of the deceased for worship and sacrifices

shěn (ㄕㄣˇ)

沈[1](瀋) shěn 沈阳(Shěnyáng),市名,在辽宁 Shenyang, name of a city in Liaoning Province

沈[2](瀋) shěn〈书 *fml.*〉汁 juice: 墨～未干。The ink is still wet.

沈[3] Shěn 姓 a surname

☞ 沉 chén on p.236

审[1](審) shěn ❶ 详细;周密 careful; meticulous: ～慎 careful; circumspect; cautious | ～视 look at sth. or sb. attentively; observe carefully ❷ 审查 examine; go over: ～阅 examine; go over | ～稿 go over a manuscript or draft and give comments ❸ 审讯 interrogate; try: ～案 try a case | 公～ public trial | 三堂会～joint trial by three departments

审[2](審、讅) shěn〈书 *fml.*〉知道 know; be aware of: ～悉 know

审[3](審) shěn〈书 *fml.*〉的确;果然 indeed; really: ～如其言。What he says is indeed true.

【审查】shěnchá 检查核对是否正确、妥当 examine(多指计划、提案、著作、个人的资历等 plans, proposals, writings, credentials, etc.): ～提案 examine proposals | ～经费 check up on the funds | ～属实。The fact was established after investigation.

【审察】shěchá ❶ 仔细观察 closely observe; closely examine ❷ 审查 examine; investigate

【审处】shěnchǔ ❶ 审判处理 try and punish ❷ 审查处理 deliberate and decide

【审订】shěndìng 审阅修订 examine and revise;

revise：～书稿 examine the manuscript of a book

【审定】shěndìng 审查决定 examine and approve; examine and finalize：～计划 examine and approve a plan

【审读】shěndú 审阅 read and evaluate (a manuscript); read：～书稿 read and finalize a manuscript

【审改】shěngǎi 审查修改 examine and revise (a manuscript); revise：～文稿 examine and revise a manuscript

【审核】shěnhé 审查核定(多指书面材料或数字材料 oft. written materials or statistics) verify; check：～经费 verify the funds|～预算 verify a budget

【审计】shěnjì 指由专设机关对国家各级政府及金融机构、企业事业组织的财务收支进行事前和事后的审查 audit; official examination and verification of financial accounts of the revenues and expenditures of governments at all levels, financial institutions, enterprises and institutions

【审结】shěnjié 审理结束，做出判决 wind up a trial and pass the verdict：这一刑事案件已经～。A court decision has been made on the criminal case following the conclusion of the trial.

【审理】shěnlǐ 审查处理(案件) try; hear：依法～ try a case according to law|这一案件的～工作正在进行。The trying of this case is now in progress.

【审美】shěnměi 领会事物或艺术品的美 aesthetics; appreciation of the beautiful：～观点 aesthetic conceptions; aesthetic standards

【审判】shěnpàn 审理和判决(案件) examine and decide (on a case); try a case

【审批】shěnpī 审查批示(下级呈报上级的书面计划、报告等 examine and write instructions (on plans, reports, etc., submitted by one's subordinates)：报请上级～ submit to the higher authorities for examination and approval

【审慎】shěnshèn 周密而谨慎 cautious and careful; circumspect：～地考虑 think carefully

【审时度势】shěn shí duó shì 了解时势的特点，估计情况的变化 judge the hour and size up the situation; take stock of the situation

【审视】shěnshì 仔细看 look closely at; examine closely：～图纸 examine the blueprints closely or carefully

【审题】shěn//tí 做文章或答题前仔细了解题目的要求 examine and consider carefully before writing an article or answering a question

【审问】shěnwèn 审讯 interrogate; question

【审讯】shěnxùn 公安机关、检察机关或法院向民事案件中的当事人或刑事案件中的自诉人、被告人查问有关案件的事实 hearing; investigation conducted by a public security organ, procuratorial organ or court of the litigants in a civil case, or of the private prosecutor and defendant, to clarify facts related to the case

【审议】shěnyì 审查讨论 examine and discuss; review; deliberate：计划草案提交大会～。The draft plan will be submitted to the session for review.

【审阅】shěnyuè 审查阅读 examine carefully and critically：～制订的方案 examine a drafted plan|～各班组送来的报告 examine the reports sent by the teams and groups

哂 shěn 〈书 *fml.*〉微笑 smile：不值一～ not worth a smile

【哂纳】shěnnà 〈客套话 *pol.*〉用于请人收下礼物 kindly accept one's gift

【哂笑】shěnxiào 〈书 *fml.*〉讥笑 laugh at; ridicule; sneer at; deride：为行家所～ to be laughed at by the experts; incurs the ridicule of the experts

矧 shěn 〈书 *fml.*〉况且 besides; moreover

谂 shěn 〈书 *fml.*〉❶ 知道 know; be aware of：～知 know; be aware of|～悉 know; be aware of ❷ 劝告 advise; urge

婶(嬸) shěn (～儿 shěnr) ❶ 婶母 wife of father's younger brother; aunt：二～ wife of father's second younger brother; second aunt|三～儿 Third Aunt ❷ 称呼跟母亲辈分相同而年纪较小的已婚妇女 form of address for a woman about one's mother's age; aunt; auntie：大～儿 Elder Aunt|张二～ Second Aunt Zhang

【婶母】shěnmǔ 叔父的妻子 wife of father's younger brother; aunt

【婶娘】shěnniáng 〈方 *dial.*〉 same as 婶母 shěnmǔ

【婶婆】shěnpó 丈夫的婶母 husband's aunt

【婶婶】shěn·shen same as 婶母 shěnmǔ

【婶子】shěn·zi same as 婶母 shěnmǔ

瞫 shěn 〈书 *fml.*〉往深处看 look deep into

shèn (ㄕㄣˋ)

肾(腎) shèn ❶ 人或高等动物的主要排泄器官，形如蚕豆，在脊柱的两侧，左右各一，表面有纤维组织构成的薄膜，有血管从内缘通入肾内。血液流过时，血内的水分和溶解在水里的物质被肾吸收，分解后形成尿，经输尿管输出。kidneys, the main excretory organ shaped like a broad bean and covered by thin membranes of fibrous tissues on either side of the spinal column, in the upper abdominal cavity of humans and other vertebrates. When blood flows through the vessels in the kidneys, both the water in the blood , and

S

the matter dissolved in the water are absorbed by the kidneys, which separate water and waste products of metabolism from the blood and excrete them as urine through the bladder and urethra; also 肾脏 shènzàng; 通称 generally called 腰子 yāo•zi; (图见 ☞ figure for 泌尿器 mìniàoqì on p. 1332) ❷〈中医 Chin. med.〉指外肾,即人的睾丸 testis; testicle

【肾囊】shènnáng〈中医 *Chin. med.*〉指阴囊 scrotum

【肾上腺】shènshàngxiàn 内分泌腺之一,共有两个,位置在两个肾脏的上端,分皮质和髓质两部分。髓质分泌肾上腺素,皮质分泌的激素总称肾上腺皮质激素,属于类固醇化合物。adrenal gland; adrenal; either of a pair of endocrine organs lying immediately above the kidneys, consisting of an inner medulla which produces epinephrine and norepinephrine and an outer cortex which produces a variety of steroid hormone; also 肾上体 shènshàngtǐ or 副肾 fùshèn; (图见 ☞ figure for 泌尿器 mìniàoqì on p. 1332)

S

【肾盂】shènyú 肾脏的一部分,是圆锥形的囊状物,下端通输尿管 renal pelvis; the funnel-shaped part of the kidney leading into the ureter

【肾脏】shènzàng same as 肾 shèn

甚[1] shèn ❶ 很;极 very; extremely: ~佳 very good | 欺人太~ bully others too much; it's going too far ❷ 超过;胜过 surpass; more than: 日~一日 get better and better; get worse and worse; get better or worse with each passing day | 他关心他人~于关心自己。He cares for others more than for himself.

甚[2] shèn〈方 *dial.*〉same as 什么 shén•me ①②③: ~事? What is it? | 有~说~。Just say what you've got to say. | 那有~要紧? What does it matter?
☞ 什 shén on p. 1704

【甚而】shèn'ér 甚至 even to the extent that; (go) so far as to

【甚或】shènhuò〈书 *fml.*〉甚至 even to the extent that; (go) so far as to; so much so that

【甚嚣尘上】shèn xiāo chén shàng 楚国跟晋国作战,楚王登车窥探敌情,对侍臣说:'甚嚣,且尘上矣。'意思是晋军喧哗纷乱得很厉害,而且尘土也飞扬起来了(见于《左传》成公十六年)。后来用'甚嚣尘上'形容对传闻之事议论纷纷。现多指某种言论十分嚣张(含贬义 derog.)。raise a hue and cry; cause a great clamour. During a war between the state of Chu and the state of Jin, the duke of Chu mounted a chariot to watch the enemy movements and told his aides: 'There is a great clamour, and the dust is rising.' He meant that there was a great clamour and confusion among the Jin troops and the dust was flying in the sky over them (see *The Zuo Commentary • Duke Cheng 16th Year*). Since then, the phrase has been used to describe a situation in which there is much talk about rumours. It is often used to refer to a widely spread rumour or opinion.

【甚至】shènzhì 提出突出的事例(有更进一层的意思) go so far as to; even to the extent that: 大院里五十多岁~六十多岁的老年人也参加了植树活动。The old people in their 50s in the compound, and even those in their 60s, took part in the tree-planting activities. also 甚至于 shènzhìyú or 甚而至于 shèn'érzhìyú

眘(昚) shèn〈书 *fml.*〉same as 慎 shèn; oft. used in the names of persons

胂 shèn 有机化合物的一类,是砷化氢分子中的氢原子部分或全部被烃基取代而成的衍生物 arsine; organic chemical compound that is a derivative of the replacement of part or all of the hydrogen atoms in the hydrogen arsenide by hydrocarbons

渗(滲) shèn 液体慢慢地透过或漏出 ooze; seep: ~水 water seeps or infiltrates | 包扎伤口的绷带上~出了血。Blood oozed out of the dressing. | 雨水都~到地里去了。The rain all seeped into the ground.

【渗沟】shèngōu 在街道下面挖掘的用以排除地面积水的暗沟 sewer; drain, built under a street, to carry off the surface water

【渗井】shènjǐng same as 渗坑 shènkēng

【渗坑】shènkēng 挖在庭院地面之下用以排除地面积水或管道污水的坑,水流入渗坑以后逐渐渗入地层 seepage pit; underground pit dug in a courtyard to drain off the surface water and sewage, which seep into the lower stratum after flowing into the seepage pit

【渗流】shènliú 液体在土壤空隙或其他透水介质中的流动,如地下水的流动、地下石油的流动 flowing of liquids through the pores of the soil or other pervious media, such as the flow of underground water, the subterranean flow of oil in an oil-bearing formation

【渗入】shènrù ❶ 液体慢慢地渗到里面去 filter through; penetrate: 融化了的雪水~大地。The melted snow water permeated the ground. ❷〈比喻 *fig.*〉某种势力无孔不入地钻进来(多含贬义 oft. derog.) (of influence, etc.) penetrate; infiltrate

【渗透】shèntòu ❶ 两种气体或两种可以互相混合的液体,彼此通过多孔性的薄膜而混合 osmosis; two gases or two liquids that can be mixed with each other pass through a porous membrane and mix together ❷ 液体从物体的细小空隙中透过 permeate; seep: 雨水~了泥土。The rainwater permeated the soil. ❸〈比喻 *fig.*〉一种事物或势力逐渐进入到其他方面(多用于抽象事物)(oft. abstract) infiltrate; penetrate: 经济~ economic infiltration |

在每一项建设工程上都～着设计人员和工人的心血。Every construction project embodies the painstaking effort of the designers and workers.

【渗析】shènxī 利用半透膜(如羊皮纸、膀胱膜)使溶胶和其中所含的杂质分离。用来提纯核酸、蛋白质等高分子化合物和精制胶体溶液。dialysis; separation of dissolved colloids from the impurities in a solution by means of a semi-permeable membrane (such as parchment, bladder membrane), used to purify high-molecular compounds like nucleic acid and protein and refine colloidal solutions; also 透析 tòuxī

葚 shèn ☞ 桑葚 sāngshèn on p.1657
☞ rèn on p.1625

椹 shèn same as 葚 shèn
☞ zhēn on p.2437

蜃 shèn 大蛤蜊 clam

【蜃景】shènjǐng ☞ 海市蜃楼 hǎi shì shèn lóu on p.757

瘆(瘮) shèn 使人害怕;可怕 scare; petrify:～人 making one's flesh creep; horrifying|夜里一个人走山路真有点儿～得慌。It's really scary for a person to climb a mountain path alone at night. *or* It really makes one's flesh creep to be walking alone on a mountain path at night.

慎 shèn ❶ 谨慎;小心 careful; cautious:不～ careless|～重 prudent; discreet; careful; cautious ❷ (Shèn)姓 a surname

【慎独】shèndú 古人的一种修养方法,指人独处的谨慎不苟 be strict with oneself in solitude; try to be blameless in one's private life — ancients' method of self-cultivation

【慎重】shènzhòng 谨慎认真 prudent; discreet; cautious; careful:～处理 handle sth. with great care|～研究 study carefully|态度～ prudent attitude

shēng(ㄕㄥ)

升[1](昇、❷陞) shēng ❶ 由低往高移动 rise; hoist; go up; ascend (跟'降'相对 as opposed to 'fall'):～旗 hoist a flag|上～ rise|旭日东～。The sun rises in the eastern sky. ❷ (等级)提高 (grades) promote; elevate; go up (跟'降'相对 as opposed to 'demote'):～级 promote to a higher grade level or rank; upgrade

升[2] shēng ❶ 公制容量的主单位,1升等于1,000毫升 litre, metric unit of measure (one litre = 1,000 millilitres); also 公升 gōngshēng; ☞ 国际公制 guójì gōngzhì on p.740 ❷ 容量单位。10合(gě)等于1升,10升等于1斗。现用市升,1市升合公制1升,即1,000毫升 *sheng*, now called *shisheng*; unit of measure (10 *ge* = 1 *sheng*, 10 *sheng* 1 *dou*; 1 *shisheng* = 1 litre, or 1,000 millilitres) ❸ 量粮食的器具,容量为斗的十分之一 *sheng*, instrument for measuring grains equal to 0.1 *dou*

【升班】shēng//bān (学生)升级 (of students) go up (one grade in school)

【升幅】shēngfú 上升的幅度 increase; margin of increase:消费品价格～较大。Consumer goods prices have risen by a big margin.

【升格】shēng//gé 身份、地位等升高 raise; promote; upgrade:公使～为大使 raise the status of their diplomatic representatives from minister to ambassador|这个县明年将～为市。The status of this county will be raised to that of a municipality next year.

【升官】shēng//guān 提升官职 get a promotion; be promoted to a higher official position

【升华】shēnghuá ❶ 固态(晶体)物质不经液态直接变为气态。樟脑、碘、萘等都容易升华。sublimate; evaporate; (of a solid such as camphor, iodine and naphthalene) become gaseous without going through an intermediate liquid state ❷〈比喻 *fig.*〉事物的提高和精炼(of sth.) rise to a higher level; distillation; sublimation:艺术不就是现实生活,而是现实生活～的结果。Art is not necessarily real life, but the distillation of it.

【升华热】shēnghuárè 单位质量的晶体直接变成气体时需要吸收的热量,叫做该固体的升华热 heat of sublimation; heat absorbed when the crystal of a unit mass changes directly to gaseous state

【升级】shēng//jí ❶ 从较低的等级或班级升到较高的等级或班级 go up one or more grades:产品～换代 updating and upgrading of products|考试及格,方可～。One can not go up to a higher grade without passing the examinations. ❷ 指战争的规模扩大、事态的紧张程度加深等 escalate; expand step by step, as from a local confrontation into a general war:战争～ escalation of a war

【升降】shēngjiàng 上升和下降 go up and down

【升降舵】shēngjiàngduò 用来调节飞机上升或下降的片状装置,装在飞机的尾部,和水平面平行 aviation elevator; pilot-controlled airfoil attached to the trailing edge of the tail section's horizontal stabilizers, used to make an aircraft go up or down and to control pitching

【升降机】shēngjiàngjī 建筑工地、多层建筑物等载人或载物升降的机械设备。由动力机和用钢丝绳吊着的箱状装置、料车或平台构成,多用电做动力。有的也叫电梯。elevator; lift; platform, cage, or box-like structure suspended by motor-operated cables for hoisting or lowering people or things in a building or mine;

also 电梯 diàntī

【升结肠】shēngjiécháng 结肠的一部分,与盲肠相连,向上行,连接横结肠 colon ascendens; part of the colon that links with the appendix and goes up to link with the transverse colon; (图见 ☞ figure for 消化系统 xiāohuà xìtǒng on p. 2100)

【升力】shēnglì 空气和物体相对运动时,空气把物体向上托的力 aviation lift; air force that lifts a thing upward; also 举力 jǔlì

【升平】shēngpíng 太平 peace: ～气象 peaceful atmosphere; peaceful life

【升旗】shēng//qí 把国旗、军旗等慢慢地拉到旗杆顶上 hoist (or raise) a flag; hoist a national flag or a military banner to the top of a flag pole: ～仪式 flag-raising ceremony

【升迁】shēngqiān 调到另一部门,职位比原来提高 be transferred and promoted

【升任】shēngrèn 提升担任(职务) be promoted: 他由排长～连长。He has been promoted from platoon leader to company commander

【升水】shēngshuǐ 调换票据或兑换货币时,因为比价的不同,比价高的一方向另一方收取一定的差额,叫升水。也指这种收取的差额。premium; amount of money charged by one party having a higher exchange rate from another party having a lower exchange rate when a bill or a currency is exchanged; also the difference paid

S

【升堂入室】shēng táng rù shì 〈比喻 *fig.*〉学问或技能由浅入深,循序渐进,达到更高的水平 pass through the hall into the inner chamber — attainment of profound scholarship; become highly proficient; reach the level of highly scholarly attainments; also 登堂入室 dēng táng rù shì

【升腾】shēngténg (火焰、气体等)向上升起 (of flames, gas, etc.) leap up; rise: 火光～。The flames leapt up. | 山头上～起白蒙蒙的雾气。A thick mist rose over the hilltop.

【升天】shēng//tiān ❶ 称人死亡(迷信) (superstition) go up to Heaven — die ❷ 升上天空 rise into the sky; take off: 卫星～。A satellite was launched into the sky.

【升温】shēngwēn 温度上升 rise of the temperature; 〈比喻 *fig.*〉事物发展程度加深或提高 warm up; thrive; be boosted: 当猪肉供不应求时,养猪业骤然～。When the pork was in short supply, the pig raising industry received a big boost all of a sudden.

【升学】shēng//xué 由低一级的学校进入高一级的学校 go to a school of a higher grade; enter a higher school

【升涨】shēngzhǎng 上升;高涨 rise; go up; shoot up: 革命潮流逐渐～。The revolutionary tide surged gradually.

【升帐】shēngzhàng 指元帅在帐中召集将士议事或发令(多见于早期白话 oft. in early vernacular) (of a marshal, or commanding general) call a meeting of generals in the commander's tent to discuss military matters or issue military orders; 现多用于比喻 (oft. used in a figurative sense) take command

【升值】shēngzhí 增加本国单位货币的含金量或提高本国货币对外币的比价,叫做升值 revalue; appreciate; raise the value of a domestic currency in foreign exchange or increase the money's gold content

生[1] shēng ❶ 生育 beget; give birth to; bear: 胎～ viviparity | 卵～ oviparity | ～孩子 give birth to a child | 优～优育 give birth to healthy babies and bring them up in a proper way ❷ 生长 grow: ～根 strike root | ～芽 sprout | 新～力量 rising force; new blood ❸ 生存;活 (跟'死'相对 as opposed to 'death') existence; life; live: 起死回～ bring back to life | 贪～怕死 cowardice; care for nothing but saving one's life; be mortally afraid of death ❹ 生计 life; livelihood: 谋～ make a living; earn a living | 营～ line of business; occupation; job ❺ 生命 life: 丧～ lose life | 舍～取义 give up one's life for justice; die a heroic death for a just cause ❻ 生平 life; all one's life: 一～一世 all one's life; lifetime | 今～今世 this life; this very life ❼ 具有生命力的;活的 living; alive: ～物 living thing | ～龙活虎 vigorous; full of vigour ❽ 产生;发生 cause; give rise to: ～病 get ill; fall ill | ～效 take effect; become effective; come into force | 惹是～非 stir up trouble; make disturbance ❾ 使柴、煤等燃烧 burn coal or firewood: ～火 light a fire | ～炉子 light a stove ❿ (Shēng)姓 a surname

生[2] shēng ❶ 果实没有成熟 (跟'熟'相对,下②③④同 as opposed to 'ripe', same as ②③④ below) unripe; green: ～柿子 green persimmon | 这西瓜是～的。The watermelon is still unripe. ❷ (食物)没有煮过或煮得不够的 (of food) uncooked or under cooked; raw: 夹～饭 half cooked rice | ～吃瓜要洗净。Melons must be washed clean before eating raw. ❸ 没有进一步加工或炼过的 unprocessed; unrefined; raw; crude: ～石膏 plaster stone | ～铁 pig iron ❹ 生疏 unfamiliar; rustic: ～人 stranger | ～字 new word | 小孩儿认～ (of a small child) be shy with strangers | 刚到这里,工作很～。I'm new here and the job is new to me too. ❺ 生硬;勉强 stiff; mechanical; rigid; unnatural: ～拉硬拽 drag one along kicking and screaming; drag sb. along against his will; stretch the meaning; make a farfetched comparison | ～搬硬套 copy or apply mechanically, follow blindly in disregard of specific conditions ❻ 很(用在少数表示感情、感觉的词的前面) [used before a few words indicating feeling or perception] very; much:～怕 very afraid|～恐 be afraid; fear|～疼 very painful

生[3] shēng ❶ 学习的人;学生 pupil; student:师～ teacher and student | 招～ enroll students|毕业～ graduate ❷〈旧时 *old*〉称读书人 intellectual, scholar:书～ intellectual, scholar ❸ 戏曲角色行当,扮演男子,有老生、小生、武生等区别 *sheng*, male role in Chinese traditional operas, including *laosheng* (role of an old or middle-aged man), *xiaosheng* (role of a young man), and *wusheng* (role of a warrior) ❹ 某些指人的名词后缀 [used as a suffix for certain nouns indicating occupations]:医～ doctor

生[4] shēng 某些副词的后缀,如'好生、怎生'等 [used as a suffix for certain adverbs, such as 好生 hǎoshēng and 怎生 zěnshēng] so; what

【生搬硬套】shēng bān yìng tào 不顾实际情况机械地搬用别人的方法、经验等 copy mechanically, disregarding specific conditions; apply or copy mechanically

【生变】shēng//biàn 发生变故 trouble arises; cause trouble:急则～ Haste gives rise to trouble.

【生病】shēng//bìng (人体或动物体)发生疾病 fall ill; get ill

【生财】shēngcái ❶ 指增加财富 make money; increase wealth:～有道 be good at making money; have the knack of making money ❷〈方 *fml.*〉指商店所用的家具杂物 furniture and miscellaneous goods used in shops

【生财有道】shēng cái yǒu dào 很有发财的办法(多含贬义 usu. derog.) know how to make money; have the knack of making money

【生菜】shēngcài ❶ 一年生或二年生草本植物,莴苣的变种。叶子狭长,花黄色。叶子可做蔬菜。romaine lettuce (*Lactuca sativa* var. *Capitata*); annual or biennial plant with edible long leaves and yellow flower ❷ 这种植物的叶子 lettuce leaves

【生产】shēngchǎn ❶ 人们使用工具来创造各种生产资料和生活资料 produce; manufacture; (of people) use tools to create means of production and subsistence:工业～ industrial production|发展～ develop production|～出更好的产品 produce still better products ❷ 生孩子 give birth to a child

【生产方式】shēngchǎn fāngshì 人们取得物质资料的方式,包括生产力和生产关系两个方面。生产方式决定社会的性质。mode of production; obtaining material goods by productive forces and production relations. The mode of production determines the nature of a society.

【生产工具】shēngchǎn gōngjù 人在生产过程中用来改变劳动对象的器具,如机器、农具、仪器等等。生产工具的发展水平标志着生产力发展的水平。tool of production; implement used by people to change the subject of labour in the course of production, such as machines, farm tools, instruments, etc. The level of development of tools of production marks the level of development of the productive force.

【生产关系】shēngchǎn guānxì 人们在物质资料的生产过程中形成的社会关系。它包括生产资料所有制的形式,人们在生产中的地位和相互关系,产品分配的形式。其中起决定作用的是生产资料所有制的形式。relations of production; production relations; social relations formed in the course of the production of material goods, including ownership of the means of production, the status of the people and their mutual relations in the course of production, and the form of product distribution; of all these it is ownership of the means of production that plays the deciding role

【生产过剩】shēngchǎn guòshèng 指商品因社会购买力不足,找不到销路而造成的剩余现象。它是资本主义经济危机的基本特征。overproduction; surplus goods caused by a shortage of social purchasing power and poor market, which is a basic feature of the capitalist economic crisis

【生产基金】shēngchǎn jījīn 企业所拥有的、处在生产领域中的那部分基金 production funds; funds owned by an enterprise and used for production

【生产力】shēngchǎnlì 具有劳动能力的人,跟生产资料(生产工具和劳动对象)相结合而构成的征服、改造自然的能力。人是生产力中具有决定性的因素。生产力是生产中最活跃最革命的要素。生产力的发展水平标志着人类征服自然界的程度。productive force; ability acquired by the working people in combination with means of production (production tools and subject of labour) to conquer and transform nature. Man is the decisive factor in the productive force, the most active and most revolutionary element in production. The level of development of the productive force marks the degree of man's conquest of nature

【生产率】shēngchǎnlǜ ❶ ☞ 劳动生产率 láodòng shēngchǎnlǜ on p. 1154 ❷ 生产设备在生产过程中的效率 efficiency of production equipment in the course of production

【生产线】shēngchǎnxiàn 指工业企业内部为生产某种产品设计的从材料投入到产品制成的连贯的工序,也指完成这些工序的整套设备 production line; continuous process from the feeding of materials to the finished product; complete set of equipment needed for a production line:电视机～ TV set production line

【生产资料】shēngchǎn zīliào 劳动资料和劳动对象的总和。是人们从事物质资料生产时所必需的物质条件。means of production; sum to-

S

tal of capital goods and the subject of labour, which is a necessary material condition for the production of material goods; also 生产手段 shēn chǎn shǒuduàn; ☞ 劳动资料 láodòng zīliào on p. 1154 and 劳动对象 láodòng duìxiàng on p. 1153

【生辰】shēngchén same as 生日 shēng·ri

【生成】shēngchéng ❶（自然现象）形成；经过化学反应而形成；产生 come or bring into being; generate; produce：台风的～必须具有一定的环境。The occurrence of typhoon calls for a certain environment.｜锌加硫酸～硫酸锌和氢气。Zinc and sulphuric acid are put together to produce zinc sulphate and hydrogen. ❷ 生就 born with, gifted with：他～一张巧嘴。He was born with a glib tongue.

【生齿】shēngchǐ〈书 *fml.*〉长出乳齿，古时把已经长出乳齿的男女登入户籍，后来借指人口、家口 growing of milk teeth. In ancient times, babies were registered only after they had developed milk teeth. The word was later used to refer to population or membership in a family：～日繁。The population is growing with each passing day.

S

【生词】shēngcí 不认识的或不懂得的词 new and unfamiliar words and phrases; new words

【生凑】shēngcòu 勉强凑成 manage to put things together; do sth. with difficulty

【生存】shēngcún 保存生命（跟'死亡'相对 as opposed to 'death'）subsist; exist; live：没有空气和水，人就无法～。Man cannot live without air and water.

【生存斗争】shēngcún dòuzhēng 达尔文学说中的一个概念，认为每个生物在生活过程中必须跟自然环境作斗争、跟同一物种的生物作斗争、跟不同物种的生物作斗争，其中以同一物种的生物之间的斗争最为剧烈；并认为在自然界里，各种生物彼此相互影响、相互制约、相互依存 struggle for survival; concept in the Darwinian theory which holds that all species of plants and animals must struggle with the natural environment, the plants and animals of their own kinds and of other species, but the struggle with the plants and animals of the same species is the fiercest, and that all plants and animals influence each other, condition each other and depend on each other

【生地】[1] shēngdì ❶ 陌生的地方 strange place; unfamiliar place ❷ 生荒 virgin soil; uncultivated land

【生地】[2] shēngdì 药名，未经蒸制的地黄的根，鲜的淡黄色，干的灰褐色 dried rhizome of rehmannia (*Rehmannia glutinosa*) that is yellowish when fresh and greyish-brown when dried; also 生地黄 shēngdìhuáng

【生动】shēngdòng 具有活力能感动人的 lively; vivid：～活泼 lively; vivid and vigorous｜～的语言 graphic language

【生发】shēngfā 滋生；发展 develop; grow：万年青默默地～着根须，把嫩芽变成宽大的绿叶。The evergreen is striking its root silently and has turned its buds into broad green leaves.

【生法】shēng//fǎ〈方 *dial.*〉设法 think of a way; try; do what one can

【生番】shēngfān〈旧时 *old*〉对开化较晚的民族的蔑称 aboriginal savage tribe; contemptuous term for ethnic peoples who are late in attaining civilization

【生分】shēng·fen（感情）疏远 estranged; not as close as before：都是自家人，一客气倒显得～了。We are family, and we don't feel close if we stand on ceremony.

【生俘】shēngfú 生擒；活捉（敌人）capture an enemy alive

【生父】shēngfù 生身父亲 biological father

【生根】shēng//gēn〈比喻 *fig.*〉事物建立起牢固的基础 take root; strike root：在群众中～ take root among the masses

【生光】shēngguāng 日食和月食的过程中，月亮阴影和太阳圆面或地球阴影和月亮圆面第二次内切时的位置关系，也指发生这种位置关系的时刻。生光发生在食甚之后。third contact (of a total solar or lunar eclipse); relationship of positions of the sun, moon and earth when the shadow of the moon cuts into the round surface of the sun or the shadow of the earth cuts into the round surface of the moon for the second time during a solar eclipse and a lunar eclipse; ☞ 食相 shíxiàng on p. 1746

【生花之笔】shēng huā zhī bǐ 传说李白少年时梦见笔头生花，从此才华横溢，名闻天下（见于五代王仁裕《开元天宝遗事》）According to *Anecdotes of Kaiyuan and Tianbao Reigns* by Wang Renyu of the Five Dynasties, Li Bai, a poet in the Tang Dynasty, saw a flower at the tip of his writing brush in a dream in his childhood and showed brilliant writing since then and became well known throughout the country;〈比喻 *fig.*〉杰出的写作才能 virtuosity; brilliant pen; brilliant style of writing

【生还】shēnghuán 脱离危险，活着回来 emerge unscathed; come back alive; survive：这次空难，旅客和机组人员无一～。None of the passengers and crew members survived this air crash.

【生荒地】shēnghuāngdì 从未耕种过的土地 virgin soil; uncultivated land; also 生地 shēngdì or 生荒 shēnghuāng

【生活】shēnghuó ❶ 人或生物为了生存和发展而进行的各种活动 life; activities of a person or living thing for survival and development：政治～ political life｜日常～ daily life; work-a-day life; day-to-day life｜观察蜜蜂和蚂蚁的～ observe the life of the bees and ants ❷ 进

行各种活动 live; carry out activities: 跟群众～在一起 live with the masses ❸ 生存 survive; exist; subsist: 一个人脱离了社会就不能～下去。One cannot survive in isolation of society. ❹ 衣、食、住、行等方面的情况 livelihood; clothes, food, housing and travelling: 人民的～不断提高。The livelihood of the people has improved steadily. ❺〈方 *dial.*〉活儿(主要指工业、农业、手工业方面的 oft. referring to industrial, agricultural, and handicraft work) work; jobs: 做～ work; do one's work; do manual work|～忙 busy with one's work

【生活费】shēnghuófèi 维持生活的费用 living expenses; cost of living; expenses to support oneself

【生活资料】shēnghuó zīliào 供人们生活需要的那部分产品,如食品、衣服、住房等 means of subsistence; means of livelihood; consumer products such as foods, clothes, housing, etc.; also 消费资料 xiāofèi zīliào

【生火】shēng//huǒ 把柴、煤等燃起来 make a fire; light a fire; burn firewood, coal, etc.: ～做饭 make a fire for cooking|～取暖 make a fire for heating

【生火】shēnghuǒ 轮船上烧锅炉的工人 stoker; person who tends a steam boiler on a ship

【生机】shēngjī ❶ 生存的机会 lease of life: 一线～ a slim chance of survival; a gleam of hope ❷ 生命力; 活力 life; vitality: ～勃勃 vibrate with life; imbued with vitality; full of vigour|春风吹过,大地上充满了～。The land is full of life in the spring breeze.

【生计】shēngjì 维护生活的办法; 生活④ means of livelihood; livelihood: 家庭～ the livelihood of a family|另谋～try to find some other means of livelihood

【生就】shēngjiù 生来就有 be born with; be gifted with: 他～一张能说会道的嘴。He was born with a glib tongue. *or* He has the gift of the gab.

【生角】shēngjué (～儿 shéngjuér) 生[3]③,通常专指老生 usu. referring to *laosheng*, the role of an old or middle-aged man in Chinese opera

【生客】shēngkè 不认识的客人 unfamiliar guest; stranger

【生恐】shēngkǒng 很怕; 唯恐 be very much afraid; fear greatly: 他～掉队,在后面紧追。Afraid of falling behind, he was trying hard to keep up.

【生圹】shēngkuàng 生前营造的墓穴; 寿穴 tomb built before one's death

【生拉硬拽】shēng lā yìng zhuài ❶ 形容用力拉扯,强使人听从自己 drag sb. along against his will ❷〈比喻 *fig.*〉牵强附会 stretch the meaning; make a farfetched comparison; also 生拉硬扯 shēng lā yìng chě

【生来】shēnglái 从小时候起 from birth; since childhood: 他～就这脾气。He has got this temperament since childhood.|这孩子身体～就结实。The child was born strong.

【生老病死】shēng lǎo bìng sǐ 佛教认为'生、老、病、死'是人生的四苦,今泛指生活中生育、养老、医疗、殡葬等事 birth, old age, sickness and death. Buddhism holds that birth, old age, sickness and death are the four sufferings of one's life. The term refers generally to maternal care, care for the old, medical service and funeral service.

【生冷】shēnglěng 指生的和冷的食物 raw or cold food: 病人忌～。Patients should avoid eating anything raw or cold.

【生离死别】shēng lí sǐ bié 很难再见面的离别或永久的离别 never to meet again; part for ever

【生理】shēnglǐ 机体的生命活动和体内各器官的机能 physiology; (of living organisms) activities in life and functions of organs: ～学 physiology|～特点 special physiological qualities

【生理学】shēnglǐxué 研究生物的功能的学科,包括人体生理学、动物生理学、植物生理学等 physiology; branch of biology dealing with the functions and vital processes of living organisms or their parts and organs, including human physiology, animal physiology, plant physiology, etc.

【生理盐水】shēnglǐ yánshuǐ 生理学实验或临床上常用的渗透压与动物或人体血浆的渗透压相等的氯化钠溶液 physiological saline; normal saline; sodium chloride solution that has the same osmotic pressure as that found in animal or human blood plasma

【生力军】shēnglìjūn ❶ 新加入作战具有强大作战能力的军队 fresh and combat-worthy troops ❷〈比喻 *fig.*〉新加入某种工作或活动能起积极作用的人员 fresh blood; new force: 青年人是祖国建设的～。The young people are the new force in building the motherland.

【生料】shēngliào 未经加工,不能直接制成产品的原料 raw materials; unprocessed materials

【生灵】shēnglíng ❶〈书 *fml.*〉指百姓 people: ～涂炭 people plunged into an abyss of misery ❷ 指有生命的东西 living thing; life: 草木～ grass and trees|这里有云雀、黄鹂、画眉,都是些可爱的小～。There are skylarks, orioles and thrushes here. They are all lovely little creatures.

【生灵涂炭】shēnglíng tútàn 形容政治混乱时期人民处在极端困苦的环境中 people plunged into an abyss of misery during political chaos

【生龙活虎】shēng lóng huó hǔ 形容很有生气和活力 doughty as a dragon and lively as a tiger; brim (or burst) with energy; full of vim and vigour

【生路】shēnglù 维护生活或生存的途径 means of livelihood; way out:另谋～ try to find another job; look for a new means of livelihood|从包围中杀出一条～ fight one's way out of enemy encirclement

【生猛】shēngměng〈方 *dial.*〉指活蹦乱跳的(鱼虾等) live fishes:～海鲜 fresh seafood

【生米煮成熟饭】shēng mǐ zhǔ chéng shú fàn〈比喻 *fig.*〉事情已经做成,不能再改变(多含无可奈何之意 oft. referring to a situation where one has no alternative) The rice is cooked. *or* What's done can not be undone.

【生命】shēngmìng 生物体所具有的活动能力,生命是蛋白质存在的一种形式 life:牺牲～ sacrifice one's life|～不息,工作不止 work unceasingly until one stops breathing; work as long as one can breathe; go on working till one breathes one's last breath◇学习古人语言中有～的东西 learn whatever is vital in the classical Chinese language

【生命力】shēngmìnglì 指事物具有的生存、发展的能力 life-force; vitality:新生事物具有强大的～。New things have great vitality.

S

【生命线】shēngmìngxiàn〈比喻 *fig.*〉保证生存和发展的最根本的因素 lifeline; lifeblood

【生母】shēngmǔ 生身母亲 biological mother

【生怕】shēngpà 生恐;很怕 be afraid of; fear:我们在泥泞的山路上小心地走着,～滑倒了。We walked on the muddy mountain path carefully for fear of falling.

【生僻】shēngpì 不常见的;不熟悉的(词语、文字、书籍等)(of words, expressions, books, etc.) uncommon; rare:～字 rarely used words|～的典故 obscure allusions

【生平】shēngpíng ❶ 一个人生活的整个过程;一辈子 all one's life:～事迹 one's life story ❷ 有生以来;平生 ever since one's birth:这幅画是他～最满意的作品。This painting is the most satisfactory work in his life.

【生漆】shēngqī 漆树树干的表皮割开后流出的树脂,乳白色,跟空气接触后逐渐变成黑色。用做涂料,也是制油漆的原料。raw lacquer; milk-white latex obtained from the lacquer trees; also 大漆 dàqī

【生气】shēng//qì 因不合心意而不愉快 take offence; get angry:孩子考试成绩很差,妈妈非常～。The mother got mad at the bad marks her child had got in the exams.|快去认个错吧,他还在生你的气呢! Go and admit your fault. He is still angry with you.

【生气】shēngqì 生命力;活力 vim; vitality:～勃勃 dynamic; vigorous; full of vitality|青年是最有～的。Young people are the most active and dynamic.

【生前】shēngqián 指死者还活着的时候 before one's death; during one's lifetime:～友好 friends of the deceased

【生擒】shēngqín 活捉(敌人、盗匪等) capture alive (enemy soldiers, bandits, etc.):～活捉 capture alive; take prisoners

【生趣】shēngqù 生活的情趣 joy of life; pleasures of life:～盎然 full of life

【生人】shēng//rén (人)出生 be born:他是1949年～。He was born in 1949.

【生人】shēngrén 不认识的人 stranger:孩子怕见～。The child was shy with strangers.

【生日】shēng·ri (人)出生的日子。也指每年满周岁的那一天 birthday ◇七月一日是中国共产党的～。July 1st is the birthday of the Communist Party of China.

【生色】shēngsè 增添光彩 add colour to; add lustre to; give added significance to:他的精彩表演使晚会～不少。His superb performance made the evening party more enjoyable.

【生涩】shēngsè (言词、文字等)不流畅,不纯熟 (of language) jerky; choppy; not smooth

【生杀予夺】shēng shā yǔ duó 指统治者掌握生死、赏罚的大权 (of the rulers) hold power over sb.'s life and property

【生身】shēngshēn 生育自己的 give birth to:～父母 biological parents

【生生世世】shēngshēngshìshì〈佛教 *Budd.*〉认为众生不断轮回,'生生世世'指每次生在世上的时候,就是每一辈子的意思。现在借指一代又一代;辈辈。(of the multitude) transmigrate continuously; generation after generation

【生石膏】shēngshígāo 石膏 plaster stone

【生石灰】shēngshíhuī 无机化合物,化学式 CaO。白色无定形固体,由石灰石煅烧而成。遇水碎裂,并放出大量的热。是常用的建筑材料,也用做杀虫剂和杀菌剂。quick lime (CaO); inorganic compound in the form of a white amorphous solid substance, obtained by roasting limestone. It breaks with water and emits a lot of heat, and is used as a common building material, and also as pesticide and germicide; also 煅石灰 duànshíhuī

【生事】shēng//shì 制造纠纷;惹事 make trouble; create a disturbance:造谣～ spread a rumour to stir up trouble|这人脾气很坏,容易～。He has a bad temper and often makes trouble.

【生手】shēngshǒu 新做某项工作,对工作还不熟悉的人 sb. new to a job; green hand

【生疏】shēngshū ❶ 没有接触过或很少接触的 not familiar:人地～ be a complete stranger; be unfamiliar with a place and have few friends there|业务～ have not much professional knowledge or training ❷ 因长期不用而不熟练 out of practice; rusty:技艺～ be impaired in skill by inaction or neglect|手法～ not feel at home with one's craft ❸ 疏远;不亲近 (of a relationship) getting distant:感情～ feel not as close as before

【生水】shēngshuǐ 没有烧开过的水 unboiled water

【生丝】shēngsī 用茧缫制成的丝，是丝纺工业的原料 raw silk; silk reeled from the cocoon, with the sericin still in it, used as a raw material in the textile industry

【生死】shēngsǐ ❶ 生存和死亡 life and death: ～关头 juncture when one's life is at stake; when one's fate hangs in the balance; critical juncture | ～与共 share a common destiny; go through thick and thin together | 同～，共患难 go through fire and water together; share difficulties and hardships ❷ 同生共死。形容情谊极深。share weal and woe, referring to profound friendship: ～弟兄 sworn friends | ～之交 friends that are ready to die for each other; people who swear eternal friendship; fast friends; sworn friends

【生死存亡】shēng sǐ cún wáng 或者生存，或者死亡。形容事关重大或形势极端危急。life or death, survival or extinction; matter of vital importance; critical situation

【生死攸关】shēng sǐ yōu guān 关系到人的生存和死亡 of life and death; of vital importance (攸 *you*: 所 about)

【生死与共】shēng sǐ yǔ gòng 生一起生，死一起死。形容情谊很深。share a common destiny; go through thick and thin together; live and die together; showing profound friendship

【生态】shēngtài 指生物在一定的自然环境下生存和发展的状态。也指生物的生理特性和生活习性。ecology; existence and development of living organisms under certain natural environments; also special physiological qualities and habits of living organisms: 保持～平衡 maintain ecological balance

【生态平衡】shēngtài pínghéng 一个生物群落及其生态系统之中，各种对立因素互相制约而达到的相对稳定的平衡。如麻雀吃果树害虫，同时它的数量又受到天敌（如猛禽等）的控制，三者的数量在自然界中达到一定的平衡，要是为了防止麻雀偷吃谷物而滥杀，就会破坏这种平衡，造成果树害虫猖獗。ecological balance; relative stability among antagonistic elements that restrict each other in a colony of living organisms and ecological system. For example, sparrow feeds on the destructive insects of fruit trees, but at the same time its population is controlled by its natural enemy (as birds of prey). The populations of the three maintain a certain balance in the natural world, and the balance is lost if sparrows are killed wantonly just to prevent them from eating grains, and as a result, fruit tree pests will go rampant.

【生态学】shēngtàixué 研究生物之间及生物与非生物环境之间相互关系的学科 ecology; branch of biology that deals with the relations between living organisms and their environment

【生铁】shēngtiě ☞ 铸铁 zhùtiě on p. 2513

【生土】shēngtǔ 未经熟化的土壤，不适于耕作 immature soil, not fit for cultivation

【生吞活剥】shēng tūn huó bō 〈比喻 *fig.*〉生硬地接受或机械地搬用（别人的理论、经验、方法等）swallow sth. raw and whole; accept sb.'s theory, experience, methods, etc. uncritically or copy them mechanically

【生物】shēngwù 自然界中由活质构成并具有生长、发育、繁殖等能力的物体。生物能通过新陈代谢作用跟周围环境进行物质交换。动物、植物、微生物都是生物。living thing; living being; organism; substance in the natural world consisting of bioplasms and having the ability to grow, develop and reproduce. An organism has material exchange with the surrounding environments through metabolism. Animals, plants and microbes are all organisms.

【生物电流】shēngwù diànliú 生物体的神经活动和肌肉运动等都伴随着很微弱的电流和电位变化，这种电流叫生物电流，如皮肤电流和心脏电流 bio-electric current; very weak electric current and potential change that accompany the nervous activities and muscular motion of an organism, such as skin current and heart current

【生物防治】shēnwù fángzhì 利用某些生物来防治对人类有害的生物的方法。如用鸭群消灭蝗蝻和稻田害虫，用寄生蜂消灭螟虫，用细菌消灭田鼠等。biological control; use of certain organisms to prevent and control organisms that are harmful to man, such as the use of flocks of ducks to eliminate the nymphs of locusts and other rice field pests, the use of parasitic bees to destroy snout moth's larva, and the use of bacteria to wipe out field rats

【生物圈】shēngwùquān 生物活动的范围和生物本身的总称。生物活动的范围包括地球大气圈的下层、岩石圈的上层和整个水圈。biosphere; general term for living organisms and their sphere of activities, including lower atmosphere, the upper layer of the lithosphere, and the whole hydrosphere

【生物武器】shēngwù wǔqì 利用生物战剂大规模伤害人和动植物的一种武器，包括生物战剂和施放生物战剂的各种武器弹药。国际公约禁止在战争中使用生物武器。biological weapon; weapon using biological agents against humans, animals and plants, including biological agents and weapons and ammunition with which to spread these agents. The use of biological weapons in war is prohibited under the International Convention. also 细菌武器 xìjūn wǔqì

【生物学】shēngwùxué 研究生物的结构、功能、发生和发展规律的学科，包括动物学、植物学、微生物学、古生物学等 biology; science that deals with the origin, history, physical characteristics, life processes, habits, etc., of plants and animals; branch of science that deals with the structure, functions, occurrence and development of animals and plants, including botany, zoology, microbiology and palaeontology

【生物钟】shēngwùzhōng 生物生命活动的周期性节律。这种节律,经过长时期的适应,与自然界的节律(如昼夜变化、四季变化)相一致。植物在每年的一定季节开花、结果,候鸟在每年的一定时间迁徙,就是生物钟的表现。biological clock; biochronometer; living clock; periodic rhythm of the life of organisms, which coincides with the natural cycles, as of days, nights, seasons. The blossoming and fruiting of plants and the migration of migratory birds during fixed periods of the year are expressions of the biological clock.

【生息】shēng//xī 取得利息 bear interest

【生息】shēngxī ❶ 生活;生存 live; exist:我们的祖先曾在这块土地上劳动～过。Our forefathers laboured, lived and multiplied on this land. ❷〈书 *fml.*〉繁殖(人口) propagate; multiply; procreate:休养～ recuperate and multiply ❸〈书 *fml.*〉使生长 cause to grow:～力量 build up one's strength

S

【生相】shēngxiàng 相貌;长相 looks; features; appearance

【生橡胶】shēngxiàngjiāo 未经硫化的橡胶。多指胶乳经过初步加工而成的半透明胶片。raw rubber; caoutchouc; unvulcanized rubber; crude, natural rubber obtained from latex; also 生胶 shēngjiāo

【生肖】shēngxiào 代表十二地支而用来记人的出生年的十二种动物,即鼠、牛、虎、兔、龙、蛇、马、羊、猴、鸡、狗、猪。如子年生的人属鼠,丑年生的人属牛等。The 12 symbolic animals representing the 12 Earthly Branches and associated with a 12-year cycle, used to denote the year of a person's birth (the 12 animals are: rat, ox, tiger, hare, dragon, snake, horse, sheep, monkey, cock, dog, and hog), such as a person born in the year of rat or in the year of ox; also 属相 shǔ·xiang

【生效】shēng//xiào 发生效力 go into effect; take effect; become effective; come into force:条约自签订之日起～。The treaty comes into force as of the date of signature.

【生性】shēngxìng 从小养成的性格、习惯 natural disposition:～活泼 have a lively disposition

【生涯】shēngyá 指从事某种活动或职业的生活 career; profession:教书～ work as a teacher; teaching career|舞台～ a stage career

【生养】shēngyǎng 生育抚养 give birth to and bring up; bear (children) and raise

【生药】shēngyào 直接从植物体或动物体采来,经过干燥加工而未精练的药物。通常所说的生药多指植物性的,如甘草、麻黄等。crude drug; dried medicinal herbs; drugs collected directly from the bodies of plants and animals, dried but not refined; crude drugs are generally herbaceous, such as licorice root and Chinese ephedra

【生业】shēngyè 赖以生活的职业 occupation; business:各安～ each being content with his occupation|不事～ have no job; be jobless; be idle

【生意】shēngyì 富有生命力的气象;生机 ② tendency to grow; life and vitality:～盎然 full of life|百花盛开,百鸟齐鸣,大地上一片蓬勃的～。With flowers in full bloom and birds singing, the land is full of life and vitality.

【生意】shēng·yi ❶ 指商业经营;买卖 business; trade:做～ do business|～兴隆。Trade is brisk. *or* Business is booming. ❷〈方 *dial.*〉指职业 job; occupation; work:停～(解雇) sack; fire; dismiss

【生意经】shēng·yijīng 做生意的方法或门路 business acumen; knack of doing business; shrewd business sense

【生硬】shēngyìng ❶ 勉强做的;不自然;不熟练 (of writing) awkward; crude:这几个字用得很～。These words are not properly used. ❷ 不柔和;不细致 stiff; rigid; harsh:态度～ be stiff in manner; take a rigid attitude|作风～ rigid style of work

【生油】[1] shēngyóu 没有熬过的油 unboiled oil

【生油】[2] shēngyóu〈方 *dial.*〉花生油 peanut oil

【生育】shēngyù 生孩子 give birth to; bear:计划～ family planning

【生员】shēngyuán 明清两代称通过最低一级考试得以在府、县学读书的人,生员有应乡试的资格 people who passed the imperial examination at the county level in the Ming and Qing dynasties, and were thus qualified for the imperial examination at the provincial level; 通称 generally known as 秀才 xiù·cai

【生源】shēngyuán 学生的来源(多就招生而言) source of students; source of school enrolment:～不足。There are not enough applicants for the school.

【生造】shēngzào 凭空制造(词语等)(words, expressions, etc.) coin:～词 coinage

【生长】shēngzhǎng ❶ 生物体在一定的生活条件下,体积和重量逐渐增加。生长是发育的一个特性。grow; increase of the size and weight of a living organism under given living conditions, which is a specific property of development:～期 growth or growing period ❷ 出生和成长;产生和增长 be born and grow:他～在北京。He was born and grew up in Beijing.|新生力量不断～。Newly forces have kept growing.

【生殖】shēngzhí 生物产生幼小的个体以繁殖后代。分有性生殖和无性生殖两种。生殖是生命的基本特征之一。reproduction; process of reproducing new individuals by animals or plants; sexual reproduction or asexual reproduction. Reproduction is one of the basic characteristics of life.

【生殖洄游】shēngzhí huíyóu 某些鱼类在产卵季节,由生活的地区游到产卵的地区去,产卵后死亡或仍回到原来的地区 breeding migration (of some fish); some fishes migrate from their living zones to their spawning zones during the spawning season, and die or migrate back to the living zones after spawning

【生殖器】shēngzhíqì 生物体产生生殖细胞用来繁殖后代的器官。高等植物的生殖器是花(包括雄蕊和雌蕊)。人和高等动物的生殖器包括雄性的精囊、输精管、睾丸、阴茎等,雌性的卵巢、输卵管、子宫、阴道等。人和高等动物的生殖器也叫性器官。reproductive organ; genitals; organ of an organism to produce cells for propagation of offspring. The reproductive organs of the higher plants are flowers (including both stamen and pistil). The reproductive organs of humans and other vertebrates include the seminal vesicle, spermatic duct, testis and penis of the male, and ovary, oviduct, womb and vagina of the female. The reproductive organs of the humans and other vertebrates are also call sexual organs.

【生殖腺】shēngzhíxiàn 人或动物体产生精子或卵子的腺体。雄性的生殖腺是睾丸,雌性的生殖腺是卵巢。gonad; gland in humans or animals that produces reproductive cells; the male gonad is the testis and the female one is the ovary; also 性腺 xìngxiàn

【生猪】shēngzhū 活猪(多用于商业 oft. used as a business term) live pig; pig; hog; pork on the hoof

【生字】shēngzì 不认识的字 words or characters new to sb.; new words or Chinese characters

声(聲) shēng ❶(～儿 shēngr)声音 sound; voice:雨～ sound of rain|小～儿说话 speak in a soft voice ❷〈量词 *classifier*〉表示声音发出的次数 [used to indicate the number of sounds]:喊了两～ call someone twice ❸ 发出声音;宣布;陈述 make a sound; announce; state:～明 state; declare|不～不响 keep quiet; keep silence; remain silent|～东击西 make a feint to the east and attack in the west ❹ 名声 reputation:～誉 reputation; fame|～望 popularity; prestige; reputation ❺ 声母 initial consonant of a Chinese syllable:双～叠韵 alliteration and vowel rhyme ❻ 字调 tone:平～ level tone|四～ four tones in classic and modern Chinese

【声辩】shēngbiàn 公开辩白;辩解 argue; justify oneself; explain away:不容～ not allow others to present their arguments|受到指责,他也不为自己～一句。He was criticised, but did not try to argue for himself.

【声波】shēngbō 能引起听觉的机械波。频率在20—20,000赫兹之间,一般在空气中传播,也可在液体或固体中传播。sound wave; acoustic wave; mechanical wave that makes sth. audible to the ear, at a frequency of between 20-20,000 Hz, usu. transmitted in the air, or through a liquid or solid

【声部】shēngbù 包含两个或两个以上同时进行的不同旋律的声乐曲或器乐曲,称为多声部音乐,其中的每一个旋律叫做一个声部。如二重唱包含两个声部,三重唱包含三个声部。part (in concert music). Vocal music or instrumental music played with two or more than two different melodies simultaneously is called multi-part music; with each melody known as a part; for example, a duet includes two parts, and a trio three parts.

【声场】shēngchǎng 媒质中存在着声波的空间范围 sound field; acoustic field

【声称】shēngchēng 声言 profess; claim; assert:他～自己与这件事无关。He asserted that he had nothing to do with this matter.

【声带】shēngdài ❶ 发音器官的主要部分,是两片带状的纤维质薄膜,附在喉部的勺状软骨上,肺内呼出气流振动声带,即发出声音 vocal cords; main part of the vocal organ consisting of two thin fibrous membranes attached to the cartilage spatulata of the larynx; producing sounds when air breathes out from the lungs to vibrate the vocal cords; (图见 ☞ figure for 人的喉 rén·dehóu on p.808) ❷ 电影胶片一侧记录着声音的部分。也指用光学方法记下的声音的纹理。soundtrack (on a film); area along one side of a film carrying its sound portion in the form of grains recorded by an optical method

【声调】shēngdiào ❶ 音调 tone; note ❷ 字调 tone of Chinese characters

【声东击西】shēng dōng jī xī 为了迷惑敌人,表面上宣扬要攻打这一边,其实是攻打另一边(语本《通典·兵典六》:'声言击东,其实击西') in order to confuse the enemy, superficially profess to attack this side, but actually attack the other side; make a feint to the east and attack in the west (*Cyclopaedia of Institutions·Military Institutions* (*VI*): 'Profess to attack in the east, but actually attack in the west.')

【声控】shēngkòng 用声音控制 sound-activated; sound-controlled:这里的部分喷泉为～,可以随着音乐频率的变化喷出不同形状的水花。Some of the fountains here are controlled by sound. They can jet different shapes and forms of water splashes with changes in the frequency of musical accompaniment.

【声口】shēngkǒu 〈方 *dial.*〉❶ 指说话的口音、语调 accent：听他的～，不是北方人。Judging from his accent, he is not a northerner. ❷ 口气；口吻 tone; vein：理直气壮的～ in a bold and confident tone

【声浪】shēnglàng ❶ 声波的旧称 old name for 声波 shēngbō ❷ 指许多人呼喊的声音 shouts of many people; many voices; clamour：喝彩的～一阵高过一阵。Waves of applause burst one after another.

【声泪俱下】shēng lèi jù xià 边诉说，边哭泣。形容极其悲恸。shedding tears while speaking; in a tearful voice：慷慨陈词，～。Tears streamed down one's cheeks while presenting one's views vehemently.

【声门】shēngmén 两片声带当中的开口。声带静止不发音时，声门呈 V 字形。glottis; opening between the vocal cords in the larynx. The glottis is V-shaped when the vocal cords do not make sounds.

【声名】shēngmíng 名声 reputation：～狼藉（形容名声极坏）have a bad name; be notorious; be utterly discredited | ～鹊起（形容名声迅速提高）rapid rise in fame

【声明】shēngmíng ❶ 公开表示态度或说明真相 state; declare; announce：郑重～ state solemnly ❷ 声明的文告 statement; declaration：发表联合～ issue a joint statement

【声母】shēngmǔ 汉语字音可以分成声母、韵母、字调三部分。一个字起头的音叫声母，其余的音叫韵母，字音的高低升降叫字调。例如'报(bào)告(gào)、丰(fēng)收(shōu)'的 b, g, f, sh 是声母；'报'和'告'的 ao，'丰'的 eng，'收'的 ou 是韵母；'报'和'告'的字调都是去声，'丰'和'收'都是阴平。大部分字的声母是辅音声母，只有小部分的字拿元音起头（就是直接拿韵母起头），它的声母叫'零声母'，如'爱(ài)'、'鹅(é)'、'藕(ǒu)'等字。initial consonant of a syllable; the pronunciation of a Chinese character consists of three parts: the initial consonant of a syllable, a vowel and a tone. The initial sound of a syllable is called initial consonant, the rest is vowel, and the rise and fall of a sound is called tone. For example, the b, g, f, sh in bàogào and fēngshōu are all initial consonants (声母) while ao in bào and gào, eng in fēng and ou in shōu are vowels (韵母). Both bào and gào are in a falling tones (去声), and fēng and shōu are in a high and level tone (阴平). Most of the initials of the syllables are consonants, and only a small number of characters are initiated by vowels, which are called 'zero initials' (零声母), such as ai for 爱(ài), e for 鹅(é) and ou for 藕(ǒu)

【声呐】shēngnà 利用超声波在水中的传播和反射来进行导航和测距的技术或设备 sonar (sound navigation and ranging); apparatus that transmits high-frequency sound waves through water and registers the vibrations reflected from an object, used in navigation, measuring distances and finding submarines

【声旁】shēngpáng ☞ 形声 xíngshēng on p. 2147

【声频】shēngpín 音频 acoustic frequency

【声谱】shēngpǔ 描绘声音成分（频率、幅度等）的图表或记录 sound spectrum; graphs or records depicting the frequencies and range of the sounds

【声气】shēngqì ❶ 消息 information：互通～ exchange information; keep in contact with each other ❷ 〈方 *dial.*〉说话时的语气、声音 voice; tone：听他说话的～像是生了气。Judging from his voice, he seemed to have got angry.

【声腔】shēngqiāng 许多剧种所共有的、成系统的腔调，如昆腔、高腔、梆子腔、皮黄等 opera tunes, as *kun* tune, *gao* (high-pitched) tune, *bangzi* tune, *pihuang* tune, etc.

【声情】shēngqíng 声音和感情 voice and expression：～并茂 remarkable in voice and expression

【声请】shēngqǐng 申请 make a formal request

【声色】[1] shēngsè 说话时的声音和脸色 voice and countenance：～俱厉 be stern in voice and countenance | 不动～ keep calm; maintain one's composure

【声色】[2] shēngsè ❶ 指诗文等艺术表现出的格调、色彩 style, colour：他的《空城计》演唱得别具～。He performed with a style of his own in *The Strategy of the Unguarded City*. ❷ 指生气和活力 vigour; spirit; vitality：这群青年人的到来给县城增添了不少～。The arrival of these young people has added much spirit to the county town.

【声色】[3] shēngsè 〈书 *fml.*〉指歌舞和女色 music and women; sensual pleasures：不近～ keep off sensual pleasures | ～犬马（指纵情淫乐的生活）music and women; keeping dogs and riding horses; sensual pleasures

【声势】shēngshì 声威和气势 prestige and power; fame and influence; impetus; momentum：虚张～ make a false show of strength | ～浩大 great in strength and impetus; powerful and dynamic

【声嘶力竭】shēng sī lì jié 嗓子喊哑，力气用尽。形容拼命叫喊、呼号。shout or cry oneself hoarse; be exhausted from shouting

【声速】shēngsù 声波传播的速度。不同的介质中声速不同，在 15℃ 的空气中每秒为 340 米。sonic speed; speed of sound, which varies from medium to medium, and measures 340 metres per second in the air at 15°C; also 音速 yīnsù

【声讨】shēngtǎo 公开谴责 denounce; condemn：愤怒～侵略者的暴行 indignantly denounce the crimes of the aggressors

【声望】shēngwàng 为众人所仰望的名声 popularity; prestige：社会～ popularity among the people|～很高 high prestige

【声威】shēngwēi ❶ 名声和威望 renown; prestige：～大震 gain great fame and high prestige ❷ 声势；威势 power; strength; momentum：摇旗呐喊，以助～。Waving flags and shouting battle cries to boost the morale

【声息】shēngxī ❶ 声音 sound; voice; noise(多用于否定 oft. in negative form)：院子里静悄悄的，没有一点～。Not a sound was heard in the quiet courtyard. ❷ 声气；消息 information; message：～相通 keep each other informed

【声响】shēngxiǎng 声音 sound; noise：山谷里洪水发出巨大的～。The flood made a deafening noise in the mountain valley.

【声学】shēngxué 研究声波的产生、传播、接收和作用等的学科 acoustics; branch of study dealing with the production, transmission, reception and function of sound waves

【声言】shēngyán 公开地用语言或文字表示 profess; claim; declare：他～不达目的，决不罢休。He declared that he would never give up until his purpose was achieved.

【声扬】shēngyáng 声张；宣扬 make public; reveal, disclose

【声音】shēngyīn 声波通过听觉所产生的印象 sound; voice：～大 high-pitched voice; big sound|他听见了敲门的～。He heard someone knocking at the door.◇报纸反映了群众的～。The newspapers reflected the voices of the masses.

【声誉】shēngyù 声望名誉 reputation; fame; prestige：有损～ harm one's reputation|～卓著 be famous; enjoy high reputation; be widely known

【声援】shēngyuán 公开发表言论支援 publicly express support for; support publicly

【声乐】shēngyuè 歌唱的音乐，可以有乐器伴奏(区别于'器乐'as compared with 'instrumental music') vocal music, sometimes accompanied by instruments

【声韵学】shēngyùnxué ☞ 音韵学 yīnyùnxué on p. 2287

【声张】shēngzhāng 把消息、事情等传出去 make public; disclose; reveal; spread (news, matters, etc.)：这个事不要～出去。Don't breathe a word about the matter. *or* Please keep quiet about this matter.

【声障】shēngzhàng 音障 sound or sonic barrier

狌 shēng 〈书 *fml.*〉 same as 鼪 shēng
☞ xīng on p. 2140

牲 shēng ❶ 家畜 livestock; domestic animal：～口 draught animal; beast of burden|～畜 livestock; domestic animal ❷〈古代 *arch.*〉祭神用的牛、羊、猪等 animal sacrifice; offering of an ox, sheep, pig, etc. as a sacrifice in ancient China：献～ offer an animal sacrifice

【牲畜】shēngchù 家畜 livestock; domestic animal：～家禽 domestic animal and fowl; livestock and poultry

【牲口】shēng·kou 用来帮助人做活的家畜，如牛、马、骡、驴等 draught animal; beast of burden; domestic animal that helps people with their work

胜 shēng ☞ 肽 tài on p. 1856
☞ shèng on p. 1723

笙 shēng 管乐器，常见的有大小数种，用若干根装有簧的竹管和一根吹气管装在一个锅形的座子上制成 *sheng*; wind instrument made of several bamboo tubes equipped with reeds and a blowpipe on a pan-shaped seat

【笙歌】shēnggē 〈书 *fml.*〉泛指奏乐唱歌 play instruments and sing songs：～达旦 with music and singing through the night

甥 shēng 外甥 nephew; sister's son

【甥女】shēngnǚ 外甥女 sister's daughter; niece

渻 shēng 人名用字 used in a person's name

鼪 shēng 〈书 *fml.*〉黄鼪 yellow weasel

shéng (ㄕㄥˊ)

渑(澠) Shéng 古水名，在今山东 Shengshui, name of an ancient river, in present-day Shandong Province
☞ miǎn on p. 1338

绳(繩) shéng ❶ (～儿 shéngr)绳子 rope; cord; string：麻～ hemp rope|线～ cotton rope|钢～ steel cable ❷〈书 *fml.*〉纠正；约束；制裁 restrict; restrain; punish：～之以法 punish sb. in accordance with the law; prosecute and punish according to law ❸〈书 *fml.*〉继续 continue; carry on ❹ (Shéng)姓 a surname

【绳锯木断】shéng jù mù duàn 〈比喻 *fig.*〉力量虽小，只要坚持不懈，事情就能成功 even if lacking in strength, ones needs only perseverance to succeed in any endeavour

【绳捆索绑】shéng kǔn suǒ bǎng 用绳索捆绑(多指对罪犯等 oft. criminals) tie or truss sb. up

【绳墨】shéngmò 木工打直线的工具 carpenter's line marker;〈比喻 *fig.*〉规矩或法度 rules; rules and regulations：不中～ not be bound by rules and regulations|拘守～ stick to the rules; ☞ 墨斗 mòdǒu on p. 1369

【绳索】shéngsuǒ 粗的绳子 rope; cord; thick string

【绳梯】shéngtī 用绳做的梯子,在两根平行的绳子中间横向而等距离地拴上许多短的木棍 rope ladder; ladder made of two parallel ropes linked by many short equidistant wooden steps in between

【绳子】shéng·zi 用两股以上的苘麻、棕毛或稻草等拧成的条状物,主要用来捆东西 cord; rope; string made by twisting together strands of crowndaisy, coir, rice straw, etc., mainly used to bind things

shěng (ㄕㄥˇ)

省[1] shěng ❶ 俭省;节约(跟'费'相对 as opposed to 'wasteful') economize; save; be frugal: ～钱 save money | ～吃俭用 save money on food and expenses; live frugally; be economical in everyday spending; be thrifty ❷ 免掉;减去 omit; delete; leave out: ～一道工序 eliminate a step from the process | 这两个字不能～。These two words cannot be deleted. ❸ (词语等)减去一部分后所剩下的 (of words and expressions) short for: '佛'是'佛陀'之～。The word *fo* is short for *fotuo* (Buddha).

S

省[2] shěng ❶ 行政区划单位,直属中央 province; administrative unit directly under the central government: 河北～ Hebei Province | 台湾～ Taiwan Province ❷ 指省会 capital of a province: 进～ go to the capital of a province | 抵～ arrive in the provincial capital ☞ xǐng on p. 2148

【省便】shěngbiàn 省事方便 convenient and trouble-free: 做事不能只图～。One should not only hanker after convenience and ease when doing things.

【省城】shěngchéng same as 省会 shěnghuì

【省得】shěng·de 不使发生某种(不好的)情况;免得 so as to avoid (some unfavourable condition): 穿厚一点,～冷。Put on more clothes, or you'll catch cold. | 你就住在这儿,～天天来回跑。You may stay here so that you won't have to make a round trip every day. | 快告诉我吧,～我着急。Tell me quickly so that I won't worry.

【省份】shěngfèn 省(不和专名连用) province (not used together with specific names): 台湾是中国的一个～。Taiwan is one of China's provinces. | 许多～连年丰收。A lot of provinces have reaped rich (or bumper) harvests for years on end.

【省会】shěnghuì 省行政机关所在地,一般也是全省的经济、文化中心 provincial capital; location of the provincial administrative organs, generally also the economic and cultural centre of the whole province; also 省城 shěngchéng

【省俭】shěngjiǎn 俭省 economical; frugal; thrifty

【省略】shěnglüè ❶ 免掉;除去(没有必要的手续、言语等) leave out; delete; omit (unnecessary procedures, words, etc.): ～这几段风景描写,可以使全篇显得更加紧凑。The descriptions of scenery in these paragraphs may be omitted to make the whole article more compact. ❷ 在一定条件下省去一个或几个句子成分,如祈使句中常常省去主语'你(们)'或'咱们',答话中常常省去跟问话中相同的词或词组 ellipsis; leaving out one or several sentence elements under certain conditions, e.g. the subject 'you' or 'we' in imperative sentences, and the word or phrase in a reply that is repeated from the question

【省略号】shěnglüèhào 标点符号(……),表示引文中省略的部分或话语中没有说完全的部分,或者表示断断续续的话语中的停顿 ellipsis; punctuation (...) that indicates the omitted or unfinished part in a quoted passage, or an intermittent pause in a speech; also 删节号 shānjiéhào

【省却】shěngquè ❶ 节省 save; economize: 这样做,可以～不少时间。Much time can be saved this way. ❷ 去掉;免除 remove; avert; rid sb. of: ～烦恼 rid sb. of worries

【省事】shěng//shì ❶ 减少办事手续 save trouble; simplify matters; make things easy; reduce the procedures for handling a situation: 办法一改就可以省许多事。We can make it much simpler by changing the method. ❷ 方便;不费事 more convenient; handy; not troublesome: 在食堂里吃饭～。It's more convenient to eat in the canteen.

【省心】shěng//xīn 少操心 save worry or anxiety: 孩子进了托儿所,我～多了。With the child entering kindergarten, I have had a load taken off my mind.

【省垣】shěngyuán 〈书 *fml.*〉 same as 省城 shěngchéng

【省治】shěngzhì 〈旧时 *old*〉 指省会 provincial capital

眚 shěng 〈书 *fml.*〉 ❶ 眼睛长白翳 cataract; film; nebula in the eye ❷ 灾异 disaster; calamity; adversity ❸ 过错 mistake; fault: 不以一～掩大德(不因为一个人有个别的错误而抹杀他的大功绩)。Do not allow a slight fault to obliterate a person's greater virtue.

shèng (ㄕㄥˋ)

圣(聖) shèng ❶ 最崇高的 holy; sacred: ～地 Holy Land; Holy City; sacred place; shrine | 神～ sacred ❷ 称学识或技能有极高成就的 sage; master; sb. highly accomplished in learning or skill: ～手 great master|诗～ Sage of Poetry; poet of genius; poet among poets ❸ 指圣人 sage; saint:～贤 sages and people of virtue ❹ 封建社会尊称帝王 emperor (of feudal society):～上 His Majesty|～旨 imperial edict ❺ 宗教徒对所崇拜的事物的尊称 holy; respectful form of addressing sth. that religious believers worship:～经 Holy Bible; the Bible; Holy Writ; (Holy) Scriptures|～灵 Holy Spirit; Holy Ghost

【圣诞】shèngdàn ❶〈旧时 *old*〉孔子的生日 birthday of Confucius ❷ 基督教徒称耶稣的生日 Christmas, birthday of Jesus Christ as celebrated by Christians

【圣诞节】Shèngdàn Jié 基督教徒纪念耶稣基督'诞生'的节日,在12月25日 Christmas; Christmas Day; birthday of Jesus Christ celebrated by Christians as a festival on December 25

【圣诞卡】shèngdànkǎ 赠送给别人用以祝贺圣诞节的纸片 Christmas card; card given to others to celebrate Christmas

【圣诞老人】Shèngdàn Lǎorén 西方童话故事人物,据说是一个白须着红袍的老人。在圣诞节晚上到各家分送礼物给儿童。西方各国在圣诞节晚上有扮成圣诞老人分送礼物给儿童的风俗。Santa Claus; Father Christmas; white-bearded old man in a red robe in Western fairy tales, who delivers presents to children in every household on Christmas Eve. It is a custom in various Western countries for some people to dress up as Santa Claus to give presents to children.

【圣诞树】shèngdànshù 圣诞节用的松树、枞树等常绿树。树上点缀着彩灯、玩具和赠送的物品等。Christmas tree; evergreen trees used at Christmas, e. g. pine, fir, etc. decorated with colourful lights, toys, gifts, etc.

【圣地】shèngdì ❶ 宗教徒称与教主生平事迹有重大关系的地方,如基督教徒称耶路撒冷为圣地,伊斯兰教徒称麦加为圣地 Holy Land; Holy City; place that has important significance in the life story of the founder of a religion, e. g. Christian believers consider Jerusalem the Holy Land, and Moslems, Mecca ❷ 指具有重大历史意义和作用的地方 sacred place; shrine; place of historical significance and function:革命～ historical site of the revolution

【圣洁】shèngjié 神圣而纯洁 holy and pure:～的心灵 pure heart

【圣经】Shèngjīng 基督教的经典,包括《旧约全书》(原为犹太教的经典,叙述世界和人类的起源,以及法典、教义、格言等)和《新约全书》(叙述耶稣言行、基督教的早期发展情况等) Holy Bible; the Bible; Holy Writ; (Holy) Scriptures; Christian classics consisting of *The Old Testament* (original classics of Judaism, recounting the origins of the world and humankind, codes, creeds, proverbs, etc.) and *The New Testament* (recounting the words and deeds of Jesus, the early development of Christianity, etc.)

【圣经贤传】shèngjīng-xiánzhuàn〈旧称 *old*〉儒家的代表性著作为圣经贤传。Confucian classics; (圣经 *shengjing*:传说经圣人手订的著作 works that are said to be personally inscribed by a sage; 贤传 *xianzhuan*:贤人阐释经书的著作 explanatory works of Confucian classics by a sage)

【圣灵】shènglíng 神灵 Holy Spirit; Holy Ghost

【圣庙】shèngmiào 奉祀孔子的庙 Confucian temple; shrine for Confucius

【圣明】shèngmíng 认识清楚,见解高明(多用来称颂皇帝 mostly used to flatter an emperor) insightful and wise

【圣母】shèngmǔ ❶ 迷信的人称某些女神 (belief of superstitious people) female deity; goddess ❷ 天主教徒称耶稣的母亲马利亚 (of Catholics) (Blessed) Virgin Mary; Madonna; mother of Jesus

【圣人】shèngrén ❶〈旧时 *old*〉指品格最高尚、智慧最高超的人物,如孔子从汉朝以后被历代帝王推崇为圣人 sage; wise man; person of the noblest character and the most outstanding wisdom. Confucius, for example, was deified by emperors of past dynasties as a sage. ❷ 封建时代臣子对君主的尊称 Your Majesty (the way for officials to respectfully address their monarch in feudal China)

【圣上】shèngshàng 封建社会称在位的皇帝 His Majesty; emperor on the throne in feudal China

【圣手】shèngshǒu 指某些方面技艺高超的人 great master; person of superb skill:国医～ divine physician of traditional Chinese medicine

【圣水】shèngshuǐ 迷信的人指用来降福、驱鬼或治病的水 holy water; (of superstitious people) water used to invoke blessings, exorcise ghosts, or cure diseases

【圣贤】shèngxián 圣人和贤人 sages and people of virtue:人非～,孰能无过? People are not saints, so how can they be free from error?

【圣药】shèngyào 迷信的人指灵验的药 (of superstitious people) elixir; panacea:灵丹～ cure-all; panacea

【圣旨】shèngzhǐ 封建社会里称皇帝的命令。现多用于比喻 imperial edict; order of the emperor in feudal China. It is oft. used in a figurative sense:他的话你就当成～啦? Do you take his words as an imperial edict?

胜[1] **(勝)** shèng ❶ 胜利(跟'负'或'败'相对 as opposed to 'defeat') victory; success:打～仗 win a battle|取～ win victory; emerge triumphant ❷ 打败(别人) win victory (over others), beat; defeat:以少

S

～多 defeat an enemy superior in number｜战～敌人 defeat the enemy ❸ 比另一个优越（后面常带'于、过'等 oft. followed by 于 yú or 过 guò）surpass；be superior to；get the better of；be better than：事实～于雄辩。Facts speak louder than words.｜实际行动～过空洞的言辞。Practical action is better than empty talk. ❹ 优美的（景物、境界等）beautiful；superb；wonderful（views，realms，etc.）：～景 beautiful scenery or landscape｜～境 place commanding a scenic view；（of a literary or artistic work）poetic embience｜引人入～ fascinating；enchanting；bewitching

胜[2]（勝）shèng（旧读 formerly pronounced shēng）能够承担或承受 can bear or stand；be equal or up to：～任 competent；equal to｜数不～数 countless；too numerous to count｜不～枚举 too numerous to mention individually or one by one

胜[3]（勝）shèng 古代戴在头上的一种首饰 hair ornament made of silk fabric in ancient China：方～ tailored headscarf made of silk fabric

☞ shēng on p. 1721

【胜朝】shèngcháo〈书 *fml.*〉指前一个朝代（被战胜而灭亡的朝代）preceding dynasty（conquered and defeated）：～遗老 diehards of the defunct dynasty

【胜地】shèngdì 有名的风景优美的地方 fabulous scenic spot：避暑～ summer resort

【胜迹】shèngjì 有名的风景优美的古迹 renowned historical site of scenic beauty；famous place of historic interest with beautiful scenery：名山～ famous mountains and historical sites

【胜景】shèngjǐng 优美的风景 beautiful scenery or landscape：园林～ beautiful landscape｜佳卉娱目，～怡情。Wonderful flowers please one's eyes，and beautiful scenery makes one feel cheerful and relaxed.

【胜境】shèngjìng ❶ 风景优美的地方 place commanding a glorious view：名山～ well-known mountains and scenic spots ❷ 极美好的意境（of a literary or artistic works）excellent embience

【胜局】shèngjú 胜利的局势或局面 victory；success；victorious prospects：～已定。The battle is as good as won. *or* Victory is a foregone conclusion. *or* The game is in the bag.

【胜利】shènglì ❶ 在斗争或竞赛中打败对方（跟'失败'相对 as opposed to 'defeat；fail'）victory；triumph；success；defeat one's opponent in a struggle or competition：抗战～ win the War of Resistance against Japan ❷ 工作、事业达到预定的目的（of a task，career，etc.）attain an intended goal：大会～闭幕。The conference has concluded successfully.｜生产任务～完成。The production target has been achieved.

【胜利果实】shènglì guǒshí 指斗争胜利所取得的成果（政权、物资等）fruits of victory；achievements made through victory in a struggle（e.g. political power，goods and materials，etc.）：保卫～ protect the fruits of victory

【胜券】shèngquàn 指胜利的把握 confidence in victory：稳操～ be assured of victory；be sure to win｜～在握。Success is within one's grasp.

【胜任】shèngrèn 能力足以担任 be competent；be qualified；be equal to：～工作 be competent at a job；prove equal to the task｜力能～ be equal to the task

【胜似】shèngsì 胜过；超过 be better than；superior to；surpass：不是亲人，～亲人 be dearer than one's own family members

【胜诉】shèngsù 诉讼当事人的一方受到有利的判决 win a lawsuit or court case；（of the litigant）receive a favourable court decision

【胜算】shèngsuàn〈书 *fml.*〉能够取得胜利的计谋 stratagem that ensures success：操～，用妙计。To be assured of victory，use a clever ruse.

【胜仗】shèngzhàng 打赢了的战役或战斗 victorious battle；victory；triumph：打了一个大～ win a big battle；score a great victory

晟 shèng〈书 *fml.*〉❶ 光明 bright；light ❷ 旺盛；兴盛 flourishing；vigorous；prosperous

☞ Chéng on p. 251

乘[1] shèng 春秋时晋国的史书叫'乘'，后来通称一般史书 historical records of the State of Jin during the Spring and Autumn Period；historical records in general：史～ historical records；annals of history｜野～ unofficial history

乘[2] shèng〈古代 *arch.*〉称四匹马拉的车一辆为一乘 war chariot drawn by four horses：千～之国 state with a thousand chariots

☞ chéng on p. 252

盛 shèng ❶ 兴盛；繁盛 flourishing；prosperous：全～时期 flourishing period；heyday；time of great power and influence；period of full bloom｜桃花～开。The peach trees are in full bloom. ❷ 强烈；旺盛 vigorous；energetic；aggressive：年轻气～ young and aggressive｜火势很～。The fire is blazing or raging. ❸ 盛大；隆重 grand；magnificent；solemn：～会 grand assembly；distinguished gathering or meeting｜～宴 grand banquet；magnificent spread；sumptuous dinner ❹ 丰富；丰盛 rich；sumptuous：～馔 feast；sumptuous meal ❺ 深厚 profound；profuse；abundant：～情 great kindness；boundless generosity；kind hospitality | ～意 great kindness; generosity; magnanimity ❻ 普遍；广泛 popular; widespread; prevalent; extensive: ～行 prevail; be very popular; be in vogue; be current or rife | ～传 be circulated extensively; be widely known; be widely rumoured; spread far and wide; be on everyone's lips ❼ 用力大；程度深 greatly; deeply: ～赞 shower praises on sb.; extol; speak of sb. or sth. in glowing terms | ～夸 highly praise; extol ❽ (Shèng)姓 a surname ☞ chéng on p. 252

【盛产】shèngchǎn 大量地出产 abound in; teem with; produce in great number: ～木材 abound in timber

【盛传】shèngchuán 广泛流传 be circulated extensively; be widely known; be widely rumoured; spread far and wide; be on everyone's lips: 这地区～着他的英雄事迹。His heroic deeds are on everyone's lips in this region.

【盛大】shèngdà 规模大,仪式隆重的(集体活动) grand; majestic; magnificent; large-scaled and grand (collective activity): ～的宴会 magnificent feast; grand banquet | ～的阅兵式 massive military parade

【盛典】shèngdiǎn 盛大的典礼 grand ceremony; grand occasion: 开国～ grand ceremony to establish a state

【盛服】shèngfú 〈书 *fml.*〉盛装 in full dress; splendid attire; rich dress; festive or formal dress

【盛会】shènghuì 盛大的会 grand assembly; distinguished gathering or meeting: 团结的～ grand gathering of unity

【盛举】shèngjǔ 盛大的活动 grand occasion or activity; great undertaking or enterprise; worthy undertaking

【盛开】shèngkāi (花)开得茂盛 (of flowers) be in full bloom: 百花～。All the flowers are in full bloom.

【盛况】shèngkuàng 盛大热烈的状况 grand occasion; spectacular event or affair: ～空前 exceptionally or unusually grand occasion | 电视台将转播大会的～。The TV station will televise the grand occasion of the conference.

【盛名】shèngmíng 很大的名望 great reputation; high fame or reputation: 享有～ enjoy a reputation

【盛名之下,其实难副】shèngmíng zhī xià, qí shí nán fù 名望很大,而实际情况难以和名望相称 fail to live up to one's high reputation

【盛年】shèngnián 壮年 robust years of one's life; prime; prime of life: 正值～ in the prime of life; in one's prime

【盛怒】shèngnù 大怒 rage; fury; in a violent rage; furious

【盛气凌人】shèng qì líng rén 傲慢的气势逼人 domineering; arrogant; pushy and overbearing; with an aggressively arrogant manner

【盛情】shèngqíng 深厚的情意 great kindness; boundless generosity; kind hospitality: ～厚谊 great hospitality and deep friendship | ～难却 it would be ungracious not to accept such a kind offer; difficult to refuse such kindness; hard to turn down such warm-hearted hospitality

【盛世】shèngshì 兴盛的时代 flourishing age; time of prosperity; heyday: 太平～ times of peace; times of peace and prosperity

【盛事】shèngshì 盛大的事情 grand occasion; great event: 文坛～ grand occasion in the literary world

【盛暑】shèngshǔ 大热天 sweltering summer heat; very hot weather; height of summer; dog days of summer

【盛夏】shèngxià 夏天最热的时候 midsummer; height of summer; peak of summer; hottest days in summer

【盛行】shèngxíng 广泛流行 prevail; be very popular; be in vogue; be current or rife: ～一时 prevalent for a time; in vogue for a time

【盛宴】shèngyàn 盛大的宴会 grand banquet; magnificent spread; sumptuous feast

【盛意】shèngyì same as 盛情 shèngqíng: ～难却。It is hard to decline a kind invitation.

【盛誉】shèngyù 很大的荣誉 great fame; high prestige: 享有～ be prestigious; be of great renown

【盛赞】shèngzàn 极力称赞 lavish praise on sb.; extol; speak of sb. or sth. in glowing terms: ～这次演出成功 gave rave review to the successful performance

【盛馔】shèngzhuàn 丰盛的饮食 feast; sumptuous meal

【盛装】shèngzhuāng 华丽的装束 glamorous dress; splendid attire; Sunday or holiday best: 姑娘们换上了节日的～。The girls changed into their holiday best.

剩(賸) shèng 剩余 surplus; remnant; leftover: ～饭 leftovers; swill; remains of a meal | ～货 surplus wares or goods | 大家都走了,只～下他一个人。With all the others gone, he was left alone.

【剩磁】shèngcí 磁性物质在外界磁场消除后保留的磁性。永久磁铁的磁化和磁性录音都是剩磁作用的应用。residual magnetism; remanence; remanent magnetism; magnetism retained in magnetic substances after the external magnetic field dissipates. For example, the magnetization of a permanent magnet and magnetic recording are the applications of residual magnetism.

【剩余】shèngyú 从某个数量里减去一部分以后遗留下来 surplus; remainder; residue; what remains after deducting a part from a total: ～物资 surplus materials|不但没有亏欠，而且还有些～。Instead of a deficit, there is a small surplus.

【剩余产品】shèngyú chǎnpǐn 由劳动者的剩余劳动生产出来的产品（跟'必要产品'相对 as opposed to 'necessary product'）surplus product; product produced by the surplus labour of workers

【剩余价值】shèngyú jiàzhí 由工人剩余劳动创造的完全被资本家所占有的那部分价值 surplus value; value created by the surplus labour of workers and fully taken by capitalists

【剩余劳动】shèngyú láodòng 劳动者在必要劳动之外所付出的劳动 surplus labour; labour expended by labourers other than necessary labour

椉 shèng〈书 *fml*.〉same as 乘 shèng ☞ chéng on p.253

嵊 Shèng 嵊州（Shèngzhōu），地名，在浙江 Shengzhou, name of a place in Zhejiang Province

shī（ㄕ）

尸（❶屍） shī ❶ 尸体 corpse; dead body; remains; carcass: 死～ corpse; dead body|僵～ rigid corpse|行～走肉 living corpse ❷〈古代 *arch*.〉祭祀时代表死者受祭的人 person representing the spirit of the deceased during the performance of a sacrificial service

【尸骨】shīgǔ ❶ 尸体腐烂后剩下的骨头 skeleton; bones of the dead (after the corpse has rotted): ～无存。Even the bones of the dead are nowhere to be found. ❷ 借指尸体 remains; dead body: ～未寒（指人刚死不久 sth. has happened when）sb.'s remains are scarcely cold yet

【尸骸】shīhái same as 尸骨 shīgǔ

【尸检】shījiǎn 指病理解剖学和法医学的尸体检查 autopsy; examination of a dead body for pathological anatomy or medical jurisprudence

【尸蜡】shīlà 埋葬多年后皮肤、肌肉等组织没有干枯腐朽的尸体 well-preserved corpse; dead body whose tissues, such as the skin and muscles, have not become wizened or decayed after being buried for many years

【尸身】shīshēn same as 尸体 shītǐ

【尸首】shī·shou 人的尸体 corpse; dead body

【尸体】shītǐ 人或动物死后的身体 corpse; carcass; cadaver; dead body of a human being or animal

【尸位】shīwèi〈书 *fml*.〉空占着职位而不做事 occupy a position without doing any work: ～误国 do a disservice to one's country by not doing any real work while holding a post

【尸位素餐】shī wèi sù cān 空占着职位，不做事而白吃饭 get paid without doing a stroke of work; neglect one's duties while in office

失 shī ❶ 失掉；丢掉（跟'得'相对 as opposed to 'get; obtain; gain'）lose; suffer loss of: 遗～ lose|丧～ lose; forsake; forfeit|～血 loss of blood; haemorrhage|坐～良机 lose a good chance; let a good opportunity slip by|不要～了信心。Don't lose heart. ❷ 没有把握住 miss; lose hold of; let slip: ～手 have a slip of the hand; accidentally drop|～足 slip; miss one's step; lose one's footing|～于检点 be indiscreet|百无一～ 100 per cent secure; foolproof ❸ 找不着 get lost: 迷～方向 lose one's bearings|～群之雁 wild goose that has wandered away from the flock ❹ 没有达到目的 fail to achieve one's ends: ～望 disappointed; discouraged; despair; lose hope; lose confidence|～意 be disappointed; be frustrated ❺ 改变（常态）deviate from the norm: ～声 lose one's voice|～色 lose colour; become discoloured; lose countenance; turn pale|～神 dejected; out of sorts; in low spirits ❻ 违背；背弃 break (a promise); go back on (one's word): ～信 break one's promise; go back on one's word; lose credibility|～约 fail to keep an appointment; break a promise ❼ 错误；过失 error; defect; mistake; mishap: ～误 fault; mistake; muff; faulty move; miss; slip up|惟恐有～ fear that there might be some mishap

【失败】shībài ❶ 在斗争或竞赛中被对方打败（跟'胜利'相对 as opposed to 'success'）be defeated; lose (a war, game, etc.); be beaten by one's opponent in a struggle or competition: 非正义的战争注定是要～的。An unjust war is doomed. ❷ 工作没有达到预定的目的（跟'成功'相对 as opposed to 'success'）fail; fizzle; not achieve the planned target: 试验～。The experiment failed.|～是成功之母。Failure is the mother of success.

【失策】shīcè ❶ 策略上有错误；失算 miscalculate; misjudge; be unwise; be ill-advised ❷ 错误的策略 miscalculation; wrong tactics

【失察】shīchá 在所负的督察责任上有疏失 neglect one's supervisory duties; commit an oversight

【失常】shīcháng 失去正常状态 abnormal; not normal; odd: 精神～ be distraught; not in one's right mind; mentally deranged|举动～ behave strangely; act oddly

【失宠】shī//chǒng 失掉别人的宠爱（含贬义 derog.）fall into disfavour; be out of favour; be in disgrace or disfavour; lose favour with sb.

【失传】shīchuán 没有流传下来 not extant; no longer existing; fail to be handed down from past generations; be lost:北曲的曲谱早已～了。The collection of tunes of *beiqu* has long fallen into oblivion.

【失聪】shīcōng 失去听力;聋 become deaf:双耳～ deaf in both ears

【失措】shīcuò 举动失常,不知怎么办才好 lose one's presence of mind; lose one's head; act oddly and be at a loss as to what to do:茫然～ be at a total loss|惊慌～ be panic-stricken; be frightened out of one's senses

【失单】shīdān 被窃、被劫和失落的财物的清单 list of stolen, robbed and lost articles; slip showing items of lost property

【失当】shīdàng 不适宜;不恰当 inappropriate; improper; indiscreet:处理～ not properly handled

【失盗】shī//dào same as 失窃 shī//qiè

【失道寡助】shī dào guǎ zhù 违背正义必然陷于孤立(语本《孟子·公孙丑下》:'得道者多助,失道者寡助')。An unjust cause finds scant support. Those who are unjust will find themselves isolated. (*Mencius · Gongsun Chou* (*II*): 'A just cause enjoys abundant support, while an unjust cause finds little support.')

【失地】shīdì ❶ 丧失国土 lose territory:～千里 lose 1,000 *li* of territory ❷ 丧失的国土 lost territory:收复～ recover lost territory

【失掉】shīdiào ❶ 原有的不再具有;没有了 lose; not have any more:～理智 lose one's mind; be out of one's mind|～联络 lose contact; be out of touch|～作用 lose effect ❷ 没有取得或没有把握住 miss; let slip:～机会 miss a chance; let an opportunity slip by

【失和】shīhé 双方由和睦变为不和睦 fail to keep on good terms; fail to get along well; become estranged; (of two parties) become disharmonious

【失衡】shīhéng 失去平衡 lose balance; unbalance; out-of-balance:产销～ imbalance between production and marketing|比例～ unbalanced proportions◇心理～ mental disequilibrium

【失欢】shī//huān 失掉别人的欢心 lose favour; be out of favour; fall into disfavour

【失悔】shīhuǐ 后悔 regret; repent; be remorseful:他～没有听从老人的劝告。He regretted not following the old man's advice.

【失魂落魄】shī hún luò pò 形容心神不定非常惊慌的样子 be panic-stricken; be driven to distraction; be scared out of one's wits; be terrified within an inch of one's life

【失火】shī//huǒ 发生火灾 catch fire; be on fire

【失计】shījì 失策;失算 miscalculate; misjudge; be unwise; be ill-advised

【失记】shījì 〈书 *fml.*〉忘记;不记得 forget; lose the memory of:年远～ have lost the memory of sth. with the passage of time

【失检】shījiǎn 失于检点 be indiscreet; commit an indiscretion; be careless in one's personal conduct:行为～ indiscreet; indiscreet in behaviour

【失脚】shī//jiǎo same as 失足 shī//zú ①

【失节】shī//jié ❶ 失去气节 forfeit one's integrity; lose one's integrity; be disloyal; be a turncoat ❷ 封建礼教指妇女失去贞操 (of a woman, according to feudal morality) lose one's chastity

【失禁】shījìn 指控制大小便的器官失去控制能力 spin incontinence; loss of control of the organs that control faeces and urine

【失敬】shījìng 〈客套话 *pol.*〉向对方表示歉意,责备自己礼貌不周 be sorry; show inadequacy; express one's regrets to sb. for inadequate hospitality

【失据】shījù 失掉凭借 lose a base of support; lose evidence or proof:进退～ be in a dilemma

【失控】shīkòng 失去控制 spin out of control; runaway:物价～ runaway prices; prices getting out of control

【失口】shī//kǒu same as 失言 shī//yán

【失礼】shīlǐ ❶ 违背礼节 breach of etiquette; impoliteness; discourtesy ❷ 自己感到礼貌有所不周,向对方表示歉意 express regrets to sb. for one's impropriety, lack of manners, etc.

【失利】shī//lì 打败仗;战败;在比赛中输了 suffer a setback; be defeated; be beaten in a match:吸取战斗～的教训,以利再战 draw lessons from setbacks in a battle so as to win battles in future|青年足球队初战～。The Youth Football Team lost the first game.

【失恋】shī//liàn 恋爱的一方失去另一方的爱情 be disappointed in love; be jilted; (of sb. in love) lose the love of the other party

【失灵】shīlíng (机器、仪器、某些器官等)变得不灵敏或失去应有的功能 (of machines, instruments, some organs, etc.) not work properly; be ineffective; be out of order; become insensitive or lose the proper functions:发动机～。The motor is out of order.|听觉～ lose one's sense of hearing◇指挥～ ineffective command

【失落】shīluò 遗失;丢失 lose:不慎～了一块手表 lose a watch out of carelessness

【失落感】shīluògǎn 精神上产生的空虚或失去寄托的感觉 sense of loss; feeling of being abandoned and alone; feeling of being left out; feeling of emptiness or loss of spiritual sustenance

【失迷】shīmí 走错(方向、道路等) lose one's way; get lost

【失密】shī//mì 泄漏机密 give away official secrets due to carelessness; leak out confidential information

【失眠】shī//mián 夜间睡不着或醒后不能再入

S

睡 suffer from insomnia; sleeplessness; loss of sleep; be unable to fall asleep after waking up at night

【失明】shī//míng 失去视力;瞎 lose one's sight; be unable to see; go blind:双目～ lose sight in both eyes; go blind in both eyes

【失陪】shīpéi 〈客套话 *pol.*〉表示不能陪伴对方 indicate that one cannot accompany sb.:你们多谈一会儿,我有事～了。Excuse me, I have to go, but please continue with your discussion.

【失窃】shī//qiè 财物被人偷走 be burgled or burglarized; have one's property stolen

【失去】shīqù same as 失掉 shīdiào:～知觉 lose consciousness|～效力 lose effect; be no longer effective; cease to be a force

【失却】shīquè same as 失掉 shīdiào

【失散】shīsàn 离散;散失 be separated from and lose touch with each other; become scattered:找到了～多年的亲人 find a family member one has lost touch with for years

【失色】shīsè ❶ 失去本来的色彩或光彩 lose colour; be discoloured; lose the original colour or lustre:壁画年久～。The murals have become discoloured with the passage of time. ❷ 因受惊或害怕而面色苍白 lose countenance; turn pale with fright or fear:大惊～ turn pale with fright|相顾～ look at each other in dismay; stare at each other in terror

【失闪】shī·shan 意外的差错或危险;闪失 mishap; accident; unexpected mistake or danger:要是有个～,可不是闹着玩的。It is no joke if anything should happen.

【失墒】shī//shāng 土壤所含的水分受到风吹日晒而蒸发,失去作物生长的湿度(of soil) lose moisture; lack moisture (for the development of crops due to evaporation and the effect of wind and sun); 通称 generally called 跑墒 pǎo//shāng or 走墒 zǒu//shāng

【失身】shī//shēn same as 失节 shī//jié

【失神】shīshén ❶ 疏忽;不注意 inattentive; negligent; absent-minded:稍一～就会出差错。Even a moment's slip of attention could result in mistakes. ❷ 形容人的精神委靡或精神状态不正常 out of sorts; in low spirits; dejected; dispirited or in an abnormal mental state

【失慎】shīshèn ❶ 疏忽;不谨慎 not cautious; not prudent; careless:行动～ act carelessly ❷〈书 *fml.*〉指失火 cause a fire through carelessness

【失声】shīshēng ❶ 不自主地发出声音 cry out despite oneself:～喊叫 cry out involuntarily|～大笑 crack up ❷ 因悲痛过度而哽咽,哭不出声来 lose one's voice; become choked with sobs due to excessive sorrow:痛哭～ be choked with tears; cry oneself hoarse ❸ 失音 aphonia; loss of voice, down to a whisper:一天喊下来,喉咙都～了。After crying the whole day, I could only talk in a whisper.

【失时】shī//shí 错过时机 miss the season; let an opportunity slip through one's fingers:播种不能～。Don't miss the sowing season.

【失实】shīshí 跟事实不符 inaccurate; untrue; inconsistent with the facts; be without foundation:传闻～。The rumour was unfounded. *or* The rumour has no foundation in fact.

【失势】shī//shì 失去权势 lose power and influence; be out of power; fall into disgrace

【失事】shī//shì 发生不幸的事故 have an accident; meet with a disaster or misfortune:飞机～ plane crash; aviation accident

【失收】shīshōu ❶ 农作物、果树等因遭受灾害而没有收成 crop failure; (of crops, fruit trees, etc.) have no crop due to a disaster or calamity:因遇大旱,夏季作物全部～。All the summer crops have failed due to the serious drought. ❷ 该收录而没有收录 (of writings) what should be included is left out:辑录《全唐诗》～的诗 collect the poems that were not included in the *Complete Tang Poetry*

【失手】shī//shǒu ❶ 因手没有把握住或没有留意,而造成不好的后果 accidentally drop; have a slip of the hand; cause an unfavourable consequence by failing to hold sth. (or out of carelessness):～伤人 hurt sb. accidentally|一～把碗摔破了 accidentally lose hold of the bowl and break it ❷〈比喻 *fig.*〉失利(多指意外的 usu. unexpected) loss or defeat:赛场～ lose the game unexpectedly

【失守】shīshǒu 防守的地区被敌方占领 (of a defensive area) fall; be taken:阵地～。The position was lost to the enemy.

【失算】shīsuàn 没有算计或算计得不好;谋划不当 miscalculate; misjudge; misread:一着～,全盘被动。One miscalculation and one could fall into a submissive overall position.

【失所】shīsuǒ 无处安身 become homeless; be displaced:流离～ wander about homeless; be uprooted and homeless

【失态】shītài 态度举止不合乎应有的礼貌 forget oneself; be ill-mannered in one's attitude or behaviour; be not one's usual self:酒后～ forget oneself in drink

【失调】shītiáo ❶ 失去平衡;调配不当 imbalance; lose balance; dislocation; improperly mixed or blended:供求～ imbalance of supply and demand|雨水～ abnormal rainfall ❷ 没有得到适当的调养 lack of proper care and rest:产后～ lack of proper care after childbirth|先天不足,后天～ born weak and later poorly nourished

【失望】shīwàng ❶ 感到没有希望,失去信心;希望落了空 lose hope; lose confidence; despair:多次抢救无效,彻底～。The case is beyond hope after repeated rescue measures have failed to work. ❷ 因为希望未实现而不愉快 be discouraged or disappointed; feel unhappy because one's wish fails to be realized:孩子不争气,真令人～。The child does not try to make a good showing, which is very disappointing.

【失物】shīwù 遗失的物品 lost article; lost property:寻找～ look for a lost article|～招领 articles found; advertise for the owner of a lost article; please contact us if found

【失误】shīwù 由于疏忽或水平不高而造成差错 fault; muff; slip up; fault; faulty move; error or mistake resulting from carelessness or incompetence:传球～ faulty pass|一着～,全盘皆输。One faulty move and the whole game is lost. *or* One faulty move can spoil the entire game.

【失陷】shīxiàn (领土、城市)被敌人侵占(of territory, cities, etc.) fall; fall into enemy hands; be lost to the enemy

【失笑】shīxiào 不自主地发笑 cannot help laughing; laugh in spite of oneself; cannot refrain from laughing:哑然～ cannot help smiling; can hardly suppress a smile

【失效】shī//xiào 失去效力 lose efficacy; lose effectiveness; cease to be effective:药剂～。The drug no longer has any effect.

【失信】shī//xìn 答应别人的事没做,失去信用 break one's promise; go back on one's word; lose credibility:～于人 break faith with sb.|准时归还,决不～。I will never go back on my word and I will return it to you on time.

【失修】shīxiū 没有维护修理(多指建筑物 usu. of buildings) fall into disrepair; become neglected:这座庙年久～,已经破败不堪了。The dilapidated thatched temple has fallen into disrepair for years. *or* The temple is crumbling due to long years of neglect.

【失学】shī//xué 因家庭困难、疾病等失去上学机会或中途退学 drop out of school; be a school dropout; be obliged to discontinue one's studies (because of financial difficulties, illness, etc.)

【失血】shīxuè 由于大量出血而体内血液含量减少 loss of blood; haemorrhage:～过多,病势危险 be critically ill due to excessive loss of blood

【失言】shī//yán 无意中说出不该说的话 make an indiscreet remark; make a slip of the tongue:一时～ let drop an inappropriate remark unintentionally; also 失口 shī//kǒu

【失业】shī//yè 有劳动能力的人找不到工作 (of a person who is able to work) lose one's job; be out of work; be unemployed

【失宜】shīyí 不得当 inappropriate; improper:处置～ handle improperly; mishandle sth.|决策～ make an inappropriate policy decision

【失意】shī//yì 不得志;不如意 be frustrated; be disappointed:情场～ be disappointed in love; be unlucky in love

【失音】shīyīn 由喉部肌肉或声带发生病变引起的发音障碍。患者说话时声调变低,声音微弱,严重时发不出声音。aphonia; loss of voice, down to a whisper; obstruction of pronunciation caused by pathological changes in the throat muscles or vocal chords, where the patient speaks in a low and feeble voice, and in serious cases cannot even produce sounds

【失迎】shīyíng 〈客套话 *pol.*〉因没有亲自迎接客人而向对方表示歉意 express one's regrets for failing to meet a guest personally

【失语】shīyǔ ❶〈书 *fml.*〉same as 失言 shī//yán ❷ 指说话困难或不能说话 difficulty in speech; inability to speak:～症 aphasia

【失约】shī//yuē 没有履行约会 fail to keep an appointment; break one's promise

【失着】shī//zhāo 行动疏忽或方法错误;失策 unwise move; wrong move; miscalculation

【失真】shī//zhēn ❶ 跟原来的有出入(指声音、形象或语言内容等 of voice, images, language contents, etc.) lack fidelity; not be true to the original:传写～。The written note is not true to the original message. ❷ 无线电技术中指输出信号与输入信号不一致。如音质变化、图像变形等。distortion; (of radio technology) inconsistency of signals transmitted and received, e.g. acoustic fidelity changes, image errors, etc; also 畸变 jībiàn

S

【失之东隅,收之桑榆】shī zhī dōng yú, shōu zhī sāng yú 〈比喻 *fig.*〉这个时候失败了,另一个时候得到了补偿(语出《后汉书·冯异传》。东隅:东方日出处,指早晨;桑榆:西方日落处,日落时太阳的余光照在桑树榆树之间,指傍晚)。suffer an earlier loss only to make up for it later (*History of Later Han · Biography of Feng Yi*; 东隅 *dongyu*: where the sun rises in the east, or morning; 桑榆 *sangyu*: where the last rays of the setting sun settle between mulberries and elms in the west, or evening)

【失之毫厘,谬以千里】shī zhī háo lí, miù yǐ qiān lǐ 开始稍微差一点儿,结果会造成很大的错误。A small discrepancy can lead to a great error.

【失之交臂】shī zhī jiāo bì 形容当面错过,失掉好机会 miss sb. by a narrow chance; lose a good opportunity (交臂 *jiao bi*:因彼此走得很靠近而胳膊碰胳膊 (of two persons) touch each others' arms when walking close):机会难得,幸勿～。Don't let such a golden opportunity slip through your fingers.

【失职】shī//zhí 没有尽到职责 negligence of one's duty; dereliction of duty:由于值班人员～,造成了严重的后果。Grave consequences were caused due to negligence of those on duty.

【失重】shī//zhòng 物体失去原有的重量。是由于物体在高空中所受地心引力变小或由于物体向地球中心方向作加速运动而引起的。如升降机开始下降时就有失重现象。weightlessness; zero gravity; loss of gravity; phenomenon of an object losing its original weight, caused by the reduction of the earth's gravitation at high altitude or accelerated motion towards the centre of the earth, e.g. the loss of gravity when an elevator starts to descend

【失主】shīzhǔ 失落或失窃的财物的所有者 owner of lost or stolen property

【失踪】shī//zōng 下落不明（多指人 oft. of a person）disappear; be missing

【失足】shī//zú ❶ 行走时不小心跌倒 lose one's footing; slip; miss one's step; fall or tumble down out of carelessness when walking：～落水 slip and fall into the water｜他一～从土坡上滑了下来。He lost his footing and slipped down from the slope. ❷〈比喻 *fig.*〉人堕落或犯严重错误 take a wrong step in life; go astray; degenerate or commit a serious error in life：一～成千古恨。One false step can bring eternal remorse.｜耐心做～青少年的教育工作 educate juvenile delinquents patiently

师[1]（師）shī ❶ 称某些传授知识技术的人 teacher; person who imparts knowledge or skills：教～ teacher; schoolteacher｜～傅 master; master worker｜～徒关系 master-apprentice relationship; teacher-student relationship ❷ 学习的榜样 model; example; guide：前事不忘，后事之～。Lessons learned from the past can guide one in the future. *or* Past lessons, if not forgotten, can guide one in the future. ❸ 掌握专门学术或技艺的人 person skilled in a certain profession or trade：工程～ engineer｜技～ technician｜医～ doctor ❹ 对和尚的尊称 honorific title of a Buddhist monk：法～ Master｜禅～ master (or teacher) of meditation ❺ 指由师徒关系产生的 of one's master's or teacher：～母 wife of one's master or teacher｜～兄 master's son who is elder than oneself or peer who began to follow the same master or teacher earlier than oneself｜～弟 master's son who is younger than oneself or peer who began to follow the same master or teacher later than oneself ❻〈书 *fml.*〉仿效；学习 follow; imitate; learn：～法 imitate; model oneself after (a great master); take as a model｜～其意不～其辞 follow sb.'s ideas without imitating his words ❼（Shī）姓 a surname

师[2]（師）shī ❶ 军队的编制单位，隶属于军或集团军，下辖若干旅或团 division (of an army); establishment for army units subordinate to an army or joint forces, with several brigades or regiments under its jurisdiction ❷ 军队 troops; army：出～ send out an army; dispatch troops to fight｜班～ order troops to withdraw from the front; (of troops) return (triumphantly) from the front

【师表】shībiǎo〈书 *fml.*〉品德学问上值得学习的榜样 paragon of virtue and learning; person of exemplary virtue：为人～ be worthy to be called teacher; be a paragon of virtue and learning

【师承】shīchéng ❶ 效法某人或某个流派并继承其传统 learn from sb. or some school and carry forward the tradition：～前贤 learn from wise and virtuous forefathers ❷ 师徒相传的系统 system of passing (knowledge, skills, etc.) on from master to disciple：这些艺人各有自己的～。These artists received their training under different masters.

【师出无名】shī chū wú míng 没有理由而出兵打仗。泛指做某件事缺乏正当理由。dispatch troops without a just cause; do sth. without a proper reason

【师弟】shīdì ❶ 称同从一个师傅学习而拜师的时间在后的人 male junior fellow apprentice or pupil; male formally apprenticed after another to a master worker to learn a skill ❷ 称师傅的儿子或父亲的徒弟中年龄比自己小的人 master's son (younger than oneself); father's apprentice or pupil (younger than oneself) ❸ 老师和学生 teacher and pupil（弟 *dì*：弟子 disciple; pupil）

【师法】shīfǎ〈书 *fml.*〉❶ 在学术或文艺上效法（某人或某个流派）imitate; model oneself after (a great master); take as a model; imitate (sb. or some school) in learning or art ❷ 师徒相传的学问和技术 knowledge or skill passed down from master to disciple

【师范】shīfàn ❶ 师范学校的简称 abbr. for 师范学校 shīfàn xuéxiào ❷〈书 *fml.*〉学习的榜样 model; example; person of exemplary virtue：为世～ be a model for the people

【师范学校】shīfàn xuéxiào 专门培养师资的学校 normal school; teacher-training school; 简称 abbr. 师范 shīfàn

【师父】shī·fu ❶ same as 师傅 shī·fu ❷ 对和尚、尼姑、道士的尊称 polite form of address to a Buddhist monk or nun, or a Taoist priest or nun

【师傅】shī·fu ❶ 工、商、戏剧等行业中传授技艺的人 master who gives instruction in any industrial or business trade, or opera, etc. ❷ 对有技艺的人的尊称 polite title for one with accomplished skill：老～ old master worker｜厨～ cook; chef｜木匠～ carpenter

【师公】shīgōng ❶ 师父的师父 master of one's master ❷ 男巫师 wizard; sorcerer

【师姐】shījiě ❶ 称从同一个师傅学习而拜师的时间在前的女子 female senior fellow apprentice or pupil; female formally apprenticed after another to a master to learn a skill ❷ 称师傅的女儿或父亲的女弟子中年龄比自己大的人 master's daughter who is older than oneself; father's female apprentice or pupil older than oneself

【师妹】shīmèi ❶ 称同从一个师傅学习而拜师的时间在后的女子 female junior fellow apprentice or pupil; female formally apprenticed after another to a master to learn a skill ❷ 称师傅的女儿或父亲的女弟子中年龄比自己小的人 master's daughter who is younger than oneself; father's female apprentice or pupil younger than oneself

【师母】shīmǔ 称自己的教师的妻子或师傅的妻子 wife of one's teacher or master

【师娘】shīniáng same as 师母 shīmǔ

【师事】shīshì 〈书 *fml.*〉拜某人做师傅或对某人以师傅的礼节相待 acknowledge sb. as one's teacher or master; treat sb. with due respect as a teacher

【师心自用】shī xīn zì yòng 固执己见，自以为是 be opinionated; be obstinate; be conceited

【师兄】shīxiōng ❶ 称从同一个师傅学习而拜师的时间在前的人 male senior fellow apprentice or pupil; male formally apprenticed before another to a master worker to learn a skill ❷ 称师傅的儿子或父亲的徒弟中年龄比自己大的人 master's son who is older than oneself; father's male apprentice or pupil older than oneself

【师爷】shī·ye 幕友的俗称 popular term for 幕友 mùyǒu：钱粮～ private assistant attending to economic and financial affairs | 刑名～ private adviser on legal matters | 包揽词讼的～ private assistant monopolizing all legal actions (for profit)

【师长】shīzhǎng 对教师的尊称 term of respect for a teacher

【师资】shīzī 指可以当教师的人才 persons qualified to teach; teachers; teaching staff：培养～ cultivate teachers | 解决～不足的问题 solve the problem of the shortage of teachers

诗 shī 文学体裁的一种，通过有节奏、韵律的语言反映生活、抒发情感 poetry; verse; poem; literary form for reflecting life and expressing or conveying emotion through rhythmical language

【诗风】shīfēng 诗歌创作的风格 style of poetry

【诗歌】shīgē 泛指各种体裁的诗 poems and songs; poetry; poems in various forms

【诗话】shīhuà ❶ 评论诗人和诗的书，多为随笔性质 notes and comments on poets and poetry; notes on classical Chinese poetry (usu. in the form of informal essays) ❷ 我国早期的有诗有话的小说，可以说唱 early Chinese stories interspersed with poems, which can be used as materials for ballad singing

【诗集】shījí 编辑一个人或许多人的诗而成的书 collection of poems; poetry anthology; book consisting of poems by one or many persons

【诗句】shījù 诗的句子，泛指诗作 verse; line; general term for poems or verses：优美动人的～ beautiful and touching poem

【诗律】shīlǜ 诗的格律 rules of prosody; rules of verse form; strict tonal pattern and rhyme scheme

【诗篇】shīpiān ❶ 诗(总称) poem (collect.)：这些～写得很动人。These poems are very touching. ❷〈比喻 *fig.*〉生动而有意义的故事、文章等 inspiring story; lively and significant story, article, etc.：光辉的～ splendid epic | 英雄的～ heroic epic

【诗情画意】shī qíng huà yì 诗画一般的美好意境 poetic beauty; idyllic; beautiful artistic mood or conception suggestive of poetry or painting：这里是一派田园景色，充满～。Here is an idyllic rural scene.

【诗人】shīrén 写诗的作家 poet; writer of poems

【诗史】shīshǐ ❶ 诗歌发展的历史 history of poetry ❷ 指反映一个时代的面貌、具有历史意义的诗歌 epic; poems reflecting the times and thus having historical significance

S

【诗坛】shītán 诗歌界 circle of poets：～领袖 leader of poetic circles | ～盛会 grand assembly of poetic circles

【诗兴】shīxìng 做诗的兴致 poetic mood; poetic inspiration; urge for poetic creation：～大发 feel greatly inspired to write poetry; feel a strong urge to compose poetry; be in an exalted, poetic mood

【诗意】shīyì 像诗里表达的那样给人以美感的意境 poetic quality or flavour; poetic sentiment; artistic mood or conception similar to poetry：富有～ rich in poetic flavour; very poetic

【诗余】shīyú 词②的别称。意思是说词是由诗发展而来的。another name for 词 cí ②, Chinese poetic genre developed from poetry

【诗韵】shīyùn ❶ 做诗所押的韵 rhyme (in poetry) ❷ 做诗所依据的韵书，一般指《平水韵》，平、上、去、入四声共106韵 rhyming dictionary; dictionary of rhyming words according to which people write poems, usu. refers to *The Pingshui Edition of Phonology*, including level, rising, falling and entering tones and 106 rhymes

【诗章】shīzhāng same as 诗篇 shīpiān

【诗作】shīzuò 诗歌作品 poems; verses

鸤 shī [鸤鸠] (shījiū) 古书上指布谷鸟 (in ancient Chinese writing) cuckoo

虱(蝨) shī 虱子 louse

【虱子】shī·zi 昆虫，灰白色、浅黄色或灰黑色，有短毛，头小，没有翅膀，腹部大，卵白色，椭圆形。

常寄生在人和猪、牛等身体上，吸食血液，能传染斑疹伤寒和回归热等疾病。louse (*Pediculus humanus*); greyish white, black, or light yellow insect with short hairs, a small head, no wings, and a large oval abdomen, often living parasitically on the bodies of people, pigs, oxen, etc., sucking blood, and able to transmit diseases such as typhus and relapsing fever

绝 shī 〈书 *fml.*〉一种粗绸子 a kind of coarse silk fabric

鸸 shī 鸟，身体长约3寸，嘴长而尖，背部苍灰色，翅膀的羽毛黑色，胸部白色，腹部淡褐色。生活在森林中，吃害虫。nuthatch (*sittidae*); bird approximately three *cun* (about 10 cm.) long, with a long and sharp beak, pale grey back, black feathers on its wings, white chest, and light brown stomach, which lives in forests and feeds on pests

狮(獅) shī 狮子 lion

【狮子】shī·zi 哺乳动物，身体长约3米，四肢强壮，有钩爪，掌部有肉块，尾巴细长，末端有一丛毛，雄狮的颈部有长鬣，全身毛棕黄色。产于非洲和亚洲西部。捕食羚羊、斑马等动物，吼声很大，有'兽王'之称。lion (*Panthera leo Linnaeus*); mammal whose body is about three metres long, with strong limbs, falculae, fleshy paws, a long thin tail with a clump of hair at the end, and light brown hair all over the body, the male having a long mane on the neck. Billed 'king of beasts,' lions are found in Africa and West Asia, prey and feed on antelopes, zebras, etc., and roar loudly.

【狮子搏兔】shī·zi bó tù 〈比喻 *fig.*〉对小事情也拿出全部力量，不轻视 'the lion pounces on the rabbit'; go all out even when tackling a minor problem; not take sth. lightly (搏 *bo*: 扑上去抓住 pounce on and catch)

【狮子大开口】shī·zi dà kāi kǒu 〈比喻 *fig.*〉要大价钱或提出很高的物质要求 'the lion opens its mouth wide'; demand an exorbitant price; make a request that can hardly be met

【狮子狗】shī·zigǒu 毛较长的巴儿狗 pug-dog; Pekinese with long hair

【狮子舞】shī·ziwǔ 流行很广的一种民间舞蹈，通常由两人扮成狮子的样子，另一人持绣球，逗引狮子舞蹈 lion dance; popular folk dance performed by two persons disguised as a lion, and another person holding a coloured silk ball for the lions to play with

【狮子座】shī·zizuò 黄道十二星座之一 Leo; Lion; one of the 12 constellations of the zodiac; ☞ 黄道十二宫 huángdào shí'èr gōng on p. 851

施 shī ❶ 施行②；施展 execute; carry out; put into practice: 实～ implement; enforce; put into effect | 措～ measure; step | ～工 construction | 无计可～ be at the end of one's resources; have no card to play ❷ 给予 exert; impose; exercise: ～礼 bow; salute | ～压力 exert pressure ❸ 施舍 give; grant; bestow; hand out: ～诊 give free medical treatment (to the poor) | ～与 grant; bestow ❹ 在物体上加某种东西 use; apply: ～粉(搽粉) powder; apply powder | ～肥 apply fertilizer; spread manure ❺ (Shī) 姓 a surname

【施暴】shībào ❶ 采取暴力行动 use violence ❷ 指强奸 rape

【施放】shīfàng 放出；发出 discharge; fire; let off: ～烟幕 throw up or lay down a smokescreen | ～毒气 discharge poisonous gas

【施肥】shī//féi 给植物上肥料 apply fertilizer; spread manure (for plants)

【施工】shī//gōng 按照设计的规格和要求建筑房屋、桥梁、道路、水利工程等 construction; building projects, of houses, bridges, roads, water conservancy etc. according to design standards and requirements

【施加】shījiā 给予(压力、影响等) exert; impose; inflict; bring to bear on (pressure, influence, etc.)

【施礼】shī//lǐ 行礼 bow; salute

【施舍】shīshě 把财物送给穷人或出家人 give or dole out alms; give charity; give one's property to the poor, or to monks and nuns

【施事】shīshì 语法上指动作的主体，也就是发出动作或发生变化的人或事物，如'爷爷笑了'里的'爷爷'，'水结成冰'里的'水'。表示施事的名词不一定做句子的主语，如'鱼叫猫吃了'里的施事是'猫'，但主语是'鱼'。doer of the action in a sentence; agent; (gram.) subject of an action, i.e. a person or thing that acts or changes, e.g. 'Grandpa' in the sentence 'Grandpa smiles', and 'water' in 'Water ices up'. A noun that serves as an agent does not necessarily have to be the subject of a sentence. For example, in 'The fish was eaten by the cat', 'cat' serves as the agent, while 'fish' is the subject of the sentence.

【施威】shīwēi 施展威风 exhibit or display one's power; show severity; throw one's weight about

【施行】shīxíng ❶ 法令、规章等公布后从某时起发生效力；执行 execute; enforce; implement; carry out; put into force; (of laws and decrees, regulations, etc.) put into effect from a certain time: 本条例自公布之日起～。These regulations will come into force upon promulgation. ❷ 按照某种方式或办法去做；实行 perform; effect; administer: ～手术 perform a surgical operation

【施用】shīyòng 使用；施④ use; employ; apply: ～化肥 apply fertilizer

【施与】shīyǔ 以财物周济人；给予(恩惠) grant

(properties) to sb.; bestow (favours) on sb.

【施斋】shī//zhāi 给出家人食物 give food to monks or nuns

【施展】shīzhǎn 发挥(能力等) display; put to good use; give full play to (one's ability, etc.): ～本领 give full play to one's talent; put one's abilities to good use | 他把全部技术都～出来了。He has given full play to his skills.

【施诊】shī//zhěn 给贫苦的人看病,不收诊费 give free medical treatment (to the poor)

【施政】shīzhèng 施行政治措施 administration; governing; governance; implementation of political measures: ～方针 administrative policies; policies or principles for running an institution or government

【施主】shīzhǔ 和尚或道士称施舍财物给佛寺或道观的人,通常用来称呼一般的在家人 almsgiver; benefactor; patron; (monks' or priests' form of address for) those who give properties to the monastery or Taoist temple; general form of address for layperson

浉(浉) Shī 浉河,水名,在河南 Shihe River, in Henan Province

葹 shī 古书上说的一种植物 Siberian cocklebur; plant in ancient writings

湿(濕、溼) shī 沾了水的或显出含水分多的(跟'干'相对 as opposed to 'dry'): ～度 wet; damp; humid; moist; humidity; moisture | 潮～ moist; damp | 地皮很～。The ground is very wet. | 衣服都给雨淋～了。The clothes got wet in the rain.

【湿度】shīdù ❶ 空气内含水分的多少,分为绝对湿度、相对湿度等,通常指绝对湿度 humidity; amount of water contained in the air, such as absolute and relative humidity, usu. referring to the former ❷ 泛指某些物质中所含水分的多少 moisture; amount of water contained in some substances: 土壤～ soil moisture

【湿冷】shīlěng 潮湿而寒冷 damp and chilly; dank; clammy

【湿淋淋】shīlínlín (～的 shīlínlín·de)形容物体湿得往下滴水 dripping wet; soaking wet; drenched: 全身被雨浇得～的 drenched through with rain

【湿漉漉】shīlūlū (～的 shīlūlū·de)形容物体潮湿的样子 wet; damp: 天气返潮,晾了一天的衣服还是～的。It is damp, and the clothes that have been drying for a whole day are still wet. also 湿渌渌 shīlùlù

【湿热】shīrè 热而湿度大 muggy; damp and hot

【湿润】shīrùn 潮湿润泽 moist; damp: ～的土地 damp soil or earth | 空气清新～。The air is fresh and moist. | 他有点激动,眼睛也～了。His eyes moistened with excitement.

蓍 shī 蓍草,多年生草本植物,茎有棱,叶子互生,羽状深裂,裂片有锯齿,花白色,结瘦果,扁平。全草入药,茎、叶含芳香油,可做香料。我国古代用它的茎占卜。alpine yarrow (*Achillea alpina*); perennial herb that has an ridged stem, alternate feather-like leaves with deep saw-toothed splits, white flowers and flat achenes, used entirely as medicine, its stem and leaves containing perfume oil and therefore used as perfume. Alpine yarrow stems were used for divination in ancient China. 通称 popularly known as 蚰蜒草 yóuyáncǎo or 锯齿草 jùchǐcǎo

酾[1](釃) shī 又 also shāi ❶〈书 *fml.*〉滤(酒) strain (wine); purify (wine) with a filter ❷〈方 *dial.*〉斟(酒) pour (wine)

酾[2](釃) shī〈书 *fml.*〉疏导(河渠) dredge (a river or canal)

嘘 shī〈叹词 *interj.*〉表示制止、驱逐等[used to stop sb. from doing sth., or to drive sb. or sth. away]: ～! 别做声。Shh! (or Hush!) Keep quiet!

☞ xū on p. 2164

鲺(鰤) shī 鱼,侧扁,背部褐色,鳍灰褐色,鳞小而圆,尾鳍分叉。生活在我国近海中。amberjack (*Seriola*); yellowtail; fish found in the coastal waters of China, laterally flat, with a greyish brown back, small round scales, and a forked tail fin

鲺 shī 节肢动物的一属,身体扁圆形,跟臭虫相似,头部有一对吸盘。寄生在鱼类身体的表面。carp louse (*Arrulus*); fish louse; arthropod with an oval body resembling that of a bedbug, and a pair of suckers on the head, which lives parasitically off the surface of a fish's body

shí(ㄕˊ)

十 shí ❶ 数目,九加一后所得 10; number obtained by adding one to nine; ☞ 数字 shùzì on p. 1791 ❷ 表示达到顶点 topmost; highest: ～足 100 per cent; complete; full | ～分 very; fully; completely; extremely; utterly | ～成 100 per cent

【十八般武艺】shíbā bān wǔyì 指使用刀、枪、剑、戟等十八种古式兵器的武艺,一般用来比喻各种技能 skill in wielding the 18 kinds of ancient Chinese weapons such as sword, spear and halberd; (fig.) skills in various fields of work

【十八罗汉】shíbā-luóhàn 佛教对如来佛的十六个弟子和降龙伏虎两罗汉的合称。多塑在佛寺里,或作为绘画的题材。18 arhats; (Budd.) title for the 16 disciples of Tathagata and the two arhats who subdued the dragon and tamed the tiger, usu. appearing in sculptures in temples or paintings

【十不闲儿】shíbùxiánr same as 什不闲儿

shíbùxiánr

【十冬腊月】shí dōng là yuè 指农历十月、十一月(冬月)、十二月(腊月),天气寒冷的季节 10th, 11th and 12th months of the lunar year — the coldest months of the year

【十恶不赦】shí è bù shè 形容罪大恶极,不可饶恕 guilty of unpardonable evil; unpardonably wicked; be too wicked to be pardoned (十恶 *shi e*: 古代刑法指不可赦免的十种重大罪名,即:谋反、谋大逆、谋叛、谋逆、不道、大不敬、不孝、不睦、不义、内乱,现在借指重大的罪行 10 major indictments that could not be pardoned according to ancient criminal law, i.e. conspiring against the state, plotting high treason, plotting a rebellion, plotting treason, being immoral, high treason by showing contempt for the monarch, failing to practise filial piety, being unfriendly, showing no benevolence, and creating internal disorder or turmoil); referring to serious crimes

【十二分】shí'èrfēn 形容程度极深(比用'十分'的语气更强(stronger in tone than 'very, fully, completely, extremely') more than 100 per cent; extremely; exceedingly; to a great degree or extent: 我对这件事感到~的满意。I am more than satisfied with it.

【十二指肠】shí'èrzhǐcháng 小肠的第一段,较粗,约有十二个横排着的指头那么长,上接胃,下接空肠。胰腺和胆囊的开口都在这里。duodenum; first segment of the small intestine, which is thick and as long as 12 fingers placed in a row, connected with the stomach above and the jejunum below, where the pancreas and gall bladder begin; (图见 ☞ figure for 消化系统 xiāohuà xìtǒng on p. 2100)

【十番乐】shífānyuè 一种民间音乐,乐队由十种乐器组成(包括管乐器、弦乐器和打击乐器) folk music played by a band with 10 different musical instruments (including wind, stringed and percussion instruments); 通称 generally called 十番锣鼓 shífān luógǔ; 简称 abbr. 十番 shífān

【十方】shífāng 〈佛教用语 *Budd.*〉,指东、西、南、北、东南、西南、东北、西北、上、下十个方位 10 directions: east, west, south, north, south-east, south-west, north-east, north-west, above and below

【十分】shífēn 〈副词 *adv.*〉很 very; fully; completely; extremely; utterly: ~满意 be very satisfied

【十锦】shíjǐn same as 什锦 shíjǐn

【十进制】shíjìnzhì 一种记数法,采用 0,1,2,3,4,5,6,7,8,9 十个数码,逢十进位。如 9 加 1 为 10,90 加 10 为 100,900 加 100 为 1,000。decimal system; decimal scale; number scale that adopts 10 numerals (0, 1, 2, 3, 4, 5, 6, 7, 8, 9). For example, 9 added to 1 is 10; 90 to 10, 100; and 900 to 100, 1,000.

【十目所视,十手所指】shí mù suǒ shì, shí shǒu suǒ zhǐ 表示监督的人很多,不允许做坏事,做了也隐瞒不住(见于《礼记·大学》)。One is not allowed to do bad things, or cannot do anything wrong without being exposed under the supervision of many people. (see *The Book of Rites·Great Learning*)

【十拿九稳】shí ná jiǔ wěn 〈比喻 *fig.*〉很有把握 90 per cent sure; practically certain; in the bag; as good as settled; also 十拿九准 shí ná jiǔ zhǔn

【十年九不遇】shí nián jiǔ bù yù 指某种情况多年难遇到 barely one out of 10; (of situation) not occurring in many years: 今年这么大的雨量,真是~。It's been many years since we last had so much rainfall as this year's.

【十年树木,百年树人】shí nián shù mù, bǎi nián shù rén 培植树木需要十年,培育人才需要百年。It takes 10 years to grow trees, but 100 to cultivate people. 〈比喻 *fig.*〉培养人才是长久之计,也形容培养人才很不容易(《管子·权修》:'十年之计,莫如树木;终身之计,莫如树人')。It is a long-term plan to cultivate people; it is a hard job to cultivate people. (*Guanzi·Writing Annals of Power*: 'It might take 10 years to grow trees, but a lifetime to cultivate people.')

【十全】shíquán 完美无缺 perfect: 人都有缺点,哪能~呢? Since everyone has shortcomings, can anyone be perfect?

【十全十美】shí quán shí měi 各方面都非常完美,毫无缺陷 be perfect in every way; be the acme of perfection; flawless and perfect; leave nothing to be desired

【十三点】shísāndiǎn 〈方 *dial.*〉❶ 形容人傻里傻气或言行不合情理 foolish; nutty; muddle-headed or unreasonable in one's words or behaviour: 这个人有点~。The guy is a little weird. ❷ 指傻里傻气,言行不合情理的人 nitwit; dunce; person who is muddle-headed or unreasonable in his words or behaviour

【十三经】Shísān Jīng 指《易经》、《书经》、《诗经》、《周礼》、《仪礼》、《礼记》、《春秋左传》、《春秋公羊传》、《春秋谷梁传》、《论语》、《孝经》、《尔雅》、《孟子》十三种儒家的经传 Thirteen Classics of Confucianism, namely *The Book of Changes*, *Classic of Documents*, *The Book of Songs*, *The Rites of Zhou*, *Book of Etiquette and Ceremonial*, *The Book of Rites*, *The Zuo Commentary*, *The Gongyang Commentary*, *The Guliang Commentary*, *Analects*, *The Book of Filial Piety*, *Er Ya* and *Mencius*

【十三辙】shísān zhé 指皮黄、鼓儿词等戏剧曲艺中押韵的十三个大类,就是:中东、江阳、衣期、姑苏、怀来、灰堆、人辰、言前、梭波、麻沙、乜邪、遥迢、由求 13 major rhyming categories of words in the Chinese theatre and ballad-singing to the accompaniment of a drum, i. e. *zhongdong*, *jiangyang*, *yiqi*, *gusu*, *huailai*, *huidui*, *renchen*, *yanqian*, *suobo*, *masha*, *miexie*, *yaotiao* and *youqiu*; also 十三道辙 shísān dàozhé

【十室九空】shí shì jiǔ kōng 十户人家九家空。形容天灾大祸使得人民流离失所的悲惨景象。nine houses out of 10 stand empty and forsaken — a miserable scene of destitute and homeless people stranded in a natural calamity or great misfortune

【十四行诗】shísìhángshī 欧洲的一种抒情诗体,每首十四行,格律上分为好几种。也译作商籁体。sonnet; 14-line European lyrics of many kinds in metre; also translated as 商籁体 shānglàitǐ

【十万八千里】shí wàn bā qiān lǐ 形容极远的距离或极大的差距 extremely long distance or a great difference: 他说了半天,离正题还差~呢! Talking for such a long time, he is still miles away from the subject. | 这两个厂相比,经济效益相差~。The two factories are poles apart in economic efficiency.

【十万火急】shí wàn huǒ jí 形容事情紧急到了极点 most urgent; post-haste; express

【十一】Shí-Yī 十月一日,中华人民共和国国庆日。一九四九年十月一日中华人民共和国成立。October 1; National Day of the People's Republic of China. The People's Republic of China was founded on October 1, 1949.

【十月革命】Shíyuè Gémìng 1917 年 11 月 7 日(俄历 10 月 25 日)俄国工人阶级和农民在以列宁为首的布尔什维克党的领导下进行的社会主义革命。十月革命推翻了俄国资产阶级临时政府,建立了世界上第一个无产阶级专政的社会主义国家。October Revolution; socialist revolution carried out by the Russian working class and peasants led by the Bolshevik Party headed by Lenin on November 7, 1917 (October 25 on the Russian calendar), overthrowing the provisional government of the Russian capitalist class, and establishing the first socialist country in the world under the dictatorship of the proletariat

【十指连心】shí zhǐ lián xīn 手指头感觉灵敏,十个手指碰伤了哪一个都感到痛得钻心 ten fingers are so sensitive that any one of them, if hurt, can cause excruciating pain; 〈比喻 *fig.*〉某人和有关的人或事具有极密切的关系 (of a person) have close relations with the people or the matter concerned

【十字架】shízìjià 罗马帝国时代的一种刑具,是一个十字形的木架,把人的两手、两脚钉在上面,任他慢慢死去。据基督教《新约全书》中记载,耶稣被钉死在十字架上。因此基督教徒就把十字架作为信仰的标记,也看做受难或死亡的象征。cross; crucifix; + -shaped wooden frame that served as an instrument of torture during the Roman Empire, to which a person was nailed by the hands and feet and left to die slowly. According to *The New Testament*, Jesus was nailed to death on the cross, which Christians therefore regard as a symbol of both their belief and of suffering or death.

【十字街头】shízì jiētóu 指道路交叉,行人往来频繁的热闹街市 intersecting streets; busy streets (with many pedestrains coming and going)

【十字路口】shízì lùkǒu (~儿 shízì lùkǒur) 两条路纵横交叉的地方 crossroads; 〈比喻 *fig.*〉在重大问题上需要对去向作出选择的境地 critical turning point when one has to make a decision on an important issue

【十足】shízú ❶ 成色纯 pure; sheer; 100 per cent; out-and-out: ~的黄金 pure gold ❷ 十分充足 full; complete: ~的理由 ample reason | 神气~ put on grand airs; be on one's high horse | 干劲~ full of energy

什 shí ❶ 〈书 *fml.*〉 same as 十 shí (多用于分数或倍数 mostly used in fractions or multiples): ~一(十分之一) one 10th | ~九(十分之九) nine 10ths | ~百(十倍或百倍) 10 fold or 100 fold ❷ 多种的;杂样的 assorted; varied; miscellaneous; sundry: ~物 odds and ends; sundries; articles for everyday use | ~件 giblets | 家~ home utensils and furniture

☞ shén on p. 1704

【什不闲儿】shíbùxiánr 曲艺的一种,由莲花落发展而成,用锣、鼓、铙、钹等伴奏 *shibuxianr*, folk art form of ballad-singing to the accompaniment of musical instruments such as gongs, drums, cymbals, developed from popular ballads sung to the accompaniment of bamboo clappers, with every stanza ending in with the wording '*lianhualao*'; also 十不闲儿 shíbùxiánr

【什件儿】shíjiànr ❶ 鸡鸭的内脏做食品时的总称 giblets; food made of a chicken's or duck's internal organs: 炒~ fried giblets ❷ 〈方 *dial.*〉箱柜、马车、刀剑等上面所附的各样起加固作用的金属装饰品 metal ornaments fixed on trunks, carriages, swords, etc., for consolidation: 黄铜~ brass accessories

【什锦】shíjǐn ❶ 多种原料制成或多种花样的 assorted; mixed; of various materials or designs: ~饼干 assorted biscuits | ~糖 assorted candy | ~锉 a set of assorted files ❷ 多种原料制成或多种花样拼成的食品 foodstuff made of various ingredients or pieced together in different patterns: 素~ assorted vegetarian delights

【什锦锉】shíjǐncuò 由各种不同横断面的小型锉刀组成的一组锉,包括扁锉、方锉、圆锉、三角锉、刀锉等 set of assorted files; set of files or rasps of various cross-sections, including flat, square, circular, triangular and knife-edged files; also 组锉 zǔcuò

【什物】shíwù 泛指家庭日常应用的衣物及其他零碎用品 odds and ends; sundries; articles for everyday use such as clothes and other things

辻 shí 日本汉字,十字路口。多用于日本姓名。Chinese character in Japanese language meaning crossroad, oft. used in Japanese names

石 shí ❶ 构成地壳的坚硬物质,是由矿物集合而成的 stone; rock; pebble; hard substances that constitute the earth's crust, made up of a collection of minerals: 花岗～ granite | 石灰～ limestone; lime-rock | ～碑 stone tablet; stele | ～板 slabstone; flagstone; flag | ～器 stone implement; stone artifact; stone vessel; ☞ 岩石 yánshí on p. 2205 ❷ 指石刻 stone inscription: 金～ inscriptions on ancient bronzes and stone tablets ❸〈古代 *arch.*〉用来治病的石针 stone needle used in ancient times to cure diseases: 药～ medicines and stone needles (for acupuncture) ❹ (Shí) 姓 a surname ☞ dàn on p. 379

【石板】shíbǎn ❶ 片状的石头,多用为建筑材料 slabstone; flagstone; flag; flaky stone usu. used as a building material ❷ 文具,用薄的方形板岩制成,周围镶木框,用石笔在上面写字 slate (for writing); stationery made of a thin square piece of slate in a wooden frame, on which one can write with a piece of slate chalk

【石版】shíbǎn 石印的印刷底版,用一种多孔质的石料制成 stone plate; lithographic printing negative made of porous stone

【石笔】shíbǐ 用滑石制成的笔,用来在石板上写字 slate chalk; chalk made of talcum, used for writing on a slate

【石沉大海】shí chén dà hǎi 像石头掉到大海里一样,不见踪影 (disappear) like a stone dropped into the sea;〈比喻 *fig.*〉始终没有消息 have no news whatsoever (about sb.); never to be seen or heard of again; disappear without a trace

【石担】shídàn 体育锻炼用的器械,在竹杠或木杠两端安着石轮 stone barbell; barbell with stone weights; sports apparatus for physical training, composed of a bamboo or wooden bar with stone wheels at both ends

【石雕】shídiāo 在石头上雕刻形象、花纹的艺术。也指用石头雕刻成的作品。stone carving; stone sculpture; art of carving images and patterns on stone; carved stone; works produced by carving on stone

【石碓】shíduì 碓(舂米用具) treadle-operated tilt hammer for hulling rice

【石方】shífāng 采石、填石或运输石头的工作通常都用立方米来计算,一立方米称为一个石方。这一类的工作叫石方工程,有时也简称石方。stonework; rock excavation; cubic metre of stonework (such as quarrying, rockfilling, or transporting stones); sometimes abbr. 石方 shífāng

【石膏】shígāo 无机化合物,化学式 $CaSO_4 \cdot 2H_2O$。透明或半透明结晶体,白色、淡黄色、粉色或灰色。大部分为天然产,用于建筑、装饰、塑造和制造水泥等。中医用做解热药,农业上用来改良碱化土壤。gypsum ($CaSO_4 \cdot 2H_2O$); plaster stone; inorganic compound that is a transparent or semi-transparent crystal white, light yellow, pink or grey in colour, most of which is produced naturally, used in construction, decoration, moulding, and production of cement, and also used as an antifebrile in traditional Chinese medicine, and in agriculture to improve alkaline soil; also 生石膏 shēngshígāo

【石膏像】shígāoxiàng 用石膏做成的人物形象,是一种美术品 plaster statue; plaster figure; figure made of plaster stone presented as artistic work

【石工】shígōng ❶ 开采石料或用石料制作器物的工作 rockwork; masonry; work in a quarry or the work of a stonemason ❷ 做这种工作的工人 stonemason; mason; worker who does such work; also 石匠 shí·jiang

【石鼓文】shígǔwén 石鼓上刻的铭文或石鼓上铭文所用的字体,叫石鼓文。石鼓是战国时秦国留存下来的文物,形状略像鼓,共有十个,上面刻有四言诗铭文。唐代初年在今陕西凤翔发现,现存北京。inscriptions, or style of calligraphy on drum-shaped stone blocks. Ten cultural relics dating back to the State of Qin during the Warring States Period, which roughly resemble drums in shape, and on which were carved inscriptions of classical poetry with four characters to a line, were unearthed in the early Tang Dynasty in present-day Fengxiang, Shaanxi Province, and are now preserved in Beijing.

【石磙】shígǔn ☞ 碌碡 liù·zhóu on p. 1247

【石灰】shíhuī 生石灰和熟石灰的统称。也特指生石灰。lime; general term for quick and slaked lime; referring in particular to slaked lime; 通称 popularly called 白灰 báihuī

【石灰质】shíhuīzhì 主要成分是碳酸钙的物质。人和动物的骨骼中都含有大量的石灰质。calcareous; calcarious; substance mainly composed of calcium carbonate; human and animal skeletons contain a great deal of such substance

【石级】shíjí 用石头砌的台阶 stone stairs or steps

【石匠】shí·jiang same as 石工 shígōng ②

【石蜐】shíjié ☞ 龟足 guīzú on p. 729

【石坎】shíkǎn ❶ 石头砌的防洪坝 flood-control stone ridge; regulating dam built of stone ❷ 石头山上凿成的台阶 steps cut into a rocky mountain; stone-hewn steps

【石刻】shíkè 刻有文字、图画的碑碣等石制品或石壁,也指上面刻的文字、图画 stone carving; stone sculpture; stone inscription; stone-engraving; steles, stone products, or rock cliffs carved with characters or pictures; the characters or pictures carved on stone

【石窟】shíkū 〈古时 *arch*.〉一种就着山崖开凿成的寺庙建筑,里面有佛像或佛教故事的壁画和石刻等,如我国的敦煌、云冈和龙门等石窟 rock cave; grotto; temple structure constructed by cutting into cliffs, in which there are images or statues of Buddhas, murals that tell Buddhist stories, and stone carvings, such as the Dunhuang, Yungang and Longmen grottoes in China

【石砬子】shílá·zi 〈方 *dial*.〉地面上突起的巨大岩石 projecting rock; crag; boulder; huge protruding rock on the ground; also 石头砬子 shí·tou lá·zi

【石料】shíliào 做建筑、筑路、雕刻等材料用的岩石或类似岩石的物质,分为天然石料(如花岗石、石灰石)和人造石料(如人造大理石、水磨石、剁斧石) stone; rock (as a building material); rock or similar substance used as raw materials in construction, road building, carving, etc., including natural stone (e.g. granite and limestone) and artificial stone (e.g. artificial marble, terrazzo and artificial stone with imitation axe-cut patterns)

【石榴】shí·liu ❶ 落叶灌木或小乔木,叶子长圆形,花红色、白色或黄色。果实球形,内有很多种子,种子的外种皮多汁,可以吃。根皮和树皮可入药。pomegranate (*Punica granatum*); deciduous bush or small arbour with oval leaves, red, white or yellow flowers, spherical fruit with many seeds, whose exosperm is juicy and edible, and velamen and bark that are used as medicine ❷ 这种植物的果实 fruit of such plants; also 安石榴 ānshí·liu

【石榴裙】shíliúqún 红裙子。借指女人。garnet-red skirt, referring to a woman

【石棉】shímián 矿物,成分是镁、铁等的硅酸盐,纤维状,多为白色、灰色或浅绿色。纤维柔软,耐高温,耐酸碱,是热和电的绝缘体。asbestos; fibrous mineral composed of the silicate of magnesium, iron, etc., usu white, grey and light green in colour, whose soft fibres, resistant to heat, acids and alkalis, are used as an insulator of heat and electricity

【石墨】shímò 矿物,成分是碳,灰黑色,有金属光泽,硬度小,熔点高,导电性强,化学性质稳定。用来制造坩埚、电极、铅笔心、润滑剂、颜料、防锈涂料等。graphite; grey-and-black mineral composed of carbon with a metallic lustre, a low level of hardness, a high melting point, strong electric conductivity and stable chemical properties, used to produce crucibles, electrodes, lead, lubricant, pigment, rust-resistant paint, etc.

【石女】shínǚ 先天性无阴道或阴道发育不全的女子 woman with a hypoplastic vagina

【石破天惊】shí pò tiān jīng 唐代李贺诗《李凭箜篌引》:'女娲炼石补天处,石破天惊逗秋雨。'形容箜篌的声音忽而高亢,忽而低沉,出人意外,有不可名状的奇境。后多用来比喻文章议论新奇惊人。*On Li Ping's Playing of Konghou*, a poem by Li He of the Tang Dynasty: 'At the place where Nü Wa melted down stones to repair the sky, / Rock shattered and heaven shook, and autumn rain fell.' The lines depict the sonorous rise and deep fall of the melody played on the *konghou* (ancient plucked instrument with five to 25 strings), which produces an indescribably wonderful ambience. The phrase is used to describe remarkably original and forceful writing or commentary.

【石器时代】shíqì shídài 考古学分期中最早的一个时代,从有人类起到青铜器的出现止共二三百万年。这时人类主要用石头制造劳动工具,还不知道利用金属。按照石器的加工情况又可分为旧石器时代、中石器时代和新石器时代。Stone Age; the earliest archaeological stage, lasting a total of two or three million years from the emergence of human beings to the appearance of bronzeware, during which time humans mainly used stone to produce tools, and did not yet know how to use metals. This period can be divided into the Old, Middle and New Stone Ages according to the level of the making of stone tools.

【石笋】shísǔn 石灰岩洞中直立的像笋的物体,常与钟乳石上下相对,是由洞顶滴下的水滴中所含的碳酸钙沉淀堆积而成的 stalagmite; object standing erect like bamboo shoots in lime caves (oft. with stalactites coming down in the opposite direction), built up through the sedimentation of calcium carbonate contained in water dripping from the top of caves

【石锁】shísuǒ 体育锻炼用的器械,形状像旧式的锁,用石料制成 stone dumb-bell in the form of an old-fashioned padlock (used for physical training)

【石炭】shítàn 〈古代 *arch*.〉指煤 coal

【石头】shí·tou same as 石 shí ①

【石头子儿】shí·touzǐr 小石块 small stone; cobble; pebble

【石硪】shíwò 用石头制成的打夯工具,圆形,周围系着几根绳子 circular stone rammer with ropes attached at the sides

【石印】shíyìn 用石版印刷。先把原稿用特制的墨写在药纸上,再轧印在石版上,涂上桃胶,干后用水擦净,然后涂油墨印刷。lithographic printing; lithography; printing process involving writing original manuscripts using special ink on medicinal paper, that is then rolled on stone plates, with peach gum applied, and wiped clean with water after drying, and then spread with printing ink for printing

【石英】shíyīng 矿物，成分是二氧化硅，质地坚硬，纯粹的石英叫做水晶，无色透明。含杂质时，有紫、褐、淡黄、深黑等颜色，一般是乳白色、半透明或不透明的结晶。工业上用来制造光学仪器、无线电器材、耐火材料、玻璃或陶瓷等。quartz; hard mineral composed of silicon dioxide. Pure quarts is called crystal, which is colourless and transparent, while that containing impurities is purple, brown, light yellow or dark in colour, but usu. it is in the form of creamy, semi-transparent or opaque crystal. Quartz is used to produce industrial products such as optical instruments, radio equipment, refractory materials, glass or ceramics.

【石英钟】shíyīngzhōng 一种计时仪器，利用石英晶体的振荡代替普通钟摆的运动。石英钟具有很高的精确性和稳定性，每天误差可小于万分之一秒。quartz clock; timepiece that replaces the movement of an ordinary pendulum with the vibration of quartz crystal, which is of high precision and stability, whose error can be less than one 10,000th of a second

S

【石油】shíyóu 具有不同结构的碳氢化合物的混合物，液体，可以燃烧，一般呈褐色、暗绿色或黑色，渗透在岩石的空隙中。从石油中可以提取汽油、煤油、柴油、润滑油、石蜡、沥青等。petroleum; oil; mixture of hydrocarbons of various structures, combustible liquid usu. brown, dark green or black in colour, integrated into the gaps of rocks, from which petrol, kerosene, diesel oil, lubricating oil, paraffin wax, pitch, etc. can be extracted

【石油气】shíyóuqì 开采石油或在炼油厂加工石油时产生的气体，主要成分是碳氢化合物和氢气。用做燃料和化工原料等。petroleum gas; gas produced when mining oil or processing it in a refinery, mainly composed of hydrocarbons and hydrogen, which is used as a fuel, chemical raw material, etc.

【石子儿】shízǐr same as 石头子儿 shí·touzǐr：碎～ crushed cobblestones

时(時) shí ❶ 指比较长的一段时间 time; times; days：古～ in ancient times｜宋～ during the Song Dynasty｜盛极一～ reach the zenith; be in vogue (for a time) ❷ 规定的时候 fixed time：按～上班 go to work on time｜列车准～到站。The train arrived at the station on time. ❸ 季节 season：四～ four seasons｜不误农～ do not miss the farming season; do farm work during the right season｜应～食品 food in season ❹ 当前；现在 present; current：～下 at present; currently｜～新 fashionable; stylish; trendy｜～事 current affairs; current events ❺ 时俗；时尚 fashion：入～ fashionable; in vogue｜合～ fashionable; in vogue ❻ 计时的单位 time unit a) 时辰 one of the 12 two-hour periods into which the day was traditionally divided, each being given the name of the 12 Earthly Branches：卯～ 5-7 a.m.｜辰～ 7-9 a.m. b) 小时(点) hour：上午八～ 8 a.m. ❼ 时机 chance; opportunity; opportune moment：失～ miss the chance; lose the opportunity｜待～而动 bide one's time ❽ 时常 occasionally; now and then; from time to time：～～ often; constantly; again and again｜～有出现 occur now and then ❾ 叠用，跟'时而…时而…'相同；有时候 [used in pairs] same as 'now ... now ...;' 'sometimes ... sometimes'：～断～续 on and off｜～快～慢 sometimes fast, sometimes slow 注意 **NOTE**：'时…时…'后面通常用单音词，'时而…时而…'没有限制。时 (shí) ... 时 ... is usu. followed by monosyllables, while 时而 (shí'ér) ... 时而 ..., has no restrictions. ❿ 一种语法范畴，表示动词所指动作在什么时候发生。很多语言的动词分现在时、过去时和将来时，有些语言分得更细。(gram.) tense; indicating the time of the action expressed by the verb; verbs in many languages are divided into the present, past or future tenses, while in others, there are even more tenses ⓫ (Shí)姓 a surname

【时弊】shíbì 当时社会的弊病 social evils of the day：切中～ strike to the core of present-day evils｜针砭～ condemn present-day evils

【时不时】shíbùshí 〈方 *dial.*〉 same as 时常 shícháng

【时不我待】shí bù wǒ dài 时间不等人，指要抓紧时间 time and tide wait for no one; one must make the best use of one's time：任务紧迫，～。As the task is urgent, we can't afford to wait.

【时差】shíchā ❶ 平太阳时和真太阳时的差。一年之中时差是不断改变的，最大正值是 +14 分 24 秒，最大负值是 -16 分 24 秒，有四次等于零。equation of time; difference between mean and true solar time, which changes constantly during a year, the maximum positive value being +14 minutes and 24 seconds, and the maximum negative value, -16 minutes and 24 seconds, with zero occurring four times ❷ 不同时区之间的时间差别 time difference between various time zones; jet lag

【时常】shícháng 常常；经常 often; frequently; again and again

【时辰】shí·chen ❶〈旧时 *old*〉计时的单位。把一昼夜平分为十二段，每段叫做一个时辰，合现在的两小时。十二个时辰用地支做名称，从半夜起算，半夜十一点到一点是子时，中午十一点到一点是午时。time unit; one of the 12 two-hour periods into which the day was traditionally divided, each being given the name of the 12 Earthly Branches. The period from 11 p.m. to 1 a.m. is called *zishi*, and that from 11 a.m. to 1 p.m. *wushi* ❷ 时间;时候 time; right time:～不早了,快睡吧。It is getting late, so let's go to bed.

【时代】shídài ❶ 指历史上以经济、政治、文化等情况为依据而划分的某个时期 times; age; era; epoch:石器～ Stone Age | 封建～ feudal period | 五四～ days of the May 4th Movement | ～潮流 trend of the times; tendency of the day ❷ 指个人生命中的某个时期 period in one's life; years:青年～ youth

【时点】shídiǎn 时间上的某一点,如说某年某月某日零点整。在计算人口、物资储备等时,都是以一个时点为限。point of time; exact time up to a certain point, with which certain data (such as deadlines for population census, material reservation, etc.) are calculated, e.g. zero hour of some day of some month of some year

【时调】shídiào 在一个地区流行的各种时兴小调、小曲,有的已发展成曲艺,有演唱,有伴奏,如天津时调 popular folk tunes or ditties (some of which have developed into folk songs with orchestral accompaniment, e.g. Tianjin tunes)

【时段】shíduàn 指某一段时间 period of time; time interval:新闻节目安排在最佳～播出。The news programme is arranged for prime time broadcast. | 秋季是该市旅游的黄金～。Autumn is the city's best tourist season.

【时而】shí'ér〈副词 *adv.*〉❶ 表示不定时地重复发生 from time to time; sometimes; occur repeatedly now and then:天空中,～飘过几片薄薄的白云。Every now and then several thick clusters of white clouds drift across the sky. ❷ 叠用,表示不同的现象或事情在一定时间内交替发生 [used in pairs] now ... now ...; sometimes ... sometimes ...; indicating the alternating of different phenomena or events within a time period:这几天～晴天,～下雨。The weather has been changeable these days — one moment it is fine, and the next it rains! | 他们兴高采烈,～引吭高歌,～婆娑起舞。They were in high spirits, now singing joyfully in loud voices, now launching themselves in dance.

【时分】shífèn same as 时候 shí·hou:三更～ at the third watch; in the dead of the night | 掌灯～ at dusk; at twilight

【时乖运蹇】shí guāi yùn jiǎn 指时运不好 down on one's luck; be born under an unlucky star; have the hand of fate against one; also 时乖命蹇 shí guāi mìng jiǎn

【时光】shíguāng ❶ 时间,光阴 time:～易逝. Time flies. | 消磨～ while or idle away one's time ❷same as 时期 shíqī:他是抗日战争～入伍的。He joined the services during the War of Resistance against Japan. ❸ 日子 times; years:过着丰衣足食的好～ enjoy a good period of ample food and clothing

【时过境迁】shí guò jìng qiān 随着时间的推移,境况发生变化 circumstances change with the passage of time

【时候】shí·hou ❶ same as 时间 shíjiān ②:你写这篇文章用了多少～? How much time did you spend writing the article? ❷ same as 时间 shíjiān ③:现在是什么～了? What time is it now? | 到～请叫我一声。Please call me when it's time.

【时机】shíjī 具有时间性的客观条件(多指有利的 oft. favourable) opportunity; opportune moment:掌握～ time | 错过～ miss a chance | 有利～ opportune time

【时价】shíjià 现时的价格 current price; going rate:～稍减 slight reduction of the current price | ～起落不大。Current prices are not rising and falling sharply.

【时间】shíjiān ❶ 物质存在的一种客观形式,由过去、现在、将来构成的连绵不断的系统。是物质的运动、变化的持续性、顺序性的表现。time; objective form in which matter exists, in a continuous system composed of the past, present and future, which shows the nature of continuity and sequence in the movement and change of matter ❷ 有起点和终点的一段时间 (the duration of) time; period of time that has both a beginning and an ending:地球自转一周的～是二十四小时。The period of one complete rotation of the earth is 24 hours. | 盖这么所房子要多少～? How long will it take to build such a house? ❸ 时间里的某一点 (a point in) time:现在的～是三点十五分。The time now is 15 minutes past 3.

【时间词】shíjiāncí 表示时间的名词,如:过去、现在、将来、早晨、今天、元旦、春季、去年、星期日等 temporal words; word denoting time, e.g. past, present, future, morning, today, New Year's Day, spring, last year, Sunday, etc.

【时间性】shíjiānxìng 事物在某一段时间内才有效、有意义或有作用的特征 timeliness; temporality; characteristic of certain matters that are only effective or significant during a certain period:新闻报道的～强,要及时发表。News reports must be released on time.

【时节】shíjié ❶ 节令;季节 season:清明～ around the Pure Brightness Festival | 农忙～ busy farming season ❷ same as 时候 shí·hou:开始学戏那～她才六岁。She was only six when she began to study opera.

【时局】shíjú 当前的政治局势 current political situation:～稳定。The situation is stable.

【时刻】shíkè ❶ same as 时间 shíjiān ③:严守～,准时到会 be strictly punctual for a meeting ❷ 每时每刻;经常 24-hour; constantly; always; at all times:时时刻刻 constantly, al-

S

ways; at all times; at every moment|～准备贡献出我们的力量 be ready at any moment to contribute our strength

【时空】shíkōng 时间和空间 time and space:～观(人们对于时间和空间的根本观点) outlook on time and space

【时来运转】shí lái yùn zhuǎn 时机来了,运气有了好转 time or luck has shifted in one's favour; fortune is smiling (on sb.)

【时令】shílìng 季节 season:～已交初秋,天气逐渐凉爽。It is already early autumn, and the weather gradually becomes cool.

【时令】shí·ling 〈方 *dial.*〉指时令病 seasonal ailment:闹～ come down with a seasonal ailment

【时令病】shílìngbìng 〈中医 *Chin. med.*〉指某一季节的多发病,如夏季的痢疾、中暑,秋季的疟疾等 seasonal ailment; diseases that occur frequently during certain seasons, such as dysentery and sunstroke in summer, malaria in autumn, etc.

【时令河】shílìnghé 季节性的河流,雨季或冰雪融化期有水,其他时期无水或断续有水 seasonal river (that has water during the rainy season or the thawing of ice and snow, and no water or intermittent water during other periods)

【时髦】shímáo 形容人的装饰衣着或其他事物入时 (of clothing, accessories or other things) fashionable; stylish; in vogue:赶～ follow the fad; keep up with the fashion

【时评】shípíng 指报刊上评论时事的文章 commentaries on current events; newspapers and periodical articles that comment on current events

【时期】shíqī 一段时间(多指具有某种特征的 mostly with certain characteristics) period; stage:抗战～ during the War of Resistance against Japan|社会主义建设～ period of socialist construction

【时气】shí·qi 〈方 *dial.*〉❶ 一时的运气,又特指一时的幸运 momentary luck:～好 really lucky|碰～ try one's luck|有～ be lucky ❷ 因气候失常而流行的疾病 epidemic due to abnormal changes of weather

【时区】shíqū ☞ 标准时区 biāozhǔn shíqū on p. 127

【时人】shírén ❶ 当时的人 people of the time:～有诗为证。We can quote poems by the people of the time as evidence. ❷〈旧时 *old*〉指社会上一个时期里最活跃的人 people most active in society during the period

【时日】shírì ❶ 时间和日期 time; date:不计～ ignore or disregard the time|延误～ miss the deadline ❷ 较长的时间 relatively long period of time:这项工程需要～。The project requires more time.

【时尚】shíshàng 当时的风尚 fashion; fad; vogue:不合～ out of fashion

【时时】shíshí 常常 often; constantly; again and again:～不忘自己是人民的公仆 often remind oneself that one is the people's public servant|二十年来我～想起这件事。I have constantly recalled the matter over the past 20 years.

【时世】shíshì ❶ same as 时代 shídài ①:艰难～ hard (or difficult) times ❷ 指当前的社会 present-day society:他对～有深刻的认识。He has a profound understanding of contemporary society.

【时事】shíshì 最近期间的国内外大事 current events; current affairs; recent major national and international event:关心～ be concerned with current affairs|～报告 report on current affairs|～述评 current-events survey

【时势】shíshì 某一时期的客观形势 current situation; trend of the times; prevailing circumstances:当时为～所迫,只好离家出走。Driven by the situation at that time, one had to run away from home.

【时俗】shísú 当时的习俗;流俗 prevalent customs of the times:囿于～ constrained by the prevalent customs of the times|不落～ depart from the prevalent customs of the times

【时速】shísù 以小时为时间单位的速度 speed per hour; hourly speed

【时务】shíwù 当前的重大事情或客观形势 current affairs; prevalent circumstances; trend of the times:不识～ show no understanding of the times; do not know what's best for one|识～者为俊杰。A wise man knows how to bow to circumstances. *or* Those who allow themselves be guided by the turn of events are real heroes.

【时下】shíxià 当前;眼下 currently; at present; right now:这是～流行的款式。This style is in fashion at present.

【时鲜】shíxiān 少量上市的应时的新鲜蔬菜、鱼虾等 small quantities of fresh vegetables, fish, shrimps, etc. in season

【时限】shíxiàn 完成某项工作的期限 deadline; time limit:～紧迫 pressed for time|以三天为～完成这项任务 fulfil the task within the time limit of three days

【时效】shíxiào ❶ 指在一定时间内能起的作用 effectiveness for a given period of time ❷〈法律 *leg.*〉所规定的刑事责任和民事诉讼权利的有效期限 limit of time; prescription; limitation; term or period of validity of criminal responsibility, and the right of civil lawsuit or action prescribed by law

【时新】shíxīn 某一时期最新的(多指服装样式 oft. referring to clothes) fashionable; stylish; trendy:～款式 latest fashion

【时兴】shíxīng 一时流行 fashionable; popular;

in vogue：这种款式～了一阵子。This style has been in vogue for a time.｜现在正～这种服装。This kind of dress is the fad now.

【时行】shíxíng same as 时兴 shíxīng

【时序】shíxù 季节变化的次序 time sequence；course of the seasons；seasons；times；sequence of seasonal changes：～推移，秋去冬来。With the change of seasons，autumn is gone and winter has now set in.

【时样】shíyàng 时新的式样 latest fashion；modern or up-to-date style

【时宜】shíyí 当时的需要 what is appropriate to the occasion；what suits the occasion：不合～ be not appropriate for the occasion；be inappropriate；be out of touch with the times

【时疫】shíyì 指某个季节流行的传染病 epidemic；infectious disease widely spread during a certain season

【时运】shíyùn 一时的运气 luck；fortune：～不济 have bad luck；be down on one's luck；luck goes against sb.；be at a low ebb

【时针】shízhēn ❶ 钟表面上的针形零件，短针指示'时'，长针指示'分'，还有指示'秒'的 hands of a clock or watch；needle-shaped parts on the surface of a clock or watch，including a short hand which indicates the hour，a long hand which shows the minute，and another one that points to the second ❷ 钟表上的短针 hour hand（of a clock or watch）；short hand of a clock or watch

【时政】shízhèng 指当时的政治情况 current political situation；current political affairs

【时钟】shízhōng 能报时的钟 clock（that gives the time）

【时装】shízhuāng ❶ 式样最新的服装 fashionable dress；latest fashion：～展览 fashion show ❷ 当代通行的服装（跟'古装'相对 as opposed to 'ancient costumes'）modern clothing：～戏 operas with performers in modern costume

识（識） shí ❶ 认识 know：～字 learn to read；become literate｜素不相～ have never met；not be acquainted with each other｜有眼不～泰山 have eyes but fail to see Taishan Mountain；entertain an angel unawares ❷ 见识；知识 knowledge；learning；insight：卓～ sagacity｜有～之士 person of insight；person with breadth of vision；knowledgeable person｜常～ general or elementary knowledge；common sense｜学～ learning；knowledge ☞ zhì on p.2472

【识别】shíbié 辨别；辨认 distinguish；discern；spot；identify：～真伪 distinguish truth and falsehood；tell the false from the genuine

【识货】shí//huò 能鉴别货物的好坏 know all about the goods；be able to tell good from bad；know what's what；be knowledgeable：不怕不～，就怕货比货。Don't worry about knowing little about the goods，for you can always make a comparison.

【识家】shíjiā 识货的人 knowledgeable customer；person who is able to tell good from bad：货卖～ sell goods to knowledgeable customers｜只要东西好，不怕没～。One need not worry about the lack of knowing customers as long as the products are good.

【识见】shíjiàn〈书 *fml.*〉知识和见闻；见识② knowledge and experience

【识荆】shíjīng〈书 *fml.*〉〈敬辞 *pol.*〉指初次见面或结识（语本李白《与韩荆州书》：'生不用封万户侯，但愿一识韩荆州'）have the honour of making your acquaintance；meet for the first time or get acquainted with sb.（The expression originated from *Letter to Han Jingzhou* by Li Bai：'I do not care about the title of a high-ranking official，all I wish is to make acquaintance with Han Jingzhou.'）

【识破】shípò 看穿（别人的内心秘密或阴谋诡计）see through；penetrate（another's secrets or a conspiracy）：～机关 see through the scheme｜～阴谋 see through a conspiracy

【识趣】shíqù 知趣 be judicious；behave or respond sensibly in a delicate situation

【识时务者为俊杰】shí shíwù zhě wéi jùnjié 能认清当前的重大事情或客观形势的才是杰出的人物（语本《三国志·蜀书·诸葛亮传》注引《襄阳记》：'识时务者，在乎俊杰'）。Whosoever understands the course of current events is a great man. *or* A wise man allows himself to bow to circumstances.（*Records of Three Kingdoms·Kingdom of Shu·Biography of Zhuge Liang*，quoting the *Notes of Xiangyang*：'A person who understands the turn of current events is a great man.'）

【识文断字】shí wén duàn zì 识字（就能力说）be able to read and write；be literate：他～，当个文化教员还能对付。He is educated and up to the job of a teacher.

【识相】shíxiàng〈方 *dial.*〉会看别人的神色行事；知趣 be sensible；showing good sense；be tactful；know how to behave by observing other's expressions：我劝你～点，别自讨没趣。You'd better be more sensible and not make yourself unwelcome.

【识羞】shíxiū 自觉羞耻（多用于否定式 oft. used in the negative）feel ashamed；have a sense of shame：好不～ so shameless

【识字】shí//zì 认识文字 learn to read；become literate：读书～ read and write｜注音～ learn to read through phonetic notation｜～课本 reading primer；elementary reader

旹 shí〈书 *fml.*〉same as 时 shí

实（實） shí ❶ 内部完全填满，没有空隙 solid；full：～心儿的铁球 solid iron ball｜把窟窿填～了 fill up the hole ❷ 真实；实

在（跟'虚'相对 as opposed to 'false'）true; real; actual; sincere:～心眼儿 honest; conscientious; honest person|～事求是 seek truth from facts; be realistic and truthful; be practical and realistic|～话～说 speak the plain truth; call a spade a spade; tell the truth; speak frankly; talk straight ❸ 实际;事实 reality; fact; actuality:传闻失～。The rumour proved unfounded.|名～相副。The reputation accords with the reality. ❹ 果实;种子 fruit; seed:芡～(鸡头米) Gorgon fruit|开花结～ blossom and bear fruit

【实报实销】shí bào shí xiāo 支出多少报销多少 be reimbursed for what one actually spends; be reimbursed for one's expenses

【实测】shícè 用工具、仪器等进行实际测量或检测 survey; inspect with tools, instruments, etc.

【实诚】shí·cheng 诚实;老实 honest; frank:～话 truth|这个人～,答应了的事一定会做到。He is an honest man who is as good as his word.

【实处】shíchù 指起实际作用的地方 where it really matters; place that has an actual effect:干劲用在～ use one's vigour where it really matters|措施落到～ put the measures into practice; carry out the measures where it matters

【实词】shící 意义比较具体的词。汉语的实词包括名词、动词、形容词、数词、量词、代词六类。notional word; words with concrete meanings, including nouns, adjectives, numerals, classifiers and pronouns in Chinese

【实打实】shí dǎ shí 实实在在 genuine; real; 100 per cent true:～的硬功夫 hard-won genuine skill|～地说吧。Tell us nothing but the truth.

【实弹】shídàn ❶ 装有枪弹或炮弹 (of a gun or cannon) be loaded:荷枪～ carry a loaded rifle ❷ 实际发射枪弹或炮弹的 live shell; live ammunition; discharging or firing bullets or shells:～演习 practise with live ammunition

【实地】shídì ❶ 在现场(做某事 do sth.) on the spot; field:～考察 carry out on-the-spot investigations|～试验 field experiment ❷ 实实在在(做某事 do sth.) in real earnest; steadfast; practical and steady:～去做 do sth. in a practical manner

【实感】shígǎn 真实的感情;实际的感受 true or genuine feelings; real sentiments:真情～ true feelings

【实干】shígàn 实地去做 get right on the job; do solid work; be steadfast in one's work:～家 person of action|发扬～精神 foster the spirit of working in earnest

【实话】shíhuà 真实的话 truth:～实说 speak the plain truth; call a spade a spade; tell the truth; speak frankly; talk straight

【实惠】shíhuì ❶ 实际的好处 real benefit; material gain:得到～ really benefit (from) ❷ 有实际的好处 substantial; solid; practical:你送他实用的东西比送陈设品要～些。It is more practical for you to send him something useful rather than something for show.

【实际】shíjì ❶ 客观存在的事物或情况 reality; practice; objective matters or situations:一切从～出发 proceed in all cases from the practice|理论联系～ integrate theory with practice ❷ 实有的;具体的 practical; realistic; concrete:举一个～的例子来说明 illustrate with a concrete example|～工作 practical work|～行动 real actions ❸ 合乎事实的 real; actual; true:这种想法不～。This idea is not realistic.|计划订得很～。The plan is very realistic.

【实际工资】shíjì gōngzī 以工人所得的货币工资实际上能购买多少生活消费品、开销多少服务费做标准来衡量的工资 real wages; wages that are measured according to the standard of how many basic consumer goods and services can be actually purchased with the money wages of a worker; ☞ 名义工资 míngyì gōngzī on p.1352

【实寄封】shíjìfēng 集邮中指经过实际投递的信封 envelope of a posted letter (in philately)

【实绩】shíjì 实际的成绩 deeds; real achievements; concrete results:考察工作～ examine the actual work

【实践】shíjiàn ❶ 实行(自己的主张);履行(自己的诺言) put (one's view) into practice; carry out (one's promise); implement ❷ 人们改造自然和改造社会的有意识的活动 practice; conscious activities carried out by people to remake nature and society:～出真知。Genuine knowledge comes from practice. *or* Practice brings knowledge.

【实景】shíjǐng 拍摄电影、电视时作为背景的真实的景物（区别于'布景' as compared with 'setting'）realistic view (serving as a background when shooting a film or television programme)

【实据】shíjù 确实的证据 substantial evidence; actual proof:真凭～ ironclad evidence

【实况】shíkuàng 实际情况 what is actually happening; actual situation:～报导 live coverage|～录像 live videotaping|转播大会～ televise a rally live

【实力】shílì 实在的力量(多指军事或经济方面 usu. military or economic) actual strength; power:经济～ economic strength|～雄厚 fully reinforced|增强～ build up strength

【实例】shílì 实际的例子 living example; concrete example:用～说明 illustrate with a concrete example

【实录】shílù ❶ 按照真实情况记载的文字 factual record; faithful record; writing that records what has actually happened:这本日记是他晚年生活的～。This diary is a faithful record of the last years of his life. ❷ 编年体史书的一种,专记某一皇帝统治时期的大事,如唐代韩愈的《顺宗实录》、宋代钱若水等的《太宗实录》等。私人记载祖先事迹的文字,有的也叫实录,如唐代李翱的《皇祖实录》。annals; records of major events during the reign of an emperor (e.g. *Records of Emperor Shunzong* by Han Yu of the Tang Dynasty, and the *Records of Emperor Taizong* by Qian Ruoshui and other writers of the Song Dynasty, etc.); personal records of the deeds of one's ancestors (e.g. *Records of the Imperial Ancestors* by Li Ao of the Tang Dynasty), some of which are also called 实录 ❸ 把实况记录或录制下来 record the facts or what has actually happened

【实落】shí·luo〈方 *dial.*〉❶ 诚实;不虚伪 honest; not false or deceitful:他有点执拗,对人心地可～。Though a little stubborn, he is honest and truthful with people. ❷ (心情)安稳踏实 (of state of mind) at peace; free from anxiety:听他这样一说,我心里才感到～。I felt relieved at his remarks. ❸ 确切 exact; precise:你究竟哪天动身,请告诉我个～的日子。Let me know the exact day of your departure. ❹ 结实;牢固 solid; firm:这把椅子做得可真～。This chair is very solidly made.

【实情】shíqíng 真实的情况 true state of affairs; actual situation; truth:了解～ find out how things stand

【实权】shíquán 实际的权力 real power:握有～ wield real power

【实生】shíshēng 直接用种子播种培育的(苗木等 of nursery stock, etc.) raised directly from planted seeds:～苗 seedling|～毛竹造林 forest grown directly from the planted seeds of *mao* bamboo

【实施】shíshī 实行(法令、政策等 of laws and decrees, policies, etc.) invoke; put into effect; implement; enforce; carry out:付诸～ put into practice|～细则 implementing regulations

【实事】shíshì ❶ 实有的事 actual thing; fact:此剧取材于京城～。This play was based on what really happened in the capital city. ❷ 具体的事;实在的事 deeds; practical work; solid work; concrete matters:少讲空话,多办～。Less empty talk, more practical deeds. *or* Say less and do more.

【实事求是】shí shì qiú shì 从实际情况出发,不夸大,不缩小,正确地对待和处理问题 seek truth from facts; be practical and realistic; deal with problems correctly by proceeding from the actual situation, neither exaggerating nor underestimating the situation

【实数】shíshù ❶ 有理数和无理数的统称 real number; general term for rational and irrational numbers ❷ 实在的数字 actual amount or number:开会的人有多少,报个～来。Give the actual attendance figure at the meeting.

【实说】shíshuō 如实地说 tell the truth; speak frankly; talk straight:实话～ speak the plain truth; tell the truth; speak frankly; talk straight; be quite blunt

【实体】shítǐ ❶ 马克思主义以前的哲学上的一个概念,认为实体是万物不变的基础和本原。唯心主义者所说的'精神'、形而上学的唯物主义者所说的'物质'都是这样的实体。substance; essence; philosophical concept predating Marxism, considered the unchangeable foundation and principle of all things, such as 'spirit' in the eyes of an idealist, and 'essence' in the eyes of a metaphysical materialist ❷ 指实际存在的起作用的组织或机构 entity; actual functioning organization or organ:经济～ economic entity|政治～ political entity

【实物】shíwù ❶ 实际应用的东西 material object; real object; thing for practical use ❷ 真实的东西 in kind; matter; real thing:～教学 object lesson ❸ 物质存在的一种基本形式,指具有相对静止状态的质量的基本粒子所组成的物质。任何实物粒子都不能脱离有关的场而独立存在。basic form of the existence of matter, i.e., substances composed of the elementary particles of a mass in relative stasis. The particles of any matter cannot be free from their relative fields and exist independently.

【实习】shíxí 把学到的理论知识拿到实际工作中去应用和检验,以锻炼工作能力 practice; fieldwork; field trip; apply and test learned theoretical knowledge in practical work to improve one's work ability

【实现】shíxiàn 使成为事实 live out; realize; fulfil; achieve; bring about; come true:理想～ realize one's ideals

【实像】shíxiàng 物体发光的光线经凹面镜、凸透镜反射或折射后会聚而形成的影像叫做实像。实像可以显现在屏幕上,能使照相底片感光。光源在主焦点以外时才能产生实像,摄影和放映电影都必须利用实像。real image; image formed by assembling the reflected or refracted luminous light from an object through a concave mirror or convex lens, which can be projected on a screen, and sensitize light-sensitive film. Real images can only be produced when the light source is outside the prime focus, and are indispensable to photography or the showing of a movie.

【实效】shíxiào 实际的效果 actual effect; substantial results:讲求～ stress actual results

【实心】shíxīn ❶ 心地诚实 sincere; honest; earnest：～话 sincere words; words from the bottom of one's heart | ～实意 honest and sincere; true and earnest ❷ (～儿 shíxīnr) 物体内部是实的 (of the inside of an object) solid; full：这个球是～的，拿着很沉。This ball is solid and heavy to hold.

【实心眼儿】shíxīnyǎnr 心地诚实，也指心地诚实的人 honest; conscientious; honest person：～的小伙子 honest young man | 他是个～，不会说假话。He is an honest man who never tells a lie.

【实行】shíxíng 用行动来实现（纲领、政策、计划等）put into practice; carry out; practise; implement; realize (a programme, policy, plan, etc.) through one's actions：～改革 carry out reforms

【实学】shíxué 塌实而有根底的学问 real learning; sound scholarship：真才～ real ability and learning

【实验】shíyàn ❶ 为了检验某种科学理论或假设而进行某种操作或从事某种活动 experiment; test; engage in an operation or activity to test a scientific theory or hypothesis ❷ 指实验的工作 experimental work; laboratory work：做～ conduct an experiment; make a test | 科学～ scientific experiment

S

【实验式】shíyànshì 用元素符号表示化合物中各元素原子数最简整数比的式子。如氯化钠的实验式是NaCl，表示氯化钠晶体中钠(Na)和氯(Cl)原子数的比例是1:1，而并不意味着有氯化钠分子存在。chemical equation; formula that indicates the integer ratio reduced to the lowest terms of the atomic number of various elements of a chemical compound by the symbol of the element, e.g. the chemical equation of sodium chloride is NaCl, which indicates that the ratio of the atomic number of Na and Cl in NaCl crystal is one to one, but does not mean the NaCl molecule actually exists; also 最简式 zuìjiǎnshì

【实业】shíyè 指工商企业 industry and commerce; business; enterprise：～家 industrialist; businessman or businessperson | 兴办～ set up a business in industry and commerce

【实益】shíyì 实在的利益 real benefit：得到～ obtain (or gain) real benefit

【实意】shíyì 心意真实 sincere; heartfelt：实心～ genuinely and sincerely; wholeheartedly

【实用】shíyòng ❶ 实际使用 practical use or application：切合～ be practical ❷ 有实际使用价值的 practical; applied; pragmatic; functional：这种家具又美观，又～。The furniture is not only beautiful but also practical.

【实用文】shíyòngwén 〈旧指 *old*〉应用文 practical writing (e.g. official documents, notices, etc.)

【实用主义】shíyòng zhǔyì 现代资产阶级哲学的一个派别，创始于美国。它的主要内容是否认世界的物质性和真理的客观性，把客观存在和主观经验等同起来，认为有用的就是真理，思维只是应付环境解决疑难的工具。pragmatism; modern capitalist philosophical school originating from the United States characterized mainly by its denial of the materiality of the world and the objectivity of truth, its equation of objective reality with subjective experience, and its belief that whatever is useful is the truth while thoughts are only tools for coping with situations and solving difficult problems

【实在】shízài ❶ 诚实；不虚假 true; real; honest; practical; not false：～的本事 real ability | 心眼儿～ be honest and down-to-earth ❷ 的确 indeed; really; honestly：～太好了 very good indeed; just wonderful; simply terrific | ～不知道 really don't know ❸ 其实 in fact; in reality; as a matter of fact：他说他懂了，～并没懂。He said he understood, when in fact he didn't.

【实在】shí·zai (工作、活儿)扎实；地道；不马虎 (of work) well done; done carefully or in real earnest：工作做得很～。The work is well done.

【实在法】shízàifǎ 西方法学家对法律的分类之一，指各国在各个历史时期制定或认可的法律(跟'自然法'相对 as opposed to 'natural law') positive law; one of the categories of law classified by Western jurists, i.e. laws formulated or approved by different countries during various historical periods

【实则】shízé 实际上；其实 actually; in fact; in reality：他满口说好，～是敷衍大家。He readily agreed, but actually he was perfunctory with us.

【实战】shízhàn 实际作战 actual combat：要从～出发，苦练杀敌本领。It is imperative to proceed from the actual needs of war and practise hard to master combat skills.

【实证】shízhèng 实际的证明 actual or concrete evidence：这些涂改过的单据是他犯罪活动的～。These doctored documents are concrete evidence of his criminal activities.

【实职】shízhí 有职位而且实际参加工作的 position with actual duties or work：～人员 person who holds a position with actual duties or work

【实质】shízhì 本质 substance; essence; gist

【实字】shízì 有实在意义的字(跟'虚字'相对 as opposed to 'empty word; function word; form word') notional word; word with substantial meaning

【实足】shízú 确定足数的 full; solid; exact：～年龄 exact age | ～一百人 no fewer than 100 people

拾[1] shí ❶ 把地上的东西拿起来；捡 pick up (from the ground); collect; gather：～

粪 gather dung; collect manure | ～麦穗儿 glean stray ears of wheat | ～金不昧 return money found ❷ 收拾 clean; put in order: ～掇 clean; tidy up; put in order

拾[2] shí '十'的大写 (capital form of the Chinese numeral) 10; ☞ 数字 shùzì on p.1791

☞ shè on p.1696

【拾掇】shí·duo ❶ 整理;归拢 clean up; tidy up; put in order: 屋里～得整整齐齐的。The room was kept clean and tidy. ❷ 修理 repair; fix; mend: ～钟表 repair watches and clocks ❸ 惩治 punish; settle with; take to task: 他要是说瞎话,得狠狠地～他! If he tells a lie, we will punish him severely!

【拾荒】shíhuāng 因生活贫困而拾取柴草、田地间遗留的谷物、别人扔掉的废品等 (of a poverty-stricken person) collect firewood or grain left in the fields or articles discarded by others, etc.

【拾金不昧】shí jīn bù mèi 拾到钱财不藏起来据为己有 not pocket the money one picks up; return money found

【拾零】shílíng 指把某方面的零碎的材料收集起来(多用于标题 usu. used in headlines) news in brief; tidbits; sidelights: 赛场～ sidelights from the competitive arena

【拾取】shíqǔ same as 拾[1] shí ①: 在海岸上～贝壳 collect shells on the beach

【拾趣】shíqù 指把某方面的有趣的材料收集起来(多用于标题 usu. used in titles) collect interesting bits and pieces : 峨眉～ 'Delights of Emei Mountain'

【拾人牙慧】shí rén yá huì 拾取人家的只言片语当做自己的话 pick up remarks from others and pass them off as one's own; steal other's idea or utterings

【拾物】shíwù 拾到的别人遗失的东西 (lost) articles found: ～招领处 lost and found (bureau); lost-property office

【拾遗】shíyí ❶ 拾取旁人遗失的东西,据为己有 appropriate lost property; pocket lost articles: 夜不闭户,道不～ (as evidence of good public order and high moral standards of a society) doors need not be bolted at night and articles left by the roadside are never appropriated ❷ 补充旁人所遗漏的事物 make good or make up for omissions: ～补阙 make up for omissions and deficiencies

【拾音器】shíyīnqì 电唱机中把唱针的振动变成电能的装置。连在放大器上由扬声器发出声音。最常见的有电磁式和晶体式两种。电磁式的由磁铁、线圈和装唱针的振动铁架构成;晶体式的用石英或酒石酸盐等有压电效应的晶体制成。pick-up; sound pick-up; adapter; device in an electric gramophone to turn the vibration of stylus into electric power, connected with a loud speaker to produce sound. The most common are electromagnetic and crystal types, the former being composed of a magnet, coil and vibrating iron frame holding the stylus, and the latter produced by piezoelectric crystals such as quartz or tartaric acid salt. also 电唱头 diànchàngtóu

食(❻蚀) shí ❶ 吃 eat: ～肉 eat meat | 应多～蔬菜。One should eat more vegetables. ❷ 专指吃饭 have a meal: ～堂 canteen; dining room; mess hall | 废寝忘～ (be so absorbed) as to forget food and sleep ❸ 人吃的东西 food (for people): 肉～ meat | 面～ food made of (wheat) flour | 主～ staple food | 副～ non-staple food | 消～开胃 help digestion and stimulate the appctite | 丰衣足～ have ample food and clothing ❹ (～儿 shír) 一般动物吃的东西;饲料 feed; things that animals eat: 猪～ pig feed | 鸡没～儿了。The chicken have no feed. | 鸟儿出来找～儿。The birds went out to look for food. ❺ 供食用或调味用的 edible; seasoning: ～物 food; edibles; eating; victuals | ～油 edible oil; cooking oil | ～盐 table salt; salt ❻ 月球走到地球太阳之间遮蔽了太阳,或地球走到太阳月球之间遮蔽了月球时,人所看到的日月亏缺或完全不见的现象 eclipse; disappearance, complete or in part, of the sun's or moon's light when the earth passes between the sun and the moon: 日～ solar eclipse | 月～ lunar eclipse

☞ sì on p.1823 and yì on p.2277

【食补】shíbǔ 吃有滋补作用的饮食补养身体 cat nutritious food (to tone up the body): 药补不如～。Eating nutritious food beats taking tonic medicine

【食不甘味】shí bù gān wèi 形容心里有事,吃东西都不知道滋味 eat without relish; have no appetite for food; find one's food tasteless; eat food without tasting anything when one is very worried about sth.

【食道】shídào same as 食管 shíguǎn

【食饵】shí'ěr 捕捉鱼虾等时用作诱饵的食物 bait; food serving as a lure when catching fish, shrimp, etc.

【食分】shífēn 发生日食或月食时,日、月被遮蔽的程度。以太阳或月球的直径为单位来计算,如日食的食分为 0.3,就是说太阳的直径被月球遮住 3/10。magnitude of eclipse; degree of obscuration of the sun or moon in a solar or lunar eclipse, calculated by the diameter of the sun or moon, so that if the magnitude of a solar eclipse is 0.3, then three 10ths of the sun's diameter is obscured by the moon

【食古不化】shí gǔ bù huà 指学了古代的文化知识不善于理解和应用,跟吃了东西不能消化一样 swallow ancient learning without digesting it; follow the ancients blindly; study ancient learning but fail to understand and use it well, as if eating without digesting

【食管】shíguǎn 连接咽头和胃的管状器官，食物经口腔从咽头进入食管，食管肌肉收缩的蠕动把食物送到胃里 esophagus; gullet; tubular organ that links the pharynx and stomach, into which food enters through the pharynx after passing through the oral cavity, its muscles tighten up, causing peristalsis to send food to the stomach; also 食道 shídào;（图见 ☞ figure for 消化系统 xiāohuà xìtǒng on p. 2100）

【食积】shíjī〈中医 *Chin. med.*〉指因饮食没有节制而引起的消化不良的病。症状是胸部、腹部胀满，吐酸水，便秘或腹泻。dyspepsia; indigestion; dyspeptic disease caused by excessive eating and drinking, with such symptoms as bloated feeling in the chest or stomach, acid regurgitation, constipation or diarrhoea

【食既】shíjì 日全食或月全食过程中，月亮阴影与太阳圆面或地球阴影与月亮圆面第一次内切时二者之间的位置关系，也指发生这种位置关系的时刻。食既发生在初亏之后。second contact of an eclipse; positional relation between the sun and the moon, or between the earth and the moon, at the first revolution of the moon's shadow with the solar disc, or of the earth's shadow with the lunar disc, during the process of a total solar or lunar eclipse; the moment when such positional relations occur after the first contact of an eclipse; ☞ 食相 shíxiàng

S

【食客】shíkè ❶〈古代 *arch.*〉寄食在贵族官僚家里，为主人策划、奔走的人 person sponging on an aristocrat; hanger-on (of an aristocrat); person who lived at the house of a nobleman or an official, intrigued and lobbied for him ❷ 饮食店的顾客 patrons or customers of a restaurant

【食口】shíkǒu 指家里吃饭的人 (of a family) number of people to provide for

【食粮】shíliáng 人吃的粮食 grain; food: ～供应 supplies of food grains ◇精神～ nourishment for the mind | 煤是工业的～。Coal is the lifeblood of industry.

【食量】shíliàng 饭量 capacity for eating; appetite

【食品】shípǐn 商店出售的经过加工制作的食物 foodstuff; food; provisions; processed food sold by shops: 罐头～ tinned or canned food | ～公司 food company

【食谱】shípǔ ❶ 介绍菜肴等制作方法的书 recipe; cookbook; book that gives the methods for cooking certain dishes ❷ 制定的每顿饭菜的单子 menu; list of dishes in a meal: 幼儿园～ menu of a kindergarten | 一周～ menu of the week

【食亲财黑】shí qīn cái hēi〈方 *dial.*〉指人贪吝自私，爱占便宜 selfish and greedy; avaricious

【食甚】shíshèn 日偏食或月偏食过程中，太阳被月亮阴影遮盖最多或月亮被地球阴影遮盖最多时，两者之间的位置关系；日全食或月全食过程中，太阳被月亮阴影全部遮盖或月亮完全走进地球阴影里而两个中心距离最近时，两者之间的位置关系。也指发生上述位置关系的时刻。食甚发生在食既之后。middle or maximum phase of an eclipse; positional relation between the sun and the moon, or between the earth and the moon, when the sun is mostly covered in the moon's shadow or the moon is mostly covered in the earth's shadow during a partial solar or lunar eclipse; positional relations of the sun and the moon, or the earth and the moon, when the sun is completely covered in the moon's shadow, or when the moon is fully covered in the earth's shadow, and the two centres are closest to each other during a total solar or lunar eclipse; the moment when such positional relations occur after the second contact of an eclipse; ☞ 食相 shíxiàng

【食堂】shítáng 机关、团体中供应本单位成员吃饭的地方 canteen; dining room; mess hall; place where an institution or organization provides meals for its staff

【食糖】shítáng 食用的糖，如白糖、红糖 sugar (such as white and brown sugar)

【食物】shíwù 可以充饥的东西 food; edibles; eating; victuals; things that can allay or appease one's hunger

【食物链】shíwùliàn 乙种生物吃甲种生物，丙种生物吃乙种生物，丁种生物又吃丙种生物…。这种一连串的食与被食的关系，叫做食物链。草食动物吃绿色植物，肉食动物吃草食动物，是最基本的食物链。food chain; food cycle; chain of relations between feeding and being fed upon, such as organism B feeding on organism A, C on B, and D on C. . . . The fundamental type of food chain involves herbivores feeding on green plants, and carnivorous animals on herbivores; also 营养链 yíngyǎngliàn

【食物中毒】shíwù zhòngdú 因吃了含有细菌或毒素的食物而引起的疾病，一般症状是呕吐、腹泻、腹痛、心脏血管机能障碍等 food poisoning; disease caused by eating food that contains germs or toxins, its common symptoms including vomiting, diarrhoea, abdominal pain, cardiac and vascular functional obstruction, etc.

【食相】shíxiàng 日食（或月食）时，月球阴影与太阳（或地球阴影与月球）的不同位置关系，也指不同位置发生的时刻。全食时，有初亏、食既、食甚、生光、复圆五种食相；偏食时有初亏、食甚、复圆三种食相。phase of an eclipse; different positional relations of the moon's shadow and the sun (or the earth's shadow and the moon) in a solar or lunar eclipse; moment of such positions. A total eclipse goes through five phases: the first contact, the second contact, the middle or maximum phase, the third contact, and the fourth contact; and a partial eclipse goes through three phases: the first contact, the maximum phase, and the last contact.

【食性】shíxìng ❶ 动物吃食料的习性。以动物为食的叫肉食性,以植物为食的叫草食性,以动物和植物为食的叫杂食性。feeding habit; eating pattern; eating habits of animals. Those feeding on animals are sarcophagy; those on plants, herbivority; and those on animals and plants, omnivory. ❷ 指各人对食物味道的爱好;口味 one's preference for food; taste

【食言】shíyán 不履行诺言;失信 go back on one's word; break one's promise: 决不~ never go back on one's word; as good as one's word

【食言而肥】shí yán ér féi 形容为了自己占便宜而说话不算数,不守信用(语本《左传》哀公二十五年:'是食言多矣,能无肥乎!') break one's promise for petty gains; break faith with sb. (*The Zuo Commentary · Duke Ai 25th Year*: 'Having gone back on his word so many times, how can he not gain advantages?')

【食盐】shíyán 无机化合物,成分是氯化钠,有海盐、池盐、岩盐和井盐四种。无色或白色晶体,有咸味。用于制染料、玻璃、肥皂等,也是重要的调味剂和防腐剂。table salt; salt; inorganic compound composed of sodium chloride, which includes four varieties: sea, lake, rock and well salt; salty colourless or white crystal used to produce dyes, glass, soaps, etc., and is also an important flavouring and antiseptic; 通称 generally called 盐 yán

【食用】shíyòng ❶ 做食物用 eat; consume; be used for food ❷ 可以吃的 edible: ~油 edible oil | ~植物 edible plant; food plant

【食油】shíyóu 供食用的油,如芝麻油、花生油、菜油、豆油等 edible oil; cooking oil (e.g. sesame, peanut, rape and soya-bean oil)

【食欲】shíyù 人进食的要求 appetite; (of a person) desire for food: ~不振 have a poor appetite; have a jaded appetite | 适当运动能促进~。Proper exercise helps improve your appetite.

【食指】shízhǐ ❶ 紧挨着大拇指的手指头 index finger; forefinger; finger next to the thumb ❷〈书 *fml*.〉〈比喻 *fig*.〉家庭人口 number of people in a family: ~众多(人口多,负担重) have a big family to support

【食茱萸】shízhūyú 落叶乔木,枝上多刺,羽状复叶,小叶披针形,花淡绿黄色。果实球形,成熟时红色,可入药,又可提制芳香油。ailanthus prickly ash (*Zanthoxylum ailanthoides*); deciduous arbour with prickly branches, pinnately compound leaves, lanceolar leaflets, and light green or yellow flowers, whose spherical fruit turns red when ripe and is used as medicine or to extract fragrant oil

蚀 shí ❶ 损失;损伤;亏耗 lose; erode; corrode: ~本 lose one's capital; lose money in business | 侵~ erode; corrode; eat into | 腐~ corrode; erode; eat into | 剥~ erode; corrode; denude; wear away ❷ same as 食 shí ⑥

【蚀本】shí//běn 赔本儿 lose one's capital; lose money in business

【蚀刻】shíkè 利用硝酸等化学药品的腐蚀作用来制造铜版、锌版等印刷版的方法 etching; method of producing copper or zinc printing plates by making use of the corrosive action of medical and chemical reagents such as hydrogen nitrate

炻 shí [炻器](shíqì)介于陶器和瓷器之间的陶瓷制品,多呈棕色、黄褐色或灰蓝色,质地致密坚硬,跟瓷器相似。如水缸、沙锅等。stone ware; ceramic product with qualities between those of porcelain and pottery, mostly brown, tawny or greyish blue, compact and hard in quality, similar to pottery, e.g. water vats, earthen pots, etc.

祏 shí〈古代 *arch*.〉宗庙中藏神主的石室 stone casket (hiding a spirit tablet in an ancient ancestral temple or shrine of a ruling house)

埘(塒) shí 在墙上凿的鸡窝 chicken roost; hen roost; chicken coop built into a wall

莳(蒔) shí [莳萝](shíluó)多年生草本植物,羽状复叶,花黄色,果实椭圆形。子实含有芳香油,可制香精。dill (*Anethum graveolens*); cumin; perennial herb with pinnately compound leaves, yellow flowers, oval fruit, and seeds containing fragrant oil and thus used to produce essence

☞ shì on p. 1762

湜 shí〈书 *fml*.〉水清见底的样子 (of water) clear; so limpid that the bottom can be seen

寔 shí〈书 *fml*.〉❶ 放置 lay; place ❷ same as 实 shí ❸ 此 this

鲥(鰣) shí 鲥鱼,背部黑绿色,腹部银白色,眼周围银白色带金光。鳞下有丰富的脂肪,肉鲜嫩,是名贵的食用鱼。属于海产鱼类,春季到我国珠江、长江、钱塘江等河流中产卵。hilsa herring (*Macrura reevesii Richardson*); reeves shad; famous marine food fish with a black-and-green back and silvery white belly, the areas around its eyes being silvery white with a golden light, with rich fat under its scales, and fresh and tender meat, and spawning in spring in China's Pearl, Yangtze and Qiantang rivers, etc.

鼫 shí 古书上指鼯鼠一类的动物 (in ancient books) animals like the flying squirrel

shǐ (ㄕˇ)

史 shǐ ❶ 历史 history: ～学 science of history; historiography | 近代～ modern history | 世界～ world history | 有～以来 since the beginning of the recorded history ❷〈古代 *arch.*〉掌管记载史实的官 official in charge of historical records ❸ (Shǐ)姓 a surname

【史部】shǐbù 我国古代图书分类的一大部类。包括各种体裁的历史著作。history as one of the important divisions of ancient Chinese library collections, including various styles of historical works; also 乙部 yǐbù; ☞ 四部 sìbù on p. 1820

【史册】shǐcè 历史记录 history; annals; historical records: 名垂～ remain immortal in the annals of history; also 史策 shǐcè

【史抄】shǐchāo 摘抄史书而成的书籍 extracts from history; book compiled from extracts of historical records

【史官】shǐguān〈古代 *arch.*〉朝廷中专门负责整理编纂前朝史料史书和搜集记录本朝史实的官 official historian; historiographer; official in an ancient court specially in charge of arranging and compiling historical materials and records of the preceding dynasty, and collecting factual historical records on the ruling dynasty

【史馆】shǐguǎn〈旧时 *old*〉指编纂国史的机构 national archives; bureau in charge of compiling national history

【史话】shǐhuà 叙述史事或某种事物发展过程的以故事的形式写成的作品(多用做书名),如《太平天国史话》、《辞书史话》historical narrative; historical account; works that recount historical events or the development of certain incidents in the form of a story, usu. used in titles of books such as *A Narrative History of the Kingdom of Heavenly Peace* and *A Narrative History of Dictionaries*

【史籍】shǐjí 历史书籍 historical records; history

【史迹】shǐjì 历史遗迹 historical sites or relics: 革命～ revolutionary relics or sites

【史剧】shǐjù 历史剧 historical play or drama

【史料】shǐliào 历史资料 historical data; historical materials

【史评】shǐpíng 评论史事或史书的著作 historical criticism; works that comment on historical events and records

【史前】shǐqián 没有书面记录的远古 prehistoric; remote antiquity of which there are no written records: ～时代 prehistoric age | ～考古学 prehistoric archaeology

【史乘】shǐshèng〈书 *fml.*〉same as 史书 shǐshū

【史诗】shǐshī 叙述英雄传说或重大历史事件的叙事长诗 epic; long narrative poem that recounts the deeds of a hero or an important historical event

【史实】shǐshí 历史上的事实 historical event: 《三国演义》中的故事,大部分都有～根据。Most stories in *Romance of Three Kingdoms* are based on historical events.

【史书】shǐshū 记载历史的书籍 history (book); historical records; book that records history

【史无前例】shǐ wú qián lì 历史上从来没有过;前所未有 without precedent in history; unprecedented; unparalleled

【史学】shǐxué 以人类历史为研究对象的科学 science of history; historical science; historiography; science that studies human history

矢1 shǐ 箭 arrow: 流～ stray arrow | 飞～ flying arrow | ～镞 metal arrowhead; arrowhead | 有的放～ shoot one's arrow at the target — have a definite goal in view; do sth. with a definite purpose in mind

矢2 shǐ〈书 *fml.*〉发誓 vow; swear; take an oath: ～口 insist; state emphatically | ～志 swear; vow; pledge oneself | ～忠 swear loyalty to

矢3 shǐ same as 屎 shǐ: 遗～ empty one's bowels; defecate | 蝇～ flyspeck

【矢口】shǐkǒu 一口咬定 insist; state emphatically: ～否认 flatly disavow; deny firmly | ～抵赖 categorically deny (one's guilt or mistake); persistently quibble and deny one's errors

【矢量】shǐliàng 有大小也有方向的物理量,如速度、动量、力等 vector; physical quantity that has a size as well as a direction, such as speed, momentum and force; also 向量 xiàngliàng

【矢石】shǐshí〈古代 *arch.*〉作武器用的箭和石头(石 *shi*: 礌石或用机械装置弹射出去的石头 stone missiles or stones shot off by a mechanical device) arrows and stones (used as weapons in ancient times): ～如雨。The arrows and stones came down like rain. | 亲冒～ brave arrows and stones in battle

【矢志】shǐzhì〈书 *fml.*〉发誓立志 swear; vow; pledge oneself: ～不渝 take an oath not to change one's mind; vow to adhere unswervingly to one's chosen course; pledge steadfast devotion to a course | ～于科学 pledge to devote oneself to science

【矢忠】shǐzhōng〈书 *fml.*〉发誓尽忠 swear loyalty to: ～于祖国 pledge loyalty to one's motherland

吏 shǐ〈书 *fml.*〉same as 史 shǐ

豕 shǐ〈书 *fml.*〉猪 pig: 狼奔～突 rush like a boar and run like a wolf — run about like wild beasts; rampage in total disorder

使[1] shǐ ❶ 派遣；支使 send; have (sb. do sth.)：～唤 order about or around｜～人去打听消息 send sb. to make enquiries ❷ 使用 use; employ; apply; exert：～拖拉机耕地 use a tractor to plough the fields｜这支笔很好～。This pen writes nicely.｜～上点肥料 use a little fertilizer ❸ 让；叫；致使 make; cause; enable; help：办事～群众满意 work to satisfy the masses｜加强质量管理，～产品合格率不断上升 tighten up quality control to ensure steady improvement in the acceptance rate of products ❹〈书 *fml.*〉假如 if; supposing

使[2] shǐ 奉使命办事的人 envoy; emissary; messenger：～节 diplomatic envoy; envoy｜大～ ambassador｜公～ minister｜特～ special envoy｜学～（科举时代派到各省去主持考试的官员）study emissary; official sent to the provinces as the chief examiner during the period of the imperial civil examination

【使绊儿】shǐ//bànr ❶ 摔跤时用腿脚勾住对方的腿脚使跌倒 (of wrestling) trip the opponent with a leg trick ❷〈比喻 *fig.*〉用不正当手段暗害别人 injure others by devious (oft. covert) means; put a spoke in sb.'s wheel; try to trip sb. up：嘴上说话比蜜甜，暗中～算计人 talk with honey on one's lips while scheming against sb. in secret ‖ also 使绊子 shǐbàn·zi

【使不得】shǐ·bu·de ❶ 不能使用 useless; cannot be used：这支笔坏了，～。This pen is broken — it can't be used.｜情况改变了，老办法～。Since circumstances have changed, the old approach no longer works. ❷ 不行；不可以 be undesirable or impermissible; must not be done：病刚好，走远路可～。You've just been ill, and mustn't walk too far.

【使得】[1] shǐ·de ❶ 可以使用 usable; can be used; will work：这支笔～使不得？Does this pen work all right? ❷ 能行；可以 workable; feasible; will do：这个主意倒～。This is quite a good idea.｜你不去如何～？I don't think it will do if you don't go.

【使得】[2] shǐ·de（意图、计划、事物）引起一定的结果 make; cause; render; (of an intention, plan, matter) bring about (a result)：科学种田～粮食产量有了大幅度提高。Scientific farming has resulted in a great increase in grain output.｜这个想法～他忘记了一切困难。This thought made him forget all the difficulties.

【使馆】shǐguǎn 外交使节在所驻国家的办公机关。外交使节是大使的叫大使馆，是公使的叫公使馆。diplomatic mission; embassy; administrative organ of a diplomatic envoy in a foreign country, such as an embassy, whose diplomatic envoy is an ambassador, and a legation, whose diplomatic envoy is a minister

【使坏】shǐ//huài 出坏主意；耍狡猾手段 be up to mischief; play a dirty trick; create trouble：暗中～ play a dirty trick in secret

【使唤】shǐ·huan ❶ 叫人替自己做事 order about or around; have sb. do sth.：孩子大了，～不动了。The child has grown up, and refuses to be ordered about. ❷ 使用（工具、牲口等 of tools, draught animals, etc.）use; handle; manage：新式农具～起来很得劲儿。The new farm implements are fit for use.｜这匹马不听生人～。This horse won't obey a stranger.

【使假】shǐ//jiǎ 以次充好；掺假 pass off inferior goods as good quality; practise fraudulence：掺杂～ mix up products of different qualities and engage in fraud

【使节】shǐjié 由一个国家派驻在另一个国家的外交代表，或由一个国家派遣到另一个国家去办理事务的代表 diplomatic envoy; envoy; diplomatic representative accredited by one country to another, or a representative sent by one country to another to handle affairs

【使劲】shǐ//jìn（～儿 shǐ//jìnr）用力 exert oneself; exert all one's strength; make efforts：～划船 exert oneself to row a boat｜我们俩使足了劲儿才把这块石头搬开。Both of us strained every muscle to move the stone out of the way.

【使命】shǐmìng 派人办事的命令，多比喻重大的责任 mission; order sb. to be sent to do sth.; (oft. fig.) important duty：历史～ historical mission｜神圣～ sacred mission

【使然】shǐrán（由于某种原因）致使这样 make it so (due to some reason); it's because：他之所以离去，实为当时处境～。His departure is really due to the situation at that time.

【使性】shǐxìng 由着脾气；任性 lose one's temper; fly off the handle; throw a tantrum：任情～ throw a tantrum wilfully｜你可不能～胡来。You should not fly off the handle and behave recklessly. also 使性子 shǐxìng·zi

【使眼色】shǐ yǎn·sè 用眼睛向别人暗示自己的意思 wink; give hints to sb. with one's eyes

【使役】shǐyì 使用（牲畜等）work (an animal); use (livestock)：～耕牛要得当。Farm cattle must be used properly.

【使用】shǐyòng 使人员、器物、资金等为某种目的服务 use; employ; apply; make use of; resort to; (of personnel, utensils, capital, etc.) serve some purpose：～干部 use cadres｜合理～资金 make rational use of the capital

【使用价值】shǐyòng jiàzhí 物品所具有的能够满足人们某种需要的属性，如粮食能充饥，衣服能御寒等 use value; property of an article that satisfies some need of people, e.g. grain can appease hunger, and clothes can keep out the cold

【使者】shǐzhě 奉使命办事的人（现多指外交人员

usu. referring to diplomats) emissary; envoy; messenger; person who handles affairs under orders

始 shǐ ❶ 最初;起头;开始(跟'终'相对 as opposed to 'end; close; finish') begin; start; commence:～祖 first ancestor; earliest ancestor|周而复～ go round and round; go round and begin again; move in cycles|从～至终 from beginning to end; from start to finish|不自今日～ nothing new; not start from today|不知～于何时 not know exactly when sth. got started|～而不解,继而恍然。At first I didn't catch on, then I suddenly saw the light. ❷〈书 *fml.*〉〈副词 *adv.*〉same as 才 cái:游行至下午五时～毕。The parade did not end until 5 p. m.|不断学习～能进步。Only persistent study brings about progress.

【始末】shǐmò (事情)从头到尾的经过 beginning and end; from start to finish; whole story:他把这件事情的～对大家说了一遍。He told us the whole story from beginning to end.

【始业】shǐyè 学业开始,特指大、中、小学的各个阶段开始 beginning of a school year; beginning of the various stages of college, middle or primary school:春季～。The school year begins in spring.|秋季～。The school year begins in autumn.

【始终】shǐzhōng 指从开始到最后 from beginning to end; from start to finish; all along; throughout:贯彻～ carry through all along|～不懈 unremitting; tireless; untiring; indefatigable

【始祖】shǐzǔ ❶ 有世系可考的最初的祖先 first ancestor; earliest ancestor (according to textual research of a pedigree) ❷〈比喻 *fig.*〉某一学派或某一行业的创始人 originator or founder (of a school of thought, trade, etc.) ❸ 指原始的(动物) primitive (animals):～鸟 archaeopteryx

【始祖马】shǐzǔmǎ 古哺乳动物,马类的祖先,身体大小与狐狸相仿,前足四趾,后足三趾 eohippus (*Hyracotherium eohippus*); dawn horse; ancient mammal that is the ancestor of the horse, having a body like a fox, with four toes on the propodeum, and three toes on the metapedes

【始祖鸟】shǐzǔniǎo 古脊椎动物,头部像鸟,有爪和翅膀,稍能飞行,有牙齿,尾巴很长,由多数尾椎骨构成,除身上有鸟类的羽毛外,跟爬行动物相似。一般认为它是爬行动物进化到鸟类的中间类型,是鸟类的祖先,出现在侏罗纪。archaeogteryx; vertebrate that can fly a little and resembles a reptile except for its bird-like feathers, appearing during the Jurassic Period, having a bird-like head, claws, wings, teeth, and a long tail composed of many caudal vertebras, generally regarded as the intermediate category between reptiles and birds and the ancestor of the bird

【始作俑者】shǐ zuò yǒng zhě 孔子反对用俑殉葬,他说,开始用俑殉葬的人,大概没有后嗣了吧!(见于《孟子·梁惠王上》) Confucius opposed the burying of terracotta figurines with the dead, and said that the first person who did so probably had no offspring (see *Mencius·Duke Hui of Liang* (*I*)).〈比喻 *fig.*〉恶劣风气的创造者 creator of a bad precedent

驶 shǐ ❶ (车马等)飞快地跑 (of a vehicle, a horse, etc.) speed; go or pass quickly:急～而过 speed by; fly past ❷ 开动(车船等) sail (a ship); drive (a vehicle):驾～ drive (a vehicle)|行～ drive (a vehicle)|轮船因故停～。The ship has been held up due to engine trouble.

屎 shǐ ❶ 从肛门出来的排泄物;粪 excrement; faeces; stool; dung; droppings; things excreted from the anus:拉～ shit; empty the bowels ❷ 眼睛、耳朵等器官里分泌出来的东西 secretion (from the eye, ear, etc.):眼～ eye discharge; gum in the eyes|耳～ earwax

【屎壳郎】shǐ·kelàng〈方 *dial.*〉蜣螂 dung beetle

shì (ㄕ)

士 shì ❶〈古代 *arch.*〉指未婚的男子 bachelor; unmarried man ❷〈古代 *arch.*〉介于大夫和庶民之间的阶层 intelligentsia; social stratum between senior officials and the common people in ancient China ❸ 士人 scholar; intelligentsia:～农工商 scholars, farmers, artisans and merchants ❹ 军人 soldier; serviceman:～兵 rank-and-file soldier; rank and file; private|～气 spirit; morale ❺ 军人的一级,在尉以下 noncommissioned officer; a rank of soldiers below junior officer:上～ (U. K.) staff sergeant; (U. S.) sergeant first class|中～ sergeant|下～ corporal ❻ 指某些种技术人员 person trained in a specified field:医～ doctor|护～ nurse|技～ junior technician|助产～ midwife ❼ 对人的美称 (commendable) person; (praiseworthy) person:烈～ martyr|勇～ brave fighter; warrior|女～ lady; madam ❽ (Shì)姓 a surname

【士兵】shìbīng 军士和兵的统称;兵③ rank-and-file soldier; rank and file; private

【士大夫】shìdàfū 封建时代泛指官僚阶层,有时也包括还没有做官的读书人 scholar-officials; literati (in feudal China); (general reference to) bureaucratic class in feudal China, sometimes also including the scholars who were not officials

【士女】shìnǚ ❶〈古代 *arch.*〉指未婚的男女,后来泛指男女 unmarried young men and women; (later generally referred to) men and women ❷ same as 仕女 shìnǚ ②

【士气】shìqì 军队的战斗意志,也泛指群众的斗争意志 morale; spirit; (of an army or troops) strong will to fight; (of the masses) strong will to struggle: ～旺盛。The morale is kept up.|鼓舞～ boost morale

【士人】shìrén 封建时代称读书人 scholar (in feudal China)

【士绅】shìshēn 绅士 gentry

【士卒】shìzú 士兵 soldiers; privates: 身先～ (of an officer) fight at the head of his men; lead the charge

【士族】shìzú 东汉魏晋南北朝时期地主阶级内部逐渐形成的世代读书做官的大族,在政治经济各方面享有特权 influential, politically and economically privileged family of a long line of scholar-officials of the landlord class (which gradually came into existence during the Eastern Han, Wei, Jin, and Northern and Southern dynasties)

氏 shì ❶ 姓(张氏是'姓张的') family name; surname (e.g. 张氏 zhāngshì person whose surname is Zhang): 张～兄弟 Zhang brothers ❷ 放在已婚妇女的姓后,通常在父姓前再加夫姓,作为称呼 née; form of address for a married woman after her surname, usu. adding the family name of the husband before that of the father: 赵王～(夫姓赵,父姓王) Mrs. Zhao, née Wang (meaning that the lady's husband is surnamed Zhao and her father is surnamed Wang) ❸ 对名人专家的称呼 form of address for a famous person or expert: 顾～(顾炎武)《日知录》Gu Yanwu's *Notes on Daily Accumulation of Knowledge*|摄～温度计 Celsius thermometer|达尔文～ Darwin ❹〈书 *fml.*〉用在亲属关系字的后面称自己的亲属 one's kinsfolk (used after the character that indicates a family relationship): 舅～(母舅) (maternal) uncle|母～ mother

☞ zhī on p. 2455

【氏族】shìzú 原始社会由血统关系联系起来的人的集体,氏族内部实行禁婚,集体占有生产资料,集体生产,集体消费 clan; collective of primitive society united by blood relationship in which marriage was forbidden, the means of production were owned collectively, and both production and consumption were conducted collectively as well; also 氏族公社 shìzú gōngshè

示 shì 把事物摆出来或指出来使人知道,表示 show; notify; produce; instruct; signify: 告～ notice|指～ instruct; indicate|显～ show; manifest; demonstrate|暗～ hint; drop a hint|～意 hint; signal; motion; gesture|～范 show; demonstrate; set an example|～威 demonstrate; hold a demonstration|～众 publicly expose; punish before the public

【示波器】shìbōqì 用来测验交流电或脉动电流波的形状的仪器,由电子管放大器、扫描振荡器、阴极射线管等组成。除观测电流的波形外,还可以测定频率、电压强度等。oscillograph; oscilloscope; equipment used to test the shape of an alternating current or pulsating current wave, composed of a valve amplifier, a scanning generator and cathode-ray tube, which, besides displaying the wave patterns of an electric current, can also be used to determine frequency, voltage intensity, etc.

【示范】shìfàn 做出某种可供大家学习的典范 show; demonstrate; set an example (for the all to learn): ～操作 demonstration operation|～作用 exemplary role

【示警】shìjǐng 用某种动作或信号使人注意(危险或紧急情况) give a warning; warn; alert to danger; make people aware of (a danger or emergency) by making some movement or giving some signal: 鸣锣～ give a warning by striking a gong; sound an alarm with a gong|举红灯～ raise an alarm by holding up a red light

【示例】shìlì 举出或做出具有代表性的例子 give typical examples; give instances; give a demonstration: ～演出 give a demonstration performance

【示人】shìrén 拿出来给人看 show sth. to others; let others have a look at sth.: 他珍藏的古董从不轻易～。He doesn't easily show his collection of antiques to others.

【示弱】shìruò 表示比对方软弱,不敢较量(多用于否定 oft. used in the negative) show signs of weakness; take sth. lying down; show one is weaker than one's opponent and dare not compete with him: 不甘～ unwilling to be outdone; refuse to yield

【示威】shìwēi ❶ 有所抗议或要求而进行的显示自身威力的集体行动 demonstrate; hold a demonstration; collective action to show power in protesting sth. or making demands: 游行～ demonstration; parade; march ❷ 向对方显示自己的力量 put on a show of force; display one's strength or prowess

【示性式】shìxìngshì 表示含有官能团的化合物分子的简化结构式,如乙醇、甲醚的示性式分别为 CH_3CH_2OH 和 CH_3OCH_3 rational formula; simplified structural formula that indicates the functioning molecular combination in a chemical compound, e.g. CH_3CH_2OH for ethanol and CH_3OCH_3 for methyl ether; ☞ 结构式 jiégòushì on p. 991

【示意】shìyì 用表情、动作、含蓄的话或图形表示意思 signal; hint; motion; gesture; show one's meaning with an expression, action, implicit word or image: 以目～ wink at sb.;

tip sb. a wink|护士指了指门,～他把门关上。The nurse motioned at him to close the door by pointing at it.

【示意图】shìyìtú 为了说明内容较复杂的事物的原理或具体轮廓而绘成的略图 sketch map (to indicate the principle or concrete outline of a complicated matter):水利工程～ sketch map of the water conservancy project|人造卫星运行～ sketch map of the orbit of a man-made satellite

【示众】shìzhòng 给大家看,特指当众惩罚犯人 publicly expose; punish before the public:游街～ parade sb. through the streets (as a punishment)

世(卋) shì ❶ 人的一辈子 lifetime; life:一生一～ lifetime; one's whole life; throughout one's life; all one's life ❷ 有血统关系的人相传而成的辈分 generation; seniority in a family or clan generation hierarchy passed on through people of blood relationship:第十～孙 the 11th in descent; descendant in the 11th generation ❸ 一代又一代 from generation to generation:～交 longstanding friendship between two families|～仇 family feud; vendetta; sworn enemy (in a family feud)|～谊 friendship dating back to two or more generations|三代祖传～医 doctor of traditional Chinese medicine with a practice spanning three generations ❹ 指有世交的关系 of people who maintain good family relations:～兄 father's friend's son who is older than oneself|～叔 younger friend of one's father ❺ 时代 age; time; era:近～ modern times|当～ nowadays; at present ❻ 社会;人间 world; society:问～ be published; come out|～人 common people; people at large|～道 manners and morals of the time; ways of the world|～上 in the world; on earth|公之于～ make sth. public; make sth. known to the world ❼ (Shì)姓 a surname

【世弊】shìbì 当代的弊病;社会上的弊病 maladies of the present-day world or society

【世变】shìbiàn 世间的变化、变故 changes in the world; vicissitudes:饱经～ having experienced the vicissitudes of life

【世仇】shìchóu 世世代代有仇的人或人家,也指世世代代的冤仇 sworn enemy (in a family feud); person or family against whom one's family has had a grudge for generations; family feud; vendetta; enmity or feud for generations

【世传】shìchuán 世世代代相传下来 be handed down through generations; be known for generations:～名医 famous doctor known for generations

【世代】shìdài ❶ (很多)年代 long period of time; many, many years:那些格言不知流传了多少～。Those adages have been in circulation for God knows how many years. ❷ 好几辈子 for generations; generation after generation:～相传 pass on from generation to generation|～务农 from a long line of farmers

【世代交替】shìdài jiāotì 某些植物和无脊椎动物有性生殖和无性生殖交替进行的现象。动物中如水螅,植物中如羊齿都有这种现象。alternation of generations; alternation of sexual generation or asexual reproduction of certain plants and invertebrates, which exist in some animals such as the hydra and some plants such as the fern

【世道】shìdào 指社会状况 manners and morals of the time; ways of the world

【世风】shìfēng 社会风气 general mood of society; public morals and mores; morals of the world; common practice of society:～日下。Public morals are deteriorating day by day.

【世故】shìgù 处世经验 ways of the world:人情～ worldly wisdom; ways of the world|老于～ worldly wisdom; versed in the ways of the world

【世故】shì·gu (处事待人)圆滑,不得罪人 worldly-wise; shrewd; crafty; (of the way one gets along with people and manages one's affairs) smooth and wily, not offending others:这人有些～,不大愿意给人提意见。This person is of a smooth character. He is reluctant to put forward suggestions.

【世纪】shìjì 计算年代的单位,一百年为一世纪 century; unit to calculate time, which is equivalent to 100 years

【世纪末】shìjìmò 原指19世纪末叶,这个时期欧洲资本主义进入腐朽阶段,各方面潜伏着危机。也泛指某一社会的没落阶段。end of the century; *fin-de-siècle*; originally referred to the end of the 19th century, during which time European capitalism entered a decadent stage, with hidden crises in various fields; (generally referring to) the declining stage of a society

【世家】shìjiā ❶ 封建社会中门第高,世代做大官的人家 aristocratic family; noble family; old and well known family; family of noble origin and a long line of great officials ❷《史记》中诸侯的传记,按着诸侯的世代编排 hereditary house of a duke (*Records of the Historian*) ❸ 指以某种专长世代相承的家族 family in which a special skill has been handed down from generation to generation:游泳～ family of swimmers|梨园～ family of Peking Opera singers

【世间】shìjiān 社会上;人间 world; society:～的事没有一成不变的。Nothing in the world remains fixed.

【世交】shìjiāo ❶ 上代就有交情的人或人家 old

family friends; person or family that has been on friendly terms for over a generation: 朱先生是我的老～。Mr. Zhu and I are old family friends. | 王家跟李家是～。The Wangs and the Lis are old family friends. ❷ 两代以上的交谊 friendship spanning two or more generations

【世界】shìjiè ❶ 自然界和人类社会的一切事物的总和 world; sum of all things in nature and the human society: ～观 world outlook | ～之大,无奇不有。It takes all sorts to make the world. ❷〈佛教用语 *Budd.*〉指宇宙 universe: 大千～ boundless universe ❸ 地球上所有地方 all over the world: ～各地 all over the world | 周游～ travel the whole world over ❹ 指社会的形势、风气 existing conditions of society; social situation and practice: 现在是什么～,还允许你不讲理? Don't you realize that the present moment does not allow you to be unreasonable? ❺ 领域;人的某种活动范围 field; scope; sphere; realm: 内心～ inner world | 主观～ subjective world | 科学～ scientific world | 儿童～ children's world

【世界观】shìjièguān 人们对世界的总的根本的看法。由于人们的社会地位不同,观察问题的角度不同,形成不同的世界观。world outlook; people's general and basic views of the world coming out of their different social status and perspective; also 宇宙观 yǔzhòuguān

【世界时】shìjièshí 以本初子午线所在时区为标准的时间。世界时用于无线电通讯和科学数据记录,以便各国取得一致。universal time; time set by the standard of the time zone of the first meridian, used in radio communication and scientific data records so that various countries have identical time standards; also 格林尼治时间 Gélínnízhì shíjiān

【世界市场】shìjiè shìchǎng 国际间进行商品交换的市场的总称 world market; general term for the international market of commodity exchange

【世界语】Shìjièyǔ 指 1887 年波兰人柴门霍夫 (Ludwig Lazarus Zamenhof) 创造的国际辅助语,语法比较简单 Esperanto; international auxiliary language created by a Pole named Ludwig Lazarus Zamenhof in 1887, which uses a simplified grammar

【世局】shìjú 世界局势 world situation; international situation: ～动荡 turbulent international situation

【世面】shìmiàn 社会上各方面上的情况 various aspects of society; society; world; situation in various segments of society: 见过～(指阅历多) have seen much of the world; be experienced

【世情】shìqíng 社会上的情况;世态人情 ways of the world: 不懂～ ignorant of the ways of the world; inexperienced in life | ～冷暖 fickleness of the world (or human relationships)

【世人】shìrén 世界上的人;一般的人 common people; people at large

【世上】shìshàng 世界上;社会上 in the world; on earth: ～无难事,只怕有心人。Nothing in the world is difficult for those who set their minds to it. *or* Perseverance is the road to success.

【世事】shìshì 世上的事 affairs of human life; affairs of the world: ～多变 changeable world affairs

【世俗】shìsú ❶ 流俗 common customs; customs and traditions; social conventions: ～之见 conventional views ❷ 非宗教的 secular; worldly; non-religious

【世态】shìtài 指社会上人对人的态度 ways of the world: ～人情 ways of the world

【世态炎凉】shìtài yán liáng 指有钱有势时,人就巴结,无钱无势时,人就冷淡 fickle or snobbish ways of the world — people curry favour with those who have money and power, and are cold towards those who have neither

【世外桃源】shì wài Táoyuán 晋陶潜在《桃花源记》中描述了一个与世隔绝的不遭战祸的安乐而美好的地方。后借指不受外界影响的地方或幻想中的美好世界。Shangri-la; 'Land of Peach Blossoms'; peaceful, happy and beautiful place isolated from the world and suffering no disaster or war, depicted by Tao Qian of the Jin Dynasty in *The Story of the Peach Blossom Valley*; place unaffected by the external world, or an imaginative beautiful world

【世袭】shìxí 指帝位、爵位等世代相传 hereditary; (of throne, rank or noble title, etc.) passing on from generation to generation

【世系】shìxì 指家族世代相承的系统 pedigree; genealogy; lineage; system that passes on from generation to generation in a family

【世兄】shìxiōng〈旧时 *old*〉对辈分相同的世交(如父亲的门生,老师的儿子)的称呼,对辈分较低的世交也尊称做世兄 father's friend's son who is older than oneself, e.g. father's disciple or teacher's son; son of one's friend or teacher

【世医】shìyī 世代为医的中医 doctor of traditional Chinese medicine with generations' experience in medical practice

【世族】shìzú 封建社会中世代相传的官僚地主家族 (in feudal society) bureaucrat-landlord family of generations' standing

仕 shì〈旧指 *old*〉做官 be an official; hold an official post: 出～ serve as an official; take up an official career

【仕宦】shìhuàn〈书 *fml.*〉指做官 be an official: ～之家 official's family | ～子弟 sons or children of officials

【仕进】shìjìn〈书 *fml.*〉指做官而谋发展 work

one's way up by embarking on an official career：不求～ have no desire for improving one's social status by entering into officialdom

【仕女】shìnǚ ❶ 宫女 maid in an imperial palace；maid of honour ❷ 以美女为题材的中国画 traditional Chinese painting of beautiful women；also 士女 shìnǚ

【仕途】shìtú〈书 *fml.*〉指做官的道路 official career：～多舛 suffer many a setback during one's official career｜～得意 be successful in one's official career

市 shì ❶ 集中买卖货物的固定场所；市场 market；regular place for buying and selling goods in a centralized manner：米～ rice market｜菜～ food or vegetable market｜夜～ night market｜上～ be on the market；(of foodstuff) be in season ❷〈书 *fml.*〉买卖货物 buying and selling；business transaction◇～惠 dispense favours in order to win popularity ❸ 城市 city；municipality：～容 appearance of a city｜～民 townspeople；urban residents｜～区 city proper；downtown area；urban district｜都～ metropolis；big city ❹ 行政区划单位，分直辖市和市。设市的地方都是工商业集中处或政治、文化的中心。municipality；administrative units including ordinary cities and those directly under the jurisdiction of the State Council，which are centres of industry and commerce，or political and cultural centres ❺ 属于市制的(度量衡单位)（unit) pertaining to the Chinese system of weights and measures：～尺 *chi*，unit of length (1/3 metre)｜～升 *sheng*，primary unit of dry measure of grain (1 litre)｜～斤 *jin*，a unit of weight (1/2 kg.)

【市布】shìbù 一种原色平纹棉布，质地比较细密 closely woven unbleached plain cotton cloth

【市场】shìchǎng ❶ 商品交易的场所 marketplace；place for product exchanges：集贸～ fair-trade market ❷ 商品行销的区域 market；bazaar；area for selling products：国内～ domestic market｜国外～ foreign market ◇悲观主义的论调，越来越没有～。Pessimistic views are losing popular support steadily.

【市场经济】shìchǎng jīngjì 由市场进行调节的国民经济 market economy；market-oriented economy；national economy regulated by the force of the market

【市电】shìdiàn 指城市里主要供居民使用的电源，电压一般是 220 伏，也有 110 伏的 electricity produced mainly supplied to urban residents，the voltage generally being 220 or 110 volts

【市房】shìfáng〈方 *dial.*〉铺面房 roadside building that houses shops

【市花】shìhuā 为某城市市民普遍喜欢、养植并经确认作为该市象征的花 city flower；local flower that is generally loved，cultivated and identified as the symbol of a city

【市徽】shìhuī 一个城市所规定的代表这个城市的标志 city emblem；prescribed emblem to represent a city

【市惠】shìhuì〈书 *fml.*〉买好儿；讨好① curry favour (with)；fawn on；dispense favours in order to win popularity

【市集】shìjí ❶ 集市 fair ❷ same as 市镇 shìzhèn

【市价】shìjià 市场价格 market price

【市郊】shìjiāo 城市所属的郊区 suburb；outskirts；suburban districts of a city

【市井】shìjǐng〈书 *fml.*〉街市；市场① market place；town：～小人 townie；vulgar villain｜～之徒（含轻视意 derog.）vulgar bumpkin

【市侩】shìkuài 本指买卖的中间人，后指唯利是图的奸商。也泛指贪图私利的人（orig.）business middleman；sordid merchant；philistine；middleman of a business；profiteer bent on profiteering；(in a broad sense) self-seeking person：～习气 sordid merchants' ways｜～作风 sordid merchants' ways

【市面】shìmiàn ❶ 街面上；做买卖的地面 market：摊贩争着占好～。Street vendors vied for a good spot at the market.｜～上很少空房空地。There are few empty houses and little unused land at the market. ❷（～儿 shìmiànr）城市工商业活动的一般状况 market conditions；business situation；general condition of industrial and commercial activities in a city：～繁荣。Business is flourishing. *or* The market is brisk.｜～萧条。Business is slack. *or* The market is slow.

【市民】shìmín 城市居民 urban residents；townspeople

【市区】shìqū 属于城市范围的地区，一般人口及房屋建筑比较集中 city proper；downtown area；urban district with high concentration of population and buildings

【市容】shìróng 城市的面貌（指街道、房屋建筑、橱窗陈列等 streets，buildings，display windows，etc.）appearance of a city：北京～比前几年更加壮观了。Beijing looks more magnificent than it did a few years ago.

【市声】shìshēng 街市上喧闹嘈杂的声音 street noise；bustling noise on a downtown street：恬静的乡村没有那种扰人的～。There is no annoying traffic and din in this quiet village.

【市树】shìshù 为某城市市民普遍喜欢、种植并经确认作为该市象征的树 city tree；local tree that is generally loved，cultivated and identified as the symbol of a city

【市肆】shìsì〈书 *fml.*〉商店 shop；store

【市招】shìzhāo same as 幌子 huǎng·zi ①

【市镇】shìzhèn 较大的集镇 small towns；towns；(big) market towns

【市政】shìzhèng 城市管理工作，包括工商业、交通、公安、卫生、公用事业、基本建设、文化教育等 municipal administration (including industry and commerce, communication, public security, public health, public service, capital construction and cultural education)

【市制】shìzhì 一种计量制度,以国际公制为基础,结合我国人民习用的计量名称制定。长度的主单位是市尺,重量的主单位是市斤,容量的主单位是市升。Chinese system of weights and measures; system of measurement based on the international metric system, formed by integrating names for measurement habitually used by Chinese people, with *chi* as the basic unit of length; *jin*, weight; and *sheng*, capacity; also 市用制 shìyòngzhì

式 shì ❶ 样式 type; style; fashion: 新～ new style; new type | 旧～ old type; old fashion | 西～ Western style ❷ 格式 form; pattern; model: 程～ pattern; form to be copied | 法～ pattern; model ❸ 仪式;典礼 ceremony; celebration; ritual: 开幕～ opening ceremony | 毕业～ graduation ceremony | 阅兵～ military parade; military review ❹ 自然科学中表明某种规律的一组符号 formula; group of symbols that indicate some rule of natural science: 分子～ molecular formula | 方程～ equation ❺ 一种语法范畴,表示说话者对所说事情的主观态度。如叙述式、命令式、条件式。mood; mode; grammatical concept indicating the subjective attitude of a speaker towards the object referred to, such as indicative, imperative and conditional moods

【式微】shìwēi 〈书 *fml.*〉指国家或世族的衰落。也泛指事物衰落(原为《诗经·邶风》篇名) (of a nation or family of traditional importance) decline in power or wealth; decline of a thing (originating from the title of a poem in *The Book of Songs · Folksongs of Bei*): 家道～ the family fortunes declined; the family has gone down in the world | 制造业日趋～。The manufacturing industry is declining on a daily basis.

【式样】shìyàng 人造的物体的形状 style; type; model; design; pattern: 各种～的服装 various styles or types of garments | 楼房～很美观。The buildings look graceful.

【式子】shì·zi ❶ 姿势 posture: 他练的这套拳,～摆得很好。He presented a good posture when practising boxing. ❷ 算式、代数式、方程式等的统称 formula; general term for equations, algebraic expressions, etc.

似 shì [似的] (shì·de) 〈助词 *aux.*〉用在名词、代词或动词后面,表示跟某种事物或情况相似 [used after a noun, pronoun, or verb to indicate similarity] be like ...; as ... as ...; as if: 像雪～那么白 as white as snow | 仿佛睡着了～ as if asleep | 乐得什么～ as happy as a lark; same as 是的 shì·de

☞ sì on p. 1822

事 shì ❶ (～儿 shìr) 事情 matter; affair; thing; business: 公～ public affairs | 家～ family affair | 国家大～ state or national affair | 新人新～ new people and new things | 老王有～请假。Lao Wang asked for leave of absence to attend to some personal business. | 这～儿容易办。This matter is easy to manage. ❷ (～儿 shìr) 事故 trouble; accident: 出～ have an accident | 平安无～。All is well. | 别怕,什么～儿也没有。Don't be afraid. There is nothing amiss. ❸ (～儿 shìr) 职业;工作 job; work: 谋～ look for a job | 找～儿 seek employment ❹ 关系或责任 responsibility; involvement: 回去吧,没有你的～了。You can go home now; we know this is not your responsibility. ❺ 〈书 *fml.*〉侍奉 be in the service of sb.; wait upon; attend upon: ～父母至孝 attend upon one's parents ❻ 从事 be engaged in: 大～宣扬 actively publicize a major event | 不～劳动 lead an idle life

【事半功倍】shì bàn gōng bèi 形容花费的劳力小,收到的成效大 achieve twice the result with half the effort

【事倍功半】shì bèi gōng bàn 形容花费的劳力大,收到的成效小 achieve half the result with twice the effort

【事必躬亲】shì bì gōng qīn 不管什么事一定亲自去做 see (or attend) to everything oneself; give personal attention to everything, big or small

【事变】shìbiàn ❶ 突然发生的重大政治、军事性事件 incident: 七七～ July 7 Incident of 1937 | 西安～ Xi'an Incident (of 1936) ❷ 政治、军事方面的重大变化 emergency; exigency; major event in politics or war ❸ 泛指事物的变化 course of events; events: 找出周围～的内部联系,作为我们行动的向导。Look into the implicit relationship of events occurring around one in all their changing aspects and use the resultant information as our guideline.

【事出有因】shì chū yǒu yīn 事情的发生有它的原因 sth. for which there is good reason; not without cause; no accident; apparently with cause

【事典】shìdiǎn ❶ 〈书 *fml.*〉专门辑录有关礼制事件的类书 encyclopaedia (of precedents, events, institutions and laws) ❷ 指辑录某方面事物的工具书,如《中华人民共和国四十年成就事典》reference book on special subjects, e.g. *Achievements of 40 Years in the People's Republic of China*

【事端】shìduān 事故;纠纷 disturbance; incident: 挑起～ provoke incidents

【事故】shìgù 意外的损失或灾祸(多指在生产、工作上发生的 usu. at work) accident; mishap: 工伤～ industrial accident | 责任～ accident arising from sb.'s negligence | 防止发生～ try to avert or prevent accidents

【事过境迁】shì guò jìng qiān 事情已经过去,客观环境也改变了 that was then, and this is now; the matter is now in the past and the situation has changed; the incident is over and the circumstances are different

【事后】shìhòu 事情发生以后,也指事情处理、了结以后 after the event; afterwards:～方知其中真相 get to know the truth of the matter after the event | 事先周密考虑,～认真总结。Consider the matter carefully before taking action and make a detailed summary after the event.

【事机】shìjī ❶ 需要保守机密的事情 affairs that should be kept secret:～败露 leak out a secret; expose ❷ 情势;行事的时机 situation; the right time to act; opportunity:延误～ miss an opportunity because of a delay

【事迹】shìjì 个人或集体过去做过的比较重要的事情 deed (of a person or a collective); merit; achievement:生平～ one's life story | 模范～ exemplary deeds

S

【事假】shìjià 因办理个人的事而请的假 leave of absence to attend to private affairs

【事件】shìjiàn 历史上或社会上发生的不平常的大事情 (unusual historical and social) event:政治～ political event

【事理】shìlǐ 事情的道理 reason; logic:明白～ be reasonable; be sensible

【事例】shìlì 具有代表性的、可以作例子的事情 example; instance:结合实际～对学生进行爱国主义教育 teach students to be patriotic by citing actual instances

【事略】shìlüè 传记文体的一种,记述人的生平大概 biographical sketch; short biographical account

【事前】shìqián 事情发生以前,也指事情处理、了结以前 before the event; in advance; beforehand:～一无所知 with no preparation at all |～做好充分准备,免得到时忙乱。Make full preparation beforehand so as to avoid chaos and confusion when the time comes.

【事情】shì·qing ❶ 人类生活中的一切活动和所遇到的一切社会现象 affair; matter; question; business:～多,忙不过来 busy at work; too much business to attend to ❷ 事故;差错 trouble; mistake:不能马虎,出了～就麻烦了。Be very careful, because if anything untoward should happen, you will be in big trouble. ❸ 职业;工作 work; job:在公司里找了一个～ find a job with a company

【事权】shìquán 处理事情的权力;职权 power; authority:下放～ transfer power to a lower level

【事实】shìshí 事情的真实情况 fact:～胜于雄辩。Facts are stronger than rhetoric. *or* Facts speak louder than words. |传闻与～不符。The rumour going around does not tally with the facts.

【事态】shìtài 局势;情况(多指坏的 usu. unfavourable) state of affairs; situation:～严重。The situation is serious. |～扩大 aggravate the situation |～有所缓和。Things have calmed down.

【事体】shìtǐ 〈方 *dial.*〉❶ same as 事情 shì·qing ②:出了啥～? What happened? ❷ same as 事情 ③:托朋友寻个～做 ask a friend to find one a job

【事务】shìwù ❶ 所做的或要做的事情 work; routine:～繁忙 have a lot (of work) to do ❷ 总务 general affairs:～科 the general affairs section |～员 staff in the general affairs section |～工作 routine work

【事务主义】shìwù zhǔyì 没有计划,不分轻重、主次,不注意方针、政策和政治思想教育,而只埋头于日常琐碎事务的工作作风 routinism; work style of paying excessive attention to daily petty matters instead of making overall plans, to the neglect of policies, principles and political education

【事物】shìwù 指客观存在的一切物体和现象 thing; object; reality

【事先】shìxiān same as 事前 shìqián:这件事～我一点也不知道。I knew nothing of this beforehand.

【事项】shìxiàng 事情的项目 item; matter:注意～ items for attention; matters needing attention; points for attention

【事业】shìyè ❶ 人所从事的,具有一定目标、规模和系统而对社会发展有影响的经常活动 cause; undertaking; career:革命～ revolutionary cause |科学文化～ scientific and cultural undertakings |～心强 dedicated to one's work ❷ 特指没有生产收入,由国家经费开支,不进行经济核算的事业(区别于'企业'as compared with 'enterprise') organization, society, foundation, etc., that is subsidized by the state and earns no income from production; institution; facilities:～费 operating expenses |～单位 public institution

【事宜】shìyí 关于事情的安排、处理(多用于公文、法令 oft. used in official documents and decrees) matters concerned; arrangements:商谈呈递国书～ discuss the presentation of a credential

【事由】shìyóu ❶ 事情的原委 origin of an incident; particulars of a matter:把～交代明白 give all the particulars about the incident ❷ 公文用语,指本件公文的主要内容(used in official documents) main content; gist ❸(～儿 shìyóur)指借口;理由 excuse, pretext:找个～离开会场 find an excuse to leave the meeting ❹〈方 *dial.*〉(～儿 shìyóur)职业;工作 job; work:找个正经～干 find a good job

【事与愿违】shì yǔ yuàn wéi 事情的发展跟主观

愿望相反 things run counter to one's wishes

【事在人为】shì zài rén wéi 事情能否成功，取决于人是否努力去做 success hinges on human effort; human effort is the decisive factor

【事主】shìzhǔ ❶ 某些刑事案件（如偷窃、抢劫等）中的被害人 victim of a crime, e. g. robbery, mugging, etc. ❷〈旧指 *old*〉办理婚丧喜事的人家 wedding or funeral ceremony held at a household

势(勢) shì ❶ 势力 power; force; influence: 威～ power and influence | 权～ power and position | 人多～众 superior strength through force of numbers; safety in numbers | 仗～欺人 rely on sb. else's power and bully people ❷ 一切事物力量表现出来的趋向 momentum; tendency: 来～甚急 come with a vengeance | ～如破竹 (of a momentum) like splitting bamboo; carry the world before one ❸ 自然界的现象或形势 outward appearance of a natural object or phenomenon: 山～ the lie of a mountain | 地～ physical features of a place | 水～汹涌 turbulent flow of water ❹ 政治、军事或其他社会活动方面的状况或情势 (political, military, social) situation; state of affairs; circumstances: 趋～ trend; tendency | 局～ situation | 守～ defensive | 大～所趋 trend of the times; general | 趁～猛追 take advantage of an opportunity to pursue sth. ❺ 姿态 sign; gesture: 手～ gesture | 姿～ posture; carriage ❻ 雄性生殖器 male genitals: 去～ castration

【势必】shìbì〈副词 *adv.*〉根据形势推测必然会怎样 certainly will; be bound to: 看不到群众的力量，～要犯错误。Failure to see the strength of the people is bound to lead to error.

【势不可挡】shì bù kě dǎng 来势迅猛，不可抵挡 irresistible; overwhelming

【势不两立】shì bù liǎng lì 指敌对的事物不能同时存在 be mutually exclusive; be extremely antagonistic; be irreconcilable

【势均力敌】shì jūn lì dí 双方势力相等，不分高低（敌 *di*: 力量相当 of equivalent strength) match each other in strength

【势力】shì·li 政治、经济、军事等方面的力量 (of politics, economy, military situation, etc.) force; power; influence

【势利】shì·li 形容看财产、地位分别对待人的表现 snobbish: ～眼 snobbery; snobbish attitude | ～小人 snob | ～之交（以权势、金钱为基础结交的朋友）friendship based on power and influence

【势利眼】shì·liyǎn ❶ 作风势利 snobbish attitude; snobbishness ❷ 作风势利的人 snob

【势能】shìnéng 相互作用的物体由于所处的位置或弹性形变等而具有的能。如水的落差和发条作功的能力都是势能。potential energy; energy of a particle or system of particles derived from position, or elastic change of form, rather than motion, e. g. the drop of water or a coiled spring has potential energy. also 位能 wèinéng

【势派】shì·pai〈方 *dial.*〉(～儿 shì·pair) ❶ 排场；气派 manner; style; air: 讲～ put on airs | 好大的～。What affectedness! ❷ 形势 situation; circumstances

【势如破竹】shì rú pò zhú 形势像劈竹子一样，劈开上端之后，底下的都随着刀刃分开了 (of a momentum) like splitting a bamboo tree — with one cut at the end, the rest splitting at the touch of the knife; like a hot knife cutting through butter;〈比喻 *fig.*〉节节胜利，毫无阻碍 win one victory after another with irresistible force

【势态】shìtài 态势；情势 position; situation: ～严重 in a serious situation

【势头】shì·tóu 形势②；情势 situation, tendency: 他一看～不对，转身就走。Sensing that the odds were against him, he immediately turned back.

【势焰】shìyàn 势力和气焰（含贬义 derog.) influence and power: ～万丈 aggressively powerful | ～熏天 overbearing arrogance (like flame darkening the sky)

【势要】shìyào〈书 *fml.*〉有权势，居要职。也指有权势、居要职的人。important and influential persons: ～之家 influential family

侍 shì 陪伴侍候 wait upon; attend upon; serve: 服～ wait upon; attend to | ～立一旁 stand at sb.'s side in attendance

【侍从】shìcóng 指在皇帝或官员左右侍候卫护的人 attendants; retinue (of an emperor or official)

【侍奉】shìfèng 侍候奉养（长辈）support and wait upon (one's elders): ～父母 support and wait upon one's parents | ～老人 look after old people

【侍候】shìhòu 服侍 wait upon; look after; attend upon: ～父母 look after one's parents | ～病人 look after a patient

【侍郎】shìláng〈古代 *arch.*〉官名。明清两代是政府各部的副长官，地位次于尚书。(official title of the Ming and Qing dynasties) vice minister, second in rank to *shangshu* or minister

【侍立】shìlì 指恭敬地站在上级或长辈左右侍候 stand in attendance (on seniors or elders); stand by respectfully: 垂手～ stand at sb.'s side respectfully in attendance

【侍弄】shìnòng ❶ 指经营、照管、喂养 tend with care (crops, domestic animals, etc.): ～猪 take care of pigs | 把荒地～成了丰产田 turn wasteland into crop fields ❷ 摆弄；修理 repair; fix: ～锄头 fix a spade | ～机器 repair a machine

【侍女】shìnǚ〈旧时 *old*〉供有钱人家使唤的年轻妇女 maidservant; maid

【侍卫】shìwèi ❶ 卫护 bodyguard ❷ 在帝王左右卫护的武官 imperial bodyguard

【侍养】shìyǎng 奉养 support and wait upon (one's elders):～老人 support and wait upon elders

【侍者】shìzhě 侍候人的人。旧时也特指旅馆、饭店中接待顾客的人。attendant; servant; waiter; (old.) page; hotel attendant

饰 shì ❶ 装饰 decorations; ornaments: 修～ decorate; adorn | 四周～上花边 with decorative borders ❷ 掩饰 hide: ～词 excuse; pretext | 文过～非 to smooth over a fault ❸ 装饰品 decoration; ornaments: 首～ women's personal ornaments; jewelry | 衣～ clothes and ornaments | 窗～ window decorations ❹ 扮演 play the role of; act the part of; impersonate: 他在京剧《空城计》里～诸葛亮。He played the role of Zhuge Liang in the Peking Opera *The Strategy of the Unguarded City*.

【饰词】shìcí 掩蔽真相的话;托词 excuse; pretext

S

【饰品】shìpǐn 首饰 ornaments; jewelry: 黄金～ gold ornaments

【饰物】shìwù ❶ 首饰 article for personal adornment; jewelry ❷ 器物上的装饰品,如花边、流苏等 ornaments; decorations such as laces and tassels

【饰演】shìyǎn same as 扮演 bànyǎn

试 shì ❶ 试验;尝试 try; test: ～行 try out | ～航 trial trip; shakedown voyage (or flight) | ～制 trial produce | 你去～～。Go and have a try. | 先这么～一下看,再做决定。Try it first and then decide. ❷ 考试 examination; test: ～题 test questions | ～场 examination hall (or room) | ～卷 examination paper | 口～ oral examination | 笔～ written examination | 初～ first try; preliminary exam | 复～ second round of examinations

【试笔】shìbǐ 试着写作或写字作画 try one's hand at writing, painting or calligraphy: 新春～ write sth. for the Spring Festival

【试表】shì//biǎo 用体温计测试体温 take sb.'s temperature: 给病人～ take the patient's temperature

【试场】shìchǎng 举行考试的场所 examination hall (or room)

【试车】shì//chē 机动车、机器等在装配好以后,正式应用之前,先进行试验性操作,看它的性能是否合乎标准 test run (of a machine, car, etc.); trial run

【试点】shì//diǎn 正式进行某项工作之前,先做小型试验,以便取得经验 make experiments; conduct tests at selected points; launch a pilot project: 先～,再推广。Do a pilot survey before putting on general release.

【试点】shìdiǎn 正式进行某项工作之前,做小型试验的地方 place where an experiment is carried out; experimental unit

【试电笔】shìdiànbǐ 检测电源相线是否带电或电气设备是否漏电的工具,形状像自来水笔,笔尖由金属制成,笔中有电阻和小灯泡。检测时,笔尖接触电源相线或电气设备上一点,并使试电笔和人体形成一个回路,如小灯泡亮了,就证明其带电或漏电。test pencil; pen-like device with a bulb and a resistor inside and a metal point at one end which, when it makes contact with a certain point of electrical wiring or apparatus, forms a circuit with the human body, and when the bulb turns on, it indicates the presense or leakage of electricity; screw driver with voltage tester; also 电笔 diànbǐ

【试飞】shìfēi ❶ 飞机在正式使用前进行试验性飞行,用来检查飞机的设备和验证飞机的性能等 (of airplane) test flight; trial flight ❷ 飞机沿着正式使用前的航线飞行 pre-flight; exploratory flight

【试工】shì//gōng (工人或佣工)在正式工作之前试做一个短时期的工作 (of a worker or servant) be hired or engaged on a provisional basis; be on probation

【试管】shìguǎn 化学实验用的圆柱形管,管底半球形或圆锥形,一般用玻璃制成 test tube; clear, cylindrical glass tube usu. open at one end and rounded at the other, used in chemical laboratory experimentation

【试航】shìháng 飞机、船只等在正式航行前进行试验性航行 trial voyage or flight; shakedown cruise or flight; trial run

【试剂】shìjì 做化学实验用的化学物质 reagent; also 试药 shìyào

【试金石】shìjīnshí ❶ 矿物,通常指黑色坚硬致密的硅质岩石。用黄金在试金石上画一条纹就可以看出黄金的成色。Lydian stone; touchstone; hard dark siliceous stone, such as basalt or jasper, that is used to test the quality of gold and silver by means of comparing the colour of a streak placed on it with that of a standard alloy ❷〈比喻 *fig.*〉精确可靠的检验方法和依据 touchstone

【试卷】shìjuàn 考试时准备应试人写答案或应试人已经写上答案的卷子 examination question sheet; paper to be completed by a test candidate; examination paper; test paper

【试看】shìkàn 试着看看;请看 try sth. and see how it works; just see: 军民团结如一人,～天下谁能敌。If the army and the people are united as one, who in the world can ever match them?

【试手】shì//shǒu (～儿 shì//shǒur) ❶ same as 试工 shì//gōng ❷ 试做 give sth. a try

【试探】shìtàn 试着探索(某种问题) probe or explore (a question); find out: 用棍子～水的深浅 fathom the depth of water with a stick

【试探】shì·tan 用含义不很明显的言语或举动引

起对方的反应，借以了解对方的意思 question (someone) in order to know (opinions, facts, etc.); sound out; feel out: 先～一下他的口气。Let's sound him out first.

【试题】shìtí 考试的题目 examination questions; test questions

【试图】shìtú 打算 attempt to (do sth.); try to (do sth.): ～闯出一条新路 try to blaze a new trail

【试问】shìwèn 试着提出问题(用于质问对方或者表示不同意对方的意见 (used when questioning the other interlocutor or when raising a different view) we should like to ask; may it be asked; may we ask: ～你这么说有什么根据? May we ask on what grounds you say this?

【试想】shìxiǎng 〈婉辞 *euph*.〉试着想想(用于质问 when reasoning with sb.) just think: ～你这样做会有好的结果吗? Think now. Will it do you any good to go on this way?

【试销】shìxiāo 新产品未正式大量生产前，先试制一部分销售，征求用户意见和检验产品质量 (before going into full production) place goods on trial sale to solicit user opinions and test product quality

【试行】shìxíng 实行起来试试 try out: ～制造 try to produce | 先～，再推广 First try out, then popularize.

【试验】shìyàn ❶ 为了察看某事的结果或某物的性能而从事某种活动 trial; experiment; test: ～新机器 try out a new machine | 新办法～后推广。The new method will be popularized after trials. ❷ 〈旧时 *old*〉指考试 examination

【试验田】shìyàntián ❶ 进行农业试验的田地 experimental plot; experimental field ❷ 〈比喻 *fig*.〉试点或试点工作 trial undertaking; work done on a trial basis

【试用】shìyòng 在正式使用以前，先试一个时期，看是否合适 on probation; try out: ～品 trial products | ～本 trial edition (edition put out to solicit comments) | ～期 probation period | ～人员 person on probation; probationer

【试纸】shìzhǐ 用指示剂或试剂浸过的干燥纸条，用来检验溶液的酸碱性和某种化合物、元素或离子的存在。如石蕊试纸、碘化钾淀粉试纸等。test paper; paper saturated with a reagent, such as litmus, used to make chemical tests

【试制】shìzhì 试着制作 trial produce; trial manufacture: 新产品～成功。The new trial production was successful.

视(眡、眎) shì ❶ 看 look at: ～力 power of vision | ～线 line of vision | 近～ near-sightedness | 熟～无睹 pay no attention to a familiar sight; turn a blind eye to ❷ 看待 regard; look upon: 轻～ despise | 重～ attach importance to | 藐～ look down upon | 一～同仁 treat equally and without discrimination ❸ 考察 inspect; watch: ～察 inspect | 巡～ make an inspection tour | 监～ keep watch on

【视差】shìchā ❶ 直接用肉眼观测时产生的误差 visual error; parallax; apparent change in the direction of an object caused by a change in observational position that provides a new line of sight ❷ 由地球表面上某一点到某天体的中心和由地心或太阳到同一天体的中心的夹角，叫做该天体的视差。由地心算起的是周日视差，由太阳算起的是周年视差。angle subtended at a celestial body, esp. a star, by the radius of the earth's orbit; annualor heliocentric parallaxis is the apparent displacement of a nearby star resulting from its observation from the earth; diurnalor geocentric parallax results from the observation of a planet, the sun, or the moon from the surface of the earth

【视察】shìchá ❶ 上级人员到下级机构检查工作 inspect ❷ 察看 watch; observe: ～地形 survey the terrain

【视而不见】shì ér bù jiàn 尽管睁着眼睛看，却什么也没有看见。指不重视或不注意。look but see not; turn a blind eye to; close (or shut) one's eyes to

【视角】shìjiǎo ❶ 由物体两端射出的两条光线在眼球内交叉而成的角。物体愈小或距离愈远，视角愈小。angle of view; visual angle formed by two rays of light inside the eyeball; angle subtended by an object at the lens of the eye. The smaller or more distant an object is, the narrower the visual angle becomes. ❷ 摄影镜头所能摄取的场面上距离最大的两点与镜头连线的夹角。短焦距镜头视角大，长焦距镜头视角小。angle formed by lines linking the lens of a camera with the farthest two points in the picture being taken. A lense with a short focal length has a wide visual angle, and one with a long focal length has a narrow visual angle ❸ 指观察问题的角度 angle from which one looks at a problem; approach; perspective: 影片以久居闹市的青年人的～反映了山区人民的文化生活。The film represented the cultural life of mountain people from an urban youth perspective.

【视觉】shìjué 物体的影像刺激视网膜所产生的感觉 visual sense; vision; sense of sight

【视力】shìlì 在一定距离内眼睛辨别物体形象的能力 vision; sight; faculty of perceiving with the eye within a given distance

【视亮度】shìliàngdù 人在地球上所看到的恒星的亮度，视亮度并不是恒星真正的亮度 (of stars) apparent brightness as observed by man on earth, which is not the actual brightness of the star being observed

【视频】shìpín 图像信号所包括的频率范围，一般在零到几个兆赫之间 video frequency; usu. ranging between zero and several MHz

【视若无睹】shì ruò wú dǔ 虽然看了却像没有看

见一样。形容对眼前事物漠不关心。take no notice of what one sees; shut one's eyes to; turn a blind eye to; ignore

【视弱】shìruò 指视力低于正常水平(多指先天性的) have (congenital) weak eyesight

【视神经】shìshénjīng 第二对脑神经,由间脑的底部发出,末端分布成眼球的视网膜。能把视觉的刺激传递给大脑皮层的视觉中枢。optic nerve; second cranial nerve, which provides a sensory pathway from the retina to the brain;(图见 ☞ figure for 眼 yǎn on p. 2210)

【视事】shìshì 〈书 *fml.*〉指官吏到职开始工作 (of officials) attend to business after assuming office; assume office

【视死如归】shì sǐ rú guī 把死看作像回家一样。形容不怕死。regard death as going home; look death calmly in the face; face death unflinchingly

【视听】shìtīng 看和听;看到的和听到的 seeing and hearing; what is seen and heard: 组织参观,以广～ arrange tours and visits so as to broaden the perspective | 混淆～ confuse the public

【视图】shìtú 根据物体的正投影绘出的图形 view; drawing based on the orthographic projection of an object

【视网膜】shìwǎngmó 眼球最内层的薄膜,是由神经组织构成的,外面跟脉络膜相连,里面是眼球的玻璃体,是接受光线刺激的部分。retina; light-sensitive membrane forming the inner lining of the posterior wall of the eyeball, composed largely of a specialized terminal expansion of the optic nerve. Images focused here by the lens of the eye are transmitted to the brain as nerve impulses;(图见 ☞ figure for 眼 yǎn on p. 2210); 简称 abbr. 网膜 wǎngmó

【视线】shìxiàn ❶ 用眼睛看东西时,眼睛和物体之间的假想直线 line of vision; view; line of sight (in surveying) ❷〈比喻 *fig.*〉注意力 attention: 转移～ divert one's attention

【视学】shìxué 督学 (formerly) educational inspector

【视野】shìyě 眼睛看到的空间范围;眼界 field of vision (or view): ～宽广 wide field of vision | 开阔～ broaden one's vision

【视阈】shìyù ❶ 能产生视觉的最高限度和最低限度的刺激强度 visual threshold; visual strength at which a stimulus is perceived ❷ 指视野 field of vision: 丰富游人的～ broaden a visitor's visual threshold; extend visitors' field of vision; also 视域 shìyù

贳 shì 〈书 *fml.*〉❶ 出赁;出借 hire out; let ❷ 赊欠 buy on credit ❸ 宽纵;赦免 pardon

【贳器店】shìqìdiàn 〈方 *dial.*〉出租婚丧喜庆应用的某些器物和陈设的铺子 shop that hires out accouterments for wedding or funeral ceremonies

柿(梯) shì ❶ 柿子树,落叶乔木,品种很多,叶子椭圆形或倒卵形,背面有绒毛,花黄白色。结浆果,扁圆形或圆锥形,橙黄色或红色,可以吃。persimmon (*Diospyros*); any of several trees of the genus *Diospyros*, typically having oval or obovate leaves with down on their back, yellowish white flowers, and edible orange-red fruit oblate or conical in shape ❷ 这种植物的果实 fruit of this plant

【柿饼】shìbǐng 用柿子制成的饼状食品 dried persimmon

【柿霜】shìshuāng 柿子去皮晾干后,表面形成的白霜,味道很甜,可入药 powder on the surface of a dried persimmon which is sweet and can be used for medicine

【柿子】shì·zi ❶ 柿子树 persimmon ❷ 柿子树的果实 fruit of the persimmon tree

【柿子椒】shì·zijiāo ❶ 辣椒的一个品种。果实近球形,略扁,表面有纵沟,味不很辣,是普通蔬菜 sweet pepper (*Capsicum frutescens grossum*); bell pepper; pepper plant with large bell-shaped fruits that have a mild pungent taste and are eaten unripe (green pepper) or ripe (red pepper) as a common vegetable ❷ 这种植物的果实 fruit of this plant

拭 shì same as 擦 cā ②: 拂～ wipe | ～泪 wipe away tears

【拭目以待】shì mù yǐ dài 擦亮眼睛等待着。形容殷切期望或等待某件事情的实现。wait and see; wait expectantly (for sth. to happen)

昰 shì same as 是 shì ,多用于人名 usu. used in personal names

是[1] shì ❶ 对;正确(跟'非'相对 as opposed to 非 fēi) correct; right: 一无～处。Nothing is right. | 自以为～ consider oneself always in the right; be self-opinionated | 实事求～ seek the truth from facts | 你说得～。You are right to put it that way. | 应当早做准备才～。Being prepared ahead of time is the right and proper thing to do. ❷〈书 *fml.*〉认为正确 praise; justify: ～古非今 praise the past and denounce the present | 深～其言 be convinced that the word is correct ❸ 表示答应的词 [used in affirmative answers] yes; right: ～,我知道。Yes. I see. | ～,我就去。Yes. I'll go right away. ❹ (Shì) 姓 a surname

是[2] shì 〈书 *fml.*〉这;这个 this; that: 如～ like this | 由～可知 from this you can see | ～可忍,孰不可忍? If this can be endured, what could not be? | ～日天气晴朗。It was sunny that day. ～可忍,孰不可忍? If this can be endured, what could not be? | ～日天气晴朗。It was sunny that day.

是[3] shì ❶ 联系两种事物,表明两者同一或后者说明前者的种类、属性 [used like 'be'

before nouns or pronouns to identify, describe or amplify the subject]:《阿Q正传》的作者～鲁迅。The author of *The True Story of Ah Q* is Lu Xun. |节约～不浪费的意思。To be thrifty means not to waste anything. ❷ 与'的'字相应,有分类的作用[used with 的·de at the end of the sentence, to indicate category, characteristic, etc.]:这张桌子～石头的。The table is made of stone. |才买来的墨水～红的。The ink just bought is red. |我～来看他的。It is him I came to see. ❸ 联系两种事物,表示陈述的对象属于'是'后面所说的情况[used to indicate the state or condition of the subject]:他～一片好心。He is of good intentions. |咱们～好汉一言,快马一鞭。What we have said cannot be unsaid. *or* Our words are those of brave and true men and should be acted upon immediately. |院子里～冬天,屋子里～春天。It was winter outdoors, but spring indoors. ❹ 表示存在,主语通常是表处所的语词,'是'后面表示存在的事物[used after nouns denoting place or position to express existence]:村子前面～一片水田。There is an expanse of paddy fields in front of the village. |他跑得满身～汗。He was bathed in sweat from running. ❺ '是'前后用相同的名词或动词,连用两个这样的格式,表示所说的几桩事物互不相干,不能混淆[used in between two identical nouns or verbs in two or more similar patterns to indicate distinction]:去年～去年,今年～今年,你当年年一个样哪!What was true last year may not be so this year; don't assume old ways always work! |说～说,做～做,有意见也不能耽误干活儿。Talking is one thing, doing is another. You can't delay the work just because you have complaints. ❻ 在上半句里'是'前后用相同的名词、形容词或动词,表示让步,含有'虽然'的意思[used to indicate concession] even though:诗～好诗,就是长了点。This is a good poem, albeit a little long. |东西旧～旧,可是还能用。Old as it is, it can still be used. |我去～去,可是不在那儿吃饭。I might go there, but I will not eat. ❼ 用在句首,加重语气[used before the subject for emphasis]:～谁告诉你的?Who on the earth told you? |～国防战士,日日夜夜保卫着祖国,咱们才能过幸福的日子。Thanks to the soldiers who keep watch over our national borders, we live a happy life. ❽ 用在名词前面,含有'凡是'的意思[used before a noun to indicate each and everyone of the kind] all; everything; anything:～有利于群众的事情他都肯干。He is ready to do anything that is good for the people. ❾ 用在名词前面,含有'适合'的意思[used before a noun] be just right:他想的很～路。His thinking is correct. |这场雨下的～时候。That fall of rain came just at the right time. |东西放的都挺～地方。Things are in their proper place. ❿ 用在选择问句、是非问句或反问句里[used in alternative, yes/no, or rhetorical questions]:你～吃米饭～吃面?What do you most like to eat, rice or noodles? |他不～走了吗?Has he not gone? |你～累了不～?Are you tired? ⓫ (必须重读)表示坚决肯定,含有'的确、实在'的意思[pronounced emphatically to indicate certainty] really; truly:我打听清楚了,他那天～没去。On specifically enquiring, I found out that he did not go yesterday. |这本书～好,你可以看看。This book is good; you should read it.

【是的】shì·de same as 似的 shì·de

【是凡】shìfán 凡是 every; any; all

【是非】shìfēi ❶ 事理的正确和错误 right and wrong:明辨～ distinguish clearly between right and wrong |～曲直 rights and wrongs; truth and falsehood ❷ 口舌 quarrel; dispute:惹起～ stir up trouble |搬弄～ stir up enmity

【是非窝】shìfēiwō 矛盾、纠纷多的地方 place where one is apt to get into trouble

【是否】shìfǒu 是不是 whether or not; whether; if:他～能来,还不一定。It's not certain whether or not he can come.

【是个儿】shì//gèr 是对手 be a match:论干力气活我不是他的个儿。I am no match for him in physical strength. |跟我下棋,你～吗?Would you take me on at chess?

【是味儿】shì//wèir ❶ (食品等)味道正;合口味(of food) have the right flavor; taste good ❷ (心里感到)好受;舒服 (of a person) feel good; feel comfortable

【是样儿】shì//yàngr 样式好看 look right or good:衣服做得很～。This suit is of a very good cut.

峙 shì 繁峙(Fánshì),地名,在山西 Fanshi, name of a place in Shanxi Province

☞ zhì on p. 2475

适[1](**適**) shì ❶ 适合 fit; suitable; proper:～当 suitable |～用 be applicable ❷ 恰好 just; right:～中 proper |～得其反 turn out to be just the opposite |～可而止 refrain from going too far ❸ 舒服 comfortable; well:舒～ easy |身体不～ feeling unwell

适[2](**適**) shì ❶ 去;往 go; follow; pursue:无所～从 not know which way to turn ❷ 〈书 *fml.*〉出嫁 (of a girl) get married; marry:～人 be married

☞ 适 kuò on p. 1134

【适才】shìcái 刚才 just now

【适当】shìdàng 合适;妥当 suitable; proper; appropriate:措辞～ appropriately worded |～的机会 opportune moment; the right moment | 由他去办这件事再～不过了。He is the best man for the task.

【适得其反】shì dé qí fǎn 结果跟希望正好相反 run counter to one's desire; be just the opposite of what one wished

【适度】shìdù 程度适当 appropriate measure; moderate degree: 繁简～ neither too simple nor too elaborate

【适逢其会】shì féng qí huì 恰巧碰到那个时机 happen to be present at the right moment (or on the occasion)

【适合】shìhé 符合(实际情况或客观要求 of actual situation or objective requirement) suit; fit: 过去的经验未必～当前的情况。Past experience is not necessarily applicable to the present situation.

【适可而止】shì kě ér zhǐ 到了适当的程度就停止(指做事不过分) stop before going too far; know when or where to stop; not overdo sth.

【适口】shìkǒu 适合口味 be agreeable to the taste; be palatable: 还是家乡菜吃起来～。One's home town dishes are the most delicious.

S

【适量】shìliàng 数量适宜 appropriate amount or quantity: 饮酒要～。Alcohol should be taken in moderation.

【适龄】shìlíng 适合某种要求的年龄(多指入学年龄和兵役应征年龄) of the right age: ～儿童都已入学。All the children of school age are attending school. | ～青年踊跃报名参军。Young people whose age qualified them to serve in the army fell over each other to sign up.

【适时】shìshí 适合时宜;不太早也不太晚 at the right moment; in good time; timely: 播种～ begin sowing in good time | ～收割 get the crops in at the right time

【适销】shìxiāo (商品)适合于消费者需要,卖得快 (of commodities) salable: 产品～对路。The products are salable.

【适宜】shìyí 合适;相宜 suitable; fit; appropriate; favourable: 浓淡～ a fit shade; (of tone, flavor, taste, etc.) neither too deep nor too light | 气候～ genial climate | 应对～ reply appropriately

【适意】shìyì 舒适 agreeable; enjoyable; comfortable

【适应】shìyìng 适合(客观条件或需要) suit; adapt to; adjust to; conform to: ～环境 adapt oneself to circumstances

【适用】shìyòng 适合使用 be suitable; be applicable: 这套耕作方法,在我们这个地区也完全～。The new method of cultivation is suitable for our area.

【适值】shìzhí 恰好遇到 just when; it so happens: 上次赴京,～全国运动会开幕。As it happened, the national games were on the last time I was in Beijing.

【适中】shìzhōng ❶ 既不是太过,又不是不及 proper; appropriate; moderate: 冷热～ of a moderate temperature | 身材～ moderate size ❷ 位置不偏于哪一面 well situated: 地点～ be well situated

恃 shì 依赖;倚仗 rely on; depend on: 有～无恐 be unscrupulous knowing one has powerful backing; feel secure in the knowledge that one has sth. to fall back upon

【恃才傲物】shì cái ào wù 依仗自己的才能而骄傲自大,轻视旁人 be inordinately proud of one's ability; be conceited and arrogant (物 *wu*: 众人 everybody)

室 shì ❶ 屋子 room: 教～ classroom | 卧～ bedroom | 休息～ lounge | ～外 outdoor ❷ 机关、工厂、学校等内部的工作单位 room as an administrative or working unit: 档案～ filing room | 图书～ library ❸ 妻子 wife: 妻～ wife | 继～ second wife ❹ 家;家族 family: 皇～ royal family | 十～九空 nine houses out of 10 are deserted — a scene of desolation (as in the aftermath of a plague or war) ❺ 器官、机器等内部的空腔 cavity: 脑～ ventricles of the brain | 心～ ventricle ❻ 二十八宿之一 one of the 28 constellations into which the celestial sphere was divided in ancient Chinese astronomy

【室内乐】shìnèiyuè 原指西洋宫廷内演奏或演唱的世俗音乐,区别于教堂音乐。现在泛指区别于管弦乐曲的各种重奏、重唱曲或独奏、独唱曲。chamber music; secular music played in Western royal palaces, as compared with church music; now referring to choral, solo instrument, or music other than orchestral

【室女】shìnǚ 〈旧时 *old*〉称未结婚的女子 unmarried girl; virgin

【室女座】shìnǚzuò 黄道十二星座之一 (astron.) Virgo (one of the 12 zodiacal constellations)
☞ 黄道十二宫 huángdào shí'èrgōng on p. 851

莳(蒔) shì ❶〈方 *dial.*〉移植(秧苗) transplant (seedlings): ～秧 transplant rice seedlings | ～田 rice paddy ❷〈书 *fml.*〉栽种 plant; cultivate: ～花 grow flowers
☞ shí on p. 1747

栻 shì 〈古代 *arch.*〉占卜用的器具 instrument of divination

轼 shì 〈书 *fml.*〉〈古代 *arch.*〉车厢前面用做扶手的横木 horizontal bar at the front of a carriage used as an armrest

逝 shì ❶ (时间、水流等)过去 (of time, water, etc.) pass: 时光易～。Time passes quickly. | ～者如斯夫。It passes this way! (a lament at what has occurred, and a warning against repetition) ❷ 死亡 die; pass away: 病～ die of illness | 长～ be gone for ever

【逝世】shìshì 去世 pass away; die

铈 shì 金属元素，符号 Ce (cerium)。是一种稀土金属。灰色，质较软，化学性质活泼，用作还原剂、催化剂，也用来制合金等。cerium (Ce); malleable ductile steel-grey element of the lanthanide series of metals, used as a reducing agent or catalyst or for the making of alloys

舐 shì 〈书 *fml.*〉舔 lick：老牛～犊 the cow licks her calf｜吮痈～痔 lick piles and suck ulcers (of sb. in power, etc.); lick sb.'s boots

【舐犊情深】shì dú qíng shēn 〈比喻 *fig.*〉对子女的慈爱 deep affection towards one's children; parental love

【舐痔】shìzhì 〈书 *fml.*〉舔别人的痔疮(语出《庄子·列御寇》：'秦王有病召医。破痈溃痤者得车一乘，舐痔者得车五乘')。*Zhuang Zi · Lie YuKou*: 'The Duke of Qin came down with an ailment and was summoning doctors. Those who lanced his ulcers would be awarded one carriage and those who licked his piles would be awarded five carriages. 〈比喻 *fig.*〉无耻的谄媚行为 lick sb. else's piles and ulcers — be a bootlicker; be obsequious

弑 shì 〈书 *fml.*〉臣杀死君主或子女杀死父母 murder (one's sovereign or parent)：～君 regicide｜～父 patricide

释[1] (釋) shì ❶ 解释 explain; elucidate：～义 explain the meaning of a word｜注～annotation ❷ 消除 clear up; dispel：～疑 dispel doubts｜涣然冰～(of doubt, misunderstanding, etc.) melt away like ice ❸ 放开；放下 let go; be relieved of：～手 relax the hold｜手不～卷 never seen without a book in hand｜爱不忍～ like sth. so much that one cannot bear to part with it ❹ 释放 release; set free：开～ release (a prisoner)｜保～ release on bail

释[2] (釋) Shì 释迦牟尼(佛教创始人)的简称，泛指佛教 Sakyamuni (founder of Buddhism); Buddhism (in a broad sense)：～门 Buddhism｜～家 Buddhist｜～子 monks

【释典】shìdiǎn 佛经 Buddhist Scripture

【释读】shìdú 考证并解释(古文字) conduct research on and explain the texts of ancient writings

【释放】shìfàng ❶ 恢复被拘押者或服刑者的人身自由 release; set free：～战俘 release prisoner of war｜刑满～ be released upon completion of a prison sentence ❷ 把所含的物质或能量放出来 release (energy matter contained in a substance)：这种肥料的养分～缓慢。The nutritious elements in this fertilizer are released slowly.｜原子反应堆能有效地～原子能。An atomic reactor releases atomic energy efficiently.

【释怀】shìhuái (爱憎、悲喜等感情)在心中消除(多用于否定 usu. used in the negative) dispel (feelings of love or hatred, sadness or happiness, etc.) from one's bosom; dismiss from one's mind：当年离别的情景使我久久不能～。I could not stop recalling the scene of our parting.

【释教】Shìjiào 佛教 Buddhism

【释然】shìrán 〈书 *fml.*〉形容疑虑、嫌隙等消释而心中平静 feel relieved; feel at ease

【释俗】shìsú 用通俗的话解释 explain in plain language：新名词要～。New terms of terminology must be explained in simple terms.

【释文】shìwén ❶ 解释文字音义(多用于书名 oft. used in book titles) annotations：《经典～》*Pronunciations and Meanings of Words in the Classics*｜《楚辞～》*Annotations of Elegies of Chu* ❷ 考订古文字(甲骨文字、金石文字等)，逐字逐句加以辨认 transcribe the text of ancient writings, such as inscriptions on oracle bones, bronzeware or stone tablets

【释疑】shìyí 解释疑难；消除疑虑 clear up (or remove) doubts; dispel suspicion：～解难 explain difficult points｜～消嫌 dispel suspicion and eliminate resentment

【释义】shìyì 解释词义或文义 explain the meaning (of a word, sentence, etc.)

【释藏】Shìzàng 佛教经典的总汇，分经、律、论三藏，包括汉译佛经和中国的一些佛教著述 Buddhist canon (consisting of scriptures, tenets, and discussions of Buddhist literature, either translated into Chinese or originally written in Chinese)

【释子】shìzǐ 〈书 *fml.*〉和尚 Buddhist monk

谥(諡) shì ❶ 君主时代帝王、贵族、大臣等死后，依其生前事迹所给予的称号。例如齐宣王的'宣'，楚庄王的'庄'；诸葛亮谥'忠武'，岳飞谥'武穆'。posthumous title (formerly bestowed on a ruler, a nobleman, or an eminent official) as apposite to the life and moral qualities of the deceased, such as *xuan* for Duke Xuan of Qi, *Zhuang* for Duke Zhuang of Chu, *zhongwu* (loyal and valiant) for Zhuge Liang, and *wumu* (valiant and solemn) for Yue Fei ❷ 称(做)；叫(做) call; name：～之为保守主义 call it conservatism

嗜 shì 特别爱好 have a liking for; be addicted to：～好 hobby｜～酒 be addicted to drink

【嗜好】shìhào 特殊的爱好(多指不良的 usu. harmful) addiction; habit：他没有别的～，就喜欢喝点儿酒。He has no addictive vices other than a liking for alcohol.

【嗜痂之癖】shì jiā zhī pǐ 《南史·刘穆之传》：'穆之孙邕，性嗜食疮痂，以为味似鳆鱼。'后来用'嗜痂之癖'形容人的乖僻嗜好。*History of Southern Dynasties · Biography of Liu Muzhi*: 'Liu Muzhi's grandson, Yong, was

S

given to eating ulcers and scab, saying that they tasted like abalone. The expression refers to eccentric proclivities. also 嗜痂成癖 shì jiā chéng pǐ

【嗜欲】shìyù 指耳目口鼻等方面贪图享受的要求 sensual desires

筮 shì〈古时 *arch.*〉用蓍草占卜 divination using the alpine yarrow

誓 shì ❶ 表示决心依照说的话实行；发誓 swear; vow; pledge: ～师 rally to pledge resolution before going to war | ～不甘休 swear not to stop until one's purpose is achieved; swear not to rest until work is done ❷ 表示决心的话 oath; vow: 宣～ take an oath | 起～ vow | 发个～ pledge

【誓词】shìcí same as 誓言 shìyán

【誓师】shìshī 军队出征前，统帅向将士宣示作战意义，表示坚决的战斗意志。也泛指群众集会庄严地表示完成某项重要任务的决心 rally to pledge resolution before going to war; solemn rally to pledge determination and resolution before taking action: ～大会 meeting to pledge mass effort; oath-taking rally

S

【誓死】shìsǐ 立下誓愿，表示至死不变 pledge one's life; dare to die: ～不屈 be willing to die rather than surrender; be unbending

【誓言】shìyán 宣誓时说的话 oath; pledge: 立下～ swear an oath

【誓愿】shìyuàn 表示决心时许下的心愿 vow

【誓约】shìyuē 宣誓时订下的必须遵守的条款 vow; pledge; solemn promise

奭 shì ❶〈书 *fml.*〉盛大的样子 grand ❷ (Shì)姓 a surname

噬 shì 咬 bite: 吞～ swallow | 反～ make a false counter charge

【噬菌体】shìjūntǐ 微生物的一类，能溶解细菌，一般呈蝌蚪状，尾部能侵入细菌体内，并在其中大量繁殖使细菌溶解。某一种噬菌体只能对相应的细菌起作用，例如伤寒杆菌噬菌体只能溶解伤寒杆菌。bacteriophage; phage; tadpole-shaped virus that is parasitic in a bacterium and multiplies massively within its host to dissolve bacteria. A phage works only on a given type of bacteria, e.g., the typhiphage can only dissolve typhoid bacillus.

【噬脐莫及】shì qí mò jí《左传》庄公六年：'若不早图，后君噬齐(齐：同'脐')，其及图之乎？'杜预注：'若啮腹齐，喻不可及'。意思是咬自己的肚脐是够不着的，后来用'噬脐莫及'比喻后悔莫及。*The Zuo Commentary · Duke Zhuang 6th Year*: 'If you fail to act before it's too late, you'll end up biting into your belly button. Isn't it too late by that time?' Du Yu's annotation of this line: 'To bite one's belly button is a figurative way to say it is too late to repent.' (fig.) One cannot bite one's own navel. *or* It is too late to save a hopeless situation. *or* Repentance is too late.

澨 shì〈书 *fml.*〉水边 water margin

螫 shì〈书 *fml.*〉蜇(zhē) sting

【螫针】shìzhēn 蜜蜂、胡蜂等尾部的毒刺，尖端有倒钩 stinger (of bees, wasps, etc.); sting

襫 shì ☞ [袯襫](bóshì) on p. 149

·shi (·ㄕ)

匙 ·shi ☞ 钥匙(yào·shi) on p. 2234
☞ chí on p. 262

殖 ·shi ☞ 骨殖 (gǔ·shi) on p. 694
☞ zhí on p. 2464

shōu (ㄕㄡ)

收(収) shōu ❶ 把外面的事物拿到里面；把摊开的或分散的事物聚拢 bring in; gather together; put in proper place; put away; take in: ～拾 put in order | ～藏 collect | ～集 bring together | ～篷 shorten sail; haul in sail | 衣裳～进来了没有? Have you brought in the clothes? ❷ 取自己有权取的东西或原来属于自己的东西 recover; retrieve: ～回 regain | ～复 recover; recapture | ～税 levy a tax | 没～ seize; confiscate | ～归国有 be nationalized ❸ 获得(经济利益) money received; receipts; income: ～入 take in; income | ～益 income; profits | ～支相抵 strike a balance in revenue and expenditure; make both ends meet ❹ 收获；收割 harvest; gather in: ～成 harvest | 秋～ autumn harvest | 麦～ wheat harvest | 今年早稻～得多。There was a good harvest of early rice this year. ❺ 接；接受；容纳 receive; accept: ～报 receive a telegram | ～留 undertake the care of | ～容 take in | ～礼物 accept a gift | ～徒弟 accept as one's apprentice ❻ 约束；控制(感情或行动) restrain; control: ～心 get into the frame of mind for work or study | 我的心像断了线的风筝似的，简直～不住了。My thoughts are like a kite flying in the wind; I simply cannot concentrate on anything. ❼ 逮捕；拘禁 arrest, take into custody: ～监 put behind bars ❽ 结束；停止(工作) bring to an end; stop: ～工 stop work for the day | ～操 bring a drill to an end | ～场 wind up

【收报】shōu//bào 用无线电或有线电等装置接收发报者发出的信号 receive a telegram: ～员 telegrapher

【收编】shōubiān 收容并改编(武装力量) incorporate into one's own forces: ～起义部队 incorporate an insurrectional army into one's own forces

【收兵】shōubīng ❶ 撤回军队，结束战斗 withdraw (or recall) troops; call off a battle: 鸣

金～ beat the gongs and withdraw the army ❷〈比喻 *fig.*〉结束工作 wind up：清理工作不可草率～。Clear orderly work should not be wound up in a rash and careless manner.

【收藏】shōucáng 收集保藏 collect and store：～文物 collect cultural relics

【收操】shōu//cāo 结束操练 bring a drill to an end

【收场】shōuchǎng ❶ 结束 wind up；end up；stop：他的话匣子一打开，就不容易～。Once he opens his trap，he just never stops. ❷ 结局；下场 end；ending；denouement：没料想事情落到这样的～。Such an ending was never expected.

【收车】shōu//chē 运输工作完毕把车辆开回或拉回 return the vehicle to the garage，terminal，etc.，and knock off：下班时间到了，该～了。It's time to knock off and drive the truck back.

【收成】shōu·cheng 庄稼、蔬菜、果品等收获的成绩。有时也指鱼虾等捕捞的成绩。harvest；crop；catch (of fish and shrimps)

【收发】shōufā ❶（机关、学校等）收进和发出公文、信件（of government departments，schools，etc.）receive and dispatch letters or documents：～室 office for incoming and outgoing mail｜～工作 receiving and dispatching ❷ 担任收发工作的人 dispatcher

【收方】shōufāng 簿记账户的左方，记载资产的增加，负债的减少和净值的减少（跟'付方'相对 as opposed to 'credit'）bookkeeping debit side；debit；also 借方 jièfāng

【收风】shōu//fēng 结束放风，让犯人回牢房 call prisoners in after letting them out for exercise

【收伏】shōufú same as 收服 shōufú

【收服】shōufú 制伏对方使顺从自己 subdue；reduce to submission；also 收伏 shōufú

【收抚】shōufǔ ❶ 收容安抚 take in and console：～难民 house refugees ❷ 收留抚养 take in and raise：～烈士遗孤 adopt the orphan of a martyr as one's own child

【收复】shōufù 夺回（失去的领土、阵地 of lost territory，battleground，etc.）recover；recapture：～失地 recover lost territory

【收割】shōugē 割取（成熟的农作物）reap；harvest；gather in：～小麦 gather in the wheat

【收工】shōu//gōng （在田间或工地上干活儿的人）结束工作（of those who work in the fields or on construction sites）stop work for the day；knock off；pack up

【收购】shōugòu 从各处买进 purchase，buy：～棉花 purchase cotton｜～粮食 buy grains｜完成羊毛～计划 fulfil the wool purchasing quotas

【收回】shōu//huí ❶ 把发出去或借出去的东西、借出去或用出去的钱取回来 take back；call in；regain；recall：～贷款 recall loans｜～成本 recoup the cost｜借出的书，应该～了。It is time to call in books that are out on loan. ❷ 撤销；取消（意见、命令等）withdraw；countermand：～原议 annul an agreement｜～成命 countermand (or retract) an order；revoke a command

【收活】shōu//huó （～儿 shōu//huór）❶（加工、修理等部门）接收顾客要加工或修理的物品 accept orders for repairs or processing ❷〈方 *dial.*〉same as 收工 shōu//gōng：赶早～ knock off early｜准时～ knock off on time

【收获】shōuhuò ❶ 取得成熟的农作物 gather (or bring) in the crops；harvest：春天播种，秋天～sow in spring and reap in autumn ❷〈比喻 *fig.*〉心得、战果等 results；gains：学习～ what one learns from study

【收集】shōují 使聚集在一起 collect；gather：～资料 collect materials｜～废品 recover waste products

【收监】shōu//jiān 指把犯人关进监牢 take into custody；put in prison

【收缴】shōujiǎo ❶ 接收；缴获 take over；capture：～武器 take over the arms ❷ 征收上交 levy：～税款 levy taxes

【收据】shōujù 收到钱或东西后写给对方的字据 receipt

【收看】shōukàn 看（电视节目）watch television：～率 audience rating｜～实况转播 watch a live broadcast

【收口】shōu//kǒu （～儿 shōu//kǒur）❶ 编织东西时把开口的地方结起来（in knitting）cast off：这件毛线衣再打几针该～了吧？How many more stitches must be cast off to bind the ribbing of this woollen sweater? ❷（伤口）愈合（of a wound）close up；heal：刀伤还没有～，要注意防止感染。The cut has not yet healed；measures must be taken to prevent infection.

【收揽】shōulǎn ❶ 收买拉拢 draw over to one's side：～民心 try to win the support of the people ❷〈书 *fml.*〉收拢把持 keep within one's grasp

【收镰】shōu//lián 指停止或结束收割工作 end the harvest season：今年麦子开镰早，～也早。The reaping of wheat began and ended early this year.

【收敛】shōuliǎn ❶（笑容、光线等 of smile，light，etc.）减弱或消失 weaken or disappear：她的笑容突然～了。Her smile suddenly disappeared.｜夕阳已经～了余晖。The radiance of the setting sun has faded. ❷ 减轻放纵的程度（指言行）restrain oneself (in deeds or words)：狂妄的态度有所～ become less arrogant and contemptuous ❸ 引起有机体组织的收缩，减少腺体的分泌 astringent：～剂 astringent

【收殓】shōuliàn 把人的尸体放进棺材 lay a body in a coffin

【收留】shōuliú 把生活困难或有特殊要求的人接收下来并给予帮助 take sb. in; have sb. in one's care: 父母死后,一位远房叔叔~了他。After his parents died, a distant relative he called 'uncle' took him in custody.

【收拢】shōulǒng ❶ 把散开的聚集起来;合拢 draw sth. in: ~队伍 muster the troops ❷ 收买拉拢 draw over to one's side: ~人心 try to win the people's support by every means

【收录】shōulù ❶ 吸收任用(人员) employ; recruit; take on: ~旧部 re-employ one's former subordinates ❷ 编集子时采用(诗文等) include (work in a collection of prose or poems):《短篇小说选》中~了他的作品。His works are included in the *Selected Short Stories*.

【收录机】shōulùjī 具有无线电收音机和录音机功能的机器 radio recorder; wireless radio with added functions of a recorder

【收罗】shōuluó 把人或物聚集在一起 collect; gather; enlist: ~人才 recruit qualified personnel|~材料 collect materials

【收买】shōumǎi ❶ same as 收购 shōugòu: ~旧书 buy used books|~废铜烂铁 recover metal scrap ❷ 用钱财或其他好处笼络人,使受利用 buy over; bribe: ~人心 buy popular support

【收纳】shōunà 收进来;收容 receive; take in: 如数~ accept a sum of money as indicated

【收盘】shōupán (~儿 shōupánr)指交易市场中营业时间终了,最后一次报告行情 closing quotation (on the exchange, etc.)

【收篷】shōu//péng〈方 *dial*.〉降下船帆 shorten sail;〈比喻 *fig*.〉结束;收场 finish: 自动~ finish doing sth. on one's own accord|趁势~ make a timely withdrawal

【收讫】shōuqì 收清(收讫这两个字常刻成戳子,加盖在发票或其他单据上) have received (goods, money, etc.) in full (the two characters oft. being carved on a seal to be stamped on an invoice or other bills)

【收清】shōuqīng 全部如数收到(多指款项) receive (money, payment, etc.) in full

【收秋】shōu//qiū 秋季收获农作物 gather in the autumn crops: 农民正忙着~。The farmers are busy with their autumn harvest.

【收取】shōuqǔ 交来(或取来)收下 get payment; receive; collect: ~手续费 collect service (or handling) charges

【收容】shōuróng (有关的组织、机构等)收留 (of an organization, government department, etc.) take in; accept; house: ~所 collecting post|~队 collecting team |~伤员 take in wounded soldiers

【收入】shōurù ❶ 收进来 take in; include: 每天~的现金都存入银行。Cash takings are deposited in the bank daily. ❷ 收进来的钱 income; revenue; receipts; earnings; proceeds: 财政~ state revenues |个人的~有所增加。Personal income has been increased.

【收审】shōushěn 拘留审查 detain for interrogation

【收生】shōushēng 指接生 midwifery: ~婆 midwife

【收生婆】shōushēngpó 以旧法接生为业的妇女 midwife

【收尸】shōu//shī 收拾尸体火化或埋葬,不使暴露 cremate or bury the dead (so as not to display the body)

【收市】shōu//shì 指市场、商店等停止交易或营业 (of markets or stores) close for the day

【收视】shōushì same as 收看 shōukàn: ~率 ratings for a TV programme |~效果 viewing effect

【收拾】shōu·shi ❶ 整顿;整理 put in order; tidy; clear away: ~残局 clear up the mess; pick up the pieces |~屋子 tidy up the room ❷ 修理 repair; mend: ~皮鞋 repair leather shoes ❸ same as 整治 zhěngzhì②: 你要不听话,看你父亲回来~你! If you don't behave yourself, your father will teach you a lesson when he comes back. ❹ 消灭;杀死 eliminate: 据点的敌人,全叫我们~了。We have wiped out the enemy stronghold.

【收受】shōushòu 接受;收取 receive; accept; take: 他不~任何礼物。He will not accept any gifts. |~贿赂 take bribes

【收缩】shōusuō ❶ (物体)由大变小或由长变短 contract; shrink; reduce: 铁受了热就会膨胀,遇到冷就会~。Iron expands when it is heated and contracts when it is cooled. ❷ 紧缩 concentrate one's forces; draw back: 把兵力~在交通线上 put all combat forces on the communication line

【收摊儿】shōu//tānr 摊贩把摆着的货收起来(of a peddler) pack up the stall;〈比喻 *fig*.〉结束手头的工作 wind up the day's business or the work at hand: 下班时间到了,~吧。It's closing time. Let's call it a day.

【收条】shōutiáo (~儿 shōutiáor) same as 收据 shōujù: 打~ make out a receipt

【收听】shōutīng 听(广播) listen to (the radio): ~天气预报 listen to a weather forecast

【收尾】shōuwěi ❶ 结束事情的最后一段;煞尾 bring to a conclusion; wind up: 麦收已到~阶段。Wheat harvesting is coming to an end. ❷ 文章的末尾 ending (of an article, etc.): 文章的~有些松懈。The ending of the story is a little slack.

【收文】shōuwén 本单位收到的公文 incoming dispatches: ~簿(登记收文的本子) register of incoming dispatches

【收效】shōu//xiào 收到效果 yield results; produce effects; bear fruit: ~显著 bring notable results

【收心】shōu//xīn 把放纵散漫的心思收起来,也指把做坏事的念头收起来 get into the frame

of mind for work or study; concentrate on more serious things: 该～用功了。It's time you settled down. | 强盗～做好人。The robbers repented and decided to go straight.

【收押】shōuyā 拘留 take into custody; detain: ～候审 be detained in anticipation of trial

【收养】shōuyǎng 把别人的儿女收下来当做自己家里的人来抚养 take in and bring up; adopt: ～弃婴 adopt and raise a foundling

【收益】shōuyì 生产上或商业上的收入 income; profit; earnings; gains: 增加～ make more profit | ～甚少 make little profit

【收音】shōuyīn ❶ 集中声波,使人听得清楚 (of an auditorium, etc.) have good acoustics: 露天剧场不～。Acoustics in an open-air theatre are poor. ❷ 接收无线电广播的 (of radio) reception: ～机 radio (set); wireless (set) | ～站 radio station | ～网 radio net | ～员 radio receptor

【收音机】shōuyīnjī 无线电收音机的通称 popular name for 无线电收音机 wúxiàndiàn shōuyīnjī

【收执】shōuzhí ❶ 公文用语,收下并保存 (of a certificate, etc.) be issued to the person concerned for safe keeping ❷ 政府机关收到税金或其他东西时发给的书面凭证 receipt (issued by a government agency as proof of tax or other objects received)

【收治】shōuzhì 收留并治疗 admit for treatment: 医院增加床位,～病人。The hospital has acquired extra beds in order to admit more patients for treatment.

shóu (ㄕㄡˊ)

熟 (shóu) same as 熟 shú
☞ shú on p. 1783

shǒu (ㄕㄡˇ)

手 shǒu ❶ 人体上肢前端能拿东西的部分 hand (图见☞ figure for 身体 shēntǐ on p. 1701) ❷ 拿着 have in one's hand; hold: 人～一册 a copy for everyone ❸ 小巧而便于拿的 handy; convenient: ～册 handbook | ～折 notebook recording deliveries ❹ 亲手 personally: ～订 personally edit | ～抄 copy by hand ❺ 手段;手法 ability: 眼高～低 have high expectations but little ability | 心狠～辣 cruel and evil ❻ (～儿 shǒur)〈量词 *classifier*〉用于技能、本领等 (for skill or dexterity): 他真有两～。He really knows his stuff. | 他有一～绝活儿。He has a unique skill. ❼ 擅长某种技能的人或做某种事的人 expert at some occupation or job: 选～ player | 能～ skilled hand | 拖拉机～ tractor driver

【手把手】shǒu bǎ shǒu 指亲自指点、传授(技艺等) personally instruct; pass on one's own knowledge and skills

【手板】shǒubǎn ❶〈方 *dial.*〉手掌 palm (of the hand) ❷ same as 手版 shǒubǎn

【手版】shǒubǎn ❶〈古时 *arch.*〉君臣在朝廷上相见时手中所拿的笏 tablet held before the breast by officials when having an audience with the emperor ❷ same as 手本 shǒuběn ① ‖ also 手板 shǒubǎn

【手背】shǒubèi 手掌的反面 back of the hand

【手本】shǒuběn ❶ 明清时代门生见老师或下属见上司所用的贴子,上面写着自己的姓名、职位等 visiting card; name card, used by students or subordinates in the Ming and Qing dynasties when they visit their teacher or superior ❷ same as 手册 shǒucè

【手笔】shǒubǐ ❶ 亲手做的文章、写的字或画的画(多指名人的) celebrated person's handwriting or painting: 这篇杂文像是鲁迅先生的～。This essay looks like Lu Xun's own handwriting. ❷ 文字技巧的造诣 literary skill: 大～(文章能手) well-known writer; master ❸ 指办事、用钱的气派 style in doing sth. or spending money: 阔～ doing things in grand style

S

【手臂】shǒubì ❶ 胳膊 arm ❷〈比喻 *fig.*〉助手 reliable helper: 他是王队长的得力～。He is team leader Wang's right-hand man.

【手边】shǒubiān (～儿 shǒubiānr) same as 手头 shǒutóu ①: 你要的那张画,不在～,等找出来给你。The picture you want is not at hand at the moment. I'll give it to you later.

【手表】shǒubiǎo 带在手腕上的表 wristwatch

【手柄】shǒubǐng 操纵机器时手握着的把儿 hand lever; hand shank; also 手把 shǒubà

【手不释卷】shǒu bù shì juàn 手里的书舍不得放下。形容读书勤奋或看书人迷。always have a book in one's hand; be very studious; be a diligent reader; (of a book) be a page-turner

【手不稳】shǒu bù wěn〈方 *dial.*〉指爱偷窃 be light-fingered; be inclined to steal or pilfer

【手册】shǒucè ❶ 介绍一般性的或某种专业知识的参考书(多用于书名 usu. used in book titles) handbook; manual:《时事～》*Handbook of Current Affairs* |《物理～》*Handbook on Physics* ❷ 专做某种记录用的本子 record book; workbook: 劳动～ worker's book

【手车】shǒuchē 用人力推动的小车,用来装运物品 handcart; pushcart; barrow; also 手推车 shǒutuīchē

【手钏】shǒuchuàn〈方 *dial.*〉same as 手镯 shǒuzhuó

【手戳】shǒuchuō (～儿 shǒuchuōr) 刻有某人姓名的图章 private seal; signet

【手搭凉棚】shǒu dā liángpéng 瞭望时用一只手平支在前额上遮阳光 use hand to shade eyes from the sun: 老大爷站在路口,～在张望。

The old man stood at the crossing, his hand raised to shade his eyes from the sun.

【手大】shǒu dà 指花钱不在乎 be liberal with money

【手到擒来】shǒu dào qín lái 手一到就把敌人捉拿过来 just stretch out the hand, capture the enemy, and draw it back; 〈比喻 *fig.*〉做事很有把握或毫不费力就能成功 sth. easily accomplishable; a piece of cake

【手底下】shǒu dǐ·xia same as 手下 shǒuxià

【手电筒】shǒudiàntǒng 利用干电池做电源的小型筒状照明用具 electric torch; flashlight; also 手电 shǒudiàn, 电筒 diàntǒng or 电棒 diànbàng

【手段】shǒuduàn ❶ 为达到某种目的而采取的具体方法 means; medium; measure; method: 革命的战争是夺取政权的～。Revolutionary war is a means of seizing political power. ❷ 指待人处世所用的不正当的方法 trick; artifice: 耍～骗人 deceit ❸ 本领;能耐 skill; finesse: ～高强 highly skilled

【手法】shǒufǎ ❶ (艺术品或文学作品的)技巧 (of art or literature) skill; technique: 白描～ line drawing technique in traditional Chinese painting | 表现～独特 have distinctive expressive skills ❷ same as 手段 shǒuduàn ②: 两面～ dual tactics

【手风琴】shǒufēngqín 风琴的一种,由金属簧、折叠的皮制风箱和键盘组成。演奏时左手拉动风箱,右手按键盘。accordion; small, portable, box-shaped reed wind instrument, with a vertical keyboard that is played with the right hand, and free metallic reeds that are made to vibrate with air generated from a set of pleated bellows operated by the left hand, that is also used to depress two or three bass harmony keys

【手感】shǒugǎn 用手抚摸时的感觉 handle; feel: 这种面料～柔和。This material is soft to the touch.

【手高手低】shǒu gāo shǒu dī 形容不用度量衡器具而用手或一般的器皿分东西时,难免稍有出入 slight differences (when dividing things up by hand instead of a measurement instrument)

【手稿】shǒugǎo 亲手写成的底稿 original (or holograph) manuscript; manuscript

【手工】shǒugōng ❶ 靠手的技能做出的工作 handwork; manual work: 做～ do handwork ❷ 用手操作 by hand; manual: ～劳动 manual labour ❸ 给予手工劳动的报酬 charge for a piece of handwork: ～很贵 high charge for manual labour | 做这件衣服要多少～? How much did it cost to tailor this garment?

【手工业】shǒugōngyè 只靠手工或只用简单工具从事生产的工业 handicraft industry; handicraft

【手工艺】shǒugōngyì 指具有高度技巧性、艺术性的手工,如挑花、刺绣、缂(kè)丝等 arts and crafts; handicraft; manual labour that calls for high skills and a keen sense of aesthetics, such as skills for cross-stitch works, embroidery, and silk weaving

【手鼓】shǒugǔ 维吾尔、哈萨克等少数民族的打击乐器,扁圆形,一面蒙皮,周围有金属片或环,常用做舞蹈的伴奏乐器 small drum similar to the tambourine (used by the Uygur, Kazakh and other ethnic peoples, usu. in accompaniment to a dance)

【手黑】shǒu hēi 手段狠毒 be unscrupulous: 心狠～ be cruel and merciless

【手疾眼快】shǒu jí yǎn kuài 形容做事机警敏捷 quick of eye and deft of hand; also 眼疾手快 yǎn jí shǒu kuài

【手记】shǒujì ❶ 亲手记录 write down notes or records ❷ 亲手写下的记录 written notes or records

【手技】shǒujì ❶ same as 手艺 shǒuyì ❷ 杂技的一种,运用手的技巧抛接、耍弄各种物件 acrobatics: juggling; jugglery

【手迹】shǒujì 亲手写的字或画的画 sb.'s original handwriting or painting: 这是鲁迅先生的～。This is an original work in the handwriting of Lu Xun.

【手脚】shǒujiǎo ❶ 指举动或动作 movement of hands or feet; motion: ～利落 nimble; agile | ～灵敏 dexterous ❷ 为了实现某种企图而暗中采取的行动(含贬义 derog.)hanky-panky; underhand method; devious device; trick: 做～ play dirty tricks on the sly; play hanky-panky with sb.

【手巾】shǒu·jīn ❶ 土布做的擦脸巾;毛巾 towel ❷ 〈方 *dial.*〉same as 手绢 shǒujuàn

【手紧】shǒu jǐn ❶ 指不随便花钱或给人东西 close-fisted; tight-fisted: 他一向～,不会买这种玩艺儿的。He is tight-fisted and won't buy stuff like this. ❷ 指缺钱用 be short of money; be hard up: 这几天～,过两天再买吧。I'm a bit hard up lately; I'll buy it later. also 手头儿紧 shǒutóur jǐn

【手卷】shǒujuàn 横幅书画长卷,只供案头观赏,不能悬挂 hand scroll

【手绢】shǒujuàn (～儿 shǒujuànr)随身携带的方形小块织物,用来擦汗或擦鼻涕等 handkerchief

【手铐】shǒukào 束缚犯人两手的刑具 handcuffs

【手快】shǒu kuài 形容动作敏捷,做事快 deft of hand: 眼疾～ quick of eye and deft of hand

【手辣】shǒu là 手段毒辣 be vicious or unscrupulous: 心狠～merciless and vicious

【手雷】shǒuléi 一种反坦克用的大型手榴弹 anti-tank grenade

【手榴弹】shǒuliúdàn ❶ 一种用手投掷的小型炸弹,有的装有木柄 hand grenade; grenade; small container filled with explosive, thrown by hand ❷ 田径运动使用的投掷器械之一,形

状跟军用的装有木柄的手榴弹一样 grenade-like apparatus used in track-and-field events

【手令】shǒulìng 亲手写的命令 orders or instructions in one's own handwriting

【手炉】shǒulú 冷天烘手用的小铜炉，多为圆形或椭圆形，直径约半尺，有提梁，盖上有许多小孔，炉中燃烧炭墼、锯末或砻糠。可以随身携带。portable hand warmer; portable tiny brass brazier for warming one's hands in winter, round or oval in shape, about 16.5 cm in diameter, having a loop handle and a lid punched with tiny holes, and fuled by charcoal briquettes, sawdust or chaff

【手锣】shǒuluó 小锣 small gong

【手慢】shǒu màn 形容动作迟缓，做事慢 slow handed; slow in movements; slow moving: 这个人～，老赶不上趟儿。This fellow is so slow that whatever his task he is always behind schedule.

【手忙脚乱】shǒu máng jiǎo luàn 形容做事慌张而没有条理。也形容惊慌失措。in a frantic rush; in a great fluster

【手面】shǒumiàn 〈方 *dial.*〉指用钱的宽紧 extent of one's spending: 你～太阔了，要节约一点才好。You spend too freely and should practise a little more thrift.

【手民】shǒumín 〈书 *fml.*〉指刻字或排字的工人 typesetter: ～之误（指印刷上发生的错误）misprint; typographical error

【手模】shǒumó same as 手印 shǒuyìn

【手帕】shǒupà 手绢儿 handkerchief; hankie

【手旗】shǒuqí 打旗语用的旗子 hand flag; semaphore flag: ～通讯 communication by flag signaling

【手气】shǒuqì 指赌博或抓彩时的运气。又特指赢钱或得彩的运气 luck at gambling, card playing: ～好 good luck (in gambling) | 有～ be lucky

【手枪】shǒuqiāng 单手发射的短枪。用于近距离射击。pistol; short-barreled handgun

【手巧】shǒu qiǎo 手灵巧；手艺高 skillful with one's hands; nimble-fingered; deft; dexterous: 心灵～ clever and deft

【手勤】shǒu qín 指做事勤快 diligent; industrious; hard-working: ～脚快 hard-working

【手轻】shǒu qīng 动作时手用力较小 have gentle hands; have a light touch; handle gently

【手球】shǒuqiú ❶ 球类运动项目之一。球场呈长方形，比赛时每队上场七人，一人守球门，用手把球掷进对方球门算得分，得分多的获胜。handball; ball game in which the ball is thrown rather than kicked on a rectangular court between two seven-member teams, with the team that scores more goals as the winner ❷ 手球运动使用的球，形状像足球，但比足球略小 handball, which is similar to, but smaller than, the soccer ball ❸ 足球运动中的犯规动作。指守门员在禁区外或其他队员故意用手或臂部携带或击、推球。handball (a foul in soccer game); offence committed when a soccer player touches the ball with his hand, or when a goalkeeper does so out of his own penalty area

【手软】shǒu ruǎn 形容不忍下手或因心慌而下手不狠 be irresolute when firmness is needed; be softhearted: 心慈～ be kind and lack the courage to do sth.

【手生】shǒu shēng 指对所做的事不熟悉或原来熟悉因长久不做而不熟练 lack practice and skill; be out of practice: 这种活儿多年没做，～了。Not having done this kind of work for years, I'm out of practice.

【手势】shǒushì 表示意思时用手（有时连同身体别的部分）所做的姿势 gesture; sign; signal: 交通警打～指挥车辆。The traffic policeman directs traffic using hand signals.

【手书】shǒushū ❶ 亲笔书写 write in one's own hand: 条幅上'天下为公'四个字乃孙中山先生～。The characters on the scroll 'The World for Everyone' were written by Dr. Sun Yat-sen. ❷ 亲笔写的信 personal letter: 今天接到了家父的～。I received my father's letter today.

【手术】shǒushù 医生用医疗器械在病人的身体上进行的切除、缝合等治疗 surgical operation; operation: 大～ major operation | 小～ minor operation | 动～ perform or undergo an operation

【手松】shǒu sōng 指随便花钱或给人东西 free with one's money; free-handed; open-handed

【手谈】shǒután 〈书 *fml.*〉下围棋 play *weiqi*

【手套】shǒutào (～儿 shǒutàor) 套在手上的物品，用棉纱、毛线、皮革等制成，用来防寒或保护手 gloves; mittens; shaped covering for the hand with individual sheaths for the fingers and thumb, made of leather or fabric

【手提包】shǒutíbāo 提包 handbag; bag

【手提箱】shǒutíxiāng 装随身用品的有提梁的轻便的箱子 suitcase

【手头】shǒutóu (～儿 shǒutóur) ❶ 指伸手可以拿到的地方 right beside one; on hand; at hand: 这部书我倒有，可惜不在～。I do have a copy of the book, but unfortunately not with me. ❷ 个人某一时候的经济情况 one's financial condition at a given time: ～宽裕 be in easy circumstances; be well off at the moment | ～紧 be short of money; be hard up ❸ 指写作或办事的能力 writing or other abilities: ～利落 neat and able

【手头字】shǒutóuzì 简体字的旧称 old term for simplified Chinese character

【手推车】shǒutuīchē same as 手车 shǒuchē

【手腕】shǒuwàn (～儿 shǒuwànr) ❶ same as 手腕子 shǒuwàn·zi ❷ same as 手段 shǒuduàn ②③: 耍～ play tricks; use artifices

【手腕子】shǒuwàn·zi 手和臂相接的部分 wrist

S

【手无寸铁】shǒu wú cùn tiě 形容手里没有任何武器 bare-handed; unarmed; defenceless

【手无缚鸡之力】shǒu wú fù jī zhī lì 形容力气很小 lack the strength to truss a chicken — physically very weak

【手舞足蹈】shǒu wǔ zú dǎo 双手舞动,两只脚也跳起来。形容高兴到极点。(of sb. at a moment of ecstasy) dance for joy

【手下】shǒuxià ❶ 领属下;管辖下 under the leadership (or guidance, direction) of; under: 他在总工程师的～当过技术员。Once he worked under the direction of the general engineer. ❷ same as 手头 shǒutóu①: 东西不在～。I don't have that thing with me. ❸ same as 手头 shǒutóu②: 用钱无计划,月底～就紧了 be short of money at the end of a month due to unplanned spending ❹ 下手的时候 take action; hit: ～留情 show mercy; be lenient; make allowances for (when meting out punishment to sb.)

【手写】shǒuxiě 用手写;亲自记录 write by hand; hand write; write by one's own hand: 口问～ ask questions and write down the responses

S

【手写体】shǒuxiětǐ 文字或拼音字母的手写形式(区别于'印刷体' as compared with 'print') handwritten form; script:

直 zhí (印刷体) print	直 *zhí* (手写体) script

【手心】shǒuxīn ❶ 手掌的中心部分 centre of the palm ❷ (～儿 shǒuxīnr)〈比喻 *fig.*〉所控制的范围 scope of control: 跳不出他的～ unable to extract oneself from sb.'s control; has sb. in the palm of one's hand

【手续】shǒuxù (办事的)程序 procedures; formalities: 报名～ entry procedure | 借款～ lending formalities | 办理转学～ go through school-transfer procedures

【手眼】shǒuyǎn same as 手段 shǒuduàn ②: ～通天 exceptionally adept at trickery

【手艺】shǒuyì 手工业工人的技术 craftsmanship; workmanship: ～人 craftsman | 这位木匠师傅的～很好。This carpenter has superb craftsmanship.

【手淫】shǒuyín 自己用手刺激生殖器以发泄性欲。成习惯后,有害健康。masturbation; self-abuse; stimulate the genital organs of oneself to achieve sexual pleasure

【手印】shǒuyìn (～儿 shǒuyìnr) ❶ 手留下的痕迹 impression of the hand ❷ 特指按在契约、证件等上面的指纹 thumbprint; fingerprint (imprinted on contract, credential, etc.)

【手语】shǒuyǔ 以手指字母和手势代替语言进行交际的方式(多用于聋哑人) sign language; dactylology

【手谕】shǒuyù〈书 *fml.*〉指上级或尊长亲笔写的指示 personally written orders or instructions

【手泽】shǒuzé〈书 *fml.*〉先人的遗物或手迹 handwriting or possessions left by one's forefathers

【手札】shǒuzhá〈书 *fml.*〉亲笔写的信 personal letter

【手掌】shǒuzhǎng 手在握拳时指尖触着的一面 palm (of the hand)

【手杖】shǒuzhàng 走路时手里拄着的棍子 walking stick; stick

【手植】shǒuzhí 亲手种植 personally plant: 这棵树乃先父～。This tree was planted by my father.

【手纸】shǒuzhǐ 解手时使用的纸 toilet paper

【手指】shǒuzhǐ 人手前端的五个分支 finger; any of the digits of the hand

【手指头】shǒuzhǐ·tou same as 手指 shǒuzhǐ

【手指头肚儿】shǒuzhǐ·toudùr 手指末端有指纹的略微隆起的部分 inner side of the fingertip

【手指字母】shǒuzhǐ zìmǔ 用手指屈伸的各种姿势代表不同的字母,可以组成文字,供聋哑人使用 manual alphabet used by the deaf or the mute; sign language alphabet

【手重】shǒu zhòng 动作时手用力较猛 use too much force: 捅火时～了些,把炉子里没烧尽的煤块儿都给捅下来了 use force to poke the stove and extract unburned coal

【手镯】shǒuzhuó 套在手腕子上的环形装饰品,多用金、银、玉等制成 bracelet, oft. made of gold, silver or jade; ornamental chain worn around the wrist

【手足】shǒuzú ❶ 指举动、动作 movement: ～无措 be disconcerted, confused; at a loss as to what to do ❷〈比喻 *fig.*〉弟兄 brothers: 情同～ brotherly affection; close as brothers

【手足无措】shǒu zú wú cuò 形容举动慌乱或没有办法应付 disconcerted; at a loss as to what to do

守 shǒu ❶ 防守(跟'攻'相对 as opposed to 'attack') guard; defend: 把～ guard | 看～ look after | ～卫 keep safe | ～住阵地 hold the position ❷ 守候;看护 keep watch: ～护 protect | 医生～着伤员。The doctor watched over (or tended) the wounded. ❸ 遵守;遵循 observe; abide by: ～法 obey or observe the law | ～约 keep a promise | ～纪律 observe discipline | ～时间 be punctual ❹ 靠近;依傍 close to; near: ～着水的地方,可多种稻子 plant more rice where there is water nearby

【守备】shǒubèi 防守戒备 perform garrison duty; be on garrison duty; garrison: 加强～ strengthen defence

【守财奴】shǒucáinú 指有钱而非常吝啬的人(含讥讽意 with a sense of irony) miser; person who hoards money or possessions, and oft. lives miserably; also 看财奴 kāncáinú

【守车】shǒuchē 货运列车中车长办公用的车厢，车身较短，挂在列车的最后 (Brit.) guard's van; (Amer.) caboose

【守成】shǒuchéng〈书 *fml.*〉在事业上保持前人的成就；守业 maintain the achievements of one's predecessors; carry on an undertaking started by one's predecessors: 保业～ carry on what has been started

【守敌】shǒudí 守备某据点的敌人 enemy holding a fortress or a strategic point

【守法】shǒu//fǎ 遵守法律或法令 abide by (or observe) the law; be law-abiding: ～户 law-abiding firm | 奉公～ obey the law

【守服】shǒufú 服丧；守孝 observe mourning for one's deceased parent

【守寡】shǒu//guǎ 妇女死了丈夫后，不再结婚 remain a widow; live in widowhood

【守恒】shǒuhéng (数值)保持恒定 conservation: 能量～conservation of energy | 动量～ conservation of momentum

【守候】shǒuhòu ❶ 等待 wait for; expect: 他～着家乡的信息。He waited for news from his home town. ❷ 看护 keep watch: 护士日夜～着伤员。The nurses kept watch over the wounded.

【守护】shǒuhù 看守保护 guard; defend: ～仓库 guard the storehouse | 战士们日夜～着祖国的边疆。Soldiers guarded the motherland border day and night.

【守活寡】shǒu huóguǎ 已婚妇女的丈夫长期外出不归，叫守活寡。有的地区也说守生寡。be a grass widow; also 守生寡 shǒu shēngguǎ in some places

【守节】shǒu//jié〈旧时 *old*〉指不改变节操。特指妇女受封建宗法的强制或封建道德观念的影响，在丈夫死后不再结婚或未婚夫死后终身不结婚。remain unmarried after the death of one's husband or fiance either in compliance with feudal patriarchal clan rules of conduct or because of the influence of feudul moral values

【守旧】[1] shǒujiù 拘泥于过时的看法或做法而不愿改变 adhere to past practices; stick to old ways; be conservative: ～思想 conservatism | 办法过于～。This method is rather out-dated.

【守旧】[2] shǒujiù 戏曲演出时挂在舞台上用来隔开前后的幕，幕上绣着跟剧情无关的图案 backdrop; large curtain hanging at the back of a stage set and embroidered with motifs not relevant to the play being staged

【守空房】shǒu kōngfáng 指丈夫外出，妻子一人住在家里 (of a married woman) stay home alone

【守口如瓶】shǒu kǒu rú píng 形容说话慎重或严守秘密 keep one's mouth shut; breathe not a single word; be close-mouthed; be reticent

【守灵】shǒu//líng 守在灵床、灵柩或灵位的旁边 stand as guards at the bier; keep vigil beside a coffin

【守门】shǒu//mén ❶ 看守门户 be on duty at the door or gate ❷ 指足球、手球、冰球等球类比赛中守卫球门 keep goal (of soccer, handball, ice hocky or other ball games)

【守门员】shǒuményuán 足球、手球、冰球等球类比赛中守卫球门的队员 goalkeeper (in football, handball, ice hockey, etc.)

【守丧】shǒu//sāng same as 守灵 shǒu//líng

【守势】shǒushì 防御敌方进攻的部署 defensive: 采取～ be on the defensive | 处于～ be on the defensive

【守岁】shǒu//suì 在农历除夕晚上不睡，直到天亮 stay up late or all night on lunar New Year's Eve: 围炉～ stay up late and sit around the stove on lunar New Year's Eve

【守土】shǒutǔ〈书 *fml.*〉保卫领土 defend the territory of one's country: ～有责 be duty-bound to defend the territory of one's country

【守望】shǒuwàng 看守瞭望 keep watch: ～塔 watchtower

【守望相助】shǒu wàng xiāng zhù 为了防御外来的侵害，邻近的村落之间互相看守瞭望，遇警互相帮助 (of neighbouring villages, etc.) keep watch and help defend each other; give mutual help and protection

【守卫】shǒuwèi 防守保卫 guard; defend: ～边疆 defend national borders

【守孝】shǒu//xiào 旧俗尊亲死后，在服满以前停止娱乐和交际，表示哀悼(old custom) observe a period of mourning for one's deceased parent, during which one is supposed to refrain from any recreational and social activities

【守信】shǒu//xìn 讲信用；不失信 keep one's word: 他是个～的人，不会失约的。He is a reliable man and would not break his promise.

【守业】shǒu//yè 守住前人所创立的事业 maintain what has been achieved by one's forefathers or predecessors; safeguard one's heritage: 不但要～，而且要创业。One must not only carry on what has been started, but also blaze a new trail.

【守夜】shǒuyè 夜间守卫 keep nightwatch; spend the night on watch: 值班～ keep watch at night

【守则】shǒuzé 共同遵守的规则 rules; regulations: 学生～ rules and regulations for students

【守职】shǒu//zhí 坚守岗位，忠于职守 stand fast at one's post; be faithful in the discharge of one's duties: ～尽责 be committed to one's duties

【守制】shǒuzhì 封建时代，儿子在父母死后，在家守孝二十七个月，谢绝应酬，做官的在这期间必须离职，叫做守制(in feudal times) observe a prescribed period of mourning (usu. 27 months) for one's deceased parent, during which officials must leave their post and shun all forms of socializing

【守株待兔】shǒu zhū dài tù 传说战国时宋国有一个农民看见一只兔子撞在树桩上死了，他便放下手里的农具在那里等待，希望再得到撞死的兔子(见于《韩非子·五蠹》)。stand by a stump waiting for more hares to come and dash themselves against it. Legend has it that during the Warring States Period a farmer of the State of Song saw a hare run into a tree and die, and he laid down his farm tool to wait for more hares to come (*Hanfeizi·Five Vermin*).〈比喻 *fig.*〉不主动地努力，而存万一的侥幸心理，希望得到意外的收获。wait for a windfall; trust in chance and strokes of luck

首[1] shǒu ❶ 头 head: 昂～ hold one's head high | 搔～ scratch one's head | ～饰 jewellery | ～级 chopped-off head ❷ 第一；最高的 first: ～相 prime minister | ～脑 head | ～席代表 chief delegate ❸ 首领 leader; head; chief: ～长 senior officer | 罪魁祸～ arch-criminal ❹ 首先 first of all: ～创 originate; initiate; pioneer | ～义 be the first to rise in revolt ❺ 出头告发 bring charges against sb.: 自～ (of a criminal) surrender oneself | 出～ inform against sb. ❻ (Shǒu)姓 a surname

首[2] shǒu〈量词 *classifier*〉用于诗词等 [for songs and poems]: 一～诗 a poem

【首倡】shǒuchàng 首先提倡 be the first to advocate; initiate; start

【首车】shǒuchē 按班次行驶的第一班车 first bus (of a regular bus service)

【首创】shǒuchuàng 最先创造；创始 originate; initiate; pioneer: 这种产品在国内还是～。This product was first pioneered in our country. | 尊重科学家们的～精神 respect scientists' creative spirit and enterprise

【首当其冲】shǒu dāng qí chōng〈比喻 *fig.*〉最先受到攻击或遭遇灾难 bear the brunt; stand in the breach (冲 *chong*: 要冲 important transportation hub)

【首都】shǒudū 国家最高政权机关所在地，是全国的政治中心 capital (of a country); seat of government of a country

【首恶】shǒu'è 作恶犯法集团的头子 chief criminal; principal culprit: ～必办。The culprits will be punished without exception.

【首犯】shǒufàn 组织、带领犯罪集团进行犯罪活动的首要分子 chief criminal; principal culprit

【首府】shǒufǔ ❶〈旧时 *old*〉称省会所在的府为首府；现在多指自治区或自治州人民政府所在地 head prefecture (the prefecture in which a provincial capital was located); now usu. referring to capital of an autonomous region or prefecture ❷ 附属国和殖民地的最高政府机关所在地 capital of a dependency or colony

【首富】shǒufù 指某个地区中最富有的人或人家 wealthiest person or family in a locality

【首告】shǒugào 出面告发(别人的犯罪行为) report (an offender); inform against (an offender)

【首户】shǒuhù same as 首富 shǒufù

【首级】shǒují〈古代 *arch.*〉指作战时斩下的人头(秦法，斩下敌人一个人头，加爵一级，后来就把斩下的敌人的头颅叫首级) (According to the law of the Qin Dynasty, soldiers who chopped off one enemy head would be awarded a feudal rank or a promotion in feudal ranking. Thus 首级, literally meaning 'head and rank', has come to refer to 'chopped-off enemy's head'.) chopped-off head in battle

【首届】shǒujiè 第一次；第一期 first occasion, term, session, etc.: ～运动会 first sports meet | ～毕业生 first graduates of a school

【首肯】shǒukěn 点头表示同意 nod approval; nod assent; approve; consent

【首领】shǒulǐng ❶〈书 *fml.*〉头和脖子 head and neck: 保全～ keep alive ❷ 借指某些集团的领导人 chieftain; leader; head: 义军～ leader of a righteous army; leader of a peasant uprising

【首脑】shǒunǎo 为首的(人、机关等)；领导人 head: 政府～ head of government | ～会议 conference of heads of state or government; summit conference

【首屈一指】shǒu qū yī zhǐ 弯下手指头计数，首先弯下大拇指，表示第一 come first on the list; be second to none

【首日封】shǒurìfēng 邮政部门发行新邮票的当天，把新邮票贴在特制的信封上，并盖上邮戳，这种信封叫做首日封 first-day cover; envelope affixed with a stamp from a commemorative set postmarked on the first day of issue

【首善之区】shǒu shàn zhī qū〈书 *fml.*〉最好的地方，指首都 best of places (i.e. the capital of a country)

【首饰】shǒu·shi 本指戴在头上的装饰品，今泛指耳环、项链、戒指、手镯等 (orig.) head ornaments or headgear; jewellery in general, such as earrings, necklace, ring, bracelet, etc.

【首鼠两端】shǒu shǔ liǎng duān 迟疑不决或动摇不定(见《史记·魏其武安侯列传》see *Records of the Historian·Biographies of Marquis Weiqi and Marquis Wu'an*) be in two minds; shilly-shally

【首途】shǒutú〈书 *fml.*〉动身；上路 set out on a journey; start a journey: ～赴任 set out to take up an official position

【首尾】shǒuwěi ❶ 起头的部分和末尾的部分 head and tail; beginning and end: ～呼应 keep the head and tail linked; make the beginning (of a piece of writing, etc.) match up with the ending ❷ 从开始到末了 from beginning to end: 这次旅行,～经过了一个多月。From start to finish the trip lasted over a month.

【首席】shǒuxí ❶ 最高的席位 seat of honour: 坐～ be seated at the head of the table; be in the seat of honour ❷ 职位最高的 chief: ～代表 chief representative (or delegate)

【首先】shǒuxiān ❶ 最先;最早 before all others; first: ～报名 sign up first ❷ 第一(用于列举事项 used in listing items) in the first place; first of all; above all: ～,是大会主席报告;其次,是代表发言。First of all the president will make his report, after which the deputies will take the floor.

【首相】shǒuxiàng 君主国家内阁的最高官职。某些非君主国家的中央政府首脑有时也沿用这个名称,职权相当于内阁总理。prime minister; head of the cabinet of a monarchy; head of a parliamentary government; chief minister of a sovereign or a state

【首选】shǒuxuǎn 以第一名当选的;首先选中的 first choice: ～药物 first choice in medicine | 该地是冬季运动会的～地点。That place is the first preference as a venue for the winter sports meet.

【首要】shǒuyào ❶ 摆在第一位的;最重要的 of primary importance; first; chief: ～任务 most important task | ～分子 ringleader ❷ 首脑 leader: 政府～ government leaders

【首义】shǒuyì 〈书 *fml.*〉首先起义 be the first to rise in revolt: 辛亥～(指辛亥革命时武昌首先起义)。Wuchang took the lead in launching the Revolution of 1911.

【首战】shǒuzhàn 第一次交战 first battle or game: ～告捷 win the very first battle or game

【首长】shǒuzhǎng 政府各部门中的高级领导人或部队中较高级的领导人 (of government departments) leading cadre; (of an army) senior officer: 部～ minister | 团～ regiment commander

【首座】shǒuzuò ❶ 筵席上最尊贵的席位 seat of honour (at a banquet); also 首坐 shǒuzuò ❷ 寺庙里地位最高的和尚 abbot, the top-ranking monk in a monastery

艏 shǒu 船的前端或前部 stem; (of a ship) bow

shòu (ㄕㄡˋ)

寿(壽、壽) shòu ❶ 活得岁数大;长命 long life; longevity; old age: 福～ good fortune and long life | 人～年丰。May people live long and harvests be fruitful. ❷ 年岁;生命 life; age: 长～ long life | ～命 lifetime ❸ 寿辰 birthday: 做～(usu. of middle-aged or elderly people) celebrate a birthday | ～面 birthday or longevity noodles ❹〈书 *fml.*〉祝人寿辰 congratulate sb. on his or her birthday ❺〈婉辞 *euph.*〉生前预备的;装殓死人的 funerary: ～材 coffin prepared before one's death; coffin | ～衣 burial clothes ❻ (Shòu)姓 a surname

【寿斑】shòubān 老年人皮肤上出现的黑斑(多指脸上的) liver-coloured spot on the face or other parts of the skin (as a result of aging); senile speckle or plaque

【寿材】shòucái 指生前准备的棺材,也泛指一般的 coffin prepared before one's death; coffin (in a broad sense)

【寿辰】shòuchén 生日(一般用于中年人或老年人 usu. elderly person) birthday: 八十～ 80th birthday

【寿诞】shòudàn same as 寿辰 shòuchén

【寿礼】shòulǐ 祝寿的礼品 birthday present (for an elderly person)

【寿面】shòumiàn 祝寿时所吃的面条 birthday noodles; longevity noodles; noodles eaten to symbolize longevity on one's birthday

【寿命】shòumìng 生存的年限 lifespan; life; 〈比喻 *fig.*〉使用的期限或存在的期限 lifespan for use: 人类平均～在不断提高。The average human lifespan is becoming longer and longer. | 延长机车的～ prolong the life of this locomotive

【寿木】shòumù same as 寿材 shòucái

【寿山石】shòushānshí 一种以叶蜡石为主要成分的石料,产于福建闽侯的寿山,是制印章的名贵材料 *Shoushan* stone; pyrophyllite stone found at Shoushan, Fujian Province, as a prized raw material for making seals

【寿数】shòu·shu 迷信的人指命中注定的岁数 (superstition) allotted lifespan of an individual: ～已尽。This life has come to an end.

【寿桃】shòutáo 祝寿所用的桃,一般用面粉制成,也有用鲜桃的。神话中,西王母做寿,设蟠桃会招待群仙,所以一般习俗用桃来做庆寿的物品。peach of longevity; fresh peaches or ones fashioned out of dough, offered as a birthday present; a Chinese custom derived from a practice of the mythological Queen Mother of the West, who made it a point to celebrate her birthday by treating various gods with peaches of longevity

【寿星】shòu·xing ❶ 指老人星,自古以来用做长寿的象征,称为寿星,民间常把它画成老人的样子,头部长而隆起 god of longevity; symbol of longevity in the image of an old man with a long and bulging head; also 寿星老儿 shòu·xinglǎor ❷ 称长寿的老人或被祝寿的人 elderly person or person whose birthday is being celebrated

【寿穴】shòuxué 生前营造的墓穴 grave prepared before one's death

【寿衣】shòuyī 装殓死人的衣服,老年人往往生前做好备用 burial clothes oft. prepared for or by elderly people when they are still alive; shroud; cerements

【寿终正寝】shòu zhōng zhèng qǐn 〈旧时 *old*〉指年老病死在家中 die of old age at home; die a natural death;〈比喻 *fig.*〉事物的消亡 end of sth.(正寝 *zheng qin*: 旧式住宅的正屋。人死后,一般停灵在正屋正中的房间。According to an old Chinese custom, when a person died, the coffin bearing his or her remains was placed in state in the central room of the house.)

受 shòu ❶ 接受 receive; accept: ～贿 take or accept bribes | ～教育 receive an education | ～到帮助 receive help ❷ 遭受 suffer; be subjected to: ～灾 be hit by a natural calamity | ～批评 be criticized | ～委屈 suffer a wrong or an injustice ❸ 忍受;禁受 stand; endure; bear: ～不了 cannot stand (or endure) | ～得住 able to withstand or bear ❹ 适合 be pleasant: ～吃(吃着有味) pleasant to the taste | ～看(看着舒服) nice looking | ～听(听着入耳) pleasant to the ear; sweet sounding

【受病】shòu//bìng 得病(多指不立即发作的) catch (or contract) a disease, oft. one that does not act up immediately; fall ill: 你身体不好,在风口站着会～的。You are not strong and could fall ill from standing in that draft.

【受潮】shòu//cháo (物体)被潮气渗入 be affected with damp: 屋子老不见太阳,东西容易～。This room gets no sun and things in it easily get damp.

【受宠若惊】shòu chǒng ruò jīng 受到过分的宠爱待遇而感到意外的惊喜 be overwhelmed by an unexpected favour; feel extremely flattered

【受挫】shòucuò 遭到挫折 be foiled; be baffled; be thwarted; suffer a setback: ～而气不馁 not lose heart despite setbacks

【受敌】shòudí 遭受敌方的攻击 be attacked by the enemy: 四面～be attacked on all sides | 腹背～ be attacked front and rear

【受罚】shòu//fá 遭到处罚 be punished: 违章～ be fined for violating the regulations

【受粉】shòu//fěn 雄蕊的花粉传到雌蕊的柱头上,就雌蕊来说,叫做受粉 be pollinated; transfer pollen from the anthers to the stigma (of a flower)

【受过】shòu//guò 承担过失的责任(多指不应承担的) bear the blame (for sb. else): 代人～ take the blame for sb.

【受害】shòu//hài 遭到损害或杀害 suffer injury; fall victim to; be affected: ～不浅 suffer not a little but a lot | 无辜～ be harmed for unwarranted reasons

【受话器】shòuhuàqì 电话机等的一个部件,能把强弱不同的电流变成声音 (telephone) receiver; component of a telephone that receives incoming electrical signals or modulated radio waves and converts them into sound; also 听筒 tīngtǒng or 耳机 ěrjī

【受贿】shòu//huì 接受贿赂 accept (or take) bribes: 贪污～ corruption and bribery

【受奖】shòu//jiǎng 得到奖励 be rewarded: 立功～ be rewarded for meritorious deeds

【受戒】shòu//jiè 〈佛教用语 *Budd.*〉在一定的宗教仪式下接受戒律。初学佛的或初出家的人,须在受戒之后才能称做正式的居士或僧尼。be initiated into monkhood or nunhood; initiation

【受惊】shòu//jīng 受到突然的刺激或威胁而害怕 be frightened; be startled

【受精】shòu//jīng ❶ 人或动物的雌性生殖细胞和雄性生殖细胞相结合。受精过程除鱼类等在体外进行外,其余都在雌性动物体内进行。在体内受精 be fertilized; be inseminated; be impregnated with semen. Except for fish, the process takes place within the body of the female of most animals. also 受胎 shòu//tāi or 受孕 shòu//yùn ❷ 植物进行有性生殖时精子和卵细胞相结合 pollination; transfer pollen from the anthers to the stigma (of a flower)

【受窘】shòu//jiǒng 陷入为难的境地 be embarrassed; be in an awkward position

【受苦】shòu//kǔ 遭受痛苦 suffer (hardships); have a rough time: ～受难 live in misery; have one's fill of suffering

【受累】shòu//lěi 受到拖累或连累 get involved on account of sb. else: 一人出事,全家～。A man in trouble could get his entire family involved.

【受累】shòu//lèi 受到劳累;消耗精神气力(也常用做客气话 oft. used in polite words) be put to much trouble; be inconvenienced: 这么远来看我,让您～了。Thank you for taking the trouble to come such a long way to see me.

【受礼】shòu//lǐ 接受别人赠送的礼物 receive gifts

【受理】shòulǐ ❶ 接受并办理 accept and handle: ～快件专递业务 handle express mail delivery ❷ 法院接受案件,进行审理 (of the court) accept and hear (a case): 法院已～此案。The court has accepted and heard the case.

【受凉】shòu//liáng 受到低温度的影响而患感冒等疾病 catch cold

【受命】shòumìng 接受命令或任务 receive instructions or assignments: ～办理 be instructed to handle (a matter)

【受难】shòu//nàn 受到灾难 suffer calamities

or disasters; be in distress: 受苦～ be in distress

【受盘】shòupán 指工商业主购买别人企业的全部财产(如房屋、机器、设备、货物等)继续经营 (of industrialists and merchants) buy up a business (including all its assets such as buildings, machines, equipment, stock, etc.) to keep business going; also 接盘 jiēpán

【受骗】shòu//piàn 被骗 be deceived (or fooled, cheated, taken in): ～上当 be taken in

【受聘】shòu//pìn ❶ 旧俗定亲时女方接受男方的聘礼(old custom) (of a bride-to-be) accept betrothal gifts ❷ 接受聘请 accept an appointment (to a post): 他～当了排球教练。He was appointed head coach of the volleyball team.

【受气】shòu//qì 遭受欺侮 be bullied; suffer wrong: 里外～ be a whipping boy at home and at work | 受了半辈子气 be humiliated for half of one's life

【受气包】shòuqìbāo (～儿 shòuqìbāor)〈比喻 *fig.*〉经常被当做抱怨或泄愤的对象的人 person upon whom anyone can vent his spite; one who always gets blamed (or takes the rap)

【受穷】shòu//qióng 遭受穷困 suffer poverty; live in poverty: 吃苦～ live in hardship and poverty

【受屈】shòu//qū 受到委屈或冤屈 be wronged

【受权】shòuquán 接受国家或上级委托有权力做某事 be authorized: 外交部～发表声明。The Ministry of Foreign Affairs is authorized to issue a statement.

【受热】shòu//rè ❶ 受到高温度的影响 be heated: 绝大部分物体～则膨胀。Most substances expand when heated. ❷ 中暑 be affected by the heat; have heatstroke (or sunstroke): 他路上～了,有点头痛。He had a heatstroke on the way here and now has a headache.

【受辱】shòu//rǔ 受到侮辱或羞辱 be insulted; be disgraced; be humiliated: 无故～ be humiliated for no reason | 当场～ be insulted on the spot

【受伤】shòu//shāng 身体或物体部分地受到破损 be injured; be wounded; sustain an injury

【受赏】shòu//shǎng 得到奖赏 be awarded: 立功～ be rewarded for meritorious deeds

【受审】shòu//shěn 接受审讯 stand trial; be tried; be on trial: 到庭～ be tried in a court of law

【受事】shòushì 语法上指动作的对象,也就是受动作支配的人或事物,如'我看报'里的'报','老鹰抓小鸡'里的'小鸡'。表示受事的名词不一定做句子的宾语,如'衣服送来了'里的'衣服'是受事,但是做句子的主语。object; grammatical term referring to sb. or sth. affected by the action of a verb. For example, 'newspaper' is the object in the sentence 'I am reading a newspaper'; 'chicken' is the object in the sentence 'The hawk caught a chicken'. A noun serving as the object of a verb is not necessarily the grammatical object. For example, in 'The clothes have been delivered', 'clothes' is the object of the verb but the subject of the sentence.

【受暑】shòu//shǔ 中暑 suffer from heatstroke (or sunstroke)

【受胎】shòu//tāi 妇女或雌性动物体内受精 become pregnant; be impregnated; conceive; also 受孕 shòu//yùn

【受托】shòu//tuō 接受人家的委托 be commissioned; be entrusted (with a task)

【受洗】shòuxǐ (基督教徒)接受洗礼 (of a Christian) be baptized; receive baptism

【受降】shòu//xiáng 接受敌方投降 accept a surrender

【受刑】shòu//xíng 遭受刑罚,特指遭受肉刑 be tortured; be put to torture

【受训】shòu//xùn 接受训练 receive (or undergo) training: 在训练班～半年 take part in a half-year training course

【受业】shòuyè〈书 *fml.*〉❶ 跟随老师学习 receive instruction ❷ 学生对老师的自称 (in letters to one's teacher) I, your pupil

【受益】shòuyì 得到好处;受到利益 profit by; benefit from; be benefited: ～良多 benefit a great deal | 水库修好后,～地区很大。A vast area will reap the benefit after the reservoir has been built.

【受用】shòuyòng 享受;得益 benefit from; profit by; enjoy: 学会这种本领,一辈子～不尽。You will benefit from the skill for the rest of your life.

【受用】shòu·yong 身心舒服(多用于否定式 usu. used in the negative) feel comfortable: 听了这番话,他心里很不～。On hearing this he felt uneasy.

【受孕】shòu//yùn same as 受胎 shòu//tāi

【受灾】shòu//zāi 遭受灾害 be hit by a natural disaster (or calamity): ～地区 disaster area; stricken (or affected) area | 赈济～群众 aid victims of the disaster

【受制】shòu//zhì〈书 *fml.*〉❶ 受辖制 be controlled: ～于人 be under others' control ❷ 受害;受罪 endure hardship, torture, rough conditions, etc.; suffer

【受阻】shòuzǔ 受到阻碍 be obstructed; meet with obstruction: 因交通～,不能按时到达。Owing to the traffic congestion we were unable to arrive on time.

【受罪】shòu//zuì 受到折磨。也泛指遇到不愉快的事。endure hardship, torture, rough conditions, etc.; (in a broad sense) have a hard time; have an unpleasant experience

狩 shòu〈书 *fml.*〉打猎,特指冬天打猎 hunting (esp. in winter)

【狩猎】shòuliè same as 打猎 dǎliè

授 shòu ❶ 交付;给予(多用于正式或隆重的场合 oft. at formal or ceremonious occasions) award; vest; confer; give: ~旗 present (sb. with) a flag | ~奖 award or confer a prize | ~权 vest sb. with authority ❷ 传授;教 teach; instruct: 讲~ lecture; impart | ~课 give lessons | 函~ teach by correspondence

【授粉】shòufěn 雄蕊的花粉传到雌蕊的柱头上,叫做授粉 pollination; transfer pollen from the anthers to the stigma (of a flower)

【授奖】shòu//jiǎng 颁发奖金、奖品或奖状 award (or give) a prize: ~大会 prize giving ceremony

【授课】shòukè 教课 give lessons; give instruction: 他在夜校每周~六小时。He teaches at night school six hours a week.

【授命】[1] shòumìng〈书 *fml.*〉献出生命 give (or lay down) one's life: 见危~ lay down one's life in a crisis | 临危~ lay down one's life at a time of danger

【授命】[2] shòumìng 下命令(多指某些国家的元首下命令 oft. by a head of state) give orders: 总统~总理组阁。The president authorized the prime minister to set up the cabinet.

【授权】shòuquán 把权力委托给人或机构代为执行 give sb. a mandate for doing sth.; empower; authorize

【授时】shòushí ❶ 某些天文台每天在一定的时间用无线电信号报告最精确的时间,这种工作叫授时 time service, referring to the work of an observatory to report the most accurate time by sending off radio signals at a given time of the day ❷〈旧时 *old*〉指政府颁行历书 (of a government or an emperor) issue the official calendar

【授首】shòushǒu〈书 *fml.*〉(叛逆、盗贼等)被斩首 (of rebels, robbers, etc.) be beheaded

【授受】shòushòu 交付和接受 grant and receive; give and accept: 私相~ give and accept in private

【授衔】shòu//xián 给予军衔或其他称号 confer a title or a military rank

【授意】shòuyì 把自己的意图告诉别人,让别人照着办(多指不公开的 oft. in secret) incite (or get) sb. to do sth.; inspire; suggest an idea (to sb.): 这件事一定是有人~他干的。He must have been put up to doing this.

【授予】shòuyǔ 给与(勋章、奖状、学位、荣誉等) confer; award

售 shòu ❶ 卖 sell: ~票 sell tickets | ~货 sell goods | 零~ sell retail | 出~ sell ❷〈书 *fml.*〉施展(奸计) make (one's plan, trick, etc.) work; carry out (intrigues): 以~其奸 carry out one's evil design | 其计不~。His plan did not work.

【售货员】shòuhuòyuán 商店里出售货物的工作人员 shop assistant; salesclerk

【售卖】shòumài same as 卖 mài ①

【售票员】shòupiàoyuán 卖票的工作人员 ticket seller; (bus, tram, etc.) conductor; booking office clerk; box-office clerk

兽(獸) shòu ❶ 哺乳动物的通称。一般指有四条腿、全身生毛的哺乳动物 mammal; beast; animal: 野~ wild animal | 禽~ birds and beasts | 走~ beast ❷〈比喻 *fig.*〉野蛮;下流 beastly; bestial: ~心 wolfish heart | ~行 brutal act

【兽环】shòuhuán 旧式大门上装的用铜或铁制成的兽头和环子,敲门或锁门时用 animal-head knocker (on doors of old-style houses)

【兽力车】shòulìchē 用牛、马、驴、骡等牲口拉的车 animal-drawn vehicle (or cart); cart drawn by an ox, horse, donkey or mule

【兽王】shòuwáng 指狮子 king of beasts — the lion

【兽行】shòuxíng ❶ 指极端野蛮、残忍的行为 brutal act; brutality ❷ 指发泄兽欲的行为 act of lust

【兽性】shòuxìng 形容极端野蛮和残忍的性情 brutish nature; barbarity

【兽医】shòuyī 治疗家畜家禽等疾病的医生 veterinary surgeon; veterinarian; vet

【兽疫】shòuyì 家畜、家禽等的传染病,如牛瘟、猪瘟、口蹄疫、鸡新城疫等 epizootic disease; epizootic, such as rinderpest, foot-and-mouth disease, Newcastle disease, etc.

【兽欲】shòuyù 指野蛮的性欲 animal (or bestial) desire

绶 shòu 绶带 silk ribbon attached to an official seal or a medal: 印~ seal adorned with a silk ribbon

【绶带】shòudài 一种彩色的丝带,用来系官印或勋章。有的斜挂在肩上表示某种身份。cordon; coloured silk ribbon, usu. attached to an official seal or a medal, sometimes slung over the shoulder to show a person's social status

瘦 shòu ❶ 脂肪少;肉少(跟'胖'或'肥'相对 as opposed to 'fat') thin; emaciated ❷ (食用的肉)脂肪少(跟'肥'相对 as opposed to 'fat') lean: 这块肉太肥,我要~点儿的。This piece of meat has too much fat on it. I want a leaner piece. ❸ (衣服鞋袜等)窄小(跟'肥'相对 as opposed to 'lose') (of clothes, shose, socks, etc.) tight: 裤子做得太~了,可以往肥里放一下。The trousers are too tight, but can be let out. ❹ (地力)薄;不肥沃 not fertile; poor: ~田 poor soil

【瘦长】shòucháng 又瘦又长 long and thin; tall and thin; lanky: ~脸 thin face | ~个儿 lanky | ~的身材 tall, slender figure

【瘦骨嶙峋】shòu gǔ línxún 形容人十分瘦 all skin and bones

【瘦果】shòuguǒ 干果的一种，比较小，里面只有一粒种子，果皮和种子皮只有一处相连接，如白头翁、向日葵、荞麦等的果实 achene; dry one-seeded indehiscent fruit developed from a single ovary, usu. having a thin pericarp attached to seed at one point only, e.g. Chinese pulsatilla, sunflower, oat, etc.

【瘦瘠】shòují ❶ 不肥胖；瘦弱 thin and weak ❷（土地）不肥沃 (of land) barren; sterile: 把～的荒山改造成富饶山区 turn barren hills into a fertile mountain area

【瘦金体】shòujīntǐ 宋徽宗赵佶的字体，笔势瘦硬挺拔 style of Chinese calligraphy originated by Emperor Huizong (Zhao Ji) of the Song Dynasty, featuring fine, sturdy strokes

【瘦溜】shòu·liu〈方 *dial.*〉形容身体瘦而细的样子 slim: 身体～，动作轻巧 be of slender build and very agile

【瘦弱】shòuruò 肌肉不丰满，软弱无力 thin and weak; emaciated; frail: 身体～ thin and weak ◇树苗～ weak sapling

【瘦小】shòuxiǎo 形容身材瘦，个儿小 thin and small: 别看他人～，力气还挺大。Despite being small and thin, he is nevertheless very strong.

【瘦削】shòuxuē 形容身体或脸很瘦 very thin; bony

【瘦子】shòu·zi 肌肉不丰满的人 lean (or thin) person

shū（ㄕㄨ）

殳 shū ❶〈古代 *arch.*〉一种兵器，用竹竿制成，有棱无刃 ancient weapon made of bamboo, with ridges but no blade ❷（Shū）姓 a surname

书（書） shū ❶ 写字；记录：书写 write: ～法 calligraphy｜大～特～ record in letters of gold｜振笔直～ take up the pen and write vigorously ❷ 字体 style of calligraphy; script: 楷～ regular script｜隶～ official script ❸ 装订成册的著作 book: 一本～ a book｜一部～ a book｜一套～ a series of books｜丛～ collection｜新～ new book｜古～ ancient books｜～店 bookshop; bookstore; bookseller's ❹ 书信 letter: 家～ letter to or from home｜～札 letters ❺ 文件 document: 证～ certificate｜保证～ guarantee｜说明～ guidebook｜挑战～ letter of challenge｜白皮～ White Paper; white book

【书案】shū'àn〈书 *fml.*〉长形的书桌 writing desk

【书包】shūbāo 布或皮革等制成的袋子，主要供学生上学时装书籍、文具用 satchel; schoolbag

【书背】shūbèi same as 书脊 shūjǐ

【书本】shūběn（～儿 shūběnr）书 ③（总称 general term for）book: ～知识 book learning; book knowledge

【书册】shūcè 装订成册的书；书本 book

【书场】shūchǎng 表演说书、弹词、相声等曲艺的场所 place of entertainment where *quyi*（曲艺）performances are given

【书橱】shūchú same as 书柜 shūguì

【书呆子】shūdāi·zi 不懂得联系实际只知道啃书本的人 pedant; bookworm; person who relies too much on academic learning or who is concerned chiefly with insignificant detail

【书丹】shūdān 刻碑前用朱笔书写碑上的文字，泛指书写碑上的文字 write an epitaph (originally in red)

【书牍】shūdú〈书 *fml.*〉same as 书信 shūxìn

【书法】shūfǎ 文字的书写艺术。特指用毛笔写汉字的艺术 penmanship; calligraphy; art of writing chinese characters with a writing brush: ～比赛 calligraphy contest｜硬笔～ calligraphic works executed with nib pens

【书坊】shūfāng〈旧时 *old*〉印刷并出售书籍的地方 bookshop attached to a printing workshop

【书房】shūfáng 读书写字的房间 study

【书稿】shūgǎo 著作的底稿 manuscript: 誊写～ copy out or transcribe a contribution

【书馆】shūguǎn ❶〈古代 *arch.*〉教授学童的处所 school-age children's private school ❷〈方 *dial.*〉(～儿 shūguǎnr) 有艺人在那里说评书的茶馆儿 teahouse featuring storytelling performances

【书柜】shūguì 放置书籍用的柜子 bookcase

【书函】shūhán ❶ same as 书套 shūtào ❷ same as 书信 shūxìn

【书号】shūhào 主管部门对正式出版物给予的编号，包括出版社的代号、书刊类别代号等 book number (issued by administrative bodies to publishers), including code numbers of the publishing house and the category of publication involved

【书后】shūhòu 写在别人著作后面，对著作有所说明或评论的文章 postscript (by the author or sb. else)

【书画】shūhuà 作为艺术品供人欣赏的书法和绘画 painting and calligraphy: ～展览会 painting and calligraphy exhibition

【书籍】shūjí 书 ③（总称 collect.）books; works; literature

【书脊】shūjǐ 书籍被钉住的一边。新式装订的书脊上一般印有书名、出版机构名称等。spine (of a book); backbone; also 书背 shūbèi

【书记】shū·ji ❶ 党、团等各级组织中的主要负责人 secretary; head of Chinese Communist Party or Chinese Communist Youth League organizations at different levels ❷〈旧时 *old*〉称办理文书及缮写工作的人员 clerk; recorder and keeper of documents

【书家】shūjiā 擅长书法的人；书法家 calligrapher; calligraphist

【书架】shūjià 放置书籍用的架子，多用木料或铁

S

制成 bookshelf; set of bookshelves; bookcase; also 书架子 shūjià•zi

【书柬】shūjiǎn same as 书简 shūjiǎn

【书简】shūnjiǎn same as 书信 shūxìn; also 书柬 shūjiǎn

【书局】shūjú 〈旧时 *old*〉印书或藏书的机构,后多用做书店的名称 publishing house; press; book company (oft. used as part of the name of a bookstore)

【书卷】shūjuàn 指书籍,古代书籍多装成卷轴,所以叫做书卷 books (in ancient times books were rolled up, hence the name)

【书卷气】shūjuànqì 指在说话、作文、写字、画画等方面表现出来的读书人的风格、气质 bookishness; scholarliness, as manifested in speech, writing, painting and calligraphy

【书刊】shūkān 书籍和刊物 books and periodicals

【书口】shūkǒu 书籍上跟书脊相对的一边,线装书在这地方标注书名、页数等 fore-edge (or foreedge); outer edge of the pages of a book

【书库】shūkù 图书馆或书店存放书刊的房屋 stockroom in library or bookshop

【书录】shūlù 有关某一部书或某些著作的版本、插图、评论及其源流等各种资料的目录 bibliography; index containing such data as the editions, illustrations, commentaries and sources of a certain book or certain publications

【书眉】shūméi 书页的上端 top of a page; top margin

【书迷】shūmí 听评弹、评书等入迷的人 storyteller's follower

【书面】shūmiàn 用文字表达的(区别于'口头'as compared with 'spoken') written; in written form; in writing: ～通知 written notice | ～答复 written reply; answer in writing | ～材料 written material

【书面语】shūmiànyǔ 用文字写出来的语言(区别于'口语' as compared with 'oral language') written language; literary language

【书名号】shūmínghào 标点符号(《》或﹏﹏,后者用在横行文字的底下或竖行文字的旁边),表示书名、篇名、报刊名等(《》or ﹏﹏) punctuation marks used to enclose the title of a book, an article, a newspaper or a periodical

【书目】shūmù ❶ 图书的目录 book list; title catalogue ❷ 曲艺上指评书、评话、弹词等说唱节目 (of folk art forms) ballad-singing and storytelling programmes; entertainment

【书皮】shūpí (～儿 shūpír) ❶ 书刊的最外面的一层,用厚纸、布、绢、皮等做成。线装书在上面贴书签,新式装订的书刊一般是把书名、作者姓名等印在上面。book cover; Book covers are made variously of thick paper, cloth, silk or leather, with title label attached (in the case of thread-bound books) or the titles and the name of the author printed on them (in the case of modern books). ❷ 读者在书皮外面再包上的一层纸,用来保护书 dust cover; book jacket: 包～ cover the bookcover of a book with paper

【书评】shūpíng 评论或介绍书刊的文章 book review

【书签】shūqiān (～儿 shūqiānr) ❶ 贴在线装书书皮上的写着或印着书名的纸或绢的条儿,有些新式装订的书也仿照它的形式直接印在书皮上 title label pasted on the cover of a Chinese-style thread-bound book ❷ 为标记阅读到什么地方而夹在书里的小片,多用纸或赛璐珞等制成 bookmark; strip or band of paper or celluloid, put between the pages of a book as a mark

【书社】shūshè ❶ 〈旧时 *old*〉文人组织的读书会 (in former times) literary guild ❷ 〈旧时 *old*〉印书的机构,后多用做出版社的名称,如齐鲁书社、岳麓书社等 (in former times) printing house; publishing house, e.g. Qilu Publishing House, Yuelu Publishing House, etc.

【书生】shūshēng 读书人 intellectual; scholar: 白面～ pale-faced intellectual

【书生气】shūshēngqì 指知识分子只顾读书,不关心生活中其他事物的习气 bookishness; bookish cast of mind

【书市】shūshì 集中出售书籍的场所,多指临时举办的、短时间的 book fair, oft. one held temperorily for a short period of time

【书套】shūtào 套在几本或一本书外面的壳子,有保护作用,多用硬纸等制成 slip case; protective case for a book or set of books that is open at one end so that only their spines are visible

【书亭】shūtíng 销售书刊的像亭子的小房子 book-kiosk; bookstall

【书童】shūtóng 〈旧时 *old*〉侍候主人及其子弟读书并做杂事的未成年的仆人 page-boy; adolescent boy waiting on a master or his schooling children and running errands for them

【书屋】shūwū 〈旧时 *old*〉供读书用的房子,现也用做书店的名称 study; now also used as the name of a bookshop

【书香】shūxiāng 指上辈有读书人的(人家 of a family) having literary or intellectual fame: ～门第 literary (or intellectual) family; family of scholars | ～子弟 person from a family of scholars | 世代～ long line of scholars; be a scholar-gentry family for generations

【书写】shūxiě 写 write: ～标语 write slogans (or posters) | ～工具 writing tools

【书写纸】shūxiězhǐ 纸张的一种,质地洁白光滑,耐水性好,适于书写 writing paper

【书心】shūxīn 书刊每页印有文字或图画的部分 type area (of a book page)

【书信】shūxìn 信 letter; written message: ～往来 keep up a correspondence | ～格式 in letter form

【书页】shūyè 书中印有文字或图片的单篇 book page; printed page

【书影】shūyǐng 显示书刊的版式和部分内容的印刷物,从前仿照原书刻印或石印,现在大多影印,有的用做插页,有的汇集成册,如《宋元书影》printed sheet, produced by block printing or lithography in old times and mostly by photocopying nowadays, that indicates the format or part of the content of a book or periodical. Such sheets are used as book inserts or bound together into books, such as *Lithographic Prints of Song and Yuan*.

【书院】shūyuàn 〈旧时 *old*〉地方上设立的供人读书、讲学的处所,有专人主持。从唐代开始,历代都有。清末废科举后,大都改为学校。academy of classical learning, established in various localities since the Tang Dynasty for studies and lectures; Most of the academies were changed into schools after the imperial examination system was abolished towards the end of the Qing Dynasty.

【书札】shūzhá 〈书 *fml.*〉same as 书信 shūxìn

【书斋】shūzhāi same as 书房 shūfáng

【书展】shūzhǎn ❶ 书籍展览 book exhibition ❷ 书法展览 calligraphy exhibition

【书证】shūzhèng ❶ 著作或注释中有关词语来历、意义、用法等的有书面出处的例证 (of works of writing and notes) written examples of the origin, meaning and usage of a word or phrase ❷ 法律上指证明案件事实的书面材料,如书信、传单、合同、账本等。通常广义的物证也包括书证在内。(law) written evidence such as letters, pamphlets, contracts, account books, etc., comprising general material evidence

【书桌】shūzhuō (～儿 shūzhuōr)读书写字用的桌子 desk; writing desk

抒 shū ❶ 表达;发表 express; give expression to; convey: 各～已见 each airs his own views | 直～胸臆 frankly express one's feelings ❷ same as 纾 shū ①

【抒发】shūfā 表达;发抒(感情) express; voice; give expression to: ～思乡之情 express longing for one's home town

【抒怀】shūhuái 抒发情怀 pour out one's heart; unburden one's feelings: 赋诗～ compose a poem to express one's feeling

【抒情】shūqíng 抒发情感 express (or convey) one's emotions: ～散文 lyric prose | 写景、叙事的诗里也往往含有～的成分。Descriptive and narrative poems often contain emotional outpourings.

【抒写】shūxiě 表达和描写 express in writing; write of; describe: 散文可以～感情,也可以发表议论。Prose is capable of emotional expression as well as argument.

纾 shū 〈书 *fml.*〉❶ 解除 relax; relieve; remove: 毁家～难(nàn) give all one has to help the state meet the crisis ❷ 延缓 procrastinate ❸ 宽裕 well-to-do

枢(樞) shū ❶ 门上的转轴 pivot; hub: 户～不蠹。A door hinge never gets worm-eaten. ❷ 指重要的或中心的部分 centre: 中～ centre | ～纽 pivot

【枢机】shūjī ❶〈旧指 *old*〉封建王朝的重要职位或机构 key government post or office in a dynasty in Chinese feudalism ❷〈书 *fml.*〉事物的关键 vital element

【枢纽】shūniǔ 事物的重要关键;事物相互联系的中心环节 pivot; hub; axis; key position: ～工程 key project | 交通～ hub of communications

【枢要】shūyào 〈书 *fml.*〉指中央行政机构 central administration

叔 shū ❶ 叔父 father's younger brother; uncle: 二～ Uncle No. 2 ❷ 称呼跟父亲辈分相同而年纪较小的男子(a form of address for a man of about one's father's age) uncle: 表～ father's younger male cousin | 李～ Uncle Li ❸ 丈夫的弟弟;小叔子 husband's younger brother: ～嫂 brother-in-law and sister-in-law ❹ 在弟兄排行的次序里代表第三 third among brothers: 伯仲～季 first, second, third and fourth sons in the family

【叔伯】shū·bai 同祖父的,有时也指同曾祖父的(弟兄姐妹) relationship between cousins of the same grandfather or great-grandfather: 他们是～弟兄。They are cousins.

【叔父】shūfù 父亲的弟弟 father's younger brother; uncle

【叔公】shūgōng ❶ 丈夫的叔叔 husband's father's younger brother ❷〈方 *dial.*〉same as 叔祖 shūzǔ

【叔母】shūmǔ 叔父的妻子 wife of father's younger brother; aunt

【叔婆】shūpó ❶ 丈夫的婶母 husband's father's younger brother's wife ❷〈方 *dial.*〉same as 叔祖母 shūzǔmǔ

【叔叔】shū·shu ❶ same as 叔父 shūfù: 亲～ father's younger brother (as compared with father's stepbrother or father's cousin) | 堂房～ father's male cousin ❷ 称呼跟父亲辈分相同而年纪较小的男子(child's form of address for any young man of one generation its senior) uncle: 刘～ Uncle Liu | 工人～ uncle worker | 解放军～ uncle PLA

【叔祖】shūzǔ 父亲的叔父 (paternal) grandfather's younger brother; grand-uncle (or great-uncle)

【叔祖母】shūzǔmǔ 父亲的叔母 wife of (paternal) grandfather's younger brother; grand-aunt (or great-aunt)

姝 shū 〈书 *fml.*〉❶ 美好 pretty; lovely ❷ 美女 pretty girl; beauty

殊 shū ❶ 不同；差异 different：～途同归 reach the same goal by different routes｜照相影印，与原本无～。A photocopy looks exactly the same as the original. ❷ 特别；特殊 outstanding; special; remarkable：～勋 outstanding merit｜～功 outstanding exploits｜～效 special effect｜～绩 distinguished service ❸〈书 *fml*.〉很；极 very much; extremely; really：～觉歉然 feel most regretful ❹〈书 *fml*.〉断；绝 cut off; sever

【殊不知】shūbùzhī ❶ 竟不知道（引述别人的意见而加以纠正）although some may say that ... this is not the case (go on to state that contrary to what others say)：有人以为喝酒可以御寒，～酒力一过，更觉得冷。Some say that drinking wine can keep out the cold, but it will actually make one feel even colder once the effect has worn off. ❷ 竟没想到（纠正自己原先的想法）little imagine, hardly realize：我以为他还在北京，～上星期他就走了。I thought he was still in Beijing and had no idea that he left last week.

【殊荣】shūróng 特殊的光荣 special honours

S

【殊死】shūsǐ ❶ 拼着性命，竭尽死力；决死 desperate; life-and-death：～战 fight to the death; fight a last-ditch battle; put up a desperate fight｜～的斗争 fight a last-ditch battle ❷〈古代 *arch*.〉指斩首的死刑 death penalty by decapitation

【殊途同归】shū tú tóng guī 通过不同道路走到同一个目的地 reach the same goal by different routes;〈比喻 *fig*.〉采取不同的方法而得到相同的结果 achieve the same result by differenf means

【殊勋】shūxūn〈书 *fml*.〉特殊的功勋 outstanding merit; distinguished service：屡建～ render one distinguished service after another

倏(倐) shū〈书 *fml*.〉极快地 suddenly; quickly：～已半年。Six months passed in a flash.

【倏地】shūdì 极快地；迅速地 suddenly; quickly：～闪过一个人影。A shadow flashed past.

【倏忽】shūhū 很快地；忽然 suddenly; quickly：～不见 suddenly (or quickly) disappear｜山地气候～变化，应当随时注意。The weather in mountainous regions changes quickly, and provision must be made for this.

【倏然】shūrán〈书 *fml*.〉❶ 忽然 suddenly：～一阵暴雨。A rainstorm came on suddenly. ❷ 形容极快 abruptly：一道流星，～而逝。A meteor shot across the sky and vanished.

菽(尗) shū 豆类的总称 beans (collet.)：不辨～麦 unable to tell wheat from beans — ignorant of common things

【菽粟】shūsù 泛指粮食 (in a broad sense) beans and grains：布帛～ cloth and grain

梳 shū ❶（～儿 shūr）梳子 comb：木～ wooden comb ❷ 梳理 comb (one's hair, etc.)：～头洗脸 comb one's hair and wash one's face｜她～着两根粗辫子。She wears her hair in two thick plaits.

【梳篦】shūbì 梳子和篦子的合称 thick and fine-toothed combs

【梳辫子】shū biàn·zi〈比喻 *fig*.〉把纷繁的事项、问题等进行分析归类 sort out matters, problems, etc.：先把存在的问题梳梳辫子，再逐个研究解决办法。Let's sort out the existing problems and then find a solution to each of them.

【梳理】shūlǐ ❶ 纺织工艺中用植有针或齿的机件使纤维排列一致，并清除其中的短纤维和杂质 carding; process of preparing the fibres of cotton, wool, etc., for spinning ❷ 用梳子整理（须、发等）comb out (one's hair); dress (one's hair)：～头发 comb the hair ◇～思路 organize one's ideas

【梳头】shū//tóu 用梳子整理头发 comb one's hair

【梳洗】shūxǐ 梳头洗脸 wash and dress：～打扮 deck oneself out

【梳妆】shūzhuāng 梳洗打扮 dress and make up：～台 dressing table

【梳子】shū·zi 整理头发、胡子的用具，有齿，用竹木、塑料等制成 comb; toothed device of metal, plastic, wood, etc., used for disentangling or arranging hair

鄃 Shū 古县名，在今山东夏津附近 Shuxian, name of an ancient county near Xiajin in present-day Shandong Province

淑 shū 温和善良；美好（of a woman) chaste and mild-mannered; refined; pure; virtuous：～女 fair maiden; virtuous maiden; noble lady

【淑静】shūjìng（女子）温柔文静 (of a woman) refined and gentle

【淑女】shūnǚ〈书 *fml*.〉美好的女子 fair maiden; virtuous maiden; noble lady：窈窕～ pretty woman

舒 shū ❶ 伸展；宽解（拘束或憋闷状态）stretch; unfold; spread; smooth out：～眉展眼 unknit the brows and open the eyes wide — be cheerful; show pleasure｜～经活血 soothe the sinews and quicken the blood｜～了一口气 heave a sigh of relief ❷〈书 *fml*.〉缓慢；从容 easy; leisurely：～徐 leisurely｜～缓 slow ❸（Shū）姓 a surname

【舒畅】shūchàng 开朗愉快；舒服痛快 happy; entirely free from worry：心情～ have ease of mind; feel happy｜车窗打开了，凉爽的风吹进来，使人非常～。Travelling in a car with its window open, one can enjoy a cool refreshing breeze.

【舒服】shū·fu ❶ 身体或精神上感到轻松愉快 comfortable：睡得很～ have a good sleep ❷

能使身体或精神上感到轻松愉快 be well：窑洞又～，又暖和。The cave dwelling is warm and comfortable.

【舒缓】shūhuǎn ❶ 缓慢 slow and unhurried; leisurely：动作～ slow and unhurried in one's movements｜节拍～的歌声 singing in a slow tempo ❷ 缓和 relaxed; mild：语调～ in a mild tone｜他的心情好像～了一些。He seemed to be in a more relaxed mood. ❸ 坡度小（of a slope）gentle; gradual：他从～的斜坡上慢慢走了下来。He walked slowly down the gentle slope.

【舒卷】shūjuǎn 〈书 *fml.*〉舒展和卷缩（多指云或烟 of clouds or smoke）curl and uncurl; roll and unroll; roll back and forth：～自如 roll back and forth freely｜白云～。White clouds amassed and scattered.

【舒散】shūsàn ❶ 活动（筋骨）stretch and flex ❷ 消除疲劳或不愉快的心情 shake off one's fatigue or cares：～心中的郁闷 shake off a gloomy mood

【舒声】shūshēng 指古汉语四声中的平、上、去三声（跟'促声'相对 as opposed to 'quick tone'）(of classical Chinese) level tone, falling-rising tone and falling tone

【舒适】shūshì 舒服安逸 comfortable; cosy; snug：环境～ easy circumstances｜～的生活 comfortable life

【舒坦】shū·tan same as 舒服 shū·fu：心里～ feel at ease

【舒心】shūxīn 心情舒展；适意 comfortable; happy：日子过得挺～ live a happy and contented life

【舒徐】shūxú 缓慢；从容不迫 leisurely; unhurried

【舒展】shū·zhǎn ❶ 不卷缩；不皱 unfold; extend; smooth out; limber up; stretch：荷叶～着，发出清香。The lotus leaves are unfolding, sending forth a delicate fragrance.｜祖父心里很高兴，脸上的皱纹也～了。The grandfather was happy, and even the wrinkles on his face smoothed out. ❷（身心）安适；舒适 comfortable; at ease

【舒张】shūzhāng 心脏或血管等的肌肉组织由紧张状态变为松弛状态 diastole; dilation of the chambers of the heart that follows each contraction, during which they are refilled with blood

疏[1]（疎）shū ❶ 清除阻塞使通畅；疏通 dredge (a river, etc.)：～导 dredge｜～浚 dredge ❷ 事物之间距离远；事物的部分之间空隙大（跟'密'相对 as opposed to 'dense'）thin; sparse; scattered：～林 sparse woods｜～星 scattered stars ❸ 关系远；不亲近；不熟悉（of family or social relations）distant; not familiar：～远 alien｜生～ unfamiliar｜亲～ close and distant ❹ 疏忽 neglect：～于防范 neglect to take precautions ❺ 空虚 scanty：志大才～ have lofty aspirations but little talent ❻ 分散；使从密变稀 disperse; scatter：～散 sparse｜仗义～财 generous in helping the poor or needy ❼（Shū）姓 a surname

疏[2] shū ❶ 封建时代臣下向君主分条陈述事情的文字；条陈 memorial to the emperor：上～ present a memorial to the emperor｜奏～ memorial to the throne ❷ 古书的比'注'更详细的注解；'注'的注 detailed annotation; annotaton on a book note：《十三经注～》*Commentaries on the Thirteen Classics*

【疏财仗义】shū cái zhàng yì ☞ 仗义疏财 zhàng yì shū cái on p. 2419

【疏导】shūdǎo ❶ 开通壅塞的水道，使水流畅通 dredge：～淮河 dredge the Huaihe River ❷ 泛指引导使畅通 remove obstructions：～交通 relieve traffic congestion｜解决思想问题一定要善于～。In order to ease the load on people's minds, one must be patient and persuasive.

【疏放】shūfàng 〈书 *fml.*〉❶ 放纵 unbridled; self-indulgent：举止～ unrestrained ❷（文章）不拘常格（of style of writing）unconventional：行文～ free and unconventional style

【疏忽】shū·hu 粗心大意；忽略 error that creeps up on sb.; carelessness; negligence; oversight：～职守 dereliction of duty｜一时～，造成错误。One oversight led to a mistake.

【疏剪】shūjiǎn 剪去树上过密的、无用的枝条 prune (trees, branches, etc.)

【疏解】shūjiě ❶ 疏通调解 mediate：由于老师从中～，他俩才消除了误会。It was the teacher's mediation that helped resolve the misunderstanding between them. ❷ 使通畅缓解 ease up; mitigate; make sth. less difficult (bitter, etc.); relieve (traffic congestion, etc.)：调集车辆，增大运输能力，～客流 muster more vehicles to expand the existing carrying capacity in order to cut down the number of stranded passengers

【疏浚】shūjùn 清除淤塞或挖深河槽使水流通畅 dredge：～航道，以利交通 dredge the waterway to facilitate water transportation

【疏狂】shūkuáng 〈书 *fml.*〉狂放不受约束 uninhibited; unrestrained; unbridled：生性～ unbridled by nature

【疏阔】shūkuò 〈书 *fml.*〉❶ 不周密 inaccurate; rough：立论～ woolly arguments ❷ 疏远（of relationship）distant：交往～ be estranged from one another ❸ 迂阔 unrealistic; impractical：～之言 pedantic views; pedantry ❹ 久别（of friends, etc.）long separated; far apart

【疏懒】shūlǎn 懒散而不惯受拘束 careless and lazy; indolent

【疏朗】shūlǎng ❶ 稀疏而清晰 thinly scattered; sparse: 须眉～ sparse beard and thin eyebrows | 夜空中闪烁着疏疏朗朗的几点星光。A few stars twinkled here and there in the night sky. ❷ 开朗 cheerful; optimistic: 胸怀渐渐～了。Little by little he (or she) cheered up.

【疏漏】shūlòu 疏忽遗漏 careless omission; slip; oversight: 工作不细心就会有～。If one works carelessly, oversights are bound to occur.

【疏略】shūlüè 〈书 *fml.*〉 ❶ 疏漏忽略 rough: ～之处甚多。There are many inaccuracies and omissions. ❷ 粗疏简略 sketchy: 记载～ sketchy record

【疏落】shūluò 稀疏零落 sparse; scattered: ～的晨星 sparse morning stars

【疏散】shūsàn ❶ same as 疏落 shūluò: ～的村落 scattered villages ❷ 把密集的人或东西散开;分散 evacuate; disperse: ～人口 evacuate residents

【疏失】shūshī 疏忽失误 careless mistake; thoughtless error; remissness: 清查库存物资,要照册仔细核对,不准稍有遗漏～。One must check the inventory against the lists carefully so as not to miss anything.

S

【疏松】shūsōng ❶ (土壤等)松散;不紧密(of soil, etc.)loose: 土质干燥～。The soil is porous. ❷ 使松散 loosen: ～土壤 loosen the soil

【疏通】shūtōng ❶ same as 疏浚 shūjùn: ～田间排水沟 dredge the irrigation ditches in the fields ❷ 沟通双方的意思,调解双方的争执 mediate between two parties: 这件事还得你从中～～。You should mediate between the parties involved in this matter.

【疏虞】shūyú 〈书 *fml.*〉same as 疏忽 shū・hu

【疏远】shūyuǎn 关系、感情上有距离;不亲近 drift apart; become estranged: 不应～有缺点的同学。We should not cold-shoulder classmates that have shortcomings.

摅(攄) shū 〈书 *fml.*〉 ❶ 表示;发表 express; set forth: 略～己意 set forth one's views ❷ 腾跃;奔腾 gallop

输[1] shū ❶ 运输;运送 transport; convey: ～出 send out | ～油管 petroleum pipeline | ～电网 power transmission network ❷ 〈书 *fml.*〉捐献(财物) contribute money; donate: ～财助战 donate money for the war

输[2] shū 在较量时失败;败(跟'赢'相对 as opposed to 'win') lose; be beaten; be defeated: 决不认～ refuse to admit defeat | ～了两个球 lose a ball game by two shots

【输诚】shūchéng 〈书 *fml.*〉 ❶ 表示诚心 express one's sincerity: ～结交 make friends in all sincerity ❷ 投降 surrender

【输出】shūchū ❶ 从内部送到外部 send out: 血液从心脏～,经血管分布到全身组织。The heart pumps blood to all parts of the body through the blood vessels. ❷ 商品或资本从某一国销售或投放到国外(of commodities or capital) export ❸ 科学技术上指能量、信号等从某种机构或装置发出 deliver output; power, signal, etc, sent from a mechanism or apparatus

【输电】shūdiàn 通过导线把电能从发电厂或变电所送到用户那里 transmit electricity; transmission of electricity from a power plant or transformer to users

【输家】shū・jiā 指赌博或比赛中失败的一方 loser (in a gambling game)

【输将】shūjiāng 〈书 *fml.*〉资助;捐献 contribute; donate: 慷慨～ make generous donations

【输精管】shūjīngguǎn 男子或雄性动物生殖器官的一部分。是把精子从睾丸输送到精囊里去的管道。spermatic duct; seminal duct; tube through which sperms travel from testicle

【输理】shū//lǐ 在道理上站不住脚 be in the wrong: 明明是你～,不要再强辩了。It's clear you are in the wrong, so stop arguing.

【输卵管】shūluǎnguǎn 女子或雌性动物生殖器官的一部分。在子宫两侧,作用是把卵巢产生的卵子输送到子宫里去。oviduct; Fallopian tube; tube through which ova are conveyed from ovary

【输尿管】shūniàoguǎn 输送尿液的管状组织,连结肾盂和膀胱,作用是把在肾脏中形成的尿输送到膀胱里去 ureter; tube that conveys urine from the kidney to the urinary bladder or cloaca (图见☞ figure for 泌尿器 mìniàoqì on p.1332)

【输入】shūrù ❶ 从外部送到内部 bring in; introduce ❷ 商品或资本从国外进入某国 import; buy or bring in (goods, services or capital) from a foreign country ❸ 科学技术上指能量、信号等进入某种机构或装置 input; energy, signal or current fed into a component or circuit

【输送】shūsòng 从一处运到另一处;运送 carry; transport; convey: ～带 conveyor belt | 植物的根吸收了肥料,就～到枝叶上去。Plants convey nutrition absorbed through the roots to their branches and leaves.

【输血】shū//xuè 把健康人的血液或血液的组成部分(如血浆、血小板等)用一定的器械输送到病人体内。有静脉、动脉和骨髓内输血三种途径。blood transfusion; intravenous, arterial or bonemarrow transfusion of blood, blood plasma, etc., into the body of a patient

【输氧】shū//yǎng 把氧气通过一定的装置输送到病人的呼吸道,使被动吸氧 oxygen therapy; use a device to supply supplementary oxygen to a patient

【输液】shūyè 把葡萄糖溶液、生理盐水等用一定的装置通过静脉血管输送到体内,以补充体液并达到治疗的目的 infusion; introduction of a glucose, saline or other solution, into a vein

【输赢】shūyíng ❶ 胜负 victory or defeat: 这两

个球队今天非见个～不可。Both teams are determined to fight it out. ❷ 指赌博时输赢的钱数 wins and losses (in gambling)：这伙赌徒，一夜就有几千元的～。These gamblers win or lose in the order of several thousand yuan or more a night.

【输油管】shūyóuguǎn 大量输送石油或石油制品的管道，通常是钢管，外面包着隔热层、保护层，有的埋在地下 petroleum pipeline; long pipe, usu. made of steel, wrapped up with heat insulating and protective materials, and usu. buried underground, used to transport oil or oil products over long distances

毹 shū ☞ [氍毹](qúshū) on p.1591

蔬 shū 蔬菜 vegetables：布衣～食 coarse clothes and simple fare

【蔬菜】shūcài 可以做菜吃的草本植物，其中以十字花科和葫芦科的植物居多，如白菜、菜花、萝卜、黄瓜、洋葱、扁豆等 vegetables; greens; greenstuff; any of various herbaceous plants having parts that are used as food, such as cabbage, cauliflower, radish, cucumber, onion, hyacinth bean, etc.

儵 shū 〈书 *fml.*〉same as 倏 shū

shú (ㄕㄨˊ)

秫 shú 高粱(多指黏高粱 oft. the sticky type) *kaoliang*; sorghum：～秸 *kaoliang* stalk｜～米 husked sorghum

【秫秸】shújiē 去掉穗的高粱秆 *kaoliang* stalk; sorghum stalk

【秫米】shúmǐ 高粱米 husked sorghum

【秫秫】shúshú 〈方 *dial.*〉高粱 *kaoliang*; sorghum

孰 shú 〈书 *fml.*〉〈疑问代词 *interrog. pron.*〉❶ 谁 who; which：人非圣贤，～能无过？No one is a saint, so who can be entirely free from error? ❷ 哪个(表示选择 indicate a choice) which; who：～胜～负？Who wins and who loses? ❸ 什么 what：是可忍，～不可忍？If this can be tolerated, what is there that cannot?

赎(贖) shú ❶ 用财物把抵押品换回 redeem; ransom：～身 redeem or ransom oneself｜把东西～回来 redeem a pledge ❷ 抵消；弥补(罪过) atone for (a crime)：立功～罪 perform meritorious services to atone for one's crime

【赎当】shúdàng 赎回抵押给当铺的东西 redeem sth. pawned; take sth. out of pledge; redeem a pledge

【赎金】shújīn 赎回抵押品或赎身所用的钱 ransom money; ransom

【赎买】shúmǎi 指国家有代价地把私营企业收归国有 redeem; buy out; buy out (private enterprises by state)

【赎身】shú//shēn 〈旧时 *old*〉奴婢妓女等用金钱或其他代价换取人身自由 (of a slave or prostitute) redeem (or ransom) oneself; buy back one's freedom

【赎罪】shú//zuì 抵消所犯的罪过 atone for one's crime：将功～ perform meritorious services to atone for one's crime｜立功～ perform meritorious services to atone for one's crime

塾 shú 〈旧时 *old*〉私人设立的教学的地方 old-style private school; family school：私～ old-style private school｜～师 tutor of an old-style private school; private tutor ☞ 私塾 sīshú on p.1815

【塾师】shúshī 私塾的教师 tutor at an old-style private school; private tutor

熟 shú ❶ 植物的果实等完全长成(跟'生[2]'相对，②至⑤同 as opposed to 'unripe', same as② through⑤) ripe：西瓜已经～了。The watermelon has ripened. ❷ (食物)加热到可以食用的程度 cooked; done：～菜 cooked food｜饭～了。The rice is done. ❸ 加工制造或锻炼过的 processed：～皮子 tanned leather｜～铁 wrought iron ❹ 因常见或常用而知道得清楚 familiar; well acquainted：～人 acquaintance｜～视无睹 pay no heed to｜这条路我常走，所以很～。I often walk along this path, so I know it well. ❺ 熟练 skilled; experienced; practised：～手 practised hand｜～能生巧。Skill comes with practice. ❻ 程度深 deeply; thoroughly：～睡 sleep soundly｜深思～虑 ponder deeply over sth.

☞ shóu on p.1767

【熟谙】shú'ān 〈书 *fml.*〉same as 熟悉 shúxī：～兵法 be well versed in military strategy and tactics

【熟菜】shúcài 已经烹调的菜。多指出售的熟肉食等。cooked food; prepared food, usu. meat, for sale

【熟道】shúdào (～儿 shúdàor) same as 熟路 shúlù

【熟地】[1] shúdì 经过多年耕种的土地 cultivated land

【熟地】[2] shúdì 药名，经过蒸晒的地黄，黑色，有滋补作用 Chinese medicine, prepared rhizome of rehmannia (*Rehmannia glutinosa*); also 熟地黄 shúdìhuáng

【熟化】shúhuà 经过深耕、晒垡、施肥、灌溉等措施，使不能耕种的土壤变成可以耕种的土壤 cultivate (land); till; till and prepare (land or soil) for cultivation of crops

【熟荒】shúhuāng 曾经耕种过后来荒芜了的土地 formerly cultivated land; abandoned cultivated land; also 熟荒地 shúhuāngdì

【熟客】shúkè 常来的客人 frequent visitor

【熟练】shúliàn 工作、动作等因常做而有经验 adept; deft; skilled; practised; proficient：～

工人 skilled worker｜业务～ be well versed in one's profession; be in practice; know one's stuff

【熟路】shúlù 常走而熟悉的道路 familiar road (or route); beaten track

【熟能生巧】shú néng shēng qiǎo 熟练了就能产生巧办法，或找出窍门 skill comes from practice; practice makes perfect

【熟年】shúnián 丰收的年头 year of good harvests; bumper year

【熟人】shúrén (～儿 shúrénr)熟识的人 acquaintance; friend

【熟稔】shúrěn〈书 *fml.*〉很熟悉 be familiar with; be conversant with

【熟石膏】shúshígāo 把石膏加热到150℃，使脱水，就成为熟石膏。是粉刷墙壁和做石膏像、石膏模型等的材料。plaster of Paris; plaster; material obtained by heating gypsum to 150℃ and dehydrating it, used as a material for whitewashing or the making of plaster statues and models

【熟石灰】shúshíhuī 无机化合物，化学式 $Ca(OH)_2$。白色粉末，由生石灰和水反应而成，它的饱和水溶液叫做石灰水。是常用的建筑材料，也用做杀菌剂和化工原料等。slaked lime ($Ca(OH)_2$); white substance (calcium hydroxide) made by adding water to quicklime, its satuated solution known as limewater, used as a common building material, disinfectant or chemical material; also 消石灰 xiāoshíhuī

【熟食】shúshí 经过加工做熟的饭菜，多指出售的做熟的肉食等 prepared food; cooked food, oft. referring to cooked meat for sale: ～专柜 cooked food display counter

【熟识】shú·shi 对某人认识得比较久或对某种事物了解得比较透彻 be well acquainted with; know well: 这批学员～水性。These trainees are expert swimmers.｜我们曾共过事，彼此都很～。We once worked together so we know each other well.

【熟视无睹】shú shì wú dǔ 指对客观事物不关心，虽然经常看见，还跟没看见一样 pay no attention to a familiar sight; turn a blind eye to; ignore

【熟手】shúshǒu 熟悉某项工作的人 old hand; practised hand

【熟睡】shúshuì 睡得很沉；睡得很香 sleep soundly; be fast asleep: 一夜～，醒来精神好多了。One feels in good spirits after a sound night's sleep.

【熟思】shúsī 周密地考虑 give serious thought to; ponder deeply; consider carefully; deliberate: 再三～ think sth. over

【熟烫】shú·tang 瓜果蔬菜等因揉搓或受热而失去新鲜的颜色或滋味 (of fruits, melons, etc.) damaged; spoiled (by heat or handling): ～味儿 smell of spoiled fruit or melons｜这些瓜都是摔打～了。These melons have all been spoiled in the process of handling.

【熟铁】shútiě ☞ 锻铁 duàntiě on p. 488

【熟土】shútǔ 熟化了的土壤，适于耕种 mellow soil, which is suitable for growing crops

【熟悉】shúxī 知道得清楚 know sth. or sb. well; be familiar with; have an intimate knowledge of: ～情况 get into the swing of things; familiarize oneself with the situation｜我～他。I know him well.｜他们彼此很～。They know each other very well.

【熟习】shúxí (对某种技术或学问)学习得很熟练或了解得很深刻 be skillful at; have the knack of; be practised in: ～业务 be practised (or well versed) in one's field of work｜他很～果树栽培知识。He has an intimate knowledge of fruit farming.

【熟橡胶】shúxiàngjiāo 硫化橡胶 vulcanized rubber

【熟语】shúyǔ 固定的词组，只能整个应用，不能随意变动其中成分，并且往往不能按照一般的构词法来分析，如'慢条斯理、无精打采、不尴不尬、乱七八糟、八九不离十'等 idiom; idiomatic phrase; group of words whose implicit meaning cannot be deduced from its constituent words, e.g. 慢条斯理 màntiáo-sīlǐ，无精打采 wú jīng dǎ cǎi，不尴不尬 bù gān bù gà，乱七八糟 luànqībāzāo and 八九不离十 bā jiǔ bù lí shí

【熟知】shúzhī 清楚地知道 have sth. at one's fingertips; know well; know intimately: ～故宫的历史变迁 have the history and vicissitudes of the Forbidden City at one's fingertips

【熟字】shúzì 已经认识了的字(跟'生字'相对 as opposed to 'strange words') words already learned; familiar words

shǔ(ㄕㄨˇ)

暑 shǔ 热(跟'寒'相对 as opposed to 'cold') heat: ～天 hot summer days｜中～ heatstroke｜受～ suffer from heatstroke｜寒来～往 as summer goes and winter comes

【暑假】shǔjià 学校中夏季的假期，在七八月间 (of school) summer vacation; summer break, usu. falling in July and August

【暑期】shǔqī 暑假期间 summer-vacation time: ～训练班 summer course

【暑气】shǔqì 盛夏时的热气 summer heat; heat of midsummer: ～逼人 threatening heat of summer

【暑热】shǔrè 指盛夏时气温高的气候 hot summer weather: ～难耐 intolerably hot summer weather

【暑天】shǔtiān 夏季炎热的日子 hot summer days; dog days of summer

黍 shǔ 黍子 broomcorn millet

【黍子】shǔ·zi ❶ 一年生草本植物，叶子线形，子实淡黄色，去皮后叫黄米，比小米稍大，煮熟后有黏性。是重要粮食作物之一，子实可以酿酒、做糕等。broomcorn millet (*Panicum miliaceum*); annual herbal plant with linear leaves and primrose seeds. When husked, the seeds are a little bigger than millet and, when steamed, are glutinous. Hence the term, glutinous millet. As one of the major cereals, the seeds are used for brewing liquor and making cakes. ❷ 这种植物的子实 seeds of this plant

属(屬) shǔ ❶ 类别 category：金～ metal ❷ 生物学中把同一科的生物群按照彼此相似的程度再分为不同的群，叫做属，如猫科有猫属、虎属等，禾本科有稻属、小麦属、燕麦属等。属以下为种。genus; category of biological classification in which biological groups of the same family are further divided into different groups according to their degree of similarity with each other, e.g. the cat family includes the cat genus and tiger genus, etc., and the grass family includes the paddy genus, wheat genus, and oat genus, etc. The category below genus is species. ❸ 隶属 be affiliated with; be subordinate to：直～ be directly under｜附～ be affiliated to｜湟中县～青海省。Huangzhong County is under the jurisdiction of Qinghai Province. ❹ 归属 belong to：胜利终～我们！The final victory is ours! ❺ 家属；亲属 family members; relatives：军～ soldier's family｜烈～ members of a revolutionary martyr's family ❻ 系；是 be：查明～实 be proven true after investigation ❼ 用十二属相记生年 one's year of birth as marked by (one of the 12 symbolic animals associated with a 12-year cycle)：哥哥～马，弟弟～鸡。Elder brother was born in the year of the horse, and younger brother in the year of the rooster. ☞ 生肖 shēngxiào on p.1718

☞ zhǔ on p.2507

【属地】shǔdì 指隶属或附属于某国的国家或地区 dependency; a country or a region affiliated to another country

【属国】shǔguó 封建时代作为宗主国的藩属的国家 (in feudal times) vassal state; dependent state

【属相】shǔ·xiang 生肖 any of the 12 animals representing the 12 Earthly Branches, used to symbolize the year in which a person is born

【属性】shǔxìng 事物所具有的性质、特点，如运动是物质的属性 property; attribute; quality and character of matter, e.g. motion is a property of matter

【属于】shǔyú 归某一方面或为某方所有 belong to; be owned by：中华人民共和国的武装力量～人民。The armed forces of the People's Republic of China belong to the people.

【属员】shǔyuán 〈旧时 *old*〉指长官所统属的官吏 government officials under the command of superiors

署[1] shǔ ❶ 办公的处所 office; workplace：海关总～ general administration of customs｜专员公～ government commissioner's office ❷ 布置 arrange：部～ deploy ❸ 署理 handle by proxy; act as deputy

署[2] shǔ 签(名)；题(名) sign; leave inscriptions on：签～ sign｜～名 put one's signature to

【署理】shǔlǐ 〈旧时 *old*〉指某官职空缺，由别人暂时代理 act as deputy; temporarily handle government affairs as a substitute when a post is vacant

【署名】shǔ//míng 在书信、文件或文稿上，签上自己的名字 sign; put one's own signature to (letter, document, or manuscript)

蜀 Shǔ ❶ 周朝国名，在今四川成都一带 Shu, a state in the Zhou Dynasty, comprising the area in and around present-day Chengdu in Sichuan Province ❷ 蜀汉 Kingdom of Shu Han (221-263) ❸ 四川的别称 another name for 四川 Sìchuān

【蜀汉】Shǔ-Hàn 三国之一，公元 221—263，刘备所建。在今四川东部和云南、贵州北部以及陕西汉中一带。为魏所灭。Kingdom of Shu Han (221-263), or Shu for short, one of the Three Kingdoms, founded by Liu Bei and comprising present-day eastern Sichuan Province, northern Yunnan and Guizhou provinces, and the Hanzhong region in Shaanxi Province, which was eliminated by the Kingdom of Wei; 简称 abbr. 蜀 shǔ

【蜀锦】shǔjǐn 四川出产的传统的丝织工艺品，用染色的熟丝织成 Sichuan brocade; traditional silk fabric produced in Sichuan, usu. woven with dyed and boiled-off silk threads

【蜀犬吠日】Shǔ quǎn fèi rì 柳宗元在《答韦中立论师道书》中说，四川地方多雾，那里的狗不常见日光，每逢日出，狗都叫起来。后来用'蜀犬吠日'比喻少见多怪。*On Teaching Methods in Response to Wei Zhongli* by Liu Zongyuan, a writer and philosopher of the Tang Dynasty: 'Shu (present-day Sichuan Province) is a misty region with little sunshine, so the dogs bark whenever they see the sun.' The phrase has since come to mean 'make a fuss about sth. that one alone finds strange'.

【蜀黍】shǔshǔ 高粱 sorghum

【蜀绣】shǔxiù 四川出产的刺绣 Sichuan school of traditional Chinese embroidery; Sichuan-style embroidery

鼠 shǔ 哺乳动物的一科，种类很多，一般的身体小，尾巴长，门齿很发达，没有犬齿，毛褐色或黑色，繁殖力很强，有的能传播鼠疫。有的地区叫耗子。mouse (*Muridae*); rat; any of numerous mammals of the family *Muridae*, with a small body, elongated tail, brown or black hair, and well-developed fore teeth but no canine teeth, and having a strong reproductive capacity, some varieties acting as vectors of plague; 通称 generally known as 老鼠 lǎoshǔ; also called 耗子 hào·zi in some regions

【鼠辈】shǔbèi 指微不足道的人（骂人的话 curse) scoundrel; nobody: 无名～ a nobody

【鼠窜】shǔcuàn〈比喻 *fig.*〉像老鼠那样的惊慌逃走 scamper off like a rat: 抱头～ scurry away like a frightened rat

【鼠肚鸡肠】shǔ dù jī cháng ☞ 小肚鸡肠 xiǎo dù jī cháng on p.2106

【鼠目寸光】shǔ mù cùn guāng〈比喻 *fig.*〉眼光短，见识浅 be short-sighted; of limited knowledge

【鼠窃狗盗】shǔ qiè gǒu dào 指小偷小摸，也比喻进行不光明的活动（语本《史记·刘敬叔孙通传》：'此特群盗鼠窃狗盗耳，何足置之齿牙间'）pilfer; (fig.) play petty tricks on the sly (*Records of the Historian·Biographies of Liu Jing and Shusun Tong*: 'Such petty tricks on the sly are not worth mentioning.'); also 鼠窃狗偷 shǔ qiè gǒu tōu

【鼠蹊】shǔxī 腹股沟 groin

【鼠疫】shǔyì 急性传染病，病原体是鼠疫杆菌，啮齿动物如鼠、兔等感染这种病之后，再由蚤传入人体。根据症状的不同可分为腺鼠疫、肺鼠疫和败血型鼠疫三种。plague; acute contagious disease caused by bacillus pestis, usu. transmitted by rodents such as rats and rabbits to humans through infected flea bites; according to different symptoms, the disease can be classified as bubonic, pneumonic, and septic plagues; also 黑死病 hēisǐbìng

数（數） shǔ ❶ 查点（数目）；逐个说出（数目）count; say aloud the numbers one by one: ～数目 count | 你去～～咱们今天种了多少棵树。Go and count how many trees we planted today. | 从十五～到三十 count from 15 to 30 ❷ 计算起来、比较起来（最突出）be reckoned as exceptionally (good or bad, etc.) by comparison: ～一～二 be reckoned as one of the best | 全班～他的功课好。He is the best in the class in terms of academic performance. ❸ 列举（罪状）；责备 enumerate (crimes, etc.); blame: ～说 scold | ～其罪 list the crimes sb. has committed | ～了一顿 blame sb. by enumerating his wrongdoings
☞ shù on p.1790 and shuò on p.1812

【数不上】shǔ·bu shàng same as 数不着 shǔ·bu zháo

【数不胜数】shǔ bù shèng shǔ 数也数不过来，形容很多 innumerable; incalculable; countless

【数不着】shǔ·bu zháo 比较起来不算突出或够不上标准 not reckoned as outstanding; not able to attain a comparable standard: 论射击技术，在我们连里可～我。I'm not counted as a good marksman in our company. also 数不上 shǔ·bu shàng

【数叨】shǔ·dao〈方 *dial.*〉same as 数落 shǔ·luo

【数得上】shǔ·de shàng same as 数得着 shǔ·de zháo: 这座建筑物的规模，在全国都是～的。This building's dimensions make it one of the outstanding structures in the country.

【数得着】shǔ·de zháo 比较突出或够得上标准 be reckoned as outstanding or be able to meet the standard: 在我们村里，她是～的插秧能手。She is one of the outstanding farmers in our village in transplanting rice seedlings. also 数得上 shǔ·de shàng

【数典忘祖】shǔ diǎn wàng zǔ 春秋时晋国的籍谈出使周朝，他回答周王的问题时没有答好，事后周王讽刺他'数典而忘其祖'，意思是籍谈说起国家的礼制掌故来，把自己祖先的职守（掌管国家的史册）都忘掉了（见于《左传》昭公十五年）。后来就用数典忘祖比喻忘掉自己本来的情况或事物的本源。give all the historical facts except those about one's own ancestors. *The Zuo Commentary·Duke Zhao 15th Year*: In the Spring and Autumn Period, when Ji Tan of the State of Jin visited the Zhou Dynasty as an envoy, he failed to field the king's questions and the king later commented that Ji Tan recounted all the social institutions and historical anecdotes but forgot his own ancestor's post in charge of the state historical documents. The phrase is used figuratively to mean 'forget one's own ancestors or origins'

【数伏】shǔ//fú 进入伏天；伏天开始 beginning of the hottest days of the year; ☞ 三伏 sānfú on p.1651

【数九】shǔ//jiǔ 进入从冬至开始的'九' beginning of the coldest days of the year following the Winter Solstice: ～寒天 the coldest days of the year; ☞ 九 jiǔ ② on p.1036

【数来宝】shǔláibǎo 曲艺的一种，用系有铜铃的牛骨或竹板打节拍，多为即兴编词，边敲边唱 *shulaibao*; form of rhythmic storytelling to the accompaniment of bamboo clappers or ox bones tied with copper bells

【数落】shǔ·luo ❶ 列举过失而指责。泛指责备 scold sb. by enumerating his wrongdoings; rebuke: 被母亲～了一顿 be rebuked by one's mother ❷ 不住嘴地列举着说 enumerate; cite one example after another: 那个老大娘～着村里的新事。The old lady recounted the village news item by item.

【数米而炊】shǔ mǐ ér chuī〈比喻 *fig.*〉做用不着做的琐细小事（见于《庄子·庚桑楚》：'简发而栉，数米而炊，窃窃乎又何足以济世哉?'）。后来也形容人吝啬或生活困窘。fuss over small things; do overly minor things (*Zhuangzi* · *Gengsang Chu*: 'How can a miser benefit the world who selects each hair before combing and counts each grain of rice before cooking?'); be miserly or living in austerity

【数说】shǔshuō ❶ 列举叙述 enumerate：把头年的事又～了一遍 enumerate over again the events of last year ❷ 责备 scold; rebuke：又被老爷子～了一顿 be scolded once again by one's father

【数一数二】shǔ yī shǔ èr 形容突出 be reckoned as one of the best：他的学习成绩在全年级都是～的。He is one of the best in academic scores in his grade.

薯(藷) shǔ 甘薯、马铃薯等农作物的统称 general designation of such crops as potato and sweet potato

【薯莨】shǔliáng ❶ 多年生草本植物，地下有块茎，地上有缠绕茎，叶子对生，狭长椭圆形，穗状花序，蒴果有三个翅。块茎的外部紫黑色，内部棕红色，茎内含有胶质，可用来染棉、麻织品。dye yam (*Dioscorea cirrhosa*); perennial herbal plant that has tuberous roots underground, twining stems on the ground, opposite oblong leaves, spica, and capsules each in three segments. Its tuberous root is dark purple outside and reddish brown inside and contains colloids which can be used for dying cotton and hemp fabrics. ❷ 这种植物的块茎 tuberous root (or tuber) of this plant ‖ also 茨莨 cíliáng

【薯莨绸】shǔliángchóu 香云纱 gambiered Canton gauze

【薯蓣】shǔyù 多年生草本植物，茎蔓生，常带紫色，块根圆柱形，叶子对生，卵形或椭圆形，花乳白色，雌雄异株。块根含淀粉和蛋白质，可以吃。Chinese yam (*Dioscorea batatas*); perennial cauligenous, usu. purple, herb that has columnar roots, opposite oblong or oval leaves, and ivory-white dioecious flowers; Its root, containing starch and protein, is edible. 通称 generally called 山药 shān·yao

曙 shǔ〈书 *fml.*〉天刚亮；晓 daybreak; dawn：～光 first ray of morning

【曙光】shǔguāng ❶ 清晨的日光 dawn; sun's glow in the early morning ❷〈比喻 *fig.*〉已经在望的美好的前景 bright prospect to be near in sight：胜利的～ dawn of victory

【曙色】shǔsè 黎明的天色 light of early dawn：从窗口透进了灰白的～。The pale light of early dawn slanted in through the window.

癙 shǔ〈书 *fml.*〉忧闷成病 have a sickness from depression：～忧 depressed

shù（ㄕㄨˋ）

术(術) shù ❶ 技艺；技术；学术 art; skill; technique：美～ fine arts | 武～ martial arts | 医～ medical skill | ～语 technical term | 不学无～ be ignorant and incompetent ❷ 方法；策略 method; tactics：战～ tactics | 权～ political trickery

☞ zhú on p. 2501

【术科】shùkē 军事训练或体育训练中的各种技术性的科目（区别于'学科' as compared with 'academic courses'）technical courses offered in military or physical training

【术士】shùshì〈书 *fml.*〉❶ 遵从儒家学说的读书人 Confucian scholar ❷ 方士 alchemist

【术语】shùyǔ 某门学科中的专门用语 technical terms for a certain subject; terminology

戍 shù（军队）防守（military）defend; garrison：卫～ garrison | ～边 defend the frontiers

【戍边】shùbiān 戍守边疆 defend the frontiers：屯垦～ station troops to reclaim wasteland in the frontiers | ～部队 garrison troops

【戍守】shùshǒu 武装守卫；防守 defend; garrison：～边疆 garrison the frontiers

束 shù ❶ 捆①；系（jì）bind; tie：腰～皮带 wear a belt round one's waist ❷〈量词 *classifier*〉用于捆在一起的东西 bundle; bunch; sheaf：一～鲜花 a bunch of flowers | 一～稻草 a sheaf of straw ❸ 聚集成一条的东西 beam：光～ light beam | 电子～ electron beam ❹ 控制；约束 control; restrain：拘～ restrain | ～手～脚 be overcautious ❺（Shù）姓 a surname

【束缚】shùfù 使受到约束限制；使停留在狭窄的范围里 tie; bind up; fetter; keep within a narrow scope：～手脚 have one's hands and feet tied; hamper the initiative of

【束身】shùshen ❶ 约束自身，不放纵 control oneself; restrain oneself from indulgence：～自爱 have self-discipline and self-respect ❷ 自缚 bind oneself

【束手】shùshǒu 捆住了手 have one's hands tied;〈比喻 *fig.*〉没有办法 be helpless：～就擒 allow oneself to be captured without putting up a fight | ～无策 throw up one's hands in horror

【束手待毙】shù shǒu dài bì〈比喻 *fig.*〉遇到危险或困难，不积极想办法解决，却坐着等死或等待失败 helplessly wait for death (when in danger or difficulties); make no efforts to find a way out but be reconciled to death or failure

【束手就擒】shù shǒu jiù qín〈比喻 *fig.*〉无法脱逃或无力抵抗 allow oneself to be captured without putting up a fight; be unable to escape or resist

【束手束脚】shù shǒu shù jiǎo〈比喻 *fig.*〉做事顾虑多,不敢放手去干 be overcautious and not courageous to act

【束脩】shùxiū〈书 *fml.*〉送给教师的报酬(古时称干肉为脩)(脩 *xiu*: referred to dried meat in ancient China) remuneration presented to a teacher

【束之高阁】shù zhī gāo gé 把东西捆起来,放在高高的架子上面 tie sth. up and place it on the top of a shelf;〈比喻 *fig.*〉扔在一边,不去用它或管它 leave sth. aside and neglect it

【束装】shùzhuāng〈书 *fml.*〉整理行装 pack up (for a journey):～就道 pack up and set off

述 shù 陈说;叙述 state; narrate:口～ dictate|重～一遍 state it once again|略～经过 give a brief account of the matter|上～各项,务须遵照执行。It's required to conform to and carry out the above-mentioned (regulations, etc.).

【述而不作】shù ér bù zuò 指只阐述他人学说而不加自己的创见 only expatiate on other's theories without stating any of one's own views

S

【述怀】shùhuái 抒发心中的感受(多用作诗文篇名 usu. used in titles of writing) express one's feeling from the heart:五十～ 'My Feelings of Turning Fifty'

【述评】shùpíng 叙述和评论,也指叙述和评论的文章 review; commentary:时事～ review of current affairs

【述说】shùshuō 陈述说明 state; recount; narrate:～身世 state one's life experiences

【述职】shù//zhí 向主管部门陈述工作情况(多用于派到外国或外地去担任重要工作的人员 usu. of personnel dispatched outside the city or abroad on important tasks) report on one's work to the authorities concerned:大使回国～。The ambassador returned to his country to report on his work.

沭 Shù 沭河,发源于山东,流入江苏 Shuhe River, originating in Shandong Province and flowing into Jiangsu Province

树(樹) shù ❶ 木本植物的通称 general term for 木本植物 mùběn zhíwù:柳～ willow|一棵～ a tree ❷ 种植;栽培 plant; cultivate:十年～木,百年～人。It takes 10 years to grow trees and 100 years to cultivate a generation of people. ❸ 树立;建立 set up; establish:建～ establish; contribute|独～一帜 develop one's own school of thought|～雄心,立壮志 have lofty ambitions; aim high ❹ (Shù)姓 a surname

【树碑立传】shù bēi lì zhuàn 原指把某人生平事迹刻在石碑上或写成传记加以颂扬,现在比喻通过某种途径树立个人威信,抬高个人声望(含贬义 derog.) glorify sb. by erecting a monument to him and writing his biography; (fig.) build up personal prestige and elevate reputation by all means

【树丛】shùcóng 丛生的树木 grove; thicket; tufted trees

【树大根深】shù dà gēn shēn〈比喻 *fig.*〉势力大,根基牢固 of great influence and with a solid foundation

【树大招风】shù dà zhāo fēng〈比喻 *fig.*〉因名气大引人注意或惹人嫉妒而生出是非 person with an attractive or enviable reputation is liable to be attacked or dragged into disputes

【树倒猢狲散】shù dǎo húsūn sàn〈比喻 *fig.*〉为首的人垮下来,随从的人无所依附也就随之而散(含贬义 derog.) when a big tree falls the monkeys scatter; when a leader falls from power, his followers disperse

【树敌】shùdí 使别人跟自己为敌 make an enemy of sb.; set others against oneself; antagonize:四面～ make enemies on all sides|～太多 antagonize too many people

【树墩】shùdūn 树身锯去后剩下的靠近根部的一段 tree stump; stump; the part of a tree remaining attached to the root after the trunk is cut; also 树墩子 shùdūn•zi

【树干】shùgàn 树木的主体部分 tree trunk; trunk; main body of a tree

【树挂】shùguà 雾凇的通称 goneral term for 雾凇 wù•sōng

【树冠】shùguān 乔木树干的上部连同所长的枝叶 crown (of a tree); topmost part of a tree including the foliage

【树行子】shùhàng•zi 排成行列的树木;小树林 rows of trees; woods

【树胶】shùjiāo 某些植物(如桃、杏等)分泌的胶质 gum; colloid secreted by some plants (e.g. peach, apricot, etc.)

【树篱】shùlí 用树密植而成的围墙 quickset; hedge; fence formed by a dense row of shrubs or low trees

【树立】shùlì 建立(多用于抽象的好的事情 usu. of abstract good things) set up; establish:～榜样 set an example|～典型 establish a model|～助人为乐的风尚 establish a habit of being ready to help others

【树凉儿】shùliángr 夏天大树底下太阳照不到的地方 cool shade of a tree (in summer); also 树阴凉儿 shùyīnliángr

【树林】shùlín 成片生长的许多树木,比森林小 wood; grove; dense growth of trees, usu. smaller in size than a forest; also 树林子 shùlín•zi

【树龄】shùlíng 树木种植的年数 tree age:院中有几株二百年以上～的古树。There are several trees over 200 years old in the courtyard.

【树苗】shùmiáo 可供移植的小树,多栽培在苗圃中 sapling; transplantable young tree, usu. cultivated in a nursery

【树木】shùmù 树(总称) trees (collect.):花草～

flowers and trees

【树身】shùshēn same as 树干 shùgàn

【树阴】shùyīn（～儿 shùyīnr）树木枝叶在日光下所形成的阴影 shade of a tree; shelter (of foliage) from the glare of sunlight

【树阴凉儿】shùyīnliángr same as 树凉儿 shùliangr

【树脂】shùzhī 遇热变软，具有可塑性的高分子化合物的统称。一般是无定形固体或半固体。分为天然树脂和合成树脂两大类。松香、安息香等是天然树脂，酚醛树脂、聚氯乙烯树脂等是合成树脂。树脂是制造塑料的主要原料，也用来制涂料、黏合剂、绝缘材料等。resin; plastic high-molecular compound that turns soft when heated; generally amorphous solid or semi-solid in two categories — natural resins (e.g. rosin and benzoin) and synthetic resins (e.g. bakelite and PVC). Resin is a major raw material for making plastics, and can be also used to make varnish, glue, and insulating materials.

【树种】shùzhǒng ❶ 树木的种类 kinds of trees：针叶～ coniferous trees｜阔叶～ broad-leaved trees ❷ 树木的种子 seeds of trees：采集～ gather the seeds of trees

【树桩】shùzhuāng ❶ same as 树墩 shùdūn; also 树桩子 shùzhuāng·zi ❷ 指树干粗而极矮的树木，枝条很少，通常用来做盆景 short, thick tree with few branches, usu. used for making miniature landscapes or bonsai

竖[1]（竪、豎）shù ❶ 跟地面垂直的（跟‘横’相对 as opposed to ‘horizontal’）vertical; upright; perpendicular：～井 vertical shaft｜～琴 harp ❷ 从上到下的；从前到后的（跟横‘相对 as opposed to ‘horizontally’）from top to bottom; vertically：画一条～线 draw a vertical line｜～着再挖一道沟 excavate another ditch from the front to the rear ❸ 使物体跟地面垂直 set upright; make an object perpendicular to the ground：～电线杆 erect a telegraph pole｜把柱子～起来 erect a pillar ❹（～儿 shùr）汉字的笔画，从上一直向下，形状是‘丨’ vertical stroke (in Chinese characters), in the shape of ‘丨’

竖[2]（竪、豎）shù〈书 *fml.*〉年轻的仆人 young servant：～子 young servant

【竖井】shùjǐng 直接通到地面的矿井，井筒是垂直的，提升矿物的叫主井，通风、排水、输送人员或材料的叫辅井 vertical shaft; mine shaft leading straight up to the ground; leading shaft; A vertical shaft for lifting minerals is a leading shaft, and one for ventilation, drainage, and transportation of personnel or materials is a supporting shaft. also 立井 lìjǐng

【竖立】shùlì 物体垂直，一端向上，一端接触地面或埋在地里 erect; stand; set upright：宝塔～在山上。The pagoda stands at the top of the mountain.｜门前～一根旗杆。A flagpole stands in front of the gate.

【竖琴】shùqín 弦乐器，在直立的三角形架上安有四十八根弦 harp; stringed instrument consisting of an upright triangle frame and 48 strings

【竖蜻蜓】shù qīngtíng〈方 *dial.*〉same as 倒立 dàolì ②

【竖子】shùzǐ〈书 *fml.*〉❶ 童仆 young servant ❷ 小子（含轻蔑意 derog.）boy; chap：～不足与谋。You, boy, do not merit consideration.

钬 shù〈书 *fml.*〉长针 long needle

恕 shù ❶ 用自己的心推想别人的心 consideration for others; presume other's thoughts based on one's own thoughts：忠～ kind-hearted｜～道 doctrine of tolerance and forgiveness ❷ 不计较（别人的）过错；原谅 forgive; pardon; forget other's faults：宽～ excuse｜饶～ forgive｜～罪 pardon a sin ❸〈客套话 *pol.*〉请对方不要计较 excuse me; beg your pardon：～不招待 excuse me for not serving you｜～难从命。We regret that we cannot comply with your wishes.

庶[1] shù ❶ 众多 numerous：～务 general affairs｜富～ rich and popular ❷〈书 *fml.*〉平民；百姓 common people：～民 common people

庶[2] shù 宗法制度下指家庭的旁支（跟‘嫡’相对 as opposed to ‘wife’）of or by a concubine：～出 be born to a concubine

庶[3] shù〈书 *fml.*〉庶几 so that; so as to：～免误会 so as to avoid misunderstanding｜～不致误 so as not to result in error

【庶出】shùchū〈旧指 *old*〉妾所生（区别于‘嫡出’、‘正生’ as compared with ‘being born to a wife’）be born to a concubine

【庶乎】shùhū〈书 *fml.*〉same as 庶几 shùjī：～可行 so that it is feasible

【庶几】shùjī〈书 *fml.*〉〈连词 *conj.*〉表示在上述情况之下才能避免某种后果或实现某种希望 so that; so as to; (only thus) can the consequences be avoided or an object realized：必须有一笔账，以便检查，～两不含糊。An accounting statement is necessary for check-up so that everybody is clear about the account. also 庶几乎 shùjīhū or 庶乎 shùhū

【庶民】shùmín〈书 *fml.*〉百姓 common people：王子犯法，与～同罪。A prince who violates the law should be sentenced in the same manner as a commoner.

【庶母】shùmǔ〈旧时 *old*〉子女称父亲的妾 concubine of one's father

【庶务】shùwù ❶〈旧时 *old*〉指机关团体内的杂项事务 general affairs (in organizations, groups, etc.) ❷〈旧时 *old*〉指担任庶务的人 person in charge of general affairs or business matters

S

【庶子】shùzǐ 指妾所生的儿子（区别于'嫡子' as compared with 'the son of a legal wife'）the son of a concubine

裋 shù ［裋褐］（shùhè）〈书 *fml.*〉粗布衣服 dress made of coarse cloth

腧（俞） shù 腧穴 acupuncture points on the human body：肺～ acupuncture points for the lungs｜胃～ acupuncture points for the stomach

☞ 俞 yú on p. 2339

【腧穴】shùxué 人体上的穴位 acupuncture points on the human body

数（數） shù ❶（～儿 shùr）数目 number; figure：人～ the number of persons｜岁～ age｜次～ the number of times｜～以万计 number tens of thousands ◇心中有～ know fairly well ❷ 数学上表示事物的量的基本概念，如自然数、整数、分数、有理数、无理数、实数、复数等（math.）number; basic concept identifying or designating the quantity of sth., e.g. natural number, whole number, fraction, rational number, irrational number, real number, complex number, etc. ❸ 一种语法范畴，表示名词或代词所指事物的数量，例如英语名词有单、复两种数（gram.）[number; amount of sth. referred to in nouns or pronouns, i.e. singular and plural for nouns in English] ❹ 天数；劫数 inexorable doom; fate; destiny：在～难逃（迷信 superstition）there is no escape ❺ 几；几个 several; a few：～十种 dozens of kinds｜～小时 a few hours ❻ 用在某些数词或量词后面表示概数 [approximate number, usu. following a numeral or a classifier]：每亩能产千～斤。The yield (of grain, etc.) per *mu* is expected to top 500 kg.

☞ shǔ on p. 1786 and shuò on p. 1812

【数表】shùbiǎo 数学用表，如三角函数表、常用对数表等 mathematical chart, e.g. trigonometric function chart, common logarithm chart, etc.

【数词】shùcí 表示数目的词。数词连用或者加上别的词，可以表示序数、分数、倍数、概数，如'第一、八成、百分之五、一千倍、十六七、二三十、四十上下'。numeral; conventional symbol that represents a number; if used together with one or more other numerals, or with other words, it can denote an ordinal number, fraction, multiple, or approximate number, e.g. 1st, 80 per cent, 5 per cent, 1000 times, 16 or 17, between 20 and 30, around 40

【数额】shù'é 一定的数目 quota; fixed number; definite amount：超出～ exceed the quota｜不足规定～ fall short of the amount required

【数据】shùjù 进行各种统计、计算、科学研究或技术设计等所依据的数值 data, usu. used as basis for calculations in statistics, planning, scientific research, technical design, etc.

【数理逻辑】shùlǐ-luó·ji 用数学方法研究推理、计算等逻辑问题的学科 mathematical logic; symbolic logic; science of developing and representing logical principles by means of mathematical approaches; also 符号逻辑 fúhào luójí

【数量】shùliàng 事物的多少 quantity; amount：要保证～，也要保证质量。Both quantity and quality should be guaranteed.

【数量词】shùliàngcí 数词和量词连用时的合称。如'三本书'的'三本'，'一群人'的'一群'，'去一次'的'一次'。numeral-classifier compound, e.g. in three books, a flock, once, etc.

【数量级】shùliàngjí 用来量度或估计某些物理量大小的一种概念。当一个物理量的数值写成以10为底的指数表达式时，指数的数目就是这个物理量的数量级。如地球赤道半径为6,378公里，可以写成 6.378×10^3 公里或 6.378×10^8 厘米。就公里来说，它的数量级是3；就厘米来说，它的数量级是8。order of magnitude; concept for measuring or estimating the magnitude of a physical quantity. When the numerical value of a physical quantity is represented as an exponent with 10 as the base number, the number of the exponent is the order of magnitude of this physical quantity. For example, the equatorial radius of the earth is 6,378 km., which can be expressed as 6.378×10^3 km. or 6.378×10^8 cm., where if counted in km., the order of magnitude is 3, while if counted in cm., the order of magnitude is 8.

【数列】shùliè 按照一定次序排列的一列数。如3,9,27,81；2,4,6,8…等。数列的项数是有限的称为有限数列，项数是无限的称为无限数列。sequence; series of numbers arranged in a certain order, e.g. 3, 9, 27, 81...; 2, 4, 6, 8..., etc.; Sequences with a finite number of terms are known as finite sequences, and sequences with an infinite number of terms are known as infinite sequences.

【数论】shùlùn 数学的一个分支，主要研究整数性质以及和它有关的规律 theory of numbers; branch of mathematics principally committed to the study of the properties of integral numbers as well as other related disciplines

【数码】shùmǎ（～儿 shùmǎr）❶ same as 数字 shùzì ❷ same as 数目 shùmù：这次进货的～比以前大得多。The amount of goods purchased this time is much more than before.

【数目】shùmù 通过单位表现出来的事物的多少 number; amount (of sth. represented in units)：你数好以后，就把～告诉他。Tell him the number after you have finished counting.

【数目字】shùmùzì same as 数字 shùzì

【数位】shùwèi 数字在数中的所在位置。如十进制数整数部分的数位从右向左依次为个位、十位、百位…，小数部分的数位从左向右依次为十分位、百分位、千分位… 。numerical digit; place of a digit in a number. In the decimal system, the numerical digits from right to left of integral numbers are ones (first place), tens (second place), hundreds (third place), etc., and the numerical digits from left to right of fractional numbers are tenths, hundredths, thousandths, etc.

【数学】shùxué 研究现实世界的空间形式和数量关系的科学，包括算术、代数、几何、三角、微积分等 mathematics; science of studying spatial configurations and quantitative relationships in the real world, including arithmetic, algebra, geometry, trigonometry, calculus, etc.

【数值】shùzhí 一个量用数目表示出来的多少，叫做这个量的数值。如 3 克的'3'，4 秒的'4'。numerical value, e.g. the 3 in '3 grams', the 4 in 'four seconds', etc.

【数制】shùzhì 记数的法则。根据进位基数的不同，有十进制、二进制、十六进制等。system of computation; can be classified as a binary system based on the number 2, a decimal system based on the number 10, or a hexadecimal system based on the number 16, etc.

【数轴】shùzhóu 规定了原点、正方向和单位长度的直线。数轴上的点和实数一一对应。number axis; straight line with an established origin, positive direction, and unit length; the points on a number axis correspond with real numbers

【数珠】shùzhū (～儿 shùzhūr) 佛教徒诵经时用来计算次数的成串的珠子 (Buddhist) beads; prayer beads; strings of beads used by Buddhists for counting while chanting scriptures; also 念珠 niànzhū

【数字】shùzì ❶ 表示数目的文字。汉字的数字有小写大写两种，'一二三四五六七八九十'等是小写，'壹贰叁肆伍陆柒捌玖拾'等是大写。written words or characters that denote amounts. Chinese characters are classified as ordinary and capital forms, i.e. 一二三四五六七八九十 are ordinary forms of 1, 2, 3, 4, 5, 6, 7, 8, 9 and 10; and 壹贰叁肆伍陆柒捌玖拾 are the capital forms. ❷ 表示数目的符号，如阿拉伯数字、苏州码子 numeral; figure; digit; symbols that denote numbers, e.g. Arabic numerals, Suzhou digits, etc. ❸ 数量 amount; quantity: 不要盲目追求～。Don't blindly pursue quantity. ‖ also 数目字 shùmùzì

【数字控制】shùzì kòngzhì 自动控制的一种方式，通常使用专门的电子计算机，操作指令以数字形式表示，机器设备按照预定的程序进行工作 numerical control; digital control; mode of automatic control in which machinery operates according to programmes predetermined through digital operation commands from specialized computers; 简称 abbr. 数控 shùkòng

【数字通信】shùzì tōngxìn 传送数字信号的通信方式。传送的一方把所要传送的信号变换成可以代表文字、图像等的数字脉冲（如二进制编码）传送，接收的一方收到后再把它们变换成原来的信号。digital telecommunications; mode of the communications that transmits digital signals, in which the sender transforms signals into digital pulses representing words and pictures, and upon receiving the digital pulses, the receiver transforms them back to the original signals

墅 shù 别墅 villa

漱 shù 含水洗（口腔）rinse (the mouth); gargle: ～口 gargle | 用药水～～ gargle with liquid medicine

澍 shù〈书 *fml.*〉及时的雨 timely rain

shuā（ㄕㄨㄚ）

刷[1] shuā ❶ (～儿 shuār) 刷子 brush: 牙～ toothbrush | 鞋～子 shoe brush ❷ 用刷子清除或涂抹 clean or paint with a brush; brush; scrub: ～牙 brush one's teeth | ～鞋 brush shoes | ～锅 clean (or scour) a pot | 用石灰浆～墙 paint the wall with limewash; whitewash a wall ❸〈比喻 *fig.*〉除名；淘汰 eliminate (through selection or competition); remove: 由于他不守劳动纪律，让厂里给～了。He was dismissed from the factory due to his failure to follow labour discipline. | 今年高考他被～了下来。He was eliminated in this year's college-entrance examinations.

刷[2]（唰）shuā〈拟声词 *onom.*〉形容迅速擦过去的声音 swish; rustle; quick sweeping sound: 风刮得树叶子～～地响。The leaves of the trees rustled in the wind. | ～～地下起雨来了。The rain came down with a swooshing sound.

☞ shuà on p. 1792

【刷拉】shuālā〈拟声词 *onom.*〉形容迅速擦过去的短促的声音 swishing sound: ～一声，柳树上飞走了一只鸟儿。Swish! A bird flew out of the willow.

【刷洗】shuāxǐ 用刷子等蘸水洗；把脏东西放在水里清洗 scrub; scour: ～地板 scrub the floor | ～锅碗 scour the pots and pans

【刷新】shuāxīn 刷洗使焕然一新 refurbish; scrub until it looks like new;〈比喻 *fig.*〉突破旧的而创出新的（记录、内容等）outdo; break through the old and make a new (record, contents, etc.): 在这次运动会上她～了一万米赛跑的世界记录。At this sports meet, she broke the world record in the 10,000-metre race.

decline|年老力～ get older and weaker|风势渐～。The wind is dying down.
☞ cuī on p. 332

【衰败】shuāibài same as 衰落 shuāiluò：家业～。Family circumstance declines. |～景象 a scene of decline

【衰惫】shuāibèi〈书 *fml.*〉衰弱疲乏 feeble and exhausted

【衰变】shuāibiàn 放射性元素自发地放射出粒子而变成另一种元素，如镭放射出 α 粒子后变成氡。decay; radioactive element spontaneously emits radioactive particles and becomes another kind of element, e.g. radium becomes radon after emitting particles of α; also 蜕变 tuìbiàn

【衰减】shuāijiǎn 减弱；减退 weaken; fail; diminish：功能～ weaken function|精力日渐～ one's energy fails with each passing day

【衰竭】shuāijié 由于疾病严重而生理机能极度减弱 failure; depletion; exhaustion; extreme weakness or failure in physiological function due to serious illness：心力～ heart failure|全身～ whole-body exhaustion

【衰老】shuāilǎo 年老精力衰弱 old and feeble; decrepit; senile：两年没见，老人显得～多了。The old man has obviously aged and weakened since I last saw him two years ago.

【衰落】shuāiluò（事物）由兴盛转向没落（of things）decline; be on the wane; come down from prosperity：家道～。The family's stars are going downhill.

【衰迈】shuāimài same as 衰老 shuāilǎo：年纪～ be aged and feeble

【衰弱】shuāiruò ❶（身体）失去了强盛的精力、机能（of body）weak; feeble; not as strong in energy and function as before：身体～ be weak|神经～ neurasthenia; nervous breakdown|心脏～ have a weak heart ❷（事物）由强转弱（of things）weaken; diminish; become weak：在我军有力反击下，敌军攻势已经～。Thanks to our army's powerful counterattack the enemy's offensive is losing momentum.

【衰替】shuāitì〈书 *fml.*〉same as 衰败 shuāibài：世风～。Public morals are on the wane.

【衰颓】shuāituí（身体、精神等）衰弱颓废（of body, spirit, etc.）weak and degenerate

【衰退】shuāituì（身体、精神、意志、能力等）趋向衰弱；（国家的政治经济状况）衰落（of body, spirit, will, capability, etc.）fall into a decline;（of a state's political and economic situation）fail; go downhill：记忆力～ be losing one's memory|经济～ economic recession

【衰亡】shuāiwáng 衰落以至灭亡 become feeble and die; decline and fall

【衰微】shuāiwēi〈书 *fml.*〉（国家、民族等）衰落；不兴旺（of a country, a nation, etc.）decline; wane：国力～。National power is on the wane.|家道～。The family's situation is declining.

【衰萎】shuāiwěi 衰败萎缩 wither; shrivel：被霜打过的野草渐渐～下来。The frost-stricken weeds are gradually withering.

【衰歇】shuāixiē 由衰落而趋于终止 come to an end after decline

【衰朽】shuāixiǔ〈书 *fml.*〉衰落；衰老 feeble and decaying; decrepit：～的王朝 decadent dynasty|～残年 decrepit old age

摔（❶踤） shuāi ❶（身体）失去平衡而倒下 lose one's balance and fall;（of body）tumble：～跤 tumble, trip and fall|～了一个跟头 have a fall ❷ 很快地往下落 hurtle down; plunge; drop quickly：敌机冒着黑烟～下来。The enemy aircraft crashed to the ground in a plume of black smoke. ❸ 使落下而破损 cause to fall and break; break：不小心把个瓶子～了 accidentally broke a bottle ❹ 扔 throw; cast：往空中～鞭炮 cast firecrackers into the air ❺ same as 摔打① shuāi·da

【摔打】shuāi·da ❶ 抓在手里磕打 beat; knock：把笤帚上的泥～～。Beat the dirt off the broom. ❷〈比喻 *fig.*〉磨练；锻炼 temper; take exercise：到社会上～～有好处。It's good for you to temper yourself in the world.

【摔跤】shuāi//jiāo ❶ 摔倒在地上 tumble; trip and fall：摔了一跤 have a fall|路太滑，一不小心就要～。The road is so slippery that it is easy to fall if one is not cautious. ❷ 体育运动项目之一，两人相抱运用力气和技巧，以摔倒对方为胜 wrestling; sport in which two individuals wrestle hand to hand using strength and technique, each attempting to subdue or unbalance the other

【摔耙子】shuāi pá·zi〈比喻 *fig.*〉扔下工作不干 throw away one's job

shuǎi（ㄕㄨㄞˇ）

甩 shuǎi ❶ 挥动；抡（lūn）fling; swing：～胳膊 swing one's arms|～辫子 swing one's braid|袖子一～就走了 fling up one's sleeve in impatience and walk off ❷ 用甩的动作往外扔 throw; fling; toss：～手榴弹 throw hand grenades ❸ 抛开 leave sb. behind; throw off：我们等他一下吧，别把他一个人～在后面。Let's wait for him, and not leave him behind alone.

【甩包袱】shuǎi bāo·fu〈比喻 *fig.*〉去掉拖累自己的人或事物 abandon one's burden (of a person or matter)

【甩车】shuǎi//chē 使列车的部分车厢或全部车厢脱离机车 uncouple some or all the coaches from the locomotive; uncouple

【甩脸子】shuǎi liǎn·zi〈方 *dial*.〉把不高兴的心情故意表现出来给别人看 pull a long face; reveal one's unhappy mood to others on purpose

【甩卖】shuǎimài 商店标榜减价,大量出售货物 disposal of goods at reduced prices; markdown sale; reduction sale:赔本大～ a great sale

【甩腔】shuǎiqiāng 拖腔 dragged tune

【甩手】shuǎi//shǒu ❶ 手向前后摆动 swing one's arms; move one's hands backward and forward ❷ 扔下不管(多指事情、工作) refuse to do (sth., a job, etc.):～不干 wash one's hands of (sth.)

【甩站】shuǎi//zhàn 指公共汽车、电车经过该停的站不停车 (of a bus, trolley, etc.) does not stop at scheduled stops

shuài (ㄕㄨㄞˋ)

帅[1](帥) shuài ❶ 军队中最高的指挥员 (mil.) commander-in-chief:元～ marshal|将～ general and commander|～旗 flag of a commander-in-chief |～印 seal of a commander-in-chief ❷ (Shuài) 姓 a surname

帅[2](帥、率) shuài 英俊、潇洒;漂亮 handsome; smart; beautiful; elegant:这个武打动作干净利落,～极了。This martial-art movement was neat and graceful.|字写得真～。He writes in a beautiful hand.

【帅才】shuàicái 指能统帅全军具有杰出指挥才能的人 born commander; talented person who is capable of commanding an entire army

率[1] shuài ❶ 带领 lead; command:～代表团离京 lead a delegation out of Beijing ❷〈书 *fml*.〉顺着;随着 follow; obey:～由旧章 act in accordance with established rules

率[2] shuài ❶ 不加思考;不慎重 rash; hasty:轻～ careless|草～ hasty ❷ 直爽坦白 frank; straightforward:直～ straightforward|坦～ candid ❸〈书 *fml*.〉大概;大抵 generally; usually:大～如此。This is usually the case.|～十日一至。Generally 10 days are counted as a period. ❹ same as 帅[2] shuài

☞ lǜ on p.1267

【率尔】shuài'ěr〈书 *fml*.〉轻率 rashly; hastily:～应战 rashly accept battle

【率领】shuàilǐng 带领(队伍或集体) lead; head (a troop, group, etc.):～队伍 command a troop|他～着一个访问团出国了。He led a visiting delegation abroad.

【率然】shuàirán〈书 *fml*.〉轻率的样子 hastily; rashly:切不可～从事。Don't act rashly.

【率先】shuàixiān 带头;首先 take the lead in doing sth.; be the first to do sth.:～发难 be the first to launch an attack|～表态 take the lead in making public one's position

【率性】shuàixìng ❶ 索性 so; fearfully:草鞋磨破了,他～赤着脚继续走。With his straw sandals tattered, he kept on walking barefooted. ❷ 由着性子;任性 do whatever one pleases; wilfully:～行事 act wilfully

【率由旧章】shuài yóu jiù zhāng 一切照老规矩办事 act in accordance with established rules

【率真】shuàizhēn 直爽而诚恳 straightforward and sincere:为人～ behave straightforwardly and sincerely

【率直】shuàizhí 直率 straightforward; unreserved:说话～ speak frankly|～的态度 straightforward attitude

蟀 shuài ☞ [蟋蟀](xīshuài) on p.2050

shuān (ㄕㄨㄢ)

闩(櫄) shuān ❶ 门关上后,插在门内使门推不开的木棍或铁棍 door bolt; latch; wood or iron piece inserted into a slot behind a closed door so that the door cannot be pushed open:门～ door bolt|上了～ fasten with a latch ❷ 用闩插上 fasten with a bolt or latch:把门～上 bolt the door|门～得紧紧的。The door is tightly bolted.

拴 shuān ❶ 用绳子等绕在物体上,再打上结 tether; tie; fasten; entwine and knot a string to an object:把马～在一棵树上 tether a horse to a tree ❷〈比喻 *fig*.〉缠住而不能自由行动 tie down; bind up; be hindered in one's free action:被琐事～住了 be tied down by trifles|这件事把大伙儿～在了一起。This matter has bound everybody together.

栓 shuān ❶ 器物上可以开关的机件 bolt; plug; switch; component that can turn on and off an appliance:消火～ fire hydrant ❷ 特指枪栓 gun bolt ❸ (瓶)塞子;也泛称形状像塞子的东西,如栓剂之类 stopper; cork; sth. resembling a stopper, e.g. suppositories

【栓剂】shuānjì 塞入肛门、尿道或阴道内的外用药,在室温下为固体,在体温下融化或软化。有的制成棒状,有的制成球状。中医叫坐药。suppository; cylindrical- or spherical-shaped external remedy, usu. solid at room temperatures but dissolving at body temperatures, for insertion into a bodily passage or cavity (such as the rectum, urethra, or vagina); known in traditional Chinese medicine as 坐药 zuòyào

【栓皮】shuānpí 栓皮栎之类树皮的木栓层。质轻而软,富于弹性,不导电,不透水,不透气,耐磨擦,隔音隔热。用来制救生圈、软木砖、隔音板、瓶塞、软木纸等。cork; suberous layer of the outer bark of an oak tree (*Quercus variabilis*) that is light, soft, strongly elastic, non-conductive, waterproof, airtight and durable, and insulates sound and heat, usu. used to make life rings, cork bricks, sound-insulation boards, bottle stoppers, cork paper, etc.; also 软木 ruǎnmù

【栓皮栎】shuānpílì 落叶乔木,叶子长圆形或长圆状披针形,叶子背面有灰白色绒毛,种子圆形。是培养木耳的主要植物,树皮的木栓层特别发达,叫做栓皮,用途很广。oriental oak (*Quercus variabilis*); deciduous tree that has oblong or needle-shaped leaves with off-white floss underneath and round seeds, and is the major plant for growing agaric. The cork layer of its bark is well developed and can be used for many purposes.

【栓塞】shuānsè 医学上指从体外侵入血管内的物质或从血管、心脏内脱落的血栓随血液流到较小的血管后,由于不能通过而将血管堵塞 embolism; sudden obstruction of a blood vessel by sth. intruding from outside the body, or thrombus from a larger blood vessel or the heart, circulating in the bloodstream

shuàn(ㄕㄨㄢˋ)

涮 shuàn ❶ 把手或东西放在水里摆动 wash; rinse hands or sth. in water: 洗洗~~ wash|~~手 wash hands ❷ 把水放在器物里面摇动,把器物冲洗干净 rinse; clean; clean the inside of a container by filling the container with water and shaking it: ~一下瓶子 rinse out the bottle ❸ 把肉片等放在开水里烫一下就取出来蘸作料吃 scald thin slices of meat in boiling water; instant-boil: ~羊肉 instant-boiled mutton ❹〈方 *dial.*〉耍弄;骗 cheat: 你别~我啦。Don't try to cheat me!

【涮锅子】shuànguō·zi 把肉片、蔬菜等放在火锅里涮着吃,这种吃法叫涮锅子 instant-boil slices of meat and vegetables in a chafing dish

shuāng(ㄕㄨㄤ)

双(雙、㕠) shuāng ❶ 两个(多为对称的,跟'单'相对 as opposed to 'single') two; both; dual: ~翅 both wings|举~手赞成 hold up both hands|男女~方 both the female and male sides ❷〈量词 *classifier*〉用于成对的东西 pair: 一~鞋 a pair of shoes|一~手 a pair of hands|买~袜子 buy a pair of socks ❸ 偶数的(跟'单'相对 as opposed to 'odd') even: ~数 even numbers|~号 even numbers ❹ 加倍的 double; twofold: ~料 extra quality|~份 twice as much; double the amount ❺(Shuāng)姓 a surname

【双棒儿】shuāngbàngr〈方 *dial.*〉same as 双胞胎 shuāngbāotāi

【双胞胎】shuāngbāotāi 同一胎内两个婴儿;两人同一胎出生 twins; two babies of the same embryo, born together as a pair

【双边】shuāngbiān 由两个方面参加的;特指由两个国家参加的 bilateral; involving two parties, esp. two countries: ~会谈 bilateral talks|~条约 bilateral treaty|~贸易 bilateral trade

【双宾语】shuāngbīnyǔ 某些动词能带两个宾语,一般是一个宾语指人,另一个宾语指事物,如'我问你一句话'。指人的一个('你')靠近动词,叫做近宾语;指事物的一个('一句话')离动词较远,叫做远宾语。double object; two objects following a verb, usu. one object referring to people while the other referring to things, e.g. 'I'm asking you a question' ('you' is closer to the verb, so it is called the near object; while 'a question' is far from the verb, so it is the far object)

【双重】shuāngchóng 两层;两方面(多用于抽象事物 usu. used for abstract things) double; dual; two-sided: ~领导 dual leadership|~任务 a double task

【双重国籍】shuāngchóng guójí 指一个人同时具有两个国家的国籍 dual nationality; (sb.) possessing the citizenship of two countries at the same time

【双重人格】shuāngchóng réngé 指一个人兼有的两种互相对立的身份、品质或态度(含贬义 derog.) dual personality; (sb.) having two opposite identities, natures, or attitudes

【双唇音】shuāngchúnyīn 双唇紧闭或接近发出的辅音,如普通话语音中的 b,p,m bilabial consonant; bilabial, e.g. p, b, m in standard Chinese

【双打】shuāngdǎ 某些球类比赛的一种方式,由每组两人的两组对打,如乒乓球、羽毛球、网球等都可以双打 doubles; a certain way of playing games (e.g. tennis, badminton, ping-pong, etc.), in which two pairs of players compete with each other

【双方】shuāngfāng 在某一件事情上相对的两个人或集体 both sides; two parties; two persons or groups in opposition to each other on some matter: 男女~ both the female and male sides|缔约国~ both signatory states

【双杠】shuānggàng ❶ 体操器械的一种。用两根木杠平行地固定在木制或铁制的架上构成。parallel bars; a pair of wooden bars fixed horizontally parallel on a wooden or iron rack, and used in gymnastics ❷ 男子竞技体操项目之一,运动员在双杠上做各种动作 an event in men's gymnastics competitions in which gymnasts execute different movements on parallel bars

【双钩】shuānggōu 用线条钩出笔画的周边,构成空心笔画的字体,如'大'(Chinese calligra-

S

phy) double thick; write a hollow character by lining the edge of strokes, e.g. 大 dà

【双关】shuāngguān 用词造句时表面上是一个意思,而暗中隐藏着另一个意思 use of a word in such a way as to express one meaning on the surface while hiding another:一语～ make a pun

【双管齐下】shuāng guǎn qí xià 本指画画时两管笔同时并用 paint a picture with two brushes at the same time;〈比喻 *fig.*〉两方面同时进行 work along two lines

【双轨】shuāngguǐ 有两组轨道的复线 double track

【双簧】shuānghuáng ❶ 曲艺的一种,一人表演动作,一人藏在后面或说或唱,互相配合 two-person folk art, with one acting in pantomime and the other hiding behind doing all the speaking or singing ❷〈比喻 *fig.*〉一方出面、一方背后操纵的活动 two-sided collaboration, with one side performing in view while the other manipulates things behind the scene ‖ also 双镄 shuānghuáng

【双簧管】shuānghuángguǎn 管乐器,由嘴子、管身和喇叭口三部分构成,嘴子上装有双簧片 oboe; double-reed woodwind instrument, composed of a double-reed mouthpiece, a tube, and a flared opening

【双肩挑】shuāng jiān tiāo〈比喻 *fig.*〉一个人在同一部门同时担任业务和行政两种工作 (of a person) shoulder both operations and administration in the same department:他在厂里既是厂长,又是工程师,是个～干部。He is not only a director but also an engineer at the factory.

【双料】shuāngliào (～儿 shuāngliàor)制造物品用的材料比通常的同类物品加倍,多用于比喻 of reinforced material; (usu. fig.) extra quality:～搪瓷盆 extra-high quality basin|～冠军 super-champion

【双抢】shuāngqiǎng 指抢收、抢种 rush-harvesting and rush-planting

【双亲】shuāngqīn 指父亲和母亲 (both) parents; father and mother

【双全】shuāngquán 成对的或相称(chèn)的两方面都具备 complete in both respects; possessing both:文武～ be well versed in both literary and martial arts|父母～。Both parents are still around.

【双人舞】shuāngrénwǔ 由两个人表演的舞蹈,可以单独表演,也可以是舞剧或集体舞中的一个部分 pas de deux; dance for two performers, which can be performed alone, or as part of a dance drama or collective dance

【双身子】shuāngshēn·zi 指孕妇 pregnant woman

【双生】shuāngshēng 孪(luán)生的通称 general term for 孪生 luánshēng

【双声】shuāngshēng 两个字或几个字的声母相同叫双声,例如'公告 gōnggào、方法 fāngfǎ' alliterative compound; compound consisting of two syllables with the same initial consonant, e.g. 公告 gōnggào, 方法 fāngfǎ

【双数】shuāngshù 正的偶数 positive even numbers

【双双】shuāngshuāng 成双成对的 in pairs:我男、女乒乓球队～获得冠军。Both our men's and women's ping-pong teams won the championship.

【双喜】shuāngxǐ 两件喜事(多指同时发生的 oft. simultaneous) double happiness:～临门。A double blessing has descended upon the house.

【双响】shuāngxiǎng (～儿 shuāngxiǎngr)一种爆竹,火药分装两截,点燃下截后发一声,升到空中后上截爆炸,又发一声。有的地区也叫二踢脚或两响。double-bang firecracker (which goes off twice, once on the ground and then again in the air); also 二踢脚 èrtījiǎo or 两响 liǎngxiǎng in some areas

【双向】shuāngxiàng 指双方互相(进行某种活动) two-way; bidirectional:～贸易 two-way trade|～服务 two-way service|～选择 two-way decision

【双薪】shuāngxīn 加倍的工资 double pay:发～ pay double salary

【双星】shuāngxīng ❶ 两个距离很近或彼此之间有引力关系的恒星叫做双星。用肉眼或望远镜能分清是两个星的叫做视双星;用分光的方法才能分清的叫做分光双星。双星中较亮的一颗叫主星,另一颗围绕主星旋转,叫伴星。double star; two stars that are very close or that gravitate towards each other. Those that can be observed with the eyes or a telescope are known as visual double stars, while those that can only be distinguished by their spectrum are known as spectrum double stars. The brighter of the double stars is called the principal star, while the other, rotating around the principal star, is the companion star. ❷ 指牛郎和织女两颗星 Altair and Vega

【双眼皮】shuāngyǎnpí (～儿 shuāngyǎnpír)沿着下缘有一条褶儿的上眼皮 double-folded eyelids

【双鱼座】shuāngyúzuò 黄道十二星座之一 Pisces, one of the 12 constellations; ☞ 黄道十二宫 huángdào shí'èrgōng on p. 851

【双语】shuāngyǔ 同时使用两种语言的 bilingual; using two languages simultaneously:～教育 bilingual education|～词典 bilingual dictionary

【双月刊】shuāngyuèkān 两个月出版一次的刊物 bimonthly; publication that is published every two months

【双职工】shuāngzhígōng 指夫妻二人都参加工作的职工 husband and wife both working; working couple

【双绉】shuāngzhòu 一种表面有绉纹的织物,常用生丝织成。质地柔软坚牢，主要用于妇女衣着。crepe de Chine; soft fabric with crinkles on the surface, usu. woven with raw silk and used as material for women's clothes

【双子座】shuāngzǐzuò 黄道十二星座之一 Gemini, one of the 12 constellations; ☞ 黄道十二宫 huángdào shí'èrgōng on p. 851

泷(瀧) shuāng 泷水(Shuāngshuǐ)，地名，在广东。今作双水。Shuangshui, name of a place in Guangdong Province; now spelled as 双水 Shuāngshuǐ
☞ lóng on p. 1250

骦 shuāng ☞ 骕骦 (sùshuāng) on p. 1833

鹴 shuāng ☞ 鹔鹴 (sùshuāng) on p. 1834

霜 shuāng ❶ 在气温降到 0℃ 以下时，接近地面空气中所含的水汽在地面物体上凝结成的白色冰晶 frost; covering of minute ice crystals formed on an object's surface from the vapour in the air near the ground as the temperature drops below zero ❷ 像霜的东西 frost-like powdery substance: 柿～ persimmon frost | 盐～ salt frosting ❸〈比喻 *fig*.〉白色 white; hoar: ～鬓(两鬓的白发) grey hair on the temples

【霜晨】shuāngchén 寒冷多霜的清晨 frosty morning

【霜冻】shuāngdòng 植物表面以及接近地面的空气温度迅速下降，使植物受到冻害的天气现象 frost; weather phenomenon in which plants suffer from frost damage because of a fast drop in temperature around the crops plant and on the soil surface

【霜害】shuānghài 农业上指由于霜冻造成的灾害 frost damage; (in agriculture) disaster caused by frost

【霜降】shuāngjiàng 二十四节气之一，在 10 月 23 日或 24 日 Frost's Descent, one of the 24 solar terms, usu. falling on October 23 or 24; ☞ 节气 jié·qi on p. 989 and 二十四节气 èrshísì jiéqì on p. 516

【霜期】shuāngqī 从第一年初霜起到第二年终霜止的时期 frost season; period from the first frost in the first year through the last frost in the second year

【霜天】shuāngtiān 指严寒的天空；寒冷的天(多指晚秋或冬天 usu. in late autumn or winter) frosty sky; freezing weather

孀 shuāng 指寡妇 widow: 孤～ orphan and widow | ～居 live as a widow | 烈士遗～ widow of a martyr

【孀妇】shuāngfù〈书 *fml*.〉same as 寡妇 guǎfù

【孀居】shuāngjū〈书 *fml*.〉守寡 live as a widow; live in widowhood: ～多年 live in widowhood for many years

骦 shuāng ☞骕骦 (sùshuāng) on p. 1833

礵 shuāng 地名用字 character esp. used in place names: 四～列岛 Sishuang Archipelago | 南～岛 Nanshuang Island | 北～岛 Beishuang Island(都在福建 all the above being in Fujian Province)

鹴 shuāng ☞ 鹔鹴 (sùshuāng) on p. 1833

shuǎng (ㄕㄨㄤˇ)

爽[1] shuǎng ❶ 明朗；清亮 bright; clear; crisp: 神清目～ uplifting to the mind and the eye | 秋高气～ clear and crisp autumn climate ❷ (性格)率直；痛快 (of sb.'s character) straightforward; open-hearted; frank: 豪～ forthright | 直～ straightforward ❸ 舒服；畅快 feel fine; comfortable: 身体不～ not feeling well | 人逢喜事精神～。Happy events always make people feel better.

爽[2] shuǎng 违背；差失 deviate: ～约 break an appointment | 毫厘不～ no deviation of the least bit | 屡试不～ be often tried and successful

【爽口】shuǎngkǒu 清爽可口 tasty and refreshing: 这个瓜吃着很～。This melon is very tasty and refreshing.

【爽快】shuǎng·kuai ❶ 舒适痛快 refreshed; comfortable: 洗个澡，身上～多了 feel much refreshed after a bath | 谈了这许多话，心里倒～了些。I feel relieved after talking things out so much. ❷ 直爽；直截了当 frank; straightforward; outright: 他是个～人。He is frank and straightforward. | 有什么事，就爽爽快快地说吧。Be frank and tell me if you have anything to say.

【爽朗】shuǎnglǎng ❶ 天气明朗，空气流通，使人感到畅快 (of weather) refreshingly clear and bright: 深秋的天空异常～。In late autumn the sky is crystal clear. | 户外比室内～得多。It's much clearer and brighter outdoors than indoors. ❷ 开朗；直爽 open-minded and straightforward: ～的笑声 hearty laughter | 这人很～，有说有笑。What a frank and open person, always talking and laughing.

【爽利】shuǎnglì 爽快；利落 brisk and neat; efficient and able: 办事～ be efficient and able in one's work | 动作～ be brisk and neat in action

【爽目】shuǎngmù 悦目 be pleasing to the eye: 清晰～ be clear and pleasing to the eye | 浅黄的楼房在蓝天的衬托下，显得格外～。The pale yellow building looks striking against the blue sky.

【爽气】shuǎngqì ❶〈书 *fml*.〉清爽的空气 cool and refreshing air ❷〈方 *dial*.〉same as 爽快 shuǎng·kuai: 她回答得十分～。She answered the question frankly.

S

【爽然】shuǎngrán 〈书 *fml.*〉茫然无主见的样子 be at a loss; confused: ～若失 not know what to do

【爽心】shuǎngxīn 心中清爽愉快 be refreshed and pleased: ～悦目 pleasing to both the eye and the mind

【爽性】shuǎngxìng same as 索性 suǒxìng

【爽约】shuǎngyuē 失约 fail to keep an appointment; break an appointment

【爽直】shuǎngzhí 直爽 straightforward: 性情～ straightforward disposition

塽 shuǎng 〈书 *fml.*〉高而向阳的地方 high and sunny place

shuí (ㄕㄨㄟˊ)

谁 shuí '谁' shéi 的又音 variant pronunciation for 谁 shéi

shuǐ (ㄕㄨㄟˇ)

水 shuǐ ❶ 最简单的氢氧化合物,化学式 H_2O。无色、无味、无臭的液体,在标准大气压下,冰点 0℃,沸点 100℃,4℃时密度最大,比重为 1。water; colourless, odourless, and tasteless liquid oxide of hydrogen (H_2O), which, under standard atmospheric pressure, freezes at 0℃ and boils at 100℃ and has a maximum density at 4℃ and a specific gravity of 1 ❷ 河流 river: 汉～ the Hanshui River | 淮～ the Huaishui River ❸ 指江、河、湖、海、洋 water; a general term for rivers, streams, lakes, seas, etc.: ～陆交通 land and water transportation | ～旱码头 water and land wharf | ～上人家 family living aboard a boat ❹ (～儿 shuǐr) 稀的汁 liquid: 墨～ ink | 药～ liquid medicine | 甘蔗的～儿很甜。The sap of sugar cane is very sweet. ❺ 指附加的费用或额外的收入 extra charges or incomes: 贴～ premium | 汇～ remittance fee | 外～ extra income ❻ 指洗的次数 times of washing: 这衣裳洗几～也不变色。These clothes do not fade despite having gone through several washings. ❼ (Shuǐ) 姓 a surname

【水坝】shuǐbà same as 坝 bà ①

【水泵】shuǐbèng 用来抽水或压水的泵,抽水的也叫抽水机 water pump; pump for drawing or pumping water; ☞ 泵 bèng on p. 94

【水笔】shuǐbǐ ❶ 写小楷用的毛较硬的毛笔。也指画水彩画的毛笔。stiff-bristled brush for Chinese calligraphy; paintbrush for watercolour painting ❷ 〈方 *dial.*〉自来水笔 fountain pen

【水表】shuǐbiǎo 记录自来水用水量的仪表,装在水管上,当用户放水时,表上指针转动指出通过的水量 water meter; instrument, usu. fitted on a water pipe, for indicating and recording the quantity of water passing through a particular outlet

【水兵】shuǐbīng 海军舰艇上士兵的统称 bluejacket; enlisted person serving on naval ships

【水波】shuǐbō 波浪 wave; ripple: ～不兴 without stirring a ripple | ～粼粼 clear waves

【水彩】shuǐcǎi 用水调和后使用的绘画颜料 watercolour; pigment mixed with water, esp. used for painting

【水彩画】shuǐcǎihuà 用水彩绘成的画 watercolour (painting); painting drawn with watercolour

【水草】shuǐcǎo ❶ 有水源和草的地方 place with water and grass: 牧民逐～而居。Herdsmen live where there is water and grass. ❷ 某些水生植物的通称,如浮萍、黑藻等 water plants, e.g. duckweed, black algae, etc.

【水产】shuǐchǎn 海洋、江河、湖泊里出产的动物、藻类等的统称,一般指有经济价值的,如各种鱼、虾、蟹、贝类、海带、石花菜等 aquatic products; general term for animals and algae of economic value produced in seas, rivers, and lakes, e.g. fish, shrimp, crabs, shellfish, kelp, agar, etc.

【水车】shuǐchē ❶ 使用人或畜力的旧式提水灌溉工具 water wagon; old-style bailing and irrigation tool using human or animal labour ❷ 以水流做动力的旧式动力机械装置,可以带动石磨、风箱等 waterwheel; old-style power device that rotates by the direct action of water, that can be used to drive a grinding mill, bellows, etc. ❸ 运送水的车 vehicle for transporting water ❹ 〈方 *dial.*〉救火车 fire truck

【水程】shuǐchéng 水路的远近 journey on waterways; voyage: 船行了六七里～就靠了岸。The boat pulled in after a three-kilometre journey.

【水到渠成】shuǐ dào qú chéng 水流到的地方自然成渠 where water flows, a channel is formed; 〈比喻 *fig.*〉条件成熟,事情自然成功 when conditions are ripe, success is inevitably achieved

【水道】shuǐdào ❶ 水流的路线,包括沟、渠、江、河等 watercourse, e.g. channel, dyke, river, stream, etc. ❷ 水路 waterway: 上海到天津打～走要两天。It takes two days to travel from Shanghai to Tianjin by water. ❸ 泳道 lanes in a swimming pool

【水稻】shuǐdào 种在水田里的稻,有粳稻和籼稻两大类 paddy; rice planting in paddy fields, usu. distinguished as round-grained rice and long-grained rice; ☞ 稻 dào on p. 401

【水滴石穿】shuǐ dī shí chuān 〈比喻 *fig.*〉力量虽小,只要坚持不懈,事情就能成功 despite weak power, unremitting efforts will lead to success; also 滴水穿石 dī shuǐ chuān shí

【水地】shuǐdì ❶ 利用灌溉系统浇水的耕地 irrigated land; field watered by an irrigation system; also 水浇地 shuǐjiāodì ❷ same as 水田 shuǐtián

【水电站】shuǐdiànzhàn 利用水力发电的机构 hydroelectric power station; installation that generates power using hydraulic power

【水貂】shuǐdiāo 哺乳动物，身体细长，四肢短，趾间有蹼，毛暗褐色，密而柔软，有光泽。善于潜入水底捕食鱼类和蛙等。皮毛珍贵，可以制衣帽等。mink; slender-bodied, short-limbed mammal that has partially webbed feet, shiny dark-brown fur and a soft thick coat, and dives into deep water to prey on fish and frogs, its fur being a valuable material for making coats or hats

【水碓】shuǐduì 利用水力舂米的器具 water-powered trip-hammer (for husking rice)

【水遁】shuǐdùn 从水里逃跑 escape by water

【水肥】shuǐféi 人粪尿等腐熟后加上水所成的肥料 liquid manure, made from adding water to discomposed night soil

【水粉】shuǐfěn ❶ 一种化妆品 a kind of cosmetic ❷〈方 *dial.*〉水浸过的粉条 soaked noodles made from beans or sweet potatoes

【水粉画】shuǐfěnhuà 用水调和粉质颜料绘成的画 gouache; picture painted with opaque watercolours

【水分】shuǐfèn ❶ 物体内所含的水 moisture content：～充足 rich in water | 植物靠它的根从土壤中吸收～。Plants absorb moisture from the soil through their roots. ❷〈比喻 *fig.*〉某一情况中夹杂的不真实的成分 exaggeration; situation in which untrue elements are included：他说的话里有很大～。His words are highly exaggerated.

【水垢】shuǐgòu same as 水碱 shuǐjiǎn

【水臌】shuǐgǔ〈中医 *Chin. med*〉指腹水 ascites

【水果】shuǐguǒ 可以吃的含水分较多的植物果实的统称，如梨、桃、苹果等 fruit; edible, succulent reproductive bodies of plants, e.g. pear, peach, apple, etc.

【水合】shuǐhé 物质跟水化合，如碳酸钠和十个水分子化合成碳酸钠的十水化合物，乙烯和水化合成乙醇 hydration; compound of water with some other substance, e.g. sodium carbonate and 10 water molecules form the decahydrate of sodium carbonate, and ethene and water put together beome ethanol; also 水化 shuǐhuà

【水鹤】shuǐhè 设在铁路旁边，给蒸汽机车加水的装置，是一个圆柱形的管子，上面弯下来的部分像鹤的头部，能左右旋转 standpipe; columniform pipe installed by a railway for supplying water to steam locomotives, its upper part bending downwards, resembling the head of a crane that can move left and right

【水红】shuǐhóng 比粉红略深而较鲜艳的颜色 bright pink; cerise

【水花】shuǐhuā (～儿 shuǐhuār) ❶ 水受到冲击而形成的许多小水泡；浪花 spray; water flying in small drops or particles upon hitting a surface：汽艇划破平静的湖面，船头堆起层层～。A motorboat streaked across the tranquil lake, its bow tossing up layer upon layer of spray. ❷〈方 *dial.*〉水痘 chickenpox; water pox：出～ suffer from chickenpox

【水患】shuǐhuàn same as 水灾 shuǐzāi

【水荒】shuǐhuāng 指水严重的缺乏 severe water shortage

【水火】[1] shuǐhuǒ ❶ 水和火两相矛盾 fire and water in contradiction to each other;〈比喻 *fig.*〉不能相容的对立物 two things diametrically opposed to each other：势如～ be opposed to each other like fire and water ❷ '水深火热'的略语 abbr. for 水深火热 shuǐ shēn huǒ rè;〈比喻 *fig.*〉灾难 calamity; extreme misery：拯救百姓于～之中 save the people from untold miseries

【水火】[2] shuǐhuǒ 指大小便（多见于早期白话 oft. in early vernacular）stool and urine

【水火无情】shuǐ huǒ wú qíng 指水灾和火灾来势凶猛，一点不容情 floods and fires occur with violent force and show no mercy

【水货】shuǐhuò 指通过水路走私的货物，泛指通过非正常途径进出口的货物 smuggled goods; goods imported or exported through illegal methods

【水碱】shuǐjiǎn 硬水煮沸后所含矿质附着在容器（如锅、壶等）内逐渐形成的白色块状或粉末状的东西，主要成分是碳酸钙、碳酸镁、硫酸镁等 thermonatrite; white lumps or powder formed from the minerals remaining on the insides of containers (e.g. pot, kettle, etc.) from boiling water, mainly composed of calcium carbonate, magnesium carbonate, and magnesium sulfate; also 水垢 shuǐgòu or 水锈 shuǐxiù

【水解】shuǐjiě 化合物跟水作用而分解，如淀粉水解生成葡萄糖 hydrolysis; decomposition of a chemical compound involving their reaction with the elements of water, e.g. starch turns into glucose upon decomposition

【水晶】shuǐjīng 纯粹的石英，无色透明，用来制光学仪器、无线电器材和装饰品等 crystal; pure quartz that is transparent and colourless, usu. used to make optical instruments, radio equipment, ornaments, etc.

【水晶宫】shuǐjīnggōng 神话里的龙王在水下居住的宫殿（in Chinese mythology）Crystal Palace of the Dragon King at the bottom of the sea

【水晶体】shuǐjīngtǐ 晶状体 crystalline lens

【水井】shuǐjǐng same as 井 jǐng ①

【水酒】shuǐjiǔ 很淡薄的酒（多用做谦辞，指请客时所备的酒 usu. used as expression of humility by a host when offering wine to guests) watery wine：请吃杯～。Please have a cup of

S

wine.

【水库】shuǐkù 拦洪蓄水和调节水流的水利工程建筑物,可以利用来灌溉、发电和养鱼 reservoir; water-conservancy work where currents are regulated, floods are controlled, and water is collected and kept in large quantities for the purposes of irrigation, power generation, and fish breeding

【水雷】shuǐléi 一种水中爆炸武器,由舰艇或飞机布设在水中,能炸毁敌方舰艇。种类很多,如漂雷、锚雷等。用于保卫领海或封锁港湾。(submarine) mine; submarine explosive weapon, esp. dropped by a ship or aircraft into the water to destroy enemy ships and safeguard a territorial sea or block a harbour, in many varieties, including the floating mine and the anchoring mine

【水力】shuǐlì 海洋、河流、湖泊的水流所产生的作功能力,是自然能源之一,可以用来做发电和转动机器的动力 water-power; hydraulic power; natural energy generated through the flow of seas, rivers, and lakes, usu. employed to generate electricity and move machinery

【水利】shuǐlì ❶ 利用水力资源和防止水的灾害 water conservancy; prevent floods by taking advantage of hydraulic resources ❷ 水利工程的简称 abbr. for 水利工程 shuǐlì gōngchéng: 兴修～ build water conservancy works

【水利工程】shuǐlì gōngchéng 利用水力资源和防止水的灾害的工程,包括防洪、排洪、蓄洪、灌溉、航运和其他水力利用工程 water conservancy project (or works); project for preventing floods and tapping hydraulic resources, including projects for controlling floods, draining off floods, storing flood water, irrigation, and shipping purposes; 简称 abbr. 水利 shuǐlì or 水工 shuǐgōng

【水利枢纽】shuǐlì shūniǔ 根据综合利用水力资源的要求,由各种不同作用的水利工程建筑所构成的整体。一般包括拦河坝、溢洪道、船闸、发电厂等。key water-control project; whole system of water-conservancy works established to meet the demand of comprehensive utilization of hydraulic resources, usu. consisting of dams, spillways, locks, power stations, etc.

【水淋淋】shuǐlīnlīn (～的 shuǐlīnlīn·de)形容物体上水往下滴 dripping wet; sopping wet: 他爬上岸来,浑身～的。He climbed onto the bank dripping wet.

【水灵】shuǐ·ling ❶ (食物)鲜美多汁而爽口 (of food) fresh and juicy: 肥城出产的桃儿很～。Peaches produced in Feicheng are fresh and juicy. ❷ (形状、容貌)漂亮而有精神 (of appearance) bright and beautiful; radiant and vivacious: 这小姑娘有两只又大又～的眼睛。This little girl has a pair of bright beautiful big eyes. | 牡丹花开得真～。The blooming peonies are really beautiful and vivacious.

【水流】shuǐliú ❶ 江、河等的统称 general term for rivers and streams ❷ 流动的水 current; flow: 河道经过疏浚,～畅通。The riverway was ensured smooth flowing after being dredged and deepened.

【水溜】shuǐliù 檐沟 eaves gutter

【水龙】[1] shuǐlóng 多年生草本植物,叶子互生,长椭圆形,有叶柄,花黄色。生在沼泽等浅水中。creeping water primrose (*Jussieua repens*); perennial herbal plant that has alternating oblong leaves with stalks, and yellow flowers, and grows in shallow waters such as marshes

【水龙】[2] shuǐlóng 救火用的引水工具,多用数条长的帆布输水管接成,一端有金属制的喷嘴,另一端和水源连接 fire hose; hose; water-drawing device designed for fire-fighting, usu. composed of several canvas tubes linked together, for conveying water with a metal spray nozzle at one end, while the other end is connected to a water source

【水龙头】shuǐlóngtóu 自来水管上的开头 (water) tap; faucet; fixture for regulating the flow of tap water from pipes

【水陆】shuǐlù ❶ 水上和陆地上 land and water: ～并进 proceed by both land and water | ～交通 land and water transportation ❷ 指山珍海味 delicacies from land and sea: ～俱陈 a feast with delicacies of every kind

【水鹿】shuǐlù 鹿的一种,身体大,耳朵大,颈较长,尾短,四肢长,全身深棕色带灰色,也有黄棕色的,臀部灰白色。雄的有角,粗大,长而有叉,鹿茸可入药。sambar (*Cervus unicolor*); black deer; large deer with big ears, a long neck, a short tail, and long limbs, its body being dark brown with a grey shade or yellow-brown, with a greyish white hip, the male having tall and thick three-pointed antlers, its hairy antlers used for medicine; also 马鹿 mǎlù or 麖 jīng

【水路】shuǐlù 水上的交通线 waterway; water route: 走陆路比～快。It's faster to travel by land than by water.

【水绿】shuǐlǜ 浅绿色 light green

【水轮机】shuǐlúnjī 涡轮机的一种,利用水流冲击叶轮转动,生产动力,是水力发电的主要动力装置,也可直接带动碾米机、磨粉机等 water turbine; turbine designed to generate dynamic power through the turning of waterwheels from the force of the current; major dynamic installation for generating hydroelectric power or driving rice mills, flour mills, etc.

【水落】shuǐluò 〈方 *dial.*〉檐沟 eaves gutter

【水落管】shuǐluòguǎn 把檐沟里的水引到地面的竖管,多用铁皮等制成 downpipe; standpipe drawing water from an eaves gutter to the ground, usu. made of sheet iron; also 雨水管

yǔshuǐguǎn

【水落石出】shuǐ luò shí chū 水落下去，石头就露出来。When the water subsides the rocks emerge.〈比喻 *fig.*〉真相大白(of sth. hidden) come to light.

【水煤气】shuǐméiqì 水蒸气通过炽热的焦炭而生成的气体，主要成分是一氧化碳和氢，有毒。用做燃料和化工原料。water gas; poisonous gaseous mixture that consists chiefly of carbon monoxide and hydrogen, that is usu. made by blowing stream through red-hot coals, used as a fuel or a raw material for the chemical industry

【水门】shuǐmén ❶ 安装在水管上的阀 water valve, a valve installed on a water pipe ❷〈方 *dial.*〉same as 水闸 shuǐzhá

【水门汀】shuǐméntīng〈方 *dial.*〉水泥，有时也指混凝土 cement or concrete

【水米无交】shuǐ mǐ wú jiāo〈比喻 *fig.*〉彼此毫无来往。特指居官清廉，跟百姓没有经济上的来往。have no relations or contact with each other; (of officials) be upright and accept no gifts from ordinary people

【水面】shuǐmiàn ❶ 水的表面 surface of the water: ～上漂着片片花瓣。Strewn petals were floating on the water surface. ❷ 水域的面积 area of a body of water: 我国可以养鱼的～很大。The waters suitable for breeding fish in our country cover a large area.

【水磨】shuǐmó 加水细磨 grind finely with water added: ～砖的墙 wall of finely polished bricks
☞ shuǐmò

【水磨工夫】shuǐmó gōng·fu〈比喻 *fig.*〉细致精密的工夫 patient and precise work

【水磨石】shuǐmóshí 一种人造石料，制作过程是用水泥、石屑或颜料等加水拌和，抹在建筑物的表面，相当凝固后，泼水并用金刚石打磨光滑 terrazzo; artificial stone stock of cement, stone fragments and pigment mixed with water, usu. plastered onto the surface of buildings, and given a high polish with diamond and water when hard set

【水墨画】shuǐmòhuà 指纯用水墨不着彩色的国画 ink and wash; traditional Chinese painting in simple ink and wash without application of colour

【水磨】shuǐmò 用水力带动的磨，多用来磨面 watermill; hydraulically driven mill, usu. used for grinding grain
☞ shuǐmó

【水能】shuǐnéng 水体运动产生的能量；水流中蕴藏的能量 water energy; energy generated in water flow or contained in currents

【水泥】shuǐní 一种建筑材料，灰绿色或棕色粉末，用石灰石、黏土等加工制成。加水拌和，干燥后坚硬。有的地区叫水门汀。cement; sage-green or brown powder of limestone and clay which is mixed with water and becomes hard when dry, and is used as a building material; also called 水门汀 shuǐméntīng in some areas

【水泥钉】shuǐnídīng 专门用来往水泥墙上钉的钢钉，硬度较高 masonry nail; high-rigidity steel nail esp. used on cement walls

【水碾】shuǐniǎn 用水力带动的碾子，多用来碾米 water-powered roller, usu. used for grinding grain

【水鸟】shuǐniǎo 在水面或水边栖息以及从水中捕取食物的鸟类的统称，如鹭鸶、野鸭、海鸥等 aquatic bird; water bird; any of the birds inhabiting water or shores, and obtaining its food from the water, e.g. bittern, widgeon, seagull, etc.

【水牛】shuǐniú 牛的一种。角很大，作新月形。毛灰黑色。暑天喜欢浸在水中。食物以青草为主。适于水田耕作。(water) buffalo (*Bubalus H. Smith*); dark-maned ox with large crescent horns that likes to stay in water on hot summer days, eats grass, and is adapted to paddy-field farming

【水牛儿】shuǐniúr〈方 *dial.*〉same as 蜗牛 wōniú

【水暖】shuǐnuǎn ❶ 锅炉烧出的热水通过暖气设备，散发热量而使室温增高的供暖方式 hot-water heating; mode of heat supply in which the hot water in a boiler emits heat and raises the indoor temperature through pipes and radiators ❷ 自来水和暖气设备的统称 water-and heat-supply equipment: ～工 plumber | ～设备 water- and heat-supply equipment

【水牌】shuǐpái 临时登记账目或记事用的漆成白色或黑色的木板或薄铁板。白色的也叫粉牌。black or white wooden board or thin iron plate for writing temporary accounts or records on; white ones are also known as 粉牌 fěnpái

【水疱】shuǐpào (～儿 shuǐpàor) 因病理变化，浆液在表皮里或表皮下聚积而成的黄豆大小的隆起 blister; bean-sized elevation of the epidermis containing watery liquid due to pathological changes

【水皮儿】shuǐpír〈方 *dial.*〉same as 水面 shuǐmiàn ①

【水平】shuǐpíng ❶ 跟水平面平行的 horizontal; level; parallel with the horizon: ～方向 horizontal direction ❷ 在生产、生活、政治、思想、文化、艺术、技术、业务等方面所达到的高度 standard; level; stature achieved in production, living, politics, thought, culture, art, skill, profession, etc.: 提高思想～和业务～ improve one's thinking and professional levels

【水平面】shuǐpíngmiàn 小范围内完全静止的水所形成的平面。也指跟这个平面平行的面。level surface; level; surface of entirely still water in a small sphere or any surface parallel to this surface

【水平线】shuǐpíngxiàn 水平面上的直线以及和水平面平行的直线 level line; any of the straight lines on or parallel to a level surface

【水平仪】shuǐpíngyí 测定水平面的仪器。由框架和装有乙醚或酒精的弧形玻璃管组成,管中留有气泡,气泡始终处于管的最高点。当水平仪处于水平位置时,气泡的位置在管上刻度的中间。spirit level; gradienter; water-level gauge; instrument for determining the levelness of a surface, usu. composed of a frame and an arc-shaped glass tube containing ether or alcohol, and having an air bladder at the summit of the tube at all times; when the gauge is at a level position, the air bladder is exactly at the middle of the calibrations on the tube; also 水准器 shuǐzhǔnqì

【水汽】shuǐqì 呈气态的水 water vapour; steam; gaseous water

【水枪】shuǐqiāng ❶ 水力采煤用的一种工具,一端有喷嘴,另一端接高压水源,水从水枪中喷射出来,能把煤层中的煤冲击下来 giant; (hydraulic) monitor; tool designed for hydraulic coal mining, connected to a high-pressure water source at one end as well as featuring a nozzle at the other end from which water is spurted out to force off the coal from coal beds ❷ 一种消防用具,由铜管和活塞构成,口小,能把水喷射到高处或远处 fire-fighting device consisting of a copper tube and a piston, and featuring a small nozzle that can spurt water high and far

【水禽】shuǐqín same as 水鸟 shuǐniǎo

【水情】shuǐqíng 水位、流量等的情况 conditions of water level, rate of flow, etc.

【水球】shuǐqiú ❶ 球类运动项目之一。球场为长方形的水池。分两队,每队七人。运动员在水中用一只手传球,把球射进对方球门算得分,得分多的获胜。water polo; goal-scoring ball game that is played in a quadrangular pool of water by two teams of seven swimmers each, with the objective of shooting a ball with one hand into the opponent's goal, where the higher-scoring team wins the game ❷ 水球运动使用的球,用皮革或橡胶等制成 ball used in the game; usu. made of leather or rubber

【水渠】shuǐqú 人工开凿的水道 canal; ditch; artificially excavated waterway

【水乳交融】shuǐ rǔ jiāo róng 水和乳汁融合在一起 blend of milk and water; milk mixed with water; 〈比喻 *fig.*〉关系非常融洽或结合十分紧密 (of relationships) well blended and perfectly harmonious

【水杉】shuǐshān 落叶大乔木,高达 35 米,叶子扁平,对生,花单性,球果近圆形,种子扁平。是世界上现存的稀有植物之一。metasequoia (*Metasequoia glyptostroboides*); large deciduous tree growing as high as 35 metres, with flat, opposing leaves, unisexual flowers, almost round strobiles, and flat seeds; a rare species in the world

【水上居民】shuǐshàng jūmín 在广东、福建、广西沿海港湾和内河上从事渔业或水上运输的居民,多以船为家 boat dwellers; people who live by fishing or water transport on inland rivers or in coastal harbours in Guangdong, Fujian, and Guangxi, and who dwell on boats; 旧称 formerly called 疍民 dànmín or 疍户 dànhù

【水上运动】shuǐshàng yùndòng 体育运动项目的一大类,包括在水上进行的各种运动,如游泳、跳水、划船运动、帆船运动等 aquatic sports; water sports; a category of sports, including various events, e.g. swimming, diving, rowing, sailing, etc.

【水筲】shuǐshāo 〈方 *dial.*〉水桶,多用木头或竹子制成 pail made of wood or bamboo strips; bucket

【水蛇】shuǐshé 生活在水边的蛇类的统称 water snake (*Enhydris*); snakes living by the water

【水蛇腰】shuǐshéyāo 指细长而腰部略弯的身材 slender stature featuring a slightly curving waist

【水深火热】shuǐ shēn huǒ rè 〈比喻 *fig.*〉人民生活处境异常艰难痛苦 (of people's living) an abyss of suffering; extreme misery and hardship

【水生植物】shuǐshēng zhíwù 植株的整体或部分浸没在水中,能适应水域环境的植物。包括水生藻类、水生蕨类和水生种子植物。如小球藻、苦草、莲、浮萍等。water (or aquatic) plant; hydrophyte; any of the plants wholly or partly growing in water, adaptable to water environment, including hydrobionic algae, ferns, and seed plants, e.g. chlorella, wild celery, lotus, duckweed, etc.

【水蚀】shuǐshí 由于水的冲击,岩石剥落,土壤被冲刷掉。多发生在山区、丘陵地带。erosion through the action of running water, causing rocks to be desquamated and soil to be washed out, usu. occurring in mountain areas and hilly terrain

【水势】shuǐshì 水流的势头 flow of water: ～湍急 rapid and turbulent flow

【水手】shuǐshǒu 船舶上负责舱面工作的普通船员 seaman; ordinary sailor in charge of the deck on ship

【水刷石】shuǐshuāshí 一种人造石料,制作过程是用水泥、石屑、小石子或颜料等加水拌和,抹在建筑物的表面,半凝固后,用硬毛刷蘸水刷去表面的水泥浆而使石屑或小石子半露 granitic plaster; man-made stone stock of cement, stone fragments, pebbles, and sometimes pigment, mixed with water, usu. plastered on building surface. When half solidified, the grout is brushed off the surface with a hard-bristled brush in order to reveal the stone fragments or pebbles. also 汰石子 tàishízǐ

【水塔】shuǐtǎ 自来水设备中增高水的压力的装置，是一种高耸的塔状构筑物，顶端有一个大水箱，箱内储水。水塔愈高，水的压力愈大，也就能把水送到更高的建筑物上。water tower; tall structure or installation for increasing water pressure in a water supply system, with a large tank at the top serving as a reservoir to store and deliver water to buildings at a required height. The higher the tower, the greater the water pressure.

【水獭】shuǐtǎ 哺乳动物，头部宽而扁，尾巴长，四肢短粗，趾间有蹼，毛褐色，密而柔软，有光泽。穴居在河边，昼伏夜出，善于游泳和潜水，吃鱼类和青蛙、水鸟等。皮毛厚而软。river otter (*Lutra Brunnich*); mammal that has a wide flat head, a long tail, short and thick limbs, webbed feet and dark brown, bushy, soft and shiny fur, lives in holes by the riverside, resting by day and coming out at night, is good at swimming and diving, and eats fish, frogs, aquatic birds, etc., its fur and hide being valuable materials for making coats, hats, etc.

【水田】shuǐtián 周围有隆起的田埂，能蓄水的耕地，多用来种植水稻 paddy field; arable field surrounded by ridges to store water, and usu. used for planting rice

【水汀】shuǐtīng〈方 *dial.*〉暖气 Chinese transliteration of the English word 'steam', meaning central heating

【水头】shuǐtóu ❶ 河流涨大水时洪峰到达的势头 flood peak; peak of flow ❷ 泛指水的来势 oncoming force of water: 打了一口～很旺的井 dug a well with plenty of water

【水土】shuǐtǔ ❶ 土地表面的水和土 water and soil on the surface of the earth: ～流失 soil erosion | 森林能保持～。Forests can help conserve water and soil. ❷ 泛指自然环境和气候 natural environment and climate: ～不服 unaccustomed to the climate of a new place; not acclimatized

【水土保持】shuǐtǔ bǎochí 用造林、种草、深耕、密植和修建梯田、沟渠、塘坝、水库等方法，蓄水分，保土壤，增加土地吸水能力，防止土壤被侵蚀冲刷 water and soil conservation; using methods including afforestation, grass planting, deep ploughing, close planting, building of terrace fields, canals and ditches, dykes and dams, and reservoirs, etc., in order to store water, conserve soil, strengthen the land's ability to absorb water, and protect soil from erosion and being washed away

【水土流失】shuǐtǔ liúshī 土地表面的肥沃土壤被水冲走或被风刮走 soil erosion; fertile soil on the earth's surface being swept away by water or blown away by wind

【水汪汪】shuǐwāngwāng（～的 shuǐwāngwāng·de）❶ 形容充满水的样子 full of water: 刚下过大雨，地里～的。A heavy rain had fallen, and the fields were flooded. ❷ 形容眼睛明亮而灵活 (of eyes) bright and intelligent: 小姑娘睁着～的大眼睛，好奇地看着我。The little girl gazed at me with curiosity, her big bright eyes open wide.

【水网】shuǐwǎng 指纵横交错的河湖港汊 web of rivers, rivulets, lakes and ponds: ～遍布 crisscrossed with rivers and lakes | 阳澄湖一带，是苏南著名的～地区。The basin of the Yangcheng Lake in southern Jiangsu Province is crisscrossed with rivers, rivulets, lakes and ponds.

【水位】shuǐwèi ❶ 江河、湖泊、海洋、水库等水面的高度（一般以某个基准面为标准）water level; altitude of the surface of rivers, lakes, seas, reservoirs, etc. (usu. with a certain base level as criterion) ❷ 地下水和地面的距离 distance between underground water and the earth's surface

【水文】shuǐwén 自然界中水的各种变化和运动的现象 hydrology; various phenomena concerning the changes and movements of water in nature: ～观测 hydrologic observation and survey

【水螅】shuǐxī 腔肠动物，身体圆筒形，褐色，口周围有触手，是捕食物的工具，体内有一个空腔。附着在池沼、水沟中的水草或枯叶上。大多雌雄同体，生殖方法有二：通常进行无性生殖（由身体长出芽体）；夏初和秋末进行有性生殖。hydra (*Hydra*); polyp; hermaphroditic coelenterate that typically has a brown hollow cylindrical body, with an opening at one end of a central mouth surrounded by tentacles as food catchers, and closed and attached at the other end to water grasses or withered leaves in ponds or marshes, and that reproduces either through parthenogenesis (producing gemma from the body itself) or by sexual reproduction in early summer and late autumn

【水洗布】shuǐxǐbù 一种经过特殊印染加工的纺织品 specially printed and dyed fabric

【水系】shuǐxì 河川流域内，干、支流的总体叫做水系。如嘉陵江、汉水、湘江、赣江等与长江干流组成长江水系。river system; hydrographic net; trunk and branches of a river valley as a whole, e.g. the Yangtze River system is composed of a trunk and branches such as the Jialing, Hanshui, Xiangjiang, and Ganjiang rivers

【水仙】shuǐxiān ❶ 多年生草本植物，地下鳞茎作卵圆形，叶子条形，伞状花序，花白色，中心黄色，有香味。供观赏，鳞茎和花可以入药。narcissus(*Narcissus*); daffodil; perennial herbal plant that has oval bulbs, strip-like leaves, and fragrant white flowers with yellow pistils in umbel. Planted ornamentally, its bulbs and flowers can also be used for medicine. ❷

这种植物的花 flower of this plant

【水险】shuǐxiǎn 水上运输事故的保险 marine insurance

【水线】shuǐxiàn 船壳外面与水平面的接触线 waterline; line, marked upon the outside of a ship, that corresponds with the surface of the water when the ship is afloat on an even keel

【水乡】shuǐxiāng 河流、湖泊多的地区 watery region; region rich in rivers and lakes: 江南～ water-bound town or country in the lower reaches of the Yangtze River

【水箱】shuǐxiāng 某些机械、交通运输工具或建筑物中盛水用的装置 water tank; water-storing device installed on a machine, vehicle, or building

【水泄不通】shuǐ xiè bù tōng 形容十分拥挤或包围得非常严密,好像连水都不能泄出 be so crowded or closely besieged that not even a drop of water could trickle through

【水榭】shuǐxiè 临水的供人游玩和休息的房屋 waterside pavilion (for sightseeing and resting)

【水星】shuǐxīng 太阳系九大行星之一,按离太阳由近而远的次序计为第一颗,绕太阳公转周期约 88 天,自转周期约 58.6 天 Mercury; planet nearest the sun, having a period of revolution of 88 days and a period of rotation of about 58.6 days ;(图见☞ figure for 太阳系 tàiyángxì on p. 1855)

【水性】shuǐxìng ❶ 游水的技能 swimming skill: 他的～不错,能游过长江。He is a good swimmer and can cross the Yangtze River by swimming. ❷ 指江河湖海的深浅、流速等方面的特点 depth, currents and other characteristics of a river, lake, etc.: 熟悉长江～ be familiar with the characteristics of the Yangtze River

【水性杨花】shuǐxìng yánghuā 形容妇女作风轻浮,用情不专一 (of a woman) of easy virtue; promiscuous

【水袖】shuǐxiù 表演古典戏曲、舞蹈的演员所穿服装的袖端拖下来的部分,用白色绸子或绢制成 water sleeves (double white silk sleeves attached to the cuffs of traditional Chinese operas or dance costumes)

【水锈】shuǐxiù ❶ same as 水碱 shuǐjiǎn ❷ 器皿盛水日久留下的痕迹 watermark; mark left on a water vessel with the passage of time

【水循环】shuǐxúnhuán 海洋、陆地、大气之间水分的大规模交换,如海面蒸发的水气进入大气,被气流带到陆地上空,以雨雪形式降落地面,汇入河流,流回海洋 hydrologic cycle; water cycle; continual large-scale exchange of water between the seas, land and atmosphere. For example, the hydrosphere evaporation from the sea joins the atmosphere and is carried by air currents to the skies over the land, and then falls as rain or snow onto the ground, eventually merging into rivers and flowing back into the sea.

【水压机】shuǐyājī 利用水传递压力的机器,多用来冲压金属 hydraulic punch; water-powered machine for conveying pressure, usu. used to punch metal

【水烟】shuǐyān 用水烟袋抽的细烟丝 shredded tobacco for water pipes

【水烟袋】shuǐyāndài 一种用铜、竹等制的吸烟用具,烟通过水的过滤而吸出,吸时发出咕噜噜的响声 water pipe; smoking utensil made of copper or bamboo through which smoke is filtered through water, emitting a gurgling sound; also 水烟筒 shuǐyāntǒng or 水烟斗 shuǐyāndǒu

【水眼】shuǐyǎn 泉眼 mouth of a spring

【水舀子】shuǐyǎo·zi 舀水的勺子 dipper; scoop (for ladling water)

【水银】shuǐyín 汞的通称 general term for 汞 gǒng

【水银灯】shuǐyíndēng 一种产生强光的照明装置。把水银充入真空的硬质玻璃管或石英玻璃管内,通电后,水银蒸气放电而发出强光。多用于摄影、晒图和街道照明等。mercury-vapour lamp; illumination device that features hard glass or quartz-glass vacuum tube filled with mercury, and, when electrified, discharges strong light through the mercury vapour, usu. used for photography, blueprint making, and street illumination; also 汞灯 gǒngdēng

【水印】[1] shuǐyìn 指我国传统的用木刻印刷绘画作品的方法。调和颜料用水,不用油质,跟一般彩印法不同,所以特称为水印。watercolour block-printing; traditional Chinese method of printing pictures using woodcarvings, in which pigments are mixed with water instead of the oil used in ordinary colour printing; also 水印木刻 shuǐyìn-mùkè

【水印】[2] shuǐyìn (～儿 shuǐyìnr) ❶ 在造纸生产过程中用改变纸浆纤维密度的方法制成的有明暗纹理的图形或文字 image or letters revealed overtly or covertly, formed by changing the density of pulp fibres in the process of paper-making ❷ 水渗在某些物体上,干后留下的痕迹 watermark; mark left by water dropped on an object that reveals itself when the object is dry

【水印】[3] shuǐyìn〈方 *dial.*〉(～儿 shuǐyìnr)〈旧时 *old*〉商店的正式图章 formal seal of a shop

【水域】shuǐyù 指海、河、湖(从水面到水底)的一定范围 river valley; water area; body of water; expanse of sea, river, lake, etc. (from the surface to the bottom)

【水源】shuǐyuán ❶ 河流发源的地方 source of a river ❷ 民用水、工业用水或灌溉用水的来源 source of water (for daily use, industry, or irrigation)

【水运】shuǐyùn 用船舶、木筏等在江河、湖泊、海洋上运输 water transport; transport on rivers, lakes, or seas by boat, ship, raft, etc.

【水灾】shuǐzāi 因久雨、山洪暴发或河水泛滥等原因而造成的灾害 flood; inundation; disaster caused by an extended period of continuous rain, mountain torrents, or overflowing of a river, etc.

【水葬】shuǐzàng 处理死人遗体的一种方法，把尸体投入水中，任其漂流，让鱼类吃掉 water burial; method of disposing of corpses in which the body is thrown into water and left to float or be eaten by fish

【水藻】shuǐzǎo 生长在水里的藻类植物的统称，如水绵、褐藻植物 algae; phycophyta growing in water, e.g. spirogyra and alginic plants

【水泽】shuǐzé 多河湖沼泽的地方 water-bound country; region with many rivers, lakes and marshes

【水闸】shuǐzhá 修建在提坝中用来控制河渠水流的水工建筑物。调节水闸开闭的大小或高低可以改变通过的水量。常见的水闸有拦河闸、分洪闸、进水闸、排水闸、挡潮闸等。sluice; water-gate; water-conservancy works built on a dam to control and change the flow of a river by regulating the width and height of the opening, e.g. barrage, flood-diversion sluice, inlet gate, drainage gate, tide lock, etc.

【水涨船高】shuǐ zhǎng chuán gāo〈比喻 *fig.*〉事物随着它所凭借的基础的提高而提高 when the water rises the boat grows tall; sth. will rise when the foundation it rests on rises; 涨 also put as 长 zhǎng

【水蒸气】shuǐzhēngqì 气态的水。常压下液态的水加热到 100℃ 时就开始沸腾，迅速变成水蒸气。steam; water vapour; water in gaseous form that evaporates when water boils by being heated to 100℃ under atmospheric pressure

【水至清则无鱼】shuǐ zhì qīng zé wú yú《大戴礼记·子张问入官篇》：'水至清则无鱼，人至察则无徒'。水太清了，鱼就无法生存，要求别人太严了，就没有伙伴。现在有时用来表示对人或物不可要求太高。*Dai De's Book of Rites · Zi Zhang's Questions on Officialdom* (of the Western Han Dynasty): 'Water that is too clean has few fish; one who is too critical has few friends.' This saying is oft. used to suggest one should not demand too much of people or things. also 水清无鱼 shuǐ qíng wú yú

【水质】shuǐzhì 水的质量(多就食用水的纯净度而言) water quality (purity of drinking water): 保护环境，改善～ protect the environment and improve water quality

【水蛭】shuǐzhì 蛭纲动物，体狭长而扁，后端稍阔，黑绿色。生活在池沼或水田中，吸食人畜的血液。leech(*Hirudinea*); dark-green hirudinean animal that typically has a long, narrow and flat body slightly broader at the end, and lives in ponds, marshes, or paddy fields by feeding on the blood of people and livestock

【水中捞月】shuǐ zhōng lāo yuè ☞ 海底捞月 hǎi dǐ lāo yuè on p. 755

【水肿】shuǐzhǒng 由于皮下组织的间隙有过量的液体积蓄而引起的全身或身体的一部分肿胀的症状 oedema; dropsy; swelling in a part of or all over the body due to an abnormal excessive accumulation of serous fluid in the sinuses between subcutaneous tissues; also 浮肿 fúzhǒng

【水准】shuǐzhǔn ❶ 地球各部分的水平面 horizontal planes at different parts on the earth ❷ same as 水平 shuǐpíng ②

【水准仪】shuǐzhǔnyí 利用水平视线直接测定地球表面两点间高度差的仪器，主要由望远镜和水平仪构成 surveyor's level; instrument designed to determine the difference in height between two points on the earth's surface by using the horizontal line of sight, usu. composed of a telescope and a gradienter

【水族】shuǐzú 我国少数民族之一，分布在贵州 the Shui people, one of China's minority peoples mainly living in Guizhou Province

【水族】Shuǐzú 生活在水中的动物，一般指形体较大行动较活跃的 aquatic animals; generally refers to large-bodied and agile animals living in water: ～馆 aquarium

【水钻】shuǐzuàn 指人造钻石 artificial diamond

shuì (ㄕㄨㄟˋ)

说 shuì 用话劝说使人听从自己的意见 try to persuade others to accept one's own view: 游～ canvass for
☞ shuō on p. 1808 and yuè on p. 2372

帨 shuì〈古时 *arch.*〉佩巾，像现在的手绢儿 piece of cloth similar to handkerchief

税 shuì ❶ 国家向征税对象按税率征收的货币或实物 tax; duty; sum of money or goods levied by the state on persons according to a tax rate: 农业～ industrial duty | 营业～ business tax | 纳～ pay a tax ❷ (Shuì) 姓 a surname

【税单】shuìdān 税收部门开给交税人的纳税收据 tax receipt; duty memo; receipt of payment of tax issued by revenue authorities to a taxpayer

【税额】shuì'é 按税率缴纳的税款数额 amount of tax to be paid according to the tax rate

【税法】shuìfǎ 国家税收的法规 (national) tax law

【税利】shuìlì 指企业单位向有关部门上缴的税款和利润 taxes and profits turned over by enterprises to the departments concerned

【税率】shuìlǜ 税收条例所规定的对某种课税对象征税时计算税额的比率 tax rate; rate of

taxation; tariff rate; rate stipulated in tax regulations, according to which the amount of tax to be levied is determined

【税卡】shuìqiǎ〈旧时 *old*〉为收税而设置的检查站或岗哨 checkpoint or a post for tax collection

【税收】shuìshōu 国家征税所得到的收入 tax revenue; income gained by the state through taxation

【税务】shuìwù 关于税收的工作 taxation affairs:～局 tax administration

【税则】shuìzé 征税的规则和实施条例 tax regulations; rules and implementation regulations of taxation

【税制】shuìzhì 国家税收的制度（state）tax system

【税种】shuìzhǒng 国家税收的种类，如农业税、工商业税 tax category, e.g. agricultural tax, industrial and commercial tax

睡 shuì 睡觉 sleep:早～早起 go to bed early and get up early|～着了 fell asleep

【睡袋】shuìdài 袋状的被子，供婴儿、幼儿或露宿的人使用 sleeping bag; bag-like quilt esp. for babies, children, or those camping out: 鸭绒～ eider-down sleeping bag

【睡觉】shuì//jiào 进入睡眠状态 sleep:该～了。It's time to go to bed.|睡了一觉 had a sleep

【睡懒觉】shuì lǎnjiào 指人贪睡，不爱起床（多指早晨晚起）be fond of sleeping and be reluctant to get up in the morning; get up late; sleep in:他就爱～，要叫几次才起床。He loves to sleep in and usually does not get up until he has been called several times.

【睡梦】shuìmèng 指睡熟的状态 sleep; slumber; be asleep:一阵敲门声把他从～中惊醒了。He was roused from his sleep by a heavy pounding on the door.

【睡眠】shuìmián 抑制过程在大脑皮层中逐渐扩散并达到大脑皮层下部各中枢的生理现象。睡眠能恢复体力和脑力。sleep; physiological phenomenon in which the process of inhibition in the pineal gradually diffuses and reaches the central nerves at the bottom of the pineal gland. Sleep can help restore the physical and mental powers of the body.

【睡魔】shuìmó〈比喻 *fig.*〉强烈的睡意 extreme sleepiness

【睡乡】shuìxiāng 指睡眠状态 the state of sleep:进入～ fall asleep

【睡眼】shuìyǎn 要睡或刚睡醒时的呈蒙眬神态的眼睛 drowsy eyes (of a person who is sleepy or just awake):～惺忪 eyes still heavy with sleep; eyes still fogged with sleep

【睡意】shuìyì 想睡觉的感觉 sleepiness; drowsiness; feeling or a readiness to fall asleep:～蒙眬 be drowsy|已经半夜了，我一点儿～也没有。It was already the middle of the night, but I was not sleepy at all.

shǔn（ㄕㄨㄣˇ）

吮 shǔn 吮吸；嘬 suck:～乳 suck milk|～痈舐痔 kiss sb.'s ass

【吮吸】shǔnxī 把嘴唇聚拢在乳头或其他有小口儿的物体上吸取东西。现多用于比喻。suck; draw sth. from a nipple or a small opening into the mouth through a suction force produced by gathered lips, often used figuratively:剥削阶级长期残酷地～着劳动人民的血汗。The exploiting classes have been cruelly sucking the blood of the labouring people for a long time.

【吮痈舐痔】shǔn yōng shì zhì 给人嘬痈疽的脓，舔痔疮 lick sb.'s ulcers and piles;〈比喻 *fig.*〉不择手段地谄媚拍马 debase oneself in trying to please sb. important or powerful; kiss sb.'s ass

楯 shǔn〈书 *fml.*〉阑干 railing
☞ dùn on p. 497

shùn（ㄕㄨㄣˋ）

顺 shùn ❶ 向着同一个方向（跟'逆'相对 as opposed to 'against'）in the same direction as; with:～风 (go) with the wind|～流而下 go downstream ❷ 依着自然情势（移动）；沿（着）along:～大道走 travel along the main road|水～着山沟流。Water runs along the ravine. ❸ 使方向一致；使有条理次序 put in order; put (sth.) in the proper sequence:把船～过来，一只一只地靠岸停下。Arrange the boats neatly, berthing them one by one.|这篇文章还得～一～。This essay needs polishing. ❹ 趁便；顺便 if convenient; at one's convenience; conveniently; on the way:～手关门。Close the door behind you.|～嘴说了出来 speak out offhandedly ❺ 适合；如意 fall in with; suit; agree with:～心 satisfactory|～眼 pleasing to the eye|不～他的意 be not as he wishes ❻ 顺利 smooth:～遂 as one wishes|这些年一直很～ has been going smoothly in recent years ❼ 依次 in sequence:～延 postpone ❽ 顺从 obey; yield to; act in submission to:归～ cross over and pledge allegiance|百依百～ docile and obedient ❾ (Shùn)姓 a surname

【顺变】shùnbiàn〈书 *fml.*〉顺应变化或变故 conform to changes or unforeseen events:节哀～ restrain one's grief and adjust to a catastrophic situation|～达权 conform to any changes according to the circumstances

【顺便】shùnbiàn（～儿 shùnbiànr）乘做某事的方便（做另一事）(do sth.) in addition to what one is doing, without much extra effort; conveniently; on the way:我是下班打这儿过，～

来看看你们。I drop in to see you guys on my way home from work.

【顺差】shùnchā 对外贸易上输出超过输入的贸易差额(跟'逆差'相对 as opposed to 'deficit') (in the international trade) favourable balance; surplus; exports exceeding imports

【顺产】shùnchǎn 医学上指胎儿头朝下经母体阴道自然娩出(区别于'难产'as compared with 'difficult labour') eutocia; natural labour; normal childbirth; childbirth process in which the embryo is naturally delivered with the head coming out first from the vagina of the mother

【顺畅】shùnchàng 顺利通畅,没有阻碍 smooth and easy; unhindered:水流~。Water runs smoothly.|交通~ smooth-moving traffic|行文~ easy style of writing

【顺次】shùncì 挨着次序 in order; in succession:~排列 be arranged in proper sequence

【顺从】shùncóng 依照别人的意思,不违背,不反抗 be obedient to (sb.); submit to; yield to; not violate or resist

【顺带】shùndài 顺便;捎带 in passing:探亲回来~捎点土产品。Bring me some local products in passing when you come back from a visit to your family.

【顺当】shùn·dang same as 顺利 shùnlì:问题解决得圆满、~。The problem was solved smoothly and to the satisfaction of all parties.|这几年日子过得顺顺当当。Life has been smooth these years.

【顺导】shùndǎo 顺着正常的发展趋向加以引导 guide or steer (a movement, etc.) along its proper course

【顺道】shùndào (~儿 shùndàor) same as 顺路 shùnlù:途经那里,~去看望一下老同学 look in to see a former schoolmate along the way

【顺耳】shùn'ěr (话)合乎心意,听着舒服 pleasing to the ear:这话听着~。This sentence is pleasing to the ear.|不能只听~的话,不~的也要听。You shouldn't listen only to what pleases you; you must listen to displeasing things as well.

【顺风】shùnfēng 车、船等行进的方向跟风向相同。也常作为祝人旅途顺利、平安的吉祥话 (of vehicles, ships, etc.) have a favourable wind; travel or sail with the wind; also used as auspicious words in wishing sb. a smooth, safe journey:今天~,船走得很快。Thanks to favourable winds today, the ship sailed very fast.|祝你一路~。Have a safe journey!

【顺风吹火】shùn fēng chuī huǒ〈比喻 *fig.*〉费力不多,事情容易做 it's like stoking the fire with the wind — get things done without much effort

【顺风耳】shùnfēng'ěr ❶ 旧小说中指能听到很远声音的人。也比喻消息灵通的人 (in classical Chinese novels) person who can hear voices a long way off; (fig.) well-informed person ❷ 旧式话筒,用铜管接成,嘴接触的地方小,末端大 old-type megaphone composed of copper tubes, small at the end near the mouth and big at the other

【顺风转舵】shùn fēng zhuǎn duò〈比喻 *fig.*〉顺着情势改变态度(多含贬义 usu. derog.) take one's cue from changing conditions; also 随风转舵 suí fēng zhuǎn duò

【顺服】shùnfú 顺从;服从 obey; yield to:人心~ public obedience|我只好~地跟在他身后。I had no choice but to follow him obediently.

【顺杆儿爬】shùn gānr pá〈比喻 *fig.*〉迎合别人的心意、言语、要求等说话或行事 speak or act to cater to sb.'s intentions, words or demands so as to please him (or her)

【顺和】shùn·he (话语、态度等)平顺缓和 (of words, attitude, etc.) gentle; affable:语气~ in a gentle tone|态度~ affable attitude

【顺脚】shùnjiǎo (~儿 shùnjiǎor) ❶ 趁车马等本来要去某个地方的方便(搭人或运货) hitch-hike:~捎回来一千斤化肥 take back 500 kg. of chemical fertilizer by hitch-hiking ❷ same as 顺路 shùnlù

【顺境】shùnjìng 顺利的境遇 easy or favourable circumstances:他中年以后,渐入~。He gradually slipped into easier circumstances in his middle age.

【顺口】shùnkǒu ❶ (词句)念着流畅 (of words) read smoothly:经他这样一改,念起来就特别~了。This reads more smoothly after being polished by him. ❷ 没有经过考虑(说出、唱出) say or sing offhandedly without thinking:~答音儿(随声附和) echo what others say ❸ (~儿 shùnkǒur)(食品)适合口味 (of food) suit one's taste:这个菜他吃着很~儿。This dish is to his taste.

【顺口溜】shùnkǒuliū 民间流行的一种口头韵文,句子长短不等,纯用口语,念起来很顺口 doggerel; jingle; popular colloquial verse that is irregular in length of lines and reads smoothly

【顺理成章】shùn lǐ chéng zhāng 形容写文章或做事条理清楚 (of writing an article or dealing with a matter) follow a rational, clear line; flow logically; put things in perspective

【顺利】shùnlì 在事物的发展或工作的进行中没有或很少遇到困难 smooth; without a hitch; (in the development of an event or the progress of work) never or seldom face difficulties:工作~ work smoothly

【顺溜】shùn·liu〈方 *dial.*〉❶ 有次序,不参差 orderly; tidy:她解开辫子,把头发梳~了,又重新编好。She loosened her braid, combed her hair neatly, and then braided it again.|这篇小文章写得很~。This essay was written neatly. ❷ 通畅顺当;没有阻拦 smooth; easy, without a hitch:这几年日子过得很~。In re-

S

cent years, life has gone very smoothly. ❸ 顺从听话 obedient; agreeable: 这几个人中间就数他脾气好,比谁都~。Of these guys, he has the best temperament and is more agreeable than any of the others.

【顺路】shùnlù (~儿 shùnlùr) ❶ 顺着所走的路线(到另一处) on the way (to somewhere else): 她在区里开完会,~到书店看了看。She stopped in at a bookstore on her way back from a meeting with the district government. ❷ 指道路没有曲折阻碍,走着方便 be a direct route; convenient route with no detours or obstacles: 这么走太绕远儿,不~。This is not a direct route, but a long way around. ‖ also 顺道儿 shùndàor or 顺脚 shùnjiǎo

【顺民】shùnmín 指归附外族侵略者或归附改朝换代后的新统治者的人(贬义 derog.) docile citizens who submit to the authority of a new regime or invaders

【顺势】shùnshì ❶ 顺着情势;趁势 take advantage of a circumstance or a trend: 见有人先退场,他也~离去。Seeing somebody exit first, he left too. ❷ 顺便;趁便 conveniently; in passing: 做午饭的时候~多加了一碗米,晚饭就不用做了。I added an extra bowl of rice as I cooked lunch, so that I wouldn't have to cook supper.

【顺手】shùnshǒu (~儿 shùnshǒur) ❶ 做事没有遇到阻碍;顺利 smooth; without a hitch; without difficulty: 事情办得相当~。It was done without a hitch.|开始试验不很~,也是很自然的。It is not surprising that an experiment will run into a snag at the beginning. ❷ 很轻易地一伸手;随手 conveniently; easily: 他~从水里捞上一颗菱角来。He easily grabbed a water chestnut from the water. ❸ 顺便;捎带着 (do sth.) as a natural sequence; simultaneously: 院子扫完了,~儿也把屋子扫一扫。After sweeping the courtyard, you may as well clean the rooms.

【顺手牵羊】shùn shǒu qiān yáng 〈比喻 *fig.*〉顺便拿走人家的东西 walk off with sth.; pick up sth. on the sly

【顺水】shùn//shuǐ 行驶的方向跟水流方向一致(跟'逆水'相对 as opposed to 'against the current') downstream; with the current: ~而下 go downstream|~推舟 push the boat along the current

【顺水人情】shùn shuǐ rénqíng 不费力的人情;顺便给人的好处 favour done at little or no cost

【顺水推舟】shùn shuǐ tuī zhōu 〈比喻 *fig.*〉顺应趋势办事 push the boat along the current; take advantage of a situation or trend to achieve a goal

【顺遂】shùnsuì 事情进行顺利,合乎心意 (of things) go one's way; go well; go smoothly: 诸事~。Everything is going smoothly.

【顺藤摸瓜】shùn téng mō guā 〈比喻 *fig.*〉沿着发现的线索追究根底 track down sb. or sth. by following clues

【顺心】shùn//xīn 合乎心意 be satisfactory: 诸事~。All is well.

【顺序】shùnxù ❶ 次序 order; sequence: ~紊乱 disorder|~颠倒 reverse order ❷ 顺着次序 in proper order; in turn; in sequence: ~前进 advance in sequence|~退场 exit in turn

【顺延】shùnyán 顺着次序向后延期 postpone; put off following the order: 划船比赛定于7月9日举行,遇雨~。The boat race is scheduled for July 9 and subject to postponement in case of rain.

【顺眼】shùnyǎn 看着舒服 be an eyeful; pleasing to the eye: 这身打扮,叫人看着不~。This style of dress is offensive to the eye.

【顺意】shùn//yì 顺心;如意 satisfactory; as one wishes: 他遇到了不~的事。He encountered unexpected mishaps.|做什么事都得顺他的意 must do everything as he wishes

【顺应】shùnyìng 顺从;适应 comply with; conform to: ~历史发展潮流 go with the tide of historical development

【顺治】Shùnzhì 清世祖(爱新觉罗福临)年号(公元1644—1661) title of the reign of Aisin Gioro Fulin (1644-1661), first emperor of the Qing Dynasty

【顺嘴】shùnzuǐ (~儿 shùnzuǐr) same as 顺口 shùnkǒu ①②

舜 Shùn 传说中上古帝王名 legendary sage king in China's remote antiquity

瞬 shùn 眼珠儿一动;一眨眼 wink; twinkling: 转~ twinkling|~间 instantaneous|~将结束 will be finished in a moment|一~即逝 disappear in a flash

【瞬间】shùnjiān 转眼之间 in the twinkling of an eye: 飞机飞上天空,~即逝。The aircraft flew towards the sky and instantly disappeared.

【瞬时】shùnshí 一瞬间 instantaneous

【瞬息】shùnxī 一眨眼一呼吸的短时间 in the momentary twinkling of an eye or a breath: 一颗流星划过天空,~便消失了。A meteor streaked across the sky and disappeared in the twinkling of an eye.

【瞬息万变】shùnxī wàn biàn 形容极短的时间内变化快而多 fast and myriad changes take place in a very short period

shuō (ㄕㄨㄛ)

说 shuō ❶ 用话来表达意思 speak; say; express oneself by words: 我不会唱歌,只~了个笑话。Since I can't sing, I just told a joke. ❷ 解释 explain: 一~就明白 catch on as soon as told ❸ 言论;主张 doctrine; theory: 学~ theory|著书立~ write books and establish a theory | 有此一～ there's such a theory ❹ 责备;批评 scold: 挨～了 be scolded | 爸爸～了他几句。His father gave him a scolding. ❺ 指说合;介绍 act as matchmaker: ～婆家 find a husband for her ❻ 意思上指 refer to; indicate: 他这段话是～谁呢? Who did his remarks refer to?

☞ shuì on p. 1805 and yuè on p. 2372

【说白】shuōbái 戏曲、歌剧中除唱词部分以外的台词 spoken parts of stage lines in an opera

【说部】shuōbù 〈旧指 *old*〉小说以及关于逸闻、琐事之类的著作 novels and anecdotal works, funny episodes, etc.

【说不得】shuō·bu·de ❶ 不能说;说不出口 unspeakable; unmentionable: 她骂得太难听了,～。She shouted in unmentionable foul-mouthed utterings. ❷ 无从说起 have no way of speaking: 他家的家务矛盾,～。It's hard to find a way to talk about the internal contradictions in his family. ❸〈方 *dial.*〉没有什么话可说 have nothing to say: ～,只好亲自走一趟。There's nothing I can say; I just have to go there personally.

【说不过去】shuō·bu guòqù 指不合情理;无法交代 cannot be justified or explained away: 你这样对待人家,太～了。It's unjustifiable for you to treat them this way.

【说不来】shuō·bu lái ❶ 双方思想感情不合,谈不到一起 cannot get along (with sb.) ❷〈方 *dial.*〉不会说 not know how to put it

【说不上】shuō·bu shàng ❶ 因了解不够、认识不清而不能具体地说出来 cannot say; cannot tell the details because of a lack of knowledge: 他也～是乡间美呢,还是城市美。He cannot say which is more beautiful, the countryside or the city. | 他也～到农场去的路怎么走。He also cannot tell you the way to the farm. ❷ 因不成理由或不可靠而无须提到或不值得提 have no ... to speak of; not worth mentioning because of unconvincing or unreliable reasons: 你这些话都～。These words of yours are not worth mentioning. | 这都是封建统治者捏造的话,～什么史料价值。These words were fabricated by the feudal rulers and have no historical value to speak of.

【说长道短】shuō cháng dào duǎn 评论别人的好坏是非 gossip

【说唱】shuōchàng 指有说有唱的曲艺,如大鼓、相声、弹词等 ballard-singing; folk art form consisting mainly of talking and singing, e.g. comic dialogue, storytelling with drum accompaniment, fiddle ballads in southern Chinese dialects, etc.

【说唱文学】shuōchàng wénxué 韵文散文兼用,可以连讲带唱的文艺形式,如古代的变文和诸宫调,现代的评弹和大鼓 a genre of popular literature partly in verse and partly in prose, e.g. Suzhou storytelling and ballad-singing, and modern storytelling and ballad-singing with drum accompaniment; also 讲唱文学 jiǎngchàng wénxué

【说穿】shuōchuān 用话揭露;说破(真相) tell what sth. really is; reveal (the truth); disclose: 他的心事被老伴儿～了。His concerns were disclosed by his wife.

【说辞】shuō·cí 辩解或推托的理由 excuse; pretext: 不妨把事儿挑明了,看他还有什么～。We might as well lay it open, and see if he still has any excuse.

【说道】shuōdào 说(小说中多用来直接引进人物说的话 used in novels to introduce direct speech of characters) say: 校长～,'应该这么办!' 'It should be done this way!' said the principle.

【说…道…】shuō…dào… 分别嵌用相对或相类的形容词、数词等表示各种性质的说话 [followed by contrasting adjectives, numerals, etc. respectively to denote speaking of different characteristics]: ～长～短 talk about right and wrong of other people | ～三～四 gossip about | ～黑～白(任意评论) remark on sth. or sb. at will | ～东～西(尽情谈论各种事物) talk about anything one likes | ～亲～热(说亲近话) have an intimate talk; sweet talk | ～千～万(话说得很多) say a lot

【说道】shuō·dao 〈方 *dial.*〉❶ 用话表达 say; tell: 你把刚才讲的在会上～～,让大家讨论讨论。Speak at the meeting about what you said just now, then everyone can discuss it. ❷ 商量;谈论 talk over; discuss: 我跟他～～再作决定。I'll talk it over with him before making a decision. ❸ (～儿 shuō·daor) 名堂;道理 reason: 他为什么突然改变主意,这里头肯定有～。There must be a reason for his sudden change of mind.

【说得过去】shuō·de guòqù 大体上合乎情理;还能令人满意 be justifiable on the whole; be generally passable: 情面上～ be justified in one's feelings | 这个活儿我做得还～吧。The job I did is passable, isn't it?

【说得来】shuō·de lái ❶ 双方思想感情相近,能谈到一块儿 can get along; be on good terms; (of two sides) be close to each other in views and sentiments: 找一个跟他～的人去动员他。Find someone who is on good terms with him to persuade him. ❷〈方 *dial.*〉会说 have a glib tongue; be talkative

【说法】shuōfǎ 讲解佛法 expound Buddhist teachings

【说法】shuō·fa ❶ 措辞 wording; way of saying a thing: 改换一个～ say it in another way | 一个意思可以有两种～。One idea can be formulated in two different ways. ❷ 意见;见解 statement; argument: '后来居上'是一种鼓舞人向前看的～。'Those who come later often surpass their predecessors' is a statement of encouragement to spur people on.

【说服】shuō//fú 用理由充分的话使对方心服 persuade; convince; move sb. by reasonable argument to believe sth. or to take some action: 只是这么几句话，～不了人。These few remarks are hardly convincing.

【说合】shuō·he ❶ 从中介绍，促成别人的事；把两方面说到一块儿 bring two parties together through introduction and other efforts: ～人 introduce two persons to each other | ～亲事 make a match ❷ 商议；商量 talk over; discuss ❸ same as 说和 shuō·he

【说和】shuō·he 调解双方的争执；劝说使和解 mediate a settlement; patch up a quarrel: 你去给他们～～。Try to patch things up between them, will you?

【说话】shuō//huà ❶ 用语言表达意思 speak; talk; say: 这人不爱～儿。This person does not like to talk. | 不要～。Don't talk. | 老乡感动得说不出话来。The farmer was too moved to say anything. ❷ (～儿 shuō//huàr) 闲谈 chat; chit-chat: 找他～儿去。Go and have a chat with him. | 说了半天话儿 have a long chat ❸ 指责；非议 censure: 要把事情做好，否则人家要～了。We should do a good job, otherwise people will start talking.

【说话】shuōhuà ❶ 说话的一会儿时间 a short while that takes one to speak (briefly); 〈比喻 *fig.*〉 时间相当短 very soon; in a minute; right away; in a jiffy: 你稍等一等，我～就来。Wait a minute. I'll be right back. ❷ 〈方 *dial.*〉 话 word; talk: 他这句～很有道理。What he said was quite right. ❸ 唐宋时代的一种民间技艺，以讲述故事为主，跟现在的说书相同 folk art form popular during the Tang and Song dynasties, similar to what is known as storytelling today

【说谎】shuō//huǎng 有意说不真实的话 tell a lie; lie; deliberately not tell the truth

【说教】shuōjiào ❶ 宗教信徒宣传教义 deliver a sermon; preach (a religious disciple) ❷ 〈比喻 *fig.*〉 生硬地、机械地空谈理论 give sb. a sermon; preach ineptly or tediously

【说开】shuōkāi ❶ 说明白；解释明白 explain clearly: 你索性把事情的原委跟他～了，免得他猜疑。You'd better clearly explain to him how all this came about, so as not to leave him in doubt. ❷ (某一词语)普遍流行起来 (of a word or expression) be in current use; become popular: 这个词儿已经～了，大家也都这么用了。This word has become popular, and everybody is using it.

【说客】shuōkè (旧读 formerly pronounced shuìkè) ❶ 善于劝说的人 persuasive talker ❷ 替别人做劝说工作的人(含贬义 derog.) lobbyist; person often engaged by others to accomplish a task through persuasion

【说口】shuō·kou 二人转等曲艺中指演员上场后的一段说白 spoken part of such forms of ballad-singing as *errenzhuan*, a song-and-dance duet popular in northeast China

【说理】shuō//lǐ ❶ 说明道理 argue; reason things out: ～的文章 persuasive article | 咱们找他～去。Let's go and reason things out with him. ❷ 讲理；不蛮横(多用于否定式 usu. used in the negative) listen to reason; be reasonable: 你这个人～不～? Won't you listen to reason?

【说媒】shuō//méi 指给人介绍婚姻 act as matchmaker

【说明】shuōmíng ❶ 解释明白 explain; illustrate: ～原因 explain the reasons | ～问题 illustrate the problem ❷ 解释意义的话 explanation; directions; caption: 图片下边附有～。There is a caption under the picture. ❸ 证明 prove; show: 事实充分～这种做法是正确的。The results clearly show that this method is correct.

【说明书】shuōmíngshū 关于物品的用途、规格、性能和使用法以及戏剧、电影情节等的文字说明 manual; brochure; booklet containing directions on the purpose, specifications, properties and usage of sth. or the gist of a drama, film, etc.

【说明文】shuōmíngwén 说明事物的情况或道理的文章 expository writing; article showing the situation or principles of a thing

【说破】shuōpò 把隐秘的意思或事情说出来 lay bare; reveal (implied or secret meanings): 这是变戏法儿，一～就没意思了。It's a conjuring trick and would be nothing if laid bare.

【说亲】shuō//qīn same as 说媒 shuō//méi

【说情】shuō//qíng (～儿 shuō//qíngr) 代人请求宽恕；给别人讲情 plead for mercy for sb.; intercede for sb.: 托人～ plead to sb. for mercy for (sb. else) | 你帮我说个情。Please put in a word for me.

【说书】shuō//shū 表演评书、评话、弹词等 storytelling; performances of storytelling, popular stories, or fiddle ballads in southern Chinese dialects

【说头儿】shuō·tour ❶ 可谈之处 sth. worthy of discussion: 这件事还有个～。This matter is worth talking about. ❷ 辩解的理由 excuse: 不管怎样，你总有你的～。No matter what, you always have an excuse.

【说戏】shuō//xì (导演等)给演员解说剧情或做示范动作 (of a film or stage director, etc.) explain (to one or more actors) the scene, or show how a part or a scene should be acted

【说闲话】shuō xiánhuà ❶ 从旁说讽刺或不满意的话 gossip; make sarcastic or critical comments: 有意见当面提，别在背后～。Make any complaints you have openly, and don't grumble behind our backs. ❷ (～儿 shuō xiánhuàr)闲谈 chat

【说项】shuōxiàng 唐代项斯被杨敬之看重,敬之赠诗有'平生不解藏人善,到处逢人说项斯'的句子,后世指为人说好话,替人讲情 put in a good word for sb.; intercede for sb. (During the Tang Dynasty, a man named Yang Jingzhi thought highly of Xiang Si and wrote him a poem which said, among other things: 'I never hide the good side of a person, so I put in a good word for Xiang Si whenever I meet somebody.')

【说笑】shuōxiào 连说带笑;又说又笑 chatting and laughing: 院子里的人,谈心的谈心,～的～。Among the people in the courtyard, some were having heart-to-heart talks, and some were just chatting and laughing.|她的性格很活泼,爱蹦蹦跳跳,说说笑笑。She is vivacious and often skips about, chatting and laughing.

【说笑话】shuō xiào·hua (～儿 shuō xiào·huar) ❶ 讲引人发笑的话或故事 tell a joke ❷ 用言语跟人开玩笑 joke; kid around using words: 他是在跟你～,你怎么就当真了呢? He was just joking. How could you take it seriously?

【说一不二】shuō yī bù èr 形容说话算数 mean what one says; stand by one's words

【说嘴】shuōzuǐ ❶ 自夸;吹牛 brag; boast: 谁也别～,咱们俩来比一比。Neither you nor I should boast — let's have a competition. ❷ 〈方 *dial.*〉争辩 argue; quarrel: 他好和人～,时常争得面红耳赤。He likes to quarrel with people and often argues intensely.

shuò (ㄕㄨㄛˋ)

妁 shuò ☞ 媒妁 méishuò on p. 1315

烁(爍) shuò 光亮的样子 bright; shining: 闪～ flicker

【烁烁】shuòshuò (光芒)闪烁 (of light) glitter; sparkle: 繁星～。Clusters of stars are glittering in the sky.

铄[1](鑠) shuò 〈书 *fml.*〉 ❶ 熔化(金属) melt (metal): ～石流金 (hot enough to) make rocks and metals melt ❷ 耗损;削弱 waste away; weaken

铄[2](鑠) shuò same as 烁 shuò

【铄石流金】shuò shí liú jīn ☞ 流金铄石 liú jīn shuò shí on p. 1241

朔[1] shuò ❶ 农历每月初一,月球运行到太阳和地球之间,跟太阳同时出没,地球上看不到月光,这种月相叫朔,这时的月亮叫新月 new moon; on the first day of every lunar month, the moon moves between the sun and the earth, and appears and disappears together with the sun, while the moon's light cannot be seen from the earth ❷ 朔日 the first day of the lunar month: ～望 the first and the 15th days of the lunar month

朔[2] shuò 北(方) north: ～方 north|～风 north wind

【朔方】shuòfāng 〈书 *fml.*〉北方 north

【朔风】shuòfēng 〈书 *fml.*〉北风 north wind: ～凛冽。The north wind was bitingly cold.

【朔日】shuòrì 农历每月初一 the first day of the lunar month

【朔望】shuòwàng 朔日和望日 the first and the 15th day of a lunar month; syzygy

【朔望月】shuòwàngyuè 月亮连续两次呈现同样的月相所经历的时间。一个朔望月等于 29 天 12 小时 44 分 2.8 秒。阴历一个月的天数为 29 天或 30 天,就是根据朔望月制定的。lunar month; lunation; synodic month; period of time, averaging 29 days, 12 hours, 44 minutes, and 2.8 seconds, spanning two successive moons of the same phase passing. The number of days in a month in the Chinese lunar calendar, 29 or 30, is established according to the synodic month.

【朔月】shuòyuè ☞ 新月 xīnyuè ② on p. 2136

硕 shuò 大 large: ～大 very large|丰～ plentiful and substantial

【硕大】shuòdà 非常大;巨大 huge; very large: ～无朋 of enormous size; gigantic|～的身躯 huge stature

【硕大无朋】shuò dà wú péng 形容无比的大 of enormous size; huge; gigantic: 整个地球可以想像为一块～的磁石。The earth as a whole can be considered a gigantic magnet. (朋 *peng*: 比 compare)

【硕果】shuòguǒ 大的果实 rich fruits; 〈比喻 *fig.*〉巨大的成绩 great achievements: 结～ bring great successes|～累累 (of trees) hung heavy with fruit; numerous significant achievements

【硕果仅存】shuòguǒ jǐn cún 〈比喻 *fig.*〉经过淘汰,留存下的稀少可贵的人或物 few worthy persons or things after a selection or contest

【硕士】shuòshì 学位的一级。大学毕业生在研究机关或高等学校学习一二年以上,成绩合格者,即可授予。master; academic degree granted to a graduate who has studied more than one year at a graduate school with acceptable grades

稍 shuò 〈书 *fml.*〉 same as 槊 shuò

蒴 shuò 蒴果 capsule: 芝麻～ sesame capsule

【蒴果】shuòguǒ 干果的一种,由两个以上的心皮构成,内含许多种子,成熟后裂开,如芝麻、百合、凤仙花等的果实 capsule; dry dehiscent, usu. multiple-seed, fruit composed of two or more carpels that crack open when ripe, e.g. the fruit of sesame, lily, balsamine, etc.

S

搠 shuò 刺；扎（多见于早期白话 usu. in early vernacular） thrust; stab

数（數） shuò〈书 *fml*.〉屡次 frequently; repeatedly：频～ frequency｜～见不鲜 be a common occurrence

☞ shǔ on p.1786 and shù on p.1790

【数见不鲜】shuò jiàn bù xiān 经常看见，并不新奇 be not uncommon; be a common occurrence and nothing new; also 屡见不鲜 lǚ jiàn bù xiān

槊 shuò〈古代 *arch*.〉兵器，杆儿比较长的矛 long spear-like ancient weapon

sī（ㄙ）

厶 sī〈书 *fml*.〉same as 私 sī

司 sī ❶ 主持；操作；经营 take charge of; manage; operate：～机 driver｜～炉 stoker｜各～其事 each manages his own affairs ❷ 中央部一级机关里的一个部门 department (under a ministerial-level organization)：人事～ Human Resources Department｜外交部礼宾～ Protocol Department of the Ministry of Foreign Affairs ❸（Sī）姓 a surname

【司铎】sīduó ☞ 神甫 shén·fu on p.1706

【司法】sīfǎ 指检察机关或法院依照法律对民事、刑事案件进行侦查、审判 administration of justice; judicature; action of investigation and trial of civil and criminal cases by a procuratorial organization or court according to law

【司号员】sīhàoyuán 军队中负责使用军号进行通信联络的士兵 bugler; trumpeter; soldier in an army who gives communication signals by sounding a bugle

【司机】sījī 火车、汽车、电车等交通运输工具上的驾驶员 driver (of transportation vehicles as train, automobile, trolley, etc.)

【司空】Sīkōng 姓 a surname

【司空见惯】sīkōng jiàn guàn 相传唐代司空（古代中央政府中掌管工程的长官）李绅请卸任和州刺史（古代一州的行政长官）刘禹锡喝酒，席上叫歌伎劝酒。刘作诗：'鬟髻（wǒtuǒ）梳头宫样妆，春风一曲杜韦娘，司空见惯浑闲事，断尽江南刺史肠。'（见唐代孟棨《本事诗》）现在用司空见惯表示看惯了就不觉得奇怪。common sight; common occurrence; According to *Original Incidents of Poems* by Meng Qi of the Tang Dynasty, Li Shen, who was a *sikong*, Minister of Works, was feasting Liu Yuxi, who had just finished his tenure as administrative governor of Hezhou Prefecture, and asked sing-song girls to urge the guest to drink. In response Liu composed this poem: 'Girls beautifully adorned in royal hairstyles,/ Singing lovely songs with smiles;/ This to Sikong a common sight,/ My heart deeply delights.'

【司寇】Sīkòu 姓 a surname

【司库】sīkù 经管财务，也指团体中做这种工作的人 cashier; treasurer; officer (in an organization) responsible for money received and spent

【司令】sīlìng ❶ 某些国家军队中主管军事的人 commander; (in certain national armies) the person in charge of military affairs ❷ 中国人民解放军的司令员习惯上也称作司令 commanding officer of the People's Liberation Army of China

【司令员】sīlìngyuán 中国人民解放军中负责军事工作的高级指挥人员，如军区司令员，兵团司令员 commander; senior commanding officer in charge of military affairs in the People's Liberation Army of China, e.g. commander of a military zone or a military unit

【司炉】sīlú 烧锅炉的工人（多指火车机车上的 oft. on a locomotive） stoker; one employed to tend a furnace and supply it with fuel

【司马】Sīmǎ 姓 a surname

【司马昭之心，路人皆知】Sīmǎ Zhāo zhī xīn, lùrén jiē zhī 《三国志·魏书·高贵乡公传》注引《汉晋春秋》，魏帝曹髦在位时，大将军司马昭专权，图谋夺取帝位。一次曹髦气愤地对大臣说：'司马昭之心，路人所知也。'后来用'司马昭之心，路人皆知'指野心非常明显，人所共知。An annotated quotation from *Annals of Han and Jin* in *Annals of the Three Kingdoms · Kingdom of Wei · Biography of Duke Gao Guixiang*: During the reign of Cao Mao, emperor of the Kingdom of Wei, known by his title as Duke Gaoguixiang before he ascended the throne, General Sima Zhao monopolized power and conspired to usurp the throne. The angry emperor said to his other ministers, 'Sima Zhao's evil intent is known to all.' The phrase has come to imply that a villain's plot or ambition is so obvious that everybody knows about it.

【司南】sīnán 我国古代辨别方向用的一种仪器。用天然磁铁矿石琢成一个勺形的东西，放在一个光滑的盘上，盘上刻着方位，利用磁铁指南的作用，可以辨别方向。是现在所用指南针的始祖。compass; device used in ancient China for the same purpose as a modern compass, determining direction by means of a spoon-shaped object of natural magnetite turning freely on a smooth plate, calibrated with directions and pointing to the magnetic south, regarded as the predecesson of modern-day compass

【司徒】Sītú 姓 a surname

【司务长】sīwùzhǎng 连队中主管装备、物资、经费、伙食等后勤工作的干部 company quartermaster; officer in an army company who takes charge of such logistics as equipment, materials, funds, and food

【司药】sīyào 医院药房里负责按处方配药、发药的人 pharmacist; druggist; chemist; person employed by a hospital pharmacy to make and dispense drugs according to prescription

【司仪】sīyí 举行典礼或召开大会时报告进行程序的人 host (or master) of ceremonies or conference chair, who announces the different items on the programme or agenda

丝(絲) sī ❶ 蚕丝 silk ❷ (～儿 sīr)像丝的物品 thread-like thing: 铁～ iron wire | 钢～ steel wire | 蜘蛛～ thread spun by a spider; cobweb | 萝卜～儿 radish shreds ❸ (某些计量单位的)万分之一 10,000th of a certain unit of measure: ～米 decimillimetre ❹ 计量单位名称 *si*, unit of measure: a)长度,10 忽等于 1 丝,10 丝等于 1 毫。通称 1 忽米为 1 丝。unit of length, equal to 10 *hu* or 0.1 *hao* or 1 *humi*; b)重量,10 忽等于 1 丝,10 丝等于 1 毫 unit of weight, equal to 10 *hu* or 0.1 *hao* ❺ 极少或极小的量 a tiny bit; very small amount: 一～不差 not a bit of difference | 一～风也没有。There isn't a single breath of wind.

【丝包线】sībāoxiàn 用丝缠绕着做绝缘层的金属导线,多用来绕制电机和电讯装置中的线圈 silk-covered wire; metal conducting wire wrapped with silk for insulation, usu. used as coils in electric machinery or telecommunication installations

【丝绸】sīchóu 用蚕丝或人造丝织成的纺织品的总称 silk; silk cloth; fabric woven of natural or artificial silk

【丝糕】sīgāo 小米面、玉米面等加水搅拌发酵后蒸成的松软的食品 steamed millet or corn cake; steamed soft food made of fermented millet or corn flour dough

【丝瓜】sīguā ❶ 一年生草本植物,茎蔓生,叶子通常三至七裂,花单性,黄色。果实长形,嫩时可供食用,成熟后肉多网状纤维,叫做丝瓜络(luò),可入药。towel gourd (*Luffa*); vegetable sponge; annual cauline herb that has three-to seven-decomposite leaves and unisexual yellow flowers, and bears long fruit which are edible when tender, and when ripe can be dried into reticular fibres to be used as sponges, or for medicine ❷ 这种植物的果实 the fruit of this plant

【丝光】sīguāng 棉织品在低温和绷紧的情况下,用浓氢氧化钠溶液浸渍,由于纤维结构发生变化,表面产生像丝一样的光彩,称为丝光 silky lustre on cotton fabrics produced by changes in fibre structure after pressure under low temperatures with caustic soda: ～毛巾 mercerized towel

【丝毫】sīháo 极小或很少;一点儿 a bit; the slightest amount or degree: ～不差 tally in every detail; be just right

【丝绵】sīmián 剥取蚕茧表面的乱丝整理而成的像棉花的东西,轻软保温,用来絮衣服、被子等 silk floss; silk wadding; floss peeled from silkworm cocoons and rearranged to resemble cotton but lighter, softer and warmer, usu used as wadding in clothes, quilts, etc.

【丝绒】sīróng 用蚕丝和人造丝为原料织成的丝织品,表面起绒毛,色泽鲜艳、光亮,质地柔软,供制妇女服装、帷幕、装饰品等 velvet; velour; fabric made of natural and artificial silks and characterized by a napped surface, bright colour and lustre, and soft quality, used for clothing, curtains, decorations, etc.

【丝丝入扣】sī sī rù kòu 织绸、布等时,经线都要从扣(筘)齿间穿过 (of the weaving of clothing, silk fabric, etc.) every warp goes through the groove of the reed; 〈比喻 *fig.*〉做得十分细腻准确(多指文章、艺术表演等)(mostly of writings or artistic performances) done with meticulous care and flawless artistry

【丝弦】sīxián ❶ 用丝拧成的弦 silk string (on a musical instrument) ❷ (～儿 sīxiánr)河北地方戏曲剧种之一,流行于石家庄一带 Hebei provincial opera, most popular in the Shijiazhuang area

【丝线】sīxiàn 用丝纺成的线 silk thread (for sewing, embroidery, etc.); silk yarn

【丝织品】sīzhīpǐn ❶ 用蚕丝或人造丝织成的纺织品 silk fabrics; any of the various fabrics woven from natural or artificial silk ❷ 用蚕丝或人造丝编织的衣物 clothes knitted with natural or artificial silk

【丝竹】sīzhú 琴、瑟、箫、笛等乐器的总称,'丝'指弦乐器,'竹'指管乐器 traditional stringed and woodwind instruments, e.g. *qin* (seven-stringed instrument), *se* (25-stringed plucked instrument), *xiao* (vertical bamboo flute), and *di* (bamboo flute). *Si* refers to stringed instruments, while *zhu* refers to woodwind instruments.

【丝锥】sīzhuī 一种加工内螺纹的刀具,形状像螺栓,沿轴向开有沟槽 tap; bolt-shaped cutting tool grooved in the axial direction for forming an internal screw thread; also 螺丝攻 luósīgōng

私 sī ❶ 属于个人的或为了个人的(跟'公'相对 as opposed to 'public') private; personal: ～事 private affairs | ～信 personal letter | ～有财产 private property ❷ 自私(跟'公'相对 as opposed to 'selfless') selfish: ～心 selfish motives | 大公无～ selfless ❸ 暗地里;私下 secret; private: 窃窃～语 whisper ❹ 秘密而不合法的 secret and illegal; illicit: ～货 smuggled goods | ～盐 contraband salt | ～通 have secret communications with

【私奔】sībēn 〈旧时 *old*〉指女子私自投奔所爱的人,或跟他一起逃走 elope; (of a woman) run away secretly to pursue the one she loves

【私弊】sībì 营私舞弊的事情 corrupt practices;

杜绝～ put an end to corrupt practices

【私产】sīchǎn 私有财产 private property

【私娼】sīchāng 暗娼 unlicensed (or unregistered) prostitute

【私仇】sīchóu 因个人利害关系而产生的仇恨 personal enmity (or grudge)：报～ satisfy a personal grudge

【私党】sīdǎng 私自纠合的宗派集团，也指这种集团的成员 clique；faction；member of a clique

【私德】sīdé 在私人生活上所表现的道德品质 private morality；individual morals in private life：～失检 unrestrained personal morals

【私邸】sīdǐ 高级官员私人所置的住所（区别于'官邸'as compared with 'official residence'）private residence (of a ranking official)

【私第】sīdì 私宅；私邸 private residence

【私法】sīfǎ 西方法学中指保护私人利益的法律，如民法、商法等（区别于'公法'as compared with 'public law'）personal law；(in Western law) laws for protecting personal interests, e.g. civil law, commercial law, etc.

【私方】sīfāng 指公私合营企业中私人的一方（跟'公方'相对 as opposed to 'public partner'）(in a joint state-private enterprise) private partner：～代表 representative of the private partner

【私房】sī·fang ❶ 家庭成员个人积蓄的（财物）private savings of a family member：～钱 private savings ❷ 不愿让外人知道的 confidential：～话 confidential talk

【私访】sīfǎng 指官吏等隐瞒身份到民间调查 (of officials) go incognito among the people to make investigations：微服～ (of officials) wear plain clothes and go incognito among the people to make investigations

【私愤】sīfèn 因个人利害关系而产生的愤恨 personal spite：泄～ vent personal spite

【私股】sīgǔ 公私合营的工商企业中，私人所有的股份 private share (in a joint state-private industrial or commercial enterprise)

【私话】sīhuà 不让外人知道的话 secret words：这是咱们的～，你别往外说。This is a secret between us, so don't go and tell others.

【私活】sīhuó（～儿 sīhuór）公务人员、集体成员所做的与公务或集体无关的活儿（of a civil servant or an employee of a collective organization) work done for others with no relation to official business or collective affairs：干～ be engaged in extraofficial business｜揽～ canvass extraofficial business

【私货】sīhuò 违法贩运的货物 smuggled goods；contraband goods：偷运～ smuggle goods ◇文章在漂亮的言词掩盖下，塞进了不少宣扬自己的～。The article is full of elements of self-aggrandizement behind a veil of flowery language.

【私见】sījiàn ❶ 个人的成见或偏见 personal prejudice or bias：不存～ have no personal bias｜克服～ overcome personal prejudice ❷ 个人的见解 personal opinion：以上～，仅供参考。The above is a personal opinion for reference only.

【私交】sījiāo 私人之间的交情 personal friendship：两人素无～。The two have never established a personal friendship.｜他们在学术上时常公开争论，但～很好。They often debate about their academic research in public, but still maintain a good personal friendship.

【私立】sīlì ❶ 私人设立（用于学校、医院等）establish and run (school, hospital, etc.) privately ❷ 私人设立的 private；privately run：～学校 private school

【私利】sīlì 私人方面的利益 private interest；personal gain：不谋～ seek no personal gain

【私了】sīliǎo 不经过司法手续而私下了结（跟'公了'相对 as opposed to 'settle in court'）settle (a case or dispute) privately；settle out of court

【私囊】sīnáng 私人的钱袋 private purse：中饱～ embezzle public money to line one's own pockets

【私念】sīniàn 私心杂念 selfish motives (or ideas)：摒除～ abandon selfish motives

【私情】sīqíng ❶ 私人的交情 personal relationships：不徇～ not swayed by personal considerations ❷ 指男女情爱的事（多指不正当的 usu. illicit) sexual relations；affairs

【私人】sīrén ❶ 属于个人或以个人身份从事的；非公家的 private；belonging to an individual person or carried on by the individual independently；non-public：～企业 private enterprise｜～资本 private capital｜～秘书 private secretary｜以前这个小城市里只有一所～办的中学。This small city formerly had only one private middle school. ❷ 个人和个人之间的 personal：～关系 personal relations；personal connections｜～感情 personal emotions ❸ 因私交、私利而依附于自己的人 one's own man：滥用～plant one's own man in a post；practise nepotism

【私商】sīshāng 用私人资本经营的商店，也指这类商人 privately owned shop；businessman；merchant；trader

【私生活】sīshēnghuó 个人生活（主要指日常生活中所表现的品质、作风 mainly referring to daily lifestyle and quality of life) personal or private life；privacy

【私生子】sīshēngzǐ 非夫妻关系的男女所生的子女 child born out of wedlock；illegitimate child

【私事】sīshì 个人的事（区别于'公事'as compared with 'public affairs' or 'official business'）private (or personal) affairs：这是我的～，与别人无关。This is my personal affair, and has nothing to do with anyone else.

【私淑】sīshū〈书 *fml.*〉未能亲自受业但敬仰其学术并尊之为师 polite respectful form of address for a master from whom one has not had direct tuition：～弟子(未亲自受业的弟子) disciple or pupil who has not been instructed personally by a master

【私塾】sīshú〈旧时 *old*〉家庭、宗族或教师自己设立的教学处所，一般只有一个教师，采用个别教学法，没有一定的教材和学习年限 private school; school set up by a family, clan, or teacher, generally with just one teacher who gives individual tuition, and that has no set textbooks and no specified time span of study：读～study at a private school | ～先生 private tutor

【私通】sītōng ❶ 私下勾结 have secret communication with：～敌寇 have secret communication with the enemy ❷ 通奸 commit adultery; have illicit intercourse

【私图】sītú〈书 *fml.*〉个人的图谋；企图(含贬义 derog.) personal scheme or attempt; selfish motives

【私吞】sītūn 私自侵吞 misappropriate：～公款 misappropriate public money

【私下】sīxià ❶ 背地里 in private; in secret：～商议 discuss a matter in private ❷ 自己进行，不通过有关部门或群众的 settle out of court or exclusive of any relevant department：～调解 meditate in private ‖ also 私下里 sīxià·li

【私枭】sīxiāo〈旧时 *old*〉指私贩食盐的人。现泛指走私或贩毒的人。traffickers of salt; now referring to smugglers or traffickers of narcotic drugs

【私心】sīxīn ❶ 个人心里；内心 selfish motives (or ideas)：他公而忘私的精神，使我～非常佩服。I admire him very much for his unselfish spirit in working for the public interest. ❷ 为自己打算的念头 selfishness：～杂念 selfish ideas and personal considerations; selfish considerations | 他～太重。He is overly selfish.

【私刑】sīxíng 指不按照法律程序加给人的刑罚 illegal punishment (meted out by a kangaroo court); lynching; punishment without due process of law

【私蓄】sīxù 个人的积蓄 private savings：动用～draw on private savings

【私学】sīxué 私人创办的学校 private school

【私营】sīyíng 私人经营 privately owned; privately run (or operated)：～企业 private enterprise

【私有】sīyǒu 私人所有 privately owned; private：～财产 private property

【私有制】sīyǒuzhì 生产资料归私人所有的制度，随着生产力的发展、剩余产品的出现和原始公社的瓦解而产生，是产生阶级和剥削的基础 private ownership; system that came into being following the development of productive forces, the incidence of surplus products, and the dissolution of primitive communes, wherein the means of production belongs to individuals, and which constitutes the basis of social classes and exploitation

【私语】sīyǔ ❶ 低声说话 whisper：窃窃～talk in whispers ❷ 私下说的话 speak in confidence

【私欲】sīyù 指个人的欲望 selfish, lustful desires：贪求～ avidly seek to satisfy selfish, carnal desires

【私章】sīzhāng 刻有个人姓名，代表个人身份的印章(区别于'公章' as compared with 'official seal') personal seal; signet; seal or chop used as a signature on documents

【私衷】sīzhōng〈书 *fml.*〉个人内心的真实想法 innermost feelings

【私自】sīzì 背着组织或有关的人，自己(做不合乎规章制度的事) privately; secretly; without permission：～逃跑 absent oneself without permission | 这是公物，不能～拿走。This is public property and must not be taken away without permission.

咝(噝) sī〈拟声词 *onom.*〉形容枪弹等在空中很快飞过的声音 whistle (the sound of flying shells and bullets)：子弹～～～地从头顶上飞过。Bullets whistled overhead.

思 sī ❶ 思考；think; consider; deliberate; same as 想 xiǎng ①：多～ think more | 深～think deeply | 寻～think sth. over | 前～后想 ponder over; think over again and again ❷ 思念；怀念；想念 miss; long for：～家 be homesick | ～亲 think affectionately of one's parents | 相～ lovesickness ❸ 希望 long to; yearn; same as 想 xiǎng③：～归 long to go home | 穷则～变。Poverty gives rise to a desire for change. ❹ 思路 reasoning; train of thought：文～ thread and flow of ideas in writing; train of thought in writing ❺ (Sī)姓 a surname

☞ sāi on p. 1648

【思辨】sībiàn ❶ 哲学上指运用逻辑推导而进行纯理论、纯概念的思考(philos.) think logically about; theorize through reasoning ❷ 思考辨析 analyse mentally; make intellectual enquiries：～能力 the ability to analyse; also 思辩 sībiàn

【思辩】sībiàn same as 思辨 sībiàn ②

【思潮】sīcháo ❶ 某一时期内在某一阶级或阶层中反映当时社会政治情况而有较大影响的思想潮流 trend of thought; prevailing ideological trend that reflects the socio-political situation of any stage or stratum of a particular period：文艺～trends of thought in art and literature ❷ 接二连三的思想活动 thoughts：～起伏 disquieting thoughts that surge through one's mind | ～澎湃 feel an upsurge of thoughts and emotions

【思春】sīchūn 怀春 harbor amorous thoughts of spring; (of young girls) have thoughts of love

【思忖】sīcǔn 〈书 *fml.*〉same as 思量 sī·liang①

【思凡】sīfán 神话小说中仙人想到人间来生活。也指僧尼等厌恶宗教生活,想过世俗生活(of an immortal) long for a life among mortals; (of a monk or a nun) tire of a life of religious seclusion and yearn for the secular life

【思古】sīgǔ 怀恋往昔;怀古 recall antiquity; meditate on the past:发～之幽情 wax nostalgic; muse over things of the remote past

【思旧】sījiù 怀念旧友;怀旧 think fondly of past times or old acquaintances

【思考】sīkǎo 进行比较深刻、周到的思维活动 think deeply; ponder over; reflect on:独立～ think things out for oneself; think independently|～问题 ponder a problem

【思恋】sīliàn 思念;怀恋 think fondly of; long for:～故乡 think fondly of one's native land

【思量】sī·liang ❶ 考虑 consider:这件事你还得好好～～。You had better think this matter over carefully. ❷〈方 *dial.*〉想念;记挂 miss; be concerned about; keep thinking about:大家正～你呢! Everyone is thinking of you!

S

【思路】sīlù 思考的线索 train of thought; thinking:别打断他的～。Don't interrupt his train of thought.|他越写越兴奋,～也越来越清晰。The more he writes, the more he warms to his subject, and his train of thought becomes ever clearer.

【思虑】sīlǜ 思索考虑 consider; contemplate; deliberate:～周到 consider everything carefully

【思摸】sī·mo 想;考虑 think; consider:我～了好几天,觉得这事还是非办不可。I have considered this matter for several days, and think something really must be done about it.

【思谋】sīmóu 思索;考虑 think; consider

【思慕】sīmù 思念(自己敬仰的人) think of sb. with respect; admire

【思念】sīniàn 想念 think of; long for; miss:～亲人 miss one's nearest and dearest|～故土 long for home

【思前想后】sī qián xiǎng hòu 形容前前后后地反复思考 ponder; turn over in one's mind; cogitate on the past and future

【思索】sīsuǒ 思考探求 think deeply; ponder:～问题 ponder a problem|用心～ do some hard thinking

【思惟】sīwéi same as 思维 sīwéi

【思维】sīwéi ❶ 在表象、概念的基础上进行分析、综合、判断、推理等认识活动的过程。思维是人类特有的一种精神活动,是从社会实践中产生的。thought; thinking; process of mental activity such as analysis, synthesis, judgement and reasoning, based on ideas and concepts, a mental faculty unique to humankind, and a product of social practice. ❷ 进行思维活动 think; consider:再三～ consider over and over again ‖ also 思惟 sīwéi

【思乡】sī//xiāng 想念家乡 be homesick

【思想】sīxiǎng ❶ 客观存在反映在人的意识中经过思维活动而产生的结果。思想的内容为社会制度的性质和人们的物质生活条件所决定,在阶级社会中,思想具有明显的阶级性。thought; thinking; ideology; sequence of thought within objective existence as reflected in human consciousness. One's ideology being determined by the nature of the social system in which one lives and the conditions of his material life. For example, in a class society, a person's ideology is characterized by the social class he or she belongs to. ❷ 念头;想法 idea; intention:她早有去农村参加农业生产的～。She has long had the idea of going to the countryside to do farm work. ❸ same as 思量 sī·liang

【思想家】sīxiǎngjiā 对客观现实的认识有独创见解并能自成体系的人 thinker; person who has an original and creative understanding of the reality and can become a school in his own right

【思想体系】sīxiǎng tǐxì ❶ 成体系的思想 ideological system ❷ 意识形态 ideology

【思想性】sīxiǎngxìng 文艺作品或其他著作中所表现的政治倾向,政治标准是衡量作品思想性的依据 ideological content (or level); political trend as reflected in works of literature, art or other works. Political criteria are the basis on which to evaluate the ideological level of a work.

【思绪】sīxù ❶ 思想的头绪;思路 train of thought; thinking:～万千 myriad of thoughts well up in one's mind|～纷乱 confused state of mind; confused train of thought ❷ 情绪 feeling:～不宁 feel perturbed

【思议】sīyì 想像和理解 conceive; think; imagine:不可～ inconceivable; unimaginable; unthinkable

虒 sī 虒亭(Sītíng),地名,在山西 name of a place in Shanxi Province

鸶(鷥) sī ☞ 鹭鸶 (lùsī) on p. 1263

偲 sī [偲偲]〈书 *fml.*〉相互切磋,互相督促 meet and chat earnestly

☞ cāi on p. 175

斯 sī ❶〈书 *fml.*〉这;此;这个;这里 this:～人 this person|～时 at this moment|生于～,长于～。This is where I was born and brought up.|以至于～ to such an extent ❷〈书 *fml.*〉于是;就 then; thus ❸ (Sī) 姓 a surname

【斯拉夫人】Sīlāfūrén 说印欧语系斯拉夫语族语言的各民族的统称。主要分布在欧洲东部,部分散居在西伯利亚和美洲。Slav; a group of

Slavic-speaking (of the Indo-European languages) peoples, mainly inhabiting eastern Europe, but also scattered throughout Siberia and the Americas

【斯文】sīwén〈书 *fml.*〉指文化或文人 culture; men of letters; scholars; literati: 敬重～look up to and respect scholars|～扫地 scholarly dignity swept into the dust; bring disgrace to the refined and educated

【斯文】sī·wen 文雅 refined; gentle: 他说话挺～的。He is a gentle speaker.|斯斯文文地坐着 sit in a refined manner

【斯文扫地】sīwén sǎo dì 指文化或文人不受尊重或文人自甘堕落 scholarly dignity swept into the dust; (men of letters) wallow in degeneracy

蛳(螄) sī ☞ 螺蛳 luó·sī on p.1279

缌 sī〈书 *fml.*〉细麻布 fine linen

榲 sī[榲仔](sīzǐ) ☞ 淋漓柯 línlíkē on p.1223

飔 sī〈书 *fml.*〉凉风 cool autumn breezes

厮[1](廝) sī ❶ 男性仆人 male servant (多见于早期白话 oft. in early vernacular): 小～ page-boy; manservant ❷ 对人轻视的称呼(多见于早期白话 usu. in early vernacular) (derog.) fellow; guy: 这～ this guy|那～that guy

厮[2](廝) sī 互相 with each other; together: ～打 tussle|～杀 fight at close quarters (with weapons)|～混 fool around (or about) with sb.; play around (or about) with sb.

【厮打】sīdǎ 相互扭打 tussle: 拼命～tussle desperately|两个人在门外～起来。Outside, the two of them began fighting.

【厮混】sīhùn ❶ 彼此生活在一起;相处(多含贬义 oft. derog.) hang out with; chum around with sb.; fool around (or about) with sb.: 他整天和那些不三不四的人～。He spends all his time fooling around with a group of rather dubious fellows. ❷ 混合;混杂 mingle; mix: 人的喊声、马的叫声、枪声～在一起。The sounds of men shouting, horses neighing, and gunshots commingled into one.

【厮杀】sīshā 相互拼杀,指战斗 fight at close quarters (with weapons): ～声 sounds of battle|跟敌人～ fight the enemy at close quarters

罳 sī ☞ 罘罳 (fúsī) on p.600

锶 sī 金属元素,符号 Sr (strontium)。银白色,质软,燃烧时发出红色光。用于制合金、光电管和烟火等。strontium (Sr); soft, malleable, ductile, bivalent, metallic element, used to make alloys, photoelectric tubes, fireworks

澌 sī〈书 *fml.*〉解冻时流动的冰 floating ice; (ice) floe

撕 sī 用手使东西(多为薄片状的)裂开或离开附着处 tear; rip; separate or pull apart by force: 把布～成两块 tear the cloth into two pieces|把书页～破了。A page in this book is torn.|把墙上的标语～下来。Rip the slogan off the wall.

【撕扯】sīchě 撕 tear: 他一怒之下把来信～成碎片。In a fit of anger he tore the letter into shreds. ◇孩子的呻吟～着母亲的心。The child's cries tore at the heart of his mother.

【撕毁】sīhuǐ ❶ 撕破毁掉 tear up; tear to shreds: ～画稿 tear up the rough sketch of a painting ❷ 单方面背弃共同商定的协议、条约等 tear up (agreement, treaty, etc.) unilaterally: ～合同 tear up a contract|～协定 tear up an agreement

【撕票】sī//piào (～儿 sī//piàor) 绑票的匪徒因勒索金钱的要求没得到满足,把掳去的人杀死,叫做撕票 (of kidnappers) kill a hostage who fails to meet their demand for ransom

嘶[1] sī〈书 *fml.*〉❶ (马)叫 neigh: 人喊马～ men shouting and horses neighing ❷ 嘶哑 hoarse: 声～力竭 be hoarse and exhausted; shout oneself hoarse

嘶[2] sī same as 咝 sī

【嘶鸣】sīmíng (骡、马等)大声叫 (of horses, mules, etc.) neigh; whinny; bray: 战马～。The warhorses neighed.

【嘶哑】sīyǎ 声音沙哑 hoarse

篪 sī[篪簩竹](sīláozhú) 竹子的一种,秆直立,顶端下垂,节间细长,皮薄,可编制家具等 a species of bamboo, with a straight stem, a drooping top, long and slender between its joints, and with a thin skin; used for making furniture

凘 sī〈书 *fml.*〉尽 drain dry; drain completely; totally disappear

【凘灭】sīmiè〈书 *fml.*〉消失干净 totally disappear

sǐ (ㄙˇ)

死 sǐ ❶ (生物)失去生命(跟'生、活'相对 as opposed to 'live' and 'alive') die; be dead: ～亡 death|～人 the deceased|这棵树～了。This tree is dead. ◇～棋 a dead piece in a game of chess|～火山 extinct volcano ❷ 不顾生命;拼死 to the death; desperately: ～战 fight to the death|～守 defend to the death; defend to the last; make a last-ditch defence ❸ 至死,表示坚决[used before verbs in the negative] stubbornly; adamantly; unyieldingly: ～不认输 stubbornly refuse to admit defeat|～也不松手 cling (or hold on, hang on) to

S

sth. like grim death ❹ 表示达到极点 extremely; to death:笑～人 extremely funny|高兴～了 be extremely happy|～顽固 diehard ❺ 不可调和的 implacable; deadly:～敌 deadly enemy; mortal enemy; implacable foe|～对头 deadly enemy; irreconcilable opponent ❻ 固定;死板;不活动 fixed; rigid; inflexible:～脑筋 one-track mind|～心眼 as obstinate as a mule; person with a one-track mind|～规矩 rigid rule|～水 stagnant water|开会的时间要定～。A time for the meeting must be fixed. ❼不能通过 inaccessible:～胡同 blind alley; dead end|～路一条 the road to ruin (or destruction)|把漏洞堵～plug the holes; stop up loopholes

【死板】sǐbǎn ❶ 不活泼;不生动 rigid; stiff:这幅画上的人物太～,没有表情。The characters in this painting are wooden and expressionless. ❷ (办事)不会变通;不灵活 inflexible:做事情不能～。Work should not be handled in a mechanical way.

【死不瞑目】sǐ bù míngmù 指人死时因心里还有牵挂,死了没有闭上眼睛多用来形容不达目的,决不甘休 not close one's eyes on dying; die with a grievance or everlasting regret; die with mission unaccomplished; die discontent; (fig.) never give up until one's goal is achieved

【死产】sǐchǎn 胎儿在分娩过程中死亡,出生后已无心跳和呼吸 stillbirth; birth of a dead foetus

【死党】sǐdǎng ❶ 为某人或某集团出死力的党羽(贬义 derog.) sworn followers ❷ 顽固的反动集团 diehard reactionary clique:结成～gang up

【死得其所】sǐ dé qí suǒ 形容死得有意义、有价值 die a worthy death(所 *suo*:处所,地方 place):一个人为人民利益而死就是～。Dying for the people is a worthy death.

【死敌】sǐdí 无论如何也不可调和的敌人 deadly enemy; mortal enemy; implacable foe

【死地】sǐdì 无法生存的境地;绝境 fatal position; death trap:置人于～ drive sb. into a fatal position|置之～而后快(恨不得把人弄死才痛快) be content with nothing less than sb.'s destruction

【死点】sǐdiǎn 机器中的活塞在汽缸内做往复运动时最左和最右(或最上和最下)的位置,叫做死点。处于死点时曲柄不能转动,而需要依靠飞轮的惯性使它通过死点,维持机器的连续运转。dead centre; either of two positions (leftmost or rightmost; or top or bottom) of a piston as it moves back and forth in a cylinder, when the crank is not revolving, and relies on the inertia of the flywheel to maintain its movement

【死对头】sǐduì·tou 无论如何也不能和解的仇敌 deadly enemy; irreconcilable opponent

【死鬼】sǐguǐ ❶ 鬼(多用于骂人或开玩笑 usu. used as a curse or jocularity) devil ❷ 指死去了的人 the deceased

【死耗】sǐhào 人死亡的消息;死讯 news of sb.'s death

【死胡同】sǐhútòng (～儿 sǐhútòngr)走不通的胡同 blind alley; 〈比喻 *fig.*〉绝路 dead end; road to ruin; impasse

【死缓】sǐhuǎn '判处死刑、缓期二年执行'的简称。到期后,根据罪犯在死缓期的悔改表现,决定执行死刑或减刑。stay of execution; short for 'death sentence with a two-year reprieve and forced labor.' When the two-year reprieve period expires, a decision is taken as to whether to carry out the execution or reduce the penalty, according to the convict's level of repentance.

【死灰】sǐhuī 熄灭的火灰 cold ashes (of an extinguished fire); dead ashes; burnt-out cinders:心如～(形容心灰意懒) one's heart being like dead ashes; hopelessly apathetic

【死灰复燃】sǐhuī fù rán 〈比喻 *fig.*〉已经停息的事物又重新活动起来(多指坏事 oft. derog.) dying cinders glowing again; resurgence; revival

【死活】sǐhuó ❶ 活得下去活不下去(用于否定句 used in negative sentence) life or death; fate:这种做法简直是不顾别人的～。This method simply takes no account of the consequences to others. ❷ 无论如何 anyway; simply:叫他别去,他～要去。I tried to dissuade him from going, but he simply insisted.|我劝了他半天,他～不答应。I spent a long time trying to persuade him, but he simply would not hear of it.

【死火山】sǐhuǒshān 在人类历史记载中没有喷发过的火山 extinct volcano; volcano having no record of a single eruption

【死记】sǐjì 强行记住;死板地记忆 memorize mechanically; learn by rote; learn without comprehending:～硬背 memorize without comprehending

【死寂】sǐjì 非常寂静;没有一点声音 deathly stillness; absolute silence:夜深了,山谷里一片～。As night wore on, a deathly silence filled the valley.

【死角】sǐjiǎo ❶军事上指在火器射程之内而射击不到的地方。也指在视力范围内而观察不到的地方(mil.) dead angle; dead space; spot within the range of a firearm but which cannot be hit; spot within the scope of vision yet hidden from view ❷ 〈比喻 *fig.*〉运动、潮流、风气等尚未影响到的地方 backwaters; spot as yet untouched by political movement, a trend, a fad, etc.:计划生育的意义要宣传到各家各户,不要留～。The significance of family planning must be disseminated to every household, leaving no stone unturned.

【死校】sǐjiào 按照原稿校对,只对原稿负责,叫死校(区别于'活校'as compared with 'flexible proof-reading') rigid proof-reading; mechanical proof-reading

【死节】sǐjié 〈书 *fml.*〉为保全节操而死;殉节 die for the sake of honour; die to preserve one's moral or political integrity:为国～ die for the country

【死结】sǐjié 不是一拉就解开的结子(区别于'活结' as compared with 'slip-knot') fast knot; a knot that (cannot be) undone by pulling it

【死劲儿】sǐjìnr ❶ 所能使出的最大的力气 all one's strength; all one's might:大伙用～来拉,终于把车子拉出了泥坑。Using all their strength, they pulled the cart out of the mud. ❷ 使出最大的力气或集中全部注意力 with all one's strength; with all one's might and main; for all one's worth:～往下压 press down for all one's worth | ～盯住他 watch him closely

【死局】sǐjú 救不活的棋局 hopeless game of chess

【死扣儿】sǐkòur same as 死结 sǐjié

【死牢】sǐláo 关押死囚的监牢 death cell; condemned cell

【死劳动】sǐláodòng 物化劳动 dead labour

【死老虎】sǐ lǎohǔ 〈贬义 *derog.*〉〈比喻 *fig.*〉失去威势没有反抗力的人 dead tiger; man who has lost his power and influence

【死力】sǐlì ❶ 最大的力量 all one's strength:下～exert one's utmost effort ❷ 使出最大的力量 with all one's strength:～抵抗 resist with might and main; fight tooth and nail

【死路】sǐlù 走不通的路 blind alley;〈比喻 *fig.*〉毁灭的途径 road to ruin (or destruction)

【死面】sǐmiàn (～儿 sǐmiànr)加水调和后未经发酵的面 unleavened dough:烙～饼 bake pancakes of unleavened dough

【死灭】sǐmiè 灭亡;死亡 die; death

【死命】sǐmìng ❶ 必然死亡的命运 doom; death:制敌人于～ send the enemy to his doom; have the enemy by the throat ❷ 拼命 desperately:～挣扎 struggle desperately

【死难】sǐnàn 遭难而死 die in an accident or a political incident (esp. for a revolutionary cause):～烈士 martyr

【死脑筋】sǐnǎojīn ❶ 不灵活的头脑;陈旧的思想意识 one-track mind; outmoded notion ❷ 指固执守旧的人 stubborn person; stickler for old ways

【死皮赖脸】sǐ pí lài liǎn 形容不顾羞耻,一味纠缠 thick-skinned; brazen and unreasonable

【死期】sǐqī 死亡的日期 date of death

【死棋】sǐqí 救不活的棋局或棋局中救不活的棋子 dead piece in a game of chess; hopeless game;〈比喻 *fig.*〉一定失败的局面 hopeless case

【死气沉沉】sǐqì chénchén 形容气氛不活泼生动 lifeless; spiritless; stagnant

【死气白赖】sǐ·qibáilài 〈方 *dial.*〉(～的 sǐ·qibáilài·de)纠缠个没完 pestering people endlessly; also 死乞白赖 sǐ·qibáilài

【死契】sǐqì 出卖房地产时所立的契约,上面写明不能赎回的叫死契 irrevocable title deed; title deed for transferring real estate incorporating a statement that such a transfer is irrevocable

【死钱】sǐqián (～儿 sǐqiánr) ❶ 指不能增息获利的钱 money without interest or profit ❷ 指定时收入的固定数额的钱 fixed regular income

【死囚】sǐqiú 已经判处死刑而尚未执行的囚犯 convict sentenced to death; convict awaiting execution

【死去活来】sǐ qù huó lái 死过去又醒过来。形容极度悲哀和疼痛。hovering between life and death; extremely sad and painful

【死伤】sǐshāng 死亡和受伤。多指死亡和受伤的人数 the dead and the wounded; casualties:～惨重 suffer heavy casualties

【死神】sǐshén 指掌管人死亡的神,多用作比喻 Death (oft. personified):经过抢救,终于把他从～手里夺了回来。After emergency treatment, he was ultimately snatched from the jaws of death.

【死尸】sǐshī 人的尸体 corpse; dead body

【死守】sǐshǒu ❶ 拼死守住 defend to the death; defend to the last; make a last-ditch defence:～阵地 defend the position to the last ❷ 固执而不知变通地遵守 obstinately cling to; rigidly adhere to:～老规矩 rigidly adhere to old rules

【死水】sǐshuǐ 不流动的池水、湖水等。常用来形容长时期没什么变化的地方 stagnant water; (fig.) place where nothing has changed for a long period of time:那里并不是一潭～。The place is by no means stagnant.

【死胎】sǐtāi 在子宫内死亡的胎儿 stillborn foetus; stillbirth

【死亡】sǐwáng 失去生命(跟'生存'相对 as opposed to 'survival') death; doom:～率 death rate; mortality

【死亡率】sǐwánglǜ 每年死亡人数在总人口中所占的比率,通常以千分之几来表示 death rate; mortality; annual proportion of deaths, usu. per thousand of the population

【死亡线】sǐwángxiàn 指危及生存的境地 verge of death:在～上挣扎 struggle on the verge of death

【死心】sǐ//xīn 不再寄托希望;断了念头 give up a notion for good; have no more illusions about the matter:失败多次,他仍不～。Although he has suffered repeated failures, he has still not given up.

【死心塌地】sǐ xīn tā dì 形容主意已定,决不改变 be dead set; be hell-bent

【死心眼儿】sǐxīnyǎnr ❶ 固执;想不开 stubborn;

as obstinate as a mule ❷ 死心眼儿的人 person with a one-track mind

【死信】[1] sǐxìn (～儿 sǐxìnr)人死了的消息 news of sb.'s death

【死信】[2] sǐxìn 无法投递的信件 dead letter; letter that the post office can neither deliver nor return

【死刑】sǐxíng 剥夺犯人生命的刑罚 death penalty; death sentence; capital punishment

【死讯】sǐxùn 人死了的消息 news of sb.'s death

【死因】sǐyīn 死亡的原因 cause of death：查明～ find out the cause of death

【死硬】sǐyìng ❶ 呆板；不灵活 stiff; inflexible ❷ 顽固 very obstinate：～分子 diehard

【死有余辜】sǐ yǒu yú gū 虽然处以死刑，也抵偿不了他的罪过。形容罪大恶极。(used when denouncing a person guilty of the most heinous of crimes) death would be too good for him; even death would not expiate all his crimes

【死于非命】sǐ yú fēi mìng 遭受意外的灾祸而死亡 die an unnatural (or a violent) death

S

【死战】sǐzhàn ❶ 关系到生死存亡的战斗或战争 life-and-death struggle or battle：决一～ fight to the death; fight to the finish ❷ 拼死战斗 fight to the death：～到底 fight to the death

【死仗】sǐzhàng 硬仗 tough (or hard-fought) battle; formidable task

【死症】sǐzhèng 无法治好的病 incurable disease

【死罪】sǐzuì ❶ 应该判处死刑的罪行 capital offence (or crime) ❷〈客套话 *pol.*〉用于请罪或道歉，表示过失很重 my fault (used to apologize)

sì (ㄙˋ)

巳(巳) sì 地支的第六位 sixth of the 12 Earthly Branches; ☞ 干支 gānzhī on p. 627

【巳时】sìshí 旧式计时法指上午九点钟到十一点钟的时间 period of the day from 9 a.m. to 11 a.m.

四[1] sì ❶〈数目 *numeral*〉三加一后所得 four; the sum of three plus one; ☞ 数字 shùzì on p. 1791 ❷ (Sì)姓 a surname

四[2] sì 我国民族音乐音阶上的一级，乐谱上用做记音符号，相当于简谱的'6' note on the scale in *gongchepu* (工尺谱), corresponding to 6 in numbered musical notation; ☞ 工尺 gōngchě on p. 664

【四…八…】sì…bā… 分别用在两个意义相近的词或词素前面，表示各方面 used before two similar characters or morphemes respectively, to show various aspects：～面～方 all directions; all quarters; all around; far and near | ～通～达 lead through at random; extend in all directions | ～平～稳 very steady

【四边】sìbiān (～儿 sìbiānr)四周(on) all four sides：房子～儿围着篱笆。The house is fenced in on all four sides.

【四边形】sìbiānxíng 同一平面上的四条直线所围成的图形 quadrilateral; polygon of four sides

【四不像】sìbùxiàng ❶ 麋鹿 Pere David's deer (*Elaphurus davidianus*); *milu* ❷〈比喻 *fig.*〉不伦不类的东西或情况 anomaly; neither fish nor fowl

【四部】sìbù 我国古代把图书按经部、史部、子部、集部划分为四大部类，合称四部。后因分库储藏，故又称四库。four bibliographic categories; four traditional divisions of a Chinese library (i.e. classics, history, philosophy, and belles-letters); As they were stored in different warehouses, they are also known as 四库 sìkù (Four Treasuries)

【四出】sìchū 到周围各地 go hither and thither; go from place to place; go around：～活动 go from place to place to engage in activities

【四处】sìchù 周围各地；到处 all around; in all directions; everywhere：～奔波 go hither and thither | 田野里～都是歌声。The fields reverberate with song.

【四大皆空】sì dà jiē kōng 佛教用语，指世界上一切都是空虚的。(印度古代认为地、水、火、风是组成宇宙的四种元素，佛教称为四大。) (Budd.) the temporal world is illusory; all physical existence is a vanity (In ancient India, the universe was thought to comprise four elements — earth, water, fire and wind, called 四大 sìdà, meaning the world.)

【四叠体】sìdiétǐ 中脑背部的四个圆形突起，是视觉和听觉反射运动的低级中枢 corpora quadrigemina; four round protuberances at the back of the midbrain, which are the lower centres of visual and auditory reflex movement; (图见☞ figure for 脑 nǎo on p. 1394)

【四方】[1] sìfāng 东、南、西、北，泛指各处 four directions (north, south, east, west); all sides; all quarters：～响应。Responses came from every quarter. | 奔走～ go hither and thither

【四方】[2] sìfāng 正方形或立方体 square; cubic：～的木头匣子 square wooden box | 四四方方的大脸 big square face

【四方步】sìfāngbù (～儿 sìfāngbùr)悠闲的、大而慢的步子 leisurely and measured steps

【四分五裂】sì fēn wǔ liè 形容分散、不完整、不团结 fall apart; be rent by disunity; split up; disintegrate

【四伏】sìfú 到处潜伏着 lurk on every side：危机～。Danger lurks on every side.

【四顾】sìgù 向四周看 look around (or about)：～无人 look around and see no one | 茫然～ look around at a loss

【四海】sìhǎi 指全国各处。也指全世界各处

four seas; whole country; whole world: 五湖～all corners of the land | ～为家 make one's home wherever one is; making one's home wherever one happens to be

【四合院】sìhéyuàn (～儿 sìhéyuànr) 一种四面是屋子，中间是院子的住房建筑 compound with houses around a square courtyard; quadrangle; also 四合房 sìhéfáng

【四呼】sìhū 按照韵母把字音分成开口呼、齐齿呼、合口呼、撮口呼四类，总称四呼。韵母是 i 或拿 i 起头的叫齐齿呼，韵母是 u 或拿 u 起头叫合口呼，韵母是 ü 或拿 ü 起头的叫撮口呼，韵母不是 i、u、ü，也不拿 i、u、ü 起头的叫开口呼。例如肝 gān(开)、坚 jiān(齐)、关 guān(合)、捐 juān(撮)。four classes of syllables, set up according to the form of the final of a syllable, i.e. 开口呼 kāikǒuhū (such as 肝 gān, the final of the syllable an without i、u、ü), 齐齿呼 qíchǐhū (such as 坚 jiān, the final of the syllable ian starts with i), 合口呼 hékǒuhū (such as 关 guān, the final of the syllable uan starts with u), and 撮口呼 cuōkǒuhū (such as 捐 juān, the final of the syllable starts with ü).

【四胡】sìhú 胡琴的一种，形状跟二胡相似，有四根弦 *sihu*; four-stringed bowed instrument, similar to the *erhu*

【四季】sìjì 春、夏、秋、冬，叫做四季，每季三个月 four seasons (spring, summer, autumn and winter), each season consisting of three months

【四郊】sìjiāo 城市周围附近的地方 suburbs; outskirts; outlying part of a city or town

【四近】sìjìn 指周围附近的地方 neighbourhood; vicinity: ～见不到一个人影。There is no one to be seen in the vicinity.

【四联单】sìliándān 一式四份的单据，形式和用处跟三联单相同 bill in four parts; similar to tripartite bill in form and function; ☞ 三联单 sānliándān on p. 1653

【四邻】sìlín 前后左右的邻居 one's near neighbours: 街坊～neighbours | 吵得～不安。The noise is so loud that all the neighbours were disturbed.

【四六体】sìliùtǐ 骈体的一种，因以四字句、六字句为主，所以有这个名称 four-six style; style of *pianti* or parallel prose, characterized by a preponderance of pairs of four-and-six-character sentences

【四面】sìmiàn 东、南、西、北。泛指周围(on) four sides (east, west, south and north); (on) all sides (in a broad sense): ～环水 surrounded by water on all four sides | ～八方 all directions; all quarters; all around; far and near

【四面八方】sì miàn bā fāng 泛指周围各地或各个方面 all directions; all quarters; all around; far and near: 人们从～来到北京。People come to Beijing from all directions. | 我们小组里的人来自～。Members of our group come from diverse places.

【四面楚歌】sìmiàn Chǔ gē 楚汉交战时，项羽的军队驻扎在垓下，兵少粮尽，被汉军和诸侯的军队层层包围起来，夜间听到汉军四面都唱楚歌，项羽吃惊地说：'汉军把楚地都占领了吗？为什么楚人这么多呢？'(见于《史记·项羽本纪》)比喻四面受敌，处于孤立危急的困境。be besieged on all sides; be utterly isolated; be in desperate straits; find oneself under fire from all quarters. During the war between the Chu and the Han, Xiang Yu's troops at Gaixia were besieged by Han troops, and soon ran out of ammunition and provisions. That night they heard the Han troops singing Chu folk songs on all sides. Xiang Yu was surprised, saying, 'Have Han troops occupied all the territory of Chu? Why are there so many Chu people?' (*Records of the Historian · Official Records of Xiang Yu*)

【四拇指】sì·muzhǐ 〈方 *dial.*〉无名指 third finger; ring finger

【四旁】sìpáng 指前后左右很近的地方 back and front, left and right; all around

【四平八稳】sì píng bā wěn 形容说话、做事、写文章稳当。有时也指做事只求不出差错，缺乏创新精神。very steady (in speaking, handling affairs, or writing); well-balanced; overcautious and lacking in initiative

【四起】sìqǐ 从周围各处出现或兴起 rise in all directions: 歌声～。The sound of singing was heard all around. | 谣言～。Rumours were heard everywhere. | 群雄～。Heroes rose up in all directions.

【四散】sìsàn 向四面分散 scatter (or disperse) in all directions: ～奔逃 disperse in all directions and flee

【四舍五入】sì shě wǔ rù 运算时取近似值的一种方法。如被舍去部分的头一位数满五，就在所取数的末位加一，不满五的就舍去，如1.3785只取两位小数是1.38，1.2434只取两位小数是1.24。round; up or down; round off; method of obtaining approximate value when calculating by disregarding decimal fractions smaller than 0.5 and counting all others, including 0.5 as 1; For instance, 1.3785 is taken as 1.38, and 1.2434 as 1.24

【四声】sìshēng ❶ 古汉语字调有平声、上声、去声、入声四类，叫做四声 four tones of classical Chinese pronunciation, i.e. level tone, rising tone, falling tone, and entering tone ❷ 普通话的字调有阴平(读高平调，符号是'ˉ')、阳平(读高升调，符号是'ˊ')、上声(读先降后升的曲折调，符号是'ˇ')、去声(读降调，符号是'ˋ')四类，也叫四声(轻声在外) four tones of modern standard Chinese pronunciation, i.e. high and level tone 'ˉ', rising tone 'ˊ', falling-rising tone 'ˇ', and falling tone

S

'丶'(neutral tone not included) ❸ 泛指字调 tones (in a broad sense)

【四时】 sìshí 四季 four seasons

【四书】 Sì Shū 指《大学》《中庸》《论语》《孟子》四种书。是儒家的主要经典。Four Books, namely, *The Great Learning*, *The Doctrine of the Mean*, *Analects*, and *Mencius*, which are the main Confucian classics

【四体】[1] sìtǐ 〈书 *fml.*〉指人的四肢 four limbs (of humans); arms and legs: ～不勤，五谷不分 can neither toil with one's limbs nor tell the five cereals apart (said of old-time intellectuals who took no part in productive labour)

【四体】[2] sìtǐ 汉字的四种主要字体，即正、草、隶、篆 four main styles of Chinese calligraphy, namely, regular script, cursive script, official script and seal characters

【四外】 sìwài 四处(多指空旷的地方 oft. referring to a large open space) all around: ～无人。Not a soul was in sight. | ～全是平坦辽阔的大草地。All around are vast expanses of grassland.

【四围】 sìwéi 周围 on all sides; all around: 村子～都是菜地。All around the village are fields of vegetables.

【四维空间】 sìwéi kōngjiān 确定任何事物都需要四个坐标(空间的三个坐标和时间的一个坐标)的空间，是三维空间和时间组成的整体。这个概念是根据任何物质都同时存在于空间和时间中，空间和时间不可分割而提出的。四维空间的几何学对相对论的广泛传播有重要作用。four-dimensional space-time; space-time continuum; Four coordinates are needed to determine matter (three for space and one for time). This concept was based on the theory that any matter exists in space and time, and that space and time are inseparable. Four-dimensional geometry plays an important role in widespread dissemination of the theory of relativity.

【四下里】 sìxià·li same as 四处 sìchù: ～一看，都是果树。Looking around, one can see a vast expanse of fruit trees. also 四下 sìxià

【四仙桌】 sìxiānzhuō 小的方桌，每边只坐一个人 four immortals table (small square table seating four people)

【四乡】 sìxiāng 城镇四周围的乡村 countryside around a town

【四言诗】 sìyánshī 我国汉代以前最通行的诗歌形式，通章或通篇每句四字。如《诗经》，多为四言。four-character verse; earliest verse form in Chinese, popular before the Han Dynasty. Most of the poems in *The Book of Songs* are four-character verses.

【四野】 sìyě 广阔的原野(就四周展望说) wilderness in all directions; surrounding country; vast expanse of open ground: ～茫茫，寂静无声。All is quiet in this vast expanse of open ground.

【四则】 sìzé 加、减、乘、除四种运算的总称 four fundamental operations of arithmetic, i. e. addition, subtraction, multiplication and division: ～题 exercises in the four arithmetic operations | 整数～ four arithmetic operations in integral numbers | 分数～ four arithmetic operations in fractions

【四肢】 sìzhī 指人体的两上肢和两下肢，也指某些动物的四条腿 four limbs; arms and legs

【四至】 sìzhì 建筑基地或耕地四周跟别的基地或耕地分界的地方 four boundaries of a piece of land or a construction site

【四周】 sìzhōu 周围 all around; on all sides; also 四周围 sìzhōuwéi

【四座】 sìzuò 指四周在座的人 people present: ～哗然。The audience burst into an uproar. | 语惊～。These words startled all present.

饲 sì 〈书 *fml.*〉same as 饲 sì

寺 sì ❶〈古代 *arch.*〉官署名 government house of ancient China: 大理～ Court of Judicial Review (an important central government agency) | 太常～ Court of Imperial Sacrifices (one of the nine 'Courts' in the central government and foremost in prestige among them) ❷ 佛教的庙宇 Buddhist temple: 碧云～ Temple of Azure Clouds | 护国～ Protecting-the-Nation Temple ❸ 伊斯兰教徒礼拜、讲经的地方 mosque; building used for public worship by Muslims: 清真～ mosque

【寺观】 sìguàn 佛教和道观。泛指庙宇。Buddhist and Taoist temple; (in a broad sense) monastery

【寺庙】 sìmiào 供神佛或历史上有名人物的处所；庙宇 temple; monastery; building for the worship of god or famous historical figures

【寺院】 sìyuàn 佛寺的总称。有时也指别的宗教的修道院。Buddhist temple; monastery of other religions

似 sì ❶ 像；如同 similar; like: 相～ resemble; be similar to; be alike | 近～ approximate; similar | 类～ similar (to); analogous (to) | ～是而非 apparently right but actually wrong ❷ 似乎 seem; appear: ～属可行 seem to be feasible | ～应从速办理。It seems as though the matter should be dealt with as soon as possible. ❸ 表示超过(used in a comparative) than: 人民生活一年强～一年。People's lives are getting better every year.
☞ shì on p. 1755

【似…非…】 sì…fēi… 嵌用同一个单音名词、形容词或动词，表示又像又不像的意思(each followed by the same word) look like but not be; smack of: ～绸～绸。It looks like silk but is not. | ～蓝～蓝 look to be blue but is not | ～笑～笑 faint smile | ～懂～懂 have only a hazy notion; not completely understand

【似乎】sì·hū〈副词 *adv.*〉仿佛;好像 as if; seemingly:他～了解了这个字的意思,但是又讲不出来。It seems as though he understands this, but is unable to express it in words.

【似是而非】sì shì ér fēi 好像对,实际上并不对 apparently right but actually wrong:这些论点～,必须认真分辨,才不至于上当。These arguments are specious; one can avoid being fooled by them only after making a serious analysis.

汜 Sì 汜河,水名,在河南 Sihe River in Henan Province

兕 sì〈书 *fml.*〉雌的犀牛 female rhinoceros

佀 sì ❶〈书 *fml.*〉same as 似 sì ❷(Sì)姓 a surname

伺 sì 观察;守候 watch; await:窥～peep at|～隙 wait for a chance|～机 watch out for one's chance

☞ cì on p. 321

【伺机】sìjī 窥伺时机 watch for one's chance:～而动 wait for an opportune moment to take action|～报复 wait for an opportunity to take revenge

【伺隙】sìxì 察看可利用的机会;伺机 wait for a chance; watch for an opportunity:～乘虚 wait for an opportunity and catch the opponent off guard|～进攻 wait for a chance to attack

祀 sì ❶祭祀 offer sacrifices to the gods or to the spirits of the dead:～天 offer sacrifices to Heaven|～孔 offer sacrifices to Confucius|～祖 offer sacrifices to one's ancestors ❷殷代特指年 year (term used in the Yin Dynasty):十有三～ the 13th year

姒 sì ❶〈古代 *arch.*〉称姐姐 elder sister ❷〈古代 *arch.*〉称丈夫的嫂子 wife of husband's elder brother ❸(Sì)姓 a surname

饲 sì ❶饲养 raise; rear:～料 forage; fodder; feed ❷饲料 forage; fodder; feed:打草储～ cut grass to store as forage

【饲料】sìliào 喂家畜或家禽的食物 forage; fodder; feed

【饲养】sìyǎng 喂养(动物) raise; rear (animals):～员 stockman; poultry raiser; husbandman

【饲育】sìyù 喂养 feed; raise; keep

泗[1] sì〈书 *fml.*〉鼻涕 nasal mucus

泗[2] Sì 泗河,水名,在山东 Sihe, name of a river in Shandong Province

【泗州戏】sìzhōuxì 安徽地方戏曲剧种之一,起源于旧泗州(州治在今安徽泗县),流行于淮河两岸。Sizhou opera; regional opera popular in the Huai River basin; named after Sizhou (present-day Sixian County, Anhui Province), its place of origin; also 拉魂腔 lāhúnqiāng

驷 sì〈书 *fml.*〉① 驷马 see below: ② 马 horse

【驷马】sìmǎ〈书 *fml.*〉同拉一辆车的四匹马 team of four horses to be harnessed to a chariot:～高车 carriage drawn by four horses|一言既出,～难追。A word once spoken cannot be taken back even by a team of four horses. *or* What is said cannot be taken back.

俟(竢) sì〈书 *fml.*〉等待 wait:～机进攻 wait for an opportunity to attack

☞ qí on p. 1511

食 sì〈书 *fml.*〉拿东西给人吃 give to; feed

☞ shí on p. 1745 and yì on p. 2277

覗 sì〈书 *fml.*〉窥视 peep

涘 sì〈书 *fml.*〉水边 riverbank:涯～ waterside; foreshore

耜 sì ❶古代的一种农具,形状像现在的锹 spade-shaped farm tool used in ancient China ❷〈古代 *arch.*〉跟犁上的铧相似的东西 sth. resembling a plowshare

笥 sì〈书 *fml.*〉盛饭或盛衣物的方形竹器 bamboo-plaited rectangular container for food or clothes

肆[1] sì 不顾一切,任意妄为 wanton; unbridled:放～ unbridled; wanton|大～攻击 wantonly vilify; launch an unbridled (or all-out) attack against

肆[2] sì '四'的大写 upper case of the numeral 4; ☞ 数字 shùzì on p. 1791

肆[3] sì 铺子 shop:茶楼酒～ teahouses and wine shops

【肆力】sìlì〈书 *fml.*〉尽力 devote all one's efforts to:～农事 devote oneself to farming

【肆虐】sìnüè 任意残杀或迫害;起破坏作用 indulge in wanton massacre or persecution; wreak havoc; run berserk:逞凶～act violently and indulge in wanton massacre

【肆扰】sìrǎo 肆意扰乱 harass recklessly

【肆无忌惮】sì wú jì dàn 任意妄为,没有一点儿顾忌 unbridled; unscrupulous; impertinent

【肆行】sìxíng 任意妄为 act recklessly:～无忌 act unscrupulously|～劫掠 plunder wantonly

【肆意】sìyì 不顾一切由着自己的性子(去做) wantonly; recklessly; wilfully:～攻击 attack wilfully|～妄为 act recklessly

嗣 sì ❶接续;继承 succeed; inherit:～位 succeed to the throne|～子 son of a wife (as compared with the son of a concubine) ❷子孙 heir; descendant:后～ descendants

【嗣后】sìhòu〈书 *fml.*〉以后 hereafter; subsequently; afterwards; later on

【嗣位】sìwèi〈书 *fml.*〉继承王位 succeed to the throne

禩 sì〈书 *fml.*〉same as 祀 sì

sōng（ㄙㄨㄥ）

忪 sōng ☞ 惺忪（xīngsōng）on p. 2142 ☞ zhōng on p. 2486

松[1] sōng ❶ 种子植物的一属，一般为常绿乔木，很少为灌木，树皮多为鳞片状，叶子针形，花单性，雌雄同株，结球果，卵圆形或圆锥形，有木质的鳞片。木材和树脂都可利用。如马尾松、油松等。pine (tree)(*Pinus*); monoecious seed plant generally in the form of an evergreen tree or bush in a few cases, with scale-like bark, needle-shaped leaves, and unisexual flowers, bearing cone-shaped or oval fruits, its timber and resin for wide use; genus includes masson pine, Chinese pine, etc. ❷ (Sōng)姓 a surname

松[2]（鬆）sōng ❶ 松散(跟'紧'相对，②③同 as opposed to 'tight', see ②③below) loose; slack：这包书捆得太～，容易散。This bundle of books has not been tied tightly enough, and is likely to fall apart. ❷ 使松 loosen; relax; slacken：～一～腰带 slacken the belt | ～口气(紧张之后，放松一下) take a breather (relax after intense efforts) | 要再接再厉，不能～劲。Redouble your efforts and never slacken. ❸ 经济宽裕 not be hard up：这个月我手头～一些，给他寄了点钱去。I am better off this month, so I have mailed him some money. ❹ 不坚实 light and flaky; soft：点心～脆适口。The pastry is light and crisp. ❺ 解开；放开 untie; unfasten; release：～绑 untie a person | 一～手，气球就飞了。As the grip on it loosened, the balloon flew away. ❻ 用鱼、虾、瘦肉等做成的绒状或碎末状的食品 dried meat (fish, shrimp) floss; dried minced meat：肉～dried minced meat

【松绑】sōng//bǎng ❶ 解开捆绑在身上的绳索 untie a person ❷〈比喻 *fig.*〉放宽约束限制 relax restrictions

【松弛】sōngchí ❶ 松[2]①；不紧张 limp; flabby; slack：肌肉～ flaccid muscles | ～的心情 a lax state of mind ❷ (制度、纪律等)执行得不严格 (of discipline, rules) lax：纪律～be under lax discipline

【松动】sōngdòng ❶ 不拥挤 become less crowded：接近终点站，车厢里～多了。As the train came nearer to its terminal, the carriage became less crowded. ❷ 宽裕；不窘 not hard up：手头～ be in easy circumstances; be quite well off at the moment ❸ (牙齿、螺丝等)不紧；活动(of teeth, screws) loose：门牙～。The front teeth have become loose. ❹ (措施、态度、关系等)灵活；改变强硬、紧张状态 show flexibility (in measures, attitude, relationship, etc.); relax：谈判中，双方口气都有了些～。In the course of negotiations, both sides have become a little more flexible.

【松花】sōnghuā 一种蛋制食品，用水混合石灰、黏土、食盐、稻壳等包在鸭蛋或鸡蛋的壳上使凝固变味而成，因蛋青上有像松针的花纹，所以叫松花。preserved egg; hen's eggs or duck's eggs preserved in a mixture of water, lime, clay, salt and rice husk, with pine needle-shaped veins (*songhua*) running through the egg whites, hence the name *songhua*; also 皮蛋 pídàn, 变蛋 biàndàn, or 松花蛋 sōnghuādàn

【松节油】sōngjiéyóu 蒸馏松脂而得的挥发性油，无色至深棕色液体，有特殊气味。油漆工业上用做溶剂，也用于医药。turpentine (oil); strong-smelling colourless or dark-brown volatile liquid extracted from the resin of pine or other coniferous trees, used esp. for thinning paint and as a solvent, also in medicine

【松紧】sōngjǐn 松或紧的程度 degree of tightness; elasticity：检查一下绳子绑的～ check the tightness of the rope

【松紧带】sōngjǐndài (～儿 sōngjǐngdàir)可以伸缩的带子，用橡胶丝或橡胶条和纱织成 elastic cord; elastic; easily stretched fabric made of yarns containing rubber

【松劲】sōng//jìn (～儿 sōng//jìnr)降低紧张用力的程度 relax one's efforts; slacken (off)：工程越接近尾声，越是不能～。The nearer the project comes to its end, the more important it is that we do not slacken our efforts.

【松口】sōngkǒu ❶ 张嘴把咬住的东西放开 unclench the jaws：猎犬叼着野兔不～。The hound is holding a rabbit in its mouth, and refuses to unclench its jaws. ❷ 不坚持(主张、意见等) soften; relent (position, proposal, etc.)：怎么劝他，他也不～。No matter how hard I tried to persuade him, he would not relent.

【松快】sōng·kuai ❶ 轻松爽快；舒畅 feel relieved：感觉～ feel relieved | 心里～多了 feel much better ❷ 宽敞 be less crowded：房间虽不大，一个人住还是～的。Although the room is not big, it is perfectly adequate for one person.

【松明】sōngmíng 燃点起来照明用的松树枝 pine torch; torch made of resinous pine branch

【松墙】sōngqiáng 栽种成行像短墙一样的桧、柏，多用于庭园布置 row of pines or junipers forming a wall, usu. used in gardening; also 松墙子 sōngqiáng·zi

【松球】sōngqiú 松树的果穗，多为卵圆形，由许多木质的鳞片组成，里面有松子。有的地区叫松塔儿。pine cone; oval-shaped fruit of the pine, comprising wooden scales and containing pine nuts; also called 松塔儿 sōngtǎr in some places

【松仁】sōngrén (～儿 sōngrénr)松子里面的仁，可以吃 edible pine nut kernels

【松软】sōngruǎn ❶ 松散绵软 soft; spongy; loose：白净～的羊毛 clean fluffy wool | 耕过的土地十分～。Ploughed soil is very soft. ❷（肢体）软而无力 become limp and weak：浑身～，瘫倒在地。His whole body became limp and weak and he collapsed.

【松散】sōngsǎn（事物结构）不紧密；（精神）不集中（of structure）loose；（of one's mind）inattentive

【松散】sōng·san 使轻松舒畅 relax; take one's ease：房里太热，出来～～。It's too hot indoors. Come outside for a breath of air.

【松手】sōng//shǒu 放开手 loosen one's grip：一～，钢笔掉在地上了。The pen dropped on the floor upon his loosening his grip. ◇工作要抓紧，不能～。Pay close attention to your work, and never slacken.

【松鼠】sōngshǔ（～儿 sōngshǔr）哺乳动物的一属，外形略像鼠，比鼠大，尾巴蓬松而特别长大，生活在松林中，有的种类毛皮珍贵 squirrel (*Sciuridae*); mammal similar to the rat in shape, but larger in size and with big bushy tail, living in pine forests, some species known for their precious fur

【松松垮垮】sōng·sōngkuǎkuǎ（～的 sōng·sōngkuǎkuǎde）❶（结构）不坚固，不紧密（of a structure）not solid or firm; unsteady：这座房子梁柱檩条～的，像是快要倒塌了。The beams, pillars and purlins of this house are unsteady; it seems likely to collapse. ❷ 懒散；松懈；不紧张 slack; sluggish：训练时～，比赛时一定打败仗。Slack training surely leads to defeat in competition.

【松塔儿】sōngtǎr〈方 *dial.*〉same as 松球 sōngqiú

【松涛】sōngtāo 松树被风吹动时所发出的像波涛一样的声音 soughing of the wind in the pines

【松香】sōngxiāng 松脂蒸馏后剩下的固体物质，淡黄色或棕色，透明，质硬而脆。用于油漆、肥皂、造纸、橡胶等工业。rosin; colophony; translucent amber or brown coloured brittle friable solid that is obtained by distillation from resin, used in making paint, soap, paper and rubber

【松懈】sōngxiè ❶ 注意力不集中；做事不抓紧 inattentive; lax; be slack ❷ 纪律不严格；意志不坚定 relax; slacken ❸ 人与人之间关系不密切；动作不协调 unharmonious relationship; unharmonious actions

【松心】sōng//xīn 不操心；使心情松快 feel relieved; have ease of mind; feel carefree and happy：家务有儿媳妇操持，婆婆就～了。The mother feels she has a weight off her mind, now that her daughter-in-law manages household affairs. | 忙完了这件事，我们就能松几天心了。After finishing this work, we can relax for a couple of days.

【松针】sōngzhēn 松树的叶子，形状像针 pine needle; pine leaf that looks like a needle

【松脂】sōngzhī 针叶树的树干上渗出的胶状液体，主要由松香和松节油组成 rosin; pine resin; sticky substance that oozes from coniferous trees, comprising mainly rosin and turpentine oil

【松子】sōngzǐ ❶（～儿 sōngzǐr）松树的种子 pine nut ❷〈方 *dial.*〉same as 松仁 sōngrén：～糖 sugar-coated pine nut kernels

【松嘴】sōng//zuǐ same as 松口 sōngkǒu

娀 sōng 有娀，古国名，在今山西运城一带 Yousong, an ancient state, located around present-day Yuncheng, Shanxi Province

凇 sōng ☞ 雾凇 wù·sōng on p. 2040 and 雨凇 yǔsōng on p. 2344

菘 sōng 古书上指白菜 ancient name for Chinese cabbage

【菘菜】sōngcài〈方 *dial.*〉白菜 Chinese cabbage

淞 sōng 吴淞江（Wúsōng Jiāng），发源于江苏，流经上海，入黄浦江 Wusong River, which originates in Jiangsu Province and joins the Huangpu River in Shanghai

嵩（崧）sōng〈书 *fml.*〉❶ 山大而高（of a mountain）big and high ❷ 高 high; lofty

sóng（ㄙㄨㄥˊ）

㞞（𡱝）sóng ❶ 精液 seminal fluid; semen ❷ 讥讽人软弱无能 weak and incompetent：～包 good-for-nothing | 这人真～。This fellow really is a good-for-nothing.

【㞞包】sóngbāo 软弱无能，也指软弱无能的人 weak and incompetent; worthless fellow

sǒng（ㄙㄨㄥˇ）

扨（㩳）sǒng ❶〈书 *fml.*〉挺立；挺起 straighten：～身 straighten one's back ❷〈方 *dial.*〉推 push

怂（慫）sǒng〈书 *fml.*〉惊惧 alarmed and panicky; terrified

【怂恿】sǒngyǒng 鼓动别人去做（某事）instigate; incite; egg sb. on; abet

耸（聳）sǒng ❶ 耸立 towering; lofty：高～入云 reach to the sky; tower into the clouds ❷ 引起注意；使人吃惊 alarm; shock：危言～听 say frightening things just to cause alarm; exaggerate just to scare people

【耸动】sǒngdòng ❶（肩膀、肌肉等）向上动（one's shoulders, muscles, etc.）raise; shrug ❷ 造成某种局面，使人震动 stir up; rouse：～视听 create a sensation

【耸肩】sǒng//jiān 微抬肩膀（表示轻蔑、疑惑、惊讶等）shrug one's shoulders（to show scorn, doubt, surprise etc.）：他耸了耸肩，现出不可理解的神情。He shrugged his shoulders, expressing incomprehension.

【耸立】sǒnglì 高高地直立 tower aloft：群山～。The mountains tower aloft.

【耸人听闻】sǒng rén tīng wén 故意说夸大或惊奇的话，使人震惊 deliberately exaggerate so as to create a sensation

悚 sǒng〈书 *fml.*〉害怕 terrified; horrified：～然 terrified; horrified

【悚惧】sǒngjù 恐惧 fear; dread

【悚然】sǒngrán 害怕的样子 terrified; horrified：毛骨～ with one's hair standing on end; absolutely terrified

竦 sǒng ❶〈书 *fml.*〉恭敬 respectful ❷ same as 悚 sǒng ❸ same as 耸 sǒng

sòng（ㄙㄨㄥˋ）

讼 sòng ❶ 在法庭上争辩是非曲直；打官司 go to law; bring a case to court：诉～lawsuit; litigation ❷ 争辩是非 dispute; argue：争～ contest a lawsuit｜聚～纷纭 argue back and forth without coming to an agreement; widely differing opinions; a welter of conflicting opinions

【讼棍】sònggùn〈旧社会 *pre-*1949〉唆使别人打官司自己从中取利的坏人 legal pettifogger; shyster; one who is professionally unscrupulous esp. in the practice of law

【讼师】sòngshī〈旧社会 *pre-*1949〉以给打官司的人出主意、写状纸为职业的人 legal pettifogger who made a living by writing plaints for others

宋[1] Sòng ❶ 周朝国名，在今河南商丘一带 Song, a state in the Zhou Dynasty, located in the present-day Shangqiu area in Henan Province ❷ 朝代 Song Dynasty a）南朝之一，公元 420—479，刘裕所建 Song Dynasty（420-479）, one of the Southern Dynasties, founded by Liu Yu; ☞ 南北朝 Nán-Běi Cháo on p. 1388 b）公元 960—1279，赵匡胤所建 Song Dynasty（960-1279）founded by Zhao Kuangyin; ☞ 北宋 Běi Sòng on p. 80 and 南宋 Nán Sòng on p. 1389 ❸ 姓 a surname

宋[2] sòng 响度单位。1 宋等于 1,000 毫宋，约相当于人耳刚能听到的声音响度的一千倍。sone; equal to 1,000 millisones; subjective unit of volume for an average listener, equal to the volume of one kilohertz at 40 decibels above the listener's own threshold of hearing; 旧作 written as 㕬 in old times

【宋江起义】Sòng Jiāng Qǐyì 北宋末年（约公元 1110 年）宋江领导的农民起义，活动于今山东、河北一带，公元 1121 年被北宋王朝所镇压 Song Jiang Uprising; peasant uprising led by Song Jiang in the late Northern Song Dynasty（c. 1110）. The rebels were active in present-day Shandong and Hebei provinces and were suppressed by the Northern Song Dynasty in 1121.

【宋体字】sòngtǐzì 通行的汉字印刷体，正方形，横的笔画细，竖的笔画粗。这种字体起于明朝中叶，叫做宋体是出于误会。另有横竖笔画都较细的字体称'仿宋体'，比较接近于宋朝刻书的字体。为了区别于仿宋体，原来的宋体字又称为'老宋体'。Song typeface, standard typeface, square-shaped, with thin horizontal strokes and thick vertical strokes, first used in the mid-Ming Dynasty but mistakenly attributed to the Song Dynasty. Another typeface with both thin horizontal and vertical strokes, is called 'imitation Song script' for its close resemblance to the Song typeface which is also called 'old Song typeface' for the purpose of differentiation.

送 sòng ❶ 把东西运去或拿去给人 deliver; carry：～报 deliver a newspaper｜～信 deliver a letter｜～公粮 deliver public grain ❷ 赠送 give as a present; give：奉～offer as a gift; give away free｜老师～我两本书。My teacher gave me two books. ❸ 陪着离去的人一起走 see sb. off or out; accompany; escort：把客人～到大门外 see a guest out of the door; walk a guest out of the gate｜～小孩儿上学 take a child to school

【送别】sòng//bié same as 送行 sòng//xíng：车站～see somebody off at the station

【送殡】sòng//bìn 出殡时陪送灵柩 attend a funeral; take part in a funeral procession

【送风机】sòngfēngjī 工厂、矿山生产中为防暑降温或保持空气清洁，向车间、矿井大量输送空气的机器 forced draught blower; blower; device that produces a current of air into a workshop or mine shaft to lower the temperature or keep it ventilated

【送礼】sòng//lǐ 赠送礼品 give sb. a present; present a gift to sb.：请客～ give dinners or send gifts（in order to curry favour）

【送命】sòng//mìng 丧失性命（含不值得的意思）；送死 lose one's life（needlessly）; be killed; go to one's doom：白白～lose one's life meaninglessly

【送气】sòngqì 语音学上把发辅音时有比较显著的气流出来叫送气，没有显著的气流出来叫不送气。普通话语音中的 b, d, g, j, z, zh 是不送气音，p, t, k, q, c, ch 是送气音。aspirated; consonant with a puff of abruptly released breath; In *putonghua*, or standard Chinese, non-aspirated sounds include b, d, g, j, z, zh; and aspirated sounds include p, t, k, q, c, ch. 送气、不送气也叫吐气、不吐气 also 吐气 tǔqì，不吐气 bùtǔqì

【送亲】sòng// qīn 结婚时女家亲属送新娘到男家(of a bride's kinsfolk) escort the bride to the groom's home

【送情】sòng// qíng ❶ 传递情意 express amorous feeling:眉目～ flash amorous glances; make eyes at sb.; ogle ❷〈方 *dial.*〉same as 送礼 sòng// lǐ

【送人情】sòng rénqíng ❶ 给人一些好处,以讨好别人 do favours at no great cost to oneself ❷〈方 *dial.*〉same as 送礼 sòng// lǐ

【送丧】sòng// sāng same as 送殡 sòng// bìn

【送审】sòngshěn 送上级或有关方面审批或审订 submit to higher level for approval or revision:～稿 manuscript submitted to a higher level for approval

【送死】sòngsǐ 自寻死路;找死 court death

【送信儿】sòng// xìnr 传递消息 send word; go and tell:大哥一到家,小妹就给妈妈～去了。No sooner had her elder brother arrived home than his younger sister went to tell their mother.

【送行】sòng// xíng ❶ 到远行人启程的地方,和他告别,看他离开 see sb. off; wish sb. bon voyage:到车站～go to the railway station to see sb. off ❷ 饯行 give a send-off party:～酒席 send-off banquet

【送葬】sòng// zàng 送死者遗体到埋葬地点或火化地点 attend a funeral; take part in a funeral procession

【送站】sòngzhàn 送人到车站 see sb. off at the station:火车开了,～的人们渐渐离去。The train started to move, and those who had come to the station to see people off gradually left.

【送终】sòng// zhōng 长辈亲属临终时在身旁照料。也指安排长辈亲属的丧事。attend upon a dying parent or other senior member of one's family; arrange the funeral of a parent or other senior member of one's family:养老～ look after one's parents in their old age and give them a proper burial upon their death

诵 sòng ❶ 读出声音来;念 read aloud; chant:朗～read aloud with expression ❷ 背诵 recite:熟读成～ read again and again until one knows by heart; learn by rote ❸ 称述;述说 state; recount; narrate:传～ be on everybody's lips; be widely read

【诵读】sòngdú 念(诗文) read aloud; chant:高声～ read aloud

唻 sòng '宋'(响度单位)旧也作唻 sone, subjective unit of loudness, formerly written as 唻

颂 sòng ❶ 颂扬 praise; extol; eulogize; laud:歌～sing praises of; laud ❷ 祝颂(多用于书信问候 usu. in letters) express good wishes:敬～大安。Wish you good health. ❸ 周代祭祀时用的舞曲,配曲的歌词有些收在《诗经》里面 sacrificial dance music of the Zhou Dynasty, some of the lyrics for which were collected in *The Book of Songs* ❹ 以颂扬为目的的诗文 song; ode; paean; eulogy:《祖国～》*Ode to Our Motherland*

【颂词】sòngcí 称赞功德或祝贺幸福的讲话或文章 speech or piece of writing praising sb. or sth.

【颂歌】sònggē 用于祝颂的诗歌 song; ode; lyric poem addressed to a person or thing

【颂扬】sòngyáng 歌颂赞扬 sing praises of; laud; extol; eulogize:大加～greatly extol｜～功绩 laud someone's contributions

sōu (ㄙㄡ)

搜(❶蒐) sōu ❶ 寻找 look for:～集 collect｜～罗 gather｜～求 seek ❷ 搜查 search; ransack; rummage:～身 search the person｜～腰 search sb's pockets｜～捕 track down and arrest｜什么也没～着。Nothing was found in the search.

【搜捕】sōubǔ 搜查与案件有关的地方并逮捕有关的人 search the associated places and arrest the involved people:～逃犯 track down and arrest escaped criminals

【搜查】sōuchá 搜索检查(犯罪的人或违禁的东西) search (a criminal or for contraband goods); ransack; rummage:～毒品 rummage for narcotic drugs

【搜肠刮肚】sōu cháng guā dù 形容费尽心思 rack one's brains:他～地想办法,却怎么也想不出好点子来。He racked his brains for a way out, but not one good idea came to him.

【搜刮】sōuguā 用各种方法掠夺(人民的财物) extort; plunder; expropriate; fleece:贪官污吏～民脂民膏。The corrupt officials lived off the flesh and blood of the people (or from ruthlessly fleecing the people).

【搜集】sōují 到处寻找(事物)并聚集在一起 hunt high and low for (things); collect; gather:～意见 solicit opinions｜～革命文物 collect revolutionary relics

【搜剿】sōujiǎo 搜索剿灭 track down and exterminate:～残敌 track down and exterminate all traces of the enemy

【搜缴】sōujiǎo 搜查收缴 search for and capture:～凶器 search for and capture a lethal weapon｜～非法出版物 search for and seize illegal publications

【搜括】sōukuò same as 搜刮 sōuguā

【搜罗】sōuluó 到处寻找(人或事物)并聚集在一起 hunt high and low for (persons or things); collect; gather; recruit:～人才 recruit qualified persons; scout for talent｜～史料 collect historical data

【搜身】sōu// shēn 搜查身上有无夹带 search

someone (for concealed articles); make a body search; frisk

【搜索】sōusuǒ 仔细寻找(隐藏的人或东西) search for; hunt for; scout around:～残敌 hunt for the remnants of enemy forces|～前进 advance and reconnoitre|四处～ferret out

【搜索枯肠】sōusuǒ kū cháng 形容竭力思索(多指写诗文)rack one's brains (for fresh ideas or apt expressions, usu. when writing poetry or an essay)

【搜寻】sōuxún 到处寻找 search for; look for; hunt for; seek:～证据 collect evidence

嗖(颼) sōu〈拟声词 *onom.*〉形容很快通过的声音 whiz:汽车～的一声开过去了。The car whizzed by.|子弹～～地从头顶飞过。Bullets whizzed overhead.

馊 sōu 饭、菜等变质而发出酸臭味(of food, dishes) turn sour; become spoiled

【馊主意】sōu zhǔ·yi 指不高明的办法 stupid suggestion; lousy idea

廋 sōu〈书 *fml.*〉隐藏;藏匿 hide; conceal

溲 sōu〈书 *fml.*〉排泄粪便,特指排泄小便 excrete stools and urine, esp. urinate

飕[1] sōu〈方 *dial.*〉风吹(使变干或变冷) dry or cool sth. by wind:别让风～干了。Don't let it dry up in the wind.

飕[2] sōu same as 嗖 sōu

【飕飗】sōuliú〈书 *fml.*〉形容风声(of wind) soughing; rustling

锼 sōu〈方 *dial.*〉镂刻(木头) engrave (on wood); carve (wood):椅背上的花纹是～出来的。The design on the back of the chair is engraved.

【锼弓子】sōugōng·zi〈方 *dial.*〉钢丝锯 fretsaw; scroll saw

螋 sōu ☞ [蠼螋](qúsōu) on p.1591

艘 sōu〈量词 *classifier*〉用于船只 for boats or ships:五～远洋货轮 five ocean-going freighters

sǒu (ㄙㄡˇ)

叟(叜) sǒu 年老的男人 old man:老～ old man|童～无欺。Neither the old nor the young shall be cheated.

瞍 sǒu〈书 *fml.*〉❶眼睛没有瞳人,看不见东西 have eyes without pupils; be blind ❷瞎子 blind person

嗾 sǒu ❶指使狗时所发的声音 whistling sound made as signal to a dog ❷〈书 *fml.*〉发出声音来指使狗 whistle to a dog ❸教唆 instigate:～使 instigate (others to do evil things); abet

【嗾使】sǒushǐ 挑动指使别人做坏事 instigate (others to do evil things); abet

薮(藪) sǒu〈书 *fml.*〉❶生长着很多草的湖 shallow lake overgrown with wild plants ❷指人或东西聚集的地方 gathering place for people or things; haunt:渊～ gathering place

擞(擻) sǒu ☞ 抖擞 dǒusǒu on p.472 ☞sòu on p.1828

sòu (ㄙㄡˋ)

嗽 sòu 咳嗽 cough:干～dry cough

擞(擻) sòu〈方 *dial.*〉用通条插到火炉里抖动,使炉灰掉下去 poke the ashes out of a stove fire; rake:～火 poke the ashes out; poke the fire|把炉子～一～give the stove fire a poking (or raking) ☞ sǒu on p.1828

sū (ㄙㄨ)

苏[1]**(蘇)** sū 植物名 perilla; beefsteak plant:紫～ purple perilla|白～ common perilla

苏[2]**(蘇)** sū 指须状下垂物 beard-shaped pendant:流～ tassel

苏[3]**(蘇、甦)** sū 苏醒 revive; come to:死而复～come back to life

苏[4]**(蘇)** Sū ❶指江苏苏州 short for Suzhou, a city in Jiangsu Province:～绣 Suzhou school or style of embroidery ❷姓 a surname

苏[5]**(囌)** sū ☞ [噜苏](lū·sū) on p.1256

苏[6]**(蘇)** sū ❶指苏维埃 short for Soviet:～区 Soviet area ❷(Sū)指苏联 short for the former Soviet Union (Union of Soviet Socialist Republics)

【苏白】sūbái ❶苏州话 Suzhou dialect ❷京剧、昆曲等剧中用苏州话说的道白 spoken parts in Suzhou dialect in *kunqu* opera and Peking Opera

【苏打】sūdá 无机化合物,化学式(Na_2CO_3)。白色粉末或颗粒,水溶液呈强碱性。是玻璃、造纸、肥皂、洗涤剂、纺织、制革等工业的重要原料,也用来软化硬水。soda ash; sodium carbonate; inorganic compound whose chemical formula is Na_2CO_3, white powder or granules, its aqueous solution strongly alkali; an important raw material for making glass, paper, soap, detergent, textiles, and tanning; also used for softening hard water; also纯碱 chúnjiǎn

【苏丹】sūdān 某些伊斯兰教国家最高统治者的称号 Arabic: sovereign ruler of certain Muslim countries [阿拉伯 Arabic: sulṭān]

【苏剧】sūjù 江苏地方戏曲剧种之一,由曲艺'苏州滩簧'发展而成。用胡琴、笛、琵琶(或弦子)、笙等伴奏 Suzhou opera; one of the local operas in Jiangsu Province, developed from *Suzhou tanhuang*, accompanied by *huqin*, bamboo flute, *pipa*, *sheng*, etc.

【苏区】sūqū 第二次国内革命战争时期的革命根据地。因根据地的政权采取苏维埃的形式,故称苏区。Chinese Soviet areas; revolutionary base areas established during the Second Revolutionary Civil War (1927-1937) whose political power adopted the Soviet form, hence the name

【苏铁】sūtiě 常绿乔木,叶子聚生在茎的顶部,有大形的羽状复叶,小叶条形,有光泽,花顶生,雌雄异株,雄花圆锥形,雌花有褐色绒毛,种子球形。产于温暖的地区,生长得很慢。sago cycad (*Cycas revolute*); evergreen tree, with large, pinnately compound, tender, linear, lustrous leaves concentrated at the top of its trunk, dioecious, apical flowers (fine brown hair grows on the female flowers, and the male flowers are cone shaped) and spherical seeds, that grows slowly and is found in warm regions; 通称 commonly known as 铁树 tiěshù

【苏维埃】sūwéi'āi 苏联中央和地方各级的国家权力机关。我国第二次国内革命战争时期曾把当时的工农民主政权组织也叫苏维埃。Soviet; central and local governing councils of the former Soviet Union; workers' and peasants' democratic political power established during China's Second Revolutionary Civil War (1927-1937) [俄 Russian: совет]

【苏醒】sūxǐng 昏迷后醒过来 revive; regain consciousness; come to; come round: 伤员已从昏迷中~。The person wounded has regained consciousness. ◇春天万物~。All things on earth come to life again in the spring.

【苏绣】sūxiù 江苏苏州出产的刺绣 embroidery in the style of Suzhou, Jiangsu Province

【苏州码子】Sūzhōu mǎ·zi 我国旧时表示数目的符号,从一到十依次写做〡、〢、〣、〤、〥、〦、〧、〨、〩、十 Suzhou numerals (from one to ten, traditionally used by shopkeepers to mark prices); also 草码 cǎomǎ

酥 sū ❶ 古代称酥油为酥 ancient name for 酥油 sūyóu ❷ (食物)松而易碎 crisp; short: 虾片一炸就很~。Prawn crackers turn crisp after being deep-fried. ❸ 面粉和油加糖制成的松而易碎的点心 shortbread; crumbly dry cake made with flour, sugar and butter: 桃~ walnut shortbread ❹ 酥软(of a person's limbs) limp; weak; soft: ~麻 weak and numb

【酥脆】sūcuì (食物)酥而且脆 (of food) crisp

【酥麻】sūmá (肢体)酥软发麻 (of a person's limbs) weak and numb: 浑身~ the whole body feeling weak and numb

【酥软】sūruǎn (肢体)软弱无力 (of a person's limbs) limp; languid: 走了一天路,累得两腿~。After walking for a whole day, (my) legs feel weak and shaky.

【酥松】sūsōng (土壤等)松散;不紧密 (of soil, etc.) loose: 泥土~ porous soil | ~的石灰层 loose lime stratum

【酥油】sūyóu 从牛奶或羊奶内提出来的脂肪。把牛奶或羊奶煮沸,用勺搅动,冷却后凝结在上面的一层就是酥油。butter; fat made by churning cow's or sheep's milk. Milk is boiled and stirred, and after it cools down a layer of butter forms on the top.

【酥油茶】sūyóuchá 藏族、蒙古族地区的一种饮料,用酥油、砖茶、盐等制成 buttered tea; drink popular in the Tibetan and Mongolian areas, made from butter, brick tea and salt

【酥油花】sūyóuhuā 藏族的一种艺术品,用搀合各种颜料的酥油雕塑成的各种人物、风景、花卉、鸟兽等 butter sculpture; Tibetan works of art depicting figures, landscapes, flowers, birds, or animals sculpted in butter mixed with the pigments of various colours

稣 sū same as 苏 sū (苏醒 sūxǐng)

窣 sū ☞ [窸窣] (xīsū) on p. 2050

sú (ㄙㄨˊ)

俗 sú ❶ 风俗 custom; convention: 土~ local custom | 移风易~ transform social traditions | 入境问~。On entering a country, enquire about its customs. ❷ 大众的;普遍流行的 popular; common: ~名 popular name | ~话 proverb; old saying | 通~ popular ❸ 庸俗 vulgar: ~气 in poor taste | ~不可耐 unbearably vulgar ❹ 指没出家的人(区别于出家的佛教徒等 as compared with 'Buddhist monks') secular; lay: 僧~ clergy and laity

【俗称】súchēng ❶ 通俗地叫做 commonly called: 马铃薯~土豆儿。马铃薯 mǎlíngshǔ (potato) is commonly called 土豆儿 tǔdòur. ❷ same as 俗名 súmíng ①

【俗话】súhuà (~儿 súhuàr) same as 俗语 súyǔ

【俗家】sújiā ❶ 僧尼道士等称其父母的家 (used by monk or nun) my parents' home ❷ 指没出家的人(对僧人道士等而言) layman (to Buddhist monks and Taoist priests): ~打扮 dressed in lay attire

【俗讲】sújiǎng 唐代寺院中用于讲解佛教经义的一种说唱形式,以佛教经义为根据,增加一些故事性成分,吸引听众 Tang-dynasty Buddhist ballad-singing; genre of entertainment in Tang-dynasty monasteries consisting mainly of talking and singing when expounding on Buddhist scriptures, plus elements of fiction, to attract an audience

【俗名】súmíng ❶ 通俗的名称，不是正式的名称（多有地方性）popular name; local name：阑尾炎～盲肠炎。The popular name for 阑尾炎 lánwěiyán (appendicitis) is mángchángyán. ❷ 僧人、道士等出家前的名字（跟'法名'相对 as opposed to 'religious name'）(of Buddhist monks or Taoist priests) secular name

【俗气】sú·qi 粗俗；庸俗 vulgar; in poor taste：这块布颜色素净，花样也大方，一点不～。The decorative pattern on this piece of cloth is subdued, in good taste, and not at all vulgar.

【俗曲】súqǔ〈旧指 *old*〉民间的通俗歌曲 folk song ‖; also 俚曲 lǐqǔ

【俗人】súrén ❶ 世俗的人；一般人（对僧、尼、道士等出家人而言 as compared with monks, priests and nuns) layman; laity ❷ 庸俗的人 vulgar person; philistine

【俗尚】súshàng 习俗所崇尚的风气 prevailing customs：不拘～ not confined by prevailing customs

【俗套】sútào ❶ 习俗上常见的使人感到无聊的礼节 boring conventional formalities ❷ 陈旧的格调 conventional pattern; convention：不落～ depart from convention ‖ also 俗套子 sútào·zi

【俗体字】sútǐzì 指通俗流行而字体不合规范的汉字，如'菓'（果）、'唸'（念）、'塟'（葬）等 non-standard forms of Chinese characters, such as 菓（果），唸（念），and 塟（葬）; also 俗字 súzì

【俗文学】súwénxué 指我国古代的通俗文学，包括歌谣、曲子、讲史、话本、变文、弹词、宝卷、鼓词、民间传说、笑话、谜语及宋元以来南北戏曲、地方戏等 popular literature in ancient China, such as ballads, songs, unofficial history, colloquial stories, *bianwen* (a form of narrative literature that flourished Buddhism in the Tang Dynasty), *tanci* (storytelling to the accompaniment of stringed instruments), *baojuan* (a form of entertainment developed from *sujiang*), *guci* (versified story sung to the accompaniment of a small drum and other instruments), folk tales, humour, riddles, local operas, etc.

【俗语】súyǔ 通俗并广泛流行的定型的语句，简练而形象化，大多数是劳动人民创造出来的，反映人民的生活经验和愿望。如：天下无难事，只怕有心人。common saying; folk adages that generally reflect the experiences, desires and beliefs of the labouring people, one example being, 'Nothing in the world is difficult for one who sets his mind to it'; also 俗话 súhuà

【俗子】súzǐ 俗人 ordinary people：凡夫～common herd

【俗字】súzì same as 俗体字 sútǐzì

sù（ㄙㄨˋ）

夙 sù〈书 *fml.*〉❶ 早 early in the morning：～兴夜寐 rise early and retire late; work hard night and day ❷ 素有的；旧有的 long-standing; old：～志 long-cherished ambition | ～愿 long-cherished wish

【夙仇】sùchóu ❶ 一向作对的仇人 long-time enemy ❷ 旧有的仇恨 long-standing enmity

【夙敌】sùdí 一向对抗的敌人 long-time enemy; also 宿敌 sùdí

【夙诺】sùnuò 以前的诺言 old promise; also 宿诺 sùnuò

【夙嫌】sùxián 旧有的嫌怨 old grudge：捐弃～ bury old grudges

【夙兴夜寐】sù xīng yè mèi 早起晚睡。形容勤劳 rise early and retire late; work hard day and night; work diligently

【夙夜】sùyè 早晨和夜晚。泛指时时刻刻 day and night; always：～忧国 be concerned about one's country day and night

【夙怨】sùyuàn 旧有的怨恨；夙嫌 old grudges; old scores：了却～ settle old scores; also 宿怨 sùyuàn

【夙愿】sùyuàn 一向怀着的愿望 long-cherished wish：～得偿 long-cherished wish fulfilled; also 宿愿 sùyuàn

诉 sù ❶ 说给人 tell; relate; inform：告～tell ❷ 倾吐（心里的话）say (what is on one's mind)：～苦 vent one's grievances | ～衷情 pour out one's heart ❸ 控告 appeal to; resort to：上～ appeal (to a higher court)

【诉苦】sù//kǔ 向人诉说自己所受的苦难 vent one's grievances; pour out one's woes：～叫屈 pour out one's woes and complain of being wronged | 无处～ have nowhere to vent one's grievances

【诉权】sùquán 起诉和诉愿的权利 right of action; the right of suing and petition

【诉述】sùshù same as 诉说 sùshuō：～经历 recount one's experiences

【诉说】sùshuō 带感情地陈述 tell; relate; recount：他在信里～着对地质工作的热爱。In his letter he told of his love for geological work.

【诉讼】sùsòng 检察机关、法院以及民事案件中的当事人、刑事案件中的自诉人解决案件时所进行的活动 lawsuit; litigation; process of bringing a dispute, claim, etc., before a court of law for settlement in civil or criminal cases; also 打官司 dǎ guān·si

【诉讼法】sùsòngfǎ 关于诉讼程序的法规，有刑事诉讼法、民事诉讼法、行政诉讼法等 procedural law; laws of judicial proceedings, including criminal procedure law, civilian procedure law, and administrative procedure law

【诉冤】sù//yuān 向人诉说自己所受的冤屈

complain of injustice; air one's grievances

【诉愿】sùyuàn 指当事人受国家机关不当的处分时,依法向原处分机关的上级机关提出申诉,请求撤消或变更原处分 complaint lodged with a high government organization against a lower one by the person to whom it has dealt inappropriately harsh punishment

【诉状】sùzhuàng 向法院提起诉讼的文书的总称 plaint; indictment; general term for written accusation submitted to the court in a lawsuit

肃(肅) sù ❶ 恭敬 respectful:～立 stand as a mark of respect ❷ 严肃 solemn:～穆 solemn and quiet ❸ 肃清 eliminate; clean up:～贪(肃清贪污行为) eliminate corruption

【肃静】sùjìng 严肃寂静 solemn silence:～无声 solemn silence

【肃立】sùlì 恭敬庄严地站着 stand as a mark of respect:奏国歌时全场～。All stood as the band struck up the national anthem.

【肃穆】sùmù ❶ 严肃安静 solemn and quiet; solemn and respectful:灵堂布置得庄严～。The mourning hall was decorated in an appropriately solemn and respectful manner. ❷ 严肃和睦 respectful and congenial

【肃清】sùqīng 彻底清除(坏人、坏事、坏思想) eliminate (bad people, matters, and ideology); clean up; mop up:～盗匪 exterminate banditry|～流毒 liquidate a pernicious influence

【肃然】sùrán 形容十分恭敬的样子 respectful:～起敬 be filled with deep veneration

【肃杀】sùshā 〈书 *fml*.〉形容秋冬天气寒冷,草木枯落 (of autumn or winter) stern; harsh:秋气～。The autumn air is harsh and raw.

素 sù ❶ 本色;白色 unbleached and undyed; white:～服 plain white clothes (esp. as mourning apparel) ❷ 颜色单纯;不艳丽 plain; simple; quiet:～净 plain and neat ❸ 蔬菜、瓜果等食物(跟'荤'相对 as opposed to 'meat') vegetables:吃～ abstain from eating meat; be a vegetarian|三荤一～ three meat dishes and one vegetable dish ❹ 本来的;原有的 native; original:～质 character; quality|～性 one's disposition ❺ 带有根本性质的物质 basic element; element:色～ pigment|毒～ toxin; poison|因～ factor|元～ element|维生～ vitamin ❻ 素来;向来 usually; habitually; always:～日 generally; usually|平～ usually|～不相识 not having met; not being acquainted|安之若～ bear (hardship, etc.) with equanimity; regard (injustice, etc.) with indifference

【素材】sùcái 文学、艺术的原始材料,就是未经总括和提炼的实际生活现象 source material (of literature and art), i.e., phenomena in everyday life yet to be summarized and refined; material; facts, information, etc., to be used in writing a book, as evidence, etc.:搜集～ collect material

【素菜】sùcài 是蔬菜、瓜果等做的菜(指不搀有肉类的) vegetable dish (without meat)

【素餐】sùcān ❶ 素的饭食 vegetarian meal ❷ 吃素 be a vegetarian ❸ 〈书 *fml*.〉不做事而白吃饭 not work for one's living; eat the bread of idleness:尸位～ hold an office and enjoy all the privileges without doing a stroke of work

【素常】sùcháng 平日;平素 usually; habitually; ordinarily:儿子结婚的那一天,老大爷把～舍不得穿的衣服都穿出来了。On his son's wedding day, the elderly gentleman wore his best clothes that he would begrudge wearing at any other time.

【素淡】sùdàn 素净;淡雅 plain; quiet:颜色～ quiet colour

【素服】sùfú 本色或白色的衣服,多指丧服 plain white clothes (esp. as mourning apparel)

【素洁】sùjié 素净洁白 white and pure:池中的白莲花是那么的～、雅致。The lotus flowers float on the pond's surface, pure and white.

【素净】sù·jing 颜色朴素,不鲜艳刺目 plain and neat; quiet:衣着～ be plainly and neatly dressed|陈设～而大方。The furnishings are simple and in good taste.

【素酒】sùjiǔ ❶ 就着素菜而喝的酒 wine served with vegetarian food ❷ 〈方 *dial*.〉same as 素席 sùxí

【素来】sùlái 从来;向来 always; usually:他的人品,是我～佩服的。I have always admired his moral qualities.

【素昧平生】sù mèi píngshēng 一向不相识 never having met; not having made sb.'s acquaintance

【素描】sùmiáo ❶ 单纯用线条描写、不加彩色的画,如铅笔画、木炭画、某种毛笔画等。素描是一切造型艺术的基础。sketch; pure linear drawing without colouration, such as pencil drawing, charcoal drawing and certain types of brushwork. Sketch is the basis for all forms of plastic art. ❷ 文学上借指文句简洁、不加渲染的朴素描写 literary sketch

【素朴】sùpǔ ❶ 朴素;不加修饰的 simple and unadorned; plain and simple:这些描绘草原人民生活的画面都很～动人。These pictures depict life on the grasslands with charming simplicity. ❷ 萌芽的;未发展的(多指哲学思想 oft. referring to philosophyical thoughts) embryonic; rudimental:～唯物主义 materialism in the embryonic stage

【素日】sùrì 平日;平常 generally; usually:他～不爱说话,今天一高兴,话也多起来了。He is usually very quiet, but today he is talkative and in high spirits.

【素食】sùshí ❶ 素的饭食和点心 vegetarian

S

food; vegetarian diet ❷ 吃素 be a vegetarian:～者(长期吃素的人) vegetarian

【素昔】sùxī 素来;往常 always; heretofore:我们～没有往来。We have hitherto never had dealings with each other.

【素席】sùxí 全用素菜不用荤菜的酒席 vegetarian feast

【素雅】sùyǎ 素净雅致 simple but elegant; plain and in good taste:衣着～be tastefully dressed in a simple style

【素养】sùyǎng 平日的修养 accomplishment; attainment:艺术～artistic accomplishment

【素油】sùyóu 指食用的植物油 vegetable oil; also 清油 qīngyóu

【素愿】sùyuàn 一向怀着的愿望 long-cherished desire, wish, or aspiration:～得偿 long-cherished wish has been fulfilled

【素志】sùzhì〈书 *fml*.〉一向怀有的志愿 long-cherished ambition:～未偿 unfulfilled long-cherished ambition | ～不改 long-cherished ambition that remains unchanged

【素质】sùzhì ❶ 指事物本来的性质 nature; peculiar and essential character ❷ same as 素养 sùyǎng:提高军事～ enhance the military quality of the troops ❸ 心理学上指人的神经系统和感觉器官上的先天的特点(psychol.) diathesis; constitutional characteristics of the human nervous system and sense organs

【素装】sùzhuāng 白色的服装;淡雅的装束 white clothes; plain dress

速[1] sù ❶ 迅速;快 fast; rapid; quick; speedy:火～at top speed | ～战～决 fight a quick battle to force a speedy decision | 加～前进 speed up one's advance ❷ 速度 speed; velocity:风～wind speed | 光～velocity of light | 声～speed of sound | 车～speed of a motor vehicle | 时～speed per hour

速[2] sù〈书 *fml*.〉邀请 invite:不～之客 uninvited (or unexpected) guest; gatecrasher

【速成】sùchéng 将学习期限缩短,在短期内很快学完 crash (course); attain a goal in a much shorter time than usual; gain a quick mastery of a course or subject:～班 accelerated course; crash course

【速冻】sùdòng 快速冷冻 quick-freeze:～食品 quick-frozen food

【速度】sùdù ❶ 运动物体在某一个方向上单位时间内所通过的距离 speed; velocity; rate of time at which sth. moves or operates ❷ 泛指快慢的程度 speed; rate; pace; tempo:高～high speed | 放慢～ slow down; decelerate

【速记】sùjì 用一种简便的记音符号迅速地把话记录下来 shorthand; stenography; method of writing rapidly, by substituting characters, abbreviations or symbols for letters, words or phrases

【速决】sùjué 迅速地解决 quick decision:速战～fight a quick battle to force a speedy decision

【速决战】sùjuézhàn 在较短时间内迅速决定胜负的战役或战斗 war (or battle) whose outcome is rapidly decided

【速率】sùlǜ 运动物体在单位时间内所通过的距离 speed; rate; speed at which sth. moves or operates

【速溶】sùróng 溶解快 be promptly soluble; instant:～奶粉 instant milk powder | ～咖啡 instant coffee

【速食面】sùshímiàn〈方 *dial*.〉方便面 instant noodles

【速算】sùsuàn 利用数与数的组成和分解以及各种运算定律、性质或它们之间的特殊关系,进行迅速简便的运算 short cut methods of accounting; rapid calculation by means of combining and breaking down numerals, as well as use of operational rules, properties or special relationships

【速效】sùxiào 见效快 quick results:～肥料 fast-acting fertilizer

【速写】sùxiě ❶ 绘画的一种方法,一边观察对象一边用简单线条把它的主要特点迅速地画出来 sketch; rough, hasty, drawing that sets out the chief features of an object or scene ❷ 一种文体,扼要描写事物的情况,及时地向读者报道 literary sketch; a short, to the point literary composition giving a brief, timely description of sth.

馃 sù〈书 *fml*.〉鼎中的食物 food in a tripod

涑 Sù 涑水,水名,在山西 Sushui River in Shanxi Province

宿[1] sù ❶ 夜里睡觉;过夜 lodge for the night; stay overnight:～舍 dormitory; hostel | ～营 camp | 住～ put up; get accommodation | 露～sleep in the open ❷ (Sù)姓 a surname

宿[2] sù〈书 *fml*.〉❶ 旧有的;一向有的 long-standing; old:～愿 long-cherished wish | ～志 cherished ambition ❷ 年老的;久于其事的 veteran; old:耆～ elderly people | ～将(jiàng) veteran general

☞ xiǔ on p. 2159 and xiù on p. 2160

【宿弊】sùbì〈书 *fml*.〉多年的弊病 long-standing abuse:～一清。Long-standing abuses have all been rooted out.

【宿逋】sùbū〈书 *fml*.〉久欠不还的债 long-standing debt

【宿娼】sù//chāng 嫖妓 visit prostitutes

【宿仇】sùchóu 旧有的仇恨 long-standing enmity

【宿敌】sùdí same as 夙敌 sùdí

【宿根】sùgēn 某些二年生或多年生草本植物的根,在茎叶枯萎以后可以继续生存,到第二年春天重新发芽,这种根叫做宿根,如芍药、薄荷等的根 perennial root; biennial root; root that exists for two or more years, producing new herbaceous growth the following year. Plants with such roots include the Chinese herbaceous peony and field mint.

【宿疾】sùjí 一向有的病;拖延很久难以治愈的病 chronic complaint; old trouble

【宿将】sùjiàng 久经战阵的指挥官;老将 experienced military commander, veteran general

【宿命论】sùmìnglùn 一种唯心主义理论,认为事物的变化和发展、人的生死和贫富等都由命运或天命预先决定,人是无能为力的 fatalism; belief that events are decided by fate; idealist theory that the change and development of events, or a person's life, death, and state of poverty or wealth, are all predestined

【宿诺】sùnuò same as 夙诺 sùnuò

【宿儒】sùrú 老成博学的读书人 learned old scholar

【宿舍】sùshè 企业、机关、学校等供给工作人员及其家属或供给学生住的房屋 hostel; living quarters; dormitory; residences provided by enterprises, institutions or schools for staff members and their families or for students

【宿世】sùshì 前生;前世 past or previous life

【宿土】sùtǔ 植物原生长地点的土壤 original soil from which a plant grows

【宿营】sùyíng 军队在行军或战斗后住宿(of troops) take up quarters; camp (after march or fight):露天～take up quarters in the open

【宿怨】sùyuàn same as 夙怨 sùyuàn

【宿愿】sùyuàn same as 夙愿 sùyuàn

【宿债】sùzhài 以前欠下的债务 long-standing debt; old debt:偿清～clear an old debt

【宿志】sùzhì 〈书 *fml.*〉一向怀有的志愿 long-standing aspiration:不忘～ do not forget long-standing aspirations

【宿主】sùzhǔ 寄主 host

骕(驌) sù ☞ below

【骕骦】sùshuāng 古书上说的一种良马 fine horse mentioned in ancient texts; also 骕骕 sùshuāng

【骕骕】sùshuāng same as 骕骦 sùshuāng

粟 sù ❶ ☞ 谷子 gǔ·zi ①② on p. 692 ❷ (Sù)姓 a surname

【粟米】sùmǐ 〈方 *dial.*〉玉米 maize; Indian corn; corn

【粟子】sù·zi 〈方 *dial.*〉☞ 谷子 gǔ·zi ①②

谡 sù 〈书 *fml.*〉起;起来 stand up, rise

【谡谡】sùsù 形容挺拔 tall and straight:～长松 tall, straight pines

嗉(膆) sù same as 嗉子 sù·zi ①

【嗉子】sù·zi ❶ 鸟类的消化器官的一部分,在食道的下部,像个袋子,用来储存食物 crop (of a bird); bag-like part of a bird's throat where food is prepared for digestion before passing into the stomach:鸡～chicken crop; also 嗉囊 sùnáng ❷ 〈方 *dial.*〉装酒的锡制的或瓷的器皿,像瓶子,底大,颈细长 tin or porcelain wine flask, with a bulbous body and a long, thin neck

塑 sù ❶ 塑造 model; mould:～像 mould a statue | 泥～木雕 like an idol carved in wood or moulded in clay; as wooden as a dummy ❷ 塑料 plastics:涂～壁纸 resin-coated wallpaper | 全～家具 all-plastic furniture

【塑封】sùfēng 为防水、耐用而用塑料膜封闭起来的 plastic-capsulated:～卡片 plastic-capsulated cards

【塑料】sùliào 以树脂等高分子化合物为基本成分,与配料混合后加热加压而成的、具有一定形状的材料。在常温下不再变形。种类很多,如电木、赛璐珞、聚氯乙烯等。一般具有质轻、绝缘、耐腐蚀、耐磨擦等特点。应用极为广泛。plastic; material made from macromolecular compounds (such as resin) mixed with a preparation of various materials under heat and pressure, which, when molded, extruded or cast into various shapes, remains unchanged under normal temperatures. Plastics come in many varieties, such as bakelite, celluloid, polyvinyl chloride, etc. Light, insulative, corrosion and wear resistant, plastics are used extensively.

【塑像】sùxiàng 用石膏或泥土等塑成的人像 statue; figure of person moulded in clay or plaster

【塑性】sùxìng 在应力超过一定限度的条件下,材料或物体不断裂而继续变形的性质。在外力去掉后还能保持一部分残余变形。plasticity; state or quality of being able to be continuously reformed without rupturing and partly retain the given form when external power is lifted; also 范性 fànxìng

【塑造】sùzào ❶ 用泥土等可塑材料塑成人物形象 model; mould:庙里～了一尊泥菩萨。A clay statue of the Goddess of Mercy was modeled at the temple. ❷ 用语言文字或其他艺术手段表现人物形象 portray; describe a person using words or other artistic means:这篇小说成功地～了一位知识分子的形象。This short story successfully portrays an intellectual.

溯(泝、遡) sù ❶ 逆着水流的方向走 go against the stream:～流而上 go upstream ❷ 往上推求或回想 trace back; recall:回～look back upon | 追～trace; recall

【溯源】sùyuán 往上游寻找发源的地方 go upstream to look for the source;〈比喻 *fig.*〉向上寻求历史根源 trace (back) to the historic source:追本～trace (back) to the source

愫 sù 〈书 *fml.*〉真实的情意;诚意 sincere feeling; sincerity:情～feeling; sentiment

鹔(鷫) sù ☞ below

【鹔鹴】sùshuāng 古书上说的一种鸟 a kind of

bird mentioned in ancient texts; also 鹔鹴 sùshuāng

【鹔鹴】sùshuāng same as 鹔鷞 sùshuāng

蔌 sù〈书 *fml.*〉蔬菜 vegetables：山肴野～ exotic mountain foods and wild vegetables

僳 sù ☞［僳僳族］(Lìsùzú) on p. 1193

觫 sù ☞［觳觫］(húsù) on p. 821

愬 sù〈书 *fml.*〉same as 诉 sù

缩 sù［缩砂密］(sùshāmì)多年生草本植物，叶子条状披针形，花粉色，蒴果椭圆形。种子棕色，椭圆形，有三个棱，入药叫砂仁。原产越南、缅甸、印度尼西亚等地。amomun (*Amomum xanthioides*); herbaceous perennial with ensiform leaves, pink flowers, oval-shaped capsule fruits bearing brown oval seeds with three ridges, called *sharen* when used in traditional Chinese medicine, found in Vietnam, Myanmar, and Indonesia; also called 缩砂 sùshā

☞ suō on p. 1842

罬 sù ☞ 罭罬(lùsù) on p. 1263

簌 sù［簌簌］❶〈拟声词 *onom.*〉形容风吹叶子等的声音 rustle; quick succession of small sounds like leaves rustling in the wind ❷ 形容眼泪等纷纷落下的样子(of tears) streaming down：～泪下。Tears streamed down. ❸ 形容肢体发抖的样子(of limbs) shiver; quiver：手指～地抖 trembling fingers

踧 sù［踧踧］〈书 *fml.*〉形容小步快走 running in small steps

suān (ㄙㄨㄢ)

狻 suān［狻猊］(suānní) 传说中的一种猛兽 legendary beast of prey

酸[1] suān ❶ 电解质电离时所生成的阳离子全部是氢离子的化合物。能跟碱中和生成盐和水，跟某些金属化合生成盐和氢气，水溶液有酸味，可使石蕊试纸变红。如盐酸、硫酸等。acid; chemical compound, such as hydrochloric acid and sulfuric acid, whose positive ions are all hydrogen ions. It neutralizes alkaline to form salt and water, and it combines with certain metals to form salt and hydrogen; in a water solution it has a sour taste, and turns blue litmus paper red. ❷ 像醋的气味或味道 sour; tart; having the taste or smell of vinegar：～菜 pickled Chinese cabbage; Chinese sauerkraut｜～枣 wild jujube｜青梅很～。Green plums are very sour. ❸ 悲痛；伤心 sick at heart; grieved; distressed：辛～ bitter; miserable｜心～ feel sad｜悲～ grieved; sad ❹ 讥讽文人迂腐 pedantic; impractical：穷～poor and pedantic｜～秀才 impractical old scholar; priggish pedant

酸[2]（痠）suān 因疲劳或疾病引起的微痛而无力的感觉 tingle; ache; a feeling of slight pain and weakness caused by fatigue or disease：腰～腿疼 have pain in the back and legs｜腿站～了。My legs ached from standing for such a long time.

【酸败】suānbài 油脂、鱼肉等由于受到空气、水分、细菌、热、光等的作用而氧化或水解，酸值增高，产生异味 rotten; putrid; fat, fish or meat becomes sour and produces an unpleasant smell in the process of oxidation or hydrolyzation owing to the effects of air, moisture, bacteria, heat and light

【酸不溜丢】suān·buliūdiū〈方 *dial.*〉(～的 suān·buliūdiūde)形容有酸味(含厌恶意 with a sense of disgust) unpleasantly sour

【酸菜】suāncài 白菜等经发酵变酸了的叫做酸菜 pickled Chinese cabbage; Chinese sauerkraut

【酸楚】suānchǔ 辛酸苦楚 grieved; distressed; miserable：心头～ heartbroken

【酸酐】suāngān 酸缩去水而成的化合物，如一个碳酸分子(H_2CO_3)缩去一分子水(H_2O)剩下的二氧化碳(CO_2)就是碳酸酐，两个醋酸分子(CH_3COOH)缩去一分子水(H_2O)剩下的$(CH_3CO)_2O$就是醋酸酐。acid anhydride; compound derived from acid by removal of water element. For instance, carbonic acid (CO_2) is derived from a carbonic molecule (H_2CO_3) by removal of water molecule (H_2O); and acetic oxide $(CH_3CO)_2O$ is derived from two acetic acid molecules (CH_3COOH) by removal of water molecule (H_2O). 简称 abbr. 酐 gān

【酸根】suāngēn 酸分子里除去氢离子后剩下的部分；酸或盐类存在于晶体或水溶液中的负离子。如硫酸根(SO_4^{2-})、硝酸根(NO_3^-)、盐酸根(Cl^-)等。acid radical; residue after removal of hydrogen ions from acid molecule; negative ions of acid or salt in crystal or water solution, such as sulfate radical (SO_4^{2-}), nitrate radical (NO_3^-), and hydrochloric radical(Cl^-)

【酸碱度】suānjiǎndù 氢离子浓度指数(pH 值) acidity; index of hydrogen ion concentration (pH value)

【酸懒】suānlǎn〈方 *dial.*〉(身体)发酸而疲倦 (body) listless and aching

【酸溜溜】suānliūliū ❶ 形容酸的味道或气味(of taste or smell) sour; pungent：这个凉菜～的，吃着挺爽口。This cold dish is piquant, and very refreshing to the taste. ❷ 形容轻微酸痛的感觉 tingle; ache：走了一天的路，腿肚子有点儿～的。My legs ached slightly after walking all day. ❸ 形容轻微嫉妒或心里难过的感觉 feel a little envious; feel a bit sad：听到被

表扬的不是自己，她心里有些～的。She felt a bit sad on hearing she was not among those commended. ❹ 形容爱引用古书词句，言谈迂腐（含讥讽意 ironical）pedantic; priggish：他就喜欢卖弄，～地来两句之乎者也。He just likes showing off, and is always spouting pedantry.

【酸梅汤】suānméitāng 把乌梅放在水里泡过或煮过再加糖制成的夏季饮料，滋味酸甜 sweet-sour plum juice; summer drink made by adding sugar to the water in which plums have been boiled or steeped

【酸牛奶】suānniúnǎi 牛奶经人工发酵而成的半固体食品，带酸味，易于消化吸收 yogurt; sour milk; fermented, slightly acid, semi-solid foodstuff made from cow's milk, easy to digest and absorb

【酸软】suānruǎn （身体）发酸而无力 aching and limp：四肢～ aching and feeble in all four limbs

【酸甜苦辣】suān tián kǔ là 指各种味道 sour, sweet, bitter, hot; all flavours; 〈比喻 *fig.*〉幸福、痛苦等种种遭遇 joys and sorrows of life

【酸痛】suāntòng （身体）又酸又痛 ache all over

【酸心】suānxīn ❶ 心里悲痛 grieve; feel sad：这出戏看了叫人～。The play was heart-rending to watch. ❷ 胃里发酸 suffer from heartburn：白薯吃多了～。Eating too many sweet potatoes causes heartburn.

【酸辛】suānxīn 辛酸 sad, bitter, miserable

【酸雨】suānyǔ 指含有一定数量酸性物质（如硫酸、硝酸、盐酸）的自然降水，包括雨、雪、雹、雾等。酸雨能腐蚀建筑物、损害植物、污染水源。acid rain; natural precipitation containing a certain amount of acid substances (such as sulfuric acid, nitric acid and hydrochloric acid), including rain, snow, hailstones, and fog; Acid rain corrodes buildings, harms plants and pollutes water sources.

【酸枣】suānzǎo ❶ 酸枣树，落叶灌木或乔木，枝上有刺，叶子长椭圆形，边缘有细锯齿，花黄绿色，果实长圆形，暗红色，肉质薄，味酸。核仁可入药。wild jujube tree; deciduous bush or tree, with thorns on its branches, oval leaves with fine tooth-like projections at their edge, yellow-green flowers, and dark red prolate fruits with a thin layer of flesh, of a tart flavour; Its kernel can be used in Chinese medicine ingredient. also called 棘 jí ❷ （～儿 suānzǎor）这种植物的果实 fruit of this plant

suàn (ㄙㄨㄢ)

蒜 suàn ❶ 多年生草本植物，花白色带紫，叶子和花轴嫩时可以做菜。地下鳞茎味道辣，有刺激性气味，可以做作料，也可入药。garlic (*Allium sativum*); herbaceous perennial plant with white, purple tinted flowers, edible leaves and floral axis, and a subterranean bulb with a strong taste and smell that is used for seasoning in cooking, and also as a medicine ingredient ❷ 这种植物的鳞茎 bulb of this plant || also 大蒜 dàsuàn

【蒜瓣儿】suànbànr 蒜的鳞茎分成瓣状，每一个瓣状部分叫做一个蒜瓣儿 garlic clove; the bulb of the garlic is divided into sections called garlic cloves

【蒜毫】suànháo （～儿 suànháor）same as 蒜薹 suàntái

【蒜黄】suànhuáng （～儿 suànhuángr）在不受日光的照射和适当的温度、湿度条件下培育出来的黄色蒜叶。做蔬菜用。blanched garlic leaves; yellow blanched leaves of the garlic cultivated under a controlled temperature and humidity; edible

【蒜苗】suànmiáo 〈方 *dial.*〉❶ 嫩的蒜薹 garlic bolt ❷ 青蒜 garlic leaves

【蒜泥】suànní 捣得非常烂的蒜，用来拌菜或蘸菜吃 mashed garlic (used as seasoning for dishes)

【蒜薹】suàntái 蒜的花轴，嫩的可以吃 garlic flower stalk (edible when tender)

【蒜头】suàntóu （～儿 suàntóur）蒜的鳞茎，略呈球形，是由许多蒜瓣构成的 head (or bulb) of garlic, comprising several cloves

筭 suàn 〈书 *fml.*〉same as 算 suàn

算(祘) suàn ❶ 计算数目 calculate; reckon; compute; figure：珠～ reckoning by the abacus | 笔～ do a sum in writing; written calculation | 心～ mental arithmetic | 预～ budget | 能写会～ good at writing and reckoning | ～了一笔账 settle a score ❷ 计算进去 include; count：明天赛球～我一个。Count me in for tomorrow's ball game. ❸ 谋划；计划 plan; calculate：失～ miscalculate | 打～ plan | 盘～ figure | 暗～ plot or conspire against | ～计 scheme ❹ 推测 guess; think; suppose：我～他今天该动身了。I guess he will have started (or be starting) out today. ❺ 认做；当做 consider; regard as; count as：他各方面都不错，可以～一个好学生。He does pretty well in all aspects, and so could be reckoned a good student. | 你们挑剩下的都～我的。I will take whatever is left after all of you have made your choice. ❻ 算数；承认有效力 carry weight; count：他说的不～，还得你说。It is not what he says, but what you say that counts. ❼ 作罢；不再计较（后面跟'了'followed by 了 ·le）let it be; let it pass：～了，别说了。That's enough! Let it go at that. *or* Forget it. | 他不愿意就～了吧，咱们两人去。If he doesn't want to go, so be it; the two of us will go. ❽ 总算 at long last; in the end; finally：最后～把这个问题弄懂了。I have at last gained a clear understanding of

S

this problem.

【算草】suàncǎo（～儿 suàncǎor）演算算题时所做的草式。如$\begin{array}{r}28\\-19\\\hline 9\end{array}$，$\begin{array}{r}5\\\times 5\\\hline 25\end{array}$ rough draft

【算尺】suànchǐ 计算尺 slide rule

【算得】suàn//dé 被认为是；算做 regard as; count as：他俩真～一对好夫妻。They are regarded as a good couple.

【算卦】suàn//guà 根据卦象推算吉凶（迷信）tell sb.'s fortune or make divinations using the Eight Trigrams (superstition)

【算计】suàn·ji ❶ 计算数目 calculate; reckon：数量之多，难以～hard to calculate an amount so large ❷ 考虑；打算 consider; plan：这件事慢一步办，还得～～。Let's put off the matter for a while. It needs more consideration. ❸ 估计 expect; figure：我～他今天回不来，果然没回来。I didn't think he would be able to return today, and, sure enough, he didn't. ❹ 暗中谋划损害别人 scheme; plot：被人～be plotted against by others

【算计儿】suàn·jir〈方 *dial.*〉计划；打算 plan：安排好生活要预先有个～。In order to arrange one's life properly, it is first of all necessary to make a plan.

【算命】suàn//mìng 凭人的生辰八字，用阴阳五行推算人的命运，断定人的吉凶祸福（迷信）fortune-telling; tell fortunes through calculation, following the formulas of *yin* and *yang* (the two opposing principles) and the five elements (metal, wood, water, fire, and earth) according to the eight characters (in four pairs, indicating the year, month, day and hour of a person's birth)

【算盘】suàn·pán ❶ 一种计算数目的用具，长方形框内装有一根横梁，梁上钻孔镶小棍儿十余根，每根上穿一串珠子，叫算盘子儿，常见的是两颗在横梁上，每颗代表五，五颗在横梁下，每颗代表一。按规定的方法拨动算盘子儿，可以做加减乘除等运算。abacus; tool for performing calculations, comprising a frame containing a dozen vertical parallel rods, and beads that slide along them, usu. separated into two sections of two beads above, each worth five, and five beads below, each worth one, used for the four fundamental operations of arithmetic ❷〈比喻 *fig.*〉计划，打算 calculation; plan; scheme：如意～ wishful thinking｜他答应这件事，是有他自己的～的。In agreeing so readily, he gave himself an axe to grind.

【算盘子儿】suàn·pánzǐr 算盘上的珠子，多为木制，扁圆形，中间有孔 beads of an abacus, usu. made of wood, oblate, with a hole through the centre

【算式】suànshì 进行数（或代数式）的计算时，所列出的式子，分为横式和竖式两种 mathematical formula or equation, set out in horizontal and vertical lines

【算是】suànshì 总算 at last：这一下～你猜着了。You have finally guessed right.｜我们早就想办这事，现在～实现了。We have long planned this, and now it has finally been achieved.

【算术】suànshù 数学的一个分支，是数学中最基础、最初等的部分。主要研究零和正整数、正分数的记数法，在加、减、乘、除、乘方、开方运算下产生的数的性质、运算法则以及在社会实践中的应用。arithmetic; basic and primary branch of mathematics that deals with the counting process of zero, positive integers and fractions, properties of numbers, and operational rules of addition, subtraction, multiplication, division, involution and evolution, and their applications in social practice

【算数】suàn//shù ❶（～儿 suàn//shùr）承认有效力 count; hold; stand：说话要～，不能翻悔。One should keep to one's word and never go back on it.｜以前的不～，从现在算起。Past events do not count; the new rules start as of now. ❷ 表示到…为止 until：学会了才～ until one has learned (a skill)

【算题】suàntí 数学的练习题 arithmetic problem; mathematical exercise

【算学】suànxué ❶ 数学 mathematics ❷ same as 算术 suànshù

【算账】suàn//zhàng ❶ 计算账目 do (or work out) accounts ❷ 吃亏或失败后和人争执较量 square (or settle) accounts with sb.; get even with sb. (after suffering a loss or defeat)：这件事得找他～，要他赔偿损失。I shall settle accounts with him on this matter, and make him compensate for my loss.

suī（ㄙㄨㄟ）

尿 suī 人或动物体内，由肾脏产生，从尿道排泄出来的液体 urine; fluid excreted by the kidney and discharged from the urethra：小孩儿又尿（niào）了一泡～。The child has pissed again!

☞ niào on p. 1415

【尿泡】suī·pāo same as 尿脬 suī·pāo

【尿脬】suī·pāo〈方 *dial.*〉膀胱 bladder; also 尿泡 suī·pāo

虽（**雖**） suī〈书 *fml.*〉〈连词 *conj.*〉❶ 虽然 though; although; even if：事情～小，意义却很大。The matter is small but significant.｜三月天气，～没太阳，也不觉得冷了。The weather in March is not cold, even on cloudy days.｜房子旧～旧，倒还干净。The house is old but clean. ❷ 纵然 even though：为人民而死，～死犹荣。Honoured though dead; to have died a glorious death.

【虽然】suīrán〈连词 *conj.*〉用在上半句，下半句往往有'可是、但是'等跟它呼应，表示承认甲事为事实，但乙事并不因为甲事而不成立[oft. used correlatively with 但是 dànshì, 可是 kěshì, etc., to indicate that A is factual, but B is not untenable due to A] though; although：现在我们～生活富裕了，但是还要注意节约。Although these days we lead more prosperous lives, we nevertheless still pay attention to thrift.｜他～工作很忙，可是对业余学习并不放松。Although he is very busy at work, he never shirks in his spare-time studies. 注意 **NOTE:** 文言里'虽然'承接上文，稍微停顿，等于白话'虽然如此'的意思。In classicalstyle writings, 虽然 is used to continue the preceding paragraph, meaning 'even so.'

【虽说】suīshuō same as 虽然 suīrán：～是开玩笑，也该有个分寸。Although it's only a joke, it should not be taken too far.｜她～才十六岁，家里地里样样活儿都能干。Although she is only 16 years old, she can do all kinds of house and farm work.

【虽则】suīzé same as 虽然 suīrán：～多费了些工夫，但是长了不少知识。Although this took a deal of time and energy, it greatly increased my knowledge.

荽 suī ☞ [芫荽](yán·suī) on p. 2202

眭 suī ❶〈书 *fml.*〉目光深注 gaze at ❷(Suī) 姓 a surname

睢[1] suī ☞ 恣睢 zìsuī on p. 2553

睢[2] Suī ❶ 睢县，在河南 Suixian County, in Henan Province ❷ 姓 a surname

濉 Suī 濉河，发源于安徽，流入江苏 Suihe River, originates in Anhui Province and flows into Jiangsu Province

suí (ㄙㄨㄟˊ)

绥 suí〈书 *fml.*〉❶ 安好 peaceful：顺颂时～。(书信结尾用语 used at the end of a letter) I avail myself of this opportunity to present my kind regards. ❷ 安抚 reassure and pacify：～靖 pacify; appease

【绥靖】suíjìng〈书 *fml.*〉安抚，使保持地方平静 pacify; appease：～四方。Every quarter is at peace.

隋 Suí ❶ 朝代，公元 581—618，杨坚所建 Sui Dynasty (581-618), founded by Yang Jian ❷ 姓 a surname

随(隨) suí ❶ same as 跟 gēn②：跟～ follow｜～着形势的发展，我们的任务更加繁重了。With the development of circumstances, our task is even more arduous. ❷ 顺从 let (sb. do as he likes)：～顺 be obedient to｜～风转舵 trim one's sails｜只要你们做得对，我都～着。As long as you are all doing the right thing, I'll go along with it. ❸ 任凭 let sb. do as he likes：～意 at will｜～便 do as one pleases｜去不去～你吧。Whether you go or not is up to you. ❹ 顺便 along with (some other action)：～手 conveniently (when doing sth.); without extra trouble ❺〈方 *dial.*〉像 look like; resemble：他长得～他父亲。He looks like his father. ❻ (Suí) 姓 a surname

【随笔】suíbǐ ❶ 一种散文体裁，篇幅短小，表现形式灵活自由，可以抒情、叙事或评论 informal essay; a type of prose, short and expressive of emotion, used as a narrative form, or to make comment or review ❷ same as 笔记 bǐjì ②

【随便】suí//biàn 按照某人的方便 do as one pleases：随你的便。Do as you please.

【随便】suíbiàn ❶ 不在范围、数量等方面加限制 random; with no limitation on scope or amount：～闲谈 chat; chit-chat｜你们活儿多，～匀给我们一些吧。As you have so much work to do, feel free to put as much our way as you like. ❷ 怎么方便就怎么做，不多考虑 casual; informal：我说话很～，请你不要见怪。Well, I'm just talking off the top of my head. Please don't take offence.｜写文章不能随随便便，要对读者负责任。Articles should not be written in a slipshod manner, as the writer has a responsibility to his readers. ❸ 任凭；无论 anyhow; any：话剧也好，京剧也好，～什么戏，他都爱看。He enjoys all kinds of plays, be it modern drama or Peking Opera.

【随波逐流】suí bō zhú liú 随着波浪起伏，跟着流水漂荡 drift with the tide (or current); go with the flow;〈比喻 *fig.*〉自己没有主见，随着潮流走 have no definite views of one's own

【随常】suícháng 平常；普通 ordinary; common; everyday：出门时就带了两件～的衣服。On setting out I took just two items of everyday clothing.

【随处】suíchù 不拘什么地方；到处 everywhere; anywhere：这个城市的建设发展很快，新的楼房～可见。Construction in this city has been rapid; there are new buildings everywhere.

【随从】suícóng ❶ 跟随(首长) accompany or follow (one's superior); attend：～师长南征北战 follow the division commander on campaigns north and south ❷ 随从人员 retinue; suite; entourage：当了一名～ serve as an attendant

【随大溜】suí dàliù (～儿 suí dàliùr) 跟着多数人说话或行事 drift (or swim) with the stream; follow (or conform to) the trend; do as others do; also 随大流 suí dàliú

【随带】suídài ❶ 随同带去 going along with, 信外～书籍一包。There is a parcel of books to go along with the letter. ❷ 随身携带 take sth. along with one: ～行李不多。I'm not taking much luggage along.

【随地】suídì 不拘什么地方 anywhere; everywhere: 随时～at any time and in any place | 公共场所禁止～乱扔果皮纸屑。Do not at any time drop litter in public places.

【随访】suífǎng 随从访问 accompany on a visit: ～记者 accompanying journalists

【随份子】suífèn·zi ❶ 拿出分摊的一份钱参加集体送礼 contribute one's share of a group gift ❷ 带着钱到别人家参加婚丧等活动 present a cash gift for a wedding, funeral, etc; also 出份子 chūfèn·zi

【随风倒】suífēngdǎo 形容无主见,看哪一边势力大就跟着哪一边走 bend with the wind; be easily swayed by whichever side has more power or influence

【随风转舵】suí fēng zhuǎn duò ☞ 顺风转舵 shùn fēng zhuǎn duò on p. 1807

【随感】suígǎn 随时的感想 random thoughts(多用作标题 oft. used in titles): ～录 collection of random thoughts |《旅欧～》*Random Thoughts on Travels in Europe*

【随行就市】suí háng jiù shì 价格随着市场的行情而变动(of prices) fluctuate in line with market conditions: 农产品充足了,价格自然会～落下来。When the supply of agricultural products is adequate, their prices will naturally drop in line with market conditions.

【随和】suí·he 和气而不固执己见 amiable; obliging: 他脾气～,跟谁都合得来。He has an amiable disposition and gets along well with everyone.

【随后】suíhòu 〈副词 *adv*.〉表示紧接某种情况或行动之后,多与'就'连用(oft. followed by 就 jiù) soon afterwards: 你先走,我～就去。You go ahead, I'll be there right away.

【随机应变】suí jī yìng biàn 跟着情况的变化,掌握时机,灵活应付 act as changing circumstances demand; suit one's actions to changing conditions; act according to circumstances

【随即】suíjí 随后就;立刻 soon after that; immediately; presently: 你们先走,我～动身。You go ahead, I'll leave presently.

【随记】suíjì 随手记录(多用作标题) random notes (oft. used as title): 参观～random notes on the visit |《采访～》*Random Notes of a Journalist on the Beat*

【随军】suíjūn 跟随军队(行动) go along with an army: ～记者 war correspondent | ～家属 camp family (i. e. an army officer's family permitted to live on an army camp)

【随口】suíkǒu 没经过考虑,随便说出 speak thoughtlessly or casually; blurt out whatever comes into one's head: ～附和 casually echo | 他对别人的要求,从不～答应。He never agrees casually to other people's demands.

【随群】suíqún (～儿 suíqúnr)举动跟大家一样 do as everybody else does; follow the crowd

【随身】suíshēn 带在身上或跟在身旁 (carry) on one's person; (take) with one: ～携带 carry on one's person | ～用品 personal necessities | ～仆从 personal servants

【随声附和】suí shēng fùhè 别人说什么,自己跟着说什么。形容没有主见。echo what others say; chime in with others; (fig.) have no definite views of one's own

【随时】suíshí ❶ 不拘什么时候 at any time; at all times: 有问题可以～来问我。Come to me any time you have problems. ❷ 有需要或有可能的时候(就做) whenever necessary; as the occasion demands: 维修工可以～上门修理。Maintenance workers are on call at all times.

【随手】suíshǒu (～儿 suíshǒur) 顺手 sth. done at sb.'s convenience; without extra effort; sth. that can be done at the same time as sth. else: 出门时请～关门。Please shut the door as you leave.

【随顺】suíshùn 依从;顺从 listen to; comply with; yield to: 怎能不加思考～别人? How can you so mindlessly obey other people?

【随俗】suísú 随顺习俗(做事) comply with convention; follow the customs; do as everybody else does: 入乡～。When in Rome do as the Romans do.

【随…随…】suí…suí… 分别用在两个动词或动词性词组前面,表示后一动作紧接着前一动作而发生[each 随 is followed by a verb, indicating that the latter action immediately follows the former]: 大家～到～吃,不用等。Everyone eat as soon as you arrive. There is no need to wait. | 这几个文件～印～发。These documents should be sent out as soon as they have been printed.

【随同】suítóng 跟着;陪着 be in company with; accompany: 几位有经验的老工人～工程师到场地查勘。Several experienced veteran workers accompany the engineer when he goes to survey the site.

【随喜】suíxǐ ❶〈佛教用语 *Budd*.〉见人做功德而乐意参加;也指随着众人做某种表示,或愿意加入集体送礼等 be happy to participate in charitable and virtuous deeds; be willing to contribute one's share to a group gift: ～拍手喝彩 join in applause and cheers | ～,～! 也算我一份儿。Let me join in the celebrations and contribute my share to a group gift. ❷〈旧指 *old*〉参观庙宇 visit a temple

【随乡入乡】suí xiāng rù xiāng 到一个地方就按照当地的风俗习惯生活 wherever you are, abide by local customs; when in Rome do as the Romans do; also 入乡随乡 rù xiāng suí xiāng

【随心】suí//xīn ❶ 随着自己的意思 follow one's inclinations: ～所欲 follow one's inclinations; have one's own way; do as one pleases ❷ 合乎自己的心愿;称心 find sth. satisfactory; be gratified: 这番话听着很～。That sounds agreeable.

【随心所欲】suí xīn suǒ yù 一切都由着自己的心意,想怎么做就怎么做 follow one's inclinations; have one's own way; do as one pleases

【随意】suí//yì 任凭自己的意思 at will; as one pleases: ～出入 come in and out at will | 请大家～点菜。Everyone order your own dishes as you please.

【随遇而安】suí yù ér ān 能适应各种环境,在任何环境中都能满足 feel at home wherever one is; be able to adapt oneself to different circumstances

【随遇平衡】suíyù-pínghéng 处于平衡的物体,在受到微小作用时,它的重心高度不变,能在任意位置继续保持平衡的现象。如水平地面上圆球的平衡状态。indifferent equilibrium; neutral balance; phenomenon where a balanced object is acted upon by minimal forces, so that its centre of gravity remains unchanged, and its balance is maintained, e.g. a ball remaining stationary on level ground

【随员】suíyuán ❶ 随同首长或代表团外出的工作人员 retinue; entourage ❷ 在驻外使馆工作的最低一级的外交官 diplomatic attaché, diplomat of the lowest ranking at an embassy

【随葬】suízàng 用财物、器具、车马等随同死者埋葬 property, tools, chariot, etc., that were buried together with a corpse: ～品 funerary objects | ～物 burial articles

遂 suí ☞ 半身不遂 bàn shēn bù suí on p. 53 ☞ suì on p. 1840

suǐ (ㄙㄨㄟˇ)

髓 suǐ ❶ ☞ 骨髓 gǔsuǐ on p. 694 ❷ 像骨髓的东西 marrow-like substance: 脑～ brains | 脊～ spinal cord ❸ 植物茎的中心部分,由薄壁的细胞组成 pith; soft spongy substance contained in the stem of certain plants, consisting of thin-walled cells

suì (ㄙㄨㄟˋ)

岁(嵗、歲、歳) suì ❶ 年 year: ～月 years | ～末 the end of the year | 辞旧～,迎新年 ring out the Old Year and ring in the New ❷〈量词 *classifier*〉表示年龄的单位 year (of age): 孩子三～了。The child is three years old. | 这匹马是六～口。This horse is six years old. ❸〈书 *fml.*〉指时间 time: ～不我与(时间不等待我们)。Time waits for no man. ❹〈书 *fml.*〉年成 year's harvest: 歉～ lean year | 丰～ bumper harvest year; good year

【岁差】suìchā 由于太阳和月亮的引力对地球赤道的作用,使地轴在黄道轴的周围作圆锥形的运动,缓慢西移,约25,800年环绕一周,同时引起春分点以每年50.2秒的速度西移,使回归年比恒星年短,这种现象叫做岁差 precession of the equinoxes. Owing to the gravitation of the sun and the moon towards the earth's equator, the earth's axis revolves around the zodiacal axis in such a way as to describe a cone, gradually moving westward. A complete cycle takes about 25,800 years, during the course of which the equinoctial point moves westward 50.2 seconds each successive year, with the result that the solar year is shorter than the sidereal year. This phenomenon is called the precession of the equinoxes.

【岁出】suìchū 国家在预算年度内的一切支出('跟岁入'相对 as opposed to 'annual income') annual expenditure in a state budget

【岁初】suìchū 年初 the beginning of the year

【岁除】suìchú〈书 *fml.*〉一年的最后一天;除夕 New Year's Eve

【岁杪】suìmiǎo〈书 *fml.*〉年底 the end of the year; year-end

【岁暮】suìmù〈书 *fml.*〉❶ 一年快完的时候 the close of the year: ～天寒。Cold weather sets in as the year draws to its close. ❷〈比喻 *fig.*〉年老 the aged; the old: ～之人 the old

【岁入】suìrù 国家在预算年度内的一切收入(跟'岁出'相对 as opposed to 'annual expenditure') annual income in a state budget; revenue

【岁首】suìshǒu〈书 *fml.*〉一年开始的时候,一般指正月 beginning of the year; first month of the lunar year

【岁数】suì·shu (～儿 suì·shur) 人的年龄 age; years: 妈是上了～的人了。Mum is getting on in years. | 他今年多大～了? How old is he?

【岁星】suìxīng 我国古代指木星。因为木星每十二年在空中绕行一周,每年移动周天的十二分之一,古人把木星所在的位置作为纪年的标准,所以叫岁星。Year Star; old name for Jupiter. Jupiter completes a revolutionary cycle every 12 years, and each year it moves 1/12 of a cycle, so ancients used the position of Jupiter to mark each passing year. Hence its name, the Year Star.

【岁修】suìxiū 各种建筑工程每年进行的有计划的整修和养护工作 annual repairs; planned repairs and maintenance of buildings each year

【岁序】suìxù〈书 *fml.*〉年份更易的顺序 sequence of the year: ～更新 beginning of a new cycle

【岁月】suìyuè 年月 years: 漫长的～long years | 艰苦斗争的～years of arduous struggle

祟 suì 原指鬼怪或鬼怪害人(迷信),借指不正当的行动 evil spirit; ghost; evildoing:鬼～ apparition; ghost|作～(of ghosts, spirits, etc.) haunt; make mischief; cause trouble; exercise evil influence

谇 suì〈书 *fml*.〉❶ 斥责;诘问 rebuke; reprimand; interrogate ❷ 谏诤 criticize sb.'s faults frankly

遂[1] suì ❶ 顺;如意 fulfil; satisfy:～心 after one's own heart; to one's liking|～愿 have one's wish fulfilled ❷ 成功 succeed:未～犯 one who attempts to commit a crime|所谋不～fail in an attempt

遂[2] suì〈书 *fml*.〉就;于是 then; thereupon:服药后腹痛～止。The patient took some medicine, upon which his stomachache stopped.

☞ suí on p.1839

【遂心】suì//xīn 合自己的心意;满意 after one's own heart; to one's liking:～如意 be perfectly satisfied|这回可遂了他的心啦! This time it was entirely to his satisfaction.

【遂意】suì//yì same as 遂心 suì//xīn

【遂愿】suì//yuàn 满足愿望;如愿 have one's wish fulfilled:称心～ perfectly satisfied; be highly satisfied

S

碎 suì ❶ 完整的东西破成零片零块 break to pieces; smash:粉～ broken to (or into) pieces|碗打～了。The bowl was smashed to smithereens. ❷ 使碎 broken:～石机 stone crusher|粉身～骨 have one's body smashed to pieces and bones ground to powder; die the most cruel death ❸ 零星;不完整 fragmentary:～布 oddments of cloth|～屑 bits; scraps; crumbs|琐～trifling ❹ 说话唠叨 garrulous; gabby:嘴太～ talk too much; be a regular chatterbox|闲言～语 sarcastic remarks; gossip

【碎步儿】suìbùr 小而快的步子 quick, short steps; also 碎步子 suìbù·zi

【碎嘴子】suìzuǐ·zi〈方 *dial*.〉❶ 说话絮烦 chatter; jabber; prate:两句话能说完的事就别犯～了。Don't talk on and on when you can say what you need to in a few words. ❷ 爱说话并且一说起来就没完的人 garrulous person; chatterbox

睟 suì〈书 *fml*.〉❶ 光润的样子 shining ❷ 颜色纯粹 pure colour

隧 suì〈书 *fml*.〉地道 tunnel

【隧道】suìdào 在山中或地下凿成的通路 underground passage; tunnel

【隧洞】suìdòng same as 隧道 suìdào

燧 suì ❶〈古代 *arch*.〉取火的器具 flint; tool which can produce sparks, used to make fire in ancient times:～石 flint ❷〈古代 *arch*.〉告警的烽火 beacon fire (in ancient China); fire lit on a hilltop as a signal:烽～ beacon fire

【燧人氏】Suìrénshì 我国古代传说中的人物。传说他发明钻木取火,教人熟食。Suiren; Producer of Fire; ruler in Chinese mythology who, according to legend, discovered fire, invented the technique to produce fire by rubbing one piece of wood against another until combustion took place, and taught the people how to use it for cooking

穗[1](❷繐) suì (～儿 suìr) ❶ 稻麦等禾本科植物的花或果实聚生在茎的顶端,叫做穗 ear of grain; spike; fruiting spike of plants of the grass family, such as rice and wheat, that grows at the top of the stem:麦～儿 ear of wheat; wheat head|谷～儿 ear of millet ❷ 用丝线、布条或纸条等扎成的、挂起来往下垂的装饰品 tassel; fringe; dangling ornament made of silk threads, cloth ribbons or paper strips:黄～红罩的宫灯 red-shaded palace lanterns fringed with yellow tassels

穗[2] Suì ❶ 广州市的别称 another name for 广州 Guǎngzhōu ❷ 姓 a surname

【穗子】suì·zi same as 穗[1] suì:高粱～ear of sorghum|锦旗的下边有许多金黄色的～。The silk banner is fringed with golden-yellow tassels.

穟 suì〈书 *fml*.〉same as 穗 suì

邃 suì〈书 *fml*.〉❶ (时间、空间)深远 (of time, space) remote:～古 remote antiquity|深～ deep; abstruse; recondite ❷ 精深 profound:精～ profound

【邃密】suìmì ❶ same as 深 shēn①:屋宇～。The houses were deep and spacious. ❷ 精深 profound:～的理论 comprehensive and profound theory

sūn (ㄙㄨㄣ)

孙(孫) sūn ❶ 孙子 son's son; grandson:祖～ grandparent and grandchild ❷ 孙子以后的各代 generations beyond that of the grandson:曾～great-grandson|玄～ great-great-grandson; grandson of one's grandson ❸ 跟孙子同辈的亲属 relatives of grandson's generation:侄～ brother's grandson; grandnephew|外～daughter's son; grandson ❹ 植物再生或孳生的 second growth of plants:稻～ new rice shoots from an old stump|～竹 new shoots of bamboo from an old stem ❺ (Sūn) 姓 a surname

〈古 *arch*.〉same as 逊 xùn

【孙女】sūn·nǚ (～儿 sūn·nǚr) 儿子的女儿 son's daughter; granddaughter

【孙女婿】sūnnǚ·xu 孙女的丈夫 granddaughter's husband; grandson-in-law

【孙媳妇】sūnxí·fu (～儿 sūnxí·fur)孙子的妻子 grandson's wife; granddaughter-in-law

【孙子】sūn·zi 儿子的儿子 son's son; grandson

荪(蓀) sūn 古书上说的一种香草 sweet-smelling grass mentioned in ancient texts

狲(猻) sūn ☞ [猢狲] húsūn on p.820

飧(飱) sūn 〈书 *fml.*〉晚饭 evening meal; supper

sǔn (ㄙㄨㄣˇ)

损 sǔn ❶ 减少 decrease; lose: ～益 increase and decrease | 增～ increase and decrease | ～兵折将 suffer heavy casualties ❷ 损害 at the expense of sb.; jeopardize: ～人利己 harm others for one's own benefit | 有益无～ can only do good, not harm ❸ 损坏 damage (objects): 破～ damaged; worn; torn | 完好无～ intact; undamaged ❹〈方 *dial.*〉用尖刻的话挖苦人 speak sarcastically; be caustic; be cutting: ～人 make caustic remarks ❺〈方 *dial.*〉刻薄;恶毒 mean; shabby: 这人办事真～。This person is ruthless in his handling of affairs. | 他说的话够～的。He is overly sarcastic.

【损兵折将】sǔn bīng zhé jiàng 兵士和将领都有损失。指作战失利。suffer heavy casualties; military reverses

【损公肥私】sǔn gōng féi sī 损害公家的利益而使私人得到好处 seek private gain at public expense; feather one's nest at public expense

【损害】sǔnhài 使事业、利益、健康、名誉等蒙受损失 do harm to (a cause, sb.'s interests, health, reputation, etc.); damage; impair: 光线不好,看书容易～视力。Reading in poor light is bad for one's eyes. | 不能～群众利益。Never do anything that harms the interests of the people.

【损耗】sǔnhào ❶ 损失消耗 loss; wear and tear: 电能的～ power loss ❷ 货物由于自然原因(如物理变化和化学变化)或运输而造成的消耗损失 wastage; spoilage: 减少水果运输中的～。Reduce the damage and spoilage incurred during the transportation of fruits.

【损坏】sǔnhuài 使失去原来的使用效能 damage (of objects): 糖吃多了,容易～牙齿。Eating too much sugar damages the teeth.

【损毁】sǔnhuǐ 损坏;毁坏 damage or destroy: ～树木近万株。Nearly 10,000 trees were damaged or destroyed.

【损人】sǔnrén ❶〈方 *dial.*〉用尖刻的话挖苦人: 你有意见直说,干吗～。If you have something to say, say it directly. Why be sarcastic? ❷ 使别人受到损失 do harm to others: ～利己 harm others to benefit oneself; benefit oneself at the expense of others

【损人利己】sǔn rén lì jǐ 使别人受到损失而使自己得到好处 harm others in order to benefit oneself; benefit oneself at the expense of others

【损伤】sǔnshāng ❶ 损害;伤害 harm; damage; injure: 工作中要注意方式方法,不要～群众的积极性。When at work, pay attention to method and style, and do not dampen the enthusiasm of the masses. ❷ same as 损失 sǔnshī: 经过两次战役,敌人的兵力～很大。After two campaigns the enemy forces suffered heavy losses.

【损失】sǔnshī ❶ 没有代价地消耗或失去 lose; suffer loss: 财产受到～ suffer a loss of property ❷ 没有代价地消耗或失去的东西 loss; damage; thing that is lost: ～巨大 suffer (or sustain) heavy losses

【损益】sǔnyì ❶ 减少和增加 increase and decrease ❷ 赔和赚;盈亏 profit and loss; gains and losses: ～相抵。The gains offset the losses.

笋(筍) sǔn 竹的嫩芽,味鲜美,可以做菜 bamboo shoot used in cooking for its fresh, delicious flavour; also 竹笋 zhúsǔn

【笋鸡】sǔnjī 做食物用的小而嫩的鸡 young chicken; broiler

隼 sǔn 鸟类的一科,翅膀窄而尖,嘴短而宽,上嘴弯曲并有齿状突起。飞得很快,善于袭击其他鸟类,是凶猛的鸟。falcon; small bird of prey having narrow and pointed wings and a short and broad beak with its upper part crooked and serrated, flying fast, and good at assaulting other birds; also 鹘 (hú)

榫 sǔn (～儿 sǔnr) same as 榫头 sǔn·tou

【榫头】sǔn·tou 竹、木、石制器物或构件上利用凹凸方式相接处凸出的部分 tenon; projecting end of a piece of bamboo, wood, or stone shaped to fit into a mortise to make a joint

【榫眼】sǔnyǎn 卯眼 mortise

【榫子】sǔn·zi same as 榫头 sǔn·tou

簨 sǔn〈古时 *arch.*〉悬挂钟鼓的架子 rack on which bells or drums are suspended

suō (ㄙㄨㄛ)

莎 suō [莎草] (suōcǎo)多年生草本植物,多生在潮湿地区或河边沙地上,叶条形,有光泽,花穗褐色。地下块根叫香附子,供药用。nutgrass flat sedge (*Cyperus rotundus*); herbaceous perennial plant, usu. growing in damp areas or riverbanks, with ensiform, lustrous leaves, brown flowers, and subterranean root tuber called *xiangfuzi* when used in medicine

☞ shā on p.1666

唆 suō 唆使 instigate; abet:教～ instigate; put sb. up to sth.|调～instigate

【唆使】suōshǐ 指使或挑动别人去做坏事 instigate; abet:受人～be instigated by someone

娑 suō ☞ below

【娑罗树】suōluóshù 常绿乔木,高30余米,叶子长卵形,花淡黄色。原产印度。木材紫褐色或淡红色,可以做建筑材料。sal tree (*Shorea robusta*); evergreen tree that originates in India and grows as tall as 30 metres, with oval leaves and pale-yellow flowers, and purplish-brown or pale-red timber that is used for construction material [梵 Sanskrit: sāla]

【娑罗双树】suōluó shuāng shù 两棵娑罗树,相传释迦牟尼涅槃于娑罗双树间 twin sal trees, between which Sakyamuni achieved nirvana

桫 suō [桫椤](suōluó)蕨类植物,木本,茎高而直,叶片大,羽状分裂。茎含淀粉,可供食用。spinulose tree fern (*Cyathea spinulosa*); pteridophyte, woody plant, with tall, straight stem that contains edible starch, and large runcinate leaves

S

梭 suō 织布时牵引纬线(横线)的工具,两头尖,中间粗,形状像枣核 shuttle; spindle-shaped device used in weaving for passing the thread of the woof between the threads of the warp; also 梭子 suō·zi

【梭镖】suōbiāo 装上长柄的两边有刃的尖刀 spear; weapon with an arrow head and a long shaft

【梭巡】suōxún 往来巡逻 keep guard; patrol to and fro:昼夜～patrol to and fro around the clock

【梭子】[1] suō·zi 梭 weaver's shuttle

【梭子】[2] suō·zi ❶ 机关枪等武器的子弹夹子 cartridge clip ❷〈量词 *classifier*〉用于子弹 clip (of bullets):一～子弹 a clip of bullets

【梭子蟹】suō·zixiè 海蟹的一类,头胸部的甲略呈梭形,螯长而大。常栖息在海底。swimming crab; marine crab with long, large pincers that lives on the seabed, whose shell resembles a shuttle; also called 蝤蛑 yóumóu

挲(抄) suō ☞ 摩挲(mósuō) on p.1363 ☞ sā on p.1647 and shā on p.1666

睃 suō 斜着眼睛看 look askance at

蓑(簑) suō 蓑衣 alpine rush or palm-bark rain cape:～笠 alpine rush rain cape and rain hat

【蓑衣】suōyī 用草或棕制成的、披在身上的防雨用具 alpine rush or palm-bark rain cape

嗦 suō ❶ ☞ [哆嗦]duō·suō on p.500 ❷ ☞ 啰嗦 luō·suō on p.1276

嘲 suō 吮吸 suck:婴儿～奶头。Babies suckle at the nipple.

羧 suō same as 羧基 suōjī

【羧基】suōjī 由羰基和羟基组成的一价原子团(-COOH) carboxyl; carboxyl group; univalent radical (-COOH) comprising hydroxyl and carboxyl

缩 suō ❶ 由大变小或由长变短;收缩 contract; shrink; shorten:紧～contract|～短 shorten|热胀冷～expand with heat and contract with cold|这布下水也不～。This cloth will not shrink on being washed. ❷ 没伸开或伸开了又收回去;不伸出 draw back; withdraw; recoil:乌龟的头老～在里面。A tortoise always tucks its head away in its shell. ❸ 后退 withdraw; recoil:退～ shrink back; flinch|畏～ recoil in fear; shrink back

☞ sù on p.1834

【缩编】suōbiān ❶(部队、机关等)缩减编制(of troops, government organs, etc.) reduce the staff:军队～ cut down on the number of troops ❷ 把作品、节目等压缩编辑,使篇幅减少 compression; abridge; condense a written or spoken work into a more concise form:将原来50集的电视连续剧～成30集 condense a 50-episode TV play into 30 episodes

【缩尺】suōchǐ 比例尺①②(专指图纸上的尺寸小于实际尺寸的) reduced scale; scale

【缩短】suōduǎn 使原有长度、距离、时间变短 shorten; cut down; cut short:～战线 shorten the front line; narrow the scope of an activity|～期限 shorten the time limit

【缩合】suōhé 两个或两个以上的有机化合物分子相互作用,同时析出水、醇、卤化氢、氢等小分子而形成另外的物质,如两个分子的乙醇析出一个分子的水而缩合成乙醚 condensation; chemical reaction involving the union of two or more organic molecules, often involving the elimination of a simple molecule (such as water, alcohol, hydrogen halide, or hydrogen) to form a new, more complex compound of a greater molecular weight. For instance, after eliminating one molecule of water, two molecules of alcohol condense to make ether.

【缩减】suōjiǎn 紧缩减少 reduce; cut:～开支 reduce (or cut) spending|～重叠的机构 streamline overlapping organizations

【缩聚】suōjù 缩合聚合,指单体结合成高分子化合物,同时析出小分子副产物。如苯酚和甲醛结合成苯酚甲醛树脂,同时产生水。condensation polymerization; polycondensation; chemical reaction in which two or more small molecules combine to form larger molecules that contain repeating structural units of the original molecules. For instance, phenol and formaldehyde combine to form phenol-formaldehyde resin by separating out water.

【缩手】suō//shǒu 手缩回来 draw back one's

hand;〈比喻 *fig.*〉不敢再做下去 shrink (from doing sth.):病势危重,几位名医都～了。The patient's condition is so critical that the most renowned of doctors are loath to take any action.

【缩手缩脚】suō shǒu suō jiǎo ❶ 因寒冷而四肢不能舒展的样子 shrink from the cold; contract ❷ 形容做事顾虑多,不大胆 be overcautious

【缩水】suō//shuǐ 将纺织品、纤维等放进水中浸泡使收缩(of cloth through getting wet) shrink:这块布缩过水了吗? Has this piece of cloth shrunk from getting wet?

【缩水】suōshuǐ 某些纺织品、纤维等下水后收缩(of textiles, fabrics, etc.) shrink; become constricted after soaking in water:这种布不～。This cloth does not shrink. also 抽水 chōu//shuǐ

【缩头缩脑】suō tóu suō nǎo ❶ 形容畏缩 be timid; be faint-hearted ❷ 形容胆小,不敢出头负责任 be timid and shrink from responsibility

【缩微】suōwēi 指利用照相技术等把文字图像缩成很小的复制品 microform; process for reproducing printed matter in a much reduced size through photography:～技术 microfilm

【缩小】suōxiǎo 使由大变小 reduce (in width, size, scope, etc.); lessen; narrow; shrink:～范围 reduce the scope; narrow the range

【缩写】suōxiě ❶ 使用拼音文字的语言中,对于常用的词组(多为专名)以及少数常用的词所采用的简便的写法 abbreviate; make briefer; in a language written in alphabetic letters, certain terms in common use are shortened by reducing them to an abridged form that stands for the whole; 缩写有几种方式。There are several forms of abbreviation. a)截取词的第一个字母来代表这个词,如C代表 carbonium (碳) by using the first letter of a word to stand for the whole, e.g. C stands for carbonium; b)截取词的前几个字母,如 Eng.代表 England (英国)或 English (英语) by using the first few letters to stand for the whole, e.g. Eng. represents England or English; c)分别截取一个词的两个部分的第一个字母,如 cm.代表 centimetre (厘米),kg.代表 kilogramme (公斤) by using the first letter of certain syllables in a word, e.g. cm. stands for centimetre, and kg. represents kilogramme; d)截取词的第一个和末一个字母,如 No.代表 numéro (号数) by using the first and last letter to stand for a word, e.g. No. stands for the Latin numéro, meaning number ❷ 把文学作品(多为长篇小说)改写,使篇幅减少 abridge; condense a written work (such as a novel) into more concise form:～本 abridged edition (or version)

【缩衣节食】suō yī jié shí ☞ 节衣缩食 jié yī suō shí on p. 990

【缩印】suōyìn 一种影印法,把书画、文件等先用照相法缩小,然后制成印刷版印刷 reprint books in a reduced format; photomechanical printing in a reduced format

【缩影】suōyǐng 指可以代表同一类型的具体而微的人或事物 epitome; miniature; typical example of a type of person or matter:作品主人公的遭遇是当时农民生活的～。The experiences of the protagonist in this work epitomize peasant life at the time.

suǒ (ㄙㄨㄛˇ)

贞 suǒ 贞乃亥(Suǒnǎihài),地名,即泽库县,在青海 Suonaihai, place name, another name for Zeku County, in Qinghai Province

所(㪽) suǒ ❶ 处所 place; location:场～ place; arena|住～dwelling place; residence; domicile|各得其～ each is in his proper place; each is properly provided for ❷ 明代驻兵的地点,大的叫千户所,小的叫百户所。现在只用于地名 places where troops were stationed in Ming Dynasty, the bigger ones called *qianhusuo*, and the smaller called *baihusuo*, now used as a place name only:海阳～(在山东) Haiyangsuo (in Shandong Province)|前～(在浙江) Qiansuo (in Zhejiang Province)|后～(在山西) Housuo (in Shanxi Province)|沙后～(在辽宁) Shahousuo (in Liaoning Province) ❸ 用做机关或其他办事地方的名称:office; bureau; institute:研究～research institute|派出～ police substation|诊疗～clinic|指挥～command post|招待～guest house ❹〈量词 *classifier*〉for houses, schools, hospitals, etc.: a)用于房屋 for houses:这～房子 this house; b)用于学校等(可以不止一所房子) for schools, etc. (not limited to one building):一～医院 one hospital|两～学校 two schools ❺〈助词 *aux.*〉a)跟'为'或'被'合用,表示被动 [used together with 为 wéi or 被 bèi in the passive voice]:为人～笑 be laughed at by others|看问题片面,容易被表面现象～迷惑。Taking a one-sided approach to problems makes one prone to being misled by outward appearances; b)用在做定语的主谓结构的动词前面,表示中心词是受事 [used before the verb in the subject-predicate structure to make it passive]:我～认识的人 people I know|大家～提的意见 opinions put forward by various people; c)用在'是…的'中间的名词、代词和动词之间,强调施事和动作的关系 [used between noun or pronoun and verb to stress the relation between the doer of an action and the action itself]:全国的形势,是同志们～关心的。The national situation is what concerns us comrades; and d)〈书 *fml.*〉

用在动词前面，跟动词构成体词结构[used before the verb to form a substantive structure]：各尽～能 each doing his best | 闻～未闻 unheard-of ❻ (Suǒ)姓 a surname

【所部】suǒbù 所率领的部队 troops under one's command

【所得税】suǒdéshuì 国家对个人和企业按一定比率从各种收入中征收的税 income tax; tax on the net income of an individual or business

【所属】suǒshǔ ❶ 统属之下的 what is subordinate to one; under one's command：命令～各部队一齐出动 order the units under one's command to set out simultaneously ❷ 自己隶属的 what one belongs to or is affiliated with：向～派出所填报户口 apply to or register with the local police station for residence;

注意 **NOTE**：后面不带名词时只有①义，如 When no noun follows, its meaning is limited to ①, for example：通令～一体遵照。All the units are to be informed that instructions should be carried out.

【所谓】suǒwèi ❶ 所说的 so-named; what is known as：～共识，就是指共同的认识。That called 'common understanding' means an understanding shared by all. ❷（某些人）所说的（含不承认意）so-called (falsely or improperly named)：难道这就是～代表作？Is this the so-called representative work?

【所向披靡】suǒ xiàng pī mǐ 〈比喻 *fig.*〉力量所到之处，一切障碍全被扫除 wherever the wind blows, the grass and trees bend with it; carry all before one; sweep away all obstacles; send the enemy fleeing helter-skelter（所向 *suo xiang*：指风吹到的地方 wherever the wind blows; 披靡 *pi mi*：草木随风倒伏 grass and trees bending at the blow of wind）

【所向无敌】suǒ xiàng wú dí 指军队等所指向的地方，谁也挡不住(of troops) invincible; all-conquering; ever-victorious; break down all enemy resistance; also 所向无前 suǒ xiàng wú qián

【所以】suǒyǐ ❶ 表示因果关系的连词 to indicate causality：a)用在下半句表示结果[used to introduce a clause of result, preceded by a clause of reason or cause]：我和他在一起工作过，～对他比较熟悉。I used to work with him so I know him pretty well. b)用在上半句主语和谓语之间，提出需要说明原因的事情，下半句说明原因[used between the subject and the predicate of a clause of result, followed by a clause of reason or cause introduced by 是因为 shì yīn・wèi or 是由于 shì yóuyú]：我～对他比较熟悉，是因为我和他在一起工作过。The reason I know him so well is because we used to work together. c)上半句先说明原因，下半句用'是…所以…的原因(缘故)'[used in the pattern 是…所以… 的原因(缘故) preceded by a clause of reason or cause] ...is the reason; is why...：我和他在一起工作过，这就是我～对他比较熟悉的原因。He and I used to work together. That's why I know him pretty well. d)'所以'单独成句，表示'原因就在这里' precisely; that is exactly the point：～呀，要不然我怎么这么说呢！Absolutely. Otherwise I wouldn't have said it! ❷ 实在的情由或适宜的举动(限用于固定词组中做宾语)[used in certain set phrases as the object of the verb, to refer to sth. indefinite but understood]：忘其～ forget oneself; be carried away by a sudden impulse | 不知～ not know why it is so

【所以然】suǒyǐrán 指为什么是这样的原因或道理 the reason why; the whys and wherefores：知其然而不知其～know the hows but not the whys | 他说了半天还是没说出个～来。He talked a lot without making one any the wiser.

【所有】suǒyǒu ❶ 领有 own; possess：～权 proprietary rights; ownership | ～制 system of ownership ❷ 领有的东西 possessions：尽其～ give everything one has; give one's all ❸ 一切；全部 all：把～的力量都贡献给祖国 dedicate all one's strength to the motherland

【所有权】suǒyǒuquán 国家、集体或个人对于生产资料或生活资料的占有权。所有权是由所有制形式决定的，它是生产关系上的所有制在立法上的表现。proprietary right; ownership; title; the right of a country, collective or individual to possess means of production or means of subsistence. The proprietary right is determined by the form of ownership, and is the formulated legal expression for ownership of production relations.

【所有制】suǒyǒuzhì 生产资料归谁占有的制度，它决定人们在生产中相互关系的性质和产品分配、交换的形式，是生产关系的基础。在人类社会的各个历史发展阶段，有各种不同性质的所有制。ownership; system of ownership of the means of production that decides the nature of production relations and form of product distribution and exchange. In various historical stages of humankind, there have been systems of ownership of various natures.

【所在】suǒzài ❶ 处所 place; location：在风景好、气候适宜的～给工人们修建了疗养院。Sanatoriums for workers are built in places with beautiful scenery and a pleasant climate. ❷ 存在的地方 where sb. or sth. is：病因～the cause of disease | 力量～ where the strength lies

索[1] suǒ ❶ 大绳子或大链子 large rope or chain：船～ ship's rigging | 绳～ thick cord | 麻～ rope made of hemp | 绞～ hangman's noose | 铁～桥 iron chain bridge ❷

(Suǒ)姓 a surname

索[2] suǒ ❶ 搜寻；寻找 search; look for; seek: 搜～ search | 遍～不得 search high and low for sth. in vain ❷ 要；取 demand; ask; exact: ～取 demand | ～还 get sth. back | ～价 ask a price

索[3] suǒ 〈书 *fml.*〉 ❶ 孤单 all alone; all by oneself: 离群～居 live in solitude; live all alone ❷ 寂寞；没有意味 dull; lonely: ～然 dull; dry; insipid

【索道】suǒdào 用钢索在两地之间架设的空中通道，通常用于运输 cableway; ropeway; air thoroughfare erected between two places by large steel cable, used for transportation: 载人架空～ manned telpher

【索贿】suǒ//huì 索取贿赂 ask for bribe: ～受贿 seek and take a bribe

【索价】suǒjià 要价 ask (or demand) a price; charge: ～过高 demand an exorbitant price

【索寞】suǒmò 〈书 *fml.*〉 ❶ 颓丧消沉 downhearted; dejected; dispirited: 神情～look dejected ❷ 寂寞萧索 lonely; desolate: 山上杂草丛生，异常～。The hill was overgrown with weeds and looked utterly desolate.

【索赔】suǒpéi 索取赔偿 claim for damages; claim indemnity: ～一千元 ask for 1,000 yuan compensation

【索取】suǒqǔ ☞ same as 要[2] yào ②: 向大自然～财富 extort wealth from nature

【索然】suǒrán 没有意味，没有兴趣的样子 dull; dry; insipid: ～寡味 flat and insipid | 兴致～ uninterested; be bored stiff

【索索】suǒsuǒ ❶〈拟声词 *onom.*〉形容轻微的声音 rustling sound: 微风吹动树叶～作响。The leaves rustled in the breeze. | 雨～地下着。You can hear the rain softly pattering down. ❷ 形容颤抖 trembling: 他吓得脸色苍白，～发抖。His face turned ashen and he trembled with fear.

【索性】suǒxìng 〈副词 *adv.*〉表示直截了当；干脆 simply; just; might as well: 既然已经做了，～就把它做完。Since you have started the job, you may as well finish it. | 找了几个地方都没有找着，～不再找了。It was nowhere to be found, so we simply gave it up for lost.

【索要】suǒyào same as 索取 suǒqǔ: ～财物 extort money and goods

【索引】suǒyǐn 把书刊中的项目或内容摘记下来，每条下标注出处页码，按一定次序排列，供人查阅的资料 index; alphabetical list of names or subjects contained in a book (usu. at the back), along with their page number, so arranged in order to make quick and easy reference; also 引得 yǐndé

【索子】suǒ·zi 〈方 *dial.*〉大绳子或大链子 large rope or large chain

唢 suǒ [唢呐](suǒ·nà)管乐器，管身正面有七孔，背面一孔 *suona* horn, a woodwind instrument with seven holes on the obverse and one on the reverse of the tube

琐 suǒ ❶ 细碎 trivial; petty: 繁～over-elaborate; tedious | ～事 trifles | ～闻 bits of news; scraps of information ❷ 卑微 petty and low: 猥～ of wretched appearance

【琐事】suǒshì 细小零碎的事情 trifles; trivial matters: 日常～daily trifles | ～缠身 be bogged down by trifles

【琐碎】suǒsuì 细小而繁多 trifling; trivial: 琐琐碎碎 trifling | 摆脱这些～的事，多抓些大问题。Break away from these trivialities, and get a better grasp of the essentials.

【琐细】suǒxì same as 琐碎 suǒsuì: ～的事务 trivial matters

【琐屑】suǒxiè 〈书 *fml.*〉same as 琐碎 suǒsuì

锁 suǒ ❶ 安在门、箱子、抽屉等的开合处或铁链的环孔中，使人不能随便打开的金属器具，一般要用钥匙才能开 lock; padlock; metal implement attached to a door, case, drawer, or links of a chain to prevent their being opened by unauthorized people, which is unlocked with a key ❷ 用锁使门、箱子、抽屉等关住或使铁链拴住 lock up; lock a door, case, drawer, etc., or secure sth. with a chain: ～门 lock the door | 把箱子～上 lock the case | 把猴子～起来 lock the monkey in ◇双眉深～ with knitted brows | 愁眉～眼 with knitted brows and lowered eyes; frowning deeply ❸ 形状像锁的东西 sth. that looks like a lock: 石～ stone dumbbell (in the form of an old-fashioned padlock) ❹ same as 锁链 suǒliàn: 枷～lock and chains ❺ 缝纫方法，用于衣物边缘或扣眼儿上，针脚很密，线斜交或钩连 lock stitch; way of sewing for the hem of garment or button hole, where close stitches are formed by interlocking threads: ～边 lock stitch a border | ～眼 do lock stitch on a buttonhole

【锁匙】suǒchí 〈方 *dial.*〉钥匙 key

【锁骨】suǒgǔ 胸腔前上部、呈S形的骨头，左右各一块，内端与胸骨相连，外端与肩胛骨相连 clavicle; collarbone; s-shaped bone located in the upper torso that articulates with the scapula; (图见☞ figure for 骨骼 gǔgé on p. 693)

【锁国】suǒguó 像锁门似的把国家关闭起来，不与外国来往 close the country to international intercourse: 闭关～ cut off one's country from the outside world

【锁链】suǒliàn (～儿 suǒliànr)用铁环连接起来的成串的东西，用来束缚人、物 fetters; trammels; chain; linked iron rings used to restrict movement of sb. or sth. ◇打断了封建的～ break the fetters of feudalism; also 锁链子 suǒliàn·zi

【锁钥】suǒyuè ❶〈比喻 *fig*.〉做好一件事的重要关键 key; factor of crucial importance in attempting to accomplish sth.:调查研究是做好各项工作的～。Investigation and research are the keys to doing a good job in all aspects. ❷〈比喻 *fig*.〉军事要地 strategic gateway (to an important centre or a major city):北门～ Key to the North Gate (the north gate of an old fort at the Badaling section of the Great Wall northwest of Beijing)

璅 suǒ〈书 *fml*.〉same as 琐 suǒ

鏁 suǒ〈书 *fml*.〉same as 锁 suǒ

S

T

tā (ㄊㄚ)

他 tā 〈代词 *pron*.〉❶ 称自己和对方以外的某个人[third person singular and male] he; him 注意 **NOTE**:'五四'以前'他'兼称男性、女性以及一切事物。现代书面语里,'他'一般只用来称男性。但是在性别不明或没有区分的必要时,'他'只是泛指,不分男性和女性。Prior to the May 4th Movement of 1919, this Chinese character 他 referred to both male and female and objects in the third person single, but in contemporary written Chinese it is used as third person single and male as we as a general reference when one is not clear about the gender of the person referred to or when it is unnecessary to clarify the gender. 如 For example:从笔迹上看不出~是男的还是女的。Judging from the handwriting there's no telling whether it is a he or a she. |一个人要是离开了集体,~就将一事无成。One can accomplish nothing if he estranges himself from the collective. ❷ 虚指(用在动词和数量词之间)[serve as a form word between a verb and a quantifier]:睡~一觉 go and get some sleep|唱~几句 sing a few lines|盖~三间瓦房 built a brick-and-tile house with three rooms ❸ 指别一方面或其他地方 something else; somewhere else:早已~去 have long left for somewhere else|留作~用 lay sth. aside for some other use ❹ 另外的;其他的 another; other:~人 other people|~乡 place away from hometown|~日 some other day

【他们】tā·men 〈代词 *pron*.〉称自己和对方以外的若干人[third person plural] they; ☞他 tā and 她们 tā·men

【他年】tānián ❶ 将来的某一年或某个时候 in the future; some other year ❷〈书 *fml*.〉过去的某个时候 some time in the past

【他人】tārén 别人 others; other people:关心~,比关心自己为重 be more concerned about others than oneself

【他日】tārì 〈书 *fml*.〉❶ 将来的某一天或某一个时期 some other time; someday ❷ 过去的某个时候 some time in the past

【他杀】tāshā 被他人杀死(区别于'自杀' as compared with 'suicide') homicide

【他山攻错】tā shān gōng cuò ☞攻错 gōngcuò on p. 673

【他乡】tāxiāng 家乡以外的地方(多指离家乡较远的 oft. a place far away from one's home town) place away from home town; alien land:流落~ be stranded in an alien land|~遇故知 come across an old acquaintance in a place away from home town.

它(牠) tā 〈代词 *pron*.〉称人以外的事物[third person singular and nonhuman] it:这杯牛奶你喝了~。Drink this cup of milk.

【它们】tā·men 〈代词 *pron*.〉称不止一个的事物[third person plural and nonhuman] they

她 tā 〈代词 *pron*.〉❶ 称自己和对方以外的某个女性[third person singular and female] she; her ❷ 称自己敬爱或珍爱的事物,如祖国、国旗等 reference to sth. beloved, such as one's motherland and national flag

【她们】tā·men 〈代词 *pron*.〉称自己和对方以外的若干女性[third person plural and female] (female) they; them 注意 **NOTE**:在书面上,若干人全是女性时用'她们',有男有女时用'他们',不用'他(她)们'。Use the phrase 她们 when referring to a group of girls or women, but 他们 when referring to a group of people that include both men and women.

趿 tā same as 趿拉 tā·la

【趿拉】tā·la 把鞋后帮踩在脚后跟下 wear cloth shoes with the backs turned in; shuffle about with the backs of one's shoes trodden down:别~着鞋走路。Don't use your shoes as slippers.|这双鞋都叫你~坏了。You have treaded this pair of shoes to pieces.

【趿拉板儿】tā·labǎnr 〈方 *dial*.〉没有帮而只有襻儿的木底鞋 wooden slippers; clogs; also 呱哒板儿 guā·dabǎnr

【趿拉儿】tā·lar 〈方 *dial*.〉拖鞋 slippers

铊 tā 金属元素,符号 Tl (thallium)。白色,质软。用来制合金光电管、温度计、光学玻璃等。铊的化合物有毒,用于医药。thallium (Tl); soft and white metal element that is used as a material for the making of alloy photoelectric cells, thermometers, optical glass, etc. Thallium-containing chemical compounds are poisonous and used for pharmaceutical purposes.

☞ 砣 tuó on p. 1961

塌 tā ❶（支架起来的东西）倒下或陷下 crumple; gave way: 倒～collapse | 六孔桥～了一孔。One of the six arches of the bridge caved in. ❷ 凹下 sink; slump: ～鼻梁 snub-nosed | 年糕越蒸越往下～。The longer rice cakes are steamed, the more they shrink. ❸ 安定; 镇定 calm down; ease: ～下心来 settle down to (work, etc.)

【塌车】tāchē 〈方 *dial.*〉一种人拉的大型两轮排子车 flatbed two-wheeled handcart; also 榻车 tàchē

【塌方】tā//fāng 因地层结构不良、雨水冲刷或修筑上的缺陷，道路、堤坝等旁边的陡坡或坑道、隧道的顶部突然坍塌 cave in; landslide; sudden collapse of road, dam, trench, tunnel, etc., caused by flawed stratigraphic structure, rainfall, or defective engineering work; also 坍方 tānfāng

【塌架】tā//jià ❶（房屋等）倒塌(of a building, etc.) collapse; topple down ❷〈比喻 *fig.*〉垮台(of a political regime) topple

【塌实】tā·shi ❶（工作或学习的态度）切实; 不浮躁(of attitude towards work or study) down-to-earth; steadfast ❷（情绪）安定; 安稳 with peace of mind; free from anxiety: 事情办完就～了。I'll feel at ease only after I've got my job done. | 翻来覆去睡不～ toss and turn in bed and can't sleep well ‖ also 踏实 tā·shi

【塌台】tā//tái 垮台 fall from power; collapse

【塌陷】tāxiàn 往下陷; 沉陷 subside; sink; cave in: 地基～。The foundation of the house is sinking.

【塌心】tā//xīn 〈方 *dial.*〉心情安定 calm down; feel at ease: 事情落实了，干活也～。With everything settled, we can work without misgivings.

【塌秧】tāyāng 〈方 *dial.*〉(～儿 tāyāngr) ❶ 花草、蔬菜等因缺水而发蔫(of flowers, grass, vegetables, etc.) wither; droop ❷ 形容垂头丧气，精神不振 dejected; crestfallen

遢 tā ☞ 邋遢(lā·tā) on p. 1138

溻 tā 〈方 *dial.*〉汗湿透(衣服、被褥等)(of clothes, bedding, etc.) be soaked with sweat: 天太热，我衣服都～了。It's sweltering and my clothes have been soaked in sweat.

禢 tā 〈书 *fml.*〉用绳索套住、捆住 tie sth. with rope

踏 tā [踏实](tā·shi) same as 塌实 tā·shi

☞ tà on p. 1849

禢1 tā 〈方 *dial.*〉在衣物上面缝(花边或绦子)(of lace or tassel) hem; sew

禢2 tā ☞ 汗禢儿 hàntār on p. 766

嗒 tā 〈书 *fml.*〉饮 imbibe; drink

tǎ（ㄊㄚˇ）

塔(墖) tǎ ❶ 佛教的建筑物，有种种形式，通常有五层到十三层不等，顶上是尖的 tower; pagoda; Buddhist building erected as a memorial or shrine, of many types, usu. with 5 to 13 storeys and a pointed rooftop: 宝～pagoda ❷ 塔形的建筑物 tower; pagoda-shaped structure: 水～water tower | 灯～beacon; lighthouse | 金字～pyramid ❸ (Tǎ) 姓 a surname

☞ ·da on p. 367

【塔吊】tǎdiào 塔式起重机。机身很高，像塔，有长臂，可以在轨道上移动，工作面较大。主要用于建筑工程。tower crane; tower-like machine that can move along rails for hoisting and moving heavy objects by means of a swinging arm

【塔灰】tǎhuī 〈方 *dial.*〉室内房顶上或墙上的尘土，多指从房顶垂下来的成串的尘土 cobwebs and dirt, usu. hanging down from a ceiling or a wall

【塔吉克族】Tǎjíkèzú ❶ 我国少数民族之一，分布在新疆 Tajiks, a minority group inhabiting the Xinjiang Uygur Autonomous Region ❷ 塔吉克斯坦共和国人数最多的民族 the largest ethnic group in the Republic of Tajikistan

【塔林】tǎlín 僧人的塔形墓群，多坐落在寺庙附近 forest of stupas; monks' cemetery, oft. located on the premises of a temple

【塔楼】tǎlóu ❶ 高层的略呈塔形的楼房 tower; high-rise building ❷ 建筑物上面的呈塔形的小楼 turret; small tower or tower-shaped projection on a building

【塔轮】tǎlún 几个直径不同的轮按大小顺序装在同一轴上构成的皮带轮，形状像宝塔。传动带挂在不同直径的轮上，轴的转动速度不同。cone pulley; stepped pulley, consisting of a number of wheels of different diameters and put together on the same axis in the shape of a pagoda, so that the turning speed of the axis can be adjusted by shifting the belt to a chosen wheel

【塔塔尔族】Tǎtǎ'ěrzú 我国少数民族之一，分布在新疆 Tartars, a minority group inhabiting the Xinjiang Uygur Autonomous Region

【塔台】tǎtái 飞机场上的塔形建筑物，设有电台，担任地面与空中的联系 aviation control tower; tower-like building fixed with radio equipment to facilitate air-land liaison at an airport

【塔钟】tǎzhōng 装在高大建筑物顶上的大型时钟 tower clock; turret clock

溚 tǎ 焦油的旧称 old term for 焦油 jiāoyóu

獭 tǎ 水獭、旱獭、海獭的统称，通常指水獭 otter; general term for water dog, marmot and sea otter, but usu, referring to water dog

【獭祭】tǎjì 〈书 *fml.*〉《礼记·月令》:'獭祭鱼。'獭贪食，常捕鱼陈列水边，称为祭鱼。后用来比喻罗列典故或堆砌典故。According to *The Book of Rites·Monthly Observances*, 'The otter holds memorial ceremonies for fish.' This refers to the habit of the otter, a rapacious animal, to spread the fish it has caught about the waterside as if offering sacrifices to heaven. Now it has become a reference to a writer's parade of allusions in literary composition in the fashion of an otter laying out fish.

鳎 tǎ 鱼类的一科，体侧扁，呈片状，长椭圆形，像舌头，有细鳞，头部短小，有绒毛状的牙，两眼生在身体的右侧，有的背鳍、臀鳍与尾鳍相连。左侧向下卧在浅海底的泥沙上，捕食小鱼。常见的有条鳎。sole (*Solea solea*); fish having an oblong laterally flat body in the shape of a tongue and covered with tiny scales, villiform teeth in a short and small mouth, both eyes on the right side, with the dorsal fins linked with anal and fail fins in some cases, oft. lying on its left side on a shallow seabed and feeding on small fish. *Solea ovata* is a common type of sole. 通称 generally known as 鳎目鱼 tǎmùyú

tà (ㄊㄚˋ)

拓(搨) tà 把碑刻、铜器等的形状和上面的文字、图形印下来，方法是在物体上蒙一层薄纸，先拍打使凹凸分明，然后上墨，显出文字、图像来 make rubbings from an inscription, patterns, etc. usu. by covering a sheet of thin paper on a stone tablet or bronzeware and patting it until the contours of the inscription or patterns show up, and then applying ink on the paper to produce the impression:～印 make rubbings|把碑文～下来 make rubbings of a text from a stone tablet

☞ tuò on p. 1962

【拓本】tàběn 把碑刻、铜器等文物的形状和上面的文字、图像拓下来的纸本 book of rubbings of the shapes of inscribed tablets and bronze ware and of the characters and images on them

【拓片】tàpiàn 把碑刻、铜器等文物的形状和上面的文字、图像拓下来的纸片 rubbing; impression of a design of stone tablet, bronzeware or other artifacts, or of the text or pictures on them, made by rubbing on paper laid over it with ink, pencil, chalk, etc.

沓 tà 〈书 *fml.*〉多而重复 crowded and repeated:杂～repeated|纷至～来 come one after another

☞ dá on p. 345

佻(㒓) tà ☞佻佻(tiāotà) on p. 1899

挞(撻) tà 〈书 *fml.*〉用鞭子、棍子等打人 flog; whip:鞭～lash at

【挞伐】tàfá 〈书 *fml.*〉讨伐 launch a punitive expedition against:大张～large-scale attack

闼(闥) tà 〈书 *fml.*〉门;小门 door; small gate:排～直入(推门就进去)push the door open and enter a house without so much as to announce oneself

汰(澾) tà 〈书 *fml.*〉滑溜(huá·liu);光滑 slippery; smooth

嗒 tà ☞ below

☞ dā on p. 343

【嗒然】tàrán 〈书 *fml.*〉形容懊丧的神情 dejected; despondent:～若丧 deeply despondent; mournful and dejected

【嗒丧】tàsàng 失意;丧气 in low spirits; dejected:～而归 return with a dejected look on one's face

遝 tà ☞杂遝 zátà on p. 2384

阘 tà ☞below

☞ dá on p. 345

【阘懦】tànuò 〈书 *fml.*〉地位低下，软弱无能 lowly and spineless

【阘茸】tàróng 〈书 *fml.*〉卑贱;低劣 mean; contemptible

榻 tà 狭长而较矮的床 couch; long and narrow bed:竹～ bamboo couch|藤～ rattan (or cane) couch

【榻车】tàchē ☞塌车 tāchē on p. 1848

漯 Tà 漯河，水名，在今山东 Tahe, name of a river in present-day Shandong Province

☞ luò on p. 1284

踏 tà ❶ 踩 tread; stamp:践～stamp on|～步 mark time|脚～实地 down-to-earth ◇～上工作岗位 begin one's career; take on a job ❷ 在现场(查勘)make onthe-spot investigation:～看 make an on-the-spot survey|～勘 survey; investigate

☞ tā on p. 1848

【踏板】tàbǎn ❶ 车、船等上面供人上下用的板 gangplank; footplate ❷ 旧式床前供上下床脚踏的板，有腿，像长而宽的矮凳。有的地区叫踏凳。long and wide footstool placed in front of an old-fashioned bed; known in some areas as 踏凳 tàdèng ❸ 运动场上供跳远起跳用的板 springboard for long jump ❹ 缝纫机、水车等下部用脚蹬的板状装置(of a sewing machine, waterwheel, etc.) treadle

【踏步】tàbù ❶ 身体站直，两脚交替抬起又着地而不迈步前进，是休操或军操的一种动作 mark time; (in gymnastics or military drill) move the feet alternately as in marching, but with-

T

out advancing：原地～marking time｜～不前 fail to make progress ❷〈方 *dial*.〉台阶 flight of steps；stairway

【踏春】tàchūn 春天到郊外散步游玩 go sightseeing when spring sets in

【踏访】tàfǎng 踏看；访查 make on-the-spot study and investigation

【踏歌】tàgē〈古代 *arch*.〉一种边歌边舞的艺术形式。舞时成群结队，连臂踏脚，配以轻微的手臂动作。现在苗、瑶等民族还有这种歌舞。rhythmic dancing；sing while stamping one's feet；a sing and dancing style that is still very much alive among the Miaos，Yaos and other minority groups

【踏勘】tàkān ❶ 铁路、公路、水库、采矿等工程进行设计之前在实地勘察地形或地质情况 make on-the-spot survey before designing a railway，highway，reservoir，mine，etc.：～油田 survey an oil field ❷ 在出事现场查看 investigate the site of an accident

【踏看】tàkàn 在现场查看 go to the spot to make an investigation：～地形 make a topographical study

【踏青】tàqīng 清明节前后到郊外散步游玩叫踏青（青：青草 green grass）go for an outing around the Qingming（Tomb-sweeping）Day

【踏足】tàzú 涉足 set foot：～影坛 set foot in the filmmaking industry｜～社会 become a member of society

艒（艪） tà〈书 *fml*.〉大船 big boat

蹋 tà ❶ 踏；踩 trample；tread ❷〈书 *fml*.〉踢 kick

tāi（ㄊㄞ）

台 Tāi 指台州（Tāizhōu），地名。天台（Tiāntāi），山名，又地名，都在浙江。Taizhou，name of a place in Zhejiang Province；Tiantai，name of a place，also name of a mountain，both in Zhejiang Province

☞ tái on p.1851

苔 tāi ☞舌苔 shétāi on p.1692

☞ tái on p.1852

胎[1] tāi ❶ 人或哺乳动物母体内的幼体 foetus；embryo：～儿 foetus｜胚～embryo｜怀～conceive ◇祸～cause of a disaster ❷ 怀孕或生育的次数 birth；farrow：头～first birth｜生过三～have given three births｜这头母猪一～下了十二个小猪。The pig delivered a litter of 12 piglets. ❸（～儿 tāir）衬在衣服、被褥等的面子和里子之间的东西 wadding；padding：棉花～cotton padding of a quilt｜这顶帽子是软～儿的。This hat is padded. ❹（～儿 tāir）某些器物的坯 blank；object ready to become a finished product：泥～儿 clay roughcast｜景泰蓝的～儿 blank of cloisonné

胎[2] tāi 轮胎 tyre：车～tyre

【胎动】tāidòng 胎儿在母体内蠕动。一般在怀孕四个月后开始。movement of the foetus which can be felt by the mother，which generally begins at the 4th month of a pregnancy

【胎毒】tāidú〈中医 *Chin. med*.〉指母体内的热毒，认为是初生婴儿所患疮疖等的病因。也指初生婴儿所患的疮疖等病。febrile toxin in the body of a mother，considered as a cause of infections of newborn infants such as boils，blisters，eczema，etc.；boils，eczema，etc. caused in an infant by febrile toxin transmitted by a mother

【胎儿】tāi'ér 母体内的幼体（通常指人的幼体，兽医学上也指家畜等的幼体）（human）foetus；（in veterinary medicine）foetus of（a domestic animal）

【胎发】tāifà 初生婴儿未剃过的头发 foetal hair；lanugo

【胎记】tāijì 人体上生来就有的深颜色的斑痕（of a human body）birthmark：他的背上有块紫色～。There is a purple birthmark on his back.

【胎教】tāijiào 指孕妇在怀孕期间，通过自身的调养和修养，给予胎儿以良好影响，如注意营养，保持心情舒畅，谨慎用药，避免辐射等 antenatal instruction；influencing the development of the foetus by a pregnant woman by such self-cultivating means as paying due attention to nutritious intake，remaining cheerful，being careful about medication，and avoiding radiation

【胎具】tāijù ❶ 制造土模、砂型或某些产品时所依据的模型 model for the making of earth or sand moulds or certain products ❷ 按产品规格、形状制造的模具 mould ‖ also 胎膜 tāimó

【胎里素】tāilǐsù 指生来就吃素的人 born vegetarian

【胎毛】tāimáo 胎发，也指初生的哺乳动物身上的毛 foetal hair；lanugo in a newborn baby or mammal

【胎盘】tāipán 介于母体的子宫内壁和胎儿之间的圆饼状组织，通过脐带和胎儿相连，是胎儿和母体的主要联系物 placenta；membranous vascular organ that develops in female mammals during pregnancy，lining the uterine wall and partially enveloping the fetus，to which it is attached by the umbilical cord

【胎生】tāishēng 人或某些动物的幼体在母体内发育到一定阶段以后才脱离母体，叫做胎生 viviparity；birth of an offspring that has develop to a certain stage inside the body of the mother

【胎位】tāiwèi 胎儿在子宫内的位置和姿势。胎位异常（如胎儿横卧或头部朝上）会引起难产。position of a foetus in the womb；The abnormal position of a foetus in the womb，such as lying decumbent or with the head facing upward, may cause dystocia.

【胎衣】tāiyī 胞衣 afterbirth

tái (ㄊㄞˊ)

台[1]（臺、❻檯、枱）tái ❶ 平而高的建筑物，便于在上面远望 deck; terrace: 瞭望～observational deck | 塔～control tower | 亭～楼阁 pavilions and towers ❷ 公共场所室内外高出地面便于讲话或表演的设备（用砖砌或用木料制成）platform; stage (built by brick or timber): 讲～podium | 舞～stage | 主席～rostrum ❸ 某些做座子用的器物 stand; support: 锅～kitchen range | 磨～grindstone | 灯～lamp stand | 蜡～candlestick ❹（～儿 táir）像台的东西 platform-like object: 井～platform of a well | 窗～儿 windowsill ❺〈量词 classifier〉: 一～戏 a theatrical performance | 一～机器 a machine ❻ 桌子或类似桌子的器物 table-like object: 写字～desk | 梳妆～dressing table | 乒乓球～table tennis table

台[2] tái〈敬辞 pol.〉〈旧时 old〉用于称呼对方或跟对方有关的动作 you; your: 兄～elder brother | ～鉴 for your perusal

台[3]（臺）Tái ❶ 指台湾省 Taiwan Province: ～胞 compatriot from Taiwan ❷ 姓 a surname

台[4]（颱）tái ☞台风 táifēng ☞ tāi on p.1850

【台本】táiběn 指经过导演加工的适用于舞台演出的剧本 playscript with stage directions

【台笔】táibǐ 放在桌子上的一种笔，笔帽的顶端与特制的底座固定在一起 table pen; pen with its cap fixed on a support to be placed on a table

【台布】táibù 桌布 tablecloth

【台步】táibù（～儿 táibùr）戏曲演员等在舞台上表演时行走的步法（in traditional opera）stage walk

【台秤】táichèng ❶ 秤的一种，用金属制成，底座上有承重的金属板 platform scale; metal scale with a weight-bearing metal pedestal; also 磅秤 bàngchèng ❷〈方 dial.〉案秤 counter scale

【台词】táicí 戏剧角色所说的话，包括对白、独白、旁白 uttering of a stage character, including dialogue, monolog and aside

【台灯】táidēng 放在桌子上用的有座子的电灯 desk lamp; table lamp; reading lamp

【台地】táidì 边缘为陡坡的广阔平坦的高地 tableland; flat, elevated land with steep edges; mesa

【台端】táiduān〈敬辞 pol.〉〈旧时 old〉称对方（多用于机关、团体等给个人的函件 oft. used in letters from a government department or organization to an individual）you: 谨聘～为本社戏剧指导。We respectfully invite you to be this association's theatrical advisor.

【台风】táifēng 发生在太平洋西部海洋和南海海上的热带气旋，是一种极强烈的风暴，中心附近最大风力达12级或12级以上，同时有暴雨 typhoon; tropical cyclone occurring in the western Pacific or the South China Sea, with the velocity reaching or exceeding 12 on the Beaufort scale near its centre, and accompanied by rainstorm

【台风儿】táifēngr 戏剧演员在舞台上表现出来的风度（of a performer）demeanour on stage: ～稳健 poised stage style | ～潇洒 show pizzazz on stage

【台甫】táifǔ〈敬辞 pol.〉〈旧时 old〉用于问人的表字［when asking sb.'s style name］Your honoured style name, please

【台驾】táijià〈敬辞 pol.〉〈旧时 old〉称对方 you; you esteemed self: 敬候～光临。I'll wait for your presence with full respect.

【台鉴】táijiàn 旧式书信套语，用在开头的称呼之后，表示请对方看信［used after the salutation on a letter in old times］attention of ...

【台阶】táijiē（～儿 táijiēr）❶ 用砖、石、混凝土等筑成的一级一级供人上下的建筑物，多在大门前或坡道上 staircase; stairway built of brick, masonry, or concrete at the front gate of a building or on a ramp ◇改进管理方法之后，该厂生产跃上新的～。Production in this factory scaled a new height after it revamped its management.（图见 ☞ figure for 房子 fáng·zi on p.550）❷〈比喻 fig.〉避免因僵持而受窘的途径或机会 chance to extricate sb. from embarrassment or predicament: 给他们找个～儿下。Give them an out.

【台历】táilì 摆在桌子上用的日历或月历 desk calendar

【台面】táimiàn〈方 dial.〉❶ 席面；桌面儿上 on the table; aboveboard: 你的话能拿到～上说吗？Can you say what you've said in public? ❷ 指赌博时桌面上的赌金总额 all the money on a gambling table: ～大 high-stakes gamble

【台盘】táipán〈方 dial.〉❶ 席面 dishes served at a banquet: 家常菜上不了～。Family fare can never make it to a banquet. ❷〈比喻 fig.〉交际应酬或公开的场合 social engagement: 扭扭捏捏的上不了～。Coyness get you nowhere in society.

【台钳】táiqián same as 老虎钳 lǎohǔqián ①

【台球】táiqiú ❶ 一种球类运动，在特制的台子上用硬木制成的杆儿击球 billiards; game played on a rectangular cloth-covered table with raised cushioned edges, in which a cue made of hardwood is used to hit balls ❷ 台球运动用的实心球，用塑料等坚韧物质制成，直径约七厘米 billiard ball; solid ball made of plastics or other hard materials for billiards ❸〈方 dial.〉乒乓球 ping-pong ball; table tennis

【台扇】táishàn 放在桌子上用的有座子的电扇

table electrical fan

【台钟】táizhōng〈方 *dial.*〉座钟 desk clock

【台柱】táizhù 戏班中的主要演员(台:戏台),借指集体中的骨干(in a performing troupe 台 tái means stage) leading star; (in an organisation) core member; mainstay; pillar; also 台柱子 táizhù·zi

【台子】tái·zi ❶ 打台球、乒乓球等时所用的特制的桌子 table; table made for special purposes such as billiards and table tennis ❷〈方 *dial.*〉桌子 table ❸ same as 台[1] tái:戏~stage|窗~windowsill

邰 Tái 姓 a surname

苔 tái 苔藓植物的一纲,属于这一纲的植物,根、茎、叶的区别不明显,绿色,生长在阴湿的地方 liverwort (*Hepaticae*), a variety of green plants growing in dampness with indistinct differences between root, stem and leaves

☞ tāi on p. 1850

【苔藓植物】táixiǎn zhíwù 隐花植物的一大类,主要分为苔和藓两个纲,种类很多,大多生长在潮湿的地方,有假根 bryophyte, a variety of cryptogam that falls into two categories, *Hepaticae* and *Musci*, coming in a big variety, oft. growing in damp places, and having rhizoid

抬(**擡**) tái ❶ 往上托;举 lift; raise:~手 raise a hand|~起头来 raise one's head ◇~价 raise the price of sth. ❷ 共同用手或肩膀搬东西(of two or more persons) carry:~担架 carry a stretcher|把桌子~过来。Move the table over here. ❸ 指抬杠 bicker; quarrel:他们两人一谈到这个问题,~起来就没完。The two of them would quarrel on and on whenever they dwelt on this topic. ❹〈量词 *classifier*〉用于两人抬的东西 a load to be carried by two persons:十~妆奁 ten loads of trousseaux

【抬爱】tái'ài 抬举爱护 favour and take good care of:多蒙~。Thanks a lot for your kindness.

【抬秤】táichèng 大型的杆秤,一次能称几百斤,用时从秤毫中穿上扁担或杠子,由两个人抬着 steelyard large enough for weighing several hundred kg. at a time, to be lifted by two persons with a shoulder pole put through the lifting cord

【抬杠】[1] tái//gàng 争辩(多指无谓的 oft. sth. not taken seriously) bicker; wrangle:~拌嘴 petty brickering; 有的地区也说抬杠子 also put as 抬杠子 táigàng·zi in some regions

【抬杠】[2] tái//gàng 指用杠抬运灵柩 carry a coffin on stout poles

【抬盒】táihé〈旧时 *old*〉赠送礼品用的大木盒,多为两层或三层,由两人抬着 two or three large wooden boxes stacked one on top of the other for containing gifts and carried by two persons with a shoulder pole

【抬肩】tái·jian 上衣从肩头到腋下的尺寸。有的地区叫抬裉。half the circumference of the sleeve where it joins the shoulder; also 抬裉 táikèn in some regions

【抬轿子】tái jiào·zi〈比喻 *fig.*〉为有权势的人捧场 curry favour with the rich and powerful; sing the praises of

【抬举】tái·ju 看重某人而加以称赞或提拔 praise or promote sb. to show favour; favour sb.:不识~ not know how to appreciate favour

【抬裉】táikèn〈方 *dial.*〉same as 抬肩 tái·jian

【抬升】táishēng 地形、气流等升高(of terrain, air current, etc.) rise:青藏高原在持续~。Qinghai-Tibet Plateau is rising all the time.|气流受山脉阻拦被迫~。The air current rises due to mountain obstruction.

【抬头】tái//tóu 把头抬起来 raise one's head;〈比喻 *fig.*〉受压制的人或事物得到伸展(of sb. or sth. under oppression) see the light of day; prevail

【抬头】táitóu ❶〈旧时 *old*〉书信、公文等行文中遇到对方的名称或涉及对方时,为表示尊敬而另起一行 begin a new line, as a token of respect, when mentioning the addressee in a letter, official correspondence, etc. ❷〈旧时 *old*〉书信、公文等行文中抬头的地方。现在一般只有在单据上写收件人或收款人的地方还叫抬头。(in a letter or official document) space for the name of the addressee; (nowadays) (on a receipt, bill, etc.) name of the buyer or payee, or space for filling in such a name

【抬头纹】táitóuwén 额上的皱纹 wrinkles on the forehead

骀 tái〈书 *fml.*〉劣马 inferior horse; broken-down nag:驽~(劣马,比喻庸才) inferior horse; (fig.) mediocre person

☞ dài on p. 370

炱 tái 由烟凝积成的黑灰 soot:煤~coal soot|松~(松烟)pine soot

鲐 tái 鲐鱼,身体纺锤形,头顶浅黑色,背部青蓝色,腹部淡黄色,两侧上部有深蓝色斑纹。生活在海里,是洄游性鱼类。chub mackerel (*Pneumatophorus japonicus*); migratory marine fish having a spindle-shaped body, gray head, bluish back, pale yellow belly, and deep blue stripes up the two flanks

臺 tái ❶ same as 台[1] tái ❷(Tái)姓 a surname

儓 tái〈古代 *arch.*〉官署中的仆役 runner in a government office

薹[1] tái 多年生草本植物,叶扁平,长约3尺,茎长3—4尺,花穗浅绿褐色,生长在水田里,叶可制蓑衣 sedge (*Cyperaceae*); perennial water plant having flat leaves about one metre long that are used as a material for the making of raincoats, a stem 1 to 1.33 metres in length, and greenish brown flowers

薹[2] tái 蒜、韭菜、油菜等生长到一定阶段时在中央部分长出的细长的茎，顶上开花结实。嫩的可以当蔬菜吃。bolt of garlic, leek, rape, etc. that is edible as vegetable when tender

tǎi (ㄊㄞˇ)

呔(奤、嚑) tǎi 〈方 *dial.*〉说话带外地口音 speak a language corrupted by an accent

☞ dāi on p.368 and 奤 hǎ on p.753

tài (ㄊㄞˋ)

太 tài ❶ 高；大 highest; greatest：～空 outer space｜～学 Imperial College｜～湖 Taihu Lake ❷ 极；最 most：～古 remote antiquity ❸ 身份最高或辈分更高的 senior; great：～老伯 great-granduncle｜～老师（老师的父亲或父亲的老师）father of one's teacher; teacher of one's father｜～夫人（尊称别人的母亲）(honor.) sb. else's mother ❹〈副词 *adv.*〉a)表示程度过分 excessively; too; over：水～热，烫手。The water is too hot — it scalds the hand.｜人～多了，会客室里坐不开。There are too many people to be seated in the reception room. b)表示程度极高 superb; super; very (用于赞叹 used positively)：这办法～好了。This method is superb.｜这建筑～伟大了。The building is most imposing. c)很(用于否定 in the negative) very：不～好 not very good｜不～够 barely enough ❺ (Tài)姓 a surname

【太白星】tàibáixīng 我国古代指金星 Grand White Star, an ancient Chinese reference to Venus or Vesper

【太半】tàibàn 〈书 *fml.*〉大半；过半 better half：敌军死伤～。The better part of the enemy have been killed or wounded.

【太仓一粟】tàicāng yī sù 〈比喻 *fig.*〉非常渺小 grain of millet in a huge granary; drop in the ocean (太仓 *taicang*：古代京城里的大粮仓 large granary in the capital city in ancient times)

【太阿倒持】Tài'ē dào chí 倒拿着太阿(宝剑名) hold the sword by the blade (*tai'e*, name of a famous sword)；〈比喻 *fig.*〉把权柄给人家，自己反而受到威胁或祸害 surrender one's power to another at one's own peril; also 倒持太阿 dào chí Tài'ē

【太公】tàigōng 〈方 *dial.*〉曾祖 great-grandfather

【太古】tàigǔ 最古的时代(指人类还没有开化的时代) remote antiquity; age in which humanity was yet to become civilized

【太后】tàihòu 帝王的母亲 empress dowager; queen mother

【太湖石】tàihúshí 江苏太湖产的石头，多窟窿和皱纹，可用来造假山，点缀庭院 Taihu rocks; boulders found on the edge of the Tai Lake in Jiangsu Province, highly prized by builders of rock gardens for their convolutions caused by weathering

【太极】tàijí 我国古代哲学上指宇宙的本原，为原始的混沌之气 the Supreme Ultimate; the Absolute in ancient Chinese cosmology, presented as the primary source of all created things

【太极拳】tàijíquán 一种传统拳术，流派很多，流传很广，动作柔和缓慢，既可用于技击，又有增强体质和防治疾病的作用 *taijiquan*; shadow boxing; school of popular traditional martial art marked for slow and graceful movements that are designed to attack or counterattack, keep fit, prevent and treat diseases

【太极图】tàijítú 我国古代说明宇宙现象的图，一种是用圆形的图像表示阴阳对立面的统一体，圆形外边附八卦方位，道教常用它做标志。另一种是宋周敦颐所画的，代表宋代理学对于世界形成问题的一种看法。他认为太极是天地万物的根源，太极分为阴阳二气，由阴阳二气产生木、火、土、金、水这五行，五行之精凝合而生人类，阴阳化合而生万物。Diagram of the Supreme Ultimate; ancient Chinese diagram on the universe, coming in two kinds. One, represented with a circular pattern surrounded by the Eight Diagrams, indicates the unity of *yin* and *yang*, and serves as the logo of Taoism. The other, drawn by Zhou Dunyi of the Song Dynasty, embodies the opinion of the Confucian school of idealist philosophy of his times that the Supreme Ultimate is the origin of the multitude of things in the universe, and consists of *yin* and *yang* that give rise to metal, wood, water, fire and earth — the Five Elements that condensed to give rise to humankind and combined to produce the multitude of things.

【太监】tàijiàn 宦官 eunuch

【太空】tàikōng 极高的天空 firmament; outer space：～飞行 space flight｜宇宙火箭射入～ launch a rocket into the space

【太庙】tàimiào 帝王祭祀祖先的庙 Imperial Ancestral Temple

【太平】tàipíng 指社会平安；安宁 (of society) peace and stability：天下～ universal peace and tranquility｜～景象 scene of a society in order｜太太平平地过日子 live in peace and contentment

【太平斧】tàipíngfǔ 消防用的长把大斧；船遇大风时用来砍断桅杆、缆绳的斧子 hydrant hatchet, a tool for firefighters; hatchet for dismasting a ship to cope with the strong

T

wind

【太平鼓】tàipínggǔ ❶ 打击乐器，舞蹈时用，在一个带柄的铁圈上蒙上羊皮，用细长的鼓槌敲打，柄的头上有十多个大小铁环，打鼓时同时发出声响 Taiping drum; a kind of drum fashioned out of an iron ring mounted with goat skin, and having a dozen or so iron rings of different sizes that jingle when the drum is beaten with a slender drumstick ❷ 民间舞蹈，多为女子表演，一边敲鼓，一边舞蹈 Taiping Drum Dance; folk dance featuring drum-beating female performers

【太平间】tàipíngjiān 医院中停放尸体的房间 mortuary

【太平龙头】tàipíng lóngtóu 消防用的自来水龙头 fire hydrant; fire plug

【太平门】tàipíngmén 戏院、电影院等公共场所为便于疏散群众而设置的旁门(of a theatre, cinema, or other public building) exit

【太平梯】tàipíngtī 仓库、公共场所、集体宿舍等楼房为万一发生火灾时便于疏散、救护而在墙外设置的楼梯 fire escape; metal stairway down an outside wall for escaping from a burning warehouse, public building, dormitory, etc.

【太平天国】Tàipíng Tiānguó 洪秀全、杨秀清等于 1851 年在广西桂平县金田村起义，建立'太平天国'，1853 年在天京(今南京)定都，建立国家政权，势力发展到十七个省。太平天国革命是我国历史上规模最大的一次农民起义。1864 年在清朝政府和帝国主义的联合镇压下失败。Taiping Heavenly Kingdom (1851-1864). In 1851, Hong Xiuquan and Yang Xiuqing proclaimed the establishment of the Taiping Heavenly Kingdom when they rose in a peasant uprising at Jintian Village in Guangxi's Guiping County, established their capital in Tianjing (present-day Nanjing) in 1853, and extended their sphere of influence to 17 provinces. This largest peasant uprising in the Chinese history was toppled in 1864 under the joint suppression of the Qing Government and imperialist powers.

【太婆】tàipó 〈方 *dial.*〉曾祖母 great-grandmother

【太上皇】tàishànghuáng ❶ 皇帝的父亲的称号，特称把皇位让给儿子而自己退位的皇帝 super sovereign; title assumed by an emperor's father who abdicated in favour of his son ❷ 〈比喻 *fig.*〉在幕后操纵，掌握实权的人 back-stage ruler

【太甚】tàishèn 太过分；太狠 too far; to the extreme: 欺人～go too far in insulting people

【太师椅】tàishīyǐ 一种旧式的比较宽大的椅子，有靠背，带扶手 old-fashioned wooden armchair

【太岁】tàisuì ❶ 〈古代 *arch.*〉天文学中假设的星名，与岁星(木星)相应，又称岁阴或太阴。古代用它围绕太阳公转的周期纪年，十二年是一周。Master of the Year; name of a hypothetic star in classic astronomy that corresponds to the planet Jupiter, used in ancient times to mark time by the number of cycles it makes around the sun, with 12 years as a cycle; also 岁阴 suìyīn or 太阴 tàiyīn ❷ 传说中神名。旧时迷信，认为太岁之神在地，与天上岁星(木星)相应而行，掘土(兴建工程)要躲避太岁的方位，否则就要遭受祸害。Master of the Year of Earth, the mythological god living underground in correspondence with the Master of the Year of Heaven (Jupiter). It is said that in spadework one has to stay away from the position of the Master of the Year of Earth, or else he is courting disaster. ❸ 〈旧社会 *pre*-1949〉对土豪的憎称 local tyrant: 镇山～Lord of the Mountain — nickname of a mountain bandit

【太岁头上动土】tàisuì tóu·shang dòng tǔ 〈比喻 *fig.*〉触犯有权势或强有力的人 break ground where Taisui (a god) presides — provoke sb. far superior in power or strength; ☞ 太岁 tàisuì ②

【太太】tài·tai ❶ 〈旧时 *old*〉通称官吏的妻子 Madame; term of address for the wife of an official ❷ 〈旧时 *old*〉仆人等称女主人 (servants' term of addressing the mistress of a household) madam; lady ❸ 对已婚妇女的尊称(带丈夫的姓)[honourific term of address for a married woman, usu. preceded by the husband's surname] Mrs.: 张～Mrs. Zhang | 王～Mrs. Wang ❹ 称某人的妻子或丈夫对人称自己的妻子(多带人称代词做定语)[oft. used with a personal pronoun] wife; Mrs.: 我～跟他～原来是同学。My wife was a classmate of his wife. ❺ 〈方 *dial.*〉称曾祖母或曾祖父 great-grandparent

【太息】tàixī 〈书 *fml.*〉叹气 heave a deep sigh

【太学】tàixué 我国古代设立在京城的最高学府 Imperial College; the highest institution of learning in ancient China, situated in the capital city

【太阳】tàiyáng ❶ 银河系的恒星之一，是一炽热的气体球，体积是地球的 130 万倍，质量是地球的 33.34 万倍，表面温度约 6,000℃，内部温度约 1,500 万℃，内部经常不断地进行原子核反应而产生大量的热能。太阳是太阳系的中心天体，距地球约 1.5 亿公里。地球和其他行星都围绕着它旋转并且从它得到光和热。sun; fixed star in the Milky Way galaxy in the form of a fiery gaseous ball 1.3 million times more than Earth in bulk, with a mass 333,400 times that of Earth, a surface temperature of approximately 6,000℃ and an interior temperature of about 15 million℃, releasing mammoth amounts of heat through constant nuclear reaction within it. The earth, approximately 150 million km. from the sun, evolves along with other planets around the sun, the center of the solar system, and receives light and heat from it. (图见 ☞ figure for 太阳系 tàiyángxì) ❷ 指太阳光 sunshine; sunlight: 今天～很好。It's a fine day today. ❸ 指太阳穴(of the human head) temples

【太阳灯】tàiyángdēng 产生紫外线的装置。在真空的石英管中封入一些水银和两个电极,通电时两极在水银蒸气中放电,产生大量紫外线。用于医疗和保健。sunlamp; sunlight lamp; device for generating ultraviolet rays, consisting of mercury and two electrodes sealed off in a vacuum quartz tube, so that when it is switched on, the electrodes releases large amounts of electricity in the vapour of mercury for medical and health-protection purposes

【太阳地儿】tàiyángdìr 太阳光照着的地方 place where there is sunshine; sunny spot

【太阳电池】tàiyáng diànchí 用半导体硅、硒等材料将太阳的光能变成电能的转换器件。具有可靠性高,寿命长,转换效率高等优点,可做人造卫星、航标灯、晶体管收音机等的电源。solar cell; battery consisting of semi-conducting silicon, selenium and other materials which can turn solar energy into electricity, and is used as a reliable, durable and efficient source of power for man-made satellites, beacons and transistor radios

【太阳风】tàiyángfēng 从太阳表面射出的高速带电粒子流 solar wind; high-speed current of electrified particles emitting from the surface of the sun

【太阳黑子】tàiyáng hēizǐ 太阳表面的气体旋涡,温度较周围区域低,从地球上看像是太阳表面上的黑斑,叫做太阳黑子。太阳黑子有很强的磁场,会影响地球上短波无线电通讯。sunspot; gaseous vortices on the surface of the sun that are relatively cooler than their surroundings and look like dark spots from Earth's perspective. The sunspots are associated with strong magnetic fields that may affect short-wave radio telecommunications on earth. also 日斑 rìbān or 黑子 hēizǐ

【太阳活动】tàiyáng huódòng 太阳表面黑子、光斑、耀斑、日珥、射电现象等的变化,平均约以11年为周期。活动强烈时,紫外线和粒子辐射增强,使地球上发生极光、磁暴、电离层扰动等现象。solar activity; changes in the sunspots, faculae, flares, solar prominence, radio, with 11 years as a cycle. In violent solar activity, the ultraviolet and particle radiation increases to induce polar lights, magnetic storms, disturbance of the ionosphere, and other phenomena on earth.

【太阳镜】tàiyángjìng 能防止太阳的紫外线伤害眼睛的眼镜,镜片多用茶色或变色玻璃等做成 sunglasses; glasses with brown lenses or glasses whose colour changes to protect the eyes from the sun's ultraviolet radiation

【太阳历】tàiyánglì 阳历 solar calendar

【太阳炉】tàiyánglú 把太阳能直接变为热能的炊事装置。常见的是由很多块平面反射材料构成一个抛物面,使阳光聚焦在锅底而产生大量热能。solar furnace; parabolic reflector consisting of a number of plane reflecting plates that focus solar radiation at the bottom of a cooking utensil to obtain large amounts of heat energy; also 太阳灶 tàiyángzào

【太阳能】tàiyángnéng 太阳所发出的辐射能,是太阳上的氢原子核发生聚变反应产生的。太阳能是地球上光和热的源泉。solar energy; energy generated from hydrogen fusion in the sun that is the source of light and heat for earth

【太阳年】tàiyángnián same as 回归年 huíguīnián

【太阳窝】tàiyángwō 〈方 *dial.*〉太阳穴(of human head) temples

【太阳系】tàiyángxì 银河系中的一个天体系统,以太阳为中心,包括太阳、九大行星及其卫星和无数的小行星、彗星、流星等 solar system; celestial system in the Milky Way galaxy, including the sun (which is in the center), the nine planets, and all other minor planets, comets and meteors

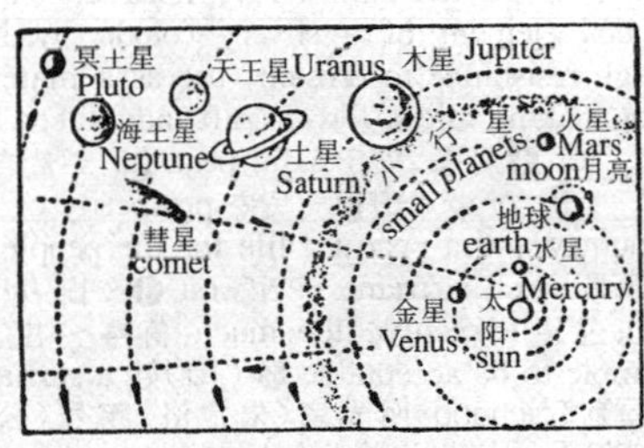

太阳系 Solar System

【太阳穴】tàiyángxué 人的鬓角前、眉梢后的部位 temple; flat region situated before the sideburn and behind the tip of the brow on either side of the forehead

【太爷】tàiyé ❶ 祖父 paternal grandfather ❷〈方 *dial.*〉曾祖父 paternal great-grandfather

【太医】tàiyī ❶ 皇家的医生 imperial physician ❷〈方 *dial.*〉医生 doctor

【太阴】tàiyīn〈方 *dial.*〉月亮 moon; lunar

【太阴历】tàiyīnlì 阴历 lunar calendar

【太子】tàizǐ 帝王的儿子中已经确定继承帝位或王位的 crown prince; male heir apparent to a throne.

汰 tài 淘汰 discard, eliminate: 裁～lay off | 优胜劣～survival of the fittest

态(態) tài ❶ 形状;状态 form; condition:形～shape; morphology|姿～posture; carriage; attitude|常～normal behaviour; normal condition|事～state of affairs; situation ❷ 一种语法范畴,多表明句子中动词所表示的动作跟主语所表示的事物之间的关系,如主动、被动等(gram.) voice; property of verbs or a set of verb inflections indicating the relation between the subject and the action expressed by the verb, such as active voice and passive voice

【态度】tài·du ❶ 人的举止神情 manner; conduct:～大方 have an easy manner|要～(发怒或急躁) lose one's temper ❷ 对于事情的看法和采取的行动 attitude:工作～attitude towards work|端正～rectify one's attitude|～坚决 resolute attitude

【态势】tàishì 状态和形势 state; stance; posture:分析敌我～analyze the stance of the enemy and our own situation

肽 tài 有机化合物,由一个氨基酸分子中的氨基与另一个氨基酸分子中的羧基缩合失去水分子形成 peptide; organic compound that is an integration of the amino group of one amino acid molecule with the carboxyl group minus the water molecule of another; also 胜(shēng)

钛 tài 金属元素,符号 Ti (titanium)。银白色,质硬而轻,耐腐蚀性强。钛合金用来制造飞机等。titanium (Ti); hard and light metal element of a silvery colour, with a high resistance to erosion, use as a material for making alloys for aircraft manufacturing

泰 tài ❶ 平安;安宁 safe; peaceful:～然自若 self-composed|国～民安 prosperity of the country and a peaceful life for the people ❷ 极;最 most; extreme:～西 west ❸〈书 *fml.*〉太;过甚 excessive; too much:简略～甚 too simple to be acceptable ❹ (Tài)姓 a surname

【泰昌】Tàichāng 明光宗(朱常洛)年号(公元1620)Taichang, title of the one-year reign of Emperor Guangzong (Zhu Changluo) of the Ming Dynasty in 1620

【泰斗】tàidǒu 泰山北斗 Mount Taishan and the North Star — man of eminence:京剧～Peking Opera guru|他算得上音乐界的～。He can be counted as a guru of the musical circles.

【泰然】tàirán 形容心情安定 composed; calm:处之～bear with equanimity|～自若 behave with perfect composure

【泰然自若】tàirán zìruò 形容镇定,毫不在意的样子 behave with perfect composure; be self-possessed:他临危不惧,神情～。In the throes of danger he was fearless and perfectly calm.

【泰山】tàishān ❶ 古人以泰山(山名,在山东)为高山的代表,常用来比喻敬仰的人和重大的、有价值的事物 Mount Taishan, regarded as the king of mountains in ancient times, now oft. a symbol of man of distinction or things of unmatched value:～北斗 guru|重于～(of one's death) weightier than Mount Taishan|有眼不识～fail to recognize someone's eminence ❷ 岳父的别称 another name for wife's father; father-in-law

【泰山北斗】tàishān běidǒu〈比喻 *fig.*〉德高望重或有卓越成就而为众人所敬仰的人 Mount Taishan and the Northern Star — person of distinction

【泰山压顶】tàishān yā dǐng〈比喻 *fig.*〉压力极大 bear down on one with the weight of Mount Taishan:～不弯腰 hold one's head high despite heavy pressure|以～之势击敌于措手不及 make a surprise attack on the enemy with the force of Mount Taishan

【泰水】tàishuǐ 岳母的别称 another name for wife's mother; mother-in-law

【泰西】Tàixī〈旧时 *old*〉指西洋(主要指欧洲) the West, mainly Europe:～各国 European countries

酞 tài 有机化合物的一类,是一个分子的邻苯二酸酐与两个分子的酚缩合的衍生物,如酚酞 phthalein; any of a group of chemical compounds formed by a reaction of monomolecular ephthalic anhydride with a bimolecular phenol, such as phenolphthalein

tān(ㄊㄢ)

坍(坤) tān 倒塌 crumble; collapse:土墙～了。The adobe wall caved in.|房～了。The house collapsed.

【坍方】tān//fāng same as 塌方 tāfāng

【坍圮】tānpǐ〈书 *fml.*〉倒塌;坍塌 crumble; cave in; collapse

【坍缩】tānsuō 天体体积缩小,密度加大(of a celestial body) shrink

【坍缩星】tānsuōxīng ☞黑洞 hēidòng on p. 793

【坍塌】tāntā (山坡、河岸、建筑物或堆积的东西)倒下来 cave in; collapse:院墙～。The wall of the courtyard collapsed.

【坍台】tān//tái〈方 *dial.*〉❶ 垮台(多指事业、局面不能继续维持 oft. of an undertaking or situation) fall; crumple ❷ 丢脸;出丑 be disgraced; eat humble pie

【坍陷】tānxiàn 塌陷 cave in; sink:地层～。The earth's stratum caved in.

贪 tān ❶ 原指爱财,后来多指贪污 defalcate; graft:～赃枉法 graft and pervert the law|～官污吏 corrupt officials|倡廉肃～advocate clean government and crack down on corruption ❷ 对某种事物欲望老不满足;求多 be greedy for; have an insatiable desire for:～玩 fond of enjoying oneself|～得无厌 be gluttonously ravenous ❸ 片面追求；贪图 covet；hanker after：～便宜 covet petty benefits

【贪杯】tānbēi 过分喜好喝酒 be excessively fond of drinking：好(hào)酒～love a drop too much|～误事 knock over a drink and cause delay in work

【贪财】tān//cái 贪图钱财 be greedy for money；be a money-grubber

【贪得无厌】tān dé wú yàn 指贪心大，老不满足 flay a flint

【贪官】tānguān 贪污受贿的官吏 corrupt officials：～污吏 corrupt officials；venal officials

【贪贿】tānhuì 贪污受贿 corruption and bribery：～无艺(艺：限度)the desire of a corrupt official for bribes knows no bound；be inordinately rapacious

【贪婪】tānlán ❶ 贪得无厌(含贬义 derog.) be avid for；greed；avarice ❷ 不知满足 be greedy for

【贪恋】tānliàn 十分留恋 cling to；hate to leave：～大都市生活 hate to give up the comfort of big-city life

【贪墨】tānmò〈书 *fml.*〉贪污 embezzle；practise graft；be corrupt

【贪青】tānqīng 农作物到了变黄成熟的时期，茎叶仍繁茂呈青绿色。多由氮肥或水分过多等引起。(of crops) remain green when it is time to yellow and ripe, an abnormality oft. caused by excessive nitrogenous fertilizer or water intake

【贪求】tānqiú 极力希望得到 seek；hanker after；covet：～无度 have an insatiable desire for|～富贵 lust for riches and honour

【贪色】tānsè 贪恋女色；好色 be fond of women；be a womanizer

【贪生】tānshēng 吝惜生命(多含贬义 oft. derog.) grudge one's life：～怕死 grudge one's life and dread death；be mortally afraid of death

【贪天之功】tān tiān zhī gōng 原指窃据上天的功绩，后泛指把不属于自己的功劳归于自己 arrogate to oneself the merits of others；claim credit for other people's achievements

【贪图】tāntú 极力希望得到(某种好处)lust for (certain benefit)：～便宜 hanker after petty gains|～凉快 want to cool off (but end up catching a cold)|～安逸 seek a life of leisure

【贪污】tānwū 利用职务上的便利非法地取得财物 embezzle；practise graft：～腐化 embezzlement and corruption|～分子 embezzler

【贪小】tānxiǎo 爱占小便宜 fond of petty gains

【贪心】tānxīn ❶ 贪得的欲望 cupidity；be a swine：～不足 insatiably greedy ❷ 贪得无厌；不知足 voracious：这人太～。No amount of wealth can satisfy this man's greed.

【贪赃】tān//zāng 指官吏接受贿赂 take bribes；practise graft：～枉法 practise graft and bend the law|～舞弊 corruption and fraudulent practices

【贪嘴】tānzuǐ 贪吃 be greedy for food；gluttonous

怹 tān〈方 *dial.*〉他(含尊敬意 term of respect) he

啴(嘽) tān［啴啴］tāntān〈书 *fml.*〉形容牲畜喘息(of draught animal) pant

☞ chǎn on p.213

猞 tān 传说中的一种兽 mythological animal

摊(攤) tān ❶ 摆开；铺平 lay out；spread out：～牌 showdown|～场 ted grain|把凉席～在床上 spread a mat on the bed ◇许多事情一～到桌面上来，是非立时分明。Who's right and who's wrong become clear once all the issues are put on the table. ❷ (～儿 tānr)设在路旁、广场上的售货处 booth；stall；vendor's stand by a road or on a square：地～儿 roadside stall|水果～儿 fruit stand ❸〈量词 *classifier*〉用于摊开的糊状物 referring to mash-like things spread out：一～血 a pool of blood|一～稀泥 a mud puddle ❹ 烹饪方法，把糊状食物倒在锅中摊开成为薄片 fry batter in a thin layer：～鸡蛋 make an omelet|～煎饼 make a pancake ❺ 分担 share；apportion：分～distribute|～派 apportion|一人仅～五元钱。It averaged only 5 yuan per person. ❻ 碰到；落到(多指不如意的事情 usu. of sth. unpleasant) befall；happen to：事情虽小，～在他身上就受不了。Though it was a minor matter, it would be too much if it happened to him.

【摊场】tān//cháng 把收割的庄稼摊开晾在场上 ted grain；spread harvested grain on a threshing ground

【摊点】tāndiǎn 一个一个的售货摊或售货点 stand；booth：街市两边设有大小～五十余处。There are some 50 stands on both sides of the street market.

【摊贩】tānfàn 摆摊子做小买卖的人 street pedlar

【摊牌】tān//pái ❶ 把手里所有的牌摆出来，跟对方比较大小，以决胜负 lay down one's cards face up；show one's cards ❷〈比喻 *fig.*〉到最后关头把所有的意见、条件、实力等摆出来给对方看 showdown；force an issue to a conclusion by presenting one's opinion or condition or showing one's strength

【摊派】tānpài 叫众人或各地区、各单位分担(捐款、任务等) apportion (donation, work, etc.)：费用按人头～。The expenses are to be apportioned on a per-capita basis.

【摊手】tān//shǒu 放开手；松手 let go：～不管 let go of sth. and see it go its natural course

【摊售】tānshòu 摆摊子出售(货物)set up a stall to sell goods：～食品要讲卫生。Vendors selling food in the streets should pay attention to hygiene.

【摊位】tānwèi 设售货摊的地方；一个货摊所占的位置 vendor's stand；booth：分配～distribute booths (at an exhibition, market, etc.)｜固定～fixed vendors' stands｜这个农贸市场有一百多个～。There are over 100 vendors' stands and booths in this rural market.

【摊子】tān·zi same as 摊 tān ②：旧货～junk vendor's stand ◇烂～(比喻难于整顿的局面) mess shambles；(fig.) situation that has gone out of control

滩(灘) tān ❶ 河、海、湖边水深时淹没、水浅时露出的地方，泛指河、海、湖边比岸低的地方 water's edge；littoral；beach：河～flood land｜海～beach；seaboard｜～地 beach land｜盐～(晒盐的海滩)saltmarsh ❷ 江河中水浅多石而水流很急的地方 shoal；rapid：险～perilous shoals and rapids

【滩地】tāndì 河滩、湖滩、海滩上较平坦的地方 beach land；flood land

【滩簧】tānhuáng 流行于江苏南部、浙江北部的一种说唱艺术。最初只是说唱故事，后来发展为表演小戏，如苏滩(苏州滩簧)、湖滩(湖州滩簧)。有的已经发展成为地方戏，如上海滩簧发展为沪剧。*tanhuang*；form of ballad singing in south Jiangsu and north Zhejiang that told stories in its early days and later developed into mini-plays (such as the *tanhuang* play of Suzhou and that of Huzhou) or local operas. The *huju* opera of Shanghai, for instance, had its origin in *tanghuang*.

【滩头】tāntóu 河、湖、海岸边的沙滩 sand bank；sandy beach：～阵地 beach position

【滩涂】tāntú 海涂 low-lying beach land

瘫(癱) tān 瘫痪 paralysed：偏～hemiplegia｜～在床上，不能下地。Bedridden with paralysis, (he) cannot be up and about once again.

【瘫痪】tānhuàn ❶ 由于神经机能发生障碍，身体的一部分完全或不完全地丧失运动的能力。可分为面瘫、单瘫、偏瘫、截瘫、四肢瘫等。paralysis；palsy；loss or impairment of the ability to move a body or a body part, usu. as a result of nerve damage, including facial palsy, monoplegia, hemiplegia, paraplegia, and the paralysis of the four limbs ❷〈比喻 *fig.*〉机构涣散，不能正常进行工作 paralysed；at a standstill；break down；(of an organization) total stoppage or severe impairment of activity

【瘫软】tānruǎn (肢体)绵软，难以动弹(of human body) become weak and limp：浑身～，一点力气也没有。It seemed all my strength had deserted me, and I feel weak all over my body.

【瘫子】tān·zi 瘫痪的人 paralytic；person suffering from paralysis

tán (ㄊㄢˊ)

坛[1](壇) tán ❶〈古代 *arch.*〉举行祭祀、誓师等大典用的台，多用土石等建成 altar；elevated place or structure, usu. built of earth or masonry, on which religious or opening ceremonies may be enacted：天～Temple of Heaven｜登～拜将 mount the altar and hold the ceremony to appoint a general ❷ 用土堆成的台，多在上面种花 terrace；flowerbed：花～flowerbed ❸ 某些会道门设立的拜神集会的组织 organization set up by a secret society to worship gods in a rally ❹ 指文艺界或体育界 literary circles；sports circles：文～literary circles｜诗～poetry circles｜影～movie world｜球～ballgame circles

坛[2](壜、罎、墰、鐔) tán (～儿 tánr) 坛子 earth jar；jug：酒～wine jar｜一～醋 a jar of vinegar

【坛坛罐罐】tántánguànguàn 泛指各种家什 pots and pans；personal possessions

【坛子】tán·zi 口小腹大的陶器，多用来盛酒、醋、酱油等 earthen jar；jug；rounded vessel of earthenware with a small mouth

昙(曇) tán 云彩密布；多云 cloudy；overcast

【昙花】tánhuā 常绿灌木，主枝圆筒形，分枝扁平呈叶状，绿色，没有叶片，花大，白色，生在分枝边缘上，多在夜间开放，开花的时间极短。供观赏。原产墨西哥。broad-leaved epiphyllum (*Epiphyllum oxypetalum*) ornamental evergreen bush native to Mexico, having a cylindrical stem, flat green leafless and lobated branches, large white flowers growing on edge of the branches and blooming briefly mostly at night

【昙花一现】tánhuā yī xiàn 昙花开放后很快就凋谢 as short-lived as the broad-leaved epiphyllum；〈比喻 *fig.*〉稀有的事物或显赫一时的人物出现不久就消逝(昙花：佛经中指优昙钵华)sth. extremely rare；transient figure；person of ephemeral importance；flower briefly as the broad-leaved epiphyllum (in Buddhism, the term *tanhua* refering to camphor flower)

倓 tán〈书 *fml.*〉安静。多用于人名。tranquil；calm；usu. for use in names

郯 tán 郯城(Tánchéng)，地名，在山东 Tancheng, name of a place in Shandong Province

谈 tán ❶ 说话或讨论 talk；discuss：漫～random talk；chitchat｜面～speak to sb. face to face｜～思想 speak one's mind ❷ 所说的话 remark；uttering：奇～strange tale｜传为美～become talk of the town｜无稽之～cook-and-bull story；unfounded statement ❸ (Tán)

姓 a surname

【谈柄】tánbǐng ❶ 被人拿来做谈笑资料的言行 laughing stock; butt of jokes ❷ 古人谈论时所执的拂尘 horsetail whisk, which some ancient men of letters held in hand when talking with one another

【谈锋】tánfēng 谈话的劲头儿 eloquence; volubility: ～甚健 be talkative; have the gift of the gab

【谈何容易】tán hé róngyì 说起来怎么这样容易,表示事情做起来并不像说的那么简单 easier said than done; by no means easy

【谈虎色变】tán hǔ sè biàn 〈比喻 *fig.*〉一提到可怕的事物连脸色都变了 turn pale at the mention of the tiger — be terrified at the mere mention of sth. horrible

【谈话】tán//huà 两个人或许多人在一起说话 chat; discuss: 他们正在屋里～。They're having a discussion in the room.

【谈话】tánhuà 用谈话的形式发表的意见(多为政治性的 oft. political in nature) statement issued in the form of an interview

【谈论】tánlùn 用谈话的方式表示对人或事物的看法 talk about: ～古今 discuss about the remote past and the present

【谈判】tánpàn 有关方面对有待解决的重大问题进行会谈 negotiate: 和平～peaceful negotiation|～破裂。The negotiation broke down.

【谈天】tántiān (～儿 tántiānr) 闲谈 chat; chitchat; shoot the bull

【谈天说地】tán tiān shuō dì 指漫无边际地闲谈 talk about everything under the sun; random talk: 人们聚在一起,～,好不热闹。People gathered together and chatted with great gusto.

【谈吐】tántǔ 指谈话时的措词和态度 attitude and choice of word during a talk: ～不俗 talk in good taste

【谈笑风生】tán xiào fēng shēng 形容谈话谈得高兴而有风趣 talk and laugh cheerfully

【谈笑自若】tán xiào zìruò 说说笑笑,跟平常一样(多指在紧张或危急的情况下 oft. under tension or in danger) go on talking and laughing as if nothing had happened; also 谈笑自如 tán xiào zìrú

【谈心】tán//xīn 谈心里话 have a heart-to-heart talk: 促膝～have a heart-to-heart talk

【谈兴】tánxìng 谈话的兴致 mode for conversation: ～正浓 be rapturously engaged in conversation; talk with great zest

【谈言微中】tán yán wēi zhòng 说话委婉而中肯 speak tactfully but to the point; make one's point through hints

【谈助】tánzhù 〈书 *fml.*〉谈资 topic of conversation: 足资～ serve as a good topic of conversation

【谈资】tánzī 谈话的资料 topic: 茶余饭后的～ things to talk about at moments of leisure

埮 tán 人名用字 Tan, for use in personal names

弹(彈) tán ❶ 由于一物的弹性作用使另一物射出去 shoot; send forth ❷ 利用机械使纤维变得松软 fluff; tease: ～棉花 fluff cotton with a bow|～羊毛 tease wool ❸ 一个指头被另一个指头压住,然后用力挣开,借这个力量触物使动 flick; flip: 把帽子上的土～去 flick dust off a hat ❹ 用手指、器具拨弄或敲打,使物体振动 play (with one's fingers or object): ～钢琴 play the piano|～琵琶 pluck the *pipa* ❺ 有弹性 elastic: ～簧 spring ❻ 抨击 accuse; impeach: 讥～laugh at sb.|～劾 impeach

☞ dàn on p. 381

【弹拨乐器】tánbō-yuèqì 指由于拨动琴弦而发音的一类乐器,如琵琶、月琴、三弦等 plucked string instrument; plucked instrument, such as *pipa*, *yueqin* and *sanxian*

【弹唱】tánchàng 一边弹奏,一边演唱 sing while playing a stringed instrument

【弹词】táncí 曲艺的一种,流行于南方各省,有说有唱,曲调、唱腔各地不同,用三弦伴奏,或再加琵琶陪衬。也指说唱弹词的底本。storytelling; *tanci*, a genre of ballad singing to the accompaniment of a *sanxian* or in addition to a *pipa*, performed in different dialects and tones, and popular in southern provinces; script for this kind of storytelling

【弹冠相庆】tán guān xiāng qìng《汉书·王吉传》:'吉与贡禹为友,世称"王阳在位,贡公弹冠",言其取舍同也'(弹冠:掸去帽子上的尘土,准备做官)。后来用'弹冠相庆'指一人当了官或升了官,他的同伙也互相庆贺将有官可做。According to *History of Han·Biography of Wang Ji*, Wang Ji and Gong Yu were good friends, and it was known to the public that upon learning that 'Wang Yang (the man's style name) was appointed to an official post, Gong flicked dust from his hat (knowing that he, too, was to become an official because of the connection). From this was derived the Chinese phrase which means 'congratulate each other in anticipation of fat jobs (upon hearing of a mutual friend's appointment to a high post)' or 'congratulate each other on the prospect of getting good appointments'

【弹劾】tánhé ❶ 君主时代担任监察职务的官员检举官吏的罪状 impeach; charge a public official with improper conduct in office before a proper tribunal ❷ 某些国家的议会抨击政府工作人员,揭发其罪状(of parliament in some countries) expose the malpractice of a government official

【弹簧】tánhuáng 利用材料的弹性作用制成的零件,在外力作用下能发生形变,除去外力后又恢复原状。常见的用合金钢制成,有螺旋形、板形等不同形状。有的地区叫绷簧。Spring; device made of elastic material that regains its original shape after being compressed or extended, usu. made of alloy steel and in spirals, plates, or other shapes; known in some regions as 绷簧 bēnghuáng

【弹簧秤】tánhuángchèng 用弹簧制成的秤，常见的是用螺旋形弹簧装在金属筒里，上端固定，下端有钩，筒上有刻度。重物悬在钩上，就可以由指针所指的刻度上得出重量。spring balance; scale fashioned out of a spring, usu. a spiral spring in a metal tube with its upper end fixed and its lower end attached to a hook, so that when an object is hanging on the hook one can read its weight from the graduation marks on the wall of the tube

【弹簧门】tánhuángmén 门框和门扇之间装有弹簧、可以自动关闭的门 swing door; door attached to its frame with springs that enable it to close automatically

【弹泪】tánlèi 挥泪，泛指伤心流泪 shed tears; cry in sorrow

【弹力】tánlì 物体发生形变时产生的使物体恢复原状的作用力 elasticity; (of an object) the property of returning to an initial form or state following deformation

【弹射】tánshè ❶ 利用弹力、压力等射出 catapult; shoot: 气压～器 air-pressed ejector; catapult ❷〈书 *fml*.〉指摘 pick faults; criticize: ～利病（指出缺点错误）pick faults; point out one's mistakes

【弹跳】tántiào （身体或物体）利用弹力向上跳起 (of body or object) bounce; spring: ～力 jumping capacity

【弹性】tánxìng ❶ 物体受外力作用变形后，除去作用力时能恢复原来形状的性质 elasticity; (of an object) the property of returning to an initial form or state following deformation ❷〈比喻 *fig*.〉事物的可多可少、可大可小等伸缩性 flexible; resilient: ～立场 resilient stand | ～外交 flexible diplomacy | ～工作制 staggered work schedule

【弹压】tányā 指用武力压制；压服 quell; crack down on; quell

【弹指】tánzhǐ〈比喻 *fig*.〉时间极短暂（as short as) the time it takes to snap one's fingers; brief: ～之间 at the snap of the fingers; in an instant | ～光阴 time zipping by

覃 tán ❶〈书 *fml*.〉深 deep: ～思（深思）deep in thought ❷（Tán）姓 a surname
☞ Qín on p. 1560

橝 tán〈方 *dial*.〉水塘。多用于地名。pond, usu. used in the name of a place

锬 tán〈书 *fml*.〉长矛 lance; spear
☞ 铦 xiān on p. 2073

痰 tán 肺泡、支气管和气管分泌出来的黏液，当肺部或呼吸道发生病变时分泌量增多，并含有某些病菌，是传播疾病的媒介物 phlegm; sputum; thick and sticky mucus secreted by the mucous membrane of the respiratory tract, which increases during pathological changes of the lungs or the respiratory duct, and, containing certain viruses, is regarded as a pestiferous medium

【痰气】tánqì〈方 *dial*.〉❶ 指精神病 mental disorder ❷ 指中风（zhòngfēng）apoplexy

【痰桶】tántǒng 形状略像桶的痰盂 spittoon

【痰盂】tányú（～儿 tányúr）盛痰用的器皿 spittoon; cuspidor

谭 tán ❶ same as 谈 tán ❷（Tán）姓 a surname

潭 tán ❶ 深的水池 deep pond: 清～limpid pool | 古～old pond | 龙～虎穴 dragon's pool and tiger's den ❷〈方 *dial*.〉坑 pit; depression

【潭府】tánfǔ〈书 *fml*.〉❶ 深渊 deep pool ❷ 深邃的府第，常用于尊称对方的住宅（honor.) your house

燂 tán〈方 *dial*.〉放在火上使热 heat sth. on a fire

澹 tán [澹台]（Tántái）姓 a two-character surname
☞ dàn on p. 383

檀 tán ❶ 落叶乔木，叶互生，卵形，花单生，果实有圆形的翅。木质坚硬，用来制造家具、农具和乐器。wingceltis (*Pteroceltis tatarinowii*); defoliating tree with alternate oval leaves, solitary flowers, and winged fruit, producing a kind of hardwood ideal for the making of furniture, farm tools and musical instrument; also 青檀 qīngtán ❷（Tán）姓 a surname

【檀板】tánbǎn 拍板，多用檀木制成 hardwood clappers oft. made of wingceltis wood

【檀越】tányuè〈佛教用语 *Budd*.〉称施主 [term of address] benefactor; almsgiver

磹 tán 磹口（Tánkǒu），地名，在福建 Tankou, name of a place in Fujian Province

镡 Tán 姓 a surname
☞ Chán on p. 211 and xín on p. 2136

醰 tán〈书 *fml*.〉酒味厚；醇（of wine) rich; mellow

tǎn（ㄊㄢˇ）

忐 tǎn [忐忑]（tǎntè）心神不定 perturbed: ～不安 be on tenterhooks

坦 tǎn ❶ 平 smooth; level: ～途 smooth sailing | 平～(of land) level; even ❷ 坦白 straightforward; be up front about sth.: ～率 forthright ❸ 心里安定 composed; calm: ～然 unperturbed

【坦白】tǎnbái ❶ 心地纯洁，语言直率 guileless: 襟怀～unselfish and magnanimous ❷ 如实地说出（自己的错误或罪行）own up to (one's mistake or crime): ～交代问题 confess one's problems|～从宽，抗拒从严 leniency to those who confess and severity to those who refuse to

【坦诚】tǎnchéng 坦率诚恳 frank and sincere：心地～open-hearted|～相见 treat sb. with sincerity|～的话语 straightforward and sincere remarks

【坦荡】tǎndàng ❶宽广平坦 broad and level：前面是一条～的大路。A broad and level road lies ahead. ❷形容心地纯洁，胸襟宽畅 be open-hearted and aboveboard：胸怀～the largeness of mind

【坦缓】tǎnhuǎn 地势平坦，倾斜度小（of land）level；smooth：～的山坡 gentle mountain slope

【坦克】tǎnkè 装有火炮、机关枪和旋转炮塔的履带式装甲战斗车辆 tank；armoured combat vehicle that is mounted with cannon and guns and a revolving turret and moves on caterpillar treads；also 坦克车 tǎnkèchē

【坦克兵】tǎnkèbīng 装甲兵 tankman；panzer force

【坦然】tǎnrán 形容心里平静，无顾虑 calm；unperturbed；having no misgivings：～无惧 composed and fearless|～自若 calmness and self-assurance

【坦实】tǎnshí same as 坦诚 tǎnchéng

【坦率】tǎnshuài 直率 straightforward；be up front about sth.：性情～of a straightforward disposition|为人～热情 treat people with candour and sincerity

【坦途】tǎntú 平坦的道路 level road；〈比喻 *fig.*〉顺利的形势或境况 smooth sailing

钽 tǎn 金属元素，符号 Ta（tantalum）。银白色，有超导电性（-268.8℃时）和延展性，耐腐蚀性强。用来制造化学器皿、真空管、医疗器械等。tantalum（Ta）；silver-white metal element with superconductivity（at -268.8℃），ductibility and high resistance to erosion，used as a material for the making of chemical apparatuses，vacuum tubes and medical equipment

袒 tǎn ❶脱去或敞开上衣，露出（身体的一部分）（of part of the body）naked；nude；being without clothing：～露 nudity|～胸露臂 décolletage；décolleté ❷袒护 be partial to：偏～be one-sided

【袒护】tǎnhù 对错误的思想行为无原则地支持或保护 be partial to：～孩子不是爱孩子。To shield a child is to harm him.

【袒露】tǎnlù 裸露 expose；uncover：～胸膛 expose one's chest ◇～心声 reveal one's inner world

菼 tǎn 〈书 *fml.*〉荻 a kind of reed（*Miscanthus sacchariflorus*）

毯 tǎn 毯子 rub；carpet；blanket：毛～woollen blanket|线～thread blanket|地～carpet|壁～tapestry

【毯子】tǎn·zi 铺在床上、地上或挂在墙上的较厚的毛织品、棉织品或棉毛混织品，大多有图案或图画 blanket；woolen，cotton or woolen-cotton fabrics used to cover a bed or floor or hung on the wall

tàn（ㄊㄢˋ）

叹（嘆、歎） tàn ❶叹气 sigh：～息 groan|可～lamentable|长吁短～moan and groan ❷吟哦 recite（a poem）：咏～intone；sing|一唱三～one sings and three others join in；sing or write with affected pathos ❸发出赞美的声音 acclaim；praise：赞～admire；praise|～为奇迹 marvel at sth. spectacular

【叹词】tàncí 表示强烈的感情以及表示招呼、应答的词，如'啊、哎、哟、哼、嗯、喂' interjection；part of speech usu. expressing emotion，greeting and response，such as Ah!，Ugh!，Hey!，Hum!，and Hello!

【叹服】tànfú 称赞而且佩服 gasp in admiration：他画的人物栩栩如生，令人～。The figures under his brush are life-like in an admirable way.

【叹观止矣】tàn guān zhǐ yǐ 春秋时吴国的季札在鲁国观看各种乐舞，看到舜时的乐舞，十分赞美，说看到这里就够了（观止矣），再有别的乐舞也不必看了（见于《左传》襄公二十九年）。后来指赞美看到的事物好到极点。hail sth. as the acme of perfection. According to *The Zuo Commentary·Duke Xiang 29th Year*，Ji Zha of the state of Wu during the Spring and Autumn Period was attending a variety show in the state of Lu. When he saw the singing and dancing of King Shun's time，he was so impressed as to say that having seen this performance there was no need for him to see other people's performances. Hence the phrase. also 叹为观止 tàn wéi guān zhǐ

【叹号】tànhào 标点符号（!），表示一个感叹句完了 exclamation mark（!），indicating the ending of an exclamatory sentence

【叹绝】tànjué 赞叹事物好到极点 admire as superb：技艺之精，让人～。The craftsmanship was so elaborate it was matchless.

【叹气】tàn//qì 心里感到不痛快而呼出长气，发出声音 sigh：唉声～sigh in dismay|叹了一口气 heave a sigh

【叹赏】tànshǎng 称赞 express admiration for：～不绝 shower praise on sb. or sth.|击节～applaud to show appreciation

【叹惋】tànwǎn〈书 *fml.*〉叹惜 sigh with regret

【叹为观止】tàn wéi guān zhǐ ☞叹观止矣 tàn guān zhǐ yǐ

【叹息】tànxī same as 叹气 tàn//qì

【叹惜】tànxī 慨叹惋惜 moan in regret：功亏一篑，令人～。It was regrettable that success slipped by when it was just a breath away.

【叹羡】tànxiàn〈书 *fml.*〉赞叹羡慕 sigh with admiration

炭(炭) tàn ❶ 木炭的通称 general term for 木炭 mùtàn ❷ 像炭的东西 sth. charcoal-like：山查～hawthorn charcoal ❸〈方 *dial.*〉煤 coal：挖～coal mining

【炭化】tànhuà 古代的植物埋藏在沉积物里，在一定的压力、温度等的作用下逐渐变成煤的过程 carbonize; palaebiochemical process of plants embedded in sedimentation being gradually turned into coal under certain pressure and temperature; also 煤化 méihuà

【炭画】tànhuà 用炭质材料绘成的画 charcoal drawing; charcoal

【炭墼】tànjī 用炭末做成的块状燃料，多呈圆柱形 charcoal briquette

【炭精】tànjīng ❶ 各种炭制品的总称 general term for charcoal products ❷〈方 *dial.*〉人造炭和石墨的总称 general term for artificial charcoal and graphite

【炭精灯】tànjīngdēng 弧光灯 arc lamp; arc light

【炭疽】tànjū 急性传染病，马、牛、绵羊等家畜和人都能感染，病原体是炭疽杆菌。病畜的症状是发高烧，痉挛，口和肛门出血，胸部、颈部或腹部肿胀。人感染后，发生脓疱、水肿或痈，也能侵入肺或胃肠。家畜的炭疽病有的地区叫癀病。anthrax; acute infectious, usu. fatal disease of horses, cattle, sheep and other domestic animals as well as human beings, caused by the bacterium Bacillus anthracis. Symptoms are high fever, convulsion, mouth and anal bleeding, tumefaction of chest, neck or belly. The bacterium can cause pustule, dropsy or carbuncle in a human being and invade the lung, stomach and intestines. Anthrax in domestic animals is known in some regions as 癀病 huángbìng.

【炭盆】tànpén 烧木炭的火盆 charcoal brazier

探 tàn ❶ 试图发现(隐藏的事物或情况)find (sth. hidden); sound：～矿 ore prospecting|～路 find out the way|～口气 sound sb. out|试～sound out; probe|钻～explore by drilling ❷ 做侦察工作的人 scout; spy：密～secret agent|敌～enemy spy ❸ 看望 call on; visit：～望 pay a call on|～亲 go home to see one's family |～病 see a patient in the hospital ❹ 向前伸出(头或上体)crane; stretch forward：～头～脑 crane one's head; pry about furtively|行车时不要～身窗外。Don't stretch your body out of the window when the bus is moving. ❺〈方 *dial.*〉过问 look into; inquire into：～闲事 be nosy about sb. else's business

【探本穷源】tàn běn qióng yuán 追本穷源 go to the root of an issue; also 探本溯源 tànběnsùyuán

【探测】tàncè 对于不能直接观察的事物或现象用仪器进行考察和测量 plumb; survey; prospect; use apparatuses to study and measure sth. that cannot be directly observed：高空～aerial survey|～海的深度 gauge the depth of the sea ◇～对方心里的秘密 sound sb.'s secret out

【探查】tànchá 深入检查或暗中查看 look over; examine; scout：剖腹～dissect the paunch for diagnosis|～敌情 reconnoitre the enemy

【探察】tànchá 探听侦察；察看 observe; look carefully at：～地形 survey the terrain|～敌人的行踪 observe the whereabouts of the enemy

【探访】tànfǎng ❶ 访求；搜寻 search; look into：～新闻 look for the leads of a news story|～善本书 search for authentic and rare book editions ❷ 探望 visit; call on：～亲友 visit relatives and friends

【探戈】tàngē 交际舞的一种，起源于非洲，流行于欧美，2/4 或 4/4 拍，速度缓慢，多为滑步，舞时变化很多。tango; ballroom dance originating in Africa and popular in Europe and America, in 2/4 or 4/4 time and a good variety of movements, oft. with glissades [西 Spanish: tango]

【探花】tànhuā 科举时代的一种称号。明清两代称殿试考取一甲(第一等)第三名的人。title conferred on the one who won third place in the highest imperial examination in the Ming and Qing Dynasties

【探监】tàn//jiān 到监狱里看望被囚禁的人(多为亲友 usu. a relative or a friend) visit a prisoner

【探井】tànjǐng 为探测矿体而开掘的小井 test well drilled for prospecting

【探究】tànjiū 探索研究；探寻追究 probe into; inquire into：～原因 look into the root causes

【探勘】tànkān same as 勘探 kāntàn

【探口气】tàn kǒu·qi 设法引出对方的话，探听他对某人某事的态度和看法 find out sb.'s opinions or feelings; also 探口风 tàn kǒufēng

【探矿】tàn//kuàng 根据矿床生成的原理，采用一定的方法寻找矿产 prospecting; prospect; search for or explore a region for mineral deposits

【探骊得珠】tàn lí dé zhū《庄子·列御寇》上说，黄河边上有人泅入深水，得到一颗价值千金的珠子。他父亲说：'这样珍贵的珠子，一定是在万丈深渊的黑龙下巴底下取得，而且是在它睡时取得的。'后来用'探骊得珠'比喻做文章扣紧主题，抓住要领。According to *Zhuangzi·Lie Yukou*, when a man dived into the depth of the Yellow River and obtained a priceless pearl, his father commented, 'This kind of valuable pearl must have been obtained from underneath the jaw of the black dragon residing in a bottomless hole while the dragon was asleep.' (fig.) probe deep and grasp the point of a theme; to the point (骊 *li*: 黑龙 black dragon)

【探马】tànmǎ 做侦察工作的骑兵(多见于早期白话 oft. in early vernacular) mounted scout

【探秘】tànmì 探索秘密或奥秘 explore the mysteries; probe the secrets:宇宙~probe the secrets of the universe

【探囊取物】tàn náng qǔ wù 伸手到袋子里取东西 take sth. out of one's pocket;〈比喻 *fig.*〉能够轻而易举地办成某件事情 as easy as taking sth. out of one's own pocket

【探亲】tàn//qīn 探望亲属,现多指探望父母或配偶 go home to see family:~假 home leave|回乡~homecoming visit

【探求】tànqiú 探索追求 pursue, search for:~学问 seek knowledge|~真理 seek truth

【探伤】tàn//shāng 通过一定装置,利用磁性、X射线、γ射线、超声波等检查和探测金属材料内部的缺陷 detect flaws in a metal material by means of magnetism, X-rays, γ-rays, or ultrasonic wave

【探身】tàn//shēn 向前伸出上体 lean forward:~向门里望了一下 lean forward to take a look at what's going on inside the door

【探胜】tànshèng〈书 *fml.*〉探寻优美的景物 go sightseeing

【探视】tànshì ❶ 看望 visit; call on:~病人 drop in on a patient ❷ 察看 observe:向窗外~look about out of a window

【探索】tànsuǒ 多方寻求答案,解决疑问 explore; probe:~人生道路 explore the ways and means to cope with life|~自然界的奥秘 probe the secrets of nature

【探讨】tàntǎo 研究讨论 inquire into; discuss:~哲学问题 discuss matters of philosophy

【探听】tàntīng 探问(多指方式比较秘密、措辞比较含蓄的 oft. secretively or using implicative verbiage) find out about sth.:~虚实 find out about an opponent|~口气 sound out sb.'s attitude

【探头】tàn//tóu 向前伸出头 pop one's head in; crane one's neck:他从窗口~看了一下,屋内不见有人。He popped his head into the window and saw nobody in the room.

【探头探脑】tàn tóu tàn nǎo (~儿 tàn tóu tàn nǎor)不断探头看,多形容鬼鬼祟祟地窥探 pop one's head in and look about:只见门外一个人~,东张西望。A man was seen prying furtively outside the door.

【探望】tànwàng ❶ 看(试图发现情况) look about (trying to find some information):四处~look all around|他不时地向窗外~。He looked out of the window from time to time. ❷ 看望(多指远道)(of sb. from afar) visit:我路过上海时,顺便~了几个老朋友。I called on a few old friends while stopping over in Shanghai on my journey.

【探问】tànwèn ❶ 试探着询问(消息、情况、意图等)make cautious inquiries about (news, situation, intention, etc.):~失散多年的亲人的下落 ask about the whereabouts of family members one hasn't heard from for many years|到处~,毫无结果。Inquires were made everywhere, but nothing came out of it. ❷ 探望,问候 call on:~病友 call on a hospital wardmate

【探析】tànxī 探讨和分析(多用做文章标题 oft. used as the title of a writing)discuss and analyze:《人口学难题~》*An Analytical Study of Difficult Issues in Demology*

【探悉】tànxī 打听后知道 find out:从有关方面~according to sources

【探险】tàn//xiǎn 到从来没有人去过或很少有人去过的地方去考察(自然界情况) explore (natural environment); adventure; tread on uncharted territory:~队 exploring team|到南极去~go on an expedition to the South Pole

【探寻】tànxún 探求;寻找seek; pursue; search for:~真理 search for truth|~地下矿藏 search for underground mineral deposits

【探询】tànxún same as 探问 tànwèn

【探幽】tànyōu〈书 *fml.*〉❶ 探索深奥的道理 unravel mysteries:~析微 inquire into the abstrusities ❷ 探寻胜境 explore scenes and sights of natural beauty:~揽胜 visit scenic spots

【探赜索隐】tàn zé suǒ yǐn 探究深奥的道理,搜索隐秘的事迹 delve into the abstruse; unravel mysteries

【探照灯】tànzhàodēng 一种用于远距离搜索和照明的装置。在军事上主要用于搜索以及照射空中、地面和水上目标。searchlight; device containing a light source and a reflector for projecting a high-intensity beam for long-distance search and lighting or the military purpose of searching and lighting targets in the sky or on the ground or a water surface

【探子】[1] tàn·zi 指在军中做侦察工作的人(多见于早期白话 oft. in early vernacular) spy

【探子】[2] tàn·zi 长条或管状的用具,用来探取东西,如蛐蛐儿探子(用来伸入穴中把蛐蛐儿撵出来)、粮食探子(用来插入袋中取出少量粮食做样品) thin tube used to drive crickets out of their holes or extract samples of grains, etc., from sacks

碳 tàn 非金属元素,符号 C (carbon)。有金刚石、石墨和无定形碳三种同素异形体。化学性质稳定,在空气中不起变化,是构成有机物的主要成分。在工业上和医药上用途很广。carbon (C); nonmetal element in three allotropes (diamond, graphite and amorphous carbon), of such stable chemical property that it does not change in air, serving as a major component in organisms, and used widely for industrial and pharmaceutical purposes

【碳化】tànhuà ☞干馏 gānliú on p. 626

【碳水化合物】tànshuǐ-huàhéwù same as 糖

táng ①

【碳酸气】tànsuānqì 二氧化碳 carbon dioxide; chokedamp

tāng (ㄊㄤ)

汤(湯) tāng ❶ 热水;开水 hot water; boiling water:温～浸种 soak seeds in warm water | 扬～止沸 stop water from boiling by scooping it up and pouring it back | 赴～蹈火 go through fire and water ❷ 专指温泉(现多用于地名 now used in the name of place) tang; a special reference to hot spring, now mostly used in place names:小～山(在北京) Lesser Tangshan Mountain (in Beijing) ❸ 食物煮后所得的汁水 water in which sth. has been boiled:米～rice soup | 鸡～chicken soup ❹ 烹调后汁儿特别多的副食 broth; soup:豆腐～soya bean soup | 菠菜～spinach soup | 四菜一～four dishes and one soup ❺ 汤药 decoction:柴胡～decoction of Chinese thorowax root ❻(Tāng)姓 a surname

☞ shāng on p. 1676

【汤池】tāngchí ❶ ☞金城汤池 jīnchéng tāngchí on p. 1004 ❷ 热水浴池 hot-water bathing pool; public bathhouse

【汤匙】tāngchí 调羹;羹匙 tablespoon; soupspoon

【汤罐】tāngguàn 旧式灶上烧热水用的罐 jug (fitted in an old-style kitchen range) used for heating up water

【汤锅】tāngguō 屠宰牲畜时煮热水煺毛的大型锅。也指屠宰场。Butcher's cauldron in a slaughterhouse; slaughterhouse

【汤壶】tānghú 盛热水后放在被中取暖的用具,多用铜合金或陶瓷、塑料制成。有的地区叫汤婆子。hot-water bottle for warming a quilt in bed, mostly made of copper alloy, pottery, or plastics; known in some regions as 汤婆子 tāngpó·zi

【汤面】tāngmiàn 加作料带汤的面条 noodles in soup

【汤婆子】tāngpó·zi 〈方 *dial*.〉same as 汤壶 tānghú

【汤泉】tāngquán 〈古代 *arch*.〉称温泉 hot spring

【汤色】tāngsè 沏茶后茶水呈现的色泽(多用于鉴定茶叶质量时) colour tone of a cup of tea (a criterion for judging the quality of tea leaves):～明亮 bright and clear colour of a kind of tea

【汤水】tāngshuǐ ❶ 食物煮后的汤儿 soup ❷〈方 *dial*.〉开水或热水 hot water; boiling water

【汤头】tāngtóu 中药多为汤剂,所以中药的配方泛称汤头。把常用的汤头编成歌诀,以便学习记忆,叫汤头歌诀。prescription for a medical decoction in traditional Chinese medicine. Prescriptions for regular uses are composed in the form of jingles for memorization. Hence the term, prescriptions in rhyme.

【汤团】tāngtuán 〈方 *dial*.〉带馅儿的汤圆 stuffed dumplings made of glutinous rice flour and served in soup

【汤药】tāngyào 〈中医 *Chin. med*.〉指用水煎服的药物 decoction of medicinal ingredients

【汤圆】tāngyuán 糯米粉等做的球形食品,大多有馅儿,带汤吃(usu. stuffed) dumplings made of glutinous rice flour and served in soup

铴(鐋) tāng [铴锣](tāngluó) 小铜锣 small brass gong

耥 tāng 用耥耙松土、除草 weed or loosen the soil in a farm plot

【耥耙】tāngbà 水稻中耕的一种农具,形状像木屐,底下有许多短铁钉,上面有长柄。在水稻行间推拉,松土除草。paddy-field harrow; farm implement in the shape of a geta with a cluster of short iron teeth beneath it and a long handle, used to break up and even off clods and weed between paddy rows

嘡 tāng 〈拟声词 *onom*.〉形容打钟、敲锣、放枪一类声音 loud ringing sound of bell, gong, gun, etc.:～～连响了两枪。Bang! Bang! There came two gunshots.

【嘡啷】tānglāng 〈拟声词 *onom*.〉金属器物等磕碰的声音 loud ringing sound; clang:～一声,脸盆掉在地上了。The washbasin fell onto the ground with a bang.

趟 tāng same as 蹚 tāng

☞ tàng on p. 1869

羰 tāng same as 羰基 tāngjī

【羰基】tāngjī 由碳和氧两种原子组合的二价原子团(>C=O) carbonyl; CO, a bivalent radical; carbonyl group; metal compound containing the CO group

镗 tāng same as 嘡 tāng

☞ táng on p. 1866

蹚[1](蹚) tāng 从浅水里走过去 wade; ford:～水过河 wade across a river

蹚[2](蹚) tāng 用犁把土翻开,除去杂草并给苗培土 turn the soil and dig up weeds with a plough:～地 plough

【蹚道】tāng//dào 〈方 *dial*.〉(～儿 tāng//dàor)探路 explore the way;〈比喻 *fig*.〉摸情况 find out about things; also 蹚路 tāng//lù

【蹚浑水】tāng húnshuǐ 〈方 *dial*.〉(～儿 tāng húnshuǐr)〈比喻 *fig*.〉跟着别人干坏事 follow sb.'s bad example

táng (ㄊㄤˊ)

饧(餳) táng 〈书 *fml*.〉same as 糖 táng

☞xíng on p. 2146

唐[1] táng ❶（言谈）虚夸 talking big; boastful:～大无验 braggadocio; sheer bragging ❷ 空;徒然 for nothing; in vain:功不～捐(功夫不白费)。The efforts will not be in vain.

唐[2] Táng ❶传说中朝代名,尧所建 Tang, legendary dynasty founded by Emperor Yao ❷ 朝代,公元618—907,李渊和他的儿子世民所建,建都长安(今陕西西安) Tang Dynasty (618-907), founded by Li Yuan and his son, Li Shimin, with the capital in Chang'an (present-day Xi'an in Shaanxi Province) ❸ 后唐 Late Tang (923-936) of the Five Dynasties Period (907-960) ❹ 姓 a surname

【唐棣】tángdì same as 棠棣 tángdì

【唐花】tánghuā 温室里养的花卉 hothouse flower; also 堂花 tánghuā

【唐人街】tángrénjiē 指海外华侨聚居并开设较多具有中国特色的店铺的街市 Chinatown; neighborhood or section of a city that is inhabited chiefly by Chinese people and clustered with Chinese shops

【唐三彩】tángsāncǎi 唐代陶器和陶俑的釉色,有黄、绿、褐、蓝等多种颜色。也指有这种釉色的陶制品,现多为仿制品。Tang-dynasty trio-coloured glazed pottery or figurines that come in such colours as yellow, green, brown, and blue. Most of the Tang-dynasty trio-coloured pottery available today is imitations.

【唐突】tángtū〈书 *fml.*〉乱闯;冒犯 be rude; be blunt; profane

堂 táng ❶ 正房 main room:～屋 main room ❷ 专为某种活动用的房屋 building for a specific purpose:礼～ auditorium | 课～ classroom | 食～ dining room; cafeteria ❸〈旧时 *old*〉官府中举行仪式、审讯案件的地方 court; main hall of a *yamen*:大～ the court | 过～ stand trial in a court ❹ 用于厅堂名称;旧时也指某一家、某一房或某一家族 [used in the name of a hall; also used in old times to refer to a certain family or clan]:三槐～ Hall of Three Pagoda Trees ❺ 用于商店牌号[used in the name of a store] *tang*:同仁～(北京的一家药店)Tongrentang; Tongren Pharmacy of Beijing ❻ 堂房[indicate relationship between cousins, etc.] with the same paternal grandfather or great-grandfather:～兄 elder cousin | ～弟 younger cousin | ～姊妹 female cousins ❼〈量词 *classifier*〉a)用于成套的家具[indicate furniture] set:一～家具 a set of furniture b)用于分节的课程,一节叫一堂[indicate school classes] class:两～课 two classes c)〈旧时 *old*〉审案一次叫一堂[indicate appearances in court]:过了两～have made two court appearances d)用于场景、壁画等[indicate stage scenes, murals, etc.]:二～内景 three indoor scenes | 一～壁画 a mural painting

【堂奥】táng'ào〈书 *fml.*〉❶ 房屋的深处 innermost recess of a house ❷ 腹地 hinterland ❸〈比喻 *fig.*〉深奥的道理或境界 profundity of thought or knowledge:窥其～get some idea about certain profound reasoning

【堂而皇之】táng ér huáng zhī ❶ 形容公开或不加掩饰 overt; make no secret of sth.:他是凭着一张伪造的出入证～进来的。He swaggered in with a forged pass. ❷ 形容体面或气派大 in state; grandiose:讲了一套～的理论 come up with an impressive theory

【堂房】tángfáng 同宗而非嫡亲的(亲属)relationship between cousins, etc. of the same paternal grandfather or great-grandfather:～弟兄、～姐妹(同祖父、同曾祖或者更疏远的弟兄姐妹)male and female cousins of the same paternal great-grandfather or an even further relationship | ～侄子、～侄女(堂房弟兄的子女) nephews and nieces — sons and daughters of one's male cousins

【堂鼓】tánggǔ 打击乐器,两面蒙牛皮,常用于戏曲乐队中 barrel-shaped drum with both ends mounted with cowhide, used as a musical instrument in traditional opera

【堂倌】tángguān〈旧时 *old*〉称饭馆、茶馆、酒店中的招待人员(in a restaurant, teahouse or inn) waiter; servant

【堂号】tánghào 厅堂的名称,旧时多指某一家、某一房或某一家族的名号 name of a hall; name of a household or clan

【堂花】tánghuā same as 唐花 tánghuā

【堂皇】tánghuáng ❶ 形容气势宏大 in state; grand:富丽～magnificent ❷ 冠冕堂皇 high-sounding; highfalutin:～的理由 high-sounding pretext

【堂会】tánghuì〈旧时 *old*〉家里有喜庆事邀请艺人来举行的演出会 performance for home celebration

【堂客】táng·kè ❶ 女客人 female guest ❷〈方 *dial.*〉泛指妇女 women ❸〈方 *dial.*〉妻 wife

【堂上】tángshàng ❶ 指父母 parents ❷〈旧时 *old*〉受审讯的人称审案的官吏(term of address to a court judge) Your Honour ❸〈旧指 *old*〉审讯问案的地方 court

【堂堂】tángtáng ❶ 形容容貌庄严大方 imposing; dignified; impressive:仪表～impeccable appearance and good manner ❷ 形容有志气或有气魄 having high aspirations and boldness of vision:～中华儿女 Chinese men and women with aspirations and verve ❸ 形容阵容或力量壮大 formidable; imposing:～之阵 formidable battle formation

【堂堂正正】tángtángzhèngzhèng ❶ 形容光明正大 be aboveboard and uphold justice:做一个～的男子汉。Be an aboveboard and dignified man ❷ 形容身材威武,仪表出众 having impeccable appearance and good manner:～的相貌 dignified look

【堂屋】tángwū ❶ 正房的居中的一间 central room of a Chinese courtyard house ❷ 泛指正房（in a broad sense）principle rooms that face south

【堂戏】tángxì ❶ 堂会上演的戏 performance at a home gathering for celebration ❷ 湖北地方戏曲剧种之一，流行于该省巴东、五峰等地 *tangxi*, a local opera popular in Badong and Wufeng in Hubei Province

【堂子】táng·zi ❶ 清朝皇室祭神的场所 place where the imperial court of the Qing Dynasty offers sacrifices to gods ❷〈方 *dial.*〉〈旧时 *old*〉妓院的别称 whorehouse; byname of a brothel

棠 táng ❶ 棠梨 birchleaf pear（*Pyrus betulaefolia*）❷（Táng）姓 a surname

【棠棣】tángdì 古书上说的一种植物 aspen-plum; Chinese bush cherry in ancient books; also 唐棣 tángdì

郿 táng 郿部（Tángwú），地名，在山东 Tangwu, name of a place in Shandong Province

塘 táng ❶ 堤岸；堤防 dyke; embankment：河～river embankment｜海～seawall ❷ 水池 pool：池～pond｜鱼～fish pond ❸ 浴池 bathing pool：洗澡～bathhouse ❹〈方 *dial.*〉室内生火取暖用的坑 brazier：火～stove chamber

【塘堰】tángyàn 在山区或丘陵地区修筑的一种小型蓄水工程，用来积蓄附近的雨水和泉水，灌溉农田 small reservoir dug in a hilly area to store rain and spring water; also 塘坝 tángbà

搪¹ táng ❶ 抵挡 ward off：～饥 allay the pang of hunger｜～风 keep out the wind｜～上一块板子就塌不下来了。It won't cave in if it is bolstered with a wood plank. ❷ 搪塞 evade; do sth. perfunctorily：～账 put off a creditor｜～差事 dillydally on one's work

搪² táng 把泥土或涂料均匀地涂在炉灶、瓷器上 plaster; daub：～炉子 line a stove with clay

搪³ táng same as 镗 táng

【搪瓷】tángcí 用石英、长石、硝石、碳酸钠等烧制成的像釉子的物质。涂在金属坯胎上，能烧制成不同颜色的图案，并可防锈。enamel; vitreous, glaze-like coating, made from quartz, feldspar, saltpeter, and sodium carbonate, protective coating in different colours, baked on metal ware in decorative patterns

【搪塞】tángsè 敷衍塞责 stall sb. off; do sth. perfunctorily：用几句话～过去 stall sb. off with a few evasive remarks

餹 táng same as 糖 táng

溏 táng 不凝结、半流动的 half congealed; viscous：～心（of cooked or salted egg）with a soft-fried yolk｜～便 semi-liquid or unformed stool

【溏便】tángbiàn〈中医 *Chin. med.*〉指稀薄的大便 semi-liquid or unformed stool

【溏心】tángxīn（～儿 tángxīnr）蛋煮过或腌过后蛋黄没有完全凝固的（of cooked or salted egg）with a soft yolk：～儿鸡蛋 soft-boiled or soft-fried egg｜～儿松花 preserved egg with jelly-like yolk

瑭 táng〈书 *fml.*〉一种玉 a kind of jade

樘 táng ❶ 门框或窗框 frame：门～door frame｜窗～window frame ❷〈量词 *classifier*〉门扇和门框或窗扇和窗框一副叫一樘[used of doors or windows, frames included]：一～玻璃门 a pair of glass doors｜四～双扇窗 four pairs of double-leaf windows

膛 táng ❶ 胸腔 thorax; chest：胸～chest｜开～cut open the chest ❷（～儿 tángr）器物的中空的部分 cavity; chamber：炉～儿 fire chamber of a stove｜枪～bore of a gun｜把子弹上了～load a gun

【膛线】tángxiàn 枪膛或炮膛内的螺旋形凹凸线，凸起的叫阳线，凹下的叫阴线。作用是使发射出的弹头旋转飞行，以增加射程、命中率和侵彻力。rifling; spiral grooves cut in a rifle barrel, with the protruding lines known as *yang* lines and the concave lines known as *yin* lines, to cause the bullet to circumgyrate while flying so as to increase the range, accuracy and piercing force; also 来复线 láifùxiàn

螗 táng 古书上指一种较小的蝉 a smaller kind of cicada in ancient books

镗 táng 用镗床切削机器零件上已有的孔眼 boring; use of a boring machine to work on a hole in a metal accessory; also 搪 táng

☞ tāng on p. 1864

【镗床】tángchuáng 金属切削机床，用来加工工件上已有的孔眼，使孔眼扩大、光洁而精确。加工时工件固定在工作台上，镗刀装在旋转的金属杆上，伸进工件的孔眼里切削。boring machine; boring lathe; borer; metal-cutting machine tool using a cutter fixed on a revolving metal rod to expand a hole in a metal accessory fixed on a workbench and make it smooth and accurate

糖（❶醣）táng ❶ 有机化合物的一类，可分为单糖、双糖和多糖三种，是人体内产生热能的主要物质，如葡萄糖、蔗糖、乳糖、淀粉等 carbohydrate; a kind of organic compound, including monosome, disaccharide and polysaccharide, a major substance derived from glucose, cane sugar, lactose, starch, etc., to produce heat in the human body; also 碳水化合物 tànshuǐ-huàhéwù ❷ 食糖的统称，包括白糖、红糖、冰糖等 general term for sugar, including white sugar, brown sugar, rock candy, etc. ❸ 糖果 confection：奶～toffee｜水果～fruit drops

【糖弹】tángdàn 糖衣炮弹的简称 abbr. for 糖衣炮弹 tángyī pàodàn

【糖房】tángfáng 制红糖、白糖等的作坊。有的地区叫糖寮或榨寮。sugar refinery; known in some regions as 糖寮 tángliáo or 榨寮 zhàliáo

【糖苷】tánggān 甙(dài) glycoside

【糖膏】tánggāo 制糖时甘蔗汁或甜菜汁蒸发浓缩后形成的赤褐色黏稠液体，是糖蜜和糖的结晶的混合物。糖膏经过分蜜后制成白糖。massecuite; fillmass; mixture of syrup and crystalline sugar in the form of a thick russet liquid, resulting from concentrated sugar cane or sugar beet juice, from which white sugar is derived

【糖瓜】tángguā (～儿 tángguār)用麦芽糖制成的瓜状食品 melon-shaped maltose

【糖果】tángguǒ 糖制的食品，其中多加有果汁、香料、牛奶或咖啡等 confectionery; candy; rich, sweet confection made with sugar and often flavoured with juice, spice, milk or coffee

【糖葫芦】tánghú·lu (～儿 tánghú·lur)一种食品，用竹签把山楂果或海棠果等穿成一串儿，蘸上熔化的冰糖、白糖或麦牙糖而制成 sugar-coated haws or crab apples on a stick; also 冰糖葫芦 bīngtáng hú·lu

【糖化】tánghuà 淀粉在酵素的作用下分解成糖 saccharify; saccharification; convert starch into sugar with the aid of yeast

【糖浆】tángjiāng ❶ 用蔗糖加蒸馏水加热溶解后制成的较稠的糖溶液。医药上用来改变某些药物的味道，使容易服用。medical syrup; syrup made from heating cane sugar in distilled water, used to change the taste of certain medicine to facilitate medication ❷ 制糖时熬成的浓度为 60% 的糖溶液，可用来做糖果等 syrup with a 60 per cent sugar content, used as a material for making candy

【糖精】tángjīng 有机化合物，化学式 $C_7H_5NO_3S$。无色晶体，难溶于水。糖精的钠盐为白色结晶粉末，易溶于水，比蔗糖甜 300—500 倍，可做食糖的代用品，但没有营养价值。saccharin ($C_7H_5NO_3S$); gluside; transparent crystalline powder having a taste 300-500 times sweeter than cane sugar, used as a calorie-free sweetener with no nutritious value

【糖萝卜】tángluó·bo ❶ 甜菜的通称 general term for 甜菜 tiáncài ❷〈方 *dial.*〉蜜饯的胡萝卜 preserved carrot

【糖蜜】tángmì 含有糖、蛋白质和色素的黏稠物体，是制糖的产物。红糖中就含有糖蜜。molasses; treacle; thick syrup containing sugar, protein and pigment, produced in refining raw sugar, also contained in brown sugar

【糖尿病】tángniàobìng 慢性病，以血糖增高为主要特征，病因是胰腺中的胰岛素分泌不足，食物中的碳水化合物的代谢不正常，变成葡萄糖从尿中排出体外。症状是食欲亢进，时常口渴，小便增多，身体消瘦等。diabetes; any of several metabolic disorders marked by high blood sugar contained in the body, caused by inadequate secretion of insulin from the pancreas and the subsequent abnormal metabolization of carbohydrate in food into glucose that is discharged together with urine, with such symptoms as excessive appetite, persistent thirst, increased discharge of urine, and loss of body weight

【糖人】tángrén (～儿 tángrénr)用糖稀吹成的人物、鸟兽，可以玩，也可以吃 sugar figurine; sculptures of figurine, bird or animal made of malt sugar that serves as toy or candy

【糖色】tángshǎi 用红糖炒至半焦而成的深棕色半流体，做肉类和其他一些食品用来上色，也指这种深棕色 melted brown sugar, brown sugar fried until it becomes a dark brown thick liquid that is used to give meat or other food a more inviting colour: 红烧肉的～不够。The braised pork would look better if more melted brown sugar was used.

【糖霜】tángshuāng ❶ 粘在食物表面上的一层白糖 icing; frosting ❷〈方 *dial.*〉白糖 white sugar

【糖稀】tángxī 含水分较多的麦芽糖，淡黄色，呈胶状，可用来制糖果、糕点等 malt sugar; maltose; light yellow glutinous syrup for the making of confectionery

【糖衣】tángyī 包在某些苦味药物表面的糖质层，作用是使药物容易吃下去 sugarcoating; coating a bitter-tasting medicine with sugar to make it easy to be taken

【糖衣炮弹】tángyī pàodàn〈比喻 *fig.*〉腐蚀、拉拢，拖人下水的手段 sugarcoated bullet; ways and means to corrupt or win over sb. or implicate sb. in a crime; 简称 abbr. 糖弹 tángdàn

【糖纸】tángzhǐ 包在一颗颗糖果外面的纸，多印有图案 candy wraps; paper oft. printed with patterns for wrapping candy

搪 táng 红色(多用于人的脸色 oft. of complexion) red: 紫～脸 cheeks with a deep tan; purple red face

螳 táng 指螳螂 mantis: ～臂当车 a mantis trying to obstruct a chariot — overrate oneself and try to hold back an overwhelmingly superior force

【螳臂当车】táng bì dāng chē 螳螂举起前腿想挡住车子前进 mantis raises its forelegs in a vain attempt to obstruct a chariot;〈比喻 *fig.*〉不估计自己的力量，去做办不到的事情，必然招致失败(语出《庄子·人间世》：'汝不知夫螳螂乎，怒其臂以当车辙，不知其不胜任也') overrate oneself and try to accomplish sth. one is not capable of. The phrase originates in the line in *Zhuangzi·Man in the World*: 'Don't you know that when the mantis, in a moment of rage, raised its arms to stop the turning wheel of a chariot, it did not know that it was doing something it was not capable of.' also 螳臂挡车 táng bì dǎng chē

【螳螂】tángláng 昆虫,全身绿色或土黄色,头呈三角形,活动灵便,触角呈丝状,胸部细长,翅两对,前腿呈镰刀状。捕食害虫,对农业有益。有的地区叫刀螂。mantis; mantid (*Paratenodera sinensis* or *Mantis religiosa*); green or yellowish brown predatory insect having a triangular head, threadlike feelers, slender chest, two pairs of wings, and sickle-shaped forelimbs, regarded as a beneficial insect because it prey on pest insects; known in some regions as 刀螂 dāoláng

【螳螂捕蝉,黄雀在后】tángláng bǔ chán, huángquè zài hòu 螳螂正要捉蝉,不知道黄雀在后面正想吃它 mantis stalks the cicada, unaware of the oriole behind it;〈比喻 *fig.*〉只看见前面有利可图,不知道祸害就在后面(语出《韩诗外传》卷十:'螳螂方欲食蝉,而不知黄雀在后,举其颈欲啄而食之也') covet gains ahead, unaware of danger behind. The phrase originates in volume 10 of *Han Ying's Illustrations of Didactic Application of the Book of Songs*: 'As the mantis was about to stalk the cicada, it was unaware that the oriole was right behind it, craning its neck and ready to peck at and prey on it.'

tǎng (ㄊㄤˇ)

帑 tǎng〈书 *fml.*〉国库里的钱财;公款 state treasury; government money: 国～ state treasury|公～public fund
〈古 *arch.*〉same as 孥(nú)

倘(儻) tǎng 倘若 if; supposing; in case: ～有困难,当再设法。If you have any difficult, we'll think about another way of doing it.
☞ cháng on p. 219

【倘或】tǎnghuò same as 倘若 tǎngruò

【倘来之物】tǎng lái zhī wù 无意中得到的或不应得而得到的钱财 windfall; sudden, unexpected piece of good fortune or personal gain

【倘然】tǎngrán same as 倘若 tǎngruò

【倘若】tǎngruò〈连词 *conj.*〉表示假设 if: 你～不信,就亲自去看看吧。If you don't believe it, you can go and take a look.

【倘使】tǎngshǐ same as 倘若 tǎngruò

淌 tǎng 往下流 drip; trickle: ～血 bleeding|～眼泪 shed tears|天气太热,身上直～汗。It was so hot that we kept dripping with sweat.|木桶漏水,～了一地。The wooden pail leaked, so that water ran all over the place.

惝 tǎng '惝'(chǎng)的又音 another pronunciation of the Chinese character 惝 chǎng

傥(儻) tǎng ❶ same as 倘(tǎng) ❷ ☞ 倜傥(tìtǎng) on p. 1886

【傥荡】tǎngdàng〈书 *fml.*〉放荡 debauch; sow one's wild oats

镋(钂) tǎng〈古代 *arch.*〉兵器,跟叉相似 weapon, resembling a fork

躺 tǎng 身体倒在地上或其他物体上。也指车辆、器具等倒在地上 recline; lie; place oneself at rest in a flat, horizontal, or recumbent position; recline; (of vehicle, object, etc.) lie flat on the ground: ～在地头休息 lie on the edge of a field for a rest|一棵大树横～在路上。A big tree lay across the road.

【躺柜】tǎngguì 一种平放的较矮的柜子,长方形,上面有盖 chest; long low box with a lid on top

【躺椅】tǎngyǐ 靠背特别长而向后倾斜的椅子,人可以斜躺在上面 deck chair; sling chair

tàng (ㄊㄤˋ)

烫(燙) tàng ❶ 温度高的物体与皮肤接触使感觉疼痛 scald; burn: ～手 feel hot to the hand|～嘴 feel hot to the mouth|别让开水～着。Be careful not to let the hot water scald you. ❷ 利用温度高的物体使另一物体温度升高或发生其他变化 heat: ～酒(用热水暖酒) warm a cup of wine in hot water|～衣裳(用热熨斗使衣服平整) iron or press clothes ❸ 物体温度高 very hot; scalding; piping hot: 这水太～。The water is too hot. ❹ 指烫发 perm; have one's hair permed: 电～permanent hair styling effected by electric rollers; electric perm

【烫发】tàng//fà 用热能或药水使头发拳曲美观 perm; give hair a permanent by using heat or certain liquid chemical

【烫花】tànghuā 烙花 pyrograph; branded flowers

【烫金】tàngjīn 在印刷品等上面烫出金色的文字或图案。方法是先把文字或图案制成金属凸版,用火或烫金电炉烘热后,在铺着金箔的印刷品等上面压印。bronzing; art to coat a book with golden letters or patterns by heating relief printing metal plate on fire or electric heater and applying it directly to a thin foil of gold or alloy of copper and zinc

【烫蜡】tàng//là 在地板、家具等表面撒上蜡屑,烤化后弄平,可以增加光泽 (of floor, furniture, etc.) polish with melted wax; wax

【烫面】tàngmiàn 用很烫的水和(huò)的面 dough made with boiling water: ～卷儿 steamed bread rolls|～饺儿 steamed dumplings made of dough prepared with boiling water

【烫伤】tàngshāng 无火焰的高温物体(如开水、热油)接触身体而引起组织的损伤 scald; injury caused by contact with a flameless object with high temperature such as boiling water and heated oil

【烫手】tàng//shǒu 〈比喻 *fig.*〉事情难办 troublesome; sticky; knotty: 他感到这个问题有些～。He felt he was confronted with a sticky business.

【烫头】tàng//tóu same as 烫发 tàng//fà

趟 tàng ❶〈量词 *classifier*〉表示走动的次数 [indicating trip or trips made]: 他到成都去了一～。He made a trip to Chengdu. | 今天夜里还有一～车。There's another train tonight. 注意 **NOTE**: 方言中不限于走动。In dialects the meaning of this word does not limit to trip or trips. For example: 看一～take a look | 洗一～have a wash | 约过他三～。(I) have made three appointments with him. ❷ (～儿 tàngr)行进的行列 procession: 跟不上～cannot catch up with the procession ❸〈方 *dial.*〉〈量词 *classifier*〉用于成行的东西 [indicating sth. in row or rows]: 半～街 half of the entire length of a street | 一～栏杆 a railing | 两～桌子 two rows of desks | 几～大字 several lines of big Chinese characters ☞ tāng on p. 1864

【趟马】tàngmǎ 戏曲表演骑着马走或跑的一套程式动作 stylized stage movements indicating trotting or galloping on horseback

tāo (ㄊㄠ)

叨 tāo 受到(好处) have the benefit of; be honoured with; receive; same as 沾 zhān ④: ～光 feel much obliged to sb. | ～教。Thanks a lot for your advice. ☞ dāo on p. 390 and dáo on p. 391

【叨光】tāo//guāng〈客套话 *pol.*〉沾光(受到好处,表示感谢) I'm much obliged to you.

【叨教】tāojiào〈客套话 *pol.*〉领教(受到指教,表示感谢) Thanks a lot for your advice.

【叨扰】tāorǎo〈客套话 *pol.*〉打扰(受到款待,表示感谢) Thanks for having us.

涛(濤) tāo 大的波浪 surging waves; billows: 波～billowing waves | 惊～骇浪 tempestuous waves

绦(縧、絛、縚) tāo 绦子 ribbon; braid: 丝～silk ribbon | ～带 ribbon

【绦虫】tāochóng 扁形动物,身体柔软,像带子,由许多节片构成,每个节片都有雌雄两性生殖器。常见的是有钩绦虫和无钩绦虫两种,都能附着在宿主的肠道里。成虫寄生在人体内,幼虫叫囊虫,多寄生在猪、牛等动物体内,也能寄生在人体内。tapeworm (*Taenia*); cestode; parasitic flatworm having a long belt-like flat body consisting of many segments each having both female and male reproductive organs, with or without a specialized organ of attachment at one end and capable of attaching itself to the host's intestines, the imago living in the human body while the larvae oft. live in the body of either a human body or the body of a pig, cattle, or other animals

【绦子】tāo·zi 用丝线编织成的圆的或扁平的带子,可以镶衣服、枕头、窗帘等的边 silk ribbon; round or flat silk lace for decorating clothing, pillow or window curtain

焘(燾) tāo '焘'(dào)的又音,多用于人名 another pronunciation of 焘 dào, used mostly in a person's name

掏(搯) tāo ❶ 用手或工具伸进物体的口,把东西弄出来 draw out; pull out; fish out: ～钱 take money from a pocket | ～耳朵 pick one's ears | ～口袋 empty one's pocket | ～麻雀窝 go sparrow nesting ❷ 挖 dig: 在墙上～一个洞 bore a hole into a wall ☞ 淘[1] táo on p. 1871

【掏底】tāo//dǐ 探明底细;摸底 find out the real intention or situation

【掏窟窿】tāo kū·long〈方 *dial.*〉〈比喻 *fig.*〉借债;负债 run, get and fall into debt

【掏心】tāoxīn 指发自内心 from the bottom of one's heart: 说句～的话,你真不该那样对他。To be honest, you shouldn't have treated him like that.

【掏腰包】tāo yāobāo ❶ 在腰包里掏(钱),多指出钱 foot the bill: 今天这顿饭我付钱,不用你～。This meal is on me — you don't have to foot the bill. ❷ 指小偷从别人腰包里偷东西 (of a thief) pickpocket

滔 tāo 大水弥漫 inundate; flood: 白浪～天 billowing whitecaps

【滔滔】tāotāo ❶ 形容大水滚滚 torrential: 白浪～,无边无际(of a lake, ocean, or river)skyfuls of white froth surging from horizon to horizon ❷ 形容连续不断(多指话多 oft. talkative) talk a blue streak: 口若悬河,～不绝 talk on and on in a flow of eloquence

【滔天】tāotiān ❶ 形容波浪极大(of waves) skyful: 波浪～skyfuls of billows ❷ 形容罪恶、灾祸极大(of crime) monstrous; heinous: 罪恶～atrocious crime | ～大祸 catastrophic trouble

韬(韜、弢) tāo〈书 *fml.*〉❶ 弓或剑的套子(of a sword) sheath; (of a bow) case ❷〈比喻 *fig.*〉隐藏 conceal; hide: ～光养晦 hide one's capacities and bide one's time ❸ 兵法 stratagem: 六～Six Strategies | ～略 strategies and tactics

【韬光养晦】tāo guāng yǎng huì〈比喻 *fig.*〉隐藏才能,不使外露 hide one's talent and bide one's time

【韬晦】tāohuì〈书 *fml.*〉收敛锋芒,隐藏行迹;韬光养晦 conceal one's true intentions or whereabouts: ～之计 the strategy of concealment

【韬略】tāolüè《六韬》、《三略》都是古代的兵书，后来称用兵的计谋为韬略 strategies and tactics, a phrase derived from the titles of two ancient Chinese books on the art of war, *Six Strategies* and *Three Tactics*

饕 tāo〈书 *fml.*〉贪财；贪食 greedy for money or food：老～（贪食者）hardened gourmand

【饕餮】tāotiè ❶ 传说中的一种凶恶贪食的野兽，古代铜器上面常用它的头部形状做装饰，叫做饕餮纹 *taotie*; vicious and rapacious animal in Chinese mythology. The *taotie*-mask, known as *taotie* pattern, is a common decorative pattern on ancient Chinese bronzeware. ❷〈比喻 *fig.*〉凶恶贪婪的人 ferocious and cruel person ❸〈比喻 *fig.*〉贪吃的人 glutton; gourmand

táo（ㄊㄠˊ）

匋 táo〈书 *fml.*〉same as 陶 táo（陶器 earthenware）

咷 táo 哭 ululate; wail：号（háo）～wail

逃（迯） táo ❶ 逃跑；逃走 escape; flee; run away：～匿 go into hiding｜～脱 make good one's escape ❷ 逃避 evade; dodge; shun：～荒 flee from famine｜～学 play truant

【逃奔】táobèn 逃走（到别的地方）run away (to another place)：～他乡 flee home and settle in another place

【逃避】táobì 躲开不愿意或不敢接触的事物 evade; shirk; run away from：～斗争 evade a struggle｜～现实 turn a blind eye to reality｜～责任 shirk one's responsibility

【逃兵】táobīng ❶ 私自脱离部队的士兵 deserter ❷〈比喻 *fig.*〉因怕困难而脱离工作岗位的人 quitter; sb. who flinches from difficulty

【逃窜】táocuàn 逃跑流窜 run away：狼狈～flee helter-skelter

【逃遁】táodùn 逃跑；逃避 flee; escape：仓皇～flee in panic

【逃反】táo//fǎn〈方 *dial.*〉跑反 flee from war or banditry

【逃犯】táofàn 未捕获或捕获后逃亡的犯人 fugitive：追捕～track down a fugitive; manhunt

【逃荒】táo//huāng 因遇灾荒而跑到外乡谋生 flee from one's famine-stricken homeland

【逃婚】táohūn 为逃避不自主的婚姻，在结婚前离家出走 run away from an arranged marriage

【逃课】táo//kè 学生有意不到课堂上课（of a student）cut classes

【逃命】táo//mìng 逃出危险的环境以保全生命 run for one's life; scramble for safety

【逃难】táo//nàn 为躲避灾难而逃往别处 flee from a disaster; be a refugee

【逃匿】táonì 逃跑并躲藏起来 go into hiding：～山林 go into hiding in a wooded mountain

【逃跑】táopǎo 为躲避不利于自己的环境或事物而离开 make good one's escape：越狱～jailbreak

【逃票】táopiào 乘车、船时有意不买票 get a bus or boat ride without buying a ticket：乘客～，照章罚款。Passengers without a ticket shall be fined according to rules.

【逃散】táosàn 逃亡失散（of a family, friends, etc.）lose contact while escaping from war or turmoil：寻找～的亲人 look for loved ones with whom one has lost contact during an escape effort

【逃生】táoshēng 逃出危险的环境以求生存 run for one's life：死里～narrowly escape death｜出外～leave home and run for one's life

【逃税】táo//shuì 逃避纳税 tax evasion; evade tax：不法商人～、漏税。Lawless merchants are given to tax evasion.

【逃脱】táotuō ❶ 逃离（险地）；逃跑 escape; make good one's escape：从虎口中～出来 escape from danger｜刚抓住的逃犯又～了。The fugitive that had just been caught escaped once again. ❷ 摆脱 shirk; evade：～罪责 evade one's responsibility for an offence

【逃亡】táowáng 逃走而流浪在外 go into exile：四散～flee in all directions｜～他乡 run away from home

【逃席】táoxí 在宴会中因怕劝酒而离开 take French leave during a banquet (to avoid being pressed to drink)：借故～leave a banquet under a pretext

【逃学】táo//xué 学生无故不上学 play truant; cut class

【逃逸】táoyì〈书 *fml.*〉逃跑 escape; run away; abscond

【逃债】táo//zhài 躲债 dodge or avoid a creditor

【逃之夭夭】táo zhī yāoyāo《诗经·周南·桃夭》有'桃之夭夭'一句，'桃'、'逃'同音，借来说逃跑，是诙谐的说法 decamp; make one's geteway, a humorous derivation from the homophonous line in *The Book of Songs*·*Folksongs of South of Zhou*·*Like the Slender Peach*: 'Like the Slender peach, lururiant and beautiful'...

【逃走】táozǒu same as 逃跑 táopǎo

洮 táo 洮水河（Táoshuǐ Hé），水名，在甘肃 Taoshuihe, name of a river in Gansu Province

桃 táo ❶ 桃树，落叶小乔木，品种很多。小枝光滑，叶长椭圆形，花单生，粉红色，果实略呈球形，表面有短绒毛，味甜，是一种常见的水果。核仁可入药。peach (*Prunus persica*); small defoliating tree that comes in a big variety, has smooth twigs, elongated oval leaves, and solitary pink flowers, and bears a ball-resembling soft, juicy fruit having yellow flesh, downy, red-tinted yellow skin, and a deeply sculptured stone that is of medical value ❷ (～儿 táor)这种植物的果实 peach; fruit of the peach tree ❸ (～儿 táor)形状像桃儿的东西 sth. resembling a peach: 棉～cotton boll ❹ 指核桃 walnut: ～酥 walnut kernel shortbread

【桃符】táofú 〈古代 *arch.*〉在大门上挂的两块画着门神或题着门神名字的桃木板,认为能压邪。后来在上面贴春联,因此借指春联。peachwood charms bearing the picture of the Guardian God of the Gate or his name, hung on the gate on lunar New Year's Eve to ward off evil; Spring Festival couplets pasted on the gate

【桃红】táohóng 像桃花的颜色;粉红 pink; colour of the peach flower

【桃花雪】táohuāxuě 桃花开时下的雪;春雪 spring snow; snowfall while peach trees are blooming

【桃花汛】táohuāxùn 桃花盛开时发生的河水暴涨 spring flood; flood occurring during the time of the year when peach trees are blooming; also 桃汛 táoxùn, 春汛 chūnxùn or 桃花水 táohuāshuǐ

【桃花源】táohuāyuán ☞ 世外桃源 shì wài táoyuán on p. 1753

【桃花运】táohuāyùn 指男子在爱情方面的运气 (of a man) luck in love

【桃李】táolǐ 〈比喻 *fig.*〉所教的学生 peaches and plums — one's students: ～盈门 have a roomful of students | ～满天下 (of a teacher's successful career) have students in every nook and cranny of the world

【桃李不言,下自成蹊】táo lǐ bù yán, xià zì chéng xī 〈比喻 *fig.*〉为人诚挚,自会有强烈的感召力而深得人心 the peach and the plum do not speak, yet a path is worn beneath them — a man of sincerity attracts admiration

【桃仁】táorén (～儿 táorénr) ❶ 桃核儿(hú r)的仁,可以入药 peach kernel, used as a medicine ❷ 核桃的仁儿 walnut meat

【桃色】táosè ❶ 粉红色 pink ❷ 形容跟不正当的男女关系有关的事情 illicit love affairs: ～新闻 grapevine story about extramarital affairs or sex scandals

【桃子】táo·zi 桃树的果实 peach

陶1 táo ❶ 用黏土烧制的材料,质地比瓷质松软,有吸水性 pottery; earthenware; absorbent ware shaped from clay and hardened by heat, and softer than porcelain: ～器 earthenware | ～俑 terracotta figurines | 彩～ painted pottery ❷ 制造陶器 pottery making: ～冶 make pottery and smelt metal ❸ 〈比喻 *fig.*〉教育、培养 cultivate; educate: 熏～ have a good influence on ❹ (Táo)姓 a surname

陶2 táo 快乐 contented and happy: ～然 happy and carefree | ～醉 revel in ☞ yáo on p. 2228

【陶瓷】táocí 陶器和瓷器的统称 ceramics; general term for pottery and porcelain

【陶管】táoguǎn 用黏土制成的管子,内外涂釉,烧制而成,主要用做排污水的管道 earthenware pipe; glazed pipe shaped from clay and hardened by heat, used for sewage-drainage purposes; 通称 generally known as 缸管 gāngguǎn

【陶钧】táojūn 〈书 *fml.*〉❶ 制陶器时所用的转轮 pottery's wheel ❷ 〈比喻 *fig.*〉造就人材 train useful people

【陶器】táoqì 陶质的器皿,现代用的陶器大多涂上粗釉 pottery; earthenware; modern pottery, usu. with coarse glaze

【陶然】táorán 形容舒畅快乐的样子 happy and carefree: ～自得 happy and content with one's lot

【陶塑】táosù 用黏土塑造后烧成的人和动物形象 ceramic sculpture in the image of people or animal; pottery figurine: ～群像 ensemble of pottery figures

【陶陶】táotáo 形容快乐 happy-to-lucky: 其乐～be delighted with sth.

【陶土】táotǔ 烧制陶器或粗瓷器的高岭土 potter's clay; pottery clay; kaolin

【陶文】táowén 〈古代 *arch.*〉陶器上的文字,多为人名、官名、地名、吉祥话、制造年月等 inscription on pottery, mostly name of people, official title, name of a place, auspicious remark, date of manufacturing, etc.

【陶冶】táoyě 烧制陶器和冶炼金属 make pottery and smelt metal; 〈比喻 *fig.*〉给人的思想、性格以有益的影响 exert a favourable influence on sb.'s thinking or character: ～情操 mould a person's temperament

【陶铸】táozhù 〈书 *fml.*〉❶ 烧制陶器和铸造金属器物 mould; cast ❷ 〈比喻 *fig.*〉造就人才 bring forth talents

【陶醉】táozuì 很满意地沉浸在某种境界或思想活动中 revel in; be intoxicated with: 自我～revel in one's own achievement | ～于山川景色之中 be delighted in the beauty of the landscape

萄 táo 指葡萄 grape: ～糖 glucose | ～酒 grape wine

梼(檮) táo ☞ below

【梼昧】táomèi 〈书 *fml.*〉愚昧 (多用做谦辞 oft. hum.) ignorant; benighted: 自惭～think oneself ignorant | 不揣～despite my ignorance

【梼杌】táowù 〈古代 *arch.*〉传说中的猛兽,借指凶恶的人 ferocious animal with man's face, tiger's paws and boar's tusks; vicious person

啕 táo 哭 wail: 号(háo)～howl; yowl

秭 táo [秭黍](táoshǔ)〈方 *dial.*〉高粱 sorghum (*Sorghum*)

淘[1] (❷掏) táo ❶ 用器物盛颗粒状的东西,加水搅动,或放在水里簸动,使除去杂质 wash (things in granules such as grain) in a sieve:～米 wash rice|～金 gold panning ❷〈方 *dial.*〉到旧货市场寻觅购买 comb second-hand markets for sth. to buy:～旧书 buy used books ❸ 从深的地方舀出污水、泥沙、粪便等 dredge; clean sewage, silt, night soil, etc. from the depth of a place:～井 dredge a well|～缸 clean a vat|～茅厕 remove night soil from a latrine

☞ 掏 tāo on p.1869

淘[2] táo ❶ 耗费 consume; tax (one's energy):～神 bothersome; trying ❷〈方 *dial.*〉顽皮 mischievous; naughty:这孩子真～! The child is really naughty.

【淘换】táo·huan 寻觅;设法寻求(某种东西)(of sth.) comb; look high and low; rifle through; search for:好不容易给你～着这本书。I've just managed to get a copy of this book for you.

【淘金】táo//jīn 用水选的方法从沙子里选出沙金。也泛指设法捞取高额的钱财。pan for gold; use an open, metal dish to separate gold from gravel by washing; gold rush; rush for high profit

【淘箩】táoluó 用来淘米或盛东西的箩 basket for washing rice in or containing sth.

【淘气】táo//qì ❶ 顽皮 naughty; mischievous:这孩子很聪明,就是有些～。The child is very bright, but a bit too mischievous.|这孩子淘起气来,净搞恶作剧。The kid is given to foul play when he gets real naughty. ❷〈方 *dial.*〉生闲气;惹气 pique; be exasperated

【淘神】táoshén 使人耗费精神 get on one's nerves; taxing:这孩子够大人～的。That kid really gets on my nerves.

【淘汰】táotài 去坏的留好的;去掉不适合的,留下适合的 dispense with; leave out; throw out:～旧产品 phase out old products|他在第二轮比赛中被～。He was eliminated in the second round of competition.

【淘汰赛】táotàisài 体育运动竞赛方式之一,按排定的次序比赛,失败者被淘汰,获胜者继续参加比赛,到定出冠军为止 knock-out rounds; elimination game; form of sports competition in which athletes compete in a prescribed order, with losers being phased out and winners retained until the champion is chosen

绹 táo ❶〈书 *fml.*〉绳索 rope ❷〈方 *dial.*〉用绳索捆 bind with rope

醄 táo ☞ [酕醄](máotáo) on p.1309

鼗(鞉、鞀) táo〈书 *fml.*〉拨浪鼓 rattle drum

tǎo (ㄊㄠˇ)

讨 tǎo ❶ 讨伐 launch a punitive expedition against:征～ mount a punitive expedition ❷ 索取;请求 come down on; ask for; request:～饭 go begging|～债 demand repayment of a debt|～饶 beg for mercy|～教 consult; seek advice ❸ 娶(of a man) marry:～老婆 take a wife ❹ 招惹 provoke:～厌 be a nuisance|～人喜欢 be likable; be lovable|自～苦吃 ask for trouble and get it ❺ 讨论 discuss:商～ consultation|研～ research|探～ explore

【讨伐】tǎofá 出兵攻打(敌人或叛逆) make war on (an enemy or rebels)

【讨饭】tǎo//fàn 要饭 beg for food; go panhandling:～的(乞丐) beggar; panhandler

【讨好】tǎo//hǎo (～儿 tǎo//hǎor) ❶ 迎合别人,取得别人的欢心或称赞 bow and scrape; lick sb.'s boots; be obsequious:～卖乖 be obsequious and show off one's cleverness|你用不着讨他的好。You don't have to ingratiate yourself with him. ❷ 得到好效果(多用于否定 oft. in the negative) have one's effort rewarded:费力不～ get no thanks for one's hard work

【讨还】tǎohuán 要回(欠下的钱、东西等) get sth. back:～血债 demand payment of a blood debt; make sb. pay for his bloody crimes

【讨价】tǎo//jià 要价 charge; ask a price

【讨价还价】tǎo jià huán jià〈比喻 *fig.*〉接受任务或举行谈判时提出种种条件,斤斤计较 bargain; haggle; also 要价还价 yào jià huán jià

【讨教】tǎojiào 请求人指教 consult; ask for advice:有个问题向您～。I'd like to ask you for advice on a problem.

【讨论】tǎolùn 就某一问题交换意见或进行辩论 confer; discuss:～会 discuss meeting|展开～ engage in a discussion|～工作计划 thrash out a work plan

【讨便宜】tǎo pián·yi 存心占便宜 seek undue advantage; try to gain sth. at the expense of others; look for a bargain

【讨平】tǎopíng 讨伐平定(叛乱) quell a rebellion; put down:～叛匪 suppress the rebel bandits

【讨乞】tǎoqǐ 向人要钱要饭等 go begging; beg alms:沿街～ go panhandling in the streets

【讨巧】tǎoqiǎo 做事不费力而占便宜 act smart to get what one wants; get the best for oneself at the least expense; choose the easy way out

【讨俏】tǎo//qiào (艺术表演、做事)使人觉得俏皮 try to be witty or humorous (in performance, doing things, etc.)

【讨亲】tǎo//qīn〈方 *dial.*〉娶亲 (of a man)

get married; take a wife

【讨情】tǎo//qíng 〈方 *dial.*〉求情 plead for sb.; beg sb. off:～告饶 plead for leniency; beg for pardon

【讨饶】tǎo//ráo 求饶 beg for mercy; ask for forgiveness

【讨生活】tǎo shēnghuó 寻求生路;混日子 eke out a living; drift along

【讨嫌】tǎo//xián 惹人厌烦 be a pain in the neck:这人整天东家长西家短的,真～! The chap is always schmoozing about what's going on in other people's families. What a nuisance! also 讨人嫌 tǎorénxián

【讨厌】tǎo//yàn ❶ 惹人厌烦 be a pain in the neck:这人说话总是这么啰唆,真～! He's always rambling like that. How annoying! ❷ 事情难办令人心烦 nasty; troublesome:这种病很～,目前还不容易彻底治好。This is a very nasty disease for which there is not complete cure. ❸ 厌恶;不喜欢 dislike; loathe:他～这地方春天的风沙。He is disgusted by the sand storm that hits the place in spring.

【讨债】tǎo//zhài 索取借给人的钱财 demand repayment of a debt:上门～confront sb. with demand for debt repayment

【讨账】tǎo//zhàng ❶ same as 讨债 tǎo//zhài ❷〈方 *dial.*〉索取买东西欠的钱 claim payment due (for purchase)

韬 tǎo [韬黍](tǎoshǔ)〈方 *dial.*〉高粱 sorghum

tào (ㄊㄠˋ)

套 tào ❶ (～儿 tàor) same as 套子 tào·zi ①:手～gloves | 书～slipcover | 封～big envelope for holding documents, books, etc. ❷ 罩在外面 cover with; slip over; encase in:～上一件毛衣 slip on a pullover ❸ 罩在外面的 cover:～鞋 galoshes | ～裤 leggings ❹ 互相衔接或重叠 overlap; interlink:～种 interplanting | ～色 colour process | ～间 apartment; flat ❺ 河流或山势弯曲的地方(多用于地名 oft. used in place names) river bend; curve in a mountain:河～Hetao (Great Bend of the Yellow River) | 葫芦～Hulutao Bend ❻〈方 *dial.*〉(～儿 tàor) same as 套子 tào·zi ②:被～cotton padding of a quilt; quilt padding | 袄～padded lining of a winter coat ❼〈方 *dial.*〉把棉花、丝绵等平整地装入被褥或袄里缝好 pad a quilt or jacket with cotton or silk floss ❽ (～儿 tàor)拴牲口的两根皮绳或麻绳,一端拴在牲口脖子夹板或轭上,另一端拴在车上 traces; harness; two side leather straps or hemp ropes connecting a harnessed draft animal to a vehicle or whiffletree:牲口～harness for a draught animal | 大车～cart harness | ～绳 lasso; noose ❾ 用套拴系 hitch up an animal to a cart:～车 harness an animal to a cart | ～马 lasso a horse ❿ 套购 purchase by fraudulent means:～外汇 illegal purchase of foreign exchange ⓫ 用绳子等结成的环状物 noose; loop ⓬ 模仿 imitate; ape:～公式 model after a formula | 这是从现成文章上～下来的。This was written in imitation of another article. ⓭ (～儿 tàor) same as 套子 tào·zi ③:～语 cliché; jargon | 客～civilities; pleasantries ⓮ 引出(真情实话) coax a secret out of sb.:想法儿～他的话 trick sb. into telling the truth ⓯ 拉拢 woo:～交情 solicit the good will of sb. | ～近乎 pay one's addresses to sb. ⓰ 事物配合成的整体 set:～装 suit | ～曲 divertimento | 成～设备 complete sets of equipment ⓱〈量词 *classifier*〉用于成组的事物 [indicating series or sets of things]:一～制度 a series of systems | 一～家具 a set of furniture | 一～课本 a set of textbooks ⓲ 用丝锥或板牙切削螺纹 [use a tap or screw die to cut a thread]

【套版】tào//bǎn 按照印刷页折叠的顺序,把印刷版排列在印刷机上 register; align plates on a printing machine

【套版】tàobǎn 套印用的版 process plate; colour plate

【套包】tàobāo 马、驴、骡拉车或碾场时,套在牲口脖子上的东西,用皮革或布制成,内装棕、糠等 collar; restraining band of leather or cloth padded with palm fibre or bran and put around the neck of an animal pulling a cart or grindstone; also 套包子 tàobāo·zi

【套裁】tàocái 裁制两件以上的服装时,在一块布料上作合理的安排,尽量减少废料 make suitable arrangements on a piece of cloth so that two or more jackets, dresses, etc. can be cut out of it

【套餐】tàocān 搭配好的成套供应的饭食 table d'hote; set meal:吃～eat table d' hote

【套车】tào//chē 把车上的套套在拉车的牲口身上 hitch up a draught animal to a cart

【套房】tàofáng ❶ 套间 inner room:一间～a room in a flat ❷ 由卧室、客厅、厨房、厕所等组成的成套住房 suite:购买豪华型～一套 purchase a suite of luxury apartment

【套服】tàofú same as 套装 tàozhuāng

【套耕】tàogēng 用两张犁同时耕地,第二张犁顺着第一张犁犁出来的沟再犁一次,目的是耕得更深 operate two ploughs simultaneously, the second one along the line of the first so as to plough deeper; also 套犁 tàolí

【套购】tàogòu 用不正当的手段购买国家计划控制的商品并从中牟利 buy up state-controlled commodities by fraud for profiteering

【套红】tàohóng 用套印方法在报刊版面的某部分印成红颜色,使醒目 print part of a newspaper or magazine page in red:～标题 print a headline in red | 报头～red-printed newspaper masthead

【套话】tàohuà ❶ 指文章、书信中按旧套套写的语句；套语 set expressions for the writing of articles or letters ❷ 特指套用现成的结论或格式而没有实际内容的话 cliché; jargon：大会发言要开门见山，～、空话都应省去。When addressing a conference, make sure to come straight to the point and avoid all the cliché and empty talks.

【套汇】tàohuì ❶ 非法购买、换取外汇 buy foreign exchange by illegal means ❷ 外汇市场上的一种投机活动，即利用不同地点的外汇市场上同一种外汇的汇价不同，在低价市场上买进，再在高价市场上卖出，取得差额收益 arbitrage; purchase of foreign exchange on one market at a lower price for immediate resale on another market at a higher price in order to profit from the price discrepancy

【套间】tàojiān（～儿 tàojiānr）住宅中几间相连的屋子的两头的房间（或衔接在相连的屋子的一头的后面），也指两间相连的屋子里头的一间，一般比较窄小，没有直通外面的门 small room opening off another; inner room

【套交情】tào jiāo·qing 跟不熟识的人拉拢感情 woo; draw in; pull sb. over to one's side

【套近乎】tào jìn·hu 和不太熟识的人拉拢关系，表示亲近（多含贬义 oft. derog.）try to chum up with sb; cotton up to; also 拉近乎 lā jìn·hu

【套裤】tàokù 套在裤子外面的只有裤腿的裤子，一般是棉的或夹的，作用是使腿部暖和而又便于行动。也有单的，用粗布、塑料、油布等做成，用来保护裤子或防雨。trouser legs; leggings; leg covering usu. cotton-padded or lined, worn over trousers to keep legs warm without impeding action, or made of coarse cloth, plastics or oilcloth to protect trousers or keep them from getting wet during a rainfall

【套犁】tàolí same as 套耕 tàogēng

【套耧】tàolóu 用旧式耧耩地而行距较宽时，为了密植，在两行中间再耩一次 sow an additional row between two rows using an old-fashioned drill barrow for close planting

【套路】tàolù 指编制成套的武术动作 prescribed sequence of martial arts movements：少林武术～serial Shaolin boxing stunts ◇改革的新～ new package of reform measures

【套马杆】tàomǎgān 牧民套牲口用的长木杆，一头拴着用皮绳做的活套 lasso; long wooden pole with a running leather noose at one end, for catching horses or other domestic animals; also 套马杆子 tàomǎgān·zi

【套曲】tàoqǔ 由若干乐曲或乐章组合成套的大型器乐曲或声乐曲 divertissement; divertimento; full-length instrumental or vocal music having a number of short movements

【套裙】tàoqún 下身是裙子的女式套装 woman's suit：西式～ Western-style woman's suit

【套色】tào//shǎi 彩色印刷的方法，用平版或凸版分次印刷，每次印一种颜色，利用红、黄、蓝三种原色重叠印刷，可以印出各种颜色 chromatography; colour process; printing method using plane or relief plates to properly position the three primitive colours of red, yellow and blue one on top of the other to produce different colours：～印刷 colour printing

【套衫】tàoshān 不开襟的针织上衣 pullover; knitwear that is put on by being drawn over the head：男～man's pullover | 女～woman's pullover; also 套头衫 tàotóushān

【套数】tàoshù ❶ 戏曲或散曲中连贯成套的曲子 sequence of songs, dramatic or non-dramatic, with one rhyme and a common set of melodies ❷〈比喻 *fig.*〉成系统的技巧或手法 series of skills or tricks ❸ same as 套子 tào·zi ③

【套套】tào·tao〈方 *dial.*〉办法；着数 methods; tricks：老～old approaches

【套问】tàowèn 不让对方察觉自己的目的，拐弯抹角地盘问 find out by asking seemingly casual questions; tactfully sound sb. out

【套鞋】tàoxié 原指套在鞋外面的防雨的胶鞋，后来泛指防雨的胶鞋 galoshes; waterproof overshoes

【套袖】tàoxiù 套在衣袖外面的、单层的袖子，作用是保护衣袖 oversleeve; single-layered sleeves worn to protect coat sleeves

【套印】tàoyìn 一种印刷书籍图画的方法。在同一版面上用颜色不同的版分次印刷 process printing; use a set of plates to print different colours on the same page：朱墨～red-and-black printing

【套用】tàoyòng 模仿着应用（现成的办法等）apply mechanically; copy：～公式 apply the formula

【套语】tàoyǔ ❶ 客套话 polite remarks; pleasantries ❷ 流行的公式化的言谈 cliché：～滥调 platitude

【套种】tàozhòng 在某一种作物生长的后期，在行间播种另一种作物，以充分利用地力和生长期，增加产量 interplanting; planting of another crop between the rows of a crop during its late stage of growth so as to make full use of the land's fertility and the farming season and increase farm yield; also 套作 tàozuò

【套装】tàozhuāng 指上下身配套设计、用同一面料制作的服装，也有用不同面料搭配制作的。一般是成套出售。suit; a set of outer clothes of the same or matching material, consisting usu. of a jacket and trousers, and sold in complete set; also 套服 tàofú

【套子】tào·zi ❶ 做成一定形状的、罩在物体外面的东西 sheath; case：伞～umbrella sheath ❷〈方 *dial.*〉棉衣、棉被里的棉絮 cotton padding; wadding：棉花～cotton padding ❸ 应酬的话；陈陈相因的办法 polite remarks; established methods：俗～conventional pattern ❹

用绳子等结成的环状物 noose;〈比喻 *fig.*〉圈套 snare; trap

tè(ㄊㄜˋ)

忑 tè ☞ [忐忑] (tǎntè) on p.1860

忒 tè〈书 *fml.*〉差错 mistake; err:差~blunder; error

☞ tēi on p.1877 and tuī on p.1947

特[1] tè ❶ 特殊;超出一般 special; particular:奇~ extraordinary|~权 prerogatives|~等 top grade|能力~强 extraordinary ability ❷ 特地 especially:~意 purposely|~为 go out of one's way to ❸ 指特务(tè·wu) secret agent; spy:匪~enemy spy|防~anti-espionage work

特[2] tè〈书 *fml.*〉只;但 but; only:不~此也。This is not the only case.

【特别】tèbié ❶ 与众不同;不普通 unusual; out of the ordinary:~的式样 special pattern|他的脾气很~。He has an unusual temperament. ❷ 格外 especially; particularly:火车跑得~快。Trains travel exceptionally fast.|这个节目~吸引观众。This program is especially appealing to the audience. ❸ 特地 go out of one's way; for a special purpose; specially:散会的时候,厂长~把他留下来研究技术上的问题。When the meeting was dismissed, the factory director made a point of having him stay behind to study some technical problems. ❹ 尤其 especially:他喜欢郊游,~是骑自行车郊游。He loves to go outing, especially by bicycle.

【特别快车】tèbié-kuàichē 指停站少、行车时间比直达快车短的旅客列车 express train; express; special express;简称 abbr. 特快 tèkuài

【特产】tèchǎn 指某地或某国特有的或特别著名的产品 special local product; speciality; specialty

【特长】tècháng 特别擅长的技能或特有的工作经验 what one is skilled in; strong point; speciality:发挥~give scope to one's special skill

【特出】tèchū 特别出众;格外突出 outstanding; prominent:~的人才 outstanding talent|~的优点 outstanding strong points

【特此】tècǐ 公文、书信用语,表示为某件事特别在这里通知、公告、奉告等等(used in a document or formal letter) hereby

【特等】tèděng 等级最高的;最优良的 special grade or class; top grade:~舱 stateroom; deluxe cabin|~功臣 one who has rendered top-grade service|~射手 top-class sharpshooter

【特地】tèdì〈副词 *adv.*〉表示专为某件事 for a special purpose; specially:他昨天~来看你,你没在。He came specially to see you yesterday, but you were not in.

【特点】tèdiǎn 人或事物所具有的独特的地方 characteristic; distinguishing feature; peculiarity; trait:快餐的~就是快。The distinguishing feature of fast food is fastness|他的~是为人直爽。His trait is frankness.

【特定】tèdìng ❶ 特别指定的 specially designated (or appointed):~的人选 person specially designated for a post ❷ 某一个(人、时期、地方等)(of a person, period of time, place, etc.) specific; specified; given:~环境 specific environment(s); specific surroundings|在~的历史时期内可以用这一办法处理。This method can be used to handle things in a given historical period.

【特工】tègōng ❶ 特务工作 secret service:~人员 special agent; secret service personnel ❷ 从事特务工作的人 special agent; secret service personnel; people engaged in the secret service

【特护】tèhù ❶ (对重病人)格外精心护理(to a patient who suffered from serious illness) special nursing:~病房 special nursing ward|经过十多天的~,他终于脱险了。He was finally out of danger after more than ten days of intensified nursing. ❷ 对病人进行特殊护理的护士 special nurse; nurse who gives special nursing to a patient

【特化】tèhuà 动物在进化过程中,为了适应环境,专门向某一方面发展。特化了的动物不能再改变发展方向,例如现代的类人猿已经特化,不能再变成人。specialization; become adapted to meet a special condition, etc. In order to adapt itself to the environments, an animal develops along a specialized line, but a specialized animal cannot change its direction of specialization once again. For example, the modern anthropoid (ape), which has been specialized, cannot change itself to a man.

【特辑】tèjí 为特定主题而编辑的文字资料、报刊或电影 special issue of a periodical devoted to a special subject or a special collection of short films

【特技】tèjì ❶ 武术、马术、飞机驾驶等方面的特殊技能 stunt; trick; special skill in the martial arts, horsemanship, piloting, etc.:~表演 stunt performance ❷ 电影用语,指摄制特殊镜头的技巧,如利用玻璃箱的装置拍摄海底的景物,叠印人物和云雾的底片表现腾云驾雾(cinematography) special effects; skill in taking trick shots, such as taking submarine sights by means of a glass-box equipment, overprinting the negatives of a person, clouds and mist to show him mounting clouds and riding mist

【特价】tèjià 特别降低的价格 special offer, bargain price:~出售 sell at a bargain price

【特刊】tèkān 刊物、报纸为纪念某一节日、事件、

T

人物等而编辑的一期或一版 special issue (or number); special issue released by a magazine or a newspaper to mark a special day or event or commemorate sb.:元旦~ New Year's Day special issue

【特快】tèkuài ❶ 速度特别快的 express:~列车 express train|~邮件 express mail|开办长途电话~业务 open long-distance telephone express service ❷ 特别快车的简称 abbr. for 特别快车 tèbié-kuàichē

【特例】tèlì 特殊的事例 special case

【特洛伊木马】Tèluòyī mùmǎ ☞ 木马计 mùmǎjì on p.1375

【特派】tèpài (为办理某项事务)特地派遣;委派 specially appoint for a special assignment:~记者 special correspondent|~专人前往接洽 send somebody specially to take up the matter

【特区】tèqū 在政治、经济等方面实行特殊政策的地区 special zone; zone where special political or economic policies are adopted:经济~ special economic zone

【特权】tèquán 特殊的权利 privilege; prerogative:享有~ enjoy privileges

【特任】tèrèn 民国时期文官的第一等,在简任以上 appoint by special presidential order; first rank in the four-echelon officialdom in the Republic of China

【特色】tèsè 事物所表现的独特的色彩、风格等 salient feature; hallmark (or quality):民族~ distinctive national features|艺术~ artistic characteristics|他们的表演各有~。There's something special about each of their performances.

【特赦】tèshè 国家对某些有悔改表现的犯人或特定犯人减轻或免除刑罚 special pardon; special amnesty; mitigation or remitment of the punishment incurred on a specific convict or one who is mending his ways

【特使】tèshǐ 国家临时派遣的担任特殊任务的外交代表 special envoy; diplomatic envoy sent by a country on a special mission

【特殊】tèshū 不同于同类的事物或平常的情况的 special; particular; exceptional; different from similar things or what is commonplace:情形~ special situation|~照顾 special attention; special care; special consideration|~待遇 special treatment

【特体】tètǐ 体形特别的,有异于常人的(多指形体特别高大或肥胖 usu. referring to exceptionally large, tall or fat people)(of build or figure) exceptional size; distiuct; exceptionally large; exceptionally fat:加工~服装 make clothes of special sizes

【特为】tèwèi 特地 for a special purpose; specially:我~来请你们去帮忙。I've come specially to ask you for help.

【特务】tèwù 军队中指担任警卫、通讯、运输等特殊任务的,如特务员、特务连、特务营 special military task (or duty), such as security, communications, transportation, etc., assigned on men, a company, or a battalion

【特务】tè·wu 经过特殊训练,从事刺探情报、颠覆、破坏等活动的人 special (or secret) agent; spy; person having received special training for collecting secret information, carrying out subversive and sabotaging activities

【特效】tèxiào 特殊的效果;特殊的疗效 specially good effect; special efficacy:~药 specific drug; specific; effective cure

【特写】tèxiě ❶ 报告文学的一种形式,主要特点是描写现实生活中的真人真事,具有高度的真实性,但在细节上也可做适当的艺术加工 feature article or story; feature; form of reportage that is truthful in its coverage of real people and real events but also allows proper artistic treatment to details ❷ 电影艺术的一种手法,拍摄人或物的某一部分,使特别放大(多为人的面部表情)(cinematography) close-up; photographic, movie or television shot of part of a figure or a thing taken at very close range:~镜头 close-up (shot)

【特性】tèxìng 某人或某事物所特有的性质 specific property or characteristic:民族~ national characteristic

【特许】tèxǔ 特别许可 specially permit:~证 special permit; letters patent|非经~,一般商店不得经销此类商品。Without a special permit, no other shops are allowed to sell this category of goods.

【特异】tèyì ❶ 特别优异 distinct; exceptionally good; excellent; superfine:成绩~ excellent record (or performance); distinct results; (pass one's exam) with flying colours ❷ 特殊 peculiar; distinctive:他们都画花卉,但各有~的风格。They all paint flowers, but they each have their own distinctive styles.

【特异质】tèyìzhì 对某些药物发生过敏性反应的体质,例如有些人服用磺胺药物后发生呕吐、恶心、皮炎等症状 idiosyncrasy; any individual allergic reaction to a drug, that is different from the reaction of most people. For example, some people vomit, feel nauseated or suffer from dermatitis after taking sulfa drugs.

【特意】tèyì 特地 specially:这块衣料是他~托人从上海买来送给你的。He specially asked someone to buy this fabric in Shanghai for you.

【特约】tèyuē 特地约请或约定 engage by special arrangement:~记者 special correspondent|~稿 special contribution to a publication

【特征】tèzhēng 可以作为事物特点的征象、标志等 characteristic; feature; trait:艺术~ artistic characteristic|这个人的相貌有什么~? What are the features of the appearance of this man?

【特制】tèzhì 特地制造 specially made (for specific purpose or by special process):～香烟 specially made cigarettes

【特质】tèzhì 特有的性质或品质 special quality:在他身上仍然保留着某些农民的淳厚朴实的～。He still has some of the simplicity and honesty characteristic of farmers.

【特种】tèzhǒng 同类事物中特殊的一种 special type; particular kind:～兵 special force; special technical troops|～工艺 special arts and crafts; special handicraft products

【特种兵】tèzhǒngbīng 执行某种特殊任务的技术兵种的统称 special technical troops; special forces; technical forces carrying out special tasks

【特种工艺】tèzhǒng gōngyì 技艺性很高的传统手工艺产品,多为供人欣赏的陈设品或装饰品,如象牙玉石雕刻、景泰蓝等 special arts and crafts; special handicraft products (of a particular place); traditional art and craft products made with fine skills, mostly for ornaments or exhibits, as ivory carvings, jade carvings, cloisonné, etc.; 简称 abbr. 特艺 tèyì

【特种邮票】tèzhǒng yóupiào 邮政部门为了达到某种宣传目的而特别发行的邮票 special stamps issued for a particular propaganda purpose

铽 tè 金属元素,符号 Tb (terbium)。是一种稀土金属。银灰色。铽的化合物用做杀虫剂,也可用来治疗某些皮肤病。terbium (Tb); a silvery-grey, rare-earth metallic chemical element. Its compounds are used as insecticides or in treating certain skin diseases.

慝 tè 〈书 *fml.*〉邪恶;罪恶;恶念 evil; wickedness; viciousness; vice:隐～(人家不知道的罪恶) hidden vice or evil (unknown to others)

螣(螣) tè 古书上指吃苗叶的害虫 destructive insect that eats leaves of seedlings as described in ancient books
☞ 螣 téng on p. 1878

·te (·ㄊㄜ)

膩 ·te '膩'·de 的又音 another pronunciation for 膩·de; ☞ [肋膩] (lē·de) on p. 1164

tēi (ㄊㄟ)

忒 tēi '忒' tuī 的又音 another pronunciation for 忒 tuī
☞ tè on p. 1875

【忒儿】tēir 〈方 *dial.*〉〈拟声词 *onom.*〉形容鸟急促地振动翅膀的声音 sound of flapping wings:麻雀～一声就飞了。With a flap of its wings, the sparrow flew off.

tēng (ㄊㄥ)

熥 tēng 凉了的熟食再蒸或烤 heat up by steaming:～馒头 heat up steamed buns|把烙饼放在铛(chēng)上～～。Heat up the pancake on the pan.

鼟 tēng 〈拟声词 *onom.*〉形容鼓声 sound of a drumbeat

téng (ㄊㄥˊ)

疼 téng ❶ same as 痛 tòng ①:头～ have a headache|脚碰得很～,不能走路。My feet were badly hurt from the bump. I can hardly walk. ❷ 心疼;疼爱 love dearly; be fond of; dote on:奶奶最～小孙子。Granny dotes on her little grandson.|这孩子怪招人～的。This child is really lovable (or lovely).

【疼爱】téng'ài 关切喜爱 love dearly; be fond of; dote on:母亲最～小女儿。Mother dotes on her younger daughter more than anyone else.

【疼痛】téngtòng same as 痛 tòng ①

腾 téng ❶ 奔跑或跳跃 gallop; jump; prance:奔～ gallop; surge forward; (of a torrent) roar down|欢～ rejoice over; rejoicing; jubilation ❷ 升(到空中) rise; soar:升～ rise; soar|飞～ fly up; climb up quickly; soar up ❸ 使空(kòng) make room; clear out; vacate:～地方 make room|～出时间温功课 find time to review the lessons ❹ 用在某些动词后面,表示反复[used after certain verbs to indicate repeated actions]:翻～ toss up and down in one's mind|折～ turn from side to side; torment; cause physical or mental suffering|倒～ do something over and over again|闹～ clamorous; noisy ❺ (Téng)姓 a surname

【腾达】téngdá 〈书 *fml.*〉❶ 上升 rise; soar ❷ 指发迹,职位高升 make rapid advances in one's career, rise to power and position

【腾飞】téngfēi ❶ 飞腾 fly swiftly upward; soar:石壁上刻着～起舞的龙。A flying and dancing dragon is carved on the stone wall. ❷ 迅速向前发展 make rapid advance; develop rapidly:经济～ rapid economic development

【腾贵】ténggui (物价)飞涨 (of prices) hike up; soar; skyrocket:百物～。Prices are hiking up.

【腾空】téngkōng 向天空上升 soar; rise high into the air; rise to the sky:烈焰～。Blazing flames rose to the sky.|一个个气球～而起。

T

Balloons soared up one after another.

【腾挪】téngnuó 挪动(多指款项或地方) transfer (funds, etc.) to other use; move sth. from one place to another:专款专用,不得任意～。Funds earmarked for specific purposes are not to be transferred at will.|把仓库里的东西～一下好放水泥。Move the things in the storehouse to make room for the cement.

【腾腾】téngténg 形容气体上升的样子 steaming; seething; rise of gases:热气～ steaming hot; piping hot|烈焰～ raging flames ◇杀气～ bellicose; murderous; sabre-rattling; with blood in one's eyes

【腾涌】téngyǒng 水流迅急 swift current; swift flow:水势～。The water rushed forward.

【腾跃】téngyuè ❶ 奔腾跳跃 prance; bounce:骏马～。The fine horse pranced. ❷〈书 *fml.*〉(物价)飞涨(of prices) go up; rise:谷价～。The rice price has jumped up.

【腾越】téngyuè 跳跃越过 jump over:～障碍物 jump over obstacles

【腾云驾雾】téng yún jià wù ❶ 传说中指利用法术乘云雾飞行 (mythology) ride the clouds and mount the mist by means of magic power ❷ 形容奔驰迅速或头脑迷糊,感到身子轻飘飘的 feel giddy (or dizzy); (of speed) very fast; feel dizzy as if one's body is floating

誊(謄) téng 誊写 transcribe (by hand); copy out:这稿子太乱,要～一遍。This draft is too messy. It must be recopied.

【誊录】ténglù 誊写;过录 transcribe (by hand); copy out:～生(缮写人员的旧称)(old Chinese term) transcriber; copier; person who transcribes (copies)|～文稿 copy out a manuscript

【誊写】téngxiě 照底稿抄写 transcribe (by hand); copy out:～社 mimeograph service|～笔记 copy out one's notes

【誊写版】téngxiěbǎn 简便的印刷版,旧时用毛笔蘸药水在特制的纸上写成,现在一般把蜡纸铺在钢版上用铁笔刻成 stencil; simple printing plate made in old times by dipping a writing brush in a liquid and writing on a special kind of paper, and now by cutting text and illustrations into a thin sheet, as of a stencil paper, with a pointed metal pen in such a way that when ink is applied to the sheet, the patterns, designs, letters, etc. are marked on the surface beneath

【誊写钢版】téngxiě gāngbǎn 刻蜡版时垫在底下的钢板,有网纹,多镶在木板上 stencil steel plate; steel plate with netted veins, mounted on a wooden block, for cutting stencils;版 also put as 板 bǎn

滕 Téng ❶ 周朝国名,在今山东滕州一带 Teng, name of a state in the Zhou Dynasty in and around present-day Tengzhou in Shandong Province ❷ 姓 a surname

螣 tèng [螣蛇](téngshé)古书上说的一种能飞的蛇 flying snake as described in ancient books

☞ 螣 tè on p.1877

縢 téng〈书 *fml.*〉❶ 封闭;约束 seal off; restrained ❷ 绳子 rope

藤(籐) téng 某些植物的匍匐茎或攀缘茎,如白藤、紫藤、葡萄等的茎。有的可以编制箱子、椅子等。vine; cane; any plant with a long, thin stem that grows along the ground or climbs a wall or other support by means of tendrils, such as rattan, Chinese wistaria (*Wistaria sinensis*) and grapevine, etc.; some of them used in weaving boxes, suitcases, and chairs

【藤本植物】téngběn zhíwù 有缠绕茎或攀缘茎的植物,通常指木本的,如葡萄、紫藤 liana; vine; any luxuriantly growing, tropical woody vine such as grape and Chinese wistaria that roots in the ground and climbs, as around tree trunks

【藤编】téngbiān 民间的一种手工艺,用某些藤本植物的茎或茎皮编制箱子、椅子和其他物品。也指用藤编制的物品。rattan weaving; folk handicraft, using the stems of certain vines or their outer covering for making boxes, suitcases, trunks, chairs, and other articles; also meaning rattan goods

【藤萝】téngluó 紫藤的通称 general term for 紫藤 zǐténg

【藤牌】téngpái 原指藤制的盾,后来泛指盾 orig. referring to cane (or rattan) shield, later referring to shields in general

【藤蔓】téngwàn 藤和蔓 vine and tendril:架子上爬满了葡萄、丝瓜、扁豆的～。The vines of grapes, luffa and hyacinth bean climb all over the pergola. ◇感情的～在他心中萌芽、蔓延。The vines of love and affection have sprouted and grown in his heart.

【藤子】téng·zi 藤 cane; rattan; vine

䲢 téng 鱼,身体黄褐色,头大而阔,眼小,下颌突出,有两个背鳍。常栖息在海底,捕食小鱼。stargazer (*Uranoscopus scaber*); big-headed, small-eyed, yellowish-brown fish with a protruding mandible and two dorsal fins, living at the sea bottom and feeding on small fish

tī (ㄊㄧ)

体(體) tī [体己](tī·ji) same as 梯己 tī·ji

☞ tǐ on p.1883

剔 tī ❶ 从骨头上把肉刮下来 clean a bone with a pointed instrument; pick:把骨头～得干干净净 pick the bones clean ❷ 从缝隙里往外挑(tiǎo) pick (as from a fissure or crack):～牙缝ル pick one's teeth|～指甲 clean the fingernails; pick one's fingernails ❸ 剔除

pick out and throw away; reject; get rid of: 挑～ nit-picking; be fastidious | 把烂了的果子～出去。Pick out the rotten fruits. ❹ 汉字的笔画,即挑(tiǎo)⑤ rising stroke (in Chinese characters)

【剔除】tīchú 把不合适的去掉 reject; get rid of: ～糟粕 reject the dross

【剔红】tīhóng 雕漆的一种 carved lacquer ware; also 雕红漆 diāohóngqī

【剔透】tītòu 明澈 bright and limpid: 晶莹～ be sparklingly bright; crystal clear | 玲珑～ exquisitely carved; beautifully wrought

【剔庄货】tīzhuānghuò 廉价出售的次货;处理品(多用于百货和服装) goods (usu. general merchandise or clothing) sold at reduced prices; shopworn or substandard goods

梯 tī ❶ 便利人上下的用具或设备,常见的是梯子、楼梯 ladder; steps; stairs; framework consisting of two parallel sidepieces connected by a series of rungs or crosspieces, enabling a person to climb up and down ❷ 作用跟楼梯相似的设备 apparatus with the same function as stairs: 电～ lift; elevator; escalator ❸ 形状像楼梯的 shaped like a staircase; terraced: ～田 terraced fields

【梯队】tīduì ❶ 军队战斗或行军时,按任务和行动顺序区分为几个部分,每一部分叫做一个梯队 echelon formation; echelon; ladder-like formation of troops with different assignments, divided into several units according to a prescribed action sequence in a battle or march, with each unit known as an echelon ❷ 指依次接替上一拨人任务的干部、运动员等 echelon or line of successor; cadres, athletes, etc. who succeed to the preceding group of cadres, successors: 加强技术人员的～建设 intensify the training of the second echelon of technical personnel | 女排第二～ bench of a women's volleyball team

【梯恩梯】tī'ēntī same as 黄色炸药 huángsè zhàyào ① T. N. T.; abbreviation of trinitrotoluene 三硝基甲苯(sānxiāojījiǎběn)

【梯河】tīhé 在较大的河流的不同地段修筑若干拦河坝,因而水流形成阶梯状,有这种水工建筑的河流叫做梯河 large river with dams built on different sections to enable the water to flow in the shape of a stair; terraced river; river with a terraced water conservancy structure

【梯级】tījí ❶ 楼梯的级 stair; step ❷ 在河流上分段拦河筑坝,使水位呈阶梯状,这种水利工程叫做梯级 build dams at different sections of a river to keep the water level in the shape of a stair; ladder-like water conservancy structure

【梯己】tī·ji ❶ 家庭成员个人积蓄的(财物) private savings of family members; same as 私房 sī·fáng ①. ～钱 private savings ❷ 亲近的;贴心的 intimate; confidential: ～人 confidant | ～话 words said in confidence ‖ also 体己 tī·ji

【梯田】tītián 沿着山坡开辟的一级一级的农田,形状像楼梯,边缘筑有田埂,防止水土流失 terraced fields; terrace; fields terraced on hill slopes, with ridges built on the fringes to prevent the loss of water and soil

【梯形】tīxíng 只有一组对边平行的四边形 trapezoid; plane figure with four sides, two of which are parallel

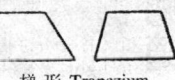

梯形 Trapezium

【梯子】tī·zi 便于人上下的用具,一般用两根长的竹子或木头并排做帮,中间横穿若干根短的竹子或木头制成 ladder; stepladder; framework made of bamboo or wood consisting of two parallel side pieces connected by a series of rungs or crosspieces enabling a person to climb up and down

锑 tī 金属元素,符号 Sb (stibium)。普通锑银白色,质硬而脆,有冷胀性。无定形锑灰色,由卤化锑电解制得。用于工业和医药上,超纯锑是重要的半导体和红外探测器材料。stibium (Sb); antimony; silvery-white, brittle, metallic element of crystalline structure with cold tension. Amorphous antimony is obtained through the electrolysis of antimony halogenate. Used in industry and medicine, superpure antimony is an important material for making semiconductors and infrared detectors.

踢 tī 抬起腿用脚撞击 kick; play (football): ～球 kick a ball | ～毽子 kick the shuttlecock | 小心牲口～人。Be careful! The cattle kicks.

【踢蹬】tī·deng ❶ 脚乱蹬乱踢 kick at random: 小孩儿爱活动,一天到晚老～。Children love to move about. They can't keep their legs still even for one minute in the day. ❷ 胡乱用钱;挥霍 waste money; squander: 这月的工资被他～光了。He has squandered up all his pay for this month. ❸ 清理;处理 handle; deal with; dispose of: 用了一个晚上才把这些琐碎事～完。It took him a whole evening to dispose of these trivial matters.

【踢脚板】tījiǎobǎn 室内四周墙壁下部的宽木条或水泥长条,用来保护墙面和墙角 skirting board; skirting; narrow board, wood or cement, placed round the margin of a floor to protect the wall surface and corners; also 踢脚线 tījiǎoxiàn

【踢皮球】tī píqiú 〈比喻 *fig.*〉互相推诿,把应该解决的事情推给别人 kick something back and forth like a ball; pass the buck; shift responsibility onto each other: 要纠正办事拖拉,～的作风。It is essential to get rid of the style of being dilatory in doing things and shifting responsibility onto each other.

【踢踏舞】tītàwǔ 主要流行于西方的一种舞蹈，以鞋底击地及各种节奏的脚的动作为其特点，舞时发出清晰的踢踏声 tap dance; dance popular in the West, which is performed with sharp, loud taps of the foot, toe, or heel at each step

【踢腾】tī·teng same as 踢蹬 tī·deng

鹛 tī ☞［䴙鹛］(pìtī) on p.1470.

擿 tī〈书 *fml.*〉揭发 expose; unmask; bring to light:发奸～伏(揭发奸邪,使无可隐藏) expose evil and crafty practices
☞ zhì on p.2479

tí(ㄊㄧˊ)

荑 tí〈书 *fml.*〉❶ 植物初生的叶芽 sprout; shoot ❷ 稗子一类的草 barnyard grass
☞ yí on p.2261

绨 tí 厚绸子 kind of thick silk:～袍 silk robe; silk gown; silk dress; dress made of thick silk
☞ tì on p.1887

提 tí ❶ 垂手拿着(有提梁、绳套之类的东西) carry in one's hand with the arm down:手里～着个篮子 carry a basket in one's hand|我去～一壶水来。I'm going to fetch a kettle of water.◇～心吊胆 be on tenterhooks; have one's heart in one's mouth ❷ 使事物由下往上移 lift; raise; promote:～高 lift; raise; heighten; improve|～升 promote ◇～神 refresh oneself; invigorate oneself; give oneself a lift ❸ 把预定的期限往前挪 move or shift to an earlier date:～前 move up a date|～早 move up to an earlier date ❹ 指出或举出 put forward; bring up; raise:～醒 remind|～意见 raise one's opinion|～问题 raise a question ❺ 提取 draw (or take) out; extract:～炼 extract; refine|～款 draw money from a bank|～货 pick up goods ❻ 把犯人从关押的地方带出来 summon (a prisoner) from the prison for interrogation:～讯 fetch a prisoner for interrogation|～犯人 summon a prisoner for interrogation ❼ 谈(起,到) mention; refer to; bring up:旧事重～ bring up an old matter|一～起这件事来他就好笑。He found it laughable once this matter was brought up.|他跟父亲～到要参加农业劳动的事。He talked to his father about participating in farm work. ❽ 舀油、酒等的器具,有很长的把儿,往往按所舀液体的斤两制成大小不等的一套 dipper; ladle; long-handled, cuplike spoon for dipping oil, wine, and other liquids, usu. in different sizes based on standard units of measurement for different purposes:油～ oil dipper|酒～ wine dipper ❾ 汉字的笔画,即挑(tiǎo)⑤ rising stroke (in Chinese characters) ❿ (Tí) 姓 a surname
☞ dī on p.413

【提案】tí'àn 提交会议讨论决定的建议 motion; proposal; draft resolution; draft proposal submitted to a meeting for discussion and making a decision

【提拔】tí·bá 挑选人员使担任更重要的职务 promote; select a person to an more important position:～干部 promote cadres to different positions

【提包】tíbāo 有提梁的包儿,用皮、布、塑料等制成 handbag; shopping bag; bag; valise; bag with a strap made of leather, cloth, plastics, etc.

【提倡】tíchàng 指出事物的优点鼓励大家使用或实行 advocate; promote; encourage; recommend; point out the good aspects or advantages of a thing and encourage everyone to use or do it:～说普通话 promote the use of *putonghua*|～勤俭节约 advocate diligence and thrift

【提成】tí//chéng (～儿 tí//chéngr)从钱财的总数中按一定成数提出来 deduct a percentage (from a sum of money, etc.):利润～ deduction of part of the profit|按百分之三～ deduct an amount at 3 per cent

【提纯】tíchún 除去某种物质所含的杂质,使变得纯净 purify; refine; make something pure by removing the impurities:～金属 refine a metal|～酒精 purify alcohol

【提词】tí//cí 戏剧演出时给演员提示台词 prompt; help an actor (who has forgotten a line) with a cue

【提单】tídān 向货栈或仓库提取货物的凭据 bill of lading (B/L); document issued for claiming goods at a depot or warehouse; also 提货单 tíhuòdān

【提调】tídiào ❶ 指挥调度 dispatch:这个车场的车辆由他一人～。He is the lone person to dispatch all the vehicles at this marshalling yard. ❷ 负责指挥调度的人 dispatcher:总～ chief dispatcher

【提纲】tígāng (写作、发言、学习、研究、讨论等)内容的要点 outline:发言～ outline for a speech|讨论～ an outline for discussion

【提纲挈领】tí gāng qiè lǐng 提住网的总绳,提住衣服的领子 take a net by the head rope or a coat by the collar;〈比喻 *fig.*〉把问题简明扼要地提示出来 concentrate on the main points; bring out the essentials

【提高】tí//gāo 使位置、程度、水平、数量、质量等方面比原来高 raise; heighten; enhance; increase; improve (position, procedure, level, standard, quantity, quality):～水位 raise the water level|～警惕 enhance (or heighten, sharpen) one's vigilance|～技术 improve the technical standards; improve one's skill; sharpen one's skill|～装载量 increase the loading capacity|～工作效率 raise the working efficiency

【提供】tígōng 供给(意见、资料、物资、条件等) provide; supply; furnish; offer (advice, data, materials, conditions, etc.):～经验 offer useful lessons; provide one's experience|～援助 give aid; provide assistance|为旅客～方便 provide convenience for the passengers; make it easier for the passengers

【提灌】tíguàn 用水泵、水车等把低处的水引到高处灌溉 irrigate by lifting water to a higher level with a water pump, waterwheel, etc.:～设备 lifting equipment for irrigation

【提行】tí//háng 书写或排版时另起一行 begin a new line (in writing or printing)

【提盒】tíhé 有提梁的盒子,多为两层或三层,形状不一,用竹、木、金属或搪瓷等制成,多用来装饭菜、糕点等 tiered food container; meal box with two or three round compartments of different shapes one above the other and a handle, made of bamboo, wood, metal, enamel, etc. for keeping food, pastries, etc.

【提花】tíhuā (～儿 tíhuār)用经线、纬线错综地在织物上织出凸起的图案 jacquard weave; raised designs woven on a fabric with skillfully arranged wefts and warps:～浴巾 jacquard bathing towel

【提货】tí//huò (从货栈、仓库等处)提取货物 pick up goods; take delivery of goods (from a depot or warehouse)

【提交】tíjiāo 把需要讨论、决定或处理的问题交有关机构或会议 submit (a problem, etc.); refer to:～大会讨论 submit sth. to the congress for discussion

【提篮】tílán (～儿 tìlánr)篮子(多指小巧的) hand-basket (small and exquisite)

【提炼】tíliàn 用化学方法或物理方法从化合物或混合物中提取(所要的东西) extract and purify; abstract; refine; obtain (something wanted) from a compound or a mixture by chemical or physical method:从野生芳香植物中～香精 extract essence from wild aromatic plants ◇科学是从无数经验中～出来的。Science is the crystallization of a wealth of experience.

【提梁】tíliáng (～儿 tíliángr)篮子、水壶、挎包等上面用手提的部分 handle (of a basket, kettle, etc.); straps (of a handbag, etc.); loop handle

【提留】tíliú 从钱财的总数中提取一部分留下来 deduct part from a sum; retain part of a sum:这笔款要～一部分做公积金。Part of this sum must be retained as public accumulation fund.

【提名】tí//míng 在评选或选举前提出有当选可能的人或事物名称 nominate (for election); name as a candidate for election or appointment; propose as a candidate for an award or honour:获得百花奖～的影片有三部。Three films have been nominated for the Hundred Flowers Award.|他被～为下届工会主席。He has been nominated for the next term of trade union presidency.

【提起】tíqǐ ❶ 谈到;说起 mention; speak of:～此人,没有一个不知道的。No one ever speaks of him without knowing him. ❷ 奋起 raise; arouse; brace up:～精神 raise one's spirits; brace oneself up ❸ 提出 file:～诉讼 file a suit

【提前】tíqián (把预定的时间)往前移 ahead of schedule; shift to an earlier date; move up (a date); advance:～动身 leave before the original schedule|～完成任务 fulfil a task ahead of time

【提挈】tíqiè 〈书 *fml.*〉 ❶ 带领;携带 lead; take with one; marshal:～全军 marshal all one's (military) forces ❷ 照顾;提拔 guide and support; give guidance and help to:～后人 give guidance and help to the younger people

【提亲】tí//qīn 受男家或女家委托向对方提议结亲 propose a marriage alliance; also 提亲事 tí qīn·shi

【提琴】tíqín 弦乐器,有四根弦,分小提琴、中提琴、大提琴、低音提琴四种 violin family; four-stringed instruments, including the violin, viola, cello, double bass and contrabass

【提请】tíqǐng 提出并请求 submit something to; propose and request:～上级批准 submit sth. to a higher authority for approval|～大会讨论通过 submit sth. to a congress for discussion and approval

【提取】tíqǔ ❶ 从负责保管的机构或一定数量的财物中取出(存放的或应得的财物) draw; pick up; collect; take something kept or due from a safekeeping institution or from a given quantity of property:～存款 draw money from a bank deposit; withdraw bank deposits|他到车站去～行李。He went to the railway station to pick up his luggage.|从技术交易净收入中～百分之十五的费用 deduct 15 per cent of the net income from technical transactions ❷ 提炼而取得 extract; abstract; recover:从油页岩中～石油 extract oil from shale

【提神】tí//shén 使精神兴奋 refresh oneself; give oneself a lift:浓茶能～。Strong tea makes you fresh; or Strong tea gives you a lift.

【提审】tíshěn ❶ same as 提讯 tíxùn ❷ 因为案情重大或其他原因,上级法院把下级法院尚未判决或已经判决的案件提来自行审判 (of a higher court) try (a case not yet tried by a lower court) or review (a case already tried by a lower court) because of its importance

【提升】tíshēng ❶ 提高(职位、等级等) promote:由副厂长～为厂长 be promoted from

deputy factory director to director ❷ 用卷扬机等向高处运送(矿物、材料等) hoist; elevate (mineral ores, materials, etc.):～设备 hoisting equipment; hoists; elevators

【提示】tíshì 把对方没有想到或想不到的提出来,引起对方注意 point out; prompt; point out what the others have not thought of or do not think of to draw their attention:向学生～课文要点 brief the students on the gist of a text

【提问】tíwèn 提出问题来问(多指教师对学生)(esp. of a teacher) put questions to (students); quiz

【提箱】tíxiāng 有提梁的轻便的箱子 suitcase (with a handle):帆布～ canvas suitcase; also 手提箱 shǒutíxiāng

【提携】tíxié ❶ 领着孩子走路 lead (a child) by the hand;〈比喻 *fig.*〉在事业上扶植后辈或后进 guide and support; give guidance and help to (younger people or less advanced):多蒙～。Many thanks for your guidance and help. ❷〈书 *fml.*〉携手;合作 join hands; cooperate:互相～ work together; help each other (in getting promotions)

【提心吊胆】tí xīn diào dǎn 形容十分担心或害怕 have one's heart in one's mouth; be on tenterhook; also 悬心吊胆 xuán xīn diào dǎn

【提醒】tí//xǐng 从旁指点,促使注意 remind; warn; call attention to:我要是忘了,请你～我。Please remind me in case I should forget.|到时候请你提个醒儿。Please remind me on time.

【提选】tíxuǎn 把认为好的选出来 select; choose:～耐旱品种 select drought-resistant varieties|我们一致～他当工会主席。We all vote for him to be the president of the trade union.

【提讯】tíxùn 把犯人从关押的地方提出来审讯 bring (a prisoner) from the prison before the court; bring (sb. in custody) to trial; fetch (a detainee) for interrogation

【提要】tíyào ❶ 从全书或全文提出要点 sum up the main points of a whole book or text; wrap up; synopsize ❷ 提出来的要点 précis; summary; abstract; epitome; synopsis (也常用做书名,如《四库全书总目提要》oft. used for the title of a book, such as the *Synopsis of the Complete Library of Four Branches of Books*)

【提议】tíyì ❶ 商讨问题时提出主张来请大家讨论 propose; suggest; move; put forward one's views for discussion at a meeting:有人～,今天暂时休会。It is suggested that the meeting be adjourned for today. ❷ 商讨问题时提出的主张 proposal; motion:大家都同意这个～。Everybody agrees to this proposal.

【提早】tízǎo 提前 shift to an earlier date; be earlier than planned or expected:～出发 leave ahead of schedule; set out earlier than planned

【提制】tízhì 提炼制造 obtain through refining; distil; extract:用麻黄～麻黄素 extract ephedrine from Chinese ephedra

【提子】tí·zi〈方 *fml.*〉same as 提 tí ⑧

啼(嗁) tí ❶ 啼哭 cry; weep aloud:～笑皆非 not know whether to laugh or cry; find something both funny and annoying|哭哭～～ keep crying and sobbing ❷(某些鸟兽)叫 (of certain birds and animals) crow; caw; screech:鸡～ Cocks crow.|月落乌～。The crows caw when the moon goes down.|虎啸猿～。Tigers howl and apes jabber.

【啼饥号寒】tí jī háo hán 因为缺乏衣食而啼哭,形容生活极端困苦 wail with hunger and cold; cry out from hunger and cold; be in dire poverty

【啼哭】tíkū 出声地哭 cry; wail:大声～ cry loudly

【啼笑皆非】tí xiào jiē fēi 哭也不是,笑也不是,形容既令人难受又令人发笑 not know whether to laugh or cry; find something both funny and annoying

遆 Tí 姓 a surname

鹈 tí [鹈鹕](tíhú)水鸟,体长可达2米,翼大,嘴长,尖端弯曲,嘴下有一个皮质的囊,可以存食,羽毛白色,翼上有少数黑色羽毛。善于游泳和捕鱼。喜群居。pelican (*Pelecanidae*); gregarious waterfowl having a two metre-long body, white feathers, large wings with few black feathers, a long beak with a bent tip and a distensible pouch which hangs from the large lower mandible and is used to scoop up or store fish, good at swimming and catching fishes; also 淘河 táohé

骎 tí ☞ [駃騠](juétí) on p. 1059

缇 tí〈书 *fml.*〉橘红色 orange-red

趧 tí [趧鴂](tíjué) 古书上指杜鹃 cuckoo as described in ancient books

题 tí ❶ 题目 topic; subject; title; problem:命～ give a topic; set an question; assign a topic|出～ set an examination paper; set a topic|离～太远 stray away from the subject|文不对～ not to the point; irrelevant to the subject; beside the point; wide of the mark; not pertinent ❷ 写上;签上 inscribe:～诗 inscribe a poem|～字 write a few words on an occasion; autograph; inscription|～名 inscribe a name; give an autograph ❸(Tí)姓 a surname

【题跋】tíbá 写在书籍、字画等前后的文字。'题'指写在前面的,'跋'指写在后面的,总称题跋。内容多为品评、鉴赏、考订、记事等。preface and postscript featuring appraisals, appreciation, corrections, memorandum, etc.; colophon (short comment, annotation, etc. on a scroll of painting or calligraphy)

【题壁】tíbì ❶ 在壁上写字或诗文 write words or a poem on a wall ❷ 写在壁上的字或诗文 inscriptions on a wall：洞里有历代文人墨客的～。There were inscriptions of literary men of all dynasties on the walls of the cave.

【题材】tícái 构成文学和艺术作品的材料，即作品中具体描写的生活事件或生活现象 subject matter; theme; material for a literary and artistic work, that is, events and phenomena of everyday life：历史～ historical theme | ～新颖 original in the choice of subject

【题词】tí//cí 写一段话表示纪念或鼓励 write a few words of encouragement, appreciation or commemoration：题个词留作纪念 write an autograph as a memento

【题词】tící ❶ 为表示纪念或勉励而写下来的话 inscription or dedication written for commemoration or encouragement ❷ 序文 foreword

【题额】tí'é 题写匾额 write an inscription on a horizontal board

【题花】tíhuā 报刊、书籍上诗文标题前面的装饰性图画 title design; decorative drawing before a poetic title in a newspaper, a magazine or a book

【题记】tíjì 写在书的正文前或文章题目下面的文字，多为扼要说明著作的内容或主旨，有的只引用名人名言 preface or words written before the text of a book or under the title of an article, usu. telling a brief summary of the content or intention of the another, sometimes just quoting a dictum of a famous person

【题解】tíjiě ❶ 供学习的书籍中解释题目含义或作品时代背景等的文字 explanatory notes on the title or background of a book ❷ 汇集成册的关于数学、物理、化学等问题的详细解答 key to exercises or problems in mathematics, physics and chemistry：《平面几何～》*Key to Exercises in Plane Geometry*

【题名】tí//míng 为留纪念或表示表扬而写上姓名 inscribe one's name; autograph：英雄榜上～ names appearing on an honour roll of heroes

【题名】tímíng ❶ 为留纪念而写上的姓名 name written as a memento ❷ 题目的名称 title

【题目】tímù ❶ 概括诗文或讲演内容的词句 title; subject; topic ❷ 练习或考试时要求解答的问题 exercise problems; examination questions：考试～ examination questions

【题签】tí//qiān 为书皮题写标签 write the title of a book on a label to be stuck on the cover

【题签】tíqiān 写在书皮上的标签 label with the title of a book on it

【题写】tíxiě 写；书写（标题、匾额等）inscribe (a title, a horizontal board)：～书名 inscribe the title of a book

【题旨】tízhǐ ❶ 文章题目的意旨 the meaning of the title of an article ❷ 文艺作品主题的意义 theme of a literary or artistic work：～深远 have a profound and far-reaching artistic meaning

【题字】tí//zì 为留纪念而写上字 write a few words of commemoration (on an autograph album, etc.)：主人拿出纪念册来请来宾～。The host took out an album and requested autographs from the guests.

【题字】tízì 为留纪念而写上的字 words written as a memento：书上有作者的亲笔～。The book is autographed by the author.

醍 tí [醍醐](tíhú)〈古时 *arch.*〉指从牛奶中提炼出来的精华，佛教比喻最高的佛法 cream, separated from milk, as described in ancient times; (fig.) the supreme Buddhist truth; ghee (used by Buddhists as a metaphor for the perfect truth of the Buddha)：如饮～ as if drinking the finest cream | ～灌顶（比喻灌输智慧，使人彻底醒悟）(fig.) be filled with wisdom; be enlightened; suddenly feel refreshed

蹄（蹏） tí 马、牛、羊等动物生在趾端的角质物，也指具有这种角质物的脚 hoof; horny covering on the feet of the horse, ox, sheep, etc.; also the entire foot of such an animal

【蹄筋】tíjīn（～儿 tíjīnr）牛、羊、猪的四肢中的筋，作为食物时叫做蹄筋 tendons of the feet of ox, sheep and pigs; The Chinese term *tijin* 蹄筋 is used only when referring to tendons as food.

【蹄髈】típǎng〈方 *dial.*〉same as 肘子 zhǒu·zi ①

【蹄子】tí·zi ❶ 蹄 hoof ❷〈方 *dial.*〉same as 肘子 zhǒu·zi ① ❸〈旧时 *old*〉骂女子的话 (of a woman) bitch

鳀（鮷） tí 鱼，体长 3—4 寸，侧扁，腹部呈圆柱形，眼和口都大，无侧线。生活在海中。幼鳀加工制成的鱼干叫海蜒。anchovy (*Engraulis*); laterally flat marine fish three to four inches long, with a cylindrical belly, a large mouth, large eyes and without a lateral line; dried young anchovies also called 海蜒 hǎiyán

tǐ（ㄊㄧˇ）

体（體、躰） tǐ ❶ 身体，有时指身体的一部分 body or part of a body：～高 height | ～重 weight | 上～ trunk | 肢～ limb | 五～投地 be on all fours; prostrate oneself before somebody (in admiration) ❷ 物体 substance or state of a substance：固～ solid | 液～ liquid | 整～ the whole; totality;

entirety|集～ collective ❸ 文字的书写形式；作品的体裁 style；form：字～ style of calligraphy|草～ scribble；characters executed swiftly and with strokes flowing together；cursive hand|文～ literary style|旧～诗 old style poetry；classical poetry ❹ 亲身(经验)；设身处地(着想) personally do or experience sth.；put oneself in another's position：～会 experience；know from experience；realise|～验 learn from practice；learn through one's experience|～谅 show understanding and sympathy for|身～力行 earnestly practise what one teaches ❺ 体制 system：政～ system of government|国～ state system ❻ 一种语法范畴，多表示动词所指动作进行的情况(gram.) aspect of a verb usu. used to indicate the progressive nature of an action

☞ tī on p.1878

【体裁】tǐcái 文学作品的表现形式。可以用各种标准来分类，如根据有韵无韵可分为韵文和散文；根据结构可分为诗歌、小说、散文、戏剧等。genre；form of literature classified by different standards，for example，verse and prose in terms of rhyme；and poetry，novel，prose and drama in terms of structure

【体操】tǐcāo 体育运动项目，徒手或借助于某些器械进行各种动作操练或表演 gymnastics；sport combining tumbling，exercises and acrobatic feats，usually done barehanded or with apparatus

【体察】tǐchá 体验和观察 experience and observe：～民情 be aware of the condition of the people

【体尝】tǐcháng 亲身尝试 have personal experience of；experience personally：仔细品味～ taste carefully|她～到了生活给自己带来的欣慰和苦涩。She personally experienced the joy and bitterness life had brought her.

【体词】tǐcí 语法上名词、代词、数词、量词的总称 substantive；general term for nouns，pronouns，numerals and measure words

【体大思精】tǐ dà sī jīng 规模宏大，思虑精密(多形容大部头著作 of a voluminous book) extensive in scope and brilliant in conception：这部小说史，～，征引宏富。This history of fiction is extensive in scope，penetrating in thought and rich in quotation.

【体罚】tǐfá 用罚站、罚跪、打手心等方式来处罚儿童的一种教育方法 corporal (or physical) punishment inflicted on school children，such as making them stand or kneel for a long time，beating the palm with a ruler：废除～ abolish corporal punishment

【体格】tǐgé ❶ 人体发育的情况和健康的情况 physique；build：检查～ give or receive a physical checkup|～健全 sound body；strong physique ❷ 泛指人和动物的体形 (in a broad sense) body form；build：古代的猛犸和现在的象～大小差不多。The mammoth in ancient times were largely the same size as the elephant of today.

【体会】tǐhuì 体验领会 know (or learn) from experience；realise；knowledge；understand：只有深入群众，才能真正～群众的思想感情。Only by maintaining close ties with the masses can you really read their minds and understand their feelings.|座谈会上大家漫谈个人的～。Everyone said a few words about his personal experience.

【体积】tǐjī 物体所占空间的大小 volume；bulk；amount of space occupied in three dimensions

【体积吨】tǐjīdūn 水运轻货时，计算运费所使用的一种计算单位。以货物占用货舱容积每1.133立方米折算为一吨，叫做一个体积吨。measurement ton；tonnage；unit of measurement used in calculating freight for transporting goods of big volume but light weight by water，with one measurement ton equal to 1.133 cubic metres of freight volume

【体检】tǐjiǎn 体格检查 physical examination：每年做一次～ have a physical examination once every year

【体力】tǐlì 人体活动时所能付出的力量 physical (or bodily) strength；physical power：消耗～ consume one's physical strength；be a drain on one's physical power|他～好，能耐久。He had good and enduring stamina.

【体力劳动】tǐlì láodòng 主要靠体力进行的生产劳动 physical (or manual) labour；productive labour done mainly by physical power

【体例】tǐlì 著作的编写格式；文章的组织形式 stylistic rules and layout；style；form of organisation of an article

【体谅】tǐ·liàng 设身处地为人着想，给以谅解 show understanding and sympathy by putting oneself in sb. else's position；make allowances for：她心肠好，很能～人。She is kindhearted and quite understanding.

【体貌】tǐmào 体态相貌 one's figure and features；general physical appearance：～特征 characteristics of one's figure and appearance

【体面】tǐ·miàn ❶ 体统；身份 dignity；face：有失～ lose one's face；lose one's dignity；loss of face；beneath his dignity ❷ 光荣；光彩 honourable；creditable；respectable：好吃懒做是不～的事。It is not respectable to love eating and hate working. ❸ (相貌或样子)好看；美丽 good-looking，handsome；beautiful；pretty：长得～ look pretty；look handsome

【体念】tǐniàn 设身处地为别人着想 give sympathetic consideration to：你要～他的难处，不要苛求于他。You should understand his difficulties. Don't be so exacting on him.

【体魄】tǐpò 体格和精力 physique：锻炼～ go in for physical training|～健壮 strong (or powerful) physique；vigorous health

【体腔】tǐqiāng 人或脊椎动物的内脏器官存在的空间，分为胸腔和腹腔两部分 body cavity; cavity of humans or vertebrates where internal organs are found, consisting of the thoracic cavity and the abdominal cavity

【体式】tǐshì ❶ 文字的式样 form of characters or letters：拼音字母有手写体和印刷体两种～。There are two forms of the Chinese phonetic alphabet, the cursive and the printed. ❷〈书 *fml.*〉same as 体裁 tǐcái

【体态】tǐtài 身体的姿态；人的体形 posture; carriage：～轻盈 have a graceful carriage｜～魁梧 big and tall

【体坛】tǐtán 体育界 sports world; sports circles：～精英 elite of the sports world; top athletes｜国际～ international sports world

【体贴】tǐtiē 细心忖度别人的心情和处境，给予关切、照顾 show consideration for; give every care to：～入微（多指对人照顾和关怀十分细致周到）look after with great care; care for with great solicitude; show every possible consideration; be extremely considerate

【体统】tǐtǒng 指体制、格局、规矩等 decorum; propriety; decency：不成～ most improper; downright outrageous

【体外循环】tǐwài xúnhuán 应用特殊机械装置把血液从身体内引到体外处理后再送回体内，如心肺体外循环是把静脉血引到体外，用人工肺脏使成为动脉血，再用人工心脏送回体内动脉，从而使全身血液暂时改道，不经过心肺 extracorporeal circulation; blood circulation by using a special mechanical device to draw the blood from inside the body for treatment and then infuse it back into the body. For example, extracorporeal cardiopulmonary circulation means drawing the venous blood from the body, using artificial lungs to turn it into arterial blood, and then using an artificial heart to send it back into the artery so that the blood flows in the whole body through a make-shift course instead of the heart and lungs.

【体位】tǐwèi 医学上指身体所保持的姿势（med.）posture; position

【体味】tǐwèi 仔细体会 appreciate; savour：～人生苦乐 savour the joys and sorrows of life

【体温】tǐwēn 身体的温度。人的正常体温为37℃左右，疾病能引起体温的变化，剧烈运动也能使体温升高。body temperature. The normal temperature of a person is around 37℃. Illness causes changes in the body temperature, and drastic body movement causes it to go up.

【体温计】tǐwēnjì 测量人或动物体温用的温度计，通常是在很细的玻璃管里装上水银制成，人用的体温计刻度从34℃开始到42℃ clinical thermometer; thermometer used to measure the temperature of a person or an animal, usu. a small glass tube with mercury, graduated from 34℃ to 42℃ for humans; also 体温表 tǐwēnbiǎo

【体无完肤】tǐ wú wán fū ❶ 形容浑身受伤 have cuts and bruises all over the body; be a mass of bruises ❷〈比喻 *fig.*〉论点被全部驳倒或文章被删改得很多（of an argument）be thoroughly refuted;（of an article）be changed beyond recognition

【体惜】tǐxī 体谅爱惜 understand and sympathize with

【体系】tǐxì 若干有关事物或某些意识互相联系而构成的一个整体 system; setup; set or arrangement of things or things so related or connected as to form an organic whole：防御～ defence structure｜工业～ industrial setup｜思想～ ideological system

【体现】tǐxiàn 某种性质或现象在某一事物上具体表现出来 embody; reflect; give expression to; of certain property or phenomenon reflected in a certain thing：说实话，办实事，～出了他的务实精神。To tell the truth and do practical things embodies his pragmatic spirit.

【体形】tǐxíng 人或动物身体的形状。也指机器等的形状。bodily form; figure; configuration of the body of a person or an animal; shape of a machine

【体型】tǐxíng 人体的类型（主要指各部分之间的比例）body type; type of build or figure; somatotype：成年人和儿童在～上有显著的区别。There is a distinctive difference in body type between adults and children.

【体恤】tǐxù 设身处地为人着想，给以同情、照顾 understand and sympathize with; show solicitude for：～孤寡老人 show solicitude for old widows and widowers

【体循环】tǐxúnhuán 血液从左心室流出，经过动脉、毛细管，把氧气和养料送到各组织，并把各组织所产生的二氧化碳或废物带走，经过静脉流回右心室。血液的这种循环叫做体循环。systematic circulation; greater circulation; circulation by which the blood flows out from the left ventricle, through the artery and capillaries, sends the oxygen and nutriments to the tissues, takes away the carbon dioxide or wastes, flows through the veins and returns to the right ventricle; also 大循环 dàxúnhuán

【体验】tǐyàn 通过实践来认识周围的事物；亲身经历 learn through practice; learn through personal experience：作家到群众中去～生活。Writers live among the masses to observe and learn from real life.｜他深深～到了这种工作的艰辛。Personal experience has driven home to him how difficult this kind of job is.

【体液】tǐyè 身体内组织间的液体 body fluid; humour

【体育】tǐyù ❶ 以发展体力、增强体质为主要任

T

务的教育，通过参加各项运动来实现 physical culture; physical training; education aimed at developing physical strength and improving the physique by taking part in different kinds of sports：～课 physical education; PE ❷ 指体育运动 sports

【体育场】tǐyùchǎng 进行体育锻炼或比赛的场地。有的设有固定看台。sports field (or ground) where physical exercises or competitions are held; stadium (with seated stands)

【体育馆】tǐyùguǎn 室内进行体育锻炼或比赛的场所。一般设有固定看台。gymnasium; gym; indoor facility for physical exercises or competitions

【体育运动】tǐyù yùndòng 锻炼身体增强体质的各种活动，包括田径、体操、球类、游泳、武术、登山、射击、滑冰、滑雪、举重、摔跤、击剑、自行车等各种项目 sports; including athletics, gymnastics, ball games, swimming, Wushu, mountaineering, shooting, skating, skiing, weightlifting, wrestling, fencing, cycling, etc.

【体针】tǐzhēn 泛指用针刺身体各部穴位的针刺疗法（区别于'耳针'、'鼻针'等 as compared with 'ear acupuncture', 'nose acupuncture', etc.) body acupuncture

【体征】tǐzhēng 医生在检查病人时所发现的异常变化，如心脏病患者心脏的杂音、阑尾炎患者右下腹部的压痛等 sign; abnormal changes discovered by a doctor in checking a patient, such as the heart murmur for a sufferer of heart disease, and sore to the touch on the lower part of the abdomen for a sufferer of appendicitis

T

【体制】tǐzhì ❶ 国家机关、企业、事业单位等的组织制度 establishment; institution; system (of organisation); structure; organisational system of a government organ, enterprise, institution, etc.：学校～ school structure | 领导～ leadership structure ❷ 文体的格局；体裁 form; pattern：五言诗的～，在汉末就形成了。The pattern of the five-character-a-line poems came into being towards the end of the Han Dynasty.

【体质】tǐzhì 人体的健康水平和对外界的适应能力 physique; constitution; health condition of a human body and its ability to adapt to the outside world：发展体育运动，增强人民～ promote physical culture and build up people's health | 各人的～不同，对疾病的抵抗力也不同。As the physique differs from person to person, so does people's resistance to diseases.

【体重】tǐzhòng 身体的重量 (body) weight

tì（ㄊㄧˋ）

屉（屜） tì ❶ same as 屉子 tì·zi ①，特指笼屉 food steamer with a whole set of removable trays of the same size, one upon the other when used; steamer tray：～帽（笼屉的盖子）lid (or cover) of a steamer | 一～馒头 a trayful of steamed buns ❷ same as 屉子 tì·zi ②：棕～ removable part of a bed made of coir ropes | 藤～ the removable part made of rattan ❸〈方 *dial.*〉抽屉 drawer：三～桌 three-drawer desk

【屉子】tì·zi ❶ 扁平的盛器，成套的屉子大小相等，可以一层层整齐地叠起来 steamer tray; food steamer with a whole set of removable trays of the same size, one atop the other when used ❷ 某些床或椅子的架子上可以取下的部分，一般用棕绳、藤皮、钢丝等编成 removable part of a chair or a bedstead, usually made of coir ropes, woven rattan, steel wires, etc. ❸〈方 *dial.*〉抽屉 drawer

剃 tì 用特制的刀子刮去（头发、胡须等）shave; cut off (hair, beard, etc.) with a special cutting instrument：～刀 razor; shaver |～光头 have one's head shaved | ～胡子 have a shave; shave oneself

【剃刀】tìdāo 剃头或刮脸用的刀子 razor; cutting instrument used to shave one's head or cheeks

【剃度】tìdù〈佛教用语 *Budd.*〉指给要出家的人剃去头发，使成为僧尼 tonsure; have one's head shaved when one wants to become a monk or a nun

【剃光头】tì guāngtóu 用剃刀刮去全部头发 have one's head shaved;〈比喻 *fig.*〉考试中一个没取或比赛中一分没得 no one passes an examination; score no points in a match

【剃头】tì//tóu 剃去头发，也泛指理发 have one's head shaved; have one's hair cut; have a haircut; tonsure

洟 tì same as 涕 tì

俶 tì［俶傥］(tìtǎng) same as 倜傥 tìtǎng ☞ chù on p. 294

倜 tì ☞ below

【倜傥】tìtǎng〈书 *fml.*〉洒脱；不拘束 elegant in a casual way; free and easy of manner; unrestrained：风流～ unrestrained and overflowing with talent; unconventional and romantic; also 俶傥 tìtǎng

【倜然】tìrán〈书 *fml.*〉❶ 超然或特出的样子 aloof; detached; distant; uncommon; extraordinary; outstanding ❷ 疏远的样子 drift apart; become estranged; keep distant

逖（逷） tì〈书 *fml.*〉远 distant; far away

涕 tì ❶ 眼泪 tears：痛哭流～ weep sadly | 感激～零 be moved to tears of gratitude ❷ 鼻涕 mucus of the nose; snivel：～泪交流 tears and snivel stream down together. *or* Tears and snivel stream down at the same time.

【涕泪】tìlèi ❶ 眼泪 tears ❷ 眼泪和鼻涕 tears and snivel：～俱下 have tears and snivel flowing down at the same time

【涕零】tìlíng 流泪 shed tears：感激～（因感激而流泪）be moved to tears of gratitude

悌 tì〈书 *fml.*〉敬爱哥哥 love and respect one's elder brother：孝～ filial piety and fraternal love

绨 tì 比绸子厚实、粗糙的纺织品，用蚕丝或人造丝做经，棉线做纬织成 silk and cotton fabric thicker and coarser than silk, using natural silk or artificial silk for the warp, and cotton yarn for weft
☞ tí on p. 1880

惕 tì 谨慎小心 be cautious; be watchful：警～ keep vigilance; be on the alert

【惕厉】tìlì 警惕；戒惧 be on the alert：日夜～ be on the alert day and night; also 惕励 tìlì

【惕励】tìlì same as 惕厉 tìlì

替1 tì ❶ 代替 take the place of; replace; substitute for：～工 work as a temporary substitute｜他没来，你～他吧！He is absent. You'll take his place.｜我～你洗衣服。Let me wash your clothes. ❷ same as 为 wèi②：大家～他高兴。Everybody is happy for him.｜同学们～他送行。His classmates went to see him off.

替2 tì〈书 *fml.*〉衰败 decline：衰～ decline; wane｜兴～ rise and fall (of dynasties)

【替班】tì//bān（～儿 tì//bānr）代替别人上班 fill in for sb.; take sb. else's place (in a work shift)：今天他生病了，得找个人～。He is ill today. We must find someonc to take his place.

【替补】tìbǔ 替代补充 substitute for：～队员 substitute (player fill in for sb.); reserve (player)

【替代】tìdài 代替 substitute for; replace; supersede

【替工】tì//gōng（～儿 tì//gōngr）代替别人做工 work as a temporary substitute：明天我有事，请你给我替一下工。I'll be away from the office tomorrow, could you work for me as a temporary substitute?

【替工】tìgong（～儿 tìgōngr）代替别人做工的人 a temporary substitute (worker)：找了个～ find a substitute; get a replacement

【替换】tì·huàn 把原来的(工作着的人、使用着的衣物等）调换下来；倒换 replace; substitute for; displace; take the place of：你去～他一下。Go and take his place for a while.｜～的衣服 change of clothes

【替身】tìshēn（～儿 tìshēnr）替代别人的人，多指代人受罪的人 substitute; replacement; stand-in; scapegoat

【替死鬼】tìsǐguǐ〈比喻 *fig.*〉代人受过或受害的人 scapegoat; fall guy; person upon whom the blame for the mistakes or crimes of others is thrust

【替罪羊】tìzuìyáng〈古代 *arch.*〉犹太教在赎罪日用做祭品的羊，表示由它替人受罪，比喻代人受过的人 scapegoat; goat over the head of which the high priest of the ancient Jews confessed the sins of the people on the Day of Atonement, after which it was allowed to escape; (fig.) person upon whom the blame for the mistakes or crimes of sb. clsc is shifted

殢 tì〈书 *fml.*〉❶ 滞留 be held up ❷ 困扰；纠缠 be perplexed and pestered

裼 tì〈书 *fml.*〉婴儿的衣服 baby clothes
☞ xī on p. 2049

薙 tì〈书 *fml.*〉❶ 除去野草 get rid of the weeds ❷ same as 剃 tì

嚏 tì〈书 *fml.*〉打喷嚏 sneeze

【嚏喷】tì·pen 喷嚏 sneeze

鬄 tì〈书 *fml.*〉same as 剃 tì

趯 tì〈书 *fml.*〉跳跃 jump; leap

tiān（ㄊㄧㄢ）

天 tiān ❶ 天空 sky; heavens：顶～立地 of gigantic stature; dauntless; indomitable｜太阳一出满～红。The sky is aglow with the rising sun. ❷ 位置在顶部的；凌空架设的 overhead：～棚 awning; canopy; ceiling｜～窗 skylight｜～桥 overhead passage; overhead crosswalk; overpass ❸ 一昼夜二十四小时的时间，有时专指白天 day (round the clock); daylight：今～ today｜每～ everyday｜第二～ the next day; the following day｜三～三夜 three days and three nights｜忙了一～，晚上早点休息吧。Having had a busy day, you should retire earlier. ❹（～儿 tiānr）一天里的某一段时间 a period of time in a day：五更～ dawn; before dawn; around four in the morning｜～儿还早呢。It's still early. ❺ 季节 season：春～ spring｜冷～ cold days; winter; cold season｜三伏～ hot summer｜黄梅～ rainy days ❻ 天气 weather：阴～ overcast｜～晴 clear; sunny; fine｜～冷了。It's getting cold. ❼ 天然的；天生的 natural; inborn; innate; inherent：～性 natural instinct; nature｜～资 natural gift; inborn gift; natural endowments｜～足 natural feet ❽ same as 自然 zìrán ①：～灾 natural calamity ❾ 迷信的人指自然界的主宰者；造物 (related to superstitious beliefs) God; Heaven; ruler of the natural world：～意 God's will; will of Heaven ❿ 迷信的人指神佛仙人所住的地方 (related to superstitious beliefs) abode of gods, Buddha, or immortals：～国

T

Heaven; kingdom of Heaven | ～堂 Heaven | 归～ die

【天宝】Tiānbǎo 唐玄宗(李隆基)年号(公元742—756) Tianbao, the reign (A. D. 742-756) title of Emperor Xuanzong (Li Longji) of the Tang Dynasty

【天崩地裂】tiān bēng dì liè 形容声响强烈或变化巨大,像天塌下、地裂开一样 heaven falling and earth rending; deafening sound; natural disaster like major earthquake or landslide; violent political or social upheavals; also 天崩地坼 tiān bēng dì chè

【天边】tiānbiān (～儿 tiānbiānr) ❶ 指极远的地方 horizon; ends of the earth; remotest places:远在～,近在眼前。Though being far away, it's close at hand. ❷ 天际 horizon

【天兵】tiānbīng ❶ 神话中指天神的兵 troops from heaven:～天将 troops and commanders from heaven ❷〈比喻 *fig.*〉英勇善战、所向无敌的军队 invincible army ❸ 封建时代指朝廷的军队 imperial troops in the feudal times

【天禀】tiānbǐng〈书 *fml.*〉天资 natural gift; talent; natural endowments:～聪颖 bright and talented

【天波】tiānbō 指离开地面,依靠电离层的反射传播的无线电波 sky wave; spatial wave; space wave; also 空间波 kōngjiānbō

【天才】tiāncái ❶ 卓绝的创造力、想像力;突出的聪明智慧 genius; talent; gift; endowment:艺术～ artistic gift; | ～的创作 ingenious creation ❷ 有天才的人 gifted person

【天差地远】tiān chā dì yuǎn〈比喻 *fig.*〉相差悬殊 be poles apart; differ in thousands of ways; also 天悬地隔 tiān xuán dì gé

【天长地久】tiān cháng dì jiǔ 跟天和地存在的时间一样长,形容永久不变(多指爱情) (of love) as enduring as heaven and earth; everlasting and unchanging

【天长日久】tiān cháng rì jiǔ 时间长,日子久 long lasting

【天车】tiānchē 一种起重机械,装在厂房上空,在高架轨道上移动。有的地区叫行(háng)车。overhead travelling crane; shop traveller; crane that is mounted right under the roof of a factory building and travels on rails; also called 行车 hángchē in some areas

【天成】tiānchéng 天然生成或形成 be wrought as if through the invisible hands of nature; springing from nature:美丽～ natural beauty | 妙趣～ natural wit and humour | ～仙境 natural wonderland; wonderland springing from nature

【天秤座】tiānchèngzuò 黄道十二星座之一 Libra; one of the 12 zodiacal constellations; ☞ 黄道十二宫 huángdào shí'èrgōng on p. 851

【天窗】tiānchuāng ❶ (～儿 tiānchuāngr)房顶上为采光开的像窗子的装置 skylight; window in a roof ❷ ☞ 开天窗 kāi tiānchuāng ② on p. 1076

【天打雷轰】tiān dǎ léi hōng 被雷电打死(多用于赌咒或发誓 usu. used in swearing) stricken to death by thunder and lightning; also 天打雷击 tiān dǎ léi jī, 天打雷劈 tiān dǎ léi pī or 天打五雷轰 tiān dǎ wǔ léi hōng

【天道】tiāndào ❶ 中国古代哲学术语。唯物主义认为天道是自然界及其发展变化的客观规律。唯心主义认为天道是上帝意志的表现,是吉凶祸福的征兆。Chinese classical philosophic term that refers to natural laws or heavenly laws. Materialism holds that natural laws are the objective laws of nature and its development and changes. Idealism holds that natural laws are a manifestation of the will of God and an omen for good luck, ill fortune, disaster or happiness. ❷〈方 *dial.*〉same as 天气 tiānqì

【天敌】tiāndí 自然界中某种动物专门捕食或危害另一种动物,前者就是后者的天敌,例如猫是鼠的天敌,寄生蜂是某些作物害虫的天敌 natural enemy; animal that specially feeds on or destroys another animal in the natural world, and thus the former being the natural enemy of the latter. For example, cat is the natural enemy of rat, and parasitic wasp is the natural enemy of certain crop pests.

【天底下】tiān dǐ·xia 指世界上 under the sun; in the world; on earth:～竟有这样的事。How could such a thing have happened under the sun!

【天地】tiāndì ❶ 天和地 heaven and earth; world; universe:炮声震动～。The earth shook with the roar of guns. ❷〈比喻 *fig.*〉人们活动的范围 field of activity; scope of operation:别有～(另有一种境界) another world; another realm | 广阔的～ broad field; broad vistas ❸〈方 *dial.*〉地步;境地 pass; plight:不料走错一步,竟落到这般～。Who could ever have expected that things could have come to such a pass just because a wrong step was taken.

【天地头】tiāndìtóu 书页上下两端的空白处,上边叫天头,下边叫地头 top and bottom margins of a page; upper and lower margins of a page

【天帝】tiāndì 我国古代指天上主宰万物的神 ancient Chinese term for the Lord of Heaven that rules the universe

【天电】tiāndiàn 大气中的电荷,对无线电的接收有干扰作用 atmospherics that disturbs radio reception

【天顶】tiāndǐng ❶ 天空 sky:飞机在～上盘旋。An airplane is circling in the sky. ❷ 将观测点的铅垂线延长与天球相交,交点就是该观测点的天顶 zenith; meeting point of the extending lead line of the observer and the celestial sphere

【天鹅】tiān'é 鸟,形状像鹅而体形较大,全身白色，上嘴分黄色和黑色两部分，脚和尾都短，脚黑色，有蹼。生活在海滨或湖边，善飞，吃植物、昆虫等。swan (*Cygnus*); any of several large-bodied, web-footed goose-like water-fowl with a long, graceful neck and, typically, pure white feathers, black and short feet with webs, a short tail, and a yellow and black upper jaw, living by the sea or a lake, feeding on plants, insects, etc., and good at flying; also 鹄(hú)

【天鹅绒】tiān'éróng 一种起绒的丝织物或毛织物，也有用棉、麻做底子的。颜色华美，大多用来做服装或帘、幕、沙发套等。velvet; rich, gorgeous fabric as of silk, wool, cotton or hemp with soft, thick piles, in gorgeous colours, and used as a material for the making of garments, curtains, screens, upholstery, etc.

【天翻地覆】tiān fān dì fù ❶ 形容变化极大 heaven and earth turning upside down; earthshaking: 这几年村里起了～的变化。Earth-shaking changes have taken place in the village in the past few years. ❷ 形容闹得很凶 raise hell; make an awful disturbance: 闹得～，四邻不安 create an awful disturbance in the neighbourhood ‖ also 地覆天翻 dì fù tiān fān

【天方】Tiānfāng 我国古代称中东一带阿拉伯人建立的国家 ancient Chinese name for Arabian countries in the Middle East:《～夜谭》*The Arabian Nights*

【天分】tiānfèn 天资 natural gift; talent; special endowments

【天府之国】tiān fǔ zhī guó 指土地肥沃、物产丰富的地方，在我国一般把四川称为'天府之国'(usu. referring to Sichuan Province) Nature's Storehouse; Land of Abundance; Land of Plenty

【天赋】tiānfù ❶ 自然赋予；生来就具备 inborn; innate; endowed by nature: ～机谋 innate resourcefulness ❷ 天资 natural gift; talent; endowments: 有～ gifted; talented | ～高 great gift; great talent; exceptionally gifted or talented

【天干】tiāngān 甲、乙、丙、丁、戊、己、庚、辛、壬、癸的总称，传统用做表示次序的符号 ten Heavenly Stems of 甲 jiǎ, 乙 yǐ, 丙 bǐng, 丁 dīng, 戊 wū, 己 jǐ, 庚 gēng, 辛 xìn, 壬 rén and 癸 guǐ, traditionally used as serial numbers; also 十干 shígān; ☞ 干支 gānzhī on p. 627

【天罡】tiāngāng 古书上指北斗星，也指北斗七星的柄 Big Dipper as described in ancient books; handle of the Big Dipper

【天高地厚】tiān gāo dì hòu ❶ 形容恩情深厚 as high as the heavens and as deep as the earth; (of kindness) profound; deep ❷ 指事物的复杂性(多用做'不知'的宾语 oft. used as an object of '不知 not know') complexity of things

【天各一方】tiān gè yī fāng 指彼此相隔遥远，难于相见(of relatives or friends) live far apart and find it difficult to see each other

【天公】tiāngōng 指自然界的主宰者；天 ruler of heaven; God: 偏偏～不作美，一连下了几天雨。Heaven is just not cooperative and it has rained for days on end.

【天公地道】tiān gōng dì dào 形容十分公平合理 absolutely fair: 多劳多得，是～的事儿。More pay for more work is an absolutely fair thing.

【天宫】tiāngōng 神话中天神的宫殿 heavenly palace (in mythology); palace of the Heavenly God

【天沟】tiāngōu 屋面和屋面连接处或屋面和高墙连接处的排水沟 gutter; trough or channel along or under the eaves of a roof, to carry off rain water

【天光】tiānguāng ❶ 天色 daylight; time of the day: ～还早。It's still early. | ～刚露出鱼肚白。The day is just breaking. ❷ 天空的光辉；日光 sunlight; sunbeam; sunshine: ～渐渐隐去。The sunlight is fading bit by bit. ❸ 〈方 *dial*.〉早晨 morning

【天癸】tiānguǐ 〈中医 *Chin. med.*〉指人体中促进生殖功能的一种物质。通常指月经。substance that promotes the reproductive function in the human body, usu. referring to menses; menstruation; period

【天国】tiānguó ❶ 〈基督教 *Christ.*〉称上帝所治理的国 Kingdom of Heaven; paradise ❷ 〈比喻 *fig.*〉理想世界 utopia; paradise

【天河】tiānhé 银河的通称 common name for 银河 yínhé

【天候】tiānhòu 天气气候和某些天文现象的统称，包括阴晴、冷暖、干湿和月相、昼夜长短、四季更替等 weather; general term for weather, climate and certain astronomical phenomena, including overcast, sunny, cold, warm, dry or wet weathers, phases of the moon, lengths of days and nights, changes of seasons, etc.

【天花】[1] tiānhuā 急性传染病，人或某些哺乳动物都能感染，病原体是天花病毒。症状是先发高热，全身出红色的丘疹，变成疱疹，最后变成脓疱，中心凹陷，十天左右结痂，痂脱落后的疤痕就是麻子。种牛痘可以预防。smallpox; acute infectious disease which infects humans or certain mammals, its pathogen being pox virus, and symptoms including high fever and eruption of pimples that turn into pustules, form scabs, and often leave pitted scars (pockmarks), when healed in about 10 days. Vaccination is a preventive measure. also 痘 dòu or 痘疮 dòuchuāng; 简称 abbr. 花 huā

【天花】[2] tiānhuā 玉米的雄花穗，因为长在植株的顶部，所以叫天花 stamen of maize; called 'skyward flower' because it grows at the top of the plant

【天花板】tiānhuābǎn 室内的天棚,讲究的有雕刻或彩绘 ceiling (of a room), which is carved or colourfully painted in certain posh houses

【天花乱坠】tiān huā luàn zhuì 传说梁武帝时云光法师讲经,感动了上天,天上的花纷纷降落下来。现在用来比喻说话有声有色,非常动听(多指夸大的或不切实际的 usu. exaggerated or impractical) A Chinese legend says that Heaven was so moved by the preaching of Monk Yunguang during the reign of Emperor Wu of the Liang Dynasty, that flowers cascaded from the sky. It is now used to metaphor an extravagantly colourful description.

【天荒地老】tiān huāng dì lǎo 指经过的时间很久 for a long, long time; also 地老天荒 dì lǎo tiān huāng

【天皇】tiānhuáng ❶ 指天子 Son of Heaven; emperor ❷ 日本皇帝的称号 emperor of Japan; Mikado

【天昏地暗】tiān hūn dì àn ❶ 形容大风时飞沙漫天的景象 murky heavens over a dark earth in a sandstorm; dark all round: 突然狂风大起,刮得～。An unexpected howling wind swept by, carrying yellow dust that darkened the sky and obscured everything. ❷〈比喻 *fig.*〉政治腐败或社会混乱 corrupt politics or social chaos ❸ 形容程度深;厉害 terribly; violently; like hell: 哭得个～ wail like hell ‖ also 天昏地黑 tiān hūn dì hēi

T

【天火】tiānhuǒ 俗指由雷电或物质氧化时温度升高等自然原因引起的大火 fire caused by lightning, the sudden rise of temperature due to the oxidation of matters or other natural phenomena

【天机】tiānjī ❶ 迷信的人指神秘的天意 Heaven's mystical will ❷〈比喻 *fig.*〉自然界的秘密,也比喻重要而不可泄露的秘密 nature's mystery; something inexplicable; important secret that cannot be revealed: 一语道破了～ lay bare the secret with one penetrating remark

【天极】tiānjí ❶ 地轴延长和天球相交的两点叫做天极。在北半天球的叫北天极,在南半天球的叫南天极。celestial pole; two points at which the extension of the earth's axis and the celestial sphere meet. The point at the northern half of the celestial sphere is called northern celestial pole, and that at the southern half is called southern celestial pole. ❷〈书 *fml.*〉天际;天边 horizon

【天际】tiānjì 肉眼能看到的天地交接的地方 horizon; place where the sky and the earth meet, which is visible to the human eye

【天骄】tiānjiāo 汉朝人称匈奴单于(chányú)为天之骄子,后来称历史上某些北方少数民族君主为天骄 The king of the Xiongnu ethnic group was called the proud son of Heaven in the Han Dynasty; later the monarchs of some minority groups in the north were also called the proud sons of Heaven.

【天经地义】tiān jīng dì yì 指非常正确不容置疑的道理 principles of heaven and earth—right and proper; perfectly justified

【天井】tiānjǐng ❶ 宅院中房子和房子或房子和围墙所围成的露天空地;院落 small yard; courtyard; space surrounded by a house or a group of combined houses or by a group of houses and an enclosure ❷ 某些地区的旧式房屋为了采光而在房顶上开的洞(对着天井在地上所挖的排泄雨水的坑叫天井沟) skylight; window in the roof or ceiling (the pit dug in the small yard to carry off the rain water is called 天井沟 tiānjǐnggōu)

【天空】tiānkōng 日月星辰罗列的广大的空间 sky; heavens: 仰望～ look up into the sky | 雄鹰在～翱翔。A powerful hawk is soaring in the sky.

【天籁】tiānlài 自然界的声音,如风声、鸟声、流水声等 sounds of nature (i. e. the sound of the wind or flowing waters, the call of the bird, etc.)

【天蓝】tiānlán 像晴朗的天空的颜色 sky blue; azure; colour of the clear sky

【天狼星】tiānlángxīng 天空中最明亮的恒星,属于大犬座。它有一个伴星,用望远镜可以看见。Sirius; the brightest star in the sky, belonging to the Canis Major (Cma; Greater Dog), having an accompanying star which can be seen by a telescope

【天老儿】tiān·laor 俗称患白化病的人 albino

【天老爷】tiānlǎo·ye 老天爷 God; Heavens

【天理】tiānlǐ ❶ 宋代的理学家认为封建伦理是客观存在的道德法则,把它叫做'天理' heavenly principles. The Confucianists in the Song Dynasty held that the feudal ethics was an objective law of ethics. ❷ 天然的道理(divine) justice: ～难容 intolerable injustice

【天理教】Tiānlǐjiào 白莲教的一个支派,是18世纪中叶白莲教武装起义失败后,由部分教徒组织起来的,曾在北京、河南发动起义。又称八卦教。Society of Heavenly Principles; a branch of the White Lotus Society, which was formed by some of the members after the armed rebellion organized by the White Lotus Society in the middle of the 18th century failed, and which started rebellions in Beijing and Henan. It was also called the Society of the Eight Trigrams.

【天良】tiānliáng 良心 conscience: 丧尽～ conscienceless; heartless

【天亮】tiān liàng 太阳快要露出地平线时天空发出光亮 daybreak; dawn; first light that appears just when the sun is about to rise above the horizon: 一觉睡到～ not wake until dawn | 鸡叫了三遍才～。The cock crows three times before dawn.

【天灵盖】tiānlínggài 指人或某些动物头顶部分的骨头 top of the skull; crown (of the head)

【天伦】tiānlún〈书 *fml.*〉指父子、兄弟等关系 natural bonds and ethical relationships among members of a family: ～之乐 family happiness

【天罗地网】tiān luó dì wǎng 上下四方都布下的罗网 nets above and snares below;〈比喻 *fig.*〉对敌人、逃犯等设下的严密包围圈 tightened encirclement for the enemy or escaped criminals

【天麻】tiānmá 多年生草本植物,地下茎肉质,地上茎杏红色,叶子呈鳞片状,花黄红色。块茎可入药。tuber of elevated gastrodia (*Gastrodia elata*); perennial herbaceous plant with a fleshy subterranean stem, apricot-red aerial stem, palta leaves, yellowish-red flowers, and tubers used for Chinese medicine

【天马行空】tiān mǎ xíng kōng 马的奔驰如同腾空飞行。多比喻诗文、书法等气势豪放,不受拘束。heavenly steed soaring across the skies; (fig.) powerful and unconstrained style of writing, calligraphy, etc.(天马:汉武帝从西域大宛国得到的汗血马称为'天马',意思是一种神马。见《史记·大宛传》)。The horse Emperor Wu of the Han Dynasty got from the Kingdom of Farghana in the Western Regions was called '天马 heavenly horse', meaning a divine horse. See *Records of the Historian·Records of Farghana*)

【天门】tiānmén ❶〈旧称 *old*〉天宫的门 Heavenly Gate; gate to the Heavenly Palace ❷ 帝王宫殿的门 gate to the imperial palace ❸ 指前额的中央 centre of the forehead ❹ 道家指心 heart or mind as refered by a Taoist

【天明】tiān míng same as 天亮 tiānliàng

【天命】tiānmìng 迷信的人指上天的意志;也指上天主宰之下的人们的命运 (superstrtion) God's will; mandate of heaven; destiny; fate

【天幕】tiānmù ❶ 笼罩大地的天空 canopy of the heavens ❷ 舞台后面悬挂的天蓝色的大布幔,演剧时配合灯光,用来表现各种天空景象 backdrop (of a stage); sky blue curtain hung at the back of a stage, used to display the sky in the stage lights

【天南地北】tiān nán dì běi ❶ 形容距离遥远,也指相距遥远的不同地方 far apart; places far from each other: ～,各在一方。They live far apart from each other. ❷ 形容说话漫无边际 talk about a wide range of subjects: 两个人～地说了好半天。The two of them chatted about everything for a long time. ‖ also 天南海北 tiān nán hǎi běi

【天年】tiānnián ❶ 指人的自然寿命 natural span of life; one's allotted span: 尽其～die a natural death; live one's full span | 安享～spend one's remaining years in contentment ❷〈方 *dial.*〉年成 year's harvest: 今年～不好,粮食歉收。Grain yield went down this year due to a crop failure. ❸〈方 *dial.*〉年头儿;时代 times; age; era: 过去那种打仗的～,家家的日子都不好过。Life was tough for every family in those years of incessant war.

【天怒人怨】tiān nù rén yuàn 形容为害作恶十分严重,引起普遍的愤怒 incur the wrath of God and the anger of men; widespread indignation and discontent over one's evil doings

【天棚】tiānpéng ❶ 房屋内部在屋顶或楼板下面加的一层东西,或用木板做成,或在木条、苇箔上抹灰,或在苇箔、秫秸上糊纸,有保温、隔音、美观等作用 ceiling; overhanging covering under a roof or a floor inside a house or a room, made of wood boards, plastered wood strips or reed matting, or papered reeds or sorghum-stalks mat, for keeping the rooms warm, sound insolating or for decoration ❷ 夏天在庭院等处搭起来遮蔽太阳的棚 awning; canopy, usu. made of reed matting propped up with bamboo poles in a courtyard in summer to shelter from the sun; also 凉棚 liángpéng

【天平】tiānpíng 较精密的衡器,根据杠杆原理制成。杠杆两头有小盘,一头放砝码,一头放要称的物体。杠杆正中的指针停在刻度中央时,砝码的重量就是所称物体的重量。多用于实验室和药房。balance; scales; precision weighing instrument built on the lever principle. There are two matched shallow pans hanging on either end of a lever supported exactly in the middle, one pan for weights and the other for sth. to be weighed. When the indicator in the middle of the lever stops at the centre of the graduation, the weight of the weights on the balance is exactly that of what is being weighed. Such instrument is usually used in laboratories and pharmacies.

【天启】Tiānqǐ 明熹宗(朱由校)年号(公元1621—1627) Tianqi, reign title of Emperor Xizong (Zhu Youxiao) (1621-1627) of the Ming Dynasty

【天气】tiānqì ❶ 一定区域一定时间内大气中发生的各种气象变化,如温度、湿度、气压、降水、风、云等的情况 weather; meteorological changes in the atmosphere over a given area at a given time, such as temperature, humidity, atmospheric pressure, precipitation, wind, cloud, etc.: ～预报 weather report; weather forecast | 今天～很好。It's a fine day today. ❷〈方 *dial.*〉指时间;时候 time: 现在是三更～。It's midnight now. | ～不早了,快回家吧! It's getting late. Let's go home.

【天气图】tiānqìtú 表示某地区或整个地球天气形势的图,图上用数字和规定的符号记录各地的气象资料。分为高空天气图和地面天气图两种,气象部门用来预测天气变化。weather map; synoptic chart; map showing the weather situation over a given area or over the whole earth, using figures and symbols to record the meteorological data in different parts of the globe. There are high-altitude weather map and ground weather map, used by meteorological institutions to forecast weather changes.

【天气预报】tiānqì yùbào 向有关地区发出的关于未来一定时间内天气变化的报告 weather forecast; report on weather changes in a given period of time, issued to areas concerned

【天堑】tiānqiàn 天然形成的隔断交通的大沟,多指长江,形容它的险要 natural chasm that cuts off traffic, usu. referring to the Yangtze River to show its strategically difficult access and importance:长江～ natural moat of the Yangtze River

【天桥】tiānqiáo ❶ 火车站里为了旅客横过铁路而在铁路上空架设的桥,也指城市中为了行人横穿马路而在马路上空架设的桥 overline bridge; platform bridge; overhead walkway; overhead crosswalk ❷ 一种体育运动设备,高而窄,形状略像独木桥,两端有梯子 bridge; sports equipment high and narrow, shaped like a single-plank bridge, with ladders at both ends

【天琴座】tiānqínzuò 北部天空中的星座,很小,在银河的西边,织女星就是其中的一颗 Lyra; tiny constellation that also includes Vega in the northern sky to the west of the Milky Way

【天青】tiānqīng 深黑而微红的颜色 reddish black

【天穹】tiānqióng 从地球表面上看,像半个球面似的覆盖着大地的天空 vault of heaven; sky which looks like a semi-sphere covering the land, viewed from the surface of the earth

【天球】tiānqiú 为研究天体位置和运动,天文学上假想天体分布在以观测者为球心,以适当长度为半径的球面上,这个球面叫做天球。以地心为球心的叫做地心天球,以太阳中心为球心的叫做日心天球。celestial sphere; imaginary sphere of infinite extent with the observer always at its centre and an appropriate length as its radius; The celestial sphere with the earth's core as its centre is called the geocentric celestial sphere, and that with the centre of the sun as its centre is called heliocentric celestial sphere.

【天球仪】tiānqiúyí 球形的天文仪器,刻画着星座、赤道、黄道等的位置 celestial globe; globe on which the stars, constellations, ecliptic, equator; etc. are marked in their respective positions in the sky

【天趣】tiānqù 自然的情趣,多指写作或艺术品的韵致 charm (of writings, paintings, etc.):～盎然 appealing; full of natural charm

【天阙】tiānquè ❶ 天上的宫阙 celestial palace ❷ 天子的宫阙,也指朝廷或京城 imperial palace; imperial court; capital city

【天然】tiānrán 自然存在的;自然产生的(区别于'人工'或'人造' as compared with 'artificial' or 'man-made') natural:～冰 natural ice|～景色 natural scenery|～财富 natural resources (or wealth)

【天然免疫】tiānrán miǎnyì 生来就有的或病后获得的免疫能力(区别于'人工免疫' as compared with 'artificial immunity') innate immunity; native immunity; natural immunity; immunity gained after an illness; also 自然免疫 zìrán miǎnyì

【天然气】tiānránqì 可燃气体,主要成分是甲烷,产生在油田、煤田和沼泽地带,是埋藏在地下的古代生物经高温、高压等作用形成的。主要用做燃料和化工原料。natural gas; inflammable gas consisting mainly of methane, found in the oilfields, coalfields and marshlands, formed by the remains of ancient animals and plants under high temperature and pressure; used mainly as fuel and in making chemicals

【天然丝】tiānránsī 指蚕丝(区别于'人造丝' as compared with 'artificial silk') silk

【天然橡胶】tiānrán xiàngjiāo 高分子化合物,由橡胶树、橡胶草等植物中取得的乳胶,经加工制成。种类很多。natural rubber; high-polymer compound made by processing the latex from rubber tree, rubber grass and other plants

【天壤】tiānrǎng 〈书 *fml.*〉❶ 天地 heaven and earth:～间 between heaven and earth ❷ 天渊 high heaven and deep sea; poles apart:～之别 as far apart as heaven and earth; worlds (or poles) apart; world of difference

【天日】tiānrì 天和太阳 sky and sun; 〈比喻 *fig.*〉光明 light:重见～ see the light of the day once again|暗无～ total absence of justice; complete darkness

【天色】tiānsè 天空的颜色,借指时间的早晚和天气的变化 colour of the sky; time of the day as shown by the colour of the sky; weather:看～怕要下雨。It looks like rain.|～还早,你再睡一会儿。It's still early. Have some more sleep.

【天上】tiānshàng same as 天空 tiānkōng

【天神】tiānshén 传说中天上的神 god; deity

【天生】tiānshēng 天然生成 born; inborn; inherent; innate:～丽质 born beautiful; naturally beautiful|～的一对 an inborn couple|本事不是～的。Ability is not inborn.

【天时】tiānshí ❶ 指宜于做某事的气候条件 weather; climate:庄稼活一定要趁～,早了晚了都不好。Farming should be done in season, neither too early nor too late. ❷ 指气候状况 weather:～转暖。It is getting warmer. ❸ 指时候;时间 time:～尚早。It's still early.

【天使】tiānshǐ ❶ 犹太教、基督教、伊斯兰教等宗教指神的使者。西方文学艺术中,天使的形象多为带翅膀的少女或小孩子,现在常用来比喻天真可爱的人(多指女子或小孩子)。angel;

messenger of God in Judaism, Christianity, Islamism and other religions. In Western literature and painting, angel is a young girl or boy with wings; (fig.) lovely and innocent person (usu. woman or child) ❷ 皇帝的使者 messenger of an emperor

【天授】tiānshòu 上天所授予(迷信)(superstition) bestowed by heaven; same as 天赋 tiānfù ①

【天书】tiānshū ❶ 天上神仙写的书或信(迷信)(superstition) book from heaven ❷〈比喻 *fig.*〉难认的文字或难懂的文章 abstruse or illegible writing ❸ 古代帝王的诏书 imperial edict (in ancient China)

【天数】tiānshù 迷信的人把一切不可解的事、不能抗御的灾难都归于上天安排的命运,称为天数 predestination; fate; superstitious people believe that all inexplicable things, all irresistible disasters are predestined by Heaven

【天顺】Tiānshùn 明英宗(朱祁镇)年号(公元1457—1464) Tianshun, the reign title of Emperor Yingzong (Zhu Qizhen) (1457-1464) of the Ming Dynasty

【天堂】tiāntáng ❶ 某些宗教指人死后灵魂居住的永享幸福的地方(跟'地狱'相对 as opposed to 'hell') paradise; heaven; place where the souls of the deceased stay and enjoy happiness ❷〈比喻 *fig.*〉幸福美好的生活环境 paradise; excellent living environments

【天梯】tiāntī 很高的梯子,多装置在较高的建筑、设备上 sky ladder; tall ladder on high buildings and installations

【天体】tiāntǐ 太阳、地球、月亮和其他恒星、行星、卫星以及彗星、流星、宇宙尘、星云、星团等的统称 celestial body; general term for the sun, the earth, the moon and the other stars, planets, satellites, comets, shooting stars, cosmic dust, nebulas, clusters, etc.

【天天】tiāntiān 每天 every day:好好学习,～向上。Study well and make progress every day.

【天条】tiāntiáo 迷信的人认为老天爷所定的戒律,人、神都要遵守 heaven's commandments that must be obeyed by the humans and the gods as superstitious people hold:违犯～ violate Heaven's commandments

【天庭】[1] tiāntíng 指前额的中央 middle of the forehead:～饱满 full forehead

【天庭】[2] tiāntíng ❶ 神话中天神居住的地方(mythology) abode of deities ❷ 帝王的住所 imperial or royal abode

【天头】tiāntóu 书页上端的空白处 top (or upper) margin of a page

【天外】tiānwài ❶ 太空以外的地方 beyond the highest heavens ❷ 指极高极远的地方 far, far away

【天外有天】tiān wài yǒu tiān 指一个境界之外,更有无穷无尽的境界,多用来表示学问、技艺、本领等是没有止境的 there is always another heaven beyond this one; there is no limit to the universe; there is no limit to learning, skills, ability, etc.

【天王】tiānwáng ❶ 指天子 epithet for the emperor ❷ 太平天国领袖洪秀全的称号 Heavenly King, title assumed by Hong Xiuquan, founder of the Taiping Heavenly Kingdom (1851-1864) ❸ 神话传说中指某些天神 (mythology) heavenly king

【天王星】tiānwángxīng 太阳系九大行星之一,按离太阳由近而远的次序计为第七颗,绕太阳公转周期约 84 年,自转周期约为 24 ± 3 小时,侧向逆转。光度较弱,用望远镜才能看到。Uranus; the 7th of the 9 major planets in the solar system in terms of distance from the sun (period of revolution, about 84 years; period of rotation, about 24 ± 3 hours), rotating from east to west, not so bright, and visible only by telescope; (图见 ☞ figure for 太阳系 tàiyángxì on p. 1855)

【天网恢恢】tiān wǎng huī huī 天道像一个广阔的大网,作恶者逃不出这个网,也就是逃不出天道的惩罚 Net of heaven has large meshes. Net of Heaven is very large, and no evildoer can escape from it or from the punishment by Heaven. (见于《老子》See *Laozi*; 恢恢 *hui hui*:形容非常广大 vast)

【天文】tiānwén 日月星辰等天体在宇宙间分布、运行等现象 astronomy

【天文表】tiānwénbiǎo 应用于天文测时或航海计时的小型计时器具 small chronometer used in measuring astronomical time and navigational time measurement

【天文单位】tiānwén dānwèi 天文学上的一种距离单位,即以地球到太阳的平均距离为一个天文单位。1 天文单位约等于 1.496×10^8 公里。astronomical unit; unit of length based on the mean distance of the earth from the sun, about 1.496×10^8 kms.

【天文馆】tiānwénguǎn 普及天文知识的文化教育机构,一般有天象仪、天文望远镜等设备 planetarium; cultural and educational establishment where astronomical knowledge is popularized, usu. equipped with a planetarium, astronomical telescopes, etc.

【天文数字】tiānwén shùzì 指亿以上的极大的数字(因为天文学上用的数字极大,如天王星和太阳的平均距离是 2.8691×10^9 公里) astronomical figure; enormous figure; any figure above 100 million (because the figures used in astronomy are very large, for example, the mean distance of the Uranus from the sun is 2.8691×10^9 km.)

【天文台】tiānwéntái 观测天体和研究天文学的机构 (astronomical) observatory; establishment for observing the celestial body and studying astronomy

【天文望远镜】tiānwén wàngyuǎnjìng 用来观测

天体的望远镜。用透镜做物镜的叫折射望远镜,用反射镜做物镜的叫反射望远镜,既用透镜又用反射镜的叫双射望远镜。astronomical telescope; telescope used to observe the celestial body. That using a concave lens as its objective lens is a refracting telescope; that using a reflector as its objective lens is a reflecting telescope; that using both an concave lens and a convex mirror is a Schmidt telescope.

【天文学】tiānwénxué 研究天体的结构、形态、分布、运行和演化等的学科,一般分为天体测量学、天体力学、天体物理学和射电天文学等。天文学在实际生活中应用很广,如授时、编制历法、测定方位等。astronomy; science of the universe in which stars, planets, etc. are studied, including their origins, evolution, composition, positions, motions, etc., covering celestial surveying, celestial mechanics, astrophysics, and radio astronomy, widely used in real life for such purposes as providing time service, issuing calendars and determining positions

【天文钟】tiānwénzhōng 确定时刻的一种天文仪器,一般是每秒摆动一次的摆钟,准确度远比一般优良的时钟为高,通常放在真空的玻璃罩中,装在恒温的地下室里 astronomical clock, astronomical instrument that determines time; clock with a pendulum that swings to and fro once every second with a degree of accuracy much higher than common good-quality clocks, usu. placed in a vacuum glass cover in a constant-temperature underground room

【天下】tiānxià ❶ 指中国或世界 land under heaven; realm; world or China:～太平 peace reigns under heaven; the world (or the country) is at peace ❷ 指国家的统治权 rule; domination:打～ seize the state power|新中国是人民的～。New China is a country where the people are their own masters. *or* The people are masters of New China.

【天仙】tiānxiān 传说中天上的仙女 goddess;〈比喻 *fig.*〉美女 beautiful young woman; beauty

【天险】tiānxiǎn 天然的险要地方 natural barrier

【天线】tiānxiàn 用来发射或接收无线电波的装置。把发射机发射出来的无线电波送到空中去的叫发射天线,接收空中无线电波传送给接收机的叫接收天线。aerial; antenna; device used in sending and receiving electromagnetic waves. That transmitting the waves from the transmitter to the air is a transmitting antenna and that receiving the waves from the air and sending them to the receiver is a receiving antenna.

【天香国色】tiān xiāng guó sè 原是赞美牡丹的话,后常用来称美女 heavenly fragrance and national beauty; orig. used in reference to peony, later used in reference to a beautiful woman; also 国色天香 guó sè tiān xiāng

【天象】tiānxiàng ❶ 天文现象 astronomical phenomena; celestial phenomena:观测～ observe the heavenly bodies; astronomical observation ❷ 天空中风、云等变化的现象 changes of wind and cloud:我国劳动人民常根据～预测天气的变化。The working people in China often forecast weather according to changes in wind and cloud.

【天象仪】tiānxiàngyí 一种特制的光学投影器,用来在半球形的幕上放映出人造星空,显示日月星辰的运行情况以及日食、月食、流星雨等天文现象 planetarium; special optical projector used to simulate the past, present or future motions or positions of the sun, moon, planets, and stars as well as the solar eclipse, lunar eclipse and meteoric shower on the inside of a large dome

【天晓得】tiān xiǎo·de 天知道 God knows; Heaven knows

【天蝎座】tiānxiēzuò 黄道十二星座之一 Scorpio; Scorpius; one of the 12 zodiacal constellations; ☞ 黄道十二宫 huángdào shí'èrgōng on p.851

【天幸】tiānxìng 濒于灾祸而幸免的好运气 providential escape from a calamity; close call; near miss

【天性】tiānxìng 指人先天具有的品质或性情 natural instincts; nature:～善良 be good and kind by nature|他～就不爱说话。He is sparing of words by nature.

【天旋地转】tiān xuán dì zhuǎn ❶〈比喻 *fig.*〉重大的变化 major change ❷ 形容眩晕时的感觉 (feel as if) the sky and earth were spinning round; dizzy:昏沉沉只觉得～feel faint and dizzy as if the earth were spinning round ❸ 形容闹得很凶 make a fierce row:吵了个～ have a hell of a row

【天悬地隔】tiān xuán dì gé ☞ 天差地远 tiān chà dì yuǎn

【天涯】tiānyá 形容极远的地方 end of the world; the remotest corner of the earth:远在～,近在咫尺。Seemingly far apart, but actually close at hand.

【天涯海角】tiān yá hǎi jiǎo 形容极远的地方或彼此之间相隔极远 ends of the earth; the remotest corners of the earth; far apart; also 天涯地角 tiān yá dì jiǎo or 海角天涯 hǎi jiǎo tiān yá

【天阉】tiānyān 男子性器官发育不完全、没有生殖能力的现象 impotency; under-developed sex organs of a male; inability to be engaged in an intercourse

【天衣无缝】tiān yī wú fèng 神话传说,仙女穿的天衣,不用针线制作,没有缝儿 seamless heavenly robe worn by a fairy woman;〈比喻 *fig.*〉事物(多指诗文、话语等)没有一点破绽 flawless (poems, speeches, etc.)

【天意】tiānyì 上天的意旨(迷信)(superstition) God's will; will of Heaven

【天鹰座】tiānyīngzuò 北部天空中的星座,其中有一个一等星、五个三等星和几十个肉眼能看到的星,大部分在银河内,其余在银河的东边,牵牛星就是其中的一颗 Aquila; northern constellation in the Milky Way having one A star, five C stars and dozens of stars visible to the human eye, most of them in the Milky Way, the others to the east of the Milky Way, the Altair being one of them

【天宇】tiānyǔ ❶ 天空 sky; heaven:歌声响彻～。The singing rang through the sky. ❷〈书 *fml.*〉天下 land under heaven—the world or China

【天渊】tiānyuān〈书 *fml.*〉上天和深渊 high heaven and deep sea; poles apart;〈比喻 *fig.*〉差别极大 great difference:～之别 as far apart as between heaven and the earth; world of difference|相去～ world of difference; poles apart

【天灾】tiānzāi 自然灾害,如水灾、旱灾、风灾、地震等 natural disaster (or calamity), as flood, drought, windstorm, earthquake, etc.

【天葬】tiānzàng 某些民族和某些宗教的信徒处理死人遗体的方法,把死尸抬到葬场或旷野,让雕、鹰、乌鸦等鸟类吃 celestial burial (by which bodies are exposed to birds of prey); practice of disposing of the dead among some ethnic groups and certain religious believers, who carry the remains to a burial ground or open country and leave them exposed to vultures, eagles, crows and birds of prey

【天造地设】tiān zào dì shè 自然形成而合乎理想 created by nature; heavenly; ideal:这里物产丰富,山水秀丽,四季如春,真是～的好地方。This place has abundant resources, beautiful scenery and a pleasant weather all the year round. It is really a heavenly tourist resort.|他们真是～的一对好夫妻。They really make a perfect match.

【天真】tiānzhēn ❶ 心地单纯,性情直率;没有做作和虚伪 innocent; simple and unaffected; artless:～烂漫 innocent and artless; simple and unaffected ❷ 头脑简单,容易被假象迷惑 simple-minded; naive:这种想法过于～。The idea is too naive.

【天知道】tiān zhī·dao 表示难以理解或无法分辩 God (or Heaven) knows; difficult to understand or distinguish:～那是怎么一回事! God knows what it's all about.

【天职】tiānzhí 应尽的职责 bounden duty; vocation:服从命令是军人的～。Obeying an order is a soldier's bounden duty.

【天轴】tiānzhóu ❶ 通过皮带和皮带轮来转动车间中全部或一组机械的总轴,多用电动机带动。过去常装在厂房的高处,所以叫天轴。line shaft; main shaft which drives all machines or a set of machines by means of a belt and a pulley, usu. driven by an electric motor. It is installed at a high place in a workshop, hence the name. ❷ 指地球自转轴无限延长与天球相交的假想轴线 celestial axis; imaginary axis line that meets the celestial sphere

【天诛地灭】tiān zhū dì miè〈比喻 *fig.*〉为天地所不容(多用于赌咒、发誓 used in cursing or taking vows) be destroyed by heaven and earth; stand condemned by God

【天竺】Tiānzhú 我国古代称印度 ancient name for India 印度

【天主】Tiānzhǔ 天主教所崇奉的神,认为是宇宙万物的创造者和主宰者(of Catholicism) God; God worshipped by Catholics as the creator and ruler of the universe

【天主教】Tiānzhǔjiào 以罗马教皇为教会最高统治者的基督教派。明代传入我国。Catholicism; Christian church headed by the Pope, introduced into China in the Ming Dynasty; Roman Catholic; also 罗马公教 Luómǎ gōngjiào; ☞ 基督教 Jīdūjiào on p.896

【天姿国色】tiān zī guó sè 形容女子容貌非常美丽,也指容貌非常美丽的女子 reigning beauty; woman of matchless beauty

【天资】tiānzī 资质 natural gift; talent; natural endowments:～聪颖 bright and talented

【天子】tiānzǐ 指国王或皇帝(奴隶社会和封建社会的统治阶级把他们的政权说成是受天命建立的,因此称国王或皇帝为天的儿子) Son of Heaven; emperor (the ruling class in the slave society and feudal society said that their regimes were established by the heavenly orders, and the kings or emperors were thus called the sons of Heaven)

【天字第一号】tiān zì dì yī hào 从前对于数目多和种类多的东西,常用《千字文》文句的字来编排次序,'天'字是《千字文》首句'天地玄黄'的第一字,因此'天字第一号'就是第一或第一类中的第一号,借指最高的、最大的或最强的 number one in the world; A-1. The characters in the sentences in the *Essay of One Thousand Characters* were often used in the past to indicate the sequence of things in great quantity or in great variety. 天 tiān is the first character in the first sentence 'Heaven is black and earth yellow' in the *Essay of One Thousand characters*. Thus the phrase means 'first' or 'number one,' indicating sth. that is the highest, the biggest or the strongest.

【天足】tiānzú〈旧时 *old*〉指妇女没有经过缠裹的脚 natural feet; unbound feet of a woman

【天尊】tiānzūn 信道教的人对神仙的尊称;信佛教的人对佛的尊称 celestial worthy; title of some deities in the Taoist pantheon; respectful term of address for the immortal by Taoists; respectful term of address for the Buddha by Buddhist believers

【天作之合】tiān zuò zhī hé 上天成全的婚姻(多用做新婚的颂词 term of congratulations on a wedding) heaven-made match

添 tiān ❶ 增添;增加 add; increase:～人 add people|～水 add water|～枝加叶 exaggerate|如虎～翼 add wings to a tiger; make something stronger or more powerful|～了三十台机器 have added thirty more machines ❷〈方 *dial.*〉指生育(后代)(of descendant) have a baby:他家～了个女儿。He had a daughter recently.

【添补】tiān·bu 补充(用具、衣裳等) replenish; get more (utensils, clothes, etc.)

【添彩】tiāncǎi 增添光彩 add colour; add lustre; bring honour to; do a credit:增色～ make more attractive|～生辉 make it more brilliant

【添仓】tiān//cāng 填仓 put grain into one's bin as a sign of good luck

【添丁】tiān//dīng〈旧时 *old*〉指生了小孩儿,特指生了男孩儿 have a baby (esp. a boy) born into the family

【添堵】tiāndǔ〈方 *dial.*〉给人增加不愉快;让人心烦、憋气 make someone unhappy; increase someone's vexation

【添加剂】tiānjiājì 为改善物质的某些性能而加入到物质中的药剂,如防老剂、增效剂、抗震剂等 additive; agent that helps to improve the properties of some substances after it is added, as antideteriorant, synergist, anti-quake agent, etc.

【添乱】tiān//luàn 增加麻烦 give more trouble to someone:人家这是在谈正事,你别在一旁～了。They are talking seriously. Don't disturb them.

【添箱】tiān//xiāng〈旧时 *old*〉指女家的亲友赠送新娘礼物或礼金 (of bride's relatives or friends) give wedding presents to bride

【添箱】tiānxiāng〈旧时 *old*〉女子出嫁时亲友所送的贺礼 wedding presents given to a bride by her relatives and friends

【添油加醋】tiān yóu jiā cù ☞ 添枝加叶 tiān zhī jiā yè

【添枝加叶】tiān zhī jiā yè 形容叙述事情或转述别人的话时,为了夸张渲染,添上原来没有的内容 add colour and emphasis to (a narration); add highly coloured details to (a story); embellish (a story); also 添油加醋 tiān yóu jiā cù

【添置】tiānzhì 在原有的以外再购置 add to one's possessions; acquire:～家具 buy more furniture|～衣服 buy more clothes

【添砖加瓦】tiān zhuān jiā wǎ〈比喻 *fig.*〉为宏伟的事业做一点小小的贡献 do what little one can to help a great cause:我们要为国家的经济建设～ do one's bit to help the country with its economic construction

黇 tiān [黇鹿](tiānlù)鹿的一种,全身毛黄褐色或带赤褐色,有白色斑纹,角的上部扁平或呈掌状,尾略长,性温顺 fallow deer (*Dama dama*); docile deer with yellowish-brown, or russet, white-striped hair all over the body, a relatively long tail, and horns whose upper part is flat or palm-shaped

tián(ㄊㄧㄢˊ)

田¹ tián ❶ 田地(有的地区专指水田 referring to paddy fields in some regions) field; farmland; cropland:水～ paddy fields|稻～ rice fields|麦～ wheat field|耕～ plough fields ❷ 指可供开采的蕴藏矿物的地带 zone with a workable mineral deposit:煤～ coalfield|油～ oilfield|气～ gas field ❸ (Tián)姓 a surname

田² tián〈书 *fml.*〉same as 畋 tián,打猎 go hunting

【田产】tiánchǎn 个人、团体等所拥有的田地 (property in the form of) land; landed property; estate

【田塍】tiánchéng〈方 *dial.*〉田埂 low bank of earth between fields; ridge

【田畴】tiánchóu〈书 *fml.*〉田地;田野 farmland; cultivated land; fields

【田地】tiándì ❶ 种植农作物的土地 field; farmland; cropland ❷ 地步 wretched situation; plight:想不到他会落到这步～! I never dreamt things would come to such a pass for him.

【田畈】tiánfàn〈方 *dial.*〉田地;土地 fields; land

【田赋】tiánfù 封建时代征收的土地税 land tax collected in the feudal times

【田埂】tiángěng 田间的埂子,用来分界并蓄水 low bank of earth between fields; ridge

【田鸡】tiánjī ❶ 鸟,形状略像鸡,体形较小,羽毛赤栗色,背部橄榄色,嘴绿褐色,脚赤色。生活在草原和水田里。sora rail (*Porzana carolina*), sora, small bird in the shape of chicken, with chestnut feathers, an olive back, a greenish-brown bill and red feet, living in grasslands and paddy fields ❷ 青蛙的通称 general term for 青蛙 qīngwā

【田家】tiánjiā 指从事农业生产的人家 farming family:～情趣 joy of life in a farming family; temperament and taste of a farming family

【田间】tiánjiān 田地里,有时借指农村 field; farm; countryside:～劳动 field work; farm work|来自～ from the country; country life

【田径赛】tiánjìngsài 田赛和径赛的合称 track and field meet

【田径运动】tiánjìng yùndòng 体育运动项目的一大类,包括各种跳跃、投掷、赛跑和竞走等 track and field; athletics; sport includes jumping, throwing, running and walking events

【田坎】tiánkǎn 田埂 low bank of earth between fields; ridge

【田猎】tiánliè 〈书 *fml.*〉打猎 go hunting

【田垄】tiánlǒng ❶ 田埂 low bank of earth between fields; ridge ❷ 田地中种植农作物的垄 ridges for planting crops in the fields

【田螺】tiánluó 软体动物,壳圆锥形,苍黑色,触角长,胎生。生长在淡水中。river snail (*Viviparus*); soft-bodied, viviparous animal with a dark-green, conical shell, a long feeler, living in fresh water

【田亩】tiánmǔ 田地(总称)(collet.) farmland

【田契】tiánqì 买卖田地时所立的契约 title deed for buying and selling farmland; land deed

【田赛】tiánsài 田径运动中各种跳跃、投掷项目比赛的总称 field events; including all jumping and throwing events

【田舍】tiánshè 〈书 *fml.*〉❶ 田地和房屋 farmland and house ❷ 农村的房子 farmhouse ❸ 田家 farming family:~翁 an old countryman|~郎 young farmer; farm boy

【田鼠】tiánshǔ 鼠的一类,有多种,体长约10厘米,生活在树林、草地、田野里,主要吃草本植物的茎、叶、种子等,对农作物有害 field vole (*Microtus arvalis*); vole; any of a number of small rodents, about 10 cm. long, which lives in the woods, grasslands and fields, and feeds on the stem, leaves and seeds of herbaceous plants, and is destructive to the farm crops

【田野】tiányě 田地和原野 field; open country:~上一片碧绿。The field is an expanse of green.

【田野工作】tiányě gōngzuò 野外工作的旧称 old term for 野外工作 yěwài gōngzuò

【田园】tiányuán 田地和园圃,泛指农村 fields and gardens; countryside:~之乐 idyllic happiness|~风光 rural scenery|~诗人 pastoral poet

【田园诗】tiányuánshī 以农村景物和农民、牧人、渔夫的劳动为题材的诗 idyll; pastoral poetry

【田庄】tiánzhuāng ❶ 田地和庄园 country estate ❷〈方 *dial.*〉庄户;农村 peasant household; countryside; rural areas:~人家 rural family; peasant family; farming family

佃 tián 〈书 *fml.*〉❶ 耕种田地 cultivate farmland ❷ same as 畋 tián, 打猎 go hunting

☞ diàn on p.441

畋 tián 〈书 *fml.*〉打猎 go hunting

畑 tián 日本汉字,旱地。多用于日本姓名。(Chinese character in the Japanese language) dryland, usu. used in the name of a Japanese

恬 tián 〈书 *fml.*〉❶ 恬静 quiet; tranquil; calm:~适 quiet and comfortable ❷ 满不在乎;坦然 not care at all; remain unperturbed:~不知耻 do not feel ashamed; have no sense of shame; be shameless|~不为怪 be not surprised at all; be not disturbed

【恬不知耻】tián bù zhī chǐ 做了坏事满不在乎,不以为耻 do not feel ashamed; have no sense of shame; be shameless

【恬淡】tiándàn ❶ 不追求名利;淡泊 indifferent to fame or gain:心怀~ remain indifferent|~寡欲 indifferent to worldly desires ❷ 恬静;安适 quiet; tranquil; peaceful:勾起对乡村~生活的回忆 call back the memory of the tranquil country life

【恬静】tiánjìng 安静;宁静 quiet; peaceful; tranquil:环境幽雅~ peaceful and pleasant environment|~的生活 peaceful life; quiet life

【恬然】tiánrán 满不在乎的样子 unperturbed; calm; nonchalant:处之~ remain unruffled|~不以为怪 be not surprised at all; be not disturbed

【恬适】tiánshì 〈书 *fml.*〉恬静而舒适 quiet and comfortable

钿 tián 〈方 *dial.*〉❶ 硬币 coin:铜~(铜钱,也泛指款子,钱财) copper (copper coin, also sum of money or money in a broad sense) ❷ same as 钱[1] qián②:几~(多少钱?) How much is it? ❸ same as 钱[1] qián ③:车~ fare

☞ diàn on p.443

畠 tián 日本汉字,旱地。多用于日本姓名。(Chinese character in the Japanese language) dryland, usually used in a Japanese name

菾 tián [菾菜] (tiáncài) same as 甜菜 tiáncài

甜 tián ❶ 像糖和蜜的味道 sweet; honeyed:这西瓜真~。This watermelon is really sweet! ◇话说得很~。The words were honeyed. ❷ 形容舒适、愉快 comfortable; pleasant:他睡得真~。He had a sound (or sweet) sleep. *or* He slept soundly.

【甜菜】tiáncài ❶ 二年生草本植物,根肥大,叶子丛生,有长柄,总状花序,花小,绿色。根含有糖质,是制糖的主要原料之一。beet (*Beta vulgaris*); biennial herbaceous plant with edible leaves in clusters and long stalks, small green flowers borne in racemes, and a thick, fleshy, white or red root that makes a major raw material for sugar refineries ❷ 这种植物的根 its root ‖ 通称 commonly called 糖萝卜 tángluó·bo; also 菾菜 tiáncài

【甜点】tiándiǎn 甜的点心 sweet snacks; sweets; pastries; dessert

【甜活儿】tiánhuór 费力少而报酬多的工作(对'苦活儿'而言 as opposed to 'hard and unprofitable job') easy and well-paid job

【甜津津】tiánjīnjīn (～的 tiánjīnjīn·de) 甜丝丝 tastefully sweet

【甜美】tiánměi ❶ same as 甜 tián ①:这种苹果多汁而～。This apple is juicy and luscious. ❷ 愉快;舒服;美好 pleasant; refreshing:音色～ sweet tone|～的生活 happy life

【甜蜜】tiánmì 形容感到幸福、愉快、舒适 sweet; happy; comfortable:孩子们笑得那么～! How merrily the children laughed! |日子过得甜甜蜜蜜 leading a very happy life together

【甜面酱】tiánmiànjiàng 馒头等发酵后制成的酱,有甜味。有的地区叫甜酱 sweet sauce made of fermented buns, etc.; in some areas also 甜酱 tiánjiàng

【甜润】tiánrùn 甜美滋润(of voice) sweet; melodious:嗓音～ sweet voice; melodious voice|清凉～的空气 cool and refreshing air

【甜食】tiánshí 甜的食品 sweet food; sweets

【甜水】tiánshuǐ 指味道不苦的水 fresh water:～井 fresh water well

【甜丝丝】tiánsīsī (～儿的 tiánsīrsīr·de) ❶ 形容有甜味 pleasantly sweet:这种菜～儿的,很好吃。This dish is sweet and delicious. ❷ 形容感到幸福愉快 quite pleased; gratified; happy:她想到孩子们都长大成人,能为祖国尽力,心里～儿的。She feels quite pleased (or happy) to think of her children all growing up and doing their bit to the country.

【甜头】tián·tou (～儿 tián·tour) ❶ 微甜的味道,泛指好吃的味道 sweet taste; pleasant flavour ❷ 好处;利益(多指引诱人的) good; benefit (as an inducement):尝到了读书的～ become aware of the benefits of going to school; come to know the good of schooling

【甜言蜜语】tián yán mì yǔ 为了讨人喜欢或哄骗人而说的好听的话 sweet words and honeyed phrases; fine-sounding words; words spoken to please or cheat others

湉 tián [湉湉]〈书 *fml.*〉形容水流平静 calm or quiet flow of water

填 tián ❶ 把凹陷地方垫平或塞满 fill; stuff; fill something into a hollow place until it is level:～坑 fill a pit|把沟～平了 fill up a ditch ❷ 补充 fill; replenish; complement; supplement:～补 fill (a vacancy) ❸ 填写 write; fill in:～表 fill in a form

【填报】tiánbào 填表上报 fill in a form and submit it to the leadership:每周～工程进度 make a weekly progress report on a project

【填补】tiánbǔ 补足空缺或缺欠 fill (a vacancy, gap, etc.); step into the breach:～缺额 fill a vacancy|～空白 fill in the gaps; fill in the blank

【填仓】tián//cāng 旧俗正月二十五日为填仓节,往粮囤里添点粮食,表示吉利,并且吃讲究的饭食(old custom) The 25th day of the 1st lunar month is the Grain-bin-filling Festival, during which time grain is put into one's bin as a sign of good luck and a good meal is served.

【填充】tiánchōng ❶ 填补(某个空间) fill up; stuff:～作用 filling effect ❷ 教学中测验的一种方法,把问题写成一句话,空着要求回答的部分,让人填写 fill in the blanks (in a test paper); test in which problems are prepared in sentences with blanks for students to fill in as their answers:～题 problems with blanks to be filled in

【填词】tián//cí 按照词的格律作词,因为必须严格地按照格律选字用韵,所以叫做填词 fill in the words to fit a given tune — compose a *ci* poem by choosing a tune and then writing words to it according to a strict tonal pattern and rhyme scheme

【填房】tián//fáng 指女子嫁给死了妻子的人 (of a woman) marry a widower

【填房】tián·fang 指前妻死后续娶的妻 woman who marries a widower

【填空】tiánkòng ❶ 填补空出的或空着的位置、职务等 fill a vacant position; fill a vacancy:～补缺 fill vacancies and supply deficiencies ❷ same as 填充 tiánchōng ②

【填料】tiánliào 搀在混凝土、橡胶、塑料等中间起填充作用的材料,通常粒状、粉末状或纤维状,如黄土、锯末、滑石、石棉、炭黑等 packing; stuffing; filling; filler; materials that are mixed with concrete, rubber, plastics, etc. with the filling effect, usually particles, powdered or fibrous, as loess, saw dust, talc, asbestos, carbon black, etc.

【填塞】tiánsè 往洞穴或空着的地方填东西,使塞满或不通 stop up; fill up; block up; fill a hole or an empty place with things:～洞隙 stop up a loophole; fill up holes and cracks ◇～心灵上的空虚 fill a spiritual vacuum

【填写】tiánxiě 在印好的表格、单据等的空白处,按照项目、格式写上应写的文字或数字 fill in or write words or figures in the blank spaces on a printed form, bills, etc.:～履历表 fill a form of personal record|～汇款通知单 fill a money order

【填鸭】tiányā ❶ 饲养鸭子的一种方法。鸭子长到一定时期,按时把做成长条形的饲料从鸭子的嘴里填进去,并减少鸭子的活动量,使它很快长肥。北京鸭多用这种方法饲养。force-feed a duck; method of raising ducks, by which long strips of prepared food are force-fed into the mouth of a duck that has grown to a certain stage. The ducks thus fed are kept from moving so that they can become fattened quickly. ❷ 用填鸭的方法饲养的鸭子 force-fed duck

阗 tián 〈书 *fml.*〉充满 be full of; fill up:喧～ noisy and crowded (with guests)

tiǎn（ㄊㄧㄢˇ）

忝 tiǎn〈书 *fml.*〉〈谦辞 *hum.*〉表示辱没他人，自己有愧 be unworthy of the honour：～列门墙（愧在师门）have the honour to be a student of somebody｜～在相知之列。I deem it an honour, though I'm unworthy of it, to be counted among your acquaintances.

殄 tiǎn 灭绝 extirpate; exterminate：暴～天物（任意糟蹋东西）waste nature's produce (esp. grains) thoughtlessly; squander natural resources

铦 tiǎn〈书 *fml.*〉勾取；探取 lure; bait; seduce

淟 tiǎn〈书 *fml.*〉污浊；肮脏 dirty; filthy muddy; turbid

惧 tiǎn〈书 *fml.*〉惭愧 be ashamed

靦 tiǎn ❶〈书 *fml.*〉形容惭愧 be ashamed：～颜 shameful look; shamefaced ❷ 厚着脸皮叫靦着脸 brazen it out

【靦颜】tiǎnyán〈书 *fml.*〉❶ 表现出惭愧的脸色 be ashamed; be shamefaced ❷ 厚颜 brazen; shameful：～惜命 save one's life at the cost of one's honour

腆 tiǎn ❶ 丰盛；丰厚 sumptuous; rich ❷〈方 *dial.*〉凸出或挺起（胸、腹）protrude; thrust out：～着胸脯 stick out one's chest｜～着个大肚子 protrude one's belly

覥 tiǎn〈书 *fml.*〉❶ 形容人脸 faced; facial：～然人面 faced; facial ❷ same as 靦 tiǎn

☞ miǎn on p.1338

舔 tiǎn 用舌头接触东西或取东西 lick; lap; pass the tongue over：～盘子 lick a plate｜猫～爪子。The cat is licking its paws.

tiàn（ㄊㄧㄢˋ）

掭 tiàn ❶ 用毛笔蘸墨后斜着在砚台上理顺笔毛或除去多余的墨汁（when preparing to write）dip a writing brush in ink and bring its tip to a fine point by twisting it gently on the inkstone ❷〈方 *dial.*〉拨动 poke：～灯心 raise the wick of a lamp

tiāo（ㄊㄧㄠ）

佻 tiāo 轻佻 frivolous：～薄 frivolous; skittish; giddy

【佻薄】tiāobó〈书 *fml.*〉轻佻 frivolous

【佻巧】tiāoqiǎo〈书 *fml.*〉❶ 轻佻巧诈 frivolous and crafty ❷（文辞）细巧而不严肃（writing）full of fine words and frivolous expressions; flowery and flippant

【佻挞】tiāotà〈书 *fml.*〉轻薄 frivolous; skittish; giddy; given to philandering：心性～ be frivolous by nature

挑1 tiāo ❶ 挑选 choose; select; pick out：～心爱的买 buy what you like ❷ 挑剔 nitpick; be hypercritical; be fastidious：～毛病 find fault

挑2 tiāo ❶ 扁担等两头挂上东西，用肩膀支起来搬运 carry (or tote) on the shoulder with a pole; shoulder：～担 carry loads on a shoulder pole｜～水 carry (or fetch) water on a shoulder pole｜～着两筐土 carry two baskets of earth on a shoulder pole ❷（～儿 tiāor）挑子 carrying pole with loads：挑～儿 shoulder a carrying pole with loads ❸（～儿 tiāor）〈量词 *classifier*〉用于成挑儿的东西 loads carried on a pole：一～儿白菜 two baskets of cabbages carried on a shoulder pole

☞ tiǎo on p.1903

【挑刺儿】tiāo//cìr 挑剔；指摘（言语行动方面的缺点）find fault; pick holes; be captious (faults in speeches and actions)

【挑肥拣瘦】tiāo féi jiǎn shòu 挑选对自己有利的（含贬义 derog.）pick the fat or choose the lean; choose whatever is to one's personal advantage：担任工作不应～。In taking assignments, one shouldn't always pick and choose.

【挑夫】tiāofū〈旧时 *old*〉指以给人挑货物、行李为业的人 porter; person who makes a living by carrying goods or luggage for others

【挑拣】tiāojiǎn same as 挑选 tiāoxuǎn

【挑脚】tiāo//jiǎo〈旧时 *old*〉指给人挑运货物或行李 carry goods or luggage on a shoulder pole：～的 person who carries goods on a shoulder pole

【挑食】tiāoshí 指对食物有所选择，有的爱吃，有的不爱吃或不吃 be choosy about what one eats; very careful in choosing what one likes to eat, what one doesn't like to eat, or what one doesn't eat

【挑剔】tiāo·tī 过分严格地在细节上指摘 nitpick; be hypercritical; be fastidious：她由于过分～，跟谁也合不来。She is too fastidious to get along with others.

【挑选】tiāoxuǎn 从若干人或事物中找出适合要求的 choose; select; pick out：～人才 select people of ability｜～苹果 select apples｜小分队的成员都是经过严格～的。All the members of the detachment were strictly chosen.

【挑眼】tiāo//yǎn〈方 *dial.*〉挑剔毛病；指摘缺点（多指礼节方面的 oft. about etiquette, etc.）fault-finding; fastidious; be fastidious

【挑字眼儿】tiāo zìyǎnr 从措辞用字上找小毛病 find fault with the choice of words; quibble

【挑子】tiāo·zi 扁担和它两头所挑的东西 carrying pole with its load; load carried on a shoulder pole：菜～ vegetables carried on a shoulder pole

【挑嘴】tiāozuǐ 挑食 be very choosy about what one eats

祧 tiāo 〈书 *fml.*〉❶ 原指祭远祖的庙,后来指继承上代 keep up one's ancestral shrine; be or become heir to:兼～ be heir to both one's father and one's uncle ❷ 把隔了几代的祖宗的神主迁入远祖的庙 move forefathers' memorial tablets into the ancestral shine:不～之祖 ancestor who does not deserve a place in the ancestral shrine

tiáo (ㄊㄧㄠˊ)

条(條) tiáo ❶ (～儿 tiáor)细长的树枝 twig:枝～ branches and twigs|荆～ twigs of the chaste tree|柳～儿 willow twigs; wicker ❷ (～儿 tiáor)条子 long narrow piece; strip; slip:面～儿 noodles|布～儿 a slip|便～儿 an informal note|金～儿 gold bar ❸ (～儿 tiáor)细长的形状 long and slender in pattern or shape; striped; streak:～纹 stripe|花～儿布 striped cloth ❹ 分项目的 item; article:～例 regulations; rules|～目 clauses and subclauses|～款 clause; article|～陈 present item by item; state point by point ❺ 层次;秩序;条理 order:有～不紊 well-organised; systematically|井井有～ in good order; in perfect order ❻〈量词 *classifier*〉a)用于细长的东西[used for long and thin things]:一～线 a thread|两～腿 two legs|三～鱼 three fish|五～黄瓜 five cucumbers|一～大街 one street b)用于以固定数量合成的某些长条形的东西[used for long things each consisting of a fixed number]:一～儿肥皂(连在一起的两块肥皂) a bar of soap (consisting of two pieces|一～儿烟(香烟一般十包合在一起叫一条) a carton of cigarettes (consisting of ten packs) c)用于分项的[used for itemized nouns]:三～新闻 three pieces of news|五～办法 five measures

【条案】tiáo'àn 一种狭长的桌子,长一丈左右,宽一尺多,放陈设品用 long narrow table, about one *zhang* (3.33 metres) long and more than one *chi* (0.33 metre) broad, to display ornaments on; also 条几 tiáojī

【条播】tiáobō 播种的一种方法,把种子均匀地播成长条,行与行之间保持一定距离 drilling; sow seeds in rows to improve growth and efficiency; plant (a field) in drills

【条畅】tiáochàng 〈书 *fml.*〉(文章)通畅而有条理(of writing) smooth and well-organised:文笔～ fluent and coherent writing

【条陈】tiáochén ❶ 分条陈述 state item by item ❷〈旧时 *old*〉向上级分条陈述意见的文件 itemized memorandum to one's superior:上了一个～ submit an itemized memorandum to one's superior

【条分缕析】tiáo fēn lǚ xī 形容分析得细密而有条理 make a careful and detailed analysis

【条幅】tiáofú 直挂的长条的字画,单幅的叫单条,成组的叫屏条 vertically hung scroll of painting or calligraphy; wall scroll; one scroll is called 单条 dāntiáo, and a set of four scrolls is called 屏条 píngtiáo

【条贯】tiáoguàn 〈书 *fml.*〉条理;系统 proper arrangement or presentation; orderlyness; systematicness

【条规】tiáoguī 由国家或集体制定的分列项目的规则 rules; regulations formulated by the state or an organization

【条件】tiáojiàn ❶ 影响事物发生、存在或发展的因素 condition; term; factor:自然～ natural conditions|创造有利～ create favourable conditions ❷ 为某事而提出的要求或定出的标准 requirement; prerequisite; qualification:讲～ negotiate terms|他的～太高,我无法答应。The conditions he proposed were too high for me to accept. ❸ 状况 conditions:他身体～很好。He is in very good physical condition.|这个工厂～好,工人素质高,设备也先进。This factory has very good conditions, high-quality workers and advanced equipment.

【条件刺激】tiáojiàn cìjī 生理学上指引起条件反射的刺激(phys.) conditioned stimulus; stimulus that occasions conditioned reflex

【条件反射】tiáojiàn fǎnshè 有机体因信号的刺激而发生的反应,例如铃声本来不会使狗分泌唾液,但是如果在每次喂食物之前打铃,经过若干次之后,狗听到铃声就会分泌出唾液来,这种因铃声这个信号的刺激而发生的反应叫条件反射,铃声就叫条件刺激 conditioned response; conditioned reflex; response from an organism occasioned by the stimulus of a signal. For example, the ringing of a bell does not give rise to the secretion of saliva in a dog, but if the bell is rung every time before the dog is fed with meat, the dog will secrete saliva when it hears the ringing of a bell. The response occasioned by the stimulus from the ringing of a bell is conditioned reflex.

【条款】tiáokuǎn 文件或契约上的条目 clause (in a formal document or deed); article; provision:法律～ legal provision

【条理】tiáolǐ 思想、言语、文字的层次;生活、工作的秩序 proper arrangement or presentation; orderliness; method:～分明 well-organized|生活安排得很有～。Good arrangements have been made for daily life.

【条例】tiáolì 由国家制定或批准的规定某些事项或某一机关的组织、职权等的法律文件,也指团体制定的章程 regulations; rules; ordinances; legal document formulated or approved by the state concerning certain matters or the setup of an organ and its functions and powers; also regulations formulated by an organization:奖惩～ rules for rewards and penalties|治安管理～ security administration regulations

【条令】tiáolìng 用简明条文规定的军队行动的准则,如战斗条令、纪律条令等 regulations for the military affairs, such as combat regulations, disciplinary regulations, etc.

【条目】tiáomù 规章、条约等的项目 clauses and subclauses (in a formal document):分列～ list of clauses and subclauses

【条绒】tiáoróng 灯心绒 corduroy

【条条框框】tiáo·tiáo kuàng·kuàng 指束缚人的各种规章制度 rules and regulations; regulations and restrictions; conventions and taboos:打破～ break free from regulations and restrictions

【条文】tiáowén 法规、章程等的分条说明的文字 article (in laws and regulations); clause

【条形码】tiáoxíngmǎ 商品的代码标记。用粗细相间的黑白线条表示数字,印在商品包装上,用于计算机识别。bar code; (U. S.) Universal Product Code (UPC); any of the patterned sets of vertical bars of varying widths imprinted on consumer products, mail, etc. and containing coded information that can be read by a computerized scanner

【条约】tiáoyuē 国家和国家签订的有关政治、军事、经济或文化等方面的权利和义务的文书 treaty; pact; document signed between two or more countries on their respective rights and obligations in political, military, economic or cultural fields:军事～ military pact|和平友好～ treaty of peace and friendship|不平等～ unequal treaty

【条子】tiáo·zi ❶ 狭长的东西 strip:纸～narrow strip of paper; a slip of paper ❷ 便条 brief informal note ❸〈方 *dial.*〉金条 gold bar

苕 tiáo 古书上指凌霄花 Chinese trumpet creeper (*Campsis grandiflora*) as described in ancient books

☞ sháo on p. 1689

岧(岹) tiáo ☞ below

【岧岧】tiáotiáo〈书 *fml.*〉形容高 high; lofty

【岧峣】tiáoyáo〈书 *fml.*〉形容山高 high (mountain)

迢 tiáo ☞ below

【迢迢】tiáotiáo 形容路途遥远 far away; remote:千里～ from a thousand *li* far; from afar

【迢远】tiáoyuǎn 遥远 remote; distant:路途～ far, far away; remote

调1 tiáo ❶ 配合得均匀合适 suit well; fit in perfectly:风～雨顺 good weather for the crops|饮食失～ have improper diet ❷ 使配合得均匀合适 mix; adjust well:～味 flavour|～配 mix; blend|牛奶里加点糖～一下。Mix some sugar into the milk. ❸ 调解 mediate:～停 mediate|～处 mediate; arbitrate|～人 mediator

调2 tiáo ❶ 挑逗 provoke; tease; tantalize:～笑 make fun of; poke fun at; tease|～戏 take liberties with (a woman); assail (a woman) with obscenities ❷ 挑拨 incite; instigate; sow discord:～词架讼(挑拨别人诉讼) abet someone in filing a suit

☞ diào on p. 447

【调拨】tiáobō 挑拨 incite, instigate; sow discord

☞ diàobō on p. 447

【调处】tiáochǔ same as 调停 tiáotíng ①:～纠纷 arbitrate a dispute; act as mediator

【调幅】tiáofú 使载波的频率保持不变,而它的振幅依照所需传递信号的变化规律而变化 amplitude modulation; changing of the amplitude of the transmitting radio wave in accordance with the signal being broadcast

【调羹】tiáogēng 羹匙 spoon

【调和】tiáo·hé ❶ 配合得适当 harmonious:色彩～ harmonious colours|雨水～。Rainfall is well distributed. ❷ 排解纠纷,使双方重归和好 mediate; reconcile:从中～ mediate; act as mediator ❸ 妥协、让步(多用于否定 usu. used in the negative) compromise; make concessions:他认为在这个原则问题上没有～的余地。He thinks that there is no room for compromise on this matter of principle.

【调和漆】tiáohéqī 人造漆的一种,用干性油、颜料等制成的叫做油性调和漆,用树脂、干性油和颜料等制成的叫做磁性调和漆 ready-mixed paint; mixed oleopaint — artificial paint consisting of drying oil and dyes; mixed varnish paint, consisting of resin, drying oil and dyes

【调护】tiáohù 调养护理 take care of a patient during convalescence; nurse:精心～ meticulous nursing

【调级】tiáo//jí 调整工资级别(多指提升 usu. upwards) adjust a wage scale

【调剂】tiáo//jì 根据医生的处方配制药物 fill a prescription

【调剂】tiáojì 把多和少、忙和闲等加以适当的调整 adjust; regulate (quantity; amount of work, etc.):～物资 regulate the supply of goods|～生活 enliven one's life|娱乐可以～精神。Recreation helps to enliven one's life (or to break the monotony of life).

【调价】tiáo//jià 调整商品价格(多指提高价格 usu. upwards) readjust or modify prices

【调教】tiáojiào ❶ 调理教导(多指幼童 usu. children) look after and guide:不服～ disobey the education and guidance ❷ 照料训练(牲畜等) feed and train (domestic animals):～劣马 break in a vicious horse|～鹦鹉 train a parrot

【调节】tiáojié 从数量上或程度上调整,使适合

要求 regulate; adjust:水能～动物的体温。Water helps to adjust the body temperature of an animal.|经过水库的～,航运条件大为改善。With the water reservoir regulating the water, navigation conditions have been greatly improved.

【调解】tiáojiě 劝说双方消除纠纷 mediate; make peace:～人 mediator|～纠纷 mediate in (or patch up) a dispute

【调经】tiáojīng 〈中医 *Chin. med.*〉指用药物调整子宫的机能,使月经正常 regulate the menstrual function of the womb

【调侃】tiáokǎn 用言语戏弄;嘲笑 ridicule; jeer at; deride

【调控】tiáokòng 调节控制 regulate and control:～地下水的水位 regulate and control of the level of the ground water|经济～失灵。The economic control has become ineffective.

【调理】tiáo·lǐ ❶ 调养;调护 nurse one's health; recuperate:病刚好,要注意～。You've just recovered. Be sure to nurse yourself. ❷ 照料;管理 take care of; look after:～伙食 take care of the diet|～牲口 look after livestock ❸ 管教;训练 subject sb. to discipline ❹〈方 *dial.*〉戏弄 make fun of; play tricks on; tease

【调料】tiáoliào 作料 condiment; seasoning; flavouring

【调弄】tiáonòng ❶ 调笑;戏弄 make fun of; tease:～妇女 dally with a woman ❷ 整理;摆弄 fix; arrange; adjust:～琴弦 adjust the strings ❸ 调唆 instigate; stir up:～是非 stir up a trouble

【调配】tiáopèi 调和,配合(颜料、药物等) mix; blend (colours, medicinal herbs, etc.)
☞ diàopèi on p.448

【调皮】tiáopí ❶ 顽皮 naughty; mischievous ❷ 不驯顺;狡猾不易对付 disobedient; unruly; tricky; recalcitrant; sly ❸ 指耍小聪明,做事不老实 insincere; scheming; dishonest

【调频】tiáopín ❶ 调整交流发电机等的输出功率,使电力系统等的频率保持在一定范围内,以保证用电设备正常工作 adjust the output of a power generator and keep the frequency of the power system within a given range to ensure normal working of the power equipment ❷ 使载波的振幅保持不变,而它的瞬时频率依照所需传递信号的变化规律而变化 frequency modulation; variation of instantaneous frequency of a carrier wave in accordance with the signal to be transmitted while keeping the amplitude of the carrier wave unchanged

【调情】tiáoqíng 男女间挑逗、戏谑 flirt; play at love

【调摄】tiáoshè 〈书 *fml.*〉调养 take good care of oneself (as in poor health or after an illness); build up one's health by taking a good rest and nutritions food; be nursed back to health

【调试】tiáoshì 试验并调整(机器、仪器等)(of machine, instrument, etc.) test run; (computer) debug:机床装好后要经过～才能投入生产。The machine tool can be put into operation only through a test run after it is installed.

【调唆】tiáo·suō 挑拨,使跟别人闹纠纷 incite; instigate; abet; stir up trouble; sow discord:他俩不知,一定有人在～。Somebody must have sown discord between them, setting the two against each other.

【调停】tiáo·tíng ❶ 调解 mediate; intervene:居中～ act as an intermediary ❷ 照料;安排(多见于早期白话 oft. in early vernacular) take care of; look after; make arrangements for

【调味】tiáo//wèi 加在食物中使滋味可口 flavour; season; add some flavourings in the food to make it tasty:～品 flavouring; dressing; seasoning; condiment|花椒、八角都可以～。Both Chinese prickly ashes and anise are good flavourings.

【调戏】tiáo·xì 用轻佻的言语举动戏弄(妇女) use frivolous language and conducts to tease (a woman); take liberties with (a woman); assail (a woman) with obscenities

【调笑】tiáoxiào 开玩笑;嘲笑 make fun of; poke fun at; tease

【调协】tiáoxié 调和;协调 coordinate; harmonize; bring into line:不相～do not cooperate well

【调谐】tiáoxié ❶ 和谐 harmonious:色彩～ harmonious colours ❷ 调节可变电容器或线圈使接收电路达到谐振 tune; tuning; adjust a radio or television receiver to a given frequency or channel so as to receive a specified station, program, etc.; tune in; tune out

【调谑】tiáoxuè same as 调笑 tiáoxiào

【调养】tiáoyǎng 调节饮食起居,必要时服用药物,使身体恢复健康 take good care of oneself (as in poor health or after an illness); build up one's health by taking rest and nourishing food; be nursed back to health:静心～ recuperate by taking a good rest and nourishing food|病后要好好～身体 take good care of one's health after illness

【调匀】tiáoyún 调和均匀 mix well:雨水～。Rainfall is well distributed.|饮食～ well blended diet

【调整】tiáozhěng 改变原有的情况,使适应客观环境和要求 adjust; regulate; revise; change the existing condition to adapt oneself to the objective environments and requirements:～物价 readjust (or modify) prices|～人力 make adjustments in the use of manpower|～作息时间 adjust the work timetable

【调制】[1] tiáo zhì 使电磁波的振幅、频率或脉冲的有关参数依照所需传递的信号而变化 modulation; modulate; alter the amplitude, frequency or pulse of an electromagnetic wave according to the variations of a signal to be transmitted

【调制】[2] tiáozhì 调配制作 prepare by blending: ～鸡尾酒 prepare a cocktail

【调治】tiáozhì 调养(身体),治疗(疾病) recuperate under medical treatment: 细心～ recuperate under meticulous medical care

【调资】tiáo//zī 调整工资(多指提升工资级别 usu. upwards) adjust wages: 评级～ grade and adjust wages accordingly

【调嘴学舌】tiáo zuǐ xué shé 指背地里说人长短,搬弄是非 tittle-tattle; tell tales; (调嘴 *tiao zui*: 耍嘴皮 talk glibly; 学舌 *xue she*: 把听到的话告诉别人 tell others what one hears); also 调嘴弄舌 tiáo zuǐ nòng shé

笤 tiáo [笤帚](tiáo·zhou)除去尘土、垃圾等的用具,用去粒的高粱穗、黍子穗等绑成,比扫帚小 whisk broom; small broom

蓨(蓚) Tiáo 古地名,在今河北景县南 Tiao, name of an ancient place south of what is present-day Jingxian County in Hebei Province

龆 tiáo 〈书 *fml.*〉儿童换牙(of a child) shed baby (or milk) teeth; grow permanent teeth: ～年(童年) childhood|～龀(指童年或儿童) childhood or child

蜩 tiáo 古书上指蝉 cicada, as described in ancient books

髫 tiáo〈古代 *arch.*〉指孩子的下垂的头发 child's hanging hair: 垂～ hanging hair|～龄 childhood

【髫龄】tiáolíng 〈书 *fml.*〉 same as 童年 tóngnián

【髫年】tiáonián 〈书 *fml.*〉 same as 童年 tóngnián

鲦(鰷、儵) tiáo [鲦鱼] ☞ [鳌鲦] (cāntiáo) on p.184

tiǎo (ㄊㄧㄠˇ)

挑 tiǎo ❶ 用竹竿等的一头支起 push something up with a pole or stick; raise: 把帘子～起来 raise the curtain ❷ 用细长的东西拨 poke with a long, slender stick; pick: ～火(拨开炉灶的盖火,露出火苗) poke a fire (move away the stove lid and expose the flame to the air|～刺 pick out a splinter ❸ 一种刺绣的方法,用针挑起经线或纬线,把针上的线从底下穿过去 method of embroidery stitch using a needle to raise a warp or weft and pull the thread on the needle through under them: ～花 a cross-stitch ❹ 挑拨;挑动 stir up; instigate: ～战 challenge|～衅 provoke|～是非 stir up trouble; foment discord ❺ 汉字的笔画,由左斜上,形状是'㇀' rising stroke in Chinese characters slanting right upward from lower left in the shape of '㇀'

☞ tiāo on p.1899

【挑拨】tiǎobō 搬弄是非,引起纠纷 instigate; incite; sow discord: ～离间(引起是非争端,使别人不和) sow discord; foment dissension; incite one against the other; drive a wedge between

【挑大梁】tiǎo dàliáng ❶ 指戏剧等艺术表演中担任主要角色或主要演员 be a leading actor or actress ❷ 泛指承担重要的、起支柱作用的工作(in a broad sense) shoulder a heavy responsibility or a demanding task: 小字辈～ young people shoulder the heavy responsibility

【挑灯】tiǎo//dēng ❶ 挑起油灯的灯心,使灯光加亮 raise the wick of an oil lamp ❷ 把灯挂在高处 hang a lantern from a pole: ～夜战 fight by torchlight; continue working by lamplight

【挑动】tiǎodòng ❶ 引起;惹起(纠纷、某种心理等) give rise to; lead to; touch off; arouse: ～是非 give rise to (or touch off) a dispute|～好奇心 arouse curiosity ❷ 挑拨煽动 provoke: ～战争 provoke a war

【挑逗】tiǎodòu 逗引;招惹 provoke; tease; tantalize

【挑花】tiǎohuā (～儿 tiǎohuār)手工艺的一种,在棉布或麻布的经纬线上用彩色的线挑出许多很小的十字,构成各种图案,一般挑在枕头、桌布、服装等上面,作为装饰 cross stitch; needlework of stitches crossing each other along the warps and wefts to form a variety of decorative patterns on pillow casc, table cloth, clothing, ctc.

【挑弄】tiǎonòng ❶ 挑拨 instigate; incite; sow discord: ～是非 give rise to (or touch off) a dispute ❷ 戏弄 make fun of; play tricks on; tease; kid

【挑唆】tiǎo·suō 调唆 incite; abet; instigate

【挑头】tiǎo//tóu (～儿 tiǎo//tóur)领头儿;带头 take the lead; be the first to do something: 他～儿向领导提意见。He was the first to voice complaints against the leadership.|谁出来挑个头,事情就好办了。If somebody takes the lead, things will be easier.

【挑衅】tiǎoxìn 借端生事,企图引起冲突或战争 provoke; do something under a pretext in an attempt to start a clash or war: 武装～ armed provocation

【挑战】tiǎo//zhàn ❶ 故意激怒敌人,使敌人出来打仗 throw down the gauntlet; challenge; incite the enemy's anger on purpose to engage the enemy in a battle ❷ 鼓动对方跟自己竞赛 challenge to a contest: 班组之间互相～应战。The teams and groups challenged each other.

T

朓 tiǎo 古书上指农历月底月亮在西方出现 appearance of the moon in the west at the end of a lunar month, as described in ancient books

窕 tiǎo ☞ 窈窕 (yǎotiǎo) on p. 2231

斢 tiǎo 〈方 *dial.*〉掉换 exchange; change; swop:～谷种 exchange grain seeds

tiào (ㄊㄧㄠˋ)

眺 tiào 眺望 look into the distance from a high place:远～ look into the distance from a high place|登高～远 climb to a higher place to enjoy a distant view

【眺望】tiàowàng 从高处往远处看 look into the distance from a high place:凭栏～ leaning on a railing to enjoy a distant view|站在山顶～ stand on the top of a mountain to see the sights

粜(糶) tiào 卖出(粮食)(跟'籴'相对 as opposed to 'buy') sell (grain):～米 sell rice

跳 tiào ❶ 腿上用力,使身体突然离开所在的地方 jump; leap; bounce; move oneself suddenly from the ground, etc. by using the leg muscles:～高 high jump|～远 long jump; broad jump|连蹦带～ bounce and jump; bounce away|～过一条沟 leap over a ditch|高兴得直～ jump for joy; leap with joy ❷ 物体由于弹性作用突然向上移动 bounce:新皮球～得高。The new rubber ball bounced high. ❸ 一起一伏地动 move up and down; beat:心～ heart beats|眼～ one's eyelids keep twitching ❹ 越过应该经过的一处而到另一处 skip; make omissions:～级 skip a grade|隔三～两 skim through (a book)
〈古 *arch.*〉same as 逃 táo

【跳班】tiào//bān same as 跳级 tiào//jí

【跳板】tiàobǎn ❶ 搭在车、船等的边沿便于人上下的长板 gangplank; narrow, movable platform or ramp forming a bridge by which to board or leave a ship or a truck ❷ 跳水池边或跳台上伸出于水面之上供跳水用的长板 diving board; springboard; springboard projecting over a swimming pool, lake, etc. for use as a takeoff in diving ❸ 朝鲜族的传统体育活动,多在节日举行。参加者均为女子。玩时两人或四人为一组,分站在跷跷板两端,交相蹬板,此起彼落,互将对方弹到空中。seesaw jumping; traditional game for Korean girls, in which one girl jumps up and down on her end of the seesaw to bounce up the girl standing on the other end, who will then take the turn to jump and bounce up the former

【跳布扎】tiào bùzhá 喇嘛教习俗,在宗教节日里喇嘛装扮成神佛魔鬼等,诵经跳舞 exorciser's dance (performed by lamas) at religious festivals to exorcise evil spirit; Lamaist custom in which the lamas dress up as gods or devils, chant sutras and dance on religious festivals; also 打鬼 dǎguǐ or 跳神 tiàoshén (布扎,藏语,恶鬼 *buzha* means evil spirit in the Tibetan language)

【跳槽】tiàocáo ❶ 牲口离开所在的槽头到别的槽头去吃食 (of cattle, etc.) leave its own manger to eat at another ❷〈比喻 *fig.*〉人离开原来的职业或单位到别的单位或改变职业 job-hop; abandon one's old job or leave one's old office to take on another or change one's profession:有的科研人员～经商去了。Some scientific researchers have left their old jobs to do business.

【跳动】tiàodòng 一起一伏地动 move up and down; beat; pulsate:只要我的心还在～,我就不会停止工作。As long as my heart still beats, I will go on working.

【跳房子】tiào fáng·zi 一种儿童游戏,在地上画几个方格,一只脚着地,沿地面踢瓦片,依次序经过各格 play hopscotch; hopscotch; children's game of hopping single-footed and kicking a tile-chip over squares drawn on the ground, one at a time until one reaches the other side of the ground; also 跳间 tiàojiān

【跳高】tiàogāo (～儿 tiàogāor)田径运动项目之一,有急行跳高、立定跳高两种。通常指急行跳高,运动员按照规则经过助跑后跳过横杆。high jump; track-and-field event in which contestants jump for height over a horizontal bar set between two upright poles. After each successful trial the bar is raised a notch higher. There are standing jump and running jump, but the official event is running jump.

【跳行】tiào//háng ❶ 阅读或抄写时漏去一行 skip a line (in reading or transcribing) ❷ 另起一行书写 start a new paragraph ❸ 改行 change one's profession (or occupation, trade)

【跳级】tiào//jí 学生越过本来应该经过的班级,如由一年级升到三年级 skip a grade, such as from Grade 1 to Grade 3; also 跳班 tiào//bān

【跳加官】tiào jiāguān 〈旧时 *old*〉戏曲开场或在演出中遇显贵到场时,加演的舞蹈节目,由一个演员戴假面具,穿红袍、皂靴,手里拿着'天官赐福'等字样的布幅向台下展示,表示庆贺 side show that is added to a performance upon the arrival of a dignitary, performed by an actor wearing a mask, a red robe and a pair of black boots and holding a cloth streamer inscribed with the wording 'Heavenly official has brought us good fortune' by way of celebrating

【跳脚】tiào//jiǎo (～儿 tiào//jiǎor)因为焦急或发怒而跺脚 stamp one's foot; stamp with anxiety or rage

【跳梁】tiàoliáng 跳跳蹦蹦;跳跃。多比喻跋扈,猖獗 jump up and down; perform antics; (fig.) be rampant:～小丑(指上蹿下跳、兴风作浪的卑劣小人) buffoon who performs antics; clown; contemptible scoundrel; also 跳踉 tiàoliáng

【跳踉】tiàoliáng same as 跳梁 tiàoliáng

【跳马】tiàomǎ ❶ 体操器械,略像马,背部无环,高低可以调节,是木马的一种 vaulting horse, gymnastic apparatus shaped slightly like a horse with no rounded handles on the back, and with an adjustable height ❷ 竞技体操项目之一,运动员用手支撑跳马的背做各种腾越动作 horse-vaulting; gymnastic event; jumping over the horse from one position to another, with the help of the hands supported on the horseback

【跳皮筋儿】tiào píjīnr 少年儿童的一种体育活动。跳时由两人分执皮筋两端,其余参加者在皮筋上来回踏跳,跳出各种式样。rubber band skipping; skipping and dancing over a chain of rubber bands; children's game in which two children each hold one end of a chained rubber bands and the other participants skip to and fro over it in a variety of movements

【跳棋】tiàoqí 棋类游艺的一种。棋盘是六角的星形,上面画着许多三角形的格子。游艺各方的棋子各占满一个犄角,根据规则,或移动,或跳越,先把自己的棋子全部走到对面的那个犄角的为胜。Chinese checkers; halma; Chinese draughts; game played on a board with many triangles arranged in the shape of a six-pointed star, by from two to six players, each occupying one corner and the winner being the one who first moves his or her set of pieces across the board by moving or skipping

【跳伞】tiào//sǎn 利用降落伞从飞行中的飞机或跳伞塔上跳下来 parachute; bale (or bail) out; parachute jumping; bale out from a flying plane or from a parachute tower

【跳伞塔】tiàosǎntǎ 训练跳伞用的塔形建筑物,高度一般为五十米 parachute tower; tower-shaped building, usu. 50 metres high, for training parachutists

【跳神】tiào//shén ❶ (～儿 tiào//shénr)女巫或巫师装出鬼神附体的样子,乱说乱舞,迷信的人认为能给人驱鬼治病 sorcerer's dance in a trance; a sorceress or sorcerer speaks and dances as if possessed to exorcise the spirit and cure illness ❷ ☞ 跳布扎 tiào bùzhá

【跳绳】tiàoshéng 一种体育活动或儿童游戏,把绳子挥舞成圆圈,人趁绳子近地时跳过去 rope skipping; jump rope; game of both adults and children in which a person keeps swinging a rope from behind his back overhead and then from forward to backward and skips over the rope when it's about to touch the ground

【跳水】tiàoshuǐ 水上体育运动项目之一。从跳台或跳板上跳入水中,身体在空中做出各种优美的动作。diving, a water sport; jump from a platform or springboard into the water with the body performing graceful stunts in the air

【跳水池】tiàoshuǐchí 专供跳水运动用的池子,池边有跳台,比游泳池深 diving pool, a pool specially built for diving, with a diving tower on one side, usually deeper than the swimming pool

【跳台】tiàotái 跳水池旁为跳水设置的台。台高一般为五米、七米五和十米,上有跳板。diving tower; diving platform. The tower is usu. five metres, seven point five metres or ten metres high and has springboards at different levels and a platform on the top.

【跳舞】tiào//wǔ ❶ 舞蹈 dance (as a performance ❷ 跳交际舞 dance (socially or in a ballroom)

【跳箱】tiàoxiāng ❶ 体操器械的一种。形状像箱,略呈梯形,高低可以调节。box horse; vaulting box slightly shaped like a trapezoid with an adjustable height ❷ 体操项目之一,运动员以种种不同的姿势跳过跳箱 unofficial gymnastic event; jumping over the box horse in various styles

【跳鞋】tiàoxié 跳高、跳远时穿的一种轻便皮鞋,和跑鞋相似,前后掌都有钉子。是钉鞋的一种。light leather shoes with spikes specially made for jumping events, which are similar to the track shoes

【跳远】tiàoyuǎn (～儿 tiàoyuǎnr)田径运动项目之一,有急行跳远、立定跳远两种,通常指急行跳远,运动员按照规则,经助跑后向前跃进沙坑内 long jump; broad jump; track-and-field event in which a contestant is required to jump into the sand pit either from a standing position or after running

【跳跃】tiàoyuè same as 跳 tiào ①:～前进 bound forward|～运动 jumping events

【跳跃器】tiàoyuèqì 体操器械的一种。形状像跳马而短,高低可以调节。可用来做腾越、全旋等动作。buck, small-sized gymnastic horse with adjustable height, used for jumping and body turning; also 山羊 shānyáng

【跳蚤】tiào·zao 昆虫,身体小,深褐色或棕黄色,有吸吮的口器,脚长,善跳跃。寄生在人或哺乳动物身体上,吸血液,是传染鼠疫、斑疹伤寒等病的媒介。也叫虼蚤(gè·zao)。有的地区叫跳虱。flea (*Siphonaptera*); small, flattened, wingless insect with large legs adapted for jumping: as adults they are bloodsucking parasites on humans or mammals and birds, and media in infecting plague, typhus fever, etc.; also called 虼蚤 gè·zao and 跳虱 tiàoshī in some areas

【跳蚤市场】tiào·zao shìchǎng 指经营廉价商

品、旧货物和古物的露天市场 flea market; bazaar usu. outdoors, dealing mainly in cheap, second-hand goods, antiques

【跳闸】tiào//zhá 电闸断路，叫做跳闸 trip; tripping

tiē (ㄊㄧㄝ)

帖[1] (贴) tiē ❶ 服从；顺从 submissive; obedient: 服～ docile; obedient; submissive ❷ 妥当；稳当 proper; appropriate: 妥～ appropriate; proper

☞ tiě on p. 1907 and tiè on p. 1909

帖[2] Tiē 姓 a surname

怗 tiē 〈书 *fml.*〉平定；平息（叛乱）quell; suppress; put down; crush (a rebellion)

贴[1] tiē ❶ 把薄片状的东西粘在另一个东西上 paste; stick; glue; attach a thin slip on something by gluing: 剪～ clip and paste | ～邮票 stick on a stamp | 把宣传画～在墙上 put up a poster on the wall ❷ 紧挨 keep close to; nestle closely to: ～身 next to the skin | ～着墙走 walk closely by the wall ❸ 贴补 subsidize; help (out) financially: 哥哥每月～他零用钱。His brother gives him some pocket money to help him out each month. ❹ same as 津贴 jīntiē ①: 米～ food allowance | 房～ housing allowance ❺ 〈量词 *classifier*〉膏药一张叫一贴 a piece of medicated plaster

贴[2] tiē same as 帖[1] tiē

【贴边】tiē//biān 挨边；沾边 have sth. to do with; be related to; be connected with; be relevant to; be involved in: 你说的话和事实贴不上边。What you've said is irrelevant.

【贴边】tiēbiān 缝在衣服里子边上的窄条，一般跟面儿用同样的料子 hem (of a garment); narrow border on the lining of a garment, usu. made by folding the edge and sewing it down

【贴标签】tiē biāoqiān 〈比喻 *fig.*〉在评论中不作具体分析，只是生搬硬套地加上一些名目 label; copy sth. mechanically in one's comment without making a concrete analysis

【贴饼子】tiēbǐng•zi 用玉米面或小米面做的长圆形厚饼，贴在锅的周围烤熟 thick, oval corn or millet cakes baked on the wall of a wok

【贴补】tiē•bǔ ❶ 从经济上帮助（多指对亲属或朋友）subsidize (one's relatives or friends); help (out) financially: 他每月～弟弟数十元钱，供弟弟上学用。He helps his younger brother in college out by giving him several dozen yuan a month as pocket money. ❷ 用积蓄的财物弥补日常的消费 use stored material or savings to cover daily needs or expenses: 还有存的料子～着用，现在先不买。We can make do with the material we've got on hand, and don't have to buy more for the time being.

【贴兜】tiēdōu 衣兜的一种样式。口袋两侧和下沿紧贴衣服。patch pocket; pocket made by sewing a patch of shaped material to the outside of a garment; also 明兜 míngdōu

【贴花】tiēhuā same as 贴画 tiēhuà ②

【贴画】tiēhuà ❶ 贴在墙上的年画、宣传画等 poster, such as New Year picture and publicity poster: 百寿图～ poster of the Chinese character that means 'longevity' in a hundred calligraphic versions ❷ 火柴盒上贴的画片；火花 picture on a matchbox

【贴换】tiē•huàn 把旧的器物折价后加一些钱跟商贩或厂家交换新的 trade in; trade sth. old in for sth. new; give in part payment when buying sth. new

【贴己】tiējǐ ❶ 亲密；亲近 intimate; close; confidential: ～话 intimate words; confidences | 她对大娘表现出十分～的样子。She seemed as if she were very close to the aunt. | 我真是错认了他，把他当成～的人。I've really mistaken him for a close friend. ❷ 〈方 *dial.*〉家庭成员个人积蓄的（财物）；梯己 private savings of family members: ～钱 private savings | 她把～首饰卖了，贴补家用。She sold her jewelry to help out with the family expenses.

【贴金】tiē//jīn 在神佛塑像上贴上金箔 cover a Buddhist statue with gold foil; gild; 〈比喻 *fig.*〉夸耀、美化 brag about; show off; prettify: 别往自己脸上～！Don't put feathers in your own cap. *or* Don't go blowing your own trumpet.

【贴近】tiējìn ❶ 紧紧地挨近；接近 press close to; nestle up against: ～生活 be close to life | 老头儿把嘴～他的耳朵边，低低地说了几句。The old man nestled his mouth close to his ears and murmured a few words. ❷ 亲近 close; intimate: 找～的人说说心里话 get a close friend for a private talk

【贴谱】tiēpǔ （讲话或做事）合乎准则或实际 proper; appropriate; sound; relevant; accord with the rule or reality: 这个分析很～。This analysis is quite to the point. | 话说得很～。The words are very appropriate. *or* The remarks are very much to the point.

【贴切】tiēqiè （措辞）恰当；确切（of words）apt; suitable; appropriate; proper: 比喻要用得～，用得通俗。It is imperatire to use metaphors in a proper and easy-to-understand way.

【贴身】tiēshēn ❶ （～儿 tiēshēnr）紧挨着身体的 next to the skin: ～儿的小褂儿 underclothes; underclothing ❷ 合身；可体 fit: 他裁的衣服穿了～。The clothes he tailored fit well. ❸ 指跟随在身边的 constantly accompanying; personal: ～丫鬟 maid servant who constantly accompanies her mistress; personal maid | ～

保镖 personal bodyguard

【贴水】tiēshuǐ ❶ 调换票据或兑换货币时,因比价的不同,比价低的一方补足一定的差额给另一方 pay an agio; pay a fee to exchange one kind of money for another or to exchange depreciated money for money of full value ❷ 调换票据或兑换货币时所补足的差额 agio; fee paid for the exchange of bills or money

【贴题】tiētí 切合题目 relevant; pertinent; to the point:着墨不多,但是十分~ brief but very much to the point

【贴息】tiēxī ❶ 用期票调换现款时付出利息 pay interest in the form of a deduction when selling a bill of exchange, etc. ❷ 用期票调换现款时所付出的利息 interest so paid; discount

【贴现】tiēxiàn 拿没有到期的票据到银行兑现或做支付手段,并由银行扣除从交付日至到期止这段时间内的利息 discount (on a promissory note); interest deducted in advance by one who buys or lends money on, a bill of exchange , promissory note, etc.

【贴心】tiēxīn 最亲近;最知己 intimate; close:~话 words spoken in confidence|~的朋友 intimate friend; bosom friend

萜 tiē 有机化合物的一类,多为有香味的液体,松节油、薄荷油等都是含萜的化合物 terpene; organic compounds, usually fragrant liquids, as turpentine, peppermint oil, etc. which are all compounds containing terpenes

tiě (ㄊㄧㄝˇ)

帖 tiě ❶ 邀请客人的通知 invitation:请~ invitation card ❷〈旧时 *old*〉写着生辰八字等的纸片 card on which are written the hour, date, month, year of one's birth (traditionally used for betrothal); age card:庚~ age card|换~ exchange the age cards ❸(~儿 tiěr)写着字的小纸片 note; card:字~儿(便条) brief note; short message ❹〈方 *dial.*〉〈量词 *classifier*〉用于配合起来的若干味汤药 (for herbal medicine):一~药 a dose (or draught) of herbal medicine

☞ tiē on p.1906 and tiè on p.1909

【帖子】tiě·zi same as 帖 tiě ①②③

铁(鐵、銕) tiě ❶ 金属元素,符号 Fe (ferrum)。银白色,质硬,延展性强,纯铁磁化和去磁都很快,含杂质的铁在湿空气中容易生锈,是炼钢的主要原料,用途很广。ferrum (Fe); iron; silvery-white, malleable, ductile, metallic element that can be readily magnetized and demagnetized, rusts rapidly in moist or salty air, and is extensively used and the main raw material in steelmaking ❷ 指刀枪等 arms; weapon:手无寸~ bare-handed; completely unarmed|动~为凶 use a weapon to murder sb. ❸ 形容坚硬;坚强;牢靠 hard; strong; solid; firm:~拳 ironfist|~汉子 man of iron will; iron man|~饭碗 iron rice bowl; secure job|铜墙~壁 solid defence; impregnable fortress; tightly fortified ❹ 形容强暴或精锐 violent; harsh; cruel; crack:~蹄 iron heel; (fig.) cruel oppression of the people|~骑 armoured horses; strong cavalry ❺ 形容确定不移 indisputable; unalterable:~定 ironclad|~的事实 hard fact; ironclad evidence|~案如山 an ironclad case ❻ 形容表情严肃 serious; solemn:他~着个脸,没有一丝笑容。He looked stern, without a faint smile. ❼(Tiě)姓 a surname

【铁案如山】tiě àn rú shān 定案像山那样不能推翻(多因证据十分确凿) case borne out by ironclad evidence; ironclad case

【铁板钉钉】tiěbǎn dìng dīng〈比喻 *fig.*〉事情已定,不能变更 that's final; be absolutely sure:这次足球赛,甲队获胜,看来是~了。It seems team A is sure to win the football match.|事实俱在,~,你抵赖不了。The evidence is conclusive and brooks no denial.

【铁板一块】tiěbǎn yī kuài〈比喻 *fig.*〉像铁板那样结合紧密的整体 monolithic block:他们不是~,内部有矛盾,有分歧。They are not a monolithic block. There are contradictions and differences among them.

【铁笔】tiěbǐ ❶ 刻图章用的小刀 cutting tool used in carving seals ❷ 刻蜡纸用的笔 stylus used for cutting stencils; stencil pen

【铁壁铜墙】tiě bì tóng qiáng ☞ 铜墙铁壁 tóng qiáng tiě bì on p.1924

【铁饼】tiěbǐng ❶ 田径运动项目之一,运动员一手平挽铁饼,转动身体,然后投出 discus throw; throwing of a discuss as a field event, in which a contestant, with the discus in one hand, is required to toss the discus forward by turning his body ❷ 田径运动使用的投掷器械之一,形状像凸镜,边沿和中心用铁制成,其余部分用木头 discus; heavy disk of metal and wood in the shape of a convex mirror, thrown for distance as a test of strength and skill

【铁蚕豆】tiěcándòu 一种炒熟的蚕豆,壳不裂开,比较硬 hard roasted broad bean

【铁杵磨成针】tiě chǔ mó chéng zhēn 传说李白幼年时,在路上碰见一个老大娘,正在磨一根铁杵,说要把它磨成一根针。李白很感动,改变了中途辍学的念头,终于得到了很大的成就(见于宋代祝穆《方舆胜览·五十三·磨针溪》)。A legend says that on his way to school when he was a child, Li Bai saw an old lady grinding an iron pestle. She told him that she was grinding it down to a needle. Greatly moved by the old woman's determination, he gave up his idea of dropping school and finally became a celebrated poet in the Tang Dynasty. (*Scenes and Sights of the Land* • *Chapter* 53 • *Needle-grinding Brook* by Zhu Mu of the Song Dynasty). 〈比喻 *fig.*〉有恒心肯努力,做任何事情都能成功 by perseverance and hard work, one can succeed in doing anything: 只要功夫深,~。As long as you work hard enough at it, you can grind an iron pestle down to a needle.

【铁窗】tiěchuāng 安上铁栅的窗户,借指监牢 bars; window with iron grating; prison: ~风味 prison life; life behind bars

【铁搭】tiědā 〈方 *dial.*〉刨土用的一种农具,有三个至六个略向里弯的铁齿 iron rake with three to six teeth; also 铁镕 tiědā

【铁镕】tiědā same as 铁搭 tiědā

【铁打】tiědǎ 用铁打成的 iron-forged; iron-wrought; 〈比喻 *fig.*〉坚固或坚强 solid; strong; firm; unshakable: ~江山 unshakable state power | ~的汉子 man of iron will; man of strong build

【铁道】tiědào same as 铁路 tiělù

【铁定】tiědìng 确定不移 ironclad; fixed; unalterable: ~的事实 hard fact; ironclad evidence | ~的局面 unalterable situation

【铁饭碗】tiěfànwǎn 〈比喻 *fig.*〉非常稳固的职业、职位 iron rice bowl; secure job

【铁杆】tiěgǎn (~儿 tiěgǎnr) ❶〈比喻 *fig.*〉十分可靠 loyal; reliable; surefire: ~卫队 loyal guards ❷ 形容顽固不化 stubborn; inveterate: ~汉奸 dyed-in-the-wool traitor

【铁工】tiěgōng ❶ 制造和修理铁器的工作 ironwork ❷ 制造和修理铁器的工人 ironworker; blacksmith

【铁公鸡】tiěgōngjī 〈比喻 *fig.*〉一毛不拔非常吝啬的人 'iron cock' (from which no feathers can be plucked); stingy person; miser

【铁轨】tiěguǐ ☞ 钢轨 gāngguǐ on p. 637

【铁汉】tiěhàn 指坚强的人 man of iron (or steel); man of iron will; strong determined person; also 铁汉子 tiěhàn•zi

【铁合金】tiěhéjīn 铁和其他金属组成的合金的统称,如锰铁、硅铁、钨铁、钼铁、钛铁等。铁合金一般很脆,不能作为金属材料使用。ferroalloy; alloy made of iron and other metals, such as ferromanganese, ferrosilicon, ferrotungsten, molybdenum iron, ferrotitanium, etc. which are very brittle and cannot be used as a metal

【铁画】tiěhuà 一种工艺品,用铁片、铁线构成图画,涂上黑色或棕红色。也指制作铁画的工艺。iron picture; handicraft product made of a thin iron sheet and iron wire that form a picture, and painted black or reddish brown; iron picture handicraft

【铁灰】tiěhuī 像铁表面氧化后那样的深灰色 dark grey; colour like that of the oxidized surface of iron

【铁活】tiěhuó ❶ 建筑物或器物上各种铁制的物件 articles and parts made of iron used on buildings or objects ❷ 制造和修理上述物件的工作 work of making and repairing such articles and parts

【铁蒺藜】tiějí•li 一种军用障碍物,用铁做成,有尖刺像蒺藜,布在要道上或浅水中,阻碍敌军人马、车辆行动 caltrop; military obstacle made of iron with spikes, placed on the ground or in shallow water to hinder the movements of the enemy troops, horses and vehicles

【铁甲】tiějiǎ ❶〈古代 *arch.*〉用铁片连缀而成的战衣 mail; armour; covering made of iron pieces to protect the body against weapons in ancient times ❷ 用厚钢板做成的车或船的外壳 armour for vessels, vehicles, etc.: ~车 armoured car; armoured vehicle

【铁甲车】tiějiǎchē 装甲车 armoured car; armoured vehicle

【铁甲舰】tiějiǎjiàn 装甲舰 ironclad warship

【铁将军】tiějiāngjūn 指锁门的锁(含诙谐意 humor.) 'General Iron'; lock: ~把门 General Iron guarding the door; the door is padlocked

【铁匠】tiě•jiang 制造和修理铁器的人 blacksmith; ironsmith; person who makes and repairs iron articles and parts

【铁脚板】tiějiǎobǎn (~儿 tiějiǎobǎnr) 指善于走路的脚,也指善于走路的人 iron soles; toughened feet; person who is good at walking

【铁军】tiějūn 顽强善战、无坚不摧的军队 iron army; invincible army

【铁路】tiělù 有钢轨的供火车行驶的道路 railway; railroad

【铁马】[1] tiěmǎ 铁骑 iron-clad (or armoured) horses; strong mounted forces: 金戈~ shining spears and armoured horses

【铁马】[2] tiěmǎ 悬挂在宫殿庙宇等屋檐下的金属片,风吹时撞击发声 tinkling pieces of metal hanging from the eaves of palaces, pagodas, temples, etc.

【铁面无私】tiě miàn wú sī 形容公正严明,不讲情面 impartial and incorruptible; strictly impartial

【铁皮】tiěpí 压成薄片的熟铁,多指铅铁或马口铁 iron sheet; usually galvanized iron or tin plate

【铁骑】tiěqí 〈书 *fml.*〉指精锐的骑兵 strong cavalry; crack mounted soldiers

【铁器时代】tiěqì shídài 青铜时代之后的一个时代,这时人类普遍制造和使用铁制的生产工具,特别是铁犁。我国在公元前5世纪,中原地区已经使用铁器。Iron Age; era following the Bronze Age characterized by the introduction and development of iron tools and weapons, iron shares in particular. Iron implements were first used in Central China in the 5th century B.C.

【铁锹】tiěqiāo 起砂、土的工具,用熟铁或钢打成片状,前一半略呈圆形而稍尖,后一半末端安有长的木把儿 spade; tool made of wrought iron or steel, with broad, deep scoop or round blade and a long handle, used in lifting and moving loose material, such as sand and earth

【铁青】tiěqīng 青黑色。多形容人恐惧、盛怒或患病时发青的脸色。ashen; livid; ghastly pale; turn livid with terror, rage or illness

【铁拳】tiěquán〈比喻 *fig.*〉强大的打击力量 iron fist; powerful striking force

【铁纱】tiěshā 用细铁丝纵横交错编成的网状物,多用来做纱窗 wire gauze; wire cloth; fine, very nice gauzelike wire netting

【铁砂】tiěshā ❶ 含铁的矿砂 iron ore ❷ 铁制小颗粒,用来清除铸件表面的砂子,也用做猎枪的子弹 shot (in a shotgun cartridge); pellets; little balls of iron for removing sand from the surface of castings

【铁石心肠】tiě shí xīncháng〈比喻 *fig.*〉心肠硬,不为感情所动 be ironhearted; have a heart of stone; be hardhearted; be heartless

【铁树】tiěshù ❶ 常绿灌木,叶聚生在茎的顶端,披针状椭圆形,花淡红色或紫色。产于热带地方。供观赏。sago cycas (*Cycas revolute*) tropical ornamental evergreen shrub with clusters of lanceolate leaves on the top of the stem and pink or purple flowers ❷ 苏铁的通称 common name for 苏铁 sūtiě

【铁树开花】tiěshù kāi huā〈比喻 *fig.*〉事情非常罕见或极难实现。苏铁原产热带,不常开花,移植北方后,往往多年才开一次。iron tree in blossom; sth. seldom seen or hardly realized. Sago cycas originally grows in the tropical zone and seldom blooms. After it is transplanted in the north, it blooms once in many years.

【铁水】tiěshuǐ 铁熔化而成的炽热液体 molten iron

【铁丝】tiěsī 用铁拉制成的线状成品 iron wire

【铁丝网】tiěsīwǎng ❶ 铁丝编成的网子 wire netting; wire meshes ❷ 一种军用障碍物,用有刺或无刺的铁丝固定在桩上,用来阻止敌人的步兵或保护禁区、仓库和建筑工地等 wire entanglement; barbed wire entanglement; military obstacle using barbed or barbless wire entanglement that is fixed on stakes to stop enemy infantry from advancing or protect an off-limit zone, warehouse or construction site

【铁算盘】tiěsuàn·pán〈比喻 *fig.*〉精细的计算,也比喻很会计算的人 careful calculation; meticulous calculation; shrewd person

【铁索】tiěsuǒ 钢丝编成的索或粗铁链 iron chain; cable: ～桥 chain bridge

【铁索桥】tiěsuǒqiáo 以铁索为主要承重构件的桥,桥面铺设或悬吊在铁索上 chain bridge; cable bridge; bridge using iron chain or cable as its bearing structure, with the surface laid on chains or suspended from chains

【铁塔】tiětǎ ❶ 用铁造的塔,也指铁色釉砖砌成的塔 iron tower; iron pagoda ❷ 指架设高压输电线的铁架子 pylon; transmission tower

【铁蹄】tiětí〈比喻 *fig.*〉蹂躏人民的残暴行为 iron heel; cruel oppression of the people

【铁腕】tiěwàn ❶ 指强有力的手段 iron hand: ～人物 ironhanded (or despotic, tyrannical) person; strong man or iron lady ❷ 指强有力的统治 strong rule (over a country)

【铁锨】tiěxiān 铲砂、土等东西的工具,用熟铁或钢打成长方形片状,一端安有长的木把儿 shovel; tool made of wrought iron or steel, with an oblong scoop and a long handle, used in lifting and moving loose material such as sand, earth, snow and gravel

【铁心】tiě//xīn 指下定决心 make up one's mind; be determined: ～务农 be devoted to do farming | 这回他可铁了心啦。He is adament in his determination this time.

【铁心】tiěxīn 电机、变压器、电磁铁等电器中的心子,多用硅钢片等材料制成 (iron) core; core made of silicon steel sheets and used in electrical machinery, transformers and electromagnetic iron

【铁锈】tiěxiù 钢铁表面上生成的红褐色的锈,主要成分是水合氧化铁 rust; reddish-brown coating formed on iron or steel by oxidization, consisting mainly of ferric hydroxide

【铁血】tiěxuè 指具有刚强意志和富于牺牲精神的 be iron-willed and ready to sacrifice oneself: ～青年 strong-willed and valiant young people | ～男儿 strong-willed and valiant man

【铁证】tiězhèng 指确凿的证据 ironclad proof; irrefutable evidence: ～如山(形容证据确凿不移) mountain of ironclad evidence; irrefutable, conclusive evidence

tiè (ㄊㄧㄝˋ)

帖 tiè 学习写字或绘画时临摹用的样本 book containing models of handwriting or painting for learners to copy: 碑～ book of rubbings (from stone inscriptions) | 法～ copy of, or rubbings from model calligraphy | 习字～ book of models of calligraphy | 画～ book of model paintings (or drawings)

☞ tiē on p. 1906 and tiě on p. 1907

餮 tiè〈书 *fml.*〉贪食 be greedy for food ☞ 饕餮 (tāotiè) on p. 1870

tīng (ㄊㄧㄥ)

厅(廳、厛) tīng ❶ 聚会或招待客人用的房间 hall (for holding meetings, concerts, receiving guests, etc.): 大～ main hall; hall; lobby | 门～ entrance hall; portico | 客～ sitting room; drawing room; living room; parlour | 餐～ dining room ❷ 大机关里一个办事部门的名称 department in a big government organization; office: 办公～ general affairs office ❸ 某些省属机关的名称 part of the name of a department in a provincial government: 教育～ provincial education department | 财政～ financial department (of a province)

【厅房】tīngfáng 〈方 *dial.*〉same as 厅 tīng ①

【厅事】tīngshì same as 听事 tīngshì ②

【厅堂】tīngtáng same as 厅 tīng ①

汀 tīng 〈书 *fml.*〉水边平地 flat; low, level land by the waterside; spit of land: 绿～ green flat | 蓼花～ knotweed flat

【汀线】tīngxiàn 海岸被海水侵蚀而成的线状的痕迹 beach line; line track of a sea shore

听[1]**(聽、聼)** tīng ❶ 用耳朵接受声音 listen; hear: ～音乐 listen to music | 耳朵聋了～不见 be deaf and cannot hear anything | 你的话我已经～清楚了。I've caught what you said. ❷ 听从(劝告);接受(意见) accept (somebody's advice); heed; obey: 言～计从 always follow what somebody says; do whatever somebody says | 我劝他,他不～。I advised him, but he wouldn't listen. ❸ 治理;判断 administer; manage; judge: ～政 administer affairs of the state; hold court | ～讼 hear a case; hold a hearing

听[2]**(聽、聼)** tīng (旧读 formerly pronounced tìng) 听凭;任凭 allow; let: ～任 allow; let (sb. do as he pleases) | ～便 as you please; do as you please | ～其自然 let things take their own course

听[3]**(聽、聼)** tīng 〈方 *dial.*〉听子 tin; can: ～装 tinned; canned | 一～香烟 a tin of cigarettes | 三～咖啡 three tins of coffee

【听便】tīng//biàn 听凭自便 do as one pleases; as one pleases: 你参加不参加这个会,～。You may be present at this meeting or not as you please.

【听差】tīngchāi ❶ 听从差使 manservant; office attendant: 他从前在衙门～。He used to be an office attendant in the government in the old times. ❷ 〈旧时 *old*〉指在机关或有钱人家里做勤杂工作的男仆人 manservant hired in a government office or a wealthy family

【听从】tīngcóng 依照别人的意思行动 act at the will of others; obey; comply with: ～指挥 obey orders | ～劝告 accept somebody's advice

【听而不闻】tīng ér bù wén 听了和没听见一样,指漠不关心 turn a deaf ear to; remain indifferent

【听风是雨】tīng fēng shì yǔ 〈比喻 *fig.*〉只听到一点儿风声就当做真的 hear the wind and mistake it for the rain; believe rumours; also 听见(到)风就是雨 tīngjiàn(dào)fēng jiùshì yǔ

【听骨】tīnggǔ 锤骨、砧骨和镫骨的合称,位置在中耳里面,作用是把鼓膜的振动传给内耳 ear bones (a general reference to malleus or hammer, incus or anvil and stapes or stirrup); three small bones in the middle ear, playing the function to transmit the vibration of the eardrum to the inner ear; (图见 ☞ figure for 耳朵 ěr·duo on p. 512)

【听喝】tīng//hē (～儿 tīng//hēr)听从别人安排,受别人使唤 do sb.'s bidding; be at somebody's beck and call: 我们只管～干活儿,别的事一概不问。We just work at the beck and call of others. *or* We don't care about other matters. | 你说怎么干就怎么干,听你喝。We'll do whatever you tell us to. We are at your beck and call.

【听候】tīnghòu 等候(上级的决定) wait for (a decision, settlement, etc. from higher authorities): ～调遣 be ready to do your bidding | ～分配 wait for one's job assignment | ～处理 pending the final decision

【听话】tīng//huà 听从长辈或领导的话 heed what an elder or superior says; be obedient: 这孩子还算～。This child behaves just well. | 他把手下不听他话的人都辞退了。He has dismissed all those under him who do not obey him.

【听话儿】tīng//huàr 等候别人给回话 wait for a reply: 同意还是不同意你去,你明天就～吧。We'll let you know tomorrow whether you will be permitted to go or not.

【听会】tīng//huì 到会场听发言、讲演等 attend a meeting as a visitor: 今天来～的人很多。There's a good turnout at the meeting today.

【听见】tīng//·jiàn 听到 hear: 听得见 can hear | 听不见 can't hear | ～打雷的声音 hear the thunder

【听讲】tīng//jiǎng ❶ 听人讲课或讲演 listen to a talk; attend a lecture: 一面～,一面记笔记 take notes while listening to a lecture ❷ 〈方 *dial.*〉听说 hear of; be told

【听觉】tīngjué 声波振动鼓膜所产生的感觉 sense of hearing; sense produced after the eardrum is vibrated by the sound wave: ～灵敏 keen sense of hearing

【听课】tīng//kè 听教师讲课 visit (or sit in on) a class; attend a lecture: ～时思想要集中。Concentrate your mind when attending a lecture. | 我听过他的课,讲得很好。I visited his class once and he gave an excellent lecture.

【听力】tīnglì 耳朵辨别声音的能力 hearing (ability)

【听命】tīngmìng ❶ 听天由命 resign oneself to one's fate; submit to the will of Heaven ❷ 听从命令 take orders from: 俯首～ be at sb.'s command; be at sb's beck and call | ～于人 be at sb's beck and call; be at sb.'s command

【听凭】tīngpíng 让别人愿意怎样就怎样；任凭 allow; let (sb. do as he pleases)：去也罢，不去也罢，～你自己作主。You decide whether or not to go. It's up to you.

【听其自然】tīng qí zìrán 任凭人或事物自然发展变化，不去干涉 let things take their own course; let matters slide; let people do in their own way

【听取】tīngqǔ 听(意见、反映、汇报等) listen to (opinion, manifest, report, etc.)：虚心～群众意见 heed the opinions of the masses open-mindedly | 大会～了常务委员会的工作报告。The session listened to the work report of the standing committee.

【听任】tīngrèn same as 听凭 tīngpíng

【听神经】tīngshénjīng 第八对脑神经，从脑桥和延髓之间发出，分布在内耳，主管听觉和身体平衡的感觉 auditory (or acoustic) nerve; the eighth pair of cranial nerves that arise in the pons and medulla oblongata and connect the inner ears and controls the sense of hearing and the sense of bodily balance; (图见 ☞ figure for 耳朵 ěr·duo on p. 512)

【听审】tīngshěn 听候审判 wait for a trial

【听事】tīngshì 〈书 *fml.*〉 ❶ 听政 (of a monarch or regent) hold court; administer affairs of state ❷ 大厅(多指官署中的) hall (in a government office); also 厅事 tīngshì

【听讼】tīngsòng 〈书 *fml.*〉指审案 try a case：～断狱 hear a case and pass a verdict

【听天由命】tīng tiān yóu mìng 任凭事态自然发展变化，不做主观努力。有时也用来比喻碰机会或听其自然。submit to the will of Heaven; (fig.) resign oneself to one's fate; trust to luck

【听筒】tīngtǒng ❶ 耳机 headphone; earphone ❷ 听诊器 stethoscope

【听闻】tīngwén 〈书 *fml.*〉指听的活动或所听到的内容 hearing; what one hears：骇人～ terrifying; appalling; shocking | 以广～ in order to widen one's knowledge

【听写】tīngxiě 语文教学方法之一，由教师发音或朗读，学生笔录，用来训练学生听和写的能力 dictation; language teaching method, by which a teacher pronounces or reads aloud for students to take notes, which is used to train the students' listening and writing abilities

【听信】tīng//xìn (～儿 tīng//xìnr) 等候消息 wait for information：今天晚上开会就决定这件事儿，你～吧。The matter will be decided at the meeting this evening. We'll let you know about it.

【听信】tīngxìn 听到而相信(多指不正确的话或消息 usu. sth. incorrect or one-sided) give credence to; believe what one hears; believe：～谣言 give much credence to rumours | ～一面之词 believe a one-sided version

【听阈】tīngyù 能产生听觉的最高限度和最低限度的刺激强度 intensity of stimulus to the upper and lower limits of hearing; threshold of audibility; threshold of hearing

【听诊】tīngzhěn 诊察的一种方法，用耳朵或听诊器来听心、肺等内脏器官的声音，以便进行诊断 auscultation; listening, by ear or with the aid of a stethoscope, to sounds in the chest, abdomen, etc, so as to determine the condition of the heart, lungs, etc.

【听诊器】tīngzhěnqì 听诊用的器械 stethoscope; also 听筒 tīngtǒng

【听证】tīngzhèng 为了解案情或其他特殊事件的真相而听取当事人的说明与证词 hear; conduct an examination or a hearing of the explanations and evidences of the litigants in order to know more about the truth of a case or other specific matters：～会 hearing

【听政】tīngzhèng (帝王或摄政的人)上朝听取臣子报告，并决定政事(of a monarch or regent) hold court; administer affairs of state：垂帘～ hold court behind a screen; administer affairs of state in the name of a child emperor

【听之任之】tīng zhī rèn zhī 听任事情自然发展，不管不问 let something (undesirable, evil, etc.) go unchecked; take a laissez-faire attitude; let somebody have his own way; let matters drift

【听众】tīngzhòng 听讲演、音乐或广播的人 audience; listeners

【听装】tīngzhuāng 用听子包装的 tinned; canned：～奶粉 tinned milk powder

【听子】tīng·zi 用镀锡或镀锌的薄铁皮做成的装食品、香烟等的筒子或罐子 tin; can; container made of tinned or galvanized iron sheet, in which foods; cigarettes or other perishable products are sealed for preservation

烃(烴) tīng 由碳和氢两种元素组成的一类有机化合物 hydrocarbon; organic compound consisting of carbon and hydrogen; also 碳氢化合物 tànqīng-huàhéwù

【烃基】tīngjī 烃分子失去一个或几个氢原子而成的基团，通常用 R 表示，如烷基、烯基、芳香基等 hydrocarbon radical; radical formed after a hydrocarbon molecule loses one or more hydrogen atoms, usu. indicated by R, such as alkyl radical, alkene radical and aromatic radical

桯 tīng ❶ 桯子 shaft of an awl ❷〈古代 *arch.*〉放置床前的小桌 small bedside table used in ancient China

【桯子】tīng·zi ❶ 锥子等的杆子 shaft of an awl：锥～ shaft of an awl ❷ 蔬菜等的花轴 floral axis of a vegetable

鞓 tīng 〈书 *fml.*〉皮革制成的腰带 waistband made of leather; leather waistband; leather belt

tíng (ㄊㄧㄥˊ)

廷 tíng 朝廷 court of a feudal ruler; seat of a monarchical government: 官～ palatial court | 清～(清朝中央政府) Qing government (central government of the Qing Dynasty)

莛 tíng (～儿 tíngr) 某些草本植物的茎 stem of a herb: 麦～儿 stalks of wheat

亭1 tíng ❶ 亭子 pavilion (in a park or beside a road for people to rest) ❷ 形状像亭子的小房子 stall; kiosk: 邮～ postal kiosk | 书～ book stall

亭2 tíng 〈书 *fml.*〉适中;均匀 well-balanced; in the middle; even: ～午 midday; noon

【亭亭】tíngtíng 〈书〉❶ 形容高耸 erect; upright: 早年种的一棵松树已长得～如盖。The pine tree planted many years ago now stands straight under a large canopy of foliage. ❷ same as 婷婷 tíngtíng

【亭亭玉立】tíngtíng yù lì 形容美女身材细长或花木等形体挺拔 (of a woman) fair, slim and graceful; (of a tree, etc.) tall and straight

【亭午】tíngwǔ 〈书 *fml.*〉正午;中午 midday; noon

【亭匀】tíngyún same as 停匀 tíngyún

【亭子】tíng•zi 盖在路旁或花园里供人休息用的建筑物,面积较小,大多只有顶,没有墙 pavilion (in a park or beside a road for people to rest), usually with a roof, but without walls

【亭子间】tíng•zijiān 〈方 *dial.*〉上海等地某些旧式楼房中的一种小房间,位置在房子后部的楼梯中间,狭小,光线较差 cubbyhole; small, dark back room tucked away behind the staircase of an old-style storeyed house in Shanghai or other cities

庭 tíng ❶ 厅堂 hall: 大～广众 before a large crowd; on a public occasion ❷ 正房前的院子 front courtyard; front yard: 前～后院 front courtyard and back garden ❸ 指法庭 law court: 民～ civil court | 刑～ criminal court | 开～ open a court session

【庭除】tíngchú 庭院 courtyard (除 *chu*: 台阶 steps): 洒扫～ sweep the courtyard

【庭审】tíngshěn 法庭审讯 try; interrogate: 进行～ conduct a trial | ～笔录 minutes of a court trial

【庭园】tíngyuán 有花木的庭院或附属于住宅的花园 flower garden; grounds

【庭院】tíngyuàn 正房前的院子,泛指院子 courtyard in front of the main building; (in a broad sense) courtyard

停1 tíng ❶ 停止 stop; cease; halt; pause: ～办 stop a business; close down | 雨～了。The rain has stopped. ❷ 停留 stop over; stay: 我在杭州～了三天,才去金华。I stopped over at Hangzhou for three days before going to Jinhua. ❸ 停放;停泊 (of cars) be parked; (of ships) lie at anchor; (of a dead body or coffin) be placed: 车～在大门口。The car is parked in front of the entrance. | 船～在江心,没有靠岸。The ship is at anchor in the middle of the river without drawing alongside. ❹ 停当 ready; settled: ～妥 be all set; be in order; be well arranged

停2 tíng (～儿 tíngr) 总数分成几等份,其中一份叫一停儿 part (of a total); portion: 三～儿去了两～儿,还剩一～儿。After two-thirds are taken from the total, only one-third is left. | 十～儿有九～儿是好的。Nine out of ten are good.

【停摆】tíng//bǎi 钟摆停止摆动 (of a pendulum) come to a standstill; (of a vehide) stop; 〈比喻 *fig.*〉事情停顿 sth. comes to a standstill: 因材料跟不上,工程已～三天了。Work on the project has ceased for three days due to short supply of materials.

【停办】tíngbàn 中途停止进行中的事业 (of a vehick) stop a business; close down

【停闭】tíngbì (工厂、商店等)歇业或停办 (a factory, shop, etc.) close a business; go out of business

【停表】tíngbiǎo ☞ 马表 mǎbiǎo on p.1287

【停泊】tíngbó (船只)停靠;停留 (of ships) on the berth: 码头上～着许多轮船。Many ships are on the berth in the harbour.

【停车】tíng//chē ❶ 车辆停留或停止行驶 (of a vehide) stop; pull up: ～十分钟 stop 10 minutes; a 10-minute stop | 因修理马路,～三天。The road is closed for repair for three days. ❷ 停放车辆 park: ～处 parking lot | ～场 car park; parking lot; parking area ❸ (机器)停止转动 (of a machine) stop operation: 三号车间～修理。No. three workshop has stopped production for an overhaul.

【停当】tíng•dang 齐备;完毕 ready; settled: 一切准备～。Everything's ready. *or* All is set.

【停顿】tíngdùn ❶ (事情)中止或暂停 stop; halt; pause; be at a standstill: 生产陷于～状态。Production was at a standstill. ❷ 说话时语音上的间歇 pause (in speaking): 他～了一下,又继续往下说。He paused, and then went on.

【停放】tíngfàng 短时间放置(多指车辆、灵柩) park (a vehicle); place (a coffin): 一辆自行车～在门前。A bicycle is parked in front of the gate.

【停航】tíngháng (轮船或飞机)停止航行 suspend air or shipping service: 班机因气候恶劣～。The flight is suspended on account of bad weather.

【停火】tíng//huǒ 交战双方或一方停止攻击 cease fire: 双方达成～协议。The two sides reached a cease-fire agreement.

【停机】tíngjī ❶ 指影片、电视片拍摄工作结束 finish shooting (a film, TV series, etc.)：该影片现已～，进入后期制作。Shooting of the film has finished. It is now in the follow-up stage of production. ❷ 停放飞机 parking airplanes：～坪 aircraft parking area; parking apron

【停刊】tíng//kān (报纸、杂志)停止刊行(of a newspaper, magazine, etc.) stop publication

【停靠】tíngkào 轮船、火车等停留在某个地方(of a train) stop; (of a ship) berth：一艘万吨货轮～在码头。A 10,000-ton freighter is on the berth at the dock.

【停课】tíng//kè (学校)因故停止上课 (of a school) suspend classes：开运动会，～一天。Classes are suspended for one day because of the school games meet.

【停灵】tínglíng 埋葬前暂时把灵柩停放在某个地方 keep a coffin in a temporary shelter before burial; rest a coffin temporarily

【停留】tíngliú 暂时不继续前进 stay for a time; stop; remain：代表团在北京～了一周。The delegation stayed in Beijing for a week.｜不能～在目前的水平上 can't remain at the present level

【停食】tíng//shí 食物停滞在胃里不消化 gastric disorder; indigestion

【停手】tíng//shǒu 停止正在做的事情 stop doing something

【停妥】tíngtuǒ 停当妥帖 be well arranged; be in order：收拾～ put things in order｜商议～ discussed and satisfactorily arranged｜准备～。All is set.

【停息】tíngxī 停止 stop; cease：雨一～，大家立即整队赶路。They dressed their ranks and hurried on with their journey as soon as the rain stopped.

【停歇】tíngxiē ❶ 歇业 close a business; go out of business：小店亏本～。The small shop closed down because it had lost money. ❷ 停止;停息 stop; cease：直到天亮，大风还没有～。The strong wind did not cease until dawn. ❸ 停止行动而休息 stop for a rest：队伍～在小树林里。The troops rested in a grove.

【停学】tíng//xué (学生)因故停止上学 stop going to school; drop out of school; quit school

【停业】tíng//yè ❶ 暂时停止营业 stop doing business：清理存货，～两天。Close for two days for clearing the inventory. ❷ 歇业 close a business; go out of business

【停匀】tíngyún 〈书 *fml*.〉均匀(多指形体、节奏 oft. of the human figure) well-proportioned; well-balanced; (of the rhythm of a melody) regular; balanced; also 亭匀 tíngyún

【停战】tíng//zhàn 交战双方停止作战 armistice; truce; cessation of hostilities：～协定 armistice; truce agreement

【停诊】tíngzhěn 停止门诊 (out-patient department of a hospital) close：节日～，急诊除外。Close on holidays except for emergent cases.

【停职】tíng//zhí 暂时解除职务，是一种处分 (as a punishment) to suspend somebody from his duties：～反省 be temporarily relieved of one's post for self-examination

【停止】tíngzhǐ 不再进行 stop; cease; halt; suspend; call off：～演习 cease the manoeuvre｜～营业 business suspended｜暴风雨～了。The storm stopped.

【停滞】tíngzhì 因为受到阻碍，不能顺利地运动或发展 stagnate; be at a standstill; bog down; no movement or development due to hindrance：～不前 stagnate; be at a standstill｜生产～。Production has come to a standstill.

葶 tíng [葶苈](tínglì)一年生草本植物，叶子卵形或长椭圆形，花小，黄色，总状花序，果实椭圆形。种子入药。draba (*Draba nemorosa* var. *hebecarpal*); annual herbal plant with ovate or oblong leaves, small, yellow flowers in racemes and elliptical fruits; the seeds are used for Chinese medicine

蜓 tíng ☞ 蜻蜓(qīngtíng) on p. 1574

渟 tíng 〈书 *fml*.〉水停滞 (of water) stagnate

婷 tíng [婷婷]〈书 *fml*.〉形容人或花木美好 (of a person or flowers, trees, etc.) graceful; also 亭亭 tíngtíng

霆 tíng 暴雷;霹雳 thunderbolt：雷～ thunderbolt; thunderclap; thunder-like rage

tǐng (ㄊㄧㄥˇ)

町 tǐng 〈书 *fml*.〉 ❶ 田界 raised path between farm fields ❷ 田亩;田地 farm fields

☞ dīng on p. 453

侹 tǐng 〈书 *fml*.〉平而直 smooth and straight

挺1 tǐng ❶ 硬而直 hard and straight; erect; stiff：笔～ well-pressed｜～立 stand upright; stand erect｜～然屹立(坚强地直立着) stand up straight; tower; stand erect ❷ 伸直或凸出(身体或身体的一部分) stick out; straighten up (physically)：～胸 thrust out one's chest; throw out one's chest; square one's shoulders｜～着脖子 with a stiffened neck ❸ 勉强支撑 endure; stand; hold out：他有病还硬～着上班。He endured illness at work. ❹ 特出;杰出 outstanding; prominent; extraordinary：英～ handsome｜～拔 towering; erect ❺ 很 very; rather; quite：这花～香。The flower has a very sweet smell.｜他学习～努力。He works hard in his studies.

挺[2] tǐng〈量词 *classifier*〉用于机关枪 [used to indicate the number of machine guns]

【挺拔】tǐngbá ❶ 直立而高耸 tall and straight; towering: 峰峦～ towering ridges and peaks | ～的白杨 tall, straight poplars ❷ 坚强有力; 强劲 forceful: 笔力～ forceful strokes in handwriting or drawing

【挺括】tǐng·guā〈方 *dial.*〉(衣服、布料、纸张等)较硬而平整 (of cloth, paper, etc.) stiff and smooth; (of clothes) neat; trim; well pressed

【挺进】tǐngjìn (军队)直向前进 (of troops) boldly drive on; press onward; push forward: ～队 advancing vanguard units; tough vanguard units | 部队马不停蹄地向前～。The troops pressed forward nonstop.

【挺举】tǐngjǔ 一种举重法,双手把杠铃从地上提到胸前,再利用屈膝等动作举过头顶,一直到两臂伸直、两腿直立为止 (of weight lifting) clean and jerk or jerk; lift in which the barbell is cleaned (or lifted from the floor to the shoulders in one continuous movement) and then thrust directly overhead so that the arms are fully extended and the legs stand upright

【挺立】tǐnglì 直立 stand upright; stand firm: 几棵老松树～在山坡上。Several old pine trees stand erect on the hillside.

【挺身】tǐng//shēn 直起身来 straighten one's back: 挺起身来 straighten one's back | ～而起 rise boldly; step forward bravely | ～反抗 stand up and fight; rise up against

【挺尸】tǐng//shī 尸体直挺挺地躺着,常用来骂人睡觉 (a corpse) lying stiff; lie sleeping like a corpse (usu. a curse at a sleeping person)

【挺脱】tǐngtuō〈方. *dial.*〉❶ 强劲; 结实 strong; sturdy; tough: 文字～ vigorous language | 这匹马真～。This is a very strong horse. ❷ 衣着挺括、舒展 (of clothes) neat; trim; well pressed

【挺秀】tǐngxiù (身材、树木等)挺拔秀丽 (of a human figure, a free, etc.) tall and graceful: 峰峦～ statuesque mountain peaks | 字体～ statuesque handwriting

珽 tǐng〈书 *fml.*〉玉笏 jade tablet held in two hands by an official when received in audience by the emperor

梃 tǐng ❶〈书 *fml.*〉棍棒 club; cudgel; bludgeon ❷ 梃子 frame: 门～ door frame | 窗～ window frame ❸〈方 *dial.*〉(～儿 tǐngr) 花梗 stalk or stem of a flower: 独～儿(只开一朵花的花梗) stalk bearing only one flower | ～折(shé)了。A stalk was broken.

☞ tìng on p. 1914

【梃子】tǐng·zi 门框、窗框或门扇、窗扇两侧直立的边框 door frame; window frame; vertical side frame by the door leaf or window leaf

脡 tǐng〈书 *fml.*〉❶ 长条的干肉 long, narrow strip of dried meat ❷ 直 straight

铤 tǐng〈书 *fml.*〉快走的样子 (walk) quickly

☞ dìng on p. 461

【铤而走险】tǐng ér zǒu xiǎn 指因无路可走而采取冒险行动 take a risk in desperation; make a reckless move; push sb. over the edge

颋 tǐng〈书 *fml.*〉正直; 直 straight; upright

艇 tǐng ❶ 指比较轻便的船,如游艇、救生艇等 light boat, such as pleasure boat, yacht and lifeboat ❷ 排水量在 500 吨以下的军用船只。潜水艇无论排水量大小,习惯上都称为艇。military vessel with a displacement below 500 tons. A submarine is customarily called a *ting* no matter what its displacement is.

tìng (ㄊㄧㄥˋ)

梃 tìng ❶ 杀猪后,在猪的腿上割一个口子,用铁棍贴着腿皮往里捅叫做梃。梃成沟之后,往里吹气,使猪皮绷紧,以便去毛除垢。poke an iron rod between the leg skin and the flesh of a slaughtered pig before blowing air into the space between the flesh and skin so as to separate them and pump up the skin for cleansing: ～猪 poke an iron rod under the leg skin of a slaughtered pig ❷ 梃猪用的铁棍 iron rod used for poking a slaughtered pig's leg skin

☞ tǐng on p. 1914

tōng (ㄊㄨㄥ)

恫(痌) tōng〈书 *fml.*〉病痛 sickness; illness; pain

☞ dòng on p. 470

【恫瘝在抱】tōng guān zài bào 把人民的疾苦放在心上 be concerned with the hardships or sufferings of the people

通 tōng ❶ 没有堵塞,可以穿过 open; through: 管子是～的。The pipe is not blocked. | 山洞快要打～了。The mountain cave will soon be tunnelled through. ◇这个主意行得～。This idea will work. ❷ 用工具戳,使不堵塞 open up or clear out by poking or jabbing: 用通条～炉子 poke the fire with a poker ❸ 有路达到 lead to; go to: 四～八达 (of railways or roads) run or extend in all directions | 火车直～北京。The train goes straight to Beijing. *or* It's a thorough train to Beijing. ❹ 连接; 相来往 connect; communicate: 沟～ communicate with; link up; connect | 串～ gang up (with) | 私～ have secret contact with (the enemy); have an illicit intercourse with | ～商 establish trade relations with | 互～有无 supply each other's needs; exchange needed goods ❺ 传达；使知道 notify; tell：～知 notify; tell; inform|～报 circulate a notice; a circular; bulletin; notify or report|～个电话 give a call; ring sb. up ❻ 了解；懂得 understand; know：～晓 be well versed in; have a thorough knowledge of|精～业务 know one's job perfectly|粗～文墨 have a little knowledge of letters|不～人情 impervious to reason; unreasonable|他～三国文字。He knows three languages. ❼ 指精通某一方面的人 expert; specialist; authority：日本～ an expert on Japan; an authority on Japan|万事～ know-all; versatile person ❽ 通顺 logical; coherent：文章写得不～。The article is incoherent. ❾ 普通；一般 common; ordinary; general：～常 usually; as usual; usual|～病 common mistake|～例 common rule; common practice; usual practice|～称 common name; general term ❿ 整个；全部 all; whole：～共 in all; altogether|～夜 the whole night; throughout the night|～盘 overall; all-round; comprehensive ⓫〈量词 *classifier*〉用于文书电报等[used for document, telegrams, etc.]：一～电报 a telegram|一～文书 a document|手书两～ two private letters ⓬(Tōng) 姓 a surname

☞ tòng on p. 1927

【通报】tōngbào ❶ 上级机关把工作情况或经验教训等用书面形式通告下级机关 circulate a notice：～表扬 circulate a notice of commendation ❷ 上级机关通告下级机关的文件 circular; document circulated among departments at a lower level ❸ 报道科学研究的动态和成果的刊物 bulletin; journal; publication reporting scientific research trends and achievements：科学～ Science Bulletin|化学～ Chemistry Journal ❹ 通知告诉(上级或主人) fill sb. in on sth.; notify or report to (one's superior or master)：请～院长一声，门外有人求见。Please tell the director that someone outside the door wanted to see him. ❺ 说出(姓名) tell one's name：～各自的姓名。Each gives the other his own name.

【通病】tōngbìng 一般都有的缺点 common mistake; common fault; common failing：娇气可以说是独生子女的～。Delicateness can be regarded the common failing of the only child.

【通才】tōngcái 兼备多种才能的人 all-round (or versatile) person; universal genius

【通常】tōngcháng 一般；平常 general; usual; normal：～的情况 normal conditions|～的方法 the usual method|他～六点钟就起床。He generally get up at six o'clock.

【通畅】tōngchàng ❶ 运行无阻 unobstructed; clear：血液循环～free circulation of the blood|道路～。The road is clear. ❷ (思路、文字)流畅(thought, writing) easy and smooth：文笔～ lucid writing

【通车】tōng//chē ❶ 铁路或公路修通，开始行车(of a railway or highway) be open to traffic：～典礼 ceremony marking the opening of (a railway or road) to traffic ❷ 有车来往 have access to transport service：我老家在山区，那儿不～。My home village is located in a mountainous area with no transport service.

【通彻】tōngchè 通晓；贯通 have a thorough knowledge of; thoroughly understand

【通称】tōngchēng ❶ 通常叫做 be generally called; be generally known as; general term; common term：乌鳢～黑鱼。*Heiyu* (black fish) is the popular name for *wuli* (snake-headed fish). ❷ 通常的名称 general (or common) term：水银是汞的～。Mercury is generally known as quicksilver.

【通诚】tōngchéng 在神、佛像前表白自己的心意 confess (before god, Buddha, etc.)：～祷告 confess and pray

【通达】tōngdá 明白(人情事理) understand things; be sensible or be reasonable：～人情 be understanding and considerate|见解～ hold sensible views; show good sense

【通道】tōngdào 往来的大路；通路 thoroughfare; passageway; passage：南北～ thoroughfare linking the south and the north

【通敌】tōng//dí 勾结敌人 collude (or collaborate) with the enemy

【通电】tōng//diàn 使电流通过 put up an electric line to link some place(s); set up an electric circuit; electrify; energize

【通电】tōngdiàn ❶ 把宣布政治上某种主张的电报拍给有关方面，同时公开发表 send a telegram to those concerned announcing certain political views and publish it openly at the same time：～全国 publish an open telegram to the whole nation ❷ 公开发表的宣布政治上某种主张的电报 open telegram announcing a certain political view：大会～ circular telegram of the conference|发出～ send a circular telegram

【通牒】tōngdié 一个国家通知另一个国家并要求对方答复的文书 diplomatic note; document of one country notifying another country and demanding a reply：最后～ ultimatum

【通都大邑】tōng dū dà yì 四通八达的大城市 large city linked by all means of transport; metropolis

【通读】[1] tōngdú 从头到尾阅读全书或全文 read over (or through) a book or an article：～课文 go over a text|书稿已～一遍。The manuscript has been read over.

【通读】[2] tōngdú 读懂；读通 understand; acquire a good knowledge of; have a good grasp of：他上过几年私塾，浅近的文言文已能～。After going to a private family school for a few years, he has been able to understand rudimental classical Chinese.

【通分】tōng//fēn 把几个分母不同的分数化成分母相同而数值不变的分数。通分后的相同分母叫做公分母,通常用各分数分母的最小公倍数作为公分母。如$\frac{1}{2}$和$\frac{1}{3}$通分后得$\frac{3}{6}$和$\frac{2}{6}$。reduction of fractions to a common denominator; change several fractions with different denominators into fractions with the same denominator and the same numerical values; After the reduction, the same denominator is called common denominator, and usu. the smallest multiple of the denominators of the different fractions is used as the common denominator, such as 3/6 and 2/6 for 1/2 and 1/3 after the reduction.

【通风】tōng//fēng ❶ 使空气流通 ventilate; aerate:～设备 ventilation equipment|把窗子打开,通通风。Open the windows to ventilate the room. *or* Open the windows to let in some fresh air. ❷ 透露消息 divulge information:～报信 furnish secret information; tip somebody off

【通风】tōngfēng 空气流通;透气儿 well ventilated:这屋子不～,闷得很。The room is not well ventilated and is very stuffy.

【通风报信】tōng fēng bào xìn 向别人暗中透露消息,多指把对立双方中一方的机密暗中告知另一方 furnish secret information; tip somebody off; usually referring to the fact that the secret of one opposing party is told to the other opposing party

【通告】tōnggào ❶ 普遍地通知 give public notice; announce (in a circular, etc.):～周知 make a public announcement ❷ 普遍通知的文告 public announcement; public notice:布告栏里贴着一张～。A notice is pasted on the notice board.

【通共】tōnggòng 一共 in all; altogether; all told:～有八个队参加比赛。Altogether eight teams have entered in the competition. *or* Eight teams take part in the competition.

【通古斯】Tōnggǔsī 西方学者对属于阿尔泰语系的某些民族的称呼,包括我国的满族、赫哲族、鄂伦春族、鄂温克族等 Tunguses; term given by Western scholars to ethnic groups belonging to the Altaic family of languages, including the Manchus, Hezhens, Oroqens Ewenkis, etc.

【通观】tōngguān 总的来看;全面地看 viewed overall; viewed in an overall way; take an overall view:～全局 take the whole situation into consideration

【通过】tōng//guò ❶ 从一端或一侧到另一端或另一侧;穿过 pass through; get past; traverse:电流～导线。Electricity passes through the wires.|队伍～了沙漠。The troops have passed through the desert.|路太窄,汽车不能～。The road is too narrow for cars to get by. ❷ 议案等经过法定人数的同意而成立 adopt; pass; endorse:～决议 adopt a resolution|该提案以四分之三的多数票获得～。The motion was carried by a majority of three fourths of the votes.

【通过】tōngguò ❶ 以人或事物为媒介或手段而达到某种目的 by means of; by way of; by; through:～老艺人收集民间故事 collect folk tales through old artisans|～座谈会征询意见 solicit suggestions and comments through informal discussions ❷ 征求有关的人或组织的同意或核准 ask the consent or approval of:～组织 get the approval from an organisation|～领导 get the approval from the leadership|这问题要～群众,才能做出决定。No decision can be made on this matter until the masses have been consulted.

【通航】tōngháng 有船只或飞机来往 be open to navigation or air traffic

【通好】tōnghǎo〈书 *fml.*〉互相友好往来(多指国与国之间 of nations) have friendly relations:累世～ have friendly relations from generation to generation

【通红】tōnghóng,又 also pronounced tònghóng 很红;十分红 very red; red through:脸冻得～。The face was bright red from the cold.|炉火～。The furnace fire was blazingly red.

【通话】tōng//huà 通电话 communicate by telephone:他刚打长途同一个朋友通了话。He just had a conversation with his friend through a long-distance call.

【通话】tōnghuà 用彼此听得懂的话交谈 converse; communicate in a language that both sides can understand:他俩用英语～。The two of them talked in English.

【通婚】tōng//hūn 结成姻亲 be (or become) related by marriage; intermarry

【通货】tōnghuò 在社会经济活动中作为流通手段的货币 currency; money; money as a medium of circulation in social and economic activities:硬～ hard currency|～膨胀(of money) inflation

【通货膨胀】tōnghuò péngzhàng 国家纸币的发行量超过流通中所需要的货币量,引起纸币贬值,物价上涨的现象 (of money) inflation; devaluation of paper money and the rise of prices as a result of oversupply of money

【通缉】tōngjī 公安或司法机关通令辖区搜捕在逃的犯人 public order for the arrest of a fugitive; list sb. as wanted; put sb. on the wanted list:～令 wanted order; wanted circular|～逃犯 order the arrest of a runaway prisoner

【通家】tōngjiā〈书 *fml.*〉❶ 指两家交谊深厚,如同一家 long and deep friendship between two families:～之好 close relationship between two families as if they were one family|～之谊 profound friendship between two families as if they were one family ❷ 指内行人 expert; professional

【通假】tōngjiǎ 汉字的通用和假借 interchangeability of Chinese characters

【通奸】tōng//jiān 男女双方没有夫妇关系而发生性行为(多指一方或双方已有配偶) commit adultery; sexual intercourse with consent between a man and a woman other than his wife, or between a married woman and a man other than her husband

【通解】tōngjiě〈书 *fml.*〉通晓;理解 thoroughly understand; have a good knowledge of; be well versed in

【通经】[1] tōng//jīng〈旧时 *old*〉指通晓儒家经典 be well versed in Confucian classics

【通经】[2] tōng//jīng〈中医 *Chin. med.*〉指用药物、针灸等使月经通畅 stimulate the menstrual flow (by emmenagogues or acupuncture)

【通栏】tōnglán 书籍报刊上,从左到右或从上到下贯通版面不分栏的编排形式 layout of a page of a book, newspaper or periodical without columns:～标题 banner (or streamer) headline; banner

【通力】tōnglì 一齐出力 put in a concerted effort:～合作 make a concerted (or united) effort; give full cooperation to

【通例】tōnglì ❶ 一般的情况;常规;惯例 general rule; usual practice:星期日休息是学校的～。It is a general rule that schools close on Sundays. ❷〈书 *fml.*〉较普遍的规律 universal law

【通连】tōnglián 接连而又相通 be connected; lead to:跟卧房～的还有一间小屋子。There is a small room off the bedroom.

【通联】tōnglián 通讯联络 communications and liaison:～工作 correspondence and liaison work

【通亮】tōngliàng 通明 well-illuminated; brightly lit:火光～。The flames lit up brightly. | 照明弹照得满天～。Star shells lit up the sky.

【通令】tōnglìng ❶ 把同一个命令发到若干地方 issue a circular or order to different places:～全国 issue a general order to all parts of the nation ❷ 发到若干地方的同一个命令 circular (or general) order issued:发出～ send a general circular

【通路】tōnglù ❶ 往来的大路 thoroughfare; passageway; route:门前有一条南北～。There is a north-south highway in front of the gate. ❷ 泛指物体通过的途径 (in a broad sense) way; channel:电流的～ the channel of the electric current

【通路子】tōng lù·zi 打通办事的途径;走门路 get something done by the back door

【通论】tōnglùn ❶ 通达的议论 well-rounded argument ❷ 某一学科的全面的论述(多用于书名 usu. used in book titles) general survey:史学～ *A General Discourse on History*

【通名】tōngmíng ❶ 说出自己的姓名(旧戏曲、小说描写武将交战时多用 used in old operas and novels describing how the generals of two opposing sides introduce themselves before a fight) introduce oneself:来将～! Announce who you are, enemy general! ❷ 通用的名称 general (or common) term

【通明】tōngmíng 十分明亮 well-illuminated; brightly lit:灯火～ be ablaze with lights; be brightly lit | 月光照着雪地,四外～。The moonlight shone over the snow-covered land, making it very bright all around.

【通年】tōngnián 一年到头;整年 throughout the year; all the year round

【通盘】tōngpán 兼顾到各个部分的;全盘;全面 overall; all-round; comprehensive:～筹划 overall planning | ～安排 comprehensive arrangement

【通票】tōngpiào 联运票 through ticket

【通铺】tōngpù (旅店、集体宿舍等)连在一起的铺位 wide bed for several people (in a small inn, dormitory, etc.)

【通气】tōng//qì ❶ 使空气流通 ventilate; aerate; same as 通风 tōngfēng ①:～孔 air vent; vent ❷ 互通声气 be in touch (or communication) with each other; keep each other informed:上下不～,工作很难开展。If information is not exchanged between the above and the below, it's very difficult to work without a hitch.

【通窍】tōng//qiào 通达事理 understand things; be sensible or reasonable:他是个～的人,用不着你去开导他。He is a sensible man. There is no need for you to tell him what is right.

【通情达理】tōng qíng dá lǐ 懂得道理,说话做事合情合理 showing good sense; understanding and reasonable; sensible

【通衢】tōngqú 四通八达的道路;大道 thoroughfare:～要道 thoroughfare | 南北～ thoroughfare between the south and the north

【通权达变】tōng quán dá biàn 为了应付当前的情势,不按照常规做事,而采取适合实际需要的灵活办法 act as the occasion requires; adapt oneself to circumstances; follow a flexible course of action; take a course of action suited to the actual needs of the situation

【通人】tōngrén〈书 *fml.*〉学识渊博通晓古今的人 person of wide knowledge and sound scholarship:～达才 versatile scholar of great learning and understanding

【通融】tōng·róng ❶ 变通办法(如放宽条件、延长期限),给人方便 stretch rules or get around regulations etc. to accommodate sb.; make an exception in somebody's favour:这事可以～。We can make an exception in this case. ❷ 指

短期借钱 accommodate sb. with a short-term loan：我想跟你～二百块钱。Could you lend me 200 yuan?

【通商】tōng//shāng（国家或地区之间）进行贸易（of nations）have trade relations：～口岸 trading port|与世界各国～ have trade relations with all countries

【通身】tōngshēn 全身；浑身 whole body：～是汗 sweat all over|～白毛的小猫 small cat with white hair all over

【通史】tōngshǐ 连贯叙述各个时代史实的史书，如《史记》、《中国通史》comprehensive history; general history; historical books narrating the historical facts of the different periods, as the *Records of the Historian*, *General History of China*

【通式】tōngshì 表示同一类化合物分子组成的化学式，如烷类化合物的通式是C_nH_{2n+2} general formula; chemical formula for the composition of the molecules of the same compound, such as C_nH_{2n+2} for all alkyl compounds

【通事】tōngshì〈旧时 *old*〉指译员 interpreter

【通书】tōngshū ❶ 历书 almanac ❷〈旧时 *old*〉结婚前男家通知女家迎娶日期的帖子 notice from the bridegroom's family to the bride's family about the date of wedding

【通顺】tōngshùn（文章）没有逻辑上或语法上的毛病（of writing）clear and coherent; smooth：文理～ coherent writing|这篇短文写得很～。This short article reads quite smoothly.

【通俗】tōngsú 浅显易懂，适合一般人的水平和需要的 popular; common; easy to understand and suited to the needs of the common people：～化 popularize|～易懂 easy to understand|～读物 books for popular consumption; popular literature

【通俗歌曲】tōngsú gēqǔ 指形式上简洁、单纯，曲调流畅，易于被社会大众接受的歌曲 pop song; popular song; song which is simple in form and fluent in tone and is easily accepted by the masses

【通体】tōngtǐ ❶ 整个物体 entire body or mass：水晶～透明。Crystal is entirely transparent. ❷ 全身；浑身 all over the body：～湿透 be soaked through; wet through

【通天】tōngtiān ❶ 上通于天，形容极大、极高 exceedingly high or great：罪恶～ be guilty of monstrous crimes|～的本事 exceptional ability; super-human skill ❷ 指能直接同最高层的领导人取得联系 have direct access to the highest authorities：～人物 person with direct access to the highest authorities

【通条】tōng·tiáo 用来通炉子或枪、炮膛等的铁条（stove）poker; cleaning rod（for a gun）

【通通】tōngtōng〈副词 *adv.*〉表示全部 all; entirely; completely：把旱地～改成了水田 turn all dry fields into paddy fields

【通同】tōngtóng 串通 collude; gang up：～舞弊 act fraudulently in collusion with somebody; gang up to cheat

【通统】tōngtǒng same as 通通 tōngtōng

【通途】tōngtú〈书 *fml.*〉大道 thoroughfare

【通侻】tōngtuō same as 通脱 tōngtuō

【通脱】tōngtuō〈书 *fml.*〉通达脱俗，不拘小节 not bother about trifles; be unconventional; also 通侻 tōngtuō

【通宵】tōngxiāo 整夜 all night; whole night; throughout the night：～不眠 sleepless night|～达旦（从天黑到天亮）all night long; from dusk till dawn; all through the night

【通晓】tōngxiǎo 透彻地了解 thoroughly understand; be well versed in; be proficient in：～音律 be well-versed in musical temperament|～多种文字 have a good command of several languages

【通心粉】tōngxīnfěn 一种中心空的面条 macaroni; pasta in the form of tubes or in various other shapes

【通信】tōng//xìn 用书信互通消息，反映情况等 communicate by letter; correspond：～处 mailing address|我们几年前曾经通过信。We had correspondence some years ago.

【通信】tōngxìn 利用电波、光波等信号传送文字、图像等 transmit scripts or images by electric wave or light wave signals：数字～ digital communication

【通信兵】tōngxìnbīng 担负通信联络任务的兵种。也称这一兵种的士兵。signal corps（or unit, troops）; signalman

【通信卫星】tōngxìn wèixīng 用于通信目的的人造地球卫星，能够把来自一个地面站的信号转发或反射给其他的地面站 telecommunication satellite; man-made earth satellite which sends or reflects signals from one earth station to another station

【通信员】tōngxìnyuán 部队、机关中担任递送公文等联络工作的人员 messenger; orderly; person in a military unit or government organization who delivers official documents and do other liaison work

【通行】tōngxíng ❶（行人、车马等）在交通线上通过（pedestrians, vehicles, horses, etc.）pass（or go）through：此巷不～ dead end; no thoroughfare|前面翻修公路，车辆停止～。Road repairs ahead. Closed to traffic. ❷ same as 通用 tōngyòng ①；流通 current; general：这是全国～的办法。This is the general rule（or current practice）throughout the country.

【通行证】tōngxíngzhèng ❶ 准许在警戒区域或规定道路通行的证件 pass; permit; safe-conduct; laissez-passer; certificate giving permission to come and go freely in a restricted area, road and street ❷ 准许在同一系统下的

各个机关通行的证件 pass; permit; certificate giving permission to move freely among the different departments under the same organization or the different organizations under the same system

【通宿】tōngxiǔ 通夜;通宵 all night; whole night; throughout the night

【通讯】tōngxùn ❶ 利用电讯设备传递消息 communications; exchanging of information through communications equipment:~班 communications squad|无线电~ radio (or wireless) communications ❷ 详实而生动地报道客观事物或典型人物的文章 news report; news dispatch; correspondence; newsletter; detailed and lively news account of an objective event or a model individual

【通讯社】tōngxùnshè 采访和编辑新闻供给各报社使用的宣传机构,如我国的新华社 news agency; news (or press) service; organization that gathers and supplies news to newspapers and other subscribers, such as the Xinhua News Agency of China

【通讯网】tōngxùnwǎng 分布很广的许多电台或通讯员所组成的整体 communication network; whole composed of many widely distributed radios or corespondents

【通讯员】tōngxùnyuán 报刊、通讯社、电台邀请的为其经常写通讯报道的非专业人员 stringer; part-time or freelance correspondent for a newspaper, news agency or radio station

【通夜】tōngyè 整夜 all night; whole night; throughout the night

【通译】tōngyì ❶〈旧时 *old*〉指在语言互不相通的人谈话时做翻译 interpret; translate oral remarks for persons who do not know each other's languages ❷〈旧时 *old*〉指做通译工作的人 interpreter; person who did interpretation in the old times

【通用】tōngyòng ❶(在一定范围内)普遍使用 in common use; current; general:国际单位制世界~。The international unit system is used in all parts of the world.|使用当地民族~的语言文字 use the language popular among the local ethnic people ❷ 某些写法不同而读音相同的汉字彼此可以换用(有的限于某一意义),如'太'和'泰','措词'和'措辞' interchangeable; certain Chinese characters written in different forms but having the same pronunciation are interchangeable (some limited to a certain meaning), such as 太 tài and 泰 tài,措词 cuò//cí and 措辞 cuò//cí

【通邮】tōngyóu (国家、地区之间)有邮件来往 accessible by postal communication

【通则】tōngzé 适合于一般情况的规章或法则 general rule:民法~ General Provisions of the Civil Law

【通知】tōngzhī ❶ 把事项告诉人知道 notify; inform; give notice:你回去~大家,明天就动工。Tell everybody after you are back that the work will start tomorrow.|你走以前~我一声。Let me know before you leave. ❷ 通知事项的文书或口信 notice; circular:把~发出去 send out the circular|口头~ oral (or verbal) notice

嗵 tōng〈拟声词 *onom.*〉:他~~地往前走。He walked ahead with heavy footsteps.|心~~直跳。The heart is thumping.

tóng(ㄊㄨㄥˊ)

仝 tóng ❶ same as 同 tóng ①-⑦ ❷(Tóng) 姓 a surname

同 tóng ❶ 相同;一样 same; alike; similar:~类 of the same kind; similar|~岁 the same age|~工~酬 equal pay for equal work|大~小异 very much the same; alike except for minor differences|条件不~ different conditions; different terms|~是一双手,我为什么干不过他? Since I also have a pair of hands, why can't I do as much as he can? ❷ 跟…相同 be the same as; be alike; be similar to:~上 the same as the above|~前 the same as the previous|'式'~'二'。'式' is the same as '二'. ❸ 共同;一齐(从事) together; in common:一~ together|会~ together with; jointly with|陪~ accompany|~甘苦,共患难 share weal and woe; go through thick and thin together ❹〈介词 *prep.*〉引进动作的对象,跟'跟'相同 [introduce the object of an action], same as '跟 gēn' (with):有事~群众商量。Consult with the masses if you have anything to do. ❺〈介词 *prep.*〉引进比较的事物,跟'跟'相同 as ... as, same as 跟 gēn:他~哥哥一样聪明。He is as clever as his elder brother.|今年的气候~往年不一样。The weather this year is not same as usual. ❻〈方 *dial.*〉〈介词 *prep.*〉表示替人做事,跟'给'相同 for; same as 给 gěi:这封信我一直~你保存着。I've kept this letter for you all this time.|你别着急,我~你出个主意。Don't worry. I'll find a way out for you. ❼〈连词 *conj.*〉表示联合关系,跟'和'相同 together with; same as 和 hé:我~你一起去。I'll go with you. ❽(Tóng) 姓 a surname

☞ tòng on p.1927

【同案犯】tóng'ànfàn 指共同参加同一犯罪案件的人 accomplice; suspect or criminal involved in the same criminal case

【同班】tóng//bān 同在一个班里 be in the same class:~同学 classmate|~战友 comrade-in-arms in the same squad

【同班】tóngbān 同一个班级的同学 classmate

【同伴】tóngbàn (~儿 tóngbànr)在一起工作、生活或从事某项活动的人 companion; person who works, lives or does things together with sb.:他进城时找了个～。He had a companion to go with him when he went to town.

【同胞】tóngbāo ❶ 同父母所生的 born of the same parents:～兄弟 full brothers|～姐妹 full sisters ❷ 同一个国家或民族的人 compatriots; fellow countryman:告全国～书 message to the compatriots of the whole nation

【同辈】tóngbèi 辈分相同 of the same generation:村里～的男子都以兄弟相称。Men of the same generation in the village call each other brothers.

【同病相怜】tóng bìng xiāng lián 〈比喻 *fig.*〉有同样不幸遭遇的人互相同情 those who have the same illness sympathize with each other; fellow sufferers commiserate with each other

【同步】tóngbù ❶ 科学技术上指两个或两个以上随时间变化的量在变化过程中保持一定的相对关系 synchronism; relative relationship maintained between two or two quantities with the quantitive change of time ❷ 泛指互相关联的事物在进行速度上协调一致(of interrelated things) coordinate in time of progress; sync with; synchronize; synchronous; in step with; keep in pace with; simultaneous:实现产值、利润和财政收入～增长 make simultaneous increases in output value, profits and revenues

【同侪】tóngchái 〈书 *fml.*〉同辈 of same generation

【同仇敌忾】tóng chóu díkài 全体一致地仇恨敌人 share a bitter hatred of an enemy; be bound by a common hatred for an enemy

【同窗】tóngchuāng ❶ 同在一个学校学习 study in the same school:～三载 study in the same class for three years|～好友 intimate classmate; intimate schoolmate; intimate friends studying in the same school ❷ 同在一个学校学习的人 schoolmate:他是我旧日的～。He was a schoolmate of mine in the past.

【同床异梦】tóng chuáng yì mèng 〈比喻 *fig.*〉虽然共同生活或者共同从事某项活动,但是各人有各人的打算 share the same bed but dream different dreams; be strange bedfellows; living or working together, but having different calculations

【同道】tóngdào ❶ 志同道合的人 people cherishing the same ideals and following the same path; people having a common goal:引为～ regard as being like-minded ❷ 同一行业的人 people of the same trade or occupation:新闻界的～ colleagues in the press ❸ 同路 travel together:～南下 travel together to the south

【同等】tóngděng 等级或地位相同 of the same class, rank, or status; on an equal basis (or footing):～重要 of equal importance|～地位 equal in status; on an equal footing

【同等学力】tóngděng xuélì 没有在某一等级的学校毕业或者没有在某一班级肄业而具有相等的知识技能的水平 same educational level:高中毕业或具有～者都可以报考。Those who are senior middle school graduates or have the same educational level can register in the exam.

【同调】tóngdiào 〈比喻 *fig.*〉志趣或主张相同的人 people having same aspiration or interest; people engaged in the same pursuit:引为～ regard sb. as a like-minded person

【同恶相济】tóng è xiāng jì 坏人跟坏人互相帮助,共同作恶 the wicked help the wicked

【同房】tóng//fáng ❶ 在同一房间住宿 roommate; live in the same room ❷ 〈婉辞 *euph.*〉指夫妻过性生活 (of husband and wife) sleep together; have sexual intercourse

【同房】tóngfáng 指家族中同一支的 of the same branch of a clan:～兄弟 brothers of the same branch of a clan

【同甘共苦】tóng gān gòng kǔ 共同享受幸福,共同担当艰苦 share weal and woe (or comforts and hardships, joys and sorrows)

【同感】tónggǎn 相同的感想或感受 same feeling (or impression):他认为这部小说的人物写得十分成功,我也有～。He feels — and so do I — that the characters of this novel are well drawn.

【同庚】tónggēng 岁数相同 of the same age:咱俩～,只是我小你两个月。We two are of the same age, but I'm only two months younger.

【同工同酬】tóng gōng tóng chóu 不分种族、民族、性别、年龄,做同样的工作,工作的质量、数量相同的,给予同样的报酬 equal pay for equal work (the same work, work of the same quality, or the same amount of work) regardless of race, nationality, sex, age; equal remuneration for work of equal value

【同工异曲】tóng gōng yì qǔ ☞ 异曲同工 yì qǔ tóng gōng on p. 2274

【同归于尽】tóng guī yú jìn 一同死亡或毁灭 perish together; end up in common ruin

【同行】tóngháng ❶ 行业相同 of the same trade or occupation:他俩～,都是学医的。The two of them are of the same occupation. They are both doctors. ❷ 同行业的人 people of the same trade or occupation:路上碰到一个～,聊了几句。I met person of the same trade and chatted with him for a while.

☞ tóngxíng on p. 1922

【同好】tónghào 爱好相同的人 like-minded; persons having similar interests or tastes:公诸～ show something to those who share the same interests

【同化】tónghuà ❶ 不相同的事物逐渐变得相近或相同 assimilate (ethnic groups, etc.); make different things like or alike:民族～

national assimilation ❷ 语言学上指一个音变得和邻近的音相同或相似。如'难免'(nánmiǎn)在口语中读成 námmiǎn,'难'字的韵尾 n 受了后面'免'字声母 m 的影响变成 m。(linguis.) assimilation; a sound pronounced the same as, or similar to, a neighbouring sound. For example, 难 nán in *nanmian* 难免 nánmiǎn is pronounced *nam* under the influence of the initial sound m of the word that follows it, 免 miǎn

【同化政策】tónghuà zhèngcè 指统治民族的统治者所实行的强制同化其他民族的政策 policy of national assimilation (as pursued by the rulers of the ruling ethnic people of a country)

【同化作用】tónghuà zuòyòng 生物体在新陈代谢过程中,从食物中摄取养料,使它转化成本身的物质,并储存能量。这个过程叫做同化作用。assimilation; change of digested food into the protoplasm of an animal; absorption and incorporation of nutritive elements by plants

【同伙】tónghuǒ ❶ 共同参加某种组织,从事某种活动(多含贬义 oft. derog.) work in partnership; collude (in doing evil); join an organization together to do a certain thing ❷ 同伙的人(多含贬义 oft. derog.) partner; confederate:供出~ give the name(s) of one's partner(s)

【同居】tóngjū ❶ 同在一处居住 live together:父母死后,他和叔父~。After his parents died, he lived with his uncle. ❷ 指夫妻共同生活。也指男女双方没有结婚而共同生活。cohabit; (man and woman) live together when not legally married

【同类】tónglèi ❶ 类别相同 of the same kind; similar:~作品 similar works|~案件 similar cases ❷ 同类的人或事物 people or things of the same category:~相从。Like draws like. *or* Like follows like.

【同僚】tóngliáo〈旧时 *old*〉称同在一个官署任职的官吏 colleague; fellow official working in the same office

【同龄】tónglíng 年龄相同或相近 of or about the same age:我和新中国~。I was born in the same year as New China.|~人 contemporary

【同流合污】tóng liú hé wū 随着坏人一起做坏事 wallow in the mire with somebody; associate with an evil person; go along with somebody in his evil deeds

【同路】tóng//lù 一路同行 go the same way

【同路人】tónglùrén 一路同行的人 fellow traveler;〈比喻 *fig.*〉在某一革命阶段在某种程度上追随或赞同革命的人 person who follows or supports the revolution to a certain degree in a certain stage of revolution

【同门】tóngmén〈书 *fml.*〉❶ 指受业于同一个老师 study under the same master ❷ 指受业于同一个老师的人 fellow disciples; disciples studying under the same master

【同盟】tóngméng ❶ 为采取共同行动而缔结盟约 form an alliance to take a joint action:~国 ally; allied nations|~军 allied forces; allies|~罢工 joint strike ❷ 由缔结盟约而形成的整体 alliance; league:结成~ form (or enter into) an alliance|军事~ military alliance|攻守~ a pact to shied each other

【同盟国】tóngméngguó ❶缔结同盟条约或参加某一同盟条约的国家 ally; allied nations; nations who conclude a treaty of alliance or party to a certain treaty of alliance ❷ 第一次世界大战时,指由德、奥等国结成的战争集团,是第一次世界大战的发动者 the Central Powers during World War I, formed by Germany and Austria ❸ 第二次世界大战期间,指反对德、意、日法西斯侵略的中、苏、美、英、法等国 the Allies against German, Italian and Japanese fascism during World War II, including China, the Soviet Union, the United States, Britain and France

【同盟会】Tóngménghuì 中国同盟会的简称 abbr. for 中国同盟会 Zhōngguó Tóngménghuì

【同盟军】tóngméngjūn 为共同的斗争目标而结成同盟的队伍 allied forces; allies; forces joining together to fight for a common objective

【同名】tóngmíng 名字或名称相同 of the same title or name:~异姓 having the same given name and a different family name|这部影片是根据~小说改编的。The film was adapted from a novel of same name.

【同谋】tóngmóu ❶ 共同谋划(做坏事) conspire (with somebody):~犯 confederate; accomplice; accessory|~作案 conspire together in a crime ❷ 共同谋划做坏事的人 person who jointly conspire to commit a crime:供出~ give the name of a confederate

【同年】tóngnián ❶ 同一年 same year:~九月大桥竣工。The bridge was completed in September of the same year. ❷〈方 *dial.*〉同岁 of the same age; peer ❸ 科举考试同榜考中的人 candidates who passed the imperial examinations in the same year

【同期】tóngqī ❶ 同一个时期 corresponding period:产量超过历史~最高水平。Output reached an all-time high of the corresponding periods. ❷ 同一届 same term, year or class (at school, etc.):~毕业 graduate of the same year

【同情】tóngqíng ❶ 对于别人的遭遇在感情上发生共鸣 feel for; commiserate with; empathize with sb.'s misfortune:~心 empathy; compassion; fellow feeling|他在青少年时期就十分~被压迫的劳苦大众。He felt for the oppressed toiling masses while still a boy. ❷ 对于别人的行动表示赞成 sympathize with; approve of or agree with sb.'s action：我们～并支持该国人民的正义斗争。We sympathize with and support the people of the country in their just struggle.

【同人】tóngrén 称在同一单位工作的人或同行业的人 colleague；person who works in the same unit or trade；also 同仁 tóngrén

【同仁】tóngrén same as 同人 tóngrén

【同上】tóngshàng 跟上面所说的相同（多用于填表 oft. used when filling out a form）ditto；*idem*；same as above

【同声相应，同气相求】tóng shēng xiāng yìng, tóng qì xiāng qiú 同类性质的事物互相感应，形容志趣相投的人自然地结合在一起（见于《周易·乾·文言》）like attracts like；similar entities respond or interact；people of the same tastes or inclinations gravitate towards one another（see *The Book of Changes・The Greative・Judgement*）

【同时】tóngshí ❶ 同一个时候 at the same time；simultaneously；concurrently；meanwhile；in the meantime：他们俩是～复员的。They demobilized at the same time.｜在抓紧工程进度的～，必须注意工程质量。While maintaining the pace of project construction, we must at the same time ensure its quality. ❷ 表示并列关系，常含有进一层的意味 moreover；besides；furthermore；in addition；coordinate relation that oft. implies a further meaning：这是非常重要的任务，～也是十分艰巨的任务。This is an extremely important task, and a arduous one as well.

【同事】tóng//shì 在同一单位工作 work in the same place；work together：我和他同过事。I once worked with him.｜我们～已经多年。We have worked together for years.

【同事】tóngshì 在同一单位工作的人 colleague；mate；fellow-worker：老～ old colleague｜～之间关系融洽。The fellow-workers get along well.

【同室操戈】tóng shì cāo gē 一家人动起刀枪来 family members drawing swords on each other；〈比喻 *fig.*〉内部相斗 internal strife；internecine feud

【同岁】tóngsuì 年龄相同 of the same age：我和他～，但他比我大几个月。He is the same age as I, but a few months older.

【同位素】tóngwèisù 同一元素中质子数相同、中子数不同的各种原子互为同位素。它们的原子序数相同，在元素周期表上占同一位置。如氢有氕、氘、氚三种同位素。isotope；one of two or more atoms in the same element in which the nuclei have the same number of protons but different numbers of neutrons and are, therefore, isotopes of one another. They are characterized by the same atom ordinals, and occupy the same position on the periodic table of elements, e.g. protium, deuterium and tritium are three isotopes of hydrogen.

【同位素量】tóngwèisùliàng 元素的同位素以原子质量单位为标准的相对质量。元素按其所含各种同位素的百分组成求得的平均同位素量，就是该元素的原子量。isotopic mass；relative quality of an isotope of an element standardized by means of the element's atomic quality unit；The percentage of the element's various isotopes constitutes its average isotopic mass, which is its atomic weight.

【同喜】tóngxǐ〈客套话 *pol.*〉用来回答对方的道喜（in response to congratulations）thank you for your congratulations

【同乡】tóngxiāng 同一籍贯的人（在外地时说 mentioned in places other than the common home）person from the same village, town or province；fellow villager, townsman and provincial

【同心】tóngxīn 齐心 of one heart；of like mind and spirit：～同德（思想、行动一致）be of one heart and one mind；be dedicated to the same cause｜～协力（统一认识，共同努力）work in full cooperation and with unity of purpose；make concerted efforts；work together with one heart

【同行】tóngxíng 一起行路 travel together：一路～ travel together all the way｜跟他～的还有两个同学。Two classmates accompanied him on the trip.

☞ tóngháng on p. 1920

【同性】tóngxìng ❶ 性别相同 of the same sex：～恋 homosexuality ❷ 性质相同 of the same nature or character；like：异性的电互相吸引，～的电互相排斥。Opposite electrical charges attract, and like ones repel.

【同性恋】tóngxìngliàn 男子和男子或女子和女子之间发生的恋爱关系，是一种心理变态 homosexuality；sexual desire for those of the same sex；also 同性恋爱 tóngxìngliàn'ài

【同姓】tóngxìng 同一姓氏 of the same surname

【同学】tóng//xué 在同一个学校学习 be in the same school；be a schoolmate of sb.：我们自幼～。We have been schoolmates since childhood.｜我和他同过三年学。He and I were classmates for three year.

【同学】tóngxué ❶ 在同一个学校学习的人 fellow student；schoolmate：老～ former schoolmate or classmate｜这位是我的同班～。This is my classmate. ❷ 称呼学生［form of address used when speaking to a student］：～，请问你到游乐场怎么走？Excuse me, could you tell me where the amusement park is?

【同样】tóngyàng 相同；一样；没有差别 same；equal；similar；alike；of no difference：～大小 of the same size｜～美观 equally beautiful｜作～处理 be dealt with on an equal basis｜他们几位做～的工作。They do the same job.

【同业】tóngyè ❶ 相同的行业 same trade or

business：～公会 trade association；trade council；guild ❷ 行业相同的人 persons of the same trade or business；fellow businessman

【同业公会】tóngyè gōnghuì〈旧时 *old*〉同行业的企业联合组成的行会组织 trade association；trade council；guild；guild jointly organized by enterprises in the same trade；简称 abbr. 公会 gōnghuì

【同一】tóngyī ❶ 共同的一个或一种 same；identical；common or one kind：～形式 same form｜向～目标前进 advance towards the same goal ❷ 一致；统一 identity；unity：～性 identity

【同一律】tóngyīlǜ 形式逻辑的基本规律之一，就是在同一思维过程中，必须在同一意义上使用概念和判断，不能混淆不相同的概念和判断。公式是：'甲是甲'或'甲等于甲'。law of identity；one of the basic laws of formal logic，where in any thinking process the concepts and judgements employed must have the same sense or meaning and not be confused with others. Its formula：'A is A' or 'A equals A.'

【同义词】tóngyìcí 意义相同或相近的词，如'教室'和'课堂'，'保护'和'保卫'，'巨大'和'宏大' synonym；word with a meaning the same as or similar to another，e. g. schoolroom and classroom，protect and defend，huge and great

【同意】tóngyì 对某种主张表示相同的意见；赞成；准许 agree；consent；approve；concur：我的意见你～吗？Do you agree with me？｜上级会～你们的要求。The higher authorities will grant your request.

【同音词】tóngyīncí 语音相同而意义不同的词，如'反攻'和'返工'（fǎngōng），'树木'和'数目'（shùmù）homonym；homophone；word pronounced the same way as another but with a different meaning，e. g. '反攻'（fǎngōng，counterattack）and '返工'（fǎngōng，redo work（that has been）poorly done）and '树木'（shùmù，tree）and '数目'（shùmù，number）

【同志】tóngzhì ❶ 为共同的理想、事业而奋斗的人，特指同一个政党的成员 comrade；persons who strive for the common ideal or cause，esp. members of the same party ❷ 人们惯用的彼此之间的称呼［customary title used between people］：女～ female comrade｜老～ senior comrade｜张～ Comrade Zhang｜～，请问您贵姓？Comrade，may I ask your name？

【同治】Tóngzhì 清穆宗（爱新觉罗载淳）年号（公元 1862—1874）Tongzhi，title of the reign（1862-1874）Emperor Muzong（Aisin Gioro Zaichun）of the Qing Dynasty

【同舟共济】tóng zhōu gòng jì〈比喻 *fig.*〉同心协力，共同渡过困难 pull together in times of trouble；（of people in the same plight）cooperate towards achieving the same aim

【同宗】tóngzōng 同一家族 of the same clan or lineage；having common ancestry：他俩同姓不～。The two of them have the same surname，but are not of the same clan.

佟 Tóng 姓 a surname

彤 tóng ❶〈书 *fml.*〉红色 red：～弓 red-painted bow ❷（Tóng）姓 a surname

【彤云】tóngyún ❶ 红霞 red clouds ❷ 下雪前密布的阴云 dark clouds（before a fall of snow）：～密布。The sky was densely clouded. *or* The sky was dark with clouds. *or* Dark clouds filled the sky.

峂 tóng 峂峪（Tóngyù），地名，在北京 Tongyu，name of a place in Beijing

侗 tóng〈书 *fml.*〉幼稚；无知 childish；ignorant

☞ Dòng on p.469 and tǒng on p.1925

垌 tóng 垌冢（Tóngzhǒng），地名，在湖北 Tongzhong，name of a place in Hubei Province

☞ dòng on p.469

茼 tóng［茼蒿］（tónghāo）一年或二年生草本植物，叶互生，长形羽状分裂，头状花序，花黄色或白色，瘦果有棱。嫩茎和叶有特殊香气，可以吃。有的地区叫蓬蒿。crowndaisy（*Chrysanthemum cormarium*）；annual or biennial herb with long alternate leaves with pinnation，capitulum，and yellow or white flowers，the edged tender stems and fragrant leaves of which are edible；also called 蓬蒿 pénghāo in some places

峒 tóng 崆峒（Kōngtóng），山名，在甘肃。又岛名，在山东。Kongtong，name of a mountain in Gansu Province and an island in Shandong Province

☞ dòng on p.469

桐 tóng ❶ 泡桐 paulownia ❷ 油桐 tung tree ❷ 梧桐 phoenix tree

【桐油】tóngyóu 用油桐的种子榨的油，黄棕色，有毒，是质量很好的干性油，用来制造油漆、油墨、油布，也可做防水防腐剂等 tung oil；yellowish brown poisonous oil extracted from the seeds of the tung tree，used as a drying agent in the production of paint and varnish，printing ink，oilcloth，waterproof materials and preservatives

砼 tóng 混凝土 concrete

烔 tóng 烔炀镇（Tóngyángzhèn），地名，在安徽 Tongyangzhen，name of a place in Anhui Province

铜 tóng 金属元素，符号 Cu（cuprum）。淡紫红色，延展性和导电、导热性能好，是工业的重要原料，用途广泛。cuprum（Cu）；copper；reddish brown ductile metal element，an excellent conductor of electricity and heat，extensively used as an industrial raw material

【铜板】tóngbǎn ❶same as 铜圆 tóngyuán ❷ 演唱快书等打拍子用的板状器具，多用铜制成 copper clappers; instrument used to beat time for quick-patter, rhythmic storytelling, generally made of copper

【铜版】tóngbǎn 用铜制成的印刷版，主要用来印刷照片、图片等 copperplate; printing plate made of copper, mainly used to print photos and pictures

【铜版画】tóngbǎnhuà 版画的一种，在以铜为主的金属版上刻画或腐蚀成图形，再印在纸上 copperplate etching or engraving; copperplate; etching or engraving impression made by carving or etching on metal plates generally made of copper, and imprinting them on paper

【铜币】tóngbì 铜制的货币 copper coin

【铜鼓】tónggǔ 南方一些少数民族的打击乐器。由古代炊具的铜釜发展而成，鼓面有浮雕图案，鼓身有花纹，视为象征统治权力的重器。明清以来，成为一般的娱乐乐器。bronze drum; percussion instrument evolved from the copper cauldron, an ancient cooking utensil, used by certain southern ethnic peoples, engraved with relief patterns on its surface and with decorative designs on its body. Originally regarded as a valuable symbol of ruling power, it has been purely a recreational instrument since the Ming and Qing dynasties.

【铜活】tónghuó ❶ 建筑物或器物上各种铜制的物件 brass or copper fittings, accessories, etc.; copper fittings on buildings or implements ❷ 制造和修理上述物件的工作 work in copper; coppersmithing; production or repair work in copper

【铜匠】tóng•jiang 制造和修理铜器的手工业工人 coppersmith; craftsman who produces and repairs copper wares

【铜筋铁骨】tóng jīn tiě gǔ 〈比喻 *fig.*〉十分健壮的身体 tough and strong; very healthy and strong; robust

【铜绿】tónglǜ 铜表面上生成的绿锈，主要成分是碱式碳酸铜，粉末状，有毒。用来制烟火和颜料、杀虫剂等。verdigris; toxic powdered patina produced on a copper surface, mainly composed of basic copper carbonate, used to produce smoke and fire, pigments, pesticides, etc.

【铜模】tóngmú 字模 matrix;(copper) mould

【铜牌】tóngpái 奖牌的一种，奖给第三名 bronze medal; medal awarded to the third best in a sports event

【铜器时代】tóngqì shídài 考古学上指石器时代后、铁器时代前的一个时代。这时人类已经能用青铜制成工具，农业和畜牧业有了很大的发展。我国在公元前 2000 年左右已能用青铜铸造器物。一般指青铜器时代。Bronze Age; archaeological period between the Stone and Iron ages, when man made tools from bronze, and great developments were achieved in agriculture and animal husbandry. The Chinese cast implements with bronze around 2000 B. C.

【铜钱】tóngqián 〈古代 *arch.*〉铜质辅币，圆形，中有方孔 copper cash; copper coin; circular fractional currency or money made of copper with a square hole through the middle, used in ancient times

【铜墙铁壁】tóng qiáng tiě bì 〈比喻 *fig.*〉十分坚固、不可摧毁的事物 solid matter that cannot be destroyed; also 铁壁铜墙 tiě bì tóng qiáng

【铜臭】tóngxiù 指铜钱、铜圆的臭味，用来讥讽惟利是图的表现 stink of copper cash or coin; term of ridicule for those seeking nothing but profit:满身～ stinking of money; filthy rich

【铜锈】tóngxiù same as 铜绿 tónglǜ

【铜元】tóngyuán same as 铜圆 tóngyuán

【铜圆】tóngyuán 从清代末年到抗日战争前通用的铜质辅币，圆形 circular fractional copper currency or money in common use from the late Qing Dynasty to the period before the War of Resistance against Japan; also 铜元 tóngyuán

【铜子儿】tóngzǐr same as 铜圆 tóngyuán

童(❸僮) tóng ❶ 儿童；小孩子 child:牧～ cowboy; cowherd; shepherd boy | 顽～ naughty boy | ～话 fairy tales; children's story; nursery story | ～谣 children's folk rhyme or song; nursery rhyme | ～年 childhood ❷ 指没结婚的 virgin; unmarried:～男 virgin man | ～女 virgin girl; virgin; maiden ❸ (～儿 tóngr)〈旧时 *old*〉指未成年的仆人 page-boy; under-age servant:书～儿 boy study attendant; boy servant waiting on a scholar (or serving in the study) | 家～ page-boy ❹ 秃 bare; bald; barren:～山 bare hill ❺ (Tóng)姓 a surname

☞ Zhuàng on p. 2527

【童便】tóngbiàn 〈中医 *Chin. med.*〉指十二岁以下健康男孩子的尿，可入药 urine of boys under 12, that is used for medical purposes

【童工】tónggōng 雇用的未成年的工人 child labor; child laborer; under-age worker

【童话】tónghuà 儿童文学的一种体裁，通过丰富的想像、幻想和夸张来编写适合于儿童欣赏的故事 fairy tales; children's story; nursery story; imaginative, mythical, oft. gothic stories that suit children's taste; children's literature

【童蒙】tóngméng 〈书 *fml.*〉年幼无知的儿童 ignorant children

【童年】tóngnián 儿童时期；幼年 childhood:～时代 childhood | 回忆～时的生活 recall one's childhood life

【童仆】tóngpú 〈书 *fml.*〉家童和仆人。也泛指仆人。houseboy and manservant; (in a broad sense) servants

【童山】tóngshān 没有树木的山 bare hills：～秃岭 bare hills and mountains

【童生】tóngshēng 明清两代称没有考秀才或没有考取秀才的读书人（in Ming and Qing dynasties）scholar who has not yet passed, or taken, the imperial examination at county level

【童声】tóngshēng 儿童未变声以前的嗓音 child's voice（before breaking on reaching adolescence）

【童心】tóngxīn 小孩子的天真纯朴的心；像小孩子那样的天真纯朴的心 heart that is innocent, honest and simple as a child's; childlike innocence：～未泯 retain a childlike heart; retain traces of childlike innocence or playfulness｜萌发了～ be possessed of childlike innocence

【童星】tóngxīng 称有名的未成年的演员、运动员 child star; precociously talented child performer or athlete

【童颜鹤发】tóng yán hè fà ☞ 鹤发童颜 hè fà tóng yán on p.792

【童养媳】tóngyǎngxí 领养人家的小女孩儿做儿媳妇，等儿子长大后再结婚。这样的小女孩儿叫做童养媳。girl brought up in the household of her future husband; child daughter-in-law; child bride

【童谣】tóngyáo 在儿童中间流行的歌谣，形式比较简短 children's folk rhyme or song; popular short nursery rhyme universally popular among children

【童贞】tóngzhēn 指没有经过性交的人所保持的贞操（多指女性 usu. of a woman）virginity; chastity; condition of never having had sex

【童真】tóngzhēn 儿童的天真稚气 childlike naivete or innocence：歌中充满～的感情。This is a song of childlike naivete.

【童装】tóngzhuāng 儿童服装 children's garment

【童子】tóngzǐ 男孩子；儿童 boy; lad

【童子鸡】tóngzǐjī〈方 *dial.*〉笋鸡 young chicken; broiler; cockerel

酮 tóng 有机化合物的一类，是羰基的两个单键分别和两个烃基连接而成的化合物 ketone; organic chemical compound connected by the two single bonds of carbonyl and two hydrocarbon radicals

铜 tóng 铜城（Tóngchéng），地名，在安徽 Tongcheng, name of a place in Anhui Province

潼 tóng 潼关（Tóngguān），地名，在陕西 Tongguan, name of a place in Shaanxi Province

橦 tóng 古书上指木棉树（in ancient books）silk cotton tree; kapok tree

曈 tóng ☞ below

【曈昽】tónglóng〈书 *fml.*〉形容太阳初升由暗而明 light at daybreak; change from darkness to light as the sun rises

【曈曈】tóngtóng〈书 *fml.*〉❶日出时光亮的样子 brilliance of the rising sun：初日～ bright rising sun ❷（目光）闪烁的样子（of eyes）glistening; flashing; glimmering

朣 tóng［朣朦］（tóngméng）〈书 *fml.*〉不明亮的样子 dim; poorly illuminated

瞳 tóng same as 瞳孔 tóngkǒng

【瞳孔】tóngkǒng 虹膜中心的圆孔，光线通过瞳孔进入眼内。瞳孔可以随着光线的强弱而扩大或缩小。pupil; aperture at center of the iris, through which light enters the eye, which can expand or diminish according to light intensity; 通称 generally called 瞳人 tóngrén.（图见 ☞ figure for 眼 yǎn on p.2210）

【瞳人】tóngrén（～儿 tóngrénr）瞳孔中有人像（就是看它的人的像），因此通称瞳人 pupil（of the eye, so called because the image of the person in front is reflected in one's pupil）; also 瞳仁 tóngrén

【瞳仁】tóngrén same as 瞳人 tóngrén

tǒng（ㄊㄨㄥˇ）

侗 tǒng ☞［侗侗］（lǒngtǒng）on p.1251 ☞ Dòng on p.469 and tóng on p.1923

统[1] tǒng ❶事物彼此之间连续的关系 interconnected system; genealogy; continuum of interrelated things：系～ system; scheme｜血～ bloodline; genealogy｜传～ tradition; heritage ❷总起来；总括；全部 all; totally; entirely; wholly; together：～筹 plan as a whole; make overall plans; coordinate in an overall manner｜～购～销 state monopoly for purchase and marketing（of grain, cotton, etc.）; unified purchase and sale by the state｜这些东西～归你用。You have all these things at your disposal. ❸统领；统管 lead; command; control：～治 rule; control; dominate｜～兵 command troops｜上级主管部门不要对企业～得过死。The department responsible for the work concerned should not exercise rigid and excessive control over enterprises.

统[2] tǒng same as 筒 tǒng ③：长～皮靴 high boots｜皮～子 fur lining for a coat

【统舱】tǒngcāng 轮船上可以容纳许多乘客的大舱，有时也用来装载货物 steerage; largest and cheapest accommodation on board a ship; cargo steerage

【统称】tǒngchēng ❶总起来叫做 be generally known as; called by a joint name; be collectively called; be grouped together under a generic or common name：陶器和瓷器～为陶瓷。Pottery and porcelain are collectively called ceramics. ❷ 总的名称 general designation or term：陶瓷是陶器和瓷器的～。Ceramics is the general term for pottery and porcelain.

【统筹】tǒngchóu 统一筹划 plan as a whole; make overall plans; coordinate in an overall manner：～兼顾 overall planning and all-round consideration; making overall plans by taking all relevant factors into consideration; unified planning with due consideration for all concerned｜～全局 take the whole situation into account and plan accordingly

【统共】tǒnggòng 一共 altogether; in all：我们小组～才七个人。There are altogether seven people in our group.

【统购】tǒnggòu 国家对某些有关国计民生的重要物资实行有计划的统一收购 state monopoly purchase (of certain important materials that concern the nation's economy and its people's livelihood)

【统管】tǒngguǎn 统一管理；全面管理 centralized control; unified management：～家务 unified management of household chores｜学校的行政和教学工作都由校长～。The president of the school has overall control of administration and teaching.

【统货】tǒnghuò 商业上指不分质量、规格、等级而按照一个价格购进或售出的某一种商品 uniformly-priced commodities; products purchased or sold at the same price, regardless of quality, specification or grade

【统计】tǒngjì ❶ 指对某一现象有关的数据的搜集、整理、计算和分析等 statistics, census; collection, organization, calculation, analysis, etc., of the relevant data of a phenomenon ❷ 总括地计算 add up; count：把人数～一下 count the number of people

【统计学】tǒngjìxué 研究统计理论和方法的学科 statistics; academic subject concerning statistical theories and methods

【统考】tǒngkǎo 在一定范围内用统一的试题进行的考试 uniform examination; general examination with a common test paper within a defined range：全国～ nationwide unified examinations｜语文～ unified examination in Chinese｜全区数学～，她取得了较好的成绩。She won an excellent score in the regional unified examination in mathematics.

【统领】tǒnglǐng ❶ 统辖率领 lead; command：～各路人马 command a joint force ❷ 统领人马的军官 leader; commander; officer in charge or command of a force

【统摄】tǒngshè 〈书 *fml.*〉 same as 统辖 tǒngxiá

【统属】tǒngshǔ 上级统辖下级，下级隶属于上级 subordination; relationship between a high authority and its subordinate, the former exercising control over the latter, and the latter is under the jurisdiction of the former：～关系 relations of subordination｜彼此不相～。Neither is subordinate to the other.

【统帅】tǒngshuài ❶ 统率全国武装力量的最高领导人 commander-in-chief; commander; supreme commander in charge of all the nation's armed forces ❷ same as 统率 tǒngshuài

【统率】tǒngshuài 统辖率领 command; lead：～全军 command or lead the whole army

【统统】tǒngtǒng 通通 all; entirely; completely

【统辖】tǒngxiá 管辖(所属单位) exercise control over; govern; have sth. or sb. under one's command：这个团归司令部直接～。This regiment is directly under the commander of the headquarters.

【统销】tǒngxiāo 国家对某些有关国计民生的重要物资实行有计划的统一销售 state monopoly marketing (of certain important goods and materials concerning the nation's economy and its people's livelihood)

【统一】tǒngyī ❶ 部分联成整体；分歧归于一致 unify; unite; integrate; combine the parts of a thing back into a unified whole; turn divergences into a common understanding：～体 entity; unity｜～战线 unified front｜大家的意见逐渐～了。They were able to gradually see eye to eye with each other. ❷ 一致的；整体的；单一的 unified; unitary; centralized：～的意见 consensus｜～调配 unified allocation｜～领导 unified leadership

【统一体】tǒngyītǐ 哲学上指矛盾的两个方面在一定条件下相互依存而结成的整体 (philos.) entity; unity; entirety of the two interdependent aspects of a contradiction formed under specific conditions

【统一战线】tǒngyī zhànxiàn 几个阶级或几个政党为了某种共同的政治目的结成的联盟。如抗日民族统一战线、人民民主统一战线、国际统一战线等。united front; alliance of several classes or parties in order to achieve a common political objective, such as the anti-Japanese national united front, the people's democratic united front, and the international united front

【统战】tǒngzhàn 统一战线的简称 abbr. for 统一战线 tǒngyī zhànxiàn：～政策 united front policy｜～工作 united front work

【统治】tǒngzhì ❶ 凭借政权来控制、管理国家或地区 rule; dominate; control and run a country or area through political power：～阶级 ruling class｜血腥～ sanguinary or bloodthirsty rule｜封建～ feudal rule ❷ 支配；控制 control; govern：～文坛 govern the literary circles

【统治阶级】tǒngzhì jiējí 掌握国家政权的阶级，有时特指占统治地位的剥削阶级 ruling class; class that wields the political power of a state; sometimes refers to a dominating exploitative class

【统制】tǒngzhì 统一控制 (unified) control; govern: 经济～economic control | ～军用物资 exercise control over military supplies

捅(挏) tǒng ❶ 戳;扎 stab; poke: ～了一刀 give sb. a stab | 他把窗户纸～了个大窟窿。He poked a big hole in the paper window pane. ❷ 碰;触动 poke; touch; nudge: 我用胳膊肘～了他一下。I gave him a nudge. ❸ 戳穿;揭露 expose; disclose; let out; give away: 他是个直性人,把看到的事儿都～出来了。He is a forthright man, and told of all he had seen.

【捅咕】tǒng·gu ❶ 碰;触动 touch ❷ 从旁鼓动人(做某种事) instigate; stir up; egg on; urge sb. to do sth.

【捅娄子】tǒng lóu·zi 引起纠纷;惹祸 make a mess of sth.; get into trouble; make a blunder

【捅马蜂窝】tǒng mǎfēngwō 〈比喻 *fig.*〉惹祸或触动不好惹的人 invite disaster; offend a person not to be trifled with

桶 tǒng 盛东西的器具,用木头、铁皮、塑料等制成,多为圆筒形,有的有提梁 barrel; tub; pail; bucket; keg; container made of wood, metal, plastic, etc., generally cylindrical and with a handle: 水～ water pail | 汽油～ petrol drum

筒(筩) tǒng ❶ 粗大的竹管 section of a thick bamboo trunk: 竹～ thick bamboo tube ❷ 较粗的管状器物 thick tube-shaped object: 笔～ brush pot | 烟～ chimney; funnel; smokestack | 邮～ mailbox; pillar box ❸ (～儿 tǒngr)衣服等的筒状部分 tube-shaped part of clothing, etc.: 袖～儿 sleeve | 袜～儿 stocking leg | 长～靴 long or high boots; also 统 tǒng

【筒裤】tǒngkù 裤腿呈直筒状的裤子,裤腿膝部和最下端肥瘦略同 straight-legged trousers; trousers with tube-shaped legs, of equal width at knee and hem

【筒裙】tǒngqún 呈筒状的裙子,上部和下部肥瘦略同,一般下摆长不过膝部,没有褶子 straight skirt; tight skirt; tube-shaped skirt of an equal width from top to bottom, whose hem is above the knee

【筒瓦】tǒngwǎ 半圆筒形的瓦 arched tile; semicircular tile

【筒子】tǒng·zi 筒 tube or tube-shaped object: 竹～ bamboo tube | 枪～ barrel of a gun | 袜～ stocking leg

【筒子楼】tǒng·zilóu 中间是过道,两边是住房,没有厨房和卫生间的楼房。这种楼房俗称筒子楼。general term for buildings with a passageway through their middle, and living rooms on either side, with no kitchen or washroom

tòng (ㄊㄨㄥˋ)

同 tòng ☞ 胡同 hú·tòng on p. 819
☞ tóng on p. 1919

恸(慟) tòng 〈书 *fml.*〉极悲哀;大哭 deep sorrow; grief; agony; wail; cry out loud

通 tòng (～儿 tòngr) 〈量词 *classifier*〉用于动作[referring to action]: 打了三～鼓 three rolls of the drums | 挨了一～儿说 get a scolding; be given a telling-off
☞ tōng on p. 1915

【通红】tònghóng '通红' tōnghóng 的又音 variant pronunciation of 通红 tōnghóng

衕 tòng ☞ [衚衕] (hú·tòng) on p. 820

痛 tòng ❶ 疾病创伤等引起的难受的感觉 ache; pain; sufferings caused by illness, injury etc.: 头～ headache | 肚子～ stomachache | 伤口很～。The wound hurts badly. ❷ 悲伤 sadness; sorrow; grief: 悲～ grief; deep sorrow | 哀～ grief; sorrow ❸ 尽情地;深切地;彻底地 extremely; deeply; bitterly; thoroughly: ～击 strike relentless blows at | ～骂 scold severely; give a good scolding; curse roundly; tell off scathingly; reproach abusively | ～歼 destroy; wipe out; annihilate | ～饮 drink one's fill; drink to one's heart's content | ～改前非 repent one's misdeeds; make a clean break with one's (past) misdeeds

【痛不欲生】tòng bù yù shēng 悲痛得不想活下去。形容悲伤到极点。be overwhelmed with sorrow; grieve to the extent of wishing to die

【痛斥】tòngchì 痛切地斥责;狠狠地斥责 bitterly attack or rebuke; make a stinging verbal attack on; scathingly denounce: ～国贼 denounce a traitor | 受了一顿～ be the subject of a blistering rebuke

【痛楚】tòngchǔ 悲痛;苦楚 pain; anguish; suffering; distress: 内心～万分 be overwhelmed by grief; be greatly grieved

【痛处】tòngchù 感到痛苦的地方;心病 sore spot; tender spot: 一句话触到他的～。These words touched him to the raw. *or* These remarks hit a sore point in him.

【痛打】tòngdǎ 狠狠地打 beat mercilessly or soundly: ～一顿 give sb. a good or sound beating; tan sb.'s hide

【痛悼】tòngdào 沉痛地哀悼 mourn deeply; grieve over: ～死难烈士 deeply mourn the martyrs

【痛定思痛】tòng dìng sī tòng 悲痛的心情平静之后,回想以前的痛苦 recall a painful experience after recovering from the grief it caused; draw a lesson from a bitter experience

【痛感】tònggǎn ❶ 深切地感觉到 keenly feel; be keenly aware (of sth.):他～自己知识贫乏。He was keenly aware of his lack of knowledge. ❷ 疼痛的感觉 sense of pain:针灸时有轻微的～。One feels a little pain when receiving acupuncture treatment.

【痛恨】tònghèn 深切地憎恨 abhor; hate bitterly; utterly detest or loathe

【痛悔】tònghuǐ 深切地后悔 lament; regret deeply; rue; bemoan

【痛击】tòngjī 狠狠地打击 bitterly hit or attack; deal a heavy or hard blow; strike relentless blows at:迎头～ strike sb. head-on; hit head-on

【痛经】tòngjīng 妇女在行经前或行经时下腹子宫部位疼痛的症状 dysmenorrhoea; menalgia; symptomatic pain in the hypogastrium of the uterus before or during menstruation; also 经痛 jīngtòng

【痛觉】tòngjué 身体组织因受破坏或受强烈的刺激所产生的感觉 sense of pain; sensation experienced when live tissue is destroyed or over stimulated

【痛哭】tòngkū 尽情大哭 wail; cry or weep bitterly:～流涕 cry bitterly; weep and wail; cry one's heart out; weep bitter tears; weep or shed bitter tears|～失声 burst out crying; be choked with tears; lose one's voice after weeping

【痛苦】tòngkǔ 身体或精神感到非常难受 pain; suffering; agony; suffering; physical suffering or mental pain:～的生活 painful life|得了这种病,非常～。This disease causes great pain and suffering.

【痛快】tòng·kuài ❶ 舒畅;高兴 happy; joyful; delighted; gratified:看见场上一堆一堆的麦子,心里真～。I was delighted at the sight of stack after stack of wheat. ❷ 尽兴 to one's heart's content; to one's great satisfaction:这个澡洗得真～。I had a very refreshing bath.|痛痛快快地玩一场 have a wonderful time ❸ 爽快;直率 straightforward; frank and direct; forthright:队长～地答应了我们的要求。The team leader readily agreed to our request.|他很～,说到哪儿做到哪儿。He is a straightforward man, and does what he says he will.

【痛切】tòngqiè 悲痛而深切;非常沉痛 intense sorrow; agonizing grief; most sorrowfully; keenly:～地认识到自己的错误 be sorrowfully remorseful of one's mistake

【痛恶】tòngwù 极端厌恶 abhor; loathe; bitterly detest; dislike intensely:不讲公德的行为,令人～。Unethical conduct is despicable.

【痛惜】tòngxī 沉痛地惋惜 deeply regret; deplore; feel remorse for:诗人英年早逝,令人～。It is a great pity that this poet should have died in his prime.

【痛心】tòngxīn 极端伤心 pained; distressed; grieved; saddened:做出这种事,真让人～。It is truly distressing that such a deed should have been committed.

【痛心疾首】tòng xīn jí shǒu 形容痛恨到极点 with bitter hatred; feel deep bitterness; with great resentment (疾首 *ji shou*:头痛 feel headache)

【痛痒】tòngyǎng ❶〈比喻 *fig.*〉疾苦 sufferings; difficulties; hardships:～相关 be closely connected; share a common lot ❷〈比喻 *fig.*〉紧要的事 importance; consequence:不关～ matter of no consequence; inconsequential trifles

【痛痒相关】tòngyǎng xiāngguān 彼此疾苦互相关联,形容关系极为密切 be closely connected; share a common lot:这事跟他～,他怎能不着急? How can he fail to be anxious about a matter of such great concern to him?

tōu(ㄊㄡ)

偷(❺媮) tōu ❶ 私下里拿走别人的东西,据为己有 steal; burglarize; pilfer; make off with:～窃 steal; pilfer|钱包被人～去了。The wallet was stolen. ❷(～儿 tōur)指偷盗的人 thief; burglar; pilferer:惯～ hardened thief ❸ 瞒着人 secretly; stealthily; covertly; surreptitiously; on the sly:～看 peep; peek; take a covert look at; steal a glance|～听 bug; tap; eavesdrop; listen in stealthily|～渡 stealthily cross (a blockaded river, etc.)|～跑 sneak; run away stealthily ❹ 抽出(时间) take (time) off; find (time):～空儿 take time off (from work to do sth. else); snatch a moment|忙里～闲 snatch a little leisure time in the midst of a busy life; allow oneself a bit of time ❺ 苟且敷衍,只顾眼前 muddle through, thinking only of the present:～安 seek temporary ease; muddle along

【偷安】tōu'ān 只顾眼前的安逸 seek temporary ease; muddle along:苟且～ seek only temporary ease and comfort

【偷盗】tōudào 偷窃;盗窃 steal; pilfer:～财物 steal property

【偷渡】tōudù 偷偷通过封锁的水域或区域 stealthily cross (a blockaded river or area)

【偷工减料】tōu gōng jiǎn liào 不按照产品或工程所规定的质量要求而暗中搀假或削减工序和用料 stint on both labour and materials; cheat in work and cut down on materials; surreptitiously adulterate or cut down on necessary amounts of work and materials for products or a project, regardless of prescribed requirements

【偷鸡摸狗】tōu jī mō gǒu ❶ 指偷盗(多指小偷

小摸 usu. petty theft) steal; pilfer; pinch ❷ 指男子乱搞男女关系 (of a man) have illicit affairs with a woman

【偷奸取巧】tōu jiān qǔ qiǎo 用狡猾的手段使自己不费力而得到好处 make a profit through craft rather than effort：他这人专会～，干事全凭一张嘴。He is a smooth talker, and resorts to chicanery for personal gain as a matter of course.

【偷空】tōu//kòng (～儿 tōu//kòngr) 忙碌中抽出时间(做别的事) take time off (from work to do sth. else); snatch a moment：前两天曾～去看过他一次。A few days ago I took time off to go and see him.

【偷懒】tōu//lǎn 贪图安逸、省事，逃避应做的事 loaf on the job; be lazy; be indolent at work, seeking ease and comfort instead of doing one's duty：从不～ never loaf on the job

【偷梁换柱】tōu liáng huàn zhù〈比喻 *fig.*〉用欺骗的手法暗中改变事物的内容或事情的性质 steal the beams and pillars and replacing them with rotten timbers; change the content or property of a thing on the sly

【偷摸】toumō 小偷小摸；偷盗 steal; pilfer; pinch; petty theft：～成性。Stealing has become his second nature.

【偷巧】tōu//qiǎo 取巧 resort to trickery to serve oneself; shirk by avoiding the difficult and time-consuming

【偷窃】tōuqiè 盗窃 steal; pilfer

【偷情】tōu//qíng〈旧指 *old*〉暗中与人谈恋爱，现多指与人发生不正当的男女关系 carry on a clandestine love affair; have a covert love affair; have illicit sexual relations

【偷生】tōushēng 苟且地活着 drag out an ignoble existence; live on without purpose：～苟安 seek temporary ease and comfort

【偷手】tōushǒu 指留有余地不把本事全显示出来 keep a trick or two in reserve (when displaying ability)

【偷税】tōu//shuì 有意不缴纳或少缴纳应该缴纳的税款 evade taxes; deliberately not pay tax, or pay less tax then required

【偷天换日】tōu tiān huàn rì〈比喻 *fig.*〉暗中玩弄手法，改变重大事物的真相来欺骗别人 cheat sb. by covertly and fraudulently changing the facts of an important matter

【偷偷】tōutōu (～儿 tōutōur) 形容行动不使人觉察 stealthily; secretly; covertly; surreptitiously; on the sly; make actions undetectable：趁人不注意，他～儿地溜走了。He sneaked away while nobody was looking.

【偷偷摸摸】tōutōumōmō 形容瞒着人做事，不敢让人知道 furtively; surreptitiously; stealthily; on the sly; do a thing covertly, not daring to let others know

【偷袭】tōuxí 趁敌人不防备时突然袭击 sneak attack; dawn raid; surprise attack (when the enemy is unprepared)：～敌营 launch a surprise attack on an enemy camp

【偷闲】tōu//xián ❶ 挤出空闲的时间 take time off; snatch a moment of leisure; find time：忙里～ snatch a little leisure time from a busy life; allow oneself a little time ❷〈方 *dial.*〉偷懒；闲着 loaf on the job; be idle

【偷眼】tōuyǎn 形容偷偷地看 steal a glance; take a furtive glance：他～看了一下母亲的神色。He stole a look at his mother's face.

【偷营】tōu//yíng 偷袭敌人的军营 make a surprise attack on an enemy camp; raid an enemy camp：～劫寨 make a surprise attack on an enemy camp

【偷嘴】tōu//zuǐ 偷吃东西 eat on the sly

tóu (ㄊㄡˊ)

头(頭) tóu ❶ 人身最上部或动物最前部长着口、鼻、眼等器官的部分 head; part of the body that contains the eyes, ears, nose, and mouth at the front of the body in animals and on the top of humans; (图见 ☞ figure for 身体 shēntǐ on p. 1701) ❷ 指头发或所留头发的样式 hair; hairstyle：剃～ have a haircut | 留～ let the hair grow long; wear one's hair long | 梳～ comb the hair | 平～ crew-cut | 分～ parted hair ❸ (～儿 tóur) 物体的顶端或末梢 top; tip; end：山～ hilltop; top of a hill | 笔～儿 pen nib; tip of a pen | 中间粗，两～儿细 thick in the middle, and thin at both ends ❹ (～儿 tóur) 事情的起点或终点 beginning; end：话～儿 thread of discourse | 提个～儿 give sb. a lead | 这样一条线一条线地，织到什么时候才是个～儿呀! When ever will you make an end, weaving thread by thread that way? ❺ (～儿 tóur) 物品的残余部分 remnant; remains; leftover; end：布～儿 odd bits of cloth; leftover of a bolt of cloth | 蜡～儿 candle end | 铅笔～儿 pencil stub or stump ❻ (～儿 tóur) 头目 head; chief; boss：李～儿 Chief Li | 他是这一帮人的～儿。He is the boss of the gang. ❼ (～儿 tóur) 方面 side; aspect：他们是一～儿的。They are on the same side. | 心挂两～ have divided loyalties ❽ 第一 first; number one：～等 first-class; first-rate | ～号 number one; size one; first-rate; top quality ❾ 领头的；次序居先的 lead; head：～车 headmost car | ～马 lead horse | ～羊 lead sheep or goat; bellwether ❿ 用在数量词前面，表示次序在前的 [used before a classifier] first：～趟 first | ～一遍 the first time | ～半本 first half part of a book | ～几个 first several | ～三天(=前面的三天) first three days ⓫〈方 *dial.*〉用在'午'或'天'前面，表示时间在先的 [used before 年 nián or 天 tiān] previous; last：～年(=去年或上一年) last year | ～天(=上一天)

the previous day; the day before|～两年(=去年和前年,或某年以前的两年) the past two years|～三天(=昨天、前天和大前天,或某天以前的三天) three days before; the past three days ⓬ 临;接近 right before; about; prior to:～五点就得动身 need to make a start before (or by) five|～鸡叫我就起来了。I got up before cockcrow.|～吃饭要洗手。Wash hands before eating. ⓭ 用在某两个数字之间,表示约数,兼表数目不大[used between two numerals] about; around; approximately; indicate a small number:十～八块 about eight or ten yuan|三～五百 approximately 300 or 500 yuan ⓮〈量词 *classifier*〉a)用于牛、驴、骡、羊等家畜[used for domestic animals such as the ox, donkey, mule and sheep]:一～牛 a head of cattle|两～驴 two donkeys b)用于蒜[used with garlic]:一～蒜 a bulb of garlic

头(頭) •tou ❶(～儿·tour)名词后缀 noun suffix a)接于名词性词根[used as a root of a noun]:木～ wood|石～ stone|骨～ bone|舌～ tongue|罐～ jar; pot; tank; tin|尺～ odd bits of cloth|苗～ suggestion of a new development; symptom of a trend b)接于动词词根[used as a root of a verb]:念～ idea; hope|扣～ discount; rebate|饶～ give gratis; throw in sth.|接～儿 contact|看～儿 worth reading or seeing|听～儿 worth listening to c)接于形容词词根[used as a root of an adjective]:有准～ have accuracy in sth.|尝了甜～儿 draw benefit from something.; learn to appreciate the good of something. ❷ 方位词后缀[suffix of a locality]:上～ above|下～ below|前～ front|后～ behind; back; rear|里～ inside; interior|外～ outside; exterior

【头筹】tóuchóu〈比喻 *fig.*〉第一位或第一名 first; championship:拔取～ come out first; win the championship|夺得～ win the championship

【头寸】tóucùn ❶ 指银行、钱庄等所拥有的款项,收多付少叫头寸多,收少付多叫头寸缺,结算收付差额叫轧(gá)头寸,借款弥补差额叫拆头寸 cash; liquidity; cash capital of a bank or money shop; 头寸多 tóucùn duō means cash received being in excess of what is paid out; 头寸缺 tóucùn quē means cash received being less than what is paid out; 轧头寸 gǎ tóucùn means balance between a cash settlement; 拆头寸 chāi tóucùn means borrow a loan to make the balance ❷ 指银根,如银根松也说头寸松,银根紧也说头寸紧 money market; money supply. 头寸松 tóucùn sōng means 'Money is plentiful.' and 头寸紧 tǒucùn jǐn means 'Money is tight.'

【头等】tóuděng 第一等;最高的 first-class; first-rate:～舱 first-class cabin|～大事 matter of primary importance; cardinal task or question|～重要任务 task of primary importance; major task

【头顶】tóudǐng 头的顶部 top or crown of the head

【头发】tóu•fa 人的前额以上、两耳以上和后颈部以上生长的毛 hair (above the human forehead, ears and nape)

【头伏】tóufú 初伏 first *fu*; first of the three ten-day periods in summer

【头骨】tóugǔ 构成头颅的骨头,包括额骨、顶骨、颞骨、枕骨、蝶骨等 skull; cranium; bone that constitutes the head, including the frontal, parietal, temporal, occipital and sphenoid bones

【头号】tóuhào ❶ 第一号;最大号 number one; size one; the largest number:～字 size one printing type|～新闻 headline news; lead story ❷ 最好的 first-rate; top quality:～面粉 top-grade flour|～货色 first-class or top-quality goods

【头家】tóujiā ❶ 指聚赌抽头的人 host of a gambling party who takes a cut of the winnings ❷ 庄家 banker in a gambling party ❸ 上家 (in mah-jong, card, dice or games, etc.) player whose turn immediately precedes ❹〈方 *dial.*〉店主;老板 shopkeeper; boss; proprietor

【头角】tóujiǎo〈比喻 *fig.*〉青年的气概或才华 brilliance or talent of a young person:崭露～ make a brilliant display of individual talent|～峥嵘 (of a youth) brilliant; very promising; outstanding

【头巾】tóujīn ❶〈古代 *arch.*〉男子裹头的纺织物;明清两代读书人裹头的纺织物 head-covering (for men in ancient times or scholars of the Ming and Qing dynasties) ❷ 现代妇女裹头的纺织物,多为正方形 scarf; kerchief; head-covering for contemporary women, usu. square-shaped

【头颈】tóujǐng〈方 *dial.*〉脖子 neck

【头盔】tóukuī 帽盔;钢盔 (steel) helmet

【头里】tóu•li ❶ 前面 in front; ahead:您～走,我马上就来。Please go ahead. I'll be right there.|工作和学习,他样样都走在～。He takes the lead in everything, be it work or study. ❷ 事前 in advance; beforehand:咱们把话说在～,不要事后翻悔。Let us make ourselves clear in advance so as not to appear to renege later. ❸〈方 *dial.*〉以前 before; ago; previously; formerly:十年～到处都唱这个歌。This song was very popular ten years ago.

【头脸】tóuliǎn ❶ 指面貌 face; features; appearance:走到跟前我才看清他的～。I did not recognize him until seeing him close up. ❷ 指面子;体面 dignity; face:他在地方上是个有～的人物。He is a local big shot.

【头领】tóulǐng 领头的人;首领 chief; leader; commander:土匪～ chief of the bandits

【头颅】tóulú 人的头 head (of a person):抛～,洒热血 lay down one's life; sacrifice oneself (for a just cause)

【头路】[1] tóulù 头等的(货物等)(of goods, etc.) first-class; first-rate; top quality; top-notch; tip-top

【头路】[2] tóulù 〈方 *dial.*〉❶ 头发朝不同方向梳时中间露出头皮的一道缝儿 hair parting; line on the scalp where the hair is combed in different directions ❷ same as 头绪 tóuxù:摸不着～ be unable to get things straight ❸ 职业、门路 job; way, connections (for getting sth. done):在这里找～可难了! Finding a job is really difficult here.

【头马】tóumǎ 马群或马帮中领头的马 head horse (of a group of horses)

【头面】tóu·mian 〈旧时 *old*〉妇女头上妆饰品的总称 woman's head ornaments or headgear:一副～ a set of headgear

【头面人物】tóumiàn rénwù 指社会上有较大势力和声望的人物 prominent figure; big shot; bigwig; magnate; powerful figure of high prestige

【头目】tóumù 某些集团中为首的人(多含贬义 oft. derog.)head of a gang; chieftain; ringleader:大～ ringleader|小～ sub-group leader in a gang; head of a small group in a gang

【头难】tóunán 〈方 *dial.*〉(做事)起头时感觉困难 difficult beginning; difficulty experienced when starting sth.:什么事情总是～,做了一阵就容易了。The first step is always difficult, but it becomes easier after some time.

【头脑】tóunǎo ❶ 脑筋;思维能力 savvy; brains; mind:有～ have a mind of one's own; have brains; be resourceful|～清楚 have a clear mind; be clear-headed|胜利冲昏～ get carried away by success; be dizzy with success; be swollen-headed with success ❷ same as 头绪 tóuxù:摸不着～(弄不清头绪) cannot make head or tail of sth.; be in the dark; be utterly puzzled ❸ 首领 head; leader; chief; chieftain

【头年】tóunián ❶ 第一年 first year:三年看～。The first year of a three-year project is crucially important. ❷ 去年或上一年 last year; previous year; the year before:～春节 last spring festival|～他曾回来过一次。He came back once last year.

【头牌】tóupái 〈旧时 *old*〉演戏时,演员的名字写在牌子上挂出来,挂在最前面的牌子叫头牌 plate or board on which the name of the leading actor or actress in a traditional opera is written:挂～ leading actor or actress announced on the board|～小生 leading beardless-youth role|～花旦 leading female role

【头皮】tóupí ❶ 头顶及其周围的皮肤 scalp; skin covering the top of the human head and surrounding area:挠着～想主意 try to think of a way out while scratching one's head ❷ 头皮表面脱落下来的碎屑 dandruff; scurf

【头前】tóuqián ❶ 前面 ahead; in front; at the head:他在～引路。He is leading the way ahead. ❷ 以前 previously; in the past:～这个地方还是很荒凉的。In the past this place was quite desolate.

【头钱】tóuqián 赌博抽头所得的钱 commission on winnings of a gambling party

【头人】tóurén 领头的人,多指部落或某些少数民族中的首领 tribal chief; headman; oft. head or chief of tribe or ethnic minority group

【头晌】tóushǎng 〈方 *dial.*〉上午 morning; before noon

【头生】tóushēng ❶ 头次生育 first birth:她这是～,不免有些紧张。It was her first birth, and she could not help but feel a little apprehensive. ❷ 第一胎生的 first born:～孩子 firstborn child ❸ (～儿 tóushēngr)第一胎生下的孩子 firstborn child

【头绳】tóushéng ❶ (～儿 tóushéngr)用棉、毛、塑料等制成的细绳子,主要用来扎发髻或辫子 thin string made of cotton, wool, plastic, etc. for binding a plait or bun ❷ 〈方 *dial.*〉毛线 knitting wool

【头饰】tóushì 戴在头上的装饰品 headgear; headdress; ornament for the head

【头套】tóutào 一种化装用具,套在头上,使头型、发式等符合某种需要 wig; actor's headgear; head dressing to make the cast of the head, hairstyle, etc., conform to a certain look

【头疼】tóuténg same as 头痛 tóutòng

【头疼脑热】tóu téng nǎo rè (～的 tóu téng nǎo rè·de)指一般的小病 slight illness:～的,着什么急呀! There is no need to worry over such a slight illness.

【头天】tóutiān ❶ 上一天 yesterday; previous day; the day before ❷ 第一天 first day

【头痛】tóutòng 头部疼痛 headache;〈比喻 *fig.*〉感到为难或讨厌 feel embarrassed or disgusted

【头痛医头,脚痛医脚】tóu tòng yī tóu, jiǎo tòng yī jiǎo 〈比喻 *fig.*〉对问题不从根本上解决,只从表面现象或枝节上应付 attending to the superficial or minor aspects only, rather than tackling the roots of a problem

【头头儿】tóu·tour 俗称某单位或某集团的为首的人 head; chief; leader; boss; head

【头头是道】tóu tóu shì dào 形容说话或做事很有条理 well-organized, clear and systematic in speech or actions

【头陀】tóutuó 指行脚乞食的和尚 mendicant Buddhist monk [梵 Sanskrit: dhūta]

【头先】tóuxiān 〈方 *dial.*〉❶ 起先;先前 before; in the past; in the beginning ❷ 前头 ahead; in the front ❸ 刚才 just now

【头衔】tóuxián 指官衔、学衔等称号 official title, academic rank or title, etc.

【头像】tóuxiàng 肩部以上的人像 head portrait or sculpture; portrait of person from shoulders up; bust

【头胸部】tóuxiōngbù 某些节肢动物(如螃蟹、虾)的头部和胸部紧连在一起,合称为头胸部 cephalothorax; (of some arthropods such as crabs and shrimps) closely connected, or fused, head and thorax

【头绪】tóuxù 复杂纷乱的事情中的条理 main threads (of a complex affair):茫无～ have no clues to follow; be in a complete mess|理不出个～ unable to disentangle

【头雁】tóuyàn 雁群中领头飞的大雁 leading wild goose; wild goose that leads the flock in a flying formation

【头羊】tóuyáng 羊群中领头的羊 bellwether; leading sheep or goat (of a group)

【头油】tóuyóu 抹在头发上的油质化妆品 hair oil; pomade; hair cosmetic

【头重脚轻】tóu zhòng jiǎo qīng 上面重,下面轻 top-heavy; dizzy; 〈比喻 *fig*.〉基础不稳固 unstable foundation

【头子】tóu·zi 首领(含贬义 derog.) boss; chief; chieftain:土匪～ bandit chief|流氓～ gang-leader

投 tóu ❶ 向一定目标扔 throw; fling; hurl; cast; toss (towards a goal):～篮 shoot (in basketball)|～手榴弹 throw a hand grenade ❷ 放进去;送进去 drop; put in; cast:～票 vote; cast a vote|～资 invest; put in (money, etc.) ❸ 跳进去(专指自杀行为 of suicidal behaviour) throw oneself into; plunge into:～河 throw oneself into a river; drown oneself in a river|～江 throw oneself into a river; drown oneself in a river|～井 throw oneself into a well; commit suicide by jumping into a well ❹ same as 投射 tóushè ②:把眼光～到他身上。(The lady) darted a glance at him.|影子～在窗户上。A shadow was cast on the window. ❺ 寄给人(书信等) send; deliver; dispatch (a letter, etc.):～书 deliver or send a letter; write to (a newspaper, etc.)|～稿 contribute (to a newspaper or magazine); submit a piece of writing for publication ❻ 找上去;参加进去 go to; seek; join; enter:～宿 put up for the night; seek temporary lodging|～考 sign up for an examination; apply for entrance examination|～军 enlist; join the army|弃暗～明 forsake darkness for light|～入战斗 throw (oneself, troops, etc.) into a battle ❼ 合;迎合 fit in with; agree with; cater to; be attracted to; be congenial to:～机 agreeable; congenial|情～意合 be attracted to each other because of having much in common; find each other congenial; fall in love with each other|意气相～ find each other congenial; be congenial in temperament; see eye to eye with|～其所好 cater to sb.'s likings or tastes ❽ 临;在…以前 approaching; before:～明(天亮以前) before dawn|～暮(天黑以前) towards dusk

【投案】tóu//àn 犯法的人主动到司法机关或公安机关交代自己的作案经过,听候处理 give oneself up or surrender oneself to the police; (of a lawbreaker) voluntarily go to a judicial or public security organ to confess to a crime in all its details, and await punishment:～自首 surrender to the police and confess one's crime

【投保】tóu//bǎo 到保险部门办理手续参加保险 insure; cover; buy insurance; go to an insurance department to fulfil the necessary formalities when taking out an insurance policy:家庭财产已经～ have one's family property insured

【投奔】tóubèn 前去依靠(别人) go to (a friend or a place) for shelter:～亲戚 go to one's relatives for help; seek refuge with relatives

【投笔从戎】tóu bǐ cóng róng 后汉班超家境穷困,在官府做抄写工作,曾经掷笔长叹说,大丈夫应当在边疆为国立功,哪能老在笔砚之间讨生活呢!(见于《后汉书·班超传》)后人把文人从军叫做投笔从戎。(of a man of letters) throw away the writing brush and take up the sword. According to *History of Later Han·Biography of Banchao*, Ban Chao, a man of the Eastern Han Dynasty who came from a poor family, was copying government documents in a local *yamen* for a living. One day, he cast aside his brush and heaved a deep sigh, saying, 'How can a man continue to make a living from the writing brush and ink slab instead of contributing to the country's efforts to defend the border regions?' He joined the army and eventually emerged as a general of the East Han Dynasty.

【投畀豺虎】tóu bì chái hǔ (把坏人)扔给豺狼老虎吃掉(见于《诗经·小雅·巷伯》)。后用来表示对坏人十分愤恨。*The Book of Songs·Odes·Palace Bulter*: throw (a vile slanderer) to feed the greed of the wolf or tiger; throw (an evildoer) to the jackals and tigers; feel righteous indignation towards an evildoer

【投鞭断流】tóu biān duàn liú 前秦的苻坚进攻东晋时骄傲地说,我这么多的军队,把每个兵的马鞭子都投到江里,就能截断水流(见于《晋书·苻坚载记》)。后用来比喻人马众多,兵力强大。When attacking the Eastern Jin Dynasty, Fu Jian of the Former Qin said arrogantly, 'My troops are so great in number that were every soldier to throw his horsewhip into the river, the current would be blocked.' (*History of Jin·Record of Fu Jian*) (fig.) have a large and powerful army

【投标】tóu//biāo 承包建筑工程或承买大宗商品时,承包人或买主按照招标公告的标准和条件提出价格,填具标单,叫做投标 submit a tender; enter a bid; (of a contractor or buyer undertaking to contract for a project or the purchase of commodities in bulk) put forward a price and fill in the letter of bidding in compliance with the listed standards and conditions of an invitation to tender

【投产】tóuchǎn 投入生产 go into operation; put into production; commission:化肥厂已建成～。The chemical fertilizer plant has been completed and commenced operation.

【投诚】tóuchéng (敌人、叛军等)归附(of enemy troops, rebels, etc.) surrender; cross over:缴械～ lay down one's arms and surrender

【投弹】tóu//dàn 空投炸弹或燃烧弹等,也指投掷手榴弹 drop a bomb or firebomb; throw a hand grenade

【投敌】tóudí 投靠敌人 go over to the enemy; defect; surrender to the enemy:叛变～go over to the enemy and turn traitor

【投递】tóudì 送(公文、信件等);递送 deliver (documents, letters, etc.):～员 postman; mailman; letter or mail carrier|信上地址不明,无法～。Owing to its unclearly written address, this letter is undeliverable.

【投递员】tóudìyuán 邮电局中负责投递邮件和电报的人员 postman; mailman; letter or mail carrier; person in charge of delivering mails and telegraphs at a post office; also 邮递员 yóudìyuán

【投放】tóufàng ❶ 投下去;放进 throw in; put in:～鱼饵 throw in the bait ❷ 把人力、物力、资金等用于工农业或商业 put manpower, resources, capital, etc., into industry, agriculture or business:～资金 invest; put money into|为兴修水力,～了大量劳力。A great deal of labor went into constructing the hydraulic project. ❸ 工商企业向市场供应商品(of industrial and commercial enterprises) put goods on the market; supply the market with commodities:夏令商品已～市场。Summer commodities have been put on the market.

【投稿】tóu//gǎo 把稿子送交报刊编辑部、出版社等,要求发表或出版 submit a piece of writing (to the editorial department of a newspaper or magazine or a publishing house) for publication; contribute (to a newspaper or magazine):欢迎～。Contributions are welcome.|他曾给报纸投过几次稿。He submitted several articles to a newspaper.

【投工】tóu//gōng 投入劳动力,使用工作日 throw in a labour force; utilize work days:修这个水库要投多少工? What amount of labour will be required to build this reservoir?

【投合】tóuhé ❶ 合得来 agree; get along:两人性情～。The two of them suited each other perfectly. *or* The two get along well. *or* The two of them hit it off.|大家谈得很～。They all talked very congenially. *or* They had a most agreeable chat. ❷ 迎合 cater to:～顾客的口味 cater to the tastes of the customers

【投壶】tóuhú 古代宴会时的一种娱乐活动,宾主依次把筹投入壶中,以投中多少决定胜负,负者须饮酒 ancient banquet game where the host and guests threw chips into a pot, with the result being determined by the number of chips thrown in, and the loser being required to drink as a penalty (壶 *hu*:古代的一种容器 an ancient container)

【投缳】tóuhuán 〈书 *fml.*〉上吊 hang oneself; put one's neck into a noose (缳 *huan*:绳索的套子 noose)

【投簧】tóuhuáng ❶ 钥匙适合锁簧 (of a key) fit (a lock) ❷〈比喻 *fig.*〉方法等切合实际,能收成效 (of a method, etc.) be practical and likely to yield results:这一剂药总算～了。This medicine finally seems to be taking effect.

【投机】tóujī ❶ 见解相同 agreeable; congenial; holding the same view; having the same opinion:话不～ disagreeable conversation|我们一路上谈得很～。We had a congenial talk during the journey. ❷ 利用时机谋取私利 speculate; be a profiteer; seize a chance to seek private gain:～取巧 be opportunistic; seize every chance to gain advantage by trickery|～分子 opportunist; careerist|～买卖 speculative business

【投机倒把】tóujī dǎobǎ 指以买空卖空、囤积居奇、套购转卖等手段牟取暴利 engage in speculation and profiteering; go profiteering by such means as buying long and selling short, hoarding and cornering, fraudulent purchase and resale

【投机取巧】tóujī qǔqiǎo 利用时机和巧妙手段谋取个人私利。也指不愿下苦功夫,凭小聪明侥幸取得成功。be opportunistic; seize every chance to gain advantage by trickery; make use of opportunity and craft in seeking private profits; achieve success by luck and petty shrewdness instead of hard work

【投井下石】tóu jǐng xià shí 见人投到井里,不但不救,反而扔下石头 throw stones at someone who has fallen down a well instead of saving him; hit a person when he is down;〈比喻 *fig.*〉乘人之危,加以陷害 take advantage of sb.'s precarious position to frame him; also 落井下石 luò jǐng xià shí

【投军】tóujūn 〈旧时 *old*〉指参军 enlist; join the army

【投考】tóukǎo 报名应试 sign up for an examination：～高等学校 sign up for the entrance examination to an institute of higher learning

【投靠】tóukào 前去依靠别人生活 seek refuge with sb.；go and seek sb.'s patronage；go and live with as a dependent：～亲友 go and seek refuge with relatives and friends｜卖身～ barter one's honour for sb.'s patronage

【投篮】tóu//lán 打篮球时向球架上的铁圈投球 shoot at a basket ball goal

【投料】tóuliào 投放原料或材料 feeding；putting in (grain) feed or raw materials：按配方～(grain) feed made up according to a formula

【投票】tóu//piào 选举的一种方式，由选举人将所要选的人的姓名写在票上，或在印有候选人姓名的选票上做出标志，投入票箱。表决议案也有用投票方式的。vote；cast a vote；way of electing where a voter writes the name of a candidate on a ballot, or marks his vote on a form printed with the names of the candidates, which then goes into the ballot box；also used when voting for a bill

【投契】tóuqì same as 投合 tóuhé and 投机 tóujī ①：他俩越谈越～。The more the two talked, the more congenial they became.

【投枪】tóuqiāng 可以投掷出去杀伤敌人或野兽的标枪 javelin；(throwing) spear used to kill enemies or beasts

T

【投亲】tóu//qīn 投靠亲戚 go and live with relatives；seek refuge with relatives：～靠友 go and seek refuge with one's relatives and friends；join relatives and friends in order to sustain a means to live

【投入】tóurù ❶ 投到某种环境里去 put into；throw into：～生产 go into operation；put into production｜新机场已经正式～使用。The new airport is now in formal operation. ❷ 聚精会神地做某事 do sth. with concentration；be engrossed (in sth.)：她演戏很～。She is completely engrossed in the performance. ❸ 指投放资金 investment；input；invest capital in：少～，多产出 input less and yield more｜教育～逐年增加。The input into education is increasing year by year.

【投射】tóushè ❶（对着目标）扔；掷 throw；fling；cast (towards a goal)：举起标枪猛力向前～ raise one's javelin and hurl it ❷（光线等）射 cast；project (a ray of light, etc.)：太阳从云海中升起，金色的光芒～到平静的海面上。The sun has risen from a sea of clouds, its golden rays casting over the calm surface of the sea.｜周围的人都对他～出惊讶的眼光。Those around gazed at him in amazement.

【投身】tóushēn 献身出力 throw oneself into；plunge：～于教育事业 dedicate oneself to educational work

【投生】tóu//shēng same as 投胎 tóu//tāi

【投师】tóu//shī 从师学习 seek instruction from a master；become a disciple of a master：～访友 learn from a master and call on friends to exchange knowledge or skills

【投石问路】tóu shí wèn lù〈比喻 *fig.*〉先以某种行动试探 throw a stone to find out whether one should proceed；sound out；send out a trial balloon

【投鼠忌器】tóu shǔ jì qì 要打老鼠又怕打坏了它旁边的器物(《汉书·贾谊传》：'里谚曰：欲投鼠而忌器') hesitate to pelt a rat for fear of smashing the dishes (beside it). According to the *History of Han · Biography of Jia Yi*, Li Yan said, 'I want to strike at a rat, but am afraid of breaking the porcelains beside it.'〈比喻 *fig.*〉想打击坏人而又有所顾忌 hold back from taking action against an evildoer for fear of involving or harming good people

【投诉】tóusù 向有关部门或有关人员申诉 complain (about an injustice to the relative departments or personnel：～信 letter of complaint｜～法院 appeal to a court｜～无门 have no one to complain to

【投宿】tóusù（旅客）找地方住宿(of a tourist) seek temporary lodging；put up for the night：到客店～ put up at an inn for the night

【投胎】tóu//tāi 人或动物(多指家畜家禽)死后，灵魂投入母胎，转生世间(迷信)(superstition) be reincarnated；when a person or animal (usu. domestic animal or fowl) dies, the soul transmigrates into a mother's womb for rebirth in the mundane world；also 投生 tóushēng

【投桃报李】tóu táo bào lǐ 他送给我桃儿，我拿李子回送他(《诗经·大雅·抑》：'投我以桃，报之以李') give a plum in return for a peach (*The Book of Songs · Epics · Admonition*)；〈比喻 *fig.*〉友好往来 friendly exchanges or contacts

【投降】tóuxiáng 停止对抗，向对方屈服 surrender；capitulate；stop resisting and yield to one's opponent：缴械～ lay down one's arms and surrender；give oneself up

【投效】tóuxiào〈书 *fml.*〉前往效力 offer one's services to：～义军 offer one's services to a righteous army

【投药】tóuyào ❶ 给以药物服用 prescribe；medicate；exhibit；offer medicine (to take) ❷ 投放毒药(多用于毒杀老鼠、蟑螂等) apply poison (usu. for killing rats, cockroaches, etc.)

【投医】tóu//yī 就医 go to a doctor；seek medical advice：～求药 seek medical treatment｜病急乱～ turn to any available doctor when critically ill；try any remedy to get out of trouble when the situation is desperate

【投影】tóuyǐng ❶ 光学上指在光线的照射下物

体的影子投射到一个面上，数学上指图形的影子投射到一个面或一条线上(optics) projection; silhouette; shadow of an illuminated object projected onto a surface; (math.) shadow of a figure projected onto a surface or a line ❷ 在一个面或一条线上投射的物体或图形的影子 shadow (of an object or a figure projected onto a surface or a line)

【投映】tóuyìng (影像)呈现在物体上 reflect; mirror: 他的身影～在平静的湖面上。His figure was reflected on the still river surface.

【投缘】tóuyuán 情意相合(多指初交 oft. of newly acquainted people) agreeable; congenial: 两人越谈越～。The more the two of them talked, the more congenial they became.

【投掷】tóuzhì 扔 throw; hurl; cast; fling; same as 投 ①: ～标枪 throw a javelin | ～手榴弹 throw a hand grenade

【投资】tóu//zī ❶ 把资金投入企业 invest; put capital into an enterprise: ～一百万元 invest one million yuan | 决定～建厂 decide to invest in building a factory; decide to invest in a factory ❷ 泛指为达到一定目的而投入资金 invest; (in a broad sense) put in money to achieve some objective: ～办学 invest in a school

【投资】tóuzī ❶ 投入企业的资金 investment; input; money or funds invested in an enterprise: 一大笔～large investment ❷ 泛指为达到一定目的而投入的钱财 investment; input; (in a broad sense) money or funds invested with a defined objective: 智力～investment in education; intellectual investment

骰 tóu [骰子](tóu·zi)〈方 *dial.*〉色子(shǎi·zi) dice

tǒu (ㄊㄡˇ)

钭 Tǒu 姓 a surname

敨 tǒu 〈方 *dial.*〉❶ 打开(包着或卷着的东西); 展平(褶子) open up or spread out (sth. wrapped or curled up); unfold (pleats) ❷ 抖搂(尘土等) shake off (dust, etc.)

tòu (ㄊㄡˋ)

透 tòu ❶ (液体、光线等)渗透; 穿透(of liquid, light, etc.) penetrate; pass through; leak or seep through: ～水 permeable; pervious to water | 阳光～过玻璃窗照进来。Sunlight came in through the windows. *or* The sun beamed through the windows. ◇～过事物的表面现象，找出它的本质 see through the surface of a matter to find out its essence ❷ 暗地里告诉 tell secretly, inform on the sly; leak or let out: ～消息 leak out the news | ～个信儿 tip sb. off ❸ 透彻 thoroughly; clearly; in a penetrating way: 把道理说～了 give a thorough explanation of the reasons | 我摸～了他的脾气。I have come to know him through and through. ❹ 达到饱满的、充分的程度 fully; completely; to the extreme; to saturation point: 雨下～了。It rained drenchingly. | 我记得熟～了。I remember it perfectly. ❺ 显露 show; appear; look: 这花白里～红。The flower is white tinged with red.

【透彻】tòuchè (了解情况、分析事理)详尽而深入(of understanding the situation or analysing reasons) penetrating; thorough; thoroughgoing: 这一番话说得非常～。These words really drove the point home. | 他对于各部分的工作内容都有～的了解。He had a deep understanding of the various parts of the job.

【透底】tòudǐ 透露底细 disclose or tell the inside story; reveal the ins and outs of a matter; reveal all: 交心～open one's heart by telling the inside story

【透雕】tòudiāo 雕塑的一种，在浮雕的基础上，镂空其背景部分 fretwork; relief sculpture executed by piercing out its background

【透顶】tòudǐng 达到极端(多含贬义 oft. derog.) extremely; absolutely; thoroughly; downright; in the extreme; through and through: 反动～thoroughly reactionary | 腐败～downright corrupt; rotten to the core; decadent in the extreme | 糊涂～downright wooly-minded

【透风】tòu//fēng ❶ 风可以通过 let in air; ventilate; aerate; allow air to circulate: 门缝儿有点～。The wind blew through a crack in the door. ❷ 把东西摊开，让风吹吹 air (sth.); spread sth. out to dry; same as 晾 liàng ①: 把箱子里的东西拿出来透透风 take out all the things in the case and let them air ❸ 透露风声 divulge a secret; leak: 这件事，他向我透了一点风。He told me something about it.

【透汗】tòuhàn 湿透全身的汗 be lathered in perspiration: 出了一身～be dripping with sweat; be in a sweat;

【透河井】tòuhéjǐng 靠近河岸挖的井，水源是靠开沟或埋管道引进河水 well that is connected to a river; well dug close to the bank of a river to draw water from the river by digging a trench or laying a pipe

【透话】tòu//huà 透露话语 hint; drop or give a hint; tip off: 他～要买这所房子。He hinted that he was about to buy the house.

【透镜】tòujìng 用透明物质(如玻璃)制成的镜片，根据镜面中央和边缘的厚薄不同，分为凸透镜和凹透镜 lens; glass or other transparent material designed to fit into spectacles, being convex or concave according to its thickness at the centre and the edge of its surface

【透亮】tòu·liàng ❶ 明亮 bright; transparent: 这间房子又向阳,又~。This room is sunny and bright. ❷ 明白 obvious; (perfectly) clear: 经你这么一说,我心里就~了。Thanks to your explanation, it is now quite clear to me now.

【透亮儿】tòu//liàngr 透过光线 allow light to pass through: 玻璃窗~。Light shines in through the window panes.

【透漏】tòulòu 透露;泄漏 divulge; reveal; leak; leak out: ~消息 leak out the news

【透露】tòulù 泄漏或显露(消息、意思等) let on about sth.; leak; divulge; reveal; disclose (news, meanings, etc.): ~风声 leak (or disclose) information|真相~出来了。The truth has been revealed.

【透明】tòumíng (物体)能透过光线的(of an object) transparent; lucid: 水是无色~的液体。Water is a colourless, transparent liquid.

【透辟】tòupì 透彻精辟 penetrating; thorough; incisive; sharp: 他的讲解很~。His explanation is very thorough.

【透气】tòu//qì (~儿 tòu//qìr) ❶ 空气可以通过;通气 ventilate; aerate; let air in or through: 门窗关着,房子不~。Keeping its door and windows closed makes the room stuffy. ❷ 指呼吸新鲜空气 breathe freely; breathe fresh air: 屋里憋得慌,到外面去透透气。The air being oppressive and stuffy. Let's go outdoors for a breath of fresh air. ❸ 通声气 tell; inform; tip off: 我得把这件事先向家里人透一点气儿。I should first of all let my family know about this.

【透墒】tòushāng 土壤中所含的水分足够农作物出苗或生长的需要(of soil) contain sufficient moisture for crops to sprout or grow

【透视】tòushì ❶ 用线条或色彩在平面上表现立体空间的方法 perspective; method of representing three-dimensional objects and depth relationships on a two-dimensional surface using lines or colours ❷ 利用X射线透过人体在荧光屏上所形成的影像观察人体内部 fluoroscopy; roentgenoscopy; X-ray examination; internal observation of the human body by an X-ray image projected onto a fluorescent screen ❸ 〈比喻 *fig.*〉清楚地看到事物的本质 grasp or see clearly the essence of sth.

【透视图】tòushìtú 根据透视的原理绘制的图,多用于机械工程和建筑工程 perspective drawing; picture or drawing made according to the principle of perspective, generally applied in mechanical and architectural engineering

【透析】tòuxī 渗析 dialysis

【透信】tòu//xìn (~儿 tòu//xìnr)透露音信 leak out news; tip off: 如果有什么变化,你最好事先给我透个信儿。If any change should occur, it would be best for you to let me know in advance.

【透雨】tòuyǔ 把田地里干土层湿透的雨 saturating, drenching rain; soaker; rainfall that soaks through to the layer of water-free soil in fields: 下了一场~。That fall of rain was a soaker.

【透支】tòuzhī ❶ 存户经银行同意在一定限额之内提取超过存款数字的款项 overdraw; overdraft; take out an overdraft; (of a depositor) draw a sum of money that exceeds the amount contained in an account within a limit agreed by the bank ❷开支超过收入 overspend; have a deficit; expenditure exceeding income ❸ 〈旧时 *old*〉职工预支工资 draw one's salary in advance

tū (ㄊㄨ)

凸 tū 高于周围(跟'凹'相对 as opposed to 'hollow', 'concave', 'sunken', 'dented') protruding; raised; bulging; convex; higher than the surrounding area: ~出 bulging; protruding; projecting; crippling|~起 swelling; bulging; doming|挺胸~肚 throw out one's chest and distend one's belly

【凸版】tūbǎn 版面印刷的部分高出空白部分的印刷版,如木版、铅版、锌版等 relief printing plate; printing plate with a raised print sheet layout, as in a printing block, or lead and zinc plates

【凸版纸】tūbǎnzhǐ 供凸版印刷用的纸,用化学纸浆制成。质量比胶版纸、凹版纸差。relief printing paper; paper made of chemical pulp for relief printing, of a quality inferior to that of offset or intaglio paper

【凸轮】tūlún 一种具有曲面周缘或凹槽的零件。种类很多,可以推动从动零件做往复运动或摆动。cam; mechanical part in many varieties, that has camber rims or concave troughs and that pushes the driven parts into reciprocal movements or swings

【凸面镜】tūmiànjìng 球面镜的一种,反射面为凸面,焦点在镜后。凸面镜所成的像为正立的缩小的虚像。convex mirror; spherical mirror with a convex reflective surface whose point of focus is behind it, and which reflects upright reduced virtual images; also 凸镜 tūjìng or 发散镜 fāsànjìng

【凸透镜】tūtòujìng 透镜的一种,中央比四周厚,平行光线透过后,向轴线的方向折射聚集于一点上。物体放在焦点以内,由另一侧看去就得一个放大的虚像。远视眼镜的镜片就属于这个类型。convex lens; a kind of lens that is thicker at the centre than the edge, through which parallel light refracts in the direction of the axis and concentrates at one point, and which reflects an enlarged virtual image of an object from the other side within its focus, used in spectacle lenses for long sight; also 会聚透镜 huìjùtòujìng; 通称 generally called 放大镜 fàngdàjìng

秃 tū ❶ (人)没有头发;(鸟兽头或尾)没有毛 bald; bare; (of a person) hairless; (of the head or tail of a bird or an animal) having no hair: ~尾巴 bare-tailed | 头顶有点~了 be going bald ❷ (树木)没有枝叶;(山)没有树木 bare; barren; (of a tree) having no branch or leaf; (of a mountain) treeless: ~树 bare trees; defoliated trees | 山是~的。The mountain is barren. ❸ 物体失去尖端 blunt; unpointed; pointless; (of an object) becoming blunt: ~笔 bald writing brush | 笔尖~了。The pen nib is worn out. *or* The pen is blunt. ❹ 首尾结构不完整 incomplete; unsatisfactory; deficient: 这篇文章煞尾处显得有点~。The article has a rather weak ending.

【秃笔】tūbǐ 没有笔尖儿的毛笔 bald writing brush; 〈比喻 *fig*.〉不高明的写作能力 poor writing ability; untalented in writing

【秃疮】tūchuāng 〈方 *dial*.〉黄癣 tinea favosa; favus of the scalp

【秃顶】tū//dǐng 头顶脱落了全部或大部分头发 bald; be going bald; (of top of the head) lose all or most of the hair

【秃顶】tūdǐng 脱落了全部或大部分头发的头顶 bald head; top of the head where all or most of the hair has fallen out

【秃鹫】tūjiù 身体大,全身棕黑色,头部颈部裸出,但有绒毛,嘴大而尖锐,呈钩状,以尸体和小动物为食物 vulture (*Neophron* or *Gypaetus*); large bird of dark brown plumage, with bare skin covered in fine hair on its head and neck, and a large hooked beak, that feeds on carrion and small animals; also 坐山雕 zuòshāndiāo

【秃噜】tū·lu 〈方 *dial*.〉❶ 松散开 come loose; come undone: 你的鞋带~了。Your shoelace has gone undone. ❷ (毛、羽毛)脱落 (of hair or feather) drop; come off; fall off or away: 这张老羊皮的毛儿都~了。The wool on this old sheepskin has worn off. ❸ 拖;坠下来 drag; droop; hang down: ~着裤子 wear drooping trousers | 裙子~地了。The skirt drags along the ground. ❹ 脱口失言 make a slip of the tongue; make an indiscreet remark: 你要留神,别把话说~了。You should take care not to shoot your mouth off. ❺ 过头 exhaust; use up: 钱一花就花~了。Money is gone once it is spent.

【秃瓢】tūpiáo (~儿 tūpiáor) 光头 (guāngtóu) baldhead: 剃了个~have a shaven head

【秃头】tū//tóu 光着头,不戴帽子 bareheaded; wearing no hat: 他秃着个头出去了。He went outside bareheaded.

【秃头】tūtóu ❶ 头发脱光或剃光的头 baldhead; shaven or baldhead ❷ 头发脱光的人 baldheaded man; bald person; person whose hair has fallen out

【秃子】tū·zi ❶ 头发脱光的人 baldhead; baldheaded man; baldy; person whose hair has fallen out ❷ 〈方 *dial*.〉黄癣 favus of the scalp

突 tū ❶ 猛冲 charge; sprint; dash forward; shoot out: ~破 break through; make a breakthrough | ~围 break through or out of an encirclement | 狼奔豕~run like wolves and rush like boars — run about like beasts ❷ 突然 suddenly; abruptly; unexpectedly: ~变 sudden change | 气温~增。The temperature suddenly rose. ❸ 高于周围 protruding; projecting; sticking out; higher than the surrounding area: ~起 rise high; tower | ~出 protruding; projecting; prominent; sticking out ❹ 〈古代 *arch*.〉灶旁突起的出烟火口,相当于现在的烟筒 long, protruding opening for letting out smoke from a fire beside a kitchen range in ancient times, equivalent to the present chimney: 灶~chimney | 曲~徙薪 clear the blocked chimney and remove the firewood; bend the chimney and remove the firewood (to prevent a possible fire); take precautions against any possible danger

【突变】tūbiàn ❶ 突然急剧的变化 sudden change: 时局~sudden change in current political situation | 神色~sudden change in expression ❷ 哲学上指飞跃 (philos.) leap

【突出】tū//chū 冲出 break through; charge out of: ~重围 break through a tight encirclement

【突出】tūchū ❶ 鼓出来 protruding; projecting; prominent; sticking out: 悬崖~ with projecting cliffs | ~的颧骨 prominent cheekbones ❷ 超过一般地显露出来 outstanding; prominent; conspicuous; salient: 成绩~outstanding achievements; conspicuous success ❸ 使超过一般 stress; emphasize; highlight; give prominence to: ~重点 lay stress on the key points | ~个人 place oneself in the spotlight; push oneself forward

【突飞猛进】tū fēi měng jìn 形容事业、学问等进展非常迅速 (of a cause, learning, etc.) advance by leaps and bounds; forge ahead rapidly; make giant strides

【突击】tūjī ❶ 集中兵力向敌人防御阵地猛烈而急速地攻击 assault; concentrate one's forces for a sudden and forceful attack on the enemy's defensive position: ~队 shock team; shock brigade; ad hoc team formed for an urgent mission ❷ 〈比喻 *fig*.〉集中力量,加快速度,在短时期内完成某项工作 make a concentrated effort to finish a job quickly; work furiously to finish a job; extend energy to complete sth.：连续～了两个晚上才把稿子写完。He worked two consecutive nights to finish the article.

【突进】tūjìn 集中兵力向一定方向或地区猛进 charge；march forward；press onward；concentrate one's forces on advancing rapidly in a certain direction or towards a particular area

【突厥】Tūjué 我国古代少数民族，游牧在阿尔泰山一带。6 世纪中叶，开始强盛起来，并吞了邻近的部落。西魏时建立政权。隋开皇二年(582)分为东突厥和西突厥。7 世纪中叶，先后被唐所灭。Tujue；Turk，an ethnic minority group of ancient China that roved the Altay Mountains in search of pasture，and which in the mid-6th century became powerful and prosperous，annexing neighbouring tribes. In 582，or the 2nd year of the Kaihuang reign of the Sui Dynasty，the Tujue divided into Eastern and Western groups，but were annihilated by the Tang Dynasty in the mid-7th century.

【突破】tūpò ❶ 集中兵力向一点进攻或反攻，打开缺口 break through；make a breakthrough；concentrate one's forces on a point of attack or counterattack：～封锁 break through a blockade｜～防线 break through defenses｜～敌人阵地 break through the enemy's position ❷ 打破(困难、限制等) surmount (difficulty)；break (limit)：～难关 overcome a difficulty；break the back of a tough job｜～定额 overfulfil a quota｜对这个问题的研究又有新的～。A new breakthrough has been made in studies of this topic.

【突起】tūqǐ ❶ 突然发生；突然兴起 break out；suddenly appear or arise；emerge or occur suddenly or unexpectedly：狂风～。A strong wind blew up.｜异军～。A new force emerged unexpectedly. *or* A new force has suddenly come to the fore. ❷ 高耸 rise high；tower：峰峦～。Ridges and peaks tower to the sky. ❸ 生物体上长的像瘤子的东西 swelling；protuberance；sth. that resembles a tumor in an organism

【突然】tūrán 在短促的时间里发生，出乎意外 abruptly；suddenly；unexpectedly；happen or occur in a short time：～袭击 surprise attack；sudden onslaught｜他来得很～。He arrived unexpectedly.

【突如其来】tū rú qí lái 突然发生 arise suddenly；come all of a sudden；come unexpectedly；happen suddenly or unexpectedly（突如 *tu ru*：突然 suddenly）

【突突】tūtū〈拟声词 *onom.*〉pit-a-pat：心～地跳 one's heart go pit-a-pat｜摩托车～地响。The motorcycle engine roared.

【突围】tū//wéi 突破包围 break through or out of an encirclement：～脱险 break through a ring of encirclement to safety

【突兀】tūwù ❶ 高耸 lofty；towering：怪峰～。Peaks thrust out in grotesque forms.｜～的山石 towering crags ❷ 突然发生，出乎意外 sudden；abrupt；unexpected：事情来得这么～，使他简直不知所措。As it all happened so suddenly，he did not know what to do.

【突袭】tūxí 用兵力出其不意地进攻；突然袭击 surprise attack；strike；rally forces for a sudden onslaught.

葖 tū ☞[蓇葖](gūtū) on p. 689

tú（ㄊㄨˊ）

图(圖) tú ❶ 用绘画表现出来的形象；图画 picture；drawing；chart；map；diagram：地～map｜蓝～blueprint｜绘～draw a picture｜插～illustration；plate｜制～make a drawing or chart｜看～识字 learn to read using pictures ❷ 谋划；谋求 plan；scheme；attempt；pursue；seek：～谋 plot；scheme；conspire｜力～try hard to；strive to ❸ 贪图 pursue；seek；desire；be after：惟利是～be after nothing but profit；desire profit above all else｜不能只～省事，不顾质量。We should not do things the easy way at the expense of quality. ❹ 意图；计划 intent；intention：良～good intention｜宏～great plan ❺〈书 *fml.*〉绘；画 draw；paint：绘影～形 draw sb.'s picture

【图案】tú'àn 有装饰意味的花纹或图形，以结构整齐、匀称、调和为特点，多用在纺织品、工艺美术品和建筑物上 pattern；design；decorative pattern or figure characterized by a regular，even and harmonious structure，mostly used on fabrics，handicrafts and buildings

【图板】túbǎn 制图时垫在图纸下面的木板，有一定的规格 drawing board；board on which to draw specifications or blueprint

【图版】túbǎn 一种印刷版，主要用于印刷照相图片、插图或表格，用铜、锌等金属制成 plate (mainly for printing photos，illustrations or figures，made of copper or zinc)

【图表】túbiǎo 表示各种情况和注明各种数字的图和表的总称，如示意图、统计表等 chart；diagram；graph；general term for charts that represent certain situations and label relevant figures，such as sketch maps and statistical graphs

【图谶】túchèn 古代关于宣扬迷信的预言、预兆的书籍 ancient book of superstitious prophecies and omens

【图钉】túdīng（～儿 túdīngr）帽大针短的钉子，用来把纸或布钉在木板或墙壁上 drawing pin；thumbtack；pin with a cap and short point，used to affix paper or cloth to a board or wall

【图画】túhuà 用线条或色彩构成的形象 drawing; picture; painting; image created with lines or colours

【图画文字】túhuà wénzì 用图画来表达意思的文字。特点是用整幅图画表示意思,本身不能分解成字,没有固定的读法。hieroglyphics; picture writing; pictographic script; writing or script that expresses meaning through pictures, an entire picture symbolizing a definition that cannot be put into words, or have a fixed pronunciation; ☞ 象形文字 xiàngxíng wénzì on p. 2098

【图籍】tújí〈书 *fml*.〉疆域图和户口册 map of territory and register of population

【图记】tújì ❶ same as 图章 túzhāng ❷ 用图形作的标志 sign; mark; symbol (composed of figures)

【图鉴】tújiàn 以图画为主而用文字解说的著作(多用做书名 usu. used in book titles) illustrated or pictorial handbook giving written explanations:《哺乳动物~》*Pictorial Handbook of Mammals*

【图解】tújiě 利用图形来分析或求解 diagram; graph; figure; analyse or seek the solution to a question through a figure or diagram:~法 graphic method

【图景】tújǐng ❶ 画面上的景物 scene in a picture or painting:他只用几笔,便勾勒出一幅海上日出的~。With just a few strokes, he portrayed the scene of sunrise over the sea. ❷ 描述的或想像中的景象 view; prospect; depicted or imaginary scene:这些民间传说反映出人们理想中的社会生活~。These folk legends reflect people's idealized scenario of social life.

【图例】túlì 地图、天文图、统计图等上面各种符号的说明 legend (of a map, astronomical figure, statistical graph, etc.); key

【图谋】túmóu ❶ 暗中谋划(多含贬义 usu. derog.) plot; scheme; conspire; plan secretly:~私利 seek personal interests|~不轨 engage in underhand activities; hatch a sinister plot; plot illegal activities ❷ 计谋 trap; stratagem

【图片】túpiàn 用来说明某一事物的图画、照片、拓片等的统称 general term for picture, photograph or rubbing used to depict an object: 古代建筑~展览 photographic exhibition of ancient buildings

【图谱】túpǔ 系统地编辑起来的、根据实物描绘或摄制的图,是研究某一学科所用的资料 collection of illustrative plates; atlas; systematically compiled pictures produced to depict real objects, used as study material: 植物~floral atlas|历史~historical atlas

【图穷匕首见】tú qióng bǐshǒu xiàn 战国时,荆轲奉燕国太子之命去刺秦王,以献燕国督亢的地图为名,预先把匕首卷在图里,到了秦王座前,慢慢把地图展开,最后露出匕首(见于《战国策·燕策》) According to *Intrigues of the Warring States·Intrigues of Yan*, during the Warring States Period, Jing Ke received orders from the prince of the state of Yan to assassinate the king of Qin. He went to the throne of the king ostensibly to present a map of Dukang of the State of Yan, in which he had secreted a dagger. He slowly unrolled the map, and eventually the dagger was revealed.〈比喻 *fig*.〉事情发展到最后,真相或本意露出来了 as the historical alta unfolds, the dagger is revealed — the true or real intention is revealed in the end; also 图穷匕见 tú qióng bǐ xiàn

【图书】túshū 图片和书刊,一般指书籍 pictures and periodicals, usu. books:~目录 catalogue of books; library catalogue|~资料 books and reference materials

【图书】tú·shu 指图章 seal; stamp

【图书馆】túshūguǎn 搜集、整理、收藏图书资料供人阅览参考的机构 library; organization that collects and sorts out books and reference materials for public reading and reference

【图说】túshuō 以图画为主而用文字加以说明的著作(多用做书名 usu. used in book titles) pictorial handbook; illustrated manual; work mainly composed of pictures with written illustrations:《天体~》*Illustrated Handbook of Celestial Bodies*

【图腾】túténg 原始社会的人认为跟本氏族有血缘关系的某种动物或自然物,一般用做本氏族的标志 totem; animal, plant or natural object believed by primitive peoples to have blood ties with their clan, and usu. used as their symbol

【图文并茂】tú wén bìng mào 图画和文字都很丰富精美(多用于同一书刊 usu. of the same book or periodical) excellent in both illustration and text

【图像】túxiàng 画成、摄制或印制的形象 picture; image; painted, produced or printed image

【图形】túxíng ❶ 在纸上或其他平面上表示出来的物体的形状 graph; figure; shape of an object expressed on paper or other surfaces ❷ 几何图形的简称 abbr. for 几何图形 jǐhé túxíng

【图样】túyàng 按照一定的规格和要求绘制的各种图形,在制造或建筑时用做样子 pattern; design; draft; drawing; mold; various graphs or figures drawn according to certain specifications and requirements, used as manufacturing or architectural prototypes

【图章】túzhāng ❶ 用小块的石头、木头、金属、象牙等做成的东西,底下一面多为方形或圆形,刻着姓名或其他名称、图案等,用来印在文件、书籍等上面,作为标记 seal; object made from a small piece of stone, wood, metal, ivory, etc., whose underside, square or circular in

T

shape, is carved with the name of a person, or other names or patterns, to be stamped on documents or books as a distinguishing mark ❷ 图章印在文件、书籍等上面的痕迹 stamp; imprint of a seal printed on a document or book

【图纸】túzhǐ 画了图样的纸;设计图 blueprint; drawing; paper on which a design is drawn; design drawing:施工～working drawing

荼 tú ❶ 古书上说的一种苦菜 one kind of bitter edible plant as described in ancient books ❷ 古书上指茅草的白花 white flower of reeds as described in ancient books:如火如～ like a raging fire

【荼毒】túdú〈书 *fml.*〉荼是一种苦菜,毒指毒虫毒蛇之类 bitter edible plant and poisonous insects or snakes;〈比喻 *fig.*〉毒害 poison; infect; defile; afflict with great suffering; torment:～生灵 plunge the people into depths of suffering; abuse and oppress the people

【荼蘼】túmí 落叶小灌木,攀缘茎,茎上有钩状的刺,羽状复叶,小叶椭圆形,花白色,有香气。供观赏。roseleaf raspberry (*Rubus rosaefolius*); small deciduous bush with climbing stems and barbed thorns, pinnately compound leaves, oval leaflets, and fragrant white flowers; also 酴醾 túmí

徒1 tú ❶ 步行 on foot:～步 on foot|～涉 ford; wade through ❷ 空的;没有凭借的 bare; empty:～手 bare-handed; unarmed ❸ 表示除此以外,没有别的;仅仅 merely; only: ～托空言 make empty promises; make a lame excuse; pay lip service|家～四壁 have nothing but the bare walls of one's house; be utterly destitute ❹ 徒然 in vain; futile; to no avail:～劳 futile effort; fruitless labor|～自惊扰 be needlessly alarmed; get into a fright for no reason ❺ (Tú) 姓 a surname

徒2 tú ❶ 徒弟;学生 apprentice; pupil; disciple:门～pupil; disciple|学～apprentice|艺～apprentice|尊师爱～respect the teacher and love the student ❷ 信仰某种宗教的人(of a religion) follower; believer:信～believer; devotee|佛教～Buddhist ❸ 同一派系的人(含贬义 derog.) gang; factionary; clique member; person of the same faction or clique:党～member of a clique or a reactionary political party; henchman ❹ 指某种人(含贬义 derog.) person; fellow:酒～drunkard; wine bibber|赌～gambler|不法之～lawbreaker|好事之～troublemaker ❺〈书 *fml.*〉指徒刑 (prison) sentence; imprisonment

【徒步】túbù 步行 on foot:～旅行 hike; travel on foot|～行军(of troops) march

【徒弟】tú·dì 跟从师傅学习的人 apprentice; pupil; disciple; person apprenticed to a master worker

【徒工】túgōng 学徒工 apprentice

【徒劳】túláo 无益地耗费劳力 futile or useless effort; fruitless labor; expend labor uselessly: ～往返 make a futile (or fruitless) trip or journey; hasten back and forth for nothing; make a trip in vain

【徒劳无功】túláo wú gōng 白费力气,没有成就或好处 make a futile effort; work to no avail; also 徒劳无益 túláo wú yì

【徒然】túrán ❶ 白白地;不起作用 futile; in vain; for nothing; to no avail:～耗费精力 waste one's energy ❷ 仅仅;只是 merely; only; simply:如果那么办,～有利于对手。To do that would be advantageous to the enemy only. *or* Such a move could only help the enemy.

【徒涉】túshè〈书 *fml.*〉蹚水过河 wade through; ford

【徒手】túshǒu 空手(不拿器械) bare-handed; unarmed:～操 free-standing exercises|～格斗 fight bare-handed or with bare hands

【徒孙】túsūn 徒弟的徒弟 disciple's disciple; pupil's pupil:徒子～disciples and followers; adherents; hangers-on and their spawn

【徒托空言】tú tuō kōng yán 只说空话,并不实行 make an empty promises; make a lame excuse; pay lip service

【徒刑】túxíng 剥夺犯人自由的刑罚,分有期徒刑和无期徒刑两种 imprisonment; (prison) sentence; punishment whereby criminals are deprived of their freedom, for set terms or life

【徒有虚名】tú yǒu xū míng 空有某种名声,指名不符实 have an unmerited reputation; enjoy undeserved fame; also 徒有其名 tú yǒu qí míng

【徒长】túzhǎng 作物在生长期间,因生长条件不协调而茎叶发育过旺。徒长影响产量。spindling; excessive growth of branches and leaves during a plant's growing period owing to uncoordinated conditions, which influences the yield

【徒子徒孙】túzǐ túsūn 徒弟和徒孙,泛指党羽 disciples and followers; adherents; (in a broad sense) hangers-on and their spawn

途 tú 道路 way; path; road; route:路～road; path|旅～trip; journey|长～long distance|道听～说 rumor; hearsay; gossip|半～而废 give up halfway ◇用～use; application; purpose

【途程】túchéng 路程(多用于比喻 usu. fig.) road; way; course:人类进化的～course of evolution of humankind|革命的～course of revolution; revolutionary course

【途次】túcì〈书 *fml.*〉旅途中住宿的地方 stopover; travelers' lodging; accommodation on a trip

【途径】tújìng 路径(多用于比喻 usu. fig.)way;

road; path; channel; approach; avenue: 寻找解决问题的～seek the solution to a problem|革新的～innovative channel

涂[1]（塗）tú ❶ 使油漆、颜色、脂粉、药物等附着在物体上 apply; anoin; smear; daub paint, colour, rouge and powder, medicine, etc., to objects: ～抹 smear; paint; daub|～饰 cover with paint, lacquer, colour wash, etc.|～脂抹粉 apply powder and paint; apply cosmetics; put on powder and rouge|～上一层油 coat with oil ❷ 乱写或乱画；随意地写字或画画 scrawl; scribble; daub: ～鸦 scrawl; poor handwriting; graffiti; chicken tracks ❸ 抹去 erase; cross or blot out: ～改 change; modify; alter; obliterate|把写错的字～掉 cross or blot out wrongly written words

涂[2]（塗）tú ❶〈书 *fml.*〉泥 mud; mire; slush: ～炭 mud and ashes-utter misery; severe suffering ❷ 海涂 beach; sea shoal; shallows: ～田 shoal field|围～造田 reclaim land from the sea ❸ same as 途 tú

涂[3]（涂）Tú 姓 a surname

【涂改】túgǎi 抹去原来的字，重新写；用白粉涂在字或画上，重新写或画 change; modify; alter; obliterate; cross out a word and rewrite it; sprinkle white powder on a word or painting and rewrite or redraw it

【涂料】túliào 涂在物体的表面，能使物体美观或保护物体防止侵蚀的物质，如油漆、绘画颜料、干性油、煤焦油等 coating; paint; matter applied to the surface of an object to make it beautiful or to prevent it from being eroded, such as paint, pigments, drying oil and coal tar

【涂抹】túmǒ ❶ same as 涂[1] tú ①: 木桩子上～了沥青。Pitch has been daubed over the wood stake. ❷ same as 涂[1] tú ②: 信笔～doodle; scribble aimlessly

【涂饰】túshì ❶ 涂上（油漆颜色）cover with (paint, lacquer, colour wash, etc.): ～木器 cover a wooden article with paint ❷ 抹（灰、泥）；粉刷 daub (plaster) on a wall; whitewash: ～墙壁 whitewash a wall

【涂炭】tútàn〈书 *fml.*〉❶ 烂泥和炭火 mud and ashes;〈比喻 *fig.*〉极困苦的境遇 utter misery; great affliction; severe suffering; ☞ 生灵涂炭 shēnglíng tútàn on p. 1715 ❷ 使处于极困苦的境遇；蹂躏 make (people) suffer (hardships); trample on: ～百姓 wreak havoc among the people

【涂写】túxiě 乱写；随意写 scribble; scrawl; doodle: 不要在墙上～标语。Do not scrawl slogans on the wall.

【涂鸦】túyā 唐代卢仝《添丁诗》：'忽来案上翻墨汁，涂抹诗书如老鸦。' 后世用'涂鸦'形容字写得很坏（多用做谦辞 usu. hum.）*Poem to a Baby Boy Born into the Family* by Lu Tong of the Tang Dynasty: 'The prepared Chinese ink on the table suddenly overturned, its spill scrawling classics as it drawing a crow'; scrawl; poor handwriting; graffiti; chicken tracks

【涂乙】túyǐ〈书 *fml.*〉涂是抹去，乙是勾画，指删改文章 cross out; erase; underline; sketch; prune (an essay, etc.); delete and change

【涂脂抹粉】tú zhī mǒ fěn 涂胭脂，抹香粉。原指妇女修饰容貌。现多比喻对丑恶事物进行粉饰。apply powder and paint; apply cosmetics; put on powder and rouge; originally referring to women dressing up and putting on make-up; (now usu. fig.) whitewash or prettify an ugly thing

菟 tú ☞ 於菟 (wūtú) on p. 2017
☞ tù on p. 1945

屠 tú ❶ 宰杀（牲畜）slaughter (animals for food): ～狗 butcher a dog|～刀 butcher's knife ❷ 屠杀 massacre; slaughter; butcher; kill indiscriminately: ～城 massacre the inhabitants of a captured city; kill all the residents of a conquered city ❸（Tú）姓 a surname

【屠城】túchéng 攻破城池后屠杀城中的居民 massacre the inhabitants of a captured city; kill all the residents of a conquered city

【屠刀】túdāo 宰杀牲畜的刀 butcher's knife; knife used to slaughter animals

【屠夫】túfū〈旧时 *old*〉指以宰杀牲畜为业的人 butcher; person who slaughters livestock by profession;〈比喻 *fig.*〉屠杀人民的人 ruthless ruler; person who slaughters the people

【屠户】túhù〈旧时 *old*〉指以宰杀牲畜为业的人或人家 butcher; person or household that slaughters livestock by profession

【屠戮】túlù〈书 *fml.*〉same as 屠杀 túshā

【屠杀】túshā 大批残杀 massacre; slaughter; butcher; kill indiscriminately; massacre or slaughter in great numbers

【屠苏】túsū〈古代 *arch.*〉一种酒名 *tusu*, name of an ancient wine

【屠宰】túzǎi 宰杀（牲畜）butcher, slaughter (livestock)

【屠宰场】túzǎichǎng 专门宰杀牲畜的处所 slaughterhouse; abattoir; butchery; place specifically for the slaughter of livestock

腯 tú〈书 *fml.*〉（猪）肥 (of pig) fat

瘏 tú〈书 *fml.*〉病 disease; illness; sickness

酴 tú〈书 *fml.*〉酿酒用的酒母 yeast for making wine

【酴醾】túmí ❶ 古书上指重酿的酒 double-fermented wine as described in ancient books ❷ same as 荼蘼 túmí

T

tǔ（ㄊㄨˇ）

土 tǔ ❶ 土壤;泥土 soil; earth:黄～loess|黏～clay|～山 earthen hill|～坡 slope|～堆 dyke; mound; windrow ❷ 土地 land; ground; territory:国～land; country's territory|领～territory; domain ❸ 本地的;地方性的 local; native; indigenous:～产 local or native product; be produced locally|～风 local ballad; local custom|～气 rustic; uncouth; countrified|～话 local dialect|这个字眼太～,外地人不好懂。This is such a localized colloquialism that anyone outside the area would find it hard to understand. ❹ 指我国民间沿用的生产技术和有关的设备、产品、人员等(区别于'洋' as compared with 'foreign', 'imported') local; indigenous; homemade; folk or popular Chinese production skills and the relevant equipment, products, personnel, etc.:～法 local method; indigenous method; traditional method|～专家 self-taught expert; local expert; indigenous expert|～洋并举 combine traditional and modern methods; use both local and foreign methods ❺ 不合潮流;不开通 crude; rustic; unenlightened; uncouth:～里～气 rustic; coarse; countrified; uncouth; cloddish|～头～脑 rustic; cloddish; countrified; unsophisticated ❻ 未熬制的鸦片(raw) opium:烟～opium ❼ (Tǔ) 姓 a surname

【土邦】tǔbāng 亚洲和非洲某些国家在帝国主义(英国)殖民统治下以独立形式存在的政权,一国之内可有若干个土邦 native state; political regime in certain Asian and African countries that is in a certain form of independence under British colonial rule, there often being several simultaneously in existence in one country

【土包子】tǔbāo·zi 指没有见过世面的人(含讥讽意 derog.) clodhopper; (country) bumpkin; yokel; coarse, unrefined person; person who has seen little of the world

【土崩瓦解】tǔ bēng wǎ jiě 〈比喻 *fig.*〉彻底崩溃 disintegrate; crumble; fall apart; fall to pieces; collapse like a house of cards

【土鳖】tǔbiē 地鳖的通称 general term for 地鳖 dìbiē

【土布】tǔbù 手工纺织的布 handwoven or handloomed cloth; homespun cloth

【土产】tǔchǎn ❶ 某地出产的 be produced locally:～品 local or native product ❷ 某地出产的富有地方色彩的产品 local or native product; produce of a place that is of a characterized local feature:这是从家乡四川带来的～。This is a local product brought from my home town in Sichuan Province.

【土地】tǔdì ❶ 田地 land; soil:～肥沃 fertile land; good soil|～改革 land reform; agrarian reform ❷ 疆域 territory; domain; area:～广阔,物产丰富 vast territory and abundant resources

【土地】tǔ·di 迷信传说中指管一个小地区的神 local god of the land; village god; god of a small area, according to old superstitions:～堂(土地庙) tiny temple housing the village god; also 土地爷 tǔ·diyé or 土地老 tǔ·dilǎo

【土地改革】tǔdì gǎigé 对封建土地所有制进行改革的运动 land reform; agrarian reform; movement to reform feudal land ownership; 简称 abbr. 土改 tǔgǎi

【土地革命战争】Tǔdì Gémìng Zhànzhēng ☞ 第二次国内革命战争 Dì Èr Cì Guónèi Gémìng Zhànzhēng on p. 429

【土豆】tǔdòu (～儿 tǔdòur) 马铃薯 potato

【土法】tǔfǎ 民间沿用的方法 indigenous method; local method; traditional method; method still in use by the people:～打井 dig a well by traditional methods

【土方】[1] tǔfāng 挖土、填土、运土的工作量通常都用立方米计算,一立方米称为一个土方。这一类的工作叫土方工程,有时也简称土方。spade work; work of digging, filling and transporting earth that is generally calculated in cubic metres of earth; known as 土方工程 tǔfānggōngchéng; sometimes abbr. 土方 tǔfāng

【土方】[2] tǔfāng (～儿 tǔfāngr) 民间流行的、不见于医药专门著作的药方 folk recipe; home remedy; traditional cure; popular folk prescription that does not appear in medical monographs

【土肥】tǔféi 用作肥料的墙土、炕土、灶土等的总称 farmyard manure; general term for the earth from walls, *kangs* and kitchen ranges that is used as fertilizer

【土匪】tǔfěi 地方上的武装匪徒 bandit; brigand; local armed gangster or robber

【土粉子】tǔfěn·zi 〈方 *dial.*〉粉刷墙壁用的白垩土 chalk (used to whitewash walls)

【土改】tǔgǎi 土地改革的简称 abbr. for 土地改革 tǔdì gǎigé

【土埂】tǔgěng 田地里稍稍高起的埂子 bank of earth that protrudes slightly from the fields; also 土埂子 tǔgěng·zi

【土棍】tǔgùn 地方上的恶棍 local rascal; local bully; ruffian; scoundrel:流氓～hooligan; gangster

【土豪】tǔháo 〈旧时 *old*〉指地方上有钱有势的家族或个人,后特指农村中有钱有势的恶霸 local tyrant or despot; originally referring to a local wealthy and influential family or individual, but later to a local wealthy and influential bully in a rural area:～劣绅 local tyrants and evil gentry; despotic landlords

【土话】tǔhuà 小地区内使用的方言 local dialect; slang; dialect spoken in a small area; also 土语 tǔyǔ

【土皇帝】tǔhuángdì 指盘踞一方的军阀或大恶霸 local despot; local tyrant; warlord or influential bully entrenched in a place

【土黄】tǔhuáng 像黄土一样的黄色 colour of loess; sallow; yellowish brown

【土货】tǔhuò 土产的物品 local product; native produce

【土籍】tǔjí 世代久居的籍贯 place where a family has lived for generations

【土家族】Tǔjiāzú 我国少数民族之一，主要分布在湖南、湖北、四川等地 Tujia or Tuchia ethnic group; one of China's ethnic minority groups mainly distributed over Hunan, Hubei and Sichuan provinces

【土木】tǔmù 指土木工程 building; construction: 大兴～go in for large-scale construction

【土木工程】tǔmù gōngchéng 房屋、道路、桥梁、海港等工程的统称 civil engineering; general term for house, road, bridge, harbour, etc., construction projects

【土牛】tǔniú 堆在堤坝上以备抢修用的土堆，从远处看去像一头头卧着的牛 mound; pile of earth on a dyke prepared for emergency repairs, known as 'earth ox' because, from a distance, it looks like a reclining ox

【土偶】tǔ'ǒu 用泥土塑成的偶像 clay idol

【土坯】tǔpī 把黏土放在模型里制成的方形土块，可以用来盘灶、盘炕、砌墙 sun-dried mud brick; adobe; block made by putting clay into a mold, used to build kitchen ranges, *kang*, and walls

【土气】tǔ·qì ❶ 不时髦的风格、式样等 rustic style; cloddish manner; uncouth bearing; unfashionable style, etc. ❷ 不时髦 rustic; countrified; uncouth; unfashionable: 穿着要像个样，不要让人家说我们太～了。Dress in a presentable way, as then people will not call us country bumpkins.

【土壤】tǔrǎng 地球陆地表面的一层疏松物质，由各种颗粒状矿物质、有机物质、水分、空气、微生物等组成，能生长植物 soil; layer of loose earth on the land surface, composed of various mineral particles, organic matter, moisture, air, microorganisms, etc., in which plants grow

【土人】tǔrén 外地人称经济、文化等不发达的原来住在本地的人（含轻视意 derog.）native; aborigine; term used by outsiders to refer to a person indigenous to an economically and culturally underdeveloped region

【土色】tǔsè 像土一样的黄色 ashen; pale; yellowish earth colour: 面如～turn deathly pale

【土生土长】tǔ shēng tǔ zhǎng 当地生长 locally born and bred, born and brought up on one's native soil or land: 他是～的山东人。He was born and bred in Shandong.

【土石方】tǔshífāng 土方、石方的总称 general term for a cubic metre of earth and stone removed

【土司】tǔsī 元、明、清各朝在少数民族地区授予少数民族首领世袭官职，以统治该族人民的制度。也指被授予这种官职的人。system of appointing headmen of national minority to a hereditary title in the Yuan, Ming and Qing dynasties; headman or chieftain holding such a title

【土俗】tǔsú ❶ 当地的习俗 local custom: ～淳朴 simple, unsophisticated custom ❷ 粗俗不雅 vulgar; coarse: ～的语言 vulgar language

【土温】tǔwēn 土壤的温度 soil temperature

【土物】tǔwù same as 土产 tǔchǎn ②

【土戏】tǔxì ❶ 土家族的戏曲剧种，流行于湖北来凤一带 Tujia Opera; traditional opera of the Tujia ethnic minority group, popular in the Laifeng area of Hubei Province ❷ 壮族戏曲剧种之一，流行于云南文山壮族苗族自治州 Zhuang Opera, popular in the Wenshan Zhuang and Miao Autonomous Prefecture, Yunnan Province; also 壮族土戏 Zhuàngzú tǔxì

【土星】tǔxīng 太阳系九大行星之一，按离太阳由近而远的次序计为第六颗，公转周期约为 29.5 年，自转周期约 10 小时 Saturn; one of the nine planets of the solar system, sixth in order of closeness to the sun, with an orbital period of 29.5 years, and a rotation period of 10 hours; （图见 ☞ figure for 太阳系 tàiyángxì on p.1855）

【土腥气】tǔ·xīngqì 泥土的气味 smell of the earth: 这菠菜没洗干净，有点儿～。The spinach was not washed clean, and had an earthy odour; also 土腥味儿 tǔ·xīngwèir

【土性】tǔxìng 土壤对植物供给养分、水分的性能 properties of soil that provide plants with nutrients and moisture

【土仪】tǔyí 〈书 *fml.*〉指用来送人的土产品 gift of a native product; native or local product presented as a gift

【土音】tǔyīn 土话的口音 local accent; accent of local dialect

【土语】tǔyǔ same as 土话 tǔhuà: 方言～ local dialect

【土葬】tǔzàng 处理死人遗体的一种方法，一般是把尸体先装在棺材里，然后再把棺材埋在地里（区别于'火葬、水葬'等 as compared with 'cremation' or 'burial at sea'）burial; interment (of the dead); way of disposing of a dead body, usually by first putting it in a coffin, and then burying it

【土政策】tǔzhèngcè 指某个地区或部门从局部利益出发制定的某些规定或办法（多与国家政策不一致 oft. at variance with a state policy）local policy; certain regulation or measure promulgated by an area or department that is partial to local interests

【土质】tǔzhì 土壤的构造和性质 soil texture; soil property:～肥沃 fertile soil

【土著】tǔzhù 世代居住本地的人 original inhabitants; aborigines; aboriginals; people who have lived in a place for generations

【土族】Tǔzú 我国少数民族之一,主要分布在青海和甘肃 Tu ethnic group; one of China's ethnic minority groups, mainly distributed in Qinghai and Gansu provinces

吐 tǔ ❶ 使东西从嘴里出来 spit; force sth. out of one's mouth:～核儿(húr) spit out pips or pits|～痰 spit; expectorate ❷ 从口儿或缝儿里长出来或露出来 emit; stick; put forth; send out; grow or expose from an opening or a seam:～穗儿 put forth ears; earing (up)|～絮 bolls opening; opening of bolls|蚕～丝。Silkworms spin silk. ❸ 说出来 say; tell; speak out; pour out:谈～style of conversation|～露 reveal; tell|～实 tell the truth|～字清楚 pronounce distinctly; enunciate clearly

☞ tù on p. 1944

【吐翠】tǔcuì〈书 *fml.*〉呈现碧绿的颜色 look fresh and green:杨柳～。The willow trees are greening.

【吐蕃】Tǔfān 我国古代少数民族,在今青藏高原。唐时曾建立政权。Tubo; Tibetan regime in ancient China; ethnic minority group in ancient China on the present Qinghai-Tibet Plateau, which established a political power during the Tang Dynasty

【吐故纳新】tǔ gù nà xīn《庄子·刻意》:'吹呴呼吸,吐故纳新'(呴 xū:吹气),本指人体呼吸,吐出碳酸气,吸进新鲜空气。现多用来比喻扬弃旧的、不好的,吸收新的、好的。*Zhuangzi·Ingrained Ideas*:'Blow out and breathe in to get rid of the stale and take in the fresh. *or* Exhale the old and inhale the new.' human respiration — emitting carbon dioxide, and absorbing oxygen; (now usu. fig.) discard the old and bad, and absorb the new and good (呴 *xu* means exhalation)

【吐话】tǔ//huà (～儿 tǔ//huàr)说出话来;发话 ① utter words; permit:要办这件事,还得领导上～才行。In order to do the work we must first get the go-ahead from the leader.

【吐口】tǔ//kǒu 开口说话,多用于表示同意或说出实情等 tell; reveal; start to talk, often used to express consent or agreement, or to tell the truth:问了半天,他就是不～。We spent a long time asking him, but he refused to tell the truth.

【吐露】tǔlù 说出(实情或真心话) reveal; tell the truth; speak one's mind:～真情 tell the truth; unburden oneself|她的心里话不轻易向人～。She does not easily pour out her heart to others.

【吐气】tǔ//qì 发泄出积在胸中的委屈或怨恨而感到痛快 feel elated after unburdening oneself of accumulated grievances or resentment:扬眉～feel elated and exultant; be proud and happy

【吐气】tǔqì 语音学上指送气(phonet.) aspirate

【吐弃】tǔqì 唾弃 spurn; reject; discard; cast aside

【吐属】tǔshǔ〈书 *fml.*〉谈话用的语句;谈吐 style and manner of conversation; type of sentences used when speaking:～不凡 unusual manner of conversation|～大方 talk with easy grace; talk naturally

【吐穗】tǔ//suì (～儿 tǔ//suìr) 抽穗 earing (up); heading (of cereal plants)

【吐絮】tǔxù 棉桃成熟裂开,露出白色的棉絮 opening of bolls; boll opening; (of cotton bolls) split open on reaching maturity, exposing white cotton fiber

【吐谷浑】Tǔyùhún 我国古代少数民族,在今甘肃、青海一带。隋唐时曾建立政权。Kokonor; ethnic minority group of ancient times that lived in present-day Gansu and Qinghai provinces, and that established political power during the Sui and Tang dynasties

【吐字】tǔzì 唱曲和说白中按照正确的或传统的音读出字音;咬字 pronounce; articulate; read words according to the received or traditional pronunciation of singing or spoken parts in an opera:～行腔 pronounce and sing (tunes)|～清楚 clear articulation

钍 tǔ 金属元素,符号 Th (thorium)。银白色,在空气中逐渐变为灰色,质软,有放射性。经过中子轰击,可得核燃料铀^{233},也可用做耐火材料、电极等。thorium (Th), soft, silvery white radioactive metal element that gradually turns grey when exposed to the air, and from which, through neutron bombardment, uranium-233 nuclear fuel can be obtained, also used for refractory material, electrodes, etc.

tù(ㄊㄨˋ)

吐 tù ❶(消化道或呼吸道里的东西)不自主地从嘴里涌出 vomit; retch; throw up; (of things in the digestive or reparatory tract) gush out from the mouth despite oneself:呕～vomit; throw up|～血 spit blood; haematemesis|上～下泻 suffer from vomiting and diarrhea ❷〈比喻 *fig.*〉被迫退还侵占的财物 disgorge; cough up; give up unwillingly; be forced to relinquish the properties occupied by force

☞ tǔ on p. 1944

【吐沫】tù·mo 唾沫 saliva; spittle; spit

【吐血】tù//xiě 内脏出血由口中吐出 spitting

blood; haematemesis; spit blood from the mouth due to internal hemorrhage; ☞咯血 kǎ// xiě on p. 1069 and 呕血 ǒu // xiè on p. 1432

【吐泻】tùxiè 呕吐和腹泻 vomiting and diarrhea

兔(兎) tù (～儿 tùr)哺乳动物，头部略像鼠，耳大，上唇中间分裂，尾短而向上翘，前肢比后肢短，善于跳跃，跑得很快。有家兔和野兔等种类。肉可以吃，毛可供纺织，毛皮可以制衣物。rabbit (*Oryetolagus cuniculus*); hare; mammal whose head slightly resembles that of a rodent, with long ears, a split upper lip, a short bob tail, and forelimbs much shorter than its hind legs, enabling it to jump and run swiftly. Rabits are either domesticated or wild, their meat is edible, their wool is a textile material, and their fur can be used to make clothes. 通称 generally called 兔子 tùzi

【兔唇】tùchún 唇裂 harelip; cleft lip

【兔毫】tùháo 用兔毛做笔头的毛笔 calligraphy brush made of rabbit hair

【兔起鹘落】tù qǐ hú luò 兔刚跑动，鹘就扑下去 the moment the hare ran out, the falcon swooped down;〈比喻 *fig.*〉动作敏捷。也比喻作画、写字、写文章等下笔迅速，没有停顿。be agile; move rapidly; paint, write words or articles rapidly without pause

【兔儿爷】tùryé 中秋节应景的兔头人身的泥制玩具 clay toy for the Mid-Autumn Festival, with a rabbit's head and human body

【兔死狗烹】tù sǐ gǒu pēng《史记·越王句践世家》:'蜚(飞)鸟尽，良弓藏；狡兔死，走狗烹。'鸟没有了，弓也就收起来不用了；兔子死了，猎狗也就被煮来吃了。*Records of the Historian · Hereditary House of Gou Jian, King of Yue*: 'When birds disappear, pack the bows away; and when all hares have been killed, stew and eat the hounds.'〈比喻 *fig.*〉事情成功以后，把曾经出过大力的人杀掉 kill trusted aides once they have outlived their usefulness

【兔死狐悲】tù sǐ hú bēi〈比喻 *fig.*〉因同类的灭亡而感到悲伤 like grieves for like; experience grief at the death of sb. of the same category: ～，物伤其类。Just as the fox grieves for the death of the hare, so one feels for one's own kind.

【兔脱】tùtuō〈书 *fml.*〉〈比喻 *fig.*〉很快地逃走 take flight; run as fleet as a hare; escape; flee

【兔崽子】tùzǎi·zi 幼小的兔子。多用做骂人的话。(oft. offens.) brat; bastard

【兔子】tù·zi 兔的通称 general term for 兔 tù

堍 tù 桥两头靠近平地的地方 ramp of a bridge; two ends of a bridge close to flat ground: 桥～end of a bridge

菟 tù [菟丝子](tùsīzǐ)一年生草本植物，茎很细，呈丝状，黄白色，茎上有吸取别的植物体养料的器官，叶子退化，开白色小花。多寄生在豆科植物上。种子黄褐色，可入药。Chinese dodder (*Cuscuta chinensis*); yellow-and-white annual parasitic vine with retrograde leaves, small white flowers, and a stem grown with organs for obtaining nutrition from other plants, oft. living off legumes, its yellowish brown seeds used as medicine; also 菟丝 tùsī

☞ tú on p. 1276

tuān (ㄊㄨㄢ)

湍 tuān〈书 *fml.*〉❶ 湍急 (of a current) rapid; torrential: ～流 torrent; rapids; swift current; rushing waters ❷ 急流的水 rapids; rushing waters: 急～rushing current

【湍急】tuānjí 水势急 (of a current) rapid; torrential: 川江险滩多，水流～。The Chuanjiang river is characterized by numerous rapids and swift currents.

【湍流】tuānliú〈书 *fml.*〉流得很急的水 torrent; rapids; swift current; rushing waters

tuán (ㄊㄨㄢˊ)

团(團、❷糰) tuán ❶ 圆形的 round; circular: ～扇 circular or round fan; moon-shaped fan | 雌蟹是～脐。Female crabs have round abdomens. ❷ 团子 dumpling: 汤～boiled rice dumpling ❸ 把东西揉弄成球形 roll into a ball; roll: ～泥球 roll a mud ball | ～纸团儿 roll paper into a ball | ～饭团子 roll a rice ball ❹ 成球形的东西 sth. shaped like a ball: 纸～儿 paper crumpled up into a ball | 棉花～儿 cotton ball ❺ 会合在一起 unite; conglomerate; rally; assemble: ～聚 reunite; gather; assemble | ～结 unite; rally ❻ 工作或活动的集体 group; society; circle; organization; collective for work or activities: 主席～presidium | 文工～art troupe; cultural troupe; song and dance ensemble | 代表～delegation; deputation; mission | 参观～visiting delegation; tour group ❼ 军队的编制单位，一般隶属于师，下辖若干营 regiment; military unit usu. subordinated to a division, and commanding several battalions ❽ 青少年的政治性组织，如儿童团、青年团等，在我国特指中国共产主义青年团 political organization for teenagers, such as Children's Corps, Youth League, etc.; Communist Youth League of China; Youth League ❾〈旧时 *old*〉某些地区相当于乡一级的政权机关 township state-agencies or organs in some areas ❿〈量词 *classifier*〉用于成团的东西 used for sth. ball-shaped: 一～毛线 a ball of knitting wool | 一

～碎纸 a ball of scraps of paper

【团拜】tuánbài（机关、学校等集体的成员）为庆祝新年或春节而聚在一起互相祝贺（of members of collective organs, schools, etc.）mutual greetings or congratulations exchanged by a group（on New Year's Day or for the Spring Festival）

【团丁】tuándīng〈旧时 *old*〉团防机构役使的壮丁 local militiaman; member of a local militia group

【团队】tuánduì 具有某种性质的集体；团体 group; team; corps; collective with some property：体育～sports team｜组织旅游～organize a tour group

【团粉】tuánfěn 烹调用的淀粉，多用绿豆或芡实制成 cooking starch（usu. made of mung beans or powdered Gorgon fruit seeds

【团伙】tuánhuǒ 纠集在一起从事不轨活动的小集团 gang; ring; small group of people who gather together to engage in illegal activities：打击流氓～crack down on criminal gangs

【团结】tuánjié ❶ 为了集中力量实现共同理想或完成共同任务而联合或结合 unite; rally; ally or combine with each other to concentrate forces in order to realize a common ideal or fulfil a common task：～朋友，打击敌人 unite with friends to strike out at the enemy｜～就是力量。Unity is strength. ❷ 和睦；友好 harmonious; united; friendly：邻里～neighbourhood unity or solidarity｜大家很～。All of us are solidly united.

【团聚】tuánjù ❶ 相聚（多指亲人分别后再相聚 oft. of family members after a separation）reunite; come or join together：夫妻～reunion of husband and wife｜全家～family reunion ❷ 团结聚集 unite; rally; gather; assemble：组织和～千千万万民众 organize and assemble thousands upon thousands of people

【团粒】tuánlì 由腐殖质和矿物颗粒等构成的团状小土粒，直径一般在1—10毫米之间。可以储存养分和水分，团粒之间的空隙便于渗水。granule; small round soil grain composed of humus and mineral particles, etc., whose diameter is 1 to 10 mm., that restores nutrient and moisture content, and between which water easily seeps

【团练】tuánliàn 宋代到民国初年，地主阶级用来镇压农民起义的地方反动武装组织 local reactionary armed forces of the landlord class that suppressed peasant uprisings from the Song Dynasty through to the early Republican years

【团圞】tuánluán〈书 *fml.*〉❶ 形容月圆（of the moon）round：一轮～的明月 a bright full moon ❷ 团圆①；团聚① reunite; gather or hold together：～到老 be together through to old age｜合家～reunion of the whole family ‖ also 团栾 tuánluán

【团弄】tuán·nong〈方 *fml.*〉❶ 用手掌搓东西使成球形 roll; roll sth. into a ball with palms ❷ 摆布；蒙蔽；笼络 manipulate; deceive; hoodwink ‖ also 抟弄 tuán·nong

【团脐】tuánqí ❶ 螃蟹肚子下面的甲是圆形的（雌蟹的特征，区别于'尖脐' as compared with the 'narrow triangular abdomen of the male crab'）abdomen of a female crab; round shell of a crab under the abdomen：今天买的螃蟹都是～的。All the crabs I bought today have round abdomens. ❷ 指雌蟹 female crab

【团扇】tuánshàn 圆形的扇子，一般用竹子或兽骨做柄，竹蔑或铁丝做圈，蒙上绢、绫子或纸 circular fan; round fan usu. with a bamboo or bone handle, and made by covering a ring of bamboo strip or iron wire with fine, durable silk, damask silk or paper

【团体】tuántǐ 有共同目的、志趣的人所组成的集体 organization; group; team; society; collective composed of people who have common goals and interests：人民～people's organization｜～活动 group activity

【团体操】tuántǐcāo 集体表演的、具有一定主题思想的体操。表演者按规定做各种体操或舞蹈动作，或进行队列变化，或组成各种有意义的图案。group calisthenics; collective gymnastic exhibition or display with a certain theme, in which the athletes perform various gymnastic exercises, dance movements, and formation changes, or create diverse, significant patterns

【团团】tuántuán ❶ 形容圆的样子 round：～的小脸儿 little round face ❷ 形容旋转或围绕的样子 round and round; all round：～转 move in a circle; go round and round｜～围住 encircle; surround completely; cluster around

【团团转】tuántuánzhuàn 来回转圈儿，多用来形容忙碌、焦急的样子（of busy or agitated appearance）move in a circle; go round and round：忙得～be up to one's ears in work｜急得～pace about in an agitated state of mind; be on tenterhooks; be anxious

【团音】tuányīn ☞ 尖团音 jiāntuányīn on p.938

【团鱼】tuányú same as 鳖 biē

【团员】tuányuán ❶ 代表团、参观团等的成员 member of a visiting group, delegation, etc.：这个代表团由团长一人～三人组成。This delegation comprises the head and three other members. ❷ 特指中国共产主义青年团团员 League member; member of the Communist Youth League of China

【团圆】tuányuán ❶（夫妻、父子等）散而复聚 reunion;（of husband and wife, father and son, etc.）gather together once more after a separation：骨肉～reunion of parents and children; family reunion｜全家～family reunion ❷ 圆形的 round; circular：这个人～脸，大眼睛。That person has a round face and big eyes.

【团圆节】Tuányuán Jié 指中秋 Mid-Autumn or Moon Festival (15th day of the 8th lunar month)

【团子】tuán·zi 米或粉做成的圆球形食物 dumpling; spherical snack made from rice or corn meal: 糯米～dumpling made of glutinous rice | 玉米面～corn dumpling

抟(摶) tuán ❶〈书 *fml.*〉盘旋 circle; hover; wheel; spiral ❷ same as 团 tuán ③

【抟弄】tuán·nong same as 团弄 tuán·nong

漙(溥) tuán〈书 *fml.*〉形容露水多dewy; with a lot of dew

tuǎn (ㄊㄨㄢˇ)

疃(畽) tuǎn 村庄;屯(多用于地名 oft. used in place names) village: 柳～(在山东) Liu Village (in Shandong Province) | 王～(在河北) Wang Village (in Hebei Province)

tuàn (ㄊㄨㄢˋ)

彖 tuàn〈书 *fml.*〉论断;判断 judge; assert: ～凶吉 judge ill or good luck

【彖辞】tuàncí《易经》中论卦义的文字 hexagram statement; commentary on the meaning of different combinations of hexagrams in *The Book of Changes*; also 卦辞 guàcí

tuī (ㄊㄨㄟ)

忒 tuī 又 also pronounced tēi〈方 *dial.*〉太 too; very; awfully: 这屋子～小,挤不下。The room is too small to squeeze in.

☞ tè on p. 1875

推 tuī ❶ 向外用力使物体或物体的某一部分顺着用力的方向移动 push; shove; thrust; concentrate strength in a forward direction to make an object or a part of an object move: ～车 push a car | ～磨 turn a millstone | ～倒 overturn; topple; push over | 我～了他一把。I gave him a push. | 门没有闩上,一～就开了。The unbolted door could be opened with the slightest push. ❷ (推磨)磨或(推碾子)碾(粮食) turn a mill or grindstone (to husk or grind grains); grind: ～了两斗荞麦 grind two *dou* of buckwheat ❸ 用工具贴着物体的表面向前剪或削 cut; pare; plane; mow; cut or pare the surface of an object by pushing a bladed tool over it in a forward direction: ～草机 mower; mowing machine | ～头 cut one's hair with (clippers) | 用刨子～光 polish with a plane ❹ 使事情开展 push forward; promote; advance; extend: ～广 spread; popularize; extend | ～销 promote sales; peddle; market; sell | ～行 pursue; introduce; carry out | 把水利建设～向高潮 advance the construction of water conservancy facilities to a climax ❺ 根据已知的事实断定其他;从某方面的情况想到其他方面 deduce; infer; form a judgement on sth. based on known facts of a separate, already established matter; consider all aspects of a situation: 类～analogize; reason by analogy | ～算 calculate; estimate; reckon | ～己及人 put oneself in the place of another; be considerate; consider others; do unto others as you would be done by ❻ 让给别人;辞让 (politely) decline; yield; give (sth. to others): ～辞 refuse; decline; turn down | ～让 yield; submit; decline (a position, favor, etc.) out of modesty | 解衣～食 give up or forgo one's own food or clothing in favor of the needy ❼ 推委;推托 shift; shirk; push away: ～三阻四 make all sorts of excuses; make excuses and create obstacles; give sb. the run-around ❽ 推迟 delay; postpone; put off: 开会日期往后～几天。The meeting has been postponed for a few days. ❾ 推崇 praise highly; hold in esteem: ～许 have a high regard for; hold in esteem | ～重 hold in esteem; think highly of ❿ 推选;推举 elect; recommend; choose: 大家～老张担任小组长。We chose Lao Zhang as our group leader. *or* We unanimously elected Lao Zhang the group leader.

【推本溯源】tuī běn sù yuán 推究根源;找原因 trace the origin; ascertain the cause; detect or find out the reason

【推波助澜】tuī bō zhù lán〈比喻 *fig.*〉促使或助长事物(多指坏的事物)的发展,使扩大影响 facilitate or foster the development of sth. (oft. bad) to expand its influence

【推测】tuīcè 根据已经知道的事情来想像不知道的事情 infer; guess; conjecture; try to imagine an unknown thing according to known facts: 无从～ have no way of inferring; be unable to infer or guess

【推陈出新】tuī chén chū xīn 去掉旧事物的糟粕,取其精华,并使它向新的方向发展(多指继承文化遗产 oft. referring to carrying on a cultural heritage) weed out the new from the old; evolve or bring forth the new out of the old; discard the dross and assimilate or select its essence, enabling it to develop in a new direction

【推诚相见】tuī chéng xiāng jiàn 用真心相待 treat with sincerity; open one's heart (to sb.); deal with sb. in good faith

【推迟】tuīchí 把预定时间向后改动 postpone; defer; delay; put off; change the time fixed to a later date: ～婚期 postpone one's wedding | 开会日期～一天。The meeting will be put off till the next day.

【推崇】tuīchóng 十分推重 extol; hold in esteem; praise highly:～备至 full of praise (for sb.)|杜甫的诗深受后世～。The poems of Du Fu have been held in high esteem by posterity.

【推辞】tuīcí 表示拒绝(任命、邀请、馈赠等) refuse; turn down; decline (an appointment, invitation, present, etc.)

【推戴】tuīdài 〈书 *fml.*〉拥护某人做领袖 support sb. (in assuming leadership):竭诚～ wholeheartedly support sb. (in assuming leadership)

【推宕】tuīdàng 拖延搁置 delay; postpone; procrastinate; put off; shelve; lay aside:借故～ find an excuse to procrastinate

【推导】tuīdǎo 数学、物理等学科中,根据已知的公理、定义、定理、定律等,经过演算和逻辑推理而得出新的结论 deduce; infer; derive; draw a new conclusion through calculations and logical inferences according to a known axiom, definition, theorem, law, etc., in subjects such as mathematics and physics

【推倒】tuī//dǎo ❶ 向前用力使立着的倒下来 overturn; topple; push over; direct one's strength forward to make a standing thing fall over:～土墙 overturn an earthen wall|他被人～在地。He was pushed to the ground. ❷ same as 推翻 tuī//fān:～前人的成说 repudiate an accepted theory formulated by antecedents|这个结论看来是推不倒的。The conclusion drawn seemed irrefutable.

【推定】tuīdìng ❶ 推举确定 elect; choose:大家～他为下一次的大会主席。He was chosen by general consensus to preside over the next meeting. ❷ 经推测而断定 infer; deduce; conclude by conjecture:一时还难以～他变卦的原因。It is difficult to infer the reason why he went back on his word.

【推动】tuī//dòng 使事物前进;使工作展开 promote; encourage; motivate; push forward; give impetus to; make sth. advance or go forward; carry out one's work:总结经验,～工作 promote work on the strength of one's own experience

【推断】tuīduàn ❶ 推测断定 infer; deduce:正确地分析事物的历史和现状,才有可能～它的发展变化。We can only deduce the developments and changes of an object by correctly analysing its past and present situation. ❷ 推测断定后所作的结论 deduction; conclusion made through inference or deduction:作出正确的～make a correct deduction

【推度】tuīduó same as 推测 tuīcè:～无据 make inferences with no proof

【推翻】tuī//fān ❶ 用武力打垮旧的政权,使局面彻底改变 overthrow; overturn; topple; smash an old regime by force in order to bring about a complete change ❷ 根本否定已有的说法、计划、决定等 repudiate; cancel; reverse; completely gainsay original wording, plan, decision, etc.:～原有结论 reverse the original conclusion|～强加给他的诬蔑不实之词。He repudiated the slander that had been spread about him.

【推服】tuīfú 〈书 *fml.*〉推许佩服 admire; have a high regard for; hold in esteem

【推广】tuīguǎng 扩大事物使用的范围或起作用的范围 popularize; spread; extend; expand the use or acting scope of a thing:～普通话 popularize *putonghua* (the common spoken Chinese)|～先进经验 spread or popularize advanced experience

【推及】tuījí 推广到;类推到 spread; extend; analogize; extend by analogy:～各处 spread or extend to various places|～其余 generalize; extend to the rest

【推己及人】tuī jǐ jí rén 用自己的心思来推想别人的心思;设身处地替别人着想 put oneself in another's place; be considerate; consider others in one's own place; do unto others as you would be done by

【推见】tuījiàn 推想出 imagine; reckon; infer; guess:从这些生活琐事上,可以～其为人。Trivial items in a person's life make it possible to infer his behaviour.

【推荐】tuījiàn 把好的人或事物向人或组织介绍,希望任用或接受 recommend; introduce a person or thing to sb. or an organization in the hope that they may be appointed or accepted:～她去当教师 recommend her as a teacher|向青年～优秀的文学作品 recommend excellent literary works to the youth

【推襟送抱】tuī jīn sòng bào 〈比喻 *fig.*〉推诚相见 treat with sincerity; open one's heart; lay one's heart bare (襟抱 *jin bao*:指心意 feeling; mind)

【推进】tuījìn ❶ 推动工作,使前进 promote; advance; push on; carry forward; give impetus to:把学科的研究～到一个新阶段 elevate studies on the subject to a new stage ❷ (战线或作战的军队)向前进 (of a front line or fighting troops) advance; drive; push; push or carry forward; press onward:主力正向前沿阵地～。The main force is advancing to a position in the forefront.

【推究】tuījiū 探索和检查(原因、道理等) examine and study (the cause, reason, etc.):～缘由 examine or study the reason or cause

【推举】tuījǔ same as 推选 tuīxuǎn:大家～他为工会小组长。We all chose him to be a group leader of the trade union.

【推理】tuīlǐ 逻辑学上指思维的基本形式之一,是由一个或几个已知的判断(前提)推出新判断(结论)的过程,有直接推理、间接推理等 inference; reasoning; ratiocination; course of directly or indirectly inferring a new judgement (or conclusion) through one or several known judgements (or premises)

【推力】tuīlì ❶ 推进的力量 incentive; motivation or driving force ❷ 物体所承受的推进的力 thrust; propulsion; motivation or driving force borne by an object

【推论】tuīlùn 用语言的形式进行推理 inference; deduction; corollary; reasoning in the form of language:根据事实～inference according to the facts

【推拿】tuīná ☞ 按摩 ànmó on p.13

【推敲】tuīqiāo 传说唐代诗人贾岛骑着驴做诗,得到'鸟宿池边树,僧敲月下门'两句。第二句的'敲'字又想改用'推'字,犹豫不决,就用手做推、敲的样子,无意中碰上了韩愈,向韩愈说明原委。韩愈想了一会儿说,用'敲'字好(见于《苕溪渔隐丛话》卷十九引《刘公嘉话》)。后人就用'推敲'来比喻斟酌字句,反复琢磨。Legend has it that Jia Dao, a poet of the Tang Dynasty, was composing a poem as he rode astride a donkey. He came up with two lines: 'The birds perched on the trees by a pond, As, in the moonlight, a monk knocked on a door,' but was unsure whether or not he should change 'knocked on' to 'pushed.' While thinking this over, and making the movements of pushing and knocking, he bumped into Han Yu, to whom he told his quandary. After thinking for a while, Han Yu said it would be better to use 'knocked on.' (See the 19th volume of *Fine Words of Duke Liu*, quoted from the *Collected Notes on a Hermit Fishing at Shaoxi Brook*); (fig.) weigh one's words and expressions; polish or refine repeatedly: 反复～weigh one's words repeatedly|～词句 weigh one's words and expressions

【推求】tuīqiú 根据已知的条件或因素来探索(道理、意图等)study; inquire; find out (from what is known); explore (a truth, intention, etc.) based on the known conditions or elements:～对方的动机 find out the motives of an opponent

【推却】tuīquè 拒绝;推辞 refuse; decline; turn down:再三～refuse over and over again

【推让】tuīràng 由于谦虚、客气而不肯接受(利益、职位等)submit; yield; decline (a favour, position, etc.) out of modesty or politeness

【推三阻四】tuī sān zǔ sì 以各种借口推托 make all sorts of excuses; make excuses and create obstacles; give sb. the run-around; also 推三推四 tuī sān tuī sì

【推事】tuīshì 〈旧时 *old*〉法院的审判员 judge (in court)

【推算】tuīsuàn 根据已有的数据计算出有关的数值 calculate; reckon; estimate; calculate the relevant numerical value on the basis of known data:根据太阳、地球、月球运行的规律,可以～日食和月食发生的时间。The time when solar and lunar eclipses occur can be calculated on the basis of regular patterns of the movements of the sun, the earth and the moon.

【推涛作浪】tuī tāo zuò làng 〈比喻 *fig.*〉促使坏事物发展,制造事端 encourage development of a bad phenomenon; stir up or make trouble; create disturbances

【推头】tuī//tóu (用推子)理发 cut sb.'s hair (with clippers); have a haircut

【推土机】tuītǔjī 在拖拉机前装有推土铲的机械,用于平整建筑场地等 bulldozer; machine comprising a mold-shovel at the front of a tractor, used to level construction sites, etc.

【推托】tuītuō 借故拒绝 plead; offer as an excuse (for not doing sth.); find an excuse to decline:她～嗓子不好,怎么也不肯唱。Pleading a sore throat, she adamantly declined to sing.

【推脱】tuītuō same as 推卸 tuīxiè:～责任 evade or shirk responsibility; shift blame onto others

【推诿】tuīwěi 把责任推给别人 shift responsibility onto others:遇事～shift responsibility onto others when confronted with a problem; also 推委 tuīwěi

【推问】tuīwèn 推究审问 question; interrogate; examine or study minutely:～案情 examine and inquire into a case

【推想】tuīxiǎng same as 推测 tuīcè

【推销】tuīxiāo 推广货物的销路 market; peddle; sell; promote the sales (of goods):～员 salesman|把大量的工业品～到农村去 sell a great number of industrial products to rural areas

【推卸】tuīxiè 不肯承担(责任)shirk; evade; shift blame; refuse to bear (a responsibility):～职责 shirk or evade one's duty

【推谢】tuīxiè 借故推辞 find an excuse to decline or refuse:～再三 repeatedly come up with excuses to decline

【推心置腹】tuī xīn zhì fù 〈比喻 *fig.*〉真心待人 treat sb. with sincerity; open one's heart to sb.:他俩～地交谈了好一阵子。They spoke to each other heart to heart for quite some time.

【推行】tuīxíng 普遍实行;推广(经验、办法等)pursue; practise; implement; carry out universally; introduce; spread or popularize (an experience, method, etc.):～新方案 carry out a new work plan|～生产责任制 implement or practise the production responsibility system

【推许】tuīxǔ 推重并赞许 hold in esteem; have a high regard for:他的见义勇为的行为受到人们的～。His deed of bravely taking up the cudgels for a just cause earned him high regard.

【推选】tuīxuǎn 口头提名选举 elect; choose; orally nominate for election:～代表 choose representatives|他被大家～为组长。He was elected group leader.

【推延】tuīyán same as 推迟 tuīchí:事情紧急,不能～。This matter is urgent and cannot be put off.|会议因故～三天。Owing to certain reasons, the meeting will be postponed for three days.

【推演】tuīyǎn 推断演绎 deduce; infer; derive

【推移】tuīyí (时间、形势、风气等)移动或发展 (of time) elapse; pass; (of a situation, common practice, etc.) develop; evolve:日月～as time passes|时局的～developments in current affairs

【推知】tuīzhī 经过推论或推算而知道 infer; reckon; deduce; learn through deductions or calculations:由此可以～其余。Other factors can be deduced from this.

【推重】tuīzhòng 重视某人的思想、才能、行为、著作、发明等,给以很高的评价 think highly of or have a high regard for sb.'s thinking, ability, behaviour, works, inventions, etc.; hold in esteem

【推子】tuī·zi 理发工具,有上下重叠的两排带刃的齿儿,使用时上面的一排齿儿左右移动,把头发剪下来。使用电力的叫电推子。hair-clippers; clippers; hairdressing tool with upper and lower overlapping bladed teeth, in which the upper blade cuts the hair as it is moved over the head; those electrically powered are called electric clippers

蓷 tuī 古书上指茺蔚(chōngwèi) motherwort (*Leonurus heterophyllus*) as described in ancient books

tuí(ㄊㄨㄟˊ)

隤 tuí〈书 *fml.*〉same as 颓 tuí

隫(隤) tuí ☞ [虺隤](huītuí) on p.857

颓 tuí ❶ 坍塌 collapse; crumble; become ruined or dilapidated:～垣断壁 crumbling walls and dilapidated houses ❷ 衰败 declining; decayed; decadent:衰～weak and in decline; on the decline; weak and degenerate|～败 decay; decline; become corrupt ❸ 委靡 dispirited; dejected; decadent:～丧 dispirited; dejected; listless|～唐 dejected; dispirited; disconsolate

【颓败】tuíbài 衰落;腐败 decay; decline; become corrupt:荒凉～的景象 scene of desolation and decay|风俗～ corrupt customs

【颓放】tuífàng〈书 *fml.*〉志气消沉,行为放纵 abandoned; dissolute; decadent; degenerate; in poor or low spirits; of unbridled behaviour

【颓废】tuífèi 意志消沉,精神委靡 dissipated; decadent; degenerate; in poor or low spirits:情绪～ decadent sentiments|～的生活 dissipated life

【颓风】tuífēng 日趋败坏的风气 degenerate or depraved manners; decadent customs; degenerative practices

【颓靡】tuímǐ 颓丧;不振作 downcast; decadent; dejected; crestfallen:士气～。Morale is low.

【颓然】tuírán〈书 *fml.*〉形容败兴的样子 dejected; disappointed:神情～have a dejected or disappointed expression

【颓丧】tuísàng 情绪低落,精神委靡 dejected; dispirited; listless; in poor or low spirits; in the dumps:他～地低着头,半天不说话。Lowering his head dispiritedly, he was silent for a long time.

【颓势】tuíshì 衰败的趋势 declining tendency; decline:扭转～turn the tide in one's favor

【颓唐】tuítáng ❶ 精神委靡 dejected; dispirited; downhearted; disconsolate ❷〈书 *fml.*〉衰颓败落 decay; decline:老境～decline of life in old age

穨 tuí〈书 *fml.*〉same as 颓 tuí

tuǐ(ㄊㄨㄟˇ)

腿 tuǐ ❶ 人和动物用来支持身体和行走的部分 leg; part of a man or animal that supports and transports the body:大～thigh|前～foreleg|后～hind leg;(图见 ☞ figure for 身体 shēntǐ on p.1701) ❷(～儿 tuǐr)器物下部像腿一样起支撑作用的部分 leg-like support (beneath an object):桌子～legs of a table|椅子～儿 legs of a chair ❸ 指火腿 ham:云～(云南火腿)Yunnan ham

【腿带】tuǐdài (～儿 tuǐdàir)束紧裤脚儿的宽而长的带子 leg wrappings; long, wide trouser leg bottom bands

【腿肚子】tuǐdù·zi 小腿后面隆起的部分,是由腓肠肌等形成的 calf (of the leg); fleshy, muscled hinder part of the leg, between the knee and ankle

【腿脚】tuǐjiǎo 指走动的能力 ability to walk:这位老人的～倒很利落。The old man still walks briskly.

【腿弯子】tuǐwān·zi〈方 *dial.*〉大腿和小腿相连的关节的后部 back of the joint connecting the thigh and calf

【腿腕子】tuǐwàn·zi 脚和小腿之间的部分 ankle; part of leg between the foot and the calf

【腿子】tuǐ·zi ❶〈方 *dial.*〉腿 leg:～发软 legs feeling like jelly ❷ 狗腿子 lackey; henchman; hired thug

tuì (ㄊㄨㄟˋ)

侻 tuì 〈书 *fml*.〉美好;相宜 beautiful; handsome; fine; agreeable; suitable
☞ tuō on p.1957

退 tuì ❶ 向后移动(跟'进'相对 as opposed to 'advance') retreat; move backwards; draw back; back up:后~retreat; draw back; fall back|倒~step up; back up|进~两难 not know whether to advance or retreat; a dilemma ❷ 使向后移动 withdraw; remove; cause to move back:~兵 retreat; withdraw troops|~敌 repulse the enemy; force the enemy to retreat or withdraw|把子弹~出来 remove a cartridge from the breech of a gun; unload a gun ❸ 退出 quit; adjourn; withdraw from; retire from:~席 leave a banquet or meeting; walk out|~职 leave a job; resign or be discharged from office|~伍 retire or be discharged from active military service; be demobilized; leave the army|~伙 withdraw from an underworld gang; withdraw from a secret society|引~resign; quit or leave office ❹ 减退;下降 decline; decrease; recede; ebb:~色 fade|~烧 bring down or lower a fever; (of a person's temperature) come down|潮水已经~了。The tidewater has receded. *or* The tide is on the ebb. ❺ 退还 return; refund; give back:~钱 refund; reimburse|~货 return products or goods|~票 return a ticket; cancel a reservation; get a refund for a ticket|把这份礼~了。Return this present. ❻ 指已定的事撤销 cancel; retract; break off:~佃(of a landlord) cancel a tenancy; evict a tenant|~婚 break off an engagement

【退避】tuìbì 退后躲避 withdraw and keep away; keep out of the way; avoid; hide from:~无地 have nowhere to hide|~不及,正好碰上 bump into someone when there is no way of avoiding him

【退避三舍】tuìbì sān shè 春秋时,晋国同楚国在城濮(在今山东鄄城西南)作战,遵守以前的诺言,把军队撤退九十里 when the state of Jin was warring with the state of Chu at Chengpu (southwest of present-day Juancheng, Shandong Province) during the Spring and Autumn Period, it retreated its troops ninety *li*, honouring a formerly made promise (舍 *she*:古时行军三十里叫一舍 unit of measurement for the mileage covered by an army in a long march in old days; one *she* equals 90 *li*);后用来比喻对人让步,不与相争 (fig.) give way to sb. to avoid a conflict

【退兵】tuì//bīng ❶ 撤退军队 retreat; withdraw troops:传令~order a retreat ❷ 迫使敌军撤退 repulse; force the enemy to retreat:~之计 plan for repulsing the enemy

【退步】tuì//bù ❶ 落后;向后退 regress; lag behind; fall behind:成绩~lag or fall behind in one's study grades|许久不练,技艺~了。Having not practised for a long time, I found my skills were not as good as they used to be. ❷ 退让;让步 give in; give way; make a concession:彼此都~,就不至于冲突起来。If both sides had made some concessions, there would have been no conflict.

【退步】tuìbù 后步 room for maneuver; leeway:留个~leave some room for maneuver; give some leeway

【退场】tuì//chǎng 离开演出、比赛等的场所 leave (a theatre, arena, sports-ground, etc.); exit:运动员~。The athletes marched out.|演出结束,请观众~。The performance is over. Goodnight everybody.

【退潮】tuì//cháo 海水在涨潮以后逐渐下降 ebb; (of sea) fall gradually after a rising tide; ebb tide; falling tide:~后,海滩上留下许多贝壳。Many shells were left on the beach after an ebb tide. also 落潮 luò//cháo

【退出】tuìchū 离开会场或其他场所,不再参加;脱离团体或组织 withdraw from; secede; quit; leave a meeting or other place and cease participation; break away from a society or an organization:~会场 walk out of a meeting|~战斗 retreat from a battle|~组织 leave an organization; withdraw or resign from an organization

【退磁】tuìcí 用加高温等方法使磁体失去磁性 demagnetize; make a magnet lose its magnetism by heating it

【退佃】tuì//diàn 地主收回租给农民种的土地 (of a landlord) cancel a tenancy; evict a tenant; (of a landlord) regain the land leased to a peasant

【退化】tuìhuà ❶ 生物体在进化过程中某一部分器官变小,构造简化,机能减退甚至完全消失,叫做退化。如鲸、海豚等的四肢成鳍状,仙人掌的叶子成针状,虱子的翅膀完全消失。degenerate; retrogress; retrograde; (of certain organs of an organism) shrink in size as their structure simplifies, and their functions decline or disappear altogether, e.g. the limbs of the whale, dolphin, etc., which have turned into fins, the leaves of the cactus which have reduced to the size of needles, and the wings of louse, which have disappeared completely ❷ 泛指事物由优变劣,由好变坏 worsen; become worse; (of a good thing) turn or become bad

【退还】tuìhuán 交还(已经收下来或买下来的东西) return (what has been accepted or bought):原物~return the original|~给本人 return sth. to its owner

【退换】tuìhuàn 退还不合适的,换取合适的(多指货物 oft. of goods) exchange or replace a purchase; replace or refund sth. in exchange for sth. more suitable:缺页或装订上有错误的书,可以～。Replacements will be forthcoming for books with missing pages or faulty binding.

【退回】tuìhuí ❶ same as 退还 tuìhuán:无法投递,～原处。Undeliverable, and so returned to sender.|把这篇稿子～给作者。Return the article to its author. ❷ 返回原来的地方 go or turn back; return to the original place:道路不通,只得～。Finding the road impassable, we had to turn back.

【退婚】tuì//hūn 解除婚约 break off an engagement

【退火】tuì//huǒ ❶ 金属工具使用时因受热而失去原有的硬度 (of metal tools) losing its original hardness when heated for use ❷ 把金属材料或工件加热到一定温度并持续一定时间后,使缓慢冷却。退火可以减低金属硬度和脆性,增加可塑性。anneal; heat metal or a workpiece to a fixed temperature for a fixed time, and allow to cool, thus making it more malleable and increasing its plasticity; also 焖火 mèn//huǒ

【退伙】[1] tuì//huǒ 〈旧时 *old*〉指退出帮会 withdraw from a secret society or underworld gang

【退伙】[2] tuì//huǒ 退出集体伙食 cancel a collective eating arrangement; withdraw from a mess

【退路】tuìlù ❶ 退回去的道路 route or line of retreat:切断敌军的～cut off the enemy's retreat ❷ 回旋的余地 room for manoeuver; leeway:留个～leave some leeway; not burn one's boats; keep options open

【退赔】tuìpéi 退还,赔偿(多指侵占的、非法取得的财物等 oft. of unlawfully obtained property) return and pay compensation:责令他～所贪污的全部公款 order him to return all embezzled public funds

【退票】tuì//piào 把已经买来的车票、船票、戏票等退还原处或转让别人,收回买票的钱 return train, bus, boat, ship, opera ticket, etc., already bought to its place of purchase, or transfer it in order to get a refund

【退坡】tuì//pō 〈比喻 *fig.*〉意志衰退,或因工作中遭到困难而后退 fall off; backslide; retrograde; step back; wane in impetus; retreat on meeting difficulty in one's work:～思想 ideological backsliding; falling off of revolutionary will or zeal

【退亲】tuì//qīn same as 退婚 tuì//hūn

【退却】tuìquè ❶ 军队在作战中向后撤退 (of troops) retreat or withdraw (from battle):全线～retreat all along the line ❷ 畏难后退;畏缩 hang back; shrink back; flinch; be apprehensive and retreat:遇到挫折也不～not retreat whatever setback may be encountered

【退让】tuìràng ❶ 向后退,让开路 make way; step back; step aside:～不及,让车撞倒 be run down before one has a chance to get out of the way ❷ 让步 make a concession; yield; give in:原则问题,一点也不能～。No concessions can be made on matters of principle.

【退色】tuì//shǎi 布匹、衣服等的颜色逐渐变淡 fade; (of cloth, clothes, etc.) gradually become lighter in colour:这种布下水后不～。This cloth will not fade after washing.

【退烧】tuì//shāo 高于正常的体温降到正常 bring down or soothe a fever; reduce a high temperature back to normal; also 退热 tuì//rè

【退守】tuìshǒu 向后退并采取守势 withdraw and stand on the defensive; retreat and make a defense

【退缩】tuìsuō 向后退或缩;畏缩 shrink back; hold back; flinch; cower:～不前 flinch; shrink back

【退庭】tuìtíng 诉讼案件的关系人(如原告人、被告人、律师、证人等)退出法庭 court adjourned; (of the parties in a case, i.e. plaintiff, defendant, lawyer, witnesses, etc.) withdraw from the court:法官宣布～。The judge declared the court adjourned.

【退位】tuì//wèi 最高统治者让出统治地位,泛指退出原有的职位或地位 give up the throne; abdicate; (of the supreme ruler) give up the dominant postion; (in a broad sense) give up hereditary position

【退伍】tuì//wǔ 指军人服满现役或由于其他原因退出军队 retire or be discharged from active military service; be demobilized; (of soldiers) leave the army when active military service is completed or for other reasons:～军人 demobilized soldier; ex-serviceman; veteran|他是两年前退的伍。He was demobilized two years ago.

【退席】tuì//xí 退出宴席或会场 leave a banquet or a meeting

【退行】tuìxíng 向后倒退;退化 retrograde; retrogress; degenerate:老年人的机体不免要产生～性改变。The body of an old person is bound to degenerate.

【退休】tuìxiū 职工因年老或因公致残而离开工作岗位,按期领取生活费用 retire; (of workers and staff members) stop working owing to advanced age or injury inflicted while on duty, receiving periodic payment of living expenses:～金 pension; retirement pay|～人员 retiree; the retired; retired personnel

【退学】tuì//xué 学生因故不能继续学习,或因严重违反纪律不许继续学习而取消学籍 leave school; discontinue one's schooling; drop out; (of a student) be unable to continue one's studies for some reason; not be permitted to go on one's studies; be struck off the school roll：因病～drop out of school owing to poor health

【退押】tuì//yā 退还押金。特指土地改革时期使地主退还佃户所缴的押金。return a deposit；（esp. of a landlord during the Land Reform Movement）return（tenant's）deposit

【退役】tuì//yì ❶ 军人退出现役或服预备役期满后停止服役 retire from active military service；be released on completing term of reserve：～军人 ex-serviceman ❷ 某种陈旧的武器不再用于军备（of outdated weapons）be taken out of service：这种型号的战斗机已经～了。This type of fighter planes is no longer in service. ❸ 泛指其他行业的人员退离专业岗位（多指运动员 of personnel of other trades, esp. of athletes）（in a broad sense）retire from special position：这个球队主力队员大半～，实力有所下降。Owing to the retirement of most of its top players, the actual strength of the team has declined.

【退隐】tuìyǐn 指官吏退职隐居（of an official）quit working to retire from public life；go into retirement：～山林 retire from public life and live in seclusion in wooded mountains

【退职】tuì//zhí 辞退或辞去职务 resign or be discharged from office；quit a job：自动～resign of one's own accord｜提前～resign ahead of time

【退走】tuìzǒu 向后退去；退却 withdraw；retreat；move backward：见势不妙，赶紧～。On encountering an adverse situation, the man hurriedly beat a retreat.

蜕 tuì ❶ 蛇、蝉等脱皮 exuviate；moult；peel；（of snakes, cicadas, etc.）slough off or shed skin：～化 slough off；exuviate ❷ 蛇、蝉等脱下的皮 slough；exuviate；（of snakes, cicadas, etc.）skin that has been shed：蛇～sloughed off snakeskin｜蝉～cicada exuviate ❸ 鸟换毛（脱毛重长）（of birds）moult

【蜕变】tuìbiàn ❶（人或事物）发生质变（of a person or thing）change qualitatively；transform；transmute；degenerate：一个优等生～为小偷，这种教训值得记取。The instance of a top student degenerating into a thief is a lesson worth remembering. ❷ 衰变 decay；degeneration

【蜕化】tuìhuà 虫类脱皮（of insects）exuviate；slough off；〈比喻 *fig.*〉腐化堕落 degenerate：～变质 degenerate

【蜕皮】tuì//pí 许多节肢动物（主要是昆虫）和爬行动物，生长期间旧的表皮脱落，由新长出的表皮来代替。通常每蜕皮一次就长大一些。exuviate；slough；moult；cast off or shed a skin；（of arthropods, mainly insects, and reptiles）replace cast-off epidermis with new growths of skin during a period of growth when the animal gets bigger

煺（焞、㨃） tuì 已宰杀的猪、鸡等用滚水烫后去掉毛 scald（a killed pig, chicken, etc.）in order to remove bristles or feathers：～毛 remove the bristles of a pig or feathers of a chicken, etc.｜～猪 remove the bristles from pigskin

褪 tuì 脱（衣服、羽毛、颜色等）take off（clothes）；shed（feathers）；（of colour）fade：～去冬衣 put aside winter clothes｜小鸭～了黄毛。The ducklings have shed their yellow down.

☞ tùn on p. 1954

【褪色】tuì//shǎi same as 退色 tuì//shǎi

tūn（ㄊㄨㄣ）

吞 tūn ❶ 不嚼或不细嚼，整个儿地或成块地咽下去 swallow；devour；gulp down；swallow sth. whole without chewing or chewing properly：囫囵～枣 swallow dates whole；read without understanding｜狼～虎咽 wolf down；gobble up；devour ravenously｜把丸药～下去 take a Chinese medicine pill or bolus at one swallow；swallow the pill ❷ 并吞 annex；seize；take（illegal）possession of；same as 吞没 tūnmò①：侵～annex；embezzle；misappropriate；swallow up｜独～take exclusive possession of｜～灭 conquer and annex；gobble up

【吞并】tūnbìng 并吞 annex；seize；gobble or swallow up；take over

【吞剥】tūnbō 侵吞剥削 embezzle and exploit；swallow up and exploit：～民财 embezzle public property；commandeer the people's property

【吞金】tūn//jīn 吞下黄金（自杀）swallow gold（to commit suicide）

【吞灭】tūnmiè 并吞消灭 conquer and annex；gobble up

【吞没】tūnmò ❶ 把公共的或代管的财物据为己有 embezzle；misappropriate；appropriate public properties or those managed on behalf of another：～巨款 embezzle or misappropriate a huge sum ❷ 淹没 swallow up；submerge；engulf：大水～了村子。Floods engulfed the village.

【吞声】tūnshēng〈书 *fml.*〉不敢出声，特指哭泣不敢出声 gulp down or suppress one's sobs；dare not cry out；choke down one's tears：忍气～swallow insults and humiliations silently；eat humble pie｜～饮泣 sob bitterly and silently；choke down one's tears

【吞食】tūnshí same as 吞 tūn ①：大鱼～小鱼。Big fish swallow small ones.

【吞噬】tūnshì 吞食；并吞 swallow；engulf；devour；gobble up

【吞吐】tūntǔ ❶ 吞进和吐出 swallow and spit；〈比喻 *fig.*〉大量地进来和出去 take in and send out in large quantities：～量 throughput capacity；handling capacity（of a harbour）；volume of freight handled | ～港 harbour；port | 北京车站昼夜不停地～着来往的旅客。There are passenger arrivals and departures at Beijing Railway Station 24 hours a day. ❷ 形容说话或行文含混不清 hesitant in speech；hum and haw；mince one's words；unclear verbal or written expression：～其词 hesitate in speech；hum and haw

【吞吞吐吐】tūntūntǔtǔ 形容有顾虑，有话不敢直说或说话含混不清 hesitant in speech；hum and haw；mutter and mumble；speak hesitantly or falteringly

【吞咽】tūnyàn same as 吞食 tūnshí：咽喉发炎，～困难 have difficulty in swallowing due to pharyngolaryngitis ◇千言万语涌到喉头，却又～了下去 hesitate as innumerable words crowd the throat

暾 tūn〈书 *fml*.〉刚出的太阳 newly-risen sun：朝～early morning sun

tún（ㄊㄨㄣˊ）

屯 tún ❶ 聚集；储存 collect；gather；stock；store up：～聚 gather together；assemble（troops）| 聚草～粮 gather straw and store up grain；collect grain and fodder（for an army）；store up army provisions ❷（军队）驻扎 station or quarter（troops）：驻～be stationed；be quartered | ～兵 station or quarter troops ❸ 村庄（多用于村庄名 oft. used in place names）village：皇姑～（在辽宁）Huanggu Village（in Liaoning Province）| 小～（在河南）Xiaotun Village（in Henan Province）
☞ zhūn on p. 2530

【屯兵】túnbīng 驻扎军队 station or quarter troops：～边城 quarter troops in a frontier town

【屯集】túnjí same as 屯聚 túnjù

【屯聚】túnjù 聚集（人马等）gather together；assemble（troops or forces）：～大量兵力 assemble a large amount of military strength or force

【屯垦】túnkěn 驻兵垦荒 station troops to open up wasteland：～戍边 station troops to guard the frontier and cultivate the frontier areas

【屯绿】túnlǜ 安徽屯溪、歙县等地产的绿茶，色泽润绿，味醇和，是绿茶中的上品 Tunxi green；quality green tea produced in Tunxi Region，Xixian County，Anhui Province，characterized by a fresh green colour，and a pure，mild taste

【屯落】túnluò〈方 *dial*.〉村庄 village

【屯守】túnshǒu 驻守 defend；garrison：～边疆 garrison the frontier

【屯田】túntián 汉以后历代政府利用兵士在驻扎的地区种地，或者招募农民种地，这种措施叫做屯田 measure adopted by the governments of dynasties following the Han Dynasty whereby soldiers or peasants were recruited to cultivate the land in a garrison area

【屯扎】túnzhā 驻扎 station or quarter troops

【屯子】tún·zi〈方 *dial*.〉村庄 village

囤 tún 储存 collect；gather；store or hoard up：～货 store goods | ～粮 hoard grain
☞ dùn on p. 496

【囤积】túnjī 投机商人为了等待时机高价出售而把货物储存起来 hoard for speculation；corner（the market）；（of speculators）store goods in order to sell them at a higher price later：～居奇 hoarding and cornering；hoarding and profiteering；hoarding and speculation

【囤聚】túnjù 储存聚集（货物）hoard；store up（goods）；gather and store：～木材 store up wood

饨 tún ☞［馄饨］（hún·tún）on p. 873

忳 tún［忳忳］〈书 *fml*.〉烦闷的样子 worried；distressed；sad

豚（豘） tún 小猪，泛指猪 suckling pig；（in a broad sense）pig

鲀 tún 河豚 globe-fish（*Tetrodontidae*）；puffer；balloonfish

臀 tún 人体后面两股的上端和腰相连接的部分，也指高等动物后肢的上端和腰相连接的部分 buttock；rump；part of human body above the legs and below the waist；uppermost hind leg of a higher animal that connects to its waist；（图见 ☞ figure for 身体 shēntǐ on p. 1701）

【臀尖】túnjiān 做食品用的猪臀部隆起处的肉 rump；pork on the fleshy part of a pig's rump suitable for cooking

【臀鳍】túnqí 鱼类肛门后面的鳍 anal fin；fin behind fish's anus；（图见 ☞ figure for 鳍 qí on p. 1513）

【臀疣】túnyóu 猴类臀部的厚而坚韧的皮，红色，不生毛 monkey's ischial callosities；monkey's seat pads；thick，tough，red and hairless skin on a monkey's rump

tǔn（ㄊㄨㄣˇ）

汆 tǔn〈方 *dial*.〉❶ 漂浮 float；drift：木板在水上～a plank adrift on the water surface ❷ 用油炸 deep-fry：油～馒头 fried steamed bun | 油～花生米 fried peanuts

tùn（ㄊㄨㄣˋ）

褪 tùn ❶ 退缩身体的某部分，使套着的东西脱离 slip out of sth.；retract a part of one's body to free it from a binding object：～套儿

break loose; free oneself; get free|～下一只袖子 slip one's arm out of a sleeve ❷〈方 *dial.*〉藏在袖子里 hide in one's sleeves:～着手 hide or keep one's hands in their sleeves|袖子里～着一封信 hide a letter up a sleeve
☞ tuì on p.1953

【褪去】tùnqù 脱去(衣服等)take off (clothes, etc.)

【褪套儿】tùn//tàor ❶ 使身体脱离缚着它的绳索 break loose (from a rope or cord constraining the body); free oneself; get oneself free:狗褪了套儿跑了。The dog broke loose and ran away. ❷〈比喻 *fig.*〉摆脱责任 shake off responsibility

tuō(ㄊㄨㄛ)

乇 tuō '托[3]'旧作乇 old written form of 托[3]

托[1] tuō ❶ 手掌或其他东西向上承受(物体) lean against the palm; hold in the palm; support (an object) with the palm; place objects on a thing with a flat surface:两手～着下巴 cup one's chin in one's hands; rest one's chin on the palm of the hand|茶盘～着茶杯和茶壶。A tea tray holds teacups and a teapot. ❷(～儿 tuōr)托子;类似托子的东西 stand; support; base; sth. serving as a support:花～flower receptacle|茶～儿 saucer|日历～儿 calendar stand ❸ 陪衬 serve as a foil; set off:衬～set off; make sth. stand out by contrast|烘云～月 paint clouds to set off the moon

托[2](託) tuō ❶ 委托;寄托① entrust; trust; ask:～儿所 kindergarten; nursery; childcare centre; creche|～人买东西 ask sb. to buy sth. ❷ 推托 plead; give as a pretext; offer as an excuse:～病 plead illness; under pretext of illness; under the pretext of being ill|～故 make an excuse; give a pretext|～词 find a pretext; make an excuse ❸ 依赖 rely on; owe to; count upon; thanks to:～福 thanks to you|～庇 rely on sb. (usu. one's elder or an influential person) for protection

托[3] tuō 压强单位,1托等于1毫米汞柱的压强,合133.32帕斯卡 torr; unit of pressure; one torr is equal to the pressure of one milli Hg, and 133.32 pascal; 旧作 formerly written as 乇 tuō

【托庇】tuōbì 依赖长辈或有权势者的庇护 rely on sb. (usu. one's elder or an influential person) for protection:～祖荫 rely on ancestors for protection

【托病】tuōbìng 以有病为借口 plead illness; on pretext of illness; under the pretext of being ill:～离席 take one's leave under the pretext of not feeling well

【托词】tuōcí ❶ 找借口 find a pretext; make an excuse:～谢绝 decline on some pretext ❷ 借口 excuse; pretext; subterfuge:他说有事,这是～,未必真有事。He said he had something to do, which was an excuse and not necessarily true.‖also 托辞 tuōcí

【托辞】tuōcí same as 托词 tuōcí

【托儿所】tuō'érsuǒ 照管婴儿或教养幼儿的处所 kindergarten; nursery; childcare center; creche; place to take care of and/or educate children

【托福】tuō//fú〈客套话 *pol.*〉意思是依赖别人的福气,使自己幸运(多用于回答别人的问候 oft. used to respond to greetings) thanks to you; have luck through relying on another's good fortune:托您的福,一切都很顺利。Thanks to you, everything is going smoothly.

【托福】tuōfú 美国'对非英语国家留学生的英语考试'英文缩写(TOEFL)的音译 transliteration of TOEFL (Test of English as a Foreign Language)

【托付】tuōfù 委托别人照料或办理 entrust (others to take care of or handle); commit (sth.) to sb.'s care:把孩子～给老师 entrust one's child to the care of the teacher|～朋友处理这件事 commit this matter to the care of a friend

【托孤】tuōgū 临终前把留下的孤儿托付给别人(多指君主把遗孤托付给大臣 oft. of a dying monarch to a minister) entrust one's child to sb.'s care (upon one's death)

【托故】tuōgù 借口某种原因 make an excuse; give a pretext:～不来 give an excuse for not coming|～早退 leave early on a pretext

【托管】tuōguǎn 由联合国委托一个或几个会员国在联合国监督下管理还没有获得自治权的地区 trusteeship; one or more United Nations (UN) member states entrusted to administer a region that have not yet achieved autonomy, under UN supervision

【托管地】tuōguǎndì 由联合国委托一个或几个会员国在联合国监督下管理的地区 trust territory; mandated territory; areas administered by one or several member states entrusted by the United Nations, under its supervision

【托疾】tuōjí〈书 *fml.*〉same as 托病 tuōbìng:～推辞 refuse or decline giving illness as an excuse

【托拉斯】tuōlāsī ❶ 资本主义垄断组织形式之一,由许多生产同类商品或在生产上有密切关系的企业合并组成。最大企业的资本家操纵领导权,其他企业主丧失了独立性,成了按股分红的股东。托拉斯的成立,是为了垄断销售市场,争夺原料产地和投资范围,以获取高额垄断利润。trust; form of capitalist monopoly organization composed of merged enterprises that produce the same products or have close production relations, in which the head of the largest enterprise holds sway, and the other owners become shareholders who receive dividends on their shares. The trust is designed to monopolize the sales market, contend for raw materials sources and the investment scope, so as to gain a huge monopoly profit ❷ 专业公司 trust; specialized company

【托门子】tuō mén·zi 为达到某种目的而找门路托人求情 try to find the appropriate channels through which to achieve a goal; solicit help from potential backers:～,拉关系 try to enlist help wherever possible and suck up to influential people

【托梦】tuō//mèng 亲友的灵魂在人的梦中出现并有所嘱托(迷信)(superstition)(of the ghost of a relative or friend) appear in a dream and make a request

【托名】tuōmíng 假借别人的名义 do sth. in sb. else's name; use sb. else's name for one's own purpose:这篇古文是～之作。This piece of classical prose was written by some one using a famous name. *or* This piece of classical prose is not genuine.

【托盘】tuōpán 端饭菜时放碗碟的盘子,也用来盛礼物 (serving) tray; plate used for bowls or dishes when serving a meal, also used to convey gifts

【托腔】tuōqiāng 指戏曲演出时演奏乐器衬托演员的唱腔 (of musical accompaniment to a Chinese opera) accompaniment suitable to complement the singing of an actor or actress:他拉胡琴没有花招,～托得极严。He never tries to show off when playing the *huqin*, instead, he does his best to complement the singing of the actor or actress.

【托儿】tuōr 〈方 *dial.*〉指从旁诱人受骗上当的人 decoy; lure to a swindle; come-on; person who lures sb. into being deceived

【托人情】tuō rénqíng 请人代为说情 ask sb. to put in a good word; also 托情 tuōqíng

【托身】tuōshēn 寄身 find accommodation or a place to live in:～之处 place to live in

【托生】tuōshēng 迷信的人指人或高等动物(多指家畜家禽)死后,灵魂转生世间 be reborn; be reincarnated; (of superstitious people) upon death the spirits of human beings or higher animals (usu. domestic animals and fowls) reincarnated (into new bodies) in the temporal world

【托熟】tuōshú 认为是熟人而不拘礼节 feel familiar enough not to bother about etiquette; not stand on ceremony owing to familiarity

【托运】tuōyùn 委托运输部门运(行李、货物等) consign for shipment; check; entrust transport departments to convey (luggage, goods, etc.):～行李 check one's baggage

【托子】tuō·zi 某些物件下面起支撑作用的部分;座儿 stand; base; support; supporting part under an object:枪～rifle butt or stock

饦 tuō ☞ [馎饦](bótuō) on p.151

拖 tuō ❶ 拉着物体使挨着地面或另一物体的表面移动 pull; drag; tug; haul; draw an object over the ground or other surface:～船 towboat; tugboat; (steam) tug|～地板 mop the floor|火车头～着十二个车皮。The railway engine pulled 12 freight trucks. ❷ 在身体后面耷拉着 trail; drag behind one's body:～着辫子 wear a pigtail|～着个尾巴 drag a tail behind one ❸ 拖延 delay; postpone; drag on; procrastinate:这件工作～得太久了。The job has been dragged on for too long.

【拖把】tuōbǎ 擦地板的工具,用许多布条或线绳绑在木棍的一头做成 mop; swab; implement for cleaning the floor, made from binding cloth strips or cotton strands to one end of a wooden rod; also 墩布 dūnbù or 拖布 tuōbù

【拖驳】tuōbó 由拖轮或汽艇牵引的驳船 lighter or barge (drawn by a tugboat or motor boat)

【拖布】tuōbù same as 拖把 tuōbǎ

【拖车】tuōchē 被牵引车拉着走的车辆,通常指汽车、电车等所牵引的车辆 trailer; vehicle drawn by a tractor, automobile, trams, etc.

【拖船】tuōchuán ❶ same as 拖轮 tuōlún ❷〈方 *dial.*〉拖轮所牵引的木船 wooden barge or lighter drawn by a tugboat

【拖带】tuōdài ❶ 牵引 tow; pull; haul:这些车辆不仅载重量大,而且～灵活,平稳安全。These vehicles not only have a large loading capacity, but are also manoeuverable in traction, stable and safe. ❷〈方 *dial.*〉牵连;牵累 be burdened by or with:受到儿女的～be burdened by one's children

【拖宕】tuōdàng 〈书 *fml.*〉same as 拖延 tuōyán:～时日 delay indefinitely

【拖斗】tuōdǒu 拖车(多指小型的、不带棚的 usu. small with no canopy) trailer

【拖粪】tuōfèn 〈方 *dial.*〉same as 拖把 tuōbǎ

【拖后腿】tuō hòutuǐ 〈比喻 *fig.*〉牵制、阻挠别人或事物使不得前进 hold up or hinder the advance of other people or matters

【拖拉】tuōlā 办事迟缓,不赶紧完成 slow; sluggish; dilatory; act slowly or not finish immediately:～作风 dilatory style of work|办事拖拖拉拉的 be dilatory in doing things; drag one's heels at work

【拖拉机】tuōlājī 主要用于农业的动力机器,种类很多,小型的用橡胶轮胎,大型的用履带。能牵引不同的农具进行耕地、播种、收割等。tractor; motor vehicle in multiple varieties mainly used in agriculture, smaller ones with rubber tires, and larger ones with crawler belts; used to draw various farm tools for land cultivation, e.g. sowing seeds, reaping etc.

【拖累】tuōlěi 牵累;使受牵累 burden; encumber; implicate; be a burden to: 受孩子～be tied down by children|不能因为我而～亲友。My relatives and friends should not be implicated by virtue of their connection with me.

【拖轮】tuōlún 装有拖曳设备,用来牵引船舶或木筏、竹排的机动船 tug; tugboat; towboat; motor-driven ship with towing equipment, used to draw ships or wooden or bamboo rafts

【拖泥带水】tuō ní dài shuǐ〈比喻 *fig.*〉说话、写文章不简洁或做事不干脆 slipshod speech or writing; slovenly

【拖欠】tuōqiàn 久欠不还 be behind in payments; be in arrears; default; be in debt for a long time: ～房租 be in arrears with the rent|～税款 be in arrears with tax payments; default in tax payments

【拖腔】tuōqiāng 指戏曲演出时唱某一个字的音拖长 make one word last over several notes when singing opera

【拖沓】tuōtà 形容做事拖拉;不爽利 dilatory; sluggish; laggard; sloppy and indecisive in action: 工作～dilatory in work|文字繁冗～dilatory and long-winded writing

【拖堂】tuō//táng 指教师拖延下课的时间(of a teacher) not dismiss class on time; exceed time allocated for class

【拖网】tuōwǎng 渔网的一种,形状像袋子,使用时抛在海底,用一只或两只渔船拖曳,兜捕底层鱼虾,如鳗鱼、小黄鱼、对虾等 trawl; trawling net; tow-net; dragnet; bag-shaped fishing net thrown to the seabed and dragged by one or two fishing boats so as to catch fish such as shrimps, eels, little yellow croakers, prawns, etc.

【拖鞋】tuōxié 后半截没有鞋帮的鞋。一般在室内穿。slippers; a pair of shoes without uppers at the back, usu. worn indoors

【拖延】tuōyán 把时间延长,不迅速办理 delay; procrastinate; put off; postpone; prolong the time, not handle immediately: ～时日 play for time; stall (for time)|期限快到,不能再～了。As the deadline is fast approaching, we cannot delay any longer.

【拖曳】tuōyè 拉着走;牵引 pull; tow; drag; draw: 信号弹～着一道长长的尾巴升起。The signal flare rose up, leaving a long tail.|拖轮～着木筏在江中航行。The tugboat sails along the river, towing a raft.

拕 tuō〈书 *fml.*〉same as 拖 tuō

侂(侘、仛) tuō〈书 *fml.*〉委托;寄托 ask; entrust

侻 tuō〈书 *fml.*〉❶简易 simple; easy ❷适当;应当 proper; appropriate; suitable ❸
☞ 通侻 tōngtuō on p. 1918
☞ tuì on p. 1951

捝 tuō〈书 *fml.*〉❶解脱 release; free or extricate oneself ❷遗漏;失误 miss; omit; err

脱 tuō ❶(皮肤、毛发等)脱落(of skin, hair, etc.) shed; drop; lose; come or fall out: ～皮 peel; exuviate; shed or slough off skin|～毛 lose hair or feathers; shed; moult|爷爷的头发都～光了。Grandpa has lost all his hair. *or* Grandpa has gone bald. ❷取下;除去 take off; cast off: ～鞋 take off one's shoes|～脂 defat; non-fat; degrease|～色 decolour; decolourize ❸脱离 get out of; break away from; escape from; extricate oneself from: 逃～succeed in escaping; make good one's escape|摆～break away from; extricate oneself from|～险 escape or be out of danger|～缰之马 bolting horse; horse that has slipped its tether and is uncontrollable; running wild ❹漏掉(文字) miss (words): ～误 omissions and errors|这一行里～了三个字。Three words are missing on this line. ❺〈书 *fml.*〉轻率;轻慢 neglect; slight: 轻～flippant|～易(轻率,不讲究礼貌) rash; indiscreet; impetuous ❻〈书 *fml.*〉倘若;或许 if; supposing; perhaps, in case: ～有不测 if anything untoward should happen|～有遗漏,必致误事。Matters are sure to be bungled should there be any omissions. ❼(Tuō)姓 a surname

【脱靶】tuō//bǎ 打靶时没有打中 miss the target in shooting practice

【脱班】tuō//bān 迟于规定接替的时间到达;晚点 be late for work; (of a bus, train, etc.) be behind schedule: 邮件～。The mail is behind schedule.|飞机～了两个小时。The plane is two hours behind schedule.

【脱产】tuō//chǎn 脱离直接生产,专门从事行政管理、党、团、工会等工作或者专门学习 be released from a production post to take on the work of administration, the Party, the Youth League, the trade union, etc., or engage in specialized studies: ～干部 cadre not engaged in production|～学习 be released from work to receive a period of training

【脱档】tuōdàng 指某种商品生产或供应暂时中断 sold out; out of stock; not in

【脱发】tuōfà 头发大量脱落,多由发癣等皮肤病引起 loss of hair; alopecia; trichomadesis, (of hair) falling out in great quantities, oft. caused by ringworm and other skin diseases

【脱肛】tuō//gāng 直肠或乙状结肠从肛门脱出的病,长期的便秘、腹泻、痔疮等都能引起脱肛 prolapse of the anus; archoptosis; prolapse of the rectum causing the sigmoid to fall out, caused by long-term constipation, diarrhea, hemorrhoids, etc.

【脱稿】tuō//gǎo (著作)写完(of a manuscript) be completed: 这本书已经～,即可付印。The book is finished and ready for printing.

【脱钩】tuō//gōu〈比喻 *fig.*〉脱离联系 cut ties with; separate or disconnect from

【脱轨】tuō//guǐ 车轮离开轨道 derail; run off the rails; (of wheels) leave the tracks: 火车～。The train derailed.

【脱货】tuō//huò 货物脱销;缺货 be in short supply; be out of stock; sold out: 这种药暂时～,四五天后才能运到。This medicine is temporarily out of stock, and new supplies won't arrive until four or five days later.

【脱胶】tuō//jiāo ❶(附着在物体上的胶质)脱落;开胶(of gel stuck to an object) come unglued; come unstuck; come apart ❷去掉附着在植物纤维上的胶质。方法很多,如用化学药剂或细菌破坏胶质,用清水浸渍,加高压蒸气,用人工捶打等。degum; get rid of gel that adheres to vegetable fibre, using methods such as destruction by chemicals or bacteria, soaking in clear water, exposing to high pressure vapor, and artificial tapping

【脱节】tuō//jié 原来连接着的物体分开,借指原来联系着的事物失掉联系,或原来应该联系的事物没有联系起来 come apart; be disjointed; be split; be out of line with; (of connected objects) be separated or parted; (of originally connected components) come adrift (from one other); (of components that are intended to be connected) fragment: 管子焊得不好,容易～。A poorly welded pipe falls apart easily. |理论与实践不能～。Theory must not be divorced from practice.

【脱臼】tuō//jiù same as 脱位 tuō//wèi

【脱口】tuōkǒu 不加思索地开口(说) blurt out; say sth. spontaneously, or unguardedly or without thinking; ready tongue: ～而出 let slip; blurt out; say unwittingly|～成章 words that flow from one's mouth as from the pen of a master; eloquent speech

【脱口而出】tuō kǒu ér chū 不加思索,随口说出 escape one's lips; blurt out; say unwittingly

【脱离】tuōlí 离开(某种环境或情况);断绝(某种联系) separate oneself from; break away from; be divorced from; leave (some environment or situation); break or cut off (some connection): ～危险 be out of danger|～旧家庭 break away from one's old-fashioned family|～实际 lose contact with reality; be divorced from reality|～群众 cut oneself off from the masses; be divorced from the masses

【脱粒】tuō//lì 把收割的庄稼放在场地上碾轧、摔打或用机器使子实脱落下来 threshing; shelling; placing harvested crops on the ground to be threshed; use machine to shell grain

【脱漏】tuōlòu 漏掉;遗漏 be left out; be omitted; be dropped; be missing: 这份抄件～的字句较多。There are numerous omissions of words and sentences in this copy.

【脱略】tuōlüè 〈书 *fml.*〉❶放任;轻慢;不拘束 unrestrained; carefree; treat disrespectfully; slight: ～形骸 unrestrained physical pleasure|举动～unrestrained behaviour ❷(文词)脱漏或省略(of writings) omission; ellipsis

【脱落】tuōluò ❶(附着的东西)掉下(of sth. attached to sth. else) drop; fall out or come away; fall off: 毛发～lose one's hair|牙齿～lose teeth|门上的油漆已经～。The paint on the door has peeled off. ❷指文字遗漏(of writings) omit: 字句～omission of words and sentences (in an article)

【脱盲】tuō//máng 指不识字的人经过学习后脱离文盲状态 become literate; overcome illiteracy; (of a person unable to read or write) overcome through study: 经过扫盲班学习,很多人都已～。Many people are able to read and write through anti-illiteracy classes.

【脱毛】tuō//máo ❶鸟兽的毛脱落(of birds and animals) lose hair or feathers; moult; shed ❷脱羽的通称 general term for 脱羽 tuōyǔ

【脱帽】tuōmào 摘下帽子(大都表示恭敬) take off or raise one's hat (usu. in respect): ～致敬 salute sb. by taking off one's hat

【脱坯】tuō//pī 用模子把泥制成土坯 mould adobe blocks

【脱皮】tuō//pí 表皮脱落 exuviate; peel; shed or slough off skin: 晒得脱了一层皮(of skin) peel after being sunburnt

【脱贫】tuōpín 摆脱贫困 quit poverty; shake off poverty; be lifted out of poverty: ～致富 quit poverty and become rich; go from rags to riches; cast off poverty and become prosperous

【脱坡】tuō//pō 堤坝等水工建筑物的斜坡被水冲塌(of a dyke or dam or other hydraulic structures) slopes that collapse or that are washed away

【脱期】tuō//qī 延误预定的日期,特指期刊延期出版 miss the deadline; (esp. of a periodical) fail to come out on time: ～交货 delay delivery|由于装订不及,造成杂志～。The magazine has failed to be published on time owing to tardy binding.

【脱色】tuō//sè ❶用化学药品去掉物质原来的色素 decolour; decolourize; eradicate the original pigment of a matter by using chemicals ❷退色 fade

【脱涩】tuō//sè 使柿子去掉涩味,通常是把它浸在温水或石灰水里 remove or take away the astringent taste of persimmon, usu. by soaking it in lukewarm water or lime water

【脱身】tuō//shēn 离开某种场合;摆脱某件事情 get away; make good one's escape (from an event or function); extricate oneself (from sth.): 事情太多,不能～too involved to get away|他正忙着,一时脱不了身。He is too involved to get away for the time being.

【脱手】tuō//shǒu ❶ 脱开手 slip out of the hand; let slip; let go:用力一扔,石块～飞出去 a powerful throw that sends a stone flying ◇ 稿子已～,即日可寄出。The manuscript is now out of my hands, and will be posted within a few days. ❷ 卖出货物(of goods) get off one's hands; dispose of; sell

【脱水】tuō//shuǐ ❶ 人体中的液体大量减少,常在严重的呕吐、腹泻或大量出汗、出血等情况下发生 deprivation or loss of body fluids; dehydration; bodily fluids seriously reduced, oft. as a result of vomiting, diarrhea, excessive sweating, or hemorrhage ❷ 物质失去所含的水分,如结晶体失去结晶水,化合物的分子中失去跟水相当的氢氧原子 dehydration; (of matter) loss of moisture content, e. g. a crystal losing crystal water; and molecules of a chemical compound losing the oxyhydrogen atoms equivalent to water ❸〈方 *dial.*〉水田里旱得没有水(of paddy fields) be parched; suffer a drought

【脱俗】tuōsú 不沾染庸俗之气 be cleansed of vulgarity; refined:超凡～stand out from the general run of people, be free from worldly cares; be not of this world; tower above the rest|房间布置得淡雅～。The room is arranged in an elegant and refined manner.

【脱胎】tuō//tāi ❶ 漆器的一种制法,在泥或木制的模型上糊上薄绸或夏布,再经涂漆磨光等工序,最后把胎脱去,涂上颜料 process of making bodiless lacquerware; method of producing lacquer ware where thin silk or grass cloth is pasted onto an earthen or wooden model, painted and polished, and the roughcast finally removed, and colour applied ❷ 指一事物由另一事物孕育变化而产生 metamorphosize (as a butterfly grub does when emerging from a chrysalis):～换骨 be reborn; cast off one's old self; thoroughly remould oneself; undergo a radical transformation

【脱胎换骨】tuō tāi huàn gǔ 原为道教修炼用语,指修道者得道,就脱凡胎而成圣胎,换凡骨而为仙骨。现在用来比喻彻底改变立场观点。be reborn; turn over a new leaf; Taoist term for a monk attaining enlightenment, and being reborn, his mortal body and bones becoming immortal; (fig.) thoroughly change one's position and viewpoint; change one's innate nature

【脱逃】tuōtáo 脱身逃走 run away; escape; flee; break free:临阵～flee from battle

【脱兔】tuōtù 逃走的兔子 fleeing hare:动如～(比喻行动迅速,像逃走的兔子一样)(fig.)run as quickly as a fleeing hare

【脱位】tuō//wèi 由于外伤或关节内部发生病变,构成关节的骨头脱离正常的位置 dislocation; bone that constitutes part of a joint knocked out of its normal position, by injury or internal joint pathology; also 脱臼 tuō//jiù

【脱误】tuōwù (文字)脱漏和错误(of writings) errors and omissions:在校样上检查出不少～之处。Quite a few omissions and errors have been found after checking the proof.

【脱险】tuō//xiǎn 脱离危险 escape or be out of danger:虎口～escape mortal danger; survive a disaster

【脱销】tuō//xiāo (某种商品)卖完,一时不能继续供应(of some product) out of stock; sold out and unable to be supplied for the time being

【脱卸】tuōxiè 摆脱;推卸(责任) shake off; shirk (responsibility):～罪责 shirk or deny responsibility for an offence or crime

【脱盐】tuō//yán 用灌水冲洗等方法除去土壤中过多的盐分 desalt; desalinize; remove excessive salt content from soil with water etc.

【脱氧】tuō//yǎng 除去物质中所含的氧。如在钢水中加入少量的硅铁、锰铁、铝等,除去所含的氧,以提高钢的质量。deoxidate; deoxidize; remove oxygen contained in matter, e. g. add silicon iron, ferromanganese, aluminum, etc., to molten steel to get rid of oxygen and improve the quality of steel

【脱颖而出】tuō yǐng ér chū 战国时代,秦兵攻打赵国。赵国平原君奉命到楚国求救,要选二十名文武双全的门客一起去,但缺一人,毛遂自动请求跟着去。平原君说,贤能的人在众人当中就像锥子放在布袋里,尖儿立刻就会露出来,你来我门下已经三年,没听到过对你的赞扬,你没什么能耐,不去吧!毛遂说,假使我毛遂早能像锥子放在布袋里似的,'乃脱颖而出,非特其末见而已',就是说,连锥子上部的环儿也会露出来的,岂止光露个尖儿!(见于《史记·平原君列传》)后来用'脱颖而出'比喻人的才能全部显示出来。According to *Records of the Historian · Biography of Lord Pingyuan*, when the Qin troops attacked the state of Zhao during the Warring States Period, Lord Pingyuan of Zhao received orders to ask the state of Chu for help. He wanted to take with him an entourage of 20 men well-versed in civil and military affairs, but could find only 19 from his retinue. A retainer by the name of Mao Sui volunteered to join up. Lord Pingyuan said to him, 'A man of talent can be spotted easily among the people, like an awl whose point is immediately exposed once it is put into a cloth bag. As I have never heard anyone praise you since you joined me three years ago, it seems you are not capable. You shan't go!' Mao Sui replied, 'If the awl had been placed into the cloth bag, then not only its point, but the ring on it as well, would have long been shining forth!' (fig.) show one's talent fully (颖 *yǐng*,据旧注,指锥子把儿上套的环 ring covering the handle of an awl, according to an old annotation)

【脱羽】tuōyǔ 鸟类的羽毛在春秋两季脱落，换新的羽毛。moult；(of birds) feathers falling out to be replaced by new plumage in the spring and autumn；通称 generally called 脱毛 tuōmáo

【脱脂】tuō//zhī 除去物质中所含的脂肪质。某些纤维和乳类常常脱脂后应用。defat；degrease；remove any fat or oil contained in certain matter, a process applied to certain fibre and milk products

【脱脂棉】tuōzhīmián 经化学处理去掉脂肪的棉花，比普通棉花容易吸收液体，是卫生用品，也用来制造硝酸纤维 absorbent cotton；cotton treated chemically to remove oil so that it more readily absorbs fluid than ordinary cotton；used as a sanitary product, and also to produce nitrocellulose

tuó（ㄊㄨㄛˊ）

驮 tuó 用背部承受物体的重量 carry or bear on the back：～运 pack；(of horses, mules, etc.) carry a load on the back｜这匹马能～四袋粮食。This horse can carry four sacks of grain.｜他～着我过了河。He carried me on his back across the river.

☞ duò on p. 501

T

【驮轿】tuójiào 驮在骡马等背上的轿子 pack sedan；sedan chair carried on the back of a mule, horse, etc.

【驮马】tuómǎ 专门用来驮东西的马 packhorse；horse specifically used for transporting goods

佗 tuó〈书 *fml*.〉负荷 carry or bear on the back

陁 tuó ☞ 盘陁 pántuó on p. 1443

陀 tuó〈书 *fml*.〉山冈 hill；hillock

【陀螺】tuóluó 儿童玩具，形状略像海螺，多用木头制成，下面有铁尖，玩时用绳子缠绕，用力抽绳，使直立旋转。有的用铁皮制成，利用发条的弹力旋转。whipping-top；children's toy conch-like in shape, symmetrical, often made of wood, with an iron tip on its base, which when wound with a length of rope and released, spins erect, and this spin maintained by whipping；also made from metal and spun by means of the elastic force of a spiral power spring

坨 tuó ❶ 面食煮熟后粘在一块儿(of food made of flour) stick together：面条～了。These noodles have stuck together. ❷（～儿 tuór）坨子 heap；lump：粉～儿 powder lump｜蜡～儿 lump of wax

【坨子】tuó·zi 成块或成堆的东西 lump；heap：泥～clod；lump of mud｜盐～lump of salt｜粉～powder lump｜礁石～reef crag

沱 tuó〈方 *dial*.〉可以停船的水湾，多用于地名，如朱家沱、石盘沱、金刚沱(都在四川) small bay in a river where ships or boats can berth, often used in place names, such as Zhujiatuo, Shipantuo and Jingangtuo (in Sichuan Province)

【沱茶】tuóchá 一种压成碗形的成块的茶，产于云南、四川 bowl-shaped compressed mass of tea leaves produced in Yunnan and Sichuan provinces

砣 tuó〈书 *fml*.〉same as 驼 tuó

驼 tuó ❶ 指骆驼 camel：～峰 hump (of a camel)｜～绒 camel's hair；camel hair cloth ❷（背）弯曲 hunchbacked；humpbacked：老爷爷的背都～了。Grandpa has a hunchback.

【驼背】tuóbèi ❶ 人的脊柱向后拱起，多由年老脊椎变形、坐立姿势不正或佝偻病等疾病引起 hunchbacked；humpbacked；(of human spine) arched forward, sometimes owing to old age, or to an improper sitting posture, or diseases such as rickets ❷〈方 *dial*.〉same as 驼子 tuó·zi

【驼峰】tuófēng ❶ 骆驼背部隆起像山峰状的部分，里面储藏大量脂肪，缺乏食物时，脂肪就供体内的消耗，因此骆驼可以较长时间不吃食物 hump (of a camel)；peak on a camel's back, where fat is stored and consumed when no food is available for external intake, enabling the camel to survive without eating for extended periods ❷ 铁路上调车用的土坡。车辆可以凭本身的重力自动溜到各股铁道上去。hump；slope on a marshalling yard where trains may automatically roll to various railways by their own force of gravity

【驼铃】tuólíng 系在骆驼颈下的铃铛，随着骆驼的行走而发出响声 camel bell；bell tied to a camel's neck, allowing its progress to be heard

【驼鹿】tuólù 哺乳动物，是最大型的鹿，毛黑棕色，头大而长，颈短，鼻长如骆驼，尾短，四肢细长，雄的有角，角上部呈铲形。我国东北大兴安岭地区有出产。有的地区叫堪达罕。elk (*Alces alces*)；moose；largest deer species；mammal with a black-and-brown hide, a large, long head, short neck and tail, a nose as long as a camel's, and long spindly limbs；the male has large flat antlers；found in the Greater Xing'an Mountains of the northeast China；called 堪达罕 kāndáhǎn or 犴 hǎn in some areas

【驼绒】tuóróng ❶ 骆驼的绒毛，用来织衣料或毯子，也可以用来絮衣裳 camel's hair (used to weave dress materials or blankets, or line clothes ❷ ☞ 骆驼绒 luò·tuoróng on p. 1280

【驼色】tuósè 像骆驼毛那样的浅棕色 colour of camel's hair；light tan

【驼子】tuó·zi 驼背的人 hunchback；humpback; hunchbacked or humpbacked person

柁 tuó 木结构屋架中顺着前后方向架在柱子上的横木 girder; horizontal beam used as a main support for the roof truss in a timber structure
☞ 舵 duò on p.502

砣(❶鉈) tuó ❶ 秤砣 movable or sliding weight of a balance or steelyard ❷ 碾砣 stone roller ❸ 用砣子打磨玉器 cut or polish jade with an emery wheel:～一个玉杯 cut jade into a cup
☞ 铊 tā on p.1847

【砣子】tuó·zi 打磨玉器的砂轮 emery wheel for cutting or polishing jade

鸵 tuó same as 鸵鸟 tuóniǎo

【鸵鸟】tuóniǎo 现代鸟类中最大的鸟,高可达3米,颈长,头小,嘴扁平,翼短小,不能飞,腿长,脚有力,善走。雌鸟灰褐色,雄鸟的翼和尾部有白色羽毛。生活在非洲的草原和沙漠地带。ostrich (*Struhio camelus*); largest contemporary flightless bird that lives on the African grasslands and in African deserts, of a maximum height of three metres, with a long neck, small head, flat beak, short small wings, long legs, and strong feet, good at running. The female are taupe in colour, and the male have white plumage on their wings and tail.

【鸵鸟政策】tuóniǎo zhèngcè 指不敢正视现实的政策(据说鸵鸟被追急时,就把头钻进沙里,自以为平安无事) ostrich policy; policy comprising a refusal to face reality (it is said that an ostrich buries its head in sand when in danger)

堶 tuó〈书 *fml.*〉砖 brick

酡 tuó〈书 *fml.*〉喝了酒脸色发红(of one's face) be flushed with drink:～然 be flushed with drink | ～颜 complexion flushed with drink

跎 tuó ☞ 蹉跎 (cuōtuó) on p.338

橐[1](槖) tuó〈书 *fml.*〉一种口袋 a kind of bag:囊～camel

橐[2](槖) tuó〈拟声词 *onom.*〉thud:～～的皮鞋声 thudding of leather boots

【橐驼】tuótuó〈书 *fml.*〉骆驼 camel

鼧 tuó [鼧鼥](tuóbá)古书上指旱獭 marmot as described in ancient books

鼍(鼉) tuó 爬行动物,吻短,体长2米多,背部、尾部有鳞甲。力大,性贪睡,穴居江河岸边。Chinese alligator (*Alligator sinensis Fauvel*); amphibious reptile with sharp teeth and powerful jaws, of a length of over two metres, with a scaly back and tail, living in caves near river banks and sleeping most of the time; also 鼍龙 tuólóng or 扬子鳄 yángzǐè; 通称 popularly known as 猪婆龙 zhūpólóng

tuǒ (ㄊㄨㄛˇ)

妥 tuǒ ❶ 妥当 appropriate; proper; suitable; sound:稳～safe; reliable | 欠～inappropriate; improper; not satisfactory | 这样处理,恐怕不～。I am afraid this is not the proper way to handle the case. ❷ 齐备;停当(多用在动词后 usu. used after a verb) ready; settled; finished; resolved:货已购～。The goods have been purchased. | 事情商量～了。The matter has been settled.

【妥便】tuǒbiàn 妥当方便 proper and convenient:这个办法～可行。This is an appropriate, convenient and feasible method.

【妥当】tuǒ·dang 稳妥适当 appropriate; suitable; proper:安排～well arranged or prepared | 这句话中有一个词用得不～。There is a misused word in this sentence.

【妥靠】tuǒkào 妥当可靠 reliable; dependable; trustworthy:为人～be reliable or trustworthy

【妥善】tuǒshàn 妥当完善 appropriate; proper; well-arranged:～安置 make appropriate arrangements

【妥实】tuǒshí 妥当;实在 appropriate; proper; well arranged; practical and reliable:需要找个～的担保人 need to find a reliable guarantor | 这样办不够～,得另想办法。This is not a proper solution. We must find another way for it.

【妥帖】tuǒtiē 恰当;十分合适 appropriate; fitting; proper; fit:用词～proper wording; appropriate choice of words | 安置得妥妥帖帖 satisfactorily arranged

【妥协】tuǒxié 用让步的方法避免冲突或争执 capitulate; compromise; avoid a conflict or dispute by making concessions:～投降 compromise and surrender | 原则问题上不能～。No compromise of principles should be made.

庹 tuǒ ❶〈量词 *classifier*〉成人两臂左右平伸时两手之间的距离,约合5尺 arm span; distance between two horizontally stretched adult arms, approximately equivalent to five *chi* ❷ (Tuǒ)姓 a surname

椭(橢) tuǒ 长圆形 oval; ellipse:～圆 ellipse; oval

【椭圆】tuǒyuán ❶ 平面上的动点A到两个定点F,F′的距离的和等于一个常数时,这个动点A的轨迹,就是椭圆。两个定点F,F′叫做椭圆的焦点。ellipse. When the sum of the distances between a moving point on plane A to the two fixed points F and F′ equals a constant, the locus of the moving point A is called an oval or ellipse, and the two fixed points F and F' are its focal points. ❷ 通常也指椭圆体 (commonly referring to) ellipsoid

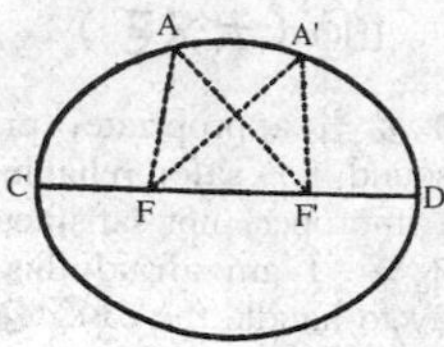

椭圆 Ellipse

【椭圆体】tuǒyuántǐ 椭圆围绕它的长轴或短轴旋转一周所围成的立体 ellipsoid; solid enclosed by an oval or ellipse revolving a circle around its long or short axis

鬌 tuǒ [鬖鬌](wǒtuǒ)〈书 *fml.*〉形容发髻美好(of a woman's coiffure) pretty; beautiful

tuò (ㄊㄨㄛˋ)

拓 tuò ❶ 开辟(土地、道路) (of land, road, etc.) open up; develop; expand; reclaim: 开～open up; develop | ～荒 open up virgin soil; reclaim wasteland | 公路～宽工程 highway broadening project ❷(Tuò) 姓 a surname ☞ tà on p. 1849

【拓荒】tuòhuāng 开荒 open up virgin soil; reclaim wasteland: ～者 pioneer; path breaker; trailblazer

【拓宽】tuòkuān 开拓使宽广 extend; broaden: ～视野 broaden one's view | ～思路 expand one's ideas; broaden one's horizon | ～路面 broaden the road surface

【拓扑学】tuòpūxué 数学的一个分支,研究几何图形在连续改变形状时还能保持不变的一些特性,它只考虑物体间的位置关系而不考虑它们的距离和大小 topology; branch of mathematics based on the invariant characteristics of geometric figures when subjected to any one-to-one continuous transformation, which is only concerned with the relationship between the locations of objects, and not their size or the distances between them

柝(檯) tuò〈书 *fml.*〉打更用的梆子 watchman's clapper or knocker

萚(蘀) tuò〈书 *fml.*〉从草木上脱落下来的皮或叶 fallen bark or leaves

唾 tuò ❶ 唾液 saliva; spittle: ～腺 salivary gland | ～壶 spittoon ❷ 用力吐唾沫 spit; expectorate: ～手可得 get or win hands down; accomplish with great ease; within easy reach ❸ 吐唾沫表示鄙视 spit; spurn (to show one's contempt): ～弃 spurn; contemn; treat with contempt; disdain and reject | ～骂 spurn; spit on and curse; revile | ～面自干 have one's face spat upon and let the spittle or saliva dry without wiping it away; drain the cup of humiliation; be utterly obsequious

【唾骂】tuòmà 鄙弃责骂 spurn; spit on and curse; revile: 当面～spit on and curse sb. to his face | 受天下人～be spurned by the general public

【唾面自干】tuò miàn zì gān 人家往自己脸上吐唾沫,不擦掉而让它自干。指受了侮辱,极度容忍,不加反抗(见于《新唐书·娄师德传》:'其弟守代州,辞之官,教之耐事。弟曰:人有唾面,洁之乃已。师德曰:未也,洁之,是违其怒,正使自干耳')。have one's face spat upon and let the spittle dry without wiping it away — meekly submit to humiliation; swallow an insult in meek submission. According to *New History of the Tang · Biography of Lou Shide*, when Lou Shide's younger brother wanted to resign from his government post as commander of Daizhou Prefecture, Lou told him to be tolerant. His brother said, 'If someone spits in your face, you've got to wipe it clean.' But Shide replied, 'No, that's not correct, for the man could become irritated if you wipe clean the spittle. The correct way to face such an insult is to let the spittle dry.'

【唾沫】tuò·mo 唾液的通称 general term for 唾液 tuòyè

【唾弃】tuòqì 鄙弃 spurn; contemn; treat with contempt; disdain and reject

【唾手可得】tuò shǒu kě dé〈比喻 *fig.*〉非常容易得到 get or win very easily; extremely easy to obtain (唾手 *tuo shou*: 往手上吐唾沫 spit on the hand)

【唾液】tuòyè 口腔中分泌的液体,作用是使口腔湿润,使食物变软容易咽下,还能分解淀粉,有部分消化作用 saliva; spittle; liquid secreted in the oral cavity with which to moisten food, making it soft and easy to swallow, and which also resolves starch and helps digestion; 通称 generally called 唾沫 tuò·mo or 口水 kǒushuǐ

【唾液腺】tuòyèxiàn 人或脊椎动物口腔内分泌唾液的腺体。人或哺乳动物有三对较大的唾液腺,即腮腺、颌下腺和舌下腺,另外还有许多小的唾液腺。salivary gland; gland in the human or animal oral cavity that secretes saliva. Man or mammal has three pairs of such big glands: parotid, submaxillary and sublingual glands, and also many small salivary glands. also 唾腺 tuòxiàn

【唾余】tuòyú〈比喻 *fig.*〉别人的无足轻重的言论或意见 other people's insignificant words or opinions: 拾人～repeat what others have said or written; parrot other's views; plagiarize

跅 tuò [跅弛](tuòchí)〈书 *fml.*〉放荡 dissolute; dissipated:～之士 dissipated person; person who leads a life of debauchery

箨(籜) tuò 竹笋上一片一片的皮 sheaths of bamboo shoots

魄 tuò '落魄'的'魄'的又音 variant for pò as in 落魄 luòpò

☞ bó on p. 151 and pò on p. 1496

T

W

wā (ㄨㄚ)

凹 wā 〈方 *dial.*〉same as 洼 wā,用于地名 used in place names:核桃～(在山西) Hetaowa (in Shanxi Province)

☞ āo on p.18

旮 wā same as 挖 wā

挖 wā ❶ 用工具或手从物体的表面向里用力,取出其一部分或其中包藏的东西 gouge sth. out; dig; excavate; remove sth. with a tool or the hands:～洞 dig a hole|～土 dig earth; do spadework|～个槽儿 dig a trough ◇ ～潜力 tap potentials ❷〈方 *dial.*〉用指甲抓 scratch with fingernails

【挖补】wābǔ 把坏的地方去掉,用新的材料补上 patch up; mend by replacing a damaged part with new material:～衣服 patch up worn-out clothes|～字画 fill in missing characters in a text or missing part in a painting

【挖方】wāfāng 土木工程施工时开挖的土石方 amount of spadework and stonework in civil engineering; cubage of excavation

【挖掘】wājué 挖;发掘 excavate; unearth:～地下的财富 bring buried treasures to light ◇ ～生产潜力 tap potentials for production|～、整理地方戏曲剧目 collect and compile repertoires of local operas

【挖空心思】wā kōng xīnsī 费尽心计(多含贬义 oft. derog.) rack one's brains

【挖苦】wā•ku 用尖酸刻薄的话讥笑(人) deride; gibe:有意见就直说,不要～人。Cut all the sarcasm — be straightforward if you have anything to say.

【挖潜】wāqián 挖掘潜力 tap the potentials

【挖墙脚】wā qiángjiǎo 拆台 pull the rug from under

【挖肉补疮】wā ròu bǔ chuāng ☞剜肉医疮 wān ròu yī chuāng on p.1972

哇 wā 〈拟声词 *onom.*〉形容呕吐声、大哭声等 sound of vomiting or crying:打得孩子～～叫。The spanking was too much for the child, who burst out crying.|～的一声把刚吃的东西全吐了 vomit all one has just eaten in a burst

☞ •wa on p.1966

【哇啦】wālā 〈拟声词 *onom.*〉形容说话或吵闹声 hullabaloo; uproar; din:～～地发议论 make a lot of noise while chatting; also 哇喇 wālā

【哇喇】wālā same as 哇啦 wālā

【哇哇】wāwā 〈拟声词 *onom.*〉形容老鸦叫声、小孩儿哭声等 cawing of a crow; crying of a baby

洼(窪) wā ❶ 凹陷 low-lying; depression:～地 depression|这地太～。This land is too low-lying to be of any use. ❷ (～儿 wār)凹陷的地方 depression:水～儿 water-logged depression

【洼地】wādì 低洼的地方 low-lying land

【洼陷】wāxiàn 凹陷(多指地面 oft. of ground) sunken; depressed:路面～。The road surface has caved in.|颧骨隆起,两眼～ protruding cheekbones and sunken eye sockets

𠰷 wā 𠰷底(Wādǐ),地名,在山西 Wadi, name of a place in Shanxi Province

窊 wā same as 洼 wā,用于地名 [used in place names]:南～子(在山西) Nanwazi (name of a place in Shanxi Province)

娲(媧) wā 女娲,我国古代神话中炼石补天的神 Nüwa, the goddess in Chinese mythology who patched up the sky with multihued stone

蛙(鼃) wā 两栖动物的一科,无尾,后肢长,前肢短,趾有蹼,善于跳跃和泅水。捕食昆虫。种类很多,青蛙是常见的蛙科动物。frog (*Rana nigromaculata*); tailless amphibian having webbed feet, with short forelegs and long hind legs adapted for leaping and swimming, preying on insects, and coming in a good variety. Frog is a commonly seen ranid.

【蛙泳】wāyǒng 游泳的一种姿势,也是游泳项目之一,运动员俯卧在水面,两臂划水,同时两腿蹬、夹水。因像蛙游的姿势而得名。breaststroke; frog style; swimming in which a person lies face down in the water and extends the arms in front of the head, then sweeps them both back laterally under the surface of the water while performing a frog kick

wá (ㄨㄚˊ)

娃 wá ❶ (～儿 wár)小孩儿 baby; child:女～ girl|男～ boy ❷〈方 *dial.*〉某些幼小的动物 newborn animal:鸡～ chick

【娃娃】wá•wa 小孩儿 baby; child:胖～ chubby child | 泥～ clay doll

【娃娃亲】wá·waqīn 指男女双方在年纪很小的时候由父母订下的亲事 nuptials pre-arranged during one's childhood; betrothal of a little boy and a little girl arranged by parents of both sides

【娃娃生】wá·washēng 戏曲中生角的一类，专演大嗓子儿童的角色，一般由年幼的演员扮演 subdivision of the young man's role in traditional opera, representing loud-voiced boys and oft. played by a child

【娃娃鱼】wá·wayú 大鲵（ní）的俗称 popular term for 大鲵 dàní

【娃子】[1] wá·zi 〈方 *dial.*〉❶ 小孩儿 baby; child ❷ 某些幼小的动物 young animal: 猪～piglet

【娃子】[2] wá·zi 〈旧时 *old*〉凉山等少数民族地区的奴隶 slave among the minority ethnic peoples in the Liangshan Mountains

wǎ（ㄨㄚˇ）

瓦[1] wǎ ❶ 铺屋顶用的建筑材料，一般用泥土烧成，也有用水泥等材料制成的，形状有拱形的、平的或半个圆筒形的等 tile; vaulted, flat or semi-cylindrical slab of hard material such as baked clay or cement, laid in rows to cover roofs ❷ 用泥土烧成的 earthen: ～盆 earthen basin | ～器 earthenware

瓦[2] wǎ 瓦特的简称 abbr. for 瓦特 wǎtè

☞ wà on p. 1965

【瓦当】wǎdāng 〈古代 *arch.*〉称瓦背向上的滴水瓦的瓦头为瓦当，呈圆形或半圆形，上有图案或文字 tile ends; eaves tile; dripping tile placed upside down, cylindrical or semi-cylindrical in shape, and with patterns or characters on it

【瓦釜雷鸣】wǎ fǔ léi míng 〈比喻 *fig.*〉无才无德的人占据高位，煊赫一时（见于《楚辞·卜居》：'黄钟毁弃，瓦釜雷鸣。'）unworthy man holding a high position. (According to *The Elegies of Chu·Divination*, 'while bronze bells were destroyed and gone, earthen crocks were left, sounding like thunder.' 瓦釜 *wa fu*: 用黏土烧制的锅 crock made from clay)

【瓦工】wǎgōng ❶ 指砌砖、盖瓦等工作 brick laying, tiling or plastering ❷ 做上述工作的建筑工人 bricklayer; tiler; plasterer

【瓦灰】wǎhuī 深灰色 dark grey

【瓦匠】wǎ·jiang same as 瓦工 wǎgōng ②

【瓦解】wǎjiě ❶〈比喻 *fig.*〉崩溃或分裂 disintegrate; collapse: 土崩～ fall apart ❷ 使对方的力量崩溃 rout: ～敌人 rout one's enemy

【瓦剌】Wǎlà 明代指我国西蒙古各部，清代叫卫拉特或额鲁特。居住在巴尔喀什湖以东以南，包括现在新疆北部及今蒙古国西部的广大地区。15 世纪时，曾一度统一蒙古各部。Oirat Mongols; branch of Mongolian people inhabiting present-day western Inner Mongolia during the Ming Dynasty; transliterated as *weilate* or *elute* in Chinese during the Qing Dynasty to refer to Mongolians inhabiting east and south of the Barkol Lake, including present-day north Xinjing and west Mongolia. The Oirat Mongols had once unified all the Mongol tribes during the 15th century.

【瓦蓝】wǎlán 蔚蓝 azure: ～的天空 azure sky

【瓦楞】wǎléng same as 瓦垄 wǎlǒng

【瓦楞纸】wǎléngzhǐ 呈瓦楞形的厚纸，多作包装用 corrugated cardboard, oft. used as packaging material

【瓦砾】wǎlì 破碎的砖头瓦片 debris; rubbles; ruins: ～堆 pile of rubbles | 一片～（形容建筑物被破坏后的景象）(of buildings that have been destroyed) in shambles

【瓦亮】wǎliàng 非常光亮 very bright: 锃光～ shining bright | 车擦得油光～。The car was polished to shine.

【瓦垄】wǎlǒng（～儿 wǎlǒngr）屋顶上用瓦铺成的凸凹相间的行列 tiles arranged on a roof in alternately convex and concave rows; also 瓦楞 wǎléng

【瓦圈】wǎquān 自行车、三轮车等车轮上安装轮胎的钢圈（of a bicycle or cart wheel）rim; circular strip of steel forming the connection between a wheel and tyre; also 车圈 chēquān

【瓦全】wǎquán 〈比喻 *fig.*〉没有节气，苟且偷生（常与'玉碎'对举 oft. used as antonym to 'broken jade'）unbroken piece of pottery — live a shameful life: 宁为玉碎，不为～ rather die on one's feet than live on one's knees

【瓦斯】wǎsī 气体，特指各种可燃气体，如煤气、沼气等 gas, esp. combustible gas such as coal gas and methane, etc.

【瓦特】wǎtè 功率单位，1 秒钟作 1 焦耳的功，功率就是 1 瓦特。这个单位名称是为纪念英国发明家瓦特(James Watt)而定的。watt; unit of power equal to 1 joule per second, named in memory of the British inventor James Watt; 简称 abbr. 瓦 wǎ

【瓦特小时计】wǎtèxiǎoshíjì 以千瓦小时为单位来计量用电量的仪表 watt-hour meter; meter measuring electricity consumed in kilowatt hour; 通称 popularly known as 电表 diànbiǎo

【瓦头】wǎtóu 滴水瓦头上下垂的边儿 drooping end of an eaves tile

佤 Wǎ ☞ 佤族 wǎzú

【佤族】Wǎzú 我国少数民族之一，分布在云南 Was; Wa people, an ethnic group inhabiting Yunnan Province

wà（ㄨㄚˋ）

瓦 wà 盖（瓦）tile (a roof): 这排房子的房顶都苫好了，就等着～瓦（wǎ）了。With their

roofs already covered with straw mats, this row of dwellings are ready for tiling.
☞ wǎ on p.1965

【瓦刀】wàdāo 瓦工所用的工具,多用铁嵌钢制成,形状略像菜刀,用来砍断砖瓦,涂抹泥灰 bricklayer's cleaver; cleaver-shaped iron tool with a steel blade for breaking bricks and plastering

袜(襪、韤) wà 袜子 socks; stockings; hose: ~底儿 sock hole | ~筒 leg of a stocking | 丝~ pantyhose | 尼龙~ nylon socks

【袜船】wàchuán 〈方 *dial.*〉没有筒儿的布袜,形状略像船 cloth slipper roughly in the shape of a boat

【袜套】wàtào (~儿 wàtàor)短筒的或没有筒的袜子,可套在袜子外面,也可单独穿 ankle socks; socks with or without short legs, worn over socks or alone

【袜筒】wàtǒng (~儿 wàtǒngr)袜子穿在脚腕以上的部分 leg of a stocking

【袜子】wà·zi 一种穿在脚上的东西,用棉、毛、丝、化学纤维等织成或用布缝成 socks; stockings; hose; footwear made of cotton yarn, wool, silk, chemical fibre, cloth, etc.

腽 wà ☞ below

【腽肭】wànà 〈书 *fml.*〉肥胖 overweight; obese

【腽肭脐】wànàqí 海狗的阴茎和睾丸,可入药 penis and testes of ursine seal, for medical use

【腽肭兽】wànàshòu ☞ 海狗 hǎigǒu on p.755

W

·wa (·ㄨㄚ)

哇 ·wa 〈助词 *aux.*〉'啊'受到前一字收音 u 或 ao 的影响而发生的变音 inflexion of 啊 ā after a word ending in u or ao: 才几天功夫~,麦子就长过了膝盖。The wheat has grown more than knee-high in only a few days' time. | 你好~? Well, how are you?
☞ wā on p.1964

wāi (ㄨㄞ)

歪 wāi ❶ 不正;斜;偏(跟'正'相对 as opposed to 'straight') off-centre; askew; inclined: ~嘴 wry mouth | ~戴着帽子 wear one's hat crooked | 这堵墙~了。This wall is a little out of the perpendicular. ❷ 不正当的;不正派的 devious; crooked: ~理 lame argument; sophistry | ~风邪气 undesirable trends; evil winds and noxious influences

【歪才】wāicái 指正业以外的某个方面的才能;不合正道的才能 perverted genius; sb. proficient at the Eclectics

【歪缠】wāichán 无理纠缠 nag; drive one up the wall; get on one's nerves: 人家都不理你了,你还一个劲地~什么。Why don't you stop nagging him, who doesn't even want to talk to you?

【歪打正着】wāi dǎ zhèng zháo (~儿 wāi dǎ zhèng zháor)〈比喻 *fig.*〉方法本来不恰当,却侥幸得到满意的结果 hit the mark by a fluke; score a lucky hit

【歪道】wāidào (~儿 wāidàor) ❶ 不正当的途径;邪道 evil ways; depraved life; vice: 年纪轻轻的,可不能走~。You are still young — on no account should you go astray. ❷ 坏主意 bad ideas: 这家伙想的尽是~。The guy can come up with nothing but bad ideas. also 歪道道儿 wāidào·daor

【歪风】wāifēng 不正派的作风;不好的风气 unhealthy trend: ~邪气 evil trends and noxious influences | 刹住铺张浪费的~。Check the trend of extravagance and waste.

【歪理】wāilǐ 强辩的、不正确的道理 falsehood; fallacy: 你这套~到哪儿也行不通。Your sophistries get you nowhere.

【歪门邪道】wāi mén xié dào 不正当的途径;坏点子 crooked ways of doing things; evil ideas

【歪七扭八】wāi qī niǔ bā 歪歪扭扭,不直 crooked; shapeless and twisted; scrawling: 字写得~。He writes a crooked hand. also 歪七斜八 wāi qī xié bā

【歪曲】wāiqū 故意改变(事实或内容) distort; misrepresent: ~事实 distort the facts | 你不要~了我的意思。Don't misinterpret what I've just said.

【歪歪扭扭】wāiwāiniǔniǔ 形容歪斜不正的样子 askew: 纸条上写着两行~的字。The slip of paper was scrawled with two lines of words.

【歪斜】wāixié 不正或不直 askew; aslant: 身子~,有点站立不稳。He kept staggering, and couldn't steady himself.

㖞(喎) wāi (嘴)歪 (of the mouth) awry: ~斜 wry mouth

【㖞斜】wāixié 嘴、眼等歪余 be wry of mouth and eyes: 口眼~ wry-mouthed and cockeyed

咼 wāi 〈叹词 *interj.*〉表示招呼 hey: ~,你住在哪儿? Hey, where do you live?

wǎi (ㄨㄞˇ)

㧟 wǎi 〈方 *dial.*〉舀 ladle out; scoop up: 从水缸里~了一瓢水 scoop a ladle of water out of a vat

崴(❸ 踒) wǎi ❶ 山路不平 bumpy mountain footpath ❷ 崴子(用于地名 used in place names) bend: 海参~ Haishenwai, the Chinese name for Vladivostok ❸ (脚)扭伤(of a foot) sprain; twist: 走路不小心,把脚给~了。I sprained my ankle in a moment of absent-mindedness on the road.
☞ wēi on p.1987

【崴泥】wǎi//ní 陷在烂泥里 bogged down in mire;〈比喻 *fig.*〉陷入困境,事情不易处理 land in trouble; in deep water; get into a fix

【崴子】wǎi·zi〈方 *dial.*〉山、水弯曲的地方(多用于地名 waizi, oft. used in place names) river bend and mountain recess:迟家~(在辽宁) Chijia Waizi, name of a place in Liaoning Province|三道~(在吉林) Sandao Waizi, name of a place in Jilin Province

wài(ㄨㄞˋ)

外[1] wài ❶ 外边;外边的(跟'内'或'里'相对 as opposed to 'in' or 'inner')out; outside:~表 appearance; looks|~伤 injury|~国 foreign country|门~outdoors|出~leave for somewhere|课~活动 extracurricular activity ❷ 指自己所在地以外的 other (than one's own):~地 other place|~埠 other city|~省 other province ❸ 外国;外国的 foreign:~文 foreign language|古今中~ past and present, Chinese and foreign|对~贸易 foreign trade ❹ 称母亲、姐妹或女儿方面的亲戚 relatives of one's mother, sister or daughter:~祖母 maternal grandmother|~甥 nephew|~孙 daughter's son; grandson ❺ 关系疏远的 not closely related:~人 outsiders|见~ treat sb. as an outsider ❻ 另外 what's more; in addition; furthermore:~加 plus; extra|~带 in addition; as well; besides ❼ 以外 besides; apart from:此~besides|除~except; excluding|六百里~ 600 *li* away ❽ 非正式的;非正规的 unofficial:~号 nickname|~传 (of news, secret, etc.) leak|《儒林~史》*The Scholars*

外[2] wài 戏曲角色行当,扮演老年男子 (in traditional opera) role for old men

【外币】wàibì 外国的货币 foreign currency

【外边】wài·bian ❶(~儿 wài·bianr)超出某一范围的地方 out there; outside:~有人敲门。Someone out there is knocking at the door.|院子~新栽了一些树。Some trees have just been planted outside the courtyard.|这事~早就传开了,我们却不知道。This has long been public knowledge — only we are kept in the dark. ❷ 指外地 place other than one's own:他刚从~来,对当地的情况不大了解。As a newcomer he knows little of the local situation. ❸ 表面 surface; exterior:行李卷儿~再包一层塑料布。Wrap a plastic sheet round the bedroll.

【外表】wàibiǎo 表面 appearance:这架机器不但构造精密,~也很美观。This machine not only is exquisite in structure, but looks nice as well.

【外宾】wàibīn 外国客人 foreign guest; foreign visitor

【外部】wàibù ❶ 某一范围以外 outward; without ❷ 表面;外表 surface; exterior; externality

【外埠】wàibù 本地以外较大的城镇 town or city other than where one is

【外财】wàicái 外快 extra gains

【外场】wàichǎng 指在外面做事所讲究的善交际、好面子、讲义气等方面的事情 be a socialite; sociable:~人儿 socialite|讲究~be a dainty socialite

【外钞】wàichāo 外国的钞票 foreign cash

【外出】wàichū 到外面去,特指因事到外地去 go out, esp. go out of town on business:~谋生 make a living away from home

【外传】wàichuán ❶ 向外传播、散布 spread; leak:这份材料只供内部参考,请勿~。This material is for internal reference. Don't let it out. ❷ 外界传说 it is said; they say

☞ wàizhuàn on p.1971

【外带】[1] wàidài 外胎的通称 popular term for 外胎 wàitāi

【外带】[2] wàidài 又加上 but also; as well:她要洗衣、做饭,~照顾老人,没有时间干别的事了。She simply has no time to spare for other things, having to do all the washing and cooking, besides looking after the elderly.

【外道】wàidào〈佛教用语 *Budd.*〉指不合佛法的教派 heterodoxy; unorthodox sect

【外道】wài·dao 指礼节过于周到反而显得疏远;见外 treat sb. too politely as if to keep sb. at arm's length; be polite to a fault:你再客气,就显得~了。If you stand on ceremony any more, you'll be treating us like strangers.

【外敌】wàidí 外来的敌人 foreign enemy

【外地】wàidì 本地以外的地方 other place:~人 settler; resident from a different region|~货 goods produced somewhere else|他到~旅游去了。He's out touring other parts of the country.

【外电】wàidiàn 国外通讯社的电讯消息 foreign news agency dispatches

【外调】wàidiào ❶ 调出;向其他地方或单位调(物资、人员) transfer (materials or personnel) to other localities or organizations:完成日用品的~任务 fulfil the task of shipping out supplies of daily necessities|有一部分机关干部要~。Some of the government functionaries will be transferred to other places. ❷ 到外地、外单位调查 investigate an internal case through outside channels:内查~ investigate within and without an organisation

【外耳】wài'ěr 耳朵最外面的一部分,由耳郭、外听道和鼓膜构成 external ear, consisting of auricle, auditory canal and eardrum;(图见 ☞ figure for 耳朵 ěr·duo on p.512)

【外耳道】wài'ěrdào 外听道 auditory canal; external auditory meatus

【外耳门】wài'ěrmén 外耳道的开口,呈圆形,内连外耳道,外连耳郭 porus austicus externus, round hole linking the auditory canal within and the auricle without; also 耳孔 ěrkǒng; popularly known as 耳朵眼儿 ěr・duoyǎnr

【外藩】wàifān 封建时代有封地的诸侯王。也泛指藩属。duke of a vassal state during the feudal times; (in a broad sense) all the dukedoms

【外分泌】wàifēnmì 人或高等动物体内,有些腺体的分泌物通过导管排出体外或引至体内其他部分,这种分泌叫做外分泌。具有外分泌功能的腺体叫外分泌腺,如唾腺、胃腺等。exocrine; external secretion; (of human beings or higher animals) secreting out of the body or to some other part of the body through a duct. There are such exocrine glands as the salivary gland and the gastric gland.

【外稃】wàifū 小麦等植物的花的外面包着的硬壳 lemma; outer or lower of the two bracts that enclose the flower in wheat and some other grass spikelets

【外敷】wàifū (把药膏等)涂抹在患处(区别于'内服' as compared with 'oral administration' or 'take orally') apply (ointment, etc.) externally

【外感】wàigǎn 〈中医 *Chin. med.*〉指由风、寒、暑、湿等侵害而引起的疾病 disease caused by such external factors as wind, cold, heat and humidity

【外港】wàigǎng 某个没有港口或没有良好港口的城市附近的较好的港口叫做这个城市的外港 outport; small port in the vicinity of a city without a port or without a fine port

【外公】wàigōng 外祖父 maternal grandfather

【外功】wàigōng (～儿 wàigōngr)锻炼筋、骨、皮的武术(区别于'内功' as compared with 'internal exercise') external exercise; exercises to benefit the muscles, bones and skin

【外骨骼】wàigǔgé 昆虫、虾、蟹等动物露在身体表面的骨骼 ectoskeleton; exoskeleton; hard outer structure, such as the shell of an insect, shrimp and crab, that provides protection or support for an organism; ☞骨骼 gǔgé on p. 693

【外观】wàiguān 物体从外表看的样子 appearance; exterior:这套家具～典雅。This set of furniture looks elegant.

【外国】wàiguó 本国以外的国家 foreign country

【外国语】wàiguóyǔ 外国的语言(包括文字) foreign language (written form included)

【外海】wàihǎi 离陆地较远的海域 pelagic sea; sea that is far away from land:开发～渔场 open up deep-sea fishery

【外行】wàiháng ❶ 对某种事情或工作不懂或没有经验 amateurish; nonprofessional; having no knowledge or experience for certain thing or work:～话 nonprofessional talk|种庄稼他可不～。He is not a novice in farming. ❷ 外行的人 nonprofessional; amateur; outsider

【外号】wàihào (～儿 wàihàor)人的本名以外,别人根据他的特征给他另起的名字,大都含有亲昵、憎恶或开玩笑的意味 nickname; descriptive name that oft. sounds endearing, derogative, or humorous, replacing the actual name of a person

【外话】wàihuà 〈方 *dial.*〉见外的话 unduly polite words that a friend is not expected to say

【外踝】wàihuái 踝部外侧的突起部分,由腓骨下端构成 external malleolus; malleolus lateralis; protruding part of the ankle consisting of the lower end of the splinter bone

【外患】wàihuàn 来自国外的祸害,指外国的侵略 foreign aggression:内忧～ home unrest and foreign aggression

【外汇】wàihuì ❶ 用于国际贸易清算的外国货币和可以兑换外国货币的支票、汇票、期票等证券 foreign exchange; foreign currency that is instrumental in settling international trade transactions, or negotiable bill such as cheque, P. O., and promissory note, that can be converted into a foreign currency ❷ 外币 foreign currency

【外货】wàihuò 从外国来的货物 imports; goods from a foreign country

【外祸】wàihuò same as 外患 wàihuàn

【外籍】wàijí ❶ 外地户籍;外地 having one's permanent residence registered elsewhere:他是～人,我是本地人。He's not a local, but I am. ❷ 外国国籍 foreign nationality:～商人 foreign businesspeople|～飞机 foreign aircraft

【外寄生】wàijìshēng 一种生物寄居在另一种生物的体表,并摄取养分以维持生活,如虱、蚤都以这种方式生活 ectoparasitic; (of an organism, such as louse and flea) living parasitically on the body of another organism for nutrients to survive

【外加】wàijiā 另外加上 extra; in addition:点了四菜一汤,～一个拼盘 have ordered four dishes and one soup, in addition to an assorted cold dish

【外家】wàijiā ❶ 指外祖父、外祖母家 maternal grandparents' ❷ 〈方 *dial.*〉娘家 married woman's parents' home ❸ 〈书 *fml.*〉指岳父母家 home of a man's parents-in-law ❹ 〈旧社会 *pre-1949*〉已婚男子在自己原来的家以外另成的家 house for a mistress or concubine ❺ 与有妻男子另外成家的妇女叫做那个男子的外家 mistress; concubine; woman who lives with a married man

【外间】wàijiān ❶ (～儿 wàijiānr)相连的几间屋子里直接通到外面的房间 outer room ❷ 指外界 external world; outside circles:～传闻,不可尽信。Hearsays from outside are to be taken with a pinch of salt.

【外交】wàijiāo 一个国家在国际关系方面的活动,如参加国际组织和会议,跟别的国家互派使节、进行谈判、签订条约和协定等 diplomacy;

activity of a country in conducting international relations, such as taking part in a world organization, attending an international conference, exchanging envoys with another country, and negotiating alliances, treaties and agreements

【外交辞令】wàijiāo cílìng 适合于外交场合的话语。借指客气、得体而无实际内容的话。diplomatic parlance; remark that sounds polite and decent enough to show one's tact and skill in dealing with people, but has no substance

【外交特权】wàijiāo tèquán 驻在国为保证他国的外交代表履行职务而给予其本人和有关人员的特权，如人身、住所不受侵犯，免受行政管辖、司法裁判，免除关税、海关检查，以及使用密码通信和派遣外交信使等 diplomatic prerogatives; privileges accorded to a diplomat and related personnel by their resident country to guarantee their right to fulfill their duty, such as inviolability of person and residence, exemption from administration restrictions, juristic judgment, customs duties and inspections, the use of secret codes for communications, and the dispatch of diplomatic messengers, etc.

【外交团】wàijiāotuán 驻在一个国家的各国使节组成的团体。外交团的活动多限于礼仪上的应酬，如祝贺、吊唁等。diplomatic corps; body of diplomatic personnel in residence at a nation's capital, formed to facilitate social intercourse, such as extending congratulations or condolences

【外界】wàijiè 某个物体以外的空间或某个集体以外的社会 outside; space outside an object; outside community：飞机的机身必须承受住～的空气压力。The fuselage of an aircraft has to withstand the external air pressure.｜～舆论 public opinions

【外景】wàijǐng 戏剧方面指舞台上的室外布景，电影方面指摄影棚外的景物(of theatre) outdoor scene; (of cinematography) scene shot on location

【外舅】wàijiù〈书 *fml.*〉岳父 wife's father; father-in-law

【外科】wàikē 医院中主要用手术来治疗体内外疾病的一科 surgical department; branch of medicine that treats injury, deformity, and disease by manual and instrumental means

【外客】wàikè 指关系较疏远的客人 visitor or guest who is an outsider

【外寇】wàikòu 指入侵的敌寇 invaders; aggressor troops：抗击～ resist foreign invaders

【外快】wàikuài 指正常收入以外的收入 extra income：捞～ make some extra money; also 外水 wàishuǐ

【外来】wàilái 从外地或外国来的；非固有的(一般用做定语 oft. used as an attribute) outside; external; foreign; extraneous：～户 settler's house; household from another place; nonnative｜～语 foreign word

【外来户】wàiláihù 从别的地方迁移来的人家 settler's house; household from another place; nonnative

【外来语】wàiláiyǔ 从别的语言吸收来的词语。如汉语里从俄语吸收来的'布拉吉'，从法语吸收来的'沙龙'，从英语吸收来的'马达、沙发'。word of foreign origin; foreign word; loanword, such as 布拉吉 bùlā·ji from the Russian word *platye*, 沙龙 shālóng from the French word *salon*, and 马达 mǎdá and 沙发 shāfā from the English words 'motor' and 'sofa'

【外力】wàilì ❶ 外部的力量 outside force ❷ 指外界作用于某一体系的力，例如其他原子对某一原子的作用力，对该原子来说就是外力 external force, such as the acting force on one atom from another

【外流】wàiliú (人口、财富等)转移到外国或外地 (of population, wealth, etc.) deplete; drain; outflow：人才～ talent drain｜资源～ depletion of resources｜黄金～ gold bullion outflow

【外路】wàilù 外地；外地来的 not local; from outside：～货 imported goods｜～人 stranger｜～口音 accent of an outsider

【外露】wàilù 显露在外 manifest; show; be an extrovert：凶相～ look fierce｜此人性格内向，不～。The man is an introvert who seldom reveals his inner feelings.

【外轮】wàilún 外国籍的轮船 foreign vessel

【外贸】wàimào 对外贸易的简称 abbr. for 对外贸易 duìwài-màoyì

【外貌】wàimào 人或物的表面形状 looks; appearance：～清秀 look comely｜这几年城市～变化较大。Big changes have taken place in the appearance of this city over the last few years.

【外面】wàimiàn (～儿 wàimianr)外表 outward appearance; exterior：这座楼房看～很坚固。The building looks rather sturdy on the surface.

【外面】wài·mian (～儿 wài·mianr)外边 outside; out：窗户～儿有棵梧桐树。There is a phoenix tree outside the window.

【外面儿光】wàimiànrguāng 仅仅外表好看 good appearance; deceptive appearance：做事要讲实际效果，不能只求～。Whatever you do it is the actual result that counts — don't ever try to be flashy.

【外婆】wàipó 外祖母 maternal grandmother

【外戚】wàiqī 指帝王的母亲和妻子方面的亲戚 relative of a king or emperor on the side of his mother or wife

【外气】wài·qi〈方 *dial.*〉因见外而客气 as polite as a stranger：咱们都是老朋友了，可不兴～。We are old friends, so don't stand on ceremony.

【外强中干】wài qiáng zhōng gān 外表上好像很强大，实际上很空虚 outwardly strong but inwardly weak; strong in appearance but weak in reality

【外侨】wàiqiáo 外国的侨民 alien; foreign national

【外勤】wàiqín ❶ 部队以及某些机关企业(如报社、测量队、贸易公司)经常在外面进行的工作 (in the army or a press, surveying team, trade company, etc.) fieldwork; work done outside the office: 跑～ do fieldwork; run errands|～记者 reporter on the beat ❷ 从事外勤工作的人 field personnel

【外人】wàirén ❶ 指没有亲友关系的人 stranger; outsider ❷ 指某个范围或组织以外的人 person not belonging to a field or organization ❸ 指外国人 foreigner

【外伤】wàishāng 身体或物体由于外界物体的打击、碰撞或化学物质的侵蚀等造成的损伤 injury; wound; damage caused to the skin or other external surface due to shock, collision, chemical erosion, etc.

【外商】wàishāng 外国商人 foreign businessman; foreign merchant

【外肾】wàishèn〈中医 *Chin. med.*〉指人的睾丸 testis; testicle

【外生殖器】wàishēngzhíqì 指男子和雄性哺乳动物的阴茎、阴囊或女子和雌性哺乳动物的阴道 external genital organs; (of man and male mammal) penis and testicles; (of woman and female mammal) vagina

【外甥】wài·sheng ❶ 姐姐或妹妹的儿子 sister's son; nephew ❷〈方 *dial.*〉外孙 daughter's son; grandson

【外甥女】wài·shengnǚ (～儿 wài·shengnǚr) ❶ 姐姐或妹妹的女儿 sister's daughter; niece ❷〈方 *dial.*〉外孙女 daughter's daughter; granddaughter

【外省】wàishěng 本省以外的省份 province other than where one is; other province

【外史】wàishǐ 指野史、杂史和以描写人物为主的旧小说之类 unorthodox history; old biographical fiction:《儒林～》*The Scholars*

【外事】wàishì ❶ 外交事务 foreign affairs: ～活动 diplomatic occasion; publicity function|～机关 government department in charge of foreign affairs ❷ 外边的事；家庭或个人以外的事 things happening in the outside world; non-personal matter

【外手】wàishǒu (～儿 wàishǒur) 赶车或操纵器械时指车或器械的右边(when driving a vehicle or operating a machine) right-hand side

【外首】wàishǒu〈方 *dial.*〉外头；外边 outside; out

【外水】wàishuǐ 外快 extra income

【外孙】wàisūn 女儿的儿子 daughter's son; grandson

【外孙女】wàisūn·nǚ (～儿 wàisūn·nǚr) 女儿的女儿 daughter's daughter; granddaughter

【外孙子】wàisūn·zi 外孙 daughter's son; grandson

【外胎】wàitāi 包在内胎外面直接与地面接触的轮胎，用橡胶和帘布制成，胎面上有凸凹的花纹 tyre; part of a wheel in direct contact with the ground, made of rubber reinforced with cord fabric and surfaced with protruding patterns; 通称 generally called 外带 wàidài

【外逃】wàitáo 指逃往外地或外国 flee to another place; flee the country

【外套】wàitào (～儿 wàitàor) ❶ 大衣 overcoat ❷ 罩在外面的西式短上衣 outer garment in the Western style

【外听道】wàitīngdào 外耳的一部分，是一个弯曲的管子，由耳郭通到鼓膜，表皮上面有绒毛，皮下有皮脂腺，能分泌出黄色的耳垢 external auditory meatus; part of the auricle in the shape of a bent tube that conducts from the outer ear to the eardrum, with downy hair on its surface, and sebaceous gland underneath, capable of secreting yellow earwax; also 外耳道 wàiěrdào;(图见☞ figure for 耳朵 ěr·duo on p.512)

【外头】wài·tou 外边 outside; out; outdoors

【外围】wàiwéi ❶ 周围 periphery ❷ 以某一事物为中心而存在的(事物) peripheral; existing around sth.: ～组织 peripheral organization

【外文】wàiwén 外国的语言或文字 foreign language

【外屋】wàiwū same as 外间 wàijiān ①

【外侮】wàiwǔ 外国的侵略和压迫 foreign aggression and oppression: 抵御～ resist foreign invaders

【外务】wàiwù ❶ 本身职务以外的事 matters having nothing to do with one's own job ❷ 与外国交涉的事务 dealings with a foreign country; foreign affairs; external affairs

【外骛】wàiwù〈书 *fml.*〉做分外的事；心不专 get involved in things which are not one's business; be absent-minded

【外弦】wàixián 拉胡琴时指靠外的比较细的那根弦 (of a fiddle) outside string which is thinner than an inside string

【外县】wàixiàn 本县或本市以外的县份 other county; county other than where one is

【外线】wàixiàn ❶ 采取包围敌方的形势的作战线 exterior line: ～作战 fight on exterior lines ❷ 在安有电话分机的地方称对外通话的线路 (of telephone) outside connections

【外乡】wàixiāng 本地以外的地方 another part of the country; some other place: ～人 outsider; person from some other place|流落～ drifting about in a strange place|～口音 accent of an outsider

【外向】wàixiàng ❶ 指人开朗活泼，内心活动易于表露出来 extroversion; being open and vivacious and ready to expose one's innermost being：性格～ be open and communicative ❷ 指面向外国市场 foreign market-oriented：～型经济 export-oriented economy

【外销】wàixiāo（产品）销售到外国或外地（of product） for sale abroad or in another part of a country：～物资 export goods； goods for sale in other areas

【外心】wàixīn ❶ 由于爱上了别人而产生的对自己的配偶不忠诚的念头，旧时也指臣子勾结外国的念头（of husband or wife） having unfaithful intentions； having the intention to two-time one's spouse； also in old times, meaning intentions of a subject to collaborate with a foreign country ❷ 三角形三条边垂直平分线相交于一点，这个点叫做三角形的外心。外心也是三角形外接圆的圆心。circumcentre； joint of vertical bisectors of the three borders of a triangle； centre of the circumcircle of a triangle

【外形】wàixíng 物体外部的形状 appearance； external form； contour

【外姓】wàixìng ❶ 本宗族以外的姓氏 not of the same surname ❷ 外姓的人 people of a different surname

【外延】wàiyán 逻辑学上指一个概念所确指的对象的范围，例如'人'这个概念的外延是指古今中外一切的人 denotation； extension； class of an object designated by a specific concept； e.g. the denotation of the concept 'man' being all people on the earth planet, dead or alive； ☞内涵 nèihán on p.1399

【外扬】wàiyáng 向外宣扬 spread； publicize：家丑不可～。Don't let the skeleton out of the closet.

【外洋】wàiyáng ❶〈旧时 *old*〉指外国 foreign countries：出使～。Go on a diplomatic mission. ❷〈旧时 *old*〉指外国货币 foreign currency ❸ 远离陆地的海洋 outer ocean：～捕鱼 fish in an outer ocean

【外衣】wàiyī 穿在外面的衣服 coat； outer garment ◇ 披着正人君子的～（of a man who is mean） wearing the cloak of a gentleman

【外溢】wàiyì ❶（财富等）外流（of wealth, etc.） outflow； drain：资金～drain of fund｜利权～。Both the benefits and power have slipped into someone else's hands. ❷ 液体从容器里流出来 spill； overflow：旅客携带的防锈漆～，引起了火灾。The anticorrosive paint carried by a passenger spilled, and caused the fire.

【外因】wàiyīn 事物变化、发展的外在原因，即一事物和他事物的互相联系和互相影响。唯物辩证法认为外因只是事物发展、变化的条件，外因只有通过内因才能起作用。external cause, referring to the connection of one matter to another and the influence of one matter on another. Materialist dialectics holds that the external cause is only the condition for the development and change of a matter and works only through the internal cause.

【外语】wàiyǔ 外国语 foreign language

【外域】wàiyù〈书 *fml.*〉外国 alien land

【外遇】wàiyù 丈夫或妻子在外面的不正当的男女关系（of husband） seeing another woman；（of wife） seeing another man； having an affair

【外圆内方】wài yuán nèi fāng〈比喻 *fig.*〉人外表随和，内心却很严正 outwardly gentle but inwardly stern； round outside but square inside

【外援】wàiyuán 来自外面的（特指外国的）援助 outside help； external assistance, esp. foreign aid

【外在】wàizài 事物本身以外的（跟'内在'相对 as opposed to 'inherent'）external； extrinsic：～因素 external factor

【外债】wàizhài 国家向外国借的债 external debt； foreign debt

【外展神经】wàizhǎn-shénjīng 第六对脑神经，从脑桥发出，分布在眼球的肌肉中，主管眼球向外侧旋转的运动 abducens； either of the 6th pair of cranial nerves that convey motor impulses to the rectus muscle on the lateral side of each eye and facilitate the outward rolling of an eyeball

【外长】wàizhǎng 外交部长 foreign minister； minister of foreign affairs

【外罩】wàizhào（～儿 wàizhàor）❶ 罩在衣服外面的褂子 outer garment； dustcoat； overall ❷ 罩在物体外面的东西 cover：钟上应加个玻璃～。The clock needs a glass cover.

【外痔】wàizhì 生在肛门外部的痔疮 external piles； external haemorrhoids

【外传】wàizhuàn〈旧指 *old*〉正史以外的传记 unauthorized biography ☞wàichuán on p.1967

【外资】wàizī 由外国投入的资本 foreign investment； foreign capital：～企业 foreign-invested enterprise｜吸收～ incorporate foreign investment

【外子】wàizǐ〈书 *fml.*〉对人称自己的丈夫 my husband

【外族】wàizú ❶ 本家族以外的人 people not of the same clan ❷ 本国以外的人；外国人 foreigner； alien ❸ 我国历史指本民族以外的民族 historical term referring to ethnic peoples other than the Han

【外祖父】wàizǔfù 母亲的父亲 maternal grandfather

【外祖母】wàizǔmǔ 母亲的母亲maternal grandmother

wān（ㄨㄢ）

弯（彎） wān ❶ 弯曲 curl； curve； winding：～路 winding road｜树枝都被

雪压～了。The branches were weighted down by the snow. ❷ 使弯曲 bend:～腰 bend one's waist|～着身子(of one's body) bend over ❸ (～儿 wānr)弯子 turn; wind:转～抹角 full of twists and turns; beat about the bush|这根竹竿有个～儿。There is a bend in the bamboo pole. ❹〈书 *fml.*〉拉(弓) pull (a bow)

【弯度】wāndù 物体弯曲的程度 curvature; (of an object) state of being curved

【弯路】wānlù 不直的路 crooked road;〈比喻 *fig.*〉工作、学习等不得法而多费的冤枉工夫 detour; roundabout course; waste of time and effort due to improper methodology in work or study

【弯曲】wānqū 不直 circuitous; anfractuous; bending:小溪弯弯曲曲地顺着山沟流下去。The tiny brook meanders its way down the valley.

【弯子】wān·zi 弯曲的部分 turn; curve; also 弯儿 wānr

剜 wān (用刀子等) 挖 gouge out (wih a knife, etc.); dig out:～野菜 dig for wild vegetables

【剜肉医疮】wān ròu yī chuāng〈比喻 *fig.*〉只顾眼前,用有害的方法来救急 cut flesh to cure a boil; use a stopgap to the jeopardy of one's long-term interests (疮 *chuang*:伤口 boil); also 剜肉补疮 wān ròu bǔ chuāng or 挖肉补疮 wā ròu bǔ chuāng

帵 wān [帵子](wān·zi)〈方 *dial.*〉剪裁衣服剩下的大片的布料,特指剪裁中式衣服挖夹肢窝剩下的那块布料 a large piece of cloth remaining after a garment has been cut out, esp. the one remaining under the armpit of a Chinese-style garment

W

塆(壪) wān 山沟里的小块平地,多用于地名 *wan*, referring to a recess in a mountain valley, oft. used as place names

湾(灣) wān ❶ 水流弯曲的地方 bend of a river:河～river bend ❷ 海湾 bay; gulf:港～ harbour|渤海～ Bohai Bay ❸ 使船停住 moor; cast anchor:把船～在那边。Moor the boat over there.

【湾泊】wānbó (船只)停留;停泊 anchor; berth:岸边～着两只大船。Two boats were anchored along the riverbank.

蜿 wān [蜿蜒](wānyán) ❶ 蛇类爬行的样子 (of a snake) wriggle; twist ❷ (山脉、河流、道路等)弯弯曲曲的延伸 (of a mountain, river, road, etc.) serpentine; meander; wind

豌 wān [豌豆](wāndòu) ❶ 一年生或二年生草本植物,羽状复叶,小叶卵形,花白色或淡紫红色,结荚果,种子略作球形。嫩荚和种子供食用。pea (*Pisum sativum*); annual or biannual herbaceous plant having pinnately compound leaves, oval-shaped leaflets, white or pale purple flowers, and bearing pods containing roughly globular seeds, with both the tender pods and seeds used for food ❷ 这种植物的荚果和种子 pea pod and seed; pea

wán (ㄨㄢˊ)

丸 wán ❶ (～儿 wánr)球形的小东西 ball; pellet:弹～pellet; bullet|鱼～fishball|肉～meatball|泥～mud ball ❷ 丸药 pill; bolus:～散膏丹 pills, pelvises, emplastrums and unguentums|牛黄清心～bezoar bolus for allaying internal heat ❸〈量词 *classifier*〉用于丸药 pill; bolus:一～药 a bolus|一次吃三～take three pills a time

【丸剂】wánjì〈中药或西药 *Chin. med. or Western med.*〉制剂的一种,把药物研成粉末跟水、蜂蜜或淀粉糊混合团成丸状 bolus; round medicinal preparation made by mixing powdered medicine with honey or starch

【丸药】wányào〈中医 *Chin. med.*〉指制成丸剂的药物 pill (or bolus)

【丸子】wán·zi 食品,把鱼、肉等剁成碎末,加上作料而团成的丸状物 meatball; round food preparation made by mixing minced fish or meat with starch and seasonings

刓 wán ❶〈书 *fml.*〉削去棱角 round off; cut off edges or angles:～方以为圆 cut a square into a round ❷ (用刀子等)挖;刻 carve with a knife; cut

汍 wán [汍澜](wánlán)〈书 *fml.*〉流泪的样子 shed tears

纨 wán〈书 *fml.*〉很细的丝织品;细绢 fine silk fabrics; thin silk:～扇 silk fan

【纨绔】wánkù same as 纨袴 wánkù

【纨袴】wánkù〈书 *fml.*〉富贵人家子弟穿的细绢做成的裤子,泛指有钱人家子弟穿的华美衣着,借指富贵人家的子弟 fine silk trousers worn by sons of a rich family; (in a broad sense) gaudy attire of rich people's children; playboy; beau; scions of the rich and powerful:～习气 bad habit of a playboy|～子弟 dandy; playboy; beau; also 纨绔 wánkù

【纨扇】wánshàn 用细绢制成的团扇 round silk fan

抏 wán〈书 *fml.*〉使受挫折;消耗 frustrate; exhaust

完 wán ❶ 完;完整 intact; whole:～好 remain intact|体无～肤 be smashed to smithereens; be refuted down to the last point|覆巢无～卵。When the nest is overturned no egg stays unbroken — in a major disaster no one can escape unscathed. ❷ 消耗尽;没有剩的 use up; run out:煤烧～了。The coal has been used up.|信纸～了 have run out of letter pads ❸ 完结 be finished; be over:事情做～了。(He) got the job done.|鱼离开水,生命

就～了。A fish is finished once it departs from water. ❹ 完成 fulfil; complete: ～工 complete a project | ～婚 consummate a marriage; get married ❺ 交纳(赋税) pay (tax): ～粮 finish delivering grain as tax in kind | ～税 pay tax ❻ (Wán)姓 a surname

【完备】wánbèi 应该有的全都有了 entire; complete; having all necessary or normal parts, components, or steps: 工具～ complete set of tools | 有不～的地方,请多提意见。Please point out whatever imperfections you have found.

【完毕】wánbì 完结 end; finish: 操练～。The drills came to an end.

【完璧归赵】wán bì guī Zhào 战国时代赵国得到了楚国的和氏璧,秦昭王要用十五座城池来换璧。赵王派蔺相如带着璧去换城。相如到秦国献了璧,见秦王没有诚意,不肯交出城池,就设法把璧弄回,派人送回赵国(见于《史记·廉颇蔺相如列传》)。return the jade intact to the state of Zhao. According to *Records of the Historian · Biographies of Lian Po and Lin Xiangru*, during the Warring States Period, the state of Zhao obtained Bian He's Jade from the state of Chu. After King Zhao of the state of Qin made an offer of 15 cities in exchange for the jade, the king of Zhao sent Lin Xiangru to Qin to conclude the deal. Upon arriving in Qin, Lin presented the jade to the duke of Qin, but soon discovered that the duke had no intention of honouring his offer of 15 cities. Lin managed to get the jade back from the duke and had it sent back to the state of Zhao. 〈比喻 *fig.*〉原物完整无损地归还本人 return sth. intact to its owner

【完成】wán//chéng 按照预期的目的结束;做成 fulfil; accomplish; finish sth. according to plan: ～任务 mission accomplished | ～作业 finish doing one's homework

【完蛋】wán//dàn 垮台;灭亡 be done for; be finished

【完稿】wán//gǎo 脱稿 finish writing an article or book; get one's manuscripts ready

【完工】wán//gōng 工程或工作完成 complete a project; finish doing sth.: 该工程已于上月底～。The project was completed towards the end of last month.

【完好】wánhǎo 没有损坏;没有残缺;完整 in perfect condition; remain intact: ～如新 as good as new | ～无缺 remain intact

【完婚】wán//hūn 指男子结婚(多指长辈为晚辈娶妻 oft. of the elders of a family arranging the marriage for a member of the younger generation) (of a man) get married

【完结】wánjié 结束;了结 end; finish: 工作～ finish one's work; get a job done

【完聚】wánjù 〈书 *fml.*〉团聚 reunite: 合家～ reunion of a family with no member missing

【完竣】wánjùn 完毕;完成(多指工程 oft. of a project) come to an end; be completed: 修建工程～。The construction project has been completed. | 整编～。The reorganization has come to an end.

【完粮】wán//liáng 交纳钱粮 pay grain as tax in kind

【完了】wánliǎo (事情)完结;结束 be over; come to an end: 等此事～,我再找你细说。I'll tell you everything after the whole thing is settled.

【完满】wánmǎn 没有缺欠;圆满 come to fruition; come to a full cycle: 问题已经～解决了。The problem has been completely solved. | 对提问回答得很～。All the questions were fielded to everyone's satisfaction.

【完美】wánměi 完备美好;没有缺点 perfect; flawless: ～无缺 perfect | ～的艺术形式 consummate art form; artistic virtuosity

【完全】wánquán ❶ 齐全;不缺少什么 complete; whole: 话还没说～ fail to spell out the entire story | 四肢～ be full-limbed ❷ same as 全部 quánbù: ～同意 agree with no reservation at all | 他的病～好了。He was completely cured of his disease.

【完全小学】wánquán xiǎoxué 指设有初级和高级两部的小学 six-grade primary school divided into junior and senior sections; 简称 abbr. 完小 wánxiǎo

【完人】wánrén 指没有缺点的人 perfect man: 金无足赤,人无～。As no gold is free from impurities, so no man is perfect. *or* There are lees to every wine.

【完善】wánshàn ❶ 完备美好 perfect; consummate: 设备～。The equipment is in perfect condition. ❷ 使完善 perfect; improve: ～管理制度 improve the management

【完事】wán//shì 事情完结 be settled; finish doing sth.: ～大吉。All is well and propitious. | 结账直到夜里十点才～。The accounts were not settled until ten at night.

【完税】wán//shuì 交纳捐税 pay taxes

【完小】wánxiǎo 完全小学的简称 abbr. for 完全小学 wánquán xiǎoxué

【完整】wánzhěng 具有或保持着应有的各部分;没有损坏或残缺 thorough; integral; unabridged; intact: 领土～ territorial integrity | 结构～ streamlined structure | 这套书是～的。This set of books comes in an unexpurgated version.

玩[1] **(顽)** wán (～儿 wánr) ❶ 玩耍 frolic; gambol; entertain oneself: ～火 play with fire | 孩子们在公园里～得很起劲。The kids were having a good time in the park. ❷ 做某种文体活动 be engaged in cultural or sporting activity: ～儿足球 play soccer | ～儿扑克 play cards ❸ 使用(不正当的方法、

手段等)resort to (oft. foul play):～花招儿 play tricks

玩[2](翫) wán ❶ 用不严肃的态度来对待;轻视;戏弄 dillydally; mess about; toy with:～弄 trifle with; toy with|～世不恭 take a cynical attitude towards life ❷ 观赏 enjoy; appreciate:～月(oft. during the Mid-Autumn Festival) enjoy the moon; let oneself be bathed in moonlight|游～ amuse oneself; go sightseeing ❸ 供观赏的东西 objects to marvel at:古～ curios and antiques

【玩忽】wánhū 不严肃认真地对待;忽视 overlook; be remiss:～职守 dereliction of duty

【玩火自焚】wán huǒ zì fén 〈比喻 *fig.*〉干冒险或害人的勾当,最后受害的还是自己 get burned by playing with fire; play with fire and perish by it

【玩具】wánjù 专供儿童玩儿的东西 toy; knickknack:电动～battery-driven toy|益智～toy designed to enhance intelligence

【玩乐】wánlè 玩耍游乐 amuse oneself:尽情～ play to one's heart's content

【玩弄】wánnòng ❶ 摆弄着玩耍 toy with:～积木 toy with building blocks|～手枪 toy with a pistol ❷ same as 戏弄 xìnòng:～女性 womanize ❸ same as 搬弄 bānnòng:该文除了～名词之外,没有什么内容。There is nothing to this article but a show of technical terms. ❹ 施展(手段、伎俩等)engage in; resort to (underhand means, tricks, etc.):～两面手法 resort to mendacity

【玩偶】wán'ǒu 供儿童玩耍的人物玩具,多用布、泥土、木头、塑料等制成 doll; children's toy made from cloth, clay, wood, plastics, etc.

【玩儿不转】wánr·bu zhuàn 没有办法;应付不了 can't handle; too much to handle:你真没用,这点小事都～。You can't handle a trifle thing like this. Are you good for anything?

【玩儿得转】wánr·de zhuàn 有办法;应付得了 can manage; be up to:几十人的饭菜,你一个人～吗? Are you up to preparing meals for several dozen people?

【玩儿命】wánrmìng 不顾一切,不顾危险,拿着性命当儿戏(含诙谐意 humor.) gamble or play with one's life; risk one's life unnecessarily

【玩儿票】wánr//piào 指业余从事戏曲表演 be engaged in theatrical performance during spare time:他是～的,不是职业演员。He's not professional — just an amateur performer.

【玩儿完】wánrwán 垮台;失败;死亡(含诙谐意 humor.)be done for; be finished

【玩赏】wánshǎng 欣赏;观赏 marvel at; enjoy:～雪景 marvel at a snowy scene|园中有很多可供～的花木。There are so many flowers and trees to be marvelled at.

【玩世不恭】wán shì bù gōng 不把现实社会放在眼里,对什么事都采取不严肃的态度 be cynical; take a hippy's attitude towards life (不恭 *bu gong*:不严肃 not serious)

【玩耍】wánshuǎ 做使自己精神愉快的活动;游戏 have fun; enjoy oneself:孩子们在大树底下～。Children were frolicking under a big tree.

【玩味】wánwèi 细细地体会其中的意味 ponder; ruminate:他的那句话值得～。His words provided a lot of food for thought.

【玩物】wánwù 供观赏或玩耍的东西 plaything; toy; thing to be enjoyed and played with

【玩物丧志】wán wù sàng zhì 只顾玩赏所喜好的东西,因而消磨掉志气 sap one's aspiration by seeking pleasure; play trough life and cherish no serious ambition

【玩笑】wánxiào ❶ 玩耍和嬉笑 play a prank on:他这是～,你别认真。He's just kidding. Don't take him seriously. ❷ 玩耍的行动或嬉笑的言语 joke; jest:开～ make fun of sb.

【玩意儿】wányìr ❶ same as 玩具 wánjù ❷ 指曲艺、杂技等,如大鼓、相声、双簧、魔术 performing art such as ballad singing and storytelling to the accompaniment of drum beats, acrobatics, comic dialogue, *shuanghuang* (two-man act with one speaking or singing while hiding behind the other who does the acting), magic, etc. ❸ 指东西;事物 thing:他手里拿的是什么～? What's that in his hand? ‖ also 玩艺儿 wányìr

顽[1] wán ❶ 愚蠢无知 foolish; obtuse; slow-witted:冥～不灵 thickheaded ❷ 不容易开导或制伏;固执 mulish; stiff-necked:～梗 bull-headed|～疾 chronic disease|～敌 inveterate foe ❸ 顽皮 impish; playful:～童 naughty child; urchin

顽[2] wán same as 玩[1] wán

【顽敌】wándí 顽固的敌人 stubborn enemy; inveterate foe

【顽钝】wándùn 〈书 *fml.*〉❶ 愚笨 dull and obtuse; thickheaded ❷ 指没有气节 impious to moral integrity ❸ 不锋利 dull; blunt

【顽梗】wángěng 非常顽固 diehard:～不化 incorrigibly stubborn

【顽固】wángù ❶ 思想保守,不愿意接受新鲜事物 obstinate; stubborn; be conservative and unwilling to accept new things:～守旧 downright conservative|～不化 be dyed in the wool ❷ 指在政治立场上坚持错误,不肯改变 diehard; refuse to change one's stand or correct one's mistake in terms of politics:～分子 diehard; diehard element ❸ 不易制伏或改变 hard nut to crack:这种病很～,要根治不容易。This kind of disease is too stubborn to be completely cured.

【顽疾】wánjí 指难治或久治不愈的疾病 stubborn disease; chronic ailment

【顽健】wánjiàn〈书 *fml.*〉〈谦称 *hum.*〉自己身体强健 I feel fine; I feel strong and healthy

【顽抗】wánkàng 顽固抵抗 be recalcitrant: 负隅～ put up a desperate struggle; fight with one's back to the wall | 凭险～ be emboldened by a stronghold and resist stubbornly

【顽劣】wánliè 顽固无知;顽皮不顺从 stubborn and stupid: 秉性～ be of a stubborn temperament | ～异常 be unusually obstinate

【顽皮】wánpí (儿童、少年等)爱玩爱闹,不听劝导 (of child, juvenile, etc.) naughty; willful: 这孩子～极了,老师也拿他没办法。The child is so willful that even his teacher doesn't know what to do with him.

【顽强】wánqiáng 坚持;强硬 tenacious; indomitable: ～的斗争 stage an indomitable fight | 他很～,没有向困难低过头。He's a tenacious man who never bows to difficulties.

【顽石点头】wánshí diǎntóu 传说晋朝和尚道生法师对着石头讲经,石头都点起头来(见于《莲社高贤传》)。后用来形容道理讲得透彻,使人心服。According to *Biographies of Great Monks of the Lotus Sect*, when Daosheng, a monk of the Jin Dynasty, preached Buddhist doctrines, his words were so impelling that even the stones in front of him nodded in agreement; (of one's persuasive power) even the insensate stones nod in agreement

【顽童】wántóng 顽皮的儿童 urchin; naughty boy

【顽症】wánzhèng 指难治或久治不愈的病症 chronic and stubborn disease; persistent ailment

烷 wán 烷烃 alkane

【烷烃】wántīng 饱和烃的一类,分子中含有单键结构的开链烃,如甲烷(CH_4)、乙烷(C_2H_6)等 any member of the homologous series of saturated, aliphatic hydrocarbons, such as methane (CH_4), and ethane (C_2H_6); also 石蜡烃 shílàtīng

wǎn (ㄨㄢˇ)

宛1 wǎn ❶ 曲折 winding; tortuous: ～转 lingering ❷ (Wǎn)姓 a surname

宛2 wǎn〈书 *fml.*〉仿佛 as if: 音容～在 as if the person were still around

【宛然】wǎnrán same as 仿佛 fǎngfú: ～在目 as if still in sight | 这里山清水秀,～江南风景。The picturesque scenery in this part of the world is evocative of the land south of the Yangtze River.

【宛如】wǎnrú 正像;好像 just like: 欢腾的人群～大海的波涛。The jubilant crowds are just like the surging waves of the sea.

【宛若】wǎnruò 宛如;仿佛 look like; be akin to: 那棵榕树枝叶繁茂,～巨大的绿伞。With its branches heaping up a luxuriant heap of foliage, the banyan tree looks like a colossal green umbrella.

【宛似】wǎnsì same as 宛如 wǎnrú

【宛转】wǎnzhuǎn ❶ same as 辗转 zhǎnzhuǎn ❷ same as 婉转 wǎnzhuǎn

挽1 (❹❺輓) wǎn ❶ 拉 draw; pull: ～弓 draw a bow | 手～着手 arm in arm; hand in hand ◇ ～留 urge sb. to stay ❷ 扭转;挽回 reverse; retrieve: ～狂澜于既倒 turn the table at a critical moment ❸ 向上卷(衣服) roll up (one's clothes): ～起袖子 roll up one's sleeves ❹ 牵引(车辆) drag; draw (vehicles): ～车 pull a cart ❺ 哀悼死者 lament; elegize the deceased: ～歌 dirge | ～联 elegiac couplet

挽2 wǎn same as 绾 wǎn

【挽歌】wǎngē 哀悼死者的歌 dirge; elegy

【挽回】wǎnhuí ❶ 扭转已成的不利局面 reverse the unfavourable situation; turn the table: ～面子 save face | ～影响 curb the impact of sth. | ～败局 turn the table ❷ 收回(利权等) retract; retrieve (economic rights and interests): 话已说出,无法～。What's said can't be unsaid.

【挽救】wǎnjiù 从危险中救回来 save; rescue: ～病人的生命 save the life of a patient

【挽具】wǎnjù 套在牲畜身上用以拉车的器具 harness (for a draught animal)

【挽联】wǎnlián 哀悼死者的对联 elegiac couplet

【挽留】wǎnliú 使要离去的人留下来 persuade sb. to stay: 再三～ try to retain sb. | ～客人 ask a guest to stay longer | ～不住 fail to retain sb.

莞 wǎn [莞尔] (wǎn'ěr)〈书 *fml.*〉形容微笑 smile: ～而笑 give a winsome smile | 不觉～ cannot help smiling

☞ guān on p. 715 and guǎn on p. 715

娩 wǎn ☞ 婉娩 wǎnwǎn on p. 1977

☞ miǎn on p. 1338

菀 wǎn ☞ 紫菀 zǐwǎn on p. 2542

☞ yù on p. 2351

晚 wǎn ❶ 晚上 evening; night: 今～ tonight | 昨～ last night | ～会 evening party | ～饭 supper | 从早到～ from morning till night ❷ 时间靠后的 late: ～稻 late rice | ～秋 late autumn | ～年 evening years; old age | ～清(清朝末年) late Qing Dynasty ❸ 比规定的或合适的时间靠后 belated; delayed; behind: 八点再去就～了。It would be too late if you go there at eight. | 今年的春天来得～。Spring came a little late this year. ❹ 后来的 later: ～辈 younger generation | ～娘 stepmother ❺ 后辈对前辈自称(用于书信 self-depreciatory term for use in correspondence) your humble... ❻〈书 *fml.*〉靠后的一段时间，特指人的晚年 latter; esp. latter life：岁～ latter part of one's life | ～节 one's moral integrity in old age | ～景 life in old age ❼（Wǎn）姓 a surname

【晚安】wǎn'ān〈客套话 *pol.*〉用于晚上道别（多见于翻译作品 mostly for use in works of translation）good night

【晚半天儿】wǎnbàntiānr〈方 *dial.*〉下午临近黄昏的时候 in the late afternoon; towards dusk; dusk; also 晚半晌儿 wǎnbànshǎngr

【晚报】wǎnbào 下午出版的报纸 evening newspaper; newspaper published in the afternoon

【晚辈】wǎnbèi 辈分低的人；后辈 younger generation; juniors

【晚场】wǎnchǎng 戏剧、电影等在晚上演出的场次（of play, film, etc.）evening show; evening performance; also 夜场 yèchǎng

【晚车】wǎnchē 晚上开出或到达的火车 night train; train that leaves or arrives at night

【晚春】wǎnchūn 春季的末期；暮春 late in the spring; late spring

【晚稻】wǎndào 插秧期比较晚或生长期比较长、成熟期比较晚的稻子 late rice; rice that ripens late because it is transplanted late or takes a longer time to grow

【晚点】wǎn//diǎn（车、船、飞机）开出、运行或到达迟于规定时间（of train, bus, boat, or plane）late; behind schedule; overdue; late start

【晚饭】wǎnfàn 晚上吃的饭 supper; dinner

【晚会】wǎnhuì 晚上举行的以文娱节目为主的集会 evening party; soirée：联欢～get-together | 营火～bonfire party

W

【晚婚】wǎnhūn 达到结婚年龄以后再推迟若干年结婚 marry late; late marriage; marry years later after one reaches the legal age for marriage

【晚间】wǎnjiān 晚上 evening; night

【晚节】wǎnjié ❶晚年的节操 integrity in one's old age：保持～uphold one's moral integrity in old age ❷〈书 *fml.*〉晚年；末期 old age：～末路 one's years are numbered

【晚近】wǎnjìn 最近若干年来 in recent years; during the past few years

【晚景】wǎnjǐng ❶傍晚的景色；夜晚的情景 nocturnal scene; evening scene ❷晚年的景况 life in old age

【晚境】wǎnjìng 晚年的境况 circumstances in old age：～凄凉 miserable life in old age

【晚年】wǎnnián 指人年老的时期 old age; one's later years：～多病 old and sick | 度过幸福的～ lead a happy life in old age

【晚娘】wǎnniáng〈方 *dial.*〉same as 继母 jìmǔ

【晚期】wǎnqī 一个时代、一个过程或一个人一生的最后阶段（of an age, process or person）late stage：肺癌～terminal lung cancer | 19 世纪～ late 19th century; latter part of the 19th century | 这是他～的作品。These are the works he did in his late years.

【晚秋】wǎnqiū ❶秋季的末期；深秋 late autumn; late in autumn ❷指晚秋作物 late-autumn crop

【晚秋作物】wǎnqiū zuòwù 在小麦、油菜等收获后复种的农作物，如玉米、甘薯、马铃薯、豆类在许多地方当做晚秋作物栽培。有的地区叫晚田。late-autumn crop; crop such as corn, sweet potato, potato, and beans, that is grown after a previous crop — wheat, rape, etc. — has been harvested; known in some regions as 晚田 wǎntián

【晚上】wǎn·shang 太阳落了以后到深夜以前的时间，也泛指夜里 evening; time between sunset and midnight; night：～要去看望一个朋友。I'm going to see a friend tonight. | 一连几个～都没有睡好觉 haven't slept well for nights on end

【晚生】wǎnshēng〈书 *fml.*〉后辈对前辈谦称自己（a junior's self-depreciatory term when addressing a senior）your humble student

【晚世】wǎnshì〈书 *fml.*〉近世 modern times

【晚熟】wǎnshú 指农作物生长期长，成熟较慢（of farm crop）late-maturing：～作物 late crop

【晚霜】wǎnshuāng 早春时降的霜。对农作物有害。late frost; frost of early spring, deemed detrimental to farm crops

【晚霞】wǎnxiá 日落时出现的霞 sunset glow; evening glow

【晚育】wǎnyù 女子婚后较晚地生育 late childbirth;（of a woman）give birth late after marriage：提倡晚婚～advocate late marriage and late childbirth

【晚造】wǎnzào 收获期较晚的作物 late crop

脘 wǎn 胃腔 gastral cavity

惋 wǎn〈书 *fml.*〉惋惜 regret; feel sorry for：叹～ sigh with regret

【惋惜】wǎnxī 对人的不幸遭遇或事物的意外变化表示同情、可惜 commiserate; sympathize; feel sorry for others' misfortunes or for the unexpected change of an event：大家对他英年早逝深感～。Everyone felt deeply sorry for his untimely death.

婉 wǎn ❶（说话）婉转（of speech）tactful：～谢 politely decline | ～言相劝 try to persuade tactfully ❷〈书 *fml.*〉柔顺 meek; sweet-tempered; tender：～顺 sweet and gracious ❸〈书 *fml.*〉美好 graceful; elegant：～丽 charming

【婉词】wǎncí same as 婉辞[1] wǎncí

【婉辞】[1] wǎncí 婉言 gentle words; euphemism; also 婉词 wǎncí

【婉辞】[2] wǎncí 婉言拒绝 graciously decline; refuse politely：他～了对方的邀请。He graciously turned down the invitation.

【婉和】wǎnhé（话语）委婉温和（of rhetoric）

tactful; mild

【婉丽】wǎnlì〈书 *fml.*〉❶ 美丽;美好 charming; lovely:姿容～ beautiful of looks and graceful of manners ❷ 婉转而优美(多指诗文 oft. of poetry) subtle and elegant:词句清新～。There is something refreshing and subtly elegant about this poem.

【婉商】wǎnshāng 婉言相商 consult with sb. tactfully and politely:经过多次～,他才同意这个方案。He finally agreed to the plan after repeated friendly consultations.

【婉顺】wǎnshùn 柔和温顺;柔顺(多用于女性 oft. of women) gentle and sweet:性情～ of a sweet disposition

【婉娩】wǎnwǎn〈书 *fml.*〉柔顺 meek; docile

【婉谢】wǎnxiè 婉言谢绝 decline graciously; politely refuse

【婉言】wǎnyán 婉转的话 tactful persuasion:～拒绝 tactful refusal

【婉约】wǎnyuē〈书 *fml.*〉委婉含蓄 subtle and implicit:古人论词的风格,分豪放和～两派。In the eyes of critics of ancient times, the *ci* poetry falls into two schools, the bold and unrestrained, and the subtle and restrained.

【婉转】wǎnzhuǎn ❶(说话)温和而曲折(但是不失本意)(of rhetoric) tactful and indirect (but retaining the meaning one wants to express):措词～ tactful choice of words ❷(歌声、鸟鸣声等)抑扬动听(of singing, bird chirping) have a sweet cadence:歌声～ sweet and melodious notes of a song ‖ also 宛转 wǎnzhuǎn

绾 wǎn 打长条形的东西盘绕起来打成结 wind up and tie a narrow strip into a knot:～个扣ル tie a knot-like button | 把头发～起来 tie up one's hair into a bun

琬 wǎn〈书 *fml.*〉美玉 fine jade

皖 Wǎn 安徽的别称 Wan, another name of Anhui Province

碗(椀、盌) wǎn ❶ 盛饮食的器具,口大底小,一般是圆形的 bowl; hemispherical vessel, wider than it is deep, used for holding food ❷ 像碗的东西 sth. bowl-like:轴～ル axle-bowl

【碗碗腔】wǎnwǎnqiāng 陕西地方戏曲剧种之一,由陕西皮影戏发展而成,流行于该省渭南、大荔一带 *wanwanqiang*, a local opera of Shaanxi evolved from the shadow play and popular in the Weinan and Dali areas

畹 wǎn〈古代 *arch.*〉称三十亩为一畹 *wan*, unit of land measurement equivalent to 30 *mu*

wàn (ㄨㄢ)

万(萬) wàn ❶〈数目 *numerical*〉十个千 ten thousand ❷ 形容很多 large number:～国 all nations | ～事 everything | ～物 multitude of things on earth | ～水千山 vastness of a country; a myriad rivers and a thousand mountains ❸ 极;很;绝对 absolutely; under all circumstances:～全 foolproof | ～不得已 last resort | ～不能行 by no means ❹ (Wàn)姓 a surname

☞ mò on p. 1365

【万般】wànbān ❶ 各种各样 all kinds ❷ 极其;非常 utterly; extremely:～无奈(没有一点办法)have no alternative; have no choice

【万变不离其宗】wàn biàn bù lí qí zōng 形式上变化很多,本质上还是没有变化 change ten thousand times without leaving the original aim or stand; change time and again, yet stay much the same

【万不得已】wàn bù dé yǐ 实在没有办法;不得不这样 out of absolute necessity; as a last resort:～,才出此下策 have no choice but to take a stupid step

【万代】wàndài same as 万世 wànshì:～传扬 carried forward through the ages | 千秋～ eternity

【万端】wànduān (头绪)极多而纷繁;各种各样 (of moods) multifarious:感慨～ a turmoil of feelings wells up in one's mind | 变化～ kaleidoscopic changes | 思绪～ overwhelmed by a swamp of thoughts

【万恶】wàn'è 极端恶毒;罪恶多端 utterly evil; downright vicious:～不赦 iniquitous; be vicious beyond redemption

【万儿八千】wàn·er-bāqiān 一万或比一万略少 ten thousand or a bit less

【万方】wànfāng ❶ 指全国各地或世界各地 every nook and cranny of the country or world ❷ 指姿态多种多样 rich and variegated:仪态～ be graceful in a bewitching way

【万分】wànfēn 非常;极其 very much; extremely:～高兴 feel elated; very happy

【万福】wànfú〈旧时 *old*〉妇女行的敬礼,两手松松抱拳重叠在胸前右下侧上下移动,同时略做鞠躬的姿势(of a woman) curtsy; gesture of respect or reverence made by a woman, in which one hand is loosely cupped in another and moves up and down before the lower-right side of the chest, with her head slightly bowed

【万古长青】wàngǔ cháng qīng 永远像春天的草木一样欣欣向荣 remain forever as fresh as the trees of spring; be everlasting; also 万古长春 wàngǔ cháng chūn

【万贯】wànguàn 一万贯铜钱。形容钱财极多。ten thousand strings of cash; great wealth:～家财 be extremely wealthy | 腰缠～ be a millionaire

【万国】wànguó 很多的国家;世界各国 all nations in the world:～博览会 world exposition

【万户侯】wànhùhóu 汉代侯爵的最高一级,享有万户农民的赋税。后来泛指高官贵爵。marquis with a fief of 10,000 families, the highest ducal rank of the Han Dynasty; (in a broad sense) high officials and noble men

【万花筒】wànhuātǒng 圆筒形玩具,两头镶着玻璃,筒的内壁装着玻璃条组成的几面镜子,筒的一端放着各种颜色和形状的碎玻璃。向着亮处转动圆筒,由于镜子的反射作用,可以从筒的另一端看到各种图案。kaleidoscope; tube-shaped toy that is rotated to produce a succession of symmetrical designs by means of mirrors reflecting the constantly changing patterns made by bits of coloured glass at one end of the tube

【万机】wànjī 指当政者处理的各种重要事情 numerous state affairs:日理～ attend to numerous state affairs on a daily basis

【万劫不复】wàn jié bù fù 表示永远不能恢复(佛家称世界从生成到毁灭的一个过程为一劫,万劫就是万世的意思) lost forever; beyond redemption. In Buddhism, the process of the world from birth to demise is known as a *kalpa* (epoch), and so 10,000 *kalpa* mean 'eternity'.

【万金油】wànjīnyóu ❶ 药名,清凉油的旧称 *Tiger Balm*, old Chinese name for cooling ointment ❷〈比喻 *fig*.〉什么都能做,但什么都不擅长的人 Jack of all trades and master of none

【万籁】wànlài 各种声音 all kinds of sounds (籁 *lai*:从孔穴里发出的声音 sound from a hole):～俱寂 all is quiet in this part of the world

【万历】Wànlì 明神宗(朱翊钧)年号(公元1573—1620) Wanli, title of the reign (1573-1620) of Emperor Shenzong (Zhu Yijun) of the Ming Dynasty

【万马齐喑】wàn mǎ qí yīn 千万匹马都沉寂无声 ten thousand horses standing mute;〈比喻 *fig*.〉人们都沉默,不说话,不发表意见(of people) keep silent; (of public opinion) muffled (喑 *yin*:哑 mute)

【万民】wànmín 广大的老百姓 broad masses of populace:～涂炭(形容广大老百姓陷入极端困苦的境地) entire population in dire misery|～欢呼。The entire nation rejoices.

【万难】wànnán ❶ 非常难于 beyond the bonds of possibility; out of the question:～照办 absolutely cannot do what one is told to|～挽回 utterly irretrievable ❷ 各种困难 all kinds of difficulties:排除～ surmount all difficulties

【万能】wànnéng ❶ 无所不能 omnipotent; all-powerful:金钱不是～的。Money cannot always make the mare go. ❷ 有多种用途的 multi-purpose:～胶 all-purpose glue|～机床 universal machine tool

【万年】wànnián 极其久远的年代 eternity:遗臭～ be consigned to an eternity of notoriety

【万年历】wànniánlì 包括很多年或适用于很多年的历书 perpetual calendar

【万念俱灰】wàn niàn jù huī 一切想法、打算都破灭了。形容失意或受到沉重打击后极端灰心失望的心情。all hope dashed to pieces; abandon oneself to despair; be utterly despondent

【万千】wànqiān ❶ 形容数量多 countless; innumerous; myriad:～的科学家 numerous scientists ❷ 形容事物所表现的方面多(多指抽象的 oft. of abstract things) multifarious:变化～ constant changes|气象～ kaleidoscopic scene|思绪～ myriads of thoughts come to mind

【万顷】wànqǐng 一万顷,形容面积大(of area) ten thousand hectares; vast stretch:碧波～ vast expanse of water|良田～ boundless fertile land

【万全】wànquán 非常周到,没有任何漏洞;非常安全 sure-fire; foolproof:～之策 foolproof strategy|计出～ work out a perfect plan

【万人空巷】wàn rén kōng xiàng 家家户户的人都从巷里出来了,多用来形容庆祝、欢迎等盛况 whole town turning out (to celebrate or to welcome sb.)

【万世】wànshì 很多世代;年代非常久远 all ages; generation after generation:千秋～ eternity|～师表 model for posterity|～不朽 immortal

【万事】wànshì 一切事情 everything; all things:～大吉(一切事情都很圆满顺利) all's well and propitious|～亨通(一切事情都很顺利)。Everything goes without a hitch.|～不求人 be self-independent; never turn to anybody for help

【万事俱备,只欠东风】wàn shì jù bèi, zhǐ qiàn dōng fēng 三国时周瑜计划火攻曹操,一切都准备好了,只差东风还没有刮起来,不能顺风放火(事见《三国演义》第四十九回)。后比喻样样都准备好了,只差最后一个重要条件。During the Three Kingdoms Period, Zhou Yu, general of the state of Wu planned to attack Cao Cao's army with fire. All was ready except that the east wind hadn't risen (see *Romance of Three Kingdoms · Chapter 49*). (fig.) All is ready or in hand except what is crucial.

【万事通】wànshìtōng 什么事情都知道的人(含讥讽意 derog.) know-all; also 百事通 bǎishìtōng

【万寿无疆】wàn shòu wú jiāng 永远生存(祝寿的话) (wish you) boundless longevity

【万水千山】wàn shuǐ qiān shān 很多的山和水。形容路途遥远险阻。ten thousand torrents and a thousand crags; trials of a long and arduous journey

【万死】wànsǐ 死一万次(夸张说法),形容受严厉惩罚或冒生命危险 die ten thousand deaths; be severely punished; risk one's life:罪该～ be so guilty as to deserve ten thousand deaths|～不辞 willing to risk a thousand deaths (for a noble cause)

【万岁】wànsuì ❶ 千秋万世，永远存在（祝愿的话）long live...（good wishes）❷ 封建时代臣民对皇帝的称呼（feudal term of address for an emperor）Your Majesty；His Majesty

【万万】wànwàn ❶ 数目，一万个万，也表示数量大 hundred million；countless ❷ 绝对；无论如何（用于否定式 used in the negative）absolutely：～想不到 have never imagined that...｜～不可粗心大意。On no account shall（we）be careless.

【万无一失】wàn wú yī shī 绝对不会出差错 perfectly safe；cannot fail under any circumstances

【万物】wànwù 宇宙间的一切事情 multitude of things in universe；all things of creation；all things on earth；myriad things

【万象】wànxiàng 宇宙间的一切事物或景象 everything in universe：～更新。Everything has taken on a new look.｜～回春。Nature awakes with spring setting in.｜包罗～ all-encapsulating

【万幸】wànxìng 非常幸运（多指免于灾难 oft. survive a disaster）by sheer luck：损失点儿东西是小事，人没有压坏，总算～。How lucky everyone survived the crash! The loss of a few things was nothing in comparison.

【万一】wànyī ❶ 万分之一，表示极小的一部分 one in ten thousand；extremely small part：笔墨不能形容其～。It simply beggars description. ❷ 指可能性极小的意外变化 eventuality；in case：多带几件衣服，以防～。Bring more clothes just in case. ❸〈连词 *conj.*〉表示可能性极小的假设（用于不如意的事 used for an unfavourable thing）in case；if by any chance：～下雨也不要紧，我带着伞呢。I've brought along an umbrella, so it doesn't matter if it rains.

【万用表】wànyòngbiǎo 测量电路或元件的电阻、电流、电压等的多量程仪表 avometer；multimeter；universal meter；apparatus for measuring resistance, current and voltage in a circuit or component part；also 万能表 wànnéngbiǎo

【万有引力】wàn yǒu yǐnlì 物体之间相互吸引的力 universal gravitation；gravitational attraction；简称 abbr. 引力 yǐnlì

【万丈】wànzhàng 形容很高或很深 lofty；bottomless；infinite：光芒～ shine in full splendour｜气焰～ overweening arrogance｜～高楼 towering building｜～深渊 abyss

【万众】wànzhòng 广大群众；千千万万的人 millions of people；the multitude：～欢腾 millions rejoice｜～一心（of a nation）united as one；of one heart and one mind

【万众一心】wànzhòng yīxīn 千千万万的人一条心 millions of people all of one mind

【万状】wànzhuàng 很多种样子，表示程度极深（多用于消极事物 of sth. negative）in all manifestations；in every way；extremely：危险～ hang by a thread；extremely dangerous｜惊恐～ utterly frightened｜痛苦～ in excruciating pain｜狼狈～ be utterly flustered

【万紫千红】wàn zǐ qiān hóng 形容百花齐放，颜色艳丽（of flowers）in a riot of colour；〈比喻 *fig.*〉事物丰富多彩或事业繁荣兴旺（of a cause, undertaking, etc.）thriving；（of things）richly variegated

沥（澫） wàn 沥尾（Wànwěi），地名，在广西防城各族自治县 Wanwei, name of a place in the Fangcheng Ethnic Autonomous County, the Guangxi Zhuang Autonomous Region

惋 wàn〈书 *fml.*〉贪 covet

腕 wàn（～儿 wànr）腕子 wrist：手～儿 wrist；（图见 ☞ figure for 身体 shēntǐ on p. 1701）

【腕骨】wàngǔ 构成手腕的骨头，每只手有八块 carpus；one of eight bones forming the joint between the forearm and the hand；carpal bone；（图见 ☞ figure for 骨骼 gǔgé on p. 693）

【腕力】wànlì ❶ 腕部的力量 wrist strength ❷〈比喻 *fig.*〉办事的能力；手腕 ability；finesse：凭他的胆识～，完全可以担负起这个责任。Given his courage, insight and ability, he can undoubtedly shoulder the responsibility.

【腕子】wàn·zi 胳膊（或小腿）下端跟手掌（或脚）相连接的可以活动的部分 wrist, the joint between the hand and the forearm；ankle, joint between the foot and the leg：手～ wrist｜脚～ ankle

【腕足】wànzú 乌贼、章鱼等生长在口的四周能蜷曲的器官，上面有许多吸盘，用来捕食并防御敌人 peduncle；tentacle；stalklike organ on the mouth of cuttlefish, octopus, etc, that curls and uncurls, and is attached to a cupula to catch food and for self-defense

蔓 wàn（～儿 wànr）细长不能直立的茎 tendrilled vine：扁豆爬～儿了。The haricot bean plant has developed tendrils.｜顺～摸瓜 follow the vine to get the melon — track down sb. or sth. by following clues

☞ mán on p.1298 and màn on p.1300

wāng（ㄨㄤ）

尪（尫） wāng〈书 *fml.*〉❶ 胫、背或胸部弯曲的病 bent calves, back or chest ❷ 瘦弱 emaciated

汪[1] wāng ❶〈书 *fml.*〉水深而广（of water）deep and vast：～洋 boundless ❷（液体）聚集（of liquid）pool：路上～了一些水。Puddles of water pooled on the road.｜眼里～着泪水 brimming eyes；tears flood one's eyes ❸

〈方 *dial*.〉小而浅的积水坑 puddle; small or shallow pool: 水牛在泥水～里打滚。Buffalos rolled in a puddle of muddy water. ❹ (～儿 wāngr)〈量词 *classifier*〉用于液体[of liquid]: 一～血 a puddle of blood | 两～眼泪 two trickles of tears ❺ (Wāng)姓 a surname

汪[2] wāng 〈拟声词 *onom*.〉形容狗叫的声音 yap; bow-wow; bark: 狗～～叫。The dog yapped.

【汪汪】wāngwāng ❶ 形容充满水或眼泪的样子 (of water or tears) brimming: 水～ brimming with water | 眼泪～ brimming eyes ❷〈书 *fml*.〉形容水面宽广 (of a water surface) vast; boundless

【汪洋】wāngyáng ❶ 形容水势浩大的样子 (of water) immense: 一片～ a vast stretch of water | ～大海 boundless sea ❷〈书 *fml*.〉形容气度宽宏 (of one's mind) magnanimous; broadminded: ～大度 immense generosity

【汪子】wāng·zi ☞汪[1] wāng ④: 一～水 a puddle of water

wáng (ㄨㄤˊ)

亡(亾) wáng ❶ 逃跑 abscond; bolt: 逃～ run away | 流～ go into exile | ～命 flee for life ❷ 失去; 丢失 lose: ～失 missing | 歧路～羊。A lamb goes astray on a forked road. ❸ 死 die; perish: 死～ death | 伤～ casualties | 阵～ die on the battlefield | 家破人～ a broken family, with members missing or dead ❹ 死去的 deceased: ～友 deceased friend ❺ 灭亡 doom: ～国 fall of a nation

〈古 *arch*.〉same as 无 wú

【亡故】wánggù 死去; 故去 die; pass away; decease

【亡国】wáng//guó 国家灭亡; 使国家灭亡 conquer a nation; doom of a nation: ～灭种 national subjugation and genocide

【亡国】wángguó 灭亡了的国家 fallen nation: ～之君 monarch of a fallen country

【亡国奴】wángguónú 指祖国已经灭亡或部分国土被侵占, 受侵略者奴役的人 enslaved people of a fallen nation or occupied territory; conquered people

【亡魂】wánghún 迷信的人指人死后的灵魂 (多指刚死不久的 oft. of the newly deceased) soul; ghost

【亡魂丧胆】wáng hún sàng dǎn 形容惊慌恐惧到了极点 be scared to death; be half dead with fright

【亡灵】wánglíng 人死后的魂灵(迷信), 多用于比喻 (superstition) soul of a deceased person; (oft. fig.) spirit; ghost; spectre

【亡命】wángmìng ❶ 逃亡; 流亡 flee; seek refuge; go into exile: ～他乡 be a fugitive ❷ (冒险作恶的人)不顾性命 (of an evildoer) desperate: ～徒 desperado

【亡失】wángshī 丢失; 散失 lost; missing: 那套书已～多年。That set of books has been missing for years.

【亡羊补牢】wáng yáng bǔ láo 羊丢失了, 才修理羊圈(语出《战国策·楚策四》: '亡羊而补牢, 未为迟也') mend the fold after the sheep is lost (according to *Intrigues of the Warring States · Intrigues of Chu* (*IV*), 'It is never late to mend the fold after the sheep is lost.'); 〈比喻 *fig*.〉在受到损失之后想办法补救, 免得以后再受损失 take remedial measures after loss is done to prevent further losses; better late than never

王 wáng ❶ 君主; 最高统治者 king; monarch: 君～ monarch | 国～ king | 女～ queen ❷ 封建社会的最高爵位 highest rank of nobility in feudal times: ～爵 prince | 亲～ prince | ～侯将相 aristocrats, generals and civil officials ❸ 首领; 头目 chieftain; ringleader: 占山为～ seize a place and become a bandit leader | 擒贼先擒～ to catch bandits first catch the ringleader ❹ 同类中居首位的或特别大的 the best or strongest of a kind: 蜂～ queen bee | 蚁～ queen ant | ～蛇 cobra | 花中之～queen of flowers ❺〈书 *fml*.〉辈分高 senior; grand: ～父(祖父) grandfather | ～母(祖母) grandmother ❻ 最强的 best; strongest: ～水 aqua regia | ～牌 trump card; ace ❼ (Wáng)姓 a surname

☞ wàng on p. 1983

【王八】wáng·ba ❶ 乌龟或鳖的俗称 popular name for tortoise or turtle ❷ 指妻子有外遇的人(骂人的话 curse) cuckold ❸〈旧 *old*〉指开设妓院的男子 man who owns a brothel

【王朝】wángcháo 朝代或朝廷 dynasty: 封建～ feudal dynasty

【王储】wángchǔ 某些君主国确定为继承王位的人 crown prince

【王道】wángdào 我国古代政治哲学中指君主以仁义治天下的政策 kingly way; benevolent government; (in ancient Chinese politics) policy to rule the country by benevolence and righteousness

【王法】wángfǎ ❶ 封建时代称国家法律 feudal term for the law of the land ❷ 指政策法令 state law and policy

【王府】wángfǔ 有王爵封号的人的住宅 mansion of a prince

【王公】wánggōng 王爵和公爵, 泛指显贵的爵位 princes and dukes; nobility: ～大臣 princes, dukes and ministers | ～贵族 aristocracy

【王宫】wánggōng 国王居住的地方 imperial palace

【王冠】wángguān 国王戴的帽子 crown

【王国】wángguó ❶ 以国王为国家元首的国家 kingdom; political or territorial unit ruled by a sovereign ◇ 独立～ independent kingdom;

private domain ❷〈比喻 *fig.*〉某种特色或事物占主导地位的领域 realm; domain:北京是自行车的～。Beijing is a world of bicycles.

【王侯】wánghóu 王爵和侯爵,泛指显贵的爵位 princes and marquises:～将相 aristocrats, generals and prime ministers

【王后】wánghòu 国王的妻子 queen consort; queen

【王蔧】wánghuì 古书上指地肤,就是扫帚菜(in ancient books) summer cypress (*Kochia scoparia*)

【王浆】wángjiāng 蜜蜂喂养幼蜂王的乳状液体。味酸甜,含有多种氨基酸和维生素,有很高的营养价值。royal jelly; sweet and sour liquid rich in a variety of amino acids and vitamins and therefore of a high nutritious value, secreted by the pharyngeal glands of worker bees that serves as food for larvae that will develop into queen bees; also 蜂王浆 fēngwángjiāng

【王母娘娘】Wángmǔ niáng·niang 西王母的通称 Queen Mother of the Western Heavens; popularly known as 西王母 xīwángmǔ

【王牌】wángpái 桥牌等游戏中最强的牌 ace; trump card;〈比喻 *fig.*〉最强有力的人物、手段等 strongest person; most effective means:～军 elite army; crack force

【王权】wángquán 君主的权力 monarchical power

【王室】wángshì ❶ 指王族 royal family:～成员 member of a royal family ❷ 指朝廷 imperial court

【王水】wángshuǐ 一体积浓硝酸和三体积浓盐酸混合而成的无色液体,迅速变黄,腐蚀性极强,能溶解金、铂等一般酸类不能溶解的金属 nitrohydrochloric acid; aqua regia; highly corrosive and volatile liquid that is a mixture of nitric and hydrochloric acids at the ration of one to three, and turns from colourless to yellow quickly, used for dissolving gold, platinum, and other metals that do not dissolve in ordinary acids

【王孙】wángsūn 封王者的子孙,也泛指一般贵族的子孙 scion of a prince; descendants of a noble man:～公子 aristocrat descendants

【王位】wángwèi 君主的地位 throne:继承～ succeed to the throne

【王爷】wáng·ye 封建时代尊称有王爵封号的人 Your Highness; His Highness; respectful address for princes and dukes

【王子】wángzǐ 帝王的儿子 king's son; prince

【王族】wángzú 王国的同族 person of royal lineage; imperial kinsman

wǎng(ㄨㄤˇ)

网(網) wǎng ❶ 用绳线等结成的捕鱼捉鸟的器具 net; openwork fabric made of threads or cords that are woven or knotted together for fishing, catching birds, or other purposes:一张～ a net|渔～ fishing net|结～ mesh a net|撒～ cast a net|张～ open a net ❷ 像网的东西 sth. resembling a net:发～ hairnet|蜘蛛～ cobweb|电～ power grid ❸ 像网一样纵横交错的组织或系统 network; netlike organization or system:通信～ telecommunications network|交通～transportation network|灌溉～irrigation network|宣传～ publicity work network ❹ 用网捕捉 catch sth. with a net:～着了一条鱼 have netted a fish ❺ 像网似的笼罩着 enmesh; entangle or catch in or as if in a mesh:眼里～着红丝 bloodshot eyes

【网点】wǎngdiǎn 指像网一样成系统地分设在各处的商业、服务业单位 network of commercial or service outlets:在新居民区增设商业～。Increase the number of stores and service centres in new residential quarters.

【网兜】wǎngdōu 用线绳、尼龙丝等编成的装东西的兜子 string bag; bag fashioned out of woven cords of cotton or nylon

【网纲】wǎnggāng 渔网上的大绳 head rope of a fishnet

【网巾】wǎngjīn 用丝结成的网状的头巾,用来拢住头发 hairnet; net-like kerchief for holding a woman's hair together

【网开三面】wǎng kāi sān miàn 把捕禽兽的网打开三面 leave three sides of the net open;〈比喻 *fig.*〉用宽大态度来对待 give the wrongdoer a chance; be lenient

【网篮】wǎnglán 上面有网子罩着的篮子,大多在出门时用来盛零星物件 basket with netting on top, for carrying odds and ends on the road

【网罗】wǎngluó ❶ 捕鱼的网和捕鸟的罗 clapnet; net for fishing or trapping birds;〈比喻 *fig.*〉束缚人的东西 trammel:陷入～be entrapped|逃出～escape and gain freedom ❷ 从各方面搜寻招致 enlist:～人才 enlist talented people

【网络】wǎngluò ❶ 网状的东西 network ❷ 指由许多互相交错的分支组成系统 setup; system consisting of interconnected branches:这个新兴城市已经形成合理的经济～。This rising city has built a balanced economic setup. ❸ 在电的系统中,由若干元件组成的用来使电信号按一定要求传输的电路和或其中的一部分,叫做网络 network; circuit or part of a circuit consisting of a number of component parts that transmit signals according to instructions

【网膜】wǎngmó ❶ 覆盖在大肠表面的脂肪质的薄膜,能使肠的表面滑润,减少磨擦,并有保护肠壁的作用 omentum; one of the aliphatic folds of the peritoneum that cover the large intestine to moisten and protect it ❷ 视网膜的简称 abbr. for 视网膜 shìwǎngmó

【网球】wǎngqiú ❶ 球类运动项目之一,球场长方形，中间有一道网，双方各占一面，用拍子来回打球。有单打和双打两种。tennis; sports game played with rackets and a light ball by two players or two pairs of players on a rectangular court divided by a net ❷ 网球运动使用的球，圆形，具有弹性。里面用橡皮，外面用毛织品等制成。tennis ball; round, elastic ball, the inside of which is made of rubber and the outside of woollen fabric

【网眼】wǎngyǎn（～儿 wǎngyǎnr）网上线绳纵横交织而成的孔，多呈菱形 mesh; oft. lozenge-shaped open spaces in a net; interstice; also 网目 wǎngmù

【网子】wǎng·zi 像网的东西。特指妇女罩头发的小网。net-like object, hair net in particular, as worn by women

枉 wǎng ❶ 弯曲或歪斜 crooked;〈比喻 *fig.*〉错误或偏差 error; excess: 矫～过正 straighten the crooked to excess ❷ 使歪曲 twist; pervert: ～法 pervert the law; bend the law ❸ 冤屈 wrong; frame sb. up: 冤～ be wronged; be framed up | ～死 die as a victim of a false charge ❹ 白白地；徒然 in vain; to no avail: ～然 in vain

【枉法】wǎngfǎ 执法的人歪曲和破坏法律（of a law executor）bend the law; take the law into one's own hands: 贪赃～ take bribes and bend the law

【枉费】wǎngfèi 白费；空费 waste; vain attempt: ～工夫 waste time and energy | ～心机 rack one's brains in vain | ～唇舌 waste one's breath

【枉顾】wǎnggù〈书 *fml.*〉〈敬辞 *pol.*〉称对方来访自己 I'm honoured by your visit

【枉驾】wǎngjià〈书 *fml.*〉〈敬辞 *pol.*〉❶ 称对方来访自己 I'm honoured by your visit ❷ 请对方往访他人 would you please be kind to see sb.

【枉然】wǎngrán 得不到任何收获；徒然 to no avail; in vain: 计划虽好，不能执行也是～。No matter how good the plan is, it's useless if it cannot be carried out.

【枉死】wǎngsǐ 含冤而死 die a victim of injustice: ～鬼 wronged soul

【枉自】wǎngzì 白白地 futile; in vain; to no purpose: ～费了半天劲，什么也没办成。They toiled for a long time to no avail.

罔1 wǎng〈书 *fml.*〉蒙蔽 deceive; trap: 欺～ hoodwink

罔2 wǎng〈书 *fml.*〉没有；无 no; not: 药石～效 beyond cure | 置若～闻 turn a deaf ear to

【罔替】wǎngtì〈书 *fml.*〉不更换；不废除 not to change; not to be replaced: 世袭～（of a aristocratic title）be eternally hereditary | 千秋万代，绵延～（of lifeline, etc.）continue for aeons of time without letup

往 wǎng ❶ 去 go: ～来 come and go | 来～ contact; associate ❷ 向（某处去）be bound for; towards; to: 一个～东，一个～西。One went east, and the other was headed west. | 这趟车开～上海。This train is bound for Shanghai. ❸ 过去的 past; previous: ～年 in former years | ～事 past events

【往常】wǎngcháng 过去的一般的日子 as usual: 今天因为有事，所以比～回来得晚。I came home later than usual because I had been occupied.

【往返】wǎngfǎn 来回；反复 to and fro: ～奔走 on the run back and forth | 徒劳～ return from a journey empty-handed | 事物的发展变化是～曲折的。Things often go back and forth along a tortuous course of development.

【往复】wǎngfù ❶ 来回；反复 repeat; back and forth: ～运动 reciprocate | 循环～ move in a perpetual cycle ❷ 往来；来往 contact; exchange: 宾主～（of friends）be each other's hosts through exchange of visits

【往还】wǎnghuán 往来；来往 dealings; contact: 他们两个经常有书信～。The two of them keep in touch through correspondence.

【往来】wǎnglái ❶ 去和来 to and fro: 大街上～的车辆很多。A lot of automobiles shuttle along the major street. ❷ 互相访问；交际 visit each other; in contact: 他们俩～十分密切。The two of them are in close contact. | 我跟他没有什么～。I'm not in close contact with him.

【往年】wǎngnián 以往的年头；从前 before; former years: 今年粮食产量超过～。Grain output this year was higher than that of previous years.

【往日】wǎngrì 过去的日子；从前 former days; bygone days: 现在的情况跟～不同了。This situation today differed from what it was in bygone days.

【往时】wǎngshí 过去的时候；从前 in the past; formerly: 他还像～一样健谈。He is as talkative as he was in the past.

【往事】wǎngshì 过去的事情 past events: 回忆～ recollect the past

【往往】wǎngwǎng〈副词 *adv.*〉表示某种情况时常存在或经常发生 more often than not; often: 他～工作到深夜。He often works late into the night.

【往昔】wǎngxī 从前 in the past; in former times: 一如～ as always

惘 wǎng 失意；精神恍惚 feel frustrated: 怅～ melancholy | ～然 disappointed

【惘然】wǎngrán 失意的样子；心里好像失掉了什么东西的样子 frustrated; disappointed: ～若失 feel lost; be listless

辋 wǎng 车轮周围的框子（of a wheel）rim; （图见 ☞ figure for 轮子 lún·zi on p. 1275）

蝄 wǎng［蝄蜽］(wǎngliǎng) same as 魍魉 wǎngliǎng

魍 wǎng［魍魉］(wǎngliǎng)〈书 *fml.*〉传说中的怪物 demons and monsters in legends：魑魅～ demons and goblins；also 蝄蜽 wǎngliǎng

wàng（ㄨㄤˋ）

王 wàng〈古代 *arch.*〉称君主有天下 govern；rule：～天下 rule supreme

☞ wáng on p.1980

妄 wàng ❶ 荒谬不合理 bizarre；nonsensical：狂～ audacious｜～人 man of audacity ❷ 非分的，出了常规的；胡乱 outrageous；reckless：～念 wild dream｜～求 unwarranted demand｜～加猜疑 harbour an unwarranted suspicion｜～作主张 make a presumptuous decision｜胆大～为 audacious to the extreme

【妄称】wàngchēng 虚妄地或狂妄地声称 make a false or presumptuous declaration

【妄动】wàngdòng 轻率地行动 rush into action：轻举～ act of indiscretion｜未经许可，不得～。Nobody is allowed to rush into action without permission.

【妄断】wàngduàn 轻率地下结论 jump to a conclusion：此事不能凭空～。On no account should any unfounded conclusion be made on this matter.

【妄念】wàngniàn 不正当或不切实际的念头 wildest fancy；improper thought

【妄求】wàngqiú 非分地要求或追求 inappropriate request；presumptuous demand

【妄取】wàngqǔ 没得到许可，擅自取用 take sth. without authorization or permission：非分的钱财，不可～。Nobody should take money that does not belong to him.

【妄人】wàngrén〈书 *fml.*〉无知妄为的人 ignorant and presumptuous person

【妄说】wàngshuō 没有根据地乱说；瞎说 talk irresponsibly；talk nonsense：无知～ ignorance and absurdity

【妄图】wàngtú 狂妄地谋划 in a vain attempt：匪徒～逃窜。The bandits tried vainly to escape.

【妄为】wàngwéi 胡作非为 act audaciously：胆大～ act wildly against law and public opinion｜恣意～ act with deliberate audacity

【妄下雌黄】wàng xià cíhuáng 指乱改文字或乱发议论 make indiscriminate changes to a text；make irresponsible comments；☞ 雌黄 cíhuáng on p.319

【妄想】wàngxiǎng ❶ 狂妄地打算 make a vain attempt to；hope vainly to do sth.：敌人～卷土重来。The enemy had the wishful thinking for a comeback. ❷ 不能实现的打算 wild fantasy；pipe dream：痴心～ wishful thinking｜你想瞒过大伙儿的眼睛，那是～。It's your widest fantasy to think that you can pull the wool over everyone's eyes.

【妄言】wàngyán same as 妄语 wàngyǔ

【妄语】wàngyǔ ❶ 说假话；胡说 tell lies；talk nonsense ❷ 虚妄的话 delusive talk

【妄自菲薄】wàng zì fěibó 过分地看轻自己 belittle oneself；be unduly humble

【妄自尊大】wàng zì zūn dà 狂妄地自高自大 be given to self-glorification；have too high an opinion of oneself；be self-important

忘 wàng 忘记 forget：喝水不～掘井人。When you drink water from the well, don't ever forget the man who dug it.｜这件事我一辈子也～不了。I'll never forget it for the rest of my life.

【忘本】wàng//běn 境遇变好后忘掉自己原来的情况和所以能得到幸福的根源 forget one's past suffering；forget where one's happiness comes from

【忘掉】wàng//diào 忘记 forget；lose sight of

【忘恩负义】wàng ēn fù yì 忘记别人对自己的恩情，做出对不起别人的事 be devoid of gratitude；be ungrateful；bite the hand that feeds one

【忘乎所以】wàng hū suǒ yǐ 由于过度兴奋或骄傲自满而忘记了一切 be carried away；be swollen-headed；also 忘其所以 wàng qí suǒ yǐ

【忘怀】wànghuái 忘记 forget；cannot remember：那次分手的情景使人不能～。It's hard to forget (our) departure last time.

【忘记】wàngjì ❶ 经历的事物不再存留在记忆中；不记得 consign to oblivion；let sth. slip from the memory：我们决不会～，今天的胜利是经过艰苦的斗争得来的。We will never forget that the victory of today came from an arduous struggle. ❷ 应该做的或原来准备做的事情因为疏忽而没有做；没有记住 overlook；neglect；fail to do sth. one should do or plans to do because of negligence：～带笔记本 forget to bring one's notebook

【忘年交】wàngniánjiāo 年岁差别大、行辈不同而交情深厚的朋友 friendship between persons who are of different generations；good friends with a striking age gap between them

【忘情】wàngqíng ❶ 感情上放得下；无动于衷（常用于否定式 oft. in the negative）callous；apathetic；detached：不能～ be emotionally attached ❷ 不能节制自己的感情 let oneself go；abandon oneself to：～地歌唱 let oneself go and sing lustily

【忘却】wàngquè 忘记 forget：这些沉痛的教训，使人无法～。These painful lessons are simply unforgettable.

【忘我】wàngwǒ 忘掉自己。形容人公而忘私。oblivious of oneself；selfless：～的精神 spirit of selflessness｜～地劳动 work selflessly；work untiringly

【忘形】wàngxíng 因为得意或高兴而忘掉应有的礼貌和应持的态度 be beside oneself (with glee, etc.); have one's head turned: 得意～ get dizzy with success

【忘性】wàng·xing 好忘事的毛病 poor memory; forgetfulness: 上了岁数的人,～大。Those who are getting old often have a poor memory

旺 wàng ❶ 旺盛 burgeoning; flourishing; going: 兴～ burgeoning | 火着得很～。The brazier in the room was burning merrily. | 花开得正～。The flowers are in full bloom. | 庄稼长得真～。The crops are thriving. ❷〈方 *dial.*〉多;充足 plentiful; bounteous: 奶水～(of a breast-feeding mother) have lots of milk | 新打的井,水～极了。The newly dug well abounds in water.

【旺季】wàngjì 营业旺盛的季节或某种东西出产多的季节(跟'淡季'相对 as opposed to 'slack season') busy season; peak period; season in which business is booming or sth. yields the most

【旺健】wàngjiàn 健旺 exude good health; vigorous and healthy: 精力～ full of vigour

【旺年】wàngnián〈方 *dial.*〉果树生长旺盛、结果多的年份 (of fruit trees) on-year

【旺盛】wàngshèng 生命力强;情绪高涨;茂盛 vigorous; exuberant: 精力～full of vigour | 槐树长得很～。The locust tree is thriving.

【旺销】wàngxiāo 畅销 sell briskly; sell like hot cakes: ～商品 commodities in big demand | 家用电器出现～势头。Indications are that household electrical appliances sell well.

W

【旺月】wàngyuè 营业旺盛的月份(跟'淡月'相对 as opposed to 'slack month') busy month in business

望1 wàng ❶ 向远处看 stretch one's eyes over (land, sea, etc.); gaze into the distance: 登山远～journey to the summit of a mountain and stretch one's eyes over many a mile of *terra incognita* | 一～无际的稻田 paddy fields that stretch from horizon to horizon ❷ 探望 look in on; drop in on; see: 拜～ call on | 看～ look in on ❸ 盼望;希望 look forward to; expect: 大喜过～ overjoyed | 丰收有～。Prospects are good for a rich harvest. | ～子成龙 (of parents) hope one's son will turn out a dragon; expect one's son to be a talent | ～准时到会 punctuality required for the meeting ❹ 名望,也指有名望的人 prestige; prestigious person: 德高～重 be of noble character and high prestige; with great virtue and a good reputation | 一乡之～ a person held in highest esteem in a place ❺ 怨 grief: 怨～ rankle ❻ 望子 shop sign: 酒～ sign of a wine shop ❼〈介词 *prep.*〉对着;朝着 to; towards: ～我点点头。(The man) nodded at me. | ～他笑了笑。(She) gave him a smile. ❽〈书 *fml.*〉(年龄)接近(of one's age) turning: ～六之年(指年近六十) turning 60 ❾ (Wàng)姓 a surname

望2 wàng ❶ 农历每月十五日(有时是十六日或十七日),地球运行到月亮和太阳之间。这天太阳从西方落下去的时候,月亮正好从东方升上来,地球上看见圆形的月亮,这种月相叫望,这时的月亮叫望月。plenilune; full moon; moon becoming visible from the earth as a fully illuminated disk on the 15th day (at times the 16th or 17th) of every lunar month), when the earth moves between the moon that happens to be rising in the east and the sun that happens to be setting in the west. This stage of the moon's movement is known in Chinese as *wang* (plenitude), and the moon at this stage, plenilune. ❷ 望日 day of plenilune; 15th day of a lunar month

【望板】wàngbǎn 平铺在椽子上面的木板 roof boarding; boards fixed on rafters

【望尘莫及】wàng chén mò jí 只望见走在前面的人带起的尘土而赶不上 so far behind that one can only see the dust of the rider ahead; 〈比喻 *fig.*〉远远落后 too far behind to catch up; too inferior to bear comparison

【望穿秋水】wàng chuān qiū shuǐ 形容盼望得非常急切 keep looking for sb. or sth. till one's eyes are strained; yearn for sth. or sb. with impatient expectancy (秋水 *qiu shui*: 比喻眼睛 referring to 'eye' in a figurative sense

【望而却步】wàng ér què bù 看到了危险或力不能及的事而往后退缩 hang back at the sight of sth. dangerous or difficult; flinch; hang back

【望而生畏】wàng ér shēng wèi 看见了就害怕 be terrified or awed by the sight of sth. or sb.

【望风】wàng//fēng 给正在进行秘密活动的人观察动静 keep watch; on the lookout (while sb. else is conducting clandestine activity); keep watch

【望风捕影】wàng fēng bǔ yǐng 捕风捉影 chase the wind and clutch at shadows: 情况没弄清楚,不要～地乱说。The situation hasn't be unravelled up yet, so don't beat the air and clutch at shadows; also 望风扑影 wàng fēng pū yǐng

【望风而逃】wàng fēng ér táo 老远看见对方的气势很盛就逃跑了 run away at the mere sight of the attacker

【望风披靡】wàng fēng pī mǐ 形容军队丧失战斗意志,老远看见对方的气势很盛就溃散了 flee pell-mell before sb.; melt away at the mere whisper of sb.'s arrival

【望楼】wànglóu 瞭望用的楼 watchtower

【望梅止渴】wàng méi zhǐ kě 曹操带兵走到一个没有水的地方,士兵们渴得很,曹操骗他们说:'前面有很大的一片梅树林,梅子很多,又甜又酸。'士兵听了,都流出口水来,不再嚷渴(见于

《世说新语·假谲》)。quench one's thirst by thinking of plums, a proverb from a story in *A New Account of Tales of the World·Falsehood and Deception*. During a march Cao Cao and his troops arrived at a place where there was no drinking water but the soldiers were very thirsty. Cao Cao said, 'Just ahead of us there is large forest of plum trees with a lot of sweet-and-sour plums.' This made the mouths of the soldiers water, and no one was complaining of thirst any more. 〈比喻 *fig.*〉用空想安慰自己 console oneself with false hopes

【望门】wàngmén 有名望的人家 distinguished family; well-established family; prominent family: 出身～ come from an old and prestigious family

【望门寡】wàngménguǎ ❶〈旧时 *old*〉女子订婚之后,未婚夫死了不再跟别人结婚,叫做守'望门寡'(of a woman) remain unmarried the rest of one's life after the death of one's fiancé ❷ 守'望门寡'的女子 woman who remains unmarried after her fiancé died

【望其项背】wàng qí xiàng bèi 能够望见别人的颈项和背脊,表示赶得上或比得上(多用于否定式 oft. in the negative) can see sb's neck and back; capable of catching up with sb.; stand comparison with sb.: 难以～ compare unfavourably with sb.

【望日】wàngrì 天文学上指月亮圆的那一天,即农历每月十五日,有时是十六日或十七日。通常指农历每月十五日。day of plenilune; day of full moon, which falls usu. on the 15th, but occasionally on the 16th or 17th, of a lunar month; generally referring to the 15th of a lunar month

【望文生义】wàng wén shēng yì 不懂某一词句的正确意义,只从字面上去附会,做出错误的解释 quote words out of the context; interpret words without understanding them

【望闻问切】wàng wén wèn qiè〈中医 *Chin. med.*〉诊断疾病的方法。望是观察病人的发育情况、面色、舌苔、表情等;闻是听病人的说话声音、咳嗽、喘息,并且嗅出病人的口臭、体臭等气味;问是询问病人自己所感到的症状,以前所患过的病等;切是用手诊脉或按腹部有没有痞块。通常这四种方法结合在一起使用,叫做四诊。watch, hear, ask and touch—a diagnosis method; four methods of diagnosis that are usu. employed together: 1) observation of physique, complexion, tongue fur, expression, etc.; 2) auscultation of voice, cough, breath and olfaction of halitosis, body odour, etc.; 3) questioning about symptoms, medical history, etc.; 4) pulse feeling and palpation or belly pressing to see if there is any lump in the abdomen

【望眼欲穿】wàng yǎn yù chuān 形容盼望殷切 bore one's eyes through by gazing anxionsly; look for with longing eyes; expect on tiptoe

【望洋兴叹】wàng yáng xīng tàn 本义指在伟大的事物面前感叹自己的藐小 lament one's inadequacy in the face of a great task; 今多比喻要做一件事而力量不够,感到无可奈何 feel powerless and frustrated at the thought of so much difficulty (望洋 *wang yang*: 抬头向上看的样子 raise one's head and look at the sky)

【望远镜】wàngyuǎnjìng 观察远距离物体的光学仪器,最简单的折射望远镜由两组透镜组成 telescope; optical device, the simplest type of which consists of two groups of lenses, used to observe distant objects

【望月】wàngyuè 望日的月亮 plenilune; full moon; also 满月 mǎnyuè

【望砖】wàngzhuān 平铺在椽子上面的较薄的砖 brick, thinner than usual, used as tiles on the rafters of a roof

【望子成龙】wàng zǐ chéng lóng 希望儿子能成为出人头地或有作为的人 long to see one's son become a dragon (i.e. win success in the world); hope one's son will amount to something when he grows up

【望子】wàng·zi 店铺标明属于某种行业的标志,多用竹竿高挂在门前,使远近都能看清 shop sign in the form of a streamer, oft. hoisted high on the top of a bamboo pole at the front gate

【望族】wàngzú 有名望、有地位的家族 long-established and distinguished family; prominent family: 名门～ family of the rich and powerful

wēi (ㄨㄟ)

危 wēi ❶ 危险;不安全(跟'安'相对 as opposed to 'safety') danger: ～急 critical; imminent danger; desperate situation | ～难 danger | 转～为安 pass from danger to safety; tide over a crisis | 居安思～ be vigilant when in peace ❷ 使处于危险境地;损害 endanger; imperil: ～害 harm | ～及生命 life-threatening ❸ 指人快要死 dying: 临～ be dying; in danger | 病～ critically ill ❹〈书 *fml.*〉高;高耸 high; towering: ～樯 tall masts | ～楼百尺 building over hundreds of feet high ❺〈书 *fml.*〉端正;正直 upright; proper: 正襟～坐 straighten one's clothes and sit properly; sit in state ❻ 二十八宿之一 *wei*, one of the 28 constellations in ancient Chinese astronomy ❼ (Wēi)姓 a surname

【危城】wēichéng ❶〈书 *fml.*〉城墙很高的城 city with towering enclosing walls ❷ 指被围困、快要被攻破的城市 beleaguered city

【危殆】wēidài〈书 *fml.*〉(形势、生命等)十分危险；危急 in great danger; in jeopardy; in a critical situation：病势～ mortally ill

【危笃】wēidǔ〈书 *fml.*〉(病势)危急 critically ill; in the throes of death

【危房】wēifáng 有倒塌危险的房屋 unsafe building：～改建 demolish dangerous houses and build new ones

【危害】wēihài 使受破坏；损害 impair; jeopardize：～生命 life-threatening｜～社会秩序 endanger social order

【危机】wēijī ❶ 指危险的根由 crisis：～四伏 beset with crisis; danger lurks everywhere ❷ 严重困难的关头 critical moment：经济～ economic crisis｜人才～ serious talent drain

【危及】wēijí 有害于；威胁到 endanger; compromise：～生命 endanger life｜～国家安全 put state security in jeopardy; compromise state security

【危急】wēijí 危险而紧急 imminent danger; desperate situation：情势～ desperate situation｜～关头 critical moment

【危局】wēijú 危险的局势 desperate situation：扭转～ turn the table and avert a dangerous situation

【危惧】wēijù 担忧害怕 worry and fear; apprehensive

【危楼】wēilóu〈书 *fml.*〉高楼 towering building：～高百尺 building of a hundred feet in height

【危难】wēinàn 危险和灾难 dire peril; calamity

【危浅】wēiqiǎn〈书 *fml.*〉(生命)垂危 mortally ill; at one's last gasp：人命～，朝不保夕 be mortally ill and may not live to the end of the day

【危如累卵】wēi rú lěi luǎn 形容形势极其危险，如同摞(luò)起来的蛋，随时都有倒下来的可能 be as precarious as a pile of eggs that may collapse any time

【危亡】wēiwáng (国家、民族)接近于灭亡的危险局势(of a nation) in perish; (fate of a country) at stake

【危险】wēixiǎn 有遭到损害或失败的可能 at risk; dangerous：～期 period of danger｜～区 danger zone｜～标志 danger signal｜预防～ precaution against danger｜山路又陡又窄，攀登的时候非常～。The mountain road is narrow and steep, and very dangerous for mountain climbers.

【危言耸听】wēi yán sǒng tīng 故意说吓人的话使听的人吃惊 resort to alarmist remarks; be sensational; exaggerate things to scare people

【危在旦夕】wēi zài dàn xī 指危险就在眼前 hang by a thread; in great danger; danger is imminent

【危重】wēizhòng (病情)严重而危险 mortally ill：抢救～病人 rescue the critically ill

【危坐】wēizuò〈书 *fml.*〉端端正正地坐着 sit in state：正襟～ straighten out one's dress and sit in state

委 wēi［委蛇］(wēiyí)〈书 *fml.*〉❶ same as 逶迤 wēiyí ❷ 形容随顺 accede to; submit to：虚与～ make a pretence of politeness, compliance, etc.

☞ wěi on p. 1996

威 wēi ❶ 表现出来的能压服人的力量或使人敬畏的态度 might; power; strength to suppress others or manner to inspire awe：～信 prestige; reputation｜～严 dignified｜示～ demonstration｜助～cheer for; root for｜狐假虎～ the fox assuming the majesty of the tiger — borrowing power to do evil ❷ 凭借威力(采取某种行动)(take certain action) by force：～逼 coerce｜～吓 intimidate｜～胁 threaten

【威逼】wēibī 用威力强迫或进逼 threaten; coerce; intimidate：～利诱 brandish both carrot and stick; by coercion and cajolery

【威风】wēifēng ❶ 使人敬畏的声势或气派 might; awe-inspiring manner：～凛凛 looking majestic｜长自己的志气，灭敌人的～ boost one's own morale and deflate the enemy's arrogance ❷ 有威风 imposing; impressive; smart：穿上军装显得很～ look smart in an army uniform

【威吓】wēihè 用威势来吓唬(xià·hu) intimidate; threaten; bully：～对方 intimidate the other party｜不怕武力～fear no threat of the use of force

【威赫】wēihè 威风显赫 powerful and influential：～一时 be powerful and influential for a time

【威力】wēilì ❶ 强大的使人畏惧的力量 power; force; awe-inspiring, powerful strength ❷ 具有巨大推动或摧毁作用的力量 mighty force, either constructive or destructive：氢弹的～比原子弹大。The hydrogen bomb is more destructive than the atom bomb.｜改革开放的政策，在发展生产中发挥着巨大的～。The policy of reform and opening up to the outside world plays a tremendous role in developing production.

【威名】wēimíng 因有惊人的力量或武功而得到的很大的名望 fame based on might or military exploits; mighty reputation：～远扬 the fame of sb. spreads far and wide

【威迫】wēipò same as 威逼 wēibī：～利诱 coerce and cajolery

【威权】wēiquán 威力和权势 authority; power：炫耀～put on a show of one's authority; flaunt one's strength

【威慑】wēishè 用武力使对方感到恐惧 deter; terrorize sb. with force：～力量 deterrent force

【威士忌】wēishìjì 一种用大麦、黑麦等制成的酒 whisky; whiskey; liquor distilled from grain, such as barley and rye, and containing approximately 40 to 50 per cent ethyl alcohol by volume

【威势】wēishì ❶ 威力和气势 power and momentum：太阳落山后，酷暑的～才稍稍减退。The heat wave let up a little bit after sunset. ❷ 威力和权势 power and influence：倚仗～ take advantage of sb. else's power and influence｜树立～ foster one's authority by force

【威望】wēiwàng 声誉和名望 prestige：国际～ international prestige｜他在文学界享有很高的～。He enjoyed a high reputation in the literary circles.

【威武】wēiwǔ ❶ 武力；权势 might；force：～不能屈 not to be intimadated by force ❷ 力量强大；有气势 powerful：～雄壮 awesome and magnificent

【威胁】wēixié 用威力逼迫恫吓使人屈服 threaten；menace：～利诱 coercion and cajolery ◇洪水正～着整个村庄。The flood is threatening the safety of the entire village.

【威信】wēixìn 威望和信誉 prestige；popular trust：～扫地 lose popular trust；have one's prestige swept into the dust｜树立～ establish one's reputation

【威严】wēiyán ❶ 有威力而又严肃的样子 stately；majestic；awe-inspiring：～的仪仗队 awe-inspiring guard of honour ❷ 威风和尊严 awe；dignity：他摆出了尊长的～。He threw his weight about as an elder.

【威仪】wēiyí 使人敬畏的严肃容貌和庄重举止 impressive and dignified manner：～凛然 awe-inspiring bearing

逶 wēi［逶迤］（wēiyí）〈书 *fml*.〉形容道路、山脉、河流等弯弯曲曲延续不绝的样子（of road，mountain，river，etc.）serpentine；meander：群山～ serpentine mountains；also 委蛇 wēiyí

偎 wēi 亲热地靠着；紧挨着 cuddle；snuggle up to：～依 nestle in｜孩子～在母亲怀里。The child snuggled up in its mother's arms.

【偎傍】wēibàng 偎依 cuddle up；lean close to

【偎依】wēiyī 偎 cuddle up：一对情人相互～着低低细语。Two lovers cuddled and muttered to each other.

隈 wēi〈书 *fml*.〉山、水等弯曲的地方（of mountain）recess；（of river）bend：山～ mountain recess｜城～ city corner

搣 wēi〈方 *dial*.〉使细长的东西弯曲 bend sth. thin and long

葳 wēi［葳蕤］（wēiruí）〈书 *fml*.〉形容枝叶繁盛（of foliage）thriving；lush

崴 wēi［崴嵬］（wēiwéi）〈书 *fml*.〉形容山高（of a mountain）lofty；towering

☞ wǎi on p.1966

椳 wēi〈书 *fml*.〉门臼（承门轴的）door socket

微 wēi ❶ 细小；轻微 tiny；little；minute：细～ minute｜～风 gentle breeze｜谨小慎～ overcautious；meticulous to a fault｜相差甚～ about the same；tiny difference ❷ 主单位的一百万分之一 one millionth part of；micro：～米 micron（pl.：microns or micra）｜～安 microampere｜～法拉 microfarad ❸ 衰落 decline：衰～ on the decline ❹ 精深奥妙 profound；abstruse：～妙 delicate；subtle｜～言大义 subtle words with profound implications；deep meaning in pithy remarks

【微波】wēibō 一般指波长从 1 米到 1 毫米（频率 300 兆赫—300,000 兆赫）的无线电波。可分为分米波、厘米波和毫米波。直线传播，方向性强，频率高，应用于导航、雷达、遥感技术、卫星通信、气象、天文等方面。microwave；high-frequency electromagnetic wave，one millimetre to one metre in wavelength，and 300 to 300,000 megahertz in frequency，that falls into decimetre wave，centimetre wave，and millimetre wave，transmits itself in straight lines，and is marked for its strong directivity and high frequency，used in such fields as navigation，radar，remote sensing，satellite telecommunications，meteorology，astronomy，etc.

【微薄】wēibó 微小单薄；数量少 meagre；scanty：～的力量 little strength｜～的收入 meagre income

【微不足道】wēi bù zú dào 非常藐小，不值得一提 negligible；insignificant

【微词】wēicí〈书 *fml*.〉隐晦的批评 complaint；veiled criticism；also 微辞 wēicí

【微辞】wēicí same as 微词 wēicí

【微电脑】wēidiànnǎo 微机的俗称 popular term for microcomputer

【微雕】wēidiāo 微型雕刻，在极小的物体上刻出字或图像等，也指用这种方法雕刻成的作品 miniature sculpture；carving letters or pictures into tiny objects；also 微刻 wēikè

【微风】wēifēng ❶ 微弱的风 gentle breeze：～拂面。A gentle breeze caresses people's faces. ❷ 气象学上指 3 级风 wind of force three on the Beaufort scale in meteorology；☞ 风级 fēngjí on p.579

【微服】wēifú〈书 *fml*.〉官吏等外出时为不暴露身份而换穿便服（of an official）incognito；in plain clothes in order to hide one's status：～私访 travel incognito on a fact-finding mission

【微观】wēiguān 深入到分子、原子、电子等构造领域的，泛指部分或较小范围的（跟'宏观'相对 as opposed to 'macrocosmic'）microcosmic；of such miniature worlds as molecule，atom，electron，etc.；general reference to part of a field：～考察 microscopic observation｜～经济 microeconomy

【微观经济学】wēiguān jīngjìxué 以单个经济单

位、个别商品作为研究对象的经济学 microeconomics; economics devoted to the study of individual economic units and individual commodities

【微观粒子】wēiguān lìzǐ 分子、原子和基本粒子的统称 microparticle; general reference to molecule, atom and electron

【微观世界】wēiguān shìjiè 指分子、原子、电子等极微小的物质粒子的领域 microcosmos; microcosm; miniature world such as molecule, atom and electron

【微乎其微】wēi hū qí wēi 形容非常少或非常小 very little; next to nothing

【微机】wēijī 微型电子计算机的简称 abbr. for 微型电子计算机 wēixíng diànzǐ jìsuànjī

【微贱】wēijiàn 指社会地位低下 humble; lowly; same as 卑贱 bēijiàn ①:出身～ of humble origin; with a humble family background

【微利】wēilì 很少的利润;很小的利益 small profit; low profit:蝇头～ petty benefit; petty profit

【微粒】wēilì 微小的颗粒,包括肉眼可以看到的,也包括肉眼看不到的分子、原子等 corpuscle; particle, including those visible as well as molecule, atoms and other tiny things that cannot be observed with naked eye

【微量元素】wēiliàng yuánsù 植物体除需要钾、磷、氮等元素作为养料外,还需要吸收极少量的硼、砷、锰、铜、钴、钼等元素作为养料,这些需要量极少的元素叫做微量元素 trace element; chemical element, such as boron, arsenic, manganese, copper, cobalt, and molybdenum, required in minute quantities other than such nutrients as kalium, phosphor, and nitrogen, by an organism to maintain proper physical functioning

W

【微茫】wēimáng 〈书 *fml.*〉隐约,不清晰 blurred; hazy:月色～ dim moonlight

【微妙】wēimiào 深奥玄妙,难以捉摸 delicate; subtle:～的关系 subtle relations|这个问题很～。This is a rather delicate problem.

【微末】wēimò 细小;不重要 paltry; of little consequence:～的贡献 contribution of no account

【微弱】wēiruò ❶ 小而弱 feeble; frail:气息～ faint breath|～的灯光 dim light ❷ 衰弱;虚弱 enfeebled; debilitated:～的身躯 emaciated body

【微生物】wēishēngwù 形体微小、构造简单的生物的统称。微生物广泛分布在自然界中,如细菌、真菌、病毒等。micro-organism; microbe; organism that is of microscopic or submicroscopic size and simple structure and that propagates rapidly and is widely distributed in nature, such as germ, eumycete and virus

【微缩】wēisuō 把物体按一定比例缩小 microform; arrangement of images reduced in size, as on microfilm or microfiche:～景区 miniature scenery; scaled-down scenery

【微调】wēitiáo ❶ 电子学上指对调谐电容做很小的变动、调整 fine tuning ❷ 指微调电容器,电容量可做精细调整的小容量电容器 trimmer capacitor; capacitor of tiny and tunable capacity; make minute change or adjustment to a capacitor ❸ 泛指做小幅度的调整 minor readjustment:工资～ slight pay raise

【微微】wēiwēi ❶ 稍微;略微 slightly; faintly:～一笑 give a wan smile ❷ 微小;细小 a little; dimly; somewhat:～的亮光 dim light

【微细】wēixì 非常细小 fine; very small:～的血管 fine blood vessel

【微小】wēixiǎo 极小 little; tiny:～的颗粒 granule|～的进步 scanty progress|个人的力量是～的。The strength of an individual is of little consequence.

【微笑】wēixiào ❶ 不显著的笑容 smile:脸上浮现一丝～。A faint smile congealed on (her) face. ❷ 不显著地、不出声地笑 laugh imperceptibly or quietly:嫣然～ give a sweet, and quiet laughter|回眸～ glance back and smile

【微行】wēixíng 帝王或大官隐蔽自己的身份改装出行(of an emperor or ranking official) travel incognito

【微型】wēixíng 体积比同类的东西小的 miniature; mini-:～汽车 minicab|～电子计算机 microcomputer

【微血管】wēixuèguǎn same as 毛细管 máoxìguǎn ①

【微言大义】wēi yán dà yì 精微的语言和深奥的道理 sublime words with profound meaning

【微音器】wēiyīnqì 把声音变成电能的器件。声波通过微音器时,微音器能使电流随声波的变化做相应的变化,用于有线和无线电广播。microphone; instrument that converts sound waves into an electric current that changes with changes in the sound waves, and is used in wired or radio broadcasting; also 传声器 chuánshēngqì;通称 popularly known as 麦克风 màikèfēng or 话筒 huàtǒng

煨 wēi ❶ 烹调法,用微火慢慢地煮 stew; simmer:～牛肉 stewed beef|～山药 stewed yam ❷ 把生的食物放在带火的灰里使烧熟 roast in fresh cinders:～白薯 roast sweet potatoes in fresh cinders

溦 wēi 〈书 *fml.*〉小雨 drizzle

薇 wēi 古书上指巢菜(in ancient books) common vetch

鳂 wēi 鱼类的一属,身体多为红色,眼大,口大而斜。生活在热带海洋。holocentrid (*Holocentrus rubber*); tropical marine fish with usu. a red body, large eyes and a large and crooked mouth

巍 wēi 形容高大 towering; lofty:～然 soaring|～峨 lofty

【巍峨】wēi'é 形容山或建筑物的高大雄伟(of mountain or building) big and majestic:～的群山 lofty mountains|～的天安门城楼 tall and stately rostrum atop the Tian'anmen Gate

【巍然】wēirán 形容山或建筑物雄伟的样子(of mountain or building) towering; majestic:～屹立 stand lofty and rock-firm|大桥～横跨在长江之上。A magnificent bridge sits astride the Yangtze River.

【巍巍】wēiwēi 形容高大 towering; lofty:～井冈山 mighty Jinggang Mountains

wéi (ㄨㄟˊ)

韦(韋) wéi ❶〈书 *fml.*〉皮革 leather ❷(Wéi)姓 a surname

【韦编三绝】wéi biān sān jué 孔子晚年很爱读《周易》,翻来覆去地读,使穿连《周易》竹简的皮条断了好几次(见于《史记·孔子世家》)。后来用'韦编三绝'形容读书勤奋。According to *Records of the Historian · Hereditary House of Confucius*, in his old age Confucius was fond of reading *The Book of Changes*, which was inscribed on bamboo slips held together with a leather cord, and because of his repeated turning of the pages, the leather cord broke three times. 'The leather cord breaks three times', the phrase derived from the story, later became a figurative term of speech to mean 'be diligent in one's studies'.

为[1](為、爲) wéi ❶ 做;作为[1] do; act:事在人～。It all depends on human effort.|敢作敢～act with courage and determination; make bold to|大有可～ have bright prospects; well worth doing|青年有～young and up-and-coming ❷ 充当 act as; serve as:选他～代表。He was elected a delegate. ❸ 变成;成 turn; become:一分～二。A whole divides into two. *or* Everything tends to divide into two.|化～乌有 come to naught; turn to dust|变沙漠～良田 turn deserts into farmlands ❹ 是 be; mean:十寸～一尺。Ten *cun* equal one *chi*.

为[2](為、爲) wéi〈介词 *prep.*〉被(跟'所'字合用)[used with 所 suǒ in passive voice]:这种艺术形式～广大人民所喜闻乐见。The broad masses of the people love to see and hear this artistic form.

为[3](為、爲) wéi〈书 *fml.*〉〈助词 *aux.*〉常跟'何'相应,表示疑问[oft. used with 何 hé in a rhetorical question]:何以家～(要家干什么)? What need have I of a home? (usu. a remark by a patriot in a national crisis)

为[4](為、爲) wéi ❶ 附于某些单音形容词后,构成表示程度、范围的副词[used after an adjective to form an adverb to indicate degree or scope]:大～高兴 very happy|广～传播 spread far and wide|深～感动 be touched deeply ❷ 附于某些表示程度的单音副词后,加强语气[used after an adverb for emphasis]:极～重要 extremely important|甚～便利 rather convenient|颇～可观 well worth seeing|尤～出色 rather outstanding

☞ wèi on p.1998

【为非作歹】wéi fēi zuò dǎi 做各种坏事 do evil; commit crimes; perpetrate outrages; commit all sorts of crimes

【为富不仁】wéi fù bù rén 靠剥削发财致富的人没有好心肠(见于《孟子·腾文公上》) Those who get rich by exploiting others are heartless, according to *Mencius · Duke Wen of Teng (I)*.

【为害】wéihài 造成损害 cause harm; cause damage:黏虫对谷子、玉米等粮食作物～最烈。Armyworms are destructive to millet, corn and other grain crops.

【为患】wéihuàn 造成祸害 bring trouble:洪水～ suffer from floods

【为力】wéilì 使劲儿;出力 put forth one's strength; exert oneself:无能～ can do nothing about it

【为难】wéinán ❶ 感到难以应付 feel embarrassed; feel awkward:～的事 awkward matter|叫人～ embarrass sb.; put sb. in an awkward situation ❷ 作对或刁难 make things difficult for:故意～ deliberately make things difficult for sb.

【为期】wéiqī 从时间、期限长短上看 for a certain period of time; by a definite date:～不远 be drawing near|～甚远。There is still a long way to go.

【为人】wéirén 指做人处世的态度 behave; conduct oneself:～正直 be upright|～忠厚 honest and tolerant; sincerely and kindly|大家都了解他的～。Everybody knows what kind of a man he is.

【为生】wéishēng (以某种途径)谋生 eke oneself through a living:捕鱼～make a living as a fisherman

【为时】wéishí 从时间的长短、早晚上看 in terms of time:～过早 premature; too early; too soon|～已晚 too late|～不多 not much time left

【为首】wéishǒu 作为领头人 with sb. as the leader; headed (or led) by:以某某～的代表团 delegation headed by so-and-so|犯罪团伙的～分子已被抓获。The ringleader of the mobsters has been busted.

【为数】wéishù 从数量多少上看 amount to;

number：～不少 amount to a considerable number; amount to quite a lot｜～甚微 amount to little｜～可观 amount to a considerable number

【为所欲为】wéi suǒ yù wéi 想干什么就干什么；任意行事（贬义 derog.）act willfully; do whatever one likes; have one's way

【为伍】wéiwǔ 同伙；做伙伴 associate with：羞与～ feel ashamed to be associated with sb.

【为止】wéizhǐ 截止；终止（多用于时间、进度等 of time, progress, etc.）up to; till：到目前～，报名的人已超过一千。The number of those who have signed up has exceeded 1,000 by now.

圩 wéi 圩子 dyke; embankment：筑～ build dykes｜～堤 flood-prevention dike in a lowland｜～埂 embankment

☞ xū on p. 2161

【圩田】wéitián 有土堤包围能防止外边的水侵入的稻田 polder; low-lying paddy fields surrounded with dykes; low-lying land that has been reclaimed from a body of water and is protected by dikes

【圩垸】wéiyuàn 滨湖地区为了防止湖水侵入而筑的堤叫圩，圩内的小圩叫垸 protective embankments in lakeside areas：～工程 embankment project

【圩子】wéi·zi ❶ 低洼地区的防水护田的堤岸 protective embankments surrounding low-lying fields ❷ same as 围子 wéi·zi ①

违（違） wéi ❶ 不遵照；不依从 disobey; violate：～背 disobey｜～反 violate｜～法 break the law｜～约 breach a contract｜～章 break rules and regulations｜阳奉阴～ comply in public but oppose in private ❷ 离别 be separated; depart：睽～ separate｜久～ have not seen sb. for ages

【违碍】wéi'ài 指触犯统治者忌讳的 taboo; anathema：～字句 prohibited words and expressions

【违拗】wéi'ào 违背；有意不依从（上级或长辈的主意）defy (one's superiors or elders); disobey

【违背】wéibèi 违反；不遵守 violate; go against; run counter to：～誓言 go back on one's word｜～规章制度 break rules and regulations

【违法】wéi∥fǎ 不遵守法律或法令 break the law; be illegal：～行为 illegal activities; unlawful practice｜～乱纪 violate law and discipline; break the law and violate discipline

【违反】wéifǎn 不遵守；不符合（法则、规程等）violate (rules, regulations, etc.); run counter to; transgress; infringe：～政策 run counter to the policy｜～纪律 violate discipline

【违犯】wéifàn 违背和触犯（法规等）violate (laws, regulations, etc.); infringe; act contrary to：～宪法 violation of the constitution

【违和】wéihé 〈婉辞 *euph.*〉称别人有病 indisposed：近闻贵体～，深为悬念。I'm quite worried to learn you are indisposed recently.

【违禁】wéijìn 违犯禁令 violate a ban：～品 contraband (goods)

【违抗】wéikàng 违背和抗拒 disobey; defy：～命令 disobey orders; act in defiance of orders

【违例】wéilì ❶ 违反惯例 breach of rules; violation ❷ 体育比赛中指违反比赛规则。如篮球比赛中带球跑、拳击球、脚踢球等。(of sports games) violation, such as walking with the ball in hand, hitting the ball with a fist, and kicking the ball in basketball

【违忤】wéiwǔ 〈书 *fml.*〉违背；不顺从 violate; go against; run counter to; disobey

【违误】wéiwù 公文用语，违反命令，耽误公事 (used in official documents) disobey orders and cause delay：迅速办理，不得～。This is to be acted upon without delay.

【违心】wéixīn 不是出于本心；跟本意相反 against one's will; contrary to one's convictions：～之论 insincere talk｜他说的是～话。What he said was against his conscience.

【违约】wéi∥yuē 违背条约或契约 break a contract; violate a treaty; break one's promise; break off an engagement

【违章】wéi∥zhāng 违反规章 break rules and regulations：～操作 in violation of the rules｜～建筑 building erected in violation of rules｜～驾驶 traffic violation

围（圍） wéi ❶ 四周拦挡起来，使里外不通；环绕 enclose; fence off; surround：包～ encircle; besiege｜突～ break an enemy encirclement｜解～ rescue sb. from a siege｜团团～住 surround completely ❷ 四周；周围 around; circumference：外～ periphery｜四～都是大山 skirted by high mountains; rimmed in big mountains ❸ 某些物体周围的长度 perimeter; girth：腰～ waistline ❹ 〈量词 *classifier*〉arm span a)两只手的拇指和食指合拢来的长度 hand span; length of the circle formed by both hands with thumbs and index fingers b)两只胳膊合拢来的长度 arm span; length of a person's two arms put together

【围脖儿】wéibór 〈方 *dial.*〉围巾 muffler; scarf

【围捕】wéibǔ 包围起来捕捉 surround and seize; round up：～逃犯 hunt down a fugitive｜～鱼群 round up a shoal of fish

【围场】wéichǎng 封建时代围起来专供皇帝贵族打猎的场地 imperial hunting park during the feudal times

【围城】wéi∥chéng 包围城市 encircle or besiege a city：～战 battle of besiegement

【围城】wéichéng 被包围的城市 besieged city; beleaguered city

【围攻】wéigōng 包围起来加以攻击 besiege; lay

siege to; jointly attack sb.: ～敌军据点 lay siege to an enemy stronghold ◇他在会上多次遭到～。He came under attack repeatedly during the meeting.

【围观】wéiguān (许多人)围着观看(of a crowd of people) watch; look on: 铁树开花,引来许多群众～。The rare blossoming of the iron tree attracted a crowd of onlookers.

【围击】wéijī same as 围攻 wéigōng

【围歼】wéijiān 包围起来歼灭 surround and annihilate: ～敌军 annihilate enemy troops under siege

【围剿】wéijiǎo 包围起来剿灭 encircle and suppress: ～残匪 roundup a remnant bandit force ◇文化～ cultural encirclement

【围巾】wéijīn 围在脖子上保暖、保护衣领或做装饰的针织品或纺织品 muffler; scarf; knitwear or textile worn around the neck for warmth, protecting the collar, or ornamentation

【围聚】wéijù 从四下里聚集 crowd around; gather round: 店门前～了不少看热闹的人。The front door of the store was mobbed by curious onlookers.

【围垦】wéikěn 用堤坝把湖滩、海滩等围起来垦殖 (build dykes to) reclaim land from marshes; enclose tideland for cultivation

【围困】wéikùn 团团围住,使处于困境 besiege; hem in; pin down: 千方百计抢救被洪水～的群众。All sorts of measures were taken to rescue those stranded by the flood.

【围猎】wéiliè 从四面合围起来捕捉禽兽 round up and hunt: 严禁～珍禽。Hunting of rare and precious species is prohibited.

【围拢】wéilǒng 从四周向某个地方聚拢 close in; surround from all sides

【围屏】wéipíng 屏风的一种,通常是四扇、六扇或八扇连在一起,可以折叠 folding screen, usu. with four, six or eight folds

【围棋】wéiqí 棋类运动的一种。棋盘上纵横各十九道线,交错成三百六十一个位,双方用黑白棋子对着,互相围攻,吃去对方的棋子。以占据位数多的为胜。go; *weiqi*; game played with black and white pieces on a square wooden board of 361 intersections formed by 19 vertical lines and 19 horizontal lines, with the party scoring more walled-in points declared as the winner

【围墙】wéiqiáng 环绕房屋、园林、场院等的拦挡用的墙 enclosure; enclosing wall around a house, a garden, a courtyard, etc.

【围裙】wéiqún 围在身前保护衣服或身体的东西,用布或橡胶等制成 apron; piece of cloth or rubber sheet worn to protect the front of one's clothes or body

【围绕】wéirào ❶ 围着转动 go round sth.; rotate: 月亮～着地球旋转。The moon rotates round the earth. ❷ 以某个问题或事情为中心 centre on an issue: 大家～着当前生产问题提出很多建议。People have raised many suggestions concerning current problems in production.

【围魏救赵】wéi Wèi jiù Zhào 公元前353年,魏国围攻赵国都城邯郸。齐国派田忌率军救赵。田忌用军师孙膑的计策,乘魏国内部空虚而引兵攻魏,魏军回救本国,齐军乘其疲惫,在桂陵(今山东菏泽)大败魏军,赵国因而解围。后来用'围魏救赵'来指类似的作战方法。In 353 B.C., the state of Wei laid siege to Handan, capital of the state of Zhao, and the state of Qi dispatched General Tian Ji and his troops to the rescue. Adopting the strategy devised by his military counsellor Sun Bin, Tian Ji launched an offensive at Wei by taking advantage of its depleted defence. When the Wei troops hurried back to save their home, they were defeated by the Qi army at Guiling (present-day Heze, Shandong Province). Zhao was thus relieved. The phrase 'besieging Wei to rescue Zhao' has since come to refer to similar strategies.

【围桌】wéizhuō 办婚丧事或祭祀时悬挂在桌子前面用来遮挡的东西,用布或绸缎制成,上面一般绣有图案。现在有些戏曲演出时仍使用。embroidered cloth or silk covering the front side of a table, used on festive, funeral or sacrificial occasions, or on the stage

【围子】wéi·zi ❶ 围绕村庄的障碍物,用土石筑成,或用密植成的荆棘做成 fence surrounding a village, built of earth and stone, or formed by thickly grown thorns: 土～ earthen fence ❷ same as 圩子 wéi·zi ① ❸ same as 帷子 wéi·zi

【围嘴儿】wéizuǐr 围在小孩子胸前使衣服保持清洁的东西,用布或塑料等制成 bib; a piece of cloth or plastic sheet worn in the front of a baby's chest to keep that part of the clothes clean

帏(幃) wéi ❶ same as 帷 wéi ❷〈古代 *arch.*〉佩带的香囊 perfume pouch

闱(闈) wéi ❶ 宫的侧门: side gate of a palace: 宫～ side gate of a palace ❷ 科举时代称考场: imperial examination site: ～墨 exemplary papers selected from imperial examinations | 春～ spring (imperial) examination | 秋～ autumn (imperial) examination

【闱墨】wéi mò 清代乡试、会试后,主考从中式(zhòngshì)的试卷中选出并刊印的文章,供后来准备应考的人阅读 papers selected from successful candidates in the imperial examinations at the county and provincial levels during the Qing Dynasty, which were printed as references for those preparing for such exams

沩(潙) wéi 沩源口(Wéiyuánkǒu)地名,在湖北 name of a place in Hubei Province

沩(溈、潙) Wéi 沩水，水名，在湖南 Weishui, name of a river in Hunan Province

浀 Wéi 浀水，水名，在湖北 Weishui, name of a river in Hubei Province

桅 wéi 桅杆 mast：船～ mast|～顶 masthead

【桅灯】wéidēng ❶ 一种航行用的信号灯 masthead light; range light ❷ 马灯 barn lantern

【桅顶】wéidǐng 桅杆的顶端 masthead

【桅杆】wéigān ❶ 船上挂帆的杆子 mast; tall vertical spar supporting the sails ❷ 轮船上悬挂信号、装设天线、支持观测台的高杆 tall pole on a ship to support signals, antennae and the observatory deck

【桅樯】wéiqiáng same as 桅杆 wéigān

涠(潿) wéi 涠洲(Wéizhōu)，岛名，在广西 Weizhou, name of an island in Guangxi Province

硙(磑) wéi [硙硙]〈书 *fml.*〉形容高 high ☞硙 wèi on p.2002

唯 wéi 同'惟[1]'，用于下列各条(属'惟[1]'的条目有时也作'唯') same as 惟 wéi when used in the following entries (sometimes exchangeable with 唯 wéi in the entries under 惟[1] wéi)
☞ wěi on p.1997

【唯物辩证法】wéiwù biànzhèngfǎ 马克思、恩格斯所创立的建立在彻底的唯物主义基础上的辩证法。唯物辩证法认为物质世界本身有着自己的辩证运动规律，任何事物都是处在普遍联系和相互作用之中；任何事物都有它产生、发展和灭亡的过程；事物发展的根本原因在于事物内部的矛盾性，矛盾着的对立面又统一又斗争，由此推动事物的运动和变化。对立统一规律，是唯物辩证法的实质和核心。materialist dialectics; dialectics established by Marx and Engels on the basis of absolute materialism. According to materialist dialectics, the material world has its own dialectic law of motion; everything is in relation with and under the influence of everything else; everything has its own process of origin, development and end; the basic cause for the development of things is its internal contradiction. It is the opposing sides of a contradiction, both unified and opposite, that promote the motion and development of things. The law of unity and opposites is the essence and core of materialistic dialectics.

【唯物论】wéiwùlùn 唯物主义 materialism

【唯物史观】wéiwù-shǐguān ☞ 历史唯物主义 lìshǐ wéiwùzhǔyì on p.1185

【唯物主义】wéiwù zhǔyì 哲学中两大派别之一，认为世界按它的本质来说是物质的，是在人的意识之外，不依赖于人的意识而客观存在的。物质是第一性的，意识是物质存在的反映，是第二性的。世界是可以认识的。唯物主义一般是先进阶级的世界观，它经历了朴素唯物主义、形而上学唯物主义和辩证唯物主义三个发展阶段。materialism; one of the two major schools of philosophy. Materialism holds that the world essentially consists of physical matter and that it is an existence independent of human consciousness. Matter is primary while consciousness is secondary. The world is accessible to human understanding. Materialism is generally the world-view of advanced classes. It has gone through three stages of development — naive, metaphysical and dialectic.

【唯心论】wéixīnlùn 唯心主义 idealism

【唯心史观】wéixīn-shǐguān ☞ 历史唯心主义 lìshǐ wéixīnzhǔyì on p.1185

【唯心主义】wéixīn zhǔyì 哲学中两大派别之一，认为物质世界是意识、精神的产物，意识、精神是第一性的，物质是第二性的。把客观世界看成是主观意识的体现或产物的叫主观唯心主义，把客观世界看成是客观精神的体现或产物的叫客观唯心主义。唯心主义一般是剥削阶级的世界观。idealism; one of the two major schools of philosophy. Idealism holds that the material world is the product of the conscious and the spirit. Consciousness and spirit are primary, while matter is secondary. Subjective idealism regards the objective world as the representation or product of subjective consciousness. Objective idealism regards the objective world as the representation or product of objective spirit. Idealism is usually the world-view of exploitive classes.

帷 wéi 帐子 net：罗～ gauze net

【帷幔】wéimàn same as 帷幕 wéimù

【帷幕】wéimù 挂在较大的屋子里或舞台上的遮挡用的幕 heavy curtain hung in a big room or on a theatric stage

【帷幄】wéiwò〈书 *fml.*〉军队里用的帐幕 army tent：运筹～ formulate strategies in a tent

【帷子】wéi·zi 围起来做遮挡用的布 curtain; cloth hung up as a kind of cover or shelter：床～ bed curtain|车～ vehicle curtain

惟[1] wéi ❶ 单单；只 only; alone：～一无二 one and one only ❷ 只是 but：他学习很好，～身体稍差。He does very well in his studies, but is a little weak in health.

惟[2] wéi〈书 *fml.*〉〈助词 *aux.*〉用在年、月、日之前 used before year, month or day：～二月既望 on the 16th of the 2nd lunar month (既望 *jiwang*：农历十六 16th day of each lunar month)

惟[3] wéi 思想 thought：思～ thinking (今多作思维 oft. 思维 sīwéi in present-day use)

【惟独】wéidú 单单 only; alone：别的事还可以放一放，～这件事必须赶快做。Other things can wait; this issue must be dealt with immediately.

【惟恐】wéikǒng 只怕 for fear that; lest:～落后 for fear that one should lag behind|～迟到 lest one should be late

【惟利是图】wéi lì shì tú 只贪图财利,别的什么都不顾 be solely bent on profit to the neglect of everything else

【惟妙惟肖】wéi miào wéi xiào 形容描写或模仿得非常好,非常逼真(of description or imitation) be remarkably good; true to life; to the turn of a hair:这幅画把儿童活泼有趣的神态画得～。The picture hit off the children's vivacious and funny mien to the turn of a hair.

【惟命是听】wéi mìng shì tīng 让做什么,就做什么,绝对服从 do whatever one is told; obey without questioning; also 惟命是从 wéi mìng shì cóng

【惟其】wéiqí 〈书 *fml.*〉〈连词 *conj.*〉表示因果关系,跟'正因为'相近 precisely because; similar to 正因为 zhèngyīn·wèi:这问题我们了解甚少,～了解甚少,所以更须多方探讨。We know little about it, and it is precisely because we know little that we must study it from various angles.

【惟我独尊】wéi wǒ dú zūn 认为只有自己最了不起 self-conceited; self-centred

【惟一】wéiyī 只有一个;独一无二 only; one and one only:这是～可行的办法。This is the only way out.|他是我～的亲人。He is my only family member.

【惟有】wéiyǒu 只有 only; except:大家都愿意,～他不愿意。Everyone is willing except him.

维[1] wéi ❶ 连接 hold together:～系 maintain ❷ 保持;保全 keep; maintain:～持 sustain|～护 preserve ❸ (Wéi)姓 a surname

维[2] wéi same as 惟[3] wéi

维[3] wéi 几何学及空间理论的基本概念。构成空间的每一个因素(如长、宽、高)叫做一维,如直线是一维的,平面是二维的,普通空间是三维的。dimension; basic concept of geometry and spatial theory; measure of spatial extent, such as width, height, or length. For example, a line is one-dimensional, a plane two-dimensional, and ordinary space three-dimensional.

【维持】wéichí ❶ 使继续存在下去;保持 maintain; keep:～秩序 maintain order|～生活 make a living|～现状 maintain the status quo ❷ 保护;维护支持 safeguard; support:亏他暗中～,才得以平安无事。Thanks to his secret support, nothing has gone wrong.

【维护】wéihù 使免于遭受破坏;维持保护 protect; uphold:～集体利益 safeguard collective interest|～法律的尊严 vindicate the dignity of law

【维纶】wéilún 合成纤维的一种,用乙炔、乙烯、醋酸、甲醛为原料合成,性质与棉纤维相近,但强度较高,较轻,吸水性较强,宜于做夏季衣服,也用来制绳索、渔网等 polyvinyl alcohol fibre; vinylon; synthetic fibre made from acetylene, ethylene, acetic acid and formaldehyde, similar to cotton fibre in texture, but more wearable, lighter and more absorbent, appropriate for summer clothes, also used to make rope and fishing net;也译作 also translated as 维尼纶 wéinílún;维尼龙 wéinílóng

【维绵布】wéimiánbù 维纶与棉花混纺后织成的布 vinylon and cotton blend

【维生素】wéishēngsù 人和动物营养、生长所必需的某些少量有机化合物,对机体的新陈代谢、生长、发育、健康有极重要作用。如果长期缺乏某种维生素,就会引起生理机能障碍而发生某种疾病。一般由食物中取得。现在发现的有几十种,如维生素A、维生素B、维生素C等。vitamin; any of various organic substances essential in minute amount for metabolism, growth and health of the body and obtained naturally from foods. Insufficient intake of certain vitamin over a long period of time will cause physiological malfunction and result in certain diseases. There are dozens of known vitamins, such as vitamins A, B and C. 旧称 fomerly called 维他命 wéitāmìng

【维他命】wéitāmìng 维生素的旧称 former term for 维生素 wéishēngsù

【维吾尔族】Wéiwú'ěrzú 我国少数民族之一,主要分布在新疆 Uygur ethnic group, or the Uygurs, mainly inhabiting the Xinjiang Uygur Autonomous Region

【维系】wéixì 维持并联系,使不涣散 maintain; hold together:～人心 maintain public morale

【维新】wéixīn 反对旧的,提倡新的。一般指政治上的改良,或改良主义运动,如我国清末的变法维新。reform; modernization; advocating the new while opposing the old; usu. referring to political reform or reformative movement, such as the Hundred Days Reform (1989) in the late Qing Dynasty

【维修】wéixiū 保护和修理 maintain and repair:～房屋 maintain a house or building|机器～得好,使用年限就能延长。Good maintenance will prolong the service life of a machine.

【维族】Wéizú 维吾尔族的简称 abbr. for 维吾尔族 Wéiwú'ěrzú

嵬 wéi 〈书 *fml.*〉高大耸立 tower high:～然 lofty|～～ towering

【嵬嵬】wéiwéi 〈书 *fml.*〉高大的样子 rising up high

鮠 wéi 鱼类的一属,身体前部扁平,后部侧扁,眼小,尾鳍分叉。生活在淡水中。leiocassis (*Leiocassis longirostris*); a genus of freshwater fish, its body flat in the front and thin in the back, with small eyes and bifurcated tail fin

潍 Wéi 潍河,水名,在山东 Weihe, name of a river in Shandong Province

wěi (ㄨㄟˇ)

伟(偉) wěi ❶ 伟大 great:雄~magnificent|~论 great theory|~绩 grand achievement ❷〈书 *fml.*〉壮美 beautiful and magnificent:~丈夫 strong and handsome man

【伟岸】wěi'àn 魁梧;高大 tall and sturdy; stalwart:身材~ of tall and sturdy stature|村头有两棵挺拔~的松树。There are two towering pine trees by the entrance to the village.

【伟大】wěidà 品格崇高;才识卓越;气象雄伟;规模宏大;超出寻常,令人景仰钦佩的 great; outstanding; magnificent; grand; extraordinary; awe-inspiring:~的领袖 distinguished leader|~的祖国 great motherland|~的事业 grand cause|~的成就 outstanding achievement

【伟绩】wěijì 伟大的功绩 great feat:丰功~ grand exploit and achievement

【伟力】wěilì 巨大的力量 mighty force

【伟论】wěilùn 宏论 grand theory

【伟人】wěirén 伟大的人物 great personage:一代~ great man of his generation

【伟业】wěiyè 伟大的业绩 illustrious exploit

伪(偽、僞) wěi ❶ 有意做作掩盖本来面貌的;虚假(跟'真'相对 as opposed to 'true')disguise; cover the original look of sth. on purpose; false:~装 disguise|~造 counterfeit|作~forge|~钞 counterfeit banknote|去~存真 remove the false and retain the true ❷ 不合法的;窃取政权、不为人民所拥护的(of a regime) illegal; unpopular:~政权 puppet regime|~军 quisling army|~组织 illegal organization

【伪钞】wěichāo 假造的纸币 counterfeit banknote

【伪君子】wěijūnzǐ 外貌正派,实际上卑鄙无耻的人 hypocrite; person who appears upright but is low in character

【伪劣】wěiliè 冒牌的、质量低劣的(of goods) fake or of low quality:~商品 shoddy goods|~书画 fake works of painting and calligraphy

【伪善】wěishàn 冒充好人 pretend to be good:~者 hypocrite|~的面孔 hypocritical face

【伪书】wěishū 作者姓名或著作时代不可靠的书 book of dubious authorship or date

【伪托】wěituō 在著述、制造等方面假托别人名义,多指把自己的或后人的作品假冒为古人的 pass off one's writing or work of art in the name of someone else, oft. referring to passing off modern works as classical ones

【伪造】wěizào 假造 fabricate:~证件 forge a certificate|~历史 fabricate history

【伪证】wěizhèng 假造的证据,指案件进行侦查或审理中,证人、鉴定人、记录人或翻译人故意做出的虚假证明、鉴定和翻译。伪证依法构成伪证罪。false evidence, provided by a witness, identifier, note-taker, or translator during investigation or trial of a case. One who supplies such testimony is guilty of perjury.

【伪装】wěizhuāng ❶ 假装 pretend; feign:~进步 pretend to be progressive ❷ 假的装扮 disguise:剥去~ strip off sb.'s mask ❸ 军事上采取措施来隐蔽自己、迷惑敌人 camouflage; take measures to hide oneself and confuse the enemy ❹ 军事上用来伪装的东西 camouflage works

【伪足】wěizú 变形虫等原生动物的运动器官和捕食器官,由身体的任一部分突出而形成,形成后可以重新缩回 pseudopodium; temporary protrusion of the surface of a protist, such as amoeba, for movement and feeding

【伪作】wěizuò ❶ 假托别人名义写作诗文或制作艺术品 create a piece of writing or art work in the name of someone else ❷ 假托别人写作的诗文或制作的艺术品 a piece of writing or art work in the name of sb. other than the real author

苇(葦) wěi 芦苇 reed

【苇箔】wěibó 用芦苇编成的帘子 reed curtain

【苇荡】wěidàng 生长大片芦苇的浅水湖 reed marsh; also 芦荡 lúdàng

【苇塘】wěitáng 生长芦苇的池塘 reed pond

【苇子】wěi·zi same as 芦苇 lúwěi

艻(蔿、蒍) Wěi 姓 a surname

尾 wěi ❶ same as 尾巴 wěi·ba ① ② ❷ 二十八宿之一 one of the 28 constellations into which the celestial sphere was divided in ancient Chinese astronomy (consisting of nine stars in the shape of a hook in Scorpio) ❸ 末端;末尾 end:排~ at the end in order|有头无~ start doing sth. without finishing it ❹ 主要部分以外的部分;没有了结的事情 remaining part; unfinished part of sth.:~数 number after a decimal point|扫~ put a finishing touch to sth. ❺〈量词 *classifier*〉用于鱼[for fish]:一~鱼 one fish

☞yǐ on p.2269

【尾巴】wěi·ba ❶ 鸟、兽、虫、鱼等动物的身体末端突出的部分,主要作用是辅助运动、保持身体平衡等 tail; posterior part of a bird, animal, insect, fish, etc., elongated and extending beyond the trunk or main part of the body, for aiding movement and keeping balance ❷ 某些物体的尾部 tail-like part of an object:飞机~ tail of an aircraft|彗星~tail of a comet ❸ 指事物的残留部分 remnant:彻底平反冤案,

不要留～。We must correct all wrong cases without exception. ❹ 指跟踪或尾随在后面的人 person who follows and reports on someone：甩掉～throw off one's tail ❺ 指没有主见、完全随声附和的人 servile follower; person who does not have his or her own opinion and always chime in with others

【尾大不掉】wěi dà bù diào〈比喻 *fig.*〉机构下强上弱，或组织庞大、涣散，以致指挥不灵 leadership rendered ineffectual by recalcitrant subordinates or by a large but cumbersome organization（掉 *diao*：摇动 wave）

【尾灯】wěidēng 装在汽车、摩托车等交通工具尾部的灯，一般用红色的灯罩，用以引起后面车辆或行人等的注意 tail light; lamp fixed on the rear part of an automobile or motorbike, usu. covered with a red lampshade to warn following vehicles or pedestrians

【尾骨】wěigǔ 人或脊椎动物脊柱的末端部分。人的尾骨是由四至五块小骨组成的。coccyx; end part of the spinal column in human beings and other vertebrates; that of the human being consisting of four to five small bones;（图见 ☞ figure for 骨骼 gǔgé on p.693）

【尾花】wěihuā 报刊、书籍上诗文末尾空白处的装饰性图画 decorative drawing to fill in blank space at the end of printed text in newspaper or book

【尾迹】wěijì 飞机等飞行时在大气中留下的痕迹。也指船只航行时在水面上留下的痕迹。wake; trail left in the atmosphere by an aircraft or that left in the water by a vessel

【尾鳍】wěiqí 鱼类尾部的鳍，是鱼类的运动器官 tail fin; caudal fin; part of the body of a fish for movement;（图见 ☞ figure for 鳍 qí on p.1513）

【尾欠】wěiqiàn ❶ 有一小部分没有偿还或交纳 owe a small balance：还了八百元，～二百元。800 yuan has been paid, with 200 yuan in balance due. ❷ 没有偿还或交纳的一小部分 small part of a balance due：～下月还清。The rest of the balance due will be cleared next month.

【尾声】wěishēng ❶ 南曲、北曲的套曲中的最后一支曲子；每出戏结束时用唢呐吹奏的曲牌 coda; last tune, of a set of tunes, played with *suona* at the end of a traditional drama of either the northern or the southern style ❷ 大型乐曲中乐章的最后一部分 coda; passage at the end of a movement or composition that brings it to a formal close ❸ 文学作品的结局部分 finishing part of a literary work ❹ 指某项活动快要结束的阶段 end of an activity：会谈接近～。The talks are going to finish soon.

【尾数】wěishù ❶ 小数点后面的数 number after a decimal point ❷ 结算账目中大数目之外剩下的小数目 odd amount in addition to the round number of settled accounts ❸ 指多位号码中末尾的数字 last number of a multi-digital figure

【尾随】wěisuí 跟随在后面 follow; tail behind：孩子们～着军乐队走了好远。The children followed the military band a long way.

【尾音】wěiyīn 一个字、一个词或一句话的最后的音 last syllable of a character, word or sentence

【尾蚴】wěiyòu 有尾巴的幼虫，身体很小，必须用显微镜才能看见，能在水中游泳，如血吸虫的幼虫 cercaria; tailed larva, small in size and observable only under a microscope, capable of swimming in water, such as the schistosome larva

【尾追】wěizhuī 紧跟在后面追赶 give chase to; chase after; follow closely behind：～不舍 follow in hot pursuit

【尾子】wěi·zi〈方 *dial.*〉❶ 事物的最后一部分 last part of sth. ❷ same as 尾数 wěishù ②

纬(緯)

wěi（旧读 formerly pronounced wèi）❶ 织物上横的方向的纱或线（跟'经'相对 as opposed to 'warp'）weft; woof; horizontal thread in a woven fabric：经～ warp and weft｜～纱 weft yarn｜～线 weft thread ❷ 纬度 latitude：南～ south latitude｜北～ north latitude ❸纬书的简称 abbr. for 纬书 wěishū：谶（chèn）～ documents and augury books

【纬度】wěidù 地球表面南北距离的度数，以赤道为零度，以北为北纬，以南为南纬，南北各 90°。通过某地的纬线跟赤道相距的度数，就是该地的纬度。latitude; angular distance north or south of the earth's equator, measured in 90 degrees respectively along a meridian; ☞ 纬线 wěixiàn ②

【纬纱】wěishā 织布时由梭带动的横纱 weft; horizontal thread pulled by the shuttle in weaving

【纬书】wěishū 汉代以神学迷信附会儒家经义的一类书，其中保存不少古代神话传说，也记录一些有关古代天文、历法、地理等方面的知识 augury books; a category of books in the Han Dynasty that provide far-fetched interpretations on Confucian classics, many containing ancient myths and legends, and knowledge in ancient astrology, calendar, geography, etc.；简称 abbr. 纬 wěi

【纬线】wěixiàn ❶ 纬纱或编织品上的横线 weft; woof; horizontal thread in weaving or knitting ❷ 假定的沿地球表面跟赤道平行的线 parallel; imaginary lines parallel to the equator of the earth; ☞纬度 wěidù

玮(瑋)

wěi〈书 *fml.*〉❶ 玉名 a kind of jade ❷ 珍奇；贵重 precious; valuable：珍珠～宝 pearls and rare treasures｜～奇（奇特）unusual

時(暐) wěi 〈书 *fml*.〉形容光很盛 (of light) bright

委1 wěi ❶ 把事交给别人去办；委任 entrust; appoint: ～托 entrust | ～派 delegate | ～以重任 assign an important task to sb. ❷ 抛弃 discard: ～弃 cast aside | ～之于地 throw sth. on the ground ❸ 推委 shift: ～过 shirk blame | ～罪 parry a crime ❹ 委员或委员会的简称 abbr. for 委员 wěiyuán or 委员会 wěiyuánhuì: 编～ editorial board | 党～ Party committee | 市～ municipal Party committee

委2 wěi 曲折 indirect; roundabout: ～曲 feel wronged | ～婉 indirect

委3 wěi 〈书 *fml*.〉 ❶ 积聚 gather; accumulate: ～积 build up ❷ 水流所聚；水的下游；末尾 accumulation of water; lower reaches of a river; end: 原～cause | 穷源竟～(追究事物的本源及其发展) trace the origin and course of development of sth.

委4 wěi 无精打采；不振作 listless; dejected: ～顿 downcast | ～靡 in low spirits

委5 wěi 〈书 *fml*.〉的确；确实 certain; for sure: ～实 actually | ～系实情。It's the true story.

☞ wēi on p. 1986

【委顿】wěidùn 疲乏；没有精神 tired; weary: 精神～ in low spirits

【委过】wěiguò same as 诿过 wěiguò

【委决不下】wěi jué bù xià 迟疑而决定不下来 hesitate to make a decision: 他一时～，跑来要我出主意。He could not make up his mind and came to me for advice.

【委靡】wěimǐ 精神不振；意志消沉 dispirited; dejected: 神志～ look spiritless | ～不振 dejected and apathetic; also 萎靡 wěimǐ

【委派】wěipài 派人担任职务或完成某项任务 appoint; delegate; designate

【委曲】wěiqū ❶ (曲调、道路、河流等)弯弯曲曲的；曲折(of road, river, etc.) winding; tortuous; (of music tune) rhythmic: ～婉转 rhythmic and pleasant | ～的溪流 winding stream ❷〈书 *fml*.〉事情的底细和原委 detail and origin of sth.: 告知～ let sb. in on the ins and outs of sth.

【委曲求全】wěi qū qiú quán 勉强迁就，以求保全；为顾全大局而暂时忍让 make concession for the sake of sth. more important; compromise to ensure overall interest

【委屈】wěi·qu ❶ 受到不应该有的指责或待遇，心里难过 feel wronged due to unjustified criticism or treatment; nurse a grievance: 诉～ vent one's grievances | 满肚子的～feel deeply aggrieved ❷ 让人受到委屈 cause sb. to feel wronged: 对不起，～你了。Sorry to have put you through this. *or* Sorry to have put you to such inconvenience.

【委任】wěirèn ❶ 派人担任职务 appoint: ～状(派人担任职务的证件) document of appointment ❷ 辛亥革命以后到解放以前文官的最末一等，在荐任以下 lowest rank of civil servant after the 1911 Revolution and before 1949, below 荐任 jiànrèn

【委身】wěishēn 〈书 *fml*.〉把自己的身体、心力投到某一方面(多指在不得已的情况下)(oft. against one's will) submit oneself to: ～事人 submit service to sb.

【委实】wěishí 实在 really; indeed: ～不容易 by no means easy

【委琐】wěisuǒ 〈书 *fml*.〉 ❶ 琐碎；拘泥于小节 petty; trivial ❷ same as 猥琐 wěisuǒ

【委托】wěituō 请人代办 entrust; delegate: 这事就～你了。I'll entrust you with the matter.

【委宛】wěiwǎn same as 委婉 wěiwǎn

【委婉】wěiwǎn (言词、声音等)婉转(of words) indirect; tactful; (of voice) rhythmic: ～动听 rhythmic and pleasant | 态度诚恳，语气～ sincere in attitude and mild in tone; also 委宛 wěiwǎn

【委员】wěiyuán ❶ 委员会的成员 member of a committee ❷〈旧时 *old*〉被委派担任特定任务的人员 envoy with a special commission

【委员会】wěiyuánhuì ❶ 政党、团体、机关、学校中的集体领导组织 committee; council; collective leadership of a party, group, organization, school, etc.: 中国共产党中央～ the Central Committee of the Communist Party of China | 体育运动～ sports committee | 校务～school committee ❷ 机关、团体、学校等为完成一定的任务而设立的专门组织 group of people officially delegated by an organization, group, school, etc. to perform a function by an organization, group, school, etc.: 招生～enrollment committee | 伙食～catering committee

【委罪】wěizuì same as 诿罪 wěizuì

炜(煒) wěi 〈书 *fml*.〉光明 bright

洧 wěi 洧川(Weichuān)，地名，在河南 Weichuan, name of a place in Henan Province

韪(韡) wěi 〈书 *fml*.〉光明；美盛 bright; magnificent

诿 wěi 把责任推给别人；推卸 put blame on sb. else; shirk: 推～skulk

【诿过】wěiguò 把过错推给别人 blame sb. else for one's own mistake: ～于人 shift the blame onto others; also 委过 wěiguò

【诿卸】wěixiè 〈书 *fml*.〉推卸 shirk

【诿罪】wěizuì 把罪名推给别人 shift blame on to sb. else; also 委罪 wěizuì

娓 wěi [娓娓]形容谈论不倦或说话动听 (speak) tirelessly or pleasantly: ～而谈 talk tirelessly in a pleasant manner | ～动听 nice to listen to

萎 wěi ❶（植物）干枯（of plant）wilt：枯～ wither｜～谢 fade ❷（口语中多读 pronounced as wēi in speech）衰落 decline：买卖～了。Business has shrunk.｜价钱～下来了。Prices have fallen.

【萎落】wěiluò ❶ 枯萎败落 wither；fade：草木～。The grass and plants have wizened. ❷ 衰落 weaken

【萎靡】wěimǐ same as 委靡 wěimǐ

【萎蔫】wěiniān 植物体由于缺乏水分而茎叶萎缩 wilt；（of plant）become flaccid due to lack of water

【萎缩】wěisuō ❶ 干枯；（身体、器官等）功能减退并缩小 wilt；shrink；wither；（of body or body organ）deteriorate in function and shrivel in size：花草～。The flowers and grass have withered.｜肢体～。The limbs have shrivelled.｜子宫～ atrophy of the uterus ❷（经济）衰退（of an economy）decline

【萎谢】wěixiè（花草）干枯凋谢（of flower and grass）wilt；fade：百花～。All the flowers have withered. ◇生命～。Life has wasted away.

唯 wěi〈书 *fml.*〉表示答应的词 yes；
☞ wéi on p. 1992

【唯唯诺诺】wěiwěinuònuò 形容一味顺从别人的意见 be blindly subservient to other people's viewpoint

痏 wěi〈书 *fml.*〉疮；伤口 sore；cut

隗 Wěi 姓 a surname
☞ Kuí on p. 1128

骫 wěi〈书 *fml.*〉曲；枉 twist；bend：～曲（委曲迁就）make compromise｜～法（枉法）pervert the law

【骫骳】wěibèi〈书 *fml.*〉曲折；屈曲 tortuous；twist

颜 wěi〈书 *fml.*〉安静。多用于人名。quiet, oft. used in personal names

猥 wěi ❶ 多；杂 many；mixed：～杂 miscellaneous ❷ 卑鄙；下流 low；obscene：～亵 indecent

【猥词】wěicí same as 猥辞 wěicí

【猥辞】wěicí 下流话；淫秽的词语 obscene words；dirty language；also 猥词 wěicí

【猥獕】wěicuī 丑陋难看；庸俗拘束（多见于早期白话 oft. in early vernacular）ugly；vulgar and ill at ease

【猥劣】wěiliè〈书 *fml.*〉卑劣 base；mean：行为～ behave in a base manner

【猥陋】wěilòu〈书 *fml.*〉低劣；卑鄙 low；base；also 猥鄙 wěibǐ

【猥琐】wěisuǒ（容貌、举动）庸俗不大方（of appearance，deportment）uncouth：举止～ conduct oneself rudely；also 委琐 wěisuǒ

【猥亵】wěixiè ❶ 淫乱；下流的（言语或行为）（of language or behaviour）licentious；obscene：言词～ speak wantonly ❷ 做下流的动作 act indecently：～妇女 harass a woman

廆 wěi 用于人名。慕容廆，西晋末年鲜卑族的首领。used in personal names, such as Murong Wei, chief of the Xianbei tribe towards the end of the Western Jin Dynasty
☞ Guī on p. 731

韪（韙） wěi ☞不韪 bùwěi on p. 167

艉 wěi 船体的尾部 stern of a ship

痿 wěi〈中医 *Chin. med.*〉指身体某一部分萎缩或失去机能的病，例如下痿、阳痿等 illness caused by decline or loss of function of a certain body part, such as paraplegia or erectile disfunction

鲔 wěi ❶ 鱼，体呈纺锤形，背黑蓝色，腹灰白色，背鳍和臀鳍后面各有七或八个小鳍。生活在热带海洋，吃小鱼等动物。Yaito tuna（*Euthynnus yaito*）；fish with a spindle-like body, dark-blue back, greyish white belly, and seven or eight small fins behind the dorsal fin and the anal fin, living in tropical seas and feeding on small fish ❷ 古书上指鲟鱼 sturgeon as mentioned in ancient books

亹 wěi［亹亹］〈书 *fml.*〉❶ 形容勤勉不倦 diligent ❷ 形容向前推移、行进 push or move forward；
☞ mén on p. 1323

wèi（ㄨㄟˋ）

卫[1]（衛、衞） wèi ❶ 保卫 defend；guard；protect：捍～ safeguard｜保家～国 protect our homes and defend our country ❷ 明代驻兵的地点，驻军人数比'所'多，后来只用于地名 location for the stationing of troops in the Ming Dynasty with a bigger number than in a '所' *suo*, which has been used only for the name of a place afterwards：威海～（今威海市，在山东）Weihaiwei（present-day city of Weihai in Shandong Province）｜松门～（今松门镇，在浙江）Songmenwei（present-day Songmen Town in Zhejiang Province）

卫[2]（衛、衞） Wèi ❶ 周朝国名，在今河北南部和河南北部一带 name of a principality in the Zhou Dynasty, now located in the southern part of Hebei Province and the northern part of Henan Province ❷ 姓 a surname

【卫兵】wèibīng 担任警卫工作的士兵 guard；bodyguard

【卫道】wèidào 卫护某种占统治地位的思想体系 defend traditional moral principles：～士 apologist｜～者 moral defender

【卫队】wèiduì 担任警卫工作的部队 squad of bodyguards；armed escort

【卫护】wèihù 捍卫保护 protect；guard

【卫拉特】Wèilātè 瓦剌在清代的称呼 Qing-dynasty transliteration of the term that denotes the Oirat Mongols

【卫冕】wèimiǎn 指竞赛中保住上次获得的冠军称号 defend one's championship; defend one's title:～成功 successfully defend one's title|男子篮球队能否～,就看这场比赛了。Whether the men's basketball team can defend its title hinges on this match.

【卫生】wèishēng ❶ 能防止疾病,有益于健康 good for one's health; hygienic; sanitary:～常识 hygienic knowledge|喝生水,不～。It's not good for health to drink unboiled water. ❷ 合乎卫生的情况 hygiene; sanitation:讲～ pay attention to hygiene|环境～ environmental hygiene

【卫生带】wèishēngdài 月经带 sanitary belt; sanitary napkin

【卫生间】wèishēngjiān 旅馆或住宅中有卫生设备的房间 toilet; washroom; room with sanitary equipment in a hotel, inn, house, etc.

【卫生裤】wèishēngkù〈方 *dial.*〉绒裤 sweat pants

【卫生球】wèishēngqiú (～儿 wèishēngqiúr)用萘制成的球状物,白色,有特殊的气味,过去放在衣物中,用来防止虫蛀 camphor ball; mothball; white balls made of naphthalene, with a special odour, which are put in clothes to prevent moth eating

【卫生设备】wèishēng shèbèi 指与上水道和下水道接通的脸盆、澡盆、抽水马桶等 sanitary equipment, as water basin, bath tub, water closet, etc., that connects with the water-supply line and the drain line

【卫生衣】wèishēngyī〈方 *dial.*〉绒衣 sweat shirt

【卫生员】wèishēngyuán 受过短期训练,具有医疗卫生基本知识和急救护理等技术的初级医务人员 medical orderly; medic; medical personnel who receive short-term medical courses and have acquired basic medical knowledge, first aid and nursing

【卫生纸】wèishēngzhǐ ❶ 手纸 toilet paper ❷ 供妇女在经期中使用的、消过毒的纸 sanitary towel;sterilized paper used by women during their menstrual period

【卫士】wèishì 卫兵,泛指担任保卫工作的人 bodyguard; (in a broad sense) people who are engaged in security work

【卫戍】wèishù 警备(多用于首都 oft. for a capital) garrison:～区 garrison command|～司令 garrison commander

【卫星】wèixīng ❶ 按一定轨道绕行星运行的天体,本身不能发光 satellite; moon; celestial body that moves around a planet along a given orbit and does not emit light by itself ❷ 像卫星那样环绕某个中心的 something that surrounds a certain centre like a satellite:～城市 satellite town ❸ 指人造卫星 artificial satellite; man-made satellite

【卫星城】wèixīngchéng 围绕大城市建设的中小城市 satellite town; small towns that are built around a big city

【卫星通信】wèixīng tōngxìn 一种通信方式,两个或几个地面站之间以人造地球卫星为中继站转发无线电信号 satellite telecommunications; form of communications by which radio signals are transmitted through space between two or more earth stations with an artificial earth satellite as its relay station

为(為、爲)

wèi ❶〈书 *fml.*〉帮助;卫护 help; defend; protect:～吕氏者右袒,～刘氏者左袒。Those who take sides with Lü please bare your right shoulder, and those take sides with Liu please bare your left shoulder. ❷〈介词 *prep.*〉表示行为的对象;替 in the interest of; for:～你庆幸 congratulate you|～人民服务 serve the people|～这本书写一篇序 write preface for the book ❸〈介词 *prep.*〉表示目的 for the purpose of; for the sake of:～大家的健康干杯。A toast to everyone's health! |～建设伟大祖国而奋斗。Strive to build up the great motherland. ❹ 对;向 to:不足～外人道 do not mention to others; not breathe about it to others ❺ 因为 because:～何? why?

☞ wéi on p.1989

【为何】wèihé 为什么 why; for what reason:～一言不发? Why didn't you say a word?

【为虎傅翼】wèi hǔ fù yì〈比喻 *fig.*〉帮助恶人,增加恶人的势力 aid an evildoer; add to the influence of a villain (傅翼 *fu yi*:加上翅膀 give wings to); also 为虎添翼 wèi hǔ tiān yì

【为虎作伥】wèi hǔ zuò chāng〈比喻 *fig.*〉做恶人的帮凶,帮助恶人做坏事 play the jackal to the tiger — help a villain do evil (伥 *chang*:鬼名 name of a ghost); ☞ 伥鬼 chāngguǐ on p.214

【为了】wèi·le 表示目的 for; for the sake of; in order to:学习是～工作 study for the sake of work|一切～人民利益 everything for the people's interests|～教育群众,首先要向群众学习。In order to educate the masses, it is, first of all, to learn from the masses. 注意

NOTE:表示原因,一般用'因为'不用'为了' to indicate a reason, usually use 因为 yīn·wèi instead of 为了 wèi·le

【为人作嫁】wèi rén zuò jià 唐朝秦韬玉《贫女》诗:'苦恨年年压金线,为他人作嫁衣裳。'The poem *Poor Girl* by Qin Taoyu of the Tang Dynasty goes:'I bitterly hate sewing with gold thread year in year out, just to make bridal clothes for others to wear.' 后来用'为人作嫁'比喻空为别人辛苦忙碌 used in later times to liken the hard toil done by a person for others without benefiting himself; sewing somebody else's trousseau — doing work for others with no benefit to oneself

【为什么】wèi shén·me 询问原因或目的 why; why (or how) is it that:～群众这么爱护解放军？因为解放军是人民的子弟兵。Why do the masses cherish the People's Liberation Army so much? It's because the People's Liberation Army is an army made up of the sons of the people.|他这么做到底是～？Why, after all, should he do this? 注意 **NOTE**:'为什么不'常含有劝告的意思，跟'何不'相同，如：这种技术很有用处，你～不学一学？为什么不 wèi shén·mebù implies an advice. It's the same as 何不 hébù. For example, this kind of skill is very useful, why don't you learn it?

【为渊驱鱼，为丛驱雀】wèi yuān qū yú, wèi cóng qū què《孟子·离娄上》:'为渊驱鱼者，獭也；为丛驱爵者，鹯也'(爵：同'雀')。意思是水獭想捉鱼吃，却把鱼赶到深渊去了；鹞鹰想捉麻雀吃，却把麻雀赶到丛林中去了。后来用这两句话比喻不善于团结人或笼络人，把可以依靠的力量赶到敌人方面去。*Mencius·Li Lou* (*I*): 'It is the otter which drives the fish into deep waters; and it is the hawk that drives the sparrows into the thickets.' It means that the otter wants to eat fish, but it drives the fish into deep water; and the hawk wants to eat sparrow, but it drives the sparrows into the thickets. The two phrases are used later to liken sb. who is not capable of uniting others or winning favour from others, but drives his friends over to the side of the enemy.

【为着】wèi·zhe same as 为了 wèi·le

未[1] wèi〈副词 *adv.*〉❶ 没(跟'已'相对 as opposed to 'have') have not; did not:～成年 be under age|健康尚～恢复 have not yet recovered one's health; not yet recovered (from illness); not yet restored to health ❷ 不 no; not:～便 not be in a position to; find it hard to|～敢苟同 not agree with; beg to differ|～可厚非 not be altogether unjustifiable; give little cause for criticism

未[2] wèi 地支的第八位 eighth of the 12 Earthly Branches; ☞ 干支 gànzhī on p. 627

【未必】wèibì 不一定 may not; not necessarily:他～知道。He doesn't necessarily know.|这消息～可靠。The news may not be reliable.

【未便】wèibiàn 不宜于；不便 not be in a position to; find it hard to:此事上级并无指示，～擅自处理。I cannot do it without authorization since there is no instruction from the higher-up.

【未卜】wèibǔ〈书 *fml.*〉不能预料；不可预知 cannot be anticipated; cannot be foreseen; unpredictable; unforeseen:前途～ unpredictable future|胜负～。It's still uncertain who will win and who will lose.

【未卜先知】wèi bǔ xiān zhī 事情发生之前不用占卜就能知道，形容有预见 know something without consulting the oracle; have foreknowledge

【未曾】wèicéng '没有'[2]('曾经'的否定 negative form of 'used to') have not; did not:这是历史上～有过的奇迹。This is a miracle unprecedented in history.

【未尝】wèicháng ❶ 未曾 have not; did not:终夜～合眼 didn't get a wink of sleep the whole night ❷ 加在否定词前面，构成双重否定，意思跟'不是(不、没)'相同，但口气更委婉 used before a negative word to make a negation of negation with the same meaning as 'no' or 'not', but in a milder tone:这～不是一个好建议。That might be a good suggestion.|你的办法固然有优点，但是也～没有缺点。It is true that your method has strong points, but it is not one without weak points.

【未婚夫】wèihūnfū 已经订婚尚未结婚的丈夫 fiancé (of a woman)

【未婚妻】wèihūnqī 已经订婚尚未结婚的妻子 fiancée (of a man)

【未几】wèijǐ〈书 *fml.*〉❶ 没有多少时候；不久 soon; before long:～即离沪北上。I'll leave Shanghai for the north very soon. ❷ 不多；无几 not many; very few

【未竟】wèijìng 没有完成(多指事业) unfulfilled; unaccomplished:～之业 unaccomplished task|～之志 unfulfilled ambition

【未决犯】wèijuéfàn 还没有经法院判决定罪的犯人 prisoner awaiting trial; culprit

【未可厚非】wèi kě hòu fēi 不可过分指责，表示虽有缺点，但是可以原谅 not be altogether unjustifiable; give little cause for criticism; also 无可厚非 wú kě hòu fēi

【未来】wèilái ❶ 就要到来的(指时间) coming; approaching; next; future:～二十四小时内将有暴雨。There will be a rainstorm in 24 hours. ❷ 现在以后的时间；将来的光景 future; tomorrow:展望～ look to the future

【未了】wèiliǎo 没有完结；没有了结 unfinished; outstanding:～事项 unsettled matters; unfinished business|～手续 formalities still to be complied with|还有一桩心愿～。There is still one unfulfilled wish.

【未免】wèimiǎn ❶ 实在不能不说是…(表示不以为然)[imply disagreement, objection] rather; a bit too; truly:你的顾虑～多了些。You are perhaps a little overcautious.|他这样对待客人，～不礼貌。He was really impolite, behaving like that towards his guest. ❷ 不免 naturally; unavoidably:如此教学，～要误人子弟。Such teaching would unavoidably mislead the younger generation.

【未能免俗】wèi néng miǎn sú 没能摆脱开自己

不以为然的习俗 be unable to rise above the convention that one does not approve; cannot but follow conventional practice

【未然】wèirán 还没有成为事实 not yet become a fact：防患于～ take preventive measures

【未时】wèishí 旧式计时法指下午一点钟到三点钟的时间 period of the day from 1 p. m. to 3 p. m. in the old Chinese time measurement

【未始】wèishǐ same as 未尝 wèicháng ②：～不可 be not that impossible

【未遂】wèisuì 没有达到(目的)；没有满足(愿望) not accomplished (a purpose); abortive; unfulfilled (wish)：～犯 one who attempts to commit a crime｜愿心～ unfulfilled wish

【未亡人】wèiwángrén〈旧时 *old*〉寡妇自称 the bereaved one (form of self-address formerly used by a widow)

【未详】wèixiáng 不知道或没有了解清楚 unknown or unclear：本书作者～。The author of the book is unknown.｜病因～。What brought on the illness is not clear.

【未央】wèiyāng〈书 *fml.*〉未尽 not ended：夜～。The night is not yet over.

【未雨绸缪】wèi yǔ chóumóu 趁着天没下雨，先修缮房屋门窗 repair the house before it rains; provide for a rainy day;〈比喻 *fig.*〉事先做好准备 take precautions

【未知数】wèizhīshù ❶ 代数式或方程中，数值需要经过运算才能确定的数。如 3x + 6 = 27 中，x 是未知数。unknown number, a number in algebraic expression or equation that should be decided through calculation, such as 'x' in the equation 3x + 6 = 27 ❷〈比喻 *fig.*〉还不知道的事情 unknown; uncertain：能否成功，还是个～。It's still uncertain whether it will be a success or not.

位 wèi ❶ 所在或所占的地方 place; location：部～ location; place; position｜座～ seat｜各就各～ on your marks ❷ 职位；地位 position：名～ fame and position ❸ 特指君主的地位 throne：即～ accede to; be enthroned;｜在～ be on the throne; reign｜篡～ usurp the throne ❹ 一个数中每个数码所占的位置 place; figure; digit：个～ single digit; unit's place｜百～ triple digit; hundred's place｜十～数 two digit number ❺〈量词 *classifier*〉用于人(含敬意 pol.) used before people：诸～ everybody｜各～ everybody｜家里来了几～客人。We have some visitors at home. ❻ (Wèi)姓 a surname

【位觉】wèijué 平衡感觉 sense of balance

【位能】wèinéng 势能 potential energy

【位移】wèiyí 物体在运动中所产生的位置的移动 displacement; difference between the later position and the original position

【位于】wèiyú 位置处在(某处) be located; be situated; lie：我国～亚洲大陆东南部。Our country is situated in the southeast of Asia.

【位置】wèi·zhi ❶ 所在或所占的地方 seat; place：大家都按指定的～坐了下来。Everybody has taken a seat as arranged for him. ❷ same as 地位 dìwèi：《狂人日记》在我国新文学中占有重要～。*A Madman's Diary* occupies an important place in the history of the new Chinese literature. ❸ 指职位 position：谋了个科员的～ get a job as a section member

【位子】wèi·zi 人所占据的地方；座位。借指职位。seat; place; position

味 wèi ❶ (～儿 wèir)物质所具有的能使舌头得到某种味觉的特性 taste; flavour; sense obtained by a touch of the tongue：～道 taste; flavour｜滋～ taste; flavour｜甜～儿 taste sweet｜津津有～(eat) with great relish ❷ (～儿 wèir)物质所具有的能使鼻子得到某种嗅觉的特性 smell; odour; sense obtained by the nose：气～ odour; smell｜香～儿 sweet smell; fragrance; perfume; aroma｜这种～儿很好闻。It smells good. ❸ 意味；趣味 interest; delight：文笔艰涩无～。The writing is dull and tasteless. ❹ 指某类菜肴、食品 delicacies：腊～ cured meat, fish, etc.｜美～ delicacy; delicious food｜野～ game as food｜山珍海～ delicacies from land and sea ❺ 辨别味道 distinguish the flavour of：体～ savour; chew; appreciate ❻〈量词 *classifier*〉用于中药 for ingredients of a Chinese medicine prescription：这个方子共有七～药。The prescription specifies seven medicinal herbs. *or* Seven medicinal herbs are prescribed.

【味道】wèi·dao ❶ same as 味 wèi ①：这个菜～好。This dish tastes good. ◇心里有一股说不出的～。There is an indescribable feeling in my heart. ❷ 指兴趣 interest：这个连续剧越看越有～。The more you see this serial play, the more you are absorbed in it. ❸〈方 *dial.*〉气味 smell, odour：他身上有一股难闻的～。There is an unpleasant smell from him.

【味精】wèijīng 调味品，成分是右旋谷氨酸的单钠盐。白色粉末状结晶，放在菜或汤里使有鲜味。monosodium glutamate; gourmet powder; MSG; dressing, white powdered crystal that makes the food or soup delicious; also 味素 wèisù

【味觉】wèijué 舌头与液体或者溶解于液体的物质接触时所产生的感觉。甜、酸、苦、咸是最基本的四种味觉。sense of taste; sense produced after the tongue touches a liquid or a substance dissolved in a liquid. Sweet, sour, bitter and salty are the four basic senses of taste.

【味蕾】wèilěi 接受味觉刺激的感受器，分布在舌头的表面，能辨别滋味 taste bud; sensory organ distributed over the surface of the tongue that receives stimulation from the sense of taste

【味同嚼蜡】wèi tóng jiáo là 形容没有味道，多指文章或讲话枯燥无味(mostly of writings, speeches, etc.) like chewing wax; insipid; tasteless; dull

畏 wèi ❶ 畏惧 fear: 大无～ dauntless; fearless; indomitable | 望而生～ be awed by the sight of; look with awe | 不～艰苦 fear no hardships ❷ 佩服 respect; admiration: 敬～ hold in awe and veneration | 后生可～。The young are to be regarded with awe.

【畏避】wèibì 因畏惧而躲避 avoid sth. out of fear; recoil from; flinch from

【畏忌】wèijì 畏惧和猜忌 have scruples; fear; dread: 相互～ have fear for each other

【畏惧】wèijù 害怕 fear; dread: 无所～ be fearless | ～心理 be in fear

【畏难】wèinán 害怕困难 be afraid of difficulty: ～情绪 fear of difficulty

【畏怯】wèiqiè 胆小害怕 cowardly; timid; chicken-hearted: 毫不～ not at all timid

【畏首畏尾】wèi shǒu wèi wěi 怕这怕那,形容疑虑过多 be full of misgivings; be overcautious

【畏缩】wèisuō 害怕而不敢向前 recoil; shrink; flinch; dare not go forward because of fear: 在困难面前毫不～ never shrink (or flinch) from difficulty

【畏途】wèitú〈书 *fml.*〉危险可怕的路途 dangerous road;〈比喻 *fig.*〉不敢做的事情 perilous undertaking; thing that one doesn't dare to do: 视为～ be regarded as a dangerous road

【畏葸】wèixǐ〈书 *fml.*〉畏惧 timid; afraid: ～不前 be too timid to go ahead; be afraid to advance

【畏友】wèiyǒu 自己敬畏的朋友 esteemed friend: 严师～ exacting teacher and esteemed friend

【畏罪】wèizuì 犯了罪怕受制裁 dread punishment for one's crime: ～潜逃 abscond to avoid punishment

胃 wèi ❶ 消化器官的一部分,形状像口袋,上端跟食道相连,下端跟十二指肠相连。能分泌胃液,消化食物。stomach; saclike organ for secreting gastric juice, storing and digesting food, its upper part linked with the esophagus and its lower part with the duodenum; (图见 ☞ figure for 消化系统 xiāohuà xìtǒng on p. 2100) ❷ 二十八宿之一 one of the 28 constellations

【胃口】wèikǒu ❶ 指食欲 appetite: ～不好 have no appetite ❷〈比喻 *fig.*〉对事物或活动的兴趣 liking; interest in things or activities: 打球他不感兴趣,游泳才对他的～。He is not interested in playing a ball game, but swimming is to his liking.

【胃酸】wèisuān 胃液中所含的盐酸,能促进蛋白质的消化,并能杀死细菌 hydrochloric acid in gastric juice, which can promote the digestion of protein and kill bacteria

【胃腺】wèixiàn 分泌胃液的腺体,密布在胃的黏膜上 gastric gland; gland that secretes gastric juice and is distributed over the mucous membrane of the stomach

【胃液】wèiyè 胃腺分泌出来的液体,呈酸性,无色透明,主要含有胃蛋白酶、盐酸和黏液。有消化食物和杀菌的作用。gastric juice; sour, colourless, transparent liquid secreted from the gastric gland, which mainly contains pepsin, hydrochloric acid and mucus and helps digestion and kills bacteria

谓 wèi ❶ 说 say: 所～ so-called | 可～神速 happen real fast ❷ 称呼;叫做 call; name: 称～ title; appellation | 何～人造卫星? What is the so-called man-made satellite?

【谓词】wèicí ❶ 数理逻辑中表示一个个体的性质和两个或两个以上个体间关系的词 predicate; word that expresses the nature of an individual or the relationship between or among two or three individuals in the mathematical logic ❷ 句子里谓语部分中主要的词 predicate; main word of the predicate part in a sentence; ☞ 谓语 wèiyǔ

【谓语】wèiyǔ 对主语加以陈述,说明主语怎样或者是什么的句子成分。一般的句子都包括主语部分和谓语部分,谓语部分里的主要的词是谓语。例如在'我们尽情地歌唱'里,'歌唱'是谓语,'尽情地歌唱'是谓语部分。有些语法书里称谓语部分为谓语,称谓语为谓词。predicate; verb or verb phrase, including any complements, objects, and modifiers, that is one of two immediate constituents of a sentence and asserts something about the subject. For example, in the sentence '我们尽情地歌唱' (We are singing to our hearts' content.), '歌唱' (singing) is 谓语 (the predicate), '尽情地歌唱' (singing to our hearts' content) is 谓语部分 (the predicate phrase). In some grammar books, 谓语部分 is called 谓语, and 谓语 is called 谓词.

W

尉 wèi ❶ 古官名 ancient official title: 太～ imperial minister in charge of military affairs ❷ 尉官 junior officer; military officer above the rank of warrant officer and below that of major ❸ (Wèi) 姓 a surname

☞ yù on p. 2352

【尉官】wèiguān 尉级军官,低于校官 junior officer; military officer above the rank of warrant officer and below that of major

遗 wèi〈书 *fml.*〉赠与;送给 offer as a gift; make a present of sth.: ～之千金 present sb. with a generous gift of money

☞ yí on p. 2263

喂[1] wèi〈叹词 *interj.*〉招呼的声音 hello; hey: ～,你上哪儿去? Hello, where are you going? | ～,你的围巾掉了。Hey, your scarf has slipped off.

喂[2](餵、餧) wèi ❶ 给动物东西吃;饲养 feed (an animal);

raise：～牲口 feed cattle｜家里～着几只鸡 raise some chickens at home ❷ 把食物送到人嘴里 send food into the mouth of a person：～奶 feed milk｜给病人～饭 feed a patient

【喂食】wèi//shí 给人或动物东西吃 feed（a person or an animal）：定时～ feed at regular times｜一天要喂两次食 feed twice a day

【喂养】wèiyǎng 给幼儿或动物东西吃，并照顾其生活，使能成长 raise；keep；feed an infant or an animal and take care of his，her or its life so as to make him，her or it grow：～牲口 feed some cattle｜精心～婴儿 feed a baby with great care

猬（蝟） wèi 刺猬 hedgehog

【猬集】wèijí〈书 *fml.*〉〈比喻 *fig.*〉事情繁多，像刺猬的硬刺那样聚在一起（of matters）as numerous as the spines of a hedgehog：诸事～ have too many things to attend to；have too many irons in the fire

渭 Wèi 渭河，发源于甘肃，经陕西流入黄河 Weihe River，rising in Gansu and flowing east into Shaanxi where it empties into the Yellow River

蔚 wèi〈书 *fml.*〉❶ 茂盛；盛大 luxuriant；grand：～成风气 become a common practice ❷ 有文采的 colourful：云蒸霞～ splendid；magnificent；gorgeous

☞ yù on p. 2353

【蔚蓝】wèilán 像晴朗的天空那样的颜色 azure；sky blue：～的天空 bright blue sky｜～的海洋 blue sea

W

【蔚起】wèiqǐ〈书 *fml.*〉兴旺地发展起来 burgeon；flourish

【蔚然】wèirán 形容茂盛、盛大：～成风 become common practice；become the order of the day｜几年前栽的树苗，现已～成林。The young saplings planted a few years ago have grown into an exuberant forest.

【蔚然成风】wèirán chéng fēng 形容一种事物逐渐发展、盛行，形成风气 become common practice；become the order of the day

【蔚为大观】wèi wéi dàguān 丰富多彩，成为盛大的景象（多指文物等 mostly referring to relics）present a splendid sight；afford a magnificent view：展出的中外名画～。There's a splendid array of Chinese and foreign famous paintings on display.

硙（硊） wèi〈方 *dial.*〉石磨（mò）millstone

☞ 硊 wéi on p. 1992

慰 wèi ❶ 使人心情安适 console；comfort：～劳 bring gifts to，or send one's best wishes to，in recognition of services rendered｜～问 express sympathy and solicitude for；extend one's regards to；convey greetings to；salute｜～唁 condole with sb. ❷ 心安 be relieved：欣～ gratified；satisfied；pleased｜得信甚～ be greatly relieved to learn about you

【慰藉】wèijiè〈书 *fml.*〉安慰 be comforted；provide a shoulder for sb.

【慰劳】wèiláo 慰问 bring gifts to，or send one's best wishes to，in recognition of services rendered：～品 gifts for people who have rendered services｜～子弟兵 bring gifts to the people's army in recognition of their services

【慰勉】wèimiǎn 安慰勉励 comfort and encourage：多方～ comfort and encourage in many ways

【慰问】wèiwèn（用话或物品）安慰问候 express sympathy and solicitude for；extend one's regards to；convey greetings to；salute：～信 letter of sympathy；sympathy note｜～灾区人民 express sympathy and solicitude for the people of disaster areas

【慰唁】wèiyàn 慰问（死者的家属）condole with（family of a deceased）

罻 wèi〈书 *fml.*〉捕鸟的网 net for catching birds

魏 Wèi ❶ 周朝国名，在今河南北部、陕西东部、山西西南部和河北南部等地 Wei，one of the states during the Zhou Dynasty，occupying what is now northern Henan，eastern Shaanxi，southwestern Shanxi，and southern Hebei ❷ 三国之一，公元 220—265，曹丕所建，领有今黄河流域各省和湖北、安徽、江苏北部，辽宁中部 Wei（220-265），one of the kingdoms during the Three Kingdoms Period（220-280），occupying the present-day provinces in the Yellow River valley and what is now northern Hubei，Anhui，and Jiangsu and central Liaoning ❸ 北魏 Northern Wei，one of the Northern Dynasties（386-581）❹（Wèi）姓 a surname

【魏碑】wèibēi 北朝碑刻的统称，字体结构严整，笔力强劲，后世作为书法的一种典范 tablet script，a general term for tablet inscriptions of the Northern Dynasties（386-581），regarded by posterity as a paragon of Chinese calligraphy；a major style of Chinese calligraphy marked for disciplined structure and forceful brushwork

【魏阙】wèiquè〈古代 *arch.*〉宫门外的建筑，是发布政令的地方，后用为朝廷的代称 building outside the gate of the imperial palace where imperial edicts were issued；later used to refer to imperial court

譌（讆、躗） wèi〈书 *fml.*〉虚妄 unfounded；fabricated：～言 unfounded remarks

霨 wèi〈书 *fml.*〉形容云起 rise of clouds

鳚 wèi 鱼类的一科，体长 2—3 寸，侧扁，无鳞，只在身体的前端有侧线。生活在近海中。blenny（*Blenniidae*）；flat，scaleless fish， two or three *cun* long, having a lateral line on the front part of the body and living in the offshore waters

wēn (ㄨㄣ)

温 wēn ❶ 不冷不热 warm; lukewarm：～带 temperate zone | ～水 lukewarm water ❷ 温度 temperature：气～ atmospheric temperature | 体～ body temperature ❸ 稍微加热 warm up：把酒～一下 warm up the wine ❹ 性情平和；温柔 mild; soft; tender：～情 tender feeling | ～驯 docile; tame; meek | ～顺 subservient; submissive; docile; meek ❺ 温习 review; revise：～书 review a book | ～课 review (or revise) one's lessons ❻ 瘟 epidemic ❼ (Wēn)姓 a surname

【温饱】wēnbǎo 吃得饱、穿得暖的生活 dress warmly and eat one's fill; have adequate food and clothing

【温标】wēnbiāo 关于温度零点和分度方法的规定。有摄氏温标、华氏温标、热力学温标等。thermometric scale; graduated scale measuring temperature, such as Celsius' thermometric scale, Fahrenheit's thermometric scale, and thermodynamic scale

【温差】wēnchā 温度的差，通常指一天中最高温度和最低温度的差 difference in temperature; range of temperature, usu. the difference between the highest temperature and lowest temperature of a day：新疆地区日照长，～大。The Xinjiang region has a long sunshine time and a great temperature difference.

【温床】wēnchuáng ❶ 冬季或早春培育蔬菜、花卉等幼苗的苗床。通常在苗床下面埋好能发酵生热的马粪、落叶、垃圾等，或利用温泉热、电热等给苗床加温，苗床上面一般装有玻璃窗或塑料薄膜。hotbed; bed for nursing vegetable and flower seedlings in winter and early spring. Usually, under the bed is a layer of horse dune, fallen leaves and garbage, etc. which generate heat by fermentation, or heat from a hot spring, electricity, etc. is used to warm up the bed. The bed is covered by glass windows or plastic films. ❷〈比喻 *fig.*〉对某种事物产生或发展有利的环境 breeding ground; hotbed：官僚主义是违法乱纪现象的～。Bureaucracy is a hotbed for violations of the law and discipline. | 海洋是孕育原始生命的～。The sea is the breeding ground for the primitive living organisms.

【温存】wēncún ❶ 殷勤抚慰(多指对异性 usu. to a person of the opposite sex) be attentive ❷ 温柔体贴 gentle; kind：性格～ be kind by character

【温带】wēndài 南半球和北半球的极圈与回归线之间的地带，气候比较温和 temperate zone; either of the two zones between the tropics and the polar circles, of relatively mild climate

【温度】wēndù 物体冷热的程度 temperature：～计 thermometer | 室内～ indoor temperature | 室外～ outdoor temperature

【温度计】wēndùjì 测量温度的仪器。常用的温度计是根据液体热胀冷缩的原理制成的，如寒暑表、体温计。工业上和科学研究上还有光学温度计、电阻温度计等。thermograph; thermometer; meter for measuring temperature. A common thermometer is made on the principle of expansion and contraction under different temperatures, as thermometer, clinical thermometer. In industry and scientific research, there are also optical thermometer, resistance thermometer, etc. also 温度表 wēndùbiǎo

【温故知新】wēn gù zhī xīn 温习旧的知识，能够得到新的理解和体会。也指回忆过去，认识现在。gain new knowledge by reviewing old; understand the present by reviewing the past

【温和】wēnhé ❶ (气候)不冷不热 (of climate) temperate; mild; moderate：昆明气候～，四季如春。Kunming has a moderate climate. It's spring in all seasons. ❷ (性情、态度、言语等)不严厉，不粗暴，使人感到亲切(of disposition, manner, speech, etc.) gentle; mild：脸色～ mild complexion | 谈吐～ talk in a gentle manner | ～的目光 tender look
☞ wēn·huo

【温厚】wēnhòu 温和宽厚 gentle and kind; good-natured：为人～ kind and sincere; gentle and kind

【温乎】wēn·hu 温和 (wēn·huo) warm; lukewarm

【温和】wēn·huo (物体)不冷不热 (of an object) warm; lukewarm：粥还～呢，快喝吧！The porridge is still warm. Drink it quickly.
☞ wēnhé

【温居】wēn//jū 指前往亲友新居贺喜 housewarming

【温觉】wēnjué 皮肤受到比体温高的温度的刺激而产生的感觉 sense of heat; sensation caused by stimulation from a temperature higher than one's body temperature

【温良】wēnliáng 温和善良 gentle and kindhearted：她举止娴雅，性情～。She has a graceful manner and a gentle disposition.

【温暖】wēnnuǎn ❶ same as 暖和 nuǎn·huo：天气～ it is warm; warm weather ◇他深深地感到集体的～。He deeply felt the warmth of the organization. ❷ 使感到温暖 warm：党的关怀，～了灾区人民的心。The concern and solicitude of the Party warmed the hearts of the people in the calamity-affected areas.

【温情】wenqíng 温柔的感情；温和的态度 tender feeling; mild manner; tender affection：一片～ a tender feeling | ～柔意 tender affection

W

【温情脉脉】wēnqíng mòmò 形容对人或事物怀有感情,很想表露出来的样子 full of tender feelings for sb. or sth. and about to express them

【温泉】wēnquán 温度在当地年平均气温以上的泉水 hot spring; spring with a temperature above the local annual average temperature

【温柔】wēnróu 温和柔顺(多形容女性)(usu. of a woman) gentle and soft:性格～ mild character|～的少女 gentle young girl

【温润】wēnrùn ❶same as 温和 wēnhé ②:性情～ gentle disposition|～的面容 kindly face ❷温暖润湿 mild (or temperate) and moist:气候～ temperate and moist climate ❸ 细润 fine and smooth:玉质～ fine and smooth jade

【温室】wēnshì 有防寒、加温和透光等设备,供冬季培育不能耐寒的花木、蔬菜、秧苗等的房间,一般利用日光照射和人工加温来保持室内适于植物生长的温度 hothouse; greenhouse; glasshouse; conservatory; room with facilities for cold-resistance, heating and lighting, used to cultivate flowers, plants, vegetables and seedlings that are vulnerable to cold. A greenhouse usually. makes use of sunshine and supplies artificial heating to maintain room temperatures that are appropriate for the growth of plants.

【温顺】wēnshùn 温和顺从 docile; meek:态度～ gentle manner

【温汤】wēntāng ❶ 温水 lukewarm water:～浸种 hot water treatment of seeds ❷〈书 *fml*.〉温泉 hot spring

【温吞】wēn·tūn same as 温暾 wēn·tūn

【温暾】wēn·tūn〈方 *dial*.〉❶(液体)不冷不热 (of liquid) lukewarm; tepid ❷(言谈、文辞等)不爽利,不着边际 (of talk, language, etc.) not to the point; irrelevant:～之谈 irrelevant talk ‖ also 温吞 wēn·tūn

【温文尔雅】wēn wén ěr yǎ 态度温和,举止文雅 (of attitude and manner) refined and cultivated

【温习】wēnxí 复习 review; revise:～功课 review one's lessons

【温馨】wēnxīn 温和芳香;温暖 cosy; warm:～的春夜 cosy spring evening|～的家 warm and sweet home

【温煦】wēnxù ❶ 暖和 warm:阳光～ warm sunshine|气候～ warm climate ❷ 温和亲切 kind and cordial:～的目光 mild and cordial look

【温血动物】wēnxuè dòngwù 恒温动物 warm-blooded animal

【温驯】wēnxùn 温和驯服 (of animals) docile; meek; tame:～的羔羊 meek lamb

榅 wēn [榅桲](wēn·po) ❶ 落叶灌木或小乔木,叶子长圆形,背面密生绒毛,花淡红色或白色。果实有香气,味酸,可以制蜜饯。quince (*Cydonia oblonga*); deciduous shrub or small tree with oblong, hairy leaves and pink or white flowers, and bearing fruits that have a fragrant smell and a sour taste and are used for making preserved fruits ❷ 这种植物的果实 fruit of the plant

辒 wēn [辒辌](wēnliáng)〈古代 *arch*.〉可以卧的车,也用做丧车 ancient carriage for sleeping, also used for mourning purposes

瘟 wēn ❶〈中医 *Chin. med*.〉指人或动物的急性传染病 acute contagious diseases ❷ 戏曲表演沉闷乏味,不够火爆 (of traditional opera) dull and insipid:这出戏情节松,人物也～。The opera has a loose plot and dull characters.

【瘟病】wēnbìng〈中医 *Chin. med*.〉对各种急性热病的统称,如春瘟、暑瘟、伏瘟等 seasonal febrile diseases, as spring fever, febrile diseases in summer, febrile diseases in hot season, etc.

【瘟神】wēnshén 传说中能散播瘟疫的恶神 legendary evil god of plague;〈比喻 *fig*.〉给人带来灾难的人或事物 person or thing that brings disaster to people

【瘟疫】wēnyì 指流行性急性传染病 pestilence; acute epidemic, contagious diseases

【瘟疹】wēnzhěn 通常指患者身上有斑或疹等症状的急性传染病,如猩红热、斑疹伤寒等 acute infectious diseases characterized by rashes, such as scarlet fever, typhus, etc.

蕰 wēn [蕰草](wēncǎo)〈方 *dial*.〉指水生的杂草,可作肥料 water weeds (*Anacharis canadensis*), used as fertilizer

鳁 wēn [鳁鲸](wēnjīng) 哺乳动物,外形像鱼,体长 6—9 米,头上有喷水孔,口内无齿,有鲸须,背鳍小,身体背面黑色,腹部带白色。生活在海洋中。sei whale (*Balaenopter a borealis Lesson*); rorqual; toothless, fish-like marine mammal, six to nine metres long, with a water injecting hole on the head, a small dorsal fin and baleen, black back and white belly

wén (ㄨㄣˊ)

文 wén ❶ 字 character; script; writing:甲骨～ inscriptions on tortoise shells or animal bones of the Shang Dynasty; oracle bone inscriptions|钟鼎～ inscriptions on bronze bells and tripods ❷ same as 文字 wénzì ②:汉～ Han language; main Chinese language|英～ English language ❸ 文章 literary composition; writing:散～ prose|韵～ verse|记叙～ narrative; narration|应用～ practical writing|～集 collection of works|～人 man of letters; literary man|～学 literature ❹ 文言 literary language; classical language:半～半白 half classical and half vernacular|这句话太～

了，不好懂。This sentence is too bookish to be understood. ❺ 指社会发展到较高阶段表现出来的状态 culture; state a society is in when it develops to a higher stage：～化 culture｜～明 civilization｜～物 cultural relic; historical relic ❻ 指文科 liberal arts：他大学里是学～的。He majored in liberal arts in the university. ❼〈旧时 *old*〉指礼节仪式 rite; ritual：虚～ mere formality｜繁～缛节 red tape; excessive formalities ❽ 非军事的（跟'武'相对 as opposed to 'military'）civilian; civil：～官 civil official｜～职 civilian post｜～武双全 be well versed both in military and civil affairs ❾ 柔和；不猛烈 mild; soft; refined：～雅 refined｜～弱 mild and weak｜～绉绉 genteel｜～火 slow fire; gentle heat ❿ 自然界的某些现象 certain natural phenomena：天～ astronomy｜水～ hydrology ⓫〈古时 *arch.*〉称在身上、脸上刺画花纹或字 tattoo; design or word marked on body and face：～身 tattoo a body｜～了双颊 have both cheeks tattooed ⓬（旧读 formerly pronounced wèn）掩饰 conceal; hide：～过饰非 gloss over one's faults; cover up (or explain away) one's errors ⓭〈量词 *classifier*〉用于旧时的铜钱［used for copper cash in old times］：一～钱 a cash｜不取分～ free of charge; not take a single coin ⓮（Wén）姓 a surname

【文本】wénběn 文件的某种本子（多就文字、措辞而言），也指某种文件 text; version：这个文件有中、英、法三种～。This document is available in Chinese, English and French. *or* There are three versions for this document, Chinese, English and French.

【文笔】wénbǐ 文章的用词造句的风格和技巧 style of writing：～辛辣 write in a pungent style｜～巧妙 write cleverly

【文不对题】wén bù duì tí 文章的内容跟题目没关系；也指答非所问或者说的话跟原有的话题不相干 irrelevant to the subject; not to the point (or mark); wide of the mark

【文不加点】wén bù jiā diǎn 形容写文章很快，不用涂改就写成 write an article from beginning to finish without changing a single word; never make the slightest change in one's writing; have a facile pen（点 *dian*：涂上一点，表示删去 to dot a word to imply omission）

【文才】wéncái 写作诗文的才能 literary talent; aptitude for writing：～出众 man of outstanding literary talent

【文采】wéncǎi ❶ 华丽的色彩 rich and bright colours ❷ 文艺方面的才华 literary grace; literary talent

【文场】wénchǎng ❶ 戏曲伴奏乐队中的管弦乐部分 one of the two divisions of the orchestra in traditional opera, consisting of stringed and wind instruments ❷ 曲艺的一种，由数人演唱，伴奏乐器以扬琴为主。流行于广西桂林、柳州一带。a kind of ballad singing in which several people sing and perform together to the accompaniment of the dulcimer and other instruments, popular in and around Guilin and Liuzhou in the Guangxi Zhuang Autonomous Region

【文抄公】wénchāogōng 指抄袭文章的人（含戏谑意 humor.）plagiarist

【文丑】wénchǒu（～儿 wénchǒur）戏曲中丑角的一种，扮演性格滑稽的人物，以念白、做工为主（in traditional opera）comedian in civil plays; clown focusing on speaking and acting instead of acrobatics and fighting

【文词】wéncí same as 文辞 wéncí

【文辞】wéncí ❶ 指文章的用字、用语等 diction; language：～优美 exquisite diction; elegant language ❷ 泛指文章 writings：以善～知名 well known for one's writings; also 文词 wéncí

【文从字顺】wén cóng zì shùn 指文章通顺 readable and fluent

【文旦】wéndàn〈方 *dial.*〉柚子（柚树的果实）pomelo fruit

【文牍】wéndú ❶ 公文、书信的总称 general term for official documents and correspondence ❷〈旧时 *old*〉称担任文牍工作的人 secretary; clerk

【文法】wénfǎ ❶ 语法 grammar ❷〈古代 *arch.*〉指法令成文 written laws and decrees

【文房四宝】wénfáng sìbǎo 指笔、墨、纸、砚，是书房中常备的四种文具 four treasures of the study (writing brush, ink stick, ink slab and paper)

【文风】wénfēng 使用语言文字的作风 style of writing：整顿～ rectify the style of writing

【文稿】wéngǎo 文章或公文的草稿 manuscript; draft of an article or an offcial document

【文告】wéngào 机关或团体发布的文件 proclamation; statement; message; document issued by a government or other organization

【文蛤】wéngé 软体动物，壳略作三角形，表面多为灰白色，有光泽，长约二三寸，生活在沿海泥沙中，以硅藻为食物 clam (*Cyclina sinensis*); soft-bodied animal enclosed in triangular, hard, greyish-white, glossy shells 6 to 9 cm in length, living in the shallows of the sea and feeding on diatom; 通称 generally called 蛤蜊 gélì

【文工团】wéngōngtuán 从事文艺演出的团体 song and dance ensemble; art troupe; cultural troupe

【文官】wénguān 指军官以外的官员 civil official

【文过饰非】wén guò shì fēi 掩饰过失、错误 gloss over one's faults; cover up (or explain away) one's errors

【文翰】wénhàn〈书〉❶ 文章 essay; article ❷

W

指公文信札 official documents and correspondence

【文豪】wénháo 杰出的、伟大的作家 literary giant; great writer; eminent writer

【文化】wénhuà ❶ 人类在社会历史发展过程中所创造的物质财富和精神财富的总和，特指精神财富，如文学、艺术、教育、科学等 civilization; culture; sum total of the material wealth and cultural wealth created by man in the course of the historical development of society, cultural wealth in particular, such as literature, arts, education, and science, etc. ❷ 考古学用语，指同一个历史时期的不依分布地点为转移的遗迹、遗物的综合体。同样的工具、用具，同样的制造技术等，是同一种文化的特征，如仰韶文化、龙山文化。(of archaeology) comprehensive body of sites and ruins left behind, which are independent of their locations, in a given historical period. The identical tools, implements and manufacturing skills are the characteristics of the same culture, as the Yangshao culture and the Longshan culture. ❸ 指运用文字的能力及一般知识 education; culture; schooling; literacy: 学习～ acquire an elementary education; learn to read and write | ～水平 cultural level; educational level

【文化层】wénhuàcéng 〈古代 *arch.*〉人类居住遗址上的土层，埋藏着古代人类遗物，如工具、用具、建筑物遗迹等 cultural stratum; earth layer above the ruins of the residences of the ancient people, where vestiges of ancient human habitation are buried, as tools, implements and ruins of buildings

【文化宫】wénhuàgōng 规模较大、设备较好的文化娱乐场所，一般设有电影院、讲演厅、图书馆等 palace of culture; large-scale, well-equipped cultural palace, usu. having a cinema, a lecture hall, a library, etc.

【文化馆】wénhuàguǎn 为了开展群众文化工作而设立的机构，也是群众进行文娱活动的场所 cultural centre; establishment where cultural work for the masses is carried out and where people take part in cultural and recreational activities

【文化人】wénhuàrén ❶ 抗日战争前后指从事文化工作的人 cultural worker; person who was engaged in the cultural work before or after the War of Resistance against Japan ❷ 指知识分子 intellectual

【文火】wénhuǒ 烹饪时用的比较弱的火 slow fire; gentle heat; cooking fire

【文集】wénjí 把某人的作品汇集起来编成的书(可以有诗有文，多用作书名 including both poems and articles, usu. used as a book title) collected works; book in which the works of a certain person are collected and compiled: 《茅盾～》*Collected Works of Mao Dun*

【文件】wénjiàn ❶ 公文、信件等 official documents, letters, etc. ❷ 指有关政治理论、时事政策、学术研究等方面的文章 articles dealing with political theories, policies on current affairs, academic research, etc.

【文教】wénjiào 文化和教育 culture and education: ～部门 cultural and educational departments | ～事业 cultural and educational work; culture and education

【文静】wénjìng (性格、举止等)文雅安静 (of character, manners, etc.) gentle and quiet

【文句】wénjù 文章的词句 sentences of an article: ～通顺。The sentences are smooth.

【文具】wénjù 指笔、墨、纸、砚等用品 writing materials; stationery, such as writing brushes, ink sticks, paper and ink slabs

【文科】wénkē 教学上对文学、语言、哲学、历史、经济等学科的统称 liberal arts; general term of such college course as literature, languages, philosophy, history, and economics

【文库】wénkù 由许多书汇编成的一套书(多用作丛书名 usu. used in book titles) a series of books issued in a single format by a publisher; library: 《世界～》*The World Library*

【文侩】wénkuài 指靠舞文弄墨投机取巧的人 literary scavenger; person who tries to gain advantage by engaging himself in phrasemongering

【文理】wénlǐ 文章内容方面和词句方面的条理 unity and coherence in content and language of a piece of writing: ～通顺 have unity and coherence; make smooth reading

【文盲】wénmáng 不识字的成年人 illiterate person; illiterate: 半～ semi-illiterate | 扫除～ wipe out illiteracy

【文庙】wénmiào 祭祀孔子的庙 Confucian temple

【文明】wénmíng ❶ same as 文化 wénhuà①: 物质～ material civilization ❷ 社会发展到较高阶段和具有较高文化的 civilized; with a higher stage of development of society and a higher level of culture: ～国家 civilized country ❸ 〈旧时 *old*〉指有西方现代色彩的(风俗、习惯、事物) modern and Western (customs, habits, things, etc.): ～结婚 Western-style wedding | ～棍儿(手杖) walking stick; stick

【文墨】wénmò ❶ 指写文章 writing: 粗通～ barely know the rudiments of writing ❷ 泛指属于脑力劳动的 of mental labour: ～人 collective name for painters, calligraphers, writers, teachers, etc. | ～事儿 mental work

【文痞】wénpǐ 舞文弄墨颠倒是非的人 literary prostitute

【文凭】wénpíng 〈旧时 *old*〉指用做凭证的官方文书，现专指毕业证书 diploma; official document used as evidence of education one has

received
【文气】wénqì 贯穿在文章里的气势;文章的连贯性 vigour of style; coherence of writing
【文气】wén·qi 文静;不粗暴 gentle and quiet
【文契】wénqì 买卖房地产等的契约 contracts concerning the buying and selling of real estate, etc.
【文人】wénrén 指会做诗文的读书人 man of letters; scholar; literati:～墨客 man of letters; scholar; literati
【文弱】wénruò 举止文雅,身体柔弱(多用来形容文人 oft. used to describe men of letters) gentle and frail-looking:～书生 frail scholar
【文山会海】wén shān huì hǎi 指过多的文件和会议 a mountain of papers and a sea of meetings — the intricate routine that a leading cadre gets bogged down in
【文身】wénshēn 在人体上绘成或刺成带颜色的花纹或图形 tattoo; design or pattern painted or marked by puncturing and inserting pigment on a human body
【文饰】wénshì ❶ 文辞方面的修饰 polish (a piece of writing):这段描写,～较少。In this passage the description shows little trace of ostentation. ❷ 掩饰(自己的过错) gloss over (one's mistakes); cover up
【文书】wénshū ❶ 指公文、书信、契约等 document; official dispatch ❷ 机关或部队中从事公文、书信工作的人员 copy clerk in an organization or in the army
【文思】wénsī 写文章的思路 thread of ideas in writing; train of thought in writing:～敏捷 have a ready pen
【文坛】wéntán 指文学界 literary world (or arena, circles); world of letters:～巨匠 giant of the literary world
【文体】[1] wéntǐ 文章的体裁 type of writing; literary form; style:就～讲,公文、书信、广告等都可以归入应用文。So far as the style of writing is concerned, official documents, letters, advertisements, etc. can all fall into the category of practical writing.
【文体】[2] wéntǐ 文娱体育的简称 abbr. for 文娱体育 wényú tǐyù:～活动 recreational and sports activities
【文恬武嬉】wén tián wǔ xī 文官图安逸,武官贪玩乐。指文武官吏一味贪图享乐,不关心国事的腐败现象。(of a corrupt regime) indolent civil officials and frivolous generals; lazy civil officials and military officers who pay no attention to state affairs
【文玩】wénwán 供赏玩的器物 objects for ornament:金石～ gold and jade ornaments
【文武】wénwǔ ❶ 文才和武艺 civil and military skills:～双全 be well versed in both polite letters and martial arts; adept with both pen and sword ❷〈书 *fml.*〉文治和武功 statecraft and military exploits:～并用,垂拱而治 employ both statecraft and military exploits to rule by laissez-faire ❸〈书 *fml.*〉文臣和武将 civil and military officials; ministers and generals:满朝～ all ministers and generals of the imperial court
【文物】wénwù 历代遗留下来的在文化发展史上有价值的东西,如建筑、碑刻、工具、武器、生活器皿和各种艺术品等 cultural relic; artifact; valuable objects in the history of cultural development left behind from the past:出土～ uncovered relics|革命～ revolutionary relics
【文戏】wénxì 以唱工或做工为主的戏(区别于'武戏' distinguished from 'military plays') (in traditional opera) civil plays characterized by singing or acting
【文献】wénxiàn 有历史价值或参考价值的图书资料 document; literature of historical value:历史～ historical documents|科技～ scientific and technical literature
【文选】wénxuǎn 选录的文章(多用作书名 usu. used in book titles) selected works; literary selections:活页～ literary selections in loose leaflets|《列宁～》*Selected Works of Lenin*
【文学】wénxué 以语言文字为工具形象化地反映客观现实的艺术,包括戏剧、诗歌、小说、散文等 literature; art of reflecting the objective reality through images by the use of written languages, including drama, poem, novel, prose, etc.
【文学革命】wénxué gémìng 指我国 1919 年五四运动前后展开的反对旧文学、提倡新文学的运动。文学革命以反对文言文,提倡白话文为起点,进而反对以封建主义为内容的旧文学,提倡反帝反封建的新文学。literary revolution; movement against old literature and for new literature around the May 4th Movement of 1919. The literary revolution started by opposing the classical writing and advocating the vernacular writing, and went further to oppose the old literature centring on feudalism and advocate the anti-imperialist and anti-feudalist new literature
【文学语言】wénxué yǔyán ❶ 标准语(偏于书面的 usu. written language) standard speech ❷ 文学作品里所用的语言 literary language; also 文艺语言 wényì yǔyán
【文雅】wényǎ (言谈、举止)温和有礼貌,不粗俗 (of talk and manner) elegant; refined; cultured; polished:谈吐～ talk in refined taste|举止～ refined in manner
【文言】wényán 指五四以前通用的以古汉语为基础的书面语 classical Chinese; written Chinese based on the ancient classical Chinese popular in China before the May 4th Movement in 1919
【文言文】wényánwén 用文言写的文章 writings in classical Chinese; classical style of writing
【文艺】wényì 文学和艺术的总称,有时特指文学或表演艺术 general term for literature and

art; sometimes esp. referring to literature or art of performance: ~团体 literary and art organizations; theatre company; theatre troupe|~作品 literary and artistic works|~会演 theatrical festival

【文艺复兴】wényì fùxīng 指欧洲(主要是意大利)从14到16世纪文化和思想发展的潮流。据说那时文化的特点是复兴被遗忘的希腊、罗马的古典文化。实际上,文艺复兴是欧洲资本主义文化思想的萌芽,是新兴的资本主义生产关系的产物。文艺复兴时期的主要思想特征是人文主义,提倡以人为本位,反对以神为本位的宗教思想。Renaissance; great revival of art, literature, and learning in Europe in the 14th, 15th and 16th centuries, based on classical sources, beginning in Italy and spreading gradually to other countries, marking the transition from the medieval world to the modern. It is said that the culture of the time was characterized by the rejuvenation of the forgotten classical culture of Greece and Rome. In fact, the Renaissance was the beginning of capitalist cultural ideas in Europe and the product of the new, rising capitalist relations of production. The major ideological feature of the Renaissance was humanism which holds that man is capable of self-fulfillment, ethical conduct, etc. without recourse to supernaturalism. ☞ 人文主义 rénwén zhǔyì on p. 1620

【文艺批评】wényì pīpíng 根据一定的美学观点对作家的作品、创作活动、创作倾向性进行分析和评论。是文艺学的组成部分。literary or art criticism; analysis and review of the works, creative activities and creative tendency of an author by given aesthetic standards; part of the study of literature and art

【文艺学】wényìxué 以文学和文学的发展规律为研究对象的科学,包括文艺理论、文学史和文艺批评 study of literature and art; branch of science dealing with literature, and the law of development of literature, including literary and art theories, history of literature, literary and art criticism

【文艺语言】wényì yǔyán same as 文学语言 wénxué yǔyán ②

【文娱】wényú 指看戏、看电影、唱歌、跳舞等娱乐 cultural recreation; entertainment, including watch a theatrical performance, film, singing, dancing, etc.: ~活动 recreational activities|~干事 person in charge of recreational activities

【文责】wénzé 作者对文章内容的正确性以及在读者中发生的作用所应负的责任 responsibility an author should assume for the accuracy of what he writes in his writings and the effect they exert on the readers; author's responsibility: ~自负。The author takes sole responsibility for what he writes.

【文摘】wénzhāi ❶ 对文章、著作所作的扼要摘述 extracts from articles and books ❷ 指选取的文章片段。也用作书刊名。abstract; digest; also used for book or magazine titles

【文章】wénzhāng ❶ 篇幅不很长的单篇作品 a piece of short writing; essay; article ❷ 泛指著作 (in a broad sense) literary works; writings ❸〈比喻 *fig.*〉暗含的意思 hidden meaning; implied meaning: 话里有~。There is an insinuation in that remark. *or* That's an insinuating remark. ❹ 关于事情的做法 way of doing sth.: 我们可以利用他们的矛盾,这里很有~可做。We can make use of their contradictions. There is still much room for improvement in this respect.|还要想到下一战略阶段的~。We must think of what we shall do in the next strategic stage.

【文职】wénzhí 文官的职务 civilian post: ~人员 non-military personnel

【文质彬彬】wén zhì bīnbīn 原形容人既文雅又朴实,后来形容人文雅有礼貌 gentle; urbane; suave

【文治】wénzhì〈书 *fml.*〉指文化教育方面的业绩 civil administration: ~武功 cultural and military achievements

【文绉绉】wénzhōuzhōu (~的 wénzhōuzhōu·de) 形容人谈吐、举止文雅的样子 genteel (manner; bearing; demeanour; conduct)

【文字】wénzì ❶ 记录语言的符号,如汉字、拉丁字母等 characters; script; writing; symbols for recording what is spoken, as Chinese characters, Latin letters ❷ 语言的书面形式,如汉文、英文等 written form of a language, as the Chinese language, English language ❸ 文章(多指形式方面 as regards form or style) writing: ~清通 lucid writing

【文字学】wénzìxué 语言学的一个部门,研究文字的性质、结构和演变 philology; branch of linguistics dealing with the nature, composition and evolution of a language

【文字狱】wénzìyù 统治者故意从作者的诗文中摘取字句,罗织罪状所造成的冤狱 literary inquisition; imprisonment or execution of an author for writing sth. (oft. taken out of context) considered offensive by the imperial court

【文宗】wénzōng〈书 *fml.*〉文章为众人所师法的人物 outstanding literary figure whose style of writing is studied and followed by a great number of people: 一代~ most outstanding literary figure of the time|海内~ domestic master writer

纹 wén ❶ (~儿 wénr)丝织品上的花纹 pattern; design on silk fabric: 绫~ satin pattern ❷ 泛指各种花纹;纹缕儿 lines; veins; grain: 指~ fingerprint; loops and whorls on a finger|螺~ thread|波~ ripple|皱~ lines (on a face); wrinkles

☞ 璺 wèn on p. 2012

【纹理】wénlǐ 物体上呈线条的花纹 veins; grain

【纹路】wén·lu (～儿 wén·lur) 物体上的皱痕或花纹 lines or grain of an object

【纹缕】wén·lü (～儿 wén·lür) 纹路 lines; grain

【纹饰】wénshì 器物上绘成或铸成的图案、花纹 decorative pattern (painted or engraved on utensils); figure: 殷周青铜器～ decorative patterns on Yin and Zhou bronzeware

【纹丝不动】wén sī bù dòng 一点儿也不动 absolutely still: 连下几镐，那块冻土还是～。After I picked several times, the frozen earth remained solid as before.

【纹银】wényín 〈旧时 *old*〉称成色最好的银子 fine silver; silver of the best quality

炆 wén 〈方 *dial.*〉用微火燉食物或熬菜 stew; cook food over a slow fire; simmer

闻 wén ❶ 听见 hear: 听而不～ turn a deaf ear to; hear but pay no attention to | 耳～不如目见。Seeing is believing. ❷ 听见的事情；消息 news; story: 见～ what one sees and hears; knowledge | 新～ news | 奇～ strange news; fantastic story ❸ 〈书 *fml.*〉有名望的 well-known; famous: ～人 famous person ❹ 名声 reputation: 令～ good name; good reputation | 秽～ ill reputation ❺ 用鼻子嗅 smell: 你～～这是什么味儿? Smell this and see what it is. ❻ (Wén) 姓 a surname

【闻达】wéndá 〈书 *fml.*〉显达；有名望 illustrious and influential; eminent: 不求～ seek neither fame nor position

【闻风而动】wén fēng ér dòng 一听到消息就立刻行动 act without delay upon hearing the news; immediately respond to a call; go into action without delay

【闻风丧胆】wén fēng sàng dǎn 听到一点风声就吓破了胆。形容对某种力量极端恐惧。become terror-stricken (or panic-stricken, terrified) at the news

【闻过则喜】wén guò zé xǐ 听到别人指出自己的缺点、错误就感到高兴。形容虚心，对自己要求严格。be glad to have one's errors or mistakes pointed out. It shows that one is modest and strict with oneself.

【闻鸡起舞】wén jī qǐ wǔ 东晋时，祖逖和刘琨二人为好友，常常互相勉励，半夜听到鸡鸣就起床舞剑(见于《晋书·祖逖传》)。后用来比喻志士及时奋发。rise at cock's crow; diligent and self-disciplined. In the Eastern Jin Dynasty, Zu Ti and Liu Kun were good friends and often encouraged each other, and both rose at cock's crow to play with their swords (see *History of Jin·Biography of Zu Ti*); (fig.) diligence of man of resolve

【闻名】wénmíng ❶ 听到名声 be familiar with sb.'s name; know sb. by repute: ～已久 known for a long time | ～不如见面。Knowing a person by repute is not as good as meeting him face to face. ❷ 有名 well known; famous; renowned: ～全国 well known throughout the country | 二万五千里长征～世界。The 25,000-*li* Long march was well known in the world. | 西湖是～的风景区。The West Lake is a famous scenic place.

【闻人】wénrén ❶ 有名望的人 well-known figure; famous man; celebrity: 社会～ social celebrities ❷ (Wénrén) 姓 a surname

【闻所未闻】wén suǒ wèi wén 听到从来没有听到过的。形容事物非常稀罕。hear what one has never heard before, referring to sth. extremely rare

蚊 wén 蚊子 mosquito: 消灭～蝇 exterminate mosquitoes and flies

【蚊虫】wénchóng 蚊子 mosquito

【蚊香】wénxiāng 含有药料，燃着后可以熏死或赶跑蚊子的线香或盘香 mosquito-repellent incense; incense sticks or coils containing insecticide to kill or drive away mosquitoes when burning

【蚊帐】wénzhàng 挂在床铺上阻挡蚊子的帐子，有伞形和长方形两种 mosquito net; net in the shape of umbrella or rectangle hanging over a bed to prevent mosquitoes

【蚊子】wén·zi 昆虫，成虫身体细长，胸部有一对翅膀和三对细长的脚，幼虫(孑孓)和蛹都生长在水中。雄蚊吸植物的汁液。雌蚊吸人畜的血液，能传播疟疾、丝虫病、流行性乙型脑炎等病。最常见的有按蚊、库蚊和伊蚊三类。mosquito (*Anopheles*, *Culex* or *Aedes*); two-winged insect with a long, slender body and three pairs of legs, the females having skin-piercing mouthparts to extract blood from humans and animals, the males extracting juice from plants. Mosquitoes can spread diseases such as malaria, filariasis, and epidemic encephalitis B. The most common varieties are malarial mosquito, culex and yellow-fever mosquito.

阌 wén 阌乡(Wénxiāng)，旧县名，在河南 Wenxiang, name of an old county in Henan Province

雯 wén 〈书 *fml.*〉有花纹的云彩 patterned cloud

螡 wén 〈书 *fml.*〉same as 蚊 wén

wěn (ㄨㄣˇ)

刎 wěn 用刀割脖子 cut one's throat: 自～ cut one's own throat

【刎颈交】wěnjǐngjiāo 指同生死共患难的朋友 friends that are ready to die for each other; also 刎颈之交 wěnjǐngzhījiāo

抆 wěn 〈书 *fml.*〉擦；拭 wipe: ～泪 wipe one's tears

W

吻(脗) wěn ❶ 嘴唇 lips：接～ kiss ❷ 用嘴唇接触人或物 kiss a person or an object ❸ 动物的嘴 animal's mouth

【吻合】wěnhé ❶ 完全符合 be identical；coincide；tally：双方意见～。Both sides have identical views. ❷ 医学上指把器官的两个断裂面连接起来 connect by anastomosis；connect broken parts of an organ of the body by surgery：肠～ intestinal anastomosis｜动脉～ artery anastomosis

【吻兽】wěnshòu 古建筑屋脊两端陶制鸱尾之类的装饰物 decorative animal sculptures on roof ridges of ancient buildings

紊 wěn（旧读 formerly pronounced wèn）紊乱 disorderly；confused：有条不～ orderly

【紊乱】wěnluàn 杂乱；纷乱 disorder；chaos；confusion：秩序～ in a state of chaos｜思路～ confused thinking

稳(穩) wěn ❶ 稳固；平稳 steady；firm：脚要站～ stand firm｜把桌子放～ make the table steady｜时局不～。The current situation is unstable.｜他的立场很～。He takes a firm stand. ❷ 稳重 steady：态度很～ steady manner｜～步前进 advance steadily ❸ 稳妥 sure；certain；reliable：十拿九～ almost certain；90 per cent sure｜～扎～打 go ahead steadily and strike sure blows (in war)；go about things steadily and surely ❹ 使稳定 stabilize；calm：你先～住他，别让他跑了。You should first try to put him at ease. Don't let him slip away.

【稳便】wěnbiàn ❶ 稳妥方便 safe and convenient：这样做恐怕不大～。It's not appropriate to do it like this, I'm afraid. ❷ 请便；任便（多见于早期白话 oft. in early vernacular）do as you wish；suit your own convenience

【稳步】wěnbù 稳重的步子 with steady steps；steadily：～前进（比喻按一定步骤推进工作）advance steadily；make steady progress；(fig.) advance work as planned｜产量～上升。Production is going up steadily.

【稳操胜券】wěn cāo shèng quàn〈比喻 *fig.*〉有胜利的把握 be certain (or confident) of success；also 稳操胜算 wěn cāo shèng suàn or 稳操左券 wěn cāo zuǒ quàn

【稳产】wěnchǎn 产量稳定 stable yields：提倡科学种田，促进农作物～高产。Encourage scientific farming to promote high, stable yields of crops.

【稳当】wěn·dang ❶ 稳重妥当 reliable；secure；safe：办事～ handle things reliably ❷ 稳固牢靠 steady；stable：把梯子放～。Put the ladder in a steady position.

【稳定】wěndìng ❶ 稳固安定；没有变动 stable；steady：水位～ water level remains stable｜情绪～。The mood is stable.｜社会～。The society is stable. ❷ 使稳定 stabilize：～物价 stabilize commodity prices｜～情绪 set sb.'s mind at rest；reassure sb.｜～局势 stabilize the situation ❸ 指物质不易被酸、碱、强氧化剂等腐蚀，或不易受光和热的作用而改变性能 stability of chemical property；substances not subject to corrosion by acid, alkaline, strong oxidants, etc., or to the change of property under the impact of light and heat

【稳定流】wěndìngliú 流体任何一处的流速、压强、密度等都不随时间改变的流动 stable current；current, the velocity, pressure and density of which do not change with the time；also 定常流 dìngchángliú

【稳定平衡】wěndìng pínghéng 处于平衡状态的物体，受到微小的外力作用后平衡状态改变，外力除去后，仍能恢复原来的平衡状态，叫做稳定平衡。如不倒翁的平衡状态。stable equilibrium；state of balance of an object changes after it is subject to the action of a minute external force and returns to the original after the external force is removed, such as the stable equilibrium of a tumbler

【稳固】wěngù ❶ 安稳而巩固 firm；stable：基础～ firm (or solid) foundation｜地位～ firm position ❷ 使稳固 make stable；stabilize：～政权 stabilize a government

【稳健】wěnjiàn ❶ 稳而有力 firm；steady：～的步子 with firm steps ❷ 稳重；不轻举妄动 steady；sure；reliable；not rash；not reckless：办事～ go about things steadily

【稳练】wěnliàn 沉稳干练 steady and proficient：办事精明～ handle things steadily and proficiently

【稳婆】wěnpó〈旧时 *old*〉以接生为业的妇女 midwife

【稳如泰山】wěn rú tàishān ☞ 安如泰山 ān rú tàishān on p.10

【稳妥】wěntuǒ 稳当；可靠 safe；reliable：这样处理，我看不够～。I think it's not safe to handle it this way.

【稳扎稳打】wěn zhā wěn dǎ ❶ 稳当而有把握地打仗 go ahead steadily and strike sure blows (in war)（扎 *zha*：扎营 pitch a camp）❷〈比喻 *fig.*〉有步骤有把握地做事 go about things steadily and surely

【稳重】wěnzhòng（言语、举动）沉着而有分寸；不轻浮 (of speech or behaviour) steady；staid；sedate：为人～ be steady and sedate｜办事～ handle matters with discretion

wèn（ㄨㄣˋ）

问 wèn ❶ 有不知道或不明白的事情或道理请人解答 ask；enquire；seek information about：询～ enquire｜～事处 enquiry desk；information desk｜不懂就～ ask if you do not know｜答非所～ answer what is not asked；

give an irrelevant answer ❷ 为表示关切而询问；慰问 ask after; enquire after：～好 send regards to｜～候 send one's respects or regards to ❸ 审讯；追究 interrogate; examine：审～ interrogate｜～案 try a case; hear a case ❹ 管；干预 hold responsible; intervene：不闻不～ be indifferent to｜概不过～ wash one's hands of the whole matter ❺ 向（某方面或某人要东西）ask (sb.) for sth.：我～他借两本书。I ask him to lend me two books. ❻（Wèn）姓 a surname

【问安】wèn//ān 问好（多对长辈 usu. to elders）wish sb. good health

【问案】wèn//àn 审问案件 try (or hear) a case

【问卜】wènbǔ 用占卜来解决疑难（迷信）(superstition) divine by the Eight Trigrams：求神～ pray to the gods and divine by the Eight Trigrams

【问长问短】wèn cháng wèn duǎn 仔细地问（多表示关心 oft. when showing one's concern for sb.）make detailed enquiries; enquire with concern about sb's well-being; ask about this and that

【问答】wèndá 发问和回答 questions and answers：～题 problems to be answered

【问道于盲】wèn dào yú máng 向瞎子问路 ask a blind man the way;〈比喻 *fig.*〉向毫无所知的人求救 seek advice from one who can offer none

【问鼎】wèndǐng 春秋时，楚子（楚庄王）北伐，陈兵于洛水，向周王朝炫耀武力。周定王派遣王孙满慰劳楚师，楚子向王孙满询问周朝的传国之宝九鼎的大小和轻重（见于《左传》宣公三年）。楚子问鼎，有夺取周王朝天下的意思。后用'问鼎'指图谋夺取政权。During the Spring and Autumn Period, King Zhuang of the state of Chu launched a northern expedition, and deployed his troops along the Luo River to show off his might to the Zhou Dynasty. King Ding of the Zhou sent Wang Sunman to bring gifts to pacify the Chu troops. King Zhuang enquired him about the size and weight of the Nine Tripods, national treasures of the Zhou Dynasty (see *The Zuo Commentary · Duke Xuan 3rd Year*). He asked about the tripods with the intention of seizing the power of the Zhou Dynasty. The phrase 'enquire about the Nine Tripods' is used to imply ambition to seize political power：～中原 have the ambition to seize the Central Plains ◇ 这次比赛主队连输几场，失去～冠军的机会。After losing several matches in a row at this tournament, we have lost the chance to win the championship.

【问寒问暖】wèn hán wèn nuǎn 形容对别人的生活十分关切 enquire with concern about sb.'s well-being; be solicitous for sb.'s welfare

【问好】wèn//hǎo 询问安好，表示关切 send one's regards to; say hello to：请向伯母～。Please give my regards to your mother. *or* Remember me to your mother.｜问同志们好！My best wishes to all of you, my comrades!

【问号】wènhào ❶ 标点符号（?），表示疑问句末尾的停顿 question mark; interrogation mark (?), indicating stop of a question ❷ same as 疑问 yíwèn：他今天晚上能不能赶到还是个～。It's still unknown whether he will be here tonight.

【问候】wènhòu same as 问好 wèn//hǎo

【问津】wènjīn 探询渡口 ask for the ferry;〈比喻 *fig.*〉探问价格或情况（多用于否定句 oft. used in the negative）make enquiries (as about prices or the situation)：无人～ no one is interested in｜书价太贵，不敢～。The book prices are too dear. No one dares even to enquire about them.

【问卷】wènjuàn 列有若干问题让人回答的书面调查材料，目的在于了解人们对这些问题的看法 questionnaire; paper with many questions to be answered in order to seek views on these questions：～调查 survey by questionnaire

【问难】wènnàn 反复质问、辩论（多指学术研究 oft. referring to academic research）raise difficult questions for discussion：质疑～ raise doubts and questions for discussions

【问世】wènshì ❶ 指著作等出版跟读者见面 (of a work) be published; come out：一部新词典即将～。A new dictionary will soon come out. ❷ same as 面市 miànshì

【问事】wènshì ❶ 询问事情 enquire; ask：～处 enquiry office; information desk ❷〈书 *fml.*〉过问事务 run affairs; be in charge

【问题】wèntí ❶ 要求回答或解释的题目 question; problem; issue：这次考试一共有五个～。There were five questions in this exam.｜我想答复一下这一类的～。I would like to answer these questions. ❷ 须要研究讨论并加以解决的矛盾、疑难 problems; contradictions; issues：思想～ ideological problem｜这种药治感冒很解决～。This drug is very effective in curing cold. ❸ 关键；重要之点 key; crucial point：重要的～在善于学习。The important problem is how to be good at studying. ❹ 事故或麻烦 trouble; mishap：那部车床又出～了。Something has gone wrong with that lathe.

【问心】wènxīn 反躬自问 examine one's conscience：～无愧 feel no qualms upon self-examination; have a clear conscience

【问讯】wènxùn ❶ same as 询问 xúnwèn：～处 enquiry office; information desk ❷ same as 问候 wènhòu ❸ 僧尼跟人应酬时合十招呼 greet someone by putting one's palms together in front of one's chest; also 打问讯 dǎ wènxùn

【问罪】wènzuì 指出对方的罪过，加以谴责或攻击；声讨 denounce; condemn：兴师～ denounce someone publicly for one's crimes

汶 Wèn 大汶河(Dàwèn Hé),水名,在山东 Dawen River, in Shandong Province; also 汶水 Wènshuǐ

揾 wèn 〈书 *fml.*〉❶ 用手指按 press or rub with fingers ❷ 擦 wipe: ~泪 wipe one's tears

璺(纹) wèn 陶瓷、玻璃等器具上的裂痕 crack (on glassware or earthenware): 碗上有一道~。The bowl has a crack in it. | 打破沙锅~到底(谐'问'璺 wèn being the pun of 问 wèn) insist on getting to the bottom of a matter; enquire persistently

☞ 纹 wén on p. 2009

wēng (ㄨㄥ)

翁 wēng ❶ 年老的男子;老头儿 old man: 渔~ old fisherman ❷ 父亲 father ❸ 丈夫的父亲 father-in-law: ~姑(公公和婆婆) woman's parents-in-law ❹ 妻子的父亲 wife's father: ~婿(岳父和女婿) father and his son-in-law ❺ (Wēng)姓 a surname

【翁仲】 wēngzhòng 原指铜铸或石雕的偶像,后来专指幕前的石人 bronze or stone image; stone statue placed in front of a tomb

嗡 wēng 〈拟声词 *onom.*〉: 蜜蜂~~地飞。Bees are buzzing all around. | 飞机~~地响。A plane is buzzing overhead.

【嗡子】 wēng·zi ☞ 京二胡 jīng'èrhú on p. 1018

滃 Wēng 滃江,水名,在广东 Wengjiang, name of a river in Guangdong Province

☞ wěng on p. 2012

鹟 wēng 鸟类的一科,身体小,嘴稍扁平,基部有许多刚毛,脚短小。大都以飞行的虫为食物,是益鸟。flycatcher (*Muscicapidae*); small passerine bird with a flat beak, bristles at the base and short legs, a beneficial bird that feeds mostly on flying insects

鳒 wēng 鱼类的一属,身体侧扁,有圆鳞,吻不尖。生活在近海。hawkfish (*Cirrhitidae*); flat fish with round scales living in coastal waters

鞥 wēng 〈方 *dial.*〉靴鞧 boot leg

【鞥靴】 wēngxuē 〈方 *dial.*〉高鞧棉鞋 cotton-padded high boots

wěng (ㄨㄥˇ)

塕 wěng 〈方 *dial.*〉❶ 形容尘土飞扬 dusty; dust being blown about ❷ 尘土 dust

蓊 wěng 〈书 *fml.*〉草木茂盛 lush; luxuriant: ~郁 lush; luxuriant

滃 wěng 〈书 *fml.*〉❶ 形容水盛 gush; abundance of water ❷ 形容云起 rise of clouds

☞ Wēng on p. 2012

wèng (ㄨㄥˋ)

瓮(甕、❶罋) wèng ❶ 一种盛东西的陶器,腹部较大 urn; earthen jar with a bulging belly: 水~ water jar | 酒~ wine jar | 菜~ jar for pickling vegetables ❷ (Wèng)姓 a surname

【瓮城】 wèngchéng 围绕在城门外的小城 barbican entrance to a city; enceinte of a city gate

【瓮声瓮气】 wèng shēng wèng qì 形容说话的声音粗大而低沉 in a low, muffled voice

【瓮中之鳖】 wèng zhōng zhī biē 〈比喻 *fig.*〉逃脱不了的人或动物 like a turtle in a jar; bottled up; trapped

【瓮中捉鳖】 wèng zhōng zhuō biē 〈比喻 *fig.*〉要捕捉的对象无处逃遁,下手即可捉到,很有把握 catch a turtle in a jar; go after an easy prey

蕹 wèng [蕹菜](wèngcài) 一年生草本植物,茎蔓生,中空,叶卵圆形或心脏形,叶柄长,花粉红色或白色,漏斗状,结蒴果,卵形。嫩茎叶可做蔬菜。water spinach (*Ipomoea aquatica*); annual herbal plant with a trailing, hollow stem, long-stalked oval or heart-shaped leaves, pink or white, funnel-shaped flowers, and ovate capsules, both its tender stem and leaves used as vegetables; also 空心菜 kōngxīncài

齆 wèng [齆鼻儿](wèngbír) ❶ 因鼻孔堵塞而发音不清 speak with a nasal twang due to a stuffy nose: 这两天伤风,说话有点儿~。I've had a cold these days and speak with a nasal twang. ❷ 齆鼻儿的人 person who speaks with a nasal twang

wō (ㄨㄛ)

挝(撾) wō 老挝(Lǎowō),亚洲国名 Laos, name of an Asian country

☞ zhuā on p. 2514

莴(萵) wō ☞ below

【莴苣】 wō·jù 一年生或二年生草本植物,叶子长圆形,头状花序,花金黄色。茎和叶子是普通蔬菜。莴苣的变种有莴笋、生菜等。lettuce (*Lactuca sativa*); annual or biennial herbal plant with oblong leaves, golden-yellow flowers in heads. Both the stem and leaves are common vegetables. The varieties include asparagus lettuce and romaine lettuce.

【莴笋】 wōsǔn 莴苣的变种,叶长圆形,茎部肉质,呈棒状,是普通蔬菜 asparagus lettuce (*Lactuca sativa* var. *angustana*); variant of lettuce with oblong leaves and fleshy rod-like stems, a common vegetable

倭 wō 我国古代称日本 ancient Chinese name for Japan

【倭瓜】wōguā〈方 *dial.*〉南瓜 pumpkin (*Cucurbita pepo*); cushaw

【倭寇】Wōkòu 14—16世纪屡次骚扰抢劫朝鲜和我国沿海的日本海盗 Japanese pirates operating in Chinese and Korean coastal waters from the 14th to the 16th century

涡(渦) wō 旋涡 whirlpool; eddy: 水～ eddies of water

☞ Guō on p.737

【涡电流】wōdiànliú same as 涡流 wōliú ③

【涡流】wōliú ❶ 流体旋转,形成旋涡的流动 circular movement of a fluid; whirling fluid; eddy; also 有旋流 yǒuxuánliú ❷ 指旋涡 eddy current; vortex flow; eddies of water ❸ 实心的导体或铁心在交流电场中由于电磁感应所产生的电流。涡流能消耗电能并使导体和铁心发热。eddy current; vortex flow; current produced from a solid conductor or an iron core in A. C. electric field due to electromagnetic induction, causing power consumption and heat in the conductor or iron core; also 涡电流 wōdiànliú

【涡轮机】wōlúnjī 利用流体冲击叶轮转动而产生动力的发动机,按流体的不同而分为汽轮机、燃气轮机和水轮机。广泛用做发电、航空、航海等的动力机。turbine; engine having a drive shaft driven either by the impulse of steam, water, air, gas, etc. against the curved vanes of a wheel or set of wheels or by the reaction of fluid passing out through nozzles located around the wheel, widely used as an engine in power generation, aviation and navigation; 简称 abbr. 轮机 lúnjī; also 透平机 tòupíngjī

喔 wō〈拟声词 *onom.*〉形容公鸡叫的声音 cock's crow

窝(窩) wō ❶ 鸟兽、昆虫住的地方(of birds, animals, insects) nest; lair; den: 鸟～ bird's nest | 狗～ dog's kennel | 蚂蚁～ ant's nest | 喜鹊搭～。Magpies are building a nest. ❷〈比喻 *fig.*〉坏人聚居的地方 place where evildoers get together; lair: 贼～ thieves' den | 土匪～ bandits' liar ❸〈方 *dial.*〉(～儿 wōr)〈比喻 *fig.*〉人体或物体所占的位置 place occupied by a human body or an object: 他不动～儿。He just stayed pit. | 这炉子真碍事,给它挪个～儿。The stove here is in the way. Let's move it to another place. ❹ (～儿 wōr) 凹进去的地方 hollow place; hollow part: 夹肢～ armpit | 酒～儿 dimple ❺ 窝藏 harbour; shelter: ～赃 harbour loot | ～主 one who harbours stolen goods ❻ 蜷缩或呆在某处不活动 curl up; huddle up: 把头～在衣领里 bury one's head in the collar | ～在家里生闷气 be in the sulks behind closed doors ❼ 郁积不得发作或发挥(be forced to) hold in: ～工 enforced idleness due to poor organization of work; holdup in the work through poor organization | ～火 be filled with anger ❽ 使弯或曲折 bend: 把铁丝～个圆圈 bend the wire into a circle ❾〈量词 *classifier*〉用于一胎所生的或一次孵出的动物(猪、狗、鸡等) used for animals as pigs, dogs, chickens, etc.; litter; brood: 一～下子五只猫 give birth to five kittens at a litter | 孵了几～小鸡 hatched broods of chickens

【窝憋】wō·bie〈方 *dial.*〉烦闷;不舒畅(多指有不如意的事情 about sth. undesirable) feel frustrated: 平白无故挨了一顿训,真～ feel frustrated to get a scolding without reason

【窝藏】wōcáng 私藏(罪犯、违禁品或赃物) harbour; shelter; give shelter to (or harbour a criminal); conceal (contraband or booty)

【窝点】wōdiǎn 坏人聚集窝藏的地方 lair; den; hideout; place where bad people hide: 贩毒～ hideout of drug dealers

【窝工】wō//gōng 因计划或调配不好,工作人员没事可做或不能发挥作用 enforced idleness due to poor organization of work; holdup in the work through poor organization

【窝火】wō//huǒ (～儿 wō//huǒr) same as 憋气 biēqì ②: 窝了一肚子火 be filled with pent-up anger; be simmering with rage; be forced to bottle up one's anger

【窝家】wōjiā same as 窝主 wōzhǔ

【窝里斗】wō·lidòu 家族或团体内部彼此钩心斗角 internal struggle in a clan or a group; infighting; internecine strife; also 窝儿里斗 wōr·lidòu

【窝里横】wō·lihèng 只敢在家里发横、不讲理 be a terror at home (but a coward outside); also 窝儿里横 wōr·lihèng

【窝囊】wō·nang ❶ 因受委屈而烦闷 feel vexed; be annoyed: ～气 petty annoyance ❷ 无能;怯懦 good-for-nothing; hopelessly stupid: 这个人真～。This man is really good-for-nothing.

【窝囊废】wō·nangfèi 怯懦无能的人(含讥讽意 derog.) good-for-nothing; worthless wretch

【窝棚】wō·peng 简陋的小屋 shack; shed; shanty

【窝铺】wōpù 供睡觉的窝棚 shed for sleeping

【窝气】wō//qì 有委屈或烦恼得不到发泄 choke with resentment; feel injured and resentful: 挨了剋,心里～ feel resentful after getting a dressing-down | 窝了一肚子气 have pent-up grievances

【窝头】wōtóu 用玉米面、高粱面或别种杂粮面做的食物,略作圆锥形,底下有个窝儿 steamed bread of corn, sorghum, etc. made in the shape of a cone with a hollow inside from the bottom up; also 窝窝头 wō·wotóu

【窝心】wōxīn〈方 *dial.*〉因受到委屈或侮辱后不能表白或发泄而心中苦闷 depressed; dejected; feel low after being wronged or insulted and not in a position to express or vent it

【窝赃】wō//zāng 故意为罪犯窝藏或转移赃物、赃款 harbour stolen goods; conceal booty:～罪 crime of concealing stolen goods; offence of harbouring the stolen goods and contrabands

【窝主】wōzhǔ 窝藏罪犯、违禁品或赃物的人或人家 person who harbours a criminal, loot or contraband goods

蜗(蝸) wō 蜗牛 snail

【蜗杆】wōgǎn 一种杆形零件,杆上有螺旋线形的槽纹,与蜗轮相啮合 worm; short, rotating screw that meshes with the teeth of a worm gear or a rack

【蜗居】wōjū〈书 *fml*.〉〈比喻 *fig*.〉窄小的住所 humble abode

【蜗轮】wōlún 一种与蜗杆相啮合,具有特殊齿形的齿轮 worm gear; worm wheel; special kind of gear that meshes with the teeth of a worm

【蜗牛】wōniú 软体动物,头部有两对触角,腹面有扁平的脚,壳略作扁圆形、球形或椭圆形,黄褐色,有螺旋纹。吃草本植物的表皮,危害植物。有的地区叫水牛ル。snail (*Macrocyclis concava*); soft-bodied animal with two pairs of feelers on the head and flat feet on the belly in a slightly oblate, spherical or oval, yellowish-brown, spiral protective shells, feeding on the cuticles of herbal plants and destructive to plants; also 水牛ル shuǐniúr in some regions

【蜗旋】wōxuán 回环旋转 spiral; helix:塔内壁有石阶,～而上。There is a staircase spiraling its way up the pagoda inside.

踒 wō (手、脚等)猛折而筋骨受伤 sprain (one's sinew or bone); strain; injury caused by a violent wrench

wǒ (ㄨㄛˇ)

我 wǒ〈代词 *pron*.〉❶ 称自己 I or me 注意 **NOTE**: a)有时也用来指称'我们'[sometimes referring to we or us]:～校 our school|～军 our army|敌～矛盾 contradiction between the enemy and ourselves b)'我、你'对举,表示泛指[when used in combination with 你 nǐ referring to people in general] ☞ 你 nǐ on p. 1406 ❷ 自己 self:自～ oneself; ego|忘～精神 selflessness

【我们】wǒ·men〈代词 *pron*.〉称包括自己在内的若干人[referring to several people including oneself] we; us; ☞ 咱们 zán·men on p. 2390

【我行我素】wǒ xíng wǒ sù 不管别人怎么说,我还是照我本来的一套去做 persist in one's old ways (no matter what others say); stick to one's old way of doing things

鬈 wǒ [鬈鬌](wǒtuǒ)〈书 *fml*.〉形容发髻美好 (of a woman's hair-coil) beautiful; pretty

wò (ㄨㄛˋ)

肟 wò 有机化合物的一类,是醛或酮的羰基和羟胺中的氨基缩合而成的衍生物 oxime; organic chemical compound derived from condensation of aldehydic or ketonic carbonyl and the amino in hydroxylamine

沃 wò ❶ 灌溉;浇 irrigate:～田 irrigate farmland|如汤～雪 like melting snow with hot water; easy job ❷ (土地)肥 fertile; rich:肥～ fertile|～土 fertile soil|～野 fertile land|肥田～地 fertile fields ❸ (Wò)姓 a surname

【沃野】wòyě 肥沃的田野 fertile soil; rich soil:～千里 a thousand *li* of fertile fields; vast expanse of fertile land

卧(臥) wò ❶ 躺下 lie:仰～ lie on the back|～倒 lie down; take a prone position|～病 be confined to bed; be laid up ❷〈方 *dial*.〉使婴儿躺下 get a baby to lie down:把小孩ル～在炕上。Lay the baby on the *kang*. ❸ (动物)趴(of animals or birds) crouch; sit:～牛 make the cow lie down|鸡～在窝里。The chickens were in the coop. ❹ 睡觉用的 for sleeping in:～室 bedroom|～房 bedroom; sleeping room|～铺 sleeping berth ❺ 指卧铺 sleeping berth:硬～ hard sleeping berth|软～ soft sleeping berth ❻〈方 *dial*.〉把去壳的鸡蛋放到开水里煮 poach (eggs):～个鸡子ル poach an egg

【卧病】wòbìng 因病躺下 be confined to bed; be laid up

【卧车】wòchē ❶ 设有卧铺的火车车厢 sleeping car; sleeping carriage; sleeper ❷ 小轿车 automobile; car; limousine; sedan

【卧床】wòchuáng 因疾病、年老等躺在床上 (of the old or the sick) lie in bed; be confined to bed:～不起 become bed-ridden; take to one's bed and never rise again

【卧底】wòdǐ 埋伏下来做内应 be a planted agent

【卧房】wòfáng same as 卧室 wòshì

【卧轨】wòguǐ 躺在铁轨上(阻止火车行驶或企图自杀) lay oneself on the railway tracks (either to commit suicide or to stop a train from moving)

【卧果ル】wò//guǒr〈方 *dial*.〉把鸡蛋去壳,整个ル放在开水里煮 poach a shelled egg:卧个果ル poach an egg

【卧果ル】wòguǒr〈方 *dial*.〉去壳后整个ル放在开水里煮的鸡蛋 poached egg, egg boiled in water without shell

【卧具】wòjù 睡觉时用的东西,特指火车、轮船上或旅馆中供给旅客的被子、毯子、枕头等 bedding (provided on a train or ship), including a quilt, blanket, pillow, etc. for use by a passenger

【卧铺】wòpù 卧车上供旅客睡觉的铺位。有的长途汽车也设卧铺。sleeping berth; sleeper; bed in a sleeping car

【卧室】wòshì 睡觉的房间 bedroom; also 卧房 wòfáng

【卧榻】wòtà 〈书 *fml.*〉床 bed: ～之侧,岂容他人鼾睡。How can one tolerate somebody snoring by one's bedside? (〈比喻 *fig.*〉不许别人侵入自己的势力范围 do not allow sb. to invade one's sphere of influence)

【卧薪尝胆】wò xīn cháng dǎn 越国被吴国打败,越王勾践立志报仇。据说他睡觉睡在柴草上头,吃饭、睡觉前都要尝一尝苦胆,策励自己不忘耻辱。经过长期准备,终于打败了吴国(《史记·越王勾践世家》只有尝胆事,苏轼《拟孙权答曹操书》才有'卧薪尝胆'的话)。形容人刻苦自励,立志为国家报仇雪耻。sleep on brushwood and taste gall. The state of Yue was defeated by the state of Wu, and Gou Jian, King of Yue, resolved to make the revenge, and he slept on brushwood and tasted a gall bladder before eating and sleeping to remind himself of the humiliation. After a long period of preparations, he finally defeated the Wu. (*Records of the Historian · Hereditary House of Gou Jian, King of Yue* only writes of the king tasting the gall bladder, and the phrase 'sleep on brushwood and taste a gall bladder' did not occur until Su Shi coined it in his *Draft Reply for Sun Quan to Cao Cao*.) The phrase refers undergoing self-imposed hardships to strengthen one's resolve to avenge a national humiliation or to accomplish an ambition.

偓 wò 偓佺(Wòquán),〈古代 *arch.*〉传说中的仙人 Woquan, legendary immortal

涴 wò 〈方 *dial.*〉弄脏,如油、泥粘在衣服或器物上 dirt; make dirty; stain oil or mud on clothes or utensils
☞ yuān on p. 2355

硪 wò 砸实地基或打桩等用的一种工具,通常是一块圆形石头或铁饼,周围系着几根绳子 flat stone or iron rammer with ropes attached at the sides, used to ram foundation or drive piles: 打～ work with a flat stone or iron rammer

握 wò ❶ 用手拿或攥 hold; grasp: 把～ hold; keep; grasp; assurance; certainty | ～笔 hold a pen or writing brush with fingers | ～手 shake hands ❷ 掌握 hold; grasp: ～有兵权 wield military power

【握别】wòbié 握手告别 shake hands at parting; part

【握力】wòlì 手握紧物体的力量 power of the hand grip; grip

【握拳】wò//quán 手指弯曲成拳头 make a fist; clench one's fist; bend one's fingers into a fist

【握手】wò//shǒu 彼此伸手相互握住,是见面或分别时的礼节,也用来表示祝贺或慰问 shake hands; clasp hands; courtesy at meeting or parting between two people, or expression of congratulation or consolation

幄 wò 〈书 *fml.*〉帐幕 tent: 帷～ military tent; commander's tent

渥 wò 〈书 *fml.*〉❶ 沾湿;沾润 wet; moisten ❷ 厚;重 strong; rich: 优～ munificent; favourable; generous; liberal

斡 wò 〈书 *fml.*〉旋转 revolve; spin; rotate

【斡旋】wòxuán same as 调解 tiáojiě: 从中～,解决两方争端 settle a dispute between two parties through one's mediation

龌 wò [龌龊](wòchuò) ❶ 不干净;脏 dirty; filthy ❷ 〈比喻 *fig.*〉人品质恶劣 base; mean: 卑鄙～ sordid; foul ❸ 〈书 *fml.*〉形容气量狭小,拘于小节 narrow-minded; fussy on small matters

wū (ㄨ)

兀 wū [兀秃](wū·tu) same as 乌涂 wū·tu
☞ wù on p. 2036

乌[1] (烏) wū ❶ 乌鸦 crow: 月落～啼。The crows cawed when the moon went down. ❷ 黑色 black; dark: ～云 dark clouds | ～木 ebony ❸ (Wū)姓 a surname

乌[2] (烏) wū 〈书 *fml.*〉何;哪里(多用于反问 oft. used in rhetorical questions) what; how: ～足道哉? What's there worth mentioning about it?
☞ wù on p. 2036

【乌飞兔走】wū fēi tù zǒu 指日月运行,形容光阴过得快(古代传说日中有三足乌,月中有玉兔) the crow flies and the rabbit runs; time flies (According to a legend, there is a crow in the sun and a rabbit in the moon. Therefore the crow and the rabbit stand for the sun and the moon respectively.)

【乌龟】wūguī ❶ 爬行动物,体扁,有硬甲,长圆形,背部隆起,黑褐色,有花纹,趾有蹼,能游泳,头尾四肢能缩入壳内。生活在河流、湖泊里,吃杂草或小动物。龟甲可入药。tortoise (*Chelonia mydas*); turtle; a kind of reptile having webbed feet and a flat, soft body encased in a hard, domed, mottled, black-and-brown shell into which the head, tail, and four legs may be withdrawn, living in rivers and lakes, and feeding on weeds and small animals, and its shell used for Chinese medicine; also 金龟 jīnguī; 俗称 popularly called 王八

wáng·ba ❷ 讥称妻子有外遇的人 cuckold; man whose wife has committed adultery

【乌合之众】wū hé zhī zhòng 指无组织纪律的一群人 disorderly band; motley crowd; rabble; mob (乌合 *wu he*:像乌鸦那样聚集 flock together like crows)

【乌黑】wūhēi 深黑 pitch-black; jet-black: ~的头发 jet-black hair | 她那一双大眼睛~发亮。Her big eyes are black and shining.

【乌呼】wūhū same as 呜呼 wūhū

【乌金】wūjīn ❶ 指煤 black gold — coal ❷ 中药上指墨 ink stick in traditional Chinese medicine

【乌桕】wūjiù 落叶乔木,叶子互生,略呈菱形,秋天变红,花单性,雌雄同株,种子的外面有白蜡层,用来制造蜡烛。叶子可以做黑色染料。树皮、叶均可入药。Chinese tallow tree (*Sapium sebiferum*); hermaphroditical deciduous tree with alternate, slightly rhombus leaves that turn red in autumn and can be used in making black dye, unisexual flowers, seeds covered in a layer of white wax which is used in making candles, with both bark and leaves being of medical value; also 桕树 jiùshù

【乌拉】wūlā ❶ 西藏民主改革前,农奴为官府或农奴主所服的劳役,主要是耕种和运输,还有种种杂役、杂差 corvée labour formerly imposed on Tibetan serfs before Democratic Reform was carried out in Tibet, mainly farming, transportation, odd jobs, etc. ❷ 服上项劳役的人 labourer in Tibet before Democratic Reform; also 乌喇 wūlā

☞ wù·la on p. 2036

W

【乌鳢】wūlǐ 鱼,身体圆柱形,头扁,口大,有齿,背部灰绿色,腹部灰白色,有黑色斑纹。性凶猛,捕食小鱼、蛙等小动物,对淡水养鱼业有害。northern snakehead (*Channa argus*); snake-headed fish; flat-headed, big-mouthed, cylindrical-bodied fish with teeth, a greyish-green back, a greyish-white belly and black spots, ferocious in nature, feeding on small fishes and frogs and thus being destructive to fresh-water fish breeding; also 乌鱼 wūyú; 通称 generally called 黑鱼 hēiyú

【乌亮】wūliàng 又黑又亮 glossy black; jet-black: ~的头发 dark, glossy hair; raven locks | 油井喷出~的石油。Glossy dark oil gushes out of an oil well.

【乌溜溜】wūliūliū (~的 wūliūliū·de)形容眼珠儿黑而灵活 (of eyes) dark and liquid; sparkling and black

【乌龙茶】wūlóngchá 半发酵的茶叶(茶叶边沿发酵,中间不发酵),黑褐色 oolong tea; dark-brown, semi-fermented tea, with the fringe of the leaves fermented while the middle part is left unfermented

【乌梅】wūméi 经过熏制的梅子,外面黑褐色,有解热、驱虫等作用 smoked plum; dark plum; dark-brown, smoked plum good for relieving internal heat and killing intestinal worms; 通称 popularly called 酸梅 suānméi

【乌木】wūmù ❶ 常绿乔木,叶子互生,椭圆形,花单性,淡黄色。果实球形,赤黄色。木材黑色,致密,用来制造精致的器具和工艺品。产于热带地区。ebony (*Diospyros ebenum*); evergreen tropical tree with alternate, elliptical leaves, yellowish, unisexual flowers, reddish-yellow, spherical fruits, and hard, heavy, dark, durable wood that serves as precious material for making exquisite furniture, utensils and decorative woodwork ❷ 这种植物的木材 wood of this plant ❸ 泛指质硬而重的黑色木材 (in a broad sense) hard, heavy and dark wood

【乌七八糟】wūqībāzāo 十分杂乱;乱七八糟 in a horrible mess; in great disorder; obscene; dirty; filthy; 乌 also put as 污 wū

【乌纱帽】wūshāmào same as 纱帽 shāmào; 〈比喻 *fig.*〉官职 official post; also 乌纱 wūshā

【乌涂】wū·tu ❶ 水不凉也不热(多指饮用的水 usu. of drinking water) lukewarm; tepid: ~水不好喝。Lukewarm drinking water is unpalatable. ❷ 不爽利;不干脆 not clear-cut; also 兀秃 wū·tu

【乌托邦】wūtuōbāng 理想中最美好的社会。本是英国空想社会主义者莫尔(Thomas More)所著书名的简称。作者在书里描写了他所想像的实行公有制的幸福社会,并把这种社会叫做'乌托邦',意即没有的地方。后来泛指不能实现的愿望、计划等。Utopia, the most idealized society of utmost perfection. In his book *Utopia* written in 1516 the English Utopian socialist Sir Thomas More described an imaginary island of happiness under public ownership, and called it 'Utopia', meaning nothing or naught. The term also refers generally to wishes, plans, etc. that cannot be realized. [新拉 Modern Latin: Utopia]

【乌鸦】wūyā 鸟,嘴大而直,全身羽毛黑色,翼有绿光。多群居在树林中或田野间,以谷物、果实、昆虫等为食物。有的地区叫老鸹、老鸦。crow (*Corvus*); any of a genus (Corvus, family Corvidae) of large, passerine birds with a big and straight beak, glossy black plumage and wings with a green sheen, living in flocks in the woods or fields, and feeding on grains, fruits, insects, etc.; also called 老鸹 lǎo·guā or 老鸦 lǎoyā in some places

【乌烟瘴气】wū yān zhàng qì 形容环境嘈杂、秩序混乱或社会黑暗 (of environment, order or society) foul; disorderly; rotten and corrupt

【乌油油】wūyōuyōu (~的 wūyōuyōu·de)形容黑而润泽 shiny black: ~的头发 black and glossy hair | 泥土~的,十分肥沃。Shiny and black, the soil is very fertile.

【乌有】wūyǒu 〈书 *fml.*〉虚幻;不存在 nothing;

naught：子虚～ made-up story；story made out of thin air｜化为～ be reduced to nothing ☞ 子虚 zǐxū on p.2541

【乌鱼蛋】wūyúdàn 作为食品的乌贼的缠卵腺（一对椭圆形的腺体，在卵巢的腹面，能分泌黏液，使卵结成块状），可以做羹 egg gland of cuttlefish (a pair of elliptical glands attached to the belly-side of the ovary, which secretes fluid, turning the eggs into lumps) used in cooking thick soup

【乌云】wūyún ❶ 黑云 black clouds；dark clouds ❷〈比喻 *fig.*〉黑暗或恶劣的形势 dark or adverse situation：战争的～ dark clouds of war ❸〈比喻 *fig.*〉妇女的黑发 black hair of a woman

【乌贼】wūzéi 软体动物，身体椭圆形而扁平，苍白色，有浓淡不均的黑斑，头部有一对大眼，口的边缘有十只腕足，腕足的内侧生有吸盘，体内有囊状物能分泌黑色液体，遇到危险时放出，以掩护自己逃跑。cuttlefish (*Sepiidae*)；pale, flat, elliptical, soft-bodied animal with spots in different hues of black colour, having a distinct head with large eyes, ten arms with suckers about the mouth, a sac in the body that ejects a dark, inklike fluid when in danger, to camouflage its escape；俗称 popularly known as 墨鱼 mòyú or 墨斗鱼 mòdǒuyú；also 乌鲗 wūzéi

【乌鲗】wūzéi same as 乌贼 wūzéi

【乌孜别克族】Wūzībiékèzú 我国少数民族之一，分布在新疆 Ozbek (Uzbek)；Ozbeks (Uzbeks), one of the Chinese ethnical groups inhabiting the Xinjiang Uygur Autonomous Region

圬(杇) wū〈书 *fml.*〉❶ 瓦工用的抹子 trowel used for plastering ❷ 抹灰；粉刷 plaster；whitewash

【圬工】wūgōng 瓦工① 的旧称 former term for 瓦工 wǎgōng ①

邬(鄔) Wū 姓 a surname

污(汙、汚) wū ❶ 浑浊的水，泛指脏东西 dirt；filth：粪～ dung｜血～ bloodstain｜去～粉 cleanser ❷ 脏 dirty；filthy；foul：～水 dirty water｜～泥 mud；mire；sludge ❸ 不廉洁 corrupt：贪官～吏 corrupt officials ❹ 弄脏 defile；smear：玷～ stain｜～辱 humiliate；insult

【污点】wūdiǎn ❶ 衣服上沾染的污垢 stain on clothes；spot ❷〈比喻 *fig.*〉不光彩的事情 blemish；smirch：历史上有～ blemish in one's record

【污垢】wūgòu 积在人身上或物体上的脏东西 dirt；filth；dirty matter deposited on the human body or on an object

【污痕】wūhén 污秽的痕迹 stain；smear；smudge：斑斑～ have countless smudges

【污秽】wūhuì〈书 *fml.*〉❶ 不干净 filthy；foul ❷ 不干净的东西 dirt；filth

【污蔑】wūmiè ❶ same as 诬蔑 wūmiè ❷ same as 玷污 diànwū

【污泥浊水】wū ní zhuó shuǐ〈比喻 *fig.*〉落后、腐朽和反动的东西 backward, rotten and reactionary things；filth and mire

【污七八糟】wūqībāzāo same as 乌七八糟 wūqībāzāo

【污染】wūrǎn ❶ 使沾染上有害物质 pollute；contaminate：～水源 pollute the water source ❷ 空气、土壤、水源等混入有害的东西 pollution of air, soil, water source, etc.：环境～ environmental pollution｜空气～ air pollution ◇精神～ spiritual pollution

【污辱】wūrǔ ❶ same as 侮辱 wūrǔ ❷ same as 玷污 diànwū

【污浊】wūzhuó ❶（水、空气等）不干净；混浊（of air, water, etc.）dirty；muddy；foul；filthy：～的水不能饮用。Dirty water cannot be used for drinking. ❷ 脏东西 dirt；filth：洗去身上的～ wash off the filth on the body

【污渍】wūzì 附着在物体上的油泥等 stain；smear；grease sticking to an object

巫 wū ❶ 指女巫、巫师 shaman；witch；wizard：小～见大～ be like a small sorcerer in the presence of a great one；be like a dwarf in the presence of a giant ❷（Wū）姓 a surname

【巫婆】wūpó same as 女巫 nǚwū

【巫神】wūshén same as 巫师 wūshī

【巫师】wūshī 以装神弄鬼替人祈祷为职业的人（多指男巫）wizard；sorcerer；man who supposedly has supernatural power by a pact with a deity or ghost to pray for others

呜(嗚) wū〈拟声词 *onom.*〉toot；hoot；zoom：～的一声，一辆汽车飞驰过去。A car zoomed past.｜轮船上的汽笛～～地直叫。The ship kept hooting its whistle.

【呜呼】wūhū ❶〈书 *fml.*〉〈叹词 *interj.*〉表示叹息 alas：～哀哉 alas ❷ 指死亡 dead and gone；all is lost：一命～ die；kick the bucket；also 乌呼 wūhū，於乎 wūhū or 於戏 wūhū

【呜呼哀哉】wūhū-āizāi〈旧时 *old*〉祭文中常用的感叹词，现在借指死了或完蛋了（含诙谐意）(formerly used in funeral orations) alas；(humor.) be dead；be finished

【呜咽】wūyè ❶ 低声哭泣 sob；whimper ❷ 形容凄切的水声或丝竹声（of stream, stringed instrument, etc.）weep；wail；lament；mourn：山泉～。The mountain spring is weeping.

於 wū〈书 *fml.*〉〈叹词 *interj.*〉表示感叹 alas

☞ Yū on p.2335 and 于[1] yú on p.2335

【於乎】wūhū same as 呜呼 wūhū

【於戏】wūhū same as 呜呼 wūhū

【於菟】wūtú 古代楚人称虎 tiger as called by people in the state of Chu in ancient times

钨(鎢) wū 金属元素,符号 W(wolfram)。灰黑色,质硬而脆,耐高温。用来制合金钢和灯丝等。wolfram (W); tungsten; hard, brittle, greyish-black, metallic chemical element, resistant to high temperature, used in making alloy steels, lamp filament, etc.

洿 wū 〈书 *fml.*〉❶ 低洼的地方 low-lying land:～池 low-lying pond ❷ 掘成水池 dig a pond

诬 wū 捏造事实冤枉人 frame sb. up; accuse falsely; fabricate facts to wrong a person:～良为盗 accuse innocent people of stealing

【诬告】wūgào 无中生有地控告别人有犯罪行为 accuse sb. falsely of committing a crime

【诬害】wūhài 捏造事实来陷害 calumniate; malign; set up by spreading false reports about:～忠良 calumniate the loyal and virtuous people

【诬赖】wūlài 毫无根据地说别人做了坏事,或说了坏话 accuse sb. without any evidence; falsely incriminate:～好人 incriminate innocent people

【诬蔑】wūmiè 捏造事实败坏别人的名誉 slander; vilify; calumniate; smear:造谣～ spread rumours in order to vilify

【诬枉】wūwǎng 诬蔑冤枉 slander; calumniate:～好人 calumniate good people

【诬陷】wūxiàn 诬告陷害 frame a case against; frame sb.:遭人～ get framed

【诬栽】wūzāi 栽赃陷害 calumniate and frame; fabricate a charge against sb.

W

屋 wū ❶ 房子 house:房～ house; housing; building|～顶 roof; housetop; rooftop ❷ 屋子:里～ inner room|外～ outer room|一间～住四个人。Four people live in one room.

【屋顶花园】wūdǐng huāyuán 高楼大厦顶上布置花木等供人游憩的场所 roof garden; garden-like place on the roof of a tall building where people take a stroll or rest

【屋脊】wūjǐ 屋顶中间高起的部分 ridge (of a roof) ◇帕米尔高原是世界的～。The Pamirs are the roof of the world. (图见 ☞ figure for 房子 fáng·zi on p. 550)

【屋架】wūjià 承载屋面的构件,多用木料、钢材或钢筋混凝土等制成,有三角形、梯形、拱形等多种形状 roof truss; framework of beams, girders, struts, bars, etc. made of wood, steel or reinforced concrete in the shape of a triangle, trapezoid, arch, etc.

【屋里人】wū·lirén 〈方 *dial.*〉妻子 wife; also 屋里的 wūlǐ·de

【屋面】wūmiàn 屋顶部分的遮盖物 roofing; materials that cover a roof

【屋上架屋】wū shàng jià wū 〈比喻 *fig.*〉机构或结构重叠,也比喻不必要的重复 build one house on top of another; overlapping organizations or structures; needless duplication

【屋檐】wūyán same as 房檐 fángyán

【屋宇】wūyǔ 〈书 *fml.*〉same as 房屋 fángwū:声震～ reverberate throughout the house

【屋子】wū·zi same as 房间 fángjiān:一间～ one room

恶(惡) wū 〈书 *fml.*〉❶ same as 乌[2] ❷ 〈叹词 *interj.*〉表示惊讶(expressing surprise) oh:～,是何言也(啊,这是什么话)! Oh! What a remark it is!

☞ ě on p. 505, è on p. 506 and wù on p. 2039

wú (ㄨˊ)

无(無) wú ❶ 没有(跟'有'相对 as opposed to 'have') nothing; nil:从～到有 start from scratch|～产阶级 proletariat|有则改之,～则加勉。Correct mistakes if you have made any, and guard against them if you have not. ❷ 不 no; not; un-; a-; in-:～论 no matter what (whether, when, where, how, etc.); regardless of; irrespective of|～须 not necessary; unnecessary; need not; not have to ❸ 不论 no matter what (whether, when, where, how, etc.); regardless of; irrespective of:事～大小,都有人负责。Everything, big and small, is properly taken care of. ❹ same as 毋 wú

☞ mó on p. 1361

【无比】wúbǐ 没有别的能够相比(多用于好的方面 usu. used in a good sense) incomparable; unparalleled; matchless; nothing else can compare with:～强大 unparalleled might; incomparably powerful|～愤慨 furiously indignant|英勇～ unrivalled in bravery

【无边】wúbiān 没有边际 boundless:一望～的大草原 boundless expanse of grassland|苦海～,回头是岸。The sea of misery (or bitterness) is boundless, repent and the shore is at hand — it is never too late to mend one's ways.

【无病呻吟】wú bìng shēnyín 〈比喻 *fig.*〉没有值得忧虑的事情而长吁短叹,也比喻文艺作品缺乏真情实感,矫揉造作 moan and groan without worries; moan and groan without illness; pine and whine for nothing; (of literature and works of art) lacking true feelings and adopting an affected pose

【无补】wúbǔ 没有益处 of no help; of no avail:空谈～于实际。Mere words won't help matters.

【无不】wúbù 没有一个不 all without exception; invariably:～为之感动。None were unmoved.

【无产阶级】wúchǎn jiējí 工人阶级。也泛指不占有生产资料的劳动者阶级。proletariat; working class; (in a broad sense) labourer class which does not own means of produc-

tion

【无产阶级专政】wúchǎn jiējí zhuānzhèng 无产阶级用暴力革命打碎资产阶级的国家机器后建立的新型国家政权。专政的主要任务是防御外部敌人的颠覆和侵略,镇压国内反动阶级、反动派和反对社会主义的分子的反抗,保证社会主义建设的顺利进行,并过渡到共产主义。dictatorship of the proletariat; proletarian dictatorship; new type of state power established after the proletariat smashed a bourgeois state machine by violent revolution. The primary task of this dictatorship is to guard against subversion and aggression by the enemy from outside, suppress resistance from the reactionary classes, reactionaries and anti-socialist elements at home and ensure the successful building of socialism and transition to communism.

【无产者】wúchǎnzhě 资本主义社会中不占有生产资料、靠出卖劳动力为生的雇佣工人 proletarian; wage labourer in the capitalist society who does not own means of production and lives by selling his labour

【无常】[1] wúcháng 时常变化;变化不定 variable; changeable:反复～ capricious; fickle; mercurial; changeable | 这里气候变化～。The weather here is changeable.

【无常】[2] wúcháng ❶ 鬼名,迷信的人相信人将死时有'无常鬼'来勾魂 name of a demon which superstitious people believe would come and take away the soul from a dying person ❷〈婉辞 *euph.*〉指人死 (of a person) die:一旦～ when death comes; once death comes

【无偿】wúcháng 不要代价的;没有报酬的 free; gratis; gratuitous:～援助 aid given gratis (or gratuitously) | ～提供各种服务 provide all kinds of services gratis; give free services

【无成】wúchéng 没有做成;没有成就 accomplish nothing:一事～ accomplish nothing | 毕生～ life of utter failure

【无耻】wúchǐ 不顾羞耻;不知羞耻 shameless; brazen; impudent:卑鄙～ base and shameless | ～吹捧 flatter sb. brazenly; shamelessly lavish praise on sb. | ～之尤(最无耻的) brazen in the extreme; height of shamelessness

【无从】wúcóng 没有门径或找不到头绪(做某件事) have no way (of doing sth.); not be in a position (to do sth.):～入手 not know where to start; not know how to set about a job | ～查考 there is no way of checking sth.; not know how to check sth. | 心中千言万语,一时～说起 have a thousand things to say but not know where to begin

【无大无小】wú dà wú xiǎo ❶ 不论大的或小的 big or small; old or young; also 无小无大 wú xiǎo wú dà ❷ 不分辈份、年龄大小,指言行过于随便,没有礼貌 regardless of seniority or age; (of young people) fail to show proper respect for elders in speaking or doing sth.

【无敌】wúdí 没有对手 unmatched; invincible; unconquerable:所向～ ever invincible; unmatched anywhere in the world; invincible

【无底洞】wúdǐdòng 永远填不满的洞(多用于比喻 oft. fig.) bottomless pit

【无地自容】wú dì zì róng 没有地方可以让自己藏起来,形容十分羞惭 find no place to hide oneself for shame; feel too ashamed to see anybody

【无的放矢】wú dì fàng shǐ 没有箭靶乱射箭 shoot an arrow without a target; shoot at random;〈比喻 *fig.*〉言语、行动没有明确目标或不切合实际 speak or act without purpose or unpractically

【无定形体】wúdìngxíngtǐ 原子、离子或分子不按一定空间次序排列而成的固体,没有规则的几何外形,没有固定的熔点和各向异性。如石蜡、玻璃等。amorphous solid; solid matter formed by atoms, ions or molecules in a mass without regular geometric stratification or crystalline structure, fixed melting point, and anisotropy, such as paraffin and glass

【无动于衷】wú dòng yú zhōng 心里一点不受感动;一点也不动心 aloof and indifferent; unmoved; untouched; unconcerned; 衷 also put as 中 zhong

【无独有偶】wú dú yǒu ǒu 虽然罕见,但是不只一个,还有一个可以成对儿(多用于贬义 oft. derog.) rare but not come singly

【无度】wúdù 没有限度;没有节制 immoderate; excessive:挥霍～ squander wantonly | 荒淫～ excessive debauchery; unbridled debauchery

【无端】wúduān 没有来由;无缘无故 for no reason at all:～生事 create a disturbance for no reason; wilfully make trouble | ～受过 get blamed for no reason at all

【无恶不作】wú è bù zuò 没有哪样坏事不干,形容人极坏 (of a very vicious person) stop at nothing in doing evils; stop at no evil; commit all manners of crimes

【无法】wúfǎ 没有办法 unable; incapable; no way:～可想。there is no way out. | 这问题是难处理,但还不是～解决。This is a difficult question, but not one that cannot be settled.

【无法无天】wú fǎ wú tiān 形容人毫无顾忌地胡作非为 defy human and divine laws; be absolutely lawless; run wild

【无方】wúfāng 不得法(跟'有方'相对 as opposed to 'in the proper way') not in a proper way; in the wrong way; not know how:经营～ mismanagement | 治家～ be unable to run a household properly; mismanage a household

【无妨】wúfáng 没有妨碍;不妨 there's no harm; may (or might) as well:提意见～直率一点儿 may as well make one's remarks straightforward

【无纺织布】wúfǎngzhībù 一种以纺织纤维为原

料，外观和用途相当于布匹的片状物，因不经过一般的纺织过程，而通过机械或化学方法使纤维黏结得名。可用做包装用布、书面用布等。adhesive-bonded fabric; non-woven fabric; fabric made of textile fibres as its material, which, equivalent to cloth in appearance and usage, is not woven but adhesive-bonded by machine or chemical method, and is used for packing or book cover; also 不织布 bùzhībù

【无非】wúfēi 只；不外乎 nothing but; no more than; simply; only：院子里种的～是凤仙花和鸡冠花。Growing in the courtyard are touch-me-not (garden balsam) and coxcomb, and nothing else.

【无风不起浪】wú fēng bù qǐ làng 〈比喻 *fig*.〉事出有因 there are no waves without wind; there's no smoke without fire

【无干】wúgān 没有关系；不相干 have nothing to do with：这是我的错儿，跟别人～。It was my fault; nobody else had anything to do with it.

【无告】wúgào ❶ 有痛苦而无处诉说。形容处境很不幸。have nobody or nowhere to turn to for help or redress; helpless; very unfortunate：穷苦～的老人 miserable and helpless old man; wretched and helpless old man ❷〈书 *fml*.〉有痛苦而无处诉说的人 wretched and helpless person：哀怜～ show pity for the helpless

【无功受禄】wú gōng shòu lù 没有功劳而得到报酬 get a reward without deserving it (禄 *lu*：古代官员的薪俸 salary for an official in ancient times)

【无辜】wúgū ❶ 没有罪 not guilty; innocent：～平民 innocent civilians; innocent people | 事实证明那个人是～的。Facts show that the person is guiltless. ❷ 没有罪的人 innocent person：株连～ implicate an innocent person

【无故】wúgù 没有缘故 without cause or reason：平白～ for no reason at all; without any reason; for no apparent reason | ～缺席 be absent without reason

【无怪】wúguài 表示明白了原因，对下文所说的情况就不觉得奇怪 [expressing understanding of sth. one did not know before] no wonder; not to be wondered at：原来炉子灭了，～屋里这么冷。The fire has gone out in the stove; no wonder it is so cold in the room. also 无怪乎 wúguàihū

【无关】wúguān 没有关系；不牵涉 have nothing to do with：此事跟他～。It has nothing to do with him. | ～紧要 of no importance; hardly relevant | ～大局 not affecting (or having no bearing on) the general situation; insignificant to the general situation; of little account

【无关宏旨】wú guān hóngzhǐ 不涉及主旨。指意义不大或关系不大。insignificant; minor; immaterial; not of cardinal principle

【无关痛痒】wú guān tòngyǎng 〈比喻 *fig*.〉与本身利害无关或无足轻重 of no consequence; immaterial; insignificant

【无轨电车】wúguǐ-diànchē 电车的一种，用橡胶轮胎行驶，不用铁轨 trackless trolley; trolleybus; electric bus that is powered from overhead wires by means of trolleys

【无何】wúhé 〈书 *fml*.〉❶ 没多久 soon; before long ❷ 没有什么；没有其他的事 nothing; nothing else

【无后坐力炮】wúhòuzuòlìpào 射击时炮身不向后坐的火炮，主要用来摧毁近距离的装甲目标和火力点 recoilless gun; gun that does not recoil or minimizes recoil when shooting and is used mainly to destroy amoured targets or firing points at short range; also 无坐力炮 wúzuòlìpào

【无华】wúhuá 没有华丽的色彩 simple and unadorned：质朴～ simple and unadorned

【无机】wújī 原来指跟非生物体有关的或从非生物体来的（化合物），现在指除碳酸盐和碳的氧化物外，不含碳原子的（化合物）inorganic; (orig.) chemical compound that is not animal or vegetable or does not have the organized structure of living things; any chemical compound not classified as carbonate and carbon oxide or not containing carbon：～盐 inorganic salts | ～肥料 inorganic fertilizer | ～化学 inorganic chemistry

【无机肥料】wújī féiliào 不含有机物质的肥料，如硫酸铵、过磷酸钙等 inorganic fertilizer; mineral fertilizer; fertilizer not containing organic matter, as ammonium sulphate, calcium superphosphate, etc.

【无机化合物】wújī huàhéwù 通常指不含碳元素的化合物，也包括一氧化碳、二氧化碳、碳酸盐、氰化物等 inorganic compound; any chemical compound not containing carbon, as carbon monoxide, carbon dioxide, carbonate, cyanide, etc.; 简称 abbr. 无机物 wújīwù

【无机化学】wújī huàxué 化学的一个分支，研究元素、单质和无机化合物的构造、性质、变化、制备、用途等 inorganic chemistry; branch of chemistry dealing with the structure, properties, changes, manufacture and uses of chemical elements, simple substances and inorganic compounds

【无稽】wújī 无从查考；毫无根据 unfounded; fantastic; absurd：荒诞～ absurd | ～之谈 unfounded statement; fantastic talk; sheer nonsense

【无及】wújí 来不及 it's too late (to do sth.); there's not enough time (to do sth.)：后悔～ too late to repent

【无几】wújǐ 没有多少；不多 very few; very little; hardly any：寥寥～ very few; very little; hardly any | 所剩～。There's very little left. | 两块试验田的产量相差～。The yields on the two experimental plots were almost the same.

【无脊椎动物】wújǐzhuī-dòngwù 体内没有脊椎骨的动物,种类很多,包括原生动物、海绵动物、腔肠动物、蠕形动物、软体动物、节肢动物和棘皮动物等 invertebrate; any animal without a backbone or spinal column, as protozoan, spongia, coelenterate, worms, mollusc, arthropod, echinoderm, etc.

【无记名投票】wújìmíng-tóupiào 一种选举方法,选举人在选票上不写自己的姓名 secret ballot; method of voting by which a voter does not write his or her name on the voting paper

【无际】wújì 没有边际 boundless; limitless; vast:一望～ stretch as far as the eye can reach|无边～ boundless; vast; limitless

【无济于事】wú jì yú shì 对于事情没有什么帮助 not help matters; of no help; of no avail; to no effect

【无价之宝】wú jià zhī bǎo 指极珍贵的东西 priceless treasure; invaluable asset

【无坚不摧】wú jiān bù cuī 能够摧毁任何坚固的东西。形容力量强大。overrun all fortifications; carry all before one; be all-conquering; very powerful

【无间】wújiàn〈书 *fml.*〉❶ 没有间隙 not keeping anything from each other; very close to each other:亲密～ be on very intimate terms with ❷ 不间断 continuously; without interruption:他每天早晨练太极拳,寒暑～。He has kept on doing *taijiquan* in the morning all the year round. ❸ 不分别 make no difference; not distinguish:～是非 not able to distinguish right from wrong

【无疆】wújiāng 没有止境;没有穷尽 boundless; limitless:万寿～(祝寿的话 a phrase used when marking the birthday of an elderly person) long life; longevity

【无尽】wújìn 没有尽头;无穷 endless; inexhaustible; infinite; limitless:～的宝藏 inexhaustible resources|感激～ many thanks; boundless gratitude

【无尽无休】wú jìn wú xiū 没完没了(含厌恶意 derog.) incessant; endless

【无精打采】wú jīng dǎ cǎi 没精打采 listless; in low spirits; lackadaisical

【无拘无束】wú jū wú shù 不受任何约束,形容自由自在 unrestrained; unconstrained; free and easy

【无可非议】wú kě fēi yì 没有什么可以指摘的,表示言行合乎情理(of speech or behaviour) blameless; reasonable

【无可厚非】wú kě hòu fēi same as 未可厚非 wèi kě hòu fēi

【无可奈何】wú kě nàihé 没有办法;没有办法可想 be helpless; there is no way out; have no alternative; have no choice

【无可无不可】wú kě wú bù kě 怎么样都行,表示没有一定的选择 not care one way or the other; either will do; it makes no difference; there is no definite choice

【无孔不入】wú kǒng bù rù〈比喻 *fig.*〉利用一切机会(多指做坏事 usu. of sb. doing sth. bad) get in by every opening; seize every opportunity

【无愧】wúkuì 没有什么可以惭愧的地方 feel no qualms; have a clear conscience:问心～ have a clear conscience|当之～ be worthy of; be well qualified for; merit the aware

【无赖】wúlài ❶ 放刁撒泼,蛮不讲理 rascally; scoundrelly; blackguardly:耍～ act shamelessly ❷ 游手好闲、品行不端的人 rascal; also 无赖汉 wúlàihàn or 无赖子 wúlàizǐ

【无理】wúlǐ 没有道理 unreasonable; unjustifiable:～强辩 insist on arguing unjustifiably|～取闹 wilfully make trouble; be deliberately provocative

【无理取闹】wú lǐ qǔ nào 毫无理由地跟人吵闹;故意捣乱 wilfully make trouble; be deliberately provocative

【无理式】wúlǐshì 有开方运算,而且被开方数含有字母的代数式。如$\sqrt{a^2+b^2}$,$\sqrt{a-x}$。irrational expression; algebraic expression with extraction operation and the radicand containing letters, as $\sqrt{a^2+b^2}$, $\sqrt{a-x}$

【无理数】wúlǐshù 无限不循环小数。如$\sqrt{2}$,$\sqrt[3]{5}$,3.1415926…。irrational number; infinite non-recurring decimal, as $\sqrt{2}$, $\sqrt[3]{5}$, 3.1415926...

【无力】wúlì ❶ 没有力量(多用于抽象事物 usu. used in abstract cases) unable; incapable; powerless:领导软弱～。The leadership is weak and incapable.|这问题事关全厂,我们车间～解决。The problem concerns the whole factory. Our workshop is unable to solve it. ❷ 没有气力 lack strength; feel weak:四肢～ feel weak in one's limbs

【无量】wúliàng 没有限量;没有止境 measureless; immeasurable; boundless:前途～ have boundless prospect|功德～ render a great service to mankind

【无聊】wúliáo ❶ 由于清闲而烦闷 feel bored for being idle:他一闲下来,便感到～。He feels bored whenever he does not have anything to do. ❷(言谈、行动等)没有意义而使人讨厌(of speech, behaviour, etc.) senseless; silly; stupid:老谈吃穿,太～了。It's very silly talking glibly about food and clothing all the time. *or* It's very silly to keep talking about food and clothing.

【无聊赖】wú liáolài〈书 *fml.*〉没有凭借或依赖,指十分无聊或潦倒失意 have nobody or nothing to rely on; extremely bored or utterly frustrated; ☞ 百无聊赖 bǎiwú liáolài on p.41

【无论】wúlùn〈连词 *conj.*〉表示条件不同而结果不变 no matter what, how, etc.; regardless of:～任务怎么艰巨,也要把它完成。No matter how difficult the task is, (we) must fulfil it.

【无论如何】wúlùn rúhé 不管怎么样,表示不管条件怎样变化,其结果始终不变[with the same result no matter how the circumstance changes] in any event; at all events; in any case; at any rate; whatever happens:这周的义务劳动我～得参加。In any event, I'll take part in the voluntary labour this week.

【无米之炊】wú mǐ zhī chuī ☞ 巧妇难为无米之炊 qiǎo fù nán wéi wú mǐ zhī chuī on p.1551

【无冕之王】wú miǎn zhī wáng 指没有权威的名义而影响、作用极大的人,现多指新闻记者 crownless king; influential person without the name of an authority; popular reference to a reporter

【无名】wúmíng ❶ 没有名称的 nameless:～肿毒 nameless sore or boil ❷ 姓名不为世人所知的 unknown:～英雄 unknown hero; unsung hero|～小辈 nobody; small potato ❸ 说不出所以然来的;无缘无故的(多指不愉快的事情或情绪 usu. indicating an unpleasant thing or mood) indefinable; indescribable:～损失 indescribable loss|～的恐惧 indefinable feeling of terror

【无名氏】wúmíngshì 不愿说出姓名或查不出姓名的人 person who is unwilling to disclose his or her name or whose name cannot be identified

【无名帖】wúmíngtiě (～儿 wúmíngtiěr)为了攻讦或恐吓别人而写的不具名的帖儿 poison-pen letter; anonymous letter; unsigned letter written in order to attack or intimidate sb.

【无名小卒】wúmíng xiǎozú〈比喻 *fig.*〉没有名气的人 nobody; nonentity

【无名英雄】wúmíng yīngxióng 姓名不为世人所知的英雄人物 unknown hero; unsung hero

【无名指】wúmíngzhǐ 靠近小指的手指 third finger; ring finger

【无名肿毒】wúmíng zhǒngdú〈中医 *Chin. med.*〉指既不像疽、又不像痈、也不像疔的毒疮 nameless sore or boil, which is unlike subcutaneous ulcer, carbuncle or malignant boil

【无明火】wúmínghuǒ 怒火 flames of anger (无明 *wuming*:佛典中指'痴'或'愚昧' meaning idiocy or ignorance in the Buddhist literature):～起(发怒) get angry; fly into a rage; also 无名火 wúmínghuǒ

【无乃】wúnǎi〈书 *fml.*〉〈副词 *adv.*〉用于反问句中,表示不以为然的意思,跟'岂不是'相近,但语气比较和缓[used in a rhetorical question to indicate mild disagreement or disapproval, similar to 岂不是 qǐbùshì]:～不可乎? That can't do, can it?

【无奈】wúnài ❶ same as 无可奈何 wú kě nàihé:出于～ have no choice but to|万般～ have no alternative but to ❷ 用在转折句的头上,表示由于某种原因,不能实现上文所说的意图,有'可惜'的意思[used at the beginning of a transitional sentence to indicate that the intention said in the preceding sentence can't be realized for some reason, with the implication of 'it's a pity' or 'unfortunately']:星期天我们本想去郊游,～天不作美下起雨来,只好作罢了。We wanted to go on an outing on Sunday, but as it rained, we had to cancel it.

【无奈何】wúnài//hé ❶ 表示对人或事没有办法,不能把…怎么样 can do nothing about:敌人无奈他何。The enemy could do nothing about him. ❷ 无可奈何 cannot help but; have no alternative; have no choice:～只得再去一趟 cannot but go once again

【无能】wúnéng 没有能力;不能干什么 incompetent; incapable:软弱～ weak and inept|腐败～ corrupt and incompetent|～之辈 incompetent person

【无能为力】wú néng wéi lì 用不上力量;没有能力或能力达不到 powerless; helpless; incapable of action

【无宁】wúnìng same as 毋宁 wúnìng

【无期徒刑】wúqī túxíng 剥夺犯人终身自由的刑罚 life sentence; punishment that deprives a criminal of personal freedom for life

【无奇不有】wú qí bù yǒu 什么稀奇的事物都有 there is no lack of strange things

【无前】wúqián ❶ 无敌;无与相比 unmatched; invincible; unconquerable:一往～ go forward with an indomitable spirit ❷ 过去没有过;空前 unprecedented:成绩～ unprecedented success

【无情】wúqíng ❶ 没有感情 unfeeling; heartless:～无义 heartless and faithless ❷ 不留情 merciless; ruthless:翻脸～ be treacherous and ruthless; turn against sb. without mercy|水火～。Water and fire are merciless.|事实是～的。The facts are inexorable.

【无穷】wúqióng 没有穷尽;没有限度 infinite; endless; boundless; inexhaustible:言有尽而意～。There may be an end to the words, but not to their message.|群众的智慧是～的。The wisdom of the masses is inexhaustible.

【无穷大】wúqióngdà 一个变量在变化过程中,绝对值永远大于任意大的已定正数,这个变量叫做无穷大,用符号∞表示。如 2^n,在 n 取值1,2,3,4…;的变化过程中就是无穷大。infinitely great; infinity; variable, the absolute value of which is always larger than an arbitrarily large set positive number in the process of varying, called infinitely great, expressed by the symbol ∞, as 2^n is the infinitely great in the process of varying when n is 1,2,3,4...; also 无限大 wúxiàndà

【无穷小】wúqióngxiǎo 一个变量在变化过程中,绝对值永远小于任意大的已定正数,即以零为极限的变量，叫做无穷小。如$\frac{1}{2^n}$，在 n 取值 1，2，3，4…的变化过程中就是无穷小。infinitely small；infinitesimal；variable，the absolute value of which is always smaller than an arbitrarily small set positive number in the process of varying，that is，variable with zero as its limit，called infinitely small. For instance，$\frac{1}{2^n}$ is the infinitely small in the process of varying when n is 1，2，3，4...；also 无限小 wúxiànxiǎo

【无缺】wúquē（器物等）没有残缺；没有缺陷（of objects）intact；whole：完好～ intact；whole｜完美～ perfect；flawless

【无任】wúrèn〈书 *fml.*〉非常；十分（用于'感激、欢迎'等 used together with 'gratitude'，'welcome'，etc.）extremely；immensely

【无日】wúrì '无日不…'是'天天…'的意思，表示不间断 all the time；not a single day without；every day；continuously：～不在渴望四个现代化早日实现。Not a single day passed without longing for the early modernization of industry，agriculture，national defence，and science and technology.

【无如】wúrú same as 无奈 wúnài：昨天本想去拜访，～天色太晚了。I wanted to see you yesterday，but it was too late.

【无伤大雅】wú shāng dàyǎ 对主要方面没有妨害 not matter much；not affect the principal aspect of a thing；not involving the major principle；immaterial

【无上】wúshàng 最高 supreme；paramount；highest：至高～ supreme；paramount；highest｜～光荣 highest honour

【无神论】wúshénlùn 否定鬼神迷信和宗教信仰的学说 atheism；doctrine that denies the existence of ghosts and God and negates religious belief

【无声】wúshēng 没有声音 noiseless；silent；still：悄然～ in silence；noiseless

【无声片儿】wúshēngpiānr 无声片 silent film

【无声片】wúshēngpiàn 只有形象没有声音的影片 silent film；film without sounds；also 默片 mòpiàn

【无声无臭】wú shēng wú xiù 没有声音，没有气味 voiceless and smell-less；〈比喻 *fig.*〉人没有名声（of a person）having no fame（or reputation）；little known；obscure

【无时无刻】wú shí wú kè '无时无刻不…'是'时时刻刻都…'的意思，表示永远，不间断 all the time；incessantly；continuously；always：我们～不在想念着你。You are constantly in our thoughts. *or* We have always been thinking of you.

【无事不登三宝殿】wú shì bù dēng sānbǎodiàn〈比喻 *fig.*〉没事不上门 never go to the temple for no reason；never visit anyone for no reason；wouldn't come to you if one had nothing. to ask（三宝殿 *sanbaodian*：指佛殿 Triratna Hall of Buddhism）：他是～，今天来，一定有原因。He never visits anyone for no reason. He wouldn't come here if he had nothing to ask of us.

【无事生非】wú shì shēng fēi 本来没有问题而故意制造纠纷 make trouble out of nothing；be deliberately provocative

【无视】wúshì 不放在眼里；漠视；不认真对待 turn a blind eye to；disregard；defy：～现实 ignore the reality｜～法纪 defy the law and disciplines｜～群众的利益 disregard the interests of the masses

【无数】wúshù ❶ 难以计数，形容极多 innumerable；countless：死伤～ countless casualties ❷ 不知道底细 not know for certain；be uncertain：心中～ not know for certain；not sure

【无双】wúshuāng 独一无二 unparalleled；unrivalled；matchless：盖世～ absolutely unrivalled

【无霜期】wúshuāngqī 每年从终霜起到初霜止的时期，是有利植物生长的季节 frost-free period；time of the year favourable for the growth of plants

【无私】wúsī 不自私 selfless；disinterested；unselfish：大公～ selfless and impartial｜～的援助 selfless aid；disinterested assistance

【无私有弊】wú sī yǒu bì 指虽然没有私弊，但因处于嫌疑之地，容易使人猜疑 be under suspicion for being in a certain position though one is innocent

【无损】wúsǔn 没有损害 cannot harm；be harmless；will not lessen：争论～于友谊。Argument does no harm to friendship. *or* Argument is not detrimental to friendship. ❷ 没有损坏 intact；whole；in good condition：完好～ intact

【无所不为】wú suǒ bù wéi 没有什么不干的。指什么坏事都干。do all manner of evil；stop at nothing

【无所不用其极】wú suǒ bù yòng qí jí 指做坏事时任何极端的手段都使得出来 resort to every conceivable means in doing sth. bad；stop at nothing；go to any extreme；go to any length

【无所不在】wú suǒ bù zài 到处都存在；到处都有 omnipresent；ubiquitous：矛盾的斗争～。Struggle among contradictions is ubiquitous.

【无所不至】wú suǒ bù zhì ❶ 没有达不到的地方 penetrate everywhere：细菌的活动范围极广，～。Bacteria are active practically everywhere. ❷ 指凡能做的都做到了（用于坏事 usu. of evildoer）spare no pains；be capable of anything；stop at nothing：威胁利诱，～ use intimidation，bribery and every other means｜摧残镇压，～ stop at nothing in destruction and suppression

【无所措手足】wú suǒ cuò shǒu zú 手脚不知放

在哪里。形容不知该怎么办才好。have nowhere to put one's hands or feet; be at a loss to know how to conduct oneself

【无所事事】wú suǒ shì shì 闲着什么事也不干 be occupied with nothing; have nothing to do; idle away one's time; keep idle; be a schmoozer

【无所适从】wú suǒ shì cóng 不知道依从谁好;不知按哪个办法做才好 not know what to do; not know whom to turn to

【无所谓】wúsuǒwèi ❶ 说不上 cannot be called; not deserve the name of:我只是来谈体会,~报告。I've come just to talk about my experience. It's not a lecture. ❷ 不在乎;没有什么关系 be indifferent; not matter:今天去还是明天去,我是~的。It makes no difference to me whether (we) go today or tomorrow.|大家都替他着急,而他自己倒好像~似的。Everyone is worried about him, but he himself doesn't seem to care.

【无所用心】wú suǒ yòng xīn 不动脑子,对什么事情都不关心 not give serious thought to anything; pay no attention to anything:饱食终日,~ be sated with food and remain idle all day

【无所作为】wú suǒ zuòwéi 不去努力做出成绩或没有做出什么成绩 attempt nothing or accomplish nothing; be in a state of inertia

【无题】wútí 诗文等有用'无题'做题目的,表示没有适当的题目可标或者不愿意标题目 [used as a title for writings for which the author cannot find, or chooses not to give, a title] no title; untitled; poem or article without title

W

【无条件】wútiáojiàn 没有任何条件;不提出任何条件 unconditional; without preconditions:~服从 obey unconditionally|~投降 unconditional surrender

【无头案】wútóu'àn 没有线索可寻的案件或事情 intricate case without a clue; unsolved mystery

【无头告示】wútóu-gào·shi 用意不明的文告。也指不得要领的官样文章。ambiguous official notice; official jargon difficult to be understood

【无往不利】wú wǎng bù lì 不论到哪里,没有不顺利的。指在各处都行得通,办得成。go smoothly everywhere; be ever successful; nothing unsuccessful

【无往不胜】wú wǎng bù shèng 不论到哪里,没有不胜的。指在各处都能成功。ever-victorious; invincible; make success everywhere

【无妄之灾】wú wàng zhī zāi 平白无故受到的损害 unexpected calamity; undeserved ill turn

【无望】wúwàng 没有希望 hopeless:事情已经~。Things are hopeless.

【无微不至】wú wēi bù zhì 形容待人非常细心周到 meticulously; in every possible way

【无为】wúwéi 顺其自然,不必有所作为,是古代道家的一种处世态度和政治思想 let things take their own course and do nothing; inaction; non-action; basic concept of Taoism; attitude towards the world and political ideology held by ancient Taoists:~而治 govern by doing nothing; govern by non-action

【无味】wúwèi ❶ 没有滋味 tasteless; unpalatable:食之~,弃之可惜。It is unpalatable, but still one would hesitate to throw it away. ❷ 没有趣味 dull; insipid; uninteresting:枯燥~ dull and uninteresting

【无畏】wúwèi 没有畏惧;不知害怕 fearless; dauntless:无私~ selfless and fearless|~的英雄气概 dauntless heroism

【无谓】wúwèi 没有意义;毫无价值 meaningless; of no value:不作~的争论 do not engage in meaningless argument

【无…无…】wú…wú… 分别用在两个意义相同或相近的词或词素前面,强调没有 [used before two words or morphemes with the same or similar meaning to stress 'no']:~影~踪(没有踪影) disappear without a trace or shadow|~缘~故(没有缘故) for no reason at all; without rhyme or reason|~拳~勇(没有武力) have no strength or courage (have no military strength)|~依~靠(没有依靠) have nobody to depend on; have nobody to turn to; helpless|~穷~尽(没有止境) endless; limitless; infinite; boundless

【无物】wúwù 没有东西;没有内容 empty; devoid of substance:眼空~ consider everyone and everything beneath one's notice; be supercilious|空洞~ devoid of content; without substance|言之~ empty talk

【无误】wúwù 没有差错 no mistake; errorless:核对~ checked and found correct

【无隙可乘】wú xì kě chéng 没有空子可钻 no crack to get in by; no loophole to exploit; no weakness to take advantage of; no chink in one's armour; also 无懈可乘 wú xiè kě chéng or 无机可乘 wú jī kě chéng

【无瑕】wúxiá 完美无疵 perfect; flawless;〈比喻 *fig.*〉没有缺点或污点 faultless; flawless:白璧~ flawless white jade; impeccable integrity|完美~ perfect; flawless

【无暇】wúxiá 没有空闲的时间 have no time; be too busy:~过问 be too busy to attend to|~顾及 have no time to attend to

【无限】wúxiàn 没有穷尽;没有限量 infinite; limitless; boundless; immeasurable:前途~光明 future of incomparable brightness; infinitely bright future

【无限公司】wúxiàn gōngsī 企业的一种组织形式,由两个以上的股东组成。股东对公司债务负有无限清偿责任。unlimited company, a form of company composed of two or more shareholders who hold unlimited liability for the company's debt liquidation

【无限小数】wúxiàn xiǎoshù 小数部分的位数是无限的小数，如 0.333…，3.14159265…。无限小数包括循环小数和无限不循环小数。infinite decimal fraction. The places of the decimal part are infinite decimals, as 0.333..., 3.14159265.... The infinite decimals include recurring decimals and infinite non-recurring decimals.

【无线电】wúxiàndiàn ❶ 用电波的振荡在空中传送信号的技术设备。因为不用导线传送，所以叫无线电。无线电广泛应用在通讯、广播、电视、远距离控制、自动化、探测等方面。radio; wireless; technology and apparatus for transmitting signals through space through the vibration of electric waves, without connecting wires. Radio is widely used in telecommunication, radio broadcast, television broadcast, remote control, automation and detection. ❷ 无线电收音机的通称 general term for 无线电收音机 wúxiàndiàn shōuyīnjī

【无线电报】wúxiàn diànbào 利用无线电波传送的电报，发报的地方把要发送的信号变成无线电波发射出去，收报的地方直接收听信号或把信号用接收机记录下来 wireless telegram; radio-telegraphy; telegraphy by radio transmitted signals. The transmitting station converts the signals into electromagnetic waves and transmits them through space, and the receiving station receives the signals or records the signals by a receiver.

【无线电波】wúxiàn diànbō 无线电技术中使用的电磁波，波长从 1 毫米到 3,000 米以上。可分为长波、中波、中短波、短波、微波等。electromagnetic waves used in radio, the wavelengths of which varying from 1 millimetre to over 3,000 metres, including long wave, medium wave, medium-short wave, short wave, microwave, etc.

【无线电话】wúxiàn diànhuà 利用无线电波传送的电话。通话的两方面各有一套无线电收发设备。radiotelephone; radiophone. The caller and receiver each have a device for sending and receiving radio signals.

【无线电视】wúxiàn-diànshì 从电视台发射的电磁波中接收图像信号的电视 cableless television; television that receives image signals from electromagnetic waves transmitted by a television station

【无线电收音机】wúxiàndiàn shōuyīnjī 接收无线电广播的装置。把空中的无线电波变为低频的电信号，经过放大而变成声音。radio receiver; radio set; receiving set; apparatus that receives radio broadcasts, changes the radio waves in the air into low frequency signals, and converts them into sounds through amplification; 通称 popularly called 无线电 wúxiàndiàn or 收音机 shōuyīnjī

【无线电台】wúxiàn-diàntái 能够发射和接收无线电信号的装置。由天线、无线电发射机和接收机等组成 radio station; apparatus that transmits and receives radio signals, which consists of antennas, transmitters and receivers; 通称 popularly called 电台 diàntái

【无线电通信】wúxiàndiàn tōngxìn 一种通信方式，利用无线电波在空间传输电信号，电信号可以代表声音、文字、图像等。按照传输内容不同可分为无线电话、无线电报、无线传真等；按照电波波长不同可分为长波通信、中波通信、短波通信等。radio communication; wireless communication; a form of communication by which radio waves are used to transmit signals through space, which represent sounds, words or images. According to what is transmitted, it is divided into radiotelephone, radio-telegraphy and radio facsimile, etc.; and according to the length of the radio waves, it is divided into long wave communication, medium wave communication, short wave communication, etc.

【无效】wúxiào 没有效力；没有效果 no avail; invalid; null and void: 过期～ invalid after the specified date | 医治～ fail to respond to medical treatment

【无懈可击】wú xiè kě jī 没有可以被攻击或挑剔的漏洞，形容十分严密 with no chink in one's armour; unassailable; invulnerable; (of articles) closely reasoned and unassailable

【无心】wúxīn ❶ 没有心思 not be in the mood for: 他心里有事，～再看电影。He was in no mood to go to the film, as he had something on his mind. ❷ 不是故意的 not intentionally; unwittingly; inadvertently: 言者～，听者有意。The remark is not intentional, but it is taken seriously.

【无行】wúxíng〈书 *fml.*〉指没有善行，品行不好 be a man of loose conduct

【无形】wúxíng ❶ 不具备某种事物的形式、名义而有类似作用的（referring to sth. abstract that functions like sth. concrete) invisible; intangible: ～的枷锁 invisible shackles | ～的战线 invisible front ❷ 无形中 unnoticeably; imperceptibly: 孩子总会有形～地受家庭的影响。Children are often perceptibly or imperceptibly influenced by their families.

【无形损耗】wúxíng sǔnhào 指机器、设备等固定资产由于科学技术进步而引起的贬值 invincible or intangible depreciation; depreciation of the machinery, equipment and other fixed assets as a result of technological advance; also 精神损耗 jīngshén sǔnhào

【无形中】wúxíngzhōng 不知不觉的情况下；不具备名义而具有实质的情况下 in reality, not in name; imperceptibly; virtually; unnoticeably: 小张～成了他的助手。Xiao Zhang has virtually become his assistant. | 大家三三两两地交谈着，～开起了小组会。They chatted in twos or threes, and virtually fell into group meetings. also 无形之中 wúxíngzhīzhōng

【无性生殖】wúxìng shēngzhí 不经过雌雄两性生殖细胞的结合、只由一个生物体产生后代的生殖方式。常见的有孢子生殖、出芽生殖和分裂生殖。此外由植物的根、茎、叶等经过压条或嫁接等方法产生新个体,也叫做无性生殖。asexual reproduction; process by which a new plant or animal is reproduced without the union of male and female germ cells, as sporogenesis, budding and fission. Moreover, production of new individuals by layering or grafting roots, stems, leaves, etc. is also called asexual reproduction.

【无性杂交】wúxìng zájiāo 不经过雌雄两性生殖细胞的结合而通过营养器官的接合,使不同个体交换营养物质,以产生杂种的一种方法。例如在动物体内移植生殖腺,对植物体进行嫁接等。asexual (or vegetative) hybridization; process of producing hybrids without the union of male and female germ cells but by joining the nutritive organs of the different individuals to exchange nutritive substances, as transplanting reproductive glands in the body of an animal and grafting a plant

【无须】wúxū 不用;不必 need not; not have to:~操心 need not worry|~大惊小怪 no need to get excited or make a fuss about nothing; also 无须乎 wúxū·hū

【无需】wúxū same as 无须 wúxū

【无烟火药】wúyān huǒyào 以硝酸纤维素或硝酸纤维素加硝化甘油为主要原料制成的火药,爆炸时只产生很少的烟。多用做枪、炮的发射药。smokeless powder; powder made of cellulose nitrate or from cellulose nitrate plus nitroglycerine, which produces little smoke during explosion, and is used as propellant powder for guns and cannons

【无烟煤】wúyānméi 煤的一种,炭化程度最高,黑色,质硬,有金属光泽,燃烧时冒烟很少或几乎没有烟。有的地区叫硬煤、红煤或白煤。anthracite; black, hard coal with metallic lustre and the highest degree of carbonization, burning with little or no smoke, called 硬煤 yìngméi, 红煤 hóngméi or 白煤 báiméi in some places

【无恙】wúyàng〈书 *fml.*〉没有疾病;没有受害 in good health; well; safe:安然~ safe and sound|别来~? Have you been all right since we met last? *or* I believe everything has been getting on well with you since we met last.

【无业】wúyè ❶ 没有职业 be out of work; be unemployed:~游民 vagrant ❷ 没有产业或财产 have no property:全然~ have no property at all; have not a stick of property

【无遗】wúyí 没有遗留;一点儿不剩 nothing left:暴露~ fully exposed|地面上的建筑已被破坏~。The ground structures (or buildings) were destroyed.

【无疑】wúyí 没有疑问 beyond doubt; undoubtedly:确凿~ well established and irrefutable

【无已】wúyǐ〈书 *fml.*〉❶ 没有休止 endlessly; incessantly:有增~ ever-growing; ever-increasing|苛责~ ceaseless severe criticism ❷ 不得已 have no alternative but to; have to

【无以复加】wú yǐ fù jiā 达到极点,不可能再增加 be in the extreme; could not be more

【无艺】wúyì〈书 *fml.*〉❶ 没有准则、法度 have no standards or regulations (to go by):用人~ have no criteria for official appointments ❷ 没有限度 unlimited:贪贿~ excessive greed for bribery

【无益】wúyì 没有好处 unprofitable; useless; no good:生气对身体~。Getting angry is bad for health.

【无意】wúyì ❶ 没有做某种事的愿望 have no intention (of doing sth.); not intend to; not be inclined to:~于此 be not interested in that; be not keen on it|他既然~参加,你就不必勉强他了。Since he has no intention of joining us, you don't have to force him to. ❷ 不是故意的 inadvertently; unwittingly; accidentally:他开荒时~中发现了一枚古钱。While reclaiming wasteland, he accidentally unearthed an ancient coin.

【无意识】wúyì·shí 指未加注意的,出于不知不觉的 unconscious; unconsciously:他说话时~地摆弄着手中的铅笔。While speaking, he unconsciously kept fiddling with his pencil.

【无翼鸟】wúyìniǎo 鸟,翅膀和尾巴都已退化,嘴长,全身有灰色细长的绒毛,腿短而粗,跑得很快。昼伏夜出,吃泥土中的昆虫。产于新西兰,是世界上稀有的鸟类。kiwi (*Apterygidae*); tailless New Zealand nocturnal bird, a rare bird in the world, with undeveloped wings, grey, hairlike feathers, big and fast-running short legs, and a long, slender bill, feeding chiefly on insects and worms in earth; also 鹬鸵 yùtuó; 通称 popularly called 几维鸟 jīwéiniǎo

【无垠】wúyín〈书 *fml.*〉辽阔无边 boundless; vast:一望~boundless; vast|~的原野 boundless prairie

【无影灯】wúyǐngdēng 医院中进行外科手术时用的照明灯。装有几个或十几个排列成环形的特殊灯泡,灯光从不同位置通过滤色器射向手术台,不会形成阴影。光线柔和而不眩目。shadowless lamp; lamp used for surgical operations in hospitals, with several or more than a dozen of special bulbs arranged in a ring so as to emit soft, non-dazzling light to the operating table through filters from different positions without forming dark shadows

【无庸】wúyōng same as 毋庸 wúyōng

【无用功】wúyònggōng 机械克服额外阻力(如起重机提起重物时起重机臂的重力以及绳索和滑

轮间的摩擦力)所做的功 useless work; work done by a machine to overcome extra resistance (as the gravity of the arm of a crane and the friction of the rope and the pulley in lifting heavy goods)

【无由】wúyóu〈书 *fml.*〉same as 无从 wúcóng

【无余】wúyú 没有剩余 nothing left: 揭露～ fully expose; thoroughly expose | 一览～ take in everything at one glance

【无与伦比】wú yǔ lún bǐ 没有能比得上的(多含褒义 commendatory) incomparable; unparalleled; peerless; unique; without equal

【无援】wúyuán 没有援助 have no support; be cut off from help: 孤立～ be isolated and cut off from support

【无缘】wúyuán ❶ 没有缘分 have no chance or luck (to do sth.); not have had the pleasure of: ～得见 have no chance to meet each other; have not had the pleasure of making one's acquaintance ❷ 无从 have no way (of doing sth.); not be in a position (to do sth.): ～分辨 have no way of differentiating (or distinguishing)

【无源之水,无本之木】wú yuán zhī shuǐ, wú běn zhī mù 没有源头的水,没有根的树木 water without a source, tree without roots; 〈比喻 *fig.*〉没有基础的事物 things without foundation

【无政府主义】wúzhèngfǔ zhǔyì ❶ 以蒲鲁东、巴枯宁为代表的一种小资产阶级的政治思潮。否定在任何历史条件下的一切国家政权,反对任何组织、纪律和权威。音译作安那其主义。anarchism; petty bourgeois trend of thought represented by Pierre-Joseph Proudhon and Mikhail Alexandrovich Bakunin, which negates all forms of government in any historical conditions and opposes any organization, discipline and authority; transliterated as 安那其主义 ānnàqí zhǔyì ❷ 指革命队伍中,不服从组织纪律的思想和行为 undisciplined behaviour or idea in the revolutionary ranks

【无知】wúzhī 缺乏知识;不明事理 ignorant: 年幼～ young and inexperienced | ～妄说 ignorant nonsense

【无中生有】wú zhōng shēng yǒu 凭空捏造 purely fictitious; fabricated

【无足轻重】wú zú qīng zhòng 无关紧要 of little importance (or consequence); insignificant; also 无足重轻 wú zú zhòng qīng

【无阻】wúzǔ 没有阻碍 without hindrance; unimpeded; unobstructed: 畅行～ be unobstructed; pass unimpeded | 风雨～ regardless of the weather; rain or shine

毋 wú ❶〈书 *fml.*〉〈副词 *adv.*〉表示禁止或劝阻,相当于'不要'[prohibit or stop by persuasion, equivalent to 'no or not']: ～妄言。Don't lie. | 宁缺～滥 be better to leave a vacancy unfilled than to give it to an incompetent; rather go without than have sth. shoddy ❷ (Wú)姓 a surname

【毋宁】wúnìng〈副词 *adv.*〉表示'不如' rather...(than); (not so much...) as: 这与其说是奇迹,～说是历史发展的必然产物。It is the necessary outcome of historical development rather than a miracle. also 无宁 wúníng

【毋庸】wúyōng 无须 need not; be unnecessary: ～讳言 to be frank | ～置疑 there is no doubt; undoubtedly; beyond doubt | 应～议。(旧时下行公文用语) (in old times words written on a document to be sent to one's inferior) This need not to be considered. also 无庸 wúyōng

芜(蕪) wú〈书 *fml.*〉❶ 草长得多而乱 overgrown with weeds: 荒～ lie waste; land overgrown with weeds ❷ 乱草丛生的地方 land overgrown with weeds: 平～ open country overgrown with weeds ❸〈比喻 *fig.*〉杂乱(多指文辞 oft. referring to diction) mixed and disorderly; miscellaneous: ～词 superfluous words; redundant words

【芜鄙】wúbǐ〈书 *fml.*〉(文章)杂乱浅陋 (of writings) disorganized and vulgar: 辞义～ poor organization and vulgar wording

【芜秽】wúhuì 形容乱草丛生 overgrown with weeds and brambles: 荒凉～ desolate and overgrown with weeds

【芜菁】wújīng ❶ 二年生草本植物,块根肉质,白色或红色,扁球形或长形,叶子狭长,有大缺刻,花黄色。块根可做蔬菜。turnip (*Brassica rapa*); biennial herbal plant of the crucifer family, with long, narrow, large incised leaves, yellow flowers, long or flat-rounded, white or red, fleshy root used as a vegetable ❷ 这种植物的块根 root of the plant; also 蔓菁 mán·jing

【芜劣】wúliè〈书 *fml.*〉(文章)杂乱拙劣 (of writing) disorderly and clumsy: 辞意～ badly written

【芜杂】wúzá 杂乱;没有条理 mixed and disorderly; confusing; jumbled: 文章内容～。The article is too wordy and poorly organized. | 昔日～的园子已经成了游览胜地。Overgrown with weeds in the past, the garden has become a place of tourist interest.

吾 wú ❶〈书 *fml.*〉我,我们(多做主语或定语) I or me; we or us: ～身 myself; my body | ～师 my teacher; my master | ～国 my or our country ❷ (Wú)姓 a surname

【吾辈】wúbèi〈书 *fml.*〉same as 我们 wǒ·men

【吾侪】wúchái〈书 *fml.*〉same as 我们 wǒ·men

【吾人】wúrén〈书 *fml.*〉same as 我们 wǒ·men

吴(吳) Wú ❶ 周朝国名,在今江苏南部和浙江北部,后来扩展到淮河流域 Wu, name of one of the Warring States into which China was divided during the Eastern Zhou Dynasty (770-256 B.C.), comprising the southern part of modern Jiangsu Province and northern part of modern Zhejiang Province and later extending to the Huai River basin ❷ 三国之一，公元 222—280，孙权所建，在长江中下游和东南沿海一带 Wu, name of one of the Three Kingdoms, which was established by Sun Quan and lasted over the period of 222-280, occupying the middle and lower reaches of the Yangtze River and part of the southeastern coastal area ❸ 指江苏南部和浙江北部一带 name for an area comprising southern Jiangsu and northern Zhejiang ❹姓 a surname

【吴牛喘月】wú niú chuǎn yuè 据说江浙一带的水牛怕热，见到月亮就以为是太阳而发喘(《世说新语·言语》：'臣犹吴牛，见月而喘') story goes that the water buffalo in Jiangsu and Zhejiang dreaded the heat of Tummer and panted at the sight of the moon because it mistook the moon for the sun ('I, your servant, pant at the sight of the moon like the water buffalo in Wu.' — *A New Account of Tales of the World · Diction*)；〈比喻 *fig.*〉因疑心而害怕 fear of sth. by mistaking it for sth. else

【吴语】wúyǔ 汉语方言之一，分布于上海、江苏东南部分和浙江大部分地区 Wu dialect; a variety of Chinese spoken in Shanghai, southeastern Jiangsu and most of Zhejiang

【吴茱萸】wúzhūyú 落叶乔木，羽状复叶，小叶对生，卵形或椭圆形，花绿黄色，伞房花序，结红色小干果。果实可入药。medicinal evodia fruit (*Evodia rutaecarpa*)；deciduous tree with compound pinnate leaves, ovate or elliptical alternate leaflets, greenish-yellow flowers borne in corymbs and orange-red nut fruits used for Chinese medicine

郚 wú 郚郚(Tángwú)，地名，在山东 Tangwu, name of a place in Shandong Province

捂 wú ☞ 枝捂 zhīwú on p. 2456
☞ wǔ on p. 2035

唔 wú ☞ 咿唔 yīwú on p. 2259
☞ 嗯 ńg on p. 1403

浯 Wú 浯河，水名，在山东 Wuhe, name of a river in Shandong Province

梧 wú 指梧桐 Chinese parasol (tree)：碧～ green parasol

【梧桐】wútóng 落叶乔木，叶子掌状分裂，叶柄长，花单性，黄绿色。木材白色，质轻而坚韧，可制造乐器和各种器具。种子可以吃，也可以榨油。Chinese parasol (tree) (*Firmiana simplex*)；phoenix tree; deciduous tree with palmately-lobed leaves, long stalk, yellowish-green unisex flowers, whose white, light and tenacious wood is used in making musical instruments and various implements, and whose seed is edible and also used for extracting oil

鹀 wú 鸟类的一属，大小和形状似麻雀，闭嘴时，上嘴的边缘不与下嘴的边缘紧密连接。雄鸟羽毛的颜色较鲜艳。吃种子和昆虫。little bunting (*Emberiza pusilla*)；one of a family (Emberizidae, esp. genera Passerina and Emberiza) of small passerine birds, the size of a sparrow that feeds on seeds and insects. When closed, the edges of its upper and lower mandibles are not closely joined. The male bird is brightly coloured.

铻 wú 锟铻(Kūnwú)，古书上记载的山名。所产的铁可以铸刀剑，因此锟铻也指宝剑。Kunwu, name of a mountain recorded in ancient books. The iron produced there was used to cast swords, hence the name Kunwu also refers to sword.
☞ yǔ on p. 2346

蜈 wú [蜈蚣](wú·gōng) 节肢动物，身体长而扁，背部暗绿色，腹部黄褐色，头部有鞭状触角，躯干由许多环节构成，每个环节有一对足。第一对足呈钩状，有毒腺，能分泌毒液。吃小昆虫。可入药。centipede (*Lithobius centipeda*)；long, flat-bodied, many-segmented, insect-eating arthropod of medical value, with a dark green back and yellowish-brown belly, whip-like feelers to the head and a pair of legs to each segment, the front, hook-like pair of legs having poison glands that secrete venom

鼯 wú [鼯鼠](wúshǔ) 哺乳动物，外形像松鼠，前后肢之间有宽大的薄膜，尾长，背部褐色或灰黑色。生活在高山树林中，能利用前后肢之间的薄膜从高处向下滑翔，吃植物的皮、果实和昆虫等。flying squirrel (*Petaurista petaurista*)；mammal, with the external form of a squirrel, a long tail and brown or greyish black back. It lives in high mountain forests and feeds on the skin, fruits of plants and insects. The wing-like folds of skin attached to the legs and body enable it to make long, gliding leaps.

wǔ (ㄨˇ)

五[1] wǔ〈数目 *num.*〉四加一后所得 five, number obtained by adding one to four; ☞ 数字 shùzì on p. 1791

五[2] wǔ 我国民族音乐音阶上的一级，乐谱上用做记音符号，相当于简谱的'6' *wu*, note of the scale of the Chinese traditional music, used as a symbol in the musical score, corresponding to '6'(la) in numbered musical notation; ☞ 工尺 gōngchě on p. 664

【五爱】wǔ'ài 指爱祖国、爱人民、爱劳动、爱科学、爱社会主义 'Five Loves', referring to love for the motherland, the people, labour, science and socialism

【五倍子】wǔbèizǐ 五倍子虫寄生在盐肤木上刺

激叶细胞而形成的虫瘿，表面灰褐色，含有单宁酸。虫在里面发育繁殖。采集下来，把虫烫死，可入药，也用于染料、制革等工业。Chinese gall (*Melaphis chinensis*); gallnut; greyish-brown gall formed by stimulation of leaf cells by the gall maker living on the Chinese sumac, which contains high tannic acid and in which the parasite grows and reproduces its offspring. The galls are gathered and the parasites are killed by heating and used for Chinese medicine, and also in the dye making and tanning industries. also 五棓子 wǔbèizǐ

【五棓子】wǔbèizǐ same as 五倍子 wǔbèizǐ

【五彩】wǔcǎi 原来指青、黄、赤、白、黑五种颜色，后来泛指多种颜色 (orig.) five colours of blue, yellow, red, white and black; (in a broad sense) multicoloured: ～缤纷 colourful; blazing with colour

【五大三粗】wǔ dà sān cū 形容人身体高大粗壮；魁梧 big and tall; tall and stalwart; strapping; tall and well-built; tall and brawny: 这个～的青年人，浑身有使不完的力气。The tall and brawny young man is brimming with unbounded energy.

【五代】Wǔ Dài 唐朝以后，后梁、后唐、后晋、后汉、后周先后在中原建立政权的时期，公元907—960。Five Dynasties (907-960), namely, the Later Liang Dynasty (907-923), Later Tang Dynasty (923-936), Later Jin Dynasty (936-946), Later Han Dynasty (947-950), and Later Zhou Dynasty (951-960)

【五帝】Wǔ Dì ☞ 三皇五帝 Sān Huáng Wǔ Dì on p.1651

【五斗米道】Wǔdǒumǐdào 道教的一派，东汉末年张道陵所创，以入道者须出五斗米而得名 Wudoumi (Five-*Dou*-of-Rice) sect of Taoism, established by Zhang Daoling towards the end of the Eastern Han Dynasty, with each member delivering five *dou* of rice as membership due, hence the name

【五短身材】wǔduǎn-shēncái 指四肢和躯干短小的身材 (of a man) short in body and limbs

【五方】wǔfāng 指东、西、南、北和中央，泛指各地 five directions (i.e. the four cardinal points, the east, west, south and north, and the centre); (in a broad sense) everywhere

【五方杂处】wǔfāng zá chǔ 形容某地的居民复杂，从各个地方来的人都有 (of a place) be inhabited by people from all parts; have a mixed or cosmopolitan population

【五分制】wǔfēnzhì 学校评定学生成绩的一种记分方法。五分为最高成绩，三分为及格。five-grade marking system, used in schools for the assessment of academic progress made by students, five being the highest mark, and three for pass

【五更】wǔgēng ❶ 从黄昏到拂晓一夜间分为五更，即一更、二更、三更、四更、五更。five watches (or periods) of the night from dusk to dawn, namely first watch, second watch, third watch, fourth watch and fifth watch ❷ 指第五更 fifth watch of the night; just before dawn: 起～，睡半夜 retire at midnight and rise before dawn

【五古】wǔgǔ 每句五字的古体诗 ancient poem with five characters to each line; ☞ 古体诗 gǔtǐshī on p.691

【五谷】wǔgǔ 古书中对五谷有不同的说法，通常指稻、黍、稷、麦、豆，泛指粮食作物 five cereals, usu. referring to rice, two kinds of millet, wheat and beans in ancient books; (in a broad sense) food crops: ～丰登 abundant harvest of all food crops; bumper grain harvest

【五官】wǔguān 指耳、目、口、鼻、舌，通常指脸上的器官 five sense organs (ears, eyes, lips, nose and tongue); facial features: ～端正 have regular features

【五光十色】wǔ guāng shí sè 形容色彩鲜艳，式样繁多 multicoloured; riot of colour; rich and varied; of all kinds; multifarious: 展品～，琳琅满目。There is a great variety of exhibits bright with many colours.

【五行八作】wǔ háng bā zuò 泛指各种行业 five professions and eight workshops; all trades and professions (作 *zuo*: 作坊 workshop)

【五湖四海】wǔ hú sì hǎi 指全国各地 all corners of the land

【五花八门】wǔ huā bā mén 〈比喻 *fig.*〉花样繁多或变幻多端 multifarious; of a wide (or rich) variety

【五花大绑】wǔ huā dà bǎng 绑人的一种方法，用绳索套住脖子并绕到背后反剪两臂 tie a person's hands behind his back with a rope that is looped round his neck

【五花肉】wǔhuāròu 作为食物的肥瘦分层相间的猪肉。有的地区叫五花儿。streaky pork; pork with different layers of lean and fat meat; also 五花儿 wǔhuār in some regions

【五黄六月】wǔ huáng liùyuè 指农历五月、六月间天气炎热的时候 hot days in the 5th and 6th months of the lunar calendar

【五荤】wǔhun 〈佛教 *Budd.*〉指大蒜、韭菜、薤(xiè)、葱、兴渠(根像萝卜，气味像蒜)五种有气味的蔬菜 five strongly flavoured vegetables of garlic, leek, scallion, shallot and *xingqu* (vegetable with a turnip-like root and the smell of garlic)

【五讲四美】wǔjiǎng-sìměi 我国人民在社会生活中总结出来的关于社会主义精神文明的行为规范。'五讲'指讲文明、讲礼貌、讲卫生、讲秩序、讲道德，'四美'指心灵美、语言美、行为美、环境美。five emphases and four beauties, norms of conduct for socialist ethics advocated in the social life of the Chinese people. The five emphases refer to emphasis on civility, cour-

W

tesy, sanitation, orderliness, and morality. The four beauties refer to beauty of soul, speech, behaviour and environment.

【五角大楼】Wǔjiǎo Dàlóu 美国国防部的办公大楼,外形为五角形,常用做美国国防部的代称 Pentagon; a set of five-sided buildings contained one in the other, in which the main offices of the U. S. Department of Defence are located; synonymous to the U. S. Department of Defence

【五金】wǔjīn 指金、银、铜、铁、锡。泛指金属或金属制品。five metals (gold, silver, copper, iron and tin); (in a broad sense) metals or hardware: ～商店 hardware store | 小～ metal fittings

【五经】Wǔ Jīng 指易、书、诗、礼、春秋五种儒家经书 Five Confucian Classics, namely, *The Book of Changes* (《易经》), *Classic of Documents* (《书经》), *The Book of Songs* (《诗经》), *The Book of Rites* (《礼记》), and *The Spring and Autumn Annals* (《春秋》)

【五绝】wǔjué 五言绝句。一首四句,每句五个字。classic poem with four five-character lines, following a strict tonal pattern and rhyme scheme
☞ 绝句 juéjù on p. 1060

【五劳七伤】wǔ láo qī shāng 中医学上五劳指心、肝、脾、肺、肾五脏的劳损;七伤指大饱伤脾,大怒气逆伤肝,强力举重,久坐湿地伤肾,形寒饮冷伤肺,忧愁思虑伤心,风雨寒暑伤形,恐惧不节伤志。泛指身体虚弱多病。(of traditional Chinese medicine) five lesions and seven injuries; 'five lesions' as of the heart, liver, spleen, lungs and kidneys, and 'seven injuries' as caused to the spleen by overeating, to the liver by rage, to the kidneys by lifting heavy weights and sitting long on wet grounds, to the lungs by wearing too little and taking cold food and drinks, to the heart by sorrow and anxiety, to the body by abrupt weather changes, and to the consciousness by immoderate fear; (in a broad sense) general debility; poor health and ailments; 劳 also put as 痨 láo

【五雷轰顶】wǔ léi hōng dǐng 〈比喻 *fig.*〉遭到巨大的打击 suffer a severe blow; be thunderstruck: 他听到这话犹如～,一下子瘫坐在椅子上。He was struck like a bolt from the blue when he heard the words, and sat in the chair as if paralysed.

【五里雾】wǔlǐwù 据说东汉张楷'好道术,能作五里雾'(见于《后汉书·张楷传》)。现在比喻迷离恍惚、不明真相的境界。thick fog. According to *History of Later Han·Biography of Zhang Kai*, Zhang Kai of the Eastern Han Dynasty was good at Taoist magic and capable of creating a thick fog over a distance of five *li*. The phrase is used figuratively to mean bewilderment: 如堕～中 completely mystified; completely bewildered

【五粮液】wǔliángyè 四川宜宾市出产的一种白酒,以五种粮食为原料 *wuliangye*; famous spirit distilled from five kinds of grain, produced in Yibin, Sichuan Province

【五岭】Wǔ Lǐng 指越城岭、都庞岭、萌渚岭、骑田岭、大庾岭,在湖南、江西南部和广西、广东北部交界处 Five Ridges, namely, Yuecheng Ridge, Dupang Ridge, Mengzhu Ridge, Qitian Ridge and Dageng Ridge, across the borders between Hunan and Jiangxi on the southern side and Guangxi and Guangdong on the northern side

【五律】wǔlǜ 五言律诗。一首八句,每句五个字。classical poem with eight five-character lines, following a strict tonal pattern and rhyme scheme; ☞ 律诗 lǜshī on p. 1267

【五伦】wǔlún 封建时代称君臣、父子、兄弟、夫妇、朋友五种伦理关系 five human relationships in feudal times, i. e. between ruler and subject, father and son, husband and wife, brothers, and friends

【五马分尸】wǔ mǎ fēn shī 古代一种残酷的刑罚,用五匹马分别拴住人的四肢和头部,把人扯开 dismemberment of a person by five horses each tied to his head or one of his four limbs, an inhumane punishment in ancient times;〈比喻 *fig.*〉把完整的东西分割得非常零碎 divide up; tear sth. to pieces; share out; also 五牛分尸 wǔ niú fēn shī

【五内】wǔnèi 〈书 *fml.*〉五脏,指内心 viscera: ～如焚(形容内心极为焦虑) feel as if one's viscera were burning; one's heart rent with grief; one's heart torn by anxiety (one's heart filled with anxieties and worries) | 铭感～ feel deeply indebted to

【五日京兆】wǔ rì jīngzhào 西汉张敞为京兆尹(官名),将被免官,有个下属知道了就不肯为他办案子,对人说:'他不过再做五天的京兆尹就是了,还能办什么案子'(见于《汉书·张敞传》)。后来比喻任职时间短或即将去职。According to *History of Han · Biography of Zhang Chang*, Zhang Chang was a metropolitan governor of the Western Han Dynasty. A subordinate of his refused to handle cases for him upon learning that he would soon be dismissed from his post. : 'He will be at the post no longer than five days,' he told others. 'How could he handle any case?' (fig.) (of an official) not expect to remain long in office; hold office only for a brief period

【五卅运动】Wǔ-Sà Yùndòng 中国人民在共产党领导下进行的反帝运动。1925 年 5 月 30 日,上海群众游行示威,抗议日本纱厂的资本家枪杀领导罢工的共产党员顾正红,到公共租界时遭到英国巡捕的开枪射击。共产党领导上海各界罢工、罢课、罢市,各地纷纷响应,形成了全国性的反帝高潮。May 30th Movement (1925);

anti-imperialist movement launched by the Chinese people under the leadership of the Communist Party of China. People in Shanghai took to the streets on May 30, 1925 in protest against a Japanese cotton mill owner's killing of Gu Zhenghong, a Communist who was leading a strike, and were fired at by British police when the procession marched to the International Settlement. The Communist Party led people in all walks of life in Shanghai on a city-wide strike involving workers, students and shopkeepers. It evoked response from all parts of the country, resulting in a nationwide anti-imperialist upsurge.

【五色】wǔsè same as 五彩 wǔcǎi:～斑斓 a riot of colour|～缤纷 blazing with colour; colourful

【五十步笑百步】wǔshí bù xiào bǎi bù 战国时候,孟子跟梁惠王谈话,打了一个比方,有两个兵士在前线上败下来,一个退了五十步,另一个退了一百步。退了五十步的就讥笑退了一百步的,说他不中用。其实两个人都是在退却,只是跑得远近不同罢了(见于《孟子·梁惠王上》)。The pot calls the kettle black. According to *Mencius·Duke Hui of Liang* (*I*), during the Warring States Period, Mencius told Duke Hui of Liang a story by way of analogy, saying that two soldiers were defeated at the battlefront and retreated, one by fifty paces and the other a hundred paces. The one who retreated fifty paces laughed at the other who retreated a hundred paces, saying that the latter was no good. As a matter of fact, Mencius concluded, they both retreated, the mere difference being only the distance.〈比喻 *fig.*〉自己跟别人有同样的缺点或错误,只是程度上轻一些,却讥笑别人 One who has the same shortcomings or mistakes as another, but to a lesser degree, laughs at the other.

【五四青年节】Wǔ-Sì Qīngnián Jié 纪念五四运动的节日。在五四运动中,我国青年充分显示了伟大的革命精神和力量。为了使青年继承和发扬这个光荣的革命传统,规定5月4日为青年节。Youth Day (May 4th), a day marking the May 4th Movement of 1919, in which the young people in China fully displayed their great revolutionary spirit and strength. In order to inherit and carry forward this glorious revolutionary tradition, May 4th was designated as Youth Day.

【五四运动】Wǔ-Sì Yùndòng 中国人民所进行的反帝、反封建的伟大的政治运动和文化运动。1919年5月4日北京学生游行示威,抗议巴黎和会承认日本接管德国侵占中国山东的各种特权的无理决定,运动很快扩大到全国。在五四运动中无产阶级作为觉悟了的独立政治力量登上政治舞台,马克思列宁主义在全国广泛传播,为中国共产党的成立做了准备。May 4th Movement; great, anti-imperialist, anti-feudal, political and cultural movement launched by the Chinese people. The students in Beijing held a parade on May 4th in 1919 in protest against the unjustified decision made at the Paris Peace Conference acknowledging Japan's take-over of Germany's privileges in Shandong, China. The movement quickly spread to the whole country. During the movement, the proletariat mounted the political stage as a conscious, independent political force, and Marxism-Leninism was widely spread in the country, thus paving the way for the founding of the Communist Party of China.

【五体投地】wǔ tǐ tóu dì 指两手、两膝和头着地,是佛教最恭敬的礼节 prostrate oneself with all limbs and the head touching the ground before sb.; most respectful form of etiquette in Buddhism;〈比喻 *fig.*〉敬佩到了极点 highest form of admiration or esteem for sb.

【五味】wǔwèi 指甜、酸、苦、辣、咸。泛指各种味道。five flavours (sweet, sour, bitter, pungent and salty); (in a broad sense) all sorts of flavours

【五线谱】wǔxiànpǔ 在五条平行横线上标记音符的乐谱 staff; stave; five horizontal lines on and between which notes are written or printed

【五香】wǔxiāng 指花椒、八角、桂皮、丁香花蕾、茴香子五种调味的香料 five spices (prickly ash, star aniseed, cinnamon, clove and fennel); spices:～豆 spiced beans

【五星红旗】Wǔxīng-Hóngqí 中华人民共和国国旗,旗面红色,长方形,长和宽为三与二之比。左上方缀五角星五颗。一星较大,居左;四星较小,环拱于大星之右,并各有一个角尖正对大星的中心点。Five-Star Red Flag, national flag of the People's Republic of China, red and rectangular, the ratio of length and breadth being three to two. Its upper left is sewn with five five-pointed stars, with the bigger one located on the left and skirted on the right by the four smaller ones cach with a point directed to the central point of the bigger star.

【五刑】wǔxíng 我国古代的主要刑罚,通常指殷、周时代的墨、劓、剕、宫、大辟 five chief forms of punishment in ancient China (tattooing the face 墨 mò, cutting off the nose 劓 yì, cutting off the feet 剕 fèi, castration 宫 gōng and decapitation 大辟 dàpì)

【五行】wǔxíng 指金、木、水、火、土五种物质。我国古代思想家企图用这五种物质来说明世界万物的起源。中医用五行来说明生理病理上的种种现象。迷信的人用五行相生相克来推算人的命运。five elements of metal, wood, water, fire and earth. Ancient Chinese thinkers tried to use these five substances to explain the origin of all things in the world. Traditional Chinese medicinal practitioners use the five elements to explain physiological and pathological phenomena. Superstitious people used the principle of the five elements producing and overcoming each other to tell the fate of a person.

【五言诗】wǔyánshī 每句五字的旧诗，有五言古诗、五言律诗和五言绝句 poem with five characters to each line, including the ancient poem with five characters to each line, classical poem with eight five-character lines and classical poem with four five-character lines, the two latter forms both following a strict tonal pattern and a rhyme scheme

【五颜六色】wǔ yán liù sè 指各种色彩 of various (or all) colours; multicoloured; colourful：～的花布 multicoloured cotton prints｜～的彩旗 colourful flags

【五一】Wǔ-Yī 五一劳动节的简称 abbr. for 五一劳动节 Wǔ-Yī Láodòng Jié

【五一劳动节】Wǔ-Yī Láodòng Jié 全世界劳动人民团结战斗的节日。1886年5月1日，美国芝加哥等地工人举行大罢工和游行示威，反对资本家的残酷剥削，要求实行八小时工作制。经过斗争，取得了胜利。1889年在恩格斯组织召开的第二国际成立大会上，决定5月1日为国际劳动节。International Labour Day; May Day; day marking the working people in the world uniting in a common fight. On May 1, 1886, workers in Chicago and other cities in the United States went on a general strike and demonstrated against brutal exploitation by capitalists, demanding an eight-hour work system. They won the struggle. At a meeting to found the Second International called by Friedrich Engels in 1889, a decision was made to designate May 1 as International Labour Day. 简称 abbr. 五一 Wǔ-Yī

【五音】wǔyīn ❶ 中国五声音阶上的五个级，相当于现行简谱上的1、2、3、5、6。古代叫宫、商、角、徵(zhǐ)、羽。five notes of the ancient Chinese five-tone scale, e.g. *gong*, *shang*, *jiao*, *zhi*, *yu*, equivalent to 1, 2, 3, 5, and 6 in the numbered musical notation ❷ 音韵学上指五类声母在口腔中的五类发音部位，即喉音、牙音、舌音、齿音、唇音 five points of consonant articulation in the oral cavity, namely, guttural sounds, dental sounds, apical sounds, dental sounds and labial sounds

【五月节】Wǔyuè Jié same as 端午 Duānwǔ

【五岳】Wǔ Yuè 指东岳泰山、西岳华山、南岳衡山、北岳恒山和中岳嵩山，是我国历史上的五大名山 Five Holy Mountains: Mount Taishan, the Eastern Holy Mountain in Shandong Province; Mount Huashan, the Western Holy Mountain in Shaanxi Province; Mount Hengshan, the Southern Holy Mountain in Hunan Province; Mount Hengshan, the Northern Holy Mountain in Shanxi Province; and Mount Songshan, the Central Holy Mountain in Henan Province

【五脏】wǔzàng 指心、肝、脾、肺、肾五种器官 viscera; five internal organs — heart, liver, spleen, lungs and kidneys

【五指】wǔzhǐ 手上的五个指头，就是拇指、食指、中指、无名指、小指 five fingers — thumb, index finger, middle finger, third or ring finger and little finger

【五中】wǔzhōng 〈书 *fml.*〉五脏，指内心 five internal organs (heart, liver, spleen, lungs and kidneys); heart：铭感～ thank sb. from the bottom of one's heart; be deeply grateful; be deeply indebted to

【五洲】wǔzhōu 指全世界各地 five continents; whole world：～四海 five continents; whole world; all parts of the world

【五子棋】wǔzǐqí 一种棋类游戏，用围棋子在围棋盘上对下，先把五个棋子连成一条直线的为胜 gobang; game of chess played between two people with black and white pieces on a board of 361 crosses and the player who first connects five pieces in a straight line being the winner

午 wǔ ❶ 地支的第七位 seventh of the 12 Earthly Branches; ☞ 干支 gānzhī on p. 627 ❷ 日中的时候；白天十二点 noon; midday：中～ noon｜上～ morning｜下～ afternoon｜～饭 lunch｜～睡 afternoon nap

【午餐】wǔcān same as 午饭 wǔfàn

【午饭】wǔfàn 中午吃的饭 midday meal; lunch

【午后】wǔhòu same as 下午 xiàwǔ

【午间】wǔjiān same as 中午 zhōngwǔ：～休息 lunch break

【午觉】wǔjiào 午饭后短时间的睡眠 afternoon nap; noontime snooze：睡～ take an afternoon nap

【午前】wǔqián same as 上午 shàngwǔ

【午时】wǔshí 旧式计时法指上午十一点钟到下午一点钟的时间 period of the day from 11 a.m. to 1 p.m., according to the old time system before the introduction of clock

【午睡】wǔshuì ❶ same as 午觉 wǔjiào ❷ 睡午觉 take (or have) a nap after lunch：大家都～了，说话请小声一些。Everybody is taking a nap, so keep down your voice if you want to talk.

【午休】wǔxiū 午间休息 noon break; midday rest; noontime rest; lunch hour

【午夜】wǔyè 半夜，夜里十二点前后 midnight; around 12 o'clock at night

伍 wǔ ❶〈古代 *arch.*〉军队的最小单位，由五个人编成，现在泛指军队 basic five-man army unit in ancient China; (in a broad sense) army：队～ ranks; contingent; troops | 入～ join the army; enlist | 行～ army; rank and file ❷ 同伙的人 company：羞与为～ feel ashamed to keep sb.'s company ❸ '五'的大写 [upper case of the numeral 5, for use on cheques, banknotes, etc. to avoid mistakes or alterations] five; ☞ 数字 shùzì on p. 1791 ❹ (Wǔ)姓 a surname

【伍的】wǔ·de 〈方 *dial.*〉等等；之类；什么的 and what not; and so on; etc.：买个篮子，装点东西～。Buy a basket and put things in it.

仵 wǔ ❶ 仵作 coroner ❷ (Wǔ)姓 a surname

【仵作】wǔzuò 〈旧时 *old*〉官府中检验命案死尸的人 coroner; public officer whose chief duty is to determine the causes of any deaths not obviously due to natural causes

迕 wǔ 〈书 *fml.*〉❶ 遇见 meet：相～ meet ❷ 违背；不顺从 violate; go against; run counter to：违～ run counter to; be defiant to

庑(廡) wǔ 〈书 *fml.*〉正房对面和两侧的小屋子 small rooms opposite to the main rooms or on the two sides of the main rooms：东～ east wing | 西～ west wing | 廊～ small side room | ～下 small side room

沅(潕、㵲) Wǔ 沅水，发源于贵州，流入湖南 Wushui, river that rises in Guizhou Province and flows into Hunan Province

怃(憮) wǔ 〈书 *fml.*〉❶ 爱怜 tender affection ❷ 失意 frustration; disappointment：～然 feel disappointed

【怃然】wǔrán 〈书 *fml.*〉形容失望的样子 feel disappointed; be frustrated

忤(啎) wǔ 不顺从；不和睦 disobedient; uncongenial：～逆 disobedient (to parents) | 与人无～ bear no ill will against anybody

【忤逆】wǔnì 不孝顺（父母）unfiial (to one's parents)：～不孝 disobedient and unfilial

妩(嫵、娬) wǔ [妩媚] (wǔmèi) 形容女子、花木等姿态美好可爱 (of a woman, flower, etc.) attractive; charming; lovely：～多姿 graceful and attractive | ～动人 lovely and charming

武1 wǔ ❶ 关于军事的 military（跟'文'相对，下②③同 as opposed to 'cultural and educational', same for ② ③ below）：～器 weapons | ～装 armed forces; arms; military equipment | ～力 force; armed force; military strength ❷ 关于技击的 of martial arts：～术 wushu; martial arts | ～艺 *wushu* skill; martial arts skill ❸ 勇猛；猛烈 brave and powerful; fierce; valiant：英～ gallant; brave; valiant | 威～ powerful; mighty; | ～火 intense fire or high heat in cooking ❹ (Wǔ)姓 a surname

武2 wǔ 〈书 *fml.*〉半步，泛指脚步 half a footstep; footstep：踵～ follow in the footsteps of sb.; follow on the heels of; follow suit; ☞ 步武 bùwǔ on p. 173

【武把子】wǔbǎ·zi 〈方 *fml.*〉❶ 指戏曲中表演武打的角色 actor or actress playing a martial role ❷ same as 把子2 bǎ·zi

【武备】wǔbèi 〈书 *fml.*〉指武装力量和武器装备；国防建设 military preparations; armed forces and weaponry (or armaments)：有文事者必有～。Administrators must have the backing of armed forces and weaponry.

【武昌起义】Wǔchāng Qǐyì 1911年在湖北武昌举行的起义 Wuchang Uprising; uprising staged in Wuchang, Hubei Province, in 1911; ☞ 辛亥革命 Xīnhài Gémìng on p. 2132

【武场】wǔchǎng 戏曲伴奏乐队中的打击乐部分 military division (one of the two divisions of the orchestra in traditional opera, consisting of percussion instruments like drums, gongs, cymbals, etc.)

【武丑】wǔchǒu (～儿 wǔchǒur)戏曲中丑角的一种，扮演有武艺而性格滑稽的人物，偏重武工 *wuchou*; (in traditional opera) clown or comedian in a military role; also 开口跳 kāikǒutiào

【武打】wǔdǎ 戏曲、影视中用武术表演的搏斗 acrobatic fighting in Chinese opera or motion picture：～片 acrobatic fighting film | ～场面 acrobatic fighting scene; acrobatic fighting performance

【武旦】wǔdàn 戏曲中旦角的一种，扮演有武艺的妇女，偏重武工 *wudan*; one of the main divisions of the *dan* or female role in traditional opera with stress on fighting skills (representing a military maiden, a princess of martial character, or a woman bandit; combining the most charming feminine virtues with bravery)

【武断】wǔduàn ❶ 只凭主观作判断 make an arbitrary decision; make a subjective conclusion：我对此事知之不详，不敢～。I don't know much about this matter. I dare not to make a subjective conclusion. ❷ 形容言行主观片面 (of speech, act) arbitrary; subjective：说话～ speak arbitrarily | 这样作决定，未免太～了。It's a bit too arbitrary to make such a decision. ❸ 〈书 *fml.*〉妄以权势裁断曲直 settle a dispute arbitrarily by one's power or authority：～乡曲 settle a local dispute arbitrarily

【武夫】wǔfū ❶ 有勇力的人 man of great physical prowess; man of valour：赳赳～ valiant and stalwart man ❷ 指军人 soldier; military man; warrior：一介～ a mere soldier

【武工】wǔgōng 戏曲中的武术表演 (in traditional opera) acrobatic feats and stage fighting performed by an actor or actress; acro-

W

batic skills; also 武功 wǔgōng

【武功】wǔgōng ❶〈书 *fml.*〉指军事方面的功绩 military accomplishments (or achievements, exploits):～赫赫 outstanding military accomplishments ❷ 武术功夫 martial arts skills:他练过～。He has learned martial arts. ❸ same as 武工 wǔgōng

【武官】wǔguān ❶ 指军官 military officer ❷ 使馆的组成人员之一,是本国军事主管部门向使馆驻在国派遣的代表,同时也是外交代表在军事问题上的顾问 military attaché; member of an embassy staff serving as a representative of the military of a country in and an adviser on military affairs

【武行】wǔháng 戏曲中专门表演武打的配角,多出现在开打的场面里 (in traditional opera) supporting roles specializing in acrobatic feats (usu. in fighting scenes)

【武火】wǔhuǒ 烹饪时用的较猛的火 intense fire or high heat (in cooking)

【武将】wǔjiàng 指军官;将领 military officer; general

【武警】wǔjǐng 武装警察的简称 abbr. for 武装警察 wǔzhuāng jǐngchá

【武库】wǔkù 储藏兵器的仓库 armoury; arsenal

【武力】wǔlì ❶ 强暴的力量 force ❷ 军事力量 military force; armed might; armed strength; force of arms

【武林】wǔlín 指武术界 martial arts circles:～新秀 new martial arts specialist|～高手 martial arts masters

【武庙】wǔmiào 供奉关羽的庙,也指关羽、岳飞合祀的庙 temple to the God of War (i.e. dedicated to Guan Yu or to Guan Yu and Yue Fei together)

【武器】wǔqì ❶ 直接用于杀伤敌人有生力量和破坏敌方作战设施的器械、装置,如刀、枪、火炮、导弹等 weapon; arms; instrument or device of any kind used to injure or kill the effective forces of the enemy and destroy the enemy's war establishments, as sabre, spear, fire gun, missile, etc. ❷ 泛指进行斗争的工具 tool used to wage struggle:思想～ ideological weapon

【武人】wǔrén 指军人 soldier

【武生】wǔshēng 戏曲中生角的一种,扮演勇武的男子,偏重开打 male role specializing in fighting feats in traditional opera, portraying valiant men, such as military heroes, high-ranking generals, and heroic outlaws

【武师】wǔshī〈旧时 *old*〉对擅长武术的人的尊称 man versed in martial arts; martial arts master

【武士】wǔshì ❶〈古代 *arch.*〉守卫宫廷的卫兵 palace guards ❷ 有勇力的人 man of prowess; warrior; knight

【武士道】wǔshìdào 日本幕府时代武士遵守的封建道德,内容是绝对效忠于封建主,甚至不惜葬送身家性命 *bushido*; chivalric code of the *samurai* of feudal Japan, emphasizing loyalty, courage and preference of death to dishonour

【武术】wǔshù 打拳和使用兵器的技术,是我国传统的体育项目 *wushu*; martial arts such as shadow-boxing, swordplay, etc. as part of Chinese traditional sports

【武松】Wǔ Sōng《水浒传》中人物之一,勇武有力,曾徒手打死猛虎,一般把他当做英雄好汉的典型 Wu Song, one of the Mount Liang heroes (梁山好汉) in the classical Chinese novel *Outlaws of the Marsh* who killed a tiger barehanded, and is regarded as a hero of heroes

【武戏】wǔxì 以武工为主的戏(区别于'文戏'as compared with 'opera focusing on singing and acting') (in traditional opera) military plays, emphasizing fighting feats

【武侠】wǔxiá 侠客 knight; swordsman; person adept in martial arts and given to chivalrous conduct (in olden times):～小说 swordsman fiction; knight-errant fiction

【武侠小说】wǔxiá xiǎoshuō 主要写侠客、义士行侠仗义故事的小说 swordsman fiction; knight-errant fiction; fiction portraying the chivalrous acts of a knight or a swordsman

【武艺】wǔyì 武术上的本领 skill in *wushu*:～高强 adept in *wushu* skills

【武职】wǔzhí 武官的职务 military post

【武装】wǔzhuāng ❶ 军事装备 arms; military equipment; battle outfit:～力量 armed forces; armed power|解除～ disarm ❷ 用武器来装备 arm; equip; provide troops with arms:缴获的武器,足够～我军两个师。The captured arms are enough to equip two divisions of our army. ◇用现代科学知识～头脑。Arm our mind with modern scientific knowledge. ❸ 用武器装备起来的队伍;军队 army; armed forces:地方～ local armed forces

【武装部队】wǔzhuāng bùduì 军队 armed forces

【武装警察】wǔzhuāng jǐngchá 国家武装力量的一部分,担负守卫国家重要工矿、企业、交通设施,维持治安,警备城市和保卫国家边疆安全等任务。也称武装警察部队的士兵。armed police; part of the state armed forces whose duty is to guard important factories, mines, enterprises and transport facilities, maintain social security, guard cities and defend the safety of the frontiers of the country; also armed policemen; 简称 abbr. 武警 wǔjǐng

【武装力量】wǔzhuāng lìliàng 国家的正规军队及其他武装组织的总称 general term for the regular troops and other armed forces of a country

侮 wǔ 欺负;轻慢 insult; bully:欺～ bully|外～ foreign aggression|御～ resist aggression; resist invasion

【侮慢】wǔmàn 欺侮轻慢 slight; treat disrespectfully:肆意～ be brazenly disrespectful to sb.

【侮蔑】wǔmiè 轻视;轻蔑 despise; look down on

【侮辱】wǔrǔ 使对方人格或名誉受到损害,蒙受耻辱 insult; humiliate; subject sb. to indignities:～人格 affront to one's dignity|遭受～ be insulted; be humiliated

捂(摀) wǔ 遮盖住或封闭起来 seal; cover; muffle:～着嘴笑 laugh with one's mouth covered|放在罐子里～起来,免得走味。Put it in a jar and seal it so as not to lose its flavour.

☞ wú on p. 2028

【捂盖子】wǔgài·zi〈比喻 *fig.*〉掩盖矛盾,不让把问题或坏人坏事揭发出来 keep the lid on; try to cover up the truth of a problem or the evil deeds of an evil person

【捂捂盖盖】wǔwǔgàigài〈方 *dial.*〉藏藏掖掖 try to cover up; hedge and dodge

牾 wǔ〈书 *fml.*〉违背;不顺从 disobedient; violate; go against:抵～ contradict|～意(违背心意) go against one's will

珷 wǔ [珷玞](wǔfū) 像玉的石块 jade-like stone; also 碔砆 wǔfū

鹉 wǔ ☞ 鹦鹉 yīngwǔ on p. 2300

碔 wǔ [碔砆](wǔfū)〈书 *fml.*〉same as 珷玞 wǔfū

舞 wǔ ❶ same as 舞蹈 wǔdǎo ①:芭蕾～ ballet|跳了一个～。(She) performed a dance. ❷ same as 舞蹈 wǔdǎo ②;做出舞蹈的动作 move about as in a dance:载歌载～ singing and dancing|手～足蹈 gesticulate merrily with hands and feet; wave one's arms and stamp one's feet in joy ◇眉飞色～ with dancing eyes and radiant face ❸ 拿着某种东西而舞蹈 dance with sth. in one's hands:～剑 perform the swordplay; play the sword|～龙灯 perform a dragon lantern dance ❹ 挥舞 wave; flourish; wield; brandish:手～双刀 brandish two swords ❺ 耍;玩弄 play with:～弊 fraudulent practice; malpractice; embezzlement|～文弄墨 engage in phrase-mongering; juggle with words ❻〈方 *fml.*〉搞;弄 get sth. going:每家出个人,这事就～起来了。If every family sends one person, this job will get started.

【舞伴】wǔbàn (～儿 wǔbànr)跟自己一起跳交际舞的人 dancing partner; person of the other sex whom one dances with

【舞弊】wǔbì 用欺骗的方式做违法乱纪的事情 fraudulent practice; malpractice; embezzlement:徇私～ fraudulence for selfish purposes

【舞步】wǔbù 跳舞的步子 dancing step:～轻盈 graceful dancing steps

【舞场】wǔchǎng 营业性的供人跳交际舞等的场所 dance hall; ballroom; large public hall for dancing

【舞池】wǔchí 供跳交际舞用的地方,多在舞厅的中心,比休息的地方略低,所以叫舞池 dance floor; floor in a dance hall for dancing, usu. in the central part of the hall, slightly lower than the surrounding places where the dancers sit after a dance, hence 舞池, which literarily means 'dance pool'

【舞蹈】wǔdǎo ❶ 以有节奏的动作为主要表现手段的艺术形式,可以表现出人的生活、思想和感情,一般用音乐伴奏 dance; rhythmic movement of the body and feet, ordinarily to music, to represent human life, and to express human thoughts and feelings ❷ 表演舞蹈 perform a dance

【舞动】wǔdòng 挥舞;摇摆 wave; brandish:～双刀 brandish two swords|柳枝在春风中～。The willow twigs are wavering in the spring breeze.

【舞会】wǔhuì 跳交际舞的集会 dance; ball

【舞剧】wǔjù 主要用舞蹈来表现内容和情节的戏剧 dance drama; ballet

【舞客】wǔkè 舞场的顾客 dance hall customer

【舞美】wǔměi 舞台美术 stage art:～设计 stage art design|～艺术 stage art

【舞迷】wǔmí 喜欢跳舞而入迷的人(多指跳交际舞 oft. referring to ballroom dance) dance fiend; dance fan

【舞弄】wǔnòng ❶ 挥舞耍弄;挥舞着手中的东西玩儿 wave; wield; brandish sth. for fun:～棍棒 brandish cudgels; play cudgels ❷〈方 *dial.*〉弄;搞 make; do:她想做个鸡笼子,可是自己不会～。She wanted to make a chicken cage, but didn't know how.

【舞女】wǔnǚ 以伴人跳舞为职业的女子,一般受舞场雇用 dancing girl; dance-hostess; taxi dancer; girl who is hired to dance with a male customer in a ballroom

【舞曲】wǔqǔ 配合舞蹈的节奏作成的乐曲,多用来为舞蹈伴奏 dance music; dance; a piece of music played as accompaniment for dancing

【舞台】wǔtái 供演员表演的台 stage; arena:～艺术 stagecraft; stage art|～生活 stage life ◇历史～ historical stage|政治～ political stage

【舞厅】wǔtīng ❶ 专供跳舞用的大厅 dance hall; ballroom ❷ same as 舞场 wǔchǎng

【舞文弄墨】wǔ wén nòng mò ❶ 歪曲法律条文作弊 pervert the law by playing with legal phraseology; tamper with the language of documents or laws for illicit purposes; also 舞文弄法 wǔ wén nòng fǎ ❷ 玩弄文字技巧 play with words; engage in play of words

【舞艺】wǔyì 舞蹈的技艺 dancing skill

【舞姿】wǔzī 舞蹈的姿态 dancer's posture and movements:～翩翩 dance gracefully

W

wù（ㄨˋ）

兀 wù〈书 *fml*.〉❶ 高高地突起 rising to a height; towering: 突～ lofty; towering; unexpectedly; suddenly ❷ 形容山秃，泛指秃 (of hill) barren; (in a broad sense) bald: ～鹫 griffon vulture
☞ wū on p. 2015

【兀傲】wù'ào〈书 *fml*.〉same as 高傲 gāo'ào: 负才～ conceited and arrogant

【兀鹫】wùjiù 鸟，身体很大，头部较小，嘴端有钩，头和颈的羽毛稀少或全秃，翼长，视觉特别敏税。生活在高原山麓地区，主要吃死尸。griffon vulture (*Gyps fulvus*); large bird of prey with a small head, a hooked beak, little or no feathers on the head and neck, long wings and a sharp vision, living in highland and mountainous regions and feeding chiefly on carrion; also 兀鹰 wùyīng

【兀立】wùlì same as 直立 zhílì: 巍然～ stand lofty and majestic | 危峰～。A precipitous peak towers in the sky.

【兀臬】wùniè same as 杌陧 wùniè

【兀自】wùzì〈方 *dial*.〉仍旧；还是 still: 想起方才的梦境，心头～突突地跳。When I thought of the dream I just had, my heart was still thumping.

勿 wù〈副词 *adv*.〉表示禁止或劝阻，相当于'不要'[used in prohibitions, admonitions, etc.] do not; never: 切～上当。Beware of swindlers. | 请～入内。No admittance.

【勿谓言之不预】wù wèi yán zhī bù yù 不要说没有预先说过。表示有言在先。do not say that you have not been forewarned; do not blame us for not having forewarned you

乌(烏) wù ☞ below
☞ wū on p. 2015

【乌拉】wù·la 东北地区冬天穿的鞋，用皮革制成，里面垫乌拉草 leather boots lined with wula sedge and worn in winter in Northeast China; also 靰鞡 wū·la
☞ wūlā on p. 2016

【乌拉草】wù·lacǎo 多年生草本植物，叶子细长，花单性，花穗绿褐色。茎和叶晒干后，垫在鞋或靴子里，可以保暖。主要产于我国东北地区。wula sedge (*Carex meyeriana*); perennial herbal plant chiefly produced in Northeast China, with long, slender leaves, unisex flowers and greenish-brown ears, its stem and leaves, after being dried, being used to fill shoes or boots to warm the feet

戊 wù 天干的第五位 5th of the 10 Heavenly Stems (天干); ☞ 干支 gānzhī on p. 627

【戊戌变法】Wùxū Biànfǎ 指 1898 年(农历戊戌年)以康有为为首的改良主义者通过光绪皇帝所进行的资产阶级政治改革，主要内容是，学习西方，提倡科学文化，改革政治、教育制度，发展农、工、商业等。这次运动遭到以慈禧太后为首的守旧派的强烈反对。这年九月慈禧太后等发动政变，光绪被囚，维新派遭捕杀或逃亡国外。历时仅一百零三天的变法终于失败。Reform Movement of 1898; bourgeois political reform initiated by reformists led by Kang Youwei through Emperor Guangxu in 1898 (the Year of Wuxu or the 5th Dog of the lunar calendar), aimed at learning from the West, promoting science and culture, reforming the political and educational system, and developing agriculture, industry and commerce. The movement met with strong opposition from the conservatives led by the Empress Dowager Cixi. In September of the same year, the Empress Dowager staged a *coup d'état*. As a result, the emperor was put under house arrest, the reformists were either arrested and killed or fled abroad. The Reform Movement lasted 103 days before meeting its defeat. also 戊戌维新 Wùxū Wéixīn or 百日维新 Bǎirì Wéixīn

务(務) wù ❶ 事情 affair; business: 事～ business; affairs | 任～ task; mission; assignment | 公～ official business; official assignment ❷ 从事；致力 be engaged in; devote one's efforts to: ～农 be engaged in farming | 好高～远 aim too high; seek for what is beyond one's ability; bite off more than one can chew ❸〈旧时 *old*〉收税的关卡现在只用于地名，如曹家务(在河北)，商酒务(在河南) taxation point [now used only as part of a geographical name, as Caojiawu (in Hebei) and Shangjiuwu (in Henan)] ❹ 务必 must; be sure to: ～须 must; be sure to | 除恶～尽。The evils must be eradicated (or rooted out). ❺ (Wù)姓 a surname

【务必】wùbì 必须；一定要 must; be sure to: 同学们都希望听你的学术报告，你～去讲一次。The students all wanted to listen to your academic lecture. Be sure to give them one.

【务工】wùgōng ❶ 从事工业或工程方面的工作 be engaged in industrial or engineering work ❷ 指投入工力 input: ～不多，收益不少。A moderate input brings a good return.

【务农】wùnóng 从事农业生产 be engaged in agricultural work (or farming); be a farmer: 回乡～ return to the home village to do farm work

【务期】wùqī 一定要 must; be sure to: ～必克 be sure to win the battle (or capture a city, etc.) | ～有成 make sure to achieve sth.

【务求】wùqiú 必须要求(达到某种情况或程度) must; be sure to have sth. done: ～善始善终 be sure to begin well and end well | ～早日完成任务。Be sure to fulfil the task as early as possible.

【务实】wù//shí ❶ 从事或讨论具体的工作 deal

with concrete matters relating to work ❷ 讲究实际，不求浮华 be pragmatic

【务须】wùxū 务必；必须 must; be sure to：～准时到达。Be sure to arrive in good time.

【务虚】wù//xū 就某项工作的政治、思想、政策、理论方面进行研究讨论 discuss principles or the political, ideological and theoretical guidelines relating to a certain field of work

【务正】wùzhèng 从事正当的职业 do honest work：不～ not do honest work | 回心～ change one's mind and do honest work

阢 wù［阢陧］(wùniè) same as 杌陧 wùniè

扤 wù〈书 *fml.*〉摭动 shake

屼 wù〈书 *fml.*〉形容山秃 bald or barren (hill)

坞(塢、隖) wù ❶ 地势周围高而中央凹的地方 depressed place：山～ col; valley ❷ 四面高而挡风的建筑物 structure tall on all sides that keep out the wind：船～ dock | 花～ sunken flower bed ❸〈书 *fml.*〉防御用的建筑物，小型的城堡 fortified building; castle; fort：村～ village fort

芴 wù 有机化合物，化学式 $C_{13}H_{10}$。白色片状晶体，不纯时有荧光，存在于煤焦油中。用来制染料、杀虫剂和药物等。fluorene ($C_{13}H_{10}$); organic chemical compound in the form of a white, flaky crystal, with fluorescent light when impure, a product of coal tar, and used in making dyes, insecticides and medicines

杌 wù same as 杌子 wù·zi

【杌凳】wùdèng (～儿 wùdèngr) 杌子 square stool

【杌陧】wùniè〈书 *fml.*〉(局势、局面、心情等)不安定 (of a situation, one's mind, etc.) unsettled; unstable; uneasy; disturbed; restless; also 阢陧 wùniè or 兀臬 wùniè

【杌子】wù·zi 凳子(多指矮小的) square stool

物 wù ❶ 东西；事物 thing; matter; substance：动～ animal | 货～ goods | ～质 matter; substance | ～尽其用 make the best use of a thing; put things to the best use ❷ 指自己以外的人或跟自己相对的环境 outside world as distinct from oneself; other people：～议 criticism from the public | 待人接～ way one gets along with people ❸ 内容；实质 content; essence; substance：言之有～ speech with substance; speak convincingly | 空洞无～ without substance; absolutely nothing in terms of content

【物产】wùchǎn 天然出产和人工制造的物品 products; produce; natural produce and manufactured goods：我国疆域广大，～丰富。Our country has a vast territory and an abundance of produce.

【物故】wùgù〈书 *fml.*〉去世 pass away; die

【物耗】wùhào 物资消耗 consumption of materials and goods：降低～ reduce the consumption of materials

【物候】wùhòu 生物的周期性现象(如植物的发芽、开花、结实，候鸟的迁徙，某些动物的冬眠等)与季节气候的关系。也指自然界非生物变化(如初霜、解冻等)与季节气候的关系。phenology; study of natural phenomena that recur periodically, as budding, blossoming and fruiting of plants, migration of birds, hibernation of certain animals, etc., and of their relation to climate and changes in season; also referring to seasonal, inorganic changes in nature, such as first frost and thaw

【物化】wùhuà〈书 *fml.*〉去世 pass away; die

【物化劳动】wùhuà láodòng 经济学上指凝结或体现在产品中的劳动(跟'活劳动'相对 as opposed to 'human labour') materialized labour; labour that is embodied in a product; also 死劳动 sǐláodòng

【物换星移】wù huàn xīng yí 景物改变了，星辰的位置也移动了。指节令变化，时间推移。things change and the stars move; change of the seasons or time; also 星移物换 xīng yí wù huàn

【物极必反】wù jí bì fǎn 事物发展到极端，就会向相反的方面转化 things turn into their opposites when they reach the extreme

【物价】wùjià 货物的价格 prices：～稳定。Prices remain stable. | ～波动 price fluctuation | 哄抬～ jack up prices

【物价指数】wùjià zhǐshù 用某一时期的物价平均数作为基数，把另一时期的物价平均数跟它相比，所得的百分数就是后一时期的物价指数，可以用它来表明商品价格变动的情况 price index; percentage obtained by taking the average price in a given period as the base number and comparing it with the average price in another period, serving as an indicator for the price changes of the commodities in the following period

W

【物件】wùjiàn 泛指成件的东西；物品 thing; article：小～ small articles | 稀罕～ rare articles

【物镜】wùjìng 显微镜、望远镜等光学仪器上对着被观察物体一端所装的透镜 objective (lens); lens mounted on the objective end of a microscope, telescope or other optical instruments; also 接物镜 jiēwùjìng

【物理】wùlǐ ❶ 事物的内在规律；事物的道理 innate laws of things：人情～ innate laws of human nature ❷ same as 物理学 wùlǐxué

【物理变化】wùlǐ biànhuà 物质变化中只是改变形态而没有生成其他物质的变化，如汽油挥发、蜡受热熔化等。发生物理变化时，物质的组成和化学性质都不改变。physical change; change leading to changes in the form of a matter without producing another matter, as the volatilization of gasoline, the melting of wax due to heat, etc. When a physical change occurs, the composition and chemical properties of a matter do not change.

【物理量】wùlǐ liàng 量度物质的属性和描述其运动状态时所用的各种量值,如重量、质量、速度、时间、温度、功、能、电压、电流等 physical quantity; attribute of a measured substance and the quantitative value used in describing its motion, as weight, mass, velocity, time, temperature, power, energy, voltage, electric current, etc.

【物理疗法】wùlǐ liáofǎ 西医的一种治疗方法。利用光、电、热泥、热蜡、不同温度的水或器械等刺激人体,通过神经反射对全身起作用,达到治疗目的。physical therapy; physiotherapy; method of Western medical treatment, by which light, electricity, hot mud, hot wax, water of different temperatures or apparatus is used to stimulate the human body and to act on the whole body through nervous reflection;简称 abbr. 理疗 lǐliáo

【物理性质】wùlǐ xìngzhì 物质不需要发生化学变化就表现出来的性质,如状态、颜色、气味、比重、硬度、沸点、溶解性等 physical property; property of a substance without the occurrence of a chemical change, as the state, colour, smell, specific gravity, hardness, boiling point, solubility, etc.

【物理学】wùlǐxué 研究物质运动最一般规律和物质基本结构的学科,是自然科学中的基础学科之一。包括力学、声学、热学、磁学、光学、原子物理学等。physics; science dealing with the most universal law of the motion of matter and the basic structure of matter; one of the basic branches of natural science, including mechanics, acoustics, thermology, magnetics, optics, atomic physics, etc.

W

【物理诊断】wùlǐ zhěnduàn 〈西医 *Western med.*〉诊断疾病的方法,如观察病人的面色、表情和发育情况,用听诊器听病人心、肺的声音,用手指敲或按病人的胸腹部,用小槌敲病人的肘、膝等关节 physical diagnosis; method of diagnosis including observing a patient's complexion, expression and development, listening to the sounds of the heart and lungs with the aid of a stethoscope, tapping or pressing the chest and abdomen with fingers, or tapping the elbow or knee with a little hammer

【物力】wùlì 可供使用的物资 material resources:爱惜人力~,避免滥用和浪费。Use manpower and material resources sparingly and avoid abuse and waste.

【物品】wùpǐn 东西(多指日常生活中应用的 oft. referring to those for daily use) article; goods:贵重~ valuables | 零星~ sundries; odds and ends

【物情】wùqíng 事物的道理 way things are; principles of things:世态~ ways of the world

【物色】wùsè 寻找(需要的人才或东西) look for; seek out; choose (qualified professional people or things needed):~演员 look for and choose actors and actresses | ~衣料 choose fabrics

【物伤其类】wù shāng qí lèi 指动物因同类遭了不幸而感到悲伤 like feels for like; all beings grieve for their fellows' misfortune;〈比喻 *fig.*〉人因同伙受到打击而伤心(多含贬义 oft. derog.)grieve for the attack one's fellow receives

【物事】wùshì ❶〈书 *fml.*〉事情 matter; affair; thing; business:作何~? What does it serve as? ❷〈方 *dial.*〉物品;东西 tangible thing; visible thing:啥~? What is it?

【物探】wùtàn 物理勘探,用物理学的原理和方法研究地质构造,测定矿体的分布情况。包括磁法勘探、重力勘探等。physical prospecting; branch of study dealing with the geological structure by applying physical principles and methods to determine the distribution of the mineral deposits, including magnetic prospecting and gravity prospecting

【物体】wùtǐ 由物质构成的、占有一定空间的个体 body; substance; object:运动~ body in motion | 透明~ transparent substance (or object)

【物外】wùwài 〈书 *fml.*〉世事之外 beyond the region of objective existence; transcendental:超然~ transcend worldly considerations; keep away from unpleasant social relations

【物象】wùxiàng ❶ 动物、器物等在不同的环境中显示的现象。我国劳动人民常根据物象作为预测天气变化的辅助手段。change in the behaviour of an animal or the property of an object, reflecting changing circumstances. The labouring people of our country often use changes in natural phenomena as a supplementary means in weather forecasting. ❷ 事物的形象 image:模写~ copy an image

【物像】wùxiàng 来自物体的光通过小孔或受到反射、折射后形成的像 reflection; visible image; image formed by the light from an object through a tiny hole or through reflection or refraction

【物以类聚】wù yǐ lèi jù 同类的东西常聚在一起,现在多指坏人跟坏人常凑在一起 like attracts like; birds of a feather flock together:~,人以群分 things of a kind come together, people of a mind fall into the same group; like attracts like; birds of a feather flock together

【物议】wùyì 〈书 *fml.*〉众人的批评 criticism from the public:免遭~ so as to avoid public censure; so as not to incur criticism by the masses

【物欲】wùyù 想得到物质享受的欲望 material

desires; desires for material benefits

【物证】wùzhèng 对查明案件事实情况有价值的物品和痕迹,如犯罪凶器、被窃财物、现场指纹等(区别于'人证'as compared with 'eyewitness')material evidence; article or trace valuable to the finding out of the facts about a case, as tools used for criminal purposes, property stolen, fingerprints on the scene, etc.

【物质】wùzhì ❶ 独立存在于人的意识之外的客观实在 matter; substance; objective being independent of the consciousness of man ❷ 特指金钱、生活资料等 material; money; means of subsistence: ～生活 material life|～奖励 material reward; material incentive|贪图～享受 seek material comforts

【物质损耗】wùzhì sǔnhào same as 有形损耗 yǒuxíng sǔnhào

【物种】wùzhǒng 生物分类的基本单位,不同物种的生物在生态和形态上具有不同的特点。物种是由共同的祖先演变发展而来的,也是生物继续进化的基础。在一般条件下,一个物种的个体不和其他物种中的个体交配,即使交配也不易产生出有生殖能力的后代。species, basic unit of classification of animals and plants. Different species of organism differ in ecology and form. Members of the same species originate from the same ancestor, which provide the basis for the continuity of revolution. Under normal conditions individuals of a species do not mate with those of another species; even if such mating happens, the offspring thus produced can hardly acquire the reproductive ability. 简称 abbr. 种 zhǒng

【物主】wùzhǔ 物资或物品的所有者,多指失落或失窃的财物的所有者 owner (esp. of lost or stolen property)

【物资】wùzī 生产上和生活上所需要的物质资料 goods and materials needed for production or life: ～交流 interflow of commodities|～丰富 amply supply of commodities; abundance of supplies; abundance of goods|战略～ strategic materials

瓟 wù ☞ 鼿瓟 nièwù on p. 1416

误(悮) wù ❶ 错误 mistake; error: ～解 misunderstanding|笔～ slip of the pen|～入歧途 be led astray ❷ 耽误 miss; delay; hinder; impede: ～点 late; behind schedule|生产学习两不～。Neither production nor study suffers. ❸ 使受损害 harm; damage: ～人子弟 mislead the younger generation|～人不浅 do no little harm to other people ❹ 不是故意地 by mistake; by accident: ～伤 injure by accident; injure sb. unintentionally|～触忌讳 break a taboo by mistake

【误差】wùchā 测定的数值或计算中的近似值与准确值的差,如用0.33代替$\frac{1}{3}$,误差为$\frac{1}{300}$ error; difference between a determined value or an approximate value in calculation and the accurate value, as 0.33 for 1/3, the error being 1/300

【误场】wù//chǎng 演出时,演员该上场而没有上场 (of an actor) fail to turn up for a performance

【误导】wùdǎo 不正确地引导 mislead; lead astray: 由于新闻媒体的～,致使读者产生误会。The misleading by the mass media led to misunderstanding among the readers.

【误点】wù//diǎn 晚点 late; overdue; behind schedule

【误工】wù//gōng 耽误工作。也指生产劳动中缺勤或迟到。delay one's work; be absent or late in work

【误会】wùhuì ❶ 误解对方的意思 misunderstand; mistake; misconstrue: 我～了他的意思。I've mistaken his meaning. ❷ 对对方意思的误解 misunderstanding: 消除～ remove misunderstanding

【误解】wùjiě ❶ 理解得不正确 misread; misunderstand: 我没这个意思,你～了。I didn't mean that. You've misunderstood it. ❷ 不正确的理解 misunderstanding: 消除～ clear up a misunderstanding

【误期】wù//qī 延误期限 exceed the time limit; be behind schedule: 必须按时完工,不能～。Work must be finished on schedule. It must not exceed the time limit.

【误区】wùqū 指较长时间形成的某种错误认识或错误做法 long-standing mistaken idea or concept: 引导青年走出～ help young people get out of the long-standing mistaken ideas

【误杀】wùshā 法律上指主观上无杀人意图,因失误而伤人致死(区别于'故杀'as compared with 'murder') legal term for manslaughter; killing of a human being by another without malice; killing of a human being by mistake

【误伤】wùshāng 无意中使人身体受伤 accidentally injure; accidental injury

【误事】wù//shì 耽误事情 cause delay in work or business; hold things up; bungle matters: 酒喝多了易～。Excessive drinking is apt to bungle matters.

【误诊】wùzhěn ❶ 错误地诊断 make a wrong diagnosis: 把肺炎～为感冒 diagnose pneumonia as a common cold ❷ 延误时间,使诊治耽搁 miss the chance for diagnosis and treatment: 离医院很远,因而～。The hospital was far away, and as a result medical treatment of the patient was delayed.

恶(惡) wù 讨厌;憎恨(跟'好'hào相对 as opposed to 'like') loathe; dislike; hate: 好～ like and dislike|深～痛绝 detest; cherish intense hatred for

☞ ě on p.505, è on p.506 and wū on p.2018

悟 wù 了解;领会;觉醒 realise; awaken: 觉～ awareness; consciousness | 若有所～ seem to realise; seem enlightened | 恍然大～ suddenly see the light | 执迷不～ obstinately stick to a wrong cause; refuse to listen to reason

【悟彻】wùchè 彻底领悟 understand thoroughly; realise completely: ～佛理 be thoroughly enlightened by the Buddha's doctrine

【悟道】wùdào 领会道理或哲理 awake to the truth; attain enlightenment: ～之言 enlightened views

【悟性】wù·xing 指人对事物的分析和理解的能力 power of understanding; comprehension: 有～ have good understanding; be intelligent; be quick-witted

晤 wù 见面 meet; interview; see: 会～ meet | ～谈 meet and talk | ～面 meet; see | 有暇请来一～。Come and see me when you are free.

【晤面】wùmiàn 见面 meet; see: 久未～,近来可好? We haven't seen each other for a long time. How have you been getting along lately?

【晤谈】wùtán 见面交谈 meet and talk; have a talk; interview: ～片刻 meet and talk for a short while

焐 wù 用热的东西接触凉的东西使变暖 warm up; warm sth. cold with a hot object: ～酒 warm the wine | 用热水袋～一～手 warm one's hands with a hot-water bottle

靰 wù [靰鞡](wù·la) same as 乌拉 wù·la

痦(疬) wù [痦子](wù·zi) 隆起的痣,半球形,红色或黑褐色 naevus; mole; red or dark-coloured, raised congenital, semicircular spot on the human skin; ☞ 痣 zhì on p.2477

婺 Wù ❶ 婺江,水名,在江西 Wujiang, name of a river in Jiangxi Province ❷ 指旧婺州,在今浙江金华一带 Wuzhou, old prefecture in and around present-day Jinhua in Zhejiang Province

【婺剧】wùjù 浙江地方戏曲剧种之一,原名金华戏,流行于该省金华(在元代以前叫婺州)地区 *Wuju* opera; local opera in Zhejiang, originally called 'Jinhua Opera', popular in and around Jinhua (known as Wuzhou before the Yuan Dynasty)

【婺绿】wùlǜ 一种绿茶,产于江西婺源 *wulü*, green tea produced in Wuyuan, Jiangxi Province

骛 wù 〈书 *fml.*〉 ❶ 纵横奔驰 move about freely and quickly; sweep through the length and breadth: 驰～ ❷ 追求 go after; seek for; same as 务 wù ②: 外～ not concentrate on one's duty (or business) | 好高～远 aim too high; reach for what is beyond one's grasp

雾(霧) wù ❶ 气温下降时,在接近地面的空气中,水蒸气凝结成的悬浮的微小水滴 fog; large mass of water vapour condensed to fine particles, at or just above the earth's surface ❷ 指像雾的许多小水点 fine spray of water: 喷～器 sprayer; atomizer

【雾霭】wù'ǎi 雾气 fog; mist; vapour: 江面上～蒙蒙。A heavy pall of mist settled on the river.

【雾沉沉】wùchénchén (～的 wùchénchén·de) 雾气浓重的样子 misty; foggy: 山上～的模糊一片。The mountaintop is hidden in the mist.

【雾茫茫】wùmāngmāng (～的 wùmāngmāngde) 雾气迷茫的样子 misty; foggy: ～的山路上什么也看不清。Everything on the mountain path is blurred in the mist. also 雾蒙蒙 wùméngméng

【雾气】wùqì same as 雾 wù ①

【雾凇】wù·sōng 寒冷天,雾凝聚在树木的枝叶上或电线上而成的白色松散冰晶 (soft) rime; white, loose, icy crystals formed by fog on twigs and leaves of trees or power wires in cold days; 通称 popularly called 树挂 shùguà

寤 wù 〈书 *fml.*〉 ❶ 睡醒 awake ❷ same as 悟 wù

鹜 wù 〈书 *fml.*〉鸭子 duck: 趋之若～ go for sth. like a flock of ducks; scramble for sth.

鋈 wù 〈书 *fml.*〉 ❶ 白铜 white copper; copper-nickel alloy ❷ 镀 plating; gilding

X

xī (ㄒㄧ)

夕 xī ❶ 太阳落的时候；傍晚 sundown; sunset; dusk: ～阳 setting sun | ～照 glow of the setting sun; evening glow | 朝发～至 set off in the morning and arrive in the evening | 朝令～改 promulgate a law in the morning and revoke it in the evening ❷ 泛指晚上 evening; night: 前～ last night | 除～ New Year's Eve (according to Chinese lunar calendar) | 风雨之～ stormy night

【夕烟】xīyān 黄昏时的烟雾 evening mist: ～缭绕 enshrouded in evening mist

【夕阳】xīyáng 傍晚的太阳 setting sun: ～西下。The sun sets in the west.

【夕照】xīzhào 傍晚的阳光 sunset glow: 西湖在～中显得格外妩媚。There is something unusually lovely about the sunset-bathed West Lake.

兮 xī 〈书 *fml.*〉〈助词 *aux.*〉跟现代的'啊'相似 akin to 啊 ā in modern Chinese: 大风起～云飞扬。The high wind rises, and the clouds scud. | 力拔山～气盖世。By uprooting the mountain by sheer muscle, the strength of man is unrivalled under heaven.

西 xī ❶ 四个主要方向之一，太阳落下去的一边 one of the four directions in which the sun sets: ～面 western | 河～ west of the river | 往～去 westward; westbound | 夕阳～下。The sun sets in the west. ❷ (Xī) 西洋；内容或形式属于西洋的 the West; (of content or form) Western; Occidental: 泰～ (old) Western countries; the West | ～医 Western medicine | ～服 Western-style suit | ～式 Western style | 学贯中～ be well-versed in both Chinese and Western learning ❸ (Xī) 姓 a surname

【西安事变】Xī'ān Shìbiàn 指1936年12月12日张学良和杨虎城两将军在西安扣押蒋介石、要求联共抗日的事件。中国共产党从中调解，在停止内战一致对外的条件下释放了蒋介石。Xi'an Incident, which took place on December 12, 1936, when generals Zhang Xueliang and Yang Hucheng took Chiang Kai-shek into custody, demanding that he unite with the Communist Party and fight against Japan. With the mediation of the Chinese Communist Party, the incident ended with the release of Chiang after he accepted the condition to cease civil war and unite with the Communists in a national war against the foreign invaders.

【西半球】xībànqiú 地球的西半部，从西经20°起向西到东经160°止。陆地包括南美洲、北美洲和南极洲的一部分。Western Hemisphere; half of the earth from longitude 20°W to 160° E, comprising South America, North America and part of the Antarctic

【西北】xīběi ❶ 西和北之间的方向 northwest ❷ (Xīběi) 指我国西北地区，包括陕西、甘肃、青海、宁夏、新疆等省区 northwest China; the Northwest, including Shaanxi, Gansu, Qinghai, Ningxia and Xinjiang

【西边】xī·bian (～儿 xī·bianr) same as 西 xī ①

【西餐】xīcān 西式的饭食，吃时用刀、叉 Western-style food, served with knife and fork instead of chopsticks

【西点】xīdiǎn 西洋式的糕点 Western-style pastry

【西法】xīfǎ 西洋的方法 Western method: ～洗染 Western method of laundering and dyeing

【西番莲】xīfānlián ❶ 藤本植物，叶子互生，掌状分裂，花多是红、黄、粉红等色，结黄色浆果。供观赏。passionflower (*Passiflora caerulea*); ornamental tendril-bearing climbing vine having alternate palmate leaves and large, showy flowers red, yellow, pink, etc. in colour, and bearing yellow berries ❷ 大丽花 dahlia

【西方】xīfāng ❶ same as 西 xī ① ❷ (Xīfāng) 指欧美各国，有时特指欧洲各国和美国 West; Occident: ～国家 Western countries ❸ 佛教徒指西天 (Budd.) Western Paradise

【西非】Xī Fēi 非洲西部，包括毛里塔尼亚、马里、塞内加尔、冈比亚、布基纳法索、几内亚比绍、几内亚、塞拉利昂、佛得角、利比里亚、科特迪瓦、加纳、多哥、贝宁、尼日尔、尼日利亚、喀麦隆、赤道几内亚、圣多美和普林西比以及加那利群岛、原西属撒哈拉等 West Africa, including Mauritania, Mali, Senegal, Gambia, Burkina Faso, Guinea-Bissau, Guinea, Sierra Leone, Cape Verde, Liberia, Cote d'Ivoire, Ghana, Togo, Benin, Niger, Nigeria, Cameroon, Equatorial Guinea, and Sao Tome and Principe, as well as Canary Islands and Western Sahara

【西风】xīfēng ❶ 指秋风 west wind; westerly wind ❷ 指西洋风俗、文化等 Western social mores and culture：～东渐。Western influence spreads eastward. ❸〈比喻 *fig.*〉日趋没落的腐朽势力 decaying influences

【西凤酒】xīfèngjiǔ 陕西凤翔柳林镇出产的一种白酒 *xifengjiu*, renowned liquor distilled in Liulin Town of Fengxiang County in Shaanxi Province

【西服】xīfú 西洋式的服装，有时特指男子穿的西式上衣、背心和裤子 Western-style clothes; suit; Western-style set of matching outer garments, especially one consisting of a coat with waistcoat and trousers

【西宫】xīgōng 皇帝的妃嫔住的地方。借指妃嫔。western-palace; residential quarters for an emperor's kept women; imperial concubines

【西瓜】xīguā ❶ 一年生草本植物，茎蔓生，叶子羽状分裂，花淡黄色。果实是大形的浆果，球形或椭圆形，果肉水分很多，味甜，是夏季很好的果品。watermelon (*Citrullus lanatus*); sprawling annual herbaceous plant having palmate leaves and light yellow flowers, and bearing large ball- or rugby-like melons that are juicy and sweet and used as a nice summer fruit ❷ 这种植物的果实 fruit of this plant

【西汉】Xī Hàn 朝代，公元前 206—公元 25，自刘邦称汉王起，到刘玄更始三年止，包括王莽称帝时期（公元 9—23）。建都长安（今陕西西安）。Western Han (206 B.C.-A.D.25), a dynasty that began in 206 B.C., when Liu Bang made himself King of Han, and ended in A.D. 25 or the 3rd year of the Gengshi reign of Liu Xuan, including the period A.D. 9-23 in which Wang Mang made himself an emperor, with Chang'an (present-day Xi'an, Shaanxi Province) as the capital; also 前汉 Qián Hàn

【西红柿】xīhóngshì same as 番茄 fānqié

【西葫芦】xīhú·lu ❶ 一年生草本植物，茎蔓生，横断面呈五角形，叶子略呈三角形，有深裂，果实长圆筒形，是普通蔬菜 summer squash (*Cucurbita pepo*); annual herbaceous plant having a crawling stem with a pentagonal cross-section, triangular leaves with drastic cracks in them, and elongated cylindrical fruit that is a common vegetable ❷ 这种植物的果实 fruit of this plant

【西化】xīhuà 欧化 Westernize

【西画】xīhuà 西洋画的简称 abbr. for 西洋画 xīyánghuà

【西晋】Xī Jìn 朝代，公元 265—317，自武帝（司马炎）泰始元年起，到愍帝（司马邺）建兴五年止。建都洛阳。Western Jin, a dynasty that began in 265, or the 1st year of the Taishi reign of Emperor Wudi (Sima Yan), to 317, or the 5th year of the Jianxing reign of Emperor Mindi (Sima Ye); with Luoyang as the capital

【西历】xīlì〈旧时 *old*〉指公历 Gregorian calendar

【西门】Xīmén 姓 a surname

【西门子】xīménzǐ 电导单位，它的数值等于导体电阻的倒数，如一个导体的电阻为 3 欧姆，它的电导就是 1/3 西门子。这个单位名称是为纪念德国电工学家西门子（William Siemens）而定的。siemens; unit of electrical conductance named in memory of the German electrotechnician William Siemens, equal to the reciprocal of the resistance of a conductor, for instance, if a conductor's resistance stands at 3 ohms, then it's electrical conductance is 1/3 siemens; also 姆欧 mǔōu

【西南】xīnán ❶ 西和南之间的方向 southwest ❷（Xīnán）指我国西南地区，包括四川、云南、贵州、西藏等省区 southwest China; the Southwest, including Sichuan, Yunnan, and Guizhou provinces and the Tibet Autonomous Region

【西南非】Xīnán Fēi 非洲西南部，包括喀麦隆、赤道几内亚、加蓬、刚果、圣多美和普林西比等国 Southwest Africa, including Cameroon, Equatorial Guinea, Gabon, Congo, and Sao Tome and Principe

【西欧】Xī Ōu 欧洲西部，狭义的指英国、爱尔兰、法国、摩纳哥、荷兰、比利时、卢森堡等国，广义的指除东欧以外的欧洲国家 Western Europe, including, in a narrow sense, the United Kingdom, Ireland, France, Monaco, Netherlands, Belgium, and Luxembourg, and in a broad sense, all the European countries except East European countries

【西皮】xīpí 戏曲声腔之一，用胡琴伴奏。跟二黄合称皮黄。*xipi*, a traditional Chinese opera tone to the accompaniment of the *erhu* fiddle, known as *pihuang* in combination with the *erhuang* tone

【西晒】xīshài 房屋门窗朝西的一面午后受阳光照射，夏季室内较热 (of a room) have a western exposure, hot on summer afternoons because of the sun

【西施】Xīshī 春秋时越王勾践献给吴王夫差的美女。后来把西施当做美女的代称。Xi Shi, name of a famed beauty during the Spring and Autumn Period, who was once presented by Gou Jian, the duke of Yue, to Fu Chai, the duke of Wu, as the decoy of a political intrigue; synonym to beauty; also 西子 Xīzǐ

【西式】xīshì 西洋的式样 Western style：～糕点 Western pastry

【西天】xītiān ❶ 我国古代佛教徒称印度（印度古称天竺，在我国西南方）Western Heaven (ancient Chinese Buddhists' name for India, a country to the southwest of China and known in ancient China as 'Tianzhu') ❷ 佛教徒指极乐世界 (Budd.) Western Paradise

【西王母】Xīwángmǔ 我国古代神话中的女神，住在昆仑山的瑶池，她园子里种有蟠桃，人吃了能长生不老 Queen Mother of the West, mythological Chinese goddess living in the Jasper Lake in the Kunlun Mountains, where peaches of longevity grow; 通称 popularly known as 王母娘娘 Wángmǔ niáng·niang

【西魏】Xī Wèi 朝代,公元 535—556。文帝元宝炬所建,建都长安。Western Wei (535-556), one of the Northern Dynasties founded by Yuan Baoju or Emperor Wendi, with Chang-an as the capital; ☞北魏 Běi Wèi on p. 81

【西西】xīxī 毫升的旧称 old transliteration of c. c., short term for cubic centimetre

【西席】xīxí〈旧时 *old*〉对幕友或家中请的教师的称呼(古时主位在东,宾位在西) man of the western seat (for a distinguished guest, whereas the eastern seat is reserved for the host); private tutor; adviser who is also a close friend

【西夏】Xī Xià 公元 1038 年党项族建立的政权,在今宁夏、陕西北部、甘肃西北部、青海东北部和内蒙古西部。公元 1227 年为元所灭。Western Xia, a dynasty that ruled a region that encompassed present-day Ningxia, north Shaanxi, northwest Gansu, northeast Qinghai and west Inner Mongolia, founded by a people of Tangut descent in 1038, and eliminated by the Yuan Dynasty in 1227

【西学】xīxué 清末称欧美的自然科学和社会、政治学说 (late Qing Dynasty term for Western natural, social and political sciences) Western learning

【西亚】Xī Yà 指亚洲西南部,包括阿富汗、伊朗、土耳其、塞浦路斯、叙利亚、黎巴嫩、巴勒斯坦、约旦、以色列、伊拉克、科威特、沙特阿拉伯、也门、阿曼、阿拉伯联合酋长国、卡塔尔、巴林等国家和地区 Southwest Asia, covering Afghanistan, Iran, Turkey, Cyprus, Syria, Lebanon, Palestine, Jordan, Israel, Iraq, Kuwait, Saudi Arabia, Yemen, Oman, the United Arab Emirates, Qatar, and Bahrain; also 西南亚 Xīnán Yà

【西洋】Xīyáng ❶ 指欧、美各国 the West; Western world: ～史 European and American history | ～文学 Western literature ❷〈古代 *arch.*〉指南洋群岛、马来半岛、印度、斯里兰卡、阿拉伯半岛、东非等地 region covering the Malay Archipelago, the Malay Peninsula, India, Sri Lanka, Arabian Peninsular, East Africa, etc.: 郑和下～ Zheng He's seven voyages to the Western Seas during the Ming Dynasty

【西洋画】xīyánghuà 指西洋的各种绘画。因工具、材料的不同,可分为铅笔画、油画、木炭画、水彩画、水粉画等 Western painting, which falls into different categories because of difference in tools and materials used, such as pencil drawing, oil painting, charcoal drawing, watercolours, and gouache; 简称 abbr. 西画 xīhuà

【西洋景】xīyángjǐng ❶ 民间文娱活动的一种装置,若干幅画片左右推动,周而复始,观众从透镜中看放大的画面。画片多是西洋画,所以叫西洋景。peep-show; Western picture show; small exhibition of a series of pictures moved left and right continuously, viewed through a magnifying lens set into a box, known also as 'Western picture show' because most of the pictures exhibited are Western ❷〈比喻 *fig.*〉故弄玄虚借以骗人的事物或手法 hanky-panky; trickery: 拆穿～ expose sb.'s tricks; strip off the camouflage ‖ also 西洋镜 xīyángjìng

【西洋参】xīyángshēn 多年生草本植物,跟人参同属,根略呈圆柱形,可入药。原产北美等地。American ginseng (*Panax quinquefolium*); perennial herbaceous plant of the same family as *Panax ginseng* (*P. schinseng*) whose roots are roughly cylindrical in shape and of high medical and tonic value; originally produced in North America

【西药】xīyào 指西医所用的药物,通常用合成的方法制成,或从天然产物中提制,如消炎片、阿司匹林、碘酊、青霉素等 Western medicine; pharmaceuticals used in Western medicine, such as sulphanilamide tablet, aspirin, tincture of iodine, and penicillin, which are usu. made synthetically or extracted from natural products

【西医】xīyī ❶ 从欧美各国传入中国的医学 Western medicine; medicine introduced to China from Europe and North America ❷ 运用上述医学理论和技术治病的医生 doctor in Western medicine; medical practitioner of Western medical theories and technology

【西域】Xīyù 汉时指现在玉门关以西的新疆和中亚细亚等地区 Western Region, a Han-dynasty term for the region west of Yumenguan Pass, including present-day Xinjiang and Central Asia

【西元】xīyuán〈旧时 *old*〉指公元 Gregorian calendar

【西乐】xīyuè 指欧美的音乐 Western music

【西崽】xīzǎi〈旧时 *old*〉称洋行、西式餐馆等行业所雇用的男仆(含轻视意 derog.) male servant doing odd jobs in a foreign company or restaurant

【西周】Xī Zhōu 朝代,公元前 1046—公元前 771,自周武王(姬发)灭商起,至周平王(姬宜臼)东迁前一年止。建都镐京(今陕西西安西南)。Western Zhou Dynasty (1046-771 B.C.), with its capital in Hao (southwest of present-day Xi'an, Shaanxi Province), beginning from the year Ji Fa, or King Wu of Zhou, eliminated the Shang Dynasty, to the year before Ji Yijiu, or King Ping of Zhou, transferred the seat of government to Luoyang

【西装】xīzhuāng same as 西服 xīfú

【西子】Xīzǐ same as 西施 Xīshī

吸 xī ❶ 生物体把液体、气体等引入体内 inhale; breathe in; (of living things) draw (liquid or gas into the body):呼～ breath|～烟 smoking ❷ 吸收 absorb; suck up:～墨纸 blotting paper|～尘器 vacuum cleaner ❸ 吸引 draw; attract:～铁石 magnet

【吸尘器】xīchénqì 清除灰尘、粉末等用的机器,一般是用电动抽气机把灰尘、粉末等吸进去 vacuum cleaner; electrical machine that cleans dust or powder by suction

【吸毒】xī//dú 吸食毒品,如鸦片、海洛因、可卡因、大麻等 doping; take drugs; be addicted to a narcotic such as opium, heroin, cocaine, and marijuana

【吸附】xīfù 固体或液体把气体或溶质吸过来,使附着在自己表面上,如活性炭吸附毒气和液体中的杂质 absorb; accumulate gases or solutes on the surface of a solid or liquid, such as active carbon absorbing toxic gases and impurities in a liquid

【吸力】xīlì 引力,多指磁体所表现的吸引力 suction; attraction; gravitation of a magnet

【吸溜】xī·liu 〈方 *dial.*〉往嘴或鼻子里吸(气体、液体等)并发出响声 slurp; loud sucking noise made in eating or drinking:冷得直～shivering with cold|～了一下鼻子 inhale noisily with one's nose|他端起一碗粥,使劲地～了一大口。He took hold of a bowl of porridge, and slurped it for all he was worth.

【吸墨纸】xīmòzhǐ 一种质地疏松、吸水性能好的纸。用来吸收墨水。blotting paper; absorbent paper used to blot a surface by soaking up excess ink

【吸盘】xīpán ❶ 某些动物用来把身体附着在其他物体上的器官,形状像圆盘,中间凹。乌贼、水蛭等都有这种器官。sucking disc (of certain animals); sucker; disc-like organ, as of the cuttlefish and leech, adapted for clinging to objects by suction ❷ 起重装卸作业中利用电磁吸力或真空吸力吸取物件的盘状装置 disc-shaped loading and unloading installation that draws objects by electromagnetic or vacuum suction

【吸取】xīqǔ 吸收采取 absorb; draw; assimilate:～养料 absorb nutrition|～力量 draw strength|～经验教训 learn experience and lessons

【吸食】xīshí 用嘴吸进(某些食物、毒物等) suck; take in (liquid foods, narcotic drugs, etc.):～滋补液 suck a tonic with a straw|～毒品 use drugs

【吸收】xīshōu ❶ 物体把外界的某些物质吸到内部,如海绵吸收水,木炭吸收气体等 absorb; imbibe; draw; suck up; take sth. in through pores or interstices, such as a sponge absorbing water, and charcoal absorbing gases ❷ 特指有机体把组织外部的物质吸到组织内部,如肠黏膜吸收养分,植物的根吸收水和无机盐等 assimilate; transform (food) into living tissue by the process of anabolism, such as the intestinal mucous membrane assimilating nutrition, and the root of a plant drawing water and inorganic salt; metabolize constructively ❸ 物体使某些现象、作用减弱或消失,如弹簧吸收震动,隔音纸吸收声音等 absorb; take in; moderate the impact of certain phenomena or the role of sth., such as a spring absorbing shock and sound-insulating paper taking in sound ❹ 组织或团体接受某人为成员 recruit; admit; enroll:～入党 be admitted into the Party|～会员 recruit new members for an association

【吸吮】xīshǔn 吮吸 suck

【吸铁石】xītiěshí ☞ 磁铁 cítiě on p.319

【吸血鬼】xīxuèguǐ 〈比喻 *fig.*〉榨取人民血汗、过着寄生生活的人 bloodsucker; vampire; parasite; person living a parasitical life off other people's sweat and toil

【吸引】xīyǐn 把别的物体、力量或别人的注意力引到自己这方面来 attract an object, force, or sb.'s attention to one's side; draw; fascinate:～力 attraction|这出戏很～观众。This opera has a strong appeal to the audience.

希腊字母表

Table of Greek Alphabets

大写 upper case	小写 lower case	名称 Chinese transliteration	大写 upper case	小写 lower case	名称 Chinese transliteration
Α	α	阿尔法 alpha	Ν	ν	纽 nu
Β	β	贝塔 beta	Ξ	ξ	克西 xi
Γ	γ	伽马 gamma	Ο	ο	奥米克戎 omicron
Δ	δ	德尔塔 delta	Π	π	派 pi
Ε	ε	艾普西隆 epsilon	Ρ	ρ	柔 rho
Ζ	ζ	泽塔 zeta	Σ	σ,s	西格马 sigma
Η	η	伊塔 eta	Τ	τ	陶 tau
Θ	θ	西塔 theta	Υ	υ	宇普西隆 upsilon
Ι	ι	约(yāo)塔 iota	Φ	ϕ	斐 phi
Κ	κ	卡帕 kappa	Χ	χ	希 chi
Λ	λ	拉姆达 lambda	Ψ	ψ	普西 psi
Μ	μ	谬 mu	Ω	ω	奥米伽 omega

汐 xī 夜间的潮 night tide; ☞ 潮汐 cháoxī on p. 230

希1 xī 希望 hope:～准时出席。It is hoped you will be present on time.|敬～读者指正。It is hoped that our readers will kindly point out our errors.

希2 xī same as 稀 xī ①

【希罕】xī•han same as 稀罕 xī•han

【希冀】xījì〈书 *fml.*〉same as 希望 xīwàng

【希腊字母】Xīlà zìmǔ 希腊文的字母。数学、物理、天文等学科常用做符号。Greek alphabet, which is often used as signs in mathematics, physics, astronomy, and many other disciplines of learning

【希奇】xīqí same as 稀奇 xīqí

【希求】xīqiú ❶ 希望得到 hope for:～大家的帮助 hope to get everybody's help ❷ 希望和要求 wish; desire:他现在除了念书,没有别的～。The only wish he has is to attend school.

【希少】xīshǎo same as 稀少 xīshǎo

【希世】xīshì same as 稀世 xīshì

【希图】xītú 心里打算着达到某种目的(多指不好的);企图 intend to; design to; attempt to (oft. sth. bad):～暴利 go profiteering|～蒙混一时 try to wangle; try to get by under false pretences

【希望】xīwàng ❶ 心里想着达到某种目的或出现某种情况 aspire; yearn; hanker; dream:他从小就～做一个医生。He has aspired to become a doctor since childhood. ❷ 希望达到的某种目的或出现的某种情况;愿望 hope; wish; dream:这个～不难实现。It's easy to turn this hope into reality. ❸ 希望所寄托的对象 sb. or sth. on which hope is placed:青少年是我们的未来,是我们的～。Our future and our hope rest with the youngsters.

【希有】xīyǒu same as 稀有 xīyǒu

昔 xī 从前 bygone days; old times; days of yore; yesterday:～日 days gone by|～年 in former years|今胜于～。The present is better than the past.

【昔年】xīnián〈书 *fml.*〉往年;从前 in years gone by; in the past

【昔日】xīrì 往日;从前 former days:～的荒山,今天已经栽满了果树。The once barren mountains are covered all over with fruit trees.

析 xī ❶ 分开;散开 divide; separate:～居 live separately|条分缕～ make meticulous analysis|分崩离～ fall to pieces ❷ 分析 analyse; dissect:剖～ dissect|解～几何 analytical geometry|奇文共欣赏,疑义相与～study a rare piece of writing and analyse its subtleties together; share the pressure of reading a rare piece of writing and discussing its subtleties ❸(Xī) 姓 a surname

【析产】xīchǎn 分割产业,指分家 divide up property, esp. family property

【析出】xīchū ❶ 分析出来 find results on analysis ❷ 固体从液体或气体中分离出来 (of solid) separate out (of a liquid or a gas):～结晶 crystallize

【析居】xījū〈书 *fml.*〉分家 (of family members) live separately:兄弟～ grownup brothers live separately

【析疑】xīyí〈书 *fml.*〉解释疑惑 resolve a doubt; clear up a doubtful point

矽 xī 硅的旧称 former term for 硅 guī

【矽肺】xīfèi 硅肺的旧称 former term for 硅肺 guīfèi

【矽钢】xīgāng 硅钢的旧称 former term for 硅钢 guīgāng

肸 xī 多用于人名。羊舌肸,春秋时晋国大夫。*xi*, a Chinese character oft. used in personal names; Yang Shexi, a high official of the state of Jin during the Spring and Autumn Period

穸 xī ☞ [窀穸](zhūnxī) on p. 2530

茜 xī 人名用字,多用于外国妇女名字的译音(人名中也有读 qiàn 的) Chinese character used in personal names, and oft. in transliteration of female personal names of foreign countries; also pronounced qiàn in a personal name

☞ qiàn on p. 1541

郗 Xī 姓 a surname

☞ Chī on p. 258

饻 xī 老解放区曾用过的一种计算货币的单位,一饻等于若干种实物价格的总和 *xi*, unit of currency in former liberated areas during the Liberation War of China; one *xi* equals the total price of a number of goods

恓 xī ☞ below

【恓惶】xīhuáng ❶〈书 *fml.*〉形容惊慌烦恼 running scared; vexed; troubled ❷〈方 *dial.*〉穷苦 be down and under

【恓恓】xīxī〈书 *fml.*〉寂寞 lonely

栖 xī [栖栖]〈书 *fml.*〉形容不安定 unsettled; restless

☞ qī on p. 1505

唏 xī〈书 *fml.*〉叹息 sigh

【唏嘘】xīxū same as 欷歔 xīxū

牺(犧) xī〈书 *fml.*〉做祭品用的毛色纯一的牲畜 beast of a uniform colour for sacrifice; sacrifice:～牛 sacrificial ox

【牺牲】xīshēng ❶〈古代 *arch.*〉为祭祀宰杀的牲畜 beast slaughtered for sacrifice; sacrifice ❷ 为了正义的目的舍弃自己的生命 give one's life for; die a martyr's death; lay down one's life:流血～ shed one's blood and lay down one's life｜为国～ lay down one's life for one's motherland｜他～在战场上。He laid down his life on the battlefield. ❸ 放弃或损害一方的利益 give up; at the expense of:～休息时间赶修机器 give up one's spare time to catch up with machine repairs

【牺牲节】Xīshēng Jié ☞ 宰牲节 Zǎishēng Jié on p. 2386

【牺牲品】xīshēngpǐn 指成为牺牲对象的人或物 victim; prey:这对青年成了包办婚姻的～。This young couple fell victim to an arranged marriage.

息 xī ❶ 呼吸时进出的气 breath:喘～ pant; gasp｜鼻～ breath｜一～尚存，此志不懈 strive for one's goal as long as one is still breathing ❷ 消息 news; information:信～information ❸ 停止 stop; cease:～怒。Don't be angry.｜～兵 cease fire; stop fighting｜自强不～strive unceasingly; continuous self-renewal｜偃旗～鼓 put away the flags and silence the drums — to cease all activities｜生命不～，战斗不止 fight on until breathing one's last ❹ 休息 rest:歇～ take a rest｜作～时间表 daily schedule; work schedule; timetable ❺ 滋生；繁殖 breed; multiply:蕃～ proliferate; multiply quickly｜生～ subsist; live ❻ 利钱；利息 interest:年～ annual interest｜月～ monthly interest｜还本付～ repay capital and interest｜减租减～ reduce rent and interest ❼〈书 *fml.*〉指子女 children:子～ one's children ❽（Xī）姓 a surname

【息肩】xījiān〈书 *fml.*〉摆脱职务，卸去责任 rest one's shoulders; lay down all the burdens

【息怒】xīnù 停止发怒 don't be angry; calm one's anger:请～，有事好商量。Don't be angry. Everything can be discussed and settled.

【息肉】xīròu 因黏膜发育异常而形成的像肉质的突起，多发生在鼻腔或肠道内 polyp; polypus; nonmalignant growth or tumor oft. protruding from the mucous lining of the nose or intestine; also 瘜肉 xīròu

【息事宁人】xī shì níng rén ❶ 从中调解，使争端平息，彼此相安 patch up a quarrel and reconcile the parties concerned; pour oil over troubled waters ❷ 在纠纷中自行让步，减少麻烦 make concessions to avoid trouble

【息讼】xīsòng 停止诉讼 withdraw or drop a lawsuit:只要他能答应提出的条件，我可以～。I may withdraw my lawsuit if he accepts the conditions that have been raised.

【息息相关】xī xī xiāng guān 呼吸相关连，比喻关系密切 (of inhaling and exhaling) be closely interrelated; (fig.) face the common fate; also 息息相通 xīxī xiāngtōng

【息影】xīyǐng〈书 *fml.*〉指退隐闲居 retire into private life:～家园 retire to one's native land｜杜门～ close the door and live in seclusion; live in complete seclusion

【息止】xīzhǐ 停止 cease:永不～地工作 work tirelessly

奚 xī ❶〈书 *fml.*〉〈疑问词 *interrog. pron.*〉何 why; how ❷（Xī）姓 a surname

【奚落】xīluò 用尖刻的话数说别人的短处，使人难堪；讥讽嘲笑 revile; sneer; taunt; jibe at; criticize in a sarcastic way to embarass sb.:受人～ be the butt of jibes｜他被～了一顿。He became the butt of their jokes.

【奚幸】xīxìng same as 傒倖 xīxìng

浠 Xī 浠水，水名，在湖北，流入长江 Xishui, name of a river that empties itself into the Yangtze River in Hubei Province

悕 xī〈书 *fml.*〉悲伤 sad; sorrow

娭 xī〈书 *fml.*〉same as 嬉 xī
☞ āi on p. 4

菥 xī［菥蓂］(xīmì)一年生草本植物，茎直立，叶子长椭圆形，花小，白色，总状花序，角果扁平。全草入药。boor's mustard (*Thlaspi arvense*); dish mustard field penny cress; wild cress; annual herbaceous plant having oblong leaves, small white botryo-flowers on an upright stem, and bearing flat pods, the whole plant useful for medical purposes

硒 xī 非金属元素，符号 Se (selenium)。灰黑色晶体或红色无定形粉末。晶体硒能够导电，导电能力随光照强度的增减而改变。用来制造光电池等，也是一种半导体材料。selenium (Se); non-metal element in the form of red amorphous powder or grayish black crystal that is electric-conductive and whose conductivity varies with changes in light intensity, used for the making of optoelectronic cells or as a semi-conductive material

晞 xī〈书 *fml.*〉❶ 干；干燥 dry:晨露未～。The morning dew is yet to dry — it is still early morning. ❷ 破晓；天亮 first light of day; daybreak:东方未～。The first rays of the sun are yet to break the eastern horizon.

欷 xī［欷歔］(xīxū)〈书 *fml.*〉哭泣后不自主地急促呼吸；抽搭 sob:相对～ sob to each other｜～不已 sob on and on; also 唏嘘 xīxū

悉[1] xī 全；尽 all; entire:～心 wholehearted; devoted｜～力 spare no effort｜～听君便。Do as you like.

悉[2] xī 知道 know; learn; be informed of:熟～ familiar｜来函敬～。I've received your letter.

【悉数】xīshǔ〈书 *fml.*〉全部数出；完全列举 reel off all the figures; enumerate in full detail:不可～ countless

【悉数】xīshù〈书 *fml.*〉全数 all; entirety:～奉还 return sth. in its entirety｜～归公 turn over all the assets to the state

【悉心】xīxīn 用尽所有的精力 devote all one's attention：～研究 immerse oneself in research work

烯 xī 烯烃 alkene

【烯烃】xītīng 不饱和烃的一类，分子中含有双键结构的开链烃，如乙烯（$CH_2=CH_2$）、丁二烯（$CH_2=CH-CH=CH_2$）等 alkene；unsaturated，open chain hydrocarbon with one or more carbon-carbon double bonds，such as ethene（$CH_2=CH_2$）and butadiene（$CH_2=CH-CH=CH_2$）

淅 xī〈书 *fml.*〉淘米 wash rice

【淅沥】xīlì〈拟声词 *onom.*〉形容轻微的风声、雨声、落叶声等 sound of light rain，breeze，falling leaves，etc.：小雨淅淅沥沥下个不停。It kept pattering all day long.

【淅淅】xīxī〈拟声词 *onom.*〉形容轻微的风、雨、雪等的声音 sound of gentle wind，light rain or snow

惜 xī ❶ 爱惜 value；cherish；treasure；use sparingly：珍～ cherish｜～寸阴 value every bit of time｜～墨如金 regard one's ink as if it were gold — one would not write or paint whimsically ❷ 可惜；惋惜 regret：痛～ regret deeply ❸ 吝惜；舍不得 grudge；stint：～别 find it hard to say good-bye to sb.｜～力 be sparing of one's effort or energy｜不～工本 do sth. at all costs；spare no expense

【惜别】xībié 舍不得分别 be reluctant to part；hate to see sb. go：依依～ be reluctant to part｜老师们怀着～的心情，送走了毕业的同学。The teachers reluctantly parted with the graduates.

【惜福】xīfú 指珍视自己的福气，不过分享受 cherish one's good fortune；not squander when one has plenty：他生平省俭～，不肯过费。Cherishing his good fortune dearly，he lived a thrifty life and never squandered his money.

【惜老怜贫】xī lǎo lián pín 爱护老年人，同情穷人 have compassion for the old and the poor；also 怜贫惜老 lián pín xī lǎo

【惜力】xīlì 舍不得用力气 be sparing of one's energy：干活不～ never spare one's effort in work

【惜墨如金】xī mò rú jīn 指写字、绘画、做文章下笔非常慎重，力求精练（of a painter，calligrapher，or writer）use ink as if it were gold — work with scrupulous care

【惜售】xīshòu 舍不得卖出 be loath to sell

【惜阴】xīyīn 爱惜光阴 cherish every minute of one's life

晰（晳） xī 清楚；明白 clear；distinct：明～ well-defined｜清～ clear

睎 xī〈书 *fml.*〉❶ 瞭望 look out over ❷ 仰慕 look up to；admire

稀 xī ❶ 事物出现得少 few and far between；rare；scarce；uncommon：～少 rare；few and far between｜～罕 rare ❷ 事物之间距离远；事物的部分之间空隙大（跟'密'相对 as opposed to 'dense'）sparse；scattered：地广人～ wide of area and sparse of population｜月明星～。The moon is bright and the stars are fading. ❸ 含水多；稀薄（跟'稠'相对 as opposed to 'thick'）liquid；watery；thin：～泥 slime｜粥太～了。The porridge is too watery. ❹ 用在'烂、松'等形容词前面，表示程度深［used before such adjectives as 烂 làn and 松 sōng］extremely；very：～烂 very pulpy｜～松 extremely loose｜～糟 rotten；very bad ❺ 指稀的东西 sth. watery or thin：糖～ syrup；molasses

【稀巴烂】xī·balàn same as 稀烂 xīlàn ②

【稀薄】xībó（空气、烟雾等）密度小；不浓厚 rarified：高山上空气～。The air over high mountains is rarified.

【稀饭】xīfàn 粥（多指用米或小米煮成的）porridge；rice or millet gruel

【稀罕】xī·han ❶ 稀奇 scarce；uncommon：骆驼在南方是～东西。Camels are a rarity in the south. ❷ 认为稀奇而喜爱 value as a rarity；cherish；treasure：谁～你那玩意儿，我们有的是。Who cares about that stuff of yours? We have plenty of it. ❸（～儿 xī·hanr）稀罕的事物 novelty；rarity；rare thing：看～儿 watch sth. or sb. with curiosity ‖ also 希罕 xī·han

【稀客】xīkè 不常来的客人 rare visitor

【稀拉】xī·la ❶ 稀疏 sparse；scanty；thinly scattered：～的枯草 a few withered grass scattered here and there ❷〈方 *dial.*〉松松垮垮；散漫 slovenly；slack：作风～ lax style of work

【稀烂】xīlàn ❶ 极烂 completely mashed；pulpy：肉煮得～。The meat was done to a pulp. ❷ 破碎到极点 smashed to smithereens：鸡蛋掉到地上，摔了个～。The egg was smashed completely when it fell on the ground. also 稀巴烂 xī·balàn

【稀朗】xīlǎng（灯火、星光）稀疏而明朗（of lights or stars）sparse or scattered but bright

【稀里糊涂】xī·lihútú ❶ 糊涂（程度略轻）；迷糊 confused（to a lesser degree）；dazed：这道题他讲了两遍，我还是～的。He explained the problem twice，but I was still confused. ❷ 马马虎虎；随便 casual；perfunctory：这件事没经过认真讨论，就～地通过了。The motion was endorsed perfunctorily，without careful discussion.

【稀里哗啦】xī·lihuālā ❶〈拟声词 *onom.*〉形容雨声、建筑物倒塌声等 sound of rain or building collapsing：雨～下了起来。The rain came pouring down.｜院墙～倒了下来。The courtyard wall fell with an elongated crash. ❷ 形容七零八落或彻底粉碎的样子 badly battered；

broken to pieces：家具被这伙人打了个～。The furniture was smashed into splinters by the gang.

【稀里马虎】xī·limǎ·hu 疏忽大意；马马虎虎 absent-minded；imprudent；neglectful：念书可不能～的。You cannot afford to be absent-minded in your studies.

【稀料】xīliào 用来溶解或稀释涂料的有机液体，常用的有汽油、酒精、松香水、香蕉水等 solvent；diluents；organic liquid such as gasoline，alcohol，rosin oil，and banana oil，used to dissolve another substance

【稀溜溜】xīliūliū （～的 xīliūliū·de）（～儿的 xīliūliūr·de）粥、汤等很稀的样子（of porridge，soup，etc.）very thin；watery

【稀奇】xīqí 稀少新奇 strange；curious：～古怪 eccentric；also 希奇 xīqí

【稀散元素】xīsàn-yuánsù 没有形成独立矿床，而以杂质状态分散在其他矿物中的元素，如硒、碲、锗、镓、铟、铊等 scattered element；element such as selenium（Se），tellurium（Te），germanium（Ge），gallium（Ga），indium（In），and thallium（Tl），that exists as impurities in mineral ores

【稀少】xīshǎo 事物出现得少 few；rare；scarce：街上行人～。There were hardly any pedestrians in the street.｜人烟～ be sparsely populated｜雨量～ sparse precipitation；also 希少 xīshǎo

【稀世】xīshì 世间很少有 rare on earth：～珍宝 rare treasure｜～之才 rare talent；also 希世 xīshì

【稀释】xīshì 在溶液中再加入溶剂使溶液的浓度降低 dilute；make thinner or less concentrated by adding a liquid

【稀疏】xīshū（物体、声音等）在空间或时间上的间隔远（of objects，sounds，etc.）few and scattered；few and far between；thin；sparse：～的头发 thin hair｜～的枪声 sporadic gunshots

【稀松】xīsōng ❶ 懒散；松懈 sloppy；lax：作风～ sloppy style of work ❷ 差劲 no good；bad：他们干起活儿来，哪个也不～。When they set to work，none of them is inattentive. ❸ 无关紧要 unimportant；trivial：别把这些～的事放在心里。Don't take such trivial matters to heart.

【稀土元素】xītǔ-yuánsù 镧、铈、镨、钕、钷、钐、铕、钆、铽、镝、钬、铒、铥、镱、镥、钇、钪 17 种元素的统称 rare-earth element；general term for the 17 elements — lanthanum（La），cerium（Ce），praseodymium（Pr），neodymium（Nd），promethium（Pm），samarium（Sm）；europium（Eu），gadolinium（Gd），terbium（Tb），dysprosium（Ds），holmium（Ho），erbium（Er），thulium（Tm），ytterbium（Yb），lutecium（Lu），yttrium（Yt），and scandium（Sc）；also 稀土金属 xītǔ-jīnshǔ

【稀稀拉拉】xī·xilālā（～的 xī·xilālā·de）稀疏的样子 sparse；thinly scattered：天上只有～的几个晨星。There were only a few stars here and there in the sky at dawn.｜会场内的掌声～，气氛一点不热烈。There was only a spattering of applauses in the meeting hall — the atmosphere was dull. also 稀稀落落 xī·xiluòluò

【稀有】xīyǒu 很少有的；极少见的 rare；unusual：～金属 rare metal｜十月下雪在这儿不是～的事。Snow in October is not uncommon in this part of the world. also 希有 xīyǒu

【稀有金属】xīyǒu jīnshǔ 通常指在自然界含量较少、比较分散的金属，如锂、钨、锗、钪、铂等 rare metal；metal that is rare and scattered in nature，such as lithium（Li），tungsten（W），germanium（Ge），scandium（Sc），and platinum（Pt）

【稀有气体】xīyǒu qìtǐ 惰性气体 noble gas；rare gas

【稀有元素】xīyǒu yuánsù 自然界中存在的数量少或很分散的元素，例如锂、铍、钽、镓、硒、碲、氪、氩、氡等 rare element；element that is rare or scattered in nature，such as lithium（Li），beryllium（Be），tantalum（Ta），gallium（Ga），selenium（Se），tellurium（Te），krypton（Kr），argon（A *or* Ar），and niton（Rn）

傒

xī［傒倖］（xīxìng）烦恼（多见于早期白话 oft. in early vernacular）vexation；annoyance；also 奚幸 xīxìng

舾

xī［舾装］（xīzhuāng）❶ 船上锚、桅杆、梯、管路、电路等设备和装置的总称 fittings of a ship，including anchor，mast，ladder，pluming，and electrical circuits ❷ 船体主要结构造完之后安装锚、桅杆、电路等设备和装置的工作 work to be done after the hull of a ship has been completed，such as the installation of anchor，mast，electrical equipment，etc.

翕

xī〈书 *fml.*〉❶ 和顺；协调 affable；agreeable；genial ❷ 收敛 furl；fold：～张 pulsate；quiver；curl and uncurl

【翕动】xīdòng〈书 *fml.*〉（嘴唇等）一张一合地动（of lips，nostrils，etc.）expand and contract rhythmically；beat；pulsate open and close alternately：嘴唇～ quivering lips｜鼻翼～ quivering nostrils；also 噏动 xīdòng

【翕然】xīrán〈书 *fml.*〉❶ 形容言论、行为一致（of opinions，actions，etc.）be in unison；be in harmony：～从之 accept without reservation ❷ 形容安定 stable；peaceful：郡境～ all is peaceful in the state

【翕张】xīzhāng〈书 *fml.*〉一合一开 pulsate：目自～ open and close one's eyes alternately

腊

xī〈书 *fml.*〉干肉 dried meat
☞ là on p.1139

粞

xī ❶〈书 *fml.*〉碎米 broken rice ❷〈方 *dial.*〉糙米碾轧时脱掉的皮，可做饲料

chaff; bran; husk, which can be used as fodder

犀 xī 哺乳动物，奇蹄目，形状略像牛，颈短，四肢粗大，鼻子上有一个或两个角。皮粗而厚，微黑色，没有毛。产在亚洲和非洲的热带森林里。rhinoceros (*Rhinocerotidae*); thick-skinned, hairless blackish mammal of the order *Perissodactyla*, looking somewhat like a bull, having a short neck, thick and large limbs, and one or two upright horns on the snout, native to tropical forests of Asia and Africa; 通称 generally known as 犀牛 xīniú

【犀角】xījiǎo 犀牛的角，由角质纤维组成，很坚硬，可入药，也用做图章或其他器物的材料 rhinoceros horn, which is made of keratin fiber, hard of texture, and used as medicine and material for making seals and other products

【犀利】xīlì （武器、言语等）锋利；锐利（of weapons, words, etc.) sharp; incisive; trenchant: 文笔～write in a trenchant style | 谈锋～ be incisive in conversation | 目光～ penetrating eyes

皙 xī 〈书 *fml*.〉人的皮肤白 fair-skinned; light-complexioned: 白～ fair

锡[1] xī ❶ 金属元素，符号 Sn (stannum)。常见的白锡为银白色，富有延展性，在空气中不易起变化，多用来镀铁、焊接金属或制造合金。有的地区叫锡镴。stannum (Sn); tin; metal oft. of a silvery colour, malleable, insusceptible to change when exposed to air, mostly used for iron-plating, welding or making alloys; known in some regions as 锡镴 xī·la ❷ (Xī)姓 a surname

锡[2] xī 〈书 *fml*.〉赐给 grant; bestow: 天～良缘 godsend union between a man and a woman

【锡伯族】Xībózú 我国少数民族之一，主要分布在新疆和辽宁 Sibos; the Sibo, a minority ethnic people distributed over the Xinjiang Uygur Autonomous Region and Liaoning Province

【锡箔】xībó 上面涂着一层薄锡的纸，多叠成或糊成元宝形，迷信的人用来焚化给鬼神 tinfoil, often folded up into shoe-shaped ingots for use as funeral offerings

【锡匠】xī·jiang 制造和修理锡器的小手工业者 tinsmith; handicraftman who makes or repairs articles of tin or tinplate

【锡剧】xījù 江苏地方戏曲剧种之一，原名常锡文戏，由无锡滩簧和常州滩簧合流而成，流行于该省南部和上海市 Wuxi opera, which is a combination of the *tanhuang* tones of Wuxi and Changzhou, popular in southern Jiangsu and Shanghai

【锡镴】xī·la 〈方 *dial*.〉❶ 焊锡 soldering tin ❷ 锡 tin

【锡杖】xīzhàng 佛教的杖形法器，头部装有锡环 (Budd.) staff topped by a tin ring, used as a ritual object

【锡纸】xīzhǐ 包装卷烟等所用的金属纸，多为银白色 tinfoil; silver paper used for packing cigarettes, etc.

傒 xī 〈书 *fml*.〉❶ 等待 wait; await ❷ same as 蹊 xī

溪 xī (旧读 formerly pronounced qī) 原指山里的小河沟，现在泛指小河沟 small stream; brook; rivulet: 清～ limpid stream | ～水 water in a stream | ～谷 mountain stream

【溪涧】xījiàn 夹在两山中间的小河沟 mountain stream; rivulet sandwiched in between two mountains

【溪流】xīliú 从山里流出来的小股水流 brook; rivulet

裼 xī 〈书 *fml*.〉敞开或脱去上衣，露出身体的一部分 unbutton or divest one's upper garment: 袒～ strip to the waist

☞ tì on p. 1887

熙 xī 〈书 *fml*.〉❶ 光明 bright; sunny ❷ 和乐 merry; cheerful: 众人～～。Every one is happy and contented. ❸ 兴盛 prosperous: ～朝(兴盛的朝代) age of prosperity

【熙和】xīhé 〈书 *fml*.〉❶ 和乐 congenial and happy ❷ 温暖 pleasantly warm; genial

【熙来攘往】xī lái rǎng wǎng same as 熙熙攘攘 xīxī rǎngrǎng

【熙攘】xīrǎng 熙熙攘攘 bustling with activity: 人群～ bustling crowd

【熙熙攘攘】xīxī rǎngrǎng 形容人来人往，非常热闹 bustling with activity; with people bustling about

豨 xī 古书上指猪 pig in ancient books

【豨莶】xīxiān 一年生草本植物，茎上有灰白色的毛，叶子对生，椭圆形或卵状披针形，花黄色，结瘦果，黑色，有四个棱。全草入药。common St. Paulswort (*Siegesbeckia orientalis*); annual herbaceous plant for medical use, having grayish hair on its stem, opposite leaves oval or lanceolate oval in shape, and yellow flowers, and bearing black four-edged achenes

蜥 xī 蜥蜴 lizard: 巨～ giant lizard

【蜥蜴】xīyì 爬行动物，身体表面有细小鳞片，有四肢，尾巴细长，容易断。雄的背面青绿色，有黑色直纹数条，雌的背面淡褐色，两侧各有黑色直纹一条，腹面都呈淡黄色。生活在草丛中，捕食昆虫和其他小动物。lizard (*Lacertidae*); reptile of the suborder *Sauria* or *Lacertilia*, characteristically having an elongated body with tiny scales and a light yellow belly, four legs, and a tapering tail that breaks easily; the male having a bluish green back with black straight stripes, the female having a light brown back with a black straight line on either side, living in weeds, and feeding on insects and tiny animals；通称 generally known as 四脚蛇 sìjiǎoshé

僖 xī〈书 *fml.*〉喜乐 happy

熄 xī 熄灭 extinguish；put out：～灯 turn off the lamp｜火势已～。The fire has gone out.

【熄灯】xī//dēng 熄灭灯火 turn off the light：～就寝 turn off the lamp and go to bed

【熄火】xī//huǒ ❶ 燃料停止燃烧（of fuel，a stove，etc.）stop burning；die out ❷ 使燃料停止燃烧 stop fuel from burning

【熄灭】xīmiè 停止燃烧；灭（灯火）（of a fire，light，etc.）go out；die out

譆 xī〈书 *fml.*〉悲叹的声音；呼痛的声音 cry of anguish；lament

磎 xī〈书 *fml.*〉same as 溪 xī

嘻 xī ❶〈书 *fml.*〉〈叹词 *interj.*〉表示惊叹［indicating admiration，wonder，etc.］alas ❷〈拟声词 *onom.*〉形容笑的声音 sound of merry laughter：～～地笑 giggle

【嘻皮笑脸】xī pí xiào liǎn same as 嬉皮笑脸 xī pí xiào liǎn

【嘻嘻哈哈】xīxī hāhā ❶ 形容嬉笑欢乐的样子 laughing and joking；laughing merrily；mirthful ❷ 形容不严肃或不认真 not serious；happy-go-lucky：对待这样的大事情，～的可不行！It is an important matter，and it won't do if you treat it casually.

噏 xī〈书 *fml.*〉❶ same as 吸 xī ❷ 收敛 contract；draw back

【噏动】xīdòng〈书 *fml.*〉same as 翕动 xīdòng

嶲 xī 越嶲（Yuèxī），地名，在四川。今作越西。Yuexi，name of a place which is now put as 越西 Yuèxī in Sichuan Province

膝 xī 大腿和小腿相连的关节的前部 knee；joint between the thigh and the lower leg；通称 popularly known as 膝盖 xīgài；（图见 ☞ figure for 身体 shēntǐ on p.1701）

【膝盖骨】xīgàigǔ ☞ 髌骨 bìngǔ on p.135

【膝下】xīxià 儿女幼时常在父母跟前，因此旧时表示有无儿女，常说'膝下怎样怎样'；给父母或祖父母写信时，也在开头的称呼下面加'膝下'两字 phrase derived from the old custom in which young children were often present at their parents' knees，now used in saying whether one has children or not；the phrase is also used in the salutations of letters to one's parents or grandparents：～犹虚（还没有儿女）have got no children yet｜父亲大人～ Dear Father

【膝痒搔背】xī yǎng sāo bèi〈比喻 *fig.*〉处事不得当或不得要领（语本《盐铁论·利议》：'议论无所依，如膝痒而搔背'）not scratch at the itch；not scratch where it itches — fail to handle a matter properly；miss the point；miss fire（Huan Kuan's *Discourses on Salt and Iron* · *For the Benefit of Argumentation*：'To make an unfounded argument is like scratching one's back while one's knee is actually itching.'）

瘜 xī［瘜肉］（xīròu）same as 息肉 xīròu

嬉 xī〈书 *fml.*〉游戏；玩耍 frolic；have a good time：～闹 gambol｜～戏 rollick

【嬉闹】xīnào 嬉笑打闹 gambol：大家～了一阵，开始安静下来。Every body began to quiet down after laughing and rollicking for a long time.

【嬉皮士】xīpíshì 指某些西方国家中具有颓废派作风的人。他们由于对现实不满而采取玩世不恭的态度，如蓄长发、穿奇装异服、吸毒等。hippie；hippy；person following a decadent lifestyle. In some Western countries，some people are so disillusioned with reality that they show their cynical attitude by wearing long hair and strange clothes，or taking drugs.

【嬉皮笑脸】xī pí xiào liǎn 形容嬉笑不严肃的样子 grinning cheekily；smiling and grimacing；also 嘻皮笑脸 xī pí xiào liǎn

【嬉戏】xīxì〈书 *fml.*〉游戏；玩耍 frolic；gambol

【嬉笑】xīxiào 笑着闹着 laughing and playing：远处传来了孩子们的～声。From the distance came the happy laughter of children at play.

熹 xī〈书 *fml.*〉❶ 天亮 daybreak；dawn：～微（of morning glow）pale；dim ❷ 明亮 brightness：星～ brightness of stars

【熹微】xīwēi〈书 *fml.*〉形容阳光不强（多指清晨的 oft. of morning sunlight）dim；pale：晨光～ faint rays of first dawn

憙 xī〈书 *fml.*〉叹声 sound of sigh

樨 xī［木樨］（mù·xi）same as 木犀 mù·xi

螅 xī ☞ 水螅 shuǐxī on p.1803

歙 xī〈书 *fml.*〉吸气 inhale
☞ Shè on p.1698

羲 Xī 姓 a surname

熺 xī〈书 *fml.*〉same as 熹 xī

窸 xī［窸窣］（xīsū）〈拟声词 *onom.*〉形容细小的摩擦声音［succession of slight，soft sounds of friction，as of leaves，silks，papers，etc.］rustle

蹊 xī〈书 *fml.*〉小路 narrow road：～径 narrow path
☞ qī on p.1507

【蹊径】xījìng〈书 *fml.*〉途径 path；way：独辟～ open a new road for oneself；blaze a trail；have a new style of one's own

蟋 xī［蟋蟀］（xīshuài）昆虫，身体黑褐色，触角很长，后腿粗大，善于跳跃。尾部有尾须一对。雄的好斗，两翅摩擦能发声。生活在阴湿的地方，吃植物的根、茎和种子，对农业有害。有的地区叫蛐蛐儿。cricket（*Gryllidae*）；insect having a darkish brown body, usu. long feelers, well-developed hind legs that enable it to hop agilely, and a pair of cercopods on its tail, living in dankness, and deemed harmful to farm crops for it feeds on roots, stalks and seeds, the male being very belligerent and capable of making a singing sound by friction of its two wings; also 促织 cùzhī; known in some areas as 蛐蛐儿 qū·qur

徯 xī ☞ 勃徯 bóxī on p.149

豀 xī ❶ same as 溪 xī ❷ ☞ 勃豀 bóxī on p.149

【豀壑】xīhè 〈书 *fml*.〉两山之间的大沟;山谷(多用于比喻 oft. fig.) gorge; gully; ravine

【豀卡】xīkǎ 西藏民主改革前属于官府、寺院和奴隶主的庄园 manor belonging to an official, slave-owner, or temple in Tibet before the democratic reform

【豀刻】xīkè 〈书 *fml*.〉尖刻;刻薄 sarcastic; scathing; mean

鸂 xī [鸂鶒](xīchì)古书上指像鸳鸯的一种水鸟 water bird akin to the mandarin duck and drake in ancient books

醯 xī 〈书 *fml*.〉醋 vinegar

曦 xī 〈书 *fml*.〉阳光(多指清晨的) sunlight (usu. of early morning):晨~ morning glow

巇 xī ☞ 险巇 xiǎnxī on p.2079

爔 xī 〈书 *fml*.〉 same as 曦 xī

鼷 xī [鼷鼠](xīshǔ)小家鼠 mouse; mice

蠵 xī [蠵龟](xīguī)海产的一种大龟,体长达一米,背面褐色,腹面淡黄色,头部有对称的鳞片,四肢呈桨状,尾短。吃鱼、虾、蟹等。loggerhead turtle (*Caretta caretta*); marine turtle having a one-metre-long body with a brown back and light yellow belly and its head covered with symmetrical scales, four oar-shaped limbs, and a short tail, and feeding on fish, shrimps, crabs, etc.

觿 xī 〈书 *fml*.〉〈古代 *arch*.〉用骨头制的解绳结的锥子 wrought-bone bodkin, for undoing knots

xí (ㄒㄧˊ)

习(習) xí ❶ 学习;复习;练习 practise; exercise; review:自~ study by oneself|实~ fieldwork|~艺 learn a skill or craft|修文~武 study literature while practising the martial arts ❷ 对某事物常常接触而熟悉 be accustomed to; be familiar with:~见 commonly seen|~闻 often hear|~以为常 be accustomed or used to ❸ 习惯 habit:积~ old habit|恶~ bad habit|相沿成~become a custom by tradition ❹ (Xí)姓 a surname

【习非成是】xí fēi chéng shì 对于某些错的事情习惯了,反认为是对的 get used to what is wrong and regard it as right

【习惯】xíguàn ❶ 常常接触某种新的情况而逐渐适应 be accustomed to; be used to; be inured to:~成自然 habit becomes second nature|对这里的生活还不~。I am yet to get used to life in this part of the world. ❷ 在长时期里逐渐养成的、一时不容易改变的行为、倾向或社会风尚 habit; custom; long-time practice, trend, or fashion that cannot be changed overnight

【习惯法】xíguànfǎ 指经国家承认,具有法律效力的社会习惯 common law; customary law; common tradition or usage so long established that it has the force or validity of law

【习好】xíhào 长期养成的嗜好 inveterate habit

【习见】xíjiàn 经常见到 commonly seen:~不鲜 not uncommon|这种情况一向为人们所~。This situation is no uncommon occurrence.

【习气】xíqì 逐渐形成的坏习惯或坏作风 unhealthy habit; bad practice:官僚~ bureaucratic style of work|不良~ undesirable trend

【习染】xírǎn 〈书 *fml*.〉❶ 沾染(不良习惯) contract (a bad habit) ❷ 坏习惯 bad habit:革除~ quit bad habits

【习尚】xíshàng 风尚 common practice; custom:社会~ social mores

【习俗】xísú 习惯和风俗 custom; customs and habits:民族~ folkways

【习题】xítí 数学上供练习用的题目 exercises (in school work):数学~ mathematical exercises|~解答 key to exercises

【习习】xíxí 形容风轻轻地吹 (of a wind) blow gently:微风~。A gentle breeze is blowing.

【习性】xíxìng 长期在某种自然条件或社会环境下所养成的特性 behaviour; habit cultivated over time under certain natural or social circumstances

【习焉不察】xí yān bù chá 习惯于某种事物而觉察不到其中的问题 too accustomed to sth. to call it in question

【习以为常】xí yǐ wéi cháng 常常做某件事,成了习惯 be used, accustomed or inured to sth.

【习艺】xíyì 学习技术、手艺 learn a trade, skill, handicraft, etc.

【习用】xíyòng 经常用;惯用 habitually use:~语 idiom

【习与性成】xí yǔ xìng chéng 指长期的习惯会形成一定的性格 habit becomes second nature

【习字】xízì 练习写字 practise penmanship; do exercises in calligraphy

【习作】xízuò ❶ 练习写作 do exercises in composition ❷ 练习的作业(指文章、绘画等) exercise in composition, drawing, etc.:每周交一篇~ deliver a composition on a weekly basis

郋 Xí 古地名，在今河南省 Xi，name of an old place in present-day Henan Province

席(❶蓆) xí ❶ 用苇蔑、竹篾、草等编成的片状物，用来铺炕、床、地或搭棚子等 mat; flat piece woven of reed or bamboo strips or straw, for use as bed (including heatable brick bed) and floor covering or for building shacks：草～ straw mat|凉～ summer mat|炕～ mat for brick bed|一领～ one mat ❷ 坐位；席位 seat：出～ be present|入～ be seated|缺～ be absent|退～leave or walk out on a banquet, meeting, etc.|硬～ (of a train) hard seat or berth|软～ soft seat or berth|来宾～ guests' seats ❸ 特指议会中的席位，表示当选的人数 seats in parliament, indicating number of people elected ❹ 成桌的饭菜；酒席 banquet; feast：摆了两桌～ lay out two tables for a banquet ❺〈量词 *classifier*〉：一～话 a talk with sb.|一～酒 a one-table banquet ❻ (Xí)姓 a surname

【席不暇暖】xí bù xiá nuǎn 坐位还没有坐热就走了，形容忙得很 not sit long enough to warm one's seat; be in a great hurry; be constantly on the go

【席次】xícì 坐位的次序 order of seats; seating arrangement; one's arranged seat：代表们按照指定～入座。The deputies were seated according to the seating arrangement.

【席地】xídì 原指在地上铺了席(坐、卧在上面)，后来泛指在地上(坐、卧) (orig.) have a mat on the ground; sit or lie on the ground：～而坐 sit on the ground

【席卷】xíjuǎn 像卷席子把东西全都卷进去 roll up like a mat; carry everything with one; take away everything：～而逃(偷了全部细软而逃跑) make away with all the belongs of sb. else

X

【席梦思】xímèngsī 一种内部装有弹簧的床垫。也指装有这种床垫的床。simmons, transliteration of a kind of innerspring mattress; mattress

【席面】xímiàn 筵席；筵席上的酒菜 dishes served at a feast：婚宴的～很丰盛。The food served during the wedding banquet was rather generous.

【席篾】xímiè 用苇子、竹子、高粱秆等的皮劈开而做成的细长的薄片，用来编席、篓子等 matting or basketry strip; thin strip of the skin of reed, bamboo or sorghum stalks for use in making mats and basketry

【席位】xíwèi 集会时个人或团体在会场上所占的座位。特指议会中的席位，表示当选的人数。seat; seat of an individual or organization at a conference, esp. in a legislative assembly, indicating the number of people elected to it

【席子】xí·zi same as 席 xí ①

觋 xí〈书 *fml.*〉男巫师 shaman; necromancer; occultist

袭[1](襲) xí ❶ 袭击；侵袭 assault; attack：夜～night raid|空～air raid|偷～hit-and-run attack; surprise attack|～取 take by surprise ◇寒气～人 chilly cold ❷ (Xí)姓 a surname

袭[2](襲) xí ❶ 照样做；依照着继续下去 copy; imitate; pattern after：抄～plagiarize|因～ follow beaten tracks; carry on (old customs, established practice, etc.)|沿～ imitate; pattern after ❷〈书 *fml.*〉〈量词 *classifier*〉用于成套的衣服 [used for counting complete suit or suits of clothing]：一～棉衣 a suit of cotton-padded clothes

【袭击】xíjī ❶ 军事上指出其不意地打击 surprise attack; attack by surprise：～敌军右侧 attack on the right flank of the enemy field ❷〈比喻 *fig.*〉突然的打击 unexpected blow; hit：遭台风～ be hit by a typhoon

【袭取】[1] xíqǔ 出其不意地夺取(多用于武装冲突 oft. in armed confrontation) take by surprise：～敌人的营地 take an enemy encampment by surprise

【袭取】[2] xíqǔ 沿袭地采取 take over (sth. long been in use)：后人～这个故事，写成了戏。People of later generations adapted this story for the stage.

【袭扰】xírǎo 袭击骚扰 harass：打退敌人的～foil enemy harassment

【袭用】xíyòng 沿袭地采用 take over (sth. long been in use)：～古方，配制丸药 take over an age-old prescriptions and make a kind of bolus of Chinese medicine

【袭占】xízhàn 袭击并占领 take (a place) by surprise

媳 xí 媳妇 daughter-in-law：婆～one's wife and mother; mother and her son's wife

【媳妇】xífù ❶ 儿子的妻子 son's wife; daughter-in-law; also 儿媳妇儿 érxí·fur ❷ 晚辈亲属的妻子(前面加晚辈称呼) wife of a relative of the younger generation：侄～ nephew's wife|孙～ grandson's wife

【媳妇儿】xí·fur〈方 *dial.*〉❶ 妻子 wife ❷ 泛指已婚的年轻妇女 married young woman

嶍(㠐) xí 嶍峨(Xí'é)，旧县名，就是现在云南的峨山彝族自治县 Xi'e, former name of a county, i.e. present-day Eshan Yi Autonomous County in Yunnan Province

隰 xí ❶〈书 *fml.*〉低湿的地方 low-lying marshy land; swamp ❷〈书 *fml.*〉新开垦的田 newly reclaimed land ❸ (Xí)姓 a surname

檄 xí ❶ 檄文 proclamation of war on (a traitor, usurper, etc.); official summons to arms：羽～ official summons to arms inscribed on a wooden strip and attached with a feather as a sign of urgency ❷〈书 *fml.*〉用

檄文晓谕或声讨 declare war on or denounce sb. in the form of a public letter：～告天下 issue a nationwide official announcement

【檄书】xíshū same as 檄文 xíwén

【檄文】xíwén〈古代 *arch.*〉用于晓谕、征召、声讨等的文书，特指声讨敌人或叛逆的文书 written document to inform, summon or, esp. denounce an enemy or traitor

霫 xí［霫霫］〈书 *fml.*〉形容下雨（of rain）patter；drip

鳛 xí 鳛水（Xíshuǐ），地名，在贵州。今作习水。Xishui, name of a place in Guizhou, written today as 习水 Xíshuǐ

xǐ（ㄒㄧˇ）

洗 xǐ ❶ 用水或汽油、煤油等去掉物体上面的脏东西 wash；clean sth. using water, gasoline, kerosene oil, etc：～脸 wash one's face | 干～ dry-clean | ～衣服 wash clothes；do one's laundry ❷ 洗礼 baptize：领～ be baptized；receive baptism | 受～ be baptized ❸ 洗雪 redress：～冤 right a wrong；redress a grievance ❹ 清除 clear away；eliminate：清～ ferret out；uproot ❺ 像用水洗净一样杀光或抢光 sack；devastate：～城 sack a city and massacre its inhabitants | ～劫 kill and loot ❻ 照相的显影定影；冲洗 develop film：～胶卷 develop a roll of film | ～相片 print photos ❼ 把磁带上的录音、录像去掉 erase a recording：那段录音已经～了。That tape of recording has been erased. ❽ 玩牌时把牌搀和整理，以便继续玩 shuffle cards in preparation for another game：～牌 give cards a shuffle；shuffle cards ❾ 笔洗 tray for washing writing brushes

☞ Xiǎn on p. 2078

【洗尘】xǐchén 设宴欢迎远道而来的人 give a dinner to greet a visitor from afar：接风～ give a welcoming dinner to a guest from afar

【洗涤】xǐdí same as 洗 xǐ ①：～器 washing machine | ～剂 detergent | ～衣物 laundry

【洗耳恭听】xǐ ěr gōng tīng 专心地听（请人讲话时说的客气话）be all ears；listen with respectful attention（polite request for sb. to speak）

【洗碱】xǐ//jiǎn 用灌水冲洗的方法除去土壤中过多的盐碱成分 irrigate a field to cleanse it of its saline-alkali content

【洗劫】xǐjié 把一个地方或一家人家的财物抢光 loot；sack：～一空（of a house, city）be plundered of all its valuables | 海盗～了一只商船。A pack of pirates raided a merchant ship and made away with all its goods.

【洗礼】xǐlǐ ❶〈基督教 *Christ.*〉接受人入教时所举行的一种宗教仪式，把水滴在受洗人的额上，或让受洗人身体浸在水里，表示洗净过去的罪恶 baptism；religious sacrament marked by splashing drops of water on the forehead of the recipient or soaking him in water to indicate atonement for his sin and admission into the community of Christians ❷〈比喻 *fig.*〉重大斗争的锻炼和考验 test of a major battle：受过战斗的～ go through the test of war

【洗练】xǐliàn（语言、文字、技艺等）简练利落（of language, writing, skill, etc.）succinct；clear：这篇小说形象生动，文字～。This short story is vivid in characterization and succinct in writing. | 剧情处理得很～。The plot in this play is well knit. also 洗炼 xǐliàn

【洗煤】xǐméi 湿法洗煤，利用各种不同成分的煤比重不同，通过水流的冲击作用，把原煤分出不同等级，并除去尘土和废石 coal washing；use water current to separate coal of different content and specific gravity, and cleanse it of dust and gangue

【洗钱】xǐqián 把非法得来的钱款，通过存入银行改变名义、性质成为合法收入，叫做洗钱 money laundering；disguise ill-earned money as legal income by depositing it in a bank

【洗三】xǐ//sān 旧俗在婴儿出生后第三天给他洗澡（old Chinese custom）give a baby a bath on the 3rd day after its birth

【洗手】xǐ//shǒu ❶〈比喻 *fig.*〉盗贼等改邪归正 wash one's hands of sth.；（of a thief, bandit, etc.）mend one's ways ❷〈比喻 *fig.*〉不再干某项职业 quit a job：～改行 quit an old job and take on a new one

【洗手间】xǐshǒujiān〈婉辞 *euph.*〉指厕所 toilet；lavatory；washroom；rest room

【洗漱】xǐshù 洗脸漱口 wash one's face and rinse one's mouth

【洗刷】xǐshuā ❶ 用水洗，用刷子蘸水刷 wash and brush；scrub ❷ 除去（耻辱、污点、错误等）wash off；clear one of（opprobrium, stigma, guilt, etc.）：～耻辱 clear oneself of opprobrium | ～冤枉 redress an injustice | ～罪名 be exonerated

【洗心革面】xǐ xīn gé miàn〈比喻 *fig.*〉彻底悔改 turn over a new leaf；thoroughly reform oneself；also 革面洗心 gé miàn xǐ xīn

【洗雪】xǐxuě 除掉（耻辱、冤屈等）wipe out（a disgrace）；redress（a wrong）

【洗衣机】xǐyījī 自动洗涤衣物的电动机械装置，是一种常用的家用电器 washing machine；common household electrical appliance for the automatic washing of clothes and linens

【洗印】xǐyìn 冲洗和印制照片或影片 develop and print photos；process

【洗澡】xǐ//zǎo 用水洗身体，除去污垢 wash and soak；have or take a bath；bathe；take a shower

【洗濯】xǐzhuó same as 洗 xǐ ①

枲 xǐ 枲麻，也泛指麻 male nettle-hemp；（in a broad sense）hemp

【枲麻】xǐmá 大麻的雄株，只开雄花，不结果实 male nettle-hemp that bears male flowers and no fruit; also 花麻 huāmá

铱 xǐ 〈书 *fml.*〉 same as 玺 xǐ

玺(壐) xǐ 帝王的印 imperial or royal seal: 玉～ imperial jade seal | 掌～大臣 seal-holding minister

缅(纚) xǐ 〈书 *fml.*〉束发帛 silk hair ribbon

☞ lí on p. 1176

铣 xǐ same as 铣削 xǐxiāo

☞ xiǎn on p. 2079

【铣床】xǐchuáng 金属切削机床,用来加工平面、曲面和各种凹槽。加工时工作台上的工件移动着跟铣刀接触,铣刀做旋转运动切削。milling machine; miller; machine tool using a revolving milling cutter to cut surfaces, curves and grooves into a metal work piece that is fixed on a worktable and moves along with the cutter

【铣工】xǐgōng ❶ 用铣床进行切削的工作 milling (work) ❷ 使用铣床工作的工人 miller; milling machine operator

【铣削】xǐxiāo 用铣床进行金属切削 work a metal piece with a milling machine

徙 xǐ ❶ 迁移 move from one place to another: 迁～ migration | ～居(搬家) move one's residence to somewhere else ❷ 〈书 *fml.*〉调动官职 (of an official) be transferred to a new post

【徙倚】xǐyǐ 〈书 *fml.*〉徘徊 pace up and down; hesitate; waver

喜 xǐ ❶ 快乐; 高兴 happy; delighted; pleased: 狂～ wild with joy | ～出望外 pleasantly surprised | 笑在脸上,～在心里 smile on one's face and rejoice in one's heart ❷ 可庆贺的; 可庆贺的事 happy event; red-letter (day): ～事 happy event | 贺～ congratulate sb. on a happy occasion | 报～ announce a piece of good news; bring good news to sb. ❸ 称怀孕为'有喜' be pregnant; have just conceived ❹ 爱好 like; have a propensity for: 好大～功 be fond of doing sth. too ambitious and unrealistic | ～新厌旧 off with the old love and on with the new; be fond of the new and tired of the old ❺ 某种生物适宜于什么环境; 某种东西适宜于配合什么东西 [referring to the environment favourable for the growth of a plant or animal, or the compatibility of sth. to sth. else]: ～光植物 photophilous plant | 海带～荤,最好跟肉一起炖。It's better to stew kelp with pork because it tastes better with meat.

【喜爱】xǐ'ài 对人或事物有好感或感兴趣 take a fancy for; be fond of; be keen to: ～游泳 be fond of swimming | 这小孩惹人～。The child is lovable.

【喜报】xǐbào 印成或写成的报喜的东西 bulletin of glad tidings: 立功～ bulletin announcing sb.'s meritorious deed | 试验成功了,快出～! The test was a success — let's hurry up and announce it in a bulletin.

【喜冲冲】xǐchōngchōng (～的 xǐchōngchōng·de)形容十分高兴的样子 look exhilarated; be in a joyful mood

【喜出望外】xǐ chū wàng wài 遇到出乎意外的喜事而特别高兴 be overjoyed (at an unexpected gain, good news, etc.); be pleasantly surprised

【喜果】xǐguǒ (～儿 xǐguǒr) ❶ 定婚和结婚时招待宾客或分送亲友的干果,如花生、枣儿等 wedding fruits; assorted nuts and dried fruits served to guests and loved ones when sb. is engaged or married ❷ 〈方 *dial.*〉same as 红蛋 hóngdàn

【喜好】xǐhào 喜欢;爱好 like; love; be fond of; be keen on: ～音乐 love music

【喜欢】xǐ·huan ❶ 对人或事物有好感或感兴趣 like; love; be fond of; be keen on: 他～文学,我～数学。He is fond of literature, while I love mathematics. ❷ 愉快;高兴 happy; elated: 喜喜欢欢过春节 have a happy Spring Festival | 快把试验成功的消息广播一下,叫大家～～。Hurry up and announce the success of the experiment on the public announcement system — everybody will be delighted by it.

【喜酒】xǐjiǔ 指结婚时招待亲友的酒或酒席 drinks offered to guests at a wedding; wedding feast: 吃～ attend a wedding banquet | 办了三桌～ throw a three-table wedding feast

【喜剧】xǐjù 戏剧的主要类别之一,用夸张手法讽刺和嘲笑丑恶、落后的现象,突出这种现象本身的矛盾和它与健康事物的冲突,往往引人发笑,结局大多是圆满的 comedy; a major genre of drama that employs hyperbole to poke fun into the ugly and the backward and dramatize their conflict with the beautiful and the healthy, and that oft. has a happy ending — to the amazement of the audience

【喜乐】xǐlè 欢喜,快乐 happiness

【喜联】xǐlián 结婚时所用的对联 wedding couplets; wedding scrolls

【喜眉笑眼】xǐ méi xiào yǎn 形容面带笑容,非常高兴 be all smiles; be smiling all over

【喜怒无常】xǐ nù wú cháng 一会儿高兴,一会儿发怒。形容人情绪变化不定。temperamental; capricious; neurotic

【喜气】xǐqì 欢喜的神色或气氛 cheerful countenance or atmosphere: 满脸～ beaming with joy | ～洋洋 jubilant; joyful

【喜气洋洋】xǐ qì yáng yáng 形容非常欢乐的样子 jubilant; joyful; full of joy

【喜钱】xǐ·qian 有喜庆的人家给人的赏钱 tips given on a happy occasion, e. g. wedding, birthday celebration, etc.

【喜庆】xǐqìng ❶ 值得喜欢和庆贺的 joyous; jubilant:～事 happy event or occasion|～的日子 red-letter day; day of jubilation; on this happy occasion ❷ 值得喜欢和庆贺的事 happy event; sth. worth celebrating

【喜鹊】xǐ·que 鸟,嘴尖,尾长,身体大部为黑色,肩和腹部白色,叫声嘈杂。民间传说听见它叫将有喜事来临,所以叫喜鹊。magpie (*Pica pica*); bird of the family *Corvidae*, having a sharp beak, a long graduated tail, and oft. black plumage that is white in the shoulders and the belly, noted for its chattering call, regarded in Chinese folklore as the harbinger of good tidings, and hence known popularly as 'happy magpie'; also 鹊 què

【喜人】xǐrén 使人喜爱 heartening; gratifying:形势～ gratifying situation|今年的小麦长势～。The wheat crop is doing splendidly.

【喜丧】xǐsāng 指高寿的人去世的丧事 funeral for sb. who lived to a venerated age

【喜色】xǐsè 欢喜的神色 happy expression; joyful look:面有～。Happiness was written on his face.

【喜事】xǐshì ❶ 值得祝贺的使人高兴的事 happy event; joyous occasion ❷ 特指结婚的事 wedding:～新办 hold one's nuptials in a new fashion

【喜糖】xǐtáng 结婚时招待亲友的糖果 wedding sweets or candy

【喜闻乐见】xǐ wén lè jiàn 喜欢听,乐意看 love to see and hear; appealing:这是一部为群众所～的文艺作品。This artistic work appeals to the populace.

【喜笑颜开】xǐ xiào yán kāi 心情愉快,满脸笑容 (of one's face) wreathed in smiles; lit up with pleasure

【喜新厌旧】xǐ xīn yàn jiù 喜欢新的,厌弃旧的(多指爱情不专一 oft. unfaithful in love) off with the old love and on with the new; be fond of the new and tired of the old

【喜形于色】xǐ xíng yú sè 抑制不住的高兴流露在脸色上 visibly pleased; beamed with happiness; (of one's face) be lit up with pleasure

【喜兴】xǐ·xing 〈方 *dial.*〉欢喜;高兴 joy; happy:～事儿 happy; joyful|今天他显得格外精神和～。The man looked exceptional today, in high spirits and a happy mood.

【喜幸】xǐxìng 〈书 *fml.*〉欢喜高兴 delighted; rejoicing

【喜讯】xǐxùn 使人高兴的消息 happy news; good news; glad tidings

【喜洋洋】xǐyángyáng 形容非常欢乐的样子 beaming with joy; radiant:新年到,过年忙,男女老少～。As New Year draws near, everybody — men and women, old and young — is beaming with joy as they are busy preparing for the Spring Festival.

【喜雨】xǐyǔ 天气干旱、庄稼需要雨水时下的雨 seasonable rain; much needed rainfall that comes during a dry spell:普降～ have a seasonable fall of rain over a wide area

【喜悦】xǐyuè 愉快;高兴 happy; joyous:～的心情 happy mood

【喜滋滋】xǐzīzī (～的 xǐzīzī·de)形容内心很欢喜 feeling greatly pleased; filled with joy:听到儿子立功的消息,她心里～的。She was immensely pleased when news came that her son had performed a meritorious deed.

【喜子】xǐ·zi same as 蟢子 xǐ·zi

葸 xǐ 〈书 *fml.*〉畏惧 dread; fear; be afraid:畏～不前 recoil in fear

蓰 xǐ 〈书 *fml.*〉五倍 fivefold:倍～(数倍) several times more than ...

屣 xǐ 〈书 *fml.*〉鞋 shoes; slippers; sandals:敝～ worn-out shoes

禧(釐) xǐ (旧读 formerly pronounced xī) 幸福;吉祥 auspiciousness; happiness; jubilation:年～Happy New Year|福～good fortune and good luck

釐 ☞ 厘 lí on p. 1175

蟢 xǐ [蟢子](xǐ·zi) 蠨蛸的通称 general term for 蠨蛸 xiāoshāo; also 喜子 xǐ·zi

鱚 xǐ 鱼,体长6寸到7寸,圆筒形,银灰色,嘴尖,眼大。生活在近海沙底。sand borer (*Sillago sihama* or *S. japonica*); fish with a silvery cylindrical body 6-7 *cun* in length, a pointed muzzle and large eyes, living in the sand bed of coastal sea; also 沙钻鱼 shāzuànyú

xì (ㄒㄧˋ)

卌 xì 四十 forty

戏(戲、戯) xì ❶ 玩耍;游戏 frolic; gambol:儿～ children's game; trifling matter|嬉～ frolic; play ❷ 开玩笑;嘲弄 joke; banter; make fun of ～弄 make fun of|～言 joke; humorous remarks; playful words ❸ 戏剧,也指杂技 drama; show; play, acrobatics:一出京～ a Beijing opera show|马～ circus|把～ gimmick|这场～演得很精彩。It was a wonderful performance.

☞ hū on p. 815

【戏班】xìbān (～儿 xìbānr)戏曲剧团的旧称 old term for 戏曲剧团 xìqǔ jùtuán; also 戏班子 xìbān·zi

【戏报子】xìbào·zi 〈旧称 *old*〉戏曲演出的招贴 show bill

【戏本】xìběn (～儿 xìběnr)戏曲剧本的旧称 old term for 戏曲剧本 xìqǔ jùběn; also 戏本子 xìběn·zi

【戏称】xìchēng ❶ 戏谑地称呼 call sb. jokingly

as ...; nickname sb. as ...:因为他说话直爽,大伙~他'炮筒子'。For his candidness he was nicknamed 'Gun Barrel'. ❷ 戏谑性的称呼 nickname:万事通是人们对他的~。Everybody nicknamed him 'Jack-of-all-trades'.

【戏出儿】xìchūr 模仿戏曲的某个场面而绘画或雕塑的人物形象,大多印成年画或制成工艺品 representation of a theatrical scene (in the form of a poster or a set of figurines)

【戏词】xìcí (~儿 xìcír)戏曲中唱词和说白的总称 (general term) actor's part

【戏单】xìdān (~儿 xìdānr)列有剧目和戏曲演员名字的单子;戏曲说明书 (theatrical) programme

【戏法】xìfǎ (~儿 xìfǎr)魔术 conjuring; jugglery; tricks; magic

【戏份儿】xìfènr 指戏曲演员每次演出按一定比例分得的报酬 bonus (for performers after a show)

【戏剧】xìjù ❶ 通过演员表演故事来反映社会生活中的各种冲突的艺术。是以表演艺术为中心的文学、音乐、舞蹈等艺术的综合。分为话剧、戏曲、歌剧、舞剧等,按作品类型又可以分为悲剧、喜剧、正剧等。drama; play; theatre; form of art acted out by actors and actresses onstage to portray conflicts in real life, regarded as a crystallization of literature, music, dance and other arts with the performing art at the core, coming in such genres as drama, opera, singing opera, dancing opera, etc. and in such categories as tragedy, comedy, and orthodox opera ❷ 指剧本 scenario; play script

【戏剧性】xìjùxìng ❶ 像戏剧情节那样曲折、突如其来或激动人心的 dramatic; spectacular; sudden and striking or exciting and impressive, like a complicated drama:局势发生了~变化。The political situation took a dramatic turn. ❷ 事情所具有的上述性质 of a dramatic nature:他们俩的悲欢离合很富有~。The joys and sorrows, and partings and reunions of the couple are nothing short of a drama.

【戏路】xìlù 指演员所能表演的角色类型 range of characterization; range of character types that an actor can portray:他~宽,正反面人物都能演。With a wide range of characterization, he plays both the hero and the villain with felicity. also 戏路子 xìlù·zi

【戏码】xìmǎ (~儿 xìmǎr)戏曲演出的剧目 (theatrical) repertoire; programme

【戏迷】xìmí 喜欢看戏或唱戏而入迷的人 theatre fan

【戏目】xìmù 剧目(theatrical) programme; repertoire

【戏弄】xìnòng 耍笑捉弄;拿人开心 make fun of; play tricks on; tease; kid

【戏曲】xìqǔ ❶ 我国传统的戏剧形式,包括昆曲、京剧和各种地方戏,以歌唱、舞蹈为主要表演手段 traditional Chinese opera predicated on singing and dancing, including the *kunqu* opera, Peking Opera and various local operas ❷ 一种文学形式,杂剧和传奇中的唱词 literary genre referring to the singing parts in *zaju* and *chuanqi* operas

【戏曲片儿】xìqǔpiānr same as 戏曲片 xìqǔpiàn

【戏曲片】xìqǔpiàn 用电影手法拍摄的戏曲演出的影片 motion-picture adaptation of a traditional or local opera

【戏耍】xìshuǎ ❶ same as 戏弄 xìnòng:~人 play tricks on sb. ❷ 玩耍 play; dillydally:终日吃喝~ squander one's time dining and wining and frolicking all day long

【戏台】xìtái 舞台 stage

【戏文】xìwén ❶ ☞南戏 nánxì on p. 1389 ❷ 戏词 actor's lines ❸ 泛指戏曲(in a broad sense) traditional opera

【戏侮】xìwǔ 戏弄侮辱 deride; chaff; insult sb. by jeering

【戏谑】xìxuè 用有趣的引人发笑的话开玩笑 banter; jest; crack jokes

【戏言】xìyán ❶ 随便说说并不当真的话 joke; joking remarks:一句~ a joking remark ❷ 开玩笑地说 jest; banter:~身后事 jest about arrangements after one's death

【戏衣】xìyī 戏曲演员演出时穿的衣服 stage costume

【戏园子】xìyuán·zi 〈旧指 *old*〉专供演出戏曲的场所 opera house; theatre

【戏院】xìyuàn 剧场 theatre

【戏照】xìzhào 穿戏装拍摄的照片 photo of a person in stage costume

【戏装】xìzhuāng 戏曲演员表演时所穿戴的衣服和靴、帽等 theatrical or stage costume, shoes and headgear included

【戏子】xì·zi 〈旧时 *old*〉称职业的戏曲演员(含轻视意 derog.) actor; actress; opera singer

饩(餼) xì 〈书 *fml.*〉❶ 谷物;饲料 cereals; fodder; feed ❷ 活的牲口;生肉 live animal; raw meat ❸ 赠送(食物) present food as a gift

系[1] (❹係 ❹—❽繫) xì ❶ 系统 system; series; line:派~ fraction | 水~ river system | 语~ language family | 世~ genealogy | 直~亲属 lineal relative ❷ 高等学校中按学科所分的教学行政单位 (of an institution of higher learning) department; faculty:哲学~ Faculty of Philosophy ❸ 年代地层单位的第三级,小于界,跟系相应的地质年代叫做纪 system; third-level division of the earth's strata, lower than erathem, with period being the corresponding geological age ❹ 联结;联系(多用于抽象的事物 mostly of sth. abstract) relate to; rely on; have to do with:维~ maintain; hold together

|名誉所～ have a bearing on one's reputation |观瞻所～ having to do with the impression a place leaves on visitors|成败～于此举。This move may make or break it. ❺ 牵挂 be concerned or anxious about:～恋 be reluctant to part from|～念 be concerned about; feel anxious about ❻ 把人或东西捆住后往上提或向下送 tie up and carry; fasten and lower down:从窖里把白薯～上来 lift crates of sweet potatoes up from a cellar ❼ 拴;绑 do up; tie; fasten:～马 tether a horse|～缚 bind up ❽ 拘禁 incarcerate; jail:～狱 be thrown into prison

系²(係) xì 〈书 *fml.*〉 same as 是³ shì:鲁迅～浙江绍兴人。Lu Xun was a native of Shaoxing, Zhejiang Province.|确～实情。This is nothing but the truth.

☞ jì on p. 918

【系词】xìcí ❶ 逻辑上指一个命题的三部分之一,连系主词和宾词来表示肯定或否定。如'雪是白的'中的'是','鲸鱼不是鱼'中的'不是'。copulative; copula; (logic) one of three parts of a proposition; (grammar) word that connects a subject and its predicate to indicate the affirmative or the negative, such as 'is' in 'Snow is white.', and 'isn't' in 'The whale isn't a fish.' ❷ 有的语法书把'是³'叫做系词 some grammar books list the word 是³ shì as a connecting word

【系缚】xìfù 〈书 *fml.*〉束缚 tie; bind up; fetter

【系恋】xìliàn 留恋;恋恋不舍 be reluctant to leave; can't bear to part (from sb. or with sth.):～家乡 find it hard to tear oneself from one's hometown

【系列】xìliè 相关联的成组成套的事物 series; set:～产品 a line of products|电视～片 TV serial

【系念】xìniàn 〈书 *fml.*〉挂念 be anxious about; worry about; feel concerned about

【系谱】xìpǔ 关于物种变化系统的记载,也指关于某动植物的世代的记载 family; genealogy; record of changes in species; record or table of the descent a certain animal or plant

【系数】xìshù ❶ 与未知数相乘的数字或文字,如 $2ax^2$ 中,$2a$ 是 x^2 的系数 coefficient; number or symbol multiplying an unknown quantity in an algebraic term, as $2a$ being the coefficient of x^2 in the $2ax^2$ ❷ 科学技术上用来表示某种性质的程度或比率的数,如膨胀系数、安全系数等 coefficient; numerical measure or rate of a certain property in science and technology, such as the coefficient of expansion and the coefficient of safety

【系统】xìtǒng ❶ 同类事物按一定的关系组成的整体 system; group of interrelated elements forming a complex whole:～化 systematize|组织～ organizational system|灌溉～ irrigation system ❷ 有条理的;有系统的 methodical; systematic:～学习 systematic study|～研究 systematic research

【系统工程】xìtǒng gōngchéng 运用先进的科学方法,进行组织管理,以求最佳效果的技术 systems engineering; technology using the most sophisticated of all methods to organize management in quest for the best possible results

【系子】xì·zi 〈方 *dial.*〉拴在器物上的绳子 string or rope tied to an object:箩筐～ rope attached to a bamboo basket|秤锤～ string for the sliding weight of a steelyard

屃(屭) xì ☞ [赑屃](bìxì) on p. 108

郄 xì 〈书 *fml.*〉 ❶ same as 隙 xì ❷ same as 郤 Xì

☞ Qiè on p. 1555

细 xì ❶ (条状物)横剖面小(跟'粗'相对,②至⑥同 ②-⑥ as opposed to 'thick') fine; thin; slender; not great in diameter or cross section:～铅丝 fine iron wire|她们纺的线又～又匀。The thread they spin is thin and smooth. ❷ (长条形)两边的距离近(of sth. long) having opposite sides close together; of little thickness; narrow; thin:画一根～线 draw a fine line|曲折的小河～得像腰带。The meandering rivulet looks as slender as a ribbon. ❸ 颗粒小 fine; in small particles:～沙 fine sand|玉米面磨得很～。The corn flour was finely ground. ❹ 音量小(of sound, voice) soft; low:嗓音～soft voice ❺ 精细 exquisite; delicate:江西～瓷 fine porcelain from Jiangxi Province|这几件象牙雕刻做得真～。These pieces of ivory carving are indeed finely chiselled. ❻ 仔细;详细;周密 meticulous; detailed:～看 peruse; see carefully|精打～算 careful calculation and strict budgeting|深耕～作 deep ploughing and careful cultivation; intensive farming|这人心很～。This is a careful man. ❼ 细微;细小 trivial; slight; petty; paltry:～节 minute detail|事无巨～ matters big and small ❽ 〈方 *dial.*〉年龄小 young; little:～妹 young girl|～娃子 little boy

【细胞】xìbāo 生物体的基本结构和功能单位,形状多种多样,主要由细胞核、细胞质、细胞膜等构成。植物的细胞膜外面还有细胞壁。细胞有运动、营养和繁殖等机能。cell; basic structural and independently functioning unit of an organism, assuming a variety of shapes, and consisting of one or more nuclei, cytoplasms and cytomembrans. The cytomembrane of a plant is surrounded by a semipermeable cell membrane. A cell has moving, nutritious, reproductive and other functions.

【细胞壁】xìbāobì 植物细胞外围的一层厚壁,包在细胞膜的外面,由纤维素构成 cell wall; membrane that consists of fibrin and surrounds the cytomembrane of a plant cell; (图

见 ☞ figure for 细胞 xìbāo)

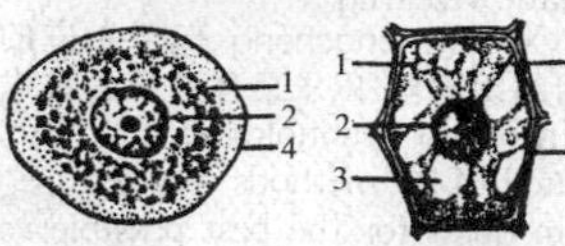

动物细胞
animal cell

植物细胞
plant cell

1.细胞质 cytoplasm　2.细胞核 nucleus
3.液泡 vacuole　4.细胞膜 cytomembrane
5.细胞壁 cell wall

细胞 Cell

【细胞核】xìbāohé 细胞的组成部分之一，在细胞的中央，多为球形或椭圆形，由核酸、核蛋白等构成 cell nucleus; situated in the centre of a cell, oft. ball- or oval-shaped, and consisting of nucleic acid and protein;（图见 ☞ figure for 细胞 xìbāo)

【细胞膜】xìbāomó 细胞的组成部分之一，是紧贴在原生质外面的一层薄膜，有控制细胞内外物质交换的作用。动植物细胞都有细胞膜。cell membrane; membrane clinging to the outer layer of bioplasm and playing a role in controlling exchange of matter within and without an animal or plant cell;（图见 ☞ figure for 细胞 xìbāo)

【细胞器】xìbāoqì 细胞质中由原生质分化而成的具有一定结构和功能的小器官，如线粒体、叶绿体、质体等 organoid; organelle; small organ differentiated from bioplasm in cytoplasm within a cell, with a certain structure of its own and performing a specific function, such as mitochondrion, chloroplast and plastid; 简称 abbr. 胞器 bāoqì

【细胞质】xìbāozhì 细胞的组成部分之一，是一种无色透明的胶状物质，在细胞核和细胞膜之间 cytoplasm; colourless and transparent jelly situated between the cell nucleus and the cell membrane as a component part of a cell;（图见 ☞ figure for 细胞 xìbāo)

【细别】xìbié ❶ 细微的差别 fine distinction; fine difference ❷ 仔细地分别 make (or draw) fine distinctions between

【细部】xìbù 制图或复制图画时用较大的比例另外画出或印出的部分，如建筑图上的卯榫，人物画上的面部 detail (of a drawing); enlarged discrete part or portion of a painting or diagram, such as the mortise and tenon of a building, and the face of a figure painting

【细布】xìbù 一种平纹棉布，质地比市布还细密 muslin; sturdy cotton fabrics of plain weave, and even more closely woven than calico (grew sheet)

【细菜】xìcài 指某个地方在某个季节供应量不多的蔬菜，如北方地区冬季的黄瓜、豆角儿、蒜苗、西红柿 fine vegetable; vegetable out of season and in short supply, such as cucumber, legume, young garlic bolt, and tomato in north China in winter

【细大不捐】xì dà bù juān 小的大的都不抛弃 reject nothing, big or small

【细点】xìdiǎn 用料、制作精细的点心 choice refreshments; dainty pastries; delicacies

【细发】xì·fa〈方 *dial.*〉细致；不粗糙 fine; smooth

【细纺】xìfǎng 把粗纱纺成细纱，是纺纱的最后一道工序 finespun, last procedure in a spinning process to turn roving into spun yarn

【细高挑儿】xìgāotiǎor〈方 *dial.*〉细长身材，也指身材细长的人 tall and slender figure; tall, slender person

【细工】xìgōng 精密细致的工作（多指手工）fine handcraft work：～活儿 fine handcraft work

【细故】xìgù 细小而值不得计较的事情 trivial matter; trifle

【细活】xìhuó（～儿 xìhuór）细致的活计，特指技术性强而消耗体力少的工作 job requiring fine workmanship or meticulous care; skilled work：慢工出～ slow work yields fine products｜他粗活～样样都能干。He is good at all work, skilled or unskilled.

【细节】xìjié 细小的环节或情节 detail; particular

【细究】xìjiū 详细推究；深究 get to the bottom of sth.：此事不必～。This matter doesn't need much probing.｜～起来，你我都负有一定责任。Both of us will be held accountable if they get to the bottom of the matter.

【细菌】xìjūn 微生物的一大类，体积微小，必须用显微镜才能看见。有球形、杆形、螺旋形、弧形、线形等多种，一般都用分裂繁殖。自然界中分布很广，对自然界物质循环起着重大作用。有的细菌对人类有利；有的细菌能使人类、牲畜等发生疾病。germ; bacterium; any fissiparous microorganism of the class *Schizomycetes*, which is so tiny as to be visible only under a microscope, round, rhabditiform, spiral, arcing and filamentous in shape, and widespread in nature, playing major roles in the material circulation in nature. Some germs are salubrious to humankind, and some are pathogenic and cause disease in humans, animals or plants.

【细菌肥料】xìjūn féiliào 人工培养的固氮菌、根瘤菌、磷细菌等制成的细菌制剂。施到土壤中，能固定空气中的氮，形成作物能吸收的物质，或把土壤中含磷、钾的物质变成作物能吸收的物质。bacterial fertilizer; synthetic bacterial preparation from azotobacter, rhizobium, phosphobacteria, applied to the soil to fixate nitrogen in air to be assimilated by far crops, or turn phosphorus- and potassium-containing matters in soil into nutrition for crops; 简称 abbr. 菌肥 jūnféi

【细菌武器】xìjūn wǔqì ☞生物武器 shēngwù wǔqì on p.1717

【细菌性痢疾】xìjūnxìng lì·ji 传染病,病原体是痢疾杆菌,症状是发烧,腹痛,里急后重,腹泻,粪便中有脓血和黏液 bacillary dysentery; contagious disease caused by shigella dysenteriae, with such symptoms as fever, stomachache, tenesmus, diarrhea and the passage of blood and mucus

【细粮】xìliáng 一般指白面和大米等食粮(区别于'粗粮' as opposed to 'coarse grain') fine grain, usu. referring to wheat flour and rice

【细毛】xìmáo 价值较高的毛皮,如水獭皮、狐皮、貂皮等 valuable fine, soft fur such as those of otter, fox and marten

【细密】xìmì ❶(质地)精细仔密 fine and closely woven; close:布织得~。The cloth is closely woven. ❷不疏忽大意;仔细 meticulous; careful:对情况进行~的分析 make a detailed analysis of the situation

【细目】xìmù 详细的项目或目录 detailed catalogue; specific item; detail

【细嫩】xìnèn (皮肤、肌肉等)柔嫩(of skin, muscle, etc.) delicate; tender:皮肤很~delicate skin

【细腻】xìnì ❶精细光滑 fine and smooth:质地~ fine texture ❷(描写、表演等)细致入微(of description, performance, etc.) exquisite; minute:感情~ delicate feelings|人物描写~而生动 detailed and graphic characterization

【细巧】xìqiǎo 精细巧妙;纤细灵巧 exquisite; dainty; delicate:石柱上雕刻着~的图案。The stone pillar is engraved with patterns in fine chisel work.

【细情】xìqíng 详细情形 details:先告诉你个大概,~等一会儿再说吧。Here's the gist of it. I'll let you in on the details later on.

【细软】xìruǎn ❶指首饰、贵重衣物等便于携带的东西 valuables; jewelry; expensive clothing and other valuables:收拾~ take stock of one's valuables|~家私 valuables and family property ❷纤细柔软 fine and soft:~的柳枝 soft willow twigs

【细润】xìrùn same as 细腻 xìnì ①:瓷质~。The porcelain is fine and glossy.

【细弱】xìruò 细小柔弱 thin and delicate; slim and fragile:声音~ feeble voice|~的柳条垂在水面上。Slim and fragile willow twigs hung low over the water.

【细纱】xìshā 粗纱再纺而成的纱,用来织布或纺线 spun yarn, for weaving cloth or twisting thread

【细水长流】xì shuǐ cháng liú ❶〈比喻 *fig.*〉节约使用财物或人力,使经常不缺 economize to avoid running short ❷〈比喻 *fig.*〉一点一滴地做某件事,总不间断 go about sth. little by little without a let-up

【细碎】xìsuì 细小零碎 in small, broken bits:~的脚步声 faint sound of shifting footsteps

【细条】xì·tiao same as 细挑 xì·tiao

【细挑】xì·tiao (身材)细长(of figure) tall and slender

【细微】xìwēi 细小;微小 slight; fine; subtle:~的变化 subtle change|~的动作 almost imperceptible movement|声音很~ slight sound

【细小】xìxiǎo 很小 very small; tiny; fine; trivial:~的雨点 tiny raindrop|~的事情 trivial matters

【细心】xìxīn 用心细密 careful; attentive:~人 careful person|~照料 take good care of

【细伢子】xìyá·zi〈方 *dial.*〉小孩儿 kid; child

【细则】xìzé 有关规章、制度、措施、办法等的详细的规则 rules and regulations:工作~ rules and regulations of work|管理~rules and regulations of management

【细账】xìzhàng 详细的账目 itemized account

【细针密缕】xì zhēn mì lǚ 针线细密,比喻工作细致 fine, close stitches; (fig.) work in a meticulous way

【细枝末节】xì zhī mò jié〈比喻 *fig.*〉事情或问题的细小而无关紧要的部分 minor details; nonessentials

【细致】xìzhì ❶精细周密 fastidious; scrupulous:工作~ fastidious work ❷细密精致 intricate; precise about details:~的花纹 intricate pattern

【细作】xìzuò〈旧指 *old*〉暗探;间谍 spy; secret agent

盻 xì〈书 *fml.*〉怒视 glare at; glower at:瞋目~之 stare at sb. angrily

郤 xì ❶ same as 隙 xì ❷(Xì)姓 a surname

绤 xì〈书 *fml.*〉粗葛布 coarse cloth

阋(鬩) xì〈书 *fml.*〉争吵;争斗 argument; affray; brawl:兄弟~于墙。The brothers brawled with each other.

舄 xì ❶〈书 *fml.*〉鞋 shoes ❷ same as 潟 xì ❸(Xì)姓 a surname

【舄卤】xìlǔ〈书 *fml.*〉same as 潟卤 xìlǔ

隙(隟) xì ❶缝隙;裂缝 crack; chink; crevice:墙~ crack in the wall|门~ crack in a door|云~ crevice between clouds ❷(地区、时间)空闲(of space and time) gap; interval:~地 open land|空~open space|农~(农闲) slack farm season ❸漏洞;机会 loophole; opportunity:无~可乘 flawless ❹(感情上的)裂痕 discord; rift; grudge:嫌~ ill will; qualms|有~ bear sb. a grudge

【隙地】xìdì 空着的地方;空隙地带 open space; unoccupied place:广场上人山人海,几无~。The square was packed with people, with little space left.|在路旁~种树 plant trees in roadside open spaces

【隙缝】xìfèng 缝隙;裂缝 crack; chink:兀鹰的

窠巢筑在悬崖峭壁的～中。Vultures build their nests in the cracks of precipices.

艴 xì〈书 *fml.*〉赤色 red

禊 xì 古代于春秋两季在水边举行的一种祭礼 waterside ritual held in spring and autumn in ancient times

隰 xì〈书 *fml.*〉same as 隙 xì

潟 xì〈书 *fml.*〉咸水浸渍的土地 salinized land

【潟湖】xìhú 浅水海湾因湾口被淤积的泥沙封闭形成的湖，高潮时可与海相通 lagoon; shallow body of water that is silted up but can be linked with the sea when the sea is surging

【潟卤】xìlǔ〈书 *fml.*〉盐碱地 saline-alkali land; also 舄卤 xìlǔ

虩 xì［虩虩］〈书 *fml.*〉形容恐惧 frightened; scared

䡾 xì〈书 *fml.*〉悲伤；痛 sorrow; pain

xiā（ㄒㄧㄚ）

呷 xiā〈方 *dial.*〉same as 喝¹ hē ①：～了一口茶 take a sip of tea

☞ gā on p. 618

虾(蝦) xiā 节肢动物，身体长，分头胸部和腹部，体外有壳质的软壳，薄而透明，腹部由多数环节构成，头部有长短触角各一对，胸部的脚第一对最大，末端的形状像钳子。生活在水中，会跳跃，捕食小虫。种类很多，如青虾、龙虾、对虾等。shrimp (*Crangon*); arthropod having an elongated body with both cephalothorax and segmented abdomen shielded in long spinelike projection of the carapace, a pair of long antennae and a pair of short feelers, with the first pair of legs being the largest and topped with pincer-like feet, living in the waters, capable of hopping and feeding in insects, in many varieties, such as freshwater shrimp, lobster and prawn

☞ há on p. 753

【虾兵蟹将】xiā bīng xiè jiàng 神话传说中龙王的兵将，比喻不中用的兵将 mythological shrimp soldiers and crab generals; (fig.) ineffective troops; hopeless soldiers

【虾米】xiā·mi ❶ 晒干的去头去壳的虾 dried, shelled shrimps ❷〈方 *dial.*〉小虾 small shrimps

【虾皮】xiāpí 晒干的或蒸熟晒干的毛虾 dried, unshelled small shrimps; also 虾米皮 xiā·mipí

【虾仁】xiārén（～儿 xiārénr）去头去壳的鲜虾 shelled fresh shrimps; shrimp meat

【虾子】xiāzǐ 虾的卵，干制后橙黄色，用做调味品 shrimp roe or egg which turns orange in colour when dried and is used as condiment

【虾子】xiā·zi〈方 *dial.*〉虾 shrimp

瞎 xiā ❶ 丧失视觉；失明 blind; sightless; unseeing; visionless：他的右眼～了。He's blind in his right eye. ❷ 没有根据地；没有来由地；没有效果地 groundlessly; futilely; to no purpose：～说 talk rubbish｜～吵 quarrel for no purposes at all｜～花钱 squander one's money｜～操心 be worried about nothing ❸ 炮弹打出去不响或爆破装置引火后不爆炸 (of a bullet, grenade, shell, or bomb) fail to detonate; be a dud：～炮 dud｜炮炮不～。Every shell went off beautifully. ❹〈方 *dial.*〉农作物种子没有发芽出土或农作物子粒不饱满 (of seeds) fail to sprout; (of farm crop) fail to bear full-grown grain ❺〈方 *dial.*〉糟蹋；损失；丢掉 waste; spoil; lose：白～了一个名额 have wasted a candidature｜一场冰雹～了多少庄稼。The hailstorm spoiled god knows how much farm crop. ❻〈方 *dial.*〉没有头绪；乱 become tangled：线绕～了。The thread has got tangled up.

【瞎掰】xiābāi〈方 *dial.*〉❶ 徒劳无益；白搭 futile; no good; no use; shoe the goose：天还没黑就让点灯，这不是～吗？Isn't it a waste to light the lamp when it hasn't turned dark? ❷ 瞎扯 talk rubbish：根本没有这事儿，你别听他～。There's nothing of the sort. Don't listen to his rubbish.

【瞎扯】xiāchě 没有中心地乱说；没有根据地乱说 gabble; prattle; whiter; waffle; talk nonsense：～一气 chatter away｜别～了，说正经的。Stop all the baloney and get down to business.

【瞎吹】xiāchuī 胡乱夸口 boast wildly; throw the bull：亩产一万斤粮食，那是～。It is sheer boast to claim a per-*mu* grain yield of 10,000 *jin*.

【瞎话】xiāhuà 不真实的话；谎话 untruth; lie：说～ tell a lie; tell a fib

【瞎火】xiāhuǒ ❶ 打不响的枪炮弹药 misfire; fail to detonate or explode：打了五发炮弹，其中有一发是～。Of the five shells, only one was a dud. ❷ 弹药失效 be a dud：子弹～了，枪没打响。The bullet was a dud. That's why the gun misfired.

【瞎奶】xiānǎi ❶ 不突起的奶头 breasts with sunken nipples ❷ 咂不出奶水的奶头 dry breasts

【瞎闹】xiānào 没有来由或没有效果地做；胡闹 act senselessly; mess about; fool around; be mischievous

【瞎炮】xiāpào 在施工爆破中，由于发生故障没有爆炸的炮 dud; ignited dynamite that fails to explode; also 哑炮 yǎpào

【瞎说】xiāshuō 没有根据地乱说 talk groundlessly or irresponsibly; talk nonsense：～一通 talk rubbish

【瞎信】xiāxìn 邮政部门指由于地址不清或写错等原因而不能投递的信件；死信 dead letter; unclaimed or undelivered letter because the address on the envelope is wrong or not clear; also 盲信 mángxìn

【瞎眼】xiā//yǎn 丧失视觉；失明 blind; lose one's eyesight ◇是我当初瞎了眼，没有看出他是个骗子。I was so blind, I did not see he was a con artist.

【瞎诌】xiāzhōu〈方 *dial.*〉说胡乱编造的话 make up wild stories; tell cock-and-bull stories

【瞎抓】xiāzhuā 没有条理地做事 do things without a plan; go about sth. in a rush

【瞎子】xiā·zi ❶ 失去视觉能力的人 blind person ❷〈方 *dial.*〉结得很不饱满的子粒 blind seed; blind ear of grain

鰕 xiā same as 虾 xiā

xiá (ㄒㄧㄚˊ)

匣 xiá (～儿 xiár) 匣子 small box or case; casket：木～ wooden box｜梳头～儿 dressing case｜两～点心 two boxes of pastry

【匣子】xiá·zi ❶ 装东西的较小的方形器具，有盖儿；盒子 small box or case with a lid; casket ❷〈方 *dial.*〉驳壳枪 Mauser pistol

【匣子枪】xiá·ziqiāng〈方 *dial.*〉驳壳枪 Mauser pistol; also 匣枪 xiáqiāng or 匣子 xiá·zi

侠(俠) xiá ❶ 侠客 knight-errant：游～ roaming swordsman｜武～ chivalrous man ❷ 侠义 chivalrous：～士 gallant｜行～仗义 perform chivalrous deeds and uphold justice

【侠肝义胆】xiá gān yì dǎn 指讲义气，有勇气，肯舍己助人的气概和行为 chivalrous deeds and fearless spirit

【侠客】xiákè〈旧时 *old*〉指有武艺、讲义气、肯舍己助人的人 person adept in martial arts and given to chivalrous conduct

【侠义】xiáyì 指讲义气，肯舍己助人的 having a high sense of justice and ready to help the down and under：～心肠 chivalrous temperament｜～行为 gallant deed

狎 xiá 亲近而态度不庄重 frivolous：～昵 be improperly familiar

【狎妓】xiájì 指玩弄妓女 see a prostitute; go whoring

【狎昵】xiánì 过分亲近而态度轻佻 be intimate in a frivolous way

柙 xiá 关野兽的笼子，旧时也用来拘禁罪重的犯人 cage for wild beasts; (old) prisoner's cage

峡(峽) xiá 两山夹水的地方(多用于地名 usu. as part of a place name) gorge; *xia*：三门～(在河南) Sanmenxia in Henan Province｜青铜～(在宁夏)Qingtongxia in Ningxia Hui Autonomous Region｜长江三～ Three Gorges of the Yangtze River

【峡谷】xiágǔ 河流经过的深而狭窄的山谷，两旁有峭壁 gorge; canyon; narrow chasm with steep cliff walls, cut into the earth by running water

狭(狹) xiá 窄(跟'广'相对 as opposed to 'broad') narrow：～小 cramped｜～路相逢 (of enemies) meet face to face on a narrow path — imminent confrontation

【狭隘】xiá'ài ❶ 宽度小 narrow：～的山道 narrow mountain path ❷ (心胸、气量、见识等)局限在一个小范围里；不宽广；不宏大 (of mind; tolerance, knowledge) narrow; limited：见闻～ narrow knowledge｜心胸～ parochial｜～的生活经验 narrow life experience

【狭长】xiácháng 窄而长 long and narrow：～的山谷 long and narrow valley

【狭路相逢】xiá lù xiāng féng 在很窄的路上遇见了，不容易让开。多指仇人相遇，难以相容。(of adversaries) meet face to face on a narrow path — in an unavoidable confrontation

【狭小】xiáxiǎo 狭窄 cramped：房屋～ narrow and small house｜气量～ narrow-minded

【狭义】xiáyì 范围比较狭窄的定义(跟'广义'相对 as opposed to 'broad sense') narrow sense：～的文艺单指文学，广义的文艺兼指美术、音乐等。The Chinese term *wenyi* denotes literature in the narrow sense of the term, and entails fine arts, music, etc. in a broad sense.

【狭窄】xiázhǎi ❶ 宽度小 contracted; cramped; narrow：～的走廊 narrow corridor｜～的小胡同 narrow alley ❷ (心胸、见识等)不宏大宽广 (of mind, knowledge, etc.) narrow; limited：心地～ intolerant; narrow-minded

祫 xiá〈古时 *arch.*〉在太庙中合祭祖先 ceremony to pay homage to ancestors in the imperial Ancestral Temple

陿(陜) xiá〈书 *fml.*〉❶ same as 狭 xiá ❷ same as 峡 xiá

硖(硤) xiá 硖石(Xiáshí)，地名，在浙江 Xiashi, name of a place in Zhejiang Province

遐 xiá〈书 *fml.*〉❶ 远 distant; far：～迩 far and wide ❷ 长久 lasting; long：～龄 venerated age

【遐迩】xiá'ěr〈书 *fml.*〉远近 far and wide：～闻名(形容名声大) be widely known; enjoy widespread renown

【遐龄】xiálíng 指人长寿；高龄 advanced age; venerated age

【遐思】xiásī same as 遐想 xiáxiǎng

【遐想】xiáxiǎng 悠远地思索或想像 in a reverie; daydreaming：～联翩 give wings to imagination｜闭目～ close one's eyes and get lost in a reverie

瑕 xiá 玉上面的斑点，比喻缺点 flaw in a piece of jade; (fig.) shortcoming; weakness：～疵 flaw; defect｜白璧微～ tiny flaw in a piece of white jade; flaw in sth. otherwise perfect|纯洁无～ pure and flawless

【瑕不掩瑜】xiá bù yǎn yú〈比喻 *fig.*〉缺点掩盖不了优点,优点是主要的,缺点是次要的 one flaw cannot mar the jade — small defects cannot obscure great virtues

【瑕疵】xiácī 微小的缺点 flaw; blemish

【瑕玷】xiádiàn〈书 *fml.*〉污点;毛病 stain; defect

【瑕瑜互见】xiá yú hù jiàn〈比喻 *fig.*〉有缺点也有优点 have defects as well as merits; have both strong and weak points

暇 xiá 没有事的时候;空闲 free time; leisure:无～兼顾 too busy to attend to something else|自顾不～ having one's hands full dealing with something

辖(❶鎋、舝) xiá ❶ 大车轴头上穿着的小铁棍,可以管住轮子使不脱落 linchpin; locking pin inserted in the end of a shaft, as in an axle, to prevent wheel from slipping off; (图见 ☞ figure for 轮子 lún•zi on p.1275) ❷ 管辖;管理 administer; govern; have jurisdiction over:直～ municipality directly under the State Council|统～ under unified command|省～市 municipality under the jurisdiction of a provincial government

【辖区】xiáqū 所管辖的地区 area under one's jurisdiction

【辖制】xiázhì 管束 control:受人～under sb.'s command or control

霞 xiá 日光斜射在天空中,由于空气的散射作用而使天空和云层呈现黄、橙、红等彩色的自然现象,多出现在日出或日落的时候。通常指这样出现的彩色的云。morning or evening glow; rosy clouds; natural phenomenon oft. occurring during sunrise or sunset, in which the sky and clouds assume yellow, orange, red and other colours as a result of air's scattering role

【霞光】xiáguāng 阳光穿透云雾射出的彩色光芒 rays of morning or evening sunlight:～万道 a myriad of sun rays

【霞帔】xiápèi 我国古时贵族妇女礼服的一部分,类似披肩 embroidered tasselled cape worn as part of ceremonial dress by noblewomen in former times

黠 xiá〈书 *fml.*〉聪明而狡猾 crafty; cunning:狡～sly|～慧 intelligent and crafty; artful

【黠慧】xiáhuì〈书 *fml.*〉狡猾聪慧 artful; smart and cunning

xià(ㄒㄧㄚˋ)

下[1] xià ❶ 位置在低处的 down:～游 lower reaches|～部 lower part|山～ at the foot of a mountain|往～看 look down ❷ 等次或品级低的 low in grade or class:～等 lower grade|～级 subordinate|～策 bad move|～品 inferior ❸ 次序或时间在后的 next; latter; late:～次 next time|～半年 latter half of the year|～不为例 not be taken as a precedent; must not happen again ❹ 向下面 downward:～达 sand down an order or announcement|～行 (of train) down; away from the capital city of Beijing ❺ 表示属于一定范围、情况、条件等 under (certain circumstances); within (a certain scope):名～ under one's name|部～ under one's command|在党的领导～ under Party leadership|在这种情况～ under these circumstances; in this situation ❻ 表示当某个时间或时节 time; time of the year:时～ at present; for the time being|节～ during a holiday or festival|年～ during the Spring Festival ❼用在数目字后面,表示方面或方位 [used after a numeral to indicate direction or position]:两～都同意。The two sides reached agreement.|往四～一看 look about oneself

下[2] xià ❶ 由高处到低处 descend; alight:～山 go downhill|～楼 go downstairs|顺流而～ sail downstream; go down the river ❷ (雨、雪等)降落 (of rain or snow) fall:～雨 raining|～雪 snowing|～霜 frosting ❸ 发布;投递 issue; deliver; send:～命令 issue an order|～通知 serve notice|～战书 deliver a letter of challenge ❹ 去;到(处所)go to:～乡 go to the countryside|～车间 go down to work in a workshop|～馆子 dine out; eat out ❺ 退场 exit; leave:八一队的五号～,三号上。No. 5 of August 1st Team was replaced by No. 3.|这一场戏你应该从右边的旁门～。During this performance you'd better go offstage from the door on the right side. ❻ 放入 put in; cast:～种 sowing|～面条 put noodles in boiled water; cook noodles|～本钱 invest|～网捞鱼 cast a fishing net ❼ 进行(棋类游艺或比赛)play (chess games):～围棋 play *weiqi*|咱们～两盘象棋吧! Let's play some games of Chinese chess. ❽ 卸除;取下 unload; take away:～装 remove one's stage makeup and costume|把敌人的枪～了 disarm one's enemy|把窗户～下来。Take down the window. ❾ 做出(言论、判断等)make (remarks); draw (a conclusion):～结论 reach a conclusion|～批语 write comments on a document or homework|～定义 give sth. a definition ❿ 使用;开始使用 use; apply:～力气 exert oneself|～工夫 make an effort|～刀 begin cutting meat|～笔 begin writing|对症～药 suit the medicine to the illness ⓫ (动物)生产 (of animals) give birth to; lay:母猪～小猪 (a pig) give birth to a litter of piglets|鸡～蛋 (of a hen) lay eggs ⑫ 攻陷 capture; take:连～数城 seize several cities at one sweep ⑬ 退让 give in; yield:相持不～ neither side would budge an inch ⑭ 到规定时间结束日常工作或学习等 finish work or study:～班 come off work; be off duty|～课 finish class; dismiss a class ⑮ 低于;少于 less than; lower than:参加大会的不～三千人。At least 3,000 people attended the meeting.

下[3] xià ❶ (～儿 xiàr)〈量词 *classifier*〉a)用于动作的次数[indicating repetition of action]:钟打了三～。The bell was tolled three times.|摇了几～旗子 wave one's flag several times b)〈方 *dial.*〉用于器物的容量[indicating capacity of a container]:瓶子里装着半～墨水。The bottle was half-filled with ink.|这么大的碗,他足足吃了三～。He ate three bowlfuls with this large bowl. ❷ (～儿 xiàr)用在'两、几'后面,表示本领、技能[used after 两 liǎng or 几 jǐ to indicate one's ability or skill]:他真有两～。He really knows a thing or two.|就这么几～,你还要逞能? That's all you can do, want to show off? ‖ also 下子 xià·zi

下 //·xià 用在动词后[when preceded by a verb] ❶ 表示由高处到低处[indicating downward motion] down:坐～ sit down|躺～ lie down|传～一道命令 send down an instruction ❷ 表示有空间,能容纳 indicating room or space:坐得～ have enough seats|这个剧场能容～上千人。This theatre is large enough to seat 1,000 people.|这间屋子太小,睡不～六个人。This room is too small for six people. ❸ 表示动作的完成或结果[indicating completion or result of an action]:打～基础 lay a foundation|定～计策 work out a strategy|准备～材料 put materials together

【下巴】xià·ba ❶ 下颌的通称 general term for 下颌 xiàhé ❷ 颏的通称 general term for 颏 kē

【下巴颏儿】xià·bakēr 颏的通称 general term for 颏 kē

【下摆】xiàbǎi 长袍、上衣、衬衫等的最下面的部分 lower hem of a gown, jacket or shirt

【下班】xià//bān (～儿 xià//bānr)每天规定的工作时间结束 knock off; get off work:每天下午六点～ knock off at 6 p.m. every day

【下板儿】xià//bǎnr〈方 *dial.*〉商店摘下门板、窗板,开始营业,叫做下板儿 take down the shutters — start the business of the day

【下半场】xiàbànchǎng 下半时 second half (of a game, concert, etc.)

【下半旗】xià bànqí 先将国旗升至杆顶,再降至离杆顶约占全杆三分之一的地方,是表示哀悼的礼节 fly a flag at half-mast, a ritual to mourn over sb.'s death; first hoist the national flag to the top of the mast, and then lower it at one third the length of the mast; also 降半旗 jiàng bànqí

【下半晌】xiàbànshǎng same as 下午 xiàwǔ

【下半时】xiàbànshí 足球、篮球等球类比赛,全场比赛分作两段时间进行,后一段时间叫下半时(of a soccer, basketball or other ball game) second half; also 下半场 xiàbànchǎng

【下半天】xiàbàntiān (～儿 xiàbàntiānr) same as 下午 xiàwǔ

【下半夜】xiàbànyè 后半夜 after midnight; latter half of the night

【下辈】xiàbèi (～儿 xiàbèir) ❶ 指子孙 children and grandchildren; offspring ❷ 家族中的下一代 younger generation of a family

【下辈子】xià bèi·zi 来世 next life

【下本儿】xià//běnr 放进本钱 invest; put in time, money and effort ◇要多打粮食就要舍得～,勤灌溉,多上肥料,加强田间管理。Don't begrudge your effort if you want to produce more grain — you've got to irrigate it often, apply more fertilizers, and tighten up farmland management.

【下笔】xià//bǐ 用笔写或画,特指开始写或画 put pen to paper; begin to write or paint:～千言 finish writing a thousand words at one go|想好了再～。Think it over before you begin writing.

【下边】xià·bian (～儿 xià·bianr) same as 下面 xià·mian

【下不来】xià·bu lái 指在人前受窘 feel embarrassed or awkward:几句话说得他脸上～。He blushed in embarrassment at the remarks.

【下不为例】xià bù wéi lì 下次不能援例,表示只通融这一次 not to be taken as a precedent; not to be repeated; just this once

【下操】xià//cāo ❶ 指出操 have drills:我们上午～,下午上课。We have drills in the morning and classes in the afternoon. ❷ 指收操 finish drilling:他刚～回来,跑得满头大汗。Beads of perspiration streamed down his face as he had just returned from the drilling ground.

【下策】xiàcè 不高明的计策或办法 bad plan or decision; worst thing to do; stupid move

【下层】xiàcéng 下面的一层或几层(多指机构、组织、阶层)(of organization; social ladder, etc.) lower levels:深入～ go down to the grass-roots level|～社会 lower rung of the social ladder

【下场】xià//chǎng ❶ 演员或运动员退场 (of performer) go off stage; (of athlete) exit the court or field ❷〈旧时 *old*〉指到考场应考 sit in an examination; take a test

【下场】xià·chǎng 人的结局(多指不好的)(oft. in the negative) end; fade; ending:没有好～ come to no good end|可耻的～ ignominious end

【下场门】xiàchǎngmén 指舞台左首(就观众说是右首)的出入口,因为角色大多从这儿下场 exit of a stage; exit and entrance at the left side of a stage (or the right side from the perspective of the audience)

【下车伊始】xià chē yī shǐ 指官吏初到任所 moment one alights from the official carriage; moment one takes up a post; immediately on arrival at a new post

【下乘】xiàchéng 本佛教用语,就是'小乘'。一般借指文学艺术的平庸境界或下品 Hinayana Buddhism; low order; inferior quality; mediocrity:~之作 inferior work; work of low order

【下处】xià·chu 出门人暂时住宿的地方 temporary lodging:找个~住下 find a place to stay for the night

【下船】xià//chuán ❶ 从船上到岸上;上岸 go ashore; disembark ❷〈方 *dial.*〉从岸上到船上;登船 get down into a junk; board; go aboard

【下存】xiàcún 支取一部分之后还存(若干数目)(of a sum) remain after deduction:这笔存款提了二百元,~八百元。200 yuan has been withdrawn, with 800 yuan left on the account.

【下达】xiàdá 向下级发布或传达(命令、指示等)make (an order, instruction, etc.) known (or transmit) to subordinates:~通知 issue a notice

【下蛋】xià//dàn (鸟类或爬行动物)产卵(of a bird or reptile) lay eggs:母鸡~。Hens lay eggs.

【下等】xiàděng 等级低的;质量低的 low grade; inferior:~货 low-grade goods

【下地】xià//dì ❶ 到地里去(干活) go to the fields:~劳动 work in the fields|~割麦 go cutting wheat in the field ❷ 从床铺上下来(多指病人 oft. of a patient) be up and about once again:他病了几个月,现在才能~。Having been ill for months, he was able to get up and move about a bit just now. ❸〈方 *dial.*〉指婴儿刚生下来 (of a newborn baby) be just delivered

【下第】xiàdì ❶〈书 *fml.*〉下等;劣等 inferior; low in quality or grade ❷ 科举时代指考试没有考中;落第 fail at imperial examinations

【下店】xià//diàn 到客店住宿 put up at an inn

【下跌】xiàdiē (水位、价格等)下降 (of water level, price, etc.) fall; drop; plunge

【下定】xià//dìng ❶〈旧时 *old*〉定婚时男方给女方聘礼 (of a bridegroom-to-be's family) give gift (to the family of the bride) ❷ 购买或租赁时预付定金 down payment (for buying or renting sth.)

【下碇】xià//dìng 把系船的石墩放到岸上或水底,使船停住。借指停船抛锚。move a stone block attached to a rope or chain on shore or drop it to the bottom of a river or sea to moor a ship; anchor; cast anchor

【下颚】xià'è ❶ 某些节肢动物的第二对(有的是第三对)摄取食物的器官,生在口两旁的下方,极小,上面长着许多短毛 (of certain arthropods) maxilla, organ for taking food into the mouth; either of the 2nd or 3rd pair of laterally moving appendages, covered with short hair and situated behind the mandibles in certain arthropods ❷ 脊椎动物的下颌 (of vertebrates) lower jaw or mandible

【下凡】xià//fán 神话中指神仙来到人世间 (of gods or immortals) descend to the world:天仙~ angel descending to the mundane world

【下饭】xià//fàn ❶ 就着菜把主食吃下去 (of dishes) go with rice ❷ 适宜于和饭一起吃 go well with the rice:这个菜下酒不~。This dish goes well with wine but does not go well with rice.

【下饭】xiàfàn 〈方 *dial.*〉指菜肴 dishes; non-staple food

【下房】xiàfáng (~儿 xiàfángr)仆人住的屋子 servant quarters; servant's room

【下放】xiàfàng ❶ 把某些权力交给下层机构(of power) be decentralized; delegate power to lower level:把经营管理权~给企业 delegate management power to enterprises ❷ 把干部调到下层机构去工作或送到农村、工厂、矿山去锻炼 send a government functionary to work at the grass-roots level, or in a rural area, factory or mine:干部~劳动 government functionary working in a factory or village

【下风】xiàfēng ❶ 风所吹向的那一方 leeward:工业区设在城市的~,就不至于污染城市的空气。Urban air pollution can be avoided by building industrial districts to the leeward of the cities. ❷〈比喻 *fig.*〉作战或比赛的一方所处的不利地位 (in war or competition) be at a disadvantage:处在~ be at a disadvantage

【下疳】xiàgān 性病,分硬性和软性两种。硬性下疳是梅毒初期,生殖器、舌、唇等形成溃疡,病灶的底部坚硬而不痛。软性下疳由软性下疳杆菌引起,生殖器外部形成溃疡,病灶的周围组织柔软而疼痛。hard or soft chancre; hard chancre — hard and insensitive lesion in the genitals, tongue, lips, etc. that is the first manifestation of syphilis; soft chancre — ulcer caused by hacmophilus ducereyi in the exterior of the genitals, with the surrounding tissues feeling soft and painful

【下岗】xià//gǎng 离开执行守卫、警戒等任务的岗位 come or go off sentry duty; be laid off:夜深了,交通警仍未~。It was late at night, yet the traffic policemen were still at their posts.◇做好~职工的安排工作。Do a good job in reallocating factory layoffs.

【下工】xià//gōng ❶ 到了规定时间停止日常劳动 come or go off work; stop work; knock off ❷〈旧时 *old*〉指解雇 fire; dismiss

【下工夫】xià gōng·fu 为了达到某个目的而花费很多的时间和很大的精力 work hard; work

with dedication; put in time and energy:要想把技术学好,就得～。You've got to work hard if you want to learn the skill well.|下过一番工夫。We've put in our time and energy in it.

【下海】xià//hǎi ❶ 到海中去 go to sea ❷(渔民)到海上(捕鱼)(of fisherman) go fishing on the sea:初次～,头晕呕吐是难免的。You can't help feeling seasick on your first trip at sea. ❸ 指业余戏曲演员成为职业演员(of amateurs in traditional opera) turn professional ❹〈旧指 *old*〉从事某些行业(如娼妓、舞女等) engage in certain trade (such as becoming a prostitute or dancer, sing-song girl, etc.) ❺ 泛指放弃原来的工作而经营商业 relinquish one's old job and go in for business; become a business person

【下颌】xiàhé 口腔的下部 lower jaw; also 下颚 xià'è; 通称 popularly known as 下巴 xià·ba; ☞ 颌 gé on p. 654

【下怀】xiàhuái 指自己的心意(原是谦辞 orig. hum.) one's heart; one's desire:正中～be just what one wants; to one's liking

【下级】xiàjí 同一组织系统中等级低的组织或人员 subordinate; lower level:～组织 lower-level organization|～服从上级。The lower level is subordinate to the higher level.

【下家】xiàjiā ❶(～儿 xiàjiār)(打牌或行酒令等)下一个轮到的人(in mahjong, card games, or in wine games) player whose turn comes next; ☞上家 shàngjiā on p. 1682 ❷〈方 *dial.*〉〈谦称 *hum.*〉自己的家 my humble family

【下贱】xiàjiàn ❶〈旧时 *old*〉指出身或社会地位低下;低贱 of humble origin; low in social status ❷ 卑劣下流(骂人的话 curse) abject; low; mean; degrading

【下江】Xiàjiāng ❶ 长江下游地区 lower reaches of the Yangtze River:～人 native of one of the provinces in the lower reaches of the Yangtze River|～官话 mandarin with a strong accent of the provinces in the lower reaches of the Yangtze River ❷ 清代指江苏 referring to Jiangsu Province in the Qing Dynasty

☞ 上江 Shàngjiāng on p. 1682

【下降】xiàjiàng 从高到低;从多到少 descend; go or come down; drop; fall; decline:地壳～ sinking of earth's crust|飞机～ descend of an aircraft|气温～ drop in the temperature|成本～ drop in production costs

【下焦】xiàjiāo〈中医 *Chin. med.*〉指胃的下口到盆腔的部分,包括肾、小肠、大肠、膀胱等脏器,主要功能是吸收和大小便 body cavity below the umbilicus, housing kidneys, bowels and bladder, whose major functions are absorption of nutrition and relieving the bowels

【下脚】xià//jiǎo (～儿 xià//jiǎor)走动时把脚踩下去 get a foothold; set one's foot in:屋子里到处是水,实在没处～。The floor was covered with water everywhere in the house, leaving nowhere to plant people's foot.

【下脚】xiàjiǎo 原材料加工、利用后剩下的碎料(of raw material) leftover bits and pieces; also 下脚料 xiàjiǎoliào

【下脚货】xiàjiǎohuò〈方 *dial.*〉卖剩下的不好的货物 unsalable leftover goods of inferior quality

【下界】xià//jiè same as 下凡 xià//fán

【下界】xiàjiè 迷信的人称天上神仙居住的地方为上界,相对把人间叫做下界(as opposed to 'immortal world') mortal world; world of man

【下劲】xià//jìn 下功夫;使劲 exert oneself; go all out:～学 be hardworking in one's studies|～干 work hard

【下九流】xiàjiǔliú〈旧时 *old*〉指社会地位低下、从事各种所谓下等职业的人,如艺人、脚夫、吹鼓手等 member of the lower walks of life; people of 'lowerly' occupations, such as performers, porters, and trumpeters

【下酒】xià//jiǔ ❶ 就着菜把酒喝下去 go with wine ❷ 适宜于和酒一起吃 go well with wine:这个菜下饭不～。This dish goes well with rice but doesn't go well with wine.

【下课】xià//kè 上课时间结束 finish class; class is dismissed or over

【下款】xiàkuǎn (～儿 xiàkuǎnr)送人的字画、给人的信件等上面所写的自己的名字 name of the donor (as inscribed on a painting or a calligraphic scroll presented as a gift); signature at the end of a letter

【下来】xià//·lái ❶ 由高处到低处来 come downward or down:他从山坡上～了。He was coming downhill. ◇昨天省里～两位干部。Two officials came down from the province yesterday. ❷ 指谷物、水果、蔬菜等成熟或收获(of grain, fruit, vegetable, etc.) be ripe or ready for harvest:再有半个月桃就～了。The peaches will be ripe in a fortnight.

【下来】//·xià//·lái ❶ 用在动词后,表示由高处向低处或由远处向近处来[used behind a verb to indicate motion toward a lower or nearer position] down (here):把树上的苹果摘～。Pick all the apples off the trees.|河水从上游流～。Water flows down the river.|又派下新任务来了。New tasks have been assigned. ❷ 用在动词后,表示从过去继续到现在或从开始继续到最后[used behind a verb to indicate continuation from past to present, or from beginning to end]:古代流传～的神话 mythology passed down from antiquity|所有参加业余培训的人都坚持～了。All those attending the part-time training persisted to the end. ❸ 用在动词后,表示动作的完成或结果[used after a verb to indicate the end or re-

X

sult of an action]：把情况记录～。Make a record of what happened.｜车渐渐停了～。The car stopped gradually.｜起下几个钉子来。Several nails have been removed. ❹ 用在形容词后，表示程度继续增加 [follow an adjective to indicate increase in degree]：天色渐渐黑～。Dusk was thickening.

【下里巴人】xiàlǐ bārén 战国时代楚国的民间歌曲（下里即乡里，巴人指巴蜀的人民，表明做歌曲的人和地方），后来泛指通俗的普及的文学艺术，常跟'阳春白雪'对举 popular literature and art; 'Songs of the Rustic Poor', title of a folk song of the state of Chu during the Warring States Period (下里 *xiali*: rural area; 巴人 *baren*: people of the ancient states of Ba and Shu); general term oft. set in contrast with 'The Spring Snow' (highbrow literature and art)

【下里】xià·li 用在数目字后面，表示方面或方位 [used after a numeral to indicate direction or position]：把敌人四～包围起来。Surround the enemy troops on all sides.

【下联】xiàlián (～儿 xiàliánr) 对联的下一半 second or latter line of a couplet

【下列】xiàliè 下面所开列的 listed below; following：预防传染病，应注意～几点。In preventing contagious diseases, attention should be paid to the following points.

【下令】xià//lìng 下达命令；发布命令 send down an order; issue an order; order：～出击 give orders to launch an attack｜～解散 issue an order to disband an organization

【下流】xiàliú ❶ same as 下游 xiàyóu：长江～ lower reaches of the Yangtze River｜黄河～ Yellow River lower reaches ❷〈旧时 *old*〉〈比喻 *fig.*〉卑下的地位 low or inferior position ❸ 卑鄙龌龊 mean-spirited; obscene; dirty：～话 obscenities; dirty words; guy talk｜～无耻 low and shameless

【下落】xiàluò ❶ 寻找中的人或物所在的地方 whereabouts：～不明 dubious whereabouts ❷ 下降 drop; descend：伞兵缓缓～。The paratroopers dropped gradually from the sky.

【下马】xià//mǎ〈比喻 *fig.*〉停止或放弃某项重大的工作、工程、计划等 dismount from a horse; (of a major project, plan, etc.) be discontinued; be given up：由于资金不足，一批建设项目将要～。A number of construction projects will be abandoned due to financial shortages.

【下马看花】xià mǎ kàn huā〈比喻 *fig.*〉较长时间地深入实际，进行调查研究 get off one's horse to look at the flowers — go deep into the realities of life and make thorough investigations

【下马威】xiàmǎwēi 原来指官吏初到任时对下属显示的威风，后泛指一开头就向对方显示的威力 severity shown by an official on assuming office; show of strength at first contact; deal sb. a head-on blow at the first encounter

【下面】xià·mian (～儿 xià·mianr) ❶ 位置较低的地方 below; under; underneath：轮船从南京长江大桥～顺流而下。The steamboat sailed downstream from underneath the Yangtze River Bridge at Nanjing.｜在山顶远望，～是一片金黄的麦田。Looking into the distance from the top of the mountain, one sees a vast track of golden wheat fields. ❷ 次序靠后的部分；文章或讲话中后于现在所叙述的部分 (of part of an article or speech) next in order; following; immediately afterwards：请看～陈列的纺织品。Now take a look at the textiles on display.｜～谈的是农业技术革新的问题。In the following let's talk about issues concerning technical renovation in agriculture. ❸ 指下级 lower level; subordinate：这个指示要及时向～传达。This instruction should be relayed to the lower levels in time.

【下奶】xià//nǎi 催奶 stimulate or increase the secretion of milk (of nursing mothers)

【下品】xiàpǐn 质量最差或等级最低的 of the lowest quality or grade

【下聘】xià//pìn 下聘礼；下定 (of a bridegroom-to-be's family) send betrothal gifts and money over to the bride-to-be

【下坡路】xiàpōlù ❶ 由高处通向低处的道路 downhill path; downhill journey ❷〈比喻 *fig.*〉向衰落或灭亡的方向发展的道路 on the decline; going downhill

【下欠】xiàqiàn ❶ 归还一部分之后还欠（若干数目）still owe (after repaying part of one's debt)：我借老王二十元，还了八元，～十二元。I borrowed 20 yuan from Lao Wang, repaid 8 yuan, and still owed 12 yuan. ❷ 下欠的款项 sum still owing or outstanding：全数还清，并无～。The debt has been paid up. Nothing outstanding.

【下情】xiàqíng ❶ 下级或群众的情况或心意 conditions at the lower levels; feelings or wishes of the people or subordinates：～上达 make the situation below known to those above｜了解～ know how things stand at the lower level ❷〈谦辞 *hum.*〉〈旧时 *old*〉对人所陈述时称自己的情况或心情 my situation, feelings and wishes

【下去】xià//·qù 由高处到低处去 go down; descend：从斜井～一百米，就到工作面。Go 100 metres down the inclined shaft, and you'll reach the working face. ◇领导干部每月要～几天。Every leading official should go down to the grass-roots units for a few days on a monthly basis.

【下去】//·xià//·qù ❶ 用在动词后，表示由高处向低处或由近处向远处去 [used after a verb to indicate motion towards a lower or farther position] down there：石头从山上滚～。

Rocks came rolling down the mountain. ◇把敌人的火力压～。Let's hold down the enemy's firepower. ❷ 用在动词后，表示从现在继续到将来［used after a verb to indicate continuation from present to future］go on; continue：坚持～ stick it out | 说不～ one's tongue failed one ❸ 用在形容词后，表示程度继续增加［used after an adjective to indicate increase in degree］grow; develop：天气可能再冷～，务必做好防冻保暖工作。It will get even colder, and a good job should be done without fail to prevent frostbite and keep warm.

【下人】xiàrén ❶〈旧时 *old*〉指仆人 servant; maid; also 底下人 dǐxiàrén ❷〈方 *dial.*〉指儿女或儿孙等晚辈 children or grandchildren

【下三烂】xiàsānlàn〈方 *dial.*〉❶ same as 下贱 xiàjiàn ❷ 指下贱、没出息的人 despicable person; ne'er-do-well ‖ also 下三滥 xiàsānlàn

【下身】xiàshēn ❶ 身体的下半部。有时专指阴部。lower part of the body; private parts; genitals ❷（～儿 xiàshēnr）指裤子 trousers; pants

【下神】xià//shén 巫婆等装神弄鬼，假称神仙附在自己身上，叫做下神（of a witch, sorceress, etc.）act as if possessed by a god or spirit

【下生】xiàshēng 出生；出世 be born

【下剩】xiàshèng 剩余 be left; remainder：留五个人打场，～的人到地里送肥料。Keep five people on the threshing job, and let the others transport manure to the fields.

【下士】xiàshì 军衔，军士的最低一级（U. S. & Brit. Army, Brit. Air Force, U. S. & Brit. Marine Corps）corporal;（U.S. Navy）petty officer third class;（Brit. Navy）petty officer second class

【下市】xià//shì ❶（季节性的货物）已过产销旺季（of seasonal products）off season：立秋后西瓜～。Watermelons go off season when autumn sets in. ❷ 结束一天的商业活动 close shop：太阳老高就～了。The shop closed way before sunset.

【下世】xià//shì 去世 leave this world — die; pass away

【下世】xiàshì 来世；来生 next life; next incarnation

【下手】xià//shǒu 动手；着手 put one's hand to; start doing sth.; set about; set to：先～为强 he who strikes first wins | 无从～ don't know where to get started | 我们还没到，人家就下了手了。We had hardly arrived when they already plunged into action.

【下手】[1] xiàshǒu（～儿 xiàshǒur）❶ 位置较卑的一侧，就室内说，一般指靠外的或靠右的（左右以人在室内而脸朝外时为准）right-hand side; seat of lower priority, oft. one close to the outside or the right side (with one's face facing outdoors); also 下首 xiàshǒu ❷ same as 下家 xiàjiā

【下手】[2] xiàshǒu（～儿 xiàshǒur）助手 assistant; aide：打～（担任助手）act as an assistant

【下首】xiàshǒu same as 下手[1] xiàshǒu ①

【下属】xiàshǔ same as 下级 xiàjí

【下水】xià//shuǐ ❶ 进入水中 enter the water; (of boat, ship, etc.) be launched：新船～典礼 launching ceremony of a new ship ❷ 把某些纺织品、纤维等浸在水中使收缩 put textiles, fabrics, etc. into water and let them shrink ❸〈比喻 *fig.*〉做坏事 fall into evil ways; take to evildoing：拖人～ involve sb. in evildoing; drag sb. into the mire

【下水】xiàshuǐ 向下游航行的 downstream; downriver：～船 downriver boat

【下水】xià·shui 食用的牲畜内脏，有些地区专指肚子（dǔ·zi）和肠子 tripe or chitterlings to be used as food, in some regions referring only to tripe：猪～ pig's tripe and chitterlings

【下水道】xiàshuǐdào 排除雨水和污水的管道 sewer; underground conduit for carrying off rain and waste water

【下榻】xiàtà（客人）住宿 stay (at a place during a trip)：～国际饭店。(He) stays at the International Hotel.

【下台】xià//tái ❶ 从舞台或讲台上下来 step down from the stage or platform ❷ 指卸去公职或交出政权 fall out of power; leave office ❸〈比喻 *fig.*〉摆脱困难窘迫的处境（多用于否定式 oft. in the negative）get out of a predicament：他这句话使我下不了台。This one remark of his put me on the spot.

【下体】xiàtǐ〈书 *fml.*〉same as 下身 xiàshēn ①

【下调】xiàtiáo（价格、利率）向下调整 reduce; lower; cut (price, interest rate, etc.)

【下同】xiàtóng 底下所说的跟这里所说的相同（多用于附注 oft. used in footnotes）similarly hereinafter; same as below

【下头】xià·tou ❶ 位置较低的地方 below; lower level：山～有个村庄。There is a village at the foot of the mountain. ❷ 指下级 subordinate：领导要耐心听取～的意见。Leaders should be patient in canvassing their subordinates' opinions.

【下晚儿】xiàwǎnr〈方 *dial.*〉近黄昏的时候 near dusk; towards evening

【下文】xiàwén ❶ 书中或文章中某一段或某一句以后的部分 what follows in the passage, paragraph, article, etc. ❷〈比喻 *fig.*〉事情的发展或结果 development; outcome; sequel：我托你的事已经好几天了，怎么还没有～？It's been days since I trusted this on you. How come nothing has happened?

【下问】xiàwèn 向地位比自己低、知识比自己少的人请教 stoop to learn from sb. of a lower status or less learned than oneself：不耻～ do not feel ashamed to ask and learn from the rank and file; be modest enough to consult one's inferiors

【下午】xiàwǔ 从正午十二点到半夜十二点的一段时间，一般也指从正午十二点到日落的一段时间 afternoon; part of day from 12 a.m. to 12 p.m. but oft. from noon until sunset

【下下】xiàxià ❶ 最下等；最差 most inferior; lowest：～策 most undesirable policy or plan ❷ 指比后一个时期更往后的(时期)(of time) after the next：～星期 the week after the next

【下弦】xiàxián 月相的一种，农历每月二十二日或二十三日，太阳跟地球的连线和地球跟月亮的连线成直角时，在地球上看到月亮呈 ◖ 形 last (or 3rd) quarter (of the moon); the moon assuming the shape of ◖ from the perspective of the earth on the 22nd or 23rd of every lunar month, when the line linking the sun and the earth is at right angle with the line linking the earth and the moon：～月 the moon at the last quarter

【下限】xiàxiàn 时间最晚或数量最小的限度(跟'上限'相对 as opposed to 'ceiling') floor; floor level; the latest; minimum

【下陷】xiàxiàn 向下或向内凹进 sunken; hollow：眼眶～ sunken eyes|地基～ subsidence of the foundation of a building

【下泻】xiàxiè ❶(水流)往下流(of water) flow down：～不畅 impeded flow ◇汇率一路～。The interest rate has been plummeting and there seems to be no end to it. ❷ 指腹泻 have loose bowels

【下泄】xiàxiè (水流)往下流或排泄 (of water current) flow or rush downward：洪峰正沿江～。The flood crest is rushing down the river.

【下行】xiàxíng ❶ 我国铁路部门规定，列车行驶方向和上行相反叫做下行。下行列车编号用奇数，如11次，103次等。down; (of trains) going from the capital to other part of the country. According to Chinese railway rules, trains going from Beijing are numbered in odd numbers, such as Train No. 11 and Train No. 103. ☞ 上行 shàngxíng on p.1686 ❷ 船从上游向下游行驶 (of boats) going downstream; downriver ❸ 公文从上级发往下级 (of official documents) being issued to the lower levels：～公文 documents issued to lower levels

【下学】xià//xué 学校一天或半天课业完毕，学生回家 after school; finish classes and leave school for the day

【下旬】xiàxún 每月二十一日到月底的日子 last ten-day period of a month; from the 21st to the last day of a month

【下腰】xià//yāo ❶ 弯下腰 bend down：她～抱起孩子。She bent down and gathered her baby into her arms. ❷ 武术上指上身尽力向后弯曲 (of martial arts) bent backwards as far as possible

【下药】xià//yào ❶(医生)用药 prescribe medicine：对症～ suit the medicine to the illness; (fig.) suit the remedy to the case; prescribe the right remedy for an illness ❷ 下毒药 put poison on or into sth.

【下野】xià//yě 执政的人被迫下台 (of a ruler) retire from the political arena; be forced to relinquish power

【下议院】xiàyìyuàn 两院制议会的组成部分。原是英国议会中的平民院的别称，后来泛指两院制中议员按人口比例或选区选举产生的议院，如美国的众议院，法国的国民议会，荷兰的二院等。House of Commons or the lower house of the British Parliament; lower house; lower chamber; branch of a bicameral legislature whose members are elected according to size of population or electorate, such as the House of Representatives of the United States, the National Assembly of the French Parliament, and the Second Chamber of the States General (*Staten Generral*) of the Netherlands; also 下院 xiàyuàn

【下意识】xiàyì·shí 心理学上指不知不觉、没有意识的心理活动。是有机体对外界刺激的本能反应。唯心主义心理学认为这种作用是潜伏在意识之下的一种精神实质，能支配人的一切思想、行动。subconscious; part of the mind below the level of conscious perception that is the reaction of the instinct of an organism to the stimulation of the outside world. Idealistic psychology holds that subconsciousness is a kind of spiritual substance that lies below perception and controls people's mind and action.

【下游】xiàyóu ❶ 河流接近出口的部分 lower reaches (of a river) ❷〈比喻 *fig.*〉落后的地位 backwardness：不可甘居～。Don't resign yourself to backwardness.

【下狱】xià//yù 关进监狱 throw into prison; imprison

【下葬】xià//zàng 把灵柩埋到土里(有的民族不用棺材，指把遗体埋到土里) be interred; bury a coffin containing the remains of a dead person; (among some ethnic people) bury the remains of the deceased into the earth

【下账】xià//zhàng 把账目登记在账本上 enter into the account book

【下肢】xiàzhī 人体的一部分，包括大腿、小腿、脚等 lower limbs; legs, including thighs, calves, and feet

【下中农】xiàzhōngnóng 占有较少生产资料，需要出卖少量劳动力，生活水平比较低下的中农 lower-middle peasant; middle peasant in the possession of relatively less means of production, having to sell some of his labour, and having a relatively low standard of living

【下种】xià//zhǒng 播种(bō//zhòng) sow

【下箸】xià//zhù 拿筷子夹东西吃 set one's chopsticks to the bowl — start eating

【下坠】xiàzhuì ❶（物体）向下坠落（of objects）fall; drop ❷（将分娩的产妇或痢疾、肠炎等病的患者）腹部感到沉重，像要大便（of woman in labour, or one who suffers dysentery or enteritis）tenesmus; straining（as at stool）

【下子】xià//zǐ（～儿 xià//zǐr）❶ 播下种子 sow seeds ❷ 产卵 lay eggs

【下子】xià·zi same as 下³ xià

【下作】xià·zuo ❶ 卑鄙；下流 low-down; mean; obscene; dirty ❷〈方 *dial.*〉（吃东西）又贪又馋 greedy（for food）; gluttonous ❸〈方 *dial.*〉助手 assistant; helper：打～（担任助手）act as an assistant

吓(嚇) xià 使害怕 intimidate; scare; frighten：～了一跳 give a start; be started｜别～着孩子。Be careful not to frighten the child.

☞ hè on p. 791

【吓唬】xià·hu 使害怕；恐吓 frighten; scare; intimidate

【吓人】xià//rén 使人害怕；可怕 spooky; frightening：山洞又深又黑，真～。It was really spooky to get into that deep and dark cave.

夏¹ xià 夏季 summer：初～ early summer｜立～（one of 24 seasonal division points）Beginning of Summer

夏² Xià ❶ 朝代，约公元前 2070—公元前 1600，禹（一说启）所建 Xia Dynasty（c. 2070-c. 16th century B.C.）, founded by King Yu（or Qi, according to another theory）❷ 指中国 China：华～ China ❸ 姓 a surname

【夏布】xiàbù 用苎麻的纤维织成的布，多用来做蚊帐或夏季服装，产于江西、湖南、四川等地 grass linen; grass cloth; cloth woven with ramie fibre, produced in Jiangxi, Hunan and Sichuan provinces, mostly for the making of mosquito nets or summer clothing

【夏侯】Xiàhóu 姓 a surname

【夏候鸟】xiàhòuniǎo 春季或夏季在某个地区繁殖、秋季飞到较暖的地区去过冬、第二年春季再飞回原地区的鸟。如家燕、杜鹃就是我国的夏候鸟。summer resident; bird that propagates in a region in spring or summer, and winters in a warm place in autumn before flying back in spring next year. Barn swallows and cuckoos, for example, are summer residents in China.

【夏季】xiàjì 一年的第二季，我国习惯指立夏到立秋的三个月时间。也指农历'四、五、六'三个月。summer; 2nd season of the year, a period that covers, according to Chinese tradition, the three lunar months from the Beginning of Summer to the Beginning of Autumn; the 4th, 5th and 6th lunar months; ☞ 四季 sìjì on p. 1821

【夏历】xiàlì same as 农历 nónglì ①

【夏粮】xiàliáng 夏季收获的粮食 summer grain crop

【夏令】xiàlìng ❶ same as 夏季 xiàjì ❷ 夏季的气候 summer weather：春行～（春天的气候像夏天）have summerlike weather in spring

【夏令营】xiàlìngyíng 夏季开设的供青少年或集体的成员短期休息、娱乐等的营地，多设在林中或海边 summer camp; camping site, mostly in a forest or by the sea, for young people or a collective to rest or entertain themselves for a short period of time in summer

【夏眠】xiàmián 某些动物（如非洲肺鱼等）在炎热和干旱季节休眠 aestivation; dormancy of certain animals, such as the African lungfish, during a hot and arid season; also 夏蛰 xiàzhé

【夏收】xiàshōu ❶ 夏季收割农作物 summer harvest ❷ 夏季的收成 summer harvest：今年～增产一成。The summer harvest this year was up 10 per cent from that of the last year.

【夏天】xiàtiān same as 夏季 xiàjì

【夏衣】xiàyī 夏季穿的衣服 summer clothing; summer wear

【夏至】xiàzhì 二十四节气之一，在 6 月 21 日或 22 日。这一天太阳经过夏至点，北半球白天最长，夜间最短。Summer Solstice; 10th of the 24 solar terms, which falls on June 21 or 22 when the sun passes the northernmost point in the ecliptic, marked by the longest day and shortest night in the Northern Hemisphere; ☞ 节气 jiéqì on p. 989 and 二十四节气 èrshísì jiéqì on p. 516

【夏至点】xiàzhìdiǎn 黄道上最北的一点，夏至这天太阳经过这个位置 Summer Solstice; northernmost point in the ecliptic reached by the sun about June 21 or 22

【夏至线】xiàzhìxiàn 北回归线 tropic of cancer; ☞ 回归线 huíguīxiàn on p. 860

【夏装】xiàzhuāng 夏季穿的服装 summer clothing; summer wear

唬 xià same as 吓（xià）

☞ hǔ on p. 822

厦(廈) xià 厦门（Xiàmén），地名，在福建 Xiamen（Amoy）, city in Fujian Province

☞ shà on p. 1667

罅 xià〈书 *fml.*〉缝隙 crack; chink; rift：云～ rift in the clouds｜石～ crack in a rock

【罅漏】xiàlòu〈书 *fml.*〉缝隙，比喻事情的漏洞 crack; chink;（fig.）loophole; shortcoming：～之处，有待订补。Shortcomings will be remedied in future editions.

【罅隙】xiàxì〈书 *fml.*〉缝隙 crack; rift; chink

xiān（ㄒㄧㄢ）

仙(僊) xiān 仙人；神仙 celestial being; immortal：成～achieve immortality | 求～ in quest of immortality; seek instruction from god

【仙丹】xiāndān 神话传说中认为吃了可以起死回生或长生不老的灵丹妙药 elixir of life; substance in mythology or fables believed to maintain life indefinitely or bring the dead back to life

【仙姑】xiāngū ❶ 女仙人 female immortal ❷ 以求神问卜等迷信活动为职业的妇女 sorceress; also 道姑 dàogū

【仙鹤】xiānhè ❶ 白鹤 Siberian white crane (*Grus leucogeranus*) ❷ 专指神话中仙人所养的白鹤 white crane kept by immortals in Chinese mythology

【仙后座】xiānhòuzuò 北部天空的一个星座，和大熊座隔着北极星遥遥相对，其中五颗主要的星可以连接成 W 形 Cassiopeia; constellation facing Triones (Great Bear) across Polaris, whose five major stars are arrayed in the shape of W in the Northern Hemisphere

【仙境】xiānjìng 神仙居住的地方。多比喻景物优美的地方。fairyland; wonderland; paradise; (fig.) place with fabulous scenery

【仙女】xiānnǚ 年轻的女仙人 angel; female celestial; fairy maiden

【仙人】xiānrén 神话和童话里指长生不老并且有种种神通的人 celestial being; immortal; man or woman in mythology or fairy tales that enjoys longevity and has divine prowess

【仙人球】xiānrénqiú 多年生植物，茎球形或椭圆形，肉质，有纵行的棱，棱上有丛生的刺，花大，红色或白色。供观赏。ball cactus (*Oreocereus intertexta*); ball-shaped or oval and fleshy perennial plant having thorny vertical ridges on it, and large flowers red or white in colour, oft. planted for ornamental purposes; also 仙人拳 xiānrénquán

【仙人掌】xiānrénzhǎng 多年生植物，茎多呈长椭圆形，稍扁平，像手掌，肉质，有刺，花黄赤色，果实椭圆形，肉质。供观赏。cactus (*Cataceae*); ornamental perennial plant having succulent, thorny flat and oblong stems that stretch out like the palm of a hand, yellowish red flowers, and fleshy oval fruit, oft. planted for ornamental purposes

【仙山琼阁】xiānshān qiónggé 〈比喻 *fig.*〉奇异美妙的境界(多指幻境) jewelled palace on the mountain of immortals — a fairyland

【仙逝】xiānshì 〈婉辞 *euph.*〉称人死 pass away

【仙子】xiānzǐ ❶ 仙女 angel; fairy ❷ 泛指仙人 immortal; celestial being

先 xiān ❶ 时间或次序在前的(跟'后'相对 as opposed to 'later') earlier: ～进 advanced | ～例 precedent | 事～ beforehand | 领～ take the lead | 争～恐后 rush off to the front; strive to be the first and fear to lag behind | 有言在～。Make it clear beforehand. ❷ 祖先；上代 ancestor; elder generation: ～人 ancestors ❸ 〈尊称 *honor.*〉死去的人 the late...: ～父 the late father | ～烈 martyrs | ～哲 great thinker of yore ❹ 先前 earlier; past: 小王的技术比～强多了。Xiao Wang's skill is much better than before. | 你～怎么不告诉我? Why didn't you tell me beforehand? ❺ (Xiān) 姓 a surname

【先辈】xiānbèi ❶ 泛指行辈在先的人 (in a broad sense) elder generation; ancestors ❷ 指已去世的令人钦佩值得学习的人 forefathers; forerunners; sb. who is deceased but is still held in high esteem and as a fine example to learn from: 继承革命～的事业 carry on with the cause of the older generation

【先不先】xiān·buxiān 〈方 *dial.*〉首先(多用于申说理由 oft. used when presenting reasons) first of all: 香山，这个礼拜去不成了，～汽车就借不到。We cannot make it to the Fragrant Hills this week. The primary reason for this is that we have failed to borrow a coach.

【先导】xiāndǎo ❶ 引导；引路 guide ❷ 引路者；向导 guide; forerunner; precursor

【先睹为快】xiān dǔ wéi kuài 以先看到为快事 consider it a pleasure to be among the first to read or see sth.

【先端】xiānduān 叶、花、果实等器官的顶部 tip (of a leaf, flower, fruit, etc.)

【先发制人】xiān fā zhì rén 先动手以制伏对方 gain the initiative by striking the first blow; forestall an opponent

【先锋】xiānfēng 作战或行军时的先头部队，旧时也指率领先头部队的将官，现在多用于比喻 vanguard; van; vanguard unit in a battle or march; officers who led the vanguard in the old times; usu. used in metaphors: ～队 vanguard | 开路～ path-breaker; pioneer | 打～ fight in the van; be a pioneer

【先河】xiānhé 古代帝王先祭祀黄河，后祭祀海，以河为海的本源(见《礼记·学记》)。后来称倡导在先的事物为先河 originating river of the sea; the beginning of sth.; sth. that is first proposed or initiated. According to the rites of ancient times, the emperors or kings offered sacrifices first to the Yellow River and then to the sea, regarding the river as the origin of the sea (*The Book of Rites · Rites of Education*): 他主演《茶花女》等西洋名剧，开国人演话剧之～。He starred in *Camille* and other Western classics to be a forerunner of the Chinese in performing the modern drama.

【先后】xiānhòu ❶ 先和后 being early or late; priority; order: 要办的事情很多，应该分个～缓急。There are many matters to be tackled, but they should be taken up in order of priority. ❷ 前后相继 successively; one after another: 新出土的文物已经～在国内外多次展出。The newly unearthed relics have been repeatedly displayed at home and abroad.

【先见之明】xiān jiàn zhī míng 事先看清问题的眼力；预见性 prophetic vision; foresight

【先进】xiānjìn ❶ 进步比较快，水平比较高，可以作为学习的榜样的 advanced; far on or ahead in progress or level and to be emulated：～工作者 advanced worker | ～水平 most advanced level ❷ 先进的人或集体 advanced individual or unit：后进赶～ those behind trying to catch up with those ahead

【先决】xiānjué 为了解决某一问题，必须先解决的 prerequisite：～条件 prerequisite; precondition

【先觉】xiānjué 在政治、社会改革方面觉悟得较早的人 person with foresight (in social and political reforms); advanced thinker：先知～ person with foresight

【先来后到】xiān lái hòu dào (～儿 xiān lái hòu dàor) 按照来到的先后而确定的次序 in the order of arrival; first come, first served

【先礼后兵】xiān lǐ hòu bīng 先讲礼貌，行不通时再使用强硬的手段 take strong measures only after courteous ones fail; try peaceful means before resorting to force

【先例】xiānlì 已有的事例 precedent：史无～ unprecedented in history

【先烈】xiānliè 对烈士的尊称 martyr：革命～ revolutionary martyr

【先期】xiānqī 在某一日期以前 earlier than a date scheduled; earlier on; in advance：代表团的部分团员已～到达。Some members of the delegation had arrived at an earlier date.

【先前】xiānqián 时间词，泛指以前或指某个时候以前 before; previously：～我和他同过学。He and I were classmates in the past. | 我们煤矿的机械化程度比～高多了。The degree of mechanization in our coal mine is much higher than before. 注意 **NOTE**：'以前'可以用在动词后面表示时间，例如'吃饭以前要洗手'，'先前'不能这样用。以前 yǐqián can be used after a verb to indicate time, such as 吃饭以前要洗手 chī // fàn yǐqián yào xǐ // shǒu (Wash your hands before having a meal), but 先前 cannot be used like this.

【先遣】xiānqiǎn 行动前先派出去担任联络、侦察等任务的(人员或组织) sent in advance; (people or group) sent in advance to do liaison or reconnaissance work：～队 advance party; advance group | ～部队 advance troops (or force)

【先秦】Xiān Qín 指秦统一以前的历史时期，一般指春秋战国时期 pre-Qin period, i.e., before 221 B.C. when Qinshihuang (First Emperor of Qin) united China; usu. referring to the Spring and Autumn Period and the Warring States Period)：～史 the pre-Qin history of China | ～诸子(指孔子、老子、墨子、庄子、孟子、荀子、韩非子等) exponents of different schools of thought in the pre-Qin times (referring to Confucius, Laozi, Mozi, Zhuangzi, Mencius, Xunzi, Hanfeizi, etc.)

【先驱】xiānqū ❶ 走在前面引导(多虚用 oft. in abstract sense) herald; harbinger：～者 pioneer; forerunner; harbinger ❷ 先驱者 pioneer; forerunner; harbinger：革命的～ revolutionary forerunner

【先人】xiānrén ❶ 祖先 ancestor; forefather ❷ 指已死的父亲 my late father

【先容】xiānróng 〈书 *fml.*〉事先为人介绍、吹嘘或疏通 speak for sb. beforehand; introduce and praise in advance：为之～ put in a good word for sb. in advance | 恳为～ requested sincerely to put in a good word in advance

【先入为主】xiān rù wéi zhǔ 先接受了一种说法或思想，以为是正确的，有了成见，后来就不容易再接受不同的说法或思想 first impressions are the strongest; prejudices die hard; preconceived ideas keep a strong hold; after taking preconceived ideas as the correct, one find it hard to accept different ideas or views

【先生】xiān·sheng ❶ same as 老师 lǎoshī ❷ 对知识分子的称呼 (of intellectuals) Mister (Mr.); gentleman; sir ❸ 称别人的丈夫或对人称自己的丈夫(都带人称代词做定语) one's husband：她～出差去了。Her husband is away on business. | 等我们～回来，我让他马上去找您。When my husband is back, I'll ask him to see you at once. ❹〈方 *dial.*〉医生 doctor ❺〈旧时 *old*〉称管账的人 bookkeeper：在商号当～ serve as bookkeeper in a trading company ❻〈旧时 *old*〉称以说书、相面、算卦、看风水等为业的人 people engaged in storytelling, fortune-telling, geomancy, etc.：算命～ fortune-teller

【先声】xiānshēng 指发生在重大事件之前的性质相同的某项事件 first signs; herald; harbinger; another event of the same nature that takes place before an important event：1789年的法国大革命是十九世纪各国资产阶级革命的～。The French Revolution of 1789 heralded other bourgeois revolutions in the 19th century.

【先声夺人】xiān shēng duó rén 先张大声势以压倒对方，多用于比喻 demoralize one's opponent by a show of strength; overawe people by displaying one's strength; usu. used in metaphors

【先世】xiānshì 祖先 forefathers; ancestors

【先是】xiān·shi 原先 before this; originally：～承认，后又反悔。He admitted it at first, but later he went back on his word.

【先手】xiānshǒu 下棋时主动的形势(跟'后手'相对 as opposed to 'defensive position') offensive position (in chess)：～棋 offensive move | 占～ take an offensive position

【先天】xiāntiān ❶ 人或动物的胚胎时期（跟'后天'相对 as opposed to 'nurture'）congenital; inborn; present in the organism：～的（胚胎时期的，生来就具有的）congenital; inborn ❷ 哲学上指先验的（in philosophy）priori; innate

【先天不足】xiāntiān bù zú 指人或动物生下来体质就不好，也泛指事物的根基差（of human or animal）congenital deficiency; inborn weakness：～，后天失调 born weak and ill cared for after birth

【先天性免疫】xiāntiānxìng miǎnyì 生来就具有的对某种疾病的抵抗能力，如婴儿出生后六个月内很少得麻疹等传染病 congenital immunity; inborn resistance to certain diseases, as an infant seldom contracted with measles or other infectious diseases in the six months after birth

【先头】xiāntóu ❶ 位置在前的（多指部队 usu. of troops）ahead; in front; in advance：～骑兵连 advance cavalry company ❷（～儿 xiāntóur）时间在前的；以前 before; formerly; in the past：～出发 set out earlier; leave ahead of others｜怎么～我没听他说过。Why haven't I heard it from him before? ❸ 前头；前面 front; in the front：首长走在队伍的～。The senior officials walked ahead of the troops.

【先贤】xiānxián〈书 *fml.*〉已经去世的有才德的人 sages of the past：～祠 temple of sages

【先行】xiānxíng ❶ 走在前面的 go ahead of the rest; start off before the others：～者 forerunner｜～官 commander of an advance unit or vanguard ❷ 先进行；预先进行 beforehand; in advance：～试办 run on a trial basis｜～通知 notify in advance ❸ 指先行官 commander of an advance unit or vanguard

【先行官】xiānxíngguān 戏曲小说中指指挥先头部队的武官 commander of an advance unit or vanguard ◇铁路运输是国民经济的～。Railway transportation is the vanguard of the national economy.

【先行者】xiānxíngzhě 首先倡导的人 forerunner：中国民主主义革命的～孙中山先生 Dr. Sun Yat-sen, forerunner of the Chinese democratic revolution

【先验论】xiānyànlùn 唯心主义的认识论。同唯物主义的反映论相对立。认为人的知识（包括才能）是先于客观存在、先于社会实践、先于感觉经验的，是先天就有的。apriorism; priori principle or method of reasoning; idealistic theory of knowledge. Opposed to the materialistic theory of knowledge, apriorism argues that the knowledge (including ability) of a person is prior to objective being, to social practice, and to perception and experience, or, to put it in a single word, innate.

【先意承志】xiān yì chéng zhì 原指不待父母明白说出就能迎合父母的心意做事，后来泛指揣摩人意，极力逢迎 anticipate and attend to the wishes of another to please him; (orig.) ability to attend to the wishes of one's parents before they say anything; fathom the intention of another to curry favour with him

【先斩后奏】xiān zhǎn hòu zòu 封建时代臣子把人杀了再报告皇帝。现在多比喻自行把问题处理了，然后报告上级或当权者。execute sb. first and report to the emperor afterwards; (fig.) handle a matter on one's own first and report it to the above authority or the person in power afterwards

【先兆】xiānzhào 事先显露出来的迹象 omen; portent; sign; indication

【先哲】xiānzhé〈书 *fml.*〉指已经去世的有才德的思想家 great thinker of the past; sage

【先知】xiānzhī ❶ 对人类或国家的大事了解得较早的人 person of foresight; who foresees the great events of mankind of a nation before others ❷ 犹太教、基督教指受上帝启示而传达上帝旨意或预言未来的人（Judaism, Christianity）religion prophet; person who speaks for God, or as though under divine guidance

【先祖】xiānzǔ〈书 *fml.*〉❶ 祖先 my forefathers ❷ 称已故的祖父 my late grandfather

纤（纖） xiān 细小 fine; minute：～尘 fine dust｜～微 tiny; minute

☞ qiàn on p.1540

【纤长】xiāncháng 细而长 long and slender：～的手指 long and slender fingers

【纤尘】xiānchén 细小的灰尘 fine dust：～不染（一点灰尘也沾染不上）without a speck of dust; untainted with evil thoughts or bad habits

【纤度】xiāndù 天然丝或化学纤维粗细的程度，用一定长度纤维的重量来表示，纤维愈细，纤度愈小。常用的单位是旦。fibre number; size. The size of a natural silk or chemical fibre is indicated by the weight of the fibre of a given length — the finer the fibre, the smaller the fibre number. The unit is denier.

【纤毫】xiānháo〈比喻 *fig.*〉非常细微的事物或部分 the least bit; the minutest detail or part：人物形象在这些牙雕艺术品里刻得～毕见。The figures on these ivory carvings are distinct in the minutest detail. *or* These ivory figures are so minutely and elaborately carved that the finest details can be distinguished.

【纤毛】xiānmáo 某些生物体的细胞上生长的纤细的毛，由原生质构成，能运动，如人的气管内壁细胞，纤毛虫和某些藻类所生的毛 cilium; short, hair-like outgrowth of certain organism cells, composed of protozoans that can produce locomotion and feeding currents, as on the inner wall of the human trachea, ciliate (or infusorians) and certain algaes

【纤巧】xiānqiǎo 细巧;小巧 dainty; delicate:饰物～精致。The ornaments are dainty and exquisite.

【纤柔】xiānróu 纤细而柔软 soft and slender; delicate and soft:～的长发 long and soft hair

【纤弱】xiānruò 纤细而柔弱 slim and fragile; delicate:身子～ slim and frail body

【纤维】xiānwéi 天然的或人工合成的细丝状物质。棉花、麻类植物的韧皮部分、动物的毛和矿物中的石棉,都是天然纤维。合成纤维用高分子化合物制成。fibre; natural or artificial slender, threadlike substance. Cotton, bast of bast fibre plants, wool of animals and asbestos in the minerals are all natural fibres. Artificial fibres are made of high-molecular compounds.

【纤维板】xiānwéibǎn 一种人造木板,把废木料分离成木纤维或木浆,经过成型、热压等工序制成 fibreboard; artificial wood board made by forming and hot-pressing wood fibres or wood pulp from waste wood

【纤维植物】xiānwéi zhíwù 能从中取得纤维的植物,如棉花、亚麻、大麻等 fibre plants; plants from which fibres are obtained, as cotton, hemp, flax, etc.

【纤悉】xiānxī〈书 *fml.*〉详细;详尽 extremely detailed:～无遗 with not a single detail left out

【纤细】xiānxì 非常细 very thin; slender; fine; tenuous:笔画～ written or drawn in a fine hand

【纤纤】xiānxiān〈书 *fml.*〉形容细长 long and slender:十指～ long and slender fingers

【纤小】xiānxiǎo 细小 fine; tenuous

氙 xiān 气体元素,符号 Xe (xenonum)。无色,无臭,无味,大气中含量极少,化学性质不活泼。具有极高的发光强度,用来填充光电管、闪光灯等。xenon (Xe); colourless, noble gaseous element without smell or taste, with extremely high intensity of illumination, which is used to fill phototubes, flash lights, etc.

【氙灯】xiāndēng 一种照明装置。把高纯度的氙气充入真空的石英玻璃管内,通电后发出的光和阳光的颜色相近。xenon lamp; lighting device in which highly pure xenon gas is filled into a vacuum quartz glass tube, which, when electricity is switched on, generates light that is close to sunlight in hue

忺 xiān 高兴;适意(唐宋诗词常用 oft. used in Tang-dynasty poetry) happy; pleased; gratified

祆 xiān [祆教](Xiānjiào)拜火教 Zoroastrianism; Mazdaism

籼(秈) xiān ☞ below

【籼稻】xiāndào 水稻的一种,茎秆较高较软,叶子黄绿色,稻穗上的子粒较稀,米粒长而细 long-grained nonglutinous rice; indica rice; species of rice with a tall and soft stem, yellowish-green leaves, loosely-grained ears and long, slender grains

【籼米】xiānmǐ 籼稻碾出的米,黏性小 polished long-grained nonglutinous rice; polished indica rice

莶(薟) xiān ☞ 豨莶 (xīxiān) on p. 2049

掀 xiān ❶ 使遮挡覆盖的东西向上离开;揭 lift (a cover, etc.):～锅盖 take the pot's lid off|～门帘 lift the door curtain|把这一页～过去 turn over this page ❷ 翻腾;翻动 rock; convulse:白浪～天。White waves heave to the sky.

【掀风鼓浪】xiān fēng gǔ làng〈比喻 *fig.*〉煽动情绪,挑起事端 raise a storm; stir up trouble

【掀起】xiānqǐ ❶ 揭起 lift; raise:～盖子 lift the lid (or cover) ❷ 往上涌起;翻腾 surge; cause to surge:大海～了波涛。Big waves surged on the sea. ❸ 使运动等大规模地兴起 set off (a movement, campaign, etc.); start:～增产节约运动新高潮。Launch a new upsurge in the campaign to increase production and practise economy.

铦(銛) xiān〈书 *fml.*〉锋利 sharp:～利 sharp

☞ 锬 tán on p. 1860

酰 xiān same as 酰基 xiānjī

【酰基】xiānjī 无机或有机含氧酸分子失去一个羟基而成的原子团 acyl; atomic group formed by the removal of an OH group from an inorganic or organic oxygen acid

跹(躚) xiān ☞ 翩跹 piānxiān on p. 1472

锨(杴、枚) xiān 掘土或铲东西用的工具,有板状的头,用钢铁或木头制成,后面安把儿 shovel; implement with a broad, deep scoop or blade made of metal or wood, and a long handle, used in digging earth or lifting and moving loose materials such as earth, snow, gravel, etc.

鲜 xiān ❶ same as 新鲜 xīnxiān ①:～肉 fresh meat|～啤酒 fresh beer ❷ same as 新鲜 xīnxiān ②:～花 fresh flower ❸ 鲜明 bright-coloured; bright:～艳 bright-coloured|～红 bright red ❹ 鲜美 delicious or tasty:味道～ taste delicious; be delicious or tasty ❺ 鲜美的食物 delicacy:时～ delicacy of the season|尝～ have a taste of the delicacy ❻ 特指鱼虾等水产食物 seafood; aquatic foods:鱼～ fresh fish ❼ (Xiān) 姓 a surname

☞ xiǎn on p. 2079

【鲜卑】Xiānbēi 我国古代民族,居住在今东北、内蒙古一带。汉末渐渐强盛起来,南北朝时曾建立北魏、北齐、北周等政权。Xianbei (Sienpi), an ancient nationality which lived in what is modern Northeast China and Inner Mongolia, rose in strength in the declining years of the Han Dynasty, and founded the Northern Wei (386-534), Northern Qi (550-577) and Northern Zhou (557-581) during the period of Southern and Northern Dynasties

【鲜果】xiānguǒ 新鲜的水果 fresh fruit

【鲜红】xiānhóng 鲜艳的红色 bright red; scarlet:～的朝霞 scarlet dawn

【鲜花】xiānhuā 新鲜的花朵 fresh flowers; flowers:一束～ a bunch of fresh flowers

【鲜货】xiānhuò 指新鲜的水果、蔬菜、鱼虾等 fresh fruit, vegetables, or seafood, etc.

【鲜丽】xiānlì 鲜艳美丽 bright-coloured and beautiful:衣着色彩～ be beautifully dressed in bright colours

【鲜亮】xiān·liang〈方 *dial*.〉❶ same as 鲜明 xiānmíng ① ❷ 漂亮 pretty; beautiful; handsome:长得～ look pretty|这一打扮就显得更～了 look even prettier when one is dressed up

【鲜灵】xiān·líng〈方 *dial*.〉形容色泽鲜明,有生气的样子;新鲜水灵 fresh; shining bright:浇了水之后,麦苗更～了。Having been watered, the wheat sprouts are looking all the more fresh.|石榴花红得那么～可爱。The pomegranate blossoms, ablaze with a fiery red, are really eye-catching.

【鲜美】xiānměi ❶(菜肴、瓜果等)滋味好(of cooked food, fruit, etc.) delicious; tasty ❷〈书 *fml*.〉(花草等)新鲜美丽(of flowers, grass, etc.) fresh and pleasing to the eye

【鲜明】xiānmíng ❶(颜色)明亮(of colour) bright:色调～ in bright colours; bright-coloured ❷ 分明而确定,一点也不含糊 clear-cut; distinct; distinctive:主题～ have a distinct theme|～的对比 sharp (striking) contrast|～的立场 clear-cut stand

【鲜嫩】xiānnèn 新鲜而嫩 fresh and tender:～的藕 fresh and tender lotus roots

【鲜血】xiānxuè 鲜红的血 (red) blood

【鲜妍】xiānyán 鲜艳 bright; bright-coloured:色彩～ in bright colours

【鲜艳】xiānyàn 鲜明而美丽 bright-coloured; gaily-coloured:～夺目 dazzlingly beautiful; resplendent

【鲜于】Xiānyú 姓 a surname

暹 xiān 暹罗(Xiānluó),泰国的旧称 Siam, old name of Thailand

騫 xiān〈书 *fml*.〉形容鸟飞(of birds) fly

xián(ㄒㄧㄢ)

闲(閒) xián ❶ 没有事情;没有活动;有空(跟'忙'相对 as opposed to 'busy') not busy; idle; unoccupied:游手好～ idle away one's time; live an idle life; loaf; lounge about|我没工夫,你找小杨吧,她～着呢。I'm busy. Please go and see Xiao Yang, who is not. ❷(房屋、器物等)不在使用中(of house, room, article, etc.) unoccupied; not in use; lying idle:～房 vacant (or unoccupied) house (or room)|不让机器～着。Don't let the machine stand idle. ❸ 闲空儿 spare or free time; leisure:农～ slack farming season|忙里偷～ steal a moment of leisure from a busy schedule ❹ 与正事无关的 having nothing to do with official business:～谈 chat; chit-chat|～话 gossip; digression; cackle

閒 ☞ 间 jiān on p. 940 and 间 jiàn on p. 952

【闲扯】xiánchě 漫无边际地随便谈话 chat; engage in chit-chat, be a schmoozer; guy-talk:两人～了一阵子。The two of them chatted for quite a while.

【闲荡】xiándàng 闲逛 saunter; stroll; loaf:～街头 loiter about in streets

【闲工夫】xiángōng·fu(～儿 xiángōng·fur)没有事情要做的时间 spare time; leisure

【闲逛】xiánguàng 闲暇时到外面随便走走;游逛 saunter; stroll; walk around in leisure time:节日期间到游乐园～了一天 spend an entire day strolling in the amusement park during the holidays

【闲话】xiánhuà ❶(～儿 xiánhuàr)与正事无关的话 digression:～少说,讨论具体问题吧! Stop digression. Let's get down to specifics. ❷ 不满意的话 complaint; gossip:注意一点,免得让人说～。Make sure to avoid gossip. ❸〈书 *fml*.〉闲谈 talk casually about; chat about:清夜～ chat in the dead of night

【闲居】xiánjū 在家里住着没有工作做 stay at home idle; lead a quiet life

【闲磕牙】xiánkēyá〈方 *dial*.〉(～儿 xiánkēyár) same as 闲谈 xiántán

【闲空】xiánkòng(～儿 xiánkòngr)没有事的时候 free time; spare time; leisure:她整天忙忙碌碌的,没有一点儿～。She was busy all day long, and had not a little free time.

【闲聊】xiánliáo 闲谈;闲扯 chat

【闲篇】xiánpiān〈方 *dial*.〉(～儿 xiánpiānr)与正事无关的话 rigmarole; meaningless talk; idle chatter:我正忙着呢,没工夫跟你扯～儿。I'm busy, and have no time to chatter with you.

【闲气】xiánqì 为了无关紧要的事而生的气 anger about trifles:怄～ be annoyed over trifles|生～ get angry about trifles (or a trivial matter)

【闲钱】xiánqián 指生活必需的费用以外多余的钱 spare cash; spare money

【闲情逸致】xián qíng yì zhì 闲适的情致 (be in) leisurely and carefree mood; (have) the leisure and (be in the) mood for enjoyment

【闲人】xiánrén ❶ 没有事情要做的人 unoccupied person; idler:现在正是农忙季节,村里一个～也没有。It's the busy season for farmers and nobody in the village is idle. ❷ 与事无关的人 persons not concerned:～免进。No admittance except on business. *or* Admittance to staff only. *or* Employees only.

【闲散】xiánsǎn ❶ 无事可做而又无拘无束 free and at leisure; at loose ends:～的日子 days of leisure ❷ 闲着不使用的(指人员或物资) unused; idle:～资金 idle capital

【闲事】xiánshì 跟自己没有关系的事;无关紧要的事 matter that does not concern one; other people's business; unimportant matter:管～ poke one's nose into another's business

【闲适】xiánshì 清闲安逸 leisurely and comfortable:～的心情 leisurely and placid mood

【闲书】xiánshū 指供消遣的书;与正业无关的书 light reading:看～ do light reading

【闲谈】xiántán 没有一定中心地谈无关紧要的话 chat; engage in chit-chat

【闲暇】xiánxiá same as 闲空 xiánkòng

【闲心】xiánxīn 闲适的心情 leisurely mood

【闲雅】xiányǎ same as 娴雅 xiányǎ

【闲言碎语】xián yán suì yǔ ❶ 与正事无关的话 idle chatter; irrelevancies:～不多讲,表一表好汉武二郎。Enough of this idle chatter, let me tell you something about the hero Younger Brother Wu. ❷ 没有根据的话;闲话 ② gossip; backbiting; groundless rumour; slander:背地里散布～ gossip behind sb.'s back|不要听了几句～就打退堂鼓。Don't beat a retreat just because of some jeering remarks.

【闲员】xiányuán 集体中没事干的人员;多余的人员 redundant staff; redundant personnel:裁汰～ reduce redundant personnel

【闲云野鹤】xián yún yě hè 〈比喻 *fig.*〉闲散安逸不受尘事羁绊的人,旧时多指隐士、道士等 (like) drifting clouds and wild storks; people who are idle and unrestrained by worldly affairs, as hermits, Taoist priests, etc.

【闲杂】xiánzá 指没有一定职务的或与某事无关的(人) without fixed duties:～人员 people without fixed duties; miscellaneous personnel

【闲章】xiánzhāng (～儿 xiánzhāngr)个人的与姓名、职务等无关的图章,印文大多是熟语或诗文的句子,如'开卷有益' seal as an object of artistic value, which is not used for practical purposes, and usu. inscribed with a motto or a line of poetry, as 'Reading is a rewarding experience.'

【闲职】xiánzhí 空闲的或事情少的职务 extremely light and easy job; sinecure; official post with little work to do

【闲置】xiánzhì 搁在一边不用 leave unused; let sth. lie idle; set aside:～设备 idle equipment

贤(賢) xián ❶ 有德行的;有才能的 virtuous and able; worthy:～明 wise and able; sagacious|～达 prominent and worthy personage|～良 able and virtuous ❷ 有德行的人;有才能的人 worthy person; able and virtuous person:圣～ sages|选～举能 recommend and appoint virtuous and able people to office|任人唯～ appoint people on their merits ❸〈敬辞 *pol.*〉用于平辈或晚辈 [used in addressing people of the same or of a younger generation]:～弟 my worthy brother|～侄 my worthy nephew

【贤达】xiándá 有才能,德行和声望的人 prominent and worthy personage:社会～ the worthies

【贤德】xiándé ❶ 善良的德行 virtue and kindheartedness ❷ 贤惠 virtuous:～女子 virtuous and kindhearted woman

【贤惠】xiánhuì 指妇女心地善良,通情达理,对人和蔼 (of a woman) virtuous; genial and prudent; kindhearted and understanding; also 贤慧 xiánhuì

【贤慧】xiánhuì same as 贤惠 xiánhuì

【贤劳】xiánláo〈书 *fml.*〉(为公事)勤劳;劳累 (for business) industrious; hardworking

【贤良】xiánliáng〈书 *fml.*〉❶ 有德行,有才能 (of a man) able and virtuous:～之士 able and virtuous men ❷ 指有德行、有才能的人 able and virtuous men:任用～ appoint able and virtuous people on their merits

【贤路】xiánlù〈书 *fml.*〉指贤能被任用的机会 channel for able and worthy people to become officials:开～ open up the channel for able and worthy people to become officials|避～ make way for able and worthy people to rise in officialdom

【贤明】xiánmíng ❶ 有才能、有见识 wise and able; sagacious:～的领袖 wise and able leader ❷ 指有才能、有见识的人 man of insight and ability:另聘～ employ another man of insight and ability

【贤能】xiánnéng ❶ 有道德,有才能 virtuous and able:～之士 virtuous and talented person ❷ 指有道德有才能的人 virtuous and talented person:另举～ recommend another virtuous and talented man

【贤契】xiánqì 对弟子或朋友子侄辈的敬称(多用于书面 usu. used in writing) term for one's junior, esp. one's pupil or a son of one's friend; my worthy pupil, nephew, etc.

【贤人】xiánrén 有才德的人 person of virtue (or merit); person of outstanding worth; worthy

【贤士】xiánshì〈书 *fml.*〉same as 贤人 xiánrén

【贤淑】xiánshū〈书 *fml.*〉same as 贤惠 xiánhuì:～的妻子 virtuous, kind and genial wife

【贤哲】xiánzhé 贤明的人 good and wise man; man of insight and ability

弦(❷絃) xián ❶ 弓背两端之间系着的绳状物,用牛筋制成,有弹性 bowstring; string; cord, made of cattle tendon, stretched from one end of the bow to the other: 弓～ bowstring ❷ (～儿 xiánr)乐器上发声的线,一般用丝线、铜丝或钢丝等制成 string of a musical instrument, usually made of silk thread, copper wire or steel wire ❸ 发条 spring (of a watch, etc.) ❹ 连接圆周上任意两点的线段 chord; straight line segment joining any two points on a circumference ❺ 我国古代称不等腰直角三角形的斜边 hypotenuse; longest side of a right triangle, located opposite the right angle

【弦歌】xiángē 用琴瑟等弦乐器伴奏而歌唱 sing to the accompaniment of stringed instruments; sing to stringed accompaniment: ～阵阵 songs sung one after another to the stringed accompaniment

【弦外之音】xián wài zhī yīn 〈比喻 *fig.*〉言外之意 overtones; implication

【弦乐器】xiányuèqì 指由于弦的振动而发音的一类乐器。如小提琴、琵琶、扬琴等。stringed instrument; instrument that produces sounds from the vibration of the strings, as violin, pipa, dulcimer, etc.

【弦子】xián·zi 三弦的通称 popular name for 三弦 sānxián

【弦子戏】xián·zixì 柳子戏 *xianzi* opera or *liuzi* opera, a local opera in Shandong Province

咸[1] xián ❶〈书 *fml.*〉全;都 all: ～受其益。Everyone benefited from it. | 老少～宜 suitable for old and young alike ❷ (Xián)姓 a surname

咸[2] **(鹹)** xián 像盐那样的味道 salted; salty: ～鱼 salt fish | 菜太～。The dish is too salty.

【咸菜】xiáncài 用盐腌制的某些菜蔬,有的地区也指某些酱菜 salted vegetable; pickles; vegetables pickled with salts; vegetables pickled in soy sauce in some regions

【咸丰】Xiánfēng 清文宗(爱新觉罗奕詝[zhǔ])年号(公元1851—1861) Xianfeng, title of the reign (1851-1861) of Emperor Wenzong (Aisin Gioro Yizhu) of the Qing Dynasty

【咸津津】xiánjīnjīn (～的 xiánjīnjīn·de)(～儿的 xiánjīnjīnr·de)味道略带点咸 with a nice saltish taste

【咸水湖】xiánshuǐhú 水中含盐分多的湖 saltwater lake; lake with water containing salt content

【咸盐】xiányán〈方 *dial.*〉盐 table salt; salt

挦(撏) xián 撕;取;拔(毛发);拉 pull out (hair); pluck: ～扯 pull and tear | ～鸡毛 pluck chicken feathers; pluck a chicken

涎 xián 口水 saliva: 垂～三尺 slobber so much that the saliva drools a metre from the mouth; have one's mouth watering; smack one's lips | 口角流～ slaver; drool; saliva drools from the corner of one's mouth

【涎皮赖脸】xián pí lài liǎn 厚着脸皮跟人纠缠,惹人厌烦的样子 brazen-faced; cheeky; shameless and loathsome

【涎水】xiánshuǐ〈方 *dial.*〉口水 saliva

【涎着脸】xián·zhe liǎn〈方 *dial.*〉(～儿 xián·zhe liǎnr)做出涎皮赖脸的样子 be brazen-faced; be cheeky

娴(嫺) xián〈书 *fml.*〉❶ 文雅 refined: ～静 gentle and refined ❷ 熟练 adept; skilled: ～熟 adept; skilled | ～于辞令 good at speech

【娴静】xiánjìng 文雅安详 gentle and refined: 举止～ gentle and refined

【娴熟】xiánshú 熟练 adept; skilled: 技术～ consummate skill

【娴雅】xiányǎ 文雅(多形容女子 of a woman) refined; elegant: 举止～ poised and elegant; also 闲雅 xiányǎ

蚿 xián 马蚿,古书上指马陆 julus, millipede of the family Julidae; 马陆 mǎlù as described in ancient books

衔[1] **(啣)** xián ❶ 用嘴含 hold in the mouth: 燕子～泥 swallows carry bits of earth in their bills | 他～着一个大烟斗。He bit a pipe between his teeth. ◇日已～山。The sun has risen over the mountain. ❷ 存在心里 harbour; bear: ～恨 harbour resentment; bear a grudge | ～冤 nurse a bitter sense of injustice ❸〈书 *fml.*〉接受;奉 receive (orders, etc.): ～命 receive an order; carry an order ❹ 相连接 link up; join: ～接 link up; connect

衔[2] xián 行政、军事、学术等系统中人员的等级或称号 rank; title (in administrative, military, academic and other systems): 头～ title | 学～ academic title | 军～ military rank | 大使～ rank of ambassador

【衔恨】xiánhèn 心中怀着怨恨或悔恨 harbour resentment; bear a grudge: ～而死 die with resentment

【衔接】xiánjiē 事物相连接 link up; join: 两个阶段必须～。The two stages must be connected.

【衔枚】xiánméi〈书 *fml.*〉〈古代 *arch.*〉军队秘密行动时,让兵士口中横衔着枚(像筷子的东西),防止说话,以免敌人发觉 (of soldiers on the march) have a wooden gag in their mouths to keep from talking to avoid discovery by the enemy: ～疾走 running swiftly with the gag between one's teeth

【衔命】xián//mìng〈书 *fml.*〉奉命;受命 carry out an order; be ordered to; receive an order

【衔铁】xiántiě 某些电器中放在电磁铁两极中间的铁块或铁片。电磁铁的线圈通电时衔铁就被吸引而移动,从而改变所连接的电路。armature; iron bar or thin, flat piece of iron connecting the two poles of a horseshoe magnet. When the coil of the magnet is energized, the armature is attracted to move, thus changing the connected circuit.

【衔冤】xiányuān 含冤 nurse a bitter sense of wrong; have a simmering sense of injustice: ～负屈 be utterly wronged in a frame-up

舷 xián 船、飞机等两侧的边儿 side of a ship or aircraft: 左～ port | 右～ starboard | ～梯 gangway ladder; ramp

【舷窗】xiánchuāng 飞机或某些船体两侧密封的窗子 porthole; hermetic window on either two sides of a passenger liner or certain ships

【舷梯】xiántī 上下轮船、飞机等用的梯子 gangway ladder; accommodation ladder (boarding); ramp

痫(癇) xián 癫痫 epilepsy

鹇(鷴) xián ☞ 白鹇 báixián on p. 38

嫌 xián ❶ 嫌疑 suspicion: 避～ avoid suspicion | 涉～ be suspected; be under suspicion ❷ 嫌怨 ill will; resentment; enmity; grudge: 消释前～ let bygones be bygones; remove previous resentment | 挟～报复 bear resentment and retaliate ❸ 厌恶;不满意 dislike; mind; complain of: 讨人～ be a nuisance; get disliked | ～贫爱富 dislike the poor and cherish the rich | 大家都～他脾气太急。Everyone dislikes him because of his hot temper. | 内容不错,文字略～啰唆。The article is good in content, only it's a bit wordy.

【嫌弃】xiánqì 厌恶而不愿接近 dislike and avoid; cold-shoulder

【嫌恶】xiánwù 厌恶 detest; loathe

【嫌隙】xiánxì 因彼此不满或猜疑而发生的恶感 ill feeling; animosity; enmity; ill will; grudge: ～消释 remove ill feeling; dispel misgivings | 素有～ harbour ill feeling for a long time

【嫌疑】xiányí 被怀疑有某种行为的可能性 suspicion; suspecting sb. of doing sth. wrong with little supporting evidence: ～犯 suspect | 不避～ unafraid of other people's suspicion

【嫌疑犯】xiányífàn 刑事诉讼中有犯罪嫌疑而未经证实的人 suspect; person suspected of committing a crime in a criminal case pending supporting evidence

【嫌怨】xiányuàn 不满的情绪;怨恨 grudge; resentment; enmity

【嫌憎】xiánzēng 嫌弃厌恶 be disgusted with; dislike intensely

鳒 xián 鱼类的一科,身体长数寸,无鳞,头扁平,口小,吻尖。生活在近海。dragonet (*Callionymus lyra Linnaeus*); small, scaleless offshore fish a few inches long, with a flat head, small mouth and pointed lips

xiǎn (ㄒㄧㄢˇ)

猕(獮) xiǎn 〈古代 *arch.*〉指秋天打猎 autumn hunting

冼 Xiǎn 姓 a surname

显(顯) xiǎn ❶ 露在外面容易看出来;明显 be apparent; be obvious; be noticeable: ～而易见 apparent; obvious; apparently; obviously; evidently; clearly | 药刚吃了一剂,效果还不很～。Since he has had only one dose, the effect of the medicine is not yet noticeable. ❷ 表现;露出 show; display; manifest: 各～其能 each displaying his ability | 大～身手 display one's skill; give full play to one's abilities ❸ 有名声有权势地位的 illustrious and influential: ～达 illustrious and influential | ～赫 illustrious; celebrated

【显摆】xiǎn·bai 〈方 *dial.*〉显示并夸耀 show off; brag about; flaunt: 她就爱在人前～自己。She always likes to show herself off. also 显白 xiǎn·bai

【显达】xiǎndá 指在官场上地位高而有名声 illustrious and influential; reputed for one's high position in officialdom

【显得】xiǎn·de 表现出(某种情形) look; seem; appear: 节日的天安门～更加壮丽。Tian'anmen looks all the more majestic during holidays.

【显贵】xiǎnguì ❶ 声名显赫,地位尊贵,指做大官 occupying a distinguished position; of high position; illustrious: ～人物 illustrious person of high position ❷ 指做大官的人 high officials (in former times): 傲视～ disdain high officials; hold high officials in disdain

【显赫】xiǎnhè (权势、名声等)盛大 illustrious; celebrated: ～一时 be once mighty | 地位～ celebrated, high position

【显花植物】xiǎnhuā-zhíwù 开花、结实、靠种子繁殖的植物的统称,如桃、菊、麦等(区别于'隐花植物' distinguished from 'cryptogam') phanerogam; general term for flowering, fruiting seed plants, as peach, chrysanthemum, wheat, etc.

【显豁】xiǎnhuò 显著明白 obvious and clear: 内容～ lucid

【显见】xiǎnjiàn 可以明显地看出 be obvious; be self-evident; be apparent: 孩子比前两年～懂事多了。The child behaves obviously better than two years ago.

【显灵】xiǎn//líng 迷信的人指神鬼现出形象,发出声响或使人感到威力 (of a ghost or spirit) (superstition) make its presence or power felt

【显露】xiǎnlù 原来看不见的变成看得见;现出 become visible; appear; manifest itself: 他脸上～出高兴的神色。A cheerful look appeared

X

on his face.

【显明】xiǎnmíng 清楚明白 obvious; manifest; distinct; marked:～的对照 sharp contrast; striking contrast

【显目】xiǎnmù same as 显眼 xiǎnyǎn

【显能】xiǎn//néng 显示自己的才能 show off one's talent or competence:你在行家面前显什么能? What have you to show off before those experts?

【显然】xiǎnrán 容易看出或感觉到;非常明显 obviously; evidently; clearly:这种说法～错误。This argument is obviously wrong.|问题很～。The problem is obvious.

【显荣】xiǎnróng 〈书 *fml.*〉显达荣耀 illustrious and glorious

【显圣】xiǎn//shèng (受崇敬的人物)死后显灵(迷信)(of the ghost of a saintly person) (superstition) make its presence or power felt

【显示】xiǎnshì 明显地表现 show; display; demonstrate; manifest:～威力 make a show of one's power; display one's strength|作品～了作者纯熟的写作技巧。The work shows the consummate writing skill of the author.

【显微镜】xiǎnwēijìng 观察微小物体用的光学仪器,主要由一个金属筒和两组透镜构成。常用的显微镜可以放大几百倍到三千倍左右。microscope; optical instrument for viewing and studying microorganisms, consisting chiefly of a metal tube and two sets of lenses. A common microscope often has a magnifying power of several hundred to three thousand times.

【显现】xiǎnxiàn 呈现;显露 manifest (or reveal) oneself; appear; show:雾气逐渐消失,重叠的山峦一层一层地～出来。As the mist lifted, the mountains revealed themselves one behind the other.

X

【显像管】xiǎnxiàngguǎn 电视接收机、示波器等设备中的一种器件,是一个高度真空的玻璃泡,一端膨大,略平,呈屏状,上面涂有荧光粉;另一端的装置能产生电子束,并使电子束在荧光屏上扫描,形成图像 picture tube; kinescope; cathode-ray tube in a TV receiver, monitor, etc. that produces visual images on its screen; high-vacuum glass tube with a large and flat fluorescent screen at one end and a device at another which is capable of producing an electron beam to form images by scanning

【显效】xiǎnxiào ❶ 显示效果 produce or show effect:这种农药～快,毒性低。This pesticide produces quick effect (or results) and is low in toxicity. ❷ 明显的效果 conspicuous result or effect:未见～。There has been no conspicuous effect.

【显形】xiǎn//xíng (～儿 xiǎn//xíngr)显露原形;露出真相(用于人时多含贬义 derog. when used of a person) show one's (true) colours; betray oneself

【显学】xiǎnxué 〈书 *fml.*〉著名的学说、学派 famous theory or school of thought

【显眼】xiǎnyǎn 明显而容易被看到;引人注目 stand out (in a crowd); conspicuous; showy; eye-catching:把布告贴在～的地方 put up the notice in a conspicuous place

【显扬】xiǎnyáng 〈书 *fml.*〉❶ 表彰 commend; extol; glorify ❷ 声誉著称 eminent; of undisputed fame:～于天下 make known throughout the world or country

【显要】xiǎnyào 官职高而权柄大,也指官职高而权柄大的人 powerful and influential:～人物 influential figure; important personage|朝中～ important figure in the imperial court; high-ranking official in the central government

【显耀】xiǎnyào ❶ 指声誉、权势等著称 be of high repute:～一时 be highly renowned for a time ❷ 夸耀;炫示 show off:～自己能干 show off one's abilities

【显影】xiǎn//yǐng 把曝过光的照相底片或相纸,用药液(酚、胺等)处理使显出影像。显影工作通常在暗室中进行。develop; immerse an exposed film, plate or printing paper in various chemical solutions usu. in a darkroom in order to make pictures visible

【显证】xiǎnzhèng 〈书 *fml.*〉明证 clear proof

【显著】xiǎnzhù 非常明显 notable; marked; striking; remarkable; outstanding:效益～ notable results|取得～成就 achieve remarkable success|发生～变化 remarkable change takes place

洗 Xiǎn 姓 a surname
☞ xǐ on p. 2053

险(險) xiǎn ❶ 地势险恶、复杂,不易通过;险要 (of terrain) dangerous; perilous; difficult of access:～地 strategic position|～隘 strategic pass; defile|～峻 dangerously steep; precipitous|山高水～。The mountain is high and the river dangerous. ❷ 地势险恶不容易通过的地方 place difficult of access; narrow pass; defile:天～ natural barrier|无～可守 have no tenable defence position; be strategically indefensible ❸ 遭到不幸或发生灾难的可能 danger; peril; risk:冒～ risk; take a risk; venture; have an adventure|保～ insure; insurance|脱～ escape from danger or risk|～症 dangerous illness or disease|巡堤查～ inspect the dam to find out the possible dangers ❹ 狠毒 sinister; vicious; venomous:阴～ sinister|～诈 sinister and sly ❺ 险些 by a hair's breadth; by inches; nearly; almost:～遭不幸 narrowly escape from death; come within an ace of death

【险隘】xiǎn'ài 险要的关口 strategic pass; defile

【险地】xiǎndì ❶ 险要的地方 strategic vantage point ❷ 危险的境地 perilous situation; dangerous circumstances

【险恶】xiǎn'è ❶（地势、情势等）危险可怕 dangerous; perilous; ominous: 山势～ difficult mountain terrain | 病情～ be dangerously ill | 环境～ dangerous or perilous surroundings ❷ 阴险恶毒 sinister; vicious; malicious; treacherous: ～用心 sinister or vicious intentions; evil motives

【险峰】xiǎnfēng 险峻的山峰 perilous peak: 攀登～ climb a dangerous peak

【险工】xiǎngōng 容易发生危险的工程 dangerous section (of a dyke or embankment)

【险固】xiǎngù 险要坚固 strategically secure; unassailable; strong in defence: 地势～。The topography makes it easy to defend.

【险关】xiǎnguān 险要的关口 strategic pass difficult of access

【险乎】xiǎn·hu 差一点(发生不如意的事) almost; nearly: ～干了件错事 nearly done a wrong thing

【险峻】xiǎnjùn ❶ (山势)高而险 dangerously steep; precipitous: 山峰～。The mountains are precipitous. ❷ 危险严峻 dangerous; critical; severe: 形势十分～。The situation is critical.

【险情】xiǎnqíng 容易发生危险的情况 dangerous state or situation: 排除～ remove the danger | 及时发现～ discover the dangers in good time

【险胜】xiǎnshèng 指体育比赛中,以接近的比分取胜 win by a narrow margin: 甲队以 31 比 30～乙队。Team A defeated Team B by a narrow margin 31-30.

【险滩】xiǎntān 江河中水浅礁石多、水流湍急、行船危险的地方 dangerous shoal; rapids; place with shoals and rapids in a river that spell danger for passing ships

【险巇】xiǎnxī 〈书 *fml.*〉形容山路危险,泛指道路艰难 (of roads, paths, etc.) dangerous and difficult; also 崄巇 xiǎnxī

【险象】xiǎnxiàng 危险的现象 dangerous sign; dangerous symptom: ～环生 dangers lurking on all sides; beset with perils

【险些】xiǎnxiē (～儿 xiǎnxiēr)差一点(发生不如意的事) narrowly (escape from sth. untoward); just barely; nearly: 马往旁边一闪,～把我摔下来。The horse suddenly shied and I was nearly thrown off.

【险要】xiǎnyào (地势)险峻而处于要冲 strategically located and difficult of access

【险韵】xiǎnyùn 指做旧体诗时用生僻字或同韵的字少的字押的韵 difficult rhyme; (of classical poetry) rhyming with difficult words or those with few matching rhyming words

【险诈】xiǎnzhà 阴险奸诈 sinister and crafty

【险症】xiǎnzhèng 危险的症候 dangerous illness

【险阻】xiǎnzǔ (道路)险恶而有阻碍,不容易过去 (of roads) dangerous and difficult: 崎岖～的山路 dangerous and difficult mountain path

蚬 xiǎn 软体动物,介壳圆形或心脏形,表面有轮状纹。生活在淡水中或河流入海的地方。little mussel (*Corbicula leana*); small clam living in fresh water or places where the rivers flow into the seas; soft-body animal in round shells or heart-shaped shells with wheel patterns on the surface

崄(嶮) xiǎn [崄巇](xiǎnxī) same as 险巇 xiǎnxī

崟(嶮) xiǎn 地名用字,周家崟,在陕西 Xian, used in geographical names, such as Zhoujiaxian in Shaanxi Province

毨(毨) xiǎn 〈书 *fml.*〉(鸟兽新生的毛)齐整 (of new-grown hair of an animal or feathers of a bird) neat; uniform

猃(玁) xiǎn [猃狁](xiǎnyǔn) same as 猃狁 xiǎnyǔn

猃(獫) xiǎn 〈书 *fml.*〉长(cháng)嘴的狗 dog with a long snout or muzzle

【猃狁】Xiǎnyǔn 我国古代北方的一个民族 Xianyun, an ancient nomadic people living in the northern part of China; also 猃狁 xiǎnyǔn

铣 xiǎn [铣铁](xiǎntiě) 铸铁 cast iron
☞ xǐ on p. 2054

筅(箲) xiǎn [筅帚](xiǎnzhǒu)〈方 *dial.*〉炊帚(多指用竹子做的) brush for cleaning pots and pans (usu. made of bamboo)

跣 xiǎn 〈书 *fml.*〉光着(脚) barefoot: ～足 with bare feet; barcfoot; barefooted

㬎 xiǎn 〈书 *fml.*〉same as 显 xiǎn

鲜(尟、尠) xiǎn 少 little; rare: ～见 rarely seen; seldom met with | ～有 rare; rarely available | ～为人知 little known | 寡廉～耻 lost to shame; brazen
☞ xiān on p. 2073

藓 xiǎn 苔藓植物的一个纲。属于这一纲的植物茎和叶子都很小,绿色,没有根,生在阴湿的地方。moss (*Musci*); any of various classes of bryophytes having tiny stems with tiny leaflike structures and without roots, and growing in velvety clusters on damp rocks, trees, moist ground, etc.

燹 xiǎn 〈书 *fml.*〉野火 wild fires; ☞ 兵燹 bīngxiǎn on p. 139

幰 xiǎn 〈书 *fml.*〉车的帷幔 curtain of a carriage

xiàn (ㄒㄧㄢˋ)

苋 xiàn same as 苋菜 xiàncài

【苋菜】xiàncài 一年生草本植物,茎细长,叶子椭圆形，有长柄，暗紫色或绿色，花绿白色，种子黑色。茎和叶子是普通蔬菜。amaranth three-coloured amaranth (*Amaranthus tricolor*); annual herbaceous plant with a long slender stem, dark purple or green elliptical long-stalked leaves, greenish-white flowers, black seeds, both stem and leaves used as vegetable

县(縣) xiàn 行政区划单位，由地区、自治州、直辖市领导 county, an administrative unit under the leadership of a prefecture, autonomous prefecture or a central municipality
〈古 *arch.*〉 same as 悬 xuán

【县城】xiànchéng 县行政机关所在的城镇 county seat; county town

【县份】xiànfèn 县(不和专名连用 not used with specific place names) county：崇信是甘肃东部的一个～。Chongxin is a county in eastern Gansu Province.

【县志】xiànzhì 记载一个县的历史、地理、风俗、人物、文教、物产等的专书 county gazetteer; general records of a county; county annals; special book recording a county's history, geography, customs, important figures, culture, education, resources, etc.

【县治】xiànzhì〈旧指 *old*〉县政府的所在地 seat of a county government; county seat

岘 Xiàn 岘山，山名，在湖北 Xianshan, name of a mountain in Hubei Province

现(❺见) xiàn ❶ 现在；此刻 present; current; existing：～状 current (or present) situation | ～任 at present hold the office of; currently in office | ～役 active service; active duty | ～行犯 active criminal ❷ 临时；当时 impromptu; extempore：～编～唱 improvise and sing simultaneously | ～做的烧饼 sesame cakes fresh from the oven ❸ 当时可以拿出来的 (of money, etc.) on hand：～货 merchandise or stock on hand | ～金 cash; ready money | ～钱 cash; ready money ❹ 现款 cash; ready money：兑～ pay cash on a check; cash a check | 贴～ discount on the rate of exchange ❺ 表露在外面，使人可以看见 show; appear; become visible：～原形 show one's true colours | 图穷匕首～。When the map is unrolled, the dagger is revealed.
☞ jiàn on p. 950

【现场】xiànchǎng ❶ 发生案件或事故的场所以及该场所在发生案件或事故时的状况 scene (of an incident)：保护～，以便进行调查。Keep the scene (of a crime or accident) intact to facilitate investigation. ❷ 直接从事生产、演出、试验等的场所 site; spot (where production, performance, experiment, etc. is going on)：～参观 visit a site | ～会议 on-the-spot meeting | ～直播 live broadcast

【现成】xiànchéng (～儿 xiànchéngr) 已经准备好，不用临时做或找的；原有的 ready-made：～饭 ready food | ～话 onlooker's unsolicited comments; kibitzer's comments | 你帮帮忙去，别净等～儿的。Go and render a hand, and don't wait until it's ready.

【现成饭】xiànchéngfàn 已经做成的饭 food ready for the table;〈比喻 *fig.*〉不劳而获的利益 unearned gain

【现成话】xiànchénghuà 不参与其事而在旁说冠冕堂皇的空话，叫说现成话 onlooker's unsolicited comments; kibitzer's comments; kibitz

【现存】xiàncún 现在留存；现有 extant; in stock：～的版本 extant edition | ～物资 goods and materials in stock

【现大洋】xiàndàyáng same as 现洋 xiànyáng

【现代】xiàndài 现在这个时代。在我国历史分期上多指五四运动到现在的时期。modern times; contemporary age; modern; contemporary; usu. the period from the May 4th Movement of 1919 to the present times in Chinese history

【现代化】xiàndàihuà 使具有现代先进科学技术水平 modernize; modernization of science and technology：国防～ modernization of national defence | ～的设备 sophisticated equipment

【现代戏】xiàndàixì 指以现代社会生活为题材的戏剧 drama with a contemporary theme

【现话】xiànhuà〈方 *dial.*〉老一套的话；废话 cliche; old same story

【现货】xiànhuò 可以当时交付的货物(跟'期货'相对 as opposed to 'futures') merchandise on hand; spots：～交易 spot transaction; over-the-counter trading | 备有～ merchandise are on hand or available

【现今】xiànjīn 现在；如今 nowadays; these days：这种式样～不时兴了。This design is no longer in vogue nowadays.

【现金】xiànjīn ❶ 现款，有时也包括可以提取现款的支票等 ready money; cash; (sometimes) payable checks：～交易 cash transaction ❷ 银行库存的货币 cash reserve in a bank

【现金账】xiànjīnzhàng 记载现金收支的会计账簿 cash account; cash book

【现局】xiànjú 现时的局面 current situation

【现款】xiànkuǎn 可以当时交付的货币 ready money; cash

【现年】xiànnián 现在的年龄 present age

【现钱】xiànqián same as 现款 xiànkuǎn

【现任】xiànrèn ❶ 现在担任(职务) at present hold the office of：他～工会主席。At present he holds the position of chairman of the trade union. ❷ 现在任职的 currently in office; incumbent：～校长是原来的教导主任。The incumbent schoolmaster used to be the head teacher.

【现如今】xiànrújīn〈方 *dial.*〉现在；如今 nowadays; at present; now

【现身说法】xiàn shēn shuō fǎ 本佛教用语，指佛力广大，能现出种种人形，向人说法。今比喻用自己的经历遭遇为例证,对人进行讲解或劝导。(Budd.) power that enables the Buddha to appear in various human forms to give advice to people; (fig.) advise sb. or explain sth. by citing one's own experience

【现时】xiànshí 现在;当前 now; at present: ~正是农忙时节。It is the busy farming season at present.

【现实】xiànshí ❶ 客观存在的事物 reality; actuality: 考虑问题,不能脱离~。Don't get divorced from reality when you think of any problem. ❷ 合于客观情况 real; actual: 这个计划不~。This plan is unrealistic. | 这是一个比较~的办法。This is a more realistic way of doing things.

【现实主义】xiànshí zhǔyì 文学艺术上的一种创作方法。通过典型人物、典型环境的描写,反映现实生活的本质。realism; method of literary creation by which to reflect the essence of the actual life through portrayal of typical persons and typical surroundings; 旧称 formerly called 写实主义 xiěshí zhǔyì

【现世】[1] xiànshì 今生;这一辈子 this life: ~报 retribution in this life

【现世】[2] xiànshì 出丑;丢脸 lose face; be disgraced; bring shame on oneself: 活~ really disgraceful (or shameful)

【现世报】xiànshìbào 迷信的人指人做了坏事今生就得到报应 (superstition) retribution in this life

【现势】xiànshì 目前的形势 current situation; trend of the times

【现下】xiànxià 现在;目前 now; at present: ~正忙,过几天再说。I'm busy now. Let's put it aside for a few days.

【现…现…】xiàn…xiàn… 嵌用两个动词,表示为了某个目的而临时采取某种行动 [used with two verbs, expressing the idea of doing sth. extempore for a certain need]: ~编~唱 make up a song as one sings | ~趸~卖 sell sth. immediately after it is bought | ~用~买 buy for immediate use | ~吃~做 cook for immediate consumption; 现 also put as 旋 xuàn

【现象】xiànxiàng 事物在发展、变化中所表现的外部的形态和联系 appearance (of things); phenomenon; external form of development and change of a thing and its relation: 社会~ social phenomenon | 自然~ natural phenomenon | 看问题不能只看~,要看本质。We should not judge problems simply by their appearance; we must grasp their essence.

【现行】xiànxíng ❶ 现在施行的;现在有效的 currently in effect; in force; in operation: ~法令 decrees in effect | ~制度 rules and regulations in force ❷ 正在进行或不久前曾进行犯罪活动的 (of a criminal) active: ~犯 active criminal

【现行法】xiànxíngfǎ 指一个国家正在施行、具有效力的法律 law in effect

【现行犯】xiànxíngfàn 法律上指正在预备犯罪、实行犯罪或犯罪后即时被发觉的罪犯 active criminal (criminal caught in, before or immediately after the act)

【现形】xiàn//xíng 显露原形 reveal one's true features; betray oneself: 《官场~记》(清末小说名) *Revealing True Colours of Officialdom* (a novel published towards the end of the Qing Dynasty)

【现眼】xiàn//yǎn 出丑;丢脸 make a spectacle (or fool) of oneself; lose face: 丢人~ make a fool of oneself | 这回差点儿现了眼,以后可得小心。You almost made a spectacle of yourself this time. Be careful in the future.

【现洋】xiànyáng 旧指银元 silver dollar in old times; also 现大洋 xiàndàyáng

【现役】xiànyì ❶ 公民自应征入伍之日起到退伍之日止所服的兵役 in active service, beginning from the day of a citizen's conscription and ending on the day of demobilization; on active duty ❷ 正在服兵役的 in active service; on active duty; active: ~军人 member of the armed forces in active service; serviceman

【现在】xiànzài 这个时候,指说话的时候,有时包括说话前后或长或短的一段时间(区别于'过去'或'将来' as distinguished from 'past' or 'future') now; at present; today; this time; at the time of speaking, sometimes including a period of short or long time before or after speaking: 他~的情况怎么样? How is he getting on now? | ~他当了厂长了。He is now director of the factory.

【现职】xiànzhí 目前正担任着的职务 incumbent; present position (or job, post): 他当过班长、排长,年初改任~。He used to be a squad leader and a platoon leader and took the present post at the beginning of this year.

【现状】xiànzhuàng 目前的状况 present (or current) situation; status quo; existing state of affairs: 打破~ break the status quo | 改变~ change the status quo | 维持~ maintain the status quo

哯 xiàn 〈书 *fml.*〉太阳出现 sunrise; appearance of the sun

限 xiàn ❶ 指定的范围;限度 limit; bounds: 界~ demarcation line | 期~ time limit | 权~ terms of reference; limits of one's authority | 以年底为~ set the end of the year as the deadline ❷ 指定范围,不许超过 set a limit; limit; restrict: ~期完工 finish a project within a time limit | 人数不~。There is no restriction (or limit) on the number of people. ❸ 〈书 *fml.*〉门槛 threshold: 门~ threshold | 户~ threshold

【限定】xiàndìng 在数量、范围等方面加以规定 prescribe (or set) a limit to; limit; restrict: ~

报名时间 set a deadline for entry|讨论的范围不～。The subject matter of the discussion is not limited.

【限度】xiàndù 范围的极限；最高或最低的数量或程度 limit；limitation：最高～ the highest limit|容忍是有～的。There is a limit to our tolerance.

【限额】xiàn'é 规定的数额 norm；quota；cap

【限界】xiànjiè 限定的界线 boundary limit

【限量】xiànliàng ❶ 限定止境、数量 limit the quantity of；set bounds to：前途不可～ have boundless prospects|～供应 limit the quantity of supply ❷ 限度 limit；limitation

【限令】xiànlìng ❶ 命令限期实行 order sb. to do sth. within a certain period of time：～三日内拆除违章建筑。A three-day limit is set for the demolition of the illegal buildings. ❷ 限定执行的命令 orders to be executed within a time limit：放宽～ extend the deadline（or time limit）

【限期】xiànqī ❶ 指定日期，不许超过 prescribe（or set）a time limit：～归还 return with the time limit|～报到 report for duty by the prescribed time ❷ 指定的不许超过的日期 time limit；deadline：～已满。The time limit has been reached.|三天的～ three-day time limit

【限于】xiànyú 受某些条件或情形的限制；局限在某一范围之内 be confined to；be limited to：～水平 limited knowledge|本文讨论的范围，～一些原则问题。The subject matter of this article is limited to a few questions of principle.

【限止】xiànzhǐ same as 限制 xiànzhì

【限制】xiànzhì ❶ 规定范围，不许超过；约束 place（or impose）restrictions on；restrict；limit；confine：～其行动自由 restrict sb.'s freedom of action|文章的字数不～。There is no restriction on the length of the article. ❷ 规定的范围 restriction；limit；confinement：有一定的～ have specified restrictions

线（綫） xiàn ❶（～儿 xiànr）用丝、棉、麻、金属等制成的细长而可以任意曲折的东西 thread；string；wire；cord；long, fine, stringlike length of material made of spun cotton, flax, silk, metal, etc.：一根～ a piece of thread|一绺～ a skein of thread|毛～ knitting wool|电～ electric wire ❷ 几何学上指一个点任意移动所构成的图形，有长，没有宽和厚。分为直线和曲线两种。（geom.）line；path of a moving point, thought of as having length, but not breadth nor thickness, whether straight or curved ❸ 细长像线的东西 sth. shaped like a line：～香 slender stick of incense ❹ 交通路线 communication line：航～ airline|运输～ transport line or route|京广～ Beijing-Guangzhou Railway|沿～各站 stations along a railway ❺ 指思想上、政治上的路线 political line：上纲上～ labeling sb. by exaggerating his flow or mistake in an ideological or political context ❻ 边缘交界的地方 demarcation line；boundary；dividing line：前～ battlefront|火～ battle line；frontline；front|防～ defence line；line of defence|海岸～ coastline|国境～ boundary line of a country；frontier ❼〈比喻 *fig.*〉所接近的某种边际 brink；verge：生命～ life line|死亡～ on the verge of death|饥饿～ on the brink of starvation ❽ 线索 clue；lead；thread：眼～ informer；spy ❾〈量词 *classifier*〉用于抽象事物，数词限用'一'，表示极少［used abstractly after 一 yī to indicate a very tiny amount］：一～光明 a gleam of light|一～希望 a ray of hope|一～生机 a slim chance of life

【线材】xiàncái 断面很小，可以卷起来的金属材料，如铁丝等 wire；metal material with a very small section, that can be coiled

【线春】xiànchūn 一种有几何图案花纹的丝织品，多用做春季衣料，浙江杭州所产的最有名 silk fabric with a geometric design（for spring wear）produced in Hangzhou, Zhejiang Province；also 春绸 chūnchóu

【线段】xiànduàn 直线上任意两点间的部分 line segment；segment of a straight line between any two points

【线桄子】xiànguàng·zi 缠线的器具，中间有轴，可以旋转 reel or spool for winding thread；also 线桄儿 xiànguàngr

【线规】xiànguī 测量金属线的直径用的工具，是一块圆形或方形的钢板，边缘有许多大小不同的开口，并标有线号或尺寸。金属线通过的开口所标的号数或尺寸就是该线的号数或直径。wire gauge；round or square steel sheet for measuring the diameter of wire, thickness of sheet metal, etc., usu. consisting of a disk with notches of graduated sizes along its edge. The size marked on one of the notches through which a metal wire passes is its exact size or diameter.

【线脚】xiànjiǎo〈方 *dial.*〉针脚 stitch：～很密 sewn with close stitches

【线粒体】xiànlìtǐ 细胞质内粒状或棒状的细胞器，能为细胞提供能量，能自行分裂，在遗传上有相对独立性 mitochondrion；chondriosome；any of various very small, usu. rodlike structures found in the cytoplasm of eucaryotic cells and serving as a centre of intracellular enzyme activity which produces the ATP needed to power the cell, capable of splitting on its own and having relative independence

【线路】xiànlù 电流、运动物体等所经过的路线 circuit；line；route；path that electric current, moving objects, etc. pass：公共汽车～ bus line or route|无线电～ radio line

【线呢】xiànní 用有颜色的纱或线按不同花型织成的棉布，质地厚实，富于弹性，外表有点像毛呢 cotton suiting；thick and cotton fabric with elasticity, woven with coloured yarn or thread to form different patterns, a bit like woollen suiting

【线坯子】xiànpī·zi 粗制的棉线,质地松,可捻成合股儿线 coarse cotton thread with loose texture, which can be twisted into plied yarn

【线圈】xiànquān 用带有绝缘外皮的导线绕制成的圈状物或筒状物,广泛应用在电机、变压器和电讯装置上 coil; spiral or loop of wire or other conducting element with insulating covering, used as an inductor, heating element, etc. in motors, transformers and communication equipment

【线索】xiànsuǒ 〈比喻 *fig.*〉事物发展的脉络或探求问题的途径 clue; thread: 故事的～ threads of a story | 找到了破案的～ find the clues for solving a case

【线毯】xiàntǎn 用棉纱、混纺纱织成的较薄的毯子 cotton (thread) blanket; thin blanket woven of thick cotton yarn or mixed yarn

【线膛】xiàntáng 有膛线的枪膛或炮膛 rifled bore: ～炮 cannon with a rifled bore

【线条】xiàntiáo ❶ 绘画时勾的或曲或直、或粗或细的线 arts line; contour; figure: 粗～ bold lines | 这幅画的～非常柔和。The lines of this painting are very soft. ❷ 人体或工艺品的轮廓 line; figure; outline

【线头】xiàntóu (～儿 xiàntóur) ❶ 线的一端 end of a thread ❷ 很短的一段线 an odd piece of thread; a bit of thread; also 线头子 xiàntóu·zi

【线香】xiànxiāng 用木屑加香料做成的细长而不带棒儿的香 slender stick of incense, made of sawdust mixed with perfume

【线形动物】xiànxíng dòngwù 无脊椎动物的一门,身体的形状像线或圆筒,两端略尖,不分环节,表面有皮,体内有消化管,大多数雌雄异体,如蛔虫、钩虫等 roundworm; invertebrate with its body shaped like a line or a round cylinder, pointed at both ends, with no segments, with skin outside the body and a digestive tract within it, most of them being dioecious, as roundworm, hookworm, etc.; also 圆形动物 yuánxíng dòngwù

【线衣】xiànyī 用粗棉线织成的上衣 cotton knitwear; clothes knitted of coarse cotton yarn

【线轴儿】xiànzhóur 缠线用的轴形物;缠着线的轴形物 reel for thread; bobbin; reel (or spool) of thread

【线装】xiànzhuāng 书籍装订法的一种,装订的线露在书的外面,是我国传统的装订法 stitch binding; thread binding; traditional technique of book binding in China: ～书 thread-bound book

宪(憲) xiàn ❶ 〈书 *fml.*〉法令 statute: ～令 laws and ordinances ❷ 宪法 constitution: 立～ constitutional; draw up a constitution | 违～ violation of the constitution; unconstitutional | ～章 charter

【宪兵】xiànbīng 某些国家的军事政治警察 gendarme; military and political police in some countries; military police; military police corps

【宪法】xiànfǎ 国家的根本法。具有最高的法律效力,是其他立法工作的根据。通常规定一个国家的社会制度、国家制度、国家机构和公民的基本权利与义务等。constitution; fundamental law of a country. It has the supreme legal effect and provides the basis for the formulation of other laws. It usually provides for the social system, state system, state organizing, structure the basic rights and obligations of the citizens of a country.

【宪警】xiànjǐng 宪兵和警察 gendarme and police

【宪章】xiànzhāng ❶ 〈书 *fml.*〉效法 follow the example of; model oneself on; learn from ❷ 〈书 *fml.*〉典章制度 institutions, decrees and regulations ❸ 某个国家的具有宪法作用的文件;规定国际机构的宗旨、原则、组织的文件 charter; document of a certain country with constitutional effect; document of an international institution providing for the purpose, principles and organization of the institution

【宪政】xiànzhèng 民主的政治 democratic government; constitutional government; constitutionalism: 实行～ practise constitutional government | ～运动 constitutional movement

粯 xiàn 〈书 *fml.*〉米屑 broken rice

【粯子】xiàn·zi 〈方 *dial.*〉粗麦粉 wholewheat; wholemeal

陷 xiàn ❶ 陷阱 pitfall; trap ❷ 掉进(泥土等松软的物体里) get stuck or bogged down (in mud or sth. soft and loose): 越～越深 sink deeper and deeper | 汽车～在泥里了。The car got stuck in the mud. ❸ 凹进 sink; cave in: 病了几天,眼睛都～进去了。After being ill for a few days, his eyes became sunken. ❹ 陷害 frame (up): 诬～ make a false charge against; frame sb. | ～人于罪 make a false charge against; frame sb. (up) ❺ 被攻破;被占领 (of a town, etc.) be captured; fall: 失～ fall | 沦～ be captured ❻ 缺点 defect; deficiency: 缺～ defect

【陷害】xiànhài 设计害人 frame (up); make a false charge against: ～好人 frame up an innocent person

【陷阱】xiànjǐng ❶ 为捉野兽或敌人而挖的坑,上面浮盖伪装的东西,踩在上面就掉到坑里 pitfall; pit; trap; snare; covered pit for use to ensnare wild animals or an enemy ❷ 〈比喻 *fig.*〉害人的圈套 trap; trick by which sb. is misled into giving themselves away

【陷坑】xiànkēng same as 陷阱 xiànjǐng

【陷落】xiànluò ❶ 地面或其他物体的表面一部分向里凹进去 subside; sink in; cave in: 许多盆地都是因为地壳～而形成的。Many basins

were formed by the subsidence of the earth's crust. ❷ same as 陷入 xiànrù ① ❸ (领土)为敌占领 (of territory) fall into enemy hands; be taken; be captured

【陷落地震】xiànluò dìzhèn 地震的一种,由地壳内岩层受水的侵蚀,形成空洞,造成局部地层陷落而引起。波及范围和破坏性都较小。depression earthquake; earthquake caused by the cave-in of rock beneath the surface of the crust after the erosion of rock by water makes it hollow. It affects a small area and is less destructive.

【陷入】xiànrù ❶ 落在(不利的境地) sink (or fall) into (a predicament); land oneself in; be caught in; get bogged down in:～重围 find oneself tightly encircled | ～停顿状态 come to a standstill ❷〈比喻 *fig.*〉深深地进入(某种境界或思想活动中) be lost in (a certain state of affairs or reverie); be immersed in; be deep in:～沉思 be lost in thought; be deep in meditation

【陷身】xiànshēn 身体陷入 fall into; land in:～囹圄(língyǔ,监狱 prison) be put into prison; be imprisoned

【陷于】xiànyú same as 陷入 xiànrù ①:～孤立 find oneself isolated | 双方谈判～僵局。The talks between the two sides were in a deadlock.

【陷阵】xiànzhèn 冲入敌阵 break through enemy lines:冲锋～ charge against the enemy lines; fight bravely in battles

馅 xiàn (～儿 xiànr) 面食、点心里包的糖、豆沙或细碎的肉、菜等 filling; stuffing; sugar, mashed red bean or minced meat and vegetables filled in the pastries:饺子～儿 stuffing for dumplings | 枣泥～儿月饼 moon cakes filled with mashed dates

X

【馅儿饼】xiànrbǐng 带馅儿的饼,用面做薄皮,包上肉、菜等拌成的馅儿,在锅上或铛上烙熟 meat pie; baked cake filled with a mixture of meat and vegetables

羡(羨) xiàn ❶ 羡慕 admire; envy:歆～ admire (with pleasure) | 艳～ great envy ❷ (Xiàn)姓 a surname

【羡慕】xiànmù 看见别人有某种长处、好处或有利条件而希望自己也有 admire; envy; desire for sb. else's strong point, benefit, advantage, etc.:他很～我有这么一个好师傅。He envies me my good master.

缐 xiàn ❶ same as 线 xiàn ❷ (Xiàn)姓 a surname

献(獻) xiàn ❶ 把实物或意见等恭敬庄严地送给集体或尊敬的人 offer; present; dedicate; donate; give an object, idea, etc. respectfully to an organisation or a esteemed person:～花 present flowers; give a bouquet | ～旗 present a banner | 贡～ contribute | 把青春～给祖国 dedicate one's youthful years to the motherland ❷ 表现给人看 show; put on; display:～技 display one's skill | ～殷勤 curry favour

【献宝】xiàn//bǎo ❶ 献出珍贵的物品 present a treasure ❷〈比喻 *fig.*〉提供宝贵的经验或意见 offer a valuable piece of advice or one's valuable experience ❸〈比喻 *fig.*〉显示自己的东西或自以为新奇的东西 show off what one treasures or what one thinks is novel

【献策】xiàn//cè same as 献计 xiàn//jì

【献丑】xiàn//chǒu〈谦辞 *hum.*〉用于表演技能或写作的时候,表示自己的能力很差 (speaking of one's own performance) show oneself up; show one's incompetence (or inadequacy)

【献词】xiàncí 祝贺的话或文字 congratulatory message:新年～ New Year message

【献花】xiàn//huā 把鲜花献给贵宾或敬爱的人 present flowers or bouquets to a distinguished guest or a respected person

【献计】xiàn//jì 贡献计策 offer advice; make suggestions; brainstorm about sth.

【献技】xiànjì 把技艺表演给大家看 show one's skill (in a performance)

【献礼】xiàn//lǐ 为了表示庆祝而献出礼物 present a gift (in token of congratulation or celebration):国庆～ greet National Day with new and outstanding successes

【献媚】xiànmèi 为了讨好别人而做出某种姿态或举动 try to ingratiate oneself with; make up to:～取宠 curry favour with

【献旗】xiàn//qí 把锦旗献给某个集体或个人,表示敬意或谢意 present a banner (to a collective or individual in token of gratitude or respect)

【献芹】xiànqín《列子·杨朱》:'昔人有美戎菽、甘枲茎、芹萍子者,对乡豪称之。乡豪取而尝之,蜇于口,惨于腹。众哂而怨之,其人大惭。'后来用'献芹'谦称赠人的礼品菲薄或所提的建议浅陋。*Liezi · Yang Zhu*: 'Someone of yore told a rich man in his village how delicious the beans, the stem of sweet moss and celery were. When the rich man took and tasted some of the celery, his mouth ached and his belly troubled. The man felt greatly ashamed as the crowd laughed and blamed him.' Afterwards, the phrase 'offering one's celery' has been used to indicate the offering of a humble gift or suggestion. also 芹献 qínxiàn

【献身】xiàn//shēn 把自己的全部精力或生命献给祖国、人民或事业 devote (or dedicate) oneself to (the cause of the motherland and the people); give one's life for (the cause of):～于教育事业几十年 have devoted oneself to the cause of education for dozens of years | 为革命而光荣～ dedicate one's life to revolution

【献艺】xiànyì same as 献技 xiànjì:登台～ go onstage to give a performance

【献殷勤】xiàn yīnqín 为了讨别人的欢心而奉

承、伺候 do everything to please; pay attentions to; pay one's addresses

腺 xiàn 生物体内能分泌某些化学物质的组织,由腺细胞组成,如人体内的汗腺和唾液腺,花的蜜腺 gland; any organ or specialized group of cells that secretes certain chemical substances, as the sweat gland and salivary gland in the human body, nectary of the flower, etc.

【腺细胞】xiànxìbāo 机体各组织的表皮中能制造和分泌某种液体物质的细胞,如构成汗腺、唾液腺等的细胞 gland cell; any cell on the epidermis of the tissues that can produce and secrete certain fluid, as the cells that form the sweat gland and salivary gland

锒 xiàn 金属线 metal wire

霰 xiàn 空中降落的白色不透明的小冰粒,常呈球形或圆锥形。多在下雪前或下雪时出现。在不同的地区有雪子(xuězǐ)、雪糁(xuěshēn)等名称。graupel; soft hail; precipitation consisting of brittle, white, spherical or cone-shaped ice particles having a snowlike structure, usu. seen before or at the time snowing; also called 雪子 xuězǐ or 雪糁 xuěshēn in some places

【霰弹】xiàndàn ☞ 榴霰弹 liúxiàndàn on p. 1245

xiāng(ㄒㄧㄤ)

乡(鄉) xiāng ❶ 乡村(跟'城'相对 opposed to 'city, town') country; countryside; village; rural area: 山~ mountain village | 下~ go to the countryside | 城~物资交流 interflow of goods between urban and rural areas; exchange of goods between city and countryside ❷ 家乡 native place; home village or town: 背井离~ leave one's native place | 回~务农 return to one's home village and take up farming ❸ 我国行政区划的基层单位,由县或县以下的区领导 township (grassroots level rural administrative unit under a county or a district of a county)

【乡巴佬儿】xiāng·balǎor 乡下人(含讥讽意),也指没有见过世面的人 (derog.) country bumpkin; country folk; person who has not seen much of the world

【乡愁】xiāngchóu 深切思念家乡的心情 homesickness: 离家多年,~与日俱增。As I have been away from home for many years, my homesickness is growing with each passing day.

【乡村】xiāngcūn 主要从事农业、人口分布较城镇分散的地方 village; countryside; rural area; area where farm production is the main occupation and the population is more scattered than in a city or town

【乡间】xiāngjiān 乡村里 in the village; in the country

【乡井】xiāngjǐng 〈书 *fml.*〉家乡 native place; home village or town: 远离~ far away from the home village

【乡里】xiānglǐ ❶ 家庭久居的地方(指小城镇或农村) home village or town: 荣归~ return to one's home village in glory ❷ 同乡的人 fellow villagers or townspeople: 看望~ pay a visit to one's fellow villagers

【乡僻】xiāngpì 离城市远而偏僻 far from town; out-of-the-way: ~之地 out-of-the-way place

【乡亲】xiāngqīn ❶ 同乡的人 person from the same village or town; fellow villager or townsman ❷ 对农村中当地人民的称呼 term of direct address for local people or villagers: ~们 folks

【乡情】xiāngqíng 对故乡的感情 affection for one's home village or home town

【乡曲】xiāngqū 〈书 *fml.*〉 ❶ 乡里 remote countryside: 横行~ act like an overlord in the village ❷ 指乡僻的地方 out-of-the-way village

【乡绅】xiāngshēn 〈旧指 *old*〉乡间的绅士 country gentleman; squire

【乡试】xiāngshì 明清两代,每三年在省城举行一次的考试,考中的人称举人 provincial examination, under the Ming-Qing civil service examination system; examination for the selection of *juren* (successful candidates at the provincial level) from among of *xiucai* (candidates who had passed such an examination at the county level), held triennially in various provincial capitals

【乡思】xiāngsī 怀念家乡的心情 homesickness; nostalgia

【乡谈】xiāngtán 指家乡话 local dialect

【乡土】xiāngtǔ 本乡本土 native soil; one's native land; local: ~观念 provincialism | ~风味 local flavour

【乡下】xiāng·xia 乡村里 countryside; village

【乡谊】xiāngyì 〈书 *fml.*〉同乡的情分 friendship between people from the same native place

【乡音】xiāngyīn 家乡的口音 accent of one's native place; local accent: ~未改 one's local accent remains unchanged

【乡愿】xiāngyuàn 〈书 *fml.*〉外貌忠诚谨慎,实际上欺世盗名的人 hypocrite; person who looks honest, but actually gains fame by dishonest means

【乡镇】xiāngzhèn ❶ 乡和镇 villages and towns ❷ 泛指较小的市镇 small towns in general

芗(薌) xiāng ❶ 古书上指用以调味的香草 fragrant herb mentioned in ancient texts ❷ 〈书 *fml.*〉 same as 香 xiāng

【芗剧】xiāngjù 流行于台湾、福建南部芗江(九龙江中游)一带的地方戏曲剧种,清末在台湾形成。台湾称之为歌仔戏。*xiangju* opera; local opera popular in Taiwan and Xiangjiang (the middle reaches of the Jiulong or Nine-Dragon River) in southern Fujian. It took shape in Taiwan towards the end of the Qing Dynasty and was called 歌仔戏 gēzǎixì on the island.

相[1] xiāng ❶ 互相 each other; one another; mutually: ～像 be alike; be similar; resemble | ～识 be acquainted with | ～距太远 be too far apart | 不～上下 almost equal; about the same ❷ 表示一方对另一方的动作 indicating an action done by one person to another: 实不～瞒 to tell you the truth | 好言～劝 coax sb. with well-meant words ❸ (Xiāng) 姓 a surname

相[2] xiāng 亲自观看(是不是合心意) see for oneself (whether sb. or sth. is to one's liking): ～亲 take a look at one's prospective son-in-law or daughter-in-law | 这件衣服她～不中。This dress is not to her liking.

☞ xiàng on p. 2097

【相安】 xiāng'ān 相处没有冲突 get along in peace: ～无事 live in peace with each other

【相帮】 xiāngbāng 〈方 *dial.*〉帮助 help; aid; assist

【相称】 xiāngchèn 事物配合起来显得合适 match; suit: 这件衣服跟他的年龄不大～。This jacket doesn't suit a person of his age.

【相成】 xiāngchéng 互相成全、配合 complement each other: 相辅～ supplement each other; complement each other | 相反～ be opposite and supplementary to each other; oppose and yet complement each other

【相持】 xiāngchí 两方坚持对立,互不相让 be locked in a stalemate: 意见～不下 each sticks to his own stand; be locked in a stalemate; neither side was ready to yield | 敌我～阶段 enemy and our side are locked in a stalemate

【相处】 xiāngchǔ 彼此生活在一起;彼此接触来往,互相对待 get along (with one another): 友好～ get along in amity; live together in friendship | 难以～ difficult to get along with

【相传】 xiāngchuán ❶ 长期以来互相传说(不是确实有据,只是辗转传说的) tradition has it that ...; according to legend; legend goes that ...; story handed down for generations among a people and popularly believed to have a historical basis, although not verifiable: ～此处是穆桂英的点将台。According to legend, this place used to be where Mu Guiying, a female general, summoned her officers and assigned them tasks. ❷ 传递;传授 pass on; hand down: 一脉～ pass on in one continuous line

【相当】 xiāngdāng ❶ (数量、价值、条件、情形等)两方面差不多;配得上或能够相抵 (of quantity, value, terms, conditions, etc.) match; balance; correspond to; be about equal to; be commensurate with: 旗鼓～ be well matched; be about equal in strength to each other | 年纪～ well-matched in age; about the same age | 拦河大坝高达一百一十米,～于二十八层的大楼。The dam stands 110 metres, or the height of a 28-storey building. ❷ 适宜;合适 suitable; fit; appropriate: 这个工作还没有找到～的人。We haven't found a suitable person for the job yet. | 他一时想不出～的字眼来。At the time he couldn't think of a suitable word for it. ❸ 〈副词 *adv.*〉表示程度高,但不到'很'的程度 [indicating a high degree, but not to the degree of 'very'] quite; fairly; considerably: 这个任务是～艰巨的。The task is quite arduous. | 这出戏演得～成功。The performance was quite a success.

【相得益彰】 xiāng dé yì zhāng 指互相帮助,互相补充,更能显出好处 each shining more brilliantly in the other's company; bring out the best in each other; complement each other

【相等】 xiāngděng (数目、分量、程度等)彼此一样 (amount, quantity, number, degree, etc.) be equal: 这两间房子的面积～。The two rooms have the same amount of floor space.

【相抵】 xiāngdǐ ❶ 互相抵消 offset; balance; counterbalance: 收支～ one's accounts balance ❷ 〈书 *fml.*〉互相抵触 conflict with each other; go against each other

【相对】 xiāngduì ❶ 指性质上互相对立,如大与小相对,美与丑相对 opposite to each other, as big is the opposite of small, and beauty the opposite of ugliness; face to face ❷ 依靠一定条件而存在,随着一定条件而变化的(跟'绝对'相对 as opposed to 'absolute') relative; dependent on given conditions: 在绝对的总的宇宙发展过程中,各个具体过程的发展都是～的。In the absolute and general process of development of the universe, the development of each particular process is relative. ❸ 比较的 relatively; comparatively: ～稳定 relatively stable | ～优势 relative advantage; relative superiority

【相对高度】 xiāngduì gāodù 以地面或选定的某个点做标准的高度 relative altitude (or height); altitude taken with the ground surface or a given point as its standard

【相对论】 xiāngduìlùn 研究时间和空间相对关系的物理学说。分为狭义相对论和广义相对论。前者认为物体的运动是相对的,光速不因光源的运动而改变,物体的质量与能量的关系为 $E=mc^2$ (E 代表能量, m 代表质量, c 代表光速)。后者认为物质的运动是物质引力场派生的,光在引力场中传播因受引力场的影响而改变方向。相对论是爱因斯坦(Albert Einstein)提出的。这个理论修正了从牛顿以来对空间、时间、引力三者互相割裂的看法以及运动规律永恒不变的看法,从而奠定了现代物理学的基础。theory of relativity; theory of physics dealing with the relative relationship between time and space, including the general theory of relativity and the special theory of relativity. The former states that there is only relative motion of matter, that the velocity of light is constant and not dependent on the motion of the source, and that the relationship between the mass and energy is $E = mc^2$ (E represents energy, m represents mass, and c represents velocity). The latter states that motion is derived from the gravitational field, and the transmission of light in the gravitational field changes its direction as affected by the gravitational field. The theory of relativity was advanced by Albert Einstein, who revised the views since Isaac Newton, that space, time and gravitation are separated and that the law of motion is constant, thus laying the foundation for modern physics.

【相对湿度】xiāngduì shīdù 空气中所含水蒸气密度和同温度下饱和水蒸气密度的比值，通常用百分数表示 relative humidity; amount of moisture in the air as compared with the saturated humidity at the same temperature, expressed as a percentage

【相对真理】xiāngduì zhēnlǐ 在总的宇宙发展过程中，人们对于在各个发展阶段上的具体过程的正确认识，它是对客观世界近似的、不完全的反映。相对真理和绝对真理是辩证统一的，绝对真理寓于相对真理之中，在相对真理中包含有绝对真理的成分，无数相对真理的总和就是绝对真理。relative truth; correct knowledge of each particular proccss of development in the general process of development of the universe. It is the near, yet incomplete reflection of the objective world. Relative truth and absolute truth are in dialectical unity. Absolute truth dwells in relative truth and relative truth contains an element of absolute truth. The sum total of innumerable relative truths constitutes absolute truth.

【相烦】xiāngfán 〈客套话 *pol.*〉烦劳 trouble (or bother) you：有事～。May I trouble you for something?

【相反】xiāngfǎn ❶ 事物的两个方面互相矛盾、互相排斥 contrary; opposite：～相成 be opposite and supplementary to each other; oppose and yet complement each other | 两个人走的方向～。The two people walked in opposite directions. ❷ 用在下文句首或句中，表示跟上文所说的意思相矛盾 used at the beginning or in the middle of the following sentence：他不但没被困难吓倒，～地，意志越来越坚强了。He is not at all scared by difficulties; on the contrary, he is more resolute than ever before.

【相反数】xiāngfǎnshù 绝对值相等，正负号相反的两个数互为相反数。如 +5 和 -5，0 的相反数是 0。When the absolute values are equal, the two numbers with the opposite positive and negative signs are opposite numbers, as +5 and -5. The opposite number of 0 is 0.

【相反相成】xiāng fǎn xiāng chéng 指相反的东西有同一性。就是说，两个矛盾方面互相排斥或互相斗争，并在一定条件下联结起来，获得同一性。identity of two opposites. In other words, the two aspects of a contradiction repel and fight each other, and join together under given conditions to acquire identity.

【相仿】xiāngfǎng 大致相同；相差不多 be similar; resemble each other; be more or less the same：年纪～ be about the same age | 颜色～ be similar in colour; be alike in colour

【相逢】xiāngféng 彼此遇见（多指偶然的）meet (by chance); come across：萍水～ meet by mere chance | 狭路～ confront each other face to face; meet face to face

【相符】xiāngfú 彼此一致 conform to; tally (or agree) with; correspond to (or with)：名实～。The name corresponds to the reality. | 他所说的话跟实际的情况完全～。What he said corresponds fully to the actual situation.

【相辅而行】xiāng fǔ ér xíng 互相协助进行或配合使用 be complementary to each other; proceed in coordination; go together

【相辅相成】xiāng fǔ xiāng chéng 互相补充，互相配合 supplement and complement each other

【相干】xiānggān 互相关连或牵涉；有关连（多用于否定式 oft. used in the negative or in a rhetorical question) have sth. to do with; be concerned with：这事跟他不～。This has nothing to do with him.

【相隔】xiānggé 相互间距离 be separated by; be apart; be at a distance of：～千里 be a thousand *li* apart; be a long way away from each other

【相顾】xiānggù 互相对看 look at each other：～无言 look at each other in silence; look at each other and keep silence

【相关】xiāngguān 彼此关连 be mutually related; be interrelated：休戚～ be bound together by common interests | 体育事业和人民健康密切～。Physical culture has a direct bearing on the people's health.

【相好】xiānghǎo ❶ 彼此亲密，感情融洽 be on intimate terms：他们几个从小就～。They have been intimate friends since childhood. ❷ 亲密的朋友 intimate friend ❸ 恋爱（多指不正当的 usu. illicit) have an affair with ❹ 指不正当的恋爱的一方 lover or mistress; in a sexual relationship, one of the partners who are not married to each other

【相互】xiānghù 两相对待的；互相 mutually；each other；one another；reciprocal：～作用 interaction；interplay｜～促进 promote each other；mutual promotion｜～间的关系 mutual relation；interrelation

【相继】xiāngjì 一个跟着一个 in succession；one after another：～发言 speak one after another

【相间】xiāngjiàn（事物和事物）一个隔着一个 alternate with：沿岸～地栽着桃树和柳树。Peach trees and willows alternate with each other along the bank. *or* Peach trees are alternated with willows along the bank.

【相交】xiāngjiāo ❶ 交叉 intersect：两线～于一点。The two lines intersect each other at one point. ❷ 互相交往；做朋友 make friends with：～多年 have been friends for years

【相近】xiāngjìn 近似；差不多 close；near：年岁～ about the same age；similar age；be similar in age｜情况～ similar situation；similar condition

【相敬如宾】xiāng jìng rú bīn 形容夫妻互相尊敬像对待宾客一样（of husband and wife）treat each other with the respect due to a guest

【相距】xiāngjù 相互间距离 be separated by（a distance of ...）；be ... apart；be ... away from：～不远 not far apart from each other｜前后～二十多年 be apart for more than twenty years

【相看】xiāng·kàn ❶ 看；注视 look at each other ❷ 看待 regard；treat：另眼～ regard sb. with special attention ❸ 亲自观看（多用于相亲 usu. for marriage，etc.）see personally；see in person

【相礼】xiānglǐ same as 襄礼 xiānglǐ

【相连】xiānglián 互相连接 be linked together；be joined：前后～（of an article，etc.）beginning and ending being coherent；front and back being connected

【相瞒】xiāngmán 隐瞒 hide sth. from sb.：实不～ to tell you the truth

【相配】xiāngpèi 配合起来合适；相称 be suited to each other；be well-matched；be a good match：一个高，一个矮，不～。One being tall and the other short，they are not well matched.｜他们两个很～。They make a perfect match.

【相亲】xiāng//qīn 定亲前家长或本人到对方家相看 size up a prospective mate in an arranged meeting

【相去】xiāngqù 互相间存在距离；相距 distance between two places：～甚远（相差很大）there is much difference between｜两地～几十里。There is a distance of several dozen *li* between the two places.

【相劝】xiāngquàn 劝告；劝解 try to persuade sb.；offer advice to sb.：好言～ persuade sb. with good intentions

【相让】xiāngràng ❶ 忍让；退让 exercise forbearance；give in；make concessions：不肯～ refuse to make concessions｜各不～。Neither would give in. ❷ 互相谦让 defer to each other politely；yield to each other modestly

【相扰】xiāngrǎo ❶ 互相打扰 interfere with or disturb each other：各不～。Neither would disturb the other. ❷〈客套话 *pol.*〉打扰 disturb；bother：无事不敢～。If it weren't something important，I wouldn't bother you with it.

【相忍为国】xiāng rěn wèi guó 为了国家和民族的利益而作一定的让步 make certain concessions for the sake of national interests；show forbearance for the sake of the nation

【相濡以沫】xiāng rú yǐ mò 泉水干涸，鱼靠在一起以唾沫相互湿润（语见《庄子·大宗师》）。后用'相濡以沫'比喻同处困境，相互救助。（of stranded fish）moisten each other with spit when spring water dries up（from *Zhuangzi·Great and Venerable Teacher*）；（fig.）help each other in time of need with meagre resources

【相商】xiāngshāng 彼此商量；商议 consult each other：有要事～。I have something important to consult you about.

【相生相克】xiāng shēng xiāng kè 我国古代关于五行之间相互作用和影响的说法，如木能生火、火能克金等 mutual promotion and restraint between the five elements（metal，wood，water，fire and earth），as wood promotes fire，fire restrains metal，etc.；concept held by the ancients to explain natural phenomena and later used in traditional Chinese medicine，etc.；☞ 五行 wǔxíng on p. 2031

【相识】xiāngshí ❶ 彼此认识 be acquainted with each other：素不～ have never met｜～多年 old acquaintance；be acquainted with each other for many years ❷ 相识的人 acquaintance：旧～ old acquaintance｜老～ old acquaintance｜成了～ become acquaintances

【相率】xiāngshuài 一个接着一个 one after another：～归附 come（or go）over to one after another；submit to the authority of sb. one after another；join

【相思】xiāngsī 彼此思念，多指男女因互相爱慕而又无法接近所引起的思念 pine with love；yearn for sb.'s love；languish with lovesickness：～病 lovesick｜两地～ lovers far apart yearn for（or miss）each other

【相似】xiāngsì same as 相像 xiāngxiàng：这两个人年貌～。These two people are alike both in age and look.

【相似形】xiāngsìxíng 对应角相等，对应边成比例的两个多边形叫做相似形 similar figures；two polygons with equal corresponding angles and the corresponding sides in proportion

【相提并论】xiāng tí bìng lùn 把不同的人或不同的事物混在一起来谈论或看待(多用于否定式 usu. used in the negative) mention different people or different things in the same breath; place different people or things on a par:鼓风机和木风箱的效力不能～。The effect of blower and wooden bellows can't be mentioned in the same breath.

【相通】xiāngtōng 事物之间彼此连贯沟通 communicate with each other; be interlinked:沟渠～。The canals and ditches are interlinked|息息～ communicate closely with each other; keep each other well informed

【相同】xiāngtóng 彼此一样,没有区别 identical; same; alike:年龄～ of the same age|内容～ of the same content|这两篇文章的结论是～的。The conclusion of the two articles are identical.|今年入学考试的科目跟去年～。The courses for the entrance examination this year are the same as last year's.

【相投】xiāngtóu (思想、感情等)彼此合得来 (of ideas, feelings, etc.)be congenial; agree with each other:气味～ be birds of a feather; be two of a kind|兴趣～ have similar (or congenial) tastes and interests; find each other congenial

【相向】xiāngxiàng ❶ 向着对方的方向 in opposite directions:～而行 go in opposite directions ❷ 向着对方 face to face; facing each other:武力～ be ready to use force against|恶言～ shout abuses to sb.

【相像】xiāngxiàng 彼此有相同点或共同点 resemble; be similar; be alike:面貌～ look alike

【相信】xiāngxìn 认为正确或确实而不怀疑 believe in; be convinced of; trust; have faith in:我～他们的试验一定会成功。I believe that they will succeed in their experiments.

【相形】xiāngxíng 相互比较 compared with each other:～失色 be outshone; seem pallid by comparison|～见绌 prove inferior by comparison|～之下,这种办法显得拙笨一些。By comparison, this method seems clumsier.

【相形见绌】xiāng xíng jiàn chù 跟另一人或事物比较起来显得远远不如 prove inferior by comparison; pale by comparison; be outshone

【相沿】xiāngyán 依着旧的一套传下来;沿袭 follow the old tradition:～成俗 become common practice through long usage|此种工艺～至今已有百余年。This craft has been passed down for more than one hundred years.

【相依】xiāngyī 互相依靠 depend on each other; be interdependent:唇齿～ be as close as lips and teeth|～为命 depend on each other for survival

【相依为命】xiāngyī wéi mìng 互相依靠着生活,谁也离不开谁 depend on each other for survival

【相宜】xiāngyí 适宜 suitable; fitting; appropriate:他做这种工作很～。He is very suitable for this job.|刚吃过饭就剧烈运动是不～的。It is not good to do violent exercise right after meal.

【相应】xiāngyīng 旧式公文用语,应该 (used as a formula for official documents in old times) ought to; should:～函达。We should inform you of this by letter.|～咨复 ought to give a reply after consultation

【相应】xiāngyìng 互相呼应或照应;相适应 corresponding; relevant; fitting; appropriate:这篇文章前后不～ the beginning and ending of the article do not correspond to each other|环境改变了,工作方法也要～地改变。Since the environment has changed, the working method should also change accordingly.

【相应】xiāng·ying 〈方 *dial.*〉便宜(pián·yi) inexpensive; cheap

【相映】xiāngyìng 互相衬托 reflect each other; set each other off; form a contrast:～生辉 set each other off wonderfully|湖光塔影,～成趣。The sparkling water of the lake and the pagoda's reflection in it make a pleasant scene.

【相与】xiāngyǔ ❶ 彼此往来;相处 get along with sb.; deal with sb.:这人是很难～的。That person is extremely difficult to get along with. ❷ 相互 each other; mutually; together:～议论 talk with each other; discuss together ❸ 〈旧时 *old*〉指相好的人 close friend

【相约】xiāngyuē 相互约定 agree (on meeting place, date, etc.); reach agreement; make an appointment:他们～明年春节聚会。They agreed to get together during the next Spring Festival.

【相知】xiāngzhī ❶ 彼此相交而互相了解,感情深厚 be well acquainted with each other; know each other well:～有素 have known each other long ❷ 相互了解,感情深厚的朋友 bosom friend; great friend:老～ old bosom friend

【相中】xiāng//zhòng 看中 take a fancy to; settle on:相得中 take fancy to|相不中 be not interested in|对象是他自己～的。The girl is his own choice.

【相助】xiāngzhù 互相帮助;协助 come to sb.'s help; aid:彼此～ help each other|～一臂之力 lend a helping hand

【相左】xiāngzuǒ 〈书 *fml.*〉❶ 不相遇 fail to meet each other ❷ 相违反;相互不一致 conflict with each other; fail to agree; be at odds with:意见～ hold different views; be at variance

香 xiāng ❶ (气味)好闻(跟'臭'相对 as opposed to 'smelly') fragrant; aromatic;

scented：～水 perfume｜～皂 toilet soap；facial soap｜这花真～。How fragrant the flower is！*or* The flower smells really sweet. ❷ 食物味道好 savoury；appetizing：饭很～。This rice is really appetizing. ❸ 吃东西胃口好 with relish；with good appetite：这两天吃饭不～。(I) have no appetite these days. ❹ 睡得塌实 (of sleep) sound：睡得正～呢 having a sound sleep ❺ 受欢迎；被看重 popular；welcome：吃～ very popular｜这种货物在农村很～。This kind of goods is very popular in the countryside. ❻ 香料 perfume or spice：檀～ sandalwood｜沉～ agalloch eaglewood｜龙涎～ ambergris ❼ 用木屑搀香料做成的细条，燃烧时，发出好闻的气味，在祭祀祖先或神佛时常用，有的加上药物，可以熏蚊子 incense；joss stick；slender stick made of sawdust mixed with fragrant materials，which wafts a fragrant smell when being burned，and is usu. used in offering sacrifices to ancestors or the Buddha，some incense，added with chemicals，is used to repel mosquitoes：线～ slender stick of incense｜蚊～ mosquito-repellent incense｜烧一炷～ burn a stick of incense ❽〈方 *dial.*〉亲吻 kiss：～面孔 kiss one's face ❾ (Xiàng)姓 a surname

【香案】xiāng'àn 放置香炉的长条桌子 long altar on which incense burners are placed；incense burner table

【香槟酒】xiāngbīnjiǔ 含有二氧化碳的起泡沫的白葡萄酒，因原产于法国香槟(Champagne)而得名 champagne；any effervescent white wine containing carbon dioxide，originally made in Champagne，France，now elsewhere

【香波】xiāngbō 专为洗头发用的肥皂或合成洗涤剂 shampoo；special soap or detergent prepared for washing hair

【香菜】xiāngcài 芫荽(yán·sui)的通称 general term for 芫荽 yán·sui

【香肠】xiāngcháng (～儿 xiāngchángr)用猪的小肠，装上碎肉和作料等制成的食品 sausage；pork or other meat，chopped fine，highly seasoned，stuffed into membranous casings made of pig's small intestines

【香椿】xiāngchūn ❶ 落叶乔木，羽状复叶，花白色。果实为蒴果，椭圆形，茶褐色。嫩枝叶有香味，可以吃。Chinese toon (*Toona sinensis*)；deciduous tree with pinnate，compound leaves，white flowers and dark brown，oval capsules，with both its leaves and stems being fragrant and edible when tender；also 椿 chūn ❷ 这种植物的嫩枝叶 tender，edible leaves and stems of this plant

【香醇】xiāngchún (气味、滋味)香而纯正 (of smell，taste) fragrant and mellow：～的美酒 mellow wine；also 香纯 xiāngchún

【香肚】xiāngdǔ 用猪的膀胱，装上碎肉和作料等制成的食品 sausage made by stuffing chopped pork and seasoning into the membranous casings of pig's bladder

【香榧】xiāngfěi 榧的通称 general term for 榧 fěi

【香馥馥】xiāngfùfù (～的 xiāngfùfù·de)形容香味浓 strongly scented；rich and fragrant

【香干】xiānggān (～儿 xiānggānr)经过熏制的豆腐干儿 bean curd smoked，dried and cut into squares

【香菇】xiānggū 寄生在栗、槲等树干上的蕈类，菌盖表面黑褐色，有裂纹，菌柄白色。有冬菇、春菇等多种。味鲜美。fragrant mushroom (*Agaricus campestris*)；mushroom growing on the trunks of chestnut，Mongolian oak and some other trees，with cracks on its dark-brown cap surface，white stem，varying in breeds，like spring and winter types，with a delicious taste；also 香蕈 xiāngxùn；香菰 xiānggū

【香菰】xiānggū same as 香菇 xiānggū

【香瓜】xiāngguā (～儿 xiāngguār)甜瓜 muskmelon

【香花】xiānghuā 有香味的花 fragrant flowers；〈比喻 *fig.*〉对人民有益的言论或作品 views，opinions，writings，artistic works，etc. useful to the people

【香灰】xiānghuī 香燃烧后剩下的灰。特指祭祀祖先或神佛烧香剩余的灰。incense ash，esp. left after sacrifices are offered to ancestors or the Buddha

【香会】xiānghuì〈旧时 *old*〉民间为朝山进香而组织的群众团体 group of Buddhists on a pilgrimage；company of Buddhist pilgrims

【香火】[1] xiānghuǒ ❶ (宗教徒或迷信的人)供佛敬神时燃点的香和灯火 (religious believers or superstitious people) joss sticks and candles burned or burning at a temple ❷ 庙宇中照料香火的人；庙祝 person who looks after incenses and candles at a temple；temple attendant ❸ same as 香烟 xiāngyān ②：断了～ be unable to continue the family line

【香火】[2] xiānghuǒ (～儿 xiānghuǒr)燃着的线香、棒香或盘香上的火 burning joss sticks，incense coil，etc.

【香蕉】xiāngjiāo ❶ 多年生草本植物，叶子长而大，有长柄，花淡黄色。果实长形，稍弯，味香甜。产在热带或亚热带地方。banana (*Musa sapientum*)；tropical or subtropical perennial herbal plant with large leaves and long stalks，yellowish flowers and long，sweet，bowlike fruits ❷ 这种植物的果实 fruit of this plant ‖ also 甘蕉 gānjiāo

【香蕉水】xiāngjiāoshuǐ 用酯类、酮类、醇类、醚类和芳香族化合物配制成的溶液，无色透明，容易挥发，有香蕉气味。用于制造喷漆和稀释喷漆等。banana oil (used as a paint solvent)；colourless，transparent，volatile solution with the smell of banana，prepared from esters，ketones，alcohol，ethers and aromatic compounds, used in making and thinning spray paint

【香精】xiāngjīng 几种香料配制而成的混合香料。有模仿花香的花香型香精、模仿果实香味的果实型香精等多种。用于化妆品、食品和烟草工业等。essence; mixture of several perfumes in the flavour of a flower or a fruit, used in making cosmetics, food, cigarettes, etc.

【香客】xiāngkè 朝山进香的人 worshipper at a Buddhist temple; Buddhist pilgrim; ☞ 朝山 cháoshān on p. 229

【香料】xiāngliào 在常温下能发出芳香的有机物质,分为天然香料和人造香料两大类。天然香料从动物或植物体中取得,如麝香、灵猫香以及玫瑰、蔷薇等的香精油,人工制造的也很多。用于化妆品和食品工业等。perfume; spice; natural or artificial organic substance that produces fragrance at constant temperature and are used in making cosmetics, foods, etc. Natural perfumes are extracted from animals or plants, as musk, civet and the essential oils from rugosa rose, rose, etc. There are also many artificial perfumes.

【香炉】xiānglú 烧香所用的器具,用陶瓷或金属制成,通常圆形有耳,底有三足 incense burner; ceramic or metal apparatus for burning incense, usu. in the shape of a round cauldron with three legs

【香喷喷】xiāngpēnpēn(～的 xiāngpēnpēn·de)形容香气扑鼻 sweet-smelling; savoury; appetizing

【香片】xiāngpiàn 花茶 scented tea

【香蒲】xiāngpú 多年生草本植物,多生在河滩上,叶子狭长,花穗上部生雄花,下部生雌花。雌花密集成棒状,成熟的果穗叫蒲棒,有绒毛。叶子可以编蒲包、蒲席、扇子等。cattail (*Typha*); perennial herbal plant growing on river beaches, with long, slender leaves and long, brown, fuzzy, cylindrical spikes bearing male flowers on the upper part and female flowers on the lower part. The female flowers cluster together and grown into fuzzy spikes with ripe fruits called *pubang* in Chinese, and its leaves are used to weave bags, mats, fans, etc.

【香薷】xiāngrú 一年或多年生草本植物,茎呈方形,紫色,有灰白色的毛,叶子对生,卵形或卵状披针形,花粉红色,果实棕色。茎和叶可以提取芳香油。全草入药。elsholtzia (*Elsholtzia*); annual or perennial herbal plant having purple, square stem with greyish-white hair, ovate or lanceolate opposite leaves, pink flowers and brown fruits. Its stem and leaves are used for extracting perfume oil. The whole plant is used for Chinese medicine.

【香水】xiāngshuǐ(～儿 xiāngshuǐr)用香料、酒精和蒸馏水等制成的化妆品 perfume; scent; cosmetic made of perfume, alcohol and distilled water

【香甜】xiāngtián ❶ 又香又甜 fragrant and sweet:这种瓜味道很～。This melon is very sweet. ❷ 形容睡得塌实,舒服(of sleep) sound:参加了一天义务劳动,晚上睡得格外～。(I) slept soundly after a day's voluntary work.

【香烟】[1] xiāngyān ❶ 燃着的香所生的烟 incense smoke:～缭绕 smoke coiling up from burning incense ❷〈旧指 *old*〉子孙祭祀祖先的事情 ancestral sacrifices; 断了～(指断绝了后代) be unable to continue the family line; discontinue one's family; also 香火 xiānghuǒ

【香烟】[2] xiāngyān 纸里包烟丝和配料卷成的条状物,供吸用 cigarette; small roll of finely cut tobacco wrapped in thin paper for smoking; also 纸烟 zhǐyān, 卷烟 juǎnyān or 烟卷儿 yānjuǎnr

【香艳】xiāngyàn 指花草芳香美丽,常用来形容词藻艳丽或内容涉及闺阁的诗文。也形容色情的小说、电影等。(of flowers, grasses, usu. used to describe flowery words or poetry or other writing dealing with young ladies, or pornographic fiction or films) amorous; flowery; sensual; voluptuous; sexy; erotic an amorous

【香胰子】xiāngyí·zi〈方 *dial.*〉same as 香皂 xiāngzào

【香油】xiāngyóu 芝麻油 sesame oil

【香橼】xiāngyuán ❶ 常绿小乔木或大灌木,有短刺,叶子卵圆形,总状花序,花瓣里面白色,外面淡紫色。果实长圆形,黄色,果皮粗而厚。供观赏,果皮可入药。citron (*Citrus medica*); small evergreen tree or large shrub with short pricks, ovate leaves, flowers borne in racemes and petals white inside and light purple outside, yellow, round, thick-skinned fruits. Citron is an ornamental tree, and its bike is used as a drug. ❷ 这种植物的果实 fruit of this plant ‖ also 枸橼 jǔyuán

【香云纱】xiāngyúnshā 一种提花丝织品,上面涂过薯莨汁液,适于做夏季衣料,主要产地是广东 gambiered Guangdong gauze; silk fabric with raised designs dyed in yam juice, suitable for summer dresses, produced chiefly in Guangdong; also 薯莨绸 shǔliángchóu or 拷纱 kǎoshā

【香皂】xiāngzào 在精炼的原料中加入香料而制成的肥皂,多用来洗脸 perfumed (or scented) soap; toilet soap; soap made from refined materials mixed with perfume, usually used for face washing

【香泽】xiāngzé〈书 *fml.*〉❶ 润发用的带有香味的油 perfumed hair cream or oil ❷ 香气 fragrance (esp. of a lady)

【香脂】xiāngzhī 一种化妆品,用硬脂酸、凡士林、杏仁油等原料制成 face cream balm; balsam; cosmetic made from stearic acid, vaseline, apricot kernel oil, etc.

【香烛】xiāngzhú 祭祀祖先或神佛用的香和蜡烛 joss sticks and candles (burned when offering sacrifices to gods or ancestors)

厢(廂) xiāng ❶ 厢房 wing (usu. of a one-storeyed house): 东～ east wing | 一正两～ one central room and two wing rooms ❷ (～儿 xiāngr)类似房子隔间的地方 place similar to a house with separated rooms: 车～儿 compartment | 包～ theatre box ❸ 靠近城的地区 vicinity outside of a city gate: 城～ city proper and the area outside its gates | 关～ neighbourhood outside a city gate ❹ 边;旁(多见于早期白话 oft. used in early vernacular) side: 这～ this side; here | 那～ that side, there | 两～ both sides

【厢房】xiāngfáng 在正房前面两旁的房屋 wing (usu. of a one-storeyed house); wing-room: 东～ east wing-room | 西～ west wing-room

葙 xiāng ☞ 青葙 qīngxiāng on p. 1564

湘 Xiāng ❶ 湘江,发源于广西,流入湖南 the Xiang River, originating in Guangxi and flowing into Hunan ❷ 湖南的别称 another name for Hunan

【湘菜】xiāngcài 湖南风味的菜肴 Hunan cuisine

【湘妃竹】xiāngfēizhú 斑竹。相传帝舜南巡苍梧而死,他的两个妃子在江湘之间哭泣,眼泪洒在竹子上,从此竹竿上都有了斑点(见于《博物志》) mottled bamboo. Legend goes that when the legendary King Shun died on a visit to Cangwu during a tour of the southern part of China, his two concubines wept between the Yangtze and Xiang rivers and their tears were splashed on the bamboo growing by them, and all the bamboo stalks have spots left on them (see *Records of Myriad Things*). also 湘竹 xiāngzhú

【湘剧】xiāngjù 湖南地方戏曲剧种之一,分长沙湘剧、衡阳湘剧、常德湘剧等 Hunan opera; local opera in Hunan Province that has branched out into Changsha Hunan opera, Hengyang Hunan opera and Changde Hunan opera

【湘帘】xiānglián 用湘妃竹制成的帘子 curtain made of bamboo of the Xiang; mottled-bamboo curtain

【湘莲】xiānglián 湖南出产的莲子 Hunan lotus seeds

【湘绣】xiāngxiù 湖南出产的刺绣 Hunan embroidery

【湘语】xiāngyǔ 汉语方言之一,分布于湖南省(西北部除外) Hunan dialect; one of the Chinese local dialects, spoken extensively in Hunan Province except its northwest

缃 xiāng 〈书 *fml.*〉浅黄色 light yellow

箱 xiāng ❶ 箱子 chest; box; case; trunk: 木～ wooden trunk; chest | 皮～ leather suitcase | 书～ book box ❷ 像箱子的东西 anything in the shape of a box: 信～ mail box | 镜～ (of a camera) darkroom or chamber; bathroom medicine cabinet whose door is faced with a mirror | 风～ bellows

【箱底】xiāngdǐ (～儿 xiāngdǐr) ❶ 箱子的内部底层 bottom of a chest ❷ 指不经常动用的财物 valuables stowed away at the bottom of a chest; one's store of valuables: ～厚 have a large store of valuables

【箱笼】xiānglǒng 泛指出门时携带的各种盛衣物的器具 (traveller's) boxes and baskets; luggage; baggage

【箱子】xiāng·zi 收藏衣物的方形器具,用皮子、木头、铁皮、塑料等制成 chest, box, case, trunk, etc. made of leather, wood, metal sheet, plastics, etc.

襄 xiāng ❶〈书 *fml.*〉帮助 assist; help: 共～义举 let everybody help to promote this worthy undertaking ❷ (Xiāng)姓 a surname

【襄礼】xiānglǐ ❶ 举行婚丧祭祀时,协助主持者完成仪式 (in former times) assist in officiating a ceremony at a wedding, funeral, etc. ❷ 担任这种事情的人 assistant master of ceremonies; officiator ‖ also 相礼 xiānglǐ

【襄理】xiānglǐ 规模较大的银行或企业中协助经理主持业务的人,地位次于协理 (in former times) assistant manager, second in rank to senior manager in a bank, enterprise, etc.

【襄助】xiāngzhù〈书 *fml.*〉从旁帮助 assist indirectly

骧 xiāng〈书 *fml.*〉❶ 马奔跑 (of horses) gallop ❷ (头)仰起;高举 rear (one's head)

瓖 xiāng〈书 *fml.*〉same as 镶 xiāng

镶 xiāng 把物体嵌入另一物体内或围在另一物体的边缘 inlay; mount; rim; set an object inside another object, or on the edge of it: ～牙 have a false tooth put in one's mouth | ～边 edge; border | 金～玉嵌 inlaid with gold and jade | 塔顶上～着一颗闪闪发亮的红星。A gleaming red star is mounted on the top of the tower.

【镶嵌】xiāngqiàn 把一物体嵌入另一物体内 inlay; mount; set an object inside another object

【镶牙】xiāng//yá 安装假牙 put in a false tooth; insert an artificial tooth

xiáng (ㄒㄧㄤˊ)

详 xiáng ❶ 详细(跟'略'相对 as opposed to 'brief')detailed: ～谈 speak in detail | 不厌

其～ go into minute detail | 这本书的注释，～略不很一致。Some of the notes on this book were given at length, while some were brief. ❷ 说明；细说 details; particulars：内～。For details, open the envelope. ❸（事情）清楚（of things）be known clearly：生卒年不～ one's dates of birth and death are unknown

【详备】xiángbèi 详细完备 detailed and all-inclusive：注释～。The comments were detailed and comprehensive.

【详尽】xiángjìn 详细而全面 detailed and complete; thorough：～的记载 detailed record

【详密】xiángmì 详细周密 elaborate; meticulous; detailed and careful：计划～ work out an elaborate plan | 分析～ analyse meticulously | ～的施工方案 meticulous construction plan

【详明】xiángmíng 详细明白 full and clear：记述～ record fully and clearly

【详情】xiángqíng 详细的情形 detailed information; details; particulars：探听～ try to find out detailed information

【详实】xiángshí same as 翔实 xiángshí

【详悉】xiángxī ❶ 详细地知道 know the details ❷ 详细而全面 detailed and complete

【详细】xiángxì 周密完备 detailed; minute; thorough and complete：～研究 study carefully | 道理讲得很～。The reasoning was exhaustive. | ～情形还不知道。Detailed information is yet unknown.

降 xiáng ❶ 投降 surrender; capitulate：～顺 yield and pledge allegiance | 诱～ lure into surrender | ～将 surrendering general | 宁死不～ rather die than surrender ❷ 降伏；使驯服 subdue; tame; vanquish：～龙伏虎 subdue the dragon and tame the tiger; overcome powerful adversaries | 一物～一物。Everything has its vanquisher.
☞ jiàng on p. 963

【降表】xiángbiǎo〈书 *fml.*〉请求投降的文书 petition of surrender

【降伏】xiáng//fú 制伏；使驯服 subdue; vanquish; tame：没有使过牲口的人，连个毛驴也～不了。One who has never worked with livestock cannot tame an animal, not even a donkey.

【降服】xiángfú 投降屈服 surrender and pledge allegiance：缴械～ surrender one's weapons and pledge allegiance

【降龙伏虎】xiáng lóng fú hǔ〈比喻 *fig.*〉战胜强大的势力 overcome powerful adversaries

【降顺】xiángshùn 归降顺从 yield and pledge allegiance to

庠 xiáng〈古代 *arch.*〉学校 schools：～序（古代乡学，泛指学校）government-run local school in ancient China

【庠生】xiángshēng 科举制度中府、州、县学的生员的别称 students of schools at prefecture and township levels under the imperial-examination system in feudal times

祥 xiáng ❶ 指吉利 auspicious; lucky：吉～ auspicious | 不～ ominous; inauspicious; unlucky ❷（Xiáng）姓 a surname

【祥和】xiánghé ❶ 吉祥平和 auspicious and peaceful：～之气 auspicious and peaceful atmosphere | ～的景象 scene of auspiciousness and peace ❷ 慈祥；和祥 kind; benign：神情～ kindly expression

【祥瑞】xiángruì 指好事情的兆头或征象 auspicious sign; propitious omen

翔 xiáng 盘旋地飞；飞 fly; hover in the air：翱～ hover over; take wing | 飞～ hover | 滑～ glide

【翔实】xiángshí 详细而确实 full and accurate：～的材料 full and accurate data | 叙述～可信。The account was full, accurate and reliable. also 详实 xiángshí

xiǎng（ㄒㄧㄤˇ）

曏（曏） xiǎng〈书 *fml.*〉从前；旧时 in the past; before

享 xiǎng ❶ 享受 enjoy：～用 enjoy the use of | 坐～其成 reap where one has not sown | 有福同～ share weal and woe ❷〈书 *fml.*〉same as 飨 xiǎng

【享福】xiǎng//fú 生活得安乐美好；享受幸福 enjoy happiness; live in ease and comfort

【享乐】xiǎnglè 享受安乐（多用于贬义 usu. derog.）lead a life of pleasure; indulge in creature comforts：～思想 hedonist philosophy | 贪图～ seek ease and comfort

【享年】xiǎngnián〈敬辞 *pol.*〉称死去的人活的岁数（多指老人）（of a deceased, generally elderly, person）die at the age of：～七十四岁 die at the age of 74

【享受】xiǎngshòu 物质上或精神上得到满足 bask in; enjoy; be satisfied materially and spiritually：贪图～ seek ease and comfort | ～权利 enjoy a right | ～公费医疗 enjoy public health services | 吃苦在前，～在后 be the first to bear hardships and the last to enjoy comforts

【享用】xiǎngyòng 使用某种东西而得到物质上或精神上的满足 enjoy; be satisfied materially or spiritually by the use of sth.：～不尽 enjoy the use of (sth.) endlessly

【享有】xiǎngyǒu 在社会上取得（权利、声誉、威望等）enjoy; attain in society (rights, prestige, reputation, etc.)：～盛名 enjoy a sterling reputation | 在我国，男女～同样的权利。In our country women enjoy equal rights with men.

响（響） xiǎng ❶ 回声 echo：～应 response | 影～ influence | 如～斯应（比喻反

应迅速）(fig.) be prompt in response ❷ 发出声音 make a sound; resound; ring: 钟～了。The bell rang.｜全场～起暴风雨般的掌声。The whole audience burst into a storm of applause. ❸ 使发出声音 make sth. emit a sound; sound: ～枪 fire a gun｜～锣 beat a gong ❹ 响亮 sonorous; loud and clear: 号声真～。The trumpet call was resounding. ❺ 声音 sound; noise: 声～ sound

【响鼻】xiǎngbí（～儿 xiǎngbír）骡马等动物鼻子里发出响声叫打响鼻儿 snort (of a horse, mule, etc.)

【响彻云霄】xiǎng chè yún xiāo 响声直达高空。形容声音十分嘹亮。resound (or reverberate) across the heavens; echo to the sky; (of sound) very loud and clear

【响当当】xiǎngdāngdāng ❶ 形容敲打的声音响亮 (of the sound made by a bell, a gong, etc.) loud and resounding ❷〈比喻 *fig.*〉出色、过硬或有名气 outstanding; competent; of resounding fame; big-name: 他是一个～的炼钢工人。He is a competent steel-worker.

【响动】xiǎng·dong（～儿 xiǎng·dongr）动作的声音；动静 sound of movement; sound of sth. astir: 夜很静，什么～也没有。The night was quiet, and nothing was astir.

【响度】xiǎngdù 听觉上感到的声音强弱的程度。单位是宋或毫宋。degree of loudness of sound; volume, expressed in units of sones or millisones; also 音量 yīnliàng

【响遏行云】xiǎng è xíng yún 声音高入云霄，把浮动着的云彩也止住了。形容歌声嘹亮。(of a sound, esp. singing) be so sonorous that it soars to the sky and stops the passing clouds

【响箭】xiǎngjiàn 射出时能发出响声的箭 whistling arrow; arrow that can sound when shot

【响雷】xiǎngléi 声音响亮的雷 resounding thunder

【响亮】xiǎngliàng（声音）宏大 (of sound) loud and clear; sonorous: 歌声～ resonant singing｜他回答得很～。He replied in a loud and clear voice.

【响马】xiǎngmǎ〈旧时 *old*〉称在路上抢劫旅客的强盗，因抢劫时先放响箭而得名 bandit; mounted highwaymen, who shot whistling arrows as a signal for attack

【响器】xiǎngqì 铙、钹、锣、鼓等打击乐器的统称 Chinese percussion instrument, e. g. cymbals, gongs, drums, etc.

【响晴】xiǎngqíng 晴朗无云 sunny and unclouded: 雪白的鸽子在～的天空中飞翔。Snow-white pigeons are flying in the clear sky.

【响儿】xiǎngr〈方 *dial.*〉same as 响声 xiǎng·shēng: 听不见～了。Not a sound was heard.

【响声】xiǎng·shēng 声音 sound; noise: 沙沙的～ rustling sound

【响头】xiǎngtóu 磕头磕出声音来叫磕响头 resonant kowtow; knock one's head on the floor with a bang: 叩了一个～ kowtow by banging one's head on the ground

【响尾蛇】xiǎngwěishé 毒蛇的一种，尾巴的末端有角质的环，摆动时能发出声音。产于美洲。吃小动物。rattlesnake (*Crotalus horridus*); venomous snake, with horny interlocking joints at the end of its tail that make a sharp rattling sound when shaken. The rattlesanke eats small animals, and is found in the Americas.

【响音】xiǎngyīn 语音学上指元音（如 a,e,o）和乐音成分占优势的辅音（如 m,n,l），有时专指乐音成分占优势的辅音 sonorant; vowels (e. g. a, e, o) in phonetics, and consonants principally occupied by tones (e. g. m, n, l)

【响应】xiǎngyìng 回声相应 echo correspondingly;〈比喻 *fig.*〉用言语行动表示赞同、支持某种号召或倡议 respond; answer; speak or take actions to show one's agreement and support to a call or a proposal: ～号召 respond to a call

【响指】xiǎngzhǐ 打榧子打出响声叫打响指 make a sound by snapping the fingers

饷 xiǎng ❶〈书 *fml.*〉用酒食等款待 entertain with food and drink ❷ 薪金（旧时多指军警等的薪金）(in old times usu. for soldiers, policemen, etc.) pay: 月～ monthly pay｜关～ official pay

【饷银】xiǎngyín〈旧指 *old*〉军饷 army pay: 克扣～ dock army pay

蚼 xiǎng [蚼虫](xiǎngchóng)〈方 *dial.*〉指浮尘子等水稻害虫 pests found in paddy, e. g. jassid

飨(饗) xiǎng〈书 *fml.*〉用酒食款待人。泛指请人享受 fete; entertain sb. with food and drink; invite sb. to enjoy sth.: ～客 fete a guest｜以～读者 cater to the readers

想 xiǎng ❶ 开动脑筋；思索 think; ponder: ～办法 try to find a way out｜～方设法 devise means｜冥思苦～ think hard ❷ 推测；认为 suppose; consider; presume; think: 我～他今天不会来。I don't think he'll be coming today. ❸ 希望；打算 hope to; want to; would like to; be going to: 我～到杭州去一趟。I want to take a trip to Hangzhou. ❹ 怀念；想念 miss; remember with longing: ～家 homesick｜朝思暮～ yearn day and night｜我们很～你。We miss you so.

【想必】xiǎngbì〈副词 *adv.*〉表示偏于肯定的推断 presumably; most likely: 这事～你知道。You most probably know this.｜他没回答我，～是没听见我的话。No response from him; presumably he didn't hear my words.

【想不到】xiǎng·bu dào 出于意料；没有料到 never expect; unexpectedly: 一年没回来，～家乡变化这么大。(I) haven't been back to my hometown for a year and never expected such great changes would have taken place here.

【想不开】xiǎng •bu kāi 不如意的事情存在心中摆脱不了 take things too seriously; take an unpleasant matter to heart

【想当然】xiǎngdāngrán 凭主观推测,认为事情大概是或应该是这样 assume sth. as a matter of course; take sth. for granted; believe sth. should be as such: 不能凭～办事 must not act on assumptions

【想得到】xiǎng •de dào 在意料中;意料得到(多用于反问 oft. in a rhetorical question) think; imagine; expect: 谁～当年的荒滩地,如今变成了米粮川。Who would have thought those desolate sands could have become fertile paddy fields?

【想得开】xiǎng •de kāi 不把不如意的事情老放在心上 take it easy; not take unpleasant things to heart

【想法】xiǎng//fǎ 设法;想办法 try a means; think of a way: ～消灭虫害 try to eliminate insect pests

【想法】xiǎng•fa 思索所得的结果;意见 idea; opinion; what one concludes after thinking: 这个～不错。This is a good idea.|有什么～可以说出来。Feel free to tell us what you have in mind.

【想方设法】xiǎng fāng shè fǎ 想尽办法 do everything possible; try all means; leave no stone unturned: ～克服工作中的困难 leave no stone unturned to overcome the difficulties in one's work

【想见】xiǎngjiàn 由推想而知道 infer; know from supposition: 从这件小事上也可以～他的为人。Just from this small matter (we) can infer what kind of person he is.

【想来】xiǎnglái 表示只是根据推测,不敢完全肯定 it can be assumed that; presumably: 从这里修涵洞～是可行的。Presumably the construction of the culvert can be started from here.

【想念】xiǎngniàn 对景仰的人、离别的人或环境不能忘怀,希望见到 miss; long to see sb. or sth. unforgettable (respected person, parting person, place, etc.): ～亲人 miss one's relatives|他们在国外,时时～着祖国。They cherished the memory of their motherland at all times while abroad.

【想儿】xiǎngr 〈方 *dial.*〉希望 hope; sth. to look forward to: 有～ have sth. to look forward to|没～ with no hope

【想入非非】xiǎng rù fēi fēi 思想进入虚幻境界,完全脱离实际;胡思乱想 indulge in fantasy; be unrealistic and go off in wild flights of fancy

【想头】xiǎng•tou ❶ 想法(xiǎng•fa);念头 idea: 我有这样一个～,你看行不行? I've got this idea, and you tell me what you think. ❷ 希望 hope: 有～ have hope|没～ there's no hope

【想望】xiǎngwàng ❶ 希望 desire; long for; yearn for: 他在上学的时候就～着做一个医生。He longed to be a doctor while still a schoolboy. ❷〈书 *fml.*〉仰慕;思慕 admire; look up to: ～风采 admire sb.'s elegant bearing

【想象】xiǎngxiàng same as 想像 xiǎngxiàng

【想像】xiǎngxiàng ❶ 心里学上指在知觉材料的基础上,经过新的配合而创造出新形象的心理过程 imagination; psychological process of creating mental images through the recombination of available perceived material ❷ 对于不在眼前的事物想出它的具体形象;设想 imagine; visualize; conceive; form a mental and visual image of sth. not present: 不难～ not hard to imagine|～不出 cannot imagine ‖ also 想象 xiǎngxiàng

【想像力】xiǎngxiànglì 在知觉材料的基础上,经过新的配合而创造出新形象的能力 imagination; ability to create mental images through the recombination of available perceived material

鲞(鮝) xiǎng 剖开晾干的鱼 dried fish, with all insides removed and the body flattened: 鳗～ dried eel|白～ dried paddlefish

【鲞鱼】xiǎngyú same as 鲞 xiǎng

xiàng (ㄒㄧㄤˋ)

向[1](❶❷❸嚮) xiàng ❶ 方向 direction: 志～ ambition|风～ wind direction ❷ 对着。特指脸或正面对着(跟'背'相对 as opposed to 'back') face; with the face or the right side towards: ～阳 turn towards the sun|面～讲台 face the podium|两人相～而行。The two persons walked in opposite directions. ❸〈书 *fml.*〉将近;接近 near upon; towards; shortly before: ～晓雨止。The rain stopped shortly before dawn. ❹ 偏袒 be partial to; side with: 穷人～穷人。Poor people side with each other. ❺〈介词 *prep.*〉表示动作的方向 towards; in the direction of: ～东看 look eastward|～先进工作者学习 learn from advanced employees|从胜利走～胜利。March from victory to victory. ❻ (Xiàng)姓 a surname

向[2] xiàng 向来 all along; always: ～有研究 have always been doing research (in sth.)|～无此例。There's no precedent for this.

【向背】xiàngbèi 拥护和反对 support and oppose: 人心～ popular support or opposition

【向壁虚构】xiàng bì xūgòu 对着墙壁,凭空想像 in the face of a wall, imagine without foun

X

dation;〈比喻 *fig.*〉不根据事实而捏造 fabricate; also 向壁虚造 xiàng bì xūzào

【向导】xiàngdǎo ❶ 带路 show sb. the way; act as a guide ❷ 带路的人 guide; person who shows the way: 登山队请了一位猎人当～。The mountaineering team engaged a hunter as a guide. ◇革命党是群众的～。The Revolutionary Party was the guide of the people.

【向迩】xiàng'ěr〈书 *fml.*〉接近;亲近 near; be close to: 不可～ unapproachable

【向火】xiàng//huǒ〈方 *dial.*〉烤火 warm oneself in front of a fire: 围炉～ warm oneself in front of a fireplace

【向来】xiànglái 从来;一向 always; all along: ～如此。It has always been so.｜他做事～认真。He's always been conscientious in his work.

【向例】xiànglì 一向的做法;惯例 usual practice: 打破～ break with the usual practice｜我们这里～起得早。Here, as a rule, we get up early.

【向量】xiàngliàng ☞矢量 shǐliàng on p. 1748

【向日】xiàngrì〈书 *fml.*〉往日 in former days; formerly

【向日葵】xiàngrìkuí 一年生草本植物,茎很高,叶子互生,心脏形,有长叶柄。开黄花,圆盘状头状花序,常朝着太阳。种子叫葵花子,可以榨油。有的地区叫转日莲。sunflower (*Helianthus annuus*); annual herbaceous plant with a tall stem, alternate heart-shaped leaves with long leafstalks, and disk-shaped yellow flower heads that face the sun, bearing seeds (known as sunflow seeds) that yield an edible oil; 朝阳花 cháoyánghuā or 葵花 kuíhuā; in some areas called 转日莲 zhuǎnrìlián

【向上】xiàngshàng 朝好的方向走;上进 make one's way up or forward; make progress: 有心～ have a mind to make one's way up｜好好学习,天天～。Study well and make progress every day.

【向使】xiàngshǐ〈书 *fml.*〉如果;假使 if; in case

【向往】xiàngwǎng 因热爱、羡慕某种事物或境界而希望得到或达到 yearn for; look forward to; desire to obtain or reach sth. or some realm out of love or admiration: 他～着北京。He yearns for Beijing.｜～着美好的未来 look forward to a bright future

【向心力】xiàngxīnlì 使物体沿着圆周或其他曲线运动的力,跟速度的方向垂直,向着圆心 centripetal force; force necessary to keep an object moving in a circular or other curving path, and directed inward towards the centre of rotation

【向学】xiàngxué 立志求学 be determined to study or pursue one's studies: 无心～ be not in the mood for study

【向阳】xiàngyáng 对着太阳,一般指朝南 be exposed to the sun; have a southern exposure: ～三间北房 three rooms with a southern exposure

【向隅】xiàngyú〈书 *fml.*〉面对着屋子的一个角落 facing one corner in a room;〈比喻 *fig.*〉非常孤立或得不到机会而失望 be disappointed due to isolation or lack of opportunity: ～而泣 weep all alone in a corner; be left to grieve out in the cold

【向着】xiàng·zhe ❶ 朝着;对着 turn towards; face: 葵花～太阳。Sunflowers face the sun. ❷ 偏袒 be partial to; side with: 哥哥怪妈妈凡事～小弟弟。The boy complained that his mother sided with his younger brother.

项[1] xiàng ❶ 颈的后部 nape of the neck ❷ (Xiàng)姓 a surname

项[2] xiàng ❶〈量词 *classifier*〉用于分项目的事物 [for itemized things]: 下列各～ the following items｜三大纪律,八～注意 Three Main Rules of Disciplines and Eight Points for Attention｜第五条第二款第一～ Item 1, Clause 2, Article 5｜改造自然是一～重大任务。The transformation of nature is a task of cardinal importance. ❷ 款项 sum (of money): 用～ sum of expenses｜存～ sum of savings ❸ 代数中不用加、减号连接的单式,如 $3a^2b$, ax^2, $4ba$等 (in algebra) unitary value, variable, unit and integer without plus or minus signs as connectors, e. g. $3a^2b$, ax^2, $4ba$, etc.

【项背】xiàngbèi 人的背影 person's background: ～相望(形容行进的人多,连续不断) walk one after another in close succession

【项链】xiàngliàn 套在脖子上垂挂胸前的链形首饰,多用金银或珍珠等制成 necklace; chain-like ornament worn around the neck, oft. made of gold, silver, pearls, etc.

【项目】xiàngmù 事物分成的门类 item: 服务～ items of service｜体育～ athletic events｜首先兴办关键性的建设～。Key construction projects should take precedence over anything else.

【项圈】xiàngquān 儿童或某些民族的妇女套在脖子上的环形装饰品,多用金银制成 chaplet; jewellery worn around the neck by children or women of certain ethnic backgrounds, oft. made of gold or silver

【项庄舞剑,意在沛公】Xiàng Zhuāng wǔ jiàn, yì zài Pèi Gōng《史记·项羽本纪》记载,刘邦和项羽在鸿门会见,酒宴上,项羽的谋士范增让项庄舞剑,乘机杀死刘邦。刘邦的谋士张良对樊哙说:'今者项庄拔剑舞,其意常在沛公也'(项庄:项羽部下的武将。沛公:刘邦)。后用来比喻说话或行动虽然表面上另有名目,其真实意图却在于对某人某事进行威胁或攻击。According to *Records of the Historian · Official Records of Xiang Yu*, Xiang Yu offered a feast at Hongmen for Liu Bang, at which Xiang

Yu's advisor Fan Zeng arranged Xiang Zhuang (a military subordinate of Xiang Yu) to perform the sword dance as a cover for his attempt on Liu Bang's life. Liu Bang's advisor Zhang Liang later said to Fan Kuai, 'Xiang Zhuang's sword dance performance was actually aimed at Liu Bang's life.' (fig.) speak or act in order to disguise a threat; attack sb. or sth. using another name on the surface as a cover

巷 xiàng 较窄的街道 lane; alley; narrow street: 深～ deep lane|陋～ slum|一条小～ a narrow alley|街头～尾 streets and lanes|街谈～议 street gossip

☞ hàng on p. 772

【巷战】xiàngzhàn 在城镇街巷内进行的战斗 street fighting; street battle

【巷子】xiàng·zi 〈方 *dial.*〉 same as 巷 xiàng: ～口 entrance to a lane|这条～里住着六户人家。This lane is home to six families.

相[1] xiàng ❶ 相貌;外貌 looks; appearance (of a person): 长～ look (of sb.)|聪明～ smart appearance|可怜～ sorry figure|狼狈～ flustered look ❷ 物体的外观 appearance of an object: 月～ phase of the moon|金～ metallurgical phase ❸ 坐、立等的姿态 bearing; posture (when sitting or standing): 站有站～,坐有坐～ know well how to stand or sit properly ❹ 相位 phase ❺ 交流电路中的一个组成部分,如三相交流发电机有三个绕组,每个绕组叫做一相 phase; component part of an alternating-current circuit, e. g. a three-phase alternator has three circuits, each of which is known as a phase ❻ same as 相态 xiàngtài ❼ 观察事物的外表,判断其优劣 estimate or decide the quality of sth. by observing its appearance: ～马 watch a horse to judge its worth ❽ (Xiàng)姓 a surname

相[2] xiàng ❶ 辅助 assist: 吉人天～(套语,用来安慰遭遇危险或困难的人 phrase to comfort people in danger or difficulties) Heaven helps a good man ❷ 宰相 prime minister: 丞～ prime minister ❸ 某些国家的官名,相当于中央政府的部长 minister (of the central government of certain countries) ❹ 〈旧时 *old*〉指帮助主人接待宾客的人 person who helps the host receive guests: 傧～ attendant of bride or bridegroom at wedding

☞ xiāng on p. 2086

【相册】xiàngcè 用来存放相片的册子 photo album

【相公】xiàng·gong ❶〈旧时 *old*〉妻子对丈夫的敬称 term of address used by a wife to her husband ❷〈旧时 *old*〉称年轻的读书人(多见于旧戏曲、小说 oft. in old dramas or novels) term of address for young men of rich or cultured families

【相机】[1] xiàngjī 照相机 camera

【相机】[2] xiàngjī 察看机会 watch for an opportunity: ～行事(看具体情况灵活办事) do as one sees fit; act flexibly in light of the specific situation|～而动 wait for an opportunity to act

【相里】Xiànglǐ 姓 a surname

【相貌】xiàngmào 人的面部长(zhǎng)的样子;容貌 (of a person) facial features; looks: ～堂堂 be elegant in appearance|～平常 be ordinary-looking

【相面】xiàng//miàn 观察人的相貌来推测祸福(迷信) (superstition) tell sb.'s fortune by reading his face

【相片儿】xiàngpiānr same as 相片 xiàngpiàn

【相片】xiàngpiàn 人的照片 photo (of a person); snapshot

【相声】xiàng·sheng 曲艺的一种,用说笑话、滑稽问答、说唱等引来观众发笑。多用于讽刺,现在也有用来歌颂新人新事的。按表演的人数分对口相声、单口相声和多口相声。comic dialogue; cross-talk; folk art in which the performers tell jokes, utter humorous questions and answers, and sing songs to make the audience laugh, oft. satirical or as tribute to new people and new things, usu. performed by two persons, and also singly or by more than two

【相书】[1] xiàngshū 〈方 *dial.*〉口技 vocal mimicry: 四川～ Sichuan vocal mimicry

【相书】[2] xiàngshū 关于相术的书 book about physiognomy

【相术】xiàngshù 指观察人的相貌,预言命运好坏的方术(迷信) (superstition) physiognomy; fortune-telling through studying sb.'s facial features

【相态】xiàngtài 同一物质的某种物理、化学状态,如水蒸气、水和冰就是三个相态 phase; physical or chemical states of the same substance, e. g., steam, water and ice constitute the three phases of one substance

【相位】xiàngwèi 作余弦(或正弦)变化的物理量,在某一时刻(或某一位置)的状态可用一个数值来确定,这种数值叫做相位 phase; numerical value determining the state of a physical quantity in cosine (or sinusoidal) variation at a certain moment (or certain location)

象[1] xiàng 哺乳动物,是陆地上现存最大的动物,耳朵大,鼻子长圆筒形,能蜷曲,多有一对长大的门牙伸出口外,全身的毛很稀疏,皮很厚,吃嫩叶和野菜等。产在我国云南南部、印度、非洲等热带地方。有的可驯养来驮运货物。elephant (*Elephantidae*); largest existing mammal on land, having large ears, a long tube-shaped trunk, two incisors in the upper jaw which can develop into large tusks, sparse hair and thick skin, eating young leaves and wild herbs, and mostly found in tropical regions such as southern Yunnan Province in China, India, and African countries, some having been domesticated to carry and transport goods

象2 xiàng ❶ 形状;样子 appearance; shape; image: 景～ scenery | 天～ astronomical phenomena | 气～ meteorology | 印～ impression | 万～更新。All things take on a new look. ❷ 仿效;摹仿 imitate: ～形 pictographic characters | ～声 imitative words

【象棋】xiàngqí 棋类运动的一种。双方各有棋子十六个,一将(帅)、两士(仕)、两象(相)、两车、两马、两炮、五卒(兵)。两人对下,各按规则移动棋子。将(jiāng)死对方的将(帅)的为胜。Chinese chess; board game for two players each moving 16 pieces — a king, two pawns, two elephants, two chariots, two horses, two cannons and five soldiers — according to fixed rules across a checkerboard and trying to checkmate the other's king; also 中国象棋 zhōngguó xiàngqí

【象声词】xiàngshēngcí 摹拟事物的声音的词,如'哗、轰、乒乓、丁东、扑哧' onomatopoeia; imitative words; vocal imitation of the sound associated with sth., e.g. 哗 huā, 轰 hōng, 乒乓 pīngpāng, 丁东 dīngdōng, 扑哧 pūchī, etc.

【象限】xiàngxiàn 平面直角坐标系的横、纵坐标轴把平面分为四个部分,每一部分叫做一个象限。右上方为第一象限,按逆时针方向旋转,依次为第二、第三、第四象限。quadrant; any of the four parts into which a plane is divided by rectangular coordinate axes lying on that plane, the upper right part being quadrant 1, and the others being, counterclockwise, quadrant 2, quadrant 3 and quadrant 4

【象形】xiàngxíng 六书之一。象形是说字描摹实物的形状。pictographic characters or pictographs — one of the six categories of Chinese characters

【象形文字】xiàngxíng wénzì 描摹实物形状的文字,每个字有固定的读法,和没有固定读法的图画文字不同 pictograph; character representing a material object in pictorial form, each having a fixed pronunciation, as distinguished from hieroglyphs, which have no fixed pronunciation; ☞ 图画文字 túhuà wénzì on p.1939

【象形文字论】xiàngxíng wénzì lùn ☞ 符号论 fúhàolùn on p.599

【象牙】xiàngyá 象的门牙,略呈圆锥形,伸出口外。质地坚硬、细致,可制工艺品。ivory; tusk of an elephant, which is hard, circular-cone-shaped, and extending out from the elephant's mouth, oft. used as material for handicrafts

【象牙之塔】xiàngyá zhī tǎ 〈比喻 *fig.*〉脱离现实生活的文学家和艺术家的小天地 ivory tower; closed circle of literati and artists who live in seclusion from real life; also 象牙宝塔 xiàngyá bǎotǎ

【象牙质】xiàngyázhì same as 牙质 yázhì ② on p.2195

【象眼儿】xiàngyǎnr 〈方 *dial.*〉斜象眼儿;菱形 rhombus

【象征】xiàngzhēng ❶ 用具体的事物表现某种特殊意义 symbolize; signify; stand for; represent or express some special meaning using a specific thing: 火炬～光明。The torch symbolizes light. ❷ 用来象征某种特别意义的具体事物 symbol; token; emblem; icon; specific thing used to symbolize some special meaning: 火炬是光明的～。The torch is a symbol of light.

銗(鋗) xiàng 〈古代 *arch.*〉储钱或投受函件的器物,入口小,像扑满,有的像竹筒 container for money or mail with a small opening, resembling a piggy bank or a thick bamboo tube

衖 xiàng 〈书 *fml.*〉same as 巷 xiàng

像 xiàng ❶ 比照人物制成的形象 likeness; portrait; picture; image made to resemble the appearance of a person: 画～ portrait | 塑～ statue | 肖～ portrait ❷ 从物体发出的光线经平面镜、球面镜、透镜、棱镜等反射或折射后所形成的与原物相似的图景。分为实像和虚像。image; optical counterpart of an object produced through reflection or refraction by an optical device (e.g. mirror, spherical mirror, lens or prism, etc.), differentiated between real and virtual images ❸ 在形象上相同或有某些共同点 take after; be like; resemble; be same or similar in image: 他的面貌～他哥哥。He takes after his elder brother. ❹ 好像 look as if; seem: ～要下雨了。It looks like rain. ❺ 比如;如 such as: ～大熊猫这样的珍稀动物,要加以保护。Rare animals such as the giant panda should be put under protection.

【像话】xiàng//huà (言语行动)合理(多用于反问 oft. used in the negative or in rhetorical questions) (of words or action) reasonable; proper; right: 他这样说还～。It's still proper for him to talk like this. | 同志们这样关心你,你还闹情绪,～吗? Aren't you ashamed to be still disgruntled while others are so concerned about you?

【像煞有介事】xiàng shà yǒu jiè shì 好像真有这回事似的。多指大模大样,好像有什么了不起。appear as if sth. really happened; make a show of being in earnest; pretend to be serious (about doing sth.); also 煞有介事 shà yǒu jiè shì

【像生】xiàngshēng ❶ 仿天然产物制成的工艺品,旧时多用绫绢、通草制成花果人物等形状 lifelike imitation; (old) handicrafts of fashioning silk fabric, rice-paper plant (*Tetrapanax papyriferus*), etc. into flowers, fruit, or figurines: ～花果 imitation flowers and fruit ❷ 宋元时期以说唱为业的女艺人 actress specializing in singing and storytelling during the Song and Yuan dynasties

【像样】xiàng//yàng (～儿 xiàng//yàngr) 有一定的水平；够一定的标准 up to the mark; presentable: 字写的挺～。The handwriting is quite presentable. also 像样子 xiàngyàng·zi

【像章】xiàngzhāng 用金属、塑料等制成的带有人像的纪念章 metal or plastic badge with sb.'s likeness on it (in honour of the person)

橡 xiàng ❶ 栎 oak ❷ 橡胶树 rubber tree

【橡胶】xiàngjiāo ❶ 高分子化合物，分为天然橡胶和合成橡胶两大类。弹性好，有绝缘性，不透水，不透气。橡胶制品广泛应用在工业和生活各方面。rubber; high-molecular compound which can be classified as natural or synthetic rubber, having useful properties such as being strongly elastic, insulative, waterproof and gas-proof. Rubber products are widely used for industrial and everyday purposes. ❷ 特指天然橡胶 esp. natural rubber

【橡胶树】xiàngjiāoshù 常绿乔木，枝细长，复叶由三个小叶构成，小叶长椭圆形，花白色，有香气，结蒴果，球形。原产巴西，现在热带地方多有栽培。是最主要的产橡胶的树种。rubber tree (*Hevea*); gum tree; evergreen tree that has slender branches, compound leaves comprised of three small oval leaves and fragrant white flowers, bearing globular capsules, originating from Brazil, mainly cultivated in tropical areas as the chief source of rubber

【橡皮】xiàngpí ❶ 硫化橡胶的通称 general term for 硫化橡胶 liúhuà xiàngjiāo ❷ 用橡胶制成的文具，能擦掉石墨或墨水的痕迹 rubber; eraser; stationery made of rubber and used to erase the marks of lead or ink

【橡皮膏】xiàngpígāo 一面涂有胶质的布条，常用来把敷料固定在皮肤上 adhesive plaster; rubberized fabric; cloth band coated with rubber on one side to fix dressings onto the skin; also 胶布 jiāobù

【橡皮筋】xiàngpíjīn (～儿 xiàngpíjīnr) 用橡胶制成的、有伸缩性的线状或环形物品，多用来捆扎东西 rubber band; elastic; elastic string or ring made of rubber, oft. used for tying things

【橡皮泥】xiàngpíní 用白石蜡、火漆、生橡胶、陶土、水泥、石膏等材料搀和颜料制成的泥，柔软有塑性，不容易干，供儿童捏东西玩儿 plasticine; modelling clay; mixture of pigments and other materials such as white paraffin, sealing wax, crude rubber, potter's clay, cement, and gypsum, which is soft, with plasticity, and not easily dried, usu. a toy for children to play and shape with their hands

【橡皮圈】xiàngpíquān ❶ 供练习游泳用的救生圈，用橡胶制成，内充空气 life buoy (for learner-swimmers), made of rubber and filled with air ❷ (～儿 xiàngpíquānr) 用橡胶、塑料制成的小型环状物，用来束住东西使不散开 rubber ring or band (for binding or tying things together)

【橡皮图章】xiàngpí túzhāng 〈比喻 *fig*.〉只有名义而无实权的人或机构 rubber-stamp; person or institution only in name but with no real power

【橡皮线】xiàngpíxiàn 外面包着橡胶的金属导线 rubber-sheathed wire; also 皮线 píxiàn

【橡实】xiàngshí 栎树的果实，长圆形，含淀粉和少量鞣酸。外壳可以制栲胶。有的地区叫橡碗子。acorn; nut of the oak tree, oval-shaped and containing starch and a bit of tannic acid, its shell used to make tanning extracts; also 橡子 xiàng·zi; called 橡碗子 xiàngwǎn·zi in some areas

xiāo (ㄒㄧㄠ)

肖 Xiāo 姓(‘萧’俗作肖) a surname (popular written form for 萧 xiāo)

☞ xiào on p. 2114

枭(梟) xiāo ❶ ☞ [鸺鹠] xiūliú on p. 2159 ❷ 〈书 *fml*.〉勇猛；强悍 brave; valiant: ～将 brave general | ～骑 valiant horse ❸ 魁首；首领 head; chief; ringleader: 毒～ drug-trafficking Kingpin ❹ 〈旧时 *old*〉指私贩食盐的人 salt smuggler: 盐～ salt smuggler | 私～ salt smuggler ❺ 〈书 *fml*.〉悬挂(砍下的人头) hang (a person's chopped-off head) for public display: ～首 cut off a person's head and hang it up | ～示 hang sb.'s head as a warning to others

【枭将】xiāojiàng 〈书 *fml*.〉勇猛的将领 brave general

【枭首】xiāoshǒu 旧时的刑罚，把人头砍下并且悬挂起来 (a punishment in old times) cut off a person's head and hang it up for public display: ～示众 cut off a person's head and hang it up as a warning to others

【枭雄】xiāoxióng 〈书 *fml*.〉强横而有野心的人物；智勇杰出的人物；魁首 powerful and ambitious person; man with outstanding wisdom and valour

枵 xiāo 〈书 *fml*.〉空虚 empty; hollow: ～肠辘辘 empty stomach

【枵腹从公】xiāo fù cóng gōng 指饿着肚子办公家的事 handle official business on an empty stomach

削 xiāo 用刀斜着去掉物体的表层 peel; pare the surface layer of an object sideways with a knife: ～铅笔 sharpen a pencil | ～苹果皮 peel an apple

☞ xuē on p. 2176

【削面】xiāomiàn ☞ 刀削面 dāoxiāomiàn on p. 390

哓(嘵) xiāo [哓哓]〈书 *fml.*〉❶ 形容争辩的声音 noise of an argument: ～不休 argue endlessly ❷ 形容鸟类因恐惧而发出的鸣叫声 twitter; bird's call in fear

骁(驍) xiāo〈书 *fml.*〉勇猛 brave; valiant: ～将 valiant general | ～勇 brave and spirited

【骁将】xiāojiàng 勇猛的将领 valiant general

【骁骑】xiāoqí〈书 *fml.*〉勇猛的骑兵 brave cavalryman

【骁勇】xiāoyǒng〈书 *fml.*〉勇猛 brave; valiant: ～善战 brave and battle-wise

逍 xiāo ☞ below

【逍遥】xiāoyáo 没有什么约束,自由自在 free and unconstrained: ～自在 free and unfettered | 独自河边垂钓,好不～。How leisurely and carefree I felt while fishing alone by the river.

【逍遥法外】xiāoyáo fǎ wài 指犯了法的人没有受到法律制裁,仍旧自由自在 (of a lawless person) get away with it; be at large; remain free from legal sanction

鸮 xiāo ☞ 鸱鸮 (chīxiāo) on p. 259

虓 xiāo〈书 *fml.*〉虎怒吼 (of tigers) roar

消 xiāo ❶ 消失 disappear; vanish: 烟～云散 vanish like smoke and clouds | 冰～瓦解 dissolve like ice and break like tiles | 红肿已～。The swelling has gone down. ❷ 使消失; 消除 cause to disappear; eliminate; dispel; remove: ～毒 disinfect | ～炎 diminish inflammation | 撤～ withdraw ❸ 度过(时间); 消遣 pass (time); spend (time); while away (time): ～夜 night snack | ～夏 pass the summer in a leisurely way ❹ 需要(前面常带'不、只、何'等 used after 不 bù, 只 zhǐ, 何 hé, etc.) need; take (time, etc.): 不～说 it goes without saying | 只～三天 takes only three days (to do sth.)

【消沉】xiāochén 情绪低落 depressed; downhearted; low-spirited: 意志～ demoralized

【消除】xiāochú 使不存在; 除去(不利的事物) put (sth.) out of existence; eliminate (harmful things); remove: ～隐患 remove hidden dangers | ～隔阂 clear up a misunderstanding | ～战争威胁 dispel a threat of war

【消磁】xiāo//cí 退磁 demagnetize

【消毒】xiāo//dú ❶ 用物理方法或化学药品杀死致病的微生物 disinfect; sterilize; destroy or kill harmful micro-organizms by the use of physical methods or chemical products: ～剂 disinfectant | 病房已经消过毒了。The sickroom has been sterilized. ❷ 指清除流毒 clear away pernicious influences

【消防】xiāofáng 救火和防火 fire-fighting and fire prevention: ～队 fire brigade; fire department | ～车 fire engine | ～器材 fire-fighting equipment

【消费】xiāofèi 为了生产或生活需要而消耗物质财富 consume; expend material wealth (or money) to meet the needs of production or living: ～品 consumer goods | 高～ high cost of living

【消费合作社】xiāofèi hézuòshè 消费者的组织, 成批购买商品,零卖给消费者 consumer cooperative; organization composed of consumers which purchases goods wholesale and then retails the goods at a lower cost to its members

【消费基金】xiāofèi jījīn 指扣除积累后用于消费的那一部分国民收入,即用于满足社会和个人的物质和文化生活需要的那部分国民收入 consumption funds; national revenues earmarked for consumption with deductions for accumulation, or the part of national revenues that is used to meet basic social and individual material, cultural and everyday needs

【消费品】xiāofèipǐn 供消费的物品。通常指人们日常生活中需要的物品。consumer goods; objects for consumption (usu. everyday necessities)

【消费资料】xiāofèi zīliào ☞生活资料 shēnghuó zīliào on p. 1715

【消耗】[1] xiāohào ❶ (精神、力量、东西等)因使用或受损失而渐渐减少 (of spirit, force, things, etc.) be gradually reduced due to use or damage; use up; expend; consume: ～精力 wear down one's vigour | ～能量 consume energy | 高产、优质、低～ high-yield, high-quality, and low-consumption ❷ 使消耗 deplete: ～敌人的有生力量 deplete the enemy's effective strength

【消耗】[2] xiāohào 音信(多见于早期白话 oft. in early vernacular) message; news: 杳无～ having not been heard from since; no news has been received for a long time

【消化】xiāohuà ❶ 食物在人或动物体内,经过物理和化学作用而变为能够溶解于水并可以被机体吸收的养料 digest food in human or animal body; (through physical and chemical functions) turn food into water-soluble nourishment to be absorbed by the body ❷〈比喻 *fig.*〉理解、吸收所学的知识 understand and absorb (knowledge and learning); digest: 一次讲得太多,学生～不了。Students may have difficulty understanding and absorbing if they are taught too much at one.

【消化系统】xiāohuà xìtǒng 人或动物体内由口腔、食管、胃、小肠、大肠等组成的系统。消化系统的作用是消化食物和吸收养料。digestive system; (in the bodies of humans or animals) system consisting of the oral cavity, esophagus, stomach, and small and large intestines, with the chief functions of digesting food and absorbing nourishment

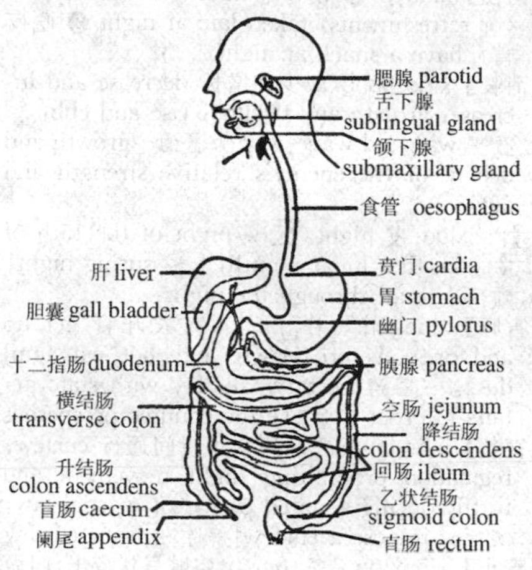

人的消化系统
Human Digestive System

【消魂】xiāohún same as 销魂 xiāohún

【消火栓】xiāohuǒshuān 消防用水的管道上的一种装置,有出水口和水门,供救火时接水龙带用 fire hydrant; part of a pipe system to discharge water for fighting fires, with a valve and drain outlet where a fire hose can be connected

【消极】xiāojí ❶ 否定的;反面的;阻碍发展的(跟'积极'相对,多用于抽象事物 as opposed to 'positive', oft. used for abstract things) negative; blocking the development: ～言论 negative statement|～影响 harmful influence|～因素 negative factor ❷ 不求进取的;消沉(跟'积极'相对 as opposed to 'active') passive; inactive; not aggressive: 态度～ take a passive attitude|～情绪 inactive mood|～防御(单纯取守势的防御) passive defence (resist using defence alone)

【消减】xiāojiǎn 减退;减少 diminish; decrease: 食欲～ decrease in appetite

【消解】xiāojiě same as 消释 xiāoshì: ～胸中的愁闷 dispel gloom from one's mind

【消弭】xiāomǐ same as 消除 xiāochú: ～隐患 eliminate hidden dangers

【消灭】xiāomiè ❶ 消失;灭亡 perish; die out; become extinct; pass away: 许多古生物,如恐龙、猛犸早已经～了。Many prehistoric forms of life, such as dinosaurs and mammoths, have long since become extinct. ❷ 使消灭;除掉(敌对的或有害的人或事物) make extinct; eliminate; abolish; wipe out; annihilate: ～蚊蝇 wipe out mosquitoes and flies|～差错 eliminate errors|～一切敢于入侵之敌 annihilate all enemies who dare to invade

【消泯】xiāomǐn 消灭;泯灭 die out; perish

【消磨】xiāomó ❶ 使意志、精力等逐渐消失 make (sb.'s will, energy, etc.) vanish gradually; wear down; fritter away: ～志气 wear down sb.'s will ❷ 度过(时间,多指虚度) pass (time) in vain; while away; idle away: ～岁月 while away the time

【消气】xiāo//qì 平息怒气 calm one's anger; cool down; be mollified: 你去赔个不是,让她消消气。You'd better go and apologize to mollify her.

【消遣】xiāoqiǎn 用自己感觉愉快的事来度过空闲时间;消闲解闷 while away time by doing sth. that can delight oneself; divert oneself

【消溶】xiāoróng same as 消融 xiāoróng

【消融】xiāoróng (冰、雪)融化 (of ice or snow) melt ◇将个人的感情～在大众的感情里。We should meld individual emotions into those of the masses. also 消溶 xiāoróng

【消散】xiāosàn (烟雾、气味、热力以及抽象事物)消失 (of smoke, fog, odour, heat, or abstract things) disappear; dissipate: 雾渐渐～了。The mist gradually lifted.

【消声器】xiāoshēngqì 降低或消除气流噪声的装置,多用于内燃机、喷气发动机、鼓风机等噪声大的机械 muffler; device to deaden or eliminate noise, often used as a part of a machine with a loud noise such as an internal-combustion engine, jet engine, blowing machine, etc.; also 消音器 xiāoyīnqì

【消失】xiāoshī (事物)逐渐减少以至没有 (of things) gradually decrease and finally disappear; vanish; die (or fade) away: 瞬间,一颗流星就从夜空中～了。A meteor vanished from the night sky in a twinkling.|脸上的笑容～了。The smile faded away from (her) face.

【消食】xiāo//shí (～儿 xiāoshír) 帮助消化 help digestion

【消逝】xiāoshì same as 消失 xiāoshī: 岁月～ time elapses|火车的隆隆声慢慢～了。The rumbling of the train slowly died away.|一抹残霞渐渐在天边～。A few stray rosy clouds are disappearing from the horizon.

【消释】xiāoshì ❶〈书 *fml.*〉消融;溶化 melt; thaw; unfreeze ❷ (疑虑、嫌怨、痛苦等)消除;解除 (of misgivings, enmity, pain, etc.) dispel; clear up: ～前嫌 dispel previous grudges|误会～。The misunderstanding has been cleared up (or ironed out).

【消受】xiāoshòu ❶ 享受;受用 (多用于否定 usu. used in the negative) enjoy; benefit from: 无福～ have no luck to enjoy ❷ 忍受;

禁(jīn)受 stand; endure; bear: ～不起 cannot stand

【消瘦】xiāoshòu (身体)变瘦 (of body) slim down; become thinner; become emaciated: 身体一天天～ get thinner with each passing day

【消暑】xiāo//shǔ ❶ same as 消夏 xiāoxià: 去北戴河度假～ take a trip to Beidaihe for the summer holiday ❷ 去暑 relieve summer heat: 喝杯冷饮消消暑。Have a cold drink to relieve the summer heat.

【消损】xiāosǔn ❶ (构成某个物体的物质)逐渐减少 (of a substance as an integral part of an object) gradually decrease; reduce bit by bit ❷ 消磨而失去; 消减损伤 fritter away; diminish and injure: 岁月～。Time has been frittered away.|锐气～。(His) dashing spirit has diminished.

【消停】xiāo·ting 〈方 *dial.*〉 ❶ 安静; 安稳 tranquil; quiet; safe and secure: 过～日子 lead a peaceful and secure life|还没住～就走了 leave after one has barely settled down ❷ 停止; 歇 let-up; stop; cease: 姐妹俩纺线不～。The two sisters kept spinning thread without a let-up.|太累了, ～一会儿再干吧。You look tired. Stop and take a break.

【消退】xiāotuì 减退; 逐渐消失 abate; subside; decrease: 太阳偏西, 暑热略略～。The summer heat is subsiding as the sun sets in the west.|笑容渐渐～了。(Her) smile gradually disappeared.

【消亡】xiāowáng 消失; 灭亡 wither away; die out

【消息】xiāo·xi ❶ 关于人或事物情况的报道 news; information; report or coverage of a person or an event ❷ 音信 news; message; tidings: 杳无～ have not heard from sb. for a long time

X

【消息儿】xiāo·xir 〈方 *dial.*〉 物件上暗藏的简单的机械装置, 一触动就能牵动其他部分 contraption; floor trap; secret spring mechanism; simple mechanical device that is hidden in an object and can affect all the other parts of the object when touched

【消夏】xiāoxià 用消遣的方式过夏天 spend summer in a leisurely way: ～晚会 summer evening party

【消闲】xiāoxián ❶ 消磨空闲的时间 while away one's leisure time; fill one's spare time: ～解闷 divert oneself from boredom during one's spare time|～遣兴 dispel boredom and while away one's leisure time ❷ 悠闲; 清闲 easy; at leisure: 别人忙得要命, 他可真～, 看戏去了。While others were all extremely busy, he was so free and easy that he went to the theatre.

【消歇】xiāoxiē 〈书 *fml.*〉 休止; 消失 cease; disappear: 风雨～。The wind and rain died down. also 销歇 xiāoxiē

【消炎】xiāoyán 使炎症消除 diminish or counteract inflammation; dephlogisticate: ～止痛 dephlogisticate and relieve pain; anti-inflammatory and pain reliever

【消夜】xiāoyè ❶ 夜宵儿 midnight snack; food (or refreshments) taken late at night ❷ 吃夜宵儿 have a snack at night

【消长】xiāozhǎng 减少和增长 decrease and increase; growth and decline; rise and ebb: ～盈虚 wax and wane|敌我力量的～growth and decline of the enemy's relative strength and ours

宵 xiāo 夜 night: 元～ night of the 15th of the first lunar month|春～ spring night|通～达旦 all through the night

【宵旰】xiāogàn 〈书 *fml.*〉 宵衣旰食 get up and dress before dawn and not eat until dusk: ～图治 be busy all day with state affairs in order to make the country prosperous

【宵禁】xiāojìn 戒严期间禁止夜间通行 curfew; regulation prohibiting night movement and traffic during a stated period of martial law: 实行～ impose a curfew|解除～ lift a curfew

【宵小】xiāoxiǎo 〈书 *fml.*〉 盗贼昼伏夜出, 叫做宵小。现泛指坏人。thieves or robbers who act under cover of night; (in a broad sense) bad people: ～行径 surreptitious action

【宵衣旰食】xiāo yī gàn shí 天不亮就穿衣起来, 天黑了才吃饭。形容勤于政务。get up and dress before dawn and not eat until dusk; be busy all day with affairs of state

绡 xiāo 〈书 *fml.*〉 ❶ 生丝 raw silk ❷ 生丝织成的绸子 raw-silk fabric

萧(蕭) xiāo ❶ 萧索; 萧条 desolate; dreary: ～瑟 bleak|～然 desolate ❷ (Xiāo)姓 a surname

【萧规曹随】Xiāo guī Cáo suí 萧何和曹参都是汉高祖的大臣。萧何创立了规章制度, 死后, 曹参做宰相, 仍照章实行。Cao Can, prime minister of Emperor Gaozu of the Han Dynasty, followed to the letter the rules and regulations set by Xiao He, his predecessor who during his lifetime had also been in the service of Gaozu; 〈比喻 *fig.*〉 后一辈的人完全依照前一辈的方式进行工作 (of the younger generation) strictly follow the rules established by the older generation

【萧墙】xiāoqiáng 〈书 *fml.*〉 照壁 screen wall facing the gate of a house; 〈比喻 *fig.*〉 内部 inside; internal; within the boundary: 祸起～ trouble arises in one's backyard|～之患 trouble from within; internal strife

【萧然】xiāorán 〈书 *fml.*〉 ❶ 形容寂寞冷落 desolate: 满目～ desolation as far as the eye can see ❷ 形容空虚 empty: 四壁～ four bare walls with nothing inside | 囊橐～。The purse is empty.

【萧洒】xiāosǎ same as 潇洒 xiāosǎ

【萧飒】xiāosà 〈书 *fml.*〉萧条冷落；萧索 desolate; bleak and chilly

【萧瑟】xiāosè ❶ 形容风吹树木的声音 rustling in the air; soughing (the sound of wind blowing through the leaves)：秋风～。The autumn wind is soughing. ❷ 形容冷落；凄凉 bleak; desolate：门庭～。There's a scene of desolation in the courtyard.

【萧森】xiāosēn 〈书 *fml.*〉❶ 形容草木凋零衰败 (of trees and grass) withered：秋树～。Trees wither in autumn. ❷ 阴森 gloomy and desolate：幽谷～ gloomy and secluded valley | 气象～ dreary and desolate atmosphere

【萧疏】xiāoshū 〈书 *fml.*〉❶ 萧条荒凉 desolate：满目疮痍，万户～。A scene of devastation met the eyes everywhere, and the entire place was evocative of a ghost town. ❷ 稀疏；稀稀落落 sparse; thinly scattered：黄叶～ sparse yellow leaves | 白发～ greying sparse hair

【萧索】xiāosuǒ 缺乏生机；不热闹 bleak and dreary; dull and desolate; lacking vital force：荒林～ desolate forest | ～的晚秋景象 bleak late-autumn scene

【萧条】xiāotiáo ❶ 寂寞冷落，毫无生气 desolate; bleak; without any vitality：荒山老树，景象十分～。Barren hills and withered trees contribute to a desolate scene. ❷ 经济衰微，即资本主义社会中紧接着周期性经济危机之后的一个阶段，工业生产处于停滞状态，物价低落，商业萎缩 (of the economy) depression; slack; (in capitalist society) phase in a cycle of periodic economic crisis, characterized by stagnant industrial production, falling prices, and declining commerce

【萧萧】xiāoxiāo 〈书 *fml.*〉❶ 形容马叫声或风声等 sound of a neighing horse or a whistling wind, etc.：马鸣～。Horses whinny and neigh. | 风～兮易水寒。The autumn wind soughing and sighing, the Yishui River presents a bleak scene. ❷ (头发)花白稀疏的样子 (of hair) grizzled and sparse：白发～ greying sparse hair

捕(㩋、㩋) xiāo 〈书 *fml.*〉敲打；敲击 beat; knock

猇 xiāo ❶ same as 虓 xiāo ❷ 猇亭(Xiāotíng)，地名，在今湖北宜昌市 Xiaoting, name of a place in present-day Yichang City, Hubei Province

硝 xiāo ❶ 泛称某些矿物盐，如硝石、硭硝等 (in a broad sense) mineral salts, e.g. nitre, mirabilite, etc. ❷ 用朴硝或硭硝加黄米面处理毛皮，使皮板儿柔软 tan; way of processing animal hide with sodium sulfate, or mirabilite mixed with glutinous-millet flour, to soften the skin：～皮子 tan animal hide into leather

【硝石】xiāoshí 矿物，成分是硝酸钾。无色、白色或灰色晶体，有玻璃光泽。用来制造炸药，也用做肥料。nitre; saltpetre; colourless, white, or grey crystal with a glasslike lustre, used as a material for dynamite or fertilizer; 通称 general term for 火硝 huǒxiāo

【硝酸】xiāosuān 无机化合物，化学式 HNO_3。无色液体，一般带微黄色，有刺激性气味，是一种强酸。用来制造火药、氮肥、染料、人造丝等，也用做腐蚀剂。nitric acid; inorganic compound (HNO_3) in the form of a colourless or light-yellow liquid with an irritant odour, a strong acid used for making gunpowder, nitrogenous fertilizer, dye, artificial silk, corrosives, etc.; 俗称 commonly called 硝镪水 xiāoqiāngshuǐ

【硝烟】xiāoyān 炸药爆炸后产生的烟雾 gun smoke; smoke produced by gunpowder after explosions：～弥漫的战场 battlefield permeated with gun smoke

【硝盐】xiāoyán 从含盐分较多的土中熬制出来的食盐 salt made from earth containing a comparatively high percentage of sodium chloride

销1 xiāo ❶ 熔化金属 melt (metal)：～金 melt gold ❷ 除去；解除 cancel; annul：撤～ withdraw | ～假 report back after a leave of absence ❸ 销售 sell; market：供～ supply and sale | 畅～ sell well | 脱～ run out of supplies | 兜～ peddle | 一天～了不少货 sell quite a lot of goods within a day ❹ 消费 spend; expend：花～ expenses | 开～ spending

销2 xiāo ❶ same as 销子 xiāo·zi ❷ 插上销子 fasten with a bolt; bolt

【销案】xiāo//àn 撤销案件 close a case

【销场】xiāochǎng 〈方 *dial.*〉same as 销路 xiāolù

【销钉】xiāodīng same as 销子 xiāo·zi

【销毁】xiāohuǐ 熔化毁掉；烧掉 destroy by melting, burning, etc.：～假货 burn counterfeit goods | ～武器 have the weapons destroyed | ～文件 destroy documents | ～证据 destroy evidence

【销魂】xiāohún 灵魂离开肉体。形容极度的悲伤、愁苦或极度的欢乐。be so distressed or happy that one's soul departs from one's body; be overwhelmed by extreme sorrow, distress or joy; also 消魂 xiāohún

【销假】xiāo//jià 请假期满后向主管人员报到 report back (to one's superior) after a leave of absence

【销路】xiāolù (商品)销售的出路 (of commodities) market; sales channels：～不畅 have a dull market | 打开～ open up the market for a product

【销纳】xiāonà 销毁和容纳（垃圾、废物等）dispose of (rubbish, waste, etc.)：解决好城市垃圾的清运和～问题 solve the problem of the transport and disposal of urban garbage

【销声匿迹】xiāo shēng nì jì 不再公开讲话，不再出头露面。形容隐藏起来或不公开出现。no longer speak or appear in public; hide oneself from the public

【销蚀】xiāoshí 消损腐蚀 corrode：～剂 corrosive｜～作用 corrosion

【销售】xiāoshòu 卖出（商品）sell (commodities)：～一空 be sold out; be snatched up

【销铄】xiāoshuò〈书 *fml.*〉❶ 熔化；消除 melt; eliminate ❷ 因久病而枯瘦 thin and frail due to a long illness：肌肤～ be all skin and bones

【销歇】xiāoxiē same as 消歇 xiāoxiē

【销行】xiāoxíng（商品）销售（of commodities) sell; market：～各地 be sold in different places｜这本书多年来在海内外～不衰。This book has sold well at home and abroad for many years.

【销赃】xiāo//zāng ❶ 销售赃物 sell stolen goods：参与盗窃～活动 take part in stealing and selling (sth.) ❷ 销毁赃物 dispose of stolen goods：～灭迹 dispose of stolen goods and destroy the evidence

【销账】xiāo//zhàng 从账上勾销 cancel or remove from an account; write off

【销子】xiāo·zi 一种形状像钉子的金属棍，横断面多呈圆形，用来插在器物中，使连接或固定 pin; bolt; dowel; nail-shaped metal bar or rod with an often round cross-section, inserted into sth. for connecting or fastening; also 销钉 xiāodīng

蛸 xiāo ☞［蟏蛸］(piāoxiāo) on p. 1476
☞ shāo on p. 1688

翛 xiāo〈书 *fml.*〉无拘无束；自由自在 free and unconstrained：～然 unconstrained

【翛然】xiāorán〈书 *fml.*〉形容无拘无束、自由自在的样子 be free and unconstrained

【翛翛】xiāoxiāo〈书 *fml.*〉羽毛残破的样子 broken feathers

箫(簫) xiāo 管乐器，古代用许多竹管排在一起做成，现代一般用一根竹管做成 *xiao*; wind instrument comprising a row of bamboo tubes in ancient times, and a single bamboo tube in modern times

潇(瀟) xiāo〈书 *fml.*〉水深而清（of water) deep and clear

【潇洒】xiāosǎ（神情、举止、风貌等）自然大方，有韵致，不拘束（of a person's expression, bearing, carriage, etc.) natural and unrestrained：风姿～ with an easy and natural bearing｜这幅画构思别致，笔墨～。This painting features a unique conception and unconstrained strokes. also 萧洒 xiāosǎ

【潇潇】xiāoxiāo ❶ 形容刮风下雨（of wind and rain) driving; whistling and pattering：风雨～ driving wind and heavy rain ❷ 形容小雨 drizzle：～微雨 fine, gentle drizzle

霄 xiāo 云；天空 clouds; sky; heaven：重～ highest heavens｜云～ skies｜九～云外 beyond the highest heavens

【霄汉】xiāohàn〈书 *fml.*〉云霄和天河，指天空 the sky：气冲～ with dauntless spirit

【霄壤】xiāorǎng 天和地 heaven and earth;〈比喻 *fig.*〉相去极远 be far apart：～之别 as different as heaven and earth

魈 xiāo ☞ 山魈 shānxiāo on p. 1670

蟏(蠨) xiāo［蟏蛸］(xiāoshāo) 蜘蛛的一种，身体细长，暗褐色，脚很长，多在室内墙壁间结网，通称喜蛛或蟢子，民间以为是喜庆的预兆 elongated cobweb-weaver (*Teraguatha*); spider with a slim dark-brown body and extra-long feet, which often spins cobwebs on interior walls; 通称 commonly called 喜蛛 xǐzhū or 蟢子 xǐ·zi; regarded as a sign of happiness

嚣(囂) xiāo 吵闹；喧哗 noisiness; clamour; din：叫～ squawk｜喧～ hullabaloo; din
☞ Áo on p. 19

【嚣杂】xiāozá 喧嚣嘈杂 noisy：～的叫卖声 noisy peddlers

【嚣张】xiāozhāng（恶势力、邪气）上涨；放肆（of an evil force or influence) rampant; rising and running wild：～一时 run rampant (or wild) for a time｜气焰～ arrogance

xiáo（ㄒㄧㄠˊ）

洨 Xiáo 洨河，水名，在河北 Xiaohe River, Hebei Province

崤 Xiáo 崤山，山名，在河南 Mount Xiaoshan, Henan Province

淆 xiáo 混杂 confuse; mix (up)：混～ mix up; confuse｜～乱 mixed up confusingly

【淆惑】xiáohuò〈书 *fml.*〉混淆迷惑 confuse and bewilder：～视听 befuddle the minds of the public

【淆乱】xiáoluàn ❶ 杂乱；混乱 mixed up and disorderly ❷ 扰乱 disorder; befuddle：～社会秩序 befuddle the social order

【淆杂】xiáozá 混杂 mixed

殽 xiáo same as 淆 xiáo

xiǎo（ㄒㄧㄠˇ）

小 xiǎo ❶ 在体积、面积、数量、力量、强度等方面不及一般的或不及比较的对象（跟'大'相对 as opposed to 'big') small; little; petty; minor; not up to the average, or not comparable in such aspects as volume, area, quantity, strength, intensity, etc.: ～河 small river|～桌子 small table|地方～ small area|鞋～了点儿。The shoes are a bit too tight.|我比你～一岁。I'm one year younger than you are.|声音太～,听不见。The sound was too low to be heard. ❷ 短时间地 of short duration: ～坐 sit for a while|～住 short stay ❸ 稍微 little; in some way; sort of: ～有才干 be sort of capable|牛刀～试 master hand's first small display ❹ 略微少于;将近 nearly; a little less than: 这里离北京有～二百里。Beijing is almost 100 kilometres from here.|编了～三十年词典 compiled dictionaries for nearly 30 years ❺ 排行最末的 last in seniority among brothers and sisters: ～儿子 youngest son|他是我的～弟弟。He is my youngest brother. ❻ 年纪小的人 younger ones; children: 一家大～ the whole family, young and old|上有老,下有～ have the old above and the young below — have parents and children to take care of ❼ 指妾① concubines: 讨～ take a concubine ❽〈谦辞 *hum.*〉称自己或与自己有关的人或事物 oneself, or sb. or sth. related to oneself: ～弟 my brother|～女 my daughter|～店 my store

【小把戏】xiǎobǎxì〈方 *dial.*〉小孩儿 little children

【小白菜】xiǎobáicài (～儿 xiǎobáicàir) same as 青菜 qīngcài ①

【小白脸儿】xiǎobáiliǎnr 指皮肤白而相貌好看的年轻男子(含戏谑意 derog.) fair-faced handsome young man

【小百货】xiǎobǎihuò 日常生活上用的轻工业和手工业的产品 small articles of daily use; products in the light and handicraft industries for use in everyday life

【小班】xiǎobān 幼儿园里由三周岁至五周岁儿童所编成的班级 junior kindergarten; class in kindergarten for children 3 to 5 years of age

【小半】xiǎobàn (～儿 xiǎobànr) 少于整体或全数一半的部分 less than half; the lesser (or smaller) half: 西瓜吃了一大半,剩下一～实在吃不下了。I have eaten more than half of the watermelon and am not able to finish the rest.

【小半活】xiǎobànhuó〈方 *dial.*〉〈旧社会 *pre-1949*〉长年出卖劳力的未成年的雇农 minor farmhand who lived by selling his labour on a long-term basis

【小报】xiǎobào 篇幅比较小的报纸 tabloid

【小报告】xiǎobàogào 指私下向领导反映的有关别人的情况(含贬义 derog.) inform on other people privately to a superior: 打～ lodge a complaint (against sb. with his superior)

【小辈】xiǎobèi (～儿 xiǎobèir) 辈分小的人 junior members of a family

【小本经营】xiǎo běn jīng yíng 本钱小、利润少的买卖 business with little capital and a narrow profit margin

【小便】xiǎobiàn ❶ (人)排泄尿 (of humans) urinate; piss; void; pass (or make) water ❷ 人尿 urine of human beings ❸ 指男子的外生殖器。也指女子的阴门。man's external genitalia or woman's vaginal orifice

【小辫儿】xiǎobiànr 短小的辫子。也泛指辫子。short braid; pigtail

【小辫子】xiǎobiàn·zi ❶ same as 小辫儿 xiǎobiànr ❷〈比喻 *fig.*〉把柄 handhold; mistake or shortcoming that may be exploited by others; vulnerable point: 抓～ capitalize on sb.'s vulnerable points; get a handle on sb.

【小冰期】xiǎobīngqī 第四纪冰期以后出现的气候明显变冷、冰川有所发展的时期。如公元1550—1850年之间的时期。medithermal; katathermal; little ice age; period following the quaternary ice age, during which the climate became distinctively cold and glaciers developed, i.e. the period between 1550 and 1850; also 小冰川期 xiǎobīngchuānqī or 小冰河期 xiǎobīnghéqī

【小不点儿】xiǎo·budiǎnr〈方 *dial.*〉❶ 形容很小 very small; tiny ❷ 指很小的小孩子 small child

【小菜】xiǎocài ❶ (～儿 xiǎocàir) 小碟儿盛的下酒饭的菜蔬,多为盐或酱腌制的 pickled vegetables; pickles; small dish of vegetables pickled in salt or soy sauce, often served with wine and meal ❷ (～儿 xiǎocàir)〈比喻 *fig.*〉轻而易举的事情 sth. extremely easy to do or manage: 电视机、电冰箱他都会修,至于修电扇,那不过是～。He can repair TV sets and refrigerators, and repairing electric fans is a piece of cake for him. ❸〈方 *dial.*〉泛指鱼肉蔬菜等 fish, meat, and vegetables in general

【小差】xiǎochāi ☞ 开小差 kāi xiǎochāi on p. 1077

【小产】xiǎochǎn 流产①的通称 general term for 流产 liú//chǎn ①

【小肠】xiǎocháng 肠的一部分,上端跟胃相连,下端跟大肠相通,比大肠细而长,约占全肠五分之四,分十二指肠、空肠、回肠三部分。主要作用是完成消化和吸收,并把食物的渣滓输送到大肠。small intestine; part of the intestine that is linked at its upper end to the stomach and at the other to the large intestine, and is slenderer and longer than the large intestine, making up four-fifths of the whole intestines and consisting of the duodenum, jejunum and ileum, its main functions being digesting food, absorbing digested nutrients and conveying food dregs to the large intestine

【小抄儿】xiǎochāor 考试作弊所夹带的纸条 crib sheet; slip of paper with facts, figures, or answers to questions, used for cheating in examinations: 打～ use a crib sheet to cheat at an examination

【小炒】xiǎochǎo（～儿 xiǎochǎor）指集体食堂里小锅单炒的菜肴（in collective canteens）dishes cooked in small pots

【小车】xiǎochē（～儿 xiǎochēr）❶ 指手推车 wheelbarrow；handbarrow；handcart；pushcart ❷ 指汽车中的小轿车 car；sedan

【小乘】xiǎochéng 早期佛教的主要流派。大乘教徒认为它教义烦琐，不能超度很多人，因此贬称它为小乘。Little Vehicle；Little Path；Hinayana；Theravada；early school of Buddhism whose doctrines are looked down upon by Mahayana（Big Vehicle）as loaded with too many trivial details to expiate the sins of all the dead；☞ 大乘 dàchéng on p. 354

【小吃】xiǎochī ❶ 饭馆中分量少而价钱低的菜（in restaurants）small and inexpensive dishes：经济～ inexpensive dish ❷ 饮食业中出售的年糕、粽子、元宵、油茶等食品的统称 snacks；refreshments；（in the food industry）pastries，e. g. rice cakes，glutinous-rice dumplings，sticky-rice balls，gruel of sweetened fried flour，etc.：～店 snack bar｜应时～ seasonal snacks｜风味～ typical local snacks ❸ 西餐中的冷盘 cold dishes（of Western-style cuisine）

【小丑】[1] xiǎochǒu（～儿 xiǎochǒur）❶ 戏曲中的丑角或在杂技中做滑稽表演的人 clown；buffoon；Jack-pudding（in the theatre）；zany（in old acrobatics）❷〈比喻 *fig.*〉举动不庄重、善于凑趣儿的人 person who behaves indecently and likes to make fun of people

【小丑（醜）】[2] xiǎochǒu 指小人 flunky；contemptible wretch；vile character：跳梁～ contemptible wretch who makes trouble

【小春】xiǎochūn〈方 *dial.*〉❶ 指农历十月 tenth lunar month；☞ 小阳春 xiǎoyángchūn ❷ 指小春时期播种的小麦、豌豆等农作物 crops（e. g. wheat，peas，etc.）sown in late autumn；also 小春作物 xiǎochūn zuòwù

【小词】xiǎocí 三段论中结论的主词 subject of conclusion（in a syllogism）；☞ 三段论 sānduànlùn on p. 1650

【小葱】xiǎocōng（～儿 xiǎocōngr）❶ 葱类的一种，分蘖性强，茎和叶较细，较短，是普通蔬菜 shallot（*Allium ascalonicum*）；spring onion；a kind of onion that is strong in tillering，and has slender，short stems and leaves，and is a common vegetable；☞ 葱 cōng on p. 323 ❷ 通常指幼嫩的葱，供移栽或食用 small and tender shallots，for transplanting or eating

【小聪明】xiǎocōng·ming 在小事情上显露出来的聪明（多含贬义 oft. derog.）cleverness shown in trivial matters；petty trickery：耍～ play petty tricks

【小道儿消息】xiǎodàor xiāo·xi 指道听途说的或非正式途径传播的消息 byway news；grapevine news；news spread in the streets or via informal approaches

【小弟】xiǎodì ❶ 小的弟弟 youngest brother ❷ 男性在朋友或熟人之间谦称自己（of males）form of self-address used among friends or acquaintances

【小调】xiǎodiào（～儿 xiǎodiàor）流行于民间的各种曲调 ditty；any of the various songs or melodies popular among the people

【小动作】xiǎodòngzuò 偷偷做的干扰别人或集体活动的动作。特指为了某种个人目的在背地搞的不正当活动，如弄虚作假、播弄是非等。mean and petty action；little trick or manoeuvre；action taken covertly to disturb others or collective activities，esp. illicit action taken privately in an attempt to achieve a personal objective，e. g. falsification，telling tales，etc.

【小豆】xiǎodòu ☞ 赤小豆 chìxiǎodòu on p. 266

【小肚儿】xiǎodǔr 用猪的膀胱，装入和（huò）有淀粉的猪肉末制成的球状食品 ball-shaped deli item made of a pig's bladder stuffed with a mixture of ground pork and corn starch

【小肚鸡肠】xiǎo dù jī cháng〈比喻 *fig.*〉气量狭小，只计较小事，不顾大局 petty；narrow-minded；be intolerant and care for trivial matters rather than the overall situation；also 鼠肚鸡肠 shǔ dù jī cháng

【小肚子】xiǎodù·zi same as 小腹 xiǎofù

【小队】xiǎoduì 队伍编制的基层单位，属中队管辖 maniple；grass-root unit of troops under the control of a lochus

【小恩小惠】xiǎo ēn xiǎo huì 为了笼络人而给人的小利 little or small favour（offered to pull sb. over to one's side）

【小儿】xiǎo'ér ❶ 儿童 children ❷〈谦称 *hum.*〉自己的儿子 my son；☞ 小儿 xiǎor

【小儿麻痹症】xiǎo'ér mábìzhèng 脊髓灰质炎的通称 general term for 脊髓灰质炎 jǐsuǐhuīzhìyán；简称 abbr. 儿麻 érmá

【小贩】xiǎofàn 指本钱很小的行商 pedlar；vendor；hawker；business person with very little capital

【小纺】xiǎofǎng 质地较薄的纺绸 very thin，soft silk fabric

【小费】xiǎofèi 顾客、旅客额外给饭馆、旅馆等行业中服务人员的钱 tip；gratuity；sum of money rendered by a customer or passenger for services performed by an attendant at a restaurant，hotel，etc.；also 小账 xiǎozhàng

【小分队】xiǎofēnduì 某些单位或团体派出执行特定任务的组织，一般人数较少，灵活机动，能力较强 small detachment；flexible and capable group sent out by an organization for a special task，usu. composed of only a few persons：民兵～ militia detachment｜文艺～ travelling art troupe

【小粉】xiǎofěn 淀粉 starch

【小腹】xiǎofù 人体肚脐以下大腿以上的部分 lower abdomen；underbelly；part of the human body above the thigh and below the navel; also 小肚子 xiǎodù·zi

【小钢炮】xiǎogāngpào ❶ 小型新式火炮的俗称 small modern steel cannon ❷〈比喻 *fig.*〉性情直爽、说话冲而直率的人（多指年轻人）straightforward, outspoken person ready to offer comments (oft. young people)

【小工】xiǎogōng（～儿 xiǎogōngr）壮工 unskilled labourer

【小姑儿】xiǎogūr ❶ 小姑子 husband's younger sister; sister-in-law ❷ 称排行最末的姑姑 one's youngest paternal aunt

【小姑子】xiǎo·gū·zi 丈夫的妹妹 husband's younger sister; sister-in-law; also 小姑儿 xiǎogūr

【小褂】xiǎoguà（～儿 xiǎoguàr）贴身穿的中式单上衣 Chinese-style upper garment worn next to the skin

【小广播】xiǎoguǎngbō 私下传播不应该传播的或不可靠的消息 rumour monger; spreading of hearsay information; grapevine; privately spread news which is not supposed to be spread or not certain

【小鬼】xiǎoguǐ ❶ 鬼神的差役（迷信）demon servant in hell (superstition) ❷ 对小孩儿的称呼（含亲昵意）little devil; child; imp (term of endearment used in addressing a child)

【小孩儿】xiǎoháir ❶ 儿童 child; also 小孩子 xiǎohái·zi ❷ 子女（多指未成年的 usu. under-age) sons and daughters: 你有几个～? How many children do you have?

【小寒】xiǎohán 二十四节气之一，在 1 月 5，6 或 7 日 Lesser Cold, the 23rd of the 24 solar terms, falling on January 5, 6, or 7; ☞ 节气 jié·qi on p. 989 and 二十四节气 èrshísì jiéqì on p. 516

【小号】[1] xiǎohào ❶（～儿 xiǎohàor）较小的型号 small size: ～中山装 size-small Mao-style uniform ❷ 商人谦称 自己的铺子 (hum.) (of merchants) my shop; our store

【小号】[2] xiǎohào 管乐器，号嘴呈碗形，一般有活塞，吹奏时声音响亮 trumpet; wind instrument with a bowl-shaped mouthpiece and a piston, issuing a sonorous sound when played

【小号】[3] xiǎohào〈方 *dial.*〉指单人牢房 single-bed ward: 关～ be imprisoned in a single-bed ward

【小户】xiǎohù ❶〈旧时 *old*〉指无钱无势的人家 family of limited means and without powerful connections ❷ 人口少的人家 small family; family with a small number of members

【小花脸】xiǎohuāliǎn 戏曲角色行当中的丑 small flowery face, another name for 丑[3] chǒu (role in traditional Chinese opera)

【小黄鱼】xiǎohuángyú 黄鱼的一种，鳞大，身体侧扁，背灰褐色，两侧黄色，鳍灰褐色。是我国主要的海产鱼类之一。little yellow croaker (*Larimichthys polyactis*); a kind of yellow croaker that has a laterally flat body, ash-colour large scales and back, and yellow sides, one of the major fishes found in China's marine areas

【小惠】xiǎohuì 微小的恩惠 small favour: 小恩～ petty favour

【小伙子】xiǎohuǒ·zi 青年男子 young man; lad; young guy

【小家碧玉】xiǎojiā bìyù 指小户人家的年轻美貌的女子 pretty young woman from a humble family

【小家伙】xiǎojiā·huo（～儿 xiǎojiā·huor）对小孩儿的称呼（含亲昵意）kid (endearing form of address)

【小家鼠】xiǎojiāshǔ 家鼠的一种，身体小，不到褐家鼠的一半大，吻部尖而长，耳朵较大，尾巴细长，全身灰黑色或灰褐色。是传播鼠疫的媒介。house mouse (*Mus musculus*); small mouse less than half the size of the sewer rat, with a long and pointed mouth, comparatively large ears, and a slender tail, and grey-black or ash-colour all over the body, a vector through which plague can spread; also 鼷鼠 xīshǔ

【小家庭】xiǎojiātíng 人口较少的家庭，通常指青年结婚后跟父母分居的家庭 small family; family with only a few members, usu. referring to a married young couple living apart from their parents

【小家子气】xiǎojiā·ziqì 形容人的举止、行动等不大方 (of a person's behaviour, action, etc.) petty; not in good taste; small-minded; also 小家子相 xiǎojiā·zixiàng

【小建】xiǎojiàn 农历的小月份，只有 29 天 lunar month of only 29 days; also 小尽 xiǎojìn

【小将】xiǎojiàng〈古代 *arch.*〉指带兵打仗的年轻将领，现多用于比喻 young general; young military commander; (oft. referring to) young pathbreaker

【小脚】xiǎojiǎo（～儿 xiǎojiǎor）指妇女缠裹后发育不正常的脚 bound feet (of women in the old days)

【小节】[1] xiǎojié 指与原则无关的琐碎的事情 small matter; trifle; unimportant thing having nothing to do with principles: 不拘～ not stick to small matters | 生活～ matters concerning daily life; everyday matters

【小节】[2] xiǎojié 音乐节拍的段落，乐谱中用一竖线隔开 (music) bar; measure; unit of music divided by a line

【小结】xiǎojié ❶ 在整个过程中的一个段落之后的临时总结，用于统计数字或综述经验等 brief summing-up; preliminary or interim summary, made when each of the phases of a whole process comes to an end, used for statistics or summing up experiences, etc.: 工作～ work summary | 思想～ brief summary of one's thoughts ❷ 做小结 summarize briefly: 把上个月的工作～一下 summarize briefly the work done last month

【小姐】xiǎo·jiě ❶〈旧时 *old*〉有钱人家里仆人称主人的女儿（in a wealthy family）term used by servants while addressing a daughter of the master ❷ 对年轻的女子的尊称 young lady；Miss

【小解】xiǎojiě（人）排泄尿（of humans）urinate；pass（or make）water

【小金库】xiǎojīnkù 指在单位财务以外另立账目的公款（of an organization）public money in an account established outside of an organization's official account

【小襟】xiǎojīn 底襟 the small inner piece on the right side of a Chinese garment that buttons on the right

【小尽】xiǎojìn 小建 lunar month of 29 days

【小九九】xiǎojiǔjiǔ（～儿 xiǎojiǔjiǔr）❶ 乘法口诀：如一一得一，一二得二，二五一十等 multiplication formula，e. g. 1 multiplied by 1 is 1，1 times 2 is 2，2 times 5 is 10，etc.；also 九九歌 jiǔjiǔgē ❷〈比喻 *fig.*〉心中的算计 plot in mind：事情怎么搞，他心中已有个～。He's got an idea in his mind for how to deal with this matter.

【小舅子】xiǎojiù·zi 妻子的弟弟 one's wife's younger brother；brother-in-law

【小开】xiǎokāi〈方 *dial.*〉称老板的儿子 old term of address for one's boss's son；young master

【小楷】xiǎokǎi ❶ 手写的小的楷体汉字 regular script in small characters（in Chinese calligraphy）：蝇头～ regular script in small characters ❷ 拼音字母的小写印刷体 lowercase letter（in printing）

【小看】xiǎokàn 轻视 look down upon；underestimate；belittle：别～这些草药，治病还真管用。Don't underestimate these medicinal herbs；they really work in treating diseases.

【小康】xiǎokāng 指可以维持中等水平生活的家庭经济状况 relatively comfortable life；well-to-do life；family's financial condition that ensures a middle-level living：家道～。The family was comfortably off.｜～人家 well off family

【小可】xiǎokě ❶〈谦称 *hum.*〉自己（多见于早期白话 oft. seen in early vernacular）I；myself：～不才 my humble self ❷ 轻微；寻常 unimportant：非同～ no small matter

【小老婆】xiǎolǎo·po same as 妾 qiè ①；有的地区叫小婆儿 also called 小婆儿 xiǎopór in some areas

【小礼拜】xiǎolǐbài 每两个星期休息三天，休息一天的那个星期或那个星期的星期日俗称小礼拜。也有每两个星期休息一天的，不休息的那个星期日俗称小礼拜。（in a schedule that offers three days off every two weeks）week or Sunday of the week with a day off；（in a schedule which offers one day off every two weeks）Sunday which is a working day

【小两口】xiǎoliǎngkǒu（～儿 xiǎoliǎngkǒur）指青年夫妇 young married couple

【小量】xiǎoliàng 少量 small amount or quantity

【小令】xiǎolìng ❶ 短的词调 short lyric；short *ci* poem with tonal patterns and rhyme schemes ❷ 散曲中不成套的曲（in 散曲 sǎnqǔ）single song

【小绺】xiǎoliǔ〈方 *dial.*〉扒手 pickpocket

【小龙】xiǎolóng 指十二生肖中的蛇（of the 12 animals used to symbolize the year in which a person is born）snake

【小炉儿匠】xiǎolúrjiàng 以锔锅、做焊活、修理铜锁等为职业的人 tinker；professional pan mender，welder，lock mender，etc.；also 小炉匠儿 xiáolújiàngr

【小萝卜】xiǎoluó·bo ❶ 萝卜的一种，生长期很短，块根细长而小，表皮鲜红色，里面白色。是普通蔬菜。radish（*Raphanus sativus*）；plant that has a very short growth period，slender roots，bright red peel，and white flesh，and is eaten as a common vegetable ❷ 这种植物的块根 root of this plant

【小锣】xiǎoluó（～儿 xiǎoluór）打击乐器，多用于戏曲伴奏 hand gong；small gong；percussion instrument，usu. played to accompany traditional operas；also 手锣 shǒuluó

【小麦】xiǎomài ❶ 一年或二年生草本植物，茎直立，中空，叶子宽条形，子实椭圆形，腹面有沟。子实供制面粉，是主要粮食作物之一。由于播种时期的不同有春小麦、冬小麦等。wheat（*Triticum*）；annual or biennial herb that has a vertical hollow stem，broad strip-like leaves，and oblong seeds with slots on the ventral sides，its seeds chiefly made into flour as a major cereal grain. Sown in different seasons，it is differentiated as spring wheat and winter wheat. ❷ 这种植物的子实 seeds of this plant

【小卖】xiǎomài ❶ 饭馆中不成桌的、分量少的菜（in restaurants）snack；dish with a small quantity，often singled out from the regular courses：应时～ seasonal snacks ❷ 做小买卖 peddle；do small business：提篮～ peddle with a basket on the arm

【小卖部】xiǎomàibù 公共场所里出售糖果、点心、冷饮、烟酒等的地方（in public facilities）outlet or counter selling candies，refreshments，cold drinks，cigarettes，etc.

【小满】xiǎomǎn 二十四节气之一，在 5 月 20，21 或 22 日 Lesser Fullness of Grain，the 8th of the 24 solar terms，falling on May 20，21，or 22；☞节气 jié·qi on p. 989 and 二十四节气 èrshísì jiéqì on p. 516

【小猫熊】xiǎomāoxióng 哺乳动物，身体长约二尺，头部棕色白色相间，背部棕红色，尾巴长而粗，黄白色相间。生活在亚热带高山上，能爬树，吃野果、野菜和竹叶，也吃小鸟等动物。是一种珍贵的动物。lesser panda (*Ailurus fulgens*); mammal with a body about two *chi* long, a brown-and-white colour head, red-brown back, and a long, thick yellow-and-white tail, mostly living on subtropical mountains, capable of climbing trees, feeding on wild fruits, wild herbs, bamboo leaves, and small animals like birds, regarded as a rare and precious animal; also 小熊猫 xiǎoxióngmāo

【小毛】xiǎomáo (～儿 xiǎomáor)短毛的皮衣料，如灰鼠皮、银鼠皮等 short-hair pelt (e. g. of the grey squirrel, snow weasel, etc.)

【小帽】xiǎomào (～儿 xiǎomàor)瓜皮帽 skull-cap

【小米】xiǎomǐ (～儿 xiǎomǐr)粟的子实去了壳叫小米 unhusked seeds of millet

【小米面】xiǎomǐmiàn ❶ 小米磨成的面 millet flour ❷〈方 *dial.*〉(～儿 xiǎomǐmiànr)糜子、黄豆、白玉米合起来磨成的面 flour made of a mixture of broom corn millet, soybeans, and white corn

【小名】xiǎomíng (～儿 xiǎomíngr) 小时候起的非正式的名字(区别于'学名' as compared with 'formal name') pet name for a child; childhood name; informal name or nickname used during one's childhood; also 乳名 rǔmíng

【小拇哥儿】xiǎo·mugēr〈方 *dial.*〉same as 小指 xiǎozhǐ

【小拇指】xiǎo·muzhǐ same as 小指 xiǎozhǐ

【小脑】xiǎonǎo 后脑的一部分，在大脑的后下方，脑桥和延髓的背面。小脑能对人体的运动起协调作用，小脑受到破坏，运动就失去正常的灵活性和准确性。cerebellum; part of the hind brain situated at the lower back part of the brain behind pons and medulla, with the function to coordinate and balance bodily movements. And if it is damaged, a person would have abnormal flexibility and accuracy of movement. (图见 ☞ figure for 脑 nǎo on p. 1394)

【小鲵】xiǎoní 两栖动物，身体的形状跟大鲵相似，但较小，尾巴扁，四肢短，牙齿呈V形，生活在水边的草地里 lesser salamander (*Hynobius chinensis*); amphibian that has a body shape similar to that of a giant salamander but smaller, a flat tail, short limbs, and V-shaped teeth, and lives in waterside meadows

【小年】xiǎonián ❶ 指农历腊月是小建的年份 lunar year in which the last month has 29 days ❷ 节日，腊月二十三或二十四日，旧俗在这天祭灶 festival on the 23rd or 24th of the 12th month of the lunar year, when sacrifices are made to the kitchen god ❸ 指果树歇枝、竹子等生长得慢的年份 off year; non-bearing year (for fruit trees, bamboo, etc.)

【小年夜】xiǎoniányè ❶ 指农历除夕前一夜 night before lunar New Year's Eve ❷〈旧指 *old*〉农历十二月二十三或二十四日 the 23rd or 24th of the 12th lunar month

【小妞儿】xiǎoniūr 小女孩儿 little girl; also 小妞子 xiǎoniū·zi

【小农】xiǎonóng 指个体农民 individual farmer: ～经济 small-scale farmer economy

【小农经济】xiǎonóng jīngjì 农民的个体经济，以一家一户为生产单位，生产力低，在一般情况下只能进行简单的再生产 small-scale farmer economy; small-scale farming by individual owners; individual economy of farmers, with households as production units, weak in productive forces, generally engaged in simple subsistence reproduction

【小女】xiǎonǚ〈谦称 *hum.*〉自己的女儿 my daughter

【小跑】xiǎopǎo (～儿 xiǎopǎor)快步走，接近于跑；小步慢跑 trot; jog in half steps; walk fast, almost at a run: 一路～ run all the way to somewhere

【小朋友】xiǎopéngyǒu ❶ 指儿童 children: 六一国际儿童节是～们的节日。The June 1st International Children's Day is a children's festival. ❷ 对儿童的称呼 (term of address used by an adult to a child) little friend; little boy or girl: ～，你喜欢唱歌吗？Little boy, do you like singing?

【小品】xiǎopǐn 原指佛经的简本，现指简短的杂文或其他短小的表现形式 originally referred to the simplified version of a sutra; short, simple literary or artistic creation; essay; sketch: 历史～ short historical sketch|广播～ broadcast sketch|戏剧～ theatrical sketch

【小品文】xiǎopǐnwén 散文的一种形式，篇幅短小，形式活泼，内容多样化 essay; form of prose that is short in length, vivid in format, and diverse in content

【小气】xiǎo·qi ❶ 吝啬 stingy; mean; miserly: ～鬼 miser; penny-pincher ❷〈方 *dial.*〉气量小 narrow-minded; petty

X

【小气候】xiǎoqìhòu ❶ 在一个大范围的气候区域内，由于局部地区地形、植被、土壤性质、建筑群等以及人或生物活动的特殊性而形成的小范围的特殊气候。如农田、城市、住宅区的气候。microclimate; essentially uniform local climate of a small area or habitat formed as a result of the special characteristics in local landforms, plants, soil, buildings, and activities of human and other living things, such as the climate of a farmland, a city or a residential quarter ❷〈比喻 *fig.*〉在一个大的政治、经济等方面的环境和条件下，由于具体地区或具体单位的特殊性而形成的特殊环境和条件 special circumstance and conditions, under macroscopic political and economic circumstances and conditions, formed as a result of the special characteristics of a specific locality or specific unit

【小器作】xiǎoqìzuō 制造并修理硬木家具、细巧木器的作坊 workshop making and repairing hardwood furniture and exquisite woodcraft

【小憩】xiǎoqì 短时间的休息 take a short rest：在树阴下～片时 take a short rest in the shade of a tree

【小前提】xiǎoqiántí 三段论的一个组成部分，含有结论中的主词，是表达具体事物的命题 minor premise in a syllogism；part of a syllogism, containing the subject of a conclusion, and serving as a proposition for a specific matter；☞ 三段论 sānduànlùn on p.1650

【小钱】xiǎoqián（～儿 xiǎoqiánr）❶ 清末铸造的质量、重量次于制钱的小铜钱。有的地区把制钱或镚子（bèng·zi）叫做小钱。copper coin made at the end of the Qing Dynasty, which is of lower quality and less weight than the required standards；copper coin or copper in some areas ❷ 指少量的钱 small amount of money：说大话，使～ talk big and spend money in small amounts ❸〈旧时 *old*〉指做贿赂用的少量钱财 small amount of money given as a bribe

【小瞧】xiǎoqiáo〈方 *dial.*〉same as 小看 xiǎokàn

【小巧】xiǎoqiǎo 小而灵巧 small and delicate：身体～（of the body）be small and delicately shaped

【小巧玲珑】xiǎoqiǎo línglóng 形容小而灵巧、精致 small and exquisite：画舫里陈设着～的紫檀桌椅。The gaily painted pleasure-boat was furnished with small and exquisite rosewood tables and chairs.｜苏州很多园林建筑得～。Many of the structures in the gardens in Suzhou were exquisitely built.

【小青年】xiǎoqīngnián（～儿 xiǎoqīngniánr）指二十岁左右的青年人 young people（around 20 years of age）

【小青瓦】xiǎoqīngwǎ 普通的中式瓦，横断面略呈弧形 small black tile；Chinese-style tile, arc-shaped on the transect；also 蝴蝶瓦 húdiéwǎ

【小秋收】xiǎoqiūshōu 指秋收前后农民对于野生动植物的采集 lesser autumn harvest（i. e. gathering of wild herbs or fruits before or after the autumn harvest）

【小区】xiǎoqū 在城市一定区域内建筑的、具有相对独立居住环境的大片居民住宅，配有成套的生活服务设施，如商业网点、学校等 residential district；an expanse of urban residences having a relatively independent living environment and a complete array of living and service facilities such as shops and schools

【小曲儿】xiǎoqǔr same as 小调 xiǎodiào

【小圈子】xiǎoquān·zi ❶ 狭小的生活范围 narrow scope of activity；small social circle：走出家庭的～，投身到火热的社会生活中去。Come out of the confinement of the family and get involved in the fervour of social life. ❷ 为个人利益而互相拉拢、互相利用的小集团 small circle（or set）of people；small clique, composed of persons who make use of one another for personal interest：搞～ organize a small clique

【小儿】xiǎor〈方 *dial.*〉❶ 指幼年 early childhood：从～ since one's early childhood｜自～ since one's early childhood ❷ 男性婴儿 baby boy：胖～ chubby baby boy；☞ 小儿 xiǎo'ér

【小人】xiǎorén ❶〈古代 *arch.*〉指地位低的人，后来地位低的人也用于自称 person of low social status；（later used by a person of a low social position to address himself）I ❷ 指人格卑鄙的人 mean man；base person；vile character；villain：～得志 small man intoxicated by success；small man having greatness thrust upon him；villains holding sway｜势利～ snob

【小人儿】xiǎorénr〈方 *dial.*〉对未成年人的爱称 baby；little one（endearing term for a young person）

【小人儿书】xiǎorénrshū 装订成册的连环画 picture-storybook；cartoon-strip book

【小人物】xiǎorénwù 指在社会上不出名、没有影响的人 unimportant person；nobody；cipher；nonentity

【小日子】xiǎorì·zi 指人口不多、经济上还过得去的家庭生活（多用于年轻夫妇 oft. of a young couple）easy life of a small family

【小嗓儿】xiǎosǎngr 京剧、昆曲等戏曲中花旦、青衣演唱时的嗓音 singing voice of young female characters in traditional operas such as Peking Opera, Kunqu opera, etc.

【小商品】xiǎoshāngpǐn 指价值一般较低的商品，如小百货、小五金及某些日常生活用品、部分文化用品等 small commodities；low-priced commodities, such as small articles of daily use, metal fittings, and stationery

【小商品经济】xiǎo shāngpǐn jīngjì 农民和手工业者以个体劳动进行商品生产的经济。生产者占有生产资料，依靠自己的劳动进行生产，并且只是为了换取自己需要的物质资料而出卖商品。small commodity economy；form of economy in which farmers and craftspeople produce commodities through individual labour. In this form of economy, producers possess the means of production, manufacture through their own labour, and sell their products only in exchange for materials for their own needs.

【小晌午】xiǎoshǎng·wu〈方 *dial.*〉将近中午的时候 late morning；time just before noon

【小舌】xiǎoshé（～儿 xiǎoshér）悬雍垂的通称 general term for 悬雍垂 xuányōngchuí

【小生】xiǎoshēng ❶ 戏曲中生角的一种，扮演青年男子 one of the main divisions of the *sheng* or male role in traditional operas ❷ 青年读书人自称（多见于早期白话 oft. in early vernacular) term used by a young student or scholar for addressing himself

【小生产】xiǎoshēngchǎn 在生产资料私有制的基础上,以一家一户为单位分散经营的生产方式 small (or small-scale) production; mode of production characterized by decentralized operation with the household as a unit and on the basis of private ownership of the means of production

【小生产者】xiǎoshēngchǎnzhě 占有简单生产工具,在自己的小块土地上或作坊里进行小规模商品生产的人,如个体农民、小手工业者 small producer; person who possesses simple production tools and produces commodities on a small scale on his own plot or in a workshop, e.g. individual farmer, handicraftsman, etc.

【小时】xiǎoshí 时间单位,一个平均太阳日的二十四分之一 hour; unit of time calculated as one of the equally divided 24 periods in a solar day

【小时候】xiǎo shí·hou (～儿 xiǎo shí·hour) 年纪小的时候 in one's childhood; when one was young: ～的一些趣事至今记忆犹新。Memories of childhood pleasures remain fresh to this day.

【小食】xiǎoshí 〈方 *dial.*〉❶ same as 小吃 xiǎochī:～铺 snack bar|卖～的 snack pedlar ❷ 零食 between-meal nibbles

【小市】xiǎoshì (～儿 xiǎoshìr)出售旧货或零星杂物的市场 secondhand or sundries market

【小市民】xiǎoshìmín ❶ 城市中占有少量生产资料或财产的居民。一般是小资产阶级,如手工业者、小商人、小房东等。town-dweller possessing a small amount of the means of production or property; urban petty bourgeois, e.g. craftspeople, small merchant, small house owner, etc. ❷ 指格调不高、喜欢斤斤计较的人 petty trader; uncultured person, who likes to haggle over every penny

【小试锋芒】xiǎo shì fēngmáng 稍微显示一下本领 display only a small part of one's talent or capability; showcase a little of one's talent or capability

【小视】xiǎoshì 小看;轻视 look down upon; underestimate; slight: 近来他技艺颇有长进,～不得。Recently he has made great progress in his skills, and this should not be downplayed.

【小手工业者】xiǎoshǒugōngyèzhě 占有少量生产资料,用手工操作进行小规模商品生产的人 small handicraftsman; person possessing a small amount of the means of production and engaged in small-scale manual production

【小手小脚】xiǎo shǒu xiǎo jiǎo ❶ 形容不大方 stingy; mean ❷ 形容不敢放手做事,没有魄力 lacking boldness; timid; not dare to do things freely

【小叔子】xiǎo·shū·zi 丈夫的弟弟 one's husband's younger brother; brother-in-law

【小暑】xiǎoshǔ 二十四节气之一,在7月6,7或8日 Lesser Heat, the 11th of the 24 solar terms, falling on July 6, 7, or 8; ☞ 节气 jié·qi on p. 989; 二十四节气 èrshísì jiéqì on p. 516

【小数】xiǎoshù 形式上不带分母的十进分数,是十进分数的特殊表现形式。如$\frac{3}{10}$可写作0.3(读作零点三),$\frac{27}{100}$可写作0.27(读作零点二七),$5\frac{1}{1000}$可写作5.001(读作五点零零一)。在小数中,符号'.'叫做小数点,小数点左边的数是小数的整数部分,右边的数是小数部分。decimal; decimal fraction; fraction or mixed number in which the denominator is a power of 10, generally expressed by the use of the decimal point, where to the left of the decimal point is integral number while to the right is the decimal number, e.g. $\frac{3}{10}$ can be expressed as 0.3; $\frac{27}{100}$ can be expressed as 0.27; $5\frac{1}{1000}$ can be expressed as 5.001.

【小水】xiǎo·shui 〈中医 *Chin. med.*〉指尿 urine

【小睡】xiǎoshuì 短时间睡眠 nap; short sleep: ～片刻 take a short nap

【小说】xiǎoshuō (～儿 xiǎoshuōr) 一种叙事性的文学体裁,通过人物的塑造和情节、环境的描述来概括地表现社会生活的矛盾。一般分为长篇小说、中篇小说和短篇小说。novel; fiction; narrative type of literature that represents social contradictions in life through portraying characters and fabricating and describing events and settings; generally classified as the novel, the novella, and the short story

【小算盘】xiǎosuàn·pan (～儿 xiǎosuàn·panr) 〈比喻 *fig.*〉为个人或局部利益的打算 selfish calculations; plot or scheme designed for personal or partial interests

【小提琴】xiǎotíqín 提琴的一种,体积最小,发音最高。旧时译作梵哑铃。violin; fiddle; bowed string instrument of the smallest size and the highest sound; transliterated in old times as 梵哑铃 fànyǎlíng

【小题大做】xiǎo tí dà zuò 〈比喻 *fig.*〉把小事当做大事来办,有不值得这样做的意思 make a fuss over a trifle; handle a small case in a manner as if it were a big deal (implying an unworthy consideration or effort)

【小同乡】xiǎotóngxiāng 指籍贯是同一县或同一村的人(对'大同乡'而言 as opposed to 'fellow provincial') fellow villagers; persons whose native places are the same county or village

【小偷】xiǎotōu (～儿 xiǎotōur) 偷东西的人 petty thief; sneak; pilferer

【小腿】xiǎotuǐ 下肢从膝盖到踝子骨的一段

shank; lower leg; the part between knee and ankle; also 胫 jìng

【小我】xiǎowǒ 指个人（跟‘大我’相对 as opposed to ‘the collective’）the individual; the self: ～服从大我 subject the self to the collective

【小巫见大巫】xiǎo wū jiàn dà wū 小巫师见了大巫师，觉得没有大巫师高明 a minor magician in the presence of a great one — feel dwarfed; 〈比喻 *fig.*〉小的跟大的一比，就显得小不如大（of a person or thing）pale in significance or size by comparison

【小五金】xiǎowǔjīn 安装在建筑物或家具上的金属器件和某些小工具的统称，如钉子、螺丝、铁丝、锁、合叶、插销、弹簧等 metal fittings and small tools fixed in buildings or furniture (e.g. nails, wires, hinges, bolts, locks, springs, etc.); hardware

【小媳妇】xiǎoxí·fu（～儿 xiǎoxí·fur）❶ 泛指年轻的已婚妇女 married young woman ❷〈比喻 *fig.*〉听支使或受气的人 one who always gets blamed or bullied

【小戏】xiǎoxì（～儿 xiǎoxìr）小型的戏曲，一般角色较少，情节比较简单 traditional operas featuring only a few roles and simple scenes

【小先生】xiǎoxiān·sheng 指学习成绩较好，给同学作辅导员的学生。也指一面跟老师学习一面教别人的人。student-teacher; student with a good academic performance playing the role of a teacher to his classmates; person teaching lessons to others while learning from a teacher

【小线儿】xiǎoxiànr〈方 *dial.*〉用棉线捻成的细绳子 thin string twisted from cotton threads

【小小不言】xiǎoxiǎo bù yán 细微而不值一提 too trivial to talk about: ～的事儿，不必计较。The matter is too small to be fussed over.

【小小子】xiǎoxiǎo·zi（～儿 xiǎoxiǎo·zir）幼小的男孩子 baby boy; little boy

X

【小鞋】xiǎoxié（～儿 xiǎoxiér）〈比喻 *fig.*〉暗中给人刁难，也比喻施加的约束、限制 difficulties created or unfair treatment given in secret; restriction imposed: 光明磊落，敢作敢为，不怕人家给～穿。He's straightforward, with the courage to act and take responsibility, and has no fear about difficulties deliberately created by others.

【小写】xiǎoxiě ❶ 汉字数目字的通常写法，如‘三、四’等（跟‘大写’相对 as opposed to the ‘capital form’）ordinary form of a Chinese numeral, e.g. 三 sān，四 sì, etc. ❷ 拼音字母的一种写法，如 a，b，c（跟‘大写’相对 as opposed to ‘uppercase’）small letter; lowercase, e.g. a, b, c, etc.

【小心】xiǎo·xīn 注意；留神；谨慎 be careful; be cautious; take care: ～火烛！Mind the fire! | 路上很滑，一不～就会跌跤。The road is slippery. Be careful or you'll slip and fall.

【小心眼儿】xiǎoxīnyǎnr ❶ 气量狭小 narrow-minded; petty: 你别太～了，为这么点儿事不值得生气！Don't be petty! It's not worth getting angry over such a small thing. ❷ 指小的心计 petty scheming: 耍～ exercise one's wits (for personal gain)

【小心翼翼】xiǎoxīn yìyì 原形容严肃虔敬的样子，现用来形容举动十分谨慎，丝毫不敢疏忽 with the greatest of care; very cautiously

【小行星】xiǎoxíngxīng 太阳系中，沿椭圆形轨道绕太阳运行而体积小，从地球上肉眼不能看到的行星。大部分小行星的运行轨道在火星和木星之间。minor planet; asteroid; planet that revolves along an elliptical orbit around the sun in our solar system but is too small to be seen from the Earth by the naked eye. Most of the minor planets travel between Mars and Jupiter. (图见 ☞ figure for 太阳系 tàiyángxì on p. 1855)

【小型】xiǎoxíng 形状或规模小的 small-sized; small-scale; miniature: ～会议 small-scale meeting | ～水利工程 small water-conservancy project

【小性儿】xiǎoxìngr〈方 *dial.*〉常因小事就发作的坏脾气 childish temper; tendency to get angry easily over trivial matters: 犯～ lose one's temper | 使～ be fretful and angry like a child

【小熊猫】xiǎoxióngmāo same as 小猫熊 xiǎomāoxióng

【小熊座】xiǎoxióngzuò 北部天空的一个星座，其中七颗主要的星排列成勺状，以 α 星（即现在的北极星）为最明亮。北半球中纬度以北地区全年可以见到这个星座。Ursa Minor; Little Bear; constellation in the northern sky, composed of the seven stars which form the Little Dipper with the North Star at the tip of the handle as the brightest. The northern half of the Northern Hemisphere is the best position to see this constellation.

【小修】xiǎoxiū 指对房屋、机器、车船等进行一般的小规模的检修 small-scale examination and repair of a house, machine, vehicle, ship, etc.

【小学】xiǎoxué ❶ 对儿童、少年实施初等教育的学校，给儿童、少年以全面的基础教育 primary school; elementary school; school giving comprehensive elementary education to children and young people ❷ 指研究文字、训诂、音韵的学问。古时小学先教六书，所以有这名称。philological studies; scholarship that studies characters, glossaries, and phonology; in ancient times, primary schools started education from the six categories of Chinese characters, hence its name

【小学生】xiǎoxuéshēng 在小学读书的学生 primary-school pupil; elementary-school student; schoolboy or schoolgirl

【小学生】xiǎo xué·sheng ❶ 年岁较小的学生 student younger in age (than others in his class) ❷〈方 *dial.*〉年岁较小的男孩子 little boy

【小雪】xiǎoxuě ❶ 二十四节气之一,在 11 月 22 日或 23 日 Lesser Snow, the 20th of the 24 solar terms, falling on November 22 or 23; ☞ 节气 jié·qi on p. 989 and 二十四节气 èrshísì jiéqì on p. 516 ❷ 指 24 小时内降雪量小于或等于 2.5 毫米的雪 light snow; snowfall that has a precipitation of 2.5mm or less within 24 hours

【小阳春】xiǎoyángchūn 指农历十月(因某些地区十月天气温暖如春) little spring (a period of mild, warm weather occurring in some parts of China in the 10th lunar month): 十月～。The 10th (lunar) month brings us the little spring.

【小洋】xiǎoyáng〈旧时 *old*〉指一角或二角的银币 silver coin of one or two *jiao* (a fractional unit of Chinese money)

【小样】xiǎoyàng ❶ 报纸的一条消息或一篇文章的校样(区别于'大样'① as distinguished from 大样 dàyàng ①) galley proof of a separate news item or an article in a newspaper ❷〈方 *dial.*〉模型;样品 model; sample: 实物～ practical model｜～产品 sample product ❸〈方 *dial.*〉(～儿 xiǎoyàngr)小家子气;小气 awkward; mean; miserly

【小业主】xiǎoyèzhǔ 占有少量资财,从事小规模的生产经营,不雇用或雇用少数工人的小工商业者 small (or petty) proprietor; small craftspeople and traders engaged in small-scale production and operations, employing no or few workers

【小叶】xiǎoyè 植物学上把复叶上的每一个叶片叫做小叶(bot.) leaflet; one of the separate blades of a compound leaf

【小叶白蜡树】xiǎoyè báilàshù 小乔木,羽状复叶,叶片卵形,圆锥花序。树皮入药叫秦皮。Chinese ash (*Fraxinus bungeana*); small tree with pinnate compound leaves, oval blades, panicles, and bark to be used as medicine known as *qinpi*; also 梣 cén

【小夜曲】xiǎoyèqǔ 西洋音乐中的一种小型声乐曲或器乐曲,多以爱情为主题 serenade; (in Western music) small vocal or instrumental composition, often devoted to love

【小衣】xiǎoyī〈方 *dial.*〉(～儿 xiǎoyīr)衬裤 underpants

【小衣裳】xiǎoyī·shang ❶ 贴身穿的单衣单裤 underclothes (worn next to the skin) ❷ 小孩儿穿的衣裳 children's clothing

【小姨儿】xiǎoyír ❶ 小姨子 one's wife's younger sister; sister-in-law ❷ 称排行最末的姨母 aunt; mother's youngest sister

【小姨子】xiǎoyí·zi 妻子的妹妹 one's wife's younger sister; sister-in-law

【小意思】xiǎoyì·si ❶ 微薄的心意(款待宾客或赠送礼物时的客气话 polite remark made while entertaining guests or presenting a gift) small token of one's regard: 这是我的一点儿～,送给你做个纪念。This is a token of my esteem, just a little keepsake for you. ❷ 指微不足道,算不了什么 mere trifle; nothing important; not worth mentioning: 这点儿故障,～,一会儿就修好。This trouble is nothing to me. I'll settle it in a while.

【小引】xiǎoyǐn 写在诗文前面的简短说明 foreword; brief or short introductory note (to a poem, essay, etc.)

【小影】xiǎoyǐng same as 小照 xiǎozhào

【小雨】xiǎoyǔ ❶ 指 24 小时内雨量达 10 毫米或一小时内雨量在 2.5 毫米以下的雨 rainfall that has a precipitation of less than 10mm within 24 hours or less than 2.5mm within a hour ❷ 指下得不大的雨 light rain; drizzle

【小月】xiǎoyuè 指阳历只有 30 天或农历只有 29 天的月份 lesser month; solar month of 30 days or a lunar month of 29 days

【小月】xiǎo·yuè 流产①的通称 general term for 流产 liúchǎn ①; also 小月子 xiǎo·yuè·zi

【小灶】xiǎozào (～儿 xiǎozàor) ❶ 集体伙食标准中最高的一级(区别于'中灶、大灶' as distinguished from 'middle or large canteen') small canteen; canteen where food of the highest grade is prepared and served to a restricted group of diners ❷〈比喻 *fig.*〉享受的特殊的对待 special treatment (enjoyed by sb.): 老师给几个学习上有困难的同学补课,开～。The teacher specially made up missed lessons for several students who lagged behind in study.

【小账】xiǎozhàng (～儿 xiǎozhàngr) same as 小费 xiǎofèi

【小照】xiǎozhào 指自己的尺寸较小的照片 small-sized photo of oneself

【小指】xiǎozhǐ 手或脚的第五指 little finger or toe

【小注】xiǎozhù (～儿 xiǎozhùr) 直行书中夹在正文中的注解,字体小于正文,多为双行 double-line notes in smaller print, incorporated in vertical text

【小传】xiǎozhuàn 简短的传记 brief biography; biographical sketch; profile; bio

【小篆】xiǎozhuàn 指笔画较简省的篆书,秦朝李斯等取大篆稍加整理简化而成 fewer-stroke seal character, simplified from 大篆 dàzhuàn by Prime Minister Li Si of the Qin Dynasty; also 秦篆 qínzhuàn

【小资产阶级】xiǎo zīchǎn jiējí 占有少量生产资料和财产,主要依靠自己劳动为生,一般不剥削别人的阶级,包括中农、手工业者、小商人、自由职业者等 petty bourgeoisie; persons (of a class) who possess a small amount of the means of production and property, and chiefly live on their own labour without exploiting others, e.g. middle peasants, craftspeople, small merchants, freelancers, etc.

【小子】xiǎozǐ〈书 *fml.*〉❶ 年幼的人 younger male generation: 后生～ young greenhorns ❷〈旧时 *old*〉长辈称晚辈;晚辈对尊长的自称 term of address used by those elder to their juniors; term referring to oneself, used by those junior to their elders or betters; I: ～识之! I understand. | ～不敏。I'm not intelligent.

【小子】xiǎo·zi ❶ 男孩子 boy: 大～ big boy | 二～ one's second son | 小～ little boy | 胖～ chubby little boy ❷ 人(用于男性)(含轻蔑意 derog.) chap; guy (for males): 这～真坏。This guy is really bad. | ～! 你敢骂人! You little twit! How dare you abuse people!

【小字辈】xiǎozìbèi (～儿 xiǎozìbèir) 指资历较浅、年龄较轻的人 younger generation; juniors; younger members; persons of lower qualifications

【小卒】xiǎozú 小兵,多用于比喻 foot soldier, usu. used in a figurative way: 马前～ pioneering solider | 无名～ nobody

【小组】xiǎozǔ 为工作、学习上的方便而组成的小集体 small group, established for the sake of convenience in work or study: 党～ Party group | 互助～ mutual-benefit group | ～讨论 group discussion

【小坐】xiǎozuò 短时间坐下来;坐一会儿 sit for a short while: ～片刻 sit for a short while

晓(曉)

xiǎo ❶ 天刚亮的时候 dawn; daybreak: 拂～ dawn | ～雾 dawn mist | 破～ daybreak | 鸡鸣报～ the crow of a rooster heralding the break of dawn | ～行夜宿 set out at daybreak and sleep at night ❷ 知道 know: 通～ be well versed in; be proficient in | 家喻户～ be widely known ❸ 使人知道 let sb. know; tell: 揭～ make known; publish | ～以利害 tell sb. clearly the advantages and disadvantages

【晓畅】xiǎochàng ❶ 精通;熟悉 be familiar with; have a deep understanding of: ～军事 be well versed in military affairs ❷ (文章)明白流畅 (of a piece of writing) smooth and clear: 该书图文并茂,语言～。The book features excellent text and pictures, and is written in a smooth and clear style.

【晓得】xiǎo·de 知道 know

【晓示】xiǎoshì 明白地告诉 explicitly tell; notify: ～众人 explicitly tell everybody

【晓市】xiǎoshì 清晨的集市;早市 morning market

【晓谕】xiǎoyù〈书 *fml.*〉晓示(用于上级对下级 of superiors to subordinates) give explicit instructions or directions: 明白～give explicit instructions or directions | ～百姓 notify the ordinary people

谀

xiǎo〈书 *fml.*〉小 small; little: ～才 petty talent | ～闻(小有名声) be more or less renowned

筱(篠)

xiǎo ❶〈书 *fml.*〉小竹子 little slender bamboo ❷ same as 小 xiǎo,多用于人名 oft. used in a person's name

xiào (ㄒㄧㄠˋ)

孝

xiào ❶ 孝顺 filial: ～子 dutiful son | 尽～ show filial piety to one's parents ❷〈旧时 *old*〉尊长死后在一定时期内遵守的礼俗 conventional mourning rites for a deceased elder member of one's family: 守～ be in mourning ❸ 丧服 mourning clothes: 穿～ dress in mourning | 带～ wear mourning for a parent or relative ❹ (Xiào)姓 a surname

【孝道】xiàodào 指奉养父母的准则 filial duty; norms of supporting parents: 尽～ fulfil one's filial duty to one's parents

【孝服】xiàofú ❶ same as 孝衣 xiàoyī ❷〈旧时 *old*〉指为尊长服丧的时期 conventional period of mourning (for a deceased elder member of one's family): ～已满。The mourning period is over.

【孝敬】xiàojìng ❶ 孝顺尊敬(长辈) be filial and respectful to one's elders; show filial respect to (one's elders): ～公婆 show filial respect to one's parents-in-law ❷ 把物品献给尊长,表示敬意 present gifts to (one's elders or superiors) to show one's respect; pay tribute or respect to: 他带了些南边的土产来～老奶奶。He brought his grandmother some native produce from the south as a gift.

【孝幔】xiàomàn 灵柩前挂的幔帐 curtain or screen before a bier

【孝顺】xiàoshùn 尽心奉养父母,顺从父母的意志 filial piety and fraternal submission; filial piety; filial obedience: ～双亲 show filial obedience to one's parents | 他是个～的孩子。He is filial towards his parents.

【孝心】xiàoxīn 孝顺的心意 filial sentiments; filial devotion: 一片～ one's filial devotion

【孝衣】xiàoyī 旧俗,在死了尊长后的一段时间穿的白色布衣或麻衣 (old custom) mourning clothes; white cloth or hemp garments worn during a conventional period of mourning for a deceased elder member of one's family

【孝子】xiàozǐ ❶ 对父母孝顺的人 dutiful son ❷ 父母死后居丧的人 son in mourning

【孝子贤孙】xiàozǐ xiánsūn 孝顺的儿子和有德行的孙子。泛指有孝行的子孙后辈(多用于比喻)。filial sons and grandsons with great virtue; (oft. fig.) worthy progeny

肖

xiào 相似;像 resemble; be like: 酷～ be much like | 逼～ be the very image of | 惟

妙惟～ remarkably true to life | 寥寥几笔，神情毕～。The figure's expression comes alive in a few brush strokes.

☞ Xiāo on p. 2099

【肖像】xiàoxiàng 以某一个人为主体的画像或相片（多指没有风景陪衬的大幅相片 usu. large and without landscape as backdrop）portrait; portraiture; painting or photo devoted to a person

【肖像画】xiàoxiànghuà 描绘具体人物形象的画 portrait-painting

咲 xiào〈书 *fml.*〉same as 笑 xiào

校1 xiào 学校 school: ～舍 schoolbuilding | ～址 location of a school | 母～ alma mater | 夜～ night school | 全～同学 all the students of the school

校2 xiào 校官 field officer; field grade officer

☞ jiào on p. 980

【校风】xiàofēng 学校的风气 school spirit; atmosphere of a school

【校服】xiàofú 学校规定的统一式样的学生服装 school uniform; student dress of a distinctive design or fashion standardized in a particular school as a means of identification

【校官】xiàoguān 校级军官，低于将官，高于尉官 field officer; field grade officer; military officer of a rank lower than general officer and higher than company officer

【校规】xiàoguī 学校制定的学生必须遵守的规则 school regulations; regulations and rules established by a school for students to follow

【校花】xiàohuā〈旧时 *old*〉指被本校公认的最漂亮的女学生（多指大学生 usu. of a college or university）campus belle; female student widely accepted to be the prettiest in a school

【校徽】xiàohuī 学校成员佩带在胸前的标明校名的徽章 school badge; standard badge showing the name of a particular school, worn on the chest by members of the school

【校刊】xiàokān 学校出版的刊物，内容包括本校各种情况的报道和本校师生所写的文章 school journal; campus paper; journal published by a school, featuring school news reports and articles written by teachers and students

【校庆】xiàoqìng 学校的成立纪念日 anniversary of the founding of a school

【校舍】xiàoshè 学校的房子 schoolhouse; school building

【校训】xiàoxùn 学校规定的对学生有指导意义的词语 school motto: 抗大的～是团结、紧张、严肃、活泼。The motto of the Chinese People's Anti-Japanese Military and Political University was unity, intensity, solemnity, and vigour.

【校友】xiàoyǒu 学校的师生称在本校毕业的人，有时也包括曾在本校任教职员的人 alumnus or alumna; term used by a school's teachers and students for addressing those who have graduated from the school or have ever been employed by the school: ～会 alumni association

【校园】xiàoyuán 泛指学校范围内的地面 campus; premises of a school

【校长】xiàozhǎng 一所学校里行政、业务方面的最高领导人（of a secondary or elementary school）principal; headmaster; (of a university or college) president; chancellor; top leader of a school in charge of administration and operations

哮 xiào ❶ 急促喘气的声音 heavy breathing; wheeze: ～喘 asthma ❷ 吼叫 roar; howl; 咆～ bluster; rave; roar

【哮喘】xiàochuǎn 气喘 asthma

笑 xiào ❶ 露出愉快的表情，发出欢喜的声音 crack a smile; smile; laugh; show a pleased expression and utter joyful sounds: ～容 smiling expression | 微～ sweet smile | 眉开眼～ be all smiles | 哈哈大～ chortle; laugh heartily; roar with laughter ❷ 讥笑 ridicule; laugh at: 耻～ mock; sneer at | 见～ laugh at

【笑柄】xiàobǐng 可以拿来取笑的资料 laughing stock; butt (of a joke); source of laughter: 传为～ be spread as a standing joke

【笑场】xiàochǎng 指演员在场上表演时失笑（of performers）cannot help laughing while performing on stage

【笑哈哈】xiàohāhā 形容笑的样子 with a laugh; laughingly

【笑呵呵】xiàohēhē（～的 xiàohēhē·de）形容笑的样子 be smiling happily; be all smiles: 日子越过越好，老人成天～的。As the days got better, the old man became all smiles.

【笑话】xiào·hua ❶（～儿 xiào·huar）能引人发笑的谈话或故事；供人当做笑料的事情 joke; jest; sth. said or done to provoke laughter or jesting: 他很会说～。He is good at cracking jokes. | 我不懂上海话，初到上海时净闹～。Through my ignorance of the Shanghai dialect, I committed a few howlers during my first days in Shanghai. ❷ 耻笑；讥笑 laugh at; ridicule: ～人 laugh at sb. | 当场出丑，让人～ make a fool of oneself on the spot and make others laugh

【笑剧】xiàojù 闹剧 farce

【笑噱】xiàojué〈书 *fml.*〉大笑；笑 laugh

【笑里藏刀】xiào lǐ cáng dāo〈比喻 *fig.*〉外表和气，心里阴险狠毒 show a gentle and friendly expression but nurse a vicious intent

【笑脸】xiàoliǎn（～儿 xiàoliǎnr）含笑的面容 smiling face: 赔～ smile obsequiously or apologetically | ～相迎 greet with a genial smile

【笑料】xiàoliào 可以拿来取笑的资料 sth. funny or laughable; laughing stock; joke: 不要把人家的生理缺陷当做～。Don't laugh at other people's physical handicaps.

【笑咧咧】xiàoliēliē（～的 xiàoliēliē·de）形容微笑时嘴角向两边伸展的样子 grin；smile with one's lips drawn back

【笑骂】xiàomà ❶ 讥笑并辱骂 deride and upbraid；taunt：～由他～，好官我自为之（讥讽官僚不顾廉耻）。Let those who want to laugh，laugh — I am a good official.（defiant，self-revealing words of a shameless official）❷ 开玩笑地骂 scold in jest（or jokingly）

【笑貌】xiàomào 含笑的面容 smiling face；smiling expression：老人去世多年了，他的音容～至今犹在眼前。The old man passed away many years ago，but his voice，smile and facial expressions remain alive and kicking today.

【笑眯眯】xiàomīmī（～的 xiàomīmī·de）形容微笑时眼皮微微合拢的样子 with a genial smile on one's face；smiling，with slightly squinted eyes：奶奶～地看孙子的立功喜报。With a genial smile on her face，the old lady read the bulletin announcing the meritorious service of her grandson.

【笑面虎】xiàomiànhǔ〈比喻 *fig.*〉外貌装得善良而心地凶狠的人 outwardly kind but inwardly cruel person

【笑纳】xiàonà〈客套话 *pol.*〉用于请人收下礼物 term used for asking sb. to kindly accept a gift

【笑容】xiàoróng 含笑的神情 smiling expression；smile：满面～ be all smiles；have a broad smile on one's face

【笑谈】xiàotán ❶ same as 笑柄 xiàobǐng：传为～ become a standing joke ❷ same as 笑话 xiào·hua ①

【笑纹】xiàowén 高兴时脸上显出的纹路 laugh lines；small ridges or furrows，esp. formed on the skin through expressing happiness：老人家喜不自禁，一脸～。The old man was unable to contain his joy and smiled until his face was all wrinkles.

【笑涡】xiàowō same as 笑窝 xiàowō

【笑窝】xiàowō（～儿 xiàowōr）酒窝儿 dimple；also 笑涡 xiàowō

【笑嘻嘻】xiàoxīxī（～的 xiàoxīxī·de）形容微笑的样子 grinning；smiling broadly

【笑星】xiàoxīng 称著名的相声演员、滑稽演员、喜剧演员等 star comedians；well-known performers of comic dialogues，farces，comedies，etc.

【笑颜】xiàoyán 笑容 smiling face：～常开 be always beaming with joy

【笑靥】xiàoyè〈书 *fml.*〉❶ 酒窝儿 dimple ❷ 笑脸 smiling face

【笑吟吟】xiàoyínyín（～的 xiàoyínyín·de）形容微笑的样子 smiling radiantly；with a winsome smile on one's face

【笑影】xiàoyǐng 微笑的神情 smiling expression；smiling face

【笑语】xiàoyǔ 指谈笑 cheerful talk interspersed with hearty laughter：欢声～ cheerful chatting and laughter

【笑逐颜开】xiào zhú yán kāi 眉开眼笑 beam with smiles；face wreathed in smiles

效¹ xiào 效果；功用 effect：功～ efficacy｜成～ effect｜无～ be of no effect；be invalid｜见～ take effect；become effective

效²（傚）xiào 仿效 imitate；follow the example of：～法 follow the example of｜上行下～ the subordinates imitate the superiors

效³（効）xiào 为别人或集团献出（力量或生命）devote（one's energy or life）to（another person or a group）：～力 render a service to｜～劳 work for｜～命 devote one's life to

【效法】xiàofǎ 照着别人的做法去做；学习（别人的长处）follow the example of；model oneself on；learn from（other's good qualities）：～前贤 follow in the footsteps of one's predecessor｜这种勇于承认错误的精神值得～。This kind of courage in acknowledging one's own mistakes is worthy of emulation.

【效仿】xiàofǎng 仿效；效法 imitate；follow the example of

【效果】xiàoguǒ ❶ 由某种力量、做法或因素产生的结果（多指好的）effect；result arising from certain strengths，approaches or factors（usu. good）：教学～ teaching results｜～显著 remarkable achievements ❷ 指演出时人工制造的风雨声、枪炮声（称音响效果）和日出、下雪（称光影效果）等（of theatrical art）artificially produced sound effects，e.g. sound of wind，rain，gunfire，or lighting effects，e.g. sunrise，snowfall，etc.

【效劳】xiào//láo 出力服务 work in the service of；work for；serve for：为国～ serve for the benefit of one's motherland

【效力】xiào//lì 效劳 serve；render a service to：为教育事业～ serve the cause of education

【效力】xiàolì 事物所产生的有利的作用 effect；favourable function of sth.：药的～很大。This medicine is effective.｜你的劝告对他没有～。Your advice had no effect on him.

【效率】xiàolǜ ❶ 机械、电器等工作时，有用功在总功中所占的百分比（of machinery，electrical appliances，etc.）ratio of useful work to the total work performed ❷ 单位时间内完成的工作量 efficiency；work accomplished in unit time：工作～ working efficiency｜用机耕比用畜耕～高得多。The efficiency of mechanized farming is much higher than that of farming using animal labour.

【效命】xiàomìng 奋不顾身地出力服务 go all out to serve sb. regardless of personal safety：～疆场 be ready to lay down one's life on the battlefield

【效能】xiàonéng 事物所蕴藏的有利的作用 efficacy; useful functions contained inside sth.: 充分发挥水利和肥料的～ make the most of irrigation and fertilizers

【效颦】xiàopín ☞ 东施效颦 Dōngshī xiàopín on p.463

【效死】xiàosǐ 尽力并且不惜牺牲生命 do one's best and not hesitate to devote one's life to sth.

【效验】xiàoyàn 方法、药剂等的如所预期的效果 (of methods, medicines, etc.) intended effect; desired result: 药吃下去，还没见～。No effect has been observed yet after the medicine was taken.

【效益】xiàoyì 效果和利益 beneficial result; effect and benefit: 社会～ social effect | 经济～ economic returns (or results, benefits) | 充分发挥水库的～ try to reap the fullest benefits that the reservoir can provide

【效益工资】xiàoyì gōngzī 职工基本工资以外，随企业、单位经济效益和本人工作成绩而浮动的那一部分工资 bonus (pay); portion of pay outside of the basic salary, varying with an enterprise's or organization's economic profits and an individual's work achievements

【效应】xiàoyìng ❶ 物理的或化学的作用所产生的效果，如光电效应、热效应、化学效应等 (physical or chemical) effect, e.g. photoelectric effect, thermal effect, chemical effect, etc. ❷ 泛指某个人物的言行或某种事物的发生、发展在社会上所引起的反应和效果 (in a broad sense) response and effect aroused in society by words or deeds of sb. or the occurrence or development of sth.: 明星～ influential effect of famous stars

【效应器】xiàoyìngqì 接受传出神经的支配，完成反射活动的组织或器官，例如肌肉、腺体等 effector; bodily tissue or organ that accepts the control of efferent nerves and acts in response to stimulation, e.g. muscles, glands, etc.

【效用】xiàoyòng 效力和作用 effective and useful; effectiveness; usefulness: 发挥～ give play to effectiveness | ～持久 long-lasting effectiveness

【效尤】xiàoyóu 明知别人的行为是错误的而照样去做 knowingly follow the example of a wrongdoer: 以儆～ serve to warn against others following a bad example

【效忠】xiàozhōng 全心全意地出力 devote oneself heart and soul to: ～于祖国 pledge loyalty to one's country; devote oneself heart and soul to the motherland

啸(嘯、歗) xiào ❶ (人)撮口发出长而清脆的声音；打口哨 (of a person) make a long and ringing sound; whistle: 登高长～ climb to a height to make a long whistle ❷ (禽兽)拉长声音叫 (of birds and beasts): 虎～ tigers roaring | 鸟～ birds screeching ❸ 自然界发出某种声响 sounds of nature: 风～ the wind howling | 海水的～声 the roaring of the sea ❹ 形容飞机、子弹等飞过的声音 whizz; the sound of a speeding object (e.g. bullet, airplane, etc.) passing through air: 枪弹的～声 the whistling of bullets | 飞机尖～着飞过顶空。An aircraft roared past overhead.

【啸傲】xiào'ào 〈书 *fml.*〉指逍遥自在，不受礼俗拘束(多指隐士生活 oft. referring to a hermit) free from worry and social conventions: ～林泉 lead a hermit's life by a brook in the woods

【啸聚】xiàojù 〈书 *fml.*〉互相招呼着聚合起来 holler to each other and band together (or gang up): ～山林 holler to each other, form a band and take to mountain forests

【啸鸣】xiàomíng ❶ 呼啸 howl; screech; whizz: 北风～。The north wind is howling. ❷ 高而长的声音 long, loud and shrill sound: 远处传来汽笛的～。The wails of the siren came from afar.

斅(斆) xiào 〈书 *fml.*〉教导 instruct ☞ xué on p.2179

xiē (ㄒㄧㄝ)

些 xiē ❶ 表示不定的数量；一些 some; indefinite amount: 有～ there are some | 这～ these | 那么～ those | 前～日子 several days ago | 买～东西 do some shopping ❷ 放在形容词后，表示略微的意思 [used after an adjective] a little more; a little: 稍大～ a little bigger | 更好～ a little better | 简单～ a little simpler

【些个】xiē·ge 一些 some; several; a few: 这～ these | 那～ those | 吃～东西 eat some food | 他是弟弟，你应该让他～。He is your younger brother, so you should yield to him a little.

【些微】xiēwēi ❶ 一点儿 slight: 一阵秋风吹来，感到～的凉意。The autumn wind sprang up, and there was a slight chill in the air. ❷ 略微 slightly; a bit; a little: 肚子～有点儿痛 have a slight stomach-ache | 字～大一点儿就好了。It would be better if the character was a bit larger.

【些小】xiēxiǎo ❶ 一点儿 a little; slightly: ～感慨 sigh slightly with emotion ❷ 细微；小 small; trivial: ～之事 trivial matters

【些须】xiēxū 些许 (多见于早期白话 oft. in early vernacular) a little; a few: ～识得几字 know a few words

【些许】xiēxǔ 一点儿；少许 a little; a few: ～小利 some small benefits

【些子】xiēzǐ 〈方 *dial.*〉一点儿；些须 a little; a few

揳 xiē 把楔子、钉子等捶打到物体里面 drive (a wedge, nail, etc.) into sth.: 榫子缝儿

里～上个楔子 drive a wedge into the slot of a tenon|墙上～个钉子 drive a nail into the wall|往地里～根橛子 drive a short wooden stake into the ground

楔 xiē ❶ (～儿 xiēr) same as 楔子 xiē·zi ①② ❷ same as 揳 xiē

【楔形文字】xiēxíng wénzì 公元前 3000 多年美索不达米亚南部苏马连人创造的文字,笔画像楔子,古代巴比伦人、亚述人、波斯人等都曾使用这种文字 sphenogram; cuneiform characters; characters featuring wedge-shaped strokes created by the Sumerians of southern Mesopotamia in 3,000 B.C. and used in Babylonia, Assyria, Persia, etc. in ancient times

【楔子】xiē·zi ❶ 插在木器的榫子缝里的木片,可以使接榫的地方不活动 wedge; piece of wood driven into the slot of a wooden tenon to keep it from moving ❷ 钉在墙上挂东西用的木钉或竹钉 peg; wood or bamboo nail hammered into a wall to be used for hanging sth. ❸ 杂剧里加在第一折前头或插在两折之间的片段;近代小说加在正文前面的片段 prologue or interlude in a poetic drama set to music; prologue in some modern novels

歇 xiē ❶ 休息 have a rest: ～礼拜 have a rest on Sunday|干累了就～一会儿。Take a short break when you feel tired. ❷ 停止 stop (work, etc.); knock off: ～工 finish work|～业 go out of business ❸〈方 *dial.*〉睡 sleep; go to bed ❹〈方 *dial.*〉很短的一段时间;一会儿 a little while; a very short period: 过了一～ after a while

【歇鞍】xiē//ān〈方 *dial.*〉歇工;休息 knock off

【歇班】xiē//bān (～儿 xiē//bānr)按照规定不上班(多用于轮班工作的人 oft. for workers on shift) be off duty; according to work schedule, be not on duty

【歇顶】xiē//dǐng 成年人因为患某种病或者随着年龄的增长,头顶的头发逐渐脱落 (of adults) get a bit thin on top; be balding; lose hair gradually on top due to disease or aging

【歇乏】xiē//fá 劳动之后休息,解除疲劳 have a rest in order to relieve fatigue after working: 下了工,老汉盘着腿儿坐在炕上～。After work, the old man sat on the bed, with his legs crossed, to relieve his fatigue.

【歇伏】xiē//fú 在伏天停工休息 stop work during the hottest days of the year

【歇工】xiē//gōng ❶ 停工休息 stop work; finish work; knock off ❷ (企业)停业;工程中止 (of enterprises) stop doing business; close down

【歇后语】xiēhòuyǔ 由两个部分组成的一句话,前一部分像谜面,后一部分像谜底,通常只说前一部分,而本意在后一部分。如'泥菩萨过江——自身难保','外甥点灯笼——照旧(舅)'。two-part allegorical saying, of which the first part, always stated, describes a riddle, while the second part, sometimes unstated, carries a message as the answer to the riddle, e.g. like a clay idol fording a river — hardly able to save oneself (let alone anyone else); the nephew lighting a lantern — illumining his uncle (this last phrase has the same pronunciation as 照旧 zhàojiù, meaning 'as before')

【歇肩】xiē//jiān 卸下担子暂时休息 take a load off one's shoulders; put down one's shoulder pole for a rest

【歇脚】xiē//jiǎo 走路疲乏时停下休息 stop on the way for a rest: 歇会儿脚再走 stop for a rest and then continue travelling; also 歇腿 xiē//tuǐ

【歇凉】xiē//liáng 乘凉 enjoy the coolness under some shade; relax in a cool place: 夏天的傍晚,人们都喜欢到湖边～。On summer evenings, people like to enjoy the coolness by the lake.

【歇气】xiē//qì 停止下来,休息一段时间 stop and take a break: 她说起话来跟连珠炮似的不～。She speaks like a rapid-fire cannon.

【歇晌】xiē//shǎng 午饭后休息(多指午睡) take a midday nap or rest

【歇手】xiē//shǒu 停止正在做的事情 stop doing sth.: 先～吃饭,下午再干。Let's stop for lunch and continue the work in the afternoon.

【歇斯底里】xiēsīdǐlǐ ❶ 癔病 hysteria ❷ 形容情绪异常激动,举止失常 be unnaturally excited or emotional

【歇宿】xiēsù 住宿 put up (somewhere) for the night; stay: 天色晚了,就在一家小客店里～。It's getting dark; let's stay at a small hotel for the night.

【歇腿】xiē//tuǐ (～儿 xiē//tuǐr) same as 歇脚 xiē//jiǎo

【歇息】xiē·xi ❶ 休息 have a rest: 病刚好,还是～几天吧。You've just recovered; you'd better rest for a few days. ❷ 住宿;睡觉 put up for the night; go to bed: 洗过澡就上床～了 go to bed after taking a bath

【歇夏】xiē//xià same as 歇伏 xiē//fú

【歇闲】xiēxián〈方 *dial.*〉停止行动而休息 stop (an action) to rest: 他一天到晚不～。He works from morning till night, without so much as taking a short rest.

【歇心】xiē//xīn ❶ 心情安闲;不操心 in a relaxed mood; free from worries: 孩子都已长大成人,老人家可以～了。Now that his children have all grown up, the old man is finally free from worries. ❷ 断了念头;死心 give up an idea forever: 几次碰壁,他还是不肯～,仍在找门路。Although rebuffed several times, he refuses to give up and is still seeking other ways.

【歇业】xiē//yè 不再继续营业 close (down) a business; not continue a business: 关门～ close (down) a business

【歇阴】xiē//yīn 〈方 *dial.*〉热天在阴凉的地方休息 rest in a cool place during the hot season

【歇枝】xiē//zhī 果树在大量结果的次年或以后几年内,结果很少,甚至不结果 (of fruit trees) after giving a large yield, bearing less or no fruit the following years

蝎(蠍) xiē same as 蝎子 xiē·zi

【蝎虎】xiēhǔ 壁虎 gecko; house lizard; also 蝎虎子 xiēhǔ·zi

【蝎子】xiē·zi 节肢动物,身体多为黄褐色,口部两侧有一对螯,胸部有四对脚,前腹部较粗,后腹部细长,末端有毒钩,用来御敌或捕食。胎生。以蜘蛛、昆虫等为食物。可入药。scorpion (*Scorpionida*); arachnid that has a russet-brown body, a pair of pincers on both sides of the mouth, four feet at the chest, a thick front belly and a long and slender rear belly, which bears a venomous sting at the tip for fighting enemies and catching food. It is regenerated by viviparity, eats spiders and insects as food, and can be used for medicine.

xié (ㄒㄧㄝˊ)

叶 xié 和洽;相合 in harmony; be in accord: ～韵 rhyme

☞ yè on p. 2239

协(協) xié ❶ 调和;和谐 harmonize; accommodate: ～调 harmonize | ～和 coordinate ❷ 共同 joint; common: ～同 in coordination with | ～力 joint efforts ❸ 协助 assist: ～理 assist in management | ～办 do sth. in assistance

【协办】xiébàn 协助办理 do sth. in assistance; assist in handling: 大奖赛由中央电视台主办,若干厂矿企业～。The tournament was sponsored by CCTV with assistance from a number of enterprises.

【协定】xiédìng ❶ 协商后订立的共同遵守的条款 agreement; accord; articles agreed upon through negotiation for both sides to follow: 停战～ truce agreement | 贸易～ trade agreement ❷ 经过协商订立(共同遵守的条款) reach an agreement on sth. (with articles to be followed by both sides); conclude a convention: 双方～共同行动纲领。The two parties reached an agreement on guidelines for common action.

【协和】xiéhé 使协调融洽 coordinate; harmonize

【协会】xiéhuì 为促进某种共同事业的发展而组成的群众团体 association; society; mass group dedicated to promoting the development of an undertaking of common interest: 作家～ writers' society | 中国人民对外友好～ Chinese People's Association for Friendship with Foreign Countries

【协理】xiélǐ ❶ 协助办理 assist in the management: ～员 assistant-management personnel | 派员前去～筹款事宜 dispatch sb. to assist the management of a fund-raising campaign ❷ 规模较大的银行、企业中协助经理主持业务的人,地位仅次于经理 assistant manager (in a bank, business enterprise, etc.), who assists the manager in doing business, and holds a position just below the manager

【协理员】xiélǐyuán 政治协理员的通称 common name for 政治协理员 zhèngzhì xiélǐyuán

【协力】xiélì 共同努力 (work) as one; unite efforts; join in a common effort: 同心～ make a concerted effort

【协商】xiéshāng 共同商量以便取得一致意见 consult; negotiate; talk things over in order to achieve agreement: 友好～ friendly negotiations | 有问题可以～解决。The problems can be solved through consultation.

【协调】xiétiáo ❶ 配合得适当 in a concerted way; balanced; harmonious; in tune: 色彩～ in harmonious colours | 国民经济各部门的发展必须互相～。Development of the different branches of the national economy should be well coordinated. ❷ 使配合得适当 coordinate; concert; harmonize; bring into line: ～产销关系 coordinate the relations between production and marketing

【协同】xiétóng 各方互相配合或甲方协助乙方做某件事 in tandem with; in coordination with; (of all the parties) work in a cooperative manner; one party cooperates with another in doing sth.: ～办理 handle (a matter, etc.) in coordination with | 各军种兵种～作战 different armed services fighting in coordination

【协议】xiéyì ❶ 协商 negotiate and agree on: 双方～,提高收购价格。The two sides agreed to raise the purchasing price. ❷ 国家、政党或团体间经过谈判、协商后取得的一致意见 agreement reached after discussion and negotiation between states, parties, or groups: 达成～ reach an agreement | 遵守～ follow an agreement | 停战～ truce agreement

【协约】xiéyuē ❶ 双方或多方协商签订条约 (of two or more sides) sign a treaty after negotiations: ～国 the Entente countries ❷ 指协商订立的条约 treaty: 两国的～期满。The treaty between the two countries has expired.

【协约国】xiéyuēguó 第一次世界大战时,指最初由英、法、俄等国结成的战争集团,随后有美、日、意等二十五国加入 Entente countries, originally composed of Great Britain, France and Russia during World War I and later joined by 25 more countries including the United States, Japan, Italy, etc.

【协助】xiézhù 帮助;辅助 assist; help: 从旁～ give assistance on the side

【协奏曲】xiézòuqǔ 指由一个独奏者(奏小提琴、钢琴等)和一个管弦乐队合作演奏的大型器乐曲,一般由三个乐章组成 concerto; full-length piece of instrumental music for a soloist (violin, piano, etc.) and an orchestra, generally composed of three different movements

【协作】xiézuò 若干人或若干单位互相配合来完成任务 (of several persons or several units) work in cooperation (to accomplish a task): 双方密切～。The two sides cooperated harmoniously.

邪 xié ❶ 不正当 evil; heretical; wicked: ～说 heretical ideas | 改～归正 give up evil and return to good ❷ 不正常 irregular; abnormal: ～门儿 abnormal | ～劲儿 perverse touch ❸〈中医 *Chin. med.*〉指引起疾病的环境因素 unhealthy environmental influence that causes disease: 风～ pathogenic factor of wind | 寒～ disease caused by cold ❹ 迷信的人指鬼神给与的灾祸 (superstition) disaster brought down by a ghost or spirit: 驱～ drive away an evil spirit

☞ yé on p. 2235

【邪财】xiécái〈方 *dial.*〉来路不正当的财物;横财 ill-gotten gains; wealth gained unexpectedly

【邪道】xiédào (～儿 xiédàor)不正当的生活道路 evil ways; depraved life: 走～ lead a depraved life

【邪恶】xié'è (性情、行为)不正而且凶恶 (of disposition, action) evil; vicious; improper and ferocious: ～势力 vicious force

【邪乎】xié·hu〈方 *dial.*〉❶ 超出寻常;厉害 terrible; extraordinary; abnormal: 这几天天气热得～。It has been extraordinarily hot these days. ❷ 离奇;玄乎 fantastic; incredible: 这事没什么,你别说得那么～。This matter is nothing big. Don't make such an incredible thing out of it.

【邪路】xiélù same as 邪道 xiédào

【邪门儿】xiéménr〈方 *dial.*〉不正常;反常 strange; odd; abnormal: 这里天气也真～,一会儿冷一会儿热。What strange weather over here — cold one minute, then hot the next!

【邪门歪道】xié mén wāi dào 指不正当的门路或途径 crooked ways; improper means (or approaches); dishonest practices (or methods)

【邪魔】xiémó 妖魔 evil spirit; demon: ～外道 evil demons and heretics

【邪念】xiéniàn 不正当的念头 evil thought; wicked idea

【邪气】xiéqì ❶ 不正当的风气或作风 perverse trend or style; evil influence: 歪风～ unhealthy trends and noxious influences | 正气上升,～下降。Healthy trends are increasing, while unhealthy ones are decreasing. ❷〈中医 *Chin. med.*〉指与人体正气相抗的多种致病因素及其病理损害 nosogenetic factors and their harmful effects that work against vital factors in the human body

【邪说】xiéshuō 有严重危害性的不正当的议论 heresy; heretical ideas; fallacy; harmful and perverse opinions: 辟～ refute heretical ideas | 异端～ heresy

【邪祟】xiésuì 指邪恶而作祟的事物 evil things that cause trouble: 驱除～ drive away evil | 战胜～ defeat evil things

【邪心】xiéxīn same as 邪念 xiéniàn

【邪行】xiéxíng 不正当的行为 evil deed; wicked conduct

【邪行】xié·xing〈方 *dial.*〉特殊;特别(多含贬义 oft. derog.) special; unusual: 天气冷得～。The weather is unusually cold. | 他们俩好得～。Those two are unusually close.

胁(脇、脅) xié ❶ 从腋下到腰上的部分 side of the human body, from the armpit to the waist: 两～ both sides of body ❷ 胁迫 coerce; force: 威～ intimidate | 裹～ coerce | ～从 be an accomplice under duress

【胁持】xiéchí 挟持 force sb. to submit

【胁从】xiécóng 被胁迫而随别人做坏事 do evil deeds as an accomplice under duress: ～分子 reluctant follower; unwilling accomplice

【胁肩谄笑】xié jiān chǎn xiào 耸起肩膀,装出笑脸。形容谄媚的丑态。shrug and show an ingratiating smile — cringe and adulate sb.; bow and scrape

【胁迫】xiépò 威胁强迫 coerce; force

挟(挾) xié ❶ 用胳膊夹住 hold sth. under the arm: ～泰山以超北海(比喻做根本办不到的事) hold Mount Taishan under the arm to surpass the Beihai Sea; (fig.) do sth. impossible; try to make the impossible possible ❷ 挟制 coerce; force sb. to submit to one's will: 要～ coerce; put pressure on (sb.) | ～天子以令诸侯 have the emperor in one's power and order the nobles about in his name; control the emperor and command the nobles ❸ 心里怀着(怨恨等) harbour (resentment, etc.): ～嫌 harbour resentment | ～恨 bear a grudge | ～仇陷害 bear hatred and make false charges against (sb.)

☞ 夹 jiā on p. 925

【挟持】xiéchí ❶ 从两旁抓住或架住被捉住的人(多指坏人捉住好人 usu. of bad people) seize sb. on both sides by the arms ❷ 用威力强迫对方服从 hold sb. under duress

【挟嫌】xiéxián〈书 *fml.*〉怀恨 harbour resentment; bear a grudge: ～报复 bear a grudge against sb. and take revenge

【挟制】xiézhì 倚仗势力或抓住别人的弱点,强使服从 take advantage of sb.'s weakness to enforce obedience: ～人 take advantage of a person's weakness to enforce obedience|受人～ be forced to do sb.'s bidding

偕 xié 一同 together with; in the company of: ～行 go in the company of sb.|相～出游 (of more than one person) travel together|不日将～夫人抵京。(He)'ll be arriving in Beijing together with his wife in a few days.

【偕老】xiélǎo 夫妻共同生活到 (of couples) live together to a ripe old age: 白头～ live together to old age in conjugal bliss|百年～ live together until old

【偕同】xiétóng 跟别人一起(到某处去) in the company of; go together with sb. (somewhere): ～前往 head some place in the company of (sb.)

斜 xié 跟平面或直线既不平行也不垂直的 oblique; slanting; inclined; tilted: 倾～ incline|～线 slanting line|～着身子坐下 sit down sideways

【斜晖】xiéhuī 〈书 *fml.*〉傍晚的日光;斜阳 slanting rays of the setting sun; sunlight at dusk

【斜楞】xié·leng 歪斜;向一边斜 slanting; inclined: ～眼 look askance|身子一～就栽倒在地上 tilt and fall to the ground

【斜路】xiélù 〈比喻 *fig.*〉错误的道路或途径 wrong path or way

【斜率】xiélǜ 一条直线与水平线相交的倾斜程度,用交角的正切来表示 slope; tangent of the angle made by a straight line with the x-axis

【斜面】xiémiàn 简单机械,是一个倾斜的平面。物体沿斜面向上移动较竖直升高省力。螺旋和劈都是斜面的变形。oblique plane; bevel (face); inclined plane used as a simple mechanical device for moving objects upward, in an attempt to save labour compared with a vertical rise. Screws and wedges are transfigurations of oblique planes.

【斜坡】xiépō 高度逐渐降低的地面 slope; ground that gradually inclines downwards

【斜射】xiéshè 光线不垂直地照射到物体上 cast oblique rays (or beams) on an object: 地球的两极地方只能受到～的日光。The earth's two polar regions can only receive oblique sunlight.

【斜视】xiéshì ❶ 眼病,由眼球位置异常、眼球肌肉麻痹等引起。当一只眼睛注视目标时,另一只眼睛的视线偏斜在目标的一边。strabismus; inability of one eye to attain binocular vision with the other because of the abnormal position of the eyeball or the absence of sensation in the muscles of the eyeball; also 斜眼 xiéyǎn ❷ 斜着眼看 look sideways; cast a sidelong glance: 目不～ look straight ahead

【斜纹】xiéwén ❶ 一根经纱和两根纬纱交错着织成的纹路,因为交织点相错,看上去是斜的 twill; textile weave in which two filling threads pass over one warp thread to give an appearance of diagonal lines ❷ (～儿 xiéwénr) same as 斜纹布 xiéwénbù

【斜纹布】xiéwénbù 一种棉织品,正面现出明显的斜纹,是普通的衣料 twilled fabric; twill; cotton fabric with a twill weave, commonly used as material for clothes

【斜象眼儿】xié·xiangyǎnr 〈方 *dial.*〉菱形 diamond (shape); lozenge; rhombus

【斜眼】xiéyǎn ❶same as 斜视 xiéshì ① ❷ (～儿 xiéyǎnr) 患斜视的眼睛 wall-eye; cross-eye; eye suffering from strabismus ❸ (～儿 xiéyǎnr) 患斜视的人 walleyed or cross-eyed person

【斜阳】xiéyáng 傍晚时西斜的太阳 setting sun

谐 xié ❶ 和谐 in harmony; in accord: ～音 consonant tones|～调 harmonize ❷ (事情)商量好;办妥(多指跟别人打交道的事情) come to an agreement (on sth.); settle: 事～之后,即可动身。We'll set off as soon as this matter is settled. ❸ 诙谐 humorous: ～谑 banter|～戏 exchange pleasantries|亦庄亦～ both solemn and humorous

【谐和】xiéhé 和谐 harmonious; concordant: 合奏～ consonant instrumental ensemble

【谐剧】xiéjù 一种介于曲艺与戏剧之间的艺术形式,流行于四川,由一人扮演角色,内容多风趣幽默 *xieju* opera; art form that combines folk opera and drama, and is usually played by one person in a comic way, popular in Sichuan Province

【谐美】xiéměi (言辞等)谐和优美 (of words) harmonious and pleasant

【谐声】xiéshēng ☞ 形声 xíngshēng on p. 2147

【谐调】xiétiáo 和谐,协调 harmonious; concerted: 色彩～ in concerted colours|游览区周围的建筑物要跟名胜古迹～。Buildings around a tourist area should be brought into line with the scenic spots and sites of historical interest.

【谐戏】xiéxì 〈书 *fml.*〉用诙谐的话开玩笑 crack a humorous joke; exchange witticisms

【谐谑】xiéxuè (语言)滑稽而略带戏弄 (of language) banter; speak in a humorous and joking manner

【谐音】xiéyīn 字词的音相同或相近 homophony

【谐振】xiézhèn 无线电接收机中调谐回路的振荡频率与无线电发射台的振荡频率相同时,接收机就可以收到发射台的无线电波,这种现象叫做谐振 resonance; phenomenon in which a receiver receives radio waves from a radio transmitter when the vibration frequency of the tuned circuits of the receiver is the same as that of the transmitter

絜 xié〈书 *fml.*〉❶ 量度物体周围的长度 measure the girth of sth. ❷ 泛指衡量 (in a broad sense) measure

☞ jié on p. 994

颉 xié ❶〈书 *fml.*〉鸟往上飞 (of birds) fly upwards ❷ (Xié)姓 a surname

☞ jié on p. 994

【颉颃】xiéháng〈书 *fml.*〉❶ 鸟上下飞 (of birds) fly up and down ❷ 泛指不相上下,相抗衡 (in a broad sense) be equally matched; rival each other

携(攜、擕) xié ❶ 携带 carry; take along: ～酒 take along a bottle of wine|～杖 carry a cane|～眷 bring one's wife and children along|～侣 take one's spouse along|扶老～幼 support the old and carry the young ❷ 拉着(手) take (or hold) sb. by the hand: ～手 join hands

【携带】xiédài ❶ 随身带着 carry; take along: ～家眷 bring along one's family members|～行李 carry luggage ❷ 提携 guide and support; promote: 多承～ be greatly indebted to one's guide and support

【携贰】xié'èr〈书 *fml.*〉有二心 be halfhearted; be disloyal; same as 离心 líxīn ①(携 *xie*: 背叛 betray): 士卒～。The soldiers were demoralized.

【携手】xié//shǒu ❶ 手拉着手 hand in hand: ～并肩 hand in hand and shoulder to shoulder|～同游 travel together ❷〈比喻 *fig.*〉共同做某事 be jointly engaged in sth.: ～合作 work jointly together

㙦 xié 麦㙦(Màixié),地名,在江西 Maixie, the name of a place in Jiangxi Province

鲑 xié 古书上指鱼类的菜肴 (in ancient books) fish dishes

☞ guī on p. 731

X

鞋 xié 穿在脚上、走路时着地的东西,没有高筒 shoe; outer foot-covering for humans to wear that touches the ground when walking, and does not generally extend above the ankle: 棉～ cotton-padded shoe|皮～ leather shoe|拖～ slipper|凉～ sandal|旅游～ sneaker|一双～ a pair of shoes

【鞋拔子】xiébá·zi 穿鞋用具,穿较紧的鞋时,放在鞋后跟里往上提,使鞋易于穿上 shoehorn; curved device used to put on tight shoes, that is forced into the back of the shoe to pull the shoe up to get the foot in it

【鞋帮】xiébāng (～儿 xiébāngr)鞋的鞋底以外的部分,有时只指鞋的两侧面 uppers of a shoe; the two sides of a shoe

【鞋底】xiédǐ (～儿 xiédǐr)鞋的着地部分 sole of a shoe; also 鞋底子 xiédǐ·zi

【鞋粉】xiéfěn 擦鞋面用的粉 shoe powder; powder for polishing shoes

【鞋匠】xié·jiang 以做鞋或修鞋为业的小手工业者 shoemaker; cobbler

【鞋脸】xiéliǎn (～儿 xiéliǎnr)鞋帮的上部和前部 upper and front part of a shoe

【鞋油】xiéyóu 擦在皮鞋或其他皮革制品上面使发光泽并起保护作用的蜡状物 shoe polish (or cream); waxen substance used for polishing and protecting leather shoes or other leather products by being applied on the surface

【鞋子】xié·zi same as 鞋 xié

撷 xié〈书 *fml.*〉❶ 摘下,取下 pick; pluck: 采～ pick ❷ same as 襭 xié

勰 xié〈书 *fml.*〉协和。多用于人名。harmonious; *xie*, oft. used as part of a person's name

缬 xié〈书 *fml.*〉有花纹的丝织品 patterned silk fabric

襭 xié〈书 *fml.*〉用衣襟兜东西 use the front of a Chinese jacket to hold sth.

鞵 xié〈书 *fml.*〉same as 鞋 xié

xiě (ㄒㄧㄝˇ)

写(寫) xiě ❶ 用笔在纸上或其他东西上做字 write; use a pen or brush to make characters on paper or other things: ～草字 write Chinese characters in a cursive hand|～对联 write couplets ❷ 写作 compose; write (an article, book, etc.): ～诗 compose a poem|～文章 write an article ❸ 描写 describe; depict: 抒～ express|～景 describe the scenery|～实 write realistically ❹ 绘画 paint; draw: ～生 sketch from nature|～真 draw a portrait

☞ xiè on p. 2123

【写本】xiěběn 抄本 handwritten copy

【写法】xiěfǎ ❶ 写作的方法 style of writing; literary style ❷ 书写文字的方法 style of handwriting; penmanship

【写景】xiějǐng 描写景物 describe scenery: 这篇散文～抒情都有独到之处。This piece of prose is distinctive in both description of scenery and expression of emotions.

【写生】xiěshēng 对着实物或风景绘画 paint or sketch from nature; do a painting of an object or a landscape: 静物～ still-life painting|室外～ outdoor sketch

【写实】xiěshí 真实地描绘事物 write or paint realistically

【写实主义】xiěshí zhǔyì 现实主义的旧称 old name for 现实主义 xiànshí zhǔyì

【写意】xiěyì 国画的一种画法,用笔不求工细,注重神态的表现和抒发作者的情趣(区别于'工笔' as distinguished from 'meticulous painting') freehand brushwork in traditional Chinese painting, characterized by bold strokes and stress on spiritual resonance and the painter's emotions

☞ xièyì on p. 2123

【写照】xiězhào ❶ 画人物的形象 portray (a person or character): 传神～ give a vivid and lifelike portrayal ❷ 描写刻画 portrayal; portraiture: '无风三尺土,有雨一街泥',这就是旧北京街道的真实～。'A thick layer of dust covers the ground even if there's no wind, and any rainfall may turn the streets muddy.' This is a true-to-life portrayal of the streets in old Beijing.

【写真】xiězhēn ❶ 画人像 portray a person; draw a portrait ❷ 画的人像 portrait ❸ 对事物的如实描绘 true-to-life depiction of sth.; faithful representation

【写字台】xiězìtái 办公、写字等用的桌子,一般有几个抽屉,有的还带小柜子 writing desk; desk for writing, handling official affairs, etc., generally with several drawers, and some with a small cabinet

【写作】xiězuò 写文章(有时专指文学创作) writing (or literary creation in particular): ～技巧 writing technique|～水平 writing level

血 xiě 义同'血'(xuè) meaning the same as 血 xuè: 流了一点～。There's a little bleeding.|吐了两口～ vomit a bit of blood

☞ xuè on p. 2181

【血糊糊】xiěhūhū (～的 xiěhūhū·de)形容流出的鲜血附着皮肉或物体的样子 bloodstained; bloody; (of skin, meat, etc.) smeared or stained with blood: ～的伤口 bloody wound|地上～的一片。There was a pool of blood on the ground.

【血淋淋】xiělīnlīn (～的 xiělīnlīn·de) ❶ 形容鲜血不断地流的样子 dripping with blood ❷〈比喻 *fig.*〉严酷或惨酷 bloody; ruthless; tragic: ～的事实 the grim truth|～的教训 bloody lesson

【血晕】xiěyùn 受伤后皮肤未破,呈红紫色 contusion; bruise; injury involving the rupture of small blood vessels, and a resulting red violet colour, without a break in the overlying skin

☞ xuèyùn on p. 2184

xiè (ㄒㄧㄝ)

写(寫) xiè ☞ below

☞ xiě on p. 2122

【写意】xièyì〈方 *dial.*〉舒适 comfortable; enjoyable

☞ xiěyì on p. 2122

灺(炧) xiè〈书 *fml.*〉蜡烛的余烬 candle drippings

泄(洩) xiè ❶ 液体、气体排出 let out (a fluid or gas); discharge; release: 排～ discharge|水～不通 fully packed; very crowded; jammed ◇气可鼓而不可～。Morale should be heightened, not dampened. ❷ 泄露 let out; leak (news, secrets, etc.):～密 divulge a secret; let the cat out of the bag|～底 reveal what is at the bottom of sth. ❸ 发泄 give vent to: ～愤 give vent to one's pent-up anger|～恨 give vent to one's pent-up resentment

【泄底】xiè//dǐ 泄露底细 reveal what is at the bottom of sth.

【泄愤】xiè//fèn 发泄内心的愤恨 give vent to one's pent-up anger: 借端～ give vent to one's anger on an excuse; find some pretext for giving vent to one's anger

【泄恨】xiè//hèn same as 泄愤 xiè//fèn

【泄洪】xiè//hóng 排泄洪水 discharge flood water: 开闸～ open sluice-gate(s) to release flood water

【泄劲】xiè//jìn (～儿 xiè//jìnr)失去信心和干劲 lose heart; lose confidence; feel discouraged; be disheartened; slacken one's efforts: 努力赶上去,别～。Keep up! Don't slacken your efforts!

【泄漏】xièlòu ❶ (液体、气体)漏出 (of a fluid or gas) leak; escape: 管道破裂,石油大量～。The pipe has broken and large amount of oil has leaked out. ❷ same as 泄露 xièlòu

【泄露】xièlòu 不应该让人知道的事情让人知道了 let out; reveal: ～机密 leak a secret|～风声 leak information; also 泄漏 xièlòu

【泄密】xiè//mì 泄露机密 divulge a secret; betray confidential matters

【泄气】xiè//qì ❶ 泄劲 lose heart; feel discouraged; be disheartened: 遇到困难也不要悲观～。Don't lose heart in the face of difficulties. ❷ 讥讽低劣或没有本领 [used to jeer at a poor performance or lack of skill] disappointing; frustrating; pathetic: 这点小故障排除不了,你也太～了。You can't get rid of even such a little trouble. What a pity!

【泄殖腔】xièzhíqiāng 某些鱼类、鸟类、两栖类和爬行动物等的肠道、输尿管和生殖腺的开口都在一个空腔里,这个空腔叫做泄殖腔 cloacal chamber; cloaca; cavity into which both the intestinal and the genitourinary tracts empty in some reptiles, birds, amphibians, and fishes

泻(瀉) xiè ❶ 很快地流 flow swiftly; rush down; pour out: 流～ flow down; rush down|倾～ pour down|河水奔腾,一～千里。The torrent rushes down for miles on end. ❷ 腹泻 have loose bowels; have diarrhoea: ～药 laxative; cathartic; purgative|上吐下～ vomit and have loose bowels

【泻肚】xiè//dù 腹泻的通称 general term for 腹泻 fùxiè

【泻湖】xièhú 潟湖的旧称 old name of 潟湖 xièhú

【泻药】xièyào 内服后能引起下泻的药物 laxative; cathartic; purgative

绁(絏、緤) xiè 〈书 *fml*.〉❶ 绳索 ropes; reins: 缧～(léixiè) rope used to tie up a criminal ❷ 捆;拴 tie; bind; fasten

契(偰) Xiè 人名,殷代的祖先,传说是舜的臣 Xie, ancestor of the Yin tribe which founded the Shang Dynasty and minister of the legendary King Shun

☞ qì on p.1525

卨(禼、离) xiè 用于人名,万俟(Mòqí)卨,宋朝人 (used in the name of a person) Moqi Xie, a man in the Song Dynasty

卸 xiè ❶ 把运输的东西从运输工具上搬下来 unload; discharge; remove the cargo from a means of transport; lay down; take off a burden (or load): ～货 unload goods ❷ 把加在人身上的东西取下来或去掉 remove; strip; take sth. off a human body: ～装 remove stage makeup and costume | ～肩 lay down one's burden; shirk one's responsibility ❸ 把牲口身上拴的套解开取下来 unhitch: ～牲口 unhitch a draught animal ❹ 把零件从机械上拆下来 remove parts from a machine: 拆～ remove parts from a machine | ～螺丝 unscrew ❺ 解除;推卸 get rid of; shirk: ～任 be relieved from one's office; be dismissed from one's office | ～责 shirk one's responsibility; shift the blame onto another

【卸包袱】xiè bāo·fu 〈比喻 *fig*.〉去掉拖累自己的事物或解除思想上的负担 remove a burden; discharge a load from one's mind

【卸车】xiè//chē 把运输的东西从车上卸下来 unload (goods, etc.) from a vehicle; unload a truck, car, etc.

【卸货】xiè//huò 把货物从运输工具上卸下来 unload (or discharge) a cargo; unload

【卸肩】xièjiān 把扛着或挑着的东西放下 lay down one's load; 〈比喻 *fig*.〉推卸责任。也比喻辞去职务。shirk one's responsibility; resign from one's office

【卸磨杀驴】xiè mò shā lǘ 〈比喻 *fig*.〉达到目的以后,就把曾给自己出过力的人除掉 get rid of sb. as soon as he has done his job; kill the donkey the moment it is released of the millstone

【卸任】xiè//rèn 指官吏解除职务 be relieved of one's office; be removed from one's office

【卸载】xiè//zài 把车、船等上面装载的货物卸下来 unload the cargo from a vehicle or a ship; also 卸儎 xiè//zài

【卸儎】xiè//zài same as 卸载 xiè//zài

【卸责】xièzé 推卸责任 shirk responsibility and shift the blame onto others: 推诿～ shift blame onto another person

【卸职】xièzhí same as 卸任 xiè//rèn

【卸妆】xiè//zhuāng 妇女除去身上的装饰 (of a female) remove ornaments and formal dress

【卸装】xiè//zhuāng 演员除去化装时穿戴涂抹的东西 (of an actor or actress) remove stage makeup and costume

屑 xiè ❶ 碎末 bits; scraps; crumbs: 铁～ iron filings; iron shavings; bits of iron | 木～ sawdust | 冰～ bits of ice ❷ 琐碎 trifling: 琐～ trifling; trivial | ～～ trivial; trifling ❸ 认为值得(做) regard it worth doing: 不～一顾 disdain to take a look

械 xiè ❶ 器械 apparatus; tool; instrument: 机～ machine; device ❷ 武器 weapon: 军～ weapons | 缴～ lay down the arms | ～斗 fight with weapons ❸ 〈书 *fml*.〉枷和镣铐之类的刑具 fetters; shackles

【械斗】xièdòu 手持棍棒等打群架 fight with weapons between groups of people

齘 xiè 〈书 *fml*.〉❶ 牙齿相磨 grinding of teeth ❷ 参差不密合 irregular teeth

猲 xiè 〈书 *fml*.〉短嘴的狗 dog with a short snout

☞ hè on p.792

亵(褻) xiè ❶ 轻慢 treat with irreverence; be disrespectful: ～渎 blaspheme; profane; pollute | ～慢 show disrespect ❷ 淫秽 obscene; indecent; salacious: 猥～ abuse sexually; be lewd | ～语 obscene utterances; obscenities

【亵渎】xièdú 〈书 *fml*.〉轻慢;不尊敬 show disrespect: ～神灵 blasphemy against gods

【亵慢】xièmàn 〈书 *fml*.〉轻慢;不庄重 show disrespect: 言语～ salacious words

渫 xiè ❶〈书 *fml*.〉除去 get rid off; remove ❷〈书 *fml*.〉泄;疏通 dredge; discharge ❸ (Xiè)姓 a surname

谢 xiè ❶ 感谢 thank: 道～ express thanks | 酬～ give a gift to sb. in token of gratitude | 这点儿小事不用～了。Don't mention such a trifle. *or* Such a trifle is not worth mentioning. ❷ 认错;道歉 make an apology; excuse oneself: ～罪 apologize for an offence | ～过 apologize for having done sth. wrong ❸ 辞去;拒绝 decline: ～绝 decline an offer (or invitation, etc.) with thanks | 敬～不敏 decline a request politely; beg to be excused for not doing something ❹ (花或叶子)脱落 (of flowers, leaves) wither: 凋～ wither; fade; wilt | 萎～ wither; fade; lose freshness ❺ (Xiè)姓 a surname

【谢病】xièbìng 〈书 *fml*.〉推脱有病 excuse oneself on grounds of illness: ～辞官 resign from one's office on the pretext of illness

【谢步】xièbù 〈旧时 *old*〉亲友前来拜访或贺喜、吊丧,事后回拜道谢,叫做谢步 pay a return visit to a relative or friend to express thanks for attending a wedding, funeral service, etc.

【谢忱】xièchén 感谢的心意 gratitude; thankfulness:聊表～ as a token of gratitude; express one's thanks for

【谢词】xiècí 在仪式上所说的表示感谢的话 thank-you speech; short address expressing thanks at a ceremony; also 谢辞 xiècí

【谢恩】xiè//ēn 感谢别人给自己的恩惠(多指臣子对君主 usu. of a minister to an emperor) express gratitude for a favour

【谢绝】xièjué 婉辞,拒绝 politely refuse; decline:～参观。Not open to visitors.|婉言～ decline politely

【谢客】xièkè ❶ 谢绝宾客 decline to receive visitors; not be seeing any visitors:闭门～ not at home to visitors ❷ 向宾客致谢 thank a guest for his visit

【谢幕】xiè//mù 演出闭幕后观众鼓掌时,演员站在台前向观众敬礼,答谢观众的盛意(of an actor or actress) answer (or respond to) a curtain call when greeted with applause at the end of a performance

【谢却】xièquè 谢绝 politely refuse; decline:婉言～ refuse or decline politely

【谢世】xièshì〈书 *fml.*〉去世 pass away; die

【谢天谢地】xiè tiān xiè dì 迷信的人认为处境顺利是受到了天地神灵的保佑,因此要感谢天地。现在多用'谢天谢地'表示感激或庆幸。thank goodness; thank heaven; (superstitious people) thank God or Heaven, believing that they are blessed and protected by God or Heaven when they are in good times; now 'thank goodness' being used to express one's gratitude or joy:～,这场灾难总算过去了。Thank goodness; the calamity is at last over.|只要他不再来找麻烦,我就～了。Only if he does not come again to make trouble, I would thank God.

【谢帖】xiètiě 受人礼物后表示答谢的回帖 note of thanks; thank-you note

【谢孝】xièxiào 旧俗指孝子等向吊唁的亲友行礼,特指服满后拜访吊唁的亲友表示感谢(old custom of a filial son having served a period of mourning for his parent) visit and thank those friends and relatives who have offered condolences

【谢谢】xiè·xie 对别人的好意表示感谢 thank sb. for his kindness

【谢意】xièyì 感谢的心意 gratitude; thankfulness

【谢罪】xiè//zuì 向人承认错误,请求原谅 apologize for an offence; offer one's apology for a fault:登门～ call someone to make an apology

屧(屟) xiè〈书 *fml.*〉木板拖鞋 wooden slippers

媟 xiè〈书 *fml.*〉狎;轻慢 flirt with (a woman); dally with (a woman):～渎(亵渎) blaspheme; profane; pollute

塮 xiè〈方 *fml.*〉指猪羊等家畜圈里积的粪便 dung from pigs, sheep and other domestic animals in their pens:猪～ pig dung|鸡～ chicken dung

解1 xiè 懂得;明白 understand; see:～不开这个道理 can't see the point

解2 xiè〈旧时 *old*〉指杂技表演的各种技艺,特指骑在马上表演的技艺 acrobatics; all kinds of acrobatics, especially the acrobatics performed on horseback:跑马卖～ earn a living by performing acrobatic stunts on horseback

解3 Xiè ❶ 解池,湖名,在山西 Xiechi, name of a lake in Shanxi Province ❷(Xiè)姓 a surname

☞ jiě on p.995 and jiè on p.1002

【解数】xièshù 指武术的架势。也泛指手段、本事 postures in martial arts; (in a broad sense) skill, art:使尽浑身～ do all one can; use all one's skill

榭 xiè 建筑在台上的房屋 pavilion or house on a terrace:水～ pavilion by the waterside; waterside pavilion|歌台舞～ platform; stage; hall for singing and dancing

榍 xiè[榍石](xièshí)矿物,成分是 $CaTi[SiO_4]O$,楔状、板状或粒状晶体,褐色或绿色,有时也呈红、黑等色,有光泽。是提炼钛的原料。titanite ($CaTi[SiO_4]O$); sphene; brown, or green, sometimes red or black crystalline mineral in the shape of a wedge, plate or particle, used for extracting titanium

薤 xiè ❶ 多年生草本植物,地下有鳞茎,叶子细长,花紫色,伞形花序。鳞茎可以吃。Chinese onion (*Allium chinense*); perennial herbaceous plant with a subterraneous stem, long, slender leaves, purple flowers borne in umbels, its stem used as a vegetable ❷ 这种植物的鳞茎 bulb of the plant ‖ also 藠头 jiào·tou

薢 xiè ☞ 萆薢(bìxiè) on p.107

嶰 xiè〈书 *fml.*〉山涧 mountain brook:～壑 ravine; gully|幽～ deep gully

獬 xiè[獬豸](xièzhì)古代传说中的异兽,能辨曲直,见人争斗就用角去顶坏人 *xiezhi*, legendary beast in ancient times which could tell right from wrong and use its horn to butt an evildoer whenever there is a fight

邂 xiè[邂逅](xièhòu)〈书 *fml.*〉偶然遇见(久别的亲友) meet by chance; run into (a close relative or friend):不期～ meet somebody unexpectedly

廨 xiè〈书 *fml.*〉官吏办事的地方 government office:公～ government office

澥1 xiè ❶(糊状物、胶状物)由稠变稀 (of paste, glue, etc.) become thin; thin down:粥～了。The porridge has become watery. | 糨糊～了。The paste has become watery. ❷〈方 *dial.*〉加水使糊状物或胶状物变稀 add water to dilute a paste or glue：糨糊太稠，加上点水～一～。The paste is too thick. Add some hot water to make it thinner.

澥[2] xiè 渤澥(Bóxiè)，渤海的古称 Boxie, ancient name of the Bohai Sea

懈 xiè 松懈 slack; lax：～怠 lax | 坚持不～ doggedly; persistently; unremittingly; perseveringly

【懈怠】xièdài 松懈懒惰 slack; sluggish：对工作尽心竭力，从不～ devote one's mind and energy to work and never slack off

【懈气】xiè//qì 放松干劲 relax one's exertions; lose one's drive; slack off：工作有了点起色，要继续努力，可不能～。Since there is some improvement in the work, you should continue to work hard. Do not slack your efforts.

燮(爕) xiè 〈书 *fml.*〉调和 mediate; harmonize; regulate：～理(协调治理) harmonize; adjust; coordinate; regulate | 调～ mediate; harmonize

蟹(蠏) xiè 螃蟹 crab：～黄 reddish-yellow crab meat | ～粉 crab meat

【蟹粉】xièfěn 〈方 *dial.*〉用来做菜或馅儿的蟹黄和蟹肉 crab meat：～狮子头 large pork-and-crab meat ball

【蟹黄】xièhuáng (～儿 xièhuángr)螃蟹体内的卵巢和消化腺，橘黄色，味鲜美 reddish-yellow crab meat (made up of the ovary and digestive glands)：～包子 steamed bun stuffed with crab and pork meat

【蟹獴】xièměng 哺乳动物，身体长约一尺，毛灰色、棕色、黑色相间。生活在水边，能游泳，捕食鱼、蟹、蛙等。毛皮珍贵。我国长江下游以南各省有出产。crab-eating mongoose (*Herpestes urva*); swimming mammal with a 33-cm-long body and alternating grey, brown and black hair, living by waterside, feeding on fishes, crabs, frogs, etc. and having a valuable fur which is produced in all provinces south of the lower reaches of the Yangtze River

【蟹青】xièqīng 像螃蟹壳那样灰而发青的颜色 greenish-grey (colour); colour similar to that of the crab shell

瀣 xiè ☞ 沆瀣 hàngxiè on p. 772

躞 xiè [躞蹀](xièdié) ☞ 蹀躞 diéxiè on p. 451

xīn (ㄒㄧㄣ)

心 xīn ❶ 人和高等动物身体内推动血液循环的器官。人的心在胸腔的中部，稍偏左方，呈圆锥形，大小约跟本人的拳头相等，内部有四个空腔，上部两个是心房，下部两个是心室。心房和心室的舒张和收缩推动血液循环全身。heart; organ that promotes the blood circulation in the body of a human or a vertebrate. The human heart is located in the middle of the thoracic cavity, slightly to the left, cone-shaped, and the size of a fist. It has four chambers: the two upper chambers are atriums and the two lower chambers are ventricles. Their expansion and contraction help promote blood circulation throughout the body. also 心脏 xīnzàng ❷ 通常也指思想的器官和思想、感情等 usu. also referring to the heart; mind; feeling; intention：～思 thought; mind; idea | ～得 what one has gained from work, study, etc. | 用～ concentrate one's mind on | 谈～ have a heart-to-heart talk | 一～一意 whole-heartedly; heart and soul ❸ 中心；中央的部分 centre; core：江～ the middle of a river; halfway across the river | 圆～ centre of a circle | 重～ centre of gravity | 灯～ lamp wick; wick ❹ 二十八宿之一 one of the twenty-eight constellations

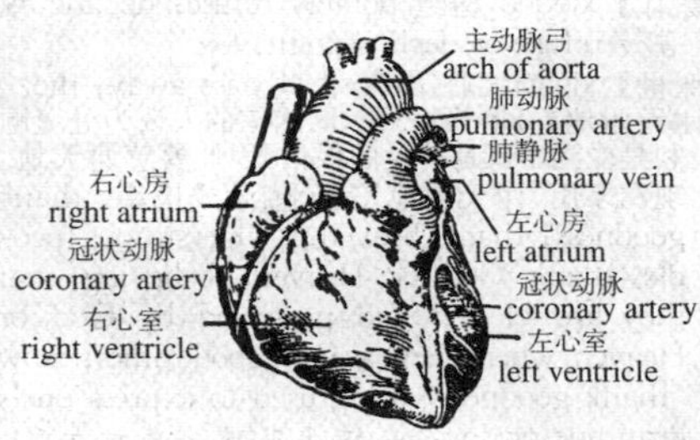

人的心 Human Heart

【心爱】xīn'ài 衷心喜爱 loved; treasured; dear to one's heart：～的人 one's beloved; loved one | ～的礼物 treasured gift

【心安理得】xīn ān lǐ dé 自信事情做得合理，心很坦然 feel at ease and justified; have an easy conscience; feel no qualm

【心包】xīnbāo 包在心脏外面的一层薄膜，心包和心脏壁的中间有浆液，能润滑心肌，使心脏活动时不跟胸腔磨擦而受伤 pericardium; thin, closed, membranous sac surrounding the heart and containing a clear serous liquid that lubricates the cardiac muscles so that the heart does not rub the thoracic cavity and get injured

【心病】xīnbìng ❶ 指忧虑或烦闷的心情 worry; anxiety：～难医。Mental worries cannot be cured by medicine. ❷ 指隐性或隐痛 sore point; secret trouble：一句话正说在她的～上。One word just hit her sore point.

【心不在焉】xīn bù zài yān 心思不在这里。指思想不集中。absent-minded; inattentive;

preoccupied with sth. else

【心材】xīncái 木材的中心，色泽较深，质地最坚硬的部分 heartwood; hardest, dark-coloured part of wood

【心裁】xīncái 心中的设计筹划（指关于诗文、美术、建筑等的）idea; conception; mental plan (about poetry, writing, painting, architecture, etc.)：独出～ be original; show originality｜别出～ try to be different

【心肠】xīncháng ❶ 用心；存心 heart; intention：～好 kindhearted｜～坏 ill-intentioned ❷ 对事物的感情状态 state of mind：～软 have a soft heart; be soft-hearted｜～硬 cold-hearted｜铁石～ stone-hearted｜菩萨～ kind-hearted ❸ 兴致；心思 mood：在车上，他一心想着厂里的生产问题，没有～去看景色。He bent himself on thinking of the problems in production in the factory and was in no mood to see the scenery in the car.

【心潮】xīncháo〈比喻 *fig.*〉像潮水一样起伏的心情 tidal surge of emotion; surging thoughts and emotions：～澎湃 feel an upsurge of emotion

【心驰神往】xīn chí shén wǎng 心神飞到（向往的地方）one's thoughts fly to (a place or person); have a deep longing for

【心传】xīnchuán ❶ 禅宗指不立文字，不依经卷，惟以师徒心心相印，传受佛法 mind-to-mind instruction from master to disciple without the aid of scriptures, a practice of the Chan Sect of Chinese Buddhism ❷ 泛指世世代代相传的某种学说（in a broad sense）doctrine or theory passed on from generation to generation

【心慈手软】xīn cí shǒu ruǎn 心地和善，不忍下手（惩治）soft-hearted and merciful

【心胆】xīndǎn ❶ 指心和胆 heart and gall bladder ❷ 指意志和胆量 determination and courage

【心得】xīndé 在工作和学习等活动中体验或领会到的知识、技术、思想认识等 knowledge, skill, thought, etc. that one has acquired from work, study, etc.：学习～ what one has learned from study｜～体会 what one has learned

【心底】xīndǐ ❶ 内心深处 the bottom of one's heart：他的一番话，让人从～里感到亲切。What he said made us feel warm from the very bottom of our hearts. ❷〈方 *fml.*〉(～儿 xīndǐr) 居心；用心 intention：这个人～好。This man means well.

【心地】xīndì ❶ 指人的内心 person's mind, character, moral nature, etc.：～坦白 candid; open｜～善良 good-natured; kind-hearted ❷ 心情；心境 state of mind：～轻松 have an ease of mind; relax

【心电图】xīndiàntú 用特别的仪器把心脏收缩和舒张时所产生的电效应放大，在纸上画出来的波状条纹的图形。可以帮助诊断心脏的各种疾病。electrocardiogram; wave-like graphic tracing drawn on a sheet of paper by a special instrument showing the variations in electric force which trigger the contractions of the heart, used in the diagnosis of heart diseases

【心毒】xīn dú 心肠狠毒 wicked; vicious; malignant：～如蛇蝎 as vicious as a viper

【心烦】xīnfán 心里烦躁或烦闷 be vexed; be perturbed：～意乱 be terribly upset; be perturbed｜这些琐碎事务叫人～。These trifles are really a bother.

【心房】xīnfáng ❶ 心脏内部上面的两个空腔，在左边的叫左心房，在右边的叫右心房。左心房与肺静脉相连，右心房与上、下腔的静脉相连。左心房接受从肺部回来的血，右心房接受从全身其他部分回来的血。心房与心室之间有带瓣膜的通路，心房收缩时血从通路流入心室。atrium (of the heart), either of the two upper chambers of the heart that receive blood. The left atrium is connected with the veins of the lungs and receives blood from the lungs, while the right atrium is connected with the veins of the upper and lower chambers and receives blood from the other parts of the body. Between the atriums and the ventricles is a valve which allows blood to flow into the ventricles when the atriums contract.（图见 ☞ figure for 心 xīn）❷ 指人的内心 heart; innermost being：亲切的话语暖人～。The kind words warmed everybody's heart.

【心扉】xīnfēi 指人的内心 the door of one's heart：叩人～ tough onc's hcart｜我愿意敞开自己的～，向她倾诉一切。I wish to open my heart and tell her everything.

【心服】xīn//fú 衷心信服 be genuinely convinced; acknowledge (one's defeat, mistake, etc.) sincerely：～口服（不但嘴里服，并且心里服）be sincerely convinced (be convinced not only in word, but from the bottom of one's heart)

【心浮】xīn//fú 心里浮躁，不塌实 flighty and impatient; unstable：～气躁 flighty and impctuous

【心腹】xīnfù ❶ 指亲信的（人）trusted subordinate; reliable agent：～朋友 bosom friend ❷ 指亲信的人 trusted follower：身边的～ henchman ❸ 藏在心里轻易不对人说的 confidential：～话 tell sb. sth. in strict confidence; confide in sb.; exchange confidences｜～事 a secret in the depth of one's heart

【心腹之患】xīnfù zhī huàn 指藏在内部的严重祸害 disease in one's vital organs — danger from within; serious hidden trouble or danger

【心甘】xīngān 甘心 willing：～情愿 be most willing to; be perfectly happy to｜为了人民的

利益,死也～。If need be, I will willingly die for the interests of the people.

【心肝】xīngān ❶ 良心;正义感 conscience; sense of justice:他不是那种没～的人。He is not that heartless person. ❷(～儿 xīngānr)称最亲热最心爱的人(多用于年幼的子女 term of endearment mostly used with one's small children) darling; dear; sweetheart; honey:～宝贝 darling baby

【心广体胖】xīn guǎng tǐ pán 心情舒畅,身体健壮 carefree and contented; fit and happy; also 心宽体胖 xīn kuān tǐ pán

【心寒】xīn hán 失望而又痛心 be bitterly disappointed

【心黑】xīn hēi ❶ 心肠歹毒 cold-blooded and ruthless ❷ 形容贪心 greedy

【心狠手辣】xīn hěn shǒu là 心肠凶狠,手段毒辣 cruel and ruthless; wicked and merciless

【心花怒放】xīn huā nù fàng 形容高兴极了 burst with joy; be wild with joy; be elated

【心怀】xīn huái 心中存有 harbour; entertain; cherish:～鬼胎(怀着不可告人的目的) have evil intentions; have sinister motives|～叵测(怀着难以窥测的恶意) harbour unfathomable evil designs; have sinister intentions

【心怀】xīnhuái ❶ 心意;心情 intention; purpose; state of mind; mood:抒写～ write of one's feelings ❷ 胸怀;胸襟 mind; nature:～坦荡 be magnanimous|～开阔 broad-minded

【心慌】xīn huāng ❶ 心里惊慌 be flustered; be nervous; get alarmed:～意乱 be nervous and flustered ❷〈方 *dial.*〉same as 心悸 xīnjì ①:～气紧 incoherent with nervousness and panting

【心慌意乱】xīn huāng yì luàn 形容心神惊慌忙乱 nervous and flustered; mentally confused

【心灰意懒】xīn huī yì lǎn 灰心丧气,意志消沉 be disheartened; be downhearted; be dispirited; also 心灰意冷 xīn huī yì lěng

【心火】xīnhuǒ ❶〈中医 *Chin. med.*〉指烦躁、口渴、脉搏快、舌头痛等症状 internal heat, symptoms of which include mental uneasiness, thirst, rapid pulse, tongue ache, etc. ❷ 心里的怒气 hidden anger:强按下～没有发作 repress one's anger; check one's anger

【心机】xīnjī 心思;计谋 thinking; scheming:枉费～ rack one's brains in vain|她年龄不大,但很有～。Young as she is, she has a mind of her own.

【心肌】xīnjī 构成心脏的肌肉,受交感神经和迷走神经的支配,是不随意的横纹肌。心肌的收缩是自动的有律的。cardiac muscle; myocardium; involuntary striated muscle that forms the heart, and is manipulated by the sympathetic nerve and vagus. The contraction of the cardiac muscle is automatic and rhythmical.

【心急】xīn jí 心里急躁;着急 impatient; short-tempered:～如焚 burning with impatience

【心急火燎】xīn jí huǒ liǎo 心里急得像火烧一样,形容非常着急 burning with impatience; in a nervous state; also 心急如焚 xīn jí rú fén or 心急如火 xīn jí rú huǒ

【心计】xīnjì 计谋;心里的打算 calculation; scheming; planning:有～ intelligently calculating|工于～ adept at scheming; very calculating

【心迹】xīnjì 内心的真实情况 the true state of one's mind; true motives or feelings:表明～ lay bare one's true feelings|剖白～ explain one's true feelings or motives

【心悸】xīnjì ❶ 由贫血、大出血或植物性神经系统机能失调等引起的心脏跳动加速、加强和节律不齐的症状 palpitation; symptom of rapid beating and irregular rhythms of heart caused by anaemia, massive hemorrhage, malfunction of autonomic nervous system, etc. ❷〈书 *fml.*〉心里害怕 be scared:令人～ terrifying; frightening

【心尖】xīnjiān ❶ 心脏的尖端 the apex of the heart; apex cordis ❷ 内心深处;心头 the bottom of one's heart; heart of hearts ❸〈方 *dial.*〉(～儿 xīnjiānr)称最喜爱的人(多指儿女 oft. of children to parents) the most beloved person; darling; dear; also 心尖子 xīnjiān·zi

【心间】xīnjiān 心上;心里 in one's mind; in one's heart:进城几年了,乡亲们的嘱托他一直记在～。Having lived in the city for a few years, he has always kept the fellow villagers' exhortations in his mind.

【心焦】xīnjiāo 由于希望的事情迟迟不实现而烦闷急躁 anxious; worried; anxiety caused by delayed fulfilment of expectations:孩子这么晚了还没回家,做父母的能不～? It's so late, but the child is not yet back home. How could the parents not be worried?

【心劲】xīnjìn (～儿 xīnjìnr) ❶ 想法;念头 thought; idea:这事正对我的～。This is exactly what I've thought of.|上上下下都是一个～,搞好教育工作。Everyone has one thought: to do the educational work well. ❷ 指思考分析问题的能力 the ability to consider and analyse problems; brains:大叔是个有胆量有～的人。Big uncle is a man of daring and brains. ❸ 兴趣;劲头;精神(jīng·shen) interest; zeal; drive; spirit:说到抓科研,他的～可足啦! Speaking of laying stress on scientific research, he is full of enthusiasm.

【心惊胆战】xīn jīng dǎn zhàn 形容非常害怕 tremble with terror; shake with fright; quake with fear; also 胆战心惊 dǎn zhàn xīn jīng

【心惊肉跳】xīn jīng ròu tiào 形容担心祸患临头,非常害怕不安 be jumpy; have the jitters

【心静】xīnjìng 心里平静 calm

【心境】xīnjìng 心情(指苦乐) state (or frame) of mind; mental state; mood:～不佳 be in a bad mood｜～好，看什么都顺眼。When in good mood, he finds everything pleasing to the eye.

【心坎】xīnkǎn（～儿 xīnkǎnr）❶ same as 心口 xīnkǒu ❷ 内心深处 bottom of one's heart：他的话说到我～上了。What he said struck a chord in my heart.

【心口】xīnkǒu 胸口 pit of the stomach

【心口如一】xīn kǒu rú yī 心里想的和嘴上说的一样。形容诚实直爽。say what one thinks; speak from the heart; be frank and forthright

【心宽】xīn kuān 心胸开阔，对不如意的事情想得开 broad-minded; tolerant of anything undesirable

【心旷神怡】xīn kuàng shén yí 心情舒畅，精神愉快 relaxed and joyful; carefree and happy

【心劳日拙】xīn láo rì zhuō 费尽心机，不但没有得到好处，反而处境越来越糟 get nothing for all one's pains; feel tired in mind and exhausted in strength

【心理】xīnlǐ ❶ 人的头脑反映客观现实的过程，如感觉、知觉、思维、情绪等 psychology; mentality; processes of reflecting objective reality by the human brains, as feelings, consciousness, thoughts, emotions, etc. ❷ 泛指人的思想、感情等内心活动（in a broad sense）thoughts; emotions; etc.：忌妒～ jealousy｜工作顺利就高兴，这是一般人的～。Joy accompanies successful work. This is how ordinary people feel about it.

【心理学】xīnlǐxué 研究心理现象客观规律的科学。心理现象指认识、情感、意志等心理过程和能力、性格等心理特征。根据不同的研究领域和任务分普通心理学、儿童心理学、教育心理学等。psychology; science classified on the basis of research fields and purposes into general psychology, children psychology and educational psychology to deal with the objective law of psychological phenomena, which refer to such psychological processes as knowledge, emotions and will and such psychological characteristics as ability and character

【心里】xīn·li ❶ 胸口内部 in the heart; at heart; in (the) mind：～发疼 one's heart aches; feel painful from the bottom of one's heart ❷ 思想里；头脑里 in the mind; in the heart：记在～ keep (or bear) sth. in the mind｜说～话 to be honest; speak one's mind; tell one's innermost thoughts and feelings; come out with what's on one's mind

【心力】xīnlì 心思和劳力 mental and physical efforts：竭尽～ make strenuous efforts｜～交瘁（精神和体力都极度疲劳）be mentally and physically exhausted

【心灵】xīn líng 心思灵敏 clever; intelligent; quick-witted：～手巧 clever and deft

【心灵】xīnlíng 指内心、精神、思想等 heart; soul; spirit：幼小的～ childish heart｜眼睛是～的窗户。The eyes are the windows of the soul.

【心领】xīnlǐng ❶ 心里领会 understand tacitly：～神会 understand tacitly; readily take a hint ❷〈客套话 *pol.*〉用于辞谢别人的馈赠或酒食招待 expressing a polite refusal (of a gift or offer of wine and food)：您的美意，我～了。I appreciate your kindness but I'm afraid I have to decline the offer.

【心领神会】xīn lǐng shén huì 不用对方明说，心里领悟其中的意思。也指深刻地领会。immediately understand what sb. wants before he or she speaks; deeply realize

【心路】xīnlù（～儿 xīnlùr）❶ 机智；计谋 wit; intelligence：斗～ battle of wits; contest of wits ❷ 气量 tolerance：～窄 narrow-minded ❸ 指人的用心、居心 motive; intention：～不正 ill-intentioned; evil motive ❹ 心思 idea; thought; mind：这话正对他的～。These words are very much to his liking.

【心律】xīnlǜ 心脏跳动的节律 rhythm of the heartbeat：～不齐 arrhythmia; any irregularity in the rhythm of the heart's beating

【心率】xīnlǜ 心脏搏动的频率。正常成年人在平静时心脏每分钟跳动 70—75 次。heart rate; frequency of the heart-throb, which beats 70-75 times per minute for a normal adult when he or she is calm

【心满意足】xīn mǎn yì zú 非常满足 be perfectly content (or satisfied)

【心明眼亮】xīn míng yǎn liàng 心里明白，眼睛雪亮。形容洞察事物，明辨是非。see and think clearly; be sharp-eyed and clear-headed; discern things clearly

【心目】xīnmù ❶ 指内心或视觉方面的感受 memory; mood; mind's eye：犹在～ remain (or is still) fresh in one's memory｜以娱～ to amuse oneself ❷ 指想法和看法 mind; view：在他的～中国家的利益高于一切。In his eyes the interests of the nation are above everything.

【心平气和】xīn píng qì hé 心里平和，不急躁，不生气 calm; even-tempered and good-humoured

【心魄】xīnpò 心灵（xīnlíng）soul：动人～ soul-stirring

【心气】xīnqì（～儿 xīnqìr）❶ 用心；想法 motive; intention：～相通 know each other's intentions ❷ 志气 aspiration; ambition：～高，干劲大 have high aspirations and work vigorously ❸ 心情 mood; frame of mind：～不顺 in a bad mood ❹ 气量 tolerance：他的～窄，说不通。He is narrow-minded. You can hardly persuade him.

【心窍】xīnqiào 指认识和思维的能力（古人以为心脏有窍，能运思，所以这样说）capacity for clear thinking (Ancients believed that the heart had an opening to the mind, hence the

X

phrase.)：财迷～ be obsessed by a lust for money|一席话真是开人～。What (you) said cleared up my thinking.

【心切】xīnqiè 心情急迫 eager; impatient; anxious：求胜～ be anxious to gain victory

【心情】xīnqíng 感情状态 frame (or state) of mind; mood：～舒畅 have ease of mind|悲伤的～ sorrowful; in a sad mood

【心曲】xīnqū ❶ same as 内心 nèixīn ①：乱我～ disturb my peace of mind ❷ 心事 sth. weighing on one's mind：畅叙～ pour out one's secret concern (or pent-up feelings); lay one's heart bare; give vent to one's grieves

【心软】xīn ruǎn 容易被外界事物感动而生怜悯或同情 be soft-hearted; be tender-hearted; be easily moved by external things and have a pity on：她这个人就是～，见不得人家伤心落泪。She is too soft-hearted to see others shed tears in grief.

【心上人】xīnshàngrén 指心里爱慕的异性；意中人 person of one's heart; one's beloved; person of the other sex cherished in one's heart

【心神】xīnshén ❶ 心思精力 thinking and energy：劳而无功，空耗～ work hard to no avail, and waste one's energy ❷ 精神状态 mind; state of mind：～不定 feel restless; be distracted

【心声】xīnshēng 发自内心的声音；心里话 heartfelt wishes; aspirations; thinking：吐露～ tell one's aspirations|这首歌表达了人民的～。This song expresses the aspirations of the people.

【心盛】xīn shèng 情绪高，干劲大 in high spirits and full of energy：求学～ seek knowledge by studying in high spirits|年轻～，敢想敢干 be young and full of vigour, and have daring to think and to do

【心事】xīn·shì 心里盘算的事(多指感到为难的) sth. weighing on one's mind; a load on one's mind; worry：～重重 be laden with anxiety; be weighed down with care|低着头想～ bend one's head with worries in the mind

【心室】xīnshì 心脏内部下面的两个空腔，在左边的叫左心室，在右边的叫右心室，壁厚，肌肉发达。左心室与主动脉相连，右心室与肺动脉相连。血液由心房压入心室后，由心室压入动脉，分别输送到肺部和全身的其他部分。ventricle; either of the two lower chambers of the heart consisting of thick walls and developed muscles. The left ventricle is connected with the aorta (the main artery) while the right ventricle is connected with the pulmonary artery. The blood is pumped into the arteries after it flows into the ventricles from the atriums, and then circulates to the lungs and the other parts of the body. (图见 ☞ figure for 心 xīn)

【心术】xīnshù ❶ 居心(多指坏的 usu. in bad sense) intention; design：～不正 harbour evil intentions (or designs) ❷ 心计；计谋 calculation; scheming; planning：他是个有～的人。He is a calculating person.

【心数】xīnshù 心计 calculation; scheming; planning

【心思】xīn·si ❶ 念头 thought; idea：坏～ wicked idea|想～(转念头) ponder over sth. ❷ same as 脑筋 nǎojīn ①：用～ do a lot of thinking; think hard|费～ think hard|挖空～ rack one's brains ❸ 想做某件事的心情 state of mind; mood：没有～下棋 be not in the mood to play chess

【心酸】xīn suān 心里悲痛 be grieved; feel sad：～落泪 feel sad and shed tears

【心算】xīnsuàn 只凭脑子而不用纸、笔、算盘等进行运算 mental arithmetic; do sums in one's head; calculate without the use of paper, pen, abacus, calculator, etc.

【心髓】xīnsuǐ 指内心深处 the depths of one's heart

【心态】xīntài 心理状态 mentality：～各异 different mentalities

【心疼】xīnténg ❶ 疼爱 love dearly：老太太最～小孙子。The old lady loves her little grandson most dearly. ❷ 舍不得；惋惜 make one's heart ache; feel sorry; be distressed：～钱 feel sorry to have the money spent lavishly|瓷瓶摔碎了，老人～极了。It made the old man's heart ache to see the porcelain vase break to pieces.

【心田】xīntián ❶ 指人的内心 heart; heart of one's hearts：同志们的关怀温暖了她的～。The concern shown by the comrades warms her heart. ❷〈方 *dial.*〉指用心；居心 intention：～好 good intention

【心跳】xīn tiào 心脏跳动。特指心脏加快地跳动，多因剧烈运动或感情激动、内心恐惧等引起，也是一种病症。palpitation; rapid heartbeat caused by violent exercises, emotional excitement, fear, etc., or as a symptom of disease

【心头】xīntóu 心上；心思 mind; heart：记在～ bear (or keep) in mind

【心土】xīntǔ 表土和底土之间的一层土壤 subsoil; the layer of soil beneath the topsoil

【心窝儿】xīnwōr 人体上心脏所在的地方 pit of the heart or stomach：后～(背上对着心脏的部位) centre of one's back (part of the back opposite to the heart)◇他的话句句都说进了大家的～里。His words struck a chord in everyone's heart.

【心无二用】xīn wú èr yòng 指做事必须专心，注意力不能分散 one cannot keep one's mind on two things at the same time; one should concentrate on one thing at a time

【心细】xīn xì 细心 careful; scrupulous：胆大～

bold but cautious

【心弦】xīnxián 指受感动而起共鸣的心 heartstrings:动人～ touching; moving; strike a chord in one's heart

【心心念念】xīnxīn niànniàn 心里一直存着某种念头(想做某件事情或得到某样东西) longingly; yearningly:他～地想当个飞行员。He is set on becoming a pilot.

【心心相印】xīn xīn xiāng yìn 彼此心意一致 have mutual affinity; be kindred spirits

【心性】xīnxìng 性情;性格 disposition; temperament:～浮华 frivolous by nature | 刚强的～ strong character

【心胸】xīnxiōng ❶ 内心深处;胸中 in the depth of one's heart; in the mind:～迸发出不可遏抑的怒火 irrepressible anger erupted from one's heart ❷ 胸怀;气量 mind; tolerance:～开阔 broad-minded; unprejudiced | ～狭窄 narrow-minded; intolerant ❸ 志气;抱负 aspiration; ambition:他有～,有气魄。He is full of vision and has high ambitions.

【心秀】xīnxiù 心里灵巧,有主意,但表面上不显露 be intelligent without looking so

【心虚】xīn xū ❶ 做错了事怕人知道 be afraid of being found out; with a guilty conscience:做贼～。A thief is always afraid of being found out. *or* A thief is always nervous. ❷ 缺乏自信心 lacking in self-confidence; diffident:刚接手做生疏的工作,不免有点儿～。I've just taken over the new job. I'm not sure whether I can do it properly.

【心绪】xīnxù 心情(多就安定或紊乱说 usu. referring to calmness or a disturbed state of mind) state of mind:～不宁 in a disturbed state of mind; in a flutter | ～乱如麻 totally upset; emotionally upset; in an emotional turmoil

【心血】xīnxuè 心思和精力 thoughts and energies; painstaking care (or effort); painstaking labour:花费～ expend one's thoughts and energies

【心血来潮】xīnxuè lái cháo 形容突然产生某种念头 be prompted by the whim of the moment; on a sudden impulse; on the spur of the moment

【心眼儿】xīnyǎnr ❶ same as 内心 nèixīn ①:大妈看到这未来的儿媳妇,打～里高兴。The aunt was very happy to see her future daughter-in-law. ❷ 心地;存心 intention; person's mind:～好 well-intentioned | 没安好～ have an evil intention ❸ 聪明机智 intelligence; cleverness:他有～,什么事都想得周到。He is clever, and thinks very carefully about everything. *or* He is intelligent and thoughtful. ❹ 对人的不必要的顾虑和考虑 unfounded doubts; unnecessary misgivings:他人不错,就是～太多。He is a good man, but is too oversensitive. ❺ 气量(小或窄) tolerance:～小 has a narrow mind; be oversensitive | 他～窄,受不了委屈。He is narrow-minded, and cannot bear being wronged.

【心仪】xīnyí 〈书 *fml.*〉心中仰慕 admire; respect:～已久 have long had a high regard for sb.

【心意】xīnyì ❶ 对人的情意 regard; kindly feelings:送上些许薄礼,略表～。A little gift is just a token of our regard. ❷ 意思 meaning; intention; purpose:我们语言不通,只好用手势来表达～。We don't understand each other's languages, so we have to make gestures to express ourselves.

【心音】xīnyīn ❶ 心脏收缩和舒张时因瓣膜关闭和血流冲击的振动而发出的声音。收缩时发出的声音低沉而长,舒张时发出的声音清晰而短。heart sounds; cardiac sounds; sounds produced due to the closing of the valves and the vibration caused by the impact from the blood flow when the heart contracts or expands. The sounds are low and heavy when the heart contracts, and distinct and short when the heart expands. ❷ 心声 heartfelt wish; aspiration

【心硬】xīn yìng 不容易被外界事物感动而怜悯或同情 hard-hearted; stone-hearted; callous; unfeeling:不是我～,让孩子从小吃点儿苦没有坏处。It's not that I'm unfeeling. It won't do any harm to let the children bear a little hardship.

【心有灵犀一点通】xīn yǒu língxī yī diǎn tōng 唐李商隐诗《无题》:'身无彩凤双飞翼,心有灵犀一点通。'(旧说犀牛是灵异的兽,它的角里有一条白纹贯通两端)原比喻恋爱着的男女心心相印,现在泛指彼此的心意相通。*No Title* by Li Shangyin in the Tang Dynasty: 'I've no wings like a phoenix,/But the hearts are linked in one beat.' (An old saying goes that rhinoceros is a divine animal and its horn has a white stripe that links the two ends.) mutual affinity between lovers; mutual understanding between two people

【心有余悸】xīn yǒu yú jì 危险的事情虽然过去了,回想起来还感到害怕 one's heart still throbbing with fear; still shudder at the thought of sth.; have lingering fears when recalling a danger

【心余力绌】xīn yú lì chù 心有余而力不足 have the intention or are willing to do sth., but have no ability to do it

【心猿意马】xīn yuán yì mǎ 形容心思不专,变化无常,好像马跑猿跳一样 restless; distracted; perturbed; a heart like a capering monkey and a mind like a galloping horse

【心愿】xīnyuàn 愿望 cherished desire; aspiration; wish; dream:美好的～ beautiful wish

【心悦诚服】xīn yuè chéng fú 诚心诚意地服从或

佩服 gladly and willingly; be completely convinced; feel a heartfelt admiration

【心脏】xīnzàng ❶ same as 心 xīn ① ❷〈比喻 *fig.*〉中心 centre:首都北京是祖国的～。Beijing, the capital, is the heart of the motherland.

【心窄】xīn zhǎi 心胸狭窄,对不如意的事情想不开 narrow-minded; intolerant of sth. undesirable

【心照】xīnzhào 不必对方明说而心中自然明白 understand without being told:彼此～ have a tacit understanding with each other|～不宣(彼此心里明白,不必明说) have a tacit understanding (understand each other without having to say anything)

【心直口快】xīn zhí kǒu kuài 性情直爽,有话就说 frank and outspoken; straightforward and plain-spoken; also 心直嘴快 xīn zhí zuǐ kuài

【心志】xīnzhì 意志 will; resolution:～不移 unflinching will

【心重】xīnzhòng 指思虑过多,遇事心里总放不下 take things too hard; oversensitive:孩子～,你不要过于责备。This child is too oversensitive. Don't scold him too much.

【心子】xīn·zi ❶ 物体中心的部分 centre (of sth.):元宵～ stuffing of a rice dumpling ❷〈方 *dial.*〉食用的动物心脏 heart of a pig, sheep, etc. as food

【心醉】xīnzuì 因极喜爱而陶醉 be charmed; be enchanted; be fascinated:～神迷 enchanting and captivating|演员的高超的艺术,令人为之～。The super artistic skills of the actors and actresses are captivating and fascinating.

芯 xīn ☞ 灯芯 dēngxīn on p.407
☞ xìn on p.2136

辛1 xīn ❶ 辣 hot (in taste, flavour, etc.); pungent:～辣 pungent ❷ 辛苦 hard; laborious:～勤 hardworking; industrious|艰～ hardships ❸ 痛苦 suffering:～酸 sad; bitter; miserable ❹ (Xīn)姓 a surname

辛2 xīn 天干的第八位 the eighth of the ten Heavenly Stems; ☞ 干支 gānzhī on p.627

【辛迪加】xīndíjiā 资本主义垄断组织形式之一。参加辛迪加的企业在生产上和法律上仍保持自己的独立性,但丧失了商业上的独立性,销售商品和采购原料由辛迪加总办事处统一办理。其内部各企业间存在着争夺销售份额的竞争。syndicate; form of capitalist monopoly organization. The enterprises which join a syndicate maintain their independence in production and in law, but lose their independence in trade, as the marketing of their products and the purchasing of raw materials are entirely controlled by the syndicate. The enterprises also compete for market shares within the syndicate. [法 French: syndicat]

【辛亥革命】Xīnhài Gémìng 孙中山领导的、推翻清朝封建统治的资产阶级民主革命。1911年(农历辛亥年)10月10日湖北武昌起义爆发后,各省相继起义响应,形成了全国规模的革命运动,终于推翻了清王朝的专制统治,结束了中国两千多年的封建君主专制制度。1912年1月1日在南京成立中华民国临时政府。由于资产阶级的妥协退让,革命果实被北洋军阀袁世凯所篡夺。Revolution of 1911; Chinese bourgeois democratic revolution led by Dr. Sun Yat-sen which overthrew the Qing Dynasty; an uprising broke out in Wuchang, Hubei Province, on October 10, 1911 (the 8th Pig Year of the lunar calendar), evoking response in all provinces and leading to a nationwide revolutionary movement which finally overthrew the autocratic rule of the Qing Dynasty and put an end to the feudal autocratic monarchy that had lasted for more than 2,000 years. The provisional government of the Republic of China was established on January 1, 1912. Due to compromises made by the bourgeoisie, the fruits of the revolution were usurped by the Northern warlord Yuan Shikai.

【辛苦】xīnkǔ ❶ 身心劳苦 hard; strenuous; toilsome; laborious:辛辛苦苦 laboriously; strenuously|他起早贪黑地工作,非常～。He works very hard from early morning till darkness. ❷〈客套话 *pol.*〉用于求人做事 ask sb. to do sth.:这事儿还得您～一趟。I'm afraid you'll have to take the trouble of going there to see about it.

【辛辣】xīnlà 辣 pungent; hot; bitter;〈比喻 *fig.*〉语言、文章尖锐而刺激性强 sharp, bitter or pungent language:～的讽刺 bitter irony; biting sarcasm

【辛劳】xīnláo 辛苦劳累 work hard; toil:日夜～ toil day and night

【辛勤】xīnqín 辛苦勤劳 industrious; hardworking:～耕耘 work hard at cultivation

【辛酸】xīnsuān 辣和酸 hot and sour;〈比喻 *fig.*〉痛苦悲伤 sad; bitter; miserable:～泪 sad tears; hot and bitter tears|～的往事 miserable past; sad (or poignant) memories

忻 xīn ❶ same as 欣 xīn ❷ (Xīn)姓 a surname

昕 xīn〈书 *fml.*〉太阳将要升起的时候 time when the sun is about to rise

欣(訢) xīn 喜悦 glad; happy; joyful:欢～ glad; happy; joyful|～喜 glad; happy; joyful|～慰 be gratified|～逢佳节 on the happy occasion of the festival

【欣忭】xīnbiàn〈书 *fml.*〉喜悦 glad; happy; joyful:不胜～ extremely happy

【欣然】xīnrán〈书 *fml.*〉愉快地 joyfully; with pleasure:～前往 go with pleasure|～接受 accept with pleasure|～命笔 ready to write; glad to start writing

【欣赏】xīnshǎng ❶ 享受美好的事物,领略其中的趣味 appreciate; enjoy; admire; feast one's eyes on sth.:音乐～ music appreciation | ～雪景 enjoy (or admire) the snow scenery ❷ 认为好;喜欢 appreciate; like:他很～这个建筑的独特风格。He appreciated the peculiar style of this architecture.

【欣慰】xīnwèi 喜欢而心安 be gratified:脸上露出～的笑容 gratifying smile on one's face

【欣喜】xīnxǐ 欢喜;快乐 glad; joyful; happy:～若狂 be wild with joy; go into raptures

【欣羡】xīnxiàn 〈书 *fml.*〉喜爱而羡慕 admire

【欣欣】xīnxīn ❶ 形容高兴 joyful; glad; happy:～然有喜色 wear a joyful expression ❷ 形容茂盛 thriving; flourishing:～向荣 thriving; flourishing; prosperous

【欣欣向荣】xīnxīn xiàng róng 形容草木茂盛 thriving; flourishing;〈比喻 *fig.*〉事业蓬勃发展 thriving; flourishing; prosperous

【欣幸】xīnxìng 欢喜而庆幸 be glad and thankful:书失而复得,实是～。It's gratifying to have the lost book returned.

炘 xīn 〈书 *fml.*〉热气盛 intense heat

莘 Xīn 莘庄,地名,在上海市 Xinzhuang, name of a place in Shanghai Municipality

☞ shēn on p. 1702

锌 xīn 金属元素,符号 Zn (zincum)。浅蓝白色。用于制合金、白铁、干电池等。zinc (Zn); bluish-white metallic chemical element used for making alloy, tin plates, dry cells, etc.; 俗称 commonly known as 白铅 báiqiān

【锌版】xīnbǎn 用锌制成的印刷版,主要用来印刷插图、表格等 zinc plate; printing plate made of zinc used chiefly to print illustrations, forms, etc.

新 xīn ❶ 刚出现的或刚经验到的(跟'旧'或'老'相对 as opposed to 'old' or 'outdated') new; fresh; up-to-date:～风气 new custom; new atmosphere | ～品种 new variety | ～的工作岗位 new job ❷ 性质上改变得更好的;使变成新的(跟'旧'相对 opposed to 'old') new; make anew; renew; fresh:～社会 the new society | ～文艺 new art and literature | 改过自～ correct one's errors and make a new start; turn over a new leaf; mend one's ways | 一～耳目 find everything fresh and different | 粉刷一～ look brand new after being whitewashed ❸ 没有用过的(跟'旧'相对 as opposed to 'used') brand new; unused:～笔 new pen | ～锄头 new hoe | 这套衣服是全～的。This suit of clothes is brand new. ❹ 指新的人或事物 new people or new things:尝～ taste sth. fresh | 花样翻～ change patterns or designs | 推陈出～ weed through the old to bring forth the new ❺ 结婚的或结婚不久的 recently married or just being married:～女婿 man newly married to one's daughter; daughter's bridegroom | ～媳妇 woman newly married to one's son; son's bride ❻ 新近;刚 newly; freshly; recently:我是～来的。I'm a new arrival. | 这几本书是～买的。These new books are newly bought. ❼ (Xīn)姓 a surname

【新潮】xīncháo ❶ 事物发展的新趋势;新的潮流 new trend; new fashion:文艺～ new trends in literature and art ❷ 符合新潮的;时髦 fashionable; modish:～发型 new hair style, modish hairdo

【新陈代谢】xīn chén dàixiè ❶ 生物的基本特征之一。生物体经常不断地从外界取得生活必需的物质,并使这些物质变成生物体本身的物质,同时把体内产生的废物排出体外,这种新物质代替旧物质的过程叫新陈代谢。metabolism, one of the basic characteristics of living organisms. A living organism constantly takes necessary matters from the outside world and converts them into its own matter and at the same time discharges the waste matter from its body. The process of supersedence of the old by the new is called metabolism. 简称 abbr. 代谢 dàixiè ❷ 〈比喻 *fig.*〉新的事物滋生发展,代替旧的事物 supersede the old by the new

【新春】xīnchūn 指春节以后的一二十天 10 to 20 days following lunar New Year's Day:欢度～ celebrate the Spring Festival | ～佳节 the happy occasion of the Spring Festival | 辞旧岁,迎～。Bid farewell to the old year and usher in the new year.

【新大陆】Xīn Dàlù 美洲的别称。因为它是到 15 世纪以后才由欧洲人殖民的,所以叫新大陆。New World; another name for the Americas. The name was given because the Europeans established colonies there after the 15th century.

【新房】xīnfáng 新婚夫妇的卧室 bridal chamber:闹～ rough house play at the wedding; play tricks on the newly-weds in their chamber

【新风】xīnfēng 刚出现的好风气;新的风尚 new custom; new trend; new practice:校园～ trend on the campus | 破旧俗,树～。Break away with the old customs and establish the new.

【新妇】xīnfù ❶ 新娘 bride ❷ 〈方 *dial.*〉指儿媳 daughter-in-law

【新官上任三把火】xīn guān shàngrèn sān bǎ huǒ 〈比喻 *fig.*〉新上任的官总要先做几件有影响的事,以显示自己的才能和胆识 A new official takes some effective measures to show his ability and insight. *or* A new broom sweeps clean.

【新贵】xīnguì 指初得势的显贵 newly appointed high official

【新欢】xīnhuān 指新的相好(多指男子的,含贬义 oft. of a man, derog.) new sweetheart: 另有～ have a new sweetheart; be seeing another woman

【新婚】xīnhūn 刚结婚 newly-married: ～夫妇 newly-married couple; newly-weds

【新纪元】xīn jìyuán 〈比喻 *fig.*〉划时代的事业的开始 new era; new epoch; beginning of an epoch-making cause: 开创人类历史的～ usher in a new epoch in the history of mankind; open a new chapter in human history

【新交】xīnjiāo ❶ 刚认识不久或交往不久 make a new acquaintance; make a new friend: 因为是～,彼此还不太了解。As they are new friends, they don't know each other too much. ❷ 新结交的朋友 new friends: 旧友～,欢聚一堂。Old and new friends held a happy get-together.

【新近】xīnjìn 不久以前的一段时期 recently; lately; in recent times: 他家～才搬到这里。He has recently moved into this new house.

【新居】xīnjū 刚建成或初迁到的住所 new home; new residence

【新郎】xīnláng 结婚时的男子 bridegroom

【新绿】xīnlǜ 初春植物现出的嫩绿 (of spring vegetation) fresh green: 五月的西山,一片～。The Western Hills in May look fresh green.

【新民主主义革命】xīn mínzhǔ zhǔyì gémìng 在帝国主义和无产阶级革命时代,殖民地半殖民地国家无产阶级领导的资产阶级民主革命。我国从1919年五四运动到1949年的革命,属于新民主主义革命。它是工人阶级经过自己的先锋队共产党领导的、以工农联盟为基础的、人民大众的、反帝、反封建、反官僚资本主义的革命。1949年中华人民共和国成立,标志了新民主主义革命阶段的基本结束和社会主义革命阶段的开始。new democratic revolution; bourgeois democratic revolution led by the proletariat in the colonial and semi-colonial countries in the era of imperialism and proletarian revolution. The revolution in China from the May 4th Movement in 1919 to the revolution of 1949 was a new democratic revolution. It was the people's anti-imperialist, anti-feudal and anti-bureaucratic capitalist revolution led by the working class through its vanguard, the Communist Party, and based on the worker-peasant alliance. In China, the founding of the People's Republic of China marked the end, by and large, of the new democratic revolution and the beginning of the stage of the socialist revolution.

【新年】xīnnián 元旦和元旦以后的几天 New Year's Day and its following days

【新娘】xīnniáng 结婚时的女子 bride; also 新娘子 xīnniáng·zi

【新奇】xīnqí 新鲜特别 strange; novel; new: ～的景象 new sight; new scene | 刚来的时候,处处觉得～。When he first came, everything struck him as new.

【新巧】xīnqiǎo 新奇而精巧 new and ingenious: 构思～ new and ingenious in conception

【新区】xīnqū 新解放的地区。特指第三次国内革命战争开始后解放的地区。newly liberated area; areas liberated during the Third Revolutionary Civil War, 1945-1949

【新人】xīnrén ❶ 具有新的道德品质的人 people of new ethic standards; people of a new type: ～新事 new people and new things ❷ 某方面新出现的人物 new talent; new personality: 文艺～ new people in the literature and art circles ❸ 指机关、团体等新来的人员 new comer; new recruit: 我们团里增加了几位～。Our group has some new recruits. ❹ 指改过自新的人 reformed person: 把失足青少年改造成为～ reform young delinquents and make them new members of society ❺ 指新娘和新郎。有时特指新娘。bride and bridegroom; newly-weds; esp. bride

【新任】xīnrèn ❶ 新任命或新担任(职务) newly appointed: ～局长 newly appointed bureau director | ～会计 newly appointed accountant ❷ 新任命或新担任的职务 new post: 星夜启程,赶赴～ leave at night to take up a new post

【新生】[1] xīnshēng ❶ 刚产生的;刚出现的 newborn; newly born: ～事物 newly emerging things; new things ❷ 新生命 new life; rebirth; regeneration: 获得～ acquire a new lease of life

【新生】[2] xīnshēng 新入学的学生 new student or pupil: ～报到处 registry for freshmen

【新诗】xīnshī 指五四运动以来的白话诗 new verse; free verse written in the vernacular after the May 4th Movement; ☞ 白话诗 báihuàshī on p. 34

【新石器时代】Xīnshíqì Shídài 石器时代的晚期,约开始于八九千年以前。这时人类已能磨制石器,制造陶器,并且已开始有农业和畜牧业。Neolithic Age; New Stone Age; late period of the Stone Age beginning about eight or nine thousand years ago, in which human beings could make stone tools and pottery and began farming and animal husbandry

【新式】xīnshì ❶ 新产生的式样 new type; latest type; new style: ～武器 latest weapons; modern weapons | 这个新建的工厂,设备和装置都是最～的。The newly established factory is equipped with the latest installations. ❷ 新的形式或仪式 new form or rite: ～婚礼 new-style wedding

【新手】xīnshǒu 初参加某种工作的人;生手 new hand; raw recruit

【新书】xīnshū ❶ 崭新的书 new book ❷ 将出版或刚出版的书(多指初版的) books to be published or just off the press: ～预告 advertisements on books to come off the press

【新四军】Xīn Sì Jūn 中国共产党领导的抗日革命武装,原是红军游击队,1937年抗日战争开始后编为新四军,是华中抗日的主力。第三次国内革命战争时期跟八路军及其他人民武装一起改编为中国人民解放军。New Fourth Army (NFA); anti-Japanese revolutionary armed forces led by the Communist Party of China, formed by regrouping Red Army guerillas after the War of Resistance against Japanese Aggression broke out in 1937 to become the main force in resistance to Japanese invaders in Central China. During the Third Revolutionary Civil War, the NFA, the 8th Route Army and the other people's armed forces were reorganized into the Chinese People's Liberation Army.

【新文化运动】xīn wénhuà yùndòng 指我国五四运动前后的文化革命运动。五四运动前,主要内容是反对科举,提倡办学校,反对旧学,提倡新学,是资产阶级旧民主主义的新文化与封建阶级的旧文化的斗争。五四运动后,成为无产阶级领导人民大众,在社会科学和文学艺术领域中反帝反封建的新民主主义的文化运动。New Culture Movement; revolutionary cultural movement around the time of the May 4th Movement in 1919. Before the May 4th Movement, it was opposed to the imperial civil examination system and the old learning, and advocated the establishment of schools and new learning. It was a struggle between the new culture of old democracy and the old culture of the feudal classes. After the May 4th Movement, it became the anti-imperialist, anti-feudal new democratic culture movement of the people led by the proletariat in social sciences and in the fields of literature and art.

【新文学】xīn wénxué 指我国自1919年五四运动以来以反帝反封建为主要内容的白话文学 new-vernacular literature on anti-imperialism and anti-feudalism since the May 4th Movement in 1919

【新闻】xīnwén ❶ 报社、通讯社、广播电台、电视台等报道的消息 news published by newspapers, news services, radios and television stations: ～记者 newsman; newspaperman; reporter; journalist | ～广播 newscast | 采访～ gather news; cover an event ❷ 泛指社会上最近发生的新事情 late occurrences; sth. new; rumor: 你刚从乡下回来,有什么～给大家说说。You are just back from the countryside. Would you tell us something new there?

【新闻公报】xīnwén gōngbào 政党或国家机关直接或委托通讯社就某一重大事件发表的新闻性公告和声明 press communiqué; news communiqué; announcement on an important event issued by a political party or a government organization directly or through an entrusted news agency

【新闻纸】xīnwénzhǐ ❶ 报纸①的旧称 old name for 报纸 bàozhǐ ① ❷ 白报纸 newsprint

【新媳妇儿】xīnxí·fur same as 新娘 xīnniáng

【新禧】xīnxǐ 新年幸福 good fortune for the new year: 恭贺～ Happy New Year; Wishing a Happy New Year

【新鲜】xīn·xiān ❶(刚生产、宰杀或烹调的食物)没有变质,也没有经过腌制、干制等 fresh: ～的水果 fresh fruit; seasonal fruit | ～的鱼虾 fresh fish and shrimps ◇～血液 new blood ❷(花朵)没有枯萎 (of flowers) not fading: ～的花朵 fresh flowers ❸(空气)经常流通,不含杂类气体 fresh (air, containing no impurities): 呼吸～空气 breathe fresh air ❹(事物)出现不久,还不普遍;少见的;稀罕 new; rare; novel; strange: ～经验 new (or fresh) experience | 电视机已经不算什么～东西啦。TV set is no longer a novelty.

【新兴】xīnxīng 最近兴起的 new and developing; rising; burgeoning: ～学科 burgeoning branch of learning | ～的工业城市 rising industrial city

【新星】xīnxīng ❶ 在短时期内亮度突然增大数千倍或数万倍,后来又逐渐回降到原来亮度的恒星 nova; variable star that suddenly increases in brightness by thousands to tens of thousands of times, and then decreases gradually to its former brightness over a period of months to years ❷ 指新出现的有名的演员、运动员等 new star; new noted actor, actress or athlete: 体坛～ new sports star | 影视～ new film or TV star

【新型】xīnxíng 新的类型;新式 new type; new pattern: ～机车 new type of engine | ～的农村妇女 new type of village woman

【新秀】xīnxiù 新出现的优秀人才 new star: 文艺～ new star in literature and art | 越剧～ new Shaoxing opera star | 体操～ new gymnastic star

【新学】xīnxué 清代末年指西学 new learning; Western learning in the last years of the Qing Dynasty

【新雅】xīnyǎ 清新典雅 fresh and elegant: 诗句～ fresh and elegant lines

【新药】xīnyào ❶ 新研制生产、投入使用的药 new drug; newly developed medicine ❷ 指西药 Western medicine

【新医】xīnyī 指西医 Wertern medicine

【新义】xīnyì 指词语新产生的意义 new meaning of a word

【新异】xīnyì 新奇 strange; novel; newfangled: 小说构思～。The novel is strange in conception.

【新意】xīnyì 新的意思;新的意境 new meaning; new conception: 追求～,力避雷同 seek for originality and avoid similarities | 文章论点,

颇有～。There's something new in the argument of the article.

【新颖】xīnyǐng 新而别致 nascent; new and original; novel: 题材～ original in choice of subject (or theme)|款式～ in a novel style

【新雨】xīnyǔ ❶ 初春的雨;刚下过的雨 rain in early spring; newly fallen rain ❷〈书 *fml.*〉〈比喻 *fig.*〉新朋友 new friend: 旧知～ friends old and new; ☞ 旧雨 jiùyǔ on p. 1040

【新月】xīnyuè ❶ 农历月初形状如钩的月亮 crescent (moon); the moon at the beginning of a lunar month: 一弯～ crescent moon ❷ 朔日的月相(人看不见) new moon (invisible to men); the moon on the first day of a lunar month; also 朔月 shuòyuè

【新张】xīnzhāng 指新商店开始营业 (of a new shop) open; begin doing business: ～志喜 congratulations on the opening of the shop

【新正】xīnzhēng 指农历的正月 the first month of the lunar year

【新址】xīnzhǐ 新的地址 the new address of an establishment: 本公司自即日起迁往～办公。The corporation moves to the new address for business as of today.

【新作】xīnzuò 新的作品 new literary or art work: 新人～ new work by a new author

歆 xīn 〈书 *fml.*〉羡慕 admire: ～羡 admire|～慕 admire

【歆慕】xīnmù 〈书 *fml.*〉same as 羡慕 xiànmù

【歆羡】xīnxiàn 〈书 *fml.*〉same as 羡慕 xiànmù

薪 xīn ❶ 柴火 firewood; faggot; fuel: 釜底抽～ take the firewood away from under the cooking cauldron|米珠～桂 rice is as expensive as pearls and fuel as cinnamon ❷ 薪水 salary: 加～ increase (or raise) the salary|发～ pay the salary|月～ monthly pay; monthly salary|年～ annual pay; annual salary

【薪俸】xīnfèng same as 薪水 xīn•shui

【薪给】xīnjǐ same as 薪水 xīn•shui

【薪金】xīnjīn same as 薪水 xīn•shui

【薪尽火传】xīn jìn huǒ chuán 前一根柴刚烧完,后一根柴已经烧着,火永远不熄 as one piece of firewood is consumed, another is lit so that the flame will burn forever;〈比喻 *fig.*〉师生传授,学问一代代地流传 the torch of learning is passed on from teacher to student

【薪水】xīn•shui 工资 salary; pay; wages

【薪饷】xīnxiǎng 军队、警察等的薪金及规定的被服鞋袜等用品 pay for soldiers, policemen, etc. and also their prescribed clothing and bedding

【薪资】xīnzī 工资 wages; pay

馨 xīn 〈书 *fml.*〉散布得远的香气 strong and pervasive fragrance: ～香 fragrance|如兰之～ heady and pervasive fragrance like the orchid's

【馨香】xīnxiāng 〈书 *fml.*〉❶ 芳香 fragrance: 桂花开了,满院～。The osmanthus is in full bloom, filling the air with its fragrance. ❷ 烧香的香味 sweet smell of burning incense: ～祷祝 burn incense and pray to the gods; earnestly pray for sth.; sincerely wish

鑫 xīn 财富兴盛(多用于人名或字号 usu. used in names of persons or shops) prosperous; making a good profit

xín (ㄒㄧㄣˊ)

镡 xín ❶〈古代 *arch.*〉剑柄的顶端部分 top part of a sword hilt ❷ 古代兵器,似剑而小 ancient weapon similar to a sword, but smaller

☞ Chán on p. 211 and Tán on p. 1860

xǐn (ㄒㄧㄣˇ)

伈 xǐn [伈伈]〈书 *fml.*〉形容恐惧 fear; frightened; scared

xìn (ㄒㄧㄣˋ)

囟(顖) xìn same as 囟门 xìnmén

【囟门】xìnmén 婴儿头顶骨未合缝的地方,在头顶的前部中央 fontanel of a baby's skull, located in the centre of the front part of the skull; any of the soft, boneless areas in the skull of a baby, which are later closed up by the formation of bone; also 囟脑门儿 xìnnǎoménr

芯(信) xìn [芯子] (xìn•zi) ❶ 装在器物中心的捻子、消息儿等的东西,如蜡烛的捻子、爆竹的引线等 fuse (as in a firecracker); wick (as in a candle) ❷ 蛇的舌头 the forked tongue of a snake

☞ xīn on p. 2132

信[1] xìn ❶ 确实 true; real: ～史 true history; authentic history; true historical account|～而有征 be reliable and borne out by evidence ❷ 信用 confidence; trust; faith: 守～ keep one's promise; live up to one's word; keep faith|失～ break faith; go back on one's word; break one's word|威～ prestige|言而有～ be as good as one's word ❸ 相信 believe: ～托 trust|～任 trust; have confidence in|～仰 believe in|别～他的话。Don't trust his words. ❹ 信奉(宗教) profess faith in; believe in: ～教 believe in a religion|～徒 religious follower; religious believer ❺ 听凭;随意;放任 at will; at random; without plan: ～步 take a stroll; walk leisurely|～口开河 talk at random; speak irresponsibly ❻ 凭据 sign; evidence: ～号 signal|～物 keepsake|印～ official seal ❼ 按照习惯的格式把要说的话写下来给指定的对象看的东西;书信 letter; missive; mail; something written down in a customary form for a designated person to know:送～ send a letter or message|介绍～ letter of introduction|证明～ certificate ❽ (～儿 xìnr)信息 message; word; information:音～ information|口～儿 oral message|通风报～ inform sb. of sth. secret; divulge secret information ❾ 引信 fuse:～管 fuse ❿ same as 芯 (xìn) ⓫ (Xìn)姓 a surname

〈古 *arch.*〉same as 伸 (shēn)

信[2] xìn 信石 arsenic:红～ red arsenic|白～ white arsenic

【信笔】xìnbǐ 没有多加考虑,随意(写或画) write at random; write without premeditation:～涂鸦 scribble along; write at random|～写来,直抒胸臆。Write without much thought as dictated by the surge of one's feelings

【信不过】xìn ·bu guò 不相信 distrust; have no trust in:他一向多疑,对谁都～。He is very dubious. He doesn't trust anyone.

【信步】xìnbù 随意走动;散步 take a leisurely walk; stroll; walk aimlessly:江边～ take a walk by the riverside|～而行 stroll casually|～来到花坛前 stroll to the flower bed

【信差】xìnchāi ❶〈旧时 *old*〉称被派递送公文信件的人 courier; messenger sent in haste or on a regular schedule with important or urgent messages ❷〈旧时 *old*〉称邮递员 postman

【信从】xìncóng 信任听从 trust and follow the advice of:盲目～ trust blindly

【信贷】xìndài 银行存款、贷款等信用活动的总称。一般指银行的贷款。credit; general term for deposits and loans in a bank; usu. bank loans

【信得过】xìn ·de guò 相信;可以信任 trust; trustworthy; dependable:我们～你。We trust you.|这家商店货真价实,～。This shop sells quality goods at a fair price. It is trustworthy.

【信而有征】xìn ér yǒu zhēng 可靠而且有证据 borne out by evidence; be reliable and borne out by evidence

【信访】xìnfǎng 指人民群众来信来访(多用于机关团体) letters and calls (i.e. letters of complaint from the people and the calls they make to lodge complaints):～工作 work related to letters and calls of complains from the people|～部门 department dealing with letters and calls of complains from the people

【信风】xìnfēng 在赤道两边的低层大气中,北半球吹东北风,南半球吹东南风,这种风的方向很少改变,叫做信风 trade winds; trades. In the lower atmospheric layer, a wind blows steadily toward the equator from the northeast in the tropics north of the equator and from the southeast in the tropics south of the equator. also 贸易风 màoyìfēng

【信封】xìnfēng (～儿 xìnfēngr)装书信的封套 envelope; folded paper container as for a letter, usu. with a gummed flap for sealing

【信奉】xìnfèng ❶ 信仰并崇奉 believe in:基督教徒～上帝。Christians believe in God. ❷ 相信并奉行 believe in and adhere to:～和平共处五项原则 believe in and adhere to the five principles of peaceful coexistence

【信服】xìnfú 相信并佩服 completely accept; be convinced:这些科学论据实在令人～。These scientific arguments are really convincing.

【信鸽】xìngē 专门训练来传递书信的家鸽 carrier pigeon; homing pigeon; homer; pigeons specially trained to carry messages

【信函】xìnhán 书信 letters:私人～ personal letters|～往来 exchange of letters

【信号】xìnhào ❶ 用来传递消息或命令的光、电波、声音、动作等 signal; sign given by light, electric wave, sound, gesture, etc. to convey information or a command:～灯 signal lamp|～枪 signal pistol|打～ give a signal; signal|发～ give a signal ❷ 电路中用来控制其他部分的电流、电压或无线电发射机发射出的电波 electric current and voltage used to control other parts of a circuit; electric wave from a radio transmitter

【信号弹】xìnhàodàn 一种发射后产生有颜色的光或烟的弹药,用于发布信号或通讯联络 signal flare; shot that produces colour light or smoke after it is fired, used to give a signal or for liaison purposes

【信号灯】xìnhàodēng 利用灯光发出各种信号的灯,多用于交通设施、电子设备等 signal lamp; semaphore; lamp that uses light to give a signal, usu. used in transport facilities, electronic devices

【信号枪】xìnhàoqiāng 发射信号弹的枪,形状像手枪 flare pistol; signal pistol; special gun in the shape of a pistol used to give signals

【信笺】xìnjiān same as 信纸 xìnzhǐ

【信件】xìnjiàn 书信和递送的文件、印刷品 letters, papers, printed matter, etc.

【信据】xìnjù 确凿可信的证据 reliable evidence; authentic evidence; absolute proof

【信口雌黄】xìn kǒu cíhuáng 不顾事实,随口乱说 make irresponsible remarks; wag one's tongue too freely; ☞ 雌黄 cíhuáng on p. 319

【信口开河】xìn kǒu kāi hé 随口乱说一气 talk irresponsibly; wag one's tongue too freely; talk at random; 河 also put as 合 hé

【信赖】xìnlài 信任并依靠 trust; count on; have faith in:他是个值得～的朋友。He is a trustworthy friend.

【信马由缰】xìn mǎ yóu jiāng 骑着马不拉缰绳,任其自由行动 ride a horse without holding the reins;〈比喻 *fig.*〉漫无目的地闲逛或随意行动 stroll about aimlessly; act as one pleases

【信念】xìnniàn 自己认为可以确信的看法 faith; belief; conviction:坚定～ firm conviction|必

胜的～ conviction that one is sure to win

【信皮儿】xìnpír same as 信封 xìnfēng

【信瓤儿】xìnrángr 〈方 *dial.*〉装在信封里的写好了的信 letter in an envelope

【信任】xìnrèn 相信而敢于托付 trust; have confidence in:她工作一向认真负责,大家都～她。She has always been responsible to the work. Everyone trusts her.

【信任投票】xìnrèn tóupiào 某些国家的议会对内阁(即政府)实行监督的方式之一。议会在讨论组阁或政府政策时,可用投票方式表示对内阁信任或不信任。vote of confidence; form of supervision exercised by a parliament over the cabinet (government) in some countries. When discussing about the formation of a cabinet or the government's policy, a parliament can express their confidence or non-confidence in the cabinet by vote.

【信赏必罚】xìn shǎng bì fá 该奖赏的一定奖赏,该处罚的一定处罚。形容赏罚严明。Due rewards and punishments will be meted out without fail.

【信石】xìnshí 砒霜,因产地信州(即今江西上饶一带)得名 arsenic; stone of Xinzhou, arsenic named after Xinzhou, an area in present-day Shangrao, Jiangxi Province

【信实】xìnshí ❶ 有信用;诚实 trustworthy; honest; reliable:为人～ be honest and reliable ❷ 真实可靠 true and reliable:史料～ true and reliable historical data

【信史】xìnshǐ 记载确实的历史 true (or authentic) history; faithful historical account

【信使】xìnshǐ 奉派传达消息或担任使命的人 courier; messenger; messenger sent in haste or on a regular schedule with important or urgent messages or missions:～往来,络绎不绝。Messengers come and go in a constant stream.

【信士】xìnshì ❶ 指信仰佛教而未出家的男人 male Buddhist devotee ❷〈书 *fml.*〉诚实的人;守信用的人 man (woman) of his (her) word; man of honour

【信誓旦旦】xìn shì dàndàn 誓言诚恳可信 pledge in all sincerity; vow solemnly

【信手】xìnshǒu 随手 do sth. spontaneously or without much thought or effort:～挥霍 squander money at will; spend money wastefully and extravagantly|～写来 write without much thought; have the words at hand; have materials, etc. at one's fingertips

【信手拈来】xìn shǒu niān lái 随手拿来。多形容写文章时词汇或材料丰富,不费思索,就能写出来。obtain off-handedly, referring to writing a paper or article with great ease because one has full command of the language or relevant information

【信守】xìnshǒu 忠诚地遵守 abide by; follow loyally:～诺言 keep one's promise to the letter

【信宿】xìnsù〈书 *fml.*〉连宿两夜,表示两夜的时间 stay of two nights; two nights' time:流连～ stay two successive nights|～可至 be expected to arrive in two days

【信天游】xìntiānyóu 陕北民歌中一类曲调的总称。一般是两句一段,短的只有一段,长的接连数十段。用同一曲调反复演唱,反复时曲调可以灵活变化。rambles in the sky — the name of a number of tunes used for the folk songs of northern Shaanxi. Usually two sentences in a paragraph, a short tune has only one paragraph, but a long one may have scores of paragraphs. It is sung to the same tune repeatedly. When it is repeated, the tune may change flexibly.

【信条】xìntiáo 信守的准则 article of creed (or faith); creed; precept; tenet

【信筒】xìntǒng 邮局在路旁等处设置的供寄信人投信的筒状设备 mailbox; pillar-box; box standing by roadside into which mail is put for collection; also 邮筒 yóutǒng

【信徒】xìntú 信仰某一宗教的人。也泛指信仰某一学派、主义或主张的人 believer; disciple; follower; adherent; devotee; a person who believes in a certain religion or an advocate of a certain school, doctrine, theory or a view:佛教～Buddhist|达尔文的～ Darwinist

【信托】xìntuō ❶ 信任人,把事情托付给他 trust; entrust:大伙儿～你,你就大胆去办吧。We all trust you. You should do it boldly. ❷ 经营别人委托购销的业务的 do some business on trust:～部 trust department|～公司 trust company

【信望】xìnwàng 威信和声望 prestige and reputation:～卓著 enjoy high prestige and reputation

【信物】xìnwù 作为凭证的物件 authenticating object; token; keepsake:定情～ keepsake for engagement; object confirming one's engagement

【信息】xìnxī ❶ 音信;消息 information; news; message:数月来一直没有得到有关他的～。For months, we haven't had any information about him. ❷ 信息论中指用符号传送的报道,报道的内容是接收符号者预先不知道的 information transmitted by signal and the content of the information not known to the recipients

【信息论】xìnxīlùn 研究信息的计量、传递、变换和储存等的科学。通过数学运算可以计算出信息传递的能力和效率,应用在通讯、生理学、物理学等学科中。information theory; study of processes of communication and transmission of messages; branch of study dealing with the measurement, transmission, and storing of information. By mathematical operation, one can calculate the capability and efficiency of information transmission and apply it to telecommunications, physiology, physics, etc.

【信箱】xìnxiāng ❶ 邮局设置的供人投寄信件的箱子 post box; mailbox; box set up by a post office, into which letters are put for collection ❷ 设在邮局内供人租来收信用的编有号码的箱子,叫邮政专用信箱。有时某号信箱只是某个收信者的代号。post-office box (P. O. B.). A numbered box for rent for receiving letters is called a special post office box. Somctimes a numbered box is just a code for a certain recipient of letters. ❸ 收信人设在门前用来收信的箱子 letter box; box put up on the door of a house for receiving letters

【信心】xìnxīn 相信自己的愿望或预料一定能够实现的心理 confidence; faith; belief that one's wish or expectation is sure to come true:满怀~ full of confidence|~百倍 fully confident; full of confidence

【信仰】xìnyǎng 对某人或某种主张、主义、宗教极度相信和尊敬,拿来作为自己行动的榜样或指南 faith; belief; conviction; firmly believe in and respect sb. or a certain view, doctrine, religion, etc. and take as an example or guidance for one's actions:宗教~ religious belief

【信义】xìnyì 信用和道义 good faith; faith:不守~ be perfidious

【信意】xìn//yì 任意;随意 at random; at will; as one pleases:~胡闹 be given to making trouble

【信用】xìnyòng ❶ 能够履行跟人约定的事情而取得的信任 trustworthiness; credit:讲~ keep one's word|丧失~ lose one's credit ❷ 不需要提供物资保证,可以按时偿付的 credit:~贷款 credit loan; unsecured loan; loan on credit ❸ 指银行借贷或商业上的赊销、赊购 bank credit; credit selling and buying ❹〈书 *fml.*〉信任并任用 trust and appoint:~奸臣 trust a treacherous court official and install him in an important position

【信用合作社】xìnyòng hézuòshè 劳动人民或居民联合起来经营信贷业务的组织,通过储蓄、借贷调剂资金,解决社员生活和生产上的困难 credit cooperative; credit organization run by working people or residents to solve the financial difficulties in livelihood and production by regulating funds through savings and credit

【信用卡】xìnyòngkǎ 银行发给储户的一种代替现款的消费凭证 credit card; card establishing the privilege of the person to whom it is issued to charge bills in place of cash for consumption

【信誉】xìnyù 信用和名誉 prestige; credit; reputation:~卓著 outstanding prestige or reputation

【信札】xìnzhá 书信 letters

【信纸】xìnzhǐ 供写信用的纸 letter paper; writing paper

衅(釁) xìn 嫌隙;争端 quarrel; dispute:挑~ provocation|寻~ seek a pretext for quarrel (or fight)

【衅端】xìnduān〈书 *fml.*〉争端 dispute; cause for a quarrel or dispute

焮 xìn ❶ 烧;灼 burning ❷〈方 *dial.*〉皮肤发炎肿痛 inflammation and aching of skin

舋 xìn〈书 *fml.*〉same as 衅 xìn

xīng (ㄒㄧㄥ)

兴(興) xīng ❶ 兴盛;流行 prosper; rise; prevail; become popular:复~ rejuvenate; revive; reinvigorate|新~ newly emerging; rising|现在已经不~这种式样了。This style is no longer in vogue. ❷ 使盛行 encourage; promote:大~调查研究之风 energetically encourage the practice of investigation and study ❸ 开始;发动;创立 start; begin:~办 run; set up; build; establish|~工 start work|~利除弊 promote what is beneficial and get rid of what is harmful|百废俱~。All neglected tasks are being undertaken. ❹ 起;起来 get up; rise:晨~(早晨起来) get up in the morning|夙~夜寐 rise early and retire late ❺〈方 *dial.*〉准许(多用于否定式 oft. used in the negative) permit; allow:说话要有根据,不~胡说。Any statement should be based on facts. Don't talk nonsense! ❻〈方 *dial.*〉或许 maybe; perhaps:明天他也~来,也~不来。He'll maybe come tomorrow, maybe not. ❼ (Xīng)姓 a surname

☞ xìng on p. 2149

【兴办】xīngbàn 创办(事业) initiate; set up:~学校 set up a school|~企业 initiate an enterprise

【兴兵】xīngbīng 起兵 start military operations; send an army:~讨伐 send a punitive expedition against; declare war on sb.

【兴奋】xīngfèn ❶ 振奋;激动 be excited ❷ 大脑皮层的两种基本神经活动过程之一,是在外部或内部刺激之下产生的。兴奋引起或增强皮层和相应器官机能的活动状态,如肌肉的收缩、腺体的分泌等。excitation; one of two basic processes of activity of the cerebral cortex resulting from external or internal stimulation. Excitation causes or increases the activity of the functions of the cortex and the corresponding organs, as contraction of the muscles and secretion of glands. ❸ 使兴奋 excite; stimulate:~剂 stimulant; excitant; dope

【兴风作浪】xīng fēng zuò làng 〈比喻 *fig.*〉挑起事端或进行破坏活动 stir up trouble or carry out sabotaging activities; make trouble; fan the flames of disorder

【兴革】xīnggé 〈书 *fml.*〉兴办和革除 initiation (of the new) and abolition (of the old); reforms

【兴工】xīnggōng 动工;开工 start work; start construction:破土～ break ground to start construction

【兴国】xīngguó 使国家振兴 rejuvenate a country:科学～ make a country strong by developing sciences; rejuvenate a country through science

【兴建】xīngjiàn 开始建筑(多指规模较大的) begin to build; construct (a large project):～钢铁基地 build an iron and steel complex

【兴利除弊】xīng lì chú bì 兴办有利的事业,除去弊端 promote what is beneficial and abolish what is harmful

【兴隆】xīnglóng 兴盛 prosperous; thriving; flourishing; brisk:生意～。Business is brisk.

【兴起】xīngqǐ ❶ 开始出现并兴盛起来 rise; give rise to; spring up; be on the upgrade:各地～绿化热潮。A tree-planting upsurge has sprung up in different parts of the country. ❷〈书 *fml.*〉因感动而奋起 rise in excitement; be aroused:闻风～ spring to action upon hearing the news

【兴盛】xīngshèng 蓬勃发展 prosper; flourish; thrive; be in the ascendant:国家～。The nation is prosperous. | 事业～。Business is thriving.

【兴师】xīngshī 〈书 *fml.*〉兴兵;起步 send an army; dispatch troops:～问罪 send a punitive expedition

【兴师动众】xīng shī dòng zhòng 发动很多人做某件事(多含不值得意) get a lot of people involved; mobilize one's forces (for sth. not worth the effort)

【兴衰】xīngshuāi 兴盛和衰落 rise and decline; rise and fall

【兴叹】xīngtàn 〈书 *fml.*〉发出感叹声 heave a sigh; lament; bemoan:望洋～ feel powerless and frustrated in the face of a great task; lament one's smallness before a vast ocean

【兴亡】xīngwáng 兴盛和灭亡(多指国家 of a nation) rise and fall:天下～,匹夫有责。Everyone of its citizens is responsible for the fate of the nation.

【兴旺】xīngwàng 兴盛;旺盛 prosper; flourish; thrive:人丁～ thriving population | 六畜～ thriving of the domestic animals

【兴修】xīngxiū 开始修建(多指规模较大的) start construction (on a large project); start building (on an extensive scale):～铁路 start railway construction | ～水利 undertake water conservancy projects

【兴许】xīngxǔ 也许;或许 perhaps; maybe:你问问老王,他～知道。Ask Old Wang. He knows it perhaps.

【兴学】xīngxué 兴办学校,振兴教育 (of individuals or groups of people) set up schools to rejuvenate education:捐资～ make donations for the setting up of schools

【兴妖作怪】xīng yāo zuò guài 〈比喻 *fig.*〉坏人进行捣乱,坏思想扩大影响 conjure up demons to make trouble; stir up trouble; make trouble or spread a pernicious idea

狌 xīng 〈书 *fml.*〉 same as 猩 xīng
☞ shēng on p.1721

星 xīng ❶ 夜晚天空中闪烁发光的天体 star; any of the luminous celestial bodies seen as points of light in the sky:～罗棋布 star-studded | 月明～稀。The moon is bright and the stars are few. *or* Few stars are seen when the moon shines brightly. ❷ 天文学上指宇宙间能发射光或反射光的天体,分为恒星(如太阳)、行星(如地球)、卫星(如月亮)、彗星、流星等 (astron.) celestial body that emits or reflects light in the space. There are stars (as the sun), planets (as the earth), satellites (as the moon), comets, shooting stars, etc. ❸ (～儿 xīngr)细碎或细小的东西 bit; particle:火～儿 spark | 一～半点儿 a tiny bit ❹ 秤杆上标记斤、两、钱的小点子 small marks on the arm of a steelyard indicating *jin* and its fractions:定盘～ starting mark (at zero weight) ❺ same as 明星 míngxīng ②:歌～ singing star | 笑～ laughing star; comedian ❻ 二十八宿之一 one of the twenty-eight constellations ❼ (Xīng)姓 a surname

【星辰】xīngchén same as 星 xīng ① (总称) (collect.) stars and constellations; the stars:日月～ the sun, the moon and the stars

【星等】xīngděng 表示星体亮度的等级,亮度越大,等数越小。根据肉眼看到的星体的亮度而定的等级,叫做视星等,如太阳的视星等为 −26.7,天狼星的视星等为 −1.6。根据星体在距离观测者 10 秒差距(即 32.6 光年)时应有的亮度而定的等级,叫做绝对星等,如太阳的绝对星等为 +4.9,天狼星的绝对星等为 +1.3。magnitude; number representing the apparent brightness of a celestial body. The brighter the star, the smaller its magnitude. The number representing the brightness of a celestial body visible to the human eye is called apparent magnitude. For example, the magnitude of the sun is −26.7 and that of the Sirius is −1.6. The apparent magnitude a star would have at a distance of 10 parsecs (or 32.6 light-years) from the observer is called absolute magnitude. For example, the absolute magnitude of the sun is +4.9 and that of the Sirius is +1.3.

【星斗】xīngdǒu same as 星 xīng ①（总称）(collect.)：满天～ star-spangled sky

【星光】xīngguāng 星的光辉 starlight：～闪烁。The stars shine brightly.

【星汉】xīnghàn〈书 *fml.*〉银河 Milky Way; Galaxy：～灿烂。Resplendent is the Milky Way.

【星号】xīnghào 加在文句上或段落之间的标志（*），多用来标示脚注或分段 asterisk（*）；starlike sign used in printing to indicate footnote, paragraphing, etc.

【星河】xīnghé 指银河 Milky Way; Galaxy

【星火】[1] xīnghuǒ 微小的火 spark：～燎原。A single spark can start a prairie fire.

【星火】[2] xīnghuǒ 流星的光，比喻急迫 shooting star; meteor; (fig.) urgent; pressing：急如～ as pressing as a shooting star; most urgent; requiring immediate action

【星火燎原】xīnghuǒ liáo yuán ☞ 星星之火，可以燎原 xīngxīng zhī huǒ, kěyǐ liáo yuán

【星际】xīngjì 星体与星体之间 interplanetary; interstellar：～空间 interplanetary space｜～旅行 space travel

【星空】xīngkōng 夜晚有星的天空 starry sky; star-studded sky; starlit sky

【星罗棋布】xīng luó qí bù 像星星似的罗列着，像棋子似的分布着。形容多而密集。scattered all over like stars in the sky, like pieces on a chessboard; spread all over the place：电力网四通八达，排灌站～。The power grid stretches to every nook and cranny of the place, with drainage and irrigation pumping stations scattered like stars in the sky.

【星期】xīngqī ❶ 我国古代历法把二十八宿按日、月、火、水、木、金、土的次序排列，七日一周，周而复始，称为'七曜'；西洋历法中也有'七日为一周'的说法，跟我国的'七曜'暗合。后来根据国际习惯，把这样连续排列的七天作为工作学习等作息日期的计算单位，叫做星期。week. In the ancient Chinese calendar, the 28 constellations are arranged in the order of the sun (日 rì), the moon (月 yuè), fire or the Mars (火 huǒ), water or the Mercury (水 shuǐ), wood or the Jupiter (木 mù), metal or the Venus (金 jīn) and earth or the Saturn (土 tǔ) in a seven-day cycle dubbed 'seven stars', which coincides with the 'seven-day week' in the Western calendar. Thus the seven-day period becomes a measurement unit for work, study and rest according to the international practice, and it is called 'week'. ❷ 跟'日、一、二、三、四、五、六、几'连用，表示一个星期中的某一天［used before 日 rì, 一 yī, 二 èr, 三 sān, 四 sì, 五 wǔ, 六 liù and 几 jǐ］ to indicate a day of the week：～日 Sunday｜～三 Wednesday｜今天～几？What day (of the week) is today? ❸ 星期日的简称 abbr. for 星期日 xīngqīrì：～休息 off on Sunday

【星期日】xīngqīrì 星期六的下一天，一般定为休息日 Sunday (Sun.); the day following Saturday; also 星期天 xīngqītiān，简称 abbr. 星期 xīngqī

【星球】xīngqiú same as 星 xīng ②

【星散】xīngsàn〈书 *fml.*〉像星星散布在天空那样，指四处分散（of family members, friends, etc.）be scattered about like the stars; be apart far and wide

【星术】xīngshù 用星象占卜吉凶的方术 astrology; divination by studying the stars

【星体】xīngtǐ 天体。通常指个别的星球，如月亮、太阳、火星、北极星。celestial body; heavenly body; usually the individual celestial bodies, as the moon, the sun, the Mars, the Northern Star

【星图】xīngtú 记录恒星位置的图。不同地点和不同季节有不同的星图。star chart; star map; star atlas; map or chart showing the positions of the stars. There are different star charts for different places and different seasons.

【星团】xīngtuán 在一个比较不大的空间区域里，数十颗至数万颗以上的恒星聚集在一起所形成的恒星集团。数十到数百颗恒星不规则地聚集在一起的叫疏散星团。数以万计的恒星密集成球状的叫球状星团。star cluster; cluster of dozens to tens of thousands of stars over not a big space. It is called 'scattered star cluster' when dozens to hundreds of stars congregate in an irregular pattern, and 'ball-like star cluster' if tens of thousands of stars cluster together like a ball.

【星系】xīngxì 恒星系的简称 abbr. for 恒星系 héngxīngxì

【星相】xīngxiàng 星象和相貌，迷信的人认为根据星相可以占定人事的吉凶 horoscope; configuration and appearance of stars, by which, superstitious people believe, one can foretell a person's fortune

【星象】xīngxiàng 指星体的明暗、位置等现象，古代迷信的人往往借观察星象，推测人事的吉凶 configuration of the stars (formerly studied for their supposed influence on human affairs)

【星星】xīngxīng 细小的点儿 tiny spot; speck：～点点 tiny spots; bits; pieces｜天空晴朗，一～薄云也没有。It's a clear and bright sky without even a tiny speck of cloud.

【星星】xīng·xing same as 星 xīng ①

【星星之火，可以燎原】xīngxīng zhī huǒ, kěyǐ liáo yuán〈比喻 *fig.*〉小乱子可以发展成为大祸害，也比喻开始时显得弱小的新生事物有旺盛的生命力和广阔的发展前途 a little trouble can develop into a big disaster; a single spark can start a prairie fire; new things, which look weak and small at the beginning, can have great vitality and a broad future for development. also 星火燎原 xīnghuǒ liáo yuán

【星宿】xīngxiù 我国古代指星座,共分二十八宿 constellation. There are 28 constellations as described in ancient China.

【星夜】xīngyè 夜晚(在野外活动) starlit (or starry) night:～行军 march in a starlit night|～奔忙 bustle around in a starlit night

【星移斗转】xīng yí dǒu zhuǎn 星斗变换位置,表示季节改变 change in the positions of the stars to indicate the change of the seasons; 〈比喻 *fig.*〉时间变化 passage of time; also 星转斗移 xīng zhuǎn dǒu yí

【星移物换】xīng yí wù huàn ☞ 物换星移 wù huàn xíng yí on p. 2037

【星云】xīngyún 指太阳系以外银河系以内像云雾的气体和尘埃状物质 nebula; cloud of interstellar gas or dust outside the solar system and within the Galaxy

【星子】xīng·zi ❶ same as 星 xīng ③:吐沫～ sputtered drops of saliva; sputter ❷〈方 *dial.*〉same as 星 xīng ①:满天的～ star-studded sky

【星座】xīngzuò 天文学上为了研究的方便,把星空分为若干区域,每一个区域叫做一个星座,有时也指每个区域中的一群星。每个星座都给以人或动物的名称,如仙后座、大熊座。现代天文学上分为八十八个星座。(astron.) constellation. For the convenience of study, the star-spangled sky is divided into areas and each area is a constellation, usu. named after a mythological being or animal, as the Cassiopeia, the Great Bear, etc. Modern astronomy devides the sky into 88 constellations.

骍 xīng〈书 *fml.*〉牛马等毛皮红色 red colour of cattle and horse

猩 xīng same as 猩猩 xīngxīng

【猩红】xīnghóng 像猩猩血那样的红色;血红 scarlet; red as the blood of orangutan; blood-red:～的榴火 deep red garnet|木棉盛开时满树～。The kapok tree is fiery red when in full bloom.

【猩红热】xīnghóngrè 急性传染病,病原体是溶血性链球菌,患者多为三岁到七岁的儿童,主要症状是发热,舌头表面呈草莓状,全身有点状红疹,红疹消失后脱皮 scarlet fever; scarlatina; acute contagious disease in children usu. between three and seven in age, caused by hemolytic streptococci and charactrerized by fever, a strawberry-like tongue surface, a scarlet rash and exuviation after the rash disappears

【猩猩】xīng·xing 哺乳动物,比猴子大,两臂长,全身有赤褐色长毛,没有臀疣。吃野果。产于南洋群岛。orangutan (*Pongo pygmaeus*); Southeast Asian mammal larger than the monkey, with long arms, long and reddish-brown hair and no seat pad, feeding on wild fruits

惺 xīng〈书 *fml.*〉❶ 聪明 intelligent; clever ❷ 醒悟;清醒 realize; come to the senses; be awake to the truth; sober

【惺忪】xīngsōng 因刚醒而眼睛模糊不清 (of eyes) not yet fully open on waking up:睡眼～ eyes still heavy with sleep; sleepy eyes; also 惺松 xīngsōng

【惺惺】xīngxīng ❶〈书 *fml.*〉清醒 clear-headed; awake ❷ 聪明,也指聪明的人 wise; intelligent; intelligent person; wise man:～惜～(泛指性格、才能或境遇等相同的人互相爱重、同情)。The wise appreciate one another. *or* Intelligent people like intelligence in others. (of people of similar disposition, ability or circumnstances) like each other and sympathize with each other ❸ ☞ 假惺惺 jiǎxīng·xīng on p. 934

【惺惺作态】xīngxīng zuò tài 装模作样,故作姿态 be affected; simulate (friendship, innocence, etc.)

腥 xīng ❶ 生肉,现指肉类鱼类等食物 raw meat or fish:荤～ dishes of meat or fish ❷ 鱼虾等的难闻的气味 having the smell of fish, seafood, etc.:放些料酒去去～ put some cooking wine in to get rid of its smell

【腥臭】xīngchòu 又腥又臭 stinking smell as of rotten fish; stench

【腥风血雨】xīng fēng xuè yǔ 风里带有腥气,血溅得像下雨一样,形容残酷屠杀的景象 a foul wind and a rain of blood — reign of terror; also 血雨腥风 xuè yǔ xīng fēng

【腥气】xīng·qi ❶ same as 腥 xīng ②:一股子～ fishy smell ❷ 有腥气 stinking; fishy:你闻闻这鱼,多～。Just smell at it. How stinky!

【腥臊】xīngsāo (气味)又腥又臊 (of smell) stench

【腥膻】xīngshān (气味)又腥又膻 the smell of fish, mutton, etc.

箵 xīng ☞ [笭箵] (língxīng) on p. 1230

xíng (ㄒㄧㄥˊ)

刑 xíng ❶ 刑罚 punishment (inflicted for a crime); penalty; sentence:死～ death sentence|徒～ imprisonment|缓～ probation|量～ measurement of penalty|判～ pass a sentence ❷ 特指对犯人的体罚 torture; corporal punishment:动～ torture; subject to torture|受～ be tortured; put to torture ❸ (Xíng)姓 a surname

【刑场】xíngchǎng 处决犯人的地方 execution-er's ground; place where criminals sentenced to death are executed

【刑罚】xíngfá 国家依据刑事法律对罪犯所施行的法律制裁 penalty (for a criminal offence); punishment

【刑法】xíngfǎ 规定什么是犯罪行为,犯罪行为应受到什么惩罚的各种法律 penal code; criminal law; body of law dealing with various crimes or offences and their legal penalities

【刑法】xíng·fa 对犯人的体罚 corporal punishment; torture: 动～ administer corporal punishment

【刑房】xíngfáng ❶〈旧时 *old*〉掌管刑事案牍的官吏 officials in charge of criminal prosecution in a yamen ❷ 用刑的房子(多指非法的 oft. illegal) torture chamber: 私设～ set up an illegal torture chamber

【刑警】xíngjǐng 刑事警察的简称 abbr. for 刑事警察 xíngshì jǐngchá

【刑具】xíngjù 用来限制自由、逼问口供或执行刑罚的器具,如手铐、脚镣、夹棍、绞架等 instruments of torture; implements of punishment used to restrict freedom, interrogate for confessions or inflict penalties, as handcuffs, shackles, clamping rods, gallows, etc.

【刑律】xínglǜ 刑法(xíngfǎ) criminal law: 触犯～ violate the criminal law

【刑名】xíngmíng ❶〈古代 *arch.*〉指法律 law (esp. criminal law): ～之学 philosophy of the legal school ❷ 刑罚的名称,如死刑、徒刑等 names of punishments (e. g. death sentence, imprisonment, etc.) ❸ 清代主管刑事的(幕僚) (in the Qing Dynasty) yamen secretary handling criminal cases: ～师爷 law secretary

【刑期】xíngqī 服刑的期限 term of imprisonment; prison term

【刑辱】xíngrǔ〈书 *fml.*〉用刑法残害凌辱 persecute and humiliate

【刑事】xíngshì 有关刑法的 criminal; penal: ～犯罪 criminal offence; criminal act | ～案件 criminal case | ～法庭 criminal court

【刑事法庭】xíngshì fǎtíng 负责审理刑事案件的法庭 criminal court; court handling criminal cases; 简称 abbr. 刑庭 xíngtíng

【刑事犯】xíngshìfàn 触犯刑法,负有刑事责任的罪犯 criminal offender; criminal

【刑事警察】xíngshì jǐngchá 刑事侦查工作人员和刑事科学技术工作人员的总称 criminal police (collect.); 简称 abbr. 刑警 xíngjǐng

【刑事拘留】xíngshì jūliú 公安机关在紧急情况下依法暂时限制现行犯或重大嫌疑分子人身自由的一种强制措施 criminal detention or custody; compulsory measure taken by a public security organ to restrict the personal freedom of an active criminal or a major criminal suspect according to law in an emergent situation

【刑事判决】xíngshì pànjué 法院就被告人是否犯罪、应否处刑、如何处刑所作的决定 court decision on a criminal case of whether the defendant is guilty and should be sentenced and how

【刑事诉讼】xíngshì sùsòng 关于刑事案件的诉讼 criminal procedure; criminal suit

【刑事责任】xíngshì zérèn 触犯刑法所必须承担的法律后果 criminal responsibility; legal consequences one has to bear after violating the criminal law

【刑庭】xíngtíng 刑事法庭的简称 abbr. for 刑事法庭 xíngshì fǎtíng

【刑讯】xíngxùn 用刑具逼供审讯 inquisition by torture; extort a confession by torture

【刑侦】xíngzhēn 刑事侦查 criminal investigation: ～人员 criminal investigator

【刑种】xíngzhǒng 刑罚的种类。一般分为主刑和从刑两大类。categories of punishsment. There are two categories: principal punishment and accessory punishment.

邢 Xíng 姓 a surname

行 xíng ❶ 走 go; walk; travel: 步～ go on foot; walk | 人～道 sidewalk; pavement | 日～千里 travel one thousand *li* a day ❷〈古代 *arch.*〉指路程 trip; journey: 千里之～始于足下。A thousand *li* journey begins with the first step. ❸ 指旅行或跟旅行有关的 travel: ～装 luggage; outfit for a journey | ～程 distance of a journey; route | ～踪 whereabouts; trace | 西欧之～ travel to West Europe ❹ 流动性的; 临时性的 temporary; makeshift: ～商 travelling trader | ～营 field headquarters ❺ 流通; 推行 be current; circulate: ～销 be on sale | 发～ issue | 风～一时 be in a vogue for a time ❻ 做;办 do; perform; carry out: 举～ hold; be held; host; stage; take place | 执～ implement; execute; carry out | 试～ trial implementation; implement on a trial basis | ～医 practise medicine | ～礼 salute | ～窃 steal | ～不通 not work; be unworkable | ～之有效 effective; effectual ❼ 表示进行某项活动(多用于双音动词前) [used before a disyllabic verb, indicating the performance of some action]: 另～通知 be notified separately; till further notice | 即～查复 check and reply immediately ❽ (旧读 formerly pronounced xìng)行为 behaviour; conduct: 品～ behaviour; conduct | 言～ words and deeds | 罪～ crime | 兽～ brutality; bestial behaviour; brutal conduct ❾ 可以 be all right; will do: ～,咱们就照这样办吧。It's all right. Let's do it as told. | 算了,把事情说明白就～了。It's okay if the matter has been made clear. ❿ 能干 capable; competent: 他样样都会,真～! He is capable of doing everything. He is really terrific! ⓫〈书 *fml.*〉将要 will; shall; be going to; be about to: ～将 will; shall | ～及半岁 will be six months old ⓬ 吃了药之后使药性发散,发挥效力 (of medicine) take effect; become effective: ～药 medicine takes effect ⓭ (Xíng) 姓 a surname

☞ háng on p. 769, hàng on p. 772 and héng on p. 797

X

【行藏】xíngcáng〈书 *fml.*〉❶ 指对于出仕和退隐的处世态度 attitude towards taking an official position and retirement; conduct; behaviour; ☞ 用舍行藏 yòng shě xíng cáng on p. 2314 ❷ 形迹;底细;来历 whereabouts; trace: 露～ show trace of one's whereabouts|看破～ see through one's background

【行草】xíngcǎo 介于行书和草书之间的字体（of Chinese calligraphy）style between the running hand and cursive hand

【行车】xíngchē 驾车行驶 drive a vehicle: ～执照 driving license or driver's license|安全～十万公里 drive 100,000 km. safely (without an accident)
☞ hángchē on p. 770

【行程】xíngchéng ❶ 路程 route or distance of travel: ～万里 travel 10,000 *li* ❷ 进程 course: 历史发展～ course of historical development ❸ ☞ 冲程 chōngchéng on p. 267

【行船】xíngchuán 驾船行驶 sail a boat; navigate: ～靠舵。Sailing a boat, one relies on the rudder. |这条河不能～。This river is not navigable.

【行刺】xíngcì (用武器)暗杀 assassinate (with a weapon): 图谋～ plot to assassinate sb.

【行道】xíngdào〈旧时 *old*〉指推行自己的政治主张 preach one's politcal doctrine; propagate one's political belief: 立身～ conduct oneself by preaching one's political doctrine
☞ háng·dao on p. 770

【行道树】xíngdàoshù 种在道路两旁的成行的树 trees that line a street

【行动】xíngdòng ❶ 行走;走动 move (or get) about: 病刚好一点儿,不宜～。You are just a bit better, and not good enough to move about. ❷ 指为实现某种意图而具体地进行活动 act; action; operation; take action: ～纲领 programme of action ❸ 行为;举动 conduct; behaviour; movement: ～自由 freedom of movement

【行都】xíngdū〈旧时 *old*〉指临时的首都 provisional capital

【行方便】xíng fāng·bian 给人以便利 make things convenient for sb.; be accommodating

【行房】xíng//fáng〈婉辞 *euph.*〉指夫妇性交 (of a married couple) have sexual intercourse; make love

【行宫】xínggōng 供帝王在京城之外居住的宫殿。也指帝王出京后临时寓居的官署或住宅。emperor's palace for short stays away from the capital; temporary dwelling place of an emperor when away from the capital

【行好】xíng//hǎo 因怜悯而给予帮助或加以原谅 act charitably; be merciful; be charitable; give help to or forgive sb. to show compassion

【行贿】xíng//huì 进行贿赂 bribe; offer a bribe; resort to bribery

【行迹】xíngjì 行动的踪迹 whereabouts; tracks (of a person); traces: ～无定 wander about; lead a vagrant life; have no fixed whereabouts

【行将】xíngjiāng〈书 *fml.*〉即将;将要 be about to; be just going to; be on the verge of: ～就道 be about to set out on a journey|～灭亡 on the verge of extinction; on the verge of destruction

【行将就木】xíngjiāng jiù mù 寿命已经不长,快要进棺材了 have one foot in the grave; be getting closer to the coffin; be fast approaching death

【行脚】xíngjiǎo (和尚)云游四方 (of a monk) travel far and wide: ～僧 itinerant monk

【行劫】xíngjié 进行抢劫 commit robbery; rob: 拦路～ waylay and rob

【行进】xíngjìn 向前行走(多用于队伍 usu. of troops) march forward; advance: ～路线 march route|稍事休息,继续～ continue the march after a short break

【行经】[1] xíngjīng 来月经 menstruate; be in the period

【行经】[2] xíngjīng 行程中经过 by way of; go (or pass) by: 火车从北京开出,～天津抵达上海。The train departed from Beijing and arrived in Shanghai by way of Tianjin.

【行径】xíngjìng 行为;举动(多指坏的 oft. negative) act; action; move: 无耻～ impudent act; shameless act

【行军】xíng//jūn 军队进行训练或执行任务时从一个地点走到另一个地点 (of troops) march; walk from one place to another in military training or military operation: 夜～ night march|急～ rapid march; forced march

【行军床】xíngjūnchuáng 可以折叠的床,用木架或金属架绷着帆布做成,多供行军或野外工作时用 camp bed; camp cot; lightweight folding bed made of wood or metal frame and canvas, usu. used at the time of a military march or field work; also 帆布床 fānbùchuáng

【行楷】xíngkǎi 介于行书和楷书之间的字体 style of handwriting between the runnng hand and the regular script

【行乐】xínglè〈书 *fml.*〉消遣娱乐;游戏取乐 indulge in pleasures; seek amusement; make merry

【行礼】xíng//lǐ ❶ 致敬礼,如鞠躬、举手等 salute (bow, raise hand, etc.) ❷〈方 *dial.*〉送礼 present or give gifts

【行李】xíng·li 出门所带的包裹、箱子等 luggage; baggage; parcel, suitcase or trunk carried for a trip

【行李卷儿】xíng·lijuǎnr 铺盖卷儿 bedroll; bedding roll; bedding pack

【行猎】xíngliè〈书 *fml.*〉打猎 go hunting: 深山～ hunting in deep mountain forests

【行令】xíng//lìng 行酒令 play drinking games：猜拳～ play drinkers' game by guessing the number of fingers；play a finger-guessing game

【行旅】xínglǚ 走远路的人 traveller；wayfarer：～往来 stream of travellers coming and going

【行囊】xíngnáng〈书 *fml.*〉出门时所带的袋子或包儿 travelling bag carried for a trip

【行期】xíngqī 出发的日期 date of departure：～在即。The date of departure is drawing near.

【行乞】xíngqǐ 向人要钱要饭 beg one's bread；beg alms；beg：沿路～ beg from door to door and from place to place along the way

【行腔】xíngqiāng 戏曲演员按个人对于曲谱的体会来运用腔调（in traditional opera）actor's rendering of an operatic tune on the basis of his own understanding of the music scores：～咬字 sing and declaim

【行窃】xíng//qiè 进行偷窃 steal；thieve

【行箧】xíngqiè〈书 *fml.*〉出门时所带的箱子 travelling box

【行人】xíngrén 在路上走的人 pedestrian；foot traveller：过往～ pedestrians；passers-by

【行人情】xíng rénqíng 指向亲友家送礼物或到亲友家贺喜、吊丧等 do what is required of social etiquette, as offering congratulations, expressing condolences, sending gifts

【行若无事】xíng ruò wú shì 指在紧急关头态度镇静如常。有时也指对坏人坏事，听之任之，满不在乎。be calm and composed at the critical moment as if nothing had happened；be indifferent to the evildoings of evildoers

【行色】xíngsè 出发前后的神态、情景或气派 circumstances or style of departure：～匆匆 be in a hurry to set out|以壮～ give a grand send-off, etc.；enable sb. to depart in style

【行善】xíng//shàn 做善事 do good；do kind deeds；practise philanthropy：积德～ do good deeds

【行商】xíngshāng 往来贩卖、没有固定营业地点的商人（区别于'坐商'as distinguished from 'tradesman'）itinerant trader；travelling merchant；pedlar

【行尸走肉】xíng shī zǒu ròu〈比喻 *fig.*〉不动脑筋、无所作为、糊里糊涂过日子的人 walking corpse — one who vegetates；utterly worthless person；the walking dead

【行时】xíngshí（事物）在当时流行；（人）在当时得势（of a thing）in vogue；be all the rage；（of a person）in the ascendant

【行使】xíngshǐ 执行；使用（职权等）exercise；perform：～国家主权 exercise state（or national）sovereignty|～公民权利 exercise the rights of a citizen

【行驶】xíngshǐ（车、船）行走（of a vehicle, ship, etc.）go；ply；travel：列车向南～。The train is going south.|长江下游可以～万吨轮船。The lower reaches of the Yangtze River are navigable for 10,000-tonners.

【行事】xíngshì ❶ 行为 behaviour；conduct：言谈～ speech and conduct ❷ 办事；做事 act；handle matters：～谨慎 act prudently|看人脸色～ act differently with different people

【行书】xíngshū 汉字字体，形体和笔势介于草书和楷书之间 running hand（in Chinese calligraphy）；style of handwriting between the cursive hand and the regular script

【行署】xíngshǔ 行政公署的简称 abbr. for 行政公署 xíngzhèng gōngshǔ

【行述】xíngshù 行状 brief biography of a deceased person（usu. accompanying an obituary notice）

【行头】xíng·tou ❶ 戏曲演员演出时用的服装 actor's costumes and paraphernalia ❷ 泛指服装（含诙谐意 implying humour）（in a broad sense）dress；clothing；apparel；outfit

【行为】xíngwéi 受思想支配而表现在外面的活动 act；action；behaviour；conduct：～不端 dishonourable behaviour；bad conduct|揭露不法～ reveal the unlawful acts

【行为能力】xíngwéi nénglì 指能够以自己的行为依法行使权利和承担义务的能力。具有行为能力的人必须首先具有权利能力，但具有权利能力的人不一定都有行为能力。capacity；capacity of disposition；disposing capacity；the capacity of exercising one's rights and assuming one's obligations according to law by one's own conduct. A person with capacity must have the capacity for rights, but a person with the capacity for rights may not necessarily have the capacity of disposition. ☞ 权利能力 quánlì nénglì on p. 1596

【行文】xíngwén ❶ 组织文字，表达意思 style or manner of writing；organization and expression of ideas：～简练 succinctly written ❷ 发公文给（某个或某些单位）（of a government office）send an official communication to other organizations：～各地。An official communication will soon be sent to all local authorities.

【行销】xíngxiāo 向各地销售 be on sale；sell：～全国 be on sale throughout the country

【行星】xíngxīng 沿不同的椭圆形轨道绕太阳运行的天体，本身不发光，只能反射太阳光。太阳系有九大行星，按离太阳由近而远的次序，依次是水星、金星、地球、火星、木星、土星、天王星、海王星和冥王星。还有许多小行星。planet；celestial body that moves around the sun along an elliptical orbit, does not emit light by itself, but reflects the light of the sun. The solar system has nine major planets：Mercury, Venus, Earth, Mars, Jupiter, Saturn, Uranus, Neptune, and Pluto, arranged in the order of their distances to the sun, from the nearest to the farthest. There are also many small planets.

【行刑】xíng//xíng 执行刑罚,特指死刑 carry out a death sentence; execute

【行凶】xíng//xiōng 指打人或杀人 commit physical assault or murder; do violence: 持刀～ assault a person with a knife (or dagger or other cutting tools) | ～作恶 commit physical assault to do evil things

【行医】xíng//yī 从事医生的业务(多指个人经营的 usu. on one's own) practise medicine: 挂牌～ practise medicine with a license; put up one's brass plate and practise medicine | 世代～ practise medicine for generations

【行营】xíngyíng 〈旧时 *old*〉指统帅出征时办公的营帐或房屋,也指专设的机构 field headquarters; field tent or house where the commanding officer holds his office on an expedition in ancient times; also as a special office

【行辕】xíngyuán same as 行营 xíngyíng

【行云流水】xíng yún liú shuǐ 〈比喻 *fig.*〉自然不拘执(多指文章、歌唱等) (of style of writing and singing) like floating clouds and flowing water; natural and unstrained

【行者】xíngzhě ❶〈书 *fml.*〉行人 passer-by ❷ 出家而未经剃度的佛教徒 Buddhist monk prior to his tonsure

【行政】xíngzhèng ❶ 行使国家权力的 administrative: ～单位 administrative unit | ～机构 adminstrative organs ❷ 指机关、企业、团体等内部的管理工作 administration: ～人员 administrative personnel (or staff) | ～费用 adminstrative expenses

【行政公署】xíngzhèng gōngshǔ ❶ 我国解放前革命根据地和解放初期部分地区设立的地方政权机关,如苏南行政公署、皖北行政公署等 administrative office (within a province); local administrative offices set up in the pre-liberation revolutionary bases and some regions in the early years of liberation, such as the South Jiangsu Administrative Office and the North Anhui Administrative Office ❷ 我国某些省、自治区设置的派出机关 representative offices set up in some Chinese provinces and autonomous regions ‖ 简称 abbr. 行署 xíngshǔ

【行政拘留】xíngzhèng jūliú 对违反治安管理行为的一种行政处罚。拘留由公安机关裁决执行。administrative detention; administrative punishment for those breaking public security rules, which is executed by a public security office

【行政区】xíngzhèngqū 设有国家政权机关的各级地区 administrative area where there is a government

【行止】xíngzhǐ 〈书 *fml.*〉❶ 行踪 whereabouts: ～无定 not know one's whereabouts ❷ 品行 conduct; behaviour: ～不检 indiscreet in one's behaviour | ～有亏。His conduct has shortcomings.

【行装】xíngzhuāng 出门时所带的衣服、被褥等 outfit for a journey; luggage: 整理～ pack (for a journey)

【行状】xíngzhuàng 〈书 *fml.*〉〈旧时 *old*〉死者家属叙述死者世系、籍贯、事迹的文章,多随讣文分送亲友 profile of a deceased person (usu. accompanying an obituary notice); also 行述 xíngshù

【行踪】xíngzōng 行动的踪迹(多指目前停留的地方 oft. place where one presently stays) whereabouts; track: ～不定 uncertain whereabouts

【行走】xíngzǒu same as 走 zǒu ①: ～如飞 walk swiftly; walk like a wind; walk as if with wings

饧(餳) xíng ❶〈书 *fml.*〉糖稀 treacle; molasses; syrup ❷ 糖块、面剂子等变软 (of dough, sweets, etc.) get soft; get sticky: 糖～了。These candies have got soft and sticky. ❸ 精神不振,眼睛半睁半闭 (of eyes) drowsy; sleepy: 眼睛发～。The eyes are sleepy.

☞ táng on p. 1864

形 xíng ❶ 形状 form; shape: 圆～ round | 方～ square | 图～ figure; graph | 地～ landform; topography; terrain ❷ 形体; 实体 body; entity: 有～ visible; tangible; physical | 无～ invisible; intangible; incorporeal; nonphysical | ～影不离 be inseparable as body and shadow; be always together ❸ 显露; 表现 appear; look: 喜～于色 look pleased; be visibly pleased; light up with pleasure | ～诸笔墨 commit to writing; express one's emotions in writing ❹ 对照 contrast; compare: 相～见绌 be overshadowed; be outshone; be inferior by comparison; pale into insignificance | 相～之下 by comparison; as compared with; when compared with

【形变】xíngbiàn 固体受到外力作用时所发生的形状或体积的改变。分为拉伸形变、扭转形变、弯曲形变和剪切形变等。deformation; change in the form or volume of a solid under external pressure. There are tensile deformation, torsion deformation, flexure deformation, shearing deformation, etc.

【形成】xíngchéng 通过发展变化而成为具有某种特点的事物,或者出现某种情形或局面 take shape; form; thing acquires a certain characteristic after it develops or changes: ～鲜明的对比 form a sharp or striking contrast

【形成层】xíngchéngcéng 植物体中的一种组织,细胞排列紧密,有不断分裂增殖的能力。形成层的细胞陆续分化而形成韧皮部和木质部,并使茎或根不断变粗。cambium; layer of formative cells between the wood and bark in dicotyledonous plants. These cells cause the girth of the stem to increase by dividing and differentiating to form new phloem and xylem tissue, which will eventually become wood and bark.

【形单影只】xíng dān yǐng zhī 形容孤独,没有伴侣 solitary form and single shadow; extremely lonely; solitary; without a companion; also 形只影单 xíng zhī yǐng dān

【形而上学】xíng'érshàngxué ❶ 哲学史上指哲学中探究宇宙根本原理的部分 metaphysics; branch of philosophy that deals with the fundamental principles of the universe ❷ 同辩证法相对立的世界观或方法论。它用孤立、静止、片面的观点看世界,认为一切事物都是孤立的,永远不变的;如果说有变化,只是数量的增减和场所的变更,这种增减或变更的原因不在事物内部而在于事物外部。metaphysics; world outlook or methodology opposed to dialectics, maintaining that things are eternally isolated from each other and immutable, and that such change as there can be is only an increase or decrease in quantity or a change of place — the cause of such an increase or decrease or change of pace is not inside things but outside them. ‖ also 玄学 xuánxué

【形格势禁】xíng gé shì jìn 指受形势的阻碍或限制 be hampered by circumstances; be in an unfavourable situation

【形骸】xínghái 〈书 *fml.*〉指人的形体 human skeleton; human body: 放浪～ be unconventional and unrestrained

【形迹】xíngjì ❶ 举动和神色 person's movements and expression: ～可疑 of suspicious appearance; suspicious-looking ❷ 痕迹;迹象 trace; mark; sign: 不留～ betray nothing in one's expression and movements ❸ 指礼貌 manners; formality; etiquete: 不拘～ without formality; not standing on ceremony

【形旁】xíngpáng ☞ 形声 xíngshēng

【形容】xíngróng ❶〈书 *fml.*〉形体和容貌 appearance; countenance; look; body; figure; shape: ～憔悴 look haggard; wan-looking; thin and pallid ❷ 对事物的形象或性质加以描述 describe: 他高兴的心情是无法～的。His joy was beyond description.

【形容词】xíngróngcí 表示人或事物的性质或状态的词,如'高、细、软、白、暖和、活泼' adjective; any of a class of words used to indicate the nature or state of a person or thing, as '高 gāo (high), 细 xì (thin or fine), 软 ruǎn (soft), 白 bái (white), 暖和 nuǎn·huo (warm), 活泼 huó·po (lively or vivacious)'

【形声】xíngshēng 六书之一。形声是说字由'形'和'声'两部分合成,形旁和全字的意义有关,声旁和全字的读音有关。如由形旁'氵(水)'和声旁'工、可'分别合成'江、河'。形声字占汉字总数的百分之八十以上。pictophonetic method for the formation of Chinese characters. As one of the six categories of Chinese characters (六书 liùshū), it consists of two elements, one indicating meaning and the other sound. For example, the meaning element '氵(水 shuǐ)' combines with the sound element 工 gōng and 可 kě respectively to form the two Chinese characters 江 jiāng and 河 hé. Pictophonetic characters account for over 80 per cent of the total number of Chinese characters. also 谐声 xiéshēng

【形胜】xíngshèng 〈书 *fml.*〉地势优越壮美 favourable and majestic geographical conditions: 山川～ magnificent mountains and rivers | ～之地 advantageous terrain

【形式】xíngshì 事物的形状、结构等 form; shape; structure: 组织～ organizational make-up | 艺术～ art form | ～逻辑 formal logic | 内容和～的统一 unity of content and form

【形式逻辑】xíngshì luó·jí 关于思维的形式及其规律的科学。形式逻辑研究概念、判断、推理等主要思维形式,研究同一律、矛盾律、排中律等思维规律。formal logic; branch of logic concerned with the forms and laws of reasoning, such as concept, judgement, deduction, law of identity, law of contradiction, law of excluded middle, etc.

【形式主义】xíngshì zhǔyì ❶ 片面地注重形式不管实质的工作作风,或只看事物的现象而不分析其本质的思想方法 formalism; style of work of paying unilateral attention to form regardless of the substance; way of thinking that pays attention to the phenomena of things without analysing its essence ❷ 19 世纪末到 20 世纪初形成的一种反现实主义的艺术思潮,主要特征是脱离现实生活,否认艺术的思想内容,只在表现形式上标新立异 formalism; anti-realistic art trend of thought that rose during the interregnum between the 19th and 20th centuries, its main characteristics being divorce from real life, negation of the ideological content of art, and obsession with unconventional forms of expression

【形势】xíngshì ❶ 地势(多指从军事角度看 usu. from a military angle) terrain; topographical features: ～险要 strategically important terrain ❷ 事物发展的状况 situation; developments of things: 国际～ international situation | 客观～ objective situation | ～逼人。The situation is pressing. *or* The situation demands immediate action. | ～好转。Things are getting better. *or* The situation has improved.

【形似】xíngsì 形式、外表上相像 likeness in form or appearance; formal likeness (or resemblance): 塑人像不仅要～,更要神似。Sculptors aim at a likeness not only in appearance, but also in spirit.

【形态】xíngtài ❶ 事物的形状或表现 form; shape; pattern; morphology: 意识～ ideology | 观念～ concept ❷ 生物体外部的形状 form and structure of an organism ❸ 词的内部变

化形式，包括构词形式和词形变化的形式 branch of linguistics that deals with changes in the internal structures and forms of words

【形态学】xíngtàixué ❶ 研究生物体外部形状、内部构造及其变化的科学 morphology; branch of biology that deals with the form and structure of animals and plants, and their changes ❷ 语法学中研究词的形态变化的部分 morphology; branch of linguistics that deals with the changes in the forms of words; also 词法 cífǎ

【形体】xíngtǐ ❶ 身体(就外观说) figure; body; shape of the body: 生物学家们塑造了～完整的中国猿人模型。Biologists have built a model of the Chinese ape-man. ❷ 形状和结构 form and structure: 文字的～ form and structure of Chinese characters

【形象】xíngxiàng ❶ 能引起人的思想或感情活动的具体形状或姿态 image; form; figure; form or posture that gives rise to thoughts or feelings of a person: 图画教学是通过～来发展儿童认识事物的能力。The use of pictures in classroom teaching helps children to understand things through images. ❷ 文艺作品中创造出来的生动具体的、激发人们思想感情的生活图景，通常指文学作品中人物的神情面貌和性格特征 literary or artistic image; imagery; vivid and lively pictures of life created in literary and art works that arouse the feelings of a person or persons: ～逼真 lifelike image | 英雄～ the image of a hero ❸ 指描绘或表达具体、生动 vivid; expressive; graphic: 语言精练而～。The language is concise and expressive.

【形象思维】xíngxiàng sīwéi 文学艺术创作过程中主要的思维方式，借助于形象反映生活，运用典型化和想像的方法，塑造艺术形象，表达作者的思想感情 thinking in (terms of) images; principal mode of thinking in the course of literary creation, about how to reflect life with the aid of images, create artistic images through models and imagination and express the author's thoughts and feelings; also 艺术思维 yìshù sīwéi

【形销骨立】xíng xiāo gǔ lì 形容身体极其消瘦 be gaunt; become emaciated; be reduced to mere skin and bones; be worn to a shadow of one's former self; be just a skeleton

【形形色色】xíngxíngsèsè 各种各样 of every hue; of all shades; of all forms; of every description

【形影不离】xíng yǐng bù lí 形容彼此关系密切 be inseparable as body and shadow; be always together; be together 24/7

【形影相吊】xíng yǐng xiāng diào 形容孤独 body and shadow comforting each other; extremely lonely; sad and solitary (吊 *diao*: 慰问 comfort)

【形制】xíngzhì 器物或建筑物的形状和构造 structure; design; form and structure of an object or building: ～古朴 design of primitive simplicity | ～奇特 unique structure | 殿宇～雄伟。The buildings of the temple are magnificent.

【形状】xíngzhuàng 物体或图形由外部的面或线条组合而呈现的外表 form; appearance; shape (of a body or graph formed by external faces or lines)

陉(陘) xíng 〈书 *fml.*〉山脉中断的地方；山口 pass; defile: 井～(地名，在河北) Jingxing (name of a place in Hebei Province)

型 xíng ❶ 模型 mould: 砂～ sand mould ❷ 类型 model; type; pattern; size: 脸～ type of a face | 血～ type of blood | 小～ small size | 大～ large size | 新～ new type | 流线～ streamline

【型钢】xínggāng 断面呈不同形状的钢材的统称。断面呈L形的叫角钢，呈凵形的叫槽钢，呈圆形的叫圆钢，呈方形的叫方钢，呈工字形的叫工字钢，呈T形的叫丁字钢。section steel; shaped steel; rolled steel with different cross-sections. The L-shaped steel is called angle steel or L steel, U steel for the U-shaped, round steel for the round-shaped, square steel for the square-shaped, I steel for the I-shaped and T steel for the T-shaped.

【型号】xínghào 指机械或其他工业制品的性能、规格和大小 model; type; properties, specifications and sizes of machines and other industial products: 品种多样，～齐全。There are a great variety and a complete away specifications.

【型砂】xíngshā 制造砂型用的主要材料，一般是二氧化硅和黏土的混合物 moulding sand; principal material for making sand moulds, usu. made of silicon dioxide and clay

【型心】xíngxīn 用来形成铸件内腔的东西，通常用型砂制成 core; part of a mould which forms the interior of a hollow casting

荥(滎) xíng 荥阳(Xíngyáng)，地名，在河南 Xinyang, name of a place in Henan Province

☞ yíng on p. 2301

钘 xíng ❶〈古代 *arch.*〉盛酒的器皿 wine vessel ❷ same as 铏 xíng

硎 xíng 〈书 *fml.*〉 ❶ 磨刀石 whetstone; grinding stone: 发～ newly-sharpened blade or knife ❷ 磨制 grind; polish

铏 xíng 〈古代 *arch.*〉盛菜羹的器皿 *xing*, three-legged vessel with two ears and a lid for holding dish and custard

xǐng (ㄒㄧㄥˇ)

省 xǐng ❶ 检查自己的思想行为 examine oneself critically: 反～ retrospection; self-examination; introspection | 内～ introspection ❷ 探望；问候（多指对尊长）visit one's parents' or elders：～亲 pay a visit to one's parents ❸ 醒悟；明白 become conscious; be aware：～悟 become conscious; be aware | 不～人事 lose consciousness; fall into a coma

☞ shěng on p.1722

【省察】xǐngchá 检查自己的思想行为 examine oneself critically; examine one's thoughts and conduct

【省墓】xǐngmù〈书 *fml*.〉祭扫尊长的坟墓 visit one's parents' or elders' graves

【省亲】xǐngqīn 回家乡或到远处看望父母或其他尊亲 pay a visit to one's parents or elders (living in another place)

【省视】xǐngshì 看望；探望 call upon; pay a visit to：～双亲 pay a visit to one's parents

【省悟】xǐngwù same as 醒悟 xǐngwù

醒 xǐng ❶ 酒醉、麻醉或昏迷后神志恢复正常状态 regain consciousness; sober up; come to：酒醉未～ be drunk and not sobered up yet ❷ 睡眠状态结束，大脑皮层恢复兴奋状态。也指尚未入睡。be awake; wake up：大梦初～ just wake up from a dream; wake up to reality | 我还～着呢，热得睡不着。I'm still awake. It's too hot for me to fall asleep. ❸ 指和(huó)好面团后，放一会儿，使面团软硬均匀 keep dough till water and flour are well mixed; keep dough till it becomes soft and even ❹ 醒悟；觉悟 become conscious; clear in mind：猛～ become sober and alert all at once | 提～ remind ❺ 明显；清楚 be striking; eye-catching：～目 conspicuous | ～豁 clear; explicit

【醒盹儿】xǐng//dǔnr〈方 *dial*.〉小睡醒过来 wake up from a nap; shake off drowsiness

【醒豁】xǐnghuò 意思表达得清楚 clear; explicit：道理说得～。The argument is clearly presented.

【醒酒】xǐng//jiǔ 使由醉而醒 dispel the effects of alcohol; sober up：～汤 broth or liquid used to remove the intoxicating effect of alcohol | 吃个梨醒醒酒。Have a pear to sober yourself up.

【醒木】xǐngmù 说评书的人为了引起听众注意而用来拍桌子的小硬木块 storyteller's gavel; small piece of hardwood used by a storyteller to pound the table to draw the listeners' attention

【醒目】xǐngmù（文字、图画等）形象明显，容易看清 (of written words or pictures) catch the eye; attract attention; be striking to the eye：大字标题十分～。The bold headlines are very eye-catching.

【醒脾】xǐngpí〈方 *dial*.〉❶ 消遣解闷 be amusing; be entertaining ❷（拿人）开心；取笑 tease; make fun of

【醒悟】xǐngwù 在认识上由模糊而清楚，由错误而正确 come to realize (or see) the truth, one's error, etc.; wake up to reality：翻然～ come to realize quickly

【醒眼】xǐngyǎn〈方 *dial*.〉❶ 醒目；显眼 (of written words or pictures) catch the eye; attract attention; be striking to the eye ❷ 醒悟；开窍 begin to realize; come to realize

擤（擤） xǐng 按住鼻孔用力出气，使鼻涕排出 blow (one's nose)：～鼻涕 blow one's nose

xìng（ㄒㄧㄥˋ）

兴（興） xìng 兴致；兴趣 interest; mood or desire to do sth.; excitement：豪～ high spirits; keep interest | 助～ add to amusemnt; make things more lively; liven up things | 败～ disappointed; dampen one's enthusiasm | 雅～ interest in refined pursuits | 游～ interest in travelling

☞ xīng on p.2139

【兴冲冲】xìngchōngchōng（～的 xìngchōngchōng·de）形容兴致很高 feel elated; (do sth.) with joy and expedition; excitedly

【兴高采烈】xìng gāo cǎi liè 兴致高，情绪热烈 in high spirits; excited; jubilant

【兴会】xìnghuì 因偶然有所感受而发生的意趣 sudden flash of inspiration; brain wave：乘一时的～，信手写了这首诗。This poem was improvised on the spur of the moment.

【兴趣】xìngqù 喜好的情绪 interest：我对下棋不感～。I'm not interested in chess. | 人们怀着极大的～参观了画展。People visited the exhibition of paintings with great interest.

【兴头】xìng·tou ❶ 因为高兴或感兴趣而产生的劲头 enthusiasm; keen interest：～十足 keen interest; be full of interest; be highly interested in ❷〈方 *dial*.〉高兴；得意 be elated; be delighted：前呼后拥，好不～。How happy he was to be accomapanied by a large number of retainers!

【兴头儿上】xìngtóur·shang 兴头正足的时候 at the height of one's enthusiasm; in high spirits：人家正在～，你干吗要泼冷水！They are now in high spirits; why should you pour cold water on their enthusiasm?

【兴味】xìngwèi 兴趣 interest：饶有～ with keen interest | ～索然 be not interested in; have no interest in; lose interest; be bored stiff

【兴致】xìngzhì 兴趣 interest; mood to enjoy：～勃勃 full of zest; in high spirits

杏 xìng ❶ 杏树，落叶乔木，叶子宽卵形，花单性，白色或粉红色，果实圆形，成熟时黄红色，味酸甜 apricot tree (*Prunus armeniaca*); deciduous tree with broad, ovatc lcaves, white or pink, unisexual flowers, and round fruits which are yellowish pink in colour when ripe and taste sour and sweet ❷ (～儿 xìngr)这种植物的果实 fruit of the plant

【杏红】xìnghóng 黄中带红，比杏黄稍红的颜色 yellowish pink; apricot pink

【杏黄】xìnghuáng 黄而微红的颜色 pinkish yellow; apricot (colour)

【杏仁】xìngrén (～儿 xìngrénr)杏核中的仁。甜的一种可以吃，苦的一种可以入药。apricot kernel; almond: the sweet kernels are used as a food, and the bitter kernels are used as medicine

【杏眼】xìngyǎn 指女子大而圆的眼睛 big and round eyes of a woman; apricot-shaped eyes: 柳眉～ willow-leaf-shaped eyebrows and apricot-shaped eyes | ～圆睁 big, round eyes widely open; beautiful eyes staring in anger

【杏子】xìng·zi 〈方 *dial.*〉杏 apricot

幸(❺倖)

xìng ❶ 幸福；幸运 happy; lucky; fortunate: 荣～ fortunate | 三生有～ extremely lucky ❷ 认为幸福而高兴 rejoice: 欣～ be happy and pleased | 庆～ rejoice | ～灾乐祸 take delight in sb.'s misfortune ❸〈书 *fml.*〉望；希望 hope: ～勿推却。Hope that you will not decline. ❹ 侥幸 lucky; fortunate: ～亏 fortunately; luckily | ～免 be lucky to avoid | ～未成灾。Fortunately, it had not caused a disaster. ❺〈书 *fml.*〉宠幸 get imperial favour: ～臣 court favourite; favourite courtier ❻〈旧时 *old*〉指帝王到达某地 (of a monarch) be present at a place or on an occasion: 巡～ imperial tour of places ❼ (Xìng) 姓 a surname

【幸臣】xìngchén 帝王宠幸的臣子(贬义 derog.) court favourite; favourite courtier

【幸存】xìngcún 侥幸地活下来 survive (an accident): ～者 survival | 飞机失事，机上人员无一～。There was no survival in the plane crash. *or* No one on the plane survived the crash.

【幸而】xìng'ér 幸亏 luckily; fortunately: ～隐患及时消除，否则后果不堪设想。Luckily, the hidden danger was removed in good time, or the consequences would have been unimaginable.

【幸福】xìngfú ❶ 使人心情舒畅的境遇和生活 happiness; well-being; circumstances and life that make one happy: 为人民谋～ work for the well-being of the people | 今天的～是先烈们流血流汗得来的。We owe our happiness of today to the toil and blood of the martyrs. ❷ (生活、境遇)称心如意 happy (life and circumstances): 随着经济的发展，人民越来越～。As a result of economic growth, life has become happier and happier for the people.

【幸好】xìnghǎo 幸亏 luckily; fortunately: ～雨不大，不然非淋成落汤鸡不可。Luckily, the rain was not heavy, otherwise (we) would all be soaked to the skin.

【幸会】xìnghuì〈客套话 *pol.*〉表示跟对方相会很荣幸 (rather formal greeting) very pleased to meet you

【幸进】xìngjìn〈书 *fml.*〉因侥幸而当官或升级 fortunate promotion

【幸亏】xìngkuī〈副词 *adv.*〉表示借以免除困难的有利情况 [indicating the favourable conditions for removing difficulties] fortunately; luckily: ～抢救及时，才保住性命。Thanks to the timely rescue, the life was secured.

【幸免】xìngmiǎn 侥幸地避免 land on one's feet; escape by sheer luck; have a narrow escape: ～于难 escape death by sheer luck; escape death by a hair's breadth

【幸甚】xìngshèn〈书 *fml.*〉❶ 表示很有希望，很可庆幸 be very lucky; be blessed indeed: 剪除奸佞，国家～。It is a good blessing for the nation to have the treacherous sycophants got rid of. ❷ 非常荣幸(多用于书信 usu. used in letters) great honour; great pleasure: 承不吝赐教，～，～。I shall be greatly honoured if you could kindly give me your advice.

【幸事】xìngshì 值得庆幸的事 a piece of good fortune; a stroke of luck; blessing

【幸喜】xìngxǐ 幸亏 fortunately; luckily: ～有热心人指点，才没有迷路。Fortunately, thanks to the advice of a kind person, I did not lose my way.

【幸运】xìngyùn ❶ 好的运气；出乎意料的好机会 good fortune; good luck; good chance: 但愿～能够降临到他的头上。I wish that good luck would befall him. ❷ 称心如意；运气好 fortunate; lucky: 买彩券得了头等奖，真是～。What a good luck that (you) have won the first prize in the lottery!

【幸运儿】xìngyùn'ér 幸运的人 fortune's favourite; lucky fellow

【幸灾乐祸】xìng zāi lè huò 别人遭到灾祸时自己心里高兴 take pleasure in (or gloat over) other people's misfortune

性

xìng ❶ 性格 nature; character; disposition: 个～ individuality; personality; personal character | 天～ natural instinct; nature | 耐～ patience ❷ 物质所具有的性能；物质因含有某种成分而产生的性质 property; quality; attribute of sth. resulting from a certain element contained in it: 黏～ viscosity | 弹～ elasticity; spring | 药～ property of a medicine | 碱～ alkalinity | 油～ greasy ❸ 在思想、感情等方面的表现 suffix designating a specified quality, property, scope, etc.: 党～ party spirit | 阶级～ class character | 纪律～ discipline ❹ 有关生物的生殖或性欲的 sexual; sexuality: ～器官 sex organs | ～行为 sexual behaviour | ～生活 have a sex or sexual intercourse; sexual life ❺ 性别 sex: 男～ male; masculine | 女～

famale; feminine|雄～ male|雌～ female ❻ 表示名词(以及代词、形容词)的类别的语法范畴。语法上的性跟事物的自然性别有时有关,有时无关。例如俄语名词有阳、阴、中三性。gender; part of linguistics dealing with the categories of nouns (as well as pronouns and adjectives) that may or may not be related to the natural gender of things, such as the three genders (masculine gender, feminine gender and neuter) of nouns in the Russian language

【性爱】xìng'ài 两性之间的爱欲(就发生性关系说) love between the sexes; sexual love; love

【性别】xìngbié 雌雄两性的区别,通常指男女两性的区别 sexual distinction; sex; distinction between the female and male sexes

【性病】xìngbìng 梅毒、淋病、软性下疳等疾病的统称,多由性交传染 venereal disease; V. D., such as syphilis, gonorrhoea, chancroid, etc.

【性感】xìnggǎn 能够引起异性情欲的;肉感 sex appeal; sexiness; appeal that tends to excite sexual desire

【性格】xìnggé 在对人、对事的态度和行为方式上所表现出来的心理特点,如英勇、刚强、懦弱、粗暴等 nature; disposition; temperament; psychological traits manifested in the attitude and behaviour of a person towards another person or a thing, as bravery, staunchiness, weakness, roughness, etc.

【性激素】xìngjīsù 由睾丸或卵巢分泌的激素,主要作用是刺激生殖器官的生长和调节生殖器的机能。男子生胡须,女子乳房发达,都与性激素有关。sex hormone; hormone secreted by testicle or ovary, the functions of which is to stimulate the growth of the sexual organs and regulate the functions of the sexual organs

【性急】xìng jí 遇事没有耐性,急于去做或急于达到目的;脾气急 impatient; short-tempered; be anxious to achieve one's purpose:养病不能～。Don't be impatient in recovering from illness.

【性交】xìngjiāo 两性之间发生性行为 sexual intercourse; make love; have sex

【性灵】xìnglíng〈书 *fml.*〉指人的精神、性情、情感等 spirituality; temperament; character; soul; mind; mood; emotion:陶冶～ mould a person's temperament, personality, etc.

【性命】xìngmìng 人和动物的生命 life (of a man or animal)

【性命交关】xìngmìng jiāoguān 关系到人的性命。形容关系重大,非常紧要。(matter) of life and death; of vital importance

【性能】xìngnéng 机械或其他工业制品对设计要求的满足程度 function (of a machine, etc.); performance; property:这种插秧机构造简单,～良好。This transplanter is simply constructed and performs satisfactorily.

【性气】xìngqì 性格;脾气 temper; temperament; character:～平和 mild-tempered

【性器官】xìngqìguān 人或高等动物的生殖器 sexual organs; genitals; ☞ 生殖器 shēngzhíqì on p. 1719

【性情】xìng·qíng 性格 disposition; temperament; temper:～急躁 short-tempered|～温和 mild-tempered; gentle disposition

【性腺】xìngxiàn ☞ 生殖腺 shēngzhíxiàn on p. 1719

【性行】xìngxíng 性格行为 character or temperament and behaviour:～暴烈 hot-tempered and violent in bahaviour

【性欲】xìngyù 对性行为的要求 sexual desire (or urge)

【性质】xìngzhì 一种事物区别于其他事物的根本属性 quality; nature; character

【性状】xìngzhuàng 性质和形状 shape and properties; properties; character:土壤的理化～ the physico-chemical properties of soil

【性子】xìng·zi ❶ 性情、脾气 temper:急～ hot-tempered|使～ lose temper|这匹马的～很烈。This is a vicious horse. ❷ 酒、药等的刺激性 (of wine, medicine, etc.) strength; potency:这药～平和。This drug is very mild. *or* This is a mild drug.

姓 xìng ❶ 表明家族的字 surname; family (or clan) name; word indicating a family:～名 full name|贵～? What's your name? *or* May I know your family name? ❷ 姓是…;以…为姓 one's family name is:你～什么? What's your family name? |他～张,不～王。His family name is Zhang, not Wang.

【姓名】xìngmíng 姓和名字 family name and given name; surname and personal name; full name

【姓氏】xìngshì 表明家族的字。姓和氏本有分别,姓起于女系,氏起于男系。后来说姓氏,专指姓。family name; surname; first name; word indicating a family. Originally there is a distinction between 姓 xìng and 氏 shì, the former originating from the female side and the latter from the male side, but now the combination means just 'family name' or 'surname'. X

荇(莕) xìng [荇菜](xìngcài)多年生草本植物,叶子略呈圆形,浮在水面,根生在水底,花黄色,蒴果椭圆形 floatingheart (*Nymphoides peltatum*); perrenial herbaceous plant with slightly round leaves floating on the water, roots growing at the bottom of the water, yellow flowers and elliptical capsules

悻 xìng ☞ below

【悻然】xìngrán 怨恨愤怒的样子 enraged

【悻悻】xìngxìng 怨恨;愤怒 angry; resentful:～而去 go away angrily; leave in a huff

婞 xìng〈书 *fml.*〉倔强固执 stubborn:～直 stubborn; obstinate

xiōng（ㄒㄩㄥ）

凶（❸❹❺❻兇）xiōng ❶ 不幸的（形容死亡、灾难等现象，跟'吉'相对 as opposed to 'auspicious'）inauspicious; ominous：～事 unfortunate events such as death, injury, accident, etc.｜～信 news of sb.'s death ❷ 年成很坏 famine; crop failure：～年 year of crop failure; year of famine ❸ 凶恶 vicious; fierce; ferocious; brutal：穷～极恶 extemely vicious and brutal; ferocious; fierce｜这个人样子真～。This chap looks really fierce. ❹ 厉害 terrible; fearful：病势很～ be terribly ill｜闹得太～。What a terrific row! ❺ 指杀害或伤害人的行为 act of violence; murder：行～ assault; murder ❻ 行凶作恶的人 murderer; criminal：正～ principal criminal｜帮～ accomplice; accessory｜元～ chief culprit; arch criminal; ring leader

【凶案】xiōng'àn 杀害人命的案件 murder case

【凶暴】xiōngbào （性情、行为）凶狠残暴 fierce and brutal (disposition, act)：脾气～ of brutal and bestial temper｜～残忍 brutal and ferocious

【凶残】xiōngcán 凶恶残暴 fierce and cruel; savage and cruel：～成性 be cruel by nature

【凶恶】xiōng'è （性情、行为或相貌）十分可怕 (of temper, appearance or behaviour) fierce; ferocious; fiendish：～的目光 fierce look in the eyes｜～的敌人 ferocious enemies

【凶犯】xiōngfàn 行凶的罪犯 one who has committed homicide or mayhem; murderer：杀人～ murderer

【凶服】xiōngfú 〈书 *fml.*〉丧服、孝衣 mourning apparel

【凶悍】xiōnghàn 凶猛强悍 fierce and tough：为人～ be fierce and tough

【凶耗】xiōnghào 人死亡的消息 news of sb.'s death; death notice

【凶狠】xiōnghěn ❶（性情、行为）凶恶狠毒 fierce and malicious：～的豺狼 ferocious jackals and wolves ❷ 猛烈 powerful; vigorous：扣球～ powerful smashes

【凶横】xiōnghèng 凶恶蛮横 fierce and arrogant; rude and ferocious：满脸～ ferocious features on one's face｜态度粗暴，说话～ speak in a rude and ferocious manner

【凶狂】xiōngkuáng 凶恶猖狂 fierce; savage; ferocious

【凶猛】xiōngměng （气势、力量）凶恶强大 (of force, strength) violent; ferocious：来势～ bear down with a devastating force｜虎豹都是～的野兽。Both tigers and leopards are ferocious beasts.

【凶年】xiōngnián 荒年 year of crop failure or famine; famine year; bad year：～饥岁 year of crop failure; year of famine

【凶虐】xiōngnüè 凶恶暴虐 brutal; tyrannical

【凶气】xiōngqì 凶狠的气势；凶恶的神色 fierce manner; ferocious expression：一脸～ with murder written on one's face

【凶器】xiōngqì 行凶用的器具 tool or weapon for criminal purposes; lethal weapon：杀人～ weapon used in murder or homicide

【凶杀】xiōngshā 杀害人命 homicide; murder：～案 murder case

【凶煞】xiōngshà same as 凶神 xiōngshén

【凶神】xiōngshén 迷信者指凶恶的神，常用来指凶恶的人 demon; fiend：～恶煞 devils; fiends

【凶手】xiōngshǒu 行凶的人 murderer; assassin; assailant (who has caused injury to sb.)

【凶死】xiōngsǐ 指被人杀害或自杀而死 die by violence; meet a violent end; get killed or kill oneself

【凶险】xiōngxiǎn ❶（情势等）危险可怕 dangerous; perilous; critical; fiendish：病情～ dangerously ill; critically ill; in a critical condition｜地势～ dangerous place; perilous terrain ❷ 凶恶阴险 ruthless and treacherous：～的敌人 treacherous enemy

【凶相】xiōngxiàng 凶恶的面目；凶恶的相貌 ferocious features; fierce look; fiendish look：～毕露 look thoroughly ferocious; fully reveal one's ferocity｜一脸的～ look fiendish

【凶信】xiōngxìn （～儿 xiōngxìnr）不好的消息，特指人死亡的消息 news of sb.'s death：报～ tell the news of sb.'s death

【凶焰】xiōngyàn 凶恶的气焰 ferocity; aggressive arrogance

【凶宅】xiōngzhái 不吉利的或闹鬼的房舍（迷信）(superstition) haunted house; unlucky abode

【凶兆】xiōngzhào 不吉祥的预兆（迷信）(superstition) ill omen; boding of evil

兄 xiōng ❶ 哥哥 elder brother：父～ father and elder brothers｜胞～ elder brother of the same parents｜从～ elder male cousin on the father's side ❷ 亲戚中同辈而年纪比自己大的男子 elder male relative of the same generation：表～ elder male cousin on the mother's side ❸ 对男性朋友的尊称 courteous form of address between male friends：仁～ my dear friend

【兄弟】xiōngdì 哥哥和弟弟 brothers; brotherhood：～二人 the two brothers ◇～单位 fraternal units (i.e. units having common purposes, interests, etc.)｜～部队 fraternal army units｜～民族 fraternal ethnic peoples

【兄弟】xiōng·di ❶ 弟弟 younger brother ❷ 称呼年纪比自己小的男子（亲切口气）(familiar form of address for a man younger than oneself) brother ❸〈谦辞 *hum.*〉男子跟辈分相同的人或对众人说话时的自称 [used by a man, usu. in a public speech] I：～我刚到这里，请

多多关照。I'm a new arrival. Please give me more advice.

【兄弟阋墙】xiōngdì xì qiáng《诗经·小雅·常棣》:'兄弟阋于墙。'兄弟在家争吵。后用来比喻内部相争。quarrel between brothers; *The Book of Songs·Odes·Brotherhood*: 'Brothers may fight within; / They fight the foes outside.' (fig.) internal strife

【兄长】xiōngzhǎng ❶ same as 兄 xiōng ① ❷ 对男性朋友的尊称 respectful form of address for one's male friend: 请～指教。You are kindly invited to give advice.

芎 xiōng [芎䓖](xiōngqióng) ☞ 川芎 chuānxiōng on p. 297

匈 xiōng〈书 *fml.*〉same as 胸 xiōng

【匈奴】Xiōngnú 我国古代民族,战国时游牧在燕、赵、秦以北。东汉时分裂为南北两部,北匈奴在一世纪末为汉所败,西迁。南匈奴附汉,东晋时曾先后建立前赵、后赵、夏、北凉等政权。Xiongnu; Huns, an ancient nomadic people in China who roved about north of the states of Yan, Zhao and Qin during the Warring States Period, split into southern and northern groups during the Eastern Han Dynasty. Defeated by the Han Dynasty towards the end of the 1st century, the northern group moved westward, and the southern group submitted to the authority of the Han. During the Eastern Jin Dynasty, the Xiongnus established the Former Zhao, Latter Han, Xia and Nothern Liang regimes.

讻(訩、哅) xiōng [讻讻]〈书 *fml.*〉same as 汹汹 xiōngxiōng ③

汹(洶) xiōng 水向上翻腾 water rushes upward: ～涌 surge

【汹汹】xiōngxiōng ❶〈书 *fml.*〉形容波涛的声音 sound of turbulent waves: 波声～ sound of waves | 波浪～ roaring waves ❷ 形容声势盛大的样子(贬义 derog.) violent; truculent: 气势～ truculent; overbearing; fierce | 来势～ come threateningly towards ❸〈书 *fml.*〉形容争论的声音或纷扰的样子 turbulent; tumultuous; noisy: 议论～ tumultuous debate; heated discussion | 天下～,干戈四起。Fighting broke out all over the country, plunging the nation into chaos. *or* Fighting has broken out all over the country and the whole nation is in upheaval. also 讻讻 xiōngxiōng

【汹涌】xiōngyǒng (水)猛烈地向上涌或向前翻滚 surging; turbulent; tempestuous: ～澎湃 surging; turbulent; tempestuous | 波涛～ turbulent waves

恟(忷) xiōng〈书 *fml.*〉恐惧;惊骇 fear; terror; panic-stricken

胸(胷) xiōng ❶ 躯干的一部分,在颈和腹之间 thorax; chest; breast; bosom; part of the trunk between the neck and the abdomen; (图见 ☞ figure for 身体 shēntǐ on p. 1701) ❷ 指心里(跟思想、见识、气量等有关) mind; heart (related to thinking, knowledge; experience, magnanimity, tolerance, etc.): 心～ mind | ～有成竹 have a ready and well-thought plan; have a ready design in one's mind | ～无点墨 not know a single letter

【胸次】xiōngcì〈书 *fml.*〉❶ 心里;心情 heart; mind; frame of mind: ～舒畅 have ease of mind; feel happy; be in a happy frame of mind ❷ 胸怀 mind: ～宽广 broad-minded

【胸骨】xiōnggǔ 人或高等动物胸腔前面正中央的一根剑形的骨头,两侧与肋骨相连。胸骨、胸椎和肋骨构成胸腔。sternum; breastbone; thin, flat structure of bone and cartilage to which most of the ribs are attached in the front of the chest in most vertebrates. The sternum, thoracic vertebra and costa constitute the thoracic cavity. (图见 ☞ figure for 骨骼 gǔgé on p. 693)

【胸怀】xiōng huái 心里怀着 mind: ～大志 cherish high ideals; have lofty aspirations | ～祖国,放眼世界。Cherish the motherland in mind and have the whole world in view.

【胸怀】xiōnghuái ❶ 胸襟 mind; heart: ～狭窄 narrow-minded | ～坦荡 open-hearted; candid; frank | 宽广的～ broad-minded ❷ 胸部;胸膛 chest; bosom; thorax: 敞着～ bare one's chest

【胸襟】xiōngjīn ❶ 抱负;气量 mind; breadth of mind; ambition; tolerance: 伟大的～ great vision | ～开阔 broad-minded; large-minded ❷ 心胸;心怀 feeling; state of mind; breadth of mind: 荡涤～ cleanse one's mind ❸ 胸部的衣襟 upper front of a jacket: ～上戴着一朵大红花。A big red flower is pinned on (his) chest.

【胸径】xiōngjìng 林业上指树干离地面高 1.3 米处的直径 diameter of a tree trunk taken at 1.3 metres above the ground

【胸口】xiōngkǒu 胸骨下端周围的部分 pit of the stomach; chest; part around the lower end of the breastbone

【胸廓】xiōngkuò 胸部的骨质支架。人的胸廓为圆锥形,由胸椎、肋骨和胸骨构成。bone frame of the chest. The frame of the human chest is cone-shaped. It consists of the thoracic vertebra, costa and sternum.

【胸膜】xiōngmó 包在肺脏表面和贴在胸腔内壁的两层浆膜。这两层薄膜两端连在一起,当中形成囊状的空腔,叫胸膜腔,腔内有少量液体,可以减少两层薄膜的摩擦。pleura; thin serous membrane that covers a lung and lines the chest cavity in mammals; two layers of membranes are linked together at both ends to form a sac with an empty cavity which contains a small amount of fluid to avoid friction between the two membranes. also 肋

膜 lèimó

【胸脯】xiōngpú (～儿 xiōngpúr) 指胸部 chest; breast: 挺着～儿 thrust out one's chest; also 胸脯子 xiōngpú·zi

【胸鳍】xiōngqí 鱼类胸部的鳍,在鳃的后面,左右各一,是鱼类的运动器官 pectoral fin; either of a pair of fins behind the gill of a fish as organs of locomotion; (图见 ☞ figure for 鳍 qí on p.1513)

【胸腔】xiōngqiāng 体腔的一部分,是胸骨、胸椎和肋骨围成的空腔,上部跟颈相连,下部有横膈膜和腹腔隔开。心、肺等器官都在胸腔内。thoracic cavity; chest cavity; part of the body cavity, surrounded by sternum, thoracic vertebra and costa, with its upper part linked with the neck and its lower part separated from the abdomenal cavity by a diaphragm. Both the heart and lungs are located in the thoracic cavity.

【胸墙】xiōngqiáng ❶ 齐胸高的矮墙 chest-high wall; low wall up to the breast ❷ 为了便于射击和减少敌人火力可能造成的损害,在掩体前面和战壕边沿用土堆砌起来的矮墙 breastwork; parapet; low wall or bank built of earth in front of a bunker, emplacement and trench and used for the convenience of shooting or to screen troops from frontal enemy fire

【胸膛】xiōngtáng same as 胸 xiōng ①: 挺起～ throw out one's chest

【胸围】xiōngwéi ❶ 围绕胸部一周的长度 chest measurement; bust ❷ 林业上指树干离地面高 1.3 米处的周长 circumference of the trunk of a tree taken at 1.3 metres above the ground

【胸无点墨】xiōng wú diǎn mò 形容读书太少,文化水平极低 unlearned; unlettered; know not a single letter

X

【胸像】xiōngxiàng 腰部以上的半身人像 bust

【胸臆】xiōngyì 指心里的话或想法 what is deep in one's heart; thoughts or feelings deep in one's heart: 直抒～ pour out one's heart | 倾吐～ pour out one's heart

【胸有成竹】xiōng yǒu chéng zhú 画竹子时心里有一幅竹子的形象(见于宋晁补之诗'与可画竹时,胸中有成竹',与可是宋代画家文同的字) bear the image of bamboo in mind when drawing bamboo. Chao Buzhi of the Song Dynasty wrote in a poem: 'When Yuke paints bamboo, he has the image of bamboo in his mind.' Yuke is the literary name of the painter Wen Tong of the Song Dynasty. 〈比喻 *fig.*〉做事之前已经有通盘的考虑 have a well-thought-out plan, stratagem, etc.; also 成竹在胸 chéng zhú zài xiōng

【胸章】xiōngzhāng ❶ 佩戴在胸前表示身份或职务的标志 badge; identification sign worn on the chest indicating one's status or position ❷ 佩带在胸前的奖章、纪念章等 pin or medal worn on one's chest

【胸中无数】xiōng zhōng wú shù 指对情况和问题了解不够,处理事情没有把握 have inadequate knowledge of the situation and problem and hesitate over how to handle a problem; also 心中无数 xīn zhōng wú shù

【胸中有数】xiōng zhōng yǒu shù 指对情况和问题有基本的了解,处理事情有一定的把握 know the situation and problem, and know how to handle the problem with certainty; also 心中有数 xīn zhōng yǒu shù

【胸椎】xiōngzhuī 胸部的椎骨,共有十二块,较颈椎大 thoracic vertebra: there are twelve thoracic vertebrae, which are bigger than cervical vertebra; (图见 ☞ figure for 骨骼 gǔgé on p.693)

xióng (ㄒㄩㄥˊ)

雄 xióng ❶ 生物中能产生精细胞的(跟'雌'相对 as opposed to 'female') male; organism that produces sperm cells; (of plants) staminate: ～性 male; masculine | ～鸡 cock | ～蕊 stamen ❷ 有气魄的 grand; imposing: ～伟 magnificent; majestic; imposing | ～心 ambition; ambitious | ～姿 heroic posture; magnificent look; majestic appearance ❸ 强有力的 mighty; powerful; forceful: ～兵 powerful army | ～辩 eloquent; convincing ❹ 强有力的人或国家 person or state having great power and influence: 英～ hero; heroine | 战国七～ seven rivalling states of the Warring States Period (475-221 B.C.)

【雄辩】xióngbiàn ❶ 强有力的辩论 convincing argument; eloquent speech: 事实胜于～。Facts speak louder than an eloquent speech. ❷ 有说服力 convincing; eloquent: 最～的莫过于事实。Nothing is more convincing than facts. | 事实～地说明,这项改革是必要的。The facts show eloquently that reform is necessary.

【雄兵】xióngbīng 强有力的军队 powerful army: ～百万 a million bold troops

【雄才大略】xióng cái dà lüè 杰出的才智和谋略 (a man of) great talent and bold vision; (a statesman or general of) rare gifts and bold strategy; extremely capable

【雄大】xióngdà (气魄)雄壮有力 full of power and grandeur

【雄风】xióngfēng ❶〈书 *fml.*〉强劲的风 strong wind ❷ 威风 awe-inspiring bearing; stately appearance: 老将～犹在。The old general is still his heroic former self. | 转战千里,～大振。Having fought here and there for a thousand *li*, the troops have greatly increased its strength and influence.

【雄蜂】xióngfēng 雄性的蜂类。特指雄性的蜜蜂,是由未受精的卵子发育而成的,身体比工蜂大,比母蜂小,头部圆形,没有毒刺,和母蜂交配后,即被工蜂赶出蜂巢。drone; male bee; bee developed from unfertilized egg, bigger than the worker, but smaller than the female, with a round head and without a sting: after mating with the female bee, it is driven out of the honeycomb by the worker

【雄关】xióngguān 险要的关口 impregnable pass:~隘口 impregnable pass

【雄厚】xiónghòu (人力、物力)充足(of strength, resources, etc.) ample; rich; solid; abundant:技术力量~ have a strong technical force|~的资金 abundant funds

【雄花】xiónghuā 只有雄蕊的单性花 male flower; staminate flower

【雄黄】xiónghuáng 矿物,成分是硫化砷,橘黄色,有光泽。用来制农药、染料等,中医入药。realgar; red orpiment; lustrous, orange-yellow mineral of arsenic sulphide, used in making insecticides, dyes, etc., and also as a Chinese medicine; also 鸡冠石 jīguānshí

【雄黄酒】xiónghuángjiǔ 搀有雄黄的烧酒,民间在端午节时饮用 realgar wine; spirit blended with realgar, to be drunk during the Dragon Boat Festival on the 5th day of the 5th lunar month to ward off poisonous creatures or effects

【雄浑】xiónghún 雄健浑厚;雄壮浑厚 vigorous and firm; forceful:笔力~ vigourous or forceful strokes in calligraphy or drawing|音调~,节奏沉稳 in a firm voice and steady rhythm

【雄健】xióngjiàn 强健有力 robust; vigorous; powerful:~的步伐 vigorous strides

【雄杰】xióngjié〈书 *fml*.〉❶ 才能出众 of exceptional ability; of great talent:~之士 man of great talent ❷ 才能出众的人物 man of great talent:一代~ greatest talent of the time

【雄劲】xióngjìn 雄壮有力 vigorous; robust; powerful:气势~ forceful; imposing; powerful

【雄赳赳】xióngjiūjiū (~的 xióngjiūjiū·de)形容威武 valiant; gallant:~,气昂昂 valiantly and in high spirits, and full of mettle

【雄蕊】xióngruǐ 花的主要部分之一,一般由花丝和花药构成。雄蕊成熟后,花药裂开,散出花粉。stamen; one of the principal parts of a flower consisting of fulament and anther. When the stamen ripens, the anther splits and gives out pollen. (图见 ☞ figure for 花 huā on p.826)

【雄师】xióngshī 雄兵 powerful army; mighty army:百万~ one million powerful troops

【雄图】xióngtú 伟大的计划或谋略 great ambition; grandiose plan

【雄威】xióngwēi 雄壮威武 full of power and grandeur; strong and imposing; awe-inspiring

【雄伟】xióngwěi ❶ 雄壮而伟大 grand; imposing and great:气魄~ imposing momentum|~的天安门 magnificent Tian'anmen Square ❷ 魁梧;魁伟 sturdy; robust; stalwart:身材~ tall and sturdy; of great stature

【雄心】xióngxīn 远大的理想和抱负 great ambitions; lofty aspirations:~壮志 lofty aspirations and high ideals|~勃勃 very ambitious

【雄性】xióngxìng 生物两性之一,能产生精子 male; one of the sexes that produces sperm:~动物 male animal

【雄主】xióngzhǔ 有雄才大略的君主 monarch of great talent and bold vision

【雄壮】xióngzhuàng ❶ (气魄、声势)强大 full of power and grandeur; magnificent; majestic:~的步伐 powerful strides|歌声~,响彻云霄。The majestic and loud singing resounds throughout the skies. ❷ (身体)魁梧强壮 sturdy; stalwart; robust:身材~ tall and stalwart

【雄姿】xióngzī 威武雄壮的姿态 majestic appearance; heroic posture:~英发 majestic and spirited; dashing and debonair|晨曦中,山海关城楼的~隐约可见。The imposing gate tower of Shanhai Pass was dimly visible in the first rays of the morning.

熊1 xióng ❶ 哺乳动物,头大,尾巴短,四肢短而粗,脚掌大,趾端有带钩的爪,能爬树。主要吃动物性食物,也吃水果、坚果等。种类很多,如棕熊、白熊、黑熊。bear (*Ursus*); mammal with a big head, a short tail, four short and bold limbs, big soles with hooked claws at the ends of the toes, capable of climbing trees, feeding mainly on animal meat, fruits and nuts. There are many kinds of bears, as brown bear, polar bear and black bear. ❷ (Xióng) 姓 a surname

熊2 xióng〈方 *dial*.〉❶ 斥责 rebuke; upbraid; scold:挨~ got a scolding|~了他一顿 give him a scolding ❷ 怯懦;没有能力 coward; timid; impotent:你也真~,一上阵就败了下来。How impotent you are! You were defeated just as you went into action.

【熊包】xióngbāo〈方 *dial*.〉讥称懦弱、无能的人 good-for-nothing; coward

【熊猫】xióngmāo ☞ 猫熊 māoxióng on p.1305

【熊瞎子】xióngxiā·zi〈方 *dial*.〉熊 bear

【熊熊】xióngxióng 形容火势旺盛 flaming; ablaze; raging:~的烈火 raging flames|大火~ blazing fire; raging fire

【熊腰虎背】xióng yāo hǔ bèi ☞ 虎背熊腰 hǔ bèi xióng yāo on p.821

xiòng (ㄒㄩㄥˋ)

诇 xiòng〈书 *fml*.〉刺探 reconnoitre; scout; pry; spy:~察(侦察) scout; reconnoitre

敻 xiòng〈书 *fml.*〉❶ 远;遥远 far; remote; distant:～若千里。It's so far as if you were a thousand *li* away. ❷ 久远 long long ago:～古 in remote antiquity

xiū(ㄒㄧㄡ)

休[1] xiū ❶ 停止;罢休(事情) cease; give up; stop:～会 adjourn|争论不～ argue endlessly ❷ 休息 rest:～养 recuperate; convalesce|～假 have days off; have a holiday; have a vacation|退～ retire ❸〈旧时 *old*〉指丈夫把妻子赶回娘家,断绝夫妻关系 terminate a marriage by sending one's wife packing:～妻 put one's wife away; discard one's wife; divorce one's wife|～书 divorce paper ❹〈副词 *adv.*〉表示禁止或劝阻(多见于早期白话 usu. in early vernacular)[indicating prohibition or dissuasion] don't:～得无理。Don't be rude. *or* Don't be unreasonable.|闲话～提。No more of this digression.|～要胡言乱语。Don't talk nonsense!

休[2] xiū〈书 *fml.*〉吉庆;欢乐 good fortune; rejoicing:～咎(吉凶) good and ill luck; weal and woe|～戚 fortune and misfortune; weal and woe; joys and sorrows

【休会】xiū//huì 会议在进行期间暂时停止开会 adjourn; close a session or a meeting for a time:～一天 adjourn the meeting for one day

【休假】xiū//jià 按照规定或经过批准后,停止一定时期的工作或学习(of workers, students, etc.) have (or take, go on) a holiday or vacation; (of soldiers, personnel working abroad, etc.) be on leave of absence:因病～ be on sick leave|休了一个月假 had a leave of one month

【休克】xiūkè ❶ 临床上常见的一种细胞急性缺氧综合症。主要症状是血压下降,血流减慢,四肢发冷,脸色苍白,体温下降,神志淡漠等。shock; common syndrome of acute oxygen deficiency in cells, characterized by a decrease in blood pressure, ineffective blood circulation, cold limbs, pale face, drop in the body temperature and apathetic look ❷ 发生休克 shock:因为流血过多,他已经～了。He has lost consciousness due to the excessive shedding of blood.

【休眠】xiūmián 某些生物为了适应环境的变化,生命活动几乎到了停止的状态,如蛇到冬季就不吃不动,植物的芽在冬季停止生长等 dormancy; be torpid in winter; in a state of suspended animation. In order to adapt themselves to the changes of the environments, certain animals and plants have almost suspended their animation, as snakes become torpid in winter and the buds stop growing in winter.

【休眠火山】xiūmián huǒshān 历史上曾经活动过,长期以来处于静止状态,但仍有可能喷发的火山 dormant volcano; once active volcano that has been in a static state but may still erupt; also 休火山 xiūhuǒshān

【休戚】xiūqī 欢乐和忧愁。泛指有利的和不利的遭遇 weal and woe; joys and sorrows:～相关(彼此间祸福互相关联) share joys and sorrows; be bound together by common interests|～与共(同甘共苦) share weal and woe; stand together through thick and thin

【休憩】xiūqì 休息 have (or take) a rest; rest:路边设有坐椅,供行人～。Benches are installed by roadsides for pedestrians who want to take a rest.

【休息】xiū·xi 暂时停止工作、学习或活动 take a breather; have (or take) a rest; rest:走累了,找个地方～～。We are tired after a walk. Let's find a place for a rest.|既要有紧张的工作,又要有适当的～。(We) should work hard on the one hand, and have proper rest on the other.

【休闲】xiūxián ❶ 休息;过清闲生活 have a leisure life:～场所 leisure place ❷(可耕地)闲着,一季或一年不种作物 lie fallow:～地 fallow (land)

【休想】xiūxiǎng 别想,不要妄想 don't imagine that it's possible:～逃脱。Don't imagine you can get away.|你要骗人,～! Don't imagine you can deceive people!

【休学】xiū//xué 学生因故不能继续学习,经学校同意,暂停学习,仍保留学籍,叫做休学 suspend one's schooling without losing one's status as a student

【休养】xiūyǎng ❶ 休息调养 recuperate; convalesce:～所 sanatorium; rest home|他到北戴河～去了。He has gone to Beidaihe for recuperation. ❷ 恢复并发展国家或人民的经济力量 revive and develop the economic strength of the state or the people:～民力 give people time to rest and recuperate

【休养生息】xiūyǎng shēngxī 指在国家大动荡或大变革以后,减轻人民负担,安定生活,发展生产,恢复元气 rest and build up strength; rejuvenate a nation from the aftermaths of a major turmoil by lessening the people's financial burdens, restoring order to life, and developing production

【休业】xiū//yè ❶ 停止营业 suspend business; be closed down:～整顿 closed for shake-up ❷ 学习单位结束一个阶段的学习(of a short-term course, etc.) come to an end; wind up

【休战】xiū//zhàn 交战双方签订协定,暂时停止军事行动 truce; cease-fire; armistice; temporary stopping of warfare following the signing of an agreement between the belligerent parties

【休整】xiūzhěng 休息整顿(多用于军队 of

troops) rest and reorganization：利用战斗空隙进行～(of troops) seize a lull in the fighting for a rest and consolidation

【休止】xiūzhǐ 停止 stop; cease; measured interval of silence between tones：这座火山已进入～状态。The volcano is inactive.

【休止符】xiūzhǐfú 乐谱中用来表示音乐停顿时间长短的符号 rest; any of various symbols indicating the length of a measured interval of silence between tones

咻 xiū〈书 *fml.*〉吵；乱说话；喧扰 make a din

【咻咻】xiūxiū〈拟声词 *onom.*〉❶ 形容喘气的声音 sound of heavy breathing：～的鼻息 noisy breathing｜～地喘气 pant noisily ❷ 形容某些动物的叫声 sound made by certain birds and animals：小鸭～地叫着。The ducklings are cheeping.

修[1] xiū ❶ 修饰 embellish; decorate：装～ paint and decorate; fit up a house or apartment; fit up the interior of a house; fix up; interior decoration｜～辞 rhetoric ❷ 修理；整治 repair; mend; overhaul：～车 repair a vehicle｜～桥补路 build bridges and repair roads｜一定要把淮河～好。We must harness the Huaihe River well. ❸ 写；编写 write; compile：～函 write a letter｜～史 compile history｜～县志 compile the historical and other records of a county ❹（学问、品行方面）学习和锻炼（of learning, character, conduct, etc.）study; cultivate：～养 cultivate｜～业 study at school｜进～ advanced study ❺ 修行（迷信）(superstition) practise Buddhism or Taoism：～炼(of Taoists) practise austerities; practise asceticism｜～仙 train and cultivate oneself to attain immortality ❻ 兴建；建筑 build; construct：～建 build｜～水库 build a reservoir｜新～了一条铁路。A new railway has been built. ❼ 剪或削，使整齐 trim; prune：～树枝 prune a tree｜～指甲 trim (or manicure) fingernails ❽ 指修正主义 revisionism：反～防～ fight and prevent revisionism ❾（Xiū）姓 a surname

修[2] xiū〈书 *fml.*〉长；高 long; tall and slender：～长 tall and slender｜～竹 tall bamboo

【修补】xiūbǔ ❶ 修理破损的东西使完好 do up; mend; fix up; patch up; repair; revamp：～轮胎 mend a tyre｜～渔网 mend a fishing net ❷ 有机体的组织发生损耗时，由体内的蛋白质来补充叫修补 repair; when a loss is caused to the tissues of an organism, it is replenished by the protein in its body

【修长】xiūcháng 细长 tall and thin; slender：～身材 slender figure

【修辞】xiūcí 修饰文字词句，运用各种表现方式，使语言表达得准确、鲜明而生动有力 rhetoric; effective use of words to make the language accurate, clear-cut, vivid and forceful by various ways of expression

【修辞格】xiūcígé 各种修辞方式，如比喻、对偶、排比等 figures of speech, such as metaphor, antithesis, parallelism, etc.

【修辞学】xiūcíxué 语言学的一个部门，研究如何使语言表达得准确、鲜明而生动有力 rhetoric; branch of phonetics dealing with the accurate, clear, vivid and effective use of words in writing and speaking

【修道院】xiūdàoyuàn 天主教和东正教等教徒出家修道的机构。在天主教会中，也指培养神甫的机构。monastery or convent; establishment where Catholics and followers of the Eastern Orthodox Church cultivate themselves in the religions. In the Catholic Church, these places are also where priests are trained.

【修订】xiūdìng 修改订正（书籍、计划等）amend; revise (books, plans, etc.)：～本 revised edition｜～教学计划 revise a teaching plan

【修短】xiūduǎn〈书 *fml.*〉长短 length：～合度 of moderate height; neither too tall nor too short

【修复】xiūfù ❶ 修理使恢复完整（多指建筑物 buildings）repair; restore; renovate：～河堤 repair a river dyke｜～铁路 repair a railway ◇～两国关系 restore or repair the relations between the two countries ❷ 有机体的组织发生缺损时，由新生的组织来补充使恢复原来的形态 repair (of destroyed cells or tissues); replacement of destroyed cells or tissues by new cells or tissues to restore it to the original form

【修改】xiūgǎi 改正文章、计划等里面的错误、缺点 revise; modify; amend; alter; change the mistakes, errors or defects in an article, plan, etc.：～初稿 revise a draft｜～章程 revise a charter｜～计划 revise a plan

【修盖】xiūgài 修建（房屋）build (houses)：～教学楼 build a classroom building

【修函】xiū//hán〈书 *fml.*〉写信 write a letter

【修好】xiū//hǎo〈方 *dial.*〉行好；行善 do good deeds：～积德 do good deeds｜你修修好吧，再宽限几天。Do me a favour by giving me a few days' grace, won't you?

【修好】xiūhǎo〈书 *fml.*〉亲善友好 foster cordial relations between states：两国～ cultivate cordial relations between two countries

【修剪】xiūjiǎn ❶ 用剪子修（枝叶、指甲等）prune; trim; clip (trees, fingernails, etc.)：～果树 prune fruit trees ❷ 修改剪接 change and cut：～影片 film editing; montage

【修建】xiūjiàn（土木工程）施工 build; construct; erect (civil engineering projects)：～铁路 build (or construct) a railway

【修脚】xiū//jiǎo 修剪脚趾甲或削去脚上的趼子

pedicure; trim the toenails or cut off the thick callus on the feet

【修旧利废】xiū jiù lì fèi 修理和利用废旧物品，使再发挥作用 repair and utilize old or discarded things

【修浚】xiūjùn 修理疏通 dredge：～河道 dredge a river

【修理】xiūlǐ ❶ 使损坏的东西恢复原来的形状或作用 repair; mend; overhaul; fix：～厂 repair shop; fix-it shop|～机车 overhaul a locomotive ❷ same as 修剪 xiūjiǎn ①; same as 整治 zhěngzhì ①：～树木 prune a tree ❸〈方 *dial.*〉same as 整治 zhěngzhì ②：把他～一顿。He was given a scolding. *or* He was taken to task.

【修炼】xiūliàn 指道家修养练功、炼丹等活动（of Taoists）practise austerities; practise asceticism; engage in alchemy to make pills of immortality

【修面】xiū//miàn〈方 *dial.*〉刮脸 shave; have a shave

【修明】xiūmíng〈书 *fml.*〉指政治清明（of a government）honest and enlightened

【修女】xiūnǚ 天主教或东正教中出家修道的女子（of Roman Catholic and Greek Orthodox churches）nun; sister

【修配】xiūpèi 修理机器等的损坏部分和配齐其中残缺的零件 make repairs and supply replacements

【修葺】xiūqì 修缮 repair; renovate：房屋～一新。The house has taken on a new look after renovation. *or* The house has been completely renovated.

【修缮】xiūshàn 修理（建筑物）repair; renovate：～厂房 repair houses

【修身】xiūshēn 指努力提高自己的品德修养 cultivate one's moral character：～养性 cultivate one's moral character and develop one's temperament

【修史】xiūshǐ〈书 *fml.*〉编写史书 compile or write history：直笔～ write history in a straightforward (or unprejudiced) way

【修士】xiūshì 天主教或东正教中出家修道的男子 monk (of the Roman Catholic and Greek Orthodox churches); brother; friar

【修饰】xiūshì ❶ 修整装饰使整齐美观 decorate; adorn; embellish：～一新 newly decorated ❷ 梳妆打扮 make up and dress up：略加～，就显得很利落。One should look quite neat with a little make-up. ❸ 修改润饰，使语言文字明确生动 polish (a piece of writing)：你把这篇稿子再～一下。Please polish this piece of writing.

【修书】xiū//shū〈书 *fml.*〉❶ 编纂书籍 compile a book ❷ 写信 write a letter：～一封 write a letter

【修仙】xiū//xiān 炼丹服药，安神养性，以求长生不老（迷信）(superstition) make pills and take them orally, calm the nerves and cultivate oneself to attain immortality

【修行】xiū·xíng 佛教徒或道教徒虔诚地学习教义，并照着教义去实行 practise Buddhism or Taoism by studying and following the tenets piously：出家～ become a Buddhist or Taoist monk or nun

【修养】xiūyǎng ❶ 指理论、知识、艺术、思想等方面的一定水平 accomplishment; training; mastery in theory, knowledge, art, ideology, etc.：理论～ mastery of theories|文学～ grounding in literature; literary taste|他是一个很有～的艺术家。He is an artist of high accomplishment (or a highly accomplished artist). ❷ 指养成的正确的待人处事的态度 accomplishment in self-cultivation; self-possession：这人有～，从不和人争吵。This man is really self-possessed, and never argues or quarrels with others.

【修业】xiūyè（学生）在校学习 study at school：～期满 one's term of schooling completed

【修造】xiūzào ❶ 修理并制造 build and repair：～农具 build and repair farm tools|～船只 build or repair ships ❷ 建造 build：～厂房 build factory premises|～花园 build a garden

【修整】xiūzhěng 修理，整治 repair and maintain：～农具 repair and maintain farm implements|～果树 prune fruit trees

【修正】xiūzhèng ❶ 修改使正确 revise; amend; correct：～错误 correct one's mistakes|最后核对材料，～了一些数字 revised some figures after checking the data ❷ 篡改（马克思列宁主义）revise; mutilate Marxism-Leninism

【修正主义】xiūzhèng zhǔyì 国际共产主义运动中披着马克思主义外衣的反马克思主义的思潮 revisionism; anti-Marxist trend in the disguise of Marxism in the international communist movement

【修筑】xiūzhù 修建（道路、工事等）(of roads, tools, etc.) build; construct; put up：～机场 build an airport|～码头 build a dock|～拦河坝 build a dam across a river

庥 xiū〈书 *fml.*〉庇荫；保护 protect; shelter; shield

脩[1] xiū〈旧时 *old*〉送给老师的薪金（原义为干肉，古代弟子用来送给老师做见面礼）dried meat as gift to a teacher in lieu of tuition：～金 tuition fee|束～ tuition fee

脩[2] xiū same as 修 xiū

羞[1] xiū ❶ 怕别人笑话的心理和表情；难为情；不好意思 shy; bashful：怕～ be shy; feel shy|害～ feel bashful; feel shy|～得低下了头 (She) lowered her head in great shyness. ❷ 使难为情 make sb. feel ashamed or embarrassed：用手指划着脸～他 shame sb. by stroking his face with a finger ❸ 羞耻 shame; disgrace：遮～ cover up one's embarrassment|～

辱 disgrace ❹ 感到耻辱 feel ashamed：～与为伍 feel ashamed to have such a friend

羞[2] xiū 〈书 *fml.*〉 same as 馐 xiū

【羞惭】xiūcán 羞愧 be ashamed：满面～ be shamefaced

【羞耻】xiūchǐ 不光彩；不体面 sense of shame; shame：不知～ lose all sense of shame

【羞答答】xiūdādā（～的 xiūdādā·de）形容害羞 coy; shy; bashful：姑娘低着头，～的不说话。The girl lowered her head in bashful silence. also 羞羞答答 xiūxiūdādā

【羞愤】xiūfèn 羞愧和愤恨 ashamed and resentful：一脸的～ extremely ashamed and resentful

【羞口】xiūkǒu 难以启齿；不好意思说 find it difficult to bring the matter up：他想说，可又感到～。He wanted to say, but found it difficult to open his mouth.

【羞愧】xiūkuì 感到羞耻和惭愧 ashamed; abashed：～难言 be ashamed beyond words

【羞赧】xiūnǎn 〈书 *fml.*〉因害臊而红了脸的样子 blush with shyness

【羞怯】xiūqiè 羞涩胆怯 shy; timid; sheepish：孩子见了生人还有几分～。The child still felt shy when he saw a stranger.

【羞人】xiū//rén 感觉难为情或羞耻 feel embarrassed or ashamed：羞死人了 simply die of shame; feel terribly embarrassed｜这话说出来多～！What a shame to say such words!

【羞人答答】xiūréndādā（～的 xiūréndādā·de）形容自己感觉难为情 feel shy or awkward

【羞辱】xiūrǔ ❶ 耻辱 shame; dishonour; humiliation：受尽～ greatly humiliated ❷ 使受耻辱 humiliate; put sb. to shame：～了他一顿 put him to shame

【羞臊】xiūsào 害臊；害羞 feel shy; feel ashamed

【羞涩】xiūsè 难为情，态度不自然 shy; bashful; embarrassed：他站在同学们中间，～地看着大家。He stood among his classmates and looked bashfully at them.

【羞恶】xiūwù 〈书 *fml.*〉对自己或别人的坏处感觉羞耻和厌恶 be ashamed of and disgusted with one's own or other people's faults：～之心 sense of shame

【羞与为伍】xiū yǔ wéi wǔ 把跟某人在一起以为是羞耻的事情 feel ashamed to have such a friend; feel ashamed to associate with sb.; think it beneath one to associate with sb.

鸺 xiū [鸺鹠]（xiūliú）鸟，羽毛棕褐色，有横斑，尾巴黑褐色，腿部白色。外形跟鸱鸺相似，但头部没有角状的羽毛。捕食鼠、兔等，对农业有益。barred owlet (*Glaucidium capense*); bird having dark brown feathers with horizontal spots, black-brown tail and white legs, similar to collared scops-owl in form but having no horn-shaped feathers on its head, feeding on rodents, rabits, etc. and therefore deemed good to farm crops; also 枭 xiāo

貅 xiū ☞ 貔貅（píxiū）on p.1468

馐 xiū 〈书 *fml.*〉滋味好的食物 delicacy; dainty：珍～ rare delicacies

髹(髤) xiū 把漆涂在器物上 coat sth. with lacquer

蟾 xiū ☞ 竹节虫 zhújiéchóng ① on p.2501

xiǔ（ㄒㄧㄡˇ）

朽 xiǔ ❶ 腐烂（多指木头 oft. of wood）rotten; decayed：～木 withered trees｜这根柱子～了。This pillar has been decayed. ◇永垂不～ eternal glory to... ❷ 衰老 age; senile：老～ old and useless

【朽败】xiǔbài 朽坏 decayed; rotten：～不堪 extremely rotten

【朽坏】xiǔhuài 腐朽毁坏 decayed; rotten：门窗～。The doors and windows are decayed.

【朽烂】xiǔlàn 腐朽；朽坏 rotten：木头～ rotten wood

【朽迈】xiǔmài 〈书 *fml.*〉 same as 老朽 lǎoxiǔ ①

【朽木】xiǔmù ❶ 烂木头 rotten wood or tree：～枯株 rotten wood and withered trees ❷〈比喻 *fig.*〉不可造就的人 hopeless case; good-for-nothing：～粪土 rotten wood and worthless soil; worthless person; useless stuff

宿 xiǔ 〈量词 *classifier*〉用于计算夜 [used for counting nights]：住了一～ stay for one night｜谈了半～ chat till midnight｜三天两～ three days and two nights｜整～没睡觉 didn't sleep for the whole night

滫 xiǔ 〈书 *fml.*〉臭泔水 stinking pigwash

xiù（ㄒㄧㄡˋ）

秀[1] xiù 植物抽穗开花（多指庄稼）(of grain crops, etc.) put forth flowers or ears：～穗 put forth ears｜六月六，看谷（粟）～。The 6th day of the 6th lunar month sees millet putting forth ears.

秀[2] xiù ❶ 清秀 elegant; beautiful：～丽 beautiful; handsome; pretty｜眉清目～ fine eyebrows and beautiful eyes｜山清水～ beautiful mountains and limpid waters｜～外慧中 beautiful and intelligent ❷ 聪明；灵巧 clever; intelligent：内～ clever without showing it; one's inner wisdom｜心～ bright without seemingly so ❸ 特别优异 excellent：优～ excellent ❹ 特别优异的人才 excellent talent; outstanding person：新～ newly emerging tal-

X

ent|后起之～ young promising person

【秀才】xiù·cai ❶ 明清两代生员的通称 *xiucai*, one who passed the imperial examination at the county level in the Ming and Qing dynasties ❷ 泛指读书人 (in a broad sense) scholar; skilful writer

【秀丽】xiùlì 清秀美丽 beautiful; handsome; pretty:容貌～ pretty look|～的桂林山水 beautiful mountains and waters of Guilin

【秀美】xiùměi 清秀美丽 graceful; elegant:仪容～ elegant looks|山川～ beautiful mountains and waters

【秀媚】xiùmèi 秀丽妩媚 pretty and charming; lovely:容貌姣好～ beautiful and pretty appearance

【秀气】xiù·qi ❶ 清秀 delicate; elegant; fine:眉眼长得很～ have beautiful eyes|他的字写得很～。He writes a beautiful hand. ❷ (言谈、举止)文雅 (of manners) refined; urbane ❸ (器物)小巧灵便 (of article of use) handy; exquisite:这把小刀儿做得真～。The knife is elegantly crafted.

【秀色】xiùsè 美好的景色或容貌 beautiful scenery or appearance:丽姿～ beautiful looks

【秀色可餐】xiùsè kě cān 形容女子姿容非常美丽或景物非常优美 be a feast to the eye (usu. said of a very attractive woman or beautiful scenery)

【秀外慧中】xiù wài huì zhōng 容貌秀美,资质聪慧(多指女子 usu. of women) beautiful and intelligent; 慧 also put as 惠 huì

【秀雅】xiùyǎ 秀丽雅致;秀丽文雅 tasteful and refined; graceful; elegant

【秀逸】xiùyì 秀丽而洒脱;俊逸 elegant and free; handsome and liberal:风姿～ elegant and free demenour|书法～ beautiful and free writing|诗句清新～。The lines are fresh and beautiful.

岫 xiù 〈书 *fml.*〉❶ 山洞 cave; cavern:白云出～。A white cloud floated out of the cave. ❷ 山 mountain peak; mountain:远～ distant peaks

臭 xiù ❶ 气味 odour; smell:乳～ smelling of milk; childish|空气是无色无～的气体。Air is a colourless and odourless gas. ❷ same as 嗅 xiù

☞ chòu on p. 280

袖 xiù ❶ (～儿 xiùr)袖子 sleeve:～口 cuff (of a sleeve)|短～儿 short sleeves ❷ 藏在袖子里 tuck inside the sleeve:～着手 hands tucked deep in the sleeves|～手旁观 stand by indifferently; look on with folded arms

【袖标】xiùbiāo 一种戴在袖子上的标志 armband or badge worn on the sleeve for identification

【袖管】xiùguǎn ❶ 袖子 sleeve ❷ 〈方 *dial.*〉袖口 cuff (of a sleeve)

【袖箭】xiùjiàn 藏在衣袖里暗中射人的箭,借着弹簧的力量发射 dart hidden in the sleeve (for throwing by a spring device)

【袖口】xiùkǒu (～儿 xiùkǒur)袖子的边缘 cuff (of a sleeve)

【袖手旁观】xiù shǒu páng guān 〈比喻 *fig.*〉置身事外或不协助别人 look on (or stand by) with folded arms; look on unconcerned

【袖筒】xiùtǒng (～儿 xiùtǒngr) same as 袖子 xiù·zi

【袖章】xiùzhāng 套在袖子上表示身份或职务的标志 armband; sleeve badge; cloth band worn around the upper arm as a symbol of status or position

【袖珍】xiùzhēn 体积较小便于携带的 pocket-size; pocket:～本 pocket edition|～词典 pocket dictionary|～收音机 pocket radio

【袖子】xiù·zi 衣服的套在胳膊上的筒状部分 sleeve; that part of a garment that covers an arm or part of an arm

绣(繡) xiù ❶ 用彩色丝、绒、棉线在绸、布等上面做成花纹、图像或文字 embroider; use colour silk, woollen or cotton threads to ornament a fabric with a design, picture or words in needlework:刺～ embroidery|～花儿 embroider a flower|～字 embroider Chinese characters ❷ 绣成的物品 embroidery:苏～ Suzhou embroidery|湘～ Hunan embroidery

【绣房】xiùfáng 〈旧指 *old*〉青年女子住的房间 young lady's bedchamber

【绣花】xiù//huā (～儿 xiù//huār)绣出图画或图案 embroider; do embroidery; embroider a picture or a design

【绣花鞋】xiùhuāxié same as 绣鞋 xiùxié

【绣花枕头】xiùhuā zhěn·tou 〈比喻 *fig.*〉徒有外表而无学识才能的人。也比喻外表好看而质量不好的货物。pillow with an embroidered case; outwardly attractive but worthless person

【绣球】xiùqiú 用绸子结成的球形装饰物 colourful ball made of rolled silk

【绣像】xiùxiàng ❶ 绣成的人像 tapestry portrait; embroidered portrait ❷ 指画工细致的人像 exquisitely drawn portrait:～小说(卷首插有绣像的通俗小说) popular novel inserted with portraits of characters

【绣鞋】xiùxié 妇女穿的绣着花的鞋 embroidered shoes

琇 xiù 〈书 *fml.*〉像玉的石头 jade-like stone

宿 xiù 我国古代天文学家把天上某些星的集合体叫做宿 ancient Chinese astronomical term for constellation:星～ constellation|二十八～ 28 constellations

锈(銹) xiù ❶ 铜、铁等金属表面在潮湿空气中氧化形成的物质 rust; matter formed by oxidation on the surface of copper, iron or other metals during exposure to air and moisture ❷ 生锈 become rusty：刀刃都～了。The blade is rusty.｜锁～住了，开不开。The lock is rusty and cannot be opened. ❸ 指锈病 rust：查～灭～。Find out the rust and eliminate it.

【锈斑】xiùbān ❶ 金属器物上生锈形成的斑痕 rusty traces formed on metalwork：刀上生了～。The knife has gone rusty. ❷ 植物的叶子和茎上因锈病而出现的铁锈色的斑点 rust spots on the leaves or stems of plants

【锈病】xiùbìng 由真菌引起的植物病害。发生病害的植物叶子和茎出现铁锈色的斑点，产量受到影响。plant disease caused by fungus. If the leaves and stems of plants are infected with the disease and have rusty spots, the yield is affected.

【锈蚀】xiùshí （金属）因生锈而腐蚀 corroded by rust; spoilt by rust：铁环～了。The iron rings are eroded by rust.｜古钟上文字清晰，没有～。The characters on the ancient bell are distinct. There is no rust erosion on it.

嗅 xiù 用鼻子辨别气味；闻 smell; scent; sniff by nose：～觉 sense of smell｜小狗在他腿上～来～去。The small dog sniffed about his legs.

【嗅觉】xiùjué 鼻腔黏膜与某些物质的气体分子相接触时所产生的感觉 sense of smell; sense produced when the mucous membrane of the nose cavity contacts the gaseous elements of certain matters：～灵敏 sharp sense of smell ◇政治～ political sense

【嗅神经】xiùshénjīng 第一对脑神经，从大脑的前下部发出，分布在鼻黏膜中，主管嗅觉 olfactory nerve; either of the first pair of cranial nerves that arise in the mucous membranes within the upper part of the nose and transmit impulses concerned with the sense of smell to the forebrain

溴 xiù 非金属元素，符号 Br（bromium）。暗棕红色发烟液体，有刺激性气味，化学性质较活泼。对皮肤和黏膜有强烈的腐蚀性。用来制染料、药品等。bromine (Br); nonmetalic chemical element usu. in the form of a dark redish-brown, corrosive liquid that has an unpleasant odour and is irritating to mucous membranes, used in making dyes, medicines, etc.

亵（褏） xiù 〈书 *fml.*〉 same as 袖 xiù

xū（ㄒㄩ）

讦 xū 〈书 *fml.*〉 ❶ 夸口 boast; brag; exaggerate ❷ 大 big; large：～谟（大计）grand plan

圩（墟） xū 湘、赣、闽、粤等地区称集市（古书中作'虚' put as 虚 xū in ancient books）country fair in Hunan, Jiangxi, Fujian, Guangdong, etc.：～市 country fair｜赶～ go to a fair｜～镇 country town
☞ wéi on p. 1990

【圩场】xūcháng 〈方 *dial.*〉集市 country fair; market

【圩日】xūrì 〈方 *dial.*〉集日 market day; also 圩期 xūqī

戌 xū 地支的第十一位 the 11th of the 12 Earthly Branches; ☞ 干支 gānzhī on p. 627
☞ ·qu on p. 1594

【戌时】xūshí 旧式计时法指晚上七点钟到九点钟的时间 time of the day from 7 p. m. to 9 p. m. in the old Chinese time measurement

吁 xū 〈书 *fml.*〉 ❶ 叹气 sigh：长～短叹 sigh and grown; moan and groan; sign ❷〈叹词 *interj.*〉表示惊异［expressing surprise or amazement］why; oh：～，是何言欤！Oh, what do you mean?
☞ yū on p. 2335 and yù on p. 2348

【吁吁】xūxū 〈拟声词 *onom.*〉形容出气的声音 sound of panting：气喘～ pant; puff hard

盱 xū 〈书 *fml.*〉睁开眼睛向上看 look up with eyes wide open

砉 xū 〈书 *fml.*〉皮骨相离的声音 sound of tearing the skin from the bone：～然嚮（响）然，奏刀騞（huō）然（见《庄子·养生主》）。the loud sound of tearing the skin from the bone, and the cracking sound of cutting with a knife (see *Zhuangzi · Nourishment of the Soul*)
☞ huā on p. 831

须[1] xū ❶ 须要 must; have to：务～ make sure to; be sure to; must; it is essential to｜必～ must, have to; it is imperative to; it is necessary to｜～知 notice; instructions; points for attention; guide｜事前～做好准备。Preparations must be made beforehand. ❷（Xū）姓 a surname

须[2] xū 〈书 *fml.*〉等待；等到 wait; await

须[3]**（鬚）** xū ❶ 原来指长在下巴上的胡子，后来泛指胡须 beard; mustache：～发 beard and hair｜～眉 beard and eyebrows; a man ❷ 须子 palpus; feeler：触～ cirrus; vibrissa; palp; barbel｜花～ pistil; stamen; tassel

【须发】xūfà 胡须和头发 beard and hair：～皆白 white hair and beard

【须根】xūgēn 根的一种，这种根没有明显的主根，只有许多细长像胡须的根。一般单子叶植物都有须根，如小麦、稻等。fibrous root; kind of root which has no main root, but many fibrous roots like mustache. Generally speaking, monocotyledons all have fibrous roots, as wheat, rice, etc.

【须鲸】xūjīng 鲸的一类，没有牙齿，有鲸须，吃甲壳动物和小鱼。如长须鲸、蓝鲸等。baleen whale (*Cetacea*); toothless whale; whale with baleen, but without teeth, as finback, blue whale etc., feeding on crustaceans and small fishes

【须眉】xūméi ❶ 胡须和眉毛 beard and eyebrows:～皆白的老人 old man with white beard and eyebrows ❷ 指男子 man:堂堂～ dignified man; man enough; real man|巾帼不让～。Women are equal with men. *or* Women are by no means inferior to men.

【须弥座】xūmízuò ❶ 指佛像的底座 Sumeru throne; pedestal of Buddha's statue ❷ 指佛塔、佛殿等的一种底座 base of Buddhist pagoda, Buddhist temple, etc.[须弥 *xumi*:古印度神话中的高山名 name of a high mountain in ancient Indian mythology; 梵 Sanskrit: Sumeru]

【须生】xūshēng ☞ 老生 lǎoshēng on p.1160

【须要】xūyào 一定要 must; have to:教育儿童～耐心。One must be patient in educating children.

【须臾】xūyú 〈书 *fml*.〉极短的时间;片刻 moment; instant:～不可离 cannot do without even for a moment|～之间,雨过天晴。In an instant the rain stopped and the sky cleared up.

【须知】xūzhī ❶ 对所从事的活动必须知道的事项(多用做通告或指导性文件的名称 oft. used in titles of notices or guidance documents) notice; announcement; points for attention:游览～tourist guide; information for tourists|考试～ instructions on examination|大会～ conference guide ❷ 一定要知道:must know; must be aware:～胜利来之不易。One must be aware that victory is hard to come by.

【须子】xū·zi 动植物体上长的像须的东西 palpus; feeler:白薯～ hair of sweet potato

胥 1 xū ❶〈书 *fml*.〉胥吏(小官吏) petty official ❷ (Xū)姓 a surname

胥 2 xū 〈书 *fml*.〉齐;皆 all; each and every:万事～备。Everything is ready.

顼 Xū 姓 a surname

虚 xū ❶ 空虚(跟'实'相对 as opposed to 'full') empty; void:～幻 unreal; illusory|～浮 impractical; superficial|乘～而入 break through at a weak point ❷ 空着 empty; void; unoccupied:～位以待 leave a seat vacant for sb. ❸ 因心里惭愧或没有把握而勇气不足 diffident; timid:胆～ timid; milk-livered|心里有点～ feel rather diffident ❹ 徒然;白白地 in vain:～度 spend one's time by doing nothing|箭不～发。Not a single arrow missed its target.|不～此行。The visit is fruitful. ❺ 虚假(跟'实'相对 as opposed to 'true') false; nominal:～伪 hypocritical|～名 false reputation|～构 frame up; fabricate; fiction ❻ 虚心 humble; modest:谦～ modest ❼ 虚弱 weak; in poor health:气～ deficiency of vital energy|血～ deficiency of blood|身子很～ be very weak physically ❽ 指政治思想、方针、政策等方面的道理 political work; ideology; policies; theory; guiding principles; abstract:务～ discuss abstract things like policies, principles and guidelines|以～带实。Let correct guidelines guide practical work. ❾ 二十八宿之一 one of the 28 constellations

【虚报】xūbào 不照真实情况报告(多指以少报多) make a false report; report untruthfully:～成绩 report one's results falsely|～冒领 make a fraudulent application and claim

【虚词】xūcí ❶ 不能单独成句,意义比较抽象,有帮助造句作用的词。汉语的虚词包括副词、介词、连词、助词、叹词、拟声词六类。function word; form word; word that cannot make a sentence alone, has abstract meaning and helps to make a sentence. The function words in the Chinese language include adverbs, prepositions, conjunctions, auxiliary verbs, interjections and onomatopes. ❷〈书 *fml*.〉same as 虚辞 xūcí

【虚辞】xūcí 〈书 *fml*.〉虚夸不实的言辞或文辞 exaggerations; empty words:空言～ empty words and exaggerations|～滥调 clichés; also 虚词 xūcí

【虚度】xūdù 白白地度过 spend time in vain; waste:～光阴 spend time in vain

【虚浮】xūfú 不切实;不塌实 impractical; superficial:～的计划 impractical plan|作风～ superficial style of work

【虚构】xūgòu 凭想像造出来 fabricate; trump up:这篇小说的情节是～的。This is a trumped-up story.

【虚汗】xūhàn 由于衰弱、患病、心里紧张等而出的汗 abnormal sweating due to general debility or nervousness

【虚怀若谷】xū huái ruò gǔ 胸怀像山谷那样深而且宽广,形容十分谦虚 have a mind as open as a valley; be extremely modest; be open-minded

【虚幻】xūhuàn 主观幻想的;不真实的(形象) unreal; illusory:～的梦境 a mere illusion (or dream)

【虚火】xūhuǒ 〈中医 *Chin. med*.〉指由身体虚弱而产生的焦躁和发热的症状 fire of defiency type marked by impatience and fever and caused by physical weakness

【虚假】xūjiǎ 跟实际不符合的 false; sham; make-believe:～现象 false appearance|做学问要老老实实,不能有半点～。Academic work calls for honesty, and tolerates no sophistry.

【虚惊】xūjīng 事后证明是不必要的惊慌 false alarm:受了一场～ be the victim of a false alarm

【虚空】xūkōng 空虚 hollow; void: 内心～ feel empty

【虚夸】xūkuā (言谈)虚假夸张 exaggerative; bombastic; boastful: 报道消息,要实事求是,切忌～。News reporting must be based on facts, and exaggerations should be avoided by all means.

【虚礼】xūlǐ 表面应酬的礼数 mere formalities; courtesies; pleasantries

【虚名】xūmíng 和实际情况不符合的名声 false reputation; undeserved reputation: 不务～。Don't seek false reputation. | 徒有～,并无实学 have a false reputation and no real learning

【虚拟】xūnǐ ❶ 不符合或不一定符合事实的;假设的 not true to the fact or not necessarily true to the fact; suppositional: ～语气 the subjunctive mood ❷ 虚构 invented; fictitious: 那篇小说里的故事情节,有的是作者～的。Part of the plot in that story was invented by the writer.

【虚胖】xūpàng 人体内脂肪异常增多而发胖,多由内分泌疾患引起 gain weight from an abnormal increase of fat in the human body, mostly caused by endocrinopathy

【虚飘飘】xūpiāopiāo (～的 xūpiāopiāo·de)形容飘飘荡荡不落实的样子 shaky; felt wobbly; unsteady: 喝了点酒,走路觉得两腿～的。After a few drinks, he found his legs unsteady while walking.

【虚荣】xūróng 表面上的光彩 vanity: ～心 vanity; vainglory | 不慕～ not affected by vanity; not vain

【虚弱】xūruò ❶ (身体)不结实 in poor health; weak; debilitated: 病后身体很～ suffer from general debility after an illness; very weak after an illness ❷ (国力、兵力)软弱;薄弱 (of national power, troops, etc.) weak; feeble

【虚设】xūshè 机构、职位等形式上虽然存在,实际上不起作用 nominal; existing in name only: 形同～ existing in name only

【虚实】xūshí 虚和实。泛指内部情况 false or true; actual situation (as of an opponent); (in a broad sense) inside information: 探听～ try to find out about an opponent, etc.; try to ascertain the strength (of an enemy) | ～莫测 unable to fathom the actual situation | 不了解～ do not know the actual situation

【虚数】xūshù ❶ 复数 $a+bi$ 中,当 $b\neq0$ 时叫做虚数,如 $1-3i$;当 $a=0$, $b\neq0$ 时叫做纯虚数,如 $5i$ imaginary number. In the complex number $a+bi$, when $b\neq0$ it is an imaginary number, as $1-3i$; when $a=0$, $b\neq0$, it is a pure imaginary number, as $5i$. ☞ 复数 fùshù on p. 611 ❷ 虚假的不实在的数字 unreliable figure

【虚岁】xūsuì 一种年龄计算法,人一生下来就算一岁,以后每逢新年就增加一岁,这样就比实际年龄多一岁或两岁,所以叫虚岁 nominal age; a person's age reckoned by the traditional method, i.e. a person becomes one year old immediately after birth and is one year older with each passing lunar new year

【虚套子】xūtào·zi 只有形式的应酬礼数 mere formalities; conventionalities: 他说话不来～,句句很实在。He spoke without formalities, so that every remark he makes sounds rather very down-to-earth. also 虚套 xūtào

【虚土】xūtǔ 〈方 *dial.*〉经过翻耕的松软的土 ploughed, soft soil

【虚脱】xūtuō ❶ 因大量失血或脱水、中毒、患传染病等而引起的心脏和血液循环突然衰竭的现象,主要症状是体温和血压下降,脉搏微细,出冷汗,面色苍白等 collapse; prostration; prostration of the heart and blood circulation caused by excessive loss of blood or bodily fluids, poisoning, or contraction of an infectious disease, characterized chiefly by decrease in the body temperature and blood pressure, feeble pulse, cold sweat, pale face, etc. ❷ 发生虚脱 collapse: 病人出汗太多,～了。The patient collapsed as a result of excessive sweating.

【虚妄】xūwàng 没有事实根据的 unfounded; fabricated; invented: ～之说 fabricated story

【虚伪】xūwěi 不真实;不实在;做假 two-faced; hypocritical: 这个人太～。That chap is a hypocrite. | 他对人实在,没有一点～。He is perfectly candid and never two-faced.

【虚位以待】xū wèi yǐ dài 留着位置等候 leave a seat vacant (or save a seat) for sb.; also 虚席以待 xū xí yǐ dài

【虚文】xūwén ❶ 具文 rules and regulations that have become a dead letter; dead letter: 一纸～ dead letter | 徒具～ merely a dead letter ❷ 没有意义的礼节 mere formality: ～浮礼 meaningless formalities; conventionalities

【虚无】xūwú 有而若无,实而若虚,道家用来指'道'(真理)的本体无所不在,但无形象可见 nihility; nothingness; there is sth., but seemingly nothing; it is true, but seemingly false. Taoists use it to indicate that the noumenon of Tao (truth) exists everywhere, but is invisible.

【虚无缥缈】xūwú piāomiǎo 形容非常空虚渺茫 purely imaginary; entirely unreal; visionary, illusory

【虚无主义】xūwú zhǔyì 一种否定人类历史文化遗产、否定民族文化,甚至否定一切的思想 nihilism; denial of the historical and cultural heritage of mankind, of national cultures and even of everything

【虚线】xūxiàn 以点或短线画成的断续的线,多用于作几何图形或标记 dotted line or line of dashes; imaginary line, usu. used as a geometric figure or sign

【虚像】xūxiàng 物体发出的光线经凹面镜、凸透镜反射或折射后，如为发散光线，它们的反向延长线相交时所形成的影像，叫做虚像。虚像不能显现在屏幕上，不能使照相底片感光。光源在主焦点以内时才能产生虚像，在放大镜、显微镜等中看到的像都是虚像。virtual image; optical image formed by the crossing of the reverse extension lines of the divergent light rays, namely, the light rays of the objects that are reflected or refracted through the concave lense and convex lense. The virtual image cannot appear on the screen or be sensitized on the film; it can be produced only when the light source is within the main focus. What are seen in the magnifying glass, microscope, etc. are virtual images.

【虚心】xūxīn 不自以为是，能够接受别人意见 open-minded; modest; ready to listen to suggestions, remarks, criticisms from others：不～ immodest | ～学习别人的长处 learn from the strong points of others | ～使人进步，骄傲使人落后。Modesty helps one to go forward, whereas conceit makes one lag behind.

【虚悬】xūxuán ❶ 悬而未决；没有着落 outstanding; unsettled：～已久的校长人选还未确定。The candidate for the post of schoolmaster, which has been vacant for a long time, is not yet decided. ❷ 凭空设想 purely made-up; entirely concocted：～的计划，没法实行。It's impossible to put an entirely concocted plan into effect.

【虚应故事】xū yìng gùshì 照例应付，敷衍了事 do sth. perfunctorily as a mere matter of form or routine

【虚有其表】xū yǒu qí biǎo 表面上看来很好，实际不是如此 look impressive but lack real worth; appear better than it is

【虚与委蛇】xū yǔ wēiyí 对人假意敷衍应酬 deal with sb. courteously but without sincerity; pretend politeness and compliance

【虚造】xūzào 凭空捏造 fabricate：向壁～ make up sth. out of one's head while facing the wall

【虚张声势】xū zhāng shēngshì 假装出强大的气势 make an empty show of strength; bluff and bluster; be swashbuckling

【虚症】xūzhèng 〈中医 *Chin. med.*〉指体质虚弱的人发生全身无力、盗汗、出虚汗等症状 symptoms like debility, night sweat, abnormal sweating; chronic disease marked by deficiency of vital energy and lowering of body immunity

【虚字】xūzì 〈古人 *arch.*〉称没有很实在意义的字，其中一部分相当于现代的虚词（跟'实字'相对 as opposed to the 'notional word'）empty word; function word; form word; also 虚字眼儿 xūzìyǎnr

谞 xū 〈书 *fml.*〉❶ 才智 wisdom; talent ❷ 计谋 scheme; strategem

媭 xū 〈古代 *arch.*〉楚国人称姐姐（term of address among people of the state of Chu in ancient times）elder sister

欻（欻） xū 〈书 *fml.*〉忽然 suddenly; all of a sudden：风雨～至。A storm came up suddenly.

☞ chuā on p. 296

湑 Xū 湑水，水名，在陕西 Xushui, name of a river in Shaanxi Province

☞ xǔ on p. 2165

墟 xū ❶ 原来有许多人家聚居而现在已经荒废了的地方 ruins; place which was once inhabited by many families formerly but is now deserted：废～ ruins | 殷～ ruins of the Imperial Palace of the Yin Dynasty ❷ same as 圩 xū

需 xū ❶ 需要 need; want; require：～求 demand | 按～分配 distribute according to need ❷ 需用的东西 necessaries; needs; goods in need：军～ military supplies

【需求】xūqiú 由需要而产生的要求 requirement; demand：人们对商品的～越来越高。There is an ever-growing demand for commodities.

【需索】xūsuǒ 〈书 *fml.*〉要求（财物）exact; extort：～无厌 make rapacious extortions

【需要】xūyào ❶ 应该有或必须有 need; want; require; demand：我们～有一支强大的科学技术队伍。We must have a strong contingent of scientists and technicians. ❷ 对事物的欲望或要求 needs：从群众的～出发 proceed from the needs of the masses

嘘 xū ❶ 慢慢地吐气 breathe out slowly：～气 exhale slowly ❷ 叹气 utter a sigh：仰天而～ staring up at the sky and sighing helplessly ❸ 火或蒸气的热力接触到物体（of cooking fire, steam, etc.）come into contact with sth.; scald; burn：掀笼屉时小心热气～着手。Don't scald your hands when you open the steamer. | 先坐上笼屉把馒头～一～。Heat steamed bread by putting it over the fire for a while. ❹ 〈方 *dial.*〉〈叹词 *interj.*〉表示制止、驱逐等 sh; hush; indicating stopping or expelling：～！轻一点，屋里有病人。Hush! Be quiet. There is a patient in the room. 注意 **NOTE**：表示制止、驱逐等，一般用 shī，也写作嘘 *shi* is usu. used when indicating stopping or expelling; also written as 嘘 ❺ 〈方 *dial.*〉发出'嘘'（xū）的声音来制止或驱逐 hiss; boo; utter the sound of '*xu*' to stop or expel sb.：大家把他～下去了。They booed him off the platform.

☞ shī on p. 1733

【嘘寒问暖】xū hán wèn nuǎn 形容对别人的生活十分关切 inquire after sb.'s well-being; be solicitous about sb.'s health（嘘寒 *xu han*：呵出热气使受寒的人温暖 breathe out hot air to warm people living in the cold)

【嘘唏】xūxī〈书 *fml*.〉same as 歔欷 xūxī

魆 xū ☞黑魆魆 hēixūxū on p. 795

歔 xū [歔欷](xūxī)〈书 *fml*.〉哽咽;抽噎 sob: 暗自～ sob secretly|～不已 keep on sobbing; also 嘘唏 xūxī

繻 xū ❶〈书 *fml*.〉彩色的缯 coloured silk fabric ❷〈古时 *arch*.〉出入关卡的凭证,用帛制成 permit made of silk for leaving and entering a country

xú (ㄒㄩˊ)

徐 xú ❶〈书 *fml*.〉慢慢地 slowly; gently: ～步 walk slowly (or leisurely); stroll|清风～来。A refreshing breeze was blowing gently. ❷ (Xú) 姓 a surname

【徐缓】xúhuǎn 缓慢 slowly: 水流～ water flows slowly|脚步～ walk slowly or leisurely; stroll

【徐图】xútú〈书 *fml*.〉慢慢地从容地谋划(做某事) plan gradually to achieve sth.: ～歼击 plan gradually to attack and destroy|～良策 seek gradually for a good plan

【徐徐】xúxú〈书 *fml*.〉慢慢地 slowly; gently: 列车～～开动。The train moved slowly.

xǔ (ㄒㄩˇ)

许¹ xǔ ❶ 称赞;承认优点 praise: 赞～ praise; commend; approve of|推～ praise; approve; have a high regard for|～为佳作 praise sth. as an excellent piece of work ❷ 答应(送人东西或给人做事) promise (to give sth. to or do sth. for sb.): ～愿 promise; make a promise; give a promise|以身～国 dedicate oneself to one's nation; pledge to serve one's country|他～过我请我看电影。He promised to invite me to see a film. ❸ 许配 (of a girl) be betrothed to; be engaged to: 姑娘～了人了。The girl is engaged. ❹ 允许;许可 allow; permit: 准～ be permitted; be allowed|特～ specially permitted|只～成功,不～失败。There must be success. It permits no failure. ❺ 也许;或许 maybe; perhaps: 她～没有这个意思。Maybe she didn't mean it.|他今天没来开会,～是不知道。He didn't come to the meeting today; perhaps he didn't know it.

许² xǔ ❶ 表示程度 indicating degree: ～多 many; a lot of; much; plenty of|～久 for a long time; for ages|少～ a little; a small amount of ❷〈书 *fml*.〉表示大约接近某个数 indicating a rough estimate: 从者百～人 followed by about 100 people|离岸一里～ about one *li* from the shore

许³ xǔ〈书 *fml*.〉处;地方 place: 何～人? Where does he come from?

许⁴ Xǔ ❶ 周朝国名,在今河南许昌东 name of a state in the Zhou Dynasty, east of present-day Xuchang in Henan Province ❷ 姓 a surname

【许多】xǔduō 很多 many; much; a great many: ～东西 a lot of things|我们有～年没见面了。We haven't seen each other for many years.|菊花有许许多多的品种。There are a lot of varieties of chrysanthemum.

【许婚】xǔhūn (女方的家长或本人)接受男方的求亲 (of a girl herself or her parents on her behalf) accept a proposal of marriage

【许久】xǔjiǔ 很久 for a long time; for ages: 他～没来了。He hasn't been here for a long time.|大家商量了～,才想出个办法来。We talked things over for a long time before we found a solution.

【许可】xǔkě 准许;容许 permit; allow: ～证 permit; license|未经～,不得动用。No one is allowed to use it without permission.

【许诺】xǔnuò 答应;应承 make a promise; promise: 他～过的事情一定会办到。He will surely carry out what he has promised.

【许配】xǔpèi 女子由家长做主,跟某人订婚 (of a girl) be betrothed to sb. (in an arranged match)

【许愿】xǔ//yuàn ❶ 迷信的人对神佛有所祈求,许下某种酬谢 make a vow to a god: 烧香～ burn incense and make a vow ❷ 借指事前答应对方将来给以某种好处 promise sb. a reward: 封官～ promise a high official post or some other favour in order to win over sb.

【许字】xǔzì〈书 *fml*.〉许婚 (of a girl) be betrothed to sb.

诩 xǔ〈书 *fml*.〉夸耀 brag; boast: 自～ boast; brag

姁 xǔ [姁姁]〈书 *fml*.〉安乐或温和的样子 peaceful and happy; gentle; mild

浒 xǔ ☞ below
☞ hǔ on p. 822

【浒墅关】Xǔshùguān 地名,在江苏 Xushuguan, name of a place in Jiangsu Province

【浒湾】Xǔwān 地名,在江西 Xuwan, name of a place in Jiangxi Province
☞ Hǔwān on p. 822

栩 xǔ [栩栩]形容生动活泼的样子 vivid; lively: ～如生 lifelike; to the life|～欲活 lifelike; to the life

湑 xǔ〈书 *fml*.〉❶ 清 clear ❷ 茂盛 luxuriant
☞ Xū on p. 2164

盨 xǔ〈古代 *arch*.〉盛(chéng)食物的铜制器皿,有盖和两个耳子 ancient bronze vessel with two ears and a lid for holding food

X

糈 xǔ〈书 *fml*.〉粮食 grains

醑 xǔ ❶〈书 *fml*.〉美酒 mellow wine; fine wine ❷ 醑剂的简称 abbr. for 醑剂 xǔjì: 樟脑～camphor spirit (or essence) | 氯仿～chloroform

【醑剂】xǔjì 挥发性物质溶解在酒精中所成的制剂 spirit; essence; preparation by dissolving a volatile substance in alcohol; 简称 abbr. 醑 xǔ

xù (ㄒㄩˋ)

旭 xù ❶〈书 *fml*.〉初出的阳光 brilliance of the rising sun: 朝～ rising sun; the morning sun ❷ (Xù) 姓 a surname

【旭日】xùrì 刚出来的太阳 rising sun: ～东升。The sun rises in the eastern sky.

芧 xù 古书上指橡实 acorn as described in ancient books

☞ zhù on p. 2508

序[1] xù ❶ 次序 order; sequence: 顺～ order; sequence | 秩～ order | 工～ work process | 程～ procedure | 井然有～ in perfect order ❷〈书 *fml*.〉排次序 arrange in order: ～次 order; sequence | ～齿 order of seniority ❸ 开头的; 在正式内容以前的 introductory; initial: ～幕 prologue | ～曲 overture; prelude ❹ 序文 preface: 写了一篇～ write a preface

序[2] xù ❶〈古代 *arch*.〉指厢房 wing room: 东～ east wing | 西～ west wing ❷〈古代 *arch*.〉由地方举办的学校 type of local school: 庠～ school

【序跋】xùbá 序文和跋文 preface and postscript

【序齿】xùchǐ〈书 *fml*.〉同在一起的人按照年纪长幼来排次序 be arranged in order of seniority: ～入座 be seated in order of seniority

【序列】xùliè 按次序排好的行列 alignment; array

【序目】xùmù (书的)序和目录 preface and table of contents

【序幕】xùmù ❶ 某些多幕剧的第一幕之前的一场戏,用以介绍剧中人物的历史和剧情发生的远因,或暗示全剧的主题 prologue (to a play); act preceding the first act of a play, introducing the heroes and heroines in the play and the background for the plot, or dropping a hint on the main theme of the whole play ❷〈比喻 *fig*.〉重大事件的开端 prologue (to a major event, etc.); prelude; beginning of a major event: 卢沟桥事变拉开了全面抗战的～。The Marco Polo Bridge Incident was the prologue to the War of Resistance against Japan.

【序曲】xùqǔ ❶ 歌剧、清唱剧、芭蕾舞剧等开场时演出的乐曲,由交响乐队演奏。也指用这种体裁写成的独立器乐曲。overture; musical introduction to an opera, oratorio, ballet, etc., played by an orchestra; independent orchestral music composed in this style ❷〈比喻 *fig*.〉事情、行动的开端 prelude (to an event, action, etc.): 预赛获胜只是夺取冠军的～。Winning the preliminary round was a prelude to winning the championship.

【序数】xùshù 表示次序的数目。汉语表示序数的方法,通常是在整数前边加'第',如'第一、第二十三'。此外还有些习惯的表示法,如'头一回、末一次、正月、初一、大女儿、小儿子'。序数后边直接连量词或名词的时候,可以省去'第',如'二等、三号、四楼、五班、六小队,1949 年 10 月 1 日'。ordinal number; ordinal; any number to indicate order in a particular series. In the Chinese language, an ordinal number is usu. indicated by adding the character 第 dì before an integer, e.g. 第一 dìyī (first) and 第二十三 dìèrshísān (23rd). Moreover, it is also indicated in other ways, e.g. 头一回 tóuyīhuí (the first time), 末一次 mòyīcì (the last time), 正月 zhēngyuè (first month of a lunar year), 初一 chūyī (first day of a month), 大女儿 dànǚér (the eldest daughter), and 小儿子 xiǎoér·zi (the youngest son). The character 第 dì is usu. omitted when an ordinal number is used directly before a classifier or a noun, e.g., 二等 èrděng (the second class), 三号 sānhào (No. 3), 四楼 sìlóu (Building No. 4), 五班 wǔbān (Class 5), 六小队 liùxiǎoduì (Squad 6), and 1949 年 10 月 1 日 yījiǔsìjiǔ nián shí yuè yī rì (October 1, 1949)

【序文】xùwén 一般写在著作正文之前的文章。有作者自己写的,多说明写书宗旨和经过。也有别人写的,多介绍或评论本书内容。preface; foreword; introduction to the text of a book. A preface is written either by the author, explaining his purpose of writing the book and how it is written, or by sb. else making an introduction to the book and giving his own comments. also 叙文 xùwén

【序言】xùyán same as 序文 xùwén; also 叙言 xùyán

呴 xù〈书 *fml*.〉same as 煦 xù, 多用于人名 usu. used in the names of persons

叙(敍、敘) xù ❶ 说;谈 talk; chat: ～家常 chitchat | 闲言少～。Cut all the meaningless disgression. ❷ 记述 narrate; recount; relate: ～事 recount an event or story | ～述 narrate ❸ 评议等级次第 assess; appraise: ～功 assess contributions | ～奖 appraise awards | 铨～ evaluate officials ❹〈书 *fml*.〉same as 序[1] xù ①②④

【叙别】xùbié 临别时聚在一块儿谈话;话别 have a farewell talk: 临行～ have a farewell talk before one's departure

【叙功】xùgōng〈书 *fml*.〉评定功绩 assess sb.'s services: ～议赏 assess sb.'s services and discuss his reward

【叙旧】xù//jiù（亲友间）谈论跟彼此有关的旧事 (of relatives and friends) talk about the old days：老同学一见面就叙起旧来了。The old classmates began talking about their old days as soon as they got together.

【叙录】xùlù 对某部书的简要介绍，包括对不同版本的校勘和对源流得失的论述 brief introduction to a book, including the collation of the different editions and remarks on the gains and losses of the sources and origin

【叙事】xùshì 叙述事情（指书面的）narrate (in writing); recount：～文 narrative|～诗 narrative poem|～曲 ballade

【叙事诗】xùshìshī 以叙述历史或当代的事件为内容的诗篇 narrative poem; ballade; poem narrating historical events or contemporary events

【叙述】xùshù 把事情的前后经过记载下来或说出来 narrate (in speech or writing); recount; relate：～了事情的经过 recounted the course of an incident; tell the story of an incident

【叙说】xùshuō 叙述（多指口头的）tell; narrate (in speech)：请把事情的经过再～一遍。Please tell the story of the incident again.

【叙谈】xùtán 随意交谈 chat; chitchat：找个时间，大家好好儿～～。Find some time and let's have a good chat.

【叙文】xùwén same as 序文 xùwén

【叙言】xùyán same as 序言 xùyán

【叙用】xùyòng 〈书 *fml*.〉任用（官吏）appoint (an official); employ (as a government official)：革去官职，永不～ removed from office and never appointed again

洫 xù 〈书 *fml*.〉田间的水道 ditch：沟～ ditches running between plots of farmland (for irrigation or drainage)

恤（卹、賉） xù ❶〈书 *fml*.〉顾虑；忧虑 anxiety; worry; misgiving：不～人言。Don't worry about the gossip. ❷ 怜悯 pity; sympathize：怜～ take pity on; have pity for|体～ understand and sympathize; show concern for; show solicitude for ❸ 救济 give relief; compensate：抚～ comfort and compensate a disabled peson or a bereaved family|～金 pension for a person disabled while on duty; pension for the dependants of a person who died while on duty

【恤金】xùjīn 抚恤金 pension for a person disabled while on duty; pension for the dependants of a person who died while on duty

【恤衫】xùshān 〈方 *dial*.〉衬衫 shirt

垿 xù 〈古代 *arch*.〉房屋的东西墙。多用于人名。east and west walls of an ancient house; *Xu*, usu. used in the name of a person

畜 xù 畜养 raise (domestic animals)：～牧 livestock breeding|～产 animal products ☞ chù on p. 295

【畜产】xùchǎn 畜牧业产品的统称 general term for animal by-products

【畜牧】xùmù 饲养大批的牲畜和家禽（多专指牲畜 oft. referring exclusively to livestock) raise (or rear) livestock or poultry：～业 animal husbandry; livestock breeding; livestock farming|从事～ go in for animal husbandry

【畜养】xùyǎng 饲养（动物）raise (domestic animals)：～牲口 raise cattle

聟 xù 〈书 *fml*.〉same as 婿 xù

酗 xù［酗酒］(xùjiǔ) 没有节制地喝酒；喝酒后撒酒疯 indulge in excessive drinking：～滋事 get drunk and create a disturbance

勖（勗） xù 〈书 *fml*.〉勉励 encourage：～勉 encourage

【勖励】xùlì 〈书 *fml*.〉勉励 encourage

【勖勉】xùmiǎn 〈书 *fml*.〉勉励 encourage; prompt：～有加（一再勉励）encourage sb. again and again|～后进 encourage those lagging behind to catch up with others

鱮（鱮） xù ☞ 鲢 lián on p. 1199

绪 xù ❶ 本指丝的头 end of a silk thread; 〈比喻 *fig*.〉事情的开端 beginning of sth.：端～ clue; thread of thought|头～ main threads of sth.; clue|千头万～ tens of thousands of loose ends; (of things) complicated and difficult to unravel ❷〈书 *fml*.〉残余 vestiges of sth.; remnants：～余 surplus; remainder|～风 vestiges of an old social custom ❸ 指心情、思想等 mental or emotional state; mood：心～ mood|情～ mood|离情别～ parting sorrow; sad feelings at parting ❹〈书 *fml*.〉事业；功业 task; cause; undertaking：续未竟之～ carry on an unfinished mission; take up where another has left off ❺ (Xù) 姓 a surname

【绪论】xùlùn 学术论著开头说明全书主旨和内容等的部分 introduction; introductory remarks of an academic writing

【绪言】xùyán 发端的话；绪论 introduction

续（續） xù ❶ 接连不断 continuous; successive：继～ continue; go on|连～ continuous; successive|陆～ one after another; in seccession; successively ❷ 接在原有的后头 continue; resume; extend; join：～编 continuation of a book; sequence|～集 continuation of a book; sequence|狗尾～貂 join a dog tail to a sable; make an unworthy continuation of a great work|这条绳子太短，再～上一截儿吧。This piece of string is too short. Join another piece onto it. ❸ 添；加 add; supply more：壶里的水是刚～的。The water in the pot was just added.|炉子该～煤了。The stove needs more coal. ❹ (Xù) 姓 a surname

【续貂】xùdiāo〈比喻 *fig.*〉拿不好的东西接到好的东西后面(多用于谦称续写别人的著作 oft. used humbly by a person who writes a sequel to another person's work) join a dog tail to a sable; make an unworthy continuation of a great work:～之讥 jeer at the unworthy continuation of a book; ☞ 狗尾续貂 gǒu wěi xù diāo on p. 683

【续航】xùháng 连续航行 (of an airplane or ship) continue (or pursue) a journey without refuelling:这种飞机不但速度远超过一般客机,～时间也很长。This type of plane not only flies faster than an ordinary one, but also flies much longer.

【续航力】xùhánglì 指舰船、飞机等一次装足燃料后能行驶或飞行的最大航程 endurance; flying range (of an airplane); cruising radius (of a ship)

【续假】xù//jià 假期满后继续请假 extend one's leave of absence; extend leave:～一周 have one's leave extended for another week|续三天假 have one's leave to be extended for three days

【续篇】xùpiān 一篇(或一部)著作完成后,接着原来的内容续写的部分 continuation of a book (or an article); sequence:小说结尾留有余味,让读者还想看～。The ending of the novel leaves a pleasant aftertaste, tempting the readers to read its sequel.

【续聘】xùpìn 继续聘任 continue to engage sb.; continue to employ sb.:聘期满后可以～。The term of employment may be extended upon expiration.

【续弦】xù//xián 男子丧妻以后再娶 remarry after the death of one's wife; second wife after the death of one's first wife

溆 xù〈书 *fml.*〉水边 waterside

絮1 xù ❶ 棉絮 (cotton) wadding:被～ wadding for a quilt ❷〈古代 *arch.*〉指粗的丝棉 coarse silk floss ❸ 像棉絮的东西 sth. resembling cotton:柳～ willow catkins|芦～ reed catkins ❹ 在衣服、被褥里铺棉花、丝棉等 wad or pad:～棉袄 line (or wad) one's clothes with cotton; wad a cotton-padded jacket|～被窝 wad a quilt

絮2 xù ❶ 絮叨 long-winded; garrulous ❷〈方 *dial.*〉腻烦 be bored; be fed up:这些话都听～了。I'm fed up with these words.

【絮叨】xù·dāo 形容说话啰唆;来回地说 (of talking) repetitive; garrulous:他说话太～了。He speaks too garrulously.|老人～起来没个完。Old people are always long-winded.

【絮烦】xù·fan 因过多或重复而感到厌烦 tired; bored:他老说这件事,人们都听～了。He was always harping on this matter, and people were bored stiff.

【絮聒】xùguō ❶ 絮叨 long-winded; garrulous; wordy ❷ 麻烦(别人) trouble (sb.)

【絮棉】xùmián 做棉被、棉衣等用的棉花,商业上叫做絮棉 cotton for wadding; commercially known as 絮棉 xùmián

【絮窝】xù//wō 鸟兽用枯草、羽毛等铺在窝里 (of birds or animals) do up a nest or lair with withered grass, feathers, etc.

【絮絮】xùxù 形容说话等连续不断 garrulous; loquacious; chattering endlessly:～不休 chatter endlessly

【絮语】xùyǔ〈书 *fml.*〉❶ 絮絮叨叨地说 prattle on ❷ 絮叨的话 endless chatter

婿(壻) xù ❶ 女婿 son-in-law:翁～ father-in-law and son-in-law ❷ 丈夫 husband:夫～ husband|妹～ younger sister's husband

蓄 xù ❶ 储存;积蓄 store up; save up:储～ save money; savings|～洪 store flood water|～电池 storage battery; accumulator ❷ 留着而不去掉 grow:～发 wear one's hair long|～须 grow a beard ❸ (心里)藏着 entertain (ideas); harbour:～意 deliberate; premeditated|～志 cherish the ambition to; harbour the resolve to; be determined to; make up one's mind to

【蓄电池】xùdiànchí 把电能变成化学能储存起来的装置。用电时再经过化学变化放出电能。storage battery; accumulator; battery of electrochemical cells for generating electric current; 通称 commonly known as 电瓶 diànpíng

【蓄洪】xùhóng 为了防止洪水成灾,把超过河道所能排泄的洪水蓄积在一定的地区 store flood water; in order to prevent the flood from becomimg a disaster, store in a given area the water in excess of the amount that can be discharged by a river

【蓄积】xùjī 积聚储存 store up; save up:水库可以～雨水。Reservoirs can store up rainwater.

【蓄谋】xùmóu 早就有这种计谋(指坏的) premeditate:～已久 long premeditated|～迫害 harbour a design of persecuting sb.

【蓄念】xùniàn 早就有这个念头 harbour an idea (or a thought, an intention):～已久 have long entertained the idea

【蓄养】xùyǎng 积蓄培养 build up; accumulate:～力量 build up (or accumulate) strength

【蓄意】xùyì 早就有这个意思(指坏的);存心 calculated; premeditated; deliberate:～进行破坏 deliberately sabotage|～挑起事端 provoke an incident deliberately

【蓄志】xùzhì 早就有这个志愿 have long cherished an ambition; have long haboured (or entertained) a resolve:～报国 make up one's mind to serve the nation whole-heartedly

煦 xù 〈书 *fml*.〉温暖 warm; balmy: ~暖 warm | 和~ warm; balmy | 拂~ (of a gentle breeze) blow warmly

湑 xù 湑仕(Xùshì),越南地名 Suc Si, name of a place in Vietnam

☞ chù on p. 296

·xu (·ㄒㄩ)

蓿 ·xu ☞ [苜蓿] (mù·xu) on p. 1378

xuān (ㄒㄩㄢ)

轩[1] xuān ❶ 高 high; lofty: ~昂 dignified; imposing | ~敞 spacious and bright | ~朗 spacious; airy and bright; open and clear; cheerful; merry; sanguine; optimistic ❷ (Xuān) 姓 a surname

轩[2] xuān ❶ 有窗的廊子或小屋子(旧时多用为书斋名或茶馆饭馆等的字号 formerly oft. used in names of studies, restaurants or teahouses) small room or veranda with windows ❷〈古代 *arch*.〉一种有帷幕而前顶较高的车 high-fronted, curtained carriage ❸〈书 *fml*.〉窗户,门 window or door

【轩昂】xuān'áng ❶ 形容精神饱满,气度不凡 dignified; imposing: 器宇~ dignified bearing; imposing manner; imposing appearance ❷〈书 *fml*.〉高大 tall and big: 佛殿~ tall, grand Buddhist temple

【轩敞】xuānchǎng (房屋)高大宽敞 (of room) spacious and bright

【轩然大波】xuānrán dà bō 〈比喻 *fig*.〉大的纠纷或风潮 great disturbance; mighty uproar; big stir

【轩轾】xuānzhì 〈书 *fml*.〉车前高后低叫轩,前低后高叫轾 high and low chariots; 〈比喻 *fig*.〉高低优劣 high or low; good or bad: 不分~ be equal; be hard to tell who or which is superior

宣 xuān ❶ 公开说出来;传播、散布出去 declare; proclaim; announce: ~传 propaganda; publicity | ~布 declare; proclaim; announce | ~誓 take a vow; take an oath; vow | 心照不~ have a tacit understanding; be understood but not expressed ❷ 宣召 (of a king, or an emperor) summon to the imperial court ❸ 疏导 give vent to; drain; lead off: ~泄 give vent to; drain; lead off ❹ (Xuān) 指安徽宣城,云南宣威 city of Xuancheng in Anhui Province, and the city of Xuanwei in Yunnan Province: ~笔 writing brushes produced in Xuancheng | ~腿 Xuanwei ham; ham produced in Xuangwei in Yunnan ❺ 指宣纸 *Xuan* paper: 玉版~(色白质坚的宣纸) white tough *Xuan* paper | 虎皮~(有浅色斑纹的红、黄、绿等色的宣纸) coloured rice paper with light stripes ❻ (Xuān) 姓 a surname

【宣笔】xuānbǐ 安徽宣城、泾县出产的毛笔,以制造精美著称 Xuan writing brush; high-quality writing brush made in Xuancheng and Jingxian in Anhui Province

【宣布】xuānbù 正式告诉(大家) declare; proclaim; announce: ~命令 announce an order

【宣称】xuānchēng 公开地用语言、文字表示;声称 assert; declare; profess: ~自己的意见是正确的 assert that one's views are correct

【宣传】xuānchuán 对群众说明讲解,使群众相信并跟着行动 do publicity work; propagate; disseminate; give publicity to: ~队 publicity team | ~交通法规 give publicity to traffic regulations and rules

【宣传弹】xuānchuándàn 散发宣传品的炮弹或炸弹,用火炮发射或飞机投掷 shell or bomb fired by a cannon or dropped from a plane to distribute leaflets

【宣传画】xuānchuánhuà 进行宣传鼓动的画,标题一般是带有号召性的文句 picture poster; posters; also 招贴画 zhāotiēhuà

【宣传品】xuānchuánpǐn 宣传用的物品,多指印刷品,如传单、招贴画等 publicity material such as leaflets and posters; promotional material; brochure

【宣德】Xuāndé 明宣宗(朱瞻基)年号(公元1426—1435) Xuande, title of the reign (1426-1435) of Emperor Xuanzong (Zhu Zhanji) of the Ming Dynasty

【宣读】xuāndú 在集会上向群众朗读(布告、文件等) read out (an announcement, a document, etc. in public): ~嘉奖令 read out an order of commendation

【宣告】xuāngào 宣布 declare; proclaim: ~成立 proclaim the founding of (a state, organization, etc.) | ~结束 declare the end of (a meeting, etc.)

【宣和】Xuānhé 宋徽宗(赵佶)年号(公元1119—1125) Xuanhe, title of the reign (1119-1125) of Emperor Huizong (Zhao Ji) of the Song Dynasty

【宣讲】xuānjiǎng 宣传讲解 publicize (a policy, decree, etc.); preach (a religion): ~交通法规 explain and publicize the traffic regulations and rules

【宣教】xuānjiào 宣传教育 publicity work and education: ~工作 publicity and educational work

【宣明】xuānmíng 明白宣布;公开表明 declare; make clear: ~观点 spell out one's view

【宣判】xuānpàn 法院对当事人宣布案件的判决 pronounce judgment: 公开~ pronounce judgment in public | 当庭~ pronounce judgment in the court

【宣示】xuānshì 公开表示;宣布 declare openly; make publicly known: ~内外 make known to people both at home and abroad; announce both at home and abroad

【宣誓】xuān//shì 担任某个任务或参加某个组织时,在一定的仪式下当众说出表示决心的话 take (or swear) an oath; make a vow; make a pledge:~就职 take an oath of office; be sworn in; be sworn into office|举手~ raise one's hand to take an oath

【宣统】Xuāntǒng 清朝最后一个皇帝(爱新觉罗溥仪)的年号(公元1909—1911) Xuantong, title of the reign (1909-1911) of the last emperor (Aisin Gioro Puyi) of the Qing Dynasty

【宣腿】xuāntuǐ 云南宣威出产的火腿 Xuanwei ham; ham produced in Xuanwei, Yunnan Province

【宣泄】xuānxiè ❶ 使积水流出去 lead off (liquids); drain:低洼地区由于雨水无法~,往往造成内涝。The low-lying lands were often waterlogged as the rainwater there could not be drained. ❷ 舒散;吐露(心中的积郁) get sth. off one's chest; unbosom oneself; give vent to one's pent-up feelings:~心中的愤懑 give vent to one's pent-up anger ❸〈书 *fml*.〉泄露 disclose; reveal; let out:事属机密,不得~。This is confidential. Don't let it out.

【宣叙调】xuānxùdiào 一种朗诵性质的曲调,节奏自由,伴奏比较简单,内容大都叙述剧情的发展,常用于歌剧、清唱剧中 recitative; type of declamatory singing, with the free rhythm and tempo of speech and simple accompaniment, usu. in the form of an introduction to the development of the plot, oft. used in the dialogue of operas and oratorios

【宣言】xuānyán ❶(国家、政党或团体)对重大问题公开表示意见以进行宣传号召的文告 (of a government, a political party or an organization) declaration; manifesto; public statement for the purpose of publicizing a major issue and issuing a call:发表~ make a declaration ❷ 宣告;声明 announcement; statement:郑重~ solemn statement; solemn declaration

【宣扬】xuānyáng 广泛宣传,使大家知道;传布 publicize; propagate; advocate; advertise:大肆~ give unlimited publicity to|~好人好事 give publicity to good people and their good deeds

【宣战】xuān//zhàn ❶ 一国或集团宣布同另一国或集团开始处于战争状态 declaring war; one country or one bloc of countries declaring war on another country or bloc of countries ❷ 泛指展开激烈斗争 (in a broad sense) fierce struggle against:他们向荒漠~,引水灌溉,植树造林。They declared war on the wasteland by diverting water for irrigation and planting trees.

【宣召】xuānzhào (帝王)宣旨召见(某人) (of a king or an emperor) summon sb. to court; summon an audience

【宣纸】xuānzhǐ 安徽宣城、泾县出产的一种高级纸张,用于写毛笔字和画国画。质地绵软坚韧,不容易破裂和被虫蛀,吸墨均匀,适于长期存放。*Xuan* paper, quality paper made in Xuancheng and Jingxian in Anhui Province, which is used for traditional Chinese painting and calligraphy, soft and tensile of texture and resistant to insect bites, absorbing ink evenly, and good for long preservation

谖 xuān〈书 *fml*.〉❶ 忘 forget ❷ 欺诈 deceive; cheat; swindle

萱(蕿) xuān ❶ 萱草 daylily ❷ 指萱堂 your mother:椿~(父母) parents; father and mother

【萱草】xuāncǎo 多年生草本植物,叶子条状披针形,花橙红色或黄红色。供观赏。daylily (*Hemerocallis*); ornamental perennial herbaceous plant with lanceolate leaves and orange-red or yellowish-red flowers

【萱堂】xuāntáng〈书 *fml*.〉指母亲 your mother

揎 xuān ❶ 捋袖子露出手臂 pull up the sleeves and bare the arms:~拳捋袖 pull up the sleeves and raise the fists; get ready to fight ❷〈方 *dial*.〉用手推 push:~开大门 push a gate open ❸〈方 *dial*.〉打 hit; beat:~了他一拳。(I) hit him with a fist.

喧(諠) xuān 声音大 noisy:~哗 confused noise; hubbub; uproar|~闹 noise and excitement; bustle; racket|锣鼓~天 deafening sound of gongs and drums

【喧宾夺主】xuān bīn duó zhǔ 客人的声音比主人的还要大 voice of the guest is louder than the host's;〈比喻 *fig*.〉客人占了主人的地位或外来的、次要的事物侵占了原有的、主要的事物的地位 presumptuous guest usurps the role of the host; the secondary supersedes the primary

【喧哗】xuānhuá ❶ 声音大而杂乱 confused noise; hubbub; uproar:笑语~ uproarious talk and laughter ❷ 喧嚷 make an uproar; make a racket:请勿~。Please keep quiet.

【喧豗】xuānhuī〈书 *fml*.〉喧闹 noise and excitement; bustle; racket

【喧闹】xuānnào 喧哗热闹 noise and excitement; bustle; racket:~的城市 bustling city

【喧嚷】xuānrǎng (好些人)大声地叫或说 make an uproar; make a racket:人声~ hubbub of voices; loud confused voices|千万别把事情~出去呀! For heaven's sake, don't leak the information!

【喧扰】xuānrǎo 喧闹扰乱 stir up a disturbance; make a commotion:市声~ hustle and bustle of the city

【喧腾】xuānténg 喧闹沸腾 noise and excitement; hubbub:工地一片~。A hubbub filled the worksite.

【喧阗】xuāntián 〈书 *fml.*〉声音大而杂；喧闹 fill the air with noises; be terribly noisy：鼓乐～。Drums and gongs made a terrible racket. | 车马～ heavy traffic

【喧嚣】xuānxiāo ❶ 声音杂乱；不清静 noisy：～的车马声 noise of dense traffic ❷ 叫嚣；喧嚷 make a clamour; make a hullabaloo; raise a din：～一时 created quite a stir

瑄 xuān 〈古代 *arch.*〉祭天用的璧 a piece of jade offered to heaven

暄1 xuān 〈书 *fml.*〉(太阳)温暖 warm and sunny：寒～ informal greetings

暄2 xuān 〈方 *dial.*〉物体内部空隙多而松软 fluffy; soft：馒头很～。The steamed bread is very fluffy. | 沙土地～，不好走。It's difficult to walk on sandy land because the soil is too soft.

【暄腾】xuān·teng 〈方 *dial.*〉松软而有弹性 soft and springy; fluffy; spongy：馒头蒸得很～。How nice and soft this steamed bread is!

煖 xuān 〈书 *fml.*〉温暖 warm
☞ 暖 nuǎn on p.1428

煊 xuān 〈书 *fml.*〉same as 暄1 xuān

【煊赫】xuānhè 形容名声很大、声势很盛 prestigious; of great renown and influence：～一时 be powerful and influential for a period | 权势～ be extremely powerful and influential

儇 xuān 〈书 *fml.*〉❶ 轻浮 frivolous：～薄 frivolous ❷ 慧黠 cunning; artful

【儇薄】xuānbó 〈书 *fml.*〉轻薄 frivolous

【儇佻】xuāntiāo 〈书 *fml.*〉轻浮；轻佻 giddy; light; frivolous

禤 Xuān 姓 a surname

谖 xuān 〈书 *fml.*〉智慧 wisdom; brilliance; sapience

懁 xuān 〈书 *fml.*〉性情急躁 bad tempered; impatient; having a quick temper

翾 xuān 〈书 *fml.*〉飞翔 fly; wing

xuán (ㄒㄩㄢˊ)

玄 xuán ❶ 黑色 black; dark：～狐 black fox ❷ 深奥 profound; abstruse：～妙 mysterious; abstruse | ～理 profound theory; theory of a philosophical sect of the Wei and Jin dynasties ❸ 玄虚；靠不住 unreliable; incredible：这话真～。This is really incredible.

【玄奥】xuán'ào 深奥 profound; abstruse：道理浅显，并不～。The meaning is not abstruse at all but easy to understand.

【玄狐】xuánhú 狐的一种，毛深黑色，长毛的尖端白色。产在北美。皮毛珍贵。black fox (*Vulpes Bowdich*); a breed of North American fox whose fur has long white-tipped black hair and is highly valued; also 银狐 yínhú

【玄乎】xuán·hu 玄虚不可捉摸 fantastic; inscrutable; subtle：他说得也太～了，天下哪有这种事！What a fantastic story he told! There is no such thing under heaven!

【玄机】xuánjī ❶〈道家 *Taoist*〉称深奥玄妙的道理 arcane truth：参悟～ meditate in order to comprehend arcane truth ❷ 神妙的机宜 abstruse plot; profound secret：不露～ not reveal one's secrets

【玄妙】xuánmiào 奥妙难以捉摸 mysterious; abstruse：～莫测 mysterious and unfathomable; too abstruse to explain

【玄青】xuánqīng 深黑色 deep black

【玄孙】xuánsūn 曾孙的儿子 great-great-grandson; grandson of one's grandson

【玄武】xuánwǔ ❶ 指乌龟 tortoise ❷ 二十八宿中北方七宿的合称 collective name for the northernmost seven of the 28 constellations ❸〈道教 *Taoism*〉所奉的北方的神 God of Northern Lunar Mansions

【玄想】xuánxiǎng 幻想 fancy; imagination：妄生～ entertain an extravagant hope; be lost in one's imagination | 闭目～ meditate with eyes closed; be lost in a reverie with eyes closed

【玄虚】xuánxū 用使人迷惑的形式来掩盖真相的欺骗手段 deceitful trick; mystery; using deceptive means to cover up the truth：故弄～ make a mystery of things; mystify; turn simple things into mysteries on purpose

【玄学】xuánxué ❶ 魏晋时代，何晏、王弼等运用道家的老庄思想糅合儒家经义而形成的一种唯心主义哲学思潮 metaphysics; branch of philosophy created by He Yan and Wang Bi of the Wei and Jin dynasties, which combines the doctrines of Taoism and Confucianism ❷ 形而上学 metaphysics

【玄远】xuányuǎn 〈书 *fml.*〉(言论、道理)深远 (of sayings and arguments) abstruse; profound

【玄之又玄】xuán zhī yòu xuán《老子》第一章：'玄之又玄，众妙之门。'后来形容非常玄妙，难以理解。mysterious and abstruse to understand. *Laozi · Chapter One*: '... The mystery of mysteries, and gateway of all subtleties.'

痃 xuán ☞ 横痃 héngxuán on p.799

悬1 (懸) xuán ❶ same as 挂 guà ①：倒～ hang upside down | ～灯结彩 be festooned with lanterns and colourful streamers ❷ 公开揭示 disclose to the public：～赏 offer a reward ❸ same as 抬 tái ①；不着地 raise; uplift; away from the ground：写大字时最好把腕子～起来。You'd better raise your

X

wrist when you practise calligraphy. ❹ 无着落;没结果 unresolved; unsettled: ～案 unsettled legal case|～而未决 unsettled|他的问题还～着。His case remains unresolved. ❺ 挂念 miss; be concerned about: ～念 be solicitous about|～望 speculate; conjecture|心～两处 be worried about both sides ❻ 凭空设想 imagine; assume; conceive; visualize: ～拟 fabricate; make up|～想 speculate; conjecture ❼ 距离远;差别大 distance; greatly different: ～隔 be separated by a great distance; be far apart|～殊 great disparity; far apart

悬[2]（懸）xuán〈方 *dial.*〉危险 dangerous: 一个人摸黑走山路,真～! It is really dangerous to go walking in the mountains in the pitch darkness.|好～,差一点儿掉到井里。How dangerous! I just missed falling into the well by a sheer chance!

【悬案】xuán'àn ❶ 没有解决的案件 unsettled legal case: 一桩～ an unsettled legal case ❷ 泛指没有解决的问题 (in a broad sense) unsettled issue; unresolved problem: 这篇文章的作者是谁,至今还是个～。It remains a riddle to this day who the writer of this article is.

【悬臂】xuánbì 某些机器、机械等伸展在机身外部像手臂的部分 cantilever; arm-like, projecting part of certain machines or mechanical instruments

【悬揣】xuánchuǎi 猜想;揣测 guess; speculate: 凭空～ conjecture without any clue

【悬垂】xuánchuí (物体)悬空下垂 (of an object) overhang: 天车的挂钩在空中～着。The pot-hook of the crane is hanging in midair.

【悬浮】xuánfú ❶ 固体微粒在流体中运动而不沉下去 suspend; (of particulate) float in liquid: 这瓶油里含有～物质。This bottle of oil contains suspended particules. ❷ 飘浮 float: 灰尘～在空中。Dust is floating in the air.

【悬隔】xuángé 相隔很远 be separated by a great distance; be far apart: 两地～。The two places are far apart.

【悬挂】xuánguà same as 挂 guà ①: ～国旗 fly the national flag ◇一轮明月～在夜空。A full, bright moon is hanging in the night sky.

【悬乎】xuán·hu〈方 *dial.*〉危险;不保险;不牢靠 scary; dangerous; unsafe; unreliable: 叫他办事可有点～。It's not safe to entrust the matter to him.

【悬壶】xuánhú〈书 *fml.*〉指行医 practise medicine

【悬空】xuánkōng ❶ 离开地面,悬在空中 hang in the air: 两手抓住杠子,身体～。Hold on to bars with your hands and let your body hang in midair. ❷〈比喻 *fig.*〉没有落实或没有着落 unsettled; unresolved: 资金还～着,说建房的事也只是空谈。With finances still unsettled, it is impractical to talk about building houses.

【悬梁】xuánliáng 在房梁上上吊 hang oneself from a beam: ～自尽 commit suicide by hanging oneself from a beam; hang oneself

【悬铃木】xuánlíngmù 落叶乔木,叶子大,掌状分裂,花淡黄绿色,果穗球形。可以作为行道树,木材供建筑用。chinar (*Platanus*); plane tree; deciduous arbour having large, palm-like leaves, pale, greenish yellow flowers and round fruit, usually planted along roads, and its wood used as a building material; also 法国梧桐 Fǎguó wútóng

【悬拟】xuánnǐ 凭空虚构 fabricate; make up; invent: 这篇小说的情节是～的。The plot of this story is fabricated.

【悬念】xuánniàn ❶ 挂念 be concerned about ❷ 欣赏戏剧、电影或其他文艺作品时,对故事发展和人物命运的关切心情 suspense; deep concern over the development of a story and the fate of characters in a play, a movie or other literary works

【悬赏】xuán//shǎng 用出钱等奖赏的办法公开征求别人帮助做某件事 offer a reward for sth.; solicit help from others by promising a reward of money, etc.: ～寻人 offer a reward for finding a missing person|～缉拿 offer a reward for the capture of a fugitive; set a price on a runaway criminal's head

【悬殊】xuánshū 相差很远 great disparity; wide gap: 众寡～ great disparity in numbers|贫富～ wide gap between the rich and the poor|敌我力量～。There's a great disparity in strength between the enemy's troops and ours.

【悬索桥】xuánsuǒqiáo same as 吊桥 diàoqiáo ②

【悬梯】xuántī 悬挂在直升飞机等上面的绳梯 ladder hanging from a helicopter, etc.

【悬腕】xuán//wàn 指用毛笔写大字时手腕子不挨着桌子 hold both wrist and elbow above the table when writing large characters with a brush

【悬望】xuánwàng 不放心地盼望 anxiously await; expect anxiously: 你办完事赶紧回来,免得家中～。Come back as soon as you're done, since the whole family is anxiously awaiting you.

【悬想】xuánxiǎng 凭空想像 imagine; fancy: 闭目～ be lost in thought with one's eyes closed

【悬心】xuán//xīn 担心 be worried about; be on tenterhooks: 写封信把情况告诉家里,免得家人～。Write to your family about yourself, so they don't worry about you.

【悬心吊胆】xuán xīn diào dǎn ☞ 提心吊胆 tí xīn diào dǎn on p. 1882

【悬崖】xuányá 高而陡的山崖 overhanging or steep cliff; precipice: ～绝壁 sheer precipices and overhanging rocks; cliffs and precipices

【悬崖勒马】xuányá lè mǎ〈比喻 *fig.*〉临到危险的边缘及时清醒回头 rein in at the brink of a precipice; wake up and escape disaster at the last moment; pull back before it is too late

【悬雍垂】xuányōngchuí 软腭后部中央向下垂的肌肉小突起，略呈圆锥形。咽东西时随软腭上升，有闭塞鼻腔通路的作用。uvula; small, roughly cone-shaped fleshy mass of tissue suspended from the centre of the soft palate, which goes up with the palate when food is swallowed, and has the function to block the nasal cavity; 通称 generally known as 小舌 xiǎoshé;（图见 ☞ figure for 人的喉 rén·de hóu on p. 808）

【悬浊液】xuánzhuóyè 微小的固体颗粒悬浮在液体中形成的混合物。悬浊液是浑浊的，静置相当时间后，固体颗粒会下降沉底，如石灰水。turbid liquid; muddy mixture of sediment or foreign particles suspended in a liquid when stirred up and sinking to the bottom when the liquid is set aside for some time, e. g. lime water; also 悬浮液 xuánfúyè

旋 xuán ❶ 旋转 revolve; circle; spin: ～绕 curl up; wind around | 盘～ hover; circle | 回～ circle around | 天～地转 feel faint and dizzy as if the sky and earth were spinning round; feel one's head swim ❷ 返回；归来 return; come back: ～里 return to one's hometown; return home | 凯～ return in triumph ❸ (～儿 xuánr) 圈儿 circle; whorl: ～涡 whirlpool; eddy; vortex; maelstrom | 老鹰在空中一个～儿一个～儿地转了半天。The eagle kept circling in the sky for a long time. ❹ (～儿 xuánr) 毛发呈旋涡状的地方 part of the scalp where the hair is whorled: 头顶上有两个～儿。There are two parts on the scalp where the hair is whorled. ❺〈书 *fml.*〉不久；很快地 soon; quickly: 入场券～即发完。All the tickets were quickly sold out. ❻ (Xuán) 姓 a surname

☞ xuàn on p. 2175

【旋即】xuánjí 不久；很快地 soon; before long; quickly: 他见事情已了结，～转身离去。Upon seeing the matter settled, he immediately turned to leave.

【旋律】xuánlǜ 乐音经过艺术构思而形成的有组织、有节奏的和谐运动。旋律是乐曲的基础，乐曲的思想情感都是通过它表现出来的。melody; rhythmically organized sequence of single tones so artistically related to one another as to create a harmonious flow of notes; as the basis of music, melody expresses the ideas and emotions of a piece of music

【旋绕】xuánrào 缭绕 curl up; wind around: 炊烟～。Smoke is curling up from the kitchen chimneys. | 歌声～。The songs reverberated throughout the area. | 求学的念头一直～在脑际。The idea of going to school kept coming into his head.

【旋塞】xuánsāi 阀的一种，一般安装在压力低、口径小的管道上，阀上有一个带孔的塞子，旋转塞子，可控制流体的通过 faucet; valve usu. fixed on a low-pressure, small-calibre pipe, having a perforated plug which revolves to control the flow of liquid

【旋梯】xuántī ❶ 体育运动器械。形状像梯子，中间有一根轴固定在铁架上，能够来回旋转。winding stairs; revolving sports equipment in the form of a ladder, with its axis fixed on an iron frame in the centre ❷ 利用旋梯的摆和旋转锻炼身体的一种体育运动 physical exercise using the winding stairs' swaying and revolving features

【旋涡】xuánwō ❶ (～儿 xuánwōr) 流体旋转时形成的螺旋形 whirlpool; vortex; eddy; maelstrom; spiral motion of revolving fluid ❷〈比喻 *fig.*〉牵累人的事情 sth. that people get caught in: 陷入爱情的～ fall head over heels in love ‖ also 漩涡 xuánwō

【旋翼】xuányì 直升机机舱上面可以旋转的机翼 rotor (wing); rotating aerofoils on the engine hold of a helicopter

【旋凿】xuánzáo〈方 *dial.*〉改锥 screwdriver

【旋踵】xuánzhǒng〈书 *fml.*〉把脚后跟转过来 turn around on one's heel;〈比喻 *fig.*〉极短的时间 in an instant; immediately: ～即逝 vanish before one has time to turn round; disappear in the twinkling of an eye

【旋转】xuánzhuǎn 物体围绕一个点或一个轴作圆周运动。如地球绕地轴旋转，同时也围绕太阳旋转。revolve; gyrate; rotate; spin; revolve around a fixed point or axis, e. g. the earth spinning on its own axis and revolving around the sun as well

【旋转乾坤】xuánzhuǎn qiánkūn 改变自然的面貌或已成的局面。形容人的本领极大。make a drastic change to the natural or established order; be earth-shaking; be earth-shattering; have the daring and resourcefulness to do sth.; also 旋乾转坤 xuán qián zhuǎn kūn

【旋子】xuán·zi 圈儿 circle; whirl: 鸟儿见了火光惊飞起来，打了几个～，消失在黑暗中。At the sight of fire, the bird flew up in panic, circled in the air several times, and vanished in the darkness.

☞ xuàn·zi on p. 2176

漩 xuán (～儿 xuánr) 回旋的水流 whirlpool; eddy: 水打着～儿向下流。The water is flowing down the river in eddies.

【漩涡】xuánwō same as 旋涡 xuánwō

璇(璿) xuán〈书 *fml.*〉美玉 fine jade

【璇玑】xuánjī ❶〈古代 *arch.*〉测天文的仪器 armillary sphere; astronomical instrument ❷

X

〈古代 *arch.*〉称北斗星的第一星至第四星 name for the first four stars in the Big Dipper

xuǎn (ㄒㄩㄢˇ)

选(選) xuǎn ❶ 挑选 select; choose; pick: 筛～ screen; sieve | ～拔 choose; select | ～派 select and send | ～种 seed selection ❷ 选举 elect: ～民 voter; electorate | 普～ general election | ～代表 select a representative ❸ 被选中了的(人或物) (person or thing) selected or chosen: 入～ be elected | 人～ candidate ❹ 挑选出来编在一起的作品 selection; anthology: 文～ anthology of essays | 诗～ selected poems | 民歌～ anthology of folk songs

【选拔】xuǎnbá 挑选(人才) select; choose (talented people): ～赛 selective trial | ～运动员 select athletes | ～基层干部 select cadres at the grass-roots level

【选拔赛】xuǎnbásài 竞赛的一种,目的是发现和挑选人员参加高一级的比赛 tryout; qualifying trial; selective trial; test to ascertain and choose qualified applicants for higher-level competitions

【选本】xuǎnběn 从一个人的或若干人的著作中选出部分篇章编辑成的书 anthology; selected works; book that incorporates selected works from several writers' or one writer's works

【选编】xuǎnbiān ❶ 从资料或文章中挑选出一部分编在一起 select excerpts from materials or articles and compile into a book: ～一本清代诗集 select Qing-dynasty poems for a collection ❷ 选编的集子(多用做书名 usu. used in book titles) selected (works); anthology: 《历代白话小说～》 *Selected Vernacular Stories of Various Dynasties*

【选材】xuǎn//cái ❶ 挑选合适的人材 select a suitable person ❷ 选择适用的材料或素材 choose suitable materials: 精于～ be skilful in selecting materials

【选调】xuǎndiào 选拔调动 recruit: 国家足球队队员是从各省市～来的。Members of the national football team are recruited from provinces and municipalities across the country.

【选读】xuǎndú ❶ 选择阅读 pick out (pieces or passages) to read; read excerpts: 这篇文章比较长,大家可以～其中的一部分。Since the article is quite long, you may pick out certain parts to read. ❷ 从一个人或若干人的著作中选出一部分编成的供阅读的书(多用做书名 usu. used in book titles) selection; selected readings; book compiled from selections of a writer's works or from different writers' works: 《古代诗歌～》 *Selected Readings of Ancient Poetry*

【选段】xuǎnduàn 从乐曲、戏曲等中间选取的片段 aria; selected passages or parts from a piece of music or an opera: 民族音乐～ selected passages of national music | 京剧～ selected arias of Peking Opera

【选集】xuǎnjí 选录一个人或若干人的著作而成的集子(多用做书名 usu. used in book titles) selection; anthology; volume of selected works of one writer or several writers

【选辑】xuǎnjí ❶ 挑选并辑录 select and compile: 他们合作～了上百万字的古汉语语法资料。They co-selected and co-compiled around one million characters of material on classical Chinese grammar. ❷ 选辑成的书(多用做书名 oft. used in book titles) selected works or writings: 《文史资料～》 *Selected Readings from Historical and Cultural Archives*

【选举】xuǎnjǔ 用投票或举手等表决方式选出代表或负责人 elect a representative or leader by ballot or a show of hands: ～工会主席 elect chairperson for the trade union

【选举权】xuǎnjǔquán ❶ 公民依法选举国家权力机关代表的权利 right to vote; franchise; suffrage; constitutional or statutory right for a citizen to elect the representatives to organs of state power ❷ 各种组织的成员选举本组织的领导人员或代表的权利 right to vote; right of members of an organization to elect its leading body or representatives

【选刊】xuǎnkān ❶ 挑选并刊载 select and publish: 从他的许多速写中,～一组,以飨读者。A collection of his works has been selected from his many writings, and published here for the appreciation of the reader. ❷ 专门选择刊载已经发表的某类作品的刊物(多用做刊物名 oft. used in titles of periodicals) magazine that specializes in selecting and publishing works that have already been published by other periodicals: 《中篇小说～》 *Selected Novelettes*

【选矿】xuǎnkuàng 把矿物中的废石、杂质和其他矿物分离出去,取得适于冶炼需要的矿石 ore dressing; mineral separation; beneficiation; getting rid of useless stones, sediments and other minerals from useful ores that are to be smelted

【选录】xuǎnlù 选择收录(文章等) select (writings, etc.): 这本散文集～当代散文一百篇。This collection has garnered 100 pieces of prose from among contemporary writers.

【选民】xuǎnmín 有选举权的公民 voter; elector; citizen who has the right to vote: ～证 elector's certificate; voter registration card

【选派】xuǎnpài 挑选合于规定条件的人派遣出去 select and appoint; detail; select qualified people and dispatch them: ～留学生 select students and send them abroad to study | ～代表参加大会 select representatives to a conference

【选票】xuǎnpiào 选举者用来填写或圈定被选举人姓名的票 vote; ballot; form on which a voter fills in or circles the chosen candidates' names

【选区】xuǎnqū 为了进行选举而按人口划分的区域 election district; electoral ward; different areas divided according to population for the purpose of elections

【选取】xuǎnqǔ 挑选采用 select; choose: ～一条近路 choose a shortcut | 经过认真考虑,他～了自学的方式。After careful consideration, he chose a method to teach himself.

【选任】xuǎnrèn 选拔任用 select a suitable person for a post; promote a qualified person; empanel

【选手】xuǎnshǒu 被选参加体育比赛的人 athlete selected for a sports meet; player; contestant: 乒乓球～ ping-pong player

【选送】xuǎnsòng 挑选推荐 select and recommend sb.: ～学员 select qualified students to recommend for admission to a school

【选修】xuǎnxiū 学生从指定可以自由选择的科目中,选定自己要学习的科目(区别于'必修' as opposed to 'prerequisite') take as an elective (course): ～科 elective course; optional course; elective | 他～的是法文。He took French as an elective.

【选用】xuǎnyòng 选择使用或运用 select and use; choose and apply: ～人才 select talented people | ～资料 choose data

【选择】xuǎnzé 挑选 choose; opt; select; pick: ～对象 choose one's boyfriend or girlfriend; select an object | ～地点 choose a location

【选种】xuǎn//zhǒng 选择动物或植物的优良品种,加以繁殖 seed selection; selecting the best breeds of animals and plants for breeding

晅 xuǎn〈书 *fml.*〉❶ 光明 bright; brilliant ❷ 干燥 dry; desiccated

烜 xuǎn 又 also xuān〈书 *fml.*〉盛大 magnificent; grand: ～赫 of great renown and influence; prestigious and influential

【烜赫】xuǎnhè〈书 *fml.*〉形容名声很大、声势很盛 of great renown and influence; prestigious and influential: ～一时 enjoy great fame and exert great influence for a period | 气势～ tremendous influence or power

癣 xuǎn 由霉菌引起的某些皮肤病的统称,如发癣、脚癣、手癣等 tinea; ringworm; general term for skin diseases caused by mildew, e. g. hair tinea, athlete's foot, tinea manus, etc.

xuàn(ㄒㄩㄢˋ)

券 xuàn 又 also quàn 拱券 arch: 发～ build an arch (into a wall) | 打～ build an arch

☞ quàn on p. 1601

泫 xuàn〈书 *fml.*〉水点下垂 (of water) drip; trickle: 花上露犹～。The flowers are still dripping with dew.

【泫然】xuànrán〈书 *fml.*〉水滴下的样子(多指眼泪 usu. tears) fall; stream down: ～泪下。Tears streamed down (his) face.

昡 xuàn〈书 *fml.*〉日光 sunshine; sunlight; daylight

炫(❷衒) xuàn〈书 *fml.*〉❶(强烈的光线)晃人的眼睛 (of strong light) dazzle; hurt one's eyes: ～目 dazzling ❷ 夸耀 show off; flaunt; vaunt: ～弄 show off | ～示 parade | 自～其能 show off one's ability

【炫目】xuànmù (光彩)耀眼 dazzling: 装饰华丽～ splendidly furnished

【炫弄】xuànnòng 炫耀卖弄 show off; display; parade: ～技巧 show off one's skill

【炫示】xuànshì 故意在人面前显示(自己的长处) show off; display; parade; make a show of (one's strengths) before others on purpose: 他有才华,但从不在人前～。He's a gifted person, but he never shows off before others.

【炫耀】xuànyào ❶ 照耀 shine; illuminate ❷ 夸耀 show off; flaunt; make a display of: ～武力 make a display of one's prowess; flaunt one's military power

【炫鬻】xuànyù〈书 *fml.*〉夸耀卖弄 make a parade of; vaunt; flaunt; show off; pique oneself on

绚 xuàn 色彩华丽 gorgeous; colourful; resplendent: ～丽 resplendent | ～烂 splendid; gorgeous

【绚烂】xuànlàn 灿烂 splendid; gorgeous; brilliant: ～的朝霞 splendid morning clouds | ～多彩 riot of colour

【绚丽】xuànlì 灿烂美丽 bright and beautiful; resplendent; magnificent: 文采～ literary grace; literary gift | ～的鲜花 gorgeous flowers

眩 xuàn ❶(眼睛)昏花 (of vision) dizzy; giddy; vertiginous: 头晕目～ feel dizzy ❷〈书 *fml.*〉迷惑;执迷 puzzled; bewildered: ～于名利 lose one's self-control over the prospect of fame and wealth; be obsessed with a desire for fame and wealth

【眩晕】xuànyùn 感觉到本身或周围的东西旋转 dizziness; whirl; feel everything to be spinning around: 突然一阵～,差一点儿摔倒 almost fall to the ground in a dizzy spell

铉 xuàn〈古代 *arch.*〉横贯鼎耳以扛鼎的器具 hook-like instrument to carry an ancient tripod by its ears

旋[1](❷❸镟) xuàn ❶ 转的 revolving; rolling; rotary; gyral; whirly: ～风 cyclone; tornado; vortex; whirlwind ❷ 用车床切削或用刀子转(zhuàn)着圈地削

cut sth. by turning on a lathe; peel circularly with a knife: ～根车轴 lathe an axle | 把梨皮～掉 peel a pear ❸ same as 旋子[1] xuàn·zi

旋[2] xuàn〈副词 *adv.*〉临时(做) at the time when sth. is needed; at the last moment: ～用～买 buy for immediate use; buy sth. when one needs it | 客人到了～做,就来不及了。It'll be too late to start preparing dinner after the guests have arrived.

☞ xuán on p. 2173

【旋风】xuànfēng 螺旋状运动的风 whirlwind

【旋子】[1] xuàn·zi ❶ 一种金属器具,像盘而较大,通常用来做粉皮等 copper plate for making sheets of bean-starch jelly, etc. ❷ 温酒时盛水的金属器具 metal hot-water container for warming wine

【旋子】[2] xuàn·zi 武术的一种动作,甩臂,拧腰,旋腿,平身跃起,双脚落地 whirlwind somersault; a type of movement in martial arts, including tossing arms, bending waist, spinning legs, jumping and landing

☞ xuán·zi on p. 2173

渲 xuàn same as 渲染 xuànrǎn ①

【渲染】xuànrǎn ❶ 国画的一种画法,用水墨或淡的色彩涂抹画面,以加强艺术效果 Chinese painting style, where washes of ink or pale colours are added to a Chinese painting to heighten artistic effect; ratchet up ❷〈比喻 *fig.*〉夸大的形容 play up; exaggerate; pile it on; heighten: 一件小事情,用不着这么～。No need to exaggerate a trifling matter like that.

楦(楥) xuàn ❶ 楦子 last: 鞋～ shoe last | 帽～ hat block ❷ 用楦子填紧或撑大鞋帽的中空部分 stuff or enlarge a shoe or a hat with a last or block: 新绱的鞋要～一～。A pair of new shoes needs lasting. ❸〈方 *dial.*〉泛指用东西填紧物体的中空部分 (in a broad sense) fill up with padding: 装完瓷器,把箱子～好。Fill up the trunk after putting the porcelain ware in.

【楦子】xuàn·zi 制鞋、制帽时所用的模型,多用木头做成 shoe last; hat block; hat or shoe mould, usu. made of wood; also 楦头 xuàn·tou

碹(镟) xuàn ❶ 桥梁、涵洞等工程建筑的弧形部分 arch of a bridge, culvert or other engineering projects ❷ 用砖、石等筑成弧形 arch built of bricks, stones, etc.

xuē (ㄒㄩㄝ)

削 xuē 义同'削'(xiāo),专用于合成词,如剥削、削减、削弱 having the same meaning as 削 xiāo, used in compound words, e.g. 剥削 bōxuē, 削减 xuējiǎn and 削弱 xuēruò

☞ xiāo on p. 2099

【削壁】xuēbì 直立的山崖,像削过的一样 precipice; cliff: 悬崖～ overhanging cliff

【削发】xuēfà 剃掉头发(出家做僧尼) tonsure; cut off one's hair (as a symbol of renouncing worldly life to become a nun or monk)

【削价】xuējià 减价;降价 cut the price; lower the price: ～处理 disposal of goods at reduced prices; clearance sale

【削减】xuējiǎn 从已定的数目中减去 cut down; reduce; slash; whittle down from a fixed number: ～不必要的开支 cut down unnecessary expenditures

【削平】xuēpíng〈书 *fml.*〉消灭;平定 wipe out; suppress; subdue: ～叛乱 quell a rebellion

【削弱】xuēruò ❶ (力量、势力)变弱 (of strength and power) weaken; die down; enfeeble: 几名主力队员离队后,这支球队实力有所～。The strength of the football team has been sapped since several top players left. ❷ 使变弱 weaken; cripple; enfeeble; undermine: ～敌人的力量 cripple or weaken an enemy

【削足适履】xuē zú shì lǚ 鞋小脚大,为了穿上鞋把脚削小 cut one's feet to fit shoes;〈比喻 *fig.*〉不合理地迁就现成条件,或不顾具体条件,生搬硬套 unreasonably conform to existing conditions; mechanically imitate regardless of specific conditions

靴(鞾) xuē 靴子 boots: 马～ riding boots | 皮～ leather boots | 雨～ rain boots | 雪地～ snow boots

【靴靿】xuēyào (～儿 xuēyàor) 靴子的筒 boot leg

【靴子】xuē·zi 帮子略呈筒状高到踝子骨以上的鞋 boot; shoe that has a taller part covering part or all of the leg

薛 Xuē 姓 a surname

xué (ㄒㄩㄝ)

穴 xué ❶ 岩洞。泛指地上或某些建筑物上的坑或孔 cave; (in a broad sense) pits in the ground or holes in some buildings: 洞～ cave | 孔～ hole | ～居 live in a cave | 空～来风。An empty cave invites the wind — weakness lends wing to rumour. ❷ 动物的窝 den; nest; lair: 巢～ nest; hideout | 虎～ tiger's lair | 蚁～ ant hole ❸ 墓穴 coffin pit: 土～ earth pit | 砖～ brick pit ❹ 医学上指人体上可以进行针灸的部位,多为神经末梢密集或较粗的神经纤维经过的地方 (med.) acupuncture point; point on the body of dense nerve bundles or relatively thick nerve fibres, where a thin needle is inserted; also 穴位 xuéwèi or 穴道 xuédào ❺ (Xué) 姓 a surname

【穴播】xuébō 播种的一种方法,把种子放在挖好的坑里并盖上土;点播 bunch planting; dibble

seeding; dibbling; way of sowing seeds in a hole and covering with soil

【穴道】xuédào same as 穴 xué ④

【穴居野处】xué jū yě chǔ 指人类没有房屋以前的生活状态 referring to people dwelling in caves in the wilds before houses were invented; lead a primitive life

【穴头】xuétóu (～儿 xuétóur)组织走穴的人 illicit broker who arranges moonlighting performances by actors or actresses from state-owned troupes

【穴位】xuéwèi ❶ same as 穴 xué ④ ❷ 墓穴的位置 location of a tomb pit

茓 xué 用茓子围起来囤粮食 store grain in a silo made of coarse matting

【茓子】xué·zi 用高粱秆、芦苇等的篾儿编制的狭而长的粗席子，可以围起来囤粮食 matting; long and narrow matting woven of sorghum stalks and reed, used to make grain silos; also 踅子 xué·zi

峃(嶨) xué 峃口(Xuékǒu)，地名，在浙江 Xuekou, name of a place in Zhejiang Province

学(學、斈) xué ❶ 学习 learn; study: ～技术 learn a skill | 勤工俭～ work-study programme; part-work and part-study system | 我跟着他～了许多知识。I've learned a lot from him. ❷ 模仿 emulate; imitate; mimic: 他～杜鹃叫，～得很像。He can give a good imitation of the cuckoo crying. ❸ 学问 learning; knowledge; scholarship: 治～ pursue one's studies; do scholarly research | 才疏～浅 of little talent and learning | 博～多能 of great learning and versatility ❹ 指学科 subject of study; branch of learning: 数～ mathematics | 物理～ physics | 政治经济～ science of political economy ❺ 学校 school: 小～ primary school | 大～ college; university | 上～ go to school

【学报】xuébào 学术团体、科研单位或高等学校定期出版的学术性刊物 journal; learned journal; academic journal regularly published by an academic institution, research institute, college, university, etc.

【学部】xuébù ❶ 清末掌管全国教育的官署 Ministry of Education towards the end of the Qing Dynasty ❷ 中国科学院和中国工程院各学科的咨询机构，由若干院士(旧称学部委员)组成，院士由院内外著名科学家担任 academic committee of the Chinese Academy of Sciences and the Chinese Academy of Engineering, composed of a number of academicians (as academic committee members were called in the past), all of whom are famous scientists working within or without the Academy

【学潮】xuécháo 指学生、教职员因对当时政治或学校事务有所不满而掀起的风潮 student strike; campus upheaval; movement sponsored by students and teachers dissatisfied with the political or school affairs of the time

【学阀】xuéfá 指凭借势力把持教育界或学术界的人 scholar-lord; scholar-tyrant; person who controls education and academia by force

【学费】xuéfèi ❶ 学校规定的学生在校学习应缴纳的费用 tuition fee; tuition; money that a student is required to pay to a school for studying there ❷ 个人求学的费用 education expenses

【学分】xuéfēn 高等学校计算课业时间的单位。一般以一学期中每周上课一小时为一学分。学生读够规定的学分才能毕业。credit; measurement unit for calculating class hours in an institution of higher learning, usu. one credit meaning one class hour a week in a semester. Students need the required amount of credits to graduate.

【学风】xuéfēng 学校的、学术界的或一般学习方面的风气 academic atmosphere; academic discipline; style of study

【学府】xuéfǔ 指实施高等教育的学校 institution of higher learning; seat of learning: 最高～ most famous university; key institution of higher learning

【学富五车】xué fù wǔ chē 形容读书多，学问大 read five cartloads of books; be learned; be erudite in learning (五车 *wu che*: 指五车书 fire cartloads of books)

【学棍】xuégùn 依仗势力在教育界为非作歹的人 educator-despot; person who uses power to do evil in the field of education

【学好】xué//hǎo 以好人好事为榜样，照着去做 learn from a good example; emulate good

【学会】xuéhuì 由研究某一学科的人组成的学术团体，如物理学会、生物学会等 society; institute; association; academic organization consisting of people in the same research field, e.g. Society of Physics, Society of Biology, etc.

【学籍】xuéjí 登记学生姓名的册子，转指作为某校学生的资格 book to register students' names; one's status as a student at a school: 保留～ retain one's status as a student; keep sb. on the school roll | 开除～ throw sb. out of school; expel sb. from school

【学监】xuéjiān 〈旧时 *old*〉学校里监督、管理学生的人员 school inspector; person who manages and supervises students

【学界】xuéjiè 指教育界 educational circles; field of education

【学究】xuéjiū 唐代科举制度有'学究一经'科(专门研究一种经书)，应这一科考试的称为学究，后来指读书人。也指迂腐的读书人。The Tang-dynasty imperial examination system had a branch of learning specializing in studying a particular Confucian classic, and people called examinees of this branch *xuejiu*, bookwormish scholar; scholar; pedant: 老～ pedantic schoolmaster; old pedant

【学科】xuékē ❶ 按照学问的性质而划分的门类,如自然科学中的物理学、化学 branch of learning; discipline; branch of knowledge classified according to the nature of knowledge, e. g. physics and chemistry in natural science ❷ 学校教学的科目。如语文、数学。course of study; school curriculum, e. g. language and mathematics ❸ 军事训练或体育训练中的各种知识性的科目(区别于'术科'as opposed to 'skills course') theoretical courses offered in military or physical training

【学理】xuélǐ 科学上的原理或法则 scientific principle or theory

【学力】xuélì 在学问上达到的程度 educational level; scholastic or academic achievements; knowledge

【学历】xuélì 学习的经历,指曾在哪些学校肄业或毕业 record of formal schooling; record of education: 招聘有大学～的人员 solicit personnel with a college background

【学龄】xuélíng 指儿童适合于入学的年龄,通常从六、七岁开始 school age; suitable age for going to school, usu. from six or seven: ～儿童 school-age children

【学名】xuémíng ❶ 入学时使用的正式名字(区别于'小名' as different from 'pet name') formal name used at school; one's registered name at school❷ 科学上的专门名称,如食盐的学名是氯化钠 scientific name, e. g. the scientific name of salt is sodium chloride

【学年】xuénián 规定的学习年度。从秋季开学到暑假,或从春季开学到寒假为一学年。academic year; from the beginning of school in the autumn to the summer holidays, or from the beginning of school in the spring to the winter holidays

【学派】xuépài 同一学科中由于学说、观点不同而形成的派别 school of thought; schools formed due to different theories and views in the same field of learning

【学期】xuéqī 一学年分为两学期,从秋季开学到寒假和从春季开学到暑假各为一个学期 term; semester; school term. One academic year is divided into two terms: one from the beginning of school in the autumn to the winter holidays, and the other from the beginning of school in the spring to the summer holidays.

【学前班】xuéqiánbān 对学龄前快要入小学的儿童进行教育所编成的班级 preschool class organized to educate children before they enter primary school

【学前教育】xuéqián-jiàoyù 指对学龄前儿童进行的教育 preschool education; infant school education; ☞ 幼儿教育 yòu'ér jiàoyù on p. 2333

【学前期】xuéqiánqī 儿童从三岁到入学前的时期 preschool period, from the age of three to entry into formal schooling

【学区】xuéqū 为了便于学生上学和对学校的业务领导,根据中、小学分布情况划分的管理区 school district; administrative precinct, divided according to the layout of secondary and primary schools to facilitate schooling and school management

【学人】xuérén 学者 scholar; learned person; person of learning: 著名～ renowned scholar

【学舌】xué//shé ❶ 模仿别人说话 imitate the words or actions of another; mechanically repeat other people's words; parrot; 〈比喻 *fig.*〉没有主见,只是跟着别人说 imitate the words or actions of another, without having one's own views: 鹦鹉～ parrot; imitate mechanically ❷ 嘴不严紧,把听到的话告诉别人 loose-tongued; gossipy

【学生】xué·sheng ❶ 在学校读书的人 student; pupil ❷ 向老师或前辈学习的人 disciple; follower ❸〈方 *dial.*〉男孩子 boy

【学生会】xuéshēnghuì 大学或中学校内全体学生的群众性组织 student union; student association; mass organization of students in a university or secondary school

【学生装】xué·shengzhuāng 一种服装,上身有三个没有盖的口袋,领子不向下翻,下身是西式长裤,过去多是学生穿的 student uniform, usu. consisting of a jacket with three pockets without flaps and a narrow stand-up collar, and a pair of Western-style trousers

【学识】xuéshí 学术上的知识和修养 learning; knowledge; scholarly attainments: ～渊博 have great learning; be erudite

【学时】xuéshí 一节课的时间,通常为四十五分钟 class hour; period, usu. lasting 45 minutes: 赵老师一周讲八个～的课。Teacher Zhao teaches eight classes a week.

【学士】xuéshì ❶ 指读书人 scholar: 文人～ literati; scholar ❷ 学位中最低的一级,大学毕业时由学校授予 bachelor; bachelor's degree; lowest degree granted by a university upon graduation

【学塾】xuéshú 私塾 private school; family school

【学术】xuéshù 有系统的、较专门的学问 systematic learning; science: ～界 academic circles|～思想 academic thought|～团体 academic organization|～性刊物 academic journal

【学说】xuéshuō 学术上的有系统的主张或见解 theory; doctrine; systematic theory of academic research

【学堂】xuétáng 〈方 *dial.*〉 same as 学校 xuéxiào

【学童】xuétóng 上学的儿童 pupil; primary school student

【学徒】xué//tú 当学徒 be apprenticed to; apprentice; serve an apprenticeship: 学了一年徒 be an apprentice for one year|他小时候在药铺～。He was a child apprentice in a pharmacy.

【学徒】xuétú 在商店里学做买卖或在作坊、工厂里学习技术的青年或少年 apprentice; trainee; youth or adolescent who learns to do business in a shop, or learns skills in a workshop or factory

【学徒工】xuétúgōng 跟随师傅(老工人)学习技术的青年工人 apprentice; young worker who learns skills from an old worker; also 徒工 túgōng

【学位】xuéwèi 根据专业学术水平由高等院校、科研机构等授予的称号,如博士、硕士、学士等 academic degree; degree; title granted by an institution of higher learning, research institute, etc., according to one's academic achievements

【学问】xué·wen ❶ 正确反映客观事物的系统知识 systematic learning; branch of knowledge; systematic knowledge that correctly reflects certain objective matters: 这是一门新兴的～。This is an emergent branch of learning. ❷ 知识;学识 knowledge; learning: 有～ be learned|～很大 be of great learning; be erudite

【学习】xuéxí ❶ 从阅读、听讲、研究、实践中获得知识或技能 learn; study; acquire knowledge or skills from reading, listening, research and practice: ～文化 acquire an elementary education; learn to read and write|～先进经验 learn from advanced experiences ❷ 效法 emulate; imitate: ～他的为人 emulate his conduct or behaviour

【学衔】xuéxián 高等学校教学人员、科研机构研究人员的专业职称,如教授、副教授、讲师、研究员、副研究员等 academic rank; academic titles of university teachers, researchers in scientific research institutes, etc., e.g. professor, associate professor, lecturer, researcher, associate researcher

【学校】xuéxiào 专门进行教育的机构 school; educational institution

【学养】xuéyǎng〈书 *fml.*〉学问和修养 learning and self-accomplishment; scholarship and self-cultivation: ～有素 well-educated and well-cultivated

【学业】xuéyè 学习的功课和作业 one's studies; school work: ～成绩 academic score; academic grades|～大有长进 make great progress in one's studies

【学友】xuéyǒu 同学 classmate; fellow student: 同窗～ schoolmate

【学员】xuéyuán 一般指在高等学校、中学、小学以外的学校或训练班学习的人 student; trainee; person who studies at a school other than post-secondary, secondary or primary schools, or takes part in a training course

【学院】xuéyuàn 高等学校的一种,以某一专业教育为主,如工业学院、音乐学院、师范学院等 college; academy; institute; institution of higher learning that specializes in certain subjects, e.g. industrial college, conservatory of music, normal school, etc.

【学长】xuézhǎng ❶ 对同学的尊称 respectful term of address for a classmate ❷〈旧时 *old*〉大学各科的负责人 dean; person in charge of a faculty: 文科～ dean of liberal arts|理科～ dean of natural science

【学者】xuézhě 指在学术上有一定成就的人 scholar; learned person; person of learning: 青年～ young scholar|访问～ visiting scholar

【学制】xuézhì 国家对各级各类学校的性质、任务、组织系统和课程、学习年限等的规定 educational system; school system; national regulations on the nature, responsibilities, administrative structure, curricula and length of semesters, etc., of schools at all levels

【学子】xuézǐ〈书 *fml.*〉学生 student: 莘莘(shēnshēn)～(很多学生) a number of students; many students; student population

敩(斅) xué〈书 *fml.*〉same as 学 xué

☞ xiào on p. 2117

踅 xué 来回走;中途折回 walk to and fro; turn back halfway: 他在大门口～来～去。He was loitering at the gate.|没走多远,就～回来了。(He) turned back after not going very far.

【踅摸】xué·mo〈方 *dial.*〉寻找 look for; search for: 想到旧书店～两本书 want to look for a couple of books in a second-hand bookstore

【踅子】xué·zi same as 茓子 xué·zi

噱 xué〈方 *dial.*〉笑 laugh: ～头 words or acts meant to amuse others|发～ speak or act to make others laugh

☞ jué on p. 1062

【噱头】xuétóu〈方 *dial.*〉❶ 引人发笑的话或举动 words or acts meant to amuse others: 相声演员～真多。The cross-talk actors really have many ways to amuse the audience. ❷ 花招 trick: 摆～(耍花招) play tricks; take cunning actions ❸ 滑稽 funny; amusing; comical: 很～ very funny|～极了 extremely amusing

xuě (ㄒㄩㄝˇ)

雪 1 xuě ❶ 空气中降落的白色结晶,多为六角形,是气温降低到0℃以下时,空气层中的水蒸气凝结而成的 snow; white crystals falling from the sky, usu. hexagonal, and formed by condensation of vapour in the atmosphere when the temperature drops below 0℃ ❷ 颜色或光彩像雪的（of colour or gloss) snow-like; snowy: ～白 snow-white | ～亮 as bright as snow ❸（Xuě）姓 a surname

雪2 xuě 洗掉（耻辱、仇恨、冤枉）wash oneself of（humiliation, animosity, or injustice）; clean: ～耻 avenge an insult; wipe out a disgrace or humiliation | ～恨 wreak vengeance; avenge | 昭～ rehabilitate; exonerate; be cleared of unfounded charges | 洗～ wipe out (a disgrace or humiliation)

【雪白】xuěbái 像雪一样的洁白 snow-white; snowy white; as white as snow: ～的墙壁 snow-white wall | 梨花盛开，一片～。Blossoming pear flowers dyed this part of the world snowy white.

【雪豹】xuěbào 豹的一种，尾巴长，毛淡青而发灰色，全身有不规则的黑斑。生活在寒冷地区的高山中。snow leopard (*Panthera uncia*); ounce; leopard with a long tail, greyish black hair and irregular speckles covering its whole body, living in the high mountains of cold areas

【雪暴】xuěbào 大量积雪或降雪随强风飞舞的现象 snowstorm; blizzard; accumulated snow or snowflakes swirling in gusts of wind

【雪崩】xuěbēng 大量积雪从高山上突然崩落下来 snow-slide; avalanche; snow-slip; great amount of accumulated snow suddenly falling from high mountains

【雪耻】xuěchǐ 洗掉耻辱 avenge an insult; wipe out a disgrace or humiliation: 报仇～ avenge sb. to wipe out a disgrace

【雪糕】xuěgāo ❶ 一种冷食，用水、牛奶、鸡蛋、糖、果汁等混合搅拌冷冻而成，形状像冰棍儿 ice lolly; popsicle; frozen food made of water mixed with milk, eggs, sugar, fruit juice, etc., in the shape of a lollipop ❷〈方 *dial.*〉冰激凌 ice cream

【雪恨】xuěhèn 洗雪仇恨 wreak vengeance; avenge: 申冤～ redress an injustice and avenge oneself

【雪花】xuěhuā 空中飘下的雪，形状像花，因此叫雪花 snowflake: 北风吹，～飘。The northern wind is blowing, and snowflakes are falling.

【雪花膏】xuěhuāgāo 一种化妆品，用硬脂酸、甘油、苛性钾和香料等制成，通常为白色，用来滋润皮肤 vanishing cream; lotion made of stearic acid, glycerine, caustic potash and fragrance, etc., usu. white, and used to moisten skin

【雪茄】xuějiā 用烟叶卷成的烟，形状较一般的香烟粗而长 cigar; thicker and longer than an ordinary cigarette; also 卷烟 juǎnyān

【雪里红】xuělǐhóng 一年生草本植物，芥（jiè）菜的变种，叶子深裂，边缘皱缩，花鲜黄色。茎和叶子是普通蔬菜，通常腌着吃。potherb mustard (*Brassica cernua*); annual herbaceous plant and a variation of mustard with saw-edged leaves and yellow flowers, its stems and leaves being a common vegetable that is usu. pickled before serving; also 雪里蕻 xuělǐhóng

【雪里蕻】xuělǐhóng same as 雪里红 xuělǐhóng

【雪连纸】xuěliánzhǐ 纸的一种，一面光滑，多用来做信笺、写公文、印招贴传单等 paper with one smooth side, mostly used as writing paper and for documents, posters, leaflets, etc.

【雪莲】xuělián 草本植物，叶子长椭圆形，花深红色，花瓣薄而狭长。生长在新疆、青海、西藏、云南等地高山中。花可入药。snow lotus (*Saussurea involucrata*); herbaceous plant having oval leaves and crimson flowers with thin, narrow and long petals, growing in high mountains in the Xinjiang Uygur Autonomous Region, the Tibet Autonomous Region, and Qinghai and Yunnan provinces, its flowers used in traditional Chinese medicine

【雪亮】xuěliàng 像雪那样明亮 as bright as snow; shiny: ～的灯光 bright light; dazzling light | 电灯把屋里照得～。The electric light illuminated the room as bright as day. ◇群众的眼睛是～的。People's eyes are discerning.

【雪柳】xuěliǔ ❶ 落叶灌木，叶子披针形或卵状披针形，有光泽，花白色，有香气。供观赏。fortune fontanesia (*Fontanesia fortunei*); deciduous shrub having needle-like or oval lanceolate leaves with a sheen, and fragrant white flowers, usu. grown for ornamental purposes; also 过街柳 guòjiēliǔ or 稻柳 dàoliǔ ❷〈旧时 *old*〉办丧事在灵前供奉或出殡用做仪仗的一种东西，用细条白纸制成，挂在木棍上 ceremonial staff wrapped around with thin strips of white paper, usu. offered before the dead in a mourning ceremony or funeral procession

【雪盲】xuěmáng 因雪地上反射的强烈的光长时间刺激眼睛而造成的损伤，症状是眼睛疼痛，怕见光，流泪 niphablepsia; snow blindness; damage to the eye caused by long exposure to strong light reflected from snow, with symptoms of sore eyes, allergy to light, and tearing

【雪泥鸿爪】xuění hóngzhǎo 鸿雁在雪泥上踏过留下的痕迹 swan goose's claw prints in mud wet from melting snow（雪泥 *xueni*: 融化着雪水的泥土 mud wet from melting snow）;〈比喻 *fig.*〉往事遗留下的痕迹 traces of past events; traces of bygone days

【雪片】xuěpiàn 纷飞的雪花，多用于比喻 flying snowflakes, oft. used in a figurative way: 各方贺电，～飞来。Congratulatory messages poured in from every direction.

【雪橇】xuěqiāo 用狗、鹿、马等拉着在冰雪上滑行的一种没有轮子的交通工具 sled; sledge; sleigh; wheelless vehicle that glides on ice or snow, and oft. pulled by draught animals such as dogs, reindeer and horses

【雪青】xuěqīng 浅紫色 lilac

【雪人】xuěrén (～儿 xuěrénr)用雪堆成的人形 snowman; snow piled up in the shape of a human being

【雪山】xuěshān 常年覆盖着积雪的山 snow-capped mountain; snowy mountain

【雪上加霜】xuě shàng jiā shuāng 〈比喻 *fig.*〉一再遭受灾难,损害愈加严重 causing more serious damage with one disaster after another

【雪糁】xuěshēn 〈方 *dial.*〉(～儿 xuěshēnr)霰(xiàn) snow pellets; graupel; also 雪糁子 xuěshēn·zi

【雪松】xuěsōng 常绿乔木,叶子针形,淡绿色、蓝绿色或银灰色,球果卵形,树冠圆锥形,是珍贵的观赏树。产于喜马拉雅山麓。木材致密,有香味。deodar (*Cedrus deodara*); cedar; evergreen coniferous tree having pale green, bluish green or silvery grey leaves, egg-shaped cones and a conical tree crown. A valuable species of tree for ornamentation, it grows at the foot of the Himalayas, producing durable, aromatic wood.

【雪条】xuětiáo 〈方 *dial.*〉冰棍儿 ice lolly; frozen sucker; popsicle

【雪线】xuěxiàn 终年积雪区域的界线。雪线的高度一般随纬度的增高而降低。snow line; altitudinal boundary, marking the extent of snow in an area that is perennially covered with snow, with the altitude of the snow line usually lowering with increase in the latitude

【雪野】xuěyě same as 雪原 xuěyuán

【雪冤】xuěyuān 洗刷冤屈 clear sb. of a false charge; redress a wrong

【雪原】xuěyuán 覆盖着深雪的原野 snowfield; plain covered with deep snow: 林海～ vast forests covered with deep snow | 茫茫～,一望无际。The snowfield is vast and boundless.

【雪中送炭】xuě zhōng sòng tàn 〈比喻 *fig.*〉在别人急需的时候给以物质上的帮助 provide timely help; provide material help to others in need

【雪子】xuězǐ 〈方 *dial.*〉(～儿 xuězǐr)霰(xiàn) snow pellets; graupel

鳕 xuě 鳕鱼,下颌有一根须,背部有许多小黑斑,有三个背鳍,腹部灰白色。肝可制鱼肝油。cod (*Gadus morrhua*); fish with an antenna on its lower jaw, small black dots on its back, three dorsal fins and an off-white belly, its liver used to make cod-liver oil; 通称 commonly called 大头鱼 dàtóuyú

xuè (ㄒㄩㄝˋ)

血 xuè ❶ 人或高等动物体内循环系统中的液体组织,暗赤或鲜红色,有腥气,由血浆、血细胞和血小板构成。作用是把养分和激素输送给体内各个组织,收集废物送给排泄器官,调节体温和抵御病菌等。blood; complex fluid circulating in the vascular system of human beings and higher animals, dark red or bright red, smelling of fish, and composed of blood plasma, corpuscles and blood platelets. As a liquid tissue, blood has such functions as transporting nutrition and hormones to all tissues of the body, gathering and delivering waste to the emunctory, adjusting body temperature and withstanding the attack of germs. also 血液 xuèyè ❷ 有血统关系的 related by blood: ～亲 relatives by blood | ～缘 blood tie ❸ 〈比喻 *fig.*〉刚强热烈 staunch; unyielding: ～性 courageous and upright | ～气 energy; sap; vigour ❹ 指月经 periods; menstruation

☞ xiě on p. 2123

【血癌】xuè'ái 白血病的俗称 popular term for 白血病 báixuèbìng

【血案】xuè'àn 凶杀案件 murder case; bloody incident: 一桩～ a murder case

【血本】xuèběn 经商的老本儿 principal; original capital: 赔了～ lose all the original capital

【血崩】xuèbēng 〈中医 *Chin. med.*〉指妇女不在行经期子宫大量出血的病,因来势急剧,故名。常因子宫病变、阴道构造异常等引起。metrorrhagia; haemorrhage or bleeding from the uterus that occurs not during menstruation. Usu. of sudden onset, the disease is oft. caused by pathological changes in the uterus or deformations of the vagina. also 崩症 bēngzhèng

【血沉】xuèchén 新鲜的血液放在特制的带有刻度的玻璃管中,静置一定时间后,红细胞即从血浆中分离出来而下沉。红细胞下沉的速度叫血细胞沉降率,通称血沉。erythrocyte sedimentation rate (ESR); speed of erythrocyte separation from blood plasma and of sedimentation after fresh blood is put into a special calibrated test tube and set aside for a time

【血仇】xuèchóu 因亲族被杀害而结下的仇恨 blood feud: 报～ wage a bloody vendetta against sb. | 结下～ become sworn enemies; start a blood feud

【血防】xuèfáng 对血吸虫病的防治 prevention and cure of schistosomiasis or snail fever

【血粉】xuèfěn 用猪、牛、羊等动物的血液制成的粉状物质,用作饲料和肥料 blood powder; powder made from the blood of pigs, cattle, sheep, etc., used as fodder or fertilizer

【血管】xuèguǎn 血液在全身中循环时所经过的管状构造,分动脉、静脉和毛细管 blood vessel; tube structures, comprising arteries, veins and capillaries, through which blood circulates in the body; ☞ 动脉 dòngmài on p. 467, 静脉 jìngmài on p. 1033 and 毛细管

máoxìguǎn on p. 1308

【血光之灾】xuè guāng zhī zāi 迷信的人指被杀的灾难 mortal danger; (omen of) being killed as believed by a superstitious person

【血海深仇】xuèhǎi shēnchóu 指因亲人被杀害而引起的极深的仇恨 blood vendetta; immense debt of blood; intense and deep-seated hatred caused by the killing of one's family members

【血汗】xuèhàn 血和汗。象征辛勤的劳动。blood and sweat; sweat and toil; hard work; industrious work: ～钱 money earned through hard work | 粮食是农民用～换来的。The grain is harvested through the toil of the peasantry.

【血红】xuèhóng 像鲜血那样的红色;鲜红 blood red; as red as blood: ～的夕阳 blood-red sun

【血红蛋白】xuèhóng dànbái 血液中一种含铁和蛋白质的红色化合物,很容易与氧气或二氧化碳结合和分离。血液借血红蛋白从肺泡里吸取氧气输送给体内各个组织,又从体内各个组织把二氧化碳带回肺脏,排出体外。血液呈红色就是由于含有血红蛋白的缘故。haemoglobin; red compound in blood that contains iron and protein, and easily combines with or separates from oxygen or carbon dioxide. Blood relies on this compound to absorb oxygen from the lungs to convey to all body tissues and then bring back carbon dioxide collected from the tissues to the lungs, which is then discharged out of the body. It is due to this compound that blood is red. also 血红素 xuèhóngsù or 血色素 xuèsèsù

【血迹】xuèjì 血在物体上留下的痕迹 bloodstain: ～斑斑 bloodstained | 衣服上有～。There are bloodstains on the clothes.

【血浆】xuèjiāng 血液中除血细胞、血小板之外的部分,无色透明的液体,含有水、无机盐、营养物、激素、尿酸等 blood plasma; colourless, transparent liquid that contains water, inorganic salt, nutrients, hormones, uric acid, etc., and is a component of blood, along with blood corpuscles and blood platelets

【血口喷人】xuè kǒu pēn rén 〈比喻 *fig.*〉用恶毒的话诬蔑别人 make unfounded and malicious attacks upon sb.; venomously slander; sling mud at sb.

【血库】xuèkù 医务部门存放血液以备输血时应用的设备 blood bank; equipment used to store blood for future transfusion

【血亏】xuèkuī 〈中医 *Chin. med.*〉指贫血 anaemia

【血泪】xuèlèi 痛哭时眼睛里流出的血 shed tears of blood when one cries with grief; 〈比喻 *fig.*〉惨痛的遭遇 painful encounter: ～家史 family history written in blood and tears

【血路】xuèlù 拼死冲杀而突破重围的道路 bloody path; escape route; road created at the cost of lives, used to break through a tight encirclement: 杀出一条～ open up a bloody path; cut an escape route

【血脉】xuèmài ❶〈中医 *Chin. med.*〉指人体内的血管或血液循环 blood vessels; blood circulation: ～流通。The blood circulation in this case is smooth and healthy. ❷ 血统 blood relationship; blood lineage: ～相通 be related by blood

【血泊】xuèpō 大摊的血 pool of blood

【血气】xuèqì ❶ 精力 energy; sap; vigour: ～方刚 full of animal spirit; full of sap; full of vigour and vitality ❷ 血性 courage and uprightness: 有～的青年 courageous and upright youth

【血亲】xuèqīn 有血统关系的亲属 relatives by blood

【血清】xuèqīng 血浆中除去纤维蛋白后的淡黄色胶状液体,在血液凝固后才能分离出来 blood serum; pale yellow glue after fibrin is separated from plasma, an operation done only after the blood has solidified

【血球】xuèqiú 血细胞 blood cell; blood corpuscle

【血肉】xuèròu ❶ 血液和肌肉 blood and flesh: ～之躯 human body | ～模糊 be badly wounded; be badly mangled ❷〈比喻 *fig.*〉特别密切的关系 of intimate relationship; as close as flesh and blood: 劳动人民～相连。The working masses maintain flesh-and-blood ties with one another.

【血色】xuèsè 皮肤红润的颜色 redness of the face; colour; ruddy complexion: 面无～ pallid face; pale face

【血色素】xuèsèsù 血红蛋白 haemochrome

【血书】xuèshū 为了表示有极大的仇恨、冤屈或决心,用自己的血写成的遗书、诉状、志愿书等 will, petition, vow, etc., written in one's own blood to express one's hatred, grievance, determination, etc.

【血栓】xuèshuān 由于动脉硬化或血管内壁损伤等原因,心脏或血管内部由少量的血液凝结成的块状物,附着在心脏或血管的内壁上 thrombus; clot formed by a tiny amount of blood, caused by arteriosclerosis or damage to the interior walls of blood vessels, and clinging to the interior walls of the heart or blood vessels

【血水】xuèshuǐ 流出来的稀薄的血 watery blood flowing out from a part of the body

【血糖】xuètáng 血液中所含的糖,通常是葡萄糖,是机体的能源之一。主要来源是食物中的淀粉和糖类。blood sugar; sugar contained in the blood, usu. glucose, one of the energy sources for the body, mainly coming from amylum and saccharides in food

【血统】xuètǒng 人类因生育而自然形成的关系,如父母与子女之间,兄弟姊妹之间的关系 blood relationship; blood lineage; extraction; naturally formed relationships due to human reproduction, e.g. the relations between parents and children, and between brothers and sisters

【血统工人】xuètǒng gōngrén 出身于工人家庭的工人(多指产业工人 oft. referring to the industrial worker) worker of working-class parentage

【血污】xuèwū 流出的血在物体上留下的污痕 bloodstain; dirty blood traces left on objects: 斑斑～ bloodstained | 抹去脸上的～ wipe away the bloodstains on the face

【血吸虫】xuèxīchóng 寄生虫,灰白色,雌雄常合抱在一起。卵随粪便到水中,在水中孵化成毛蚴,进入钉螺体内变成尾蚴。尾蚴离开钉螺,遇到入水的人、畜就钻入皮肤,侵入体内,变成成虫。成虫主要寄生在肝脏和肠内,引起血吸虫病。血吸虫病的症状是发热、起风疹块、腹泻、有腹水、肝和脾肿大等。血吸虫病有的地区叫罗汉病。blood fluke; schistosome; elongated trematode of the genus *Schistosoma*, greyish parasitic, the male and female oft. clinging to each other, releasing eggs that are excreted together with feces out of the body of man or other mammals and hatch miracidia in water. The miracidia enter the snails, and after they have grown into cercarias, they leave the snails, penetrate the skin of man or mammals bathing or swimming in water, and grow into blood flukes that live parasitically in livers and intestines and cause schistosomiasis, or snail fever, which is known in some regions as 罗汉病 luóhànbìng. Symptoms of snail fever are fever, wheals, diarrhea, ascites, hepatomegaly, splenomegaly, etc.

【血洗】xuèxǐ 像用血洗了某个地方一样,形容残酷地屠杀人民 bloodbath; massacre; merciless slaughter

【血细胞】xuèxìbāo 血液中的细胞,由红骨髓、脾脏等制造出来,分白细胞和红细胞两种 blood corpuscle; blood cell produced by the red marrow and the spleen, classified as leucocyte or white blood cells, and erythrocyte or red blood cells; also 血球 xuèqiú; ☞ 白细胞 báixìbāo on p. 38 and 红细胞 hóngxìbāo on p. 805

【血象】xuèxiàng 用化验的方法把血液中所含红细胞、白细胞、血小板等的数目计算出来制成的图表,用做诊断的资料 haemogram; blood picture; chart to show the test-based numbers of white blood cells, red blood cells and platelets in the blood, used as reference data for diagnosis

【血小板】xuèxiǎobǎn 血液的组成部分之一,比血细胞小,形状不规则。有帮助止血和凝血的作用。blood platelet; one of the constituents of blood, smaller than blood corpuscles, and irregularly shaped, with the functions of stopping bleeding and promoting blood-clotting

【血腥】xuèxīng 血液的腥味 reeking of blood; bloody;〈比喻 *fig.*〉屠杀的残酷 sanguinary: ～统治 sanguinary rule; bloodstained rule | ～镇压 bloody crackdown; ruthless subjugation

【血型】xuèxíng 血液的类型,根据血细胞凝结现象的不同而分成 O,A,B 和 AB 四种。输血时,除 O 型可以输给任何型,AB 型可以接受任何型外,必须用同型的血。blood group; blood type, classified as Type O, Type A, Type B and Type AB, according to the different phenomena in blood corpuscle clotting. When blood transfusion is conducted — other than Type O, which is applicable to all blood types, and Type AB, which can receive any other blood types — a blood receiver can use only the same blood type as his own.

【血性】xuèxìng 刚强正直的气质 courageous and upright: ～汉子(有血性的人) courageous and upright man | ～男儿 courageous and upright youth

【血循环】xuèxúnhuán 血液从心脏流出,经动脉、毛细管,把氧、养料、激素等输送给全身各部组织,并把组织中的二氧化碳等废物经静脉带回心脏,再经肺动脉带入肺内,进行气体交换后,经肺静脉流回心脏,如此循环不已,叫做血循环 blood circulation; blood flows out of the heart into arteries and capillaries, transporting oxygen, nutrients and hormones to all body tissues, and bringing back waste such as carbon dioxide to the heart via the veins, and continuing forward via the pulmonary artery to the lungs where air exchange is conducted, and finally back to the heart via the pulmonary vein. Blood circulates continuously in the body.

【血压】xuèyā 血管中的血液对血管壁的压力,由于心脏收缩和主动脉壁的弹性作用而产生。心脏收缩时的最高血压叫收缩压。心脏舒张时的最低血压叫舒张压。blood pressure; pressure exerted by the blood against the walls of the blood vessels, produced by the strength of the heartbeat and the elasticity of the arterial walls. The highest pressure (when the heart contracts) is called systolic pressure, and the lowest pressure (when the heart dilates), diastolic pressure.

【血样】xuèyàng (～儿 xuèyàngr) 用做化验样品的少量的血 blood sample; blood specimen; a tiny amount of blood to be used for blood tests

【血液】xuèyè ❶ same as 血 xuè ① ❷〈比喻 *fig.*〉主要的成分或力量等 lifeblood; lifeline; primary element and strength: 石油是工业的～。Petroleum is the lifeblood of industry. | 这批青年工人的到来为工厂增加了新鲜～。The arrival of this batch of young workers has added new life to the factory.

【血衣】xuèyī 杀人者或被杀者的沾血的衣服 bloodstained garment; clothes covered with gore

【血印】xuèyìn（～儿 xuèyìnr）same as 血迹 xuèjì

【血缘】xuèyuán 血统 ties of blood; consanguinity; relationship by birth：他们名义上是兄妹，但没有～关系。They are brother and sister in name, but not related by blood.

【血晕】xuèyùn〈中医 *Chin. med.*〉指产后因失血过多而晕厥的病症 coma after childbirth due to excessive loss of blood

☞ xiěyùn on p. 2123

【血债】xuèzhài 指残杀人民的罪行 debt of blood; crime of slaughter：～累累 have heavy blood debts; commit a string of murders｜偿还～ pay debts of blood

【血战】xuèzhàn ❶ 指非常激烈的战斗 bloody battle; extremely fierce fight：一场～ a sanguinary battle ❷ 进行殊死的战斗 fight an extremely fierce battle; wage a life-and-death battle：～到底 fight to the last drop of one's blood; fight to the bitter end

【血证】xuèzhèng 作为杀人证据的带有被害者血迹的衣物等 bloodstained evidence, such as clothes stained with the blood of a murder victim

【血脂】xuèzhī 血液中所含的脂类，包括脂肪、胆固醇、磷脂和游离脂肪酸 blood fat, including fat, cholesterol, phosphatide, free fatty acids

【血肿】xuèzhǒng 血管壁破裂，血液流出血管，聚积在软组织内所形成的肿块 haematoma; swelling containing coagulated blood in the parenchyma, formed by accumulated blood flowing out of broken blood vessels

【血渍】xuèzì 血迹 bloodstain：～斑斑 full of bloodstains; bloodstained｜满身～。Bloodstains covered every inch of the body.

谑 xuè〈书 *fml.*〉开玩笑 crack a joke; banter; tease：戏～ make fun of｜谐～ humorous joke; wisecrack; pleasantries｜～而不虐 banter

【谑而不虐】xuè ér bù nüè 开玩笑而不至于使人难堪 lightly tease; banter; tease without hurt or embarrassment

xūn（ㄒㄩㄣ）

荤 xūn［荤粥］（Xūnyù）same as 獯鬻 Xūnyù

☞ hūn on p. 871

勋（勳） xūn ❶ 功勋 merit; meritorious service; achievement：～业 contribution; merit; exploit｜～劳 meritorious service｜屡建奇～ perform one meritorious service after another ❷ 勋章 medal; decoration：授～ confer titles or medals

【勋绩】xūnjì 勋劳 meritorious service; outstanding contribution：光辉的～ glorious achievements; remarkable achievements

【勋爵】xūnjué ❶ 封建时代朝廷赐予功臣的爵位 Lord; title of nobility conferred to a man of great merit by the royal court in feudal society ❷ 英国贵族的一种名誉头衔，由国王授予，可以世袭 honourary, hereditary title for the British aristocracy conferred by the king

【勋劳】xūnláo 很高的功劳 meritorious service; great contribution：～卓著 outstanding contribution; eminent achievements

【勋业】xūnyè〈书 *fml.*〉功勋和事业 meritorious service; great achievement：建立～ make remarkable contributions｜不朽的～ immortal meritorious deeds; monumental service

【勋章】xūnzhāng 授给对国家有贡献的人的一种表示荣誉的证章 medal; badge; emblem of honour awarded by the state to a person who has made great contributions

埙（壎） xūn〈古代 *arch.*〉吹奏乐器，多用陶土烧制而成，形状像鸡蛋，有一至六个音孔 *xun*, egg-shaped ancient wind instrument made of pottery, clay, with one to six holes

熏（❶❷燻） xūn ❶（烟、气等）接触物体，使变颜色或沾上气味 smoke; fumigate; subject things to smoke, gases, etc., in order to change their colour or smell：烟把墙～黑了。The wall was blackened by soot.｜臭气～天 stink to the sky; be horribly stinking ◇利欲～心 be blinded by greed; be obsessed with the desire for gain ❷ 熏制（食品）smoke (food)：～鱼 smoked fish｜～鸡 smoked chicken ❸〈书 *fml.*〉和暖 pleasantly warm; genial; mild：～风 warm, southerly breeze

☞ xùn on p. 2190

【熏风】xūnfēng〈书 *fml.*〉和暖的南风 warm, southerly breeze

【熏沐】xūnmù 迷信的人在斋戒占卜前烧香、沐浴，表示对神虔诚 (of a superstitious person) have a bath and burn incense before divination or fasting, to express devotion to a deity

【熏染】xūnrǎn 长期接触的人或事物对生活习惯逐渐产生某种影响（多指坏的）extended contact with a certain person or thing exerting a gradual (usu. corrupting) influence on sb.'s lifestyle

【熏陶】xūntáo 长期接触的人对生活习惯、思想行为、品行学问等逐渐产生好的影响 edify; nurture; exert a gradual, uplifting influence on sb.'s lifestyle, thinking, behaviour, moral character, learning, etc.：在父母的～下，他从小喜爱音乐。Under the nurturing influence of his parents, he developed a love for music at a young age.

【熏蒸】xūnzhēng 形容闷热使人难受 sultry;

sweltering; stifling; suffocating: 暑气～ sweltering summer weather; stifling summer heat

【熏制】xūnzhì 食品加工的一种方法,用烟火或香花熏食品,使带有某种气味 smoking; way of processing food by curing with smoke or fragrant flowers, so as to let it produce a certain flavour

窨 xūn 同'熏',用于窨茶叶。把茉莉花等放在茶叶中,使茶叶染上花的香味。same as 熏 xūn, used only in the phrase 窨茶叶 xūn cháyè, meaning put jasmine flowers into tea leaves for fragrance

☞ yìn on p. 2297

薰[1] xūn〈书 *fml*.〉一种香草。也泛指花草的香。a kind of fragrant grass; (in a broad sense) fragrance of flowers and grasses

薰[2] xūn same as 熏 xūn

【薰莸不同器】xūn yóu bù tóng qì 香草和臭草不能收藏在一个器物里 Fragrant herbs and stinking weeds must be kept in separate vessels;〈比喻 *fig*.〉好和坏不能共处 The good and the bad cannot mix with each other. also 薰莸异器 xūn yóu yì qì

獯 xūn [獯鬻](Xūnyù) 我国古代北方的一个民族 Xunyu, name of a people in ancient northern China; also 荤粥 Xūnyù

纁 xūn〈书 *fml*.〉浅红色 light pink

曛 xūn〈书 *fml*.〉❶ 日落时的余光 last glow of the setting sun ❷ 昏黑; 暮 dusk; nightfall

醺 xūn 酒醉 drunk: 微～ tipsy | 醉～～ heavily drunk; dead drunk; as drunk as a fiddler (or lord)

xún (ㄒㄩㄣˊ)

旬 xún ❶ 十日为一旬,一个月分上中下三旬 period of ten days, with a month made up of three such periods: 兼～(二十天) 20 days | 三月上～ the early period of March ❷ 十岁为一旬 ten years in a person's age: 八～老母 80-year-old mother | 年过七～ over 70 years old

【旬刊】xúnkān 每十日出版一次的刊物 periodical published every ten days

【旬日】xúnrì 十天 ten days

寻[1] (尋) xún ❶〈古代 *arch*.〉长度单位,八尺叫一寻 measure of length, equal to 8 *chi* ❷ (Xún) 姓 a surname

寻[2] (尋) xún 找 look for; search; seek: ～求 pursue | ～觅 look for | ～人 look for sb. | 搜～ search

【寻查】xúnchá 寻找;查找 search; look for; seek: ～失散的亲人 look for lost family members

【寻常】xúncháng 平常(古代八尺为'寻',倍寻为'常',寻和常都是平常的长度) common; ordinary; usual (in ancient times, eight *chi* equalled one *xun*, two *xun* was one *chang*, both *xun* and *chang* being common units of length): ～人家 ordinary family | 拾金不昧,在今天是～的事了。It is not uncommon today for people to return to its owner money they pick on the road.

【寻短见】xún duǎnjiàn ('寻'口语中多读 xín oft. pronounced xín in spoken Chinese) 自杀 commit suicide; take one's own life

【寻访】xúnfǎng 寻找探问;寻找访查 look for; try to locate; make enquiries about; ask for: 四处～ make enquiries everywhere | ～故友 try to locate the whereabouts of a friend

【寻根】xúngēn ❶ 寻找根底;寻找根源 get to the bottom of sth.; investigate deeply into: ～溯源 trace sth. to its source ❷ 特指寻找祖籍宗族 search for the roots of one's family: ～祭祖 search for the roots of one's family and make offerings to one's ancestors

【寻根究底】xún gēn jiū dǐ 追究根底。泛指弄清一事的来龙去脉。get to the root of sth.; get to the bottom of things; investigate deeply into; investigate thoroughly; also 寻根问底 xún gēn wèn dǐ

【寻花问柳】xún huā wèn liǔ 指狎妓;嫖娼 frequent houses of ill repute; go whoring; visit brothels

【寻机】xúnjī 寻找机会 look for or seek an opportunity: ～报复 seek an opportunity to retaliate

【寻开心】xún kāixīn ('寻'口语中多读 xín oft. pronounced xín in spoken Chinese)〈方 *dial*.〉逗乐儿;开玩笑 make fun of; poke fun at; joke; kidding

【寻觅】xúnmì 寻找 seek; look for: 四处～ look around everywhere

【寻摸】xún·mo same as 寻找 xúnzhǎo

【寻求】xúnqiú 寻找追求 seek; explore; go in quest of: ～知识 seek knowledge | ～真理 seek truth

【寻事】xúnshì 找麻烦;故意引起争端 invite trouble; seek a quarrel; pick a fight on purpose: ～挑衅 pick a fight deliberately

【寻死】xún//sǐ ('寻'口语中多读 xín oft. pronounced xín in spoken Chinese) 自杀或企图自杀 commit suicide; try to commit suicide; attempt suicide

【寻死觅活】xún sǐ mì huó ('寻'口语中多读 xín oft. pronounced xín in spoken Chinese) 企图自杀。多指用寻死来吓唬人。threaten to commit suicide

【寻思】xún·si ('寻'口语中多读 xín oft. pronounced xín in spoken Chinese) 思索;考虑 think; consider; ponder: 独自～ mull over sth. by oneself | 你～～这件事该怎么办。

What do you think we should do about it?

【寻索】xúnsuǒ ❶ 寻找 look for; search; seek: ～他的踪迹 search for traces of him ❷ 寻求探索 search for clues; explore; probe into: ～答案 search for an answer

【寻味】xúnwèi 仔细体会 chew sth. over; ruminate; think over; mull over: 耐人～ be thought-provoking

【寻隙】xúnxì ❶ 故意挑毛病,引起争端 find fault with sb. with the purpose of causing a dispute: ～闹事 kick up a row by nit-picking ❷ 找空子;找机会 look for a chance; seek an opening: ～行窃 look for a chance to steal

【寻衅】xúnxìn 故意找事挑衅 pick a quarrel; provoke: ～逞凶 kick up a row and act violently

【寻章摘句】xún zhāng zhāi jù 读书时只摘记一些漂亮词句,不深入研究;也指写作只堆砌现成词句,缺乏创造性 cull phrases and cite passages without doing further research; write in clichés without originality

【寻找】xúnzhǎo 找 seek; look for: ～失物 look for lost articles|～真理 seek truth

纠 xún 〈书 *fml.*〉绦子 silk ribbon

巡(廵) xún ❶ 巡查;巡视 patrol; make one's rounds; inspect: ～夜 make night rounds|～逻 patrol|出～ go on an inspection tour ❷〈量词 *classifier*〉遍(用于给全座斟酒) time; round of drinks (served to all present): 酒过三～。The wine has gone round three times.

【巡捕】xúnbǔ ❶ 清代总督、巡抚等地方长官的随从官员 entourage of local officials, such as provincial viceroy and imperial inspector, in the Qing Dynasty ❷〈旧时 *old*〉称租界中的警察 police or policeman in former foreign concessions: ～房 police station (in former foreign concessions)

X

【巡捕房】xúnbǔfáng〈旧社会 *pre-1949*〉帝国主义者在上海等商埠的租界里为压制中国人民而设立的巡捕办事机关,相当于旧中国的警察局 agency set up in foreign concessions in port cities by foreign imperialists in order to suppress the Chinese people, having the same function as a police station in pre-1949 China; also 捕房 bǔfáng

【巡查】xúnchá 一面走一面查看 go on a tour of inspection; make one's rounds: ～堤防 inspect the embankment

【巡察】xúnchá 巡视考察;巡行察访 go on an tour of inspection; make an inspection tour: ～各地 make an inspection tour of various localities

【巡风】xúnfēng 来回走着望风 keep watch: ～瞭哨 stand sentry and keep watch

【巡抚】xúnfǔ〈古代 *arch.*〉官名,明代称临时派遣到地方巡视和监督地方民政、军政的大臣,清代称掌管一省民政、军政的长官 ancient official title; imperial inspector of the Ming Dynasty temporarily sent to inspect and supervise local civil and military affairs; provincial governor in charge of civil and military affairs in a province in the Qing Dynasty

【巡航】xúnháng 巡逻航行 cruise: 飞机每天～护林。The plane flies through the forest every day.|乘小艇在港湾～ cruise the bay in a cockboat

【巡回】xúnhuí 按一定路线到各处(活动) go the rounds; tour; make a circuit of: ～展览 exhibition tour|～演出 performing tour|～医疗 mobile medical treatment

【巡警】xúnjǐng〈旧时 *old*〉指警察。现在指巡逻、维持治安的警察。police officer; oft. referring to a policeman on patrol to maintain public order

【巡礼】xúnlǐ ❶ 朝拜圣地 visit a sacred land; go on a pilgrimage ❷ 借指观光或游览 tour; sightseeing: 市场～ visiting a market; roundup of the market situation

【巡逻】xúnluó 巡查警戒 go on patrol; patrol: 有专人值夜～。There are people specially assigned for night patrol.

【巡哨】xúnshào (负警戒任务的小部队等)巡行侦察 (of a small troop in charge of security) go on patrol; patrol

【巡视】xúnshì ❶ 到各处视察 make an inspection tour; tour: 师首长～哨所。The division commander inspected the sentries. ❷ 往四下里看 look round: ～着四周的听众 look around at the audience

【巡天】xúntiān 巡游天空 tour the universe: ～遨游 roam the universe

【巡行】xúnxíng 沿着一定路线行进;巡回 go the rounds; tour; make a circuit of: ～市区 make one's rounds in an urban district|～各地 make a circuit of all areas

【巡幸】xúnxìng〈书 *fml.*〉指帝王出巡,到达某地 (of an emperor) go on an inspection tour with a certain destination: ～江南 go on tour south of the Yangtze River

【巡洋舰】xúnyángjiàn 主要在远洋活动,装备大口径火炮和厚装甲的大型军舰。一般用于护航、炮击敌航船和岸上目标,支援登陆兵作战等。装备有导弹的巡洋舰叫导弹巡洋舰。cruiser; big warship mainly travelling to distant seas, equipped with large-calibre cannons and heavily armoured, that convoys other warships, fights enemy warships, attacks shores with cannons and supports soldiers who land to combat. A cruiser equipped with missiles is called a missile cruiser.

【巡夜】xúnyè 在夜间巡查警戒 go on night patrol: 值班～ keep night watch

【巡弋】xúnyì (军舰)在水域巡逻 (of a warship) cruise; ply the waters

【巡游】xúnyóu ❶ 出外游玩；闲逛 saunter; stroll; roam; idle about; ramble: ～各地 roam from place to place ❷ 巡行(察看) patrol: 巡逻哨在村外～。People are on patrol outside the village.

【巡诊】xúnzhěn 巡回治病 (of a doctor) make a round of visits; go on one's rounds

郇 Xún ❶ 周朝国名,在今山西临猗西 Xun, name of a state of Zhou, to the west of present-day Linyi, Shanxi Province ❷ 姓 a surname

☞ Huán on p. 845

询 xún 询问 ask; enquire: 查～ enquire about | 咨～ consult; seek advice from

【询查】xúnchá 查询 enquire about; demand; make enquiries

【询问】xúnwèn 征求意见;打听 ask about; enquire about; pry into; solicit opinions: 他用～的目光望着大家。He looked enquiringly at all present. | 向经理～公司的情况 ask the manager about the situation of the company

郇(鄩) xún 斟郇(Zhēnxún),古国名,在今山东潍坊西南 Zhenxun, name of an ancient state, located to the southwest of present-day Weifang, Shandong Province

荀 Xún 姓 a surname

荨 xún [荨麻疹] (xúnmázhěn,旧读 formerly pronounced qiánmázhěn) 皮肤病,症状是局部皮肤突然成块地红肿,发痒,几小时后消退,不留痕迹。常常复发。药物、寄生虫、血清、细菌感染、接触刺激性物质等都能引起这种病。nettle rash; urticaria; skin disease with symptoms of sudden turgescence and itching in certain parts of the body, which fade away several hours later without any trace. The ailment attacks frequently, and is easily caused by medicine, parasites, serum, bacterial infection, contact with stimulants, etc. also called 风疹块 fēngzhěnkuài;有的地区叫鬼风疙瘩 in some places also called 鬼风疙瘩 guǐfēng gē•da

☞ qián on p. 1532

哔(噚) xún 又 also yīngxún; 英寻旧也作哔 also 英寻 yīngxún formerly written as 哔 xún

峋 xún ☞ 嶙峋 línxún on p. 1224

洵 xún 〈书 *fml.*〉诚然;实在 truly; indeed; to be sure: ～属可贵 truly valuable

浔[1](潯) xún ❶ 〈书 *fml.*〉水边 waterside: 江～ riverside ❷ (Xún)江西九江的别称 another name for Jiujiang, a city in Jiangxi Province

浔[2](潯) xún 又 also hǎixún; 海寻旧也作浔 also 海寻 hǎixún formerly written as 浔 xún

恂 xún 〈书 *fml.*〉❶ 诚实;恭顺 honest; faithful; respectful and submissive: ～谨 sincere ❷ 恐惧 dread; afraid: ～然 terrified

珣 xún 〈书 *fml.*〉玉名 name of a jade

玽(璕) xún 〈书 *fml.*〉一种美石 a kind of fine stone

栒 xún [栒子木] (xún•zimù) 落叶灌木,叶子卵形,花白色,果实球形,红色,供观赏 cotoneaster (*Cotoneaster*); deciduous shrub, having oval leaves, white flowers and round red fruit, and frequently cultivated for ornamentation

循 xún 遵守;依照;沿袭 follow; abide by; be in line with: 遵～ abide by | 因～ be in line with sth. | ～例 follow the usual practice; follow a precedent | ～规蹈矩 observe rules; conform to convention

【循规蹈矩】xún guī dǎo jǔ 遵守规矩 observe rules; conform to convention; toe the line; obey docilely

【循环】xúnhuán 事物周而复始地运动或变化 circle; cycle; (of a thing) move or change in cycles: ～往复 move in a circle | 血液～ blood circulation | ～小数 cycled or repeated decimal

【循环论】xúnhuánlùn 形而上学的认识论,认为事物只是周而复始的循环运动,没有发展和本质的变化 cyclical theory; metaphysical epistemology that believes things move in endless cycles without development or intrinsic change

【循环论证】xúnhuán lùnzhèng 逻辑学上指由前提甲推出结论乙,又拿乙做前提来证明甲,这样的论证叫循环论证,是不能成立的 circular argument; arguing in a circle; untenable way of argumentation in logic, which makes conclusion B from premise A, and then takes B as a premise to prove A

【循环赛】xúnhuánsài 体育运动竞赛方式之一,参加者相互轮流比赛,按全部比赛中得分多少决定名次 round robin; method of sports competition, in which players compete with each other by turns, and the scores they accumulate after all matches are completed decide their places

【循环系统】xúnhuán xìtǒng 人或某些动物体内由心脏、血管、血液、淋巴等组成的系统,血液由心脏压出去流到全身各部再回到心脏 circulatory system; system consisting of the heart, blood vessels, blood, lymph, etc. in human or animal bodies. Via this system, blood is pumped out of the heart to flow to every part of the body and then back to the heart. ☞ 体循环 tǐxúnhuán on p. 1885 and 肺循环 fèixúnhán on p. 563

【循例】xúnlì 依照常例 in accordance with common practice: ～办理 deal with sth. in line with established practice

X

【循名责实】xún míng zé shí 要求实质跟名称或名义相符 demand that reality matches up to the name; expect reality to correspond to the name

【循序】xúnxù 顺着次序 in proper order or sequence: ～渐进 follow in order and advance step by step; proceed in an orderly way step by step

【循序渐进】xúnxù jiànjìn (学习、工作)按照一定的步骤逐渐深入或提高 (of study or work) follow in order and advance step by step; proceed in an orderly and gradual way

【循循善诱】xúnxún shàn yòu 善于有步骤地引导别人学习 be good at giving systematic guidance; teach with skill and patience (循循 *xunxun*:有步骤的样子 in a systematic way; step by step)

鲟(鱘、鱏) xún 鲟鱼,背部黄灰色,口小而尖,背部和腹部有大片硬鳞。生活在淡水中,有些入海越冬。sturgeon (*Acipenseridae*); fish with a yellowish grey back, a small and pointed mouth, and large hard scales on the back and belly, living in fresh water and sometimes swimming to the sea for the winter

xùn (ㄒㄩㄣˋ)

训 xùn ❶ 教导;训诫 talking to; instruct; admonish; teach: 教～ teach sb. a lesson|～告 instruct|～话 give sb. a lesson|～词 admonition; instruction|～了他一顿 give him a dressing-down|挨了一通～ be given a good talking to ❷ 教导或训诫的话 admonition; instruction: 家～ family precept|遗～ teachings of the deceased ❸ 训练 train; drill: 培～ train; cultivate|轮～ train in turn|军～ military training ❹ 准则 rule; guideline; standard: 不足为～ not fit to serve as a model ❺ 词义解释 explanation of a word; interpretation of a text: ～诂 explanations of words in ancient books; gloss; textual exegesis

【训斥】xùnchì 训诫和斥责 reprimand; rebuke; dress down: 他让父亲～了一顿。His father gave him a good dressing-down.

【训词】xùncí 训话时所说的话 admonition; instructions

【训导】xùndǎo 教育训诫 instruct and admonish

【训迪】xùndí 〈书 *fml.*〉教诲开导 instruct and enlighten

【训诂】xùngǔ 对古书字句的解释 explanation of words and sentences in ancient books; exegetical studies of ancient texts; exegesis

【训话】xùn//huà 上级对下级讲教导和告诫的话 give a dressing-down to one's subordinates

【训诲】xùnhuì 〈书 *fml.*〉教导 instruct; teach

【训戒】xùnjiè same as 训诫 xùnjiè

【训诫】xùnjiè ❶ 教导和告诫 admonish; advise: ～部下 give an admonishing lecture to one's subordinates ❷ 一种最轻的刑罚,人民法院以国家的名义对犯罪者进行公开的批评教育 admonishment; the lightest punishment, including criticism and teaching a law-breaker in public, conducted by a people's court in the name of the state ‖ also 训戒 xùnjiè

【训练】xùnliàn 有计划有步骤地使具有某种特长或技能 train; drill; help sb. grasp certain skill in a planned and systematic way: ～班 training class|业务～ professional training|～救护人员 train ambulance personnel|警犬都是受过～的。All these police dogs are well trained.

【训令】xùnlìng 机关晓谕下属或委派人员时所用的公文 mandate; ordinance; written instructions to subordinates; accreditation documents

【训示】xùnshì 上级对下级或长辈对晚辈的指示 allocution; instructions or orders to subordinates from a superior, or to younger members of a family from elders

【训育】xùnyù 〈旧时 *old*〉指学校里的道德教育 moral education at school

【训谕】xùnyù 〈书 *fml.*〉same as 训喻 xùnyù

【训喻】xùnyù 〈书 *fml.*〉训诲;开导 instruct; teach; also 训谕 xùnyù

讯 xùn ❶ 询问 enquire; ask: 问～ ask after; enquire about; send one's regards to ❷ 审问 interrogate; question: 审～ interrogate ❸ 消息;信息 news; information; message; dispatch: 通～ communication|音～ news|新华社～ dispatch from Xinhua News Agency

【讯号】xùnhào ❶ 通过电磁波发出的信号 radio signal; signal ❷ 泛指信号 (in a broad sense) signal

【讯实】xùnshí 审讯属实 prove sth. to be true through interrogation

【讯问】xùnwèn ❶ same as 问 wèn ①: ～病状 ask about the condition of a patient|～原委 enquire about the details ❷ 审问 interrogate; question: ～案件 hear a case

汛 xùn 河流定期的涨水 seasonal flood; high water; regular swelling of a river: 桃花～ spring flood|伏～ summer flood|秋～ autumn flood|凌～ winter flood; ice run|防～ flood control; flood prevention

【汛期】xùnqī 江河水位定时性的上涨时期 flood season; high-water season

【汛情】xùnqíng 汛期水位涨落的情况 flood situation; water level in flood season

迅 xùn 迅速 fast; swift: ～跑 run swiftly|～捷 fast; rapid; agile; quick|～猛 sudden and violent

【迅步】xùnbù 〈书 *fml.*〉快步 walk fast; hurry：～追赶 follow sb. in a hot pursuit

【迅即】xùnjí 立即 immediately; at once：～处理 take immediate action to deal with sth.

【迅急】xùnjí 急速 very fast; rapidly; at high speed; in haste：～回家 hurry back home

【迅疾】xùnjí 迅速 swiftly; rapidly：动作～ act swiftly; be quick in movement

【迅捷】xùnjié 迅速敏捷 fast; agile; quick：行动～ be quick in action | 他们～地做好了准备。They got themselves ready in no time.

【迅雷不及掩耳】xùn léi bù jí yǎn ěr〈比喻 *fig.*〉动作或事件突然而来，使人来不及防备 (of an action or event) as sudden as a flash of lightning, leaving no time for people to make preparations; as sudden as a thunderbolt

【迅猛】xùnměng 迅速而猛烈 swift and violent：来势～ come suddenly and violently; come with the momentum of an avalanche

【迅速】xùnsù 速度高；非常快 rapid; swift; speedy; prompt：动作～ be quick in action | ～前进 march forward at high speed | 高等教育发展～。Higher education has made rapid development.

驯 xùn ❶ 顺服的；善良 tame and docile; obedient; kind-hearted：温～ gentle and obedient | ～顺 tame and docile; submissive ❷ 使顺服 tame; domesticate：善于～虎 be good at taming tigers

【驯服】xùnfú ❶ 顺从 docile; tame; tractable：猫是很～的。Cats are very docile. ❷ 使顺从 tame; break; domesticate; bring sb. under control：这匹野马终于被他～了。He finally succeeded in breaking in the wild horse.

【驯化】xùnhuà ❶ 野生动物经人长期饲养后逐渐改变原来的习性，听从人的指挥。如野牛、野马等经过驯化，成为家畜。domesticate; tame; train or adapt a wild animal to obey human instructions by gradually changing its wild behaviour over a long period of rearing, e. g. the domestication of wild bulls and horses ❷ 野生植物经过引种培育并不断选择，逐渐成为人类所需要的栽培植物 domesticate; adapt a species of wild plant by breeding and selection so that it becomes a cultivated plant meeting the demands of humans

【驯良】xùnliáng 和顺善良 tractable; docile; tame and gentle：性情～ tame and gentle temperament

【驯鹿】xùnlù 哺乳动物，毛栗棕色，头长，耳短，颈长，尾短，雌雄都有角。性温顺，能耐寒。毛皮可做衣物，鹿茸可入药。reindeer (*Rangifer tarandus*); mammal with chestnut-coloured hair, long head, short ears, long neck, short tail, and antlers for both the male and the female, gentle and docile, and resistant to cold, its fur used to make clothes and its antlers of medical value; 俗称 popularly known as 四不像 sìbùxiàng

【驯熟】xùnshú ❶ 驯顺 tame and docile：～的小巴儿狗 tame and docile puppy ❷ 熟练；纯熟 experienced; skilful; well versed; proficient：技艺～ be well versed in skills; be very skilful

【驯顺】xùnshùn 驯服顺从 tame and docile; submissive：他～得像头绵羊。He's as tame and docile as a sheep.

【驯养】xùnyǎng 饲养野生动物使逐渐驯服 domesticate; tame; make wild animals fit for human use by raising and training them：～猴子 tame a monkey | ～麋鹿 raise and train David's deer

徇(狥) xùn ❶ 依从；曲从 give in to; submit to; comply with：～情 act out of personal considerations | ～私 act dishonestly for one's own benefit ❷〈书 *fml.*〉对众宣示 declare; proclaim; announce officially or publicly ❸〈书 *fml.*〉same as 殉 xùn ②

【徇情】xùnqíng〈书 *fml.*〉徇私 act wrongly out of personal considerations; act dishonestly for one's own benefit; practise favouritism：～枉法 bend the law to help one's friends or relatives

【徇私】xùnsī 为了私情而做不合法的事 bend the law to help one's friends or relatives; break the law for personal considerations

逊(遜) xùn ❶ 让出(帝王的位子) abdicate; (of an emperor) give up the throne：～位 abdicate ❷ 谦虚；谦恭 unassuming; modest：谦～ be modest | 出言不～ utter imprudent remarks ❸〈书 *fml.*〉差；比不上；不及 inferior to：～色 be inferior to | 稍～一筹 be a shade or cut inferior; be slightly inferior

【逊色】xùnsè ❶ 不及之处 be inferior：毫无～ be in no way inferior ❷ 差劲 not good; badly：大为～ be paled or overshadowed | 并不～ be in no way inferior

殉(❷徇) xùn ❶ 殉葬 be buried alive with the dead ❷ 因为维护某种事物或追求某种理想而牺牲生命 sacrifice one's life for protecting sth. or pursuing an ideal：～难 die for a just cause | 以身～职 die at one's post; die in line of duty; die in the course of performing one's duty

【殉国】xùn//guó 为国家的利益而牺牲生命 give one's life for one's country：壮烈～ die in a heroic way for one's country

【殉节】xùn//jié ❶ 指战争失败或国家灭亡后因不愿投降而牺牲生命 die out of loyalty to one's country; die rather than surrender after losing a war or after the fall of one's country：慷慨～ die in dignity for a just cause ❷〈旧时 *old*〉指妇女因抗拒凌辱而牺牲生命 (of a woman) die in defence of one's chastity ❸〈旧时 *old*〉指妇女受封建礼教毒害，因丈夫死

而自杀 (of a widow) commit suicide rather than remarry

【殉难】xùn//nàn (为国家或正义事业)遇难牺牲生命 give one's life (for one's country or a just cause); die a martyr: 他是在抗战中～的。He laid down his life for his country in the War of Resistance against Japan.

【殉情】xùnqíng 因恋爱受到阻碍而自杀 die for love

【殉葬】xùnzàng 古代的一种风俗,逼迫死者的妻妾、奴隶等随同埋葬,也指用俑和财物、器具随葬 be buried alive with the dead; ancient custom which forced a dead person's wife, concubines and slaves to be buried together with his remains; also referring to the custom of burying carved figures, property and utensils with the dead: ～品 funerary object; sacrificial object

【殉职】xùn//zhí (在职人员)为公务而牺牲生命 die at one's post; die in the course of performing one's duty; die in line of duty: 在爆破施工中他不幸～。He died at his post in an explosion.

浚(濬) Xùn 浚县,在河南 Xunxian County, in Henan Province

☞ jùn on p. 1067

巽 xùn 八卦之一,卦形是☴,代表风 one part of the Eight Trigrams, with the sign ☴, representing the wind; ☞ 八卦 bāguà on p. 22

熏 xùn 〈方 *dial.*〉(煤气)使人窒息中毒 be poisoned or suffocated by coal gas: 炉子安上烟筒,就不至于～着了。Install a chimney over the stove, and you won't be suffocated by coal gas.

☞ xūn on p. 2184

蕈 xùn 高等菌类。生长在树林里或草地上。地下部分叫菌丝,能从土壤里或朽木里吸取养料。地上部分由帽状的菌盖和杆状的菌柄构成,菌盖能产生孢子,是繁殖器官。种类很多,有的可以吃,如香菇,有的有毒,如毒蝇蕈。gill fungus (*Agaricaceae*); higher fungus growing in forests or on grasslands. Its underground part is called mycelium, which can absorb nutrients from the soil or decayed wood, and its above-ground part is comprised of a cap-shaped pileus and bacilliform stipe, with the former being the generative organ producing spores. There are a variety of fungus, some being edible, such as mushrooms, while others are poisonous, such as toadstools.

噀(潠) xùn 〈书 *fml.*〉含在口中而喷出 hold water in the mouth and spurt it out: ～水 spurt water

Y

yā（丨丫）

丫 yā ❶ 上端分叉的东西 bifurcation; fork: 枝～fork of a tree branch ❷〈方 *dial.*〉女孩子 girl: 小～little girl

【丫巴儿】yā·bar〈方 *dial.*〉东西分叉的地方 fork; bifurcation; crotch: 树～fork of a tree | 手～crotch between the fingers of a hand

【丫杈】yāchà same as 桠杈 yāchà

【丫鬟】yā·huan 婢女 slave girl; servant girl; also 丫环 yā·huan

【丫髻】yājì 女孩梳在头顶两边的发髻 girl's coiffure with a loop on either side of the head

【丫头】yā·tou ❶ 女孩子 girl ❷ 丫鬟 servant girl

压（壓） yā ❶ 对物体施压力（多指从上向下）press; push down; hold down; weigh down; bring the pressure to bear on: ～碎 crush to pieces | 用铜尺把纸～住 hold a piece of paper in place with a copper paperweight bar ◇泰山～顶不弯腰 be so dauntless as to refuse to yield to any pressure even if it had the weight of Mount Taishan ❷ 超越；胜过 surpass; outdo: 才不～众 have mediocre talent | 技～群芳 be unmatched in skill ❸ 使稳定；使平静 stabilize; hold back; keep under control: ～咳嗽 hold back a cough | ～住阵脚 dig oneself in; hold one's ground | ～不住火儿 fail to hold back one's anger | 这出戏很精彩，一定～得住台。This performance is good enough to hold the audience enthralled, no question about it. ❹ 压制 suppress; quell: 镇～crack down on | 别拿大帽子～人。Stop labeling people. *or* Stop intimidating people with political labels. ❺ 逼近 draw near; close in on; approach: ～境（of enemy troops）close in on the border of a country | 太阳～树梢。The sun has risen above the top of the trees. ❻ 搁着不动 set aside; shelve; pigeonhole: 积～stockpile | 这件公文要赶紧处理，别～起来。Don't pigeonhole this document, which needs to be handled without delay. ❼ 赌博时在某一门上下注（of a gambler）bet; stake

☞ yà on p. 2198

【压宝】yā//bǎo 赌博的一种。赌博的人猜测宝上所指的方向下注。stake; gambling game played with dice under a bowl, in which a gambler lays down a stake by guessing the direction on the dice; also 押宝 yā//bǎo

【压场】yā//chǎng ❶ 控制住场面 have（a meeting, an audience, etc.）under control: 他说话没人听，压不住场。He couldn't keep the situation under control because nobody listened to him. ❷ 在一次演出中把某个节目排在最后演出 last performance in a variety or theatrical show: ～戏 finale to a performance | 以他独创的唢呐演奏～。The performance concluded with the solo of a *suona* horn he had invented.

【压秤】yāchèng ❶ 物体称起来分量大（多就同体积的而言）be relatively heavy per unit volume: 劈柴太湿，～。This firewood is too wet and weighs much more than usual. | 稻草不～，一大捆才十来斤。Dry straw doesn't weigh much, and a big bundle of it amounts to a little more than a dozen *jin*. ❷ 过秤时有意压低所称物品的分量 deliberately under-weigh sth.: 收购时严禁～、压价。When purchasing farm products, it is forbidden to under-weigh and underpay the peasants.

【压船】yā//chuán 由于装卸不及时或气候变化，船不能按时离开码头 boats being held up in a habour because of delay in loading and unloading or bad weather

【压倒】yā//dǎo 力量胜过或重要性超过 overwhelm; overpower; prevail over: ～一切 overriding; of paramount importance | 以～多数的选票当选 be elected by an overwhelming majority

【压低】yādī 使降低 keep down; lower; reduce: ～售价 keep prices down | 他怕别人听见，便～声音说话。He lowered his voice in case someone else would hear him.

【压顶】yādǐng 由头顶上方压下来，多用于比喻（oft. fig.）bear down on one; weigh heavily on one: 乌云～。Dark clouds hung overhead. | 泰山～志不移 remain staunch even if Mount Taishan were bearing down

【压队】yā//duì 跟在队伍后面保护或监督 bring up the rear; also 押队 yā//duì

【压服】yā//fú 用强力制伏；迫使服从 whip sb. into line; force（or compel）sb. to submit: ～众人 force people to submit | 要说服，不要～。Use persuasion, rather than coercion, if you want to convince people. also 压伏 yā//fú

【压价】yā//jià 强使价格降低 force prices down; demand a lower price

【压惊】yājīng 用请吃饭等方式安慰受惊的人 help sb. get over a shock (by treat him to dinner, etc.)

【压境】yājìng (敌军)逼近边境(of enemy troops) press on to the border: 大军～。A large enemy force is bearing down upon the border.

【压卷】yājuàn 评为第一、压倒其余的某篇诗文 a piece of writing that surpasses all the others: ～之作 the best work that has ever been written

【压库】yā//kù ❶ 货物卖不出去,积压在仓库里 overstock ❷ 减少库存积压 reduce the stocks: 限产～。Curtail the output and reduce the stocks.

【压力】yālì ❶ 物体所承受的与表面垂直的作用力 pressure; force applied uniformly over a surface ❷ 制伏人的力量 overwhelming force; pressure: 舆论～pressure of public opinion | 施加～bring pressure to bear on sb. ❸ 承受的负担 burden; strain: 交通～strain on transportation | 人口～burden of a large population

【压力锅】yālìguō 高压锅 pressure cooker

【压路机】yālùjī 用来压实道路或场地的机器,有很重的圆筒形轮子,用蒸汽机或内燃机做动力机 road roller; roller; machine equipped with a steam engine or internal-combustion engine and a heavy, revolving cylinder that is used to press and smooth a road or a place

【压迫】yāpò ❶ 用权力或势力强制别人服从 oppress; keep down by severe and unjust use of force or authority: ～人 oppression of people | 反抗～struggle against oppression ❷ 对有机体的某个部分加上压力 constrict; compress: 肿瘤～神经而引起疼痛。The tumour constricts the nerves and causes pain.

【压气】yā//qì (～儿 yā//qìr)使怒气平息 calm sb.'s anger: 说几句好话给他压压气儿。Say a few agreeable words to calm him down.

【压强】yāqiáng 物体单位面积上所受的压力 intensity of pressure; pressure; force applied over a surface, measured as force per unit of area

【压青】yāqīng 把绿肥作物或采集的野草、树叶埋到田地里做肥料 green manuring; green dressing; apply green manure to farmland; bury weeds or tree leaves in the soil as manure

【压岁钱】yāsuìqián 过阴历年时长辈给小孩儿的钱 money given to children as a lunar New Year gift

【压缩】yāsuō ❶ 加上压力,使体积缩小 compress; condense: ～空气 compressed air | ～饼干 ship biscuit; hardtack ❷ 减少(人员、经费、篇幅等) reduce; cut down on; down-size (personnel, funding, size, etc.): ～编制 down-size the staff | ～开支 cut down on expenses | ～篇幅 condense a piece of writing, etc.

【压缩空气】yāsuō kōngqì 用气泵把空气压入容器而形成的压力高于大气压的空气,可以用来开动机具等 compressed air; air under greater than atmospheric pressure, to be used to power a mechanical device

【压台】yā//tái ❶ same as 压场 yā//chǎng ②: ～戏 last number on a repertoire | 这次演出由她的独唱～。Her solo singing will be the finale to the performance. ❷ 指稳住局面,使局势平静 keep the situation under control and restore it to peace

【压台戏】yātáixì 指一场戏曲演出中排在最后的节目 last and most important item in a theatrical performance

【压条】yātiáo 把植物(如葡萄)的枝条的一部分埋入土中,尖端露出地面,目的是等它生根以后把它和母株分开,使另成一个植株 layering; fasten down a shoot, as of grapevine, to take root while attached to the parent plant; also 压枝 yāzhī

【压痛】yātòng 医学上指用手轻轻地按身体的某一部分时所产生的疼痛或异常的感觉(med.) tenderness; soreness felt when part of the body is pressed lightly with a hand

【压蔓】yā//wàn (～儿 yā//wànr)把瓜类等作物匍匐在地面上的蔓每隔一定距离用土压住。压蔓可以促使蔓上长出不定根,多吸收养分。fasten down the vines of a creeping plant by covering them with earth at regular intervals for facilitating the growth of adventitious roots or absorbing more nutrition

【压延】yāyán 加压力使金属伸延成一定形状。大多数金属要加热到一定程度进行压延。mangle; bring a metal into shape by means of heated rollers; Most metals can be mangled only after they have been heated to a certain temperature.

【压抑】yāyì 对感情、力量等加以限制,使不能充分流露或发挥(of feelings, strength, etc.) constrain; inhibit; depress; hold back: ～感 feeling of being constrained; sense of pressure | 心情～feel constrained

【压韵】yā//yùn same as 押韵 yā//yùn

【压榨】yāzhà ❶ 压取物体里的汁液 extract (juice, etc.) by pressure; press; squeeze: 用甘蔗制糖,一般分～和煎熬两个步骤。Refining sugar generally calls for two steps, first, squeezing sugarcanes to obtain the juice, and second, boiling the juice to condense it. ❷ 〈比喻 *fig.*〉剥削或搜刮 exploit; plunder; expropriate; extort

【压阵】yā//zhèn ❶ 排在或走在队列的最后;压队 bring up the rear: 他～掩护大家脱险。He brought up the rear and provided the cover for us to break through the danger zone. ❷ 压住阵脚,多用于比喻 (oft. fig.) keep one's troops in battle array; keep the situation under control; boost the morale:为了这场比赛取胜,队长亲自上场～。The captain personally played in the game in order to boost the morale of his team and get a win.

【压制】[1] yāzhì 竭力限制或制止;抑制 suppress; stifle; inhibit:不要～批评 make sure not to muzzle criticism|～不住自己的愤怒 cannot contain one's anger

【压制】[2] yāzhì 用压的方法制造 make sth. by pressing:～砖坯 make adobe by pressing

【压轴戏】yāzhòuxì 压轴子的戏曲节目 finale; the last item on the repertoire of a theatrical performance;〈比喻 *fig.*〉令人注目的、最后出现的事件 last of a chain of events that is the most eye-catching

【压轴子】yāzhòu·zi ❶ 把某一出戏排做一次戏曲演出中的倒数第二个节目(最后的一出戏叫大轴子)(the last item on a theatrical performance is called 大轴子 dàzhòu·zi) present the last item but one on a theatrical performance ❷ 一次演出的戏曲节目中排在倒数第二的一出戏 the last but one item staged during a theatrical performance

呀 yā ❶〈叹词 *interj.*〉表示惊异[expressing surprise] ah; oh:～,下雪了! Oh, it's snowing. ❷〈拟声词 *onom.*〉:门～的一声开了。The door opened with a creak.

☞ 呀·ya on p. 2198

押[1] yā ❶ 把财物交给对方作为保证 give as security; mortgage; pawn; pledge:抵～ mortgage|～租 rent sth. with a pledge|～金 deposit; down payment ❷ 暂时把人扣留,不准自由行动 detain; take into custody:拘～ take sb. into custody|看～keep sb. under detention ❸ 跟随着照料或看管 escort:～车 escort a vehicle in transportation|～运 transport goods under escort|～送 take a prisoner, etc. under escort ❹ same as 压 yā;用于'押宝','押队'、'押韵'等 used in such phrases as 押宝 yā// bǎo, 押队 yā// duì and 押韵 yā// yùn, etc. ❺ (Yā) 姓 a surname

押[2] yā ❶ 在公文、契约上签字或画符号,作为凭信 sign (a document or contract); put one's mark in lieu of a signature:～尾 sign at the end of a document ❷ 作为凭信而在公文、契约上所签的名字或所画的符号 signature; mark made on a document or contract in the place of a signature:花～signature|画～put one's mark on a document or contract

【押宝】yā// bǎo same as 压宝 yā// bǎo

【押车】yā// chē 随车看管(物品等)escort goods on a train, truck, etc.

【押当】yā// dàng 拿衣物向当铺抵押借钱 pawn; give or deposit (clothes or other personal property) in a pawnshop as security for repaying the money borrowed

【押当】yādàng 小当铺 small pawnshop

【押队】yā// duì same as 压队 yā// duì

【押解】yājiè ❶ 押送犯人或俘虏 escort; send (a criminal or captive) under escort ❷ 押运 escort sth. in transport:～货物 escort goods being shipped|～礼品 escort gifts to be delivered

【押金】yājīn ❶ 做抵押用的钱 cash pledge; deposit ❷ same as 押款 yākuǎn ②

【押款】yā// kuǎn 用货物、房地产或有价证券等做抵押向银行或钱庄借款 borrow money on security; borrow money from the bank or a money shop by using goods, real estate, or securities as pledge

【押款】yākuǎn ❶ 指用抵押的方式所借得的款子 mortgaged loan ❷ 指预付的款项 loan on security; secured loan

【押送】yāsòng ❶ 押着(犯人或俘虏)送交有关方面 escort; send (a prisoner or captive) under escort ❷ same as 押运 yāyùn:～军粮 escort army provisions

【押头】yā·tou〈方 *dial.*〉做抵押用的东西 security; pledge; collateral

【押尾】yāwěi 在文书、契约的末尾画押 sign or mark in lieu of signature at the end of a document or contract

【押运】yāyùn 运输货物时随同照料 escort goods being transported:～粮草 transport provisions and fodder under escort

【押韵】yā// yùn 诗词歌赋中,某些句子的末一字用韵母相同或相近的字,使音调和谐优美 rhyme; (of poem or verse) use of words with the same vowel or similar vowels at the end of lines to make them sound harmonious and pleasant to the ear; also 压韵 yā// yùn

【押账】yāzhàng 借钱时用某种物品做抵押 leave (or offer) sth. as security for a loan

【押租】yāzū〈旧时 *old*〉租用土地或房屋时交付的保证金 rent deposit; caution money paid when renting land or a house

垭(埡) yā〈方 *dial.*〉两山之间可通行的狭窄地方;山口。多用于地名,如马头垭、荀家垭(都在湖北)。moutain pass; strip of land that provides passage between two mountains, mostly used in place names, such as Matouya and Xunjiaya in Hubei

【垭口】yākǒu〈方 *dial.*〉山口 mountain pass

鸦(鴉) yā 鸟类的一属,全身多为黑色,嘴大,翼长,脚有力。常见的有乌鸦、寒鸦等。crow; bird usu. black in colour and having a large beak, long wings and vigorous limbs. Corbie and jackdaw are two common crow breeds.

【鸦片】yāpiàn 用罂粟果实中的乳状汁液制成的一种毒品 narcotic made of inspissated juice of opium poppies; also 阿芙蓉 āfúróng; 通称 popularly known as 大烟 dàyān; ☞ 阿片 āpiàn on p. 1

Y

【鸦片战争】Yāpiàn Zhànzhēng 1840—1842年英国以我国禁止英商贩卖鸦片为借口对我国发动的侵略战争。战争开始后虽然有林则徐等人领导广东爱国军民的坚决抵抗,但腐败无能的清政府一再向侵略者谋求妥协,致使侵略军先后攻陷厦门、宁波、上海等地,兵临南京城下。在英军的武力威迫下,清政府向侵略者屈膝投降,和英国签订了我国近代史上第一个丧权辱国的《南京条约》。从此,中国逐渐沦为半殖民地半封建的国家,我国人民的反帝国主义、反封建主义的民主革命也从此开始。Opium War (1840-1842); the First Opium War; war of aggression launched by Britain against China under the pretext of China's sanctions on opium sales by British merchants. At the beginning the invaders met with the staunch resistance of patriotic Chinese armymen and civilians under the leadership of Lin Zexu and others, but owing to repeated compromises made by the decadent and inept Qing government, the invading troops were able to sack Xiamen, Ningbo and Shanghai, and arrive at Nanjing. Under British military intimidation the Qing government buckled and signed the Treaty of Nanjing of 1842, an unequal treaty that infringed upon state sovereignty of China and humiliated the Chinese people. The war marked the beginning of China's degeneration into a semi-colonial, semi-feudal country, and gave rise to the Chinese people's anti-imperialist, anti-feudal democratic revolution. also 第一次鸦片战争 Dì Yī Cì Yāpiàn Zhànzhēng

【鸦雀无声】yā què wú shēng 形容非常静 not even a crow or sparrow could be heard; all is quiet

哑(啞) yā same as 呀 yā ☞ yǎ on p. 2196

【哑哑】yāyā 〈拟声词 *onom.*〉形容乌鸦的叫声、小儿的学语声等 crow; babble; cries of a crow; babble; sound of a baby learning to speak

桠(椏、枒) yā 桠杈 fork (of a tree): 树～tree fork

【桠杈】yāchà ❶ 树枝分出的地方 fork of a tree ❷ 形容树枝歧出(of tree branches) crotched; forked ‖ also 丫杈 yāchà

【桠枝】yāzhī 枝桠 tree fork

鸭 yā 鸟类的一科,嘴扁腿短,趾间有蹼,善游泳,有家鸭、野鸭两种。肉供食用,毛(rǒng)毛用来絮被子、羽绒服或填充枕头。通常指家鸭。duck (*Anas domestica*); drake; duckling; wild or domesticated swimming bird of the family *Anatidae*, characterized by a flat bill, short limbs and webbed feet, whose meat is used as food and whose down is a material for padding quilts, snow jackets or pillows. The term usually refers to a domesticated duck.

【鸭蛋青】yādànqīng 极淡的青色 pale blue

【鸭蛋圆】yādànyuán 〈方 *dial.*〉(～儿 yādànyuánr)椭圆 oval

【鸭黄】yāhuáng 〈方 *dial.*〉孵出不久的小鸭,身上有淡黄色的毛(rǒng)毛 duckling; young duck whose body is covered with light yellow down

【鸭儿梨】yārlí ❶ 梨的一个品种,果实卵圆形,皮薄而光滑,淡黄色,有棕色斑点,味甜,脆而多汁 egg-shaped pear (*Pyrus*); a strain of pear with brown-speckled pale yellow skin that is thin and smooth, and meat that is sweet, crunch and juicy ❷ 这种植物的果实 pear

【鸭绒】yāróng 加工过的鸭毛(rǒng)毛,有很强的保温能力 duck's down; eiderdown; highly warmth-preserving processed duck's down: ～被 down-padded quilt

【鸭舌帽】yāshémào 帽顶的前部和月牙形帽檐扣在一起的帽子 peaked cap; cap with its foreside stuck with its crescent moon-shaped bill

【鸭子】yā·zi same as 鸭 yā

【鸭子儿】yāzǐr 〈方 *dial.*〉鸭蛋 duck's egg

【鸭嘴笔】yāzuǐbǐ 制图时画墨线的用具,笔头由两片弧形的钢相向合成,略呈鸭嘴状 drawing pen; ruling pen; cartographic pen with two curved steel pieces put together facing each other to form a tip in the shape of the duck's bill

【鸭嘴兽】yāzuǐshòu 哺乳动物,身体肥而扁,尾巴短而阔,嘴像鸭嘴,毛细密,深褐色,卵生。雌兽无乳头,乳汁由腹部的几个乳腺流出。穴居河边,善游泳,吃昆虫和贝类。产在大洋洲。platypus (*Ornithorhynchus anatinus*); duck-billed platypus; duckbill; semiaquatic egg-laying mammal of Oceania, having a deep brown plump and flat body covered with fine hair, a broad flat tail, webbed feet, and a snout resembling a duck's bill, a good swimmer that lives in riverside holes and feeds on insects and shellfish. The female duckbill does not have nipples, and its milk flows out from a number of milk glands in its belly.

雅 yā same as 鸦 yā ☞ yǎ on p. 2197

【雅片】yāpiàn same as 鸦片 yāpiàn

yá (ㄧㄚˊ)

牙[1] yá ❶ 牙齿 tooth: 门～ incisor; front tooth | 镶～insert an artificial tooth | ～医 dentist ❷ 特指象牙 ivory: ～筷 ivory chopstick | ～章 ivory seal ❸ 形状像牙齿的东西 sth. tooth-like: ～子 serrated edge ❹ (Yá) 姓 a surname

牙[2] yá '牙子'[2]〈旧时 *old*〉middleman; broker: ～行 brokerage

【牙碜】yá·chen ❶ 食物中夹杂着砂子,嚼起来牙齿不舒服(of food) gritty：菜没有洗干净，有点儿～。The vegetable wasn't washed properly, and was a kind of gritty. ❷〈比喻 *fig*.〉言语粗鄙不堪入耳(of language) coarse; jarring：你能说出这样的话来，也不嫌～。Fancy you could talk like that. Don't you feel ashamed?

【牙齿】 yáchǐ 齿的通称 general term for 齿 chǐ

【牙床】[1] yáchuáng 齿龈的通称。有的地区也叫牙床子。general term for 齿龈 chǐyín; known in some areas as 牙床子 yáchuáng•zi

【牙床】[2] yáchuáng 有象牙雕刻装饰的床。也泛指装饰精美的床。elaborately carved ivory-inlaid bed; (in a broad sense) finely crafted bed

【牙雕】 yádiāo 在象牙上雕刻形象、花纹的艺术 ivory carving; art of carving images and patterns on ivory; 也指用象牙雕刻成的工艺品 ivory carving; handicraft product of ivory carving

【牙粉】 yáfěn 刷牙用的粉状物，主要用碳酸钙、肥皂粉、香料、杀菌剂等制成 tooth powder; powder for brushing teeth, composed mainly of calcium carbonate, soap powder, perfume, and disinfectant

【牙膏】 yágāo 刷牙用的膏状物，用甘油、牙粉、白胶粉、水、糖精、淀粉等制成，装在金属或塑料的软管里 toothpaste; cream-like substance made from glycerin, tooth powder, white glue powder, water, gluside, starch, etc. contained in soft metal or plastic tube

【牙根】 yágēn same as 牙床[1] yáchuáng：～疼 pain in one's gum ◇咬定～clench one's teeth (and refuse to say anything)

【牙垢】 yágòu 牙齿表面黑褐色或黄色的污垢。有的地区叫牙花。tartar; dental calculus; hard, dark brown or yellowish deposit on the teeth, consisting of organic secretions and food particles deposited in various salts; known in some areas as 牙花 yáhuā

【牙关】 yáguān 指上颌(hé)和下颌之间的关节 mandibular joint：～紧闭 lockjaw | 咬紧～grit one's teeth

【牙行】 yáháng〈旧时 *old*〉提供场所、协助买卖双方成交而从中取得佣金的商号或个人 middleman; broker; broker house; brokerage

【牙花】 yáhuā〈方 *dial*.〉❶ same as 牙垢 yágòu ❷ 齿龈 gums ‖ also 牙花子 yáhuā•zi

【牙具】 yájù 刷牙漱口的用具 tooth-cleaners, e.g. toothbrush, toothpaste, etc.

【牙口】 yá•kou ❶ 指牲口的年龄(根据牲口的牙齿多少可以判定牲口的年龄) age of a draught animal as shown by the number of its teeth：这头牛～不老。Judging from its teeth this ox is not old at all. ❷ (～儿 yá•kour)指老年人牙齿的咀嚼能力 chewing ability of an old person's teeth：您老人家的～还好吧？I suppose your teeth are still in a good condition, aren't they?

【牙侩】 yákuài〈书 *fml*.〉same as 牙子[2] yá•zi

【牙轮】 yálún 齿轮的通称 general term for 齿轮 chǐlún

【牙牌】 yápái 骨牌 dominoes made of ivory, wrought bone, etc.

【牙婆】 yápó〈旧时 *old*〉以介绍人口买卖为业从中取利的妇女 woman engaged in the trafficking of young women and children

【牙签】 yáqiān (～儿 yáqiānr)剔除牙缝中食物残屑用的细棍儿 toothpick

【牙色】 yásè 近似象牙的淡黄颜色 ivory-coloured; creamy white

【牙石】[1] yáshí 结成硬块的牙垢 tartar

【牙石】[2] yáshí ☞ 缘石 yuánshí on p. 2364

【牙刷】 yáshuā (～儿 yáshuār)刷牙的刷子 toothbrush; also 牙刷子 yáshuā•zi

【牙牙】 yáyá〈书 *fml*.〉〈拟声词 *onom*.〉形容婴儿学说话的声音 baby talk; babble：～学语 babble one's first sounds; learn to speak

【牙医】 yáyī 给人镶牙、拔牙、治疗牙病的医生 dentist

【牙龈】 yáyín same as 齿龈 chǐyín

【牙质】 yázhì ❶ 以象牙为质料的 made of ivory：～的刀把 ivory knife handle ❷ 牙齿的主要组成部分，比骨坚硬而致密，在齿髓的外面，釉质的里面，由许多纤细的小管构成 dentin; hard, calcareous tissue consisting of numerous tiny tubes, denser and harder than bone, that is found between tooth pulp and enamel; also 象牙质 xiàngyázhì

【牙子】[1] yá•zi 物体周围雕花的装饰或突出的部分 serrated fringe; ornamental carving along the edges of an object：桌椅的～做工精细。The chairs and tables are adorned with finely crafted serrated fringes. | 马路～curbstone

【牙子】[2] yá•zi〈旧时 *old*〉为买卖双方撮合从中取得佣金的人(通常卖方为农民、渔民等小生产者，买方为收购商或消费者) middleman; broker; one that acts as an agent in a business transaction in return for a commission. Usually a seller is a peasant, fisherman or small-time producer, and the buyer is a businessman or consumer.

伢 yá〈方 *dial*.〉小孩儿 child; kid

芽 yá (～儿 yár) ❶ 植物刚长出来的可以发育成茎、叶或花的部分 sprout; shoot：麦子发～儿了。The wheat is sprouting. ❷ 形状像芽的东西 sth. that looks like a sprout：肉～(伤口愈合后多长出的肉) granulation tissue; outgrowths of new capillaries on the surface of a wound that is healing

【芽茶】 yáchá 极嫩的茶叶 young tea leaves; bud-tea

【芽豆】 yádòu 用水泡后长出短芽的蚕豆，做菜吃 sprouted broad bean

【芽接】 yájiē 嫁接的一种方法，用植物的幼芽嵌在砧木上扎紧 bud grafting; budding; unite a shoot or bud with a growing plant by insertion; ☞ 嫁接 jiàjiē on p. 937

【芽体】yátǐ 低等生物出芽生殖时所生出的芽状体 gem; sprout; bud; gemmule

【芽眼】yáyǎn 块茎上凹进去可以生芽的部分 eye; bud of a tuber

岈 yá 嵖岈(Cháyá),山名,在河南 Chaya, name of a mountain in Henan Province

玡(琊) yá 琅玡(Lángyá),山名,在山东 Langya, name of a mountain in Shandong Province

蚜 yá 蚜虫 aphid; aphis; plant louse: 棉～ cotton aphid | 烟～tobacco aphid

【蚜虫】yáchóng 昆虫,身体卵圆形,绿色、黄色或棕色,腹部大。吸食植物的汁液,是农业害虫。种类很多,如棉蚜、烟蚜。aphid (*Aphididae*); aphis; plant louse; insect with a green, yellow or brown oval body and big belly, and regarded as a pest for it sucks on the juice of farm crops; of various kinds, such as cotton aphid, tabacco budworm, etc.; 通称 popularly called 腻虫 nìchóng; 有的地区叫蜜虫 known in some regions as 蜜虫 mìchóng

崖(厓、崕) yá (又读 also pronounced ái) ❶ 山石或高地的陡立的侧面 precipice; cliff: 山～cliff | 悬～overhanging cliff | 摩～cliff carving ❷ 边际 limit; bound; boundary: ～略 general idea

【崖画】yáhuà 岩画 cliff painting

【崖刻】yákè 山崖上刻的文字 cliff inscription

【崖略】yálüè 〈书 *fml.*〉大略;概略 gist; outline; general idea: 言其～。Here is the gist of the idea.

涯 yá 水边 water margin; 泛指边际 margin; limit: 天～海角 corner of heaven and end of the earth | 一望无～boundless

【涯际】yájì 边际 limit; boundary: 漫无～的海洋 boundless sea

睚 yá 〈书 *fml.*〉眼角 corner of the eye

【睚眦】yázì 〈书 *fml.*〉发怒时瞪眼睛 angry stare; 借指极小的仇恨 small grievance: ～之怨 trifling (or trivial) grievance

【睚眦必报】yázì bì bào 像瞪了自己一眼那样的极小仇恨也要报复。形容心胸极其狭窄。seek revenge just for an angry look; narrow-minded

衙 yá same as 衙门 yá·men: ～役 *yamen* runner

【衙门】yá·men 〈旧时 *old*〉官员办公的机关 *yamen*, government office

【衙内】yánèi 唐代称担任警卫的官员,五代及宋初多以大臣子弟充任,后来泛指官僚的子弟 imperial bodyguard, a Tang-dynasty official title. During the Five Dynasties and the early Song Dynasty, this position was mostly taken by sons of major officials. Hence the term, *yanei*, a bureaucrat's child.

【衙役】yá·yi 衙门里的差役 *yamen* runner

yǎ (ㄧㄚˇ)

疋 yǎ same as 雅 yǎ
☞ 匹 pǐ on p. 1468

哑(啞) yǎ ❶ 由于生理缺陷或疾病而不能说话 mute; dumb; lacking the power of speech due to physiological handicap or illness: 聋～deaf-mute◇～剧 pantomime; mummery; dumb show | ～口无言 be tongue-tied; be rendered speechless ❷ 嗓子干涩发不出声音或发音低而不清楚 husky; hoarse: 沙～hoarse | ～嗓子 husky voice | 嗓子都喊～了 shout oneself hoarse ❸ 因发生故障,炮弹、子弹等打不响(of a shell, bomb, etc.) fail to explode: ～炮 dud | ～火 dud; (of a person) quiet
☞ yā on p. 2194

【哑巴】yǎ·ba 由于生理缺陷或疾病而不能说话的人 dumb person; mute; speech-impaired person

【哑巴亏】yǎ·bakuī ☞吃哑巴亏 chī yǎ·bākuī on p. 258

【哑场】yǎ//chǎng same as 冷场 lěng//chǎng ②

【哑剧】yǎjù 不用对话或歌唱而只用动作和表情来表达剧情的戏剧 pantomime; theatrical performance that tells a story not by dialogue or singing but by action and facial expression

【哑铃】yǎlíng 体育运动的辅助器械,用木头或铁等制成,两头呈球形,中间较细,用手握住做各种动作 dumbbell; wooden or iron weight consisting of a short bar with a metal ball or disk at either end that is lifted for various physical exercises

【哑谜】yǎmí 隐晦的话 puzzling remark; 〈比喻 *fig.*〉难以猜透的问题 enigma; riddle: 打～keep somebody guessing

【哑炮】yǎpào ☞ 瞎炮 xiāpào on p. 2060

【哑然】[1] yǎrán 〈书 *fml.*〉❶ 形容寂静 soundless; silent: ～无声 all is quiet | 全场～。Silence prevailed over the entire meeting hall. ❷ 形容惊异得说不出话来 struck speechless: ～失惊 dumbfounded

【哑然】[2] yǎrán ('哑'旧读 formerly pronounced è)〈书 *fml.*〉形容笑声 sound of laughter: ～失笑 cannot help laughing; unable to stifle a laugh

【哑语】yǎyǔ 手语 sign language; dactylology: 打～communicate with the sign language

【哑子】yǎ·zi 〈方 *dial.*〉same as 哑巴 yǎ·ba

痖(瘂) yǎ same as 哑 yǎ

雅[1] yǎ ❶〈书 *fml*.〉合乎规范的 standard; proper; correct:～正 please be so kind as to point out any mistakes in my work ❷ 高尚的;不粗俗的 graceful; polished; stylish:文～ gentle and cultivated|～致 tasteful|～座(of a restaurant, etc.) private room ❸ 西周朝廷上的乐歌,《诗经》中诗篇的一类 ode; court hymns of the Western Zhou Dynasty; ode, one of the genres of verse in *The Book of Songs* ❹〈敬辞 *pol*.〉用于称对方的情意、举动 your (feelings or behaviour):～意 your kindness|～教 your esteemed advice

雅[2] yǎ〈书 *fml*.〉❶ 交情 friendship; companionship:无一日之～ not have the pleasure of knowing sb. ❷ 平素 usually; often:～善鼓琴 often play the zither and play it well ❸ 很;极 very much; extremely:～以为美 really consider it beautiful

☞ yā on p. 2194

【雅观】yǎguān 装束、举动文雅(多用于否定式 oft. in the negative) refined (in manner, etc.); seemly; in good taste:坐的姿势很不～ unseemly sitting posture

【雅号】yǎhào ❶ 高雅的名号(多用于尊称人的名字 oft. honor.) your elegant name ❷ 指绰号(含诙谐意 humor.) nickname:我倒不晓得他还有这么一个～呢! Really, I didn't know he had such a nickname!

【雅教】yǎjiào〈敬辞 *pol*.〉称对方的指教 your esteemed opinion; your excellent advice

【雅静】yǎjìng ❶ 雅致而清静 unostentatious; tasteful and quiet:～的房间 elegant and peaceful room ❷ 文静 gentle and quiet:这位姑娘很～。The young woman looks rather gentle and quiet.

【雅量】yǎliàng ❶ 宽宏的气度 broadmindedness; magnanimity; generosity:要有倾听批评意见的～。You've got to have a big heart to listen to criticisms. ❷ 大的酒量 great capacity for liquor

【雅趣】yǎqù 高雅的意趣 refined taste:～盎然 be imbued with a cultivated taste

【雅人】yǎrén 高雅的人。旧时多指吟风弄月的文人。person of refined tastes; (old) scholar who shuns politics and the mundane world by indulging in literary pursuits

【雅士】yǎshì 高雅的人 man of refinement; 多指读书人 scholar:文人～ men of letters and refined scholars

【雅俗共赏】yǎ sú gòng shǎng 文化高的人和文化低的人都能欣赏(of a work of art or literature) appeal to all; suit both refined and popular tastes

【雅兴】yǎxìng 高雅的兴趣 stylish interest; good taste:～不浅 show depth in a tasteful pursuit

【雅驯】yǎxùn〈书 *fml*.〉(文辞)典雅(of diction or language) refined; elegant

【雅意】yǎyì ❶ 高尚的情意 kindly consideration; tender regards:高情～ lofty sentiments|有负～。I'm sorry to have failed to live up to your kindness. ❷〈敬辞 *pol*.〉称对方的情意或意见 your kindness; your opinion

【雅正】yǎzhèng ❶〈书 *fml*.〉合规范:纯正 standard; pure ❷ 正直 upright; righteous ❸〈敬辞 *pol*.〉把自己的诗文书画等送给人时,表示请对方指教 [when presenting sb. with one's work of painting, calligraphy, writing, etc.] please be so kind as to point out my inadequacies

【雅致】yǎ·zhi (服饰、器物、房屋等)美观而不落俗套(of attire, objects, dwelling, etc.) look beautiful in an ingenious way; have some pretensions to good taste

【雅座】yǎzuò (～儿 yǎzuòr)指饭馆、酒店、澡堂中比较精致而舒适的小房间 private room (in a restaurant, public bath, etc.)

yà (丨Ỳ)

轧[1] yà ❶ 碾;滚压 roll; run over:～棉花 gin cotton ❷ 排挤 eject; throw out; unseat; dispossess; disinherit:倾～ conflict; discord ❸ (Yà)姓 a surname

轧[2] yà〈拟声词 *onom*.〉形容机器开动时发出的声音 rumble; click; sound of a running machine:机声～～。The machines rumbled away.|缝纫机～～～地响着。The sewing machine clicked away.

☞ gá on p. 618 and zhá on p. 2404

【轧场】yà//cháng 用碌碡等压平场院或滚压摊在场上的谷物使脱粒 level a threshing ground with a stone roller; thresh grain on a threshing ground with a stone roller

【轧道车】yàdàochē 铁路上巡查或检修用的车,多用电瓶或柴油机做动力 line inspection trolley; track-testing trolley, usu. powered with battery or diesel engine

【轧道机】yàdàojī〈方 *dial*.〉压路机 road roller; roller

【轧花机】yàhuājī 用来分离棉子和棉絮的机器,有锯齿式和皮辊式两种 sawtooth- or roller-type cotton gin; machine that separates the seeds and seed hulls from the fibers of cotton; also 轧棉机 yàmiánjī

亚[1](亞) yà ❶ 较差 inferior; shabby:他的技术不～于你。He's by no means inferior to you in skill. ❷ 次一等 substandard:～军 runner-up|～热带 subtropical zone; subtropics ❸ 原子价较低的 of lower atomic valence;酸根或化合物中少含一个氢原子或氧原子的 acid radical or compound minus one hydrogen or oxygen atom:硫酸～铁 ($FeSO_4$) ferrisulphas |～氨基(NH) imino group |～硫酸(H_2SO_3) sulphurous acid

亚²(亞) Yà 指亚洲 Asia; short for 亚洲

【亚当】Yàdāng《圣经》故事中人类的始祖 Adam, the first man according to the Bible [希伯来 Hebrew: Ādhām]

【亚军】yàjūn 体育、游艺项目等的竞赛中评比出来的第二名 second place (in a sports contest); runner-up

【亚麻】yàmá ❶一年生草本植物,茎细长,叶子互生,披针形或条形,花浅蓝色,结蒴果,球形。纤维用亚麻的茎皮含纤维很多,可以做纺织原料。flax (*Linum usitatissimum*); annual herbaceous plant having a slender stem, alternate lanceolate or strip leaves, and pale blue flowers, bearing spherical capsules, and its fibrous stem being a raw material for the textile industry ❷纤维用亚麻的茎皮纤维 flax fibre

【亚热带】yàrèdài 热带和温带之间的过渡地带。与热带相比,有显著的季节变化,气温比温带高,植物在冬季仍能缓慢生长。subtropical zone; subtropics; semitropics; transitional zone between the tropical and temperate zones, marked for more distinct seasonal changes than the tropical zone and higher temperatures than the temperate zone so that plants can grow slowly in winter; also 副热带 fùrèdài

压(壓) yà ☞ below
☞ yā on p. 2191

【压板】yàbǎn 〈方 *dial.*〉跷跷板(qiāoqiāo-bǎn) seesaw; teeterboard; teeter-totter

【压根儿】yàgēnr 根本;从来 from the start; in the first place; altogether(多用于否定句 usu. in the negative):他全忘了,好像～没有这回事。He's clean forgotten about it, as if it had never happened.

讶 yà 〈书 *fml.*〉诧异 be astonished; wonder: 惊～surprise; yipe|～然 be surprised; be astonished

迓 yà 〈书 *fml.*〉迎接 welcome; greet: 迎～面 greet

砑 yà 用卵石或弧形的石块碾压或摩擦皮革、布匹等,使密实而光亮 press and smooth (leather, cloth, etc.) with pebbles or stones with curving services; calender: 把牛皮～光 calender a piece of cowhide

挜(掗) yà 〈方 *dial.*〉硬把东西送给对方或卖给对方 force sb. to take or buy sth.

娅(婭) yà ☞姻娅 yīnyà on p. 2288

氩(氬) yà 气体元素,符号 Ar(argonium)。无色无臭无味,是大气中含量最多的稀有气体,化学性质很不活泼。放电时发出蓝色的光,在电弧焊接不锈钢、镁、铝等时用作保护气体,也用来填充灯管和灯泡。argon (Ar); colourless, odorless, inert gaseous element and the most abundant rare gas in the earth's atmosphere, emitting blue light when discharging electricity, used as an inert gas shield in arc welding of stainless steel, magnesium, aluminum, etc., and also for use in electric light bulbs, fluorescent tubes, and radio vacuum tubes

揠 yà 〈书 *fml.*〉拔 pull up; tug upward: ～苗助长 try to help shoots grow by pulling them up

【揠苗助长】yà miáo zhù zhǎng 古时候宋国有个人,嫌禾苗长得太慢,就一棵棵地往上拔起一点,回家还夸口说:'今天我帮助苗长了!'他儿子听说后,到地里一看,苗都死了(见于《孟子·公孙丑》)。后来用来比喻违反事物的发展规律,急于求成,反而坏事。According to *Mencius·Gongsun Chou*, a man from the State of Song became impatient with the slow growth of grain seedlings in his fields and pulled them up a little one by one. When he went home he bragged, 'Today I've helped the seedlings grow a bit higher!' His son heard what he was saying, and went to the fields to take a look. It turned out that all the seedlings had died. (fig.) try to help seedlings grow by pulling them up—spoil things by excessive enthusiasm; also 拔苗助长 bá miáo zhù zhǎng

猰(貐) yà [猰貐](yàyǔ)古代传说中的一种吃人的猛兽 *yayu*, mythological man-eating beast

·ya (·丨丫)

呀 ·ya 〈助词 *aux.*〉'啊'受前一字韵母 a,e,i,o,ü 的影响而发生的变音[used in place of 啊 when the preceding character ends in sound a, e, i, o, or ü]: 马跑得真快～! Ah, how fast the horse runs! |大家快去～! Come on, let's go quickly! |你怎么不学一学～! Why don't you try to learn it? |这个瓜～,甜得很! This melon is, indeed, very sweet.
☞ yā on p. 2193

yān (丨ㄢ)

咽 yān 口腔后部主要由肌肉和黏膜构成的管子。咽分成三部分,上段跟鼻腔相对叫鼻咽,中段跟口腔相对叫口咽,下段在喉的后部叫喉咽。咽是呼吸道和消化道的共同通路。pharynx; alimentary canal consisting mainly of muscle and mucous membrane in the rear of the mouth. The pharynx consists of three sections: nasopharynx (the upper part of the pharynx above the soft palate that is continuous with the nasal passages), oropharynx (the middle part of the pharynx between the soft palate and the epiglottis) and laryngopharynx (the lower portion of the pharynx just above the larynx). Pharynx is the canal for both the respiratory tract and the esophagus. also 咽头 yāntóu

☞ yàn on p. 2214 and yè on p. 2241

【咽喉】yānhóu ❶ 咽头和喉头 pharynx and larynx; throat ❷〈比喻 *fig.*〉形势险要的交通孔道 strategic (or vital) passage; key junction (or link):～要地 place of strategic interest

【咽头】yāntóu same as 咽 yān

恹(懨、懕) yān [恹恹]〈书 *fml.*〉形容患病而精神疲乏 weak and weary through illness; run-down:～欲睡 feel weak and sleepy

殷 yān〈书 *fml.*〉赤黑色 blackish red; dark red

☞ yīn on p. 2288 and yǐn on p. 2294

【殷红】yānhóng 带黑的红色 blackish red; dark red:～的血迹 blackish red bloodstains|～的鸡冠子 dark red cockscombs

胭(臙) yān 胭脂 rouge:～粉 rouge and powder|～红 carmine; rouge

【胭红】yānhóng 像胭脂的红色 carmine; rouge:～的野百合 carmine flowers of the wild lily|～的朝霞 rosy morning sunglow

【胭脂】yān·zhi 一种红色的化妆品,涂在两颊或嘴唇上。也用做国画的颜料。rouge; red or pink cosmetic for colouring the cheeks or lips, also used as a pigment in traditional Chinese painting

【胭脂鱼】yān·zhiyú 鱼,体长而侧扁,背部隆起,成鱼全身粉红、黄褐或暗褐色,供食用。分布在长江上游。有的地区叫黄排。Chinese sucker (*Myxocyprinus asiaticus Bleeker*); slender and laterally flat food fish with a hunched back, turning pink or yellowish or dark brown when fully grown, found in the upper reaches of the Yangtze River; known in some regions as 黄排 huángpái

烟(煙、❹菸) yān ❶ 物质燃烧时产生的混有未完全燃烧的微小颗粒的气体 smoke; vaporous gas made up of small particles of carbonaceous matter in the air, resulting mainly from the incomplete burning of organic material ❷ 像烟的东西 sth. smoke-like:～雾 mist|～霞 mist and clouds ❸ 由于烟的刺激使眼睛流泪或睁不开 (of eyes) be irritated by smoke:～了眼睛了。My eyes were irritated by the smoke. ❹ 烟草 tobacco:～叶 tobacco leaves|烤～ flue-cured tobacco ❺ 纸烟、烟丝等的统称 tobacco; cigarette:香～ cigarette|旱～ tobacco smoked in a long-stemmed Chinese pipe|～瘾 crave for tobacco|请勿吸～。No smoking. ❻ 指鸦片 opium:～土 raw opium ❼ 烟子 soot:松～ pine soot

☞ yīn on p. 1501

【烟霭】yān'ǎi〈书 *fml.*〉云雾 mist and clouds:～朦胧 ethereal mist and clouds

【烟波】yānbō 烟雾笼罩的江湖水面 mist-covered waters:～浩淼 vast expanse of misty, rolling waters

【烟草】yāncǎo ❶ 一年生草本植物,叶子大,长圆状披针形,总状花序生在茎的顶端,花冠漏斗形,筒部粉红色或白色,裂片红色,结蒴果,卵圆形。叶是制造烟丝、香烟等的主要原料。tobacco (*Nicotiana spp.*); annual herbaceous plant having large ovate lanceolate leaves that are a major raw material for making cut tobacco and cigarettes, and raceme flowers growing atop the stalk with funnel-shaped corolla, pink or white tubes and red lobes, and bearing elliptical capsules ❷ 指烟叶 tobacco leaves:～市场 tobacco market

【烟尘】yānchén ❶ 烟雾和尘埃 smoke and dust:～滚滚 thick pall of smoke and dust ❷ 烽烟和战场上扬起的尘土。旧时指战火。beacon smoke and dust of war; (old) battle; war; flames of war ❸〈书 *fml.*〉指人烟稠密的地方 densely populated place

【烟囱】yāncōng 烟筒 chimney; funnel; stovepipe:～林立 jungle of chimneys

【烟袋】yāndài 吸烟的用具,有旱烟袋和水烟袋两种。特指旱烟袋。long-stemmed pipe; water pipe; pipe, esp. long-stemmed pipe; ☞ 旱烟袋 hànyāndài on p. 767 and 水烟袋 shuǐyāndài on p. 1804

【烟蒂】yāndì same as 烟头 yāntóu

【烟斗】yāndǒu ❶ 吸烟用具,多用坚硬的木头制成,一头装烟叶,一头衔在嘴里吸 (tobacco) pipe; device for smoking, consisting of a tube oft. of hardwood with a small bowl at one end containing burning tobacco, and a mouthpiece at the other ❷ 鸦片烟枪上的陶质球状物,顶端奶头状的部分有小孔 (of an opium pipe) ceramic ball with a nipple-shaped protrusion that has a hole in it

【烟斗丝】yāndǒusī 装在烟斗中吸的烟丝 pipe tobacco; also 斗烟丝 dǒuyānsī

【烟膏】yāngāo 烟土熬成的膏 prepared opium paste

【烟鬼】yānguǐ 讥称吸鸦片成瘾的人。也指吸烟瘾头很大的人。opium addict; heavy smoker

【烟海】yānhǎi 烟雾弥漫的大海,多用于比喻 foggy or misty sea, often used figuratively:浩如～ ocean of mist — vast and voluminous|如堕～ as if lost in an immense fog; be all at sea

【烟花】[1] yānhuā ❶〈书 *fml.*〉指春天艳丽的景物 lovely spring scene ❷〈旧时 *old*〉指妓女,也指跟娼妓有关的 prostitute; prostitution:沦为～ become a whore|～女 prostitute; whore|～巷 red-light district

【烟花】[2] yānhuā same as 烟火 yān·huo:～爆竹

fireworks and firecrackers

【烟灰】yānhuī 烟吸完后剩下的灰 tobacco or cigarette ash

【烟火】yānhuǒ ❶ 烟和火 smoke and fire：动～(指生火做饭) raise a fire and prepare food|建筑工地严禁～。Smoking and lighting fires are strictly banned on the construction site. ❷ 烟火食 cooked food：不食人间～do not eat cooked food；live the life of an immortal ❸〈书 *fml*.〉烽火；战火 signal fire；flames of war ❹〈旧时 *old*〉指祭祀祖先的事。借指后嗣。matters associated with a sacrificial ritual for ancestors；(fig.) offspring；progeny：绝了～ have no male offspring to carry on a family line

【烟火】yān·huo 燃放时能发出各种颜色的火花而供人观赏的东西，主要是在火药中搀入锶、锂、铝、钡、镁、钠、铜等金属盐类，并用纸裹成，种类不一。燃放时发出火花，同时变幻出各种景物。firework；device made by wrapping in paper a mixture of powder and salts of such metals as strontium，lithium，aluminum，barium，magnesium，natrium and copper，and when set off，emitting sparks that form a variety of spectacular sights

【烟火食】yānhuǒshí 指熟食 cooked food

【烟具】yānjù 吸烟的用具，如烟嘴、烟盒、烟灰缸等 smoking paraphernalia；smoking set，including cigarette holder，cigarette case，and ashtray

【烟卷儿】yānjuǎnr same as 香烟[2] xiāngyān

【烟煤】yānméi 煤的一种，暗黑色，有光泽，燃烧时冒烟。可分为焦煤、肥煤、瘦煤、气煤等。除用做燃料外，也是炼焦的原料。bituminous coal；soft coal；shiny blackish mineral coal with a high percentage of volatile matter that burns with a smoky yellow flame，coming in such varieties as coking coal，'fat' coal，'lean' coal，and gas coal，used as fuel and raw material for coking

【烟幕】yānmù ❶ 用化学药剂造成的浓厚的烟雾，作战时用来遮蔽敌人的视线 smokescreen；mass of dense artificial smoke created with chemicals to conceal military operations from an enemy ❷ 燃烧某些燃料或化学物质而造成的浓厚的烟雾，农业上用来防止霜冻 thick pall of smoke produced from chemicals to protect farm crops from frost ❸〈比喻 *fig*.〉掩盖真相或本意的言语或行为 smokescreen；action or statement used to conceal truth or actual plans or intentions：以和谈作～use peace talks as a smokescreen

【烟幕弹】yānmùdàn ❶ 爆炸时可以形成烟幕的炮弹或炸弹等 smoke shell；smoke bomb；also 发烟弹 fāyāndàn ❷〈比喻 *fig*.〉掩盖真相或本意的言语或行为 smokescreen；deed or word used to cover up truth or intention

【烟农】yānnóng 以种烟草为主的农民 tobacco grower

【烟屁股】yānpì·gu same as 烟头 yāntóu

【烟色】yānsè 像烤烟那样的深棕色 colour of tobacco；dark brown

【烟丝】yānsī 烟叶加工成的细丝 cut tobacco；pipe tobacco

【烟筒】yān·tong 炉灶、锅炉上出烟的管状装置 chimney；funnel；stovepipe

【烟头】yāntóu (～儿 yāntóur)纸烟吸到最后剩下的部分 cigarette end，stub，butt and stump

【烟土】yāntǔ 未经熬制的鸦片 crude opium

【烟雾】yānwù 泛指烟、雾、云、气等 smoke；mist；vapour；smog；smoke and vapour：～弥漫 enshrouded in mist|～腾腾 filled with steam and smoke

【烟霞】yānxiá 烟雾和云霞 mists and clouds：～缥缈 ethereal mist and clouds

【烟霞癖】yānxiápǐ〈书 *fml*.〉❶ 游山玩水的癖好 love for the beauty of nature with its mists and clouds；rambling propensity ❷ 借指吸食鸦片的嗜好 addiction to opium smoking；opium habit

【烟消云散】yān xiāo yún sàn〈比喻 *fig*.〉事物消失净尽 vanish like smoke and disperse like clouds；completely vanish；also 云消雾散 yún xiāo wù sàn

【烟叶】yānyè 烟草的叶子，是制造烟丝、香烟等的原料 tobacco leaf；leaf tobacco，raw material for making cut tobacco and cigarettes

【烟瘾】yānyǐn 吸烟的瘾。旧时多指吸鸦片烟等的瘾。crave for smoking；(old) crave for opium

【烟雨】yānyǔ 像烟雾那样的细雨 misty rain

【烟云】yānyún 烟气和云雾 smoke，mists and clouds：～缭绕 be lost in clouds that keep curling and uncurling

【烟柱】yānzhù 烈火燃烧时直向上升的呈柱状的浓烟 column of thick，ascending smoke produced by a raging fire

【烟子】yān·zi 烧火或熬油时的烟上升而聚成的黑色物质，可以制墨 soot；fine black particles chiefly composed of carbon，produced by incomplete combustion of coal，oil，wood，or other fuels，used as a material for making ink

【烟嘴儿】yānzuǐr 吸纸烟用的短管子 cigarette holder

焉 yān〈书 *fml*.〉❶ 跟介词'于'加代词'是'相当[similar to the meaning of the preposition 于 yú followed by the pronoun 是 shì] here；this：心不在～with one's attention elsewhere；absent-minded|乐莫大～。There's no greater happiness than this. ❷ 哪里；怎么(多用于反问 oft. in a rhetorical question) how；how come；why：～有今日？How could I become what I am today (without your help)？|～能不去？How could I choose not to go？|不入虎穴，～得虎子？How can you catch tiger cubs without entering the tiger's lair？❸

乃；才 not unless; only then：必知乱之所自起，～能治之。Only by locating the cause of the trouble can it be properly handled. ❹〈语助词 *aux*.〉：有厚望～。There are great expectations on you. | 因以为号～use this as the signal

崦 yān [崦嵫](Yānzī) ❶ 山名，在甘肃 Yanzi, name of a mountain in Gansu Province ❷〈古代 *arch*.〉指太阳落山的地方 where the sun sets：日薄～。The sun is setting beyond the horizon.

阉 yān ❶ 阉割 castrate; spay：～鸡 capon | ～猪 barrow; hog ❷〈书 *fml*.〉指宦官 eunuch：～党 clique of eunuchs

【阉割】yāngē ❶ 割掉睾丸或卵巢，使失去生殖能力 geld; emasculate; castrate; spay; remove the testicles of (a male) ❷〈比喻 *fig*.〉抽掉文章或理论的主要内容，使失去作用或改变实质 deprive an article or theory of its essence; emasculate

【阉人】yānrén 指被阉割的人。也用做宦官的代称。castrated person; eunuch

【阉寺】yānsì〈书 *fml*.〉指宦官 eunuch

阏 yān [阏氏](yānzhī)汉代匈奴称君主的正妻 Han-dynasty term of address for the wife of a Hun (Xiongnu) chief

☞ è on p. 507

淹(❶ 渰) yān ❶ 淹没 flood; submerge; inundate：～死 die from drowning | 庄稼遭水～了。The crops were inundated. ❷ 汗液等浸渍皮肤使感到痛或痒 tingling or smarting from sweat：胳肢窝被汗～得难受。My armpits are tingling from sweat. ❸〈书 *fml*.〉广 broad; wide：～博 wide-read ❹〈书 *fml*.〉久；迟延 delay; tarry：～留 stay for a long time

【淹博】yānbó〈书 *fml*.〉广博 well-read; of great learning：学问～ have encyclopedic knowledge

【淹灌】yānguàn 灌溉的一种方法，在田里蓄水供作物的根部吸收，适用于水稻等 basin irrigation; form of irrigation, suitable for paddy rice cultivation, etc., by storing water to be absorbed by crop roots in the fields

【淹留】yānliú〈书 *fml*.〉长期逗留 stay for a long period：～他乡。Have been away from one's native land for a long time.

【淹埋】yānmái（淤泥、沙土）盖过；埋住（of mud, sand, etc.) flow or blow over and cover completely：铁路被淤泥～了。The railway was buried in mud.

【淹没】yānmò（大水）漫过，盖过 submerge; flood; inundate; drown：河里涨水，小桥都～了。The river flooded and submerged the small bridge. ◇掌声～了他的讲话。His speech was drowned out by the applause.

腌(醃) yān 把鱼、肉、蛋、蔬菜、果品等加上盐、糖、酱、酒等 preserve fish, meat, egg, vegetable, fruit, etc. in salt, sugar, soy sauce, wine, etc.; pickle; salt

☞ ā on p. 2

【腌渍】yānzì same as 腌 yān

湮 yān〈书 *fml*.〉❶ 埋没 fall into oblivion; bury in oblivion：～没 fall into oblivion | ～灭 bury in obscurity ❷ 淤塞 clog up; stop

☞ 洇 yīn on p. 2287

【湮灭】yānmiè same as 湮没 yānmò

【湮没】yānmò 埋没 be neglected; be forgotten：～无闻 sink into oblivion; fall into obscurity

鄢 Yān 姓 a surname

嫣 yān〈书 *fml*.〉容貌美好 handsome; beautiful

【嫣红】yānhóng〈书 *fml*.〉鲜艳的红色 bright red：姹紫～beautiful flowers of brilliant purples and reds

【嫣然】yānrán〈书 *fml*.〉美好的样子 engaging; sweet：～一笑 give a winsome smile

燕 Yān ❶ 周朝国名，在今河北北部和辽宁南部 Yan, a state during the Eastern Zhou Dynasty in present-day northern Hebei and southern Liaoning ❷ 指河北北部 northern Hebei ❸ 姓 a surname

☞ yàn on p. 2216

yán (丨ㄢˊ)

延 yán ❶ 延长 prolong; extend; protract：蔓～spread | 绵～be continuous; run uninterrupted; stretch long and unbroken | ～年益寿 prolong one's life | 苟～残喘 eke out a miserable life; be on one's last legs ❷（时间）向后推迟 postpone, put off：迟～delay; retard | ～期 postponement | 大会遇雨顺～。The meeting shall be put off in case it rains. ❸〈书 *fml*.〉聘请；邀请 engage; invite：～聘 employ; hire | ～师 hire a tutor | ～医 send for a doctor | ～至其家 invite sb. to one's family ❹（Yán）姓 a surname

【延长】yáncháng 向长的方面发展 elongate; lengthen; prolong; extend：～生命 extend one's life | 路线～一百里 extend a route for 100 *li* | 会议～了三天。The meeting was extended for another three days.

【延迟】yánchí 推迟 delay; defer; postpone：会议～三天召开。The conference has been put off for three days.

【延宕】yándàng 拖延 procrastinate; delay; keep putting off：～时日 be delayed for days on end

【延搁】yángē 拖延耽搁 delay; procrastinate

【延缓】yánhuǎn 延迟；推迟 delay; postpone; put off：工程进度不容～。On no account should this construction be delayed.

【延颈企踵】yán jǐng qǐ zhǒng 伸长脖子，抬起脚跟。形容急切盼望。crane one's neck and stand on tiptoe; look forward to on tiptoe; anxiously expect; yearn for

【延揽】yánlǎn〈书 *fml*.〉延聘招揽;聘请 enlist the services of:～人才 enlist the services of able people|～天下贤士 recruit worthy people from all over the country

【延绵】yánmián 绵延 extend uninterruptedly; be continuous

【延纳】yánnà〈书 *fml*.〉接待;接纳 accommodate; recruit; admit

【延年益寿】yán nián yì shòu 增加岁数,延长寿命(of tonics, etc.) prolong life; promise longevity

【延聘】yánpìn〈书 *fml*.〉聘请 engage; invite (sb. to do sth. in a particular capacity)

【延期】yán//qī 推迟原来规定的日期 postpone; defer; put off:会议～举行。The meeting has been postponed.

【延请】yánqǐng 请人担任工作(多指临时的) invite (sb. to do a particular job); engage:～律师 hire a lawyer|～家庭教师 hire a family tutor

【延烧】yánshāo 火势蔓延燃烧(of a fire) spread:这场大火～房屋数十间。The fire spread to such an extent that it burned down several dozen houses.

【延伸】yánshēn 延长;伸展 extend; stretch; elongate:这条铁路一直～到国境线。The railway line stretches right to the border.

【延髓】yánsuǐ 后脑的一部分,上接脑桥,下接脊髓。舌咽神经、迷走神经、舌下神经等都由延髓发出。延髓中有呼吸、循环等中枢,主管呼吸、血液循环、唾液分泌等。medulla oblongata; part of the tritocerebrum (hind-brain) attached to the mesocephalon (pons) and continuous with the spinal cord. The glossopharyngeal nerve, pneumogastric nerve and the hypoglossal nerve begin at the medulla oblongata, which also contains respiratory, circulation and other nerve centers that control such functions as breathing, blood circulation, and salivation (图见 ☞ figure for 脑 nǎo on p. 1394)

【延误】yánwù 迟延耽误 morra; incur loss through delay:～时日 lose time because of delay

【延性】yánxìng 物体可以拉成细丝而不断裂的性质。金属多具有延性。ductility; (of a metal) capable of being drawn into wire; pliable, not brittle. Most metals are ductile.

【延续】yánxù 照原来样子继续下去;延长下去 continue; go on; last:会谈～了两个小时。The talks lasted for two hours.

【延展】yánzhǎn 延伸;扩展 extend; stretch:公路一直～到江边。The highway extends all the way to the riverside.

芫 yán [芫荽](yán·suī)一年生草本植物,叶互生,羽状复叶,茎和叶有特殊香气,花小,白色。果实圆形,用做香料,也可入药。嫩茎和叶用来调味。coriander (*Coriandrum sativum*); cilantro; annual herbaceous plant having alternately-pinnate compound leaves and stem that both emit a peculiar fragrance, tiny white flowers, and round fruit used as spice and medicine; 通称 popularly called 香菜 xiāngcài; also 胡荽 húsuī

☞ yuán on p. 2357

严(嚴) yán ❶ 严密;紧密 tight; close:～紧 strict; stern|～戒 strictly forbid|谨～circumspect; scrupulous|把瓶口封～了 seal up a bottle|他嘴～,从来不乱说。He is tight-lipped and never makes irresponsible remarks. ❷ 严厉;严格 strict; stern:庄～solemn|威～dignified; stately|～办 deal with sth. sternly|～加管束 bring under stern discipline|纪律很～strict in discipline|坦白从宽,抗拒从～。Leniency to those who confess and severity to those who refuse to do so. ❸ 程度深;厉害 severe, heavy; extreme:～冬 severe winter|～寒 severe cold|～刑 torture ❹ 指父亲 father:家～my father ❺ (Yán)姓 a surname

【严办】yánbàn 严厉惩办 deal with severely; punish with severity:依法～punish strictly according to law

【严惩】yánchéng 严厉处罚 punish severely:～凶犯 mete out stern punishment on a criminal|～不贷 punish without leniency (贷 *dai*:宽恕 mercy)

【严词】yáncí 严厉的话 strong terms; stern words:～拒绝 give a stern rebuff; sternly refuse

【严冬】yándōng 极冷的冬天 severe winter; hard winter

【严防】yánfáng 严格防止;严密防备 strictly guard against; take strict precautions against:～破坏 take strict precautions against sabotage|～事故发生 take strict precautions against accidents

【严格】yángé 在遵守制度或掌握标准时认真不放松 strict; rigorous; rigid; stringent:～遵守 observe (discipline, law, etc.) strictly|他对自己要求很～。He is very strict with himself.

【严寒】yánhán (气候)极冷 severe frigidity; bitter cold:天气～frigid weather

【严紧】yán·jǐn ❶ 严格;严厉 tight; close:管得～些才对。It's only right to be strict with these people. ❷ same as 严密 yánmì:窗户糊得挺～。The window is sealed real tight.

【严谨】yánjǐn ❶ 严密谨慎 rigorous; strict; careful and precise:办事～be meticulous and precise in work ❷ 严密细致;严格 compact;

well-knit：格律～strict tonal pattern and rhyme scheme｜文章结构～。The essay is well-knit.

【严禁】yánjìn 严格禁止 strictly forbid (or prohibit)：库房重地，～烟火。Important warehouse. Smoking strictly prohibited.

【严峻】yánjùn ❶ 严厉；严肃 stern；severe；rigorous；grim：～的考验 severe test；rigorous test｜～的现实 stern reality｜～的神情 stern expression ❷ same as 严重 yánzhòng：形势～grave situation

【严酷】yánkù ❶ 严厉；严格 implacable；harsh；bitter；grim：～的教训 bitter lesson ❷ 残酷；冷酷 brutal；ruthless：～的压迫 brutal oppression｜～的剥削 cruel exploitation

【严厉】yánlì 严肃而厉害 strong；stern；severe：～打击 telling blow｜态度～stern attitude｜措辞～stern verbiage

【严令】yánlìng 严格命令 give strict orders：～禁止 issue strict orders to prohibit sth.

【严密】yánmì ❶ 事物之间结合得紧，没有空隙 tight；close：瓶子盖得很～。The bottle is tightly sealed.｜小说结构～，文字流畅。The novel is well-conceived in structure and fluent in language. ❷ 周到；没有疏漏 well-conceived；tight：消息封锁得很～。The news blackout is real tight.｜～注视形势的发展 closely follow the development of the situation ❸ 使严密 tighten up：～规章制度 tighten up the rules and regulations

【严明】yánmíng ❶ 严肃而公正 strict and impartial(多指法纪 oft. of law and discipline)：赏罚～be strict and impartial in meting out rewards and punishments｜纪律～highly disciplined；well-discipline；observe strict discipline ❷ 使严明 tighten up；enforce strictly：～军纪 tighten up the enforcement of military discipline｜要～纪律，制止不正之风。It is imperative to tighten up discipline and check unhealthy trends.

【严命】yánmìng〈书 *fml.*〉❶ same as 严令 yánlìng：～缉查 issue strict orders to apprehend the criminal and bring him to justice ❷ 指父亲的命令 father's instruction：～难违 father's word is the final

【严师】yánshī 指对学生要求严格的老师 demanding teacher：～诤友 demanding teacher and friend who gives unpalatable advice｜～出高徒 a strict teacher produces outstanding students

【严实】yán·shi〈方 *dial.*〉❶ same as 严密 yánmì ①：门关得挺～。The door's shut real tight.｜河里刚凿通的冰窟窿又冻～了。The hole that had just been bored into the river was frozen solidly again. ❷ 藏得好，不容易找到 hide sth. carefully so that it is hard to find；hide sth. in safety

【严守】yánshǒu ❶ 严格地遵守 observe strictly：～纪律 observe strict discipline｜～中立 observe strict neutrality ❷ 严密地保守 guard closely；strictly guard：～国家机密 strictly guard state secrets

【严丝合缝】yán sī hé fèng 指缝隙密合 fit together perfectly；join tightly；dovetail

【严肃】yánsù ❶（神情、气氛等）使人感到敬畏的（of expression，atmosphere，etc.）stern；grave；serious；keep a straight face：他是个很～的人，从来不苟言笑。A serious man，he is reticent and reserved.｜会场的气氛既～又隆重。The atmosphere of the meeting was both serious and grand. ❷（作风、态度等）严格认真（of style of work and attitude）strict；earnest：～处理 handle something in real earnest ❸ 使严肃 tighten up：～党纪 tighten up Party discipline｜～法制 tighten up the legal system

【严刑】yánxíng 极厉害的刑法（xíng·fa）或刑罚 cruel torture；severe punishment：～拷打 subject somebody to brutal torture；cruelly beat up

【严阵以待】yán zhèn yǐ dài 摆好严整的阵势，等待来犯的敌人 in full battle array；in combat readiness

【严整】yánzhěng ❶ 严肃整齐（多指队伍 usu. of troops）in neat formation：军容～。The troops are in gallant array. ❷ 严谨；严密 strict；well-conceived：治家～run one's family in a meticulous way｜画儿的布局～。The painting has a well-conceived composition.

【严正】yánzhèng 严肃正当 solemn and just；serious and principled；stern：～声明 solemn statement｜～的立场 solemn stand

【严重】yánzhòng 程度深；影响大；情势危急 serious；grave；critical：病情～be mortally ill｜问题～the gravity of a problem｜～的后果 grave consequence

言 yán ❶ 话 speech；word：～语 words；remark｜语～language｜格～motto；maxim；adage；apophthegm｜诺～promise｜发～deliver a speech｜有～在先 have a piece of advice to offer；let it be understood beforehand｜～外之意 implication；what is actually meant ❷ 说 say；talk；speak；describe：～之有理 sound reasonable；be convincing｜畅所欲～express with zest and gust；get sth. off one's chest｜知无不～，～无不尽 say all you know and say it without reserve ❸ 汉语的一个字叫一言（in the Chinese language）character；word：五～诗 five-character verse｜万～书 letter of 10,000 words｜全书近二十万～。The whole book amounts to nearly 200,000 words. ❹（Yán）姓 a surname

【言必有中】yán bì yǒu zhòng 一说就说到点子上 when one speaks，one speaks to the point；whenever one says something one hits the

mark

【言不及义】yán bù jí yì 只说些无聊的话，不涉及正经道理 never say anything serious; talk frivolously

【言不尽意】yán bù jìn yì 说的话未能表达出全部意思。表示意犹未尽(多用于书信结尾 usu. when concluding a letter) I've got to end this letter now though I have so much more to tell you

【言不由衷】yán bù yóu zhōng 说的话不是从内心发出来的。指心口不一致。speak insincerely; speak with tongue in cheek

【言出法随】yán chū fǎ suí 宣布之后立即按法执行(of a law) be strictly enforced upon promulgation

【言传】yánchuán 用言语来表达 explain in words: 只可意会，不可～only to be sensed, not explained

【言传身教】yán chuán shēn jiào 一面口头上传授，一面行动上以身作则。指言语行动起模范作用。teach by personal example as well as verbal instruction; teach by precept and example

【言词】yáncí same as 言辞 yáncí

【言辞】yáncí 说话所用的词句 words; utterance: ～尖刻 poignant words | ～恳切 sincere remarks; also 言词 yáncí

【言多语失】yán duō yǔ shī 话说多了就难免出错 he who talks too much is prone to error

【言归于好】yán guī yú hǎo 彼此重新和好 make it up (with sb.); become reconciled

【言归正传】yán guī zhèng zhuàn 说话写文章回到正题上来(评话和旧小说中常用的套语 jargon in storytelling and old stories) come back to our story; return to the subject

【言过其实】yán guò qí shí 说话过分，不符合实际 exaggerate; overstate

【言和】yánhé 讲和 make peace; become reconciled; bury the hatchet: 握手～shake hands and patch it up

【言欢】yánhuān 说笑；愉快地交谈 chat amiably; talk and laugh: 握手～shake hand and talk merrily | 杯酒～have a pleasant talk over a cup of wine

Y

【言简意赅】yán jiǎn yì gāi 言语简单而意思概括 concise and comprehensive; compendious

【言教】yánjiào 用讲说的方式教育、开导人 teach by word of mouth; give verbal directions: 不仅要～，更要身教。Deed speaks louder than word. *or* Example is better than precept.

【言近旨远】yán jìn zhǐ yuǎn 话说得浅近，而含义却很深远 simple words but deep meaning; simple in language but profound in meaning

【言路】yánlù 向政府或领导提出批评或建议的途径(从政府或领导的角度说 from the perspective of a government or leader) channels through which criticisms and suggestions may be communicated: 广开～provide more and better means for people to air their views

【言论】yánlùn 关于政治或一般公共事务的议论 opinion on public affairs; expression of one's political views; speech: 发表～make one's opinion heard | 进步的～progressive opinion

【言情】yánqíng 描写男女爱情的(作品 of works) romantic: ～小说 romance; romantic fiction; romantic or sentimental novel

【言人人殊】yán rén rén shū 每人所说的话各不相同。指对同一事物各人有各人的见解。different people, different versions; each person has a different story

【言声儿】yán//shēngr 说话；吭声儿 give a yell; utter a sound or a word: 不言一声儿 do not say a word | 你缺什么，只管～。If you are in need of something, just give me a yell.

【言说】yánshuō 说 put into words; say: 不可～cannot be conveyed in word | 难以～beyond description; indescribable

【言谈】yántán 说话。也指说话的内容和态度。the way one speaks; what one says: ～举止 speech and deportment | ～风雅 be graceful in one's speech and deportment | 不善于～not have the gift of the gab; awkward in speech

【言听计从】yán tīng jì cóng 说的话，出的主意，都听从照办。形容对某个人非常信任。listen to sb.'s words and follow his counsels; always follow sb.'s advice; act upon whatever sb. says; have implicit faith in sb.

【言外之意】yán wài zhī yì 话里暗含着的没有直接说出的意思 what is actually meant; real meaning; implication; between the lines

【言为心声】yán wéi xīn shēng 言语是思想的表达 words are the voice of the mind; speech is the picture of the mind; what the heart thinks the tongue speaks

【言笑】yánxiào 说和笑；谈笑 speak and laugh; talk animatedly: 不苟～(形容人态度庄重) be serious in speech and manner | ～自若 be at ease in one's deportment

【言行】yánxíng 言语和行为 words and deeds; statements and actions: ～一致 the deeds match (or square with) the words; one's actions are in keeping with one's promises; one's deeds are consistent with one's words; be as good as one's word

【言犹在耳】yán yóu zài ěr 形容别人的话说过不久，或者虽然说过很久，但是还记得很清楚 words still ring (or reverberate) in one's ears

【言语】yányǔ 说的话 spoken language; speech: ～粗鲁 speak rudely | ～行动 word and deed

【言语】yán·yu 〈方 *dial.*〉说；说话 say; speak: 你走的时候～一声儿。Let me know when you leave. | 问你话呢，你怎么不～？I'm asking you a question. Why don't you say something?

【言喻】yányù〈书 *fml.*〉用语言来说明(多用于否定 oft. in the negative) describe:不可～indescribable|难以～beyond words; difficult to say

【言责】yánzé ❶ 君主时代臣下对君主进谏的责任 subject's responsibility of offering advice to the ruler ❷ 指对自己发表的言论的责任 responsibility for what one says:～自负 be accountable for what one says

【言者无罪,闻者足戒】yánzhě wú zuì, wénzhě zú jiè 尽管意见不完全正确,提出意见的人并没有罪,听取意见的人即使没有对方所说的错误,也可以拿听到的话来警惕自己 blame not the speaker but be warned by his words; blame not the critic, heed what he says

【言重】yánzhòng 话说得过重 overstate; exaggerate

【言状】yánzhuàng 用言语来形容(多用于否定 oft. in the negative) describe or depict sb. or sth. in words:难以～indescribable; beyond description

阽 yán '阽' diàn 的又音 variant pronunciation of 阽 diàn

妍 yán〈书 *fml.*〉美丽 charming; enchanting; beautiful(跟'媸'相对 as opposed to 'ugly'):春光明媚,百花争～。The spring scene is bright and beautiful, with a hundred flowers contending in beauty.

【妍媸】yánchī 美和丑 beautiful and ugly:不辨～unable to tell the beautiful from the ugly

岩(巖、嵒) yán ❶ 岩石 rock; stone:～层 rock formation|水成～ aqueous rock; hydrogenic rock|花岗～ granite ❷ 岩石突起而成的山峰 cliff; crag:七星～(在广西) Seven-Star Cliff, a scenic spot in the Guangxi Zhuang Autonomous Region

【岩层】yáncéng 地壳中成层的岩石 rock stratum; rock formation

【岩洞】yándòng 泛指岩层中曲折幽深的大洞 stone cave, esp. a winding and deep one in a rock stratum

【岩画】yánhuà 刻画在岩石或崖壁上的图画 rock painting; also 崖壁画 yábìhuà or 崖画 yáhuà

【岩浆】yánjiāng 地壳下面含有硅酸盐和挥发成分的高温熔融物质 magma; substance under the earth's crust, containing silicate and volatile molten rock material

【岩溶】yánróng 可溶性岩石,特别是碳酸盐类岩石(如石灰岩等),受含有二氧化碳的流水溶蚀,并加上沉积作用而形成的地貌。往往形状奇特,有洞穴也有峭壁。我国广西、云南、贵州等地有这种地貌。现以喀斯特为正名。karst; strange-looking landform of soluble rock, esp. carbonate-type rock (such as limestone), in which erosion and sedimentation have produced cliff-like fissures and caverns. The karst landform is found in the Guangxi Zhuang Autonomous Region, and Yunnan and Guizhou provinces.

【岩石】yánshí 构成地壳的矿物的集合体,分为火成岩、沉积岩和变质岩三大类 rock; natural aggregate of mineral matter constituting a significant part of the earth's crust, in three categories: igneous rock, sedimentary rock, and metamorphic rock

【岩心】yánxīn 进行地质勘探时用管状的机件从地层中取得的柱状岩石标本 core; cylindrical mass drilled vertically into the earth and removed from it to determine composition or presence of oil or gas

【岩盐】yányán 地壳中沉积的成层的盐,是古代的海水或湖水干涸后形成的 rock salt; halite; sedimentary salt occurring in layers in the earth's crust, resulting from dried sea or lakebeds in arid climates, to be mined or gathered for use as table salt; also 矿盐 kuàngyán or 石盐 shíyán

炎 yán ❶ 极热(指天气) scorching; burning hot:～热 burning hot; sweltering|～夏 sultry summer days; hot summer ❷ 炎症 inflammation:发～inflammation|肠胃～enterogastritis ❸〈比喻 *fig.*〉权势 power; influence:趋～附势 fawn on the rich and powerful; curry favour with the powerful; play up to those in power ❹ (Yán)指炎帝 Yandi, a legendary ruler of China:～黄子孙 descendants of Yandi and Huangdi; the Chinese people

【炎帝】Yándì ☞炎黄 Yán-Huáng

【炎黄】Yán-Huáng 指炎帝神农氏和黄帝轩辕氏,是我国古代传说中的两个帝王,借指中华民族的祖先 Yandi (also known as Shen Nong [Divine Peasant]) and Huangdi (Xuan Yuan, also known as Yellow Emperor), legendary rulers of China in remote antiquity; ancestors of the Chinese people:～子孙 descendants of Yangdi and Huangdi; the Chinese people

【炎凉】yánliáng 热和冷 hot and cold;〈比喻 *fig.*〉对待地位不同的人或者亲热攀附,或者冷淡疏远 blowing hot and cold; fawning on the rich and powerful and snub the underprivileged:世态～fickleness of the world; ways of the world blowing hot and cold all the time

【炎热】yánrè (天气)很热(of weather) scorching; blazing; burning hot:～的夏天 sweltering summer days

【炎日】yánrì 炎热的太阳 burning (or scorching) sun:～当空 with the sun blazing overhead; the sun is an overhead scorcher

【炎暑】yánshǔ ❶ 夏天最热的时候 hot summer; sweltering summer days; dog days:时值～in the height of summer ❷ 指暑气 summer heat:～逼人 scorching summer heat|冒～,顶烈日 brave the heat of summer and the burning sun

【炎夏】yánxià 炎热的夏天 torrid or scorching summer:～盛暑 dog days

【炎炎】yányán ❶ 形容夏天阳光强烈 scorching; sweltering; blazing:赤日～scorching sun ❷ 形容火势猛烈(of fire) blazing:～的烈火 raging fire

【炎症】yánzhèng 机体受到较强烈刺激后的反应现象,多有红、热、肿、痛、机能障碍等症状 inflammation; localized protective reaction of tissue to strong irritation, characterized by redness, heat, swelling, pain, and impaired function

沿(沿) yán ❶ 顺着(江河、道路或物体的边) along (river, road, or the edge of sth.):～途 along the way|～街 along the street|～着河边走 walk along a river ❷ 依照以往的方法、规矩、式样等 follow (established ways of doing things, practice, or pattern):～袭 inherit; carry on; continue; follow|相～成习 become a custom through long usage; it has long been customary to... ❸ 顺着衣物的边再镶上一条边 trim:～鞋口 trim the top of a shoe ❹ (～儿 yánr)边(多用在名词后 oft. preceded by a noun) edge:边～edge|沟～edge of a ditch|炕～儿 edge of a brick platform bed|缸～儿 edge of a jar|前～front-line

【沿岸】yán'àn 靠近江、河、湖、海一带地区 along the bank of a river or lake or the coast of the sea:黄河～along the Yellow River|洞庭湖～along the shore of the Dongting Lake

【沿边儿】yán//biānr 把窄条的布或绦子等缝在衣物边上 trim (a coat, etc. with tape or ribbon)

【沿革】yángé (事物)发展和变化的历程 course of change and development; evolution:社会风俗的～evolution of folklore|历史～地图 map of historical changes and developments

【沿海】yánhǎi 靠海的一带 coastal; seaboard:～城市 seaboard city

【沿江】yánjiāng 靠江(多指长江)的一带 along a river (esp. the Yangtze River); riparian; riverine

【沿街】yánjiē 顺着街道 along the street:～叫卖 peddle; hawk|～乞讨 go panhandling along the street

【沿例】yánlì 沿用旧例 follow an old practice; follow established precedents

【沿路】yánlù 顺着路边上;一路上 along the road; on the way:～寻找 search for sb. or sth. along the way|～景色迷人。The scenery along the road is fabulous.

【沿条儿】yántiáor 沿边儿用的绸布条儿 trimming tape or ribbon

【沿途】yántú same as 沿路 yánlù

【沿袭】yánxí 依照旧传统或原有的规定办理;因袭 carry on as before; follow; inherit:～成规 follow old conventions|～前人成说 adopt a theory accepted by predecessors

【沿线】yánxiàn 靠近铁路、公路或航线的地方 along the line (i.e. a railway, highway, air or shipping line)

【沿用】yányòng 继续使用(过去的方法、制度、法令) continue to use (an old method, system, legislation, etc.):～原来的名称 retain the original name

研 yán ❶ 细磨(mó) grind; pestle:～墨 rub an inkstick on an inkslab (to prepare ink for painting or writing with a brush)|把药～成粉 grind medicine ❷ 研究 research; study:钻～业务 study professional knowledge; hone one's skill|～习书法艺术 study the art of calligraphy

☞ yàn on p. 2214

【研读】yándú 钻研阅读 delve into; study carefully:～史书 delve into history books

【研究】yánjiū ❶ 探求事物的真相、性质、规律等 study; research; look into:～语言 linguistics studies|学术～academic research|调查～study and investigation ❷ 考虑或商讨(意见、问题) consider; discuss; deliberate (opinions and issues):今天的会议,只～三个重要问题。There are only three major issues for us to deliberate at today's meeting.|这个方案领导上正在～。The higher-ups are considering this plan.

【研究生】yánjiūshēng 经考试录取在高等学校或科学研究机关里通过研究工作进修的人。有规定的修业年限。postgraduate (student); graduate student; one who is engaged in a fixed number of years' advanced study in an institution of higher learning or research institute after graduation from college

【研究员】yánjiūyuán 科学研究机关中的高级研究人员 research fellow; senior researcher in a research institute

【研磨】yánmó ❶ 用工具研成粉末 grind; pestle:把药物放在乳钵里～grind medicine in a mortar ❷ 用磨料磨擦器物使变得光洁 abrade; polish:～粉 abrasive powder

【研讨】yántǎo 研究和讨论;研究和探讨 deliberate; study and discuss:学术～会 seminar; symposium|深入～其发展规律 study the law of development of sth. in a deep-going way

【研习】yánxí 研究学习 study; research:～山水画 study landscape painting

【研制】yánzhì 研究制造 trial-produce; develop:～新产品 trial-produce a new product

盐(鹽) yán ❶ 食盐的通称 table salt; salt:精～refined salt|井～well salt ❷ 由金属离子(包括铵离子)和酸根离子组成的化合物。常温时一般为晶体,绝大多数是强电解质,在水溶液中和熔融状态下都能电离。salt; chemical compound made up of metal ions (ammonium ions included) and acid radicalions, generally in a crystalline form under normal temperatures, and mostly being strong electrolytes capable of ionization when dissolved in water

【盐巴】yánbā〈方 *dial.*〉食盐 table salt; salt

【盐场】yánchǎng 制盐的场所 saltern; saltworks

【盐池】yánchí 出产食盐的咸水湖 salt lake; salt pond

【盐分】yánfèn 物体内所含的盐 salt content; salinity：汗流得过多，会造成体内～和水份的不足。Excessive sweating tends to cause inadequate salt and water content in the body.

【盐湖】yánhú 含盐量很高的咸水湖 salt lake; lake of salt water

【盐花】yánhuā ❶ (～儿 yánhuār)极少量的盐 a little salt; a pinch of salt：汤里搁点儿～儿。Put just a little salt in the soup. ❷〈方 *dial.*〉same as 盐霜 yánshuāng

【盐碱地】yánjiǎndì 土壤中含有较多盐分的土地，不利于植物生长 saline and alkaline land; soil containing too much salt and therefore detrimental to the growth of farm crops

【盐井】yánjǐng 为汲取含盐质的地下水而挖的井 salt well; brine pit

【盐卤】yánlǔ 熬盐时剩下的液体，是氯化镁、硫酸镁和氯化钠的混合物，黑色，味苦，有毒。可以使豆浆凝结成豆腐。bittern; poisonous, bitter, black liquid that is a mixture of magnesium chloride, magnesium sulfate and sodium chloride. Bittern can cause soybean milk to coagulate and become beancurd. also 卤水 lǔshuǐ; 简称 abbr. 卤 lǔ.

【盐汽水】yánqìshuǐ 加盐的汽水，主要供高温下工作的人饮用 salt soda water, a drink for those working under high temperatures

【盐泉】yánquán 矿泉的一种，泉水中含有大量盐分，用这种泉水可制得食盐 brine (or salt) spring; mineral spring water with a high salt content that can be used to produce salt

【盐霜】yánshuāng 含盐分的东西干燥后表面呈现的白色细盐粒 salt frosting; salt efflorescence; salt frost; deposit of white minute salt crystals formed when something that contains salt dries up

【盐酸】yánsuān 无机化合物，化学式 HCl。是氯化氢的水溶液，无色透明，含杂质时为淡黄色，有刺激性气味，是一种强酸。广泛用于化学、冶金、石油、印染等工业。hydrochloric acid (HCl); clear, colourless, fuming, highly acidic aqueous solution of hydrogen chloride, used widely in chemical, metallurgical, petrochemical, and printing and dyeing industries; also 氢氯酸 qīng lǜsuān

【盐滩】yántān 用来晒盐的海滩、湖滩 beach for making sea salt

【盐田】yántián 用海水或盐湖水晒盐时挖的一排排的四方形的浅坑 salt pan; salina; saltworks consisting of row upon row of shallow square pits for sunning sea or salt lake water to obtain the salt

【盐土】yántǔ 含可溶性盐类过多，不利于作物的生长的土壤 solonchak; saline soil; soil containing an excess of soluble salts that are detrimental to the growth of farm crops

【盐坨子】yántuó·zi 露天的盐堆 pile of salt in the open

【盐枭】yánxiāo〈旧时 *old*〉私贩食盐的人，大多有武装 salt smuggler who is oft. armed

铅 yán 铅山(Yánshān)，地名，在江西 Yanshan, name of a place in Jiangxi Province

☞ qiān on p. 1531

阎(❷閆) yán ❶〈书 *fml.*〉里巷的门 entrance to a lane ❷ (Yán)姓 a surname

【阎罗】Yánluó〈佛教 *Budd.*〉称管地狱的神 Yama; King of Hell; also 阎罗王 yánluó·wáng，阎王 yán·wang, and 阎王爷 yán·wangyé [阎魔罗阇之省，梵 abbreviation for 閻魔罗阇 yánmóluóshé, Sanskrit: *yamaraja*]

【阎王】Yán·wang ❶ 阎罗 Yama; King of Hell ❷〈比喻 *fig.*〉极严厉或极凶恶的人 devil incarnate; brute; terror

【阎王账】Yán·wangzhàng 指高利贷 usurious loan; shark's loan; also 阎王债 yán·wangzhài

蜒 yán ❶ [蜒蚰](yányóu)〈方 *dial.*〉蛞蝓(kuòyú) slug (*Limax*); small snaillike, gastropod mollusk having a slow-moving elongated body with no shell or only a flat rudimentary shell on or under the skin ❷ ☞ 蚰蜒 yóuyán on p. 2323 and 海蜒 hǎiyán on p. 758

筵 yán 古人席地而坐时铺的席。泛指筵席。mat spread on the floor for people to sit in ancient times; widely used to refer to feast or banquet：喜～ wedding feast | 寿～ birthday banquet

【筵席】yánxí 指宴饮时陈设的座位。泛指酒席。seat arranged around a banquet table; (in a broad sense) banquet

揅 yán〈书 *fml.*〉same as 研 yán

颜 yán ❶ 脸；脸上的表情 face; countenance：容～ looks; appearance | 和～悦色 cheerful countenance; amiable manners and a pleasant countenance | 笑逐～开 beaming with smiles ❷ 体面；面子 grace; face：无～见人 not have the face to look people in the eye ❸ 颜色 colour：～料 dye | 五～六色 colourful; a riot of colour ❹ (Yán)姓 a surname

【颜料】yánliào 用来着色的物质，种类很多，如朱砂、锌白等 pigment; colouring, which comes in a good variety, such as vermilion and zinc white

【颜面】yánmiàn ❶ 脸部 face：～神经 facial nerve ❷ 体面；面子 decency；face：顾全～面 save face

【颜容】yánróng 容颜；面容 facial expression；complexion；countenance：～枯槁 look gaunt；wear a haggard look

【颜色】yánsè ❶ 由物体发射、反射或透过的光波通过视觉所产生的印象 colour；hue；visual impression of an object or substance with respect to light waves emitted or reflected by it or infiltrating it：～鲜艳 bright colour｜彩虹有七种～。The rainbow has seven spectral colours in it. ❷〈书 *fml.*〉指面貌；容貌 complexion；countenance；looks：～憔悴 look haggard ❸ 指脸上的表情 facial expression：现出羞愧的～blush with shame ❹ 指显示给人看的厉害的脸色或行动 stern look on one's face as a warning；action taken as a punishment：给他一点～看看 make it hot for him；teach him a lesson

【颜色】yán·shai 颜料或染料 pigment；dyestuff

【颜体】Yán tǐ 唐代颜真卿所写的字体，参用篆书笔意写楷书，浑厚挺拔，开阔雄伟 Yan style. Yan Zhenqing of the Tang Dynasty incorporated suggestions of the seal characters in the regular script，thereby creating a style of Chinese calligraphy which is marked for well-spaced and magnificent brushwork and the full-bodied solidity and statuesque grace of characters

檐(簷) yán ❶（～儿 yánr）屋顶向旁伸出的边沿部分 eaves；projecting overhang at the lower edge of a roof：房～eves｜廊～eaves of a veranda｜～下 under the eaves｜～前 in front of the eaves（图见 ☞ figure for 房子 fáng·zi on p.550）❷（～儿 yánr）某些器物上形状像房檐的部分 ledge；brim：帽～儿 bill；brim of a hat

【檐沟】yángōu 房檐下面横向的槽形排水沟，作用是承接屋面的雨水，然后由竖管引到地面。有的地区叫水落。eaves gutter；trough fixed under the eaves for draining rainwater from a roof and diverting it to the ground through a standpipe；know in some regions as 水落 shuǐluò

【檐口】yánkǒu 房檐边滴水的地方 cornice；end sprout of a eaves gutter

【檐溜】yánliù 顺着房檐往下流的雨水或雪水 rainwater or snowmelt that flows along the eaves

【檐子】yán·zi 房檐 eaves

yǎn（丨ㄢˇ）

奄 yǎn〈书 *fml.*〉❶ 覆盖；包括 cover；include：～有四方 survey every nook and cranny of the country ❷ 忽然；突然 all of a sudden；suddenly：～忽 quickly｜～然 unexpectedly

〈古 *arch.*〉same as 阉 yān

【奄忽】yǎnhū〈书 *fml.*〉忽然；倏忽 suddenly；all of a sudden；all at once

【奄然】yǎnrán 忽然；奄忽 suddenly；quickly

【奄奄】yǎnyǎn 形容气息微弱 breathing feebly：～一息 at one's last gasp；on one's last leg

兖 yǎn 兖州（Yǎnzhōu），地名，在山东 Yanzhou，name of a place in Shandong Province

龑(龑) yǎn 五代时南汉刘龑为自己名字造的字 Yan，a Chinese character coined by Liu Yan of the Southern Han of the Five Dynasties as his own given name

俨(儼) yǎn〈书 *fml.*〉❶ 庄重 majestic；solemn；dignified ❷ 很像 just as；like

【俨然】yǎnrán〈书 *fml.*〉❶ 形容庄严 solemn；dignified：望之～look dignified ❷ 形容齐整 neat：屋舍～houses laid out neatly ❸ 形容很像 just like：这孩子说起话来～是个大人。This child speaks just like a grownup.

【俨如】yǎnrú 十分像 just like：日光灯下～白昼。Under the fluorescent lamp it looks as bright as day.

衍¹ yǎn〈书 *fml.*〉❶ 开展，发挥 extend；develop；amplify：推～elaborate；popularize｜敷～gloss things over；do the routine work superficially；muddle with one's duty ❷ 多余（指字句）redundant；superfluous：～文 redundancy；tautology due to misprinting or miscopying

衍² yǎn〈书 *fml.*〉❶ 低而平坦的土地 low-lying flatland：广～沃野 vast expanse of fertile land ❷ 沼泽 marsh；swamp；bog

【衍变】yǎnbiàn 演变 develop；evolve

【衍化】yǎnhuà 发展变化 evolve；develop：这个药方是综合几个秘方～而来的。This prescription is developed by incorporate elements from a number of secret recipes.

【衍射】yǎnshè 波在传播时，如果被一个大小近于或小于波长的物体阻挡，就绕过这个物体，继续进行；如果通过一个大小近于或小于波长的孔，则以孔为中心，形成环形波向前传播。这种现象叫衍射。diffraction，phenomenon exhibited by the transmission of waves that，when obstructed by an object close to or smaller than the wave length，bypass the object and continue，or，when passing a hole close to or smaller than the wave length，become circular waves with the hole as the centre and continue their transmission；also 绕射 ràoshè

【衍生】yǎnshēng ❶ 较简单的化合物中的原子或原子团被其他原子或原子团置换而生成较复

杂的化合物 derive; obtain a more complex compound by replacing the atoms or radicles of a simple compound with other atoms or radicles ❷ 演变发生;产生 evolve; produce

【衍文】yǎnwén 因缮写、刻版、排版错误而多出来的字句 redundancy due to misprinting or miscopying

弇 yǎn〈书 *fml.*〉覆盖;遮蔽 cover; overlay

【弇陋】yǎnlòu〈书 *fml.*〉见识浅陋 (of knowledge) superficial

剡 yǎn〈书 *fml.*〉❶ 削尖 sharpen:~木为楫 fashion an oar out of wood ❷ 锐利 sharp; pointed

☞ Shàn on p.1674

厣(厴) yǎn ❶ 螺类介壳口圆片状的盖,由足部表皮分泌的物质形成 operculum; disc-shaped lid on the horny shell of snails or mollusks, formed with the secretion of the foot scarfskin ❷ 蟹腹下的薄壳 operculum; lid covering the belly of a crab

掩(揜) yǎn ❶ 遮盖,掩蔽 cover up; hide:~口而笑 hide one's smile | ~人耳目 muzzle the public; throw dust in to people's eyes | ~着怀(上衣遮盖着胸膛而不扣纽扣) cover one's chest with one's coat without buttoning it ❷ 关;合 shut; close:~卷 close a book | 虚~着房门 door left closed but unlocked ❸〈方 *dial.*〉关门或合上箱盖等物时被夹住 get squeezed or pinched by a door or lid:手被门~了一下 get one's hand caught in a door ❹〈书 *fml.*〉乘人不备(袭击、捕捉) attack by surprise:~杀 attack by surprise; pounce on | ~捕 arrest sb. by surprise

【掩鼻】yǎnbí 捂住鼻子,指对肮脏的东西或丑恶的行为非常厌恶 hold one's nose; detest:~而过 pass by sth. nauseating holding one's nose

【掩蔽】yǎnbì ❶ 遮蔽;隐藏 screen; shelter; cover:~部 shelter ❷ 遮蔽的东西或隐藏的地方 shield; cover; screen:河边的堤埂很高,正好做我们的~。The embankment of the river was high enough to shield us.

【掩蔽部】yǎnbìbù 保障人员免受敌方炮火伤害的掩蔽工事,一般构筑在地下 shelter; oft. underground defense work that protects people from enemy fire

【掩藏】yǎncáng 隐藏 hide; conceal; sweep sb. or sth. under the carpet:~内心的痛苦 conceal mental trauma in one's heart

【掩耳盗铃】yǎn ěr dào líng 把耳朵捂住去偷铃铛 plug one's ears while stealing a bell;〈比喻 *fig.*〉自己欺骗自己,明明掩盖不了的事偏要设法掩盖 deceive oneself; bury one's head in the sand

【掩盖】yǎngài ❶ same as 遮盖 zhēgài ①:大雪~着田野。The fields were cocooned under a mantle of snow. ❷ 隐藏;隐瞒 conceal; cover up:~罪行 cover up one's crime | ~不住内心的喜悦 be unable to conceal one's joy

【掩护】yǎnhù ❶ 对敌采取警戒、牵制、压制等手段,保障部队或人员行动的安全 screen; shield; cover; protect the safety of one's army or personnel by guarding against or containing an enemy ❷ 采取某种方式暗中保护或不使暴露 cover; protect or shield from exposure, harm, loss, or danger:打~shield sb. ❸ 指作战时遮蔽身体的工事、山岗、树木等 shield; protective device or structure, such as defense works, mountains, trees that serve to conceal one during a battle

【掩埋】yǎnmái 用泥土等盖在上面;埋葬 bury:~尸体 bury a corpse

【掩人耳目】yǎn rén ěr mù 遮着别人的耳朵和眼睛 muzzle sb. up;〈比喻 *fig.*〉以假象蒙骗别人 deceive the public; hoodwink people

【掩杀】yǎnshā〈书 *fml.*〉乘人不备而袭击 make a surprise attack; pounce on (the enemy)

【掩饰】yǎnshì 设法掩盖(真实的情况) cover up (faults, mistakes, etc.); gloss over; conceal:~错误 gloss over one's mistake | ~不住内心的喜悦 unable to contain one's joy

【掩体】yǎntǐ 供单个火器射击或技术器材操作的掩蔽工事,如机枪掩体、雷达掩体等 blindage; bunker; emplacement; camouflaged defense work for a sniper or equipment such as machine-gun and radar

【掩眼法】yǎnyǎnfǎ 障眼法 cover-up; camouflage

【掩映】yǎnyìng 彼此遮掩而互相衬托 (of things screening part of each other from view); show off (each other); set off (one another):桃红柳绿相互~。Pink peach flowers and green willows set off each other in a picturesque fashion.

郾 yǎn 郾城(Yǎnchéng),地名,在河南 Yancheng, name of a place in Henan Province

眼 yǎn ❶ 人或动物的视觉器官 eye; human or animal organ of vision or of light sensitivity; 通称 generally called 眼睛 yǎn·jing ❷ (~儿 yǎnr) 小洞;窟窿 small hole; aperture:泉~opening of a spring | 炮~porthole; dynamite hole | 拿针扎一个~儿 pierce a hole with a needle ❸ (~儿 yǎnr) 指事物的关键性所在 key point:节骨~儿 critical juncture ❹ 围棋用语,成片的白子或黑子中间的空儿,在这个空儿中对手不能下成活棋(*weiqi*) trap; empty space in the middle of patches of black or white pieces, where an opponent has no way of manoeuvring ❺ 戏曲中的拍子 unaccented beat in traditional Chinese music:二黄慢板,一板三~one accented beat and three unaccented beats in an *erhuang* melody ❻〈量词 *classifier*〉用于井、窑洞[used of wells, cave

dwellings, etc].:～～井 a well | ～～旧窑洞 an old cave dwelling

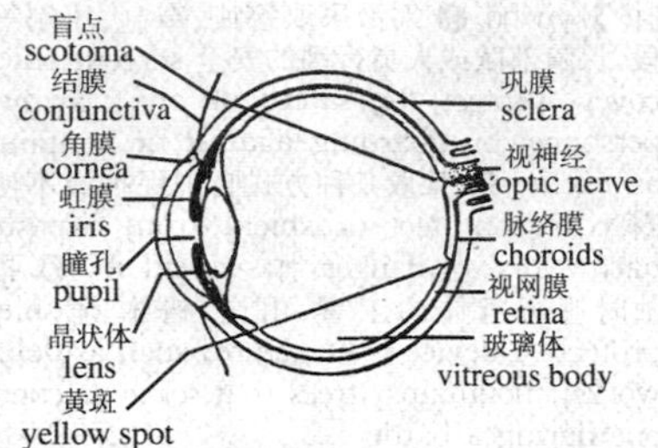

人的眼

The Human Eye

【眼巴巴】yǎnbābā (～的 yǎnbābā·de) ❶ 形容急切地盼望 on tiptoe; eager; anxious: 大家～地等着他回来。Everybody was expecting eagerly for him to return. ❷ 形容急切地看着不如意的事情发生而无可奈何 feel helpless while sth. bad happens: 他～地看着老鹰把小鸡抓走了。He helplessly looked on when the hawk snatched the chick away.

【眼白】yǎnbái 〈方 *dial.*〉白眼珠儿 white of the eye

【眼波】yǎnbō 形容流动如水波的目光(多指女子的 usu. of a young lady) glances

【眼岔】yǎnchà 〈方 *dial.*〉看错;认错 mistake one for another: 刚才看见的不是蝎子,是我～了。What I saw just now is not a scorpion. My eyes cheated me.

【眼馋】yǎnchán 看见自己喜爱的事物极想得到 cast covetous eyes at sth.; eye sth. covetously

【眼眵】yǎnchī ☞眵 chī on p. 259

【眼袋】yǎndài 指下眼皮微微凸起的部分 eyebag

【眼底】yǎndǐ ❶ 医学上指用某种器械通过瞳孔所能观察到的眼内构造。如脉络膜、视网膜、视神经乳头等。eyeground; fundus of the eye (fundus oculi), including venation membrane, retina and optic nerve papilla ❷ 眼睛跟前;眼里 in one's eyes; in sight: 登楼一望,全城景色尽收～。Mount the pavilion and you get an overview of the city.

【眼底下】yǎn dǐ·xia ❶ 眼睛跟前 right before one's eyes: 他的眼睛近视得厉害,放到～才看得清。He is so nearsighted that he can only see clearly things placed right before his eyes. ❷ 目前 at the moment: 以后的事以后再说,～的事要紧。Let's settle the business on hand first and leave the other matters alone for the moment. ‖ also 眼皮底下 yǎnpí dǐ·xia

【眼点】yǎndiǎn 某些低等生物的感觉器官,通常是红色的小圆点,能感受温度和光线的刺激 eyespot (of a protozoan); small, light-sensitive patch of pigment, usu. in the form of a tiny red dot, in certain algae and unicellular organisms

【眼福】yǎnfú 看到珍奇或美好事物的福分 good fortune of seeing sth. rare or beautiful: ～不浅 a feast for the eye | 以饱～ feast one's eyes on sth.

【眼高手低】yǎn gāo shǒu dī 自己要求的标准高,而实际工作的能力低 have high standards but little ability; be fastidious but incompetent

【眼格】yǎngé 〈方 *dial.*〉same as 眼界 yǎnjiè

【眼光】yǎnguāng ❶ 视线 eye: 大家的～都集中到他身上。Everyone turned their eyes on him. ❷ 观察鉴别事物的能力;眼力 sense of judgment; sight; foresight; insight; vision: 这辆车挑得好,你真有～。You've chosen a good car — evidence of your good sense of judgment. ❸ 指观点 point of view: 老～old viewpoint | 用发展的～看问题 observe things from a developmental point of view

【眼黑】yǎnhēi 〈方 *dial.*〉黑眼珠儿 pupil (of the eye)

【眼红】yǎnhóng ❶ 看见别人有名有利或有好的东西时非常羡慕、忌妒,自己也想得到 covet; be envious; be jealous: 看哥哥买辆新车,弟弟有点～。The man was somewhat jealous when his elder brother bought a new car. ❷ 激怒的样子 furious; eyes burning with fury: 仇人见面,分外～。When two foes meet, their eyes flash fire.

【眼花】yǎnhuā 看东西模糊不清 have dim eyesight; have blurred vision: 头昏～feel dizzy; one's head swims

【眼花缭乱】yǎnhuā liáoluàn 眼睛看见复杂纷繁的东西而感到迷乱 be dazzled

【眼犄角儿】yǎnjījiǎor 〈方 *dial.*〉same as 眼角 yǎnjiǎo

【眼疾手快】yǎn jí shǒu kuài ☞手疾眼快 shǒu jí yǎn kuài on p. 1768

【眼尖】yǎn jiān 眼力好,视觉锐敏 be sharp-eyed; have sharp eyes; have keen sight: 还是你～,一眼就认出了他。You are really sharp-eyed to know who the man was the moment you set your eyes on him.

【眼睑】yǎnjiǎn 眼睛周围能开闭的皮,边缘长着睫毛。眼睑和睫毛都有保护眼球的作用。eyelid; skin around an eye that can be opened and closed, with its edges covered with eyelashes — both the eyelid and the eyelashes serve to protect the eyeball; also 睑 jiǎn; 通称 popularly known as 眼皮 yǎnpí

【眼见】yǎnjiàn 马上;眼看 soon; in no time: ～就要立冬了,棉衣还没做好。Winter is setting in, yet the cotton-padded coats haven't been made.

【眼见得】yǎnjiàn·de 〈方 *dial.*〉显然(多用于不如意的事情 oft. of sth. unpleasant) evident; clear: 病人～不行了。Evidently the patient isn't likely to pull through.

【眼角】yǎnjiǎo（～儿 yǎnjiǎor）眦的通称，内眦叫大眼角，外眦叫小眼角 general term for 眦 zì；内眦 is called 大眼角 dàyǎnjiǎo inner canthus；外眦 is 小眼角 xiǎoyǎnjiǎo outer canthus

【眼睫毛】yǎnjiémáo 睫毛 eyelash

【眼界】yǎnjiè 所见事物的范围，借指见识的广度 field of vision (or view)；outlook：～开阔 wide field of vision｜大开～widen one's horizon；be an eye-opener

【眼镜】yǎnjìng（～儿 yǎnjìngr）戴在眼睛上矫正视力或保护眼睛的透镜 eyeglasses；glasses；spectacles；pair of lenses which serve to correct the eyesight or protect the eyes

【眼镜蛇】yǎnjìngshé 毒蛇的一种，颈部很粗，上面有一对白边黑心的环状斑纹，像一副眼镜。毒性很大。吃小动物。产在热带和亚热带地区。cobra (*Naja naja*)；venomous snake native to tropical and subtropical regions, having a thick neck with a pair of ringlike dapples that resemble a pair of spectacles, and feeding on small animals

【眼睛】yǎn·jing 眼的通称 general term for 眼 yǎn

【眼看】yǎnkàn ❶ 马上 soon；in a moment：鸡叫三遍，天～就要亮了。The rooster has crowed three times, and it'll be daybreak soon. ❷ 听凭（不如意的事情发生或发展）look on helplessly (sth. unpleasant to happen or develop)：天再旱，我们也不能～着庄稼干死。No matter how severe the dry spell is, we cannot let the crops perish without doing anything about it.

【眼眶】yǎnkuàng ❶ 眼皮的边缘所构成的框儿 eye socket；eyepit；orbit：～里含着泪水 eyes brimming with tears ❷ 眼睛周围的部位 rim of the eye：他揉了揉～。He rubbed his eyes. ‖ also 眼眶子 yǎnkuàng·zi

【眼泪】yǎnlèi 泪液的通称 general term for 泪液 lèiyè

【眼离】yǎnlí〈方 *dial.*〉指视觉一时错乱而产生幻象 have hallucinations；see things：牲口一～就惊了。The animal shied the moment it began to see things.

【眼力】yǎnlì ❶ 视力 eyesight；vision：～越来越差了。My eyesight is going from bad to worse. ❷ 辨别是非好坏的能力 sense of judgment：他的～不错，找到了一个好帮手。Showing a good sense of judgment, he found a good assistant for himself.

【眼力见儿】yǎnlìjiànr〈方 *dial.*〉见机行事的能力 sensible；able to see what's happening：这孩子真有～，看见我扫地，就把簸箕拿过来了。So sensible is the kid, he fetched me the dustpan the moment he saw me sweeping the floor.

【眼帘】yǎnlián 指眼皮或眼内（多用于文学作品 oft. used in literary works）eyes：垂下～close one's eyes｜一片丰收的景色映入～。A lovely scene of bumper harvest met the eye.

【眼眉】yǎnméi〈方 *dial.*〉眉毛 eyebrow

【眼面前】yǎnmiànqián〈方 *dial.*〉（～儿 yǎnmiànqiánr）❶ 眼前；跟前 before one's eyes；at the moment：～几件事就够他忙的了。The things at hand are enough to keep him busy.｜他刚从我～过去。He went past before my eyes a moment ago. ❷ 指日常使用的；常见的 common；everyday：虽说他文化低，～的一些字还认识。Though he hasn't received much schooling he knows quite a few common words.

【眼明手快】yǎn míng shǒu kuài 眼力好，动作快。形容反应快。quick of eye and deft of hand；sharp-eyed and deft-handed

【眼目】yǎnmù ❶ 指眼睛 eyes：强烈的灯光炫人～。Strong lights dazzle the eyes. ❷ 为人暗中察看情况并通风报信的人 spy；one who spies for sb. else：安插～plant a spy to keep sb. under surveillance

【眼泡】yǎnpāo（～儿 yǎnpāor）上眼皮 upper eyelid：肉～儿 heavy eyelid｜～儿哭肿了 cry one's eyes swollen

【眼皮】yǎnpí（～儿 yǎnpír）眼睑的通称 general term for 眼睑 yǎnjiǎn

【眼皮底下】yǎnpí dǐ·xia 眼底下 right before one's eyes；also 眼皮子底下 yǎnpí·zi dǐ·xia

【眼皮子】yǎnpí·zi ❶ same as 眼皮 yǎnpí：困得～都睁不开了 too drowsy to keep one's eyes open ❷ 指眼界，见识 outlook；experience：～高 ambitious；cocky；hard to please｜～浅 short sighted

【眼前】yǎnqián ❶ 眼睛前面；跟前 before one's eyes：～是一片金黄色的麦田。A stretch of golden wheat fields lay before our eyes. ❷ 目前 for the time being；at the moment；at present

【眼前亏】yǎnqiánkuī 指当时就会受到的损害 imminent trouble：好汉不吃～。Discretion is the better part of valour. *or* A wise man never runs his head against a brick wall.

【眼浅】yǎnqiǎn 见识浅；眼光短 short-sighted

【眼球】yǎnqiú 眼的主要组成部分，呈球形，外部由角膜、巩膜、脉络膜、视网膜等薄膜构成，内部有水状液、晶状体和玻璃体，中央有一个圆形的瞳孔。眼球通过视网膜上的视神经末梢与中枢神经系统联系，外界物体在视网膜上构成物像刺激视神经发生兴奋，传递到大脑皮层即产生视觉。eyeball；major part of the eye, consisting externally of cornea, sclera, choroids, and retina, and internally of hydatoid, lens, and vitreous body；通称 generally known as 眼珠子 yǎnzhū·zi

【眼圈】yǎnquān（～儿 yǎnquānr）same as 眼眶 yǎnkuàng

【眼热】yǎnrè 看见好的事物而希望得到 cast covetous eyes at sth.；eye sth. covetously：她

见了这些花布怪～的。She eyed the printed cloths covetously.

【眼色】yǎnsè ❶ 向人示意的目光 hint given with the eyes; a meaningful glance; wink:递了个～cast a meaningful glance|使了个～wink at sb.; tip sb. the wink|看他的～行事。Take your cue from his wink. ❷ 指见机行事的能力 ability to adapt to circumstances:做买卖要多长～。In doing business you've got to be more adaptable to the market situation.|你这没～的糊涂虫! You dumb idiot!

【眼梢】yǎnshāo 〈方 *dial.*〉靠近两鬓的眼角 corner of the eye close to the temple

【眼神】yǎnshén ❶ 眼睛的神态 looks in one's eyes; expression in one's eyes:人们都用异样的～看着他。People looked at him with curious eyes. ❷〈方 *dial.*〉(～儿 yǎnshénr) same as 眼力 yǎnlì ①:我～儿不好,天一黑就看不清了。My eyesight fails me the moment it gets dark.

【眼神】yǎn·shen 〈方 *dial.*〉(～儿 yǎn·shenr) same as 眼色 yǎnsè

【眼生】yǎnshēng 看着不认识或不熟悉 look unfamiliar:这人看着有点～。The man looks unfamiliar.|几年不到这儿来,连从前最熟的路也～了。I have been away for only a few years, but even those places I knew quite well look strange to me now.

【眼时】yǎnshí 〈方 *dial.*〉目前 at the moment; at present; nowadays

【眼屎】yǎnshǐ 〈方 *dial.*〉眵 gum (in the eyes)

【眼熟】yǎnshú 看着好像认识;见过而想不起是在哪儿见过 look familiar:这人看着很～。The man looks familiar, but I cannot tell who he really is.

【眼跳】yǎntiào 眼睑的肌肉紧张而跳动,多由眼睛疲劳或严重的沙眼所引起 twitching of the eyelid, an eye disease caused by fatigue or serious trachoma

【眼窝】yǎnwō (～儿 yǎnwōr)眼球所在的凹陷的部分 eye socket; eyehole; orbit

【眼下】yǎnxià 目前 at the moment; at present; now:～秋收大忙,农民天不亮就下地了。The autumn harvest is now at its peak, and the farmers begin work in the fields before daybreak.

【眼线】[1] yǎnxiàn 化妆时在上下眼皮边沿画的线条(多为黑色) eye-line; mostly black lines drawn along the upper and lower eyelids:描～draw eye-lines

【眼线】[2] yǎnxiàn 暗中侦察情况、必要时担任向导的人 stool pigeon

【眼影】yǎnyǐng 妇女涂在眼皮上的一种装饰,有蓝色、淡褐色、粉红色等 eye-shadow; ornamentation applied on a woman's eyelids, in such colours as blue, light brown and pink:～膏 eye-shadow ointment|～粉 eye-shadow powder

【眼晕】yǎnyùn 因视觉关系而发晕 dizziness (owing to defective vision)

【眼罩儿】yǎnzhàor ❶ 给牲畜戴的遮眼的东西 eyeshade; blinkers for a draught animal ❷ 戴在眼睛上起遮蔽或保护作用的东西。旧时也指风镜。eyeshade; visor fastened about the eyes and used for protection against glare; (old) goggle ❸ 用手平放在额上遮住阳光叫打眼罩儿 raise a hand across one's forehead to block the glare of the sun:他打起～向远处望去。He looked in the distance with one hand across his forehead.

【眼睁睁】yǎnzhēngzhēng (～的 yǎnzhēngzhēng·de)睁着眼睛,多形容发呆、没有办法或无动于衷(look on) in a daze, helplessly or indifferently

【眼中钉】yǎnzhōngdīng 〈比喻 *fig.*〉心目中最痛恨、最讨厌的人 thorn in one's flesh or side

【眼珠子】yǎnzhū·zi ❶ same as 眼球 yǎnqiú; also 眼珠儿 yǎnzhūr ❷〈比喻 *fig.*〉最珍爱的人或物品 apple of one's eye

【眼拙】yǎnzhuō 〈客套话 *pol.*〉表示没认出对方是谁或记不清跟对方见过面没有 my bad eyes; my bad memory:恕我～,您贵姓? Excuse me for my bad memory, but would you please tell me what your name is?

偃 yǎn 〈书 *fml.*〉❶ 仰面倒下;放倒 fall on one's back; lay down:～卧 lie supine; lie on one's back|～旗息鼓 lower the flags and stop beating the drums ❷ 停止 desist; cease:～武修文 lay down arms to cultivate the arts of peace

【偃旗息鼓】yǎn qí xī gǔ 放倒军旗,停击战鼓。指秘密行军,不暴露目标。也指停止战斗。也比喻停止批评、攻击等。furl all the banners and silence the drums — to cover up a secret military operation and avoid exposure to the enemy, or to stop fighting; (fig.) cease hostility, criticism, or attack

【偃武修文】yǎn wǔ xiū wén 停止武备,提倡文教 desist from war and encourage the arts of peace; desist from military activities and encourage culture and education

琰 yǎn 〈书 *fml.*〉一种玉 a kind of jade

棪 yǎn 古书上说的一种树,果实像柰。多用于人名。a kind of tree described in ancient books, bearing apple-like fruit; *yan*, oft. used in personal names

晻 yǎn 〈书 *fml.*〉阴暗不明 gloomy; dim ☞ àn on p. 15

扊 yǎn [扊扅](yǎnyí)〈书 *fml.*〉门闩 door bolt; door bar

罨 yǎn ❶〈书 *fml.*〉捕鸟或捕鱼的网 net for catching birds or fish ❷ 覆盖;敷 cover:热～(一种医疗方法)hot compress, a therapeutical technique|拿湿布～在伤口上 apply a wet towel on the wound

演 yǎn ❶ 演变;演化 develop; evolve: ～进 evolution; gradual progress ❷ 发挥 exert; act: ～说 deliver a speech | ～绎 deduction ❸ 依照程式(练习或计算) exercise; calculate: ～算 make mathematical calculation; do sums | ～武 practice martial arts | ～兵场 drilling ground; parade ground ❹ 表演技艺;扮演 perform: ～奏 play a musical instrument in a concert | 她～过白毛女。She once played the role of the White-haired Girl.

【演变】yǎnbiàn 发展变化(指历时较久的 of sth. time-honoured) evolution: 宇宙间一切事物都是在不断～的。Everything in the universe changes constantly.

【演播】yǎnbō (通过广播电台、电视台)表演并播送(节目) (radio) broadcast a play, etc.; telecast a television program: ～设施 broadcasting facility | ～室 broadcasting or television studio; studio

【演唱】yǎnchàng 表演(歌曲、戏曲) sing in a performance: ～会 concert of singing | ～京戏 act in Beijing opera

【演出】yǎnchū 把戏剧、舞蹈、曲艺、杂技等演给观众欣赏 perform (opera, dances, ballad singing and storytelling, acrobatics, etc.) for an audience

【演化】yǎnhuà 演变(多指自然界的变化 oft. of changes in nature) evolution: ～过程 process of evolution | 生物的～ evolution of living things

【演技】yǎnjì 表演技巧,指演员运用各种技术和手法创造形象的能力 acting skill; ability of a performer to foster an image with various techniques

【演讲】yǎnjiǎng 演说;讲演 give a lecture; make a speech; lecture: 登台～take the podium and deliver a speech

【演进】yǎnjìn 演变进化 gradual progress; evolution

【演练】yǎnliàn 训练演习;操练 drill: ～场 drill ground | 运动员们正在～各种技巧动作。The athletes are practicing all kinds of sports acrobatics.

【演示】yǎnshì 利用实验或实物、图表把事物的发展变化过程显示出来,使人有所认识或理解 explain and illustrate; demonstrate; help people understand the process of development of sth. by experiments, examples, or diagrams

【演说】yǎnshuō 就某个问题对听众说明事理,发表见解 deliver a speech; make an address: ～词 text of a speech | 发表～deliver a speech

【演算】yǎnsuàn 按一定原理和公式计算 perform mathematical calculations: ～习题 do sums

【演武】yǎnwǔ 指练习武艺 practise traditional martial arts: ～厅 hall for practicing martial arts

【演习】yǎnxí 实地练习(多指军事的 oft. military) exercise; drill; practice: 海军～naval exercise | 实弹～live ammunition manoeuvre | 消防～fire drill

【演戏】yǎn//xì 表演戏剧 put on a play; act in a play: 登台～go onstage for a performance

【演义】yǎnyì ❶〈书 *fml*.〉敷陈义理而加以引申 extend the meaning on the basis of a text: 此剧是取书中若干章节加以编排贯串,～而成。This play is compiled and adapted on the basis of some chapters of a book. ❷ 以一定的历史事迹为背景,以史书及传说的材料为基础,增添一些细节,用章回体写成的小说,如《三国演义》、《隋唐演义》等 historical novel; historical romance; novel written in chapters, with historical facts as the background and history books and legends as the basis, and with the dramatization of certain details, examples being *Romance of Three Kingdoms* and *Romance of Sui and Tang*

【演绎】yǎnyì 一种推理方法,由一般原理推出关于特殊情况下的结论。三段论就是演绎的一种形式(跟'归纳'相对 as opposed to 'sum up') deduction; a priori; infer from a general principle; derive a conclusion for special circumstances from a general principle

【演员】yǎnyuán 参加戏剧、电影、电视、舞蹈、曲艺、杂技等表演的人员 performer; actor; actress; person who plays a part in theatre, movie, television, dance, ballad-singing and storytelling, acrobatics, etc.

【演奏】yǎnzòu 用乐器表演 give an instrumental performance; play a musical instrument (in a performance): ～小提琴 play the violin

缜 yǎn〈书 *fml*.〉延长 extend; prolong

魇(魘) yǎn ❶ 发生梦魇 have a nightmare: ～住了 have a nightmare ❷〈方 *dial*.〉说梦话 talk in one's sleep

蝘 yǎn 古书上指蝉一类的昆虫 cicada and similar insects as described in ancient books

巘(巘) yǎn〈书 *fml*.〉山峰;山顶 mountain peak; summit: 绝～(极高的山顶) summit (soaring mountain peak)

黡(黶) yǎn〈书 *fml*.〉黑色的痣 black mole (on the skin)

甗 yǎn 古代炊具,中部有箅子 ancient cooking vessel with a grid in it

鼹(鼴) yǎn 哺乳动物,毛黑褐色,嘴尖,眼小。前肢发达,脚掌向外翻,有利爪,适于掘土,后肢细小。白天住在土中,夜晚出来捕食昆虫,也吃农作物的根。mole (*Talpa europaea*); small burrowing insectivorous mammal of the family *Talpidae*, usu. living underground during the daytime and coming out to feed on insects and the roots of farm crops at night, having dark brown fur, pointed muzzle, small rudimentary eyes, and strong forefeet with soles turned outward for burrowing; 通称 popularly known as 鼹鼠 yǎnshǔ

yàn (丨㔾)

厌(厭) yàn ❶ 满足 satisfied; satiated: 贪得无～have insatiable greed; be insatiably avaricious; flay a flint ❷ 因过多而不喜欢 be fed up with; be tired of: 看～了 be tired of reading sth. ❸ 憎恶 detest; be disgusted with: ～恶 disgust; abhor; abominate | ～弃 spurn; be wearied with sb. or sth.

【厌烦】yànfán 嫌麻烦而讨厌 be wearied with sb. or sth; be sick of; be fed up with: 话说了一遍又一遍，都叫人听～了。People are sick and tired of listening to the same remark repeated over and over again.

【厌恨】yànhèn 厌恶痛恨 abhor, loathe

【厌倦】yànjuàn 对某种活动失去兴趣而不愿继续 be weary of; be tired of: 下围棋，他早就～了。He's long been tired of playing *weiqi*.

【厌弃】yànqì 厌恶而嫌弃 spurn; turn one's nose up at: 遭人～be detested and rejected | 对成绩差的学生不应～而应热情帮助。We should warmly help those students who are not doing well in their studies rather than spurn them.

【厌食】yànshí 食欲不振，不想吃东西 loss of appetite; anorexia: 这种新药主治小儿～。This new drug applies to anorexia in children.

【厌世】yànshì 悲观消极，厌弃人生 be world-weary; be pessimistic: 悲观～be pessimistic and sick of life

【厌恶】yànwù（对人或事物）产生很大的反感 abhor; abominate; be disgusted with; detest: 大家都～他。Everybody is disgusted with him. | 这种无聊的生活令人～。This kind of humdrum life is simply disgusting.

【厌战】yànzhàn 厌恶战争 be weary of war; be war-weary: ～情绪 war-weariness

赝 yàn 赝口（Yànkǒu），地名，在浙江 Yankou, name of a place in Zhejiang Province

研 yàn same as 砚 yàn
☞ yán on p. 2206

砚 yàn ❶ 砚台 inkstone; inkslab: 笔～writing brush and inkslab | 端～Duanxi inkslab; inkstone produced in Duanxi, Guangdong Province ❷〈旧时 *old*〉指有同学关系的（因同学常共笔砚，同学也称'同砚'）fellow student; classmate, a term derived from the fact that classmates sharing the same desk often shared their writing brushes and inkslabs: ～兄 senior fellow student | ～友 classmate

【砚池】yànchí same as 砚台 yàn·tai

【砚滴】yàndī 水注 small receptacle for holding water for use on an inkslab

【砚台】yàn·tai 研墨的文具，有石头的，有瓦的 inkstone; brick inkslab

咽(嚥) yàn 使嘴里的食物或别的东西通过咽头到食道里去 swallow; cause food or sth. else to pass through the mouth and throat into the stomach: ～唾沫 swallow one's own saliva | 细嚼慢～chew one's food well before swallowing it | 狼吞虎～eat voraciously; gobble up; wolf down ◇ 话到嘴边，又～回去了。He wanted to say something but thought better of it.
☞ yān on p. 2199 and yè on p. 2241

【咽气】yàn//qì 指人死断气 die; breath one's last

彦 yàn〈古代 *arch.*〉指有才德的人 man of virtue and ability

艳(艶、豔) yàn ❶ 色彩光泽鲜明好看 gorgeous; colourful; gaudy: ～丽 gorgeous | 娇～pretty and charming | 百花争～flowers in full bloom; flowers in a riot of colour | 这布的花色太～了，有没有素一点的？The cloth is too gaudy. Is there anything simpler? ❷ 指关于爱情方面的；香艳 amorous: ～情 romance | ～史 love story ❸〈书 *fml.*〉羡慕 envy: ～羡 admire; envy

【艳福】yànfú 指男子得到美女欢心的福分 man's good fortune in love affairs

【艳丽】yànlì 鲜明美丽 gorgeous; splendid: 色彩～splendid colour | ～夺目 dazzling | ～的彩虹 dazzling rainbow

【艳情】yànqíng 指关于男女爱情的 erotic: ～小说 erotic fiction | ～故事 erotica

【艳诗】yànshī 指描写男女爱情的诗 love poem; erotic poem

【艳史】yànshǐ 指关于男女爱情的故事 merry romance; amorous story

【艳羡】yànxiàn〈书 *fml.*〉十分羡慕 great envy

【艳阳】yànyáng ❶ 明亮的太阳 bright sun: ～高照。The sun rides high in the sky. ❷ 明媚的风光，多指春天 sunny sky; spring day: ～桃李节 spring peach and plum flower festival | ～天（明媚的春天）sunny spring day; bright and warm spring

晏 yàn ❶ 迟 late: ～起 sleep in; get up late ❷ same as 宴 yàn ③ ❸（Yàn）姓 a surname

【晏驾】yànjià 君主时代称帝王死（of an emperor) die; pass away

唁 yàn 对遭遇丧事的表示慰问 offer condolences: 慰～express sympathy with the bereaved | 吊～pay respect to the deceased and offer condolences to the bereaved | ～电 message of condolences

【唁电】yàndiàn 慰问死者家属的电报 telegram

or cable of condolence; message of condolence

【唁函】yànhán 慰问死者家属的信 letter or message of condolence

宴 yàn ❶ 请人吃酒饭;聚会在一起吃酒饭 fete; entertain sb. at a feast:～客 throw a banquet to guests|欢～feast ❷ 酒席;宴会 banquet; feast:设～give a banquet|赴～attend a banquet|盛～grand banquet|国～state banquet ❸ 安乐;安闲 ease and comfort:～安(安逸)ease and comfort|～乐(安乐) live in ease and comfort

【宴安鸩毒】yàn'ān zhèn dú 贪图享乐等于喝毒酒自杀 seeking pleasure is like drinking poisoned wine; voluptuous comfort is poison

【宴尔】yàn'ěr 〈书 *fml*.〉安乐。《诗经·邶风·谷风》有'宴尔新昏(婚)'的诗句。后来就用'宴尔'指新婚。ease and comfort; be a happy newlywed (*The Book of Songs·Folksongs of Bei·Spring Breeze*: 'Happy you are at your wedding now,/With guests as brothers elder and younger'):～之乐 joy of wedding; also 燕尔 yàn'ěr

【宴会】yànhuì 宾主在一起饮酒吃饭的集会(指比较隆重的) banquet; feast; dinner party:举行盛大～hold a grand banquet

【宴请】yànqǐng 设宴招待 fete:～外宾 fete a foreign guest; hold a banquet in honour of foreign guests

【宴席】yànxí 请客的酒席 banquet; feast:承办～undertake banquets

验(驗、騐) yàn ❶ 察看;查考 inspect; examine; check:～货 check goods|～血 blood test|查～examine|考～exam; examination|试～test ❷ 产生预期的效果 prove effective; produce an expected result:灵～effective|应～be borne out; come true|屡试屡～prove successful in every test ❸ 预期的效果 intended effect; desired result:效～intended result

【验方】yànfāng 临床经验证明有疗效的现成的药方 proved recipe; ready prescription

【验关】yàn//guān 人员出入境时,由海关官员检验其证件及携带的物品等 customs examination; customs inspection of the credentials and luggage of those entering or exiting a country:办理～手续 go through customs formalities|在机场等候～wait for customs inspection at an airport

【验光】yàn//guāng 检查眼球晶状体的屈光度 optometry; examine the dioptre of the lenses in eyeballs

【验看】yànkàn 察看;检验 examine; inspect:～指纹 examine fingerprints|～护照 examine a passport

【验墒】yàn//shāng 检查或测定土壤的湿度 check the moisture of the soil

【验尸】yàn//shī (司法人员)检验人的尸体,确定死亡的原因和过程 postmortem; autopsy; medical examination of a dead body to ascertain the cause and process of death

【验收】yànshōu 按照一定标准进行检验而后收下 acceptance examination; check upon delivery:～工作 acceptance appraisal work|大桥竣工～后才能交付使用。After its completion the bridge can be opened to traffic only after passing acceptance examinations.

【验算】yànsuàn 算题算好以后,再用另外的方法演算一遍,检验已得出的运算结果是否正确。验算多用逆运算,如减法算题用加法,除法算题用乘法。checking computations; verify the result of a mathematical calculation that has been performed by using a different method of computation. Checking computations are mostly conducted by reciprocal operations, such as addition for subtraction, and multiplication for division.

【验证】yànzhèng same as 证验 zhèngyàn①:～数据 verify data

谚 yàn 谚语 proverb; saying; adage:古～old saying|农～farmers' adage

【谚语】yànyǔ 在群众中间流传的固定语句,用简单通俗的话反映出深刻的道理。如'三个臭皮匠,赛过诸葛亮','三百六十行,行行出状元','天下无难事,只怕有心人'。proverb; popular short, pithy saying that expresses a profound precept, such as 'Three fools make one wise man', 'Every profession produces its own leading authority', and 'Where there is an ill, there is a way'.

堰 yàn 较低的挡水建筑物,作用是提高上游水位,便利灌溉和航运 weir; low dam built across a river to raise the water and facilitate irrigation and shipping

雁(鴈) yàn 鸟类的一属,形状略像鹅,颈和翼较长,足和尾较短,羽毛淡紫褐色。善于游泳和飞行。常见的有鸿雁。wild goose (*Anser cygnoides*); wild bird resembling a domesticated goose, characteristically having a long neck and wings, short feet and tail, and light purplish brown feathers, and being good at swimming and flying. The swan goose is a common type of wild goose.

【雁过拔毛】yàn guò bá máo 〈比喻 *fig*.〉对经手的事不放过任何机会牟取私利 pluck feathers from each goose as it passes by; spare no effort in taking advantage of what one puts his hand on

【雁行】yànháng 鸿雁飞时整齐的行列 swan geese flying in a line; 借指弟兄 brothers

【雁阵】yànzhèn 雁高飞时排成的队形 flying formation of wild geese

喭 yàn 〈书 *fml*.〉❶ 粗鲁 rude; boorish ❷ same as 唁 yàn

焰(燄) yàn 火苗 flame; blaze:火～fire ◇气～ arrogance

【焰火】yànhuǒ same as 烟火 yān·huo

【焰口】yàn·kou 〈佛教用语 *Budd.*〉形容饿鬼渴望饮食,口吐火焰。和尚做法事向饿鬼施食叫放焰口。*ulka-mukha* (Sanskrit); fire-spitting hungry ghost. The monastic ritual to offer food to these fire-spitting ghosts is known as 'feeding ulka-mukha ceremony'.

【焰心】yànxīn 火焰最里面的部分,这部分气体还没有氧化,不发光 flame core; innermost part of a flame, where the gas has not been oxygenated and become luminescent yet

焱 yàn 〈书 *fml.*〉火花;火焰。多用于人名。spark; fire; *yan*, oft. used in a personal name

滟(灩) yàn 滟滪堆(Yànyù Duī),长江瞿塘峡口的巨石。1958 年整治航道时已炸平。Yanyudui Crag, a mammoth monolith lying at the entrance to the Qutang Gorge of the Yangtze River, which was demolished in 1958 to dredge and straighten the navigation lane

堰 yàn ❶〈方 *dial.*〉两山之间的山地 clearance between two mountains ❷ same as 堰 yàn

酽(釅) yàn (汁液)浓;味厚(of liquid) thick; strong: 这碗茶太~了。This bowl of tea tastes a bit too strong.|墨磨得~~的。The inkstick had been ground meticulously on the inkstone until the ink became thick and black.

餍(饜) yàn 〈书 *fml.*〉❶ 吃饱 have enough (food) ❷ 满足 be satiated

【餍足】yàn zú 〈书 *fml.*〉满足(多指私欲) satisfy (esp. selfish desires)

鷃(鴳) yàn [鷃雀](yànquè) 古书上说的一种小鸟 a kind of tiny bird as described in ancient books

焰 yàn 〈书 *fml.*〉same as 焰 yàn

谳(讞) yàn 〈书 *fml.*〉审判定罪 decide a law case: 定~pass judgment on a criminal case

燕[1](鷰) yàn 鸟类的一科,翅膀尖而长,尾巴分开像剪刀。捕食昆虫,对农作物有益。春天飞到北方,秋天飞到南方,是候鸟。常见的有家燕。swallow (*Hirundo*); migrant passerine bird of the family *Hirundinidae*, having long, pointed wings and a forked tail, feeding on insects, noted for their regular migrations to the north in spring and the south in autumn. Those habitually building their nests in human dwellings are a common type of swallows.

燕[2](讌、❶醼) yàn ❶ same as 宴 yàn ①② ❷ same as 宴 yàn ③

☞ Yān on p. 2201

【燕尔】yàn'ěr same as 宴尔 yàn'ěr

【燕麦】yànmài ❶ 一年生或二年生草本植物,叶子细长而尖,花绿色,小穗有细长的芒。子实可以吃,也可以做饲料。oats (*Avena sativa*); annual or biannual herbaceous plant having slender and pointed leaves, green flowers, tiny ears with awns, and seeds that can be used as food or animal feed ❷ 这种植物的子实 seed of the plant

【燕雀】yànquè 鸟,身体小,嘴圆锥形,喉和胸褐色,雄的头和背黑色,雌的头和背暗褐色,边缘浅黄色。吃昆虫等。brambling (*Fringilla montifringilla*); tiny bird feeding on insects, and having a tapered beak and brown throat and chest, the male having a black head and back, the female having a dark brown head and back with pale yellow fringes

【燕雀处堂】yàn què chǔ táng 燕子和麻雀在堂上筑窝,自以为十分安全,房子着了火,燕子和麻雀仍然在窝里作乐,不知道大祸已经临头(见于《孔丛子·论势》) Swallows and sparrows were building nests in a hall, feeling happy about having found good refuge. When the hall caught fire, they were still wallowing in the warmth and comfort of their nests, oblivious to the imminent danger (*Kongcong zi·On Situation*); 〈比喻 *fig.*〉安居而失去警惕 live in peace and lose sight of danger

【燕尾服】yànwěifú 男子西式晚礼服的一种,黑色,前身较短,后身较长而下端分开像燕子尾巴 tails; swallow-tailed coat; tailcoat; man's black evening dress with a short front part, and cutaway over the hips and descending in a pair of tapering skirts behind

【燕窝】yànwō 金丝燕在海边岩石间筑的巢,是金丝燕吞下海藻后吐出的胶状物凝结而成的,是一种珍贵的食品 edible bird's nest; teacup-like nest of the esculent swift, formed of the alga-eating bird's saliva on seaside rocks, and used as a delicacy of the Chinese cuisine

【燕子】yàn·zi 家燕的通称 generally known as 家燕 jiāyàn

赝(贋) yàn 〈书 *fml.*〉伪造的 counterfeit; spurious; fake: ~品 forgery; fake

【赝本】yànběn 假托名人手笔的书画 spurious copy of a famous work of calligraphy or painting

【赝币】yànbì 〈书 *fml.*〉伪造的货币(多指硬币 oft. coin) counterfeit currency

【赝鼎】yàndǐng 〈书 *fml.*〉伪造的某个鼎 counterfeit tripod; 泛指赝品 art forgery

【赝品】yànpǐn 伪造的文物或艺术品 fake artifact; art forgery

嬿 yàn 〈书 *fml.*〉美好 lovely; charming

yāng (|九)

央[1] yāng 恳求 implore; entreat: ~求 beg|~人作保 ask sb. to stand guarantor

央[2] yāng 中心 core; centre: 中～central authorities

央[3] yāng 〈书 *fml*.〉终止;完结 terminate; end: 夜未～。The night is not yet spent. | 长乐未～lasting peace and happiness

【央告】yāng·gao same as 央求 yāngqiú

【央求】yāngqiú 恳求 importune; beseech: 再三～,他才答应。He consented only after we had pleaded with him desperately.

【央托】yāngtuō 请托 entrust; entreat sb. to do sth.: ～一位朋友办理。A friend was entrusted to handle the matter.

【央中】yāngzhōng 〈旧时文书用语 *fml*. *arch*.〉请某人做中人 request sb. to be an intermediary

泱 yāng [泱泱]〈书 *fml*.〉❶ 水面广阔(of water) extensive; vast: 湖水～vast expanse of water in a lake; large lake ❷ 形容气魄宏大 magnificent; great: ～大国 great country

殃 yāng ❶ 祸害 calamity; disaster; misfortune: 灾～disaster | 遭～ suffer retribution; fall victim to a disaster ❷ 使受祸害 bring disaster to; harm: 祸国～民 bring calamity to the country and the people

【殃及池鱼】yāng jí chí yú ☞城门失火,殃及池鱼 chéngmén shī huǒ, yāng jí chí yú on p. 251

鸯 yāng ☞鸳鸯 yuān·yāng on p. 2354

秧 yāng ❶ (～儿 yāngr)植物的幼苗 seedling; sprout: 树～儿 sapling | 白菜～儿 cabbage seedling | 黄瓜～儿 cucumber sprout ❷ 特指水稻的幼苗 rice seedling: ～田 rice seedling bed | 插～transplant rice seedlings ❸ 某些植物的茎 vine: 瓜～melon vine | 豆～bean seedling | 白薯～sweet potato vine ❹ 某些饲养的幼小动物 young; fry: 鱼～fry ❺〈方 *dial*.〉栽培;畜养 cultivate; raise; breed: ～几棵树 have planted several tree saplings | ～了一池鱼 have raised a pond of fish

【秧歌】yāng·ge 主要流行于北方广大农村的一种民间舞蹈,用锣鼓伴奏,有的地区也表演故事,跟小歌舞剧相似。跳这种舞叫扭秧歌或闹秧歌。yangko; *yangge* dance; folk dance popular in rural north China, performed to the accompaniment of gongs and drums, or in a simple opera form in some areas. Performing the *yangge* dance is called 扭秧歌 niǔ yāng·ge or 闹秧歌 nào yāng·ge.

【秧歌剧】yāng·gejù 由秧歌发展而成的歌舞剧,演出简单,能迅速反映现实。如抗日战争时期演的《兄妹开荒》就是秧歌剧。*yangge* opera; opera developed from the *yangge* dance, which is simple in form and therefore appropriate for reflecting current affairs. *Brother and Sister Reclaiming Wasteland*, which was created during the War of Resistance against Japan, is a *yangge* opera.

【秧龄】yānglíng 水稻的幼苗在秧田中生长的时期 length of time when rice seedlings grow in seedling beds until they are transplanted

【秧苗】yāngmiáo 农作物的幼苗,通常指水稻的幼苗 seedling; (oft. referring) paddy rice seedling

【秧田】yāngtián 培植水稻秧苗的田 rice seedling bed

【秧子】yāng·zi ❶ same as 秧 yāng ①: 树～tree sapling ❷ same as 秧 yāng ③: 花生～peanut seedling ❸ same as 秧 yāng ④: 猪～piglet ❹〈方 *dial*.〉〈比喻 *fig*.〉某种人(多含贬义 oft. derog.) certain type of person: 病～weakling; valetudinarian; sickman | 奴才～ yes man; toady; flunkey

鞅 yāng (旧读 formerly pronunced yǎng)〈古代 *arch*.〉用马拉车时安在马脖子上的皮套子 leather collar for a horse
☞ yàng on p. 2225

yáng (丨尢)

扬[1](揚、敭) yáng ❶ 高举;往上升 raise; hoist: 飘～flutter; fly | 趾高气～strut about and give oneself air; put on an extremely haughty and arrogant air | ～帆 set sail ❷ 往上撒 throw up and scatter; winnow: ～场 winnowing | 把种子晒干～净 dry the seeds in the sun and get rid of the chaff by winnowing ❸ 传播出去 spread; make known: 表～commend; praise | 颂～eulogize | 赞～praise | ～言 boast; threaten ❹ 指容貌好看 good-looking: 其貌不～look homely

扬[2](揚) Yáng ❶ 指江苏扬州 Yangzhou, a city in Jiangsu Province ❷ 姓 a surname

【扬长】yángcháng 大模大样地离开的样子 swashbuckling: ～走了 leave with a swagger | ～而去 stalk off; stride off; walk out on sb.

【扬长避短】yáng cháng bì duǎn 发扬长处,避开短处 show one's strong points and hide one's weaknesses; maximize favourable factors and minimize unfavourable ones: 知人善任,～be good at judging people and know how to use their strengths while avoiding their weaknesses | 因地制宜,～,利用当地资源,发展商品生产。Adapt our policies to reality, give full scope to our strengths and overcome our weaknesses, and tap local resources to boost commodities production.

【扬场】yáng//cháng 把打下来的谷物、豆类等用机器、木锨等扬起,借风力吹掉壳和尘土,分离出干净的子粒 winnow; toss grain or beans high into the air by machine or wooden shovel to get rid of the chaffs and dust by the force of the wind

【扬程】yángchéng 水泵向上扬水的高度 lift of

a pump; a pump's power or force available for raising

【扬帆】yáng//fān 扯起帆(开船) hoist the sails; set sail:～远航 set sail for a long journey

【扬幡招魂】yáng fān zhāo hún 挂幡招回死者的魂灵(迷信)。现多用于比喻。fly a funeral banner to summon the soul; (oft. fig.) try to resurrect sth. that is dead, obsolete, or wrong

【扬花】yánghuā 水稻、小麦、高粱等作物开花时,花药裂开,花粉飞散(of paddy rice, wheat, sorghum, or other farm crops) flowering, during which time the anther (pollen-bearing part of the stamen) splits open, allowing the pollen to be scattered in the air and blown away by the wind

【扬剧】yángjù 江苏地方戏曲剧种之一,原名维扬戏,流行于扬州一带 Yangzhou opera, originally known as *weiyang* opera, one of the local operas of Jiangsu Province that is popular in and around Yangzhou

【扬厉】yánglì 〈书 *fml.*〉发扬 carry forward; develop:铺张～ extremely extravagant

【扬眉吐气】yáng méi tǔ qì 形容被压抑的心情得到舒展而快活如意 feel elated; feel proud and elated; stand up holding one's head high

【扬名】yáng//míng 传播名声 make a name for oneself; become famous:～天下 become world-famous; become renowned across the land

【扬旗】yángqí 铁路信号的一种,设在车站的两头,在立柱上装着活动的板,板横着时表示不准火车进站,板向下斜时表示准许进站 railway semaphore; visual signaling apparatus installed at either end of a railway station, with a mechanically moving arm that signals 'no entrance' when horizontal, and 'entrance permitted' when slanting downwards

【扬弃】yángqì ❶ 哲学上指事物在新陈代谢过程中,发扬旧事物中的积极因素,抛弃旧事物中的消极因素 sublate; (in metabolism) develop what is positive and discard what is negative ❷ 抛弃 negate; deny; discard

【扬琴】yángqín 弦乐器,把许多根弦安在一个梯形的扁木箱上,用竹制的富有弹性的小槌击弦而发声 dulcimer; musical instrument with wire strings of graduated lengths stretched over a flat trapeziform wooden sound box, played by striking with two tiny bamboo hammers; also 洋琴 yángqín

【扬清激浊】yáng qīng jī zhuó ☞ 激浊扬清 jī zhuó yáng qīng on p.900

【扬榷】yángquè 〈书 *fml.*〉略举大要;扼要论述 expound the gist of piece of writing:～古今 succinct review of past and present events

【扬声器】yángshēngqì 把电能变成声音的器件,常见的一种是由磁铁、线圈、纸盆等构成的,电流通过线圈时使纸盆作相应的振动而发出声音。用在收音机和扩音机上。loudspeaker; device installed in a radio or amplifier to convert electric signals to audible sound. A common type consists of a permanent magnet, a voice coil and a cone-shaped diaphragm, and when the current flows through the voice coil, the diaphragm vibrates to produce sound waves.

【扬水】yángshuǐ 用水泵提水 elevate water to a higher place by a pump:～站 pumping station

【扬汤止沸】yáng tāng zhǐ fèi 把沸水舀起来再倒回去,想叫它不沸腾 try to stop water from boiling by skimming it off and pouring it back;〈比喻 *fig.*〉办法不彻底,不能从根本上解决问题 use an ineffectual remedy; apply a palliative

【扬威】yángwēi 显示威风 make a show of force:耀武～bluff and bluster

【扬言】yángyán 故意说出要采取某种行动的话(多含贬义 oft. derog.) threaten (that one is going to take action):～要进行报复 threaten to retaliate

【扬扬】yángyáng 得意的样子 triumphantly; complacently:～得意 be immensely proud with success; look triumphant; also 洋洋 yángyáng

【扬子鳄】yángzǐ'è 鼍(tuó),因产于扬子江(长江)而得名 Yangtze alligator (*Alligator sinensis*); Chinese alligator, named after its habitat, the Yangtze River

羊 yáng ❶ 哺乳动物,反刍类,一般头上有一对角,分山羊、绵羊、羚羊等多种 sheep; goat; usu. horned ruminant mammal in such varieties as goat, sheep and antelope ❷ (Yáng)姓 a surname

【羊肠线】yángchángxiàn 羊的肠子制成的线,用于缝合体腔内的伤口或切口 catgut suture; tough, thin cord made from the treated and stretched sheep intestines, and used for surgical ligatures

【羊肠小道】yángcháng xiǎodào 曲折而极窄的路(多指山路 oft. refer to mountain road) narrow winding trail; meandering footpath; byway

【羊肚儿手巾】yángdǔr shǒu•jin 〈方 *dial.*〉毛巾 towel

【羊羔】yánggāo ❶ 小羊 lamb ❷〈古代 *arch.*〉汾州(在今山西省)出产的名酒 *yanggao*, famous liquor produced in Fenzhou in present-day Shanxi Province

【羊羹】yánggēng 用赤小豆粉、琼脂、砂糖等制成的一种点心 red-bean cake; sweet gelatinized red-bean cake made from red-bean flour, agar, granulated sugar, etc.

【羊工】yánggōng 放羊的雇工 hired herdsman

【羊倌】yángguān (～儿 yángguānr)专职放羊的人 shepherd

【羊毫】yángháo 有羊毛做笔头的毛笔,比较柔软 soft writing brush made of goat's hair

【羊角】yángjiǎo 〈书 *fml.*〉指弯曲而上的旋风

cyclone in the shape of a ram's horn

【羊角风】 yángjiǎofēng 癫痫的通称 general term for 癫痫 diānxián

【羊毛】 yángmáo 羊的毛,通常指用做纺织原料的 wool, a raw material for the textile industry

【羊膜】 yángmó 人或哺乳动物包裹胎儿的膜,由外胚层和中胚层的一部分组成 amnion; membranous sac that encloses the fetus of a woman or a mammal, consisting of the ectoderm and part of the mesoblast

【羊皮纸】 yángpízhǐ ❶ 用羊皮做成的像纸的薄片,用于书写 parchment; sheep or goat skin prepared as a material on which to write or paint ❷ 经硫酸处理而制成的纸,厚而结实,不透油和水,用来包装物品 thick, tough, and oil- and waterproof paper treated with sulfuric acid, used as wrapping material

【羊绒】 yángróng 指山羊腹部的绒毛,纤维柔细,是较好的纺织原料 cashmere; fine, downy wool growing on the belly of the Cashmere goat, used as a quality textile material: ~衫 cashmere sweater

【羊水】 yángshuǐ 羊膜中的液体。羊水能使胎儿不受外界的震荡,并能减少胎儿在子宫内活动时对母体的刺激。amniotic fluid; fluid that fills the amnion, in which the embryo is suspended and thus protected from shock from the outside, and which reduces the irritation caused to the mother by the movement of the fetus in the womb

【羊痫风】 yángxiánfēng 癫痫的通称 general term for 癫痫 diānxián

【羊眼】 yángyǎn 装在镜框、门窗等上面的金属零件,一端成圆环形,一端有螺纹,便于悬挂或固定 screw eye; screw with a loop for passing cord through, used to hang a picture frame or fix doors and windows

阳(陽) yáng ❶ 我国古代哲学认为存在于宇宙间的一切事物中的两大对立面之一(跟阴相对,下②到⑦同 as opposed to 阴 yīn in the following cases of ② through ⑦)(in Chinese dualistic philosophy) *yang*, active, masculine cosmic principle: 阴~二气 *yin* and *yang* ❷ 太阳;日光 sun; sunlight: ~光 sunshine | ~历 Gregorian calendar; solar calendar | ~坡 hillside exposed to the sun | 朝~ be exposed to the sun; sunny side | 向~ facing the sun; sunny ❸ 山的南面;水的北面 south of a mountain; north of a river: 衡~(在衡山之南) Hengyang, name of a place situated south of the Hengshan Mountain | 洛~(在洛河之北) Luoyang, name of a city situated north of the Luohe River ❹ 凸出的 in relief: ~文 characters or designs carved in relief ❺ 外露的;表面的 open; overt; outward: ~沟 open ditch | ~奉阴违 agree in public but oppose in private ❻ 指属于活人和人世的(迷信 superstition) of this world; of this life: ~宅 residence; dwelling | ~间 human world | ~寿 lifespan ❼ 带正电的(of electricity) positive: ~电 positive electricity | ~极 positive pole ❽ 指男性生殖器 male genitals ❾ (Yáng) 姓 a surname

【阳春】 yángchūn 指春天 spring: ~三月 third lunar month in spring

【阳春白雪】 yángchūn báixuě 战国时代楚国的一种高雅的歌曲。后来泛指高深的、不通俗的文学艺术,常跟'下里巴人'对举。'Spring Snow', a kind of melody that belonged to the élite in the State of Chu during the Warring States Period; (in a broad sense) highbrow literature and art, as opposed to the 'Songs of the Rustic Poor', meaning popular literature and art

【阳电】 yángdiàn 正电 positive electricity

【阳奉阴违】 yáng fèng yīn wéi 表面上遵从,暗地里不执行 double-dealing; overtly agree but covertly oppose; comply in public but oppose in private; feign compliance

【阳刚】 yánggāng 指男子在风度、气概、体魄等方面表现出来的刚强气质 manly; virile; masculine; doughty quality in mannerism, spirit, and physique that belongs to or befits a man: ~之气 manliness; virility

【阳沟】 yánggōu 露在地面上的排水沟 open drain; ditch

【阳关道】 yángguāndào 原指古代经过阳关(在今甘肃敦煌西南)通向西域的大道,后来泛指通行便利的大路 broad road; thoroughfare, esp. the one leading to the Western Region by way of Yangguan Pass to the southwest of present-day Dunhuang, Gansu Province, in ancient times; 〈比喻 *fig.*〉有光明前途的道路 road to a bright future: 你走你的~,我过我的独木桥。You take the open road, I'll cross the log bridge — you go your way, I'll go mine. also 阳关大道 yángguān dàdào

【阳光】 yángguāng 日光 sunlight; sunshine: ~灿烂 bright sunshine | ~充足 adequate sunlight

【阳极】 yángjí ❶ 电池等直流电源中吸收电子带正电的电极。干电池中间的炭精棒就是阳极。positive pole; positive electrode; anode; positively charged electrode in a direct-circuit electrical source, such as the carbon rod of a battery; also 正极 zhèngjí ❷ 电子器件中吸收电子的一极。电子管和各种阴极射线管中都有阳极,接受阴极放射的电子,这一极跟电源的正极相接。electrically charged pole in an electronics device; Vacuum tubes and various types of cathode ray tubes all contain such a pole that receives electrons released from the cathode and is linked with the anode of an electrical source.

【阳间】 yángjiān 人世间(对'阴间'而言 as opposed to 'afterworld') this world

【阳狂】 yángkuáng same as 佯狂 yángkuáng

【阳离子】yánglízǐ 正离子 positive ion; cation

【阳历】yánglì ❶ 历法的一类，以地球绕太阳1周的时间(365.24219天)为1年，平年365天，闰年366天，1年分12个月。公历是阳历的一种。Gregorian calendar; a kind of solar calendar which puts the time it takes for the earth to move around the sun (365.24219 days) as a year, with a common year containing 365 days, and a leap year consisting of 366 days, and each year containing 12 months; also 太阳历 tàiyánglì ❷ 公历的通称 general term for 公历 gōnglì

【阳面】yángmiàn (～儿 yángmiànr)(建筑物等)向阳的一面(of buildings) sunny side

【阳平】yángpíng 普通话字调的第二声，主要由古汉语平声字中浊音声母字分化而成 rising tone (the second of the four tones in modern standard Chinese pronunciation); ☞ 四声 sìshēng on p.1821

【阳畦】yángqí 苗床的一种，设在向阳的地方，四周用土培成框，北面或四周安上风障，夜间或气温低时，在框上盖席或塑料薄膜来保温 sunny seed bed; rectangular ridged seed bed set up at the sunny side of a place, with windbreaks erected around it or on its northern side, and covered with matting or plastic sheets at night or when the weather becomes cold

【阳伞】yángsǎn 遮太阳光用的伞。有的地区叫旱伞。parasol; sunshade; known in some regions as 旱伞 hànsǎn

【阳世】yángshì 人世间 human world

【阳寿】yángshòu 迷信的人指人活在人世的寿数 (superstition) lifespan in the human world

【阳燧】yángsuì 〈古代 *arch.*〉利用太阳光取火的器具，用铜制成，略像镜子 bronze mirror-like implement used to obtain fire from the sun

【阳台】yángtái 楼房的小平台，有栏杆，可以乘凉、晒太阳或远望 balcony; tiny platform that projects from the wall of a building and is surrounded by a railing, where people can enjoy the cool, sun themselves, or enjoy the scenery

【阳痿】yángwěi 成年男子性功能障碍的病，阴茎不能勃起或勃起不坚而不能性交。多由前列腺炎症或神经机能障碍等引起。impotence; man's sexual dysfunction mostly caused by prostatitis or dysneuria, characterized by failure to get an erection or an adequate erection to facilitate intercourse

【阳文】yángwén 印章或某些器物上所刻或所铸的凸出的文字或花纹(跟'阴文'相对 as opposed to 'intaglio') relief; inscription or design cut in relief

【阳性】yángxìng ❶ 诊断疾病时对进行某种试验或化验所得结果的表示方法。说明体内有某种病原体存在或对某种药物有过敏反应，例如注射结核菌素后有红肿等反应时叫做结核菌素试验阳性。positive, a medical indication of the result of a chemical test for the diagnosis of diseases, indicating the presence of a particular disease or allergy to a certain medicine. For instance, when an injection of tuberculin has caused the skin to swell, it is known as 'tuberculin test positive'. ❷ 某些语言里名词(以及代词、形容词)分别阴性、阳性，或阴性、阳性、中性 masculine gender; grammatical category used to categorize nouns (as well as pronouns and adjectives) in some languages into feminine and masculine genders, or feminine, masculine and neutral genders; ☞ 性 xìng ⑥ on p.2151

【阳性植物】yángxìng zhíwù 在阳光充足的条件下才生长得好的植物，如松树和一般的农作物 heliotrope; plant that grows well only under adequate sunshine, such as the pine and ordinary farm crops; also 喜光植物 xǐguāng zhíwù

【阳韵】yángyùn 音韵学家根据古韵母的性质，把字音分成三类：韵尾是b,d,g的叫入声；韵尾是m,n,ng的叫阳韵；入声和阳韵以外的叫阴韵。阳韵和阴韵的字调各有平声、上声、去声三类。In phonology, the sounds of word fall into three categories according to the nature of classical vowels of Chinese syllables: *rusheng* or entering tone ending with b, d, or g; *yangyun* or masculine terminal sound with m, n, or ng; and *yinyun* or feminine sound, including terminal sounds that are neither *rusheng* nor *yangyun*. Both *yangyun* and *yinyun* sounds are further classified into level tone, rising tone and falling tone.

【阳宅】yángzhái 迷信的人称住宅(对'阴宅'而言 as opposed to 'residence in the netherworld') (superstition) residence; dwelling in the human world

玚(瑒) yáng 古代的一种玉 a kind of jade in ancient times; ☞ chàng on p.223

杨(楊) yáng ❶ 杨树，落叶乔木，叶子互生，卵形或卵状披针形，柔荑花序，种类很多，有银白杨、毛白杨、小叶杨等 poplar (*Populus*), deciduous tree having alternate oval or ovate lanceolate leaves and catkin, coming in a good variety such as abele, Chinese white poplar (*Populus tomentosa*) and *Populus simonii* ❷ (Yáng)姓 a surname

【杨辉三角】Yáng Huī sānjiǎo 二项式(a+b)的n(n=0,1,2,3,...)次方展开式的系数依次可排列成一个三角形的数表 Yang Hui Triangle; the coefficients of the binomial $(a+b)^n$, where n=1,2,3..., can be arranged a triangle of numbers as follows; known in the West as Pascal's triangle:

1
1 1
1 2 1
1 3 3 1
1 4 6 4 1
1 5 10 10 5 1

这个数表见于我国南宋数学家杨辉的《详解九章算法》,后来叫做杨辉三角。因《详解九章算法》指出北宋数学家贾宪已用这个数表开高次方,所以也叫贾宪三角。This chart can be seen in *Detailed Annotations of Mathematics in Nine Sections* by Yang Hui, a mathematician of the Southern Song Dynasty, later called the Yang Hui Triangle. According to the book, Jia Xian, a mathematician of the Northern Song Dynasty, had used this chart in the extraction of high-degree roots, therefore it is also called the Jia Xian Triangle.

【杨柳】yángliǔ ❶ 杨树和柳树 poplar and willow ❷ 泛指柳树 (in a broad sense) willow

【杨梅】yángméi ❶ 常绿灌木或乔木,叶子狭长,花褐色,雌雄异株。果实表面有粒状突起,紫红色或白色,味酸甜,可以吃。red bayberry (*Myrica rubra*); evergreen shrub or tree, with long narrow leaves and brown flowers; dioecious plant having purplish-red or white edible fruit that has granular bumps and tastes sweet and sour ❷ 这种植物的果实 fruits of this plant ❸〈方 *dial.*〉草莓 strawberry ❹〈方 *dial.*〉梅毒 syphilis

【杨梅疮】yángméichuāng〈方 *dial.*〉梅毒 syphilis

旸(暘) yáng〈书 *fml.*〉❶ 日出 sunrise ❷ 晴;晴天 fine; fine day

【旸谷】yánggǔ 古书上指日出的地方 (in ancient books) where the sun rises

飏(颺) yáng 飞扬;飘扬 be blown about by the wind; fly (about)

炀(煬) yáng〈书 *fml.*〉❶ 熔化金属 smelt (metals) ❷ 火旺 in flames; blazing

钖(鍚) yáng〈书 *fml.*〉马额上的装饰物 ornaments on a horse's forehead

佯 yáng 假装 pretend; feign; sham: ~死 feign death; play dead | ~攻 feign (or simulate) an attack; make a feint

【佯攻】yánggōng 虚张声势地进攻 feign (or simulate) attack; make a feint

【佯狂】yángkuáng〈书 *fml.*〉假装疯癫 feign madness; pretend to be insane; also 阳狂 yángkuáng

【佯言】yángyán〈书 *fml.*〉诈言;说假话 allege falsely; tell lies; lie; pretend

【佯装】yángzhuāng 假装 pretend; feign: ~惊诧 pretend to be surprised

疡(瘍) yáng ❶〈书 *fml.*〉疮 sore ❷ 溃烂 fester; ulcerate: 溃~ ulcer

垟 yáng〈方 *dial.*〉田地。多用于地名,如翁垟、黄垟(都在浙江)。land, often used in place names, e.g. Wengyang and Huangyang (both in Zhejiang Province)

徉 yáng ☞ 徜徉 chángyáng on p. 221

洋 yáng ❶ 盛大;丰富 vast; multitudinous: ~溢 be permeated with; brim with ❷ 地球表面上被水覆盖的广大地方,约占地球面积的十分之七,分成四个部分,即太平洋、大西洋、印度洋、北冰洋 ocean; vast bodies of salt water that cover seven tenths of the surface of the globe, i.e., the Pacific Ocean, Atlantic Ocean, Indian Ocean, and Arctic Ocean ❸ 外国的;外国来的 foreign: ~人 foreigner | ~货 foreign goods; imported goods ❹ 现代化的(区别于'土' as compared with 'old-fashioned') modern: ~办法 modern method | 土~结合 combine old-fashioned and modern methods ❺ 洋钱;银元 silver dollar or coin: 大~ silver dollar | 小~ silver coin | 罚~一百元 impose a fine of one hundred silver dollars

【洋白菜】yángbáicài 结球甘蓝的通称 general term for 结球甘蓝 jiéqiú gānlán

【洋布】yángbù 旧指机器织的平纹布 olden machine-woven cloth; calico

【洋财】yángcái 指跟外国做买卖得到的财物,泛指意外得到的财物 wealth obtained from trading with foreigners; unexpected large fortune; windfall: 发~ make a large fortune

【洋场】yángchǎng 指旧时洋人较多的都市,多指上海(含贬义 derog.) metropolis infested with foreign adventurers, often referring to pre-liberation Shanghai: 十里~ a ten-*li*-long street infested with foreign adventurers

【洋车】yángchē ☞ 人力车 rénlìchē ②

【洋瓷】yángcí 搪瓷 enamel

【洋葱】yángcōng ❶ 多年生草本植物,花茎细长,中空,花小,色白。地下有扁球形的鳞茎。白色或带紫红色,是普通蔬菜。onion (*Allium cepa*); herbaceous perennial with a hollow, long thin stem, small white flowers, and oblate-spherical subterranean bulbs that are white or purplish red and edible ❷ 这种植物的鳞茎 the bulb of this plant ‖ also 葱头 cōngtóu

【洋缎】yángduàn 一种棉织品,表面光洁,像缎子。主要用来做鞋帽沿条和服装衬里。foreign satin; cotton fabric as smooth as satin, mainly used to make ribbon to trim shoes and hats, and to line garments

【洋房】yángfáng 指欧美式样的房屋 foreign-style house; Western-style house

【洋橄榄】yánggǎnlǎn 油橄榄的通称 general term for 油橄榄 yóugǎnlǎn

【洋镐】yánggǎo 鹤嘴镐的通称 general term for 鹤嘴镐 hèzuǐgǎo

【洋鬼子】yángguǐ·zi〈旧时 *old*〉憎称侵略我国的西洋人 foreign devil

【洋行】yángháng〈旧时 *old*〉指外国资本家在中国开设的商行。也指专跟外国商人做买卖的商行。foreign firm; firms that specialize in trade with foreign businesspeople

【洋红】yánghóng ❶ 粉红色的颜料 crimson

pigment ❷ 较深的粉红色 carmine

【洋灰】yánghuī 水泥的俗称 popular name for 水泥 shuǐní

【洋货】yánghuò 指从外国进口的货物 foreign goods; imported goods

【洋碱】yángjiǎn〈方 *dial.*〉肥皂 soap

【洋流】yángliú 海洋中朝着一定方向流动的水 ocean current; water moving continuously in a certain direction in the ocean; also 海流 hǎiliú

【洋码子】yángmǎ·zi〈方 *dial.*〉指阿拉伯数字 Arabic numerals

【洋奴】yángnú 指崇洋媚外、甘心供外国人驱使的人 slave of a foreign master; flunkey of imperialism; worshipper of everything foreign

【洋盘】yángpán〈方 *dial.*〉对都市中普通的或时髦的事物缺乏常识、经验的人 greenhorn; one who knows little about common or fashionable things in cities

【洋气】yáng·qi ❶ 指西洋的式样、风格、习俗等 foreign flavour; Western style ❷ 带洋气的 in an ostentatious Western style: 打扮得十分～ be dressed in an ostentatious Western style; be stylishly dressed

【洋钱】yángqián 银元 silver dollar

【洋琴】yángqín same as 扬琴 yángqín

【洋人】yángrén 外国人(多指西洋人 usu. Westerner) foreigner

【洋嗓子】yángsǎng·zi 用西洋发声方法唱歌的嗓音 Western-style of singing voice

【洋纱】yángshā ❶〈旧时 *old*〉用机器纺的棉纱 machine-spun cotton yarn ❷〈旧时 *old*〉用细棉纱织成的一种平纹细布,质地轻薄,多用来做手绢、蚊帐和夏季服装等 plain cloth; calico; muslin; plain-woven sheer cotton fabric, oft. used to make handkerchiefs, mosquito nets and summer garments

【洋铁】yángtiě 镀锡铁或镀锌铁的旧称(old name for) galvanized iron; tinned iron

【洋娃娃】yángwá·wa 儿童玩具,模仿外国小孩儿的相貌、服饰做成的小人儿(Western-style) doll; figurine of a foreign child used as a child's toy

【洋文】yángwén 指外国的语言文字(多指欧美的 oft. European and American) foreign language

【洋务】yángwù ❶ 清末指关于外国的和关于模仿外国的事务(in the late Qing Dynasty) foreign affairs ❷ 香港等地指以外国人为对象的服务行业(in Hong Kong, etc.) service trades targeted at foreigners

【洋相】yángxiàng ☞ 出洋相 chū yángxiàng on p. 288

【洋洋】yángyáng ❶ 形容众多或丰盛 numerous; copious: ～万言 run to ten thousand words; very lengthy | ～大观 spectacular; grandiose; imposing ❷ same as 扬扬 yángyáng

【洋洋大观】yángyáng dà guān 形容事物繁多,丰富多彩 spectacular; grandiose; imposing

【洋洋洒洒】yángyángsǎsǎ ❶ 形容文章或谈话丰富明快,连续不断(of writing or speech) voluminous; of great length ❷ 形容规模或气势盛大 spectacular; grandiose; imposing

【洋溢】yángyì (情绪、气氛等)充分流露(of mood, atmosphere, etc.) be permeated with; brim with: 热情～ zealous | 节日的校园,～着欢乐气氛。The school was permeated with a joyous atmosphere during the holidays.

【洋油】yángyóu〈方 *dial.*〉煤油 imported oil; kerosene

【洋芋】yángyù〈方 *dial.*〉马铃薯 potato

【洋装】[1] yángzhuāng 西服 Western-style clothes

【洋装】[2] yángzhuāng 西式的装订方法,装订的线藏在书皮里面 Western-style binding, with the binding threads hidden inside the cover: ～书 book with Western-style binding

烊 yáng〈方 *dial.*〉熔化;溶化 melt; go soft ☞ yàng on p. 2225

蛘 yáng〈方 *dial.*〉(～儿 yángr)指米象一类的昆虫 rice weevil; also 蛘子 yáng·zi

yǎng (丨尤)

仰 yǎng ❶ 脸向上(跟'俯'相对 as opposed to 'bow') face upward: ～视 look up | ～望 look up | ～天大笑 laugh sardonically ❷ 敬慕 admire; respect; look up to: ～慕 admire; respect; look up to | 敬～ revere | 信～ faith, believe ❸ 依靠;依赖 rely on: ～仗 rely on; look to sb. for support | ～人鼻息 be dependent on the whims of others; be slavishly dependent ❹〈旧时 *old*〉公文用语。上行文中用在'请、祈、恳'等字之前,表示恭敬;下行文中表示命令,如'仰即遵照'。used before 请, 祈 or 恳 in old times, in submitting official documents to a superior to show respect, and in transmitting orders or requests to a subordinate: 仰即遵照。We hope that you will act accordingly at once. ❺ (Yǎng) 姓 a surname

【仰八叉】yǎng·bachā 身体向后跌倒的姿势,也泛指仰卧的姿势(fall) on one's back; lie on one's back; lie supine: 摔了个～ fall flat on one's back; also 仰八脚儿 yǎng·bajiǎor

【仰承】yǎngchéng ❶〈书 *fml.*〉依靠;依赖 rely on; count on ❷〈敬辞 *pol.*〉遵从对方的意图 in compliance with your wishes: ～意旨 in compliance with your wishes

【仰给】yǎngjǐ 仰仗别人供给 count on sb. for support: ～于人 rely on others for support

【仰角】yǎngjiǎo 视线在水平线以上时,在视线所在的垂直平面内,视线与水平线所成的角叫做仰角 angle of elevation; angle formed by the line of sight and the horizontal plane for an

object above the horizontal line

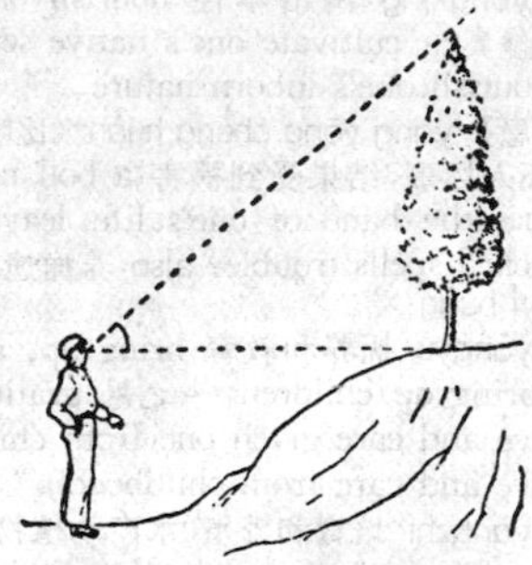

仰 角 Angle of Elevation

【仰壳】yǎngké〈方 *dial*.〉(～儿 yǎngkér) same as 仰八叉 yǎng·bachā：摔了个大～ fall flat on one's back; also 后仰壳 hòuyǎngké

【仰赖】yǎnglài 依靠 rely on：～他人 rely on others

【仰面】yǎngmiàn 脸朝上 face upward：～跌倒 fall on one's back

【仰慕】yǎngmù 敬仰思慕 admire; look up to：～已久。I've long been looking forward to meeting you.

【仰人鼻息】yǎng rén bíxī〈比喻 *fig*.〉依赖人，看人的脸色行事 be dependent on the whims of others; be slavishly dependent

【仰韶文化】Yǎngsháo wénhuà 我国黄河流域新石器时代的一种文化，因最早发现于河南渑池仰韶村而得名。遗物中常有带彩色花纹的陶器，所以也曾称为彩陶文化。Yangshao Culture; culture of the Neolithic Age in the Yellow River Valley, named after Yangshao Village, Mianchi County, Henan Province, where relics of this culture were first found; also called the Painted Pottery Culture because its relics abound in pottery painted with colourful patterns

【仰视】yǎngshì 抬起头向上看 look up：～天空 look up at the sky

【仰天】yǎngtiān 仰望天空 look up to heaven：～长叹 look up to heaven and heave a deep sigh

【仰望】yǎngwàng ❶ 抬着头向上看 look up at：～蓝天 look up at the blue sky ❷〈书 *fml*.〉敬仰而有所期望 respectfully seek guidance or help from; look up to：万众～ be admired by millions of people

【仰卧】yǎngwò 脸朝上躺着 lie on one's back; lie supine

【仰泳】yǎngyǒng 游泳的一种姿势，也是游泳项目之一。身体仰卧水面，用臂划水，用脚打水。backstroke; swimming style, and also a swimming event, where one lies back on the water's surface and uses the arms to stroke and the feet to beat the water

【仰仗】yǎngzhàng 依靠；依赖 rely on; look to sb. for support (or backing)：此事还得～诸位大力支持。We rely on your energetic support in this matter.

养(養) yǎng ❶ 供给生活资料或生活费用 support; provide for：抚～ foster | 赡～ support | ～家活口 support a family ❷ 饲养(动物)；培植(花草) raise (animals); grow (plants)：～猪 raise pigs | ～蚕 raise silkworms | ～花 grow flowers ❸ 生育 give birth to：她～了一个儿子。She gave birth to a boy. ❹ 抚养的(非亲生的) foster; adoptive：～子 adopted son | ～女 adopted daughter | ～父 foster father | ～母 foster mother ❺ 培养 form; acquire; cultivate：他从小～成了爱劳动的习惯。He has cultivated a good habit of loving physical labour. ❻ 使身心得到滋补或休息，以增进精力或恢复健康 rest; convalesce; recuperate one's health; heal：保～ take good care of one's health | 休～ recuperate | 疗～ convalesce | 营～ nutrition | ～料 nourishment | ～精蓄锐 conserve strength and store up energy ❼ 修养 accomplishment：教～ train, educate, bring up | 学～有素 well trained in learning and cultivation ❽ same as 养护 yǎnghù ①：～路 maintain a road or railway ❾ (毛发)留长；蓄起不剪 let (one's hair) grow ❿ 扶植；扶助 support; help：以农～牧，以牧促农 use agriculture to support animal husbandry, and use animal husbandry to promote agriculture

【养兵】yǎng//bīng 指供养和训练士兵 maintain an army：～千日，用兵一时。The maintenance of an army for a thousand days boils down to the use of a single battle.

【养病】yǎng//bìng 因患病而休养 take rest and nourishment to regain one's health; recuperate：安心～ ease one's mind and recuperate

【养地】yǎng//dì 采取施肥、轮作等措施提高土地肥力 increase soil fertility (through fertilization, crop rotation, etc.)

【养分】yǎngfèn 物质中所含的能供给有机体营养的成分 nutrient; something that nourishes or promotes growth of organic life

【养父】yǎngfù 指抚养自己的非生身父亲 foster father; man who gives parental care to sb. not related by blood

【养虎遗患】yǎng hǔ yí huàn〈比喻 *fig*.〉纵容敌人，给自己留下后患 to rear a tiger is to court calamity; appeasement brings disaster

【养护】yǎnghù ❶ 保养维护 maintain; conserve：～公路 maintain a highway | 加强设备～工作 strengthen the maintenance of equipment | 精心～古树名木 take good care of famous ancient trees ❷ 调养护理 curing：经过一段时间～，伤口就愈合了。After a period of curing, the wound has healed.

【养活】yǎng·huo ❶ 供给生活资料或生活费用 support; provide for: 他还要～老母亲。He has, among other things, to provide for his old mother. ❷ 饲养(动物) raise (animals): 农场今年～了上千头猪,上万只鸡。This year the farm has raised over 1,000 pigs and 10,000 chickens. ❸〈方 *dial.*〉生育 give birth to

【养家】yǎng//jiā 供给家庭成员生活所需 raise a family; support one's family: 挣钱～ earn money to support one's family | ～糊口 support one's family

【养老】yǎng//lǎo ❶ 奉养老人 provide for the aged (usu. one's parents): ～送终 look after one's parents in their old age and give them a proper burial after they die ❷ 指年老闲居休养 live out one's life in retirement: 居家～ live out one's retirement at home

【养老院】yǎnglǎoyuàn 由公家或集体办的收养孤独老人的机构 old people's home; nursing home for the elderly run by the state or collective; also 敬老院 jìnglǎoyuàn

【养廉】yǎnglián〈书 *fml.*〉培养廉洁的操守 (of government officials) nourish honesty; refrain from corruption and graft: 俭以～ nourish honesty by living a frugal life

【养料】yǎngliào 能供给有机体营养的物质 nutriment; nourishment; something that nourishes or promotes growth of organic life

【养路】yǎng//lù 养护公路或铁路 maintain a road or railway: ～工 road maintenance worker | ～费 road toll

【养母】yǎngmǔ 指抚养自己的非生身母亲 foster mother; woman who gives parental care to sb. not related by blood

【养女】yǎngnǚ 指领养的女儿 adopted daughter

【养气】yǎngqì〈书 *fml.*〉❶ 培养品德;增进涵养功夫 foster moral value (by cultivation or through a moral life) ❷〈古代 *arch.*〉道家的一种修炼方法 conserve one's vital powers (by avoiding conflict with the unchangeable laws of nature, as practised by Taoists)

【养人】yǎngrén 对人体有保养作用 nourishing: 喝粥～。Eating porridge is nourishing.

【养伤】yǎng//shāng 因受伤而休养 nurse one's injuries or wounds

【养神】yǎng//shén 保持身体和心理的平静状态,以消除疲劳 rest to attain mental tranquility; repose: 闭目～ sit in repose with one's eyes closed

【养生】yǎngshēng 保养身体 care for life; conserve one's vital powers; preserve one's health; keep in good health: ～之道 way to care for life (or conserve one's vital powers); the way to stay healthy

【养媳妇】yǎngxífù〈方 *dial.*〉童养媳 child bride; girl taken into a family as an intended daughter-in-law

【养性】yǎngxìng 陶冶本性 nourish one's nature: 修真～ cultivate one's native sensibility and nourish one's inborn nature

【养痈成患】yǎng yōng chéng huàn〈比喻 *fig.*〉姑息坏人坏事,结果受到祸害 a boil neglected becomes the bane of one's life; leaving evil unchecked spells trouble; also 养痈遗患 yǎng yōng yí huàn

【养育】yǎngyù 抚养和教育 bring up; rear: ～子女 bring up children | ～之恩 gratitude for the love and care given one from childhood; the love and care from childhood

【养殖】yǎngzhí 培育和繁殖(水产动植物) breed (aquatics): ～业 fish breeding and poultry raising; aquaculture | ～海带 cultivate kelp

【养子】yǎngzǐ 指领养的儿子 adopted son

【养尊处优】yǎng zūn chǔ yōu 生活在优裕的环境中(多含贬义 usu. derog.) enjoy high position and live in comfort; live in clover

氧 yǎng 气体元素,符号 O (oxygenium)。无色无臭无味,能助燃,化学性质很活泼。氧在空气中约占 1/5,是人和动植物呼吸所必需的气体,在工业上用途很广。oxygen (O); active combustion-supporting gaseous chemical element that is colourless, tasteless and odourless, and makes up one fifth of the atmosphere; essential gas for the respiration of human beings, animals and plants, and widely used in industry; 通称 commonly called 氧气 yǎngqì

【氧割】yǎnggē 用氧炔吹管的火焰来切割金属制品 oxyacetylene metal-cutting; cutting metallic objects with a flame from an oxyacetylene blowpipe

【氧化】yǎnghuà 指物质跟氧化合。也泛指物质在化学反应中失去电子或电子对偏离。如铁生锈、煤燃烧等。氧化和还原是伴同发生的。oxidize; oxidate; combine a substance with oxygen; increase the positive valence or decrease the negative valence of elements or ions in chemical reaction; remove an electron from an atom or an ion, as in the rusting of iron or the burning of coal; oxidation and reduction occur concurrently

【氧化剂】yǎnghuàjì 在氧化还原反应中得到电子或电子对偏近的反应物。氧化剂能氧化其他物质而自身被还原。oxidizer; oxidant; oxidizing agent; reactant that gains an electron in oxidation-reduction reactions; an oxidizer can oxidize other substances through its own reduction

【氧气】yǎngqì 氧的通称 general term for 氧 yǎng

【氧炔吹管】yǎngquē chuīguǎn 用氧和乙炔做燃料的吹管,产生的火焰温度可达 3,500℃,工业上多用来焊接和切割金属 oxyacetylene blowpipe; blowpipe using oxygen and acetylene as fuel, whose flame can reach 3,500℃, and used to weld or cut metal; ☞ 吹管 chuīguǎn on p. 307

痒(癢) yǎng 皮肤或黏膜受到轻微刺激时引起的想挠的感觉 itch; tickle; an uneasy irritating sensation on the upper surface of the skin resulting from mild stimulation of pain receptors

【痒痒】yǎng·yang 痒 itch; tickle

yàng (丨尢`)

怏 yàng ☞ below

【怏然】yàngrán ❶〈书 *fml.*〉形容不高兴的样子 unhappy: ～不悦 be discontented and unhappy ❷ 形容自大的样子 swollen with pride: ～自足 complacent

【怏怏】yàngyàng 形容不满意或不高兴的神情 disgruntled; sullen: ～不乐 unhappy about sth.; morose|～不得志 disgruntled

样(樣) yàng (～儿 yàngr) ❶ same as 样子 yàng·zi ①: ～式 form|模～ appearance, look|图～ design|新～儿的 new-style ❷ same as 样子 yàng·zi ②: 两年没见,他还是那个～儿。It's two years since I last saw him, but he still looks the same. ❸ same as 样子 yàng·zi ③: ～品 sample product|～本 sample copy|货～ sample goods|榜～ example ❹〈量词 *classifier*〉表示事物的种类 kind; type: 四～儿点心 four kinds of pastries|他的功课～～儿都好。He does well in every subject.|商店虽小,各～货物俱全。Small as it is, the shop stocks all kinds of wares. ❺ same as 样子 yàng·zi ④: 看～儿我们队今天要输。It seems that today our team is likely to lose the match.

【样板】yàngbǎn ❶ 板状的样品 sample plate; proof plate ❷ 工业或工程上指供比照或检验尺寸、形状、光洁度等用的板状工具 template; screed; a plate-shaped tool in industry or engineering used to gauge specification, shape, smoothness, etc. ❸〈比喻 *fig.*〉学习的榜样 model; prototype; example

【样本】yàngběn ❶ 商品图样的印本或剪贴纸张、织物而成的本子 sample book; book printed with samples of commodities, or book pasted with samples of paper or fabrics ❷ 出版物的作为样品的本子 sample; a copy used as a representative of a batch of publications

【样稿】yànggǎo 作为样品的部分书稿,用来征求意见或送有关的人审阅 sample manuscript; part of a manuscript used to solicit opinions, or submitted to relevant personnel for examination and evaluation

【样机】yàngjī 制造出来作为样品的机器 prototype of a machine

【样款】yàngkuǎn 样式;款式 form; pattern; type; style

【样片】yàngpiàn 摄制出来供审查的电影片或电视片 sample copy of a film or TV programme (for examination and evaluation)

【样品】yàngpǐn 做样子的物品(多用于商品推销或材料试验 oft. promotional merchandise or trial materials) sample product; sample; specimen: 服装～ sample garments

【样式】yàngshì 式样;形式 pattern; type; style; form: ～美观 beautiful design|建筑～新颖 in a novel architectural style

【样书】yàngshū 作为样品的书 sample book

【样张】yàngzhāng ❶ 印刷出来作为样品的单页、散页 specimen page ❷ 指绘有服装样式的大张纸样 pattern; large-format paper printed with patterns for tailoring: 衣服～ tailoring pattern

【样子】yàng·zi ❶ 形状 appearance; shape: 这件衣服～很好看。This garment is well cut. ❷ 人的模样或神情 manner; air: 小姑娘的～真爱人儿。This little girl has a lovable manner.|高高兴兴的～ look happy ❸ 作为标准或代表,供人看或模仿的事物 sample; model; pattern: 鞋～ shoe pattern; outline of a sole|就照这个～做。Model it after this. ❹ 形势;趋势 tendency; likelihood: 天要下雨的～。It looks like rain.|看～今天观众要超过三千人。It seems likely that today's audience will exceed 3,000.

恙 yàng〈书 *fml.*〉病 ailment; illness: 偶染微～ feel slightly indisposed ◇安然无～(没受损伤或没发生意外) safe and sound; (escape) unscathed

烊 yàng ☞ 打烊 dǎ//yàng on p. 352
☞ yáng on p. 2222

鞅 yàng ☞ 牛鞅 niúyàng on p. 1421
☞ yāng on p. 2217

漾 yàng ❶ 水面微微动荡 ripple; (of water's surface) undulate mildly: 荡～ ripple; undulate ❷ 液体太满而向外流 brim over; overflow: ～奶 throw up milk|眼里～着泪 with tears in one's eyes|这碗汤盛得太满,都～出来了。The bowl is so full that the soup is brimming over. ◇脸上～出了笑容 face brimming with smiles ❸〈方 *dial.*〉小的湖泊 lakelet; pool; pond

【漾奶】yàng//nǎi 婴儿吃过奶后吐出,多因一次吃得太多 (of a baby) throw up milk, oft. from drinking too much

yāo (丨幺)

幺(么) yāo ❶ 数目中的'1'叫'幺'(只能单用,不能组成合成数词,也不能带量词,旧时指色子和骨牌中的一点,现在说数字时也用来代表'1') one (used alone, cannot be combined with other numerals, nor be followed by a classifier); (old-time) 'one dot' on a dice or domino; (now) one (used in place of '1') ❷〈方 *dial.*〉排行最小的 the youngest: ～叔 the youngest uncle | ～妹 the youngest sister ❸〈书 *fml.*〉细;小 petty; insignificant; paltry: ～小 small | ～麽 insignificant ❹ (Yāo) 姓 a surname

么☞ 嘛 ·ma, 吗 ·ma on p. 1292 and ·me on p. 1312

【幺蛾子】yāo'ézi〈方 *dial.*〉鬼点子;坏主意 wicked idea; devilish trick: 他就会出～戏弄人。He is full of wicked ideas to tease others.

【幺麽】yāomó〈书 *fml.*〉微小 insignificant: ～小丑(指微不足道的坏人) a despicable wretch

夭[1] **(殀)** yāo 夭折 die young: ～亡 die young | 寿～(长寿与夭折;寿命长短) lifespan; duration of life

夭[2] yāo〈书 *fml.*〉形容草木茂盛 (of trees and grass) luxuriant: ～桃秾李 beautiful peach and plum blossoms; pretty girls; beautiful young ladies

【夭矫】yāojiǎo〈书 *fml.*〉屈曲而有气势 sprightly; alive; moving gracefully: ～婆娑的古柏 vibrant ancient cypress

【夭亡】yāowáng 短命 die young; short-lived; same as 夭折 yāozhé ①

【夭折】yāozhé ❶ 未成年而死 die young ❷〈比喻 *fig.*〉事情中途失败 come to a premature end

吆(吆) yāo 大声喊 cry out: ～牲口 loudly urge an animal on | ～五喝六 hubbub of gambling; arrogant

【吆喝】yāo·he 大声喊叫(多指叫卖东西、赶牲口、呼唤等) cry out; yell; hawk (oft. to urge to buy, hurry, etc.): ～牲口 loudly urge on (an animal) | 小贩沿街～。The vendor hawks his wares in the streets. | 你去～几个人来搬行李。You go and get some hands to carry the luggage.

【吆五喝六】yāo wǔ hè liù ❶ 掷色子时的喊叫声(五、六是色子的点子)。泛指赌博时的喧哗声。shout out the number when throwing dice in a gamble (five and six refer to the dots on a dice); hubbub of gambling ❷〈方 *dial.*〉形容盛气凌人的样子 arrogant: 整天～地抖威风 throw one's weight about all the time

约 yāo 用秤称 weigh on a balance (or a scale): ～一斤肉 weigh out one pound of meat | ～一～有多重。See how much it weighs.

☞ yuē on p. 2368

妖 yāo ❶ 妖怪 goblin; demon; evil spirit: ～魔 demon | ～精 evil spirit ❷ 邪恶而迷惑人的 evil and fraudulent: ～言 heresy; fallacy | ～术 sorcery | ～道 Taoist sorcerer; witchcraft | ～人 sorcerer; enchanter ❸ 装束奇特,作风不正派(多指女性 oft. female) seductive: ～里～气 be seductive; sexy ❹〈书 *fml.*〉艳丽;妩媚 bewitching; seductively charming: ～娆 enchanting; fascinating; bewitching

【妖风】yāofēng 神话中妖魔兴起的风。今比喻邪恶的风气、潮流。evil wind (in mythology); (fig.) noxious trend; pernicious tendency

【妖怪】yāo·guài 神话、传说、童话中所说形状奇怪可怕、有妖术、会害人的精灵 (in mythology, legend, fairytales) monster; bogy; goblin; demon; evil spirit that uses sorcery to harm people

【妖精】yāo·jing ❶ same as 妖怪 yāo·guài ❷〈比喻 *fig.*〉以姿色迷人的女子 seductress; siren

【妖媚】yāomèi 妩媚而不正派 seductively charming; bewitching; sexy

【妖魔】yāomó same as 妖怪 yāo·guài

【妖魔鬼怪】yāo mó guǐ guài 妖怪和魔鬼 demons and ghosts; monsters of every description;〈比喻 *fig.*〉各色各样的邪恶势力 all manner of evil forces

【妖孽】yāoniè〈书 *fml.*〉❶ 怪异不祥的事物 person or event associated with evil or misfortune ❷ 指妖魔鬼怪 monster; bogy; goblin; demon ❸〈比喻 *fig.*〉专做坏事的人 evildoer

【妖娆】yāoráo〈书 *fml.*〉娇艳美好 enchanting; fascinating; bewitching

【妖物】yāowù 妖怪一类的东西 evil spirit; monster

【妖言】yāoyán 迷惑人的邪说 heresy; fallacy: ～惑众 spread fallacies to deceive people

【妖艳】yāoyàn 艳丽而不庄重 seductive; bewitching

【妖冶】yāoyě 艳丽而不正派 seductive; bewitching

要 yāo ❶ 求 demand; ask: ～求 demand ❷ 强迫;威胁 force; coerce: ～挟 coerce; put pressure on; threaten ❸ same as 邀 yāo ❹ (Yāo) 姓 a surname

〈古 *arch.*〉same as 腰 yāo

☞ yào on p. 2233

【要功】yāogōng same as 邀功 yāogōng

【要击】yāojī same as 邀击 yāojī

【要买】yāomǎi same as 邀买 yāomǎi

【要求】yāoqiú ❶ 提出具体愿望或条件,希望得到满足或实现 ask; demand; require; claim; ask or call for something as one's right or due: ～转学 ask to transfer from one school to another | 严格～自己 set strict demands on oneself; be strict with oneself ❷ 所提出的具体愿望或条件 requirement; demand; claim: 满足了他的～ satisfied (or met) his demands | 符合规定的～ accord with prescribed requirements

Y

【要挟】yāoxié 利用对方的弱点，强迫对方答应自己的要求 coerce; put pressure on the other party; threaten; enforce; bring sb. in line by force or threat

㴘 yāo 地名用字 place name：寨子～（在山西）Zhaiziyao, name of a place in Shanxi Province

喓 yāo［喓喓］〈书 *fml.*〉虫叫的声音 cry of insects

腰 yāo ❶ 胯上胁下的部分，在身体的中部 waist; the small of the back：弯～ bend down; stoop｜两手叉～ arms akimbo; with one's hands on one's hips and one's elbows turned outward;（图见 ☞ figure for 身体 shēntǐ on p. 1701）❷ 裤腰 waist (of a garment)：红裤子绿～ red trousers with a green waist ❸ 指腰包或衣兜 pocket：我～里还有些钱，足够我们零用的。I've still got enough money in my pocket for our minor purchases. ❹ 事物的中间部分 middle：山～ halfway up the mountain; mountainside｜树～ middle of a tree trunk｜故事说到半中～就不说了。He broke off in the middle of the story. ❺ 中间狭小，像腰部的地势 waist-like topography, which is narrow in the middle：土～ isthmus｜海～ strait ❻（Yāo）姓 a surname

【腰板儿】yāobǎnr ❶ 人的腰和背（就姿势说）human back and waist (posture)：挺着～ straighten one's back ❷ 借指体格 physique; build：他虽然六十多岁了，～倒还挺硬朗的。He is well over sixty, but his physique is still quite strong.

【腰包】yāobāo 指钱包 purse; pocket：掏～ pay out of one's own pocket; foot a bill; pick sb.'s pocket

【腰缠万贯】yāo chán wàn guàn 形容人极富有 have a myriad of strings of cash tied around the waist; (fig.) be very rich

【腰带】yāodài 束腰的带子；裤带 belt; girdle

【腰杆子】yāogǎn·zi ❶ 指腰部 back：挺着～ straighten one's back, be confident and fearless ❷〈比喻 *fig.*〉靠山 backing; support：～硬（有人支持）have strong backing; also 腰杆儿 yāogǎnr

【腰鼓】yāogǔ ❶ 打击乐器，短圆柱形，两头略小，挂在腰间敲打 waist drum; cylindrical percussion instrument that tapers at both ends, and is hung on the waist ❷ 一种民间舞蹈，腰间挂着腰鼓，一边跳舞，一边敲打 waist-drum dance; folk dance where performers beat drums hung on their waists

【腰锅】yāoguō 云南景颇族、傈僳族、白族、彝族等使用的一种锅，用生铁铸成，形如葫芦 waist cauldron; gourd-shaped cauldron cast from pig iron, used by the Jingpo, Lisu, Bai, Yi, etc., peoples inhabiting Yunnan Province

【腰果】yāoguǒ ❶ 常绿乔木，叶子互生，倒卵形，花粉红色，果实肾脏形。果仁可以吃，果壳可以榨油。原产南美，我国广东等地也有栽植。cashew (*Anacardium*); evergreen tree with egg-shaped alternate leaves, pink flowers, and kidney-shaped nuts, whose kernel is edible and whose shell can be pressed to obtain oil, originally grown in South America, and now also cultivated in Guangdong Province, etc. ❷ 这种植物的果实 fruit of this plant

【腰花】yāohuā（～儿 yāohuār）作菜用的猪、羊等的腰子，多切成齿状花纹 pork, lamb, etc., kidneys for cooking, and often scalloped

【腰身】yāo·shēn 指人体腰部的粗细。也指长袍、上衣等腰部的尺寸。waistline; waist; waist measurement of a robe, coat, etc.; girth

【腰围】yāowéi ❶ 腰部周围的长度 waistline; waist measurement ❷ 束腰的宽带子 girdle

【腰眼】yāoyǎn（～儿 yāoyǎnr）❶ 腰后胯骨上面脊椎骨两侧的部位 either side of the small of the back ❷〈比喻 *fig.*〉关键 key：您这一句话算是点到～上了。This remark of yours makes the point exactly.

【腰斩】yāozhǎn ❶ 古代的酷刑，从腰部把身体斩为两段 cutting sb. in two at the waist (a form of capital punishment in ancient times) ❷〈比喻 *fig.*〉把同一事物或相联系的事物从中割断 cut sth. in half; sever

【腰椎】yāozhuī 腰部的椎骨，共有 5 块，较胸椎大 lumbar vertebra; vertebrae at the waist, five altogether, larger than the thoracic vertebrae;（图见 ☞ figure for 骨骼 gǔgé on p. 693）

【腰子】yāo·zi 肾的通称 general term for 肾 shèn

邀 yāo ❶ 邀请 invite; ask：～客 invite guests｜特～代表 specially invited representatives｜应～出席 attend a function at sb.'s invitation ❷〈书 *fml.*〉求得 solicit; seek：～准 seek approval; ask permission｜谅～同意。Your agreement is earnestly requested. ❸ 拦住 intercept：～击 intercept (the enemy); waylay

【邀宠】yāochǒng 迎合别人，求得宠爱 try to win sb.'s favour; curry favour with sb.

【邀功】yāogōng 把别人的功劳抢过来当作自己的 take credit for someone else's achievements：～请赏 take credit and seek rewards for someone else's achievements; also 要功 yāogōng

【邀击】yāojī 在敌人行进中途加以攻击 intercept (the enemy); waylay; also 要击 yāojī

【邀集】yāojí 把较多的人邀请到一起 invite (many people) to meet together; call (people) together：～同学成立了一个读书会 call schoolmates together to establish a reading club

【邀买】yāomǎi 收买 buy (popularity)：～人心 buy popular support; court popularity; also 要买 yāomǎi

【邀请】yāoqǐng 请人到自己的地方来或到约定的地方去 invite; request (sb.) to be present or participate

【邀请赛】yāoqǐngsài 由一个单位或几个单位联合发出邀请,有许多单位参加的体育比赛 invitational tournament; sports competition joined by many teams at the invitation of one or several sponsors

【邀约】yāoyuē 约请 invite; send an invitation to: 盛情～ warmly invite | ～友人 invite friends

yáo (丨幺ˊ)

爻 yáo 组成八卦的长短横道,'—'为阳爻,'- -'为阴爻 lines in the Eight Trigrams, where the solid line represents positive, and the broken line represents negative

尧(堯) Yáo ❶ 传说中上古帝王名 Emperor Yao, legendary sage-king in remote antiquity ❷ 姓 a surname

【尧舜】Yáo-Shùn 尧和舜,传说是上古的贤明君主。后来泛指圣人。Emperor Yao and Emperor Shun, legendary sage-kings in remote antiquity; ancient sages

【尧天舜日】Yáo tiān Shùn rì〈比喻 *fig.*〉太平盛世 the days of Yao and Shun; golden age; age of prosperity and peace

侥(僥) yáo ☞ 僬侥 jiāoyáo on p. 973
☞ jiǎo on p. 975

肴(餚) yáo 鱼肉等荤菜 meat and fish dishes: 菜～ cooked dishes | 酒～ wine and delicacies

【肴馔】yáozhuàn〈书 *fml.*〉宴席上的或比较丰盛的菜和饭 sumptuous courses at a meal or a banquet

垚 yáo〈书 *fml.*〉山高。多用于人名。mountain high, oft. used in a person's name

轺 yáo〈书 *fml.*〉轺车 light horse-drawn carriage: 乘～行于湖边 travel along the lakeshore by a light horse-drawn carriage

【轺车】yáochē〈古代 *arch.*〉一种轻便的车 light horse-drawn carriage

峣(嶢) yáo〈书 *fml.*〉形容高峻 high; lofty

姚 Yáo 姓 a surname

珧 yáo 蚌、蛤的甲壳,古时用做刀、弓等上的装饰物 pen shell, used as ornaments on knives and bows in ancient times

陶 yáo 皋陶(Gāoyáo),上古人名 Gaoyao, name of person of remote antiquity
☞ táo on p. 1871

铫 yáo ❶ 古代的一种大锄 large hoe (in ancient times) ❷ (Yáo)姓。铫期,东汉人。Yao, a surname; Yao Qi, a person in the Eastern Han Dynasty
☞ diào on p. 450

窑(窰、窯) yáo ❶ 烧制砖瓦陶瓷等物的建筑物 kiln; oven, furnace or heated enclosure used for processing bricks, tiles or ceramics, by burning, firing or drying: 砖～ brick kiln | 石灰～ lime kiln ❷ 指土法生产的煤矿 coal pit that mines coal using old-fashioned methods: 煤～ coal pit ❸ 窑洞 cave dwelling ❹〈方 *dial.*〉指妓院 brothel: ～姐儿 prostitute

【窑变】yáobiàn 指烧制陶瓷时,因坯体所涂不同釉浆互相渗透变化,釉面出现意外的特异颜色和花样 furnace transmutation; kiln transformation; unexpected special colours and designs appearing on ceramic caused by the interactions of different glazes in the process of being fired in a kiln

【窑洞】yáodòng 我国西北黄土高原地区就土山的山崖挖成的洞,供人居住 cave dwelling; dwelling dug out of an earthen hill on the Loess Plateau of northwest China

【窑姐儿】yáojiěr〈方 *dial.*〉妓女 prostitute

【窑坑】yáokēng 为取土制砖瓦等而挖成的坑 pit left after earth is dug out for making bricks or tiles

【窑子】yáo·zi〈方 *dial.*〉妓院 brothel

谣 yáo ❶ 歌谣 ballad; rhyme: 民～ folk rhymes | 童～ children's folk rhymes ❷ 谣言 rumour: ～传 rumour; hearsay | 造～ start a rumour

【谣传】yáochuán ❶ 谣言传播 it is rumoured that; rumour has it that: ～他出事了。It is rumoured that he met with a mishap. ❷ 传播的谣言 rumour; hearsay: 听信～ believe rumours

【谣言】yáoyán 没有事实根据的消息 rumour; unfounded report; groundless allegation: 散布～ spread (or circulate) rumours | 不要轻信～。Give no credence to rumours.

【谣诼】yáozhuó〈书 *fml.*〉造谣诬蔑的话 slander; calumny

摇 yáo 摇摆;使物体来回地动 shake; wave; rock; turn: 动～ waver | ～晃 rock; sway; shake | ～手 wave hands | ～铃 ring a bell | ～橹 scull | ～纺车 turn a spinning wheel

【摇摆】yáobǎi 向相反的方向来回地移动或变动 sway; swing; rock; vacillate; move back and forth: 池塘里的荷叶迎风～。Lotus leaves in the pond swayed in the breeze.

【摇车】yáochē〈方 *dial.*〉❶ (～儿 yáochēr)小孩用的睡车;摇篮 cradle; a bed or a cot for a baby, often on rockers or pivots ❷ 旧式纺纱用的器具 old-style spinning wheel

【摇唇鼓舌】yáo chún gǔ shé 指利用口才进行煽动、游说或大发议论(含贬义 derog.) flap one's lips and beat one's tongue; wag one's tongue; have a loose tongue; engage in loose talk (to stir up trouble)

【摇荡】yáodàng 摇摆动荡 rock; sway: 小船随波～。The small boat rocked along with the tide.

【摇动】yáo//dòng 摇东西使它动 shake; wave: 摇得动 shakeable|摇不动 unshakeable|用力～木桩 exert oneself to shake the woodpile

【摇动】yáodòng ❶ same as 摇摆 yáobǎi: 柳枝在水面上～。Willow twigs swayed over the surface of the water. ❷ 动摇 waver: 人心～ popular anxiety|信念从未～。There has never been any wavering in his conviction.

【摇鹅毛扇】yáo émáoshàn 旧小说戏曲描写的军师、谋士多手拿羽毛扇。后来用'摇鹅毛扇'比喻背后出谋划策。wave a goose-feather fan; (fig.) mastermind a plot behind the scenes; give counsel (in old novels and dramas, a military adviser oft. holds a goose-feather fan)

【摇滚乐】yáogǔnyuè 西方流行的一种音乐,由称为布鲁斯的爵士乐演变而来,音响丰富,节奏强烈 rock and roll; rock (music); Western popular music developed from Jazz, or blues, played on electronically amplified instruments and characterized by a persistent heavily stressed beat, much repetition of simple phrases, and often with country, folk and blues elements

【摇撼】yáo·hàn 摇动(树木、建筑物等) give a violent shake to (a tree, building, etc.); shake to the roots or foundation; rock

【摇晃】yáo·huàng same as 摇摆 yáobǎi: 灯光～ flickering light|摇摇晃晃地走着 walk with faltering steps

【摇惑】yáohuò ❶ 动摇迷惑 waver and confuse: 人心～ popular anxiety ❷ 使动摇迷惑 resort to demagoguery: ～人心 resort to demagoguery|～视听 confuse public opinion

【摇篮】yáolán ❶ 供婴儿睡的家具,形状略像篮子,多用竹或藤制成,可以左右摇动,使婴儿容易入睡 cradle; basket-like device for a baby to sleep, often made of bamboo or rattan, that can be rocked to help a baby fall asleep ❷〈比喻 *fig.*〉幼年或青年时代的生活环境或文化、运动等的发源地 cradle; living environment of one's childhood or youth; place where a culture or movement begins or is nurtured: 井冈山是中国革命的～。The Jinggang Mountains is the cradle of the Chinese revolution.|黄河流域是我国古代文化的～。The Yellow River Valley is the cradle of ancient Chinese culture.

【摇篮曲】yáolánqǔ 催婴儿入睡时唱的小歌曲,以及由此发展而成的形式简单的声乐曲或器乐曲 cradlesong; lullaby; *berceuse*; soothing songs to lull a baby to sleep, and the simple vocal or instrumental music developed from these songs

【摇耧】yáo//lóu 用耧播种时,扶耧的人不断摇晃耧把,使种子均匀地漏下 rock a drill barrow in sowing; sow with a drill barrow

【摇蜜】yáo//mì 把削去盖的蜂房放在特制的装置中转动,利用离心力使蜂蜜从蜂房中分离出来 extract honey; put wax cells of a honeycomb into a special revolving device, to separate out the honey using centrifugal force

【摇旗呐喊】yáo qí nà hǎn ❶〈古代 *arch.*〉打仗的时候,后面的人摇着旗子呐喊,给前面作战的人助威 wave flags and shout battle cries (to boost the morale of fighters) ❷〈比喻 *fig.*〉替别人助长声势 bang the drum for others

【摇钱树】yáoqiánshù 神话中的一种宝树,一摇晃就有许多钱落下来。后来多用来比喻借以获取钱财的人或物。legendary tree that sheds coins when shaken; (oft. fig.) ready source of money

【摇身一变】yáo shēn yī biàn 神怪小说中描写人物或妖怪一晃身就变成别的形体。现指坏人改换面目出现。(in mythology) give oneself a shake and change into another form; (derog.) suddenly change one's identity

【摇手】yáo//shǒu 把手左右摇动,表示阻止或否定 shake one's hand in admonition or disapproval

【摇手】yáoshǒu 机械上用手旋转的、使轮子等转动的把儿 handle on a machine (for turning a wheel, etc.)

【摇头】yáo//tóu 把头左右摇动,表示否定、不以为然或阻止 shake one's head, in admonition, disagreement or disapproval

【摇头摆尾】yáo tóu bǎi wěi 形容得意或轻狂的样子 shake the head and wag the tail; assume an air of complacency or levity

【摇头晃脑】yáo tóu huàng nǎo 形容自得其乐或自以为是的样子 wag one's head; look pleased with oneself; assume an air of self-approbation or self-satisfaction

【摇尾乞怜】yáo wěi qǐ lián 狗对主人的姿态,形容用谄媚姿态求取别人的欢心 (of dogs) wag the tail ingratiatingly; (fig.) fawn obsequiously

【摇摇欲坠】yáoyáo yù zhuì 形容非常危险,就要掉下来或垮下来 tottering; crumbling; on the verge of collapse

【摇曳】yáoyè 摇荡 flicker; sway: ～的灯光 flickering light|垂柳～ swaying willow branches

【摇椅】yáoyǐ 一种能够前后摇晃的椅子,构造的特点是前腿儿和后腿儿连成弓形,弓背着地,供休息时坐 rocking chair; chair mounted on rockers, on which one can sit and rock to relax or rest

徭(傜) yáo 劳役 corvée; conscript labour

【徭役】yáoyì〈古时 *arch.*〉统治者强制人民承担的无偿劳动 corvée; conscript labour imposed on the people by rulers

遥 yáo 遥远 distant; remote; far: ～望 look into the distance | 千里之～ at a distance of a thousand *li*; a thousand *li* away | 路～知马力。Distance tests a horse's strength.

【遥测】yáocè 运用现代化的电子、光学仪器对远距离的事物进行测量 telemetering; use modern electronic or optical instruments to measure quantities of remote objects

【遥感】yáogǎn 使用空间运载工具和现代化的电子、光学仪器探测和识别远距离的研究对象 remote sensing; use space carriers and modern electronic or optical instruments to explore and identify remote targets for research

【遥控】yáokòng 通过有线或无线电路的装备操纵一定距离以外的机器、仪器等。遥控广泛应用在操纵水电站、飞机、飞行武器和自动化生产等方面。remote control; telecontrol; control a remote machine or instrument through wire or wireless radio, widely applied in the control of hydroelectric stations, aircraft, missiles, automated production, etc.

【遥望】yáowàng 往远处望 look into the distance: ～天边,红霞烂漫。Look at the horizon, where the rosy clouds shine brilliantly.

【遥相呼应】yáo xiāng hūyìng 远远地互相配合 echo each other at a distance; coordinate with each other from afar

【遥想】yáoxiǎng 想像(久远的将来);回想(久远的过去) imagine; fancy; visualize (the remote future); recall; recollect; reminisce: ～未来 predict the remote future | ～当年 recall the good old days

【遥遥】yáoyáo ❶ 形容距离远 far away; a long way off: ～相对 stand far apart facing each other | ～领先 be far ahead; hold a safe lead ❷ 形容时间长久 for a long time: ～无期 not realisable within the foreseeable future

【遥远】yáoyuǎn 很远 distant; remote; faraway: 路途～ a long journey; a long way to go | ～的将来 distant (or remote) future

猺 yáo ☞ 黄猺 huángyáo on p. 854 and 青猺 qīngyáo on p. 1564

瑶 yáo〈书 *fml*.〉❶ 美玉 precious jade; jasper: 琼～ precious jade | ～琴(镶有玉饰的琴) lute with jasper mountings ❷ 形容美好、珍贵 fine; precious: ～浆(美酒) fine delicious wine

【瑶池】Yáochí 神话中称西王母所住的地方 Emerald Lake (dwelling-place of the Queen Mother of the West)

【瑶族】Yáozú 我国少数民族之一,分布在广西、湖南、云南、广东和贵州 Yao people, or the Yaos, one of China's ethnic minority peoples inhabiting the Guangxi Zhuang Autonomous Region, and Hunan, Yunnan, Guangdong and Guizhou provinces

飖 yáo ☞ 飘飖 piāoyáo on p. 1476

繇 yáo〈书 *fml*.〉❶ same as 徭 yáo ❷ same as 谣 yáo

☞ yóu on p. 2325 and zhòu on p. 2498

鳐 yáo 鱼类的一科,身体扁平,略呈圆形或菱形,表面光滑或有小刺,口小,牙细小而多。生活在海中。skate (*Raja batis L.*); ray; a family of marine fish having a round or dorsoventrally flat body, whose surface is smooth or has small spikes, and a small mouth with many fine teeth

yǎo (ㄧㄠˇ)

杳 yǎo〈书 *fml*.〉远得不见踪影 distant and out of sight: ～然 disappear | ～无音信 there has been no news whatsoever (about somebody); never been heard of since | ～无踪迹 disappear without a trace; vanish

【杳渺】yǎomiǎo〈书 *fml*.〉形容遥远或深远 distant and indistinct; also 杳眇 yǎomiǎo

【杳然】yǎorán〈书 *fml*.〉形容沉寂或不见踪影 quiet; still; disappeared: 音信～ never been heard of since

【杳如黄鹤】yǎo rú huánghè 唐代崔颢《黄鹤楼》诗:'黄鹤一去不复返,白云千载空悠悠。'后来用'杳如黄鹤'比喻人或物下落不明。leave like the yellow crane; (fig.) leave never to return; be gone for ever. *Yellow Crane Tower* by the Tang-dynasty poet Cui Hao: 'The yellow crane, once gone, will never again come, /But white clouds of a thousand years go aimlessly on and on.'

咬(齩、鱙) yǎo ❶ 上下牙齿用力对着(大多为了夹物体或使物体的一部分从整体分离 mostly to catch things or tear a part off a whole being) bite; snap at; seize, pierce or cut with teeth: ～紧牙关 grit (or clench) one's teeth; endure with dogged determination | 用嘴～住绳子 grip the rope with one's mouth | 让蛇～了一口 be bitten by a snake | ～了一口苹果。(He) took a bite of an apple. ❷ 钳子等夹住或齿轮、螺丝等互相卡住 (of gears, screws, etc.) bite; catch; (of pincers) grip: 螺丝母勚(yì)了,～不住。The nut is worn and won't catch. ❸ (狗)叫 (of dogs) bark: 鸡叫狗～ cocks crow and dogs bark ❹ 受责难或审讯时牵扯别人(多指无辜的) incriminate sb. (oft. innocent) when blamed or interrogated: 反～一口 trump up a countercharge against one's accuser ❺〈方 *dial*.〉油漆等使皮肤、衣物损伤 corrode (metals); irritate (the skin): 碱水把铝盆～坏了。Alkaline water has corroded the aluminum basin. | 我最怕漆～。I'm allergic to paint. ❻ 正确地念出(字的音);过分地计较(字句的意义) pronounce; articulate; be nitpicking (about the use of words): ～字 articulate | ～

字眼儿 be nitpicking over words｜～文嚼字 pay excessive attention to wording ❼ 追赶进逼；紧跟不放 close in on；advance on；press on towards：双方比分～得很紧。The score was very close throughout the match.｜火炮始终～住目标。The cannons are closing in on the targets.

【咬定】yǎodìng 说了就不改口，指话说得十分肯定 assert emphatically；insist：一口～ assert positively；state categorically

【咬耳朵】yǎo ěr·duo 凑近人耳边低声说话，不使别人听见 whisper in sb.'s ear；whisper (so as not to let others hear)

【咬群】yǎoqún ❶ 某个家畜常跟同类争斗 (of a domestic animal) be prone to fight within the herd ❷〈比喻 *fig.*〉某个人常跟周围的人闹纠纷 (of a person) be apt to pick a quarrel within a group

【咬舌儿】yǎoshér ❶ 说话时舌尖常接触牙齿，因而发音不清 lisp；utter falteringly ❷ 说话咬舌儿的人 lisper；also 咬舌子 yǎoshézi

【咬文嚼字】yǎo wén jiáo zì 过分地斟酌字句(多用来指死抠字眼儿而不领会精神实质) pay excessive attention to wording (oft. in finding fault with the choice of words rather than understanding the essence of the matter)

【咬牙】yǎo//yá ❶ 由于极端愤怒或忍住极大的痛苦而咬紧牙齿 grit (or set, clench, gnash) one's teeth (in hatred or pain)：恨得直～ gnash one's teeth in hatred｜～忍痛 grit one's teeth in pain ❷ 熟睡时上下牙齿相磨发声，由消化不良等原因引起 grind one's teeth (in sleep, caused by indigestion, etc.)

【咬牙切齿】yǎo yá qiè chǐ 形容极端愤恨或仇视 gnash one's teeth in rage or in hatred

【咬字儿】yǎozìr 按照正确的或传统的音念出文章或唱出歌词、戏词中的字 pronounce；articulate；utter every word distinctly while reading an article or singing a song：～清楚。(Her) pronunciation is clear.

【咬字眼儿】yǎo zìyǎnr 在措辞方面挑毛病(多指对别人说的话 usu. of sb. else) be nitpicking over words

舀 yǎo 用瓢、勺等取东西(多指液体 oft. liquid) ladle out；spoon up (or out)：～一瓢水 scoop up a ladle of water

【舀子】yǎo·zi 舀水、油等液体用的器具，底平，口圆，有柄，多用铝或铁皮制成 dipper；ladle；scoop；handled container with a flat bottom and round mouth for fetching water, oil or other liquids, often made of aluminum or other sheet metal；also 舀儿 yǎor

窅 yǎo〈书 *fml.*〉形容深远 far and deep

窈 yǎo〈书 *fml.*〉❶ 深远 far and deep ❷ 昏暗 remote and obscure

【窈窕】yǎotiǎo〈书 *fml.*〉❶ (女子)文静而美好；(妆饰、仪容)美好 (of a woman) milling-willing；sweet and fair；chaste and modest；graceful；(of adornment, looks) beautiful ❷ (宫室、山水)幽深 (of palaces, landscapes, etc.) secluded

yào (丨幺)

疟(瘧) yào 义同'疟'(nüè)，只用于'疟子' same as 疟 nüè in meaning, used only in 疟子 yào·zi (malaria)

☞ nüè on p.1429

【疟子】yào·zi 疟疾 malaria：发～ have an attack of malaria；suffer from malarial fever

药(藥) yào ❶ 药物 medicine；drug；remedy ❷ 某些有化学作用的物质 certain chemicals：火～ gunpowder｜炸～ explosive (charges)；dynamite｜焊～ flux ❸〈书 *fml.*〉用药治疗 cure with medicine：不可救～ incurable；incorrigible；hopeless ❹ 用药毒死 kill with poison：～老鼠 kill rats with poison｜～虫子 kill insects with pesticide

【药材】yàocái 指中药的原料或饮片 medicinal materials；crude drugs

【药草】yàocǎo 用做药物的草本植物 medicinal herbs

【药叉】yàochā ☞ 夜叉 yè·chā on p.2240

【药典】yàodiǎn 国家法定的记载药物的名称、性质、形状、成分、用量以及配制、贮藏方法等的书籍 pharmacopoeia；a book describing the names, properties, appearance, ingredients, dosage, storage and preparation of drugs and chemicals, issued by an officially recognised authority and serving as a standard

【药店】yàodiàn 出售药品的商店；药铺 drugstore；pharmacy；chemist's shop；apothecary (old)

【药方】yàofāng (～儿 yàofāngr) ❶ 为治疗某种疾病而组合起来的若干种药物的名称、剂量和用法 prescription；written instruction for a therapeutic or corrective agent, especially one for the preparation and use of a medicine：开～ write out a prescription ❷ 写着药方的纸 recipe；a paper with a written prescription

【药房】yàofáng ❶ 出售西药的商店，有的能调剂配方，有的兼售中药的成药 drugstore；pharmacy；chemist's shop；apothecary (old) ❷ 医院或诊疗所里供应药物的部门 hospital pharmacy；dispensary

【药粉】yàofěn 粉末状的药 medicinal powder

【药膏】yàogāo 膏状的外敷药 ointment；salve

【药罐子】yàoguàn·zi ❶ 熬中药用的罐子 pot for decocting herbal medicine ❷〈比喻 *fig.*〉经常生病吃药的人(含嘲笑意 satirical) chronic invalid

【药衡】yàohéng 英美重量制度，用于药物（区别于'常衡、金衡' as compared with 'avoirdupois weight' and 'troy weight'）apothecaries' measure or weight

【药剂】yàojì 据药典或处方配成的制剂 medicament; drug prepared according to pharmacopoeia or prescription

【药检】yàojiǎn ❶ 对药品的质量进行化验检查 drug inspection; inspection on the quality of drugs ❷ 对参加体育比赛的运动员进行是否服用违禁药物的检测 drug test; testing of an athlete to see whether he or she has taken contraband drugs

【药酒】yàojiǔ 用药材浸制的酒 medicinal liquor

【药理】yàolǐ 药物在机体内所起的变化、对机体的影响及其防治疾病的原理 pharmacology; pharmacodynamics; science dealing with the reactions between drugs and living organisms; the properties and reactions of drugs with relation to their therapeutic value

【药力】yàolì 药物的效力 efficacy of a drug (or medicine)

【药棉】yàomián 医疗上用的消过毒的脱脂棉 absorbent cotton; sterilized cotton used in medical treatment

【药面】yàomiàn (～儿 yàomiànr) same as 药粉 yàofěn

【药捻儿】yàoniǎnr ❶ 用来点燃火药、爆竹的引线 fuse (for igniting an explosive charge or firecracker) ❷ same as 药捻子 yàoniǎn·zi

【药捻子】yàoniǎn·zi 带药的纸捻或纱布条,外科治疗时用来放入伤口或疮口内 slender roll of medicated paper or gauze (to be applied on wounds, boils, etc.)

【药农】yàonóng 以种植或采集药用植物为主的农民 peasant who cultivates or collects medicinal herbs as a major occupation; medicinal herb grower or gatherer; herbalist

【药片】yàopiàn (～儿 yàopiànr) 片状的制剂 (medicinal) tablet

【药品】yàopǐn 药物和化学试剂的总称 (general term for) medicines and chemical reagents

【药铺】yàopù 出售中药的商店,主要按中医药方配药,有的兼售西药 herbal medicine shop; apothecary; shop mainly selling herbal medicines, sometimes also Western medicine as a sideline

【药膳】yàoshàn 配有中药的菜肴或食品,如参芪鸡、虫草鸭、银耳羹等 medicated food; medicinal dishes; food cooked with medicinal herbs, e.g. chicken stewed with ginseng and astragalus, duck stewed with Chinese caterpillar fungi, white jelly-fungus soup, etc.

【药石】yàoshí 〈古时 *arch.*〉指药和治病的石针 medicines and stone acupuncture needles; remedies: ～罔效 All medical treatment has failed. ◇～之言(劝人改过的话) unpalatable but salutary advice

【药水】yàoshuǐ (～儿 yàoshuǐr)液态的药 liquid medicine; medicinal liquid; lotion

【药筒】yàotǒng 枪弹或炮弹后部装发射火药的圆筒,多用金属制成 shell case; cartridge case; cylindrical case, most made of metal, at the end of a bullet or shell containing explosive charges; 通称 commonly called 弹壳 dànké

【药丸】yàowán (～儿 yàowánr)制成丸状的药物 pill; bolus; medicine in a wax ball; also 药丸子 yàowán·zi

【药味】yàowèi ❶ 中药方中的药(总称) herbal medicines in a prescription (collect.) ❷ (～儿 yàowèir)药的气味或味道 smell or taste of a drug

【药物】yàowù 能防治疾病、病虫害等的物质 pharmaceuticals; materia medica; medicines; drugs; medicaments

【药械】yàoxiè 农业、林业等施药用的器械,如喷雾器、喷粉器等 insecticide-application devices (used in agriculture, forestry, etc., e.g. sprayer, duster)

【药性】yàoxìng 药的性质 properties of a medicine: ～平和 the medicinal properties are quite mild

【药性气】yào·xing·qi 药的气味 the flavour of medicinal decoctions

【药引子】yàoyǐn·zi 中药药剂中另加的一些药物,能加强药剂的效力 an ingredient added to enhance the efficacy of a dose of medicine; a medicinal supplement

【药皂】yàozào 用脂肪酸盐和石炭酸、来苏等化学药品制成的肥皂,略有消毒作用 medicated soap; soap containing chemicals such as fatty acid salt, carbolic acid, lysol, etc., as slight disinfectants

【药疹】yàozhěn 由药物引起的皮疹。长期大量使用某种药物,或患者对某种药品过敏,都会引起药诊。drug rash; drug eruption; reaction caused by long-term usage of certain drugs, or allergy to certain drugs

要1 yào ❶ 重要 important; essential: 主～ principal; major | 紧～ critical; crucial; vital | 险～ strategically located and difficult to access | ～事 important matter | ～点 main points; essentials; gist ❷ 重要的内容 main points; essentials: 纲～ outline; sketch | 摘～ summary; abstract; precis | 提～ summary; synopsis; precis | 择～记录 note down the essential points

要2 yào ❶ 希望得到;希望保持 want; wish to keep; desire: 他～一个口琴。He wants a harmonica. | 这本书我还～呢! I want to keep this book. ❷ 因为希望得到或收回而有所表示;索取 demand; claim: ～账 demand repayment of a debt | 小弟弟跟姐姐～钢笔用。The younger brother asked his elder sister for permission to use her pen. ❸ 请求 ask for: 她～我替她写信。She asked me to write a letter for her. ❹ 表示做某件事的意志 want to; wish to: 他～学游泳。He wants to learn to swim. ❺ 须要;应该 must; should; it is necessary (or imperative, essential)：路很滑，大家～小心！The road is slippery, be careful, everybody! |早点儿睡吧，明天还～起早呢！Let's go to bed now, since we have to get up early tomorrow morning. ❻ 需要 need; take：我做件上衣～多少布？How much cloth do I need to make a jacket? |由北京到天津坐汽车～两个小时。It takes two hours to travel from Beijing to Tianjin by bus. ❼ 将要 will; be going to：我们～参加劳动竞赛了。We are going to take part in a labour competition. |～下雨了。It's going to rain. ❽ 表示估计，用于比较[used in comparisons to indicate an estimate]：夏天屋子里太热，树阴底下～凉快得多。In summer, it is much cooler under a tree than inside the room.

要[3] yào〈连词 *conj.*〉❶ 如果 if; suppose; in case：明天～下雨，我就不去了。If it rains tomorrow, I won't go. ❷ 要么 or; either ... or ...：～就去打球，～就去溜冰，别再犹豫了。Let's go either to play ball or to skate. Don't be so indecisive.

☞ yāo on p. 2226

【要隘】yào'ài 险要的关口 strategic pass：扼守～ hold the strategic pass

【要案】yào'àn 重要的案件 important case

【要不】yàobù〈连词 *conj.*〉❶ 不然；否则 otherwise; or else; or：从上海到武汉，可以搭长江轮船，～绕道坐火车也行。From Shanghai to Wuhan, one may go by boat on the Yangtze River, or make a detour by train. ❷ same as 要么 yào·me：今天的会得去一个人，～你去，～我去。In any case one person must attend today's meeting, so either you go or I go. also 要不然 yàobùrán

【要不得】yào·bu·de 表示人或事物不好，不能同意或容忍 be no good; be intolerable：你这种想法～。An idea such as yours cannot be tolerated.

【要冲】yàochōng 全国的或某一个地区的重要道路会合的地方 communications centre (or hub) of a country or region：兰州向来是西北交通的～。Lanzhou has always been the communications hub of northwestern China.

【要道】yàodào ❶ 重要的道路 thoroughfare; main road：交通～ important transportation line; vital communications line ❷ 重要的道理、方法 important ways or methods

【要得】yàodé〈方 *dial.*〉好 good; fine; desirable(用来表示同意或赞美 used to express agreement or praise)：这个计划～，我们就这样办。That's a good plan, so let's just do it that way.

【要地】yàodì ❶ 重要的地方(多指军事上的 oft. military) important place; strategic point：徐州是历史上的军事～。Xuzhou has been well known in history as a hotly contested strategic point. ❷〈书 *fml.*〉显要的地位 important position：身处～ hold an important post

【要点】yàodiǎn ❶ 话或文章等的主要内容(of a speech or article) main points; essentials; gist：摘录～ make extracts of the main points |抓住～ grasp the main points ❷ 重要的据点 key strongpoint：战略～ strategic point

【要端】yàoduān 重要的事项 essentials; same as 要点 yàodiǎn ①：举其～ list its (or the) essentials

【要犯】yàofàn 重要的罪犯 important or principal criminal

【要饭】yào//fàn 向人乞求饭食或财物 beg (for food or money)：～的(乞丐) beggar

【要害】yàohài ❶ 身体上能致命的部位 vital part; crucial point：一拳击中～ hit the vital part with one blow◇一句话点到～。Make the crucial point in one sentence. ❷〈比喻 *fig.*〉重要的部分或军事上重要的地点 key part; strategic point：～部门 key department| 地处～ be located at a strategic point

【要好】yàohǎo ❶ 指感情融洽；也指对人表示好感，愿意亲近 be on good terms; be close friends：她们两人从小就很～。The two of them have been close friends since childhood. ❷ 努力求好；要求上进 be eager to improve oneself; try hard to make progress：这孩子很～，从来不肯无故耽误功课。This child is eager to make progress, and never misses a class without reason.

【要好看】yào hǎokàn (～儿 yào hǎokànr) 使出丑 embarrass：要我当众表演，简直是要我的好看儿。Making me perform in public is simply asking me to make a fool of myself.

【要谎】yào//huǎng 向顾客要价超过实价叫要谎 (of a seller) ask an exorbitant price

【要价】yào//jià ❶ (～儿 yào//jiàr)做买卖的人向顾客说出货物的售价 ask a price; charge：漫天～，就地还钱。The seller can charge any way he wants, and the buyer can make a down-to-earth offer. *or* The price asked is as high as heaven, and the offer as low as the earth. ❷〈比喻 *fig.*〉谈判或接受某项任务时向对方提出条件 demand conditions of the other party in negotiating or accepting a task

【要价还价】yào jià huán jià ☞ 讨价还价 tǎo jià huán jià on p. 1872

【要件】yàojiàn ❶ 重要的文件 an important document ❷ 重要的条件 an important condition

【要津】yàojīn ❶ 冲要的渡口。泛指水陆交通要道。strategically important ferry crossing; (gen.) key land and water hub ❷〈比喻 *fig.*〉显要的地位 key post：位居～ hold a key post

【要紧】yàojǐn ❶ 重要 vital; important; essential：这段河堤～得很，一定要加强防护。This section of the riverbank is very important, and we must reinforce and protect its embankments. ❷ 严重 be critical; be serious; matter: 他只受了点儿轻伤,不～。He was only slightly injured, nothing serious. ❸〈方 *dial.*〉急着(做某件事) be in a hurry to; be anxious to (do sth.): 我～进城,来不及和他细说。I was in a hurry to go to town, so there was no time to tell him in detail.

【要诀】yàojué 重要的诀窍 important tricks of the trade; knack

【要领】yàolǐng ❶ same as 要点 yàodiǎn ①: 不得～ fail to grasp the main point; not see what sb. is driving at ❷ 体育和军事操练中某项动作的基本要求 essentials (of a military or athletic exercise): 掌握～ grasp the essentials

【要略】yàolüè 阐述要旨的概说 outline; summary (多用于书名 oft. used in book titles): 《中国文法～》*Outline of Chinese Grammar*

【要么】yào·me〈连词 *conj.*〉表示两种情况或两种意愿的选择关系 or; either ... or ... (to show choice between two conditions or two desires): 你赶快拍个电报通知他,～打个长途电话。Send him a telegram at once, or call him long-distance. |～他来,～我去,明天总得当面谈一谈。Either he comes here or I go there; in any case we've got to talk face to face tomorrow. also 要末 yào·me

【要面子】yào miàn·zi 爱面子 be keen on face-saving; be anxious to keep up appearances

【要命】yào//mìng ❶ 使丧失生命 drive sb. to his death; kill: 一场重病,差点儿要了命 almost died of a serious illness ❷ 表示程度达到极点 confoundedly; extremely; awfully; terribly: 痒得～ itch terribly | 好得～ very good ❸ 给人造成严重困难 nuisance (着急或抱怨时说 used when one is anxious or complaining): 这人真～,火车都快开了,他还不来。That man is quite impossible. The train is leaving any minute and there's still no sign of him.

【要目】yàomù 重要的条目或篇目 important clauses or contents: 图书～ Bibliography | 本报今日～ Main Items of This Issue

【要强】yàoqiáng 好胜心强,不肯落在别人后面 be eager to excel; be anxious to outdo others

【要人】yàorén 指有权势有地位的人物 very important person (VIP); important personage

【要塞】yàosài 在军事上有重要意义的、有巩固的防御设备的据点 fort; fortress; fortification; strategically important stronghold equipped with defense works

【要事】yàoshì 重要的事情 important matter: 有～相商 have something important to consult about

【要是】yào·shi 如果;如果是 if; suppose; in case: ～你想参加,我可以当介绍人。If you want to join, I can serve as your sponsor. | 这事～叫他知道了,一定会发生争吵。Once he gets wind of this, there would be a quarrel.

【要死】yàosǐ 表示程度达到极点 extremely; awfully; terribly: 疼得～ ache terribly | 怕得～ be scared to death | 这菜咸得～。The dish tastes awfully salty.

【要素】yàosù 构成事物的必要因素 essential factor; key element: 一般来说,每个汉字都有形、音、义三个～。Generally speaking, a Chinese character has three essential factors: form, pronunciation and meaning.

【要图】yàotú 重要的规划 important plan (or programme)

【要闻】yàowén 重要的新闻 important news: 国际～ important international news | 一周～ important news of the week

【要务】yàowù 重要的事务 important affairs: ～在身 be charged with important tasks

【要言不烦】yào yán bù fán 说话、行文简明扼要、不烦琐 (of speech or writing) terse; succinct; pithy

【要义】yàoyì 重要的内容或道理 essentials: 阐明～ expound the essentials

【要员】yàoyuán 重要的人员(多用于委派时 oft. used during appointment) VIP; very important official: 政府～ important government officials

【要职】yàozhí 重要的职位 an important post: 身居～ hold an important post

【要旨】yàozhǐ 主要的意思 main idea; gist

【要子】yào·zi ❶ 用麦秆、稻草等临时拧成的绳状物,用来捆麦子、稻子等 straw cord for bundling up rice or wheat stalks, etc. ❷ 捆货物用的或打包用的条状物 baling strap or hoop: 铁～ iron baling strap

钥(鑰) yào 钥匙 key
☞ yuè on p. 2372

【钥匙】yào·shi 开锁用的东西,有的锁用了它才能锁上 key; instrument by which a lock is opened, and in some cases is also locked

袎 yào〈书 *fml.*〉same as 靿 yào

靿 yào (～儿 yàor) 靴或袜子的筒儿 leg of a boot or sock: 靴～儿 leg of a boot | 高～儿袜子 stockings

鹞 yào 雀鹰 sparrow hawk (*Accipiter nisus*)

【鹞鹰】yàoyīng 雀鹰的通称 general term for 雀鹰 quèyīng

【鹞子】yào·zi ❶ 雀鹰的通称 general term for 雀鹰 quèyīng ❷〈方 *dial.*〉纸鹞;风筝 kite

藥 yào ❶ ☞ 药 yào on p. 2231 ❷ (Yào) 姓 a surname

曜 yào〈书 *fml.*〉❶ 日光 sunlight ❷ 照耀 shine; illuminate ❸ 日、月、星都叫曜,日、月和火、水、木、金、土五星合称七曜,旧时分别用来称一个星期的七天,日曜日是星期天,月曜日是星期一,其余依次类推 luminary (i. e.

the sun, the moon, or the stars; used in old names of the days of the week, such as 日曜日 Sunday, 月曜日 Monday, 火曜日 Tuesday, 水曜日 Wednesday, 木曜日 Thursday, 金曜日 Friday, and 土曜日 Saturday)

燿 yào 〈书 *fml.*〉 same as 耀 yào

耀 yào ❶ 光线强烈地照射 shine; illuminate; dazzle: 照～ shine | 光芒～眼 dazzling ❷ 炫耀 flaunt, show off: ～武扬威 make a show of one's strength; swagger around; throw one's weight around ❸ 光芒;光辉 rays of light; radiance: 光～ brilliant light ❹ 光荣 honour; credit: 荣～ honour; glory

【耀斑】 yàobān 太阳表面突然出现在太阳黑子附近的发亮区域。持续时间从几分钟到几小时。它的出现跟太阳黑子的活动有密切关系。太阳上出现耀斑时,常引起磁暴现象。solar flare; sudden, short-lived (lasting from several minutes to several hours) increase of intensity in the light of the sun, in the vicinity of sunspots, closely linked with sunspot activity, and oft. accompanied by large increases in cosmic rays, X-rays, etc., and by resultant magnetic storms

【耀武扬威】 yào wǔ yáng wēi 炫耀武力,显示威风 make a show of strength; swagger around; throw one's weight around

【耀眼】 yàoyǎn 光线强烈,使人眼花 dazzling; overpower or dim one's vision with very bright light

yē (ㄧㄝ)

耶 yē ☞ below
☞ yé on p. 2236

【耶和华】 Yēhéhuá 希伯来人信奉的犹太教中最高的神。基督教《旧约》中用做上帝的同义词。Jehovah (an Old Testament name for the Christian God); supreme deity of Judaism as followed by Hebrews

【耶稣】 Yēsū 基督教徒所信奉的救世主,即基督 Jesus; Jesus Christ; founder of Christianity, worshipped as the Saviour by Christian followers

【耶稣教】 Yēsūjiào 我国称基督教的新派。耶稣教于19世纪初传入我国。Protestantism; New School of Christianity, introduced to China in the early 19th century; ☞ 基督教 Jīdūjiào on p. 896

倻 yē ☞ 伽倻琴 jiāyēqín on p. 926

掖 yē 塞进(衣袋或夹缝里) tuck in; thrust in between: 把书～在怀里 tuck a book into one's bosom | 把纸条从门缝里～进去 slip a note under the door
☞ yè on p. 2241

椰 yē same as 椰子 yē·zi

【椰雕】 yēdiāo 在椰子壳上雕刻形象、花纹的艺术。也指用椰子壳雕刻成的工艺品。coconut-shell carving; handicrafts carved out of coconut shell

【椰蓉】 yēróng 椰子的果肉晾干后制成的粉状物,用来做糕点的馅儿 finely grated coconut (used as a filling for cakes): ～月饼 coconut moon-cake (with such a filling)

【椰子】 yē·zi ❶ 常绿乔木,树干直立,不分枝。叶子丛生在顶部,羽状复叶,小叶细长,肉穗花序,花单性,雌雄同株。核果椭圆形,外果皮黄褐色,中果皮为厚纤维层,内果皮为角质的硬壳,果肉白色多汁,含脂肪。果肉可吃,也可榨油,果肉内的汁可做饮料。coconut palm (*Cocos nucifera*); coconut tree; coco; evergreen tree, with single straight trunk, and long narrow, pinnate compound leaves growing at its top, monoecist, with spadix, unisexual flowers, and oval fruit consisting of a thick and fibrous brown oval husk under which there is a thin hard shell enclosing a layer of edible white meat that contains fat and can be pressed to obtain oil and a hollow centre filled with a sweet, milky fluid that is used as a drink ❷ 这种植物的果实 coconut; the fruit of this plant

暍 yē 〈书 *fml.*〉 中暑 suffer heatstroke

噎 yē ❶ 食物堵住食管 choke; have the oesophagus blocked by food: 因～废食 give up eating for fear of choking; refrain from doing what one should for fear of a risk | 吃得太快,～着了。I choked because of eating too fast. ❷ 因为迎风而呼吸困难 breathe with difficulty against the wind ❸ 〈方 *dial.*〉 说话顶撞人或使人受窘没法接着说下去 render sb. speechless by saying sth. blunt or rude; choke off: 他一句话就把人家给～回去了。The other person was just about to say something when that one remark of his choked him off.

yé (ㄧㄝˊ)

邪 yé ❶ [莫邪] (mòyé) same as 镆铘 mòyé ❷ same as 耶 yé
☞ xié on p. 2120

爷(爺) yé ❶ 〈方 *dial.*〉 父亲 father: ～娘 father and mother ❷ 〈方 *dial.*〉 祖父 grandfather ❸ 对长一辈或年长男子的尊称 (a respectful form of address for an elderly man) uncle: 大～(dà·ye) Uncle | 李～ Uncle Li | 四～ Fourth Uncle ❹ 〈旧时 *old*〉 对官僚、财主等的称呼 (address for an official or rich man) sir; master; lord: 老～ Lord | 太～

district magistrate ❺ 迷信的人对神的称呼 worshipper's form of address for a deity：土地～ God of the Land｜阎王～ Yama；King of Hell

【爷们】yé·men〈方 *dial.*〉❶ 男人(可以用于单数 can be used as a singular noun) man；menfolk：老～ man ❷ 丈夫 husband

【爷们儿】yé·menr〈方 *dial.*〉❶ 爷儿们 collective term for men of two or more generations ❷ 男人之间的互称(含亲昵意) form of address between men (to show intimacy)

【爷儿】yér 长辈男子和男女晚辈的合称,如父亲和子女,叔父和侄子、侄女,祖父和孙子、孙女(后面常带数量词 oft. followed by 俩 liǎ,几个 jǐ·ge, etc.) senior male member of a family together with one or more junior members, e.g. a father with sons or daughters, an uncle with a nephew or niece, or a grandfather with his grandchildren：～俩 the two of (us, them, you)｜～几个在院子里乘凉。The grandfather and his grandchildren were enjoying the cool of the courtyard.

【爷儿们】yér·men 长辈男子和晚辈男子的合称 collective term for men of two or more generations

【爷爷】yé·ye ❶ 祖父 (paternal) grandfather ❷ 称呼跟祖父辈分相同或年纪相仿的男人 grandpa (a respectful form of address for a man whose seniority or age is similar to one's grandfather)

耶 yé〈书 *fml.*〉〈助词 *aux.*〉表示疑问的语气 [used at the end of a question to show query or doubt]：是～非～? Is it or isn't it? *or* Yes or no?
〈古 *arch.*〉same as 爷 yé
☞ yē on p. 2235

揶 yé [揶揄] (yéyú)〈书 *fml.*〉嘲笑 ridicule；deride：受人～ be mocked at

铘 yé ☞ 镆铘 mòyé on p. 1370

yě (ㄧㄝˇ)

也[1] yě〈书 *fml.*〉〈助词 *aux.*〉❶ 表示判断或解释的语气 [used at the end of a sentence] indicating an explanation or a judgment：孔子,鲁人～。Confucius was a native of the State of Lu.｜非不能～,是不为～。This is a case of choosing not to, not of being unable to. ❷ 表示疑问或反诘的语气 [used at the end of a question or counter-question]：何～? How is that? *or* Why so?｜是可忍也,孰不可忍～? If this can be tolerated, then what cannot be? ❸ 表示句中的停顿 [used in the middle of a sentence, marking off a sentence element about which there is to be a statement]：大道之行～,天下为公。When the Great Tao prevailed, the whole world was one community.｜地之相去～,千有余里。The two places are more than 1,000 *li* apart.

也[2] yě〈副词 *adv.*〉❶ 表示同样 also；too；either：水库可以灌溉、发电,～可以养鱼。Reservoirs can be used for irrigation and power generation, and also for fish breeding. ❷ 叠用,强调两事并列或对待 (reduplicated to show two parallel things) as well as：他～会种地,～会打铁。He is good at both farming and forging iron.｜游客里面～有坐车的,～有步行的。Among the tourists, there are those who take buses as well as those who go on foot. ❸ 叠用,表示无论这样或那样;不以某种情形为条件 (reduplicated) whether... or...；no matter whether：你去我～去,你不去我～去。Whether you go or not, I'll go anyway.｜他左想～不是,右想～不是。He thinks this way and that, and still it is not right. ❹ 表示转折或让步(常跟上文的'虽然、即使'等呼应 oft. used correlatively with 虽然 suīrán,即使 jíshǐ, etc., indicating aversion or concession) still；yet：我虽然没见过,～听人说过。I've heard about it, though I have never seen it.｜即使你不说,我～知道。You don't have to tell me. I know already. ❺ 表示委婉 [used in a hesitant or guarded statement]：倒～罢了。Let it pass.｜～只好如此。We'll have to leave it at that. ❻ 表示强调(常跟上文的'连'字呼应 used correlatively with 连 lián, indicating emphasis)：连爷爷～乐得合不拢嘴。Even Grandpa was so happy that he grinned from ear to ear.

【也罢】[1] yěbà 表示容忍或只得如此,有'算了'或'也就算了'的意思(单用多见于戏曲 oft. used alone in drama) [used to express forbearance, resignation, etc.] well；all right：这种事情不知道～,知道了反倒难为情。It's quite all right that you don't know this kind of things. It would be embarrassing had you known it.｜～,你一定要走,我送你上车。All right, I'll see you to the bus, since you insist on going.

【也罢】[2] yěbà〈助词 *aux.*〉两个或几个连用,表示不以某种情形为条件 (reduplicated) whether... or...；no matter whether：你去～,不去～,反正是一样。It makes no difference whether you go or not.

【也许】yěxǔ〈副词 *adv.*〉表示不很肯定 perhaps；probably；maybe：你仔细找一找,～能找到。Make a careful search, perhaps you can find it.

冶[1] yě ❶ 熔炼(金属) smelt (metal)：～金 metallurgy ❷ (Yě) 姓 a surname

冶[2] yě〈书 *fml.*〉形容女子装饰艳丽(含贬义 derog.) seductively dressed or made up;

妖～ seductive; bewitching|～容 seductive looks

【冶金】yějīn 冶炼金属 metallurgy:～工业 metallurgical industry

【冶炼】yěliàn 用焙烧、熔炼、电解等方法把矿石中所需要的金属提取出来 smelt; separate metals from their ores by smelting, refining or electrolysis

【冶容】yěróng〈书 *fml*.〉❶ 打扮得很妖媚 be seductively made up ❷ 妖媚的容貌 seductive looks

【冶艳】yěyàn〈书 *fml*.〉妖艳 seductive and bewitching

【冶游】yěyóu 原指男女在春天或节日里外出游玩,后来专指嫖妓 (orig.) men and women go on a spring or holiday outing; (now) frequent brothels; go whoring

野(埜) yě ❶ 野外 open country; the open:旷～ wilderness|～地 wild country; wilderness|～火 prairie fire; bush fire|～战 field operations ❷ 界限 limit; boundary:视～ field of vision (view)|分～ dividing line ❸ 指不当政的地位(跟'朝'相对 as opposed to 'court') not in power; out of office:下～ retire from the political arena; be forced to relinquish power|在～ not be in office; be out of office ❹ 不是人工饲养或培植的 (of plants or animals) wild; uncultivated; undomesticated; untamed:～兽 wild beast|～兔 hare|～菜 edible wild herbs|～花 wild flowers|～草 weeds ❺ 蛮横不讲理;粗鲁没礼貌 rude; rough:～蛮 uncivilized; savage|粗～ rough; boorish; uncouth|撒～ act wildly; behave atrociously|这人说话太～。This person speaks rudely. ❻ 不受约束 unrestrained; abandoned; unruly:～性 wild nature; unruliness|放了几天假,心都玩～了。After the fun they had during the holidays, they can't concentrate on their school work.

【野菜】yěcài 可以做蔬菜的野生植物,如马齿苋、苣荬菜等 edible wild herbs, e. g. purslane, endive, etc.

【野餐】yěcān ❶ 带了食物到野外去吃 picnic; hold or attend a picnic ❷ 带到野外去吃的一顿饭 picnic; pleasure outing at which a meal is eaten outdoors

【野炊】yěchuī 在野外烧火做饭 cook in the open air

【野地】yědì 野外的荒地 wild country; wilderness:荒山～ barren hills and wild country

【野火】yěhuǒ 荒山野地燃烧的火 prairie fire; bush fire

【野鸡】yějī ❶ 雉[1]的通称 general term for 雉[1] zhì ❷〈旧时 *old*〉指沿街拉客的私娼 street walker; unlicensed prostitute ❸ 指不合规章而经营的 enterprise or undertaking that is illegal, unethical, irregular, or unauthorized:～大学 diploma mill|～汽车 plying taxi|～公司 unauthorized company

【野景】yějǐng 野外的景致 wild scenery

【野马】yěmǎ 哺乳动物,体形似家马,毛浅棕色,腹部毛色较浅,尾毛长而多。群栖于沙漠、草原地带。产于我国西北及蒙古,数量很少。wild horse (*Equus przewalskii*); untamed horse; Przhevalski's horse (*Equus przewalski*), mammal looking like a domestic horse, having pale-brown hair but paler on the abdomen, and a thick long-haired tail, living in herds on deserts or grasslands, originating in northwestern China and Mongolia, in very small numbers

【野蛮】yěmán ❶ 不文明;没有文化 uncivilized; savage ❷ 蛮横残暴 barbarous; cruel; brutal:～屠杀 brutal massacre|举止～ savage behaviour

【野猫】yěmāo ❶ 无主的猫 stray cat ❷〈方 *dial*.〉same as 野兔 yětù

【野牛】yěniú 哺乳动物,形状跟家牛相似,身体高大,毛褐色,头部和颈部有长毛,背部隆起。吃树皮、树叶等。有好几种,分别产于亚洲、欧洲和美洲,现存不多,是一种珍奇的动物。wild ox (*Bos gaurus*); mammal looking like a domestic ox, tall, with brown hair, and long hair on the head and neck, and a humped back, in several species, living in Asia, Europe and America, a rare animal

【野禽】yěqín 家禽以外的鸟类 wild poultry

【野人】yěrén ❶〈古时 *arch*.〉指田野间的人;平民 farmers in the fields; commoner ❷ 指未开化的人 savage; barbarian ❸ 指性情粗野的人 an uncouth person; rustic

【野生】yěshēng 生物在自然环境里生长而不是由人饲养或栽培 wild; undomesticated; uncultivated; feral:～植物 wild plant

【野食儿】yěshír ❶ 禽兽在野外找到的食物 animals' food foraged in the wilds ❷〈比喻 *fig*.〉本分以外所得的财物 ill-gotten (or illicit) gains

【野史】yěshǐ 指旧时私家著的史书 (old-time) unofficial history:稗官～ books of anecdotes

【野兽】yěshòu 家畜以外的兽类 wild beast; wild animal

【野兔】yětù 生活在野地里的兔类,身体一般较家兔略大,耳长大,毛很密,多为茶褐色或略带灰色。吃草、蔬菜等。有的地区叫野猫。hare (*Lepus*); rabbit living in the wild, bigger in size than domestic rabbit, with long ears, thick hair, mostly brown or slightly grey, living on grass and vegetables; called 野猫 yěmāo in some areas

【野外】yěwài 离居民点较远的地方 where the wild things are; open country; field; place far from settlements:荒郊～ desolate place outside a town; wilderness

【野外工作】yěwài gōngzuò 指科学技术工作者

在野外进行的调查、勘探、测量、发掘等工作 fieldwork; field operation; work of investigation, prospecting, surveying or excavation in the field by scientific or technical personnel, e.g. geologist, botanist, etc.; 旧称 formerly called 田野工作 tiányě gōngzuò

【野味】yěwèi 猎得的做肉食的鸟兽 game; wild birds or animals hunted for use as food

【野心】yěxīn 对领土、权力或名利的大而非分的欲望 wild ambition; careerism; strong and inordinate desire to gain territory, power or fame: ～家 careerist|～勃勃 be overweeningly ambitious; be obsessed with ambition|狼子～ be full of wild ambitions

【野性】yěxìng 不驯顺的性情 wild nature; unruliness

【野鸭】yěyā 野生的鸭,形状跟家鸭相似,雄的头部绿色,有亮光,背部黑褐色,两翼有蓝色斑点。雌的全身褐色。吃小鱼、贝类及植物的种子等。wild duck (*Anas platyrhynchos platyrhynchos*); duck living in the wilds, looking like a domestic duck, the males having a green lustrous head and dark-brown back, with blue spots on the wings, and the females brown all over the body, living on small fish, shells, seeds, etc.; also 凫 fú or 绿头鸭 lǜtóuyā

【野营】yěyíng 到野外搭了营帐住宿,是军事或体育训练的一种项目 camp; bivouac; stay in a tent put up in the wilderness as part of military or athletic training: ～训练 camp and field training|明天我们到西山～去。Tomorrow we are going to have camp and field training in the Western Hills.

【野战】yězhàn 在要塞和大城市以外进行的战斗 field operations; battle waged away from a fortress or big cities

【野战军】yězhànjūn 适应广大区域机动作战的正规军 field army; regular army suited for quick battle in vast areas

【野猪】yězhū 哺乳动物,全身长黑褐色粗毛,犬齿突出口外,耳和尾短小。性凶猛,昼伏夜出,吃蚯蚓、蛇、甲虫和蔬菜、甘薯等。对农业危害很大。wild boar (*Sus scrofa*); nocturnal mammal having a black-brown hairy coat, long snout, sharp protruding canine teeth, and short ears and tail; ferocious, living on earthworms, snakes, beetles, vegetables, sweet potatoes, etc., very harmful to agriculture

埜 yě 〈书 *fml.*〉 same as 野 yě

yè(丨せ)

业[1](業) yè ❶ 行业 line of business; trade; industry: 工～ industry|农～ agriculture|林～ forestry|畜牧～ animal husbandry|饮食～catering trade|各行各～ all trades and professions; all walks of life ❷ 职业 occupation; profession; employment; job: 就～ employment|转～ (of armymen) be transferred to civilian work|～余 spare time; after-work ❸ 学业 course of study: 肄～ study in school|修～ study in school|毕～ graduate|结～ complete a course ❹ 事业 cause; enterprise: 功～ exploits; achievements|创～ start an undertaking; do pioneering work|～绩 outstanding achievement ❺ 产业;财产 estate; property: 家～ family property|～主 owner (of an enterprise or estate); proprietor ❻ 佛教徒称一切行为、言语、思想为业,分别叫做身业、口业、意业,合称三业,包括善恶两面,一般专指恶业 (Buddhism) karma; deed, speech and ideology are called the three karmas by Buddhists, including both good and evil; generally refers to evil ❼ 从事(某种行业) engage in (a profession): ～农 engage in farming|～商 engage in commerce ❽ (Yè)姓 a surname

业[2](業) yè 已经 already: ～已 already|～经 already

【业海】yèhǎi 〈佛教 *Budd.*〉 使人沉沦的无边的罪恶 endless crimes; sea of retribution

【业绩】yèjì 建立的功劳和完成的事业;重大的成就 accomplishment; contributions and exploits; outstanding achievement

【业界】yèjiè 〈方 *dial.*〉 指企业界。也指企业界中各行业或某个行业。business circles; various trades or a certain trade in business circles

【业经】yèjīng 已经(多见于公文 oft. used in official documents) already: ～呈报在案 already reported to a higher level for the record

【业师】yèshī 称教过自己的老师 one's (former) teacher

【业务】yèwù 个人的或某个机构的专业工作 vocational work; professional work; business: ～能力 professional ability|～学习 vocational study|～范围 scope of business|发展～ develop business

【业已】yèyǐ 已经(多见于公文 oft. used in official documents) already: ～调查属实 already verified to be true|～准备就绪 preparations are already complete

【业余】yèyú ❶ 工作时间以外的 spare time; after-work: ～时间 spare time|～学校 spare-time school ❷ 非专业的 nonprofessional; amateur: ～歌手 amateur singer|～剧团 an amateur theatrical troupe|～文艺活动 amateur literary and artistic activities

【业余教育】yèyú jiàoyù 为提高工人、农民、干部等的政治、文化和科学、技术水平,在业余时间进行的教育 continuing education; spare-time education; education carried out during after-work hours to raise the political, cultural, scientific and technical level of workers, peasants and cadres

【业障】yèzhàng ❶〈佛教 *Budd.*〉指妨碍修行的罪恶 retribution in this life for the sins of a previous existence ❷〈旧时 *old*〉长辈骂不肖子弟的话 (used to curse one's children) medium of retribution

【业主】yèzhǔ 产业或企业的所有者 owner (of an enterprise or estate); proprietor

叶[1]**(葉)** yè ❶(~儿 yèr) 植物的营养器官之一,通常由叶片和叶柄组成 leaf; foliage; one of the nutritive organs of plants, usu. consisting of a blade and stalk; 通称 commonly known as 叶子 yè·zi ❷ 像叶子的 leaf-like thing: 百~窗 shutter | 千~莲 multiple-petal lotus ❸ same as 页 yè ❹ (Yè) 姓 a surname

叶[2]**(葉)** yè 较长时期的分段 part of a historical period: 清朝末~ the closing period of the Qing Dynasty | 20 世纪中~ (in) middle of the 20th century; mid-20th century

☞ xié on p. 2119

【叶柄】yèbǐng 叶子的组成部分之一,连接叶片和茎,长条形。有的叶子没有叶柄,叶片直接和茎连接。petiole; leafstalk; slender stem connecting the leaf blade and stalk. Some leaves do not have leafstalks, and blades are linked directly to the stalk.

【叶公好龙】Yè Gōng hào lóng 据说古代有个叶公,非常爱好龙,器物上画着龙,房屋上也刻着龙。真龙知道了,就到叶公家来,把头探进窗户。叶公一见,吓得面如土色,拔腿就跑(见于汉代刘向《新序·杂事》)。比喻说是爱好某事物,其实并不真爱好。Lord Ye professed to love dragons; originally from *New Preface·Miscellany* by Liu Xiang of the Han Dynasty: In ancient times it was said that Lord Ye loved dragons so much that he adorned his whole house with drawings and carvings of them. A real dragon in heaven heard of this and paid a visit, and when Lord Ye saw the real dragon thrusting its head through his study window, he turned pale with fright and ran away at once. (fig.) professed love of what one really fears.

【叶绿素】yèlǜsù 植物体中的绿色物质,是一种复杂的有机酸。植物利用叶绿素进行光合作用制造养料。chlorophyll; green matter found in plants, which is a kind of complex organic acid. Plants use chlorophyll to produce nutrients through photosynthesis.

【叶绿体】yèlǜtǐ 植物细胞质中的一种细胞器,内含叶绿素、酶和脱氧核糖核酸,能自行分裂,在遗传上有相对独立性 chloroplast; plastid in the cytoplasm of plants, which contains chlorophyll, enzymes and DNA, is capable of self-division, and has relatively independence in propagation

【叶轮】yèlún 涡轮机里带有叶片的轮,叶片受蒸汽或水流等的作用,使轴旋转而产生动力。也指水泵、鼓风机等机器里带有叶片的轮,转动时使流体运动。impeller; vane wheel; turbine with blades, propelled by steam or water current, turning the axle to generate power; wheel with vanes in a water pump, air-blower, etc., that keeps fluid moving when it revolves

【叶落归根】yè luò guī gēn〈比喻 *fig.*〉事物有一定的归宿。多指客居他乡的人终究要回到本乡。falling leaves return to their roots; people residing elsewhere will finally return to their ancestral home

【叶脉】yèmài 叶片上分布的细管状构造,主要由细而长的细胞构成,分布到叶片的各个部分,作用是输送水分、养料等 leaf vein; vascular tissues mainly consisting of long thin cells, forming the framework of a leaf blade, and conveying water and nutrition

【叶片】yèpiàn ❶ 叶的组成部分之一,通常是很薄的扁平体,有叶肉和叶脉,是植物进行光合作用的主要部分 leaf blade; flat, expanded part of leaf consisting of mesophyll and leaf veins, and the main site of photosynthesis ❷ 涡轮机、水泵、鼓风机等机器中形状像叶子的零件,许多叶片构成叶轮 vane; leaf-like part in a turbine, water pump and air-blower, many vanes forming the vane wheel

【叶鞘】yèqiào 稻、麦、莎草等植物的叶子裹在茎上的部分 leaf sheath; leaf base covering the stems of plants, e.g. rice, wheat, sedge, etc.

【叶肉】yèròu 叶片表皮里面除去叶脉以外所剩下的部分,主要由薄壁的细胞构成 mesophyll; leaf blade with no veins, mainly composed of thin-walled cells

【叶序】yèxù 叶子在茎上排列的形式,常见的有互生、对生、轮生等 phyllotaxy; the appearance of the leaf arrangement on a stem, common ones including alternate, opposite and verticillate

【叶芽】yèyá 发育后长成新枝条的芽 leaf bud; a bud from which only stems and leaves develop

【叶腋】yèyè 叶的基部和茎之间所夹的角 leaf axil; the upper angle formed by the leaf and stem

【叶枝】yèzhī ❶ 果树上只长叶子不结果实的枝 leafy branch; branch of a fruit tree that grows only leaves, without bearing fruit ❷ 棉花植株上只长叶子不长棉桃的枝 branch of a cotton plant that grows only leaves, without bearing cotton bolls

【叶子】yè·zi ❶ 植物的叶的通称 common name for leaf; foilage ❷〈方 *dial.*〉纸牌 (playing) card ❸〈方 *dial.*〉指茶叶 leaf (tea leaf)

【叶子烟】yè·ziyān 晒干或烤干而未进一步加工

的烟叶 dried tobacco leaves

页(頁、葉、箂) yè ❶ 张(指纸) page or leaf: 册～ album of paintings or calligraphy|活～ loose-leaf ❷〈量词 *classifier*〉〈旧时 *old*〉单面印刷的书本中的一张纸,现在一般指两面印刷的书本中一张纸的一面,但作为印刷术语时仍指一张 page; an entire leaf of a book; one side of a leaf of a book; referring to an entire leaf when used as a printing term

【页码】yèmǎ (～儿 yèmǎr) 书籍每一页上标明次第的数目字 page number; number marked on each page to show the order of the pages

【页心】yèxīn 版心 type page

曳(拽、抴) yè 拖;拉;牵引 drag; haul; tug; tow: ～光弹 tracer bullet|弃甲～兵 (of routed troops) throw away armour and trail weapons ☞ 拽 zhuāi on p. 2515 and zhuài on p. 2515

【曳光弹】yèguāngdàn 一种弹头尾部装有能发光的化学药剂的炮弹或枪弹,发射后能发光,用以显示弹道和指示目标 tracer bullet or shell; tracer; ammunition containing a chemical composition to mark the flight of projectiles with a trail of fire, or to indicate the target

邺(鄴) Yè ❶ 古地名,在今河北临漳 Ye, place name in ancient times, in present-day Linzhang, Hebei Province. ❷ 姓 a surname

夜(亱) yè ❶ 从天黑到天亮的一段时间(跟'日'或'昼'相对 as opposed to 'day' or 'daytime') night; evening; the time from dusk to dawn: ～晚 night|白天黑～ day and night|三天三～ three days and three nights|冬天昼短～长。In winter, the days are short and the nights are long. ❷〈方 *dial.*〉指天黑;入夜 night is falling: 天快～了。It is getting dark.

【夜班】yèbān 夜里工作的班次 night shift: 值～ be on night shift

【夜半】yèbàn 夜里十二点钟前后;半夜 in the middle of the night; midnight; 12 o'clock at night

【夜不闭户】yè bù bì hù 夜间不用关闭门户睡觉,形容社会安宁,风气良好 doors are not bolted at night; (fig.) law and order prevail

【夜餐】yècān 夜间吃的饭 midnight snack

【夜叉】yè·chā〈佛教 *Budd.*〉指恶鬼。后来用来比喻相貌丑陋、凶恶的人。yaksha (malevolent spirit); (fig.) hideous, ferocious person; also 药叉 yàochā [梵 Sanskrit: yakṣa]

【夜长梦多】yè cháng mèng duō〈比喻 *fig.*〉时间拖长了,事情可能发生不利的变化 a long night is fraught with dreams; (fig.) a long delay means trouble

【夜场】yèchǎng 晚场 evening show; evening performance

【夜车】yèchē ❶ 夜里开出、夜里到达或者夜里经过的火车 night train; a train that departs, arrives or passes through at night ❷ ☞ 开夜车 kāi yèchē on p. 1077

【夜饭】yèfàn〈方 *dial.*〉晚饭 supper; dinner

【夜工】yègōng 夜间的活儿 night work; night job: 做～ work at night|打～ do a night job

【夜光表】yèguāngbiǎo 指针和标志时刻的数字或符号能发荧光的表,在黑暗中也可以看时刻 luminous watch; fluorescent watch; watch whose hands and dial-face symbols glow and can be seen in the dark

【夜壶】yèhú 便壶(多指旧式的 oft. old style) chamber pot

【夜间】yè·jiān same as 夜里 yè·li

【夜景】yèjǐng 夜晚由灯光、景物等组成的景色 night scene (or view)

【夜空】yèkōng 夜晚的天空 the night sky

【夜来】yèlái〈书 *fml.*〉❶ 昨天 yesterday ❷ same as 夜间 yè·jiān

【夜阑】yèlán〈书 *fml.*〉夜深 late at night: ～人静 in the dead of night; in the still (or quiet) of the night

【夜郎自大】Yèláng zìdà 汉代西南邻国中,夜郎国(在今贵州西部)最大。夜郎国的国君问汉朝使臣道:'你们汉朝大呢?还是我们夜郎国大呢?'(见于《史记·西南夷列传》)后来用'夜郎自大'比喻妄自尊大。ludicrous conceit of the King of Yelang; (fig.) parochial arrogance. According to *Records of the Historian · Accounts of Southwestern Tribes*, among the small kingdoms in southwestern China, Yelang (in present-day western Guizhou) was the largest, where one day the King of Yelang asked an envoy from the Han Dynasty, 'Which is bigger, your Han Dynasty or our Yelang Kingdom?'

【夜里】yè·li 从天黑到天亮的一段时间 at night; the time from dusk to dawn

【夜盲】yèmáng 病,主要由缺乏维生素A引起,症状是在夜间光线弱的地方视力很差或完全不能看见东西。有的地区叫雀盲眼。nyctalopia; night blindness; disease characterized by the decreased ability to see at night in reduced light, caused by a deficiency of vitamin A; also called 雀盲眼 qiǎo·mangyǎn in some areas

【夜猫子】yèmāo·zi〈方 *dial.*〉❶ 猫头鹰 owl ❷〈比喻 *fig.*〉喜欢晚睡的人 night owl; person who goes to bed late

【夜明珠】yèmíngzhū 古代传说黑暗中能放光的珍珠(as found in ancient legends) night-luminescent pearl; pearl that glows in the dark

【夜幕】yèmù 在夜间,景物像被一幅大幕罩住一样,因此叫做夜幕 the curtain (or veil) of night; gathering darkness: ～笼罩着大地。The land is shrouded in a curtain of darkness.

【夜儿个】yèr·ge〈方 *dial.*〉昨天 yesterday

【夜色】yèsè 夜晚的景色 the dim light of night：～苍茫 in the gathering dusk|～深沉 the night is dark|朦胧的～ hazy night view

【夜生活】yèshēnghuó 指夜间的交际应酬、文化娱乐等活动 nightlife; activities of socializing and entertainment at night

【夜市】yèshì ❶ 夜间做买卖的市场 night market ❷ 夜间的营业 night business operation：一个～可收入百十来元。One night of operation can bring in an income of about 100 yuan.

【夜晚】yèwǎn 夜间；晚上 night; evening

【夜消】yèxiāo same as 夜宵 yèxiāo

【夜宵】yèxiāo（～儿 yèxiāor）夜里吃的酒食、点心等 food, wine, snacks, etc., taken late at night; midnight snack; also 夜消 yèxiao

【夜校】yèxiào 夜间上课的学校，多半是业余学校 night (or evening) school, mostly classes taken after work; also 夜学 yèxué

【夜以继日】yè yǐ jì rì 日夜不停 day and night; round the clock; also 日以继夜 rì yǐ jì yè

【夜莺】yèyīng 文学上指歌鸲（qú）一类叫声清脆婉转的鸟 nightingale (*Luscinia*); philomel; (in literary writing) birds with clear and melodious singing

【夜游神】yèyóushén 迷信传说中夜间巡行的神。比喻喜欢深夜在外游荡的人。legendary deity patrolling at night; (fig.) person who is up and about at night; night owl

【夜战】yèzhàn 夜间作战。也指夜间加班工作。night fighting; night work：挑灯～ fight by torchlight (in ancient times); continue working by lamplight

【夜总会】yèzǒnghuì 大都市中供人们夜间吃喝玩儿乐的场所 nightclub; cabaret; place of entertainment open at night, usu. serving food and liquor, having a floor show, and providing music and space for dancing

【夜作】yèzuò ☞ 打夜作 dǎ yèzuò on p. 352

咽 yè 声音受阻而低沉 low and deep voice due to hoarseness：哽～ choke with sobs|喇叭声～。The sound of the horn ran deep. ☞ yān on p. 2199; yàn on p. 2214

晔(曄) yè〈书 *fml.*〉光 (of light) bright

烨(燁、爗) yè ❶ 火光；日光 firelight or sunlight ❷ 光盛 (of light) bright

掖 yè 用手搀扶别人的胳膊。借指扶助或提拔。support sb. by the arm; help; assist; promote：扶～ support; help|奖～ reward and promote; encourage by rewarding and promoting. ☞ yē on p. 2235

【掖县】Yè Xiàn 地名，在山东。现改名莱州。Yexian County, name of a place in Shandong Province, now called Laizhou

液 yè 液体 liquid; fluid; juice：汁～ juice|血～ blood|溶～ solution

【液果】yèguǒ 指多汁或多肉质的果实，如浆果、核果等 juicy fruit; pulpy fruit (e.g. berries, drupes, etc.)

【液化】yèhuà ❶ 气体因温度降低或压力增加而变成液体 liquefaction; the process of change from gas to liquid due to a drop of temperature or an increase of pressure：～石油气 liquefied petroleum gas (LPG) ❷ 有机体的某些组织因发生病理变化而变成液体 pathological changes in certain tissues causing them to become liquefied

【液化热】yèhuàrè 单位质量的某种气体变成液体时所放出的热量，叫做这种气体的液化热 liquefaction heat; heat released in a liquefaction process, of gas per unit

【液晶】yèjīng 液态晶体，是具有液体的流动性和表面张力，又具有晶体的光学性质的物体。可用做电子工业中的显示材料，也用于无损探伤和医疗诊断等。liquid crystal; object having both the physical properties of a liquid, such as fluidity and surface tension, and the optical properties of a crystal, used for display materials in the electronics industry, and also in non-intrusive examination and medical diagnosis, etc.

【液泡】yèpào 细胞质中泡状的结构，内含液体，周围有薄膜使液泡与细胞质分开 vacuole; fluid-filled cavity in the cytoplasm, surrounded by a membrane to separate the cavity from the cytoplasm

【液态】yètài 物质的液体状态，是物质存在的一种形态 liquid state; state in which matter exists

【液体】yètǐ 有一定的体积、没有一定的形状、可以流动的物质。在常温下，油、水、酒、水银等都是液体。liquid; substance that flows readily and assumes the shape of its container but retains its independent volume. Under normal atmospheric temperatures, oil, water, liquor and mercury are all liquid.

【液压机】yèyājī 利用液体传递压力的机器的统称，如水压机、油压机 hydraulic press; general term for machines that are operated by the pressure created when a liquid is forced through an aperture, tube, etc., e.g. water hydraulic press and oil hydraulic press

谒 yè〈书 *fml.*〉谒见 call on (a superior or an elderly person); pay one's respects to：拜～ pay a formal visit|进～ call on (sb. holding high office)|～黄帝陵 pay homage at the Yellow Emperor's mausoleum

【谒见】yèjiàn 进见（地位或辈分高的人）call on; have an audience with (a superior or a senior in the clan hierarchy)

腋 yè ❶ same as 腋窝 yèwō ❷ 其他生物体上跟腋类似的部分 axil; upper angle formed by a leaf, twig, etc., and the stem from which it grows：～芽 axilliary bud

【腋臭】yèchòu 腋窝狐臭 underarm odour
【腋毛】yèmáo 人腋部生长的毛 armpit hair
【腋生】yèshēng 着生在叶腋或枝腋上 axillary; of, in or growing from an axil: ～穗状花序 axillary spike
【腋窝】yèwō 上肢和肩膀连接处靠底下的部分，呈窝状 armpit; junction of the arm and shoulder; 通称 commonly called 夹肢窝 gāzhiwō
【腋芽】yèyá ☞ 侧芽 cèyá on p.196

馌 yè 〈书 *fml*.〉往田野送饭 deliver meals to the fields

靥(靨) yè 酒窝 dimple: 酒～ dimple | 笑～ dimple; smiling face

yī (丨)

一[1] yī ❶ 数目，最小的正整数 one; the smallest positive integer; ☞ 数字 shùzì on p.1791 ❷ 同一 same: ～视同仁 treat equally without discrimination | 咱们是～家人。We are of the same family. | 你们～路走。You are going the same way. | 这不是～码事。They are not the same thing. ❸ 另一 also; otherwise: 番茄～名西红柿。'*Fanqie*' (tomato) is also called '*xihongshi*' in Chinese. ❹ 全；满 whole; all; throughout: ～冬 the whole winter; all winter; throughout the winter | ～生 all one's life | ～路平安 have a good journey; bon voyage | ～屋子人 a roomful of people | ～身的汗 soaked with sweat ❺ 专一 concentrated; wholehearted: ～心～意 single-minded; concentrated ❻ 表示动作是一次，或表示动作是短暂的，或表示动作是试试的 [used to indicate that an action occurs just once or lasts for a short time, or is being attempted]: a)用在重叠的动词(多为单音)中间 [used in the middle of a reduplicated verb, oft: a single syllable]: 歇～歇 have a rest | 笑～笑 give a smile | 让我闻～闻。Let me smell it. b)用在动词之后，动量词之前 [used between a verb and a verbal measure]: 笑～声 give a laugh | 看～眼 take a look | 让我们商量～下。Let's talk it over. ❼ 用在动词或动量词前面，表示先做某个动作(下文说明动作结果) [used before a verb or a verbal measure to indicate an action to be followed by a result]: ～跳跳了过去 get over in one jump | ～脚把它踢开 move it away with one kick | 他在旁边～站，再也不说什么。He stood by the side, and did not say any more. ❽ 一旦；一经 once; as soon as: ～失足成千古恨。A single slip can cause a lasting sorrow. ❾ 〈书 *fml*.〉〈助词 *aux*.〉用在某些词前加强语气 [used before certain words for emphasis]: ～何速也! How fast it is! | 为害之甚，～至于此! To think that it has caused such serious harm! ‖ 注意 **NOTE**: '一'字单用或在一词一句末尾念阴平，如'十一、一一得一'，在去声字前念阳平，如'一半、一共'，在阴平、阳平、上声字前念去声，如'一天、一年、一点'。本词典为简便起见，条目中的'一'字，都注阴平。when used alone, or used at the end of a word or sentence, 一 is pronounced with the first tone, e.g. 十一 shíyī and 一一得一 yīyīdéyī; when used before a character with a falling tone, 一 is pronounced with the second tone, e.g. 一半 yíbàn and 一共 yígòng; when used before a character with the first, second or third tone, it is pronounced with the fourth tone, e.g. 一天 yìtiān, 一年 yìnián, and 一点 yìdiǎn; for convenience, 一 in all the entries is marked with the first tone.

一[2] yī 我国民族音乐音阶上的一级，乐谱上用做记音符号，相当于简谱的'7' note in the traditional Chinese musical scale called *gongchepu*, corresponding to 7 in numbered musical notation; ☞ 工尺 gōngchě on p.664
【一把手】yī bǎ shǒu ❶ 作为参加活动的一员 party to an undertaking; member; hand: 咱们搭伙干，你也算上～。Let's pool our efforts, and count you in. ❷ 能干的人 good hand: 要说干活儿，他可真是～。He is really a good hand at work. also 一把好手 yī bǎ hǎo shǒu ❸ same as 第一把手 dì yī bǎ shǒu
【一把死拿】yī bǎ sǐ ná 〈方 *dial*.〉(～儿 yī bǎ sǐ nár) 形容固执成法，不肯变通 inflexible; stubborn
【一把抓】yī bǎ zhuā ❶ 对一切事都不放手，都要自己管 take everything into one's own hands ❷ 做事不分轻重缓急，一齐下手 try to tackle all problems at once regardless of their relative importance and urgency
【一百一】yībǎiyī 〈方 *dial*.〉形容好到极点，无可挑剔 perfect; faultless; ideal: 他是～的好人。He is a perfect gentleman. | 他侍候病人可说是～。He attends to the patients with the best of care.
【一败涂地】yī bài tú dì 形容败得不可收拾 fail completely; suffer a crushing defeat; be routed
【一般】yībān ❶ 一样；同样 same as; just like: 哥儿俩长得～高。The two brothers are the same height. | 火车飞～地向前驰去。The train flashed past like lightning. ❷ 一种 sort; kind: 别有～滋味 have a distinct taste ❸ 普通；通常 general; ordinary; common: ～性 generality; common quality | ～化 vague generalization | ～情况 ordinary circumstances | 他一早出去，～要到天黑才回来。He goes out in the early morning, and usually does not return till dusk. | ～地说，吃这种药是很见效的。Generally speaking, taking this type of medi-

cine is very effective.

【一般见识】yībān jiàn·shi 不跟知识、修养较差的人争执,叫做不跟他一般见识 (lower oneself to) the same level as sb. (used negatively when not wanting to argue with sb. less knowledgeable or accomplished)

【一斑】yībān 指豹身上的一块斑纹 one spot (on a leopard);〈比喻 *fig.*〉相类似的许多事物中很小的一部分 one of a number of similar things: 管中窥豹,可见～。Look at one spot on a leopard through a bamboo tube and you can visualize the whole animal; (fig.) conjure up the whole thing through seeing a part of it; ☞ 管中窥豹 guǎn zhōng kuī bào on p. 717

【一板一眼】yī bǎn yī yǎn 〈比喻 *fig.*〉言语行为有条理,合规矩,不马虎 following a prescribed (or set) pattern in speech or action; scrupulous and methodical; ☞ 板眼 bǎn yǎn on p. 50

【一半】yībàn (～儿 yībànr)二分之一 one half; half: 把菜子分给他们～儿,咱们有～儿也就够了。Let's give them half the vegetable seeds; half is enough for us.

【一…半…】yī…bàn… 分别用在同义词或近义词前边,表示不多或不久 [used with synonymous words, forming a phrase implying not much or many, or not a long time]: ～鳞～爪 odd bits; fragments | ～年～载 in a year or so; in about a year | ～时～刻 a short time; a little while | ～星～点儿 a tiny bit | ～知～解 have a smattering of knowledge; have a little knowledge

【一半天】yī bàn tiān 一两天 in a day or two: 过～就给你送去。I'll return it to you in a day or two.

【一包在内】yī bāo zài nèi 一切都包括在里面 and all; all included: 车钱、店钱、饭钱,～,花了五十块钱。I spent 50 yuan, fares, hotel, meals and all.

【一辈子】yībèi·zi 一生 all one's life; throughout one's life; as long as one lives; a lifetime

【一本万利】yī běn wàn lì 形容本钱小,利润很大 a small investment brings a ten-thousand-fold profit; make big profits with a small capital

【一本正经】yī běn zhèng jīng 形容很规矩,很庄重 in all seriousness; in dead earnest

【一鼻孔出气】yī bíkǒng chū qì 比喻持有同样的态度和主张(含贬义 derog.) breathe through the same nostrils; (fig.) sing the same tune

【一笔带过】yī bǐ dài guò 对事情只简单一提,不着重叙说或描述 mention casually; make a casual remark in passing

【一笔勾销】yī bǐ gōuxiāo 把账一笔抹去。比喻把一切完全取消。write off at one stroke; cancel

【一笔抹杀】yī bǐ mǒshā 〈比喻 *fig.*〉轻率地把优点、成绩等全部否定 blot out at one stroke; condemn out of hand; totally negate

【一臂之力】yī bì zhī lì 指其中的一部分力量或不大的力量 helping hand; instrumental part: 助你～ lend you a hand

【一边】yībiān (～儿 yībiānr) ❶ 东西的一面;事情的一方面 one side; side: 这块木料有～儿不光滑。One side of this piece of wood is not smooth. | 两方面争论,总有～儿理屈。In a dispute between two parties, there is always one which is in the wrong. ❷ 旁边 beside: 我们打球,他坐在～看书。We play ball, and he sits to the side reading a book. ❸ 表示一个动作跟另一个动作同时进行 at the same time; simultaneously: a)单用 used alone: 他慢慢往前走,～儿唱着歌儿。He sang as he slowly strolled along. b)连用 used consecutively: 他～儿答应,～儿放下手里的书。He put down the book in his hand as he responded. ❹〈方 *dial.*〉同样 the same; same as 一般 yībān ①: 他俩～高。The two of them are the same height. | 天下乌鸦～黑。All crows under the sun are black; Evil people all over the world are bad.

【一边倒】yī biān dǎo 指完全倾向于对立双方中的一方 lean to one side; side with sb. without reservation

【一表非凡】yī biǎo fēi fán 形容人的仪表出众,很不寻常 be unlike the common run of men; handsome and spirited; remarkable-looking

【一表人才】yī biǎo rén cái 形容人相貌英俊、风度潇洒 person of striking appearance and demeanour

【一并】yībìng 〈副词 *adv.*〉表示合在一起 along with all the others; lumped all together: ～办理 be handled together | ～报销 be reimbursed together

【一波三折】yī bō sān zhé 原指写字笔画曲折多姿,后形容文章结构曲折起伏。也比喻事情进行中阻碍、变化很多。(orig.) written Chinese character with many cranking strokes; (later) article with complicated plots; (fig.) full of twists and turns, or ups and downs; throw many obstacles in the way; with unexpected changes

【一波未平,一波又起】yī bō wèi píng, yī bō yòu qǐ 〈比喻 *fig.*〉波折多,一个问题还没有解决,另一个问题又发生了 hardly has one wave subsided when another rises; one trouble follows another

【一…不…】yī…bù… ❶ 分别用在两个动作前面,表示动作或情况一经发生就不改变 [used before two verbs to indicate the inalterability of a situation]: ～定～易 unalterable | ～去～返 gone never to return | ～蹶～振 never recover from a setback ❷ 分别用在一个名词和一个动词前面,表示强调或夸张 (used before a noun and a verb, to indicate emphasis or exaggeration) not a single; not the slightest: ～言～发 not utter a word|～字～漏 without missing a single word|～钱～值 not worth a penny; utterly worthless; mere trash|～毛～拔 unwilling to give up even a hair; very stingy

【一不做,二不休】yī bù zuò,èr bù xiū 事情已经开始了,就索性干到底 carry sth. through, whatever the consequences; in for a penny, in for a pound

【一步登天】yībù dēng tiān〈比喻 *fig*.〉一下子达到最高的境界或程度。也比喻地位一下子升得很高。reach the sky in a single bound; attain the highest level in one step; experience a meteoric rise

【一步一个脚印儿】yī bù yī gè jiǎo yìnr〈比喻 *fig*.〉做事塌实 every step leaves its print; work steadily and make solid progress

【一差二错】yī chā èr cuò 可能发生的意外或差错 possible mistake or mishap: 万一有个～,就麻烦了。Just in case there is a slip somewhere, it would be troublesome.

【一刹那】yīchànà 极短的时间 in an instant; in a flash; ☞ 刹那 chànà on p. 206

【一划】yīchàn ❶〈方 *dial*.〉一概;全部 all; without exception: ～都是新的。All are new. ❷ 一味;总是(多见于早期白话 usu. in early vernacular) always; constantly: ～地残害忠良 constantly persecute the faithful and upright

【一场空】yī cháng kōng 希望和努力完全落空 all in vain; futile

【一倡百和】yī chàng bǎi hè 一人首倡,百人附和。形容附和的人极多。when one starts singing, the others join in; meet with general approval; also 一唱百和 yī chàng bǎi hè

【一唱一和】yī chàng yī hè〈比喻 *fig*.〉互相配合,互相呼应(多含贬义 oft. derog) sing in chorus with sb.; chime in with sb.

【一朝天子一朝臣】yī cháo tiānzǐ yī cháo chén 指一个人上台,就另换一班人马 new emperor brings in a new court of officials; *or* new boss reshuffles the leadership

【一尘不染】yī chén bù rǎn ❶ 佛家称色、声、香、味、触、法为六尘,修道的人不被六尘所玷污,叫做一尘不染。泛指人品纯洁,丝毫没沾染坏习气。not soiled by a speck of dust; maintain one's pure character. Buddhists call objects of the senses (form, sound, smell, taste, touch, and perception of character) the 'six worldly environments,' and a Buddhist not contaminated by these six worldly environments is described as '一尘不染.' ❷ 借指环境非常清洁 spotlessly clean; very clean: 屋子里窗明几净,～。The room is spotlessly clean, with bright windows and clean tables.

【一成不变】yī chéng bù biàn 一经形成,永不改变 immutable and frozen; invariable; unalterable: 任何事物都是不断发展的,不是～的。All matters develop continuously, and nothing is immutable.

【一程子】yīchéng·zi〈方 *dial*.〉一些日子 a number of days: 我母亲来住了～,昨天刚走。My mother was here with us for a number of days. She left only yesterday.

【一筹】yī chóu 计数的一根竹签。借指一着(zhāo)。chip used as a counter; move: 略逊～ be slightly inferior|他的思维能力比一般人高出～。His thinking ability is better than that of ordinary people.

【一筹莫展】yī chóu mò zhǎn 一点计策也施展不出;一点办法也想不出 can find no way out; be at one's wits' end; be at the end of one's tether

【一触即发】yī chù jí fā〈比喻 *fig*.〉形势非常紧张,马上会发生严重的事情 may break out at any moment; be on the verge of breaking out: 矛盾～。A conflict may break out at any moment.

【一触即溃】yī chù jí kuì 一碰就崩溃 collapse at the first encounter: 敌军士气涣散,～。The enemy was demoralized and collapsed at the first encounter.

【一锤定音】yī chuí dìng yīn〈比喻 *fig*.〉凭某个人的一句话做出最后决定 set the tune with one beat of the gong; give the final word; 锤 also put as 椎 chuí

【一锤子买卖】yī chuí·zi mǎi·mai 不考虑以后怎样,只做一次的交易(多用于比喻 oft. used in a figurative way) a one-time deal; the one and only business deal to be made with sb. regardless of future consequences

【一次能源】yī cì néngyuán 指存在于自然界的天然能源,如煤炭、石油、天然气、水力、铀矿等 primary energy; natural energy resources existing in nature, e. g. coal, petroleum, natural gas, waterpower, uranium, etc.

【一次性】yīcìxìng 只一次的;不须或不做第二次的 once only; one-time (without a second chance): 发给～补助金 one lump-sum grant|对某些滞销商品作～削价处理 cut-rate disposal of unmarketable commodities

【一从】yīcóng 自从 since: ～别后,音信杳然。No word has come from him since he left.

【一蹴而就】yī cù ér jiù 踏一步就成功。形容事情轻而易举,一下子就能完成。reach the goal in one step; accomplish one's aim in one move

【一搭两用儿】yī dā liǎng yòngr 一样东西当两样用 one thing serving two purposes: 带件大衣,白天穿,晚上当被盖,～。Take an overcoat with you. You can wear it during the day and use it as a quilt at night, letting it serve two purposes.

【一带】yīdài 泛指某处及其附近地方 area around a particular place: 北京～ Beijing area|江南～雨量充足。The area south of the

Yangtze River enjoys plentiful rainfall.

【一旦】yīdàn ❶ 一天之间(形容时间短) in a single day; in a very short time: 毁于～ be destroyed overnight ❷ 不确定的时间词,表示有一天 one day: a) 用于已然,表示'忽然有一天' used for one day in the past: 相处三年,～离别,怎么能不想念呢? After being together for three years, how can they not miss each other after parting? b)用于未然,表示'要是有一天' used for one day in the future: 理论～为群众所掌握,就会产生巨大的物质力量。Once grasped by the masses, theory will generate a tremendous material force.

【一刀两断】yī dāo liǎng duàn 〈比喻 *fig.*〉坚决断绝关系 sever with one stroke; make a clean break

【一刀切】yīdāoqiē 〈比喻 *fig.*〉不顾实际情况,用同一方式处理问题 cut it all evenly with one stroke; make everything rigidly uniform regardless of the actual situation; impose uniformity in all cases; prescribe a single solution for diverse problems; also 一刀齐 yīdāoqí

【一道】yīdào (～儿 yīdàor) 一同 together; side by side; alongside; same as 一路 yīlù ③: ～走 go together|～工作 work together

【一得之功】yī dé zhī gōng 一点微小的成绩 just an occasional, minor success: 不能沾沾自喜于～,一孔之见。Don't feel so self-satisfied over a minor success or a narrow view.

【一得之愚】yī dé zhī yú 〈谦辞 *hum.*〉指自己对于某一问题的见解 my humble opinion: 这是我的～,供你参考。This is my humble opinion, for your reference only.

☞ 千虑一得 qiān lǜ yī dé on p. 1528

【一点儿】yīdiǎnr ❶ 表示不定的数量 indefinite amount: 我没活儿做了,你分给我～吧。I have no work to do, so please give me a bit. ❷ 表示很小或很少 tiny; a little: 我以为有多大呢,原来只有这么～。I had thought it quite big, actually it is so tiny. |只有那么～,够用吗? That's all that is left. Is it enough? |几年过去了,他的毛病～都没改。Several years have passed, but his shortcomings have not changed a bit.

【一丁点儿】yīdīngdiǎnr 〈方 *dial.*〉极少的或极小的一点儿 a wee bit

【一定】yīdìng ❶ 规定的;确定的 fixed; specified; certain; regular: 每天工作几小时,学习几小时,休息几小时,都有～。There are fixed hours for a day's work, study and rest. ❷ 固定不变;必然 surely; necessarily: 文章的深浅跟篇幅的长短,并没有～的关系。The depth of an article is not necessarily associated with its length. ❸ 表示坚决或确定;必定 must; certainly: ～要努力工作。It is imperative to work hard. |这半天还不回来,～是没搭到车。He must have missed the train, not to have come back yet all this time. ❹ 特定的 given; particular; certain: ～的文化是～社会的政治和经济的反映。A particular culture is the reflection of a particular society's politics and economy. ❺ 相当的 proper; fair; due: 我们的工作已经取得了～的成绩。We have made some due achievements in our work. |他的思想感情起了～程度的变化。He has experienced changes in his thoughts and feelings to a fair extent.

【一定之规】yīdìng zhī guī 一定的规则。多比喻已经打定的主意。fixed pattern; (oft. fig.) one's own way; one's set views

【一动】yīdòng (～儿 yīdòngr) 动不动 easily; frequently; at every turn: ～就发脾气 lose one's temper frequently|～儿就哭 weep easily

【一度】yī dù ❶ 一次;一阵 once: 一年～的春节又到了。The once-a-year Spring Festival is coming. |经过～紧张的战斗,洪水终于被战胜了。After an intense struggle, the flood was finally beaten off. ❷ 有过一次 on one occasion; for a time: 他～休学。He stopped going to school for a time.

【一端】yī duān (事情的)一点或一个方面 one aspect (or side) of the matter: 此其～。This is one aspect of the matter.

【一多半】yīduōbàn (～儿 yīduōbànr) 超过半数 the greater part; same as 多半 duōbàn ①: 小组成员～是年轻人。Most of the members of this group are young people.

【一…而…】yī…ér… 分别用在两个动词前面,表示前一个动作很快产生了结果 [used before two verbs to indicate that one action follows another as an immediate result]: ～哄～散 break up in a hubbub|～怒～去 go away in a temper; leave in anger|～痛～绝 be deeply grieved|～望～知。It can be seen at one glance. |～扫～光 make a clean sweep of|～挥～就。Just one flourish of the pen and it's done.

【一而再,再而三】yī ér zài,zài ér sān 反复多次;再三 again and again; time and again; repeatedly

【一二】yī'èr 一两个;少数 one or two; just a few; just a little: ～知己 a few close friends|略知～(自谦所知不多 term of self-depreciation) know a little about

【一…二…】yī…èr… 分别加在某些双音节形容词的两个词素前面,表示强调 [used before the two morphemes of certain disyllabic adjectives to indicate emphasis]: ～干～净 neat and tidy|～清～楚 perfectly clear|～清～白 very clean

【一二·九运动】Yī'èr-Jiǔ Yùndòng 1935 年 12 月 9 日,北平(今北京)学生在中国共产党领导下,发动的抗日救国运动。目标是反对日本帝国主义对华北的进一步侵略和国民政府的不抵抗政策,号召全国人民起来抗日救国。运动很快发展到全国各地，为1937年开始的抗日战争准备了条件。December 9th Movement; demonstration staged on December 9, 1935 by Beiping (present-day Beijing) students under the leadership of the Chinese Communist Party, the aim being to oppose further invasion of North China by Japanese imperialism and the non-resistance policy of the Kuomintang government, and to call for resistance to Japanese aggression and for national salvation. The movement soon spread across the nation, paving the way for the War of Resistance against Japan that started in 1937.

【一发】yīfā ❶ 更加 all the more; even more: 如果处理不当，就～不可收拾了。If not handled properly, the situation will become even more hopeless. ❷ 一同；一并 together; along with all the others: 你先把这些急用的材料领走，明天～登记。Take these urgent materials first, and register along with all the others tomorrow.

【一发千钧】yī fà qiān jūn 一根头发上系着千钧的重量 hundredweight hanging by a hair; 〈比喻 *fig*.〉极其危险 be in imminent peril; hang by a thread; also 千钧一发 qiān jūn yī fà

【一帆风顺】yī fān fēng shùn 〈比喻 *fig*.〉非常顺利，毫无挫折 plain sailing; smooth sailing

【一反常态】yī fǎn cháng tài 完全改变了平时的态度 depart from one's normal behaviour; act out of character

【一风吹】yīfēngchuī 〈比喻 *fig*.〉一笔勾销 scatter to the winds; dismiss all charges, etc.; cancel the whole thing

【一概】yīgài 〈副词 *adv*.〉表示适用于全体，没有例外 one and all; without exception; totally; categorically: 过期～作废 become invalid after the specified date without exception

【一概而论】yīgài ér lùn 用同一标准来对待或处理(多用于否定 usu. used in the negative) treat (different matters) as the same: 不能～ not to be lumped together; not to be mentioned in the same breath

【一干】yīgān 所有跟某件事(多指案件)有关的 all those involved: ～人 all those involved | ～人犯 the criminals and all those involved in the case

【一竿子到底】yī gān·zi dào dǐ 〈比喻 *fig*.〉直接贯彻到底 carry (a task or directive) right down to the grass-roots level; carry sth. through to the end; also 一竿子插到底 yī gān·zi chā dào dǐ

【一个巴掌拍不响】yī·ge bā·zhang pāi bù xiǎng 〈比喻 *fig*.〉矛盾和纠纷不是单方面引起的 one hand alone can't clap; it takes two to make a quarrel

【一个劲儿】yī·gejìnr 表示不停地连续下去 continuously; persistently: 雨～地下。It kept on raining nonstop. | 他～地直往前跑。He continuously runs ahead.

【一个萝卜一个坑儿】yī·ge luó·bo yī gè kēngr 〈比喻 *fig*.〉每人各有岗位，各有职责 Each has his own task, and nobody is dispensable.

【一个心眼儿】yī·ge xīnyǎnr ❶ 指专心一意 have one's heart set on sth.; devotedly; stubbornly: ～为集体 wholehearted devotion to the collective ❷ 〈比喻 *fig*.〉固执不知变通 stubborn; inflexible

【一共】yīgòng 〈副词 *adv*.〉表示合在一起 altogether; in all; all told: 三个小组～是十七个人。The three groups have a total of 17 members.

【一股劲儿】yīgǔjìnr 表示从始至终不松劲；一口气 without a break; at one go; at a stretch: ～地干 do sth. without a break

【一股脑儿】yīgǔnǎor 〈方 *dial*.〉通通 completely; lock, stock and barrel; root and branch: 她兴奋得很，把要讲的话～都讲出来了。She got so excited that she poured out all she had to say at once. also 一古脑儿 yīgǔnǎor

【一鼓作气】yī gǔ zuò qì 《左传》庄公十年：'夫战，勇气也。一鼓作气，再而衰，三而竭。'意思是打仗靠勇气，擂一通鼓，勇气振作起来了，两通鼓，勇气就衰了，三通鼓，勇气就完了。后来用来比喻趁劲头大的时候一下子把事情完成。press on to the finish without letup; get sth. done in one vigorous effort. *The Zuo Commentary* · *Duke Zhuang 10th Year*: 'To fight relies on courage. The fighting spirit aroused by the first roll of drum is depleted by the second and exhausted by the third.'

【一贯】yīguàn (思想、作风等)一向如此，从未改变 (of thinking, style of work, etc.) consistent; persistent; all along: 谦虚、朴素是他～的作风。He consistently maintains a modest and simple style.

【一棍子打死】yī gùn·zi dǎ sǐ 〈比喻 *fig*.〉对人或事物不加分析，全盘否定 knock sb. down with one stroke; finish off with one blow; completely negate

【一锅端】yī guō duān 〈比喻 *fig*.〉全部消灭或尽其所有 wipe out; get rid of the whole lot; give away all one has: 把这伙贩毒分子来个～。Wipe out this band of drug traffickers completely. | 各种各样的意见，～地往外倒。Various opinions are pouring out without reservation.

【一锅粥】yī guō zhōu 形容混乱的形象；一团糟 a pot of porridge; (fig.) complete mess; all in a muddle: 乱成～ in a mess; in utter confusion

【一锅煮】yī guō zhǔ 〈比喻 *fig*.〉不区别情况，对不同的事物作同样的处理 cook all things in one pot; treat different persons or things in the same way; also 一锅烩 yī guō huì or 一勺烩 yī sháo huì

【一国三公】yī guó sān gōng 《左传》僖公五年：'一国三公，吾谁适从？'一个国家有三个主持政事的人，我听从谁？后来泛指事权不统一。state with three rulers; (fig.) divided leadership; power that is not unified. *The Zuo Commentary·Duke Xi 5th Year*: 'In a state with three rulers, whom should I obey?'

【一呼百应】yī hū bǎi yìng 形容响应的人很多 hundreds respond to a single call; be ready to go into action in their hundreds

【一忽儿】yīhūr〈方 *dial.*〉一会儿 a little while

【一晃】yīhuǎng（～儿 yīhuǎngr）很快地一闪 flash：窗外有个人影，～儿就不见了。A figure flashed past the window, and disappeared in no time.

【一晃】yīhuàng 形容时间过去得快（有不知不觉的意思）(of time) pass in a flash (without one's realising it)：～就是五年，孩子都长这么大了。Five years passed in a flash, and the children have grown so big.

【一会儿】yīhuìr ❶ 指很短的时间 a little while：～的工夫 a little while｜咱们歇～。Let's rest for a while. ❷ 指在很短的时间之内 in a moment; presently：～厂里还要开会。Our factory will have a meeting in a moment.｜你妈妈～就回来了。Your mother will come back soon.｜～地上就积起了三四寸厚的雪。Soon the ground was covered with a layer of snow three to four inches thick. ❸ 叠用在两个反义词的前面，表示两种情况交替［reduplicated before a pair of antonyms］now... now...; one moment... the next...：天气～晴～阴。The weather is one moment clear, the next cloudy.｜他～出，～进，忙个不停。He is busy all the time, going out one moment and coming in the next.

【一己】yījǐ 自身；个人 oneself; personal：～之私 one's own selfish interests

【一技之长】yī jì zhī cháng 指某一种技术特长 proficiency in a particular line (or field); professional skill; specialization; speciality

【一家之言】yī jiā zhī yán 指有独特见解、自成体系的学术论述。也泛指一个学派或个人的理论、说法。distinctive doctrine or theory; original system of thought of a school or individual

【一见如故】yī jiàn rú gù 初次见面就很相投，像老朋友一样 feel like old friends at the first meeting; hit it off right from the start

【一见钟情】yī jiàn zhōngqíng 一见面就产生了爱情 fall in love at first sight

【一箭双雕】yī jiàn shuāng diāo〈比喻 *fig.*〉一举两得 shoot two hawks with one arrow; kill two birds with one stone; serve a double purpose

【一经】yījīng〈副词 *adv.*〉表示只要经过某个步骤或者某种行为（下文说明就能产生相应的结果）as soon as; once (a certain step or action is taken to bring about a corresponding result)：～解释，就恍然大悟。He sees the light as soon as an explanation is made.

【一径】yījìng ❶ 径直 straight; directly; straightaway：他没有跟别人打招呼，～走进屋里。He went straight into the room without so much as to greet anyone. ❷〈方 *dial.*〉一直；连续不断 always：她～在微笑。She always has a smile on her face.｜他～是做教师的。He has always worked as a teacher.

【一…就…】yī…jiù… 表示两事时间上前后紧接 (one matter follows the other) no sooner... than...; the moment...; as soon as; at once：a)同一主语的 of the same subject：～学～会 catch on as soon as one learns｜～开～谢 (a flower) withers as soon as it blossoms｜～吃～吐 throw up as soon as one eats; b)不同主语的 of different subjects：～教～懂 learn as soon as one is taught｜～请～到 arrive as soon as one is invited｜～说～成 agree upon being persuaded｜～推～倒 fall upon being pushed

【一举】yījǔ 一种举动；一次行动 at one fling; with one effort; in one action; one stroke; one fell swoop：多此～ make an unnecessary move｜成败在此～。Success or failure hinges on this one action.｜～捣毁敌人的巢穴 destroy the enemy's lair in one stroke

【一举两得】yī jǔ liǎng dé 做一件事情，得到两种收获 gain two ends at once; kill two birds with one stone：荒山造林，既能生产木材，又能保持水土，是～的事。Planting trees on barren hills can both produce timber and conserve water and soil, killing two birds with one stone.

【一蹶不振】yī jué bù zhèn〈比喻 *fig.*〉一遭到挫折就不能再振作起来 collapse after a single setback; be unable to recover after a setback

【一刻】yīkè 指短暂的时间；片刻 a short while, an instant：～千金（形容时光非常宝贵）one moment is worth a thousand pieces of gold; time is precious

【一空】yīkōng 一点不剩 nothing is left：销售～ sold out｜抢劫～ robbed of everything one has

【一孔之见】yī kǒng zhī jiàn 从一个小窟窿里面所看到的 peephole view;〈比喻 *fig.*〉狭隘片面的见解（多用作谦词 oft. as a self-depreciatory expression）narrow view; very limited outlook

【一口】yīkǒu ❶ 纯一（指说话的口音、腔调）manner of speech：这孩子普通话说得很流利，可半年前还是～的广东话呢。This child speaks fluent Mandarin, but half a year ago all he could spoke was the Guangdong dialect. ❷ 表示口气坚决 with certainty; readily; flatly：～否认 flatly deny｜～咬定 cling to one's view; stick to what one says

【一口气】yī kǒu qì（～儿 yī kǒu qìr）❶ 一口气息 one breath：只要她还有～，就要尽力抢救。As long as there is a breath left in her, we must do our best to save her. ❷ 不间断地(做某件事) in one breath; without a break; at one go; at a stretch; breathlessly: ～儿说完 finish a narration without a break | ～跑到家 run home at one go

【一块儿】yīkuàir ❶ 同一个处所 at the same place: 他俩过去在～上学,现在又在～工作。In the past they studied at the same school, and now they are at the same workplace. ❷ 一同 together: 他们～参军。They joined the army together.

【一来二去】yī lái èr qù 指互相交往、接触后渐渐产生某种情况 in the course of frequent contact; in the course of time: 两家住在一个院子里,～地孩子们也都熟了。The two families live in the same courtyard, and over time the children got to know one another quite well.

【一览】yīlǎn 用图表或简明的文字做成的关于概况的说明(多用做书名 oft. used in book titles) general survey; bird's-eye view:《北京名胜古迹～》*A Guide to the Historical Sites and Scenic Spots of Beijing*

【一览表】yīlǎnbiǎo 说明概况的表格 table; schedule: 行车时间～ (train or bus) timetable

【一揽子】yīlǎn·zi 对各种事物不加区别或不加选择的 wholesale; package: ～计划(总的计划) package plan (overall plan) | ～建议(或者全部接受或者全部拒绝的建议) recommendation package; package deal (to be either totally accepted or totally rejected)

【一劳永逸】yī láo yǒng yì 辛苦一次,把事情办好,以后就不再费事了 by one supreme effort gain lasting repose; settle a matter once and for all

【一力】yīlì 尽全力;竭力 do one's best; do all one can: ～成全 do one's best to help (sb. to achieve his aim) | ～主持 do one's best to preside over | ～承担 do one's best to take charge

【一例】yīlì 一律;同等 same; alike: ～看待 treat in the same way

【一连】yīlián 〈副词 *adv.*〉表示动作继续不断或情况连续发生 in a row; in succession; running: ～下了三天雨。It rained for three days running. | 今天～运到了四五批货。Today four or five batches of goods have arrived in succession.

【一连串】yīliánchuàn (行动、事情等)一个紧接着一个 a succession of (actions, issues, etc.); a series of; a string of; a chain of (events, etc.): ～的胜利 a string of victories | ～的打击 a series of blows

【一连气儿】yīliánqìr 〈方 *dial.*〉一连 in a row; in succession; running: ～唱了四五个歌。She sang four or five songs in a row.

【一了百了】yī liǎo bǎi liǎo 由于主要的事情了结了,其余的事情也跟着了结 all troubles end when the main trouble ends

【一鳞半爪】yī lín bàn zhǎo 〈比喻 *fig.*〉零星片段的事物 odd bits; fragments; also 东鳞西爪 dōng lín xī zhǎo

【一零儿】yīlíngr 〈方 *dial.*〉零头 fraction: 我知道的这一点儿,连人家的～也比不上啊。What little I know isn't even a fraction of what he knows.

【一流】yīliú ❶ 同一类;一类 a kind; the same kind: 他是属于新派～人物。He belongs to the avant-garde school. ❷ 第一等 of the best quality; first-class; first-rate; top-notch: ～作品 a first-rate work

【一溜风】yīliùfēng 形容跑得很快 like a gust of wind; very quickly: 他～地从山上跑下来。He runs down the hill like a gust of wind.

【一溜儿】yīliùr ❶ 一排;一行 row: 这～十间房是集体宿舍。This row of ten rooms is the dormitory. ❷ 附近一带 nearby area; vicinity; neighbourhood: 反正就是那～,准在哪儿我就说不清了。Anyway, it's over there, though I'm not sure exactly where.

【一溜歪斜】yīliù-wāixié 〈方 *dial.*〉形容走路脚步不稳,不能照直走 (walk, etc.) unsteadily in a zigzag: 他挑着一挑儿水,～地从河边走上来。He staggered up the slope from the river, carrying two buckets of water on a shoulder pole.

【一溜烟】yīliùyān (～儿 yīliùyānr)形容跑得很快 be gone in a blur; streak off; quick as a wisp of smoke: 他说了一声再会,就骑上车,～地向东去了。After saying goodbye, he got on his bicycle and streaked off eastward.

【一路】yīlù ❶ 在整个行程中;沿路 all the way; throughout the journey: ～平安 bon voyage | ～顺风 have a good journey | ～上庄稼长势很好,一片丰收景象。The crops along the way are doing well, promising a bumper harvest. | ～上大家说说笑笑,很热闹。People chat cheerfully all the way, and the atmosphere was very lively indeed. ❷ 同一类 of the same kind (type; category; sort): ～人 the same kind of people; birds of a feather | ～货 the same type of goods | 老王是拘谨～,小张是旷达～。Old Wang belongs to the category of the overcautious, while Little Zhang belongs to the category of the broadminded. ❸ 一起(来、去、走) go the same way; take the same route: 咱们～走。Let's go the same way. | 我跟他～来的。He and I came the same way. ❹ 〈方 *dial.*〉一个劲儿;一直 continuously; persistently: 铝价～下跌。The price of aluminum keeps dropping.

【一律】yīlǜ ❶ 一个样子;相同 same; alike; uniform: 千篇～ stereotyped; following the same pattern | 强求～ seek rigid uniformity ❷ 适用于全体,无例外 all; without exception: 我国各民族～平等。All peoples of our country are equal.

【一落千丈】yī luò qiān zhàng 形容地位、景况、声誉等下降得很厉害(of status, situation, reputation, etc.) drop a thousand *zhang* in one fall; suffer a drastic decline

【一马当先】yī mǎ dāng xiān 作战时策马冲锋在前。形容领先;带头。gallop at the head; take the lead; be in the forefront

【一马平川】yī mǎ píng chuān 能够纵马疾驰的平地 wide expanse of flat land; wide stretch of flat country:翻过山岗,就是~了。After crossing the ridge there is a wide expanse of flat land.

【一脉相传】yī mài xiāng chuán 由一个血统或一个派别传下来 come down in one continuous line; can be traced to the same origin; in a direct line of descent (or succession); also 一脉相承 yī mài xiāng chéng

【一毛不拔】yī máo bù bá《孟子·尽心》:'杨子取为我,拔一毛而利天下,不为也。'unwilling to give up even a hair;〈比喻 *fig*.〉非常吝啬 very stingy. In *Mencius · Exhaustion of Mental Constitution*: 'Master Yang is an egotist, unwilling to give up even a hair for the benefit of others in the world.'

【一门心思】yī mén xīn·si 一心一意;集中精神 heart and soul; wholeheartedly; with great concentration:他~搞技术革新。He throws himself wholeheartedly into technological innovation.|老汉在~地磨着镰刀。The old man is sharpening his sickle with great concentration.

【一面】yī miàn ❶(~儿 yīmiànr)物体的几个面之一 one side (of an object):缎子~光~毛。Satin is lustrous on one side and dull on the other.|这房子朝北的~只开了一个小窗。The house has only a small window on the north side. ❷一个方面 one aspect:~倒 lean to one side|~之词 the statement of only one of the parties|独当~ assume responsibility for a certain task or field of work ❸表示一个动作跟另一个动作同时进行 at the same time; simultaneously: a)单用[used alone]:说着话,~朝窗户外面看。So saying, he looked out of the window. b)连用[used consecutively]:~走,~唱 singing while walking ❹〈书 *fml*.〉见过一次面 have met once before:~之识 have met once|未尝~ have never met before

【一面儿理】yīmiànrlǐ 一方面的理由;片面的道理 one party's version; a biased account; lopsided (or one-sided) argument

【一面之词】yī miàn zhī cí 争执双方的一方所说的话 the statement of only one of the parties

【一面之交】yī miàn zhī jiāo 只见过一次面的交情 have met only once; be casually acquainted; also 一面之雅 yī miàn zhī yǎ

【一鸣惊人】yī míng jīng rén《史记·滑稽列传》:'此鸟不飞则已,一飞冲天;不鸣则已,一鸣惊人。'比喻平时没有特殊的表现,一干就有惊人的成绩。(of an obscure person) amaze the world with a single brilliant feat; set the world on fire; originally from *Records of the Historian · Biographies of Jesters*: 'This bird does not fly unless it is able to soar up into the sky in one swoop; and it does not cry unless it is able to amaze the world'.

【一命呜呼】yī mìng wūhū 指死(含诙谐意 humour.) die; kick the bucket; give up the ghost

【一模一样】yī mú yī yàng 形容完全相同,没有什么两样 exactly alike; like two peas in a pod

【一木难支】yī mù nán zhī〈比喻 *fig*.〉艰巨的事业不是一人之力所能胜任的 a single post cannot support a mansion; it is difficult for a person to do much single-handed:众擎易举,~。With many people it's easy to lift a load; one person cannot do it alone.

【一目了然】yī mù liǎorán 一眼就能看清楚 be clear at a glance

【一目十行】yī mù shí háng 形容看书极快 take in ten lines at a glance; read quickly

【一年到头】yī nián dào tóu (~儿 yī nián dào tóur)从年初到年底;整年 throughout the year; all year round:~不得闲 be busy all year round

【一年生】yīniánshēng 在当年之内完成全部生活周期的(种子萌发、长出根、茎、叶,开花,结果,植物体死亡),如大豆、花生、水稻等植物都是一年生的 annual (plant); complete the life cycle within a year, e. g. sprouting seeds, growing roots, stems and leaves, blossoming, bearing fruit, and dying. Beans, peanuts, paddy rice, etc., arc aunnal plants.

【一念之差】yī niàn zhī chā 一个念头的差错(引起严重的后果) wrong decision made in a moment of weakness; momentary slip with serious consequences

【一诺千金】yī nuò qiān jīn《史记·季布栾布列传》:'得黄金百,不如得季布一诺'。后来用'一诺千金'形容诺言的信用极高。promise worth a thousand pieces of gold; promise that can be counted on. *Records of the Historian · Biographies of Ji Bu and Luan Bu*: 'Obtaining 100 pieces of gold is not as good as obtaining a promise from Ji Bu.'

【一拍即合】yī pāi jí hé 一打拍子就合上了曲子的节奏 beat time to the rhythm of music;〈比喻 *fig*.〉双方很容易一致 fit in readily; chime in easily

【一盘棋】yī pán qí〈比喻 *fig*.〉整体或全局 game of chess or chessboard; overall situation:全国~ coordinate efforts all over the country as on a single chessboard|~观点 overall view-point

【一盘散沙】yī pán sǎn shā〈比喻 *fig*.〉分散的、不团结的状态 sheet of loose sand; state of disunity

【一旁】yīpáng 旁边 one side：站在～看热闹 stand by watching the fun

【一炮打响】yī pào dǎ xiǎng〈比喻 *fig*.〉第一次行动就获得很大成功 get sth. done at one fling; accomplish with one effort; get off to a good start

【一偏】yīpiān 偏于一方面的 one-sided：～之见 one-sided view｜～之论 one-sided argument

【一片冰心】yī piàn bīng xīn 形容心地纯洁，不羡慕荣华富贵（语本唐王昌龄《芙蓉楼送辛渐》诗：'洛阳亲友如相问，一片冰心在玉壶'）moral purity; do not envy high position and great wealth. *Seeing Off Xin Jian at Furong Tower* by the Tang-dynasty poet Wang Changling: 'If relatives and friends in Luoyang ask about me, I have nothing but a pure heart.'

【一瞥】yīpiē ❶ 用眼一看 quick glance;〈比喻 *fig*.〉极短的时间 very short time：就在这～之间，我已看出他那激动的心情。In a quick glance I noticed his agitation. ❷ 一眼看到的概况（多用做文章题目 oft. used in titles of articles）glimpse; brief survey：边城市场～ A Glimpse of a Border-Town Market

【一贫如洗】yī pín rú xǐ 形容穷得一无所有 penniless; utterly destitute

【一品锅】yīpǐnguō ❶ 一种类似火锅的用具，用金属制成，上面是锅，下面是盛炭火的座子 covered tureen; utensil similar to a hot-pot, made of metal, where the upper part is a pot, and the lower part a base for holding charcoal ❷ 菜名，把鸡、鸭、火腿、肘子、香菇等放在一品锅里做成 name of a dish, with chicken, duck, ham, upper leg of pork, mushrooms, etc., cooked in covered tureen

【一品红】yīpǐnhóng 落叶灌木，叶子互生，下部的叶子椭圆形或披针形，绿色，顶端的叶片较狭小，鲜红色，很像花瓣。花小，单性，没有花被。供观赏。poinsettia (*Euphorbia pulcherrima*); deciduous shrub with alternate leaves, the lower leaves being green and oval or lanceolate, and the top leaves narrow, red, petal-like, and the flowers small, unisex, and without a perianth, grown as an ornamental plant

【一暴十寒】yī pù shí hán《孟子·告子》：'虽有天下易生之物也，一日暴之（'暴'同'曝(pù)'），十日寒之，未有能生者也。'比喻时而勤奋，时而懈怠，没有恒心。have one day's sun and then 10 days' cold; *Mencius·Gaozi*: 'Even with the most easily growing thing in the world, if you let it have one day's genial heat, and then expose it for 10 days to cold, it will not be able to grow.' (fig.) work by fits and starts, lacking perseverance

【一齐】yīqí〈副词 *adv*.〉表示同时 at the same time; simultaneously; in unison：队伍～出动。The troops are going into action simultaneously.｜全场～鼓掌。The audience started clapping in unison.｜人和行李～到了。The luggage arrived at the same time as the passengers.

【一起】yīqǐ ❶ 同一个处所 in the same place：坐在～ sit in the same place ❷ 一同 together; in company：张大叔明天进城，你～去吧。Uncle Zhang will go downtown tomorrow. Would you like to go along with him? ❸〈方 *dial*.〉一共 altogether; in all：这几件东西～多少钱？How much is that altogether?

【一气】yīqì ❶（～儿 yīqìr）不间断地（做某件事）at one go; without a break; at a stretch：～儿跑了五里地 run five *li* at a stretch ❷ 声气相通；成为一伙（多含贬义 oft. derog.）of the same gang; hand in glove：串通～ gang up; collaborate｜他们通同～。They act in collusion. ❸ 一阵（多含贬义 oft. derog.）spell; fit：瞎闹～ raise hell; kick up a row｜乱说～ talk nonsense

【一气呵成】yīqì hē chéng ❶〈比喻 *fig*.〉文章的气势首尾贯通（of writing）form a coherent whole; make smooth reading ❷〈比喻 *fig*.〉整个工作过程中不间断，不松懈 get sth. done at one go; carry sth. through without stopping

【一窍不通】yī qiào bù tōng〈比喻 *fig*.〉一点儿也不懂 do not know the first thing about; know nothing about (a subject); be utterly ignorant of; be beyond one's depth when it comes to something

【一切】yīqiè ❶ 全部的 all; every：调动～积极因素 bring every positive factor into play ❷ 全部的事物 everything; all：人民的利益高于～。The interests of the people are above everything.｜夜深了，田野里的～都是那么静。It was late at night, and all was quiet in the fields.

【一清早】yīqīngzǎo（～儿 yīqīngzǎor）清晨 early in the morning

【一穷二白】yī qióng èr bái 形容基础差，底子薄 poor and blank; poor economic foundation (穷 *qiong*：指工农业不发达 referring to underdeveloped industry and agriculture; 白 *bai*：指文化科学水平不高 referring to low cultural and scientific levels)

【一丘之貉】yī qiū zhī hé 同一个山丘上的貉 jackals from the same lair; birds of a feather;〈比喻 *fig*.〉彼此相同，没有差别（专指坏人 of bad people）be alike and have no difference

【一人得道，鸡犬升天】yī rén dé dào, jī quǎn shēng tiān 传说汉代淮南王刘安修炼成仙，全家升天，连鸡狗吃了仙药也都升了天（见于汉代王充《论衡·道虚》）。后来用'一人得道，鸡犬升天'比喻一个人得势，他的亲戚朋友也跟着沾光。when a man attains immortality, even his pets ascend to heaven; Legend goes that when Liu An, Prince of Huainan of the Han Dynasty, cultivated himself and became an immortal, all members of his family ascended to Heaven, and even his chickens and dogs ascended to Heaven by taking his pills of immortality (*Discourses Weighted in the Balance·On Falsehood* by Wang Chong in the Han Dynasty). (fig.) when a man gets to the top, all his friends and relations get there with him; 升天 shēng tiān also 飞升 fēi shēng

【一任】yīrèn 〈书 *fml.*〉听凭 allow; let

【一仍旧贯】yī réng jiù guàn 完全按照旧例 stick to the old practice; follow the old routine

【一日千里】yī rì qiān lǐ 形容进展极快 thousand *li* a day; at a tremendous pace; with giant strides

【一日三秋】yī rì sān qiū《诗经·王风·采葛》:'一日不见,如三秋兮。'一天不见,就好像过了三年。形容思念人的心情非常迫切。One day's separation seems as long as three years (from *The Book of Songs·Folksongs of the Capital·Picking Vine Flowers*); miss somebody very much

【一日之雅】yī rì zhī yǎ 一天的交情。指交情不深。a day's acquaintance: 无～ not have the pleasure of knowing somebody

【一如】yīrú (同某种情况)完全一样 just like; the same as; just as: ～所见 just like what we've seen|～所闻 just as what we've heard|～所请 just as we've requested

【一如既往】yīrú jìwǎng 完全跟过去一样 just as in the past; as before; as always

【一色】yīsè ❶ 一样的颜色 of the same colour: 水天～ the waters and the sky blend in the same colour ❷ 全部一样的;不混杂别的种类或式样的 of the same type; uniform: ～的大瓦房 brick-and-tile houses of a uniform style|～的江西瓷器 porcelain ware of the same style from Jiangxi

【一霎】yīshà 一会儿;短时间 in an instant; in a moment: ～间 in a flash|～时 quick as flash|就～工夫 just a moment

【一身】yīshēn ❶ 全身;浑身 whole body; all over the body: ～是劲 feel vigorous all over the body|～是胆 one's whole body is all pluck —know no fear; be absolutely fearless ❷ (～儿 yīshēnr)一套(衣服) a suit: ～工作服 a suit of work clothes ❸ 一个人 a single person: 独自～ solitary; all alone|～二任 hold two posts at the same time

【一身两役】yī shēn liǎng yì 一个人同时担任两件工作 hold two jobs at the same time; serve in a dual capacity

【一身是胆】yī shēn shì dǎn 形容胆量极大 one's whole body is all pluck; know no fear; be absolutely fearless

【一神教】yīshénjiào 只信奉一个神的宗教,如基督教、伊斯兰教等(区别于'多神教'as compared with'polytheism') monotheism; belief that there is only one god, such as Christianity, Islamism

【一审】yīshěn same as 第一审 dìyīshěn

【一生】yīshēng 从生到死的全部时间 all one's life; throughout one's life

【一失足成千古恨】yī shīzú chéng qiāngǔ hèn 一旦堕落或犯了严重错误,就成为终身的恨事 one false step brings everlasting grief; single slip may cause lasting sorrow; a moment's error can bring a lifelong regret

【一时】yīshí ❶ 一个时期 a period of time: 此～彼～。Times have changed.|～无出其右。For sometime nobody could outshine him. ❷ 短时间;暂时 for a short while; temporary; momentary; ephemeral: ～半刻 a short time; a short while|～还用不着 not needed for the time being|这是～的和表面的现象。This is a transient and superficial phenomenon. ❸ 临时;偶然 temporary; offhand; accidental; by chance: ～想不起他是谁 can't recall who he is for the moment|～高兴,写了两首诗。I happened to be in a good mood and wrote two poems. ❹ 叠用,跟'时而'相同 [used reiteratively like 时而 shí'ér] now... and now...; this moment ..., and the next ...: 高原上气候变化大,～晴,～雨,～冷,～热。The climate on the highland is changeable: it's now clear and now rainy, now cold and now hot.

【一时半会儿】yī shí bàn huìr 指短时间 short time; short moment; short while: 这场雨～停不了。The rain will not stop for a short while.

【一时一刻】yī shí yī kè 每时每刻 every moment: 我～也不能忘记这个教训。I shall never forget this lesson.

【一世】yīshì ❶ 一辈子 all one's life; lifetime: 他～没出过远门。All his life he's never been far away from home. ❷ 一个时代 an age: ～之雄 hero of an age

【一事】yīshì 〈方 *dial.*〉业务或组织上有关系的;一起的 related (organisationally or professionally); belong to the same organisation; be one and the same outfit: 这家药铺和城里同仁堂药铺是～。This drug store and the Tongrentang Pharmacy downtown are of the same organisation.

【一事无成】yī shì wú chéng 连一样事情也没做成;什么事情都做不成 accomplish nothing; get nowhere

【一视同仁】yī shì tóng rén 同样看待,不分厚薄 treat equally without discrimination

【一是一,二是二】yī shì yī, èr shì èr 根据事情本来的情况,应该怎样就怎样。多形容对事情认真,一丝不苟。unequivocally; use plain and blunt words; one is one, and two is two; call a spade a spade

【一手】yīshǒu ❶（～儿 yīshǒur）指一种技能或本领 proficiency; skill: 留～ hold back (or retain) one or two tricks ❷（～儿 yīshǒur）指要的手段 trick; move: 你可不能跟我来这～。Don't play the trick on me. ❸ 指一个人单独地 single-handed; all by oneself; all alone: ～造成 of one's own doing|～包办 keep everything in one's own hands; take everything on oneself

【一手一足】yī shǒu yī zú 指单薄的力量 one hand and one foot; a single person; a single effort

【一手遮天】yī shǒu zhē tiān 形容倚仗权势，玩弄骗人手法，蒙蔽众人耳目 hide the truth from the masses by relying on one's position and influence; hoodwink the public by deception

【一水儿】yīshuǐr〈方 *dial.*〉same as 一色 yīsè ②: 屋里～红木家具。The furniture in the room is made of nothing but mahogany.

【一顺儿】yīshùnr 同一个方向或顺序 in the same direction or order: 村里新盖的房子，～都是朝南的瓦房。All the new houses in the village are brick-and-tile ones and they all face south.

【一瞬】yīshùn 转眼之间。形容时间极短。an instant; a flash; twinkling of an eye: 火箭飞行，～千里。The rocket flies one thousand *li* in a flash.

【一丝】yīsī 形容极小或很少；一点儿 tiny bit; trace: 脸上露出了～笑容。There is a faint smile on his face.

【一丝不苟】yī sī bù gǒu 形容办事认真，连最细微的地方也不马虎 not be the least bit negligent; be scrupulous about every detail; be conscientious and meticulous

【一丝不挂】yī sī bù guà 形容赤身裸体 not have a stitch on; be stark naked

【一丝一毫】yī sī yī háo 丝毫 a tiny bit; an iota; a trace

【一死儿】yīsǐr〈方 *dial.*〉非常固执地（要怎么样）very obstinately; very stubbornly: 不让他去，他～要去。He was told not to go, but he insisted.

【一似】yīsì〈书 *fml.*〉一如；好像 just like; the same as

【一塌刮子】yītāguā·zi〈方〉❶ 通通 all; entirely; completely ❷ 总共加在一起 in all; altogether

【一塌糊涂】yītāhútú 乱到不可收拾；糟到不可收拾 in a hopeless mess; in an awful (or terrible) state: 闹得～ make a terrible row|烂得～ totally rotten

【一潭死水】yī tán sǐshuǐ〈比喻 *fig.*〉没有生气或停滞不前的沉闷局面 a pool of stagnant water; stagnant or lifeless condition

【一体】yītǐ ❶ 关系密切，如同一个整体 an organic (or integral) whole ❷ 全体 the whole; all people concerned; to a man: ～周知 be made known to all people concerned|～遵照 be observed by all

【一天】yī tiān ❶ 一昼夜 a day: ～二十四小时 twenty-four hours a day ❷ 一个白天 day: ～一夜 one day and one night ❸ 泛指过去某一天 one day (in the past): ～，他谈起当演员的经过。One day, he talked of how he became an actor. ❹〈方 *dial.*〉一天到晚 the whole day; all (the) day; from morning till night

【一天到晚】yī tiān dào wǎn 整天；成天 from morning till night; from dawn to dusk; all day long

【一条龙】yītiáolóng ❶〈比喻 *fig.*〉一个较长的行列 one continuous line: 十几辆汽车排成～。A dozen trucks stood in a long line. ❷〈比喻 *fig.*〉生产程序或工作环节上的紧密联系和配合 be streamlined; in a streamlined fashion; a coordinated process: 产运销～ integrate production, transportation and marketing in a streamlined fashion

【一条藤儿】yītiáoténgr〈方 *fml.*〉〈比喻 *fig.*〉串通一气的一伙儿 gang

【一条心】yī tiáo xīn 意志相同 be of one mind; be at one

【一同】yītóng〈副词 *adv.*〉表示同时同地做某件事 together; at the same time and place: ～出发 set out together|～欢度新年 spend the New Year's Day together

【一通】yītòng（～儿 yītòngr）一阵；一次 once; for one time: 胡扯～ sheer nonsense|他和我吵过～。He quarrelled with me once.|这～打真不轻。The beating this time was not light.

【一统】yītǒng 统一（国家）unify (a country): ～天下 unified country

【一头】yītóu ❶ 表示同时进行几件事；一面 [indicate several things being done simultaneously] at the same time; simultaneously: 他～走，～说。He talked as he walked. ❷ 表示动作急；径直 [indicate quickness] directly; straightly: 打开车门，他～钻了进去。He opened the door and dived into the car. ❸ 突然；一下子 all of a sudden; all at once: 刚进门，～碰见了他。I bumped into him the moment I came in. ❹ 头部突然往下扎或往下倒的动作 headlong: ～扑进水里 plunge headlong into the water|～倒在床上 collapse into the bed ❺（～儿 yītóur）一端 one end: 扁担的～挑着篮子，另～挂着水罐。A basket was being carried at one end of the shoulder pole, and a water pitcher at the other. ❻ 相当于一个头的高度 a head: 他比你高出～。He is a head taller than you are. ❼（～儿 yītóur）同一个方面；一伙 in a group; on one side: 昨天打桥牌，我和老王～，小张和小李～。We played bridge yesterday, Lao Wang and I on one side against Little Zhang and Little Li on the other. ❸〈方 *dial.*〉一块 together：他们是～来的。They came together.

【一头儿沉】yītóurchén〈方 *fml.*〉❶ 书桌或办公桌的一种构造形式，一头有柜子或抽屉，另一头没有。也指这种形式的桌子。heavy-at-one-end; desk or table with a cupboard or drawers at one end ❷〈比喻 *fig.*〉进行调解时偏袒一方 be partial (in mediation)

【一团和气】yī tuán héqì 态度温和，没有原则 keep on good terms with everyone (at the expense of principle); keep on the right side of everyone

【一团漆黑】yī tuán qīhēi ☞ 漆黑一团 qīhēi yī tuán on p. 1507

【一团糟】yītuánzāo 形容异常混乱，不易收拾 complete mess; chaotic state

【一退六二五】yī tuì liù èr wǔ 本是一句珠算斤两法口诀，十六除一是 0.0625，借用做推卸干净的意识。'退'是'推'的谐音，有时就说成'推'。'When one is divided by 16, it is 0.0625,' an abacus rhyme used figuratively to mean 'evade or deny all responsibility.' 退 (retreat) is the homophonic sound for 推 (evade), sometimes it is replaced by 推.

【一碗水端平】yī wǎn shuǐ duān píng〈比喻 *fig.*〉办事公道，不偏袒任何一方 hold a bowl of water level—be impartial

【一网打尽】yī wǎng dǎ jìn〈比喻 *fig.*〉全部抓住或消灭 catch the whole lot in a dragnet; round up a whole gang at one fell swoop

【一往情深】yī wǎng qíng shēn 指对人或事物有深厚的感情，十分向往留恋 be deeply attached; be passionately devoted; be head over heels in love

【一往无前】yī wǎng wú qián 指不怕困难，奋勇前进 press forward with an indomitable will

【一望无际】yī wàng wú jì 一眼看不到边。形容辽阔。stretch as far as the eye can see; stretch to the horizon：麦浪翻滚，～。The fields of wheat billowing like waves stretch as far as the eye can see.

【一味】yīwèi〈副词 *adv.*〉单纯地 purely; blindly; persistently：～迁就 make endless concessions; make one concession after another｜～推托 find one excuse after another for not doing sth.

【一文不名】yī wén bù míng 一个钱也没有 not have a penny to one's name; be penniless (名 *míng*：占有 possess)

【一窝蜂】yīwōfēng 形容许多人乱哄哄地同时说话或行动 like a swarm of bees

【一无】yīwú 全无；毫无 nothing at all; not in the least：～所获 achieve nothing; get nothing｜～所知 know nothing about; not have the least inkling of; be absolutely ignorant of; be completely in the dark｜～所有 not own a thing in the world; not have a thing to one's name

【一无是处】yī wú shì chù 一点对的地方也没有 without a single redeeming feature; devoid of any merit; no saving grace：不要把人说得～。Don't make him out to be without a saving grace.

【一无所有】yī wú suǒ yǒu 什么都没有。多形容非常贫穷。not own a thing in the world; not have a thing to one's name

【一五一十】yī wǔ yī shí 数数目时往往以五为单位，一五，一十，十五，二十…数下去，因此用'一五一十'比喻叙述时清楚而无遗漏 narrate systematically and in full detail; in counting numbers, five is often used as one unit, as five, ten, fifteen, twenty . . . , therefore 一五一十 (one five one ten) is used to indicate that every detail is told in one's narration

【一物降一物】yī wù xiáng yī wù 某种事物专门制伏另一种事物，或者某种事物专门有另一种事物来制伏 one thing conquers another; everything has its superior

【一息尚存】yī xī shàng cún 还有一口气儿，表示直到生命的最后阶段 so long as one still has a breath left; till one's last gasp：～，决不懈怠。I'll never relax my efforts as long as I live.

【一席话】yī xí huà 一番话 what one says during a conversation：你这～对我很有启发。What you said was a great inspiration to me.

【一席之地】yī xí zhī dì〈比喻 *fig.*〉极小的一块地方或极小的一个位置 a very small place or a very small position

【一系列】yīxìliè 许许多多有关联的或一连串的(事物) a series of：～问题 a whole series of questions｜引起了～变化 bring about a number of changes｜采取了～措施 have taken a series of measures

【一下】yīxià (～儿 yīxiàr) ❶ 用在动词后面，表示做一次或试着做 [used after a verb to indicate one action or one try]：看～儿 have a look｜打听～ make some inquiries｜研究～ think it over; mull it over ❷ 表示短暂的时间 in a short while; all at once; all of a sudden：灯～儿又亮了。After a little while the lights went on again.｜这天气，～冷，～热。Look at this weather. It's cold one moment and hot the next. ‖ also 一下子 yīxià·zi

【一线】[1] yī xiàn ❶ 战争的最前线 war front; front line ❷ 指直接从事生产、教学、科研等活动的岗位 forefront (of production, teaching or scientific research)：深入车间慰问～工人 go to the workshops and extend solicitude to the workers at the forefront of production

【一线】[2] yīxiàn 形容极其细微 a ray of; a gleam of：～阳光 a ray of sunlight｜～光明 a ray (or gleam) of light｜～希望 a gleam of hope｜～生机 a slim chance of survival

【一相情愿】yī xiāng qíng yuàn 处理彼此有关的事情时，只管自己愿意，不管对方愿意不愿意；泛指办事时全从主观愿望出发，不考虑客观条件 one-sided wish; one's own wishful thinking; in handling matters concerning each other, a person thinks of only his own wish, but not the other's; handle things according to one's subjective wish without taking the objective conditions into account; 相 also 厢 xiāng

【一向】yīxiàng ❶ 过去的某一段时期 earlier on; lately: 前～雨水多（指较早的一段时期）。There was quite a lot of rain earlier on (referring to an earlier period). | 这～工程的进度很快（指最近的一段时期）。Fast progress has been made in the work lately (referring to a recent period). ❷〈副词 *adv.*〉a) 表示从过去到现在 [indicating a period from the past to the present] always; consistently: ～俭朴 always thrifty and simple | ～好客 always hospitable b) 表示从上次见面到现在 [indicating a period from the last meeting to the present] all along: 你～好哇！How have you been all along?

【一小儿】yīxiǎor〈方 *dial.*〉从小 since childhood: 他～就喜欢画画儿。He has loved to paint ever since childhood.

【一笑置之】yī xiào zhì zhī 笑一笑就把它搁在一旁，表示不拿它当回事 dismiss with a laugh (or smile); laugh off

【一些】yīxiē ❶ 表示不定的数量 indicating an indefinite number or quantity; a number of; a certain amount or number of sth.; some; a few; a little: 这些活儿你做不完，分～给我。You can't finish that much work. Give some of it to me. ❷（～儿 yīxiēr）表示数量少 indicating a small amount: 只有这～儿了，怕不够吧？There's only this much left. Is it enough? ❸ 表示不止一种或一次 indicating more than one or once: 他曾担任过～重要的职务。He held some important posts in the past. ❹ 放在形容词、动词或动词性词组后，表示略微的意思 [used after an adjective, verb or verbal phrase to indicate a slight change in degree]: 好～ a bit better | 留神～ be more careful | 想开～ take it easier.

【一泻千里】yī xiè qiān lǐ 形容江河水流迅速。也形容文笔奔放、流畅。(of a river) rush down a thousand *li*; flow powerfully; (of a writing style) bold and flowing

【一蟹不如一蟹】yī xiè bùrú yī xiè 艾子来到沿海的地方，看见一物扁而圆，有很多腿。他不认识，就问当地居民，当地人告诉他那是一种螃蟹。后来艾子又看到了好几种螃蟹，但一种比一种小，艾子叹了口气说：'怎么一蟹不如一蟹呢！'（见于托名苏轼的《艾子杂说》）后来比喻一个比一个糟。each crab is smaller than the last. When Ai Zi came to a coastal place, he saw a creature that was flat and round with many legs. He did not know what it was and asked local residents. He was told it was a species of crab. Later, he saw some other species, but each was smaller than the last. Aizi said with a sigh: 'Why is each crab smaller than the last?' (*The Miscellanies of Aizi*, compiled in the name of Su Shi) (fig.) each one is worse than the last.

【一心】yīxīn ❶ 专心；全心全意 wholeheartedly; heart and soul: ～为公 serve the public whole-heartedly (or heart and soul) ❷ 齐心；同心 of one mind; at one: 万众～ the people of the whole country are united as one | 全国～。The whole country is of one mind.

【一心一德】yī xīn yī dé 同心同德 be of one heart and one mind; be dedicated to the same cause

【一心一意】yī xīn yī yì 心思、意念专一 heart and soul; wholeheartedly

【一新】yīxīn 完全变成新的 become completely new; brand new: 整修～ take on a new look after renovation

【一星半点儿】yīxīngbàndiǎnr 极少 tiny bit; very small amount: 为大伙儿做～的事情，不值得一提。It's not worth mentioning to do such a tiny bit for the public.

【一星儿】yīxīngr 极少的一点儿 tiny bit

【一行】yīxíng 一群（指同行的人）a group (travelling together); party: 参观团～十二人已于昨日起程。A 12-member visiting group left yesterday.

【一言既出，驷马难追】yī yán jì chū, sì mǎ nán-zhuī 一句话说出了口，就是套四匹马的车也追不上。形容话说出之后，无法再收回。a word once spoken cannot be taken back even by a team of four horses; what is said cannot be unsaid

【一言堂】yī yán táng ❶〈旧时 *old*〉商店挂的匾额，上写'一言堂'三个字，表示不二价 horizontal shop sign board inscribed with the words 'no bargaining' in old times ❷ 指领导缺乏民主作风，不能听取群众意见，特别是不能听相反的意见（跟'群言堂'相对 as opposed to 'the conference hall where everybody has a say'）conference hall where one person has all the say; one person alone has the say; one person lays down the law. It implies that the leadership adopts an undemocratic style of work and refuses to listen to criticisms and suggestions from his juniors.

【一言以蔽之】yī yán yǐ bì zhī 用一句话来概括 to sum up in a word

【一氧化碳】yīyǎnghuàtàn 无机化合物，化学式 CO。无色无味的气体，比空气轻，有剧毒，燃烧时发出蓝色火焰，并放出大量的热。用做燃料，也是化工原料。煤气中含有一氧化碳。carbon monoxide (CO); colourless, odourless, poisonous inorganic compound gas, which is lighter than air, emits a blue flame when burning, gives out plenty of heat, and is used as a fuel and a raw material for making chemicals. The coal gas contains carbon monoxide.

【一样】yīyàng 同样;没有差别 the same; alike; make no different; as...as...:哥儿俩相貌～,脾气也～。The two brothers are alike both in appearance and in temperament.|他们两个人打枪打得～准。They both shoot accurately.

【一叶蔽目】yī yè bì mù《鹖冠子·天则》:'一叶蔽目,不见太山。''a leaf before the eye shuts out Mount Tai.'(*Heguanzi·Law of Heaven*);〈比喻 *fig.*〉为局部的或暂时的现象所迷惑,不能认清事物的全貌或问题的本质 baffled by a local or temporary phenomenon; fail to see the whole picture of a thing or the essence of a question clearly; have one's view of the important overshadowed by the trivial; also 一叶障目 yī yè zhàng mù

【一叶知秋】yī yè zhī qiū 看见一片落叶就知道秋天的来临 falling of one leaf heralds the autumn; it is a straw in the wind;〈比喻 *fig.*〉发现一点预兆就料到事物发展的趋向 a small sign can indicate a great trend

【一一】yīyī 一个一个地 one by one; one after another:临行时妈妈嘱咐了好些话,他～记在心里。He remembers everything his mother said to him on his departure.

【一…一…】yī…yī… ❶ 分别用在两个同类的名词前面[used before two nouns of the same kind] a) 表示整个[indicating the whole] all; the whole:～心～意 whole-heartedly|～生～世(人的一生) one's whole life; all one's life b)表示数量极少[indicating a very small amount] each; every; single:～针～钱 a single needle or piece of thread|～草～木 every grass and tree|～言～行 every word and deed ❷ 分别用在不同类的名词前面[used before two nouns of different kinds] a)用相对的名词表明前后事物的对比 use two relative nouns to indicate contrast:～薰～莸(比喻好的和坏的有区别) a fragrant herb and a blade of stinking grass(fig.) there is difference between the good and the bad; b)用相关的名词表示事物的关系[use two related nouns to indicate their relationship]:～本～利(指本钱和利息相等) capital and profit; profit proportionate to the capital ❸ 分别用在同类动词的前面,表示动作是连续的[used before two verbs of similar meaning to indicate two successive actions]:～瘸～拐 limping along|～歪～扭 twist and crook ❹ 分别用在相对的动词前面,表示两方面的行动协调配合或两种动作交替进行[used before two relative verbs to indicate the coordination or alternation of the two actions]:～问～答 one asking and the other answering|～唱～和 one singing and the other echoing; sing the same tune; collude with each other|～起～落 rise and fall in turn; up and down|～张～弛 alternate tension with relaxation ❺ 分别用在相反的方位词、形容词等的前面,表示相反的方位或情况[used before two words of direction opposite in meaning to indicate opposite directions or situations]:～上～下 one above, one below|～东～西 one east, one west; poles apart|～长～短 one long, one short

【一衣带水】yī yī dài shuǐ 水面像一条衣带那样窄;形容一水之隔,往来方便 a narrow strip of water; two neighbouring countries separated by a narrow strip of water

【一意孤行】yī yì gū xíng 不听劝告,固执地照自己的意思行事 cling obstinately to one's course; act wilfully; refuse to listen to sb.'s advice and insist on having one's own way

【一应】yīyīng 所有一切 all; everything:～俱全 everything needed is there|～工具、材料都准备好了。All the tools and materials are ready.

【一隅】yīyú〈书 *fml.*〉❶ 一个角落 a corner:～之地 a very small area|偏安～ keep a small area safe under enemy threat ❷ 偏于一方面的 one-sided; limited; narrow:～之见 a very narrow (or limited) view

【一隅三反】yī yú sān fǎn ☞ 举一反三 jǔ yī fǎn sān on p.1049

【一语破的】yī yǔ pò dì 一句话就说明关键 hit the mark with a single comment (的 *dì*:箭靶 target; 比喻关键 (fig.) key; crucial point)

【一元化】yīyuánhuà ❶ 由多样向单一发展;由分散向统一发展 integration; centralization ❷ 指集中统一 centralized; unified:～领导 unified (or centralized) leadership

【一元论】yīyuánlùn 认为世界只有一个本原的哲学学说。认为物质是世界本原的是唯物主义的一元论。认为精神是世界本原的是唯心主义的一元论。monism; doctrine that there is only one ultimate substance or principle in the world. The belief that matter is the ultimate substance or principle of the world is materialist monism, and that mind is the ultimate substance or principle is idealist monism.

【一再】yīzài 一次又一次 time and again; again and again; repeatedly:～声明 state again and again|～表示 express again and again

【一…再…】yī…zài… 分别放在同一个动词前面,表示该动作多次重复 used separately before the same verb to indicate the repetition of the same action:～误～误 delay time and again|～错～错 keep on making mistakes|～拖～拖 postpone again and again

【一早】yīzǎo ❶ (～儿 yīzǎor)清晨 early in the morning:今天～他就下乡去了。He went to the countryside early this morning. ❷〈方 *dial.*〉很早；早先 long ago; earlier：这是他现在的表现呢，还是～就如此呢？Has he always behaved like his or differently before?

【一朝】yīzhāo same as 一旦 yīdàn

【一朝一夕】yī zhāo yī xī 一个早晨或一个晚上。指非常短的时间。in one morning or evening; overnight; in one day：非～之功 not the work of a single day

【一针见血】yī zhēn jiàn xiě〈比喻 *fig.*〉说话简短而能说中要害 brief and to the point; pierce to the truth with one pertinent remark; hit the nail on the head

【一枕黄粱】yī zhěn huáng liáng ☞ 黄粱梦 huáng liáng mèng on p. 852

【一阵】yīzhèn (～儿 yīzhènr)动作或情形继续的一段时间 a burst; a fit; a peal：～掌声 a burst of applause | ～狂风 a violent gust of wind; a blast (of wind) | 说～笑～ now talking, now laughing; also 一阵子 yīzhèn·zi

【一阵风】yīzhènfēng ❶ 形容动作快 like a whirlwind：同学们～地冲了上来。The students rushed forth like a whirlwind. ❷〈比喻 *fig.*〉行动短暂，不能持久 transient; in a flash; very briefly：搞科学实验，不能～。Making scientific experiments must not be a transient thing.

【一知半解】yī zhī bàn jiě 知道得不全面，理解得不透彻 not know much about; have a smattering of knowledge of; have scanty knowledge of

【一直】yīzhí〈副词 *adv.*〉❶ 表示顺着一个方向不变 indicating one direction; straight：～走，不拐弯。Go straight ahead. Don't turn. | ～往东，就到了。Go straight east, and you'll get there. ❷ 表示动作始终不间断或状态始终不变 indicating an uninterrupted action or a constant state：雨～下了一天一夜。It had been raining for one day and one night. | 他干活儿～很卖力。He has been working very hard. ❸ 强调所指的范围 referring to the given limits; all the way：全村从老人～到小孩都非常热情。The people of the whole village, old and young, are very enthusiastic.

【一纸空文】yī zhǐ kōng wén 指没有效用的文书 a mere scrap of paper

【一致】yīzhì ❶ 没有分歧 showing no difference; identical; unanimous; consistent：看法～ unanimous view; identical view | 步调～ march in step; act in unison ❷ 一同；一齐 together：～对外 unite to deal with outsiders, foreigners, an enemy, etc.

【一掷千金】yī zhì qiān jīn 原指赌博时下一次注就多达千金，后用来形容任意挥霍钱财 stake a thousand pieces of gold on one throw; throw away money like dirt; spend money like water

【一准】yīzhǔn〈副词 *adv.*〉必定 sure; surely; certainly：明儿我～进城。I'll surely go to the city tomorrow.

【一字长蛇阵】yī zì chángshézhèn 排列成一长条的阵势。泛指排列成一长条的人或物。single-line battle array; single-line formation; a single line of people or things

【一字千金】yī zì qiān jīn 秦相吕不韦叫门客著《吕氏春秋》，书写成后出布告，称有能增减一字的，就赏给千金(见于《史记·吕不韦传》)。后来用'一字千金'称赞诗文精妙。each word is worth a thousand pieces of gold; a highly finished literary product. Lü Buwei, prime minister of the State of Qin in the late Warring States Period, asked his hangers-on to write the *Lü's Spring and Autumn Annals*. After it was finished, he announced that whoever could add or delete one word, he would be awarded one thousand pieces of gold (*Records of the Historians · Biography of Lü Buwei*). Since then, 'each word is worth a thousand pieces of gold' has been used to praise a fine piece of literary work.

【一字一板】yī zì yī bǎn 形容说话从容清楚 speak unhurriedly and clearly

【一总】yīzǒng ❶ (～儿 yīzǒngr)合并(计算) altogether; all told; in all：～要二十个人才够分配。Altogether, twenty people will be enough for disposition. | 钱请你再垫一下，过后～算吧。Please pay the money for me. We'll settle our accounts altogether later. ❷ 全都 all：这些工作～交给我们小组去完成。Give all this work to our group.

伊[1] yī ❶〈书 *fml.*〉〈助词 *part.*〉用于词语的前面[used before a phrase]：下车～始 as soon as one alights from his official carriage | ～于胡底。Where will it all end? | ～谁之力？To whom should the credit go? ❷ (Yī) 姓 a surname

伊[2] yī 他或她 he or she 注意 **NOTE**：五四前后有的文字作品中用'伊'专指女性，后来改用'她'。'伊' was used especially in some literary works around the May 4th Movement of 1919 to refer to the female sex, and was later changed to 她 tā

【伊甸园】yīdiànyuán 犹太教、基督教圣经中指人类祖先居住的乐园 the Garden of Eden; paradise where the forefathers of mankind lived as described in the Holy Bibles of Judaism and Christianity [伊甸，希伯来 Hebrew: 'edēn]

【伊人】yīrén〈书 *fml.*〉那个人(多指女性 esp. referring to a woman) that person

【伊始】yīshǐ〈书 *fml.*〉开始 beginning：新春～ beginning of the new year | 下车～ as soon as one alights from one's official carriage

【伊斯兰教】Yīsīlánjiào 世界上主要宗教之一，公元7世纪初阿拉伯人穆罕默德所创，盛行于亚洲西部和非洲北部。唐代传入我国。在我国也叫清真教、回教。Islam; Islamism; Muslim religion; one of the main religions in the world, founded by an Arab called Mohammed in the early 7th century; popular in West Asia and North Africa and introduced to China during the Tang Dynasty; also 清真教 Qīngzhēnjiào or 回教 Húijiào [伊斯兰,阿拉伯 Arabic: Islām]

【伊斯兰教历】Yīsīlánjiàolì 伊斯兰教的历法,是阴历的一种。1 年分为 12 个月,单月为大月,每月 30 天,双月为小月,每月 29 天。平年 354 天,闰年 355 天。30 年中有 11 个闰年,不设置闰月。纪元以公元 622 年 7 月 16 日(即穆罕默德入麦地那的第二天)为元年元旦。我国也叫回历。Muslim Calendar; one of the lunar calendars that divides a year into 12 months, with the odd months each having 30 days and the even months each having 29 days. The common year has 354 days and the leap year has 355 days. There are 11 leap years every 30 years, but there is no leap month, and July 16th of A. D. 622 (namely the day following Mohammed's entry into Medina) was the New Year's Day of the first year. It is also called 回历 huílì in China.

【伊于胡底】yī yú hú dǐ 〈书 *fml.*〉到什么地步为止(对不好的现象表示感叹)。[when signing over an undesirable trend] Where will it all end?

衣 yī ❶ 衣服 clothing; clothes; garment: 上～ jacket; upper outer garment | 内～ underclothes; underwear | 大～ overcoat | 丰～足食 be well-clad and well-fed; have ample clothing and food ❷ 包在物体外面的一层东西 coating; covering: 炮～ gun cover | 笋～ tender bamboo covers | 糖～ sugar-coating ❸ 胞衣 afterbirth; secundines ❹ (Yī) 姓 a surname

☞ Yì on p. 2273

【衣摆】yībǎi 衣服的下摆 lower hem of a jacket, gown, coat

【衣包】yībāo 旧俗祭奠时烧给死者的纸衣和装着纸钱的纸袋(old custom) paper clothes and paper bag containing paper money burned as offerings to the dead

【衣胞】yī·bao ☞ 胞衣 bāoyī on p. 63

【衣钵】yībō 原指佛教中师父传授给徒弟的袈裟和钵,后泛指传授下来的思想、学术、技能等 mantle and alms bowl handed down by a Buddhist monk's to his favourite disciple; legacy; thinking, learning, skills, etc. handed down: 继承～ inherit the mantle of somebody | ～相传 hand down the cassock and bowl; hand down the legacy

【衣不解带】yī bù jiě dài 形容日夜辛劳,不能安稳休息 sleep without taking off one's clothes; be too tired to have proper sleep due to hard work

【衣兜】yīdōu (～儿 yīdōur) 衣服上的口袋 pocket; also 衣袋 yīdài

【衣服】yī·fu 穿在身上遮蔽身体和御寒的东西 clothing; clothes

【衣冠楚楚】yīguān chǔchǔ 形容穿戴整齐、漂亮 neatly and immaculately dressed

【衣冠禽兽】yīguān qínshòu 穿戴着衣帽的禽兽。指行为卑劣,如同禽兽的人。beast in human clothing; person as vile as a brute

【衣冠冢】yīguānzhǒng 只埋着死者的衣服等遗物的坟墓 tomb containing personal effects of the deceased, whose remains are either missing or buried elsewhere; also 衣冠墓 yīguānmù

【衣架】yījià ❶ (～儿 yījiàr) 挂衣服用的家具,用木材、金属等制成 coat hanger; clothes-rack; clothes tree; clothes stand ❷ 指人的身材;身架 stature; figure: 他的～好,穿上西服特别精神。He has a good figure and looks smart in a Western suit. also 衣架子 yījià·zi

【衣襟】yījīn 上衣、袍子前面的部分 the one or two pieces making up the front of a Chinese jacket

【衣锦还乡】yī jǐn huán xiāng 〈古时 *arch.*〉指做官以后,穿了锦绣的衣服,回到故乡向亲友夸耀 return to one's native place in silken robes (after acquiring wealth and position); also 衣锦荣归 yī jǐn róng guī

【衣料】yīliào (～儿 yīliàor) 做衣服用的棉布、绸缎、呢绒等材料 material for clothing; dress material

【衣帽间】yīmàojiān 公共场所中暂时存放衣物的地方 (British English) cloakroom; (American English) checkroom; coatroom; coatcheck

【衣衫】yīshān 泛指衣服 clothes: ～不整 not properly dressed | ～褴褛 in rags; shabbily dressed; out at elbows

【衣裳】yī·shang same as 衣服 yī·fu

【衣食】yīshí 衣服和食物。泛指基本生活资料 clothing and food; basic means of subsistence: ～丰足 have ample clothing and food | ～不周 be ill clad and fed; be short of clothing and food; live in poverty

【衣食住行】yī shí zhù xíng 穿衣、吃饭、住宿、行路。指生活上的基本需要。food, clothing, shelter and transportation — daily necessities

【衣物】yīwù 指衣着和日常用品 clothing and other articles of daily use

【衣鱼】yīyú 昆虫,体形长而扁,头小,触角鞭状,无翅,有三条长尾毛。常躲在黑暗的地方。蛀食衣服、书籍等。fish moth (*Lepisma saccharina*); silverfish; bookworm; wingless insect with a long and flat body, small head, whip-shaped feelers and three long strands of tail hair, often hiding itself in dark places and feeding on clothing and books; also 蠹鱼 dùyú or 纸鱼 zhǐyú

【衣装】yīzhuāng ❶ 衣服装束 dress; attire ❷ 衣服和行李 clothes and luggage

【衣着】yīzhuó 指身上的穿戴,包括衣服、鞋、袜、帽子等 clothing, headgear and footwear:～华丽 brightly dressed | 从～看,他像个商人。From his clothes, he looks like a merchant.

医(醫、毉) yī ❶ 医生 doctor (of medicine):军～ medical officer; army doctor; army surgeon | 牙～ dentist | 延～诊治 call in a doctor for diagnosis and treatment ❷ 医学 medicine; medical science: 中～ traditional Chinese medicine | 西～ Western medicine | ～科 medical courses in general; medicine | 他是学～的。He majors in medicine. ❸ 医治 cure; treat: 把我的病～好了 cure me of my illness | 头痛～头,脚痛～脚,不是根本办法。It's not the essential way to treat the head when the head aches and treat the foot when the foot hurts.

【医道】yīdào 治病的本领(多指中医 usu. of Chin. med.) art of healing; medical knowledge; physician's skill: ～高明 be a highly skilled doctor

【医德】yīdé 医务人员应该具备的品德 medical ethics: ～高尚 be an ethical doctor

【医护】yīhù 医治和护理 treatment and nursing: ～工作 medical service; medical work | ～人员 doctors and nurses | 经精心～,病情大有好转。After careful treatment and nursing, the patient's condition has greatly improved.

【医家】yījiā 指医生(多指中医 usu. in traditional Chinese medicine) physician: 收集各地～祖传秘方 collect secret prescriptions handed down along family lines

【医科】yīkē 教学上对有关医疗、药物、公共卫生等方面的学科的统称 medicine; medical sciences; medical education, including medical treatment, pharmaceuticals, public hygiene, etc.

【医理】yīlǐ 医学上的道理或理论知识 principles of medical science; medical knowledge: 深通～ have a profound knowledge of medicine

【医疗】yīliáo 疾病的治疗 medical treatment: ～队 medical team | ～机构 medical establishment (or institution) | ～设备 medical apparatus and instruments

【医生】yīshēng 掌握医药知识、以治病为业的人 doctor; medical man

【医师】yīshī 受过高等医学教育或具有同等能力、经国家卫生部门审查合格的负主要医疗责任的医务工作者 certified doctor; person who has received higher medical education or has the equivalent ability and is qualified after examination by a state medical department for the medical responsibility

【医士】yīshì 受过中等医学教育或具有同等能力、经国家卫生部门审查合格的负医疗责任的医务工作者 practitioner with secondary medical school education, medical practioner who has the equivalent ability and is qualified after examination by a state medical department for medical responsibility

【医书】yīshū 讲述医学的书籍(多指中医的 usu. of traditional Chinese medicine) medical book

【医术】yīshù 医疗技术 medical skill; art of healing: ～高明 have superb medical skill

【医务】yīwù 医疗事务 medical matters: ～工作者 medical worker

【医学】yīxué 以保护和增进人类健康、预防和治疗疾病为研究内容的科学 medical science; medicine; science and art of diagnosing, treating, curing, and preventing disease, relieving pain, and improving and preserving health; ☞ 中医 zhōngyī on p. 2485 and 西医 xīyī on p. 2043

【医药】yīyào 医疗和药品 medicine: ～费 medical expenses (or costs) | ～常识 general medical knowledge | ～卫生 medicine and hygiene

【医院】yīyuàn 治疗和护理病人的机构 hospital; establishment for treating and nursing patients

【医治】yīzhì 治疗 cure; treat; heal: 急性病应该赶快～。An acute disease should be treated quickly.

【医嘱】yīzhǔ 医生根据病情和治疗的需要对病人在饮食、用药、化验等方面的指示 doctor's advice (or orders) on a patient's diet, drug taking and laboratory tests

依 yī ❶ same as 依靠 yīkào ①: 唇齿相～ depend on each other like lips and teeth; share a common fate ❷ 依从; 同意 comply with; listen to; yield to: 劝他休息,他怎么也不～。No matter how I asked him to have a rest, he didn't listen. ❸ 按照 according to; in the light of; judging by: ～次前进 advance in order | ～法惩处 punish according to law | ～样画葫芦 draw a gourd according to the model; copy mechanically | ～我看,这样办可以。I would say it's okay to do it this way. ❹ (Yī)姓 a surname

【依傍】yībàng ❶ same as 依靠 yīkào ①: 无可～ with nobody to rely on ❷ 摹仿(多指艺术、学问方面 oft. concerning art, scholarship, etc.) imitate; model oneself on: ～前人 model oneself on one's predecessors

【依次】yīcì 按照次序 in proper order; successively: ～入座 take their seats in proper order | ～就诊 consult doctors in proper order

【依从】yīcóng 顺从 comply with; yield to: 万难～ be impossible to comply with

【依存】yīcún (互相)依附而存在 depend on sb. or sth. for existence; be interdependent

【依法】yīfǎ ❶ 按照成法 according to fixed rule: ～炮制 prepare a Chinese medicine according to a prescribed method ❷ 按照法律 according to law; in conformity with legal provisions; in accordance with the law:～惩办 punish according to law; deal with in accordance with the law; bring to justice

【依附】yīfù ❶ 附着 be attached to:凌霄花～在别的树木上。Chinese trumpet creepers grow attached to other trees. ❷same as 依赖 yīlài ①;从属 depend on; attach oneself to; become an appendage to:～权贵 attach oneself to bigwigs

【依归】yīguī ❶ 出发点和归宿 starting point and destination; what one turns to for guidance or support:以民族的利益为～ take the interests of the nation as the starting point and the end for one's work ❷ 依托;依靠 dependence; reliance:无所～ with no one to depend on; be helpless

【依旧】yījiù 照旧 remain the same:风物～。The landscape remains unchanged.|别人都走了,他～坐在那里看书。He still sat there reading after everybody had left.

【依据】yījù 根据 according to; in the light of; on the basis of; judging by

【依靠】yīkào ❶ 指望(别的人或事物来达到一定目的) fall back on; rely on (other people or things to reach certain purpose); depend on:～群众 depend on the masses|～组织 depend on the organisation ❷ 可以依靠的人或东西 a person or thing on whom or which one can depend on:女儿是老人唯一的～。The daughter is the only support of the old man.

【依赖】yīlài ❶ 依靠别的人或事物而不能自立或自给 rely on; be dependent on:～性 dependence|不～别人。Do not rely on others. ❷ 指各个事物或现象互为条件而不可分离 interdependent:工业和农业是互相～、互相支援的两大国民经济部门。Industry and agriculture are the two major sectors of the national economy which depend on and support each other.

【依恋】yīliàn 留恋;舍不得离开 be reluctant to leave; feel regret at parting from:～故园 be reluctant to leave one's native place|～之情 feeling of attachment

【依凭】yīpíng ❶ 依靠 rely on; depend on:孤身在外,无所～。He lives abroad alone and helpless. ❷ 指证据;凭证 evidence; certificate; voucher

【依然】yīrán 依旧 still; as before:～如故 remain as before; remain the same|风景～。The landscape is just the same as before.

【依顺】yīshùn 顺从 be obedient; comply with:他说得有理,也就～了他。What he said was reasonable and I complied with him.

【依随】yīsuí 顺从 agree to; yield to; comply with:丈夫说什么她都～。She agrees to whatever her husband says.

【依托】yītuō ❶ 依靠 rely on; depend on:无所～ with no one or nothing to depend on ❷ 为达到一定目的而假借某种名义 pretext; excuse:～古人 in the name of ancients|～鬼神,骗人钱财 use ghosts or gods to cheat people of their money

【依偎】yīwēi 亲热地靠着;紧挨着 snuggle up to; lean close to:孩子～在奶奶的怀里。The child snuggled up to her grandmother.

【依违】yīwéi 〈书 *fml.*〉依从或违背。指模棱、犹豫。comply with or go against; equivocal; undecided:～两可 be equivocal; be ambiguous|～不决 be undecided; shilly-shally

【依稀】yīxī 模模糊糊 vaguely; dimly:～可辨 dimly discernable|～记得 vaguely remember|远处楼台,～可见。The buildings in the distance are faintly visible.

【依循】yīxún 依照;遵循 follow; abide by

【依样葫芦】yī yàng húlú 照葫芦的样子画葫芦 draw a gourd according to the model;〈比喻 *fig.*〉单纯模仿,不加改变 copy mechanically; also 依样画葫芦 yī yàng huà húlú

【依依】yīyī ❶〈书 *fml.*〉形容树枝柔弱,随风摇摆(of tree branches and twigs) frail and tender; swaying in the wind:杨柳～。The twigs of the willows are swaying in the gentle breeze. ❷ 形容留恋,不忍分离 be reluctant to separate or part:～不舍 be reluctant to part; cannot bear to part|～惜别 be reluctant to say goodbye|～之感 feel reluctant to part

【依允】yīyǔn 依从;应允 assent; consent:他点头～了孩子的要求。He nodded assent to the child's demand.

【依仗】yīzhàng same as 倚仗 yǐzhàng

【依照】yīzhào 以某事物为根据照着进行;按照 according to; in accordance with; in the light of:～他说的去做 do as he says|～原样复制一件 make a copy of the original

祎(禕) yī〈书 *fml.*〉美好(多用于人名 usu. used in personal names) fine

咿(吚) yī ☞ below

【咿唔】yīwū〈拟声词 *onom.*〉形容读书的声音 sound of reading aloud

【咿呀】yīyā ❶〈拟声词 *onom.*〉squeak; creak:芦苇里传出～的桨声。The squeak of oars in oarlocks were heard from the reeds.|隔壁发出咿咿呀呀的胡琴声。Squeaky notes of a Chinese violin came from the other side of the wall. ❷ 小孩子学话的声音 prattle; babble:～学语 babbling baby

洢 Yī ❶ 洢水,水名,在湖南 Yishui, name of a river in Hunan Province ❷ 古水名,即今伊河,在河南 name of an ancient river, namely the present-day Yihe River in Henan Province

椸 yī ☞［移椸］（yíyī）on p.2262

铱 yī 金属元素，符号 Ir（iridium）。银白色，质硬而脆，化学性质稳定，用来制科学仪器。iridium（Ir）; hard, brittle silver-white metallic chemical element with stable chemical properties used in making scientific instruments.

猗 yī〈书 *fml.*〉❶〈助词 *aux.*〉相当于'啊' equivalent to 啊 ā：河水清且涟～。The clear river ripples on. ❷〈叹词 *interj.*〉表示赞美 expressing approval：～欤休哉。Happy! Joyful!

壹（弌） yī '一'的大写 one（used as the numeral 一 on cheques, banknotes, etc. to avoid mistakes or alterations）; ☞数字 shùzì on p.1791

椅 yī ☞山桐子 shāntóngzǐ on p.1670
☞ yǐ on p.2270

欹 yī〈书 *fml.*〉same as 猗 ② yī
☞ qī on p.1507

揖 yī〈书 *fml.*〉拱手行礼 make a bow with hands clasped

【揖让】yīràng〈书 *fml.*〉作揖和谦让，是古代宾主相见的礼节（of host and guest）bow and make way for each other

毉 yī［毉娩］（yīní）〈书 *fml.*〉婴儿 baby

漪 yī〈书 *fml.*〉水波纹 ripples：～澜 ripples｜清～ clear ripples

【漪澜】yīlán〈书 *fml.*〉水波 ripples

鷖 yī 古书上指鸥 gull as described in ancient books

噫 yī〈叹词 *interj.*〉❶〈书 *fml.*〉表示悲痛或叹息［expressing grief or regret］alas ❷ 表示惊异 expressing surprise：～，他今天怎么来了？How come he came here today?

【噫嘻】yīxī〈书 *fml.*〉〈叹词 *interj.*〉表示悲痛或叹息 expressing grief or regret

繄 yī〈书 *fml.*〉❶ 惟 only; alone：～我独无！Only I have none! ❷ 是 be tantamount to

Y

黟 Yī 黟县，在安徽 Yixian County, in Anhui Province

yí（丨）

一 yí ☞一 yī on p.2242

匜 yí〈古代 *arch.*〉盥洗时舀水用的器具，形状像瓢 ladle for dipping water in the shape of a gourd

仪[1]（儀） yí ❶ 人的外表 appearance; bearing：～表 appearance; bearing｜～容 looks; appearance｜威～ impressive manner; dignified bearing ❷ 礼节；仪式 ceremony; rite：司～ master of ceremonies｜行礼如～ salute ceremoniously ❸ 礼物 present; gift：贺～ present or gift（for wedding, birthday, etc.）｜谢～ a gift in token of gratitude; a thank-you gift; a gift for expressing gratitude（or thanks）❹〈书 *fml.*〉倾心；向往 admire; look forward to; yearn for：心～已久 admire somebody for a long time ❺（Yí）姓 a surname

仪[2]（儀） yí 仪器 apparatus; instrument：～表 metre｜地动～ seismograph（as invented by the Chinese scientist Zhang Heng 张衡 in A.D. 132）｜半圆～ protractor; semi-circle instrument

【仪表】[1] yíbiǎo 人的外表（包括容貌、姿态、风度等，指好的）（positive meaning, referring to one's looks, deportment and demeanour）appearance; bearing：～堂堂 dignified in appearance; impressive-looking

【仪表】[2] yíbiǎo 测定温度、气压、电量、血压等的仪器，形状或作用像计时的表 metre; instrument for measuring temperature, atmospheric pressure, electric quantity, blood pressure, etc.; its form and function are similar to that of a time-piece

【仪器】yíqì 科学技术上用于实验、计量、观测、检验、绘图等的比较精密的器具或装置 instrument; apparatus

【仪容】yíróng same as 仪表[1] yíbiǎo（多就容貌说）looks; appearance：～俊秀，举止大方 handsome and poised

【仪式】yíshì 举行典礼的程序、形式 ceremony; rite; function：授勋～ ceremony for awarding decorations｜～隆重 solemn and grand ceremony

【仪态】yítài〈书 *fml.*〉same as 仪表[1] yíbiǎo（多就姿态说）bearing; deportment：～万方（姿态美丽多姿）（of a beauty）appear in all her gracefulness

【仪仗】yízhàng ❶〈古代 *arch.*〉帝王、官员等外出时护卫所持的旗帜、伞、扇、武器等 insignia carried before the emperor; flags, umbrellas, fans, weapons carried by the guard of honour when a king, emperor, or high official is out ❷ 国家举行大典或迎接外国贵宾时护卫所持的武器。也指游行队伍前列举着的较大的旗帜、标语、图表、模型等。weapons carried by guards of honour at a grand state ceremony or welcoming ceremony for foreign guests; flags, slogans, charts, models, etc. carried in front of a procession

【仪仗队】yízhàngduì ❶ 由军队派出的执行某种礼节任务的小部队，有时带有军乐队，用于迎送国家元首、政府首脑等，也用于隆重典礼 guard of honour; honour guard; small unit sometimes with a military band for ceremonial occasions ❷ 走在游行队伍前，由手持仪仗的人员组成的队伍 guard of honour carrying flags and marching at the head of a parade

圯 yí〈书 *fml.*〉桥 bridge

夷1 yí〈书〉❶ 平坦;平安 smooth; safe: 化险为～ turn danger into safety ❷ 破坏建筑物(使成为平地) raze: 烧～弹 incendiary shell | ～为平地 level to the ground; raze ❸ 灭掉;杀尽 exterminate; wipe out: ～灭 exterminate; wipe out | ～族 extermination of an entire family (a punishment in ancient times)

夷2 yí ❶ 我国古代称东方的民族。也泛指周边的民族。*yi*, ancient term for tribes in the east or neighbouring regions: 淮～ ethnic groups living along the Huai River | 四～ all the ethnic minorities living around China (in ancient times) ❷〈旧时 *old*〉泛指外国或外国人 foreign country; foreigner: ～情 international situation | 华～杂处 inhabited by Chinese and foreigners

貤 yí〈书 *fml.*〉移动;移 move; shift
☞ yì on p. 2275

沂 Yí 沂河,发源于山东,流入江苏 Yihe River, rising in Shandong and flowing through northern Jiangsu into the Yellow Sea

诒(詑、訑) yí [诒诒]〈书 *fml.*〉自满自足的样子 self-satisfied and self-contented

诒 yí〈书 *fml.*〉same as 贻 yí

迤(迆) yí ☞ 逶迤 wēiyí on p. 1987
☞ yǐ on p. 2269

饴 yí 饴糖 maltose; malt sugar: 高粱～ sorghum maltose | 甘之如～ as sweet as sugar

【饴糖】yítáng 用米和麦芽为原料制成的糖。主要成分是麦芽糖、葡萄糖和糊精。maltose; malt sugar; sugar made from rice and malt, its chief contents including malt sugar, glucose and dextrin

怡 yí〈书 *fml.*〉快乐;愉快 happy; joyful; cheerful: 心旷神～ be cheerful; feel happy and relaxed

【怡然】yírán 形容喜悦 happy and contented: ～自得 be happy and pleased with oneself; feel a glow of happiness

宜 yí ❶ 合适 suitable; appropriate; fitting: 相～ suitable | 适～ appropriate | 权～之计 expedient; makeshift device; stopgap measure | 因地制～ suited to local conditions ❷ 应当(今多用于否定式 oft. used in the negative) should; ought to: 事不～迟。No more delays. *or* The matter needs immediate attention. | 不～操之过急。Don't act in haste. ❸〈书 *fml.*〉当然;无怪 of course; no wonder: ～其无往而不利。There's no doubt that they will meet success wherever they go. ❹ (Yí)姓 a surname

【宜人】yírén 适合人的心意 pleasant; delightful: 景物～ attractive (or charming) scenery | 气候～ pleasant (or delightful) weather

荑 yí〈书 *fml.*〉除去田地里的野草 clear the fields of weeds; weed: 芟～ weed; clear the fields of weeds
☞ tí on p. 1880

椸(杝) yí 古书上指一种像白杨的树 tree looking like poplar as described in ancient books
☞ duò on p. 502 and lí on p. 1175

咦 yí〈叹词 *interj.*〉表示惊异 (expressing surprise) well; why: ～,你什么时候来的? Well, when did you come here? | ～,这是怎么回事? Why, what's all this about?

贻 yí〈书 *fml.*〉❶ 赠送 make a gift of something; present: ～赠 make a gift of something; present | 馈～ make a gift of something; present ❷ 遗留 bequeath; leave behind; hand down: ～害 leave a legacy of trouble | ～患 leave a legacy of trouble

【贻害】yíhài 留下祸害 leave a legacy of trouble: ～无穷 entail untold troubles; involve endless trouble

【贻人口实】yí rén kǒushí 给人以利用的借口;让人当做话柄 provide one's critics with a handle; give occasion for talk

【贻误】yíwù 错误遗留下去,使受到坏的影响;耽误 affect adversely; bungle; leave mistakes behind to affect others adversely: ～后学 mislead the young students | ～战机 bungle the chance of winning a battle; forfeit a chance for combat | ～农时 miss the farming season

【贻笑大方】yíxiào dàfāng 让内行见笑 make a laughing stock of oneself before experts; incur the ridicule of experts

迻 yí〈书 *fml.*〉same as 移 yí

【迻录】yílù〈书 *fml.*〉抄录;誊录 copy out; transcribe

【迻译】yíyì〈书 *fml.*〉翻译 translate; also 移译 yíyì

姨 yí ❶ 姨母 mother's sister; maternal aunt; aunt: 二～ mother's second sister | ～夫 husband of mother's sister ❷ 妻子的姐妹 wife's sister; sister-in-law: 大～子 wife's elder sister | 小～子 wife's younger sister

【姨表】yíbiǎo 两家的母亲是姐妹的亲戚关系(区别于'姑表' as compared with 'the relationship between the children of sister and brother') relationship between the children of sisters; maternal cousins; cousinship: ～亲 maternal relatives | ～兄弟 male maternal cousins

【姨夫】yí·fu 姨母的丈夫 husband of mother's sister (or maternal aunt); uncle; also 姨父 yí·fu

【姨父】yí·fu same as 姨夫 yí·fu

【姨姥姥】yílǎo·lao 外祖母的姐妹 sister of one's maternal grandmother; great-aunt

【姨妈】yímā 姨母(指已婚的) (married) maternal aunt; aunt

【姨母】yímǔ 母亲的姐妹（married）maternal aunt; aunt

【姨奶奶】yínǎi·nai ❶ 祖母的姐妹 sister of one's paternal grandmother; great-aunt ❷ 姨太太 concubine

【姨娘】yí·niáng ❶〈旧时 *old*〉子女称父亲的妾 term of address for father's concubine ❷〈方 *dial.*〉same as 姨母 yímǔ

【姨儿】yír〈方 *dial.*〉same as 姨母 yímǔ：三～ mother's third sister

【姨太太】yítài·tai 妾 concubine

【姨丈】yízhàng same as 姨夫 yí·fu

栘 yí［栘棯］(yíyī) 常绿乔木，叶子椭圆形或卵状披针形，花白色，果实卵形。树皮和果实可入药。delavay docynia (*Docynia delavayi*); evergreen tree with ovate or lanceolate leaves, white flowers, and oval fruits, and both bark and fruits used for traditional Chinese medicine

眙 yí 盱眙(Xūyí)，地名，在江苏 Xuyi, name of a place in Jiangsu Province
☞ chì on p. 266

胰 yí 人或高等动物体内的腺体之一，在胃的后下方，形状像牛舌。能分泌胰液，帮助消化，又能分泌胰岛素，调节体内糖的新陈代谢。pancreas; gland in the shape of a bovine tongue in man or vertebrates in the rear lower side of the stomach, secreting juice to help digestion and insulin to regulate metabolism of sugar in the body; also 胰腺 yíxiàn or 胰脏 yízàng；旧称 formerly called 膵脏 cuìzàng

【胰岛素】yídǎosù 胰腺分泌的一种激素，能促进肝脏和肌肉内动物淀粉的生成，加速组织中葡萄糖的氧化和利用，从而调节体内血糖的含量。胰岛素分泌量减低时即引起糖尿病。insulin; hormone secreted by the pancreas which can promote the formation of the animal starch in the liver and muscles and accelerate the oxidation and utilization of the glucose in the tissues, thereby regulating the content of the blood sugar in the body. Reduced secretion of insulin causes diabetes.

【胰腺】yíxiàn 胰 pancreas;（图见☞ figure for 消化系统 xiāohuà xìtǒng on p. 2100）

【胰液】yíyè 胰腺分泌的一种消化液，无色透明，碱性，内含碳酸氢钠、胰蛋白酶、胰脂酶、胰淀粉酶等。由胰腺分泌出来之后，经导管流入小肠。pancreatic juice; colourless, transparent, digestive juice secreted by the pancreas, which contains sodium bicarbonate, trypsin, pancreatic lipase, amylopsin, etc., and flows from the pancreas to the small intestine through a duct.

【胰子】yí·zi ❶ 猪羊等的胰 pancreas (of pigs, sheep, etc.) ❷〈方 *dial.*〉肥皂 soap：香～ toilet soap｜药～ medicated soap

宧 yí〈旧时 *old*〉指屋子里的东北角 north-eastern corner of a room

扅 yí ☞［扊扅］(yǎnyí) on p. 2212

蛇 yí ☞［委蛇］(wēiyí) on p. 1986
☞ shé on p. 1693

移 yí ❶ 移动 move; remove; shift：转～ transfer; divert; shift｜迁～ move; migrate; remove｜把菊花～到花盆里去 move the chrysanthemum into the flowerpot ❷ 改变；变动 change; alter：～风易俗 change prevailing habits and customs; transform social traditions; reform the ways and manners of the people｜贫贱不能～ neither poverty nor humbleness can make one swerve from principle

【移动】yídòng 改换原来的位置 move; shift：冷空气正向南～。The cold air is moving southward.｜汽笛响后，船身开始～了。The ship began to move after the siren whistled.

【移防】yífáng 在某地驻防的军队移到另一地驻防 be shifted from one place to another for garrison duty

【移风易俗】yí fēng yì sú 改变旧的风俗习惯 change prevailing habits and customs; transform social traditions; reform the ways and manners of the people

【移花接木】yí huā jiē mù 把带花的枝条嫁接在别的树木上 graft one twig on another;〈比喻 *fig.*〉使用手段，暗中更换人或事物 stealthily substitute one person or thing for another

【移交】yíjiāo ❶ 把人或事物转移给有关方面 turn over; transfer：把罪犯～法庭审讯 deliver a criminal to the court for trial｜工程竣工后已～使用单位。The project has been transferred to the user after it was completed. ❷ 原来负责经管的人离职前把所管的事物交给接手的人 settler; migrant; hand over one's job to a successor before leaving the post：新会计刚到，账目还没有～。The new accountant has just come, and the accounts have not yet been handed over.

【移解】yíjiè 把犯人从原关押的地方押送到另一个地方 transfer a prisoner from one place to another under escort

【移居】yíjū 改变居住的地方；迁居 move one's residence; migrate：～外地 move to another place

【移民】yí//mín 居民由一地或一国迁移到另一地或另一国落户 migrate; emigrate or immigrate; move from one place to another or from one country to another：～海外 migrate abroad｜～政策 immigration policy

【移民】yímín 迁移到外地或外国去落户的人 settler; migrant; person who has migrated to another place or another country：安置～ find settlements for immigrants; settle an immigrant

【移山倒海】yí shān dǎo hǎi 改变山和海的位

置。形容人类征服自然的力量和气魄的伟大。move mountains and drain seas; exercise magic powers; transform nature; the great power and momentum with which man conquers Nature

【移师】yíshī 移动军队 move the troops: ～北上 move the troops northward ◇获出线资格的球队将～上海参加决赛。The teams qualified for the next round will move to Shanghai for the finals.

【移译】yíyì〈书 *fml.*〉same as 迻译 yíyì

【移易】yíyì〈书 *fml.*〉改变 change; alter; transform: 措辞精当,一字不可～。The wording is precise and appropriate. Not a single word should be altered.

【移用】yíyòng 把用于别方面的方法、物资等拿来使用 divert (materials, funds, etc.) from one use to another: 专款专用,不得～。The special fund is set for special use. It should not be used for another purpose.

【移植】yízhí ❶ 把播种在苗床或秧田里的幼苗拔起或连土掘起种在田地里 transplant; pull up seedlings from the seedling beds or plots or dig them out with earth and plant them in the fields; transplant seedlings◇近年来京剧从各种地方戏曲～了不少优秀剧目。In recent years many outstanding local operas have been adapted to the Peking Opera. ❷ 将机体的一部分组织或器官补在同一机体或另一机体的缺陷部分上,使它逐渐长好 transplanting; grafting; transplant a piece of skin, bone, cornea, blood vessel or other living tissue from one part of a body to another part of the same body or from one body to another, where it grows and becomes a permanent part

【移樽就教】yí zūn jiù jiào 端着酒杯到别人跟前共饮,以便求教。泛指主动前去向人请教。take one's wine cup and go to sb.'s table to ask for advice; go to sb. for advice

痍 yí〈书 *fml.*〉创伤 wound; trauma: 疮～ wound; devastation; ruins

遗 yí ❶ 遗失 lose ❷ 遗失的东西 something lost: 路不拾～ No one picks up or pocket anything lost on the road. ❸ 遗漏 omit: ～忘 forget | 补～ addendum ❹ 留下 leave behind; keep back; not give: ～迹 ruins; historical remains; traces; vestiges | ～憾 regret | 不～余力 spare no efforts ❺ 专指死人留下的 leave behind at one's death; bequeath; hand down: ～容 looks of the deceased; portrait of the deceased | ～嘱 will; testament | ～著 posthumous work of a deceased ❻ 排泄大小便或精液(多指不自主的 oft. involuntarily) involuntary discharge of urine, etc.: ～矢 empty one's bowels; defecate | ～尿 enuresis; bed-wetting | ～精 (seminal) emission

☞ wèi on p. 2001

【遗产】yíchǎn ❶ 死者留下的财产,包括财物、债权等 legacy; inheritance; heritage; property left behind after one's death, including property, creditor's rights ❷ 借指历史上遗留下来的精神财富或物质财富 legacy; heritage; cultural wealth or material wealth left down in history: 文学～ literary legacy | 医学～ medical heritage | 经济～ economic heritage

【遗臭万年】yí chòu wàn nián 坏名声流传下去,永远为人唾骂 leave a name that will stink to eternity; go down in history as a byword for infamy

【遗传】yíchuán 生物体的构造和生理机能等由上代传给下代 heredity; inheritance of the structure and physiological functions of living organisms from the previous generation to the current generation or from the current generation to the next generation

【遗传工程】yíchuán gōngchéng 一种遗传学技术,借助生物化学的手段,将一种生物细胞中的遗传物质取出来,在体外进行切割和重新组合,然后引入另一种生物的活细胞内,以改变另一种生物的遗传性状或创造新的生物品种 genetic engineering; branch of biology dealing with the taking by biochemical means, splicing, and recombining of specific genetic units from the DNA of a living organism to be used in the living cells of another living organism to modify the existing genetic codes and produce new, or improved, species, valuable biochemicals, etc.; also 基因工程 jīyīn gōngchéng

【遗传学】yíchuánxué 研究生物体遗传和变异规律的学科 genetics; branch of study dealing with the heredity and variation in similar or related animals and plants

【遗存】yícún ❶ 遗留 be left over; be handed down: 这些石刻～至今已有千年。These stone inscriptions have been in existence for over a thousand years. ❷ 古代遗留下来的东西 things left over from ancient times; remnants; remains: 古代文化～ remains of the ancient culture | 北京周口店有人类化石～。Zhoukoudian in Beijing is a site of man's fossil remains.

【遗毒】yídú 遗留下来的有害的思想、风气等 evil legacy; harmful tradition; pernicious influence: 肃清～ eradicate vestiges of pernicious influences

【遗风】yífēng 某个时代留传下来的风气 traditions and customs handed down from a certain age: 古代～ ancient customs | ～余韵 remaining grace of an old tradition

【遗腹子】yífùzǐ 父亲死后才出生的子女 a posthumous child

【遗稿】yígǎo 死者生前没有发表的文稿 a manuscript left unpublished by the author at his death; a posthumous manuscript

【遗孤】yígū 某人死后遗留下来的孤儿 orphan: 烈士～ orphan of a martyr | 抚养～ support organs

【遗骸】yíhái 遗体;遗骨 remains (of the dead): 生物～ remains of living organisms | 迁葬烈士～ remove and bury the remains of the martyrs

【遗憾】yíhàn ❶ 遗恨 regret; pity: 一时失足成了他终生的～。The error of a moment becomes his lifelong regret. ❷ 不称心;大可惋惜(在外交文件上常用来表示不满和抗议 usu. used to express displeasure and protest) regret: 功亏一篑,令人～。It's a pity to fall short of success for lack of a final effort. | 对此,我们深感～。We deeply regret at this.

【遗恨】yíhèn 到死还感到悔恨或不称心的事情 eternal regret; lifelong regret: 死无～ die without regret; there is no regret when one dies

【遗患】yíhuàn 留下祸患 leave a legacy of trouble: 养虎～ rear a tiger to invite disaster | ～无穷 leave endless trouble

【遗祸】yíhuò 留下祸患,使人受害 leave a legacy of trouble

【遗迹】yíjì 古代或旧时代的事物遗留下来痕迹 historical remains; traces; vestiges: 历史～ historical remains; historical ruins | 古代村落的～ the remains of ancient villages

【遗教】yíjiào 死者遗留下的学说、主张、著作等 teachings, views, works, etc. of the deceased

【遗精】yí//jīng 未经性交而在无意中流出精液。男子在夜间有时遗精是正常的生理现象,但次数过多的遗精是病理现象。(seminal) emission; involuntary discharge of semen without an intercourse. It's a normal physiological phenomenon for a man to have an occasional emission at night, but a pathological phenomenon to have frequent emissions.

【遗老】yílǎo ❶ 指改朝换代后仍然效忠前一朝代的老年人 adherent of a former dynasty; old fogy; old diehard: 前朝～ adherent of the preceding dynasty ❷〈书 *fml.*〉指经历世变的老人 old people who have witnessed big social changes

【遗留】yíliú (以前的事物或现象)继续存在;(过去)留下来 leave over; hand down: 解决～问题 solve problems left over from the past | 许多历史遗迹一直～到现在。Many historical remains have been in existence till today.

【遗漏】yílòu 应该列入或提到的因疏忽而没有列入或提到 omit; leave out: 名册上把他的名字给～了。His name is missing from the list. | 他回答完全,一点也没有～。He made a complete answer without leaving out anything.

【遗民】yímín 指改朝换代后仍然效忠前一朝代的人。也泛指大乱后遗留下来的人民。adherent of a former dynasty; survivor of a great upheaval

【遗墨】yímò 死者遗留下来的亲笔书札、文稿、字画等 letters, manuscripts, scrolls of painting or calligraphy, etc. left behind by the deceased

【遗尿】yí//niào 不自主的排尿。三岁以前的遗尿是生理性的。三岁以后的遗尿是一种不正常的现象。不正常的遗尿多发生于夜间,所以也叫夜尿症。enuresis; bed-wetting; involuntary discharge of urine. It's a physiological phenomenon for a baby under three years old to have problems of urinating during sleep, but abnormal for those above three. As abnormal bedwetting occurs at night, it is also called 'urinating during sleep'.

【遗篇】yípiān 前人遗留下来的诗文 poems and articles left behind by the deceased

【遗弃】yíqì ❶ 抛弃 abandon; forsake; desert; walk out on: 敌军～辎重无数。The enemy abandoned (or left behind) countless supplies. ❷ 对自己应该赡养或抚养的亲属抛开不管 forsake one's wife and children

【遗缺】yíquē 因原任人员死亡或去职而空出来的职位 vacancy (caused by somebody's death, resignation, transfer, etc.); a vacated post

【遗容】yíróng ❶ 人死后的容貌 looks of the deceased: 瞻仰～ pay one's respects to the remains of somebody ❷ same as 遗像 yíxiàng

【遗少】yíshào 指改朝换代后仍然效忠前一朝代的年轻人 a young man with the mentality of an old fogy; a young diehard; a young adherent of a former dynasty

【遗失】yíshī 由于疏忽而失掉(东西) lose: ～证件 lose one's card

【遗矢】yíshǐ〈书 *fml.*〉拉屎 empty one's bowels; defecate

【遗事】yíshì 前代或前人留下来的事迹 anecdotes of past ages; deeds of those now dead: 前朝～ anecdotes of former dynasties | 革命烈士的～ deeds of revolutionary martyrs

【遗书】yíshū ❶ 前人留下而由后人刊印的著作(多用做书名 usu. used in book titles) surviving works; posthumous works; collected writings published after the author's death ❷ 死者临死前留下的书信 letter or note left by one immediately before death ❸〈书 *fml.*〉散失的书 lost books

【遗属】yíshǔ 死者的眷属 members of the deceased's family; family dependants of the deceased

【遗孀】yíshuāng 某人死后,他的妻子称为某人的遗孀 widow; relict; a woman whose husband has died

【遗体】yítǐ ❶ 死者的尸体(多用于所尊敬的人) remains (of sb. held in esteem) ❷ 动植物死后的残余物质 remnants of animals and plants after they die

【遗忘】yíwàng 忘记 forget：童年的生活，至今尚未～。I still remember how I spent my childhood.

【遗闻】yíwén 遗留下来的传闻 tales of old times：～轶事 tales of old times and anecdotes

【遗物】yíwù 古代或死者留下来的东西 things left behind by the deceased; relic

【遗像】yíxiàng 死者生前的相片或画像 photograph or portrait of the deceased

【遗训】yíxùn 死者生前所说的有教育意义的话 teachings of the deceased

【遗言】yíyán 死者死前留下来的话 words of the deceased; (a person's) last words：临终～ last words of the deceased

【遗业】yíyè ❶ 前人遗留下来的事业 unfulfilled cause; work left unfinished by one's predecessor or ancestor ❷ same as 遗产 yíchǎn

【遗愿】yíyuàn 死者生前没有实现的愿望 unfulfilled wish of the deceased; last wish; behest：实现先烈的～ carry out the behests of the revolutionary martyrs

【遗诏】yízhào 皇帝临死时留下的诏书 testamentary edict left by a dying emperor

【遗照】yízhào 死者生前的相片 photograph of the deceased

【遗址】yízhǐ 毁坏的年代较久的建筑物所在的地方 site：圆明园～ the site of the Yuanmingyuan (the old Summer Palace in Beijing burned down by the British and French aggressor troops in 1860)

【遗志】yízhì 死者生前没有实现的志愿 unfulfilled wish; behest; work bequeathed by the deceased：继承先烈～ carry out the behest of the martyrs; continue the work left by the martyrs

【遗嘱】yízhǔ ❶ 人在生前或临死时用口头或书面形式嘱咐身后各事应如何处理 make a will orally or in writing; leave one's last words ❷ 关于上述内容的话或字据 testament; will; dying words

【遗族】yízú 死者的家族 the family of the deceased

颐1 yí 〈书 *fml.*〉颊；腮 chin or cheek：支～(手托住腮) hold up one's cheeks with both hands; cheeks in palms|解～(面现笑容) smile on the cheeks; smile on a face

颐2 yí 〈书 *fml.*〉保养 nourish; take good care of one's health：～神 preserve one's vital energy |～养 keep fit; take good care of one's health

【颐养】yíyǎng 〈书 *fml.*〉保养 keep fit; take good care of oneself：～天年 take good care of oneself so as to fulfil one's allotted life span

【颐指气使】yí zhǐ qì shǐ 不说话而用面部表情来示意。指有权势的人傲慢的神气。order people about by gestures; be insufferably arrogant

椸(箷) yí 〈书 *fml.*〉衣架 clothes stand; clothes rack; coat hanger

疑 yí ❶ 不能确定是否真实；不能有肯定的意见；不信；因不信而猜度；怀疑 doubt; disbelieve; suspect; be not sure if it is true or not：～惑 doubt|～心 suspicion|～虑 misgivings|迟～ hesitate|猜～distrust|半信半～ half believing, half doubting ❷ 不能确定的；不能解决的 doubtful; uncertain：～问 question; doubt|～案 a doubtful (or disputed) case; an open question; mystery|～义 doubt; doubtful point

【疑案】yí'àn ❶ 真相不明，证据不足，一时难以判决的案件 doubtful (or disputed) case; case on which it is difficult to make a decision for the time being for insufficient evidence ❷ 泛指情况了解不够、不能确定的事件或情节 an open question; mystery

【疑兵】yíbīng 为了虚张声势、迷惑敌人而布置的军队 troops deployed to mislead an enemy; deceptive deployment (of soldiers)

【疑点】yídiǎn 怀疑的地方；不太明了的地方 doubtful (or questionable) point; uncertain (or unclear) point：听了他的解释我仍有许多～。After hearing his explanations, I was still not quite clear about many points.|把书上的～画出来请教老师 underline the doubtful points in the book and ask your teacher for explanations

【疑窦】yídòu 〈书 *fml.*〉可疑之点 doubtful points; cause for suspicion; suspicion：～丛生 full of suspicions

【疑惑】yíhuò 心里不明白；困惑 feel uncertain; not be convinced：～不解 feel puzzled; have doubts

【疑忌】yíjì 因怀疑别人而生猜忌 be suspicious：心怀～ feel suspicious|～功臣 distrust and have misgivings about ministers and generals who have performed distinguished merits

【疑惧】yíjù 疑虑而恐惧 apprehensive, worried and nervous：面露～ look apprehensive

【疑虑】yílǜ 因怀疑而顾虑 misgivings; doubts：消除～ clear one's mind of doubt; free somebody from doubts and misgivings

【疑难】yínán 有疑问而难于判断或处理的 difficult; knotty：～问题 hard nut to crack; knotty problem|～杂症(各种病理不明或难治的病) difficult and complicated cases (of illness)

【疑神疑鬼】yí shén yí guǐ 形容人多疑 be terribly suspicious; be even afraid of one's own shadow：人家没议论你，别那么～的。No one talked about you. Don't be suspicious.

【疑似】yísì 似乎确实又似乎不确实 doubtful：～之间 doubtful|～之词 ambiguous words

【疑团】yítuán 积聚的怀疑；一连串不能解决的问题 clouds of suspicion; doubts and suspicion; have sb. in a wing：满腹～ be full of doubts and suspicions; have sb. in a swing|～难解。

It's difficult to clear up the doubts.

【疑问】yíwèn 有怀疑的问题；不能确定或不能解释的事情 query; question; doubt; doubtful question; something that is uncertain or cannot be explained

【疑问句】yíwènjù 提出问题的句子，如'谁来了?''你愿意不愿意?''你是去呢还是不去?''我们坐火车去吗?'在书面上，疑问句后边用问号。interrogative sentence; sentence that asks a question, such as 'Who has come or who is there?' 'Are you willing?' 'Are you going or not?' 'Shall we take a train?' In writing, an interrogative sentence ends with a question mark.

【疑心】yíxīn ❶ 怀疑的念头 suspicion：人家是好意，你别起～。They did this out of good intentions, so don't be suspicious. ❷ same as 怀疑 huáiyí ②：我一走进村子，全变了样，我真～自己走错路了。When I came to the village and found everything changed, I indeed began to wonder if I'd come to a wrong place.

【疑心病】yíxīnbìng 指多疑的心理 suspicious frame of mind

【疑义】yíyì 可以怀疑的道理；可疑之点 doubt; doubtful point; doubtful argument

【疑云】yíyún 像浓云一样聚集的怀疑 misgivings or suspicions clouding one's mind：驱散～ dispel one's misgivings | ～难消 hard to dispel one's misgivings

【疑阵】yízhèn 为了使对方迷惑而布置的阵势或局面 deceptive battle array to mislead the enemy; decoy

嶷 yí 九嶷(Jiǔyí)，山名，在湖南 Jiuyi, name of a mountain in Hunan Province; also 九疑 Jiǔyí

簃 yí〈书 *fml.*〉楼阁旁边的小屋 small hut beside a storeyed building (多用做书斋的名称 usu. used as the name of a study)

彝[1]（彞）yí ❶ 古代盛酒的器具。也泛指祭器。ancient wine vessel; also a sacrificial vessel：～器 sacrificial vessel | 鼎～ a wine vessel with two handles and three legs ❷〈书 *fml.*〉法度；常规 law; rule：～准 common law

彝[2]（彞）Yí same as 彝族 Yízú

【彝剧】yíjù 彝族戏曲剧种，在彝族歌舞艺术的基础上发展而成。流行于云南楚雄彝族自治州。*yiju* opera; local opera of the Yi people, developed on the basis of its folk songs and dances and popular among the Chuxiong Yi Autonomous Prefecture

【彝族】Yízú 我国少数民族之一，主要分布在四川、云南、贵州和广西 the ethnic Yi people; the Yis, an ethnic people distributed over Yunnan, Sichuan, and Guizhou provinces, and the Guangxi Zhuang Autonomous Region

黟 yí [黟黟]〈书 *fml.*〉形容兽角锐利 sharp and pointed (horn of a beast)

yǐ (丨)

乙[1] yǐ ❶ 天干的第二位 2nd of the 10 Heavenly Stems (天干)；☞ 干支 gānzhī on p. 627 ❷ (Yǐ)姓 a surname

乙[2] yǐ 我国民族音乐音阶上的一级，乐谱上用做记音符号，相当于简谱的'7' a note of the scale in *gongchepu* (工尺谱), corresponding to 7 in numbered musical notation; ☞ 工尺 gōngchě on p. 664

乙[3] yǐ 画'乙'字形状的记号，从前读书写字时常常用到，例如读书读到一个地方暂时停止，在上面画个'∠'形的记号，或是写字有颠倒、遗漏，用曲折的线勾过来或把补写的字勾进去，都叫做'乙'。古书没有标点，到一段终了而下无空格时，有时也画个'∠'形记号，表示第二行起是另一段。draw a mark like '乙' oft. when reading or writing. For example, when you pause after reading to a certain place, you mark with a '∠' at the place; when two Chinese characters are printed in wrong order or there is a word missing, transpose the two characters or insert the missing word with the same mark of '乙'. As no punctuation marks were used in the ancient books, when you come to the end of a paragraph with no space, a '∠' mark was used to indicate the next line as a new paragraph.

【乙部】yǐbù 史部 division of history

【乙种粒子】yǐzhǒng lìzǐ 某些放射性物质衰变时放射出来的高速运动的电子，带负电 beta particle; electron with negative electricity, ejected at high velocity from the nucleus of an atom undergoing beta decay; also 贝塔粒子 bèitǎ lìzǐ

【乙种射线】yǐzhǒng shèxiàn 放射性物质衰变时放射出来的乙种粒子流 beta ray; a stream of beta particles; also 贝塔射线 bèitǎ shèxiàn

【乙状结肠】yǐzhuàng-jiécháng 结肠的一部分，与降结肠相连，在左髂骨附近，形成'乙'字形，下连直肠 sigmoid; sigmoid colon; part of the colon linked with the descending colon near the ilium to form the shape of '乙'; also S-shaped 结肠；(图见 ☞ figure for 消化系统 xiāohuà xìtǒng on p. 2100)

已 yǐ ❶ 停止 stop; cease; end：争论不～ argue endlessly; be bogged down in endless argument | 有加无～ more and more; increasingly ❷ 已经 (跟'未'相对 as opposed to 'not yet') already：时间～过。It's past the closing time. | 此事～设法解决。Something has been done to settle the matter. ❸〈书 *fml.*〉后来；过了一会儿 thereafter; afterwards：～而 then; afterwards | ～忽不见 disappear afterwards ❹〈书 *fml.*〉太；过 too：不为～甚 not go to extremes

〈古 *arch*.〉also same as 以[2] yǐ

【已而】yǐ'ér〈书 *fml*.〉❶ 不久;继而 then; afterwards:突然雷电大作,～大雨倾盆。Suddenly it thundered and lightened, and then rain fell in torrents. ❷ 罢了;算了 that's all; simply that; no more

【已经】yǐ·jing〈副词 *adv*.〉表示事情完成或时间过去 already:任务～完成。The task has been fulfilled. | 他们～来了。They have already come. | 天～黑了,他们还没有收工。It's already dark, but they haven't knocked off yet.

【已决犯】yǐjuéfàn 经法院判决定了罪的犯人 convicted prisoner; convict

【已然】yǐrán ❶ 已经 already:事情～如此,还是想开些吧。It's already so. Don't take it too much to heart. ❷ 已经这样;已经成为事实 be already so; have already become a fact:与其补救于～,不如防止于未然。To forestall is better than to amend. *or* Prevention is better than cure.

【已往】yǐwǎng 以前;过去 before; previously; in the past:今天的农村跟～大不一样了。Today's countryside is much different from the past.

以[1] yǐ ❶ 用;拿 with; by means of:～少胜多 defeat an opponent superior in number | 喻之～理 reason with sb.; try to make sb. see reason | 赠～鲜花 present sb. with a bouquet ❷ 依;按照 according to:～次就座 take seats in order | ～时启闭 open and close according to schedule ❸ 因 because of:何～知之? How do you know? | 不～人废言。Don't reject a view because you dislike the speaker. ❹ 表示目的 in order to; so as to:～广视听 so as to make it known to more people | ～待时机 wait for a chance ❺〈书 *fml*.〉于;在(时间) at; on; in:中华人民共和国～1949年10月1日宣告成立。The founding of the People's Republic of China was proclaimed on October 1, 1949. ❻〈书 *fml*.〉〈连词 *conj*.〉跟'而'相同 same as 而 ér:城高～厚,地广～深。The city wall is high and thick and the area is wide and deep.

以[2] yǐ 用在单纯的方位词前,组成合成的方位词或方位结构,表示时间、方位、数量的界限[used before certain localizers to form compound localizers to indicate time, position and limit of quantity]:～前 before | ～上 above | 三日～后 three days later; in three days | 县级～上 above the county level | 长江～南 south of the Yangtze River | 五千～内 within five thousand | 二十岁～下 under twenty years of age

【以暴易暴】yǐ bào yì bào 用凶暴的代替凶暴的,表示统治者改换了,可是暴虐的统治方式依然不变 replace one tyranny by another; replace a brutal force by another to indicate that the ruler has changed, but the tyrannical rule has not.

【以便】yǐbiàn〈连词 *conj*.〉用在下半句的开头,表示使下文所说的目的容易实现 so that; in order to; so as to; with the aim of; for the purpose of:请在信封上写清邮政编码,～迅速投递。Please write the postal code on the envelope clearly so that the letter will be quickly delivered.

【以次】yǐcì ❶ 依照次序 in proper order:～入座 take seats in order ❷ 次序在某处以后的;以下 the following:～各章,内容从略 the following chapters are omitted

【以德报怨】yǐ dé bào yuàn 用恩惠回报与别人之间的仇恨 return good for evil; repay evil with good; requite ingratitude with kindness

【以毒攻毒】yǐ dú gōng dú 用毒药来治疗毒疮等疾病 fight poison with poison; use poison as an antidote for poison;〈比喻 *fig*.〉利用恶人来制恶人或利用不良事物本身的矛盾来反对不良事物 use evil people to check evil people; use the contradiction in an evil thing to oppose it.

【以讹传讹】yǐ é chuán é 把本来就不正确的话又错误地传出去,结果越传越错 incorrectly relay an erroneous message (so that it becomes increasingly distorted); spread an error or a falsehood

【以后】yǐhòu 现在或所说某时之后的时期 after; afterwards; later; hereafter:从今～ from now on | 五年～ five years later; five years afterwards; in five years | 毕业～ after graduation | ～,我们还要研究这个问题。We'll discuss this question again later.

【以还】yǐhuán〈书 *fml*.〉过去某个时期以后 after a certain period in the past; since; after; until:海禁～ since the ban was imposed on maritime trade with foreign countries ... | 隋唐～,方兴科举。The imperial examination system was not instituted until the Sui and Tang dynasties.

【以及】yǐjí〈连词 *conj*.〉连接并列的词或词组 as well as; along with; and:院子里种着大丽花、矢车菊、夹竹桃～其他的花木。Dahlias, cornflowers, oleanders and other flowers and trees are planted in the yard.

【以己度人】yǐ jǐ duó rén 拿自己的心思来衡量或揣度别人 judge others against one's own value; measure others' corn with one's own bushel

【以近】yǐjìn 指铁路、公路、航空等路线上比某个车站或机场近的。例如从北京经过石家庄、郑州到武汉,石家庄、郑州都是武汉以近的地方。up to; rail, road or air transportation route up to a certain station or airport. For example, on the transportation line from Beijing via Shijiazhuang and Zhengzhou to Wuhan, both Shijiazhuang and Zhengzhou are within the distance up to Wuhan

【以儆效尤】yǐ jǐng xiào yóu 用对一个坏人或一件坏事的严肃处理来警告那些学做坏事的人 punish a wrong-doer or handle a bad deed seriously as a warning to others

【以来】yǐlái 表示从过去某时直到现在的一段时期 since：自古～ since antiquity；since ancient times｜长期～ for a long time past｜有生～ since birth｜解放～ since liberation｜开春～ since the beginning of spring

【以邻为壑】yǐ lín wéi hè 拿邻国当做大水坑，把本国洪水排泄到那里去 use one's neighbour's field as a drain；〈比喻 *fig.*〉把灾祸推给别人 shift one's troubles onto others

【以卵投石】yǐ luǎn tóu shí 用蛋打石头 throw an egg against a rock；〈比喻 *fig.*〉不自量力，自取灭亡 court defeat by fighting against overwhelming odds；also 以卵击石 yǐ luǎn jī shí

【以貌取人】yǐ mào qǔ rén 只根据外表来判断人的品质或能力 judge people solely by their appearance

【以免】yǐmiǎn〈连词 *conj.*〉用在下半句话的开头，表示目的是使下文所说的情况不至于发生 in order to avoid；so as not to；lest：工地上应该加强安全措施，～发生工伤事故。Safety measures should be tightened up on the worksite to avoid injuries.｜借阅的书籍应该在限期之内归还，～妨碍流通。The borrowed books should be returned within the time limit in order not to hinder the circulation.

【以内】yǐnèi 在一定的时间、处所、数量、范围的界限之内 within；less than；within a given time，position，number，scope. etc.：本年～ within this year｜长城～ within the Great Wall｜五十人～ less than fifty people

【以期】yǐqī 用在下半句话的开头，表示下文是前半句所说希望达到的目的［used at the beginning of the second half of a sentence to indicate that the following is the aim one hopes to achieve as said in the first half of the sentence］in the hope of：再接再厉，～全胜。Make still greater efforts in the hope of winning a complete victory.

【以前】yǐqián 现在或所说某时之前的时期 before；formerly；previously：解放～ before liberation｜三年～ three years ago｜很久～ long，long ago｜～他是个学生。He was a student before.

【以人废言】yǐ rén fèi yán 因为某人不好或不喜欢某人而不管他的话是否有道理，概不听取 reject an opinion because the speaker is not good or the person one doesn't like no matter what he says is right or not

【以上】yǐshàng ❶ 表示位置、次序或数目等在某一点之上 more than；over；above；indicating the position，order，number，etc. is above a given point：半山～石级更陡。From halfway up the mountain，the stone steps become even steeper.｜县级～干部 cadres at and above the county level ❷ 指前面的（话），总括上文 the above；the foregoing；the aforementioned：～所说的是方针问题。What I've said in the foregoing is a question of principle.

【以身试法】yǐ shēn shì fǎ 以自己的行为来试试法律的威力。指明知法律的规定而还要去做触犯法律的事。defy the law personally；break the law knowingly

【以身作则】yǐ shēn zuò zé 用自己的行动做榜样 set a good example with one's own conduct；set an example

【以汤沃雪】yǐ tāng wò xuě 把开水浇在雪上，雪很快就融化 melt snow with hot water；〈比喻 *fig.*〉轻而易举 easily done

【以外】yǐwài 在一定的时间、处所、数量、范围的界限之外 beyond；outside；other than；beyond a given time，position，number，scope，etc.：十天～ more than ten days｜办公室～ outside the office｜五步～ farther than five strides｜除此～，还有一点要注意。There is something else I have to draw your attention to.

【以往】yǐwǎng 从前；过去 before；formerly；in the past：产品的质量比～大有提高。The quality of the products is much better than in the past.｜这地方～是一片荒野。This place used to be a vast expanse of wasteland.

【以为】yǐwéi 认为 think；believe；consider：不～然 disagree；object to｜不～苦，反～乐 regard sth. not as a hardship，but a pleasure｜这部电影我～很有教育意义。I think the film is very educational.｜我～是谁呢，原来是你。I thought it was other than you.

【以下】yǐxià ❶ 表示位置、次序或数目等在某一点之下 below；under；indicating that the position，order，number，etc. is below a given point：气温已降到零度～。The temperature has dropped to below zero.｜请勿携带三岁～儿童入场。No admittance for children under three. ❷ 指下面的（话）the following；hereafter：～就要谈谈具体办法。Now I'm coming to the concrete measures.

【以眼还眼，以牙还牙】yǐ yǎn huán yǎn，yǐ yá huán yá〈比喻 *fig.*〉用对方所使用的手段还击对方 an eye for an eye and a tooth for a tooth；counter attack a person by the means he uses

【以一当十】yǐ yī dāng shí 一个人抵挡十个人。形容军队勇敢善战。pit one against ten；troops fight heroically

【以逸待劳】yǐ yì dài láo 指作战的时候采取守势，养精蓄锐，等待来攻的敌人疲劳后再出击 wait at one's ease for an exhausted enemy

【以远】yǐyuǎn 指铁路、公路、航空等路线上比某个车站或机场远的。例如从北京经过济南往南去上海或往东去青岛，上海和青岛都是济南以远的地方。beyond；rail，road or air line extending beyond a certain station or airport. For example, on a transportation line from Beijing southward to Shanghai and eastward to Qingcao via Jinan, both Shanghai and Qingdao are stations beyond Jinan.

【以怨报德】yǐ yuàn bào dé 用仇恨回报别人对自己的恩惠 return evil for good; repay good with evil; requite kindness with ingratitude; bite the hand that feeds one

【以至】yǐzhì〈连词 *conj.*〉❶ 表示在时间、数量、程度、范围上的延伸 [used to indicate the extension of time, number, degree, scope, etc.] down to; up to: 实践、认识、再实践、再认识,这种形式,循环往复～无穷,而实践和认识之每一循环的内容,都比较地进到了高一级的程度。Practice, knowledge, again practice, and again knowledge. This form repeats itself in endless cycles, and with each cycle the content of practice and knowledge rises to a higher level. ❷ 用在下半句话的开头,表示由于前半句话所说的动作、情况的程度很深而形成的结果 [used at the beginning of the second half of a sentence to indicate the result of an action or situation expressed in the first half of the sentence] to such an extent . . . as; so . . . that: 他非常用心地写生,～野地里刮起风沙来也不理会。He was so bent on his painting that he totally ignored the sand blown up by the wind in the fields.| 情势的发展十分迅速,～使很多人感到惊奇。The situation grew so fast that many people were caught by surprise. ‖ also 以至于 yǐzhìyú

【以致】yǐzhì〈连词 *conj.*〉用在下半句话的开头,表示下文是上述的原因所形成的结果(多指不好的结果 oft. referring to negative results) [used at the beginning of the second part of a sentence to indicate the second part is the result of the first part] so that; consequently; as a result: 他事先没有充分调查研究,～做出了错误的结论。He didn't make adequate investigation beforehand, and consequently made a wrong conclusion.

【以子之矛,攻子之盾】yǐ zǐ zhī máo, gōng zǐ zhī dùn 用你的矛来刺你的盾 set a person's spear against his own shield;〈比喻 *fig.*〉用对方的观点、方法或言论等来反驳对方 refute sb. with his own argument; ☞ 矛盾 máodùn on p. 1308

目 yǐ〈书 *fml.*〉same as 以 yǐ

钇 yǐ 金属元素,符号 Y (yttrium)。是一种稀土金属。暗灰色,用来制合金和特种玻璃等。yttrium (Y), dark grey rare-earth metal, used in making alloys and special glass

苡 yǐ 薏苡 Job's tears

【苡米】yǐmǐ ☞ 薏米 yìmǐ on p. 2281

【苡仁】yǐrén ☞ 薏米 yìmǐ on p. 2281

尾 yǐ (～儿 yǐr) ❶ 特指马尾上的毛 hairs on a horse's tail: 马～罗(以马尾毛为筛绢的筛子) sieve with a fabric woven from horsetail hairs ❷ 特指蟋蟀等尾部的针状物 spikelets on a cricket's tail: 三～儿(雌蟋蟀) cricket with three spikelets

☞ wěi on p. 1994

矣 yǐ〈古汉语 *arch.*〉〈助词 *aux.*〉❶ 用在句末,跟'了'相同 [used at the end of a sentence like 了·le]: 由来久～ it's been a long time; go back to a long time ago| 悔之晚～。It's too late for regrets. ❷ 表示感叹 [used in exclamatory sentences] how; what: 大～哉! How great!

苢 yǐ ☞ [芣苢] (fúyǐ) on p. 594

迤(迆) yǐ 往;向(表示在某一方向上的延伸) go (or extend) towards: 天安门～西是中山公园,～东是劳动人民文化宫。To the west of Tian'anmen rostrum is Zhongshan (Sun Yat-sen) Park and to the east is the Cultural Palace of the Working People.

☞ yí on p. 2261

【迤逦】yǐlǐ〈书 *fml.*〉曲折连绵 winding; tortuous; meandering: 队伍沿着山道～而行。The troops marched along a winding mountain path.

蚁(蟻、螘) yǐ ❶ 昆虫的一科,种类很多,一般体小,呈黑、褐、红等色,触角丝状或棒状,腹部球状,腰部细。营群居生活,分雌蚁、雄蚁、工蚁和兵蚁。雌蚁和雄蚁都有单眼,有翅。工蚁和兵蚁都没有翅,生殖器官不发达。工蚁担任筑巢、采集食物、抚养幼虫等工作。兵蚁负责守卫。ant (*Oecophylla smaragdina*); one of a variety of insects having a tiny body that is black, brown or red in colour, silky or rod-shaped feelers, a thin waist and a big belly. Ants are gregarious, and classified into female ants, male ants, workers and soldiers. Both the male and female ants have simple eyes and wings. The workers and soldiers have no wings but underdeveloped sexual organs. The workers' job is to build nests, collect food and rear young ants. The soldiers are responsible for keeping guard. ❷ (Yǐ)姓 a surname

舣(艤、檥) yǐ〈书 *fml.*〉使船靠岸 pull in a boat to shore

酏 yǐ 酏剂 elixir: 芳香～ aromatic elixir [拉 Latin: elixir]

【酏剂】yǐjì 含有糖和挥发油或另含有主要药物的酒精溶液的制剂 elixir; alcoholic solution containing sugar and volatile oil or plus drugs

倚 yǐ ❶ 靠着 lean on or against; rest on or against: ～门而望 lean against the door and look into the distance| ～马千言 dash off a thousand words at the side of a horse ❷ 仗恃 rely on; count on:～势欺人 take advantage of one's position to bully people|～老卖老 flaunt one's seniority ❸〈书 *fml.*〉偏;歪 biased; partial:不偏不～ impartial

【倚傍】yǐbàng same as 依傍 yībàng

【倚靠】yǐkào ❶ 依赖;依靠 rely on; depend on ❷ 身体靠在物体上 lean on or against; rest on or against

【倚赖】yǐlài same as 依赖 yīlài

【倚老卖老】yǐ lǎo mài lǎo 仗着年纪大,卖弄老资格 take advantage of one's seniority or old age (to ignore manners, regulations, etc.); flaunt one's seniority

【倚马可待】yǐ mǎ kě dài 形容文思敏捷,写文章快 can write at the side of a horse; be nimble-minded and write fast; ☞ 倚马千言 yǐ mǎ qiān yán

【倚马千言】yǐ mǎ qiān yán 晋朝桓温领兵北征,命令袁虎靠着马拟公文,一会儿就写成七张纸,而且作得很好(见于《世说新语·文学》)。形容文思敏捷,写文章快。dash off a thousand words at the side of a horse—write with great facility. According to *A New Account of Tales of the World·Letters and Scholarship*. During a northern expedition the Jin Dynasty commander Huan Wen asked a man by the name of Yuan Hu to draft a document. The man, leaning against his horse, dashed off seven pieces of paper in no time, and came up with a good piece of writing. Hence the phrase.

【倚仗】yǐzhàng 靠别人的势力或有利条件;依赖 rely on; count on:～权势 rely on one's power and position; count on one's powerful connections|～力气大 rely on one's physical strength

【倚重】yǐzhòng 依靠,器重 rely heavily on somebody's service:～贤才 rely on the able people

扆 yǐ ❶ 古代的一种屏风 a kind of ancient screen ❷ (Yǐ)姓 a surname

椅 yǐ 椅子 chair:藤～ rattan chair|躺～ reclining chair; deck chair|桌～板凳 table, chair, bench and stool

☞ yī on p.2260

【椅披】yǐpī 披在椅背上的装饰品,多用大红绸缎或布料制成,有的还绣花,与椅垫、桌围成套,现在戏曲演出时还用 colourful silk chair cover; ornamental chair back, mostly made of red silk or cotton fabric, some with embroidered designs, making up a set with the chair cushion and table curtain, still in use in theatrical performances

【椅子】yǐ·zi 有靠背的坐具,主要用木头、竹子、藤子等制成 chair, chiefly made of wood, bamboo, rattan, etc.

顗(顗) yǐ〈书 *fml.*〉安静(古时多用于人名 usu. used in personal names in ancient times) quiet

蛾 yǐ〈书 *fml.*〉same as 蚁 yǐ

☞ é on p.504

旖 yǐ[旖旎](yǐnǐ)〈书 *fml.*〉柔和美好 charming; enchanting:风光～ enchanting scene

踦 yǐ〈书 *fml.*〉用力抵住 support; prop up; sustain; withstand

齮 yǐ〈书 *fml.*〉咬 bite:～龁 bite; gnaw; nibble

【齮龁】yǐhé〈书 *fml.*〉❶ 咬;啃 bite; gnaw; nibble ❷ 忌恨;倾轧 hate out of envy; engage in internal strife

yì (丨)

一 yì ☞ 一 yī on p.2242

乂 yì〈书 *fml.*〉治理;安定 pacify; govern; administer:～安(太平无事) peace and stability

弋 yì ❶〈书 *fml.*〉用带有绳子的箭射鸟 shoot a retrievable arrow with a string attached to it:～获 hit; catch; capture|～凫与雁 catch wild ducks and wild geese by shooting ❷〈书 *fml.*〉用来射鸟的带有绳子的箭 stringed arrows for shooting birds ❸ (Yì)姓 a surname

【弋获】yìhuò〈书 *fml.*〉❶ 射中(飞禽) hit (birds) by shooting ❷ 捕获(逃犯、盗匪) capture; arrest (criminals, bandits, etc.)

【弋阳腔】yìyángqiāng 戏曲声腔之一,起源于江西弋阳,流行地区很广。由一人独唱,众人帮腔,用打击乐器伴奏。*yiyang* tune; opera tune which originated in Yiyang, Jiangxi Province, and is popular in many places, characterized by solo singing with the aid of a chorus to the accompaniment of percussion instruments; also 弋腔 yìqiāng

亿(億) yì ❶〈数目 *numeral*〉一万万 hundred million ❷〈古代 *arch.*〉指十万 a hundred thousand

【亿万】yìwàn 泛指极大的数目 hundreds of millions; millions upon millions:～斯年 (for) billions of years; (for) aeons; time without end; eternity

【亿万斯年】yì wàn sī nián 形容无限长远的年代 (for) aeons; time without end; eternity

义[1](義) yì ❶ 正义 justice; righteousness:道～ morality and justice|大～灭亲 uphold justice and righteousness at the sacrifice of one's blood relations|～不容辞 be duty-bound; have an unshirkable duty ❷ 合乎正义或公益的 righteous; equitable; just:～举 a righteous deed; a magnanimous act undertaken for the public good|～演 benefit performance ❸ 情谊 human ties; relationship; fraternity; friendship; friendly feelings: 情～ friendship; mutual affection between friends, relatives|忘恩负～ be ungrateful; show ingratitude for ❹ 因抚养或拜认而成为亲属的 adopted or adoptive: ～父 adoptive father|～女 adopted daughter ❺ 人工制造的(人体的部分) artificial; false: ～齿 false teeth|～肢 artificial limb ❻ (Yì) 姓 a surname

义[2](**義**) yì 意义 meaning; significance: 字～ the meaning of a word|定～ definition

【义不容辞】yì bù róng cí 道义上允许推辞 be duty-bound; have an unshirkable duty

【义仓】yìcāng 〈旧时 *old*〉地方上为防备荒年而设置的公益粮仓 public granary for storing relief grain in case of a famine

【义齿】yìchǐ 假牙 false tooth; artificial tooth

【义地】yìdì 〈旧时 *old*〉埋葬穷人的公共墓地。也指由私人或团体购置,专为埋葬一般同乡、团体成员及其家属的墓地。cemetery; free burial ground for the destitute; burial ground bought privately or by an organisation for fellow provincials, members and their family dependents

【义愤】yìfèn 对违反正义的事情所产生的愤怒 righteous indignation; moral indignation: 满腔～ be enraged; filled with righteous indignation|～填膺 be filled with righteous indignation

【义愤填膺】yìfèn tián yīng 胸中充满义愤 be filled with righteous indignation

【义和团】Yìhétuán 19 世纪末我国北方人民自发组织的反对帝国主义侵略的团体 Yihetuan, anti-imperialist organisation formed by peasants and handicraftsmen in north China at the end of the 19th century

【义举】yìjǔ 指疏财仗义的行为 righteous deed; philanthropic act undertaken for the public good; undertaking in the interest of the public

【义军】yìjūn 起义的或为正义而战的军队 uprising army; army fighting for a just cause

【义理】yìlǐ 言论或文章的内容和道理 reason and good sense; argumentation (of a speech or essay)

【义卖】yìmài 为正义或公益的事情筹款而出售物品,出售的物品往往是捐献的,售价比市价高 charity sales; sale of goods for charity or other worthy causes; the goods on sale are often donated and their prices are above the market level

【义旗】yìqí 义军的旗帜 the banner of an army fighting a just war; banner of righteousness: ～所向,势不可当。The troops fighting for a just cause are irresistible wherever they go.

【义气】yì·qi ❶ 指由于私人关系而甘于承担风险或牺牲自己利益的气概 code of brotherhood; personal loyalty; quality of bearing a risk or sacrificing one's own interests for private reasons: 讲～ be loyal (to one's friends)|～凛然 inspire awe by holding justice ❷ 有这种气概或感情 quality and sentiment of being loyal to one's friends: 你看他多么慷慨,多么～。Look, how loyal and generous he is!

【义师】yìshī 义军 army fighting a just war; righteous army

【义士】yìshì 〈旧时 *old*〉指能维护正义的或侠义的人 high-minded or chivalrous person; person who upholds justice; righteous man

【义塾】yìshú same as 义学 yìxué

【义无反顾】yì wú fǎn gù 在道义上只有勇往直前,绝对不能退缩回顾 honour permits no turning back; be duty-bound not to turn back; 反 also put as 返 fǎn

【义务】yìwù ❶ 公民或法人按法律规定应尽的责任,例如服兵役(跟'权利'相对 as opposed to 'right') duty; obligation; the responsibility undertaken by a citizen or legal person according to law, such as serving in the army ❷ 道德上应尽的责任 moral obligation: 我们有～帮助学习较差的同学。We are duty bound to help classmates who are not doing well in their studies ❸ 不要报酬的 volunteer; voluntary: ～劳动 voluntary labour|～演出 benefit performance

【义务兵】yìwùbīng 按义务兵役制服役的士兵 compulsory serviceman

【义务兵役制】yìwù bīngyìzhì 公民依照法律在一定年龄内有服一定期限兵役义务的制度 compulsory military service; conscription; military service system under which eligible citizens have the obligation to serve in the army

【义务教育】yìwù jiàoyù 国家在法律中规定一定年龄的儿童必须受到一定程度的教育 compulsory education; education that a child up to a prescribed age is compelled to receive under the state law

【义项】yìxiàng 字典、词典中同一个条目内按意义分列的项目 items in a dictionary entry arranged according to their meanings

【义形于色】yì xíng yú sè 义愤之气显露在脸上 with righteous indignation written on one's face

【义学】yìxué 〈旧时 *old*〉由私人集资或用地方公益金创办的免费的学校 private or community-run school charging no tuition; free school

【义演】yìyǎn 为正义或公益的事情筹款而举行演出 benefit performance; fund-raising performance; fund-raiser

【义勇】yìyǒng 为正义事业而勇于斗争的 righteous and courageous: ～军 volunteers; army of volunteers|～之气 bravery in fighting a just war

【义勇军】yìyǒngjūn 人民为抗击侵略者自愿组织起来的队伍。特指我国抗日时期人民自动组织起来的一种抗日武装。army of volunteers; volunteers; army organised by the people on a voluntary basis for the purpose of fighting against aggressors, especially the armed anti-Japanese forces during China's War of Resistance Against Japan

【义战】yìzhàn 正义的战争 just war

【义诊】yìzhěn ❶ 为正义或公益的事情筹款而设门诊给人治病 set up a clinic to provide medical consultation to raise funds for justice and public welfare ❷ 医生无报酬地给人治病 (of a doctor) free medical consultation

【义正词严】yì zhèng cí yán 道理正当,措词严肃 speak out sternly from a sense of justice; speak with the force of justice; 词 also put as 辞 cí

【义肢】yìzhī 装在残疾人身上的假的上肢或下肢 artificial limb (fitted on a disabled person who has lost his limb)

【义冢】yìzhǒng 〈旧时 *old*〉埋葬无主尸骨的坟墓 a burial ground for the remains of unidentified persons

艺(藝) yì ❶ 技能;技术 skill:工～ art craft; craft; technology | 手～ skill | 园～ gardening; horticulture | ～高人胆大 person with superb skill has dauntless courage; boldness of execution stems from superb skill ❷ 艺术 art:文～ literature and art | 曲～ folk art forms including bollad singing, storytelling, clapper talks, cross talks, etc. | ～人 folk artist; craftsman; artisan ❸ 〈书 *fml.*〉准则;限度 limit; rule; norm:贪贿无～。There's no limit to greed for bribes.

【艺林】yìlín ❶ 指图书典籍荟萃的地方 place where collections of classical books are kept ❷ 指文艺界 the world of art; art circles:驰誉～ well reputed in the world of art | ～盛事 great event for the art world

【艺龄】yìlíng 演员从事艺术活动的年数 length of sb.'s stage career

【艺名】yìmíng 艺人为从艺起的别名 stage name (of an actor or actress)

【艺人】yìrén ❶ 戏曲、曲艺、杂技等演员 actor or entertainer (in opera, storytelling, acrobatics, etc.) ❷ 某些手工艺工人 artisan; handicraftsman

【艺术】yìshù ❶ 用形象来反映现实但比现实有典型性的社会意识形态,包括文学、绘画、雕塑、建筑、音乐、舞蹈、戏剧、电影、曲艺等 art; way of reflecting reality by way of reflecting social ideology more typical than in reality through images, including literature, painting, sculpture, architecture, and music, etc. ❷ 指富有创造性的方式、方法 artistically minded, way of doing things; skill; art; craft:领导～ art of leadership ❸ 形状独特而美观的 conforming to good taste:这棵松树的样子挺～。This pine tree looks very artistic.

【艺术家】yìshùjiā 从事艺术创作或表演而有一定成就的人 artist; person accomplished in artistic creation or performing art

【艺术品】yìshùpǐn 艺术作品。一般指造型艺术的作品。work of art; usually work of plastic art

【艺术体操】yìshù tǐcāo 体操运动项目之一。女运动员在音乐伴奏下做走、跑、跳、转体、平衡等各种动作,富于艺术性。rhythmic gymnastics; discipline of gymnastics in which a woman gymnast performs such movements as walking, running, jumping, turning, balancing, etc. in artistic forms; also 韵律体操 yùnlǜ tǐcāo

【艺术性】yìshùxìng 文学艺术作品通过形象反映生活、表现思想感情所达到的准确、鲜明、生动的程度以及形式、结构、表现技巧的完美的程度 artistic attainment; artistry; degree of accuracy, distinctiveness and vividness, and degree of perfection in form, structure and technique in reflecting life through images and portraying thoughts and feelings

【艺徒】yìtú 〈方 *dial.*〉学徒工 apprentice

【艺文志】yìwénzhì ❶ 我国纪传体史书和政书、方志等记载的图书目录 catalogue of biographical history, political literature and local annals; bibliography ❷ 指方志中所辑录的诗文 poems and essays collected in local records

【艺苑】yìyuàn 文学艺术荟萃的地方。泛指文学艺术界 realm of art and literature; art and literary circles:～奇葩 exquisite works of art

刈 yì 〈书 *fml.*〉割(草或谷类) mow; cut down (grass or grain crops):～麦 reap wheat; cut down wheat | ～草 mow grass

忆 yì 回想;记得 recall; recollect; remember:回～ recall; recollect | 记～ remember

【忆想】yìxiǎng 回想 recall; recollect; call to mind:～往事 recollect past events | ～当年 recall what happened at some point of the past

艾 yì 〈书 *fml.*〉❶ same as 乂 yì ❷ 惩治 punish:惩～ punish

☞ ài on p. 5

仡 yì [仡仡]〈书 *fml.*〉❶ 强壮勇敢 strong and brave ❷ 高大 tall and large

☞ gē on p. 649

议(議) yì ❶ 意见;言论 opinion; view:提～ propose | 建～ suggest | 异～ object to ❷ 商议 discuss; exchange views on; talk over:～论 discuss; talk; comment | ～定 discuss and decide | ～会 parliament | 会～ meeting; conference | 自报公～ self-assessment and public discussion | 这件事大家先～一～。Let's discuss this matter first. ❸ 议论;评说 comment; remark:物～ public comment;

public criticism or censure | 无可非～ beyond reproach; above criticism; indisputable

【议案】yì'àn 列入会议议程的提案 proposal; motion

【议程】yìchéng 会议上议案讨论的程序 agenda

【议定】yìdìng 商议决定 decide through consultation; agree on: ～书 protocol | 当面～价款 discuss and decide a price in sb.'s presence

【议定书】yìdìngshū 一种国际文件,是缔约国关于个别问题所取得的协议,通常是正式条约的修正或补充,附在正式条约的后面,也可作为单独的文件。有时也把国际会议对某问题达成协议并经签字的记录叫做议定书。protocol; international document concerning agreement reached by signatory nations on a certain issue that usually amends or adds to the official treaty and is attached to it, or that can also be a separate document. Sometimes, a record of agreement on a certain issue reached at an international conference and signed by all parties is also called a protocol.

【议和】yìhé 进行和平谈判;通过谈判,结束战争 hold peace talks and end the war through negotiation

【议会】yìhuì ❶ 某些国家的最高立法机关,一般由上、下两院组成。议会成员由选举产生。parliament; congress; legislative assembly; highest legislative body in certain countries, usually consisting of two chambers — the upper house and the lower house. The members of the legislative body, parliament or congress are elected by vote; also 议院 yìyuàn ❷ 某些国家的最高权力机关 the highest state organ in certain countries ‖ also 国会 guóhuì

【议会制】yìhuìzhì ☞ 代议制 dàiyìzhì on p. 370

【议价】yì//jià 买卖双方或同业共同议定货品价格 negotiate a price; negotiated price; negotiable price

【议决】yìjué 会议对议案经过讨论后做出决定 resolve after deliberation; pass a resolution

【议论】yìlùn ❶ 对人或事物的好坏、是非等表示意见 comment; talk; discuss: ～纷纷 carry on endless discussions; all sorts of comments; widespread comment | 大家都在～这件事。Everybody is talking about the matter. ❷ 对人或事物的好坏、是非等所表示的意见 comment; remark: 大发～ speak at great length

【议事】yìshì 商讨公事 discuss official business: ～日程 agenda; order of the day

【议题】yìtí 会议讨论的题目 item on the agenda; subject under discussion; topic for discussion: 确定～ decide subjects for discussion | 中心～ central topics

【议席】yìxí 议会中议员的席位 seat in a legislative assembly

【议员】yìyuán 在议会中有正式代表资格,享有表决权的成员 member of a legislative assembly having the right to vote; assemblyman; (in Great Britain) member of parliament (MP); (in U. S.) congressman or congresswoman

【议院】yìyuàn same as 议会 yìhuì ①: 上～ upper house | 下～ lower house

【议长】yìzhǎng 议会中的领导人 speaker (of a legislative body); president

【议政】yìzhèng 议论政事;对政府的方针政策和管理工作等提出意见和建议 discuss affairs of government; make suggestions and comments on government principles and policies and administrative work

屹 yì 〈书 *fml.*〉山峰高耸的样子 towering like a mountain peak: ～立 stand towering like a giant; stand erect

☞ gē on p. 649

【屹立】yìlì 像山峰一样高耸而稳固地立着,常用来比喻坚定不可动摇 stand towering like a mountain peak; stand erect; (oft. fig.) firmness and unshakability: ～不动 stand firm and erect | 人民英雄纪念碑～在天安门广场上。The Monument to the People's Heroes stands erect on the Tian'anmen Square.

【屹然】yìrán 屹立的样子 towering; majestic: ～不动 stand firm and erect

亦 yì ❶ 〈书 *fml.*〉也(表示同样);也是 also; too: 反之～然 and the reverse is also true; and vice versa | 人云～云 repeat what others say; parrot ❷ (Yì) 姓 a surname

【亦步亦趋】yì bù yì qū 《庄子·田子方》:'夫子步亦步,夫子趋亦趋。'意思是老师走学生也走,老师跑学生也跑。ape somebody at every step; imitate somebody's every move; blindly follow suit; *Zhuangzi · Tian Zifang*: 'When the teacher walks, the students also walk. When the teacher runs, the students also run.' 〈比喻 *fig.*〉自己没有主张,或为了讨好,每件事都顺从别人,跟着人家走 follow sb. in every move for having no idea of one's own or pleasing others.

【亦庄亦谐】yì zhuāng yì xié 形容既庄重,又诙谐 serious and comical at the same time; seriocomic

衣 yì 〈书〉穿(衣服);拿衣服给人穿 wear; clothe: ～布衣 wear cotton clothes | 解衣～我。(He) doffed his own garment to clothe me.

☞ yī on p. 2257

异(異) yì ❶ 有分别;不相同 different: ～口同声 with one voice; in unison | 大同小～ with little difference; slightly different; almost the same; very much the same | 日新月～ change with each passing day | 求同存～ seek common ground while reserving differences ❷ 奇异;特别 strange; unusual; extraordinary: ～香 rare fragrance; rarely sweet odour; peculiar fragrance | ～闻 extraordinary news ❸ 惊奇;奇怪 surprise: 惊～

surprise|深以为～ be greatly surprised ❹ 另外的；别的 other；another：～日 another day|～地 another place ❺ 分开 separate：离～ separate；divorce|～爨（亲属分家）（of brothers）divide up the family property and form separate families

【异邦】yìbāng 外国 foreign country；alien land

【异彩】yìcǎi 奇异的光彩 extraordinary（or radiant）splendour；〈比喻 *fig.*〉突出的成就或表现 outstanding accomplishments or performances：大放～ blossom in radiant splendour；in great brilliance|～纷呈 a varied colourful splendour

【异常】yìcháng ❶ 不同于寻常 aberrant；unusual；abnormal：神色～ not be one's usual self|情况～ abnormal condition|～现象 abnormal phenomenon ❷ 非常；特别 exceptionally；greatly；unusually；very：～激动 exceptionally excited|～美丽 exceedingly beautiful|～反感 very antipathetic to

【异词】yìcí same as 异言 yìyán

【异地】yìdì 他乡；外乡 place far away from home；strange land：流落～ lead a wretched life away from home|～相逢 meet in an alien place

【异读】yìdú 指一个字在习惯上具有的两个或几个不同的读法，如'谁'字读 shéi 又读 shuí variant pronunciation of one character，such as the character'谁' which reads either as shéi or shuí

【异端】yìduān 指不符合正统思想的主张或教义 heterodoxy；heresy：～邪说 heresies；heretical beliefs；unorthodox opinions

【异国】yìguó 外国 foreign country（or land）：～情调 smack of a distant land；exotic atmosphere|～他乡 alien land

【异乎】yìhū 不同于 different from：～寻常 unusually；extraordinarily

【异化】yìhuà ❶ 相似或相同的事物逐渐变得不相似或不相同 similar or identical things gradually become not similar or not identical ❷ 哲学上指把自己的素质或力量转化为跟自己对立、支配自己的东西（philos.）alienation；transformation of one's quality or strength into sth. that is opposed to and controls oneself ❸ 语音学上指连发几个相似或相同的音，其中一个变得和其他的音不相似或不相同 dissimilation；process of linguistic change in which one of several similar or identical phonemes within a word or phrase becomes dissimilar to or different from the others

Y

【异化作用】yìhuà zuòyòng 生物体在新陈代谢过程中，自身的组成物质发生分解，同时放出能量，这个过程叫做异化作用 dissimilation；process of metabolism in which components of a living organism dissolve and emit energy

【异己】yìjǐ 同一集体中在立场、政见或重大问题上常跟自己有严重分歧甚至敌对的人 dissident；alien；sb. in one's group who differs greatly or even holds an antagonistic stand or political view on major issues：～分子 dissident；alien|排除～ discriminate against those who hold different views；get rid of dissidents

【异军突起】yì jūn tū qǐ〈比喻 *fig.*〉与众不同的新派别或新力量突然兴起 a new faction or new force suddenly coming to the fore

【异口同声】yì kǒu tóng shēng 形容很多人说同样的话 with one voice；in unison

【异类】yìlèi ❶〈旧时 *old*〉称外族 foreign peoples ❷ 指鸟兽、草木、神鬼等（对'人类'而言 as opposed to 'humans'）alien class or species such as birds，beasts，plants，gods or ghosts，etc.

【异曲同工】yì qǔ tóng gōng 不同的曲调演得同样好 different tunes sung with equal skill；〈比喻 *fig.*〉不同的人的辞章或言论同样精彩，或者不同的做法收到同样的效果 different people write or speak equally well；different writing or speeches having the same good effect；different approaches but equally satisfactory results；also 同工异曲 tóng gōng yì qǔ

【异趣】yìqù ❶ 不同的志趣、情趣 different in taste and interest ❷ 不同于一般的趣味 peculiar taste：点画之间，多有～。There is something peculiar to the brushwork of this work of calligraphy.

【异日】yìrì〈书 *fml.*〉❶ 将来；日后 some other day：委之～ be entrusted some other day|留待～再决 leave it till some other day for a decision ❷ 从前；往日（in）former days：谈笑一如～ chat and laugh as before

【异体】yìtǐ ❶ 不同的形体 variant：～字 variant form of a Chinese character ❷ 不同属一个身体或个体 not belonging to the same body or individual：～组织移植 alien tissue transplant|雌雄～ gonochorism；dioecism

【异体字】yìtǐzì 跟规定的正体字同音同义而写法不同的字，如'攷'是'考'的异体字，'隄'是'堤'的异体字 variant form of a Chinese character；Chinese character which has the same pronunciation and same meaning as its standardized form but is written in a different way，e.g.，攷 kǎo is the variant form of 考 kǎo，and 隄 tí is the variant form of 堤 tí.

【异同】yìtóng ❶ 不同之处和相同之处 similarities and differences：分别～ differentiate between the similarities and differences ❷〈书 *fml.*〉same as 异议 yìyì

【异味】yìwèi ❶ 不同寻常的美味；难得的好吃的东西 rare delicacy ❷ 不正常的气味 peculiar odour：食物已有～，不能再吃。The food has a peculiar smell，and it is not eatable any more.

【异物】yìwù ❶ 不应进入而进入或不应存在而

存在于身体内部的物体，通常多指非生物体，例如进入眼内的沙子、掉进气管内的玻璃球等 foreign matter; foreign body; substance that is not an organic part of a body, usu. referring to non-organisms, such as a fine grit in an eye or a glass ball in the trachea ❷〈书 *fml.*〉指死亡的人 dead person; ghost: 化为～ give up the ghost; die ❸〈书 *fml.*〉奇异的物品 a rare object

【异乡】yìxiāng 外乡；外地(就做客的人而言 as far as a guest is concerned) foreign land; strange land: 客居～ live in a foreign land

【异香】yìxiāng 异乎寻常的香味 unusually sweet smell; rare perfume: ～扑鼻。Strong whiffs of rare perfume assailed the nostrils.

【异想天开】yì xiǎng tiān kāi 形容想法离奇，不切实际 indulge in the wildest fantasy; have a most fantastic idea

【异心】yìxīn 不忠实的念头 infidelity; disloyalty: 怀有～ harbour disloyalty

【异型】yìxíng 通常指某些材料截面形状不同于常见的方形、圆形的形状 shapes of the cross sections of certain materials different from the common square and round shapes; irregular shape; special shape: ～钢 special-shaped steel | ～砖 irregular bricks

【异性】yìxìng ❶ 性别不同的人 opposite sex: 追求～woo sb. of the opposite sex ❷ 性质不同 different in nature: ～的电互相吸引，同性的电互相排斥。Unlike electric charges attract each other, while like electric charges repel each other.

【异姓】yìxìng 不同姓 different family names: ～兄弟 brothers of different family names

【异言】yìyán 表示不同意的话 dissenting words: 并无～ raise no objection

【异样】yìyàng ❶ 两样；不同 difference: 多年没见了，看不出他有什么～。We haven't seen each other for many years, but he doesn't look any different. ❷ 不同寻常的；特殊 unusual; peculiar: 人们都用～的眼光打量他。Everyone sized him up with curious eyes.

【异议】yìyì 不同的意见 objection; dissent: 提出～ raise an objection; take exception to; challenge

【异域】yìyù ❶ 外国 a foreign country ❷ 他乡；外乡 an alien land; a strange land

【异族】yìzú 外族 a different race or nation

苅(苅) yì same as 刈 yì

杙 yì〈书 *fml.*〉小木桩 small wooden stake

抑[1] yì 向下按；压制 press down; restrain; repress; curb: ～制 check; curb; restrain | ～郁 depressed; dejected | 压～ feel depressed | ～强扶弱 restrain the powerful and help the weak | ～恶扬善 suppress the bad and commend the good

抑[2] yì〈书 *fml.*〉〈连词 *conj.*〉❶ 表示选择，相当于'或是'、'还是'[indicating a choice] or: 求之欤，～与之欤? Is it asked for or is it given? ❷ 表示转折，相当于'可是'、'但是'、'然而'[indicating a turn] but; however: 多则多矣，～君似鼠。Despite his great achievements, the monarch acted as timidly as a mouse. *or* The monarch had many accomplishments, but he acted like a mouse. ❸ 表示递进，相当于'而且'[indicating progressive advance] moreover; besides: 非惟天时，～亦人谋也。It's not only a matter of Heaven-sent occasions but also a matter of human endeavour.

【抑或】yìhuò〈书 *fml.*〉〈连词 *conj.*〉表示选择关系 or: 不知他们是赞成，～是反对。I wonder if they are for or against this.

【抑扬】yìyáng (声音)高低起伏 (of sound) rise and fall; modulate

【抑扬顿挫】yìyáng dùncuò (声音)高低起伏和停顿转折 cadence; modulation in tone

【抑郁】yìyù 心有愤恨，不能诉说而烦闷 depressed; despondent; gloomy: 心情～ be depressed

【抑止】yìzhǐ same as 抑制 yìzhì ②

【抑制】yìzhì ❶ 大脑皮层的两种基本神经活动过程之一。是在外部或内部刺激下产生的，作用是阻止皮层的兴奋，减弱器官机能的活动。睡眠就是大脑皮层全部处于抑制的现象。inhibition; one of the two basic processes of nervous activity of the cerebral cortex, caused by external or internal stimulation; function being to check the excitation of the cortex and reduce the activities of the organs. Sleep is exactly a complete inhibition of the cerebral contex. ❷ 压下去；控制 restrain; control; check: 他～不住内心的喜悦。He couldn't check his joy.

呓(囈、讛) yì 呓语 talk in one's sleep: 梦～ talk in one's sleep

【呓语】yìyǔ 梦话 talk in one's sleep; crazy talk; ravings

邑 yì ❶ 城市 town; city: 城～ city | 通都大～ big city ❷〈古时 *arch.*〉县的别称 *yi*, another term for county: ～境 county area | ～宰(县令) county magistrate

駯 yì〈书 *fml.*〉重叠；重复 overlapping; repetition; duplication
☞ yí on p. 2261

佚 yì same as 逸 yì

役 yì ❶ 需要出劳力的事 labour; service: 劳～ corvée; forced labour | 徭～ corvée ❷ 兵役 military service: 服～ serve in the army | 现～ active service | 退～ retire from military service | 预备～ reserve service ❸ 役使 use as a servant: 奴～ enslave ❹〈旧时 *old*〉指供使

唤的人 servant：仆～ domestic servant｜衙～ yamen runner ❺ 战争；战役 battle；campaign：平型关之～ Battle of Pingxingguan (September 1937)

【役畜】yìchù ☞ 力畜 lìchù on p. 1183

【役龄】yìlíng ❶ 指适合服兵役的年龄 enlistment age ❷ 服兵役的年数 years of military service

【役使】yìshǐ 使用(牲畜)；强迫使用(人力) work (an animal)；use：～骡马 draft animals｜～奴婢 work servants

译(譯) yì 翻译 translate；interpret：口～ interpret｜笔～ translate｜直～ literal translation｜编～ edit and translate｜～文 translation

【译本】yìběn 翻译成另一种文字的本子 translated version (of a book)；translation：这部著作已有两种外文～。The book has been translated into two foreign versions.

【译笔】yìbǐ 指译文的质量或风格 the quality or style of a translation：～流畅。The translation reads smoothly.

【译名】yìmíng 翻译出来的名称 translated term or name

【译文】yìwén 翻译成的文字 translated text；translation

【译意风】yìyìfēng 会场或电影院使用的一种翻译装置。译员在隔音室里把讲演人或影片里的对话随时翻译成各种语言，听的人可以用座位上的耳机从中挑选自己懂得的语言。常在国际会议或多民族参加的会议上使用。simultaneous interpretation installation；interpretation installation used in a conference hall or cinema, through which an interpreter in a soundproof room interprets a speech or the dialogues in a film into a desired language simultaneously and a listener uses an earphone to listen to the translated speech by choosing a selected channel：it is commonly used at international conferences or multi-national conferences.

【译音】yìyīn ❶ 把一种语言的语词用另一种语言中跟它发音相同或近似的语音表示出来，例如'большевик'译成'布尔什维克'，'sofa'译成'沙发' transliterate；write or spell (words, letters, etc.) in corresponding characters of another alphabet, e.g. 'Bolshevic' is transliterated as '布尔什维克'，'sofa' is transliterated as '沙发' ❷ 按译音法译成的音 transliteration

【译员】yìyuán 翻译人员(多指口译的) interpreter (orally)

【译制】yìzhì 翻译制作(电影片、电视片等) dub (a film, TV film, etc.)

【译注】yìzhù 翻译并注解 translate and annotate：～古籍 translate and annotate ancient books｜《孟子～》*Annotations to Mencius*

【译作】yìzuò 翻译的作品 translations

易[1] yì ❶ 做起来不费事的；容易(跟'难'相对 as opposed to 'difficult') have no difficulty in doing things；easy：简～ simple｜轻～ easily｜～如反掌 as easy as turning over one's hand｜显而～见 obviously；apparently｜得来不～ be hard-won；has not come easily；be hard earned；not easy to earn ❷ 平和 amiable：平～近人 be amiable and easy of approach ❸〈书 *fml.*〉轻视 despise

易[2] yì ❶ 改变；变换 change：变～ change｜～名 change one's name｜移风～俗 change the established social customs｜不～之论 irrefutable argument ❷ 交换 exchange：贸～ trade｜交～ deal；business；｜～货协定 barter trade agreement｜以物～物 barter ❸ (Yì) 姓 a surname

【易拉罐】yìlāguàn 一种装饮料或其他流质食品的金属罐，封闭罐口的一块儿金属片很容易拉开，所以叫易拉罐 pop-top；pull-top；flip-top；a metal tin holding drink or liquid food with a pull opening on the top

【易如反掌】yì rú fǎn zhǎng 像翻一下手掌那样容易 as easy as turning one's hand over；as easy as falling off a log；〈比喻 *fig.*〉事情极容易办 very easy

【易手】yìshǒu (政权、财产等)更换占有者 change hands：他家原先的住宅早已～他人。The house where his family had lived changed hands long ago.

【易于】yìyú 容易 be easy to：这个办法～实行。This method is easy to carry out.

【易帜】yìzhì 国家或军队更换旗子。指政权性质发生变化或投向敌方。change the banner (of a government or an army)；change the nature of a political power or one's allegiance

峄(嶧) yì 峄山，山名，在山东 Yishan, name of a mountain in Shandong Province

佾 yì〈古代 *arch.*〉乐舞的行列 procession of singers and dancers in a performance

泆 yì〈书 *fml.*〉❶ 放纵 indulgent ❷ same as 溢 yì

怿(懌) yì〈书 *fml.*〉欢喜；高兴 pleased；happy；joyful

诣 yì〈书 *fml.*〉❶ 到某人所在的地方；到某个地方去看人(多用于所尊敬的人) go to (a place)；call on (sb. one respects)：～烈士墓参谒 go to the graves of revolutionary martyrs to pay one's respects ❷ (学业、技术等)所达到的程度 (academic or technical) attainments：造～ attainments｜苦心孤～ toil or endeavour single-heartedly；make extraordinarily painstaking efforts

驿(驛) yì 驿站。现在多用于地名。post station；*yi*, now used mainly as part of a place name：龙泉～(在四川) Longquanyi (in Sichuan Province)｜郑家～(在湖南) Zhengjiayi (in Hunan Province)

【驿道】yìdào〈古代 *arch.*〉传递政府文书等的道路,沿途设有驿站 post road; an ancient road with post stations, over which government documents were delivered

【驿站】yìzhàn〈古代 *arch.*〉供传递政府文书的人中途更换马匹或休息、住宿的地方 post station, where government messengers changed horses or took rest or stayed; courier station

绎(繹) yì〈书 *fml.*〉抽出或理出事物的头绪来 unravel; sort out: 寻～ unravel; inquire into | 演～ deduction | 抽～ sort things out; get things into shape

枻(栧) yì〈书 *fml.*〉桨 oar

轶 yì same as 逸 yì ④ ⑤

昳 yì [昳丽](yìlì)〈书 *fml.*〉容貌美丽 pretty; beautiful (looks)

☞ dié on p. 450

食 yì 用于人名,郦食其(Lì Yìjī),汉朝人 used in personal names, such as Li Yiji, a man of the Han Dynasty

☞ shí on p. 1745 and sì on p. 1823

狭 yì ☞ 林狭 línyì on p. 1221

疫 yì 瘟疫 epidemic disease; pestilence: 鼠～ plague | 时～ epidemic | 防～ epidemic prevention (or control)

【疫病】yìbìng 流行性的传染病 epidemic disease: ～流行。An epidemic disease is spreading.

【疫苗】yìmiáo 能使机体产生免疫力的病毒、立克次氏体等制剂,如牛痘苗、麻疹疫苗等。通常也包括能使机体产生免疫力的细菌制剂、抗毒素、类毒素。vaccine; virus that enables the body to produce immunity, rickettsia, and other preparations, such as bovine vaccine and measles virus vaccine, usu. also including bacterial preparations, antitoxins, and toxoids

【疫情】yìqíng 疫病的产生和发展情况 information about and appraisal of an epidemic; epidemic situation: 控制～ keep the epidemic under control | ～报告站 a station for reporting incidence of epidemic diseases

弈 yì〈书 *fml.*〉❶ 围棋 weiqi, a game played with black and white pieces on a board of 361 crosses; go ❷ 下棋 play chess: 对～ play chess (between two people) | ～棋 play chess

奕 yì ❶〈书 *fml.*〉盛大 grand; great ❷ (Yì) 姓 a surname

【奕奕】yìyì 精神饱满的样子 grand; great; radiating power and vitality: 神采～ glowing with radiance and vitality

斁(斁) yì〈书 *fml.*〉厌弃;厌倦 loathe; be tired of

☞ dù on p. 483

羿 yì ❶ 上古人名,传说是夏代有穷国的君主,善于射箭 Yi, who was a legendary king of the Youqiong State in the Xia Dynasty and a master archer ❷ (Yì)姓 a surname

挹 yì〈书〉❶ 舀 ladle out; scoop up: ～取 ladle out; scoop up | ～彼注兹(从那里舀出来倒在这里头) ladle out from there to pour in here; draw from one to make good the deficits of another ❷ 牵引;拉 pull

【挹取】yìqǔ〈书 *fml.*〉舀 ladle out; scoop up

【挹注】yìzhù〈书 *fml.*〉〈比喻 *fig.*〉从有余的地方取些出来以补不足的地方 draw from one to make good the deficits of another

唈 yì〈书 *fml.*〉same as 悒 yì

益1 yì ❶ 好处(跟'害'相对 as opposed to 'disadvantage') benefit; profit; advantage: 利～ interest; benefit | 公～ public interest; public benefit | 权～ rights and interests | 受～不浅 benefit greatly ❷ 有益的(跟'害'相对 as opposed to 'harmful') beneficial: ～友 friend and mentor | ～鸟 beneficial bird | ～虫 beneficial insect ❸ (Yì) 姓 a surname

益2 yì ❶ 增加 increase: 增～ increase; add | 延年～寿 prolong life ❷ 更加 all the more; increasingly: 多多～善 the more the better | 精～求精 keep improving; make constant improvements; be a perfectionist

【益虫】yìchóng 直接或间接对人有利的昆虫,如吐丝的蚕,酿蜜和传播花粉的蜜蜂,捕食农业害虫的螳螂、瓢虫、蜻蜓等 beneficial insect; insect that is directly or indirectly beneficial to the humans, such as silkworm (a moth caterpillar) that produces cocoons of silk, bee that makes honey and disseminates pollen, and mantis, ladybug, dragonfly, etc. that catch and feed on insects destructive to farm crops

【益处】yì·chu 对人或事物有利的因素;好处 benefit; advantage; factor beneficial to humans or things

【益发】yìfā 越发;更加 all the more; even more: 自他病倒以后,家里的日子～艰难了。Since he fell ill, the days of the family have become all the more difficult.

【益母草】yìmǔcǎo 二年生草本植物,茎直立,方形,基部的叶子有长柄,略呈圆形,茎部的叶子掌状分裂,裂片狭长,花淡紫红色,坚果有棱。茎叶和子实均可入药。motherwort (*Leonurus heterophyllus*); biennial herbal plant with a straight, square stem, long-stalk, slightly round leaves at the base, palmately-lobed leaves on the stem, long and narrow lobes, pale-purple flowers and edged nuts, the stem, leaves and seeds used for Chinese medicine. also 茺蔚 chōngwèi

【益鸟】yìniǎo 捕食害虫、害兽,直接或间接对人类有益的鸟类,如燕子、杜鹃、猫头鹰等 beneficial bird; birds that catch and feed on destructive insects or destructive animals, and are directly or indirectly beneficial to man, such as swallow, cuckoo, owl, etc.

【益友】yìyǒu 对自己思想、工作、学习有帮助的朋友 friend and mentor; friend who is helpful to one's thinking, work and study: 良师～ good teacher and helpful friend

浥 yì〈书 *fml.*〉沾湿 wet; soak

悒 yì〈书 *fmlk.*〉忧愁不安 sad; worried: 忧～ depressed; despondent; gloomy | 郁～ depressed; despondent; gloomy | ～～不乐 feel depressed; mope

谊 yì 交情 friendship: 友～ friendship | 情～ friendship | 深情厚～ profound friendship

埸 yì〈书 *fml.*〉❶ 田间的界限 low bank of earth between fields; ridge ❷ 边境 boundary; border: 疆～ border

勚 yì ❶〈书 *fml.*〉劳苦 toil; hard work ❷ 器物的棱角、锋芒等磨损 wear and tear; (of an edge, point, etc.) become worn; become dull or blunt: 螺丝扣～了。The thread of the screw was worn.

逸 yì ❶ 安乐;安闲 ease; leisure: 安～ leisure | 以～待劳 wait at ease for an exhausted enemy; conserve one's strength while the enemy or opponent is tired out after a long march or travel | 一劳永～ get sth. done once and for all ❷ 逃跑 escape; flee; run away: 奔～ gallop away | 逃～ escape; run away ❸ 避世隐居 live in seclusion: 隐～ lead the life of a hermit | ～民 hermit ❹ 散失;失传 be lost: ～文 ancient essay no longer extant | ～书 ancient books that have been partly lost or in private collection; ancient works no longer extant | ～事 anecdote; episode | ～闻 anecdote ❺ 超过一般 excel: 超～ free from material desires; above worldly desires | ～群 outstanding; head and shoulders above others; absolutely superior

【逸乐】yìlè 闲适安乐 comfort and pleasure

【逸民】yìmín〈古代 *arch.*〉称避世隐居不做官的人。也指亡国后不在新朝代做官的人。hermit; recluse; person who refuses to take an official post by living in solitude, or who refuses to assume an official post in a new dynasty

【逸事】yìshì 世人不大知道的关于某人的事迹，多指不见于正式记载的 anecdote; little known, entertaining facts of history or biography, usually not seen in official records: 这部书里记载了很多名人～。This book contains anecdotes of many celebrities.

【逸闻】yìwén 世人不大知道的传说，多指不见于正式记载的 anecdote; little known, entertaining facts of legends, usually not seen in official records

Y

【逸豫】yìyù〈书 *fml.*〉安逸享乐 idleness and pleasure: ～亡身。Idleness and pleasure lead to ruin.

翊 yì〈书 *fml.*〉辅佐;帮助 assist (a ruler): ～戴(辅佐拥戴) assist and support (a ruler) | ～赞(辅助) assist (a monarch)

翌 yì〈书 *fml.*〉次于今日、今年的 immediately following in time; next: ～日 next day | ～年 next year | ～晨(第二天早晨) the next morning

【翌日】yìrì〈书 *fml.*〉次日 next day; the following day

晹 yì〈书 *fml.*〉太阳在云中忽隐忽视 the sun keeps disappearing and appearing in the floating clouds

嗌 yì〈书 *fml.*〉咽喉 throat; ☞ ài on p. 7

鹝(鶂) yì〈书 *fml.*〉same as 鹢 yì

【鹝鹝】yìyì〈书 *fml.*〉形容鹅叫的声音 sound of goose crying

肄 yì 学习 study: ～业 study in school or at college | ～习(学习) study

【肄业】yìyè 学习(课程)。指没有毕业或尚未毕业。study in school or at college: ～生 student who fails to complete his education in a school | 高中～ not finishing one's senior middle schooling | 他曾在北京大学物理系～两年。He studied in the physics department of the Beijing University for two years.

裔 yì ❶〈书 *fml.*〉后代 descendants; posterity: 后～ descendants | 华～ foreign citizen of Chinese origin ❷〈书 *fml.*〉边远的地方 distant land; remote region: 四～borderlands; frontiers ❸ (Yì)姓 a surname

意 yì ❶ 意思 meaning; idea; thought: 同～ agree; consent | 来～ one's purpose of coming or visit | 词不达～ the words fail to convey the meaning; the language fail to express the idea ❷ 心愿;愿望 wish; desire; intention: 中～ be to one's taste; be to one's liking | 任～ at will; at random; wilfully | 满～ satisfactory; be satisfied with ❸ 意料;料想 anticipate; expect: ～外 unexpectedly | 出其不～ catch somebody by surprise

【意表】yìbiǎo 意想之外 what one expects; expectation: 出人～ catch somebody by surprise

【意会】yìhuì 不经直接说明而了解(意思) perceive by intuition; sense: 只可～，不可言传 can be sensed, but not explained in words

【意见】yì•jiàn ❶ 对事情的一定的看法或想法 idea; view; opinion; suggestion: 你的～怎么样？What's your opinion? *or* What do you think of it? | 咱们来交换交换～。Let's exchange our ideas. ❷ (对人、对事)认为不对因而不满意的想法 objection; differing opinion; complaint: 我对于这种办法有～。I strongly object to this method. *or* I take vigorous exception to this approach. | 人家对他的～很多。People have a lot of complaints about him.

【意匠】yìjiàng 指诗文、绘画等的构思设计 artistic conception (of a poem, painting, etc.); artistic design: 别具～ show originality in artistic conception

【意境】yìjìng 文学艺术作品通过形象描写表现出来的境界和情调 mood of a literary work or a work of art; artistic conception; artistic mood

【意料】yìliào 事先对情况、结果等的估计 anticipate; expect: ～之中 as expected | 出乎～ beyond expectation; unexpected; out of expectation | ～不到的事 something that nobody has expected

【意念】yìniàn 念头；想法 idea; thought: 这时每人脑子里都只有一个～：'胜利!' At that moment victory was the only idea that occupied everyone's mind. *or* Everybody had only one thought in mind at the moment: Victory!

【意气】yìqì ❶ 意志和气概 will and spirit: ～高昂 high-spirited; in high spirits | ～风发 in high spirits ❷ 志趣和性格 temperament and interest: ～相投 be congenial in temperament; hit it off with each other; see eye to eye ❸ 由于主观和偏激而产生的情绪 personal feelings or prejudice: 闹～ give vent to personal feelings | ～用事 be carried away by personal feelings

【意气风发】yìqì fēngfā 形容精神振奋，气概昂扬 in high spirits; high-spirited and vigorous; daring and energetic

【意气用事】yìqì yòngshì 只凭感情办事，缺乏理智 be swayed by personal feelings

【意趣】yìqù 意味和兴趣 interest and charm (of a literary work or a work of art); temperament and taste; flavour; mood: ～盎然 full of interest

【意识】yì·shí ❶ 人的头脑对于客观物质世界的反映，是感觉、思维等各种心理过程的总和，其中的思维是人类特有的反映现实的高级形式。存在决定意识，意识又反作用于存在。consciousness; awareness. The reflection of the objective material world in man's mind is the sum total of sensation, thinking and other psychological processes, and thinking is a high form of reflection of reality peculiar to man. Being determines consciousness, and consciousness reacts on being. ❷ 觉察(常与'到'字连用 usu. used with 到 dào) be conscious (or aware) of; awake to; realise: 天还冷，看见树枝发绿才～到已经是春天了。It's still cold. Only at the sight of the green twigs did I realise that it's already spring.

【意识形态】yì·shí xíngtài 在一定的经济基础上形成的，人对于世界和社会的有系统的看法和见解，哲学、政治、艺术、宗教、道德等是它的具体表现。意识形态是上层建筑的组成部分，在阶级社会里具有阶级性。ideology; man's systematic views on the world and society formed on a certain economic basis. Philosophy, politics, art, religion and morality are its concrete manifestations. Ideology is a component part of the superstructure, and it has class character in a class society. also 观念形态 guānniàn xíngtài

【意思】yì·si ❶ 语言文字的意义；思想内容 meaning; idea: '节约'就是不浪费的～。'Thrift' means no waste. | 要正确地了解这篇文章的中心～。One should correctly understand the central idea of this article. | 你这句话是什么～? What do you mean by this sentence? ❷ 意见；愿望 opinion; wish; desire: 大家的～是一起去。Everyone wants to go together. | 我想跟你合写一篇文章，你是不是也有这个～? I want to write an article together with you. Do you have the same wish? ❸ 指礼品所代表的心意 a token of affection, appreciation, gratitude, etc.: 这不过是我的一点～，你就收下吧! Please accept this little gift as a token of my appreciation. ❹ 指表示一点心意 as a mere token: 大家受累了，得买些东西～一下。Everyone has taken the trouble to help me. I'll buy you something as a token of my thanks. ❺ 某种趋势或苗头 suggestion; hint; trace: 天有点要下雨的～。It looks like rain. | 天气渐渐暖了，树木有点儿发绿的～了。It's getting warm, and the trees look like sprouting. ❻ 情趣；趣味 interest; fun: 这棵松树长得像座宝塔，真有～。It's very interesting to see the pine tree look like a pagoda. | 他看着工业展览会上的新产品，感觉很有～。He found the new products at the industrial exhibition very interesting.

【意图】yìtú 希望达到某种目的的打算 intention; intent: 主观～ subjective intention | 他的～很明显，是想要那本书。His intention is obvious. He wants that book.

【意外】yìwài ❶ 意料之外 unexpected; unforeseen: 感到～ be surprised; be taken by surprise | ～事故 accident ❷ 意外的不幸事件 accident; mishap: 煤炉子一定要装烟筒，以免发生～。The coal stove must have smoke pipes so as to avoid accidents.

【意味】yìwèi ❶ 含蓄的意思 meaning; significance; implication: 话里含有讽刺～ words imply sarcasm ❷ 情调；情趣；趣味 interest; overtone; flavour: ～无穷 of unlimited interest | 富于文学～ imbued with a literary flavour

【意味着】yìwèi·zhe 含有某种意义 signify; mean; imply; be the stamp of: 生产率的提高～劳动力的节省。Increased productivity means reduced labour power.

【意想】yìxiǎng 料想；想像 imagine; expect: ～

不到 unexpected|比赛结果在～之中。The result of the match was as expected.

【意向】yìxiàng 意图；目的 intention; purpose:～不明 intentions are not clear|该厂有扩大生产规模的～。The factory has the intention to expand its production scale.

【意向书】yìxiàngshū 在经济活动中签署的表明双方意向的文书 letter of intent, signed by the two parties in economic activities

【意象】yìxiàng 意境 images; imagery:这首民歌～新颖。This folk song is conceived with originality.

【意兴】yìxìng 兴致 interest; enthusiasm:～索然 have lost all interest in sth.; be no longer interested in sth.|～勃勃 be highly enthusiastic

【意义】yìyì ❶ 语言文字或其他信号所表示的内容 meaning; sense; significance ❷ 价值；作用 value; effect:革命的～ revolutionary significance|人生的～ meaning of life|一部富有教育～的影片 a film with high educational value; a very educative film

【意译】yìyì ❶ 根据原文的大意来翻译，不作逐字逐句的翻译（区别于'直译' as compared with 'transliteration'） free translation; translation by rough idea, not verbation ❷ 根据某种语言词语的意义译成另一种语言的词语（区别于'音译' as compared with 'transliteration'） translate words of one language into the words of another language on the basis of their meanings

【意愿】yìyuàn 愿望；心愿 wish; desire; aspiration:尊重本人的～ respect one's own wish

【意蕴】yìyùn 内在的意义；含义 meaning; implication; connotation:～丰富 rich connotation|反复琢磨，才能领会这首诗的～。Only after a lot of thinking can one grasp the inner meaning of the poem.

【意在言外】yì zài yán wài 言词的真正用意是暗含着的，没有明白说出 the meaning is implied

【意旨】yìzhǐ 意图（多指应该遵从的 oft. sth. that should be followed） intention; wish; will:秉承～ acting according to sb.'s wish

【意志】yìzhì 决定达到某种目的而产生的心理状态，往往由语言和行动表现出来 will; willpower; determination:～薄弱 weak-willed|～坚强 strong-willed|不屈不挠的～indomitable will

【意中人】yìzhōngrén 心里爱慕的异性 person one is in love with; person of one's heart; beloved one

溢 yì ❶ 充满而流出来 overflow; spill:充～ overflowing|洋～ brim with; be full of|河水四～。The river overflowed. ❷ 过分 excessive:～美 excessive praise; overpraise 〈古 arch.〉 same as 镒 yì

【溢洪道】yìhóngdào 水库建筑物的防洪设备，多筑在水坝的一侧，像大槽子。当水库的水位超过安全限度时，水就从溢洪道向下游流出。spillway; a passageway or channel beside dam; flood prevention installation to drain excess water from a reservoir when the water level exceeds the safety limit

【溢美】yìměi 〈书 *fml.*〉过分夸赞 excessive praise; fulsome praise; undeserved praise:～之词 excessive praise

【溢于言表】yì yú yán biǎo （感情）流露在言辞、神情上（of feelings） show clearly in one's words and manner:愤激之情，～。Indignation showed clearly in his words and manner.

缢 yì 〈书 *fml.*〉用绳子勒死；吊死 die or be put to death by hanging:自～ hang onself to death

蓺 yì 〈书 *fml.*〉种植 plant; grow:～菊 grow chrysanthemums|树～五谷 grow all food crops

蜴 yì ☞ 蜥蜴 xīyì on p.2049

鮨 yì 鱼类的一科，体侧扁，红色或褐色，有斑纹，口大，牙细而尖。大部分种类生活在海洋中。comber (*Serranus cabrilla*); red or brown fish with a flat, striped body, a big mouth and small and pointed teeth, most of them living in the sea

廙 yì 〈书 *fml.*〉恭敬（多用于人名 usu. used in personal names） respect

瘗（瘞） yì 〈书 *fml.*〉掩埋；埋藏 bury

潩 yì 清潩河，水名，颍河支流，在河南 Qingyi River, tributary of the Yinghe River in Henan Province

嫕 yì 〈书 *fml.*〉性情和善可亲 amiable; affable:婉～（和婉柔顺） pliant and amiable

鹝 yì same as 鹢 yì

镒 yì 〈古代 *arch.*〉重量单位，合二十两（一说二十四两） unit of weight equal to 20 or 24 taels:黄金百～ one hundred *yi* of gold

饐 yì 〈书 *fml.*〉食物腐败变味（of food） decompose and rot

毅 yì 坚决 firm; resolute; staunch:～力 determination; will power; will;|刚～ resolute and steadfast|沉～ determined; resolute; steadfast

【毅力】yìlì 坚强持久的意志 willpower; will; stamina; tenacity:学习没有～是不行的。It's impossible to study well without strong will power.

【毅然】yìrán 坚决地；毫不犹疑地 resolutely; firmly; determinedly:～决然 resolutely; determinedly|～献身祖国的科学事业 dedicate oneself to scientific development of one's motherland with determination

鹢 yì 古书上说的一种水鸟 water bird as described in ancient books

熠 yì 〈书 *fml*.〉光耀;鲜明 bright; brilliant

【熠熠】yìyì 〈书 *fml*.〉形容闪光发亮 sparkling; glittering:光彩～ brilliant splendour

薏 yì ☞ below

【薏米】yìmǐ 去壳后的薏苡的子实,白色,可供食用,也可入药 seed of Job's tears. After the husk is removed, the white seed is used for food or medicine; also 薏仁米 yìrénmǐ, 苡仁 yǐrén or 苡米 yǐmǐ

【薏仁米】yìrénmǐ same as 薏米 yìmǐ

【薏苡】yìyǐ 多年生草本植物,茎直立,叶披针形,颖果卵形,灰白色。果仁叫薏米。Job's tears (*Coix lacryma-jobi*); perennial herbal plant with a straight stem, lanceolate leaves and greyish-white, ovate caryopsis

瞖 yì 〈书 *fml*.〉 same as 翳 yì

殪 yì 〈书 *fml*.〉❶ 死 die ❷ 杀死 kill

曀 yì 〈书 *fml*.〉天阴沉 cloudy; overcast

螠 yì 无脊椎动物的一纲,雌雄异体,身体呈圆筒状,不分节,有少数刚毛。生活在海底泥沙中。Echiuroid; dioecious group of invertebrates having cylinder-shaped, non-segmented bodies with a few setae, and living on muddy sea floors

劓 yì 〈古代 *arch*.〉割掉鼻子的酷刑 punishment of cutting off the nose

燚 yì 人名用字 *yi*, used as part of a person's name

翳 yì ❶〈书 *fml*.〉遮蔽 screen; conceal:阴～ hide|～蔽 conceal ❷ 眼睛角膜病变后遗留下来的疤痕 nebula; a slight cloudy opacity of the cornea

臆(肊) yì ❶ 胸 chest:胸～ heart; one's feelings ❷ 主观地 subjectively:～测 conjecture; surmise; guess|～造 fabricate

【臆测】yìcè 主观地推测 conjecture; surmise; guess; subjectively suppose

【臆断】yìduàn 凭臆测来断定 assume; judge according to one's subjective conjecture:主观～ form a subjective judgment

【臆度】yìduó 〈书 *fml*.〉 same as 臆测 yìcè

【臆见】yìjiàn 主观的见解 a subjective view

【臆说】yìshuō 主观推测的说法 assumption; (subjective) supposition

【臆想】yìxiǎng 主观地想像 a wishful imagination

【臆造】yìzào 凭主观的想法编造 fabricate; concoct on the basis of wishful thinking:凭空～ sheer fabrication

瘱 yì 〈书 *fml*.〉 same as 呓 yì

翼 yì ❶ 鸟类的飞行器官,由前肢演化而成,上面生有羽毛。有的鸟翼退化,不能飞翔。wing; feathered appendages, evolved from forelimbs, by means of which a bird is able to fly. Some birds, with degenerated wings, cannot fly; 通称 commonly known as 翅膀 chìbǎng ❷ 飞机或滑翔机等飞行工具两侧伸出像鸟翼的部分,有支撑机身、产生升力等作用 wings of an aircraft (e. g. airplane, glider, etc.); airfoils that extend like a bird's wings, and function to support aircraft and generate forces for takeoff, etc. ❸ 侧 flank; side:两～阵地 bastions on both sides|由左～进攻 attack from the left flank ❹ 二十八宿之一 one of the 28 constellations into which the celestial sphere was divided in ancient Chinese astronomy ❺〈书 *fml*.〉帮助;辅佐 help; assist:～助 render assistance to sb.|扶～ support and assist ❻〈书 *fml*.〉 same as 翌 yì:～日 the next day ❼ (Yì) 姓 a surname

【翼侧】yìcè 作战时部队的两翼 flank; (in the battlefield) one of two wings of a troop formation:左～ left flank|右～ right flank; also 侧翼 cèyì

【翼翅】yìchì 翅膀 wing

【翼翼】yìyì 〈书 *fml*.〉❶ 严肃谨慎 serious and cautious:小心～ cautiously; with great care ❷ 严整有秩序 in orderly array; in neat formation ❸ 繁盛;众多 thriving; abundant

虉 yì same as 虉草 yìcǎo

【虉草】yìcǎo 多年生草本植物,叶子条形,圆锥花序。嫩时可作饲料,秆可用来编织器物。reed canarygrass (*Phalaris arundinacea*); perennial herb that has ribbon-shaped leaves and bears flowers in panicles, used as feed when tender, and its stalks used for weaving articles

镱 yì 金属元素,符号 Yb (ytterbium)。是一种稀土金属。银白色,质软。用来制特种合金,也用作激光材料等。ytterbium (Yb); silvery white, soft, rare-earth metallic element, used for making special alloys or as a laser material

癔 yì [癔病](yìbìng) 精神病,多由精神受重大刺激引起。发作时大叫大闹,哭笑无常,言语错乱,或有痉挛、麻痹、失明、失语等现象。hysteria; psychoneurosis mostly caused by mental irritation and marked by emotional excitability such as yelling, half crying and half laughing, and verbal confusion, sometimes accompanied by jerking, paralysis, blindness, aphasia, etc. also 歇斯底里 xiēsīdǐlǐ

懿 yì 〈书 *fml*.〉美好(多指德行 esp. of moral integrity) virtuous; exemplary:～德 admirable virtue; moral excellence|～范 virtuous example|嘉言～行 virtuous speaking and exemplary conduct

【懿旨】yìzhǐ 指皇太后或皇后的命令 decree of an empress or an empress dowager

yīn (丨ㄣ)

因 yīn ❶〈书 *fml.*〉沿袭 follow; carry on: ～循 follow (old customs, etc.) | 陈陈相～ do (sth.) in a customary way; follow a set routine ❷〈书 *fml.*〉凭借;根据 rely on; accord with: ～势利导 guide a matter along its course of development | ～陋就简 make do with whatever is available | ～地制宜 take measures tailored to actual conditions | ～人成事 depend on sb. else for success in one's work ❸ 原因(跟'果'相对 as opposed to 'effect') reason; cause: ～由 reason | 事出有～。There's good reason for it. | 前～后果 cause and effect ❹ 因为 because (of); as a result of: ～病请假 call in sick; ask for sick leave | 会议～故改期。The meeting has been postponed for some reason.

【因材施教】yīn cái shī jiào 针对学习的人的能力、性格、志趣等具体情况施行不同的教育 teach (a student) according to his (or her) aptitude, disposition, interest, etc.; suit instruction (or education) to a student's level

【因此】yīncǐ 因为这个 so; therefore; for this reason; consequently: 他的话引得大家都笑了,室内的空气～轻松了很多。What he said made everyone laugh, and consequently the atmosphere in the room lightened up a lot.

【因地制宜】yīn dì zhì yí 根据不同地区的具体情况规定适宜的办法 take measures tailored to individual local conditions; suit measures to different local conditions

【因而】yīn'ér〈连词 *conj.*〉表示结果 as a result; therefore; thus: 下游河床狭窄,～河水容易泛滥。The riverbed in the lower reaches is narrow, and as a result the river is prone to overflow.

Y

【因果】yīnguǒ ❶ 原因和结果,合起来说,指二者的关系 cause and effect: ～关系 causality | 互为～ interact as both cause and effect ❷〈佛教 *Budd.*〉指事物的起因和结果,今生种什么因,来生结什么果,善有善报,恶有恶报 karma; preordained fate; the force generated by a person's actions, believed to perpetuate transmigration and in its ethical consequences to determine destiny in one's next existence: ～报应 retribution; karma

【因陋就简】yīn lòu jiù jiǎn 就着原来简陋的条件 do things simply and thriftily; make do with whatever is available: 要提倡～、少花钱多办事的精神。We should advocate the spirit of doing things thriftily and making maximum achievements with minimum spending.

【因明】yīnmíng 古代印度关于论证和反驳的学说,类似现在的逻辑学,随佛教传入中国。'因'是立论的根据,'明'是一门科学的意思。*hutu-vidya*; doctrine of the ancient Hindus about argumentation and contradiction, similar to modern logic, introduced to China with Buddhism. *Hutu* 因 means the basis for the proposition and *vidya* 明 denotes knowledge

【因人成事】yīn rén chéng shì 依赖别人的力量办成事情 depend on others for success in one's work

【因式】yīnshì 一个多项式能够被另一个整式整除,后者就是前者的因式。如 a+b 和 a-b 都是 a^2-b^2 的因式。factor; polynomial that divides another polynomial, e.g. a+b and a-b are both factors of a^2-b^2; also 因子 yīnzǐ

【因势利导】yīn shì lì dǎo 顺着事情的发展趋势加以引导 guide a matter along its course of development; channel one's action according to circumstances

【因数】yīnshù same as 约数 yuēshù②

【因素】yīnsù ❶ 构成事物本质的成分 factor; elements that constitute the substance of a matter ❷ 决定事物成败的原因或条件 factor; reasons or situations that determine success or failure of a thing: 学习先进经验是提高生产的重要～之一。Learning from advanced experiences is one of the important factors in increasing production.

【因为】yīn·wèi〈连词 *conj.*〉表示原因或理由 because: ～今天事情多,所以没有去。I didn't go because I was terribly busy today.

【因袭】yīnxí 继续使用(过去的方法、制度、法令等);模仿(别人) follow (old methods, systems, acts, etc.); copy (others): ～陈规 follow the beaten track; stick in the old rut

【因循】yīnxún ❶ 沿袭 follow; continue in the same old tracks: ～旧习 follow the old customs | ～守旧 be fettered by old conventions ❷ 迟延拖拉 procrastinate: ～误事 cause delay in work or business

【因循守旧】yīn xún shǒu jiù 不求变革,沿袭老的一套 stick to old ways without any request for reforms; follow the old routine

【因噎废食】yīn yē fèi shí 因为吃饭噎住了,索性连饭也不吃了 give up eating for fear of choking;〈比喻 *fig.*〉因为怕出问题,索性不干 refrain from doing what one should for fear of running a risk

【因由】yīnyóu (～儿 yīnyóur) 原因 reason; cause; origin: 问明～ find out the origin; investigate the reasons

【因缘】yīnyuán ❶〈佛教 *Budd.*〉指产生结果的直接原因和辅助促成结果的条件或力量 *hutu-pratyaya*; primary cause and secondary cause of a result ❷ 缘分 predestined relationship; fated tie

【因子】yīnzǐ ❶ same as 因数 yīnshù ❷ same as

因式 yīnshì

阴(陰、隂) yīn ❶ 我国古代哲学认为存在于宇宙间的一切事物中的两大对立面之一（跟'阳'相对，下②⑤⑦⑧⑩⑪同 as opposed to '*yang*', same as in ②⑤⑦⑧⑩⑪）(in ancient Chinese philosophy) *yin*; feminine or negative principle, one of the two opposites that exist in all things under the heaven ❷ 指太阴，即月亮 the moon: ～历 lunar calendar ❸ 我国气象上，天空 80%以上被云遮住时叫做阴。泛指空中云层密布，不见阳光或偶见阳光的天气。overcast; (in Chinese meteorology) weather in which dense clouds cover more than 80 per cent of the sky and keep out the sunlight ❹ 不见阳光的地方 shade; a place sheltered from the glare of sunlight: 树～ arbour | 背～儿 in the shade ❺ 山的北面；水的南面 north of a hill or south of a river: 华～(在华山之北) Huayin (a county situated on the north side of Mount Huashan) | 江～(在长江之南) Jiangyin (a county situated on the south side of the Yangtze River) ❻ 背面 back side: 碑～ the back of a stone tablet ❼ 凹进的 in intaglio: ～文 characters engraved in intaglio ❽ 隐藏的；不露在外面的 hidden; secret: ～沟 culvert | ～私 shameful secret | 阳奉～违 overtly agree but covertly oppose ❾ 阴险；不光明 sinister: ～谋 conspiracy | 这个人真～。This person is very sinister. ❿ 指属于鬼神的；阴间的(迷信) (superstition) of the netherworld; of ghosts: ～司 Hades | ～曹 of the netherworld ⓫ 带负电的 negative: ～电 negative electricity | ～极 negative pole ⓬ 生殖器，有时特指女性生殖器 private parts, esp. of the female ⓭ (Yīn) 姓 a surname

【阴暗】yīn'àn 暗；阴沉 dark; gloomy: 地下室里～而潮湿。It's dark and damp in the basement. | 天色～。The sky is dark. ◇～心理 mentality marked by antipathy and gloom | ～的脸色 glum face

【阴暗面】yīn'ànmiàn〈比喻 *fig.*〉思想、生活、社会风气等不健康的方面 dark (or unhealthy) side of thoughts, living, social ethos, etc.: 揭露～ disclose the seamy side of sth.

【阴部】yīnbù 外生殖器官(通常指人的 usu. of human) private parts; genitals; pudenda

【阴曹】yīncáo 阴间 netherworld; Hades

【阴沉】yīnchén 天阴的样子 cloudy; overcast; gloomy: 天色～。The sky is cloudy (or grey). ◇脸色～ have a sombre countenance; look glum

【阴沉沉】yīnchénchén (～的 yīnchénchén·de) 形容天色或脸色等阴暗 (of sky, countenance, etc.) dark; gloomy: 天空～的，像要下雨。The sky is dark, and looks like it will rain. | 他脸上～的，一点儿笑容也没有。He looked glum, without a trace of a smile on his face.

【阴错阳差】yīn cuò yáng chā〈比喻 *fig.*〉由于偶然因素而造成了差错 accidental mistake or error; also 阴差阳错 yīn chā yáng cuò

【阴丹士林】yīndānshìlín ❶ 一种有机染料，有多种颜色，最常见的蓝色。耐洗、耐晒，能染棉、丝、毛等纤维和纺织品。indanthrone; an organic dye in various colours, mostly blue, washable and sun-fast, capable of dyeing cotton, silk, wool, etc., fabrics ❷ 用阴丹士林蓝染的布 cotton cloth dyed with indanthrone

【阴道】yīndào 女性或某些雌性动物生殖器官的一部分，管状。人的阴道在子宫颈的下方，膀胱和直肠的中间。vagina; tube-shaped part of the reproductive organs of women or some female animals. A woman's vagina is situated below the cervix and between the bladder and the rectum.

【阴德】yīndé 暗中做的好事；迷信的人指在人世间所做的而在阴间可以记功的好事 good deeds done in secret; hidden acts of merit; (superstition) good deeds done in the land of living will be recorded as a merit for the netherworld

【阴电】yīndiàn 负电 negative electricity

【阴毒】yīndú 阴险毒辣 insidious; sinister and ruthless: 手段～ sinister and ruthless means

【阴风】yīnfēng ❶ 寒风 cold wind ❷ 从阴暗处来的风 ill wind; wind from a dark place ◇煽～，点鬼火 use an evil wind to fan the ghost flames

【阴干】yīngān 东西在通风而不见太阳的地方慢慢地干 be placed in the shade to dry; dry sth. in a place full of fresh air but sheltered from the sun

【阴功】yīngōng same as 阴德 yīndé

【阴沟】yīngōu 地面下的排水沟 sewer; covered drain

【阴魂】yīnhún 迷信指人死后的灵魂，今多用做比喻(oft. used in a figurative way) (superstition) ghost; spirit of the dead: ～不散 the ghost lingers on; the evil influence remains

【阴极】yīnjí ❶ 电池等直流电源放出电子带负电的电极 negative pole; negative electrode; electrode of a direct-current supply (e. g. from a battery, etc.) that emits negative electricity; also 负极 fùjí ❷ 电子器件中放射电子的一极。电子管和各种阴极射线管中都有阴极。cathode; terminal of an electronic device, e. g. electron tube or any of the various cathode-ray tubes, that emits electrons

【阴极射线】yīnjí shèxiàn 装着两个电极的真空管，增加电压时，从阴极向阳极高速运动的电子流，叫做阴极射线。一般情况下，按直线前进，受磁力作用而偏转。能使荧光物质或磷光物质发光。示波管、显像管、电子显微镜等都是阴极射线的应用。cathode ray; stream of high-speed electrons projected from the cathode of a vacuum tube to the anode under the propulsion of a strong electric field, generally moving along a straight line, deviating with the influence of magnetic forces, and capable of radiating fluorescent or phosphorescent substances, used for making oscilloscope tubes, kinescopes, electron microscopes, etc.

【阴间】yīnjiān 迷信指人死后灵魂所在的地方 (superstition) netherworld; (the kingdom of) Hades; the place housing spirits of the dead; also 阴曹 yīncáo or 阴司 yīnsī

【阴茎】yīnjīng 男子和某些雄性哺乳动物生殖器官的一部分,内有三根柱状的海绵体。中间有尿道。penis; a part of the reproductive organs of men and some male mammals, comprised of three column-shaped spongy bodies and the urethra in the centre

【阴冷】yīnlěng ❶ 阴暗而寒冷 gloomy and cold: 天气～ gloomy and cold weather | 朝北的房间～～的。Rooms with north-facing windows are usually dark and cold. ❷ (脸色)阴沉而冷酷 (of a person's look) sombre and stern; glum and cold

【阴离子】yīnlízǐ 负离子 negative ion

【阴历】yīnlì ❶ 历法的一类。以月亮绕地球1周的时间(29.53059天)为1月,大月30天,小月29天,12个月为1年,1年354天或355天。伊斯兰教历是阴历的一种。lunar calendar; a calendar where a month is set by the time — 29 or 30 days (29.53059 days on average) — it takes for the moon to revolve once around the earth, and 12 months constitute a year of 354 or 355 days; the Islamic calendar being a lunar calendar; also 太阴历 tàiyīnlì ❷ 农历的通称 general term for 农历 nónglì

【阴凉】yīnliáng ❶ 太阳照不到而凉爽的 shady and cool: ～的地方 shady and cool place ❷ (～儿 yīnliángr)阴凉的地方 cool place; shade: 找个～儿歇一歇。Let's find a shady place for a rest.

【阴霾】yīnmái 霾的通称 general term for 霾 mái

【阴门】yīnmén 阴道的口儿 vulva; vaginal orifice; also 阴户 yīnhù

【阴面】yīnmiàn (～儿 yīnmiànr) (建筑物等)背阴的一面 (of buildings, etc.) shady side; back side: 石碑的～有字。There are inscriptions on the back of the stone tablet.

【阴谋】yīnmóu ❶ 暗中策划(做坏事) conspire; plot; scheme (to do bad deeds): ～暴乱 plot a rebellion | ～陷害好人 scheme to frame an innocent person ❷ 暗中做坏事的计谋 conspiracy; plot; scheme (to do bad deeds in secret): 耍～ play a plot | ～诡计 schemes and intrigues

【阴囊】yīnnáng 包藏睾丸的囊状物,在腹部的下面,两股根部的中间 scrotum; the external pouch, under the belly and between the upper ends of the two thighs of most male mammals, that contains the testes

【阴蜃】yīnnì 〈中医 *Chin. med.*〉指一种妇科病,症状是外阴部瘙痒疼痛,白带增多等 pruritus vulvae; women's ailment characterized by symptoms of itching and pain around the vulva and an increase of leucorrhoea; also 阴蚀 yīnshí or 阴痒 yīnyǎng

【阴平】yīnpíng 普通话字调的第一声,主要由古汉语平声字中的清音声母字分化而成 high and level tone; the first of the four tones in modern standard Chinese pronunciation, chiefly developed from the aphonic initial consonant of ancient Chinese level-tone characters; ☞ 四声 sìshēng ② on p. 1821

【阴森】yīnsēn (地方、气氛、脸色等)阴沉,可怕 (of places, atmosphere, looks, etc.) gloomy; gruesome; ghastly: ～的树林 deep, dark forest | ～的古庙 ghastly old temple

【阴山背后】yīnshān bèihòu 指偏僻冷落的地方 a remote and desolate place

【阴寿】yīnshòu ❶ 旧俗为已故长辈逢十周年生日祝寿,叫做阴寿 (old custom) celebrate every 10th birthday of a deceased elder in a family ❷ 迷信的人指死去的人在阴间的寿数 (superstition) age of a dead person in the netherworld

【阴司】yīnsī same as 阴间 yīnjiān

【阴私】yīnsī 不可告人的坏事 shameful secret act

【阴损】yīnsǔn ❶ 阴险尖刻 sinister and vicious: 说话～ speak sinisterly and viciously ❷ 暗地里损害 hurt secretly: 当面装笑脸,背后～人 overtly smile at but hurt people behind their backs

【阴文】yīnwén 印章上或某些器物上所刻或所铸的凹下的文字或花纹(跟'阳文'相对 as opposed to 'relief') characters or designs cut or cast in intaglio on seals or other wares; intaglio

【阴险】yīnxiǎn 表面和善,暗地不存好心 insidious; kind on the surface but sinister underneath: 狡诈～ deceitful and insidious | ～毒辣 sinister and ruthless

【阴性】yīnxìng ❶ 诊断疾病时对进行某种试验或化验所得结果的表示方法,说明体内没有某种病原体存在或对某种药物没有过敏反应。例如注射结核菌素后并无红肿等反应时叫做结核菌素试验阴性。negative; (in diagnosis of disease) a denotation of the results of an examination or test, not showing the existence of a pathogeny or allergic reaction to certain drugs, e.g. a negative TB test indicates that the patient has no reactions like redness, swelling, etc., after an injection of tuberculin ❷ 某些语言里名词(以及代词、形容词)分别阴性、阳性,或阴性、阳性、中性 feminine gender; (in some languages) nouns, pronouns and adjectives are distinguished as feminine and masculine in gender, or feminine, masculine, and neuter; ☞ 性 xìng ⑥ on p. 2151

【阴阳】yīnyáng ❶ 我国古代哲学指宇宙中贯通物质和人事的两大对立面 *yin* and *yang* in ancient Chinese philosophy, two opposing principles existing in substances, people, and all things under the heaven ❷〈古代 *arch.*〉指日、月等天体运转规律的学问 ancient Chinese astronomy; study of the movements of the celestial bodies ❸ 指星相、占卜、相宅、相墓的方术 occult arts, including astrology, geomancy, etc.; same as 阴阳生 yīnyángshēng

【阴阳怪气】yīn yáng guàiqì (～的 yīn yáng guàiqì·de)(性格、言行等)乖僻,跟一般的不同 (of a person's disposition, manner of speaking and acting, etc.) mystifying; enigmatic; eccentric; different from the usual: 他说话～的,没法跟他打交道。He speaks in a deliberately ambiguous manner, and it's hard to get along with him. ◇天气老是这样～的,不晴也不雨。What mystifying weather — neither sunny nor rainy!

【阴阳历】yīnyánglì 历法的一类,以月亮绕地球一周的时间为一月,但设置闰月,使一年的平均天数跟太阳年的天数相符,因此这类历法与月相符合,也与地球绕太阳的周年运动相符合。农历是阴阳历的一种。lunisolar calendar; calendar where a month is set by the period the moon revolves once around the earth, and with leap months added to years, having as many days as those of a solar year on average, and therefore conforming to both the lunar and solar calendars established according to the movement of the earth around the sun. The traditional Chinese calendar is a form of lunisolar calendar.

【阴阳人】yīnyángrén ❶ 两性人 bisexual person; hermaphrodite ❷ 阴阳生 *yin-yang* adept (e. g. astrologer, diviner, geomancer, etc.)

【阴阳生】yīnyángshēng〈旧时 *old*〉指以星相、占卜、相宅、相墓等为业的人。特指以办理丧葬中相墓、选择吉日等事务为业的人。*yin-yang* adept (e. g. astrologer, diviner, geomancer, etc.); person engaged in the professions of astrology, divination, geomancy, etc., esp. those involved in the business of deciding the location of tombs and choosing auspicious days for funerals

【阴阳水】yīnyángshuǐ〈中医 *Chin. med.*〉指凉水和开水,或井水和河水合在一起的水,调药或服药时用 *yin-yang* water; mixture of unboiled and boiled water, or of river and well water, used for the preparation or administration of medicine

【阴翳】yīyì same as 荫翳 yīnyì

【阴影】yīnyǐng (～儿 yīnyǐngr)阴暗的影子 shadow: 树木的～ shadows of trees | 肺部有～ have a shadow on the lung | 月球的表面有许多高山的～。There are many shadows of mountains on the surface of the moon. ◇新的冲突使和谈蒙上了～。The new conflicts cast shadows on the peace talks.

【阴雨】yīnyǔ 天阴又下雨 overcast and rainy: ～连绵 cloudy and drizzly for days on end; an unbroken spell of wet weather

【阴郁】yīnyù ❶ (天气)低沉郁闷;(气氛)不活跃 (of weather) gloomy; dismal; (of atmosphere) not lively: ～的天色 gloomy weather | 笑声冲破了室内～的空气。The laughter broke the dismal atmosphere in the room. ❷ 忧郁,不开朗 depressed; closed and gloomy: 心情～ feel depressed

【阴云】yīnyún 天阴时的云 dark clouds: ～密布。The sky is covered with dark clouds. ◇战争的～ dark clouds of war

【阴韵】yīnyùn ☞ 阳韵 yángyùn on p. 2220

【阴宅】yīnzhái 迷信的人称坟墓 (superstition) grave; tomb

【阴鸷】yīnzhì〈书 *fml.*〉阴险凶狠 sinister and ruthless

【阴骘】yīnzhì 原指默默地使安定,转指阴德 secretly seek stability through doing good deeds for merit in the netherworld: 积～ do good deeds for the sake of the netherworld

茵(裀) yīn 垫子或褥子 mattress or cushion: 绿草如～ a carpet of green grass

荫(蔭) yīn 树阴 arbour: 绿树成～ (of a place) sheltered by green foliage of trees

【荫蔽】yīnbì ❶ (枝叶)遮蔽 (of branches and foliage) shade or hide: 茅屋～在树林中。The hutch is tucked away among the trees. ❷ 隐蔽 cover; conceal

【荫翳】yīnyì ❶ same as 荫蔽 yīnbì ①: 柳树～的河边 riverside shaded by the foliage of willows ❷ 枝叶繁茂 (of foliage) flourishing; thriving; lush: 桃李～。Peach and plum trees are flourishing.

音 yīn ❶ 声音 sound: ～律 temperament | ～乐 music | 口～ accent | 乐～ tone | 杂～ noise ❷ 消息 news; tidings: 佳～ good news | ～信 message ❸ 指音节 syllable: 单～词 monosyllabic word | 复～词 polysyllabic word ❹ 读(某音) read: '区'字作姓时～欧。When used as a surname, 区 is pronounced Ōu.

【音标】yīnbiāo 语音学上用来记录语音的符号,如国际音标 phonetic alphabet; (phonetics) symbols that show the pronunciation of a word, e. g. the international phonetic alphabet

【音波】yīnbō 声波 sound wave

【音叉】yīnchā 用钢材制成的发声仪器,形状像叉子,用小木槌敲打发出声音。音叉的长短厚薄不同,能产生各种音高的声音,可以用来调整乐器和帮助歌唱者定出音高。tuning fork; fork-shaped steel implement that gives a fixed tone when struck by a small wood hammer. Varying in length and thickness, it can produce tones of different pitch and is used to tune musical instruments and help singers ascertain a standard pitch

【音长】yīncháng 声音的长短,是由发声体振动持续时间的长短决定的 the duration of a sound, determined by the length of time of the vibration produced by a sounding body

【音程】yīnchéng 两个乐音之间的音高关系。用'度'来表示。以简谱为例,从 1 到 1 或从 2 到 2 都是一度,从 1 到 3 或从 2 到 4 都是三度,从 1 到 5 是五度。interval; difference in pitch between two tones, marked by degree, e.g. in numbered musical notation, the intervals between 1 and 1 and between 2 and 2 are both 1 degree, between 1 and 3 and between 2 and 4 are 3 degrees, and between 1 and 5 are 5 degrees

【音带】yīndài 录音磁带,多指盒式录音带 audio tape; cassette (tape); magnetic sound-recording tape

【音调】yīndiào 声音的高低 tone; the pitch of a sound

【音读】yīndú (字的)念法;读音 (of a character) pronunciation

【音符】yīnfú 乐谱中表示音长或音高的符号。五线谱上用空心或实心的小椭圆形和特定的附加符号。简谱上用七个阿拉伯数字,1 2 3 4 5 6 7,和特定的附加符号。musical note; written symbol used to indicate the duration and pitch of a tone by its shape and position on a music score. The notes on the staff are hollow or solid oblong symbols with special annexes, and those on a numbered musical notation are 7 Arabic numerals (1 2 3 4 5 6 7) with some special annexes.

【音高】yīngāo 由于发声体振动频率的不同所造成的声音的属性,频率越高,声音越高 pitch; the property of a sound, and esp. a musical tone that is determined by the vibrational frequency produced by a sounding body, where the higher the frequency, the higher the pitch

【音耗】yīnhào 音信;消息 news; message; information: 不通～。No news has been received. |杳无～。No news has been received for a long time.

【音阶】yīnjiē 以一定的调式为标准,按音高次序向上或向下排列成的一组音 scale; a graduated series of musical tones ascending or descending in order of pitch according to a specified scheme of intervals

【音节】yīnjié 由一个或几个音素组成的语音单位。其中包含一个比较响亮的中心。一句话里头,有几个响亮的中心就是有几个音节。在汉语里,一般地讲,一个汉字是一个音节,一个音节写成一个汉字(儿化韵一个音节写成两个字,儿不自成音节,是例外)。syllable; unit of spoken language consisting of one or more phonemes and containing a more resonant core (vowel). The number of more resonant cores in a sentence suggests the number of syllables in the sentence. In Chinese language, each character is pronounced as a syllable and each syllable can be written as a character. An exception is that a word ending with *r* which is not itself a syllable, can be written as two characters. also 音缀 yīnzhuì

【音节文字】yīnjié wénzì 一种拼音文字,它的字母表示整个音节,例如梵文和日本文的假名 syllabic language; alphabetic script composed of letters that denote an entire syllable each, e.g. Sanskrit and Japanese kana

【音量】yīnliàng 声音的强弱;响度 volume of sound

【音律】yīnlǜ 指音乐上的律吕、宫调等 temperament; tuning pitch-pipes and modes of music; also 乐律 yuèlǜ

【音名】yīnmíng ❶ 律吕的名称,如黄钟、大吕等 (in ancient Chinese music) the name of a tuning pitch-pipe, e.g. yellow bell, great bell, etc. ❷ 西洋音乐中代表不同音高的七个基本音律的名称,即 C、D、E、F、G、A、B (in Western music) musical alphabet; names of the seven basic musical scales that mark different pitches: C、D、E、F、G、A、B

【音频】yīnpín 人的耳朵能听见的振动频率(20—20,000 赫兹) audio frequency; tone frequency; the vibrational frequency that can be heard by the human ear (usu. 20-20,000 HZ)

【音品】yīnpǐn same as 音色 yīnsè

【音强】yīnqiáng 声音的大小,是由声波振幅的大小决定的 intensity of sound, determined by the amplitude of the sound wave; also 音势 yīnshì

【音区】yīnqū 音域中按音高和音色特点划分出的若干部分,一般分高音区、中音区、低音区三种 range; any of the parts of a musical range, classified as high range, medium range, and low range according to the pitch and timbre of the music

【音儿】yīnr 〈方 *dial.*〉 ❶ (说话的)声音 (of speaking) voice: 他急得连说话的～都变了。He was so anxious that even his voice changed. ❷ 话里边微露的意思 implication; implied meaning (in words or sentences): 听话听～。When listening to some one, we should try to get what he really means.

【音容】yīnróng 声音容貌 voice and facial expression: ～笑貌 one's voice and expression

【音容宛在】yīn róng wǎn zài 声音和容貌仿佛还在耳边和眼前。多形容对死者的怀念。voice and face still seem to linger within hearing and sight (oft. when thinking fondly of a dead person)

【音色】yīnsè 由于波型和泛音的不同所造成的声音的属性。每个人的声音以及钢琴、提琴、笛子等各种乐器所发出的声音的区别,就是由音色不同造成的。tone colour; timbre; the quality of tone distinctive of a particular singing voice or musical instrument (e.g. piano, violin, flute, etc.), due to differences in wave patterns and overtones; also 音品 yīnpǐn or 音质 yīnzhì

【音势】yīnshì same as 音强 yīnqiáng

【音素】yīnsù 语音中最小的单位,例如 mǎ 是由 m,a 和上声调这三个音素组成的 phoneme; the smallest unit of speech, e.g. mǎ is composed of the following three phonemes: m, a, and the third tone of Chinese pronunciation

【音素文字】yīnsù wénzì 一种拼音文字,它的字母表示语言中的音素,如俄文、英文 phonemic language; alphabetic language with letters denote phonemes e.g. Russian, English, etc.

【音速】yīnsù ☞ 声速 shēngsù on p.1720

【音位】yīnwèi 一个语言中能够区别意义的最简单的语音单位 phoneme; (of a language) simplest unit of speech that conveys distinct meaning

【音问】yīnwèn 音信 news; tidings: 不通～。No news has been received. | ～断绝。News is cut off. *or* All channels of communication have been severed.

【音息】yīnxī 音信;消息 message; news: 渺无～ no news has been received for a long time

【音响】yīnxiǎng ❶ 声音(多就声音所产生的效果说 oft. of the effect produced by sounds) sound; acoustics: 剧场～条件很好。The theatre features good acoustics. ❷ 录音机、电唱机、收音机及扩音器等的统称 stereo set, including tape recorder, record player, radio, loudspeaker, etc.: 组合～ music centre

【音像】yīnxiàng 录音和录像的合称 audiovisual; sound and video recording: ～制品 audiovisual goods | ～教材 audiovisual teaching materials

【音信】yīnxìn 往来的信件和消息 (in communications) mail; message; news: 互通～ communicate with each other; be in correspondence with each other | 杳无～ have not been heard from (sb.) since

【音讯】yīnxùn same as 音信 yīnxìn

【音义】yīnyì ❶ 文字的读音和意义 pronunciation and meaning (of a character) ❷〈旧时 *old*〉关于文字音义方面的注解 (多用做书名 oft. used in book titles) annotation of pronunciation and meaning of written Chinese characters:《毛诗～》*Pronunciation and Meaning of Poems of Mao Heng and Mao Chang* (Mao Heng 毛亨 and Mao Chang 毛苌 were poets of the early Western Han Dynasty)

【音译】yīnyì same as 译音 yìyīn ①(区别于'意译'as compared with 'paraphrase')

【音域】yīnyù 指某一乐器或人声(歌唱)所能发出的最低音到最高音之间的范围 range; compass; register; range between the lowest and the highest tones that a musical instrument or a singer can produce: ～宽 wide range of voice

【音乐】yīnyuè 用有组织的乐音来表达人们的思想感情、反映现实生活的一种艺术。它的最基本的要素是节奏和旋律。分为声乐和器乐两大部门。music; art that expresses people's ideas and sentiments, and reflects true life through organisation of tones or sounds, its basic elements being rhythm and melody, featuring vocal and instrumental sectors

【音韵】yīnyùn ❶ 指和谐的声音;诗文的音节韵律 harmonious sound; syllabic rhyme and rhythm (of poetry): ～悠扬 melodious rhyme ❷ 指汉字字音的声、韵、调 sound, rhyme and tone of a written Chinese character

【音韵学】yīnyùnxué 语言学的一个部门,研究语音结构和语音演变 phonology; branch of linguistics that studies the structure and evolvement of sound; also 声韵学 shēngyùnxué

【音障】yīnzhàng 高速飞行的物体(如飞机、火箭)速度增加到接近音速时,物体前方的空气因来不及散开而受到压缩,密度、温度突然增加,阻碍该物体向前飞行,这种现象叫做音障 sound (or sonic) barrier; sudden large increase in the density and temperature of the compressed air in front of a high-speed flying object (e.g. aircraft or rocket) that occurs as the speed of the flying object approaches the speed of sound and retards the object's forward flight

【音值】yīnzhí 指人们实际发出或听见的语音,对音位而言。例如 dài(代)里 a 的跟 dà(大)里的 a,音值上有些不同,但在汉语普通话里是一个音位。value; sound that a human can produce or hear, as compared with the phoneme, e.g. the value of the 'a' in 'dài' and that of the 'a' in 'da' is somewhat different from each other, but in standard Chinese, the two are of the same phoneme

【音质】yīnzhì ❶ same as 音色 yīnsè ❷ 录音或广播上所说的音质,不仅指音色的好坏,也兼指声音的清晰或逼真的程度 (of tape-recording or radio) acoustic fidelity

【音缀】yīnzhuì same as 音节 yīnjié

【音准】yīnzhǔn 音乐上指音高的准确程度 (of music) accuracy in pitch; pitch accuracy

洇(湮) yīn 液体落在纸上向四外散开或渗透;浸 (of liquid) spread or penetrate on paper; immerse: 这种纸写字容易～。This paper is vulnerable to ink blots. | 用水把

土～湿 wet earth by spreading water
☞'湮' yān on p.2201

姻(婣) yīn ❶ 婚姻 marriage: 联～ related by marriage ❷ 由婚姻结成的、比较间接的亲戚关系,如称弟兄的岳父、姐妹的公公为'姻伯',称姐妹的丈夫的弟兄、妻子的表兄弟为'姻兄、姻弟'等 indirect relationship by marriage, e.g. one calls a brother's or sister's father-in-law *yinbo*, and brother-in-law's brother or his wife's cousin *yinxiong* or *yindi*

【姻亲】yīnqīn 由婚姻而结成的亲戚,如姑夫、姐夫、妻子的兄弟姐妹以及比这些更间接的亲戚 relationship by marriage; affinity, e.g. sibling of one's wife, uncle, or brother-in-law, as well as even more distant relatives

【姻亚】yīnyà same as 姻娅 yīnyà

【姻娅】yīnyà 〈书 *fml.*〉亲家和连襟。泛指姻亲。relatives by marriage; husbands of sisters; affinity (in general); also 姻亚 yīnyà

【姻缘】yīnyuán 指婚姻的缘分 marriage put together by luck: 结～ be married | 美满～ happy marriage

骃 yīn 古书上指一种浅黑带白色的马 (in ancient books) white-striped darkish horse

细 yīn [细缊](yīnyūn) same as 氤氲 yīnyūn

氤 yīn [氤氲](yīnyūn)〈书 *fml.*〉形容烟或云气浓郁 (of smoke or mist) dense; thick; enshrouding: 云烟～ enshrouding mists; also 细缊 yīnyūn or 烟煴 yīnyūn

殷[1] yīn 〈书 *fml.*〉❶ 丰盛;丰富 plenteous; plentiful: ～实 rich | ～富 wealthy ❷ 深厚 ardent; profound: ～切 eager and profound | 期望甚～ cherish high hopes ❸ 殷勤 hospitable: 招待甚～ offer cordial hospitality

殷[2] Yīn ❶ 朝代,公元前 1300—公元前 1046,是商代迁都于殷(今河南安阳市西北小屯村)后改用的称号 Yin Dynasty (1300 B.C.-1046 B.C.), name of the Shang Dynasty after it moved its capital to Yin (present-day Xiaotun Village, northwest of Anyang, Henan Province) ❷ 姓 a surname

☞ yān on p.2199 and yǐn on p.2294

【殷富】yīnfù 殷实富足 wealthy; well-off: 家道～ wealthy family

【殷鉴】yīnjiàn《诗经·大雅·荡》:'殷鉴不远,在夏后之世。'意思是殷人灭夏,殷人的子孙应该以夏的灭亡作为鉴戒。*The Book of Songs·Epics·Warnings*: 'The downfall of the Xia be seen,/ As a warning to you (纣 Zhòu, the 31st and last king)!' This line implies that the Yin people had overthrown the Xia Dynasty and that the last king of the Yin Dynasty should draw a lesson from the downfall of the Xia. 后来用来泛指可以作为后人鉴戒的前人失败之事 failure of a predecessor serving as a warning: 可资～ may serve as a warning (or lesson)

【殷切】yīnqiè 深厚而急切 eager and profound; ardent: ～的期望 ardent expectations

【殷勤】yīnqín 热情而周到 solicitous and thoughtful: ～招待 entertain sb. solicitously; also 慇懃 yīnqín

【殷实】yīnshí 富裕 well-off; rich; of substance: ～人家 well-off family | 家道～ be a person of substance; be from a family of substance

【殷墟】Yīnxū 商代后期的都城遗址,在今河南安阳小屯村附近。1899 年在这个地方发现甲骨刻辞。Yin ruins; ruins of the capital of the late Yin (or Shang) Dynasty, near Xiaotun Village in present-day Anyang, Henan Province, where oracle-bone inscriptions of the Shang Dynasty were unearthed in 1899

【殷殷】yīnyīn ❶ 形容殷切 ardent; sincere: ～期望 entertain ardent hopes | ～嘱咐 sincerely enjoin ❷〈书 *fml.*〉形容忧伤 distressed; be laden with sorrow: 忧心～ care-laden; anxiety-ridden

【殷忧】yīnyōu 深深的忧虑 great worries; deep anxieties: 内怀～ be anxious about; be worried about; be anxiety-ridden

烟 yīn [烟煴](yīnyūn) same as 氤氲 yīnyūn
☞ yān on p.2199

铟 yīn 金属元素,符号 In (indium)。银白色,质软。用来制低熔合金、轴承合金、半导体、电光源等。indium (In); soft, silvery-white metallic element, used for making low-melting alloys, alloys for making bearings, semiconductors, electric light sources, etc.

堙 yīn 〈书 *fml.*〉❶ 土山 mound ❷ 堵塞;填塞 block up; stop up

喑(瘖) yīn 〈书 *fml.*〉❶ 嗓子哑,不能出声;失音 mute; dumb; hoarse; lose one's voice: ～哑 mute ❷ 缄默,不做声 keep silent: 万马齐～。Ten thousand horses stand mute. *or* All fall mute.

【喑哑】yīnyǎ 嗓子干涩发不出声音或发音低而不清楚 cannot produce a sound; speak in a low, unclear voice (because of a dry and hoarse throat)

闉 yīn ❶ 古代瓮城的门 (in ancient China) gate of the defence enclosures outside a city gate ❷〈书 *fml.*〉堵塞 block up; jam

愔 yīn [愔愔](yīnyīn)〈书 *fml.*〉安静无声;默默无言 silent; without saying a single word

歅 yīn 用于人名,九方歅,春秋时人,善相马 part of a person's name, esp. Jiu Fangyin, from the Spring and Autumn Period, famous for his good judgement of the worth of a horse

溵 yīn 溵溜(Yīnliù),地名,在天津市 Yinliu, a place in Tianjin Municipality

禋 yīn ❶ 古代祭天的祭名 name of a ceremony of offering sacrifices to Heaven ❷ 泛指祭祀 offer sacrifices to deities or ancestors

慇 yīn [慇懃](yīnqín) same as 殷勤 yīnqín

yín (ㄧㄣˊ)

圻 yín 〈书 *fml*.〉 same as 垠 yín
☞ qí on p. 1508

吟(唫) yín ❶ 吟咏 chant; recite: ～诗 recite a poem | 抱膝长～ recite (a poem, etc.) with knees held in the arms (or arms wrapped around the knees) ❷ 〈书 *fml*.〉 呻吟;叹息 groan; moan ❸ 古典诗歌的一种名称 song (usu. used for the name of a type of a classical poetry):《秦妇～》*Song of a Qin Lady* | 水龙～ *Shuilongyin*, name of tune for a certain type of *ci* poem
☞ 唫 jìn on p. 1016

【吟哦】yín'é same as 吟咏 yínyǒng

【吟风弄月】yín fēng nòng yuè 〈旧时 *old*〉有的诗人做诗爱用风花雪月做题材,因此称这类题材的写作为吟风弄月(多含贬义 oft. derog.) write sentimental verse; a type of writing in which poems are devoted to the wind and the moon; also 吟风咏月 yín fēng yǒng yuè

【吟咏】yínyǒng 有节奏地诵读诗文 recite (poetry) with a cadence; chant: ～古诗 recite ancient poetry with a cadence

垠 yín 〈书 *fml*.〉界限;边际 boundary; limit: 一望无～ as far as the eye can see | 平沙无～。A vast expanse of desert stretches from horizon to horizon.

狺 yín [狺狺]〈书 *fml*.〉 狗叫的声音 yap; yelp; bark of a dog: ～狂吠 bark frenziedly

訚 yín [訚訚]〈书 *fml*.〉 形容辩论时态度好 with a good manner when arguing

崟(崯) yín ☞ [嵚崟](qīnyín) on p. 1559

银 yín ❶ 金属元素,符号 Ag (argentum)。白色,质软,延展性强,导电、导热性能好,化学性质稳定。用途很广。argentum (Ag); silver; white metallic element that is ductile and very malleable, possesses high electrical and thermal conductivity, and stable chemical properties, and can be used for many purposes; 通称 generally called 银子 yín·zi or 白银 báiyín ❷ 跟货币有关的 relating to currency or money: ～行 bank | ～根 money ❸ 像银子的颜色 silver-coloured: ～灰色 silver grey | 红地～字的匾 plaque with silver characters on a red background ❹ (Yín) 姓 a surname

【银白】yínbái 白中略带银光的颜色 silvery white: 一场大雪把大地变成了～世界。After a heavy snowfall, the ground became a silvery white world.

【银杯】yínbēi 体育竞赛用的银质杯形奖品 (of sport games) silver cup; silver trophy

【银本位】yínběnwèi 用白银做本位货币的货币制度 silver standard; monetary standard under which the basic unit of currency is defined by a stated quantity of silver

【银币】yínbì 银制的货币 silver coin

【银锭】yíndìng ❶ (～儿 yíndìngr)银元宝 silver ingot; sycee (silver) ❷ 用锡箔折成或糊成的假元宝,迷信的人焚化给鬼神用 (superstition) tinfoil folded as, or pasted on a shoe-shaped object resembling, a silver ingot to be burnt for ghosts

【银耳】yín'ěr 真菌的一种,生长在枯死或半枯死的栓皮栎等树上,白色,半透明,富于胶质。用做滋养品。tremella (*Tremella fuciformis*); semi-transparent white fungus that grows on withered or half-dead cork oaks, rich in colloids, and can be used for nourishment; also 白木耳 báimù'ěr

【银发】yínfà 白头发 silver (or silvery) hair: 满头～ silver-haired

【银粉】yínfěn 铝粉的俗称 common name for aluminium powder

【银根】yíngēn 指市场上货币周转流通的情况。市场需要货币多而流通量小叫银根紧,市场需要货币少而流通量大叫银根松。money supply; money; situation of money turnover in a market; the market situation in which demand for money exceeds turnover is known as tight money 银根紧 yíngēnjǐn, while the situation in which turnover of money exceeds demand is known as easy money 银根松 yíngēnsōng

【银汉】yínhàn 〈书 *fml*.〉银河 Milky Way: ～横空。The Milky Way stretches across the sky.

【银行】yínháng 经营存款、贷款、汇兑、储蓄等业务的金融机构 bank; financial institute handling such business as deposits, loans, exchange, savings, etc.

【银号】yínhào 〈旧时 *old*〉指规模较大的钱庄 a large banking house; ☞ 钱庄 qiánzhuāng on p. 1537

【银河】yínhé 晴天夜晚,天空呈现出一条明亮的光带,夹杂着许多闪烁的小星,看起来像一条银白色的河,叫做银河。银河由许许多多的恒星构成。Milky Way; broad luminous band of light that appears in the sky on a clear night and that looks like a milky river, composed of a myriad of fixed stars; 通称 commonly called 天河 tiānhé

【银河系】yínhéxì 宇宙中的一个大的恒星系,由1,000亿颗以上的大小恒星和无数星云、星团构成,形状像怀表,中心厚,直径为10万光年。太阳是银河系中的许多恒星之一,距离银河中心约有3万光年。我们平常在夜晚看到的天空的银河，就是银河系的密集部分在天球上的投影。Milky Way galaxy; large galaxy in the universe composed of 100 billion fixed stars (big and small) and countless nebulae and clusters, in the shape of a pocket watch, thick at the centre, and 100,000 light years in diameter. The sun is one of the myriad of stars in the Milky Way galaxy, about 30,000 light years from the centre of the galaxy. The Milky Way we see in the night sky is the projection of the dense part of the Milky Way galaxy on the celestial sphere.

【银红】yínhóng 在粉红色颜料里加银朱调和而成的颜色 pale rose colour; the colour of a mixture of pink pigment and vermilion

【银灰】yínhuī 浅灰而略带银光的颜色 silver grey

【银婚】yínhūn 欧洲风俗称结婚二十五周年为银婚 silver wedding; (in European custom) 25th wedding anniversary

【银匠】yínjiàng 制造金银饰物、器具的工人 silversmith; artisan who makes gold and silver ornaments and articles

【银两】yínliǎng〈旧时 *old*〉用银子为主要货币，以两为单位，因此做货币用的银子称为银两(总称) silver, chiefly used as currency in the unit of *liang*, hence the name (collect.)

【银楼】yínlóu 制造和买卖金银首饰和器皿的商店 silverware shop; shop that makes and sells gold and silver ornaments and vessels

【银幕】yínmù 放映电影或幻灯时，用来显示影像的白色的幕 (motion-picture or movie) screen; projection screen; white surface on which the images of a film or transparency are projected or reflected

【银牌】yínpái 奖牌的一种，奖给第二名 silver medal; medal as a prize for the second-place winner

【银屏】yínpíng 电视机的荧光屏。也借指电视节目。(fluorescent) screen of a TV set; TV programme

【银钱】yínqián 泛指钱财 money

【银杏】yínxìng ❶ 落叶乔木，雌雄异株，叶片扇形。种子椭圆形，外面有橙黄色带臭味的种皮，果仁可以吃，也可以入药。木材致密，可供雕刻用。是我国的特产。ginkgo (*Ginkgo biloba*); gingko; deciduous dioecious tree with fan-shaped leaves, oblong seeds, orange-yellow odorous seed coat, and edible fruit, unique to China, its fruit used for medicine, and its timber being of a fine texture and suitable for woodcarving; also 公孙树 gōngsūnshù ❷ 这种植物的果实 fruit of this plant ‖ also 白果 báiguǒ

【银洋】yínyáng same as 银圆 yínyuán

【银样镴枪头】yín yàng là qiāng tóu〈比喻 *fig.*〉表面看起来还不错，实际上不中用，好像颜色如银子的锡镴枪头一样 pewter spearhead that shines like silver; (of a person) impressive-looking but useless

【银鹰】yínyīng〈比喻 *fig.*〉飞机(多指战斗机 oft. referring to a fighter plane) aircraft：祖国的～在天空翱翔。Fighter plane of the motherland were hovering in the sky.

【银元】yínyuán same as 银圆 yínyuán

【银圆】yínyuán〈旧时 *old*〉使用的银质硬币，圆形，价值相当于七钱二分白银 silver dollar; round silver coin used in old times, worth 0.72 tael of silver; also 银元 yínyuán

【银朱】yínzhū 无机化合物，鲜红色粉末，有毒。用做颜料和药品等。vermilion; inorganic compound in the form of vermeil powder, poisonous, used for making pigment, medicine, etc.

【银子】yín·zi 银的通称 general term for 银 yín

淫(婬) yín ❶ 过多或过甚 excessive; extra：～雨 excessive rains | ～威 despotic power ❷ 放纵 wanton：骄奢～逸 extravagant and dissipated | 乐而不～，哀而不伤 be joyful but not wanton, be sorrowful but not despondent ❸ 指不正当的男女关系 illicit sexual relations; lewd; lascivious：奸～ adultery | ～乱 (sexually) promiscuous; licentious

【淫荡】yíndàng 淫乱放荡 loose in morals; lascivious; licentious; lewd

【淫秽】yínhuì 淫乱或猥亵 obscene; risqué; salacious; bawdy：～书刊 pornographic literature

【淫乱】yínluàn 在性行为上违反道德准则 (of sexual behaviour) against moral standards; promiscuous; licentious

【淫威】yínwēi 滥用的威力 abuse of power; despotic power：横施～ flagrantly abuse power

【淫猥】yínwěi same as 淫秽 yínhuì

【淫雨】yínyǔ 连绵不停的过量的雨 excessive rains：～成灾。Excessive rains caused a flood. also 霪雨 yínyǔ

【淫欲】yínyù 指色欲 lechery; lust

寅 yín 地支的第三位 3rd of the 12 Earthly Branches (地支)；☞ 干支 gānzhī on p.627

【寅吃卯粮】yín chī mǎo liáng 寅年就吃了卯年的口粮 eat the food of next year;〈比喻 *fig.*〉入不敷出，预先支用了以后的收入 live beyond one's income; anticipate later income; also 寅支卯粮 yín zhī mǎo liáng

【寅时】yínshí 旧式计时法指夜里三点钟到五点钟的时间 (old) period of the day from 3 a.m. to 5 a.m.

龂 yín〈书 *fml.*〉❶ same as 龈 yín ❷［龂龂］形容争辩 argue; debate

鄞 yín 鄞县，在浙江 Yinxian County, in Zhejiang Province

龈 yín 齿龈 gum
☞ 啃 kěn on p. 1100

夤 yín〈书 *fml*.〉❶ 敬畏 hold sb. in respectful awe; revere: ～畏 revere ❷ 深 deep: ～夜 in the depth of night

【夤夜】yínyè〈书 *fml*.〉深夜 in the depth of night; at the dead of night

【夤缘】yínyuán〈书 *fml*.〉攀附上升 climb up;〈比喻 *fig*.〉拉扰关系,向上巴结 take advantage of one's connections to make one's way up; try to advance one's career by currying favour with important people: ～而上 take advantage of one's connections to make one's way up

蟫 yín 古书上指衣鱼(as recorded in ancient books) silverfish; fish moth; bookworm

嚚 yín〈书 *fml*.〉❶ 蠢而顽固 ignorant and hard-headed ❷ 奸诈 fraudulent; crafty

霪 yín [霪雨](yínyǔ) same as 淫雨 yínyǔ

yǐn (丨ㄣˇ)

尹 yǐn ❶〈旧时 *old*〉官名 official title: 府～ prefectural magistrate | 道～ prefectural magistrate | 京兆～ capital officials ❷ (Yǐn) 姓 a surname

引 yǐn ❶ 牵引;拉 draw; pull: ～弓 draw a bow | ～车卖浆 pull a cart to sell soya bean milk ❷ 引导 guide; lead: ～路 lead the way | ～港 pilot a ship (into or out of a harbour) ❸ 离开 leave: ～避(因避嫌而辞官) keep clear of; make way for (i. e. quit an official position to avoid arousing suspicion) | ～退 retire from post ❹ 伸着 stretch: ～领 crane one's neck to look into the distance | ～颈 stretch one's neck ❺ 引起;使出现 induce; attract; make appear: 用纸～火 kindle a fire with paper | 抛砖～玉 throw out a brick in order to get a jade; break the ice ❻ same as 惹 rě ③: 他这一句话,～得大家笑了起来。His remark set everybody laughing. ❼ 用来做证据或理由 quote; cite: ～书 cite a book (as proof) | ～证 cite as evidence ❽ 旧俗出殡时牵引棺材的白布 (old custom) white cloth esp. used to pull along the coffin during a funeral procession: 发～ pull along the coffin with white cloth ❾ 长度单位。10 丈等于 1 引,15 引等于 1 里。*yin*, a traditional unit of length, where to 1 *yin* equals 10 *zhang* (丈) and 15 *yin* equals 0.5 km.

【引爆】yǐnbào 用发火装置使爆炸物爆炸 ignite; detonate; cause (a fuel mixture) to burn by a lighting device: ～装置 igniter; igniting device | ～了一颗炸弹 detonate a bomb

【引柴】yǐnchái 引火用的小木片、小竹片或秫秸等 kindling; slender wood chips, bamboo strips, sorghum stalks, etc. used for kindling a fire; also 引火柴 yǐnhuǒchái

【引产】yǐnchǎn 指妊娠后期用药物、针刺、手术等方法引起子宫收缩,促进胎儿产出 induced labour; artificial labour; (in the later stage of pregnancy) induce contractions of the uterus and delivery of a baby by means of drugs, acupuncture, surgery, etc.

【引导】yǐndǎo ❶ same as 带领 dàilǐng ①: 主人～记者参观了几个主要车间。The host showed the reporters around several major workshops. ❷ 带着人向某个目标行动 instruct and guide sb. in actions towards a certain goal: 老师对学生要善于～。Teachers should be good at giving guidance to students.

【引得】yǐndé same as 索引 suǒyǐn

【引动】yǐndòng 引起;触动(多指心情) cause; arouse; stir up (feelings): 一席话～我思乡的情怀。The words stirred up my homesickness.

【引逗】yǐndòu 挑逗;引诱 tease; lure; entice

【引渡】yǐndù ❶ 引导人渡过(水面); 指引 lead sb. across (water); direct: ～迷津 direct sb. through a maze ❷ 甲国应乙国的请求,把乙国逃到甲国的犯人拘捕,解交乙国 extradite; State A, at the request of State B, arrests an alleged criminal of State B who escaped to State A and deliver the criminal back to State B

【引而不发】yǐn ér bù fā 射箭时拉开弓却不把箭放出去 draw the bow but not release the arrow;〈比喻 *fig*.〉善于引导或控制,也比喻做好准备,待机行动 be good at guidance or control; get ready and wait for a chance for action

【引发】yǐnfā 引起;触发 initiate; trigger; spark off; touch off: 天象表演～了大家对天文学的浓厚兴趣。The astronomical-phenomena show triggered the audience's strong interest in astronomy.

【引港】yǐngǎng ☞ 领港 lǐnggǎng on p. 1233

【引吭高歌】yǐn háng gāo gē 放开喉咙高声歌唱 sing joyfully in a loud voice; sing heartily

【引航】yǐnháng 由熟悉航道的人员引导(或驾驶)船舶进出港口或在内海、江河一定区域内航行 (of a person who knows the water routes well) pilot a ship (into or out of a harbour or through a certain stretch of an inland waterway or river); also 引水 yǐnshuǐ

【引号】yǐnhào 标点符号(横行文字用" "、' ';竖行文字开始时用﹁、﹃,结束时用﹂、﹄),表示文中直接引用的部分。有时也用来表示需要着重论述的对象或具有特殊含义的词语等。quotation marks (" " or ' ' used in writings in horizontal layout, and ﹁﹃ and ﹂﹄ used in vertical writing); pair of punctuation marks used to indicate the beginning and the end of a quotation, in which the exact phraseology of another text is directly cited, and also occasionally used to highlight the addressed object or words of special meaning

【引河】yǐnhé ❶ 为引水灌溉而开挖的河道 irrigation channel; water course dug for irrigation ❷ 减河 diversion canal

【引火】yǐn//huǒ 把燃料点着,特指用燃烧着的东西把燃料点着 light fuel with sth. burning: 引个火 kindle a fire | ～煤 kindling coal; lighting coal; coal lighter | 用木柴～ light a fire with firewood

【引火烧身】yǐn huǒ shāo shēn ❶ ☞ 惹火烧身 rě huǒ shāo shēn on p.1611 ❷〈比喻 *fig.*〉主动暴露自己的问题,争取批评帮助 criticize oneself or reveal one's problems on one's own initiative in an attempt to invite criticism and help

【引见】yǐnjiàn 引人相见,使彼此认识 introduce and get people acquainted with one another: 经友人～,得以认识这位前辈。I was presented by a friend to this senior person.

【引荐】yǐnjiàn 推荐(人) recommend (a person)

【引酵】yǐnjiào 酵子 leaven; leavening dough

【引进】yǐnjìn ❶ same as 引荐 yǐnjiàn ❷ 从外地或外国引入(人员、资金、技术、设备等) introduce from elsewhere; import (personnel, capital, technology, equipment, etc.): ～良种 introduce a fine breed | ～人才 introduce talents | ～外资 introduce foreign capital

【引经据典】yǐn jīng jù diǎn 引用经典中的语句或故事 quote sentences or stories from the classics; quote authoritative works

【引颈】yǐnjǐng 伸长脖子 crane one's neck: ～企待 eagerly look forward to | ～受戮 stick out one's neck for execution

【引咎】yǐnjiù 把过失归在自己身上 hold oneself responsible for a mistake; take the blame: ～自责 hold oneself responsible for a mistake and condemn oneself | ～辞职 take the blame and resign

【引狼入室】yǐn láng rù shì〈比喻 *fig.*〉把敌人或坏人引入内部 invite disaster by letting in the wolf

【引力】yǐnlì 万有引力的简称 abbr. for 万有引力 wàn yǒu yǐnlì

【引例】yǐn//lì 在书、文章中引用例证 cite an example or illustration in a book or an article

【引例】yǐnlì 在书、文章中引用的例证 example or illustration cited in a book or an article

【引领】yǐnlǐng ❶ 引导;带领 lead; guide: 由当地人～,穿过丛林 go through a jungle with the guidance of a local person ❷〈书 *fml.*〉伸直脖子(远望),形容盼望殷切 crane one's neck to look into the distance — eagerly look forward to sth.

【引流】yǐnliú 用外科手术把体内病灶的脓液排出来 drainage; surgical operation for drawing out pus from a focus

【引路】yǐn//lù 带路 lead the way: 在前～ lead the way

【引起】yǐnqǐ 一种事情、现象、活动使另一种事情、现象、活动出现 give rise to; lead to; cause; arouse; (of a thing, phenomenon, or activity) make (another thing, phenomenon, or activity) appear: ～注意 catch sb.'s attention | ～争论 evoke dispute

【引桥】yǐnqiáo 连接正桥和路堤的桥 bridge approach; bridge connecting a principal bridge with the embankment

【引擎】yǐnqíng 发动机,特指蒸汽机、内燃机等热机 engine, esp. heat engine, e.g. gas engine, internal-combustion engine, etc.

【引人入胜】yǐn rén rù shèng 引人进入佳境(指风景或文章等 of scenery, literary works, etc.) fascinating; enchanting; bewitching

【引蛇出洞】yǐn shé chū dòng〈比喻 *fig.*〉运用计谋诱使坏人进行活动,使之暴露 use tact to draw a villain and his activities out into the open

【引申】yǐnshēn (字、词)由原义产生新义,如'鉴'字本义为'镜子','可以作为警戒或引为教训的事'是它的引申义 (of words) new meaning as an extension of the original, e.g. 鉴 originally meant 'mirror' and has by extension come to mean 'warning'

【引述】yǐnshù 引用(别人的话或文字)叙述 quote (sb.'s words or writing): ～专家的评论 quote an expert's comments

【引水】yǐnshuǐ same as 引航 yǐnháng

【引退】yǐntuì 指辞去官职 retire from an official position; resign

【引文】yǐnwén 引自其他书籍或文件的语句 sentence or passage quoted from another book or document; quotation; also 引语 yǐnyǔ

【引线】yǐnxiàn ❶ 线状的引信 wire-like fuse ❷ 做媒介的人或东西 go-between ❸〈方 *dial.*〉缝衣针 sewing needle

【引信】yǐnxìn 引起炮弹、炸弹、地雷等爆炸的一种装置 detonator; fuse; device designed to explode cannonballs, bombs, landmines, etc. also 信管 xìnguǎn

【引言】yǐnyán 写在书或文章前面类似序言或导言的短文 foreword; introduction; preface; brief comments written to introduce a book or an article

【引用】yǐnyòng ❶ 用别人说过的话(包括书面材料)或做过的事作为根据 quote; cite; take sb.'s words (including written ones) or deeds as example or proof: ～古书上的话 quote from an ancient book ❷ 任用;援引(人) appoint; recommend (sb.): ～私人 appoint one's own person

【引诱】yǐnyòu ❶ 诱导。多指引人做坏事。lure; seduce (others to do bad things): 受坏人～走

上邪路 lured by villains into evil ways ❷ 诱惑 entice; tempt: 经不起金钱的～ cannot stand the temptation of money

【引玉之砖】yǐn yù zhī zhuān 〈谦辞 *hum.*〉〈比喻 *fig.*〉为了引出别人高明的意见而发表的粗浅的、不成熟的意见 superficial, immature ideas put forth esp. to induce others to come up with brilliant ideas; ☞ 抛砖引玉 pāo zhuān yǐn yù on p. 1448

【引证】yǐnzhèng 引用事实或言论、著作做根据 quote or cite a truth, speech, or literary work as proof or evidence

【引致】yǐnzhì 引起;导致 induce; cause

【引种】yǐnzhǒng 把别的地区的动植物优良品种引入本地区,选择适于本地区条件的加以繁殖推广 introduce a fine breed of animal or plant from elsewhere, and reproduce and popularize this breed in accordance with local conditions

【引种】yǐnzhòng 把外地的优良品种引入本地种植 plant a fine variety introduced from other places

【引子】yǐn·zi ❶ 南曲、北曲的套曲中的第一支曲子 (in southern and northern tunes of Chinese opera) the first of a series of melodies ❷ 戏曲角色初上场时所念的一段词句,有时唱和念相间 (in traditional opera) performer's opening words, either spoken or sung ❸ 某些乐曲的开始部分,有酝酿情绪、提示内容等作用 introductory music; beginning part of some music, intended to incite the audience's emotions or introduce the content of the music ❹〈比喻 *fig.*〉引起正文的话或启发别人发言的话 comments that introduce texts; words that inspire others to speak: 这一段话是下文的～。This paragraph is an introduction to what follows. | 我简单说几句做个～,希望大家多发表意见。I'll just say a few words to start the ball rolling. ❺ 药引子 added ingredient (to enhance the efficacy of medicines)

吲 yǐn [吲哚](yǐnduǒ)有机化合物,化学式 C_8H_7N,无色或淡黄色片状结晶。存在于煤焦油和腐败的蛋白质中。用来制香料、染料和药物。indole, organic compound (C_8H_7N), in the form of a colourless or light-yellow tabular crystal, chiefly found in coal tars and rotten proteins, and oft. used for making perfumes, dyestuffs, and medicines

饮 yǐn ❶ 喝,有时特指喝酒 drink; (sometimes esp.) drink wine or liquor: ～料 drink | ～食 food and drink | 痛～ swig; booze; drink to one's heart's content | ～水思源 when you drink from the stream, remember the source ❷ 可以喝的东西 drinks; beverages; anything to drink: 冷～ cold drinks ❸ 饮子 decoction of medical herbs to be taken cold: 香苏～ medical broth ❹〈中医 *Chin. med.*〉指稀痰 thin phlegm ❺ 心里存着;含着 keep in one's heart; nurse; harbour: ～恨 cherish a grievance; nurse a grievance
☞ yìn on p. 2297

【饮弹】yǐndàn 身上中(zhòng)了子弹 be hit by a bullet: ～身亡 be killed by a bullet

【饮恨】yǐnhèn 〈书 *fml.*〉抱恨含冤 cherish a grievance: ～而终 die with a grievance in one's heart

【饮料】yǐnliào 经过加工制造供饮用的液体,如酒、茶、汽水、橘子水等 beverage; drink; processed liquid for drinking, e. g. wine, tea, soda pop, orange juice, etc.

【饮片】yǐnpiàn 供制汤剂的中药,多指经过炮制的 prepared herbal medicine in small pieces ready for decoction

【饮泣】yǐnqì 泪流满面,流到口里去。形容悲哀到了极点。tears flow into the mouth; be extremely sorrowful: ～吞声 swallow one's tears; weep silent tears

【饮食】yǐnshí ❶ 吃的和喝的东西 food and drink: 注意～卫生 pay attention to dietetic hygiene ❷ 吃东西和喝东西 eat and drink: ～起居 eating, drinking and living; daily life

【饮食疗法】yǐnshí liáofǎ 调配病人的饮食以治疗某些疾病的方法,例如治疗胃溃疡的方法,每日多吃几顿饭,每顿饭要少吃,吃容易消化的食物 dietotherapy; therapy for certain illnesses involving a special diet for patients to follow, e. g. patients with gastric ulcers should have many small meals of easily digestible foods

【饮食业】yǐnshíyè 从事饮食品的烹制加工,并提供就地消费的场所和设备的行业 catering service; business preparing and providing food and the facility for the consumption of it

【饮水】yǐnshuǐ 喝的和做饭用的水 drinking water; potable water; water for drinking and cooking

【饮水思源】yǐn shuǐ sī yuán 喝水的时候想到水的来源 when drinking water, think of its source;〈比喻 *fig.*〉人在幸福的时候不忘掉幸福的来源 (of people) while living in happiness, keep in mind the source of it

【饮誉】yǐnyù 享有盛名;受到称赞 enjoy a sterling reputation; be lauded: ～全球 be globally well-known | 他的作品～文坛。His works enjoy a good reputation in literary circles.

【饮鸩止渴】yǐn zhèn zhǐ kě 用毒酒解渴 drink poison to quench thirst;〈比喻 *fig.*〉只求解决目前困难而不计后果 seek quick relief (of present problems or difficulties) regardless of the consequences

【饮子】yǐn·zi 宜于冷着喝的汤药 decoction of medical herbs to be taken cold

蚓 yǐn 蚯蚓 earthworm (*Lumbricidae*); fishworm; angleworm

Y

殷 yǐn〈书 *fml*.〉〈拟声词 *onom*.〉形容雷声 thunder：～其雷 clap of thunder
☞ yān on p. 2199 and yīn on p. 2288

隐(隱) yǐn ❶ 隐藏不露 hide from view; conceal：～蔽 conceal｜～士 hermit ❷ 潜伏的；藏在深处的 latent; hidden; lurking：～情 hidden facts｜～患 hidden trouble (or danger) ❸ 指隐秘的事 secret things：难言之～ sth. difficult to speak out

【隐蔽】yǐnbì ❶ 借旁的事物来遮掩 conceal; take cover; with the cover of sth.：游击队～在高粱地里。The guerrillas took cover in the sorghum fields. ❷ 被别的事物遮住不易被发现 covert; be concealed from exposure：地形～ concealed geographical position｜手法～ by covert means

【隐避】yǐnbì 隐藏躲避 evade and conceal：～在外 evade and conceal (oneself) somewhere

【隐藏】yǐncáng 藏起来不让发现 hide; conceal; keep out of sight：～在树林中 hide in the woods

【隐恶扬善】yǐn è yáng shàn 隐瞒人的坏处，而表扬他的好处。这是古代提倡的一种为人处世的态度。conceal sb.'s wickedness and publicize his goodness; overlook faults of others and praise their good ones, as a recommended attitude in conducting oneself in ancient China

【隐伏】yǐnfú 隐藏；潜伏 lie concealed; lie hidden：～在黑暗角落里 lie hidden in a dark corner｜～着危机 lurking crisis

【隐花植物】yǐnhuā-zhíwù 不开花结实、靠孢子、配子或细胞分裂繁殖的植物的统称，如藻类、菌类、蕨类、苔藓类（区别于'显花植物' as compared with 'phanerogam'） cryptogam; plant reproducing by spores, gametes, or cell division, and not producing flowers or seeds, e.g. alga, fungus, pteridophyte or moss

【隐患】yǐnhuàn 潜藏着的祸患 hidden trouble; hidden danger：消除～ remove a hidden peril

【隐讳】yǐnhuì 有所顾忌而隐瞒不说 avoid mentioning due to some worry or qualm：毫无～ without avoiding mention｜他从不～自己的缺点和错误。He never glossed over his shortcomings or faults.

【隐晦】yǐnhuì（意思）不明显（of meaning） obscure; ambiguous：这些诗写得十分～，不容易懂。The poem is too obscure, and difficult to understand.

【隐疾】yǐnjí 不好向别人说的病，如性病之类 unmentionable disease, e.g. VD

【隐居】yǐnjū 由于对统治者不满或有厌世思想而住在偏僻地方，不出来做官 withdraw from official positions and live in a secluded place because of world-weariness or dissatisfaction toward the establishment

【隐君子】yǐnjūnzǐ 原指隐居的人，后来借以嘲讽吸毒成瘾的人（隐、瘾谐音）(orig. referred to) hermit; (later used to sneer at) drug addicts (a pun on 隐 yǐn 'retired' and 瘾 yǐn 'addicted')

【隐括】yǐnkuò same as 檃栝 yǐnkuò

【隐瞒】yǐnmán 掩盖真相，不让人知道 conceal; hide; cover up; hold back the facts from revealing：～错误 conceal one's mistakes｜大家都知道了，他还想～。Everybody knows, but he still wants to hide it.

【隐秘】yǐnmì ❶ 隐蔽不外露 hide; keep from disclosure：～不说 not disclose a secret｜地道的出口开在～的地方。The exit of the tunnel is concealed. ❷ 秘密的事 secret; covert thing：刺探～ pry into sb.'s secrets

【隐没】yǐnmò same as 隐蔽 yǐnbì ①；渐渐看不见 hide and gradually disappear; immerge：远去的航船～在雨雾里。The ship disappeared into the distance in the rainy mist.

【隐匿】yǐnnì〈书 *fml*.〉隐藏；躲起来 conceal; hide

【隐僻】yǐnpì ❶ 偏僻 out of the way：～的角落 remote corner ❷ 隐晦而罕见 ambiguous and rare：用典～ cite (words or paragraphs) from an ambiguous and rare source

【隐情】yǐnqíng 不愿告诉人的事实或原因 facts or reasons one wishes to hide; secrets：说出～ tell secrets

【隐然】yǐnrán 隐隐约约的样子 dim; faint：～可见 dimly visible｜～可闻 faintly audible

【隐忍】yǐnrěn 把事情藏在内心，勉强忍耐 bear patiently; forbear：～不言 forbear from speaking

【隐射】yǐnshè 暗射；影射 innuendo; insinuate; allude

【隐身草】yǐnshēncǎo（～儿 yǐnshēncǎor）〈比喻 *fig*.〉用来遮掩自己的人或事物 person or thing acting as a cover

【隐士】yǐnshì 隐居的人 hermit; recluse

【隐私】yǐnsī 不愿告人的或不愿公开的个人的事 one's secrets; private matters one does not want to publish; privacy; intimacy

【隐痛】yǐntòng ❶ 不愿告诉人的痛苦 secret anguish ❷ 隐隐约约的疼痛 indistinct pain; dull pain; obtuse pain

【隐现】yǐnxiàn 时隐时现；不清晰地显现 be in and out of visibility; be dimly visible：水天相接，岛屿～。The water merges with the sky; the islands are dimly visible.

【隐形飞机】yǐnxíng-fēijī 指用雷达、红外线或其他探测系统难以发现的飞机 stealth aircraft; aircraft difficult to be detected by radar, infrared rays, or other detection systems

【隐形眼镜】yǐnxíng-yǎnjìng 角膜接触镜的通称 contact lens

【隐姓埋名】yǐn xìng mái míng 隐瞒自己的真实姓名 conceal one's identity; live incognito

【隐血】yǐnxuè 因体内某部分出血而在粪便或脑脊液中出现的血液，用肉眼或显微镜都不能查出,必须用化学试剂或试纸才能测出来 occult blood; blood appearing in one's excrement or cerebrospinal fluid due to internal bleeding, not visible to the naked eye or a microscope but verifiable using chemical reagents or test papers; also 潜血 qiánxuè

【隐逸】yǐnyì〈书 *fml.*〉避世隐居。也指隐居的人。withdraw from society and live in seclusion; hermit (or recluse): 山林～ live in a mountain forest as hermit

【隐隐】yǐnyǐn 隐约 indistinct; faint: ～的雷声 distant sound of thunder | 青山～。The green hills are dimly visible. | 筋骨～作痛 feel a dull pain in one's bones and muscles

【隐忧】yǐnyōu 深藏的忧愁;潜藏的忧虑 secret worry; hidden worry

【隐语】yǐnyǔ ❶ 不把要说的意思明说出来,而借用别的话来表示,古代称做隐语,类似后世的谜语 wording that does not express a meaning frankly, but uses borrowed words; enigmatic language; insinuating language; riddle ❷ 黑话;暗语 cant; argot; code word

【隐喻】yǐnyù 比喻的一种,不用'如''像''似''好像'等比喻词,而用'是''成''就是''成为''变为'等词,把某事物比拟成和它有相似关系的另一事物。如'少年儿童是祖国的花朵','荷叶成了一把把撑开的小伞'。metaphor; figure of speech in which an object or idea is compared to another to suggest a likeness or analogy between them, by the use of such words as 是 shì 成 chéng 就是 jiùshì 成为 chéngwéi or 变为 biànwéi instead of figurative words as 如 rú 像 xiàng 似 sì 好像 hǎoxiàng, etc., e.g. 'Children are the flowers of the country.' and 'Lotus leaves have transformed into open umbrellas.' also 暗喻 ànyù

【隐约】yǐnyuē 看起来或听起来不很清楚;感觉不很明显 indistinct; faint (to the eye or ear): 远处的高楼大厦～可见。High buildings in the distance could be faintly seen. | 歌声隐隐约约地从山头传来。Singing could be heard faintly from the top of the mountain.

【隐衷】yǐnzhōng 不愿告诉人的苦衷 feelings or difficulties that one is reluctant to mention

靷 yǐn〈书 *fml.*〉引车前行的皮带 leather strap for pulling a cart

谶(讔) yǐn〈书 *fml.*〉隐语;谜语 riddle; insinuating language

歈 yǐn〈书 *fml.*〉same as 饮 yǐn

檃(㯆、櫽) yǐn [檃栝](yǐnkuò)〈书 *fml.*〉❶ 矫正木材弯曲的器具 straightening machine; apparatus for rectifying warping timber ❷ (就原有的文章、著作)剪裁改写 adapt; tailor and rewrite (based on the original article or work) ‖ also 隐括 yǐnkuò

瘾(癮) yǐn ❶ 由于神经中枢经常接受某种外界刺激而形成的习惯性 addiction; habitual craving formed as a result of the central nervous system's repeated exposure to a stimulus: 烟～ craving for tobacco | 他喝酒的～真大。He's too fond of alcohol. ❷ 泛指浓厚的兴趣 (in a broad sense) strong interest: 球～ passion for ballgames | 他看书看上～了。He's crazy about books.

【瘾头】yǐntóu (～儿 yǐntóur)瘾的程度 degree of addiction; strong interest: 你们下棋的～儿可真不小。You people are certainly keen on playing chess.

螾 yǐn same as 蚓 yǐn

缦 yǐn〈方 *dial.*〉绗(háng) sew with long stitches

yìn (丨ㄣˋ)

印 yìn ❶ 政府机关的图章。泛指图章。(in a broad sense) seal; stamp; esp. official seals of government organizations: 盖～ affix a seal; stamp a seal | 钢～ steel seal ❷ (～儿 yìnr) same as 印子 yìn·zi ①: 烙～ brand | 脚～儿 footprint ❸ 留下痕迹。特指文字或图画等留在纸上或器物上。print; leave marks; esp. characters or pictures left on paper or wares: ～书 print books | 排～ typesetting and printing | 石～ lithography | ～花儿布 calico ❹ 符合 tally; conform: ～证 confirm | 心心相～ be kindred spirits; have mutual affinity ❺ (Yìn)姓 a surname

【印把子】yìnbà·zi 指行政机关的图章的把儿 knob of the official seal of an administrative organ; 〈比喻 *fig.*〉政权 authority; power: 掌握～ hold the authority; wield political power

【印本】yìnběn 印刷的书本(区别于'抄本' as compared with 'transcribed copy') printed copy

【印鼻】yìnbí 印纽 knob (or handle) of a seal

【印次】yìncì 图书每一版印刷的次数。从第一版第一次印刷起连续计算。如内容经重大修订而再版,就另行计算印次。impression; all the copies (as of a book) printed in one continuous operation from a single edition, subject to consideration if the book is amended and reprinted

【印第安人】Yìndì'ānrén 美洲最古老的居民,皮肤红黑色,从前称为红种人。大部分住在中、南美各国。(American) Indian; native, aboriginal and indigenous Americans; original inhabitants of the Americas characterized by red-black skin, previously called Red Indian, now mostly living in Central and Southern Americas

【印度教】Yìndùjiào 经过改革的婆罗门教,现在流行于印度、尼泊尔等国 Hinduism; reformed Brahmanism, popular in India, Nepal, etc.

【印发】yìnfā 印刷散发 print and distribute: ～传单 print and distribute leaflets|把这些材料～给各科室。Print these materials and distribute them to all the departments.

【印痕】yìnhén 痕迹 mark of print; trace

【印花】yìn//huā (～儿 yìn//huār) 将有色花纹或图案印到纺织品等上去 printing; decorating cloth with colourful patterns or designs all over its surface by a machine

【印花】[1] yìnhuā (～儿 yìnhuār)印有花纹的 printed; patterned: ～儿布 calico|～绸 silk print

【印花】[2] yìnhuā 由政府出售,规定贴在契约、凭证等上面,作为税款的一种特制印刷品。全称印花税票。fiscal stamp; revenue stamp; government-sold stamp to affix on documents (e.g. deed, contract, warrant, etc.) for use as evidence of payment of a tax; full name for 印花税票 yìnhuā shuìpiào

【印花税】yìnhuāshuì 国家税收的一种,各项契约、簿据、凭证上须按税则贴政府发售的印花 stamp duty; stamp tax; national tax collected by means of a government-sold stamp to affix to a document (e.g. deed, voucher; receipt; promissory note, or credence)

【印记】yìnjì ❶〈旧指 *old*〉钤记 seal or stamp of a government organization ❷ 印迹 impression of a seal; trace; mark: 公章一按,留下了鲜红的～。Once pressed, the official seal left a red impression. ◇他的每篇作品都带有鲜明的时代～。Each of his works was imprinted with a mark of the times. ❸ 把印象深刻地保持着 impress deeply in one's mind; (of sth.) made a deep impression: 他一直把那次约会的情景～在脑海里。That date has been deeply ingrained in his mind.

【印迹】yìnjì 痕迹 trace; mark; vestige

【印鉴】yìnjiàn 为防假冒,在支付款项的机关留供核对的印章底样。支领款项时,所用的印章要与所留的印章底样相符。specimen seal impression left with the payment recipient office for checking, in order to avoid fraud. When making payment, the seal used should conform to the specimen seal impression

【印泥】yìnní 盖图章用的颜料,一般用朱砂、艾绒和油制成,印出来是红色 red ink paste used for seals; palette used for seals, generally made of vermilion, moxa, and oil, giving a red impression

【印纽】yìnniǔ〈古代 *arch.*〉印章上端雕刻成龟、虎、狮等形象的部分,有孔,可以穿带子 knob of a seal; upper end of a seal, carved in the shape of a tortoise, tiger, or lion, with a hole to wear on a belt; also 印鼻 yìnbí or 印钮 yìnniǔ

【印谱】yìnpǔ 汇集古印或名家所刻印章而成的书 collection of impressions of seals by famous seal-engravers

【印染】yìnrǎn 纺织品的印花和染色 printing and dyeing of textiles: ～技术 printing and dyeing techniques

【印色】yìn·se same as 印泥 yìnní

【印绶】yìnshòu〈旧时 *old*〉称印信和系印的丝带 official seal and the ribbon attached to it

【印刷】yìnshuā 把文字、图画等做成版,涂上油墨,印在纸张上。近代印刷用各种印刷机。我国的手工印刷,多用棕刷子蘸墨刷在印版上,然后放上纸,再用干净的棕刷子在纸背上用力擦过,所以叫做印刷。printing; process in which a plate engraved with characters or pictures is pasted with ink and printed on paper. Compared with modern printing, which uses machines, traditional Chinese manual printing is a process in which a printing plate is daubed with ink using a coir brush and then covered with a sheet of paper and finally brushed over with great force by a clean coir brush on the back of the paper

【印刷品】yìnshuāpǐn 印刷成的书报、图片等 printed books, papers, pictures, etc.; printed matter

【印刷体】yìnshuātǐ 文字或拼音字母的印刷形式(区别于'手写体' as compared with 'script') block letter; print form of characters or phonetic alphabets; ☞ 手写体 shǒuxiětǐ on p. 1770

【印台】yìntái 盖图章(主要是橡皮图章或木戳)所用的印油盒 ink pad; stamp pad (for rubber or wood seals); also 打印台 dǎyìntái

【印堂】yìntáng 指额部两眉之间 space between the eyebrows

【印铁】yìntiě 在镀锡的薄铁皮或铝皮上印刷图案文字 tin-plate printing; print characters or patterns on a tinned thin iron or aluminium sheet

【印相纸】yìnxiàngzhǐ 印相片的感光纸,上面涂有卤化银乳剂 photographic paper; sensitive paper for developing photos, coated with emulsion of silver halide

【印象】yìnxiàng 客观事物在人的头脑里留下的迹象 impression; mark or imprint left by an objective matter in people's mind: 深刻的～ deep impression|他给我的～很好。He left me with a good impression.

【印信】yìnxìn 政府机关的图章(总称) official seal; seal of a government organization (collect.)

【印行】yìnxíng 印刷并发行 print and distribute: ～单行本 print and distribute a separate edition|那本书已～上百万册。That book has a press run of over a million copies.

【印油】yìnyóu 专供印台用的液体,有红、蓝、紫等色 stamp-pad ink, in red, blue, purple, etc.

【印张】yìnzhāng 印刷书籍时每一本所用纸张数量的计算单位，以一整张平板纸(通称新闻纸或报纸)为两个印张 printed sheet; unit for counting the amount of paper used for printing each copy of a book, equal to a half sheet of printing paper (general term for printing paper or newsprint)

【印章】yìnzhāng 印和章的合称 seal; signet; stamp

【印证】yìnzhèng ❶ 证明与事实相符 confirm; verify; corroborate; do a fact-check (prove correspondence to actual facts): 材料已～过。The material has been verified. ❷ 用来印证的事物 matters used as proof for confirmation

【印子】yìn·zi ❶ 痕迹 mark; trace; print: 地板上踩了好多脚～。Many footprints well left on the floor. ❷ 指印子钱 usury: 放～ practise usury | 打～(借印子钱) borrow from a usurer

【印子钱】yìn·ziqián 高利贷的一种，把本钱和很高的利息加在一起，约定期限，由债务人分期偿还，每还一期，在折子上盖印为记 usury; high-interest loan in which the borrower amortizes the principal as well as an exorbitant rate of interest within an established time limit, with a seal imprinted as a mark upon each periodic reimbursement; 简称 abbr. 印子 yìn·zi

饮 yìn 给牲畜水喝 give (animals) water to drink; water: ～牲口 water an animal | 马～过了。The horse has been watered.

☞ yǐn on p. 2293

【饮场】yìnchǎng 〈旧时 *old*〉戏曲演员在台上喝水润嗓 opera singer drink water onstage to moisten his throat

茚 yìn 有机化合物，化学式 C_9H_8，无色液体，化学性质活泼。用来制造合成树脂，与其他液态烃混合可做油漆的溶剂。indene (C_9H_8); organic compound in the form of colourless liquid, with active chemical properties, used esp. in making synthetic resins or paint solvents by mixing with other liquid hydrocarbons

荫(蔭、❷❸廕) yìn ❶ 没有阳光；又凉又潮 sunless; damp and chilly: 南屋太～，这边坐吧。The room with northern exposure is too damp and chilly; come sit here. ❷〈书 *fml.*〉荫庇 shelter; protect ❸ 封建时代由于父祖有功而给予子孙入学或任官的权利 (in feudal dynasties) official rank or privilege in school entrance granted to sb. as a recognition of the merits of his ancestors

☞ yīn on p. 2285

【荫庇】yìnbì 大树枝叶遮蔽阳光，宜于人们休息 shelter; protect; thick foliage offering shade from sunlight for people to rest; 〈比喻 *fig.*〉尊长照顾着晚辈或祖宗保佑着子孙 the old take care of the young; ancestors bless the offspring

【荫凉】yìnliáng 因没有太阳晒着而凉爽 shady and cool, with no exposure to the sun: 这屋子～得很。It's very shady and cool in this room.

胤 yìn 〈书 *fml.*〉后代；后嗣 offspring; posterity

垽 yìn 〈书 *fml.*〉沉淀物；沉淀物的痕迹 sediment (or precipitate); mark of sediment

鮣 yìn 鱼，身体细长，灰黑色，圆柱形，头和身体前端的背部扁平，有一长椭圆形吸盘，鳞小而圆。生活在海洋中，常用吸盘吸在其他大鱼身体下面或船底下。sharksucker (*Echeneis naucrates Linnaeus*); suckerfish; remora; marine fish that has a dark slender cylinder-shaped body, a flat head and a flat front part of the back, small and round scales, and an oblong sucker by means of which it clings to the bottom of other large fish or ships

窨 yìn 地窨子；地下室 cellar; basement

☞ xūn on p. 2185

【窨井】yìnjǐng 上下水道或其他地下管线工程中，为便于检查或疏通而设置的井状建筑物 inspection shaft; inspection well; (in water-supply plumbing, sewers, or other underground pipes) well-like structure set up for the convenience of inspection or dredging

慭(憖) yìn 〈书 *fml.*〉❶ 愿；宁愿 prefer; would rather ❷ 损伤；残缺 injure; fragmentary

【慭慭】yìnyìn 形容小心谨慎 cautious; attentive

yīng (丨ㄥ)

吋 yīngcùn，又 also cùn 英寸旧也作吋 inch (英寸) formerly as 吋 yīngcùn

呎 yīngchǐ，又 also chǐ 英尺旧也作呎 foot (英尺) formerly as 呎 yīngchǐ

应[1](應) yīng ❶ 答应 answer; respond: 喊他不～。I called him, but he didn't answer. ❷ 答应(做) agree (to do sth.); promise: 这事是我～下来的，由我负责。I'm the one who took on the job, so let me take care of it. ❸ (Yīng)姓 a surname

应[2](應) yīng 应该 should; ought to: ～有尽有 have everything one expects to find | 发现错误，～立即纠正。When a mistake is discovered, it should be corrected at once.

☞ yìng on p. 2305

【应当】yīngdāng same as 应该 yīnggāi

【应分】yīngfèn 分内应该 be part of one's job (or duty): 帮他点忙，也是我们～的事。It's part of our job to help him out.

【应该】yīnggāi 表示理所当然 should; ought to: ～爱护公共财产 one should take good care of public property｜为了大伙的事，我多受点累也是～的。It was in everybody's interest that I went to so much trouble. I'm only doing my duty.

【应届】yīngjiè 本期的 this year's; this term's (只用于毕业生 exclusive term for a graduate)：～毕业生 graduate (of this term or year); this year's graduate

【应名儿】yīng//míngr 用某人的名义(办某事)；挂某种虚名 by the name of sb. (to do sth.); hold a title but have no real power or responsibility：你应个名儿吧，反正费不了多大事儿。Hold the title, since it won't require much from you.

【应名儿】yīngmíngr 仅仅在名义上(是) only in name; nominally：他们～是亲戚，实际上不大来往。Nominally they're relatives, but they don't see much of each other.

【应声】yīng//shēng (～儿 yīng//shēngr)出声回答 answer; respond：敲了一阵门，里边没有人～儿。I knocked and knocked, but no one answered.｜问了半天，你也该应一声。I've been asking you all this time; you should at least give me an answer.

☞ yìngshēng on p. 2306

【应许】yīngxǔ ❶ 答应(做) agree (to do sth.); promise：他～明天来谈。He agreed to come and talk it over with us tomorrow. ❷ 允许 permit; allow：谁～他把写字台搬走的？Who permitted him to take the desk away?

【应有尽有】yīng yǒu jìn yǒu 应该有的全都有了，表示一切齐备 have everything that one could wish for

【应允】yīngyǔn 应许 assent; consent：点头～ nod assent; nod approval

英1 yīng ❶〈书 *fml.*〉花 flower; petal：落～缤纷。Petals fell in riotous profusion. ❷ 才能或智慧过人的人 outstanding person in talent or intelligence：～豪 outstanding figures｜群～大会 gathering of heroes ❸ (Yīng) 姓 a surname

英2 Yīng 指英国 Great Britain; United Kingdom：～尺 foot｜～镑 pound sterling

【英镑】yīngbàng 英国的本位货币 pound sterling, standard currency of Great Britain

【英才】yīngcái ❶ 才智出众的人(多指青年 oft. of youth) person of outstanding ability; person of superior talent：一代～ a generation of talented people ❷ 杰出的才智 outstanding talent and ability：～盖世 unparalleled talent

【英尺】yīngchǐ 英美制长度单位，1 英尺等于 12 英寸，合 0.3048 米，0.9144 市尺 foot; British and American measure of length comprising 12 inches and equal to 0.3048 m. or 0.9144 *chi*；旧也作 formerly as 呎 yīngchǐ

【英寸】yīngcùn 英美制长度单位，1 英寸等于 1 英尺的 1/12 inch; British and American measure of length equal to 1/12 foot；旧也作 formerly as 吋 cùn

【英豪】yīngháo 英雄豪杰 hero; outstanding figure：各路～ heroes from different places

【英魂】yīnghún 英灵 spirit of the brave departed; spirit of a martyr

【英杰】yīngjié 英豪 hero; outstanding figure：一代～ a generation of outstanding figures

【英俊】yīngjùn ❶ 才能出众 brilliant; eminently talented：～有为 brilliant and promising ❷ 容貌俊秀又有精神 handsome; good-looking and vigorous：～少年 handsome young chap

【英里】yīnglǐ 英美制长度单位，1 英里等于 5,280英尺，合 1.6093 公里 mile; British and American measure of length comprising 5,280 feet and equal to 1.6093 km.；旧也作 formerly as 哩 lǐ

【英两】yīngliǎng 盎司的旧称 old name for 盎司 àngsī；旧也作 formerly as 唡 liǎng

【英烈】yīngliè ❶ 英勇刚烈 heroic and fiery; valiant：～女子 heroic woman ❷ 英勇牺牲的烈士 martyr：祭奠～ hold a memorial ceremony for martyrs

【英灵】yīnglíng 受崇敬的人去世后的灵魂 spirit of the brave departed; spirit of a martyr：告慰先烈～may the souls of our martyrs rest in peace; also 英魂 yīnghún

【英名】yīngmíng 指英雄人物的名字或名声 illustrious name; name or reputation of a hero：～永存 illustrious name existing forever

【英明】yīngmíng 卓越而明智 outstanding and wise; brilliant：～果断 wise and determined｜～的领导 brilliant leader

【英模】yīngmó 英雄模范 heroes and model workers：～报告会 meeting of heroes and models

【英亩】yīngmǔ 英美制地积单位，1 英亩等于 4,840平方码，合 4,046.86平方米 acre; British and American measure of land equal to 4,840 square yards or 4,046.86 square metres；旧也作 formerly as 啩 mǔ

【英年】yīngnián 英气焕发的年龄，一般指青壮年时期 in the prime of life; youthful years：正当～ right in the prime of one's life｜～早逝 pass away when one is young

【英气】yīngqì 英俊、豪迈的气概 heroic spirit：～勃勃 full of heroic spirit

【英石】yīngshí 广东英德所产的一种石头，用来叠假山 limestone produced in Yingde County, Guangdong Province, used for constructing rockeries

【英特耐雄纳尔】Yīngtènàixióngnà'ěr '国际'('国际工人协会'的简称)的音译。在《国际歌》中指国际共产主义的理想。Internationale (transliteration of an abbr. of the International Workers Association). It refers to the ideal of communism in the song *Internationale*. [法 French: Internationale]

【英武】yīngwǔ〈书 *fml.*〉英俊威武 handsome

and mighty

【英雄】yīngxióng ❶ 才能勇武过人的人 hero; talented and brave person: ～好汉 hero | 自古～出少年。Heroes display their talent and bravery in their youth. This has always been true since ancient times. ❷ 不怕困难,不顾自己,为人民利益而英勇斗争,令人钦敬的人 person who never fears difficulties and struggles bravely for the sake of the people's interests, thus winning the respect of the people: 人民～ people's heroes | 劳动～ labour heroes | 民族～ national heroes ❸ 具有英雄品质的 heroic; with qualities of a hero: ～的中国人民 heroic Chinese people

【英雄无用武之地】yīngxióng wú yòngwǔ zhī dì 形容有本领的人得不到施展的机会 (of a capable person) have no scope for the exercise of his or her abilities

【英寻】yīngxún 英美制计量水深的单位,1 英寻等于 6 英尺,合 1.828 米 fathom; British and American measure of the depth of water, equal to 6 feet or 1.828 m.; 旧也作 formerly as 㖊 xún

【英勇】yīngyǒng 勇敢出众 exceptionally brave; heroic; valiant: ～杀敌 fight heroically against the enemy | ～的战士 brave soldiers

【英制】yīngzhì 单位制的一种,以英尺为长度的主单位,磅为质量的主单位,秒为时间的主单位。盎司、码、英亩、加仑等都是英制单位。British system of units in which the foot is the principal unit of length, the pound the principal unit of weight, and the second the principal unit of time. Other British units include the ounce, yard, acre, and gallon.

【英姿】yīngzī 英俊威武的风姿 heroic bearing: ～焕发 dashing and spirited | 飒爽～ valiant and heroic in bearing; bold and brave

㖊 yīngxún, 又 also xún 英寻旧也作㖊 fathom (英寻) formerly as 㖊 yīngxún

莺(鶯、鸎) yīng 鸟类的一科,身体小,多为褐色或暗绿色,嘴短而尖。叫的声音清脆。吃昆虫,对农业和林业有益。warbler (*Acanthizinae*); oriole; small-bodied, brown or dark greenish bird with a short and pointed beak, twittering clearly and melodiously, feeding on insects and therefore beneficial to agriculture and forestry

【莺歌燕舞】yīng gē yàn wǔ 黄莺歌唱,燕子飞舞。形容大好春光或比喻大好形势 orioles sing and swallows dance — (fig.) joy of spring; scene of prosperity: 大地春回,～。Spring has returned to the land, bringing scenes of joy.

唡(啢) yīngliǎng, 又 also liǎng, 盎司的旧称 old term for ounce

哩 yīnglǐ, 又 also lǐ 英里旧也作哩 mile (英里) formerly as 哩 yīnglǐ

☞ lǐ on p. 1174 and •li on p. 1193

䓨(罃) yīng 〈书 *fml.*〉 same as 罂 yīng

婴[1] yīng 婴儿 baby; infant: 妇～ women and infants | 溺～ infanticide by drowning

婴[2] yīng 〈书 *fml.*〉 触犯,缠绕 offend; harass; pester: ～疾(得病) fall ill; be pesterd by illness

【婴儿】yīng'ér 不满一岁的小孩儿 baby; infant; child who is not yet a year old

【婴孩】yīnghái 婴儿 baby; infant

媖 yīng 〈书 *fml.*〉 妇女的美称 laudatory term for a woman

瑛 yīng 〈书 *fml.*〉 ❶ 美玉 beautiful jade ❷ 玉的光彩 jade lustre

煐 yīng 人名用字 character used specially in a person's name

嘤 yīngmǔ 又 also mǔ 英亩旧也作嘤 acre (英亩) formerly as 嘤 yīngmǔ

锳 yīng 〈书 *fml.*〉 铃声 ring

蘡 yīng [蘡薁] (yīngyù) 落叶藤本植物,枝条细长有棱角,叶子阔卵形,有三到五个深裂,圆锥花序,浆果黑紫色。茎的纤维可以做绳索。wild grape (*Vitis adstricta*); deciduous liana that has slender hanging branches with edges and corners, broad and oval leaves with three to five deep lobes, panicled flowers, and dark purple pulpy fruit, its stem fibres useful for making rope

撄 yīng 〈书 *fml.*〉 ❶ 接触;触犯 oppose; run against: ～其锋 blunt the thrust (of an attacking force) | ～怒 incur sb.'s displeasure ❷ 纠缠;扰乱 disturb; stir up; bug

嘤 yīng 〈书 *fml.*〉〈拟声词 *onom.*〉 形容鸟叫声 chirp; twitter

罂(甖) yīng 〈书 *fml.*〉 小口大肚的瓶子 small-mouthed, big-belly container; jar

【罂粟】yīngsù 二年生草本植物,全株有白粉,叶长圆形,边缘有缺刻,花红色、粉色或白色,果实球形。果实未成熟时划破表皮,流出汁液,用来制取阿片。果壳可入药,花供观赏。opium poppy (*Papaver somniferum*); biennial herb covered all over in white powder, having oblong, notch-edged leaves, and red, pink or white flowers. When the peel of its capsular fruits is lacerated before ripening, a milky juice seeps out, which is the source of opium. Its shell can be used medicinally, and its flowers are cultivated for ornamentation

缨 yīng ❶ 〈古代 *arch.*〉 帽子上系在颔下的带子。也泛指带子。ribbon of a hat, usu. fastened below the chin ❷ (～儿 yīngr) same as 缨子 yīng•zi ①: 红～枪 red-tasselled spear ❸ (～儿 yīngr) same as 缨子 yīng•zi ②: 芥菜～儿 mustard leaves

【缨帽】yīngmào 清朝官吏所戴的帽子,帽顶上有红缨子 official hat with red tassels at the top

(worn by officials of the Qing Dynasty)

【缨子】yīng·zi ❶ 系在服装或器物上的穗状饰物 tassels as ornamentation on costumes or articles：帽～ hat tassels ❷ 像缨子的东西 sth. shaped like a tassel：萝卜～ radish leaves

璎 yīng〈书 *fml.*〉似玉的石头 jade-like stone; gem

【璎珞】yīngluò〈古代 *arch.*〉用珠玉穿成的戴在颈项上的装饰品 pearl and jade necklace

樱 yīng ❶ 指樱桃 cherry ❷ 指樱花 cherry blossom

【樱花】yīnghuā ❶ 落叶乔木，叶子椭圆形，总状花序或伞房花序，花白色或粉红色，略有芳香，果实球形，黑色。原产日本。供观赏。cherry blossom (*Prunus serrulata*); ornamental cherry; deciduous tree having oblong leaves, white or pink flowers in raceme or corymb with a slight fragrance, and black spherical fruit, originally from Japan, and usu. cultivated for ornamental purposes ❷ 这种植物的花 flower of this plant

【樱桃】yīng·táo ❶ 落叶乔木，叶子长卵圆形，花白色略带红晕。果实近于球形，红色，味甜，可以吃。cherry (*Prunus*); deciduous tree having oblong leaves, white flowers with red haloes, and almost spherical red fruit that tastes sweet ❷ 这种植物的果实 fruit of this plant

霙 yīng 古书上指雪花 (as recorded in ancient books) snowflake

鹦 yīng ☞ below

【鹦鹉】yīngwǔ 鸟，头部圆，上嘴大，呈钩状，下嘴短小，羽毛美丽，有白、赤、黄、绿等色。生活在热带树林里，吃果实。能模仿人说话的声音。parrot (*Psittacidae*); bird that has a round head, a large hooked upper bill, a short small lower bill, and bright feathers in white, red, yellow or green, living in tropical forests, eating fruits, and being capable of mimicking human voice; also 鹦哥 yīnggē

【鹦鹉学舌】yīngwǔ xuéshé 鹦鹉学人说话 a parrot repeating a person's words;〈比喻 *fig.*〉别人怎样说，也跟着怎样说（含贬义 derog.）echo another's words without thinking or understanding; repeat whatever another person says

膺¹ yīng〈书 *fml.*〉胸 chest; breast：义愤填～ be filled with moral indignation

膺² yīng〈书 *fml.*〉❶ 承受；承当 bear; take：荣～勋章 be honoured with a medal ❷ 讨伐；打击 crusade against; strike：～惩 send armed forces to suppress

【膺惩】yīngchéng〈书 *fml.*〉讨伐；打击 send armed forces to suppress; send a punitive expedition against

【膺选】yīngxuǎn〈书 *fml.*〉当选 be elected

鹰 yīng 鸟类的一科，一般指鹰属的鸟类，上嘴呈钩形，颈短，脚部有长毛，足趾有长而锐利的爪。性凶猛，捕食小兽及其他鸟类。hawk (*Accipitridae*); eagle; bird of the Aquila category that has a hooked upper beak, short neck, and long-feathered feet with long and sharp claws; distinguished by its fierce character, preying on small animals and other birds for food

【鹰鼻鹞眼】yīng bí yào yǎn 形容奸诈凶狠的人的相貌 having a nose like an eagle's beak and eyes of a sparrow hawk; facial features of a sinister and fierce person

【鹰犬】yīngquǎn 打猎所用的鹰和狗 falcons and hounds;〈比喻 *fig.*〉受驱使、做爪牙的人 hired thug; button man

【鹰隼】yīngsǔn〈书 *fml.*〉鹰和隼，都捕食小鸟和别种小动物 hawks and falcons, both preying on birds and small animals for food;〈比喻 *fig.*〉凶猛或勇猛的人 fierce or brutal person

【鹰洋】yīngyáng〈旧时 *old*〉曾在我国市面上流通过的墨西哥银币，正面有凸起的鹰形 Mexican silver dollar with an eagle in relief on its face, circulated for a time in old China

【鹰爪毛儿】yīngzhǎomáor 一种短毛羊皮，因毛像鹰爪而得名 short-wool sheepskin, so named because of its eagle-claw-like wool

膺 yīng〈书 *fml.*〉same as 应 yīng ☞ yìng on p. 2309

yíng（ㄧㄥˊ）

迎 yíng ❶ 迎接 welcome; greet; go to meet：欢～ welcome｜～新会 welcome meeting for newcomers ❷ 对着；冲着 against; towards：～面 in the face｜～风 against the wind｜～击 repulse attacks

【迎春】yíngchūn 落叶灌木，羽状复叶，小叶卵形或长椭圆形，花单生，黄色，早春开花。供观赏。winter jasmine (*Jasminum nudiflorum*); deciduous bush having pinnate compound leaves, oval or oblong small leaves, and solitary yellow flowers which bloom in early spring, chiefly grown for ornamentation

【迎风】yíng//fēng ❶ 对着风 against the wind：这里坐着正～，很凉爽。It's nice and cool to sit here against the wind. ❷ 随风 downwind; with the wind：红旗～招展。Red flags fluttered in the breeze.

【迎合】yínghé 故意使自己的言语或举动适合别人的心意 cater to; purposely tailor one's own words or behaviour to others' intentions：～上司 cater to the wishes of one's superior｜～观众 cater to the audience

【迎候】yínghòu 到某个地方等候迎接（到来的人）await the arrival of (a guest) at a place

【迎击】yíngjī 对着敌人来的方向攻击 repulse enemy's attacks; counterattack against an approaching enemy：奋勇～ bravely repulse｜～

进犯之敌 counterattack an invading enemy

【迎接】yíngjiē 到某个地点去陪同客人等一起来 meet；welcome：到车站去～贵宾 meet a distinguished guest at a railway station ◇～劳动节 welcome Labour Day｜～即将到来的战斗任务 meet an upcoming fighting task

【迎面】yíng//miàn（～儿 yíng//miànr）冲着脸 head-on；in one's face：西北风正～儿刮着。The northwest wind is blowing in my face.｜～走上去打招呼 step forward to greet (sb.)

【迎亲】yíng//qīn 旧俗结婚时男家用花轿鼓乐等到女家迎接新娘（old custom）party dispatched by the bridegroom to meet the bride at the bride's home and escort her in a bridal sedan chair by beating drums and playing wind instruments to the bridegroom's home for the wedding

【迎娶】yíngqǔ 娶妻（of a man）get married

【迎刃而解】yíng rèn ér jiě 用刀劈竹子，劈开了口儿，下面的一段就迎着刀口自己裂开（见于《晋书·杜预传》）bamboo splits as it meets the edge of a knife (see *History of Jin·Biography of Du Yu*)；〈比喻 *fig.*〉主要的问题解决了，其他有关的问题就可以很容易地得到解决 once the principal problem is solved, the related problems can be readily solved

【迎头】yíng//tóu（～儿 yíng//tóur）迎面；当头 head-on；in one's face：～痛击 deal a head-on blow

【迎头赶上】yíngtóu gǎnshàng 加紧追上最前面的 try hard to catch up (with those ahead)

【迎新】yíngxīn 欢迎新来的人 welcome new arrivals：～晚会 evening party to welcome newcomers

【迎迓】yíngyà〈书 *fml.*〉same as 迎接 yíngjiē

【迎战】yíngzhàn 朝着敌人来的方向上前去作战 fight head-on against (an approaching enemy)：～敌军 meet the enemy head-on ◇我队在决赛中将～欧洲劲旅。Our team will meet a forceful team from Europe in the finals.

茔(塋) yíng〈书 *fml.*〉坟地 grave：～地 graveyard；cemetery｜祖～ ancestors' grave

荥(滎) yíng 荥经（Yíngjīng），地名，在四川 Yingjing, a place in Sichuan Province

☞ xíng on p. 2148

荧(熒) yíng〈书 *fml.*〉❶ 光亮微弱的样子 glimmering；shimmering：一灯～然。A light is glimmering. ❷ 眼光迷乱；疑惑 dazzled；perplexed：～惑 confused

【荧光】yíngguāng 某些物质受光或其他射线照射时所发出的可见光。光和其他射线停止照射，荧光随之消失。荧光灯和荧光屏都涂有荧光物质。fluorescence；fluorescent light；(of some substances) emission of, or the property of emitting, visible light as a result of being exposed to and absorbing light or certain other radiation, disappearing without the irradiation of light and other rays. Fluorescent lamps and fluorescent screens are oft. coated with such substances.

【荧光灯】yíngguāngdēng 灯的一种，在真空玻璃管里充入水银，两端安装电极，管的内壁涂有荧光物质。通电后水银蒸气放电，同时产生紫外线，激发荧光物质而发光。常见的荧光灯光和日光相似。fluorescent lamp；daylight lamp；vacuum-tubular lamp, fitted with electrodes at both ends, having a coating of fluorescent material on its inner surface and containing mercury vapour whose bombardment by electrons from the cathode provides ultraviolet light which causes the material to emit visible light, the light produced by the common type of such a lamp being akin to sunlight；also 日光灯 rìguāngdēng

【荧光屏】yíngguāngpíng 涂有荧光物质的屏，眼睛看不见的爱克斯射线、紫外线、阴极射线照射在荧光屏上能发出可见光。如示波器和电视机上都装有荧光屏，用来把阴极射线变为图像。fluorescent screen；screen coated with fluorescent material, which emits visible light when irradiated by x-rays, ultraviolet light, or cathode rays, used as part of an oscillograph or TV set to turn cathode rays into pictures

【荧惑】yínghuò ❶〈书 *fml.*〉迷惑 bewilder；confuse：～人心 confuse people's minds ❷ 我国古代天文学上指火星（in Chinese ancient astronomy）Mars

【荧屏】yíngpíng 荧光屏。特指电视荧光屏，也借指电视 fluorescent screen；TV screen in particular；also referring to TV：六集连续剧下周即可在～上和观众见面。A six-part serial play will be shown on TV next week.

【荧荧】yíngyíng 形容星光或灯烛光 starlight, lamplight, or candlelight：明星～ twinkling stars｜一灯～ shimmering light of a lamp

盈 yíng ❶ 充满 be full of；be filled with：充～ plentiful｜丰～ plentiful｜车马～门 be jammed with carriages and horses｜恶贯满～ face retribution for a life of crime ❷ 多出来；多余 surplus；have a surplus of：～余 surplus｜～利 profit

【盈亏】yíngkuī ❶ 指月亮的圆和缺 the waxing and waning of the moon ❷ 指赚钱或赔本 profit or loss：自负～ be responsible for one's own profits or losses

【盈利】yínglì same as 赢利 yínglì

【盈千累万】yíng qiān lěi wàn 形容数量多 thousands upon thousands；in a great number：参观展览的人～。Thousands upon thousands of people visited the exhibition.

【盈盈】yíngyíng ❶ 形容清澈 clear；limpid：春水～ clear spring water｜荷叶上露珠～。The lotus leaves glistened with dewdrops. ❷ 形容

仪态美好（of one's manner）delicate；dainty：～顾盼 look about gracefully ❸ 形容情绪、气氛等充分流露（of mood，atmosphere，etc.）brimming over；plentiful：喜气～ brimming over with joy｜笑脸～ face brimming over with smiles ❹ 形容动作轻盈（of movements）lissom；graceful：～起舞 dancing gracefully

【盈余】yíngyú ❶ 收入中除去开支后剩余 surplus；part of income that remains of expenses：～二百元 have a surplus of 200 yuan ❷ 收入中除去开支后剩余的财物 profit；gain；surplus property of income after the deduction of expenditures：有二百元的～ with a profit of 200 yuan ‖ also 赢余 yíngyú

莹（瑩） yíng〈书 *fml*.〉❶ 光洁像玉的石头 stone as bright and smooth as jade；jade-like stone ❷ 光亮透明 lustrous and transparent：晶～ sparkling and crystal-clear

萤（螢） yíng 昆虫，身体黄褐色，触角丝状，腹部末端有发光的器官，能发带绿色的光。白天伏在草丛里，夜晚飞出来。firefly（*Luciola terminalis*）；glow-worm；lightning bug；insect having a russet-brown body，thread-like antennae，and a luminescent organ at the bottom of its belly which emits greenish light，staying in thick grass during daytime and flying out at night；also 萤火虫 yínghuǒchóng

营[1]（營） yíng ❶ 谋求 seek：～生 earn a living｜～救 rescue ❷ 经营；管理 operate；run：～造 construct｜～业 do business｜国～ state-owned｜公私合～ joint state-private ownership ❸（Yíng）姓 a surname

营[2]（營） yíng ❶ 军队驻扎的地方 camp；barracks；military residence：军～ military camp｜安～ pitch a camp；encamp ❷ 军队的编制单位，隶属于团，下辖若干连 battalion；military unit subordinate to a regiment and composed of several companies

【营办】yíngbàn 操持办理；承办 handle；undertake

【营地】yíngdì 部队扎营的地方 encampment；campsite

【营房】yíngfáng 专供军队驻扎的房屋及其周围划定的地方 barracks；houses and surroundings esp. for lodging soldiers in garrison

【营火】yínghuǒ 露营时燃起的火堆 campfire；bonfire used esp. during camping

【营火会】yínghuǒhuì 一种露天晚会，参加者多是青少年，围着火堆谈笑歌舞 campfire party；open-air evening party featuring often young participants who talk，sing and dance around a bonfire

【营建】yíngjiàn 营造；建造 construct；build：～宿舍楼 construct a dormitory building

【营救】yíngjiù 设法援救 rescue；manage to save：～遇险船员 rescue the sailors in danger

【营垒】yínglěi ❶ 军营和四周的围墙 barracks and the enclosing walls ❷ 阵营 camp：革命～ revolutionary camp

【营利】yínglì 谋求利润 seek profits

【营盘】yíngpán 军营的旧称 old term for military camp

【营区】yíngqū 指军队扎营的地区 camping area；location of a military camp

【营生】yíngshēng 谋生活 earn a living；make a living：船户们长年都在水上～。Boat dwellers make a living on water all the year round.

【营生】yíng·sheng〈方 *dial*.〉（～儿 yíng·shengr）职业工作 job；profession：找个～ look for a job｜地里的～他都拿得起来。He has a command of all kinds of farmwork.

【营私】yíngsī 谋求私利 seek private gain；feather one's nest：结党～ gang up for selfish interests｜～舞弊 engage in malpractices for selfish ends；practise graft

【营养】yíngyǎng ❶ 有机体从外界吸取需要的物质来维持生长发育等生命活动的作用 nourish；（of organisms）absorb needed substances from the outside to sustain and promote vital activities for growth ❷ 养分 nutrient content；nutrition：水果富于～。Fruits are nutritious.

【营养素】yíngyǎngsù 食物中具有营养的物质，包括蛋白质、脂肪、糖类、维生素、矿物质、膳食纤维素和水等 nutrient；nutritive substances or ingredients of food，including proteins，fats，sugars，vitamins，mineral matters，dietary fibres，water，etc.

【营养元素】yíngyǎng yuánsù 农作物生长所不可缺少的元素。主要的是氮、磷、钾，此外还有碳、氢、氧、钙、镁、硫、硅、铅、铜、锰、锌、硼、钼等。nutritive elements；elements indispensable for the growth of crops，including mainly nitrogen，phosphorus，potassium，and also carbon，hydrogen，oxygen，calcium，magnesium，sulphur，silicon，lead，copper，manganese，zinc，boron，molybdenum，etc.

【营业】yíngyè（商业、服务业、交通运输业等）经营业务（in commerce，service industries，communications，transportation，etc.）in business：～额 turnover；volume of business｜开始～ start business｜扩充～ expand business

【营业税】yíngyèshuì 国家税收的一种，工商业部门遵照政府规定的分类法，按营业额的大小向政府交纳税款。我国于 1958 年将营业税并入工商统一税。business tax；transactions tax；turnover tax；sales tax；national tax requiring industrial and commercial branches to pay a sum of money to the government according to the state tax system and the volume of their business；China merged its business tax into industrial and commercial consolidated tax in 1958

【营业员】yíngyèyuán 售货员和收购员的统称 shop employees including buyers and shop assistants

【营运】yíngyùn ❶（车船等）营业和运行；运营（of vehicles, ships, etc.）business and operation：这条新船即将投入～。This new ship will soon go into operation. ❷ 经营，一般指经商（多见于早期白话 oft. in early vernacular）do business

【营造】yíngzào ❶ 经营建筑 construct; build：～住宅 build a residential house ❷ 有计划地造（林）plant (trees) according to design：～防护林 plant a windbreak forest ❸ 有目的地造（气氛、环境）deliberately create (an atmosphere or an environment)：～宽松和谐的氛围 create a relaxed and harmonious atmosphere

【营造尺】yíngzàochǐ 清代工部营造所用的尺，合0.32米。为当时的标准长度单位。standard unit of length adopted by the Department of Palace Construction of the Ministry of Public Works during the Qing Dynasty (equal to 0.32m.)

【营寨】yíngzhài〈旧时 *old*〉驻扎军队的地方；军营 military camp; barracks：偷袭～ launch a surprise attack on a military camp

【营帐】yíngzhàng 军队或野外工作者等用的帐篷 tent esp. for military or fieldwork purposes

萦（縈） yíng〈书 *fml.*〉围绕；缠绕 entangle; encompass：琐事～身 be preoccupied with trivialities; get bogged down in petty matters

【萦怀】yínghuái（事情）牵挂在心上（of things）occupy one's mind：离思～ homesickness occupying one's mind｜此事使人梦寐～。This matter has been occupying our minds and dreams.

【萦回】yínghuí 回旋往复；曲折环绕 hover; linger：当年情景，～脑际。The scene of that year still lingers in my mind.｜青山环抱，绿水～（of a place）be skirted by green mountains, with a limpid stream meandering its way across the land

【萦绕】yíngrào same as 萦回 yínghuí：泉石～。Spring waters hover over the rocks.｜云雾～。Clouds and mists hover around.

【萦系】yíngxì 记挂；牵挂 worry：思乡之念～心头。Homesickness worried me.

【萦纡】yíngyū〈书 *fml.*〉旋绕弯曲；萦回 linger; wind around

滢（瀅） yíng 地名用字 *ying*, esp. used in place names：～湾镇（在湖南长沙）Yingwan Town (in Changsha, Hunan Province)｜～溪（在四川南充）Yingxi (in Nanchong, Sichuan Province)

蓥（鎣） yíng 华蓥（Huáyíng），山名，在四川东部和重庆西北部 Huaying, a mountain in Sichuan Province

楹 yíng ❶ 堂屋前部的柱子 columns (or pillars) at the front of the main hall of a building：～联 couplet written on scrolls and hung on the pillars of a hall ❷〈书 *fml.*〉〈量词 *classifier*〉房屋一间为一楹 bay unit of measurement for buildings：园内有小舍三～。There is a three-bay small house in the courtyard.

【楹联】yínglián 挂或贴在楹上的对联。泛指对联。couplet written on scrolls and hung on the pillars of a hall; couplet

滢（瀅） yíng〈书 *fml.*〉清澈 crystal clear; limpid

蝇（蠅） yíng 苍蝇 fly：～拍 fly swatter; fly flap｜～蛹 fly pupa｜灭～ exterminate flies

【蝇甩儿】yíngshuǎir〈方 *dial.*〉拂尘 horsetail whisk

【蝇头】yíngtóu〈比喻 *fig.*〉非常小 very small; tiny：～小楷 small characters the size of a fly's head; very small handwritten characters｜～微利 pittance of profit; petty profit

【蝇营狗苟】yíng yíng gǒu gǒu 像苍蝇那样飞来飞去，像狗那样苟且偷生 fly about like a fly or drag out an ignoble existence like a dog;〈比喻 *fig.*〉人不顾廉耻，到处钻营 shamelessly seek personal gain; also 狗苟蝇营 gǒu gǒu yíng yíng

【蝇子】yíng·zi 苍蝇 fly (*Musca domestica*)

潆（瀠） yíng ☞ below

【潆洄】yínghuí 水流回旋（of current）swirl around

【潆绕】yíngrào 水流环绕（of current）circle：清溪～clear streams circle around

嬴 Yíng 姓 a surname

赢 yíng ❶ 胜（跟'输'相对 as opposed to 'lose'）win：足球比赛结果，甲队～了。Team A won the football game.｜这盘棋他一定～。He'll certainly win this game of chess. ❷ 获利 gain profit：～余 profit

【赢得】yíngdé 博得；取得 win; gain：～时间 win time｜～信任与支持 obtain trust and support｜精彩的表演～全场喝彩。The wonderful performance drew applause from the whole audience.

【赢家】yíng·jiā 指赌博或比赛中获胜的一方 winner; winning party in gambling or a competition

【赢利】yínglì ❶ 企业单位的利润 profits (of enterprises or other units) ❷ 获得利润 earn a profit ‖ also 盈利 yínglì

【赢余】yíngyú same as 盈余 yíngyú

瀛 yíng ❶〈书 *fml.*〉大海 sea; ocean ❷（Yíng）姓 a surname

【瀛海】yínghǎi〈书 *fml.*〉大海 sea; ocean

【瀛寰】yínghuán〈书 *fml.*〉指全世界 the world as a whole

籯(籯) yíng 〈书 *fml*.〉❶ 箱笼一类的器具 bamboo box or chest ❷ 放筷子的笼子 basket for holding chopsticks

yǐng (丨ㄥˇ)

郢 Yǐng 楚国的都城,在今湖北江陵北 capital of the state of Chu of the Warring States Period, north of present-day Jiangling in Hubei Province

颍 Yǐng 颍河,发源于河南,流入安徽 Yinghe River, originating from Henan Province and flowing through Anhui Province

颖 yǐng 〈书 *fml*.〉❶ 某些禾本科植物子实的带芒的外壳 glume; husk with awns on the seed of some graminaceous plants: ～果 caryopsis ❷ 指某些小而细长的东西的尖端 point; tip of sth. small and slender: 短～羊毫(笔) short-tip writing brush made of goat's hair ❸ 聪明 clever: 聪～ clever

【颖果】yǐngguǒ 干果的一种,种皮和果皮合而为一,里面只有一粒种子。禾本科植物的果实都是颖果,如稻、麦的果实。caryopsis; dry one-seeded fruit in which the seed coat and peel fuse in a single grain. The fruit of all graminaceous plants (e. g. rice, wheat) are caryopses.

【颖慧】yǐnghuì 〈书 *fml*.〉聪明(多指少年 oft. of youth) clever; bright; intelligent

【颖悟】yǐngwù 〈书 *fml*.〉聪明(多指少年 oft. of youth) clever; bright

【颖异】yǐngyì 〈书 *fml*.〉❶ 指聪明过人 be extraordinarily clever: 自幼～ be extraordinarily clever since childhood ❷ 新颖奇异 novel; strange: 构思～ novel design

影 yǐng ❶ (～儿 yǐngr) same as 影子 yǐng·zi ①: 树～ shadow of a tree | 阴～ shadow ❷ (～儿 yǐngr) same as 影子 yǐng·zi②: 倒～ inverted image ❸ (～儿 yǐngr) same as 影子 yǐng·zi ③: 人～儿 trace of a person's presence ❹ 照片 picture; photo: 小～ small picture | 合～ group photo ❺ 〈旧时 *old*〉指祖先的画像 figure or portrait of one's ancestor ❻ 指电影 movie; film: ～评 film review | ～院 cinema ❼ 指皮影戏 shadow play: 滦州～ Luanzhou shadow play ❽ 〈方 *dial*.〉隐藏;遮蔽 hide; conceal: 一只野兔～在草丛里。There was a hare hiding in the grass. | 把棍子～在背后 hide a stick behind the back ❾ 描摹 copy; trace: ～宋本 facsimile edition of a Song-dynasty book

【影壁】yǐngbì ❶ 大门内或屏门内做屏蔽的墙壁。也有木制的,下有底座,可以移动,上面像屋脊。screen wall; wall erected behind a gate to block the view; movable wooden screen with a base and a roof-like top ❷ 照壁 screen wall (facing the gate inside or outside a traditional Chinese courtyard) ❸ 指塑有各种形象的墙壁 wall carved with various figures

【影碟】yǐngdié 〈方 *dial*.〉视盘 video disc; VCD

【影格儿】yǐnggér 小孩儿初学毛笔字时放在纸下模仿着写的字样子 copy-slip for tracing over (for children or new learners in brush writing)

【影集】yǐngjí 用来贴照片的本子 photograph (or picture, photo) album

【影剧院】yǐngjùyuàn 供放映电影、演出戏剧、歌舞、曲艺等的场所 theatre; facility for showing films or giving performances of dramas, songs and dances, folk art forms, etc.

【影迷】yǐngmí 喜欢看电影而入迷的人 film (or movie) fan; person enthused about and fascinated with film

【影片儿】yǐngpiānr same as 影片 yǐnpiàn

【影片】yǐngpiàn ❶ 用来放映电影的胶片 cine film; film stock used for projecting film; ☞ 拷贝 kǎobèi on p. 1086 ❷ 放映的电影 film; movie: 故事～ feature film | 科学教育～ scientific and educational film

【影评】yǐngpíng 评论电影的文章 film review; article devoted to commentary on a film

【影射】yǐngshè 借甲指乙;暗指(某人某事) allude; hint obliquely at; innuendo; refer to sb. or sth. indirectly, with the use of sb. or sth. else: 小说的主角～作者的一个同学。The hero of this novel alludes to one of the author's classmates.

【影视】yǐngshì 电影和电视 film and television: ～圈 show business; film and television circles | ～明星 film and TV star

【影戏】yǐngxì ❶ 皮影戏 shadow play; leather-silhouette show ❷ 〈方 *dial*.〉电影 film; movie

【影响】yǐngxiǎng ❶ 对别人的思想或行动起作用(如影之随形,响之应声) influence; affect; produce an impact over other's thinking or actions (from the idiom 'Shadows form after the image and sound echoes the voice.'): 父母应该用自己的模范行为去～孩子。Parents should influence their children by personal example. ❷ 对人或事物所起的作用 effect; influence exerted over sb. or sth.: 他爱好音乐是受了一位老师的～。His love of music resulted from the influence of a teacher. ❸ 传闻的;无根据的 hearsay; groundless: 模糊～之谈 speaking from hearsay

【影像】yǐngxiàng ❶ 肖像;画像 portrait; figure ❷ 形象 image: 他的～时刻在我眼前浮现。His image appears in my mind now and then. ❸ 物体通过光学装置、电子装置等呈现出来的形状 the shape or form of an object presented by an optical or electronic device, etc.

Y

【影星】yǐngxīng 电影明星 film (or movie) star

【影印】yǐngyìn 用照相的方法制版印刷，多用于翻印书籍或图表 photomechanical printing; photo-offset process; plate-making and printing by photomechanical methods, often used for printing books or graphs

【影影绰绰】yǐngyǐngchuòchuò (～的 yǐngyǐngchuòchuò·de)模模糊糊；不真切 vague; dim; indistinct; not real：天刚亮，～地可以看见墙外的槐树梢儿。In the first glimmers of dawn, the tops of the Chinese scholartree loomed outside the wall.

【影院】yǐngyuàn 电影院(多用做电影院的名称 oft. used as part of the name of a cinema) cinema

【影展】yǐngzhǎn ❶ 摄影展览 photo exhibition ❷ 电影展览 film exhibition

【影子】yǐng·zi ❶ 物体挡住光线后，映在地面或其他物体上的形象 shadow：树～ shadow of a tree ❷ 镜中、水面等反映出来的物体的形象 reflection; image of an object reflected in a mirror or a water surface ❸ 模糊的形象 trace; vague impression：那件事我连点儿～也记不得了。I do not even have the vaguest recollection of that matter.

【影子内阁】yǐng·zi nèigé 某些国家的在野党在其议会党团内部按照内阁形式组成的准备上台执政的班子。始于英国。shadow cabinet; group of leaders of a parliamentary opposition who constitute the probable membership of the cabinet if their party assumes power, a political phenomenon that first appeared in Great Britain

瘿 yǐng ❶〈中医 *Chin. med.*〉指生长在脖子上的一种囊状的瘤子，主要指甲状腺肿大等病症 goitre; struma; enlargement of the thyroid gland visible as a swelling of a cystiform tumour at the front of the neck ❷ ☞ 虫瘿 chóngyǐng on p. 270

yìng (丨ㄥˋ)

应(應) yìng ❶ 回答 answer; respond; reply：答～ answer|呼～ echo ❷ 满足要求；允许；接受 comply with; meet the demand; permit; accept：有求必～ grant whatever is requested|～邀 at the invitation of (somebody) ❸ 顺应；适应 suit; respond to：～时 in season|～景 do something for the occasion|得心～手 with facility ❹ 应付 deal with; cope with：～变 deal with a contingency|～急 cope with an emergency|～接不暇 have too many visitors or too much business to deal with

☞ yīng on p. 2297

【应变】[1] yìngbiàn 应付突然发生的情况 cope with an emergency (or contingency)：随机～ act according to circumstances|他的～能力很强。He is very capable in handling emergencies.

【应变】[2] yìngbiàn 物体由于外因(受力、温度变化等)或内在缺陷，它的形状尺寸所发生的相对改变 strain; deformation or change of shape and size of a material body under the action of applied forces, changes in temperature, etc., or some inherent flaws

【应承】yìngchéng 答应(做) agree (to do something); promise; consent：满口～ agree without hesitation to do something|把事情～下来 promise to do something

【应城】Yìngchéng 地名，在湖北 Yingcheng, a place in Hubei Province

【应酬】yìng·chou ❶ 交际往来；以礼相待 have social intercourse with; treat with courtesy：～话 social remarks|不善～ socially inept ❷ 指私人间的宴会 social engagement; person-to-person feast or party：今天晚上有个～。I have been invited to a dinner this evening.

【应从】yìngcóng 答应并顺从 assent to; comply with：他点头～了大家的建议。He nodded his assent to our suggestion.

【应答】yìngdá 回答 reply; answer：～如流 reply readily and fluently

【应敌】yìngdí 应付敌人 deal the enemy：～计划 plan for dealing the enemy|现有兵力不足以～。The available military force is not strong enough to deal with the enemy.

【应典】yìng//diǎn〈方 *dial.*〉指实践自己说的话 carry out one's words; make good one's promise; also 应点 yìng//diǎn

【应对】yìngduì 答对 reply; answer：善于～ be good at repartee|～如流 reply readily and fluently

【应付】yìng·fù ❶ 对人对事采取措施、办法 handle; cope with; adopt measures to deal with sb. or sth.：～局面 deal with a situation|～事变 handle an incident|事情太多，难于～。There are too many things to be dealt with at once. ❷ 敷衍了事 do sth. perfunctorily; gloss over things：～事儿 go through the motions ❸ 将就；凑合 make do：这件衣服今年还可以～过去。I can make do with this dress again this year.

【应和】yìnghé (声音、语言、行动等)相呼应 (of sound, language, action, etc.) echo each other：同声～ echo simultaneously

【应急】yìng//jí 应付迫切的需要 meet an urgent need; handle an emergency：～措施 emergency measure|你先借我点儿钱应应急。Would you please lend me a small sum for an emergency?

【应接不暇】yìngjiē bù xiá《世说新语·言语》：'从山阴道上行，山川自相映发，使人应接不暇。''应接不暇'指一路上风景优美，看不过来。*A New Account of Tales of the World · Diction*：'Walking along the northern side of the mountain, one came upon a rapid succession of peaks and streams which set each other off and was too much for the eye to take in.' 后来也形容来人或事情太多,接待应付不过来 have more (visitors or business) than one can attend to:图书馆挤满了人,有还书的,有借书的,工作人员~。The library was crowded, and the staff were having their hands full handling those who came to return or borrow books.

【应景】yìng//jǐng (~儿 yìng//jǐngr)为了适应当前情况而勉强做某事 do sth. reluctantly for the occasion or situation:他本来不大会喝酒,可是在宴会上也不得不应个景儿。He hardly ever drinks, but at banquets he has to drink a little for the occasion.

【应景】yìngjǐng (~儿 yìngjǐngr)适合当时的节令 seasonable:~果品 seasonable fruits|端午吃粽子是~儿。It is customary to eat *zongzi* during the Dragon Boat Festival.

【应举】yìngjǔ 指参加科举考试,明清两代指参加乡试 attend imperial examinations; provincial civil service examinations during the Ming and Qing dynasties

【应考】yìngkǎo 参加招考的考试 take (or sit for) an entrance examination:踊跃~ sit eagerly for an entrance examination|今年~人数超过往年。More candidates sat for the examination this year than in any of the previous years.

【应力】yìnglì 物体由于外因或内在缺陷而产生形变时,在它内部任一截面单位面积上两方的相互作用力 stress; mutual constraining force or influence from two sides on the surface of any section of an object, deformed due to external forces or internal defects

【应卯】yìng//mǎo〈旧时 *old*〉官厅每天卯时(早晨五点到七点)查点到班人员,点名时到班的人应声叫应卯。现比喻到场应付一下 (at government offices) answer the roll call for the 5 a.m. - 7 a.m. period; (fig.) put in a routine appearance:上班时他应个卯就走了。He usually puts in a routine appearance early during office hours and then leaves.

【应门】yìng//mén 管开关门户 answer the door; take charge of opening and closing the door

【应募】yìngmù 接受招募 respond to a call for recruits; enlist; join up:~从戎 respond to a call and join the army

【应诺】yìngnuò 答应;应承 agree (to do sth.); promise; undertake:连声~ agree coherently|慨然~ promise generously

【应聘】yìngpìn 接受聘请 accept an offer of employment:他~到广州教书。He accepted a teaching post in Guangzhou.

【应山】Yìngshān 地名,在湖北 Yingshan, name of a place in Hubei Province

【应声】yìngshēng 随着声音 happen right at the sound of sth.:~而至 show up as the sound draws near|一枪打去,猛兽~而倒。The fierce beast fell at the report of a shotgun.

☞ yīng//shēng on p.2298

【应声虫】yìngshēngchóng〈比喻 *fig.*〉随声附和的人 yes man; person who agrees with everything that is said to him

【应时】yìngshí ❶ 适合时令的 seasonable; in season:~小菜 seasonable vegetables|~货品 seasonable goods ❷〈方 *dial.*〉符合规定时间 in accordance with a fixed time or schedule:他一连多日没吃过~饭,没睡过安生觉。He has not had meals on schedule or slept restfully for several days in a row. ❸ 立刻;马上 at once; immediately:车子一歪,~他就摔了下来。He fell down immediately after the cart tilted.

【应市】yìngshì (商品)适应市场需要上市出售 (of commodities) go on the market; be offered for sale:新产品即将~。The new product will soon be put on the market.|大批水产品节前~。A large amount of aquatic products will be put on the market before the festival.

【应试】yìngshì 应考 take (or sit for) an entrance examination

【应县】Yìng Xiàn 地名,在山西 Yingxian County in Shanxi Province

【应验】yìngyàn (预言、预感)和后来发生的事实相符 (of predictions or presentiments) come true; be confirmed; be fulfilled; tally with what later actually happens:他的预测果然~了。What he predicted has finally come true.

【应邀】yìngyāo 接受邀请 accept sb.'s invitation; on invitation; at the invitation of sb.:~前往 head for somewhere on invitation

【应用】yìngyòng ❶ 使用 apply; use:~新技术 apply new technology|这种方法~得最为普遍。This is a most widely used method. ❷ 直接用于生活或生产的 applied (in life or production):~文 practical writing|~科学 applied science

【应用科学】yìngyòng kēxué 跟人类生产、生活直接联系的科学,如医学、农学 applied science; science (e.g. medical science, agricultural science, etc.) that has a direct relation to production and the lives of people

【应用卫星】yìngyòng wèixīng 供地面上实际业务应用的人造地球卫星,如气象卫星、通信卫星、导航卫星、侦察卫星、预警卫星等 applied satellite; man-made earth satellite that offers practical application for life on earth, e.g. weather satellite, communications satellite, navigation satellite, reconnaissance satellite, early-warning satellite, etc.

【应用文】yìngyòngwén 指日常生活或工作中经

常应用的文件，如公文、书信、广告、收据等 practical writing, esp. used in daily life or official affairs (e.g. official documents, letters, advertisements, receipts, etc.)

【应援】yìngyuán（军队）接应 (of the military) respond to a call for help; come to sb.'s aid

【应运】yìngyùn 原指应天命（而降生），泛指顺应时机 be born of destiny; conform to one's destiny; (in a broad sense) temporize; comply with the situation or trends: ～而生 rise to the moment; emerge as the times demand

【应战】yìng//zhàn ❶ 跟进攻的敌人作战 engage the enemy: 沉着～ calmly engage the enemy ❷ 接受对方提出的挑战条件 accept (or take up) a challenge: 我坚决～，保证按时完成生产指标。I firmly accepted the challenge and promised to fulfil the production target on schedule.

【应招】yìngzhāo 接受招考、招募等 respond to a call for recruits or candidates

【应诊】yìngzhěn 接受病人，给予治疗 (of a doctor) see patients and offer treatment: ～时间 patient hours; appointment hours | 节假日照常～。Medical care is available as usual during holidays.

【应征】yìngzhēng ❶ 适龄的公民响应征兵号召 (of citizens of the appropriate age) respond to a call and be recruited into the army: ～入伍 be recruited into the army ❷ 泛指响应某种征求 respond to a call for sth.: ～稿件 respond to a call for contributions

【应制】yìngzhì 指奉皇帝的命令而写作诗文 write poems in compliance with an emperor's orders: ～诗 emperor-ordered poem

映 yìng 因光线照射而显出物体的形象 silhouette; reflect; mirror; shine: 反～ reflect | 放～ project | 垂柳倒～在水里。Weeping willows are mirrored in the water.

【映衬】yìngchèn ❶ 映照；衬托 set off: 红墙碧瓦，互相～。The red walls and green tiles set each other off beautifully. ❷ 修辞方式，并列相反的事物，形成鲜明的对比。如'为人民利益而死，就比泰山还重；替法西斯卖力，替剥削人民和压迫人民的人去死，就比鸿毛还轻'. antithesis; rhetorical contrast of opposing things or ideas by means of parallel arrangements of words, clauses, or sentences, e.g. 'Dying for the good of the people is weightier than Mount Taishan, but dying for fascism or those who exploit and oppress the people is lighter than a feather.'

【映带】yìngdài 〈书 *fml.*〉景物相互衬托 (of scenery) enhance each other's beauty; set off each other: 湖光山色，～左右。The shining lake next to the scenic mountain, each enhancing the other's beauty.

【映山红】yìngshānhóng 杜鹃（植物）azalea (bot.)

【映射】yìngshè 照射 shine upon; cast light upon: 阳光～在江面上。The sun shines upon the river.

【映现】yìngxiàn 由光线照射而显现；呈现 appear due to the illumination of rays; show: 轮船驶向海岸，热带岛国的景色～眼前。As the ship approached the coast, the scenery of a tropical island came into view. | 当年的情景再次在脑海中～。The situation of that year once again appeared in my mind.

【映照】yìngzhào 照射 shine upon; cast light upon: 晚霞～ glory of the dusk shines upon (sth.)

硬 yìng ❶ 物体内部的组织紧密，受外力作用后不容易改变形状（跟'软'相对 as opposed to 'soft'）hard; stiff to the touch; (of an object) not easily yielding to the pressure of an external force because of its tight texture: 坚～ hard | ～木 hardwood | ～煤 hard coal ❷（性格）刚强；（意志）坚定；（态度）坚决或执拗 (of character) unyielding; (of will) firm; (of attitude) resolved and obstinate: 强～ strong and tough | ～汉子 strong man | 话说得～ express oneself in strong terms | 不让他去，他～要去。Although he was not allowed, he obstinately wanted to go. ❸ 勉强 be reluctant: ～撑 force oneself to go on doing sth. | 他一发狠，～爬上去了。He made a determined effort and finally climbed up. ❹（能力）强；（质量）好 (of ability) strong; (of quality) good: ～手 skilled (or good) hand | 货色～ goods of high quality | 功夫～ be skilled

【硬邦邦】yìngbāngbāng（～的 yìngbāngbāng·de）形容坚硬结实 very hard; very stiff

【硬棒】yìng·bang 〈方 *dial.*〉硬；结实有力 hard; strong; sturdy: 有了这根～的拐棍儿，上山就得力了。Thanks to this sturdy walking stick, I found it easier to climb the mountain. | 老人的身体还挺～。The old man is still hale and hearty.

【硬包装】yìngbāozhuāng ❶ 用马口铁、玻璃瓶等质地较硬的包装材料密封包装 put a package in hard packaging materials such as a tinplate, glass bottle, etc. ❷ 指用来密封包装商品的质地较硬的材料，如马口铁罐、玻璃瓶等 hard materials (such as a tinplate, glass, etc.) used for packing commodities

【硬笔】yìngbǐ 指笔尖坚硬的笔，如钢笔、圆珠笔等（对笔尖柔软的毛笔而言 in contrast to 'soft brush'）hard-point pen, e.g. pen, ball-point pen, etc.: ～书法 pen calligraphy

【硬币】yìngbì 金属的货币 coin; specie

【硬磁盘】yìngcípán 指固定在电子计算机内的磁盘 hard disc, fixed in an electronic computer; 简称 abbr. 硬盘 yìngpán

【硬度】yìngdù ❶ 固体坚硬的程度，也就是固体对磨损和外力所能引起的形变的抵抗能力的大小 hardness; rigidity; quality or state of being hard, or the capability of a solid to resist abrasion or deformation caused by external forces ❷ 水中含钙盐、镁盐等盐类的多少,叫做水的硬度 hardness of water, determined by the content of salts (e.g. calcium salts, magnesium salts, etc.)

【硬腭】yìng'è 腭的前部,是由骨和肌肉构成的 hard palate; front part of the palate, composed of bones and muscle; (图见☞ figure for 人的喉 rén•dehóu on p. 808)

【硬弓】yìnggōng 拉起来费力大的弓 strong bow

【硬骨头】yìnggǔ•tou 〈比喻 *fig.*〉坚强不屈的人 dauntless, unyielding person

【硬汉】yìnghàn 坚强不屈的男人 dauntless, unyielding man; man of iron; also 硬汉子 yìnghàn•zi

【硬化】yìnghuà ❶ 物体由软变硬 (of objects) harden; become hard: 生橡胶遇冷容易～,遇热容易软化。Raw rubber is apt to harden when subjected to low temperatures and to soften at high temperatures. | 血管～ vascular sclerosis ❷〈比喻 *fig.*〉思想停止发展;僵化 ossify; become rigid or inflexible in thinking, opinions, etc.

【硬件】yìngjiàn ❶ 计算机系统的一个组成部分,是构成计算机的各个元件、部件和装置的统称 computer hardware; component part of a computer system, consisting all the elements, units, and devices of a computer; also 硬设备 yìngshèbèi ❷ 借指生产、科研、经营等过程中的机器设备、物质材料等 mechanical equipment, or materials esp. used in production, scientific research, management, etc.

【硬结】yìngjié ❶ 结成硬块;变硬 indurate; harden ❷ 硬块 scleroma: 外痔在肛门周围结成～。External piles turned into scleromas around the anus.

【硬撅撅】yìngjuējuē 〈方 *dial.*〉(～的 jìngjuējuē•de) ❶ 形容很硬 (含厌恶意 derog.) very stiff; very rigid: 衣服浆得～的,穿着不舒服。Starched clothing is stiff and uncomfortable to wear. ❷ 形容生硬 harsh: 他说话～的,让人接受不了。He spoke in a harsh manner that was hard to accept.

【硬拷贝】yìngkǎobèi 指能够永久保存的信息记录,如电子计算机打印的数据文本 hard copy; readable and preservable record of information produced on paper, e.g. data or document printed from computer storage

【硬朗】yìng•lang ❶ (老人)身体健壮 (of old people) hale and hearty: 大爷身板还挺～。The old man is hale and hearty. ❷ 坚强有力 strong and forceful: 几句话,他说得十分～。He put his few sentences forcefully.

【硬煤】yìngméi 〈方 *dial.*〉无烟煤 hard coal; anthracite

【硬面】yìngmiàn (～儿 yìngmiànr)用少量水和成的面或发酵的面搀入干面和成的面 hard dough; dough as a mixture of lesser water to flour, or a mixture of fermented dough and flour: ～馒头 hard steamed bread

【硬木】yìngmù 坚实细致的木材,多指紫檀、花梨等 hardwood; firm and delicate wood, e.g. padauk wood, rosewood, etc.

【硬盘】yìngpán 硬磁盘的简称 abbr. for 硬磁盘 yìngcípán

【硬碰硬】yìng pèng yìng 硬的东西碰硬的东西 confront the tough with toughness; meet force with force; 〈比喻 *fig.*〉用强硬的态度对付强硬的态度 tit for tat

【硬片】yìngpiàn ☞ 干板 gānbǎn on p. 625

【硬气】yìng•qi 〈方 *dial.*〉❶ 刚强;有骨气 strong-willed; unyielding: 为人～ be strong-willed ❷ 有正当理由,于心无愧(多在用钱、吃饭上说 oft. with regard to spending money or having meals) have no qualms; feel justice is on one's side: 她觉得自己挣的钱用着～。She had no qualms about spending money she had earned herself.

【硬任务】yìngrènwù 在时间、数量、质量等方面有明确要求,不能通融、改变的任务 hard task; non-negotiable, non-alterable task that has definite requirements on time, amount, quality, etc.

【硬是】yìngshì ❶〈方 *dial.*〉实在是;真的是 actually; really ❷ 就是(无论如何也是…) just; simply (at any rate): 他虽然身体不好,可～不肯休息。He is not physically well, but just wouldn't rest.

【硬实】yìng•shi 〈方 *dial.*〉壮实;硬棒 strong; sturdy; robust

【硬手】yìngshǒu (～儿 yìngshǒur)能手;强手 skilled (or good) hand: 这人真是把～儿,干活又快又细致。This man is really a good hand, swift and meticulous in his work.

【硬水】yìngshuǐ 含有较多钙、镁盐类的水,味道不好,并容易形成水垢 hard water; water that does not taste good and is apt to scale due to its high content of calcium and magnesium salts

【硬挺】yìngtǐng 勉强支撑 force oneself to go on doing (sth.); endure with all one's will: 有了病不要～,应该早点儿治。Don't just try to put up with your illness. Go and see a doctor as early as possible.

【硬通货】yìngtōnghuò 在国际上能广泛作为计价、支付、结算手段使用的货币 hard currency; currency used internationally as a means of valuation, payment, and settling accounts

【硬卧】yìngwò 火车上的硬席卧铺 hard berth; hard sleeper (on a train)

【硬武器】yìngwǔqì 指用来直接杀伤敌人或摧毁敌方军事目标的武器,如枪炮、地雷、导弹等 lethal weapons; weapons used to directly kill and wound enemies or destroy enemy military targets

【硬席】yìngxí 火车上设备比较简单的、硬的坐位或铺位 hard seats or berths (on a train)

【硬性】yìngxìng 不能改变的；不能通融的 rigid; stiff; inflexible：～规定 hard and fast rules

【硬仗】yìngzhàng 正面硬拼的战斗；艰苦激烈的战斗 tough (or hard-fought) battle; formidable task：打～ fight a hard battle

【硬着头皮】yìng•zhe tóupí 不得已勉强做某事 force oneself to do sth. against one's own will：这首诗实在难译，他还是～译下去。That poem was really difficult to translate, but he forced himself through it.

【硬挣】yìng•zheng〈方 *dial.*〉❶ 硬而有韧性 hard and tenacious; tough：这种纸很～，可以做包装。This paper is very tough and can be used for packing. ❷ 坚强；强硬有力的 strong; forceful：找个～搭档 look for a strong partner

【硬指标】yìngzhǐbiāo 有明确而严格的要求，不能通融、改变的指标 mandatory quota; inflexible target with strict, definite requirements：每月生产五十台机床，这是必须完成的～。A monthly production of 50 machine tools is a mandatory target that must be accomplished.

【硬着陆】yìngzhuólù 人造卫星、宇宙飞船等不经减速控制而以较高速度降落到地面或其他星体表面上 hard landing; (of man-made satellites, space shuttles, etc.) land on Earth or other planets at a fast speed without any attempt to decelerate

【硬座】yìngzuò 火车上的硬席坐位 hard seat (on a train)

暎 yìng〈书 *fml.*〉same as 映 yìng

媵 yìng〈书 *fml.*〉❶ 陪送出嫁 accompany a bride to her new home ❷ 陪嫁的人 maid accompanying a bride to her new home ❸ 妾 concubine

膺 yìng〈书 *fml.*〉same as 应 yìng
☞ yīng on p. 2300

yō (ㄧㄛ)

育 yō ☞［杭育］hángyō on p. 770
☞ yù on p. 2348

哟 yō〈叹词 *interj.*〉表示轻微的惊异（有时带玩笑的语气）(sometimes with a humorous tone) expressing slight surprise：～，你踩我脚了。Oh! You've stepped on my foot.
☞ •yo on p. 2309

唷 yō ☞ 哼唷 hēngyō on p. 797

•yo (•ㄧㄛ)

哟 •yo〈助词 *aux.*〉❶ 用在句末表示祈使的语气 [used at the end of a sentence to express an imperative tone]：大家一齐用力～！Everybody, let's pool our energy together! ❷ 用在歌词中做衬字 [used as a syllable filler in a song]：呼儿嗨～！Hu-er-hei-yo!
☞ yō on p. 2309

yōng (ㄩㄥ)

佣(傭) yōng ❶ 雇用 hire：雇～ hire|～工 hired labourer ❷ 仆人 servant：女～ maidservant; woman servant
☞ yòng on p. 2314

【佣工】yōnggōng 受雇为人做工的人 hired labourer; servant

拥(擁) yōng ❶ 抱 hold in one's arms; embrace; hug：～抱 embrace ❷ 围着 gather around; wrap around：前呼后～ with a large retinue|一群青年～着一位老师傅走出来。An old master came out surrounded by a group of young people. ❸（人群）挤着走 (of crowd) throng; swarm：一～而入 roll in|大家都～到前边去了。The crowd has swarmed to the front. ❹ 拥护 support：～戴 support|～军优属 support the army and give preferential treatment to families of revolutionary soldiers and martyrs ❺〈书 *fml.*〉拥有 possess; have：～兵百万 possess an army of one million

【拥抱】yōngbào 为表示亲爱而相抱 embrace; hug; hold in one's arms to express affection

【拥戴】yōngdài 拥护推戴 support (sb. as leader)：深受群众～ enjoy great support from the masses

【拥护】yōnghù 对领袖、党派、政策、措施等表示赞成并全力支持 uphold; endorse; agree to and fully support (a leader, party, policy, measure, etc.)

【拥挤】yōngjǐ ❶（人或车船等）挤在一起 (of people, vehicles, ships, etc.) push or squeeze (together)：按次序上车，不要～。Get on the bus in order. Don't push! ❷ 地方相对地小而人或车船等相对地多 (of people, vehicles, ships, etc.) be crowded; be packed：星期天市场里特别～。The market is especially crowded on Sundays.

【拥军优属】yōng jūn yōu shǔ 拥护人民军队，优待革命军人家属 (of civilians) support the army and give preferential treatment to families of revolutionary soldiers and martyrs

【拥塞】yōngsè 拥挤的人马、车辆或船只等把道路或河道堵塞 jam; (of people, vehicles, ships, etc.) congest a road, street, waterway, etc.：城门口～得水泄不通。The entrance to the city gate was so jammed as to be impassable.

【拥有】yōngyǒu 领有；具有（大量的土地、人口、财产等）possess; have; own (a great deal of land, population, property, etc.)：柴达木盆地～二十二万平方公里的面积。The Qaidam Basin covers an area of 220,000 square km.｜我国～巨大的水电资源。China abounds in hydroelectric power resources.

【拥政爱民】yōng zhèng ài mín 军队拥护政府，爱护人民 (of the army) support the government and cherish the people

痈(癰) yōng 皮肤和皮下组织化脓性的炎症，病原体是葡萄球菌，多发生在背部或项部，症状是局部红肿，形成硬块，表面有许多脓泡，有时形成许多小孔，呈筛状，非常疼痛，常引起发烧、寒战等，严重时并发败血症 carbuncle; painful purulent inflammation of the skin and subcutaneous tissues, caused by staphylococcus bacteria, attacking the back or neck, with symptoms of local swelling, solid mass, and multiple sieved-shaped openings for the discharge of pus, prone to cause fever or chills, or to be complicated by blood poisoning when serious

【痈疽】yōngjū 毒疮 ulcer; poisoned sore

邕 Yōng ❶ 邕江，水名，在广西 Yongjiang, name of a river in Guangxi ❷ 广西南宁的别称 another name for 南宁 Nánníng

【邕剧】yōngjù 广西地方戏曲剧种之一，流行于广西说粤语的地区 *yongju* opera; local opera popular in the Cantonese-speaking areas of Guangxi

庸1 yōng ❶ 平凡；平庸 commonplace; mediocre：～言～行（平平常常的言行）commonplace words and deeds ❷ 不高明；没有作为 inferior; not brilliant; unaccomplished：～人（平庸没有作为的人）mediocre person｜～医 quack｜～～碌碌 mediocre and unambitious

庸2 yōng 〈书 *fml.*〉❶ 用（用于否定式 used in the negative）need：无～细述。This needn't be related in detail.｜毋～讳言。There is no need to avoid speaking up. ❷〈疑问词 *interrog.*〉表示反问；岂［used in rhetorical questions］how; in what way：～有济乎？How could this be of any help?｜～可弃乎？How could this possibly be relinquished?

【庸才】yōngcái 〈书 *fml.*〉指能力平常或能力低的人 mediocre person; person of mediocre ability; mediocrity

【庸夫】yōngfū 没有作为的人 mediocre person

【庸碌】yōnglù 形容人平庸没有志气，没有作为 (of a person) mediocre and unambitious：～无能 mediocre and incompetent｜庸庸碌碌，随波逐流 be mediocre and unambitious and go with the crowd

【庸人自扰】yōng rén zì rǎo《新唐书·陆象先传》：'天下本无事，庸人扰之为烦耳。' *New History of Tang*：*Biography of Lu Xiangxian*：'There's nothing troublesome under heaven, but mediocre people bring troubles upon themselves.' 今泛指本来没有问题而自己瞎着急或自找麻烦 worry about nothing; alarm oneself needlessly; be unreasonably worried about sth. although it's not a problem in reality

【庸俗】yōngsú 平庸鄙俗；不高尚 vulgar; crude; of low tastes：～化 vulgarize｜作风～ in vulgar ways｜趣味～ have unrefined tastes

【庸医】yōngyī 医术低劣的医生 quack; poor-skilled doctor

【庸中佼佼】yōng zhōng jiǎojiǎo 指平常人中比较特出的（佼佼 jiǎojiǎo：美好 nice; outstanding) person distinguished from the common run

喁(噰) yōng［喁喁］〈书 *fml.*〉〈拟声词 *onom.*〉形容鸟叫声 singing of birds

鄘 Yōng 周朝国名，在今河南卫辉市 Yong, a state during the Zhou Dynasty in present-day Weihui, a city in Henan Province

雍 yōng ❶〈书 *fml.*〉和谐 harmony ❷ (Yōng) 姓 a surname

【雍容】yōngróng 形容文雅大方，从容不迫 graceful and poised; elegant and in good taste：～华贵 (of a woman) elegant and poised; stately｜态度～ have a dignified bearing

【雍正】Yōngzhèng 清世宗（爱新觉罗胤禛）年号（公元 1723—1735）Yongzheng (1723-1735), title of the reign of Emperor Shizong (Aisin Gioro Yinzhen) of the Qing Dynasty

滽 Yōng 滽水，水名，在江西 Yongshui, a river in Jiangxi Province

墉(墉) yōng〈书 *fml.*〉城墙；高墙 city wall; high wall

慵 yōng〈书 *fml.*〉困倦 weary; lethargic; languid; same as 懒 lǎn②：～困 weary and sleepy

镛 yōng 古乐器，奏乐时表示节拍的大钟 large bell used as an ancient musical instrument to denote rhythms while music was being played

壅 yōng ❶ 堵塞 obstruct; jam：～塞 be congested｜～蔽 hide from view; conceal ❷ 把土或肥料培在植物根上 heap soil or fertilizer over and around the roots of plants and trees：～土 heaped-up soil｜～肥 heap fertilizer around the roots

【壅塞】yōngsè 堵塞不通 be clogged up; be jammed; be congested：泥沙～。The mud and sand blocked up the way.

【壅土】yōngtǔ ❶ 培土 heap soil over and around the roots of plants ❷ 指用机具耙地或播种时土聚集起来妨碍耕作的现象，多由草根或作物根茬阻挡、耙齿过密、土壤较湿等引起 hilling; phenomenon in which the earth piled up during harrowing or sowing obstructs farming, often as a result of a blockage of grass or crop roots, overcrowded harrow points, wet soil, etc.

臃 yōng 〈书 *fml.*〉肿 swelling

【臃肿】yōngzhǒng ❶ 过度肥胖,转动不灵 too overweight to move agilely:身躯~,步子缓慢 be stout in stature and slow in steps ❷〈比喻 *fig.*〉机构庞大,调度不灵 overstaffed; (of an organization) large and cumbersome

雝 yōng same as 雍 yōng

鳙 yōng 鳙鱼,身体暗黑色,鳞细,头大,眼睛靠近头的下部。生活在淡水中,是重要的食用鱼。bighead carp (*Hypopthalmichthys nobilis*); variegated carp; dark black fish with small scales, big head, and eyes close to the lower part of its head, living in fresh water and used for food; also 胖头鱼 pàngtóuyú

饔 yōng〈书 *fml.*〉熟食。有时专指早饭。cooked food, esp. that for breakfast

【饔飧不继】yōng sūn bù jì〈书 *fml.*〉指吃了上顿没有下顿 not know where the next meal will come from (饔飧 *yong sun*:早饭和晚饭 breakfast and supper)

yóng (ㄩㄥˊ)

喁 yóng〈书 *fml.*〉鱼口向上,露出水面 fish sticking its mouth out of the water
☞ yú on p. 2340

【喁喁】yóngyóng〈书 *fml.*〉〈比喻 *fig.*〉众人景仰归向的样子 the way everyone looks up to sb.; ☞ yúyú on p. 2340

颙 yóng〈书 *fml.*〉❶ 大 big; large ❷ 仰慕 look up to; respect; revere:~望 look up to

yǒng (ㄩㄥˇ)

永 yǒng 永远;久远 perpetually; forever; always:~久 forever|~恒 eternal|~世 forever

【永别】yǒngbié 永远分别,多指人死 part never to meet again; part forever; be parted by death

【永垂不朽】yǒng chuí bù xiǔ (姓名、事迹、精神等)永远流传,不磨灭 (memory of sb.'s name, deeds, spirit, etc.) live forever; be immortal:人民英雄~! Eternal glory to the people's heroes! *or* Immortal are the people's heroes! |~的杰作 masterpiece that will last forever

【永存】yǒngcún 永久存在;长存不灭 everlasting; evergreen:友谊~ everlasting friendship|烈士的英名和业绩~。The brilliant names and exploits of the martyrs are everlasting.

【永恒】yǒnghéng 永远不变 eternal; perpetual:~的友谊 eternal friendship

【永嘉】Yǒngjiā 晋怀帝(司马炽)年号(公元307—313) Yongjia (307-313), title of the reign of Emperor Huai (Sima Chi) of the Jin Dynasty

【永久】yǒngjiǔ 永远;长久 abiding; lasting; permanent; perpetual; everlasting; forever; for good (and all)

【永诀】yǒngjué〈书 *fml.*〉same as 永别 yǒngbié:岂料京城一别,竟成~。When we parted in the capital city, I never thought that we were never to meet again in this world.

【永乐】Yǒnglè 明成祖(朱棣)年号(公元1403—1424) Yongle (1403-1424), title of the reign of Emperor Chengzu (Zhu Di) of the Ming Dynasty

【永眠】yǒngmián〈婉辞 *euph.*〉指人死 die; be dead

【永生】yǒngshēng ❶ 原为宗教用语,指人死后灵魂永久不灭,现在一般用做哀悼死者的话 (orig. religions) eternal life; be immortal (usu. used in mourning for the dead); live forever:为争取民族解放而牺牲的烈士们~! Those who died for national liberation shall live forever in our memory. ❷ 终生;一辈子 all one's life; for life:~难忘 never forget for one's life|真善美是他~的追求。The true, the good and the beautiful are what he has pursued for all his life.

【永生永世】yǒngshēng yǒngshì same as 永远 yǒngyuǎn:您的教诲我将~铭记在心。I'll always keep your instructions in my memory.

【永世】yǒngshì 永远,也指终生 forever; for life:~长存 live forever; be everlasting; be immortal|~不忘 will never forget it for the rest of one's life

【永逝】yǒngshì ❶ 永远消逝 pass away; be gone forever:青春~。My youthful days are gone forever|~的韶光 beautiful time that has passed forever ❷ 指人死 die

【永远】yǒngyuǎn〈副词 *adv.*〉表示时间长久,没有终止 always; forever; ever:先烈们的革命精神~值得我们学习。The revolutionary spirit of the martyrs is always something we should learn from.

甬 Yǒng ❶ 甬江,在浙江,流经宁波 Yongjiang, name of a river in Zhejiang Province, which flows through Ningbo ❷ 宁波的别称 another name for 宁波 Níngbō

【甬道】yǒngdào ❶ 大的院落或墓地中间对着厅堂、坟墓等主要建筑物的路,多用砖石砌成 brick-paved path leading to a main hall in a large courtyard, a tomb, etc.; also 甬路 yǒnglù ❷ 走廊;过道 corridor

咏(詠) yǒng ❶ 依着一定腔调缓慢地诵读 recite; chant; intone:歌~ sing and chant|吟~ recite; chant ❷ 用诗词等来叙述 express or narrate in poetic form:~

雪 Ode to Snow|～梅 Ode to the Plum Blossom|～史 singing of historical personages or events

【咏怀】yǒnghuái 抒发情怀抱负 singing from one's heart (literary subgenre); express one's feelings and aspirations in poetic form:～诗 poems of one's heart (in which the poet reveals his innermost feelings); poems expressing one's innermost feelings|借物～ use something to express one's sentiments and aspirations in poetic form

【咏叹】yǒngtàn 歌咏;吟咏 intone; chant; sing:反复～ sing something repeatedly

【咏叹调】yǒngtàndiào 富于抒情的独唱歌曲,用管弦乐器或键盘乐器伴奏,能集中表现人物内心情绪,通常是歌剧、清唱剧和大合唱曲的组成部分 aria; operatic solo; air or melody in an opera, cantata, or oratorio expressing the innermost feelings, especially for solo voice to the accompaniment of wind and string or keyboard instruments

泳 yǒng 游泳 swim:仰～ backstroke|蛙～ breaststroke|自由～ freestyle

【泳程】yǒngchéng 游泳的距离 swimming distance:这次横渡,～五公里。The cross-river swimming covered five km.

【泳道】yǒngdào 游泳池中供游泳比赛的分道,每道宽 2.5 米。分道线由单个白色浮标连接而成,分道线两端各 5 米的浮标为红色。lane (in a swimming race); swimming lane, the separated courses in a swimming pool, each course 2.5 metres wide, the line separating two courses is a string of connected white buoys and the buoys at the two five-metre ends are red.

俑 yǒng 古代殉葬的偶像 wooden or earthen human figure buried with the dead in ancient times; tomb figure; figurine:陶～ pottery figurine|女～ terracotta female figurine

勇 yǒng ❶ 勇敢 brave; valiant; courageous:～武 valiant|奋～ bravely|越战越～ one's courage mounts as the battle progresses|智～双全 with both wisdom and courage ❷ 清朝称战争时期临时招募,不在平时编制之内的兵 temporary recruits in times of war during the Qing Dynasty:散兵游～ stragglers and disbanded soldiers ❸ (Yǒng) 姓 a surname

【勇敢】yǒnggǎn 不怕危险和困难;有胆量 brave; courageous:机智～ resourceful and brave|～作战 courageous and skilful in battle

【勇悍】yǒnghàn 勇猛强悍 brave and fierce

【勇决】yǒngjué 〈书 *fml.*〉勇敢而有决断 brave and resolute

【勇力】yǒnglì 勇气和力量 courage and strength:～过人 exceptional courage and strength

【勇猛】yǒngměng 勇敢有力 bold and powerful; full of valour and vigour:～冲杀 rush ahead and fight fiercely

【勇气】yǒngqì 敢作敢为毫不畏惧的气魄 courage; nerve:鼓起～ pluck up (or muster up) one's courage

【勇士】yǒngshì 有力气有胆量的人 brave and strong man; warrior

【勇往直前】yǒng wǎng zhí qián 勇敢地一直往前进 march forward courageously; advance bravely

【勇武】yǒngwǔ 英勇威武 valiant

【勇于】yǒngyú 在困难面前不退缩;不推诿(后面跟动词)[followed by a verb] be brave in; be bold in; have the courage to:～负责 be brave in shouldering responsibilities|～承认错误 have the courage to admit one's mistakes

埇 yǒng 石埇(Shíyǒng),地名,在广西 Shiyong, name of a place in the Guangxi Zhuang Autonomous Region

涌 yǒng ❶ 水或云气冒出 (of water or clouds) gush; pour; surge:泪如泉～ tears welling up in the eyes and streaming down the cheeks|风起云～ wind rising and clouds gathering ❷ 从水或云气中冒出 rise; spring; well; emerge (from water or clouds):雨过天晴,～出一轮明月。It cleared up after rain, and the bright moon rose from the clouds.◇脸上～出了笑容。A smile rose on his face. ❸ 波峰呈半圆形,波长特别大、波速特别高的海浪 huge, exceptionally long, semicircular, speedy sea wave:一个大～滚过来。A huge sea wave rolled by.
☞ chōng on p.270

【涌流】yǒngliú 急速地流淌 flow rapidly; pour:江水～。The river tumbles on.

【涌现】yǒngxiàn (人或事物)大量出现 (of people or things) emerge in large numbers; spring up; come to the fore:新人新作不断～。New people and new works are emerging in a constant stream.

恿(慂) yǒng ☞ 怂恿 sǒngyǒng on p.1825

湧 yǒng ❶ same as 涌 yǒng ❷ (Yǒng) 姓 a surname

蛹 yǒng 完全变态的昆虫由幼虫变为成虫的过渡形态。幼虫生长到一定时期,就不再吃东西,内部组织和外形发生变化,最后变成蛹,一般为枣核形。蛹在条件适合的情况下变为成虫。pupa; insect in the transitional form of development from larva to adult. After growing to a certain stage, the larva stops feeding, undergoes anatomical changes in its internal tissues and external form, and finally becomes a pupa in the form of a date stone. The pupa then becomes an adult under appropriate conditions.

踊(踴) yǒng 往上跳 leap up; jump up: ～跃 eagerly; vie with each other to do sth.

【踊跃】yǒngyuè ❶ 跳跃 leap; jump: ～欢呼 leap and cheer ❷ 形容情绪热烈,争先恐后 vying with one another; eagerly; enthusiastically: ～参加 be eager to take part | 座谈会上发言非常～。People took the floor one after another at the forum.

鲬 yǒng 鱼的一类,身体长形,扁而平,黄褐色,一般头部扁而宽,有黑褐色斑点,无鳔。生活在海中。flathead (*Platycephalus indicus L.*); sand gurnard; yellowish-brown fish with a long, flat body and a flat, wide head dotted with blackish-brown spots, having no air bladder, living in the sea

yòng (ㄩㄥˋ)

用 yòng ❶ 使用 use; employ; apply: ～具 appliance; utensil; implement | ～力 exert oneself (physically); put forth one's strength | ～兵 use military force; employ military forces; resort to arms | 公～ public use | 大材小～ large material used for insignificant purposes; assign petty jobs to people of great ability | ～笔写字 write with a pen ❷ 费用 expense: ～项 item of expenditure | 家～ family expenses; housekeeping money ❸ 用处 use: 功～ function | 多少总会有点～ be useful more or less; be of some use more or less ❹ 需要 (多用于否定 usu. in the negative) need; have to: 天还很亮,不～开灯。It's still bright enough. There's no need to put on the light. | 东西都准备好了,您不～操心了。Everything is ready. You don't have to worry about it. ❺ 吃、喝 eat; drink (含恭敬意 in polite speech): ～饭 have a meal | 请～茶。Have tea, please. ❻ 〈书 *fml.*〉因此 for this reason; same as 因 yīn ④ (多用于书信 oft. in correspondence): ～特函达。It is for this reason that I'm writing you.

【用兵】yòng//bīng 使用军队作战 use military forces; employ military forces; resort to arms: 善于～ be well-versed in the art of war | ～如神 direct military operations with miraculous skill; be a superb military commander

【用材林】yòngcáilín 人工经营的以培育木材为主要目的的森林 commercial forest; timber forest

【用场】yòngchǎng same as 用途 yòngtú: 派～ put to uses | 有～ be useful

【用处】yòng·chu same as 用途 yòngtú: 水库的～很多。A reservoir has many uses.

【用度】yòngdù 费用(总括各种 of all kinds) expenditure; expense; outlay: 他家人口多,～较大。He has a big family and many expenses.

【用法】yòngfǎ 使用的方法 use; usage: 虚词～ usages of function words | 商品～可看说明书。Read the directions for the use of the commodity.

【用饭】yòng//fàn 〈敬辞 *pol.*〉吃饭 have a meal: 您请～。Please have your meal.

【用费】yòngfèi 某一件事上的费用 expense; cost: 日常～ daily expenses | 一应～由我负担。I'll cover all your expenses.

【用工】yònggōng 指招收工人或使用工人 recruit and use (workers): 改革～制度 reform the system of recruitment

【用工夫】yòng gōng·fu 指练得勤,费的精力多,花的时间多 study or work hard; spend time and energy: 他对太极拳很～。He works very hard at *Taijiquan*. | 他在这门学问上用过不少工夫。He has spent a lot of time and energy on this branch of learning.

【用功】yòng//gōng 努力学习 study hard; hardworking; diligent; studious: 他正在图书馆里～。He is working hard in the library.

【用功】yònggōng 学习努力 diligent; hardworking; studious: 读书很～ be very studious; study very hard

【用户】yònghù 指某些设备、商品的使用者或消费者 user; consumer: 竭诚为～服务。Do our best to provide good service for our customers.

【用劲】yòng//jìn same as 用力 yòng//lì: 一齐～ exert ourselves together; put all our efforts together | 多用一把劲,就多一分成绩。One more effort means one more achievement.

【用具】yòngjù 日常生活、生产等所使用的器具 utensil; apparatus; appliance; gear: 炊事～ kitchen (or cooking) utensils

【用力】yòng//lì 用力气;使劲 exert oneself (physically); put forth one's strength: ～喊叫 shout at the top of one's voice | ～把门推开 push the door open with an effort

【用命】yòngmìng 〈书 *fml.*〉服从命令;效命 obey an order; follow an instruction: 将士～。Officers and men serve wholeheartedly.

【用品】yòngpǐn 应用的物品 articles for use: 生活～ articles for daily use; daily necessities | 办公～ office goods; office articles

【用人】yòng//rén ❶ 选择与使用人员 choose and use personnel: ～不当 not choose the right person for the job | 善于～ know how to choose the right person for the right job; know how to make proper use of personnel; know how to employ people to the best advantage ❷ 需要人手 need hands: 现在正是～的时候。Now is the time when we are in need of personnel.

【用人】yòng·ren 仆人 servant: 女～ maid; woman servant; maidservant

【用舍行藏】yòng shě xíng cáng《论语·述而》:'用之则行,舍之则藏。'被任用就出仕,不被任用就退隐,是儒家对于出处进退的态度。*Analects·Being a Transmitter*:'Try to carry out your propositions when you are employed in the government; stop doing so when you are not thus employed.' Going forward when employed and staying out of sight when set aside is a Confucian attitude towards officialdom. also 用行舍藏 yòng xíng shě cáng

【用事】yòngshì ❶〈书 *fml.*〉当权 be in power:奸臣~ treacherous officials in power ❷(凭感情、意气等)行事 act:意气~ be swayed by one's feelings and act rashly|感情~ act impetuously or impulsively; be swayed by one's emotions in action ❸〈书 *fml.*〉引用典故 make literary allusions; quote literary allusions

【用途】yòngtú 应用的方面或范围(of aspect or range) use; application; purpose:橡胶的~很广。Rubber has many uses.|一套设备,多种~。One set of equipment serves many purposes.

【用武】yòngwǔ 使用武力;用兵 use military force; resort to arms ◇英雄无~之地 have no scope for displaying one's abilities

【用项】yòngxiàng 费用 items of expenditure; expenditures:今年厂里要添不少机器,~自然要增加一些。A lot of machinery will be added in the factory this year, and items of expenditure will naturally be increased.

【用心】yòng//xīn 集中注意力;多用心力 diligently; attentively; with concentrated attention:学习~ concentrate on one's studies; study diligently|~听讲 listen attentively to a lecture

【用心】yòngxīn 居心;存心 motive; intention:~良苦 have really given much thought to the matter; have expended much care and thought on something|险恶~ have vicious intentions; harbour sinister motives|别有~ out of ulterior motives

Y

【用刑】yòng//xíng 动用刑具;施加刑法(xíng·fa) put sb. to torture; torture

【用意】yòngyì 居心;企图 intention; purpose:我说这话的~,只是想劝告他一下。I said all that just to give him some advice.

【用印】yòng//yìn 盖图章(用于庄重的场合 on a solemn occasion) affix an official seal (to a document); seal (a document)

【用语】yòngyǔ ❶措辞 choice of words; wording; diction:~不当 inappropriate choice of words; incorrect wording ❷某一方面专用的词语 phraseology; term:军事~ military terms|外交~ diplomatic terms

佣 yòng same as 佣金 yòngjīn; ☞ yōng on p. 2309

【佣金】yòngjīn 买卖时付给中间人的报酬 commission; brokerage; middleman's fee

【佣钱】yòng·qian same as 佣金 yòngjīn

yōu (丨又)

优[1](優) yōu ❶优良;美好(跟'劣'相对 as opposed to 'inferior') excellent:~美 graceful; elegant; fine; exquisite|~等 top-grade; first-class; top-class; excellent ❷〈书 *fml.*〉充足;富裕 ample; abundant; affluent; plentiful:~渥 liberal; munificent; favourable|~裕 affluent; abundant ❸优待 give preferential (or favoured, special) treatment:拥军~属 support the army and give preferential treatment to army dependents

优[2](優) yōu〈旧时 *old*〉称演戏的人 actor or actress:~伶 actor and actress|名~ famous actor

【优待】yōudài ❶给以好的待遇 give preferential (or favoured, special) treatment:~烈属 give favoured treatment to martyrs' families ❷好的待遇 preferential (or favoured, special) treatment:受到了特别的~ receive preferential treatment

【优等】yōuděng 优良的等级;上等 high-class; first-rate; excellent:~生 top student|成绩~ excellent marks; excellent results

【优点】yōudiǎn 好处;长处(跟'缺点'相对 as opposed to 'demerit') merit; strong (or good) point; advantage; virtue:勇于负责是他的~。One of his merits is to shoulder responsibility without demure.|这个办法有很多~。This method has many advantages.

【优抚】yōufǔ 指对烈属、军属、残废军人等的优待和抚恤 give special care to disabled servicemen, and to family members of revolutionary martyrs and servicemen:做好~工作 do well the job of giving special care to disabled servicemen, and to family members of revolutionary martyrs and servicemen

【优厚】yōuhòu (待遇等)好 (of remuneration, etc.) munificent; liberal; favourable; generous:月薪~ generous monthly pay

【优化】yōuhuà 加以改变或选择使优良 optimize:~组合 optimization grouping or regrouping|~设计 optimize designing|~环境 optimize the environments|~产品结构 optimize the product mix

【优惠】yōuhuì 较一般优厚 preferential; favourable:~条件 favourable terms|~贷款 loan on favourable terms|价格~ preferential price

【优惠待遇】yōuhuì dàiyù 在国际商务关系中,一国对另一国给予比对其他国更优厚的待遇,如放宽进口限额、减免关税等 preferential treatment; favoured treatment; more favourable treatment given by one country to another country than to other countries in international trade relations, e. g. increased import quotas, tariff reduction or exemption

【优良】yōuliáng (品种、质量、成绩、作风等)十分好(of variety, quality, results, style, etc.) fine; good:～的传统 fine tradition

【优伶】yōulíng〈旧时 *old*〉称戏曲演员 theatrical actor or actress

【优美】yōuměi 美好 graceful; fine; exquisite:风景～ fine scenery|姿态～ graceful postures|～的民间艺术 exquisite folk arts

【优容】yōuróng〈书 *fml.*〉宽待;宽容 treat with leniency

【优柔】yōuróu ❶〈书 *fml.*〉宽舒;从容 leisurely; unhurried:～不迫 in a leisurely and unhurried manner ❷〈书 *fml.*〉平和;柔和 gentle; amiable ❸ 犹豫不决 weak in character; hesitant:～的性格 irresolute character|～寡断 irresolute and hesitant; indecisive

【优柔寡断】yōuróu guǎ duàn 办事迟疑,没有决断 irresolute and hesitant; indecisive

【优生】yōushēng 生育素质优良的孩子 give birth to healthy babies:提倡少生、～,控制人口数量,提高人口素质 encourage fewer but healthier births, control the population and improve population quality

【优生学】yōushēngxué 生物学的一个分支,研究如何改进人类的遗传性 eugenics; branch of biology dealing with the improvement of the hereditary factors of human beings

【优胜】yōushèng 成绩优异,胜过别人 winning; superior:他在这次比赛中获得～奖。He won an award for excellence in this match.

【优势】yōushì 能压倒对方的有利形势 superiority; preponderance; dominant position:集中～兵力 concentrate the superior forces|上半场的比赛主队占～。The host team played better in the first half of the match.

【优渥】yōuwò〈书 *fml.*〉same as 优厚 yōuhòu

【优先】yōuxiān 在待遇上占先 have priority; take precedence (in treatment):～权 priority; preference|～录取 priority in getting admitted

【优秀】yōuxiù (品行、学问、成绩等)非常好 (of conduct, character, learning, results, etc.) outstanding; excellent; splendid; fine:～作品 (literary or artistic) works of excellence|成绩～ get excellent results or marks

【优选】yōuxuǎn 选择出好的 select the best:对各种方案进行～,确定出最佳方案 decide on the best of all programmes available through optimization

【优选法】yōuxuǎnfǎ 对生产和科学试验中提出的问题,根据数学原理,通过尽可能少的试验次数,迅速求得最佳方案的方法 optimum seeking method; optimization; method of seeking the optimum answer or answers to the questions raised in production and scientific tests through the minimum number of tests in accordance with the principles of mathematics

【优雅】yōuyǎ ❶ 优美雅致 graceful; exquisite; elegant; in good taste:唱词～ elegant lyrics|演奏合拍,～动听。The playing was harmonious, beautiful and pleasant to the ear.|～宽敞的大厅 elegantly furnished and spacious hall ❷ 优美高雅 beautiful and elegant:～的姿态 graceful postures|举止～ elegant manners; graceful manners

【优异】yōuyì 特别好 excellent; outstanding; exceedingly good:成绩～ brilliant results

【优游】yōuyóu〈书 *fml.*〉❶ 生活悠闲 leisurely and carefree:～岁月 spend one's days in carefree leisure|～自得 leisurely and carefree ❷ 悠闲游乐 have leisurely fun; amuse oneself in a leisurely way:～林下 enjoy oneself in the woods in a leisurely manner

【优育】yōuyù 以优良条件抚育婴幼儿 provide children with the best possible health care and education:优生～ give birth to healthy babies and provide them with the best possible health care and education

【优裕】yōuyù 富裕;充足 affluent; abundant:生活～ be well-off; be well-to-do; live in affluence

【优遇】yōuyù same as 优待 yōudài:格外～ accord exceptionally good treatment|以示～ so as to show our preferential treatment (of sb.)

【优越】yōuyuè 优胜;优良 superior, advantageous:～的条件 favourable conditions|地理位置十分～。The geographic position is very advantageous.

【优越感】yōuyuègǎn 自以为比别人优越的意识 sense of superiority; superiority complex

【优质】yōuzhì 质量优良 high (or top) quality; high grade:～皮鞋 high-quality leather shoes

攸 yōu〈书 *fml.*〉所 used like the particle 所 in certain phrases:责有～归 responsibility should lie where it belongs|利害～关 affect one's interests

忧(憂) yōu ❶ 忧愁 worry about; be worried:～闷 feel depressed; dejected; feel low|～伤 distressed; upset ❷ 使人忧愁的事 sorrow; anxiety; concern; care:～患 suffering; misery; hardship|高枕无～ sleep sound with no worries ❸ 担心;忧虑 worry; be concerned with:杞人～天 haunted by imaginary fears|～国～民 be concerned about one's country and one's people ❹〈书 *fml.*〉指父母的丧事 funeral services of one's parents:丁～ afflicted with the misfortune that one's parents has passed away

【忧愁】yōuchóu 因遭遇困难或不如意的事而苦闷 worried; troubled, depressed

【忧烦】yōufán 忧愁烦恼 worried; vexed; dejected

【忧愤】yōufèn 忧闷愤慨 worried and indignant:～而死 die of worry and indignation

【忧患】yōuhuàn 困苦患难 suffering; misery; hardship:饱经～ have gone through a good deal of misery and hardships

【忧惧】yōujù 忧虑害怕 worried and apprehensive:～不安 worried and disturbed

【忧虑】yōulǜ 忧愁担心 be worried; be anxious; be concerned:病情令人～。The patient's condition is worrisome.

【忧闷】yōumèn 忧愁烦闷 depressed; feeling low; weighed down with cares:心中～ feel depressed

【忧戚】yōuqī〈书 *fml.*〉same as 忧伤 yōushāng

【忧伤】yōushāng 忧愁悲伤 distressed; weighed down with sorrow; laden with grief:神情～ look distressed or dejected|极度的～摧残了他的健康。Extreme distress has impaired his health.

【忧心】yōuxīn ❶ 忧愁;忧虑 anxiety; worry:大家都替他的身体～。We are all worried about his health. ❷〈书 *fml.*〉忧愁的心情 troubled heart:～忡忡 heavy-hearted; care-laden; weighed down with anxieties

【忧心如焚】yōu xīn rú fén 忧愁得心里像火烧火燎一样 burning with anxiety; extremely worried

【忧悒】yōuyì〈书 *fml.*〉忧愁不安 anxious and restless

【忧郁】yōuyù 忧伤,愁闷 melancholy; heavy-hearted; dejected:神情～ look dejected

呦 yōu〈叹词 *interj.*〉表示惊异 expressing surprise:～!怎么你也来了? Hey! How come you are here? *or* Fancy seeing you here.

【呦呦】yōuyōu〈书 *fml.*〉鹿鸣声 cry of a deer

幽[1] yōu ❶ 深远;僻静;昏暗 deep and remote; secluded; dim:～静 quiet; still|～谷 deep and secluded valley ❷ 隐蔽的;不公开的 secret; hidden:～居 live secluded|～会 (lovers) tryst ❸ 沉静 quiet; tranquil; serene:～思 muse; ponder; meditate ❹ 囚禁 imprison:～囚 put under house arrest; imprison|～禁 put under house arrest; imprison ❺ 阴间 nether world:～灵 hobgoblin; ghost; spirit; spectre

幽[2] Yōu ❶ 古州名,大致在今河北北部和辽宁南部 name of an ancient prefecture, roughly comprising the north of present-day Hebei Province and the south of present-day Liaoning Province ❷ 姓 a surname

【幽暗】yōu'àn 昏暗 dim; dark; gloomy:光线～ dim light|～的角落 dark corner

【幽闭】yōubì ❶ same as 幽禁 yōujìn ❷ 深居家中不能外出或不愿外出 confine oneself indoors

【幽愤】yōufèn 郁结在心里的怨愤 hidden resentment

【幽谷】yōugǔ 幽深的山谷 deep and secluded valley:密林～ dense forest and deep valley

【幽会】yōuhuì 相爱的男女秘密相会 secret meeting of lovers; lovers' rendezvous; tryst

【幽魂】yōuhún 人死后的灵魂(迷信 superstition) soul of a deceased; ghost; spectre; spirit; hobgoblin

【幽寂】yōujì 幽静;寂寞 secluded and lonely:～的生活 secluded and lonely life

【幽禁】yōujìn 软禁;囚禁 put under house arrest; imprison

【幽静】yōujìng 幽雅寂静 quiet and secluded; peaceful:～的环境 quiet and peaceful surroundings|树影婆娑,夜色分外～。With the shadows of the trees dancing, it is a particularly quiet and peaceful night.

【幽灵】yōulíng same as 幽魂 yōuhún

【幽美】yōuměi 幽静美丽;幽雅 secluded and beautiful:景色～ secluded and beautiful sights|～的庭院 secluded and beautiful courtyard

【幽门】yōumén 胃与十二指肠相连的部分,是胃下端的口儿,胃中的食物通过幽门进入十二指肠 pylorus; part connecting the stomach and duodenum, the opening at the lower end of the stomach, through which the food in the stomach passes into the duodenum;(图见☞ figure for 消化系统 xiāohuà xìtǒng on p.2100)

【幽眇】yōumiǎo〈书 *fml.*〉精微 profound and subtle:义趣～ profound implication; profound significance

【幽明】yōumíng〈书 *fml.*〉阴间和阳间 nether world and this world:～永隔。The dead and the living are separated forever.

【幽冥】yōumíng ❶ same as 幽暗 yōu'àn ❷ 指阴间 nether world

【幽默】yōumò 有趣或可笑而意味深长 humour:言词～ humourous words|～画 humourous painting

【幽期】yōuqī same as 幽会 yōuhuì

【幽情】yōuqíng 深远的感情 exquisite feelings:发思古之～ muse over things of the remote past

【幽囚】yōuqiú 囚禁 imprison; put in jail; keep in captivity

【幽趣】yōuqù 幽雅的趣味 delightful serenity of seclusion

【幽深】yōushēn (山水、树林、宫室等)深而幽静 (of mountains, rivers, forests, palaces, etc.) deep and serene; deep and quiet:～的峡谷 deep gorge|山林～ deep mountain forests

【幽思】yōusī ❶ 沉静地深思 ponder; muse; meditate ❷ 隐藏在内心的思想感情 deep contemplation; melancholy brooding; hidden sentiments

【幽邃】yōusuì〈书 *fml.*〉same as 幽深 yōushēn

【幽婉】yōuwǎn（文学作品、声音、语调等）含意深而曲折（of literary works, voices, intonation, etc.）subtle and delicate; exquisite:～的诗篇 exquisite poems|～的歌声 exquisite singing; also 幽宛 yōuwǎn

【幽微】yōuwēi ❶（声音、气味等）微弱（of sound, smell, etc.）faint; weak:～的呼唤 faint shout|～的花香 faint flower fragrance ❷〈书 *fml.*〉深奥精微 profound and exquisite:涵义～ profound meaning

【幽闲】yōuxián ❶ same as 幽娴 yōuxián ❷ same as 悠闲 yōuxián

【幽娴】yōuxián（女子）安详文雅（of a woman）gentle and serene:气度～ serene-looking

【幽香】yōuxiāng 清淡的香气 delicate (or faint) fragrance:～四溢 give out a delicate fragrance; delicate fragrance permeate the air

【幽敻】yōuxiòng〈书 *fml.*〉深远 profound

【幽雅】yōuyǎ 幽静而雅致（of a place）quiet and tastefully laid out; elegant:景致～ quiet and elegant scenery|环境～ fine surroundings

【幽咽】yōuyè〈书〉❶ 形容低微的哭声 whimpering; sobbing ❷ 形容低微的流水声 babbling; murmuring:泉水～ murmuring spring

【幽忧】yōuyōu〈书 *fml.*〉忧伤 distressed; weighed down with sorrow; laden with grief

【幽幽】yōuyōu ❶ 形容声音、光线等微弱（of sound or light）faint:～啜泣 sob quietly|～的路灯 dim street lamps ❷〈书 *fml.*〉深远 looming in the distance:～南山。The southern mountain looms indistinctly in the distance.

【幽远】yōuyuǎn same as 幽深 yōushēn:意境～ of profound implications|～的夜空 quiet and remote night sky

【幽怨】yōuyuàn 隐藏在内心的怨恨（多指女子的与爱情有关的 oft. of a young woman thwarted in love）hidden bitterness:深闺～ sorrow of a woman in the depth of her boudoir

悠[1] yōu ❶ 久;远 long-drawn-out; remote in time or space:～久 long; long-standing; age-old|～扬 rising and falling; melodious; mellifluous ❷ 闲适;闲散 leisurely:～闲 leisurely and carefree|～然 carefree and leisurely

悠[2] yōu 悠荡 swing; sway:站在秋千上来回～ standing on the swing and swaying back and forth|他抓住杠子,一～就上去了。He held on to the bar and swung up into the air.

【悠长】yōucháng 长;漫长 long; long-drawn-out:～的岁月 long years|～的汽笛声 drawn-out sound of a siren

【悠荡】yōudàng 悬在空中摆动 swing (to and fro); sway (back and forth):坐在秋千上来回～ swaying back and forth on the swing

【悠忽】yōuhū〈书 *fml.*〉形容悠闲懒散 lazy and idle

【悠久】yōujiǔ 年代久远 time-honoured; long; long-standing; age-old:历史～ have a long history|～的文化传统 age-old cultural tradition

【悠谬】yōumiù〈书 *fml.*〉荒诞无稽 fantastic, absurd; incredible; also 悠缪 yōumiù

【悠然】yōurán 悠闲的样子 carefree and leisurely:～自得 be carefree and content|～神往 turn one's thoughts to things remote

【悠闲】yōuxián 闲适自得 leisurely and carefree:态度～ leisurely and carefree|他退休后过着～的生活。He lives a leisure life after retirement.

【悠扬】yōuyáng 形容声音时高时低而和谐（of sound）rising and falling; melodious; mellifluous:～的歌声 melodious singing

【悠悠】yōuyōu ❶ 长久;遥远 long; long-drawn-out; remote:～长夜。It seemed a long, dragging night. *or* The night seemed to drag.|～岁月 long years|～山川。Oh, this vast, everlasting land! ❷〈书 *fml.*〉众多 a multitude of; a great number of; myriad:～万事 a myriad of events ❸ 形容从容不迫 leisurely; unhurriedly:～自得 carefree and content ❹〈书 *fml.*〉荒谬 absurd; preposterous:～之谈 preposterous statement|～之论 absurd argument

【悠游】yōuyóu ❶ 从容移动 move about unhurriedly:小艇在荡漾的春波中～。The small boat was sailing leisurely on the rippling lake in spring. ❷ same as 悠闲 yōuxián:～自在 leisurely and carefree|～从容的态度 in a leisurely and unhurried manner

【悠远】yōuyuǎn ❶ 离现在时间长 long time ago; long ago; distant:～的童年 childhood of the long past ❷ 距离远 far off (or away), remote; distant:山川～ mountains and rivers far, far away

【悠着】yōu·zhe〈方 *dial.*〉控制着不使过度 take things easy:～点劲儿,别太猛了。Easy! Don't go at it so hard.

麀 yōu 古书上指母鹿 doe described in ancient books

鄾 Yōu 周朝国名,在今湖北襄樊北 You, name of a state in the Zhou Dynasty, north of present-day Xiangfan, Hubei Province

耰 yōu ❶ 古代的一种农具,弄碎土块,平整田地用 *you*, rake-like ancient farm implement, used for breaking earth lumps and levelling the fields ❷ 播种后用耰翻土、盖土 turn up the soil with a rake and cover the seeds with soil after sowing

yóu（丨ㄡˊ）

尤[1]（尢）yóu ❶ 特异的;突出的 outstanding; remarkable; conspicuous:择

～ pick out the best | 拔其～ select and promote those of outstanding ability | 无耻之～ extremely shameless; shameless in the extreme ❷ 更;尤其 particularly; especially: ～甚 more so; especially | ～妙 particularly wonderful | 此地盛产水果,～以梨桃著称。The place abounds with fruit, especially pears and peaches. ❸ (Yóu) 姓 a surname

尤[2]**(尢)** yóu ❶ 过失 fault; mistake: 效～(模仿别人做坏事) follow the example of a wrongdoer ❷ 怨恨;归咎 have a grudge against; blame: 怨天～人 blame everyone and everything but oneself

【尤其】yóuqí 〈副词 *adv*.〉表示更进一步 especially; particularly: 我喜欢图画,～喜欢国画。I love paintings, especially traditional Chinese painting.

【尤为】yóuwéi 〈副词 *adv*.〉用在双音节的形容词或动词前,表示在全体中或跟其他事物比较时特别突出 used before a disyllabic adjective or verb to indicate sth. is particularly outstanding in the whole or in comparison with other things: ～奇妙 particularly marvellous | ～惊慌 particularly panic-stricken | ～不满 particularly dissatisfied

【尤物】yóuwù 〈书 *fml*.〉指优异的人或物品(多指美女 oft. applied to a beauty) rare thing; extraordinary person; woman of great beauty

【尤异】yóuyì 〈书 *fml*.〉优异;优秀 excellent; outstanding: 政绩～ outstanding achievements in performing one's official duties

由 yóu ❶ 原由 cause; reason: 因～ because; as | 事～ cause of a matter; origin of a matter | 理～ reason; ground ❷ 由于 because of; due to; owing to: 咎～自取 trouble of one's own making; have only oneself to blame ❸ 经过 pass through; go by way of: 必～之路 the only way; road one must follow ❹ 顺随;听从 be up to somebody; rest with sb.: 事不～己。Things are beyond one's control. *or* Things are getting out of hand. | ～着性子 do as one pleases ❺ 〈介词 *prep*.〉(某事)归(某人去做) (done) by sb.: 准备工作～我负责。I'll be responsible for the preparatory work. | 队长～你担任。You'll be the team captain. ❻ 〈介词 *prep*.〉表示凭借 because of; due to: ～此可知 know from this; thus it can be seen; this shows; that proves | 人体是～各种细胞组织成的。The human body is composed of various kinds of cells. ❼ 〈介词 *prep*.〉表示起点 starting point: ～表及里 from the outside to the inside; from the surface to the centre | ～北京出发 set off from Beijing ❽ (Yóu) 姓 a surname

【由不得】yóu·bu·de ❶ 不能依从;不能由…做主 not be up to sb. to decide; be beyond the control of: 这件事～你。It's not up to you. ❷ 不由自主地 cannot help: 相声的特点就是叫人～发笑。The characteristic of cross talk is such that you could not help laughing.

【由打】yóudǎ 〈方 *dial*.〉❶ 自从;从 since; from: ～入冬以来,这里没下过雪。It has never snowed since winter began. | ～家乡来 come from one's home village ❷ 经由 passing by: 黄河水～这儿往北,再向东入海。The Yellow River bends from here to the north, then turns to the east, and finally empties itself into the sea.

【由得】yóu·de 能依从;能由…做主;允许 be up to; allow; permit: 辛辛苦苦种出来的粮食,～你作践糟蹋吗! How could you be allowed to waste the grain produced by toil and sweat?

【由来】yóulái ❶ 从发生到现在 up to now; so far: ～已久 long-standing; time-honoured ❷ 事物发生的原因;来源 origin; source: 查清这次火警的～ find out the origin of the fire alarm

【由头】yóu·tou (～儿 yóu·tour) 可作为借口的事 pretext: 找～ find a pretext

【由于】yóuyú 表示原因或理由 owing to; thanks to; as a result of; due to; in virtue of: ～老师傅的耐心教导,他很快就掌握了这一门技术。Thanks to patient teaching on the part of the veteran masters, he learnt the skill very quickly.

【由衷】yóuzhōng 出于本心 from the bottom of one's heart; sincere; heartfelt: ～之言 words from the bottom of one's heart; sincere words | 言不～ insincere words | 表示～的感激 extend one's heartfelt thanks

邮(郵) yóu ❶ 邮寄;邮汇 post; mail: ～封信 post (or mail) a letter | 上月给家里～去五十元。I remitted home fifty yuan by mail last month. ❷ 有关邮务的 postal; mail: ～电 post and telecommunications | ～局 post office | ～票 stamp ❸ 指邮票 stamps: 集～ collect stamps; go in for philately | ～展 philatelic exhibition

【邮包】yóubāo (～儿 yóubāor) 由邮局寄递的包裹 postal parcel; parcel

【邮编】yóubiān 邮政编码的简称 abbr. for 邮政编码 yóuzhèng biānmǎ

【邮差】yóuchāi 邮递员的旧称 postman; old term of address for a postman

【邮船】yóuchuán 海洋上定线、定期航行的大型客运轮船。因过去水运邮件总是委托这种大型快速客轮运载,故名。ocean liner; liner; packet ship; large ocean-going passenger ship that travels a regular route at regular interval. The mail carried by water was usually entrusted to this kind of large, fast passenger boat, hence the name.

【邮戳】yóuchuō (～儿 yóuchuōr) 邮局盖在邮件上,注销邮票并标明收发日期的戳子 postmark; post-office mark stamped on a piece of mail, nullifying the postage stamp and recording the dates of sending and receiving

【邮袋】yóudài 邮政部门用来装邮件的袋子,多用帆布做成 mailbag; postbag; (mail) pouch; bag made of canvas for holding mail

【邮递】yóudì 由邮局递送(包裹、信件等) send by post (or mail); postal (or mail) delivery

【邮递员】yóudìyuán 投递员 postman; mailman

【邮电】yóudiàn 邮政、电信的合称 post and telecommunications

【邮电局】yóudiànjú 办理邮政和电信业务的机构 post and telecommunications office

【邮费】yóufèi same as 邮资 yóuzī

【邮购】yóugòu 通过邮递购买(售货部门接到汇款后把货物寄给购货人) mail-order; purchase by mail (a selling department mail the goods to the purchaser after receiving the remittance

【邮花】yóuhuā〈方 *dial.*〉same as 邮票 yóupiào

【邮汇】yóuhuì 通过邮局汇款 remit money by post

【邮集】yóují 收集、保存邮票的册子 stamp album:精美~ exquisite stamp album

【邮寄】yóujì 通过邮局寄递 send by post; post

【邮件】yóujiàn 由邮局接收、运送、投递的信件、包裹等的统称 postal matter; post; mail

【邮局】yóujú 办理邮政业务的机构 post office

【邮轮】yóulún same as 邮船 yóuchuán

【邮票】yóupiào 邮局发卖的、用来贴在邮件上表明已付邮资的凭证 postage stamp; stamp

【邮亭】yóutíng 邮局在街道、广场等处设立的收寄邮件的处所。多是木头建造的小屋,有的像亭子。postal kiosk; small house set up by a post office at a street or square for posting letters, usu. built of wood, some in the shape of a pavilion

【邮筒】yóutǒng 信筒 pillar box; postbox; mailbox

【邮箱】yóuxiāng same as 信箱 xìnxiāng ①

【邮展】yóuzhǎn 集邮展览 philatelic exhibition:国际~ international philatelic exhibition

【邮政】yóuzhèng 邮电业务的一大部门,主要业务是寄递信件和包裹,办理汇兑,发行报刊等 postal service, whose chief business is to mail or deliver letters and parcels, handle remittances and distribute newspapers and magazines

【邮政编码】yóuzhèng biānmǎ 邮政部门为了分拣、投递方便、迅速,按地区编成的号码。我国邮政编码采用六位数。(Brit.) postcode; (Amer.) zip code; zip; (China) postal code, in six digits and used for easy sorting and delivery

【邮政局】yóuzhèngjú same as 邮局 yóujú

【邮资】yóuzī 邮局按照规定数额向寄邮件的人所收的费用 postage; official amount charged for a letter or package

犹(猶) yóu〈书 *fml.*〉❶ 如同 just as; like:虽死~生 still live in the hearts of the people though dead | 过~不及 going too far is as bad as not going far enough ❷ 还;尚且 still:记忆~新 remain fresh in one's memory | 困兽~斗 cornered beast would still fight

【犹大】Yóudà 据基督教《新约·马太福音》的传说,是受了三十块银币出卖自己老师耶稣的叛徒,一般用做叛徒的同义语 Judas; synonym for traitor or betrayer; *New Testament · the Gospel According to Matthew*: Judas Iscariot, the disciple who betrayed Jesus for thirty silver dollars [希腊 Greek: Ioudas]

【犹然】yóurán 仍然;照旧 still; just as before:虽然时隔多年,那事他~记得很清楚。After so many years, he still remembers it clearly. | 大家都离去了,只有她~坐在那里不走。Everyone has left, but she still sat there alone.

【犹如】yóurú 如同 just as; like; as if:灯烛辉煌,~白昼。The place was lit up as bright as day.

【犹太教】Yóutàijiào 主要在犹太人中间流行的宗教,奉耶和华为唯一的神,基督教的《旧约》原是它的经典 Judaism; religion popular among Jews who regard Jehovah as God, and *The Old Testament* as its classic

【犹太人】Yóutàirén 古代聚居在巴勒斯坦的居民,曾建立以色列和犹太王国,后来为罗马所灭,人口全部向外迁徙,散居在欧洲、美洲、西亚和北非等地。1948 年,有一部分犹太人在地中海东南岸(巴勒斯坦部分地区)建立了以色列国。Jews; residents who lived in Palestine in ancient times and founded the Kingdom of Israel and Judah. It was later wiped out by Rome and the whole population migrated outside and settled in Europe, America, West Asia, and North Africa. Some of them established the state of Israel on the southeastern bank of the Mediterranean (part of Palestine) in 1948. [犹太,希伯来 in Hebrew, Judah is spelled as Yěhūdhi]

【犹疑】yóu·yi same as 犹豫 yóuyù

【犹豫】yóuyù 拿不定主意 hesitate; be irresolute:~不定 hesitate; remain undecided | 犹犹豫豫 hesitate

【犹之乎】yóuzhīhū〈书 *fml.*〉如同 just as:人离不开土地,~鱼离不开水。Man cannot leave the soil just as fish cannot leave the water.

【犹自】yóuzì 尚且;仍然 still:现在提起那件事,~叫人心惊肉跳。Even to this day, I still shudder at the very mention of it.

油 yóu ❶ 动植物体内所含的液态脂肪或矿产的碳氢化合物的混合液体。通常把固态的动物脂肪也叫油。oil; fat; grease; petroleum; liquid fat contained in animals and plants, or mixed mineral liquids of hydrocarbon compounds. Usually, animal fat in the solid state is also called 油 yóu. ❷ 用桐油、油漆等涂抹 apply tung oil, varnish, or paint to:～窗户 paint the windows|这扇门去年～过一次。This door was painted last year. ❸ 被油弄脏 be stained or smeared with oil or grease:衣服～了。The coat is smeared with oil. ❹ 油滑 oily; glib:～腔滑调 glib; oily|这个人～得很。That chap is much too slippery (or tricky).

【油泵】yóubèng 用来抽油或压油的泵,多用于油类的输送以及在润滑和传动系统的管道中产生压力 oil pump; pump used to draw or press oil, usu. used to produce pressure in the conveyance of oils and the pipes of the lubricating and driving systems

【油饼】[1] yóubǐng 油料作物的种子榨油后饼状的渣滓,如豆饼、花生饼等,多用做饲料和肥料 oil cake; dregs of crushed soya bean, peanut, etc. from which oil has been extracted, used as animal feed or fertilizer; also 枯饼 kūbǐng or 油枯 yóukū

【油饼】[2] yóubǐng (～儿 yóubǐngr)油炸的一种面食,扁而圆,多用做早点 deep-fried dough cake; round and flat, used usu. for breakfast

【油驳】yóubó 运输散装油类的驳船 oil barge; barge for holding and transporting oil in bulk

【油布】yóubù 涂上桐油的布,用来防水防湿 oilcloth; oilskin; tarpaulin, used for preventing water and moisture

【油彩】yóucǎi 舞台化装用的含有油质的颜料 greasepaint, used by actors and actresses

【油菜】yóucài ❶ 一年生或二年生草本植物,茎直立,绿色或紫色,叶子互生,下部的叶有柄,边缘有缺刻,上部的叶长圆形或披针形。总状花序,花黄色,果实为角果,种子可以榨油,是我国重要油料作物之一。rape (*Brassica napus*); annual or biennial herbal plant with a straight, green or purple stem, alternate leaves, the incised leaves under having stems and leaves above being ovate or lanceolate, yellow flowers in racemes, and two-carpel pods, its seeds used for extracting oil. Rape is one of the major oil-bearing crops in China. also 芸薹 yútái ❷ 二年生草本植物,略像白菜,叶子浓绿色,叶柄淡绿色,是普通蔬菜 green rape (*Brassica chinensis*); biennial herbal plant slightly like the Chinese cabbage, with dark green leaves, light green stem, used as a common vegetable

【油层】yóucéng 积聚着石油的地层 oil-bearing formation; oil reservoir; oil layer

【油茶】[1] yóuchá 常绿灌木,叶子互生,椭圆形,花白色,果实内有黑褐色的种子。种子榨的油叫茶油。油茶是我国的特产,湖南、江西、福建等省种植最多。tea-oil tree (*Camellia oleifera*); oil-tea camellia; evergreen shrub with alternate, obovate leaves, white flowers and dark brown seeds in fruits. The oil extracted from the seeds is called tea oil. Tea-oil tree is a special product in China, and grown mostly in Hunan, Jiangxi and Fujian provinces.

【油茶】[2] yóuchá 用油茶面儿冲成的糊状食品 gruel of sweetened, fried flour

【油茶面儿】yóuchámiànr 一种食品,面粉内搀牛骨髓或牛油炒熟,加糖、芝麻等物制成。吃时用滚水冲成糊状,叫油茶。flour fried with bone marrow of the bull or in beef fat with sugar and sesame. It is made into *youcha*, a gruel when boiled water is mixed with fried flour before eating.

【油船】yóuchuán same as 油轮 yóulún

【油灯】yóudēng 用植物油做燃料的灯 oil lamp; lamp using vegetable oil as its fuel

【油底子】yóudǐ·zi 指盛油容器底部较黏稠的油。有的地区叫油脚。oil dregs; thick oil left at the bottom of the oil vessel; called 油脚 yóujiǎo in some regions

【油坊】yóufáng 榨植物油的作坊 oil mill; mill for extracting vegetable oil

【油橄榄】yóugǎnlǎn ❶ 常绿小乔木,叶子对生,长椭圆形,花白色,气味很香。果实椭圆形,成熟后黑色,加工后可以吃,又可以榨油。原产欧洲,西洋用它的枝叶作为和平的象征。olive (*Olea europaea*); small evergreen tree originating in Europe, with opposite, oblong leaves, heavily scented white flowers and ovate fruits, black when ripe, edible as a food and used for extracting oil, its branch regarded as a symbol of peace in the West ❷ 这种植物的果实 fruit of this plant ‖ also 齐墩果 qídūnguǒ,通称 commonly known as 橄榄 gǎnlǎn or 洋橄榄 yánggǎnlǎn

【油垢】yóugòu 含油的污垢;油泥 greasy filth; greasy dirt:他刚修完车,满手～。He had just repaired his car and that's why his hands were stained with greasy filth.

【油光】yóuguāng 形容光亮润泽 glossy; shiny; varnished:～闪亮 shiny; glossy|～碧绿的树叶 shiny green leaves

【油耗】yóuhào (车辆、机器等)机油、柴油、汽油等的消耗量 (of vehicles, machines, etc.) oil consumption; consumption of engine oil, diesel oil, gas, etc.:降低～ reduce the oil consumption

【油乎乎】yóuhūhū (～的 yóuhūhū·de)形容物体上油很多的样子 oily; greasy:～的糕点 oily cakes and pastries|工作服～的。The overalls are smeared with oil.

【油葫芦】yóu·hulǔ 昆虫,体形像蟋蟀,比蟋蟀大,黑褐色,有油光,触角大,腹部肥大,有一对尾须,雌虫另有一个赤褐色的产卵管,雄虫的翅能互相摩擦发声。昼伏夜出,吃豆类、谷类、瓜类等。large field cricket (*Gryllus testaceus*); blackish-brown, shiny insect like common cricket, but larger, with a pair of large feelers, a big, fat belly and a pair of cerci, the female also having a russet ovipositor and the male producing sounds when its wings rub each other. It is a nocturnal insect that feeds on beans, cereals, melons, etc.

【油花】yóuhuā (～儿 yóuhuār) 汤或带汤食物表面上浮着的油滴 drops of oil floating on the surface of soup; blobs of fat

【油滑】yóuhuá 圆滑；世故；不诚恳 slippery; foxy; slick：为人～ wily person | 说话～ speaks slickly

【油画】yóuhuà 西洋画的一种，用含油质的颜料在布或木板上绘成 oil painting; Western-style painting done on a piece of canvas or wood board with oily paints

【油灰】yóuhuī 桐油和石灰的混合物，用来填充器物上的缝隙 putty; soft, plastic mixture of tung oil and lime, used to secure glass panes, fill small cracks, etc.

【油煎火燎】yóu jiān huǒ liǎo 形容非常焦急 on pins and needles; in a stew; burning with anxiety：孩子发高烧，病得很重，母亲急得～的。The child was seriously ill and running a high fever, and the mother was on pins and needles.

【油井】yóujǐng 开采石油时用钻机从地面打到油层而成的井 oil well; well drilled with a drilling machine through the ground to an oil-bearing formation

【油锯】yóujù 以内燃机为动力的锯，主要用来伐木 chain saw, powered by an internal combustion engine and used chiefly for tree

【油矿】yóukuàng ❶ 蕴藏在地下的石油矿床 oil deposit ❷ 开采石油的地方 oilfield

【油亮】yóuliàng 油光(多叠用 oft. reduplicated) glossy; shiny：刚下过雨，花草树木的叶子绿得～～的。The rain had just stopped, and the leaves of plants and trees all have turned shiny green.

【油料作物】yóuliào zuòwù 种子含有多量油脂的作物，如花生、油菜、大豆、蓖麻、芝麻、胡麻、向日葵 oil-bearing crop; oil crop, including peanuts, rape seeds, soya bean, castor seeds, sesame seeds, flaxseeds, sunflower seeds

【油篓】yóulǒu 口小腹大的篓子，用竹篾、荆条等编成，里面糊纸，并涂上桐油和其他涂料，用来盛油等 small-mouthed and big-bellied basket woven of bamboo strips or chaste tree twigs, coated with tung oil or other coating material, and lined with oil paper, used to contain oil

【油绿】yóulǜ 有光泽的深绿色 glossy dark green：雨后，麦田一片～。The wheat fields were all glossy dark green after the rain.

【油轮】yóulún 设有装液体的货舱、专用于运输散装油类的轮船 oil tanker; tanker; oil carrier; ship with large tanks in the hull for carrying a cargo of oil; also 油船 yóuchuán

【油麦】yóumài same as 莜麦 yóumài

【油毛】yóumáo ☞ 原毛 yuánmáo on p. 2359

【油毛毡】yóumáozhān same as 油毡 yóuzhān

【油门】yóumén (～儿 yóuménr) 内燃机上调节燃料供给量的装置，油门开得越大，机器转动得越快 throttle; accelerator; device fitted on an internal combustion engine for regulating fuel supply. The bigger the throttle is, the faster the machine runs.

【油苗】yóumiáo 地壳内的石油在地面上的露头，是寻找石油资源的重要标志之一 oil seepage; oil that seeps from the earth crust to the ground surface, an important sign for discovering petroleum deposits

【油墨】yóumò 印刷用的黏性油质，是用胡麻子油、松脂油、矿物油、硬胶等加入各种颜料或油烟调和制成的 printing ink; oily and sticky ink for printing, prepared by adding flaxseed oil, rosin oil, mineral oil, hard gum, etc.

【油泥】yóuní 含油的泥垢 greasy filth：满手～ hands smeared with greasy filth

【油腻】yóunì ❶ 含油多的 greasy; fatty; oily：他不爱吃～的东西 not care for greasy (or fatty, oily) food ❷ 含油多的食物 greasy food; fatty food; oily food：忌食～ avoid greasy food

【油皮】yóupí 〈方 *dial.*〉(～儿 yóupír) ❶ 皮肤的最外层 outermost layer of skin; epidermis：擦破一块～。It's only a scratch. ❷ same as 豆腐皮 dòu·fupí ①

【油漆】yóuqī ❶ 泛指油类和漆类涂料 paint ❷ 用油或漆涂抹 cover with paint, paint：把门窗～一下 have the doors and windows painted ❸ 用矿物颜料(如铅白、锌白)和干性油、树脂等制成的涂料，涂在器物的表面，能保护器物，并增加光泽 coat objects with mineral paint (as white lead, zinc white) and dry oil, resin, etc. for protection and adding lustre

【油气】yóuqì 油田伴生气 associated gas

【油气田】yóuqìtián 既可开采石油又可开采天然气的地带 oil and gas field

【油气显示】yóuqì xiǎnshì 石油或天然气的露头。包括天然的和人工的。oil and gas indications, including both natural and artificial

【油腔滑调】yóu qiāng huá diào 形容人说话轻浮油滑 glib; unctuous

【油然】yóurán ❶ 形容思想感情自然而然地产生(of feelings) spontaneously; involuntarily：敬慕之心，～而生。Respect and admiration well up in one's heart. ❷ 形容云气上升 (of clouds) gathering：～作云 clouds beginning to gather

【油石】yóushí 用磨料制成的各种形状的研磨工具，质地细致，用来磨精致的刀具，磨时放上油 oilstone (for sharpening cutting tools); grinding tool made of abrasives in various shapes and of fine quality for sharpening cutting tools with oil applied on it

【油饰】yóushì 用油漆涂饰门窗家具等 cover or decorate with paint; paint; varnish：门窗～一

新。The doors and windows are freshly painted or varnished.

【油水】yóu·shui ❶ 指饭菜里所含的脂肪质 grease ❷〈比喻 *fig*.〉可以利己的好处(多指不正当的额外收入 oft. referring to extra income through tricky means) pickings; profit: 捞～ pick up a few crumbs; make a profit

【油酥】yóusū 和面时加食油,烙熟后发酥的 short; crisp; flaky; Cooking oil is added when flour and other ingredients are worked together into a soft dough, and the food is short and crisp after it is baked: ～烧饼 short baked cakes

【油田】yóutián 可以开采的大面积的油层分布地带 oilfield; zone with a large area of workable oil formations

【油田伴生气】yóutián bànshēngqì 伴随石油从油井中出来的气体,主要成分是甲烷、乙烷,也含有相当数量的丙烷、丁烷、戊烷等。用作燃料和化工原料。associated gas; gas associated with oil that gushes out of an oil well, its main elements being methane, ethane, but also a fair amount of propane, butane, pentane, used as fuel and chemical raw material; also 油田气 yóutiánqì or 油气 yóuqì

【油条】yóutiáo ❶ 一种油炸的面食。长条形,多用做早点。long, deep-fried, twisted dough sticks, usu. served as breakfast ❷ 讥称处事经验多而油滑的人 sly person; old fox; slick person with much experience in handling affairs

【油头粉面】yóu tóu fěn miàn 形容人打扮过分而显轻浮(多指男子 usu. referring to a man) sleek-haired and creamy-faced; heavily made-up; dressy or foppish

【油头滑脑】yóu tóu huá nǎo 形容人狡猾轻浮 slick; smooth; oily; shifty-looking

【油汪汪】yóuwāngwāng (～的 yōuwāngwāng·de) ❶ 形容油多 dripping with oil; full of grease ❷ same as 油光 yóuguāng

【油污】yóuwū same as 油垢 yóugòu: 满身～ covered all over with greasy dirt

【油香】yóu·xiang 伊斯兰教徒的一种食物,用温水和面,加盐,制成饼状,再用香油炸熟 salted cake fried in sesame oil (a Moslem food)

【油箱】yóuxiāng 装油用的容器。特指飞机、汽车上盛燃料油用的。fuel tank, especially the tank in an airplane or vehicle containing fuel oil

【油鞋】yóuxié 外面涂桐油的旧式雨鞋 oiled shoes (for wet weather)

【油性】yóuxìng 物质因含油而产生的性质 oiliness; greasiness: 这种果仁～大。This kind of kernel is oily.

【油压机】yóuyājī 利用矿物油传递压力的机器,多用来冲压金属 hydraulic press; oil press; pressing machine using mineral oil for the transmission of pressure, mostly used to punch metals

【油烟】yóuyān 油类没有完全燃烧所产生的黑色物质,主要成分是碳,可以用来制墨、油墨等 lampblack; soot; black substance produced from half-burned oils, chiefly carbon, used in making ink sticks and printing ink; also 油烟子 yóuyānzi

【油印】yóuyìn 一种简便的印刷方法。用刻写或打字的蜡纸做版,用油墨印刷 mimeograph; a simple printing method, using a cut or typewritten stencil as the block and ink for printing

【油炸鬼】yóuzháguǐ 油炸的面食,有长条、圆圈等形状。deep-fried dough strips or rings; 有的地区也叫 also called 油鬼 yóuguǐ in some regions

【油毡】yóuzhān 用动物的毛或植物纤维制成的毡或厚纸坯浸透沥青后所成的建筑材料,有韧性,不透水,用来做屋顶、地下室墙壁、地基等的防水、防潮层 asphalt felt; building material made from animal hair or plant fibre, or from thick paperboard soaked with asphalt, tough and waterproof, and used for building roofs, basement walls and foundations for preventing water and moisture; also 油毛毡 yóumáozhān

【油脂】yóuzhī 油和脂肪的统称 general term for oil; fat

【油脂麻花】yóu·zhimáhuā〈方 *dial*.〉(～的 yóu·zhimáhuā·de)形容衣物上油泥很多的样子 smeared or spotted with grease; grease-stained: 看你的衣服～的,也该洗洗了。Look, your clothes are all covered with greasy filth. You should wash them.

【油纸】yóuzhǐ 涂上桐油的纸,能防潮湿,常用来包东西 oil paper; paper waterproofed with tung oil, often used for wrapping

【油渍】yóuzì 粘在衣物等上的油垢 grease stains on clothes, etc.: 满手～ hands stained with greasy filth

【油子】yóu·zi ❶ 某些稠而黏的东西,多为黑色 black sticky substance: 膏药～plaster | 烟袋～tar inside a tobacco pipe ❷ 指阅历多,熟悉情况而狡猾的人 foxy person; sly person: 老～old foxy man

【油嘴】[1] yóuzuǐ ❶ 说话油滑,善于狡辩 glib: ～滑舌 glib-tongued ❷ 油嘴的人 glib talker

【油嘴】[2] yóuzuǐ 喷嘴 spray nozzle; spray head

【油嘴滑舌】yóu zuǐ huá shé (～的 yóu zuǐ huáshé·de)形容说话油滑 glib-tongued

柚 yóu [柚木](yóumù) 落叶乔木,叶子大,卵形或椭圆形,表面粗糙,背面有褐色绒毛,花序圆锥状,花白色或蓝色,核果略作球形。木材暗褐色,坚硬,耐腐蚀,用来造船、车、家具,也供建筑用。产于印度、印度尼西亚等地。teakwood (*Tectona grandis*); teak; deciduous tree produced in India, Indonesia, etc., having large, ovate or elliptical leaves with a rough surface and brown hairy back, white or blue flowers in panicles, and spherical drupes, its hard, corrosion-resistant, dark brown wood used in making boats, vehicles and furniture as well as in buildings

☞ yòu on p.2334

疣(肬) yóu 皮肤病,病原体是一种病毒,症状是皮肤上出现跟正常的皮肤颜色相同的或黄褐色的突起,表面干燥而粗糙,不疼不痒,多长在面部、头部或手背等处 wart; skin disease caused by a virus, characterized by a protuberance on the skin, of the normal skin colour or yellowish-brown, with a dry and rough surface, neither painful nor itchy, usu. growing on the face, head or the back of the hand; also 肉赘 ròuzhuì;通称 commonly called 瘊子 hóu·zi

斿 yóu 〈书 *fml.*〉❶ 旌旗上面的飘带 ribbons of a banner or flag ❷ same as 游 yóu

莜 yóu [莜麦](yóumài) ❶ 一年生草本植物,和燕麦极相似,但小穗的花数较多,种子成熟后容易与外壳脱离。生长期短,子实可磨成面供食用。naked oats (*Avena nuda*); annual herbal plant similar to oats, but its small ears have more flowers and its seeds are liable to fall away from the hulls. Its growth period is short, and its seeds are gathered and milled into flour for food ❷ 这种植物的子实 seed of the plant; also 油麦 yóumài

莸(蕕) yóu ❶ 落叶小灌木,叶子卵形或披针形,聚伞花序,花蓝色,蒴果成熟后裂成四个小坚果。供观赏。common bluebeard (*Caryopteris incana*); ornamental deciduous shrub with ovate or lanceolate leaves, blue flowers in cymes, its capsules split into four small nuts after ripening ❷ 古书上指一种有臭味的草 stinking grass mentioned in ancient texts;〈比喻 *fig.*〉坏人 evil man; bad man:薰~不同器(比喻好人和坏人搞不到一块儿)。Good people and bad people never mix together.

铀 yóu 金属元素,符号 U (uranium)。银白色,有放射性,主要用于原子能工业,做核燃料。uranium (U), silver-white, radioactive metallic element used chiefly as a nuclear fuel in the atomic energy industry

蚰 yóu ❶ [蚰蜒](yóu·yán) 节肢动物,像蜈蚣而略小,黄褐色,触角和脚都很细,生活在阴湿的地方。common house centipede (*Thereuopoda*); arthropod-like centipede, yellowish-brown in colour, with small feelers and legs, living in dark and damp places ❷ ☞ 蜒蚰 yányóu on p.2207

鱿 yóu [鱿鱼](yóuyú) 枪乌贼的通称 squid; calamary; common name for 枪乌贼 qiāngwūzéi

游(❷❸❹ 遊) yóu ❶ 人或动物在水里行动 swim; man or animals move in water:~泳 swim|鱼在水里~。Fish swim in water. ❷ 各处从容地行走;闲逛 rove around; saunter; stroll; travel; tour:~览 go sightseeing; tour; visit|~历 travel for pleasure; tour; visit|~园 attend a garden party; attend celebrations in a park; visit a park or garden|~玩 play; stroll about; go sightseeing|~人 tourist|周~天下 tour the country; tour the world ❸〈书 *fml.*〉交游;来往 associate with; make acquaintances with; make friends with ❹ 不固定的;经常移动的 move around; move about; rove:~牧 nomadic|~民 vagrant; vagabond|~击 guerilla warfare|~资 idle fund; floating capital; idle money ❺ 江河的一段 section of a river; reach:上~ upper reach|中~ middle reach|下~ lower reach ❻ (Yóu)姓 a surname

【游伴】yóubàn 游玩时的伴侣 travel companion

【游标】yóubiāo 某些度量器具上可以滑动的部分,有指示数字等作用,如计算尺上的游标、标尺上的游标 vernier; vernier scale; short graduated scale that slides along a longer graduated instrument, and used to indicate fractional parts of divisions, such as the vernier on a slide rule and the vernier on the surveyor's rod

【游标卡尺】yóubiāo kǎchǐ 用来测量机器零件或工件的内外直径或厚度等的量具,精密度可达 0.02 毫米 vernier calliper; implement for measuring the internal or external diameter or thickness of a machine part or workpiece to the precision of 0.02 millimetres; 简称 abbr. 卡尺 kǎchǐ

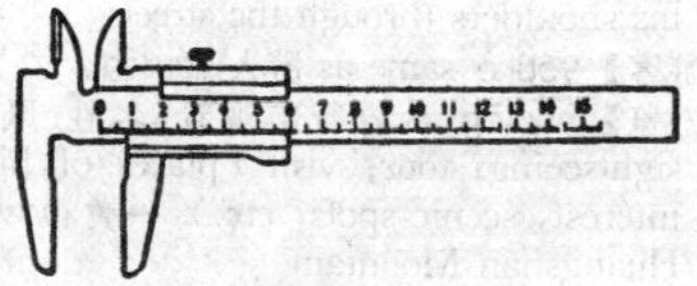

游标卡尺 Vernier Calliper

【游程】yóuchéng ❶ 游泳的距离 distance of swimming:比赛的~是一千米。The distance of the swimming race is 1,000 m. ❷ 游玩的路程;旅游的路程 route of travel:一日~ one-day tour; one-day trip|~三千里 travel or tour covers 3,000 *li* ❸ 旅游的日程 itinerary:时间有限,把~排得紧一点。As the time is limited, we'll have a tight tour schedule.

【游船】yóuchuán 游览用的船 pleasure boat

【游荡】yóudàng ❶ 闲游放荡,不务正业 idle; loaf about; loiter; wander ❷ 闲游;闲逛 stroll; saunter:独自一人在田野里~。Stroll alone in the fields ❸ 飘浮晃荡 float:船在湖心随风~。The boat is floating on the lake.

【游方】[1] yóufāng 云游四方 roam all around the world:~僧 itinerant (roving) monk|~和尚 itinerant (roving) monk

【游方】[2] yóufāng 苗族男女青年的社交方式。多在节日或农闲时进行,通常是男女对歌,相邀谈话，互赠信物等。social gathering for young people of the ethnic Miao people on festive occasions or during slack seasons, where young people are involved in antiphonal singing, engaging each other in conversation, or exchanging mementos

【游舫】yóufǎng same as 游船 yóuchuán

【游逛】yóuguàng 游览；为消遣而闲走 go sightseeing; stroll about：出外～ go out sightseeing｜～名山大川 visit famous mountains and great rivers

【游击】yóujī 对敌人进行分散的出没无常的袭击 guerrilla warfare against enemy troops

【游击队】yóujīduì 执行游击作战任务的非正规武装组织 guerrilla forces; guerrilla detachment

【游击战】yóujīzhàn 灵活、分散的小部队，在敌后用袭击、伏击、破坏、扰乱等手段进行的战斗 guerrilla war; guerrilla warfare; any member of a small defensive force of irregular soldiers, usually volunteers, making surprise raids, especially behind the lines of an invading enemy army

【游记】yóujì 记述游览经历的文章 travel notes; travels

【游街】yóu//jiē 许多人在街上游行，多押着犯罪分子以示惩戒，有时拥着英雄人物以示表扬 parade a criminal or a hero through the streets：～示众 parade a criminal through the streets to expose him to the public｜披红～ parade somebody with red silk draped over his shoulders through the streets

【游客】yóukè same as 游人 yóurén

【游览】yóulǎn 从容行走观看（名胜、风景）go sightseeing; tour; visit (places of historical interest, scenic spots, etc.)：～黄山 visit the Huangshan Mountain

【游廊】yóuláng 连接两个或几个独立建筑物的走廊 covered corridor (linking two or more buildings); veranda

【游乐】yóulè 游玩嬉戏 make merry; amuse oneself：～场 amusement park｜青年们在森林公园尽情～。The young people amused themselves to their hearts' content in the Forest Park.

【游离】yóulí ❶ 一种物质不和其他物质化合而单独存在，或物质从化合物中分离出来，叫做游离 free; substance not united or combined with other substances or a substance freed from a compound ❷〈比喻 *fig.*〉离开集体或依附的事物而存在 dissociate; drift away; independent of a collective or a thing to which it is attached：～分子 one who quits the collective｜～状态 free state

【游离态】yóulítài 元素以单质存在的形态 free state

【游历】yóulì 到远地游览 travel for pleasure; travel; tour：～名山大川 visit famous mountains and great rivers

【游民】yóumín 没有正当职业的人 vagrant; vagabond

【游民无产者】yóumín wúchǎnzhě ☞ 流氓无产者 liúmáng wúchǎnzhě on p.1241

【游牧】yóumù 从事畜牧，不在一个地方定居的 move about in search of pasture; rove around as a nomad：～民族 nomadic tribe｜～生活 nomadic life

【游憩】yóuqì 游玩和休息 stroll about or have a rest; play and relax

【游禽】yóuqín 鸟的一类。这类鸟会游泳，通常在水上生活，趾间有蹼，嘴宽而扁平，吃鱼虾等，如雁、鸳鸯、野鸭 natatorial bird; swimming bird; waterfowl, such as the wild goose, mandarin duck and wild duck, with webbed feet, a broad and flat beak, and feeding on fish and shrimps

【游人】yóurén 游览的人 visitor; sightseer; tourist：～如织 throngs of visitors; crowds of tourists

【游刃有余】yóu rèn yǒu yú 厨师把整个的牛分割成块，技术熟练，刀子在牛的骨头缝里自由移动着，没有一点阻碍（见于《庄子·养生主》）handle a cleaver with skill; a cook cut the whole beef into pieces with great skill and move his cleaver freely at the bones without any hindrance (see *Zhuangzi · Nourishment of the Soul*)；〈比喻 *fig.*〉做事熟练，轻而易举 do a job with skill and ease; be more than equal to a task

【游手好闲】yóu shǒu hào xián 游荡成性，不好劳动 idle about; loaf; dislike working

【游水】yóu//shuǐ 在水里游；游泳 swim

【游说】yóushuì 古代叫做'说客'的政客，奔走各国，凭着口才劝说君主采纳他的主张，叫做游说 lobby; go about selling an idea; go about drumming up support for an idea; go canvassing; In ancient times, lobbyists went about among different states to sell political views and drum up support from a monarch

【游丝】yóusī ❶ 蜘蛛等所吐的飘荡在空中的丝 (of a spider) gossamer; filmy cobweb floating in the air ❷ 装在仪表指针的转轴上或钟表等的摆轮轴上的弹簧，是用金属线卷成的，能控制转轴或摆轮做往复运动 hairspring; a very slender, hairlike coil that controls the regular movement of the revolution axis or balance wheel in a watch or clock

【游艇】yóutǐng same as 游船 yóuchuán

【游玩】yóuwán ❶ same as 游戏 yóuxì ❷ 游逛 go sightseeing; stroll about

【游戏】yóuxì ❶ 娱乐活动，如捉迷藏、猜灯谜等。某些非正式比赛项目的体育活动，如康乐球等也叫游戏。recreation; game; play games, such as hide-and-seek game, guessing riddles, etc. Some non-competition sports, as caroms, etc. are also called 游戏 yóuxì。❷ 玩耍 play：几个孩子正在大树底下～。Some children are playing under a big tree.

【游侠】yóuxiá 〈古代 *arch*.〉称好交游、轻生死、重信义、能救人于急难的人 roving brave; knight-errant; person who was fond of making friends, valued honour more than life and helped people in great distress

【游仙诗】yóuxiānshī 古代借描述仙境以寄托个人怀抱的诗歌 ancient poem which portrayed mystical excursions into the realm of the immortals to express one's ideal or wish

【游乡】yóu//xiāng ❶ 许多人在乡村中游行,多押着有罪的人以示惩戒 parade sb. (a criminal or guilty person for punishment) around the villages ❷ 在乡村中流动着兜揽生意 (of a pedlar) go from village to village soliciting customers

【游行】yóuxíng ❶ 行踪无定,到处漫游 rove about:～四方 rove about ❷ 广大群众为了庆祝、纪念、示威等在街上结队而行 parade; march; demonstration for celebration, commemoration or protest:～示威 demonstration| 上午十时～开始。The parade began at ten in the morning.

【游兴】yóuxìng 游逛的兴致 interest in going on an excursion or sightseeing:～大发 arouse great interest in sightseeing

【游学】yóuxué 〈旧时 *old*〉指离开本乡到外地或外国求学 study away from home or abroad

【游移】yóuyí ❶ 来回移动 float:浮云在空中～。Clouds are floating in the sky. ❷ (态度、办法、方针等)摇摆不定 (of attitude, method, policy, etc.) waver; vacillate; wobble:～不决 hesitate and cannot decide; remain undecided

【游弋】yóuyì ❶ (兵船等)巡逻 (of warships) cruise ❷ 泛指在水中游动 swim; move about in the water:几只野鸭在湖心～。Some wild ducks are swimming in the middle of the lake.

【游艺】yóuyì 游戏娱乐 entertainment; recreation; amusement:～室 recreation room|～会 entertainment gathering (for watching performances and playing games)

【游艺会】yóuyìhuì 以文艺表演、游戏等为内容的集会 entertainment gathering (for watching performances and playing games)

【游泳】yóuyǒng ❶ 人或动物在水里游动(of man or animals) swim; move in the water ❷ 体育运动项目之一,人在水里用各种不同的姿势划水前进 a sport; people move ahead in the water in different styles

【游泳池】yóuyǒngchí 人工建造的供游泳用的水池子,分室内、室外两种 swimming pool; water pool built indoors or outdoors for swimming

【游勇】yóuyǒng ☞ 散兵游勇 sǎnbīng yóuyǒng on p.1655

【游园】yóuyuán 在公园或花园中游览、观赏 visit a garden or park:～活动 mass celebrations in parks or gardens

【游园会】yóuyuánhuì 在公园或花园里举行的联欢会,规模较大的游园会有各种文艺表演 garden gathering; garden carnival; garden party; party or gathering held in a park or garden where various shows are presented

【游资】yóuzī 从生产过程中游离出来的、没有用于扩大再生产的资金 idle fund; idle money; floating capital; capital or fund not used for expanded reproduction

【游子】yóuzǐ 〈书 *fml*.〉离家在外或久居外乡的人 man travelling or residing in a place far away from home:海外～ people residing abroad

【游子】yóu·zi same as 圝子 yóu·zi

楢 yóu 古书上指一种质地柔软的树木 a kind of tree with soft timber as mentioned in ancient books

輶 yóu ❶〈古代 *arch*.〉一种轻便的车 a kind of light carriage ❷〈书 *fml*.〉轻 light

鲉 yóu 鱼类的一科,体侧扁,头部有许多棘状突起,生活在海中 scorpionfish(*Scorpaenidae*); flat marine fish with many spiny protuberances on its head

猷 yóu 〈书 *fml*.〉计划;谋划 plan; scheme:鸿～(大计划) great plan

蝣 yóu ☞ [蜉蝣] fúyóu on p.600

蝤 yóu [蝤蛑] (yóumóu) 梭子蟹 swimming crab

☞ qiú on p.1586

繇 yóu 〈书 *fml*〉same as 由 yóu ⑥⑦

☞ yáo on p.2230 and zhòu on p.2498

圝 yóu [圝子] (yóu·zi) 用已捉到的鸟把同类的鸟引来,这种起引诱作用的鸟叫圝子 decoy; bird used to lure other birds into a trap; also 游子 yóu·zi

yǒu (丨ㄡˇ)

友 yǒu ❶ 朋友 friend:好～ good (or great) friend|战～ comrade in arms ❷ 相好;亲近 friendly:～爱 friendship|～好 friendly ❸ 有友好关系的 having friendly relations:～人 friend|～邦 friendly nation (or country)|～军 friendly army

【友爱】yǒu'ài 友好亲爱 friendly affection; fraternal love:兄弟～ fraternal affection|团结～ fraternal unity

【友邦】yǒubāng 友好的国家 friendly nation (or country)

【友好】yǒuhǎo ❶ 好朋友 close friend; friend:生前～ friends of the deceased ❷ 亲近和睦 friendly; amicable:团结～ fraternal unity; unity and friendship|～邻邦 friendly neighbouring country

【友军】yǒujūn 与本部队协同作战的部队 friendly forces; friendly army

【友情】yǒuqíng 朋友的感情;友谊 friendly sentiments; friendship:深厚的～ profound friendship

【友人】yǒurén 朋友 friend:国际～ foreign friend

【友善】yǒushàn 〈书 *fml*.〉朋友之间亲近和睦 friendly; amicable:素相～ has always been amicable and friendly|～相处 live together amicably

【友谊】yǒuyì 朋友间的交情 friendship:深厚的～ profound friendship

【友谊赛】yǒuyìsài 为了增进友谊、交流经验、提高技术而举行的体育比赛 friendly match; match for enhancing friendship, exchanging experience and improving skills

有 yǒu ❶ 表示领有(跟'无'或'没'相对,下②③同 as opposed to 'have not', same with the following ② and ③) have; possess:我～《鲁迅全集》。I have the *Collected Works of Lu Xun*.|～热情,～朝气 full of enthusiasm and vigour ❷ 表示存在 there is; exist:屋里～十来个人。There are about a dozen people in the room. ❸ 表示估量或比较 indicating estimation or comparison:水～一丈多深。The water is about more than one *zhang* deep.|他～他哥哥那么高了。He is now as tall as his elder brother is. ❹ 表示发生或出现 indicating occurrence or emergence:他～病了。He is ill.|形势～了新发展。There are new developments in the situation.|他在大家的帮助下～了很大的进步。He has made tremendous progress with the help of everybody. ❺ 表示多,大 indicating much and big:～学问 be well-learned|～经验 be experienced|～了年纪 be getting on in age ❻ 泛指,跟'某'的作用相近 [be used in a general sense, indicating 'certain' or 'some']:～一天他来了。He came one day.|～人这么说,我可没看见。Someone put it that way, but I didn't see it. ❼ 用在'人、时候、地方'前面,表示一部分 [used before 'person, time, place' to indicate a part]:～人性子急,～人性子慢。Some are hot-tempered and some are placid.|这里～时候也能热到三十八九度。The temperature here sometimes can also go up to 38℃ or 39℃.|这场雨～地方下到了,～地方没下到。The rain fell in some areas, but not in others. ❽ 用在某些动词的前面组成套语,表示客气 [used before certain verbs to form polite formulas]:～劳 may I trouble you; sorry to bother you|～请 ask someone politely into a room ❾ 〈书 *fml*.〉〈前缀 *prefix*〉用在某些朝代名称的前面 used before the names of certain dynasties:～夏 the Xia Dynasty|～周 the Zhou Dynasty|～宋一代 the Song Dynasty

☞ yòu on p. 2334

【有板有眼】yǒu bǎn yǒu yǎn 〈比喻 *fig*.〉言语行动有条不紊,富有节奏或章法 (of speech or action) rhythmical; measured; orderly

【有备无患】yǒu bèi wú huàn 事先有准备就可以避免祸患 where there is precaution, there is no danger; preparedness averts peril; preparedness ensures security:有了水库,雨天可以蓄水,旱天可以灌溉,可说是～了。Since there is the reservoir, it can store water in rainy days and irrigate fields in dry season. It can be said that preparedness ensures security.

【有鼻子有眼儿】yǒu bí·zi yǒu yǎnr 形容把虚构的事物说得很逼真,活灵活现 with every detail described; describe sth. fictitious in vivid detail:听他说得～的,也就信了。He described it so vividly that we all believed it.

【有差】yǒuchā 〈书 *fml*.〉有区别;不同 differentiate; distinguish:赏罚～ differentiate in awards and punishments

【有偿】yǒucháng 有代价的;有报酬的 with compensation; compensated; paid:～服务 paid service

【有成】yǒuchéng 〈书 *fml*.〉成功 achieve success:三年～ achieve success in three years|双方意见已渐接近,谈判可望～。Since the two sides are beginning to see eye to eye, the talks are expected to be a success.

【有待】yǒudài 要等待 remain (to be done); await:这个问题～进一步的研究。This problem awaits further discussion and study.

【有得】yǒudé 有心得;有所领会 what one has learned from work, study, etc.:学习～ have gained something from study|读书～ have gained something from reading

【有的】yǒu·de 人或事物中的一部分(多叠用 oft. used reiteratively) some; part of a group of people or things:～人记性好。Some people have good memory.|十个指头,～长,～短。Of the ten fingers, some are long and some are short.

【有的是】yǒu·deshì 强调很多(不怕没有) have plenty of; there's no lack of:立功的机会～。There are plenty of chances to perform merits.

【有底】yǒu//dǐ 知道底细,因而有把握 know how things stand and feel confident of handling them; be fully prepared for what is coming:心里～ know well what to do

【有的放矢】yǒu dì fàng shǐ 对准靶子射箭 shoot the arrow at the target;〈比喻 *fig*.〉言论、行动目标明确 have a definite objective in speech or action

【有点】yǒudiǎn (～儿 yǒudiǎnr) ❶ 表示数量不大或程度不深 a bit; some; a little:锅里还～剩饭。There is still some rice left in the pot.|看来～希望。There seems to be some hope.

❷〈副词 *adv.*〉表示略微；稍微(多用于不如意的事情 mostly used for unhappy event) slightly：今天他～不大高兴。He is somewhat unhappy today. *or* He seems a bit out of sorts today.｜这句话说得～叫人摸不着头脑。This remark is rather baffling.

【有方】yǒufāng 得法（跟'无方'相对 as opposed to 'in the wrong way'）in the right way：领导～ right leadership；good leadership｜计划周详，指挥～ well-thought plan and correct guidance

【有关】yǒuguān ❶ 有关系 have something to do with；have a bearing on；relate to；concern：～方面 parties concerned｜～部门 department concerned｜这些问题都跟哲学～。All these questions are associated with philosophy. ❷ 涉及到 related；concerned；relevant；pertinent：他研究了历代～水利问题的著作。He has studied works of all dynasties related to water conservancy.

【有光纸】yǒuguāngzhǐ 一种一面光一面毛的纸，质薄，可用来单面书写或印刷 glazed paper；thin paper with one side glazed for writing or printing on

【有过之无不及】yǒu guò zhī wú bù jí （相比起来）只有超过的，没有不如的(多用于坏的方面 usu. of sth. bad) go even farther than；outdo

【有恒】yǒuhéng 有恒心，能坚持下去 persevering；with perseverance

【有会子】yǒuhuì·zi 表示时间已经不短 quite a long while；quite some time：他出去可～啦！He's been out for quite a while. also 有会儿 yǒuhuìr

【有机】yǒujī ❶ 原来指跟生物体有关的或从生物体来的(化合物)，现在指除碳酸盐和碳的氧化物外，含碳原子的(化合物) organic；originally referring to compounds related to organisms or originating from organisms；now referring to compounds containing carbon atoms in addition to carbonates and carbon oxides：～酸 organic acid｜～化学 organic chemistry ❷ 指事物构成的各部分互相关连协调，而具有不可分的统一性，就像一个生物体那样 organic；intrinsic；mutually related and coordinated components of an inseparable whole, just like an organism

【有机玻璃】yǒujī bō·lí 由甲基丙烯酸甲酯聚合而成的高分子化合物，透明性好，质轻，不易破碎，有热塑性。可用做玻璃的代用品，制航空窗玻璃、仪表盘等。也用来制日常用品。organic glass；polymethyl methacrylat obtained by polymerizing methyl methacrylate；high-molecular compound polymerized from methacrylic acid and methyl ester, transparent, lightweight, thermoplastic and not easily breakable, used as a substitute for glass for aircraft canopies, instrument panels, etc., or in making articles for daily use

【有机肥料】yǒujī féiliào 含有机物质的肥料，如厩肥、堆肥、绿肥等 organic fertilizer；manure；fertilizers containing organic matters, as barnyard manure, compost, green manure, etc.

【有机合成】yǒujī héchéng 用化学合成方法把无机物或简单的有机物制成较复杂的有机物，如用煤、石油、天然气制成合成纤维、合成橡胶、合成染料 organic synthesis；make complicated organic substances from inorganic compounds or simple organic substances by chemical synthesis, such as making synthetic fibre, synthetic rubber, synthetic dyes, etc. from coal, petroleum or natural gas

【有机化合物】yǒujī huàhéwù 指含有碳元素的化合物。有机物中除碳元素以外，通常还含有氢、氧、氮、硫、磷、卤素等。organic compound；compound containing carbon elements, usu. in addition to hydrogen, oxygen, nitrogen, sulphur, phosphorus, halogen, etc.；简称 abbr. 有机物 yǒujīwù

【有机化学】yǒujī huàxué 化学的一个分支，研究有机化合物的结构、性质、变化、制备、用途等 organic chemistry；branch of chemistry dealing with the structure, properties, changes, preparations and uses of organic compounds

【有机染料】yǒujī rǎnliào 做染料用的有机化合物的统称，有天然的和人造的两种，如靛蓝、海昌蓝 organic dyestuffs；general term for organic compounds both natural and artificial, used for making dyestuffs, such as indigo blue and hydron blue

【有机体】yǒujītǐ 机体 organism

【有机物】yǒujīwù 有机化合物的简称 abbr. for 有机化合物 yǒujī huàhéwù

【有机质】yǒujīzhì 一般指植物体和动物的遗体、粪便等腐烂后变成的物质，里面含有植物生长所需要的各种养料。肥沃的土壤含有机质较多。有机质经过微生物的作用转化生成腐殖质。organic matter (or substance)；matter usu. turned from the decomposed plants and animals, dung, etc., which contains nutrients needed for the growth of plants. Fertile soil abounds in organic matters, which are transformed into humus by the action of microbes

【有价证券】yǒujià zhèngquàn 表示对货币、资本、商品或其他资产等有价物具有一定权利的凭证，如股票、公债券、各种票据、提货单、仓库营业者出具的存货栈单等 negotiable securities；securities；evidence of one's rights to money, capital, commodities or other assets, as stocks, bonds, bills, bills of lading warehouse stock warrants, etc.

【有劲】yǒu//jìn ❶（～儿 yǒu//jìnr）有力气 have great physical strength：这人真～，能挑起二百斤重的担子。This chap has great physical strength and can carry a load of 100 km. ❷ 指兴致浓；有趣 enthusiasm；interest：大家谈得

非常～。We all talked with great enthusiasm. |今天的球赛真精彩，越看越～。The ball game today was really exciting. The longer we watched, the more we were absorbed.

【有旧】yǒujiù〈书 *fml.*〉过去曾相交好；有老交情 used to be friends

【有救】yǒu//jiù 有可能挽救或补救 curable; can be saved, cured, or remedied：有了这药，病就～了！With this drug, the illness will be cured.

【有口皆碑】yǒu kǒu jiē bēi〈比喻 *fig.*〉人人称赞 win universal praise; be universally acclaimed

【有口难分】yǒu kǒu nán fēn 形容很难分辩 find it hard to defend or vindicate oneself

【有口无心】yǒu kǒu wú xīn 嘴上爱说，心里不存什么 be sharp-tongued but not malicious; one's bark is worse than his bite

【有赖】yǒulài 表示一件事要依赖另一件事的帮助促成（常跟'于'usu. used with 于 yú) depend on; fulfilment of one thing depends on the help from another：任务是否能提前完成，～于大家努力。Whether the task can be fulfilled ahead of schedule depends upon the hard work of all.

【有劳】yǒuláo〈客套话 *pol.*〉用于拜托或答谢别人代自己做事 may I trouble you; sorry to bother you：这件事～您了。Sorry to have bothered you with this matter. |～您代我买一本书。May I trouble you to buy a book for me?

【有理】yǒulǐ 有道理；符合道理 reasonable; justified; in the right：言之～ speaking in a convincing way; talk reasonably |～走遍天下。With justice on one's side, one can go anywhere.

【有理式】yǒulǐshì 没有开方运算，或有开方运算但被开方数不含字母的代数式。如 a^2+b，$\frac{\sqrt{2}}{x-y}$。rational expression; algebraic expression with or without the extraction of a root but the radicand having no letters, as a^2+b, $\frac{\sqrt{2}}{x-y}$

【有理数】yǒulǐshù 整数（正整数、负整数和零）和分数（正分数、负分数）的统称 rational number; general term for integer (positive integer, negative integer and zero) and fraction (positive fraction, negative fraction)

【有力】yǒulì 有力量；分量重 strong; powerful; forceful; energetic; vigorous：领导～ strong leadership |～的回击 powerful counter-attack |这篇文章写得简短～。This article is terse and forceful.

【有利】yǒulì 有好处；有帮助 advantageous; beneficial; favourable：～可图 be profitable; have good prospects of profit; stand to gain | 积极储蓄既～于国家建设，又～于个人。To be active to save up is beneficial to both national construction and individuals.

【有两下子】yǒu liǎng xià·zi 有些本领 have real skill; know one's stuff：他干活又快又好，真～。He works fast and well; he obviously knows his stuff.

【有零】yǒulíng 用在整数后，表示附有零数；挂零 used after an integer to indicate an odd; odd：一千～ just over a thousand

【有门儿】yǒu//ménr 有希望 find the beginning of a solution; be hopeful (of success)

【有名】yǒu//míng 名字为大家所熟知；出名 well-known; famous; celebrated：他是～的登山运动健将。He is a famous master in mountaineering.

【有名无实】yǒu míng wú shí 空有名义或名声而没有实际 in name but not in reality; merely nominal; titular

【有目共睹】yǒu mù gòng dǔ 人人都看见，极其明显 be obvious to anyone who has eyes; be perfectly obvious; also 有目共见 yǒu mù gòng jiàn

【有目共赏】yǒu mù gòng shǎng 看见的人都赞赏 have a universal appeal; appeal to all alike

【有奶便是娘】yǒu nǎi biàn shì niáng〈比喻 *fig.*〉贪利忘义，谁给好处就投靠谁 whoever suckles me is my mother; submit to whoever feeds one; forget moral principles in hankering for personal gains; seek the patronage of anyone who gives a few coins; lick the hand of anyone who throws a few crumbs

【有年】yǒunián〈书 *fml.*〉已经有许多年 for years：习艺～，渐臻纯熟。Having been practising the art for years, he is growing highly skilled.

【有盼儿】yǒu//pànr〈方 *dial.*〉有希望 things have become hopeful; sth. nice is going to happen：孩子快大学毕业了，您总算～了。With the child about to graduate from college, things are finally becoming hopeful to you.

【有谱儿】yǒu//pǔr〈方 *dial.*〉心中有数；有一定的计划 know exactly what to do; have a ready idea or plan：做这样的事你心里～没有？Do you know exactly how to do this job?

【有期徒刑】yǒuqī túxíng 有期限的徒刑，在刑期内剥夺犯人的自由 fixed-term imprisonment, by which a criminal is stripped of his freedom during the term

【有气无力】yǒu qì wú lì 形容无精打采的样子 feeble; weak; faint; listless

【有顷】yǒuqǐng〈书 *fml.*〉一会儿；片刻 after a little while; not long after; soon after

【有请】yǒuqǐng〈客套话 *pol.*〉表示主人请客人相见 ask the visitor in

【有求必应】yǒu qiú bì yìng 只要有人请求就一定答应 respond to every plea; grant whatever is requested

【有趣】yǒuqù（～儿 yǒuqùr）能引起人的好奇心或喜爱 interesting；fascinating；amusing：～故事 interesting story｜这孩子活泼～。The child is lively and amusing.

【有人家儿】yǒu rénjiār 指女子已经定婚（of a girl）be engaged

【有日子】yǒurì·zi ❶ 指有好些天 for quite a few days；for days：咱们～没见面了！We haven't seen each other for quite a few days. ❷ 有确定的日期 have fixed a date：你们结婚～了没有？Have you fixed the date for the wedding?

【有如】yǒurú 就像；好像 just like；as if；as though：他的身躯～一棵青松。His body looks as robust as a green pine tree.

【有色金属】yǒusè jīnshǔ 工业上黑色金属（铁、锰、铬）以外的所有金属的统称，如金、银、铜、锡、汞、锌、锑等 nonferrous metal；metals other than the ferrous metals（iron，manganese，chromium），including gold，silver，copper，tin，mercury，zinc，and antimony

【有色人种】yǒusè rénzhǒng 指白种人以外的人种 coloured race（or people）；races other than the white

【有色眼镜】yǒusè yǎnjìng〈比喻 *fig.*〉妨碍得出正确看法的成见或偏见 preconceived idea or prejudice that hinders the conception of correct ideas

【有身子】yǒushēn·zi 指妇女怀孕 be pregnant；be in a family way

【有神论】yǒushénlùn 承认神的存在的学说。认为神是世界万物的创造者，能操纵自然变化和干预人的生活。有神论是宗教信仰的根据。theism；belief in God；theory that regard God as the creator of the universe who is capable of manipulating the changes in Nature and intervening with human life. Theism is the basis for religious belief.

【有生力量】yǒushēng-lìliàng ❶ 指军队中的兵员和马匹 effective troop strength；effectives ❷ 泛指军队（in a broad sense）army

【有生以来】yǒu shēng yǐlái 从出生到现在 since birth：这种事我～还是第一次听见。This is the first time I've ever heard of this.

【有生之年】yǒu shēng zhī nián 指人还活在世上的岁月 one's remaining years

【有声片儿】yǒushēngpiānr same as 有声片 yǒushēngpiàn

【有声片】yǒushēngpiàn 既有形象又有声音的影片 sound film；talkie

【有声有色】yǒu shēng yǒu sè 形容表现得十分生动 full of sound and colour；vivid and dramatic

【有时】yǒushí 有时候 sometimes；at times；now and then：那里的天气，～冷，～热。The weather there is now cold, now hot.

【有始无终】yǒu shǐ wú zhōng 指人做事不能坚持到底 start sth. but unable to carry it through to the end

【有始有终】yǒu shǐ yǒu zhōng 指人做事能坚持到底 carry sth. through to the end

【有恃无恐】yǒu shì wú kǒng 因有所依仗而不害怕 have nothing to fear because of strong backing；when one has sth. to fall back upon one has nothing to fear；feel secure in the knowledge that sb. is behind one

【有数】yǒu//shù（～儿 yǒu//shùr）知道数目。指了解情况，有把握 know exactly how things stand；have a definite idea of what one's doing；be certain：两个人心里都～儿。Both of them know what they should do.

【有数】yǒushù 表示数目不多 not many：只剩下～的几天了，得加把劲儿。There are only a few days left. We must get a move on.

【有司】yǒusī〈书 *fml.*〉指官吏 government official

【有丝分裂】yǒusī-fēnliè 植物细胞繁殖的一种方式。细胞成熟时，细胞核内出现一定数量的染色体，并形成细丝，密集在细胞的两极，排成纺锤形。后期染色体向两极移动形成两个新细胞。高等植物的细胞繁殖主要以有丝分裂的方式进行。mitosis；method of reproduction of plant cells. When cells mature, the nuclear chromatin appears as long threads which shorten and thicken to form a certain number of chromosomes, each of which splits lengthwise to double in number, with half of each set then moving toward opposite poles of the cell to be reorganized into two new nuclei with the normal number of chromosomes. The cells of higher plants are propagated chiefly by mitosis；also 间接分裂 jiànjiē-fēnliè

【有条不紊】yǒu tiáo bù wěn 有条理，有次序，一点不乱 in an orderly way；methodically；systematically

【有头无尾】yǒu tóu wú wěi 只有开头，没有结尾。指做事不能坚持到底。have a beginning but no end；start sth. but not finish it；leave sth. unfinished；give up sth. halfway

【有头有脸】yǒu tóu yǒu liǎn（～儿 yǒu tóu yǒu liǎnr）〈比喻 *fig.*〉有名誉，有威信 have reputation and prestige；command respect：他在村里是个～的，说话很有分量。He is a prestigious figure in his village and what he says carries a lot of weight.

【有头有尾】yǒu tóu yǒu wěi 既有开头，又有结尾。指做事能坚持到底。have a beginning and an end；do sth. from beginning to end

【有望】yǒuwàng 有希望 hopeful：丰收～。There's hope of a bumper harvest.

【有为】yǒuwéi 有作为 promising：奋发～ hard-working and promising｜～的青年 promising young person

【有…无…】yǒu…wú… ❶ 表示只有前者而没有后者 indicating there is only the former but not the latter：～行～市（过去通货膨胀时，有货价却无成交）have price quotations, but no actual business|～己～人(自私自利,只顾自己,不顾别人) have in mind only oneself, but no others; be so selfish as to think of no one but oneself|～口～心(指心直口快) be sharp-tongued but not malicious; be frank and outspoken|～利～弊 have all the advantages but not a single disadvantage|～名～实 in name but not in reality; merely nominal; titular|～始～终 start sth. but fail to carry it through to the end|～头～尾 have a beginning but no end; give up sth. halfway|～眼～珠 have eyes but see not; possess no sense of judgement|～益～损 have profit but no loss|～勇～谋 have courage but no tactics ❷ 表示有前者没有后者(强调的说法) [indicating emphatically that there is the former but not the latter]:～过之～不及 go even farther than; outdo|～加～已 be ever-increasing|～增～减 ever-growing; ever-increasing ❸ 表示有了前者就可以没有后者 indicating that with the former there is no need for the latter:～备～患。Where there is precaution, there is no danger.|～恃～恐 have nothing to fear because of strong backing ❹ 表示似有似无 [indicating that sth. may or may not exist]:～意～意 consciously or unconsciously; wittingly or unwittingly

【有喜】yǒu//xǐ 指妇女怀孕 be pregnant; be expecting; be in a family way

【有戏】yǒu//xì 〈方 *dial.*〉有希望 hopeful; there is hope

【有隙可乘】yǒu xì kě chéng (事情)有漏洞可以利用 there is a crack to squeeze through—there is a loophole to exploit

【有限】yǒuxiàn ❶ 有一定限度 limited; finite:～性 limit|～责任 limited liability ❷ 数量不多;程度不高 not many in number; not high in degree:为数～ limited in number; not many|我的文化水平～。I have had little schooling.

【有限公司】yǒuxiàn gōngsī 企业的一种组织形式,由两个以上的股东组成,股东所负的责任以他认定的股本为限 limited company; limited-liability company; Form of enterprise organization, comprising two or more shareholders who are legally responsible for the company only to the extent of the share they invested.

【有限小数】yǒuxiàn xiǎoshù 小数部分的位数是有限的小数 finite decimal. The places of the decimal part are finite decimals, such as 0.28, 0.333, 3.1416.

【有线电报】yǒuxiàn diànbào 靠导线传送信号的电报,在发报和收报装置之间有导线连接。普通电报大多是有线电报。wire telegraph; cablegram telegraphy by wire-transmitted signals. A transmitter is connected to a receiver by wire, and common telegraphs are mostly wire telegraphs.

☞ 电报 diànbào on p.435

【有线电话】yǒuxiàn diànhuà 靠导线传送的电话,在通话的两地之间有导线连接。普通电话大多是有线电话。wire (or wired) telephone; telephone operating by wire-transmitted signals. Telephones at two places are connected by wire, and common telephones are mostly wire telephones.

【有线广播】yǒuxiàn guǎngbō 靠导线传送的广播,把声音通过放大器放大,由导线送到装在各处的扬声器发送出去 wire (or wired) broadcasting; rediffusion on wire; broadcasting by wire, the sound or voice is diffused through an amplifier and transmitted to the loudspeakers installed at different places

【有线通信】yǒuxiàn tōngxìn 一种通信方式,利用导线传输电信号,电信号可以代表声音、文字、图像等。按照传输内容不同可分为有线电话、有线电报、有线传真等;按照传输线路不同可分为明线通信、电缆通信等。wired telecommunications; method of communication by which wire is used to transmit signals, which represent sounds, words or images. According to what is transmitted, it is divided into wire telephone, wire telegraph and wire facsimile, and according to the different lines, it is divided into outdoor wire communication and cable communication, etc.

【有效】yǒuxiào 能实现预期目的;有效果 efficacious; effective; be good for; valid:～方法 effective method|～措施 effective measures|这个方法果然～。This method proved really effective.

【有效期】yǒuxiàoqī ❶ 条约、合同等有效的期限 (of treaty, contract, etc.) term (or period) of validity ❷ 化学物品、医药用品以及某些特殊器材在规定的使用与保管的条件下,其性能不变而有效的期限。一般由原生产单位规定,有时由使用部门自行规定。time of efficacy; period of time in which the properties or performances of chemicals, drugs and certain special equipment remain unchanged under prescribed conditions for their use and keeping. Usually, the time of efficacy is prescribed by producer or user.

【有效射程】yǒuxiào shèchéng 指弹头射出后能获得可靠射击效果的距离 effective range; distance for the reliable shooting result after a bullet or warhead is shot

【有效温度】yǒuxiào wēndù 某种植物生长所需的最低温度为10℃,某天的平均温度为15℃,两个温度之差为5℃。这个相差的温度对这种植物的生长起积极作用,叫做这种植物的有效温度。effective temperature. If the minimum temperature needed for the growth of a certain plant is 10℃, and if the average temperature on a given day is 15℃, then the difference between them is 5℃. This temperature difference, which plays a positive role in the growth of plants, is called effective temperature.

【有些】yǒuxiē ❶ 有一部分;有的 part; some:今天来参观的人～是从外地来的。Some of the visitors today came from other parts of the country. | 列车上～人在看书,～人在谈天。Some people on the train were reading and some were chatting. ❷ 有一些(表示数量不大 indicating a small number of sth.) some; not many:我～旧书想捐给图书馆。I want to donate some of my old books to the library. ❸ 〈副词 *adv.*〉表示略微,稍微 somewhat; rather:他心里～着急。He is rather worried.

【有心】yǒuxīn ❶ 有某种心意或想法 have a mind to; set one's mind on:～人 person who sets his mind on doing sth. useful ❷ 故意 intentionally; purposely:～捣鬼 play dirty tricks intentionally

【有心人】yǒuxīnrén 有某种志愿,肯动脑筋的人 person with aspirations and determination; observant and conscientious person:世上无难事,只怕～。Nothing in the world is difficult for a person who sets his mind on it.

【有形】yǒuxíng 感官能感觉到的 tangible; visible; physical

【有形损耗】yǒuxíng sǔnhào 指机器、厂房等固定资产由于使用或自然力作用(生锈、腐烂)而引起的损耗 material loss; loss caused to machines, factory premises and other fixed assets by use or natural force (e. g. rust or rot); also 物质损耗 wùzhì sǔnhào

【有幸】yǒuxìng 很幸运 be lucky to; have the good fortune to:我～见到了海市蜃楼的奇妙景象。I was happy to see the wonderful sight of mirage.

【有性生殖】yǒuxìng shēngzhí 经过雌雄两性生殖细胞的结合而形成新个体的一种生殖方式,是生物界中最普遍的一种生殖方式 sexual reproduction; zoogamy; method of reproduction in which reproductive cells of both sexes are united to form a new individual, the most common method of reproduction in the biosphere; also 两性生殖 liǎngxìng shēngzhí

【有性杂交】yǒuxìng zájiāo 使雌雄两性的生殖细胞相结合的杂交。动物的有性杂交是使不同种、属或品种的动物交配产生新的一代。植物的有性杂交是用人工授粉的方法使不同种、属或品种的植物产生新品种。sexual hybridization; hybridization by which the reproductive cells of both sexes are united. The sexual hybridization of animals is the mating of animals of different breeds, genera or strains to reproduce a new generation while the sexual hybridization of plants is the use of artificial pollination to make plants of different strains, genera or variety produce new varieties.

【有血有肉】yǒu xuè yǒu ròu 〈比喻 *fig.*〉文艺作品的描写生动,内容充实 lifelike; true to life; vivid:这篇报道写得生动具体,～。This news report is full of vivid details.

【有言在先】yǒu yán zài xiān 已经有话讲在头里。指事前打了招呼。make it clear beforehand; forewarn

【有眼不识泰山】yǒu yǎn bù shí TàiShān 〈比喻 *fig.*〉认不出地位高或本领大的人 have eyes but not see Mount Taishan; entertain an angel unawares

【有眼无珠】yǒu yǎn wú zhū 〈比喻 *fig.*〉没有识别能力 have eyes but see not; possess no true discernment

【有一搭没一搭】yǒuyīdā-méiyīdā ❶ 表示没有话找话说 find sth. to say when there is nothing to say; try to begin a conversation ❷ 表示可有可无,无足轻重 of little importance; of no significance

【有一得一】yǒu yī dé yī 不增不减,有多少是多少 no more, no less; just that much

【有益】yǒuyì 有帮助;有好处 profitable; beneficial; useful:运动对健康～。Exercises are good for health.

【有意】yǒuyì ❶ 有心思 have a mind to; be inclined (or disposed) to:我～到海滨游泳,但是事情忙,去不了。I wanted to go to the sea beach for swimming, but was too busy for that. ❷ 指男女间有爱慕之心 take a fancy to someone; be attracted sexually:小王对小李～,可一直没有机会表白。Little Wang took a fancy to Little Li, but he found no chance to say so. ❸ 故意 intentionally; deliberately; purposely:他这是～跟我作对。He set himself against me intentionally by doing so.

【有意识】yǒu yì·shí 主观上意识到的;有目的有计划的 consciously; purposely; in a planned way:他这样做完全是～的。He did it quite consciously.

【有意思】yǒu yì·si ❶ 有意义,耐人寻味 significant; meaningful:他的讲话虽然简短,可是非常～。What he said was concise, but very significant (or interesting). ❷ same as 有趣 yǒuqù:今天的晚会很～。The party tonight was most enjoyable. ❸ 指男女间有爱慕之心 be attracted sexually; take a fancy to:她对你～,你没看出来? Don't you see that she has shown fondness for you?

【有…有…】yǒu…yǒu… ❶ 分别用在意思相反或相对的两个名词或动词前面,表示既有这个又有那个,两方面兼而有之[used before two nouns or two verbs with opposite or contrastive meaning to indicate that both are present]:～利～弊 have both advantages and disadvantages | ～头～尾 have a beginning and an end ❷ 分别用在意思相同或相近的两个名词或动词(或一个双音名词或动词的两个词素)前面,表示强调[used before two nouns or verbs with the same or similar meaning (or two morphemes of a disyllabic noun or verb) to indicate emphasis]:～板～眼 measured; rhythmical; orderly systematic|～鼻子～眼儿 with every detail vividly described|～尽(jǐn)～让(互相谦让) decline an offer politely|～棱～角 have both edges and corners|～情～义 affectionate and faithful|～声～色 vivid and dramatic|～说～笑 talk and laugh|～偏～向 be partial|～凭～据 have evidence|～条～理 be reasonable|～头～绪 have a clue or clues; have the main threads (of a complicated thing)|～血～肉 have flesh and blood; vividly described; true to life

【有余】yǒuyú ❶ 有剩余;超过足够的程度 have a surplus; have enough to spare; have more than enough:绰绰～ more than enough ❷ same as 有零 yǒulíng:他比我大十岁～。He is ten odd years older than I.

【有缘】yǒuyuán 有缘分 be predetermined by fate; be predestined; have a bond; have an affinity

【有朝一日】yǒu zhāo yī rì 将来有一天 someday; should the day come when ...; if by chance ...

【有着】yǒu·zhe 存在着;具有 possess; have:五四运动～伟大的历史意义。The May 4th Movement is of great historical significance. |他～别人所没有的胆识。He possesses the courage and insight the others don't have.

【有枝添叶儿】yǒu zhī tiān yèr ☞ 添枝加叶 tiānzhī jiā yè on p. 1896

【有志者事竟成】yǒu zhì zhě shì jìng chéng 只要有决心有毅力,事情终究会成功 where there's a will there's a way; as long as one has the determination and willpower, one will finally succeed.

【有致】yǒuzhì 富有情趣 full of interest; of taste; appealing:错落～ in picturesque disorder; in tasteful disarray

【有种】yǒuzhǒng 指有胆量,有骨气 have guts; be plucky; be gritty

酉 yǒu 地支的第十位 the 10th of the 12 Earthly Branches (地支); ☞ 干支 gānzhī on p. 627

【酉时】yǒushí 旧式记时法指下午五点钟到七点钟的时间 period of the day from 5 p.m. to 7 p.m. in the old time measurement

卣 yǒu 古代盛酒的器具,口小腹大 *you*; ancient small-mouthed, big-bellied wine vessel

羑 yǒu 羑里(Yǒulǐ),古代地名,在今河南汤阴一带 Youli, name of an ancient place, in and around present-day Tangyin, Henan Province

莠 yǒu ❶ 狗尾草 green bristlegrass ❷〈书 *fml.*〉〈比喻 *fig.*〉品质坏的(人) bad; vicious; undesirable (person):良～不齐 the good and the bad are intermingled

铕 yǒu 金属元素,符号 Eu (europium)。是一种稀土金属。灰白色,在核反应堆中做中子吸收剂,也用来做激光材料。europium (Eu); greyish-white rare-earth metallic chemical element used as a neutron absorbent in the nuclear reactor, and also used as a laser material

槱 yǒu〈书 *fml.*〉聚积木柴以备燃烧 collect firewood for a fire

牖 yǒu〈书 *fml.*〉窗户 window

黝 yǒu ☞ below

【黝黯】yǒu'àn 没有光亮;黑暗 with no light; dark:～的墙角 dark corner; also 黝暗 yǒu'àn

【黝黑】yǒuhēi 黑 dark; swarthy; same as 黑暗 hēi'àn ①:胳膊晒得～ with sunburnt arms

yòu (丨又)

又 yòu〈副词 *adv.*〉❶ 表示重复或继续 indicating repetition or continuation; again:他拿着这封信看了～看。He took the letter and read it again and again. |人类社会的生产活动,是一步～一步地由低级向高级发展。The production activities of the human society developed step by step from a lower stage to a higher stage. ❷ 表示几种情况或性质同时存在 [indicating the simultaneous existence of more than one situation or property] a) 单用 [used singly]:五四运动是反帝国主义的运动,～是反封建的运动。The May 4th Movement was an anti-imperialist movement, and an anti-feudal one at that. b) 连用 [used continuously]:～快～好 both quick and good |～香～脆 both sweet and crisp ❸ 表示意思上更进一层 [indicating a deeper meaning]:冬季日短,～是阴天,夜色早已笼罩了整个市镇。The winter day is short, and moreover, it was overcast and the whole town was already shrouded in darkness. ❹ 表示在某个范围之外有所补充 [indicating an addition to a given scope]:生活费之外,～发给五十块钱做零用 give 50 yuan as pocket money in addition to the daily allowance ❺ 表示整数之外再加零数 [indicating an odd number in addition to a whole number]:一～二分之一 one and a half ❻ 表示有矛盾的两件事情(多叠用 oft. used reiteratively) indicating two contradictory things:她～想去,～想不去,拿不定主意。She hesitated over whether she would go or not. ❼ 表示转折,有'可是'的意思 [indicating a turning of meaning to 'but']:刚才有个事儿要问你,这会儿～想不起来了。I just wanted to ask you about something, but I couldn't remember it for the moment. ❽ 用在否定句或

反问句里，加强语气［used in a negative sentence or a rhetorical question to make it more emphatic］：我～不是客人，还用你老陪着吗？I'm not a guest. Why should you keep me company all the time?

【又及】yòují 附带再提一下。信写完并已署名后又添上几句，往往在这几句话下面注明'又及'或'某某又及'。postscript (PS)；又及 yòují or 某某又及 mǒumǒu yòují is indicated below the few words added to a finished letter with one's signed name

右 yòu ❶ 面向南时靠西的一边（跟'左'相对，下②⑤同 as opposed to 'the left or the left side', same as the following ② and ⑤) right side; right：～方 on the right; to the right｜～手 right hand; to the right｜靠～走 keep to the right ❷ 西 west：山～（太行山以西的地方，后专指山西）west of the mountain (areas west of the Taihang Mountain, specifically Shanxi Province) ❸ same as 上[1] shàng ① ②（古人以右为尊 the right side was regarded as the side of precedence in ancient times）：无出其～ second to none ❹〈书 *fml.*〉崇尚 uphold; advocate：～文 stress culture and learning ❺ 保守的；反动的 conservative; reactionary：～派 rightist｜～倾 Right deviation ❻〈书 *fml.*〉same as 佑 yòu

【右边】yòu·bian（～儿 yòu·bianr）靠右的一边 right (or right-hand) side; right

【右面】yòumiàn same as 右边 yòu·bian

【右派】yòupài 在阶级、政党、集团内，政治上保守、反动的一派。也指属于这一派的人。Right; right wing; Rightist (conservative or reactionary faction in a class, political party, or political group)

【右倾】yòuqīng 思想保守的；向反动势力妥协或投降的 Right deviation; ideologically conservative; compromise with or surrender to the reactionary forces

【右倾机会主义】yòuqīng jīhuì zhǔyì ☞ 机会主义 jīhuì zhǔyì on p. 890

【右手】yòushǒu ❶ 右边的手 right hand ❷ same as 右首 yòushǒu

【右首】yòushǒu 右边（多指坐位 oft. referring to seats) right-hand side; right：那天他就坐在我的～。He sat to my left that day. also 右手 yòushǒu

【右翼】yòuyì ❶ 作战时在正面部队右侧的部队 right wing; right flank; troops flanking the front troops on the right when fighting ❷ 政党或阶级、集团中在政治思想上倾向保守的一部分 right wing; Right; political and ideological conservatives in a political party, class, or group

幼 yòu ❶（年纪）小；未长成 young; under age：～年 childhood; infancy｜～儿 child; infant｜～苗 seedling｜～虫 larva ❷ 小孩儿 child; infant; children; the young：扶老携～ help the old along and lead the young by the hand

【幼虫】yòuchóng 昆虫的胚胎在卵内发育完成后，从卵内孵化出来的幼小生物体。如孑孓是蚊子的幼虫，蛆是苍蝇的幼虫。也指某些寄生虫的幼体。larva; early, immature form of an insect that is hatched after its embryo becomes developed in the egg, e.g. wriggler is the larva of a mosquito and maggot is the larva of a fly; also larvae of certain parasites

【幼儿】yòu'ér 幼小的儿童 child; infant

【幼儿教育】yòu'ér jiàoyù 对幼儿进行的教育，包括思想、体育、语言、认识环境、图画、手工、音乐、计算等 pre-school education; education for pre-school children, including ideology, physical education, language, the environment for cognition, drawing, handwork, music, calculation, etc.

【幼儿园】yòu'éryuán 实施幼儿教育的机构 kindergarten; nursery school; infant school

【幼功】yòugōng 戏曲演员、杂技演员等童年练成的功夫 skills (of actors, acrobats, etc.) acquired during childhood

【幼教】yòujiào 幼儿教育的简称 abbr. for 幼儿教育 yòu'ér jiàoyù：～事业 cause of pre-school education｜～工作 pre-school educational work

【幼林】yòulín 由小树形成的树林。幼林长大就形成森林。forest of young trees, which form forest in the true sense of the term after they grow up

【幼苗】yòumiáo 种子发芽后生长初期的幼小植物体 seedling; young plants after seeds sprout and grow

【幼年】yòunián 三岁左右到十岁左右的时期 childhood; infancy; between three to ten in age

【幼体】yòutǐ 在母体内或脱离母体不久的小生物 the young; larva; little organism still in the mother's body or having just left the mother's body

【幼小】yòuxiǎo 未成年；未长成 young and small; immature：～的心灵 immature mind｜～的果树 young fruit trees

【幼稚】yòuzhì ❶ 年纪小 young ❷ 形容头脑简单或缺乏经验 childish; puerile; naive：～的想法 naive ideas

【幼稚病】yòuzhìbìng 看问题或处理问题简单化，不作深入分析的思想毛病 infantile disorder; view and handle problems in an oversimplified way and fail to making deep analysis

【幼稚园】yòuzhìyuán 幼儿园的旧称 old name for 幼儿园 yòu'éryuán

【幼株】yòuzhū 初生的植物体（指种子植物）young plant; seedling; seed plant

【幼子】yòuzǐ 最小的儿子；幼小的儿子 youngest son：弱妻～ frail wife and little children

有 yòu〈书 *fml.*〉same as 又 yòu：三十～八年 thirty-eight years

☞ yǒu on p. 2326

佑(祐) yòu 保佑 help; protect; bless

侑 yòu〈书 *fml.*〉劝人(吃、喝) press sb. to eat or drink; urge：～食 press somebody to eat | ～觞(劝人饮酒) urge somebody to drink

狖 yòu 古书上说的一种猴 a kind of monkey as described in ancient books

柚 yòu ❶ 常绿乔木,叶子大而阔,卵形,花白色,很香,果实大,冬季成熟,球形或扁圆形,果皮淡黄,果肉白色或粉红色,是普通的水果。产于我国南部地区。shaddock (*Citrus grandis*); pomelo; evergreen tree with large ovate leaves, white, fragrant flowers and big fruits. The fruit ripens in winter, is round or flat round in shape, has a pale-yellow rind, white or pink juicy pulp, and is a common fruit growing in south China. ❷ 这种植物的果实。有的地区叫文旦。fruit of the plant; called 文旦 wéndàn in some regions ‖ 通称 common name as 柚子 yòu·zi

☞ yóu on p. 2323

囿 yòu〈书 *fml.*〉❶ 养动物的园子 animal farm; enclosure; park：鹿～ deer farm; deer park | 园～ animal farm ❷ 局限;拘泥 limited; hampered：～于成见 be blinded by prejudice

宥 yòu〈书 *fml.*〉宽恕;原谅 excuse; pardon; forgive：原～excuse; pardon; forgive | 宽～excuse; pardon; forgive | 尚希见～。Please accept my apologies.

诱 yòu ❶ 诱导 guide; lead; induce：循循善～ be good at giving systematic guidance; teach with skill and patience ❷ 使用手段引人随从自己的意愿 lure; seduce; entice：引～ induce; lure | ～敌深入 lure the enemy in deep

【诱捕】yòubǔ 引诱捕捉 trap (animals)：用灯光～害虫 trap injurious insects by the use of light

【诱导】yòudǎo ❶ 劝诱教导;引导 guide; lead; induce：对学生要多用启发和～的方法 give more guidance and induction to students | 这些故事的结局很能～观众进行思索。The ending of these stories is thought-provoking. ❷ 物理学上指感应 (phys.) induction ❸ 大脑皮层中兴奋过程引起抑制过程的加强,或者抑制过程引起兴奋过程的加强 process of excitation giving rise to the process of inhibition, or process of inhibition giving rise to the process of excitation of the cerebral cortex

【诱饵】yòu'ěr 捕捉动物时用来引诱它的食物 bait; anything used as a lure ◇用金钱作～拖人下水 use money as a bait to trap sb.

【诱发】yòufā ❶ 诱导启发 bring out (sth. potential or latent); induce; cause to happen：～人的联想 (of something) connect in one's mind; spark immagination ❷ 导致发生(多指疾病) bring out (a disease); cause to occur：～肠炎 precipitate enteritis (oft. by complication)

【诱供】yòugòng 用不正当的方法诱使刑事被告人按侦查、审判人员的主观意图或推断进行陈述 secure a confession by trickery; trap a person (a defendant) into confessing by improper means as desired by investigators and judges; induce a person to make a confession

【诱拐】yòuguǎi 用诱骗的方法把别人家的妇女或儿童弄走 abduct; carry off (a woman) by fraud; kidnap (a child)

【诱惑】yòuhuò ❶ 使用手段,使人认识模糊而做坏事 entice; tempt; seduce; lure ❷ 吸引;招引 attract; allure：窗外是一片～人的景色。It's a captivating sight outside the window. *or* The window opens onto a charming view.

【诱奸】yòujiān 用欺骗的手段使异性跟自己发生性行为 entice a person of the opposite sex into unlawful sexual intercourse; seduce

【诱骗】yòupiàn 诱惑欺骗 inveigle; cajole; trap; trick

【诱杀】yòushā 引诱出来杀死 trap and kill; lure to destruction：用灯光～棉铃虫 lure bollworms to their death with lamps

【诱降】yòuxiáng 引诱敌人投降 lure into surrender

【诱胁】yòuxié 利诱威胁 cajole and coerce

【诱因】yòuyīn 导致某种事情发生的原因(多指疾病 oft. of an illness) cause

【诱致】yòuzhì 导致;招致(不好的结果) lead to; cause (negative result)

蚴 yòu 绦虫、血吸虫等动物的幼体 larva of a tapeworm or cercaria of a schistosome：尾～ cercaria | 毛～ miracidium

釉 yòu same as 釉子 yòu·zi

【釉质】yòuzhì 齿冠表面的一层硬组织,主要成分是磷酸钙和碳酸钙,此外还含有氟和一些有机质。有保护牙齿免受磨损的作用。enamel; layer of hard tissues covering the crown of a tooth, which consists chiefly of calcium phosphate and calcium carbonate, and also fluorine and organic matters, and helps to protect the tooth from wear; also 珐琅质 fàlángzhì; (图见 ☞ figure for 齿 chǐ on p. 263)

【釉子】yòu·zi 以石英、长石、硼砂、黏土等为原料,磨成粉末,加水调制而成的物质,用来涂在陶瓷半成品的表面,烧制后发出玻璃光泽,并能增加陶瓷的机械强度和绝缘性能 glaze; substance prepared from powdered quartz, feldspar, borax and clay blended with water, and used to coat the surface of semi-finished ceramic ware, giving a glassy finish and increasing the mechanical strength and insulation of a ceramic product after firing

鼬 yòu 哺乳动物的一科,身体细长,四肢短小,尾较粗,唇有须,毛有黄褐、棕、灰棕等色。如黄鼬、紫貂。weasel (*Mustela sibirica*); mammal with a long, slender body, short legs, a bushy tail, moustache about the mouth, and yellowish brown, brown or greyish-brown hair, such as yellow weasel and sable

yū (ㄩ)

迂 yū ❶ 曲折;绕弯 circuitous; winding; roundabout:～回 circuitous; winding; roundabout|～道访问 make a detour to call on somebody ❷ 迂腐 clinging to outworn rules and ideas; pedantic:～论 pedantic view|这人～得很。He's a very pedant man.

【迂夫子】yūfūzǐ 迂腐的读书人 pedant scholar

【迂腐】yūfǔ (言谈、行事)拘泥于陈旧的准则,不适应新时代 (of speeches or actions) stubbornly clinging to outworn rules and ideas; pedantic:～之谈 pedantic talk

【迂缓】yūhuǎn (行动)迟缓;不直截 (of movement) slow; dilatory

【迂回】yūhuí ❶ 回旋;环绕 circuitous; tortuous; roundabout:～曲折 circuitous; tortuous; roundabout ❷ 绕到敌人侧面或后面(进攻敌人) outflank(the enemy and attack):～包抄 outflank and envelop|～战术 outflanking tactics

【迂阔】yūkuò 不切合实际 high-sounding and impracticable:～之论 impractical views

【迂曲】yūqū 迂回曲折 tortuous; circuitous:山路～难行 tortuous and difficult mountain path

【迂执】yūzhí 迂腐固执 pedantic and obstinate:生性～ pedantic and obstinate by nature

【迂拙】yūzhuō 迂阔笨拙 impractical and stupid

吁 yū 〈拟声词 *onom.*〉吆喝牲口的声音 whoa; command to an animal to stop or slow down

☞ xū on p.2161 and yù on p.2348

纡 yū ❶ 弯曲;曲折 winding; tortuous:萦～ wind around ❷ 〈书 *fml.*〉系;结 tie, bind:～金佩紫(指地位显贵) wear a gold ornament and a purple gown (symbolic of high official rank)

【纡回】yūhuí 〈书 *fml.*〉same as 迂回 yūhuí ①

【纡徐】yūxú 〈书 *fml.*〉从容缓慢的样子 unhurried; leisurely

於 Yū 姓 a surname

☞ wū on p.2017 and 于[1] yú on p.2335

淤(❹瘀) yū ❶ 淤积 become silted up; be choked with silt:大雨过后,院子里～了一层泥。The courtyard was silted up after a heavy rain. ❷ 淤积起来的 silt:～泥 silt|～地 alluvial land ❸ 淤积的泥沙;淤泥 silt; sediment; mud:河～ sludge from a riverbed|沟～ drainage silt ❹ (血液)不流通 (of blood) stasis:～血 extravasated blood ❺ 〈方 *dial.*〉液体沸腾溢出 spill; overflow:米汤～了一锅台。The boiling rice split all over the kitchen range.

【淤灌】yūguàn 在洪水期放水灌溉,让洪水带来的泥沙和养分淤积在田地里,以改善土壤的性质,增加土壤的肥力 warping; irrigate fields with flood water to deposit silt and nutrients in the fields during the flood season so as to improve the soil and increase its fertility

【淤积】yūjī (水里的泥沙等)沉积 (of mud, sand, etc. in water) silt up; deposit ◇忧愁～在心头。Worry was pent up in his heart.

【淤泥】yūní 河流、湖沼、水库、池塘中沉积的泥沙 silt; sludge; ooze in a river, lake, water reservoir or pond

【淤塞】yūsè (水道)被沉积的泥沙堵塞 silt up; be choked with silt:河床～。The riverbed was silted up.

【淤血】yūxuè 凝聚不流通的血 extravasated blood

【淤滞】yūzhì ❶ (水道)因泥沙沉积而不能畅通 (of the flow of a river, etc.) be retarded by silt; silt up:疏通～的河道 dredge a silted watercourse ❷ 〈中医 *Chin. med.*〉指经络血脉等阻塞不通 stasis (of blood or other bodily fluids)

yú (ㄩˊ)

于[1](於) yú ❶ 〈介词 *prep.*〉a)在 in; on; at:她生～1949年。She was born in 1949.|黄河发源～青海。The Yellow River rises in Qinghai. b)向 towards; to:问道～盲 ask a blind man for the way|告慰～知己 feel it a great relief to tell one's friend|求救～人 ask somebody for help c)给 to:嫁祸～人 shift the blame to others|献身～科学事业 dedicate oneself to science d)对;对于 to:忠～祖国 be loyal to the motherland|有益～人民 be beneficial to the people|形势～我们有利。The situation is favourable to us. c)自;从 from:青出～蓝 the disciple outdoes the master|出～自愿 voluntarily f)表示比较 [to indicate comparison]:大～ bigger than|少～ less than; fewer than|高～ higher than; above; over|低～ lower than; below; under g)表示被动 [in passive voice] by:见笑～大方之家 be laughed at by experts ❷ 后缀 postfix; suffix a)动词后缀[suffix after a verb]:合～ conform to; accord with; tally with|属～ belong to|在～ lie in|至～ as for b)形容词后缀 [suffix after an adjective]:勇～负责 dare to be responsible for; have the courage to bear responsibility

for|善～调度 good at dispatching|易～了解 easy to understand|难～实行 difficult to carry out

☞ 於 wū on p. 2017 and Yū on p. 2335

于[2] Yú 姓 a surname

【于今】yújīn ❶ 到现在 up to the present; since: 故乡一别,～十载。It's ten years since we parted at our native village. ❷ 如今 nowadays; today; now: 这城市建设得非常快,～已看不出原来的面貌。The city has been built up really fast — it's changed beyond recognition.

【于思】yúsāi〈书 *fml.*〉形容胡须很多(多叠用 oft. used in a repetitive way) heavily bearded

【于是】yúshì〈连词 *conj.*〉表示后一事紧接着前一事,后一事往往是由前一事引起的[indicating that the latter immediately following the former, and that the latter is often led to by the former] so; then; thereupon; hence: 大家一鼓励,我～恢复了信心。With your encouragement, I've regained my confidence. also 于是乎 yúshìhū

与(與) yú same as 欤 yǔ

☞ yǔ on p. 2342 and yù on p. 2346

予 yú〈书 *fml.*〉我 I; me

☞ yǔ on p. 2342

【予取予求】yú qǔ yú qiú 原指从我这里取,从我这里求(财物)(见于《左传》僖公七年),后用来指任意索取 take from me whatever you please; take whatever one wants (see *The Zuo Commentary · Duke Xi 7th Year*); take freely; make unlimited demands

邪 Yú 周朝国名,在今河南沁阳西北 Yu, name of a state during the Zhou Dynasty in northwest of present-day Qinyang in Henan Province

伃 yú ☞ 倢伃 jiéyú on p. 994

玙(璵) yú〈书 *fml.*〉美玉 beautiful jade

余[1] yú ❶ 我 I; me ❷ (Yú) 姓 a surname

余[2](餘) yú ❶ 剩下 surplus; spare; remaining: ～粮 surplus grains|～钱 spare money (or cash)|不遗～力 spare no efforts|收支相抵,尚～一百元。After paying all the expenses, there is a balance of one hundred yuan. ❷ 大数或度量单位等后面的零头 more than; odd; over: 五百～斤 five hundred odd *jin*|一丈～ more than one *zhang* ❸ 指某种事情、情况以外或以后的时间 time beyond or after an event: 业～ spare time|兴奋之～,高歌一曲 raise one's voice to sing a song in excitement

【余波】yúbō 指事件结束以后留下的影响 aftermath; repercussions: 纠纷的～aftermath of a dispute|～未平。The repercussions are still being felt.

【余存】yúcún (出入相抵后)剩余;结存 balance; remainder: 核对销售数量和～数量 check the amount of sales and stock

【余党】yúdǎng 未消灭尽的党羽 remnants of an overthrown clique (or gang); remaining confederates

【余地】yúdì 指言语或行动中留下的可回旋的地步 leeway; margin; room; latitude: 不留～ leave no room; leave no margin|有充分考虑的～ room for full consideration

【余毒】yúdú 残留的毒素或祸害 residual poison; vestige of sth. pernicious; pernicious influence: 肃清～ eliminate the pernicious influence

【余额】yú'é ❶ 名额中余下的空额 vacancies yet to be filled ❷ 账目上剩余的金额 remaining sum; balance; surplus

【余风】yúfēng 遗留下来的风气 lingering remnants of an old custom

【余割】yúgē ☞ 三角函数 sānjiǎo hánshù on p. 1652

【余晖】yúhuī 傍晚的阳光 sunset glow; evening glow: 夕阳的～last rays of the setting sun; afterglow|晚霞的～last rays of the setting sun; afterglow; also 余辉 yúhuī

【余悸】yújì 事后还感到的恐惧 lingering fear: 心有～ still have a lingering fear

【余角】yújiǎo 平面上两个角的和等于一个直角(90°),这两个角就互为余角 complementary angle; either of two angles whose sum is 90°

【余烬】yújìn ❶ 燃烧后剩下的灰和没烧尽的东西 ashes; embers: 纸烟～ cigarette ash ❷〈比喻 *fig.*〉战乱后残存的东西 ruins; wreckage: 劫后～ruins of war

【余力】yúlì 剩余的力量;多余的精力 surplus energy or strength: 不遗～ spare no efforts; spare no pains; do one's utmost|没有～顾及此事 have no pains to attend to this matter

【余利】yúlì 指工商业所得的利润 profit

【余沥】yúlì〈书 *fml.*〉剩余的酒 heeltap; leftover liquor;〈比喻 *fig.*〉分到的一点小利 fringe benefit; small share of profit: 分沾～ share the fringe benefit

【余粮】yúliáng 吃用之外余下的粮食 surplus grain

【余年】yúnián 晚年 one's remaining years: 安度～ spend one's remaining years in peace

【余孽】yúniè 残余的坏人或恶势力 remaining evil element; leftover evil; surviving supporter of an evil cause: 封建～ dregs of feudalism|铲除～ root out the remnant evil elements

【余切】yúqiē ☞ 三角函数 sānjiǎo hánshù on p. 1652

【余缺】yúquē 富余和缺欠 surplus and deficiency：互通有无，调剂～ each making up the other's deficiency his own surplus

【余热】yúrè ❶ 生产过程中剩余的热量（of a production process）surplus energy：利用～取暖 use surplus energy for heating purposes ❷〈比喻 *fig*.〉离休、退休以后的老年人的精力和作用 old people's capacity for work：老专家要发挥～，为社会多做贡献。Old experts should do what they can in their old age to make contributions to society.

【余生】yúshēng ❶ 指晚年 remainder of one's life; evening years; one's remaining years：安度～ spend one's remaining years in peace ❷（大灾难后）侥幸保全的生命 survival（after a disaster）：劫后～ survive a disaster; survival of a war（or disaster）| 忧患～ one who has survived a great misfortune | 虎口～ survival of a tiger's jaws; survival of a great disaster; escape from a misfortune

【余剩】yúshèng 剩余 surplus：去年收成好，今年有～。The good harvest last year being good, there is a surplus this year.

【余数】yúshù 整数除法中，被除数未被除数整除所剩的大于0而小于除数的部分。如27÷6=4…3，即不完全商是4，余数是3。remainder（after division）; what is left when a smaller number is subtracted from a larger number; what is left undivided when one number is divided by another that is not one of its factors, as 27÷6=4…3, i.e., the incomplete quotient is 4 and the remainder is 3.

【余外】yúwài〈方 *dial*.〉除此之外 besides; apart from this：荒野里只见几个坟头，～什么也看不到。Nothing but a few graves could be seen in the wilderness.

【余威】yúwēi 剩余的威力 remaining prestige or influence：～犹存 one's prestige（or influence）remains | 傍晚，地面仍发散着烈日的～。The heat of the scorching sun remains on the surface in the evening.

【余味】yúwèi 留下的耐人回想的味道 agreeable aftertaste; pleasant impression：歌声美妙，～无穷。The beautiful singing left a lasting and pleasant impression.

【余暇】yúxiá 工作或学习之外的空闲时间 spare time; leisure time; leisure

【余下】yúxià 剩下 remaining：一共一千元，用去六百元，还～四百元。There was 1,000 yuan in total. After spending 600 yuan, one has 400 yuan left.

【余弦】yúxián ☞ 三角函数 sānjiǎo hánshù on p.1652

【余兴】yúxìng ❶ 未尽的兴致 lingering interest; wish to prolong a pleasant diversion：～未尽 have a lingering interest ❷ 会议或宴会之后附带举行的文娱活动 entertainment after a meeting or a dinner party：会议到此结束，～节目现在开始。So much for the meeting. The entertainment now begins.

【余音】yúyīn 指歌唱或演奏后好像还留在耳边的声音 lingering sound（of singing or music）：～缭绕。The music lingered in the air.

【余音绕梁】yú yīn rào liáng 歌唱停止后，余音好像还在绕着屋梁回旋。形容歌声或音乐优美，耐人回味。sound of music lingering around the beams; music lingering in the air long after the performance; the singing or music is so beautiful as to leave the listeners an aftertaste

【余勇可贾】yú yǒng kě gǔ 还有剩余力量可以使出来 with plenty of mettle left in one; with strength yet to spare

【余裕】yúyù 富裕 enough and to spare; ample：～的时间 time to spare | ～的精力 ample energy | 这几年吃穿不但不愁，而且还有～。We not only have no worries about food and clothing these years, but have enough and to spare.

【余韵】yúyùn 遗留下来的韵致 remaining grace：饶有～ as graceful as before

【余震】yúzhèn 大地震之后紧跟着发生的小地震。较大的余震也能造成破坏。aftershock; minor earthquake immediately following a major one at the same place or nearby. A major aftershock may also cause destruction.

欤（歟） yú〈书 *fml*.〉〈助词 *aux*.〉❶ 表示疑问或反问，跟'吗'或'呢'相同 expressing doubt, surprise, etc., same as 吗·ma or 呢·ne：子非三闾大夫～？Aren't you the cabinet minister Qu Yuan? | 呜呼，是谁之咎～？Alas, who is to blame? ❷ 表示感叹，跟'啊'相同［used in an exclamation］same as 啊·a：论者之言，一似管窥虎～！Indeed, the speaker's argument was as one-sided as looking at a tiger through a bamboo tube.

妤 yú ☞［婕妤］jiéyú on p.994

盂 yú（～儿 yúr）盛液体的敞口器具 broad-mouthed receptacle for holding liquid; jar：水～ water jar; water basin | 痰～ spittoon | 漱口～儿 mouth cleansing cup

【盂兰盆会】yúlánpén huì 农历七月十五日佛教徒为超度祖先亡灵所举行的仪式，有斋僧、拜忏、放焰口等活动 Ullambana; Buddhist ceremony held on the 15th of the 7th lunar month to redeem the souls of one's deceased ancestors, including such activities as offering vegetarian's food to monks, praying for sb.'s redemption, and exorcising the *ulkamukha*（flaming-mouth hungry ghosts）; Buddhist name of the Ghost Festival［盂兰盆，梵 Sanskrit: ullambana］

臾 yú ☞ 须臾 xūyú on p.2162

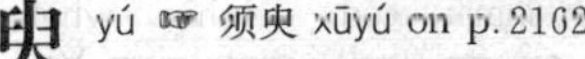

鱼(魚) yú ❶ 生活在水中的脊椎动物,体温随外界温度而变化,一般身体侧扁,有鳞和鳍,用鳃呼吸。种类极多,大部分可供食用或制鱼胶。fish (*Pisces*), vertebrate with a flat body living in water and having permanent gills for breathing, scales, and fins, its body temperature changing with the outside temperature, coming in many species, most of which are used for food or making fish glue ❷ (Yú) 姓 a surname

【鱼白】[1] yúbái ❶ 鱼的精液 fish sperm; milt ❷ 〈方 *dial.*〉same as 鱼鳔 yúbiào

【鱼白】[2] yúbái same as 鱼肚白 yúdùbái: 东方一线~,黎明已经到来。A streak of light appeared over the east horizon, heralding the dawn.

【鱼鳔】yúbiào 鱼腹内白色的囊状器官。鳔的胀缩可以调节身体的浮沉。鱼鳔可以制鱼胶。air bladder; swim bladder; white bladder organ in the fish belly, which can be used in making fish glue. Expansion and contraction of the bladder help to regulate the floating and sinking of the fish body.

【鱼舱】yúcāng 渔船上供装载鱼、虾等的船舱 cabin in a fishing boat for holding fishes, shrimps, etc.

【鱼池】yúchí 养渔的池塘 fish pond

【鱼翅】yúchì 鲨鱼的鳍经过加工之后,其软骨条叫做鱼翅,是珍贵的食品 shark's fin (referring to the cartilage obtained by processing shark's fins, used as a delicacy); also 翅 chì or 翅子 chì·zi

【鱼唇】yúchún 海味,用鲨鱼的唇加工而成 shark's lip (as food)

【鱼刺】yúcì 鱼的细而尖的骨头 fishbone, which is thin and pointed

【鱼肚】yúdǔ 食品,用某些鱼类的鳔制成 fish maw (as food), made from the air bladders of some fishes

【鱼肚白】yúdùbái 像鱼肚子的颜色,白里略带青。多指黎明时东方天的颜色。whitish colour of a fish's belly; grey dawn: 天边现出了~。The first whitish rays have appeared above the horizon.

【鱼饵】yú'ěr 钓鱼用的鱼食 (fish) bait; food for fish

【鱼粉】yúfěn 鱼类或鱼类加工后剩下的头、尾、内脏等经过蒸干、压榨、粉碎等工序而制成的产品,含有丰富的蛋白质,是良好的饲料 fish meal; product made by drying, pressing and crushing the head, tail and internal organs of fishes, a good feed rich in protein

【鱼肝油】yúgānyóu 从鲨鱼、鳕鱼和海豚、鲸等的肝脏中提炼出来的脂肪,黄色,有腥味,主要含有维生素A和维生素D。常用于夜盲症、佝偻病等。cod-liver oil; yellow fat extracted from the livers of shark, cod, dolphin, whale, etc., with a strong smell, containing Vitamin A and Vitamin D, and often used for treating night blindness, rickets, etc.

【鱼鼓】yúgǔ same as 渔鼓 yúgǔ

【鱼鼓道情】yúgǔ dàoqíng ☞ 道情 dàoqíng on p. 400

【鱼贯】yúguàn 像游鱼一样一个挨一个地接连着(走) one following the other like the swimming fish; in single file: ~而行 walk in a single line; file in | ~入场 enter a hall in a single line

【鱼花】yúhuā same as 鱼苗 yúmiáo

【鱼胶】yújiāo ❶ 用鱼鳔或用鱼鳞、鱼骨熬成的胶。熔化后黏性强,用做黏合剂,也用来制胶片。fish glue; isinglass; glue made from fish bladder, fish scales or fishbones ❷ 〈方 *dial.*〉鱼的鳔,特指黄鱼的鳔 air bladder; swim bladder (esp. that of yellow croakers)

【鱼具】yújù same as 渔具 yújù

【鱼雷】yúléi 一种能在水中自行推进、自行控制方向和深度的炸弹。略呈圆筒形,由舰艇发射或飞机投掷,用来攻击敌方的舰艇或破坏港口的建筑物。torpedo; large, cylindrical-shaped, self-propelled, underwater projectile with self-controlled direction and depth, for launching against enemy ships or harbour buildings from a submarine or airplane

【鱼雷艇】yúléitǐng 以鱼雷为主要武器的小型舰艇,能迅速而灵活地逼近敌舰,发射鱼雷 torpedo boat; small, fast, manoeuverable warship for attacking with torpedo as its main weapon; also 鱼雷快艇 yúléi kuàitǐng

【鱼鳞】yúlín 鱼身上的鳞片,可以制鱼胶 fish scale; scale: it is used in making fish glue

【鱼鳞坑】yúlínkēng 为蓄水或种树而在山坡上挖的坑,交错排列像鱼鳞 fish-scale pits; pits arranged like fish scales, dug on mountain slopes for holding water or planting trees

【鱼龙混杂】yú lóng hùnzá 〈比喻 *fig.*〉坏人和好人混在一起 dragons and fishes jumbled together; good and bad people mixed up

【鱼米之乡】yú mǐ zhī xiāng 指盛产鱼和大米的富庶的地方 land of fish and rice; water-bound place where fish and rice abound

【鱼苗】yúmiáo 由鱼子孵化出来供养殖用的小鱼 (fish) fry; newly hatched fish for feeding

【鱼目混珠】yú mù hùn zhū 拿鱼眼睛冒充珍珠 pass off fish eyes as pearls; 〈比喻 *fig.*〉拿假的东西冒充真的东西 pass off sth. sham as genuine

【鱼漂】yúpiāo (~儿 yúpiāor)钓鱼时拴在线上的能漂浮的东西,作用是使鱼钩不致沉底。鱼漂下沉,就知道鱼已上钩。cork on a fishing line; float: it prevents the fishing hook from sinking to the bottom. If the float sinks, it means the fish is already hooked.

【鱼肉】yúròu《史记·项羽本纪》:'人为刀俎,我为鱼肉。'(刀俎指宰割的器具,鱼肉指受宰割者) 后来比喻用暴力欺凌,残害 'be meat on sb's chopping block' (*Records of the Historian · Official Records of Xiang Yu*); be at sb.'s mercy; (fig.) ruthlessly persecute; cruelly oppress: 土豪横行乡里,～百姓。The local tyrants rode roughshod and savagely oppressed the people in the countryside.

【鱼水】yúshuǐ 鱼和水 fish and water; 〈比喻 *fig.*〉彼此亲密 be close to each other: ～情深 close relationship between fish and water; inseparable

【鱼水情】yúshuǐqíng 形容极其亲密的情谊,就像鱼和水不能分离一样 inseparable relationship between fish and water; close relationship

【鱼死网破】yú sǐ wǎng pò 〈比喻 *fig.*〉斗争双方同归于尽 either the fish dies or the net gets torn — life-and-death struggle: 拼个～ fight at the risk of mutual destruction

【鱼松】yúsōng 用鱼类的肉加工制成的绒状或碎末状的食品 dried fish floss; flosslike or minced food made from fish meat; also 鱼肉松 yúròusōng

【鱼网】yúwǎng same as 渔网 yúwǎng

【鱼尾纹】yúwěiwén 人的眼角与鬓角之间的像鱼尾的皱纹 crow's feet; wrinkles that develop at the outer corners of the eyes of adults

【鱼鲜】yúxiān 指鱼虾等水产食物 seafood like fish, shrimp, etc.

【鱼汛】yúxùn 某些鱼类由于产卵、越冬等原因在一定时期内高度集中在一定海域,适于捕捞的时期 fishing season; some fishes congregate themselves in a given sea area and given period for spawning and surviving winter; also 渔汛 yúxùn

【鱼雁】yúyàn 〈书 *fml.*〉〈比喻 *fig.*〉书信(古时有借鱼腹和雁足传信的说法) letters (there is an ancient saying that the fish belly and wild goose' feet were used to carry messages): 频通～ often write to each other | ～往还 exchange letters

【鱼秧子】yúyāng·zi 比鱼苗稍大的小鱼 fingerling; small fish slightly bigger than fish fry

【鱼鹰】yúyīng ❶ 鹗的通称 general term for 鹗 è ❷ 鸬鹚的通称 general term for 鸬鹚 lúcí

【鱼游釜中】yú yóu fǔ zhōng 〈比喻 *fig.*〉处境危险,快要灭亡 like fish swimming in a cooking pot; in imminent peril

【鱼子】yúzǐ 鱼的卵 (fish) roe: ～酱 caviar

禺 yú 古书上说的一种猴 a kind of monkey as described in ancient books

竽 yú 古乐器,形状像现在的笙 *yu*, ancient wind instrument shaped like the modern *sheng*, but slightly bigger than it

舁 yú 〈方 *dial.*〉共同抬东西 (of two or more persons) carry

俞 yú ❶ 文言叹词,表示允许 [an interjection in classical Chinese indicating consent] ❷ (Yú)姓 a surname
☞ 腧 shù on p.1790

【俞允】yúyǔn 〈书 *fml.*〉允许 accede to (a request); consent; approve; permit; allow

旟(旗) yú 〈古代 *arch.*〉一种军旗 military banner

馀 yú ☞ [犰狳] qiúyú on p.1583

馀 yú ❶ ☞ 余² yú on p.2336。在余和馀意义上可能混淆时,仍用馀 The character 馀 is still used when 余 yú and 馀 yú are confused in meaning: ～年无多。I've few years left. ❷ (Yú) 姓 a surname

谀 yú 〈书 *fml.*〉谄媚;奉承 flatter: 阿(ē)～ flatter | ～辞 flattering words; flattery

【谀辞】yúcí 阿谀奉承的话 flattering words; flattery; also 谀词 yúcí

娱 yú ❶ 使快乐 give pleasure to; amuse: 聊以自～ just to amuse oneself ❷ 快乐 joy; pleasure; amusement: 欢～ joy; pleasure; amusement | 耳目之～ pleasures of the senses

【娱乐】yúlè ❶ 使人快乐;消遣 amusement; entertainment; recreation: ～场所 public place of entertainment ❷ 快乐有趣的活动 recreational activities; hobby: 下棋是他爱好的～。Chess is his favourite amusement.

萸 yú ☞ [茱萸] zhūyú on p.2499

雩 yú 〈古代 *arch.*〉求雨的祭礼 sacrificial rite to pray for rain

渔(𩺰) yú ❶ 捕鱼 fishing; fishery: ～捞 fishery | ～船 fishing boat; fishing vessel | ～翁 old fisherman | ～业 fishery | 竭泽而～ dry up the pond to catch the fish in it ❷ 谋取(不应得的东西) take sth. one is not entitled to: ～利 seek illegal gains

【渔霸】yúbà 占有渔船、鱼网等或开鱼行剥削、欺压渔民的恶霸 local despot who forcibly possesses others' fishing boats and fishing nets, exploiting and bullying fishermen, and monopolizes the fishing market

【渔产】yúchǎn 渔业产品 aquatic products: 沿海～丰富。There is an abundance of fishes along the coast.

【渔场】yúchǎng 海上集中捕鱼的区域,一般为鱼群密集的地方 fishing ground; fishery; place where fishes are bred and caught

【渔船】yúchuán 用于捕鱼的船 fishing boat

【渔村】yúcūn 渔民聚居的村庄 fishing village; village where fishermen live

【渔夫】yúfū 以捕鱼为业的男子 fisherman

【渔港】yúgǎng 停泊渔船的港湾 fishing port (or harbour)

【渔歌】yúgē 渔民所唱的、反映渔民生活的歌曲 fisherman's song

【渔鼓】yúgǔ ❶ 打击乐器,在长竹筒的一头蒙上薄皮,用手敲打。是演唱道情的主要伴奏乐器。percussion instrument made of a long bamboo tube with one end covered with a piece of thin animal hide, used to accompany the chanting of folk tales ❷ 指道情,因用渔鼓伴奏而得名 chanting of folk tales to the accompaniment of a bamboo percussion instrument; ☞ 道情 dàoqíng on p. 400 ‖ also 鱼鼓 yúgǔ

【渔鼓道情】yúgǔ dàoqíng ☞ 道情 dàoqíng on p. 400

【渔火】yúhuǒ 渔船上的灯火 lights on fishing boats: 入夜，江上～点点。There were myriads of lights on fishing boats on the river when night fell.

【渔家】yújiā 以捕鱼为业的人家 fisherman's family

【渔具】yújù 捕鱼或钓鱼的器具 fishing tackle; also 鱼具 yújù

【渔利】yúlì ❶ 趁机会谋取不正当的利益 seek illegal profit: 从中～ exploit others to benefit oneself ❷ ☞ 渔人之利 yú rén zhī lì

【渔猎】yúliè ❶ 捕鱼打猎 fishing and hunting ❷〈书 *fml.*〉掠夺 plunder; loot: ～百姓 plunder the common people ❸〈书 *fml.*〉贪求并追逐 hanker after; pursue: ～女色 seek carnal pleasure

【渔轮】yúlún 捕鱼的轮船 fishing vessel

【渔民】yúmín 以捕鱼为业的人 fisherman; fisherfolk

【渔人之利】yú rén zhī lì〈比喻 *fig.*〉第三者利用双方的矛盾冲突而取得的利益 fisherman's gains; profit reaped by a third party: 坐收～ reap a ready profit from fighting between two other parties; ☞ 鹬蚌相争，渔人得利 yùbàng xiāng zhēng, yúrén dé lì on p. 2354

【渔网】yúwǎng 捕鱼用的网 fishnet; fishing net; also 鱼网 yúwǎng

【渔翁】yúwēng 称年老的渔夫 old fisherman

【渔汛】yúxùn same as 鱼汛 yúxùn

【渔业】yúyè 捕捞或养殖水生动植物的生产事业 fishery; industry of catching or raising fish

【渔舟】yúzhōu〈书 *fml.*〉same as 渔船 yúchuán

隅 yú ❶ 角落 corner; nook: 墙～ corner | 城～ corner of a city wall | 向～ face a corner in a room; sit alone in a corner | 一～之地 tiny place; corner of a country ❷ 靠边沿的地方 edge; outlying place; border: 海～ seaboard

揄 yú〈书 *fml.*〉牵引；提起 draw; raise

【揄扬】yúyáng〈书 *fml.*〉❶ 赞扬 praise: 极口～ laud ❷ 宣扬 publicize; advocate: ～大义 advocate justice

喁 yú〈书 *fml.*〉应和的声音 echoing sound ☞ yóng on p. 2311

【喁喁】yúyú〈书 *fml.*〉❶ 随声附和 echo ❷ 形容说话的声音(多用于小声说话) talk in an undertone; whisper: ～私语 talk privately in a low voice

☞ yóngyóng on p. 2311

嵎 yú ❶ 山弯儿 mountain curve ❷ same as 隅 yú

嵛 yú 昆嵛(Kūnyú)，山名，在山东 Kunyu, name of a mountain in Shandong Province

畬 yú〈书 *fml.*〉开垦过两年的田地 fields that have been cultivated for two years; fields in the third year of cultivation

☞ shē on p. 1692

逾(❶**踰**) yú ❶ 超过；越过 exceed; go beyond: ～期 expire; exceed the time limit; be overdue | ～限 exceed the limited period; exceed the time limit; be overdue | ～额 exceed the allowed amount | 年～六十 over sixty years old ❷ 更加 even more: ～甚 even more

【逾常】yúcháng 超过寻常 out of the ordinary; unusual: 欣喜～ be overjoyed

【逾分】yúfèn 过分 excessive; undue: ～的要求 excessive demands

【逾期】yú//qī 超过所规定的期限 exceed the time limit; be overdue: ～未归 fail to return when the leave is over | ～三天 be three days overdue; exceed the time limit by three days

【逾越】yúyuè 超越 exceed; go beyond: ～常规 depart from the usual practice | 不可～的障碍 insurmountable barrier; obstacle that cannot be crossed over

腴 yú ❶ (人)胖 fat; plump: 丰～ fat; plump ❷ 肥沃 fertile: 膏～ fertile

渝[1] yú 改变(多指态度或感情) (of one's attitude or feeling) change: 始终不～ always remain unchanged | 坚贞不～ remain loyal to

渝[2] Yú 重庆市的别称 another name for 重庆 Chóngqìng

愉 yú 愉快 pleased; happy; joyful; cheerful: ～悦 happy; cheerful | 面有不～之色 wear an annoyed expression; look displeased

【愉快】yúkuài 快意；舒畅 happy; joyful; cheerful: ～的微笑 happy smile | 心情～ in a happy mood; in a cheerful frame of mind | 生活过得很～ live a happy life

【愉悦】yúyuè 喜悦 joyful; cheerful; delighted: 怀着十分～的心情 be highly delighted; be very much pleased

觎 yú〈书 *fml.*〉紫色的马 purple horse

瑜 yú〈书〉❶ 美玉 beautiful jade; fine jade; gem ❷ 玉的光彩 lustre of gems, 〈比喻 *fig.*〉优点 virtues; good points: 瑕不掩～ one flaw cannot obscure the splendour of the jade; *or* the defects cannot obscure the virtues | 瑕～互见。Both defects and virtues are obvious.

【瑜伽】yújiā 印度的一种传统健身法。'瑜伽'意为'结合'，指修行。强调呼吸规则和静坐，以解除精神紧张，修身养性。yoga; a system of exercising involving the postures, breathing, etc. by which one seeks to ease tension, cultivate oneself, and keep fit, with emphasis on rules of breathing and sitting in deep meditation; also 瑜珈 yújiā [梵 Sanscrit: Yoga]

榆 yú 榆树,落叶乔木,叶子卵形,花有短梗。翅果倒卵形,通称榆钱。木材可供建筑或制器具用。elm (*Elmus*); deciduous tree with ovate leaves, short-stemmed flowers, obovate samara that is commonly called *yuqian* (elm seeds), and wood used in buildings or in making implements and utensils

【榆荚】yújiá 榆树的果实 elm seeds

【榆钱】yúqián (～儿 yúqiánr)榆荚,形状圆而小,像小铜钱 elm seeds, small and round, which looks like a small copper coin

虞1 yú ❶ 猜测;预料 supposition; prediction: 不～ unexpected; not anticipated ❷ 忧虑 anxiety; worry: 兴修水利,水旱无～ build water conservancy works so as to ward off scourges of drought and flood | 无冻馁之～ be secure against hunger and cold ❸ 欺骗 deceive; cheat; fool: 尔～我诈 mutual deception; each trying to cheat the other

虞2 Yú ❶ 传说中的朝代名,舜所建 Yu, name of a legendary dynasty founded by King Shun ❷ 周朝国名,在今山西平陆东北 Yu, name of a state in the Zhou(周) Dynasty to the northeast of present-day Pinglu in Shanxi Province ❸ (Yú) 姓 a surname

愚 yú ❶ 愚笨;傻 foolish; stupid: ～人 foolish man | ～不可及 couldn't be more foolish; be hopelessly stupid; height of folly | 大智若～。A man of great wisdom looks like a fool. ❷ 愚弄 fool; make a fool of: 为人所～ be fooled by others ❸ 用于自称的谦辞 [humble way of addressing oneself] I: ～兄 your unworthy elder brother — I | ～见 in my humble opinion | ～以为不可。I don't agree; I don't think you should do it.

【愚笨】yúbèn 头脑迟钝,不灵活 foolish; stupid; clumsy

【愚不可及】yú bù kě jí《论语·公冶长》:'宁武子,邦有道则知(智);邦无道则愚。其知可及也,其愚不可及也。'原指人为了应付不利局面假装愚痴,以免祸患,为常人所不及。后用来形容人极端愚蠢。*Anelects · Gongye Chang*: 'Ah, Ning Wuzi! He displayed great wisdom when his state was well-governed and enjoying the piping times of peace; he acted the part of a fool when his state was ill-governed and out of good order. People can match his wisdom, but none can equal his foolishness.'; couldn't be more foolish; be hopelessly stupid; height of folly; there can be no greater folly than this

【愚痴】yúchī 愚笨痴呆 stupid; idiotic; folly; silly

【愚蠢】yúchǔn 愚笨;不聪明 stupid; foolish; silly: ～无知 foolish and ignorant | 这种做法太～。This way of doing things is too stupid.

【愚钝】yúdùn 愚笨;不伶俐 slow-witted; stupid: 天资～ slow-witted; stupid

【愚公移山】Yúgong yí shān 传说古代有一位老人名叫北山愚公,家门前有两座大山挡住了路,他下决心要把山平掉,另一个老人河曲智叟笑他太傻,认为不可能。愚公回答说:'我死了有儿子,儿子死了还有孙子,子子孙孙是没有穷尽的。这两座山可不会再增高了,凿去一点就少一点,终有一天要凿平的。'(见于《列子·汤问》) Legend goes that there was an old man in ancient times who was known as the Foolish Old Man of North Mountain, who was determined to remove the two great mountains that stood beyond his doorway and obstructed the way. Another greybeard, known as the Wise Old Man, laughed at him for his foolishness of attempting to accomplishing the impossible. The Foolish Old Man replied: 'When I die, my sons will carry on; when they die, there will be my grandsons, and then their sons and grandsons, and so on to infinity. High as they are, the mountains cannot grow any higher and with every bit we dig, they will be that much lower. The day will finally come when they are cleared away.' (*Yin Tang's Questions*); 〈比喻 *fig*.〉做事有毅力,不怕困难 do things with dogged perseverance and fear no difficulty

【愚陋】yúlòu 愚昧鄙陋 stupid and ignorant: ～之见 stupid idea

【愚鲁】yúlǔ 愚笨 dull-witted; stupid: 自愧～ feel ashamed of one's foolishness | 生性～ stupid and dull-witted by nature

【愚昧】yúmèi 缺乏知识;愚蠢而不明事理 ignorant; benighted: ～无知 benighted; unenlightened; ignorant

【愚氓】yúméng 愚蠢的人 fool

【愚蒙】yúméng same as 愚昧 yúmèi

【愚民政策】yúmín zhèngcè 统治者为了便于统治人民而实行的愚弄人民,使人民处于愚昧无知和闭塞状态的政策 policy of keeping the people in ignorance; obscurantist policy; obscurantism

【愚弄】yúnòng 蒙蔽玩弄 deceive; hoodwink, make a fool of; dupe: 被人～ be fooled by others

【愚懦】yúnuò 愚昧怯懦 stupid and timid: 生性～ stupid and timid by nature

【愚顽】yúwán 愚昧而顽固 ignorant and stubborn

【愚妄】yúwàng 愚昧而狂妄 ignorant but self-important; stupid but conceited: ～可笑 ignorant and ridiculous

【愚拙】yúzhuō same as 愚笨 yúbèn

艅 yú [艅艎](yúhuáng)〈古时 *arch*.〉一种木船 a kind of wooden boat

覦 yú ☞ 觊覦 jìyú on p. 920

歈 yú 〈书 *fml.*〉❶ 歌 song ❷ same as 愉 yú

輿1 yú 〈书 *fml.*〉❶ 车 carriage; chariot: ～马 coach horse | 舍～登舟 change from a carriage to a boat ❷ 车上可以载人载物的部分 part of a carriage for passengers or goods ❸ 指轿 sedan chair: 肩～ sedan chair | 彩～ decorated sedan chair

輿2 yú 地 area; territory: ～地 territory; area | ～图 map

輿3 yú 众人的 public; popular: ～论 public opinion | ～情 public sentiment; popular feelings

【輿论】yúlùn 群众的言论 public opinion: ～界 the media; press circles | 社会～ public opinion | 国际～ world opinion | ～哗然 public outcry

【輿情】yúqíng 群众的意见和态度 public sentiment; popular feelings: 洞察～ know public sentiment well | ～激昂 seething public opinion

【輿图】yútú 〈书 *fml.*〉地图(多指疆域图) map (territorial map)

窬(踰) yú 〈书 *fml.*〉从墙上爬过去 climb over a wall: 穿～ get over a wall

褕 yú ☞ 襜褕 chānyú on p. 209

蝓 yú ☞ 蛞蝓 kuòyú on p. 1134

髃 yú 〈中医 *Chin. med.*〉指肩的前部 front part of a shoulder

yǔ (ㄩˇ)

与1(與) yǔ ❶ 给 give; offer; grant: 赠～ give; grant | ～人方便 give help to others; make things easy for others | 信件已交～本人。The letter has been given to the person concerned. ❷ 交往 get along with; be on good terms with: 相～ be on good terms with | ～国(友邦) friendly country; allied state ❸ 赞许;赞助 commend; support: ～人为善 well-intentioned; well-meaning ❹〈书 *fml.*〉等待 wait for; await: 岁不我～(时光不等我)。Time and Tide wait for no man.

与2(與) yǔ ❶〈介词 *prep.*〉跟 with: ～虎谋皮 ask a figer for its skin; attempt the impossible | ～困难作斗争 struggle against difficulties ❷〈连词 *conj.*〉和 and: 工业～农业 industry and agriculture | 批评～自我批评 criticism and self-criticism

☞ yú on p. 2336 and yù on p. 2346

【与共】yǔgòng 在一起 together: 生死～ share a common destiny; go through thick and thin together | 朝夕～ be together from morning till night | 荣辱～ share honour and dishonour (or disgrace)

【与虎谋皮】yǔ hǔ móu pí 跟老虎商量取下它的皮来 ask a tiger for its skin; 〈比喻 *fig.*〉所商量的事跟对方(多指坏人)利害冲突,绝对办不到 it's impossible to expect sb. (usu. an evil person) to act against his own interests

【与其】yǔqí 〈连词 *conj.*〉比较两件事的利害得失而决定取舍的时候,'与其'用在放弃的一面(后面常用'毋宁、不如'呼应) [used usu. with 毋宁 wùníng and 不如 bùrú] rather than; better than: ～扬汤止沸,不如釜底抽薪。The best way to stop water from boiling is to withdraw the burning firewood. *or* To stop water from boiling, withdrawing the burning firewood is better than scooping the water up and pouring it back again.

【与人为善】yǔ rén wéi shàn 原指赞助人学好,现多指善意帮助别人 well-intentioned; well-meaning; originally meaning to help others learn from good examples, now meaning to help others at good will

【与日俱增】yǔ rì jù zēng 随着时间的推移而不断增长 grow with each passing day; be steadily on the increase

【与世长辞】yǔ shì cháng cí 指人去世 depart from the world for ever; pass away

予 yǔ 给 give; grant; bestow: 授～奖状 award a certificate of merit | 免～处分 exempt sb. from punishment | 请～批准。Please give your endorsement.

☞ yú on p. 2336

【予人口实】yǔ rén kǒushí 给人留下指责的把柄 give people a handle

【予以】yǔyǐ 给以 give; grant: ～支持 give support | ～警告 give a warning | ～表扬 commend sb. | ～批评 give a reprimand; criticize sb.

屿(嶼) yǔ (旧读 formerly pronounced xù) 小岛 small island; islet: 岛～ islands; islands and islets

伛(傴) yǔ 曲(背);弯(腰) bow (to show respect): ～着背 hunchbacked; humpbacked | ～下腰 bow (to show respect)

【伛偻】yǔlǚ 〈书 *fml.*〉腰背弯曲 hunchbacked; humpbacked; bow (to show respect)

宇 yǔ ❶ 房檐。泛指房屋。eaves; house: 屋～ house; building | 栋～ house; building; mansion ❷ 上下四方,所有的空间;世界 space; universe; world: ～宙 space | ～内 in the world | 寰～ space; universe; world ❸ 年代地层单位的最高一级,跟宇相应的地质年代叫做宙 eonothem, the highest-level divison of geologic time, as corresponding to 'eon' ❹ 风度;气质 poise; temperament; bearing; manner: 眉～ features; manner | 神～ appearance; temperament | 器～ bearing; carriage; deportment ❺ (Yǔ)姓 a surname

【宇航】yǔháng ❶ 宇宙航行。指人造地球卫星、宇宙飞船等在太阳系内外空间航行。space navigation; astronavigation; flight of earth satellites and spacecraft in the space of the solar system ❷ 跟宇航有关的 astronavigation-related：～员 astronaut

【宇文】Yǔwén 姓 a surname

【宇宙】yǔzhòu ❶ 包括地球及其他一切天体的无限空间 universe; cosmos; infinite space including the earth and all other celestial bodies ❷ 一切物质及其存在形式的总体（'宇'指无限空间，'宙'指无限时间）。哲学上也叫世界。total of all matters and their forms of existence (*yu* refers to infinite space and *zhou* refers to infinite time); also called 'the world' in philosophy; ☞ 空间 kōngjiān on p. 1103, 时间 shíjiān on p. 1739 and 世界 shìjiè on p. 1753

【宇宙尘】yǔzhòuchén 散在宇宙空间的微粒状物质，密集像云雾，常作剧烈的回旋运动 cosmic dust; small particles of matter distributed throughout space which usu. form interplanetary or interstellar clouds that reflect and absorb light and often make violent cyclonic movements

【宇宙飞船】yǔzhòu fēichuán 用多级火箭做运载工具，从地球上发射出去能在宇宙空间航行的飞行器 spacecraft; spaceship; flying vehicle launched from the earth by means of multi-stage rocket as a carrier, which can navigate in the space

【宇宙观】yǔzhòuguān 世界观 world view; world outlook

【宇宙火箭】yǔzhòu huǒjiàn 可以脱离地心引力，发射到其他星球或星际空间的火箭 space rocket; rocket that can be sent to other planets or interplanetary space by breaking away from the terrestrial gravity

【宇宙空间】yǔzhòu kōngjiān 指地球大气层以外的空间 cosmic space; outer space; also 外层空间 wàicéng kōngjiān

【宇宙射线】yǔzhòu shèxiàn 从宇宙空间辐射到地球上的射线。能量极大，穿透力比爱克斯射线和丙种射线更强。cosmic rays; cosmic radiation; rays of high-energy charged particles from outer space, which have an ever stronger penetrating force than the X-rays and gamma rays; also 宇宙线 yǔzhòuxiàn

【宇宙速度】yǔzhòu sùdù 物体能够克服地心引力的作用离开地球进入星际空间的速度。宇宙速度分为三级，即第一宇宙速度、第二宇宙速度、第三宇宙速度。cosmic velocity; velocity at which a substance can leave the earth and enter the outer space by overcoming the effect of the terrestrial gravity. The cosmic velocity is classified into three grades: first cosmic velocity or circular velocity; second cosmic velocity or earth escape velocity; and third cosmic velocity or solar escape velocity.

羽[1] yǔ ❶ same as 羽毛 yǔmáo ① ❷ 鸟类或昆虫的翅膀 wings (of birds or insects)：振～ flap the wings ❸〈量词 *classifier*〉用于鸟类 used for birds：一～信鸽 a homing pigeon; a carrier pigeon

羽[2] yǔ 古代五音之一，相当于简谱的'6' tone of the ancient Chinese five-tone scale, corresponding to 6 in the numbered musical notation; ☞ 五音 wǔyīn on p. 2032

【羽缎】yǔduàn 光滑像缎子的棉织品，常用来做外衣和大衣的里子 sateen; smooth, glossy cloth of cotton made to imitate satin and often used in making the lining of outer garment and overcoat; also 羽毛缎 yǔmáoduàn

【羽冠】yǔguàn 鸟类头顶上的竖立的长羽毛，例如孔雀就有羽冠 crest (of a bird); long, feathered tuft on certain birds, as of a peacock

【羽化】[1] yǔhuà ❶ 古人说仙人能飞升变化，把成仙叫做羽化 (in ancient times) ascend to Heaven and become an immortal ❷〈婉辞 *euph.*〉道教徒称人死 (used by Taoists) pass away; die

【羽化】[2] yǔhuà 昆虫由蛹变为成虫 eclosion; change of an insect from pupa to an adult

【羽毛】yǔmáo ❶ 鸟类身体表面所长的毛，有保护身体、保持体温、帮助飞翔等作用 feather; plume; covering growth on the body of a bird, which protects the body, keeps the temperature and helps it fly ❷ 鸟类的羽和兽类的毛 feathers of birds and hair of animals;〈比喻 *fig.*〉人的名誉 reputation：爱惜～ cherish one's reputation

【羽毛球】yǔmáoqiú ❶ 球类运动项目之一，规则和用具大体上像网球 badminton, ball game whose rules and equipment are roughly similar to those of tennis ❷ 羽毛球运动使用的球，用软木包羊皮装上羽毛制成。也有用塑料制的。shuttlecock (or bird); feathered cork covered with sheepskin; birds made of plastics

【羽毛未丰】yǔmáo wèi fēng〈比喻 *fig.*〉还没有成熟，还没有成长壮大 unfledged; young and immature

【羽绒】yǔróng 禽类腹部和背部的绒毛。特指经过加工处理的鸭、鹅等的羽毛。fine soft feathers; eiderdown; down：～服 down jacket | ～制品 down products

【羽纱】yǔshā 一种薄的纺织品，用棉跟毛或丝等混合织成，多用来做衣服里子 camlet; thin fabric of cotton blended with wool or silk; used as the lining of a garment

【羽扇】yǔshàn 用鸟翅膀上的长羽毛制成的扇子 feather fan：～纶（guān）巾 feather fan and silk kerchief

【羽翼】yǔyì 翅膀 wing;〈比喻 *fig.*〉辅佐的人或力量 assistant; supporter; support

雨 yǔ 从云层中降向地面的水。云里的小水滴体积增大到不能悬浮在空气中时，就落下成为雨。rain; water that precipitates from the clouds. When small waterdrops in the clouds expand to such an extent that they can no long float in the air, they fall down to become rain.

☞ yù on p. 2348

【雨布】yǔbù 指可以遮挡雨的布，如油布、胶布、塑料布等 waterproof cloth, waterproof, plastic sheet, etc.

【雨点】yǔdiǎn（～儿 yǔdiǎnr）形成雨的小水滴 raindrop

【雨刮器】yǔguāqì 刮去汽车挡风玻璃上雨水的装置 windscreen (or windshield) wiper (of a car); also 雨刷 yǔshuā

【雨后春笋】yǔ hòu chūnsǔn 春天下雨后竹笋长得很多很快 (spring up like) bamboo shoots after a spring rain;〈比喻 *fig*.〉新事物大量出现(of new things) mushroom; spring up

【雨花石】yǔhuāshí 一种光洁的小卵石，有美丽的色彩和花纹，可供观赏，主要出产在南京雨花台一带 *yuhua* pebbles; colourful and fine-grained pebbles found in the Yuhuatai area at Nanjing)

【雨季】yǔjì 雨水多的季节 rainy season

【雨脚】yǔjiǎo 指像线一样一串串密密连接着的雨点 thick and fast raindrops

【雨具】yǔjù 防雨的用具，如雨伞、雨衣、雨鞋、油布 rain gear (i. e. umbrella, raincoat, galoshes, waterproof cloth, etc.)

【雨量】yǔliàng 在一定时间内，降落在水平地面上的未经蒸发、渗透或流失的雨水所积的深度，通常以毫米为单位 rainfall; precipitation; depth of the rain water accumulated on the level ground without vaporization, seepage or loss in a given period of time, usually measured in millimetre

【雨林】yǔlín 热带或亚热带暖热湿润地区的一种森林类型。由高大常绿阔叶树构成繁密林冠，多层结构，并包含丰富的木质藤本和附生高等植物。包括热带雨林、亚热带雨林、山地雨林等。rainforest; dense, evergreen forest having abundant rainfall throughout the year; forest in tropical or subtropical warm, damp regions, consisting of tall, large, evergreen, broad-leaved trees with a dense, multi-layered canopy and including rich woody liana and epiphyte. There are tropical rainforests, subtropical rainforests and mountain rainforests.

【雨露】yǔlù 雨和露 rain and dew;〈比喻 *fig*.〉恩惠 favour; grace; bounty: ～之恩 favour and kindness

【雨幕】yǔmù 雨点密密麻麻，景物像被幕罩住一样，因此叫做雨幕 curtain of rain; dense rain

【雨披】yǔpī 防雨的斗篷 waterproof cape; rain cape

【雨前】yǔqián 绿茶的一种，用谷雨前采摘的细嫩芽尖制成 *yuqian* tea; green tea prepared from small, tender leaves picked before Grain Rain (about mid-April)

【雨情】yǔqíng 某个地区降雨的情况 rainfall (in a given area)

【雨伞】yǔsǎn 防雨的伞，用油纸、油布、锦纶或塑料布等制成 umbrella; screen made of oilpaper, oil cloth, polyamide fibre or plastic sheet

【雨刷】yǔshuā 雨刮器 windscreen wiper

【雨水】[1] yǔshuǐ 由降雨而来的水 rainwater; rainfall; rain: ～调和。The rainfall is just right. | ～足，庄稼长得好。With adequate rainfall, the crops grow well.

【雨水】[2] yǔshuǐ 二十四节气之一，在2月18，19或20日 Rain Water; 2nd of the 24 solar terms, the day marking the beginning of the 2nd solar term, which falls on February 18, 19 or 20; ☞ 节气 jié·qi on p. 989, 二十四节气 èrshísì jiéqì on p. 516

【雨水管】yǔshuǐguǎn ☞ 水落管 shuǐluòguǎn on p. 1800

【雨丝】yǔsī 像一条条丝的细雨 very light rain; drizzle; fine rain: 空中飘着～。It is drizzling.

【雨凇】yǔsōng 雨落在0℃以下的地表或地面物体上，或过冷的水滴和物体(如电线、树枝、飞机翼面等)互相接触而形成的冰层 verglas; thin layer of ice formed when rain fell on the ground or the surfaces of objects on the ground below zero Centigrade or when excessive cold water drops and objects (like cables, tree branches or airplane wings) contact each other; 通称 popularly called 冰挂 bīngguà

【雨雾】yǔwù 像雾一样的细雨 misty rain: ～茫茫 vast blur in the misty rain | ～笼罩了江面。A misty rain shrouded the river.

【雨鞋】yǔxié 下雨天穿的不透水的鞋 galoshes; rubbers

【雨靴】yǔxuē 防水的靴子，用橡胶、塑料等制成 rubber or plastic boots; rain boots; waterproof boots

【雨衣】yǔyī 用油布、胶布或塑料等制成的防雨外衣 raincoat; waterproof made of oil cloth, rubberized fabric or plastic

【雨意】yǔyì 要下雨的征兆 signs of approaching rain: 阴云密布，～正浓。It is overcast and threatens to rain. | 天空万里无云，没有一丝～。It is clear all over the sky. There is no sign of rain.

俣 yǔ [俣俣]〈书 *fml*.〉身材高大 of large and tall stature

禹 Yǔ ❶ 传说中的古代部落联盟首领，曾治平洪水 King Yu, legendary leader of an ancient tribe union who successfully tamed a major flood ❷ 姓 a surname

语 yǔ ❶ 话 language; tongue; words: ～言 language | ～音 speech sounds; pronunciation|汉～ Chinese language; Han language|外～ foreign language|成～ idiom; set phrase|千言万～ innumerable words ❷ 说 speak; say: 细～ speak in details|低～ speak in a low voice; whisper|不言不～ speak nothing; be mute; keep silence|默默不～ speak nothing; be mute; keep silence ❸ 谚语; 成语 proverb; saying set phrase: ～云, '不入虎穴, 焉得虎子。' As the saying goes: 'How can one catch tiger cubs without venturing into the tiger lair?' ❹ 代替语言表示意思的动作或方式 nonlinguistic means of communicating ideas; sign; signal: 手～ sign language; dactylology|旗～ flag signal; semaphore|灯～ lamp signal ☛ yù on p. 2349

【语病】yǔbìng 措词上的毛病(多指不通顺、有歧义或容易引起误会的) faulty wording or formulation that are incoherent, ambiguous or misleading

【语词】yǔcí 指词、词组一类的语言成分 words and phrases

【语调】yǔdiào 说话的腔调,就是一句话里语音高低轻重的配置 intonation; system of significant levels and variations in pitch sequences within an utterance

【语法】yǔfǎ ❶ 语言的结构方式,包括词的构成的变化、词组和句子的组织 grammar; branch of the study of language that deals with forms and structure of words, with their customary arrangement in phrases and sentences ❷ 语法研究 study of grammar: 描写～ descriptive grammar|历史～ historical grammar|比较～ comparative grammar

【语法学】yǔfǎxué 语言学的一个部门,研究语法结构规律 grammar; branch of linguistics that deals with the rules of sentence structures

【语感】yǔgǎn 言语交流中指对词语表达的理解、使用习惯等的反映 instinctive feel for the language; understanding of expressions in words and phrases and their habitual usages in speaking and writing a language

【语汇】yǔhuì 一种语言的或一个人所用的词和短语的总和 vocabulary; all the words of a language or all the words used by a particular person: 汉语的～是极其丰富的。Chinese has a very rich vocabulary.|～贫乏是写不出好文章的。One can hardly write good articles with a poor vocabulary.

【语句】yǔjù 泛指成句的话 sentence: ～不通 incoherent sentence

【语库】yǔkù 汇集并保存语料的地方 language data bank; also 语料库 yǔliàokù

【语料】yǔliào 语言材料,是编写字典、词典和进行语言研究的依据 language data or material, basis for dictionary compilation and language study

【语料库】yǔliàokù same as 语库 yǔkù

【语录】yǔlù 某人言论的记录或摘录 recorded utterance; quotation

【语气】yǔqì ❶ 说话的口气 tone; manner of speaking: 听他的～,这事大概有点不妙。From the way he spoke about the matter, I gathered something had gone wrong. ❷ 表示陈述、疑问、祈使、感叹等分别的语法范畴 mood; a category of grammar indicating a fact (indicative mood), a question (interrogative mood), a command (imperative mood) or an exclamation (exclamatory mood)

【语塞】yǔsè 由于激动、气愤或理亏等原因而一时说不出话 unable to utter a word (due to excitement, anger, etc.); tongue-tied: 悲愤之下,一时～ be rendered speechless with grief and indignation

【语素】yǔsù 词素 morpheme

【语体文】yǔtǐwén 白话文 prose written in the vernacular

【语文】yǔwén ❶ 语言和文字 Chinese (as a subject of study or a means of communication); spoken language and written language: ～程度(指阅读、写作等能力) degree of one's language (one's reading and writing aptiude) ❷ 语言和文学 language and literature: 中学～课本 language and literature textbook for middle school

【语无伦次】yǔ wú lúncì 话讲得很乱,没有条理层次 speak incoherently

【语系】yǔxì 有共同来源的一些语言的总称。如汉藏语系、印欧语系。同一语系又可以根据关系疏密分成好些语族,如印欧语系可以分成印度、伊朗、斯拉夫、日耳曼、罗马等语族。family of languages; language family; group of languages with the same source, such as the Han-Tibetan family and the Indo-European family. One family may be divided into several branches, e.g. the Indo-European family may be divided into the Indian, Iranian, Slavic, Germanic and Roman branches.

【语序】yǔxù 词序 word order

【语焉不详】yǔ yān bù xiáng 说得不详细 not speak in detail; not elaborate; (of a statement) be rather too brief or sketchy

【语言】yǔyán ❶ 人类所特有的用来表达意思、交流思想的工具,是一种特殊的社会现象,由语音、词汇和语法构成一定的系统。'语言'一般包括它的书面形式,但在与'文字'并举时只指口语。language; tool peculiar to mankind, used for the expression and communication of thoughts and feelings, a special social phenomenon, a particular system consisting of speech sounds, vocabulary and grammar. 语言 (language) generally includes its written form, but only refers to the spoken language when it is used together with 文字 (written language). ❷ 话语 language or spoken language: ～乏味 dull language|由于文化水平和职业的差异,他们之间缺少共同的～。They have no common language between them because of their difference in education and profession.

【语言学】yǔyánxué 研究语言的本质、结构和发展规律的科学 linguistics; philology; branch of science dealing with the nature, structure and development, etc., of a particular language

【语义学】yǔyìxué 语言学的一个部门，研究词语的意义及其演变 semantics; branch of linguistics that deals with the meaning of words and phrases and their development

【语意】yǔyì 话语所包含的意义 meaning of words：～深长。The remarks are full of meaning.

【语音】yǔyīn 语言的声音，就是人说话的声音 speech sounds; pronunciation

【语音学】yǔyīnxué 语言学的一个部门，研究的对象是语音 phonetics; branch of linguistics that deals with the speech sounds

【语源学】yǔyuánxué 语言学的一个部门，研究语词的语音和意义的演变，并应用比较语言学的方法考求某个语词的最初的语音和意义 etymology; branch of linguistics that deals with the development of the speech sound and meaning of a word, and applies the method of comparative linguistics to exploring the original speech sound and meaning of a certain word

【语种】yǔzhǒng 语言按语音、词汇和语法特征、性质的不同而划分的种类 languages; kind of language; classification of languages on the basis of the different characteristics and nature of the speech sounds, vocabulary and grammar

【语重心长】yǔ zhòng xīn cháng 言辞诚恳，情意深长 sincere words and earnest wishes

【语助词】yǔzhùcí 汉语和另外一些语言中专门表示各种语气的助词，一般位于句子的末尾或句中停顿的地方 auxiliary word; word that indicates mood in the Chinese language and some other languages, and usu. used at the end or a pause of a sentence; also 语气助词 yǔqì zhùcí

【语族】yǔzú ☞ 语系 yǔxì

圄 yǔ ☞ 囹圄 língyǔ on p. 1228

敔 yǔ 古乐器，奏乐将终，击敔使演奏停止 *yu*, ancient percussion instrument, which is struck to stop a performance

圉 yǔ〈书 *fml.*〉养马的地方 stable：～人（掌管养马的人）stable boy (or lad); stableman

偊 yǔ〈书 *fml.*〉形容独行 walk alone

郚 Yǔ 周朝国名，在今山东临沂 Yu, name of a state in the Zhou Dynasty in present-day Linyi, Shandong Province

庾 yǔ ❶〈书 *fml.*〉露天的谷仓 open-air granary; enclosure for storing grain ❷（Yǔ）姓 a surname

铻 yǔ ☞［钽铻］jǔyǔ on p. 1049
☞ wú on p. 2028

貐（貐） yǔ ☞［猰貐］yàyǔ on p. 2198

瑀 yǔ〈书 *fml.*〉像玉的石头 jade-like stone

瘐 yǔ ☞ below

【瘐毙】yǔbì same as 瘐死 yǔsǐ

【瘐死】yǔsǐ〈古代 *arch.*〉指犯人在监狱中因饥寒而死。后来也泛指在监狱中病死。(of a prisoner) die of hunger and cold; die of disease

龉 yǔ ☞［龃龉］jǔyǔ on p. 1049

窳 yǔ〈书 *fml.*〉(事物)恶劣；坏 evil; bad：～败 corrupt | ～劣 bad; inferior; of poor quality | 良～(优劣) good or bad

【窳败】yǔbài〈书 *fml.*〉败坏；腐败 corrupt; rot

【窳惰】yǔduò〈书 *fml.*〉懒惰 lazy and dissipated

【窳劣】yǔliè〈书 *fml.*〉粗劣；恶劣 inferior; of poor quality：器具～ inferior tools and equipment

yù（ㄩˋ）

与（與） yù 参与 take part in; participate in：～会 attend a meeting; be present at a meeting
☞ yú on p. 2336 and yǔ on p. 2342

【与会】yùhuì 参加会议 participate in a conference：～国 countries attending a conference; participating countries | ～人员 conferee; participant

【与闻】yùwén 参与并且得知(内情) have a participant's knowledge of; be let into (a secret, etc.)：～其事 have a participant's knowledge of a matter; be in the know; also 预闻 yùwén

玉 yù ❶ 矿物，硬玉和软玉的统称，质地细而有光泽，可用来制造装饰品或做雕刻的材料 jade; general name for hard jade and soft jade; lustrous mineral of fine quality, used for ornaments or carving ❷〈比喻 *fig.*〉洁白或美丽 pure; fair; handsome; beautiful：～颜 beautiful features | 亭亭～立 have a graceful figure; slim and pretty; fair; handsome ❸〈敬辞 *pol.*〉指对方身体或行动 your：～音 your message; your reply; your letter | ～照 your photo ❹（Yù）姓 a surname

【玉版宣】yùbǎnxuān 一种色白质坚的宣纸，比一般宣纸厚 tenacious white *xuan* paper, usu. thicker than common *xuan* paper

【玉版纸】yùbǎnzhǐ 一种文化用纸，供书写或作簿籍用。产于湖南。fine-quality paper produced in Hunan Province for writing or notebooks

【玉帛】yùbó〈古时 *arch.*〉国与国间交际时用做礼物的玉器和丝织品 jade objects and silk fabrics, used as state gifts：化干戈为～（变战争为和平）turn swords into ploughshares；turn war into peace；cease hostilities and make peace；turn hostility into friendship

【玉成】yùchéng〈敬辞 *pol.*〉成全 kindly help secure the success of sth.：深望～此事。It's my earnest hope that you'll kindly help to secure the success of this matter.

【玉带】yùdài〈古代 *arch.*〉官员所用的玉饰腰带 jade belt worn by ranking officials

【玉雕】yùdiāo 在玉上雕刻形象、花纹的艺术。也指用玉雕刻成的工艺品。jade carving；jade sculpture；art of carving figures，designs，etc. on a piece of jade

【玉皇大帝】Yùhuáng Dàdì 道教称天上最高的神 Jade Emperor（Supreme Deity of Taoism）；also 玉帝 Yùdì

【玉茭】yùjiāo〈方 *dial.*〉same as 玉米 yùmǐ；also 玉茭子 yùjiāo•zi

【玉洁冰清】yù jié bīng qīng〈比喻 *fig.*〉高尚纯洁 pure as jade and chaste as ice；pure and noble；also 冰清玉洁 bīng qīng yù jié

【玉兰】yùlán ❶ 落叶乔木，叶子倒卵形，背面有柔毛，花大，多为白色或紫色，有香气，花瓣长倒卵形，果实圆筒形。供观赏。*yulan* magnolia（*Magnolia denudata*）；ornamental deciduous tree with obovate leaves，soft hair on the back of the leaf，big，fragrant，white or purple flowers，obovate petals and cylindrical fruits ❷ 这种植物的花 flowers of the plant

【玉兰片】yùlánpiàn 晒干了的白色嫩笋片，供食用 dried slices of tender bamboo shoots used as food

【玉麦】yùmài〈方 *dial.*〉same as 玉米 yùmǐ

【玉米】yùmǐ ❶ 一年生草本植物，茎高 2—3 米，叶子长而大，花单性，雌雄同株，子实比黄豆稍大，可供食用或制淀粉等 corn（*Zea mays*）；annual herbal plant with a stem 2-3 metres long，big，long leaves，unisexual，hermaphroditic flowers，seeds slightly bigger than soya beans and used for food or for the making of starch ❷ 这种植物的果实 ear of maize（or corn）‖ also 玉蜀黍 yùshǔshǔ；在不同地区有老玉米、玉茭、玉麦、包谷、包米、棒子、珍珠米等名称 in different regions also called 老玉米 lǎoyùmǐ，玉茭 yùjiāo，玉麦 yùmài，包谷 bāogǔ，包米 bāomǐ，棒子 bàng•zi，珍珠米 zhēnzhūmǐ etc.

【玉米面】yùmǐmiàn 玉米磨成的面 corn flour；cornmeal

【玉佩】yùpèi 用玉石制成的装饰品，古时多系在衣带上 jade pendant；jade ornament tied usu. on the waistband in ancient times

【玉器】yùqì 用玉石雕琢成的各种器物。多为工艺美术品。jade article；jade object；jadeware；jade artworks

【玉搔头】yùsāotóu same as 玉簪 yùzān

【玉色】yù•shai〈方 *dial.*〉淡青色 jade green；light bluish green

【玉石】yù•shí 玉 jade：这座人像是～的。This human statue is carved out of jade.

【玉石俱焚】yù shí jù fén 美玉和石头一齐烧毁了 burn jade and stone together；〈比喻 *fig.*〉好的和坏的一同毁掉 destroy the good and the bad together；throw out the baby with the bath water；total destruction

【玉碎】yùsuì〈比喻 *fig.*〉为保持气节而牺牲（常与'瓦全'对举 oft. used antithetically to 'intact tile'）resemble a broken piece of jade；die in glory；die a heroic death；sacrifice one's life to maintain integrity：宁为～，不为瓦全。I would rather die in integrity than live in humiliation.

【玉兔】yùtù〈书 *fml.*〉指月亮，传说中月中有兔 Jade Hare；the moon：traditional Chinese legend has it that there is a hare on the moon，hence the name Jade Hare for the moon：～东升。The moon is rising in the east.

【玉玺】yùxǐ 君主的玉印 imperial jade seal

【玉音】yùyīn 尊称对方的书信、言词（多用于书信 oft. used in correspondences）your answer；your reply；your letter：伫候～。I'm looking forward to hearing from you.

【玉宇】yùyǔ ❶ 传说中神仙住的华丽的宫殿（in a legend）grand palace where immortals live：琼楼～ fabulously residence；magnificent building；richly decorated jade palace ❷ 指天空。也指宇宙。sky；universe：～澄清 clear sky

【玉簪】yùzān 用玉做成的簪子 jade hairpin；also 玉搔头 yùsāotóu

【玉照】yùzhào〈敬辞 *pol.*〉称别人的照片 your photograph

驭 yù ❶ 驾驭 drive：～车 drive a carriage｜～马 ride a horse｜～手 soldier in charge of pack animals；driver of a chariot ❷〈书 *fml.*〉统率；控制 control；dominate；command；be master of：～下无方 be unable to manage sth. well；lack ability to do sth.

【驭手】yùshǒu 使役牲畜的士兵 soldier in charge of pack animals；driver of a chariot；also 御手 yùshǒu

芋 yù ❶ 多年生草本植物，块茎椭圆形或卵形，叶子略呈卵形，有长柄，花穗轴在苞内，雄花黄色，雌花绿色。块茎含淀粉很多，供食用。taro（*Colocasia esculenta*）；dasheen；perennial herb，having oval or egg-shaped tubers，egg-shaped leaves，long stems，spikestalks inside its buds，yellow male flowers and green female flowers, its edible tubers high in starch ❷ 这种植物的块茎 tuber crops of this plant ‖ 通称 generally known as 芋头 yù·tou ❸ 泛指马铃薯、甘薯等植物 potatoes and sweet potatoes: 洋～ potato | 山～ sweet potato

【芋艿】yùnǎi same as 芋 yù ①②

【芋头】yù·tou ❶ 芋①②的通称 general term for taro, dasheen and their tubers ❷〈方 *dial.*〉甘薯 sweet potato

吁(籲) yù 为某种要求而呼喊 appeal; plead; call on: ～请 appeal and request; petition | ～求 appeal earnestly for | 呼～ appeal; call on

☞ xū on p. 2161 and yū on p. 2335

【吁请】yùqǐng 呼吁并请求 call on; appeal and request; petition: ～有关部门采取有效措施 call on relevant departments to adopt efficient measures

【吁求】yùqiú 呼吁并恳求 call on; appeal earnestly for; petition: ～各界人士捐款救灾 call on all walks of life to donate for the relief of disaster-stricken people

聿 yù〈古汉语助词 *arch. aux.*〉用在句首或句中 [used at the beginning of or in a sentence] then; and then

谷 yù ☞ 吐谷浑 Tǔyùhún on p. 1944

☞ gǔ on p. 692

饫 yù〈书 *fml.*〉饱 be full; be well-fed

妪(嫗) yù〈书 *fml.*〉年老的女人 old woman; old lady: 老～ old woman | 翁～ old couple

雨 yù〈书 *fml.*〉下(雨、雪等)(of rain, snow, etc.) fall: ～雪。The snow is falling.

☞ yǔ on p. 2344

郁[1] yù ❶ 香气浓厚 of strong fragrance; highly fragrant: 馥～ rich fragrance | ～烈 strong aroma ❷ (Yù) 姓 a surname

郁[2](鬱) yù ❶ (草木)茂盛 (of grass and plants) luxuriant; lush: 葱～ lush; verdant ❷ (忧愁、气愤等)在心里积聚不得发泄 (of sorrow, anger, etc.) pent-up; gloomy; depressed: 忧～ gloomy; melancholy | 抑～ despondent; depressed; gloomy | ～闷 gloomy; depressed

【郁愤】yùfèn 忧愤 worried and indignant: 满腔～ extremely worried and indignant; burning with anxiety

【郁积】yùjī 郁结 pent-up; smouldering: 哀怨～ pent-up grief and resentment | 发泄心中～的愤怒 give vent to pent-up anger

【郁结】yùjié 积聚不得发泄 smouldering; pent-up; unable to vent what's building up in one's heart: ～在心头的烦闷 pent-up vexation; smouldering with frustration

【郁金香】yùjīnxiāng ❶ 多年生草本植物，叶阔披针形，有白粉，花通常鲜红色，花心黑紫色，花瓣倒卵形，结蒴果。供观赏，根和花可入药。tulip (*Tulipa gesneriana*); perennial herbaceous plant, having lanceolate broad leaves covered with a layer of white powder, flowers usu. bright red with black purple pistils and petals in the shape of an egg put upside down, and yielding capsules, its roots and flowers used in medicine ❷ 这种植物的花 tulip; flower of this plant

【郁闷】yùmèn 烦闷；不舒畅 gloomy; depressed: ～不乐 be in low spirits; be dejected; be downcast | 排解胸中的～ relieve one's pent-up frustration

【郁热】yùrè 闷热 hot and suffocating; sultry; stuffy; muggy; sweltering: 天气～。The weather is muggy.

【郁血】yùxuè 由于管腔堵塞或管外的压迫等原因，血液郁积在静脉管内 stagnation of the blood; venous stasis; blood accumulating in the venous ducts due to blockage of or exterior pressure on the ducts

【郁悒】yùyì〈书 *fml.*〉忧愁；苦闷 depressed; dejected; melancholy: 心境～ feel depressed; feel dejected

【郁郁】[1] yùyù〈书 *fml.*〉❶ 文采显著 elegant; refined; of elegant literary talent: 文采～ overflowing with literary elegance ❷ 香气浓厚 strong fragrance; rich perfume; strong aroma; rich scent

【郁郁】[2] yùyù〈书 *fml.*〉❶ (草木)茂密 (of grass and trees) lush and green; exuberant; luxuriant: ～葱葱 verdant; lush and green ❷ 心里苦闷 depressed; melancholy; gloomy: ～不乐 depressed; gloomy | ～寡欢 depressed; melancholy

【郁郁葱葱】yùyùcōngcōng (草木)苍翠茂盛 (of grass and trees) lush and green; also 郁郁苍苍 yùyùcāngcāng

育 yù ❶ 生育 give birth to; labour: 节～ birth control ❷ 养活 raise; bring up; rear: ～婴 raise a baby | ～苗 grow seedlings | 封山～林 seal off mountains to facilitate afforestation; seal off hills to grow trees ❸ 教育 educate: 德～ moral education | 智～ intellectual education | 体～ physical education

☞ yō on p. 2309

【育才】yùcái 培养人才 cultivate talent; train people

【育雏】yùchú 喂养幼小的鸟类 raise young birds; feed young birds

【育肥】yùféi ☞ 肥育 féiyù on p. 561

【育林】yùlín 培植森林 plant trees; cultivate woods; afforest: 封山～ seal off mountains to cultivate forests

【育龄】yùlíng 指适合生育的年龄 childbearing

age：～夫妇 couple of childbearing age

【育苗】yù//miáo 在苗圃、温床或温室里培育幼苗，以备移到地里去栽种 grow seedlings; raise seedlings in a nursery garden, seedbed or greenhouse, which are to be transplanted to the fields

【育秧】yù//yāng 培育秧苗 raise rice seedlings：温室～ raise rice seedlings in a greenhouse

【育婴堂】yùyīngtáng〈旧时 *old*〉收养无人抚育的婴儿的机构 orphanage; foundling hospital

【育种】yù//zhǒng 用人工方法培育新的品种。常用的作物育种方法有单穗或单株选种、有性杂交、无性杂交等。breeding; cultivating new breeds in artificial ways, including the common ways of single-spike or single-plant seed selection, sexual hybridization, asexual hybridization, etc.

昱 yù〈方 *dial.*〉❶ 日光 sunlight; sunshine ❷ 照耀 shine; illuminate

狱(獄) yù ❶ 监狱 prison; jail：牢～ prison | 下～ be thrown into jail; be put behind bars | 入～ go to jail ❷ 官司；罪案 lawsuit; case：冤～ frame-up unjust charge; unjust verdict | 文字～ literary inquisition; persecution of authors for writing sth. considered offensive by the imperial court

【狱警】yùjǐng 看管监狱的警察 prison guard; jailer

【狱吏】yùlì〈旧时 *old*〉管理监狱的小官 warder; prison warden; jailer; gaoler

【狱卒】yùzú〈旧时 *old*〉称监狱看守人 prison guard; turnkey

语 yù〈书 *fml.*〉告诉 tell; inform; notify; wise up：不以～人 keep sth. from others

☞ yǔ on p. 2345

彧 yù〈书 *fml.*〉有文采 of literary elegance; overflowing with literary talent

峪 yù 山谷(多用于地名 oft. used in place names) valley：马兰～(在河北) Malan Valley (in Hebei Province) | 嘉～关(在甘肃) Jiayu Pass (in Gansu Province)

钰 yù〈书 *fml.*〉珍宝 treasure

鴥 yù〈书 *fml.*〉形容鸟飞得快 (of birds) fly quickly

浴 yù 洗澡 take a bath; bathe：沐～ take a bath | 淋～ have a shower | ～室 bathroom; shower room | 海水～ sea bathing ◇日光～ sunbathing

【浴场】yùchǎng 露天游泳场所 outdoor bathing place：海滨～ bathing beach

【浴池】yùchí ❶ 供许多人同时洗澡的设备，形状像池塘，用石头或混凝土筑成 bathing pool; public pool made of stone or concrete where people bathe together ❷ 借指澡堂(多用做澡堂的名称 oft. used in the name of a bathhouse) public bathhouse; public bath

【浴缸】yùgāng 新式的大澡盆 Western-style bathtub

【浴巾】yùjīn 洗澡时用的长毛巾 bath towel; long towel used for drying a bather's body

【浴盆】yùpén 澡盆 bathtub of traditional Chinese style(不包括新式的大澡盆 excluding Western style)

【浴室】yùshì ❶ 有洗澡设备的房间 bathroom; shower room ❷ 澡堂 public bathhouse; public bath

【浴血】yùxuè 形容战斗激烈 (of a fierce battle) bathed in blood; bloody; sanguinary：～奋战 fight a bloody battle

【浴衣】yùyī 专供洗澡前后穿的衣服 bathrobe; bathing-gown; bathing-wrap

预[1] yù 预先；事先 in advance; beforehand：～备 prepare; get ready | ～测 predict; foresee; forecast | 天气～报 weather forecast | ～祝成功 wish sb. great success | 勿谓言之不～。Do not tell me that you have not been forewarned. *or* Don't blame us for not informing you beforehand.

预[2] yù same as 与 yù

【预案】yù'àn 为应付某种情况的发生而事先制订的处置方案 plan or means worked out in advance for the arrival of a possible event

【预报】yùbào 预先报告(多用于天文、气象方面 oft. used in astronomy and meteorology) forecast; prediction：天气～ weather forecast

【预备】yùbèi 准备 prepare; get ready：～功课 prepare lessons | 春节你～到哪儿去玩儿? Where do you plan to go during the Spring Festival?

【预备役】yùbèiyì 随时准备根据国家需要应征入伍的兵役。服满现役退伍的军人和依法应服兵役而未入伍的公民，按规定编入预备役。reserve duty or service; section of a military force ready to enter service at any time of need for the country, including retired veterans and citizens who should have entered the service but haven't yet

【预卜】yùbǔ 预先断定 augur; foretell; predict：前途未可～。It is difficult to predict future developments.

【预测】yùcè 预先推测或测定 predict; forecast; foresee：市场～ market predictions; market forecasting

【预产期】yùchǎnqī 预计的胎儿出生的日期。预产期的计算方法是从最后一次月经的第一日后推九个月零七天。expected date of childbirth; date on which a baby is expected to be born, calculated nine months and seven days after the first day of an expectant mother's last period

【预订】yùdìng 预先订购 subscribe; book; place an order：～报纸 subscribe to a newspaper | ～酒席 book a banquet table

【预定】yùdìng 预先规定或约定 fix in advance;

predetermine; schedule: ～计划 predetermine a plan|～时间 fix the time in advance|这项工程～在明年完成。The project is scheduled for completion next year.

【预断】yùduàn 预先断定 prejudge; predict; anticipate: 发展前景还很难～。It is hard to predict the development prospects.

【预防】yùfáng 事先防备 take precautions against; guard against; prevent: ～传染病 prevent of contagious diseases|～自然灾害 take precautions against natural disasters

【预付】yùfù 预先付给(款项) pay (money) in advance: ～租金 pay rent in advance; pay a deposit

【预感】yùgǎn ❶ 事先感觉 have a premonition about sth.; forebode: 天气异常闷热,大家都～到将要下一场大雨。It was extremely sultry, and everyone had a foreboding that there would be a downpour. ❷ 事先的感觉 premonition; presentiment; foreboding; presage: 不祥的～ ominous premonition of sth.; ominous presentiment of sth.

【预告】yùgào ❶ 事先通告 announce in advance; herald: 这场大雪～了来年农业的丰收。The big snowfall heralded good agricultural harvests for next year. ❷ 事先的通告(多用于戏剧演出、图书出版等 oft. used in theatrical announcements, publications, etc.) advance notice: 新书～ notice of forthcoming books; publication notice|电视节目～ TV programme notice

【预购】yùgòu 预先购买或订购 place an order or purchase in advance: ～农产品 purchase agricultural produce in advance|～返程机票 buy a return airplane ticket in advance

【预后】yùhòu 对于某种疾病发展过程和最后结果的估计 prognosis; estimation of the developing course and final results of a disease: ～不良 unfavourable prognosis

【预会】yùhuì same as 与会 yùhuì

【预计】yùjì 预先计算、计划或推测 estimate; calculate, plan or predict in advance: ～十天之内就可以完工。It is estimated that (it) will be completed within ten days.

【预见】yùjiàn ❶ 根据事物的发展规律预先料到将来 foresee; predict; tell the future of sth. according to its laws of development: 可以～,我厂的生产水平几年内将有很大的提高。It can be predicted that the production level of our plant will be greatly improved within several years. ❷ 能预先料到将来的见识 foresight; prevision; ability to have advance knowledge of the future: 科学的～ scientific foresight

【预警】yùjǐng 预先告警 early-warning; forewarning: ～卫星 early-warning satellite|～雷达 early-warning radar

【预科】yùkē 为高等学校培养新生的机构,附设在高等学校里,也有单独设立的 preparatory school; prep school; independent institution or institution affiliated to a school of higher learning to prepare students for college study

【预料】yùliào ❶ 事先推测 expect; predict; anticipate: ～这个地区农业方面可以比去年增产百分之十。It is anticipated that agricultural production for this area will increase by 10 per cent over last year. ❷ 事先的推测 prediction; anticipation: 果然不出他的～。Sure enough, it has turned out as he predicted.

【预谋】yùmóu 做坏事之前有所谋划。特指犯人做犯法的事之前有所谋划。premeditate; plan beforehand; make a plan before doing a bad thing; (esp. of a criminal) plan before committing a crime

【预期】yùqī 预先期待 expect; anticipate; predict: 达到～的目的 achieve the expected results

【预赛】yùsài 决赛之前进行的比赛。在预赛中选拔参加决赛的选手或单位。preliminary contest; preliminary heats; preliminary; trial match; ☞ 决赛 juésài on p. 1058

【预审】yùshěn ❶ 法院正式开庭审判前对刑事被告人所进行的预备性审讯活动 preliminary or first hearing; pretrial; preparatory interrogation to the accused, conducted by the court before the opening of formal trial ❷ 侦查阶段对刑事案件被告人进行的讯问 interrogating the accused during the investigation of a criminal case

【预示】yùshì 预先显示 betoken; indicate; presage; forebode: 灿烂的晚霞～明天又是好天气。The splendid evening glow indicates another fine day tomorrow.

【预收】yùshōu 预先收取(款项) collect (money) in advance: ～定金 collect a deposit

【预算】yùsuàn 国家机关、团体和事业单位等对于未来的一定时期内的收入和支出的计划 budget; plan of revenues and expenses for state organs, organizations and institutions within a certain period in the future

【预闻】yùwén same as 与闻 yùwén

【预习】yùxí 学生预先自学将要听讲的功课 (of students) prepare lessons before class; review (lessons)

【预先】yùxiān 在事情发生或进行之前 in advance; beforehand: ～声明 state explicitly beforehand|～通知 notify in advance|～布置 make arrangements in advance

【预想】yùxiǎng 预料;事前推想 anticipate; expect; envisage: 事情并不像～的那么简单。It turns out to be not as easy as anticipated.

【预行】yùxíng 预先施行 carry out ahead of schedule: ～警报 early warning

【预选】yùxuǎn 在正式选举前,为确定候选人而进行的选举 primary election; primaries; preliminary election to determine the candidates before a formal election

【预言】yùyán ❶ 预先说出(将来要发生的事情) prophesy; predict; foretell; tell in advance (what will happen in the future): 科学家~人类在征服宇宙方面将有新的突破。Scientists predict that humans will make new breakthroughs in their efforts in exploring the universe. ❷ 预先说出的关于将来要发生什么事情的话 prophecy; prediction; words that predict future happenings in advance: 科学家的~已经变成了现实。The prediction of the scientists has become reality.

【预演】yùyǎn 在正式演出前试演 preview (of a performance or motion picture)

【预约】yùyuē 事先约定(服务时间、购货权利等) reserve; make an appointment; make a reservation (for service time, purchase rights, etc.): ~挂号 make an appointment with a doctor; register to see a doctor

【预展】yùzhǎn 在展览会正式开幕前先行展览,请人参观,以便提出意见,加以改进,然后再正式展出 preview of an exhibition, when people are invited to give their opinions so as to improve it before its official opening

【预兆】yùzhào ❶ 预先显露出来的迹象 omen; presage; sign; harbinger: 不祥的~ inauspicious omen ❷ (某种迹象)预示将要发生某种事情 (of certain phenomenon) indicate; foreshow; forerun; tell the happening of certain thing in advance: 瑞雪~来年丰收。An auspicious snow presages a good harvest next year.

【预支】yùzhī 预先付出或领取(款项) pay in advance; get payment in advance: ~一个月的工资 obtain an advance on a month's salary; get a monthly payment in advance

【预知】yùzhī 预先知道 predict; foresee; foreknow: 云能够帮助我们~天气变化。Clouds can help us know a change in the weather beforehand.

【预制构件】yùzhì gòujiàn 按照设计规格在工厂或现场预先制成的钢、木或混凝土构件 prefabricated components prepared either in a factory or on the spot; steel, wood or concrete components made beforehand according to design and specifications

域 yù ❶ 在一定疆界内的地方;疆域 land within certain boundaries; territory; region: 区~ area; district | 异~ foreign land; strange land | ~外 outside the country | 绝~ inaccessible area; remote area hard to reach ❷ 泛指某种范围 domain; sphere; range: 境~ situation; circumstances | 音~ range; register; compass; gamut

堉 yù 〈书 *fml.*〉肥沃的土地 fertile land

菀 yù 〈书 *fml.*〉茂盛 flourishing; exuberant; prosperous

☞ wǎn on p. 1975

欲(❶慾) yù ❶ 欲望 desire; longing; wish; yearning: 食~ appetite | 求知~ thirst for knowledge ❷ 想要;希望 want; hope; wish; yearn; long (for): 畅所~言 speak without reservation; speak out what's in one's heart | 从心所~ get what one wants; do what one desires ❸ 需要 need; require; demand: 胆~大而心~细。(You) should be at once bold and careful. ❹ 将要 will; be about to; be just going to; be on the point of: 摇摇~坠 be on the verge of collapse; tottering; crumbling | 山雨~来风满楼。The rising wind around the tower foretold the imminent arrival of a storm.

【欲罢不能】yù bà bù néng 想停止也不能停止 unable to stop doing sth. even though one wants to; try to stop but cannot; cannot help going on and on

【欲盖弥彰】yù gài mí zhāng 想要掩盖事实的真相,结果反而更加显露出来(指坏事) the more one tries to hide, the more one is exposed; try to cover up a misdeed, only to make it more conspicuous; protest too much; the harder one tries to conceal a thing, the more attention one attracts

【欲壑难填】yù hè nán tián 形容贪得的欲望太大,很难满足 greed is a valley that can never be filled; avarice knows no bounds

【欲火】yùhuǒ 〈比喻 *fig.*〉强烈的欲望(多指情欲 oft. sexual desire) fire of lust; lewd desire; burning desire

【欲加之罪,何患无辞】yù jiā zhī zuì, hé huàn wú cí 想要给人加上罪名,何愁找不到借口。指以种种借口诬陷人。if you are out to condemn sb., you can always trump up a charge; condemn sb. by fabricating all kinds of charges; frame a case against sb.; give a dog a bad name and hang him

【欲念】yùniàn same as 欲望 yùwàng

【欲擒故纵】yù qín gù zòng 为了要捉住他,故意先放开他,使他放松戒备 leave sb. at large the better to apprehend him; allow sb. more latitude first to keep a tighter rein on him afterwards; 〈比喻 *fig.*〉为了更好地控制,故意放松一步 play cat and mouse with sb.; give sb. enough line or rope

【欲速则不达】yù sù zé bù dá 过于性急反而不能达到目的 desire to have things done quickly prevents them from being done thoroughly; haste does not bring success; more haste, less speed

【欲望】yùwàng 想得到某种东西或想达到某种目的的要求 desire; wish; lust: 求知的~ desire to acquire knowledge; thirst for knowledge

阈 yù〈书 *fml.*〉门坎儿。泛指界限或范围。threshold; doorsill; limits; confines: 视～ visual range; visual threshold | 听～ audibility range; aural threshold

淯 Yù 淯河,发源于河南,流入湖北 Yuhe River, originating in Henan Province and flowing into Hubei Province

谕 yù 告诉;吩咐(用于上级对下级或长辈对晚辈 of superior to subordinate, or senior to junior) instruct; tell; behest; enjoin: ～知 announce by edict; notify in a decree | 面～ give orders personally; instruct face to face | 手～ hand-written directive | 上～(旧时称皇帝的命令 imperial order; (old) emperor's order)
〈古 *arch.*〉same as 喻 yù

【谕旨】yùzhǐ 皇帝对臣子下的命令、指示 imperial edict; imperial decree; order or instruction issued by an emperor to his subjects

尉 yù ☞ below
☞ wèi on p. 2001

【尉迟】Yùchí 姓 a surname

【尉犁】Yùlí 地名,在新疆 Yuli, name of a county in the Xinjiang Uygur Autonomous Region

棫 yù 古书上说的一种植物 a kind of plant in ancient books

遇 yù ❶ 相逢;遭遇 meet; encounter: 相～ meet each other; run across each other | ～雨 be caught in a rain | ～险 meet with a mishap; be landed in danger | 不期而～ chance encounter; meet by chance ❷ 对待;款待 treat; receive: 待～ treatment; remuneration; pay | 优～ give special treatment; treat well | 冷～ be treated coldly ❸ 机会 chance; opportunity: 机～ favourable circumstance; luck; opportunity | 际～ good opportunity; favourable turn in life; spell of good fortune ❹ (Yù)姓 a surname

【遇刺】yùcì 被暗杀 be attacked by an assassin: ～身亡 be assassinated

Y 【遇害】yù//hài 被杀害 be murdered: 不幸～ be murdered

【遇合】yùhé ❶ 相遇而彼此投合 meet and hit it off; meet and get on well ❷ 遇见;碰到 come across; run into; encounter

【遇见】yù//·jiàn 碰到 meet; run into; come across; encounter

【遇救】yù//jiù 得到援救 be rescued; be saved: ～脱险 be rescued out of danger

【遇难】yù//nàn ❶ 遭受迫害或遇到意外而死亡 be persecuted to death; die in an accident: 他在一次飞机失事中～。He died in an air crash. ❷ 遭遇危难 face danger; be in trouble: ～成祥(遭遇危难而化为吉祥)。Misfortune has turned into good luck.

【遇事生风】yù shì shēng fēng 一有机会就搬弄是非 sow discord whenever possible; tell tales at every opportunity

【遇险】yù//xiǎn 遭遇危险 meet with a mishap; be in danger; be in distress: 船在海上～。The ship met with a mishap on the sea.

喻 yù ❶ 说明;告知 explain; make clear; inform: 晓～ enlighten; persuade | ～之以理 reason with sb. | 不可理～ be perverse; refuse to listen to reason ❷ 明白;了解 understand; know: 家～户晓 be a household name; be known to every household; widely known | 不言而～ be self-evident; it goes without saying ❸ 比方 analogy; figure of speech: 比～ analogy; metaphor; simile ❹ (Yù) 姓 a surname

【喻世】yùshì 告诫世人,使明白道理 admonish people; exhort people; persuade people to be reasonable

【喻义】yùyì 比喻的意义 meaning of an analogy

御1 yù ❶ 驾御车马;赶车 drive; ride: ～者 carriage driver ❷ 封建社会指上级对下级的管理或支配(of a superior to a subordinate in feudal society) manage; control; dominate: ～下 control one's subordinates | ～众 dominate the masses ❸ 封建社会指与皇帝有关的 related to an emperor in the feudal society; royal; imperial: ～赐 bestowed, granted or conferred by an emperor | ～前 in His Majesty's presence | 告～状 file a suit directly to the emperor

御2(禦) yù 抵挡 resist; keep; ward off; defend: 防～ defend | ～寒 keep out the cold; keep warm | ～敌 ward off the enemy; resist the enemy

【御笔】yùbǐ 指皇帝亲笔写的字或画的画 imperial brush; handwriting or painting of the emperor

【御寒】yùhán 抵御寒冷 keep out the cold: ～用品 articles to keep warm

【御驾】yùjià 皇帝的马车 emperor's carriage; His Majesty's carriage: ～亲征(皇帝亲自带兵出征) expedition led or commanded by an emperor in person

【御林军】yùlínjūn 禁军 imperial guards

【御手】yùshǒu same as 驭手 yùshǒu

【御侮】yùwǔ 抵抗外侮 resist foreign invasion

【御用】yùyòng ❶ 皇帝所用 hired by the emperor; for the use of an emperor ❷ 为反动统治者利用而做帮凶的 serve as a tool for reactionary forces; be in the pay of: ～文人 hired scribbler; hack writer | ～学者 hired scholar

鹆 yù ☞ 鸲鹆 qúyù on p. 1590

寓(庽) yù ❶ 居住 reside; live; inhabit; dwell: ～居 make one's home in; settle down | ～所 residence; abode; dwelling ❷ 住的地方 residence; dwelling; abode: 客～ guest house | 公～ apartment; flat | 赵～ the

Zhaos' residence ❸ 寄托 imply; place; contain: ～意 implication; implied meaning

【寓邸】yùdǐ 高级官员的住所 residence of a high official

【寓公】yùgōng〈古时 *arch.*〉指寄居他国的诸侯、贵族。后泛指失势寄居他乡的官僚、绅士等。vassal or aristocrat living in a foreign country; (in a broad sense) bureaucrat or gent in exile

【寓居】yùjū 居住（多指不是本地人 oft. of a non-native resident）make one's home in a place other than one's native place: 他晚年～上海。He settled down in Shanghai in his old age.

【寓目】yùmù〈书 *fml.*〉过目 look over or examine for approval: 室内展览品我已大致～。I've looked over all the items on display in the room.

【寓所】yùsuǒ 寓居的地方 residence; abode; dwelling

【寓言】yùyán ❶ 有所寄托的话 parable; allegory; sayings or words that contain a deeper meaning ❷ 用假托的故事或自然物的拟人手法来说明某个道理或教训的文学作品，常带有讽刺或劝诫的性质 literary work illustrating an argument or a lesson by means of a story or the personification of things in nature, oft. satirical and dissuasive

【寓意】yùyì 寄托或隐含的意思 implied meaning; implication; connotative import: ～深长 be pregnant with meaning; have a profound moral

【寓于】yùyú 包含在(其中) entail; be contained in; reside in; be implied; lie in: 矛盾的普遍性～矛盾的特殊性之中。It is precisely in the particularity of contradictions that the universality of contradictions resides.

裕 yù ❶ 丰富；宽绰 abundant; plentiful; affluent; ample: 富～ well-off; well-to-do; affluent | 宽～ well-off; plentiful | 充～ ample; plentiful | 余～ well-to-do; comfortably off ❷〈书 *fml.*〉使富足 enrich; make affluent: 富国～民 enrich the country and its people ❸ (Yù)姓 a surname

【裕固族】Yùgùzú 我国少数民族之一，分布在甘肃 Yugur (Yugu) people, or the Yugurs (Yugus), one of China's minority peoples living in Gansu Province

【裕如】yùrú ❶ 形容从容不费力 effortlessly; with ease: 应付～ handle the situation with ease; be equal to the occasion ❷ 形容丰足 well-off; plentiful; abundant; affluent: 生活～ a well-to-do life

粥 yù ❶〈书 *fml.*〉生养 give birth to; bear ❷ same as 鬻 yù

☞ zhōu on p. 2496

矞 yù〈书 *fml.*〉象征祥瑞的彩云 auspicious colourful clouds

蒮 yù ☞ 薯蒮 shǔyù on p. 1787

罭 yù〈书 *fml.*〉捕捉小鱼的细网 fine net for catching small fish

愈[1]（❶瘉、癒）yù ❶（病）好 (of illness) heal; recover; be cured: 痊～ recover | 病～ be cured ❷ 较好；胜过 be better than; overpass; overtake: 彼～于此。That is better than this.

愈[2] yù 叠用，跟'越…越…'相同 [used reiteratively, same as 越 yuè…越 yuè] the more... the more: 山路～走～陡，而风景～来～奇。The further we went, the steeper the mountain path became, and the more beautiful the scenery. | ～是情况紧急，～是需要沉着冷静。The tenser the situation becomes, the calmer we should be.

【愈合】yùhé（伤口）长好 (of a wound) heal: 等伤口～了才能出院。(You) can leave the hospital only after the wound heals.

【愈加】yùjiā 越发 even more; still more; all the more: 由于他的插手，事情变得～复杂了。With his interference, things have become even more complicated.

【愈演愈烈】yù yǎn yù liè（事情、情况）变得越来越严重 (of a matter, situation or condition) intensify; become increasingly serious; grow in intensity; go from bad to worse

【愈益】yùyì 愈加 all the more; even more; further; increasingly: 在科学技术日益发达的今天，学科分类～细密了。Today, as science increasingly develops, subject classifications have become even more specific.

煜 yù〈书 *fml.*〉照耀 illuminate; shine

澦 yù ☞ 滟澦堆 Yànyù Duī on p. 2216

誉（譽）yù ❶ 名誉 reputation; fame: 荣～ honour; glory | ～满全国 known across the nation ❷ 称赞 laud; praise; extol; eulogize; compliment; applaud; acclaim: 毁～ blame or praise | ～不绝口 praise profusely; praise sb. to the skies; be full of praises

蔚 Yù 蔚县，在河北 Yuxian County in Hebei Province

☞ wèi on p. 2002

蜮（魊）yù 传说中在水里暗中害人的怪物 legendary monster hidden in water to harm people: 鬼～ water demon

毓 yù ❶〈书 *fml.*〉生育；养育 give birth; nurture; bring up: 钟灵～秀。A favourable environment nurtures great talent. ❷ (Yù)姓 a surname

隩 yù〈书 *fml.*〉河岸弯曲的地方 bend of a river
☞ ào on p. 20

蒮 yù ☞ [蘡蒮] (yīngyù) on p. 2299

澦 yù〈书 *fml.*〉水涌 (of water) gush; surge

熨 yù [熨贴] (yùtiē) ❶ (用字、用词)贴切;妥贴 (of wording) apt; fitting; appropriate; proper ❷ 心里平静 calm; composed; placid; peaceful; tranquil: 这一番坦诚的谈话,说得他心里十分~。The sincere discussion put him at ease. ❸〈方 *dial.*〉舒服 comfortable; at ease; well: 他身上不~,要回家躺一会儿。He's not feeling well; he is going home to have a rest. ❹〈方 *dial.*〉(事情)完全办妥 (of a matter or business) be settled; be well done; do a good job: 这事不办~,我不能走。I can't go if it's not settled.
☞ yùn on p. 2382

遹 yù〈书 *fml.*〉遵循 follow; be in line with; be in accordance with

豫1 yù〈书 *fml.*〉❶ 欢喜;快乐 happy; pleased; delighted; glad; jubilant; joyful: 面有不~之色。An unhappy expression showed on (his) face. ❷ 安适 comfortable; at ease; contented: 逸~亡身。Over-indulgence spells ruin.

豫2 yù same as 预[1] yù

豫3 Yù 河南的别称 another name for Henan Province

【豫剧】yùjù 河南地方戏曲剧种之一,流行于河南全省和陕西、山西等地 Henan opera, one of the local operas in Henan Province, popular in Henan and parts of Shaanxi and Shanxi provinces; also 河南梆子 Hénán bāng•zi

噢 yù〈书 *fml.*〉same as 燠 yù

燠 yù〈书 *fml.*〉暖;热 warm; hot: ~热 sweltering; hot and suffocating | 寒~失时 unreasonable weather

【燠热】yùrè〈书 *fml.*〉闷热 sweltering; hot and suffocating; sultry; close and hot: 天气~。The weather is sultry.

燏 yù〈书 *fml.*〉火光 flame; blaze; fire light

鹬 yù 鸟的一属,体色暗淡,嘴细长,腿长,趾间没有蹼。常在浅水边或水田中吃小鱼、贝类、昆虫等,是候鸟。sandpiper (*Scolopacidae*); snipe; migratory bird, having grey feathers, a long thin bill, long legs, and feet not webbed, feeding on small fish, shells, insects, etc. on shores or in paddy fields

【鹬蚌相争,渔人得利】yù bàng xiāng zhēng, yúrén dé lì 蚌张开壳晒太阳,鹬去啄它,被蚌壳钳住了嘴,两方面都不肯相让。渔翁来了,把两个都捉住了(见于《战国策•燕策》)。*Intrigues of the Warring States • Intrigues of Yan*: A clam was basking in the sun when a snipe pecked at it. The clam caught the snipe's bill between its shells, and both sides refused to give in. A fisherman came and caught them both.〈比喻 *fig.*〉双方相争持,让第三者得了利。when two dogs fight over a bone, a third runs away with it; when two sides fight, a third party gains

鬻 yù〈书 *fml.*〉卖 sell; vend; be on sale: ~歌 make a living by singing | ~画 sell a painting | ~文为生 make a living by writing | 卖官~爵 sell official posts and titles

yuān (ㄩㄢ)

鸢 yuān 老鹰 kite; hawk; gled: ~飞鱼跃 hawks circling in the sky and fish diving

帑 yuān ☞ [缗帑] (fányuān) on p. 534

眢 yuān〈书 *fml.*〉❶ 眼睛干枯下陷 (of eyes) dry and sunken ❷ 枯竭 drained; dry; exhausted; depleted: ~井(干枯的井) dry well

鸳 yuān 指鸳鸯 mandarin duck ◇~侣(比喻夫妻 affectionate couple; (fig.) husband and wife

【鸳鸯】yuān•yāng 鸟,像野鸭,体形较小,嘴扁,颈长,趾间有蹼,善游泳,翼长,能飞。雄鸟有彩色羽毛,头后有铜赤、紫、绿等色的长冠毛,嘴红色。雌鸟羽毛苍褐色,嘴灰黑色,雌雄多成对生活在水边。文学上用来比喻夫妻。mandarin duck (*Aix galericulate*); bird shaped like a wild duck but smaller, having a flat beak, a long neck, webbed feet, and long wings, able to fly and good at swimming, the male bird having colourful feathers and a long reddish brown, purple or green aigrette, while the female has dark brown feathers and a dark grey beak, oft. living in couples at the waterside, and symbolizing affectionate husband and wife

冤(寃) yuān ❶ 冤枉;冤屈 wrong; injustice; grievance: ~情 truth or facts of an injustice; grievance | 鸣~ call to redress a wrong; complain of an injustice | 伸~ redress a grievance; right a wrong | 含~负屈 be wronged; be unfairly treated ❷ 冤仇 grievance; hatred; enmity; rancour: ~家 opponent and foe; enemy | 结~ start a feud; become foes; incur hatred ❸ 上当;吃亏 swallow the bait; be not worth the effort, time or money; in vain; for nothing: 花~钱 spend money in vain | 白跑一趟,真~! (I) went all the way there for nothing, what a waste of time! ❹〈方 *dial.*〉欺骗 cheat; befool; deceive; pull sb.'s leg: 你别~人! Don't kid me!

【冤案】yuān'àn 误判的冤屈案件；被人诬陷，妄加罪名的案件 unjust case; injustice; wrong: 平反～ overturn a wrong verdict; redress an injustice; right a wrong

【冤仇】yuānchóu 受人侵害或侮辱而产生的仇恨 rancour; enmity; hatred resulting from being harmed or insulted

【冤大头】yuāndàtóu 枉费钱财的人（含讥讽意 satirical）blockhead in money matters; foolish spender; sucker

【冤魂】yuānhún 称死得冤枉的人的魂灵（迷信）（superstition）spirit of someone who died of an injustice

【冤家】yuān·jia ❶ 仇人 enemy; foe: ～对头 opponent and foe; enemy ❷ 称似恨而实爱、给自己带来苦恼而又舍不得的人（旧时戏曲或民歌中多用来称情人 term used to address one's sweetheart in traditional Chinese operas or folk songs）one's destined love; sweetheart; lover (term to address a lover who has brought agony and whom one at once loves and hates and is reluctant to part with)

【冤家路窄】yuānjiā lù zhǎi 仇人或不愿意相见的人偏偏容易相逢，无可回避 the road of enemies is narrow; one can't avoid one's enemy as much as one wants to

【冤孽】yuānniè 冤仇罪孽 enmity and sin

【冤情】yuānqíng 受冤枉的情况 facts or truth of an injustice: ～大白。The truth of the injustice eventually came to light. | 申诉～ appeal to sb. to redress a wrong

【冤屈】yuānqū ❶ same as 冤枉 yuān·wang①② ❷ 不公平的待遇；不应受的损害 unfair treatment; injustice: 受～ be framed; be wronged; be unfairly treated; suffer an injustice

【冤头】yuāntóu 仇人 enemy; foe

【冤枉】yuān·wang ❶ 受到不公平的待遇；被加上不应有的罪名 be treated unfairly; be wronged with fabricated charges: ～官司 unjust verdict; uncalled-for lawsuit | 把这过错加在我头上，真是～。It's so unfair to blame me for this mistake. ❷ 使无罪者有罪；没有事实根据，给人加上恶名 treat sb. unfairly or unjustly; wrong; charge an innocent person with fabricated crimes: 别～好人。Don't wrong an innocent person. ❸ 不值得；吃亏 not worthwhile; not being repaid for effort; in vain; for nothing: 这个钱花得真～！(I) really didn't get my money's worth!

【冤枉路】yuān·wanglù 本来不必走而多走的路 vain trip; roundabout way; long way

【冤枉钱】yuān·wangqián 本来不必花而花的钱 money spent in vain; not worth the money spent

【冤狱】yuānyù 冤屈的案件 unjust charge or verdict; miscarriage of justice; frame-up: 平反～ redress a wrong; right a wrong; reverse an unjust verdict

渊（淵） yuān ❶ 深水；潭 deep water; deep pool: 深～ deep pool | 鱼跃于～ fish springing up to the surface of a deep pool | 天～之别 as far apart as heaven from earth; poles apart; worlds apart ❷ 深 deep: ～泉 deep spring | ～博 erudite; learned ❸ (Yuān)姓 a surname

【渊博】yuānbó （学识）深而且广 (of knowledge) broad and profound; erudite; learned: 知识～ erudite; learned; knowledgeable | ～的学者 erudite scholar

【渊海】yuānhǎi 深渊和大海 abyss and ocean; 〈比喻 *fig.*〉内容广而深 (of content) deep and vast; profound and extensive: 笔墨～ of great literary talent

【渊深】yuānshēn （学问、计谋等）很深 (of knowledge, stratagems, etc.) profound; deep; erudite: 学识～ be erudite and profound in knowledge

【渊薮】yuānsǒu 〈比喻 *fig.*〉人或事物聚集的地方 gathering place of people and things（渊 *yuan*: 深水，鱼所聚处 deep water where fish gather; 薮 *sou*: 水边草地，兽所聚处 waterside marshland where beasts assemble）: 罪恶的～ hotbed or breeding ground of crime; sink of iniquity

【渊源】yuānyuán 〈比喻 *fig.*〉事情的本原 origin; source: 历史～ historical origins | 家学～（家世学问的传授有根源）long tradition of family learning

涴 yuān 涴市(Yuānshì)，地名，在湖北 city of Yuanshi, in Hubei Province
☞ wò on p. 2015

痟 yuān 〈书 *fml.*〉❶ 酸痛 ache; sore ❷ 忧郁 melancholy

蜎 yuān 〈书 *fml.*〉孑孓 wiggler; wriggler

【蜎蜎】yuānyuān 〈书 *fml.*〉形容虫子爬行 (of a worm) wriggling; twisting

鹓 yuān [鹓鶵](yuānchú) 古书上说的凤凰一类的鸟 legendary bird like the phoenix in ancient books

篼 yuān ☞ below

【篼篼】yuāndōu 〈方 *dial.*〉same as 篼箕 yuānjī

【篼箕】yuānjī 〈方 *dial.*〉竹篾等编成的盛东西的器具 basketry; basket; basket woven of thin bamboo strips, etc.

yuán（ㄩㄢˊ）

元[1] yuán ❶ 开始的；第一 first; primary; initial: ～始 genesis | ～旦 New Year's Day | ～月 first lunar month; January | ～年 first year (of an era or of an emperor's reign) | 纪～ beginning of an era or an epoch ❷ 为首

的；居首的 chief; principal; leading：～首 head of state; monarch|～老 founding member|～帅 marshal|～勋 founding father; person who has rendered pre-eminent meritorious service|～凶 culprit|状～ first place in the imperial examination ❸ 主要；根本 basic; fundamental：～素 element|～音 vowel ❹ 元素 element; essential factor：一～论 monism|二～论 dualism ❺ 构成一个整体的 unit; component：单～ unit

元[2] yuán 货币单位 unit of money; same as 圆 yuán ⑥⑦

元[3] Yuán ❶ 朝代。蒙古孛儿只斤·铁木真于1206年建国。1271年忽必烈定国号为元。1279年灭宋。定都大都(今北京)。Yuan Dynasty (1271-1368), first founded in 1206 by Temujine, who was none other than Chenghis Khan, and renamed Yuan in 1271 by Kublai Khan, who brought an end to the Song Dynasty in 1279 and made Dadu (present-day Beijing) the capital ❷ 姓 a surname

【元宝】yuánbǎo 〈旧时 *old*〉较大的金银锭，两头翘起中间凹下，银元宝一般重五十两，金元宝重五两或十两 gold or silver ingot, with upturned ends and concave middle part; a silver ingot weighs 50 taels, while gold is 5 or 10 taels

【元宝枫】yuánbǎofēng 落叶乔木，羽状复叶，小叶长椭圆形，花黄绿色，果实两旁有直立的翅，像元宝，可栽培做行道树 Chinese wingnut (*Pterocarya stenoptera*); deciduous arbour, having pinnated compound leaves with oval-shaped leaflets, yellowish green flowers, and ingot-shaped samaras with vertical wings, oft. planted along roads; also 柜柳 jǔliǔ

【元旦】Yuándàn 新年的第一天 New Year's Day

【元恶】yuán'è 〈书 *fml.*〉首恶 chief criminal; principal culprit or offender

【元件】yuánjiàn 构成机器、仪表等的一部分，常由若干零件组成，可以在同类装置中调换使用 element; component; cell; unit of a machine or an instrument, often made of a few parts and used in the same type of equipment

【元老】yuánlǎo 称政界年辈资望高的人 senior leader; elder statesman; founding member; senior and prestigious person in the field of politics：三朝～ minister to three emperors; official who takes powerful positions under different rulers

【元麦】yuánmài 青稞 highland barley

【元煤】yuánméi same as 原煤 yuánméi

【元谋猿人】Yuánmóu yuánrén 中国猿人的一种，大约生活在一百七十万年以前，化石在1965年发现于云南元谋 Yuanmou Man; apelike people in China, who lived about 1.7 million years ago and whose fossils were found in Yuanmou, Yunnan Province in 1965; also 元谋人 Yuánmóurén

【元年】yuánnián 帝王或诸侯即位的第一年或帝王改元的第一年，如隐公元年，贞观元年。又指纪年的第一年，如公元元年，回历元年。有时指政体改变或政府组织上的大改变的第一年，如周代共和元年。first year of an emperor's reign or a new era named by an emperor, e.g. first year of the Yingong reign and of the Zhenguan reign; first year of an epoch, e.g. first year of the Christian or Islamic calendar; first year of a newly established regime or government, e.g. first year of the Gonghe reign of the Zhou Dynasty

【元配】yuánpèi 指第一次娶的妻子 first wife; also 原配 yuánpèi

【元气】yuánqì 指人或国家、组织的生命力 vitality; vigour of a person, a country or an organisation：～旺盛 full of vim and vigour|不伤～ not sapping one's vitality; not undermining one's constitution|恢复～ regain one's strength or health; recover from illness

【元曲】yuánqǔ 盛行于元代的一种文艺形式，包括杂剧和散曲，有时专指杂剧 Yuan drama, including proto-drama and lyric verse forms popular in the Yuan Dynasty; also sometimes used to refer to proto-drama; ☞ 杂剧 zájù on p.238 and 散曲 sǎnqǔ on p.1656

【元日】yuánrì 一年的第一天(旧指农历正月初一) New Year's Day; 1st day of the lunar New Year

【元戎】yuánróng 〈书 *fml.*〉主将 supreme commander

【元首】yuánshǒu ❶〈书 *fml.*〉君主 monarch ❷ 国家的最高领导人 head of state：国家～ head of state; sovereign

【元书纸】yuánshūzhǐ 一种文化用纸，供书写或作薄籍用，产于浙江 writing paper produced in Zhejiang Province

【元帅】yuánshuài ❶ 军衔，高于将官的军官 marshal; military rank higher than general ❷〈古时 *arch.*〉称统率全军的主帅 supreme commander who ruled all the army in a country

【元素】yuánsù ❶ 要素 element; essential factor ❷ 在代数学中组成联合的各个部分，如723,312中的7,2,3,1。在几何学中构成图形的各个部分，如构成三角形的边和角。element; elements in algebra, e.g. 7,2,3 and 1 in 723,312, and elements in geometry that form a figure, e.g. lines and angles in a triangle ❸ 化学元素的简称 abbr. for 化学元素 huàxué yuánsù

【元素符号】yuánsù fúhào 用来表示元素的化学符号。通常用元素的拉丁文名称的第一个字母(大写)来表示，如第一个字母与其他元素相同，就附加后面的一个字母(小写)来区别。如氧的元素符号是 O，铁的元素符号是 Fe。element symbol; symbol representing a chemical element and expressed by the first capitalized letter of the Latin name of the element, where if a letter is used by several chemical elements then a lower-case letter is added so as to differentiate them, e.g., the element symbol of oxygen is O, while that of iron is Fe

【元宵】yuánxiāo ❶ 农历正月十五日夜晚。因为这一天叫上元节,所以晚上叫元宵。night of the 15th of the 1st lunar month (Lantern Festival). Since the day is called the Shangyuan Festival, the night is *yuanxiao* (night of the Shangyuan Festival). ❷ 用糯米粉等做成的球形食品,有馅,多煮着吃。是元宵节的应时食品。rice dumpling; stuffed sweet, round dumplings made of glutinous rice flour specially prepared for the Lantern Festival

【元宵节】Yuánxiāo Jié 我国传统节日,在农历正月十五日。从唐代起,在这一天夜晚就有观灯的风俗。Lantern Festival; traditional Chinese festival falling on the 15th of the 1st lunar month, on which lantern displays are held at night, a custom handed down from the Tang Dynasty; also 灯节 Dēng Jié and 上元节 Shàngyuán Jié

【元凶】yuánxiōng 祸首 culprit; arch criminal

【元勋】yuánxūn 立大功的人 person of great merit; founding father: 开国~ founding father (or founder) of a state

【元夜】yuányè 〈书 *fml.*〉same as 元宵 yuánxiāo ①

【元音】yuányīn 声带颤动,气流在口腔的通路上不受到阻碍而发出的声音,如普通话语音的 ɑ, e, o, i, u, ü 等。也叫母音。发元音时鼻腔不通气,要是鼻腔也通气,发的元音就叫鼻化元音。普通话语音中 ng 尾韵儿化时元音变成鼻化元音。vowel; speech sound created by the relatively free passage of breath through the larynx and oral cavity, e.g. ɑ, e, o, i, u and ü in standard Chinese. Usually in pronouncing a vowel the nasal cavity is not open to air, but if it is open to air, the vowel is called a nasalized vowel. In standard Chinese 'ng', if added with the pronunciation of 'er', becomes a nasalized vowel.

【元鱼】yuányú same as 鼋鱼 yuányú

【元元本本】yuányuánběnběn same as 原原本本 yuányuánběnběn

【元月】yuányuè 指农历正月。也指公历一月。January; first month of the lunar calendar

芫 yuán [芫花](yuánhuā) 落叶灌木,叶子长圆形,花淡紫色,结核果。供观赏,花蕾可入药。lilac daphne (*Daphne genkwa*); deciduous shrub, having oval leaves and light purple flowers, and yielding drupes, grown for ornamental and medicinal purposes

☞ yán on p. 2202

园(園) yuán ❶ (~儿 yuanr) 种蔬菜、花果、树木的地方 garden; plot; plantation; land for growing vegetables, flowers, fruits and trees: 花~儿 flower garden | 果~ orchard | ~艺 horticulture ❷ 供人游览娱乐的地方 place of recreation; park; garden: 公~ park | 动物~ zoo; zoological garden

【园地】yuándì ❶ 菜园、花园、果园等的统称 garden plot; plot; general term for vegetable garden, flower garden, orchard, etc.: 农业~ agricultural plot; experimental farm ❷ 〈比喻 *fig.*〉开展某种活动的地方 field; scope; place to organize activities: 文化~ field of culture | 艺术~ art field

【园丁】yuándīng ❶ 从事园艺的工人 gardener ❷ 〈比喻 *fig.*〉教师(多指小学的 oft. of primary school) teacher

【园林】yuánlín 种植花草树木供人游赏休息的风景区 garden; park; area where flowers and trees are planted for people to enjoy and take a rest: ~艺术 art of landscaping; horticulture; gardening

【园圃】yuánpǔ 种蔬菜、花果、树木的场所 garden; plot for growing vegetables, flowers, fruits and trees; nursery

【园田】yuántián 种菜的田地 vegetable garden: 耕作~化(精耕细作) garden-style cultivating of farmland; intensive cultivation

【园艺】yuányì 种植蔬菜、花卉、果树等的技术 horticulture; gardening; landscaping: ~师 horticulturist; landscaper

【园囿】yuányòu 〈书 *fml.*〉供游玩的花园或动物园 garden; zoo

【园子】yuán·zi ❶ same as 园 yuán①: 菜~ vegetable garden; vegetable farm ❷ 指戏园子 theatre

员 yuán ❶ 指工作或学习的人 person engaged in some field of work or study; staff member: 教~ teacher | 学~ student; trainee | 演~ actor; actress | 职~ staff member; clerk | 炊事~ cook | 指挥~ commander | 战斗~ combatant | ~工 staff; personnel | 人~ personnel ❷ 指团体或组织中的成员 member of a group or an organization: 党~ Party member | 团~ member of the Communist Youth League of China; League member | 会~ member of an organization | 队~ team member ❸ 〈量词 *classifier*〉用于武将 [used to describe a brave soldier]: 一~大将 a valiant general; one vigorous man

☞ yún on p. 2377 and Yùn on p. 2380

【员额】yuán'é 人员的定额 specified number of personnel: 缩减~ reduce the number of personnel

【员工】yuángōng 职员和工人 staff; personnel; clerk; worker: 铁路~ railway workers and staff; railway employees

【员司】yuánsī 〈旧时 *old*〉指政府机关的中下级

人员 junior clerks or functionaries in government offices

【员外】yuánwài ❶〈古时 *arch*.〉官职(全称为'员外郎',是在郎官的定员之外设置的) counsellor; official title (whole name being 员外郎 yuánwàiláng, an official post set outside of the fixed number of officials) ❷ 指地主豪绅(多见于早期白话 oft. used in early vernacular) landlord; squire

沅 Yuán 沅江,发源于贵州,流入湖南 Yuanjiang River, originating in Guizhou Province and flowing into Hunan Province

垣 yuán ❶〈书 *fml*.〉墙 wall: 城～ city wall | 颓～断壁 dilapidated wall; debris; ruins ❷〈书 *fml*.〉城 city: 省～(省城) provincial capital ❸ (Yuán) 姓 a surname

爰 yuán〈书 *fml*.〉❶ 何处;哪里 where: ～其适归? Where to go? ❷ 于是 hence; therefore; thereupon; so; consequently: ～书其事以告。Therefore, (I) am writing to tell you about it.

袁 Yuán 姓 a surname

【袁头】yuántóu 指民国初年发行的铸有袁世凯头像的银元 silver coin minted in the early years of the Republic of China with the head of Yuan Shikai on the reverse side; also 袁大头 yuándàtóu

原[1] yuán ❶ 最初的;开始的 primary; original; inceptive; at the very beginning: ～始 primitive | ～人 primitive man | ～生动物 protozoan ❷ 原来;本来 original; former: ～地 same place | ～作者 original writer | ～班人马 same crew members; former staff | ～有人数 former number of people ❸ 没加工的 unprocessed; crude; raw: ～棉 raw cotton | ～煤 raw coal | ～油 crude oil ❹ (Yuán) 姓 a surname

原[2] yuán 原谅 excuse; pardon: ～宥 forgive; pardon | 情有可～ excusable; forgivable; pardonable

原[3] yuán ❶ 宽广平坦的地方 open country; plain; level and extensive land: 平～ plain | 高～ plateau | 草～ grassland; prairie | ～野 open country; champaign ❷ same as 塬 yuán

【原版】yuánbǎn ❶ 书籍原来的印本 original edition ❷ 指音像部门原出版的录音带、录像带(区别于'盗版'或翻录的 as compared with 'pirate' or 'duplicate') original cassettes and video tapes

【原本】[1] yuánběn ❶ 底本;原稿(区别于传抄本 as compared with 'hand-written copy') original manuscript; master copy ❷ 初刻本(区别于重刻本 as compared with 'block reprint') original block-printed edition ❸ 翻译所根据的原书 original version from which a translation is made

【原本】[2] yuánběn 原来;本来 originally; formerly: 他～是学医的,后来改行搞戏剧。He originally majored in medicine and later changed to drama.

【原材料】yuáncáiliào 原料和材料 raw and processed material

【原初】yuánchū 起初;原先 originally; formerly; at first: 她～不像现在这样爱说爱笑。At first she wasn't as talkative and cheerful as she is now.

【原动机】yuándòngjī 利用热能、水力、风力等产生动力的机械 prime power; prime motor; mechanism employed to make use of heat, energy of water, wind, etc., to produce motive power

【原动力】yuándònglì 产生动力的力,如水力发电的水力 motivity; motive power or force, e.g. water energy used to generate electricity

【原封】yuánfēng (～儿 yuánfēngr)没有开封的。泛指保持原来的样子,一点不加变动的。with the seal unbroken; intact: ～烧酒 distilled liquor with the seal intact | ～不动 remain untouched; be left intact | ～退回 return sth. unopened

【原稿】yuángǎo 写成后没有经过他人修改增删的稿子;出版部门据以印刷出版的稿子 original manuscript; master copy; manuscript unpolished by others; manuscript according to which a book will be published

【原告】yuángào 向法院提出诉讼的人或机关、团体 (in civil cases) plaintiff; (in criminal cases) prosecutor; person, organ or organization who files a suit in court; also 原告人 yuángàorén

【原鸽】yuángē 鸽的一种,身体的上部灰色,颈部有绿紫色的光泽,腹部淡灰色,善飞行。吃谷物及其他植物的种子。wild pigeon (*Columba livia*), having a grey upper body, green and purple neck, and light grey belly; good at flying, and feeding on grains or other plant seeds; also 野鸽 yěgē

【原故】yuángù same as 缘故 yuángù

【原鸡】yuánjī 鸟,体形和家鸡相似而小,是家鸡的远祖。雄鸡羽毛颜色美丽,体上部多红色,下部黑褐色。雌鸡体上部暗褐色,尾短。栖息在云南、广西南部及海南岛等山区密林中。jungle fowl (*Gallus gallus jabouillei*); jungle rooster or hen, remote ancestor of the domesticated chicken, but smaller in physique, with the male having beautifully coloured feathers, a red-feathered upper body and a dark brown lower body, and the female having a dark brown upper body and a short tail, mainly found in the deep forests of Yunnan Province, southern Guangxi Zhuang Autonomous Region, and Hainan Island

【原籍】yuánjí 原先的籍贯(区别于'寄籍、客籍'

as compared with 'migrant home' and 'temporary home') ancestral home：～浙江，寄籍北京。His ancestral home is in Zhejiang Province, and he has now settled down in Beijing.

【原价】yuánjià 原来的价格 original price; former price：按～打八折出售 sell at 20 per cent off; give a 20 per cent discount on the marked price

【原件】yuánjiàn 未经改动或变动的文件或物件；翻印文件、制作复制品所依据的原来的文件或物件 original manuscript; master copy; unpolished or unchanged document or object; original document or object from which a replica is made：～退回 return the master copy

【原矿】yuánkuàng 开采后未经加工的矿石 raw ore; run-of-mine ore; crude ore

【原来】yuánlái ❶ 起初；没有经过改变的 originally; formerly：我们能够学会我们～不懂的东西。We can learn and master what we formerly didn't understand.｜他还住在～的地方。He still lives in the same place. ❷ 表示发现真实情况 so; it turns out：～是你。So it's you.｜我说夜里怎么这么冷，～是下雪了。So it's snowing. I was just wondering why it was so cold tonight.

【原理】yuánlǐ 带有普遍性的、最基本的、可以作为其他规律的基础的规律；具有普遍意义的道理 principle; theory; universal and fundamental law that can be the basis of other laws; principle of universal significance

【原粮】yuánliáng 没有经过加工的粮食，如没有碾成米的稻谷，没有磨成面粉的小麦 unprocessed grain; unhusked grain, e.g. unhusked rice and unground wheat

【原谅】yuánliàng 对人的疏忽、过失或错误宽恕谅解，不加责备或惩罚 forgive; pardon; excuse; not blame or punish sb. for negligence, error or mistake

【原料】yuánliào 指没有经过加工制造的材料，如用来冶金的矿砂，用来纺织的棉花 raw material; unprocessed material, e.g. raw ore, unprocessed cotton

【原麻】yuánmá 纺织上指用做原料的麻类植物的纤维 hemp used in the textile industry

【原毛】yuánmáo 纺织上指未经加工的兽毛，如兔毛、羊毛等 raw wool or fur, e.g. rabbit hair, fleece, etc.; also 油毛 yóumáo

【原貌】yuánmào 原来的面貌；本来的样子 original appearance or look; original state：保持～ keep sth. as it is; leave sth. in its original state

【原煤】yuánméi 从矿井开采出来，没有经过筛、洗、选等加工程序的煤 raw coal; extracted coal that hasn't been sifted, washed, selected, etc.; also 元煤 yuánméi

【原蜜】yuánmì 没有经过加工的蜂蜜 unprocessed honey; raw honey

【原棉】yuánmián 纺织上指用做原料的皮棉 unprocessed cotton

【原木】yuánmù 采伐后未经加工的木料 log; unprocessed wood

【原配】yuánpèi same as 元配 yuánpèi

【原人】yuánrén 指猿人 apeman

【原色】yuánsè 能配合成各种颜色的基本颜色。颜料中的原色是红、黄、蓝，蓝和黄可以配合成绿，红和蓝可以配合成紫。色光中的原色是红、绿、蓝，红和绿可以配合成黄，红和蓝可以配合成紫。primary colour; basic colours that combine to produce different shades of colour. In pigment, red, yellow and blue are the primary colours, and blue and yellow combine to produce green while red and blue combine to produce purple. In light, the primary colours are red, green and blue, and red and green combine to produce yellow while the combination of red and blue produces purple. also 基色 jīsè

【原审】yuánshěn 对案件进行第二次审判时，称前一次审判为原审 first trial

【原生动物】yuánshēng-dòngwù 最原始最简单的动物，生活在水中或其他生物体内，大都是单细胞动物，有的由多数个体组织成群体生活 protozoan; most primitive, simplest creature living in water or in the bodies of other organisms, mostly single-cell and some living in groups

【原生矿物】yuánshēng-kuàngwù 矿床中保持其生成时的形态和成分的矿物，如辉石、石英、方铅矿等 primary mineral; mineral that maintains its original state and elements, e.g. augite, quartz, galenite, etc.

【原生林】yuánshēnglín 从来未经人工采伐和培育的天然森林 primeval forest; virgin forest; undeveloped natural forest; also 原始林 yuánshǐlín

【原生质】yuánshēngzhì 细胞中有生活力的组成部分，是生命的物质基础，由蛋白质、核酸、脂肪、碳水化合物、无机盐、水等构成 protoplasm; vital part of a cell, which is the basic material of life, including protein, nucleic acid, fat, carbohydrate, inorganic salt, water, etc.

【原声带】yuánshēngdài 指乐队或演员直接在录音棚里录制的磁带（区别于转录的磁带 as compared with 'duplicate tape'）original sound track; master tape; tape that directly recorded the performance by a band or actor in a recording studio

【原始】yuánshǐ ❶ 最初的；第一手的 primal; original; first-hand; initial; primordial：～记录 original record｜～资料 first-hand data ❷ 最古老的；未开发的；未开化的 undeveloped; primitive; primeval：～动物 primitive animal｜～社会 primitive society｜～森林 primeval forest; virgin forest

【原始公社】yuánshǐ gōngshè 人类社会历史上

最早阶段的社会组织，延续了数十万年。包括母系氏族公社和父系氏族公社两个阶段。primitive commune; social organization in the earliest period of human history, which lasted hundreds of thousands of years and included two periods, of matrilineal clan commune and patrilineal clan commune; ☞ 原始社会 yuánshǐ shèhuì

【原始积累】yuánshǐ jīlěi 指在资本主义大生产方式建立以前，剥削阶级通过对农民、小生产者和殖民地人民的残酷掠夺而进行的资本积累 primitive accumulation; capital accumulation of the exploiting class by mercilessly robbing peasants, small begetters and people in colonies, before the establishment of the capitalist mass production mode

【原始群】yuánshǐqún 原始社会初期，人类为了共同劳动和抵御敌人，由有血统关系的人自然形成的集体。这时生产能力极低，以采集野生植物和狩猎为生，没有固定居住的地方。后来原始群发展成氏族。primitive horde or nomadic tribes. In the early period of primitive society, to work together and fight enemies, people related to each other by kinship formed groups, and productivity being extremely low, made a living by hunting and gather, without fixed habitats. Later the primitive horde developed into clans.

【原始社会】yuánshǐ shèhuì 人类历史上最早的社会，从原始群的形成开始，经过母系氏族公社、父系氏族公社直至原始公社的解体。原始社会生产力极低，生产资料公有，人们共同劳动，共同消费，没有剥削，没有阶级。后被奴隶社会所取代。primitive society; earliest form of society in human history, starting from the formation of primitive groups through to the matrilineal clan commune, the patrilineal clan commune, and ending with the disintegration of the primitive commune; primitive society, in which social productivity was very low, productive materials were collectively owned, and people worked and consumed together without exploitation or the existence of classes, later replaced by slave society

【原诉】yuánsù 在诉讼过程中，被告对原告提出反诉时，称原告提起的诉讼为原诉 original suit; original suit filed by the accuser, so called when the accused countercharges the accuser

【原索动物】yuánsuǒ-dòngwù 脊索动物的一个亚门。背部有柔软的脊索，以支持身体，如文昌鱼等。protochordate; prochordate; chordate subphylum, having a soft notochord on the back to support the body, e.g. lancelet

【原汤】yuántāng 指煮熟某种食物后的汤汁 original soup or juice left of food being cooked

【原田】yuántián 〈方 *dial.*〉高原上的田地 farmland on a plateau

【原委】yuánwěi 事情从头到尾的经过；本末 whole story; all the details: 说明～ tell the whole story; give all the details

【原文】yuánwén ❶ 翻译时所根据的词句或文章 original; words and phrases or articles from which a translation is based on: 译笔能表达出～精神。The translation can convey well the meaning of the original. ❷ 征引或转写所依据的文字 original text; master copy; text quoted or transcribed: 引用～要加引号。Put quoted text in quotation marks. | 抄完之后要跟～校对一下。Please check the copy against the original after the transcription is done.

【原先】yuánxiān 从前；起初 original; former: 照～的计划做 do according to the original plan | 他～是个文盲，现在已经成了业余作家。He was illiterate in the past, but he has now become an amateur writer.

【原线圈】yuánxiànquān 感应圈、变压器内接电源的线圈 primary coil; coil whose inductor and transformer are connected with an electrical source; also 初级线圈 chūjíxiànquān

【原形】yuánxíng 原来的形状；本来面目（贬义 derog.）original form; true features; true appearance beneath the disguise: 现～ show one's true colours; betray oneself | ～毕露 show one's true colours; be revealed for what one is

【原型】yuánxíng 原来的类型或模型。特指叙事性文学作品中塑造人物形象所依据的现实生活中的人。model; prototype; original type or model; esp. referring to persons in real life, on whom the characters in narrative literary works are based

【原盐】yuányán 只经过初步晒制或熬制的食盐，一般含杂质较多，多用做工业原料 crude salt; salt initially manufactured through drying or decocting, generally containing lots of residues, and often used as raw industrial material

【原样】yuányàng（～儿 yuányàngr）原来的样子；老样子 original appearance or state; same old way: 照实物～复制 replicate according to the original appearance of the object | 几年没见，你还是～，一点不见老。It's years since we met last time, but you look just the same and haven't aged at all.

【原野】yuányě 平原旷野 open country; champaign; weald: 辽阔的～ vast open country | 山下是肥沃的～。At the foot of the mountain is a stretch of fertile open country.

【原意】yuányì 原来的意思或意图 meaning; original meaning or intention: 有背～ go against the original meaning | 不要曲解～。Don't distort the meaning.

【原因】yuányīn 造成某种结果或引起另一件事情发生的条件 cause; reason; condition that brings about a certain result, or accounts for a certain occurrence：丰收的～ reason for a bumper harvest｜成功的～ reason for success｜检查生病的～ examine the cause of illness

【原由】yuányóu same as 缘由 yuányóu

【原油】yuányóu 开采出来未经提炼的石油 crude oil；unrefined petroleum

【原宥】yuányòu 原谅 pardon；forgive；excuse for：敬希～。(I) wish to ask for your pardon. *or* (I) hope you will forgive me.

【原原本本】yuányuánběnběn 从头到尾地（叙述）(relate) from beginning to end：我把这件事～讲给他们听。I told them the whole story exactly as it had happened. 原 yuán also as 源 yuán or 元 yuán

【原则】yuánzé ❶ 说话或行事所依据的法则或标准 principle；tenet；criterion by which one speaks or acts：～性 of principle｜～问题 matter of principle｜坚持～ stick or adhere to principle；live up to one's principles｜基本～ basic principle ❷ 指总的方面；大体上 in principle；in general：他～上赞成这个方案，只在个别细节上提了些具体意见。He agreed to the plan in principle and only put forward some suggestions on one or two specific details.

【原职】yuánzhí 原来的职务 former post：官复～ be rehabilitated to one's former post

【原址】yuánzhǐ 原来的地址 former address；original site：该公司已迁回～。The company has moved back to its former address.

【原纸】yuánzhǐ 用来制造各种加工纸的原料纸。质量根据加工要求而不同，如钢纸原纸要求结构松软，吸收液体性能好；誊写蜡纸原纸要求纸质柔韧，纤维细长。body paper；body stock；base paper；raw stock；raw paper of different qualities used to manufacture all other kinds of paper for different purposes. Body paper for making vulcanized fibre paper should be soft and absorb liquid easily, while stencil paper needs pliable, long and fine fibres

【原种】yuánzhǒng 原来的品种；保持原来的特性、没有变易的品种 protospecies；stock；breed that has retained its original features without any changes：～肉鸡 stock chicken；stock table hen

【原主】yuánzhǔ（～儿 yuánzhǔr）原来的所有者 original owner or proprietor：物归～ return sth. to its owner

【原著】yuánzhù 著作的原本（对译本、缩写本、删节本、改编本而言 as opposed to 'translated', 'simplified', 'abridged', or 'adapted' versions) original work；original：翻译作品要忠实于～。Translation should be faithful to the original.

【原装】yuánzhuāng ❶ 原来装配好的 factory-assembled；factory-packed：～名牌电器 factory-packed brand-name home appliances ❷ 原来包装好的 original packing：～名酒 liquor in its original packing

【原状】yuánzhuàng 原来的样子 original state；previous condition；status quo ante：恢复～ restore to its former state

【原子】yuánzǐ 构成化学元素的基本单位，是物质化学变化中的最小微粒，由带正电的原子核和围绕原子核运动的电子组成 atom；basic unit forming a chemical element, which is the tiniest particle in chemical combination of substances, comprising a positively charged nucleus with electrons moving round it

【原子弹】yuánzǐdàn 核武器的一种，利用铀、钚等原子核分裂所产生的原子能进行杀伤和破坏。爆炸时产生冲击波、光辐射、贯穿辐射和放射性沾染。atom bomb；atomic bomb；A-bomb；explosive nuclear weapon of great destructive power, derived from the rapid release of energy in the fission of heavy atomic nuclei, as of uranium, plutonium, etc. When exploding, it produces shock waves, radiation, penetrating radiation, and radioactive contamination.

【原子反应堆】yuánzǐ fǎnyìngduī 使铀、钚等的原子核裂变的链式反应能够有控制地持续进行，从而获得原子能的装置 atomic reactor；atomic pile；chain reactor；nuclear reactor；apparatus in which a nuclear-fission chain reaction can be initiated, sustained and controlled, for generating atomic energy；also 核反应堆 héfǎnyìngduī；简称 abbr. 反应堆 fǎnyìngduī

【原子核】yuánzǐhé 原子的核心部分，由质子和中子组成。原子核只占原子体积的极小部分，而原子的质量几乎全部集中在原子核上。atomic nucleus；nucleus；positively charged central core of an atom, composed of protons and neutrons, and containing almost all of the mass of the atom though forming only a fraction of the atomic volume

【原子价】yuánzǐjià ☞ 化合价 huàhéjià on p.835

【原子量】yuánzǐliàng 元素原子的相对质量。将质量数为12的碳原子的质量定为12，其他元素的原子量就是该元素质子质量和这种碳原子质量的比值。如氢的原子量为1.0079，氧的原子量为15.9994。atomic weight；average mass of an atom of an element, generally expressed relative to the mass of carbon 12, which is assigned a 12 atomic mass unit, e.g. the atomic weight of hydrogen is 1.0079, while that of oxygen is 15.9994

【原子能】yuánzǐnéng 原子核发生裂变或聚变反应时产生的能量，广泛用于工业、军事等方面 atomic energy；A-energy；nuclear energy；energy released by rearrangement of atomic nuclei, as in nuclear fission or fusion, with wide industrial and military uses; also 核能 hénéng

【原子团】yuánzǐtuán 几个不同种的原子结合成的集团,在许多化学反应中作为一个整体参加,如氢氧根(OH)、硫酸根(SO_4)、烷基(CH_3)等 atomic group; formed of several different atoms and taking part in many chemical reactions as a group, e. g. hydroxyls (OH), vitriol (SO_4), alkyls (CH_3), etc.

【原子武器】yuánzǐ wǔqì ☞ 核武器 héwǔqì on p.790

【原子序数】yuánzǐ xùshù 元素周期表中,元素按原子的核电荷数从小到大顺序排列的号码 atomic number; number of positive charges in the nucleus of an atom of a given element, arranged from lesser to greater in the periodic table of elements

【原子质量单位】yuánzǐ zhìliàng dānwèi 计量原子质量的单位。它的数值相当于碳同位素原子$^{12}_{6}C$质量的1/12,约等于1.6606×10^{-27}千克。atomic mass unit, whose numerical value is equal to 1/12 of the mass of carbon isotope $^{12}_{6}C$, or 1.6606×10^{-27} kg.

【原子钟】yuánzǐzhōng 利用铯、铷等原子的稳定振荡频率制成的极精密的计时器,计时误差每日可小于百万分之一秒 atomic clock; extremely accurate clock regulated by the steady vibration frequency of atoms of certain substances, e. g. caesium, rubidium, etc., measuring the time of a day with a tolerance of less than 1/1,000,000 second

【原罪】yuánzuì 〈基督教 *Christ.*〉指人类始祖亚当和夏娃在伊甸园偷吃了上帝禁吃的智慧之果而犯下的罪。传给后世子孙,成为一切罪恶和灾祸的根源。original sin; according to Christianity, sin committed by the first humans, Adam and Eve in Eden, who stole and ate the fruit of knowledge, which was forbidden by God, a sin then passed on to their posterity and being the source of all evil and disaster

【原作】yuánzuò ❶ 诗文唱和的最初的一篇 master or primary copy; first poem that is responded to by many other poems ❷ 译文或改写本所根据的原文 original work; original version; original

圆 yuán ❶ 圆周所围成的平面 round; circular; spherical: ～桌 round table | ～柱 round pillar | ～筒 round tube ❷ 圆周的简称 abbr. for 圆周 yuánzhōu ❸ 像球的形状 ball-shaped: 滚～ round as a ball | 滴溜～ extremely round ❹ 圆满;周全 tactful; satisfactory: 这话说得不～。This remark is not tactful. | 这人做事很～,各方面都能照顾到。He was very tactful and took all aspects into consideration. ❺ 使圆满;使周全 make perfect; justify; make complete: ～场 smooth things over | ～谎 make a lie sound plausible | 自～其说 make one's statement consistent; justify oneself ❻ 我国的本位货币单位,一圆等于十角或一百分 standard Chinese currency unit, with one yuan equal to 10 *jiao* or 100 *fen*; also 元 yuán ❼ 圆形的货币 round coin: 银～ silver dollar | 铜～ copper coin; also 元 yuán ❽ (Yuán) 姓 a surname

【圆白菜】yuánbáicài 结球甘蓝的通称 general term for 结球甘蓝 jiéqiú gānlán

【圆场】yuán//chǎng 为打开僵局而从中解说或提出折衷办法 mediate; help to effect a compromise; smooth things over: 这事最好由你出面说几句话圆圆场。This would be best settled by you standing up and saying a few words.

【圆场】yuánchǎng ☞ 跑圆场 pǎo yuánchǎng on p.1450

【圆成】yuánchéng 成全 help sb. attain his or her aim: ～好事 help sb. achieve sth.

【圆雕】yuándiāo 雕塑的一种,用石头、金属、木头等雕出的立体形象 sculpture-in-the-round; solid image sculpted with stone, metal, wood, etc.

【圆房】yuán//fáng 〈旧指 *old*〉童养媳和未婚夫开始过夫妇生活 consummating of a marriage between a child bride and her husband when they come of age

【圆坟】yuán//fén 旧俗在死人埋葬三天后去坟上培土 (old custom) add soil onto a tomb three days after the burial

【圆鼓鼓】yuángǔgǔ (～的 yuángǔgǔ·de)形容圆而凸起的样子 round and bulging; rotund: 挺着～的肚子 protruding round belly | ～的豆粒 round bean

【圆光】yuánguāng 〈旧时 *old*〉江湖术士利用迷信心理骗人的一种方法,先念咒语,叫小孩看镜子里或白纸上有什么形象出现,胡说凭所见形象就可以知道失物所在或预测凶吉、祸福 round light image; method employed to cheat superstitious people by wizards, who chant incantations and ask a child to look in a mirror or on white paper for images, which are claimed to give clues for lost property or fortune-telling

【圆规】yuánguī 两脚规的一种,一脚是尖针,另一脚可以装上铅笔芯或鸭嘴笔头,是画圆和弧的用具 compasses; bow compass; dividers; implement having two legs, with one fixed with a needle and the other with a lead or pen point, used to draw circles or arcs

【圆滚滚】yuángǔngǔn (～的 yuángǔngǔn·de)形容非常圆 very round; rounded: ～的脸蛋儿 chubby face | ～的小肥猪 podgy piglet

【圆号】yuánhào 管乐器,管身圈成圆形,号嘴的形状像漏斗,装有活塞。音色沉静、柔和。French horn; valved brass wind instrument that produces a mellow tone from a long, narrow tube coiled in a circle with a funnel-like mouthpiece.

【圆滑】yuánhuá 形容人只顾各方面敷衍讨好，不负责任 tactful; wily; slick and sly

【圆谎】yuán//huǎng 弥补谎话中的漏洞 patch up a lie; make a lie sound plausible: 他想～，可越说漏洞越多。He wanted to explain his lie away but the more he explained, the more gaffes he made.

【圆浑】yuánhún ❶（声音）婉转而圆润自然（of voice）rich; mellow: 语调～ in a round, mellow voice | 这段唱腔流畅而～。This aria is fluent and melodious. ❷（诗文）意味浓厚，没有雕琢的痕迹（of writing）natural and smooth; beautifully written with profound meaning

【圆寂】yuánjì〈佛教用语 *Budd.*〉称僧尼死亡（of monks or nuns）pass away; die

【圆笼】yuánlóng 放饭菜或送饭菜用的圆形大提盒 large round basket for holding food

【圆颅方趾】yuán lú fāng zhǐ《淮南子·精神篇》：'故头之圆也象天，足之方也象地' *Huainanzi · On Spirit*: 'So the round head resembles the sky and the square foot the earth.' 后来用'圆颅方趾'指人类 referring to human being

【圆满】yuánmǎn 没有缺欠、漏洞，使人满意 satisfactory; perfect: ～的答案 satisfactory answer | 两国会谈～结束。The talks between the two countries came to a successful end.

【圆梦】yuán//mèng 解说梦的吉凶（迷信）（superstition）oneiromancy; divination by dreams

【圆盘耙】yuánpánbà 碎土、平地的农具，也可用来灭茬，由一个个边缘锋利的钢制圆盘组成，用拖拉机或畜力牵引 disc harrow; farm implement consisting of steel disks with sharp teeth, used to break up and even off ploughed earth and clean the stubble

【圆圈】yuánquān（～儿 yuánquānr）圆形的圈子 circle; ring

【圆全】yuán·quan〈方 *dial.*〉圆满；周全 thoughtful; considerate: 想得～ be very considerate; be thoughtful | 事情办得～。The matter has been thoughtfully handled.

【圆润】yuánrùn ❶ 饱满而润泽 mellow and full: ～的歌喉 a sweet, mellow voice ❷（书、画技法）圆熟流利（of skills in calligraphy and painting）fluid; smooth: 他的书法～有力。His calligraphy is flowing and powerful.

【圆实】yuán·shi 圆而结实 round and solid; plump: 西瓜长得挺～。The watermelons are growing round and plump. | 莲子饱满～。The lotus seeds are plump.

【圆熟】yuánshú ❶ 熟练；纯熟 skilful; proficient; dexterous: 笔体～ skilful brushwork | 演技日臻～。Their performance skills are improving with each passing day. ❷ 精明练达；灵活变通 astute; tactful; flexible: 处事极～ be astute in one's behaviour; be sophisticated in dealing with people or matters

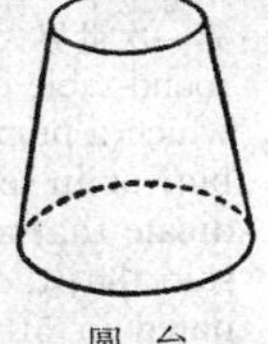

圆台
Frustum of a Cone

【圆台】yuántái 圆锥的底面和平行于底面的一个截面间的部分，叫做圆台 frustum of a cone; truncated cone; part between the underside of a cone and a parallel section; also 圆锥台 yuánzhuītái

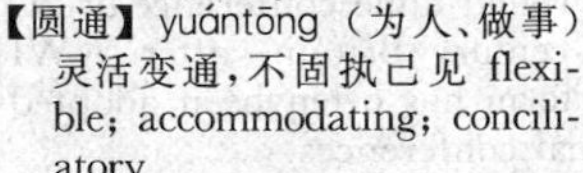

【圆通】yuántōng（为人、做事）灵活变通，不固执己见 flexible; accommodating; conciliatory

【圆舞曲】yuánwǔqǔ 一种每节三拍的民间舞曲，起源于奥地利民间，后来流行很广 waltz; folk dance in triple time, originating in Austria and later popular in other parts of the world

【圆心】yuánxīn 圆的中心；跟圆周上各点距离都相等的一点 centre of a circle, which is equidistant from any point on its circumference

【圆凿方枘】yuán záo fāng ruì ☞ 方枘圆凿 fāng ruì yuán záo on p. 545

【圆周】yuánzhōu 平面上一动点以一定点为中心，一定长为距离运动一周的轨迹 circumference; boundary of a circle; 简称 abbr. 圆 yuán

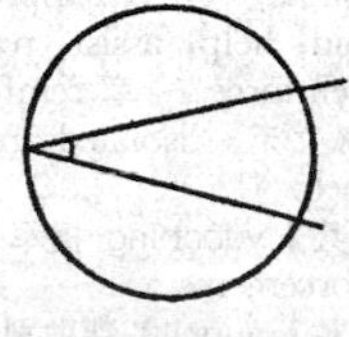

圆周角
Circumferential Angle

【圆周角】yuánzhōujiǎo 顶点在圆周上，两条边都与圆相交的角 circumferential angle; angle that has its vertex on the circumference and its two lines intersecting with a circle

【圆周率】yuánzhōulǜ 圆周长度与圆的直径长度的比，圆周率的值是3.14159265358979323846…，通常用'π'表示。计算中常取3.1416为它的近似值。pi; ratio of the circumference of a circle to its diameter, or 3.14159265358979323846…, written as 'π', oft. rounded off to 3.1416 for use in practical calculations

【圆珠笔】yuánzhūbǐ 用油墨书写的一种笔，笔芯里装有油墨，笔尖是个小钢珠，油墨由钢珠四周漏下 ballpoint pen; ball-pen; pen having an ink refill and a point comprising a tiny steel ball, from around which the writing ink leaks out when in use

【圆柱】yuánzhù 以矩形的一边为轴使矩形旋转一周所围成的立体 cylinder; solid figure generated by a line of a rectangle tracing a closed curve

【圆锥】yuánzhuī 以直角三角形的一直角边为轴旋转一周所围成的立体 circular cone; cone; solid figure generated by a straight line of a right-angled triangle tracing a closed curve

【圆桌】yuánzhuō 桌面是圆形的桌子 round table

【圆桌会议】yuánzhuō huìyì 一种会议形式，用圆桌或把座位排成圆圈，以表示与会各方席次不分上下一律平等。相传创始于5世纪的英国。第一次世界大战后，国际会议常采用这种形式。round-table conference; a type of meeting at which a number of people sit at a round table, or in seats arranged in a circle, to indicate that all participants are equal. It is said that the round-table conference originated in 5th-century Britain; after WWI this meeting form has often been adopted at international conferences.

【圆桌面】yuánzhuōmiàn（～儿 yuánzhuōmiànr）圆形桌面，可以安放在方桌上，当圆桌用 detachable round table top which can be put on a square table so that a round table is made

【圆子】yuán·zi ❶ 糯米粉等做成的一种食品，大多有馅儿 dumpling; stuffed glutinous rice flour dough ❷〈方 *dial.*〉丸子 meat or fish ball

黿(黿) yuán same as 黿鱼 yuányú

【黿鱼】yuányú 鳖 soft-shelled turtle (*Pelochelys bibroni*); also 元鱼 yuányú

援 yuán ❶ 以手牵引 pull by hand; hold: 攀～ climb ❷ 引用 quote; cite: ～用 cite; quote|～例 cite a precedent ❸ 援助 support; aid; help; assist; rescue: 支～ support|增～ reinforce|～军 reinforcements; relief troops|孤立无～ isolated and separated from outside help

【援兵】yuánbīng 援军；救兵 relief troops; reinforcements

【援救】yuánjiù 帮助别人使脱离痛苦或危险 rescue; save; deliver sb. from danger; help sb. to get away from pain or danger: ～灾民 deliver disaster-stricken people from danger

【援军】yuánjūn 增援的军队 relief troops; reinforcements

【援例】yuán//lì 引用成例 quote or cite a precedent: ～处理 dispose or deal with sth. by following a precedent|我们不能援这个例。We cannot follow this precedent.

【援手】yuánshǒu〈书 *fml.*〉救助（语出《孟子·离娄上》：'嫂溺，援之以手'）aid; save; rescue. *Mencius·Li Lou (I)*: 'When his sister-in-law was drowning, he reached out his hand to save her.'

【援外】yuánwài（在经济、技术等方面）支援外国 give (economic, technological, etc.) aid to another country; aid a foreign country: ～物资 material aid for a foreign country

【援引】yuányǐn ❶ 引用 quote; cite: ～条文 quote a regulation|～例证 cite an example ❷ 提拔；引荐 promote; recommend or appoint sb. to a post: ～贤能 recommend the capable and virtuous

【援用】yuányòng ❶ 引用 quote; cite; invoke: ～成例 cite a precedent ❷ 引荐任用 recommend and appoint sb.: ～亲信 appoint one's favourite

【援助】yuánzhù 支援；帮助 help; support; aid; assist: 国际～ international support|经济～ economic aid|～受难者 help the victims

湲 yuán ☞ 潺湲 chányuán on p.211

媛 yuán ☞ 婵媛 chányuán on p.210
☞ yuàn on p.2368

缘 yuán ❶ 缘故 reason; cause: ～由 reason|无～无故 without rhyme or reason; for no reason at all ❷ 因为；为了 because; for: ～何到此？Why did you come here? ❸ 缘分 predestined relationship or affinity: 人～ one's relations with others|姻～ marriage|有～ predestined to have an affinity|不解之～ indissoluble bond ❹ 沿着；顺着 along: ～溪而行 walk along the brook ❺ 边 edge; rim; brink; fringe: 边～ rim; edge

【缘簿】yuánbù 僧道向人化缘的册子 records of contributions kept at Buddhist or Taoist temples

【缘分】yuánfèn 迷信的人认为人与人之间由命中注定的遇合的机会；泛指人与人或人与事物之间发生联系的可能性（superstition）predestined affinity or relationship; (in a broad sense) lot or luck by which people are brought together; possibility of affinity between people or between people and things: 咱们俩又在一起了，真是有～。It must be fate that brought us together again.|烟、酒跟我没有～。Smoking and drinking don't appeal to me.

【缘故】yuángù 原因 reason; cause: 他到这时候还没来，不知什么～。I wonder why he hasn't come yet. also 原故 yuángù

【缘何】yuánhé〈书 *fml.*〉为什么；因何 why; for what reason: ～避而不见？What's the reason for avoiding me?

【缘木求鱼】yuán mù qiú yú《孟子·梁惠王上》：'以若所为，求若所欲，犹缘木而求鱼也。'用那样的办法来追求那样的目的，就像爬到树上去找鱼一样。*Mencius·King Hui of Liang* (I): 'To obtain your goal in such a way is like climbing a tree to catch a fish.'〈比喻 *fig.*〉方向、方法不对，一定达不到目的 wrong approach will defeat the purpose

【缘起】yuánqǐ ❶ 事情的起因 cause; origin ❷ 说明发起某件事情的缘故的文字 account of the reasons for sponsoring sth.: 成立学会的～ reasons for establishing an association

【缘石】yuánshí 砌在车行道与人行道交界线上的长条形砖或混凝土块，通常略高出车行道的路面 guiding curb (kerb); rim built of joined bricks or concrete, forming an edge for a sidewalk and separating it from the vehicle lane; also 牙石 yáshí

【缘由】yuányóu 原因 cause; reason: 他这样做不是没有～的。There must be reasons for him acting this way. also 原由 yuányóu

塬 yuán 我国西北黄土高原地区因流水冲刷而形成的一种地貌，呈台状，四周陡峭，顶上平坦 tableland; terrace; physiognomy formed by water erosion on the Loess Plateau in China's northwest, which is shaped like a platform, with a level top and steep walls

猿（猨）yuán 哺乳动物，跟猴相似，比猴大，种类很多，没有颊囊和尾巴，有的形状跟人类很相似。生活在森林中。如猩猩和长臂猿。ape (*Pongidae*); mammal resembling a monkey but larger, without a tail or cheek pouches, with a variety of kinds, some looking very similar to human beings, and living in forests, e.g. orangutan and gibbon

【猿猴】yuánhóu 猿和猴 ape and monkey

【猿人】yuánrén 最原始的人类。猿人还保留猿类的某些特征，但已能直立行走，并产生了简单的语言，能制造简单的生产工具，知道用火熟食等。apeman (*Pithecanthropus*); primitive human being, still retaining certain characteristics of the ape, but already able to walk with a straight body, use simple language, make simple tools, use fire to cook food, etc.

源 yuán ❶ 水流起头的地方 source of a river; fountainhead: 河～ source of a river | 泉～ fountainhead | 发～ originate from | ～远流长 long river with a distant source | 饮水思～。When you drink from the stream, remember the source. ❷ 来源 source; cause; root: 货～ source of supplies | 资～ resources | 病～ cause of a disease ❸ (Yuán) 姓 a surname

【源流】yuánliú 水源和水流 source and course of a river; 〈比喻 *fig.*〉事物的起源和发展 origin and development: 七言诗的～ origins of the seven-characters-per-line poem

【源泉】yuánquán 泉源 source; fountainhead; well-spring: 知识是力量的～。Knowledge is the fountainhead of strength. | 生活是创作的～。Life is the sourcc of creativity.

【源头】yuántóu 水发源的地方 fountainhead; source: 黄河～ source of the Yellow River ◇ 民歌是文学的一个～。Folk songs are one of the sources of literature.

【源源】yuányuán 继续不断的样子 in a steady stream; continuously: ～不绝 in an endless flow; incessantly | ～不竭 in an endless stream | ～而来 come in a steady or endless flow; keep pouring in

【源源本本】yuányuánběnběn same as 原原本本 yuányuánběnběn

【源远流长】yuán yuǎn liú cháng ❶ 源头很远，流程很长 distant source and long river: 长江是一条～的大河。The Yangtze River is a long river with a distant source. ❷〈比喻 *fig.*〉历史悠久 time-honoured; of long standing

嫄 yuán 用于人名，姜嫄，传说是周朝祖先后稷的母亲 used in people's names, e.g. Jiang Yuan, mother of Hou Ji, ancestor of the Zhou Dynasty, according to legend

辕 yuán ❶ 车前驾牲畜的两根直木 two shafts of a cart or carriage: 一匹马驾～，一匹马拉套。One horse is harnessed between the shafts, and another pulls in front. ❷ 指辕门。借指衙署。outer gate of a government office in ancient times; government office: 行～ field headquarters

【辕骡】yuánluó 驾辕的骡子 mule between the shafts; shaft-mule

【辕马】yuánmǎ 驾辕的马 horse between the shafts; shaft-horse

【辕门】yuánmén〈古时 *arch.*〉军营的门或官署的外门 outer gate of a government office or barracks

【辕子】yuán·zi same as 辕 yuán ①: 车～ shafts of a cart

橼 yuán ☞ 香橼 xiāngyuán on p. 2091

螈 yuán ☞ [蝾螈] (róngyuán) on p. 1631

圜 yuán same as 圆 yuán
☞ huán on p. 845

羱 yuán 羱羊 ibex

【羱羊】yuányáng ☞ 北山羊 běishānyáng on p. 80

yuǎn (ㄩㄢˇ)

远（遠）yuǎn ❶ 空间或时间的距离长（跟'近'相对 as opposed to 'near'）far away in time or space; distant; remote: ～处 in the distance | 路～ long journey | 广州离北京很～。Guangzhou is far away from Beijing. | ～古 remote antiquity | ～景 distant view | 久～ ages ago; far back | 为时不～ not far from | 眼光要看得～。One should be far-sighted. ❷ (血统关系) 疏远 (of blood relationship) distant: ～亲 distantly related; distant relative | ～房 distantly related ❸ (差别) 程度大 (of difference) (by) far: 差得～ far inferior to | ～～超过 far exceed ❹ 不接近 keep away from: 敬而～之 keep a respectful distance from sb. ❺ (Yuǎn) 姓 a surname

【远程】yuǎnchéng 路程远的 long-range; long-distance: ～运输 long-distance transportation | ～航行 long voyage

【远大】yuǎndà 长远而广阔，不限于目前 long-range; broad; ambitious: 前途～ have a bright future | 眼光～ be far-sighted; have a broad vision|～的理想 lofty ideal

【远道】yuǎndào 遥远的道路 long way; long journey: ～而来 come a long way; come from afar

【远地点】yuǎndìdiǎn 月球或人造地球卫星绕地球运行的轨道上离地球最远的点 apogee; farthest point from the earth in the orbit of the moon or a man-made satellite that circles around the earth

【远东】Yuǎndōng 欧洲人指亚洲东部地区 Far East Asia from the perspective of Europe

【远方】yuǎnfāng 距离较远的地方 distant place: ～的来客 guest from afar

【远房】yuǎnfáng 血统疏远的(宗族成员) distantly related (kinsman); remote (kinsfolk): ～叔父 distant uncle|～兄弟 distant cousin

【远古】yuǎngǔ 遥远的古代 remote antiquity; time immemorial: '女娲补天'是从～流传下来的神话。'Nüwa patching up the sky' is a legend passed down from time immemorial.

【远海】yuǎnhǎi 距离陆地较远的海域 distant seas; high or open seas: ～航行 take a long-distance sea voyage

【远航】yuǎnháng 远程航行 take a long voyage: 扬帆～ sail to a distant place

【远见】yuǎnjiàn 远大的眼光 foresight; far-sightedness; vision: ～卓识 foresight and sagacity; breadth of vision

【远交近攻】yuǎn jiāo jìn gōng 联络距离远的国家,进攻邻近的国家。本来是战国时秦国采用的一种外交策略,秦国用它达到了统一六国、建立统一王朝的目的。befriend distant states while attacking those nearby; strategy for dealing with foreign countries, used by the state of Qin during the Warring States Period to achieve the goal of vanquishing the six rival states and establishing a unified dynasty; 后来也指待人、处世的一种手段 means to deal with people and conduct oneself in life

【远郊】yuǎnjiāo 离城区较远的郊区 outer suburbs; outskirts; exurbs

【远近】yuǎnjìn ❶ 多远多近;远近的程度 far and near; distance: 这两条路的～差不多。The distance is about the same by either road.|这里离市中心有十公里～。This place is 10 km. from downtown. ❷ 远处和近处 far and wide; far and near; everywhere: ～闻名 be known far and wide

【远景】yuǎnjǐng ❶ 远距离的景物 distant view; long-range perspective; prospect: 眺望～ look at the distant landscape|用色彩的浓淡来表示画面前景和～的分别。Different shades of colour are adopted to depict the difference between the foreground and the distant view. ❷ 将来的景象 future; prospects: ～规划 long-range plan

【远客】yuǎnkè 远方来的客人 guest from afar

【远虑】yuǎnlǜ 长远考虑 from the long run; from a long-term point of view: 深谋～ think profoundly and plan carefully; be circumspect and far-sighted|人无～,必有近忧。One who lacks foresight will face danger close at hand. *or* Those who fail to plan for the future will find trouble at their doorstep.

【远略】yuǎnlüè 深远的谋略 long-term strategy: 有～ be far-sighted; have a long-term strategy

【远门】yuǎnmén ❶ 离家到很远的地方去叫出远门 travel far away from home; go on a long journey ❷ 远房 distantly related: ～兄弟 distant cousin

【远谋】yuǎnmóu 深远的谋划;长远的打算 long-term plan: ～深算 map out a well-conceived long-term plan

【远亲】yuǎnqīn 血统关系或婚姻关系疏远的亲戚,也指居住相隔很远的亲戚 distant relative; remote kinsman; distant relation by blood or marriage; relative that lives far away: ～不如近邻。A distant relative is of less help than a neighbour close by. *or* Close neighbours mean more than distant relatives.

【远日点】yuǎnrìdiǎn 行星或彗星绕太阳公转的轨道上离太阳最远的点 aphelion; farthest point from the sun in the orbit of a planet or a comet that revolves around the sun

【远视】yuǎnshì ❶ 视力缺陷的一种,能看清远处的东西,看不清近处的东西。远视是由于眼球的晶状体和视网膜间的距离过短或晶状体折光力过弱,使进入眼球中的影像不能正落在视网膜上而落在网膜的后面。long sight; hyperopia; hypermetropia; abnormal condition of the eye in which vision is better for distant objects than near objects, resulting from the distance between the lens of the eyeball to the retina being too short or weak refraction of the lens, causing images to be focused behind the retina ❷ 眼光远大 be far-sighted: 她在生活中保持了平和～的乐观态度。She has kept a peaceful, far-sighted and optimistic attitude in life.

【远水解不了近渴】yuǎnshuǐjiěbùliǎojìnkě 〈比喻 *fig.*〉缓慢的解决办法不能满足急迫的需要 distant waters can't quench present thirst; aid is too slow in coming to be of any help; a distant well is no help to a thirsty person; also 远水不解近渴 yuǎn shuǐ bù jiě jìn kě

【远水救不了近火】yuǎnshuǐjiùbùliǎojìnhuǒ 〈比喻 *fig.*〉缓慢的解决办法不能满足急迫的需要 distant waters won't put out a fire close at hand; a slow remedy cannot meet an urgent need; while the grass grows, the horse starves; also 远水不救近火 yuǎn shuǐ bù jiù jìn huǒ

【远扬】yuǎnyáng (名声等)传播很远 (of fame, reputation, etc.) spread far and wide: 臭名

～ be notorious｜声威～ be known far and wide; enjoy great prestige far and wide

【远洋】yuǎnyáng 距离大陆远的海洋 ocean; sea waters that are far away from the continent: ～轮船 ocean-going ship｜～捕鱼 deep-sea or pelagic fishing｜～航行 oceangoing voyage

【远因】yuǎnyīn 不是直接造成结果的原因(区别于'近因' as compared with 'direct cause') remote cause; indirect cause

【远征】yuǎnzhēng 远道出征或长途行军 expedition; long-distance march: ～军 expeditionary army or force｜出师～ go on an expedition

【远志】[1] yuǎnzhì 远大的志向 lofty ideal; noble aspiration; great ambition: 胸怀～ cherish high aspirations

【远志】[2] yuǎnzhì 多年生草本植物,茎细,叶子互生,条形,总状花序,花绿白色,蒴果卵圆形。根可入药。narrow-leaved polygala (*Polygala tenuifolia*); perennial herb having thin stems, alternate strip leaves, raceme of greenish white flowers, egg-shaped capsules, and roots of medicinal value

【远走高飞】yuǎn zǒu gāo fēi 远远地离开,到别的地方。多指逃往远处。fly far and high; be off to a distant place; flee to a faraway place

【远足】yuǎnzú 比较远的徒步旅行 excursion; outing; hike; pleasure trip on foot

【远祖】yuǎnzǔ 许多代以前的祖先 remote ancestor

yuàn（ㄩㄢˋ）

苑 yuàn ❶〈书 *fml.*〉养禽兽植林木的地方(多指帝王的花园 oft. referring to an imperial garden) enclosed ground for growing trees and keeping animals: 鹿～ deer park｜御～ imperial garden ❷〈书 *fml.*〉(学术、文艺)荟萃之处 (learning, art) centre: 文～ centre of literature; field of literature｜艺～ arts centre ❸ (Yuàn) 姓 a surname

怨 yuàn ❶ 怨恨 resentment; enmity; hatred; discontent: 抱～ complain｜结～ incur sb.'s hatred or enmity ❷ 责怪 blame; complain: 任劳任～ work hard without any complaint; work hard and be not upset by criticism｜事情没办好只能～我自己。I have only myself to blame for failing to get things done.

【怨不得】yuàn·bu·de 怪不得; 难怪 cannot blame; no wonder

【怨敌】yuàndí 仇敌 foe; enemy

【怨毒】yuàndú〈书 *fml.*〉仇恨 enmity; hatred; animosity

【怨怼】yuànduì〈书 *fml.*〉same as 怨恨 yuànhèn

【怨愤】yuànfèn 怨恨愤怒 discontent and indignation: 满腔～ full of indignation and discontent

【怨府】yuànfǔ〈书 *fml.*〉大家怨恨的对象 target of public indignation

【怨恨】yuànhèn ❶ 对人或事物强烈地不满或仇恨 bear a grudge against sb.; hate; resent; be extremely dissatisfied with sb. or sth.: 我对谁也不～,只恨自己不争气。I won't blame anybody but myself for the failure. ❷ 强烈的不满或仇恨 resentment; grudge; enmity: 一腔～ be full of hatred

【怨偶】yuàn'ǒu〈书 *fml.*〉不和睦的夫妻 estranged husband and wife

【怨气】yuànqì 怨恨的神色或情绪 grievance; complaint; resentment; indignant expression or mood: ～冲天 towering resentment｜一肚子～ be full of grievances or complaints

【怨声载道】yuàn shēng zài dào 怨恨的声音充满道路。形容群众普遍不满。cries of discontent fill the roads; complaints or voices of discontent are heard everywhere

【怨天尤人】yuàn tiān yóu rén 抱怨天,埋怨别人。形容对不如意的事情一味归咎于客观。grumble against heaven and lay the blame upon other people; blame everyone but oneself

【怨望】yuànwàng〈书 *fml.*〉same as 怨恨 yuànhèn

【怨言】yuànyán 抱怨的话 complaint; grumble: 毫无～ without a word of complaint

【怨艾】yuànyì〈书 *fml.*〉怨恨 resentment; grudge; hatred: 深自～ deeply blame oneself for sth.

院 yuàn ❶ (～儿 yuànr) 院子 courtyard; yard; compound: 场～ threshing ground; level open space｜四合～儿 courtyard｜～里种了许多花。There are many flowers in the yard. ❷ 某些机关和公共处所的名称 designation for certain government organizations and public places: 法～ court｜国务～ State Council｜科学～ academy of science｜博物～ museum｜电影～ movie theatre ❸ 指学院 college; university; academy; institute of higher learning: 高等～校 institutes of higher learning ❹ 指医院 hospital: 住～ be hospitalized｜出～ be discharged from hospital ❺ (Yuàn) 姓 a surname

【院本】yuànběn 金、元时代行院(hángyuàn)演唱用的戏曲脚本,明清泛指杂剧、传奇 drama script of the Jin and Yuan dynasties; poetic drama and romance drama in the Ming and Qing dynasties

【院画】yuànhuà 院体画的简称 abbr. for 院体画 yuàntǐhuà

【院落】yuànluò same as 院子 yuàn·zi

【院士】yuànshì 某些国家科学院、工程院部分高级研究人员的称号 academician; title for certain senior researchers in the national academy of sciences and engineering in some countries

【院体画】yuàntǐhuà 指我国封建时代宫廷画家作品,题材多以花鸟、山水或宗教内容为主 imperial-court paintings, often with themes of flowers, birds, landscapes and religion; 简称 abbr. 院画 yuànhuà

【院子】yuàn·zi 房屋前后用墙或栅栏围起来的空地 courtyard; yard; compound; fenced open ground in front of or behind a house or building

垸 yuàn〈方 *dial.*〉same as 垸子 yuàn·zi: 堤～ dyke; embankment; dam|～田(在湖边淤积的地方作成的圩田) lakeside farm fields with protective embankments

【垸子】yuàn·zi 湖南、湖北等地,在沿江、湖地带围绕房屋、田地等修建的像堤坝的防水建筑物 levee; dyke; dam; protective embankment built around houses, fields, etc., by the riverside and lakeside in places like Hunan and Hubei provinces

衙 yuàn ☞[衙衙](hángyuàn) on p. 771

掾 yuàn〈书 *fml.*〉属员 minor official; subordinate

媛 yuàn〈书 *fml.*〉美女 beautiful woman ☞ yuán on p. 2364

瑗 yuàn〈书 *fml.*〉大孔的璧 round, flat jade with a big hole in the centre

愿[1] yuàn〈书 *fml.*〉老实谨慎 honest and cautious: 谨～ prudent and faithful; honest|诚～ honest and sincere

愿[2](願) yuàn ❶ 愿望 hope; wish; desire: 心～ cherished desire; wish|志～ aspiration|如～ as one wishes; one's dream comes true|平生之～ lifelong wish ❷ 愿意 be willing; be ready: 情～ be willing to do sth.|自觉自～ of one's own will|我～参加篮球比赛。I'm willing to take part in the basketball match. ❸ 愿心 vow; declare solemnly: 许～ make a vow|还～ fulfil one's promise; fulfil a vow to a deity

【愿望】yuànwàng 希望将来能达到某种目的的想法 desire; wish; aspiration; idea to achieve a certain goal in the future: 主观～ wishful thinking; subjective desire|他终于实现了上大学的～。His wish to go to university has finally come true.

【愿心】yuànxīn ❶ 迷信的人对神佛有所祈求时许下的酬谢 vow made to a deity or Buddha when a superstitious person prays for blessings ❷ 泛指愿望、志向 (in a broad snese) desire; hope; wish: 他从小就有做一番事业的～。He has hoped to amount to something since his childhood.

【愿意】yuàn·yì ❶ 认为符合自己心愿而同意(做某事) be willing; be ready; agree to do sth. one sees as in line with one's wish or desire: 送你去学习,你～不～? If we send you to study at school, would you agree or not? ❷ 希望(发生某种情况) hope; wish; like; want (sth. to happen): 他们～你留在这里。They hope that you will stay here.

yuē (ㄩㄝ)

曰 yuē〈书 *fml.*〉❶ 说 say: 其谁～不然。Who could be against it? ❷ 叫做 call; name: 名之～农民学校(给它个名字,叫做农民学校) name it Farmers' School

约 yuē ❶ 提出或商量(须要共同遵守的事) make an appointment; arrange: 预～ make an appointment in advance; book; reserve|～定 agree on; arrange|～期 agree on a date or time; fix or set a date ❷ 邀请 invite in advance; engage: 特～ be specially invited|～请 invite; ask|～他来 invite him to come here ❸ 约定的事;共同订立、须要共同遵守的条文 agreement; pact; treaty; regulations that both sides agree on and should abide by: 践～ keep an appointment; keep one's word|条～ treaty|和～ peace treaty|有～在先 have a prior agreement ❹ 限制使不越出范围;拘束 restrict; restrain; confine: ～束 restrain; keep within bounds|制～ restrict; check ❺ 俭省 economical and frugal; thrifty: 节～ economical; thrifty|俭～ thrifty and frugal ❻ 简单;简要 simple; concise; brief; succinct: 由博返～ arrive at simplicity through complexity ❼ 大概 about; around; approximate: 大～ about|～计 amount approximate to|～数 approximate number|年～十七八 about 17 or 18 years old|～有五十人。There are about 50 people. ❽ 约分 reduction of a fraction: $\frac{5}{10}$可以～成$\frac{1}{2}$。Five tenths can be reduced to one half.

☞ yāo on p. 2226

【约定】yuēdìng 经过商量而确定 agree after discussion; appoint; arrange: 大家～明天在公园会面。We arranged to meet in the park tomorrow.

【约定俗成】yuē dìng sú chéng 指某种事物的名称或社会习惯是由人们经过长期实践而认定或形成的 (of a certain name or social habit) established or sanctioned by popular usage; accepted through common practice

【约法】yuēfǎ 暂行的具有宪法性质的文件。如我国辛亥革命后制定的《中华民国临时约法》。provisional constitution; document that serves as temporary constitution, e. g. *Provisional Constitution of the Republic of China* promulgated after the Revolution of 1911

【约法三章】yuē fǎ sān zhāng《史记·高祖本纪》:'与父老约,法三章耳:杀人者死,伤人及盗抵罪。'指订立法律,与人民相约遵守。后来泛指订立简单的条款。agree on a three-point rule; originally from *Records of the Historian · Official Records of Emperor Gaozu*: 'Make three rules with the populace: anyone who kills shall be sentenced to death; anyone who hurts others or steals shall be punished accordingly.' It refers to lay down a few simple rules to be observed by all concerned.

【约分】yuē//fēn 用分子和分母的公约数同时除分子和分母，使分子、分母都比原来较小而分数值不变。如$\frac{16}{64}$约分成$\frac{1}{4}$。reduction of a fraction; where the numerator and denominator of a fraction are divided by a common divisor so that the numerator and denominator become smaller but the fraction's value remains unchanged, e. g. 16 over 64 can be reduced to one fourth

【约会】yuē·huì ❶ 预先约定相会 arrange a meeting; make an appointment: 大伙儿～好在这儿碰头。We've arranged to meet here.|他们～过我，我没去。They invited me, but I didn't go. ❷ (～儿 yuē·huìr)预先约定的会晤 appointment; date; engagement: 订个～儿 make an appointment|我今天晚上有个～儿。I've got an engagement tonight.

【约集】yuējí 请人到一起；邀集 invite to meet; call together; gather: ～有关人员开个会 gather the people involved for a meeting

【约计】yuējì 约略计算 count roughly; come roughly to: ～有百十来人。There are about 100 people.

【约见】yuējiàn 约定时间会见(多用于外交场合 oft. used for diplomatic occasions) make an appointment to meet: ～该国驻华大使。Make an appointment to meet the country's ambassador to China. *or* Summon the country's ambassador to China.

【约据】yuējù 合同、契约等的统称 general term for contract and deed

【约略】yuēlüè ❶ 大致；大概 rough; approximate: 这件事的经过我也～知道一些。I've got a rough idea about what happened. ❷ 依稀；仿佛 vaguely; dimly; seemingly; as if; as though: ～听得见窗外的雨点声。(I) vaguely heard the rain pattering outside my window.

【约莫】yuē·mo 大概估计 about; roughly; approximately: 我们等了～有一个小时的光景。We've waited for one hour or so. also 约摸 yuē·mo

【约摸】yuē·mo same as 约莫 yuē·mo

【约期】yuēqī ❶ 约定日期 fix or set a date; appoint a time; set a time: ～会谈 set a date for talks ❷ 约定的日子 fixed date; set time: 误了～。(We) missed the fixed date. ❸ 契约的期限 term or duration of an agreement: ～未满。The contract has not yet expired.

【约请】yuēqǐng 邀请 invite; ask: ～几位老同学到家里聚一聚 invite several old classmates home for a party

【约束】yuēshù 限制使不越出范围 keep within bounds; restrain; restrict; bind: 受纪律的～ be restricted by discipline|这种口头协议～不了他们。This kind of oral agreement won't be enough to restrain them.

【约数】yuēshù ❶ (～儿 yuēshùr)大约的数目 approximate number ❷ 一个数能够整除另一数，这个数就是另一数的约数。如 2，3，4，6 都能整除 12，因此 2，3，4，6 都是 12 的约数。divisor; number divided exactly by another, with the latter being the divisor, e. g. 12 can be divided exactly by 2, 3, 4 and 6, so 2, 3, 4 and 6 are divisors of 12; also 因数 yīnshù

【约同】yuētóng 邀请一起去 ask sb. to go together: ～前往 let's go together

【约言】yuēyán 约定的话 promise; vow; pledge: 履行～ fulfil one's promise; redeem one's promise|遵守～ keep one's promise or word|违背～ break one's promise; go back on one's word

彟 yuē 〈书 *fml.*〉尺度 yardstick; measure; scale; measurement

蒦(彠) yuē 〈书 *fml.*〉❶ 尺度 yardstick; measure; scale; measurement ❷ 用秤称 measure; weigh (今口语说 yāo，写作'约' pronounced yāo in present oral Chinese and written as 约 yuē)

yuě (ㄩㄝˇ)

哕(噦) yuě ❶ 〈拟声词 *onom.*〉呕吐时嘴里发出的声音 sound of vomiting: ～的一声，吐了。With a belch, (he) vomited. ❷ 呕吐 vomit; throw up; disgorge: 干～ retch|刚吃完药，都～出来了。All the medicine that had just been taken was thrown up.
☞ huì on p. 868

yuè (ㄩㄝˋ)

月 yuè ❶ 月球；月亮 moon: ～食 lunar eclipse|～光 moonlight|赏～ enjoy the beauty of the moon ❷ 计时的单位，公历 1 年分为 12 个月 month; one year being divided into 12 months ❸ 每月的 monthly: ～刊 monthly|～产量 monthly output ❹ 形状像月亮的；圆的 full-moon-shaped; round: ～琴 *yueqin* (four-stringed moon-shaped Chinese mandolin)|～饼 moon cake

【月白】yuèbái 淡蓝色 bluish white; pale blue: ～竹布褂 shirt made of pale blue fine cloth

【月半】yuèbàn 一个月的第十五天 15th day of a month

【月报】yuèbào ❶ 每月出版一次的报刊(多用做刊物名 oft. used in the name of a periodical) monthly magazine; monthly; magazine that is published once a month:《新华～》*Xinhua*

Monthly ❷ 按月的汇报 monthly report：～表 monthly statistical report

【月饼】yuè·bing 圆形有馅的点心，中秋节应时的食品 moon cake；stuffed round cake especially made for the Mid-Autumn Festival

【月城】yuèchéng〈书 *fml*.〉瓮城 barbican entrance to a city；crescent moon-shaped enclosure for defence purposes outside a city gate

【月初】yuèchū 一个月的开头几天 beginning of a month

【月底】yuèdǐ 一个月的最后几天 end of a month

【月洞门】yuèdòngmén 月亮门儿 moon gate；lunar gate

【月度】yuèdù 作为计算单位的一个月 monthly：～计划 monthly plan｜最高～运输量 highest monthly freight volume

【月份】yuèfèn（～儿 yuèfènr）指某一个月 month：七～的产量比六～提高百分之十五。The output in July increased by 15 per cent over that of June.

【月份牌】yuèfènpái（～儿 yuèfènpáir）旧式的彩画单张年历，现在也指日历 single-sheet colour-printed calendar；calendar

【月工】yuègōng 论月雇用的工人 worker employed by the month；monthly worker

【月宫】yuègōng 传说中月亮里的宫殿，也作为月亮的代称 legendary palace on the moon；moon

【月光】yuèguāng 月亮的光线，是由太阳光照到月亮上反射出来的 moonlight；moonbeam；moonshine produced by the moon reflecting the light of the sun

【月桂树】yuèguìshù 常绿乔木，叶互生，披针形或长椭圆形，花带黄色，伞形花序，浆果卵形，暗紫色。供观赏，叶子可做香料。laurel（*Laurus nobilis*）；bay tree；bay；decorative evergreen arbour，having lanceolate or oval alternate leaves，yellowish flowers，in umbel inflorescence，and oval dark purple berries，its leaves used as a spice

【月黑天】yuèhēitiān 指没有月光的漆黑的夜晚 moonless night；pitch-dark night；also 月黑夜 yuèhēiyè

【月华】yuèhuá ❶〈书 *fml*.〉月光 moonlight；moonshine；moonbeam：～如水 watery moonbeam；flood of translucent moonlight ❷ 月光通过云中的小水滴或冰粒时发生衍射，在月亮周围形成的彩色光环，内紫外红 lunar corona；colourful halo around the moon，having a purple interior and red exterior，and formed by moonlight diffracting through water droplets or ice crystals in the clouds

【月季】yuèjì ❶ 常绿或半常绿小灌木，茎有刺，羽状复叶，小叶阔卵形，花红色、粉红或近白色，夏季开花。供观赏。园艺上变种很多。Chinese rose（*Rosa chinensis*）；decorative evergreen or semi-evergreen underbrush，having thorns on its stems，pinnated leaves，with the leaflets in a broad oval shape，red，pink or nearly white flowers that blossom in summer，and a variety of breeds in horticulture ❷ 这种植物的花 Chinese rose；flowers of this plant

【月经】yuèjīng ❶ 生殖细胞发育成熟的女子每二十八天左右有一次周期性的子宫出血，出血时间持续三到七天，这种生理现象叫做月经 menses；menstruation；period；catamenia；menstrual flow；monthly flow of blood from the uterus in women who ovulate，usu. lasting three to seven days and in a cycle of 28 days ❷ 月经期间流出的血 menses；menstruation；menstrual blood

【月刊】yuèkān 每月出版一次的刊物 monthly；monthly magazine

【月老】yuèlǎo 月下老人 matchmaker；go-between；god who unites man and woman in marriage

【月历】yuèlì 一月一页的历书 monthly calendar

【月利】yuèlì 按月计算的利息 monthly interest

【月例】yuèlì ❶ 月钱 monthly payment；monthly allowance：～银子 monthly allowance in silver ❷〈婉辞 *euph*.〉指月经（for menstruation）period；monthlies；that time of the month

【月亮】yuè·liang 月球的通称 general term for 月球 yuèqiú；（图见 ☞ figure for 太阳系 tàiyángxì on p.1855）

【月亮门儿】yuè·liangménr 院子里的墙上的圆形的门 moon gate；lunar gate；round gate in a courtyard

【月令】yuèlìng 农历某个月的气候和物候 weather and phenology in a certain lunar month

【月轮】yuèlún 指圆月 full moon

【月杪】yuèmiǎo〈书 *fml*.〉月底 end of a month

【月末】yuèmò same as 月底 yuèdǐ

【月票】yuèpiào 按月购买的乘公共汽车、电车或游览公园等使用的票 monthly ticket；monthly pass；ticket bought by the month for buses，streetcars，park entrance，etc.

【月钱】yuè·qian 按月付给家庭成员、学徒等的零用钱 monthly allowance；monthly pocket money given to family members，apprentices，etc.

【月琴】yuèqín 弦乐器，用木头制成，琴身为扁圆形或八角形，有四根弦或三根弦 *yueqin*；four- or three-stringed wooden musical instrument with a flat-round or octagonal soundbox

【月球】yuèqiú 地球的卫星，表面凹凸不平，本身不发光，只能反射太阳光，直径约为地球直径的1/4，引力相当于地球的1/6 moon；satellite of the earth，not shining itself but reflecting the sun's light，having a rugged surface，one fourth of the earth's diameter，and one sixth of the earth's gravitation；通称 generally known as 月亮 yuè·liang

【月色】yuèsè 月光 moonlight; moonshine; moonbeam: 荷塘～ the moon over a lotus pond|～溶溶 flood of translucent moonlight

【月石】yuèshí 中药上指硼砂 (Chin. med.) borax

【月食】yuèshí 地球运行到月亮和太阳的中间时，太阳的光正好被地球挡住，不能射到月亮上去，月亮上就出现黑影，这种现象叫月食。太阳光全部被地球挡住时，叫月全食；部分被挡住时，叫月偏食。月食一定发生在农历十五日或十五日以后一两天。lunar eclipse. When the earth moves to a position between the moon and the sun, the sun's light is blocked by the earth and cannot reach the moon, so that a shadow appears on the moon, this phenomenon being called a lunar eclipse. When the sun's light is completely blocked by the earth, it is called a total lunar eclipse, and when a part is blocked, it is called a partial lunar eclipse. Lunar eclipses take place on the 15th, 16th or 17th days of a lunar month.

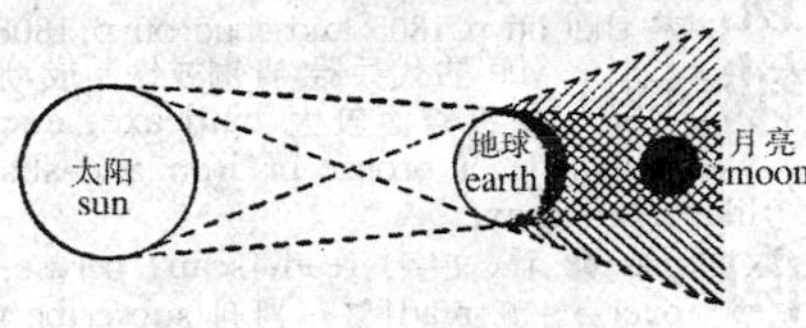

月食 Lunar Eclipse

【月台】yuètái ❶〈旧时 *old*〉为赏月而筑的台 terrace built for admiring the moon ❷ 正殿前方突出的台，三面有台阶 terrace in front of a main hall, with stairs on its three sides ❸ 站台 railway platform

【月台票】yuètáipiào 站台票 platform ticket

【月头儿】yuètóur ❶ 满一个月的时候（多用于财物按月的支付 oft. used as time for monthly payment) full month: 到～了，该交水电费了。It's time to pay the month's water and electricity bills. ❷ 月初 beginning of a month

【月尾】yuèwěi 一个月的最后几天；月末 end of a month; last few days of a month

【月息】yuèxī same as 月利 yuèlì

【月下老人】yuèxià lǎorén 传说唐朝韦固月夜里经过宋城，遇见一个老人坐着翻检书本。韦固往前窥视，一个字也不认得，向老人询问后，才知道老人是专管人间婚姻的神仙，翻检的书是婚姻簿子（见于《续幽怪录·定婚店》）。后来因此称媒人为月下老人 God of Marriage. According to a story in *Sequence to Mysterious Tales · The Broker of Betrothals* of the Tang Dynasty, Wei Gu passed by the city of Songcheng on a moonlit night and ran across an old man who sat looking through some books, and Wei Gu went up to have a look but could not read a character. After enquiring from the old man, he learned that the old man was the god in charge of marriage in the earthly world and the books he was looking through were marriage documents. Thus the name for a matchmaker or go-between. also 月下老儿 yuèxià lǎor or 月老 yuèlǎo

【月相】yuèxiàng 指人们所看到的月亮表面发亮部分的形状。主要有朔、上弦、望、下弦四种。phases of the moon; shapes of the shining part of the moon that people see in its different phases, mainly including the crescent moon, the first quarter, the full moon, and the last quarter

【月薪】yuèxīn 按月发给的工资 salary; monthly payment

【月牙】yuèyá（～儿 yuèyár）新月① crescent; also 月芽 yuèyá

【月夜】yuèyè 有月光的夜晚 moonlit night

【月晕】yuèyùn 月光通过云层中的冰晶时，经折射而成的光的现象。成彩色光环，内红外紫。月晕常被认为是天气变化的预兆。lunar halo; halo; circular band of coloured light around the moon, caused by the refraction of moonlight through ice particles suspended in the intervening atmosphere and often regarded as an omen of weather change; also 风圈 fēngquān

【月氏】Yuèzhī 汉朝西域国名 Scyths; name of a state in the Western Regions during the Han Dynasty

【月中】yuèzhōng 一个月的中间几天 middle of a month

【月终】yuèzhōng same as 月底 yuèdǐ

【月子】yuè·zi ❶ 妇女生育后的第一个月 first month of confinement after giving birth to a child: 坐～ be in confinement|她还没出～。She's still in confinement. ❷ 分娩的时期 time of childbirth; confinement: 她的～是二月初。She's expecting her baby at the beginning of February.

·【月子病】yuè·zibìng 产褥热的通称 general term for puerperal fever

乐(樂) yuè ❶ 音乐 music: 奏～ play music|～器 musical instrument ❷ (Yuè)姓 a surname (与 Lè 不同姓 different from the surname Lè, also written as 乐)

☞ lè on p. 1164

【乐池】yuèchí 舞台前面乐队伴奏的地方，有矮墙跟观众席隔开 orchestra pit; orchestra; area in front of the stage where an orchestra play music, separated from the audience by a sunken boundary

【乐队】yuèduì 演奏不同乐器的许多人组成的集体 orchestra; band; group formed of people who play different musical instruments

【乐府】yuèfǔ 原是汉代朝廷的音乐官署，它的主要任务是采集各地民间诗歌和乐曲。后世把这类民歌或文人模拟的作品也叫做乐府。Music

Bureau of the Han Dynasty, responsible for collecting folk songs and ballads; folk songs, ballads or their imitations by literati in the Han style

【乐歌】yuègē ❶ 音乐与歌曲 music and songs ❷ 有音乐伴奏的歌曲 song with musical accompaniment

【乐户】yuèhù 〈古代 *arch.*〉妇女因犯罪或受牵累而被逮入官府充当奏乐的官妓,叫做乐户,后来也用来称妓院 singsong girl; female criminal or suspect who was forced to serve as a musician in a yamen; brothel

【乐理】yuèlǐ 音乐的一般基础理论 music theory

【乐律】yuèlǜ ☞ 音律 yīnlǜ on p. 2286

【乐谱】yuèpǔ 歌谱或器乐演奏用的谱子,有简谱、五线谱等 music score; sheet music; music, including numbered musical notation, staff, etc.

【乐器】yuèqì 可以发出乐音,供演奏音乐使用的器具,如钢琴、胡琴、笛子、板鼓等 musical instrument; instrument that people play to produce music, e.g. piano, *huqin* (two-stringed traditional Chinese instrument), flute, small drum for marking time, etc.

【乐清】Yuèqīng 地名,在浙江 Yueqing, name of a place in Zhejiang Province

【乐曲】yuèqǔ 音乐作品 musical composition; music

【乐师】yuèshī 指从事音乐演奏的人 musician; musical player

【乐坛】yuètán 音乐界 music circles: 誉满～ enjoy a widespread reputation in the music world

【乐团】yuètuán 演出音乐的团体 philharmonic society: 广播～ broadcast symphony orchestra | 交响～ philharmonic orchestra

【乐舞】yuèwǔ 有音乐伴奏的舞蹈 dance with musical accompaniment

【乐音】yuèyīn 有一定频率,听起来比较和谐悦耳的声音,是由发音体有规律的振动而产生的(区别于'噪音'as compared with 'noise') musical sound; tone; rhythmical, harmonious, pleasant sound produced by the regular vibration of sth.

【乐章】yuèzhāng 成套的乐曲中具有一定主题的独立组成部分,一部交响曲一般分为四个乐章 movement; independent part in a piece of music, with a theme, e.g. a symphony is usually divided into four movements

刖(跀) yuè 〈古代 *arch.*〉砍掉脚的酷刑 cruel punishment of chopping off a person's feet

軏 yuè 〈古代 *arch.*〉车辕与横木相连接的关键 joint of the crossbar of a carriage with either one of the shafts

抈 yuè 〈书 *fml.*〉❶ 动摇 shake ❷ 折断 break

玥 yuè 〈古代 *arch.*〉传说中的一种神珠 legendary magic pearl

岳(❶嶽) yuè ❶ 高大的山 high mountain; towering mountain: 五～ Five Holy Mountains in China ❷ 称妻的父母及伯父、叔父 wife's parents and uncles: ～父 father-in-law | ～母 mother-in-law | 叔～ uncle; wife's uncle ❸ (Yuè)姓 a surname

【岳父】yuèfù 妻子的父亲 wife's father; father-in-law; also 岳丈 yuèzhàng

【岳家】yuèjiā 妻子的娘家 wife's parents' home

【岳母】yuèmǔ 妻子的母亲 wife's mother; mother-in-law

【岳丈】yuèzhàng same as 岳父 yuèfù

栎(櫟) yuè 栎阳(Yuèyáng),地名,在今陕西临潼 Yueyang, name of a place in present-day Lintong, Shaanxi Province
☞ lì on p. 1192

钥(鑰) yuè 钥匙 key: 北门锁～(北方重镇) northern town of strategic importance
☞ yào on p. 2234

说 yuè same as 悦 yuè
☞ shuì on p. 1805 and shuō on p. 1808

钺(戉) yuè 古代兵器,青铜或铁制成,形状像板斧而较大 battleaxe; ancient weapon made of bronze or iron and shaped like a broad axe

阅 yuè ❶ 看(文字) read; scan; peruse; go over: ～览 read | 订～期刊 subscribe to a journal | 翻～文件 read documents ❷ 检阅 review; inspect: ～兵 review or inspect troops ❸ 经历;经过 undergo; pass through: ～历 experience | 试行已～三月。It has been three months since the trial operation began.

【阅兵】yuè//bīng 检阅军队 review or inspect troops: ～式 military parade

【阅读】yuèdú 看(书报)并领会其内容 read (books and newspapers) and comprehend: 他认识了两千多字,已能～通俗书报。He has learned more than 2,000 characters and can read popular books and newspapers.

【阅卷】yuè//juàn 评阅试卷 go over examination papers and give grades; read and mark examination papers

【阅览】yuèlǎn 看(书报) read (books and newspapers): ～室 reading room

【阅历】yuèlì ❶ 亲身见过、听过或做过;经历 see, hear or do for oneself; experience: ～过很多事 experience many things; pass through many events | 他应该出去～一番。He should go out to get some life experience. ❷ 由经历得来的知识 experience: ～浅 have little experience; inexperienced

【阅世】yuèshì 〈书 *fml.*〉经历世事 see the world: ～渐深 gradually gain deeper experience of life

悦 yuè ❶ 高兴；愉快 joyous；happy；pleased；delighted；merry；gay：喜～ happy；joyous｜不～ unhappy｜和颜～色 be kind and affable；be amiable；have a genial expression ❷ 使愉快 please；delight：～耳 pleasing to the ear｜～目 pleasing to the eye ❸（Yuè）姓 a surname

【悦耳】 yuè'ěr 好听 sweet；pleasing to the ear；sweet-sounding：歌声婉转～。The song sounded sweet and pleasant to the ear.

【悦服】 yuèfú 从心里佩服 admire from the bottom of one's heart：四方～ be deeply admired by people from all directions

【悦目】 yuèmù 看着愉快；好看 pleasing to the eye；good-looking：赏心～ pleasing both to the mind and eye｜天空几抹晚霞，鲜明～。The afterglow of the sky looked splendid and pleasing to the eye.

跃（躍） yuè 跳 leap；jump；bounce；spring：跳～ jump｜飞～ leap｜一～而过 jump over at one go

【跃进】 yuèjìn ❶ 跳着前进 leap forward；make a leap：避开火力，向左侧～。Make a leap to your left to avoid the firepower of the enemy. ❷〈比喻 *fig.*〉极快地前进 leap forward；jump：生产～ big increase in production｜从感性认识～到理性认识 proceed from perceptual knowledge to rational knowledge

【跃迁】 yuèqiān 原子、分子等由某一种状态过渡到另一种状态，如一个能级较高的原子发射一个光了而跃迁到能级较低的原子 transition；process of one atom or molecule transiting from one state to another, e. g. a high-energy atom firing a photon and becoming an atom of lower energy

【跃然】 yuèrán 形容活跃地呈现 appear vividly：义愤之情～。Righteous indignation was clearly apparent in the writing.

【跃跃欲试】 yuèyuè yù shì 形容心里急切地想试试 be eager to have a try；itch for action；be anxious to have a go

越[1] yuè ❶ 跨过（阻碍）；跳过 get over；jump over；stride over；leap over：～墙 jump over the wall｜翻山～岭 climb over hills ❷ 不按照一般的次序；超出（范围） exceed；overstep；go beyond：～级 skip a rank；bypass one's immediate superior｜～权 exceed one's powers；overstep one's authority ❸（声音、情感）昂扬（of voice or emotion）be at a high pitch；vigorous：激～ be excited｜声音清～。The voice is clear and far-reaching. ❹〈书 *fml.*〉抢夺 rob；loot；plunder：杀人～货 kill a person and seize property；rob and kill

越[2] yuè 叠用，表示程度随着条件的发展而发展（跟'愈…愈…'相同）[used reduplicated to express deepening of degree, same as 'the more ... the more']：脑子～用～灵。The more you use your brain, the cleverer you become.｜争论～认真，是非～清楚。The more earnestly people argue, the clearer the truth becomes. 注意 **NOTE**：'越来越…'表示程度随着时间发展，如：天气～来～热了。越来越 yuèláiyuè expresses a deepening of degree over the passage of time, e. g., The weather is becoming hotter and hotter.

越[3] Yuè ❶ 周朝国名，原来在今浙江东部，后来扩展到江苏、山东 state of Yue of the Zhou Dynasty, originally covering the eastern part of present-day Zhejiang Province and later expanding to what is today's Jiangsu and Shandong provinces ❷ 指浙江东部 east Zhejiang ❸（Yuè）姓 a surname

【越冬】 yuèdōng 过冬（多指植物、昆虫、病菌 oft. of plants, insects and germs）live through or survive winter：～作物 winter crop；overwintering crop｜有些昆虫的卵潜伏在土内～。Eggs of some insects survive winter by hiding under the earth.

【越冬作物】 yuèdōng zuòwù 秋季播种，幼苗经过冬季，到第二年春季或夏季收割的农作物，如冬小麦 winter crop；overwintering crop；crop that is sown in autumn and harvested the next spring or summer, e. g. winter wheat；also 过冬作物 guòdōng zuòwù

【越发】 yuèfā ❶ 更加 even more；all the more；still more：过了中秋，天气～凉快了。It has become even cooler after the Mid-Autumn Festival. ❷ 跟上文的'越'或'越是'呼应，作用跟'越…越…'相同（用于两个或更多的分句前后呼应的场合）[used correlatively after 越 yuè or 越是 yuèshì, in two or more clauses] the more ... the more：观众越多，他们演得～卖力气。The larger the audience, the more earnestly they perform.｜越是性急，～容易出差错。The more impatient you are, the more mistakes you'll make.

【越轨】 yuè//guǐ（行为）超出规章制度所允许的范围 exceed the bounds；transgress；go beyond the limits：～的行为 behaviour of aberration；transgression；act of indiscretion

【越过】 yuè//guò 经过中间的界限、障碍物等由一边到另一边 cross；surmount；negotiate；go from one place to another by crossing boundaries and overcoming hindrances：～高山 negotiate high mountains｜～一片草地 traverse a stretch of grasslands

【越级】 yuè//jí 不按照一般的次序，越过直属的一级到更高的一级 bypass the immediate leadership and go directly to higher levels：～上诉 bypass the immediate leadership and present one's appeals and complaints to higher authorities

【越界】 yuèjiè 超越界限或边界 overstep the boundary；cross the border

【越境】yuè//jìng 非法入境或出境（多指国境）cross the border illegally; sneak in or out of a country

【越剧】yuèjù 浙江地方戏曲剧种之一，起源于嵊县，由当地民歌发展而成，主要流行于江浙、上海一带 Shaoxing opera; local opera in Zhejiang Province, that originated in Shengxian and developed from local folk songs, and is popular mainly in Jiangsu and Zhejiang provinces and the city of Shanghai

【越礼】yuèlǐ 不合规定的礼节；不守礼法 improper; indecorous: ～行为 improper behaviour

【越权】yuè//quán（行为）超出权限（of behaviour) exceed or overstep one's power or authority; *ultra vires*

【越位】yuèwèi ❶ 超越自己的职位或地位 exceed or overstep one's position or status: 僭权～（指超越职权和地位行事）act in excess of one's position, power and status ❷ 在足球赛中，攻方的队员踢球，同队的另一队员如果在对方半场内，并在球的前方或攻方队员与对端线（球场两端的界线）之间、对方队员少于二人，都是越位。此外，冰球、橄榄球、曲棍球赛中也有判越位的规定。offside (in soccer matches, before one member of the offensive team kicks the ball, another member of the same team runs ahead of the ball or there are less than two players of the other team between the member of the offensive team and the bottom line); also refers to offside in games like ice hockey, football and field hockey

【越野】yuèyě 在野地、山地里行进 cross-country: ～车 cross-country vehicle | ～赛跑 cross-country race

【越野赛】yuèyěsài 自行车、汽车、摩托车运动比赛项目之一。在有天然障碍的复杂地形中进行比赛。(of cycle, car and motorcycle) cross-country race, held on complex terrain with natural obstacles

【越野赛跑】yuèyě sàipǎo 在运动场以外进行的中长距离赛跑。通常在野外或公路上举行。cross-country race; long-distance running contest held in the open country or on a highway, instead of in a stadium

【越狱】yuè//yù（犯人）从监狱里逃走（of criminals) escape from prison; make a jailbreak: ～潜逃 escape from prison and abscond

【越俎代庖】yuè zǔ dài páo 厨子不做饭，掌管祭祀神主的人不能越过自己的职守，放下祭器去代替厨子做饭（见于《庄子·逍遥游》）。一般用来比喻超过自己的职务范围，去处理别人所管的事情。If a cook doesn't do his job, the person in charge of a sacrificial ceremony cannot overstep his responsibility and put down his work to take the cook's place to prepare food (*Zhuangzi·Transcendent Bliss*). (fig.) exceed one's authority and meddle in other people's affairs; take sb. else's job into one's own hands; do things outside one's area of responsibility

粤 Yuè ❶ 指广东、广西 Guangdong and Guangxi provinces: 两～ Guangdong and Guangxi provinces ❷ 广东的别称 Yue, another name for Guangdong Province: ～剧 Guangdong opera

【粤菜】yuècài 广东风味的菜肴 Guangdong dishes; Cantonese cuisine

【粤剧】yuèjù 广东地方戏曲剧种之一，用广州话演唱，主要流行于说粤语的地区 Guangdong opera; one of the local operas in Guangdong Province, sung in Guangzhou dialect and mainly popular in areas where people speak Guangdong dialect

箢 yuè same as 籰 yuè

鸑（鷟） yuè［鸑鷟］(yuèzhuó) 古书上说的一种水鸟 a kind of water bird recorded in ancient books

樾 yuè〈书 *fml.*〉树阴 shade of a tree

龠[1] yuè〈古代 *arch.*〉容量单位，等于半合(gě) ancient unit of capacity (equal to 0.5 *ge*)

龠[2]**（籥）** yuè〈古代 *arch.*〉一种乐器，形状像箫 ancient musical instrument, similar to the flute

黦 yuè〈书 *fml.*〉黄黑色 yellowish black

瀹 yuè〈书 *fml.*〉❶ 煮 boil; cook: ～茗（烹茶）boil tea; make tea; prepare tea ❷ 疏通（河道）dredge (a river)

爚 yuè〈书 *fml.*〉火光 flame; firelight

籰（篗） yuè〈方 *dial.*〉籰子，绕丝、纱、线等的工具 reel; spool; device used to reel silk, yarn, thread, etc.

yūn（ㄩㄣ）

晕 yūn ❶ same as 晕 yùn ①，用于'头晕、晕头晕脑、晕头转向'等［used in phrases like 头晕 tóu yūn, 晕头晕脑 yūn tóu yūn nǎo and 晕头转向 yūn tóu zhuàn xiàng］❷ 昏迷 swoon; faint; pass out; lose consciousness: ～倒 pass out; fall down in a faint | ～厥 syncope; faint ☞ yùn on p. 2380

【晕厥】yūnjué 昏厥 syncope; faint

【晕头转向】yūn tóu zhuàn xiàng 形容头脑昏乱，迷失方向 dizzy; giddy; muddle-headed; confused and disoriented; in a daze: 风浪很大，船把我摇晃得～。The strong wind and surging waves tossed the boat, leaving me giddy. ◇这道算题真难，把我搞得～。The math problem was so difficult that it made me dizzy.

缊 yūn［细缊］(yīnyūn) ☞［氤氲］(yīnyūn) on p. 2288
☞ yùn on p. 2381

氲 yūn ☞［氤氲］(yīnyūn) on p. 2288

煴 yūn〈书 *fml.*〉微火；无焰的火 slow fire; fire without flames
☞ yùn on p. 2382

赟 yūn〈书 *fml.*〉美好 fine; nice; beautiful

yún (ㄩㄣˊ)

云[1] yún ❶ 说 say; speak: 人～亦～ repeat what others say; parrot | 不知所～ do not understand what other people say or mean ❷ 古汉语助词 (auxiliary word in classical Chinese): 岁～暮矣。The year is drawing to its end.

云[2]（雲）yún 在空中悬浮的由水滴、冰晶聚集形成的物体 cloud; airborne matter formed of water droplets and ice particles

云[3]（雲）Yún ❶ 指云南 Yunnan Province: ～腿（云南宣威一带出产的火腿）Yunnan ham (produced in Xuanwei in Yunnan Province) ❷ 姓 a surname

【云板】yúbǎn〈旧时 *old*〉打击乐器，用长铁片做成，两端作云头形，官署和权贵之家多用做报时报事的器具 percussion instrument, made of a pair of long strips of sheet iron with cloud patterns on both ends, and used in the old times to give the correct time or announce an event in government offices or influential families; also 云版 yúnbǎn

【云豹】yúnbào 哺乳动物，四肢较短，尾较长。毛淡黄色，略带灰色。有云块状斑纹，因而得名。毛皮柔软，花纹美观，可制衣物。clouded leopard (*Neofelis nebulosa*); mammal with relatively short limbs and a long tail, greyish yellow fur with cloud-shaped spots, its soft, beautifully patterned fur used to make garments; also 猫豹 māobào

【云鬓】yúnbìn〈书 *fml.*〉妇女多而美的鬓发 thick, beautiful hair over the temples of a woman

【云彩】yún·cai 云 cloud: 蓝蓝的天上没有一丝～。There is not a speck of cloud in the totally blue sky.

【云层】yúncéng 成层的云 cloud layer: 许多山峰高出～。Many towering peaks reach high above the clouds. | 灰色的～低低压在大森林上面。The grey clouds pressed down over the forest.

【云豆】yúndòu same as 芸豆 yúndòu

【云端】yúnduān 云里 high in the clouds: 飞机从～飞来。An airplane is flying out from behind the clouds.

【云朵】yúnduǒ 呈块状的云 fluffy cloud; mass of cloud; cloud

【云贵】Yún-Guì 云南贵州两省的合称 Yunnan-Guizhou; combined name for Yunnan and Guizhou provinces: ～高原 Yunnan-Guizhou Plateau

【云海】yúnhǎi 从高处下望时，平铺在下面的像海一样的云 sea of clouds; stretch of clouds that look like a sea from far above: ～苍茫 vast sea of clouds

【云汉】yúnhàn〈书 *fml.*〉❶ 天河 Milky Way ❷ 指高空 high sky: 冉冉入～ go slowly up into the sky

【云集】yúnjí〈比喻 *fig.*〉许多人从各处来，聚集在一起 congregate; gather; converge; come to a meeting from all directions: 各地代表～首都。Representatives from every corner of the country gathered in the capital.

【云锦】yúnjǐn 我国一种历史悠久的高级提花丝织物，色彩鲜艳，花纹瑰丽如彩云 cloud-pattern brocade; high-quality silk jacquard with a long history in China, of bright colours and magnificent cloud patterns

【云谲波诡】yún jué bō guǐ 汉代扬雄《甘泉赋》:'于是大厦云谲波诡。'形容房屋构造就像云彩和波浪那样千姿百态。后多用来形容事态变幻莫测。*Sweet Spring Rhapsody* by the Han-dynasty writer Yang Xiong: 'The structure of the building is as varied in shapes and postures as the clouds and waves.' (oft. of the development of an event) unpredictable; capricious; fickle; bewilderingly changeable; also 波谲云诡 bō jué yún guǐ

【云锣】yúnluó 打击乐器，用十个小锣编排而成，第一排一个，以下三排各三个，装置在小木架上。各个锣的大小相同而厚薄不同，所以发出的声音不同。最上面的一个不常用，因此也叫九音锣。现在云锣有所发展，已不止十个。chiming gongs; Chinese gong chimes; percussion instrument that used to consist of ten gong-shaped pieces of brass of the same diameter, one in the first row and three for each of the following three rows. The gongs were hung in a wooden frame and were of varying thickness so that different notes were produced, and because the gong in the first row is seldom used, it is also called 九音锣 jiǔyīnluó; today, this instrument has been developed using more than 10 gongs.

【云母】yúnmǔ 矿物，主要成分是硅酸盐，白色、黑色，带有深浅不同的褐色或绿色。耐高温，不导电，能分成透明的可以弯曲的薄片，是重要的电气绝缘材料。mica; mineral, consisting mainly of silicate, which comes in different colours, with white and black tinted with different shades of brown or green. Highly heat-resistant and insulating, it can be made

into translucent and flexible sheets, an important insulation material.

【云泥之别】yún ní zhī bié 相差像天空的云和地下的泥 as far apart as clouds in the sky and mud on the ground;〈比喻 *fig.*〉高低差别悬殊 big difference between the high and the low

【云片糕】yúnpiàngāo 用米粉加糖和核桃仁等制成的糕,切做长方形薄片 a kind of cake in thin layers, made of glutinous rice, sugar and walnuts

【云气】yúnqì 稀薄游动的云 thin, floating cloud

【云雀】yúnquè 鸟,羽毛赤褐色,有黑色斑纹,嘴小而尖,翅膀大,飞得高,叫的声音好听 skylark (*Alauda arvensis*); russet-feathered bird, having black spots on its body, a small pointed beak, and large wings, that flies high and chirps pleasantly

【云散】yúnsàn 像天空的云那样四处散开 disperse like clouds; a)〈比喻 *fig.*〉曾在一起的人分散到各地 (of people) scatter to different places: 旧友～。Old friends scattered like clouds. b)〈比喻 *fig.*〉事物四散消失 disappear; vanish; dissolve: 烟消～ melt into thin air; vanish like smoke; disappear like clouds

【云山雾罩】yún shān wù zhào ❶ 形容云雾弥漫 misty; cloud-enshrouded; enveloped in cloud; permeating mist; under a thickening pall of mist ❷ 形容说话漫无边际,使人困惑不解 (of talk) make sb. feel completely at sea; confusing; perplexing; discursive; rambling

【云梯】yúntī 攻城或救火时用的长梯 scaling ladder; long ladder used when attacking a city or in fire-fighting

【云天】yúntiān 高空;云霄 sky; welkin: 响彻～ sound throughout the sky; make the welkin ring|高耸～ tower into the sky|高峰直插～。The high peaks reached towards the sky.

【云头】yúntóu 看起来成团成堆的云 cloud cluster; cloud; heap of clouds: 看这～像有雨的样子。From the look of the clouds, it is going to rain.

【云头儿】yúntóur 云状的图案花纹 cloud pattern

【云图】yúntú 云的图片,记录着某时某地云的情况和形状,是气象研究和预报的参考资料 cloud atlas; cloud chart; cloud picture that records the state and shape of clouds at a certain time in a certain place, serving as reference material for study and forecast of weather

【云雾】yúnwù 云和雾,多比喻遮蔽或障碍的东西 cloud and mist; mist; (fig.) veil; coverage; blockade; hindrance: 拨开～见青天 see blue sky again after the clouds have dispersed

【云霞】yúnxiá 彩云 rosy clouds; pink clouds

【云消雾散】yún xiāo wù sàn ☞ 烟消云散 yān xiāo yún sàn on p. 2200

【云霄】yúnxiāo 极高的天空;天际 sky; heaven: 响彻～ reverberate through the sky; echo to the clouds; make the heavens ring|直上～ soar to the sky; skyrocket; rise or fly into the sky

【云崖】yúnyá 高耸入云的山崖 steep cliffs towering into the sky

【云烟】yúnyān 云雾和烟气 cloud and mist; mist: ～缭绕 wreathed in clouds and mists; enveloped in mist|～过眼(比喻事物很快就消失了) fleeting clouds; (fig.) things passing quickly; transient

【云翳】yúnyì ❶ 阴暗的云 black cloud: 清澄的蓝天上没有一点～。There was not a speck of cloud in the azure sky. ◇脸上罩上了忧郁的～。(His) face became clouded with gloom. ❷ 眼球角膜发生病变后遗留下来的疤痕组织,影响视力 nebula; scar left by pathological changes to the cornea of an eyeball, which affects eyesight

【云游】yúnyóu 到处遨游,行踪无定(多指和尚、道士 oft. of a Buddhist monk or Taoist priest) wander about; roam about: ～四海 roam from place to place; wander the world over

【云雨】yúnyǔ 宋玉《高唐赋》叙宋玉对楚襄王问,说楚怀王曾游高唐,梦与巫山神女相会,神女临去说自己'旦为朝云,暮为行雨' *Gaotang Rhapsody* by Song Yu: Song Yu told King Xiang of Chu that once King Huai of Chu visited Gaotang and had a dream in which he met the Goddess of Wushan Mountain. Before the goddess left, she described herself as 'clouds in the morning and rain in the evening'. 后世因以指男女合欢(多见于旧小说 oft. seen in traditional Chinese fiction) later, clouds and rain used to refer to sexual intercourse; love-making

【云云】yúnyún〈书 *fml.*〉如此;这样(引用文句或谈话时,表示结束或有所省略)[used at the end of a speech or quotation to indicate an ending or omission] and so on; and so on and so forth; etc.: 他来信说读了不少新书,很有心得～。He wrote to say that he had read many new books and learned a lot from them, and so on.

【云蒸霞蔚】yún zhēng xiá wèi 形容景物灿烂绚丽 (of scenery) splendid; gorgeous; magnificent; effulgent; also 云兴霞蔚 yún xīng xiá wèi

匀 yún ❶ 均匀 even; equitable: 颜色涂得不～。The colour is not evenly applied. ❷ 使均匀 even up; divide evenly: 把粉～～ even out the powder|这两份多少不均,再～一～吧。The two portions are not equal; please even them up. ❸ 抽出一部分给别人或做别用 take from sth. and give to sb.; take from sth. for some other use; spare: ～出一部分粮食支援灾区 spare a portion of grain to the disaster-stricken areas|工作太忙，～不出时间干家务 be too busy with one's work to spare time for housework

【匀称】yún·chèn 均匀；比例和谐 well proportioned; well balanced; symmetrical: 穗子又多又～。The ears have come out abundantly and uniformly.|字写得很～ write in a neat hand|这人身段～。The man is of a well-proportioned build.

【匀兑】yún·dui 匀出来；抽出一部分让给别人 spare; take from sth. and give to others: 给他～一间屋子。Please arrange to give him a spare room.

【匀和】yún·huo (～儿 yún·huor) ❶ 均匀 even; equal; uniform: 刚才还在喘气，现在呼吸才～了。(He) was panting just a moment ago, but he's breathing steadily now. ❷ 使均匀 even up; divide evenly: 这些苹果大的大，小的小，得～～再分。There are big and small apples; mix them up first and then divide them evenly. also 匀乎 yún·hu

【匀净】yún·jing 粗细或深浅一致；均匀 (of thickness or colour) uniform; even; neat: 这块布染得很～。This cloth is evenly dyed.|线纺得非常～。The yarn is evenly spun.

【匀脸】yún//liǎn 化装时用手搓脸使脂粉匀净 rub powder and paint evenly on the face; apply rouge and powder evenly on one's face

【匀溜】yún·liu (～儿 yún·liur)大小、粗细或稀稠等适中 of the right size, thickness, consistency, etc.: 这线纺得真～。The yarn is spun so neatly, all of the same thickness!

【匀实】yún·shi 均匀 even; neat; uniform: 瞧这布多细密多～。Look! How close and uniform the texture of the cloth is!|麦苗出得很～。The wheat seedlings have come out in uniform density.

【匀速运动】yúnsù yùndòng 物体在单位时间内所通过的距离相等的运动 uniform motion; (of an object) covering an equal distance within a unit of time; also 等速运动 děngsù yùndòng

【匀整】yún·zhěng 均匀整齐 neat and well-spaced; tidy; even and orderly: 字写得～very neat handwriting|～的脚步 regular strides

芸[1] yún same as 芸香 yúnxiāng

芸[2]（**蕓**）yún ☞ 芸薹 yúntái

【芸豆】yúndòu 菜豆的通称 general term for 菜豆 càidòu; also 云豆 yúndòu

【芸薹】yúntái same as 油菜 yóucài ①

【芸香】yúnxiāng 多年生草本植物，茎直立，叶子互生，羽状分裂，裂片长圆形，花黄色，果实为蒴果。全草有香气，可入药。rue (*Ruta*); perennial herb, having erect stems, alternate pinnated oval leaves with ovate lobes, and yellow flowers that yield capsules. The whole plant is fragrant, and can be used in medicine.

【芸芸】yúnyún〈书 *fml.*〉形容众多 numerous; multitudinous; a great many; large amount of: 万物～ myriad of things|～众生 common populace; all mortal beings; all living things

【芸芸众生】yúnyún zhòng shēng〈佛教 *Budd.*〉指一切有生命的东西。一般也用来指众多的平常人。all living things; all mortal things; common populace

员 yún 用于人名，伍员(即伍子胥)，春秋时人 used in a person's name, e. g. Wu Yun (Wu Zixu) in the Spring and Autumn Period ☞ yuán on p. 2357 and Yùn on p. 2380

沄[1] yún [沄沄]〈书 *fml.*〉形容水流动 (of water) flowing

沄[2]（**澐**）yún〈书 *fml.*〉大波浪 great wave; torrential waves; surging waves

妘 Yún 姓 a surname

纭 yún [纭纭]形容多而乱 numerous and disorderly; diverse and confused

昀 yún〈书 *fml.*〉日光 sunlight; sunshine; daylight; light

畇 yún [畇畇]〈书 *fml.*〉形容田地整齐 (of fields) neatly arranged; neat; tidy

郧 Yún ❶ 郧县，在湖北 Yunxian County, in Hubei Province ❷ 姓 a surname

耘 yún 田地里除草 weed: ～田 weed the fields|春耕夏～，秋收冬藏。Plough in spring, weed in summer, harvest in autumn, and store in winter.

【耘锄】yúnchú 除草和松土用的锄头 hoe; farm tool for weeding and turning up the soil

【耘耥】yúntāng 耘稻和耥稻。指在水稻分蘖期间进行中耕除草。furrow and weed paddy fields during the tillering stage of the paddy rice

涢 Yún 涢水，水名，在湖北 Yunshui River, in Hubei Province

筠 yún〈书 *fml.*〉❶ 竹子的青皮 green bamboo skin ❷ 借指竹子 bamboo ☞ jūn on p. 1066

篔 yún [篔筜](yúndāng)〈书 *fml.*〉生长在水边的大竹子 tall bamboo growing by the waterside

鋆 yún (在人名中也读 jūn also pronounced jūn if used in a person's name)〈书 *fml.*〉金子 gold

yǔn (ㄩㄣˇ)

允[1] yǔn 允许 permit; allow; consent; grant: 应～ agree; promise|不～ refuse to give consent or permission

允² yǔn 公平；适当 fair; appropriate; suitable: ～当 proper; suitable | 公～ fair | 平～ fair and just; equitable

【允当】yǔndàng 得当；适当 proper; suitable: 繁简～ just the right degree of simplicity

【允诺】yǔnnuò 应许 promise; consent; undertake: 欣然～ readily consent

【允许】yǔnxǔ 许可 permit; allow; grant; approve: 得到～，方可入内。One is allowed in only with permission.

【允准】yǔnzhǔn 允许；许可 give the go-ahead to; approve; permit; allow; consent; give permission to: ～开业 be allowed to do business

狁 yǔn ☞ 猃狁 Xiǎnyǔn on p. 2079

陨 yǔn 陨落 fall from the sky or outer space: ～石 aerolite; stony meteorite

【陨落】yǔnluò（星体或其他在高空运行的物体）从高空掉下（of meteorites or other objects) fall from the sky or outer space

【陨灭】yǔnmiè ❶ 物体从高空掉下而毁灭（of objects) fall from the sky or outer space, and burn up ❷ 丧命 meet one's death; perish; die; also 殒灭 yǔnmiè

【陨石】yǔnshí 含石质较多或全部为石质的陨星 aerolite; stony meteorite; meteorite consisting of pure or mainly stone

【陨铁】yǔntiě 含铁质较多或全部是铁质的陨星 siderite; iron meteorite; meteorite consisting of pure or mainly iron

【陨星】yǔnxīng 流星体经过地球大气层时，没有完全烧毁而落在地面上的部分叫做陨星，有纯铁质的、纯石质的和铁质石质混合的 meteorite; rock of pure iron or stone, or a mixture of iron and stone, formed from a meteor to reach the earth's surface without burning up completely in the atmosphere

殒 yǔn 死亡 perish; die: ～身 be killed; perish; meet one's death | ～命 die; expire; meet one's death

【殒灭】yǔnmiè same as 陨灭 yǔnmiè ②

【殒命】yǔnmìng〈书 *fml.*〉丧命 die; expire; meet one's death; be killed

【殒身】yǔnshēn〈书 *fml.*〉丧命；死亡 be killed; perish; meet one's death

yùn（ㄩㄣˋ）

孕 yùn ❶ 怀胎 pregnant: ～育 give birth to; be pregnant with; breed ◇～穗 booting ❷ 身孕 pregnancy: 有～ be pregnant; be in the family way

【孕畜】yùnchù 怀孕的牲畜 pregnant domestic animal

【孕妇】yùnfù 怀孕的妇女 pregnant woman

【孕期】yùnqī 妇女从受孕到产出胎儿的一段时间，通常为 266 日，自末次月经的第一日算起则为 280 日 pregnancy; gestation; period from conception in a woman to the birth of her baby, usually of 266 days, or 280 days if counted from the first day of the last menstruation

【孕穗】yùnsuì 水稻、小麦、玉米等作物的穗在叶鞘内形成而尚未抽出来，叫做孕穗 booting; ear of rice, wheat, corn, etc., forming in its sheath and not yet coming out

【孕吐】yùntù 孕妇在妊娠初期食欲异常、恶心、呕吐的现象 morning sickness; vomiting during pregnancy; phenomena of altered eating habits, nausea and vomiting during the early period of pregnancy

【孕育】yùnyù 怀胎生育 be pregnant (with); breed; be conceived;〈比喻 *fig.*〉既存的事物中酝酿着新事物 (of existing thing) brew new things; give rise to; deliberate upon: 海洋是～原始生命的温床。The ocean is the nursery for primitive life.

运¹（運）yùn ❶ same as 运动 yùndòng ①: ～行 move; be in operation ❷ 搬运；运输 carry; transport; ship: ～货 transport or ship goods | 客～ passenger transport | 水～ water transport | 空～ air transport; airlift | 这批货～到哪儿去？Where will this batch of goods be transported? ❸ 运用 use; wield; utilize; apply: ～笔 write or paint with a brush | ～思 put one's ideas into words ❹ (Yùn) 姓 a surname

运²（運）yùn 运气 fortune; luck; fate; destiny; lot: 幸～ fortunate; lucky | 好～ good luck

【运笔】yùnbǐ 运用笔（写或画）；动笔 wield the pen (to write or paint); start writing: 时而搁笔沉思，时而～如飞。One minute, (he) put down the pen, lost in thought; the next minute, (he) was wielding the pen with rapid, vigorous strokes.

【运筹】yùnchóu 制定策略；筹划 draw up a plan; devise strategies

【运筹帷幄】yùnchóu wéiwò《汉书·高帝纪》：'上（刘邦）曰：夫运筹帷幄之中，决胜于千里之外，吾不如子房（张良）。' *History of Han · Biography of Emperor Gaodi*: 'Liu Bang said: "As for planning strategies within a command tent to ensure victory on a battlefront a thousand *li* away, I would be no match for Zifang (alias of Zhang Liang)."' 后因以称在后方决定作战策略，也泛指筹划决策。devise strategies from the home front; (in a broad sense) devise strategies and make decisions

【运筹学】yùnchóuxué 利用现代数学，特别是统计数学的成就，研究人力物力的运用和筹划，使能发挥最大效率的学科 operational research; operations research; subject studying how to make the best use of labour and material resources to make them most efficient by means of modern mathematics, esp. statistical mathematics

【运单】yùndān 托运人在托运货物时填写的单据,是运输部门承运货物的依据 booking note or list; form that a shipper fills when entrusting goods to a transport department, which will undertake the transporting of goods accordingly

【运道】yùn·dao〈方 *dial.*〉运气(yùn·qi) fortune; luck: 交上了好~。(He) was lucky.

【运动】yùndòng ❶ 物体的位置不断变化的现象。通常指一个物体和其他物体之间相对位置的变化,说某物体运动常是对另一物体而言。motion; movement; continuous change of location of an object, usu. referring to the change of location of a certain object in relation to others ❷ 指宇宙所发生的一切变化和过程,从简单的位置变动到复杂的人类思维,都是物质运动的表现 motion; movement; all changes and processes in the universe, from a simple change in location to complex human thought processes ❸ 体育活动 sports; athletics; exercise: 田径~ track and field sports; athletics|~健将 master sportsman ❹ 政治、文化、生产等方面有组织、有目的而声势较大的群众性活动 movement; campaign; drive; political, cultural or productive mass activities done in an organized way and with a clear purpose: 五四~ May 4th Movement|技术革新~ technical innovation movement

【运动】yùn·dong 为求达到某种目的而奔走钻营 go lobbying; canvass; make arrangements to accomplish certain purposes or secure personal gains: ~官府 canvass or drum up support from the authorities

【运动场】yùndòngchǎng 供体育锻炼和比赛的场地 sports venue; athletic ground; playground; stadium; venue for sports exercises and competitions

【运动会】yùndònghuì 多项体育运动的竞赛会 sports meet; athletic meeting; games

【运动健将】yùndòng jiànjiàng 我国对符合技术等级标准的运动员授予的最高称号 master of sports; master sportsman or sports woman; highest title granted to an athlete for his or her achievement in sports in China

【运动量】yùndòngliàng 指体育运动所给予人体的生理负荷量。由强度、密度、时间、数量及运动项目的特点等因素构成。amount of physical exercise, decided by the degree of intensity and consistency, time, amount, and the characteristics of sports or physical exercises; also 运动负荷 yùndòng fùhè

【运动神经】yùndòngshénjīng ☞ 传出神经 chuánchū shénjīng on p. 299

【运动学】yùndòngxué 体育科学的一门学科,以人体解剖学和力学来解释各种体育活动 kinesiology; branch of physical culture that studies different kinds of sports from the perspective of anatomy and mechanics

【运动员】yùndòngyuán 参加体育运动竞赛的人 sportsman or sportswoman; athlete; player; participant in sports matches

【运动战】yùndòngzhàn 主要指正规兵团在长的战线和大的战区上面,从事于战役和战斗上的外线的、速决的进攻战的形式 mobile war or warfare; quick offensive on the exterior lines by regular troops in a campaign or a battle

【运费】yùnfèi 运载货物时支付的费用 transportation expenses; freight; carriage; freightage

【运河】yùnhé 人工挖成的可以通航的河 canal; river dug out by human labour and open to navigation

【运脚】yùnjiǎo〈方 *dial.*〉运费 transportation expenses; freight; carriage

【运斤成风】yùn jīn chéng fēng 楚国郢人在鼻尖抹了一层白粉,让一个名叫石的巧匠用斧子把粉削去,石便挥动斧子顺着风势削掉白粉,那人的鼻子却毫无损伤(见于《庄子·徐无鬼》)。后来就用'运斤成风'比喻手法熟练,技艺高超。whirl the hatchet with a noise like the wind; *Zhuangzi · Xu Wugui*: A man from the state of Chu smeared a layer of white powder on his nose and asked a craftsman named Shi to scrub it off with a hatchet, at which point Shi wielded his hatchet, produced the noise of soughing wind, and cleared away the white powder without causing any injury to the nose. (fig.) perform an uncanny feat; have superb skill

【运力】yùnlì 运输力量 means of transport: 提高~ improve the means of transport|安排~,抢运救灾物资 make arrangements for rush-transport for emergency supply of disaster relief

【运气】yùn//qì 把力气贯注到身体某一部分 focus one's strength to a certain part of the body: 他一~,把石块搬了起来。He took a deep breath and, through focus of exertion, lifted the stone.

【运气】yùn·qi ❶ 命运 destiny; fate; odds; lot: ~不佳 be unlucky; have a bad lot ❷ 幸运 odds; luck; fortune: 你真~,中了头等奖。You're lucky, you've won first prize.

【运输】yùnshū 用交通工具把物资或人从一个地方运到另一个地方 transport; transportation; carriage; conveyance; moving materials or people from one place to another in vehicles

【运输机】yùnshūjī 专门用来载运人员和物资的飞机 transport plane; air-freighter; airplane specializing in transporting personnel and materials

【运输舰】yùnshūjiàn 专门担负军事运输任务的军舰 naval or military cargo ship; naval transport

【运思】yùnsī 运用心思（多指诗文写作 oft. in poetry）put one's thought into words：执笔～ take up the pen and concentrate one's mind on writing｜～精巧 refined writing

【运送】yùnsòng 把人或物资运到别处 transport; ship; convey：～肥料 transport（or ship）fertilizer

【运算】yùnsuàn 依照数学法则，求出一个算题或算式的结果 operation; solving a math problem according to mathematical rules

【运算器】yùnsuànqì 电子计算机中用来进行算术运算或逻辑运算的部件 computer arithmetic unit; unit in a computer that does arithmetical operations or Boolean calculations

【运销】yùnxiāo 把货物运到别处销售 transportation and sale（of commodities）：～全国 transport and sale of sth. across the country｜～水果 transport and sale of fruit

【运行】yùnxíng 周而复始地运转（多指星球、车船等）（of planets）revolve in cycle;（of ships and vehicles）move year round; be in motion; be in action; be in operation：人造卫星的～轨道 orbit of a man-made satellite｜列车～示意图 sketch map of train routes｜缩短列车的～时间 shorten the time for a train to get from one place to another

【运营】yùnyíng ❶（车船等）运行和营业（of buses, ships, etc.）be in operation; open for service; put into operation：地下铁道开始正式～。The subway was formally launched into operation. ❷〈比喻 *fig.*〉机构有组织地进行工作（of an institution）operate（or run）in an organized way：改善一些工矿企业低效率～的状况 overcome inefficiency in mining and other industrial enterprises

【运用】yùnyòng 根据事物的特性加以利用 use; apply; make use of sth. according to its characteristics：～自如 have a perfect command of sth.; handle sth. skilfully｜灵活～ apply in a flexible way

【运载】yùnzài 装载和运送 deliver; carry：～工具 means of delivery; carrier｜～货物 deliver goods｜增加货车的～量 increase the carrying capacity of a truck

【运载火箭】yùnzài huǒjiàn 把人造卫星或宇宙飞船等运送到预定轨道的火箭 carrier rocket; rocket that delivers a man-made satellite, space shuttle, etc., into a pre-designated orbit

【运转】yùnzhuǎn ❶ 沿着一定的轨道行动 revolve; turn round; move in an orbit：行星绕着太阳～。The planets revolve round the sun. ❷ 指机器转动（of machines）work; operate：发电机～正常。The generator is working properly. ❸〈比喻 *fig.*〉组织、机构等进行工作（of organizations, institutions, etc.）be in operation; run; operate：这家公司前不久宣告成立，开始～。The company, which was established not long ago, has started operation.

【运作】yùnzuò（组织、机构等）进行工作；开展活动（of organizations, institutions, etc.）be in operation; operate; run：改变现行的～方式 change the current operating mode; change the existing mode of implementation｜保证海关机构的正常～ guarantee normal work procedures in the customs office

员 Yùn 姓 a surname

☞ yuán on p. 2357 and yún on p. 2377

郓 Yùn ❶ 郓城，地名，在山东 Yuncheng, name of a place in Shandong Province ❷ 姓 a surname

恽 Yùn 姓 a surname

晕 yùn ❶ 头脑发昏，周围物体好像在旋转，人有要跌倒的感觉 dizzy; giddy; faint; having a feeling that everything around is whirling：～船 seasick｜眼～ have a giddy spell｜他一坐汽车就～。He feels sick whenever he travels by car. ❷ 日光或月光通过云层中的冰晶时经折射而形成的光圈 halo; circular band of colour light around the sun or moon, caused by the refraction of light by ice particles suspended in the intervening atmosphere; ☞ 日晕 rìyùn on p. 1628 and 月晕 yuèyùn on p. 2371 ❸ 光影、色彩四周模糊的部分 halo or haze around some light or colour：墨～ running ink｜红～ blush｜灯光黄而有～。The light is yellow and has a halo.

☞ yūn on p. 2374

【晕场】yùn//chǎng 考生在考试或演员在演出时由于过度紧张或其他原因而头晕，影响考试或演出的正常进行（of sb. taking an exam or giving a performance）have stage fright; feel dizzy due to excessive nervousness or other reasons

【晕车】yùn//chē 坐车时头晕、呕吐 feel sick when travelling by a vehicle; be carsick

【晕池】yùn//chí（到池汤中洗澡的人）因温度过高、湿度过大、体质较弱等原因而昏厥（of a person taking a bath in a public bathhouse）faint due to high temperature, high humidity, physical weakness, etc.; also 晕堂 yùn//táng

【晕船】yùn//chuán 坐船时头晕、呕吐 be seasick; feel dizziness and nausea when travelling by boat

【晕高儿】yùn//gāor〈方 *dial.*〉登高时头晕心跳 feel dizzy when climbing high; suffer from fear of heights

【晕机】yùnjī 坐飞机时头晕、呕吐 suffer from airsickness; be airsick

【晕针】yùnzhēn 针刺后病人面色苍白，头晕，目眩，心烦欲呕等，叫做晕针 become pale and feel dizzy and sick after taking an injection; be afflicted with vertigo when receiving an injection

酝(醞) yùn〈书 *fml.*〉❶ 酿酒 ferment; brew: ～酿 brew; ferment; deliberate on | 春～夏成。(of a beverage) start brewing in spring and become ready in summer. ❷ 指酒 wine: 佳～ good wine

【酝酿】yùnniàng 造酒的发酵过程 ferment; brew ;〈比喻 *fig.*〉做准备工作 make preparations; deliberate on: ～候选人名单 consider and discuss the list of candidates | 大家先～一下,好充分发表意见。We should deliberate on it first and then express our opinions in full.

愠 yùn〈书 *fml.*〉怒 angry; irritated; infuriated; annoyed; indignant; furious: 微～ look slightly irritated | ～色 angry look; irritated look

【愠色】yùnsè〈书 *fml.*〉恼怒的脸色 angry look; irritated look: 面有～ look irritated

缊 yùn〈书 *fml.*〉❶ 碎麻 bits of hemp, flax, etc. ❷ 新旧混合的丝绵絮 silk wadding made of old and new floss: ～袍 floss-padded robe

☞ yūn on p. 2375

韫(韞) yùn〈书 *fml.*〉包含;蕴藏 comprise; include; imply; contain; hold in store

韵(韻) yùn ❶ 好听的声音 agreeable sound; pleasing sound: 琴～悠扬 sweet music | 松声竹～ soughing of pine trees and bamboo; melodious sound of the wind blowing through pine and bamboo ❷ 韵母 simple or compound vowel: 押～ rhyme with; be in rhyme | 叠～ rhyming couplet | ～文 verse; prose ❸ 情趣 charm; appeal; delight: 风～ be charming | ～味 charm; interest; implicit richness | ～致 graceful bearing; grace ❹ (Yùn)姓 a surname

【韵白】yùnbái ❶ 京剧中指按照传统念法念出的道白,有的字音和北京音略有不同 spoken part in Peking Opera, recited according to traditional pronunciation, sometimes a bit different from Beijing dialect ❷ 戏曲中句子整齐押韵的道白 rhyming spoken parts in an opera

【韵调】yùndiào 音调 musical tone: ～优美 beautiful tone | ～悠扬 sweet melody

【韵腹】yùnfù 指韵母中的主要元音 essential vowel in a compound vowel in Chinese; ☞ 韵母 yùnmǔ

【韵脚】yùnjiǎo 韵文句末押韵的字 rhyming word at the end of a verse line; rhyme

【韵律】yùnlǜ 指诗词中的平仄格式和押韵规则 metre and rhyme scheme in poetry; prosody; rhythm; rules of rhyming

【韵律体操】yùnlǜ tǐcāo 艺术体操 rhythmic gymnastics

【韵母】yùnmǔ 汉语字音中声母、字调以外的部分。韵母又可以分成韵头(介音)、韵腹(主要元音)、韵尾三部分。如'娘'niáng 的韵母是 iang,其中 i 是韵头,a 是韵腹,ng 是韵尾。每个韵母一定有韵腹,韵头和韵尾则可有可无。如'大'dà 的韵母是 a,a 是韵腹,没有韵头、韵尾;'瓜'guā 的韵母是 ua,其中 u 是韵头,a 是韵腹,没有韵尾;'刀'dāo 的韵母是 ao,其中 a 是韵腹,o 是韵尾,没有韵头。simple or compound vowel in a Chinese syllable, the other two parts being consonant and tone. A vowel may be divided into three parts: a head vowel, essential vowel and tail vowel, e.g. the 'iang' in 娘 niáng is the vowel, within which 'i' is the head vowel, 'a' is the essential vowel and 'ng' is the tail vowel; each compound vowel has an essential vowel but may or may not have a head or a tail vowel, e.g. 大 dà has an essential vowel of 'a', but doesn't have a head or tail vowel; 'ua' is the compound vowel of 瓜 guā, with 'u' as the head vowel, and 'a' the essential vowel, but without a tail vowel; 'ao' in 刀 dāo is the compound vowel, with 'a' as the essential vowel and 'o' the tail vowel, but no head vowel. ☞ 声母 shēngmǔ on p. 1720

【韵目】yùnmù 韵书把同韵的字归为一部,每韵用一个字标目,按次序排列,如通用的诗韵上平声分为一东、二冬、三江、四支等,叫做韵目 category in a dictionary of rhyming words, represented by a Chinese character and arranged in order, e.g. for the level tone of all-purpose rhymes, there are categories of 一东 yīdōng, 二冬 èrdōng, 三江 sānjiāng, 四支 sìzhī, etc.

【韵事】yùnshì 风雅的事 romantic or anecdotal event: 风流～ romantic affair; love affair

【韵书】yùnshū 为写作韵文押韵用的同韵、同音字典,如《广韵》、《集韵》、《中原音韵》等 dictionary of rhyming words and homophones, e.g. *Comprehensive Phonology* (Song Dynasty), *The Revised Comprehensive Phonology* (Song Dynasty), *Phonetic Tones and Rhymes of Central Plain* (Yuan Dynasty), etc.

【韵头】yùntóu 介音 head vowel; ☞ 韵母 yùnmǔ

【韵尾】yùnwěi 指韵母的收尾部分,例如韵母 ai、ei 的 i,韵母 ao 的 o, 韵母 ou 的 u,韵母 an、en 的 n, 韵母 ang、eng 的 ng tail vowel or terminal nasal consonant in a compound vowel, e.g. 'i' in 'ai' and 'ei', 'o' in 'ao', 'u' in 'ou', 'n' in 'an' and 'en', and 'ng' in 'ang' and 'eng'; ☞ 韵母 yùnmǔ

【韵味】yùnwèi ❶ 声韵所体现的意味 charm or appeal implied by sound and rhythm; implicit richness: 他的唱腔很有～。His singing has a special pleasing charm. ❷ 情趣;趣味 charm; appeal; interest: 这首诗～很浓。This poem is written in a style of implicit poetic appeal. | 古塔古树相互映衬,平添了古朴的～。

The age-old pagoda and trees that set off each other so harmoniously lent a simple and unsophisticated charm to the whole place.

【韵文】yùnwén 有节奏韵律的文学体裁，也指用这种体裁写成的文章，包括诗、词、歌、赋等（区别于'散文' as compared with 'prose'）verse; literary genre in rhyme; literary composition in rhyme, including poetry, *ci* poetry, songs, rhapsody, etc.

【韵语】yùnyǔ 押韵的语言，指诗、词和唱词、歌诀等 rhymes, including poetry, *ci* poetry, song lyrics, etc.

【韵致】yùnzhì 风度韵味；情致 grace; charm; appeal: 水仙另有一种淡雅的～。The narcissus has a natural and graceful bearing about it.

煴 yùn〈书 *fml.*〉same as 熨 yùn
☞ yūn on p. 2375

蕴 yùn〈书 *fml.*〉❶ 包含；蓄积 accumulate; hold in store; contain: ～藏 contain; store ❷ 事理深奥的地方 profoundness: 底～ depth of sth.; profundity; hidden strength

【蕴藏】yùncáng 蓄积而未显露或未发掘 hold in store; contain: 大沙漠下面～着丰富的石油资源。The boundless desert is rich in oil reserves. | 他们心中～着极大的爱国热情。They have a vast reservoir of patriotic ardour in their hearts.

【蕴含】yùnhán same as 蕴涵 yùnhán ①

【蕴涵】yùnhán ❶ 包含 contain; embrace; hold in store: 这段文字不长，却～着丰富的内容。This paragraph, short as it is, has rich content. also 蕴含 yùnhán ❷ 判断中前后两个命题间存在的某一种条件关系叫做蕴涵，表现形式是'如果…则…'。例如'如果温度增高则寒暑表的水银柱上升'。implication; certain relationship between two propositions, in the forms of 'if ..., then ...', e.g. 'If the temperature increases, the mercury in a thermometer will go up.'

【蕴藉】yùnjiè〈书 *fml.*〉（言语、文字、神情等）含蓄而不显露 (of speech, language, expression, etc.) temperate and refined; cultured and restrained; implicit: 意味～ implicit meaning | ～的微笑 modest smile

【蕴蓄】yùnxù 积蓄或包含在里面而未表露出来 lie hidden and undeveloped; be latent; be implicit: 青年人身上～着旺盛的活力。The youths are remarkably energetic.

熨 yùn 用烙铁或熨斗烫平 iron; press: ～衣服 iron or press clothes
☞ yù on p. 2354

【熨斗】yùndǒu 形状像斗，中间烧木炭，用来烫平衣物的金属器具。用电发热的叫电熨斗。iron; flat iron; square or drum-like metal implement used to press clothes with the heat from the charcoal placed inside it, called an 'electric iron' if heated through electricity

Z

zā (ㄗㄚ)

扎(紮、紥) zā ❶ 捆；束 do up (a package); tie; bind; bunch: ～彩 hang up festoons and streamers | ～裤脚 bind the bottom of one's trouser legs | 腰里～着一条皮带 tie a leather belt around one's waist ❷〈方 *dial.*〉〈量词 *classifier*〉用于捆起来的东西 bundle: 一～干草 a bundle of hay

☞ zhā on p. 2402 and zhá on p. 2403

匝(帀) zā〈书 *fml.*〉❶ same as 周[1] zhōu ①；圈 circle; circumference: 绕树三～ circle a tree three times ❷ 环绕 surround; encircle; revolve around: 清渠～庭堂。The houses are skirted by a limpid stream. ❸ 遍；满 all over; complete; full: ～地 all around; everywhere

【匝地】zādì〈书 *fml.*〉遍地；满地 all over the ground; everywhere: 柳荫～。The willow trees cast their shadows all around.

【匝月】zāyuè〈书 *fml.*〉满一个月 full month

咂 zā ❶ 用嘴唇吸 sip; suck: ～了一口酒 take a sip of wine ❷ 咂嘴 smack one's lips ❸ 仔细辨别(滋味) taste or savour carefully (the flavour)

【咂摸】zā·mo〈方 *dial.*〉仔细辨别(滋味、意思等) taste or savour carefully; weigh (meaning, etc.) carefully: ～着酒的香味 carefully savour the bouquet of a wine | 你再～～他这话是什么意思。You must weigh his words carefully again.

【咂嘴】zā//zuǐ (～儿 zā//zuǐr) 舌尖抵住上腭发出吸气音，表示称赞、羡慕、惊讶、为难、惋惜等 smack one's lips (in praise, admiration, surprise, bewilderment, regret, etc.)

拶 zā〈书 *fml.*〉逼迫 force; coerce: 逼～ force; compel

☞ zǎn on p. 2390

臜 zā ☞ [腌臜] (ā·zā) on p. 2

zá (ㄗㄚˊ)

杂(雜、雜、襍) zá ❶ 多种多样的 miscellaneous; sundry; mixed; varied; diverse: 复～ complicated; complex | ～色 variegated; varicoloured; particoloured; motley | ～技 acrobatics ❷ 正项以外的；正式的以外的 extra; irregular: ～费 miscellaneous expenses | ～项 sundry items; miscellaneous items | ～牌儿 less-known or inferior brand ❸ 混合在一起；搀杂 mix; mingle: 夹～ mingle | 草丛中还～有粉红色的野花。The grove of grass was dotted with pink wildflowers.

【杂拌儿】zábànr ❶ 搀杂在一起的各种干果、果脯等 assorted preserved fruits; mixed sweetmeats ❷〈比喻 *fig.*〉杂凑而成的事物 mixture; miscellany; medley; hotchpotch: 这个集子是个大～，有诗，有杂文，有游记，还有短篇小说。This collection is miscellaneous, including poetry, essays, travels and short stories.

【杂处】záchǔ 来自各地的人在一个地区居住 (of people from different places) live in one area: 五方～。People from different places mingle in the area.

【杂凑】zácòu 不同的人或事物勉强合在一起 put (different people or things) together at random; jumble up; knock together

【杂费】záfèi ❶ 主要开支以外的零碎费用 incidental or miscellaneous expenses; incidentals: 节约开支，减少～ save on expenses and cut down on incidentals ❷ 学校为杂项开支而向学生收的费用 sundry fees that schools charge students in addition to tuition fee; extras

【杂感】zágǎn ❶ 零星的感想 random thought ❷ 写零星感想的一种文体 literary genre that records the writer's random thoughts

【杂烩】záhuì ❶ 用多种菜合在一起烩成的菜 mixed stew; hotchpotch ❷〈比喻 *fig.*〉杂凑而成的事物 mixture; miscellany; medley; hotchpotch

【杂活儿】záhuór 零碎的工作；各种各样的力气活 odd jobs; sundry duties

【杂货】záhuò 各种日用的零星货物 sundry goods; groceries; various household supplies

【杂和菜】zá·huocài 把多种剩菜搀和在一起的菜 mixed stew of leftovers

【杂和面儿】zá·huomiànr 搀少量豆类磨成的玉米面儿 corn flour mixed with a little soyabean flour

【杂记】zájì ❶ 记载风景、琐事、感想等的一种文体 literary genre that records scenery, trivial matters, random thoughts, etc.; miscellanies ❷ 零碎的笔记 jottings; notes: 学习～ study notes | 旅途～ travel notes; travels

【杂技】zájì 各种技艺表演(如车技、口技、顶碗、走钢丝、狮子舞、魔术等)的总称 acrobatics (including trick-cycling, vocal mimicry, pagoda of bowls, lion dance, magic, etc.)

【杂家】zájiā ❶ 先秦时期融会各家学说而成一家之言的学派 Eclectics; school of thought that combined various schools of thoughts into one and flourished during the pre-Qin period ❷ 指知识面广,什么都懂一点儿的人 eclectic; jack-of-all-trades; person who knows a little of everything

【杂交】zájiāo 不同种、属或品种的动物或植物进行交配或结合 (of animals or plants of different species, genus or breeds) hybridize; crossbreed; ☞ 有性杂交 yǒuxìng zájiāo on p. 2331; 无性杂交 wúxìng zájiāo on p. 2026

【杂居】zájū 指两个或两个以上的民族在一个地区居住 (of two or more nationalities) live in one area

【杂剧】zájù 宋代以滑稽调笑为特点的一种表演形式。元代发展成戏曲形式,每本以四折为主,有时在开头或折间另加楔子。每折用同宫调同韵的北曲套曲和宾白组成。如关汉卿的《窦娥冤》等。流行于大都(今北京)一带。明清两代也有杂剧,但每本不限四折。comic performance in the Song Dynasty, which evolved into a poetic drama in the Yuan Dynasty, consisting of four acts and occasionally a prelude before the first act or an interlude between acts, with each act comprising northern opera melodies of the same tune and rhyme and spoken parts, e. g. *The Injustice to Dou Oh* by Guan Hanqing, which was very popular in Dadu (present-day Beijing); poetic drama in the Ming and Qing dynasties, which was not limited to only four acts

【杂粮】záliáng 稻谷、小麦以外的粮食,如玉米、高粱、豆类等 coarse cereals; coarse food grains other than wheat and rice, e.g. maize, sorghum, legumes, etc.

【杂乱】záluàn 多而乱,没有秩序或条理 chaotic; untidy; disorderly; in a jumble; messy; in a mess: 院子里～地堆着木料、砖瓦。Timber, bricks and tiles were piled higgledy-piggledy in the yard.

【杂乱无章】záluàn wú zhāng 又多又乱,没有条理 higgledy-piggledy; messy; in a mess

【杂念】zániàn 不纯正的念头,多指为个人打算的念头 distracting thoughts; selfish considerations: 摒除～ banish distracting thoughts from one's mind | 私心～ selfish or personal considerations

【杂牌】zápái (～儿 zápáir)非正规的;非正牌的 less-known or inferior brand: ～军 miscellaneous troops; troops of miscellaneous allegiances | ～货 goods of inferior brands

【杂品】zápǐn 商业上指各种日用的零星物品 odds and ends for daily use; groceries; sundry goods

【杂七杂八】zá qī zá bā 形容多而杂 mixed; assorted; miscellaneous; motley

【杂糅】záróu 指不同的事物混杂在一起 (of different things) mix; mingle; blend: 古今～ blending of the ancient and modern

【杂食】záshí ❶ 以各种动物植物为食物 omnivorous; eating different kinds of both meat and plants: ～动物 omnivorous animal; omnivore ❷〈书 *fml.*〉零食 snack; between-meal nibbles

【杂史】záshǐ 只记一事始末和一时见闻的史书或私家记述有关掌故的史书 history book that records the beginning and end of a single event, or gives an eyewitness account of a single event; private record of anecdotes

【杂事】záshì (～儿 záshìr)琐碎的事;杂七杂八的事 trivial matters; sundry matters

【杂书】záshū ❶ 科举时代指与科举考试无直接关系的书籍 book not directly related to the subjects of the imperial examination ❷ 指与本人专业无直接关系的书籍 book not directly related to one's profession

【杂耍】záshuǎ (～儿 záshuǎr)指曲艺、杂技等 miscellaneous theatrical performances; vaudeville, including ballad singing, acrobatics, comic dialogue, etc.

【杂税】záshuì 指在正税以外征收的各种各样的税 miscellaneous levies; sundry taxes: 苛捐～ exorbitant taxes and levies

【杂说】záshuō ❶ 各种各样的说法 different views; different opinions: ～不一 diverse versions of sth. ❷〈书 *fml.*〉零碎的论说文章 miscellaneous writings of argumentation ❸〈书 *fml.*〉正统学说以外的各种学说 unorthodox theory

【杂碎】zá·sui 煮熟切碎供食用的牛羊等的内脏 chopped cooked entrails of sheep, oxen, etc.: 牛～ chopped cooked ox entrails | 羊～ chopped cooked sheep entrails

【杂沓】zátà 杂乱 confused; disorderly: 门外传来～的脚步声。The clatter of disorderly footsteps could be heard outside the gate. also 杂遝 zátà

【杂遝】zátà same as 杂沓 zátà

【杂文】záwén 现代散文的一种,不拘泥于某一种形式,偏重议论,也可以叙事 essay; satirical essay; modern prose genre, which is not limited to one form, stresses argumentation and narrates stories as well

【杂务】záwù 专门业务以外的琐碎事务 odd jobs; sundry duties

【杂项】záxiàng 正项以外的项目 sundry items; miscellaneous items

【杂音】záyīn 人或动物的心、肺等或机器装置等因发生障碍或受到干扰而发出的不正常的声音 noise; heart murmur; abnormal noise produced by the heart of an animal or a human being, or by a machine that runs irregularly because of malfunction or interference

【杂院儿】záyuànr 有许多户人家居住的院子 compound shared by many households; also 大杂院儿 dàzáyuànr

【杂志】zázhì ❶ 刊物 magazine: 报章～ newspapers and magazines ❷ 零碎的笔记(多用做书名 oft. used in a book title) random notes; records

【杂质】zázhì 某种物质中所夹杂的不纯的成分 impurity; foreign matter or substance

【杂种】zázhǒng ❶ 不同种、属或品种的动物或植物杂交而生成的新品种。杂种具有上一代品种的特征。hybrid; cross-breed; new breed derived from cross-breeding among animals or plants of different species, genus or breeds, and maintaining the features of the last-generation breed ❷ 骂人的话(curse) bastard; son of a bitch

【杂字】zázì 汇集在一起的各类日常用字(多用做书名 oft. used in a book title) collection of words in common use:《农村四言～》*Book of Four-Character Rhymes for Rural Usage*

咱(喒、偺) zá [咱家](zájiā)我(多见于早期白话 oft. seen in early vernacular) I; me
☞ zán on p.2390 and ·zan on p.2391

砸 zá ❶ 用沉重的东西对准物体撞击;沉重的东西落在物体上 pound; tamp; thump against sth. using a heavy thing; (of a heavy object) drop on another object: ～核桃 crack walnuts | ～地基 tamp the foundation solid | 搬石头不小心,～了脚了。(He) moved a stone and carelessly dropped it on his foot. ❷ 打破 break; smash: 碗～了。The bowl is broken. ❸〈方 *dial.*〉(事情)失败 fail; lose; be defeated: 事儿办～了。The job was bungled. | 戏演～了。The performance was a fiasco.

【砸饭碗】zá fànwǎn 〈比喻 *fig.*〉失业 lose one's job; be dismissed; be unemployed; be fired; get sacked

【砸锅】zá//guō 〈方 *dial.*〉〈比喻 *fig.*〉办事失败 fail; fall through; be bungled: 让他去办这件事儿,准～。It would surely be a total failure if he were sent to deal with it.

【砸锅卖铁】zá guō mài tiě 〈比喻 *fig.*〉把自己所有的都拿出来 give away all one has; spend one's entire fortune

zǎ (ㄗㄚˇ)

咋(嚍) zǎ 〈方 *dial.*〉怎;怎么 how; why; what: ～样? How is it? | ～办? What shall we do? | 你～不去? Why aren't you going?
☞ zé on p.2399 and zhā on p.2403

zāi (ㄗㄞ)

灾(災) zāi ❶ 灾害 catastrophe; calamity; disaster: 旱～ drought | 水～ flood | 防～ take precautionary measures against natural disasters | 救～ provide relief and assistance for a disaster-stricken area; help people through a natural disaster | ～区 disaster-stricken area ❷ 个人遭遇的不幸 personal misfortune; ill luck; adversity: 招～惹祸 court disaster or invite trouble | 没病没～ good health and good luck

【灾害】zāihài 旱、涝、虫、雹、战争等所造成的祸害 catastrophe; calamity; disaster; damage caused by drought, floods, pests, hail, war, etc.

【灾患】zāihuàn 灾害;灾难 calamity; disaster; mischance; catastrophe

【灾荒】zāihuāng 指自然给人造成的损害(多指荒年 oft. referring to a lean year) damage caused by nature; famine due to crops failure: 闹～。Famine hit the area.

【灾祸】zāihuò 自然的或人为的祸害 disaster; calamity; catastrophe; natural or man-made adversity

【灾民】zāimín 遭受灾害的人 victims of a natural calamity; afflicted people

【灾难】zāinàn 天灾人祸所造成的严重损害和痛苦 suffering; calamity; disaster; catastrophe; severe damage and pain caused by natural disasters or man-made calamities: ～深重 disaster-ridden | 遭受～ be hit by a disaster; fall a victim to a disaster

【灾情】zāiqíng 受灾的情况 damages and losses caused by a disaster

【灾殃】zāiyāng 灾难;祸殃 suffering; calamity; disaster

【灾异】zāiyì 指自然灾害和某些特异的自然现象,如水灾、地震、日食等 natural disasters and unusual natural phenomena, e.g. floods, earthquakes, solar eclipses, etc.

甾 zāi 有机化合物的一类,广泛存在于动植物体内,一般具有重要的生理作用,如胆固醇、胆酸、维生素 D 和性激素等 steroid; organic compound widely found in bodies of animals and plants and usually having important physiological functions, e.g. cholesterol, cholic acid, Vitamin D, hormones, etc.; also 类固醇 lèigùchún

哉 zāi 〈书 *fml.*〉❶ 语气词,表示感叹[modal particle, used in exclamations]: 呜呼哀～! Alas! | 快～此风! Alas! What a pleasant breeze! ❷ 语气词,跟疑问词合用,表示疑问或反诘[modal particle, used after an interrogative to indicate doubt or to form a rhetorical question]: 何足道～! It is really not worth mentioning! | 如此而已,岂有他～!

Z

That's all there is to it!

栽[1] zāi ❶ 栽种 plant; grow: ～树 plant trees|～花 grow flowers ❷ 插上 erect; insert; plant: ～绒 tufted fabric|～刷子 tufting brush ❸ 硬给安上 impose sth. on sb.; force sth. on sb.: ～赃 plant stolen or contraband goods on sb.; fabricate a charge against sb.; frame sb.|～上了罪名 be falsely charged ❹ 栽子 young plant; seedling: 桃～ peach seedling

栽[2] zāi ❶ 摔倒;跌倒 tumble; fall; topple: ～了一跤。(He) fell down. ❷〈方 *dial.*〉〈比喻 *fig.*〉受挫 suffer a setback; be frustrated

【栽跟头】zāi gēn·tou ❶ 摔跤;跌倒 tumble; fall; topple ❷〈比喻 *fig.*〉失败或出丑 come to grief; come a cropper; be defeated

【栽培】zāipéi ❶ 种植,培养 cultivate; grow; tend: ～水稻 cultivate rice|～果树 plant fruit trees ❷〈比喻 *fig.*〉培养、造就人才 foster; train; educate: 感谢老师的～ thank one's teacher for education ❸ 官场中比喻照拂、提拔 help sb. advance in career; patronize

【栽绒】zāiróng 一种织物,把绒线织入以后割断,再剪平,绒都立着 tufted fabric, woven of woollen yarn, which is cut and smoothened so that the yarn stands up

【栽赃】zāi//zāng 把赃物或违禁物品暗放在别人处,诬告他犯法 frame sb.; fabricate a charge against sb.: ～陷害 plant a stolen article on sb. in order to frame him or her

【栽植】zāizhí 把植物的幼苗种在土壤中 plant; transplant: ～葡萄 transplant grapes

【栽种】zāizhòng 种植(花草树木等) plant or grow (flowers, grass, trees, etc.): ～苹果 plant apple trees

【栽子】zāi·zi 供移植的植物幼苗 young plant; seedling: 树～ tree seedling

䘚 zāi〈书 *fml.*〉same as 灾 zāi

zǎi (ㄗㄞˇ)

载[1] zǎi 年 year: 一年半～ six months to one year|三年五～ three to five years|千～难逢 occurring only once in a thousand years; once in a blue moon; rare

载[2] zǎi same as 记载 jìzǎi ①; 刊登 put down in writing; record: 登～ publish; carry|刊～ publish in a magazine|转～ reprint

☞ zài on p. 2389

宰[1] zǎi ❶ 主管;主持 control; rule; reign; be in charge of; govern: 主～ dominate; have the final say ❷〈古代 *arch.*〉官名 title of an official position: 县～ county magistrate|邑～ county magistrate

宰[2] zǎi ❶ 杀(牲畜、家禽等) slaughter; butcher (animals, poultry, etc.): 屠～ butcher|杀猪～羊 slaughter pigs and sheep ❷〈比喻 *fig.*〉向买东西或接受服务的人索取高价 overcharge; soak; fleece; charge more than a customer should pay: 挨～ be forced to pay more than one has to; be fleeced|～人 overcharge sb.

【宰割】zǎigē〈比喻 *fig.*〉侵略、压迫、剥削 invade, oppress and exploit: 不能任人～ not allow oneself to be trampled on

【宰杀】zǎishā 杀(牲畜、家禽等) slaughter; butcher (animals, poultry, etc.); put down: 禁止随意～耕牛。Slaughtering cattle at random is banned.

【宰牲节】Zǎishēng Jié 伊斯兰教重要节日之一,在伊斯兰教历12月10日。这一天,伊斯兰教徒要宰牛、羊、骆驼等献礼。*'Id al-Adha*; *'Id al-kurban*; important Islamic festival which falls on December 12 on the Islamic calendar, when Islamic people sacrificially slaughter cattle, sheep, camels, etc.; also 古尔邦节 Gǔ'ěrbāng Jié or 牺牲节 Xīshēng Jié

【宰相】zǎixiàng 我国古代辅助君主掌握国事的最高官员的通称 prime minister; chancellor; general term for the highest official in ancient China who helped a monarch in administering state affairs

崽(仔) zǎi〈方 *dial.*〉❶ 儿子 son ❷ 男青年 young man: 华～ young Chinese man|打工～ working man ❸ (～儿 zǎir)幼小的动物 young animal; whelp: 猪～儿 piglet

☞ 仔 zī on p. 2536 and zǐ on p. 2541

【崽子】zǎi·zi same as 崽 zǎi ③(多用做骂人的话 oft. curse)

zài (ㄗㄞˋ)

再 zài ❶〈副词 *adv.*〉a) 表示又一次(有时专指第二次 sometimes meaning 'again') once more; again; one more time: ～版 second impression of printing; second edition|～接～厉 work ceaselessly|一而～,～而三 over and over again; time and again; again and again|学习,学习,～学习。Study, study, and study again. 注意 **NOTE**: 表示已经重复的动作用'又',表示将要重复的动作用'再', 又 yòu is used to indicate repeated action, while 再 zài is used to indicate an action that will be repeated in future, e.g.: 这部书前几天我又读了一遍,以后有时间我还要～读一遍。I read the book once more several days ago, and I'll read it again when I have time. b) 表示更加 to a greater extent or degree: 高点儿,～高点儿 higher, still higher|～多一点儿就好了。It would be great if there was more. c) 表示如

果继续下去就会怎样［indicating what will happen if such is allowed to continue］：学习～不努力，就得留级了。You'll fail to go up to the next grade if you still don't study hard.｜离开车只剩半个钟头了，～不走可赶不上了。There is only half an hour left. We'll miss the train if we delay any longer. d)表示一个动作发生在另一个动作结束之后［indicating one action taking place after the completion of another］：咱们看完了这个节目～走。We'll leave after we watch the performance.｜你把材料整理好～动笔。Sort out the materials before setting pen to paper. e)表示另外有所补充［indicating additional information］：～则 moreover; in addition; furthermore; besides｜～不然 or; or else｜院子里种着迎春、牡丹、海棠、石榴，～就是玫瑰和月季。The garden has winter jasmine, peonies, crab apple trees, pomegranates, as well as roses and Chinese roses. ❷〈书 *fml.*〉再继续；再出现 continue; return; reappear：青春不～。One's youth never returns.｜良机难～。Opportunity knocks but once.

【再版】zàibǎn （书刊）第二次出版。有时也指第二次印刷。(of books) second edition; second printing; second impression

【再不】zài·bu 要不然 if not; or else; or：我打算让老吴去一趟，～让小王也去，俩人好商量。I'll send Lao Wu there; if that won't do, let Xiao Wang go too, so they can consult each other.

【再次】zàicì 第二次；又一次 second time; once more; once again：～获奖 win awards once again

【再度】zàidù 第二次；又一次 once more; second time; once again：机构～调整 re-adjust the structure｜谈判～破裂。Negotiations broke down once again.

【再会】zàihuì 再见 goodbye; see you (again); adieu; farewell; until we meet again

【再婚】zàihūn 离婚或配偶死后再结婚 remarry; marry again

【再嫁】zàijià （妇女）再婚 (of a woman) remarry

【再见】zàijiàn 〈客套话 *pol.*〉用于分手时 goodbye; see you again; so long

【再醮】zàijiào 〈旧时 *old*〉称寡妇再嫁 (of a widow) remarry

【再接再厉】zài jiē zài lì 一次又一次地继续努力 make persistent efforts; continue to exert oneself; work ceaselessly and unremittingly

【再三】zàisān 一次又一次 over and over again; time and again; again and again; repeatedly：～再四 over and over again｜言之～ repeat sth. time and again｜考虑～ consider over and over again｜～挽留 repeatedly urge sb. not to quit; press sb. to stay on

【再审】zàishěn ❶重新审查 review; examine again ❷法院对已经审理终结的案件依法重新审理 retrial; reopening of a case; fresh trial

【再生】zàishēng ❶死而复生 revive; rise again ❷机体的组织或器官的某一部分丧失或受到损伤后，重新生长。如创口愈合，水螅被切成两段后长成两个水螅等。regenerate; reproduce; regrow, or cause new tissue to regrow to replace lost or injured tissue, e.g. the healing of an wound or a polypus, which if cut into two, will grow into two polypi ❸对某种废品加工，使恢复原有性能，成为新的产品 reprocess; recycle; regenerate; process certain waste materials in order to recover its former function and become a new product：～纸 recycled paper｜～橡胶 regenerated or reclaimed rubber｜～材料 recycled material

【再生产】zàishēngchǎn 指生产过程不断重复和经常更新。有两种形式，即按原规模重复的简单再生产和在扩大的规模上进行的扩大再生产。reproduce; continuously repeat or renew production. Reproduction comes in two forms: simple reproduction, which is repeated production on the former production scale, and extended reproduction, which is production on an expanded production scale.

【再生父母】zàishēng fùmǔ 指对自己有重大恩情的人。多指救命的恩人。one's great benefactor; one's second parent, said with gratitude, often a person who has saved one's life, or showed great kindness; also 重生父母 chóngshēng fùmǔ

【再世】zàishì ❶来世 next life ❷〈书 *fml.*〉再次在世上出现 reappear; reincarnate; revive; same as 再生 zàishēng ①：华佗～ Hua Tuo reincarnated

【再衰三竭】zài shuāi sān jié《左传》庄公十年：'一鼓作气，再而衰，三而竭' *The Zuo Commentary·Duke Zhuang 10th Year*: 'The morale of warriors is aroused by the first roll of drums, depleted by the second, and exhausted by the third.' 形容士气低落，不能再振作 be dispirited; be weakened and demoralized

【再说】zàishuō ❶表示留待以后办理或考虑 talk about sth. later; not deal with sth. till some time later; put off until some time later：这事先搁一搁，过两天～。Let's put the matter aside for a couple of days. ❷表示推进一层 what's more; besides：去约他，来不及了，～他也不一定有工夫。It's too late to make an appointment with him; besides, he may not have time.

【再现】zàixiàn （过去的事情）再次出现 (of a past event) reappear; be reproduced

【再造】zàizào 重新给予生命（多用来表示对于重大恩惠的感激 oft. used to express one's gratitude for a major favour bestowed) give sb. a new lease of life：恩同～ favour tantamount to giving (me) a new lease of life

【再则】zàizé 表示更进一层或另外列举原因、理由 moreover; furthermore; besides; in addition: 兴修水利可灌溉农田,~还能发电。The construction of water conservancy works can irrigate the farm fields, and in addition, can generate electricity. | 他学习成绩差,原因是不刻苦,~学习方法也不对头。The reasons for his low grades lie not only in his laziness but also his improper methods.

【再者】zàizhě same as 再则 zàizé

在 zài ❶ 存在;生存 exist; be alive: 精神永~。The spirit lives on. | 留得青山~,不怕没柴烧。As long as green mountains exist, there will be no shortage of firewood. *or* While there is life, there is hope. | 父母都~。Both his parents are still around. ❷ 表示人或事物的位置 indicating where a person or a thing is: 我今天晚上不~厂里。I won't be in the factory tonight. | 你的钢笔~桌子上呢。Your pen is on the desk. ❸ 留在 remain: ~职 on the regular payroll | ~位 be on the throne ❹ 参加(某团体);属于(某团体) join or belong to (an organization): ~党 be a member of a party | ~组织 be a member of an organization ❺ 在于;决定于 lie in; depend on; rest with; rely on: 事~人为。Human effort is the decisive factor. | 学习好,主要~自己努力。Getting good results in one's studies lies mainly in hard work. ❻ '在'和'所'连用,表示强调,下面多连'不' [used together with 所 suǒ and usu. followed by 不 bù to indicate emphasis]: ~所不辞 will not decline under all circumstances | ~所不惜 regardless of cost or sacrifice | ~所不计 regardless of the risk; whatever the cost | ~所难免 be unavoidable; can hardly avoid ❼ 〈介词 *prep.*〉表示时间、处所、范围等 [indicating time, place, scope, etc.]: 事情发生~去年。It happened last year. | ~礼堂开会 hold a meeting in the auditorium | 这件事~方式上还可以研究。The ways to deal with this matter can be discussed. ❽ 正在 [indicating an action in progress]: 风~刮,雨~下。The wind is howling; the rain is falling. | 姐姐~做功课。Elder Sister is doing her homework.

【在案】zài'àn 公文用语,表示某事在档案中已经有记录,可以查考 (officialese) be recorded in archives; be on record: 记录~ be put (or placed) on record

【在编】zàibiān (人员)在编制之内 be on the payroll; be on the permanent staff: ~人员 those on the regular payroll; permanent staff | 他已退休,不~了。He's retired and not on the permanent staff.

【在册】zàicè (登记)在名册内 registered; on the name list: 登记~ registered | ~职工 staff member on a name list

【在场】zàichǎng 亲身在事情发生、进行的地方 be on the scene; be on the spot; be present: 事故发生时他不~。He was not present when the accident happened. | 当时~的人都可以作证。Anyone who was at the scene can testify.

【在行】zàiháng (对某事、某行业)了解底细,富有经验 be expert at sth.; know the ropes; excel in sth.; same as 内行 nèiháng ①: 修电器他十分~。He's good at repairing home appliances. | 做生意我可不~。I'm no expert at business.

【在乎】zài·hu ❶ 在于 lie in; rest with; depend on: 东西不~好看,而~实用。The value of a thing does not lie in its beautiful appearance but in its practicality. ❷ 在意;介意(多用于否定式 oft. used in the negative) care about; mind; take to heart: 满不~ could not care less; not care at all | 只要能学会,多学几天倒不~。I don't mind studying for a few more days as long as I can master it.

【在即】zàijí (某种情况)在最近期间就要发生 (of certain events) be near at hand; shortly; soon; be in sight: 毕业~ will soon be graduating | 大赛~。The competition will be held before long.

【在家】zàijiā ❶ 在家里;在工作或住宿的地方;没有出门 be at home; be in ❷ 对僧、尼、道士等'出家'而言,一般人都算在家 remain a layman, as opposed to 'leave one's family behind and become a monk, nun, Taoist, etc.': ~人 layperson; person of the earthly world

【在教】zàijiào ❶ 信仰某一宗教 believe in a religion ❷ 特指信仰伊斯兰教(esp.) believe in Islam; be a Muslim

【在劫难逃】zài jié nán táo 命中注定要遭受祸害,逃也逃不脱(迷信)。现在借指坏事情一定要发生,要避免也避免不了。(superstition) be doomed; be impossible to escape one's doom; what is destined cannot be avoided

【在理】zàilǐ 合乎道理;有理 reasonable; sensible; right: 老王这话说得~。What Lao Wang said is perfectly reasonable.

【在谱】zàipǔ (~儿 zàipǔr)(说话)符合实际或公认的准则 conform to the general norm; be to the point: 你看我说的~不~? Don't you think my view is to the point?

【在世】zàishì 活在世上;生存;存在 be living; exist; be alive: 当年的老人~的不多了。Not many old people of that time are living now.

【在逃】zàitáo (犯人)已经逃走,还没有捉到 (of a criminal) be at large; have escaped; be on the run: ~犯 criminal at large; fugitive; escaped convict

【在天之灵】zài tiān zhī líng 〈尊称 *honor.*〉逝世者的心灵、精神 soul or spirit of the deceased

【在望】zàiwàng ❶ 远处的东西在视线以内,可以望见 be within the range of vision; be in sight; be in view; be visible: 大雁塔隐隐～。The Greater Wild Goose Pagoda loomed in the distance. ❷ (盼望的好事情)即将到来,就在眼前 (of an expected good thing) will soon materialize; be round the corner; be in sight; be in the offing: 丰收～。A bumper harvest is in the offing.

【在位】zàiwèi ❶ 居于君主的地位;做君主 be on the throne; reign; be a monarch ❷ 居于官位。现多指居于某个领导岗位。hold an official post; be a leader

【在握】zàiwò 有把握;在手中 be in one's hands; be within one's grasp; be under one's control: 全局在胸,胜利～。With a clear picture of the overall situation in the mind, victory is near at hand.

【在下】zàixià 〈谦辞 *hum.*〉自称(多见于早期白话 oft. used in early vernacular) I: 先生过奖,～实不敢当。I'm flattered, and wish I could deserve your compliments. *or* It's really kind of you to say so, but it is more than I deserve.

【在先】zàixiān ❶ 从前;早先 formerly; in the past; before: ～我年纪小,什么事也不明白。I was young at the time, so I didn't understand anything. ❷ 预先;事先 in advance; beforehand: 不论做什么事,～都要有个准备。No matter what one does, one must make preparations beforehand.

【在心】zài//xīn 留心;放在心上 feel concerned; mind; be attentive: 你说什么,他都不～。No matter what you say, he just isn't concerned.

【在押】zàiyā (犯人)在拘留监禁中 (of a convict) be under detention; be in custody; be in prison

【在野】zàiyě 原指不担任朝廷官职,后来也借指不当政 not be in office; be out of office; be in opposition: ～党 opposition party; party not in office

【在业】zàiyè 指已经参加工作;就业 be employed; be on the job: ～人口 working population | ～工人 worker on the job

【在意】zài//yì 放在心上;留意(多用于否定式 oft. used in the negative) take notice of; care about; mind; take to heart: 这些小事,他是不大～的。He won't take such trifling matters to heart.

【在于】zàiyú ❶ 指出事物的本质所在,或指出事物以什么为内容 [used to point out the essence or contents of sth.] lie in; consist in: 先进人物的特点～他们总是把集体利益放在个人利益之上。A hallmark of advanced workers lies in that they always give priority to the collective interest over their own. ❷ 决定于 depend on; rest with; be determined by: 去不去～你自己。It's up to you to decide whether to go or not.

【在在】zàizài 〈书 *fml.*〉处处 everywhere; in all aspects; all over: ～皆是 can be seen everywhere

【在职】zàizhí 担任着职务 in office; incumbent; be at one's post; be on the job: ～干部 cadre at his or her post

【在座】zàizuò 在聚会、宴会等的座位上。泛指参加聚会或宴会。be seated at a meeting or a banquet; (in a broad sense) be present at a meeting or a banquet

载[1] zài ❶ 装载 carry; hold; be loaded with: ～客 carry passengers | ～货 be loaded with goods ◇～誉归来 return with great honour ❷ 充满(道路) along all the roads; everywhere along the way: 风雪～途。The snowstorm blocked the way. | 怨声～道。Discontent is rife. *or* Popular grievances are openly voiced. ❸ (Zài)姓 a surname

载[2] zài 〈书 *fml.*〉又;且 and; as well as; at the same time; while: ～歌～舞 sing and dance joyously

☞ zǎi on p. 2386

【载波】zàibō 在有线电和无线电技术中,把不直接发射的音频(低频)信号加在高频电波上,以便发出去,这种方法叫做载波 carrier wave; carrier; high-frequency electromagnetic wave modulated in amplitude or frequency to convey a signal

【载歌载舞】zài gē zài wǔ 又唱歌,又跳舞。形容尽情欢乐。sing and dance joyously; enjoy to one's heart's content

【载荷】zàihè same as 负荷 fùhè ②

【载体】zàitǐ ❶ 科学技术上指某些能传递能量或运载其他物质的物质。如工业上用来传递热能的介质,为增加催化剂有效表面,使催化剂附着的浮石、硅胶等都是载体。carrier; substance used to transfer energy or convey other substances, e.g. carriers that transfer heat, float-stone and silica gel and strengthen the appendiculate capacity of catalysts, etc. ❷ 承载知识或信息的物质形体 carrier; thing that carries knowledge or information: 语言文字是信息的～。Languages are the carriers of information.

【载运】zàiyùn 运载 transport; ship; carry: ～量 carrying capacity | ～货物 transport goods

【载重】zàizhòng (交通工具)负担重量 load; carrying capacity: ～量 loading capacity; dead-weight capacity | ～汽车 heavy-load truck; truck; lorry | 一节车皮～多少吨? How many tons is the loading capacity of a train wagon?

儎 zài ❶ 运输工具所装的东西 cargo; load: 卸～ unload; land a cargo (of goods) | 过～ be overloaded ❷ 〈方 *dial.*〉一只船装运的货物叫一儎 cargo carried by a ship

zān (ㄗㄢ)

篸(篸) zān 〈书 *fml*.〉 same as 簪 zān
☞ cǎn on p. 188

糌 zān [糌粑](zān·ba) 青稞麦炒熟后磨成的面。吃时用酥油茶或青稞酒拌和，捏成小团。是藏族人的主食。*zanba*; staple food for Tibetans, prepared by mixing roasted barley flour with buttered tea or barley wine into small balls

簪 zān ❶ (～儿 zānr)簪子 hairpin: 扁～ flat hairpin | 玉～ jade hairpin ❷ 插在头发上 wear (sth.) in one's hair: ～花 wear flowers in one's hair

【簪子】zān·zi 别住发髻的条状物，用金属、骨头、玉石等制成 hair-clasp; hairpin; oblong object to pin one's hair, made of metal, bone, jade, etc.

zán (ㄗㄢˊ)

咱(喒、偺) zán ❶ 咱们 we; us: 哥哥，～回家吧。Elder brother, let's go home. | ～穷人都翻身了。We poor people have stood up and become our own masters. ❷ 〈方 *dial*.〉我 I; me: ～不懂他的话。I don't understand his words.
☞ zá on p. 2385 and ·zan on p. 2391

【咱们】zán·men 〈代词 *pron*.〉 ❶ 总称己方(我或我们)和对方(你或你们) we or us (including both the speaker and the person or people spoken to): ～是一家人。We're family. | 你来得正好，～商量一下。You came at the right time. Let's discuss it. [注意] NOTE: 包括谈话的对方用'咱们'，不包括谈话的对方用'我们'，如：我们明天参加义务劳动，你要是没事，～一块儿去。不过说'我们'也可以包括谈话的对方。咱们 is used to include both the speaker and the person or persons spoken to while 我们 wǒ·men may refer to the speaker only or both the speaker and the person or persons spoken to, e.g.: We're going to take part in obligatory labour tomorrow. If you're free, let's go together. ❷ 借指我或你 borrowed to mean 'I' or 'you': ～是个直性子，说话不会曲里拐弯(指我)。I'm a straightforward person and won't beat around the bush when talking. | ～别哭，妈妈出去就回来(对小孩儿说，指你)。Don't cry. Mom will be back in a minute. (when a mother speaks to her child, *zan* here means 'you')

zǎn (ㄗㄢˇ)

拶(桚) zǎn 压紧 press hard; squeeze forcibly
☞ zā on p. 2383

【拶指】zǎnzhǐ 〈旧时 *old*〉用拶子夹手指的酷刑 torture in old China, of squeezing a person's fingers between sticks

【拶子】zǎn·zi 〈旧时 *old*〉夹手指的刑具 sticks for squeezing a person's fingers (as a torture in old China)

昝 Zǎn 姓 a surname

噆 zǎn 〈书 *fml*.〉 ❶ 叼；衔 hold in the mouth ❷ 咬；叮 bite; sting

攒(儹) zǎn 积聚；储蓄 accumulate; hoard; save; scrape up: 积～ save; collect bit by bit | ～粪 accumulate manure | 把节省下来的钱～起来。Put aside the money (we) saved.
☞ cuán on p. 331

趱 zǎn ❶ 赶(路)；快走(多见于早期白话 oft. used in early vernacular) hurry or rush through: 紧～了一程 rush through one leg of a journey ❷ 催促；催逼 urge; hasten: ～马向前 urge on a horse

zàn (ㄗㄢˋ)

暂 zàn ❶ 时间短(跟'久'相对 as opposed to 'long') of short duration; transient; brief: 短～ short; fleeting ❷ 暂时 temporary; transient; for the time being: ～停 suspend | ～住 stay with sb. temporarily | ～行条例 provisional regulation; interim regulation | ～不答复 put off replying | 工作～告一段落。The work has been brought to a temporary end.

【暂缓】zànhuǎn 暂且延缓 postpone; put off; defer: ～执行 put off the implementation | ～一时 postpone for the time being

【暂且】zànqiě 暂时；姑且 for the time being; for the moment; temporary; transient: ～如此。Let it be like this for the moment. | 这是后话，～不提。We'll come to this topic again later. *or* More on this topic later.

【暂时】zànshí 短时间之内 in a short period; temporary; transient; for the time being; for the moment: ～借用 borrow and use for a short time | 因翻修马路，车辆～停止通行。The road under reconstruction is temporarily closed to traffic.

【暂停】zàntíng ❶ 暂时停止 suspend; stop for the time being: ～施工。Construction is suspended. | 会议～。The meeting is adjourned. ❷ 某些球类比赛中指暂时停止比赛 time-out; temporary stop in certain ball games

【暂星】zànxīng 我国古代指新星 nova (as called in ancient China)

【暂行】zànxíng 暂时实行的(法令规章) provisional; temporary; interim (laws, rules and

Z

regulations)：～条例 provisional or interim regulation

趲 zàn〈书 *fml*.〉same as 暂 zàn

錾 zàn ❶ 在砖石上凿；在金银上刻 engrave on gold or silver; carve; chisel; incise: ～花 carve flowers or patterns | ～字 engrave characters | ～金 engrave in gold ❷ 錾子；錾刀 engraving tool; chisel; graver

【錾刀】zàndāo 雕刻金银用的小刀 graver; engraving tool; chisel

【錾子】zàn·zi 凿石头或金属的小凿子 chisel for cutting stone or metal; graver: 石～ chisel for cutting stone | 油槽～ oil groove chisel

赞(賛、❷❸讚) zàn ❶ 帮助 help; assist; aid: ～助 aid; assistance; support ❷ 称赞 applaud; acclaim; compliment; eulogize; extol; praise: ～许 praise; approve of; commend; endorse | ～扬 eulogize | ～不绝口 be full of praise; praise unceasingly ❸ 旧时的一种文体，内容是称赞人或物的 eulogy; old literary genre used to praise a person or as an ode to sth.: 像～ inscription eulogizing the subject of a portrait

【赞成】zànchéng ❶ 同意(别人的主张或行为) approve of; favour; agree with; assent; be for sth.; endorse (others' opinions or actions): ～这项提议的请举手。Raise your hand if you agree with this proposal. | 他的意见我不～。I don't buy his opinion. ❷〈书 *fml*.〉帮助使完成 help sb. finish sth.: ～其行 help accomplish the task

【赞歌】zàngē 赞美人或事物的歌曲或诗文 paean; hymn; song or poem in praise of a person or a thing: 唱～ sing the praises of | 英雄～ paean to the heroes

【赞礼】zànlǐ ❶〈旧时 *old*〉举行婚丧、祭祀仪式时在旁宣读仪式项目 perform the duty of master of ceremonies at a wedding, funeral or sacrificial rite ❷ 赞礼的人 master of ceremonies

【赞美】zànměi 称赞；颂扬 praise; eulogize: ～金色的秋景 praise the golden landscape of autumn | 助人为乐的精神受到人们的～。(His) readiness to help others is widely praised.

【赞美诗】zànměishī 基督教徒赞美上帝或颂扬教义的诗歌 hymn; psalm; canticle; chant; poem that Christian believers sing in praise of God and Christian doctrines; also 赞美歌 zànměigē

【赞佩】zànpèi 称赞佩服 esteem; admire; hold in esteem: 由衷～ admire from the bottom of one's heart

【赞赏】zànshǎng 赞美赏识 appreciate; admire; think highly of: 击节～ admire immensely; clap and applaud; show appreciation by beating time with one's hand

【赞颂】zànsòng 称赞颂扬 extol; eulogize; sing the praises of: ～祖国的大好河山 sing the praises of the beautiful landscape of one's motherland

【赞叹】zàntàn 称赞 gasp in (or with) admiration; highly praise: 演员高超的演技，令人～。People gasped with admiration at the superb skill of the performers.

【赞同】zàntóng 赞成；同意 approve of; agree with; endorse; consent; accede: 全厂职工一致～这项改革。All the staff members of the factory unanimously approved of this reform.

【赞许】zànxǔ 认为好而加以称赞 speak favourably of; praise; commend

【赞扬】zànyáng 称赞表扬 speak highly of; praise; commend; applaud: ～好人好事 sing the praises of kind people and good deeds | 孩子们爱护公共财物的事迹受到了人们的～。The deeds of children protecting public property won praise from the people.

【赞语】zànyǔ 称赞的话 praise; compliment; words of praise

【赞誉】zànyù 称赞 praise; acclaim; commend: 交口～ be widely acclaimed

【赞助】zànzhù 赞同并帮助(现多指拿出财物帮助 oft. referring to monetary or material aid) support; assistance; aid: ～单位 supporting unit | 这笔奖金全部用来～农村教育事业。The prize will be all used to support the cause of education in the countryside.

酂 Zàn 古地名，在今湖北光化一带 ancient name of a place in present-day Guanghua, Hubei Province

☞ Cuó on p. 339

濽 zàn〈方 *dial*.〉溅 splash; spatter: ～了一身水。Water splashed all over me.

瓒 zàn〈古代 *arch*.〉祭祀时用的玉勺子 jade ladle used at a sacrificial ceremony

·zan (·ㄗㄢ)

咱(噜、偺) ·zan〈方 *dial*.〉用在'这咱、那咱、多咱'里，是'早晚'两字的合音 [used in 这咱 zhè·zan, 那咱 nà·zan and 多咱 duō·zan, as a combined pronunciation of 早 zǎo and 晚 wǎn]

☞ zá on p. 2385 and zán on p. 2390

zāng (ㄗㄤ)

赃(贜、贓) zāng 赃物 stolen goods; booty; spoils; loot: 贼～ stolen goods; loot | 追～ recover stolen money or goods | 退～ disgorge the spoils | 贪～枉法 take bribes and bend the laws

【赃官】zāngguān 贪污、受贿的官吏 corrupt official; dishonest official

Z

【赃款】zāngkuǎn 贪污、受贿或盗窃得来的钱 embezzled money; accepted bribes; stolen money; illicit money: 追回～ recover illicit money

【赃物】zāngwù 贪污、受贿或盗窃得来的财物 bribe; stolen goods; booty; spoils

【赃证】zāngzhèng 可以用来证明贪污、受贿或盗窃事实的证据 evidence of bribery, embezzlement, theft or robbery

脏(髒) zāng 有尘土、汗渍、污垢等;不干净 dirty; filthy; unclean: ～衣服 dirty clothes ◇～话 obscene language

☞ zàng on p. 2392

【脏病】zāngbìng 性病的俗称 popular name for venereal disease

【脏话】zānghuà 下流的话 obscene, dirty or foul language; dirty word; swear word; four-letter word: 不说～ don't talk dirt; don't use filthy and dirty words

【脏土】zāngtǔ 尘土、垃圾等 rubbish; garbage; dust; dirt

【脏字】zāngzì (～儿 zāngzìr)粗俗下流的字眼儿 obscene word; swear word; dirty word; vulgar word: 说话别带～儿。Don't swear when talking. *or* Don't be foul-mouthed.

牂 zāng〈书 *fml.*〉母羊 ewe

【牂牁】Zāngkē 古代郡名,在今贵州境内 Zangke, name of an ancient prefecture in present-day Guizhou Province

【牂牂】zāngzāng〈书 *fml.*〉草木茂盛的样子 (of grass and trees) exuberant; luxuriant; lush: 其叶～。The leaves are lush.

臧 zāng ❶〈书 *fml.*〉善;好 good; right; kind ❷ (Zāng) 姓 a surname

〈古 *arch.*〉same as 藏 cáng

【臧否】zāngpǐ〈书 *fml.*〉褒贬;评论 appraise; comment on; judge; review: ～人物 pass judgment on a person; make comments on the merits and demerits of a person

zǎng (ㄗㄤˇ)

驵 zǎng〈书 *fml.*〉壮马;骏马 steed; stallion; fine horse; courser

【驵侩】zǎngkuài〈书 *fml.*〉马匹交易的经纪人。泛指经纪人。horse trader; horse-coper; (in a broad sense) broker

Z

zàng (ㄗㄤˋ)

脏(臟) zàng 内脏 internal organs of the body; bowels; entrails; guts; viscera: 心～ heart | 肾～ kidneys | 五～六腑 internal organs of the body; guts; viscera

☞ zāng on p. 2392

【脏腑】zàngfǔ〈中医 *Chin. med.*〉对人体内部器官的总称。心、肝、脾、肺、肾叫脏,胃、胆、大肠、小肠、膀胱等叫腑。viscera; internal organs of the body, consisting of the heart, liver, spleen, lungs and kidneys, which are known as 脏 zàng, as well as the stomach, gall, small and large intestines, bladder, etc., which are known as 腑 fǔ

奘 zàng ❶〈书 *fml.*〉壮大。用于人名,如唐代和尚玄奘。strong; robust; used in a person's name, as in 玄奘 xuánzàng, a famous monk of the Tang Dynasty ❷〈方 *dial.*〉说话粗鲁,态度生硬 rude; crude in manner; surly; boorish in manner and speech

☞ zhuǎng on p. 2525

葬 zàng ❶ 掩埋死者遗体 bury; inter: 埋～ bury | 安～ bury ❷ 泛指依照风俗习惯用其他方法处理死者遗体 (in a broad sense) disposal of the body of the deceased according to local customs and certain methods: 火～ cremation | 海～ sea-burial; burial at sea

【葬礼】zànglǐ 殡葬仪式 funeral; funeral or burial rites: 举行～ hold a funeral

【葬埋】zàngmái 埋葬 entomb; bury; inter

【葬身】zàngshēn 埋葬尸体,多用于比喻 (oft. fig.) be buried: 敌机～海底。The enemy plane was swallowed up by the waves of the sea.

【葬送】zàngsòng 断送 ruin; put an end to; wreck: 封建的婚姻制度不知～了多少青年的幸福。The feudal marriage system robbed many young people of their happiness.

藏[1] zàng ❶ 储存大量东西的地方 storage; depository: 宝～ hidden treasures; valuable deposits ❷ 佛教或道教的经典的总称 general term for Buddhist or Taoist scriptures: 道～ Taoist scriptures | 大～经 Tripitaka; complete collection of Buddhist scriptures

〈古 *arch.*〉same as 脏(臟) zàng

藏[2] Zàng ❶ 指西藏 Tibet: ～香 joss stick produced in Tibet | 川～公路 Sichuan-Tibet highway ❷ 藏族 Tibetan people: ～历 Tibetan lunar calendar | ～医 doctor in Tibetan medicine

☞ cáng on p. 190

【藏蓝】zànglán 蓝中略带红的颜色 purplish blue

【藏历】Zànglì 藏族的传统历法,是唐代从内地传过去的。基本上跟农历相同,但为了使十五那天一定是月圆以及宗教上的理由,往往把某一天重复一次,或把某一天减掉,例如有时有两个初五而没有初六等。藏历用五行和十二生肖纪年,如火鸡年、土狗年。Tibetan calendar; lunar calendar used by the Tibetan people, which came to Tibet from inland China during the Tang Dynasty, and is basically the same as the lunar calendar used by the Han Chinese except that, for religious reasons and to have the 15th day fall on a full moon, a certain day is perhaps repeated and another day deducted. For example, there are maybe two 5th days and no 6th day in certain months. The Tibetan lunar calendar is marked by the five elements of metal, wood, water, fire and earth, and the 12 animals representing the 12 Earthly Branches, hence the Year of the Fire Chicken and the Year of the Earth Dog.

【藏青】zàngqīng 蓝中带黑的颜色 dark blue

【藏戏】zàngxì 藏族戏曲剧种,流行于西藏地区 local Tibetan opera, popular in Tibetan areas

【藏香】zàngxiāng 西藏一带所产的一种线香,原料用檀香、芸香、艾等,颜色有黑、黄两种,藏族用来敬佛 joss stick made in Tibet from sandalwood, rue, wormwood, etc., in two colours of black and yellow, and offered to the Buddha as a sign of respect

【藏医】zàngyī ❶ 藏族的传统医学 traditional Tibetan medicine ❷ 用藏族传统医学理论和方法治病的医生 doctor who treats patients with traditional Tibetan medicine

【藏族】Zàngzú 我国少数民族之一,分布在西藏和青海、四川、甘肃、云南 Tibetan ethnic group; one of China's ethnic groups living in the Tibet Autonomous Region, and Qinghai, Sichuan, Gansu and Yunnan provinces

zāo (ㄗㄠ)

遭[1] zāo 遇到(多指不幸或不利的事 oft. disaster or misfortune) meet with; suffer; sustain: ～难 be killed|～殃 run into disaster|～了毒手 be killed; be murdered

遭[2] zāo (～儿 zāor)〈量词 *classifier*〉❶ 回;次 time; turn: 一～生,两～熟。Strangers at first meeting, friends by the second. *or* Green the first time, experienced the second. *or* Uncomfortable the first time, familiar the second.|一个人出远门,我还是第一～。This is the first time I am setting out on a long journey alone. ❷ 周;圈儿 round: 用绳子绕两～ circle the rope round it twice|跑了一～儿 run round once

【遭逢】zāoféng 碰上;遇到 meet with; come across; encounter: ～盛世 live in prosperous times; live in an age of prosperity|～不幸 suffer or meet with misfortune

【遭际】zāojì〈书 *fml.*〉❶ 境遇;经历 circumstances; lot ❷ same as 遭遇 zāoyù ①: ～艰危 be confronted with difficulties and dangers

【遭劫】zāo//jié 遇到灾难 meet with catastrophe; come face to face with calamity

【遭难】zāo//nàn 遭遇灾难;遇难 meet with misfortune; suffer disaster; be killed in an accident; be murdered

【遭受】zāoshòu 受到(不幸或损害) suffer; be subjected to; sustain; undergo: ～打击 suffer an attack|～失败 suffer a failure|身体～摧残。(His) health suffered.

【遭殃】zāo//yāng 遭受灾殃 suffer disaster; suffer

【遭遇】zāoyù ❶ 碰上;遇到(敌人,不幸的或不顺利的事等) meet with; encounter; run up against (an enemy, misfortune, difficulties, etc.): 我军先头部队和敌人～了。Our advance unit encountered the enemy.|工作中～了不少困难。(We've) encountered many difficulties in the work. ❷ 遇到的事情(多指不幸的) experience (oft. bitter); misfortune; bad luck: 不幸的～ bad luck; adversity|童年的～ bitter experience in one's childhood

【遭罪】zāo//zuì 受罪 endure hardships, tortures, rough conditions, etc.; have a difficult time

糟 zāo ❶ 做酒剩下的渣子 distillers' grains; grains; brewers' grains ❷ 用酒或糟腌制食物 pickle food in wine or with grain: ～肉 pickled meat|～鱼 pickled fish ❸ 腐烂;腐朽 rotten, decayed; worn out: 木头～了。The wood is rotten. ❹ 指事情或情况坏 in a wretched state; in a mess: 事情搞～了。(You)'ve made a pretty bad mess of the whole thing.|他身体很～,老生病。He is very frail and easily gets sick.

【糟改】zāogǎi〈方 *dial.*〉讽刺挖苦;戏弄 make caustic or ironic remarks; ridicule; make fun of; play tricks on

【糟糕】zāogāo 指事情、情况坏得很 how terrible; what bad luck; too bad; in a terrible mess: 真～,把钥匙锁在屋里,进不去了。Oh no, I've locked the key in the room and cannot get in.

【糟害】zāo·hài〈方 *dial.*〉糟蹋损害,多指禽兽糟蹋庄稼等 spoil; damage; lay waste to; make havoc of; (of birds or beasts) damage crops

【糟践】zāo·jian 糟蹋 spoil; lay waste to; ruin; waste; befool; trample on; insult: 别～粮食。Don't waste grain.|说话可不要随便～人。Don't casually insult people when you speak.

【糟糠】zāokāng 酒糟、米糠等粗劣食物,旧时穷人用来充饥 lees; pot ale; distillers' grains; husk; coarse food, e.g. lees, rice chaff, etc., eaten in old times by the poor to relieve hunger: ～之妻(指贫穷时共患难的妻子) wife of 'chaff and husk days' (who has shared her husband's hard lot)

【糟粕】zāopò 酒糟、豆渣之类的东西 waste matter; dross; dregs; distillers' grains; bean dregs;〈比喻 *fig.*〉粗劣而没有价值的东西 shoddy and flimsy thing: 弃其～,取其精华 discard (or get rid of) the dross and absorb (or select) the essence

【糟踏】zāo·tà same as 糟蹋 zāo·tà

【糟蹋】zāo·tà ❶ 浪费或损坏 waste; ruin; spoil; destroy: 这阵大风～了不少果子。The typhoon winds have damaged a great deal of fruit. | 小心剪裁，别把料子～了。Cut the material carefully, so as no to spoil it. ❷ 侮辱；蹂躏 insult; trample on; violate; rape ‖ also 糟踏 zāo·tà

【糟心】zāoxīn 因情况坏而心烦 vexed; annoyed; dejected: 偏这个时候车又坏了，真叫人～。The car broke down right at that moment; it was really annoying.

záo (ㄗㄠˊ)

凿[1] (**鑿**) záo ❶ 凿子 chisel: 扁～ flat chisel; plain chisel | 圆～ circular chisel ❷ 打孔；挖掘 bore a hole; chisel; dig: ～井 dig, sink or bore a well | ～一个窟窿 bore a hole

凿[2] (**鑿**) záo (也有读 also pronounced zuò)〈书 *fml.*〉卯眼 mortise; hole: 方枘圆～ square peg in a round hole; incompatible

凿[3] (**鑿**) záo (也有读 also pronounced zuò)〈书 *fml.*〉明确；真实 certain; sure; authentic: 确～ irrefutable; beyond doubt

【凿空】záokōng (也有读 also pronounced zuòkōng)〈书 *fml.*〉穿凿 forced; far-fetched; implausible: ～之论 far-fetched argument; irrelevant talk

【凿枘】záoruì (也有读 also pronounced zuòruì)〈书 *fml.*〉❶ 凿是卯眼，枘是榫头，凿枘相应 mortise and tenon;〈比喻 *fig.*〉彼此相合 compatible; in harmony ❷ 圆凿方枘的略语，比喻格格不入 short term for 圆凿方枘 yuán záo fāng ruì; (fig.) incompatible; square peg in a round hole; at variance with each other ‖ also 枘凿 ruìzáo

【凿岩机】záoyánjī 在岩石中开凿深孔用的风动工具，利用压缩空气做动力使活塞往复运动，冲击钎子。多用于打炮眼。rock drill; charge; tool used to drill holes in rocks, powered by compressed air to make pistons move back and forth, and hence its name; often used to make holes for dynamite; also 风钻 fēngzuàn

Z

【凿凿】záozáo (也有读 also pronounced zuòzuò)〈书 *fml.*〉确切；确实 authentic; reliable; true; certain; verified: 言之～ say sth. with certainty | ～有据 supported by irrefutable evidence

【凿子】záo·zi 手工工具，长条形，前端有刃，使用时用重物砸后端。用来挖槽或打孔。chisel; long hand tool with a blade at the front to chamfer or bore a hole by using a hammer to hit its back end

zǎo (ㄗㄠˇ)

早 zǎo ❶ 早晨 morning: 清～ early morning | ～饭 breakfast | 从～到晚 from morning to night; from dawn till dusk ❷ 很久以前 long ago: 他～走了。He left long ago. | 这件事我们～商量好了。We'd already discussed this matter long before. ❸ 时间在先的 (as in a time sequence) former; previous; early: ～期 early time; early phase; early stage | ～稻 early rice ❹ 比一定的时间靠前 earlier than scheduled or planned; beforehand; in advance; early: ～熟 early ripening; early maturing | ～婚 marrying too early; early marriage | 你～点儿来。You should come early. | 忙什么，离开演还～呢。Don't worry, it's still too early for the performance to begin. ❺ 问候的话，用于早晨见面时互相招呼 [greeting words, used to greet each other in the morning]: 老师～! Good morning, teacher!

【早半天儿】zǎobàntiānr〈方 *dial.*〉中午以前；上午 in the morning; before noon; also 早半晌儿 zǎobànshǎngr

【早操】zǎocāo 早晨做的体操 morning exercises

【早茶】zǎochá 早晨吃的茶点 morning tea: 粤式～ Guangdong-style breakfast

【早产】zǎochǎn 怀孕28周后，胎儿尚未足月就产出。多由孕妇子宫口松弛、胎膜早破或患严重疾病等引起。premature delivery; (of a baby) be born before the end of the full term of gestation, often caused by laxness of the uterus, early breaking of the caul, or other serious ailments

【早场】zǎochǎng 戏剧、电影等在上午演出的场次 morning show (at a cinema, theatre, etc.)

【早晨】zǎo·chen 从天将亮到八、九点钟的一段时间。有时从午夜十二点以后到中午十二点以前都算是早晨。morning; period of time from dawn to eight or nine o'clock, or the period from midnight to noon

【早春】zǎochūn 春季的早期；初春 early spring

【早稻】zǎodào 插秧期比较早或生长期比较短、成熟期比较早的稻子 early (season) rice; rice that is planted early, or has a short growth period, and ripens early

【早点】zǎodiǎn 早晨吃的点心；早饭 breakfast; snack eaten in the morning

【早饭】zǎofàn 早晨吃的饭 breakfast

【早婚】zǎohūn 身体未发育成熟或未达到法定结婚年龄而结婚 marry underage or before one becomes eligible for marriage

【早年】zǎonián ❶ 多年以前；从前 many years ago; in the past: ～这里没见过汽车。There were no cars here in the past. ❷ 指一个人年轻的时候 when one is young; at a tender age: ～丧父 lose one's father when one is young

【早期】zǎoqī 某个时代、某个过程或某个人一生的最初阶段 early stage; early phase; initial stage of an era, a process, or a person's life: 清代～ early Qing Dynasty | 注意～病人的治疗 stress early treatment to a patient | 他～的作品，大多描写农村生活。His early works mostly described country life.

【早期白话】zǎoqī báihuà 指唐宋至五四运动前口语的书面形式 early vernacular; vernacular used from the Tang and Song dynasties to the May 4th Movement of 1919

【早起】zǎo·qi〈方 *dial.*〉same as 早晨 zǎo·chen

【早秋】zǎoqiū 秋季的早期；初秋 early autumn

【早日】zǎorì ❶ 早早儿；时间提早 at an early date; early; soon: ～完工 complete the work as soon as possible | 祝你～恢复健康。I hope you'll recover as soon as possible. ❷ 从前；先前 in the past; previously: 他人老了，也失去了～的那种威严了。He's getting old and has lost his former stateliness.

【早上】zǎo·shang same as 早晨 zǎo·chen

【早市】zǎoshì ❶ 早晨做买卖的市场 morning market: 逛～ go to the morning market ❷ 早晨的营业 morning business: 一个～有三千元的营业额。Morning business can bring a turnover of 3,000 yuan

【早熟】zǎoshú ❶ 生理学上指由于脑上体退化过早，引起性腺过早发育，从而使生长加速，长骨和骨骺(hóu)提早融合的现象。早熟儿童常比同龄儿童长得高，但到成年时，长得反而比常人矮。precocity; physiological phenomena of a child growing unnaturally fast, and the long bone and epiphysis inosculating unnaturally early due to the premature growth of the sex glands, caused by the premature degradation of the pineal body. A precocious child grows taller than his or her peers but will be shorter than average at maturity ❷ 指农作物生长期短、成熟较快 early maturing; early ripening; (of crop) have a short growing period and ripen quickly: ～品种 early-maturing variety; early variety

【早衰】zǎoshuāi (生物体)提前衰老 (of organisms) premature senility or decrepitude; early ageing

【早霜】zǎoshuāng 晚秋时降的霜 early frost; frost in late autumn

【早退】zǎotuì (工作、学习或参加会议)未到规定时间提前离开 leave earlier than scheduled (from work, study or a meeting); leave early: 上班不得随意迟到～。Coming late for work and leaving early will not be permitted.

【早晚】zǎowǎn ❶ 早晨和晚上 morning and evening: 他每天～都练太极拳。He practises *taijiquan* every morning and evening. ❷ 或早或晚 sooner or later: 这事瞒不了人，～大家都会知道的。(We) cannot hide the matter forever. Sooner or later, people will know. ❸ 时候 time: 多～(多咱) time | 他一清早就走了，这～多半已经到家了。He left in the early morning; he's perhaps at home by this time. ❹〈方 *dial.*〉指将来某个时候 some time in the future; some day: 你～上城里来，请到我家里来玩。When you come to town some day in the future, please come to hang out at my place.

【早先】zǎoxiān 以前；从前 previously; before; in the past: 看你写的字，比～好多了。Your handwriting looks much better than before.

【早已】zǎoyǐ ❶ 很早已经；早就 long ago; for a long time: 你要的东西，我～给你准备好了。I've prepared what you wanted a long time ago. ❷〈方 *dial.*〉早先；以前 previously; before; in the past: 现在大家用钢笔写字，～都用毛笔。Today everyone uses pens to write but in the past people all used brushes.

【早育】zǎoyù 过早地生育 early child-bearing

【早早儿】zǎozǎor 赶快；提早 as early as possible; well in advance: 要来，明天～来。If you want to come, then come early tomorrow. | 决定办，就～办。Since we've decided to do it, let's do it as soon as possible.

【早造】zǎozào 收获期较早的作物 early-harvested crop

枣(棗) zǎo ❶ 枣树，落叶灌木或乔木，幼枝上有成对的刺，叶子卵形或长圆形，花黄绿色。结核果，暗红色，卵形、长圆形或球形，味甜，可以吃。jujube (*Zizyphus*); date; deciduous bush or tree, having pairs of thorns on its tender twigs, egg-shaped or oval leaves, yellowish green flowers, yielding egg-, oval- or ball-shaped dark red drupe fruit, which is sweet and edible ❷ (～儿 zǎor)这种植物的果实 date; fruit of this tree

【枣红】zǎohóng 像红枣儿的颜色 purplish red; claret

【枣泥】zǎoní 把枣儿煮熟后去皮去核捣烂制成的泥状物，做馅儿用 jujube paste; mashed date or jujube, peeled and pitted, used as filling: ～月饼 moon cake with jujube paste filling

【枣子】zǎo·zi〈方 *dial.*〉same as 枣 zǎo ②

蚤 zǎo 跳蚤 flea

〈古 *arch.*〉same as 早 zǎo

澡 zǎo 洗(身体) wash (one's body): 洗～ take a bath; take a shower | 擦～ rub oneself down with a damp towel; take a sponge bath | ～盆 bathtub

【澡盆】zǎopén 洗澡用的盆 bathtub

【澡堂】zǎotáng 供人洗澡的地方(多指营业的机构 oft. run as a business) public bath; bathhouse; also 澡堂子 zǎotáng·zi

Z

【澡塘】zǎotáng ❶ same as 浴池 yùchí ① ❷ same as 澡堂 zǎotáng

璪 zǎo〈古代 *arch.*〉皇冠前下垂的装饰，是用彩色丝线穿起来的成串的玉石 ornamental strings of silk-threaded jade and stone hanging on the front of a crown

藻 zǎo ❶ 藻类植物 algae：水～ algae | 海～ algae ❷ 泛指生长在水中的绿色植物，也包括某些水生的高等植物，如金鱼藻、狸藻等 aquatic plants, including certain higher aquatic plants such as hornwort and bladderwort ❸ 华丽的文辞 flowery language：辞～ ornate diction

【藻井】zǎojǐng 宫殿、厅堂的天花板上一块一块的装饰，多为方格形，有彩色图案 caisson ceiling; ceiling of a palace or a hall with square decorative colour pictures

【藻类植物】zǎolèi zhíwù 隐花植物的一大类，由单细胞或多细胞组成，用细胞分裂、孢子或两个配子体相结合进行繁殖。植物体没有根、茎、叶的区分，绝大多数是水生的，极少数可以生活在陆地的阴湿地方。主要有红藻、褐藻、绿藻、蓝藻等几种。algae; a family of cryptogam, single-celled or multi-celled, multiplying by cell division, spores or two gametes combining, having no distinction between roots, stems and leaves. Most types of algae live in water and a very few live in dank areas on land. Main types include red algae, brown algae, green algae, blue algae, etc.

【藻饰】zǎoshì〈书 *fml.*〉修饰（多指文章）embellishments in writing：词句朴实无华，不重～ simple and straightforward language free of literary embellishment

zào（ㄗㄠˋ）

皂（皁） zào ❶ 黑色 black：～鞋 black shoes | ～白 black and white; right and wrong ❷ 差役 yamen runner：～隶 yamen runner ❸ 肥皂 soap：香～ toilet soap | 药～ medicated soap

【皂白】zàobái 黑白 black and white;〈比喻 *fig.*〉是非 right and wrong：～不分 make no distinction between right and wrong

【皂化】zàohuà 原指用油脂在碱的作用下制取肥皂，现泛指酯在碱的作用下水解成羧酸盐和醇 saponification; process of turning fat or oil into soap by reaction with an alkali; (in a broad sense) converting an ester to carboxylate and alcohol by reaction with an alkali

灶（竈） zào ❶ 用砖、坯、金属等制成的生火做饭的设备 kitchen range; cooking stove; equipment made of bricks, blocks of soil and metal, for making a fire and cooking：炉～ stove | 煤气～ gas stove ❷ 借指厨房 kitchen ❸ 指灶神 Kitchen God：祭～ make offerings to the Kitchen God | 送～ see off the Kitchen God

【灶火】zào·huo〈方 *dial.*〉❶ 厨房 kitchen ❷ same as 灶 zào ①：～上蒸了一锅饭。A pot of rice is steaming on the stove.

【灶神】Zàoshén 迷信的人在锅灶附近供的神，认为他掌管一家的祸福财气 Kitchen God; god a superstitious person pays homage to near the kitchen, believing that he controls a family's fortune; also 灶君 Zàojūn and 灶王爷 Zàowángyé; ☞ 祭灶 jì//zào on p. 921

【灶膛】zàotáng 灶内烧火的地方 chamber of a kitchen range or a stove

【灶头】zào·tou〈方 *dial.*〉same as 灶 zào ①

【灶屋】zàowū〈方 *dial.*〉厨房 kitchen

埠 zào〈方 *dial.*〉山坳 col

唣（唕） zào ☞［啰唣］(luózào) on p. 1278

造[1] zào ❶ 做；制作 make; build; manufacture; create; construct：创～ create | 建～ build; construct | ～船 construct a boat | ～纸 manufacture paper | ～预算 draw up (or make) a budget | ～名册 compile a register of names ❷ 假编；捏造 invent; cook up; concoct; fabricate：～谣 cook up a story; spread a rumour

造[2] zào ❶ 指相对两方面的人，法院里专用于诉讼的两方 one of the two parties in a legal agreement or a lawsuit：两～ both parties | 甲～ first party ❷ 农作物的收成或收成的次数 crop; time of harvesting：早～ early crop | 晚～ late crop | 一年三～皆丰收。(We) reaped three bumper crops this year.

造[3] zào ❶ 前往；到 go to; arrive at：～访 pay a visit to sb.'s house; call on | 登峰～极 reach great heights; reach the peak of perfection ❷ 成就 achievement; attainment; accomplishment：～诣 academic achievement; artistic accomplishments | 深～ pursue advanced studies; do further specialized training ❸ 培养 train; cultivate：可～之才 talented person of promise; promising young person

【造次】zàocì〈书 *fml.*〉❶ 匆忙；仓促 hurried; hasty：～之间 in a hurry; in a moment of haste ❷ 鲁莽；轻率 rash; impetuous; impertinent; indiscrete; imprudent; flippant：～行事 act rashly | 不可～。Don't be so impetuous.

【造反】zào//fǎn 发动叛乱；采取反抗行动 rise in rebellion; rebel; revolt; take action in resistance

【造访】zàofǎng〈书 *fml.*〉拜访 pay a visit or call; call on：登门～ call at sb.'s house; pay sb. a visit

【造福】zàofú 给人带来幸福 bring benefit to; benefit; do good for：～后代 bring benefit to; benefit | 为人民～ work for the benefit or well-being of the people

【造化】zàohuà ❶ 自然界的创造者，也指自然 the Creator; Nature ❷ 创造，化育 create; nurture; breed

【造化】zào·hua 福气；运气 good luck; good fortune：有～ be born under a lucky star; be lucky

【造价】zàojià 建筑物、铁路、公路等修建的费用或汽车、轮船、机器等制造的费用 cost for constructing buildings, railways, highways, etc., or for manufacturing cars, ships, machines, etc.：降低～ reduce the cost

【造就】zàojiù ❶ 培养使有成就 bring up; train; cultivate：～人才 train competent personnel ❷ 造诣；成就（多指青年人的 oft. of young people）accomplishment; achievement; attainment：在技术上很有～。(He)'s made great accomplishments in technology.

【造句】zào//jù 把词组织成句子 make a sentence

【造林】zào//lín 在大面积的土地上种植树苗，培育成为森林 afforestation; plant trees on a large stretch of land and cultivate it into a forest

【造孽】zào//niè ❶〈佛教用语 *Budd.*〉做坏事（将来要受报应）commit a sin; do evil (to be punished in the future) ❷〈方 *dial.*〉可怜 poor; pitiable; pitiful：这孩子从小没了娘，真～。What a poor child! He lost his mother at a very tender age. ‖ also 作孽 zuò//niè

【造物】zàowù 古人认为有一个创造万物的神力，叫做造物 divine force that created the universe, as believed by ancient people

【造物主】zàowùzhǔ 基督教徒认为上帝创造万物，因此称上帝为造物主 the Christian God; the Creator (as Christians believe that God created the universe)

【造像】zàoxiàng 用泥塑成或用石头、木头、金属等雕成的形象 statue; image sculpted from clay, stone, wood, metal, etc.

【造型】[1] zàoxíng ❶ 创造物体形象 modelling; mould-making：～艺术 plastic arts ❷ 创造出来的物体的形象 model; mould; create image of an object; form：这些玩具～简单，生动有趣。These toys are simple in form, yet vivid and interesting. ‖ also 造形 zàoxíng

【造型】[2] zàoxíng 制造砂型 moulding

【造型艺术】zàoxíng yìshù 占有一定空间、构成有美感的形象、使人通过视觉来欣赏的艺术，包括绘画、雕塑、建筑等 plastic arts; art forms that occupy a defined space and form aesthetic images pleasing to the human eye, including painting, sculpture, architecture, etc.; also 美术 měishù

【造谣】zào//yáo 为了达到某种目的而捏造消息，迷惑群众 cook up a story; spread a rumour; fabricate news to confuse listeners in order to achieve a certain purpose：～生事 start a rumour to create trouble; stir up trouble by rumour-mongering | ～中伤 spread slanderous rumours

【造诣】zàoyì 学问、艺术等所达到的程度（academic, artistic, etc.）attainment or accomplishment：～很高 of great attainments

【造影】zàoyǐng 通过口服或注射某些X射线不能透过的药物，使某些器官在X射线下显示出来，以便检查疾病 radiography; X-ray imaging of certain organs through patients imbibing or being injected with certain medicine that the X-ray cannot penetrate：钡餐～ barium-meal radiography

【造作】zàozuò 制造；制作 make; manufacture

【造作】zào·zuo 做作 affected; artificial; unnatural：矫揉～ be affected in manner

慥 zào [慥慥]〈书 *fml.*〉忠厚诚恳的样子 honest and sincere

噪(❷譟) zào ❶ 虫或鸟叫（of insects or birds）chirp：蝉～ chirping of cicadas | 鹊～ chirping of a magpie | 群鸦乱～。Flocks of crows were cawing. ❷ 大声叫嚷 make an uproar; clamour：聒～ make an uproar ❸（名声）广为传扬 become well known：名～一时 be very popular for a period of time | 声名大～ win great fame

【噪声】zàoshēng 在一定环境中不应有而有的声音。泛指嘈杂、刺耳的声音。noise; din; discordant sound in certain environments; also 噪音 zàoyīn

【噪音】zàoyīn ❶ 音高和音强变化混乱、听起来不谐和的声音。是由发音体不规则的振动而产生的（区别于'乐音' as compared with 'music'）noise; discordant low and high sounds, produced by the irregular vibration of sounding objects ❷ same as 噪声 zàoshēng

簉 zào〈书 *fml.*〉副的；附属的 secondary; subsidiary：～室（指妾）concubine

燥 zào 缺少水分；干燥 dry; lacking water; arid：～热 hot and dry | 山高地～。It is arid in the high mountains.

【燥热】zàorè（天气）干燥炎热（of weather）dry and hot：这里冬季干冷，夏季～。Winters here are dry and cold, while summers are dry and hot.

躁 zào 性急；不冷静 rash; impetuous; restless：烦～ irritable; agitated; upset; restless | 急～ impetuous; rash; impatient | 不骄不～ neither arrogant nor rash; neither conceited nor impetuous | 性子～ hot-tempered; quick-tempered

【躁动】zàodòng ❶ 因急躁而活动 move restlessly; be jittery：一听这话，心中顿时～起来，坐立不安。When (he) heard this, (he) became instantly agitated as if (he) had ants in his pants. ❷ 不停地跳动 keep moving; pulsate; throb：胎儿～。The fetus kept moving up and down in the womb.

Z

zé (ㄗㄜˊ)

则[1] zé ❶ 规范 standard; norm; criterion: 准～ criterion; standard | 以身作～ set an example by one's own conduct ❷ 规则 rule; decree; regulation: 总～ general rules | 细～ procedural provisions | 法～ law; rule ❸〈书 *fml*.〉效法 take as an example; imitate; emulate; follow ❹〈量词 *classifier*〉用于分项或自成段落的文字的条数 item; paragraph or piece of writing: 试题三～ three examination questions | 新闻两～ two news items | 寓言四～ four fables

则[2] zé〈书 *fml*.〉❶〈连词 *conj*.〉a)表示两事在时间上相承 [indicating one action follows another]: 每一巨弹堕地,～火光迸裂。Each fall of the huge bomb was accompanied by an explosion of light and fire. b)表示因果或情理上的联系 [indicating relationship between cause and effect]: 欲速～不达。More haste, less speed. *or* Haste makes waste. | 物体热～胀,冷～缩。Objects expand when heated and contract when cooled. c)表示对比 [indicating contrast]: 旧的制度已经腐朽,新的制度～如旭日东升。The old system is decaying, while the new one is rising like the morning sun in the eastern sky. d)用在相同的两个词之间表示让步 [used between two identical words to indicate concession]: 好～好,只是太贵。Good as it is, it's too expensive. ❷ 用在'一、二(再)、三'等后面,列举原因或理由 [used after 一 yī, 二(再) èr(zài) and 三 sān to enumerate causes or reasons]: 墨子在归途上,是走得较慢了,一～力乏,二～脚痛,三～干粮已经吃完,难免觉得肚子饿,四～事情已经办妥,不像来时的匆忙。Mozi walked slowly on his way back because, first, he was tired; second, his feet hurt; third, he was running out of solid food and naturally felt hungry; and fourth, he was not in as much a hurry as when he came because he had finished his task. ❸〈书 *fml*.〉是;乃是 be: 此～余之过也。This is my fault.

【则声】zéshēng 做声 make a sound; utter a word: 不敢～ dare not utter a word

责 zé ❶ 责任 duty; responsibility; liability; obligation: 职～ duty | 负～ take responsibility; be responsible | 尽～ do one's duty; fulfil one's responsibility | 专～ specific responsibility | 保卫祖国,人人有～。It is every citizen's duty to safeguard our motherland. ❷ 要求做成某件事或行事达到一定标准 demand; exact; require sb. to finish a thing or reach certain standard: ～成 enjoin; instruct; charge | 求全～备 demand perfection; nit-pick | ～人从宽,～己从严 be tolerant towards others and be strict with oneself ❸ 诘问;质问 ask; interrogate; question closely; call sb. to account: ～问 ask reprovingly; call sb. to account | ～难 censure; blame ❹ 责备 accuse; blame; remonstrate; reproach: 斥～ scold in a severe tone
〈古 *arch*.〉same as 债 zhài

【责备】zébèi 批评指摘 accuse; blame; remonstrate; reproach: 受了一通～ be blamed | ～几句就算了。Just give him a few reproaches, and then leave it at that.

【责编】zébiān 责任编辑的简称 abbr. for 责任编辑 zérèn biānjí

【责成】zéchéng 指定专人或机构负责办好某件事 put a special person or an organization in charge of sth.: ～公安部门迅速破案 instruct the public security department to crack the case as soon as possible

【责罚】zéfá 处罚 punish; fine

【责怪】zéguài 责备;埋怨 blame; accuse; remonstrate; reproach: 是我没说清楚,不能～他。Don't blame him; it was me who didn't make it clear.

【责令】zélìng 责成(某人或某机构)做成某事 instruct (sb. or some institution) to finish sth.; order; enjoin; charge: ～有关部门查清案情 order relevant departments to make a clear investigation of the case

【责骂】zémà 用严厉的话责备 scold; rebuke; dress down: 父亲～了他一顿。His father gave him a good dressing down.

【责难】zénàn 指摘非难 censure; reproach; blame: 备受～ be accused in all possible ways

【责任】zérèn ❶ 分内应做的事 duty; responsibility; obligation: 尽～ do one's duty; fulfil one's task ❷ 没有做好分内应做的事,因而应当承担的过失 responsibility for a fault; failure to fulfil an obligation: 追究～ ascertain where the responsibility lies

【责任编辑】zérèn biānjí 出版部门负责对某一稿件进行审阅、整理、加工等工作的编辑人员 copy editor; editor who is charge of checking and approving a manuscript, etc., and coordinating the entire editing process prior to publication; 简称 abbr. 责编 zébiān

【责任感】zérèngǎn 自觉地把分内的事做好的心情 sense of responsibility; sense of duty; also 责任心 zérènxīn

【责任事故】zérèn shìgù 由于工作上没有尽到责任而造成的事故 accident due to negligence; accident involving criminal or civil liability

【责问】zéwèn 用责备的口气问 call or bring sb. to account; ask in a reproachful tone: 厉声～ call sb. to account in a severe tone

【责无旁贷】zé wú páng dài 自己的责任,不能推卸给别人 be duty-bound; have a responsibility one cannot shirk (贷 *dai*: 推卸 shift; shirk)

【责有攸归】zé yǒu yōu guī 责任各有归属(推卸

不了 unshirkable) responsibility rests where it belongs

择(擇) zé 挑选 select; choose; pick: 选～ choose; select | ～善而从 choose and embrace what is good | 饥不～食。Hunger finds no fault with the cooking. *or* Beggars can't be choosers. | 两者任～其一 choose either of the two

☞ zhái on p.2407

【择吉】zéjí 指为婚嫁、丧葬、店铺开业等挑选好日子 choose or select an auspicious day (for a wedding, funeral, opening of business, etc.): ～迎娶 select an auspicious day for the wedding | ～开张 select an auspicious day for opening a business

【择交】zéjiāo 选择朋友 choose friends: 慎重～ choose one's friends with care

【择偶】zé'ǒu 选择配偶 choose one's spouse

【择期】zéqī 选择日期 select a day or time: ～完婚 select a day for the wedding ceremony

【择优】zéyōu 选择优秀的 select the superior (person or thing); select the best: ～录取 employ or enroll on the basis of competitive merit; enroll the best

咋 zé 〈书 *fml.*〉咬住 bite; grip between one's teeth

☞ zǎ on p.2385 and zhā on p.2403

【咋舌】zéshé 〈书 *fml.*〉形容吃惊、害怕,说不出话 be struck dumb; be left speechless or breathless in surprise or fear: 闻者～。The listeners were all struck dumb.

迮 zé ❶〈书 *fml.*〉狭窄 narrow: ～狭 narrow ❷ (Zé) 姓 a surname

泽(澤) zé ❶ 聚水的地方 pool; pond; swamp: 沼～ marsh; swamp | 湖～ lake | 深山大～ jumble of mountains and big lakes ❷ 湿 humid; wet; moist; damp: 润～ moisten ❸ 金属、珠玉等的光 gloss; sheen; lustre of metals, pearls, jade, etc.: 光～ lustre; gloss; sheen | 色～ colour and lustre ❹ 恩惠 favour; beneficence; largesse; kindness: 恩～ favour; kindness | ～及枯骨(施恩惠及于死人)。Benevolence reaches even the deceased.

【泽国】zéguó 〈书 *fml.*〉❶ 河流、湖泊多的地区 land that abounds in rivers and lakes: 水乡～ watery region; area that abounds in rivers and lakes ❷ 受水淹的地区 inundated area; flooded area: 沦为～ become submerged; become inundated

啧 zé 形容咂嘴声 click of the tongue; smack of the lips

【啧有烦言】zé yǒu fán yán 很多人说不满意的话 complaints from a number of people; complaints all around

【啧啧】zézé ❶ 形容咂嘴或说话声 clicking the tongue; chattering: ～称羡 be profuse or generous in one's praise | 人言～。There is a great deal of public criticism. ❷〈书 *fml.*〉形容鸟叫的声音 chirping: 雀声～。Sparrows are chirping.

帻 zé 古代的一种头巾 man's headdress in ancient China

笮 Zé 姓 a surname

☞ zuó on p.2572

舴 zé [舴艋](zéměng)〈书 *fml.*〉小船 small boat

箦 zé 〈书 *fml.*〉床席 bed mat made of woven strips of bamboo

赜 zé 〈书 *fml.*〉精微;深奥 profound; subtle; abstruse: 探～索隐 search for hidden meanings; explore what is subtle and abstruse

齰(齚) zé 〈书 *fml.*〉咬 bite

zè (ㄗㄜˋ)

仄[1] zè ❶狭窄 narrow: 逼～ narrow; cramped ❷ 心里不安 upset; uneasy: 歉～ feel sorry or apologetic

仄[2] zè 指仄声 oblique tones

【仄声】zèshēng 指古四声中的上、去、入三声(区别于'平声' as compared with 'level tone') oblique tone, such as the falling-rising tone, the falling tone and the rising tone in classical Chinese pronunciation

昃 zè 〈书 *fml.*〉太阳偏西 sun inclining to the west; afternoon

侧 zè same as 仄[2] zè

☞ cè on p.195 and zhāi on p.2406

zéi (ㄗㄟˊ)

贼[1] zéi ❶ 偷东西的人 thief; burglar ❷ 做大坏事的人(多指危害国家和人民的人 oft. person who hurts the interest of his or her country and people) traitor; enemy; evildoer: 工～ scab; strike-breaker | 卖国～ traitor ❸ 邪的;不正派的 wily; crooked; wicked; evil; furtive: ～心 evil intention or design | ～眉鼠眼 look like a sly old fox; wear a thievish expression | ～头～脑 thievish-looking; furtive ❹ 狡猾 crafty; sly; cunning; deceitful: 老鼠真～。Rats are really cunning. ❺〈书 *fml.*〉伤害 injure; harm; maim: 戕～ harm; injure

贼[2] zéi 〈方 *dial.*〉〈副词 *adv.*〉很;非常(多用于令人不满意的或不正常的情况 oft. used to endicate dissatisfaction or abnormality) extremely; disagreeably; exceedingly: ～冷 terribly cold | ～亮 uncomfortably bright

【贼风】zéifēng 指从檐下或门窗缝隙中钻进的风 wind that blows in from under the eaves or

Z

through cracks in doors or windows

【贼喊捉贼】zéi hǎn zhuō zéi 自己是贼还喊捉贼 thief crying 'Stop thief';〈比喻 *fig.*〉为了逃脱罪责,故意混淆视听,转移目标 deliberately confuse what others see and hear so as to distract their attention and to shirk one's responsibility for an offense

【贼寇】zéikòu 强盗。也指入侵的敌人。robber; bandit; housebreaker; invader; aggressor

【贼眉鼠眼】zéi méi shǔ yǎn 形容神情鬼鬼祟祟 wear a thievish look; look like a sly old fox

【贼人】zéirén ❶ 偷东西的人 thief; burglar ❷ 干坏事的人 evildoer

【贼死】zéisǐ〈方 *dial.*〉用作补语,表示程度极深,使人难于忍受[used as a complement to indicate degree of seriousness or unbearableness] extremely: 累得~ extremely tired; completely exhausted | 气了个~ extremely angry

【贼头贼脑】zéi tóu zéi nǎo 形容举动鬼鬼祟祟 thievish; furtive; stealthy

【贼心】zéixīn 做坏事的念头;邪心 evil design; evil intention: ~不死 refuse to give up one's evil design; still harbour ill intentions

【贼星】zéixīng 流星的俗称 popular name for 流星 liúxīng

【贼眼】zéiyǎn 神情鬼祟、不正派的眼睛 shifty eyes; furtive glance

【贼赃】zéizāng 盗贼偷到或抢到的财物 stolen goods; booty; spoils: 搜出~ seek out stolen goods

【贼子】zéizǐ〈书 *fml.*〉危害国家、残害百姓的坏人 traitor; person who harms the country and oppresses the people: 乱臣~ rebellious subjects and undutiful son; traitors and usurpers

【贼走关门】zéi zǒu guān mén〈比喻 *fig.*〉出了事故才采取防范措施 shut the gate after the cows have gone; take preventive measures after harm is done; also 贼去关门 zéi qù guān mén

鲗 zéi [乌鲗](wūzéi) same as 乌贼 wūzéi

zěn (ㄗㄣˇ)

怎 zěn 怎么 why; how: 你~不早说呀? Why didn't you say so earlier? | 任务完不成,我~能不着急呢? How can I refrain from worrying when the task isn't done?

【怎地】zěn·di same as 怎的 zěn·di

【怎的】zěn·di〈方 *dial.*〉怎么;怎么样 what; why; how: 大哥~不见? How come I don't see Elder Brother? | 我偏不去,看你能把我~? What can you do with me if I just don't go? also 怎地 zěn·di

【怎么】zěn·me〈疑问代词 *interrog. pron.*〉❶ 询问性质、状况、方式、原因等[used to enquire about the nature, condition, manner, cause, etc., of sth.]: 这是~回事? What's the matter? | 这个问题该~解决? How shall we resolve this problem? | 他~还不回来? Why hasn't he come yet? ❷ 泛指性质、状况或方式[used to indicate the general nature, condition or manner of sth.]: 你愿意~办就~办。Do as you like. ❸ 有一定程度(用于否定式 oft. in the negative)[used to indicate inadequacy]: 这出戏他刚学,还不~会唱(=不大会唱)。He's just started to learn the aria, so he's still not able to sing it well yet.

【怎么样】zěn·meyàng〈疑问代词 *interrog. pron.*〉❶ 怎样 how about; what about ❷ 代替某种不说出来的动作或情况(只用于否定式,比直说委婉 euph., only used in the negative)[replace an unnamed action or condition]: 他画得也并不~(=并不好)。He doesn't paint particularly good either. *or* He's not much of a painter either. | 那是他一时的糊涂,也不好~他(=责罚他)。Since he was so confused at the time we couldn't be too hard on him.

【怎么着】zěn·me·zhe〈疑问代词 *interrog. pron.*〉❶ 询问动作或情况[used to enquire about actions or conditions]: 你~? How about you? | 我们都报名参加了,你打算~? All of us signed up for it. What about you? | 她半天不做声,是生气了还是~? She didn't utter a word for a long time. Was she angry or what? ❷ 泛指动作或情况[referring generally to actions or conditions]: 一个人不能想~就~。One cannot just do what one pleases.

【怎奈】zěnnài 无奈 but; however: 办法虽好,~行不通。Good as the method is, it is unworkable.

【怎样】zěnyàng〈疑问代词 *interrog. pron.*〉❶ 询问性质、状况、方式等[used to enquire about the nature, condition, manner, etc., of sth.]: 你们的话剧排得~了? What about the play you're rehearsing? | 步兵和炮兵~配合作战? How shall the infantry and artillery cooperate in the battle? ❷ 泛指性质、状况或方式[referring to general nature, condition or manner of sth.]: 要经常进行回忆对比,想想从前~,再看看现在~。It is necessary to frequently remember the past, look hard at the present, and compare between them. | 人家~说,你就~做。Do as you're told. ‖ also 怎么样 zěn·meyàng

zèn (ㄗㄣˋ)

谮 zèn〈书 *fml.*〉诬陷;中伤 frame a case against; falsely charge; slander; calumniate: ~言 slander; calumny

zēng（ㄗㄥ）

曾 zēng ❶ 指中间隔两代的亲属关系 relationship between great-grandchildren and great-grandparents：～祖 great-grandfather｜～孙 great-grandson ❷（Zēng）姓 a surname 〈古 *arch.*〉same as 增 zēng

☞ céng on p. 198

【曾孙】zēngsūn 孙子的儿子 great-grandson

【曾孙女】zēngsūn·nǚ（～儿 zēngsūn·nǚr）孙子的女儿 great-granddaughter

【曾祖】zēngzǔ 祖父的父亲 great-grandfather

【曾祖母】zēngzǔmǔ 祖父的母亲 great-grandmother

增 zēng ❶ 增加 increase；add；aggrandize；augment；enhance；gain：～高 increase one's height；become taller or higher｜～强 augment；enhance｜～兵 throw in more troops；augment one's forces；reinforce｜有～无减 keep growing；keep increasing｜产量猛～。Output increased sharply. ❷（Zēng）姓 a surname

【增补】zēngbǔ 加上所缺的或漏掉的（人员、内容等）；增添补充 augment；supplement；add (personnel，content，etc.) that is lacking or omitted：～本 enlarged edition｜人员最近略有～。The staff has been slightly augmented recently.

【增产】zēng//chǎn 增加生产 increase production：努力～ work hard to increase production｜～节约 increase production and practise economy｜～措施 measures to increase production

【增订】zēngdìng 增补和修订（书籍内容）revise and enlarge（the contents of a book）：～本 revised and enlarged edition

【增多】zēngduō 数量比原来增加 grow in number or quantity；increase；become larger：轻工业产品日益～。There is an increase in light industrial products with each passing day.

【增幅】zēngfú 增长的幅度 increasing range；growth rate：产值～不大。The growth rate of the output value is not large.

【增高】zēnggāo ❶ 增加高度 get higher；rise；increase：身量～ grow in height｜水位～。The water level rose. ❷ 提高 improve；elevate；heighten；increase：～地温 increase the ground temperature

【增光】zēng//guāng 增添光彩 add lustre to；do credit to；add to the prestige of：为国～ do credit to one's country；bring glory to one's country

【增辉】zēnghuī 增添光彩 add lustre to；do credit to：～生色 add lustre to

【增加】zēngjiā 在原有的基础上加多 increase；raise；add；augment：～品种 increase the variety of sth.｜～抵抗力 build up one's resistance to disease｜在校学生已由八百～到一千。The number of students at the school has increased from 800 to 1,000.

【增进】zēngjìn 增加并促进 enhance；promote；further；amp up：～友谊 promote or further friendship｜～健康 improve one's health｜～食欲 whet one's appetite

【增刊】zēngkān 报刊逢纪念日或有某种需要时增加的篇幅或另出的册子 supplement（to a newspaper or periodical）；supplementary issue；enlarged edition or supplementary issue to newspapers and periodicals on commemorative days or to meet certain demands：新年～ supplementary issue for the New Year｜国庆～ supplementary National Day issue

【增强】zēngqiáng 增进；加强 strengthen；heighten；enhance；reinforce：～体质 build up one's health｜～信心 heighten one's confidence｜实力大大～。Its strength has been substantially reinforced.

【增色】zēngsè 增添光彩、情趣等 add colour to；add beauty to；add lustre to：新修的假山为公园～不少。The newly built artificial hill has made the park more beautiful.

【增删】zēngshān 增补和删削 alterations；additions and deletions：新版本的文字略有～。Some modifications were made in the new edition.

【增设】zēngshè 在原有的以外再设置 establish an additional or new（organization，unit，course，etc.）：～门市部 set up a salesroom｜～选修课 offer selective courses

【增生】zēngshēng 生物体某一部分组织的细胞数目增加，体积扩大，例如皮肤经常受摩擦，上皮和结缔组织变厚 hyperplasia；proliferation；multiplication；cells of certain tissue of an organism increasing in quantity and expanding in bulk，e. g. the epidermis and connective tissues becoming thicker due to frequent rubbing of the skin；also 增殖 zēngzhí

【增收】zēngshōu 增加收入 increase income：～节支 increase revenue，and cut or reduce expenditure

【增添】zēngtiān 添加；加多 add；increase；augment：～设备 get additional equipment｜～麻烦 put sb. to trouble

【增益】zēngyì ❶ 增加；增添 increase；add ❷ 放大器输出功率与输入功率比值的对数，用来表示功率放大的程度。也指电压或电流的放大倍数。gain；logarithm of the ratio of output power to input power of an amplifier，used to indicate the degree of power amplification；also the amount of voltage or electric current being amplified

【增援】zēngyuán 增加人力、物力来支援（多用于军事 oft. used in military matters）reinforce：火速～ send or dispatch reinforcements

at top speed|～部队 reinforcements; reinforcing unit

【增长】zēngzhǎng 增加;提高 increase; rise; grow: ～知识 broaden or enrich one's knowledge|～才干 enhance or develop one's abilities|产值比去年约～百分之十。Output value has increased by about 10 per cent over last year.

【增值】zēngzhí 资产价值增加 rise (or increase) in value; appreciation; increment; value added: ～税(以企业的增值额为征税依据的税种) value added tax (VAT, tax levied on the basis of the increment of an enterprise)

【增殖】zēngzhí ❶ 增生 hyperplasia; proliferation; multiplication ❷ 繁殖 breed; reproduce; multiply; propagate: ～率 rate of propagation; rate of increase|～耕牛 breed cattle

憎 zēng 厌恶;恨 hate; detest; abhor: ～恶 detest; abhor; loathe|爱～分明 be clear about what to love and what to hate|面目可～ repulsive or repellent look

【憎称】zēngchēng 表示憎恨、厌恶的称呼,如鬼子 term of condemnation; derogatory name for sb. one hates or loathes, e.g. 'devil'

【憎恨】zēnghèn 厌恶痛恨 detest; hate; loathe: 热爱人民,～敌人。Love the people and hate the enemy.

【憎恶】zēngwù 憎恨;厌恶 abhor; loathe; abominate; be disgusted with; detest: 令人～ detestable

缯 zēng 古代对丝织品的统称 ancient term for silk fabrics

☞ zèng on p. 2402

罾 zēng 一种用木棍或竹竿做支架的方形鱼网 square-shaped fishing net supported by wooden or bamboo sticks

矰 zēng〈古代 *arch.*〉射鸟用的拴着丝绳的箭 arrow tied with silk string and used to shoot at birds

zèng (ㄗㄥˋ)

综 zèng (旧读 formerly pronounced zòng) 织布机上使经线交错着上下分开以便梭子通过的装置 heddle; heald; part of a loom that divides the warp threads to let the shuttle pass through

☞ zōng on p. 2554

锃 zèng 器物经擦或磨后,闪光耀眼 (of utensils, etc.) shiny, after being polished: ～光 shiny|～亮 shiny

【锃光瓦亮】zèng guāng wǎ liàng 锃亮 shiny: 铜火锅擦得～的。A good shine was put on the bronze hotpot.

【锃亮】zèngliàng 形容反光发亮 shiny: 通明～ transparent and shiny|皮鞋擦得～。The pair of leather shoes has been polished to a shine.

缯 zèng〈方 *dial.*〉绑;扎 tie; bind; fasten: 竹竿儿裂了,把它～起来。The bamboo pole is cracked and has to be bound together.

☞ zēng on p. 2402

赠 zèng 赠送 give as a present; present as a gift; donate: 捐～ donate|～阅 complimentary copy; (of a book) given free by the publisher|～言 words of advice or encouragement|～款 donation

【赠答】zèngdá 互相赠送、酬答 present each other with gifts, poems, etc.

【赠礼】zènglǐ 礼物 gift; present: 接受～ accept a gift

【赠品】zèngpǐn 赠送的物品 (complimentary) gift; give-away

【赠送】zèngsòng 无代价地把东西送给别人 give as a present; present as a gift: ～生日礼物 give a birthday present

【赠言】zèngyán 分别时说的或写的勉励的话 words of advice or encouragement given to a friend at parting: 临别～ words of encouragement given at parting

【赠阅】zèngyuè 编辑或出版机构把自己出的书刊赠送给人 complimentary copy; (of a book, periodical, etc.) given free by the publisher

甑 zèng ❶ 古代炊具,底部有许多小孔,放在鬲(lì)上蒸食物 ancient earthen implement for steaming food, with many small holes at the bottom ❷ 甑子 rice steamer ❸ 蒸馏或使物体分解用的器皿 implement for distilling water or breaking things down: 曲颈～ retort; vessel with a long tapering neck that is bent down, used for distillation

【甑子】zèng·zi 蒸米饭等的用具,略像木桶,有屉子而无底 rice steamer that is bottomless and shaped somewhat like a wooden bucket

zhā (ㄓㄚ)

扎(❸紥、紮) zhā ❶ 刺 prick; push a needle into: ～手 prick the hand|～针 give (or have) acupuncture treatment ❷〈方 *dial.*〉钻(进去) dive (into): ～猛子 dive|扑通一声,他就～进水里去了。With a splash, he dived into the water.|～到人群里 disappear in(to) a crowd ❸ 驻扎 be stationed; be quartered: ～营 pitch a camp; camp

☞ zā on p. 2383 and zhá on p. 2403

【扎堆】zhāduī (～儿 zhāduīr)(人)凑集到一处 (of people) gather around; get together; congregate: ～聊天 chat in groups; get together to gossip

【扎耳朵】zhā ěr·duo (声音或话)听着令人不舒服;刺耳 (of sound or words) grate or jar on the ear; be ear-piercing; be unpleasant;

sound harsh：电锯的声音真～。The electric saw made an ear-piercing racket.｜这些泄气的话，我一听就～。Such discouraging words jar on my ears.

【扎根】zhā//gēn ❶ 植物的根向土壤里生长 take root；(of a plant) grow roots into the ground ❷〈比喻 *fig*.〉深入到人群或事物中去，打下基础 be rooted in；take or strike root (among the masses or in sth.)；make a foundation：～基层 take root in the grass-roots｜他在农村扎了根。He settled down in the countryside.

【扎花】zhā//huā〈方 *dial*.〉(～儿 zhā//huār)刺绣 embroider

【扎猛子】zhā měng·zi〈方 *dial*.〉游泳时头朝下钻到水里 dive；swim with one's head in the water

【扎煞】zhā·shā〈方 *dial*.〉same as 挓挲 zhā·shā

【扎实】zhā·shi ❶ 结实 sturdy；strong；robust：把行李捆～了。Bind the luggage tightly. ❷(工作、学问等)实在；塌实 (of work, study, etc.) solid；sound；down-to-earth；firm：功底～ has sound basic knowledge｜干活儿～ do a solid piece of work｜没有听到确实的消息，心里总不～。My mind won't be at ease until (I) receive news of confirmation.

【扎手】zhā//shǒu ❶ 刺手 prick the hand：玫瑰花梗有刺，留神～。The rose is thorny；mind you don't prick your hands. ❷〈比喻 *fig*.〉事情难办 (of an affair) difficult to handle；thorny：事情～。This is really a hard nut to crack.

【扎眼】zhāyǎn ❶ 刺眼 dazzling；offending to the eye；loud；garish：这块布的花色太～。This cloth is too garish. ❷ 惹人注意(含贬义 derog.)offensively conspicuous：她这身穿戴实在～。She's dressed really too loudly.

【扎营】zhā//yíng 军队安营驻扎 (of troops) pitch a camp；camp

【扎针】zhā//zhēn 用特制的针刺入穴位治疗疾病 give (or have) acupuncture treatment；sticking of specialized needles into the skin during acupuncture to treat an ailment；☞ 针灸 zhēnjiǔ on p. 2434

吒 zhā 用于神话中人名，如金吒、木吒等 used in names of mythical beings, e.g. 金吒 jīnzhā，木吒 mùzhā, etc.
☞ 咤 zhà on p. 2405

咋 zhā ☞ below
☞ zǎ on p. 2385 and zé on p. 2399

【咋呼】zhā·hu〈方 *dial*.〉❶ 吆喝 shout in a blustering voice；cry out loudly：你瞎～什么？Why are you shouting so loudly? ❷ 炫耀；张扬 show off；make a fuss；be fussy about ‖ also 咋唬 zhà·hu

挓 zhā [挓挲](zhā·shā)〈方 *dial*.〉(手、头发、树枝等)张开；伸开 (of hands, branches, etc.) spread；stretch out；(of hair) stand on end；also 扎煞 zhā·shā

查(查) zhā ❶ ☞ 山查 shānzhā on p. 1671 ❷ (Zhā)姓 a surname
☞ chá on p. 203

奓 Zhā 奓山、小奓河、小奓湖，都在湖北 Zhashan Mountain, Xiaozha River and Xiaozha Lake, all in Hubei Province
☞ zhà on p. 2405

哳 zhā ☞ [啁哳](zhāozhā) on p. 2422

揸(摣、䶥) zhā〈方 *dial*.〉❶ 用手指撮东西 pick up sth. with the fingers；take a pinch of sth. ❷ 把手指伸张开 spread one's fingers：～开五指 spread one's five fingers

喳 zhā ❶〈旧时 *old*〉仆役对主人的应诺声 [used by servants in old times to indicate polite attentiveness] aye ❷〈拟声词 *onom*.〉：喜鹊～～地叫。Magpies are tweeting.
☞ chā on p. 201

渣 zhā (～儿 zhār) ❶ same as 渣滓 zhā·zǐ ①：油～儿 scrap｜豆腐～ soya-bean residue after making bean curd ❷ 碎屑 broken bits；crumb；dross；chipping：面包～儿 crumbs

【渣滓】zhā·zǐ ❶ 物品提出精华后剩下的东西 dregs；sediment；residue；leftover after the essence has been taken out ❷〈比喻 *fig*.〉品质恶劣对社会起破坏作用的人，如盗贼、骗子、流氓 dregs；riff-raff；bad person who is harmful to society, e.g. thief, swindler or ruffian：社会～ dregs of society

【渣子】zhā·zi 渣 dregs；sediment；residue；broken bits：甘蔗～ bagasse｜点心～ cake crumbs

楂(樝) zhā ☞ 山楂 shānzhā on p. 1671
☞ chá on p. 204

劄 zhā same as 扎 zhā ①③
☞ zhá on p. 2404

齇(皻) zhā 鼻子上的红斑，就是酒渣鼻的渣 blotchy redness on the nose (from drinking)

zhá (ㄓㄚˊ)

扎 zhá [扎挣](zhá·zheng)〈方 *dial*.〉勉强支撑 struggle to (maintain)；deal with sth. with difficulty (due to physical weakness)：病人～着坐了起来。The patient struggled to sit up.
☞ zā on p. 2383 and zhā on p. 2402

札 zhá ❶〈古代 *arch*.〉写字用的小而薄的木片 thin piece of wood used for writing on in ancient China ❷ 信件 letter；correspondence：书～ letter；correspondence｜信～ letter；correspondence｜手～ personal letter

【札记】zhájì 读书时摘记的要点和心得 reading notes or commentary; important points or comments written down when reading; also 劄记 zhájì

轧 zhá 压(钢坯) roll (billet): ～钢 steel rolling
☞ gá on p.618 and yà on p.2197

【轧钢】zhá//gāng 把钢坯压制成一定形状的钢材 steel rolling; steel that moulds billets into certain shapes

【轧辊】zhágǔn 轧机上的主要装置,是一对转动方向相反的辊子,两个辊子之间形成一定形状的缝或孔,钢坯由缝或孔中通过,就轧成钢材 roll; roller; major installation on a rolling mill consisting of a pair of cylinders that revolve in opposite directions, between which steel ingots pass to become rolled steel

【轧机】zhájī 轧钢用的机器。主要由几组轧辊构成,钢坯通过轧辊就成为一定形状的钢材。rolling mill; machine on which ingots pass between groups of rollers to give them a certain thickness and a cross-section form

闸(牐) zhá ❶ 水闸 floodgate; sluicegate; water-locks: 开～放水 open the sluice ❷ 把水截住 dam up a stream, river, etc.: 水流得太猛,～不住。The water runs too swiftly to dam it up. ❸ 制动器的通称 general term for 制动器 zhìdòngqì: 踩～ step on the brakes ❹ 电闸 switch: 拉～限电 switch it off so as not waste electricity

【闸盒】zháhé (～儿 zháhér)电路中装有保险丝的小盒 fuse box; small box that contains the fuse in an electrical circuit

【闸口】zhákǒu 闸门开时水流过的孔道 sluiceway

【闸门】zhámén 水闸或管道上调节流量的门 sluice-gate; lock-gate; watergate; gate to regulate water volume; throttle valve along pipelines

炸(煠) zhá ❶ 烹调方法,把食物放在煮沸的油里弄熟 fry in deep fat or oil; deep-fry: ～糕 fried cake | ～油条 fried dough ❷〈方 *dial.*〉焯(chāo) scald: 把菠菜～一下 scald the spinach in hot water
☞ zhà on p.2405

铡 zhá ❶ 铡刀 (hand) hay cutter; fodder chopper ❷ 用铡刀切 cut up with a hay cutter: ～草 chop hay

【铡刀】zhádāo 切草或切其他东西的器具,在底槽上安刀,刀的一头固定,一头有把,可以上下活动 (hand) hay or straw cutter; fodder chopper; knife fixed at the bottom groove at one end and with a handle at the other so that one can move it up and down, for cutting hay or other things

喋 zhá ☞ [唼喋](shàzhá) on p.1667
☞ dié on p.451

劄 zhá same as 劄子 zhá·zi
☞ zhā on p.2403

【劄记】zhájì same as 札记 zhájì

【劄子】zhá·zi〈古代 *arch.*〉一种公文,多用于上奏。后来也用于下行。official documents in ancient China (used to refer to documents submitted to one's superior and later also to documents dispatched to subordinates)

zhǎ (ㄓㄚˇ)

苲 zhǎ [苲草](zhǎcǎo) 指金鱼藻等水生植物 water weed (*Anacharis*); water plant, e.g. hornwort, etc.

拃(搩) zhǎ ❶ 张开大拇指和中指(或小指)来量长度 span; measure by stretching one's thumb and middle finger or little finger: 用手～了～桌面。(He) used his hands to measure the surface of the desk. ❷〈量词 *classifier*〉表示张开的大拇指和中指(或小指)两端间的距离 span; distance between one's stretching thumb and middle finger or little finger: 这块布有三～宽。This cloth is three spans wide.

眨 zhǎ (眼睛)闭上立刻又睁开 (of eyes) blink; wink: ～眼 blink one's eyes | 眼睛也不～一～ without batting an eyelid; one's eyes wide open

【眨巴】zhǎ·ba〈方 *dial.*〉眨 blink: 孩子的眼睛直～,想是困了。The child is blinking his eyes; he must be sleepy.

【眨眼】zhǎ//yǎn ❶ 眼睛快速地一闭一睁 blink; wink; twinkle: ～示意 gesture by winking one's eye ❷ 形容时间极短;瞬间 very short time; in a wink; in the twinkling of an eye: 小燕儿在空中飞过,一～就不见了。The swallow flew across the sky and disappeared in a twinkling of an eye.

砟 zhǎ (～儿 zhǎr) same as 砟子 zhǎ·zi: 道～ small stone; cobblestone | 焦～ coking cinders | 炉灰～儿 cinder

【砟子】zhǎ·zi 小的石块、煤块等 tiny fragments of stone, coal, etc.

鲊 zhǎ ❶ 腌制的鱼 salted fish ❷ 用米粉、面粉等加盐和其他作料拌制的切碎的菜,可以贮存 chopped vegetables seasoned with salted ground rice, wheat flour and other condiments, easy to store: 茄子～ eggplants in salted ground rice and other condiments | 扁豆～ beans in salted ground rice and other condiments

【鲊肉】zhǎròu〈方 *dial.*〉米粉肉 pork steamed with ground glutinous rice

鲝 zhǎ ❶ same as 鲊 zhǎ ❷ same as 苲 zhǎ。鲝草滩 (Zhǎcǎotān),地名,在四川 Zhacaotan, name of a place in Sichuan

Province

zhà(ㄓㄚˋ)

乍 zhà ❶ 刚刚开始;起初 first; for the first time: 分别多年,～一见都不认识了。After so many years of separation, (we) didn't recognize each other at first. ❷ 忽然;突然 suddenly; abruptly; all of a sudden: ～冷～热 (temperature) change abruptly | 山风～起。The mountain wind rose suddenly. ❸ 同'奓',张开 same as 奓 zhà; spread; extend: ～翅 spread wings ❹ (Zhà) 姓 a surname

【乍猛的】zhàměng·de 〈方 *dial.*〉突然;猛然 suddenly; unexpectedly: 他～问我,倒想不起来了。When he asked me so suddenly, I had a mental black and couldn't give an answer.

诈 zhà ❶ 欺骗 cheat; swindle; deceive; befool: 欺～ cheat; swindle | ～财 get money by fraud; cheat or swindle sb. out of his or her money | ～取 lay one's hands on sth. by cheating | 兵不厌～。In war there can never be too much deception. ❷ 假装 pretend; feign: ～降 pretend to surrender | ～死 pretend to be dead; play dead ❸ 用假话试探,使对方吐露真情 bluff sb. into giving information: 他是拿话～我,我一听就知道。As soon as he opened his mouth, I realized he was trying to draw me out.

【诈唬】zhà·hu 蒙哄吓唬 bluff; bluster: 他这是～你,别理他。Don't pay any attention to him; he's trying to bluff you.

【诈骗】zhàpiàn 讹诈骗取 defraud; swindle: ～钱财 cheat or swindle sb. out of his or her money and property; get money and property by fraud

【诈尸】zhà//shī ❶ 迷信的人指停放的尸体忽然起来(superstition) (of a corpse) suddenly rise before being buried ❷〈方 *dial.*〉指突然叫嚷或做出像发狂似的动作(骂人的话 curse) scream suddenly or behave as if mad

【诈降】zhàxiáng 假投降 pretend to surrender; feign surrender

【诈语】zhà·yǔ 骗人的话;假话 lie; falsehood; fabrication; deceit

柞 zhà 柞水 (Zhàshuǐ), 地名,在陕西 Zhashui, name of a place in Shaanxi Province

☞ zuò on p. 2578

栅(柵) zhà 栅栏 fence; railings; paling; bars; palisade: 铁～ iron railings; metal rails; iron bars | 木～ paling; palisade | ～门(栅栏门) fence gate

☞ shān on p. 1672

【栅栏】zhà·lan (～儿 zhà·lanr)用铁条、木条等做成的类似篱笆而较坚固的东西 fence; railings; paling; bars; palisade; solid fence made of iron or wood bars: ～门 fence gate | 工地四周围着～儿。The construction site is surrounded by fencing.

【栅子】zhà·zi 〈方 *dial.*〉用竹子、芦苇等做成的类似篱笆的东西,有的带顶,多用来圈住家禽 enclosure fenced with bamboo, reeds, etc., sometimes with a roof, for keeping poultry

奓 zhà 〈方 *dial.*〉张开 spread; extend: ～着头发 with dishevelled hair | 这衣服下摆太～了。The hem of the dress is too outspread.

☞ Zhā on p. 2403

【奓着胆子】zhà·zhe dǎn·zi 〈方 *dial.*〉勉强鼓着勇气 pluck up one's courage; collect one's courage; sum up one's courage: 他～走过了独木桥。He plucked up his courage and walked across the single plank bridge.

咤(吒) zhà ☞ 叱咤 chìzhà on p. 264
☞ 吒 zhā on p. 2403

炸 zhà ❶ (物体)突然破裂 (of an object) burst; blast; explode: 爆～ explode | 这瓶子一灌开水就～了。The bottle burst as it was being filled with hot water. ❷ 用炸药爆破;用炸弹轰炸 blow up; blast; bomb: ～碉堡 blow up the blockhouse ❸ 因愤怒而激烈发作 fly into a rage; flare up; explode with rage: 他一听就气～了。He exploded with anger at the words. ❹ 因受惊而四处乱逃 scamper; flee in terror in all directions: ～市 (of a group of people) flee in terror through crowded streets; run away in all directions | ～窝 be thrown into confusion

☞ zhá on p. 2404

【炸弹】zhàdàn 一种爆炸性武器,通常外壳用铁制成,里面装有炸药,触动信管就爆炸。一般用飞机投掷。bomb; explosive weapon, consisting of an iron exterior filled with explosives inside, blowing up if its fuse is touched. Generally planes are used to drop bombs on targets.

【炸雷】zhàléi 〈方 *dial.*〉声音响亮的雷 loud thunderbolt

【炸群】zhà//qún 成群的骡马等由于受惊而四处乱跑 (of mules, horses, etc.) scamper; stampede; flee in terror in all directions: 马～了! The horses stampeded in fright!

【炸市】zhà//shì 集市上的人因受惊而四处乱跑 (of people in a marketplace) run in terror in all directions

【炸窝】zhà//wō ❶ 鸟或蜂群受惊扰从巢里向四处乱飞 (of birds, bees, etc.) flee in fright ❷〈比喻 *fig.*〉许多人由于受惊而乱成一团 (of frightened people) be thrown into panic; be in disarray

【炸药】zhàyào 受热或撞击后发生爆炸,并产生大量的能和高温气体的物质,如黄色炸药、黑色火药等 explosive; dynamite; substance that explodes when heated or struck, producing voluminous energy and high-temperature gas, e.g. TNT, gunpowder, etc.

痄 zhà [痄腮](zhà·sai) 流行性腮腺炎的通称 general term for mumps

蚱 zhà ☞ below

【蚱蝉】zhàchán 身体最大的一种蝉,前、后翅基部黑褐色,斑纹外侧呈截断状。夏天鸣声大,幼虫蜕的壳可入药。cicada (*Cicadidae*); the largest kind of cicada, dark brown at the base of front and rear wings with exterior sides of their spots and stripes looking as if segmented, producing a high-pitched droning sound in summer, the carapace of its larva used in medicine; 俗称 popularly known as 知了 zhīliǎo

【蚱蜢】zhàměng 昆虫,像蝗虫,常生活在一个地区,不向外地迁移。危害禾本科、豆科等植物,是害虫。grasshopper (*Orlhoptera*); pest similar to the locust, living in one area without moving to other areas, harmful to grasses, beans, etc.

蛇 zhà〈方 *dial.*〉海蜇 jellyfish; nettle-fish

溠 Zhà 溠水,水名,在湖北 Zhashui, name of a river in Hubei Province

榨(❶搾) zhà ❶ 压出物体里的汁液 press; extract; squeeze out liquid from sth.:~油 press oil from a oil-bearing crop|~甘蔗 extract juice from sugarcanes ❷ 压出物体里汁液的器具 apparatus used to extract juice out of sth.:油~ oil press|酒~ wine press

【榨菜】zhàcài ❶ 二年生草本植物,芥(jiè)菜的变种,叶子椭圆形或长卵形。茎膨大成瘤状,可以吃。mustard tuber (*Brassica juncea* var. *tsatsai*); biennial herb, a variation of mustard, having oval or egg-shaped long leaves and large edible tubers ❷ 用这种植物的茎加辣椒、香料等腌制成的副食品 tuber of mustard preserved in pepper, spices, etc.

【榨取】zhàqǔ ❶ 压榨而取得 squeeze; extort:~汁液 squeeze juice out of something ❷〈比喻 *fig.*〉残酷剥削或搜刮 ruthlessly exploit; extort:~民财 extort money and property from the people

砟 zhà 大水砟 (Dàshuǐzhà),地名,在甘肃 Dashuizha, name of a place in Gansu

蜡(禮) zhà〈古代 *arch.*〉一种年终祭祀 year-end sacrificial rite

☞ là on p.1140

霅 Zhá 霅溪,水名,在浙江。现在叫东苕溪。Zhaxi River in Zhejiang Province; now called Dongtiaoxi

醡 zhà same as 榨 zhà②, 就是酒榨的榨 wine press

·zha (·ㄓㄚ)

馇 ·zha ☞ [饹馇](gē·zha) on p.650

☞ chā on p.202

zhāi (ㄓㄞ)

侧 zhāi〈方 *dial.*〉倾斜;不正 lean; tilt; slant:~歪 incline

☞ cè on p.195 and zè on p.2309

【侧棱】zhāi·leng〈方 *dial.*〉向一边斜 lean; incline; slant:~着耳朵听 prick up one's ears|~着身子睡 sleep on one's side

【侧歪】zhāi·wai〈方 *dial.*〉倾斜 tilt; slant; incline:车在山坡上~着开。The vehicle tilted while moving forward on a hillside.|帽子~在一边儿 wear one's hat tilted to one side

斋[1](齋) zhāi ❶ 斋戒 fast; abstain from certain foods, esp. as a religious discipline ❷ 信仰佛教、道教等宗教的人所吃的素食 vegetarian diet (of Buddhist, Taoist or other religious believers):吃~ be on a vegetarian diet ❸ 舍饭给僧人、道人 give alms to a monk or a Taoist:~僧 give alms to a monk

斋[2](齋) zhāi 屋子,常用做书房、商店的名称,学校宿舍也有叫斋的 room or building; used mostly in the names of studies, shops or school dormitories:书~ study|新~ new building|第三~ No. 3 Building|荣宝~ Rongbao Study

【斋饭】zhāifàn ❶ 僧尼向人化缘得来的饭 food given to Buddhist monks as alms ❷ 寺庙里素的饭食 vegetarian meal in a temple

【斋果】zhāiguǒ〈方 *dial.*〉供品 offerings

【斋醮】zhāijiào 僧道设坛向神佛祈祷 (of Buddhist and Taoist priests) set up an altar for prayer rituals

【斋戒】zhāijiè ❶〈旧时 *old*〉祭祀鬼神时,穿整洁衣服,戒除嗜欲(如不喝酒、不吃荤等等),以表示虔诚 fast; show one's piety when making offerings to gods and spirits, e.g. by wearing clean clothes, abstaining from meat, wine, etc. ❷ 封斋 day of fasting

【斋月】zhāiyuè 伊斯兰教在封斋期间的一个月,即伊斯兰教历的九月 Islam's Ramadan (Ramazan); month of fasting which falls on the ninth month of the Islamic calendar

摘 zhāi ❶ 取(植物的花、果、叶或戴着、挂着的东西) pick; pluck (a flower, fruit, leaf); take off (sth. worn on one's body, or hanging):~梨 pick pears|~一朵花 pluck a flower|~帽子 take off one's hat|把灯泡~下来。Remove the bulb, please. ❷ 选取 select; choose; make extracts from:~要 make a summary; make an abstract|~录 take passa-

Z

ges; make extracts; extract ❸ 摘借 borrow money when in urgent need: ～了几个钱救急 borrow some money to meet an urgent need

【摘编】zhāibiān ❶ 摘录下来加以编辑 select and edit; extract and compile: 将资料～成书 select and edit the materials into a book ❷ 摘录下来加以编辑而成的文字资料 extracted and edited written materials; extracts: 言论～ extracts from speeches

【摘除】zhāichú 摘去;除去(有机体的某些部分) excise; remove (certain parts of an organism): 白内障～ cataract extraction | 长了虫的果子应该尽早～。Fruits that develop bugs should be removed as soon as possible.

【摘登】zhāidēng (报刊)摘要登载 publish excerpts or extracts of something.: ～一周电视节目 a week's TV programmes in excerpts

【摘记】zhāijì ❶ 摘要记录 take notes: 报告很长,我只～几个要点。The report was rather long. I just jotted down the main points. ❷ 摘录 extract; excerpt; summary

【摘借】zhāijiè 有急用时临时向人借钱 borrow money when in urgent need

【摘录】zhāilù 从书刊、文件等里头选择 部分写下来 take passages (from); make extracts; extract: 这篇文章很好,我特地～了几段。The article is well written, and I've extracted a few paragraphs from it.

【摘要】zhāiyào ❶ 摘录要点 make a summary; make an abstract: ～发表 publish excerpts or extracts of something ❷ 摘录下来的要点 summary; excerpt; extract: 谈话～ extracts of the speech | 社论～ summary of an editorial

【摘引】zhāiyǐn 摘录引用 quote; quotation: ～别人的文章要注明出处。When quoting other people's writings it is necessary to give credit to the sources.

【摘由】zhāi//yóu 摘录公文的主要内容以便查阅(因为公文的主要内容叫事由) key extracts of a document kept for later reference (main content of a document is called 事由 shìyóu in Chinese, hence 摘由 zhāi//yóu)

zhái (ㄓㄞˊ)

宅 zhái 住所;住宅 residence; house; abode; dwelling: 家～ residence; dwelling | 深～大院 imposing dwelling and spacious courtyard

【宅第】zháidì 〈书 *fml*.〉住宅(多指较大的 oft. large) house; mansion

【宅基】zháijī 住宅的地基 foundations of a house; site of a house: ～地 house site

【宅门】zháimén ❶ 深宅大院的大门 gate of a large old-style house ❷ (～儿 zháiménr)借指住在深宅大院里的人家 family living in a mansion with spacious courtyards: 这胡同里有好几个～儿。There are several families living in imposing mansions on the lane.

【宅院】zháiyuàn 带院子的宅子。泛指住宅。house with a courtyard; (in a broad sense) house

【宅子】zhái·zi 住宅 residence; house; abode; dwelling: 一所～ a residence

择(擇) zhái 义同'择'(zé),用于以下各条 having the same meaning as 择 zé and used in the following entries

☞ zé on p. 2399

【择不开】zhái·bu kāi ❶ 分解不开 unable to disentangle or undo; impossible to unravel; past untangling: 线乱成了一团,怎么也～了。The thread is all entangled. It's simply impossible to unravel it. ❷ 摆脱不开;抽不出身 cannot get away from: 一点儿工夫也～ not have a moment to spare; be fully occupied

【择菜】zhái//cài 把蔬菜中不宜吃的部分剔除,留下可以吃的部分 trim vegetables for cooking; get rid of the inedible parts of vegetables and retain what is edible

【择席】zháixí 在某个地方睡惯了,换个地方就睡不安稳,叫择席 be unable to sleep well in a new place

翟 Zhái 姓 a surname

☞ dí on p. 416

zhǎi (ㄓㄞˇ)

窄 zhǎi ❶ 横的距离小(跟'宽'相对 as opposed to 'wide') narrow: 狭～ narrow | 路～ narrow road | ～胡同 narrow alley ❷ (心胸)不开朗;(气量)小 petty-minded; petty; small-minded: 心眼儿～ petty-minded ❸ (生活)不宽裕 hard up; badly off; straitened: 他家的日子过得挺～。His family lived in very straitened circumstances.

鉙 zhǎi 〈方 *dial*.〉(～儿 zhǎir)残缺损伤的痕迹(指某些器皿、衣服、水果上的) blemish; flaw (on certain wares, clothes and fruit): 碗上有点～儿。The bowl has a flaw on it. | 没～儿的苹果 apple without a blemish

zhài (ㄓㄞˋ)

债 zhài 欠别人的钱 debt: 借～ borrow money | 欠～ be in debt; get into debt | 还～ pay (back) one's debts | 公～ government bond ◇血～要用血来偿。Debts of blood must be paid in blood.

【债户】zhàihù 借别人钱财付给利息的人;借债的人 debtor; one who borrows money or property from and pays interest to others

【债利】zhàilì 放债所得的利息 interest on loans

【债权】zhàiquán 依法要求债务人偿还钱财和履行一定行为的权利 creditor's rights; legal

rights to demand a debtor pay back money and property and fulfil certain obligations

【债权人】zhàiquánrén 根据法律或合同的规定，有权要求债务人履行义务的人 creditor; person who has the right to demand a debtor to fulfil obligations according to law or contract

【债券】zhàiquàn ❶ 公债券 public or government bond ❷ 企业、银行或股份公司发行的债权人领取本息的凭证 bond; debenture; voucher issued by enterprises, banks or stock companies to creditors for reclaiming principal and interest

【债台高筑】zhài tái gāo zhù 战国时代周赧(nǎn)王欠了债，无法偿还，被债主逼得逃到一座宫殿的高台上。后人称此台为'逃债之台'(见于《汉书·诸侯王表序》及颜师古引服虔注)。后来就用'债台高筑'形容欠债极多。be heavily in debt; be up to one's ears (or neck) in debt; be saddled with huge debts; be debt-ridden. According to *History of Han · Preface to Biographies of Princes and Vassals*, during the Warring States Period, King Nan of the state of Zhou was unable to meet his debts and was forced to flee from creditors to a high deck in his palace. Later generations call this 'Deck of the Dodging Debtor'.

【债务】zhàiwù 债户所负还债的义务。也指所欠的债。debt; liabilities: 偿还～ pay back a debt; meet one's debts

【债务人】zhàiwùrén 根据法律或合同的规定，对债权人承担义务的人 debtor; person who fulfils his or her obligations to a creditor according to laws or contracts

【债主】zhàizhǔ 借给别人钱财收取利息的人；放债的人 creditor; person who draws interest by lending money or property to others

砦 zhài ❶ same as 寨 zhài: 鹿～ enclosure for deer ❷ (Zhài)姓 a surname

祭 Zhài 姓 a surname
☞ jì on p. 921

寨 zhài ❶ 防守用的栅栏 stockade; fence: 山～ mountain fortress; fortified mountain village; mountain fastness ❷〈旧时 *old*〉驻兵的地方 camp: 营～ military camp | 安营扎～ encamp; pitch a camp ❸ 强盗聚居的地方；山寨 mountain stronghold; mountain fortress; place where bandits gather and live: ～主 brigand chief ❹ 寨子 stockaded village: 本村本～ home village

【寨子】zhài·zi ❶ 四周的栅栏或围墙 stockade; fence; boundary wall ❷ 四周有栅栏或围墙的村子 stockaded village

瘵 zhài〈书 *fml.*〉病 illness; sickness; disease

搩 zhài〈方 *dial.*〉把衣服上附加的物件缝上 sew accessories onto clothes: ～花边 trim a dress with lace

zhān (ㄓㄢ)

占 zhān ❶ 占卜 practise divination; divine: ～卦 practise divination; divine ❷ (Zhān) 姓 a surname
☞ zhàn on p. 2411

【占卜】zhānbǔ 古代用龟、蓍等，后世用铜钱、牙牌等推断祸福，包括打卦、起课等(迷信)(superstition) practise divination; try to discover one's destiny through turtle's shells, alpine yarrow, etc., in ancient times, and later by means of copper coins, dominoes, the Eight Trigrams, or tossing coins, etc.

【占卦】zhān//guà 打卦；算卦 divine by means of the Eight Trigrams

【占课】zhān//kè 起课 divine by tossing coins

【占梦】zhān//mèng 圆梦 divination by interpreting dreams; oneiromancy

【占星】zhān//xīng 观察星象来推断吉凶(迷信)(superstition) divine by astrology; cast a horoscope

沾(❶❷ 霑) zhān ❶ 浸湿 soak; welter; wet; damp; moisten: 泪流～襟。Tears soaked the front of the garment. ❷ 因为接触而被东西附着上 be stained with; be soiled with: ～水 be soaked by water ❸ 稍微碰上或挨上 touch: ～边儿 be somehow related to somebody or with something | 脚不～地 one's feet not touching the ground; walk very fast; run very fast; be extremely busy ❹ 因发生关系而得到(好处) gain by association with sb. or sth.; benefit from some kind of relationship: ～光 benefit from association with somebody or something; cash in on one's connection with somebody | 利益均～ have an equal share of benefits; share benefits equally ❺〈方 *dial.*〉行；好；可以 alright; okay: 不～(不行，不成) will not do; do not work; be not workable

【沾边】zhān//biān (～儿 zhān//biānr) ❶ 略有接触 touch on (or upon) only lightly: 这项工作他还没～儿。He hasn't got his hand on the job yet. ❷ 接近事实或事物应有的样子 be close to what it should be; be relevant; be pertinent: 你讲的一点儿也沾不上边儿。What you say is completely irrelevant. | 他唱的这几句还～儿。These few lines he sang sounded as they should.

【沾光】zhān//guāng 凭借别人或某种事物而得到好处 benefit from association with sb. or sth.; cash in on one's connection with sb.; gain from the support or influence of sb.

【沾亲】zhān//qīn 有亲戚关系(多指关系较远的 oft. distantly related) be somewhat related: 我跟他沾点儿亲。He and I are distantly related.

【沾染】zhānrǎn ❶ 因接触而被不好的东西附着

上 be infected with：创口～了细菌。The wound was infected with germs. ❷ 因接触而受到不良的影响 be contaminated by; be tainted with：不要～坏习气。Don't become tainted with bad habits.

【沾手】zhān//shǒu ❶ 用手接触 touch with one's hand：雪花一～就化了。Snowflakes melt the moment they fall on one's hand. ❷〈比喻 *fig.*〉参与某事 have a hand in; get involved in; butt in; intervene; interfere：这事一～就甩不掉。You cannot throw it off once you get involved.

【沾沾自喜】zhānzhān zì xǐ 形容自以为很好而得意的样子 feel complacent; be pleased with oneself; feel self-satisfied

毡(氈、氊) zhān 毡子 felt：～帽 felt hat | ～靴 felt boots | 擀～ felt; make into felt

【毡房】zhānfáng 牧区人民居住的圆顶帐篷，用毡子蒙在木架上做成 yurt; rotund tent made of felt covering a wooden structure, used as a dwelling by pastoral people

【毡条】zhāntiáo〈方 *dial.*〉成张的毡子，用来铺或垫 felt; felt rug

【毡子】zhān·zi 用羊毛等压成的像厚呢子或粗毯子似的东西 felt; felt rug; felt blanket; sth. made of pressed wool like box cloth or a coarse blanket

栴 zhān [栴檀](zhāntán) 古书上指檀香 sandalwood; white sandalwood, as recorded in ancient Chinese books

旃[1] zhān〈书 *fml.*〉same as 毡 zhān

旃[2] zhān〈书 *fml.*〉〈助词 *aux.*〉'之焉'的合音 contraction of 之 zhī and 焉 yān：勉～! Hope you'll do a good job of it. *or* Do your best!

【旃檀】zhāntán 古书上指檀香 sandalwood; white sandalwood, as recorded in ancient Chinese books

粘 zhān ❶ 黏的东西附着在物体上或者互相连接 glue; stick; paste; (of a sticky substance) cling to an object; be joined to sth.：麦芽糖～在一块儿了。The malt sugar got glued together. ❷ 用黏的东西使物件连接起来 glue; join or connect objects with a sticky substance：～信封 seal up an envelope

☞ nián on p. 1411

【粘连】zhānlián ❶ 身体内的黏膜或浆膜，由于炎症病变而粘在一起，例如腹膜发炎时，腹膜和肠管的浆膜粘在一起 adhesion; mucous membrane or chorion joining together due to inflammation, e.g. adhesion of the peritoneum and chorion of the intestines when the peritoneum is affected by inflammation ❷〈比喻 *fig.*〉联系；牵连 link; involvement; relation：这件事跟他们没什么～。This doesn't have anything to do with them.

【粘贴】zhāntiē 用胶水、糨糊等使纸张或其他东西附着在另一种东西上 glue; stick; paste; use glue to attach a piece of paper or an object to another object：～标语 put up or paste slogans

詹 Zhān 姓 a surname

谵 zhān〈书 *fml.*〉说胡话 rave; rant; be delirious：～语 delirious speech; ranting and raving; wild talk

【谵妄】zhānwàng 由发烧、酒醉、药物中毒以及其他疾患引起的意识模糊、短时间内精神错乱的症状，如说胡话、不认识熟人等 delirium; temporary state of mental confusion and clouded consciousness resulting from high fever, inebriation, overdose of medicine, or other causes; characterized by incoherent speech, disorientation, etc.

【谵语】zhānyǔ〈书 *fml.*〉❶ 说胡话 rave; rant; be delirious ❷ 胡话 delirious speech; wild talk; ranting and raving

馇(飦) zhān〈书 *fml.*〉稠粥 thick porridge; congee

邅 zhān ☞ [迍邅](zhūnzhān) on p. 2530

瞻 zhān ❶ 往前或往上看 look forward; look up：观～ sight; view | 高～远瞩 look far ahead and aim high; be far-sighted ❷ (Zhān) 姓 a surname

【瞻顾】zhāngù〈书 *fml.*〉❶ 向前看，又向后看；思前想后 look ahead and behind; consider carefully; weigh the pros and cons; take into account both past experience and future possibilities：徘徊～ hesitate and think carefully time and again ❷ 照应；看顾 look after; take care of

【瞻礼】zhānlǐ ❶ 天主教徒称宗教节日 festival as observed by Catholic followers ❷ 天主教徒称星期日为主日，一星期中除主日以外的六天顺序称为'瞻礼二'至'瞻礼七' weekdays aside from Sunday (or Lord's Day). Monday through Saturday are respectively called 瞻礼二 zhānlǐ'èr, 瞻礼三 zhānlǐsān, 瞻礼四 zhānlǐsì, 瞻礼五 zhānlǐwǔ, 瞻礼六 zhānlǐliù and 瞻礼七 zhānlǐqī. ❸〈书 *fml.*〉瞻仰礼拜(神佛等) worship (the Buddha, deities); go to church

【瞻念】zhānniàn 瞻望并思考 think of; look ahead：～前途 think of the future

【瞻前顾后】zhān qián gù hòu ❶ 看看前面再看看后面。形容做事以前考虑周密谨慎。look ahead into the future and back into the past; think twice before taking action; weigh the pros and cons; take into account both past experience and future possibilities ❷ 形容顾虑过多，犹豫不决 be overcautious and indecisive

【瞻望】zhānwàng 往远处看；往将来看 look forward; look far ahead: 抬头～ look into the distance|～前途 look to the future

【瞻仰】zhānyǎng 恭敬地看 look at with reverence; pay homage to: ～遗容 pay respects to somebody's remains

鹯 zhān 古书上指一种猛禽 bird of prey, as recorded in ancient books

鳣 zhān 古书上指鲟一类的鱼 sturgeon as recorded in ancient books

zhǎn (ㄓㄢˇ)

斩 zhǎn ❶ 砍 chop; cut; slay; kill: ～草除根 cut the weeds and dig up the roots|披荆～棘 break through brambles and thorns|～断侵略者的魔爪 chop off the claws of the invaders ❷〈方 *dial.*〉〈比喻 *fig.*〉敲竹杠;讹诈 blackmail; fleece; extort

【斩草除根】zhǎn cǎo chú gēn〈比喻 *fig.*〉彻底除掉祸根,不留后患 cut the weeds and dig up the roots; stamp out the source of trouble

【斩钉截铁】zhǎn dīng jié tiě 形容说话办事坚决果断,毫不犹豫 resolute and decisive; categorical

【斩假石】zhǎnjiǎshí ☞ 剁斧石 duòfǔshí on p. 502

【斩首】zhǎnshǒu 杀头 behead; decapitate

琖(琖) zhǎn〈书 *fml.*〉same as 盏 zhǎn

飐 zhǎn〈书 *fml.*〉风吹使颤动 quiver in the wind; flicker in the wind

盏(盞) zhǎn ❶ 小杯子 small cup: 酒～ small wine cup ❷〈量词 *classifier*〉用于灯 [used for lamps]: 一～电灯 an electric lamp

展 zhǎn ❶ 张开;放开 open up; spread out; unfold; unfurl: 舒～ unfold; extend; comfortable|伸～ spread; stretch|开～ develop; launch; carry out|愁眉不～ knit one's brows in anxiety; wear a worried frown ❷ 施展 put to good use; give full play to: 一筹莫～ be at one's wits' end ❸ 展缓 postpone; extend; prolong; delay; put off: ～期 postpone; extend a time limit|～限 extend a time limit; extend a deadline ❹ 展览 exhibit; display; show: ～出 put on display; be on show; exhibit|预～ preview|画～ exhibition of paintings ❺ (Zhǎn)姓 a surname

【展播】zhǎnbō 以展览为目的而播放(广播或电视节目) broadcast (TV or radio programmes) for publicity purposes: 电视台举办迎春文艺节目～。The TV station is going to broadcast Spring Festival theatrical performances.

【展翅】zhǎnchì 张开翅膀 spread the wings; get ready for flight: ～高飞 soar to great heights; soar into the sky

【展缓】zhǎnhuǎn 推迟(日期);放宽(限期) put off; postpone; extend; prolong; extend a time limit: 行期一再～。The date for departure was postponed again and again.|限期不得～。The time limit cannot to be extended.

【展开】zhǎn//kāi ❶ 张开;铺开 spread out; unfold; open up; roll out; unroll: ～画卷 unroll a scroll painting ❷ 大规模地进行 launch; develop; carry out: ～竞赛 launch a competition|～辩论 set off a debate

【展宽】zhǎnkuān (道路、河床等)扩展加宽 (of a road, riverbed, etc.) expand; broaden; widen: ～马路 widen the road

【展览】zhǎnlǎn 陈列出来供人观看 put on display; exhibit; show: ～馆 exhibition hall|～会 exhibition|摄影～ exhibition of photographs

【展露】zhǎnlù 展现;显露 exhibit; display; show: ～才华 display one's talent

【展品】zhǎnpǐn 展览的物品 exhibit; item on display

【展期】[1] zhǎnqī 把预定的日期往后推迟或延长 extend a time limit; postpone: 报名工作～至五月底结束。The application deadline is to be extended to the end of May.

【展期】[2] zhǎnqī 展览的时期;展览的期限 exhibition period; schedule of an exhibition: ～为十五天。The exhibition will last 15 days.

【展示】zhǎnshì 清楚地摆出来;明显地表现出来 reveal; show; lay bare; put on show: ～图纸 demonstrate a blueprint|作品～了人物的内心活动。The work reveals the character's inner world.

【展望】zhǎnwàng ❶ 往远处看;往将来看 look into the distance; look ahead; look to the future: 他爬上山顶,向四周～。He climbed to the mountaintop and looked into the distance in all directions.|～未来 look to the future|～世界局势 look to the future of the world situation ❷ 对事物发展前途的预测 forecast; prospect: 21世纪～ 21st century in prospect

【展现】zhǎnxiàn 显现出;展示 unfold before one's eyes; emerge; show; appear: 走进大门,～在眼前的是一个宽广的庭院。On entering the gate, a spacious courtyard unfolded before our eyes.

【展限】zhǎnxiàn 放宽限期 extend a time limit; extend a deadline; (in law) grant a moratorium: 借款到期不再～。The loan's time limit won't be extended again.

【展销】zhǎnxiāo 以展览的方式销售(多在规定的日期和地点 oft. within a designated period and location) display and sell goods: ～会 commodities fair|服装～ garment fair

【展性】zhǎnxìng 物体可以压成片状而不断裂的性质,金属多具有展性 malleability; quality of being capable of being pressed into flakes without rupturing; most metals having malleability

【展转】zhǎnzhuǎn same as 辗转 zhǎnzhuǎn

崭 zhǎn ❶〈书 *fml.*〉高峻；高出 towering; high and steep ❷〈方 *dial.*〉优异；好 outstanding; excellent; good: 滋味真～。It's really delicious.

【崭露头角】zhǎn lù tóujiǎo〈比喻 *fig.*〉突出地显露出才能和本领（多指青少年 oft. of young people）begin to show one's brilliant talents; begin to distinguish oneself; cut a striking figure; stand out conspicuously

【崭然】zhǎnrán〈书 *fml.*〉形容高出一般的样子 towering; outstanding

【崭新】zhǎnxīn 极新；簇新 nascent; brand new; completely new: ～的大楼 new building | ～的衣服 brand new clothes | ～的时代 new age; new epoch

搌 zhǎn（用松软干燥的东西）轻轻擦抹或按压，吸去湿处的液体 wipe or dab (with a soft dry object) to sop up liquid: ～布 rag; dishcloth; dish towel | 纸上落了一滴墨，拿吸墨纸来～一～。A drop of ink has fallen on the paper. Soak it up with a piece of blotting paper.

【搌布】zhǎn·bù 擦器皿用的布；抹（mā）布 rag; dishcloth; dish towel

晰 zhǎn〈方 *dial.*〉眼皮开合；眨眼 wink; blink

辗 zhǎn ☞ below
☞ 碾 niǎn on p. 1413

【辗转】zhǎnzhuǎn ❶（身体）翻来覆去（of a body）toss and turn; toss about (in bed): ～反侧 toss and turn restlessly; toss about (in bed) | ～不眠 toss and turn (in bed); be unable to go to sleep; lie in bed wide awake ❷ 经过许多人的手或经过许多地方；非直接地 pass through many hands or places; indirectly: ～流传 spread from place to place, or hand to hand ‖ also 展转 zhǎnzhuǎn

【辗转反侧】zhǎnzhuǎn fǎn cè 形容心中有事，躺在床上翻来覆去地不能入睡 toss and turn restlessly; toss about (in bed); lie in bed but be unable to go to sleep due to a heavy heart

黵 zhǎn〈方 *dial.*〉弄脏；沾污 befoul; make dirty; dirty; soil: 墨水把纸～了。The paper is stained with ink. | 黑布禁（jīn）～。Dark cloth doesn't show dirt easily.

zhàn（ㄓㄢˋ）

占（佔） zhàn ❶ 占据 occupy; seize; take: 霸～ take by force | 强～ seize by force | 攻～ conquer ❷ 处在某一种地位或属于某一种情形 hold a certain status; be in a certain situation: ～优势 be superior to; have the advantage; hold all the trumps | ～上风 get the upper hand; have the edge over; turn the tables on | 赞成的～多数。Most people are in favour of it.
☞ zhān on p. 2408

【占据】zhànjù 用强力取得或保持（地域、场所等）seize, occupy, hold or take by force (a region, place, etc.): ～地盘 occupy an area

【占领】zhànlǐng ❶ 用武装力量取得（阵地或领土）capture; occupy; seize; use force to seize (a position or territory) ❷ 占有 take possession of; possess; have; own: ～市场 capture a market | 开拓和～新的科技领域 exploit and capture new scientific and technological fields

【占便宜】zhàn pián·yi ❶ 用不正当的方法，取得额外的利益 gain extra advantage by unfair means; profit at other people's expense; take an undue advantage of ❷〈比喻 *fig.*〉有优越的条件 be advantageous; be favourable: 你个子高，打篮球～。A tall fellow like you has an advantage in playing basketball.

【占先】zhàn//xiān 占优先地位 take precedence; take the lead; get ahead of: 这个月的竞赛，被他们小组占了先。Their group took the lead in this month's competition.

【占线】zhàn//xiàn 指对方电话线路被占用，电话打不进去（of a phone line）busy; engaged: 一连拨了几次，他家的电话都～。His family's phone line was so busy that I dialed several times but couldn't get through.

【占用】zhànyòng 占有并使用 occupy and use: 不能随便～耕地。It is illegal to occupy cultivated land and put it to other uses without authorization. | ～一点儿时间，开个小会。Let's take some time to have a short meeting.

【占有】zhànyǒu ❶ 占据 own; possess; have ❷ 处在（某种地位）be in (a certain status); occupy; hold: 农业在国民经济中～重要地位。Agriculture holds an important position in the national economy. ❸ 掌握 grasp; hold; master; learn thoroughly: 科学研究必须～大量材料。Scientific research requires thorough learning of a vast amount of materials.

组 zhàn〈书 *fml.*〉缝补 sew and mend

栈（棧） zhàn ❶ 养牲畜的竹、木栅栏 shed; pen; fold: 马～ stable | 羊～ sheep pen; sheepfold ❷ 栈道 plank road built along the face of a cliff with wooden brackets fixed into the cliff ❸ 栈房 storehouse; warehouse: 货～ warehouse | 客～ inn

【栈道】zhàndào 在悬崖绝壁上凿孔支架木桩，铺上木板而成的窄路 plank road built along the face of a cliff by fixing wooden brackets into holes bored into it

【栈房】zhànfáng ❶ 存放货物的地方；仓库 warehouse; storehouse ❷〈方 *dial.*〉旅馆；客店 inn

【栈桥】zhànqiáo 火车站、港口、矿山或工厂的一种建筑物，形状略像桥，用于装卸货物，港口上

Z

的栈桥也用于上下旅客 landing stage (in a port); loading bridge (at a railway station); bridge-shaped structure in railway stations, ports, mines or factories, used to load and unload goods or for passengers to embark and disembark

战[1](戰) zhàn ❶ 战争;战斗 war; warfare; battle; fight; combat: 宣～ declare war|停～ ceasefire; armistice|持久～ protracted war◇商～ commercial war ❷ 进行战争或战斗 fight, battle; engage in war: ～胜 conquer; overcome; defeat; vanquish; surmount; triumph over|百～百胜 be invincible; win every fight|愈～愈勇 grow ever more brave in fighting ◇～天斗地 brave the elements; fight heaven and earth; combat nature ❸ (Zhàn) 姓 a surname

战[2](戰) zhàn 发抖 shiver; tremble; shudder: 寒～ shiver with cold|冷得打～ shiver with cold|胆～心惊 tremble with fear; be scared out of one's wits

【战败】zhànbài ❶ 打败仗;在战争中失败 be defeated; be vanquished; suffer a defeat; lose a battle or war: ～国 vanquished or defeated nation|铁扇公主～了。The Iron Fan Princess was defeated. ❷ 战胜(敌人);打败(敌人) defeat; vanquish; beat; triumph over: 孙行者～了铁扇公主。The Monkey King triumphed over the Iron Fan Princess.|孙行者把铁扇公主～了。The Monkey King defeated the Iron Fan Princess.

【战报】zhànbào 战时由司令部或其他有关方面发表的关于战争情况的报道。也用于比喻。war communiqué; battlefield report; report on a war issued by wartime headquarters or other relevant departments; also used figuratively: 工地～ reports from the construction site

【战备】zhànbèi 战争准备 war preparedness; combat readiness; preparation for war: 加强～ step up efforts in combat readiness

【战表】zhànbiǎo 向敌方宣战或挑战的文书(多见于旧小说、戏曲 oft. found in traditional novels or plays) written challenge to war; letter declaring war; letter of challenge: 下～ send a letter to declare war ◇市篮球队已经递来了～。The municipal basketball team has already submitted a letter of challenge.

【战场】zhànchǎng 两军交战的地方,也用于比喻 battlefield; battleground; battlefront; also used figuratively: 开赴～ go to the war front|抗洪～ anti-flood battlefront

【战刀】zhàndāo 马刀 sabre

【战地】zhàndì 两军交战的地区,也用于比喻 battlefield; battleground; combat zone; also used figuratively: ～医院 field hospital|参赛队已大半抵达～。Most of the participating teams have arrived in the arena.

【战抖】zhàndǒu 发抖;哆嗦 tremble; shiver; shudder; shake: 浑身～ shiver all over

【战斗】zhàndòu ❶ 敌对双方所进行的武装冲突,是达到战争目的的主要手段 fight; battle; combat; military conflict between antagonistic parties, the main means to achieve the objectives of a war ❷ 同敌方作战 fight; combat; campaign: ～力 combat effectiveness or capability; fighting capacity|～英雄 combat hero ❸ 泛指斗争 fight; struggle; battle; contend: ～性 militancy|～的唯物主义 militant materialism|投入抢险～ be engaged in the efforts to deal with an emergency

【战斗机】zhàndòujī 歼击机的旧称 old name for 歼击机 jiānjījī

【战斗力】zhàndòulì 军队作战的能力 combat effectiveness, strength or capability; fighting capacity: 提高～ improve fighting capacity

【战犯】zhànfàn 发动非正义战争或在战争中犯严重罪行的人 war criminal; person who launches an unjust war or commits serious crimes in a war

【战俘】zhànfú 战争中捉住的敌方人员 prisoner of war; POW; same as 俘虏 fúlǔ ②: 遣返～ repatriate POWs

【战歌】zhàngē 鼓舞士气的歌曲 battle song; fighting song; song to enhance soldiers' morale

【战功】zhàngōng 战斗中所立的功劳 meritorious military service; outstanding military exploit; achievements in battle: 屡立～ distinguish oneself time and again in action; perform meritorious deeds in the battlefield|～显赫 perform many meritorious deeds in the battlefield; win great distinction in a war; achieve miraculous feats in a war

【战鼓】zhàngǔ 〈古代 *arch.*〉作战时为鼓舞士气或指挥战斗而打的鼓。现多用于比喻。war drum; battle drum; drum used in ancient battles to rouse morale or to give orders; oft. used figuratively now

【战国】Zhànguó 我国历史上的一个时代(公元前475—公元前221) Warring States Period (475-221 B.C.) in Chinese history

【战果】zhànguǒ 战斗中获得的成果,也指工作中取得的成绩 result of a battle; combat success; victory; achievement in one's work: ～辉煌 splendid results in the battlefield; brilliant combat performance

【战壕】zhànháo 作战时为掩护而挖的壕沟 trench; entrenchment; military works dug to shelter soldiers in a battle

【战火】zhànhuǒ 指战争(就其破坏作用和带来的祸害而言) (in terms of damage and disaster a war causes) flames of war: ～纷飞。Flames of war raged everywhere.

【战祸】zhànhuò 战争带来的祸害 disaster of war; scourge of war: ～连年 be subjected to the scourge of war for years on end

【战机】[1] zhànjī ❶ 适于战斗的时机 opportunity for combat：抓住～ seize the opportunity for combat ❷ 战事的机密 credential information about military actions；military secrets：泄露～ leak military secrets

【战机】[2] zhànjī 作战用的飞机 fighter plane；fighter：出动～拦截 call out fighters to block the way of enemy fighters

【战绩】zhànjì 战争中获得的成绩，也用于比喻 military success，exploit or feat；combat achievements；also used figuratively：以全胜～夺冠 win the championship by sweeping the board

【战舰】zhànjiàn 作战舰艇的统称 general term for warship

【战局】zhànjú 某一时期或某一地区的战争局势 war situation in a certain period or area：扭转～ turn the tables on the enemy

【战具】zhànjù 指武器装备 weapon；arms：～精良 highly sophisticated weapon

【战利品】zhànlìpǐn 作战时从敌方缴获的武器、装备等 spoils of war；captured equipment；war trophies or booty

【战例】zhànlì 战争、战役或战斗的事例 specific example of a battle (in military science)：光辉～ glorious example of a battle|淝水之战是我国历史上以少胜多的著名～。The Feishui Battle is a famous example of the few defeating the many in Chinese history.

【战栗】zhànlì 战抖 tremble；shiver；shudder；also 颤栗 zhànlì

【战列舰】zhànlièjiàn 一种装备大口径火炮和厚装甲的大型军舰，主要用于远洋战斗活动，因炮战时排成单纵队的战列线而得名 battleship；ship-of-the-line；large warship that is heavily armoured and equipped with heavy-calibre cannons，mainly serving in battles on the ocean and having got this Chinese name because warships line up to fight in a battle

【战乱】zhànluàn 指战争时期的混乱状况 chaos caused by war；war turmoil

【战略】zhànlüè ❶ 指导战争全局的计划和策略 strategy；overall plan and tactics for a war ❷ 有关战争全局的 strategic；concerning the overall situation of a war：～部署 strategic deployment；strategic disposition|～防御 strategic defense ❸〈比喻 *fig*.〉决定全局的策略 strategy that determines the overall trends of a situation：革命～ revolutionary strategy|全球～ global strategy

【战略物资】zhànlüè wùzī 与战争有关的重要物资，如粮食、钢铁、石油、橡胶、稀有金属等 strategic goods and materials；important materials related to war，e. g. grain，steel，petroleum，rubber，rare metals，etc.

【战马】zhànmǎ 经过特殊训练，用于作战的马 battle steed；war-horse；horse that is specially trained for battle

【战勤】zhànqín 直接支援军队作战的各种勤务，如运送物资、伤员，带路送信，站岗放哨，维护交通，押送俘虏等 civilian war services；various services that give direct support to an army to fight a war，e. g. delivering supplies and caring for the wounded，scouting and sending messages，standing sentry，maintaining communications，escorting captives，etc.

【战区】zhànqū 为便于执行战略任务而划分的作战区域 war zone；theatre of operations；theatre of war；war zones divided for strategic purposes

【战胜】zhànshèng 在战争或比赛中取得胜利 defeat；triumph over；vanquish；overcome；conquer：～顽敌 rout a tough enemy|～乙队 defeat Team B ◇～困难 overcome (or surmount) difficulties

【战士】zhànshì ❶ 军队最基层的成员 soldier；armyman；member at the grass-roots level of the army；foot soldier：解放军～ PLA soldier|新入伍的～ new recruit ❷ 泛指从事某种正义事业或参加某种正义斗争的人 (in a broad sense) those who are engaged in a certain just cause，or join a certain just struggle；champion；warrior；fighter：白衣～ medical worker|无产阶级～ proletarian fighter

【战事】zhànshì 有关战争的各种活动，泛指战争 all activities concerning war；(in a broad sense) war；hostilities：～频繁。Battles erupt frequently.

【战术】zhànshù ❶ 进行战斗的原则和方法 principle and method for a battle；(military) tactics ❷〈比喻 *fig*.〉解决局部问题的方法 methods for solving partial questions

【战天斗地】zhàn tiān dòu dì 指同大自然作斗争 fight against heaven and earth；combat nature；brave the elements

【战线】zhànxiàn 敌对双方军队作战时的接触线 battle lines；battlefront；front；frontline：缩短～ shorten the battle lines ◇农业～ agricultural front|思想～ ideological front

【战役】zhànyì 为实现一定的战略目的，按照统一的作战计划，在一定的方向上和一定的时间内进行的一系列战斗的总和 campaign；battle；the sum total of fights waged in a certain direction and at a certain time，under a unified fighting plan to achieve a certain strategic target：渡江～ Campaign to Cross the Yangtze River

【战鹰】zhànyīng 指作战的飞机(含喜爱意) fighting eagle (pet name for a fighter plane)：只见四只～直冲云霄。Four fighting eagles (or four fighter planes) soared into the sky.

【战友】zhànyǒu 在一起战斗的人 battle companion；comrade-in-arms：老～ old-time comrade-in-arms|亲密～ close comrade-in-arms

【战云】zhànyún〈比喻 *fig.*〉战争的气氛 war clouds; atmosphere of war: ～密布 gathering war clouds

【战战兢兢】zhànzhànjīngjīng ❶ 形容因害怕而微微发抖的样子 trembling with fear; with fear and trepidation ❷ 形容小心谨慎的样子 gingerly; with caution

【战争】zhànzhēng 民族与民族之间、国家与国家之间、阶级与阶级之间或政治集团与政治集团之间的武装斗争 war; warfare; armed struggle waged between nations, states, classes, or political groups

站[1] zhàn 直着身体,两脚着地或踏在物体上 stand; get up; be on one's feet; take a stand: 请大家坐着,不要～起来。Please sit down, no need to stand up.|交通警～在十字路口指挥来往车辆。The traffic policeman stands in the middle of the intersection to direct traffic. ◇～稳立场 uphold the standpoint

站[2] zhàn ❶ 在行进中停下来;停留 stop; come to a halt: 不怕慢,只怕～。Fear not slowness, but fear standing still.|车还没～稳,请别着急下车。The bus has not come to a full stop yet, please don't be in such a rush to get down. ❷ 为乘客上下或货物装卸而设的停车的地方 station; stop; place set for passengers to get on or get off the bus or train, or place for loading and unloading goods: 火车～ railway station|汽车～ bus station; bus stop; bus halt|北京～ Beijing Railway Station|车到～了。The bus has reached the station. ❸ 为某种业务而设立的机构 station or centre for rendering certain services: 粮～ grain supply centre|供应～ supply centre|保健～ health centre|气象～ meteorological station

【站队】zhàn//duì 站成行列 line up; fall in; stand in line: ～入场。Line up to go in please.

【站岗】zhàn//gǎng 站在岗位上,执行守卫、警戒任务 stand or mount guard; stand sentinel; stand sentry; be on sentry duty; stand at the post to keep watch

【站柜台】zhàn guìtái 指营业员站在柜台跟前接待顾客 serve as a shop assistant; serve behind the counter

【站立】zhànlì 站 stand; rise; be on one's feet: 他默默地～在烈士墓前。He stood in respectful silence before the martyr's tomb. ◇中国人民～起来了。The Chinese people have stood up.

【站票】zhànpiào (剧院、火车站等)出售的没有座位只能站着的票 (of theatre, train, etc.) ticket for standing room only; standing ticket: 打～ buy a ticket for standing room only

【站台】zhàntái 车站上下乘客或装卸货物的高于路面的平台 platform (in a railway station); platform where passengers get on or off the train, and goods are loaded and unloaded; also 月台 yuètái

【站住】zhàn//·zhù ❶ (人马车辆等)停止行动 (of people, horses, cars, etc.) come to a stop; stop; halt: 听到有人喊他,他连忙～了。On hearing someone yelling at him, he suddenly came to a stop. ❷ 站稳(多就能不能说,下同 oft. of possibility, same below) stand firmly on one's feet; keep one's footing: 他病刚好,腿很软,站不住。He has just recovered from an illness, and feeling weak in his legs, could hardly stand. ❸ 在某个地方待下去 stand or hold one's ground; consolidate one's position ❹ (理由等)成立 (of reasons, etc.) hold water; be valid; be tenable: 这个论点实在站不住。This theory is untenable. ❺〈方 *dial.*〉(颜色、油漆等)附着而不掉 (of colour, paint, etc.) remain fast: 墙面太光,抹的灰站不住。The wall is too smooth to hold lime mortar.

【站住脚】zhàn//·zhù jiǎo ❶ 停止行走 stop moving; stop; come to a stop; halt: 他跑得太快,一下子站不住脚。(He) was running too fast to stop suddenly. ❷ 停在某个地方(多就能不能说,下同 oft. of possibility, same below) able to stay put: 忙得站不住脚。(He) was so busy (he) could not stay in one place. ❸ 在某个地方待下去 able to keep or hold one's ground; able to consolidate one's position: 这个店由于经营得好,在这里～了。Because the shop is doing well, (he) has finally gained a footing here. ❹ (理由等)成立 (of arguments, etc.) hold water; be valid; be tenable: 那篇文章的论点是能～的。The viewpoint of this article is valid.

绽 zhàn 裂开 split; tear; burst: 破～ flaw; weak point|皮开肉～。The skin is torn and the flesh gapes open.|鞋开～了。The shoe has split. ◇脸上～出了微笑。A smile crept across (his) face.

湛 zhàn ❶ 深 profound; deep; thorough: 精～ superb; consummate ❷ 清澈 crystal clear; limpid: 清～ limpid ❸ (Zhàn) 姓 a surname

【湛蓝】zhànlán 深蓝(多用来形容天空、湖海等) (of the sky, sea, lake, etc.) azure blue; azure

【湛清】zhànqīng 清澈 limpid; clear: 河水～见底。The water in the river is so clear that one can see the bottom.

颤 zhàn 发抖 tremble; shiver; shudder ☞ chàn on p. 214

【颤栗】zhànlì same as 战栗 zhànlì

蘸 zhàn 在液体、粉末或糊状的东西里沾一下就拿出来 dip in (liquid, powder or paste): ～水钢笔 dip pen|～糖吃 eat sth. by dipping it in sugar|大葱～酱 scallions dipped in thick sauce

【蘸火】zhàn//huǒ 淬火的通称 general term for 淬火 cuì//huǒ

zhāng (ㄓㄤ)

饧(餦) zhāng [饧馆] (zhānghuáng) 〈书 *fml*.〉❶ 干的饴糖 malt sugar; maltose ❷ 一种面食 a kind of cooked wheaten food

张(張) zhāng ❶ 使合拢的东西分开或使紧缩的东西放开 open; spread; draw; stretch: ～嘴 open one's mouth|～翅膀儿 spread the wings|～弓射箭 draw a bow to shoot|一～一弛 tension alternating with relaxation ❷ 陈设;铺排 lay out; display: ～灯结彩 be decorated with lanterns and coloured streamers|大～筵席 lay out a feast ❸ 扩大;夸张 magnify; exaggerate; amplify: 虚～声势 make a show of strength ❹ 看;望 look; glance: 东～西望 glance around; look this way and that; look around in all directions ❺ 商店开业 open a new shop: 新～ new start|开～ open a business ❻ 〈量词 *classifier*〉 a) 用于纸、皮子等 [of paper, paintings, leather, etc.]: 一～纸 a piece of paper|两～画 two paintings|十～皮子 10 sheets of leather|三～铁板 three steel plates b) 用于床、桌子等 [of beds, tables, etc.]: 一～床 one bed|四～桌子 four tables|七～犁 seven ploughs c) 用于嘴、脸 [of mouth and face]: 两～嘴 two sharp tongues|一～脸 a face d) 用于弓 [of bow]: 一～弓 a bow ❼ 二十八宿之一 one of the 28 constellations ❽ (Zhāng) 姓 a surname

【张榜】zhāng//bǎng 贴出文告 put up a notice; post a notice; put up a proclamation: ～招贤 put up a proclamation to recruit talented people

【张本】zhāngběn ❶ 为事态的发展预先做的安排 anticipatory action ❷ 作为伏笔而预先说在前面的话 hint foreshadowing later developments in a story; anticipatory remark

【张楚】Zhāng Chǔ 秦末农民起义领袖陈胜于公元前 209 年在陈县（今河南淮阳）建立的革命政权 revolutionary political power established in Chenxian (present-day Huaiyang, Henan Province) in 209 B.C. by Chen Sheng, leader of a peasant uprising towards the end of the Qin Dynasty

【张大】zhāngdà 〈书 *fml*.〉扩大;夸大 magnify; exaggerate; publicize widely: ～其事 publicize widely|～其词 overstate the case; exaggerate

【张挂】zhāngguà (字画、帐子等)展开挂起 hang up (a picture, curtain, etc.): ～地图 hang up a map|～蚊帐 hang up a mosquito net

【张冠李戴】Zhāng guān Lǐ dài 姓张的帽子戴到姓李的头上 put Zhang's hat on Li's head; 〈比喻 *fig*.〉弄错了对象或弄错了事实 confuse one thing with another; attribute sth. to the wrong person

【张皇】zhānghuáng 〈书 *fml*.〉惊慌;慌张 alarmed; scared; flurried; flustered: 神色～ look scared|～失措(慌慌张张，不知所措) be in a frenzy of alarm; lose one's head; get into a panic

【张口】zhāng//kǒu 张嘴 open one's mouth (to say sth.): 气得他半天没～。He was struck speechless with rage.|向人借钱,我实在张不开口。I really cannot open my mouth to borrow money from others.

【张口结舌】zhāng kǒu jié shé 张着嘴说不出话来，形容理屈或害怕 be agape and tongue-tied; be at a loss for words; be unable to say anything

【张狂】zhāngkuáng 嚣张;轻狂 impudent; insolent; arrogant: 举止～ behave arrogantly

【张力】zhānglì ☞ 拉力 lālì ② on p.1138

【张罗】zhāng·luo ❶ 料理 take care of; get busy about; attend to: 要带的东西早点儿收拾好，不要临时～。Get your things ready in good time to avoid a last-minute rush. ❷ 筹划 raise (funds); collect (money, etc.): ～一笔钱 raise a sum of money|他们正～着婚事。They are preparing for the wedding. ❸ 应酬;接待 greet and entertain (guests); attend to (customers, etc.): 顾客很多,一个售货员～不过来。There were too many customers for one shop assistant to attend to.

【张目】zhāngmù ❶ 睁大眼睛 open one's eyes wide: ～注视 watch wide-eyed ❷ 助长某人的声势叫'为某人张目' inflate sb.'s arrogance; boost sb.'s arrogance; build up another

【张三李四】Zhāng Sān Lǐ Sì 泛指某人或某些人 (in a broad sense) Zhang, Li or anybody; any Tom, Dick or Harry

【张贴】zhāngtiē 贴(布告、广告、标语等) put up (a notice, poster, etc.): ～告示 post a notice

【张望】zhāngwàng 从小孔或缝隙里看;向四周或远处看 peep (through a crack, etc.); look around: 探头～ crane one's neck and look around|四顾～ look around

【张牙舞爪】zhāng yá wǔ zhǎo 形容猖狂凶恶的样子 bare fangs and brandish claws; make threatening gestures; engage in sabre-rattling

【张扬】zhāngyáng 把隐秘的或不必让众人知道的事情声张出去;宣扬 come out into the open; make widely known; make public; publicize: 四处～ publicize everywhere; spread (a story) all over the place

【张嘴】zhāng//zuǐ ❶ 把嘴张开,多指说话 open one's mouth (to say sth.): 你一～,我就知道你要说什么。The moment you started talking, I knew what you were going to say. ❷ 指向人借贷或有所请求 ask for a loan or a favour：向人～，怪难为情的。It is very embarrassing to ask anyone for a favour.

章[1] zhāng ❶ 歌曲诗文的段落（of book，poetry，music，etc.）chapter；section，division：乐～ movement（of a symphony，etc.）|～节 section；chapter | 全书共分三十六～。The book has 36 chapters. ❷ 条目 clause and subclause：约法三～ agree on a three-point law；make a few simple rules to be observed by all concerned ❸ 条理 order；orderliness：杂乱无～ disorderly and unsystematic ❹ 章程 rules；regulations，charter；constitution：党～ Party Constitution | 团～ Constitution of the Youth League | 简～ general regulations | 规～ rules；regulations；constitution ❺ 奏章 memorial to the throne ❻（Zhāng）姓 a surname

章[2] zhāng ❶ 图章 seal；stamp；signet：印～ seal；stamp；signet | 盖～ affix a seal；seal；stamp ❷ 佩带在身上的标志 badge；insignia；medal；armband：领～ collar badge；insignia | 臂～ armband

【章草】zhāngcǎo 草书的一种，笔画保存一些隶书的笔势，相传为汉元帝时史游所作，以其用于奏章，所以叫做章草（in Chinese calligraphy）memorial script；a type of the cursive script（草书 cǎoshū），which retains some techniques of the official script（隶书 lìshū），reputedly developed by Shi You of the Han Dynasty，so called due to its use in memorials

【章程】zhāngchéng 书面写定的组织规程或办事条例 written rules；regulations；constitution

【章程】zhāng·cheng〈方 *dial.*〉指办法 solution；way：心里还没个准～。（I）'m not sure yet what the best way to go about it is.

【章法】zhāngfǎ ❶ 文章的组织结构 organization and structure of a piece of writing；art of composition ❷〈比喻 *fig.*〉办事的程序和规则 orderly ways；methodicalness：他虽然很老练，这时候也有点乱了～。Although he is capable and experienced，this incident threw him off balance.

【章回体】zhānghuítǐ 长篇小说的一种体裁，全书分成若干回，每回有标题，概括全回的故事内容 a type of traditional Chinese novel with each chapter headed by a couplet giving the gist of its content

【章节】zhāngjié 文章的组成部分，通常一本书分为若干章，一章又分为若干节 chapters and sections；parts of an article or a book

【章句】zhāngjù ❶ 古书的章节和句读 chapters，sections，sentences and phrases in ancient writings ❷ 指对古书章句的分析解释 syntactic and semantic analysis of ancient texts；philological study：～之学 analysis and interpretation of ancient writings

【章则】zhāngzé 章程规则 rules and regulations：违反～ violate rules and regulations

【章子】zhāng·zi〈方 *dial.*〉图章 seal；stamp：刻～ engrave a seal | 盖～ affix one's seal

鄣 Zhāng 周朝国名，在今山东东平东 Zhang，name of a state of the Zhou Dynasty eastern of present-day Dongping，Shandong Province

獐（**麞**） zhāng smae as 獐子 zhāng·zi

【獐头鼠目】zhāng tóu shǔ mù 獐子的头小而尖，老鼠的眼睛小而圆，形容相貌丑陋猥琐而神情狡猾（多指坏人 oft. referring to bad people）with the head of a river deer and the eyes of a rat；repulsively ugly and sly-looking

【獐子】zhāng·zi 哺乳动物，形状像鹿而较小，身体上面黄褐色，腹部白色，毛较粗，没有角。皮可以制革。Chinese river deer（*Hydropotes inermis Swinhoe*）；mammal which looks like a deer but is much smaller，with yellowish-brown fur on its back and white fur on its belly，coarse hair and no horns，its hide being a material for leather tanning；also 牙獐 yázhāng

彰 zhāng ❶ 明显；显著 clear；evident；conspicuous：昭～ clear；manifest；evident | 欲盖弥～ try to hide a mistake | 相得益～ each shining more brilliantly in the other's company；complement each other ❷ 表彰；显扬 cite（in dispatches）；commend：～善瘅恶 commend good and denounce evil ❸（Zhāng）姓 a surname

【彰明较著】zhāng míng jiào zhù 非常明显，容易看清 very obvious；conspicuous；very evidently（较 *jiao*：明显 obvious）

【彰善瘅恶】zhāng shàn dàn è 表扬好的，憎恨坏的 praise good and denounce evil；uphold virtue and condemn vice

漳 Zhāng ❶ 漳河，水名，发源于山西，流入卫河 Zhanghe，name of a river originating in Shanxi Province and emptying into the Weihe River ❷ 漳江，水名，在福建 Zhangjiang，name of a river in Fujian Province

嫜 zhāng〈书 *fml.*〉丈夫的父亲 husband's father；father-in-law：姑～（婆婆和公公）husband's parents；parents-in-law

璋 zhāng 古代的一种玉器，形状像半个圭 jade tablet

樟 zhāng 樟树，常绿乔木，叶子椭圆形或卵形，花白色略带绿色，结暗紫色浆果。全株有香气，可以防虫蛀。木材致密，适于制家具和手工艺品，枝叶可以提制樟脑。camphor tree（*Cinnamomum camphora*）；evergreen arbour with oval or egg-shaped leaves，white and greenish flowers，and dark purple berry，the entire tree being fragrant and mothproof，its wood having a fine texture and good for making furniture and arts and crafts，and its leaves used to produce camphor；also 香樟 xiāngzhāng

【樟脑】zhāngnǎo 有机化合物，化学式 $C_{10}H_{16}O$。

无色晶体，味道辛辣，有清凉的香气，容易挥发和升华。通常用樟树枝叶提制而成。日常用来防虫蛀，也用来制赛璐珞、炸药、香料等，医药上用做强心剂和防腐剂。camphor ($C_{10}H_{16}O$); organic compound in the form of a colourless crystal with a pungent taste and a cool refreshing smell, easy to volatilize and sublimate, usu. processed from camphor leaves, used to keep away moths in daily life, make celluloid, explosives, perfume, etc., and medically as a cardiac stimulant or preservative; also 潮脑 cháonǎo

【樟脑丸】zhāngnǎowán〈方 *dial.*〉用樟脑制成的丸状物，用来防腐或防虫蛀等 camphor balls used as a preservative and to keep away moths; mothball

蟑 zhāng [蟑螂] (zhāngláng) 昆虫，体扁平，黑褐色，能发出臭味。常咬坏衣物，并能传染伤寒、霍乱等疾病，是害虫。cockroach (*Blatta orientalis*); roach; harmful insect with a flat, dark brown body giving forth an offensive odour, eating clothes, and spreading disease such as typhoid fever and cholera; also 蜚蠊 fěilián

zhǎng (ㄓㄤˇ)

长[1] (長) zhǎng ❶ 年纪较大 older; elder; senior: 年～ a senior | 他比我～两岁。He is two years older than I am. ❷ 排行最大 eldest; oldest: ～兄 eldest brother | ～子 eldest son ❸ 辈分大 older generation: 师～ teacher | ～亲 elders | 叔叔比侄子～一辈。An uncle is one generation older than his nephew. ❹ 领导人 chief; head; leader: 部～ minister | 校～ president; school headmaster; principal | 乡～ township head | 首～ leading cadre; senior officer

长[2] (長) zhǎng ❶ 生 come into being; spring up; form: ～锈 get rusty | 山上～满了青翠的树木。The mountains are overgrown with green trees. ❷ 生长；成长 grow; develop: 杨树～得快。The poplar trees grow fast. | 这孩子～得真胖。What a chubby child! ❸ 增进；增加 boost; enhance; increase: ～见识 increase one's knowledge; gain experience | ～力气 increase strength | 吃一堑，～一智。A fall into a pit, a gain in wit.

☞ cháng on p. 215

【长辈】zhǎngbèi 辈分大的人 elder member of a family; elder; senior

【长膘】zhǎng//biāo 上膘 (of a domestic animal) get fat; put on flesh; flesh out

【长房】zhǎngfáng 家族中长子的一支 eldest branch of a family or a clan

【长官】zhǎngguān〈旧时 *old*〉指行政单位或军队的高级官吏 senior officer or official; commanding officer

【长机】zhǎngjī 编队飞行中，率领和指挥机群或僚机执行任务的飞机 (of military) lead aircraft; leader; lead aircraft commanding other aircraft in flight formation; also 主机 zhǔjī

【长进】zhǎngjìn 在学问或品行等方面有进步 make good progress in one's studies or morality: 技艺大有～ make major progress in one's skill

【长老】zhǎnglǎo ❶〈书 *fml.*〉年纪大的人 elder ❷ 对年纪大的和尚的尊称 elder (respectful term of address for an old monk) ❸ 犹太教、基督教指本教在地方上的领袖 (in Judaism and Christianity) local religious leader; elder

【长脸】zhǎng//liǎn 增加体面；使脸上增添光彩 do credit to; make a name for: 这部片子获得大奖，真为咱们制片厂～。This film has won the first prize and made a name for our studio.

【长门】zhǎngmén same as 长房 zhǎngfáng

【长年】zhǎngnián〈方 *dial.*〉船主人 owner of a ship

☞ chángnián on p. 217

【长亲】zhǎngqīn 辈分大的亲戚 senior relatives

【长上】zhǎngshàng ❶ 长辈 elder member of a family; elder; senior ❷ 上司 superior; boss

【长势】zhǎngshì (植物)生长的状况 the way a crop is growing; growth: 小麦～喜人。The wheat is coming along fine.

【长孙】zhǎngsūn ❶ 长子的长子，现在也指排行最大的孙子 eldest son's eldest son; eldest grandson ❷ (Zhǎngsūn) 姓 a surname

【长尾巴】zhǎng wěi·ba 俗称小孩儿过生日 popular term for child's birthday

【长相】zhǎngxiàng (～儿 zhǎngxiàngr) 相貌 looks; features; appearance: 从他们的～上看，好像兄弟俩。They look like brothers.

【长者】zhǎngzhě ❶ 年纪和辈分都高的人 elder; senior ❷ 年高有德的人 venerable elder

【长子】zhǎngzǐ ❶ 排行最大的儿子 eldest son ❷ (Zhǎngzǐ) 地名，在山西 Zhangzi, name of a place in Shanxi Province

仉 Zhǎng 姓 a surname

涨 (漲) zhǎng (水位)升高；(物价)提高 (of water, prices, etc.) rise; surge; go up; become higher: 水～船高。When the water rises, the boat will rise. | 河水暴～。The water in the river rises quickly. | 物价上～。Prices are going up.

☞ zhàng on p. 2420

【涨潮】zhǎng//cháo 潮水升高 rising tide; flood tide

【涨风】zhǎngfēng 物价上涨的情势 trend of price hikes

【涨幅】zhǎngfú (物价等)上涨的幅度 (of price, etc.) margin or rate of rise; rise: 物价～不

大。The rise in prices is not great.

掌 zhǎng ❶ 手掌 palm：鼓～ clap one's hands；applaud｜易如反～ as easy as turning one's hand over；easy as pie｜摩拳擦～ be eager for a fight；itch to have a go ❷ 用手掌打 strike with the palm of the hand；slap：～嘴 slap sb. on the face ❸ 掌管；掌握 hold in one's hand；be in charge of；control；wield：～舵 be the helmsman；operate the rudder；steer a boat｜～印 keep the seal；take control；be in power｜～权 wield (or hold) power ❹ 某些动物的脚掌 bottom of certain animals' feet；pad；sole：熊～ bear's paw｜鸭～ duck's webbed feet ❺ 马蹄铁 horseshoe：这匹马该钉～了。It's time for the horse to be shod. ❻ (～儿 zhǎngr)钉或缝在鞋底前部、后部的皮子等 shoe sole or heel：前～儿 front sole｜后～儿 heel｜钉一块～儿 have a shoe soled ❼〈方 *dial.*〉钉补鞋底 mend the sole of a shoe：～鞋 mend the sole of a shoe ❽〈方 *dial.*〉加上(油盐等) put in (cooking oil, salt, etc.)：～点酱油 put in some soy sauce ❾〈方 *dial.*〉same as 把 bǎ：～门关上。Close the door. ❿ (Zhǎng)姓 a surname

【掌厨】zhǎng// chú 主持烹调 chef

【掌灯】zhǎng// dēng ❶ 手里举着灯 hold a lamp in one's hand ❷ 上灯；点灯(指油灯) light an oil lamp：天黑了，该～了。It's getting dark；the lamp should be lit.

【掌舵】zhǎng// duò ❶ 行船时掌握船上的舵 be at the helm；operate the rudder；take the tiller；steer a boat ❷〈比喻 *fig.*〉掌握方向 be at the helm

【掌舵】zhǎngduò 掌舵的人 helmsman；steersman

【掌骨】zhǎnggǔ 构成手掌的骨头，每个手掌有五根 metacarpal bone；(图见 ☞ figure for 骨骼 gǔgé on p. 693)

【掌故】zhǎnggù 历史上的人物事迹、制度沿革等 (of historical figures, social evolution, etc.) anecdotes；tales：文坛～ literary anecdotes

【掌管】zhǎngguǎn 负责管理；主持 be in charge of；administer：各项事务都有专人～。Everything is taken care of by specially assigned people.

【掌柜】zhǎngguì ❶〈旧时 *old*〉称商店老板或负责管理商店的人 shopkeeper；manager (of a shop) ❷〈方 *dial.*〉〈旧时 *old*〉佃户称地主 form of address of a landlord by tenant farmers ❸〈方 *dial.*〉指丈夫 husband ‖ also 掌柜的 zhǎngguì·de

【掌权】zhǎng// quán 掌握大权 be in power；wield power；exercise control

【掌上明珠】zhǎng shàng míngzhū〈比喻 *fig.*〉极受父母宠爱的儿女，也比喻为人所珍爱的物品 pearl in the palm；apple of one's eye；beloved child；one's treasures；also 掌珠 zhǎngzhū，掌上珠 zhǎng shàng zhū or 掌中珠 zhǎng zhōng zhū

【掌勺儿】zhǎng// sháor 主持烹调 prepare a banquet；do the cooking：～的(饭馆、食堂中主持烹调的厨师) chef；chief cook of a restaurant or a canteen

【掌握】zhǎngwò ❶ 了解事物，因而能充分支配或运用 grasp；master；know well；learn thoroughly：～技术 master techniques｜～理论 grasp theory｜～原则 have a good grasp of the principles｜～规律 learn the rules thoroughly ◇～自己的命运 take one's destiny into one's own hands；be master of one's own destiny ❷ 主持；控制 have in hand；take into one's hands；control：～会议 preside over a meeting｜～政权 wield political power

【掌心】zhǎngxīn 手心 centre (or hollow) of the palm；sphere of control

【掌印】zhǎng// yìn ❶ 掌管印信 keep the seal ❷〈比喻 *fig.*〉主持事务或掌握政权 take control；be in power

【掌灶】zhǎng// zào 在饭馆、食堂或办酒席的人家主持烹调 cook；prepare food (in a restaurant, canteen, or a family that is giving a feast)：～儿的(掌灶的人) chef；chief cook

【掌子】zhǎng·zi 采矿或隧道工程中掘进的工作面 (in mining or tunnelling) face；area；also 礃子 zhǎng·zi and 掌(礃)子面 zhǎng·zimiàn

【掌嘴】zhǎng// zuǐ 打嘴巴 slap sb.'s face；box sb.'s ears

礃 zhǎng [礃子] (zhǎng·zi) same as 掌子 zhǎng·zi

zhàng (ㄓㄤˋ)

丈[1] zhàng ❶ 长度单位，10 尺等于 1 丈，10 丈等于 1 引 *zhang*, a unit of length, where 10 *chi* equals 1 *zhang*, and 10 *zhang* equals 1 *yin* ❷ 丈量(土地) measure (a piece of land)：清～ make an exact measurement of the land｜春耕前要把地～完。We must finish measuring the land before spring ploughing.

丈[2] zhàng ❶〈古时 *arch.*〉对老年男子的尊称 respectful form of address for an old man：老～ venerable old man ❷ 丈夫(用于某些亲戚的尊称 used in certain kinship terms) husband：姑～(姑夫) husband of one's father's sister；uncle｜姐～(姐夫) husband of one's sister

【丈夫】zhàngfū 成年男子 man：大～ true man｜～气 manliness

【丈夫】zhàng·fu 男女两人结婚后，男子是女子的丈夫 husband

【丈量】zhàngliáng 用步弓、皮尺等量土地面积或距离 measure the area or dimensions of a piece of land using paces, tape, etc.：～地亩 measure land；take the dimensions of a field

【丈母】zhàng·mu 岳母 wife's mother；mother-in-law；also 丈母娘 zhàng·muniáng

【丈人】zhàngrén〈古时 *arch.*〉对老年男子的尊称 respectful form of address for an old man

【丈人】zhàng·ren 岳父 wife's father; father-in-law

仗[1] zhàng ❶ 兵器的总称 (collect.) weaponry; weapons: 仪～ flags, weapons, etc. carried by a guard of honour|明火执～ carry torches and weapons in a robbery; robbery in broad daylight ❷ 拿着(兵器) hold (a weapon): ～剑 hold a sword ❸ 凭借; 倚仗 rely on; depend on: 狗～人势 like a dog threatening people on the strength of its master's power; be a bully with the support of a powerful person|～势欺人 abuse one's power and bully people; play the bully on the strength of one's powerful connections or position

仗[2] zhàng 指战争或战斗 fight; battle; war: 打胜～ win a battle; triumph over|打败～ be defeated in a battle; suffer a defeat|这一～打得真漂亮。This is really a brilliant victory. ◇打好春耕生产这一～ make a success of this spring's ploughing and sowing

【仗胆】zhàng//dǎn (～儿 zhàng//dǎnr)壮胆 by dint of one's courage

【仗势】zhàng//shì 倚仗某种权势(做坏事) take advantage of one's own or others' power: ～欺人 take advantage of one's own or sb. else's power to bully people; bully people on the strength of one's powerful connections or position; abuse one's power and bully people

【仗恃】zhàngshì 倚仗; 依靠 rely on; depend on: ～豪门 by dint of one's powerful connections

【仗义】zhàngyì ❶〈书 *fml.*〉主持正义 uphold justice: ～执言 speak out to uphold justice ❷ 讲义气 be loyal to (one's friends)

【仗义疏财】zhàng yì shū cái 讲义气,轻钱财,多指拿出钱来帮助有困难的人 be loyal to one's friends and generous in helping the poor and needy

【仗义执言】zhàng yì zhí yán 为了正义说公道话 speak out to uphold justice

杖 zhàng ❶ 拐杖; 手杖 cane; stick: 扶～而行 walk with a stick ❷ 泛指棍棒 (in a broad sense) rod or staff used for a specific purpose: 擀面～ rolling pin|拿刀动～ carry swords and rods

【杖子】zhàng·zi 障子(多用于地名 oft. used in place names) barrier made of weeds, sorghum stalks, etc.: 大～(在河北) Dazhangzi (in Hebei Province)|宋～(在辽宁) Songzhangzi (in Liaoning Province)

帐(帳) zhàng ❶ 用布、纱或绸子等做成的遮蔽用的东西 curtain; tent; canopy; shelter made out of cloth, yarn, silk, etc.: 蚊～ mosquito net|营～ tent|～篷 canopy ◇青纱～ green curtain of tall crops ❷ same as 账 zhàng

【帐幕】zhàngmù 帐篷(多指较大的 usu. of large size) tent

【帐篷】zhàng·peng 撑在地上遮蔽风雨、日光的东西,多用帆布、尼龙布等做成 tent made of canvas, nylon, etc., and pitched on the ground as shelter from wind, rain and sunlight

【帐子】zhàng·zi 用布、纱或绸子等做成的张在床上或屋子里的东西 bed-curtain; mosquito net; sth. made out of cloth, yarn, silk, etc. to hang on a bed or in a room

账(賬) zhàng ❶ 关于货币、货物出入的记载 account: 记～ keep accounts|查～ check (or audit, or examine) accounts ❷ 指账簿 account book: 一本～ an account book ❸ 债 debt; credit: 欠～ owe a debt|还～ repay a debt|放～ buy or sell on credit

【账本】zhàngběn (～儿 zhàngběnr) 账簿 account book

【账簿】zhàngbù 记载货币、货物出入事项的本子 account book

【账册】zhàngcè same as 账簿 zhàngbù

【账单】zhàngdān 记载货币、货物出入事项的单子 bill; check; account

【账房】zhàngfáng (～儿 zhàngfángr) ❶〈旧时 *old*〉企业或有钱人家中管理银钱货物出入的处所 accountant's office; place where enterprises or rich families used to handle money and goods ❷ 在账房管理银钱货物出入的人 accountant; person in charge of receiving and paying out money, bills or goods

【账号】zhànghào 单位或个人跟银行建立经济关系后,银行在账上给该单位或个人编的号码 account number the bank gives an unit or individual after they have established economic relations with the bank

【账户】zhànghù 会计上指账簿中对各种资金运用、来源和周转过程等设置的分类 accounts; classifications made in an account book about the use, source and turnover of capital, etc.

【账面】zhàngmiàn (～儿 zhàngmiànr) 指账目(对实物而言) items of an account (in kind): 先把～弄清,再去核对库存 sort out the accounts before checking the stock

【账目】zhàngmù 账上记载的项目 items of an account; accounts: 清理～ square accounts|定期公布～ publish the accounts regularly

胀(脹) zhàng ❶ 膨胀 grow in size; expand; distend: 热～冷缩 expand when heated and contract when cooled ❷ 身体内壁受到压迫而产生不舒服的感觉 swell; be bloated: 肚子发～ feel bloated in the stomach

【胀库】zhàngkù 仓库库存饱和 fully stocked: 猪肉～ storehouse full of pork

【胀闸】zhàngzhá 自行车制动装置的一种,由两个半圆形的圈和弹簧构成,装在车轴轴套的内部,使用时半圆形的圈撑开,与轴套摩擦,起制动作用 damper brake; hub brake; control device on a bicycle, formed with two semicircles and a spring and fixed on the inside of the axle sleeve. When in use the semicircles stretch to rub the axle sleeve to enable control and braking.

涨(漲) zhàng ❶ 固体吸收液体后体积增大 of solids swell after absorbing water, etc.: 豆子泡～了。The beans swelled up after being soaked. ❷ (头部)充血 (of the head) be swelled by a rush of blood: 头昏脑～ feel one's head swim | 他的脸～得通红。His face went red. ❸ 多出;超出(用于度量衡或货币的数目) (of weight and measures, etc.) be more, larger, etc., than expected: 钱花～了(超过收入或预计) spent more money (than one got or planned to) | 把布一量,～出了半尺。When the cloth was measured, it was found to be half a *chi* longer than expected.

☞ zhǎng on p. 2417

障 zhàng ❶ 阻隔;遮挡 hinder; obstruct; impede: ～碍 barrier; block | ～蔽 block; obstruct; shut out ❷ 用来遮挡的东西 screen; block; barrier: 屏～ screen

【障碍】zhàng'ài ❶ 挡住道路,使不能顺利通过;阻碍 hinder; block; obstruct: ～物 obstacle; barrier; entanglement, hindrance ❷ 阻挡前进的东西 obstacle; obstruction; barrier; impediment: 排除～ remove an impediment | 扫清～ clear away obstacles

【障蔽】zhàngbì 遮蔽;遮挡 block; obstruct; shut out: ～视线 block the sight; obstruct one's view

【障眼法】zhàngyǎnfǎ 遮蔽或转移人的目光使看不清真相的手法 cover-up; camouflage; disguise; also 遮眼法 zhēyǎnfǎ or 掩眼法 yǎnyǎnfǎ

【障子】zhàng·zi 用芦苇、秫秸等编成的或利用成行的树木做成的屏障 hedge; fence; barrier made of reeds, sorghum stalks, closely planted shrubs, etc.: 树～ tree hedge | 篱笆～ bamboo or twig fence

幛 zhàng 幛子 a large, oblong sheet of silk with appropriate messages attached, presented at a wedding, birthday or funeral: 贺～ large silk sheet with an inscription of congratulations on it | 寿～ large sheet of silk inscribed with good wishes for a birthday | 喜～ large sheet of silk with an appropriate message attached, presented at a wedding | 挽～ large silk sheet inscribed with condolences, presented at a funeral

【幛子】zhàng·zi 题上词句的整幅绸布,用做祝贺或吊唁的礼物 large, oblong sheet of silk with appropriate messages attached, presented at a wedding, birthday or funeral

嶂 zhàng 直立像屏障的山峰 screen-like mountain peak: 层峦叠～ peaks rising each higher than the other

瘴 zhàng 瘴气 miasma: ～疠 communicable subtropical diseases, e.g. pernicious malaria, etc.

【瘴疠】zhànglì 指亚热带潮湿地区流行的恶性疟疾等传染病 communicable subtropical diseases, e.g. pernicious malaria, etc.

【瘴气】zhàngqì 热带或亚热带山林中的湿热空气,从前认为是瘴疠的病原 miasma; damp and hot air in tropical or subtropical forests, formerly believed to be the cause of communicable diseases

zhāo (ㄓㄠ)

钊 zhāo 〈书 *fml.*〉勉励。多用于人名。(oft. used in given names) encourage; exhort; urge; spur

招[1] zhāo ❶ 举手上下挥动 beckon; gesture: ～手 wave hands | ～之即来 come at sb.'s beckoning; be at sb.'s beck and call ❷ 用广告或通知的方式使人来 recruit; enlist; enroll: ～领 announce the finding of lost property | ～考 give public notice of an entrance examination; employ by examination | ～生 enroll new students; recruit students ❸ 引来(不好的事物) attract (sth. bad); incur; court: ～苍蝇 attract flies | ～灾 court disaster; invite calamity ❹ same as 惹 rě ②; 招惹 provoke; tease: 这孩子爱哭,别～他。He's a cry-baby. Don't tease him. ❺ same as 惹 rě ③: 这孩子真～人喜欢。What a loveable child! ❻ 〈方 *dial.*〉传染 infect; be contagious: 这病～人,要注意预防。This disease is contagious, and must be guarded against. ❼ (Zhāo)姓 a surname

招[2] zhāo 承认罪行 confess; own up: ～供 confess; confess one's crime(s) | ～认 make a confession of one's crimes; plead guilty | 不打自～ make a confession without prompting

招[3] zhāo same as 着 zhāo ①②

【招安】zhāo'ān 〈旧时 *old*〉指统治者用笼络的手腕使武装反抗者或盗匪投降归顺 (of feudal rulers) offer amnesty to rebels or bandits, and enlist their services

【招标】zhāo//biāo 兴建工程或进行大宗商品交易时,公布标准和条件,招人承包或承买叫做招标 invite tenders; invite bids (or public bidding); before construction of a large project, or a large transaction of commodities, standards and conditions are given to invite tenders

【招兵】zhāo//bīng 招募人来当兵 recruit soldiers; raise troops

【招兵买马】zhāo bīng mǎi mǎ 组织或扩充武装力量。也比喻扩大组织或扩充人员。recruit

men and buy horses to raise or expand an army; (fig.) recruit followers

【招待】zhāodài 对宾客或顾客表示欢迎并给以应有的待遇 receive (guests); entertain; wait on; serve (customers):～客人 entertain guests|记者～会 press conference

【招待所】zhāodàisuǒ 机关、厂矿等所设接待宾客或所属单位来往的人住宿的处所 guest house; hostel; residence operated by an institution, factory or mine for receiving guests and people from its branches

【招风】zhāo//fēng 指惹人注意而生出是非 catch the wind; attract too much attention and invite trouble

【招抚】zhāofǔ same as 招安 zhāo'ān

【招供】zhāo//gòng (罪犯)供出犯罪事实 make a confession of one's crime(s); confess:从实～ make a clean breast of

【招股】zhāo//gǔ 企业用公司组织形式募集股金 raise capital by floating shares

【招呼】zhāo·hu ❶ 呼唤 call; shout; beckon:远处有人～你。Someone is beckoning at you in the distance. ❷ 用语言或动作表示问候 hail; greet; say hello to:乡亲们都围上来,我不知～谁好。I really didn't know whom I should say hello to when so many villagers mobbed me. ❸ 吩咐;关照 ask; notify; tell:～他赶快做好了送来。Tell him to finish and send it over quickly. ❹ 照料 take care of; look after:医院里对病人～得很周到。The hospital looks after the patients well. ❺〈方 *dial.*〉留神 watch; mind, take care:路上有冰,～滑倒了。The road is icy. Mind you don't slip.

【招魂】zhāo//hún 招回死者的魂(迷信),现多用于比喻 (superstition) call back the spirits of the dead; (oft. fig.) revive

【招集】zhāojí 招呼人们聚集;召集 call together; convene

【招架】zhāojià 抵挡 ward off blows; hold one's own:～不住 be unable to hold one's own; unable to withstand|来势凶猛,难于～ be unable to hold one's own as the attack becomes fierce

【招考】zhāokǎo 用公告的方式叫人来应考 give public notice of an entrance examination; admit (students, applicants, etc.) by examination:～新生 enrol students by examination|～学徒工 recruit apprentices

【招徕】zhāolái same as 招揽 zhāolǎn:～顾客 solicit customers

【招揽】zhāolǎn 招引(顾客) solicit (customers or business); canvass:～生意 canvass; seek business orders; drum up trade

【招领】zhāolǐng 用出公告的方式叫丢失物品的人来领取 announce the finding of lost property:～失物 Found (in a notice)

【招募】zhāomù 募集(人员) recruit; enlist:～新兵 recruit new soldiers

【招女婿】zhāonǚ·xu same as 招亲 zhāoqīn ①

【招牌】zhāo·pai 挂在商店门前写明商店名称或经售的货物的牌子,作为商店的标志。也比喻某种名义或称号。shop sign; signboard; (fig.)certain fame or title

【招盘】zhāopán 工商业主因亏损或其他原因,把企业的货物、器具、房屋、地基等作价,招人承购,继续经营 because of loss or other reasons, an enterprise assessing its goods, utensils, houses, land, etc., for sale so as to keep the business going

【招聘】zhāopìn 用公告的方式聘请 engage through public notice; invite applications for a job:～技术人员 advertise for technicians

【招亲】zhāo//qīn ❶ 招人到自己家里做女婿 take a man into the family as a son-in-law ❷ 到人家里做女婿;入赘 marry into and live with one's bride's family

【招惹】zhāo·rě ❶ (言语、行动)引起(是非、麻烦等) (of speech and action) provoke; incur; court (trouble):～是非 beg for trouble; bring trouble on oneself ❷〈方 *dial.*〉(用言语、行动)触动,逗引(多用于否定式 oft. used in the negative) using speech and action to tease; provoke:别～他。Don't provoke him.|这个人～不得。You'd better not provoke that person.

【招认】zhāorèn (罪犯)承认犯罪事实 confess one's crime(s); plead guilty

【招生】zhāo//shēng 招收新学生 enrol new students; recruit students:～简章 school admission brochure

【招事】zhāo//shì 惹是非 bring trouble on oneself; invite trouble:他爱多嘴,好～。He is in the habit of shooting his mouth off and bringing trouble on himself as a consequence.

【招收】zhāoshōu 用考试或其他方式接收(学员、学徒、工作人员等) recruit; take in; enrol (students, apprentices and staff members) through an examination

【招手】zhāo//shǒu 举起手来上下摇动,表示叫人来或跟人打招呼 wave one's hand as a signal; beckon; wave:～示意 wave one's greetings; wave back in acknowledgement

【招数】zhāoshù same as 着数 zhāoshù

【招贴】zhāotiē 贴在街头或公共场所,以达到宣传目的的文字、图画 poster; placard; bill; written notice or picture put up in the street or public places in order to give publicity

【招贴画】zhāotiēhuà 宣传画 pictorial poster (or placard)

【招贤】zhāoxián 招纳有才德的人 (of a ruler) summon people of worth to serve their country:张榜～ put up posters to recruit talents|～纳士 invite men of virtue and wisdom

【招降】zhāo//xiáng 号召敌人来投降 summon sb. to surrender

【招降纳叛】zhāo xiáng nà pàn 招收接纳敌方投降、叛变过来的人。现多指网罗坏人,结党营私。recruit deserters and traitors; form factions, and recruit turncoats and renegades

【招笑儿】zhāoxiàor〈方 *dial.*〉引人发笑 laughable; funny

【招眼】zhāoyǎn 惹人注意 attract people's attention; show; be ostentatious: 大红的外衣很～。The red overcoat is too ostentatious.

【招摇】zhāoyáo 故意张大声势,引人注意 act ostentatiously; show off: ～过市 swagger through the streets; blatantly seek publicity | 这样做,太～了。Doing it that way is too ostentatious.

【招摇过市】zhāoyáo guò shì 故意在公众场合张大声势,引人注意 swagger through the streets; blatantly seek publicity

【招摇撞骗】zhāoyáo zhuàngpiàn 假借名义,到处炫耀,进行诈骗 browbeat and swindle; bluff one's way around

【招引】zhāoyǐn 用动作、声响或色、香、味等特点吸引 draw; induce; attract with action, sound, colour, fragrance, etc.: ～顾客 attract customers

【招灾】zhāo//zāi 引来灾祸 court disaster; invite trouble: ～惹祸 court disaster; bring trouble on oneself

【招展】zhāozhǎn 飘动;摇动(引人注意) move to and fro; flutter; wave (to attract the attention of others): 红旗迎风～。Red flags flutter in the breeze. | 花枝～ be gorgeously dressed

【招致】zhāozhì ❶ 招收;搜罗(人才) recruit (talents); seek and employ ❷ 引起(后果) result in; bring about (a certain result); lead to: ～意外的损失 cause unexpected losses

【招赘】zhāozhuì 招女婿 have the groom move into the bride's house after marriage

【招子】zhāo·zi ❶ 招贴 poster; placard; bill ❷ 挂在商店门口写明商店名称的旗子或其他招揽顾客的标志 flag with the shop's name on it hung at the doorway of a shop, or other signs for attracting customers ❸ 着儿;办法、计策或手段 device; move; means; stratagem

【招租】zhāozū 招人租赁(房屋) (of a house) ask for lodgers; attract lodgers; to let: ～启事 notice asking for lodgers

Z

昭 zhāo ❶ 明显;显著 clear; obvious; evident: ～彰 clear; manifest; obvious; evident | ～著 clear; evidently manifest ❷〈书 *fml.*〉表明;显示 show; demonstrate: 以～信守 demonstrate one's good faith

【昭然】zhāorán 很明显的样子 clear and obvious; obvious; manifest; very clear: 天理～。Heavenly principles are obvious to all. | ～若揭(指真相大明) abundantly clear; all too clear; clear as daylight

【昭示】zhāoshì 明白地表示或宣布 make clear to all; declare publicly: ～后世 make it clear to posterity | ～国人 declare to the whole people of the country

【昭雪】zhāoxuě 洗清(冤枉) exonerate; rehabilitate; redress: 平反～ redress and exonerate

【昭彰】zhāozhāng 明显;显著 clear; manifest; evident: 罪恶～ commit flagrant crimes

【昭昭】zhāozhāo〈书 *fml.*〉❶ 明亮 bright; light; well-lit: 日月～。The sun and the moon shine brightly. ❷ 明白 clear; obvious; plain: 以其昏昏,使人～。It is clear the ignorant cannot enlighten others.

【昭著】zhāozhù 明显 clear; evident; obvious: 恶名～ of ill repute; notorious | 罪行～ obvious crimes

啁 zhāo [啁哳](zhāozhā)〈书 *fml.*〉形容声音烦杂细碎 twitter; also 嘲哳 zhāozhā

☞ zhōu on p. 2496

着(❶❷招) zhāo ❶ (～儿 zhāor) 下棋时下一子或走一步叫一着 a move in a chess game: 高～儿 clever move | 别支～儿。Don't tell about it. *or* Don't reveal the move. ❷ (～儿 zhāor)〈比喻 *fig.*〉计策或手段 trick; device; move: 使花～ play tricks | 我没～儿了。I am at my wit's end. | 这一～厉害。That was really a stroke of brilliance. ❸〈方 *dial.*〉放;搁进去 put in; add: ～点儿盐 put some salt in it. ❹〈方 *dial.*〉用于应答,表示同意 all right; OK: 这话～哇! That says it all! | ～,咱们就这么办。OK, that's what we'll do then.

☞ zháo on p. 2423, ·zhe on p. 2432 and zhuó on p. 2534

【着数】zhāoshù ❶ 下棋的步子 move in chess ❷ 武术的动作 movement in wushu ❸〈比喻 *fig.*〉手段或计策 trick; device ‖ also 招数 zhāoshù

朝 zhāo ❶ 早晨 early morning; dawn; morning: ～阳 morning sun | 一～一夕 overnight | ～令夕改 issue an order in the morning and rescind it in the evening ❷ 日;天 day: 今～ today | 一～有事 if something happens one day

☞ cháo on p. 228

【朝不保夕】zhāo bù bǎo xī 保得住早上,不一定保得住晚上。形容情况危急。not know at dawn what may happen by dusk; be in a precarious state; also 朝不虑夕 zhāo bù lǜ xī

【朝发夕至】zhāo fā xī zhì 早晨出发晚上就能到达。形容路程不远或交通便利。start at dawn and arrive at dusk; a day's journey

【朝晖】zhāohuī 早晨太阳的光辉 morning sunlight

【朝令夕改】zhāo lìng xī gǎi 早晨发布了命令,晚上又改变了。形容主张或办法经常改变,一会儿一个样。issue an order at dawn and rescind it at dusk; make unpredictable changes in policy

【朝露】zhāolù 〈书 *fml.*〉早晨的露水 morning dew; 〈比喻 *fig.*〉存在时间非常短促的事物 short-lived; ephemeral; transitory

【朝气】zhāoqì 精神振作,力求进取的气概(跟'暮气'相对 as opposed to 'lethargy' and 'apathy') youthful spirit; vigour; vitality: ～蓬勃 full of youthful spirit; full of vigour and vitality; imbued with vitality|富有～ full of vigour

【朝乾夕惕】zhāo qián xī tì 形容一天到晚很勤奋,很谨慎 work hard and conscientiously from morning till night (乾 *qian*:勉力 make an effort)

【朝秦暮楚】zhāo Qín mù Chǔ 一时倾向秦国,一时又依附楚国 serve the State of Qin in the morning and the State of Chu in the evening; 〈比喻 *fig.*〉人反复无常 change one's allegiance frequently; be inconstant; be temperamental

【朝日】zhāorì 早晨的太阳 morning sun: ～初升。The morning sun has just risen.

【朝三暮四】zhāo sān mù sì 有个玩猴子的人拿橡实喂猴子,他跟猴子说,早上给每个猴子三个橡子,晚上给四个,所有的猴子听了都急了;后来他又说,早上给四个,晚上给三个,所有的猴子就都高兴了(见于《庄子·齐物论》)。原比喻聪明人善于使用手段,愚笨的人不善于辨别事情,后来比喻反复无常。Three in the morning, four in the evening. *Zhuangzi · The Sorting which Evens Things Out*: A monkey trainer fed monkeys with acorns, saying to them, 'I'll give each of you three acorns in the morning and four acorns in the evening.' On hearing this, all the monkeys became annoyed. Then the man changed this around to say: 'I'll give each of you four acorns in the morning and three acorns in the evening.' Then all the monkeys felt happy. (orig. fig.) The wise are good at playing tricks, while the foolish are slow to perceive; change one's mind frequently

【朝夕】zhāoxī ❶ 天天;时时 morning and evening; from morning till night; day and night; daily: ～相处 be together from morning till night; be closely associated ❷ 形容非常短的时间 shortly; very short time: ～不保 feel uneasy day and night|只争～ seize the day, seize the hour; seize every minute

【朝霞】zhāoxiá 日出时东方的云霞 rosy clouds of dawn; rosy dawn

【朝阳】zhāoyáng 初升的太阳 rising sun; morning sun

☞ 朝阳 cháoyáng on p. 229

嘲 zhāo [嘲哳] (zhāozhā) same as 啁哳 zhāozhā

☞ cháo on p. 229

zháo (ㄓㄠˊ)

着 zháo ❶ 接触;挨上 touch; contact: 上不～天,下不～地 touch neither the sky nor the earth ❷ 感受;受到 feel; suffer: ～风 be chilled by the wind; become unwell through being in a draught|～凉 catch cold; catch a chill ❸ 燃烧,也指灯发光(跟'灭'相对 as opposed to 'extinguished') burn; be ignited; be lit: 炉子～得很旺。The stove is burning strong.|天黑了,路灯都～了。It's dark, and the streetlights are all on. ❹ 用在动词后,表示已经达到目的或有了结果 [used after a verb to indicate the result of reaching the goal or the action]: 睡～了 fall asleep|打～了 hit the target|猜～了 guess right|灯点～了。The lamp is lit. ❺ 〈方 *dial.*〉入睡 fall asleep: 一上床就～了。He fell asleep the moment he got into bed.

☞ zhāo on p. 2422, ·zhe on p. 2432 and zhuó on p. 2534

【着慌】zháo//huāng 着急;慌张 get nervous; get alarmed; become flustered (or jittery); be thrown into a panic: 大家都急得什么似的,可他一点儿也不～。Everyone panicked, but he was not worried in the slightest.

【着火】zháo//huǒ 失火 catch fire; be on fire

【着火点】zháohuǒdiǎn same as 燃点[2] rándiǎn

【着急】zháo//jí 急躁不安 get worried; feel anxious; have ants in one's pants: 别～,有问题商量着解决。Don't worry. Let's talk it over and work out a solution.|时间还早,着什么急? It's still early, why worry?

【着凉】zháo//liáng 受凉 catch cold; catch a chill: 外面挺冷,当心～。It's chilly outside; be careful not to catch cold.|我夜间着了一点儿凉。I caught a cold at night.

【着忙】zháo//máng ❶ 因感到时间紧迫而加快动作 be in a hurry; be in a rush: 事先收拾好行李,免得临上车～。Get all the luggage ready so as to avoid a last-minute rush when you get on the train.|时间还早着呢,你着的什么忙? It's still early, why are you in such a rush? ❷ 着急;慌张 worry; feel anxious; panic: 别～,等我说完了你再说。Don't worry, you can talk after I finish.|听说孩子病了,她心里有点～。Hearing her child was ill, she felt worried.

【着迷】zháo//mí 对人或事物产生难以舍弃的爱好;入迷 be fascinated; be captivated; be enchanted: 老爷爷讲的故事真动人,孩子们听得都～了。The story the old man told was so interesting, the children listened spellbound.

【着魔】zháo//mó 入魔 be bewitched; be possessed; be entranced

【着三不着两】zháo sān bù zháo liǎng 指说话

Z

或行事考虑不周，轻重失宜 scatter-brained; thoughtless

zhǎo (ㄓㄠˇ)

爪 zhǎo ❶ 动物的脚趾甲 claw; talon: 乌龟趾间有蹼，趾端有～。A turtle has webs in between its toes and a talon at the tip of each toe. ❷ 鸟兽的脚 claw; paw: 前～ front paws | 鹰～ hawk's talons | 张牙舞～ bare fangs and brandish claws; make threatening gestures; engage in sabre-rattling

☞ zhuǎ on p. 2515

【爪牙】zhǎoyá 爪和牙是猛禽、猛兽的武器 talons and fangs;〈比喻 *fig.*〉坏人的党羽 lackeys; underlings

找1 zhǎo 为了要见到或得到所需求的人或事物而努力 look for; try to find; seek: ～人 look for sb. | ～材料 try to find materials | ～出路 seek a way out | 钢笔丢了，到处～不着。He lost his pen and looked for it everywhere in vain.

找2 zhǎo 把超过应收的部分退还；把不足的部分补上 give change: ～钱 give change | ～齐 make uniform; even up; balance; make complete; make up for a deficiency

【找病】zhǎo//bìng 自找生病 look for illness;〈比喻 *fig.*〉自寻苦恼 invite trouble; ask for it; bring vexation to oneself

【找补】zhǎo•bu 把不足的补上 make up a deficiency: 不够再～点儿。We'll make it up if there's any shortage. | 话没说完，还得～几句。As I haven't made myself sufficiently clear, I would like to add a few more words.

【找茬儿】zhǎo//chár 故意挑毛病 find fault; pick holes; pick a quarrel: ～打架 find some excuse and start a fight; also 找碴儿 zhǎo//chár

【找麻烦】zhǎo má•fan (给自己或别人)添麻烦 look for trouble; ask for trouble; cause sb. trouble

【找平】zhǎo//píng (瓦工砌墙、木工刨木料等)使高低凹凸的表面变平 (of bricklaying, planing, etc.) make level; level up or down: 右手边儿还差两层砖，先～了再一起往上砌。The right side needs two more layers of bricks. Make it level before laying more bricks.

【找齐】zhǎoqí ❶ 使高低、长短相差不多 make uniform; even up; balance: 篱笆编成了，顶上还要～。The top of the fence needs to be made even. ❷ 补足 make complete: 今儿先给你一部分，差多少明儿～。We'll pay you part of the money today, and make up the balance tomorrow.

【找钱】zhǎo//qián 收到币值较大的钞票或硬币，超过应收的数目，把超过的部分用币值小的钱币退还 give change; receive a bank note or a coin of a larger sum than what one should get, and give the surplus back in a bank note or a coin of a smaller sum

【找事】zhǎo//shì ❶ 寻找职业 look or hunt for a job; seek employment: 你替他找个事干干。Why don't you find a job for him. ❷ 故意挑毛病，引起争吵；寻衅 kick up a row; pick a quarrel: 他是故意来～的，别理他。He came here to pick a quarrel. Just ignore him.

【找死】zhǎosǐ 自找死亡(多用于责备人不顾危险 oft. used to reproach sb. for disregarding their own safety) court death

【找头】zhǎo•tou 找回的钱 change (from money paid)

【找寻】zhǎoxún 寻找 try to find; look for; seek

【找辙】zhǎo//zhé〈方 *dial.*〉❶ 找借口 find an excuse; use a pretext: 我实在坐不住了，于是～离去。I really could not sit there any longer, and I quickly found an excuse to leave. ❷ 想办法；找门路 find a solution; seek a way out: 厂里停工待料，领导都忙着～呢。The work is held up due to a lack of materials in the factory, and the factory leaders are busy trying to look for a way out.

沼 zhǎo 天然的水池子 natural pond: 池～ pond; pool | ～泽 marsh; swamp; bog

【沼气】zhǎoqì 池沼污泥中埋藏的植物体发酵腐烂生成的气体，也可用粪便、植物茎叶加甲烷细菌发酵制得。主要成分是甲烷。用做燃料或化工原料。marsh gas; firedamp; methane; sewage gas; sludge gas; gases produced by burying plants in the sludge of a pond to let them ferment and rot, or by putting excrement, urine and plants' stems and leaves together and adding some methane germs to let them ferment, the main element being methane, which is used as a fuel or raw material in chemical industry

【沼泽】zhǎozé 水草茂密的泥泞地带 marsh; swamp; bog

zhào (ㄓㄠˋ)

召1 zhào ❶ 召唤 call together; convene; summon; gather: ～集 call together; convene; assemble ❷ (Zhào) 傣族姓 a surname of the Dai people

召2 zhào 寺庙，多用于地名，如乌审召，罗布召，都在内蒙古 temple; monastery; often used in place names, e.g. Wushenzhao and Luobuzhao (in Inner Mongolia) [蒙 Mongolian]

☞ Shào on p. 1691

【召唤】zhàohuàn 叫人来(多用于抽象方面 usu. abstract) call; summon: 新的生活在～着我们。New life is calling us.

【召集】zhàojí 通知人们聚集起来 call together;

convene; assemble: ～人 convener | 队长～全体队员开会。The team leader called all his members together for a meeting.

【召见】zhàojiàn ❶ 上级叫下级来见面 call in (one's subordinates) ❷ 外交部通知外国驻本国使节前来谈有关事宜 summon (an envoy of a foreign country) to an interview

【召开】zhàokāi 召集人们开会;举行(会议) convene; hold; convoke (a meeting, conference)

兆[1] zhào ❶ same as 预兆 yùzhào ①: 征～ sign; omen; portent | 不吉之～ ill (or evil) omen ❷ 预示 augur; portend; foretell: 瑞雪～丰年。A timely snow augurs a good harvest. ❸ (Zhào) 姓 a surname

兆[2] zhào 数目 number; amount a) 一百万 million; mega b) 〈古代 *arch*.〉指一万亿 million million; trillion

【兆头】zhào·tou same as 预兆 yùzhào ①: 好～ good omen | 坏～ bad omen | 暴风雨的～ signs of an impending storm

诏 zhào ❶ 〈书 *fml*.〉告诉;告诫 instruct; admonish; warn; exhort ❷ 诏书 imperial edict: 下～ issue an imperial edict

【诏书】zhàoshū 皇帝颁发的命令 imperial edict

赵(趙) Zhào ❶ 周朝国名,在今山西北部和中部,河北西部和南部 Zhao; one of the states of Zhou Dynasty, in present-day western and southern Hebei Province and northern and central Shanxi Province ❷ 旧诗文中指今河北南部 (used in classical writings to refer to) southern part of present-day Hebei Province ❸ 姓 a surname

【赵体】Zhào tǐ 元代赵孟頫(fǔ)所写的字体,圆润清秀,结构谨严 Zhao style; an exquisite, strict style of Chinese calligraphy created by Zhao Mengfu during the Yuan Dynasty

炤 zhào same as 照 zhào

笊 zhào [笊篱] (zhào·lí) 用金属丝、竹篾或柳条等制成的能漏水的用具,有长柄,用来捞东西 strainer made of wire, bamboo, or wicker, which has a long handle and is used to dredge things up from water

棹(櫂、艄) zhào 〈方 *dial*.〉❶ 桨 oar ❷ 划(船) row (a boat)

旐 zhào 〈古代 *arch*.〉一种旗子 a kind of flag

照 zhào ❶ 照射 shine; illuminate; light up; radiate: 日～ sunshine | 阳光～在窗台上。The sun shines on the window. | 用手电筒～一～ light up with a torch ❷ 对着镜子或其他反光的东西看自己的影子;有反光作用的东西把人或物的形象反映出来 reflect; mirror: ～镜子 look in the mirror | 湖面如镜,把岸上的树木～得清清楚楚。Like a mirror, the lake reflected clearly the trees on the banks. ❸ 拍摄(相片、电影) take a picture; photograph; film: 这张相片～得很好。This picture is well-taken. ❹ 相片 photograph; picture: 小～ small-sized photo | 玉～ your photograph ❺ 执照;政府所发的凭证 license; permit: 车～ licence (of a car, bicycle, etc.) | 护～ passport | 牌～ licence plate; number-plate | 取缔无～摊贩 ban pedlars who have no licence ❻ 照料 take care of; look after; attend to: ～管 take care of | ～应 look after ❼ 通知 inform; notify: 关～ look after; keep an eye on | ～会 note ❽ 比照 compare; contrast: 查～ please note | 对～ contrast, check (against sth. else) ❾ 知晓;明白 make out; understand: 心～不宣 have a tacit understanding ❿ 对着;向着 in the direction of; towards: ～这个方向走 go in this direction ⓫ 依照;按照 according to; in conformity with: ～章办事 act in accordance with the regulations | ～这个样子做 handle it accordingly

【照搬】zhàobān 照原样不动地搬用(现成的方法、经验、教材等) indiscriminately imitate; mechanically copy (methods, experiences, teaching materials, etc.): 学习先进经验要因地制宜,不能盲目～。We must learn advanced experiences in line with our local conditions, rather than copy them indiscriminately.

【照办】zhào//bàn 依照办理 act ditto; act accordingly; act in accordance with; act upon; comply with; follow: 碍难～ find it difficult to comply | 您吩咐的事都一一～了。I have done all you asked.

【照本宣科】zhào běn xuān kē 〈比喻 *fig*.〉不能灵活运用,死板地照现成文章或稿子宣读 read item by item from the text; repeat what the book says

【照壁】zhàobì 大门外对着大门做屏蔽用的墙壁 screen wall facing the gate of a house; also 照墙 zhàoqiáng or 照壁墙 zhàobìqiáng

【照常】zhàocháng 跟平常一样 as usual: ～工作 work as usual | ～营业 do business as usual | 一切～。Everything is the same as usual.

【照抄】zhàochāo ❶ 照原来的文字抄写或引用 copy word for word; copy verbatim: 这一段～新华社的电讯。This paragraph is copied from the Xinhua News Agency. ❷ 照搬 indiscriminately imitate; mechanically copy

【照登】zhàodēng 文稿、信件等不加修改地刊载 publish (manuscripts, letters, etc.) without alteration: 来函～。Letters will be published verbatim.

【照发】zhàofā ❶ 照这样发出(公文、电报等),多用于批语 approved for distribution (used for documents, telegrams, etc.) ❷ 照常发给 be paid as usual: 带职学习,工资～。Salary will be paid in full when one goes to receive on-the-job training.

【照拂】zhàofú 照料;照顾 look after; care for; attend to

【照顾】zhào·gù ❶ 考虑(到);注意(到) give

consideration to; show consideration for; make allowance(s) for: ～全局 take the whole thing into account; consider the situation as a whole | ～各个部门 take every department into consideration ❷ 照料 keep an eye on; look after: 我去买票，你来～行李。I'll go to buy the tickets, you keep an eye on the luggage. ❸ 特别注意，加以优待 look after; care for; attend to: ～病人 look after a patient | 老幼乘车，～座位。Please give the seats to the elderly and children. ❹ 商店或服务行业等管顾客前来购买东西或要求服务叫照顾(of a customer) patronize; customer, client, or patron — how shops, service trades, etc., refer to those who come to buy things or request services

【照管】zhàoguǎn 照料管理 look after; tend; be in charge of: ～孩子 look after a child; mind a child | ～器材 tend the equipment | 这件事由他～。Let him take charge of this matter.

【照葫芦画瓢】zhào hú·lu huà piáo 〈比喻 *fig*.〉照样子模仿 copy; imitate; draw a dipper with a gourd as a model

【照护】zhàohù 照料护理(伤员、病人等) look after (patients, the wounded, etc.): ～老人 look after the elderly | 细心～ carefully attend

【照会】zhàohuì ❶ 一国政府把自己对于彼此有关的某一事件的意见通知另一国政府 (government of a country) present (or deliver, address) a note (about a certain matter, to the government of another country) ❷ 上述性质的外交文件 above-mentioned diplomatic document

【照旧】zhàojiù 跟原来一样 as before; as usual; as of old: 我们休息了一下，～往前走。After a short rest, we marched on as usual. | 这本书再版时，体例可以～，资料必须补充。When this book is published again, the style and layout can remain intact, but the contents should be enriched.

【照看】zhàokàn 照料(人或东西) look after; attend to; keep an eye on (a person or a thing): ～孩子 attend to the children | 你放心去吧，家里的事有我～。You just set your mind at rest and go. I will look after things at home.

Z

【照理】zhàolǐ ❶ 按理 in the ordinary course of events; normally: ～他现在该来了。Normally, he would have been here. ❷ 〈方 *dial*.〉照料；料理 look after; attend to: ～家务 attend to household chores

【照例】zhàolì 按照惯例；按照常情 as a rule; as usual; usually: 春节～放假三天。As a rule we have a three-day holiday during the Spring Festival. | 扫帚不到，灰尘～不会自己跑掉。Where the broom doesn't reach, dust will never run away.

【照料】zhàoliào 关心料理 take care of; attend to: ～病人 look after patients

【照临】zhàolín (日、月、星的光)照射到 shine on; illuminate; light up (of the light of the sun, the moon and stars): 曙光～大地。The rising sun bathes the land in light.

【照猫画虎】zhào māo huà hǔ 〈比喻 *fig*.〉照着样子模仿 draw a tiger with a cat as a model; copy sth. without capturing its spirit

【照面儿】zhào//miànr ❶ 面对面地不期而遇叫打个照面儿 encounter; come across; come face to face with sb.; run into sb. ❷ 露面；见面[多用于否定式 oft. used in the negative] put in an appearance; show up; turn up: 始终没有～。He never showed up. | 互不～ avoid each other

【照明】zhàomíng 用灯光照亮室内、场地等 illumination; lighting: ～设备 lighting equipment | 舞台～ stage illumination

【照明弹】zhàomíngdàn 一种特制的炸弹或炮弹，弹体内装有发光药剂，有的有小降落伞，能在空中发出强光。用于夜间观察或指示攻击目标。flare; star shell; specially made bombs or shells loaded with luminous powder, some of which have small parachutes and give out a powerful light in the sky to help observe or illuminate a target for attack at night

【照排】zhàopái 用电子计算机照相排版 phototype setting; photocomposition; filmsetting: 激光～ laser phototype setting

【照片儿】zhàopiānr same as 照片 zhàopiàn

【照片】zhàopiàn 把感光纸放在照相底片下曝光后经显影、定影而成的人或物的图片 photograph; picture developed from film by presenting the film and sensitive paper to the actinic rays of light

【照墙】zhàoqiáng same as 照壁 zhàobì

【照射】zhàoshè 光线射在物体上 shine; illuminate; light up; irradiate: 植物需要阳光～。Plants need sunshine.

【照实】zhàoshí 按照实情 according to the facts: 你做了什么，～说好了。Tell us all you've actually done.

【照说】zhàoshuō 按说 ordinarily; generally; as a rule: 他补习了几个月，～这试题应该能做出来。He has taken remedial lessons for several months. Generally he should be able to work out these test questions.

【照相】zhào//xiàng 摄影 ① 的通称 general term for 摄影 shèyǐng ①

【照相版】zhàoxiàngbǎn 应用摄影术制成的印刷版的统称，种类很多，如三色版、珂罗版等 process plate; the general term for photo-offset process plates of different kinds, e.g. three-colour, halftone collotype, etc.

【照相机】zhàoxiàngjī 照相的器械，由镜头、暗箱、快门以及测距、取景、测光等装置构成 camera; device for taking pictures, consisting of a lens, magazine, shutter, range finder, viewfinder, etc.; also 摄影机 shèyǐngjī

【照相纸】zhàoxiàngzhǐ 印相纸和放大纸的统称 (general term for) photographic paper

【照样】zhào//yàng (～儿 zhào//yàngr) 依照某个样式 after a pattern or model: 照着样儿画 draw from a model | 照这个样儿做 do it this way

【照样】zhàoyàng (～儿 zhàoyàngr) 照旧 in the same old way; as before; all the same; as usual: 天气尽管很冷,工地上～热火朝天。Although it was very cold, the construction site was bustling with activity all the same.

【照妖镜】zhàoyāojìng 旧小说中所说的一种宝镜,能照出妖魔原形。现在也用于比喻。(in old novels) mirror that shows up the monster for what it is; monster-detector (also used in a figurative way)

【照耀】zhàoyào (强烈的光线)照射 (of strong rays) shine; radiate; illuminate: 阳光～着大地。The sun shines over the land.

【照应】zhàoyìng 配合;呼应 coordinate; correlate: 互相～ be well coordinated | 前后～ be well organised

【照应】zhào·ying 照料 look after; take care of: 一路上乘务员对旅客～得很好。The attendants took good care of the passengers.

【照直】zhàozhí ❶ 沿着直线(前进) (go) straight on: ～走。Go straight ahead. | ～往东,就是菜市。Go straight east and you'll find the market. ❷ (说话)直截了当 straightforward; direct: 有话就～说,不要吞吞吐吐的。Say directly what you have to say. Don't hem and haw.

罩 zhào ❶ 遮盖;扣住;套在外面 cover; overspread; envelop; wrap: 笼～ envelop; shroud | 天空阴沉沉地～满了乌云。The sky is covered with dark clouds. | 棉袄外面～着一件蓝布褂儿 wear a blue dust-coat over a cotton-padded coat ❷ (～儿 zhàor) 罩子 cover; shade; hood; casing: 灯～儿 lampshade | 口～儿 gauze mask ❸ (～儿 zhàor)外罩;罩衣 outer garment; wrap; dust-coat; overall: 袍～儿 outer garment of a robe (or gown) ❹ 养鸡用的笼子 small cage or coop for raising chickens ❺ 捕鱼用的竹器,圆筒形,上小下大,无顶无底 tube-shaded bamboo fish trap, with the upper part being small and the lower part big, topless and bottomless

【罩棚】zhàopéng 用芦苇、竹子等搭在门前或院子里的棚子 reed or bamboo-made awning over a gateway or a courtyard

【罩衫】zhàoshān 〈方 *dial.*〉 same as 罩衣 zhàoyī

【罩袖】zhàoxiù 〈方 *dial.*〉 套袖 oversleeve; sleevelet

【罩衣】zhàoyī 穿在短袄或长袍外面的单褂 outer garment; dust-coat; overall; also 罩褂儿 zhàoguàr

【罩子】zhào·zi 遮盖在物体外面的东西 cover; shade; hood; casing

鲱 zhào 鱼类的一科,全身无鳞,头部扁平,有的种类胸部前方有吸盘。生活在溪水中。sisorid catfish (*Sisoridae*), a kind of scaleless fish with a flat head, some having a sucking disc on their front chests, and living in streams

肇(肈) zhào ❶ 发生;引起 cause (trouble, etc.); lead to: ～事 make trouble; stir up a disturbance | ～祸 bring trouble; cause an accident ❷ 〈书 *fml.*〉 开始 start; commence; initiate: ～始 begin; start | ～端 beginning; origin ❸ (Zhào) 姓 a surname

【肇端】zhàoduān 〈书 *fml.*〉 开端 beginning; origin

【肇祸】zhàohuò 闯祸 cause trouble; cause an accident

【肇始】zhàoshǐ 〈书 *fml.*〉 开始 start; commence; initiate

【肇事】zhàoshì 引起事故;闹事 cause trouble; create a disturbance: 追查～者 find out the troublemaker

曌 zhào same as 照 zhào。唐代武则天为自己名字造的字。written Chinese character created by Wu Zetian of the Tang Dynasty for her own given name

zhē (ㄓㄜ)

折 zhē ❶ 翻转 roll over; turn over: ～跟头 turn or throw a somersault; loop a loop ❷ 倒过来倒过去 pour back and forth between two containers: 水太热,用两个碗～一～就凉了。The water's boiling hot. Pour it from one cup to another to cool it.

☞ shé on p. 1693 and zhé on p. 2428

【折箩】zhēluó 〈方 *dial.*〉 指酒席吃过后倒在一起的剩菜 leftovers from a feast

【折腾】zhē·teng ❶ 翻过来倒过去 turn from side to side; toss about: 凑合着睡一会儿,别来回～了。Just find a place and sleep for a while. Don't keep tossing and turning. ❷ 反复做(某事) do sth. over and over again: 他把收音机拆了又装,装了又拆,～了几十回。He time and again took the radio apart, and then put it back together dozens of times. ❸ 折磨 cause physical or mental suffering; torment: 慢性病～人。A chronic disease can cause such torment.

蜇 zhē ❶ 蜂、蝎子等用毒刺刺人或动物 (of bees, scorpions, etc.) sting; prick with a sting ❷ 某些物质刺激皮肤或黏膜使发生微痛 cause sharp pain; smart; sting: 切洋葱～眼睛。Your eyes will smart when you cut on-

Z

ions.|这种药水擦在伤口上～得慌。You will feel a sharp sting when this iodine is applied to the cut.

☞ zhé on p.2430

嗻 zhē ☞ [哳嗻](chēzhē) on p.233

☞ zhè on p.2432

遮 zhē ❶ 一物体处在另一物体的某一方位，使后者不显露 hide from view; cover; screen; conceal: 山高～不住太阳。High mountains cannot shut out the sunlight. ❷ 拦住 hinder; block; obstruct; impede: 横～竖拦 impede in every possible way ❸ 掩盖 cover up; cloak: ～丑 gloss over one's blemishes; hide one's shame; cover up one's defects|～人耳目 throw dust in people's eyes; hoodwink (or fool) the public|～不住内心的喜悦 cannot conceal one's delight

【遮蔽】zhēbì same as 遮 zhē ①: ～风雨 keep out wind and rain|树林～了我们的视线，看不到远处的村庄。The trees blocked our view, so we could not see the village in the distance.

【遮藏】zhēcáng 遮蔽；掩藏 hide; conceal; cover up

【遮丑】zhē//chǒu 用言语或行动遮掩缺点、错误和不足 gloss over one's blemishes; hide one's shame; cover up one's defects

【遮挡】zhēdǎng ❶ 遮蔽拦挡 shelter from; keep out: ～寒风 keep out the cold wind|窗户用布帘～起来 cover the window with a curtain ❷ 可以遮蔽拦挡的东西 sth. used as a cover; shelter: 草原上没有什么～。There was nothing to obstruct the view on the grassland.

【遮盖】zhēgài ❶ 从上面遮住 cover; overspread: 路给大雪～住了。The road is covered by snow. ❷ same as 掩盖 yǎngài ②；隐瞒 hide; conceal; cover up: 错误是～不住的。Mistakes can never be hidden.

【遮拦】zhēlán 遮挡；阻挡 block; obstruct; impede: 防风林可以～大风。The wind-break serves to keep out wind and sand.

【遮羞】zhē//xiū ❶ 把身体上不好让人看见的部分遮住 cover one's private parts ❷ 做了丢脸的事用好听的话来掩盖 hush up a scandal; cover up one's embarrassment: ～解嘲 make excuses to get out of a scrape

Z

【遮羞布】zhēxiūbù ❶ 系在腰间遮盖下身的布 loincloth; fig leaf ❷ 借指用来掩盖羞耻的事物 disguise; veil; cover-up

【遮掩】zhēyǎn ❶ 遮蔽 cover; overspread; envelop; block; same as 遮盖 zhēgài ①: 远山被雨雾～，变得朦胧了。The distant hills were clouded up in clouds and mist and became blurred. ❷ 掩饰 cover up; hide; conceal: ～错误 gloss over one's mistakes|极力～内心的不安 try to conceal the uneasiness in one's heart

【遮眼法】zhēyǎnfǎ 障眼法 cover-up; camouflage

【遮阳】zhēyáng 指帽檐或形状像帽檐那样可以遮阳光的东西 sunshade; things that can give shade from sunshine like the brim of a hat, etc.

zhé (ㄓㄜˊ)

折[1] zhé ❶ 断；弄断 fracture; break; snap: 骨～ fracture ❷ 损失 suffer the loss of; lose: 损兵～将 suffer heavy casualties ❸ 弯；弯曲 bend; twist; turn: 曲～ twists and turns|百～不挠 be unbending; be undaunted by repeated setbacks ❹ 回转；转变方向 turn back; change direction: 转～ turn in the course of an event|刚走出大门又～了回来 turn back after walking out of the gate ❺ 折服 be convinced; be filled with admiration: 心～ be deeply convinced; be filled with heartfelt admiration ❻ 折合；抵换 convert into; amount to: ～价 convert into money; assess the cash value|～账 pay a debt in kind|～变 sell off (one's property) ❼ 折扣 discount; rebate: 打九～ give a 10% discount|不～不扣 without the slightest discount; 100 per cent; out and out; to the letter ❽ 北曲每一个剧本分为四折，一折相当于后来的一场 There are four acts in a *beiqu* musical drama, where one act equals one scene in modern drama.

折[2] zhé ❶ 折叠 fold: ～扇 folding fan|～尺 folding ruler|她把信～好，装在信封里。She folded the letter and put it in an envelope. ❷ (～儿 zhér)折子 book or booklet used for keeping accounts, etc.: 奏～ memorial or memorandum (presented to an emperor)|存～儿 deposit book; bankbook

☞ shé on p.1693 and zhē on p.2427

【折半】zhébàn 减半；对折 reduce (a price) by half; give a 50% discount: 处理品按定价～出售 sell at a 50% discount; sell at half price

【折变】zhébiàn 变卖 sell off: ～家产 sell off one's property

【折尺】zhéchǐ 可以折叠起来的木尺，长度多为一米 folding wooden ruler (usu. about 1-metre long)

【折冲】zhéchōng 〈书 *fml.*〉制敌取胜 defeat or subdue the enemy: ～御侮 repel foreign aggression|～千里之外 use stratagem or diplomacy to vanquish the enemy long before they get close

【折冲樽俎】zhéchōng zūnzǔ 在酒席宴会间制敌取胜，指进行外交谈判 outmanoeuvre an enemy over glasses of wine; win by superior diplomacy; engage in diplomatic negotiations

（樽俎 *zunzu*：古时盛酒食的器具 ancient wine vessel）

【折叠】zhédié 把物体的一部分翻转和另一部分紧挨在一起 fold; bend or close sth. over upon itself：～衣服 fold the clothes｜把被褥～得整整齐齐 fold the quilt neatly

【折兑】zhéduì 兑换金银时按成色、分量折算 convert; exchange gold or silver for money

【折服】zhéfú ❶ 说服；使屈服 subdue; bring into submission; convince：强词夺理不能～人。You cannot convince people by sophistry.｜艰难困苦～不了我们。No hardship can daunt us. ❷ 信服 be convinced; be filled with admiration：令人～ compel admiration｜大为～ filled with great admiration

【折福】zhé//fú 迷信的人指过分享用或不合情理地承受财物而减少福分（superstition）ruin one's happy lot either through the acquisition of an undeserved fortune or through enjoying comfort to excess

【折干】zhé//gān（～儿 zhé//gānr）指赠送礼品时用钱来代替 give money in place of a present; present sb. with money as a gift

【折光】zhéguāng ❶（物质）使通过的光线发生折射（of water, glass, etc.）refract light ❷ 指折射出来的光 refracted light;〈比喻 *fig.*〉被间接反映出来的事 物的本质特征 indirect reflection of the essence of things：时代的～ reflection of the times｜现实生活的～ reflection of real life

【折合】zhéhé ❶ 在实物和实物间、货币和货币间、实物和货币间按照比价计算 convert into; calculate according to rates of exchange between different objects, between different currencies, or between an object and a currency：当时的一个工资分～一斤小米。One wage point converted into one *jin* of millet at that time. ❷ 同一实物换用另一种单位来计算 amount to; be equivalent to：水泥每包五十公斤，～市斤，刚好一百斤。Each bag of cement weighs 50 kilograms, that is, 100 *jin*.

【折回】zhéhuí 半路返回 turn back (halfway)

【折价】zhé//jià 把实物折合成钱 convert into money; assess the cash value：损坏公物要～赔偿。If you damage public property, you must pay for it.

【折旧】zhéjiù 补偿固定资产所损耗的价值 depreciation (in value of property)：～费 depreciation charge

【折扣】zhé·kòu 买卖货物时，照标价减去一个数目，减到原标价的十分之几叫做几折或几扣，例如标价一元的减到九角叫做九折或九扣，减到七角五分叫做七五折或七五扣 discount; rebate. When a price is reduced by a certain percentage in doing business, it is called a certain per cent discount, e.g. if the price is 1 yuan and then reduced to 90 cents, it is called a 10 per cent discount, while if the price is reduced to 75 cents, it is a 25 per cent discount.

【折磨】zhé·mó 使在肉体上、精神上受痛苦 cause physical or mental suffering; torment; torture：受～ be tortured; be in torment｜这病真～人。It is a torturing illness.

【折辱】zhérǔ〈书 *fml*〉使受挫折和污辱 humiliate; insult

【折扇】zhéshàn（～儿 zhéshànr）用竹、木、象牙等做骨架，上面蒙上纸或绢而制成的可以折叠的扇子 folding fan; fan with a bamboo, wood, ivory, etc. frame, covered with paper or silk, that can be folded

【折射】zhéshè ❶ 光线、声波从一种媒质进入另一种媒质时传播方向发生偏折的现象 refraction; refracting phenomenon light and sound waves produce when they spread from one medium to another ❷〈比喻 *fig.*〉把事物的表象或实质表现出来 reveal; reflect：用白描的手法～不同人物的不同心态 reveal the different mentality of different characters through the method of plain sketches

【折实】zhéshí ❶ 打了折扣，合成实在数目 reckon the actual amount after a discount ❷ 把金额折合成某种实物价格计算 adjust payment in accordance with the price index of certain commodities

【折寿】zhé//shòu 迷信的人指因享受过分而减损寿命 (superstition) have one's allotted portion of life span reduced by having or getting more than one deserves

【折受】zhé·shou〈方 *dial.*〉因过分尊敬或优待而使人承受不起 flatter; treat sb. better than deserved

【折算】zhésuàn 折合；换算 convert

【折头】zhé·tou〈方 *dial.*〉折扣 discount; rebate：打～ give a discount

【折线】zhéxiàn 不在同一直线上而顺次首尾相连的若干线段组成的图形 broken line

【折腰】zhéyāo〈书 *fml.*〉弯腰行礼。也指屈身事人。bend one's back; bow in obeisance; cringe

【折账】zhé//zhàng 用实物抵偿债款 pay a debt in kind

【折纸】zhézhǐ 儿童手工的一种，用纸折叠成物体的形状 origami; paper folding

【折中】zhézhōng 对几种不同的意见进行调和 aim at the golden mean; medium; compromise：～方案 compromise proposal｜～的办法 compromise method; also 折衷 zhézhōng

【折衷】zhézhōng same as 折中 zhézhōng

【折衷主义】zhézhōng zhǔyì 一种形而上学思想方法，把各种不同的思想、观点和理论无原则地、机械地拼凑在一起 eclecticism; metaphysical method of thinking, by which different thoughts, ideas and theories are put together unconditionally and mechanically

【折皱】zhézhòu 皱纹 wrinkle; lines：满脸～

have a wrinkled face

【折子】zhé·zi 用纸折叠而成的册子，多用来记账 booklet in accordion form with a slipcase, often used for keeping accounts

【折子戏】zhé·zixì 只表演全本中可以独立演出的一段情节的戏曲，（区别于'本戏'）。例如演整本《牡丹亭》是本戏，只演《春香闹学》或《游园惊梦》是折子戏。aria; scene or excerpt from a traditional opera; highlight from an opera (as compared with 'whole opera'), e. g. *The Peony Pavilion* is the whole opera, while 'Chun Xiang Raises Hell at School' or 'A Dream in the Garden' are arias of it.

哲(喆) zhé ❶ 有智慧 wise; sagacious; intelligent: ～人 philosopher; sage ❷ 有智慧的人 wise man; sage: 先～ great thinker of the past; sage of old

【哲理】zhélǐ 关于宇宙和人生的原理 philosophic theory; philosophy: 人生～ philosophy of life | 富有～的诗句 philosophical poem

【哲人】zhérén〈书 *fml.*〉智慧卓越的人 sage; philosopher

【哲学】zhéxué 关于世界观的学说。是自然知识和社会知识的概括和总结。哲学的根本问题是思维和存在、精神和物质的关系问题，根据对这个问题的不同回答而形成唯心主义哲学和唯物主义哲学两大对立派别。philosophy; theory concerning world outlook, and the generalization and summarization of natural and social knowledge. The fundamental question of philosophy is that of the relationship between thought and existence, and between spirit and matter, and the different answers to this question give rise to two antagonistic schools of philosophy: metaphysical idealism and materialism.

辄(輒) zhé〈书 *fml.*〉总是；就 always; often; regularly; as soon as; soon after: 动～得咎 be blamed for whatever one does | 浅尝～止 stop studying soon after getting a smattering of a subject

晢(晣) zhé〈书 *fml.*〉明亮 bright; shining

詟(讋) zhé〈书 *fml.*〉惧怕 fear; awe; apprehension; dread: ～服（慑服）surrender (or yield) in fear | ～惧（恐惧）be frightened

Z

蛰(蟄) zhé 蛰伏 prick with a sting; sting: 惊～ Waking of Insects (3rd solar term) | ～如冬蛇 look like a hibernating snake | 久～乡间 live in seclusion in the country

【蛰伏】zhéfú ❶ 动物冬眠，潜伏起来不食不动 (of animals) dormancy; hibernation ❷ 借指蛰居 live in seclusion or solitude

【蛰居】zhéjū〈书 *fml.*〉像动物冬眠一样长期躲在一个地方，不出头露面 live in seclusion like animals in hibernation: ～山村 live in seclusion in a mountain village

蜇 zhé ☞ 海蜇 hǎizhé on p. 759
☞ zhē on p. 2428

箬 zhé [箬子] (zhé·zi)〈方 *dial.*〉一种粗的竹席 a kind of bamboo mat

谪(謫) zhé〈书 *fml.*〉❶ 封建时代把高级官吏降职并调到边远地方做官 relegate a high official to a minor post in a remote region (as a form of punishment in feudal times); banish; exile: 贬～ relegate; banish from the court | ～居 (after being banished) settle or live in exile ❷ 指神仙受了处罚，降到人间（迷信）(of immortals) be banished from Heaven: 有人把李白称为～仙人。Some people dubbed Li Bai a 'Banished Immortal'. ❸ 责备；指摘 censure; blame: 众人交～ be censured by everybody

【谪居】zhéjū 被贬谪后住在某个地方 (of officials in former times) live in banishment: 苏东坡曾～黄州。At one time Su Dongpo lived at Huangzhou in banishment.

摺 zhé same as 折[2] zhé

磔[1] zhé 古代的一种酷刑，把肢体分裂 (as a punishment in ancient China) dismember the body; tear limb from limb; draw and quarter

磔[2] zhé〈书 *fml.*〉汉字的笔画，即捺 (nà) right-falling stroke in Chinese written characters, also known as 捺 nà

辙 zhé (～儿 zhér) ❶ 车轮压出的痕迹；车辙 the track of a wheel; rut: 覆～ take the road where carts have overturned; repeat the same mistakes | 如出一～ follow the same track; be exactly the same | 前头有车，后头有～。A cart leaves tracks behind it. ❷ 行车规定的路线方向 direction of traffic: 上下～ up the road, then down the road | 顺～儿 go in the right direction; follow the track | 戗 (qiāng) ～儿 drive in the wrong direction (against traffic regulations) ❸ 杂曲、戏曲、歌词所押的韵 rhyme (in a song, poetic drama, etc.): 十三～ 13 rhymes | 合～ in rhyme; in agreement ❹〈方 *dial.*〉办法；主意（多用在'有、没'后面 usu. used after 有 yǒu or 没 méi) way; idea; wit: 想～ think of a way | 你来得正好，我正没～呢。You came at the right time. I am really at my wits' end.

【辙口】zhékǒu same as 辙 zhé ③: 这一段词儿换换～就容易唱了。A change in the rhyme of these lines will certainly make singing them easier.

zhě (ㄓㄜˇ)

者[1] zhě〈助词 *aux.*〉❶ 用在形容词或动词后面，或带有形容词或动词的词组后面，表示

有此属性或做此动作的人或事物[used after a verb or adjective, or a verb or adjective phrase, to indicate a class of persons or things]: one (or those) who; the thing (or things) which: 强～ the strong|老～ old man|作～ writer|读～ reader|胜利～ winner|未渡～ those who have not crossed the river|卖柑～ orange seller|符合标准～ those who have reached the standard ❷ 用在某某工作、某某主义后面,表示从事某项工作或信仰某个主义的人[used after a noun phrase ending with 'work' or 'ism' to indicate the person or persons doing the stated work or holding the stated doctrine] -er; -ist: 文艺工作～ literary and art workers|共产主义～ communist ❸〈书 *fml.*〉用在'二、三、数'等数词后面,指上文所说的几件事物[used with the numbers 二 èr、三 sān、数 shù, etc., to refer to things mentioned above]: 二～必居其一。It must be one or the other.|两～缺一不可。Neither is dispensable. ❹〈书 *fml.*〉用在词、词组、分句后面表示停顿[used after a word, phrase, or clause to mark a pause, as in giving definitions]: 风～,空气流动而成。Wind is formed because of the flow of the air. ❺ 用在句尾表示希望或命令的语气(多见于早期白话 oft. used in early vernacular to give force) command: 路上小心在意～。Do take care while on your way.

者[2] zhě〈代词 *pron.*〉义同'这'(多见于早期白话 oft. used in early vernacular) this: ～番 this|～边 (over) here; this side

锗 zhě 金属元素,符号 Ge (germanium)。灰白色,质脆,有单向导电性,自然界分布极少。是重要的半导体材料。germanium (Ge); metal element with a greyish white colour, that is a brittle, one-way conductive, and very rare in the natural world

赭 zhě 红褐色 reddish brown; burnt ochre: ～石 ochre (a mineral)

【赭石】zhěshí 矿物,主要成分是三氧化二铁。一般呈暗棕色,也有土黄色或红色的,主要用做颜料。ochre; mineral reddish brown in colour, with some being yellowish or red, mainly used as pigment

褶(襵) zhě (～儿 zhěr) 褶子 pleat; crease: 百～裙 pleated skirt|裤子上有一道～儿 a crease in the trousers

【褶皱】zhězhòu ❶ 由于地壳运动,岩层受到压力而形成的连续弯曲的构造形式 fold; continuous bending structure of rock formed by pressure from movement of the earth's crust ❷ 皱纹 wrinkle (in the skin): 满脸～ wrinkled face

【褶子】zhě·zi ❶(衣服上)经折叠而缝成的纹 (of clothes) pleat: 裙子上的～ pleats in the skirt ❷(衣服、布匹、纸张上)经折叠而留下的痕迹 (of clothes, cloth and paper) crease; fold; wrinkle: 用熨斗把～烙平。Iron out the wrinkles. ❸ 脸上的皱纹 wrinkles on the face

zhè (ㄓㄜˋ)

这(這) zhè ❶〈指示代词 *demons. pron.*〉指示比较近的人或事物[indicating close persons or things]: a)后面跟量词或数词加量词,或直接跟名词[followed by a classifier or a numeral plus a classifier, or directly by a noun]: ～本杂志 this magazine|～几匹马 these horses|～孩子 this child|～地方 this place|～时候 this time b)单用[used independently]: ～叫什么? What is this called?|～是我们厂的新产品。This is a new product by our factory. 注意 **NOTE**: 在口语里,'这'单用或者后面直接跟名词时,说 zhè;'这'后面跟量词或数词加量词时,常常说 zhèi。以下【这程子】、【这个】、【这会儿】、【这些】、【这样】各条在口语里都常常说 zhèi- 。In spoken language, when 这 zhè is used independently or followed directly by a noun, it is pronounced 'zhè'; when 这 zhè is followed by a classifier or a numeral plus a classifier, it is pronounced 'zhèi'; in the following examples of 这程子 zhèchéng·zi,这个 zhè·ge,这会儿 zhèhuìr,这些 zhèxiē and 这样 zhèyàng, it is pronounced 'zhèi-'. ❷ 这时候 now; then: 他～才知道运动的好处。Only now does he see the value of taking physical exercises.|我～就走。I'm leaving right now.

【这程子】zhèchéng·zi〈方 *dial.*〉这些日子 these days; lately; of late; recently: 你～到哪儿去了? Where have you been these last few days?

【这个】zhè·ge ❶ 这一个 this one; this: ～孩子真懂事。This child is sensible.|～比那个沉,我们两个人抬。This one is heavier than that one. Let us two carry it. ❷ 这东西;这事情 this: 你问～吗? 这叫哈密瓜。Are you asking about this? This is called Hami melon.|他为了～忙了好几天。He's been busy with this for quite a few days. ❸ 用在动词、形容词之前,表示夸张[used before a verb or adjective to give it force] so; such: 大家～乐啊! How happy everyone was!

【这会儿】zhèhuìr 这时候 now; at the moment; at present: ～雪下得更大了。It is snowing harder at the moment.|你～又上哪儿去呀? Where are you going now? also 这会子 zhèhuì·zi

【这里】zhèlǐ〈指示代词 *demons. pron.*〉指示比较近的处所[used as a demonstrative pronoun] over here; here: ～没有姓洪的,你走错了吧? No one is surnamed Hong over here. You must have got the wrong place.|我们～

Z

一年种两季稻子。We grow two crops of rice a year here.

【这么】zhè·me〈指示代词 *demons. pron.*〉指示性质、状态、方式、程度等[indicating nature, state, way, degree, etc.]：有～回事。Yes, that's true.|大家都～说。So everyone says.|～好的庄稼。What good crops they are! also 这末 zhè·me 注意 **NOTE**：在口语里常常说 zè·me，以下四条同。In spoken language，这么 zhè·me is often pronounced zè·me. The following four entries are as the same as this one.

【这么点儿】zhè·mediǎnr 指示数量小 such a tiny bit：～水，怕不够喝。I'm afraid so little water won't be enough to drink.|～路一会儿就走到了。It is so close, we can walk there in a very short time.

【这么些】zhè·mexiē 指示一定的数量(多指数量大 oft. large quantity) so much; that many：～人坐得开吗？Is there enough seating for that many people?|就～了，你要都拿去。This is all we have. Take all this with you.

【这么样】zhè·meyàng 这样 like this; this way

【这么着】zhè·me·zhe〈指示代词 *demons. pron.*〉指示动作或情况 this way; like this：～好。It's better this way.|瞄准的姿势要～，才打得准。Only when you take aim in the correct posture can you become a crack shot.

【这儿】zhèr ❶ 这里 here ❷ 这时候(只用在'打、从、由'后面)[used only after 打 dǎ，从 cóng or 由 yóu] now; then：打～起我每天坚持锻炼。From now on I am going to do physical training every day.

【这山望着那山高】zhè shān wàng·zhe nà shān gāo〈比喻 *fig.*〉不满意自己的环境、工作，老觉得别的环境、别的工作好 it's always the other mountain that looks higher; the grass is always greener on the other side; never feel satisfied with one's lot

【这些】zhèxiē〈指示代词 *demons. pron.*〉指示较近的两个以上的人或事物[indicating two or more persons or things]these：～就是我们的意见。These are our opinions.|～日子老下雨。It has been raining these days. also 这些个 zhèxiē·ge

【这样】zhèyàng (～儿 zhèyàngr)〈指示代词 *demons. pron.*〉指示性质、状态、方式，程度等[indicating nature, state, way, degree, etc.] such; so; like this; this way：他就是～一个大公无私的人。He is such an unselfish man.|他的认识和态度就是～转变的。His view and attitude changed like this.|担负～重大的责任，够难为他的。It's really difficult for him to undertake such a big responsibility.|～，就可以引起同学们爬山的兴趣。This way can arouse the interest of the students in climbing the mountain. also 这么样 zhè·meyàng 注意 **NOTE**：'这(么)样'可以用做定语或状语，也可以用做补语或谓语。'这么'只能用做定语或状语。这(么)样 zhè(·me)yàng can be used as an attribute, adverbial modifier, complement, or predicate, whereas 这么 zhē·me can only be used as attribute, or adverbial modifier

Z

柘 zhè 落叶灌木或乔木，树皮灰褐色，有长刺，叶子卵形或椭圆形，花小，排列成头状花序，果实球形。叶子可以喂蚕，木材中心为黄色，质坚而致密，是贵重的木料。three-bristle cudrania (*Cudrania tricuspidata*); deciduous bush or arbour, having grey brown bark, long thorns, egg-shaped or oval leaves, small flowers in capitulum, and round fruits, its leaves used for raising silkworms, the central part of the trunk being a precious yellow timber with a hard solid texture

浙(淛) Zhè 指浙江 (Zhèjiāng)，我国的一省 Zhejiang Province in china

蔗 zhè 甘蔗 sugarcane：～糖 sucrose|～田 sugarcane field|～农 sugarcane grower

【蔗农】zhènóng 从事甘蔗生产的农民 sugarcane grower

【蔗糖】zhètáng ❶ 有机化合物，化学式 $C_{12}H_{22}O_{11}$。白色结晶，有甜味，甘蔗和甜菜中含量特别丰富。日常食用的白糖或红糖中主要成分是蔗糖。sucrose ($C_{12}H_{22}O_{11}$); white crystal that tastes sweet, found in abundance in sugarcane and beet. The main element of white and brown sugar is sucrose ❷ 用甘蔗榨汁熬成的糖 cane sugar

【蔗渣】zhèzhā 甘蔗榨汁后剩下的渣滓，是造纸、酿酒的原料 bagasse; raw material for making paper and brewing wine

嗻 zhè〈旧时 *old*〉仆役对主人或宾客的应诺声[said by a servant in reply to the master's command] yes; yeah; alright

☞ zhē on p.2428

鹧 zhè [鹧鸪](zhègū)鸟，背部和腹部黑白两色相杂，头顶棕色，脚黄色。吃昆虫、蚯蚓、植物的种子等。francolin (*Francolinus*); partridge; bird with black and white feathers on its back and breast, brown feathers on its head, and yellow claws; eating insects, earthworms, seeds, etc.

䗪 zhè [䗪虫](zhèchóng) 地鳖 ground beetle

·zhe (·ㄓㄜ)

著 ·zhe same as 着 ·zhe

☞ zhù on p.2512 and zhuó on p.2534

着 ·zhe ❶ 表示动作的持续[indicating the continuation of an action] be doing：他打～红旗在前面走。He is holding a red flag and walking in the front.|他们正谈～话呢。They are having a talk. ❷ 表示状态的持续[indicatind the continuation of a state]：大门敞～。The gate is wide open.|茶几上放～一瓶花。A vase of flowers is placed on the tea table. ❸ 用在动词或表示程度的形容词后面，加强命令或嘱咐的语气[used after a verb or an adjective to strengthen the tone of an order or exhortion]：你听～。Just listen.|步子大～点儿。Quicken your steps, please.|快～点儿写。Write quickly.|手可要轻～点儿。Do it lightly. ❹ 加在某些动词后面，使变成介词[used after certain verbs to form a preposition]：顺～ along|沿～ alongside|朝～ towards|照～ follow the example|为～ for (the sake of)

☞ zhāo on p.2422, zháo on p.2423 and zhuó on p.2534

【着哩】·zhe ·li 〈方 *dial.*〉same as 着呢 ·zhe ·ne

【着呢】·zhe·ne 表示程度深[used to indicate degree] very; quite：街上热闹～。The streets are full of noise and excitement.|这种瓜好吃～。This melon is very good.|他画得可像～。He draws quite well.

zhèi (ㄓㄟˋ)

这(這) zhèi '这'(zhè)的口语音 variant pronunciation for 这 zhè, in spoken Chinese ☞ 注意 **NOTE** for 这 zhè on p.2431

zhēn (ㄓㄣ)

贞[1] zhēn ❶ 忠于自己所信守的原则；坚定不变 loyal; faithful; staunch：忠～ loyal|坚～ staunch ❷ 封建礼教指女子的贞节(feudal ethical code) chastity or virginity：～女 virgin; chaste girl|～妇 chaste woman

贞[2] zhēn 〈书 *fml.*〉占卜 divination

【贞操】zhēncāo same as 贞节 zhēnjié：保持～ maintain one's virginity

【贞观】Zhēnguàn 唐太宗(李世民)年号(公元627—649) Zhenguan, title of the reign (627-649) of Li Shimin, 2nd emperor of the Tang Dynasty, called reverently Emperor Taizong after death

【贞节】zhēnjié ❶ 坚贞的节操 moral integrity; loyalty ❷ 封建礼教所提倡的女子不失身、不改嫁的道德 chastity or virginity, i.e. remaining chaste and faithful to one's husband or betrothed, even after his death, as demanded by the feudal moral code

【贞洁】zhēnjié 指妇女在节操上没有污点(of a woman) chaste

【贞烈】zhēnliè 封建礼教中指妇女坚守贞操，宁死不屈(of a woman) would rather die than lose one's chastity

针(鍼) zhēn ❶ (～儿 zhēnr)缝衣物用的工具，细长而小，一头尖锐，一头有孔或钩，可以引线，多用金属制成 needle; tiny, thin long sewing tool, mostly made of metal, with one end being sharp and the other having a hole or a hook for putting thread through：绣花～ embroidering needle|缝纫机～ sewing needle ❷ 细长像针的东西 anything like a needle：松～ pine needle|指南～ compass; compass needle|表上有时～、分～和秒～。A watch has hour, minute and second hands. ❸ 针剂 injection; shot：防疫～ inoculation|打～ get an injection ❹ 〈中医 *Chin. med.*〉刺穴位用的特制的金属针。也指用这种针按穴位刺入体内医治疾病。acupuncture; specially made metal needle used in traditional Chinese medical science to tumilate the acupoint：～灸 acupuncture and moxibustion

【针鼻儿】zhēnbír 针上引线的孔 eye of a needle

【针砭】zhēnbiān 砭是古代治病的石头针，使用方法已失传。*Bian* is a wrought-stone needle used for an ancient form of acupuncture, whose method has been lost.'针砭'比喻发现或指出错误，以求改正 find or point out mistakes so as to correct them; criticize; refute：痛下～ resolutely correct one's mistakes

【针刺麻醉】zhēncì-mázuì 我国一种独特的麻醉技术。用毫针扎在病人的某些穴位上，达到镇痛目的，使病人在清醒的状态下接受手术。acupuncture anaesthesia; unique Chinese technique using needles to pierce the acupoints of the patient to ease pain, so that an operation can be done while the patient is conscious; 简称 abbr. 针麻 zhēnmá

【针对】zhēnduì 对准 be directed against; be aimed at; be targeted at; take into consideration：～儿童的心理特点进行教育 educate children by taking into consideration their psychological characteristics|这些话都是～着这个问题说的。These remarks are aimed at this problem.

【针锋相对】zhēn fēng xiāng duì 针尖对针尖 tit for tat; measure for measure; 〈比喻 *fig.*〉双方策略、论点等尖锐地对立 in direct opposition to; two sides diametrically opposed to each other in strategy, viewpoint, etc.

【针箍】zhēngū 〈方 *dial.*〉(～儿 zhēngūr)顶针儿 thimble

【针管】zhēnguǎn 注射上盛药水的管子，有刻度，用玻璃等制成 needle tube; graduated tube to hold liquid medicine for injections, made of glass, etc.; also 针筒 zhēntǒng

【针剂】zhēnjì 注射用的药物 injection

【针尖儿对麦芒儿】zhēnjiānr duì màimángr 指争执时针锋相对 a pin against an awn; confront eyeball to eyeball; diamond cutting diamond：两个人你一句，我一句，～，越吵越厉害。The two quarrelled like diamond cutting diamond.

【针脚】zhēn·jiao ❶ 衣物上针线的痕迹 line of stitches：棉袄上面有一道一道的～。There are lines of stitches on the cotton-padded overcoat.｜顺着线头找～（比喻寻找事情的线索）find the stitches by tracing the thread;（fig.）find the clue to the matter ❷ 缝纫时前后两针之间的距离 stitch：～太大了。The stitches are too long.｜她纳的鞋底～又密又匀。The shoe sole she made has small, neat stitches.

【针灸】zhēnjiǔ 针法和灸法的合称。针法是把毫针按一定穴位刺入患者体内，用捻、提等手法来治疗疾病。灸法是把燃烧着的艾绒按一定穴位靠近皮肤或放在皮肤上，利用热的刺激来治疗疾病。针灸是我国医学的宝贵遗产。acupuncture and moxibustion. Acupuncture puts filiform needles into the patient's body according to certain acupoints, treating ailments by twisting and pulling the needles, while moxibustion puts burning moxa close to or on the skin according to certain acupoints, using stimulation of the heat to treat ailments. Acupuncture and moxibustion are valuable legacies of traditional Chinese medicine

【针头】zhēntóu 安在注射器上的针状金属管 syringe needle

【针头线脑】zhēn tóu xiàn nǎo（～儿 zhēn tóu xiàn nǎor）缝纫用的针线等物 needle and thread; sewing kit;〈比喻 *fig.*〉零碎细小的东西 odds and ends; trivial things

【针线】zhēn·xian 缝纫刺绣等工作的总称 needlework; needlecraft：～活儿 needlework｜学～ learn to do needlework

【针眼】zhēnyǎn ❶ 针鼻儿 eye of a needle; needle's eye ❷（～儿 zhēnyǎnr）被针扎过之后所留下的小孔 pinprick

【针眼】zhēn·yan 麦粒肿的通称 general term for 麦粒肿 màilìzhǒng

【针叶树】zhēnyèshù 叶子的形状像针或鳞片的树木，如松、柏、杉（区别于'阔叶树' as compared with 'broadleaf trees'）coniferous tree; conifer; trees with needle-like or scale-like leaves, e.g. pine, cypress, and fir

【针织品】zhēnzhīpǐn 用针编织的物品，如线袜子、线手套、线围巾等。分机织的和手工织的两种。knitted goods; knitwear; hosiery; knitted items like socks, gloves, scarves, etc. produced with a machine or by hand

Z

【针黹】zhēnzhǐ〈书 *fml.*〉针线 needlework

侦 zhēn 暗中察看；调查 detect; scout; investigate：～探 spy; do detective work｜～查 investigate

【侦办】zhēnbàn 侦查并办理（案件）investigate and handle (a case)

【侦查】zhēnchá 检察机关或公安机关为了确定犯罪事实和犯罪人而进行调查 investigate a crime or criminal act through a procuratorial organ or public security organ：～案情 investigate a case｜立案～ enter a case on file for investigation

【侦察】zhēnchá 为了弄清敌情、地形及其他有关作战的情况而进行活动 reconnoitre; scout; reconnaissance to gather intelligence about the enemy, including the topography of the enemy's position and strategy：～兵 scout｜火力～ reconnaissance by firing｜～飞行 reconnaissance flight

【侦获】zhēnhuò 侦查破获；侦破 investigate and crack

【侦缉】zhēnjī 侦查缉捕 track down and arrest：～队 tracking team｜～盗匪 track down and arrest bandits

【侦破】zhēnpò 侦查并破获 investigate and crack; break：这是一个没有线索、难于～的案件。This is a case without clues, therefore very hard to break.

【侦探】zhēntàn ❶ 暗中探寻机密或案情 do detective work; spy：～敌情 spy on the enemy ❷ 做侦探工作的人；间谍 detective; spy

【侦探小说】zhēntàn xiǎoshuō 描写刑事案件的发生和破案经过的小说 detective story; detective fiction; crime novel

珍（珎）zhēn ❶ 宝贵的东西 treasure; riches：奇～异宝 rare treasures｜山～海味 delicacies from land and sea; choice food of every kind｜如数家～ as if enumerating one's family valuables ❷ 宝贵的；贵重的 treasured; precious; valuable; rare：～品 treasure; curiosity; curio｜～禽 rare bird ❸ 看重 value highly; set great store by：～视 treasure; prize; value; set store by｜～重 prize; cherish; treasure; value highly｜～惜 treasure; cherish; value; prize

【珍爱】zhēn'ài 重视爱护 treasure; love dearly; be very fond of：孩子深受祖父的～。The child is deeply loved by his grandfather.｜他～这幅字，不轻易示人。He treasures this work of calligraphy and doesn't easily show it to others.

【珍宝】zhēnbǎo 珠玉宝石的总称，泛指有价值的东西 jewellery; treasure; riches：如获～ as if one had found hidden riches｜勘探队正在寻找地下～。The prospecting team is looking for underground treasure.

【珍本】zhēnběn 珍贵而不易获得的书籍 rare edition; rare book

【珍藏】zhēncáng ❶ 认为有价值而妥善地收藏 collect (rare books, art treasures, etc.)：～多年，完好无损 be stored for many years and still in good condition ❷ 指收藏的珍贵物品 rare and valuable articles collected or stored as treasure：把家中的～献给博物馆 donate all rare and valuable articles collected in the house to the museum

【珍贵】zhēnguì 价值大；意义深刻；宝贵 valuable; precious: ～的参考资料 valuable reference data | ～的纪念品 precious mementos

【珍品】zhēnpǐn 珍贵的物品 treasure: 艺术～ art treasure

【珍奇】zhēnqí 稀有而珍贵 rare: 大熊猫是～的动物。The panda is a rare animal.

【珍禽】zhēnqín 珍奇的鸟类 rare birds: ～异兽 rare birds and animals

【珍摄】zhēnshè 〈书 *fml.*〉书信套语,指保重(身体) [used in letters] take good care of yourself; look after yourself

【珍视】zhēnshì 珍惜重视 treasure; cherish; prize; value; set store by: ～友谊 treasure the friendship | 教育青年人～今天的美好生活。Teach young people to prize the happy life they lead today.

【珍玩】zhēnwán 珍贵的供玩赏的东西 rare curios

【珍闻】zhēnwén 珍奇的见闻(多指有趣的小事 oft. human-interest stories) news tidbits; fillers: 世界～ world briefs (or miscellany)

【珍惜】zhēnxī 珍重爱惜 treasure; value; cherish: ～时间 value one's time

【珍稀】zhēnxī 珍贵而稀有 rare and precious: 大熊猫、金丝猴、野牦牛是我国的～动物。The panda, golden monkey and wild yak are rare animals in our country.

【珍羞】zhēnxiū same as 珍馐 zhēnxiū

【珍馐】zhēnxiū 〈书 *fml.*〉珍奇贵重的食物 delicacies; dainties: ～美味 delicacies; dainties; also 珍羞 zhēnxiū

【珍重】zhēnzhòng ❶ 爱惜;珍爱(重要或难得的事物) (of important or rare matters) prize; cherish; treasure; value highly: ～人才 value personnel highly ❷ 保重(身体) take good care of yourself; look after yourself: 两人紧紧握手,互道～。They clasped hands, each asking the other to take good care of himself.

【珍珠】zhēnzhū 某些软体动物(如蚌)的贝壳内产生的圆形颗粒,乳白色或略带黄色,有光泽,是这类动物体内发生病理变化或外界砂粒和微生物等进入贝壳而形成的。多用做装饰品。pearl; round-shaped beads grown in the shells of certain molluscs like the oyster, of a white or light yellow colour, and shiny, formed through pathological changes inside the mollusc, or through the entry of external elements like sand and microbes into the shells, usu. used for ornamentation; also 真珠 zhēnzhū

【珍珠贝】zhēnzhūbèi 能产珍珠的贝类,如珠母贝等 pearl shell; pearl oyster; shellfish that can produce pearls e.g. pearl shell, pearl oyster, etc.

【珍珠米】zhēnzhūmǐ 〈方 *dial.*〉玉米 maize; (Indian) corn

帧 zhēn (旧读 formerly pronounced zhèng) 〈量词 *classifier*〉幅(用于字画等 of painting and calligraphy, etc.) painting

胗 zhēn (～儿 zhēnr) 鸟类的胃 gizzard: 鸡～儿 chicken's gizzard | 鸭～儿 duck's gizzard

溱 Zhēn 溱水,水名,在广东 Zhenshui River, in Guangdong Province

真 zhēn ❶ 真实(跟'假、伪'相对 as opposed to 'false, fake') true; real; genuine: ～心诚意 sincerely, genuinely | 千～万确 absolutely true | 去伪存～ eliminate the false and retain the true | 这幅宋人的水墨画是～的。This is a genuine Song-dynasty painting. ❷ 的确;实在 really; truly; indeed: 时间过得～快! How time flies! | '人勤地不懒'这话～不假。It is really true that 'hard work in the fields brings in a good harvest'. ❸ 清楚确实 clearly; distinctly; unmistakably: 字音咬得～ pronounce words distinctly | 黑板上的字你看得～吗? Can you see the characters on the blackboard clearly? ❹ 指真书 (in Chinese calligraphy) regular script: ～草隶篆 regular, cursive, official, and seal scripts ❺ 人的肖像;事物的形象 portrait; image: 传～ fax; facsimile | 写～ draw a portrait ❻ 〈书 *fml.*〉本性;本原 nature; natural state: 返朴归～ recovering one's original simplicity; back to nature ❼ (Zhēn)姓 a surname

【真诚】zhēnchéng 真实诚恳;没有一点虚假 with all one's heart; sincere; genuine; true: ～的心意 sincerity | ～的帮助 sincere help

【真传】zhēnchuán 指在技艺、学术方面得到的某人或某一派传授的精髓 essence of a craft or knowledge imparted by a master or a school

【真谛】zhēndì 真实的意义或道理 true essence; true meaning: 探索人生的～ seek the true meaning of life

【真格的】zhēngé·de 实在的 serious; real; true: ～,你到底去不去? Seriously, do you want to go or not? | 你别再装着玩儿啦,说～吧! Stop joking and tell me the truth!

【真个】zhēngè 〈方 *dial.*〉的确;实在 really; truly; indeed: 这地方～是变了。This place has really changed.

【真果】zhēnguǒ 果实的一类,果实的果肉是由子房壁发育而成的,如桃、杏 true fruit; a kind of fruit, the flesh of which develops from the wall of the ovary, e.g. peach and apricot

【真迹】zhēnjì 出于书法家或画家本人之手的作品(区别于临摹的或伪造的 as compared with 'copy' or 'fake') authentic work (of painting or calligraphy): 这一幅画是宋人的～。This is an authentic Song-dynasty painting.

【真金不怕火炼】zhēn jīn bù pà huǒ liàn 〈比喻 *fig.*〉坚强或正直的人经得住考验 true gold fears no fire — person of integrity can stand the severest tests

【真菌】zhēnjūn 低等生物,菌丝体中有明显的细胞核，以有性或无性的孢子进行繁殖。主要靠菌丝体吸收外界现成的营养物质来维持生活。通常寄生在其他物体上，自然界中分布很广，例如酵母菌，制造青霉素用的青霉菌，食品中的蘑菇和松蕈，衣物发霉时长的毛绒状的东西，以及某些病原体。eumycete; fungus; category of lower organism, with an obvious nucleus in the mycelium, propagating through sexual or asexual spores, living mainly by absorbing existing nutrition from the outside world. As a parasitic plant, it is widespread in the natural world, e.g. saccharomycete, the mould used to make penicillin, edible fungus, pine mushrooms, mould growing from mildewed lichen, and certain pathogens.

【真空】zhēnkōng ❶ 没有空气或只有极少空气的状态 space with little or no air ❷ 真空的空间 vacuum; situation characterised by emptiness

【真空泵】zhēnkōngbèng 用来抽气以获得真空的风泵 vacuum pump; vacuum cleaner; air exhauster; air extractor; air pump; also 抽气机 chōuqìjī

【真理】zhēnlǐ 真实的道理，即客观事物及其规律在人的意识中的正确反映 truth; the correct reflection of objective things and objective laws in the minds of human beings
☞ 绝对真理 juéduì zhēnlǐ on p. 1060 and 相对真理 xiāngduì zhēnlǐ on p. 2087

【真皮】zhēnpí 人或动物身体表皮下面的结缔组织，比表皮厚，含有许多弹性纤维 derma; corium; the connective tissue beneath the epidermis of a human being's or animal's body, thicker than the epidermis and having many resilient fibres; (图见 ☞ figure for 皮肤 pífū on p. 1464)

【真品】zhēnpǐn 真正出于某个时代、某地或某人之手的物品（对仿制的或伪造的物品而言 as opposed to 'imitation' or 'counterfeit'）genuine piece; authentic work

【真凭实据】zhēn píng shí jù 真实可靠的凭据 genuine evidence; hard evidence; conclusive proof

【真切】zhēnqiè ❶ 清楚确实；一点不模糊 vivid; clear; distinct; graphic: 看不～ can't see clearly | 听得～ hear distinctly ❷ 真诚恳切；真挚 sincere; genuine: 情意～ genuine feeling | ～的话语 sincere remarks

【真情】zhēnqíng ❶ 真实的情况 real or true situation; facts; actual state of affairs; truth: ～实况 real situation | 了解～ find out the truth ❷ 真诚的心情或感情 true feelings; real sentiments: ～实感 real feelings | ～流露 revelation of one's true feelings

【真确】zhēnquè ❶ 真实 true; real; authentic: ～的消息 authentic news ❷ same as 真切 zhēnqiè ①: 看得～ see clearly | 记不～ cannot remember clearly

【真人】zhēnrén ❶ 道教所说修行得道的人，多用做称号，如'太乙真人'、'玉鼎真人' true man; person and immortal (sb. who has attained enlightenment or immortality through practising Taoism, oft. a form of address) e.g. True Man of Grand Unity, True Man of the Jade Tripod ❷ 真实的非虚构的人物 real people: ～真事 real people and real events

【真实】zhēnshí 跟客观事实相符合；不假 real; true; actual; authentic: ～情况 real situation | ～的感情 true feelings; real sentiments

【真是】zhēn·shi 实在是（表示不满意的情绪）(used in complaints) really; indeed: 雨下了两天还不住，～！What a shame! The rain has continued for two days without a let-up. | 你们俩也～，戏票都买好了，你们又不去了。Really, you two! We bought tickets for you but you don't want to go.

【真释】zhēnshì 真实的正确的解释 faithful and correct explanation or interpretation

【真书】zhēnshū 楷书 (in Chinese calligraphy) regular script

【真数】zhēnshù ☞ 对数 duìshù on p. 493

【真率】zhēnshuài 真诚直率；不做作 sincere; candid; unaffected; straightforward

【真丝】zhēnsī 指蚕丝（区别于'人造丝' as compared with 'artificial silk'）pure silk; 100% silk

【真相】zhēnxiàng 事情的真实情况（区别于表面的或假造的情况 as compared with 'superficial' or 'false situation'）real situation; actual state of affairs; facts; truth: ～大白。The truth is out. *or* The facts are clear now. | 弄清问题的～ clarify the truth of the matter

【真心】zhēnxīn 真实的心意 wholehearted; heartfelt; sincere: ～话 sincere words; words from the bottom of one's heart | ～实意 genuinely and sincerely; truly and wholeheartedly

【真性】zhēnxìng ❶ 真的（区别于表面上相似而实际上不是的 as compared with 'sham'）true; genuine: ～霍乱 cholera ❷〈书 *fml.*〉本性 nature; natural instincts

【真影】zhēnyǐng 祭祀时张挂的祖先的画像 portrait of one's deceased ancestors (to be put up during ceremonial offerings)

【真章儿】zhēnzhāngr〈方 *dial.*〉真实的行动；切实有效的办法 effective solution; real action: 你这回要不拿出点～来，他们不会放过你。They will not let you off if you fail to come up with a feasible solution.

【真正】zhēnzhèng ❶ 实质跟名义完全相符 genuine; true; real: 群众是～的英雄。The masses are the true heroes. | ～的吉林人参 genuine Jilin ginseng ❷ 的的确确；确实 truly; really; in earnest: 这东西～好吃。This is really delicious.

【真知】zhēnzhī 正确的认识 genuine (or real) knowledge: ～灼见 real knowledge and deep insight | 一切～都是从直接经验发源的。All real knowledge comes from practice.

【真知灼见】zhēn zhī zhuó jiàn 正确而透彻的见解（不是人云亦云）(not echoing other's views) real knowledge and deep insight; penetrating judgement

【真挚】zhēnzhì 真诚恳切(多指感情 oft. of feelings) sincere; cordial: ～的友谊 sincere friendship

【真珠】zhēnzhū same as 珍珠 zhēnzhū

【真主】Zhēnzhǔ 伊斯兰教所崇奉的唯一的神，认为是万物的创造者，人类命运的主宰者 Allah; principal Muslim name for God; the one Supreme Being

桢 zhēn 〈古时 *arch*.〉筑墙时所立的柱子 terminal posts used in building a wall

【桢干】zhēngàn 〈书 *fml*.〉〈比喻 *fig*.〉能担当重任的人才 core; key member; backbone; mainstay: 国家～ pillar of the state

砧(碪) zhēn 捶或砸东西时垫在底下的器具，有铁的(砸钢铁材料时用)、石头的(捶衣物时用)、木头的(即砧板) hammering block; anvil; heavy iron, stone or wood block on which metals are hammered during forging; wooden block on which clothes in washing are beaten

【砧板】zhēnbǎn 切菜用的木板 chopping block

【砧骨】zhēngǔ 听骨之一，形状像铁砧，外端跟锤骨相连，内端跟镫骨相连(图见 ☞ figure 耳朵 ěr·duo on p. 512) incus; anvil; anvil-shaped bone between the malleus and the stapes in the mammalian middle ear

【砧木】zhēnmù 嫁接植物时把接穗接在另一个植物体上，这个植物体叫砧木，例如把梨树枝接在杜梨树上，梨树枝是接穗，杜梨树是砧木 stock; rooted plant into which a scion is inserted during grafting, e. g. when pear is grafted onto a birch-leaf pear, the pear is the scion and the birch-leaf pear is the stock

【砧子】zhēn·zi same as 砧 zhēn

祯 zhēn 〈书 *fml*.〉吉祥 auspicious; propitious

蓁 zhēn [蓁蓁]〈书 *fml*.〉❶ 草木茂盛的样子 luxuriant; exuberant ❷ 荆棘丛生的样子 overgrown with brambles

斟 zhēn 往杯子或碗里倒(酒、茶) pour (tea or wine): 自～自饮 help oneself to wine; drink by oneself | ～了满满一杯酒 poured a full cup of wine

【斟酌】zhēnzhuó 考虑事情、文字等是否可行或是否适当 consider; deliberate: 再三～ consider carefully again and again | ～字句 weigh one's words | 这件事请你～着办吧。It's up to you to act as you see fit.

椹 zhēn same as 砧 zhēn
☞ shèn on p. 1711

甄 zhēn ❶〈书 *fml*.〉审查鉴定(优劣、真伪) discriminate; distinguish; examine: ～选 select | ～录 examine and then employ ❷ (Zhēn)姓 a surname

【甄别】zhēnbié ❶ 审查辨别(优劣、真伪) examine and distinguish; screen; discriminate ❷ 考核鉴定(能力、品质等) test and assess

【甄审】zhēnshěn 甄别审查 examine; screen

獉 zhēn [獉狉](zhēnpī)〈书 *fml*.〉same as 榛狉 zhēnpī

溱 Zhēn 古水名，在今河南 Zhen, name of an ancient river in present-day Henan Province
☞ qín on p. 1561

榛 zhēn ❶ 落叶乔木，叶子互生，圆形或倒卵形，雄花黄褐色，雌花鲜红色，结球形坚果。果仁可以吃，又可榨油。hazel (*Corylus*); deciduous shrub or low tree, having round or oval serrated alternate leaves, ochre staminate flowers and scarler pistillate flowers, and edible round brown oil-bearing nuts ❷ 这种植物的果实 hazelnut; nut of this plant ‖ 通称 commonly known as 榛子 zhēn·zi

【榛莽】zhēnmǎng 〈书 *fml*.〉丛生的草木 luxuriant vegetation

【榛狉】zhēnpī 〈书 *fml*.〉狉榛 densely wooded and frequented by wild animals; also 獉狉 zhēnpī

【榛榛】zhēnzhēn 〈书 *fml*.〉形容草木丛杂 be overgrown with plants or trees

【榛子】zhēn·zi ❶ 榛树 hazel ❷ 榛树的果实 hazelnut

禛 zhēn 〈书 *fml*.〉吉祥，多用于人名 (oft. used in a person's name) auspiciousness; happiness; luck

箴 zhēn 〈书 *fml*.〉❶ 劝告；劝诫 admonish; exhort: ～言 admonition; exhortation; maxim ❷ 古代的一种文体，以规劝告诫为主 didactic literary style; ancient style of writing focusing on persuasion and exhortation

【箴言】zhēnyán 〈书 *fml*.〉劝诫的话 admonition; exhortation; maxim

臻 zhēn 〈书 *fml*.〉❶ 达到(美好的境地) attain (excellence); become better: 渐～佳境 gradually attain perfection | 交通工具日～便利。Transportation and communication facilities are becoming more convenient day by day. ❷ 来到 arrive; come: 百福并～。May a hundred blessings descend on you!

鱵 zhēn 鱼，身体呈圆柱形，下颌特长，呈针状，鳞呈圆形，尾鳍分叉。栖息在近海中，也进入淡水。halfbeak (*Hemiramphidae*); any marine and freshwater teleost fish, having an elongated body with short upper jaw and long protruding lower jaw

zhěn (ㄓㄣˇ)

诊 zhěn 诊察 examine (a patient): ～断 diagnose | 门～ outpatient service | 出～ (of a

doctor) visit a patient at home | 会～ group consultation of doctors

【诊察】zhěnchá 为了了解病情而进行检查 examine (a patient)

【诊断】zhěnduàn 在检查病人的症状之后判定病人的病症及其发展情况 diagnose: ～书 medical certificate

【诊疗】zhěnliáo 诊断和治疗 make a diagnosis and give treatment: ～室 consulting room | ～器械 medical instruments

【诊脉】zhěn//mài 医生用手按在病人腕部的动脉上，根据脉搏的变化来诊断病情 feel the pulse; (of a doctor) press the artery at the wrist of a patient and make a diagnosis according to the pulse; also 按脉 àn//mài and 号脉 hào//mài

【诊视】zhěnshì 诊察 examine (a patient)

【诊室】zhěnshì 医生为病人看病的房间 consulting room

【诊所】zhěnsuǒ ❶ 个人开业的医生给病人治病的地方 private clinic; dispensary ❷ 规模比医院小的医疗机构 small hospital

【诊治】zhěnzhì 诊疗 make a diagnosis and give treatment: 有病应及早～。When ill, one should see a doctor as soon as possible.

枕 zhěn ❶ 枕头 pillow: ～套 pillowcase | 凉～ summer pillow ❷ 躺着的时候把头放在枕头上或其他东西上 rest the head on: ～戈待旦 maintain combat readiness | 他～着胳膊睡着了。He fell asleep, his head on his arm.

【枕戈待旦】zhěn gē dài dàn 枕着兵器等待天亮，形容时刻警惕敌人，准备作战 lie with one's head pillowed on a spear, waiting for daybreak — be ready for battle; maintain combat readiness

【枕骨】zhěngǔ 构成颅腔底部与后部的骨头，在头部后面正下方，底部有一孔，是脑与脊髓连接的地方，孔外有两块卵圆形突起，与第一颈椎构成关节，使头部可以俯仰活动 occipital bone; saucer-shaped bone that forms the back part of the skull and part of its base, located right beneath the rear part of the head, with a hole at its bottom, serving to join the brain and spinal cord, and two oval projections outside the hole, forming the joint of the first cervical vertebra upon which the head can move up and down

Z 【枕藉】zhěnjiè 〈书 *fml.*〉(很多人)交错地倒或躺在一起 (many people) lying about; lying higgledy-piggledy

【枕巾】zhěnjīn 铺在枕头上面的用品，多为毛巾一类的针织品 towel used to cover a pillow

【枕木】zhěnmù 横铺在铁路路基的道砟上、用来垫平和固定铁轨的方柱形木头 railway sleeper; tie; also 道木 dàomù

【枕套】zhěntào 套在枕心外面的套子，多用布或绸子做成 pillowcase; pillow-slip; also 枕头套 zhěn·toutào

【枕头】zhěn·tou 躺着的时候，垫在头下使头略高的东西 pillow; cloth case stuffed with feathers, foam rubber, etc., used to support the head when lying down

【枕头箱】zhěn·touxiāng 收藏首饰、契约等贵重物品的小箱子。常放在卧房中。pillow casket; a small box for valuables, oft. a found in the bedroom

【枕席】zhěnxí ❶〈书 *fml.*〉指床榻 bed ❷ (～儿 zhěnxír)铺在枕头上的凉席 mat used to cover a pillow; pillow mat; also 枕头席儿 zhěn·touxír

【枕心】zhěnxīn 枕套中间的囊状物，里面装着木棉、蒲绒或荞麦皮等松软的东西 pillow; cloth case stuffed with loose soft things like kapok, rush, buckwheat husks, etc.; also 枕头心儿 zhěn·touxīnr

紾 zhěn 〈书 *fml.*〉扭；转 turn; rotate

轸[1] zhěn ❶〈书 *fml.*〉车后横木，借指车 the cross board at the rear of an ancient carriage; carriage ❷ 二十八宿之一 the last of the 28 constellations into which the celestial sphere was divided in ancient Chinese astronomy (consisting of four stars in Corvus)

轸[2] zhěn 〈书 *fml.*〉悲痛 sorrowful; distressed: ～悼 mourn with deep grief | ～怀 sorrowfully cherish the memory of sb.

【轸念】zhěnniàn 〈书 *fml.*〉悲痛地怀念；深切地思念 sorrowfully cherish the memory of sb.; think anxiously about

畛 zhěn 〈书 *fml.*〉田地里的小路 raised paths between fields

【畛域】zhěnyù 〈书 *fml.*〉界限 boundary: 不分～ regardless of distinctions

疹 zhěn 病人皮肤上起的很多的小疙瘩，通常是红色的，小的像针尖，大的像豆粒，如丘疹、疱疹等 bleb; rash; any skin eruption, e.g. herpes; papule, etc.

【疹子】zhěn·zi 麻疹的通称 common name for 麻疹 mázhěn

袗 zhěn 〈书 *fml.*〉❶ 单衣 unlined garment ❷ 华美 (of clothes) gorgeous: ～衣 gorgeous dress

缜(**稹**) zhěn 〈书 *fml.*〉细致 careful; painstaking; meticulous: ～密 careful; detailed

【缜密】zhěnmì 周密；细致(多指思想 oft. thought) careful; meticulous; deliberate: 文思～ meticulously written | ～的分析 careful (or minute) analysis | 事先经过了～的研究。Detailed research has been done beforehand.

鬒(**黰**) zhěn 〈书 *fml.*〉头发稠而黑 (of hair) thick and black

zhèn (ㄓㄣˋ)

圳(**甽**) zhèn 〈方 *dial.*〉田野间的水沟 ditch between fields

阵[1] zhèn ❶〈古代 *arch*.〉战术用语，指作战队伍的行列或组合方式 battle array (or formation)：严～以待 be ready in full battle array｜摆了个一字长蛇～ string out in a long line ❷ 阵地 position; front：上～杀敌 go into battle to kill the enemy

阵[2] zhèn (～儿 zhènr) ❶ 一段时间 period of time：这～儿 these days; recently｜那～儿 in those days; then｜他病了一～儿。He was ill for some time. ❷〈量词 *classifier*〉表示事情或动作经过的段落 short period; spell：几～雨 spatter of rain｜一～风 a gust (or blast) of wind｜一～剧痛 an attack of gnawing pain｜一～热烈的掌声 a burst of warm applause

【阵地】zhèndì 军队为了进行战斗而占据的地方，通常修有工事 position; front; place where troops occupy in a battle and defence works are built：～战 positional warfare｜占领敌军～ take an enemy position ◇文艺～ art and literary fronts｜思想～ ideological front

【阵风】zhènfēng 指短时间内风向变动不定，风速剧烈变化的风。通常指风速突然增强的风。gust (of wind); sudden blast of wind speeding up in changing directions

【阵脚】zhènjiǎo 指所摆的阵的最前方，现多用于比喻 front line; (oft. fig.) condition; situation：压住～ secure one's position｜～大乱 be thrown into confusion

【阵容】zhènróng ❶ 作战队伍的外貌 battle array (or formation) ❷ 队伍所显示的力量，多比喻人力的配备 strength displayed by an army; (oft. fig.) people deployed; lineup：～整齐 well-balanced cast｜～强大 have a strong lineup

【阵势】zhèn·shì ❶ 军队作战的布置 battle array (or formation); disposition of combat forces ❷ 情势；场面 situation; condition; circumstances：面对这种～，他惊得目瞪口呆。In the face of this kind of situation, he was dumbstruck.

【阵痛】zhèntòng ❶ 分娩时因子宫一阵一阵地收缩而引起的疼痛的感觉 labour pains; throes (of childbirth) ❷〈比喻 *fig*.〉新事物产生过程中出现的暂时困难 birth pangs; throes of giving birth to sth. new; temporary difficulties before a new thing is born

【阵亡】zhènwáng 在作战中牺牲 be killed in action; fall in battle

【阵线】zhènxiàn 战线，多用于比喻 (oft. fig.) front; ranks; alignment：革命～ alignment of revolutionary forces｜民族统一～ national united front

【阵营】zhènyíng 为了共同的利益和目标而联合起来进行斗争的集团 group of people who pursue a common interest; camp

【阵雨】zhènyǔ 指降雨时间较短，雨的强度变化很大，开始和停止都很突然的雨。有时伴有闪电和雷声，多发生在夏天。shower; brief period of rain, hail, sometimes with thunder and lightning, and often in summer

【阵子】zhèn·zi〈方 *dial*.〉same as 阵[2] zhèn

纼 zhèn〈方 *dial*.〉拴牲口的绳 tether for tying domestic animals; also 纼子 zhèn·zi

鸩（❷❸酖）zhèn ❶ 传说中的一种有毒的鸟，用它的羽毛泡的酒，喝了能毒死人 legendary bird with poisonous feathers, which when soaked in wine can kill the drinker ❷ 毒酒 poisoned wine：饮～止渴 drink poisoned wine to quench thirst — seek immediate relief regardless of consequences ❸〈书 *fml*.〉用毒酒害人 kill sb. with poisoned wine

【鸩毒】zhèndú〈书 *fml*.〉毒酒 poisoned wine：宴安～。Seeking pleasure is like drinking poisoned wine.

振 zhèn ❶ 摇动；挥动 shake; flap：～翅 flap the wings; flutter｜～笔疾书 wield the pen furiously ❷ 振动 vibrate：共～ resonance｜谐～ resonance｜～幅 amplitude of vibration ❸ 奋起；振作 rise with force and spirit; brace up; boost：～奋 be high-spirited｜～起精神来 rouse oneself｜听说比赛开始，观众精神一～。Upon learning the game was to begin, the audience became spirits-lifted.

【振拔】zhènbá〈书 *fml*.〉从陷入的境地中摆脱出来，振奋自立 extricate oneself from a predicament and brace up：及早～ extricate oneself as soon as possible｜不自～ cannot extricate oneself

【振臂】zhènbì 挥动胳膊，表示奋发或激昂 raise one's arm：～高呼 raise one's arm and shout (slogans, etc.)｜～一呼，应者云集。People followed in the tens of thousands when he raised his arm and called for action.

【振荡】zhèndàng ❶ 振动 vibration; periodic motion about an equilibrium position, such as the regular displacement of air in the propagation of sound ❷ 电流的周期性变化 oscillation; regular changes in an alternating current

【振动】zhèndòng 物体通过一个中心位置，不断作往复运动。摆的运动就是振动。vibration; oscillation; regular fluctuation in value, position, or state, around a mean value, such as the variation in an alternating current or the regular swinging of a pendulum; also 振荡 zhèndàng

【振奋】zhènfèn ❶（精神）振作奋发 rouse oneself; rise with force and spirit; be inspired with enthusiasm; feel it refreshing to：人人～，个个当先。Full of vigour, everyone forges ahead. ❷ 使振奋 inspire; stimulate：～人心 inspire people; fill people with enthusiasm

【振幅】zhènfú 振动过程中，振动物体离开平衡位置的最大距离 amplitude (of vibration); maximum displacement from zero; mean po-

Z

sition of a periodic motion or curve

【振聋发聩】zhèn lóng fā kuì ☞ 发聋振聩 fā lóng zhèn kuì on p. 521

【振刷】zhènshuā〈书 *fml.*〉振作 bestir (or exert) oneself; display vigour: ～精神 rouse oneself

【振兴】zhènxīng 大力发展,使兴盛起来 rejuvenate; revitalize; invigorate: ～工业 rejuvenate industry|～中华 rejuvenate China

【振振有词】zhènzhèn yǒu cí 形容理由似乎很充分,说个不休 speak plausibly and volubly (in self-justification); 词 cí also put as 辞 cí

【振作】zhènzuò 使精神旺盛,情绪高涨;奋发 bestir (or exert) oneself; display vigour: ～精神 bestir oneself; brace (or cheer) up|～起来 pull oneself together; be in high spirits

朕[1] zhèn 秦以前指'我的'或'我',自秦始皇起专用做皇帝自称 I, the sovereign; we, our (used by royalty in proclamations instead of 'I' or 'my' from the time of Qinshihuang, the founding emperor of the Qin Dynasty)

朕[2] zhèn〈书 *fml.*〉先兆;预兆 sign; omen: ～兆 sign; omen

【朕兆】zhènzhào〈书 *fml.*〉兆头;预兆 sign; omen; portent

赈 zhèn 赈济 relieve; aid: ～灾 provide relief to people in a disaster-stricken area|以工代～ aid disaster victims by providing them with work; provide work-relief|开仓～饥 distribute food to aid disaster-stricken people

【赈济】zhènjì 用钱或衣服、粮食等救济(灾民) provide relief (to people in stricken areas); aid (the victims of natural calamities)

【赈灾】zhènzāi 赈济灾民 provide relief to people in stricken areas: 开仓～ distribute grain from state stores to disaster-stricken people

揕 zhèn〈书 *fml.*〉用刀剑等刺 stab with a sword, knife, etc.

瑱 zhèn〈书 *fml.*〉戴在耳垂上的玉 jade earring

震 zhèn ❶ 震动 shake; shock; vibrate; quake: 地～ earthquake |～耳欲聋 deafening ◇威～四方 be renowned far and wide ❷ 情绪过分激动 be excited; be shocked: ～惊 be astonished |～怒 be enraged ❸ 八卦之一,卦形是'☳',代表雷 one of the Eight Trigrams, symbolizing thunder; ☞ 八卦 bāguà on p. 22

【震波】zhènbō 地震波 seismic wave; earthquake wave

【震颤】zhènchàn 颤动;使颤动 tremble; quiver: 浑身～ tremble all over |噩耗～着人们的心。People were stunned by the tragic news.

【震荡】zhèndàng 震动;动荡 shake; shock; vibrate; quake: 社会～ social upheaval |回声～,山鸣谷应。The sound echoed throughout the valley.

【震动】zhèndòng ❶ 颤动;使颤动 shake; shock; vibrate; quake: 火车～了一下,开走了。The train pulled out with a jerk. |春雷～着山谷。Spring thunder shook the valley. ❷ (重大的事情、消息等)使人心不平静 shock; stir; astonish; excite: ～全国。The whole nation was shocked.

【震耳欲聋】zhèn ěr yù lóng 耳朵都快震聋了,形容声音很大 deafening; very loud (as if deafening one's ears)

【震感】zhèngǎn 对地震产生的感觉 seismaesthesia: 离震源二百公里外的地方都有～。The earthquake was felt two hundred kilometres from the focus.

【震古烁今】zhèn gǔ shuò jīn 形容事业或功绩伟大,可以震动古人,显耀当世 (of great achievements, etc.) surpassing the ancients and amazing contemporaries

【震撼】zhènhàn 震动;摇撼 shake; shock; vibrate: ～人心 stirring; thrilling |滚滚春雷,～大地。The rumbling spring thunder shakes the earth.

【震级】zhènjí 地震震级的简称 abbr. for 地震震级 dìzhèn zhènjí

【震惊】zhènjīng ❶ 使大吃一惊 shock; amaze; astonish: ～世界 shock the world ❷ 大吃一惊 be surprised; be shocked; be stunned: 大为～ be greatly shocked

【震怒】zhènnù 异常愤怒;大怒 be enraged; be furious

【震慑】zhènshè 震动使害怕 awe; frighten; intimidate: ～敌人 terrify the enemy

【震悚】zhènsǒng〈书 *fml.*〉因恐惧而颤动;震惊 tremble with fear; be terrified; be frightened

【震源】zhènyuán 地球内部发生地震的地方 focus (of an earthquake); point beneath the earth's surface at which an earthquake originates

【震中】zhènzhōng 震源正上方的地面叫做震中。地震时震中所受破坏最大。epicentre; point on the earth's surface directly above the focus of an earthquake, where the damage is the most serious

镇[1] zhèn ❶ 压;抑制 press down; keep down; ease: ～纸 paperweight|～痛 ease pain |他一说话,就把大家给～住了。His words calmed everyone down. ❷ 安定 calm; stable; tranquil; at ease: ～静 calm; composed; cool |～定 calm; unruffled ❸ 用武力维持安定 keep peace by force; garrison: ～守 garrison; guard |坐～ assume personal command ❹ 镇守的地方 garrison post: 军事重～ key military post ❺ 行政区划单位,一般由县一级领导 town; administrative division generally under the jurisdiction of a county ❻ 较大的市集 comparatively large trading centre ❼ 把食物、饮料等同冰块放在一块儿或放在冷水里使凉 cool sth. with cold water or ice：冰～汽水 iced soda | 把西瓜放在冷水里～一～ put a watermelon in cold water for a while to chill it ❽ (Zhèn)姓 a surname

镇2 zhèn ❶ 时常(多见于早期白话 oft. used in the early vernacular) often; frequently：十年～相随。For ten years we were often together. ❷ 表示整个的一段时间(多见于早期白话 oft. used in the early vernacular) whole period：～日 all day long

【镇尺】zhènchǐ 直尺状的镇纸，多用金属制成 paperweight oft. made of metal and in the shape of a ruler

【镇定】zhèndìng ❶ 遇到紧急的情况不慌不乱 calm; cool; composed; unruffled：神色～ be calm and collected; show composure and presence of mind ❷ 使镇定 calm down：竭力～自己 try hard to calm oneself down

【镇反】zhènfǎn 镇压反革命 suppress counter-revolutionaries

【镇静】zhènjìng ❶ 情绪稳定或平静 calm; cool; composed; unruffled：故作～ pretend to be calm | 他遇事不慌不忙，非常～。He is always composed in an emergency. ❷ 使镇静 calm down：～剂 tranquillizer | 尽力～自己 try hard to calm oneself down; try hard to keep composed

【镇静剂】zhènjìngjì 对大脑皮层有抑制作用的药物，如溴化钠、溴化钾、鲁米那等 sedative; tranquillizer; drug that calms a person without affecting clarity of consciousness, e.g. sodium bromide, potassium bromide, luminal, etc.

【镇守】zhènshǒu 指军队驻扎在军事上重要的地方防守 guard (a strategically important place); garrison：～边关 guard a strategic pass on the frontier

【镇星】zhènxīng 我国古代指土星 old Chinese name for Quelling Star

【镇压】zhènyā ❶ 用强力压制，不许进行活动(多用于政治 oft. politically) suppress; repress; put down：～反革命 crack down on counter-revolutionaries ❷ 处决(反革命分子) execute (a counter-revolutionary) ❸ 压紧播种后的垄或植株行间的松土，目的是使种子或植株容易吸收水分和养分 rolling; compacting; tamping; pressing hard the ridges after sowing seeds or the loose soil between plants so as to make it easy for seeds or plants absorb water and nutrients

【镇纸】zhènzhǐ 写字画画儿时压纸的东西，用铜、铁或玉石等制成 paperweight; made of copper, iron, jade, etc., used to keep the paper steady when painting or writing

【镇子】zhèn·zi 〈方 *dial.*〉集镇 small town; market town

zhēng (ㄓㄥ)

丁 zhēng [丁丁]〈书 *fml.*〉〈拟声词 *onom.*〉形容伐木、下棋、弹琴等声音 sound of chopping wood, playing chess, plucking strings (of a musical instrument, etc.)：伐木～。Clang, clang goes the woodman's axe.
☞ dīng on p. 452

正 zhēng 正月 first month of the lunar year; first moon：新～ first month of the lunar new year; first moon
☞ zhèng on p. 2445

【正旦】zhēngdàn〈书 *fml.*〉农历正月初一日 lunar New Year's Day
☞ zhèngdàn on p. 2447

【正月】zhēngyuè 农历一年的第一个月 first month of the lunar year; first moon

争1 zhēng ❶ 力求得到或达到；争夺 compete; contend; vie; strive：～冠军 strive for the championship | 力～上游 aim high; aim for the best | 分秒必～ make good use of every minute | 大家～着发言。People vied with each other to take the floor. ❷ 争执；争论 argue; dispute; wrangle：～吵 quarrel; argue | ～端 dispute; controversy | 意气之～ dispute caused by personal grudges | 意见已经一致，不必再～了。Let's stop arguing since we have reached an agreement. ❸〈方 *dial.*〉差(chà)；欠缺 short of; wanting：总数还～多少？How many more are needed to make up the total? | ～点儿摔了一跤 almost fall down

争2 zhēng 怎么(多见于诗、词、曲 oft. seen in poetry and lyrics) how; why：～知 how does one know | ～奈 unfortunately; however | ～忍 how can one bear to; how can one bring oneself to (do sth.)

【争辩】zhēngbiàn 争论；辩论 argue; debate; contend：据理～ argue on just grounds

【争吵】zhēngchǎo 因意见不合大声争辩，互不相让 quarrel; wrangle; squabble：无谓的～ pointless quarrel | ～不休 bicker (or squabble) endlessly

【争持】zhēngchí 争执而相持不下 refuse to give in; stick to one's guns：为了一件小事双方～了半天。Neither side was willing to give in over a trifle.

【争宠】zhēngchǒng 使用手段争着取得别人对自己的宠爱 strive for sb.'s favour

【争斗】zhēngdòu ❶ 打架 fight ❷ 泛指对立的一方力求克服另一方的活动 (in a abroad sense) struggle; contend

【争端】zhēngduān 引起争执的事由 controversial issue; dispute; conflict：国际～ international dispute | 消除～ settle a dispute

【争夺】zhēngduó 争着夺取 fight (or contend,

scramble) for; enter into rivalry with sb. over sth.; vie with sb. for sth.: ～市场 scramble for markets | 阵地～战 battle for a position | ～出线权 strive to qualify for the next round of competition

【争分夺秒】zhēng fēn duó miǎo 不放过一分一秒，形容对时间抓得很紧 race (or work) against time; make every minute and second count

【争风吃醋】zhēng fēng chī cù 指因追求同一异性而互相忌妒争斗 fight for the affections of a man or woman; be jealous (of a rival in love)

【争光】zhēng//guāng 争取光荣 win honour (or glory) for: 为国～ win honour for our homeland; bring credit to (or be a credit to) our country

【争衡】zhēnghéng 〈书 *fml.*〉较量高低 scramble for supremacy; strive for mastery; be in rivalry with

【争竞】zhēng·jing 〈方 *dial.*〉计较；争论 haggle over; fuss about

【争脸】zhēng//liǎn 争取荣誉，使脸上有光彩 try to win credit or honour: 把书念好，给家乡～。Study well in school and win credit for your hometown. also 争面子 zhēngmiàn·zi

【争论】zhēnglùn 各执己见，互相辩论 controversy; dispute; debate; contention: ～不休 endless debate

【争鸣】zhēngmíng 〈比喻 *fig.*〉在学术上进行争辩 contend (over academic issues): 百家～ contentions among the exponents of various schools of thought

【争气】zhēng//qì 发愤图强，不甘落后或示弱 try to make a good showing; try to win credit for; try to bring credit to: 孩子真～，每次考试都名列前茅。The child makes a good showing, coming out on top in all tests.

【争取】zhēngqǔ ❶ 力求获得 strive for; fight for; win over: ～时间 race (or work) against time | ～主动 try to gain the initiative; contend for the initiative | ～彻底的胜利 fight for a complete victory ❷ 力求实现 try to realise: ～提前完成计划 do one's best to finish the plan ahead of time

【争权夺利】zhēng quán duó lì 争夺权柄和利益 scramble for power and gain; fight each other for power

【争胜】zhēngshèng (在竞赛中)争取优胜 compete for first place: 好(hào)强～ seek to outdo others

【争先】zhēngxiān 争着赶到别人前头 try to be the first to do sth.: 个个奋勇～ everyone try to take the lead | 大家～发言。Everyone tried to be the first to speak.

【争先恐后】zhēng xiān kǒng hòu 争着向前，唯恐落后 strive to be the first and fear to lag behind; fall over each other to do sth.

【争议】zhēngyì same as 争论 zhēnglùn

【争战】zhēngzhàn 打仗 fight; war: 两军～ war between two armies

【争执】zhēngzhí 争论中各持己见，不肯相让 disagree; dispute; stick to one's position (or guns): ～不下 each stands (or holds) his ground; each sticks to his own position; each sticks to his guns | 双方在看法上发生～。The two sides have different views, leading to disputes.

【争嘴】zhēng//zuǐ 〈方 *dial.*〉❶ 在吃东西上争多论少或占别人的份儿 scramble for a bit to eat ❷ 吵嘴 quarrel; row

征[1]

zhēng ❶ 走远路(多指军队) (of an army) go on a journey: ～途 the road to be travelled; journey | 二万五千里长～ 25,000 *li* Long March ❷ 征讨 go on an expedition (or a campaign): 出～ go out to battle | 南～北战 fight in both the north and south

征[2](徵)

zhēng ❶ 政府召集人民服务 levy (troops); call up; draft: ～兵 conscription | 应～入伍 be drafted into the army ❷ 征收 levy (taxes); collect; impose: ～税 impose a tax | ～粮 impose grain levies ❸ 征求: ～稿 solicit contributions (to a journal, etc.) | ～文 solicit essays or articles

征[3](徵)

zhēng ❶ 证明；证验 evidence; proof: 文献足～。There are historical documents as proof. | 信而有～ be borne out by evidence | 有实物可～。There is solid evidence. ❷ 表露出来的迹象；现象 sign; portent: ～候 sign | 象～ sign; symptom | 特～ characteristic

☞ 徵 zhǐ on p. 2470

【征兵】zhēng//bīng 政府召集公民服兵役 conscription; draft; call-up

【征尘】zhēngchén 在远行的路途中身上沾染的尘土 dust which settles on one during a journey

【征程】zhēngchéng 征途 journey: 万里～ journey of 10,000 *li*

【征调】zhēngdiào 政府征集和调用人员、物资 (of government) requisition; call up; draft: ～粮食及医务人员支援灾区 requisition food supplies and draft medical personnel to aid a disaster-stricken area

【征订】zhēngdìng 征求订购 solicit subscriptions: ～单 subscription list

【征发】zhēngfā 〈旧时 *old*〉指政府征集民间的人力和物资 (of government) make requisition for supplies and personnel

【征伐】zhēngfá 讨伐 go on a punitive expedition: ～叛逆 dispatch a punitive expedition against rebels

【征帆】zhēngfān 〈书 *fml.*〉远行的船 ship bound for distant climes; ship on a long voyage

【征服】zhēngfú 用武力使(别的国家、民族)屈服 conquer; subjugate ◇ ～自然 conquer nature

【征稿】zhēnggǎo 征求投稿 solicit contributions (to a journal, etc.): ～启事 notice soliciting contributions

【征购】zhēnggòu 国家根据法律向生产者或所有者购买(农产品、土地等) government purchase (of agricultural products, land, etc.)

【征候】zhēnghòu 发生某种情况的迹象 sign: 病人已有好转的～。The patient shows signs of a turn for the better.

【征婚】zhēng//hūn 公开征求结婚对象 marriage seeking: ～启事 lonely-heart ad

【征集】zhēngjí ❶ 用公告或口头询问的方式征集 collect or solicit publicly; gather or collect through public channels or oral inquiry: ～文史资料 collect historical documents ❷ 征募 draft; call up; recruit: ～新兵 recruitment

【征募】zhēngmù 招募(兵士) enlist; recruit

【征聘】zhēngpìn 招聘 give public notice of vacancies to be filled; invite applications for jobs; advertise for (a secretary, teacher, etc.): ～科技人员 advertise for researchers and technicians

【征求】zhēngqiú 用书面或口头询问的方式访求 solicit; seek; ask for: ～意见 solicit (or seek) opinions; ask for criticisms

【征实】zhēngshí 指田赋征收实物 levies in kind; grain levies (or tax)

【征收】zhēngshōu 政府依法向个人或单位收取(公粮、税款等) levy; collect; impose (taxes, etc.): ～商业税 impose business taxes

【征讨】zhēngtǎo 出兵讨伐 go on a punitive expedition

【征途】zhēngtú 远行的路途;行程 journey: 踏上～ start on a journey; set out | 艰难的～ perilous journey

【征文】zhēngwén 报章杂志为某一主题而公开征集诗文稿件 (of a newspaper or magazine) solicit articles or essays on a certain theme

【征象】zhēngxiàng 征候 sign; symptom; indication: 煤气中毒的～是头痛、恶心和心跳加速等。Symptoms of gas poisoning are headaches, nausea, and fast heartbeat.

【征询】zhēngxún 征求(意见) consult; seek the opinion of

【征引】zhēngyǐn 引用;引证 quote; cite

【征用】zhēngyòng 政府依法使用个人或集体的土地、房产等 take over (legally, by government) for public use; commandeer; requisition

【征战】zhēngzhàn 出征作战 go on an expedition (or a campaign)

【征召】zhēngzhào ❶ 征(兵) call up; enlist; draft; conscript: ～入伍 enlist in the army | 响应～ answer the call to enlist in the army ❷〈书 *fml*.〉授官职;调用 appoint to an official position

【征兆】zhēngzhào 征候;先兆 sign; omen; portent; indication: 不祥的～ bad omen

怔 zhēng ☞ below
☞ zhèng on p. 2451

【怔忡】zhēngchōng〈书 *fml*.〉心悸 palpitations

【怔营】zhēngyíng〈书 *fml*.〉惶恐不安 in a state of alarm (or trepidation); be terrified and uncertain; be seized with fear and terror

【怔忪】zhēngzhōng〈书 *fml*.〉惊恐 alarmed and panicky; terrified; scared; panic-stricken; seized with terror

挣 zhēng [挣扎](zhēngzhá)用力支撑 struggle; battle: 垂死～ last-ditch struggle | 他～着从病床上爬了起来。He struggled to his feet from the sickbed.
☞ zhèng on p. 2452

峥 zhēng [峥嵘](zhēngróng) ❶ 高峻 lofty and steep; towering: 山势～ mountains towering high | 怪石～ lofty and bizarre rocks | 殿宇～ soaring palaces and halls ❷〈比喻 *fig*.〉才气、品格等超越寻常;不平凡 (of talent, personality, etc.) outstanding; extraordinary: 头角～ (of a youth) brilliant | ～岁月 eventful years; memorable years (of one's life)

狰 zhēng [狰狞](zhēngníng) 面目凶恶 (of appearance) ferocious; savage; hideous: ～可畏 hideous and repulsive

钲 zhēng〈古代 *arch*.〉行军时用的打击乐器,有柄,形状像钟,但比钟狭而长,用铜制成 bell-shaped percussion instrument, used in ancient times by marching bands

症(癥) zhēng〈中医 *Chin. med*.〉指腹腔内结块的病 lump in the abdomen
☞ zhèng on p. 2453

【症结】zhēngjié〈中医 *Chin. med*.〉指腹腔内结块的病 lump in the abdomen;〈比喻 *fig*.〉事情弄坏或不能解决的关键 crux; crucial cause

烝 zhēng〈书 *fml*.〉众多 multitude; great number: ～民 masses of people

睁 zhēng 张开(眼睛) open (one's eyes): ～眼 open (one's eyes) | 风沙打得眼睛～不开 cannot open one's eyes in the sandstorm

【睁眼瞎子】zhēngyǎn xiā·zi〈比喻 *fig*.〉不识字的人;文盲 blind person with eyes wide open — sb. who does not know how to read and write; illiterate; also 睁眼瞎 zhēngyǎnxiā

铮 zhēng ☞ below
☞ zhèng on p. 2453

【铮纵】zhēngcōng〈书 *fml*.〉〈拟声词 *onom*.〉形容金属撞击的声音 clank; clang; make a loud resounding noise, as metal when struck

【铮铮】zhēngzhēng〈拟声词 *onom*.〉形容金属

撞击所发出的响亮声音 clank; clang：～悦耳 make pleasant clangs | 铁中～(比喻胜过一般人的人) remarkable person; (fig.) outstanding person

筝 zhēng ❶ ☞ 古筝 gǔzhēng on p. 691 ❷ ☞ 风筝 fēngzheng on p. 584

蒸 zhēng ❶ 蒸发 evaporate：～气 vapour ❷ 利用水蒸气的热力使食物变熟、变热 steam：～馒头 steam *mantou* | 把剩饭～一～ warm up the leftovers in the steamer

【蒸发】zhēngfā 液体表面缓慢地转化成气体 evaporate; change or cause to change from a surface liquid to vapour

【蒸馏】zhēngliú 把液体混合物加热沸腾,使其中沸点较低的组分首先变成蒸气,再冷凝成液体,以与其他组分分离或除去所含杂质 distillate; separate or remove impurities, or concentrate, by heating and boiling a substance so that the component with a lower boiling point evaporates first, to be then cooled and condensed into a separate liquid

【蒸馏水】zhēngliúshuǐ 用蒸馏方法取得的水,清洁而不含杂质,多用于医药和化学工业 distilled water, clean and without impurities, used in medicine and chemical industries

【蒸笼】zhēnglóng 用竹篾、木片等制成的蒸食物用的器具 food steamer (usu. made of bamboo or wood splints)

【蒸气】zhēngqì 液体或固体(如水、汞、苯、碘)因蒸发、沸腾或升华而变成的气体 vapour; gaseous state of a substance that is liquid or solid (e. g. water, mercury, iodine, etc.) under normal conditions：水～ aqueous vapour | 苯～ benzene vapour

【蒸气田】zhēngqìtián 蕴藏着高温天然水蒸气的地热田 vaporous field; field containing natural vapour; also 热气田 rèqìtián

【蒸汽】zhēngqì 水蒸气 steam

【蒸汽锤】zhēngqìchuí 利用水蒸气产生动力的锻锤 steam hammer; also 汽锤 qìchuí

【蒸汽机】zhēngqìjī 利用水蒸气产生动力的发动机,由供应水蒸气的装置、汽缸和传动机构组成。多用做机车的发动机。steam engine; engine that uses the thermal energy of steam to produce mechanical movement, esp. one in which steam from a boiler is expanded in cylinders to drive reciprocating pistons

Z

【蒸食】zhēng·shi 馒头、包子、花卷等蒸熟了吃的面食的总称 (collect.) steamed wheaten foods

【蒸腾】zhēngténg (气体)上升 (of steam) rising：热气～ steaming

【蒸蒸日上】zhēngzhēng rì shàng 〈比喻 *fig.*〉事业天天向上发展 becoming more prosperous every day; flourishing; thriving; make rapid progress

鬇 zhēng [鬇鬡](zhēngníng)〈书 *fml.*〉头发蓬松 (of hair) fluffy

鲭 zhēng〈书 *fml.*〉鱼跟肉合在一起的菜 dishes made of fish and other meat ☞ qīng on p. 1574

zhěng (ㄓㄥˇ)

拯 zhěng 救 save; rescue; deliver：～救 save; deliver | ～民于水火之中 deliver the people from an abyss of misery

【拯救】zhěngjiù 救 save; rescue; deliver：～被压迫的人民 liberate the oppressed people

整 zhěng ❶ 全部在内,没有剩余或残缺;完整(跟'零'相对 as opposed to 'fractional') whole; complete; full; entire：～天 whole day | ～套设备 complete set of facilities | 一年～ a whole year | 十二点～ at 12 o'clock sharp | 化～为零 break up the whole into parts ❷ 整齐 in good order; neat; tidy：～洁 clean and tidy | ～然有序 be in good order | 仪容不～ untidy in appearance ❸ 整理;整顿 put in order; rectify：～风 rectify incorrect styles of work; rectification campaign | ～装待发 all packed up and ready to set out ❹ 修理 repair; mend; renovate：～修 rebuild; recondition | ～旧如新 repair sth. old and make it as good as new ❺ 使吃苦头 make sb. suffer; punish; castigate：旧社会～得我们穷人好苦! What a miserable life we had in the old days! ❻〈方 *dial.*〉搞;弄 do; make; work：绳子～断了。The rope was broken. | 这东西我看见人～过,并不难。I once saw someone make it; it's not very difficult.

【整备】zhěngbèi 整顿配备(武装力量) reorganize and outfit (troops)：～兵力 reorganise and equip the troops

【整编】zhěngbiān 整顿改编(军队等组织) reorganise (troops)：～机构 restructure the organisational setup | ～起义部队 reorganise the rebel troops

【整补】zhěngbǔ 整顿补充(武装力量) reorganise and bring (an armed force) up to full strength

【整饬】zhěngchì ❶ 使有条理;整顿 put in order; strengthen：～纪律 strengthen discipline | ～阵容 maintain the required standards for a soldier's bearing and appearance ❷ 整齐;有条理 in good order; neat; tidy：服装～ neatly dressed | 治家～ neatly manage the household

【整除】zhěngchú 两个整数相除,所得的商是整数,叫做整除 be divided with no remainder; divide exactly

【整地】zhěng//dì 播种前,进行耕地、耙地、平地等工作。有时也包括开沟、做畦。soil preparation (i. e. preparation of land for sowing or planting by ploughing, harrowing, levelling, etc.)

【整队】zhěng//duì 整顿队伍使排列有次序 get

(or bring) the ranks into orderly alignment; line up: ～入场 file into an arena, auditorium, etc.

【整顿】zhěngdùn 使紊乱的变为整齐;使不健全的健全起来(多指组织、纪律、作风等 oft. of organisation, discipline, work style, etc.) rectify; consolidate; reorganize: ～队形 rearrange the formation|～文风 rectify the style of writing|～基层组织 overhaul and consolidate grass-roots units of an organisation

【整风】zhěng//fēng 整顿思想作风和工作作风 rectification of incorrect styles of work or thinking: ～运动 rectification movement

【整改】zhěnggǎi 整顿并改革 reform and consolidate: ～措施 measures of reform and consolidation|经过～,工作效率明显提高。After reform and consolidation, the efficiency at work is much higher.

【整个】zhěnggè (～儿 zhěnggèr)全部 whole; entire: ～上午 entire morning|～会场 whole meeting hall|～社会 whole of society

【整洁】zhěngjié 整齐清洁 clean and tidy; neat; trim: 衣着～ neatly dressed|房间收拾得很～。The room is kept clean and tidy

【整理】zhěnglǐ 使有条理秩序 put in order; straighten out; arrange; sort out; same as 收拾 shōu·shi ①: ～行装 pack up for a journey; pack (for a trip)|～房间 put a room in order; tidy a room|～账目 check accounts|～文化遗产 sort out cultural heritage

【整料】zhěngliào 合乎一定尺寸,可以单独用来制造一个物件或其中的一个完整部分的材料 whole piece of material; material of a required size for the making of sth.

【整流】zhěngliú 利用一定的装置把交流电变成直流电 rectification; convert (alternating current) into direct current

【整流器】zhěngliúqì 把交流电变成直流电的装置,由具有单向导电性的电子元件和有关电路元件组成 rectifier; electronic device, e.g. a semiconductor diode or valve, that converts an alternating current to a direct current by suppression or inversion of alternate half cycles

【整齐】zhěngqí ❶ 有秩序;有条理;不凌乱 in good order; neat; tidy; trim and well-groomed: ～划一 uniform; alike|服装～ neatly dressed|步伐～ march in step ❷ 使整齐 put sth. in order; keep sth. in good order: ～步调 make sb. walk in step ❸ 外形规则、完整 even; regular: 山下有一排～的瓦房。There are well laid-out blocks of tile-roofed houses at the foot of the hill. ❹ 大小、长短相差不多 even; level; regular; alike: 出苗～ evenly grown seedlings|字写得清楚～ neat handwriting ◇这个队人员的技术水平比较～。The members of this team are at the same level in their technical know-how.

【整儿】zhěngr 〈方 *dial.*〉 same as 整数 zhěngshù ②: 把钱凑个～存起来。Let's make it a round sum and put it in the bank.

【整容】zhěng//róng 修饰容貌。特指给有缺陷的面部施行手术,使变得美观 face-lift; cosmetic surgery for tightening sagging skin and smoothing unwanted wrinkles on the face: ～手术 face-lift surgery

【整式】zhěngshì 没有除法运算,或有除法运算但除式中不含字母的有理式。如 x^2+2x-4, $xy-\sqrt{5}y^2+\frac{x}{3}$, $5a$。integral expression, rational expression containing no division or containing divisions that contain no letters, such as x^2+2x-4, $xy-\sqrt{5}y^2+\frac{x}{3}$ and $5a$

【整数】zhěngshù ❶ 正整数(1,2,3,4,5…)、负整数(-1,-2,-3,-4,-5…)和零的统称 integer; whole number; any rational number that can be expressed as the sum or difference of a finite number of units, being a member of the set ...-3, -2, -1, 0, 1, 2, 3... ❷ 没有零头的数目,如十、二百、三千、四万 round number; round figure, e.g. ten, two hundred, three thousand, forty thousand, etc.

【整肃】zhěngsù 〈书 *fml.*〉 ❶ 严肃 strict; rigid: 军容～ soldiers drawn up in strict formation|法纪～ solemn law and discipline ❷ 整顿;整理 rectify; consolidate: ～衣冠 tidy up one's clothing

【整套】zhěngtào 完整的或成系统的一套 complete (or whole) set of: ～设备 complete set of equipment

【整体】zhěngtǐ 指整个集体或整个事物的全部(跟各个成员或各个部分相对待 as opposed to 'individual member' or 'part') whole; entirety: ～规划 overall plan|～利益 overall interests

【整形】zhěng//xíng 通过外科手术使人体上先天的缺陷(如兔唇、腭裂)或后天的畸形(如瘢痕、眼睑下垂)恢复正常外形或生理机能 plastic surgery; branch of surgery concerned with therapeutic or cosmetic repair or re-formation of missing, injured, or malformed tissues or parts (e.g. harelip, cleft palate, scars, sagging eyelids, etc.)

【整修】zhěngxiū 整治修理(多用于工程 oft. of engineering projects) rebuild; renovate; recondition: ～水利工程 rebuild water conservancy projects|～梯田 reinforce terraced fields|～底片 touch up a negative

【整训】zhěngxùn 整顿和训练 train and consolidate (troops, etc.): ～干部 train and consolidate cadres

【整整】zhěngzhěng 达到一个整数的 whole; full: ～忙活了一天 be busy for the whole day|到北京已经～三年了。(I) have been living in Beijing for three years.

【整枝】zhěng//zhī 修剪植物的枝叶，使能更好地生长 prune; remove (dead or superfluous twigs, branches, etc.) from (a tree, shrub, etc.), esp. by cutting

【整治】zhěngzhì ❶ 整理；修理 renovate; repair; dredge (a river, etc.): ～河道 dredge a waterway | 机器出了毛病都是他自己～。He fixes the machine whenever it is out of order. ❷ 为了管束、惩罚、打击等，使吃苦头 punish; fix; make to suffer: ～坏人 punish scoundrels | 这匹马真调皮，你替我好好～～它。The horse is really skittish. You must break it in for me. ❸ 进行某项工作；搞；做 do; perform; work at: ～饭(做饭) prepare food | ～庄稼(做田间管理工作) field management

【整装待发】zhěng zhuāng dài fā 整理行装，等待出发 get ready for a journey or a march; be ready to start out

zhèng (ㄓㄥˋ)

正 zhèng ❶ 垂直或符合标准方向(跟'歪'相对 as opposed to 'crooked') straight; upright: ～南 due south | ～前方 directly ahead | 前后对～ line up the front and back | 这幅画挂得不～。This picture is not hanging straight. ❷ 位置在中间(跟'侧、偏'相对 as opposed to 'by the side') in the centre; main: ～房 principal or main rooms (in a courtyard, usu. facing south) | ～院儿 main courtyard ❸ 用于时间，指正在那一点上或在那一段的正中 (of time) punctually; sharp: ～午 high noon | 十二点～ at 12 o'clock sharp ❹ 正面(跟'反'相对 as opposed to 'reverse') front; obverse; right(side): 这张纸～反都很光洁。Both the front and the back of the paper are smooth. ❺ 正直 honest; upright; impartial: ～派 upright; honest; decent | 公～ impartial | 方～ straightforward ❻ 正当 correct; right: ～路 correct path | ～理 valid reason ❼ (色、味)纯正 (of colour, flavour, etc.) pure; right: ～红 pure red | ～黄 pure yellow | 颜色不～。This is not the right colour. | 味道不～ not the right flavour ❽ 合乎法度；端正 regular; standard: ～楷 regular script | ～体 standard form of a Chinese character ❾ 基本的；主要的(区别于'副' as compared with 'secondary', or 'vice') principal; chief: ～文 main body (of a book, etc.); text | ～编 original part (of a book) | ～本 original (of a document, etc.) | ～副主任 director and deputy director ❿ 图形的各个边的长度和各个角的大小都相等的 (of figures, designs, etc.) regular; (of a polygon) equilateral and equiangular: ～方形 square | ～六边形 regular hexagon ⓫ 大于零的(跟'负'相对 as opposed to 'negative') positive; plus; measured in a direction opposite to that regarded as negative: ～数 positive number | ～号 positive sign | 负乘负得～。A negative multiplied by another negative makes a positive. ⓬ 指失去电子的(跟'负'相对 as opposed to 'negative') positive; plus; (of an electric charge) have an opposite polarity to the charge of an electron and the same polarity as the charge of a proton: ～电 positive | ～极 positive polar ⓭ 使位置正；使不歪斜 rectify; straighten; set right: ～一～帽子 put one's cap straight ⓮ 使端正 set to rights; rectify: ～人先～己。Those who wish to make others upright must be upright themselves first. ⓯ 改正；纠正(错误) make right; correct: ～误 correct (typographical) errors | ～音 correct one's pronunciation ⓰ 恰好 just; right; precisely; exactly: ～中下怀 precisely to one's liking | 时钟～打十二点。The clock is striking the 12. ⓱ 表示动作的进行、状态的持续 be doing; just (doing sth.); just now: ～下着雨呢。It is raining. ⓲ (Zhèng)姓 a surname ☞ zhēng on p.2441

【正本】zhèngběn ❶ 备有副本的图书，别于副本称为正本 original (of a document, as opposed to a duplicate) ❷ 文书或文件的正式的一份 formal copy of a document or letter

【正本清源】zhèng běn qīng yuán 从根源上进行改革 radically reform; thoroughly overhaul: ～的措施 measures for thorough-going reform

【正比】zhèngbǐ ❶ 两个事物或一事物的两个方面，一方发生变化，其另一方随之起相应的变化，如儿童随着年龄的增长，体力也逐渐增长，就是正比 direct proportion; relationship between two things or the two aspects of sth., in which changes in one thing or aspect cause changes in the other, e.g. a child's age growing in direct proportion to his or her weight ❷ 一个数对另一个数的比，如 9∶3 ratio (e.g. 9∶3); ☞ 反比 fǎnbǐ on p.535

【正比例】zhèngbǐlì 两个量(a 和 b)，如果其中的一个量(a)扩大到若干倍，另一个量(b)也随着扩大到若干倍，或一个量(a)缩小到原来的若干分之一，另一个量(b)也随着缩小到原来的若干分之一，这两个量的变化关系叫做正比例，记作 $a \propto b$ direct proportion; relationship that maintains a constant ratio between two variable quantities (when one is multiplied or divided by a certain number, the other changes by the same ratio), e.g. item a increasing in direct proportion to item b, marked as $a \propto b$

【正步】zhèngbù 队伍行进的一种步法，上身保持立正姿式，两腿绷直，两脚着地时适当用力，两臂摆动较高。通常用于检阅。parade step; goose step; military march step in which the leg is swung rigidly to an exaggerated height

【正餐】zhèngcān 指正常的饭食，如午餐、晚餐等

Z

(区别于小吃、早点、夜宵等 as compared with 'snacks', 'midnight snacks', etc.) regular meal, e.g. lunch, dinner, etc.

【正茬】zhèngchá 某个地区轮种的各茬作物中主要的一茬 main crop (in crop rotation): ～麦 main crop of wheat|力争小麦回茬赶～ strive for as much yield in the second crop of the year as the main crop of wheat

【正常】zhèngcháng 符合一般规律或情况 normal; usual; regular: 精神～ in sound mental condition|生活～ lead a regular life|～进行 go on normally

【正出】zhèngchū 〈旧指 *old*〉正妻所生(区别于'庶出' as compared with 'be born of a concubine') be born of the legal wife

【正大】zhèngdà (言行)正当,不存私心 upright; honest; aboveboard: 光明～ open and aboveboard|～的理由 justifiable reasons

【正旦】zhèngdàn 戏曲角色行当,青衣的旧称,有些地方剧种里还用这个名称 old name for 青衣 qīngyī, which is still used in some local operas in China
☞ zhēngdàn on p.2441

【正当】zhèngdāng 正处在(某个时期或阶段) just when; just as; just the time for: ～春耕之时 just the time for spring ploughing

【正当年】zhèngdāngnián 正在身强力壮的年龄 in the prime of life; in one's prime: 十七十八力不全,二十七八～。A man is not yet fully grown in his late teens; in his late twenties he is in the prime of his life.

【正当时】zhèngdāngshí 正在合适的时令 right season or time: 白露早,寒露迟,秋分种麦～。It is too early to sow wheat at White Dew, and too late at Cold Dew. The Autumnal Equinox is the right time for sowing wheat.

【正当中】zhèngdāngzhōng 正中 right in the middle or centre of sth.: 院子的～有一个花坛。There is a flowerbed right in the centre of the courtyard.

【正当】zhèngdàng ❶ 合理合法的 proper; appropriate; correct; legitimate: ～行为 correct behaviour|～的要求 rightful claim (or demand) ❷ (人品)端正 upright; just; honest

【正道】zhèngdào ❶ 正路 right way (or course); correct path ❷ 正确的道理 correct principle; correct way

【正德】Zhèngdé 明武宗(朱厚照)年号(公元1506—1521) Zhengde, title of the reign of Zhu Houzhao (1506-1521), Emperor Wuzong of the Ming Dynasty

【正点】zhèngdiǎn (车、船、飞机)按规定时间开出、运行或到达 (of ships, trains, airplanes, etc.) on schedule; on time; punctually: ～起飞 take off on time|～到达 arrive on time (or punctually)

【正电】zhèngdiàn 物体失去电子时表现出带电现象,这种性质的电叫做正电 positive electricity; (of an electric charge) having an opposite polarity to the charge of an electron and the same polarity as the charge of a proton; also 阳电 yángdiàn

【正殿】zhèngdiàn 宫殿或庙宇里位置在中间的主要的殿 main hall (in a palace or temple, usu. situated in the middle)

【正多边形】zhèngduōbiānxíng 各边相等,各角也相等的多边形 regular polygon

【正法】zhèngfǎ 执行死刑 execute (a criminal): 就地～ execute a convict on the spot

【正反应】zhèngfǎnyìng 通常指向生成物方向进行的化学反应 positive reaction; chemical reaction leading to the formation of a new substance

【正犯】zhèngfàn 共犯中直接参加实施犯罪行为的人 principal offender

【正方】[1]zhèngfāng 呈正方形或立方体的 square or cubic: ～盒子 square box

【正方】[2]zhèngfāng 指辩论中对某一论断持赞成意见的一方(跟'反方'相对 as opposed to 'opposition') (of debate) those holding an affirmative view

【正方体】zhèngfāngtǐ 立方体 cube

【正方形】zhèngfāngxíng 四边相等,四个角都是直角的四边形。正方形是矩形和菱形的特殊形式。square; plane geometric figure having four equal sides and four right angles

【正房】zhèngfáng ❶ 四合院里位置在正面的房屋,通常是坐北朝南的 principal rooms (in a courtyard, usu. facing south); also 上房 shàngfáng ❷ 指大老婆 legal wife (as distinguished from 'concubine')

【正告】zhènggào 严正地告诉 earnestly admonish; sternly warn; warn in all seriousness: ～一切侵略者,玩火者必自焚。We want to warn all aggressors in all seriousness that those who play with fire will burn themselves.

【正割】zhènggē ☞ 三角函数 sānjiǎo hánshù on p.1652

【正宫】zhènggōng 皇后居住的宫室,也指皇后 empress' palace; empress

【正骨】zhènggǔ 〈中医 *Chin. med.*〉指用推、拽、按、捺等手法治疗骨折、脱臼等疾病的医术 bone-setting; traditional Chinese surgery to treat fractures and dislocations

【正规】zhèngguī 符合正式规定的或一般公认的标准的 regular; standard; conforming to a recognised standard: ～军 regular army|～方法 standard methods

【正规军】zhèngguījūn 按照统一的编制组成,有统一的指挥,统一的制度,统一的纪律和统一的训练的军队 regular army; professional long-term personnel in military units

【正轨】zhèngguǐ 正常的发展道路 right (or correct) path: 纳入～ lead onto the correct path; put on the right track|走上～ put on a regular basis; regularize

【正果】zhèngguǒ 〈佛教 *Budd*.〉把修行得道叫做成正果 right fruit — proper consequence of a regulated life in this world

【正好】zhènghǎo ❶ 恰好(指时间、位置不前不后,体积不大不小,数量不多不少,程度不高不低等[of time, position, size, quantity, degree, etc., as neither too little nor too much] just in time; just right; just enough: 你来得~。You've come just in time.|皮球~掉到井里。The ball fell right in the well.|这双鞋我穿~。This pair of shoes fits me just right.|那笔钱~买台抽水机。This is just enough money for a pump.|天气不冷不热,~出去旅行。It's neither too hot nor too cold — just the right weather for an outing. ❷ 恰巧遇到机会 happen to; chance to; as it happens: 这次见到王老师,~当面向他请教。When I see Teacher Wang, I'll have a chance to ask for his advice.

【正极】zhèngjí same as 阳极 yángjí ①

【正教】Zhèngjiào 基督教的一派。11 世纪中叶,随着罗马帝国的分裂,基督教分裂为东西两部,以东罗马帝国首都君士坦丁堡为中心的东部教会自命为'正宗的教会',故称正教或东正教。Orthodox Church (also Byzantine Church, Eastern Orthodox Church, Greek Orthodox Church); collective term for those Eastern Churches that were separated from the Western Church in the 11th century when the Roman Empire fell and are in communion with the Greek patriarch of Constantinople

【正襟危坐】zhèng jīn wēi zuò 理好衣襟端端正正地坐着。形容严肃或拘谨的样子。straighten one's clothes and sit properly; sit bolt upright; become completely serious

【正经】zhèngjīng 〈旧时 *old*〉指十三经 old name for 十三经 Shísān Jīng: ~正史 Confucian canon and official history; ☞ 十三经 Shísān Jīng on p. 1734

【正经】zhèng·jing ❶ 端庄正派 decent; respectable; honest: ~人 decent person ❷ 正当的 serious; proper; right: ~事儿 serious affairs|我们的钱必须用在~地方。Our money must be put to right uses. ❸ 正式的;合乎一定标准的 formal; standard: ~货 standard goods ❹ 〈方 *dial*.〉确实;实在 really; truly; indeed: 黄瓜长得~不错呢! The cucumbers are truly growing well!

【正经八百】zhèngjīng-bābǎi 〈方 *dial*.〉正经的;严肃而认真的 serious; earnest; 百 bǎi also put as 摆 bǎi

【正剧】zhèngjù 戏剧主要类别之一,兼有悲剧与喜剧的因素。以表现严肃的冲突为内容,剧中矛盾复杂,便于多方面反映社会生活。serious drama; serious plays that combine comic and tragic elements to express serious and complex social conflicts

【正楷】zhèngkǎi 楷书(in Chinese calligraphy) regular script

【正理】zhènglǐ 正确的道理 correct principle; valid reason (or argument); right thing to do

【正梁】zhèngliáng ☞ 脊檩 jǐlǐn on p. 911

【正路】zhènglù 做人做事的正当途径 right way (or course); correct path: 走~ take the right path; do the right thing

【正论】zhènglùn 正确合理的言论 just opinion; valid argument; right thing to say

【正门】zhèngmén 整个建筑物(如房屋、院子、公园)正面的主要的门 front door (or gate); main entrance

【正面】zhèngmiàn ❶ 人体前部那一面;建筑物临广场、临街、装饰比较讲究的一面;前进的方向(区别于'侧面' as compared with 'flank') front; frontage; facade; face of the building, usu. facing a street or square and more meticulously ornamented: ~图 front view|大楼的~有八根大理石的柱子。The facade of the building has eight marble pillars.|一连从~进攻,二连、三连侧面包抄。The first company launched an attack on the front while the second and third companies outflanked the enemy from the other sides. ❷ 片状物主要使用的一面或跟外界接触的一面 obverse side; right side: 牛皮纸的~比较光滑。The right side of kraft paper is smooth. ❸ 好的、积极的一面(跟'反面'相对 as opposed to 'negative') positive: ~人物 positive character|~教育 educate by positive measures or examples; positive education ❹ 事情、问题等直接显示的一面 obvious side (of events, issues, etc.): 不但要看问题的~,还要看问题的反面。We should not only look at issues at their face value, but also at what is hidden as well. ❺ 直接 directly; openly; straightforwardly: 有问题~提出来,别绕弯子。Please ask your question directly. Don't beat about the bush.

【正牌】zhèngpái (~儿 zhèngpáir)正规的;非冒牌的 genuine; regular; quality product: ~货 genuine goods

【正派】zhèngpài (品行、作风)规矩,严肃,光明 (of personality, style, etc.) upright; honest; decent: ~人 decent person|为人~ be honest and upright|作风~ work in an honest style

【正片儿】zhèngpiānr same as 正片 zhèngpiàn

【正片】zhèngpiàn ❶ 经过晒印带有图像的照相纸 positive; print or slide showing a photographic image whose colours or tones correspond to those of the original subject ❷ ☞ 拷贝 kǎobèi on p. 1086 ❸ 电影放映时的主要影片(区别于加映的短片 as compared with 'short') feature (film)

【正品】zhèngpǐn 质量符合规定标准的产品 certified products (or goods); quality products (or goods)

【正气】[1] zhèngqì ❶ 光明正大的作风或风气 healthy atmosphere (or tendency): ~上升,

Z

邪气下降。A healthy atmosphere prevails when morbid practices are curbed. ❷ 刚正的气节 unyielding integrity; moral courage: ～凛然 awe-inspiring rectitude

【正气】[2] zhèngqì 〈中医 *Chin. med.*〉指人体的抗病能力 vital energy

【正桥】zhèngqiáo 大型桥梁的主要部分,横跨在河床交叉的道路上面,两端与引桥相连 main structure of a bridge (laying across a river or a road, with both ends linked with approaches to it)

【正巧】zhèngqiǎo 刚巧;正好 happen to; chance to; as it happens; just in time; in the nick of time; just at the right time: 你来得～,我们就要出发了。You've come just in time. We were just about to leave.

【正切】zhèngqiē ☞ 三角函数 sānjiǎo hánshù on p. 1652

【正取】zhèngqǔ 正式录取(区别于'备取' as compared with 'be waitlisted') be admitted or enrolled: ～生 enrolled student

【正确】zhèngquè 符合事实、道理或某种公认的标准 correct; right; proper: 答案～ correct answer|～的意见 correct opinion|实践证明这种方法是～的。Practice has proved that this is the right way.

【正人君子】zhèngrén-jūnzǐ 指品行端正的人 person of honour; person of integrity; gentleman

【正日】zhèngrì 正式举行某种仪式的一天 date for a ceremony; also 正日子 zhèngrì·zi

【正色】[1] zhèngsè 〈书 *fml.*〉纯正的颜色,指青、黄、赤、白、黑等色 primary colours, i. e. blue, yellow, red, white and black

【正色】[2] zhèngsè 态度严肃;神色严厉 with a stern countenance: ～拒绝 sternly refuse|～直言 claim in grave tones

【正身】zhèngshēn 指确是本人(并非冒名顶替的人) true identity; in person; not by proxy: 验明～ make a positive identification of a criminal before execution

【正史】zhèngshǐ 指《史记》、《汉书》等纪传体史书 history books written in biographical style, e. g. *Records of the Historian*, *History of Han*, etc.

【正式】zhèngshì 合乎一般公认的标准的;合乎一定手续的 formal; official; regular: ～比赛 formal contest|～结婚 officially registered as married|～工作人员 full-time worker|～会谈 official discussions

【正事】zhèngshì 正经的事 one's proper business: 大家不要闲扯了,谈～吧。Stop chatting everyone, and let's get down to business.

【正视】zhèngshì 用严肃认真的态度对待,不躲避,不敷衍 face squarely; face up to; look squarely at: ～现实 look reality in the face|～自己的缺点 acknowledge one's shortcomings

【正室】zhèngshì ❶ 大老婆 legal wife (as distinguished from 'concubine') ❷ 〈书 *fml.*〉嫡长子 eldest son born by one's legal wife

【正书】zhèngshū 指楷书 regular script

【正数】zhèngshù 大于零的数,如 +3, +0.25 positive number; number greater than zero, e. g. +3, +0.25

【正题】zhèngtí 说话或写文章的主要题目;中心内容 subject (or topic) of a talk or essay: 转入～ get to the subject|离开～ digress

【正体】zhèngtǐ ❶ 规范的汉字字形 standard form of a Chinese character ❷ 楷书 regular script ❸ 拼音文字的印刷体 block letter

【正厅】zhèngtīng ❶ 正中的大厅 main hall (in the middle) ❷ 剧场中楼下正对舞台的部分 stalls (in a theatre); area of seats on the ground floor of a theatre or cinema nearest to the stage or screen

【正统】zhèngtǒng ❶ 指封建王朝先后相承的系统 legitimism; monarchist who supports the rule of a legitimate dynasty or of its senior branch ❷ 指党派、学派等从创建以来一脉相传的嫡派 orthodox; (of religion, behaviour, attitudes, etc.) conforming with established or accepted standards

【正统】Zhèngtǒng 明英宗(朱祁镇)年号(公元1436—1449) Zhengtong, title of the reign (1436-1449) of Zhu Qizhen, Emperor Yingzong of the Ming Dynasty

【正投影】zhèngtóuyǐng 物体在一组平行光线的照射下在面上的投影叫正投影。投影的光线和投影面垂直。orthographic projection; style of engineering drawing in which true dimensions are represented as if projected from infinity on three planes perpendicular to each other, avoiding the effects of perspective

【正文】zhèngwén 著作的本文(区别于'注解'、'附录'等 as compared with 'annotations', 'appendices', etc.) text; main body (of a book, etc.)

【正午】zhèngwǔ 中午十二点 high noon

【正误】zhèngwù 勘正错误 correct (typographical) errors: ～表 errata; corrigenda

【正弦】zhèngxián ☞ 三角函数 sānjiǎo hánshù on p. 1652

【正项】zhèngxiàng 正式的项目;正规的项目 main project; regular project

【正凶】zhèngxiōng 凶杀案件中的主要凶手 principal murderer

【正眼】zhèngyǎn 眼睛正着(看) look sb. or sth. in the eye; look squarely

【正业】zhèngyè 正当的职业 regular occupation; proper duties: 不务～ neglect one's business; not attend to one's proper duties

【正义】[1] zhèngyì ❶ 公正的、有利于人民的道理 justice: 伸张～ let justice prevail|主持～ uphold justice ❷ 公正的、有利于人民的 just; righteous; benefiting the people: ～的事业

just cause|～的战争 just war

【正义】[2] zhèngyì (语言文字上)正当的或正确的意义。也用做书名,如《史记正义》。correct meaning; (also used in book titles) orthodox or rectified interpretation (of ancient texts), e. g. *Rectified Interpretation of the Records of the Historian*

【正音】zhèng//yīn 矫正语音 correct one's pronunciation

【正音】zhèngyīn 标准音 standard pronunciation

【正在】zhèngzài 〈副词 *adv.*〉表示动作在进行或状态在持续中 in the process of; in the course of: 他们～开会。They are having a meeting. |温度～慢慢上升。The temperature is rising.

【正直】zhèngzhí 公正坦率 honest; upright; fair-minded: 他襟怀坦白,为人～。He is aboveboard and upright.

【正职】zhèngzhí ❶ 正的职位 position of the chief of an office, department, etc.: 这些干部有担任～的,也有担任副职的。Some of these officials are chiefs and others are deputies. ❷ 主要的职业 main occupation or profession; full-time job

【正中】zhèngzhōng 中心点 right in the middle (or centre); also 正当中 zhèng dāngzhōng

【正中下怀】zhèng zhòng xià huái 正好符合自己的心愿 be just what one hopes for; fit in exactly with one's wishes; be precisely to one's liking or tastes; be up to one's expectations

【正字】zhèng//zì 矫正字形,使符合书写或拼写规范 correct a wrongly written character or a misspelt word

【正字】zhèngzì ❶ 楷书 regular script ❷ 指正体,即标准字形 standard form of a Chinese character

【正字法】zhèngzìfǎ 文字的书写或拼写规则 orthography; study of spelling; what is considered to be correct spelling

【正宗】zhèngzōng ❶ 原指佛教各派的创建者所传下来的嫡派,后来泛指正统派 Buddhist doctrines handed down in direct line of the founder of a school; orthodox school ❷ 正统的;真正的 authentic; genuine: ～川菜 genuine Sichuan cooking

【正座】zhèngzuò (～儿 zhèngzuòr)剧场中正对舞台的坐位 central seats that directly face the stage; stalls

证(證) zhèng ❶ 证明 testify to; prove; demonstrate: ～人 witness|～书 certificate|～实 confirm; verify|论～ expound and prove ❷ 证据;证件 evidence; proof; certificate; card: 工作～ employee's ID card|出入～ pass|以此为～。This serves as certification. *or* Take this as evidence.

【证词】zhèngcí 对某个案件或某种事情提供证明的话 testimony; statement of fact for a certain case or thing

【证婚】zhènghūn 在结婚仪式上为结婚人做证明 witness a wedding: ～人 chief witness at a wedding ceremony

【证件】zhèngjiàn 证明身份、经历等的文件,如学生证、工作证、毕业证书等 credentials; papers; certificate (e.g. student or work credentials, diploma, etc.)

【证据】zhèngjù 能够证明某事物的真实性的有关事实或材料 evidence; proof; testimony: ～确凿 irrefutable evidence

【证明】zhèngmíng ❶ 用可靠的材料来表明或断定人或事物的真实性 prove; testify; bear out; verify: ～人 evidence|～书 certificate; testimonial|～信 credential; papers|事实～这个判断是正确的。The facts bear out this judgment. ❷ 证明书或证明信 certificate; identification; testimonial: 开个～ write out a certificate

【证券】zhèngquàn 有价证券 bond; securities: ～市场 stock market|～交易所 stock exchange; stock market

【证人】zhèng•ren ❶ 法律上指除当事人外能对案件提供证据的非当事人 witness; person who testifies, esp. in a court of law, to events or facts within his or her own knowledge ❷ 对某种事情提供证明的人 person who has seen or can give firsthand evidence of a certain event

【证实】zhèngshí 证明其确实 confirm; verify; bear out: 通过实践而发现真理,又通过实践而～真理。Truth is discovered in practice and borne out by practice.

【证书】zhèngshū 由机关、学校、团体等发的证明资格或权利等的文件 certificate; testimonial; credentials; document issued by government organs, schools and other organizations to prove one's qualification or right, etc.: 结婚～ marriage certificate|毕业～ diploma

【证物】zhèngwù 能证明有关案件事实的物件 exhibit (produced in court as evidence)

【证言】zhèngyán 证人就所知道的与案件有关的事实、情节所作的陈述 testimony; statement made by a witness, esp. orally in court under oath, of affirmation of facts and circumstances relative to a case

【证验】zhèngyàn ❶ 通过试验使得到证实 verify: 实习可以～课堂学习的知识。Practice can test and verify what one has learned in classroom. ❷ 实际的效验 real results; efficacy

【证章】zhèngzhāng 学校、机关、团体发给本单位人员证明身份的标志,多用金属制成,佩在胸前 badge; distinguishing emblem or mark worn on the chest to signify membership, employment, achievement, etc., often made of metel

郑(鄭) Zhèng ❶ 周朝国名，在今河南新郑一带 Zheng, one of the warring states into which China was divided during the Zhou Dynasty (1066-256 B. C.), located around present-day Xinzheng in Henan Province ❷ 姓 a surname

【郑重】zhèngzhòng 严肃认真 serious; solemn; earnest: ～其事 seriously; in earnest | ～声明 solemnly declare | 话说得很～ speak in earnest

怔 zhèng〈方 *dial.*〉发愣；发呆 be stumped for words; stare blankly; be in a daze; be in a trance: 我一看诊断书，顿时～住了，不敢对他明说。At a glance of the medical certificate, I was stumped for words, and I dared not tell him the truth.

☞ zhēng on p. 2443

【怔怔】zhèngzhèng〈方 *dial.*〉形容发愣的样子 stare blankly; be in a daze; be in a trance: ～地站着 stand there as if in a trance; stand there staring blankly

诤 zhèng〈书 *fml.*〉直爽地劝告 criticize sb.'s faults frankly; admonish; expostulate: ～友 friend who will give forthright criticism | ～言 forthright criticism

【诤谏】zhèngjiàn〈书 *fml.*〉直爽地说出人的过错，劝人改正 criticize sb.'s faults frankly

【诤言】zhèngyán〈书 *fml.*〉直爽地规劝人改正过错的话 frank criticism; forthright admonition

【诤友】zhèngyǒu〈书 *fml.*〉能直言规劝的朋友 friend who gives forthright criticism

政 zhèng ❶ 政治 politics; political affairs: ～党 political party | ～府 government | ～策 policy | ～务 administrative affairs | ～权 political power ❷ 国家某一部门主管的业务 certain administrative aspects of government: 财～ finance administration | 民～ civil administration | 邮～ postal service ❸ 指家庭或团体的事务 affairs of a family or an organisation: 家～ household management | 校～ school administration ❹ (Zhèng) 姓 a surname

【政变】zhèngbiàn 统治集团内部一部分人采取军事或政治手段造成的国家政权的突然变更 coup d'état; coup; sudden violent or illegal seizure of a government, militarily or politically launched by some people within the ruling group: 发动～ stage a coup d'état | 宫廷～ palace coup

【政柄】zhèngbǐng〈书 *fml.*〉政权 political or state power; regime

【政策】zhèngcè 国家或政党为实现一定历史时期的路线而制定的行动准则 policy; plan of action adopted or pursued by a government, party, etc., to fulfil a political line for a certain historical period: 民族～ policy towards ethnic peoples | 按～办事 do things according to government policies

【政党】zhèngdǎng 代表某个阶级、阶层或集团并为实现其利益而进行斗争的政治组织 political party; an organisation representing a certain class, social strata or group and struggling for its interests

【政敌】zhèngdí 指在政治上跟自己处于敌对地位的人 political opponent

【政法】zhèngfǎ 政治和法律的合称 politics and law

【政府】zhèngfǔ 国家权力机关的执行机关，即国家行政机关，例如我国的国务院（中央人民政府）和地方各级人民政府 government; e. g. in China, the State Council (i. e. the Central People's Government) and the People's Government at different levels

【政纲】zhènggāng 政治纲领，它说明一个政党的政治任务和要求 political programme; programme that explains the political task and requirement of a party; platform

【政工】zhènggōng 政治工作 political work: ～人员 political worker

【政纪】zhèngjì 国家行政机关所制定的为行政机关人员必须遵守的纪律 government discipline

【政绩】zhèngjì 指官员在职期间办事的成绩 achievements in one's official career

【政见】zhèngjiàn 政治主张；政治见解 political view

【政界】zhèngjiè 指政治界 political circles; government circles

【政局】zhèngjú 政治局势 political situation; political scene: 稳定～ stabilize the political situation

【政客】zhèngkè 指从事政治投机，玩弄权术，谋取私利的人 politician; person who engages in politics out of a wish for personal gain, as realised by holding a public office

【政令】zhènglìng 政府公布的法令 government decree (or order)

【政论】zhènglùn 针对当时政治问题发表的评论 political comment: ～文章 political essay

【政派】zhèngpài 政治上的派别 political grouping (or faction)

【政权】zhèngquán ❶ 政治上的统治权力，是阶级专政的工具 political (or state) power; regime (as means of class dictatorship) ❷ 指政权机关 regime; organs of state (or political) power

【政审】zhèngshěn 政治审查 examine sb.'s political behaviour or record: 干部～ examine cadres' political behaviour | ～合格 pass political examinations

【政事】zhèngshì 政府的事务 government affairs

【政体】zhèngtǐ 国家政权的构成形式。政体和国体是相适应的，我国的政体是人民代表大会制。system of government; form of government, e. g. system of the People's Congress as the form of government of China

【政通人和】zhèng tōng rén hé 政事顺遂，人民和乐。形容国泰民安。government is efficient and the people are united; country prospers and the people live in contentment

【政委】zhèngwěi 政治委员的简称 abbr. for 政治委员 zhèngzhì wěiyuán

【政务】zhèngwù 关于政治方面的事务，也指国家的管理工作 government affairs; government administration

【政务院】zhèngwùyuàn 某些国家的最高行政机关。在1954年9月以前我国中央人民政府用此名称，后改称国务院。Administrative Council (i. e. Central People's Government of the People's Republic of China, replaced in September 1954 by the State Council)

【政协】zhèngxié 政治协商会议的简称 abbr. for 政治协商会议 zhèngzhì xiéshāng huìyì

【政要】zhèngyào 政界要人 important person in politics

【政治】zhèngzhì 政府、政党、社会团体和个人在内政及国际关系方面的活动。政治是经济的集中表现，它产生于一定的经济基础，并为经济基础服务，同时极大地影响经济的发展。politics; practice of a government, political party, social organisation and individuals in civil affairs and international relations. A centraled manifestation of economics, politics is born of a certain economic base, serves this economic base, and exert a considerable impact on economic growth.

【政治避难】zhèngzhì bìnàn 一国公民因政治原因逃亡到别国，取得那个国家给予的居留权后，住在那里 political refuge; political asylum; right of abode and protection afforded by one country to an exiled citizen of another nation for political reasons

【政治犯】zhèngzhìfàn 由于从事某种政治活动被政府认为犯罪的人 political offender; political prisoner

【政治家】zhèngzhìjiā 有政治见识和政治才能并从事政治活动的人，多指国家的领导人物 statesman; person who has political foresight and talent and is engaged in political activity, oft. referring to a leader of a country

【政治教导员】zhèngzhì jiàodǎoyuán 中国人民解放军营一级的政治工作人员，和营长同为营的首长 political instructor (of a PLA battalion); 通称 commonly known as 教导员 jiàodǎoyuán

【政治经济学】zhèngzhì-jīngjìxué 研究社会的生产关系及其发展规律的学科。政治经济学是经济学中最重要的一门学科，具有强烈的阶级性。political economics; social science concerned with the relations of production and laws of their development. An important branch of economics, political economics has a strong class nature.

【政治面目】zhèngzhì miànmù 指一个人的政治立场、政治活动以及和政治有关的各种社会关系 political affiliation and background, and his various social relations associated with politics

【政治权利】zhèngzhì quánlì 公民依法在政治上享有的权利，如选举权、被选举权和言论、出版、集会、结社、通信、人身、居住、迁徙、宗教信仰及游行、示威等自由 political rights, e.g. right to elect and be elected, freedom of speech, press, assembly, association, housing, expression, religious belief, demonstration, etc.

【政治委员】zhèngzhì wěiyuán 中国人民解放军团以上部队或某些独立营的政治工作人员，通常是党委日常工作的主持者，和军事指挥员同为该部队首长。political commissar (of a PLA unit at and above the regimental level, usu. executive of daily Party committee work, holding the same rank as the commander of that unit); commissar; 简称 abbr. 政委 zhèngwěi

【政治协理员】zhèngzhì xiélǐyuán 中国人民解放军在团以上机关部门根据需要设立的政治工作人员，在所在单位政治机关和首长领导下，进行本单位机关部门的党的工作和政治工作 political assistant (of a PLA unit at and above the regimental level, who is engaged in Party and political work under the leadership of the political department and commanders of this unit); 通称 commonly known as 协理员 xiélǐyuán

【政治协商会议】zhèngzhì xiéshāng huìyì 我国人民民主统一战线的组织形式。全国性的组织是'中国人民政治协商会议'，各地方也有地方性的各级政治协商会议。Chinese People's Political Consultative Conference (CPPCC); organisational form of the united front of the people's democrary of China, which comprises a national council, and local branches at all levels; 简称 abbr. 政协 zhèngxié

【政治学】zhèngzhìxué 研究各种社会政治现象、政治思想、政治关系及其发展规律的学科 political science; science concerned with political phenomena, political ideology, political relations, and the laws of their development

【政治指导员】zhèngzhì zhǐdǎoyuán 中国人民解放军连一级的政治工作人员，和连长同为连的首长。political instructor (of a PLA company holding the same rank as a company leader); 通称 commonly known as 指导员 zhǐdǎoyuán

挣[1] zhèng 用力使自己摆脱束缚 struggle to get free; try to throw off: ～脱枷锁 throw off the shackles | 把捆绑的绳子～开了 wrenched oneself free of the bonds

挣[2] zhèng 用劳动换取 earn; make; scrape for: ～钱 make money; earn money

☞ zhēng on p. 2443

【挣揣】zhèngchuài 〈书 *fml.*〉挣扎 (zhēngzhá) struggle; strive hard

【挣命】zhèngmìng 为保全生命而挣扎 struggle to save one's life

阐 zhèng [阐阐] (zhèngchuài) same as 挣揣 zhèngchuài

症(證) zhèng 疾病 disease; malady; illness: 病～ disease; illness | 急～ acute disease | 不治之～ incurable disease | 对～下药 fit the medicine to the illness; suit the remedy to the case

☞ zhēng on p. 2443

【症候】zhèng·hòu ❶ 疾病 disease ❷ 症状 symptom

【症候群】zhènghòuqún 因某些有病的器官相互关联的变化而同时出现的一系列症状 syndrome; any combination of signs and symptoms that are indicative of a particular disease or disorder; also 综合征 zōnghézhēng

【症状】zhèngzhuàng 有机体因发生疾病而表现出来的异常状态，如咳嗽、盗汗、下午发烧等是人的肺结核病的症状 symptom; any sensation or change in bodily function experienced by a patient that is associated with a particular disease, e.g. coughing, night sweats and afternoon low fever as symptoms of TB

铮 zhèng 〈方 *dial*.〉(器物表面)光亮耀眼 (of polished utensils, etc.) dazzling; shining: 玻璃擦得～亮。The windowpanes have been polished to shine.

☞ zhēng on p. 2443

zhī (ㄓ)

之[1] zhī 〈书 *fml*.〉往 go; leave for: 由京～沪 leave Beijing for Shanghai | 君将何～? Where are you bound for?

之[2] zhī 〈书 *fml*.〉〈代词 *pron*.〉❶ 代替人或事物(限于做宾语) [used in place of an objective noun or pronoun]: 求～不得 (of an opportunity, gain, etc.) all that one can hope for; most welcome | 取～不尽 inexhaustible | 操～过急 too hasty | 言～成理 hold water; sound reasonable; speak in a convincing way | 取而代～ replace someone | 有过～无不及 go even farther than | 反其道而行～ act in a diametrically opposite way ❷ 虚用，无所指 (used in certain set phrases without a definite designation): 久而久～ with the passage of time | 不觉手之舞～，足之蹈～ dance with joy ❸ 这；那 this or that: ～二虫 these two creatures | ～子于钓 that man fishing

之[3] zhī 〈书 *fml*.〉〈助词 *aux*.〉❶ 用在定语和中心词之间，组成偏正词组 [used between an attribute and the word it modifies]: a) 表示领属关系 to indicate that one thing belongs to another: 赤子～心 pure-heartedness; pure heart of a newborn baby | 钟鼓～声 sound of drums and the tolling of bells | 以子～矛，攻子～盾 beat sb. with his own weapon b) 表示一般的修饰关系 to indicate a descriptive phrase: 光荣～家 glorious family | 无价～宝 treasure of treasures | 缓兵～计 stalling tactics | 千里～外 thousand miles away | 意料～中 within expectations | 十分～九 nine tenths ❷ 用在主谓结构之间，取消它的独立性，使变成偏正结构 [used between the subject and the predicate in a S-P structure so as to nominalise]: 中国～大 the vastness of China | 战斗～烈 the fierceness of the battle | 大道～行也，天下为公。When the great doctrine is followed, all the world belongs to the people. | 如因势利导，则如水～就下，极为自然。If we guide the matter along its course of development, it will proceed as naturally as water flows downwards.

【之后】zhīhòu ❶ 表示在某个时间或处所的后面 later; after; afterwards: 三天～我们又分手了。Three days later we parted again. | 文艺大队走在煤矿工人队伍～。The team of artists marched after the coal miners. 注意 **NOTE**: 多指时间，少指处所 之后 zhīhòu is oft. used to indicate time and occasionally location. ❷ 单独用在句子头上，表示在上文所说的事情以后 (independently used at the beginning of a sentence) afterwards; later: ～，他们又提出了具体的计划。Then they put forward their plan.

【之乎者也】zhī hū zhě yě '之、乎、者、也'是文言文里常用的语助词，常用来形容半文不白的话或文章 often used particles in literary Chinese — pedantic terms; literary jargon; archaisms

【之前】zhīqián 表示在某个时间或处所的前面 before; prior to; ago: 吃饭～要洗手。Wash your hands before eating. | 一个月～我还遇到过他。I saw him only a month ago. | 他们站在队旗～举手宣誓。They swore allegiance in front of the Young Pioneer's Flag. 注意 **NOTE**: 多指时间，少指处所。之前 zhīqián is oft. used to indicate time and occasionally location.

支[1] zhī ❶ 撑 prop up; put up: ～帐篷 put up a tent | 把苇帘子～起来 prop the reed curtain | 他用两手～着头正在想什么。He was meditating with his head in both hands. ❷ 伸出；竖起 protrude; raise; prick up: 两只虎牙朝两边～着 with two upper canine teeth protruding sideways | ～着耳朵听 prick up one's ears to listen ❸ 支持 support; sustain; bear: ～援 aid | ～应 handle; manage | 体力不～ too weak physically to do sth. | 乐不可～ overwhelmed with joy | 疼得实在～不住 can't bear the pain ❹ 调度；指使 send away; put sb. off; order about: ～配 allocate; control | ～使 order about | 把人～走 put sb. off; send sb. away ❺ 付出或领取(款项) pay or withdraw (money): ～出 expense | ～取 withdraw

Z

(money) | ～钱 withdraw money; receive money ❻ (Zhī)姓 a surname

支2 zhī ❶ 分支;支派 branch; offshoot: ～流 tributary | ～队 detachment | ～线 branch line | ～店 branch store ❷〈量词 *classifier*〉a) 用于队伍等 [for troops, fleets, etc.]: 一～军队 an army | 一～文化队伍 a team of cultural workers b) 用于歌曲或乐曲 [for songs or musical compositions]: 两～新的乐曲 two new melodies c) 用于电灯的光度 [for the illuminating power of electric light watt]: 四十～烛光 40 watt | 二十五～光的灯泡 25-watt bulb d) 纱线粗细程度的计算单位,用单位重量的长度来表示,如 1 克重的纱线长 100 米,就叫 100 支(纱)。纱线愈细,支数愈多。(for the size or quality of yarncount) (where 100-count refers to 100 metres of yarn weighing 1 gram) e) same as 枝 zhī ③

支3 zhī 地支 twelve earthly branches; ☞ 干支 gānzhī on p. 627

【支边】zhī//biān 支援边疆 support the border areas; go assist in the development of the border regions: ～工作 management of assistance for the border regions | 科技～ support the border areas through science and technology

【支部】zhībù ❶ 某些党派、团体的基层组织 grass-roots level branch of a party, society, etc. ❷ 特指中国共产党的基层组织 branch of the Chinese Communist Party

【支撑】zhī·chēng ❶ 抵抗住压力使东西不倒塌 prop up; hold up; sustain; support: 坑道里用柱子～着。The pillars hold up the roof of the pit. ❷ 勉强维持 be barely able to; maintain; shore up: 他～着坐起来,头还在发晕。He propped himself into a sitting position, still feeling dizzy. | 一家的生活由他一人～。He barely manages on his own to provide for the family.

【支持】zhīchí ❶ 勉强维持;支撑 sustain; hold out; bear: 累得～不住了 be too tired to hold on ❷ 给以鼓励或赞助 support; back; stand by: 互相～ support each other | ～合理化建议 in favour of proposals for rationalization; be all for proposals for improvement

【支出】zhīchū ❶ 付出去;支付 pay (money); expend; disburse ❷ 支付的款项 expenses; expenditure; outlay; disbursement: 尽量控制非生产性的～ try to minimize non-productive expenditures

【支绌】zhīchù (款项)不够支配 (of funds) not enough; insufficient: 经费～ funds are insufficient; ☞ 左支右绌 zuǒ zhī yòu chù on p. 2573

【支点】zhīdiǎn ❶ 杠杆上起支撑作用,绕着转动的固定点 fulcrum; pivot about which a lever turns ❷ 指事物的中心或关键 strongpoint; fortified point; stronghold: 战略～ strategic stronghold

【支队】zhīduì ❶ 军队中相当于团或师的一级组织,如独立支队、游击支队等 detachment; corresponding to a regiment or division, e. g. independent detachment, guerrilla detachment, etc. ❷ 作战时的临时编组,如先遣支队 military unit organised temporarily for a certain purpose, e. g. advance military unit

【支付】zhīfù 付出(款项) pay (money); defray: ～现金 pay cash

【支架】zhījià ❶ 支持物体用的架子 support; stand; trestle ❷ 支撑;架起 prop up; hold up: ～屋梁 prop up the roof | ～锅灶 hold up the cooking pan ❸ 招架;抵挡 ward off (blows); withstand: 寡不敌众,～不住 fight against hopeless odds

【支解】zhījiě same as 肢解 zhījiě

【支离】zhīlí ❶ 分散;残缺 fragmented; broken; disorganised: ～破碎 fragmented; broken up ❷ (语言文字)烦琐而凌乱 (of writing) trivial and jumbled; incoherent: ～错乱,不成文理 incoherent and absurd (of writing)

【支离破碎】zhīlí pòsuì 形容事物零散破碎,不成整体 fragmented; shattered; torn to pieces; broken up

【支流】zhīliú ❶ 流入干流的河流 tributary; affluent ❷〈比喻 *fig.*〉伴随主要事物而出现的次要事物 minor aspects; nonessentials

【支炉儿】zhīlúr 烙饼的器具,用沙土制成,面上有许多小孔,用时扣在火炉上 earthen pan with many small holes, used over an oven for baking cakes

【支脉】zhīmài 山脉的分支 offshoot (of a mountain range); branch range: 伏牛山是秦岭的～。The Funiu Mountains are an offshoot of the Qinling Mountains.

【支派】zhīpài 分出来的派别;分支 branch; sect; offshoot

【支派】zhī·pài 支使;调动 order; send; dispatch: ～人 boss over others

【支配】zhīpèi ❶ 安排 arrange; allocate; budget: 合理～时间 be good at budgeting time | ～劳动力 allocate the labour force | 不听～ not obey orders ❷ 对人或事物起引导和控制的作用 control; dominate; govern: 思想～行动 thought governs actions

【支票】zhīpiào 向银行支取或划拨存款的票据 cheque; check; bill of exchange drawn on a bank by the holder of a current account; payable on demand if not crossed, or into a bank account if crossed

【支气管】zhīqìguǎn 气管的分支,分布在肺脏内 bronchus; either of the two main branches of the trachea, which contain cartilage within their walls; (图见 ☞ figure for 肺 fèi on p. 563)

【支渠】zhīqú 从干(gàn)渠引水到斗(dǒu)渠的渠道 branch (irrigation) canal

【支取】zhīqǔ 领取(款项) withdraw (money):～存款 withdraw one's savings (from a bank)

【支使】zhī·shi 命令人做事 order about; send away; put sb. off:～人 order others about|把他～走 send him away

【支书】zhīshū 支部书记,是党团支部的主要负责人 Secretary of a Party or League branch; branch secretary

【支吾】zhī·wú 说话含混躲闪;用含混的话搪塞 equivocate; prevaricate; hum and haw:～其词 speak evasively; hum and haw|一味～ be evasive throughout

【支线】zhīxiàn 交通线路的分支(跟'干线'相对 as opposed to 'trunk line') branch line; feeder (line)

【支应】zhīyìng ❶ 应付 cope with; deal with; manage:一个人～不开。One person alone is not enough to cope with it. ❷ 供应 supply:～粮草 supply with rations and fodder ❸ 守候;听候使唤 wait on; attend to:～门户 look after household affairs|今天晚上我来～,你们去睡好了。I will attend to everything here tonight. You may all go to bed.

【支援】zhīyuán 用人力、物力、财力或其他实际行动去支持和援助 support; assist; aid; help:～灾区 give aid (or send relief) to disaster areas|互相～ support each other

【支着儿】zhī//zhāor 从旁给人出主意(多用于看下棋 oft. of a chess game) watch and give advice; kibitz; also 支招儿 zhī//zhāor

【支柱】zhīzhù ❶ 起支撑作用的柱子 pillar; prop ❷〈比喻 *fig.*〉中坚力量 pillar; mainstay:～行业 mainstay industry|国家的～ pillar of the state

【支子】zhī·zi ❶ 支撑物体的东西 stand; support:火～(炉灶上支锅、壶等的东西,圈形,有足,用铁制成) trivet; stand, usually three-legged and made of iron, on which cooking vessels are placed over a fire|车～ kickstand of a bicycle ❷ 一种铁制的架在火上烤肉的用具,像箅子而带腿 gridiron (as a cooking utensil)

【支嘴儿】zhī//zuǐr〈方 *dial.*〉从旁给人出主意 give advice; suggest ideas; make suggestions:他爱看人家下棋,可从来不～。He loves to watch chess games, but he never gives advice to players.|咱们别～,让他自己多动动脑筋。We should not give any suggestions; let him think by himself.

氏

zhī ☞[阏氏](yānzhī) on p.2201 and 月氏(Yuèzhī) on p.2371

☞ shì on p.1751

只(隻)

zhī ❶ 单独的 single; one only:～身 by oneself|片纸～字 brief message|独具～眼 sharp-eyed ❷〈量词 *classifier*〉a)用于某些成对的东西的一个[for one of certain paired things]:两～耳朵 two ears|两～手 two hands|一～袜子一～鞋 a sock and a shoe b)用于动物(多指飞禽、走兽)(oft. birds or beasts)[for animals]:一～鸡 a chicken|两～兔子 two rabbits c)用于某些器具[for certain furniture]:一～箱子 a suitcase d)用于船只[for boats or ships]:一～小船 a boat

☞ zhǐ on p.2465

【只身】zhīshēn 单独一个人 alone; by oneself:～独往 go there alone|～在外 be away from home all by oneself

【只言片语】zhī yán piàn yǔ 个别的词句;片段的话 a word or two; a few isolated words and phrases

卮(巵)

zhī〈古代 *arch.*〉盛酒的器皿 wine vessel:漏～ leaky drinking vessel

汁

zhī(～儿 zhīr) 含有某种物质的液体 juice:乳～ milk|胆～ bile|牛肉～ beef extract|橘子～ orange juice|墨～儿(prepared Chinese) ink

【汁水】zhī·shui〈方 *dial.*〉汁儿 juice:这种果子～很多。This fruit is very juicy.

【汁液】zhīyè 汁儿 juice

芝

zhī ❶ 古书上指灵芝 glossy ganoderma ❷ 古书上指白芷 root of eumenol angelica (*Angelica anomala*) as recorded in ancient books

【芝兰】zhīlán 芝和兰是两种香草,古时比喻德行的高尚或友情、环境的美好等 irises and orchids; (fig.) noble character; true friendship; beautiful surroundings (in old times):～之室 room full of fragrant orchids; good society

【芝麻】zhī·ma ❶ 一年生草本植物,茎直立,下部为圆形,上部一般为四棱形,叶子上有毛,花白色,蒴果有棱,种子小而扁平,有白、黑、黄、褐等不同颜色。是重要的油料作物。sesame (*Sesamum indicum*); annual herb having upright stems that are round at the base and with four ridges on the top, hairy leaves, white flowers, and ridged pods with small, flat seeds white, yellow, or brown in colour, an important source of oil ❷ 这种植物的种子,可以吃,也可以榨油 sesame seeds, which are edible and a source of oil ‖ also 脂麻 zhī·ma

【芝麻官】zhī·maguān 指职位低、权力小的官(含讥讽意 ironicle.) sesame official; petty official:小小～ petty official|七品～ petty government official of the 7th rank (in dynastic times)

【芝麻酱】zhī·majiàng 把芝麻炒熟、磨碎而制成的酱,有香味,用做调料 sesame paste, made by roasting and crushing sesame, fragrant and used as seasoning; also 麻酱 májiàng

【芝麻油】zhī·mayóu 用芝麻榨的油,有特殊的香味,是普通的食用油 sesame-seed oil; sesame oil; also known as 香油 xiāngyóu or 麻油

máyóu

吱 zhī 〈拟声词 *onom.*〉 creak：是什么在～～叫？What is making that creaking noise?｜车～的一声停住了。The cart creaked to a stop.

☞ zī on p.2536

枝 zhī ❶ (～儿 zhīr)枝子 branch；twig：树～twig｜柳～儿 willow branches ❷〈量词 *classifier*〉用于带枝子的花朵［for flowers with stems intact］：一～梅花 a spray of plum blossoms ❸〈量词 *classifier*〉用于杆状的东西［for long, thin, inflexible objects］：一～枪 a rifle｜三～钢笔 three pens｜一～蜡烛 a candle

【枝杈】zhīchà 植物上分杈的小枝子 branch；twig

【枝节】zhījié ❶〈比喻 *fig.*〉有关的但是次要的事情 branches and knots；minor matters；minor aspects；side problems：～问题随后再解决。Side problems will be solved later.｜不要过多地注意那些枝枝节节。Don't pay too much attention to the minor issues. ❷〈比喻 *fig.*〉在解决一个问题的过程中发生的麻烦 complication；unexpected difficulty：横生～ deliberately complicate an issue；raise unexpected difficulties

【枝解】zhījiě same as 肢解 zhījiě

【枝蔓】zhīmàn 枝条和藤蔓 branches and tendrils；〈比喻 *fig.*〉烦琐纷杂 complicated and confused：文字～，不得要领。The writing is confused, and the main points are not clear.

【枝条】zhītiáo same as 枝子 zhī·zi

【枝捂】zhīwú same as 枝梧 zhīwú

【枝梧】zhīwú〈书 *fml.*〉same as 支吾 zhīwú；also 枝捂 zhīwú

【枝丫】zhīyā 枝杈 branch；twig；also 枝桠 zhīyā

【枝桠】zhīyā same as 枝丫 zhīyā

【枝叶】zhīyè 枝子和叶子，也比喻琐碎的情节或话语 branches and leaves；(fig.) nonessentials；trifles

【枝子】zhī·zi 由植物的主干上分出来的较细的茎 branch；twig

知 zhī ❶ 知道 know；realise；be aware of：～无不言 say all one knows｜～其一不～其二 be aware of one aspect of a thing but ignorant of another｜这话不～是谁说的。We don't know who said this. ❷ 使知道 inform；notify；tell：通～ inform｜～会 notify｜～单 invitation ❸ 知识 knowledge：求～ seek knowledge｜无～ ignorant ❹〈书 *fml.*〉知己 intimate friend：新～ new friend｜～友 close friend ❺〈旧指 *old*〉主管 administer；be in charge of：～县 county magistrate｜～客 person in charge of reception at ceremonies

〈古 *arch.*〉same as 智 zhì

【知宾】zhībīn〈方 *dial.*〉same as 知客 zhīkè ①

【知单】zhīdān〈旧时 *old*〉常用的请客通知单，上边开列被邀请的人的名字，由专人持单依次通知，被邀请的人如果能到，一般在自己名下写'知'字，表示已经知道。如果不能到，一般在自己名下写'谢'字，表示谢绝。notice of invitation with a list of the names of those invited (who are supposed to write against their names a 'notified' to indicate a promise to attend or a 'thanks' to indicate refusal)

【知道】zhī·dào 对于事实或道理有认识；懂得 know；realise；be aware of：他～的事情很多。He is a knowledgeable person.｜你的意思我～。I know what you mean.

【知底】zhī∥dǐ 知道根底或内情 know the inside story；know the background；be in the know：知根～ know sb.'s background｜这事我也不～。I don't know the inside story of this matter.

【知法犯法】zhī fǎ fàn fǎ 懂得某项法令、规章而故意违犯 knowingly violate the law；deliberately break the law

【知府】zhīfǔ 明清两代称一府的长官 (in the Ming and Qing dynasties) prefect

【知根知底】zhī gēn zhī dǐ 知道根底或内情 know sb.'s background；know sb. thoroughly：我们是老朋友啦，彼此都～。We are old friends and know each other very well.

【知会】zhī·hui 通知；告诉 tell (verbally)：你先去～他一声，让他早一点儿准备。Go and tell him so that he can get ready in time.

【知己】zhījǐ ❶ 彼此相互了解而情谊深切的 intimate；understanding：～话 intimate words；heart-to-heart talk｜～的朋友 bosom (or intimate) friend ❷ 彼此相互了解而情谊深切的人 bosom (or intimate) friend；sb. who knows one's worth：海内存～，天涯若比邻。A bosom friend brings a distant land near.

【知己知彼】zhī jǐ zhī bǐ《孙子·谋攻》：'知彼知己，百战不殆' *Sunzi · Attack by Stratagem*：'If one knows one's opponent as well as oneself, one will never lose a battle.' 一般都说'知己知彼'，指对自己的情况和对方的情况都有透彻的了解 know one's own situation and that of one's opponent

【知交】zhījiāo 知己的朋友 bosom (or intimate) friend：他是我中学时代的～。He was my close friend when we were in middle school.

【知近】zhījìn 彼此相互了解而关系亲近 intimate：～的朋友 intimate friend

【知觉】zhījué ❶ 反映客观事物的整体形象和表面联系的心理过程。知觉是在感觉的基础上形成的，比感觉复杂、完整。perception；psychological process that reflects the relationship between the whole image of a subjective object and its external appearance. Perception is formed on the basis of sensations but is more complex and complete. ❷ same as 感觉 gǎnjué ①：失去了～ lose consciousness；pass out

【知客】zhīkè ❶〈旧时 *old*〉帮助办喜事或丧事的人家招待宾客的人。有的地区叫知宾。person in charge of receiving guests at a wedding or a funeral; also known as 知宾 zhībīn in some regions ❷ 寺院中主管接待宾客的和尚 monk in charge of reception at a monastery; also 知客僧 zhīkèsēng

【知了】zhīliǎo 蚱蝉的俗称,因叫的声音像'知了'而得名 popular name of cicada that is mimetic to the thrilling sound it produces

【知名】zhīmíng 著名;有名(多用于人 oft. of people) well known; noted; celebrated; famous: 海内～ be well-known at home | ～人士 personage with a prestige; eminent person; public figure; celebrity | ～作家 noted writer

【知名度】zhīmíngdù 指某人或某事物被社会、公众知道熟悉的程度 popularity; fame: 他是个～很高的人。He enjoys great popularity.

【知命】zhīmìng〈书 *fml.*〉❶ 了解天命;认识命运 understand the will of Heaven; know one's destiny: 乐天～ be contented with one's lot ❷《论语·为政》:'五十而知天命。'后来用'知命'指人五十岁 age of fifty. *Analects · Governance*: 'At fifty I understood the Decree of Heaven.': ～之年 at the age of fifty

【知青】zhīqīng 知识青年 educated youth

【知情】zhī//qíng 对别人善意行动的情谊表示感激 feel grateful to sb.; appreciate sb.'s kindness: 对于你的热情帮助,我很～。I'm very grateful to you for your kind help. | 你为他操心,他会知你的情的。He will be grateful to you for your thoughtfulness.

【知情】zhīqíng 知道事件的情节(多用于有关犯罪事件 oft. of illegal happenings) know the facts of a case or the details of an incident; be in the know: ～人 insider; person in the know | ～不报 misprision; failure to report what one knows of a case

【知情达理】zhī qíng dá lǐ 通人情,懂事理 reasonable; sensible

【知趣】zhīqù 知道进退,不惹人讨厌 know how to behave in a delicate situation; be sensitive; be tactful: 人家拒绝了,他还一再去纠缠,真不～。He had been refused and yet he still pestered them. He really doesn't know how to behave.

【知人之明】zhī rén zhī míng 能认识人的品行和才能的眼力 ability to appreciate a person's character and capability; keen insight into a person's character

【知识】zhī·shi ❶ 人们在改造世界的实践中所获得的认识和经验的总和 knowledge; facts and experiences known by people in their practice to transform the objective world ❷ 指有关学术文化的 pertaining to learning or culture; intellectual: ～分子 intellectual | ～界 intellectual circles; the intelligentsia

【知识产业】zhī·shi chǎnyè 指传播知识、提供知识的产业,如教育部门、科研部门、信息服务部门等 knowledge industry (institutions of higher learning, research, information service, etc.); also 智力产业 zhìlì chǎnyè

【知识分子】zhī·shi fènzǐ 具有较高文化水平、从事脑力劳动的人。如科学工作者、教师、医生、记者、工程师等。intellectual; intelligentsia; person who is well educated and engages in mental labour, e.g. scientist, teacher, doctor, journalist, engineer, etc.

【知识青年】zhī·shi qīngnián 指受过学校教育,具有一定文化知识的青年人 school graduates; educated youth

【知事】zhīshì 民国初年称一县的长官 (in the early Republican years) county magistrate; also 县知事 xiànzhīshì

【知书达理】zhī shū dá lǐ 有知识,懂礼貌。指人有文化教养。be well-educated and sensible; also 知书识礼 zhī shū shí lǐ

【知疼着热】zhī téng zháo rè 形容对人非常关心爱护(多用于夫妻之间 oft. between husband and wife) love tenderly

【知悉】zhīxī 知道 know; learn; be informed of: 详情～ be informed of the details of the matter | 无从～ have no way of finding out about sth.

【知县】zhīxiàn 宋代多用中央机关的官做县官,称'知某县事',简称知县,明清两代用做一县长官的正式名称 (in ancient times) county magistrate. In the Song Dynasty, most county magistrates were officials in the central government and referred to as 知某县事 zhī mǒu xiàn shì (knowing the situation of a certain county), which later became 知县 zhīxiàn for short. In the Ming and Qing dynasties, 知县 zhīxiàn became a formal address for county magistrate.

【知晓】zhīxiǎo 知道;晓得 know; be aware of; understand

【知心】zhīxīn same as 知己 zhījǐ ①: ～话 intimate words; heart-to-heart talk | ～朋友 intimate (or bosom) friend

【知音】zhīyīn 伯牙弹琴,弹到描写高山的曲调时,在旁听琴的钟子期就说:'善哉峨峨兮若泰山。'弹到描写流水的曲调时,钟子期就说:'善哉洋洋兮若江河。'钟子期死后,伯牙不再弹琴,认为没有人比钟子期更懂得他的音乐(见于《列子·汤问》)。后来用'知音'指了解自己特长的人。sb. who is keenly appreciative of one's talents; understanding friend; alter ego ('good ear for music', originally from *Liezi · Yin Tang's Questions*: when Boya, a good musician, played the zither with his mind on climbing a lofty mountain, Zhong Ziqi, who was sitting by his side and listening, said, 'How nice! It sounds as lofty as Mount Taishan.' When Boya played a tone portraying flowering waters, Zhong said, 'How nice! It

sounds as immense as the Yellow River and the Yangtze River.' After Zhong died, Boya quitted playing music altogether, believing that no one in this world could understand his music better than his deceased friend.

【知友】zhīyǒu 相互了解的朋友 close friend; intimate friend

【知遇】zhīyù 指得到赏识或重用 have found a patron or superior appreciative of one's ability: ～之感 debt of gratitude for sb.'s recognition and appreciation

【知照】zhīzhào 通知;关照 inform; notify; tell: 你去～他一声,说我已经回来了。Please go and tell him I've returned.

【知州】zhīzhōu 宋代多用中央机关的官做州官,称'权知某军州事',简称知州。明清两代用做一州长官的正式名称。magistrate of a prefecture; prefect. In the Song Dynasty, most prefects were officials of the central government and referred to as 权知某军州事 quán zhī mǒu jūn zhōu shì (kowing the situation of a certain prefecture), which later became 知州 zhīzhōu for short. In the Ming and Qing dynasties, 知州 zhīzhōu became the formal address for prefect.

【知足】zhīzú 满足于已经得到的(指生活、愿望等) be content with one's lot: ～常乐。Contentment brings happiness.|～无求 ask for no more than what one has

肢 zhī 人的胳膊、腿;某些动物的腿 limb: ～体 limbs and trunk|上～和下～ upper limbs and lower limbs; arms and legs

【肢解】zhījiě 〈古代 *arch.*〉割去四肢的酷刑。现多用于比喻。cruel punishment to remove the limbs of a person; dismember; often used figuratively to mean partition; also 支解 zhījiě and 枝解 zhījiě

【肢势】zhīshì 家畜四肢站立时的姿势,是评定家畜役使能力的重要依据 standing (or erect) posture (of domestic animals)

【肢体】zhītǐ 四肢,也指四肢和躯干 limbs; limbs and trunk

泜 Zhī 泜河,水名,在河北 Zhihe, name of a river in Hebei Province

织(織) zhī ❶ 使纱或线交叉穿过,制成绸、布、呢子等 weave; produce (fabric) by interweaving (yarn, thread, etc.), esp. on a loom: 纺～ spinning and weaving|～布 weave cloth|棉～物 cotton fabrics|丝～物 silk fabrics|毛～物 woollen textiles ❷ 用针使纱或线互相套住,制成毛衣、袜子、花边、网子等 knit; make (a garment, etc.) by looping and entwining (yarn, esp. wool) by hand by means of long eyeless needles (knitting needles): 编～ plait; weave|～渔网 weave a fishing net|针～品 knitting

【织补】zhībǔ 用纱或线仿照织布的方式把衣服上破的地方补好 darning; invisible mending

【织锦】zhījǐn ❶ 织有彩色花纹的缎子;锦缎 brocade ❷ 一种织有图画、像刺绣似的丝织品,有彩色的,也有单色的。是杭州等地的特产。multicolour or singlecolour picture woven in silk (a local specialty of Hangzhou and other areas)

【织女】zhīnǚ ❶ 〈旧指 *old*〉织布、织绸的女子 weaving-girl; weaving-maid; girl weaver ❷ 指织女星 Weaving-girl; Spinning Damsel; Vega (star)

【织女星】zhīnǚxīng 天琴座中最亮的一颗星,是零等星,隔银河与牵牛星相对 Vega; the most brilliant star of magnitude 0, in the constellation Lyra, facing Altair ('Cowherd' in the Chinese legend of the lovers the Cowherd and the Weaving-girl) across the Milky Way

【织品】zhīpǐn 指纺织品 textile; fabric

【织物】zhīwù 用棉、麻、丝等织成的衣物的总称 (collect.) fabric; fabrics; general term for clothes made of cotton, flax, silk, etc.

【织造】zhīzào 用机器织成织物 weave with a machine

栀(梔) zhī [栀子](zhī·zi) ❶ 常绿灌木或小乔木,叶子对生,长椭圆形,有光泽,花大,白色,有强烈的香气,果实倒卵形。花供观赏,果实可做黄色染料,也可入药。有的地区叫水横枝。cape jasmine (*Gardenia jasminoides*); widely cultivated gardenia shrub or small tree having long oval, lustrous opposite leaves, and highly fragrant large white flowers, grown for ornamentation, its oval fruit used as yellow dye and medicine; also known as 水横枝 shuǐhéngzhī in some regions ❷ 这种植物的果实 fruit of this plant

胝 zhī ☞ 胼胝 piánzhī on p.1473

祗 zhī 〈书 *fml.*〉恭敬 venerate; esteem; respect: ～仰(敬仰) venerate|～候光临。We request the pleasure of your company.

脂 zhī ❶ 动植物所含的油质 fat; grease; tallow: ～肪 fat|松～ pine resin ❷ 胭脂 rouge: ～粉 rouge and powder

【脂肪】zhīfáng 有机化合物,由三个脂肪酸分子和一个甘油分子化合而成,存在于人体和动物的皮下组织以及植物体中。脂肪是储存热能最高的食物,能供给人体中所需的大量热能。fat; any of a class of naturally occurring soft greasy solids that are esters of one glycerol molecule and three fatty acid molecules, present in some plants and in the adipose tissue of humans and animals. As the highest energy-containing nutrient, it provides large amounts of heat energy for the human body.

【脂肪酸】zhīfángsuān 有机化合物的一类,低级的脂肪酸是无色液体,有刺激气味,高级的脂肪酸是蜡状固体。天然油脂中含量很多。fatty acid; any of a class of aliphatic carboxylic acids, e.g. palmitic acid, stearic acid, and oleic acid, that form part of a lipid molecule. The lower form of a fatty acid is a colourless liquid with an offensive smell and the higher form is a wax-like solid. Natural oil is rich in fatty acids. also 脂酸 zhīsuān

【脂粉】zhīfěn 胭脂和粉，旧时借指妇女 rouge and powder; cosmetics; (old) woman: ～气 womanlike ways; femininity

【脂膏】zhīgāo ❶ 脂肪 fat; grease ❷〈比喻 *fig.*〉人民的血汗和劳动果实 fruits of the people's labour; wealth of the people

【脂麻】zhī·ma same as 芝麻 zhī·ma

【脂油】zhīyóu〈方 *dial.*〉板油 leaf fat; leaf lard: 香～ fragrant lard | ～饼 pancake with lard

椥 zhī 槟椥(Bīnzhī)，越南地名 Binzhi, Chinese transliteration of 'Ben Tre', the name of a place in Viet nam

胝 zhī ☞ [胼胝](piánzhī) on p. 1473

稙 zhī 庄稼种得早些或熟得早些 (of crops) early planting, or early maturing: ～庄稼(种得早) early-planting crops | ～谷子(种得早) early-planting millet | 白玉米～(熟得早)。White corn ripens early.

槠 zhī〈书 *fml.*〉❶ 柱下的木础或石础 wooden or stone base of a column ❷ 支撑 prop up; strut

蜘 zhī [蜘蛛](zhīzhū) 节肢动物，身体圆形或长圆形，分头胸和腹两部，有触须，雄的触须内有精囊，有脚四对。肛门尖端的突起能分泌黏液，黏液在空气中凝成细丝，用来结网捕食昆虫。生活在屋檐和草木间。spider (*Araneae*); any predatory silk-producing arachnid of the order *Araneae*, having four pairs of legs and a rounded or oval unsegmented body consisting of an abdomen and cephalothorax, the male having cirrus containing seminal vesicles, whose spinnerets produce a mucus that in the air turns into fine silk to form a web to catch insects, living under eaves or among plants; 通称 commonly known as 蛛蛛 zhū·zhu

zhí (ㄓˊ)

执(執) zhí ❶ 拿着 hold; grasp: ～笔 have a pen in hand; do the actual writing | 手～红旗 hold (or carry) a red banner ❷ 执掌 take charge of; direct; manage: ～政 be in office | ～教 teach; be a teacher ❸ 坚持 stick to (one's views, etc.); persist: ～意不肯 obstinately refuse | 各～一词。Each has his or her own view. *or* Each tells his or her own story. ❹ 执行;施行 carry out; observe: ～法 enforce law and decrees ❺〈书 *fml.*〉捉住 catch; capture: 战败被～ be held captive after being defeated in battle ❻ 凭单 written acknowledgement: 回～ note to acknowledge receiving sth. | 收～ receipt ❼〈书 *fml.*〉执友 intimate friend: 父～ good friend of one's father ❽ (Zhí)姓 a surname

【执笔】zhíbǐ 用笔写，指写文章，特指动笔拟订集体名义的文稿 write; do the actual writing (in the name of a group, etc.)

【执导】zhídǎo 担任导演;从事导演工作 be a director; direct (a film, etc.): 他～过不少优秀影片。He directed many fine films. | 在戏剧界～多年。He has been a theatre director for many years.

【执法】zhífǎ 执行法令、法律 enforce or execute laws and decrees: ～如山 strictly enforce the law; uphold the law firmly (如山 *ru shan*: 比喻坚定不动摇 unswerving) | ～不阿(ē) enforce laws with a high sense of justice

【执绋】zhífú 原指送葬时帮助牵引灵柩，后来泛指送殡 (orig.) help pull a bier in a funeral procession; (later) take part in a funeral procession

【执教】zhíjiào 担任教学任务;当教练 be a teacher or coach; teach: 他在外贸学院～多年。He has been teaching in the Foreign Trades Institute for many years. | 他们曾携手～中国女排。Once they were coaches of the Chinese Women's Volleyball Team.

【执迷不悟】zhí mí bù wù 坚持错误而不觉悟 obstinately stick to a wrong course; refuse to come to one's senses

【执泥】zhíní 固执;拘泥 obstinate; stubborn; bigoted; stubbornly and rigidly adhere to (sth.): 不可～一说 should not stubbornly and rigidly stick to one theory

【执牛耳】zhí niú'ěr 古代诸侯订立盟约，要每人尝一点牲血，主盟的人亲手割牛耳取血，故用'执牛耳'指盟主。后来指在某一方面居领导地位。In a ceremony marking the conclusion of an alliance in ancient times, the duke who cuts the ears of a sacrificial bull to draw the blood to be drunk by members is the lord of the alliance. (later) be the acknowledged leader; occupy a leading position

【执拗】zhíniù 固执任性，不听从别人的意见 stubborn; pigheaded; wilful: 脾气～ be bigoted

【执勤】zhí//qín 执行勤务 be on duty

【执事】zhí·shi〈旧时 *old*〉俗称仪仗 flags, weapons, etc. carried by a guard of honour: 打～的 guard of honour

【执行】zhíxíng 实施;实行(政策、法律、计划、命令、判决中规定的事项) carry out; execute; implement: 严格～ strictly carry out | ～任务 fulfil a task | ～计划 carry out a plan | ～命令 execute an order

【执行主席】zhíxíng zhǔxí 开大会时由主席团中推举的轮流主持会议的人 executive (or presiding) chairman

【执意】zhíyì 坚持自己的意见 insist on; be de-

Z

termined to; be bent on: ～要去 insist on leaving | ～不肯 firmly refuse

【执友】zhíyǒu 〈书 *fml.*〉志同道合的朋友 intimate friend; bosom friend

【执掌】zhízhǎng 掌管;掌握(职权) wield; be in control of: ～大权 wield power

【执照】zhízhào 由主管机关发给的准许做某项事情的凭证 licence; permit (issued by administrative organs): 施工～ builders' licence | 驾驶～ driving licence

【执政】zhí//zhèng 掌握政权 be in power; be in office; be at the helm of the state: ～党 party in power (or in office); ruling (or governing) party

【执著】zhízhuó 原为佛教用语,指对某一事物坚持不放,不能超脱。后来指固执或拘泥,也指坚持不懈 persistent; persevering; inflexible; rigid; work unflaggingly: 性情古板～ be rigid and inflexible | 不要～于生活琐事。Don't be inflexible about trivial matters. | ～地献身于祖国的教育事业 devote oneself to the motherland's education cause; also 执着 zhízhuó

【执着】zhízhuó same as 执著 zhízhuó

直 zhí ❶ 成直线的(跟'曲'相对 as opposed to 'crooked') straight: 笔～ bolt straight | 马路又平又～。The streets are smooth and straight. | 你把铁丝拉～。Straighten that piece of wire. ❷ 跟地面垂直的(跟'横'相对 as opposed to 'horizontal') vertical: ～升机 helicopter ❸ 从上到下的;从前到后的(跟'横'相对 as opposed to 'horizontal') vertical; perpendicular: ～行的文字 characters written from top to bottom | 屋子很大,～里有两丈,横里有四丈。The room is spacious, measuring two *zhang* in length and four *zhang* in width. ❹ 挺直;使笔直 straighten: ～起腰来 straighten one's back; stand up straight ❺ 公正的;正义的 just; upright: 正～ upright; fair-minded | 理～气壮 feel confident with justice on one's side ❻ 直爽;直截 candid; frank; straightforward: ～性子 straightforward; downright | 心～口快 plain-spoken and straightforward | ～呼其名 call sb. by name | ～言不讳 admit frankly; own up readily | 他嘴～,藏不住话。He is outspoken and never hides anything. ❼ 汉字的笔画,即'竖[1]'④ vertical stroke (in Chinese characters); same as 竖[1] shù ④ ❽ 一直;径直;直接 directly; straight: 列车～达北京。The train goes straight to Beijing. | 游艺会～到中午才结束。The garden party did not come to an end until noon. ❾ 一个劲儿;不断地 continuously: 他看着我～笑。He just smiled at me. | 我冷得～哆嗦。I was so cold that I kept shivering. ❿ 简直 just; simply: 痛得～像针扎一样难受 feel a piercing pain ⓫ (Zhí)姓 a surname

【直拨】zhíbō 电话不经过总机可直接拨通外线或长途线路 direct dialing; make a local or distance call without the need to call an operator first: ～电话 direct-dial telephone | 很多城市之间的电话可以～通话。Direct-dial calls are available in many cities.

【直播】[1] zhíbō 不经过育苗,直接把种子播种到田地里 direct seeding

【直播】[2] zhíbō 广播电台不经过录音或电视台不经过录像而直接播送 (radio or TV) live transmission; live broadcast: 现场～大会的实况 make a live broadcast of the conference

【直肠】zhícháng 大肠的最末段,上端与乙状结肠相连,下端与肛门相连,作用是吸收水分。当粪便到达直肠时,直肠收缩,肛门周围的括约肌张开,粪便就从肛门排出。rectum; lower part of the alimentary canal, between the sigmoid flexure of the colon and the anus, whose function is to absorb water. When excrement reaches the rectum, the rectum contracts and the sphincter of the anus dilates so as to discharge the excrement. (图见 ☞ figure for 消化系统 xiāohuà xìtǒng on p. 2100)

【直肠子】zhícháng·zi 〈比喻 *fig.*〉直性子或性情爽直的人 straightforward person

【直达】zhídá 不必在中途换车换船而直接到达 go straight to one's destination without transfer: ～车 through train | 从北京坐火车～广州 take a through train from Beijing to Guangzhou

【直达快车】zhídá kuàichē 指停站少(一般不停小站)、行车时间少于普通列车的旅客列车 through express train; passenger train that stops at fewer stations (usu. small stations) and takes less time to reach its destination; 简称 abbr. 直快 zhíkuài

【直待】zhídài 一直等到(某个时间、阶段等) wait until (a certain time or a certain period, etc.): ～天黑才回家 do not go home until it is dark

【直到】zhídào 一直到(多指时间 oft. time) until: 这事～今天我才知道。We didn't know this until today.

【直瞪瞪】zhídēngdēng (～的 zhídēngdēng·de)形容两眼直视发怔 stare blankly: 他～地望着地面,神情木然。He fixed his gaze on the ground, with a dazed look in his eyes.

【直裰】zhíduō 僧道穿的大领长袍 loose robe worn by a Buddhist monk or a Taoist priest

【直根】zhígēn 比较发达的粗而长的主根。一般双子叶植物如棉花、白菜都有直根。taproot; relatively developed, long thick main root of plants; roots of dicotyledons like cotton or cabbage

【直贡呢】zhígòngní 一种精致、光滑的斜纹毛织品或棉织品,质地厚实,多用来做大衣和鞋的面子 venetian; thick cotton or woollen cloth used for overcoats and shoes

【直观】zhíguān 用感官直接接受的;直接观察的

direct perception (through the senses); audio-visual (AV): ～教具 teaching aids; audio-visual aids|～教学 hands-on teaching

【直角】zhíjiǎo 两条直线或两个平面垂直相交所成的角。直角为 90°。right angle; angle formed by the perpendicular intersection of two straight lines or two planes; angle of 90 degrees

【直接】zhíjiē 不经过中间事物的(跟'间接'相对 as opposed to 'indirect') direct; immediate: ～关系 direct relationship|～领导 direct leadership|～阅读外文书籍 read foreign language books in the original (and not in translation)

【直接经验】zhíjiē jīngyàn 亲自从实践中取得的经验(跟'间接经验'相对 as opposed to 'indirect experience') direct experience

【直接税】zhíjiēshuì 由纳税人直接负担的税,如所得税、土地税、房产税等 direct tax; tax paid by the person or organization on which it is levied, e.g. income tax, land tax, estate tax, etc.

【直接推理】zhíjiē tuīlǐ 由一个前提推出结论的推理 immediate reasoning

【直接选举】zhíjiē xuǎnjǔ 选民直接参加选举代表或领导成员,不经过复选手续的选举 direct election; election in which voters vote directly for their representatives or leaders without a second election

【直截】zhíjié same as 直截了当 zhíjié-liǎodàng; also 直捷 zhíjié

【直截了当】zhíjié-liǎodàng (言语、行动等)简单爽快 (of speech, action, etc.) straightforward; blunt; point-blank

【直径】zhíjìng 通过圆心并且两端都在圆周上的线段叫做圆的直径;通过球心并且两端都在球面上的线段叫做球的直径 diameter; straight line connecting the centre of a geometric figure, esp. a circle or sphere, with two points on the perimeter or surface

【直撅撅】zhíjuējuē 〈方 *dial.*〉(～的 zhíjuējuē·de) 形容挺直 straight and stiff

【直觉】zhíjué 未经充分逻辑推理的直观。直觉是以已经获得的知识和累积的经验为依据的,而不是像唯心主义者所说的那样,是不依靠实践、不依靠意识的逻辑活动的一种天赋的认识能力。intuition; direct perception of truth, fact, etc., independant of any reasoning process, but on the basis of already acquired knowledge and accumulated experience

【直快】zhíkuài 直达快车的简称 abbr. for 直达快车 zhídá kuàichē

【直来直去】zhí lái zhí qù ❶ 径直去径直回 go and return directly: 这次去广州是～,过不几天就回来了。I will go to Guangzhou and then come back directly in a few days. ❷ 指心地直爽,说话不绕弯子 frank and outspoken; blunt: 他是个～的人,想到什么,就说什么。He's a blunt man, and always says what's on his mind.

【直立】zhílì 笔直地站着或竖着 stand erect; stand upright

【直立茎】zhílìjīng 直立向上生长的茎。大多数植物的茎都是直立茎,如松、柏、甘蔗的茎。erect stem; stems of most plants, e.g. that of the pine, cypress, sugar cane, etc. that are erect

【直溜】zhí·liu (～儿 zhí·liur)形容笔直 perfectly straight: 你看这棵小树,长得多～儿。Look at this small tree — standing so erect.

【直溜溜】zhíliūliū (～的 zhíliúliū·de) 形容笔直的样子 perfectly straight: ～的大马路 straight broad avenue

【直流电】zhíliúdiàn 方向不随时间而改变的电流 direct current (DC); continuous electric current that flows in one direction only, without substantial variation in magnitude

【直眉瞪眼】zhí méi dèng yǎn ❶ 形容发脾气 fume; stare in anger ❷ 形容发呆 stare blankly; be in a daze; be stupefied: 他～地站在那里,也不说话。He stood there staring blankly, saying nothing.

【直面】zhímiàn 面对;正视 look sb. in the eye; face squarely; look squarely at: ～人生 look at life in the face; face the realities of life

【直升机】zhíshēngjī 能直升直落的飞机,螺旋桨装在机身的上部,作水平方向旋转,能停留在空中,可在小面积场地起落 helicopter; copter; aircraft capable of hovering, vertical flight and horizontal flight in any direction, and taking off and landing from small areas, getting the lift and propulsion from the rotation of an overhead propeller

【直书】zhíshū 〈书 *fml.*〉据实写 write what has actually happened; give a truthful account of an event: 秉笔～ wield the pen to record the truth, and the truth only

【直抒】zhíshū 直率地发抒 express freely; state frankly: ～己见 state one's views frankly; be plainspoken

【直属】zhíshǔ ❶ 直接隶属 directly under; directly subordinate to; affiliated to: 这个机构是～文化部的。This organisation is directly affiliated to the Ministry of Culture. ❷ 直接统属的 under the jurisdiction (of a superior organisation, etc.): ～部队 troops under direct command|国务院～机关 departments directly under the State Council

【直率】zhíshuài same as 直爽 zhíshuǎng: 生性～ be straightforward by nature

【直爽】zhíshuǎng 心地坦白,言语、行动没有顾忌 frank; candid; straightforward; forthright: 性情～ forthright in character|他是个～人,心里怎么想,嘴上就怎么说。He is a straightforward man and says what he thinks.

【直挺挺】zhítǐngtǐng (～的 zhítǐngtǐng·de)形容僵直的样子 straight; stiff, bolt upright: ～地站着 stand ramrod straight|～地躺在床上 lie stiff in bed

【直筒子】zhítǒng·zi 〈比喻 *fig.*〉直性子或思想单纯的人 straightforward person：他是个～，说话做事从来不会拐弯抹角。He is a straightforward man who never beats around the bush whatever he says or does.

【直系亲属】zhíxì qīnshǔ 指和自己有直接血统关系或婚姻关系的人，如父、母、夫、妻、子、女等 directly related members of one's family, e. g. parents, spouse, children, etc.

【直辖】zhíxiá 直接管辖的 directly under the jurisdiction of：～市 municipality directly under the central government｜～机构 organization directly under the jurisdiction of a certain department

【直辖市】zhíxiáshì 由中央直接领导的市 municipality directly under the central government

【直线】zhíxiàn ❶ 一个点在平面或空间沿着一定方向和其相反方向运动的轨迹；不弯曲的线 straight line; track left by a dot moving on a surface or in a space in certain direction and the opposite ❷ 指直接的或没有曲折起伏的 direct; steep; sharp (rise or fall)：～电话 direct-dial telephone｜～运输 direct transport｜～联系 direct connection｜～上升 rise sharply

【直心眼儿】zhíxīnyǎnr ❶ 心地直爽 open; frank; straightforward ❷ 指心地直爽的人 straightforward person

【直性】zhíxìng (～儿 zhíxìngr)性情直爽 straightforward; downright; forthright：他是个～人，有什么说什么。He is a straightforward man and says what he thinks.

【直性子】zhíxìng·zi ❶ same as 直性 zhíxìng ❷ 直性的人 straightforward person

【直言】zhíyán 毫无顾忌地说出来 speak bluntly; state outright：～不讳 speak without reservation; not mince words

【直译】zhíyì 指偏重于照顾原文字句的翻译(区别于'意译' as compared with 'free translation') word-for-word translation; verbatim translation

【直音】zhíyīn 我国传统的一种注音方法，就是用一个比较容易认识的字来标注跟它同音的字，例如'蛊，音古'，是说'蛊'字和'古'字同音；'冶，音也'，是说'冶'字和'也'字同音 traditional method of indicating the pronunciation; of a Chinese character by citing another character with the same pronunciation; For example, the Chinese character 蛊 gǔ is homonymous to the character 古 gǔ, and 冶 yě to 也 yě

【直至】zhízhì same as 直到 zhídào

侄(姪)

zhí (～儿 zhír)侄子 brother's son; nephew：表～ son of a male cousin on the woman's side; nephew｜内～ son of one's wife's brother; wife's nephew

【侄妇】zhífù 〈书 *fml.*〉 same as 侄媳妇 zhíxí·fu

【侄女】zhí·nǚ (～儿 zhí·nǚr)弟兄或其他同辈男性亲属的女儿。也称朋友的女儿。brother's daughter; niece; also used to address a friend's daughter

【侄女婿】zhínǚ·xu 侄女的丈夫 husband of one's brother's daughter; niece's husband

【侄孙】zhísūn 弟兄的孙子 brother's grandson; grand-nephew

【侄孙女】zhísūn·nǚ (～儿 zhísūn·nǚr)弟兄的孙女 brother's granddaughter; grand-niece

【侄媳妇】zhíxí·fu (～儿 zhíxí·fur)侄子的妻子 wife of one's brother's son; nephew's wife

【侄子】zhí·zi 弟兄或其他同辈男性亲属的儿子。也称朋友的儿子。brother's son; nephew; also used to call a friend's son

值

zhí ❶ 价格；数值 value：币～ currency value｜比～ ratio; specific value｜总产～ total output value ❷ 货物和价钱相当 be worth; what a specific sum of money can buy：这双皮鞋～五十块钱。This pair of leather shoes is worth 50 yuan. ❸ 用数字表示的量或数学运算所能得到的每一个结果，如 *a* 取值 10，*b* 取值 8，则代数式 *ab* 的值为 10×8 = 80 value; particular magnitude, number, or amount, e. g. if the value of *a* is 10 and the value of *b* is 8, then the equation *ab* stands for the value 80, i. e. 8 × 10 = 80 ❹ 指有意义或有价值；值得 worth; worthwhile：不～一提 not worth mentioning｜走一趟，～了。Travelling there is worthwhile. ❺ 遇到；碰上 happen to：正～国庆，老友重逢，真是分外高兴。It's a delight to see an old friend, and even more so to see one on National Day. ❻ 轮流担任一定时间内的工作 be on duty; take one's turn at sth.：～班 be on duty; be on shift｜～日 be on duty

【值班】zhí//bān (轮流)在规定的时间担任工作 be on duty (in turn)

【值当】zhídàng 〈方 *dial.*〉值得；合算；犯得上 be worthwhile; be to one's advantage：为些鸡毛蒜皮的事生气，太不～。It is not worth getting angry over such trifling matters.

【值得】zhí//·dé ❶ 价钱相当；合算 be worth the money：这东西买得～。It is worth buying.｜东西好，价钱又便宜，～买。This is of good quality and inexpensive; it is worth buying. ❷ 指这样去做有好的结果；有价值，有意义 be worth; merit; deserve：不～ not worthy｜值不得 not worthwhile｜～研究 deserve to be studied｜～推广 deserve to be promoted

【值钱】zhíqián 价钱高；有价值 costly; valuable; of great value; expensive：把～的东西交给柜台保管 entrust valuables to the counter｜这只戒指很～。The ring is expensive.

【值勤】zhí//qín 部队中的人员或负责治安保卫、交通等工作的人员值班 (of army, police, etc.) be on duty; be on point duty：～人员 personnel on duty｜今天晚上该我～。I will be on duty tonight.

【值日】zhírì 在轮到负责的那一天执行任务 be on duty for the day; be one's turn to be on duty: ～生 student on duty | 今天该谁～? Who is on duty today?

【值星】zhíxīng 部队中各级行政负责干部(营里由连长,连里由排长),在轮到负责的那一周带队和处理一般事务 (of a company commander in a battalion, or a platoon leader in a company) be on duty for the week: ～排长 platoon leader on duty this week | 本周是王连长～。Company commander Wang is the officer of the week.

【值夜】zhí//yè 夜间值班 be on night duty; be on the night shift: 分组轮流～ be divided into groups, with each on night duty by turns

【值遇】zhíyù 〈书 *fml*.〉遭逢 meet with; come across; encounter: ～不幸 encounter disaster; come upon misfortune

埴 zhí 〈书 *fml*.〉黏土 clay

职(職) zhí ❶ 职务;责任 duty; job: 尽～ carry out one's duty | ～分 obligatory duty | 天～ bounden duty | 有～有权 entrust sb. with the responsibility and authority that go with sb.'s position ❷ 职位 post; office: 调～ be transferred to another post | 在～ be at one's post | 就～ assume office; take office | 兼～ hold two or more posts concurrently | 撤～ be removed from office | 辞～ resign ❸ 〈旧时 *old*〉公文用语,下属对上司的自称 [used in official reports to superiors] I: ～等奉命 your humble subordinate acts on your instructions ❹ 掌管 manage; direct: ～掌 take charge ❺ 〈书 *fml*.〉由于 because of: ～是之故 for this particular reason | ～此而已。It is for this reason alone.

【职别】zhíbié 职务的区别 official rank

【职称】zhíchēng 职务的名称 title of a technical or professional post (e.g. engineer, professor, lecturer, etc.): 技术～ technical titles | 评定～ evaluate professional titles

【职分】zhífèn ❶ 职务上应尽的本分 duty ❷ 官职 official post; position

【职工】zhígōng ❶ 职员和工人 staff and workers; workers and staff members: ～代表大会 conference of workers and administrative staff ❷ 〈旧时 *old*〉指工人 workers; labourers: ～运动 labour movement; trade union movement

【职能】zhínéng 人、事物、机构应有的作用;功能 function: 货币的～ functions of money | 政法部门是执行国家专政～的机关。Procuratorial and judicial departments are functional organs of state power.

【职权】zhíquán 职务范围以内的权力 powers (or authority) of office: 行使～ exercise one's functions and powers

【职守】zhíshǒu 工作岗位 post; duty: 擅离～ AWOL; away without leave | 忠于～ be faithful in the discharge of one's duties; be devoted to one's duty

【职位】zhíwèi 机关或团体中执行一定职务的位置 position; post

【职务】zhíwù 职位规定应该担任的工作 post; duty; job; position

【职衔】zhíxián ❶ 职位和军衔(如中校团长,团长是职,中校是衔) post and military rank, e.g. regiment commander with the rank of lieutenant colonel ❷ 〈书 *fml*.〉官衔 official title

【职业】zhíyè ❶ 个人在社会中所从事的作为主要生活来源的工作 occupation; profession; vocation; a person's regular work or profession; job or principal activity as the means of livelihood ❷ 专业的;非业余的 professional: ～剧团 professional theatrical troupe | ～运动员 professional athlete

【职业病】zhíyèbìng 由于某种劳动的性质或特殊的劳动环境而引起的慢性疾病。如矿工和陶瓷工业工人易患的尘肺,吹玻璃的工人易患的肺气肿等。occupational disease; chronic disease caused by certain work or work environment, e.g. pneumoconiosis for miners and porcelain workers, pulmonary emphysema for glass-blowers, etc.

【职员】zhíyuán 机关、企业、学校、团体里担任行政或业务工作的人员 office worker; staff member; functionary

【职责】zhízé 职务和责任 duty; obligation; responsibility: 应尽的～ obligation | 保卫祖国是每个公民的神圣～。Safeguarding our motherland is the sacred mission of every citizen.

【职掌】zhízhǎng 掌管 be in charge of: ～生杀大权 possess the power of life and death over

皇 zhí same as 埴 zhí。用于人名。*zhi*, used in people's names

植 zhí ❶ 栽种 plant; grow: 种～ plant; grow | 培～ cultivate | 移～ transplant | ～树 plant trees ◇～皮 skin grafting | 断肢再～ replantation of a severed limb ❷ 树立 set up; establish: ～党营私(结党营私) form a clique to further one's own selfish interests ❸ 指植物 plant; flora: ～被 vegetation | ～株 plant | ～保 plant (or crop) protection ❹ (Zhí)姓 a surname

【植保】zhíbǎo 植物保护的简称 abbr. for 植物保护 zhíwù bǎohù

【植被】zhíbèi 覆盖在某一个地区地面上、具有一定密度的许多植物的总和 vegetation; plant life as a whole, esp. the plant life of a particular region

【植苗】zhí//miáo 移植苗木 transplant seedlings

【植皮】zhí//pí 移植皮肤 skin grafting; ☞ 移植 yízhí ② on p. 2263

【植物】zhíwù 生物的一大类，这一类生物的细胞多具有细胞壁。一般有叶绿素，多以无机物为养料，没有神经，没有感觉。plant；flora；any living organism that typically synthesizes its food from inorganic substances，possessing cellulose cell walls，and having no nerves and sense organs

【植物保护】zhíwù bǎohù 指防治和消灭病、虫、鸟、兽、杂草等对农林植物的危害，使植物能够正常发育 plant (or crop) protection，including prevention of diseases，insects，birds，pests，weeds，etc. 简称 abbr. 植保 zhíbǎo

【植物群落】zhíwù qúnluò 在某一地区内，常结合成一定关系而生存的许多同种的或不同种的植物 plant community；phytocoenosis；various species of plants oft. forming certain relationships in certain areas

【植物人】zhíwùrén 指严重脑外伤、脑出血等引起的大脑皮层丧失活动能力，完全没有知觉的人 (of a human being) vegetable；person who has completely lost mental faculties，as from serious injury，brain damage，etc.

【植物纤维】zhíwù xiānwéi 直接从植物体上取得的纤维，如棉、麻的纤维 vegetable fibre，e.g. fibre from cotton，hemp，etc.

【植物性神经】zhíwùxìng shénjīng 周围神经系的一部分，从延髓、中脑、脊髓发出，分布在内脏器官上，包括传入和传出两种神经纤维，通过这两种神经纤维跟脑和脊髓发生联系，调节内脏器官活动。包括交感神经与副交感神经两个部分。因为不受意志支配，所以叫做植物性神经。autonomic nerve；part of the vertebrate nervous system that branches from the medulla，midbrain and spinal cord to be distributed through internal organs，regulates involuntary actions，as of the intestines，heart，glands，and spinal cord，and is divided into the sympathetic nervous system and the parasympathetic nervous system；also 自主神经 zìzhǔ shénjīng

【植物学】zhíwùxué 研究植物的构造、生长和生活机能的规律、植物的分类、进化、传播以及怎样利用植物的学科 botany；study of plants，including their structure，the laws of growth and vital functions，as well as their classification，evolution，spread，and their utilization

【植物油】zhíwùyóu 从植物种子或果实中压榨或提炼出来的油，如豆油、桐油、花生油、蓖麻油、椰子油等。有的供食用，有的是制造润滑油、油漆的重要原料。vegetable oil；any of a group of oils that are esters of fatty acids and glycerol and are obtained from plants，e.g. tung oil，peanut oil，castor oil，coconut oil，etc.，some being edible，and others being major raw materials for lubricants and paints

【植物园】zhíwùyuán 栽培各种植物，供学术研究或观赏的地方 botanical garden，where plants are grown，exhibited and studied

【植株】zhízhū 成长的植物体，包括根、茎、叶等部分 plant ready for transplantation，including root，stems，leaves，etc.

殖 zhí 繁殖；孳生 breed；multiply；propagate：生～ breed；reproduce | 牲畜增～计划 plan to propagate livestock

☞ ·shi on p. 1764

【殖民】zhímín 原指强国向它所征服的地区移民。在资本主义时期，指资本主义国家把经济政治势力扩张到不发达的国家或地区，掠夺和奴役当地的人民。establish a colony；colonize；establish a body of people who settle in a distant country but maintain ties with their homeland. In the period of capitalism，such practice aims at extending capitalist countries' economic and political power to underdeveloped countries and regions，and at exploiting and enslaving the local people

【殖民地】zhímíndì 原指一个国家在国外侵占并大批移民居住的地区。在资本主义时期，指被资本主义国家剥夺了政治、经济的独立权力，并受它管辖的地区或国家。colony；area which is occupied by an invading country and to which large numbers of settlers are moved；in the period of capitalism，a region or country that was robbed of political and economic independence，and under the control of a capitalist country

【殖民主义】zhímín zhǔyì 资本主义强国对力量弱小的国家或地区进行压迫、统治、奴役和剥削的政策。殖民主义主要表现为海外移民、海盗式抢劫、奴隶贩卖、资本输出、商品倾销、原料掠夺等。colonialism；policy exercised by capitalist powers to enslave and exploit weaker and smaller countries by means of settlement，slave trade，capital export，commodities dumping，and pillage of raw materials，etc.

絷(縶) zhí〈书 *fml.*〉❶ 拴；捆 tie up；fasten ❷ 拘禁 take into custody ❸ 马缰绳 horse reins

跖 zhí same as 蹠 zhí

摭 zhí〈书 *fml.*〉拾取；摘取 pick up：～拾 gather；muster

【摭拾】zhíshí〈书 *fml.*〉拾；捡（多指袭用现成的事例或词句 oft. of examples or set phrases）pick；gather；collect：～故事 collect anecdotes of the past

踯(躑) zhí［踯躅］(zhízhú)〈书 *fml.*〉same as 徘徊 páihuái ①

蹠 zhí ❶ 脚面上接近脚趾的部分 metatarsus ❷〈书 *fml.*〉脚掌 sole of the foot ❸〈书 *fml.*〉踏 tread

【蹠骨】zhígǔ 构成脚掌的小型长骨，跟掌骨相似，共有5块，上端与跗骨相接，下端与趾骨相连 metatarsal bones；skeleton of the human foot between the toes and the tarsus，consisting of five long bones (图见 ☞ figure for 骨骼 gǔgé on p. 693)

Z

蹢 zhí [蹢躅](zhízhú)〈书 *fml*.〉same as 踯躅 zhízhú
☞ dí on p.416

zhǐ (ㄓˇ)

止 zhǐ ❶ 停止 stop; halt; cease; desist: ～步 halt; stop|～境 end; limit|不达目的不～ refuse to give up without attaining one's objective ❷ 拦阻;使停止 prohibit; check; hold back: 禁～ prohibit|制～ check|～血 stop bleeding|～痛 relieve pain|～得住 be able to stop|～不住 be unable to stop ❸ (到、至…)截止 to; till: 展览从10月1日起至10月14日～。The exhibition is open October 1 through 14. ❹ 仅;只 only: ～此一家。This is the only shop.|这话你说过不～一次了。You have said this more than once.

【止步】zhǐ//bù 停止脚步 halt; stop; go no further: ～不前 halt; stand still; make no headway|游人～(公共游览场所用来标明非游览部分 of part of a public place) no visitors; out of bounds; off limits

【止境】zhǐjìng 尽头 end; limit: 学无～。There is no end to learning.|科学的发展是没有～的。There is no limit to the development of science.

【止息】zhǐxī 停止 cease; stop: 永无～。There will be no end to it.

只(衹、祇) zhǐ ❶〈副词 *adv*.〉表示限于某个范围 only; just; merely: ～知其一,不知其二 know only one aspect of a matter but be ignorant of another|～见树木,不见森林 be unable to see the wood for the trees ❷ 只有;仅有 all that there is; only: 家里～我一个人。I'm alone at home.
☞ zhī on p.2455 and 祇 qí on p.1511

【只得】zhǐdé 不得不 have no alternative but to; be obliged to; have to: 河上没有桥,我们～涉水而过。There being no bridge, we had no choice but to wade across the river.

【只顾】zhǐgù ❶〈副词 *adv*.〉表示专一不变 be absorbed in: 他话也不答,头也不回,～低着头干他的事。He didn't reply, nor turn his head, being so engrossed in his work. ❷ 仅仅顾到 care only for; pay attention only to: ～一方面不行,还要顾别的方面。One should not pay attention to only one side; but consideration should be given to the other aspects as well.

【只管】zhǐguǎn〈副词 *adv*.〉❶ 尽管 by all means; feel free to: 你有什么针线活儿,～拿来,我抽空帮你做。If you have any clothes that need mending, feel free to bring them to me and I will find time to mend them for you. ❷ same as 只顾 zhǐgù ①: 他不会使桨,小船～在湖中打转。He didn't know how to use the oars, so the boat just turned round and round on the lake.

【只好】zhǐhǎo 不得不;只得 cannot but; have to; be forced to: 我等了半天他还没回来,～留个条子就走了。I waited for a long time and he did not return, so I had to leave him a note and go.

【只是】zhǐshì ❶ 仅仅是;不过是 only; just; merely; nothing but: 我今天进城,～去看看朋友,逛逛书店,没有别的事儿。Today I'm going to town just to see friends and visit bookshops. ❷ 表示强调限于某个情况或范围 simply: 大家问他是什么事,他～笑,不回答。When asked what had happened, he simply laughed without replying. ❸ 但是(口气较轻)(of a relatively mild tone) but; however: 本来预备今天拍摄外景,～天还没有晴,不能拍摄。We planned to shoot a scene on location today, but we couldn't do it because the weather did not clear up.

【只消】zhǐxiāo 只需要 all one has to do is; you only need to: 这点活儿,～几分钟就可以干完。This will be done only in a few minutes.

【只许州官放火,不许百姓点灯】zhǐ xǔ zhōu guān fàng huǒ, bù xǔ bǎixìng diǎn dēng 宋代田登做州官,要人避讳他的名字,因为'登'和'灯'同音,于是全州都把灯叫做火。到元宵节放灯时,出布告说,本州依例放火三日(见于陆游《老学庵笔记》卷五)。后来用来形容专制蛮横的统治者,为所欲为,不许人民有一点儿自由。也泛指胡作非为的人不许别人有正当的权利。'Tian Deng, a prefect of the Song Dynasty, forbad the use of any characters with the pronunciation of *deng*, including that for 'lamp' and 'lantern'. Thus all the people in his prefecture had to call 'lamp' and 'lantern' 'fire', which is pronounced *huo*. At the Lantern Festival, the prefect's public notice announced that fires (actually lanterns) were to be lit for three days. (See *Notes of Old Learner's Study·Volume 5* by Lu You) Thus the phrase 'While the prefect is free to commit arson, the common people are forbidden even to light lamps' or 'One may steal a horse while another may not look over the hedge'. It is used to depict tyrannical rulers who limit the people's freedom to the extreme. It also refers to evildoers who deprive others of their lawful rights.

【只要】zhǐyào〈连词 *conj*.〉表示充足的条件(下文常用'就'或'便'呼应 usu. used correlatively with 就 jiù or 便 biàn) if only; as long as; provided: ～肯干,就会干出成绩来。So long as one works hard, one is bound to make achievements.|～功夫深,铁杵磨成针。If you work at it hard enough, you can grind an iron rod into a needle.

【只要功夫深,铁杵磨成针】 zhǐyào gōng · fu shēn, tiě chǔ mó chéng zhēn 〈比喻 *fig.*〉人只要有毅力,肯下工夫,就能把事情做成功 If you work at it hard enough, you can grind an iron rod into a needle. *or* Perseverance spells success.

【只有】zhǐyǒu 〈连词 *conj.*〉表示必需的条件(下文常用'才'或'方'呼应 usu. used correlatively with 才 cái or 方 fāng) only if; provided that: ~同心协力,才能把事情办好。Only if we work in concert can we do a good job.

旨[1] zhǐ 〈书 *fml.*〉滋味美 tasty; delicious: ~酒 fragrant wine | 甘~ delicacies

旨[2] (❶恉) zhǐ ❶ 意义;用意;目的 purpose; aim; purport: 主~ purport | 要~ gist; main idea or point | 宗~ aim; purpose | 会议通过了一系列~在进一步发展两国科学技术合作的决议。The meeting adopted a series of resolutions aimed at further strengthening cooperation between the two countries in the field of science and technology. ❷ 意旨,特指帝王的命令 decree; order; esp. imperial decree: 圣~ imperial decree (or edict)

【旨趣】zhǐqù 主要目的和意图;宗旨 main purpose; objective: 本刊的~在发刊词中已经说过了。The purpose of this publication has already been stated in the foreword.

【旨意】zhǐyì 意旨;意图 design; intention: ~何在? What is the point of this instruction?

址(阯) zhǐ 建筑物的位置;地基 location; site: 地~ address | 住~ home address | 校~ location of a school or university | 厂~ location of a factory | 新~ new address | 遗~ ruins; relics

芷 zhǐ ☞ 白芷 báizhǐ on p. 39

抵 zhǐ 〈书 *fml.*〉侧手击 flank attack with one's hand

【抵掌】zhǐzhǎng 〈书 *fml.*〉击掌(表示高兴) clap (one's hands to show appreciation): ~而谈 talking while clapping one's hands rhythmically; have a heart-to-heart talk |

注意 **NOTE**: '抵'不作'抵',也不念dǐ抵 cannot be written as 抵 dǐ, nor pronounced as dǐ

Z

沚 zhǐ 〈书 *fml.*〉水中的小块陆地 islet; small piece of land in a body of water

纸(帋) zhǐ ❶ 写字、绘画、印刷、包装等所用的东西,多用植物纤维制造 paper; substance made from cellulose fibres derived from rags, wood, etc., oft. with other additives, and formed into flat thin sheets suitable for writing, painting or printing on, or for decorating walls, wrapping, etc. ❷ 〈量词 *classifier*〉书信、文件的张数 [for letters, documents, etc.]: 一~公文 an official document | 一~禁令 a prohibition notice; a ban | 单据三~ three receipts; three bills

【纸板】zhǐbǎn 板状的纸。质地粗糙,较厚而硬,用来制作纸盒、纸箱等。paperboard; cardboard; thick, stiff paper, used for making boxes, cartons, signs, etc.

【纸币】zhǐbì 纸制的货币,一般由国家银行或政府授权的银行发行 paper money; paper currency; note; generally issued by a state bank or any bank with government authorization

【纸浆】zhǐjiāng 芦苇、稻草、竹子、木材等经过化学或机械方法处理,除去杂质后剩下的纤维素,是造纸的原料 paper pulp; pulp; moist mixture of cellulose fibres, as obtained from reeds, straw, bamboo, wood, etc., chemically or mechanically processed and purified, from which paper is made

【纸老虎】zhǐlǎohǔ 〈比喻 *fig.*〉外表强大凶狠而实际空虚无力的人或集团 paper tiger; sb. or some group that is outwardly strong but inwardly weak

【纸马】zhǐmǎ ❶ (~儿 zhǐmǎr) 迷信用品,印有神像供焚化用的纸片 paper painted with pictures of idols and burned at altars, used in superstitious ceremonies ❷ 〈方 *dial.*〉迷信用品,用纸糊成的人、车、马等形状的东西 human figures, carriages, horses, etc., made of paper for superstitious use

【纸媒儿】zhǐméir same as 纸煤儿 zhǐméir

【纸煤儿】zhǐméir 引火用的很细的纸卷儿 paper rolled into a thin stick used to light sth.; also 纸媒儿 zhǐméir

【纸捻】zhǐniǎn (~儿 zhǐniǎnr) 用纸条搓成的像细绳的东西 spill of rolled paper; (paper) spill

【纸牌】zhǐpái 牌类娱乐用具,用硬纸制成,上面印着各种点子或文字,种类很多。playing cards; poker; entertainment tool made of cardboard printed with different kinds of dots or words, of various types; also 扑克牌 pūkèpái

【纸钱】zhǐqián (~儿 zhǐqiánr) 迷信的人烧给死人或鬼神的铜钱形的圆纸片,中间有方孔。也有用较大的纸片,上面打出一些钱形做成。paper made to resemble money (round in shape, with a square hole at the centre) and burned by superstitious people as an offering to the dead or idols; paper printed with images of coins

【纸上谈兵】zhǐ shàng tán bīng 在文字上谈用兵策略 talk about stratagems only on paper; be an armchair strategist; 〈比喻 *fig.*〉不联系实际情况,发空议论 engage in idle theorizing

【纸头】zhǐtóu 〈方 *dial.*〉纸 paper

【纸型】zhǐxíng 浇铸铅版的模子。用特制的纸覆在排好的版上压制成。paper mould; paper matrix; mould in which printing type is cast, and which is produced by placing a special kind of paper on a set type and then pressing it

【纸烟】zhǐyān 香烟 cigarette
【纸样】zhǐyàng 按衣服等的式样、尺寸用纸裁成的标准样式 paper pattern for making clothes, etc.
【纸鹞】zhǐyào〈方 *dial.*〉风筝 kite
【纸叶子】zhǐyè·zi〈方 *dial.*〉same as 纸牌 zhǐpái
【纸鸢】zhǐyuān〈书 *fml.*〉风筝 kite
【纸张】zhǐzhāng 纸(总称)(collect.) paper
【纸醉金迷】zhǐ zuì jīn mí 形容叫人沉迷的奢侈繁华的环境 (a life of) luxury and dissipation; also 金迷纸醉 jīn mí zhǐ zuì

祉 zhǐ〈书 *fml.*〉幸福 blessedness; felicity; weal: 福～ happiness; blissfulness

枳 zhǐ 落叶灌木或小乔木,茎上有刺,叶为复叶,有小叶三片,小叶倒卵形或椭圆形,花白色,浆果球形,黄绿色,味酸苦 trifoliate orange (*Poncirus trifoliata*); wild orange; fast-growing, spiny small deciduous Chinese orange tree, bearing compound leaves with three inverted-egg or oval-shaped leaf blades, white flowers, and yellowish green round berries which taste bitter; also 枸橘 gōujú
【枳椇】zhǐjǔ 拐枣 raisin tree (*Hovenia*); Japanese raisin tree; honey tree

轵 zhǐ〈书 *fml.*〉车轴的末端 axle end

指 zhǐ ❶ 手指头 finger: 食～ index finger; forefinger | 首屈一～ second to none | 屈～可数 can be counted on one's fingers; few and far between; very few | 天黑得伸手不见五～。It's so dark that you can't even see your hand in front of you. ❷ 一个手指头的宽度叫'一指',用来计算深浅宽窄等 (unit for measuring depth or width, etc.) finger-width; digit; finger; finger's width: 下了三～雨。We had rain about 3 inches deep. | 这双鞋大了一～。This pair of shoes is a finger too large. | 两～宽的纸条 a slip of paper of two-finger width ❸ (手指头、物体尖端)对着;向着 (with a finger or pointed end) indicate the position or direction of; point to; point (a finger, stick, etc.) at: 用手一～ point to | 时针正～十二点。The hour hand is pointing to 12. ❹ (头发)直立 (of hair) stand stiffly on end; bristle; straighten up: 发～ get one's hackles up; boil with anger ❺ 指点 give directions or guidance: ～导 instruct; give guidance; direct; coach; tutor; supervise; guide | ～示 indicate; point out; instruct; order | ～出正确方向 point out the right way | ～出缺点 point out sb.'s shortcomings ❻ 意思上指着 refer to; direct: 这不是～你说的,是～他的。The remarks are not meant for you, but for him. ❼ 仰仗;依靠 depend on; rely on; count on; lean upon; calculate on; reck on on: ～望 expect; count on; reckon on; bank on; figure on | 单～着一个人是不能把事情做好的。You can't possibly get a good job done counting on one person alone.
【指标】zhǐbiāo 计划中规定达到的目标 target; index; quota; norm: 数量～ quota | 质量～ quality index | 生产～ output quota; production target
【指拨】zhǐ·bō ❶ 指点;点拨 give directions or guidance: 我工作上没有经验,请您多～。I'm a novice at the job; your guidance will be most appreciated. ❷ 指示;调度 order; instruct; dispatch: 我只听队长的,你甭想～我! I take orders from nobody except the team leader!
【指不定】zhǐ·bu dìng 没有准儿;说不定 there is no telling; not sure: 你别等他了,他～来不来呢。You don't have to wait for him; maybe he won't come.
【指不胜屈】zhǐ bù shèng qū 形容数量很多,扳着指头数也数不过来 too many to be counted on the fingers; a great many
【指斥】zhǐchì 指摘;斥责 reprove; reprimand; condemn; impugn; chide; tax; denounce: ～时弊 denounce the maladies of the time
【指导】zhǐdǎo 指示教导;指点引导 direct; guide; instruct; coach; supervise; tutor: ～员 instructor | 教师正在～学生做实验。The teacher is supervising his students in conducting the experiment.
【指导员】zhǐdǎoyuán ❶ 担任指导工作的人员 instructor ❷ 政治指导员的通称 general term for 政治指导员 zhèngzhì zhǐdǎoyuán
【指点】zhǐdiǎn ❶ 指出来使人知道;点明 give directions or guidance; point out; give tips (to sb.): 他～给我看,哪是织女星,哪是牵牛星。He pointed out where the stars Vega and the Altair were located. | 大家都朝他～的方向看。All of us looked in the direction he pointed at. | 老大爷～我怎样积肥选种。The old man showed me how to collect manure and select seeds. ❷ 在旁边挑剔毛病;在背后说人不是 point one's finger at; gossip about sb.; talk behind sb.'s back; find fault with; pick on; trip up; crab at
【指定】zhǐdìng 确定(做某件事的人、时间、地点等) appoint; specify; designate; assign; name: ～他做大会发言人。He was named as the spokesman of the conference. | 各组分头出发,到～的地点集合。All the groups started off separately and assembled at the designated place.
【指法】zhǐfǎ 指戏曲、舞蹈表演中手指动作的方式;演奏管弦乐器时用手指的技巧 (in the performance of traditional opera, dance, and musical instruments) fingering: ～熟练 skilful fingering
【指骨】zhǐgǔ 构成手指的小型长骨,每只手有14根,大拇指有2根,其余四个手指各有3根 phalanx; one of the digital bones of the

hand, with each hand having 14 such bones: 2 for the thumb and 3 for each of the four other fingers;(图见☞ figure for 骨骼 gǔgé on p.693)

【指画】[1] zhǐhuà 挥动手指;指点 point to; point at:孩子们～着,'看,飞机!三架!又三架!' The children pointed with their fingers, 'Look! Planes! Three of them! And another three!'

【指画】[2] zhǐhuà 国画中用指头、指甲和手掌蘸水墨或颜色画出的画 finger-painting; technique of Chinese painting by applying colour or ink to paper with the fingers, nails or palm

【指环】zhǐhuán 戒指 (finger) ring

【指挥】zhǐhuī ❶ 发令调度 command; direct:～部 headquarters; command|～所 command post|～作战 direct a battle ❷ 发令调度的人 commander; director ❸ 在乐队或合唱队前面指示如何演奏或演唱的人 conductor; person who directs an orchestra or chorus

【指挥棒】zhǐhuībàng ❶ 乐队指挥、交通警等指挥时用的小棒 baton; wand used by a conductor or traffic police ❷ 借指起导向作用的事物(多含贬义 oft. derog.) sth. that serves to command:他要大家都得随着他的～转。He wants all of us to dance to his baton.

【指挥刀】zhǐhuīdāo 指挥士兵作战、演习或操练时用的狭长的刀 commander's sword with which to direct battles, military exercises or drills

【指挥员】zhǐhuīyuán ❶ 中国人民解放军中担任各级领导职务的干部 commander (in the Chinese People's Liberation Army) ❷ 泛指在某项工作中负责指挥的人员(in a broad sense) person who directs the work of an undertaking

【指鸡骂狗】zhǐ jī mà gǒu ☞指桑骂槐 zhǐ sāng mà huái

【指甲】zhǐ·jia (口语中多读 in spoken Chinese oft. pronounced zhī·jia)指尖上面的角质物,有保护指尖的作用 nail; horny covering on the upper surface of the tip of the finger

【指甲盖儿】zhǐ·jiagàir (口语中多读 in spoken Chinese oft. pronounced zhī·jiagàir) 指甲连着肌肉的部分 lunula of a fingernail

【指甲心儿】zhǐ·jiaxīnr (口语中多读 in spoken Chinese oft. pronounced zhī·jiaxīnr) 指甲跟指尖肌肉相接连的地方 nail root; root of a fingernail

【指教】zhǐjiào ❶ 指点教导 give directions or guidance; instruct; teach; indoctrinate; coach:在教练的耐心～下,运动员的进步很快。The athletes made rapid progress under the patient instruction of the coach. ❷〈客套话 *pol.*〉用于请人对自己的工作、作品提出批评或意见 used to ask sb. to give advice or comments:希望多多～。Your comments would be much appreciated. *or* Kindly give us your advice.

【指靠】zhǐkào 依靠(多指生活方面的 oft. for a living) depend on; rely on; count on; look to sb.:生活有了～ have sth. to rely on in life|要学会自立,不能～别人。You should learn to stand on your own two feet, since you cannot always depend on others.

【指控】zhǐkòng 指责和控诉 accuse sb. of; charge sb. with; be indicted on a charge of (a crime); bring a charge against sb.; make a charge against sb.:提出～ bring up a charge; file a charge|～他造谣中伤。He was charged with slander.

【指令】zhǐlìng ❶ 指示;命令 instruct; order; direct; command ❷〈旧时 *old*〉公文的一类,上级机关因下级机关呈请而有所指示时称为指令 written instruction or directive by a superior on a submitted document; command; order; injunction

【指鹿为马】zhǐ lù wéi mǎ 秦朝二世皇帝的时候,丞相赵高想造反,怕别的臣子不附和,就先试验一下。他把一只鹿献给二世,说:'这是马。'二世笑着说:'丞相错了吧,把鹿说成马了。'问旁边的人,有的不说话,有的说是马,有的说是鹿。事后赵高就暗中把说是鹿的人杀了(见于《史记·秦始皇本纪》)。call a deer a horse; According to *Records of the Historian·Official Records of Qinshihuang*, during the reign of the second emperor of the Qin Dynasty, Prime Minister Zhao Gao wanted to rebel, but the first thing he did was to sound the other ministers out for fear that some of them might refuse to follow his line. During a court session, he presented a deer to the second emperor, saying, 'This is a horse.' 'You are wrong, my Prime Minister,' the second emperor said, laughing. 'You've mistaken the deer for a horse.' When opinions were canvassed from those present, some remained silent, some said it was a horse, and some insisted it was a deer. Afterwards Zhao Gao had all those who called the deer a deer put to death.〈比喻 *fig.*〉颠倒是非 call white black; turn right into wrong; confound right and wrong

【指名】zhǐmíng (～儿 zhǐmíngr) 指出人或事物的名字 mention by name; designate:～要我发言。I was designated to make a speech.|～道姓(直接说出姓名) name names; mention by name

【指明】zhǐmíng 明确指出 show clearly; point out; demonstrate; designate:～方向 show a way out

【指南】zhǐnán〈比喻 *fig.*〉辨别方向的依据 guide; directory; manual:行动～ guide to action|考试～ examinee's guide

【指南车】zhǐnánchē 我国古代用来指示方向的车。在车上装着一个木头人,车子里面有很多齿轮,无论车子转向哪个方向,木头人的手总是指着南方。compass vehicle; ancient Chinese vehicle equipped with many gear wheels and a wooden figure that always pointed south no matter which direction the vehicle went

【指南针】zhǐnánzhēn ❶ 利用磁针制成的指示方向的仪器,把磁针支在一个直轴上,可以作水平旋转,由于磁针受地磁吸引,针的一头总是指着南方 compass; device used to determine geographic direction, consisting of a magnetic needle which is horizontally suspended and free to pivot until aligned with the earth's magnetic field and pointing to the south ❷〈比喻 *fig.*〉辨别正确发展方向的依据 sth. that guides people along the right direction

【指派】zhǐpài 派遣(某人去做某项工作 send a certain person on a mission) assign; appoint; designate; name; call on:受人～ be dispatched|～他担当这个任务 assign him to this duty; entrust a task on him

【指认】zhǐrèn 指出并确认(某人的身份、某事物的情况等) point out and affirm; identify; recognize:经多人～,此人就是作案者。A number of people identified him as the man responsible for the crime.|在车上我试着～记忆里当年城关一带的景物。On the train I tried to relive my memories of the scenery around the city gate in those past years.

【指日可待】zhǐ rì kě dài (事情、希望等)不久就可以实现(of success, hopes, etc.) be realized very soon; can be expected soon; be just around the corner:计划的完成～。The completion of the plan is just around the corner.

【指桑骂槐】zhǐ sāng mà huái〈比喻 *fig.*〉表面上骂这个人,实际上骂那个人 pretend to be telling one person off when it is another person one is digging at; point at one but scold another; also 指鸡骂狗 zhǐ jī mà gǒu

【指使】zhǐshǐ 出主意叫别人去做某事 incite; prompt; provoke; instigate; prod; egg on:这件事幕后有人～。There must be someone who stirred things up behind the scenes.|有人～他这样做的。He acted on someone's instigation. *or* He was incited to act like this.

【指示】zhǐshì ❶ 指给人看 show; indicate:～剂 indicator|～代词 demonstrative pronoun ❷ 上级对下级或长辈对晚辈说明处理某个问题的原则和方法(of a superior or an elder) give directives or instructions:局长～我们必须按期完成任务。The director instructed us in the necessity of completing the project on schedule. ❸ 指示下级或晚辈的话或文字 instruction; directive; order:执行上级的～ carry out instructions from one's superior

【指事】zhǐshì 六书之一。指事是说字由象征性的符号构成。如:'上'字古写作'二','下'字古写作'＝'。one of the six categories of Chinese characters, showing that a Chinese character is composed of certain symbols, e. g. 上 shàng was originally written as 二, and 下 xià written as ＝

【指手画脚】zhǐ shǒu huà jiǎo 形容说话时兼用手势示意。也形容轻率地指点、批评。(of a person) talk with lots of animated gestures; gesticulate; (of a person) make imprudent remarks or criticisms; throw one's weight around

【指数】zhǐshù ❶ 表示一个数自乘若干次的数字,记在数的右上角,如 3^2,4^3,6^n 的 2,3,n exponent; exponential; index; power; number denoting the number of times a quantity is multiplied by itself, placed to the right upper corner of another number, e.g. 2, 3, n, in the expressions of 3^2, 4^3, 6^n ❷ 某一经济现象在某时期内的数值和同一现象在另一个作为比较标准的时期内的数值的比数。指数表明经济现象变动的程度,如生产指数、物价指数、劳动生产率指数。此外,说明地区差异或计划完成情况的比数也叫指数。index; index number; indicator; ratio of a certain economic value at certain times to a value of similar kind over a chosen standard period of time, which shows certain variations of an economic event, e. g. the index of production, price index, index of productivity; ratio that show differences between regions or completion of plans

【指头】zhǐ·tou (口语中多读 in spoken Chinese oft. pronounced zhí·tou) 手前端的五个分支,可以屈伸拿东西。也指脚趾。one of the five digits of the hand; finger; also referring to 脚趾 jiǎozhǐ

【指头肚儿】zhǐ·toudùr (口语中多读 in spoken Chinese oft. pronounced zhí·toudùr)〈方 *dial.*〉手指头上有螺纹的鼓起的部分 fingertip; front of the fingertip

【指望】zhǐ·wang ❶ 一心期待;盼望 bank on; look forward to; expect; pin one's hopes on; hope for:～今年有个好收成 look forward to a good harvest for the year ❷ (～儿 zhǐ·wangr)所指望的;盼头 hope; expectation:这病还有～儿。There is still hope for a cure for the disease.

【指纹】zhǐwén 手指肚上皮肤的纹理,也指这种纹理留下来的痕迹 fingerprint; loops and whorls on a finger; dactylogram; finger mark

【指引】zhǐyǐn 指点引导 lead; show the way; direct; guide:～航向 steer a ship along the right course; direct the course of a ship|猎人～他通过了林区。The hunter showed him the way through the forest.

【指印】zhǐyìn (～儿 zhǐyìnr) 手指肚留下的痕迹。有时特指按在契约、证件、单据等上面的指纹。fingerprint; finger mark (esp. the one made on a contract, certificate, bill of document, etc.)

【指责】zhǐzé 指摘;责备 censure; condemn; rebuke; blame; criticize; accuse; reproach; reprehend; exclaim against; find fault with; throw stones at; give sb. flak for doing sth.: 大家～他不爱护公物。He was censured for not protecting public property.

【指摘】zhǐzhāi 挑出错误,加以批评 pick fault and criticize: 严厉～ severely criticize|无可～ faultless; unimpeachable

【指战员】zhǐzhànyuán 指挥员和战斗员的合称 officers and men; commanders and soldiers (collect.)

【指仗】zhǐzhàng 〈方 *dial.*〉仰仗;依靠 rely on; depend on; count on: 这里农民一年的生计就～地里的收成。The farmers here depend for their whole year's livelihood on the harvest from the land.

【指针】zhǐzhēn ❶ 钟表的面上指示时间的针,分为时针、分针、秒针;仪表指示度数的针 hand of a clock or watch pointing to the hour, minute or second; indicator; needle; pointer; index (on a meter) ❷〈比喻 *fig.*〉辨别正确方向的依据 guideline; guiding principle

【指正】zhǐzhèng ❶ 指出错误,使之改正 point out mistakes so that they can be corrected ❷〈客套话 *pol.*〉用于请人批评自己的作品或意见 used to invite sb. to make comments or critical remarks: 有不对的地方请大家～。Your pointing out of errors needing correction would be much appreciated.

咫 zhǐ 〈古代 *arch.*〉称八寸为咫 measurement of length, equal to eight *cun* (寸)

【咫尺】zhǐchǐ 〈书 *fml.*〉〈比喻 *fig.*〉距离很近 very near or close: ～之间 very near, as if a few feet away|近在～ very close or near

【咫尺天涯】zhǐchǐ tiānyá 指距离虽然很近,但很难相见,就像在遥远的天边一样 though within walking distance, yet difficult to meet as if oceans apart; see little of each other though living close together

趾 zhǐ ❶ 脚指头 toe: ～骨 phalanx|鹅鸭之类～间有蹼。Geese and ducks have webbed feet. ❷ 脚 foot: ～高气扬 be high and mighty; strut

【趾高气扬】zhǐ gāo qì yáng 高高举步,神气十足。形容骄傲自满,得意忘形。walk with pompous bearing; be high and mighty; strut (proudly); be above oneself; be on one's high horse; be puffed up with pride

【趾骨】zhǐgǔ 构成脚趾的小型长骨,每只脚有 14 块,大脚趾有 2 块,其余四个脚趾各有 3 块 phalanx; phalange; bone of a toe, each foot having 14 such bones, with the big toe having two and the remaining four toes having three each; (图见☞ figure for 骨骼 gǔgé on p. 693)

【趾甲】zhǐjiǎ 脚指甲 toenail

黹 zhǐ 〈书 *fml.*〉缝纫;刺绣 stitch-work; needlework; embroidery: 针～ needlework

酯 zhǐ 有机化合物的一类,是酸分子中能电离的氢原子被烃基取代而成的化合物。是动植物油脂的主要部分。ester; organic compound, formed through the process of replacing the hydrogen atoms which can be ionized in an acid molecule by an alkyl; major component of vegetable oil

徵 zhǐ 古代五音之一。相当于简谱的'5'。note of the ancient Chinese five-note scale, corresponding to 5 in numbered musical notation; ☞ 五音 wǔyīn on p. 2032
☞ 征 zhēng on p. 2442

zhì (㞢)

至 zhì ❶ 到 reaching; to; until: ～今 so far; up to now; to this day; to date; hitherto|自始～终 from beginning to end; all the way|～死不屈 not yield until death ❷ 至于 to such an extent; as for; as to; as regards: 甚～ even; go so far as ❸ 极;最 very; most: 欢迎之～ warmest welcome|三个人不够,～少需要五个。Three people still won't be enough; at least five are needed.|你要早来,～迟下星期内一定赶到。You'd better come early; arrive no later than next Sunday.

【至宝】zhìbǎo 最珍贵的宝物 most valuable treasure: 如获～ as if one has acquired a rare treasure; get what one has dreamed of for a long time

【至诚】zhìchéng 诚心诚意 complete sincerity; full earnestness: 一片～ in all sincerity; with all one's heart; wholeheartedly|出于～ from the bottom of one's heart; in all sincerity|～待人 treat sb. with all sincerity

【至诚】zhì·cheng 诚恳 sincere; honest; wholehearted; cordial: ～的朋友 honest friend|他是个～人,从来不说空话。He is an honest man who never makes empty promises.

【至此】zhìcǐ ❶ 到这里 here and now; at this point; up to here; hereto; hereunto; thus far: 文章～为止。The article ends at this point. ❷ 到这个时候 until now; up to this time; by now: ～,事情才逐渐有了眉目。Only now have things begun to take shape. ❸ 到这种地步 to such an extent: 事已～,只好就这样了。Now that things have gone this far, we have no choice but to accept them.

【至多】zhìduō 〈副词 *adv.*〉表示最大的限度 at most; at best; not more than; at the utmost; (of time) at the longest: 他～不过四十岁。He can't be more than 40 years old.|老师～是从头到尾讲一遍,要纯熟还得靠自己多练习。The teacher at best lectures from the beginning to end, so you will have to do extra exercises to improve your skills.

【至高无上】zhì gāo wú shàng 最高;没有更高的 supreme; sovereign

【至好】zhìhǎo same as 至交 zhìjiāo

【至极】zhìjí 达到极点 attaining the greatest or highest degree; to the utmost point; extremely; exceedingly: 可恶～ outrageous; extremely abhorrent

【至交】zhìjiāo 最相好的朋友 close friend; best friend; bosom friend; pal; intimate; confidant: ～好友 hail-fellow; confidant | 他们俩是～。They are bosom friends.

【至今】zhìjīn 直到现在 so far; until now; up to now; to this day; to date; hitherto: 他回家以后～还没有来信。Since he went back home, I haven't heard from him up to now.

【至理名言】zhìlǐ-míngyán 最正确、最有价值的话 wisdom; most truthful remarks

【至亲】zhìqīn 关系最近的亲戚 close relative; close kin: ～好友 beloved family and friends; close relatives and good friends; kith and kin | 骨肉～ one's own flesh and blood

【至上】zhìshàng (地位、权力等)最高 (of status, power, etc.) supreme; sovereign; paramount: 顾客～。Customers come first. | 国家利益～ put national interest above all else

【至少】zhìshǎo 〈副词 *adv*.〉表示最小的限度 at least: 今天到会的～有三千人。There are at least three thousand people attending the conference today. | 从这儿走到学校,～要半个小时。It takes at least half an hour to walk from here to the school.

【至于】zhìyú ❶ 表示达到某种程度 (go) so far as to; to such an extent: 他说了要来的,也许晚一些,不～不来吧? He said he would come maybe a bit late, but would he go so far as to not show up at all? ❷ 表示另提一事 as for; as to; as regards: 这两年来,村里新盖的瓦房就有几百间,～村民添置的电器、日用品,就不可胜数了。In the last couple of years several hundred new houses have been built in the village, and as for the household appliances and daily necessities the villagers have bought, they are just too numerous to be counted.

【至嘱】zhìzhǔ 极恳切的嘱咐(多用于书信 oft. used in letter writing) sincere hope

【至尊】zhìzūn ❶ 最尊贵 most honoured and revered: ～无上 most distinguished ❷ 封建时代称皇帝为至尊 (in feudal times) emperor

志[1] zhì ❶ 志向;志愿 ambition; ideal; aspiration; will; wish: 立～ aspire (to be or become); have an ambition | 得～ achieve one's ambition; have one's ambitions fulfilled | ～同道合 be in the same camp; be like-minded ❷ (Zhì)姓 a surname

志[2] zhì 〈方 *dial*.〉称轻重;量长短、多少 weigh; measure: 用秤～～ weigh sth. on a steelyard | 拿碗～一～ measure sth. out with a bowl

志[3] (**誌**) zhì ❶ 记 remember; keep in mind: ～喜 (of sth. or some event that serves as) celebration or congratulations | ～哀 expression of mourning | 永～不忘 forever bear in mind ❷ 文字记录 written or printed documents; records; annals; chronicles: 杂～ magazine; journal | 县～ annals of a county | 《三国～》 *Records of Three Kingdoms* ❸ 记号 mark; token; sign: 标～ mark; symbol; label; stamp; flag

【志哀】zhì'āi 用某种方式表示哀悼 expression of mourning

【志大才疏】zhì dà cái shū 志向虽然大,可是能力不够 have high aspirations but low competence; hitch one's wagon to a star

【志气】zhì·qì 求上进的决心和勇气;要求做成某件事的气概 aspiration; spirit; ambition; backbone: 有～ have aspirations; aspire (to do sth.) | ～昂扬 be high-spirited; have one's spirits uplifted

【志趣】zhìqù 行动或意志的趋向;志向和兴趣 aspirations and interests; inclination; turn of mind; bent: ～相投 like-minded

【志士】zhìshì 有坚决意志和节操的人 person of ideals and integrity: ～仁人 people of purpose and virtue; people with high aspirations | 革命～ committed revolutionaries | 爱国～ patriotic people with noble minds

【志同道合】zhì tóng dào hé 志向相同,意见相合 share the same ideals and thoughts; be in the same camp; be like-minded

【志向】zhì·xiàng 关于将来要做什么事,要做什么样人的意愿和决心 ambition; ideal; aspiration: 远大的～ far-reaching aspiration; lofty ideal

【志愿】zhìyuàn ❶ 志向和愿望 aspiration and wish; ideal; will: 立下～ make a wish | 他的～是当个教师。He wishes to be a teacher. ❷ 自愿 volunteer (to do sth.): ～军 volunteers (who fight in another country)

【志愿兵】zhìyuànbīng 自愿服兵役的士兵,我国专指服满一定年限的兵役后自愿继续服役的士兵 volunteer (soldier); (in China) soldier who volunteers to stay in the army after serving a term of service

【志愿兵制】zhìyuànbīngzhì 自愿参军的制度。中国共产党领导的人民军队,1954 年前一直实行志愿兵制;1955 年开始实行义务兵役制;1978 年起,实行义务兵与志愿兵相结合的兵役制度。volunteer service system. The people's army under the leadership of the Chinese Communist Party utilized a volunteer military service system until 1954. In 1955 a compulsory military service system was put into operation, and then since 1978 a new system of selective and volunteer service has been in place.

【志愿军】zhìyuànjūn 一国或数国人民，因自愿参加另一国家的对外战争或国内战争而组成的军队，多指为了帮助另一国抵抗武装侵略而组成的 volunteers; people from one or more countries who volunteer to join an army to fight for another country in a foreign or civil war; (oft.) those who volunteer to assist another country to resist an armed invasion

【志子】zhì·zi 〈方 *dial.*〉称轻重或量长短、多少的简单器具 implement for weighing or measuring

豸 zhì 〈书 *fml.*〉没有脚的虫 legless insect: 虫～ insects

忮 zhì 〈书 *fml.*〉嫉妒 envy; jealousy: ～刻(忌刻) penetrating jealousy | 不～不求 be neither envious of nor greedy for what others have

识(識) zhì 〈书 *fml.*〉❶ 记 remember; bear in mind: 博闻强～ be well-read and have a retentive mind ❷ 记号 mark; sign; symbol: 款～ inscriptions (on an ancient bronze vessel, e.g. bell, etc.) | 标～ sign; mark

☞ shí on p.1741

厔 zhì 盩厔(Zhōuzhì)，地名，在陕西。今已改作周至。Zhouzhi, name of a place in Shaanxi province; now named 周至 Zhōuzhì

郅 zhì ❶〈书 *fml.*〉极；最 most; extreme ❷ (Zhì) 姓 a surname

帜(幟) zhì ❶ 旗子 flag; banner: 旗～ banner; standard; ensign; oriflamme | 独树一～ develop a style of one's own; be unique ❷〈书 *fml.*〉标记 mark; sign

帙 zhì 〈书 *fml.*〉❶ 书画外面包着的布套 cloth slip case for a book or a painting ❷〈量词 *classifier*〉用于装套的线装书 used for slip-cased, thread-bound book(s)

制(❶製) zhì ❶ 制造 make; manufacture; produce; turn out; fabricate: ～版 plate making | ～革 leather making | ～图 charting; drawing; mapping; cartography | 炼～ refine; melt; temper with fire | 缝～ tailor ❷ 拟订；规定 work out; draw up or out; mark out; formulate; stipulate; prescribe: ～定 constitute; establish; frame; formulate; map; lay down; set down | 因地～宜 adjust measures to local conditions ❸ 用强力约束；限定；管束 rule; control; inhibit; restrict; restrain; limit; hold in: 压～ inhibit; suppress; stifle; put a lid on | 限～ restrict; limit; confine | 管～ control; put under surveillance | 节～ abstain from; deny oneself; refrain from; abstinence; continency; abstention; sobriety; temperateness | ～伏 fight down; tame; overwhelm; overmaster; override; subdue ❹ 制度 system; institution: 全民所有～ ownership by the whole people | 民主集中～ democratic centralism

【制版】zhì//bǎn 制造各种印刷上用的版 plate making: ～车间 plate-making workshop

【制备】zhìbèi 化学工业上指经过制造而取得 (in chemical industry) preparation

【制裁】zhìcái 用强力管束并惩处，使不得胡作非为 apply or impose sanctions against; crack down on: 法律～ legal sanction; punishment by law | 经济～ economic sanctions

【制导】zhìdǎo 通过无线电装置，控制和引导导弹等，使其按一定轨道运行 control and guidance of a missile, etc., by means of remote control, so that it follows a certain course

【制订】zhìdìng 创制拟定 draw up; work out; formulate; map out; stipulate for; block in (or out): ～汉语拼音方案 work out the Scheme for the Chinese Phonetic Alphabet

【制定】zhìdìng 定出(法律、规程、计划等) establish; map out; formulate; institute; lay down; set down: ～宪法 establish a constitution | ～学习计划 work out a study plan | ～学会章程 formulate the constitution for an association, society, etc.

【制动器】zhìdòngqì 使运行中的运输工具、机器等减低速度或停止运动的装置 brake; device designed to make a vehicle or machine in motion slow down or stop; 通称 generally called 闸 zhá

【制度】zhìdù ❶ 要求大家共同遵守的办事规程或行动准则 system; institution; rules; regulations: 工作～ work rules and regulations | 财政～ fiscal regulations ❷ 在一定历史条件下形成的政治、经济、文化等方面的体系 system; institution formed under certain historical conditions in the political, economic and cultural fields: 社会主义～ socialist system | 封建宗法～ patriarchal clan system of feudalism

【制伏】zhì//fú 用强力压制使驯服 fight down; tame; overwhelm; overmaster; override; check; subdue; bring under control; also 制服 zhì//fú

【制服】zhì//fú same as 制伏 zhì//fú

【制服】zhìfú 军人、机关工作者、学生等穿戴的有规定式样的服装 uniform (as worn by an army personnel, office worker, student, etc.)

【制服呢】zhìfúní 用粗毛纱织成的呢子。多半是斜纹的，质地紧密，两面都有绒毛，主要用来做秋冬季制服。woollen uniform coating, made with woollen yarn, diagonal and firm textured, having fuzzy surfaces on both sides, mostly used to make autumn and winter wear

【制高点】zhìgāodiǎn 军事上指能够俯视、控制周围地面的高地或建筑物等 (in military affairs) commanding elevation or height; high point, e. g. highland or building from which one can have a bird's-eye view and control of the surroundings

【制海权】zhìhǎiquán 海军兵力在一定时间、一定海区所掌握的主动权 thalassocracy; command of the seas; mastery of the seas

【制剂】zhìjì 生药或化学药品经过加工制成的药物,如水剂、酊剂、血清、疫苗 preparation; medicament prepared from natural or chemical ingredients, e. g. aqua, tincture, blood serum, and vaccine

【制件】zhìjiàn ☞ 作件 zuòjiàn on p. 2575

【制空权】zhìkōngquán 空军兵力在一定时间、一定空间范围内所掌握的主动权 air supremacy; mastery of the sky; control of the air

【制冷】zhìlěng 用人工方法取得低温 refrigeration

【制品】zhìpǐn 制造成的物品 products; goods; wares: 乳～ dairy products | 塑料～ plastic articles; plastic wares | 化学～ chemical products

【制钱】zhìqián 明清两代称由本朝铸造通行的铜钱 copper coins made in the Ming and Qing dynasties

【制胜】zhìshèng 取胜;战胜 gain or get the upper hand; subdue; beat; ace: 出奇～ win by surprise; have an ace in the hole | ～敌人 subdue the enemy; defeat the enemy

【制式教练】zhìshì-jiàoliàn 按照条令规定进行的军人队列动作的教练 formation drill master

【制图】zhì//tú 把实物或想像的物体的形象大、小等在平面上按一定比例描绘出来(多用于机械、工程等设计工作 oft. used in mechanical design, engineering, etc.) charting; drawing; mapping; cartography; protraction

【制约】zhìyuē 甲事物本身的存在和变化以乙事物的存在和变化为条件,则甲事物为乙事物所制约 condition; restrict; restrain; limit: 互相～ condition each other; interact

【制造】zhìzào ❶ 用人工使原材料成为可供使用的物品 make; manufacture; produce; fabricate; turn out: ～机器 manufacture machines | ～化肥 produce (chemical) fertilizer ❷ 人为地造成某种气氛或局面等(含贬义 derog.) concoct; stir up; create: ～纠纷 make trouble; give rise to dissension | ～紧张气氛 create tensions

【制止】zhìzhǐ 强迫使停止;不允许继续(行动) prevent; stop; deter; check; interdict; refrain; curb; hold out; put down; put a stay on; put a stop to: ～侵略 put an end to aggression | 我做了一个手势,～他再说下去。I made a gesture to restrain him from saying any more. *or* I motioned for him to stop talking.

【制作】zhìzuò same as 制造 zhìzào: ～家具 make furniture

质[1](質) zhì ❶ 性质;本质 character; nature; quality; property; essence: 实～ essence; substance | 变～ deteriorate; metamorphose; turn; transmute; go bad; become off | 量的变化能引起～的变化。A quantitative change will possibly lead to a qualitative change. ❷ same as 质量 zhìliàng ②: ～量并重(质量和数量并重) pay equal attention to quality and quantity | 保～保量 guarantee both quality and quantity ❸ 物质 matter; substance; material thing: 铁～的器具 ironware; iron utensils | 流～的食物 liquid diet ❹ 朴素;单纯 simple; natural; plain: ～朴 unaffected; simple; plain

质[2](質) zhì 询问;责问 ask; question; bring or call to account: ～疑 oppugn; question; call sth. into question; challenge | ～问 interrogate; enquire; query; assail; interpellate

质[3](質) zhì 〈书〉❶ 抵押 pawn; mortgage; pledge; guaranty: 以衣物～钱 pawn one's clothes for money ❷ 抵押品 pledge; gage; guarantee; security; hostage: 以此物为～ with this as security or collateral

【质变】zhìbiàn 事物的根本性质的变化。是由一种性质向另一种性质的突变。qualitative change; fundamental change in the quality of sth.; abrupt change into a different thing in quality; ☞ 量变 liàngbiàn on p. 1210

【质地】zhìdì ❶ 某种材料的结构的性质 quality of a material; character; texture; grain: ～坚韧 tenacious | ～精美 of exquisite texture; of fine quality ❷ 指人的品质或资质 (a person's) character; quality; aptitude

【质点】zhìdiǎn 在说明物体运动状态时,不考虑物体的大小和形状,认为它只是具有质量的点,这个物体叫做质点 particle; matter having finite mass but whose dimensions and shape are negligible when accounting for the matter's state of movement

【质对】zhìduì 对证;对质 confrontation; counterpoint: 当面～ confront sb. with a question; challenge sb. face to face

【质感】zhìgǎn 指艺术品所表现的物体特质的真实感 (of a work of art which gives people) a sense of reality: 这幅作品用多种绘画手段,表现了不同物体的～。The painting gives a realistic feel to different objects by using diverse pictorial techniques.

【质量】zhìliàng ❶ 量度物体惯性大小的物理量。数值上等于物体所受外力和它获得的加速度的比值。有时也指物体中所含物质的量。质量是常量,不因高度或纬度变化而改变。physical capacity measuring a body's inertia, equal to the ratio of an outside force upon a body to changes in the speed; also the quantity of matter a body contains. The mass of a body is a constant, and not changed by altitude or latitude ❷ 产品或工作的优劣程度 quality of a product or work：工程～ quality of a project | 教学～ quality of teaching | 这布～好，又好看，又耐穿。The cloth is of fine quality; it looks nice and stands wear and tear.

【质料】zhìliào 产品所用的材料 material：这套衣服的～很好。This suit is made of very good fabric.

【质朴】zhìpǔ 朴实；不矫饰 unaffected; simple; plain; guileless：为人～忠厚 be simple and honest; be guileless and unsophisticated | 文字平易～ written in a simple and plain style

【质数】zhìshù 在大于1的整数中，只能被1和这个数本身整除的数，如2,3,5,7,11 prime number; positive integer not divisible without a remainder by any positive integer other than itself and 1, e.g. 2, 3, 5, 7, 11; also 素数 sùshù

【质问】zhìwèn 依据事实问明是非；责问 interrogate; enquire; query; assail; interpellate (about a policy or government business)：提出～ bring or call sb. to account

【质心】zhìxīn 物体内各点所受的平行力产生合力，这个合力的作用点叫做这个物质的质心 centre of mass; barycentre; centroid; point at which the entire mass of a body is concentrated and at which the resultant of parallel forces on various points in the body lands

【质询】zhìxún 质疑询问 enquiry; interpellation; interrogatory

【质疑】zhìyí 提出疑问 question; query; oppugn; call sth. into question; challenge：～问难 seek solutions to a thorny problem

【质疑问难】zhì yí wèn nàn 提出疑难问题来讨论；提出疑问以求解答 raise difficult questions for discussion; raise doubts to seek solutions

【质因数】zhìyīnshù 一个数是质数，又是另一数的因数，这个数叫做另一数的质因数。如6=2×3中，2和3都是6的质因数。prime factor; factor which is also a prime number, e.g. 6=2×3, 2 and 3 are both prime factors of 6; also 素因数 sùyīnshù

【质证】zhìzhèng 诉讼中对证人证言进一步提出问题，要求证人作进一步的陈述，以解除疑义；对质 (in court) question the witness; cross-examine; challenge the witness：当面～ challenge the witness face to face

【质子】zhìzǐ 构成原子核的基本粒子之一，带正电，所带电量和电子相等，质量为电子的1,836.5倍。各种原子所含的质子数不同。proton; one of the elementary particles of the atomic nucleus, positively charged with the same amount of electricity as an electron, but having a mass 1,836.5 times that of an electron; the number of protons varies in different atoms

炙 zhì ❶ 烤 broil; grill; roast; parch (corn); torrefy (ores); carbonado (scored fish or meat); spitchcock (a split eel)：烈日～人。The sun is scorching. ❷〈书 *fml.*〉烤熟的肉 barbecue; grill; roast; rotisserie; kabob

【炙热】zhìrè 像火烤一样的热，形容极热 broiling heat; scorching heat：～的阳光 scorching sun

【炙手可热】zhì shǒu kě rè 手一挨近就感觉得热 burning to the touch;〈比喻 *fig.*〉气焰很盛，权势很大 haughty arrogance of sb. with great power

治 zhì ❶ 治理 rule; govern; control; manage; administer：～家 run a household | ～国 govern a country; manage state affairs | 自～ self-government; autonomy; self-rule | ～标 adopt a temporary solution; seek temporary relief | ～本 effect a permanent cure | ～淮(淮河) harness the Huai River ❷ 指安定或太平 stability and peace：～世 age of order and peace | 天下大～ great order and peace in the world ❸ 旧称地方政府所在地 (old term for) site of a local government：县～ county seat | 府～ government office | 省～ provincial capital ❹ 医治 treat; cure; heal：～病 treat an illness | 我的病已经～好了。My illness has been cured. ❺ 消灭(害虫) eliminate; wipe out; kill (pests)：～蝗 exterminate locusts | ～蚜虫 exterminate aphids ❻ 惩办 punish：～罪 bring sb. to justice; punish sb. for his crime | 惩～ punish; mete out punishment to | 处～ punish ❼ 研究 study or research：～学 pursue one's studies ❽ (Zhì)姓 a surname

【治安】zhì'ān 社会的安宁秩序 public order; public security; peace：维持～ maintain or keep public order

【治本】zhìběn 从根本上加以处理(跟'治标'相对 as opposed to 'seek temporary relief') effect a permanent cure; seek a radical solution to a problem; get at the root (of a problem, etc.)

【治标】zhìbiāo 就显露在外的毛病加以应急的处理(跟'治本'相对 as opposed to 'permanently cure') adopt a temporary solution; seek temporary relief; take stopgap measures

【治病救人】zhì bìng jiù rén〈比喻 *fig.*〉针对某人的缺点和错误进行批评，帮助他改正 cure the sickness to save the patient; help sb. mend his ways; point out sb.'s mistake and help him correct it; prevent sb. from going astray

【治国安民】zhì guó ān mín 治理国家，使人民各安其业 run the state well and have people live and work in peace and contentment

【治理】zhìlǐ ❶ 统治；管理 rule; govern; control; manage; administer：～国家 govern or administer a country; run a state ❷ 处理;整修 (recondition or renovate in order to prevent trouble or disaster) harness; bring under control: ～淮河 harness the Huai River

【治疗】zhìliáo 用药物、手术等消除疾病 (by means of medicine, operation, etc.) treat; cure: 长期～ long-term treatment | 隔离～ put sb. in or under quarantine for treatment; place sb. into quarantine | 他的病必须住院～。He has to be hospitalized.

【治丧】zhìsāng 办理丧事 make funeral arrangements: ～委员会 funeral committee

【治水】zhì//shuǐ 疏通水道,消除水患 dredge a watercourse to prevent floods; water control: ～工程 water-control project | 大禹～。Yu the Great brought the waters under control.

【治丝益棼】zhì sī yì fén 理丝不找头绪,结果越理越乱 try to sort out silk threads only to tangle them; 〈比喻 *fig.*〉解决问题的方法不对头,反而使问题更加复杂 mess up sth. due to mishandling

【治外法权】zhìwài fǎquán 国家间彼此授予对方外交官员的特权,包括人身、住所的不可侵犯,不受当地司法、行政的管辖,免除捐税和服役等。出国访问的国家元首和政府首脑,一般也都享有治外法权。extraterritoriality; exterritoriality; privilege granted to foreign diplomats between countries, including the inviolability of person and residence, exemption from local legal jurisdiction including exemption from taxes, army service, etc.; A head of state or a government leader on a visit abroad will generally also be entitled to such privileges.

【治学】zhìxué 研究学问 study and research; pursue one's studies: ～严谨 be a rigorous scholar; seek precision in one's studies | 实事求是,才是～的正确态度。Seeking truth from facts is the correct approach in academic pursuits.

【治印】zhì//yìn 刻图章 engrave a seal: ～艺术 art of seal engraving

【治装】zhìzhuāng 备办行装 purchase things necessary for a journey; get things ready for a journey; prepare luggage for a journey

【治罪】zhì//zuì 给犯罪人以应得的惩罚 bring sb. to justice for a crime; punish: 依法～ mete out legal punishment to sb. for a crime; punish sb. by law

轶 zhì 〈书 *fml.*〉缝;补缀 sew; mend

栉(櫛) zhì 〈书 *fml.*〉❶ 梳子、篦子等梳头发的用具 things used for combing hair; comb ❷ 梳(头发) comb (hair): ～发 comb one's hair | ～风沐雨 be combed by the wind and washed by the rain; travel (or work) rain or shine

【栉比】zhìbǐ 〈书 *fml.*〉像梳子齿那样密密地排着 be placed closed side by side (like the teeth of a comb): 鳞次～ (of buildings, etc.) stand cheek by jowl | 厂房～ row upon row of workshops

【栉比鳞次】zhì bǐ lín cì ☞ 鳞次栉比 lín cì zhì bǐ on p.1224

【栉风沐雨】zhì fēng mù yǔ 风梳头,雨洗发。形容奔波劳碌,不避风雨。be combed by the wind and washed by the rain; keep traveling or working rain or shine

峙 zhì 〈书 *fml.*〉耸立;屹(yì)立 stand erect; stand towering; rise high; tower like a mountain peak; lift; tower over; on top of: 对～ stand facing each other; confront each other

☞ shì on p.1761

庤 zhì 〈书 *fml.*〉储备 put by; store up; lay in

陟 zhì 〈书 *fml.*〉登高 ascend; go uphill; rise up; climb up (a height)

桎 zhì 〈书 *fml.*〉脚镣 fetters; shackles; anklets: ～梏 shackles

【桎梏】zhìgù 〈书 *fml.*〉脚镣和手铐 fetters and manacles; 〈比喻 *fig.*〉束缚人或事物的东西 sth. that restricts, confines or hampers; shackles

贽(贄) zhì 〈书 *fml.*〉初次拜见长辈所送的礼物 gift presented to an elder on one's first visit as a mark of esteem: ～见(拿着礼物求见) call on sb. with gifts | ～敬(旧时拜师送的礼) ceremonial gift presented to a master or teacher on one's first courtesy call in old times

挚(摯) zhì 〈书 *fml.*〉诚恳 earnest; sincerity; pure-heartedness: 真～ sincerity; good faith | 恳～ earnest; sincerity | ～爱 sacred fire; affections; deep love; true love

【挚爱】zhì'ài 真挚的爱 sacred fire; affections; true love; deep love; profound love; flame of passion: 深情～ deep love | 他的作品洋溢着对祖国的～之情。His works brim with love for his motherland.

【挚友】zhìyǒu 亲密的朋友 bosom friend; intimate friend; close friend

致1 zhì ❶ 给与;向对方表示(礼节、情意等) extend; send; deliver (respects, good wishes, etc.): ～函 send a letter to sb.; write to sb. | ～电慰问 send a message of condolence by telegraph; send a telegram of condolence | ～欢迎词 deliver a welcome speech | 向大会～热烈的祝贺 extend one's warm congratulations to the conference ❷ 集中(力量、意志等)于某个方面 put (one's efforts, attention, etc.) into sth.; concentrate on; devote to; focus on: ～力 devote one's efforts to sth.; work for; commit oneself to sth.; bend oneself to sth.; be devoted to; dedicate one's time to | 专心～志 wholeheartedly; with great presence of mind; devote heart and soul to sth.; put one's back into sth.; be fully absorbed in sth. ❸ 达到;实现 achieve; reach; arrive at; live up to; attain; obtain: ～富 become rich | 学以～用 study sth. in order to apply it ❹ 招致 incur; invite; induce; bring on; lead to; beget: ～病 cause a disease ❺ 以致 so as to; that: ～使 bring about; result in; lead to; render | 由于粗心大意,～将地址写错。He was so careless that he took down a wrong address.

致[2] zhì 情趣 sentiment and interest: 兴～ interest | 景～ scenery; view; scene | 别～ novel; original; unique; with a difference | 错落有～ in picturesque disarray | 毫无二～ without a bit of difference; completely the same | 故事曲折有～。The story is full of ups and downs and unfolds in an intriguing way.

致[3]**(緻)** zhì 精密;精细 precision; exactitude; nicety; finesse: 细～ careful; precise | 精～ delicacy; finesse; refinement | 工～ delicate; exquisite; refined

【致词】zhì//cí same as 致辞 zhìcí

【致辞】zhì//cí 在举行某种仪式时说勉励、感谢、祝贺、哀悼等的话 make or deliver a speech (of encouragement, acknowledgement, congratulations, condolences, etc.): 由大会主席～。The chairman addressed the conference. also 致词 zhì//cí

【致富】zhìfù 实现富裕 become rich; make a fortune; acquire wealth: 勤劳～ get rich through hard work | ～之路 road to prosperity

【致敬】zhìjìng 向人敬礼或表示敬意 honour; horray for sb.; pay one's respects to sb.; pay tribute to: ～信 letter of greetings; letter of courtesy | 举手～ raise one's hand to salute sb.

【致力】zhìlì 把力量用在某个方面 devote one's efforts to sth.; work for; commit oneself to sth.; bend oneself to sth.; be devoted to; dedicate or devote oneself to: ～革命 commit oneself to the cause of revolution | ～写作 devote oneself to writing

【致密】zhìmì 细致精密 fine and close; compact: ～的网 fine net | ～的观察 close observation | 结构～ refined texture; compact texture

【致命】zhìmìng 可使丧失生命 causing death; fatal; mortal; deadly; life-threatening; lethal; murderous; pestilent; virulent: ～伤 deadly wound; fatal wound ◇～的弱点 fatal weakness; Achilles' heel; mortal weakness

【致使】zhìshǐ 由于某种原因而使得;以致 cause; bring about; lead to; result in; render: 由于字迹不清,～信件无法投递。The letter cannot be delivered because the address is illegible.

【致死】zhìsǐ 导致死亡 (beat, stab, etc., sb.) to death; cause death: 因伤～ die from injuries

【致意】zhìyì 表示问候之意 send one's regards; pay one's respects; extend one's greetings; present one's compliments: 再三～ greet sb. repeatedly; send one's regards repeatedly | 点头～ nod at sb. (in greeting)

轾 zhì ☞ 轩轾 xuānzhì on p.2169

秩[1] zhì 〈书 *fml.*〉 ❶ 次序 order; sequence: ～序 order ❷ 俸禄,也指官的品级 official salary or rank: 厚～ high official salary | 加官进～ promotion and salary raise

秩[2] zhì 〈书 *fml.*〉 十年 decade: 七～大庆 70th anniversary

【秩序】zhìxù 有条理、不混乱的情况 maintain freedom from disorder through respect for the established system or authority; order: ～井然 in good order; orderly | 遵守会场～ observe order in the meeting room

猘(猘) zhì 〈书 *fml.*〉 (狗)疯狂 (of a dog) become mad or rabid

桎 zhì 桎木山 (Zhìmùshān), 地名,在湖南 place in Hunan Province

掷(擲) zhì 扔;投 throw; cast; fling; toss: 投～ throw; fling; cast; toss; pelt; pitch | 弃～ cast aside; throw away | ～铁饼 discus throw | ～铅球 shot-put | 手榴弹～远比赛 grenade-throwing competition

【掷弹筒】zhìdàntǒng 一种发射炮弹的小型武器,炮弹从筒口装入,射程较近 grenade launcher; short-range small weapon with bullets fed from the muzzle

【掷地有声】zhì dì yǒu shēng 形容话语豪迈有力 (of speech) forceful and impressive; resounding

【掷还】zhìhuán 〈客套话 *pol.*〉请人把原物归还自己 (used to ask sb. to return sth.) please return: 前请审阅之件,请早日～为荷。Please return at your earliest convenience the manuscript submitted for your approval.

鸷(鷙) zhì 〈书 *fml.*〉 凶猛 ferocious: ～鸟 birds of prey

【鸷鸟】zhìniǎo 凶猛的鸟,如鹰、雕 birds of prey, e.g. hawks, vultures

畤 zhì 〈书 *fml.*〉 祭天地及古代帝王的处所 place where heaven and earth and ancient emperors are worshipped

铚 zhì 〈书 *fml.*〉 ❶ 短的镰刀 sickle ❷ 割禾穗 cut down grain; reap crops

袠 zhì 〈书 *fml.*〉 same as 帙 (zhì)

痔 zhì 病,肛门或直肠末端的静脉由于郁血扩张而形成的突起的小结节。分为内痔、外痔和内外混合痔。症状是发痒,灼热,疼痛,大便带血等。haemorrhoids; piles; swollen mass of dilated veins around the anus or lower part of the rectum, including internal, external and mixed swellings, having such symptoms as itching, soreness, pain, and bloody stools, etc.; 通称 commonly called 痔疮 zhìchuāng

窒 zhì 阻塞不通 obstruct; block; congest; plug up: ～碍 obstacle; impediment; holdback; obstruction|～息 be suffocated

【窒碍】zhì'ài 〈书 *fml.*〉有阻碍;障碍 obstacle; handicap; block; holdback; impediment; obstruction; encumbrance: ～难行 difficult to advance because of many obstacles in the way

【窒息】zhìxī 因外界氧气不足或呼吸系统发生障碍而呼吸困难甚至停止呼吸 (laboured or interrupted breathing caused by a lack of oxygen or block in the respiratory system) suffocation; asphyxia; suffocate; stifle

蛭 zhì 环节动物的一纲,体一般长而扁平,无刚毛,前后各有一个吸盘。生活在淡水中或湿润的地方,大多营半寄生生活,如水蛭、蚂蟥等。leech (*Hirudinea*); class of annelids, characterized by an elongated and flat body, having no bristles, with an acetabulum on either the front or back end, living in fresh water or humid areas, and mostly clinging to other animals, e. g. bloodsuckers, etc.

智 zhì ❶ 有智慧;聪明 wisdom; wit; intelligence; brightness; resourcefulness: 明～ wise; sensible; advisable|～者千虑,必有一失。Even the wise make mistakes sometimes. *or* No one is infallible. ❷ 智慧;见识 brainpower; insight: 足～多谋 resourceful; be full of resources|～勇双全 be both brave and resourceful|吃一堑,长一～。A fall into a pit, a gain in wit. ❸ (Zhì)姓 a surname

【智齿】zhìchǐ 口腔中最后面的臼齿,一般在十八至三十岁才长出来,有些人的智齿终生长不出来 wisdom tooth; one of the four rearmost molars on each side of the upper and lower jaw in humans, which generally appears between the age of 18 to 30, or in some people never; also 智牙 zhìyá

【智多星】zhìduōxīng 《水浒》中吴用的绰号。泛指计谋多的人。wizard; nickname for Wu Yong, the resourceful strategist of the peasant army in *Outlaws of the Marsh*; (in a broad sense) resourceful person; mastermind; the brains (behind sth.)

【智慧】zhìhuì 辨析判断、发明创造的能力 wisdom; intelligence; brightness; wits; sagacity; brains: 人民的～是无穷的。The people provide an endless source of wisdom. |领导干部要善于集中群众的～。Leaders should know better how to pool the wisdom of the masses.

【智力】zhìlì 指人认识、理解客观事物并运用知识、经验等解决问题的能力,包括记忆、观察、想像、思考、判断等 intelligence; intellect; brains; mind; wit; ability to learn, understand, reason and apply knowledge, including the faculties of memory, observation, imagination, thinking, judgement, etc.

【智龄】zhìlíng 智力年龄。某一年龄儿童的智龄,根据对一定数量同龄儿童进行测验的平均成绩确定。智龄超过实足年龄越多,智力发展水平越高。intelligence age; IA; mental age. The mental age of a child at a certain age is determined by the average score of the intelligence tests for a given number of children of the same age, where the greater the margin of the score above a child's chronological age, the higher the developmental intelligence

【智略】zhìlüè 智谋和才略 resourcefulness and talent; wisdom and ability: ～过人 of unusual wisdom and talent; be unusually intelligent and resourceful

【智谋】zhìmóu 智慧和计谋 wisdom and stratagem; resourcefulness: 人多～高。The more people, the greater the pool of wisdom.

【智囊】zhìnáng 〈比喻 *fig.*〉计谋多的人。特指为别人划策的人 resourceful person; mastermind; the brains; back-room boy: ～团 brainpower; brain trust; think-tank; shadow cabinet

【智能】zhìnéng ❶ 智慧和能力 aptitude; brainpower; capacity; intelligence: ～双全 be intelligent and competent|培养～ develop (foster or cultivate) one's intellect and ability|发展学生～ develop the intellectual ability of the students ❷ 具有人的某些智慧和能力的 having human-like brains or ability; intelligent: ～机器人 intelligent robot

【智商】zhìshāng 智力商数。智商=智龄÷实足年龄×100。如果一儿童的智龄与实足年龄相等,则智商为100,说明其智力中等。智商在120以上的叫做'聪明',在80以下的叫做'愚蠢'。一般认为智商基本不变,如两个五岁儿童,智商一个为80,另一个为120,几年后,他们的智商基本上仍分别为80和120。intelligence quotient; IQ; According to the equation, IQ = mental age ÷ chronological age × 100, if a child's mental age is equal to his or her chronological age, his or her IQ is 100, which means average intelligence. A person is billed 'intelligent' if his IQ is above 120, and 'of low intelligence' if his IQ stands below 80. Generally a person's IQ is presumed to be stable, e. g. two five-year-old children with different IQs of 80 and 120 will still maintain the same IQ results a few years later.

【智术】zhìshù 权术 trickery; stratagem; scheme

【智育】zhìyù 发展智力的教育。有时也单指文化科学知识的教育。intellectual education; intellectual development; mental development; also education for knowledge in general

痣 zhì 皮肤上生的青色、红色或黑褐色的斑痕或小疙瘩。多由先天性血管瘤或淋巴管瘤引起,也有由皮肤色素沉着引起的,不痛不痒。

naevus; mole; lentigo; beauty spot; blue, red or dark brown spot or small protuberance on the skin, often caused by congenital haemangioma or lymphangioma, occasionally by skin pigmentation, having no symptoms like pain or itching

滞(滯) zhì 停滞;不流通 stagnant; motionless; sluggish: ～货 unsaleable goods; poor sellers; arrears of stock; dead stock; drug on the market|～销 unsaleable; not readily marketable; slow-moving|～留 be stopped; be detained; be held up

【滞洪】zhìhóng 在洪水期利用河流附近的湖泊、洼地等蓄积洪水 flood detention; store water by detaining a flood by means of nearby lakes, basins, etc., during a flood season: ～区 detention basin; retarding basin

【滞后】zhìhòu (事物)落在形势发展的后面 (of things) lag behind: 由于电力发展～,致使电力供应紧张。Because development of the power industry falls short of the demand, there is a shortage in power supply.

【滞留】zhìliú 停留不动 be stopped; be detained; be held up; settle: ～一夜 be held up for a night|～他乡 be detained in a strange land

【滞纳金】zhìnàjīn 因逾期缴纳税款、保险费或水、电、煤气等费用而需额外缴纳的钱 fine for delayed payment (of taxes, insurance premiums, or water, electricity, gas, etc.); late fee

【滞销】zhìxiāo (货物)不易售出;销路不畅 unsaleable; not readily marketable; slow-moving: ～商品 unsaleable goods; deadstock; drug on the market|产品～。The market for the goods is sluggish. *or* There is a poor market for the goods.

【滞胀】zhìzhàng 指通货膨胀下的经济停滞 stagflation; sluggish economic growth coupled with a high rate of inflation

骘 zhì 〈书 *fml.*〉安排;定 arrange; fix: 评～ evaluate; appraise|阴～ perform good deeds while keeping people in the dark about it

彘 zhì 〈书 *fml.*〉猪 pig; swine

礩(礩) zhì 〈书 *fml.*〉柱下石 base stone of a pillar

置 zhì ❶ 搁;放 place; put; set; keep: 安～ resettlement; allocation; aftercare; help settle down; nestle; put; position; plant; install; find a place for|搁～ lay aside; set aside|漠然～之 be indifferent to sth.; have a disregard for|～之不理 wave aside; brush aside; turn one's back on|～诸脑后 dismiss sth. from one's mind; consign sth. to oblivion; turn one's back on ❷ 设立;布置 set up; form; establish; lay; dispose: 装～ install; fix; set|设～ setup; setting ❸ 购置 purchase; buy: 添～ buy; purchase|～一些用具 purchase some appliances

【置办】zhìbàn 采买;购置 buy; purchase: ～年货 make purchases for the Spring Festival|这笔钱是～农具的。The money is for the purchase of farming tools.

【置备】zhìbèi 购买(设备、用具) purchase (equipment, appliances, etc.): ～家具 buy furniture|小的农具可以就地～。Small farming tools can be purchased in local places.

【置辩】zhìbiàn 辩论;申辩(用于否定 used in the negative) argue; justify: 不屑～ think it useless to argue; scorn or disdain to argue; scorn or disdain arguing|不容～ indisputable; allow for no excuses

【置换】zhìhuàn 一种单质跟一种化合物经过化学反应生成另一种单质和另一种化合物,如镁和硫酸铜反应生成铜和硫酸镁 displacement; replacement; chemical reaction in which a simple substance and a compound are replaced by another simple substance and compound, e.g. magnesium and blue stone are replaced by copper and bitter salt through chemical reaction

【置换】zhì·huàn ❶ 替换 displace; replace; substitute; swap; shift; switch (from sth. to): 通用件是可以互相～的。General parts are mutually interchangeable. ❷〈方 *dial.*〉购置 buy; purchase: 结婚前家具已经～齐了。All the furniture was purchased before the wedding.

【置喙】zhìhuì 〈书 *fml.*〉插嘴(多用于否定 oft. used in the negative) cut in; get a word in; interrupt; chip in: 不敢妄自～ not dare to rashly interrupt

【置若罔闻】zhì ruò wǎng wén 放在一边儿不管,好像没听见一样 turn a deaf ear to; ignore completely

【置身】zhìshēn 把自己放在;存身(于) place oneself; stay: ～于群众之中 place oneself in the midst of the masses; stay with the masses

【置身事外】zhì shēn shì wài 把自己放在事情之外,毫不关心 keep oneself out of it; stay out of it; stay aloof from sth.

【置信】zhìxìn 相信(多用于否定 oft. used in the negative) believe; give credit to: 不可～ cannot believe it; (of sth.) incredible; unbelievable|难以～ unbelievable; incredible

【置疑】zhìyí 怀疑(用于否定 used in the negative) doubt: 不容～ allow no doubt; beyond doubt; indubitable; unassailable|无可～。There is no doubt about it. *or* It's unquestionable.

【置之不理】zhì zhī bù lǐ 放在一边儿不理不睬 wave aside; brush aside; turn one's back on;

dismiss sth. from one's mind; close one's eyes to; ignore; pay no attention to

【置之度外】zhì zhī dù wài 不(把生死、利害等)放在心上 set everything else (death, loss, etc.) aside; give no thought to; disregard; regardless of

锧(鑕) zhì〈书 *fml.*〉❶ 砧板 chopping block ❷ 铡刀(古代刑具)座 (an ancient instrument of torture) guillotine block: 斧～ axe and block

雉[1] zhì 鸟,形状像鸡,雄的尾巴长,羽毛很美丽,多为赤铜色或深绿色,有光泽,雌的尾巴稍短,灰褐色。善走,不能久飞。尾部羽毛可做装饰品。pheasant (*Phasianidae*); gallinaceous bird; the male characteristically having a long tail and brilliantly coloured glossy plumage, often copper red or dark green and used for ornamental purposes, while the female has a short tail and is greyish brown, capable of walking long distances but unable to fly for a long time; 通称 commonly called 野鸡 yějī; 有的地区叫山鸡 in some places known as 山鸡 shānjī

雉[2] zhì〈古代 *arch.*〉城墙长三丈高一丈叫一雉 parapet section of an ancient city wall, 30 *chi* high and 10 *chi* long (1 *chi* equal to 1/3 metre)

【雉堞】zhìdié〈古代 *arch.*〉在城墙上面修筑的矮而短的墙,守城的人可借以掩护自己 crenelation; battlements; parapet or cresting consisting of a regulation of merlons and crenels for defence purposes

稚(穉) zhì 幼小 childish; young: ～子 (innocent) child | 幼～ childish; babyish; infantile; infant; untutored; green; vealy; puerile

【稚嫩】zhìnèn ❶ 幼小而娇嫩 young and tender: ～的童音 child's tender voice | ～的心灵 innocent heart ❷ 幼稚;不成熟 immature; green: 初学写作,文笔难免～。My style is still green, which is unavoidable for what I am, a new writer.

【稚气】zhìqì 孩子气 childishness: 一脸～ young and innocent look

滍 zhì 滍阳 (Zhìyáng),地名,在河南 name of a place in Henan Province

寘 zhì〈书 *fml.*〉放置 place; lay; put

疐(疐) zhì〈书 *fml.*〉❶ 遇到障碍 meet with an obstacle; encounter obstruction ❷ 跌倒 fall; slip up; tumble: 跋前～后(进退两难) difficult either to go ahead or step back; in a dilemma; between the devil and the deep blue sea; up a tree; in a box; in a spot

瘈 zhì〈书 *fml.*〉疯狂 crazy; mad
☞ chì on p. 266

踬(躓) zhì〈书〉❶ 被东西绊倒 trip; stumble: 颠～ trip over sth. ❷〈比喻 *fig.*〉事情不顺利;失败 fail; be frustrated; suffer a setback: 屡试屡～ tried and failed repeatedly

膣 zhì 阴道的旧称 old name of 阴道 yīndào

觯(觶) zhì〈古时 *arch.*〉饮酒用的器具 drinking vessel

擿 zhì〈书 *fml.*〉same as 掷 zhì
☞ tī on p. 1880

螲 zhì ☞蝼螲(lóuzhì) on p. 1253
☞ dié on p. 452

zhōng (ㄓㄨㄥ)

中 zhōng ❶ 跟四周的距离相等;中心 centre; middle: ～央 centre; middle; midst | 华～ central China | 居～ in the middle; at the centre ❷ (Zhōng) 指中国 China: ～文 Chinese | 古今～外 at all times and in all countries; in the past or present, in China or anywhere else ❸ 范围内;内部 in; among; amid; amidst: 家～ in the family; at home; in the house | 水～ in the water | 山～ in the mountains | 心～ at heart; in mind; on one's mind | 队伍～ in the procession; within the ranks ❹ 位置在两端之间的 middle; mid: ～指 middle finger | ～锋 centre forward | ～年 middle age; mid-life; middle-aged | ～秋 Mid-Autumn (Festival) | ～途 halfway; midway ❺ 等级在两端之间的 medium; intermediate: ～农 middle peasant (political term used before or after the liberation in China to refer to self-sufficient farmers) | ～学 middle school; high school; secondary school | ～型 medium; medium-sized | ～等 medium; moderate; average; secondary ❻ 不偏不倚 impartial; even-handed; neutral: ～庸 mean; middle of the road; middlebrow; golden mean | 适～ moderate ❼ 中人 go-between; mediator; middleman: 作～ act as an intermediary; be a middleman ❽ 适于;合于 suitable for; fit for; good for; equal to: ～用 be helpful; be of use; be useful | ～看 be pleasant to the eye; be presentable; look nice | ～听 be pleasant to the ear ❾〈方 *dial.*〉成;行;好 all right; okay; OK; fine; good: ～不～? Is it all right? | 这办法～。It works! | 饭这就～了。Dinner is ready. ❿ 用在动词后表示持续状态(动词前有'在'字) [with 在 zài before the verb, used after a verb to indicate continuity] in the course of; in the process of: 列车在运行～。The train is running. | 工厂在建设～。The factory is under construction. *or* The factory is being built.
☞ zhòng on p. 2490

【中班】zhōngbān 幼儿园里由四周岁至五周岁的儿童所编成的班级 middle class in a kindergarten (composed of children four or five years old)

【中饱】zhōngbǎo 经手钱财,以欺诈手段从中取利 swindle money entrusted to one's care; embezzle: 贪污～ embezzle | ～私囊 feather one's nest; line one's pockets

【中保】zhōngbǎo 中人和保人 middleman and guarantor

【中表】zhōngbiǎo 跟祖父、父亲的姐妹的子女的亲戚关系,或跟祖母、母亲的兄弟姐妹的子女的亲戚关系 cousins; any children of one's grandfather's or father's sisters, or children of one's grandmother's or mother's sisters or brothers

【中波】zhōngbō 波长 3,000 米—200 米的无线电波(频率 100—1,500 千赫)。以地波和天波的方式传播,用于无线电广播和电报通讯等方面。medium wave; radio wave of medium length between 3,000m -200m, with frequency between 100-1,500 kilohertz; Medium-wave broadcast is transmitted by means of surface waves and airwaves, and used for radio and telegraph communication, etc.

【中不溜儿】zhōng·buliūr 〈方 *dial.*〉不好也不坏;不大也不小;中等的;中间的 medium (in size, quality, level, etc.) mediocre; middling: 成绩～ middling score | 不要太大的,挑个～的。I don't want anything too big. Get me one of average size. also 中溜儿 zhōngliūr

【中餐】zhōngcān 中国式的饭菜(区别于'西餐' as compared with 'Western food') Chinese cuisine; Chinese food

【中策】zhōngcè 不及上策而胜过下策的计策或办法 second best plan or method

【中层】zhōngcéng 中间的一层或几层(多指机构、组织、阶层等 oft. of organization, class, stratum, etc.) middle-level; middle-ranking: ～干部 middle-level cadres

【中产阶级】zhōngchǎn jiējí 中等资产阶级,在我国多指民族资产阶级 middle class; middle bourgeoisie (in China it oft. refers to the national bourgeoisie)

【中常】zhōngcháng 中等;不高不低;不好不坏 middling; average; moderate: 成绩～ average score | ～年景 average harvest

【中辍】zhōngchuò (事情)中途停止进行 cease mid-course; stop (doing sth.) halfway; give up halfway: 学业～ leave school (before graduation); drop out of school; discontinue one's studies

【中词】zhōngcí 三段论中大前提和小前提所共有的名词 middle term (a term common to both the major premise and minor premise in a syllogism); ☞三段论 sānduànlùn on p. 1650

【中档】zhōngdàng 质量中等,价格适中的(商品) (of a commodity) of middling quality or price: ～茶叶 tea of average quality

【中道】zhōngdào ❶ 半路;中途 halfway; midway: ～而废 give up halfway; leave sth. unfinished ❷〈书 *fml.*〉中庸之道 golden mean; happy medium; middle of the road; ☞中庸 zhōngyōng

【中稻】zhōngdào 插秧期或生长期和成熟期比早稻稍晚的稻子 semi-late rice; middle-season rice

【中等】zhōngděng ❶ 等级介于上等、下等之间或高等、初等之间的 medium; moderate; middling; average; secondary: ～货 goods of average quality or price | ～教育 secondary education; secondary school education ❷ 不高不矮的(指身材) (of a person) of medium height: ～个儿 be of medium height

【中等教育】zhōngděng jiàoyù 在初等教育的基础上,培养学生全面发展,或培养学生具有某类专业知识的教育 secondary education; secondary school education designed for the all-round development of students or training them in certain professional know-how

【中东】Zhōngdōng 指亚洲西南部和非洲东北部,包括近东和伊朗、阿富汗 Middle East (south-west Asia and north-east Africa, including Near East, Iran and Afghanistan); ☞近东 Jìndōng on p. 1014

【中短波】zhōngduǎnbō 波长 200 米—50 米(频率 1,500—6,000 千赫)的无线电波,以地波和天波的方式传播,用于无线电广播和电报通讯等方面 intermediate wave; medium-short wave; radio wave of intermediate length between 200m and 50m, with a frequency between 1,500-6,000 kilohertz; Medium-short-wave broadcast is transmitted through surface waves and airwaves, and used for radio and telegraph communications, etc.

【中断】zhōngduàn 中途停止或断绝 interrupt; discontinue; suspend; intermit; break off: 供应～。The supply was cut. | 联系～ lose contact (with sb.); be out of touch (with sb.) | ～两国关系 suspend relations between the two countries

【中队】zhōngduì ❶ 队伍编制,由若干小队(分队)组成,属大队管辖 detachment; unit composed of a number of squads (or branches), under the control of a brigade ❷ 军队中相当于连的一级组织 squadron; military unit corresponding to a company

【中耳】zhōng'ěr 外耳和内耳之间的部分,内有三块互相连接的听骨(锤骨、砧骨和镫骨) eardrum; middle ear; tympanum; space between the outer and inner ear that contains the three auditory ossicles (malleus, anvil and stapes); (图见☞ figure for 耳朵 ěr·duo on p. 512)

【中幡】zhōng·fān 杂技的一种,表演时舞弄顶上有幡的高大旗杆 flagpole waving; acrobatic performance waving a high pole with a long narrow flag attached to the top of it

【中饭】zhōngfàn 午饭 midday meal; lunch

【中锋】zhōngfēng 篮球、足球等球类比赛的前锋之一，位置在中间（as in basketball, football, etc.）centre forward; centre

【中缝】zhōngfèng ❶ 报纸左右两版之间的狭长的部分，有的报纸在这里刊登广告或启事等 column on the folding line of a newspaper (oft. reserved for advertisements, notices, etc.) ❷ 木版书每一页中间的狭长部分，折叠起来是书口 middle strip in the page of a wooden book, which can be folded to become the fore-edge ❸ 衣服背部中间的竖缝 line sewn down the back of a jacket

【中伏】zhōngfú ❶ 夏至后的第四个庚日，是三伏的第二伏 1st day of the 2nd of the three *fu* (the three 10-day hottest periods of the year), which starts from the 4th *gengri* (day designated by combining the 7th of the 10 Heavenly Stems with one of the Earthly Brandes) after the Summer Solstice ❷ 通常也指从夏至后第四个庚日起到立秋后第一个庚日前一天的一段时间 period of the hot season from the 4th *gengri* after the Summer Solstice to the day before the first *gengri* right after autumn begins ‖ also 二伏 èrfú; ☞三伏 sānfú on p. 1651

【中耕】zhōnggēng 作物生长期中，在植株之间进行锄草、松土叫做中耕 weeding and scarification between crop plants during growth; intertill

【中古】zhōnggǔ ❶ 较晚的古代，在我国历史分期上多指魏晋南北朝隋唐这个时期 middle ancient period (in Chinese history, from the 3rd to the 9th century A. D., encompassing the Wei, Jin, North and South, Sui, Tang dynasties) ❷ 指封建社会时代 period of feudalism

【中国工农红军】Zhōngguó Gōng Nóng Hóngjūn 第二次国内革命战争时期，中国共产党领导的人民军队。1928年4月秋收起义部队——工农革命军，与南昌起义的一部分部队在井冈山会师，改称中国工农红军第四军。此后，党所领导的各地武装力量，都改称中国工农红军。抗日战争时期改称八路军、新四军。是中国人民解放军的前身。Chinese Workers' and Peasants' Red Army; Red Army; the people's army led by the Chinese Communist Party during the Second Revolutionary Civil War; In April 1928, the army from the Autumn Harvest Uprising and the Workers' and Peasants' Revolutionary Army, joined forces with a part of the army from the Nanchang Uprising and was renamed the Fourth Army of the Chinese Workers' and Peasants' Red Army. Henceforth, all the local armed forces led by the CCP were renamed the Chinese Workers' and Peasants' Red Army, and during the War of Resistance against Japan, the CWPRA was separately renamed the Eighth Route Army and New Fourth Army. It was the predecessor of the Chinese People's Liberation Army. 简称 abbr. 红军 Hóngjūn

【中国话】zhōngguóhuà 中国人民的语言，特指汉语 Chinese language; esp. mandarin Chinese

【中国画】zhōngguóhuà 国画 traditional Chinese painting

【中国人民解放军】Zhōngguó Rénmín Jiěfàngjūn 中华人民共和国的国家武装力量。1927年8月1日开始建军，第二次国内革命战争时期称中国工农红军，抗日战争时期称八路军和新四军，第三次国内革命战争时期改称中国人民解放军。Chinese People's Liberation Army (PLA); national armed forces of the People's Republic of China, founded on 1 August 1927, which was named the Chinese Workers' and Peasants' Red Army during the Second Revolutionary Civil War, renamed the Eighth Route Army and the New Fourth Army during the War of Resistance against Japan, and assumed the present name during the Third Revolutionary Civil War

【中国同盟会】Zhōngguó Tóngménghuì 1905年孙中山在日本东京成立的中国资产阶级革命政党。其政治纲领是'驱逐鞑虏，恢复中华，创立民国，平均地权'。中国同盟会成立后，积极进行反清革命斗争，领导辛亥革命，推翻了清王朝的封建统治，建立了中华民国。1912年中国同盟会改组为中国国民党。United League; Chinese bourgeois revolutionary party founded by Sun Yat-sen in Tokyo in 1905, whose political programme was to 'expel the Manchus, restore order to China, found the Republic, and redistribute land ownership equally'. Active in the revolutionary struggle against the Qing Dynasty, the United League launched the Revolution of 1911, overthrew the Qing Dynasty and founded the Republic of China. In 1912 it was regrouped and became the Kuomintang of China. 简称 abbr. 同盟会 Tóngménghuì

【中国字】zhōngguózì 中国的文字，特指汉字 Chinese written language; esp. Chinese characters

【中果皮】zhōngguǒpí 果实的中间一层果皮，如桃、梅等多汁可以吃的部分就是中果皮 mesocarp; middle fleshy layer of a fruit, such as the edible flesh of a peach, plum, etc.

【中和】zhōnghé ❶ 酸和碱经过化学反应生成盐和水，如盐酸和氢氧化钠反应生成氯化钠和水，所生成的物质失去酸和碱的性质 neutralization; chemical reaction between an acid and a alkali that yields a salt and water, e.g. the combination of hydrochloric acid and sodium hydroxide yields sodium chloride and water, substances lacking acidity and alkalinity ❷ 使中和 neutralize ❸ 抗毒素或抗毒血清跟毒素起作用，产生其他物质，使毒素的毒性消失 detoxify; (of an antitoxin or antitoxic blood serum) counteract or destroy the poisonous properties of a toxin ❹ 物体的正电量和负电量相等,不显带电现象的状态叫中和 neutralization; process occurring when the positive electric charge of an object is equal to its negative electric charge, counteracting the electrical effect

【中华】Zhōnghuá 〈古代 *arch.*〉称黄河流域一带为中华,是汉族最初兴起的地方,后来指中国 Yellow River Valley, where the Han nationality originated and flourished; (later) China

【中华民族】Zhōnghuá Mínzú 我国各民族的总称,包括五十六个民族,有悠久的历史,灿烂的文化遗产和光荣的革命传统 Chinese nation, having 56 ethnic peoples, a long history, a splendid cultural heritage, and a glorious revolutionary tradition

【中级】zhōngjí 介于高级和初级之间的 intermediate; mid-level: ～人民法院 intermediate people's court

【中继线】zhōngjìxiàn 接在各个电话交换台之间的导线。例如电话局各个分局之间的连接线、电话局和使用单位总机的连接线以及长途电话局和市内电话局之间的连接线。relay line; junction line; line connecting switchboards, such as any of the connection lines between various branches of a telephone exchange service, between the telephone exchange service and its client units, and between the long distance telephone exchange and the local telephone exchange

【中继站】zhōngjìzhàn ❶ 在运输线中途设立的转运站 (in transport) relay point; relay station ❷ 在无线电通讯中,设置在发射点与接收点中间的工作站,作用是把接收的信号放大后再发射出去 (in radio telecommunications) relay station; work station set up between a transmitting station and a receiving station, which acts to amplify the strength of a transmitted signal and relay it

【中坚】zhōngjiān 在集体中最有力的并起较大作用的成分 nucleus; spark plug; backbone; hard core: ～力量 nucleus; hard core; mainstay|～分子 spark plug; elite

【中间】zhōngjiān ❶ 里面 among; between: 那些树～有半数是李树。Half of those trees are plum trees. ❷ same as 中心 zhōngxīn: 湖底像锅底,越到～越深。The bottom of a lake is like a cooking pot getting deeper toward the centre. ❸ 在事物两端之间或两个事物之间的位置 between: 地球走到太阳和月亮～就发生月食。When the earth moves between the sun and the moon there will be lunar eclipse. |从我家到工厂,～要换车。I have to change buses to go from my home to the factory.

【中间派】zhōngjiānpài 指动摇于两个对立的政治力量之间的派别。有时也指中间派的人。middle-of-the-roader; fence-sitter

【中间人】zhōngjiānrén same as 中人 zhōngrén ①

【中间儿】zhōngjiānr same as 中间 zhōngjiān

【中将】zhōngjiàng 军衔,低于上将,高于少将 (US & Brit. Army; US Air Force; US & Brit. Marine Corps) lieutenant general; (US & Brit. Navy) vice-admiral; (Brit. Air Force) air marshal

【中焦】zhōngjiāo 〈中医 *Chin. med.*〉指胃的上下口之间的一段,主要功能是管消化 middle warmer; middle burner; part of the stomach that spans the upper and lower openings, with digestion as its major function

【中介】zhōngjiè 媒介 medium; intermediary; intermedium; agent; vehicle; instrumentality: ～人 agent; intermediary|～作用 act as an agent or intermediary

【中局】zhōngjú 象棋、国际象棋竞赛中指开局与残局之间的比赛阶段 middle phase (of a chess game)

【中楷】zhōngkǎi 手写的不大不小的楷体汉字 regular script of medium-sized Chinese characters

【中看】zhōngkàn 看起来很好 pleasing to the eye; presentable: ～不中吃 look good but taste bad; be pleasing to the eye but not to the tongue

【中馈】zhōngkuì 〈书 *fml.*〉❶ 指妇女在家里主管的饮食等事 cooking attended to by a housewife: 主～ do the cooking ❷ 借指妻 wife: ～犹虚(没有妻室) (of a man) be unmarried

【中栏】zhōnglán 男女径赛项目之一,规定距离为400米,男子所用栏架高91.4厘米,女子为76.2厘米 intermediate hurdles; 400m. track event with 91.4cm.-high hurdles for men, and 76.2cm.-high hurdles for women

【中立】zhōnglì 处于两个对立的政治力量之间,不倾向于任何一方 neutral; cross-bench; non-aligned: 严守～ observe strict neutrality

【中立国】zhōnglìguó ❶ 指在国际战争中奉行中立政策的国家,它对交战国任何一方不采取敌视行为,也不帮助 neutral nation; nation non-aligned with either side in a war ❷ 由国际条约保证,永远不跟其他国家作战,也不承担任何可以间接把它拖入战争的国际义务的国家 neutral nation that has signed an international treaty never to start a war with any other country, nor take on any international obligations that may indirectly involve it in a war

【中流】zhōngliú ❶ 水流的中央 midstream: ～砥柱 tower of strength; mainstay ❷ same as 中游 zhōngyóu: 长江～ middle reaches of the Yangtze River ❸ same as 中等 zhōngděng: ～社会 middle society

【中流砥柱】zhōngliú Dǐzhù 〈比喻 *fig.*〉坚强的、能起支柱作用的人或集体,就像立在黄河激流中的砥柱山(在三门峡)一样 (of a person or a group) be an unyielding support just like Mount Dizhu (in the Sanmenxia Gorge), standing firm in the rip tides of the Yellow River; tower of strength; mainstay

【中路】zhōnglù (～儿 zhōnglùr) 质量中等;普通 (of goods) of middling quality; mediocre: ～货 mediocre goods

【中路梆子】zhōnglù-bāng·zi same as 晋剧 jìnjù

【中落】zhōngluò (家境)由盛到衰 (of family fortunes) decline; ebb: 家道～。The family is on the decline.

【中拇指】zhōng·muzhǐ same as 中指 zhōngzhǐ

【中脑】zhōngnǎo 脑的一部分,在大脑与后脑之间,包括四叠体和大脑脚,主要作用是纠正身体姿势和掌握头部转动方向 mesencephalon; midbrain; middle portion of the brain in front of the cerebrum and hindbrain, comprising the corpora quadrigemina and cerebral peduncle, which serves to rectify body posture and direct head movement

【中年】zhōngnián 四五十岁的年纪 middle age; mid-life: ～男子 middle-aged man|人到～ (of sb.) reach middle age

【中农】zhōngnóng 经济地位在富农和贫农之间的农民。多数占有土地,并有部分生产工具,生活来源靠自己劳动,一般不剥削人,也不出卖劳动力。特指介乎上中农和下中农之间的农民。middle peasant; peasant whose economic status is between the rich peasant and the poor peasant, who generally owns land and some means of production, and is self-supporting, neither exploiting nor selling labour; esp. peasant with an economic status between the upper-middle-peasant and the lower-middle-peasant; ☞ 上中农 shàngzhōngnóng on p. 1687 and 下中农 xiàzhōngnóng on p. 2068

【中跑】zhōngpǎo 中距离赛跑。包括男子 800 米、1,500 米、3,000 米,女子 800 米、1,500 米。middle-distance race (including men's 800m., 1,500m. and 3,000m. races, and women's 800m. and 1,500m. races)

【中篇小说】zhōngpiān xiǎoshuō 篇幅介于长篇和短篇小说之间的小说,叙述不很铺张,但是可以对社会生活作广泛的描写 novelette; novella; medium-length novel with limited length of narration but a broad depiction of social life

【中频】zhōngpín ❶ 在超外差收音机中,把射频信号变成预定信号,以便放大,这个预定信号叫做中频 intermediate frequency; predetermined frequency in a superheterodyne receiver, which signals carried by radio frequency change into before they are amplified ❷ 指 300—3,000 千赫范围内的频率 frequency between 300-3,000 kilohertz

【中期】zhōngqī ❶ 某一时期的中间阶段 middle period; metaphase: 20 世纪～ mid-20th century|加强棉花～管理 strengthen the mid-period management of cotton growth ❷ 时期的长短在长期和短期之间 medium term: ～贷款 medium-term loan

【中气】zhōngqì ❶ 太阳每年在黄道上移动 360°,从冬至起,每隔 30°为一中气。农历把一年二十四节气分为节气和中气两种,雨水、春分、谷雨、小满、夏至、大暑、处暑、秋分、霜降、小雪、冬至、大寒为十二个中气。12 of the 24 solar terms; Every year the sun moves 360 degrees along the ecliptic, with every 30 degrees as a division (中气 *zhongqi*) starting with the Winter Solstice. In the traditional Chinese lunar calendar, the year is divided into 24 solar terms, with 12 *jieqi* (节气), and 12 *zhongqi*, which are Rain Water, Vernal Equinox, Grain Rain, Grain Budding, Summer Solstice, Great Heat, Limit of Heat, Autumnal Equinox, Frost's Descent, Slight Snow, Winter Solstice and Great Cold ❷ 〈中医 *Chin. med.*〉指中焦脾胃之气,对食物的消化、身体的营养,都有作用 vitality of the cavity between the diaphragm and the umbilicus, housing the spleen, stomach, etc., which facilitates digestion and nutrition ❸ 戏曲演唱上指呼吸量,唱的时候呼吸量大,能够自由控制,叫做中气足 (in the singing of traditional Chinese opera) volume of breath; If a performer's singing is sufficient in breath and control, he is considered as having enough volume of breath.

【中秋】Zhōngqiū 我国传统节日,在农历八月十五日,这一天有赏月、吃月饼的风俗 Mid-Autumn Festival, which falls on the 15th day of the 8th lunar month, when people observe such customs as enjoying the bright full moon and eating moon cakes

【中人】zhōngrén ❶ 为双方介绍买卖、调解纠纷等并做见证的人 middleman; go-between; mediator; intermediary ❷ 〈书 *fml.*〉在身材、相貌、智力等方面居于中等的人 ordinary person; average person (in terms of size, appearance, intellect, etc.): ～以上 (of sb.) above average|不及～ (of sb.) below average

【中山狼】zhōngshānláng 古代寓言,赵简子在中山打猎,一只狼中箭而逃,赵在后追捕。东郭先生从那儿走过,狼向他求救。东郭先生动了怜悯之心,把狼藏在书囊中,骗过了赵简子。狼活命后却要吃救命恩人东郭先生(见于明马中锡《东田集·中山狼传》)。originally from an ancient fable 'The Collected Tales from Dongtian · Wolf of Zhongshan' from Ma Zhongxi's *The Collected Tales from Dongtian* (Ming Dynasty): While Zhao Jianzi was pursuing a wolf he had wounded with an arrow shot on a hunting tour in a place called Zhongshan, the wolf stopped Master Dongguo, who happened to be walking by, and asked him for help. Master Dongguo had mercy on the wolf and hid it in his book bag, a ploy that fooled Zhao Jianzi and saved

the wolf's life. However, no sooner had the hunter gone than the wolf threatened to eat the man who had saved its life. 〈比喻 *fig.*〉 恩将仇报,没有良心的人 person who returns evil for good; one who bites the hand that feeds one

【中山装】zhōngshānzhuāng 一种服装,上身左右各有两个带盖子和扣子的口袋,下身是西式长裤,由孙中山提倡而得名 Chinese suit; Sun Yat-sen uniform; suit with a jacket having two flapped and buttoned pockets, a pair of Western-style trousers, named after Sun Yat-sen, who promoted its wear

【中石器时代】Zhōngshíqì Shídài 旧石器时代和新石器时代之间的石器时代。这时人类使用的工具以打制石器为主,并发明了弓箭。Mesolithic Period; Middle Stone Age; cultural period of the Stone Age between the Paleolithic and Neolithic periods, marked by the emergence of microlithic tools, bows and arrows

【中士】zhōngshì 军衔,低于上士,高于下士 (US & Brit. Army, Brit. Air Force) sergeant; (US Navy) petty officer second class; (Brit. Navy) petty officer first class; (US Air Force) staff sergeant

【中世纪】zhōngshìjì 欧洲历史上指封建社会时代 Middle Ages; period in European history between antiquity and the Renaissance, oft. dated from 476 A.D. to 1453

【中式】zhōngshì 中国式样 Chinese style: ~服装 Chinese-style clothing
☞ zhòng// shì on p. 2491

【中枢】zhōngshū 在一事物系统中起总的主导作用的部分 centre; backbone; hub: 电讯~ telecommunications centre | 交通~ transportation hub

【中枢神经】zhōngshū shénjīng 神经系统的主要部分,包括脑和脊髓,主管全身感觉运动和条件反射、非条件反射等 central nervous system (including the brain and spiral cord, governing body and sensory movements and conditioned reflexes); ☞脑 nǎo on p. 1394 and 脊髓 jǐsuí on p. 912

【中堂】zhōngtáng ❶ 正房居中的一间;堂屋 central room (of a traditional Chinese house) ❷ 悬挂在客厅正中的尺寸较大的字画 central scroll (of painting or calligraphy) hung in the middle of the wall of the main room

【中堂】zhōng·tang 明清两代内阁大学士的别称 alternate name for a Grand Secretary in the Ming and Qing Dynasties

【中提琴】zhōngtíqín 提琴的一种,体积比小提琴稍大,音比小提琴低五度 viola; stringed instrument of the violin family, slightly larger than a violin, tuned a fifth lower

【中听】zhōngtīng (话)听起来满意 (of remarks) pleasant to the ear; agreeable: 这话~。His remarks sound agreeable.

【中途】zhōngtú 半路 halfway; midway: 在回家的~下开了大雨。He was caught in a heavy rain on his way home. | 他原先是学建筑工程的,~又改行搞起地质来了。At first he studied architecture, but later switched to geology.

【中外】zhōngwài 中国和外国 China and foreign countries: 古今~ at all times and in all over the world | 闻名~ be well-known at home and abroad | ~人士 Chinese and foreign people

【中卫】zhōngwèi 足球、手球等球类比赛的后卫之一,位置在中间 (of football, handball, etc.) centre halfback

【中尉】zhōngwèi 军衔,低于上尉,高于少尉 (military rank) (US Army, Air Force & Marine Corps) first lieutenant; (Brit. Army & Marine Corps) lieutenant; (US Navy) lieutenant junior grade; (Brit. Navy) sublieutenant; (Brit. Air Force) flying officer

【中文】Zhōngwén 中国的语言文字,特指汉族的语言文字 Chinese language; esp. Chinese, the language of the Han people

【中午】zhōngwǔ 指白天十二点左右的一段时间 noon; midday

【中西】zhōngxī 中国和西洋 Chinese and Western: ~合璧 mixture of Chinese and Western styles | ~医结合 combine traditional Chinese and Western medicine; combination of traditional Chinese medicine and Western medicine

【中线】zhōngxiàn ❶ 三角形的一顶点与对边中点的连线 median line; line drawn from an angle of a triangle to the middle of the opposite side ❷ 球场中间画的一条横线,是双方的界限 (in football) halfway line; (in basketball and volleyball) centre line

【中校】zhōngxiào 军衔,低于上校,高于少校 (military rank) (US & Brit. Army, US Air Force, US & Brit. Marine Corps) lieutenant colonel; (US & Brit. Navy) commander; (Brit. Air Force) wing commander

【中心】zhōngxīn ❶ 跟四周的距离相等的位置 centre; middle; heart; core; hub; focus; epicentre: 在草地的~有一个八角亭子。There is an octagonal pavilion in the centre of the lawn. ❷ 事物的主要部分 main; chief; body: ~思想 main idea | ~问题 central issue | ~工作 central task ❸ 在某一方面占重要地位的城市或地区 centre (city or area of certain importance): 政治~ political centre | 文化~ cultural centre ❹ 设备、技术力量等比较完备的机构和单位(多作单位名称 oft. used in the name of a business or organization) institution or organization with a complete set of facilities, technology, etc.: 维修~ service centre | 研究~ research centre | 科技信息~ centre of technology and information

【中兴】zhōngxīng 由衰微而复兴(多指国家 oft. of a nation) resurgence; rejuvenation

【中型】zhōngxíng 形状或规模不大不小的 medium-sized; medium: ～汽车 medium-sized car or automobile

【中性】zhōngxìng ❶ 化学上指既不呈酸性又不呈碱性的性质 (chemistry) neutral ❷ 某些语言里名词(以及代词、形容词等)分别阴性、阳性、中性 (neither masculine nor feminine in gender, of a noun, pronoun, adjective, etc. in certain languages) neuter; ☞ 性 xìng ⑥ on p. 2150 ❸ 指词语意义不含褒贬色彩 (of a word) neither positive nor negative; neutral; neuter: ～词 neutral word; neuter word; neuter | ～注释 neutral note

【中休】zhōngxiū 在一段工作或一段路程的中间休息 break (taken from work or journey)

【中学】[1] zhōngxué 对青少年实施中等教育的学校 middle school; high school; secondary school

【中学】[2] zhōngxué 清末称我国传统的学术 (in late Qing Dynasty) Chinese traditional learning

【中学生】zhōngxuéshēng 在中学读书的学生 middle-school student; high-school student

【中雪】zhōngxuě 指24小时内雪量达2.5—5毫米的雪 moderate snowfall (a snowfall of 2.5-5mm. in 24 hours)

【中旬】zhōngxún 每月十一日到二十日的十天 middle ten days of a month

【中央】zhōngyāng ❶ 中心地方 centre; middle: 湖的～有个亭子。There is a pavilion at the centre of the lake. ❷ 特指国家政权或政治团体的最高领导机构 highest leading body of a state or party: 党～ Party Central Committee | 团～ Central Committee of the Youth League

【中药】zhōngyào 中医所用的药物,以植物为最多,但也包括动物和矿物 traditional Chinese medicines (generally referring to herbs and plants, but also including animal and mineral substances)

【中叶】zhōngyè 中期 middle period: 唐代～ middle period of the Tang Dynasty; mid-Tang | 清朝～ middle period of the Qing Dynasty; mid-Qing | 20世纪～ mid-20th century; middle of the 20th century

【中医】zhōngyī ❶ 中国固有的医学 traditional Chinese medical science ❷ 用中国医学的理论和方法治病的医生 practitioner of traditional Chinese medicine

【中庸】zhōngyōng ❶ 儒家的一种主张,待人接物采取不偏不倚,调和折中的态度 golden mean; way of wisdom of the Confucian school, which advocates impartiality, reconciliation and compromise in one's approach to people or matters: ～之道 golden mean ❷ 〈书 *fml*.〉指德才平凡 (of a person) mediocre; average; middling: ～之才 person of mediocre ability

【中用】zhōngyòng 顶事;有用(多用于否定 oft. used in the negative) of use; useful: 这点事情都办不好,真不～。Messing up such a small task, you're really useless.

【中游】zhōngyóu ❶ 河流中介于上游与下游之间的一段 middle reaches (of a river) ❷〈比喻 *fig*.〉所处的地位不前不后;所达到的水平不高不低 (of a rank or level) middling; so-so; mediocre: 要力争上游,不能甘居～。Strive for the upper rungs of the ladder, and don't settle for a mediocre position.

【中雨】zhōngyǔ 指24小时内雨量达10—25毫米的雨 moderate rain (with a precipitation of 10-25mm. in 24 hours)

【中元节】Zhōngyuán Jié 指农历七月十五日,旧俗有烧衣包、祭祀亡故亲人等活动 Zhongyuan Festival, which falls on the 15th day of the 7th lunar month, when the old custom was to burn paper clothes or paper money as sacrificial offerings to the dead

【中原】Zhōngyuán 指黄河中下游地区,包括河南的大部分地区、山东的西部和河北、山西的南部 Central Plains; the middle and lower reaches of the Yellow River, including most of Henan, western Shandong, and southern Hebei and Shanxi provinces

【中允】zhōngyǔn 〈书 *fml*.〉公正 fairness; equity; impartiality: 貌似～ seemingly impartial

【中灶】zhōngzào 集体伙食的标准中的第二级(区别于'大灶'、'小灶' as compared with 'mess' and 'special mess' for ranking officials) canteen for medium-ranking officials

【中正】zhōngzhèng 〈书 *fml*.〉公正;公平 equity; impartiality; justice

【中止】zhōngzhǐ (做事)中途停止 (of work or activity) discontinue; suspend; abate; cease: ～比赛 suspend the game | 刚做了一半就～了。The work was suspended halfway.

【中指】zhōngzhǐ 第三个指头 middle finger; also 将指 jiàngzhǐ

【中州】Zhōngzhōu 〈旧时 *old*〉指现在河南省一带 Zhongzhou, name for the region in and around present-day Henan Province

【中州韵】zhōngzhōuyùn 我国近代戏曲韵文所根据的韵部。'中州'指现在的河南省一带,'中州韵'是以北方话为基础的,分韵的方法各地不完全一样,都跟皮黄戏的'十三辙'很相近。*zhongzhouyun*; rhyme schemes for modern Chinese opera verse that are rooted in Zhongzhou (in and around present-day Henan Province) and based on the northern dialect; its methodology may differ in various localities, but it bears a close resemblance to that of *shisanzhe*, or the 13 rhyme schemes for the *pihuang* opera; ☞ 十三辙 shísān zhé on p. 1734

【中转】zhōngzhuǎn ❶ 交通部门指中途转换交

通运输工具 transit；change from one station，route，etc.，to another on a journey：～旅客 transfer passengers ❷ 中间转手 change hands：产销直接挂钩，减少～环节。A direct channel should be established between production and sales so as to cut down on intermediate links.

【中装】zhōngzhuāng 中国旧式服装（区别于'中山装、西装'等 as compared with 'Sun Yat-sen uniform' and 'Western suits'，etc.）traditional Chinese clothing

【中子】zhōngzǐ 构成原子核的基本粒子之一，质量约和质子相等。不带电，容易进入原子核，可以用来轰击原子核，引起核反应。neutron；one of the elementary particles composing the atomic nucleus，having a mass approximating that of a proton，and electrically uncharged The particle can enter into the structure of the atomic nucleus and bombard the atomic nucleus to produce a nuclear reaction

【中子弹】zhōngzǐdàn 核武器的一种，爆炸时释放大量的高能中子，靠中子辐射起杀伤作用，穿透力较强，冲击波、热辐射和放射性沾染较其他核武器为小。在有效范围内能杀伤一般坦克内或建筑物内的人员。可作战术核武器使用。neutron bomb；nuclear bomb that can produce a great amount of high-energy neutrons to destroy life by neutron radiation. Highly penetrating but producing less blast，heat radiation and radioactive contamination than other nuclear weapons，within its effective range the neutron bomb is capable of destroying enemy personnel inside tanks or buildings，and can be used as a tactical nuclear weapon

【中子态】zhōngzǐtài 物质存在的一种形态，这种形态下的物体密度极大，电子和质子大量结合成中子 neutron state；form of a substance in which an object has a high density，with its electrons and protons integrated into the neutrons

【中子星】zhōngzǐxīng 中子态的恒星，由质量相当大的恒星演变而来。自转速度很快，周期性地发射出脉冲辐射。neutron star；celestial body composed of neutrons，which has evolved from the remains of a massive star that has collapsed. It rotates at a high speed and periodically sends off pulse radiation.

Z

忪(伀) zhōng ☞ 怔忪 zhēngzhōng on p. 2443

☞ sōng on p. 1824

忠 zhōng 忠诚 loyalty；faithfulness；fidelity；adherence：～心 good faith；loyalty；devotion｜～言 sincere advice｜效～ vow loyalty and devotion to｜～于人民 be loyal to the people；be true to the people

【忠臣】zhōngchén 忠于君主的官吏 loyal court official

【忠诚】zhōngchéng（对国家、人民、事业、领导、朋友等）尽心尽力（towards country，people，cause，leader，friends，etc.）faithful；loyal；true；staunch：～老实 honest and faithful｜对事业无限～ be wholeheartedly devoted to one's career

【忠告】zhōnggào ❶ 诚恳地劝告 sincerely advise；admonish；counsel；expostulate；exhort：一再～ give sb. repeated advice ❷ 忠告的话 advice；admonition；counsel：接受～ take sb.'s advice

【忠厚】zhōnghòu 忠实厚道 honest and kind-hearted：～长者 a kind and tolerant elder｜待人～ be honest and kind-hearted

【忠良】zhōngliáng ❶ 忠诚正直 faithful and upright ❷ 忠诚正直的人 person of good faith and integrity：陷害～ frame a loyal person of integrity

【忠烈】zhōngliè ❶ 指对国家或人民无限忠诚而牺牲生命 lay down one's life out of boundless loyalty to one's country and people：～之臣 loyal court official who is ready to give his life for a noble cause ❷ 指有这种行为的人 martyr：缅怀～ cherish the memory of the martyrs

【忠实】zhōngshí ❶ 忠诚可靠 faithful and trustworthy；loyal；true；true-hearted；dutiful；devoted；staunch；dog-like：～的信徒 faithful disciple｜～的朋友 devoted（or faithful，loyal）friend ❷ 真实 true；truthful；real：～的记录 truthful record｜～的写照 true representation or portrayal

【忠顺】zhōngshùn 一心顺从（今多用于贬义 oft. derog.）wholeheartedly obedient；loyal and meek：～的奴仆 willing servant

【忠心】zhōngxīn 忠诚的心 good faith；devotion；loyalty；dedication：～耿耿 be devoted or dedicated；have steadfast faith in；be firmly faithful｜赤胆～ sheer loyalty；true blue

【忠言】zhōngyán 诚恳劝告的话 sincere advice：～逆耳。Good advice is harsh to the ear.

【忠言逆耳】zhōngyán nì ěr 诚恳劝告的话，往往让人听起来不舒服 Good advice is harsh to the ear；Faithful words grate on the ear：良药苦口利于病，～利于行。Good medicine tastes bitter but cures；likewise，good advice sounds harsh but works.

【忠义】zhōngyì ❶ 忠诚，讲义气 loyalty；righteousness：～之士 loyal person ❷〈旧指 *old*〉忠臣义士 loyal court official：表彰～ commend a loyal person

【忠勇】zhōngyǒng 忠诚而勇敢 loyal and brave；faithful and courageous；staunch and valiant：～的战士 loyal and valiant fighter

【忠于】zhōngyú 忠诚地对待 loyal to；faithful to；true to；devoted to：～祖国 be loyal to one's country｜～人民的事业 be devoted to the cause of the people

【忠贞】zhōngzhēn 忠诚而坚定不移 allegiance; steadfast loyalty; single-mindedness; fealty: ～不贰 have loyalty that can stand the test of time|～不屈 be staunch and unyielding|～不渝 be steadfastly loyal

终 zhōng ❶ 最后;末了(跟'始'相对 as opposed to 'beginning') end: ～点 end; end point; goal|告～ end up; reach an end|自始至～ from beginning to end; from start to finish; from first to last; all the way; throughout; all through ❷ 指人死 death: 临～(人将死) when one is dying; on one's deathbed; on the threshold of death ❸ 终归;到底 in the end; eventually: ～将见效 will eventually take effect|～必成功 will certainly succeed in the end ❹ 自始至终的整段时间 whole; entire; all; throughout: ～日 all day|～年 throughout the year; all year round|～生 all one's life|～身 lifelong; throughout one's life ❺ (Zhōng)姓 a surname

【终场】zhōngchǎng ❶ (戏)演完;(球赛)结束 end (of a performance or game): 当～落幕的时候,在观众中响起了热烈的掌声。When the curtain fell on the show, the audience erupted in warm applause.|～前一分钟,主队又攻进一球。Just one minute before the end of the match, the host team scored another goal. ❷ 〈旧时 *old*〉指分几场考试时考完最后的一场 final session of an examination

【终点】zhōngdiǎn ❶ 一段路程结束的地方 end (of a journey); terminal; destination: ～站 terminal station; terminal; terminus ❷ 特指径赛中终止的地点 finishing line (of a track event)

【终端】zhōngduān 电子计算机等系统中用来发指令或接收信息的装置 (computer, etc.) terminal; apparatus for transmission of messages in a computer system

【终伏】zhōngfú 末伏 last ten days of the hottest period of the year

【终古】zhōnggǔ 〈书 *fml.*〉久远;永远 forever: 这虽是一句老话,却令人感到～常新。This is an old saying, but it always rings fresh in the ear.

【终归】zhōngguī 毕竟;到底 eventually; in the end; after all: ～无效 eventually prove useless|技术无论怎样复杂,只要努力钻研,～能够学会的。However complicated the technology might be, if you work hard at it you can learn it in the end.

【终极】zhōngjí 最终;最后 final; ultimate: ～目的 ultimate aim

【终结】zhōngjié 最后结束 end; terminate; conclude; end; wind-up; expiry; finality; finis

【终究】zhōngjiū 毕竟;终归 eventually; in the end; after all: 一个人的力量～有限。The strength of one individual is limited after all.

【终久】zhōngjiǔ same as 终究 zhōngjiū: 纸包不住火,假面具～要被揭穿。No one can wrap up fire in paper; the mask will be eventually destroyed.

【终局】zhōngjú 结局;终了 ending; finale

【终老】zhōnglǎo 指度过晚年直到去世 spend one's last years: ～山林 spend one's last years in a mountain forest|～故乡 spend one's last years in one's home town

【终了】zhōngliǎo (时期)结束;完了 (of a period) come to an end: 学期～ end of the (school) term

【终南捷径】Zhōngnán jiéjìng 唐代卢藏用曾经隐居在京城长安附近的终南山,借此得到很大名声而做了大官(见于《新唐书·卢藏用传》) Zhongnan short cut to officialdom. *New History of Tang·Biography of Lu Zangyong*: the close proximity of Zhongnan Mountain, where Lu Zangyong lived in seclusion, to the capital city of Chang'an helped propel him to great popularity, and the fame he thus attained eventually enabled him to land a major official post; 后来用'终南捷径'比喻求官的最近便的门路,也比喻达到目的的便捷途径 (fig.) short cut to high office; short cut to success

【终年】zhōngnián ❶ 全年;一年到头 all year round; throughout the year: ～积雪的高山 mountains perennially covered with snow ❷ 指人去世时的年龄 age at which one dies: ～八十岁。He died at the age of 80.

【终日】zhōngrì 从早到晚;整天 all the day; all day long; all day: 奔走～,苦不堪言。It pains me extremely to spend all day on the run.|参观展览的人～不断。All day long there is an endless flow of visitors going to the exhibition.

【终身】zhōngshēn 一生;一辈子(多就切身的事说 oft. of sth. personal) lifelong; life; lifetime; all one's life; for life: ～之计 lifelong plan|～大事(关系一生的大事情,多指婚姻) (oft. referring to marriage, which affects one's whole life) once in a lifetime event

【终审】zhōngshěn ❶ 法院对案件的最后一级审判 last instance; final judgement: ～判决 final judgement ❷ 对影视作品或书刊稿件进行最后一级的审查 final censoring (of a film, TV programme, book, etc.): ～定稿后即可发稿。As soon as the news dispatches are finalized by the censor they will be distributed.

【终生】zhōngshēng 一生(多就事业说 oft. used when speaking of a career) all one's life: 奋斗～ struggle or strive all one's life

【终霜】zhōngshuāng 入春后最晚出现的一次霜 latest frost (in spring)

【终天】zhōngtiān ❶ same as 终日 zhōngrì: ～发愁 be worried all day long|～不停地写

keep writing all day long ❷〈书 *fml.*〉终身(就遗恨无穷说 indicating eternal regret) all one's life：～之恨 lifelong regret; eternal regret|抱恨～ have a gnawing regret all one's life

【终于】zhōngyú〈副词 *adv.*〉表示经过种种变化或等待之后出现的情况 finally; at last; in the end; eventually; at length; in the event; ultimately; in the course of time; in time; lastly：试验～成功了。They finally succeeded in the experiment.|她多次想说，但～没说出口。She wanted to speak for many times, but in the end didn't utter a word.

【终止】zhōngzhǐ 结束；停止 stop; end; cease; suspend; halt; conclude; wind up; be over; close：～活动 put an end to the activity; bring activities to a close

柊 zhōng ☞ below

【柊树】zhōngshù 常绿灌木或小乔木，叶子卵形，花白色，有香气。供观赏。evergreen shrub or small arbour, having egg-shaped leaves, white fragrant flowers, which is grown as an ornamental plant

【柊叶】zhōngyè 多年生草本植物，根茎块状，叶子长圆形，似芭蕉，花紫色。根和叶可入药，叶片可用来包粽子。*Phrynimu placentarium*; perennial hebaceous plant having a massive root, long round banana-like leaves, and purple flowers, its root and leaves used to make medicine, and its leaves to wrap *zongzi*, a pyramid-shaped glutinous rice dumpling

盅 zhōng (～儿 zhōngr) 饮酒或喝茶用的没有把儿的杯子 handle-less cup：酒～儿 wine cup|小茶～ teacup

【盅子】zhōng·zi 盅 goblet; handle-less cup

钟[1]（鐘） zhōng ❶ 响器，中空，用铜或铁制成 bell; hollow metallic vessel made of copper or iron, which gives forth a ringing sound when struck ❷ 计时的器具，有挂在墙上的，也有放在桌上的 clock, timepiece hanging on the wall or placed on a table：挂～ wall clock|座～ desk clock|闹～ alarm clock ❸ 指钟点、时间 time as measured by hours or minutes：六点～ 6 o'clock|由这儿到那儿只要十分～。It takes only 10 minutes to go there from here.

钟[2]（鍾） zhōng ❶（情感等）集中 (of affections, etc.) focus on; concentrate on：～爱 love; cherish|～情 be deeply in love with sb.; be soft on sb.; set one's affections on sb. ❷ (Zhōng)姓 a surname

钟[3]（鍾） zhōng same as 盅 zhōng

【钟爱】zhōng'ài 特别爱(子女或其他晚辈中的某一人) dote on; love; cherish (one's offspring, etc.)：祖母～小孙子。The grandmother especially dotes on her little grandson.

【钟摆】zhōngbǎi 时钟机件的一部分，是根据单摆的原理制成的，左右摆动，通过一系列齿轮的作用，使指针以均匀的速度转动 pendulum; clockwork part, made on the basis of the single pendulum theory, swinging to and fro so that the hands of a clock move around steadily under the actions of a gear system

【钟表】zhōngbiǎo 钟和表的总称 clocks and watches; timekeepers; timepieces; horologes

【钟点】zhōngdiǎn (～儿 zhōngdiǎnr) ❶ 指某个一定的时间 time at which sth. happens or gets done：到～儿了，快走吧！It's time; hurry and let's go! ❷ 小时；钟头 hour：等了一个～，他还没来。I've been waiting for him for an hour, but he hasn't turned up yet.

【钟鼎文】zhōngdǐngwén ☞ 金文 jīnwén on p. 1006

【钟馗】Zhōngkuí 传说中能打鬼的神，旧时民间常挂钟馗的像，认为可以驱除邪祟 Zhongkui; legendary god who chases demons; In old times Zhongkui's pictures were often found on the walls of people's houses, meant to drive away evil spirits

【钟离】Zhōnglí 姓 a two-character surname

【钟灵毓秀】zhōng líng yù xiù 指美好的自然环境产生优秀的人物 (of a place) nurture or produce talent because of its beautiful natural environment (毓 *yu*：养育 nurture)

【钟楼】zhōnglóu ❶〈旧时 *old*〉城市中设置大钟的楼，楼内按时敲钟报告时辰 bell tower; belfry; campanile ❷ 安装时钟的较高的建筑物 clock tower

【钟鸣鼎食】zhōng míng dǐng shí 敲着钟，列鼎而食。旧时形容富贵人家生活奢侈豪华。dine with a rich meal and resonant bells; (of an affluent family in old times) live an extravagant life

【钟情】zhōngqíng 感情专注(多指爱情 oft. referring to love relationships) be deeply in love with; be soft on sb.; set one's affections on sb.：一见～ fall in love at first sight

【钟乳石】zhōngrǔshí 石灰岩洞中悬在洞顶上的像冰锥的物体，常与石笋上下相对，由含碳酸钙的水溶液逐渐蒸发凝结而成 stalactite; icicle-shaped object, hanging from the roof of a calcific cavern, often facing a stalagmite below, formed from calciferous water solution through gradual sedimentation; also 石钟乳 shízhōngrǔ

【钟头】zhōngtóu 小时 hour：这出戏演了三个半～还没完。The play has been on for three and a half hours, and still has not finished.

衷 zhōng ❶ 内心 heart; inner feelings：言不由～ speak insincerely; talk tongue-in-cheek|无动于～ be apathetic; not be moved at the least ❷ same as 中 zhōng; ☞ 折中 zhézhōng on p. 2429 ❸ (Zhōng)姓 a surname

【衷肠】zhōngcháng 〈书 *fml.*〉内心的话 words from one's heart: 倾吐～ pour out one's feelings|畅叙～ have a heart-to-heart talk

【衷情】zhōngqíng 内心的情感 inner feelings: 久别重逢,互诉～。They opened their hearts to each other upon meeting after a long separation.

【衷曲】zhōngqǔ 〈书 *fml.*〉衷情;心事 heartfelt emotion; inner feelings: 倾吐～ pour out one's feelings; open one's heart

【衷心】zhōngxīn 出于内心的 heartfelt; hearty: ～拥护 give hearty support|～的感谢 thank from the bottom of one's heart

螽 zhōng [螽斯](zhōngsī)昆虫,身体绿色或褐色,触角呈丝状,有的种类无翅。雄虫的前翅有发音器,雌虫尾端有剑状的产卵管。善于跳跃,一般以其他小动物为食物,有的种类也吃庄稼,是害虫。katydid (*Microcentrum*); green grasshopper having thread-like antenna (with some species having no wings), the male equipped with soniferous organs on its forewings, and the female having a sword-shaped ovipositor on its tail. A good hopper, the katydid feeds on other minor insects, but some species within the family feed on crops and are harmful.

zhǒng (ㄓㄨㄥˇ)

肿(腫) zhǒng 皮肤、黏膜或肌肉等组织由于局部循环发生障碍、发炎、化脓、内出血等原因而突起 swollen; tumescent; tumid; bloated; distended; puffed; puffy; bulging of the skin, mucous membrane, muscle, etc., due to local circulation obstruction, inflammation, festering, internal bleeding, etc.

【肿瘤】zhǒngliú 机体的某一部分组织细胞长期不正常增生所形成的新生物。对机体有危害性,可分为良性肿瘤和恶性肿瘤。tumour; abnormal new mass of tissue produced through a long process which is harmful to the body; a tumour can be benign or malignant; also 瘤子 liú·zi

【肿胀】zhǒngzhàng 肌肉、皮肤或黏膜等组织由于发炎、郁血或充血而体积增大 swelling; tumescence

种(種) zhǒng ❶ 物种的简称 abbr. for 物种 wùzhǒng: 小麦是单子叶植物禾本科小麦属的一～。Wheat is a monocotyledon grain of the *Triticum* family.|猫是哺乳动物猫科猫属的一～。The cat is a mammal of the *Felidae* family. ❷ 人种 race: 黄～ yellow race|黑～ black race|白～ white race ❸ (～儿 zhǒngr) 生物传代繁殖的物质 seed; breed; strain: 高粱～ sorghum seed|麦～ wheat seed|传～ (of an animal or plant) reproduce; propagate; multiply|配～ hybridization ❹ 指胆量或骨气(跟'有、没有'连用 used with 有 yǒu, 没有 méiyǒu) guts; spunk; nerve; courage; strength of character ❺〈量词 *classifier*〉表示种类,用于人和任何事物 kind; sort; type; variety; class; category; breed; species: 两～人 two kinds of people|三～布 three types of cloth|各～情况 various situations; all sorts of things|菊花的颜色有好几～。Chrysanthemum comes in several colours. ❻ (Zhǒng)姓 a surname

☞ Chóng on p. 271 and zhòng on p. 2492

【种差】zhǒngchā 指在同属中,某个种不同于其他种的属性 differentia; attribute that distinguishes one species from others of the same genus

【种畜】zhǒngchù 配种用的公畜或母畜 stock male or female domestic animal; stud stock

【种蛋】zhǒngdàn 为繁殖家禽用来孵化的蛋,从健康高产的家禽所产的蛋中选出 breeding egg; egg laid by healthy, productive poultry and chosen for breeding

【种类】zhǒnglèi 根据事物本身的性质或特点而分成的门类 kind; sort; type; variety; class; category: 花的～很多。There are a large variety of flowers.

【种禽】zhǒngqín 配种用的雄性家禽或雌性家禽 fowl for breeding

【种群】zhǒngqún 指生活在同一地点、属于同一物种的一群生物体 population; all the organisms that constitute a specific group or occur in a specified habitat

【种仁】zhǒngrén 某些植物的种子中所含的仁 kernel; stone of the seeds of certain plants

【种条】zhǒngtiáo 繁殖用的树木的枝条 branch or twig for layering

【种姓】zhǒngxìng 某些国家的一种世袭的社会等级。种姓的出现与阶级社会形成时期的社会分工有关。在印度,种姓区分得最为典型,最初分为四大种姓,即婆罗门(僧侣和学者)、刹帝利(武士和贵族)、吠舍(手工业者和商人)和首陀罗(农民、仆役)。种姓和种姓之间不能通婚,不通交往。后来又在种姓之外分出一个社会地位最低的'贱民'阶层。caste; (in some countries) hereditary social classes, which emerged from the social division of labour when classes were formed; India is a country having typical caste divisions, where originally there were four castes, i.e. Brahmans (monks and scholars), Kshatriyas (warriors and aristocrats), Vaisyas (handicraftsmen and merchants) and Sudras (farmers and servants), with members of a caste not allowed to intermarry or mix with those not of their own caste. Over time, a new caste sprung up outside those castes, the Pariahs, 'untouchables' or 'outcastes'

【种鱼】zhǒngyú 亲鱼 parent fish

【种种】zhǒngzhǒng 各种各样 all kinds or sorts of; various; a variety of: 克服～困难 overcome all kinds of difficulties | 遇到～问题 be faced with all kinds of problems; encounter all sorts of problems

【种子】zhǒng·zi ❶ 显花植物所特有的器官，是由完成了受精过程的胚珠发育而成的，通常包括种皮、胚和胚乳三部分。种子在一定条件下能萌发成新的植物体。seed; pip; apparatus particular to a phanerogam, which grows from an impregnated ovule; a seed consists of a coat, embryo and albumen, which can bud and grow into a new plant under certain conditions ◇革命的～ seeds of revolution ❷ 比赛中，进行分组淘汰赛时，被安排在各组里的实力较强的运动员叫做种子。同样，以队为单位参加比赛时，被安排在各组的实力较强的队，叫做种子队。seed; more-skilled contestants arranged in various groups during the elimination heat of a tournament. Likewise, more skilled teams placed among various groups are called seed teams

【种族】zhǒngzú 人种 race (of people)

【种族歧视】zhǒngzú qíshì 对不同种族或民族采取敌视、迫害和不平等对待的行为 racial discrimination; racialism; racism; colour bar

【种族主义】zhǒngzú zhǔyì 鼓吹种族歧视的反动理论，它宣扬各种族生来就分为优等和劣等，前者负有统治后者的使命 racism; racialism; theory preaching racial discrimination and the belief that races are born unequal, with one particular race superior to others and destined to rule the others

冢(塚) zhǒng 坟墓 tomb; grave; last home; sepulchre; narrow cell; narrow house; urn: 古～ ancient tomb | 荒～ abandoned tomb | 衣冠～ tomb containing personal effects of the deceased

踵 zhǒng〈书 *fml.*〉❶ 脚后跟 heel: 举～ on tiptoe | 接～ follow on sb.'s heels ❷ 亲到 call on sb.: ～门道谢 pay a personal visit to thank sb. ❸ 跟随 follow close behind; follow close on the heels (of sb.): ～至(跟在后面来到) arrive close on the heels of sb.; come right after sb.

Z

【踵事增华】zhǒng shì zēng huá 继续以前的事业并更加发展 carry on a predecessor's undertaking and make it flourish; take over and carry forward a cause

【踵武】zhǒngwǔ〈书 *fml.*〉跟着别人的脚步走，比喻效法 follow in sb.'s footsteps; imitate; emulate; follow an example; follow the lead of sb.; follow suit: ～前贤 follow the example of virtuous predecessors

穜 zhǒng〈书 *fml.*〉same as 种(種) zhǒng ☞ zhòng on p.2494

zhòng (ㄓㄨㄥˋ)

中 zhòng ❶ 正对上；恰好合上 fit exactly; hit: ～选 be selected; be chosen | 猜～了 guess right; hit it on the nose | 三枪都打～了目标。None of the three shots missed the target. ❷ 受到；遭受 be affected by; be hit by; undergo; suffer: ～毒 poisoning; toxication; toxicosis | ～暑 collapse from sunstroke; heatstroke; sunstroke; insolation; calenture; siriasis; thermic fever | 胳膊上～了一枪。(He) was shot in the arm.

☞ zhōng on p.2479

【中标】zhòng//biāo 投标得中 get the bid; win the tender: 第一建筑公司夺魁～。The First Building Company got the tender.

【中毒】zhòng//dú 医学上指人或动物由于毒物进入体内而发生组织破坏、生理机能障碍或死亡等现象。症状是恶心，呕吐，腹泻，头痛，眩晕，呼吸急促，瞳孔异常等。poisoning; toxication; toxicosis; (of a person or animal who suffers from) tissue impairment, physiological obstruction or death caused by poison or a toxic substance, characterized by nausea, vomiting, diarrhea, headache, fainting, breathlessness, corectopia, etc.

【中风】zhòng//fēng 患中风 (zhòngfēng) 病 have a stroke; also 卒中 cùzhòng

【中风】zhòngfēng 病，多由脑血栓、脑溢血等引起。初起时突然头痛，眩晕，短时间内失去知觉。得病后半身不遂或截瘫，严重时很快死亡。apoplexy; stroke; palsy; disease often caused by cerebral thrombosis, cerebral haemorrhage, etc., with early symptoms characterized by sudden headache, fainting and temporary loss of consciousness; victims may suffer hemiplegia or paralysis, or even die in severe cases; also 卒中 cùzhòng

【中奖】zhòng//jiǎng 奖券、有奖储蓄券等的号码跟抽签等所得号码相同，可以获得奖金，叫做中奖 win a lottery; give a prize to the holder of a lottery ticket or save a ticket whose number is chosen at random

【中肯】zhòngkěn (言论)抓住要点；正中要害 (of a statement or speech) hit the nail on the head; relevant; pertinent; to the point: 他的话很～。What he said hit the nail right on the head.

【中签】zhòng//qiān 分期还本的公债券号码跟用抽签办法得出的本期还本的公债券号码相同。中签的公债券可以领取本息。be the lucky number; process in which the number of a treasury bond is chosen at random and the person who gets the chosen number is repaid with the capital and interest

【中伤】zhòngshāng 诬蔑别人使受损害 sling, fling and throw mud at sb.; backbite; slander; calumniate; vilify; traduce; asperse; cast aspersions on; libel: 造谣～ spread calumnious rumours | 恶意～ calumniate; malign

【中式】zhòng//shì 科举时代考试合格 (in feudal China) pass the imperial examination ☞ zhōngshì on p. 2484

【中暑】zhòng//shǔ 患中暑(zhòngshǔ)病。有的地区叫发痧。suffer sunstroke; in some places known as 发痧 fā//shā

【中暑】zhòngshǔ 病,由于长时间受烈日照射或室内温度过高、不通风引起。症状是头痛,耳鸣,严重时昏睡,痉挛,血压下降。heatstroke; sunstroke; insolation; calenture; siriasis; thermic fever; disease caused by overexposure to the sun, or too much heat or absence of draught indoors, characterized by headache, tinnitus, or in severe cases, coma, convulsions, and decline in blood pressure

【中选】zhòng//xuǎn 选举或选择时被选上 be chosen; be selected

【中意】zhòng//yì 合意;满意 catch sb.'s fancy; be to sb.'s liking; please: 这几种颜色的布她都不～。None of these kinds of multicolour cloth is to her liking. | 这件衣服很中她的意。The dress is just to her taste.

仲 zhòng ❶ 地位居中的 middle; intermediate: ～裁 arbitrate; intercede; mediate; referee; umpire ❷ 指农历一季的第二个月 second month of a season according to lunar calendar: ～秋 mid-autumn; ☞孟 mèng on p. 1327 and 季 jì on p. 918 ❸ 在弟兄排行里代表第二 (of a brother) second in order of birth: ～兄 second eldest brother | ～弟 second youngest brother | 伯～叔季 eldest, second eldest, younger, and youngest brothers ❹ (Zhòng)姓 a surname

【仲裁】zhòngcái 争执双方同意的第三者对争执事项做出决定,如国际仲裁、海事仲裁等 arbitrate; (of two parties engaged in a dispute) choose a third party to settle an issue by making a judgement or decision; arbitration, e.g. international arbitration, marine arbitration, etc.

【仲春】zhòngchūn 春季的第二个月,即农历二月 2nd lunar month of spring; mid-spring; February

【仲冬】zhòngdōng 冬季的第二个月,即农历十一月 2nd lunar month of winter; 11th lunar month

【仲家】Zhòngjiā 布依族和云南部分壮族的旧称 Zhongjia, old name for the Buyi ethnic group and, part of the Zhuang ethnic group in Yunnan Province

【仲秋】zhòngqiū 秋季的第二个月,即农历八月 2nd month of autumn; mid-autumn; August

【仲夏】zhòngxià 夏季的第二个月,即农历五月 2nd lunar month of summer; midsummer; May

众(衆) zhòng ❶ 许多(跟'寡'相对 as opposed to 'few') many; numerous: ～多 numerous; in great numbers | ～人 many people; everybody | 寡不敌～ the few cannot resist the many; be outnumbered | ～志成城。Unity is strength. ❷ 许多人 many people; crowd; multitude: 听～ audience; listeners | 观～ audience; viewers; spectators | 群～ the masses; crowd; multitude | ～所周知 it's well-known that; as is well-known; it's common knowledge that

【众多】zhòngduō 很多(多指人 oft. of people) numerous; in great numbers: 人口～ have a large population; populous

【众口难调】zhòng kǒu nán tiáo 吃饭的人多,很难适合每个人的口味 it's difficult to cater to all tastes; 〈比喻 *fig.*〉不容易使所有的人都满意 it's difficult to please everyone

【众口铄金】zhòng kǒu shuò jīn 原来比喻舆论的力量大,后来形容人多口杂,能混淆是非 voice of the masses can melt metals; public clamour can confound right and wrong (铄 *shuo*: 熔化 melt)

【众口一词】zhòng kǒu yī cí 形容许多人说同样的话 unanimous; with one voice

【众目睽睽】zhòng mù kuíkuí 大家的眼睛都注视着 eyes of the public are fixed on sth.; under the gaze of people; under people's eyes

【众目昭彰】zhòng mù zhāozhāng 群众的眼睛看得很清楚 the public have discerning eyes

【众怒】zhòngnù 众人的愤怒 public wrath or rage: ～难犯。It's dangerous to outrage the public. *or* One cannot afford to antagonize the masses.

【众叛亲离】zhòng pàn qīn lí 众人反对,亲信背离。形容十分孤立。be forsaken by one's friends and relatives; be utterly isolated

【众擎易举】zhòng qíng yì jǔ 许多人一齐用力,就容易把东西托起来 many people, if they work together, will easily lift a load; 〈比喻 *fig.*〉大家同心合力,就容易把事情做成功 many hands make light work; what is supported by many people is easily finished

【众人】zhòngrén 大家;许多人 everybody; many people: ～拾柴火焰高(比喻人多力量大) many people make a big fire by adding wood to it; (fig.) the more people, the more strength

【众生】zhòngshēng 一切有生命的,有时专指人和动物 all living creatures; all flesh; mouse and man: 芸芸～ mouse and man; common herd

【众生相】zhòngshēngxiàng 许多人的各自不同的表情或表现 various looks or manners of people; portrayal of many people

【众矢之的】zhòng shǐ zhī dì 〈比喻 *fig.*〉大家攻击的对象 target of public criticism (or censure)

【众说】zhòngshuō 各种各样的说法 public opinion; different versions of (an event):～纷纭 opinions vary; there are many different versions of a story

【众所周知】zhòng suǒ zhōu zhī 大家全都知道 it's well-known that; as is known to all; it's common knowledge that

【众望】zhòngwàng 众人的希望 people's expectations; popular confidence: 不孚～ fall short of people's expectations|～所归 enjoy popular confidence

【众望所归】zhòngwàng suǒ guī 众人的信任、希望归向某人。多指某人得到大家的信赖,希望他担任某项工作。enjoy popular confidence; command popular respect or support; oft. of sb. who is trusted and expected by all to take on a task

【众议院】zhòngyìyuàn ❶ 两院制议会的下议院名称之一 one of the names of the lower house or chamber of a bicameral system; (US, Australia, Japan, etc.) House of Representatives; (Italy, Mexico, Chile, etc.) Chamber of Deputies; ☞下议院 xiàyìyuàn on p. 2068 ❷ 实行一院制的国家的议会也有叫众议院的,如卢森堡的议会 name of the parliament of some unicameral country, e.g. Chamber of Deputies in Luxembourg

【众志成城】zhòng zhì chéng chéng 大家同心协力,就像城墙一样的牢固 joint efforts construct an insurmountable wall; 〈比喻 *fig.*〉大家团结一致,就能克服困难,得到成功 unity is strength; the will of many is a formidable force

种(種) zhòng 种植 grow; plant; crop; put in: ～田 engage in farming; be a farmer; farm; do farm work|～麦子 plant wheat|～棉花 grow cotton ◇～牛痘 vaccination against smallpox

☞ Chóng on p. 271 and zhǒng on p. 2489

【种地】zhòng//dì 从事田间劳动 engage in farming; be a farmer: 他在家种过地。He used to be a farmer in his home town.

【种痘】zhòng//dòu 把痘苗接种在人体上,使人体对天花产生自动免疫作用 vaccination; inoculation with a vaccine in order to produce immunity to smallpox; also 种牛痘 zhòngniúdòu; 有的地区叫种花 in some regions known as 种花 zhòng//huā

Z

【种瓜得瓜,种豆得豆】zhòng guā dé guā, zhòng dòu dé dòu 〈比喻 *fig.*〉做了什么样的事,就得到什么样的结果 reap what one has sown; as a man sows, so he shall reap; you must reap what you have sown

【种花】zhòng//huā ❶ (～儿 zhòng//huār)培植花草 cultivate or grow flowers; floriculture ❷〈方 *dial.*〉(～儿 zhòng//huār) same as 种痘 zhòng//dòu ❸〈方 *dial.*〉种棉花 grow cotton

【种田】zhòng//tián same as 种地 zhòng//dì

【种植】zhòngzhí 把植物的种子埋在土里;把植物的幼苗栽到土里 plant; grow; crop; put in: ～果树 plant fruit saplings; grow fruit; cultivate fruit|～花草 plant flowers and grass

重 zhòng ❶ 重量;分量 weight; heft: 举～ weightlifting|这条鱼有几斤～? What's the weight of the fish? *or* How much does the fish weigh? ❷ 重量大;比重大(跟'轻'相对 as opposed to 'light') heavy; weighty; hefty; ponderous: 体积相等时,铁比木头～。Given equal volume, iron is weightier than wood. ◇工作很～ have a heavy workload; overwork|脚步很～ walk heavily; walk with loud footsteps|话说得太～了。That's putting it too strongly. ❸ 程度深 deep; serious: 情意～ deep feelings or affections|病势很～ (of a patient) be in a serious condition; be seriously ill|受了～伤 be gravely wounded ❹ 重要 important: 军事～地 place of military importance|身负～任 be on an important commission ❺ 重视 attach importance to; lay stress on; lay or set store by: 敬～ respect deeply; regard highly; regard sb. with reverence; hold sb. in esteem; stand in awe of sb.; think a great deal of sb.|尊～ respect; regard; defer to; have a high regard for; have a high opinion of; value|看～ think a lot of; value; attach importance to|器～ regard highly; hold sb. in high regard; have a high opinion of|为人所～ be highly respected|～男轻女是错误的。It's wrong to regard men as superior to women. ❻ 不轻率 prudent; discreet: 自～ self-respect|慎～ discreet; prudent; circumspect; gingerly|老成持～ experienced and prudent

☞ chóng on p. 271

【重办】zhòngbàn 严厉地处罚(罪犯) severely punish (a criminal)

【重臂】zhòngbì 阻力臂的旧称 old name for 阻力臂 zǔlìbì

【重兵】zhòngbīng 力量雄厚的军队 large number of forces: ～把守 be heavily guarded|～压境 be heavily pressed by the enemy forces on the border

【重彩】zhòngcǎi 浓重的色彩(描绘) strong colours (used in painting): 浓墨～ (paint in) dark ink and rich colours

【重创】zhòngchuāng 使受到严重的损伤 inflict heavy losses on; maul heavily; plaster: ～敌人 inflict heavy casualties on the enemy

【重大】zhòngdà 大而重要(用于抽象事物 used for abstract things) of great importance; significant; great; fateful; fatal; eventful; life-and-death; weighty; momentous: ～问题 big issue; vital problem|意义～ of great significance; significant

【重担】zhòngdàn 沉重的担子 heavy load; heavy burden; 〈比喻 *fig.*〉繁重的责任 great responsibility; difficult task; challenging work: 千斤～ weighty mission, task, or burden | 勇挑～ ready to shoulder heavy burdens | ～在肩 be under a heavy burden

【重地】zhòngdì 重要而需要严密防护的地方 important location (usu. closely guarded) 工程～ construction site | 军事～ place of military importance

【重点】zhòngdiǎn ❶ 阻力点的旧称 old name for 阻力点 zǔlìdiǎn ❷ 同类事物中的重要的或主要的 key; important; major; emphasis; focal point: ～试验区 important experimental section or area | ～工作 focus of work | 工业建设的～ key industrial constructions ❸ 有重点地 give priority to; lay emphasis on; stress: ～推广 give priority to the popularization of sth. | ～发展 lay emphasis on the development of sth. | ～进攻 attack on key sectors

【重读】zhòngdú 把一个词或一个词组里的某个音节或语句里的某几个音节读得重些,强些。例如'石头、棍子'两个词里,第一个音节重读。'老三'这个词里,第二个音节重读。'过年'里'过'字重读是'明年'的意思;'年'字重读是'过新年'的意思。stress; emphasis placed on a syllable spoken in a word or a phrase, or on several syllables in a sentence, e.g. the stress for 石头 shí·tou and 棍子 gùn·zi is put on the first syllable, but for 老三 lǎosān, the stress is on the second syllable; when 过 guò is stressed in 过年 guò·nian, this means 'next year (明年 míngnián)', while if 年 nián is spoken forcefully the same word means 'celebrate the new year (过新年 guò xīnnián)' ☞ chóngdú on p. 271

【重犯】zhòngfàn 犯有严重罪行的犯人 felon; offender who has committed a grave crime

【重负】zhòngfù 沉重的负担 heavy burden: 如释～ feel as if relieved of a heavy load; feel a sense of relief; breathe again; breathe freely

【重工业】zhònggōngyè 以生产生产资料为主的工业,包括冶金、电力、煤炭、石油、基本化学、建筑材料和机器制造等工业部门 heavy industry; industry which focuses on the means of production, e.g. metallurgy, electric power, coal-mining, petroleum, basic chemicals, building materials, machine-building, etc.

【重话】zhònghuà 分量过重,使人难堪的话 harsh words; offensive remarks: 他俩结婚多年,互敬互爱,连句～都没说过。They got married years ago, and ever since they have loved and respected each other, and never spoken a harsh word.

【重活】zhònghuó (～儿 zhònghuór)指费力气的体力劳动 heavy manual labour

【重机关枪】zhòngjīguānqiāng 机关枪的一种,装有三脚或轮式枪架,射击稳定性好,有效射程一般为 1,000 米 heavy machine-gun; machine-gun set on a tripod or trundled rack, capable of steady firing, good for a range of 1,000 m.

【重价】zhòngjià 很高的价钱 high price: ～收买 pay a high price for sth. | ～征求 solicit a high price | 不惜～ not hesitate to pay a high price

【重奖】zhòngjiǎng ❶ 巨额奖金或贵重的奖品 handsome reward (large sum of money or costly goods): 对有突出贡献的科技人员将给予～。Those who make outstanding achievements in the field of science and technology will be highly rewarded. ❷ 给予重奖 highly reward sb.; offer rich rewards to sb.: ～有突出贡献的科技人员 highly reward those who have made outstanding contributions to science and technology

【重金】zhòngjīn 巨额的钱;重价 huge sum of money; high price: ～收买 buy over sb. with a large sum of money | ～聘请 offer a high salary for sb.; employ sb. at a high pay

【重金属】zhòngjīnshǔ 通常指比重大于 5 的金属,如铜、镍、铅、锌、锡、钨等 heavy metal; metal with a specific gravity greater than 5.0, e.g. copper, nickel, tin, lead, etc.

【重力】zhònglì ❶ 地心引力 gravity; gravitation; gravitational force; gravitational attraction ❷ 泛指任何天体吸引其他物体的力,如月球重力、火星重力等 gravitational force of any celestial body, e.g. moon's gravity, Mars' gravity, etc.

【重利】zhònglì ❶ 很高的利息 heavy interest; high rate of interest; usury: ～盘剥 exploit by usury; usury; usuriousness ❷ 很高的利润 great profit; huge profit: 牟取～ obtain huge profits ❸〈书 *fml.*〉看重钱财 value material gains: ～轻义 put material gains above justice

【重量】zhòngliàng 物体受到的重力的大小叫做重量。重量随高度或纬度变化而有微小差别。在高处比在低处小一些,在两极比在赤道大一些。weight; heft; quantity of heaviness of a mass, which varies slightly at different heights or latitudes, where the weight of an object at a higher position is smaller than that at a lower position, so at either pole the object will be heavier than at the equator

【重炮】zhòngpào 重型大炮,如榴弹炮、加农炮、高射炮等 heavy gun; heavy artillery; heavy artillery piece, e.g. howitzer, cannon, anti-aircraft artillery, etc.

【重氢】zhòngqīng 氘 (dāo) deuterium; diplogen; heavy hydrogen

【重任】zhòngrèn 重大的责任;重要的任务 important task; great commitment; heavy responsibility: 身负～ hold a position of great responsibility; be on a important commission

|委以～ entrust sb. with an important task

【重伤】zhòngshāng 身体受到的严重的伤害 severe injury; grievous bodily harm (GBH)

【重身子】zhòngshēn·zi ❶ 指怀孕 be pregnant ❷ 指怀孕的妇女 pregnant woman

【重视】zhòngshì 认为人的德才优良或事物的作用重要而认真对待;看重 attach importance to; think much of; put, lay and place emphasis on; lay store by; set store by; regard highly; think highly of; lay stress on: ～学习 give priority to one's studies; attach great importance to the acquisition of knowledge|～群众的发明创造 attach due importance to the creativity and inventiveness of the masses

【重听】zhòngtīng 听觉迟钝 hard of hearing: 他有点～,你说话得大声点儿。You have to raise your voice for he is hard of hearing.

【重头戏】zhòngtóuxì 指唱工和做工很重的戏 traditional opera involving much singing and action

【重托】zhòngtuō 重大的委托 great trust: 不负～ live up to the great trust placed on one; deserve one's great trust

【重武器】zhòngwǔqì 射程远、威力大,转移时多需车辆装载、牵引的武器。如高射炮、迫击炮、火箭炮等,坦克、装甲车也属于重武器。heavy weapons; armament having a longer range and more firepower, which is movable (either loaded on or pulled by a vehicle), e.g. antiaircraft artillery, trench mortar, etc., as well as tank and armoured car

【重孝】zhòngxiào 最重的孝服,如父母死后子女所穿的孝服 dress worn in deep mourning, esp. after the death of a parent

【重心】zhòngxīn ❶ 物体内各点所受的重力产生合力,这个合力的作用点叫做这个物体的重心 barycentre; centre of mass; centre of gravity; centroid; point in a body at which the mass of various points within the same body may be considered to be concentrated and at which external forces may be considered to be applied ❷ 三角形三条中线相交于一点,这个点叫做三角形的重心 median point; intersection of the three medians of a triangle ❸ 事情的中心或主要部分 heart; focus; core; crux: 工作～ the focus of work|问题的～ crux of a problem; heart of a matter

【重型】zhòngxíng (机器、武器等)在重量、体积、功效或威力上特别大的 heavy (machine, weaponry, etc.): ～汽车 heavy vehicle|～车床 heavy-duty lathe|～坦克 heavy tank

【重要】zhòngyào 具有重大的意义、作用和影响的 important; significant; major; critical; vital; crucial; momentous: ～人物 VIP; dignitary; prominent figure|～问题 big issue; major problem|这文件很～。This document is very important.

【重音】zhòngyīn ❶ 指一个词、词组或句子里重读的音 stress; accent (of a word); ☞重读 zhòngdú ❷ 乐曲中强度较大的音,是构成节奏的主要因素 mark giving emphasis or prominence to a musical note or chord, which is a major component of rhythm

【重用】zhòngyòng (把某人)放在重要工作岗位上 put sb. in an important position: ～优秀科技人员 reserve important positions for those outstanding technical staff|他在单位很受～。He is given an important position in his workplace.

【重元素】zhòngyuánsù 原子量较大的元素,如铀、锎、钔等 heavy element (e.g. uranium, californium, mendelevium, etc.)

【重责】zhòngzé ❶ 重大的责任 heavy responsibility: 身负～ bear heavy responsibilities ❷ 严厉斥责或责罚 severely reprimand or punish: 因工作失职,受到～ be severely reproached for breach of duty

【重镇】zhòngzhèn 军事上占重要地位的城镇,也泛指在其他方面占重要地位的城镇 town of military importance; town of strategic importance; (in a broad sense) town of certain importance: 战略～ strategic town; strategic place|工业～ important industrial town

【重资】zhòngzī 数额巨大的资金 large sum of money; great deal of capital: 投下～ make a huge investment|不惜～购买设备 be ready to offer a larger sum of money for equipment purchase

【重子】zhòngzǐ 质子和质量重于质子的基本粒子的统称 baryon; heavy particle; name for proton and any of the elementary particles having a mass greater than that of a proton

蚛 zhòng〈书 *fml*.〉虫咬 insect bite

穜 zhòng〈书 *fml*.〉same as 种(種) zhòng ☞ zhǒng on p. 2490

zhōu(ㄓㄡ)

舟 zhōu〈书 *fml*.〉船 boat: 轻～ light boat|小～ small boat|一叶扁～ a small boat

【舟车】zhōuchē 船和车,借指旅途 boat and carriage; vessel and vehicle; journey: ～劳顿 exhausted by a long journey

【舟楫】zhōují〈书 *fml*.〉船只 vessel

州 zhōu ❶ 旧时的一种行政区划,所辖地区的大小历代不同,现在这名称还保留在地名里,如苏州、德州 (old) prefecture; administrative division, the area of which varies in size in different dynasties; this term still survives in some names of present-day places, e.g. 苏州 Sūzhōu, 德州 Dézhōu ❷ 指自治州 autonomous prefecture

诌(謅) zhōu 编造(言辞) fabricate (a story, etc.); make up; cook up; invent: 胡～ tall story; fabrication; spin a yarn; fabricate wild tales|瞎～ talk trash

侜 zhōu〈书 *fml.*〉诳 deceive; cheat; befool: ～张 defraud

【侜张】zhōuzhāng〈书 *fml.*〉欺骗;作伪 deceive; beguile; defraud; hoodwink; fake: ～为幻 mislead; entrap; also 诪张 zhōuzhāng

周[1](週) zhōu ❶ same as 圈子 quān·zi ①: 全体运动员绕场一～。All the athletes did a lap around the field.|地球绕太阳一～是一年。It takes a year for the earth to move around the sun once. ❷ 周围 circumambience; circumference: 圆～ circle; circumference|房屋的四～是用篱笆拦起来的。The house is fenced all around. ❸ 绕一圈 make a circuit; make a circle: ～而复始 move in cycles; go round and round ❹ 普遍;全 all; whole: ～身 all over the body|众所～知 as is known to all; as is well-known ❺ 完备;周到 with no detail missing; thoughtful: ～密 careful; thorough|由于计划不～,所以走了一些弯路。We've made some detours because our plan was not a thorough one. ❻ 星期 week: 上～ last week|下～ next week|～末晚会 weekend party ❼ 周波的简称 abbr. for 周波 zhōubō

周[2] zhōu 接济 give financial help to; help out: ～济 help out; relieve

周[3] Zhōu ❶ 朝代,公元前 1046—公元前 256,姬发所建 Zhou Dynasty (1046B. C. - 256 B. C.), which was founded by Jifa; ☞ 西周 Xī Zhōu on p. 2043 and 东周 Dōng Zhōu on p. 464 ❷ 北周 Northern Zhou of the Northern Dynasties ❸ 后周 Later Zhou of the Five Dynasties (951—960) ❹ 姓 a surname

【周报】zhōubào 周刊(用做刊物名 used in names of periodicals) weekly newspaper or periodical; weekly:《北京～》*Beijing Review*

【周边】zhōubiān same as 周围 zhōuwéi: ～地区 surrounding areas|～国家 neighbouring countries

【周波】zhōubō ❶ 交流电的变化或电磁波的振荡从一点开始完成一个过程再到这一点,叫做一个周波 cycle; one complete performance of current alternation or electric oscillation (starting from a point and going back to it after a periodic process) ❷ 电磁波频率单位,一周波等于 1 周/秒 unit of electric frequency, which is equal to one cycle per second; hertz; Hz; 简称 abbr. 周 zhōu

【周到】zhōu·dào 面面都照顾到;不疏忽 thoughtful; considerate; attentive; wary: 服务～ offer good service|他考虑问题很～。He is very considerate when it comes to problems.

【周而复始】zhōu ér fù shǐ 一次又一次地循环 move in cycles; go round and round

【周济】zhōujì 对穷困的人给予物质上的帮助 relieve; help out

【周角】zhōujiǎo 一条射线以端点为定点在平面上旋转一周所成的角。角的两条边重合在一起。周角为 360°。perigon; round angle; angle of 360 degrees

【周刊】zhōukān 每星期出版一次的刊物 weekly; weekly publication

【周密】zhōumì 周到而细密 thorough and careful: 计划～ thorough plan; well-conceived plan|～的调查 close investigation

【周末】zhōumò 一星期的最后的时间,一般指星期六 weekend

【周年】zhōunián 满一年 anniversary: ～纪念 anniversary|建国三十～ the 30th anniversary of the founding of the republic

【周期】zhōuqī ❶ 事物在运动、变化的发展过程中,某些特征多次重复出现,其接续两次出现所经过的时间叫周期 cycle; interval during which a series of events or operations recur regularly, oft. leading back to the starting point ❷ 物体作往复运动或物理量作周而复始的变化时,重复一次所经历的时间 cycle; time during which an object completes a reciprocal movement, or a physical quantity completes a transformation process and starts a repeated one ❸ 元素周期表中元素的一种分类。具有相同电子层数的一系列元素按原子序数递增顺序排列的一个横行为一个周期。同周期元素从左到右,金属性逐渐减弱,非金属性逐渐增强。classification of elements (as in the periodic table); (in the periodic table) horizontal row of elements, which have equal number of electrons and are arranged in an increasing order of atomic number; the metallicity of each row of elements declines, while their non-metallicity increases, from left to right

【周全】zhōuquán ❶ 周到;全面 thorough; comprehensive: 计划要订得～些。The plan should be made more comprehensive. ❷ 指成全,帮助 help sb. to fulfil their wishes: ～这件好事 help make this happy event come true

【周身】zhōushēn 浑身;全身 all over the body; all over; at every pore; from head to foot: ～都淋湿了 be wet all over; be soaked through; be soaked to the skin

【周岁】zhōusuì 年龄满一岁 one full year of life; exactly one year in age: 今天是孩子的～。Today the child is exactly one year old.|他已经三十二～了。He is 32 years old.

【周围】zhōuwéi 环绕着中心的部分 circumambience; circumference: ～地区 surrounding areas|屋子～是篱笆。There is a fence around the house.|关心～的群众 have concern for the masses

【周围神经】zhōuwéi shénjīng 分布在全身皮肤、肌肉、内脏等处的神经,由脑和脊髓所发出的许多神经构成,包括脑神经、脊髓神经和植物性神经,是身体各个器官与中枢神经联系的桥梁 peripheral nerves; nerves distributed all over the skin, muscle, bowels, etc., which start from the brain and spinal cord, including the cranial nerves, spinal nerves, and autonomic nerves, and serve as a bridge between any of the various organs and central nerves

【周详】zhōuxiáng 周到而详细 comprehensive; detailed; thorough; complete:他考虑得十分～。He has taken everything into consideration.

【周恤】zhōuxù〈书 *fml*.〉对别人表示同情并给予物质的帮助 sympathize and give help to

【周旋】zhōuxuán ❶ 回旋;盘旋 whirl; circle around; convolve; hover; orbit; whorl ❷ 交际应酬;打交道 engage in social intercourse; deal with; interact with; mix with (sb.):成天跟人～,真累人。It's tiring to deal with people day in, day out. ❸ 与敌人较量,相机进退 contend with one's enemy so as to choose to advance or withdraw to the best advantage; flexibly fight (the enemy)

【周延】zhōuyán 一个判断的主词(或宾词)所包括的是其全部外延,如在'所有的物体都是运动的'这个判断中,主词(物体)是周延的,因为它说的是所有的物体 distribution; in a sentence giving judgement, what the subject covers is called the extension, e. g. in 'All bodies are moving.' The subject includes all individuals, because it indicates all bodies.

【周游】zhōuyóu 到各地游历;游遍 go on a circuit; travel around; take a journey around:～世界 go world-trotting; trot the globe; travel around the world|孔子～列国。Confucius travelled to many states.

【周缘】zhōuyuán 周围的边缘 outer edge (usu. circular); rim:车轮的～叫轮辋。The circular outer part of a wheel is called 轮辋 lúnwǎng (rim).

【周遭】zhōuzāo 四周;周围 around; all around:～静悄悄的,没有一个人。It was very quiet all around, with nobody in sight.

【周章】zhōuzhāng〈书 *fml*.〉❶ 仓皇惊恐 scared; startled; frightened; in a panic; in a fluster:狼狈～ get into a panic|～失措 be scared witless ❷ 周折;苦心 setbacks; painstaking; trouble:煞费～ go to a lot of trouble; take great pains; be full of twists and turns

【周折】zhōuzhé 指事情进行往返曲折,不顺利 twists and turns; setbacks:大费～ it takes a lot of trouble; it's painstaking (to do sth.)

【周正】zhōu·zhèng〈方 *fml*.〉端正 straight; regular:模样～ have a regular face|把帽子戴～。Put your hat on straight.|桌子做得～。The desk is neatly made.

【周至】zhōuzhì (做事、思考)周到 (of a person's actions or thinking) thoughtful; considerate:叮咛～ give thoughtful advice

【周转】zhōuzhuǎn ❶ 企业的资金从投入生产到销售产品而收回货币,再投入生产,这个过程一次又一次地重复进行,叫做周转。周转所需的时间,是生产时间和流通时间的总和。turnover; repeated business process, from investment, production and sales to the return of the invested capital; the time taken for a turnover is the sum of productive time plus circulating time ❷ 指个人或团体的经济开支调度的情况或物品轮流使用的情况 (of an individual or organization) able to manage financial expenses or use sth. in turn:～不开 not have enough money (to cover an expense); be short of sth. that is needed

洲 zhōu ❶ 一块大陆和附近岛屿的总称。地球上有七大洲,即亚洲、欧洲、非洲、北美洲、南美洲、大洋洲、南极洲。continent; one of the principal land masses of the earth and its surrounding islands. On the earth there are seven continents: Asia, Europe, Africa, North America, South America, Oceania, and Antarctica. ❷ 河流中由沙石、泥土淤积而成的陆地 land of sand, stones or silt built up in a river; sandbar:沙～ sandbar|三角～ delta

【洲际导弹】zhōujì dǎodàn 射程在8,000公里以上的导弹。可从一大洲袭击另一大洲的目标。intercontinental ballistic missile; IBM; ballistic missile capable of travelling from one continent to another and hitting the target, having a range of above 8,000 km.

诪(譸) zhōu〈书 *fml*.〉❶ 诅咒 curse; damn; execrate ❷ same as 侜 zhōu

【诪张】zhōuzhāng same as 侜张 zhōuzhāng

辀 zhōu〈书 *fml*.〉车辕 thill

掫(擫) zhōu〈方 *dial*.〉从一侧或一端托起沉重的物体 lift sth. heavy from one side or end:费了九牛二虎之力,也没把箱子～起来。He tried with tremendous effort to lift the box, but failed.

啁 zhōu [啁啾](zhōujiū)〈书 *fml*.〉〈拟声词 *onom*.〉形容鸟叫的声音(of a bird) twitter; tweet; chirp; warble; chatter

☞ zhāo on p. 2422

鸼 zhōu ☞[鹘鸼](gǔzhōu) on p. 697

喌 zhōu〈拟声词 *onom*.〉唤鸡的声音 cry used to call chickens

赒 zhōu same as 周² zhōu

粥 zhōu 用粮食或粮食加其他东西煮成的半流质食物 porridge; congee; gruel:江米～ glutinous rice porridge|八宝～ eight-treasure porridge (cooked from eight nutritious ingredients)

☞ yù on p. 2353

【粥少僧多】zhōu shǎo sēng duō〈比喻 *fig*.〉东西少而人多,不够分配 too little porridge for too many monks; (of sth.) not enough to satisfy everyone; also 僧多粥少 sēng duō zhōu shǎo

盩 zhōu 盩厔(Zhōuzhì),地名,在陕西。今已改作周至。place in Shaanxi Province, now written as 周至 Zhōuzhì

zhóu (ㄓㄡˊ)

妯 zhóu [妯娌](zhóu·li) 哥哥的妻子和弟弟的妻子的合称 brothers' wives; sisters-in-law: 她们三个是~。The three of them are sisters-in-law. | 你们~俩去吧! You two sisters should go!

轴 zhóu ❶ 圆柱形的零件,轮子或其他转动的机件绕着它转动或随着它转动 axis; shaft; spindle; axle-tree: 车~ axle; axle-tree | 轮~ axle; axle-tree | 多~自动车床 multi-axle automatic lathe; (图见☞ figure for 轮子 lún·zi on p. 1275) ❷ 把平面或立体分成对称部分的直线 axis; line along which a figure or a cube is symmetric ❸ (~儿 zhóur) 圆柱形的用来往上绕东西的器物 spool; roller: 线~儿 spool; bobbin | 画~ Chinese scroll painting ❹〈量词 *classifier*〉用于缠在轴上的线以及装裱带轴子的字画 amount of thread wound on a spool; Chinese scroll painting or calligraphy: 两~丝线 two spools of silk thread | 一~泼墨山水 a scroll landscape painting in Chinese ink

☞ zhòu on p. 2498

【轴承】zhóuchéng 支承轴的机件,轴可以在轴承上旋转,按摩擦的性质不同可分为滑动轴承、滚动轴承等 bearing; machine part supporting a rotating axle there are sliding bearings and rolling bearings, according to the type of friction involved

【轴瓦】zhóuwǎ 滑动轴承和轴接触的部分,非常光滑,一般用减摩合金、塑料等制成 axle bush; machine part between a sliding bearing and an axle, lubricious and made of friction-reducing alloy, plastic, etc.; also 轴衬 zhóuchèn

【轴线】zhóuxiàn 绕在线轴上的棉线或丝线等 spool thread; spool cotton

【轴子】zhóu·zi ❶ 安在字画的下端便于悬挂或卷起的圆杆儿 roller (fixed to the bottom end of a scroll painting or calligraphy for the convenience of hanging or rolling up) ❷ 弦乐器上系弦的小圆杆儿,用来调节音的高低 peg (of a stringed instrument); tuning peg

碡 zhóu ☞[碌碡](liù·zhóu) on p. 1247

zhǒu (ㄓㄡˇ)

肘 zhǒu ❶ 上臂和前臂相接处向外面突起的部分;胳膊肘儿 elbow; protruding joint between the forearm and the upper arm; (图见☞ figure for 身体 shēntǐ on p. 1701) ❷ (~儿 zhǒur) same as 肘子 zhǒu·zi ①: 后~ hind leg of pork | 酱~ pork leg in sauce

【肘窝】zhǒuwō 肘关节里侧凹下去的部分 crook of the arm

【肘腋】zhǒuyè〈书 *fml*.〉胳膊肘儿和夹肢窝 elbow and armpit;〈比喻 *fig*.〉极近的地方(多用于祸患的发生 oft. of a disaster) close at hand: 变生~ unavoidable accident | ~之患 trouble close at hand

【肘腋之患】zhǒuyè zhī huàn〈比喻 *fig*.〉发生在身旁或极近地方的祸患 disaster which occurs close to one; trouble coming from those closest to one

【肘子】zhǒu·zi ❶ 作为食物的猪腿的最上部 upper part of a leg of pork ❷ (~儿 zhǒu·zir) same as 肘 zhǒu ①: 胳膊~ elbow

帚(箒) zhǒu 除去尘土、垃圾、油垢等的用具 broom; tool to remove dust, rubbish, grease, etc.: 扫~ broom | 炊~ pot-scouring brush

zhòu (ㄓㄡˋ)

纣[1] zhòu〈书 *fml*.〉后鞧(qiū) crupper (canvas or leather trap around the rump of a shaft-horse)

纣[2] Zhòu 商(殷)朝末代君王,相传是个暴君 Zhou, last ruler of the Shang Dynasty, who, according to legend, was a tyrant: 助~为虐 help a tyrant to do evil

【纣棍】zhòugùn (~儿 zhòugùnr) 系在驴马等尾下的横木,两端用绳子连着鞍子,防止鞍子往前滑 crupper of a saddle; wooden bar fixed under the tail of a horse or a donkey, which is joined to a saddle by ropes attached to the both ends of it, and keeps the saddle from slipping forward

伷 zhòu〈书 *fml*.〉same as 胄[1] zhòu。多用于人名。usu. used in a person's name

㑇(㑳) zhòu 俊俏;乖巧(多见于早期白话 oft. used in early vernacular) pretty; cute; lovely

咒(呪) zhòu ❶ 信某些宗教的人以为念着可以除灾或降灾的语句 incantation; spell; conjuration; curse; malediction: 念~ chant incantations ❷ 说希望人不顺利的话 damn; curse; execrate

【咒骂】zhòumà 用恶毒的话骂 curse; damn; swear

Z

㤘(㥮) zhòu〈方 *dial.*〉固执 obstinate; stubborn: 性情～ tough-minded; straight-laced | ～脾气 obstinacy

宙 zhòu ❶ 指古往今来的时间 time conceived as past, present and future; ☞宇宙 yǔzhòu on p. 2343 ❷ 地质年代分期的最高一级,跟宙相应的年代地层单位叫做宇 aeon; eon; highest order of geological time division, with eonothem being the corresponding stratum

绉(縐) zhòu same as 绉纱 zhòushā

【绉布】zhòubù 织出皱纹的棉织品 cotton crepe; crepe

【绉纱】zhòushā 织出皱纹的丝织品,用起收缩作用的捻合线做纬线织成,质地坚牢,常用来做衣服、被面等 crepe; crape; fabric made of silk with a crinkled surface and long-lasting texture, usu. used to make dresses, bedcovers, etc.

荮 zhòu〈方 *dial.*〉❶ 用草包裹 wrap with straw ❷〈量词 *classifier*〉用草绳绑扎的碗、碟等,一捆叫一荮 bundle (of dishes, bowls, etc., tied up with a straw rope)

轴 zhòu ☞大轴子 dàzhòu·zi on p. 367 and 压轴子 yāzhòu·zi on p. 2193

☞ zhóu on p. 2497

胄[1] zhòu〈古代 *arch.*〉称帝王或贵族的子孙 descendants of ancient emperors or aristocrats: 贵～ descendants of aristocrats

胄[2] zhòu〈古代 *arch.*〉打仗时戴的保护头部的帽子 helmet: 甲～ armour and helmet

咮 zhòu〈书 *fml.*〉鸟嘴 beak

昼(晝) zhòu 从天亮到天黑的一段时间;白天(跟'夜'相对 as opposed to 'night') day; daytime; daylight: ～夜 day and night | 白～ day; daytime; daylight

【昼夜】zhòuyè 白天和黑夜 24-hour; day and night; round the clock: ～兼程 hurry one's journey day and night | 机器轰鸣,～不停。The machine keeps roaring day and night.

酎 zhòu〈书 *fml.*〉重酿的醇酒 double-fermented wine

【酎金】zhòujīn〈书 *fml.*〉诸侯给皇帝的贡金,供祭祀之用 contributions of feudal vassals to an emperor for sacrificial purposes

皱(皺) zhòu ❶ 皱纹 wrinkle; furrow; rimple; crumple; pucker; rugosity: 上了年纪脸上就会起～。When people get on in years, their faces will become wrinkled. ❷ 起皱纹 (of a person) wrinkle; furrow; shrivel: 眉头一～,计上心来。Knit one's brow and an idea comes to one's mind. | 衣裳～了。The dress is crumpled.

【皱巴巴】zhòubābā (～的 zhòubābā·de) 形容皱纹多,不舒展 crumpled; wrinkled: ～的瘦脸 small and wrinkled face | 衣服～的 crumpled dress

【皱襞】zhòubì〈书 *fml.*〉褶儿;皱纹 fold; pleat; wrinkle

【皱胃】zhòuwèi 反刍动物胃的第四部分,内壁能分泌胃液。食物由重瓣胃进入皱胃,消化后进入肠管。abomasum; fourth stomach; fourth division of the stomach in a ruminant animal, the wall of which can excrete gastric juices to digest the food from the omasum, and the digested food will then move on into the intestines

【皱纹】zhòuwén (～儿 zhòuwénr) 物体表面上因收缩或揉弄而形成的一凸一凹的条纹 wrinkle; furrow; rimple; crumple; pucker; rugosity: 脸上布满～ face full of wrinkles; furrowed face

甃 zhòu〈方 *dial.*〉❶ 井壁 wall of a well ❷ 用砖砌(井、池子等) build (a well, pond, etc.) with bricks

㑇 zhōu ☞[僝㑇](chánzhòu) on p. 211

繇 zhòu〈古时 *arch.*〉占卜的文辞 auspicial words

☞ yáo on p. 2230 and yóu on p. 2325

骤 zhòu ❶ (马)奔跑 (of a horse) trot: 驰～ gallop ❷ 急速 violently quick or rapid: 暴风～雨 violent storm ❸ 突然;忽然 sudden: 狂风～起。A gale suddenly came up. | 脸色～变。His expression suddenly changed.

【骤然】zhòurán 突然,忽然 suddenly; abruptly: ～一惊 be startled | 掌声～像暴风雨般响起来。A storm of applause suddenly broke out.

籀 zhòu〈书 *fml.*〉❶ 读书;讽诵 read aloud; recite ❷ 指籀文 Zhou-dynasty style of Chinese calligraphy

【籀文】zhòuwén〈古代 *arch.*〉一种字体,就是大篆 seal script of calligraphy in use during the Zhou Dynasty

zhū (ㄓㄨ)

朱(❷硃) zhū ❶ 朱红 vermilion; vermeil: ～笔 brush dipped with red ink ❷ 朱砂 cinnabar ❸ (Zhū)姓 a surname

【朱笔】zhūbǐ 蘸红色的毛笔,批公文,校古书,批改学生作业等常用红色,以区别于原写原印用的黑色 brush dipped in red ink, which is used to endorse official documents, proofread ancient scripts, and correct students' schoolwork, to distinguish from the original in black ink

【朱红】zhūhóng 比较鲜艳的红色 vermilion; vermeil; bright red

【朱鹮】zhūhuán 鸟,全身羽毛白色,额和眼睛周围朱红色,嘴黑色,长而略弯,腿和爪红色。生活在水田和沼泽地区。是珍贵鸟类。Japanese crested ibis (*Nipponia nippon*); bird, having white plumage, vermeil forehead and around the eyes, black downward-curving bill, and red legs and claws, living in paddy fields and wetlands; a rare bird

【朱槿】zhūjǐn 落叶灌木,叶子阔卵形,先端尖,花红色,蒴果卵圆形。供观赏。Chinese hibiscus (*Hibiscus rosa-sinensis*); defoliate shrub having broad egg-shaped leaves pointed at the top ends, red flowers, and oval-shaped capsules; grown as an ornamental plant; also 扶桑 fúsāng

【朱门】zhūmén 红漆的大门,旧时指豪富人家 showy gate painted vermilion; wealthy family: ～酒肉臭 behind the red gates of the rich, meat and wine are left to rot (referring to a life of debauchery and dissipation)

【朱墨】[1] zhūmò 红黑两色 red and black: ～加批 endorsed with red and black | ～套印 printed in red and black

【朱墨】[2] zhūmò 用朱砂制成的墨 ink made of cinnabar

【朱鸟】zhūniǎo ☞朱雀[2] zhūquè

【朱批】zhūpī 用朱笔写的批语 comments written in red with a brush

【朱漆】zhūqī 红漆 red paint; red lacquer: ～大门 vermilion gate | ～家具 red-lacquered furniture

【朱雀】[1] zhūquè 鸟,形状跟麻雀相似,雄鸟红色或暗褐色,雌鸟橄榄褐色。生活在山林中,吃果实等。rosefinch (*Carpodacus*); bird which looks like a sparrow, with the male having a red or dark brown colour, and the female being olive brown, living in mountain trees, eating fruit, etc.; also 红麻料儿 hóngmáliàor

【朱雀】[2] zhūquè ❶ 二十八宿中南方七宿的合称 name for the seven southern mansions of the 28 lunar mansions in ancient astronomy ❷〈道教 *Taoism*〉所奉的南方的神 God of Southern Lunar Mansions ‖ also 朱鸟 zhūniǎo

【朱砂】zhūshā 无机化合物,化学式 HgS。红色或棕红色,无毒。是炼汞的主要矿物,也用做颜料,中医入药。cinnabar; red or brownish red nonpoisonous; inorganic compound (HgS), the principal ore for mercury, and also used as a pigment and in Chinese medicine; also 辰砂 chénshā or 丹砂 dānshā

【朱文】zhūwén 印章上的阳文(跟'白文'相对 as opposed to 'intagliated characters') characters carved in relief on a seal

邾 Zhū ❶ 周朝邹国本来叫邾 Zhu, original name for the state of Zou during the Zhou Dynasty ❷ 姓 a surname

侏 zhū [侏儒](zhūrú) 身材异常矮小的人。这种异常的发育多由脑垂体前叶的功能低下所致。dwarf; midget; manikin; gnome; pygmy; Lilliputian; abnormally small person, oft. due to the hypofunction of the fore lobe of the pituitary gland

诛 zhū〈书 *fml.*〉❶ 杀(有罪的人) put (a criminal) to death: 伏～ be executed | 罪不容～ death does not atone for the gravity of an offence; be guilty of crimes for which death alone is insufficient punishment ❷ 谴责处罚 punish: 口～笔伐 condemn verbally and in writing

【诛戮】zhūlù〈书 *fml.*〉杀害 kill; put to death: ～忠良 kill the faithful and upright

【诛求】zhūqiú〈书 *fml.*〉勒索 make exorbitant demands; extort; exact: ～无厌 demand greedily; be insatiably avaricious

【诛心之论】zhū xīn zhī lùn 揭穿动机的批评 penetrating criticism; exposure of sb.'s ulterior motives

茱 zhū [茱萸](zhūyú) ☞ 山茱萸 shānzhūyú on p. 1671, 吴茱萸 wúzhūyú on p. 2028 and 食茱萸 shízhūyú on p. 1747

洙 zhū 洙水河(Zhūshuǐ Hé), 洙溪河(Zhūxī Hé), 水名,都在山东 Zhushui River and Zhuxi River, both in Shandong Province

珠 zhū ❶ 珠子 pearl: ～宝 pearls and jewels; jewelry | 夜明～ night-luminescent pearl ❷ (～儿 zhūr) 小的球形的东西 bead: 眼～儿 eyeball; apple of sb.'s eye | 泪～儿 teardrop | 水～儿 a drop of water | 滚～儿 ball (of ball bearing)

【珠宝】zhūbǎo 珍珠宝石一类的饰物 pearls and jewels; jewelry: ～店 jeweler's (shop) | 满身～ resplendent with jewels; bedecked with jewels

【珠翠】zhūcuì 珍珠翠玉,泛指用珍珠翠玉做成的各种装饰品 pearls and jade; ornaments made of pearls and jade: ～满头 be richly decked with head ornaments made of pearls and jade

【珠光宝气】zhū guāng bǎo qì 形容服饰、陈设等非常华丽 resplendent with jewels; bedecked with jewels

【珠玑】zhūjī〈书 *fml.*〉❶ same as 珠子 zhū·zi: 万粒～ ten thousand pearls ❷〈比喻 *fig.*〉优美的文章或词句 beautifully-written article; exquisite diction: 字字～ exquisitely worded piece of writing | 满腹～ be possessed of profound learning

【珠联璧合】zhū lián bì hé 珍珠串在一起,美玉合在一块儿 strings of pearls and girdles of jade;〈比喻 *fig.*〉美好的事物凑在一起 perfect pair; happy combination

【珠算】zhūsuàn 用算盘计算的方法 reckoning by the abacus; calculation using an abacus

【珠圆玉润】zhū yuán yù rùn 像珠子那样圆,像玉石那样滑润。形容歌声婉转优美或文字流畅明快。round as pearls and smooth as jade; excellent singing voice or fluid lucid writing style

【珠子】zhū·zi ❶ 珍珠 pearl ❷ 像珍珠般的颗粒 bead: 汗～ beads of sweat

株 zhū ❶ 露在地面上的树木的根和茎 trunk of a tree; stem of a plant: 守～待兔 wait under a tree, in the hope that a hare might run headlong into its trunk and kill itself ❷ 植株 individual plant; plant: ～距 row spacing|幼～young plant; sapling ❸〈量词 *classifier*〉棵 [used for plants]: 院子里种了两～枣树。In the courtyard grow two jujube trees.

【株距】zhūjù 同一行中相邻的两个植株之间的距离 spacing between two plants in a row

【株连】zhūlián 指一人有罪,牵连别人;连累 involve (others) in a criminal case; implicate: ～九族 implicate nine generations of a family

【株守】zhūshǒu 〈书 *fml*.〉死守不放 hold on stubbornly to (a silly idea, etc.); ☞ 守株待兔 shǒu zhū dài tù on p.1772

诸[1] zhū ❶ 众;许多 all; various: ～位 ladies and gentlemen; all of you|～君 everybody|～侯 dukes or princes under an emperor; feudal princes|～子百家 different philosophers and authors, particularly during the Spring and Autumn and Warring States periods; various schools of thought and their exponents from pre-Qin times to the early years of the Han Dynasty ❷ (Zhū)姓 a surname

诸[2] zhū 〈书 *fml*.〉'之于(於)'或'之乎'的合音 fusing of 之于 zhīyú or of 之乎 zhīhū: 付～实施(=之于) put into effect|数易其稿,而后公～社会(=之于)。It went through several drafts before being published.|有～(=之乎)? Is this true?

【诸多】zhūduō 许多;好些个(用于抽象事物 used for abstract matters) a good deal; a lot of: ～不便 quite a lot of trouble; rather inconvenient|～妨碍 quite a number of obstacles

【诸葛】Zhūgě 姓 a surname

【诸葛亮】Zhūgě Liàng 三国时蜀汉政治家,字孔明,辅佐刘备建立蜀汉。《三国演义》对他的智谋多所渲染,一般用来称足智多谋的人。Zhuge Liang (181-234), style name Kongming, a statesman and strategist during the Three Kingdoms Period (220-265) who helped Liu Bei establish the kingdom of Shu; His wisdom is described in *Romance of Three Kingdoms*, and in Chinese folklore he is regarded as the personification of resourcefulness and wisdom; person of great wisdom and resourcefulness; mastermind

【诸宫调】zhūgōngdiào 宋、金、元的一种说唱文学,以韵文为主要组成成分,夹杂散文说白,叙述一个故事。韵文部分用不同宫调的多组套曲连成很长的篇幅。如金董解元的《弦索西厢》。ballad popular in the Song, Jin and Yuan dynasties, whose long verses are sung to various melodies, and, interspersed with narration, tell a story; Examples include Dong Jieyuan's 'The West Chamber to the Accompaniment of a Stringed Instrument' of the Jin Dynasty.

【诸侯】zhūhóu 〈古代 *arch*.〉帝王统辖下的列国君主的统称 general term for dukes and princes serving an emperor

【诸如】zhūrú 举例用语,放在所举的例子前面,表示不止一个例子[used before examples cited] such as: 他非常关心群众,做了不少好事,～访问职工家属,去医院看病人,等等。He is deeply concerned about the masses and has done a lot of good work, such as visiting the families of workers, and going to see patients in hospital, etc.

【诸如此类】zhū rú cǐ lèi 与此相似的种种事物 whatnot; things of that sort; and suchlike; of that like: ～,不胜枚举。Such instances are too numerous to mention.

【诸位】zhūwèi 〈敬辞 *pol*.〉总称所指的若干人 [used when addressing a group of people] ladies and gentlemen; you: ～同志 comrades|～有何意见,请尽量发表。Your unreserved and honest opinions are appreciated.

铢 zhū 〈古代 *arch*.〉重量单位,一两的二十四分之一 ancient unit of weight, equal to 1/24 *liang*

【铢积寸累】zhū jī cùn lěi 一点一滴地积累 accumulate little by little; build up bit by bit

【铢两悉称】zhūliǎng xī chèn 形容两方面轻重相当或优劣相等 carry the same weight; be exactly equal

猪(豬) zhū 哺乳动物,头大,鼻子和口吻都长,眼睛小,耳朵大,脚短,身体肥。肉供食用,皮可制革,鬃可制刷子和做其他工业原料。pig (*Sus scrofa* var. *domestica*); hog; swine; mammal with large head, long snout, small eyes, big ears, short legs, cloven hooves, and a fleshy body; Its meat is edible, its hide used to make leather, and its bristles to make brushes and as industrial raw materials

【猪倌】zhūguān (～儿 zhūguānr)专职养猪的人 swineherd

【猪獾】zhūhuān 哺乳动物,背部淡黑色或灰色,四肢棕黑色,头部有一条白色纵纹,颈、喉、耳朵和尾部白色。毛皮可以制褥子。hog-badger (*Arctonyx collaris F. cuvier*); mammal with a black or grey back and brownish-black legs, a white strip over its head, and white neck, throat, ears and tail; Its fur can be used to make mattresses. also 沙獾 shāhuān; 有的地区叫獾猪 in some areas called 獾猪 huānzhū

【猪猡】zhūluó 〈方 *dial*.〉猪 pig; swine; hog

【猪排】zhūpái 炸着吃或煎着吃的大片猪肉 pork chop; slice of pork for frying or deep-frying

【猪鬃】zhūzōng 猪的脖颈子上的较长的毛,质硬而韧,可用来制刷子(hog) bristles; long, stiff, hair that grows on the neck of a hog, used to make brushes

蛛 zhū 指蜘蛛 spider:～网 spider web; cobweb|～丝马迹 the thread of a spider and the tracks of a horse; (fig.) clues; traces

【蛛丝马迹】zhū sī mǎ jì〈比喻 *fig.*〉查究事情根源的不很明显的线索 thread of a spider and tracks of a horse; clues; traces

【蛛网】zhūwǎng 蜘蛛结成的网状物。结网的丝是蜘蛛肛门尖端分泌的黏液遇空气凝结而成的。蜘蛛利用蛛网捕食昆虫。spider web; cobweb; web spun by a spider, mucus emanating from the tip of a spider's anus that coagulates into stringy filament, used to trap other insects for food.

【蛛蛛】zhū·zhu 蜘蛛的通称 common name for 蜘蛛 zhīzhū

槠 zhū 常绿乔木,叶子长椭圆形,花黄绿色,果实球形,褐色,有光泽。木材坚硬,可制器具。sweet oak; evergreen tree, with long, oval leaves, yellow-green flowers, spherical lustrous brown fruits, and hard timber that is used to make utensils

潴(瀦) zhū〈书 *fml.*〉❶(水)积聚(of water) collect; accumulate; store:停～stagnate|～积 store up ❷ 水积聚的地方 puddle; pool

【潴留】zhūliú 医学上指液体聚集停留(of fluid) retention:尿～ retention of urine; urinary retention

橥(櫫) zhū〈书 *fml.*〉拴牲口的小木桩 small wooden pile for tethering animals

zhú(ㄓㄨˊ)

术 zhú ☞ 白术 báizhú on p. 39, 苍术 cāngzhú on p. 189 and 莪术 ézhú on p. 504
☞ shù on p. 1787

竹 zhú ❶ 竹子 bamboo:～林 bamboo forest; groves of bamboo|～园 bamboo garden|修～千竿 a thousand tall bamboos ❷(Zhú)姓 a surname

【竹板书】zhúbǎnshū 曲艺的一种,说唱者一手打呱嗒板儿,一手打节子板(用七块小竹板编穿而成) clapper talk; story recited to the rhythm of bamboo clappers, where the performer holds a large, two-piece bamboo clapper in his left hand and a smaller seven-piece clapper in his right; form of Chinese *quyi* (a collective term for Chinese folk art forms including ballad singing, storytelling, comic dialogues, clapper talk, crosstalk, etc.)

【竹编】zhúbiān 用竹篾编制的工艺品,如果盒、提篮等 bambo basketry; bamboo woven articles, such as fruit bowl, hand-basket, etc

【竹帛】zhúbó 竹简和绢,古时用来写字,因此也借指典籍 bamboo slips and silk (used as writing materials in ancient times); ancient books:功垂～ go down in history in gold letters

【竹布】zhúbù 通常指淡蓝色的布纹致密的棉布,用来做夏季服装。也有白色的,叫白竹布。light blue cotton cloth for making summer clothes; also in white, known as 白竹布 báizhúbù

【竹材】zhúcái 竹子采伐后经过初步加工的材料 bamboo wood; bamboo that has undergone initial processing after felling:利用～代替木材 substitute bamboo for timber

【竹雕】zhúdiāo 在竹子上雕刻形象、花纹的艺术。也指用竹子雕刻成的工艺品 bamboo carving; handicrafts carved out of bamboo

【竹竿】zhúgān(～儿 zhúgānr)砍下来的削去枝叶的竹子 bamboo pole:把衣服晾在～上 hang washing out on a bamboo pole to dry

【竹黄】zhúhuáng 一种工艺品。把竹筒去青、煮、晒、压平后,里面向外胶合或镶嵌在木胎上,然后磨光,刻上人物、山水、花鸟等。产品以果盒、文具盒等为主。handicraft articles made from bamboo after its green outer coating has been removed, when it is then boiled, dried, and pressed flat, then pasted or inlaid onto a wooden surface with its inside facing outwards. It is then polished, and carved with patterns such as figures, landscapes, or flowers and birds. Such handicrafts are generally in the form of fruit bowls and stationery receptacles; also 翻黄(翻簧) fānhuáng or 竹簧 zhúhuáng

【竹簧】zhúhuáng same as 竹黄 zhúhuáng

【竹简】zhújiǎn〈古代 *arch.*〉用来写字的竹片 bamboo slip (used for writing)

【竹节虫】zhújiéchóng ❶ 昆虫,身体细长。形状像竹节或树枝,绿色或褐色。头小,无翅。生活在树上,吃树叶。stick insect; phasmid; wingless, stick-like insect, with a small head, and a long narrow body, green or brown in colour, that lives in trees and feeds on leaves; also 蛐 xiū ❷ 蛣(jié) skeleton shrimp

【竹刻】zhúkè 在竹制的器物上雕刻文字图画的艺术 bamboo carving; bamboo engraving; art of carving patterns or texts on bamboo articles

【竹马】zhúmǎ(～儿 zhúmǎr)❶ 儿童放在胯下当马骑的竹竿 bamboo horse; bamboo stick used as a toy horse ❷ 一种民间歌舞用的道具,用竹片、纸、布扎成马形,可系在表演者身上 bamboo hobby horse; horse made of bamboo strips, paper and cloth that is tied to the body of a performer in folk dancing

【竹排】zhúpái 放在江河里的成排地连起来的竹材,使顺流而下,运输到各地 bamboo raft; flat structure consisting of bamboo poles fastened together that floats and that can be used to transport goods as it drifts downstream

【竹器】zhúqì 用竹子做的器物,如竹篮、竹筐、竹椅等 bamboo ware; articles made of bamboo,

such as bamboo baskets, bamboo chairs, etc.

【竹笋】zhúsǔn 笋 bamboo shoots

【竹筒倒豆子】zhútǒng dào dòu·zi 〈比喻 *fig*.〉把事实全部说出来，没有隐瞒 pour beans out of a bamboo tube; own up to (one's crime, wrongdoing, etc.)

【竹叶青】[1] zhúyèqīng 毒蛇的一种，身体绿色，从眼的下部沿着腹部两旁到尾端有黄白色条纹，尾端红褐色。生活在温带和热带地方的树上。green bamboo snake (*Trimeresurus stejnegeri*); venomous snake with a green body and yellow and white stripes from eye to tail, the tip of which is reddish-brown, found living in trees in temperate and tropical zones

【竹叶青】[2] zhúyèqīng ❶ 以汾酒为原酒加入多种药材泡制成的一种略带黄绿色的酒 bamboo leaf green liqueur; pale green liqueur made of Fen Liquor in which medicinal ingredients have been steeped ❷ 绍兴酒的一种，淡黄色 light yellow Shaoxing wine

【竹枝词】zhúzhīcí 〈古代 *arch*.〉富有民歌色彩的诗，形式是七言绝句，语言通俗，音调轻快。最初多是歌唱男女爱情的，以后常用来描写某一地区的风土人情。ancient folk songs with love as their main theme, in the form of a heptasyllabic quatrain, featuring simple language and light tones; a form of poetry in the classical style oft. used for the portrayal of local topics

【竹纸】zhúzhǐ 用嫩的竹子制成的纸 bamboo paper; paper made from young bamboo

【竹子】zhú·zi 常绿植物，茎圆柱形，中空，有节，叶子有平行脉，嫩芽叫笋。种类很多，如淡竹、苦竹。茎可供建筑和制器具用，笋可以吃。bamboo (*Bambuso ideae*); perennial evergreen plant with jointed stems that are woody, hard, springy and hollow, leaves that have parallel veins, and young shoots that are called *sun*, in many varieties, such as henon bamboo (*Phyllostacys nigra* var. *Henonis*) and bitter bamboo (*Pleioblastus amarus*). Its stems are used in construction, and for making furniture, walking sticks, etc., and its young shoots are edible.

竺 Zhú 姓 a surname

逐 zhú ❶ 追赶 pursue; chase: 追～pursue; chase | ～鹿 chase the deer — contend for the throne; bid for state power | 随波～流 drift with the tide; go with the stream ❷ 驱逐 drive out; expel: ～客令 order guests to leave | ～出门外 drive out of the door ❸ 挨着(次序) one by one: ～年 year by year | ～日 day by day | ～条说明 explain item by item

【逐步】zhúbù 一步一步地 step by step; progressively: ～深入 deepen step by step | 工作～开展起来了。The work is carried out step by step.

【逐个】zhúgè 一个一个地 one by one: ～清点 sort and count one by one | ～检查产品的质量 check the quality of the products one by one

【逐渐】zhújiàn 渐渐；逐步 gradually; by degrees: 影响～扩大。The influence is gradually expanding. | 事业～发展。The undertaking is gradually developing. | 天色～暗了下来。It is getting darker and darker.

【逐客令】zhúkèlìng 秦始皇曾经下令驱逐从各国来的客卿，后来称赶走客人为下逐客令 show sb. the door; order guests to leave; Emperor Qinshihuang once issued orders to expel all foreign-born government officials, and the expression *xia zhukeling* is now used to mean asking a visitor to leave.

【逐鹿】zhúlù 〈书 *fml*.〉《史记·淮阴侯列传》:'秦失其鹿，天下共逐之' *Records of the Historian · Biography of Marquis of Huaiyin*: 'The Qin had lost the stag (imperial power) and all the world pursued it.' chase the deer; 〈比喻 *fig*.〉争夺天下 contend for the throne; bid for state power: ～中原 chase the deer over the Central Plains—try to seize control of the empire | 群雄～ feudal lords vying for the throne; powerful politicians fighting for supremacy

【逐年】zhúnián 一年一年地 on a yearly or annual basis; year by year; year after year: 产量～增长。Production has increased year upon year.

【逐日】zhúrì 一天一天地 on a daily basis; daily; day by day; every day: 废品率～下降。The reject rate for the products drops day by day.

【逐一】zhúyī same as 逐个 zhúgè: ～清点 check and sort out one by one | 对这几个问题～举例说明。Illustrate all these problems using examples, one by one.

【逐字逐句】zhú zì zhú jù 挨次序一字一句地 word for word and sentence by sentence; word for word: ～仔细讲解 explain sth. in detail, word for word, sentence by sentence

烛(燭) zhú ❶ 蜡烛 candle: 火～ things that may cause fire | 洞房花～ wedding candles burning in a bridal chamber; wedding festivities ❷ 〈书 *fml*.〉照亮；照见 illuminate; light up: 火光～天。The blaze lit up the sky. ◇洞～其奸 see through sb.'s tricks ❸ 俗称多少烛的电灯泡，指灯泡的瓦特数，如 50 烛的灯泡就是 50 瓦特的灯泡 common name for 瓦特 watt, e.g. a 50 candelas is a 50-candela bulb

【烛花】zhúhuā 蜡烛燃烧时烛心结成的花状物 snuff; charred end of a candlewick

【烛泪】zhúlèi 指蜡烛燃烧时淌下的蜡油 gluttenings of a candle

【烛台】zhútái 插蜡烛的器具，多用铜锡等金属制成 candlestick; cupped or spiked holder for a candle or candles, generally made of metal such as copper or tin

【烛照】zhúzhào〈书 *fml.*〉照亮 illuminate; light up:阳光～万物。The sun illuminates all things on earth.

舳 zhú [舳舻](zhúlú)〈书 *fml.*〉指首尾衔接的船只 convoy of ships, sailing in stem-to-stern formation (舳 *zhu*: 船尾 stern; 舻 *lu*: 船头 stem): ～相继 convoy of ships, stem-to-stern|～千里。The fleet stretches from stem to stern for a thousand *li*.

瘃 zhú〈书 *fml.*〉冻疮 chilblain: 冻～chilblain

蠋 zhú 蝴蝶、蛾等的幼虫 larva of a butterfly or moth

躅(蠾) zhú ☞ [踯躅](zhízhú) on p. 2464

zhǔ(ㄓㄨˇ)

主 zhǔ ❶ 接待别人的人(跟'客、宾'相对 as opposed to 'guest' or 'visitor') host: 宾～guest and host|东道～ host ❷ 权力或财物的所有者 owner: 物～owner of property|车～owner of a car|物归原～return sth. to its rightful owner ❸ 旧社会中占有奴隶或雇用仆役的人(跟'奴、仆'相对 as opposed to 'slave' or 'servant') master: ～仆 master and servant|奴隶～slave owner ❹ 当事人 person or party concerned: 失～owner of lost property|事～ victim of a crime|卖～seller|～顾 customer; client ❺ 基督教徒对上帝、伊斯兰教徒对真主的称呼(*Christ.*) God; Lord; (*Islam*) Allah ❻ 最重要的;最基本的 main; primary: ～要 main|～力 main force; main strength of an army ❼ 负主要责任;主持 manage; direct; be in charge of: ～办 sponsor|～讲 give a lecture ❽ 主张 advocate: ～战 advocate war|～和 advocate peace; stand for negotiation|力～改革 do one's utmost to advocate reform ❾ 预示(吉凶祸福、自然变化等) indicate; signify (one's fate or changes of nature): 左眼跳～财,右眼跳～灾。(迷信) (superstition) Twitching of the left eyelid signifies fortune; and twitching of the right signifies calamity.|早霞～雨,晚霞～晴。Rosy morning clouds indicate rain, and a rosy sunset means fine weather. ❿ 对事情的确定的见解 hold a definite view about sth.: 他心里没～。He did not know what to do. ⓫ 从自身出发的 subjective: ～动 initiative|～观 subjective ⓬ 死人的牌位 memorial tablet of the deceased: 神～spirit tablet|木～ sacred wooden tablets ⓭ (Zhǔ)姓 a surname

【主办】zhǔbàn 主持办理;主持举办 direct; sponsor; host: ～世界杯足球赛 host the World Cup football tournament|展览会由我们单位～。The exhibition is sponsored by our unit.

【主笔】zhǔbǐ 指报刊编辑部中负责撰写评论的人,也指编辑部的负责人 chief commentator (of the editorial board of a publication); editor-in-chief (of an editorial board)

【主币】zhǔbì 本位货币(跟'辅币'相对 as opposed to 'fractional currency') standard currency; standard money

【主编】zhǔbiān ❶ 负编辑工作的主要责任 supervise the publication (of a newspaper, magazine, etc.); edit: 他～一本语文杂志。He edits a Chinese language magazine. ❷ 编辑工作的主要负责人 chief editor (or compiler); editor-in-chief: 他是这本语文杂志的～。He is the editor-in-chief of this Chinese language magazine.

【主场】zhǔchǎng 体育比赛中,主队所在地的场地对主队来说叫主场 home court; host arena; arena of the host team in a sports competition

【主持】zhǔchí ❶ 负责掌握或处理 take charge (or care) of; manage; direct: ～人 anchorperson|～会议 preside over a meeting; take the chair ❷ 主张;维护 uphold; stand for: ～公道 uphold justice|～正义 uphold justice

【主词】zhǔcí 一个命题的三部分之一,表示思考的对象,如'糖是甜的'这个命题中的'糖'是主词 subject term; subject; one of the three parts of a proposition, indicating the object for thinking. For instance, in the proposition 'Sugar is sweet,' sugar is the subject.

【主次】zhǔcì 主要的和次要的 primary and secondary: 分清～differentiate what is primary from what is secondary

【主从】zhǔcóng 主要的和从属的 principal and subordinate: ～关系 relationship between the principal and the subordinate

【主刀】zhǔdāo (医生)主持并亲自做手术 operate; act as surgeon (in a surgical operation): 由外科主任亲自～。The director of the surgical department personally carries out surgical operations.

【主导】zhǔdǎo ❶ 主要的并且引导事物向某方面发展的 leading; dominant; guiding: ～思想 dominant ideas; guiding ideology|～作用 leading role ❷ 起主导作用的事物 leading factor: 我国国民经济的发展以农业为基础,工业为～。Development of our national economy takes agriculture as its base and industry as the leading factor.

【主动】zhǔdòng ❶ 不待外力推动而行动(跟'被动'相对 as opposed to 'passive') initiative; act without outside impetus: ～性 initiative|～争取 take the initiative to win over ❷ 能够造成有利局面,使事情按照自己的意图进行(跟'被动'相对 as opposed to 'be thrown into passivity') take the initiative; do sth. of one's own accord: ～权 initiative|争取～try to gain the initiative; contend for the initiative | 处于～地位 find oneself in an advantageous position

【主动脉】zhǔdòngmài 人体内最粗大的动脉，从左心室发出，向上向右再向下略呈弓状，再沿脊柱向下行，在胸腹等分出很多较小的动脉。是向全身各部输送血液的主要导管。aorta; large artery that constitutes the main trunk of the systemic arterial system, arising from the base of the left ventricle of the heart, and turning up, right, and back down in the shape of an arch, running down along the vertebra, and dividing to form smaller arteries at the chest cavity; carries blood to all parts of the body; also 大动脉 dàdòngmài

【主动脉弓】zhǔdòngmàigōng 主动脉从左心室向上行，然后向右，再沿脊柱向下行，这一段主动脉略呈弓状，叫主动脉弓 arch of the aorta; aorta that rises from the base of the left ventricle of the heart, turns right, and then downward along the vertebra, in the shape of an arch; also 动脉弓 dòngmàigōng; (图见 ☞ figure for 心 xīn on p. 2126)

【主队】zhǔduì 体育比赛中，和客队比赛的本单位或本地、本国的体育代表队叫主队 home team; host team; the team representing a local unit, region or country, that plays a visiting team in a sports competition

【主伐】zhǔfá 砍伐已经长成可以利用的森林。主伐不仅为获取木材，同时还为了森林更新，培育后一代森林。final felling (or cutting); The aim of felling mature trees is not only to gain timber, but also to renew a forest.

【主犯】zhǔfàn 在共同犯罪中起主要和组织作用的罪犯（区别于'从犯' as compared with 'accessory' to a crime) prime culprit; principal criminal (or offender); principal

【主峰】zhǔfēng 山脉的最高峰 highest peak in a mountain range

【主父】Zhǔfù 姓 a surname

【主妇】zhǔfù 一家的女主人 housewife; hostess: 家庭～housewife

【主干】zhǔgàn ❶ 植物的主要的茎 trunk; main stem of a plant ❷ 主要的、起决定作用的力量 main force; mainstay: 中青年教师是教育战线的～。Middle-aged and young teachers are the mainstay of the educational front.

【主根】zhǔgēn 植物最初生长出来的根，是由胚根突出种皮后发育而成的，通常是垂直向地下生长，并长出许多侧根，组成根系 main root; taproot; primary root that develops from the radicle after breaking through the seed coat, and that grows vertically downward, from which small lateral roots grow outwards to form the root system

【主攻】zhǔgōng 集中主要兵力在主要方向上进攻（区别于'助攻' as compared with 'holding or secondary attack') main attack; attack in the main direction along with concentrated main force: ～部队 main attack force | 指战员纷纷请战，要求担负～任务。Officers and men alike requested battle assignments one after another, demanding to serve as the main attack force.

【主顾】zhǔgù 顾客 customer; client: 老～regular customer | 招揽～solicit customers

【主观】zhǔguān ❶ 属于自我意识方面的（跟'客观'相对 as opposed to 'objective') subjective; arising from conditions within the brain or sense organs and not directly caused by external stimuli: ～愿望 subjective desire; wishful thinking | ～能动性 subjective initiative; conscious activity ❷ 不依据实际情况，单凭自己的偏见的（跟'客观'相对 as opposed to 'objective') subjective; peculiar to a particular individual: 看问题不要～片面。When considering a problem, try to avoid being subjective or partisan.

【主观能动性】zhǔguān néngdòngxìng 人的主观意识和行动对于客观世界的反作用。辩证唯物主义认为主观能动性是人在实践中认识客观规律，并根据客观规律自觉地改造世界，推动事物发展的能力和作用。subjective initiative; conscious activity; reaction of the human subjective consciousness to the objective world and resultant human action. Dialectical materialists hold that subjective initiative is a human ability and function, through whose practice they come to understand objective laws, according to which they consciously transform the world, and promote the development of things.

【主观唯心主义】zhǔguān wéixīn zhǔyì 唯心主义哲学的一个派别，否认世界的物质性，认为存在只是'我'的感觉，物质世界只是人的主观意识的体现或产物 subjective idealism; school of idealist philosophy that denies the existence of the material world, regarding existence as nothing but a sensation of 'ego,' and a mere reflection or product of human subjective consciousness.

【主观主义】zhǔguān zhǔyì 一种唯心主义的思想作风，特点是不从客观实际出发，而从主观愿望和臆想出发来认识和对待事物，以致主观和客观分离，理论和实践脱节。主观主义有时表现为教条主义，有时表现为经验主义。subjectivism; idealist style of thinking that rejects objective realities, treating matter solely on the basis of idealist wishes and conjecture, resulting in a departure of the subjective from the objective, and of practice from theory. Subjectivism might manifest itself as dogmatism, or as empiricism.

【主管】zhǔguǎn ❶ 负主要责任管理（某一方面）be responsible for; be in charge of: ～部门 department responsible for the work | ～原料收购和产品销售 be responsible for the purchase of raw materials and marketing of products ◇听神经～听觉和身体平衡的感觉。The sensations of hearing and balance come under the auspices of the acoustic nerve. ❷ 主管的人员 person in charge：财务～treasurer

【主婚】zhǔhūn 主持婚礼 preside over a wedding ceremony：～人 person who presides over a wedding ceremony

【主机】zhǔjī ❶ 长机（zhǎngjī）lead aircraft；leader ❷ 成套动力设备中起主要作用的机器，如轮船上的动力系统的发动机、汽轮发电机组中的汽轮发电机 main engine；machine that plays the main role in a complete set of powered equipment, such as the engine in the dynamic system of a ship, and the turbo-generators in a turbo-generating set

【主祭】zhǔjì 主持祭礼 officiate at funeral or sacrificial rites：～人 one who officiates at funeral or sacrificial rites

【主见】zhǔjiàn（对事情的）确定的意见 ideas or thoughts of one's own；one's own judgment；definite view：众说纷纭，他也没了～。As general opinions vary, he has no definite views of his own.

【主讲】zhǔjiǎng 担任讲授或讲演 be the speaker；give a lecture：王教授～隋唐文学。Professor Wang is to give a lecture on the literature of the Sui and Tang dynasties.｜这次动员大会由他～。He will speak at the mobilization meeting.

【主将】zhǔjiàng ❶ 主要的将领 chief commander；commanding general：中军～commanding general of the middle army ❷〈比喻 *fig.*〉在某方面起主要作用的人 one who plays the main role in a certain field of endeavour：鲁迅是中国文化革命的～。Lu Xun was a leading figure in the cultural revolution of China.

【主教】zhǔjiào 天主教、东正教的高级神职人员，通常是一个地区教会的首领。新教的某些教派也沿用这个名称。bishop；Anglican, Eastern Orthodox, or Roman Catholic clergyman of a higher order than a priest, that usu. governs a diocese. Certain divisions of the Protestant church also use this title.

【主角】zhǔjué（～儿 zhǔjuér）❶ 指戏剧、电影等艺术表演中的主要角色或主要演员 leading role；lead；protagonist (in a drama or movie) ❷〈比喻 *fig.*〉主要人物 main personages：那次事变的几个～已先后去世。The main personages involved in that incident have since died, one after another.

【主考】zhǔkǎo ❶ 主持考试 be in charge of an examination：校长亲临考场～。The headmaster personally invigilated the examination. ❷ 主持考试的人 chief examiner (in a school, etc.)

【主课】zhǔkè 学习的主要课程 major；main subject；major course：语文、数学、政治、外语是中学的～。Chinese, mathematics, politics and foreign language are the main subjects in a middle school curriculum.

【主力】zhǔlì 主要力量 main force；main strength of an army：～军 main force｜～部队 principal force｜～队员 principal member (of a team)｜球队～top player of a ball team

【主力舰】zhǔlìjiàn〈旧时 *old*〉指海上作战的主力战舰，包括战列舰和巡洋舰 capital ship, including battleships and cruisers

【主力军】zhǔlìjūn ❶ 担负作战主力的部队 main force (of an army) ❷〈比喻 *fig.*〉起主要作用的力量 force that plays a major role

【主粮】zhǔliáng 各地区生产和消费的粮食中占主要地位的粮食，如长江流域的主粮是大米 staple food grain；food grain that occupies the leading position in the production and consumption of grain in a given region, e. g. rice is the main staple food grain of the Yangtze River Valley

【主流】zhǔliú ❶ 干流 trunk stream；mainstream ❷〈比喻 *fig.*〉事情发展的主要方面 essential or main aspect；main trend：我们必须分清～和支流，区别本质和现象。It is essential to distinguish the main aspect from the minor, and the essence from mere appearance.

【主楼】zhǔlóu 楼群中主要的一幢楼。楼群中其他楼房的设计、位置等与主楼相配合。main building；main building in a group. The buildings surrounding the main building are required to match it in design and layout.

【主麻】zhǔmá 伊斯兰教徒做集体礼拜，在每周的星期五午后举行，伊斯兰教定星期五为礼拜日，称主麻日。伊斯兰教徒习惯称一周为一个主麻。Djumah (Friday)；gathering of Islamic believers each Friday afternoon. Moslems consider Friday as a day of worship (Day of Djumah). By habit Moslems regard a week as a 'djumah.' [阿拉伯 Arabian：jum'a]

【主谋】zhǔmóu ❶ 共同做坏事时做主要的谋划者 head a conspiracy；be chief plotter ❷ 主谋的人 chief instigator

【主脑】zhǔnǎo ❶ 主要的、起决定作用的部分 control centre；centre of operations ❷ 首领 leader；chief

【主权】zhǔquán 一个国家在其领域内拥有的最高权力。根据这种权力，国家按照自己的意志决定对内对外政策，处理国内国际一切事务，而不受任何外来干涉。sovereign rights；sovereignty；supreme power of a country exercised within its territory. With this power, the country decides its domestic and foreign policies and handles all domestic and international affairs, free from external interference.

【主儿】zhǔr ❶ 指主人 master；employer ❷ 指

Z

某种类型的人 person of a specified type：这～真不讲理。This guy is utterly unreasonable.｜他是说到做到的～。He is a person who lives up to his word. ❸ 指婆家 husband or fiancé：她快三十了，也该找～了。She is about thirty, and it is time she found a husband.

【主人】zhǔ·rén ❶ 接待客人的人（跟'客人'相对 as opposed to 'guest'）host; one that receives guests ❷〈旧时 *old*〉聘用家庭教师、账房等的人；雇用仆人的人 master; head of a household that hires private tutors, accountants, etc.; one who employs servants ❸ 财物或权力的所有人 owner (of property or power)：磨坊～mill owner

【主人公】zhǔréngōng 指文艺作品中的中心人物 leading character (in a novel, etc.); hero or heroine; protagonist

【主人翁】zhǔrénwēng ❶ 当家做主的人 master：劳动人民成了国家的～。The working people have become the masters of the country. ❷ same as 主人公 zhǔréngōng

【主任】zhǔrèn 职位名称，一个部门或机构的主要负责人 director; head; chairman (of a department or an organisation)：办公室～office director｜车间～head of the workshop｜居民委员会～chairman of the neighbourhood committee

【主食】zhǔshí 主要食物，一般指用粮食制成的，如米饭、馒头等 staple food; principal food, usu. a cereal, such as rice or steamed buns

【主使】zhǔshǐ 出主意使别人去做坏事；指使 instigate; incite; abet：受人～under sb.'s instigation; act on sb.'s instigation

【主事】zhǔ//shì (～儿 zhǔ//shìr)主管事情 be in charge; take charge：～人 person in charge｜当家～be master of one's own house｜前几年他还主过事。He was in charge several years ago.

【主视图】zhǔshìtú 由物体正前方向后做正投影得到的视图 front view; elevation; a view obtained by making an orthographic projection of an object from the front

【主诉】zhǔsù 医疗机构指病人看病时对自己病情的陈述 chief complaint; when a patient describes his or her own ailment to a doctor in a medical institution

【主题】zhǔtí ❶ 文学、艺术作品中所表现的中心思想，是作品思想内容的核心 theme (of a literary or art work); subject; motif; leitmotiv ❷ 泛指谈话、文件等的主要内容 main contents (of a speech, document, etc.)：～词 subject term｜年终分配成了人们议论的～。Year-end distribution has become the main subject of discussion among the people.

【主题词】zhǔtící 用来标明图书、文件等主题的词或词组 theme word; catch phrase; word or phrase that indicates the subject of a book or document

【主题歌】zhǔtígē 电影、歌剧、话剧、电视剧中能概括地表现主题的歌曲 theme song; the song preceding a movie, opera, or stage or TV play, that epitomizes its theme

【主体】zhǔtǐ ❶ 事物的主要部分 centrepiece; main body; main part; principal part：工人、农民和知识分子是国家的～。Workers, peasants and intellectuals constitute the main body of the country.｜中央的十层大厦是这个建筑群的～。The ten-storey tower at the centre is the centrepiece of the complex. ❷ 哲学上指有认识和实践能力的人（philos.）subject; one that has the capability to understand and practise; ☞ 客体 kètǐ ①on p.1098 ❸ 法律上指依法享有权利和承担义务的自然人、法人或国家 subject; natural person, legal person or state that enjoys rights and performs duties according to law; ☞ 客体 kètǐ ② on p.1098

【主文】zhǔwén 判决书的结论部分 concluding part of a court verdict

【主席】zhǔxí ❶ 主持会议的人 chairman (of a meeting) ❷ 某些国家、国家机关、党派或团体某一级组织的最高领导职位名称 chairman; president (of an organisation, institution, party or state)

【主席团】zhǔxítuán 委员会或会议的集体领导组织 presidium; collective leading body of a committee or conference

【主线】zhǔxiàn 指贯穿事物发展过程的主要线索。特指文艺作品故事情节发展的主要线索。thread; an element suggestive of a thread for its continuity; main thread (of a novel, etc.)

【主心骨】zhǔxīngǔ (～儿 zhǔxīngǔr) ❶ 可依靠的人或事物 backbone; mainstay; pillar：你来了，我可有了～了！You have come, and now I have someone to depend on. ❷ 主见；主意 definite view; one's own judgment：事情来得太突然，一时间我也没了～。It happened suddenly, and for a moment I did not know what to do.

【主星】zhǔxīng 双星中较亮的一颗，伴星围绕着它旋转 primary (component); the brighter of a binary star, around which its companion orbits

【主刑】zhǔxíng 可以独立应用的刑罚，如有期徒刑、无期徒刑等（区别于'从刑' as compared with 'accessory penalty'）principal penalty; penalty that can be meted out independently, such as fixed-term imprisonment, life imprisonment, etc.

【主旋律】zhǔxuánlǜ ❶ 指多声部演唱或演奏的音乐中，一个声部所唱或所奏的主要曲调，其他声部只起润色、丰富、烘托、补充的作用 main melody; the main theme within concerted songs or music, to which others are complementary ❷〈比喻 *fig.*〉主要精神；基本观点 theme; gistname of the game：改革是这个报

告的～。The theme of this report is reform.

【主演】zhǔyǎn ❶ 扮演戏剧或电影中的主角 act the leading role (in a play or film); star:他一生～过几十部电影。He starred in dozens of films during his lifetime. ❷ 指担任主演工作的人 leading performer

【主要】zhǔyào 有关事物中最重要的;起决定作用的 main; chief; principal; major:～原因 main reasons|～目的 major objective|～人物 major characters

【主义】zhǔyì ❶ 对客观世界、社会生活以及学术问题等所持有的系统的理论和主张 -ism; systematic doctrine or theory on the objective world, society, or academic issues:马克思列宁～Marxism-Leninism|达尔文～Darwinism|现实～realism|浪漫～ romanticism ❷ 思想作风 ideological style:本位～selfish departmentalism|自由～liberalism|主观～ subjectivism ❸ 一定的社会制度;政治经济体系 social system; politico-economic system:社会～socialism|资本～capitalism

【主意】zhǔ·yi ❶ 主见 idea; plan:大家七嘴八舌地一说,他倒拿不定～了。With so many people trying to get a word in all at once, he was quite at a loss as to a definite plan. ❷ 办法 decision; definite view:出～offer advice|馊～ stupid suggestion; lousy idea|这个～好。That's a good idea. |人多～多。The more people there are, the greater the ferment of ideas will occur.

【主语】zhǔyǔ 谓语的陈述对象,指出谓语说的是谁或者是什么的句子成分。一般的句子都包括主语部分和谓语部分,主语部分里的主要的词是主语。例如在'我们的生活很幸福'里,'生活'是主语,'我们的生活'是主语部分(有些语法书里称主语部分为主语,称主语为主词)。subject; element of a sentence, about which something is said in the predicate. In general, a sentence comprises a subject part and a predicate part; the major word in the subject part is the subject. For instance, in the sentence 'Our life is happy,' 'life' is the subject, and 'our life' is the subject part. (In some grammar books, the subject part is called the subject, and the subject is called *zhuci*.)

【主宰】zhǔzǎi ❶ 支配;统治;掌握 dominate; dictate; decide:～万物 dominate all things in creation|迷信的人总以为人的命运是由上天～的。The superstitious hold that humankind's destiny is dominated by providence. ❷ 掌握、支配人或事物的力量 force that dominates the destiny of people or determines the development of matters:思想是人们行动的～。A man's actions are determined by his thinking. |中国人民已经成为自己命运的～。The Chinese people have become masters of their own fate.

【主张】zhǔzhāng ❶ 对于如何行动持有某种见解 advocate; stand for; maintain; hold:他～马上动身。He advocates starting immediately. ❷ 对于如何行动所持有的见解 view; position; stand; proposition:自作～act on one's own; decide for oneself|这两种～都有理由。Both propositions are reasonable.

【主旨】zhǔzhǐ 主要的意义、用意或目的 purport; substance; gist:文章的～不清楚。The gist of this article is not clear.

【主轴】zhǔzhóu 指机械中从发动机或电动机接受动力并将动力传给其他机件的轴 principal axis; main shaft; spindle; shaft that receives power from an engine or electric motor and transmits it to other parts of a machine

【主子】zhǔ·zi 〈旧时 *old*〉奴仆称主人,现多比喻操纵、主使的人 master; boss; manipulator

讠(詝) zhǔ 〈书 *fml.*〉智慧 wisdom

拄 zhǔ 为了支持身体用棍杖等顶住地面 lean on (a stick, etc.):～着拐棍儿走 walk with the help of a stick

渚 zhǔ 〈书 *fml.*〉水中间的小块陆地 islet; small piece of land surrounded by water

煮 zhǔ 把食物或其他东西放在有水的锅里烧 boil; cook; stew; heat food or other things in a container filled with water:～饺子 boil jiaozi|饭还没～好。The rice is not yet cooked. |病人的碗筷每餐之后要～一下。Patients' bowls and chopsticks should be boiled after each use.

【煮豆燃萁】zhǔ dòu rán qí 相传魏文帝曹丕叫他弟弟曹植做诗,限他在走完七步之前做成,否则就要杀他。曹植立刻就做了一首诗:'煮豆持作羹,漉豉以为汁。萁在釜下燃,豆在釜中泣。本自同根生,相煎何太急'(见于《世说新语·文学》)。比喻兄弟间自相残害。burn beanstalks to cook beans; (fig.) fratricidal strife. It is said that Cao Pi, Emperor Wendi of the kingdom of Wei, demanded of his younger brother Cao Zhi that he compose a poem in the time it took him to walk seven paces, promising that his life would be spared if he succeeded. Cao Zhi improvised immediately: 'They were boiling beans on a beanstalk fire,/ Came a plaintive voice from the pot,/ "O why, since we sprung from the selfsame root,/ Should you kill me with anger hot?"' (*A New Account of Tales of the World·Letters and Scholarship*)

【煮鹤焚琴】zhǔ hè fén qín 把鹤煮了吃,拿琴当柴烧 cook a crane for meat and burn a stringed instrument for fuel;〈比喻 *fig.*〉做杀风景的事 destroy sth. valuable; spoil sth. nice

属(屬) zhǔ 〈书 *fml.*〉❶ 连缀;连续 join; combine:～文 compose a piece of prose writing|前后相～(of two parts) join together ❷（意念）集中在一点 fix (one's mind) on; centre (one's attention, etc.) upon：～意 fix one's mind on sb. or sth. (as one's choice, favourite, etc.)｜～望 centre one's hopes on; look forward to ❸〈古 *arch.*〉same as 嘱 zhǔ

☞ shǔ on p. 1785

【属望】zhǔwàng〈书 *fml.*〉期望；期待 hope; look forward to

【属意】zhǔyì 意向专注于（某人或某事物）fix one's mind on sb. or sth. (as one's choice, favourite, etc.)：他兴趣转移后，不再～诗文。Since his interest was diverted, poetry is no longer his main pursuit.

【属垣有耳】zhǔ yuán yǒu ěr 有人靠着墙偷听 walls have ears; beware of eavesdroppers

褚 zhǔ〈书 *fml.*〉❶ 丝绵 silk floss; silk wadding ❷ 在衣服里铺丝绵 pad with silk wadding ❸ 口袋 bag; satchel

☞ Chǔ on p. 294

劚（斸、斲） zhǔ〈书 *fml.*〉砍；斫 chop; cut; hack

嘱（囑） zhǔ 嘱咐；嘱托 enjoin; advise; urge：叮～urge again and again; exhort｜遗～testament; will｜医～doctor's advice; doctor's orders

【嘱咐】zhǔ·fù 告诉对方记住应该怎样，不应该怎样 enjoin; advise; urge：再三～exhort again and again; din sth. into sb.｜～孩子好好学习 urge a child to study hard

【嘱托】zhǔtuō 托（人办事）；托付 entrust：妈妈出国之前，～舅舅照应家事。Before going abroad, my mum entrusted my uncle to take care of household affairs.

麈 zhǔ 古书上指鹿一类的动物，尾巴可以做拂尘 elk; a species of deer as described in ancient books, the tail of which can be made into a whisk or swatter

瞩（矚） zhǔ 注视 gaze; look steadily：～目 fix one's eyes upon; focus one's attention upon｜～望 look forward to｜高瞻远～stand tall and see afar; take a broad and long view; show great foresight

【瞩目】zhǔmù〈书 *fml.*〉注目 fix one's eyes upon; focus one's attention upon：举世～be the focus of worldwide attention｜万众～attract the attention of millions of people

【瞩望】zhǔwàng〈书 *fml.*〉❶ same as 属望 zhǔwàng ❷ 注视 gaze at; look long and steadily upon：举目～raise the eyes to gaze at

zhù（ㄓㄨˋ）

伫（佇、竚） zhù〈书 *fml.*〉伫立 stand for a long while：～候 stand waiting｜～听风雨声 stand still and listen to the sound of wind and rain

【伫候】zhùhòu〈书 *fml.*〉站着等候，泛指等候 stand waiting; wait：～佳音 look forward to your good news｜～光临。I look forward to your coming.

【伫立】zhùlì〈书 *fml.*〉长时间地站着 stand still for a long while：凝神～stand still in deep concentration｜～窗前 stand still before the window

苎（苧） zhù［苎麻］(zhùmá) ❶ 多年生草本植物，茎直立，高可达 7 尺，叶子互生，卵圆形或心脏形，花绿色，单性，雌雄同株。茎皮纤维洁白有光泽，拉力和耐热力强，是纺织工业的重要原料。ramie (*Boehmeria nivea*); herbaceous monoecious perennial that grows as tall as 7 *chi*, with oval, alternate leaves, and green unisexual flowers. Its bast fibre is white and lustrous, with a strong pulling force and high heat-durability, and is an important raw material in the textile industry. ❷ 这种植物的茎皮纤维 bast fibre of this plant.

☞ 苧 níng on p. 1417

芧 zhù〈书 *fml.*〉same as 苎 zhù

☞ xù on p. 2166

助 zhù 帮助；协助 help; assist; aid：互～help each other｜～人为乐 take pleasure in helping others; delight in helping others｜爱莫能～be willing to help but unable to do so｜～我一臂之力 lend me a hand

【助产士】zhùchǎnshì 受过助产专业教育，能独立接生和护理产妇的中级医务人员 midwife; intermediate-level medical worker qualified to practise midwifery, having specialized training in gynecology and child care, and the ability to carry out emergency measures in the absence of medical help

【助词】zhùcí 独立性最差、意义最不实在的一种特殊的虚词，包括：auxiliary word, an unstressed form word, e.g. a)结构助词，如'的、地、得、所' performing the grammatical functions of structure, such as 的·de, 地·de, 得·de, 所 suǒ b)时态助词，如'了、着、过' performing the grammatical functions of tense, such as 了·le, 着·zhe, 过·guo c)语气助词，如'呢、吗、吧、啊' performing the grammatical functions of mood, such as 呢·ne, 吗·ma, 吧·ba, 啊·a.

【助动词】zhùdòngcí 动词的一类，表示可能、应该、必须、愿望等意思，如'能、会、可以、可能、该、应该、得(děi)、必须、要、肯、敢、愿意'。助动词通常用在动词或形容词前边。'我要糖'、'他会英文'里的'要、会'是一般动词。auxiliary verb that expresses 'maybe, should, must, or wish', such as 能 néng, 会 huì, 可以 kěyǐ, 可能 kěnéng, 该 gāi, 应该 yīnggāi, 得 děi, 必须 bìxū, 要 yào, 肯 kěn, 敢 gǎn, 愿意 yuànyì. In general, an auxiliary verb is placed before a verb or an adjective. In the sentences '我要

糖(I want candy)' and '他会英文(He knows English),' 要 yào and 会 huì are ordinary verbs.

【助攻】zhùgōng 以部分兵力在次要方向上进攻(区别于'主攻' as compared with 'main attack') holding (or secondary) attack

【助教】zhùjiào 高等学校中职别最低的教师 assistant (the lowest rank of college faculty)

【助桀为虐】zhù Jié wéi nüè 〈比喻 *fig.*〉帮助坏人做坏事 aid King Jie in his tyrannical rule; aid and abet an evil-doer; also 助纣为虐 zhù Zhòu wéi nüè (桀是夏朝的末了一个王,纣是商朝的末了一个王,相传都是暴君 Both King Jie, the last monarch of the Xia Dynasty, and King Zhou, the last monarch of the Shang Dynasty, were tyrants.)

【助理】zhùlǐ 协助主要负责人办事的(多用于职位名称 usu. used in titles) assistant; one who assists:～人员 assistant personnel|～编辑 assistant editor|～研究员 assistant research fellow|部长～assistant minister

【助跑】zhùpǎo 体育运动中有些项目,如跳高、跳远、投掷标枪或手榴弹,在跳、投等开始前先跑一段,这种动作叫助跑 run-up; approach; the taking of preliminary steps in certain sports events, such as high jump, long jump, javelin, and hand grenade

【助燃】zhùrán 一种物质,本身不能燃烧,在其他物质燃烧时能提供燃烧所需的氧,叫做助燃 combustion-supporting; substance that does not itself burn but that can provide the oxygen needed to help other substances burn

【助手】zhùshǒu 不独立承担任务,只协助别人进行工作的人 assistant; helper; aide; person who helps others at work:得力～capable assistant; right-hand man

【助听器】zhùtīngqì 辅助听觉的一种器械,利用声学原理,把声波集中起来送入耳内,或者利用电学原理,把受话器或话筒所接收的声波放大后送入耳内,使重听的人听到声音 audiphone; hearing aid; deaf-aid; device designed to bring sound more effectively into the ear. It works on acoustic principles, concentrating sound waves as they enter the ear, or electric principles, amplifying sound waves through a receiver before they enter the ear.

【助威】zhù//wēi 帮助增加声势 boost the morale of; cheer (for):呐喊～shout encouragement

【助兴】zhù//xìng 帮助增加兴致 liven things up; add to the fun:席间有杂技表演～。Acrobatics will be performed at the banquet for added entertainment.|您来段京剧给大伙儿助助兴吧! Sing us a Peking Opera aria, and liven things up a little.

【助学金】zhùxuéjīn 政府发给学生的补助金 stipend; grant-in-aid; a fixed sum of money for students provided by the government

【助战】zhù//zhàn ❶ 协助作战 assist in fighting (a battle) ❷ 助威 bolster sb.'s morale

【助长】zhùzhǎng 帮助增长(多指坏的方面 oft. derog.) encourage; abet; put a premium on:姑息迁就,势必～不良风气的蔓延。Overindulgence or being too accommodating encourages evil tendencies.

【助纣为虐】zhù Zhòu wéi nüè ☞ 助桀为虐 zhù Jié wéi nüè

住 zhù ❶ 居住;住宿 live; reside; stay:你～在什么地方? Where do you live?|～了一夜 stay overnight ❷ 停住;止住 stop; cease:～手 stop; hands off|～嘴 shut up|雨～了。The rain has stopped. ❸ 做动词的补语[used after a verb as complement] a)表示牢固或稳当 firmly:拿～hold tight|捉～seize hold of sth. or sb.|把～了方向盘 hold the steering wheel firmly|牢牢记～老师的教导。Keep firmly in mind the teacher's instructions. b)表示停顿或静止 to a stop:一句话把他问～了。He was stumped by this question.|当时他就愣～了。He was immediately struck dumb. c)跟'得'(或'不')连用,表示力量够得上(或够不上);胜任[used after 得 dé or 不 bù to express 'capable' or 'incapable']:支持不～cannot stand; cannot hold out|禁得～风吹雨打 be able to withstand wind and rain

【住持】zhùchí ❶ 主持一个佛寺或道观的事务 take charge of affairs in a Buddhist or Taoist temple ❷ 主持一个佛寺或道观的僧尼或道士 (Buddhist or Taoist) abbot; abbess; highest ranking officiator at a monastery or nunnery

【住处】zhù·chù 住宿的地方;住所 residence; dwelling (place); lodging; quarters

【住地】zhùdì 居住的地方 dwelling (place); lodging

【住读】zhùdú (学生)住在学校里上学(of a student) board at school:～生 boarder

【住房】zhùfáng 供人居住的房屋 housing; lodgings

【住户】zhùhù 定居在某处的家庭或有单独户口的人 household; resident; a social unit comprising a family or a person with independently registered permanent residence:院子里有三家～。There are three households in the compound.

【住家】zhùjiā ❶ 家庭居住(在某处) (of one's family) live; reside in:他在郊区～。He lives with his family in the suburbs. ❷ (～儿 zhùjiār)住户 household; resident:楼里不少～都要求改善环境卫生。A large number of the residents in the building demand improvements to environmental sanitation.

【住居】zhùjū 居住 live; reside; inhabit:少数民族～的地区 region inhabited by minority ethnic groups

【住口】zhù//kǒu 停止说话 stop talking:不～地

夸奖孩子 heap praises on a child | 你胡说什么，快给我～！Nonsense, hold your tongue!

【住手】zhù//shǒu 停止手的动作；停止做某件事 stay one's hand; stop：他不做完不肯～。He will not stop until he has finished everything. | 快～，这东西禁不起摆弄。Stop what you are doing, this thing cannot withstand any meddling.

【住宿】zhùsù 在外居住（多指过夜 oft. overnight）stay; put up; get accommodation：安排～find lodgings; arrange accommodation | 今天晚上到哪里～呢？Where will we put up tonight?

【住所】zhùsuǒ 居住的处所（多指住户的 oft. of a family）dwelling place; residence; domicile

【住院】zhù//yuàn 病人住进医院治疗 be hospitalized

【住宅】zhùzhái 住房（多指规模较大的 oft. of large scale）residence; dwelling：～区 residential quarters | 居民～ residences

【住址】zhùzhǐ 居住的地址（指城镇、乡村、街道的名称和门牌号数 name of street, village or town, and house number）address：家庭～ home address

纻（紵） zhù 〈书 *fml.*〉指苎麻纤维织的布 ramie fabrics：～衣 ramie clothes

杼 zhù ❶ 筘 reed ❷〈古代 *arch.*〉也指梭 shuttle

【杼轴】zhùzhóu 〈书 *fml.*〉杼和轴，旧式织布机上管经纬线的两个部件 reed and shaft, two parts of an old-style loom, the former separating the warp and the latter the weft threads;〈比喻 *fig.*〉文章的组织构思 plot of a literary work

贮（貯） zhù 储存；积存 store; save; lay aside：～木场 lumber yard | ～草五万斤 lay up 50,000 *jin* of forage grass | 缸里～满了水。The vat is full of water.

【贮备】zhùbèi 储备 store up; have in reserve; lay aside

【贮藏】zhùcáng 储藏 store up; lay in

【贮存】zhùcún 储存 store; keep in storage

注[1] zhù ❶ 灌入 pour; fill：～射 inject | 大雨如～。It's pouring with rain. ❷（精神、力量）集中（spirit, strength）concentrate; fix：～视 look attentively at; gaze at | ～意 pay attention to; take note (or notice) of | ～目 gaze at; fix one's eyes on | 贯～ concentrate on; be absorbed in ❸ 赌注 stakes (in gambling)：下～lay down a stake (in gambling) | 孤～一掷 stake everything on a single throw; (fig.) risk everything on a single venture ❹〈方 *dial.*〉〈量词 *classifier*〉多用于款项或交易[for deals or sums of money]：一～买卖 a deal | 十来～交易 about ten transactions

注[2]（註） zhù ❶ 用文字来解释字句 annotate; explain with notes：批～ annotate and comment on ❷ 解释字句的文字 annotations：附～notes appended to a book | 脚～footnotes | 正文用大字，～用小字。The text is to be in a large typeface, and the notes in a smaller one. ❸ 记载；登记 record; register：～册 register | ～销 cancel; write off

【注册】zhùcè 向有关机关、团体或学校登记备案 register; to enroll formally in an organisation, institute or school：～商标 registered trademark | 新生报到～从9月1日开始。Registration of new students starts on September 1.

【注定】zhùdìng（某种客观规律或所谓命运）预先决定 be doomed; be destined：命中～decreed by fate; predestined | ～灭亡 be doomed to destruction

【注脚】zhùjiǎo same as 注解 zhùjiě②

【注解】zhùjiě ❶ 用文字来解释字句 annotate; explain through notes：～古籍 annotate ancient books ❷ 解释字句的文字（explanatory）note; annotation：凡是书内难懂的字句，都有～。All the sentences in the book that are difficult to understand carry explanatory notes.

【注目】zhùmù 把视线集中在一点上 gaze at; fix one's eyes on：引人～spectacular | 这个小县城当时成了全国～的地方。This small county town became the focus of attention of the whole country at that time.

【注射】zhùshè 用注射器把液体药剂输送到有机体内 inject; force a fluid into an organism with a hypodermic syringe

【注射剂】zhùshèjì 针剂 injection

【注射器】zhùshèqì 注射液体药剂的小唧筒状的器具，多用玻璃制成，一端装有针头 injector; syringe; instrument for injecting medicine or withdrawing bodily fluids, that consists of a hollow tube (usu. made of glass) fitted with a plunger and a hollow needle

【注视】zhùshì 注意地看 look attentively at; gaze at：他目不转睛地～着窗外。He looked fixedly out of the window.

【注释】zhùshì same as 注解 zhùjiě

【注疏】zhùshū 注解和解释注解的文字合称注疏 commentary and sub-commentary：《十三经～》*Commentary on the Thirteen Classics*

【注塑】zhùsù 将熔化状态的塑料原料压注到模具内成型 mold plastics; produce plastic articles by injection molding

【注文】zhùwén 注解的文字 explanatory notes; notes

【注销】zhùxiāo 取消登记过的事项 cancel; write off：～户口 cancellation of household registration | 这笔账已经～了。The account has been written off.

【注意】zhù//yì 把意志放到某一方面 pay attention to; take note (or notice) of; keep one's eyes peeled for：～力 attention|～安全 pay attention to safety|提请～call sb.'s attention to sth.

【注音】zhù//yīn 用符号表明文字的读音 phonetic notation；mark the text with phonetic symbols

【注音字母】zhùyīn zìmǔ 在汉语拼音方案公布以前用来标注汉字字音的音标，采用笔画简单的汉字，有的加以修改。有二十四个声母，即ㄅㄆㄇㄈ ㄪ ㄉㄊㄋㄌㄍㄎ ㄫ ㄏㄐㄑ ㄬ ㄒㄓㄔㄕㄖㄗㄘㄙ(其中ㄪㄫㄬ是拼写方言用的)，十六个韵母，即ㄚㄛㄜㄝㄞㄟㄠㄡㄢㄣㄤㄥㄦㄧㄨㄩ。national phonetic alphabet (in use before publication of the Scheme for the Chinese Phonetic Alphabet, or pinyin), created by substituting Chinese characters for simple strokes, comprising 24 syllable initials, i.e. ㄅㄆㄇㄈㄪㄉㄊㄋㄌㄍㄎㄫㄏㄐㄑㄬㄒㄓㄔㄕㄖㄗㄘㄙ (among them, ㄪ, ㄫ and ㄬ are used for dialects), and 16 syllable finals, i.e. ㄚㄛㄜㄝㄞㄟㄠㄡㄢ ㄣㄤㄥㄦㄧ ㄨㄩ; also 注音符号 zhùyīn fúhào

【注重】zhùzhòng 重视 lay stress on; pay attention to; attach importance to：～调查研究 pay attention to investigation and study|～对孩子的教育 attach importance to the education of children

驻 zhù ❶ 停留 halt; stay：～足 make a temporary stay ❷ (部队或工作人员)住在执行职务的地方；(机关)设在某地(of troops or personnel) be stationed; encamp：～京办事处 resident office in Beijing; Beijing Agency|部队～在村东的一个大院里。The troops are stationed in a big courtyard in the eastern part of the village.

【驻跸】zhùbì 〈书 *fml.*〉帝王出行时沿途停留暂住(of a monarch on a tour) stay temporarily; stop over; put up

【驻地】zhùdì ❶ 部队或外勤工作人员所驻的地方 place where troops, etc., are stationed ❷ 地方行政机关的所在地 seat (of a local administrative organ)

【驻防】zhù//fáng 军队在重要的地方驻扎防守 be on garrison duty; garrison

【驻军】zhùjūn ❶ 军队在某地驻扎 (of troops) be stationed troops; be quartered：～云南 station troops in Yunnan ❷ (在某地)驻扎的军队 station troops; base troops：云南～Yunnan garrison troops

【驻守】zhùshǒu 驻扎防守 garrison; defend：～边疆 garrison the frontier

【驻屯】zhùtún 驻扎(of troops) be stationed; be quartered

【驻扎】zhùzhā (军队)在某地住下(of troops) be stationed; be quartered

【驻足】zhùzú 停止脚步 halt; stop; go no further：精美的工艺品吸引了许多参观者～观看。The exquisite arts and crafts have attracted large numbers of visitors to stop and take a close look.

柱 zhù ❶ 柱子 post; upright; pillar; column：梁～beam and pillar|支～ pillar ❷ 像柱子的东西 sth. shaped like a column：水～water column|花～style|脊～spinal column; vertebral column; backbone; spine

【柱石】zhùshí 柱子和柱子下面的基石 pillar and its foundation; 〈比喻 *fig.*〉担负国家重任的人 pillar; mainstay：中国人民解放军是我国人民民主专政的～。The Chinese People's Liberation Army is the pillar of the country and the people's democratic dictatorship.

【柱头】zhùtóu ❶ 柱子的顶部 column cap; column head ❷〈方 *dial.*〉柱子 post; pillar ❸ 雌蕊的顶部，是接受花粉的地方 stigma; part of the pistil of a flower which receives the pollen grains; (图见☞ figure for 花 huā on p.826)

【柱子】zhù·zi 建筑物中直立的起支持作用的构件，用木、石、型钢、钢筋混凝土等制成 post; pillar; a firm upright support for a superstructure, made of wood, stone, shaped steel, or reinforced concrete, etc.; (图见☞ figure for 房子 fáng·zi on p.550)

炷 zhù ❶〈书 *fml.*〉灯心 wick (of an oil lamp)：灯～ wick of an oil lamp ❷〈书 *fml.*〉烧(香) burn (joss sticks) ❸〈量词 *classifier*〉用于点着的香 used for burning joss sticks：一～香 a burning joss stick

祝[1] zhù ❶ 表示良好愿望 express good wishes; wish：～你健康。I wish you the best of health.|～两国的友谊万古常青。May the friendship between our two countries be everlasting! ❷ (Zhù)姓 a surname

祝[2] zhù 〈书 *fml.*〉削；断绝 cut off：～发为僧(剃去头发当和尚)shave one's head and become a monk

【祝词】zhùcí ❶〈古代 *arch.*〉祭祀时祷告的话 prayers at sacrificial rites in ancient times ❷ 举行典礼或会议时表示良好愿望或庆贺的话 congratulatory speech (at a ceremony, etc.); congratulations：新年～New Year's message‖also 祝辞 zhùcí

【祝辞】zhùcí same as 祝词 zhùcí

【祝祷】zhùdǎo 祝愿祷告；祷祝 pray; say one's prayers

【祝福】zhùfú ❶ 原指祈求上帝赐福，后来指祝人平安和幸福 blessing; benediction：～你一路平安。Bon voyage. *or* Have a pleasant journey.|请接受我诚恳的～。Please accept my heartfelt blessings. ❷ 我国某些地区的旧俗，除夕祭祀天地，祈求赐福 New Year's sacrifice (held on New Year's Eve, an old custom in certain areas of China)

【祝告】zhùgào 祝祷；祷告 pray; say one's

prayers：焚香～burn incense and pray|～上天 pray to Heaven

【祝贺】zhùhè 庆贺 congratulate：～你们超额完成了计划。Let me congratulate you on exceeding your planned production figure.|向会议表示热烈的～。Warm congratulations are extended to the meeting.

【祝捷】zhùjié 庆祝或祝贺胜利 celebrate a victory：～大会 victory celebration (meeting)

【祝酒】zhù//jiǔ 向人敬酒，表示祝愿、祝福等 drink a toast；toast：～词 toast|主人向宾客频频～。The host proposed toast after toast to his guests.

【祝寿】zhùshòu 在老年人过生日时向他祝贺 congratulate (an elderly person) on his or her birthday

【祝颂】zhùsòng 表示良好愿望 express good wishes：宴会中宾主互相～。During the banquet，host and guests expressed good wishes to each other.

【祝愿】zhùyuàn 表示良好愿望 wish：衷心～ with best wishes|～大家身体健康，万事如意。Wishing everyone the best of health and good luck.

砫 zhù 石砫(Shízhù)，地名，在重庆。今作石柱。Shizhu，name of a place in Chongqing，now written as 石柱 shízhù

疰 zhù [疰夏](zhùxià) ❶〈中医 *Chin. med.*〉指夏季长期发烧的病，患者多为小儿。多由排汗机能发生障碍引起。症状是持续发烧，食欲不振，消瘦，口渴，多尿，皮肤干热，天气愈热体温愈高等。a summer disease，usu. contracted by children，caused by malfunction of the sweat glands，whose symptoms are fever，loss of appetite，weight loss，thirst，polyuria，hot，dry skin，and body temperature that rises as the weather gets hotter ❷〈方 *dial.*〉苦夏 loss of appetite and weight in summer

著 zhù ❶ 显著 marked；outstanding：昭～ evident；obvious|卓～distinguished；outstanding；eminent|彰明较～ very obvious；conspicuous；easily seen ❷ 显出 show；prove：～名 famous；well-known|颇～成效 prove most effective ❸ 写作 write：编～compile|～书立说 write books and formulate a theory；become an author ❹ 著作 work；book；writing：名～ famous work；famous book|新～sb.'s latest work|译～translations ☞ ·zhe on p. 2432 and zhuó on p. 2534

【著称】zhùchēng 著名 celebrated；famous：杭州以西湖～于世。Hangzhou is world-famous for its West Lake.

【著录】zhùlù 记载；记录 put down in writing；record

【著名】zhùmíng 有名 famous；celebrated；well-known：李时珍是明代的～药物学家。Li Shizhen was a famous pharmacologist of the Ming Dynasty.|吐鲁番的葡萄很～。The grapes produced in Turpan are extremely well-known.

【著述】zhùshù ❶ same as 著作 zhùzuò ①；编纂 write；compile：专心～devote oneself to writing or compiling scholarly works ❷ 著作和编纂的成品 book；work：先生留下的～不多。This gentleman left few works of his own.

【著者】zhùzhě 书或文章的作者 author；writer

【著作】zhùzuò ❶ 用文字表达意见、知识、思想、感情等 write；to express one's opinion，knowledge，thinking，or emotion in writing：从事～多年 be engaged in writing for years ❷ 著作的成品 work；book；writings：学术～ academic works|经典～classical works|～等身(形容著作极多)an author with many books to his credit

【著作权】zhùzuòquán 著作者按照法律规定对自己的著作所享有的权利 copyright (of the author)；author's lawful rights to his work

【著作人】zhùzuòrén 编书或写文章的人；著者 author；writer

蛀 zhù ❶ 蛀虫 moth or any other insect that eats books，clothes，wood，etc. ❷(蛀虫)咬(of moths，etc.) eat；bore through：～蚀 worm；corrode|毛料裤子让虫～了。This pair of woollen pants is moth-eaten.

【蛀齿】zhùchǐ 龋(qǔ)齿 decayed tooth；dental caries

【蛀虫】zhùchóng 指咬树干、衣服、书籍、谷粒等的小虫，如天牛、衣蛾、衣鱼、米象 insect that eats wood，clothes，books or grain，such as the long-horned beetle，moth，silverfish，termite，and rice weevil ◇贪污分子是社会主义建设事业的～。Embezzlers are termites in the cause of socialist construction.

【蛀蚀】zhùshí 由于虫咬而受损伤 worm-eaten：这座房屋的大部分梁柱已被白蚁～。Most of the beams and pillars of this house have been worm-eaten by white ants. ◇～灵魂 corrode the souls

铸(鑄) zhù 铸造 casting；founding：～工 foundry work；founder|～件 foundry goods；casting|这口钟是铜～的。This bell is of cast copper.

【铸币】zhùbì 金属铸成的货币 coin；cast metal currency

【铸错】zhù cuò〈书 *fml.*〉造成重大错误。《资治通鉴》唐纪八十一记载，唐末哀帝天佑三年，天雄节度使罗绍威手下有从六个州招募来的牙军(自卫队)几千人，素不服从他的管辖，他暗中勾结朱全忠，里应外合，突然袭击，把牙军全部消灭了。朱全忠为此居功，向他要这要那，罗绍威苦于供应，后悔地对人说：'合六州四十三县铁，不能为此错也'。commit blunders；commit grave mistakes. According to the *Comprehensive Mirror for Aid in Government·81 Tang Annals*，during the 3rd year of the

Tianyou reign of Emperor Aidi of the late Tang Dynasty, the military commissioner of Tianxiong, Luo Shaowei, had under his command several thousand troops recruited from six prefectures that did not obey his orders. He secretly colluded with Zhu Quanzhong, who acted from the inside, and launched a surprise attack on these troops, wiping them out. Zhu Quanzhong claimed all the credit for this, and demanded all manner of goods from Luo. Unable to meet the demand, Luo said with regret, 'All of the iron collected from 43 counties in these six prefectures is not enough to cast this file.' (错 *cuo*: 锉刀,双关指错误 the Chinese character meaning 'file' is a homonym of 'error')

【铸工】zhùgōng ❶ 铸造器物的工作 foundry work; 通称 commonly called 翻砂 fānshā ❷ 铸造器物的技术工人 foundry worker; founder

【铸焊】zhùhàn 把熔化的金属液浇铸在外有模型的工件连接处,使结合在一起。主要用于连接钢轨等。cast joint; cast-weld; aluminothermic welding; pour molten metal into a mould placed at the joint of work pieces to combine them, mainly used to cast welded rails

【铸件】zhùjiàn 铸造的工件 foundry goods; casting

【铸模】zhùmú 铸造用的模具 mould for casting; matrix; also 铸型 zhùxíng

【铸铁】zhùtiě 用铁矿石炼成的铁。含碳量在1.7—4.5%之间,并含有磷、硫、硅等杂质。质脆,不能锻压。是炼钢和铸造器物的原料。pig iron; crude iron that is the direct product of the blast furnace, whose carbon content is between 1.7 and 4.5 percent, and contains impurities such as phosphorus, sulfur, and silicon. Fragile and nonmalleable, it may be refined to produce steel, and is a raw material for casting; also 生铁 shēngtiě or 铣铁 xiǎntiě

【铸造】zhùzào 把金属加热熔化后倒入砂型或模子里,冷却后凝固成为器物 casting; founding; give shape to a substance by pouring molten metal into a mould and allowing to solidify: ～机器零件 cast machine parts|～车间 foundry; casting shop

【铸字】zhù//zì 铸造铅字 type founding; typecasting

筑[1](築) zhù 建筑;修建 build; construct: ～路 construct a road|～堤 build a dyke|修～build; put up|构～construct; build

筑[2] zhù 〈古代 *arch*.〉弦乐器,像琴,有十三根弦,用竹尺敲打 *zhu*, ancient 13-stringed musical instrument similar to the zither, played by tapping its strings with bamboo strips

筑[3] Zhù (旧读 formerly pronounced Zhú) 贵州贵阳的别称 another name for Guiyang in Guizhou Province

【筑室道谋】zhù shì dào móu 自己要造房子,却在路上和过路人商量 ask every passerby how to build one's house; 〈比喻 *fig*.〉自己没有主见或毫无计划,东问西问,结果人多言杂,不能成事 have no idea or plan of one's own (and accomplish nothing)

翥 zhù 〈书 *fml*.〉(鸟)向上飞 (of birds) fly; soar: 龙翔凤～。The dragon soars, and the phoenix flies aloft.

箸(筯) zhù 〈方 *dial*.〉筷子 chopsticks

zhuā (ㄓㄨㄚ)

抓 zhuā ❶ 手指聚拢,使物体固定在手中 grab; seize; clutch: 一把～住 take hold of sth. or sb. by grabbing|他～起帽子就往外走。He grabbed (or snatched up) his cap and headed for the door. ❷ 人用指甲或带齿的东西或动物用爪在物体上划过 scratch; scrape with sth. sharp or jagged, such as claws or fingernails: ～痒痒 scratch an itch|他手上被猫～破一块皮。On his hand was a graze where the cat had scratched him. ❸ 捉拿;捕捉 arrest; bust; nick; catch: ～土匪 catch a bandit|老鹰～走了一只小鸡儿。The eagle swooped down and snatched away a chicken. ❹ 加强领导,特别着重(某方面) stress (certain aspect); take charge of; be responsible for: ～重点 stress the essentials|他分工～农业。According to labour divisions, he is in charge of agriculture. ❺ 抢着做 vie with each other to do sth.: 三～两～就把工作～完了。The work is accomplished by the concerted effort of several divisions. ❻ 吸引(人注意) attract (attention); draw; fascinate: 这个演员一出场就～住了观众。The actor commanded the audience's attention as soon as he appeared on stage.

【抓辫子】zhuā biàn·zi 揪辫子 seize on sb.'s mistake or shortcoming; capitalize on sb.'s vulnerable point; catch sb. out

【抓膘】zhuā//biāo 采取加强饲养管理并注意适当使用等措施,使牲畜肥壮 fatten (pigs, cattle, etc., through strengthening management of feeding and proper usage): 放青～ fatten the livestock by putting them out to graze

【抓兵】zhuā//bīng 〈旧时 *old*〉指抓人去当兵 pressgang a man into military service

【抓茬儿】zhuā//chár 〈方 *dial*.〉故意挑别人的小毛病;找茬儿 find fault; pick holes; pick a quarrel

【抓耳挠腮】zhuā ěr náo sāi ❶ 形容焦急而又没办法的样子 tweak one's ears and scratch one's cheeks (as a sign of anxiety) ❷ 形容欢喜而

不能自持的样子 tweak one's ears and scratch one's cheeks (as a sign of delight)

【抓哏】zhuā//gén 戏曲中的丑角或相声演员在表演时,即景生情地临时编出本来没有的台词来逗观众发笑(of a comedian, clown, etc.) ad lib; speak impromptu lines

【抓工夫】zhuā gōng·fu 挤时间;抽空 make good use of one's time; find time (to do sth.)

【抓获】zhuāhuò 逮住;捕获 catch (a criminal, etc.); capture; seize:凶手已被~。The murderer has been arrested.

【抓髻】zhuā·ji same as 髽髻 zhuā·ji

【抓紧】zhuā//jǐn 紧紧地把握住,不放松 firmly grasp; pay close attention to:~时间 make the best use of one's time|~学习 attend to one's studies in earnest; study hard|~生产 pay close attention to production

【抓阄儿】zhuā//jiūr 从预先做好记号的纸卷或纸团中每人取一个,以决定谁该得什么东西或谁该做什么事 draw lots; cast lots; the use of lots made from crumpled or rolled strips of marked paper as a means of deciding who should do sth.; also 拈阄儿 niān//jiūr

【抓鬏】zhuā·jiu same as 髽鬏 zhuā·jiu

【抓举】zhuājǔ 一种举重法,两手把杠铃从地上举过头顶,一直到两臂伸直为止,不在胸前停顿 snatch; a method of weightlifting in which the weight is raised from the floor directly to an overhead position, usu. with a lunge or squat under the weight

【抓空儿】zhuā//kòngr 抓工夫 find time (to do sth.):过两天我~去一趟。I'll find the time to go there in a few days. also 抓空子 zhuā//kòng·zi

【抓挠】zhuā·nao〈方 *dial.*〉❶ 搔 scratch:~几下就不痒了。Scratch it and it won't itch any more. ❷ 乱动东西,致使凌乱 mess about:好孩子,别~东西!There's a good boy. Don't mess about with things. ❸ 打架 come to blows; fight:他们俩又~起来了,你赶快去劝劝吧!The two of them have got into a fight again. Come on, try to patch things up between them. ❹ 忙乱地赶着做;弄 prepare sth. hastily:一下子来了这么多的人吃饭,炊事员怕~不过来吧!I doubt whether the cook will be able to rustle up a meal for so many people arriving all at once. ❺ 挣;获得(钱) earn; make (money):庄稼人靠副业~俩活钱儿。The peasants rely on sideline production to earn extra money. ❻ (~儿 zhuā·naor)指可用的东西或可凭借依靠的人 sb. or sth. that one can rely on:东西都让人借走了,自己反倒弄得没~了。We have loaned ours to someone else, and we have nothing that can be used instead.|最好派个负责人来,咱好有个~。It would be best to have someone sent here to take charge, that we can go to with our problems. ❼ (~儿 zhuā·naor)指对付事情的办法 solution to a difficulty:事前要慎重考虑,免得发生问题时没~。Think it over carefully beforehand, so as to be prepared for all eventualities.

【抓拍】zhuāpāi 拍摄时不是特意摆设场景、安排人物姿态等,而是抓住时机把现场实际发生的事情摄入镜头,叫做抓拍 take a candid photograph (or picture); photography whose subjects are in natural or spontaneous, rather than prepared poses

【抓破脸】zhuā pò liǎn〈比喻 *fig.*〉感情破裂,公开争吵 scratch each other's faces; quarrel openly; also 撕破脸 sī pò liǎn

【抓瞎】zhuā//xiā 事前没有准备而临时忙乱着急 find oneself at a loss; be in a rush and a muddle; be thrown off balance:早点儿做好准备,免得临时~。Arrange everything in advance so that you won't be in a rush at the last moment.

【抓药】zhuā//yào ❶ 中药店按照顾客的药方取药,也指医院的药房为病人取中药(a traditional Chinese medicine shop, or pharmacy in a hospital) make up (or fill) a prescription of Chinese herbal medicine ❷ 拿着药方到中药店买药 have a prescription of Chinese herbal medicine made up (or filled):抓一服药 buy a dose of Chinese herbal medicine

【抓周】zhuā//zhōu (~儿 zhuā//zhōur)旧俗,婴儿周岁时,父母摆上各种物品任其抓取,用来试探婴儿将来的志向、爱好等 (old custom) grabbing test on the occasion of a baby's first birthday (in which various articles—e. g. a book, a writing brush, an ink-stone, workman's tools, playthings and eatables, cosmetics, and unusual gadgets—are assembled and spread out before the baby, and the particular article he or she picks is supposed to indicate his or her future character and life style, career and behaviour, and habits and pastimes)

【抓壮丁】zhuā zhuàngdīng〈旧时 *old*〉官府抓青壮年男子去当兵 pressgang able-bodied men; compel able-bodied men to render military service

【抓总儿】zhuāzǒngr 负责全面工作;拿总儿 assume overall responsibility (in carrying out a project, etc.)

挝(撾) zhuā ❶〈书 *fml.*〉敲;打(鼓) knock at; beat:~鼓 beat a drum ❷ same as 抓 zhuā(多见于早期白话 mostly in early vernacular)

☞ wō on p. 2012

檛(檛、簻) zhuā〈书 *fml.*〉马鞭子 whip

髽 zhuā ☞ below

【髽髻】zhuā·ji 梳在头顶两旁的髻 hair worn in two buns:~夫妻(结发夫妻) husband and wife by first marriage; also 抓髻 zhuā·ji

【髽鬏】zhuā·jiu same as 髽髻 zhuā·ji; also 抓鬏 zhuā·jiu

zhuǎ (ㄓㄨㄚˇ)

爪 zhuǎ 义同'爪'(zhǎo)②,用于以下各条 same as 爪(zhǎo)② in meaning, used in the following entries

☞ zhǎo on p. 2424

【爪尖儿】zhuǎjiānr 用做食物的猪蹄 pig's trotters; pettitoes

【爪儿】zhuǎr ❶ 爪子 paw of a small animal:老鼠～rat's paws ❷ 某些器物的脚 foot of a utensil:三～锅 three-legged pan

【爪子】zhuǎ·zi 动物的有尖甲的脚 claw; paw; talon:鸡～chicken's feet|猫～cat's paw

zhuāi (ㄓㄨㄞ)

拽[1] zhuāi 〈方 *dial*.〉扔;抛 fling; throw; hurl:拿砖头～狗 throw a brick at a dog|把皮球～得老远 fling a ball far away

拽[2] zhuāi 〈方 *dial*.〉胳膊有毛病,活动不灵便 strained arm muscles

☞ 曳 yè on p. 2240 and zhuài on p. 2515

zhuǎi (ㄓㄨㄞˇ)

转(轉) zhuǎi 转文 lard one's speech with literary allusions; show off one's learning:他平时好～两句。He likes to lard his speech with archaisms.|说大白话就行,用不着～。Just talk normally, there is no need for such pseudo-intellectual expressions.

☞ zhuǎn on p. 2518 and zhuàn on p. 2521

【转文】zhuǎi//wén '转文'(zhuǎn//wén)的又音 variant pronunciation for 转文 zhuǎn//wén

跩 zhuǎi 〈方 *dial*.〉身体肥胖不灵活,走路摇晃 waddle; walk with an awkward clumsy swaying gait:鸭子一～一～地走着。Ducks walk in a waddle.

zhuài (ㄓㄨㄞˋ)

拽(擺) zhuài 拉 pull; drag; haul:生拉硬～drag sb. along against his will; strain an interpretation; over-analogize|一把～住不放 catch hold of sb. or sth. and not let go

☞ 曳 yè on p. 2240 and zhuāi on p. 2515

zhuān (ㄓㄨㄢ)

专(專、❶❷耑) zhuān ❶ 集中在一件事上的 a particular person, occasion, purpose, etc.; focus on one thing; special:～心 concentrate one's attention|～题 special subject; special topic|～门 special; specialized|～业 specialty; discipline|～款 special fund|～科 special field of study ❷ 独自掌握和占有 monopolize:～制 autocracy|～权 monopolize power|～利 patent|～卖 monopoly ❸ (Zhuān)姓 a surname

☞ 耑 duān on p. 483

【专案】zhuān'àn 专门处理的案件或重要事件 special case for investigation; case

【专差】zhuānchāi ❶ 指特地出去办某件公事 special mission (or errand):他～去北京。He went to Beijing on a special mission. ❷ 指特地出去办某件公事的人 person sent on a special mission

【专长】zhuāncháng 专门的学问技能;特长 speciality; special skill or knowledge:学有～have specialized knowledge of a subject; be expert in a particular field of study|发挥各人的～give full play to each person's professional knowledge or skill

【专场】zhuānchǎng ❶ 剧场、影院等专为某一部分人演出的一场 special performance; show intended for a limited audience:学生～ special show for students ❷ 一场里专门演出一种类型的若干节目 performance of a certain type of programme:相声～special performance of comic dialogues|曲艺～ special performance of *quyi*

【专车】zhuānchē ❶ 在例行车次之外专为某人或某事特别开行的火车或汽车 special train or car (for a person or a mission out of regular service) ❷ 机关单位或个人专用的汽车 automobile for an organisation or an individual

【专诚】zhuānchéng 特地(表示非顺便) for a particular purpose; specially:～拜访 pay a special visit to sb.

【专程】zhuānchéng 专为某事而到某地 special trip:～看望 make a special trip to visit sb.|～前去迎接客人 make a special trip to greet a guest

【专电】zhuāndiàn 记者专为本报社报道新闻而由外地用电话、电报、电传发来的稿子(区别于通讯社供稿 as compared with manuscripts provided by news agencies) special dispatch (sent by a reporter to a newspaper by means of telephone, telegram, or telex)

【专断】zhuānduàn 应该会商而不会商,单独做出决定 make an arbitrary decision; act arbitrarily:～独行 act arbitrarily regardless of others' opinions

【专访】zhuānfǎng ❶ 只就某个问题或对某个人进行采访 special coverage; interview with sb. on a certain topic:接受记者～ accept a reporter's exclusive interview ❷ 这样采访写成的文章 special article (written after an interview):登载了一篇关于他的模范事迹的～

carried a special article about his exemplary deeds

【专攻】zhuāngōng 专门研究(某一学科) specialize in; do specialized research on:他是～水利工程的。He specializes in hydraulic engineering.

【专柜】zhuānguì 商店中专门出售某一种类或某一地区商品的柜台 special counter; counter in a store dealing in specific commodities or commodities from a certain region:床上用品～ special counter for bedding

【专号】zhuānhào 以某项内容为中心而编成的一期报刊 special issue (of a periodical):妇女问题～ special issue on women's problems|《红楼梦》研究～ special issue on research on *A Dream of Red Mansions*

【专横】zhuānhèng 任意妄为;专断强横 imperious; peremptory; domineering:～跋扈 imperious and despotic; arrogant and domineering

【专机】zhuānjī ❶ 在班机之外专为某人或某事特别飞行的飞机 special plane; plane arranged for a special person, or a special mission ❷ 某人专用的飞机 private plane

【专集】zhuānjí ❶ 只收录某一作者作品的集子 collection (of a certain author's works) ❷ 就某一文体或某一内容编成的集子 collection (of writings of a certain literary style or of a particular content):论文～ collection of treatises

【专家】zhuānjiā 对某一门学问有专门研究的人;擅长某项技术的人 expert; specialist; person very skilled or highly trained and informed in some special field

【专刊】zhuānkān ❶ 报刊以某项内容为中心而编辑的一栏或一期 special issue or column (of a periodical or newspaper) ❷ 学术机构出版的以一个问题的研究结果为内容的单册著作 monograph; book published by an academic organization on the research into a specific topic

【专科】zhuānkē ❶ 专门科目 specialty; special field of study; specialized subject:～医生 medical specialist|～词典 specialized dictionary ❷ 指专科学校 college for professional training; training school:～毕业 graduate of a professional training college

【专科学校】zhuānkē xuéxiào 实施专业教育的学校,修业年限一般为二至三年。如农业专科学校、师范专科学校、医学专科学校等。vocational school; school for professional training, whose courses are generally two-to-three-years in length, such as agricultural school, normal school, or medical school

【专款】zhuānkuǎn 指定只能用于某项事务的款项 special fund; fund earmarked for a special purpose:教育～education fund|～专用 earmark a fund for a specific purpose

【专栏】zhuānlán 报刊上专门登载某类稿件的一部分篇幅 special column; special department or feature in a newspaper or a periodical

【专利】zhuānlì 法律保障创造发明者在一定时期内由于创造发明而独自享有的利益 patent; monopoly right granted to an inventor by law to produce, sell or make profit from an invention for a specific number of years:～权 patent right

【专列】zhuānliè 专为某人或某事特别增开的列车 special train (for a person or an assignment)

【专卖】zhuānmài 国家指定的专营机构经营某些物品,其他部门非经专营机构许可,不得生产和运销 monopoly; exclusive privilege to engage in a particular business or provide a service, granted by the state:烟草～公司 tobacco monopoly company

【专美】zhuānměi 〈书 *fml.*〉独自享受美名 have an exclusive claim to fame; be the sole possessor of an honour:青年演员钻研表演艺术,不让上代艺人～于前。Challenging their predecessors' exclusive claim to fame, young actors now strive to hone their skills.

【专门】zhuānmén ❶ 特地 specially:我是～来看望你的。I come specially to see you. ❷ 专从事某一项事的 specialized:～人才 people with professional skill; specialized personnel|他是～研究土壤学的。He specializes in pedology. ❸〈方 *dial.*〉表示强调经常做某类事情 frequently:他～会讲风凉话。He often makes sarcastic remarks.

【专名】zhuānmíng 指人名、地名、机关团体名之类,如'鲁迅、长春、北京大学' proper noun; name of a specific individual, place or organization, such as Lu Xun, Changchun, Beijing University, etc.

【专名号】zhuānmínghào 标点符号(——),用在横行文字的底下或竖行文字的旁边,表示人名、地名、机关团体名之类 line under or beside a word to show that it is a proper noun, such as the name of an individual, place or organization

【专区】zhuānqū 我国省、自治区曾经根据需要设立的行政区域,包括若干县、市。1975 年后改称地区。prefecture; administrative region under the jurisdiction of a province or autonomous region, under which are a number of counties and cities; renamed 地区 dìqū after 1975.

【专权】zhuānquán 独揽大权 arrogate all powers to oneself; monopolize power:～误国。Autocracy spells danger for a country.

【专人】zhuānrén ❶ 专门负责某项工作的人 person specially assigned to a task or job ❷ 临时派遣专办某件事的人 person temporarily assigned to a task

【专任】zhuānrèn 专门担任(区别于'兼任'as compared with 'part-time') full-time; regular:～教员 full-time teacher

【专擅】zhuānshàn〈书 *fml.*〉擅自做主,不向上级请示或不听上级指示 usurp authority; act without the authorization of one's superior

【专史】zhuānshǐ 各种专门学科的历史,如哲学史、文学史、经济史等 history of a particular subject (e.g. history of philosophy, literature or economics)

【专使】zhuānshǐ 专为某件事而派遣的使节 special envoy; envoy for a special mission

【专书】zhuānshū 就某一专题而编写的书;专著 monograph; book on a specific topic

【专署】zhuānshǔ 专员公署的简称 abbr. for 专员公署 zhuānyuán gōngshǔ

【专题】zhuāntí 专门研究或讨论的题目 special subject; special topic:～报告 report on a special topic|～讨论 seminar|～调查 investigation of a special topic

【专文】zhuānwén 专门就某个问题写的文章 article on a certain topic:这一事件的始末另有～披露。Details of the incident are disclosed in another article.

【专席】zhuānxí 专为某人或某类人设置的席位 special seat:来宾～seats especially for the guests|孕妇～special seats for pregnant women

【专线】zhuānxiàn ❶ 较大的厂矿铺设的自用铁路线 special-purpose railway line (of a large factory or mine) ❷ 电话局为重要机关或首长设置的专用电话线 special telephone line; line for the exclusive use of important organs or leading cadres

【专项】zhuānxiàng 特定的某个项目 special item:～训练 specialized training|～检查 specialized checkup

【专心】zhuānxīn 集中注意力 concentrate one's attention; be absorbed:～一意 with intense concentration|学习必须～。Study requires undivided attention.

【专心致志】zhuān xīn zhì zhì 一心一意;集中精神 complete absorption; with single-minded dedication:要创造条件让科学家～地做研究工作。We must create conditions for scientists to devote wholeheartedly to research.

【专修】zhuānxiū 集中学习某种课业 major in; specialize in (a subject):～科(大学中附设的实施短期专业教育的班级) crack course (at university)

【专业】zhuānyè ❶ 高等学校的一个系里或中等专业学校里,根据科学分工或生产部门的分工把学业分成的门类 special field of study; specialized subject; specialty; discipline:～课 specialized courses|中文系汉语～specialty of Chinese language in the Chinese Department ❷ 产业部门中根据产品生产的不同过程而分成的各业务部分 specialized trade or profession; special line:～化 specialize|～生产 production along specialized lines ❸ 专门从事某种工作或职业的 specialized; professional personnel:～户 specialized household|～文艺工作者 professional literary and art workers; writers and artists

【专业户】zhuānyèhù 我国农村中专门从事某种农副业的家庭或个人 rural family engaged in farming or a sideline occupation along a specialized line; specialized household:养鸡～household that specializes in raising chickens

【专业课】zhuānyèkè 高等学校中,使学生具有必要的专门知识和技能的课程 specialized course; course provided in schools of higher learning that teaches specialized knowledge and skills

【专一】zhuānyī 专心一意;不分心 single-minded; concentrated:心思～with concentrated attention|爱情～be constant in love

【专用】zhuānyòng 专供某种需要或某个人使用 for a special purpose or a person:～电话 telephone for special use|专款～earmark a fund for its specified purpose only

【专员】zhuānyuán ❶ 省、自治区所派的地区负责人(administrative) commissioner (of a prefecture assigned by a province or autonomous region) ❷ 担任某项专门职务的人员 assistant director; attaché; person with special duties

【专员公署】zhuānyuán gōngshǔ 我国省、自治区曾经根据需要设置的派出机构 prefectural commissioner's office, set up by a province or autonomous region; 简称 abbr. 专署 zhuānshǔ

【专责】zhuānzé 专门担负的某项责任 specific responsibility:分工明确,各有～。The division of labour is clear-cut, and each is charged with specific responsibilities.

【专政】zhuānzhèng 占统治地位的阶级对敌对阶级实行的强力统治。一切国家都是一定阶级的专政。dictatorship; rule imposed on an antagonistic class by the ruling class. A state is inevitably the dictatorship of a certain class.

【专职】zhuānzhí 由专人担任的职务 full-time (position):～工会干部 full-time trade union cadre

【专制】zhuānzhì ❶(君主)独自掌握政权 autocracy:～政体 autocracy|～帝王 autocratic monarch; despotic emperor|君主～autocrat ❷ 凭自己的意志独断独行,操纵一切 autocratic; despotic; act arbitrarily according to one's own will and monopolize all power

【专注】zhuānzhù 专心注意 concentrate one's attention on; be absorbed in; devote one's mind to:心神～ be wholly absorbed; with single-minded dedication

【专著】zhuānzhù 就某方面加以研究论述的专门著作 monograph; treatise; book on a special subject

肫(腖)

zhuān〈方 *dial.*〉鸟类的胃;胗 gizzard; stomach of a bird:鸡～

chicken's gizzard

砖(磚、甎、塼) zhuān ❶ 把黏土等做成的坯放在窑里烧制而成的建筑材料，多为长方形或方形 brick; handy-sized unit of building material, made from moist clay baked in a kiln, generally in the shape of a rectangular or square block ❷ 形状像砖的东西 sth. shaped like a brick: 茶～tea brick | 煤～brick-shaped briquet | 冰～ice-cream brick

【砖茶】zhuānchá 压紧后形状像砖的茶叶块儿 brick tea; rectangular mass of compressed tea leaves; also 茶砖 cházhuān

【砖坯】zhuānpī 没有经过烧制的砖；砖的毛坯 unfired brick

【砖头】zhuāntóu 不完整的砖；碎砖 fragment of a brick

【砖头】zhuān·tou 〈方 *dial.*〉砖 brick

【砖窑】zhuānyáo 烧砖的窑 brick kiln

颛 zhuān 〈书 *fml.*〉❶ 愚昧 ignorant; benighted ❷ same as 专 zhuān

【颛孙】Zhuānsūn 姓 a surname

【颛顼】Zhuānxū 传说中的上古帝王名 Emperor Zhuanxu, a legendary ruler in remote antiquity

【颛臾】Zhuānyú 春秋时的一个小国，在今山东费县一带 Zhuanyu, name of a state of the Spring and Autumn Period, located in present-day Feixian County, Shandong Province

zhuǎn (ㄓㄨㄢˇ)

转(轉) zhuǎn ❶ 改换方向、位置、形势、情况等(of orientation, position, situation, condition, etc.,) turn; shift; change: ～身 turn round | ～脸 turn one's face | ～换 change; transform | ～移 shift; transfer | 好～ turn for the better; improve | 向左～turn left | 向后～about turn | ～败为胜 turn defeat into victory | 由阴～晴 change from overcast to fine ❷ 把一方的物品、信件、意见等传到另一方 pass on; transfer (objects, letters, opinions, etc): ～达 pass on; convey | ～交 pass on; transmit | ～送 pass on | 这封信由我～给他好了。Let me pass the letter on to him.

☞ zhuǎi on p. 2515 and zhuàn on p. 2521

【转氨酶】zhuǎn'ānméi 生物体内能转移氨基酸的氨基的酶，在氨基酸代谢中有重要作用 glutamic-pyruvic transaminase (GPT); aminotransferase; enzyme that causes the transfer of an amino group from one molecule to another through the action of a transaminase, and which performs an important function in the metabolism of amino acids

【转变】zhuǎnbiàn 由一种情况变到另一种情况 change; transform: 思想～change in one's ideology | 风向～了。The wind has changed direction. | ～态度 change one's attitude

【转播】zhuǎnbō (广播电台、电视台)播送别的电台或电视台的节目 relay (a radio or TV broadcast)

【转产】zhuǎn//chǎn 企业停止原来产品的生产而生产别的产品(of an enterprise) switch to the manufacture of a different line of products; change the line of production

【转车】zhuǎn//chē 中途换车 change trains or buses; transfer to another train or bus: 从北京到宁波去，可以在上海～。When travelling from Beijing to Ningbo, one can change trains at Shanghai. | 他住在市郊，回家要转两次车。He lives in the suburbs, and has to change buses twice to get home.

【转达】zhuǎndá 把一方的话转告给另一方 pass on; convey; communicate: 我对老人的心意请你代为～。Please convey my regards to the elderly folk. | 你放心走吧，我一定把你的话～给他。You can go and rest assured that I will pass on your message to him.

【转道】zhuǎndào 绕道经过 make a detour; go by way of: 从上海～武汉进京 go from Shanghai to Beijing by way of Wuhan

【转调】zhuǎndiào 一个乐曲中，为了表达不同内容的需要和丰富乐曲的表现力，从某调过渡到另一个调 modulation; transposition; a change from one tonality to another by regular melodic or chord succession (to express diverse content and enrich the appeal of the music); also 变调 biàndiào or 移调 yídiào

【转动】zhuǎndòng 转身活动；身体或物体的某部分自由活动 turn; move; turn round: 伤好后，腰部～自如。After the wound has healed, you can move and turn your waist freely.

☞ zhuàndòng on p. 2521

【转发】zhuǎnfā ❶ 把有关单位的文件转给下属单位 transmit; transmit documents received from a relevant unit to subordinate units ❷ 报刊上发表别的报刊上发表过的文章 re-publish; reprint articles published in other publications ❸ 把接收到的从某个地点发射来的无线电信号发射到别的地点 relay; transmit radio signals from one place to an other: 通信卫星电视信号～测试 TV signal communications satellite transmission test

【转告】zhuǎngào 受人嘱托把某人的话、情况等告诉另一方 pass on (word); communicate; transmit: 他让我～你，他明天不能来了。He asked me to let you know that he can't come tomorrow.

【转关系】zhuǎn guān·xi 党派或团体的成员在调动时转移组织关系 transfer the registration of party or organization membership from one unit to another

【转轨】zhuǎn//guǐ ❶ 转入另一轨道(运行) switch to another track; orbital transfer ❷ 〈比喻 *fig.*〉改变原来的体制等 change the original operation mechanism: 工厂从单一生

产型向生产经营型～。The factory has switched from unitary production to production and marketing.

【转行】zhuǎn//háng ❶ 从一个行业转到另一个行业；改行 change one's profession ❷ 写字、打字或排版等，从一行转到下一行 move to the next line (in writing, typing or composition)：抄稿时，标点符号尽量不要～。When copying a manuscript, do your best to avoid putting punctuation marks on the following line.

【转化】zhuǎnhuà ❶ 转变；改变 change; transform ❷ 矛盾的双方经过斗争，在一定的条件下，各自向着和自己相反的方面转变，向着对立方面所处的地位转变。如主要矛盾和次要矛盾、对抗性矛盾和非对抗性矛盾等在一定条件下都可以互相转化。transform into one's antithesis; change into the reverse through struggle. Under certain conditions, the two sides of a contradiction change into each other's opposites. For instance, the principal contradiction and the secondary contradiction, and the antagonistic contradiction and the non-antagonistic contradiction can, under certain conditions, change into their opposites.

【转圜】zhuǎnhuán ❶ 挽回 save (a situation)：事已至此，难以～了。Things having gone this far, it will be hard to save the situation. ❷ 从中调停 mediate：他们俩的矛盾由你出面～比较好些。It would be much better for you to mediate between the two over their differences.

【转换】zhuǎnhuàn 改变；改换 change; transform：～方向 change direction｜～话题 change the subject of a conversation; switch to another subject of conversation

【转机】zhuǎnjī 好转的可能（多指病症脱离危险或事情能挽回 of a disease or crisis） favourable turn of events; turn a corner; take a turn for the better：事情还有～。It is possible that the matter could take a turn for the better.｜病入膏肓，已无～。The disease has attacked the vitals and is beyond treatment.

【转嫁】zhuǎnjià ❶ 改嫁（of women） marry again; remarry ❷ 把自己应承受的负担、损失、罪名等加在别人身上 shift; transfer (burden, losses, blame) to someone else：不能把事故的责任～于人。One should not shift one's responsibility on others.

【转交】zhuǎnjiāo 把一方的东西交给另一方 pass on; transmit：这个小包裹是她托我～给你的。She asked me to pass this small parcel on to you.

【转角】zhuǎnjiǎo（～儿 zhuǎnjiǎor）街巷等的拐弯处 street corner; corner

【转借】zhuǎnjiè ❶ 把借来的东西再借给别人 lend a borrowed thing to someone else ❷ 把自己的证件等借给别人使用 lend one's personal certificate to sb. else：借书证不得～他人。There should be no lending out of library cards to people who are not library members. *or* The library card is not transferable.

【转科】zhuǎn//kē ❶ 病人从医院的某一科转到另一科去看病（of a patient） transfer from one department of the hospital to another ❷ 学生从某一科转到另一科去学习（of a student） transfer from one specialty to another

【转口】zhuǎnkǒu 商品经过一个港口运到另一个港口或通过一个国家运到另一个国家 transit; entrepot; conveyance of commodities from one port to another or from one country to another：～贸易 entrepot trade

【转脸】zhuǎnliǎn（～儿 zhuǎnliǎnr）〈比喻 *fig*.〉时间很短 in no time; in the twinkling of an eye：他刚才还在这里，怎么～就不见了？He was here just now, how did he disappear so quickly?

【转捩点】zhuǎnlièdiǎn same as 转折点 zhuǎnzhédiǎn

【转录】zhuǎnlù 把磁带上已录好的录音、录像录到空白磁带上 copy; dub; make a copy of a pre-recorded cassette tape or videotape

【转卖】zhuǎnmài 把买进的东西再卖出去（of merchandise） resell：倒手～sell what one has bought

【转年】zhuǎn//nián 到了下一年 coming year; next year

【转年】zhuǎnnián〈方 *dial*.〉❶ 某一年的第二年（多用于过去 oft. in past tense） following year ❷ 明年 coming year; next year

【转念】zhuǎnniàn 再一想（多指改变主意 oft. change of one's mind） have second thoughts; think better of：他刚想开口，但一～，觉得还是暂时不说为好。He was just about to speak, but thought better of it for the time being.

【转让】zhuǎnràng 把自己的东西或应享有的权利让给别人 transfer the ownership of; make over：～房屋 transfer the ownership of real estate｜技术～technology transfer

【转身】zhuǎnshēn（～儿 zhuǎnshēnr）〈比喻 *fig*.〉时间很短 in no time：刚说好了的，一～就不认账。On having just agreed, he turned around and denied doing so.

【转生】zhuǎnshēng〈佛教 *Budd*.〉认为人或动物死后，灵魂依照因果报应而投胎，成为另一个人或动物，叫做转生 reincarnation; transmigration; upon death of the earthly body, rebirth into a new body or form, according to one's karma; also 转世 zhuǎnshì

【转世】zhuǎnshì ❶ 转生 reincarnation ❷〈喇嘛教 *Lamaism*〉寺院集团决定活佛继承人的制度。始于13世纪。活佛死后，通过占卜、降神等活动，寻找在活佛死时出生的若干婴儿，从中选一个作为活佛的转世，定为继承人。reincarnation; system that started in the 13th century, whereby the successor to the living Buddha of a monastery is chosen. When a living Buddha dies, several soul boys born on the day of his death are selected through divinations and seances, and one of whom is selected as his reincarnation.

【转手】zhuǎn//shǒu 从一方取得或买得东西交给或卖给另一方 pass on; sell on what one has bought: ～倒卖 resell | 你就直接交给他,何必要我转个手呢? Give it directly to him, why go through me?

【转述】zhuǎnshù 把别人的话说给另外的人 report; relate sth. as told by sb. else: 我这是～老师的话,不是我自己的意思。I am merely reporting what the teacher said; it is not my personal opinion.

【转瞬】zhuǎnshùn 转眼 in the twinkling of an eye; in an instant; in a flash: ～间,来这儿已有十几天了。A couple of days have gone by in the twinkling of an eye since I arrived here. | 国庆节～就要到了。National Day will be here before we know it.

【转送】zhuǎnsòng ❶ 转交 pass on; transmit onwards: 这是刚收到的急件,请你立即～给他。This urgent document has just been received. Please pass it on to him immediately. ❷ 转赠 make a present of what one has been given: 这本书是老张送给他的,他又～给我了。This book was a present to him from Lao Zhang, and he later made a gift of it to me.

【转托】zhuǎntuō 把别人托给自己的事再托给另外的人 ask sb. else to do what has been asked of oneself: 这件事我虽然没法帮忙,但可以设法替你～一个人。Although I cannot personally help you, I can try to get someone else to take care of it for you.

【转弯】zhuǎn//wān (～儿 zhuǎn//wānr) ❶ 拐弯儿 turn a corner; make a turn: ～抹角 full of twists and turns; beat about the bush | 这儿离学校很近,一～儿就到了。The school is close by, just turn the corner and you're there. ❷〈比喻 *fig.*〉改变认识或想法 change one's viewpoint or concept: 他感到太突然了,一时转不过弯儿来。He was taken by surprise, and could not think straight for a moment.

【转弯抹角】zhuǎn wān mò jiǎo (～儿 zhuǎn wān mò jiǎor) ❶ 沿着弯弯曲曲的路走 walk along a winding road: 汽车～开进了村子。The car drove into the village along a tortuously winding road. ❷ 形容路弯弯曲曲 (of road) full of twists and turns; zigzagging; winding: 这条路～的,可难走了。This road is full of twists and turns that make it hard going. ❸〈比喻 *fig.*〉说话、做事不直截了当 beat about the bush; speak in a roundabout way: 有什么意见就痛快说,别这么～的。Say what you have to say and don't beat about the bush.

【转弯子】zhuǎn wān·zi same as 转弯 zhuǎnwān ②

☞ zhuàn wān·zi on p. 2522

【转危为安】zhuǎn wēi wéi ān (局势、病情等)从危急转为平安 (situation, patient's condition, etc.) take a turn for the better and be out of danger; pull through

【转文】zhuǎn//wén, 又 also zhuǎi//wén 说话时不用口语,而用文言的字眼儿,以显示有学问 lard one's speech with literary allusions; show off one's learning: 说大白话就可以了,何必～呢! Just speak normally, there is no need for such pseudo intellectual expressions.

【转向】zhuǎnxiàng ❶ 转变方向 change direction: 上午是东风,下午～了,成了南风。This morning an east wind was blowing, and this afternoon it became a southerly. ❷〈比喻 *fig.*〉改变政治立场 change one's political stance

☞ zhuàn//xiàng on p. 2522

【转学】zhuǎn//xué 学生转往另一个学校学习 (of a student) transfer from one school to another

【转眼】zhuǎnyǎn 形容极短的时间 in the twinkling of an eye; in an instant; in a flash: 冬天过去,～又是春天了。Winter passed, and spring arrived in the twinkling of an eye.

【转业】zhuǎn//yè 由一种行业转到另一种行业。特指中国人民解放军干部转到地方工作。change one's profession; (of an armyman) transfer to civilian work

【转移】zhuǎnyí ❶ 改换位置,从一方移到另一方 shift; transfer; divert: ～阵地 move to another position | ～方向 divert the orientation | ～目标 distract people's attention from sth. or sb. | ～视线 divert sb.'s attention ❷ 改变 change; transform: 客观规律不以人们的意志为～。Objective laws are independent of human will.

【转译】zhuǎnyì 不直接根据某种语言的原文翻译,而根据另一种语言的译文翻译,叫做转译 re-translation; translating from a language other than the original

【转院】zhuǎn//yuàn 病人从一个医院转到另一个医院治疗 (of a patient) transfer from one hospital to another

【转运】zhuǎn//yùn 运气好转(迷信) (superstition) have a change of luck; luck takes a turn in one's favour

【转运】zhuǎnyùn 把运来的东西再运到另外的地方去 transport; transfer; trans-ship: ～站 transfer post | ～物资 trans-shipment material

【转载】zhuǎnzǎi 报刊上刊登别的报刊上发表过的文章 reprint sth. that has been published elsewhere; reprint: 几种报纸都～了《人民日

报》的社论。Several newspapers have reprinted the *People's Daily* editorial.

【转载】zhuǎnzài same as 过载 guòzài ②

【转赠】zhuǎnzèng 把收到的礼物赠送给别人 make a present to sb. of a gift one has received

【转战】zhuǎnzhàn 连续在不同地区作战 fight in one place after another:～千里 fight successively for a thousand *li*｜～大江南北 fight successively in different parts north and south of the Yangtze River

【转账】zhuǎn//zhàng 不收付现金,只在账簿上记载收付关系 transfer money from one account to another; non-cash transaction:～支票 transfer check; check paid into an account

【转折】zhuǎnzhé ❶(事物)在发展过程中改变原来的方向、形势等 turn in the course of events:～点 turning point ❷ 指文章或语意由一个方向转向另一方向 transition (of an essay); adversative

【转折点】zhuǎnzhédiǎn 事物发展过程中对改变原来方向起决定作用的事情;事物发展过程中改变原来方向的时间 turning point; point at which a significant change occurs; critical point in the course of development; also 转捩点 zhuǎnlièdiǎn

【转正】zhuǎn//zhèng 组织中的非正式成员成为正式成员(of a probationary member of an organization) become a full member after completion of a probationary period:预备党员～become a full Party member on having served a probationary period｜临时工～(of a temporary worker) become a regular worker

【转注】zhuǎnzhù 六书之一。许慎《说文解字·叙》:'转注者,建类一首,同意相受,考、老是也。'后人的解释很分歧,比较可信的是清代戴震、段玉裁的说法。他们认为转注就是互训,意义上相同或相近的字彼此互相解释。如《说文》'老'字的解释是'考也','考'字的解释是'老也',以'考'注'老',以'老'注'考',所以叫转注。synonymous characters sharing the same radical that can explain each other; one of the six categories of Chinese characters. *Discourses on Words and Explanations of Characters·Narration* by Xu Shen: 'The term *zhuanzhu* refers to words sharing the same radical and thus belonging to the same category that are synonymous to and can explain each other, such as 老 lǎo (old age) and 考 kǎo (long life, aged).' Explanations of this line by later scholars vary. Those of Dai Zhen and Duan Yucai of the Qing Dynasty are relatively reliable. They held that *zhuanzhu* means mutually explanatory or synonymous characters, e. g. 老 lǎo (old age) and 考 kǎo (long life, aged).

zhuàn (ㄓㄨㄢˋ)

传(傳) zhuàn ❶ 解释经文的著作 commentaries on classics:经～Confucian classics and commentaries on them｜《春秋公羊～》*The Gongyang Commentary* ❷ 传记 biography:列～collected biographies of ancient dynastic histories｜别～supplementary biography (not contained in official collected biographies)｜外～unauthorized biographies｜自～autobiography｜《三国志》上有诸葛亮的～。*Records of Three Kingdoms* contains a biography of Zhuge Liang. ❸ 叙述历史故事的作品(多用做小说名称 usu. used in titles) story or novel:《水浒～》*Outlaws of the Marsh*｜《吕梁英雄～》*Heroes of the Lüliang Mountain*

☞ chuán on p. 298

【传记】zhuànjì 记录某人生平事迹的文字 biography; written account of a person's life; life story:名人～biographies of famous persons｜～文学 biographical literature

【传略】zhuànlüè 比较简略的传记 brief biography; biographical sketch:《孙中山～》*A Brief Biography of Sun Yat-sen*

沌 Zhuàn 沌河,水名,在湖北。沌口(Zhuànkǒu),地名,在湖北。Zhuanghe River, in Hubei Province; Zhuankou, name of a place in Hubei Province.

☞ dùn on p. 496

转(轉) zhuàn ❶ 旋转 turn; rotate:轮子～得很快。The wheel turns very quickly. ❷ 绕着某物移动;打转 take a lap around sth.; revolve; rotate; circle:～圈子 circle; go round and round｜～来～去 hang around ❸〈方 *dial.*〉〈量词 *classifier*〉绕一圈儿叫绕一转 revolution

☞ zhuǎi on p. 2515; zhuǎn on p. 2518

【转动】zhuàndòng ❶ 物体以一点为中心或以一直线为轴作圆周运动 turn; revolve; rotate; turn around a central point or axis:水可以使磨～。Water can set a mill in motion. ❷ 使转动 turn:～辘轳把儿 turn the crank of a windlass

☞ zhuǎndòng on p. 2518

【转筋】zhuàn//jīn〈中医 *Chin. med.*〉称肌肉(通常指小腿部的腓肠肌)痉挛 experience a cramp (esp. in the leg); have a twisted muscle; systremma:～霍乱 cramp owing to cholera morbus; cramp of the gastrocnemius muscles owing to excessive loss of water from severe vomiting and diarrhea

【转铃】zhuànlíng (～儿 zhuànlíngr)自行车车铃的一种,按动时铃盖转动发声 revolving bell for bicycles

【转炉】zhuànlú 冶炼炉的一种,炉体有圆筒形、梨形等形状，架在一个水平轴架上，可以转动。用来炼钢，也用来炼铜等。converter; smelting furnace, cylindrical or pear shaped, that rotates on a horizontal shaft bracket; used to smelt steel or copper

【转门】zhuànmén 门扇能旋转的门，由几扇门扇连在中间的一个转轴上构成 revolving door; door consisting of several vanes hinged on a central axl, that revolves when being pushed

【转磨】zhuàn//mò〈方 *dial.*〉绕着磨转，也指着急时想不出办法直转圈子 go round and round a millstone; (fig.) be at a loss as to what to do

【转盘】zhuànpán ❶ 某些器械(如唱机)上能够旋转的圆盘 turntable (as on a record player); circular rotating platform ❷ 便于机车或其他在轨道上行驶的车辆掉转方向的圆盘形设备，车辆开到圆盘上，用机器或人力转动圆盘，使车辆对着要去的方向 turntable; circular rotating platform carrying the track necessary for a locomotive to turn around ❸ 指交叉路口中间的环形岛 roundabout; traffic circus; circle at the intersection of three or more streets where vehicles travel in one direction only, designed to facilitate the flow of traffic

【转圈】zhuàn//quān (～儿 zhuàn//quānr)围绕某一点运动 circle; go round and round: ～看了大家一眼 make a circuit and have a look at all those present|我转了三个圈儿也没找着他。I made three circuits but still could not find him.

【转日莲】zhuànrìlián〈方 *dial.*〉向日葵 sunflower

【转速】zhuànsù 转动物体在单位时间内转动的圈数。通常用每分钟转动的圈数来表示。rotational speed; speed of revolution per unit of time, usu. revolutions per minute (r.p.m.)

【转台】zhuàntái ❶ 中心部分能够旋转的舞台。在这种舞台上演出，能够缩短换景的时间。revolving stage; stage whose central section revolves, used to shorten the time taken to change the stage scenery and props ❷ 餐桌上安放的较小的圆台，可以转动，用来放菜盘等，使就餐方便 revolving platform; small circular rotating platform on a dining table for the convenience of diners

【转梯】zhuàntī 台阶呈扇形，沿着主轴旋转而上的楼梯 spiral stairs; stairs that are circular in plan and consist entirely of winders or wedge-shaped steps that ascend from a central axis

【转弯子】zhuàn wān•zi〈比喻 *fig.*〉说话不直截了当；不直爽 beat about the bush: 他心眼儿多，说话爱～。He is oversensitive, and when speaking tends to beat about the bush.
☞ zhuǎn wān•zi on p.2520

【转向】zhuàn//xiàng 迷失方向 lose one's bearings; get lost: 晕头～ confused and disoriented; feel dizzy and giddy
☞ zhuǎnxiàng on p.2520

【转椅】zhuànyǐ ❶ 一种能够左右转动的椅子 swivel chair; chair whose seat revolves horizontally from a pivot at its base ❷ 儿童体育活动器械，在转盘上安上若干椅子，儿童坐在椅子上，随着转盘旋转 roundabout; recreational equipment for children, comprising a number of seats fixed to a revolving platform

【转悠】zhuàn•you ❶ 转动 turn; move from side to side: 眼珠子直～ roll one's eyes ❷ 漫步；无目的地闲逛 stroll; saunter; take a leisurely walk: 星期天我上街～了一下。On Sunday I took a stroll through the streets. ‖ also 转游 zhuàn•you

【转游】zhuàn•you same as 转悠 zhuàn•you

【转轴】zhuànzhóu ❶ 能转动的轴 axle ❷〈方 *dial.*〉(～儿 zhuànzhóur)〈比喻 *fig.*〉主意或心眼儿 idea; plan

【转子】zhuànzǐ 电机、涡轮机或泵中的转动部分 rotor; rotating part of a motor, turbine or pump

啭(囀) zhuàn〈书 *fml.*〉鸟婉转地叫(of birds) twitter; sing: 啼～ warble; trill

瑑 zhuàn〈书 *fml.*〉玉器上隆起的雕刻花纹 relief engravings on jadeware

赚 zhuàn ❶ 获得利润(跟'赔'相对 as opposed to 'lose') make a profit; gain: ～钱 make money; make a profit ❷ (～儿 zhuànr)利润 profit: 有～profitable ❸〈方 *dial.*〉挣(钱) earn (money): 做一天工，～十块 earn ten yuan for a day's work.
☞ zuàn on p.2568

【赚头】zhuàn•tou 利润 profit: 本小利微，～不大。A small business earns a small profit.

譔 zhuàn same as 撰 zhuàn

撰 zhuàn 写作 write; compose: ～文 write an essay|～稿 write articles

【撰述】zhuànshù ❶ 撰写；著述 write; compile: ～文章 write articles ❷ 撰述的作品 book; work: ～甚多 have written many books

【撰写】zhuànxiě 写作 write; compose: ～碑文 write an inscription for a tablet|～论文 write a thesis

【撰著】zhuànzhù 写作 write; compose: ～中国通史 write a general history of China

篆 zhuàn ❶ 汉字形体的一种 seal script (a style of Chinese calligraphy): ～书 seal character (a style of Chinese calligraphy)|～体 seal script|大～greater seal character|小～lesser seal character|真草隶～ regular script, cursive script, official script and seal character ❷ 写篆书 inscribe in the seal script: ～额(用篆字写在碑额上) inscribe seal characters on the head of a tablet ❸ 指印章 seal

【篆刻】zhuànkè 刻印章(因印章多用篆文)(seal characters are thus named because this style of Chinese calligraphy is oft. used on seals) seal cutting

【篆书】zhuànshū 汉字字体,秦朝整理字体后规定的写法 seal script (a style of Chinese calligraphy, standard Qin-dynasty script)

【篆字】zhuànzì same as 篆书 zhuànshū

馔 zhuàn 〈书 *fml.*〉饭食 food:酒～food and drink|盛(shèng)～ sumptuous dinner; feast

篹 zhuàn 〈书 *fml.*〉 ❶ same as 馔 zhuàn ❷ same as 撰 zhuàn

☞ zuǎn on p.2567

篡(簒) zhuàn 〈书 *fml.*〉 ❶ same as 馔 zhuàn ❷ same as 撰 zhuàn

☞ zuǎn on p.2567

zhuāng (ㄓㄨㄤ)

妆(妝、粧) zhuāng ❶ 化妆 apply makeup; make up:梳～ dress and make up ❷ 女子身上的装饰;演员的装饰 woman's personal adornments; stage makeup and costume:红～ bright feminine attire; young woman|卸～(of woman) remove ornaments and formal dress; remove stage makeup and costume ❸ 指嫁妆 trousseau; dowry:～奁 trousseau; dowry|送～(运送嫁妆)transport dowry

【妆奁】zhuānglián ❶ 女子梳妆用的镜匣 toilet case used by women in ancient China ❷ 借指嫁妆 trousseau; dowry

【妆饰】zhuāngshì ❶ 打扮 adorn; dress up; be decked out:精心～dress up elaborately ❷ 打扮出来的样子 makeup:～俏丽 be smartly attired

【妆新】zhuāngxīn 〈方 *dial.*〉 ❶ 新婚前把新婚所用的衣服、被褥、枕头等摆放在新房里 arrange complete sets of clothing and bedding for newly-weds in their bridal chamber ❷ 指新婚时所用的衣服、被褥、枕头等 complete outfit for newly-weds (including clothing and bedding)

庄[1](莊) zhuāng ❶(～儿 zhuāngr)村庄 village:～户 peasant household|农～farmstead|王家～Wang Family Village ❷ 封建社会里君主、贵族等所占有的成片土地 manor; land owned by monarch and nobles under the feudal system:皇～fields owned by royal families|～田 fields let out to tenant farmers by imperial families, etc.|～园 manor ❸ 规模较大或做批发生意的商店 place of business; wholesale shop:钱～old-style Chinese private bank|布～shop for clothing materials|茶～tea shop|饭～restaurant ❹ 庄家 banker (in a gambling game):做～be banker by turns|是谁的～? Who's the banker? ❺ (Zhuāng)姓 a surname

庄[2](莊) zhuāng 庄重 serious; grave; sedate:～严 solemn; stately|端～ dignified; sedate|亦～亦谐 seriocomic; serious and comical at the same time

【庄户】zhuānghù 指农户 peasant household:～人 peasant|～人家 peasant family

【庄家】zhuāng·jia 某些牌戏或赌博中每一局的主持人 banker (in a gambling game)

【庄稼】zhuāng·jia 地里长着的农作物(多指粮食作物 usu. cereal crops) crops; agricultural plants growing in the field

【庄稼地】zhuāng·jiadì 田地;农田 cropland; fields

【庄稼汉】zhuāng·jiahàn 种庄稼的男人 farmer; peasant

【庄稼活儿】zhuāng·jiahuór 农业生产工作(多指田间劳动 usu. in the field) farm work

【庄稼人】zhuāng·jiarén 种庄稼的人;农民 peasant; farmer

【庄田】zhuāngtián ❶ 皇室、官僚、寺院等雇人耕种或租给佃户的土地 fields let out to tenant farmers by imperial families, bureaucrats, monasteries, etc. ❷ 田地;农田 field; farmland; cropland:千里平原好～。The thousand-*li* plain makes good farmland.

【庄严】zhuāngyán 庄重而严肃 solemn; dignified; stately:态度～dignified in manner|～地宣誓 make a solemn vow|雄伟、～的人民英雄纪念碑 magnificent and solemn Monument to the People's Heroes

【庄园】zhuāngyuán 封建主占有和经营的大片地产,包括一个或若干个村庄,基本上是自给自足的经济单位。以欧洲中世纪早期的封建领主庄园最典型,我国封建时代皇室、贵族、大地主、寺院等占有和经营的大田庄,也有叫庄园的。manor; finca; medieval landed estate held by a feudal lord under the feudal system and worked by serfs or tenant farmers as a largely self-sufficient economic unit, chiefly in Western Europe; fields let out to tenant farmers by imperial families, nobles, big landlords or monasteries, etc. during China's feudal times

【庄重】zhuāngzhòng (言语、举止)不随便;不轻浮 serious; grave; solemn; sedate:态度～solemn in manner|在严肃的场合你要放～点儿。Be serious on a solemn occasion.

【庄子】zhuāng·zi ❶ 村庄 village; hamlet:他是我们～里的人。He is a fellow villager of ours. ❷ 田庄 country estate

桩(樁) zhuāng ❶ 桩子 stake; pile:木～ wood stake|桥～bridge stake|打～pile driving|拴马～ hitching post ❷〈量词 *classifier*〉件(用于事情 of things) piece:一～心事 a matter on one's mind

Z

【桩子】zhuāng·zi 一端或全部埋在土中的柱形物,多用于建筑或做分界的标志 stake; pile; pillar-shaped object sunk into the ground, usu. part of a building, or for marking a boundary

装[1](裝) zhuāng ❶ 修饰;打扮;化装 dress up; attire; deck out; play the part (or role) of; act:~饰 decorate|~点 deck|他~老头儿。He plays the part of an old man. ❷ 服装 outfit; clothing:新~new clothes|冬~winter dress (or clothes)|军~ military uniform|中山~ Chinese tunic suit ❸ 行装 outfit for a journey; luggage:整~待发 get ready for a journey; be ready to start out|轻~简从 (of an important person) travel with little luggage and few attendants; travel light ❹ 演员化装时穿戴涂抹的东西 stage makeup and costume:卸~(of an actor or actress) remove stage makeup and costume ❺ 假装 pretend; feign; make believe:~模作样 be affected; attitudinize|不懂就是不懂,不要~懂。If you don't know, just say so; don't pretend to know about something you don't.

装[2](裝) zhuāng ❶ 把东西放进器物内;把物品放在运输工具上 load; pack; hold; put sth. into a vessel; put into or upon a carrier:~箱 pack a box; put sth. in a crate; crate|~车 load a truck (or cart) ❷ 装配;安装 install; fit; assemble:~订 bookbinding|~电灯 install electric lights|机器已经~好了。The machine has been installed.

【装扮】zhuāngbàn ❶ 打扮 dress up; attire; deck out:节日的广场~得分外美丽。On holidays the square is particularly beautifully decked out. ❷ 化装 disguise; masquerade:他~成算命先生进城侦察敌情。He disguised himself as a fortune-teller and entered the city to gather intelligence on the enemy. ❸ 假装 pretend; feign:巫婆~神仙欺骗人。The sorceress pretended to be an immortal so as to cheat people.

【装备】zhuāngbèi ❶ 配备(武器、军装、器材、技术力量等) equip; fit out (weapons, uniforms, equipment, technical force, etc.):这些武器可以~一个营。These weapons are sufficient to equip a battalion. ❷ 指配备的武器、军装、器材、技术力量等 equipment; outfit (weapons, uniforms, equipment, technical force, etc.):现代化~modern equipment

【装裱】zhuāngbiǎo 裱褙书画并装上轴子等 mount (a picture, etc.) on a scroll:~字画 mount calligraphy and painting

【装点】zhuāngdiǎn 装饰点缀 decorate; dress; deck:~门面 put on a facade; keep up appearances

【装订】zhuāngdìng 把零散的书页或纸张加工成本子 binding; bookbinding; fasten together the printed pages (of a book) and enclose them in a protective cover:~成册 bind into a volume|~车间 bookbindery; bindery

【装疯卖傻】zhuāng fēng mài shǎ 故意装做疯癫痴呆的样子 feign madness and act like an idiot

【装裹】zhuāng·guo ❶ 给死人穿衣服 dress a corpse; wrap (a corpse) in a shroud ❷ 死人入殓时穿的衣服 shroud; burial clothes

【装潢】zhuānghuáng ❶ 装饰物品使美观(原只指书画,今不限) (orig.) mount (a picture, book); decorate; dress:~门面 window dress; put on a facade; keep up appearances|墙上挂着红木镜框~起来的名画。On the wall hang famous paintings mounted in mahogany frames. ❷ 物品的装饰 decoration; mounting; packaging:这个茶叶罐的~很讲究。This tea caddy is tastefully decorated.

【装甲】zhuāngjiǎ ❶ 装有防弹钢板的 armoured:~车 armoured car; armoured vehicle|~舰 ironclad warship; armoured ship ❷ 装在车辆、船只、飞机、碉堡等上面的防弹钢板 plate armour (covering vehicles, vessels, planes, blockhouses, etc.)

【装甲兵】zhuāngjiǎbīng 以坦克、自行火炮和装甲输送车为基本装备的兵种。也称这一兵种的士兵。armoured forces; army whose basic equipment comprises tanks, self-propelled guns and armoured carriers; soldiers of this combat branch; also 坦克兵 tǎnkèbīng

【装甲车】zhuāngjiǎchē 作战用的装有防弹钢板和武器的汽车或列车 armoured car; armoured vehicle; motor vehicle or train covered with plate armour and equipped with weapons; also 铁甲车 tiějiǎchē

【装甲舰】zhuāngjiǎjiàn 19世纪后半期出现的一种火力和防护力很强的军舰。船壳是钢质,火炮有炮塔防护,两舷、甲板都有装甲。ironclad; a warship appeared in the latter half of the 19th century that was built to be equipped with powerful firearms, and was securely protected by armour plating. Its shell was of steel, and its guns kept within a turret; its two sides and deck were covered with armour plate. also 铁甲舰 tiějiǎjiàn

【装假】zhuāng//jiǎ 实际不是那样而装做那样 pretend; feign; make believe:这孩子很老实,不会~。This child is honest and never pretends.

【装殓】zhuāngliàn 给死人穿好衣裳,放到棺材里 dress and lay a corpse in a coffin

【装门面】zhuāng mén·mian〈比喻 *fig.*〉为了表面好看而加以粉饰点缀 put up a front; maintain an outward show; keep up appearances

【装模作样】zhuāng mú zuò yàng 故意做作,装出某种样子给人看 indulge in histrionics; be affected; attitudinize; put on an act; behave in an affected way

【装配】zhuāngpèi 把零件或部件配成整体 assemble; fit together (parts of a machine, etc.):～工 assembler; fitter|～车间 assembly shop; fitting shop|发电机已经～好了。The generator has been assembled.

【装配线】zhuāngpèixiàn 在流水作业法的生产过程中,按次序在不同的工作区把各个零件或部件装配成整体,这种工作组织叫装配线 assembly line; grouping of machines, equipment and workers in such a way as to streamline the process of production until the product is assembled

【装腔作势】zhuāng qiāng zuò shì 故意做作,装出某种情态 give oneself airs; be affected or pretentious; strike a pose; put on airs:我们应该老老实实地办事,不要靠～来吓人。We should do things honestly, and never rely on pretence in order to intimidate people.

【装神弄鬼】zhuāng shén nòng guǐ ❶ 装扮成鬼神(骗人) make oneself out to be a supernatural being (to cheat people) ❷〈比喻 *fig.*〉故弄玄虚 purposely make a mystery out of simple matters; deliberately mystify:他～糊弄人。He purposely mystifies simple matters so as to fool people.

【装饰】zhuāngshì ❶ 在身体或物体的表面加些附属的东西,使美观 decorate; adorn; ornament; deck:～品 ornaments|～图案 decorative pattern|她向来朴素,不爱～。She has always been plain and modest, and does not care much for ornamentation. ❷ 装饰品 ornaments:建筑物上的各种～都很精巧。The ornamentation on this building is exquisite.

【装束】zhuāngshù ❶ 打扮 dress; attire:～朴素 be simply dressed|～入时 be fashionably dressed ❷〈书 *fml.*〉整理行装 pack up (for a journey)

【装蒜】zhuāng//suàn 装糊涂;装腔作势 pretend not to know; feign ignorance:你比谁都明白,别～啦! Don't plead ignorance; you know more about this than anyone else.

【装相】zhuāng//xiàng (～儿 zhuāng//xiàngr) 装模作样 pretend; put on an act

【装卸】zhuāngxiè ❶ 装到运输工具上和从运输工具上卸下 load and unload:～货物 load and unload a truck, ship, etc.; load and unload goods ❷ 装配和拆卸 assemble and disassemble:他会～自行车。He can take a bicycle apart and put it back together again.

【装修】zhuāngxiū ❶ 在房屋工程上抹面、粉刷并安装门窗、水电等设备 fit up (a house, etc., including plastering, whitewashing, fitting doors and windows, installing plumbing, and putting in electrical wiring):～门面 fit up a shop front|内部～,暂停营业。Business will be suspended until completion of internal refurbishment. ❷ 房屋工程上抹的保护层和安装的门窗、水电等设备 fixtures (of a house, including protective plastering, doors, windows, and plumbing and electrical equipment)

【装样子】zhuāng yàng·zi 装模作样 put on an act; do sth. for appearance's sake

【装运】zhuāngyùn 装载并运输 load and transport; ship:～货物 ship cargo

【装载】zhuāngzài 用运输工具装(人或物) load; put (goods or passengers) into or upon a carrier

【装帧】zhuāngzhēn 指书画、书刊的装潢设计(书刊的装帧包括封面、版面、插图、装订形式等设计)(of a painting, book, magazine, etc., including covers, title page and illustrations) binding and layout design:～考究 beautifully designed and bound

【装置】zhuāngzhì ❶ 安装 install; fit:降温设备已经～好了。The cooling equipment has been installed. ❷ 机器、仪器或其他设备中,构造较复杂并具有某种独立的功用的物件 installation; unit; device; plant; complex apparatus for a specific function:自动化～ automatic device

zhuǎng(ㄓㄨㄤˇ)

奘 zhuǎng〈方 *dial.*〉粗而大 big and thick; stout, robust:身高腰～tall and robust|这棵树很～。The tree is very tall and thick.
☞ zàng on p. 2392

zhuàng(ㄓㄨㄤˋ)

壮[1](壯) zhuàng ❶ 强壮 strong; robust:健～strong and healthy|身体～have a strong physique|年轻力～young and robust ❷ 雄壮;大 magnificent; grand:～观 grand (or magnificent) sight|～志 great aspiration; lofty ideal|理直气～ with justice on one's side, one feels bold and assured ❸ 加强;使壮大 strengthen; make better:以～声势 to lend impetus and strength; to make sth. appear more dynamic and impressive|～～胆子 build up sb.'s courage; boost sb.'s courage ❹〈中医 *Chin. med.*〉艾灸,一灼叫一壮 one moxa-cone; one moxa-cone is called a *zhuang*, the number of moxa cones used are taken as measurement for moxibustion

壮[2](壯) Zhuàng 壮族。原作僮。the Zhuang ethnic group; originally 僮 zhuàng

【壮大】zhuàngdà ❶ 变得强大 grow in strength; expand:力量日益～。Forces are growing steadily. ❷ 使强大 strengthen:～队伍 expand the ranks ❸ 强壮粗大 thick and strong; bulky:手脚～have thick and strong arms and legs

【壮胆】zhuàng//dǎn 使胆大 build up sb.'s

courage; boost sb.'s courage：走夜路唱歌，自己给自己～。Sing a song to bolster one's courage when walking alone at night.

【壮丁】zhuàngdīng〈旧时 *old*〉指青壮年的男子（多指达到当兵年龄的人 oft. of a person eligible for conscription）able-bodied man

【壮工】zhuànggōng 从事简单体力劳动的没有专门技术的工人 unskilled labourer

【壮观】zhuàngguān ❶ 雄伟的景象 grand (or magnificent) sight：这大自然的～，是我从来没有见过的。I have never seen such a magnificent natural phenomenon. ❷ 景象雄伟 magnificent：用数不清的红旗装饰起来的长江大桥，显得格外～。The Yangtze River Bridge, decorated with countless red flags, is a splendid sight.

【壮怀】zhuànghuái〈书 *fml.*〉豪放的胸怀；壮志 great aspiration; lofty ideal：仰天长啸，～激烈。Raising my eyes toward heaven, I heave a long sigh, my wrath not yet appeased.

【壮健】zhuàngjiàn 健壮 healthy and strong; robust：身体～ be healthy and strong

【壮锦】zhuàngjǐn 壮族妇女用手工编织的锦，经线一般用白色棉纱，纬线用彩色丝绒 Zhuang brocade; fabric woven by Zhuang women on hand looms, with a white cotton warp and colourful silk weft

【壮举】zhuàngjǔ 伟大的举动；壮烈的行为 magnificent feat; heroic undertaking：史无前例的～unparalleled feat

【壮阔】zhuàngkuò ❶ 雄壮而宽广 vast; magnificent; grandiose：波澜～ surging forward with grand momentum; unfolding on a magnificent scale ❷ 宏伟；宏大 great; grand：规模～grand in scale

【壮丽】zhuànglì 雄壮而美丽 majestic; magnificent; glorious：山河～。The landscape is spectacular.

【壮烈】zhuàngliè 勇敢有气节 heroic; brave：～牺牲 heroically give one's life; die a hero's death

【壮年】zhuàngnián 三四十岁的年纪 robust years of a person's life (between thirty and fifty); prime of life

【壮士】zhuàngshì 豪壮而勇敢的人 brave man; heroic man; hero; warrior

【壮实】zhuàng·shi（身体）强壮结实 sturdy; robust：这小伙子长得多～！What a sturdy young chap!

【壮戏】zhuàngxì 壮族戏曲剧种之一，流行于广西壮族自治区和云南壮族聚居地区。由壮族山歌、说唱发展而成。Zhuang Opera; drama originating in folk songs and ballads of the Zhuang ethnic group, popular in the Guangxi Zhuang Autonomous Region and areas in Yunnan where the Zhuang people live in compact communities

【壮心】zhuàngxīn 壮志 high aspirations; lofty (or noble) ideal：～不已。The heart of a hero is stout for ever.

【壮志】zhuàngzhì 伟大的志向 great aspiration; lofty ideal：雄心～lofty aspirations and high ideals｜～凌云 with soaring (or high) aspirations｜～未酬 one's as yet unrealized high aspirations

【壮族】Zhuàngzú 我国少数民族之一，分布在广西和云南、广东、贵州、湖南等地 Zhuang ethnic group, or the Zhuangs; one of China's ethnic peoples inhabiting the Guangxi Zhuang Autonomous Region, and Yunnan, Guangdong, Guizhou and Hunan provinces

状(狀) zhuàng ❶ 形状；样子 form; shape：～态 state; condition; state of affairs｜奇形怪～grotesque or fantastic in shape or appearance｜惊恐万～in a great panic; convulsed with fear ❷ 情况 state; condition：～况 state; condition｜病～symptom of disease｜罪～facts about a crime; charges in an indictment ❸ 陈述或描摹 describe; depict：～语 adverbial modifier; adverbial｜不可名～ beggar description; be indescribable; be beyond description ❹ 陈述事件或记载事迹的文字 account; record：供～written confession; deposition｜行～ brief biography of a deceased person (usu. accompanying an obituary notice) ❺ 指诉状 written complaint; plaint：～纸 written complaint; plaint｜告～ bring a lawsuit against sb. ❻ 褒奖、委任等文件 certificate：奖～certificate of merit｜委任～certificate of appointment

【状况】zhuàngkuàng 情形 condition; state; state of affairs：经济～(a person's) financial situation; (a country's) economic situation｜健康～physical condition; state of health; health

【状态】zhuàngtài 人或事物表现出来的形态 state; condition; state of affairs：心理～state of mind; psychology｜液体～liquid state｜病人处于昏迷～。The patient is in a coma.

【状语】zhuàngyǔ 动词、形容词前边的表示状态、程度、时间、处所等等的修饰成分。形容词、副词、时间词、处所词都可以做状语。例如'你仔细看'的'仔细'（状态），'天很热'的'很'（程度），'我前天来的'的'前天'（时间），'你这儿坐'的'这儿'（处所）。状语有时候可以放在主语前边，例如'昨天我没有出门'的'昨天'，'忽然他对我笑了笑'的'忽然'。adverbials modifier; adverbials; word used generally to modify a verb, or adjective, by expressing time, place, manner, or degree. Adjectives, adverbs, and words expressing time and place can be used adverbially. For instance, in the sentences 'Look carefully,' 'It is very hot,' 'I came the day before yesterday' and 'Take your seat here,' the words 'carefully' (manner), 'hot' (degree), 'the day before yesterday' (time) and 'here' (place) are all adverbials. Sometimes an adverbial word or phrase is placed before the subject. For instance, in the sentences 'Yesterday I did not go out' and 'Suddenly he smiled at me,' the adverbials 'yesterday' and 'suddenly' are placed before the subject.

【状元】zhuàng·yuan ❶ 科举时代的一种称号。唐代称进士科及第的第一人,有时也泛称新进士。宋代主要指第一名,有时也用于第二、三名。元代以后限于称殿试一甲(第一等)第一名。Number One Scholar; title conferred on the person with the best score in the highest imperial examination. During the Tang Dynasty, this title referred to the number one metropolitan graduate with honours (designating the national civil service recruitment examination graduate with the highest marks), and sometimes to new metropolitan graduates. During the Song Dynasty, it referred to the number one metropolitan graduate, and sometimes also to those in second and third place. During the Yuan and following dynasties, it referred to the candidate for the palace examinations (the final stage in any sequence of civil service recruitment examinations) with the highest marks. ❷〈比喻 *fig.*〉在本行业中成绩最好的人 the very best (in any field):养鸡～champion chicken-farmer | 行行出～。Each profession has its peerless master.

【状纸】zhuàngzhǐ ❶ 印有规定格式供写诉状用的纸 old official form for filing a lawsuit ❷ 诉状 written complaint; plaint; indictment

【状子】zhuàng·zi 诉状 written complaint; plaint; indictment

僮 Zhuàng 我国少数民族壮族的壮字原作僮 old form of 壮 Zhuàng, name of an ethnic group in China
☞ 童 tóng on p. 1924

撞 zhuàng ❶ 运动着的物体跟别的物体猛然碰上 knock; bump into; run into; strike; collide:～钟 toll (or strike) a bell | 别让汽车～上。Don't get run over by a car. | 两个人～了个满怀。The two ran full tilt into each other. ❷ 碰见 meet by chance; bump into; run into:不想见他,偏～上他。I wanted to avoid him, but as it happened I ran into him. ❸ 试探 take one's chance:～运气 try one's luck; take a chance ❹ 莽撞地行动;闯 rush; dash; barge:横冲直～barge around; dash about

【撞车】zhuàng//chē ❶ 车辆相撞 collision of vehicles:～事故 traffic accident ❷〈比喻 *fig.*〉互相矛盾;互相冲突 clash (of opinions, interests or meetings, etc.):安排不周,两个会～了。Not having been properly planned, the two meetings clashed.

【撞击】zhuàngjī same as 撞 zhuàng ①:波浪～岩石。The breakers dashed against the rocks.◇这突如其来的消息猛烈地～着她的心扉。The abruptness of the news had a terrific impact on her.

【撞见】zhuàngjiàn 碰见 meet or discover by chance; run across; catch sb. in the act

【撞骗】zhuàngpiàn 到处找机会行骗 seek a chance of defrauding; swindle:招摇～swindle and bluff; bluff one's way through sth.

【撞墙】zhuàng//qiáng〈比喻 *fig.*〉碰壁 run up against a wall; be rebuffed

【撞锁】zhuàng//suǒ 上门找人时,人不在家,门锁着,叫做撞锁 find that sb. is not at home and that the door is locked

【撞锁】zhuàngsuǒ 安在门上的一种锁,把门一关不必用钥匙就能锁上 spring lock; lock in which the bolt is shot automatically by a spring; also 碰锁 pèngsuǒ

【撞针】zhuàngzhēn 枪炮里撞击子弹或炮弹底火的机件 firing pin; part in the bolt or breech of a firearm which strikes the primer and explodes the charge

幢 zhuàng〈方 *dial.*〉〈量词 *classifier*〉房屋一座叫一幢 measure word for house
☞ chuáng on p. 305

戆 zhuàng〈书 *fml.*〉same as 戆直 zhuàngzhí
☞ gàng on p. 639

【戆直】zhuàngzhí 憨厚而刚直 blunt and tactless; simple and honest:为人～ be simple and honest

zhuī(ㄓㄨㄟ)

隹 zhuī 古书上指短尾巴的鸟 short-tailed birds mentioned in ancient books

追 zhuī ❶ 追赶 chase (or run) after; pursue:～兵 pursuing troops | 急起直～ summon all one's energies in an effort to catch up; do one's utmost to overtake ❷ 追究 trace; look into; get to the bottom of:～问 question closely | ～赃 order the return of stolen money or goods | 一定要把这事的根底～出来。We are determined to get to the bottom of the matter. ❸ 追求 court (a woman); woo:～名逐利 seek fame and wealth | 两个小伙子都在～这位姑娘。Both young men are courting this girl. ❹ 回溯 recall; reminisce:～念 think back, recall | ～悼 mourn over a person's death | ～述 relate; recount ❺ 事后补办 retroactively; posthumously:～加 add to (the original amount) | ～认 recognize retroactively

【追奔逐北】zhuī bēn zhú běi 追击败逃的敌军 give chase to a routed enemy. also 追亡逐北 zhuī wáng zhú běi

【追逼】zhuībī ❶ 追赶进逼 pursue closely (a

fleeing enemy):敌军不战而逃,我军乘胜～。The enemy fled without so much as putting up a fight, and in pursuing and routing them our troops claimed a resounding victory. ❷ 用强迫的方式追究或索取 press for (repayment); extort (a confession):～债款 press for the repayment of debt | ～他说出实情 force him to tell the truth

【追补】zhuībǔ ❶ 在原有的数额以外再增加;追加 add to (the original amount):～预算 supplement a budget ❷ 事后补偿 make up; remedy; make good:不可～的遗憾 irremediable regret

【追捕】zhuībǔ 追赶捉拿 pursue and capture:～逃犯 pursue and capture an escaped convict

【追查】zhuīchá 根据事故发生的经过进行调查 investigate; trace; find out:～责任 find out where the responsibility lies | ～事故原因 investigate the causes of an accident

【追悼】zhuīdào 沉痛地怀念(死者) mourn over a person's death:～会 memorial gathering | ～死难烈士 hold a memorial service for martyrs

【追肥】zhuī//féi 在农作物生长期内施肥 top-dress; spread manure during the crop growth period; apply fertilizer

【追肥】zhuīféi 在农作物生长期内施的肥 topsoil dressing; fertilizer applied during crop growth period

【追赶】zhuīgǎn ❶ 加快速度赶上前去打击或捉住 pursue; accelerate one's pace in order to pursue and attack, or capture:～敌人 pursue the enemy | ～野兔 chase the hare ❷ 加快速度赶上(前面的人或事物) accelerate one's pace in order to catch up; run after; pursue:～部队 run after the troops | ～世界先进水平 measure up to advanced world levels

【追根】zhuīgēn 追究根源 get to the root (or bottom) of sth.:～究底 get to the bottom of the affair | ～溯源 trace sth. to its source | 这孩子什么事都爱～。This child does not give up until he gets to the bottom of something.

【追怀】zhuīhuái 回忆;追念 call to mind; recall; reminisce:～往事 reminisce about the old days

【追悔】zhuīhuǐ 追溯以往,感到悔恨 repent; regret:～莫及 too late to repent

【追击】zhuījī 追赶着攻击 pursue and attack; follow up:乘胜～follow up a victory with a pursuit that routs the enemy

【追记】zhuījì ❶ 在人死后给他记上(功勋) cite (or award) posthumously:为烈士～特等功 posthumously award a martyr special-class merit citation ❷ 事后记录或记载 record retroactively:会后,他～了几个发言的主要内容。After the meeting, he gave a brief account of the gists of several speeches. ❸ 事后的记载 (多用做文章标题 usu. used in titles) accounts of events after they have occurred, or from memory:世界杯足球赛～'World Cup Soccer Tournament in Retrospect'

【追加】zhuījiā 在原定的数额以外再增加 add to (the original amount):～预算 supplement a budget; make a supplementary budget | ～基本建设投资 make an additional investment in capital construction

【追缴】zhuījiǎo 勒令缴回(非法所得的财物) recover (property illegally obtained):～赃款 recover illicit money

【追究】zhuījiū 追问(根由);追查(原因、责任等) look into (the origin); find out; investigate (causes, responsibilities, etc.):～原由 investigate the cause of sth. | ～责任 investigate, and affix responsibility; find out who is to blame | 不予～no action will be taken against sb.

【追求】zhuīqiú ❶ 用积极的行动来争取达到某种目的 seek; pursue; try to acquire or gain; aim at:～真理 seek truth; in pursuit of truth | ～进步 strive to make progress | ～名利 seek fame and wealth ❷ 特指向异性求爱 try to win the love of; court (a woman); woo

【追认】zhuīrèn ❶ 事后认可某项法令、决议等 (of a decree, decision, etc.) subsequently confirm or endorse; recognize retroactively ❷ 批准某人生前提出的参加党、团组织的要求 admit or confer posthumously (as a member of the Communist Party, the Communist Youth League, etc.)

【追述】zhuīshù 述说过去的事情 talk about events from the past; relate; recount:王大爷向孩子们～当时的欢乐情景。Uncle Wang recounted to the children that joyful scene of so long ago.

【追思】zhuīsī 追想;回想 recall; reminisce:～往事 recall the past

【追诉】zhuīsù 司法机关或有告诉权的人对有犯罪行为的人在其犯罪后一定期限内,依法提起诉讼,追究刑事责任 prosecute; institute legal proceedings, or conduct criminal court proceedings, within a certain period of time after a crime has been committed

【追溯】zhuīsù 逆流而上,向江河发源处走,比喻探索事物的由来 sail against the current to where the river originates; (fig.) trace back to; date from:两国交往的历史可以～到许多世纪以前。Contacts between the two countries can be traced back over the centuries.

【追随】zhuīsuí 跟随 follow:～左右 follow sb. closely | ～潮流 go with the tide

【追尾】zhuīwěi 机动车在行驶中,后一辆车的前部撞上前一辆车的尾部 tailgate; run into the back of the preceding car:保持车距,严防～。No tailgating. *or* Keep a safe distance from the car ahead to aviod bumping.

【追问】zhuīwèn 追根究底地问 question closely; make a detailed inquiry; examine minutely: ～下落 question closely on the whereabouts|他既然不知道,就不必再～了。As he does not know, there is no need to question him.

【追想】zhuīxiǎng 追忆;回忆 recall; reminisce

【追叙】zhuīxù ❶ 追述 talk of the past; relate; recount ❷ 写作的一种手法,先写出结果,然后再倒回头去叙述经过 flashback; narration of earlier episodes

【追寻】zhuīxún 跟踪寻找 pursue; search; track down: ～走散的同伴 search for lost companions ◇～美好的人生 pursue a beautiful life

【追忆】zhuīyì 回忆 recollect; recall; look back: ～往事,历历在目。As I look back, scenes of the past leap before my eyes.

【追赃】zhuī//zāng 勒令罪犯缴回赃款、赃物 order the return of stolen money or goods; recover stolen money or goods; make sb. relinquish his spoils

【追赠】zhuīzèng 在人死后授予某种官职、称号等 confer posthumously (a title, etc.)

【追逐】zhuīzhú ❶ 追赶 pursue; chase: ～野兽 pursue wild beasts ❷ 追求 seek; quest: ～名利 seek fame and wealth

【追踪】zhuīzōng 按踪迹或线索追寻 follow the trail of; track; trace: 边防战士沿着脚印～潜入国境的人。The frontier guards tracked down illegal immigrants by following their footprints.

骓 zhuī 〈书 *fml*.〉毛色青白相杂的马 piebald horse

椎 zhuī 椎骨 vertebra: 脊～ vertebra | 颈～ cervical vertebra| 胸～thoracic vertebra ☞ chuí on p.309

【椎骨】zhuīgǔ 构成脊柱的短骨,根据所处部位,依次分为颈椎、胸椎、腰椎、骶椎和尾椎。除第一、二颈椎外,每两椎骨中间有一椎间盘。人的椎骨共有 33 块,即颈椎 7 块,胸椎 12 块,腰椎 5 块,骶椎 5 块,尾椎 4 块。vertebra; any of the single bones or segments of the spinal column, consisting of cervical vertebra, thoracic vertebrae, lumbar vertebrae, sacral vertebrae, and caudal vertebra. Except for the first and second cervical vertebrae, there is an intervertebral disk between every two adjacent vertebrae. A man has 33 vertebrae, including 7 cervical vertebrae, 12 thoracic vertebrae, 5 lumbar vertebrae, 5 sacral vertebrae, and 4 caudal vertebrae. 通称 commonly called 脊椎骨 jǐzhuīgǔ

【椎间盘】zhuījiānpán 连接相邻两个椎骨椎体的圆盘状软垫,中央是灰白色富有弹性的胶状物,四周是坚韧的软骨环。有承受压力、缓冲震荡并使脊柱能活动等作用。intervertebral disk; layer of disk-shaped fibrous connective tissue, interposed between the bodies of adjacent vertebrae, composed of an outer fibrous part that surrounds a central gelatinous mass. It can bear weight, absorb shock and enables the spinal column to be flexible.

锥 zhuī ❶ 锥子 awl ❷ 形状像锥子的东西 anything shaped like an awl: 冰～icicle| 圆～体 circular cone ❸ 用锥子或锥子形的工具钻 bore; drill; make a hole with an awl: 上鞋时先用锥子～个眼儿。In order to stitch the sole to the upper of a shoe, first make a hole with an awl.

【锥处囊中】zhuī chǔ náng zhōng 锥子放在口袋里,锥尖就会露出来 awl in a bag; 〈比喻 *fig*.〉有才智的人终能显露头角,不会长久被埋没 talent will reveal itself despite temporary obscurity

【锥度】zhuīdù ❶ 柱形物体的横剖面向一端逐渐缩小的形式 coning; tapering; gradual decrease in breadth or thickness of one end of an elongated object; also called 梢 sào ❷ 横剖面缩小的数值,如锥度1∶50,即每长 50 个单位缩小 1 个单位 taper ratio; numerical value of the decrease in breadth or thickness. For instance, the taper ratio 1∶50 signifies a rate of reduction in breadth of one unit of thickness per 50 units.

【锥子】zhuī·zi 有尖头的用来钻孔的工具 awl; small, pointed tool for making holes

zhuì (ㄓㄨㄟˋ)

坠(墜) zhuì ❶ 落 fall; drop: ～马 fall off a horse| ～楼 fall down a building |摇摇欲～ tottering; crumbling ❷ (沉重的东西)往下垂;垂在下面(heavy things) weigh down: 石榴把树枝～得弯弯的。The branches bent with the weight of pomegranates .|他的心里像～上了千斤的石头。The matter weighs on his mind as heavily as a thousand-kilo stone. ❸ (～儿 zhuìr)垂在下面的东西 weight; hanging object: 扇～儿 fan pendants| 耳～儿 eardrops

【坠地】zhuìdì 〈书 *fml*.〉指小孩子初生(of a child) be born: 呱呱(gūgū)～(of a child) be born

【坠毁】zhuìhuǐ (飞机等)落下来毁坏(of a plane, etc.) fall and break; crash

【坠落】zhuìluò 落;掉 fall; drop; pitch: 陨星～ falling of a meteorite|被击中的敌机冒着黑烟,～在大海里。The shot enemy plane fell, black smoke billowing from it, into the sea.

【坠琴】zhuìqín 弦乐器,有蟒皮面和桐木板面两种。前者琴筒像四胡而较短,后者琴筒像小三弦。原来是河南坠子的专用乐器,后来逐渐用于其他曲艺、戏曲等。*zhuiqin*, a kind of bowed instrument. There are two main types: one made with boa skin, and another plated with Chinese parasol tree wood. The former looks like a *sihu*, but shorter, and the latter looks like a *xiaosan xian*. This instrument was originally played exclusively for accompaniment to Henan *zhuizi* (ballads) and later also for musical accompaniment to other folk performing arts; also known as 坠子 zhuì·zi, 坠胡 zhuìhú or 二弦 èrxián

【坠子】[1] zhuì·zi 〈方 *dial*.〉 same as 坠 zhuì ③, 也专指耳坠子 weight; plummet; pendant; eardrop

【坠子】[2] zhuì·zi ❶ 流行于河南的一种曲艺，因主要伴奏乐器是坠琴而得名。*zhuizi*; ballad singing to the accompaniment of *zhuiqin* (坠琴), popular in Henan Province. 通称 commonly called 河南坠子 Hénán zhuì·zi ❷ same as 坠琴 zhuìqín

缀 zhuì ❶ 用针线等使连起来 sew; stitch: ～网 weave net | 补～mend (clothes); patch | 你的袖子破了，我给你～上两针。Your sleeve is torn; I'll put a few stitches in it for you. ❷〈书 *fml*.〉组合字句篇章 put words together correctly; compose: ～辑 compose | ～字成文 put words together to produce a piece of writing ❸ 装饰 embellish; decorate: 点～embellish; ornament; adorn

【缀合】zhuìhé 连缀；组合 put together; make up; compose: 作者把几件事稍加铺张，～成篇。The author produced a piece of writing by putting together several issues and elaborating on them.

【缀文】zhuìwén 〈书 *fml*.〉写文章；作文 compose an essay; write a composition

惴 zhuì 〈书 *fml*.〉形容又发愁又害怕的样子 anxious and fearful: ～栗 shudder; tremble with fear | ～～不安 be anxious and fearful; be alarmed; be on tenterhooks

【惴栗】zhuìlì 〈书 *fml*.〉恐惧战栗 shudder; tremble with fear

缒 zhuì 用绳子拴住人或东西从上往下送 let down (with a rope): ～城而出 let oneself or sb. down a city wall with a rope | 从阳台上把篮子～下来 lower a basket down from the balcony with a rope

锻 zhuì 〈书 *fml*.〉赶马杖上端用来刺马的铁针 needle; iron pin fixed to a rod used to spur on a horse

膇 zhuì 〈书 *fml*.〉脚肿 swelling of the foot

赘 zhuì ❶ 多余的；无用的 superfluous; redundant: 累～burdensome; cumbersome | ～疣 wart | ～言 redundancy; superfluous words ❷ 入赘；招女婿 (of a man) go to live in the household of one's in-laws on getting married; (of the bride's parents) gain a son-in-law in such a manner: ～婿 son-in-law who lives in the home of his wife's parents | 招～ take a man into the family as a son-in-law ❸〈方 *dial*.〉使受累赘 be burdensome; be cumbersome: 孩子多了真～人。Having lots of children is a great burden.

【赘瘤】zhuìliú same as 赘疣 zhuìyóu ②

【赘述】zhuìshù 多余地叙述 give unnecessary details; say more than is needed: 不须～。It is unnecessary to go into such detail.

【赘婿】zhuìxù 入赘的女婿 son-in-law who lives in the home of his wife's parents

【赘言】zhuìyán 〈书 *fml*.〉❶ 说不必要的话；赘述 go into unnecessary detail; say more than is needed: 不再～。No more need be said. ❷ 不必要的话 redundancy; superfluous words

【赘疣】zhuìyóu ❶ 疣 wart ❷〈比喻 *fig*.〉多余而无用的东西 anything superfluous or useless

醊 zhuì 〈书 *fml*.〉祭奠 make offerings to the spirits of the dead

zhūn (ㄓㄨㄣ)

屯 zhūn [屯遭] (zhūnzhān) 〈书 *fml*.〉 same as 迍邅 zhūnzhān

☞ tún on p. 1954

迍 zhūn [迍邅] (zhūnzhān) 〈书 *fml*.〉❶ 形容迟迟不进 procrastinate in one's advance; be delatory: ～途次 stay for too long during a stopover on a journey ❷ 困顿不得志 in a predicament: ～坎坷 full of frustrations ‖ also 屯遭 zhūnzhān

肫[1] zhūn 〈书 *fml*.〉诚恳 sincere; genuine: ～挚 sincere | ～～(诚恳的样子)sincere

肫[2] zhūn 鸟类的胃 gizzard (of a fowl): 鸡～chicken gizzard | 鸭～duck gizzard

窀 zhūn [窀穸] (zhūnxī) 〈书 *fml*.〉墓穴 grave; tomb

谆 zhūn 恳切 earnest; sincere: ～嘱 give earnest exhortations

【谆谆】zhūnzhūn 形容恳切教导 earnest and tireless: ～告诫 repeatedly admonish; tirelessly exhort | ～嘱咐 give earnest exhortations | 言者～，听者藐藐(说的人很诚恳，听的人却不放在心上)。The speaker is in earnest, but his listeners are indifferent. *or* The words are earnest, but fall on deaf ears.

衠 zhūn 〈方 *dial*.〉纯粹；纯 pure

zhǔn (ㄓㄨㄣˇ)

准[1] zhǔn 准许 allow; grant; permit: 批～approve; sanction | 不～迟到或早退。Neither arriving late nor leaving early is permitted.

准[2] (準) zhǔn ❶ 标准 standard; norm; criterion: ～绳 criterion | 水～level | ～则 norms; standard | 以此为～。Take

Z

this as the standard (or criterion). ❷ 依据；依照 in accordance with; follow：～此办理。Settle by following this precedent. ❸ 准确 accurate; exact：瞄～ aim at｜钟走得不～。This clock does not keep good time.｜他投球很～。He is an accurate basketball shooter. ❹ 一定 definitely; certainly：我明天～去。I'll definitely be there tomorrow.｜他不～能来。He may be unable to come.｜任务～能完成。The task is sure to be accomplished. ❺ 程度上虽不完全够，但可以作为某类事物看待的 quasi-; para-：～将 (U. S. Army, Air Force and Marine Corps) brigadier general; (British Army and Marine Corps) brigadier; (U. S. and British Navy) commodore; (British Air Force) air commodore｜～平原 paraplain

【准保】zhǔnbǎo 〈副词 *adv.*〉表示可以肯定或保证 certainly; for sure：～没错儿 for sure｜他～不会来。He will definitely not be coming.

【准备】zhǔnbèi ❶ 预先安排或筹划 prepare; get ready; arrange or plan in advance：精神～ mental preparation｜～发言提纲 prepare the outline of a speech｜～一个空箱子放书 prepare an empty case for books ❷ 打算 intend; plan; think：春节我～回家。I intend to return home during the Spring Festival.｜昨天我本来～去看你，因为临时有事没去成。I planned to see you yesterday, but failed to because I was temporarily occupied.

【准点】zhǔndiǎn (～儿 zhǔndiǎnr)准时 on time; on the dot

【准定】zhǔndìng〈副词 *adv.*〉表示可以肯定；一定 certainly; undoubtedly; for sure：吃下这药～会好。You will surely recover if you take this medicine.｜我～去，你就放心好了。I will go for sure, please set your mind at rest.

【准稿子】zhǔngǎo·zi 准谱儿 certain; sure; definite：办事心里要有个～才行。One must be certain when handling affairs.

【准话】zhǔnhuà (～儿 zhǔnhuàr)确定的话 definite message or information：什么时候定好日子，我再给您个～。I'll give you a definite answer when we fix the date.

【准将】zhǔnjiàng 某些国家军衔的一级，在少将之下，校官之上 brigadier general; a grade of military rank in some countries, lower than a major general or rear admiral, and higher than a field officer

【准平原】zhǔnpíngyuán 隆起的地面经长期剥蚀而形成的平原 paraplain; plain forming after long-term erosion of the hilly ground

【准谱儿】zhǔnpǔr 准儿 certain; sure：下一步怎么个搞法儿，至今还没～。We are not yet certain what the next step is.

【准确】zhǔnquè 行动的结果完全符合实际或预期 accurate; exact; precise; (of the result of an action) fully conform to reality or expectations：～性 accuracy; precision; preciseness｜计算～ be precise in calculations｜～地击中目标 hit the target accurately

【准儿】zhǔnr 确定的主意、方式、规律等(大多用在'有、没有'后面 mostly following 有 yǒu or 没有 méiyǒu) certain; sure; positive; definite (idea, method, law, etc.)：心里有～ feel sure; know what one is doing; be quite positive about｜他到底来不来，还没有～。We are not sure yet whether he will come.

【准绳】zhǔnshéng 测定平直的器具 yardstick; tool to determine straightness;〈比喻 *fig.*〉言论、行动等所依据的原则或标准 principle or criterion serving as the basis of one's statements, actions, etc.

【准时】zhǔnshí 按规定的时间 punctual; on time; on schedule; according to the prescribed time：～出席 come on time｜列车～到达。The train arrived on schedule (or at the scheduled time).

【准头】zhǔn·tou (～儿 zhǔn·tour)射击、说话等的准确性 (of marksmanship, choice of words, etc.) accuracy：枪法挺有～ shoot well; be a good or crack shot; be an expert marksman; shoot with great accuracy｜说话没个～ speak without accuracy

【准尉】zhǔnwèi 某些国家军衔的一级，在上士之上，少尉之下 warrant officer; a grade of military rank in some countries, higher than a sergeant and lower than a captain or lieutenant

【准信】zhǔnxìn (～儿 zhǔnxìnr)准确可靠的消息 accurate information; definite and reliable information：你哪天能来，赶快给我个～。Let me know as soon as possible exactly when you can come.

【准星】zhǔnxīng ❶ 秤上的定盘星 zero point on a steelyard ◇他心眼儿太活，说话没～。He is too unpredicative, and his words are not reliable. ❷ 枪上瞄准装置的一部分，在枪口上端 front sight (of a gun); cross-hairs, the part of a gun-sighting device on the top of the muzzle

【准许】zhǔnxǔ 同意人的要求 permit; allow; grant：～通行 permit or allow to go through｜～办理出境手续 permit to go through the formalities for leaving a country

【准予】zhǔnyǔ 公文用语，表示准许 (used in official documents) grant; permit; approve; allow：成绩合格，～毕业。With the qualifying grades, one's graduation should be approved.

【准则】zhǔnzé 言论、行动等所依据的原则 norm; standard; criterion; principle that serves as the basis for one's statements, actions, etc.：行动～ code of conduct｜国际关系～ basic norms of international relations

埻 zhǔn〈书 *fml.*〉箭靶的中心 bull's-eye (of a target)

zhuō (ㄓㄨㄛ)

拙 zhuō ❶ 笨 clumsy; awkward; dull; stupid: 手～ be all thumbs | 眼～ slow to see and react | 勤能补～ can make up for lack of skill with industry | 弄巧成～ try to be clever only to end up with a blunder; outsmart oneself | ～于言辞 inarticulate; be clumsy in expressing oneself; be unable to communicate one's ideas adequately ❷ 〈谦辞 *hum.*〉 称自己的(文章、见解等) my (writing, opinion, etc.): ～著 my writing | ～作 my works | ～见 my humble opinion

【拙笨】zhuōbèn 笨拙 clumsy; dull; unskilful; awkward; dull: 口齿～ clumsy of speech

【拙笔】zhuōbǐ 〈谦辞 *hum.*〉 称自己的文字或书画 my (poor) writing, painting or calligraphy

【拙见】zhuōjiàn 〈谦辞 *hum.*〉 称自己的见解 my humble opinion

【拙劣】zhuōliè 笨拙而低劣 clumsy; inferior: 文笔～ poor writing | ～的表演 clumsy or poor performance; bad show

【拙涩】zhuōsè 拙劣晦涩 clumsy and obscure: 译文～ clumsy and obscure translation

捉 zhuō ❶ 握;抓 clutch; hold; grasp; grab: ～笔 hold a pen | ～襟见肘 pull together one's lapels to conceal raggedness only to expose one's elbows ❷ 使人或动物落入自己的手中 catch; capture; seize; ensnare; make people or animals fall into one's hands: 捕～ catch; capture | 活～ capture sb. alive | ～拿 catch; arrest; apprehend | ～贼 catch a thief | 猫～老鼠。Cats catch rats.

【捉刀】zhuōdāo 〈书 *fml.*〉 曹操叫崔琰(yǎn)代替自己接见匈奴使臣,自己却持刀站立床头。接见完毕,叫人问匈奴使臣:'魏王何如?'回答说:'魏王雅望非常,然床头捉刀人,此乃英雄也。'(见于《世说新语·容止》) 后来把代别人做文章叫捉刀。ghost-write. According to *A New Account of Tales of the World·Demeanours*, Cao Cao asked Cui Yan to greet a Xiongnu envoy in his place, while he himself stood by the bed with a sword. When the reception was over, he sent someone to ask the envoy, 'What do you think about the king of the state of Wei?' The envoy answered, 'The king of Wei looks elegant, but the man holding a sword by the bed is a hero.' The phrase later refers to ghost-write.

【捉对】zhuōduì (～儿 zhuōduìr) 一个对一个;两两成对 in pairs: ～厮杀 fight in pairs

【捉奸】zhuō//jiān 捉拿正在通奸的人 catch adulterers in the act; catch sb. committing adultery (in flagrante): ～捉双。To prove adultery, catch the pair.

【捉襟见肘】zhuō jīn jiàn zhǒu 拉一下衣襟就露出胳膊肘儿,形容衣服破烂。也比喻困难重重,应付不过来。pull one's lapels together to conceal raggedness only to expose one's elbows; (fig.) have too many difficulties to cope with at the same time

【捉迷藏】zhuō mícáng ❶ 儿童游戏,一人蒙住眼睛,摸索着去捉在他身边来回躲避的人 blindman's buff; children's game in which a blindfolded child gropes to catch others moving back and forth to avoid him or her ❷ 〈比喻 *fig.*〉 言语、行为故意迷离恍惚,使人难以捉摸 be tricky and evasive; play hide-and-seek; hedge; beat about the bush; (of one's speech or action) intentionally bewilder to make it difficult to ascertain: 你直截了当地说吧,不要跟我～了。Get straight to the point. Don't beat about the bush.

【捉摸】zhuōmō 猜测;预料(多用于否定句 oft. used in the negative) predict; ascertain; fathom; conjecture: 难以～ difficult to ascertain; hard to make head or tail of something | ～不定 unpredictable; elusive; difficult to conjecture 注意 **NOTE**: 反复思索的意思应该作'琢磨'(zuó·mo)。'think or ponder over and over' meaning 琢磨 zuó·mo

【捉拿】zhuōná 捉(犯人) catch (a criminal); arrest; apprehend: ～凶手 arrest a murderer | ～逃犯 arrest an escaped prisoner

【捉弄】zhuōnòng 对人开玩笑,使为难 tease; make fun of; make a fool of; play tricks on; play pranks on: 你别～人,我才不上你的当呢! Don't make fun of me; I will not be taken in.

桌 zhuō ❶ (～儿 zhuōr) 桌子 table; desk: 书～ writing desk; desk | 餐～ dining table | 八仙～ old-fashioned square table for eight persons | ～椅板凳 tables, chairs and benches; ordinary household furniture ❷ 〈量词 *classifier*〉: 一～菜 a table of dishes | 三～客人 three tables of guests

【桌布】zhuōbù 铺在桌面上做装饰和保护用的布或类似布的东西 tablecloth; cloth or similar material that is spread over a tabletop for decoration or protection

【桌灯】zhuōdēng 台灯 desk or table lamp

【桌面】zhuōmiàn (～儿 zhuōmiànr) 桌子的面儿,包括固定的和活动的 top of a table; tabletop (including fixed and movable ones): 圆～儿 circular tabletop | ～儿是大理石的。The top of the table is made of marble.

【桌面儿上】zhuōmiànr·shang 〈比喻 *fig.*〉 互相应酬或公开商量的场合 on the table; (put sth. out) for discussion on a social occasion or in public: ～的话(听起来既有理由而又不失身份的话) polite and unimpeachable remarks (that sound both reasonable and compatible with one's status) | 有什么问题最好摆

到～来谈。We'd better place problems on the table. *or* It's better to bring problems out into the open.

【桌椅板凳】zhuō yǐ bǎndèng 泛指一般的家具 (in a broad sense) ordinary household furniture

【桌子】zhuō·zi 家具,上有平面,下有支柱,在上面放东西或做事情 table; desk; furniture with a flat surface on the top and legs at the bottom, on which things may be put or one may do sth.:一张～ a table or desk

倬 zhuō〈书 *fml.*〉显著;大 notable; striking; great; marked; remarkable

棁 zhuō〈书 *fml.*〉梁上的短柱 joist; short post on a roof beam

涿 zhuō 涿州(Zhuōzhōu),涿鹿(Zhuōlù),地名,都在河北 Zhuozhou and Zhuolu, names of places in Hebei Province

焯 zhuō〈书 *fml.*〉明显;明白 clear; evident; obvious; distinct

☞ chāo on p. 228

镯 zhuō〈方 *dial.*〉(用镐)刨地或刨茬儿 dig the ground; dig out the stubble (of grain) with a pick:～玉米 dig out maize stubble with a pick|～高粱 dig out sorghum stubble with a pick

【镯钩】zhuō· gou〈方 *dial.*〉镐 pick; pickaxe

zhuó(ㄓㄨㄛˊ)

灼 zhuó ❶ 火烧;火烫 burn; scorch; sear; broil:烧～ burn|～伤 burn ❷ 明亮 bright; luminous; shining

【灼见】zhuójiàn 透彻的见解 profound view; penetrating insight:真知～ profound knowledge and penetrating insight; wise judgement

【灼热】zhuórè 像火烧着、烫着那样热 scorching hot; as hot as a burning fire:～的炼钢炉 scorching hot steel-smelting furnace

【灼灼】zhuózhuó〈书 *fml.*〉形容明亮 bright; brilliant; shining; dazzling:目光～ with keen, sparkling eyes

茁 zhuó (草木)发芽,也指植物旺盛生长 (of plants) sprout; grow vigorously; grow luxuriantly; grow lushly:～壮 vigorous; sturdy; healthy and strong

【茁实】zhuó·shi〈方 *dial.*〉壮实 sturdy; robust; healthy and strong

【茁长】zhuózhǎng (植物、动物)茁壮地生长 (of plants or animals) grow vigorously; grow luxuriantly; grow sturdily:两岸花草丛生,竹林～。Flowers and plants grow thickly, and a forest of bamboo grows lushly on both banks.

【茁壮】zhuózhuàng (年轻人、孩子、动植物)强壮;健壮 (of young people, children, animals and plants) vigorous; sturdy; healthy and strong:一代新人～成长。A new generation is growing healthily and vigorously.|托儿所里的孩子们又～又活泼。The children in the kindergarten are both vigorous and active.|牛羊～ sturdy cattle and sheep|小麦长得十分～。The wheat is growing vigorously.

卓 zhuó ❶ 高而直 tall and erect; upright:～立 stand erect; stand upright ❷ 高明 eminent; outstanding; remarkable:～见 brilliant idea; excellent understanding or view ❸ (Zhuó)姓 a surname

【卓尔不群】zhuó'ěr bù qún 优秀卓越,超出常人 stand head and shoulders above the common run; be outstanding; be preeminent; rise above the common herd

【卓见】zhuójiàn 高明的见解 brilliant idea; excellent understanding or view

【卓绝】zhuójué 程度达到极点,超过一切 outstanding; extreme; unsurpassed; of the highest degree:英勇～ extremely brave|坚苦～ extremely hard and bitter; most arduous

【卓荦】zhuóluò〈书 *fml.*〉超绝 outstanding; unsurpassed; extraordinary; eminent; preeminent:英才～ outstanding talent; also 卓跞 zhuóluò

【卓跞】zhuóluò〈书 *fml.*〉same as 卓荦 zhuóluò

【卓然】zhuórán 卓越 outstanding; remarkable; eminent; brilliant:成绩～ outstanding achievements; remarkable achievements

【卓识】zhuóshí 卓越的见识 judicious judgment; sagacity; outstanding insight:远见～ foresight and sagacity

【卓异】zhuóyì 高出于一般;与众不同 out of the ordinary; outstanding; remarkable; unique:政绩～ outstanding or remarkable achievements in a political career

【卓有成效】zhuó yǒu chéngxiào 成绩、效果显著 very fruitful; highly effective

【卓越】zhuóyuè 非常优秀,超出一般 outstanding; brilliant; remarkable; preeminent:～的成就 remarkable achievements; splendid or brilliant achievements|～的贡献 outstanding contributions; extraordinary or singular contributions|～的科学家 outstanding scientist; brilliant (or distinguished) scientist

【卓著】zhuózhù 突出地好 distinguished; outstanding; eminent; illustrious:成效～ outstanding results|战功～ render meritorious or illustrious military service|信誉～ outstanding reputation

斫 zhuó 用刀斧砍 hack; cut; chop (with a sword or axe)

浊(濁) zhuó ❶ 浑浊(跟'清'相对 as opposed to 'clear or pure') turbid; muddy; murky:～流 muddy stream; turbid current|污～ dirty; foul; filthy ❷ (声音)低

沉粗重 (of voices) deep and thick; muddy: ～声～气 in a deep, raucous voice ❸ 混乱 confused; chaotic; disorderly: ～世 corrupt world; chaotic or turbulent times

【浊世】zhuóshì ❶〈书 *fml.*〉黑暗或混乱的时代 corrupt world; chaotic or turbulent times ❷〈佛教 *Budd.*〉指尘世 mortal world

【浊音】zhuóyīn 发音时声带振动的音 voiced sound; sound articulated by vibrating the vocal chords; ☞ 带音 dàiyīn on p. 372

酌 zhuó ❶ 斟(酒);饮(酒) pour (wine); drink (wine): 对～ (two people) have a drink together | 自斟自～ drink alone; enjoy a glass of wine by oneself ❷〈书 *fml.*〉酒饭 meal with wine or alcohol: 菲～ simple meal | 便～ informal dinner ❸ 斟酌;考虑 deliberate; weigh and consider; mull over: ～办 act according to one's judgement; do as one thinks fit | ～定 make a decision as one sees fit; decide according to one's judgement; use one's discretion | ～情 take into consideration the circumstances; act according to the circumstances; use one's discretion | ～予答复 consider (the above points) and favour us with a reply | ～加修改 make any alterations as one may think fit

【酌量】zhuó·liáng 斟酌;估量 consider; deliberate; use one's judgment; give due consideration: ～补助 offer allowances at one's discretion | ～调拨 transfer and allocate (goods or funds) at one's discretion | 你～着办吧。You may handle the matter as you think fit.

【酌情】zhuóqíng 斟酌情况 take into consideration the circumstances; act according to the circumstances; use one's discretion: ～处理 settle a matter as one sees fit; act at one's discretion; deal with matters on the merits of each case

浞 zhuó 淋;使湿 pour; drench: 让雨～了 be drenched with rain | 一潲雨,桌子上的书全～湿了。All the books on the table got drenched when the rain slanted in.

诼 zhuó〈书 *fml.*〉毁谤 slander; calumny; gossip; defamation: 谣～ smear; many rumours; rumour-mongering and mud-slinging

著¹ zhuó same as 着¹ zhuó

著² zhuó same as 着² zhuó ☞ ·zhe on p. 2432 and zhù on p. 2512

啄 zhuó 鸟类用嘴取食物 peck; (of birds) take food with the beak: ～食 peck at food | 鸡～米。The chicken pecked at the rice.

【啄木鸟】zhuómùniǎo 鸟,脚短,趾端有锐利的爪,善于攀缘树木,嘴尖而直,能啄开木头,用细长而尖端有钩的舌头捕食树洞里的虫,尾羽粗硬,啄木时支撑身体。是益鸟。woodpecker (*Picidae*); beneficial bird with short legs and sharp-tipped claws, good at climbing trees, which can peck open wood with its sharp and straight beak and catch insects in holes in trees with its long thin hook-tipped tongue, and whose thick, hard tail feathers can support its body; also 䴕 liè

着¹ zhuó ❶ 穿(衣) wear (clothes); dress: 穿～ dress; apparel | 吃～不尽 have as much food and clothing as one wants ❷ 接触;挨上 touch; contact: 附～ adhere to | ～陆 land; touch down | 不～边际 irrelevant; wide of the mark; not to the point; neither here nor there ❸ 使接触别的事物;使附着在别的物体上 apply; attach; contact or touch another thing; adhere to another object: ～笔 set pen to paper; begin to write or paint | ～眼 view or see from the angle of; have something in mind; consider a certain aspect; take as the basis | ～手 begin; set about; put one's hand to | ～色 colour; apply colour | ～墨 paint; ink in; describe in writing | 不～痕迹 leave no trace ❹ 着落 whereabouts: 寻找无～ whereabouts unknown; nowhere to be found

着² zhuó ❶ 派遣 send; dispatch: ～人前来领取 send someone here for it ❷ 公文用语,表示命令的口气 [used in official documents, to indicate an imperative tone]: ～即施行 to be enforced immediately

☞ zhāo on p. 2422, zháo on p. 2423 and ·zhe on p. 2432

【着笔】zhuóbǐ 用笔;下笔 set pen to paper; begin to write or paint

【着力】zhuólì 使力气;用力;致力 put forth effort; make an effort; exert oneself: 无从～ fail to see where to direct one's efforts | 这部小说～地描绘了农村的新面貌。This novel takes great pains to describe the new features of the countryside.

【着陆】zhuó//lù (飞机等)从空中到达陆地 (of a plane, etc.) arrive on land from the air; land; touch down: 安全～ safe landing

【着落】zhuóluò ❶ 下落 whereabouts: 遗失的行李已经有了～了。The whereabouts of the missing luggage are known. ❷ 可以依靠或指望的来源 assured source; source that one may depend or count on: 这笔经费还没有～。The funds are still unavailable. ❸ 事情责成某人负责办理 fall on; rest with; order or instruct sb. to be in charge of handling certain affairs: 这件事情就～在你身上了。This matter has fallen on you. ❹ 安放(多见于早期白话 oft. used in early vernacular) lay; settle: ～停当 settled; properly laid

【着墨】zhuómò 指用文字来描述 describe in writing: 剧中这个人物～不多,却令人感到真实可信。Although sketchily described in the novel, the character is credible and true to life.

【着色】zhuó//sè 涂上颜色 colour; apply colour

【着实】zhuóshí ❶ 实在;确实 really; truly; indeed:这孩子～讨人喜欢。The child is really lovely. ❷(言语、动作)分量重;力量大 severely; sharply; (of one's words or actions) weighty; great in strength:～批评了他一顿 lecture him severely; reprove him sharply

【着手】zhuóshǒu 开始做;动手 begin; set about; put one's hand to:～编制计划 start drawing up a plan|提高生产要从改进技术～。To improve production, we must start with technical innovations.

【着手成春】zhuó shǒu chéng chūn 称赞医生医道高明,一下手就能把垂危的病人治好 [to praise a doctor whose great skill has quickly cured a dying patient] have magic hands that bring back life; also 妙手回春 miào shǒu huí chūn

【着想】zhuóxiǎng (为某人或某事的利益)考虑 consider (the interests of sb. or sth.); set one's mind on; take into consideration; think about:他是为你～才劝你少喝酒的。It was for your own good that he advised you to drink less alcohol.|我们应该为增加生产～。We should set our mind on increasing production.

【着眼】zhuóyǎn (从某方面)观察;考虑 view or see (from the angle of); have sth. in mind; consider a certain aspect; take as the basis:～点 focus of attention; starting point; point of departure|大处～,小处下手 bear larger interests in mind (or keep the general goal in view), while going about solving practical problems|积极培养年轻选手,～于将来的世界大赛 actively cultivate young players, for future international competition

【着意】zhuóyì ❶ 用心 strive; take pains; spare no pains; exert oneself:～经营 manage with diligent care|～刻画人物的心理活动 concentrate on the depiction of the psychological activities of the character ❷ 在意;留心 take seriously; mind:他听了这话,也不～。He didn't seem to mind much what was said.

【着重】zhuózhòng 把重点放在某方面;强调 stress; emphasize; underline; put emphasis on a certain aspect:～说明 emphatically indicate (or explain); stress|～指出 point out emphatically; emphasize|工作的～点 focal point of the work

【着重号】zhuózhònghào 标点符号(·),用在横行文字的下边或竖行文字的右边,标明要求读者特别注意的字、词、句 mark of emphasis; punctuation (·) used under Chinese characters written in horizontal lines or on the right of characters in vertical lines, to mark the character(s), word(s) or sentence(s) to which readers should pay special attention

【着装】zhuózhuāng ❶ 指穿戴衣帽等 put on (clothes, headgear, etc.):～完毕 be dressed; finish dressing oneself ❷ 衣着 clothing; accessories (headgear and footwear):整理～ straighten out one's clothing|检查每个战士的～ examine the clothing of every solider

琢 zhuó 雕刻玉石,使成器物 chisel; carve; grind; cut; carve jade into articles:精雕细～ work at something with great care|玉不～,不成器。If jade is not cut and polished, it cannot be made into anything; one cannot become useful without being educated.|翡翠～成的小壶 small carved jadeite pot

☞ zuó on p. 2572

【琢磨】zhuómó ❶ 雕刻和打磨(玉石) carve and polish (jade) ❷ 加工使精美(指文章等) (of writing, etc.) improve; polish; refine (to make more elegant)

☞ zuó·mo on p. 2572

斮 zhuó 〈书 *fml.*〉斩;削 cut; chop; hack

椓 zhuó 〈古代 *arch.*〉割去男性生殖器的酷刑 castration; cruel or savage torture of cutting a man's genital organs

禚 Zhuó 姓 a surname

斲 zhuó 〈书 *fml.*〉砍;削 chop; cut; hack:～木为舟 make a boat out of tree trunk; make a dugout canoe

【斲轮老手】zhuó lún lǎo shǒu《庄子·天道》:'是以行年七十而老斲轮' *Zhuangzi · Way of Heaven*: 'So he became an expert wheelwright at the age of 70.'(斲轮 *zhuo lun*:砍木头做车轮 chop wood to make a wheel);后来称对某种事情富有经验的人为'斲轮老手' old hand; person who is very experienced in sth.

【斲丧】zhuósàng 〈书 *fml.*〉伤害,特指因沉溺酒色以致伤害身体 destroy one's health, esp. by indulging in wine and womanizing

鸑 zhuó ☞[鸑鷟](yuèzhuó) on p. 2374

缴 zhuó 〈书 *fml.*〉系在箭上的丝绳,射鸟用 silk rope tied to an arrow for shooting birds

☞ jiǎo on p. 978

擢 zhuó 〈书 *fml.*〉❶ 拔 extract; pull out:～发难数 (of crimes) be as uncountable as the hair on one's head; be innumerable ❷ 提拔 raise; promote; advance (in rank):～拔 promote; select|～升 promote; raise (to a higher position or rank)

【擢发难数】zhuó fà nán shǔ 〈比喻 *fig.*〉罪恶多得像头发那样,数也数不清 (of crimes) be as uncountable as the hair on a head; be innumerable

【擢升】zhuóshēng 〈书 *fml.*〉提升 promote; raise (to a higher position or rank)

Z

【擢用】zhuóyòng〈书 *fml.*〉提升任用 promote; raise or assign sb. to a post:～贤能 promote people of virtue and talent

濯 zhuó〈书 *fml.*〉洗 wash:～足 wash one's feet

【濯濯】zhuózhuó〈书 *fml.*〉形容山上光秃秃的,没有树木 (of mountains) bare (of trees); bald; denuded:童山～ bare or treeless hills

镯(鋜) zhuó 镯子 bracelet:手～ bracelet|玉～ jade bracelet

【镯子】zhuó·zi 戴在手腕或脚腕上的环形装饰品 bracelet; anklet; circular ornament that one wears around the wrist or ankle:金～ gold bracelet

zī (ㄗ)

仔 zī [仔肩](zījiān)〈书 *fml.*〉责任;负担 official burdens or responsibilities

☞ 崽 zǎi on p. 2386 and zǐ on p. 2541

吱 zī〈拟声词 *onom.*〉多形容小动物的叫声 squeak; chirp; cry of a small animal:老鼠～～地叫。Mice are going squeak-squeak.

☞ zhī on p. 2456

【吱声】zī//shēng〈方 *dial.*〉做声 make or utter a sound; speak:问他几遍,他都没～。He was asked several times, but he didn't say a word.

孜 zī ☞ below

【孜孜】zīzī 勤勉 diligent; industrious; hardworking; studious:～不倦 diligently; indefatigably; industriously; assiduously; persist in one's studies or work with untiring vigour|～不息地工作 diligently work without rest; work hard without a break; also 孳孳 zīzī

【孜孜矻矻】zīzī kūkū〈书 *fml.*〉形容勤勉不懈怠的样子 industrious; diligent; working or studying hard and attentively

咨 zī ❶ 跟别人商量 consult; take counsel; seek advice; discuss with others:～询 consult; seek advice from; hold counsel with ❷ 咨文 report on state affairs delivered by the head of a government

【咨文】zīwén ❶〈旧时 *old*〉指用于平行机关的公文 official communication (between government offices of equal rank) ❷ 指某些国家(如美国)元首向国会提出的关于国事情况的报告 report on state affairs delivered by the head of a government (e.g. US president):国情～ (US) State of the Union Message

【咨询】zīxún 征求意见(多指行政当局向顾问之类的人员或特设的机关征求意见 oft. administrative authorities seeking advice from consultants or similar personnel or special organs) consult; hold counsel with; seek advice from:法律～ seek legal advice|～机关(备咨询的机关) advisory body (organ that offers consulting services)

姿 zī ❶ 容貌 looks; appearance:～容 appearance; looks|～色 (of a woman) good looks; charm ❷ 姿势 gesture; bearing; carriage; posture:～态 posture; carriage; bearing; deportment|舞～ dancer's posture and movements

【姿容】zīróng 容貌 looks; appearance:～秀美 good-looking; pretty

【姿色】zīsè (妇女)美好的容貌 (of a woman) good looks; charm

【姿势】zīshì 身体呈现的样子 posture; carriage; gesture (of the body):～端正 regular posture|立正的～ position of attention

【姿态】zītài ❶ 姿势;样儿 posture; carriage; bearing; deportment:～优美 have an elegant or graceful carriage ❷ 态度;气度 attitude; gesture; pose:做出让步的～ make a concessionary gesture|以普通劳动者的～出现 (of a cadre) appear among the masses as an ordinary worker

兹(茲) zī〈书 *fml.*〉❶ 这个 this:～事体大(这是件大事情)。This is indeed a serious matter.|念～在～(念念不忘某件事) always remember this; bear this in mind ❷ 现在 now; at present; at this time:于～已有三载。Three years have passed since then.|～订于9月1日上午9时在本校礼堂举行开学典礼。This is to announce the school's opening ceremony at the assembly hall at 9 a.m. on September 1. ❸ 年 year:今～ this year|来～ next year

☞ cí on p. 317

赀 zī〈书 *fml.*〉❶ 计算 estimate; calculate; reckon:所费不～ incur a considerable expense ❷ same as 资[1] zī

资[1] zī ❶ 钱财;费用 money; fund; expenses:投～ invest; put money in|工～ wages; pay|川～ travelling expenses|合～购买 purchase by joint investment ❷ 资助;助 subsidize; support; help; aid:～敌 support the enemy; give provisions to the enemy ❸ 提供 provide; supply; serve:可～借鉴 can serve as an example|以～参考 use for reference ❹ (Zī)姓 a surname

资[2] zī ❶ 资质 endowment; intelligence; aptitude; natural ability:天～ aptitude; native intelligence; natural endowments ❷ 资格 qualifications; seniority; record of service:～历 qualifications; seniority; record of service|论～排辈 promotion goes by seniority; give top priority to seniority (in the selection of cadres)

【资本】zīběn ❶ 用来生产或经营以求牟利的生产资料和货币 capital; materials and money used in production or management to pursue profit ❷〈比喻 *fig.*〉牟取利益的凭借 sth. to capitalize on; sth. used to one's own advantage; sth. used to make profit: 政治～ political capital

【资本家】zīběnjiā 占有资本、剥削工人的剩余劳动的人 capitalist; person who holds capital and exploits workers' surplus labour

【资本主义】zīběn zhǔyì 资本家占有生产资料并用以剥削雇佣劳动、榨取剩余价值的社会制度。资本主义的生产社会化和生产资料资本家占有制，是资本主义社会的基本矛盾。资本主义发展到最高阶段，就成为垄断资本主义，即帝国主义。capitalism; social system by which capitalists hold the means of production to exploit wage labour and extract surplus value; capitalist productive socialization and ownership of means of production are the basic contradictions of capitalist society. When capitalism reaches the highest stage it inevitably becomes monopoly capitalism, i. e. imperialism.

【资材】zīcái 物资和器材 materials and equipment: 调剂～ redistribute goods and materials

【资财】zīcái 资金和物资；财物 funds and goods; capital and goods; assets: 清点～ make an inventory of the assets

【资产】zīchǎn ❶ 财产 property; estate ❷ 企业资金 capital; capital fund (of an enterprise) ❸ 资产负债表所列的一方，表示资金的运用情况 assets; items listed in a balance sheet to indicate the application of capital; ☞ 资产负债表 zīchǎn fùzhài biǎo

【资产负债表】zīchǎn fùzhài biǎo 会计定期核算时以货币形式总括地反映企业的资金运用及其来源的报表。表中采用资产和负债两方的平衡式，资产方表示资金的运用，负债方表示资金的来源。从表上可以分析企业的财务情况和检查资金的使用情况。statement of assets and liabilities; balance sheet; report form in which an accountant summarizes the application of capital and its sources for an enterprise in monetary form for accounting, which adopts a balance of assets and liabilities, the former indicating the application of capital, and the latter, its sources, by which one can analyse the financial condition of an enterprise and examine the application of its capital

【资产阶级】zīchǎn jiējí 占有生产资料，剥削工人的剩余劳动的阶级 capitalist class; bourgeoisie; class that holds the means of production and exploits worker's surplus labour

【资产阶级革命】zīchǎn jiējí gémìng 由资产阶级领导的反对封建社会制度的革命。资产阶级革命胜利的结果是国家政权由封建地主阶级手中转到资产阶级手中，建立资产阶级专政的国家。bourgeois revolution; revolution led by the capitalist class to oppose the system of feudal society, whose victory resulted in the transfer of state power from the feudalist landlord class to the capitalist class, and the establishment of countries with a dictatorship of the bourgeoisie

【资方】zīfāng 指私营工商业中的资本家一方 those representing capital (in private industry and commerce); capitalist; owner of a private enterprise: ～代理人 agent of a capitalist

【资格】zī·gé ❶ 从事某种活动所应具备的条件、身份等 qualifications; conditions, status, etc., for engaging in a certain activity: 审查～ examine the qualifications | 取消～ be disqualified from ❷ 由从事某种工作或活动的时间长短所形成的身份 seniority; status accumulated due to the length of time engaging in certain work or activity: 老～ (have) seniority | 他在我们车间里是～最老的了。He has the most seniority in our workshop.

【资金】zījīn ❶ 国家用于发展国民经济的物资或货币 funds; materials or money of a state for national economic development ❷ 指经营工商业的本钱 capital (for industrial and commercial management)

【资力】zīlì ❶ 财力 financial strength: ～雄厚 have a great deal of capital; be financially powerful ❷ 天资和能力 talent and ability: ～有限 limited talent and ability

【资历】zīlì 资格和经历 qualifications; seniority; record of service: ～浅 have little previous experience

【资料】zīliào ❶ 生产、生活中必需的东西 means; necessary materials for production or life: 生产～ means of production; capital goods | 生活～ means of livelihood or subsistence; consumer goods ❷ 用做参考或依据的材料 data; material; information: 收集～ collect data; gather materials | 参考～ reference material | 统计～ statistical data | 谈笑的～ subject of conversation

【资深】zīshēn 资历深或资格老 senior; having high credentials or seniority: ～望重 have a distinguished reputation

【资源】zīyuán 生产资料或生活资料的天然来源 resources; natural resources (of means of production or livelihood): 地下～ underground resources | 水力～ water-power resources◇旅游～ tourist resources

【资质】zīzhì 人的素质；智力 (of a person) aptitude; natural endowments; intelligence; crendential: ～高 highly intelligent

【资助】zīzhù 用财物帮助 subsidize; aid financially; give financial aid: 解囊～ loosen the purse strings to provide assistance; assist financially; help sb. generously with money

菑 zī ❶〈古代 *arch.*〉指初耕的田地 newly cultivated land ❷〈书 *fml.*〉除草 weeding

〈古 *arch.*〉same as 灾 zāi

谘 zī same as 咨 zī ①

淄 Zī 淄河,水名,在山东 Zihe River, name of a river in Shandong Province

缁 zī〈书 *fml*.〉黑色 black:～衣 black coat

辎 zī〈古代 *arch*.〉的一种车 ancient wagon

【辎重】zīzhòng 行军时由运输部队携带的军械、粮草、被服等物资 impedimenta; baggage and other supplies of an army; materials carried by transport troops on the march, e.g. armaments, army provisions, bedding, clothing, etc.

嗞 zī same as 吱 zī

嵫 zī ☞ [崦嵫](Yānzī) on p. 2201

粢 zī〈古代 *arch*.〉供祭祀的谷物 sacrificial grain
☞ cī on p. 315

孳 zī 繁殖 multiply; propagate:～生 multiply; propagate; breed | ～乳 (of mammals) breed; propagate; multiply

【孳乳】zīrǔ〈书 *fml*.〉❶(哺乳动物)繁殖 (of mammals) breed; propagate; multiply ❷ 泛指派生 (in a broad sense) derive

【孳生】zīshēng same as 滋生 zīshēng ①

【孳孳】zīzī same as 孜孜 zīzī

滋[1] zī ❶ 滋生 grow; multiply; propagate:～蔓 grow and spread; grow vigorously; grow quickly | ～事 make or cause trouble; provoke a dispute ❷ 增添;加多 increase; wax:～益 increase interest or profits

滋[2] zī〈方 *dial*.〉喷射 burst; spurt; spout:往外～水 spurt water | 电线～火。The electric wire is sending out a spray of sparks.

【滋补】zībǔ 供给身体需要的养分;补养 nourishing; nutritious; taking nutrients providing for the needs of one's body; taking a tonic or nourishing food to build up one's health:鹿茸是～身体的药品。Pilose antler is a tonic that builds up one's health.

【滋蔓】zīmàn〈书 *fml*.〉生长蔓延 grow and spread; grow vigorously; grow quickly:湖中水藻～。Algae grew and spread quickly in the lake.

Z

【滋润】zīrùn ❶ 含水分多;不干燥 moist; humid; of high moisture content; not dry:雨后初晴,空气～。After the shower, the sky cleared and the air was moist. | 皮肤～ soft skin ❷ 增添水分,使不干枯 moisten; increase moisture content so as not to become dry:附近的湖水～着牧场的青草。The lake nearby provides moisture for the green grass of the pasture. ❸〈方 *dial*.〉舒服 comfortable; well off:小日子过得挺～ lead a very comfortable life

【滋生】zīshēng ❶ 繁殖 multiply; breed; grow; propagate:及时清除污水、粪便,防止蚊蝇～ clean waste water, excrement and urine in time to prevent the multiplication of flies and mosquitoes; also 孳生 zīshēng ❷ 引起 cause; create; provoke; bring:～事端 cause (or stir up) trouble; create (or raise) a disturbance

【滋事】zīshì 惹事;制造纠纷 make or cause trouble; provoke a dispute:酗酒～ make trouble under the influence of alcohol; kick up a row when one is drunk

【滋味】zīwèi (～儿 zīwèir) ❶ 味道 taste; flavour; relish; savour:菜的～不错。The dish tastes quite good. ❷〈比喻 *fig*.〉某种感受 experience; feeling:挨饿的～不好受。Starvation is a bitter experience. | 听了这话,心里真不是～。Hearing this, one really feels upset.

【滋芽】zī//yá〈方 *dial*.〉(～儿 zī//yár)发芽 sprout; germinate

【滋养】zīyǎng ❶ 供给养分 nourish; supplying nutriment:～品 nutriment; nourishment; nourishing food | ～身体 be nourishing; take nourishment to regain one's health (or to recuperate) ❷ 养分;养料 nutriment; nourishment:吸收～ assimilate nutriment | 丰富的～ rich nutriment (or nourishment)

【滋长】zīzhǎng 生长;产生(多用于抽象事物 oft. of abstract things) grow; develop; engender:有了成绩,要防止～骄傲自满的情绪。One should guard against arrogance and conceit after achieving success.

趑(趦) zī [趑趄](zījū)〈书 *fml*.〉❶ 行走困难 walk with difficulty; lumber along; plough one's way ❷ 想前进又不敢前进 falter; hesitate to advance:～不前 hesitate to advance; hesitate to act (or choose one's course); hang back

觜 zī 二十八宿之一 one of the 28 constellations
☞ zuǐ on p. 2568

訾 zī ❶〈书 *fml*.〉same as 赀 zī ① ❷ (Zī) 姓 a surname
☞ zǐ on p. 2542

锱 zī〈古代 *arch*.〉重量单位,一两的四分之一 unit of weight, equal to one fourth of a *liang*

【锱铢】zīzhū 指很少的钱或很小的事 small amount of money; trifle; farthing:～必较 be excessively mean in one's dealings; haggle over every penny; argue about little details; fight over the smallest trifles; dispute over trivialities

龇(呲) zī 露(牙) bare; show (one's teeth):～着牙 show or bare one's teeth | ～牙咧嘴 show one's teeth; look ferocious
☞ 呲 cī on p. 315

【龇牙咧嘴】zī yá liě zuǐ ❶ 形容凶狠的样子 bare one's teeth; look ferocious ❷ 形容疼痛难忍的样子 contort one's face in agony; grimace with pain

镃 zī [镃镇](zījī)〈书 *fml.*〉大锄 big hoe; also 镃基 zījī

鼒 zī〈书 *fml.*〉口小的鼎 tripod tapering off towards the top

髭 zī 嘴上边的胡子 moustache (above the mouth): ～须 moustache; whiskers | 短～ short moustache

鲻 zī 鲻鱼,身体长,前部圆,后部侧扁,头短而扁,吻宽而短,眼大,鳞片圆形,没有侧线。生活在浅海或河口咸水和淡水交汇处。是常见的食用鱼。mullet (*Mugilidae*); fish with a long body, circular front section, laterally flat back, short flat head, wide short snout, big eyes, circular scales, and no lateral lines, living in continental seas or at the convergence of salt and fresh water at river mouths, being a common food fish

zǐ (ㄗˇ)

子1 zǐ ❶〈古代 *arch.*〉指儿女,现在专指儿子 child; son and daughter; (usu. referring to) son: 父～ father and son | ～女 sons and daughters; children | 独生～ only son ❷ 人的通称 general term for human beings: 男～ man; male person | 女～ woman; female person ❸〈古代 *arch.*〉特指有学问的男人,是男人的美称 ancient term of respect for a learned man; laudatory term for a man: 夫～ master | 孔～ Confucius | 诸～百家 various schools of thought and their exponents during the period from pre-Qin times to the early Han Dynasty ❹〈古代 *arch.*〉指你 you: 以～之矛,攻～之盾 pierce your shield with your own spear — shoot oneself in the foot; beat sb. with his own weapon; refute sb. with his or her own argument ❺〈古代 *arch.*〉图书四部分类法(经史子集)中的第三类 'philosophy', third of the four traditional categories of ancient Chinese writings (as distinct from 'Confucian Classics' 经, 'history' 史, and 'belles-letters' 集): ～部 'philosophy', third of the four traditional categories of the ancient Chinese writings, which contains works by the exponents of the various schools of thought other than Confucianism from the Spring and Autumn Period onwards | ～书 works of ancient philosophers other than Confucius, which belong to the third traditional category of Chinese writings ❻ (～儿 zǐr) 种子 seed: 瓜～儿 melon seeds | 结～儿了 bear seeds; go to seed ❼ 卵 egg: 鱼～ roe | 鸡～儿 hen's egg ❽ 幼小的;小的;嫩的 young; small; tender: ～猪 piglet; shoat | ～城 satellite town; extension of the old city | ～姜 tender ginger ❾〈比喻 *fig.*〉派生的、附属的 subsidiary: ～公司 subcompany; subsidiaries ❿ (～儿 zǐr) 小而坚硬的块状物或粒状物 small hard lump or thing in grain: 棋～儿 (chess) piece; chessman | 枪～儿 bullet | 算盘～儿 abacus bead | 石头～儿 pebble; small stone ⓫ (～儿 zǐr) 铜子儿;铜元 copper coin; copper: 大～儿(旧时当二十文的铜元) big coin (equivalent to 20 coppers in old times) | 小～儿(旧时当十文的铜元) copper (equivalent to 10 coppers in old times) | 一个～儿也不值(一钱不值) worthless; not worth a copper ⓬ (～儿 zǐr)〈量词 *classifier*〉用于能用手指掐住的一束细长的东西 [used for a bundle of sth. that can be gripped with the hand]: 一～儿线 a hank of thread | 一～儿挂面 a bundle of fine dried noodles ⓭ (Zǐ) 姓 a surname

子2 zǐ 封建五等爵位的第四等 viscount; fourth ranking of the five feudal titles of nobility: ～爵 viscount

子3 zǐ 地支的第一位 first of the 12 Earthly Branches; ☞ 干支 gānzhī on p. 627

子 ·zi ❶ 名词后缀 [used after a noun as a suffix] a) 加在名词性词素后 [used after a noun]: 帽～ cap | 旗～ flag | 桌～ table; desk | 命根～ one's very life; lifeblood b) 加在形容词或动词性词素后 [used after an adjective or verb]: 胖～ fatty; fat person | 矮～ short person; shorty; dwarf | 垫～ cushion; mat | 掸～ duster ❷ 某些量词后缀 [used after a classifier as a suffix]: 这档～事 this matter | 一下～认不出来 fail to recognize somebody at first glance | 来了一伙～人。A group of people came.

【子部】zǐbù 我国古代图书分类的一大部类。包括诸子百家的著作。'philosophy', one of the categories of the ancient Chinese books, which contains works by the exponents of the various schools of thought other than Confucianism from the Spring and Autumn Period onwards; also 丙部 bǐngbù; ☞ 四部 sìbù on p. 1820

【子城】zǐchéng 指大城所附的小城,如瓮城 satellite town; extension of the old city; minor division of a metropolitan city, e.g. city-gate enceinte

【子畜】zǐchù 幼小的牲畜 young animal; newborn animal; also 仔畜 zǐchù

【子代】zǐdài ☞ 亲代 qīndài on p. 1558

【子弹】zǐdàn 枪弹 bullet; cartridge

【子埝】zǐdì same as 子埝 zǐniàn

【子弟】zǐdì ❶ 弟弟、儿子、侄子等 younger brothers, sons, nephews, etc.: 职工～ children of the workers and staff (of a factory, etc.) ❷ 指年轻的后辈 younger generation;

children; juniors: ～兵 army made up of the sons of the people; people's own army|工农～ army of the workers and peasants

【子弟兵】zǐdìbīng 原指由本乡本土的子弟组成的军队,现在是对人民军队的亲热称呼 army made up of the sons of the people of the native land; (now used as a term of endearment) people's own army

【子弟书】zǐdìshū 盛行于清代的一种曲艺,由鼓词派生而成,为满族八旗子弟所创 *zidishu*, a popular form of *quyi* storytelling of the Qing Dynasty, derived from the words of *dagu* (musical storytelling to the accompliment of a small drum and other instruments), which originated with the descendants of the 'Eight Banners' of the Manchus in the Qing Dynasty

【子房】zǐfáng 雌蕊下面膨大的部分,里面有胚珠。子房发育成果实,胚珠发育成种子。ovary; expanding part under a pistil filled with ovules, which develops into fruit, with ovules developing into seeds; (图见 ☞ figure for 花 huā on p.826)

【子宫】zǐgōng 女子或雌性哺乳动物的生殖器官,形状像一个囊。在膀胱和直肠中间,有口通阴道,子宫底部两侧与输卵管相通。卵子受精后,在子宫内发育成胎儿。uterus; womb; bag-shaped reproductive organ in a woman or female mammal between the urinary bladder and rectum, whose opening is connected with the vagina and its two sides at the bottom are connected to the oviducts, in which a fertilized egg can develop into a foetus

【子宫颈】zǐgōngjǐng 医学上指子宫下部较狭窄的部分,上接子宫体,下连子宫外口 (med.) cervix (of a womb); cervix uteri; narrow lower part of womb, whose upper part is connected with the corpus uteri, and the lower part with the outer opening of the womb; 简称 abbr. 宫颈 gōngjǐng

【子规】zǐguī 杜鹃(鸟名) cuckoo (*Cuculidae*) (name of a bird)

【子鸡】zǐjī 刚孵化出来的小鸡 chick (that has just been hatched); also 仔鸡 zǐjī

【子金】zǐjīn 利息(对'母金'而言 as compared with 'principal') interest

【子口】zǐ·kou 瓶、罐、箱、匣等器物上跟盖儿相密合的部分 opening; mouth; part of a bottle, jar, box, casket, etc., that seals closely with the lid or cover

【子粒】zǐlì 子实 seed; grain; kernel; bean; also 籽粒 zǐlì

【子棉】zǐmián 摘下来以后还没有去掉种子的棉花 unginned cotton; cotton from which seeds have not been removed after being stripped; also 籽棉 zǐmián

【子母弹】zǐmǔdàn 榴霰弹 cluster bomb

【子母扣儿】zǐmǔkòur 纽扣的一种,用金属制成,一凸一凹的两个合成一对 snap button; snap fastener; popper; press stud; a pair of metal concave and convex buttons; also 摁扣儿 ènkòur

【子母钟】zǐmǔzhōng 大型企业、商场、车站等处用的成组的计时钟。其中控制、带动其他钟运转的精确的钟叫母钟,受母钟控制的钟叫子钟。secondary and primary clocks; a group of clocks at a large enterprise, market, station, etc., among which the precision clock operating others is called the primary clock, and the ones controlled by it, the secondary clocks

【子目】zǐmù 细目 specific item; subtitle: 丛书～索引 index of the subtitles of a series of books|表册上共有六个大项目,每个项目底下又分列若干～。There are six large projects on the collected statistical form, with several subtitles under each of them.

【子囊】zǐnáng 某些植物体内藏孢子的器官 ascus; internal organ of certain plants, that hides spores

【子埝】zǐniàn 洪水上涨接近堤顶时,为了防止洪水漫溢决口,在堤顶上临时加筑的小堤 small dyke added on top of the original dyke to prevent a flood from overflowing and breaching when it rises close to the top of the dyke; also 子堤 zǐdī

【子女】zǐnǚ 儿子和女儿 children; sons and daughters

【子时】zǐshí 旧式计时法指夜里十一点钟到一点钟的时间 hour-counting method, referring to the period of the day from 11 p.m. to 1 a.m.

【子实】zǐshí 稻、麦、谷子、高粱等农作物穗上的种子;大豆、小豆、绿豆等豆类作物豆荚内的豆粒 grain; kernel; seed (on ears of crops such as rice, wheat, millet, sorghum, etc.); beans (in pods of legumes such as soya bean, red bean, mung bean, etc.); also 籽实 zǐshí or 子粒 zǐlì

【子兽】zǐshòu 初生的幼兽 newborn animal; young animal; also 仔兽 zǐshòu

【子书】zǐshū 〈古代 *arch*.〉图书四部分类法的一类书,如《老子》、《墨子》、《荀子》、《韩非子》等书 'philosophy', one of the four traditional categories of ancient Chinese writings, e.g. *Laozi*, *Mozi*, *Xunzi* and *Hanfeizi*

【子嗣】zǐsì 〈书 *fml*.〉指儿子(就传宗接代说) son; male offspring (to carry on the family name)

【子孙】zǐsūn 儿子和孙子,泛指后代 children and grandchildren; (in a broad sense) descendants: ～万代 generation after generation|不肖～ unworthy descendant|炎黄～ descendants of Emperors Yandi and Huangdi — Chinese people

【子午线】zǐwǔxiàn 为测量地球而假设的南(午)北(子)方向的线,即通过地面某点的经线 meridian (line); hypothetical north-south line to measure the earth, i. e. the meridian (line) crossing some point on the ground; ☞ 本初子午线 běnchū-zǐwǔxiàn on p. 89

【子息】zǐxī ❶ 子嗣 son; male offspring ❷〈书 *fml*.〉利息 interest

【子细】zǐxì same as 仔细 zǐxì

【子弦】zǐxián 较细的丝弦,做三弦、琵琶、南胡的外弦用 fine silk strings used for the outer strings of the *sanxian* (three-stringed Chinese guitar), *pipa* (four-stringed Chinese lute), and *nanhu* (two-stringed bowed instrument)

【子虚】zǐxū〈书 *fml*.〉汉朝司马相如有《子虚赋》,假托子虚先生、乌有先生和亡(pronounced wú,〈古 *arch*.〉same as 无 wú)是公三人互相问答。后世因此用'子虚'、'子虚乌有'指虚构的或不真实的事情。nil, a term originating in *Rhapsody of Master Nil* by Sima Xiangru of the Han Dynasty, in which commentaries are made through a dialogue between Zixu (Master Nil), Wuyou and Wushi; later referring to fictitious, imaginary or nonexistant things: 事属～。It is sheer fiction.

【子婿】zǐxù〈书 *fml*.〉女婿 son-in-law

【子叶】zǐyè 种子植物胚的组成部分之一,是种子萌发时的营养器官。单子叶植物的胚只有一枚子叶,双子叶植物的胚有一对子叶,裸子植物的胚有两个或两个以上的子叶。cotyledon; one of the component parts of the embryo of a seed plant, which serves as a nutritional organ when the seed sprouts. The embryo of a monocotyledon has only a single cotyledon, that of a dicotyledon has a pair, and that of gymnosperm has two or more cotyledons.

【子夜】zǐyè 半夜 midnight

【子音】zǐyīn 辅音 consonant

【子鱼】zǐyú 刚孵化出来的小鱼 spawn; newborn fish; also 仔鱼 zǐyú or 稚鱼 zhìyú

【子侄】zǐzhí 儿辈和侄辈的统称 general term for sons and nephews

【子猪】zǐzhū 初生的小猪 piglet; shoat; newborn little pig; also 苗猪 miáozhū or 仔猪 zǐzhū

仔 zǐ 幼小的(多指牲畜、家禽等 oft. of domestic animals, poultry, etc.) the young: ～猪 piglet; shoat | ～鸡 chick
☞ 崽 zǎi on p. 2386 and zī on p. 2536

【仔畜】zǐchù same as 子畜 zǐchù

【仔鸡】zǐjī same as 子鸡 zǐjī

【仔密】zǐmì 纺织品、针织品等纱与纱之间、线与线之间距离近,空隙小 closely woven or knitted; of a close texture; (of fabric or knitwear) having little space between sheers or threads: 这双袜子织得很～。The socks are tightly knit.

【仔兽】zǐshòu same as 子兽 zǐshòu

【仔细】zǐxì ❶ 细心 careful; attentive; meticulous: 他做事很～。He does everything carefully. | ～领会文件的精神 carefully understand the spirit of the document ❷ 小心;当心 be careful; look out; watch out; be cautious; take care: 路很滑,～点儿。Watch your step! The road is very slippery. ❸〈方 *dial*.〉俭省 economical; thrifty; frugal: 日子过得～ live frugally; be frugal with one's expenses ‖ also 子细 zǐxì

【仔鱼】zǐyú same as 子鱼 zǐyú

【仔猪】zǐzhū same as 子猪 zǐzhū

姊 zǐ 姐姐 elder sister; sister: ～妹 sisters; elder and younger sisters

【姊妹】zǐmèi 姐妹 sisters; elder and younger sisters ◇～篇 companion volume or piece | ～城 sister cities; twin cities; twinning of cities

耔 zǐ〈书 *fml*.〉培土 earth up; hill up

茈 zǐ 茈湖口(Zǐhúkǒu),地名,在湖南 Zihukou, name of a place in Hunan Province
☞ cí on p. 317

呰 zǐ〈书 *fml*.〉❶ same as 訾 zǐ ❷ same as 呰 zǐ

虸 zǐ [虸蚄](zǐfāng)〈方 *dial*.〉黏虫 army worm

秭 zǐ ❶〈古时 *arch*.〉数目名,一万亿 billion (as in the UK and Germany); thousand billion or trillion (as in the US and France) ❷ 秭归(Zǐguī),地名,在湖北 Zigui, name of a place in Hubei Province

籽 zǐ (～儿 zǐr) 某些植物的种子 seed (of certain plants): 棉～儿 cotton seed | 菜～儿 vegetable seed | 花～儿 flower seed | ～棉 unginned cotton

【籽粒】zǐlì same as 子粒 zǐlì

【籽棉】zǐmián same as 子棉 zǐmián

【籽实】zǐshí same as 子实 zǐshí

笫 zǐ〈书 *fml*.〉竹篾编的席 mat made of thin bamboo strips: 床～ bed mat

梓 zǐ ❶ 梓树,落叶乔木,叶子对生,稍有掌状浅裂,圆锥花序,花黄白色。木材可以做器具。Chinese catalpa (*Catalpa ovata*); deciduous tree, having opposite leaves with small palm-shaped lobes, panicles, and yellow and white flowers, its wood used to make utensils ❷ same as 刻板 kèbǎn ①: 付～ send to the printers

【梓里】zǐlǐ〈书 *fml*.〉指故乡 home town; ☞ 桑梓 sāngzǐ on p. 1657

呰 zǐ [呰窳](zǐyǔ)〈书 *fml*.〉懒惰 laziness

紫 zǐ ❶红和蓝合成的颜色 purple; violet; colour made by mixing red and blue: ～红 purplish red | 青～ green and purple; dark purple | 玫瑰～ rosy; rose-red ❷ (Zǐ)姓 a sur-

Z

name

【紫菜】zǐcài 甘紫菜的通称 general term for purple laver (*Porphyra*), an edible algae

【紫貂】zǐdiāo 貂的一种，比猫略小，耳朵略呈三角形，毛棕褐色。能爬树，吃野兔、野鼠或鸟类，有时也吃野菜、野果和鱼。毛皮柔软，是我国东北特产之一。sable(*Martes zibellina*); a kind of marten that is a little smaller than a cat, with slightly triangular ears and sepia fur, climbing trees, feeding on hares, field rats, birds, and sometimes edible wild herbs, fruit and fish, its fur being soft and one of the special products of northeast China; also 黑貂 hēidiāo

【紫毫】zǐháo 一种毛笔，笔锋用深紫色的细而硬的兔毛做成，比羊毫硬 writing brush made of dark purple, thin hard rabbits' hair, being harder than those made of goats' hair

【紫河车】zǐhéchē 中药上指胞衣 (Chin. med.) dried human placenta

【紫红】zǐhóng 深红中略带紫的颜色 purplish red; dark red touched with purple

【紫花】zǐ·huā 淡赭色 light reddish brown: ～布(一种粗布) nankeen (a type of coarse cloth) | ～裤子 light reddish brown trousers

【紫荆】zǐjīng 落叶灌木或小乔木，叶子略呈圆形，表面有光泽，花紫红色，荚果扁平。供观赏，木材和树皮都入药。Chinese redbud (*Cercis chinensis*); deciduous bush or small tree, having slightly circular leaves, lustrous on the surface, purplish red flowers, and flat pods. An ornamental plant, its timber and bark can also be used as medicine.

【紫罗兰】zǐluólán ❶ 二年生或多年生草本植物，叶子长圆形或倒披针形，总状花序，花紫红色，也有淡红、淡黄或白色的，果实细长。供观赏。violet (*Matthiola incana*); common stock; biennial or perennial herb with oval or inverted lanceolate leaves, raceme, purplish red, light red, light yellow or white flowers, and long thin fruit, being an ornamental plant ❷ 这种植物的花 flower of such a plant

【紫砂】zǐshā 一种陶土，产于江苏宜兴。质地细腻，含铁量高，烧制后呈赤褐、紫黑等色。主要用来烧制茶壶。boccaro ware; delicate potter's clay produced in Yixing City, Jiangsu Province, containing a high iron content, which after being burned turns russet, purplish black, etc., mainly used to make tea pots

【紫檀】zǐtán ❶ 常绿乔木，羽状复叶，小叶卵形，花黄色，结荚果。木材坚硬，带红色，可以做贵重的家具或美术品。padauk (*Pterocarpus indicus*); red sandalwood; evergreen tree with pinnately compound leaves, oval leaflets, yellow flowers and pods, whose hard reddish timber can be used to make valuable furniture or art works ❷ 这种植物的木材 timber of such a plant

【紫糖】zǐtáng 黑而红的颜色(多形容脸色 oft. of complexion) swarthy touched with red: ～脸 dark red face

【紫藤】zǐténg 落叶木本植物，缠绕茎，羽状复叶，小叶长椭圆形，总状花序，花紫色，荚果长大而硬，表面有绒毛。供观赏。Chinese wistaria (*Wistaria sinensis*); deciduous woody plant with vines, pinnately compound leaves, long oval leaflets, raceme, purple flowers, and long and hard pods covered with fine hair, used as an ornamental plant; 通称 generally called 藤萝 téngluó

【紫铜】zǐtóng 纯质的铜，紫红色，所含杂质不超过1%，是电和热的良导体。耐腐蚀性好，用来制造电线、冷藏器的零件等。red copper; pure purplish red copper containing no more than one per cent impurities, a good conductor of electricity and heat, with excellent corrosion resistance, used to produce wires, spare parts of refrigerators, etc.; also 红铜 hóngtóng

【紫外线】zǐwàixiàn 波长比可见光短的电磁波，波长约 0.39—0.04 微米，在光谱上位于紫色光的外侧。可使磷光和荧光物质发光，能透过空气，不易穿过玻璃，有杀菌能力，对眼睛有伤害作用。用于治疗皮肤病、矿工的保健以及消毒等。ultraviolet ray; electromagnetic wave on the outer side of purple light on the spectrum, whose wavelength (about 0.39-0.04 microns) is shorter than visible light, which can cause phosphorescent and fluorescent substances to emit light, penetrate the air but cannot pass through glass easily, and which kills bacteria, and hurts the eyes, applied in the treatment of skin diseases, health care of miners, sterilization, etc.; also 紫外光 zǐwàiguāng

【紫菀】zǐwǎn 多年生草本植物，叶子椭圆状披针形，头状花序，边缘的小花雌性，呈舌状，蓝紫色，中央的小花两性，呈管状，黄色，瘦果有毛。根和根茎可入药。aster (*Aster tataricus*); perennial herb with oval lanceolate leaves, capitulum, bluish violet tongue-shaped small female flowers on the edges, and yellow tube-shaped hermaphrodite flowers in the middle, and hairy achenes, whose root and rhizome can be used as medicine

【紫药水】zǐyàoshuǐ 龙胆紫溶液的通称 general term for gentian violet solution, used as an antiseptic

訾 zǐ 〈书 *fml*.〉说人坏话 slander; smear; calumniate; speak ill of others: ～议 criticize; censure; impeach; discuss the failings of others; find fault with | ～毁 defame; vilify ☞ zī on p. 2538

【訾议】zǐyì 〈书 *fml*.〉评论人的短处 criticize; censure; impeach; discuss the failings of others; find fault with: 无可～ above criticism; unimpeachable

滓 zǐ ❶ 沉淀的杂质 dregs; lees; sediment: 渣～ dregs | 泥～ dirt ❷ 污浊 dirty; muddy: 垢～ dirt | ～浊 dirt

zì (ㄗˋ)

自[1] zì ❶ 自己 self; oneself; one's own: ～动 voluntary; of one's own accord | ～卫 defending oneself; self-defence | ～爱 self-respect; proper respect for oneself | ～力更生 bootstrap oneself; (pull or haul oneself up) by one's own bootstrap; relying on oneself | ～言～语 talk to oneself; speak one's thoughts aloud; think aloud; soliloquize | ～给～足 self-sufficiency; autarky | ～告奋勇 offer to do (something difficult); volunteer to undertake (a difficult task) | ～顾不暇 have trouble even in taking care of oneself; be busy enough with one's own affairs; be unable even to fend for oneself (much less look after others) | 不～量力 overestimate oneself or one's own strength or ability; overrate oneself; do something beyond one's ability ❷ 自然; 当然 naturally; certainly: ～不待言 it goes without saying; it is self-evident; needless to say; it is taken for granted; it is axiomatic | 公道～在人心。People have a natural sense of justice. *or* A sense of justice is shared by all people. | 两人久别重逢,～有许多话说。Having reunited after a long departure, the two of them certainly have a lot to talk about.

自[2] zì 从;由 from; since: ～小 since childhood | ～此 since then; from then on | ～古 since ancient times; since antiquity; from time immemorial | ～远而近 from the distant to the near | 选～《人民日报》excerpted from the *People's Daily* | 来～各国的朋友 friends from different countries

【自爱】zì'ài 爱惜自己的身体、名誉 self-respect; proper respect for oneself; cherishing one's own health or reputation: 不知～ have no (sense of) self-respect

【自傲】zì'ào 自以为有本领而骄傲 arrogant; self-conceited; feeling proud of one's assumed ability: 居功～ become arrogant because of one's meritorious service

【自拔】zìbá 主动地从痛苦或罪恶中解脱出来 free oneself (from pain or evil-doing); extricate oneself: 越陷越深,无法～ get increasingly involved and be unable to extricate oneself

【自白】zìbái 自己说明自己的意思;自我表白 make clear one's meaning or position; vindicate oneself: ～书 written confession | 无以～ cannot find a way to justify oneself

【自暴自弃】zì bào zì qì 自己甘心落后,不求上进 give oneself up as hopeless; be self-abandoned; fall behind and have no urge to make progress; be resigned to one's backwardness

【自卑】zìbēi 轻视自己,认为不如别人 abject; feel oneself inferior (to others); be self-abased: ～感 sense of inferiority; inferiority complex | 不自满,也不～ neither self-satisfied nor self-abased

【自便】zìbiàn 随自己的方便;按自己的意思行动 act at one's convenience; do as one pleases; suit oneself: 听其～。Let (him) do as (he) pleases. | 您～吧,别陪着了。Please go and do as you like. Don't waste time for me.

【自裁】zìcái 〈书 *fml.*〉 自杀;自尽 kill oneself; commit suicide; take one's own life

【自残】zìcán 自己残害自己;自相残害 injure oneself; kill each other (in the same group); autotomy: ～肢体 autotomy of limbs | 骨肉～ fratricidal fight

【自惭形秽】zì cán xíng huì 原指因自己容貌举止不如别人而感到惭愧,后来泛指自愧不如别人 feel ashamed at one's inferior appearance or manners; (in a broad sense) have a sense of inferiority or inadequacy

【自沉】zìchén 〈书 *fml.*〉 投水自尽 drown oneself; commit suicide by throwing oneself into a river, well, etc.

【自称】zìchēng ❶ 自己称呼自己 call oneself; style oneself: 项羽～西楚霸王。Xiang Yu styled himself 'Lord of Western Chu'. ❷ 自己声称 claim to be; profess; declare oneself to be: 他们～是当地生产效益最好的单位。They claimed to be the unit with the best production results in the local area.

【自成一家】zì chéng yī jiā 在某种学问上或技术上有独创的见解或独特的做法,能自成体系 (in a certain branch of learning or technology) have a unique view or practice, which can become a school of one's own

【自乘】zìchéng 一个数自身和自身相乘,也就是两个或两个以上相同的数相乘,如求 3^4 $(3\times3\times3\times3)$ 的运算就是自乘 involution; squaring; multiplication of a number by itself, i.e., multiplication of two or more same numbers, e.g. calculation of the 4th power of 3 $(3\times3\times3\times3)$

【自持】zìchí 控制自己的欲望或情绪 control oneself; exercise self-restraint; keep one's desires or emotions under control: 清廉～ be honest, upright and self-restrained | 激动得不能～ too excited to control oneself; can hardly contain one's excitement

【自出机杼】zì chū jīzhù 〈比喻 *fig.*〉 诗文的构思和布局别出心裁、独创新意 (of poetic prose) be original in conception and overall arrangement; ☞ 机杼 jīzhù on p. 892

【自吹自擂】zìchuī-zìléi 自己吹喇叭,自己打鼓 blow one's own trumpet or horn; beat one's own drum;〈比喻 *fig.*〉自我吹嘘 brag; praise oneself; self-glorification

【自从】zìcóng〈介词 *prep.*〉表示时间的起点(指过去) since (referring to a starting point in time, in the past):我～参加了体育锻炼,身体强健多了。I have become much stronger and healthier since doing physical training.

【自打】zìdǎ〈方 *dial.*〉自从(某时以后) since (a certain time):儿子～离家以后,没有回来过。The son has not returned since leaving his home.

【自大】zìdà 自以为了不起 self-important; arrogant; conceited; feeling proud of oneself: 自高～ conceited; arrogant; self-important; full of vainglory|骄傲～ conceited and arrogant; swollen with pride

【自得】zìdé 自己感到得意或舒适 contented; self-satisfied; self-complacent; pleased with oneself; feeling complacent:洋洋～ smug; complacent|安闲～ carefree and contented; contentedly take one's leisure

【自动】zìdòng ❶ 自己主动 voluntary; of one's own accord:～参加 participate voluntarily|～帮忙 help voluntarily ❷ 不凭借人为的力量的 automatic; automated; spontaneous:～燃烧 spontaneous combustion|水～地流到田里。Water flows into the fields automatically. ❸ 不用人力而用机械装置直接操作的 automation; self-action; self-motion:～化 automation|～控制 automatic control; auto-control|～装置 automatic assembly; automatic device; automaton; automatics

【自动步枪】zìdòng bùqiāng 能够连续发射的步枪。装有快慢机的,可连发射击,也可单发射击。automatic rifle; rifle that can be fired continuously. Those equipped with regulators can shoot in bursts or single shots.

【自动化】zìdònghuà 最高程度的机械化。机器、设备和仪器能全部自动地按规定要求和既定程序进行生产,人只需要确定控制的要求和程序,不用直接操作。automation; highest degree of mechanization, in which all machines, equipment and instruments can produce automatically according to prescribed requirements and set procedures, and people only need to determine the control requirements and procedures instead of engaging in direct operation

【自动控制】zìdòng kòngzhì 通过自动化装置控制机器,使按照预定的程序工作 automatic control; auto-control; control a machine through automatics to make it work according to predetermined procedures; 简称 abbr. 自控 zìkòng

【自动炮】zìdòngpào 能够连续发射的火炮 automatic gun; gun that can be fired continuously

【自动铅笔】zìdòng qiānbǐ 铅笔的一种,形状跟自来水笔相似,可以随意调节,使笔铅露出或缩进 retractable pencil; a kind of pencil similar to a fountain pen in shape, which can be regulated freely to expose or retract the pencil lead

【自动线】zìdòngxiàn 一套能自动连续进行生产的设备所组成的生产线 production line made up by a set of automatic equipment that can be engaged in production continuously

【自发】zìfā 由自己产生,不受外力影响的;不自觉的 spontaneous; self-generating, not caused by external influence; unconsciously:～性 spontaneity|～势力 spontaneous forces|这个科研小组是他们几个人～地组织起来的。They launched this scientific research group by themselves.

【自肥】zìféi 经手财物时用不正当的手段从中取利 line one's pocket; make money for oneself in a way that is disapproved of; enrich oneself by misappropriating funds or material that one handles:中饱～ divert public money to feather one's nest

【自费】zìfèi 自己负担费用 at one's own expense:～生 self-funded student; self-supporting student|～留学 study abroad at one's own expense|～旅行 travel at one's own expense|孩子看病是～。The child saw the doctor at his parents' expense.

【自焚】zìfén 自己烧死自己 burn oneself to death; self-immolation ◇玩火～。Those who play with fire will get burned (or will be consumed by fire).

【自分】zìfèn〈书 *fml.*〉自己估量自己 estimate one's own ability or strength; make a self-appraisal or self-assessment:～不足以当重任 come to the conclusion after a self-appraisal that one is not up to an important task

【自封】[1] zìfēng 自己给自己加头衔;自命(含贬义 derog.) proclaim or style oneself:～为专家 proclaim oneself an expert

【自封】[2] zìfēng 限制自己 confine oneself; isolate oneself:故步～ be satisfied with old practices; be conservative and complacent; remain in a rut

【自奉】zìfèng〈书 *fml.*〉自己生活享用 provide the necessities of life for oneself:～甚俭 lead an extremely simple life; lead a plain and simple life

【自负】[1] zìfù 自己负责 be responsible for one's own actions; hold oneself responsible:～盈亏 (of an enterprise) assume sole responsibility for one's own profits and losses; be held economically responsible|文责～。The author takes sole responsibility for his views.

【自负】[2] zìfù 自以为了不起 think highly of oneself; be conceited; pride oneself (on one's talent):这个人很～。This person is rather conceited.

【自高自大】zì gāo zì dà 自以为了不起,看不起

Z

别人 self-important; conceited; arrogant; thinking highly of oneself while looking down upon others

【自告奋勇】zì gào fèn yǒng 主动地要求承担某项艰难的工作 offer to undertake (a difficult task); volunteer (to do sth. difficult)

【自个儿】zìgěr 〈方 *dial.*〉自己 oneself; by oneself; also 自各儿 zìgěr

【自各儿】zìgěr same as 自个儿 zìgěr

【自耕农】zìgēngnóng 土地改革以前,自己耕种自己的土地的农民,多指中农 owner-peasant; land-holding peasant; peasant who cultivated his own land before land reforms; middle peasants

【自供】zìgòng 自己招供 confess; confess on one's own to a crime: ～状 confession|～不讳 confess without hiding anything; candidly confess

【自古】zìgǔ 从古以来;从来 since ancient times; since antiquity; from time immemorial: 这个群岛～就是中国的领土。This group of islands has been part of Chinese territory from ancient times.

【自顾不暇】zì gù bù xiá 照顾自己都来不及(哪里还能顾到别人) have trouble even in taking care of oneself; be busy enough with one's own affairs; be unable even to fend for oneself (let alone look after others)

【自豪】zìháo 因为自己或者与自己有关的集体或个人具有优良品质或取得伟大成就而感到光荣 be bristled with pride; be proud of or take pride in the excellent qualities or great achievements of oneself, or the collective, or an individual concerned with oneself: ～感 sense of pride|以此～ be proud of this

【自己】zìjǐ ❶〈代词 *pron.*〉复指前头的名词或代词(多强调不由于外力)[referring to the preceding noun or pronoun, oft. to exclude an external factor in an emphatic way]: ～动手,丰衣足食 get ample food and clothing by working with one's own hands; be well-fed and well-clothed through one's own work|鞋我～去买吧。I will buy the shoes myself.|瓶子不会～倒下来,准是有人碰了它。The bottle cannot have fallen down by itself; someone must have knocked it over.|这种新型客机是我国～制造的。The new passenger plane was produced by our country. ❷ 亲近的;关系密切的 one's own; closely related to oneself: ～人 person on one's own side; people in one's own circles; one of us|～弟兄 one's own brothers

【自己人】zìjǐrén 指彼此关系密切的人;自己方面的人 people on one's own side; people in one's own circles; one of us; people closely related to each other: 老大爷,咱们都是～,别客气。Uncle, we are all family, so make yourself at home.|老刘是～,你有什么话,当他面说不碍事。Lao Liu is one of us, so don't hesitate to speak frankly in his presence.

【自给】zìjǐ 依靠自己的生产满足自己的需要 self-sufficient; self-supporting; self-contained; rely on one's own productivity to satisfy one's own needs: ～自足 self-sufficiency; autarky|粮食～有余 be more than self-sufficient in grain; be self-sufficient and achieve a surplus in grain

【自家】zìjiā 〈方 *dial.*〉自己 oneself

【自尽】zìjìn 自杀 kill oneself; commit suicide; take one's own life

【自经】zìjīng 〈书 *fml.*〉自缢 hang oneself

【自刭】zìjǐng 〈书 *fml.*〉自刎 commit suicide by cutting one's throat; cut one's own throat

【自疚】zìjiù 对自己的过失感到惭愧不安 guilty conscience; compunction; feel guilty and uneasy over one's own culpability: 深感～ have a bad conscience; be pricked by conscience

【自咎】zìjiù 〈书 *fml.*〉自己责备自己 blame oneself; rebuke or reproach oneself: 悔恨～ deeply regret and blame oneself

【自救】zìjiù 自己解救自己 save oneself; support oneself; provide for and help oneself: 生产～ support oneself by engaging in production; provide for and help oneself by engaging in production

【自居】zìjū 自以为具有某种身份 consider oneself to be; pose as; call oneself; consider oneself to have some status: ～名士 consider oneself to be a person of literary talent; pose as a person with a literary reputation|以功臣～ pose as one who has rendered great service; consider oneself to be someone who has rendered great service; put on heroic airs

【自决】zìjué 自己决定自己的事 self-determination; matter decided by oneself: 民族～权 right to national self-determination

【自觉】zìjué ❶ 自己感觉到 realize; be aware of: 肺结核的初期,病症不很显著,病人常常不～。Due to the hidden symptoms, patients suffering from pulmonary tuberculosis (TB) are often unaware of the disease at the early stages. ❷ 自己有所认识而觉悟 consciously; on one's own initiative: ～自愿 voluntarily; willingly; of one's own free will or volition|～地遵守纪律 observe discipline consciously (or on one's own initiative)

【自觉自愿】zì jué zì yuàn 自己认识到应该如此而甘心情愿(去做) voluntarily; willingly; of one's own free will or volition; realize sth. by oneself, and do it willingly

【自绝】zìjué 做了坏事而不愿悔改,因此自行断绝跟对方之间的关系 alienate oneself; unwilling to repent and mend one's ways for an evil deed, and thus cut oneself off from the other party: ～于人民 alienate or isolate oneself from the people

【自控】zìkòng 自动控制的简称 abbr. for 自动控制 zìdòng kòngzhì

【自夸】zìkuā 自己夸耀自己 sing one's own praises; build oneself up; blow one's own trumpet

【自郐以下】zì kuài yǐ xià 吴国的季札在鲁国看周代的乐舞，对各诸侯国的乐曲都发表了意见，从郐国以下他就没有评论（见于《左传》襄公二十九年）*The Zuo Commentary · Duke Xiang 29th Year*: Ji Zha of the state of Wu, when watching a dance to the accompaniment of Zhou-dynasty music in the State of Lu, aired his views about the music of various dukedoms, but stopped short at the mention of Kuai and the other states to follow;〈比喻 *fig.*〉从…以下就不值得一谈 none is worth mentioning except...

【自来】zìlái 从来；原来 from the beginning; originally; in the first place; from the outset: 这里～就是交通要道。It is a vital communication line from the very beginning.

【自来火】zìláihuǒ〈方 *dial.*〉❶ 火柴 matches ❷ 打火机 cigarette lighter; lighter

【自来水】zìláishuǐ ❶ 供应居民生活、工业生产等方面用水的设备。把取自水源的水经过净化、消毒后，加压力，通过管道输送给用户。equipment that supplies residents and factories, etc. with water; facility that fetches water from a water source, purifies, disinfects, and pressurizes it before sending it to users through pipelines ❷ 从自来水管道中流出来的水 running water; tap water; water flowing from water pipes

【自来水笔】zìláishuǐbǐ 钢笔的一种，笔杆内有贮存墨水的装置，吸一次墨水可以连续使用一段时间 fountain pen; a kind of pen whose shaft is equipped with a device to store ink to be used for a period of time

【自理】zìlǐ ❶ 自己承担 provide for oneself: 费用～ at one's own expenses ❷ 自己料理 take care of oneself: 他卧病在床，生活不能～。Confined to bed by illness, he is unable to take care of himself in daily life.

【自力更生】zì lì gēng shēng 不依赖外力，靠自己的力量把事情办起来 rely on one's own efforts; develop sth. by depending on one's own efforts instead of outside forces

【自立】zìlì 不依赖别人，靠自己的劳动而生活 self-supporting; earn one's own bread; stand on one's own (two) feet; earn one's own living instead of relying on others: ～谋生 earn one's own living | 孩子小，在经济上还不能～。The child is too young to support himself economically.

【自量】zìliàng 估计自己的实际能力 estimate one's own actual ability or strength: 不知～ overrate one's abilities; fail to take a proper measure of oneself | 我～还能胜任这项工作。I believe that I am capable of doing this work.

【自流】zìliú ❶ 自动地流 (of water, etc.) flow automatically; flow by itself: ～井 artesian well | ～灌溉 gravity irrigation ❷〈比喻 *fig.*〉在缺乏领导的情况下自由发展 take its natural course; do as one pleases; develop freely without leadership: 放任～ let things drift along; let people act as they like; do whatever one likes | 听其～ let people act freely without leadership; let things drift along

【自流井】zìliújǐng 自动地喷出水来的井 artesian well; well that spouts water automatically

【自留地】zìliúdì 我国在实行农业集体化以后留给农民个人经营的少量土地，产品归个人所有 plot of land for personal needs; family plot; private plot; small amount of land alloted to peasants after agricultural collectivization in China, with the produce belonging to the peasants

【自律】zìlǜ〈书 *fml.*〉自己约束自己 self-discipline; restrain oneself: ～甚严 discipline oneself very strictly

【自卖自夸】zì mài zì kuā 自己卖什么就夸什么好 praise the goods one sells; praise one's own wares;〈比喻 *fig.*〉自我吹嘘 indulge in (or be given to) self-glorification; blow one's own trumpet

【自满】zìmǎn 满足于自己已有的成绩 complacent; self-satisfied; self-contented; smug; satisfied with one's own achievements: 骄傲～ arrogant and complacent; conceited and self-satisfied | ～情绪 complacency; self-satisfaction | 他虚心好学，从不～。Modest and eager to learn, he is never self-satisfied.

【自鸣得意】zì míng déyì 自己表示很得意（多含贬义 oft. derog.）be very pleased with oneself; preen oneself; feel smug

【自鸣钟】zìmíngzhōng 指自动报时的钟 chime clock; clock that gives the correct time automatically: 一架～ a striking clock; a chime clock

【自命】zìmìng 自以为有某种品格、身份等 regard oneself as; consider oneself (to have some character, identity, etc.): ～清高 profess to be above worldly considerations; act as if one is morally better than other people; claim to keep aloof from politics and material pursuits | ～不凡（自以为不平凡）pride oneself on being out of the ordinary; consider oneself above the crowd; be self-important; think no end of oneself

【自馁】zìněi 失去自信而畏缩 lose confidence; lose heart; be discouraged; be disheartened: 再接再厉，绝不～ make persistent efforts, never losing confidence

【自欺欺人】zì qī qī rén 用自己都难以置信的话

Z

或手法来欺骗别人；既欺骗自己也欺骗别人 deceive others by words or means even incredible to oneself; cheat or deceive oneself and others

【自戕】zìqiāng〈书 *fml.*〉自杀 kill oneself; commit suicide; take one's own life

【自强】zìqiáng 自己努力向上 strive to become stronger:～不息 make unremitting efforts to improve oneself; strive unceasingly to become stronger|男儿当～。A man should strive to improve himself constantly.

【自强不息】zì qiáng bù xī 自己努力向上，永远不懈怠 constantly strive to become stronger; make unremitting (or unceasing) efforts to improve oneself

【自然】zìrán ❶ 自然界 natural world; nature: 大～ nature ❷ 自由发展；不经人力干预 naturally; in the natural course of events; develop naturally without artificial interference:～免疫 natural immunity; native immunity; innate immunity|听其～ let things run their course|～而然 naturally; of oneself; spontaneously; automatically; as a matter of course|你先别问，到时候～明白。Don't ask now. You'll understand in due course. ❸ 表示理所当然 naturally; certainly; of course:只要认真学习，～会取得好成绩。You will certainly get good grades if you study hard.

【自然】zì·ran 不勉强；不局促；不呆板 natural; unaffected; at ease; not feeling embarrassed; not rigid:态度很～。The attitude is quite natural.|他是初次演出，但演得挺～。Although it was his debut on stage, he performed quite well.

【自然村】zìráncūn 自然形成的村落 natural village; hamlet; village that forms naturally

【自然而然】zìrán ér rán 不经外力作用而如此 naturally; of oneself; spontaneously; automatically; as a matter of course; as such without any outside force or power:我们长期在一起工作，～地建立了浓厚的友谊。A deep friendship has naturally developed between us, who have worked together for a long time.

【自然法】zìránfǎ 西方法学家对法律的分类之一，认为自然法是自然存在、永恒不变并为一切人所遵守的行为规则(跟'实在法'相对 as opposed to 'positive law') natural law; law of nature; *jus naturae*; one of the categories of law according to Western jurisprudence, that believes that the laws of nature are a natural and eternal law observed by all people

【自然光】zìránguāng 不直接显示偏振现象的光，一般光源直接发出的光都是自然光，如阳光、灯光等 natural light; light that does not directly show the polarizing phenomenon. What is emitted by ordinary light sources is natural light, e.g. sunlight, lamplight, etc.

【自然规律】zìrán guīlǜ 存在于自然界的客观事物内部的规律 natural law; law of nature; internal laws of objective matter in nature; also 自然法则 zìrán fǎzé

【自然界】zìránjiè 一般指无机界和有机界。有时也指包括社会在内的整个物质世界。natural world; nature; inorganic and organic world; the whole material world, society included

【自然经济】zìrán jīngjì 只是为了满足生产者本身或经济单位（如氏族、庄园）的需要而进行生产的经济，也就是自给自足的经济 natural economy; economy whose production is to meet the needs of the producers themselves or an economic unit (e.g. clans and manors), i.e., self-sufficient economy

【自然科学】zìrán kēxué 研究自然界各种物质和现象的科学。包括物理学、化学、动物学、植物学、矿物学、生理学、数学等。natural science; science that studies various matters and phenomena in nature, including physics, chemistry, zoology, botany, mineralogy, physiology, mathematics, etc.

【自然力】zìránlì 可以利用来代替人力的自然界的动力，如风力、水力 natural forces; natural power that can be used to replace human power or labour, e.g. wind power, water power, etc.

【自然人】zìránrén 法律上指在民事上能享受权利和承担义务的公民（区别于'法人'as compared with 'juristic person')(leg.) natural person; citizen who can enjoy the rights and undertake the duties relating to civil laws

【自然数】zìránshù 大于零的整数，即 1，2，3，4，5，… natural number; integer greater than zero, i.e. 1, 2, 3, 4, 5, etc.

【自然物】zìránwù 天然存在，没经过人类加工的东西，如禽兽、虫鱼、草木、矿物等 unprocessed thing; natural thing that has not been processed by humans, e.g. birds and beasts, insects, fish, plants, minerals, etc.

【自然选择】zìrán xuǎnzé 达尔文学说认为生物在自然条件的影响下经常发生变异，适于自然条件的生物可以生存、发展，不适于自然条件的生物被淘汰，这种适者生存的过程叫做自然选择 natural selection; survival of the fittest; Darwin's theory of evolution which believes that organisms often undergo transformations under the influence of natural conditions, and those fit for certain particular natural conditions can survive and evolve, while those that unfit are eliminated through a process of natural selection

【自然灾害】zìrán zāihài 水、旱、病、虫、鸟、兽、风、雹、霜冻等自然现象造成的灾害 natural calamity or disaster; calamity or disaster caused by natural phenomena, e.g. flood, drought, disease, insects, birds, beasts, wind, hail, frost, etc.

【自然主义】zìrán zhǔyì ❶ 文学艺术创作上的一

种不良倾向,着重描写现实生活中个别现象和琐碎细节,但不能正确地反映社会的本质 naturalism; unhealthy trend in literary and artistic creation, which emphatically depicts individual phenomena and trifling details in practical life, but cannot properly reflect the real nature of society ❷ 19 世纪产生于法国的一种采取自然主义创作手法的文艺流派,以左拉(Émile Zola)为代表 naturalism; literary and artistic school adopting the naturalist mode of writing developed in the 19th century, represented by Émile Zola

【自燃】zìrán 物质在空气中缓慢氧化而自动燃烧,如白磷能够自燃,大量堆积的煤、棉花、干草等在通风不良的情况下也能自燃 spontaneous combustion or ignition; self-ignition of a substance gradually oxidized in the air, e.g. white phosphorus may ignite spontaneously, just as a great deal of piled-up coal, cotton, hay, etc., may when poorly ventilated

【自如】zìrú〈书 *fml.*〉❶ 活动或操作不受阻碍 freely; smoothly; with ease; with facility: 旋转～ revolve or rotate freely | 操纵～ operate with facility | 运用～ wield skilfully; use with facility; handle and use (a tool) with skill ❷ 自若 composed; with composure; self-possessed; calm and at ease: 神态～ appear calm and at ease

【自若】zìruò 不拘束;不变常态 composed; with composure; self-possessed; calm and at ease; not feeling ill at ease; remaining in a natural state: 神态～ appear calm and at ease | 谈笑～ talk and laugh imperturbably

【自杀】zìshā 自己杀死自己 commit suicide; take one's own life

【自身】zìshēn 自己(强调非别人或别的事物 instead of sb. or sth. else) self; oneself: 不顾～安危 regardless of one's own safety

【自食其果】zì shí qí guǒ 指做了坏事,结果害了自己;自作自受 eat one's own bitter fruit; reap what one has sown

【自食其力】zì shí qí lì 凭自己的劳力养活自己 support oneself by one's own labour; earn one's own living

【自食其言】zì shí qí yán 不守信用,说了话不算数 go back on one's word; break one's promise; break faith with sb.

【自始至终】zì shǐ zhì zhōng 从开始到末了 from beginning to end; from start to finish: 大会～充满着团结欢乐的气氛。The conference was held from beginning to end in a pervading atmosphere of solidarity and cheerfulness.

【自视】zìshì 自己认为自己(如何如何) consider (or think, imagine) oneself: ～甚高 think highly of oneself; be self-important

【自是】[1] zìshì 自然是 naturally; of course: 久别重逢,～高兴。It was of course a delight for them to meet again after such a long separation.

【自是】[2] zìshì 自以为是 consider oneself (always) in the right; regard oneself as infallible; be opinionated: 他既很～又很顽固。He is always very opinionated and obstinate.

【自恃】zìshì〈书 *fml.*〉❶ 过分自信而骄傲自满;自负 overconfident and conceited ❷ 倚仗;仗恃 be self-assured for having sth. or sb. to rely on; count on; capitalize on: ～功高 capitalize on one's achievements

【自首】zìshǒu (犯法的人)自行向司法机关或有关部门交代自己的罪行 (of a criminal) voluntarily surrender oneself; confess one's crime; give oneself up: 投案～ surrender oneself to the juridical department

【自赎】zìshú 自己弥补罪过 redeem oneself; atone for one's crime: 立功～ perform meritorious services to atone for one's crime

【自述】zìshù ❶ 自己述说自己的事情 account in one's own words: 序言里作者～了写书的经过。The author gave an account of how he wrote the book in the foreword. ❷ 关于自己情况的叙述 account of one's experience; autobiography: 他写了一篇～。He wrote an autobiography.

【自私】zìsī 只顾自己的利益,不顾别人 selfish; self-centred; preoccupied with one's own interests and having little or no concern for others

【自诉】zìsù 刑事诉讼的一种方式,由被害人自己向法院起诉(区别于'公诉' as compared with 'public prosecution') private prosecution; action initiated by an injured party without the participation of the public prosecutor

【自外】zìwài 有意识地站在某个范围之外,或者站在对立的方面 stand by as an outsider; regard oneself as an outsider or opponent

【自卫】zìwèi 保卫自己 defend oneself; self-defence: ～战争 war of self-defence | 奋力～ do all one can to defend oneself

【自为阶级】zìwèi jiējí 指进入自觉斗争阶段的无产阶级。这时无产阶级在反对资产阶级的实际斗争过程中已成长起来,具有鲜明的阶级意识,创立了革命理论,建立了自己的政党,意识到本阶级的历史使命。class-for-itself; the proletariat in the stage of waging conscious struggles. The proletariat in this stage has grown up in the actual struggle against the bourgeoise, fostered distinct class consciousness, established its revolutionary theory and founded its own political party, and is aware of its historical mission.

【自慰】zìwèi 自己安慰自己 console oneself: 聊以～ just to console oneself

【自刎】zìwěn 割颈部自杀;抹脖子 commit suicide by slitting one's throat; cut one's throat

【自问】zìwèn ❶ 自己问自己 ask oneself; examine oneself: 反躬～ examine oneself; examine one's conscience | 扪心～ search one's heart; examine one's conscience ❷ 自己衡量(得出结论) reach a conclusion after weighing a matter：我～还能胜任这项工作。I think I'm still competent for this work.

【自我】zìwǒ ❶ 自己(用在双音动词前面,表示这个动作由自己发出,同时又以自己为对象)[used before disyllabic verbs to indicate an act by the self and upon the self] self; oneself：～批评 self-criticism | ～介绍 introduce oneself ❷ 指人们对于自身的把握和认识 be conscious of oneself; be understanding of oneself：～意识 self-consciousness | 追求～ assert one's own value as a constructive member of society, etc.

【自我作古】zì wǒ zuò gǔ 由自己创始,不依傍前人或旧例 be the founder or originator of sth.; initiate sth. without depending on the predecessors or precedents

【自习】zìxí 学生在规定时间或课外自己学习(of students) study by oneself in scheduled time or free time

【自相…】zìxiāng… 指自己跟自己或集体内部的相互之间(存在某种情况)[indicating certain state of affairs existing] in oneself; in a collective：～矛盾 self-contradiction; self-contradictory; contradictory to each other; one's words, ideas, etc. that contradict each other | ～惊扰 alarm one's own group, etc.; create a disturbance within one's ranks; raise false alarms | ～残害 injure or kill each other

【自新】zìxīn 自觉地改正错误,重新做人 turn over a new leaf; make a fresh start：悔过～ repent and make a new start | ～之路 new leaf of life; road to start afresh

【自信】zìxìn 相信自己 self-confident; confident：～心 confidence; self-confidence; self-assurance | ～能够完成这个任务 confident of being able to fulfil this task; be sure one can fulfil the task

【自行】zìxíng ❶ 自己(做) of one's own accord; by oneself：～解决 settle (a problem) by oneself | ～办理 handle (a matter) or go through (the formalities) by oneself ❷ same as 自动 zìdòng ①：～脱落 fall away automatically | ～退出 withdraw from of one's own accord

【自行车】zìxíngchē 一种两轮交通工具,骑在上面用脚蹬着前进。在不同的地区有脚踏车、单车等名称。bicycle; bike; two-wheeled vehicle equipped with foot pedals; also called 脚踏车 jiǎotàchē or 单车 dānchē in different regions

【自行火炮】zìxíng huǒpào 装在履带式、半履带式或轮胎式车辆上能自行运动的火炮 self-propelled gun mounted on a caterpillar, semi-caterpillar or wheeled vehicle

【自行其是】zì xíng qí shì 按照自己认为对的去做(不考虑别人的意见) go one's own way; act wilfully; act as one thinks right without giving a thought to others' opinions

【自修】zìxiū ❶ 自习(of students) study by oneself; self-study ❷ 自学 study on one's own; study independently：～数学 teach oneself mathematics

【自序】zìxù ❶ 作者自己写的序言 author's preface; preface ❷ 叙述自己生平经历的文章 autobiographic note; brief account of oneself ‖ also 自叙 zìxù

【自叙】zìxù same as 自序 zìxù

【自选动作】zìxuǎn-dòngzuò 某些体育项目比赛时,由运动员按照规定要求的难度和数量自己编选的整套或单个的动作。如花样滑冰、竞技体操等。optional exercise; in some sports, athletes choose their own exercises or sets of exercises with the required number and degrees of difficulty, as in figure skating, gymnastics, etc.

【自学】zìxué 没有教师指导,自己独立学习 study on one's own; study independently; teach oneself：～成材 be self-taught | 他～了高中的课程。He taught himself senior middle school courses.

【自已】zìyǐ 抑制住自己的感情(多用于否定式 usu. in a negative sense) control one's emotions：不能～ can't help controlling one's emotions | 思乡之情难以～。I can't help controlling my homesickness.

【自以为是】zì yǐ wéi shì 认为自己的看法和做法都正确,不接受别人的意见 consider oneself (always) in the right; regard oneself as infallible; be opinionated

【自缢】zìyì 〈书 *fml.*〉上吊自杀 hang oneself

【自用】zìyòng ❶〈书 *fml.*〉自以为是 obstinately holding to one's own views; opinionated; self-willed：刚愎～ stubborn; obstinate; self-willed | 师心～ conceited; opinionated; self-conceited; self-opinionated ❷ 私人使用 for private use; personal：～摩托车 private motorcycle

【自由】zìyóu ❶ 在法律规定的范围内,随自己意志活动的权利 freedom; liberty; right to act as one pleases within the limits of law：～平等 freedom and equality ❷ 哲学上把人认识了事物发展的规律性,自觉地运用到实践中去,叫做自由(philo.) freedom; consciously apply the law of the development of things one knows in practice ❸ 不受拘束;不受限制 free; unrestrained; unrestricted：～参加 participate or attend freely; free to participate | ～发表意见 express one's views unreservedly

【自由港】zìyóugǎng 一种港口,在划定的区域内商品的输出、输入和转口都可以免税 free port; port or zone where goods may be unloaded, stored and reshipped without payment of customs or duties if they are not imported

【自由价格】zìyóu jiàgé 由买卖双方自由协商议

定的价格 free price; price negotiated between the buyer and seller

【自由竞争】zìyóu jìngzhēng 商品生产者之间在生产和销售方面进行的不受限制的竞争。在竞争中,大资本排挤吞并小资本,使生产日益集中,发展到一定阶段,就形成垄断。free competition; unrestricted competition among commodity producers in production and marketing. In the course of competition, big capital pushes out and annexes small capital so that production is more and more concentrated and becomes monopoly after it develops to a certain stage.

【自由落体运动】zìyóu luòtǐ yùndòng 物体只受重力作用而从静止开始下落的运动。在同一地点,做自由落体运动的物体的加速度都相同。free fall; drop of a static object under the impact of its own gravity. In a given place the rate of acceleration is the same for all objects in a free fall.

【自由民】zìyóumín 指奴隶社会占有土地的农民和占有生产资料的手工业者。他们和奴隶不同,享有人身自由。freeman; person not in slavery or bondage; person with full civil and political rights; peasant who owns land or a handicraft person who owns means of production in a slave society. Different from slaves, a free man enjoys personal freedom.

【自由诗】zìyóushī 结构自由、有语言的自然节奏而没有一定格律的诗,一般不押韵 free verse; unorthodox verse; vers libre; poetry without regular metre, rhyme, or stanzaic forms

【自由市场】zìyóu shìchǎng 农贸市场的俗称 popular name for 农贸市场 nóngmào shìchǎng

【自由体操】zìyóu tǐcāo 竞技体操项目之一,运动员在地板、地毯或垫子上徒手做各种动作 floor exercise; free callisthenics; gymnastic event in which a gymnast performs compulsory or optional exercises bare-handedly on the floor, carpet or mattress

【自由王国】zìyóu wángguó 哲学上指人在认识和掌握客观世界规律之后,自由地运用规律改造客观世界的境界(philos.) realm of freedom; realm in which man applies the law of the objective world freely to remould the objective world after knowing and grasping the law of the objective world; ☞ 必然王国 bìrán wángguó on p.104

【自由泳】zìyóuyǒng ❶ 游泳项目之一,运动员可以用任何姿势游泳 freestyle (swimming); swimming event in which contestants may use any stroke ❷ 爬泳 crawl

【自由职业】zìyóu zhíyè 〈旧时 *old*〉指知识分子凭借个人的知识技能从事的职业。如医生、教师、律师、新闻记者、著作家、艺术家所从事的职业。profession; vocation or occupation requiring advanced education and training, and involving intellectual skills, as medicine, teaching, law, journalism, writing, art, etc.

【自由主义】zìyóu zhǔyì ❶ 19世纪和20世纪初期的一种资产阶级政治思想。自由主义者代表资产阶级的利益,反对政治的、社会的和宗教的束缚,在历史上曾经起过进步的作用。但在资产阶级取得政权后,自由主义就成了掩饰资产阶级统治的幌子。liberalism; bourgeois political philosophy in the 19th century and early 20th century. The liberalists represented the interests of the bourgeoisie and opposed the political, social and religious shackles, and played a progressive role in history. However, after the bourgeoisie took power, liberalism became cover for the bourgeois rule. ❷ 革命队伍中的一种错误的思想作风,主要表现是缺乏原则性,无组织,无纪律,强调个人利益等 liberalism; erroneous ideology and tendency in the revolutionary ranks, chiefly characterized by lack of principle, organization and discipline, and stress on personal interests

【自圆其说】zì yuán qí shuō 使自己的论断或谎话没有破绽 make one's statement valid; justify oneself; make one's lie flawless

【自怨自艾】zì yuàn zì yì 本义是悔恨自己的错误,自己改正(艾:治理;惩治),现在只指悔恨 repent on one's mistake and correct it on his own; 艾 *yì* meaning 'rectify or punish;' (now) repent; be full of remorse

【自愿】zìyuàn 自己愿意 voluntary; of one's own accord; of one's own free will; on a voluntary basis: 自觉~ voluntarily; willingly|~参加 voluntary participation; participate, attend or join on a voluntary basis|出于~ on a voluntary basis; of one's free will

【自在】zìzài 自由;不受拘束 free; unrestrained: 逍遥~ take life easy

【自在】zì·zai 安闲舒适 comfortable; at ease: 他们俩的小日子过得挺~。The couple is leading a free and easy life.

【自在阶级】zìzài jiējí 指处在自发斗争阶段的无产阶级。这时无产阶级还没有显著的阶级觉悟和自己的政党。class-in-itself; proletariat in the stage of waging spontaneous struggles, showing no distinct class consciousness, and having no political party of its own; ☞ 自为阶级 zìwéi jiējí

【自知之明】zì zhī zhī míng 了解自己(多指缺点)了解得透彻的能力(常跟'有、无'连用)[oft. used together with 有 yǒu or 无 wú] knowledge of oneself; ability to know oneself (oft. one's own defects) thoroughly

【自制】[1] zìzhì 自己制造 made by oneself: ~糕点 home-made pastry | ~玩具 home-made toys

【自制】[2] zìzhì 克制自己 self-control; self-restraint: ~力 ability to control oneself|难以~ difficult to control oneself

【自治】zìzhì 民族、团体、地区等除了受所隶属的国家、政府或上级单位领导外,对自己的事务行使一定的权力 autonomy; self-government;

ethnic people, organization or region exercising certain power over its own affairs apart from the leadership of the state, government or the higher-up authority:～区 autonomous region|民族区域～ ethnic regional autonomy

【自治机关】zìzhì jīguān 行使民族自治权力的机关,如自治区、自治州、自治县的人民代表大会和人民政府 organ of self-government; organ that exercises the power of ethnic autonomy, as the people's congress and people's government of an autonomous region, prefecture or county

【自治领】zìzhìlǐng 英联邦的成员国的一种组织形式,有独立的立法权和行政权,并可以派遣外交代表,但承认英国皇帝为元首,它的首脑总督是英皇派驻自治领的代表。如新西兰、加拿大等都是英联邦内的自治领。self-governing dominion; dominion; form of organization of a member state of the British Commonwealth, which has independent legislative power and administrative power and can appoint its own diplomatic representatives, but recognizes the British king as its head of state. Its governor is the representative the British king sends to a dominion. New Zealand, Canada, etc. are all dominions within the British Commonwealth.

【自治区】zìzhìqū 相当于省一级的民族自治地方,如内蒙古自治区、新疆维吾尔自治区等 autonomous region; ethnic autonomous region corresponding to the provincial level, as the Inner Mongolia Autonomous Region, the Xinjiang Uygur Autonomous Region, etc.

【自治县】zìzhìxiàn 相当于县一级的民族自治地方,如青海省的门源回族自治县 autonomous county; autonomous area corresponding to the county level, as the Menyuan Hui Autonomous County in Qinghai Province

【自治州】zìzhìzhōu 介于自治区和自治县之间的民族自治地方,如湖南省的湘西土家族苗族自治州 autonomous prefecture; ethnic autonomous region area corresponding to the level between the autonomous region and autonomous county, as the Xiangxi Tujia and Miao Autonomous Prefecture in Hunan Province

【自重】[1] zìzhòng ❶ 注意自己的言行 behave oneself with dignity; mind one's own conduct and words:自爱～ behave oneself with dignity and self-respect|请～些! Please behave yourself! *or* Mind your conduct! ❷〈书 *fml.*〉抬高自己的身份、地位 enhance one's status or position; extend one's influence:拥兵～ extend one's influence with military power

【自重】[2] zìzhòng 机器、运输工具或建筑物承重构件等的本身的重量 dead weight; weight of a machine, vehicle or structural part of a building itself

【自主】zìzhǔ 自己做主 act on one's own; decide for oneself; keep the initiative in one's own hands:独立～ independently|婚姻～ marry sb. of one's own choice; freedom of marriage|不由～ can't help; involuntarily; unconsciously

【自助餐】zìzhùcān 一种由用餐者自取菜肴、主食的用餐方式 buffet meal; buffet; meal at which diners serve themselves from a buffet or table

【自传】zìzhuàn 叙述自己的生平经历的书或文章 autobiography; a book or piece of writing recounting one's life story or experiences

【自转】zìzhuàn 天体绕着自己的轴心而转动。地球自转一周的时间是一昼夜;月亮自转一周的时间是农历一个月。rotation; spinning motion around the axis of a celestial body. It is one day and one night when the earth moves around its axis in one cycle, and one lunar month when the moon moves around its axis in one cycle.

【自尊】zìzūn 尊重自己,不向别人卑躬屈节,也不容许别人歧视、侮辱 self-respect; self-esteem; proper pride:～心 self-respect

【自作聪明】zì zuò cōngmíng 自以为挺聪明,轻率逞能 think oneself clever (in making suggestions, etc.); try to be smart (by acting on one's own, etc.)

【自作自受】zì zuò zì shòu 自己做错了事,自己承受不好的后果 reap the fruit of one's actions; suffer from one's own actions; stew in one's own juice

字 zì ❶ 文字 word; character:汉～ Chinese|识～ learn to read and write|～体 form of written or printed character|～义 meaning of a word|常用～ everyday words ❷(～儿 zìr)字音 pronunciation (of a word or character):咬～儿 pronounce|～正腔圆 pronounce every word correctly and in a sweet, mellow voice|他说话～～清楚。He pronounced every word clearly. ❸ 字体 form of a written or printed character; style of handwriting; printing type:篆～ seal character|柳～ style of calligraphy of Liu Gongquan|宋体～ Song typeface|美术～ artistic calligraphy ❹ 书法作品 scripts; writings:～画 calligraphy and painting|一幅～ a piece of calligraphy or a painting ❺ 字眼;词 word:革命人民的字典中没有'屈服'这个～。There is no such word as 'submit' in the dictionary of the revolutionary people. ❻(～儿 zìr)字据 receipt; written pledge:立～为凭 give a written pledge|收到款子,写个～儿给他。Write him a receipt when you get the money from him. ❼ 根据人名中的字义,另取的别名叫'字' style name:孔明是诸葛亮的～。Zhuge Liang styled himself Kongming.|岳飞～鹏举。Yue Fei styled himself Pengju. ❽ 俗指电表、水表等指

示的数量 number indicated on an electric meter, water meter, etc.:这个月电表走了五十个~,水表走了十二个~。As indicated on the electric meter and water meter, 50 kilowatt-hours of electricity and 12 tons of water were used this month. ❾〈书 *fml.*〉许配 (of a girl) be betrothed:待~闺中 not betrothed yet

【字典】zìdiǎn 以字为单位,按一定次序排列,每个字注上读音、意义和用法的工具书 dictionary; book of characters and words listed in a given order, with pronunciations, meanings, usage and other information provided

【字调】zìdiào 字音的高低升降 tones of Chinese characters; also 声调 shēngdiào; ☞ 四声 sìshēng on p. 1821

【字符】zìfú 电子计算机或无线电通信中字母、数字和各种符号的统称 general term for the letters, numbers and other symbols used in the electronic computer or wireless telecommunications

【字幅】zìfú 写成条幅或横幅的书法作品 horizontal or vertical scroll of calligraphy

【字号】zì·hao ❶ 商店的名称 name of a shop:这家商店是什么~? What's the name of this shop? ❷ 指商店 shop; store:这是一家老~。This is an old, reputable shop.|这家~名气大。This shop has a great reputation.

【字画】zìhuà 书画 calligraphy and painting:名人~ calligraphy and painting of a celebrity

【字汇】zìhuì 字典一类的工具书 glossary; wordbook; lexicon

【字迹】zìjì 字的笔画和形体 handwriting; writing; strokes and form of a character:~工整 neat writing|墓碑上的~模糊不清。The inscription on the gravestone is illegible.

【字句】zìjù 文章里的字眼和句子 words and expressions; writing:~通顺 coherent and smooth writing|锤炼~ refine one's writing; hone one's writing skill to excellence

【字据】zìjù 书面的凭证,如合同、收据、借条 written pledge (e.g. contract, receipt, IOU, etc.):立~ give a written pledge|写了一张~ write out a pledge

【字里行间】zì lǐ háng jiān 字句中间 between the lines:~充满了乐观主义精神 be imbued with optimism between the lines

【字码儿】zìmǎr same as 数码 shùmǎ ①:阿拉伯~ Arabic numerals

【字谜】zìmí 用字做谜底的谜语。如'拿不出手',谜底是'合'。riddle about a character or word, e.g., the answer to the riddle '拿不出手 ná bùchū shǒu' is the character '合 hé'

【字面】zìmiàn (~儿 zìmiànr)文字表面上的意义(不是含蓄在内的意义) literal; superficial meaning of words or phrases:这句话从~上看没有指摘的意思。This sentence does not contain suggestion of harsh criticism literally.

【字模】zìmú 浇铸铅字的模型,用紫铜或锌合金制成 (type) matrix; die or mould for casting types, made of red copper or zinc alloy; also 铜模 tóngmú

【字母】zìmǔ ❶ 拼音文字或注音符号的最小的书写单位 letters of an alphabet; letter:拉丁~ Latin alphabet|注音~ phonetic alphabet ❷ 音韵学上指声母的代表字,如'明'代表 m 声母 (in phonology) character representing an initial consonant (声母), as 明 míng for the initial m

【字幕】zìmù ❶ 银幕或电视机的荧光屏上映出的文字 captions (of motion pictures, etc.); subtitles ❷ 演戏时为了帮助观众听懂唱词而配合放映的文字 captioned songs for operas shown on a screen, used to help theatre-goers understand the singing

【字书】zìshū 解释汉字的形体、读音和意义的书,如《说文解字》wordbook; lexicon; dictionary; book of forms, pronunciations and definitions of Chinese characters, as *Discourses on Words and Explanations of Characters*

【字体】zìtǐ ❶ 同一种文字的各种不同形体,如汉字手写的楷书、行书、草书,印刷的宋体、黑体 script; typeface; different forms of a written or printed character of a language, as the handwriting styles 楷书 (regular script), 行书 (running script), 草书 (cursive style) and the printing types 宋体 (Song type) and 黑体 (boldface type) ❷ 书法的派别,如欧体、颜体 style of calligraphy as that of Ouyang Xiu, and that of Yan Zhengqing ❸ 字的形体 handwriting; writing:~工整匀称 neat handwriting

【字条】zìtiáo (~儿 zìtiáor)写上简单话语的纸条 note; brief note; short message:他走时留了一个~儿。He left a note when he departed.

【字帖儿】zìtiěr 写着简单的话的纸片,多为通知、启事之类 brief note; slip of paper with a brief message, usu. a notice, announcement, etc.

【字帖】zìtiè 供学习书法的人临摹的范本,多为名家墨迹的石刻拓本、木刻印本或影印本 copybook (for calligraphy); book containing models of handwriting for others to copy, mostly books of stone inscription rubbings, woodcut printing or photoprinting

【字形】zìxíng 字的形体 character pattern; font:标准~ standard font|~规范 standardization of font

【字眼】zìyǎn (~儿 zìyǎnr)用在句子中的字或词 wording; diction:挑~ find faults with wording; be fastidious about wording|抠~ find faults with wording; be fastidious about wording|激动的心情,使我找不出适当的~来形容。I can't find appropriate words to describe my excitement.

【字样】zìyàng ❶ 文字形体的规范 model of written characters:《九经～》*Model Characters of the Nine Classics* ❷ 用在某处的词语或简短的句子 printed or written words or phrases:门上写着'卫生模范'的～。On the door are inscribed with the words 'Model in Hygiene'.

【字义】zìyì 字所代表的意义 meaning of a word:解释～ interpret or explain the meaning of a word

【字音】zìyīn 字的读音 pronunciation:注明～ marked with phonetic symbols

【字斟句酌】zì zhēn jù zhuó 对每一字、每一句都仔细推敲。形容说话或写作的态度慎重。choose one's words with care; weigh every word

【字纸】zìzhǐ 有字的废纸 waste paper with characters written or printed on it:～篓儿 wastepaper basket

剚(倳) zì〈书 *fml.*〉用刀刺进去 pierce with a knife, dagger, etc.; stab

牸 zì 雌性的牲畜(一般用于牛) female livestock (usu. used to refer to cow):～牛 cow

恣 zì ❶ 放纵;没有拘束 abandoned; throw off restraint; do as one pleases:～意 unscrupulous; reckless; unbridled; wilful ❷〈方 *dial.*〉(～儿 zìr)舒服;自在(zì·zai) comfortable; at ease:～得很 very comfortable; live comfortably

【恣情】zìqíng ❶ 纵情 to one's heart's content; as much as one likes:～享乐 seek pleasure as much as one pleases; indulge in creature comforts to one's heart's content|～欢笑 laugh heartily ❷ 任意 wanton; arbitrary; wilful:钱拿到手别～胡花。Don't spend your money wastefully once you get it. *or* Don't squander away your money once you get it.

【恣肆】zìsì〈书 *fml.*〉❶ 放纵 unrestrained; self-indulgent; wanton:骄横～ arrogant and wilful ❷(言谈、写作等)豪放不拘 (of speech, writing style, etc.) forceful and untrammelled; free and natural:文笔～ free and natural writing; write in a free and natural style

【恣睢】zìsuī〈书 *fml.*〉任意胡为 reckless; unbridled:暴戾～ unbridled cruelty

【恣意】zìyì 任意;任性 unscrupulous; reckless; unbridled; wilful:～妄为 act wilfully and wildly; behave unscrupulously

眦(眥) zì 上下眼睑的接合处,靠近鼻子的叫内眦,靠近两鬓的叫外眦 canthus; either corner of the eye where the eyelids meet. The canthus close to the nose is called the inner canthus and that close to the temples is the outer canthus;通称 commonly called 眼角 yǎnjiǎo

渍 zì ❶ 浸;沤;沾 steep; soak; ret:～麻 ret flax, jute, etc.|白衬衣被汗水～黄了。The white shirt has yellowed with sweat. ❷ 地面的积水 floodwater on a low-lying land:内～ waterlogging|防洪排～ prevention of floods and drainage of floodwater ❸ 油泥等积在上面难以除去 be soiled (with grease, etc.):烟斗里～了很多的油子。The pipe is caked with tar.|他每天擦机器,不让～一点泥。He cleans every day to keep dirt off the machine. ❹〈方 *dial.*〉积在物体上面难以除去的油泥等 stain; sludge:油～ greasy filth|茶～ tea stains; tea sludge

胾 zì〈书 *fml.*〉切成的大块肉 large piece of meat

胔 zì〈书 *fml.*〉腐烂的肉 rotten meat; putrid meat

zōng(ㄗㄨㄥ)

纵(㙡) zōng ☞ 鸡纵 jīzōng on p. 894

枞(樅) zōng 枞阳(Zōngyáng),地名,在安徽 Zongyang, name of a place in Anhui Province

☞ cōng on p. 323

宗¹ zōng ❶ 祖宗 ancestor:列祖列～ successive generations of ancestors ❷ 家族;同一家族的 clan; of the same clan:同～ of the same clan|～兄 elder brother of the same clan ❸ 宗派;派别 sect; faction; school:正～ orthodox school|禅～ Chan Sect of Chinese Buddhism; Zen Sect of Japanese Buddhism ❹ 宗旨 principal aim; purpose:开～明义 make clear the purpose and main theme from the very beginning|万变不离其～。Ten thousand different methods may be used, but the purpose remains the same. ❺ 在学术或文艺上效法 (in academic or artistic work) take as one's model:他的唱工～的是梅派。In opera singing he takes Mei Lanfang as his model. ❻ 为众人所师法的人物 model; great master:文～ literary master; master writer|一代词～ great literary master of one's time; great master in *ci* poetry of one's time ❼〈量词 *classifier*〉:一～心事 sth. that worries one; long-cherished wish|大～款项 a large sum of money ❽ (Zōng) 姓 a surname

宗² zōng 西藏地区旧行政区划单位,大致相当于县 old administrative unit in the Tibet region, roughly corresponding to the county

【宗祠】zōngcí same as 祠堂 cítáng ①

【宗法】zōngfǎ ❶〈旧时 *old*〉以家族为中心,按血统远近区别亲疏的法则 patriarchal clan rules and regulations; rules of a clan in

Z

which closeness of relationship is determined by the order of blood lineage：～制度 patriarchal clan system｜～社会 patriarchal society ❷ 师法；效法 take as a model or example; model on; follow：他的字～柳体。His handwriting is modelled on the calligraphic style of Liu Gongquan.

【宗匠】zōngjiàng 在学术或艺术上有重大成就而为众人所敬仰的人 great master (in academic or artistic work and respected by other people of the same profession)：词家～ great master in *ci* poetry｜一代～ greatest master of one's time

【宗教】zōngjiào 一种社会意识形态，是对客观世界的一种虚幻的反映，要求人们信仰上帝、神道、精灵、因果报应等，把希望寄托于所谓天国或来世 religion; a social ideology and an imaginary reflection of the objective world which urges people to believe in God, ghosts, spirits and retribution for sin, and places hope on the so-called Kingdom of Heaven or next life

【宗庙】zōngmiào 帝王或诸侯祭祀祖宗的处所 ancestral temple (or shrine) of a ruling house

【宗派】zōngpài ❶ 政治、学术、宗教方面的自成一派而和别派对立的集团（今多用于贬义 usu. derog) faction; sect; political, academic or religious group antagonistic to other factions：～活动 factional activities; sectarian activities ❷〈书 *fml.*〉宗族的分支 branch of a patriarchal clan

【宗派主义】zōngpài zhǔyì 主观主义在组织关系上的一种表现，特点是思想狭隘，只顾小集团的利益，好闹独立性和做无原则的派系斗争等 sectarianism; factionalism; manifestation of subjectivism in organizational relations, characterized by narrow-mindedness, caring only for the interests of one's small group, being given to one's 'independence' and unprincipled factional strife

【宗师】zōngshī 指在思想或学术上受人尊崇而可奉为楷模的人 master of great learning and integrity; person who is respected and modelled on in ideology or academic field：一代～ greatest master of one's time

【宗室】zōngshì 帝王的宗族 imperial (or royal) clan; imperial (or royal) clansman

Z 【宗祧】zōngtiāo〈旧时 *old*〉指家族相传的世系 family line：继承～ carry on the family line

【宗仰】zōngyǎng〈书 *fml.*〉（众人）推崇；景仰 hold in esteem：海内～ be held in esteem throughout the country｜远近～ be held in esteem far and near

【宗旨】zōngzhǐ 主要的目的和意图 aim; purpose：本学会以弘扬祖国文化为～。This society aims at developing the national culture.

【宗主国】zōngzhǔguó 封建时代直接控制藩属国的外交和国防，从而使藩属国处于半独立的状态的国家。在资本主义时代，殖民国家对殖民地也自称宗主国。suzerain (state); metropolitan state; state which directly controlled the diplomacy and defence of a vassal state in the feudal times, thus subjecting the vassal state in a status of semi-independence. In the capitalist times, a colonial state calls itself a suzerain state to its colonies.

【宗主权】zōngzhǔquán 宗主国对藩属国、殖民地享有的支配或统治的权力 suzerainty; suzerain power that a suzerain state enjoys to dominate or rule a vassal state or a colony

【宗族】zōngzú ❶ 同一父系的家族 patriarchal clan：～制度 patriarchal clan system ❷ 同一父系家族的成员（不包括出嫁的女性）(not including married women) clansman

综 zōng 总起来聚在一起 put together; sum up：～合 sum up; synthesize｜错～ intricate; criss-cross

☞ zèng on p. 2402

【综观】zōngguān 综合观察 make a comprehensive survey：～全局 take a broad view of the whole situation

【综合】zōnghé ❶ 把分析过的对象或现象的各个部分、各属性联合成一个统一的整体（跟'分析'相对 as opposed to 'analyse'）synthesize; form a whole by bringing together the separate parts and attributes of the analysed objects or phenomena ❷ 不同种类、不同性质的事物组合在一起 synthesis; gathering together of parts or elements of different kinds or different properties; synthetical; comprehensive; multiple; composite：～治理 tackle a problem in a comprehensive way｜～平衡（各方面之间的平衡）(strike an) overall balance｜～大学 university｜戏剧是一种～艺术，它包括文学、美术、音乐、建筑各种艺术的成分。Drama is a comprehensive art that embraces literature, fine art, music, architecture and other elements.

【综合大学】zōnghé dàxué 多科系的高等学校，一般设有哲学社会科学（文科）和自然科学（理科）方面的各种专业 university; educational institution of the highest level with a good number of professional schools (colleges), usu. having philosophy and social science (liberal arts) and natural science

【综合利用】zōnghé lìyòng 对资源实行全面、充分、合理的利用 make multiple, full and reasonable use of resources

【综合语】zōnghéyǔ 词与词之间的语法关系主要是靠词本身的形态变化来表示的语言，如俄语。词的形态变化也叫屈折，所以综合语也叫屈折语。synthetic language; inflectional language; language in which the grammar relationships between or among words is chiefly indicated by morphological changes of the words, e.g. Russian; change in the forms of words

【综计】zōngjì 总计 sum up; add up

【综括】zōngkuò 总括 sum up

【综述】zōngshù 综合叙述 summarize; sum up: 新闻～ news summary; news roundup | 社论～了一年来的经济形势。The editorial summed up the economic situation the year that had just gone by.

棕(椶) zōng ❶ 棕榈 palm ❷ 棕毛 palm fibre; coir: ～绳 coir rope | ～毯 coir rug | ～刷子 coir brush

【棕绷】zōngbēng 用棕绳穿在木框上制成的床屉子 wooden bed frame strung with criss-cross coir ropes: ～床 wooden bed frame strung with criss-cross coir ropes; also 棕绷子 zōngbēng·zi

【棕榈】zōnglǘ 常绿乔木，茎呈圆柱形，没有分枝，叶子大，有长叶柄，掌状深裂，裂片呈披针形，花黄色，雌雄异株，核果长圆形。木材可以制器具。palm (*Palmae*); evergreen, dioecious, unbranched tree with a cylindrical trunk, large, long-stalked, palmately- and lanceolate-lobed leaves, yellow flowers, and long, round nuts, its wood used in making implements; 通称 popularly known as 棕树 zōngshù

【棕毛】zōngmáo 棕榈树叶鞘的纤维，包在树干外面，红褐色，可以制蓑衣、绳索、刷子等物品 palm fibre; reddish-brown fibre of the leaf sheath of the palm tree, covering the trunk, used to make rain capes, ropes, brushes, etc.

【棕色】zōngsè 像棕毛那样的颜色 brown; colour of the palm fibre

【棕熊】zōngxióng 哺乳动物，身体大，肩部隆起，毛色一般是棕褐色，但随地区不同而深浅不一。能爬树，会游泳，吃果、菜、虫、鱼、鸟、兽等，有时也伤害人畜。胆可入药。brown bear; large-trunked mammal with bridged shoulders and tan to dark brown hair, capable of climbing trees and swimming, feeding on fruits, vegetables, insects, fishes, birds and beasts, and preying on humans and domestic animals occasionally. Bear paws and meat are used as food, its skin is used to make fur-lined mattress, and its gall bladder is used for Chinese medicine. also 马熊 mǎxióng or 罴 pí, 通称 popularly called 人熊 rénxióng

腙 zōng 有机化合物的一类，是醛或酮的羰基与肼或取代肼缩合而成的化合物 hydrazone; organic chemical compound condensed from aldehyde or ketone carbonyl with hydrazine or by replacing it

骔(騌) zōng 马鬃 horse's mane

踪(蹤) zōng 脚印；踪迹 footprint; track; trace: ～影 trace; sign | 失～ be missing | 跟～ tail; shadow | 无影无～ disappear without any trace; vanish into thin air

【踪迹】zōngjì 行动所留的痕迹 trace; track: 各个角落都找遍了，仍然不见～。It was looked for in every nook and cranny, but there is still no trace of it.

【踪影】zōngyǐng 踪迹(指寻找的对象，多用于否定式 usu. in the negative) trace; sign: 毫无～。There is no trace at all. | 好几天看不见他的～。I haven't seen a trace of him for several days now.

鬃 zōng 马、猪等颈上的长毛 bristle; hair on the neck of a horse, pig, etc.: 马～ horse's mane | 猪～ pig bristle | ～刷 bristle brush

zǒng (ㄗㄨㄥˇ)

总(總、總) zǒng ❶ 总括；汇集 assemble; put together; sum up: ～之 in short | 汇～ collect; gather | ～其成 assume the responsibility for completing a task | ～起来说 to sum up | 把两笔账～到一块儿 settle the two accounts together ❷ 全部的；全面的 general; overall; total: ～账 general account; general ledger | ～动员 general mobilization | ～攻击 general offensive | ～罢工 general strike | ～的情况对我们非常有利。The whole (or general) situation is very favourable to us. ❸ 概括全部的；为首的；领导的 chief; head; general: ～纲 general programme | ～则 general rules | ～店 main store; general office | ～工会 federation of trade unions | ～路线 general line | ～司令 commander-in-chief | ～书记 general secretary ❹ 一直；一向 always; invariably: 天～不放晴。It's always cloudy or rainy. | 晚饭后他～是到湖边散步。He always takes a walk along the lakeside after supper. ❺ 毕竟；总归 anyway; after all; eventually; sooner or later: 冬天～要过去，春天～会来临。Winter will be over anyway, and spring will come eventually. | 小孩子～是小孩子，哪能像大人那样有力气。After all, a child is a child. How can he possibly be as strong as a grown-up?

【总裁】zǒngcái ❶ 清代称中央编纂机构的主管官员和主持会试的大臣 (in the Qing Dynasty) minister in charge of the imperial editing staff and the imperial civil service examination in the capital ❷ 某些政党或大型企业领导人的名称 director-general (of a political party); president (of a company); governor (of a bank)

【总产值】zǒngchǎnzhí 用价值形式计算的物质生产部门、生产单位在一定时期内生产的各种产品的总量 gross output value; total output value; total output of all material production departments and production units calculated in terms of value in a given period

【总称】zǒngchēng 统称 general term: 医、卜、星相之类过去～为方技 *Fangji* was the general term for medicine, necromancy, clairvoyance, astrology, physiognomy, etc. in the past.|舰艇是各种军用船只的～。Warship is the general term for all kinds of military vessels.

【总得】zǒngděi same as 必须 bìxū ①:这件事～想个办法解决才好。There must be some solution to this matter.|我想他今天～来一趟。He's bound to come today.

【总动员】zǒngdòngyuán ❶ 国家把全部武装力量由和平状态转入战时状态,并把所有的人力、物力动员起来以备战争需要的紧急措施 general (or total) mobilization; emergent measure to bring all armed forces from peacetime service to wartime service and mobilize all manpower and material power into the active service of a war ❷ 为完成某项重要任务动员全部力量 call up all forces to fulfil an important task

【总督】zǒngdū ❶ 明初在用兵时派往地方巡视监察的官员,清朝始正式成为地方最高长官,一般管辖两省的军事和政治,也有管三省或只管一省的 high official dispatched to make wartime inspection and supervision tours of the provinces during the early Ming Dynasty; viceroy in the Qing Dynasty ❷ 英国、法国等国家驻在殖民地的最高统治官员(in British colonies and dominions) viceroy; governor-general; governor; highest British and French ruler in a colony ❸ 英国国王派驻自治领的代表 governor-general; representative of the British King to a dominion

【总队】zǒngduì 军队中相当于团或师的一级组织 general detachment; army unit corresponding to a regiment or division

【总额】zǒng'é (款项)总数 total:存款～ total deposits|工资～ total wages; payroll|销售～ total sales; total sales volume

【总而言之】zǒng ér yán zhī 总括起来说;总之 in short; to put it in a nutshell; in brief; to make a long story short:～,要主动,不要被动。In short, you must take the initiative. Don't take a passive position.|大的、小的、方的、圆的,～,各种形状都有。Big or small, square or round, in a word, we have all shapes.

【总纲】zǒnggāng 总的原则、要点;总的纲领 general programme; general principles

【总攻】zǒnggōng 军事上指全线出击或全面进攻 general offensive:～令 order for a general offensive|发起～launch a general offensive

【总共】zǒnggòng 一共 in all; altogether; in the aggregate:他家～三口人。There are three people altogether in his family.|我们场里～养了两千多头奶牛。Our farm has raised more than 2,000 milk cows in all.

【总管】zǒngguǎn ❶ 全面管理 take overall responsibility; be in full charge of:校内事务一时无人～。No one takes the overall responsibility for school affairs for the time being.|后勤工作由老张～。Lao Zhang is in full charge of the logistics. ❷ 全面管理事务的人 person in full charge; manager ❸〈旧时 *old*〉富豪人家管理奴仆和各项事务的人 chief steward; head servant; butler; person in charge of servants and household affairs in a wealthy family

【总归】zǒngguī〈副词 *adv.*〉表示无论怎样一定如此;终究 anyway; after all; eventually:事实～是事实。Facts are facts, after all.

【总合】zǒnghé 全部加起来;合在一起 sum up; add up:把各种力量～起来 put all forces together

【总和】zǒnghé 全部加起来的数量或内容 sum; total; sum total:力量的～ total forces|三个月产量的～ total output of the three months

【总后方】zǒnghòufāng 指挥整个战争的领导机关所在的后方 rear area (in wartime)

【总汇】zǒnghuì ❶(水流)会合(of streams) come or flow together:～入海 flow into the sea together ❷ 汇合在一起的事物 confluence; concourse; aggregate:人民是智慧的海洋,力量的～。The people are a sea of wisdom and the aggregation of strength.

【总机】zǒngjī 供机关、企业等内部使用的交换机,可以接通许多分机和外线 switchboard; telephone exchange; exchange used in an office, enterprise, etc., which connects both inside and outside extensions

【总集】zǒngjí 汇集许多人的作品而成的诗文集,如萧统《文选》、郭茂倩《乐府诗集》(区别于'别集' as compared with 'collected works of an individual author') general collection; general anthology, e.g. Xiao Tong's *Selections of Refined Literature* compiled in the Liang Dynasty(502-557), and Guo Maoqian's *Anthology of Yuefu Poems* compiled in the Song Dynasty

【总计】zǒngjì 合起来计算 grand total; amount to; add up to; total:观众～有十万人。The audience totalled 100,000. *or* There were 100,000 spectators in all.|这个村粮食产量～为一百万斤。The total grain output of this village is one million *jin*.

【总角】zǒngjiǎo〈书 *fml.*〉〈古代 *arch.*〉未成年的人把头发扎成髻,借指幼年 child's hair twisted in a knot; childhood:～之交(幼年就相识的好朋友) childhood friend

【总结】zǒngjié ❶ 把一阶段内的工作、学习或思想中的各种经验或情况分析研究,做出有指导性的结论 sum up; summarize:～工作 summarize one's work|～经验 sum up one's experience ❷ 指总结后概括出来的结论 summary; summing-up:年终～ year-end summary|工作～ work summary

【总括】zǒngkuò 把各方面合在一起 sum up:～

起来说 to sum up; to state succinctly|对各方面的情况加以～ sum up all aspects of the situation

【总览】zǒnglǎn 全面地看;综观 overview; take an overall view:～全局 make an overall survey of the whole situation

【总揽】zǒnglǎn 全面掌握 assume overall responsibility; take on everything:～大权 have overall authority; assume a dominant role

【总理】zǒnglǐ ❶ 我国国务院领导人的名称 premier, title of the leader of the State Council of China ❷ 某些国家政府首脑的名称 prime minister, title of the head of government in some countries ❸ 某些政党领导人的名称 title of the leader of a political party ❹〈旧时 *old*〉某些机构、企业负责人的名称 general manager, title of a leader of institutions or corporations :学校～ school master|分公司的～ general manager of a subsidiary company ❺〈书 *fml.*〉全面主持管理 assume overall responsibility; take full charge of:～其事 take full charge of the affairs|～军务 assume overall responsibilities for the military affairs

【总领事】zǒnglǐngshì 领事中的最高一级的 consul general; ☞ 领事 lǐngshì on p. 1234

【总路线】zǒnglùxiàn 在一定历史时期指导各方面工作的最根本的方针 general line; fundamental principle guiding all aspects of work in a given historical period

【总目】zǒngmù 总的目录 general table of contents; general catalogue:四库全书～ General Catalogue for the *Complete Library of Four Branches of Books*|全书分订五册,除分册目录外,第一册前面还有全书～。The book is in five volumes. There is a table of contents for each volume, and also a general one for the whole book in the first volume.

【总评】zǒngpíng 总的评价、评论或评比 general comment; overall appraisal

【总鳍鱼】zǒngqíyú 鱼的一类,有肺,可以在水外呼吸,鳍强壮有力。生活在古生代,是陆生脊椎动物的祖先,为鱼类进化成两栖类的过渡类型,现在仍有残存。crossopterygian (*Crossopterygii*); fish with strong fins and lungs which allow it to breathe outside water; living in the Palaeozoic Era as the precursors of terrestrial vertebrates and regarded as the transitional precursors which evolved from fishes to amphibians. There are still some survivors today.

【总数】zǒngshù 加在一起的数目 total; sum total:资产～ total assets|与会人员～不足一百。Less than one hundred people were present at the meeting.

【总司令】zǒngsīlìng 全国或一个方面的军队的最高统帅 commander in chief; supreme commander of the whole national army or a field army

【总算】zǒngsuàn〈副词 *adv.*〉❶ 表示经过相当长的时间以后某种愿望终于实现 indicating that a certain wish finally came true after a fairly long period of time; at long last; finally:一连下了六七天的雨,今天～晴了。It clears up at long last today after raining for six or seven successive days.|他白天想,夜里想,最后～想到了一个好办法。He mulled it over day and night and finally came to a good solution. ❷ 表示大体上还过得去 considering everything; all things considered; on the whole:小孩子的字能写成这样,～不错了。For a child's handwriting, it's quite good.

【总体】zǒngtǐ 若干个体所合成的事物;整体 overall; total:～规则 overall plan|～设计 master design

【总统】zǒngtǒng 某些共和国的元首的名称 president (of a republic); title of the head of state in some republics

【总务】zǒngwù ❶ 机关学校等单位中的行政杂务 general affairs; general services:～科 general affairs section|～工作 general service work ❷ 负责总务的人 person in charge of general affairs

【总星系】zǒngxīngxì 银河系和所有已经发现的河外星系的总称,是人类迄今为止所观测到的恒星世界 metagalaxy; hypergalaxy; assemblage of all galaxies, including all intergalactic matter; measurable material universe; stellar world observed so far by man

【总则】zǒngzé 规章条例的最前面的概括性的条文 general rules; general principles; general provisions

【总长】zǒngzhǎng ❶ 北洋军阀时期中央政府各部的最高长官 cabinet minister of the central government during the Northern Warlords period (1912-1927) ❷ 总参谋长 chief of the general staff

【总账】zǒngzhàng 簿记中主要账簿之一,按户头分类登记一切经济及财政业务。根据总账所记账目编制资产负债表。general ledger; general account; one of the major books in bookkeeping, which records all economic and financial entries according to the accounts to which they belong. A balance sheet is prepared according to the entries in the general ledger.

【总之】zǒngzhī 表示下文是总括性的话 [indicating that the following is a summary remark] in a word; in short; in brief:政治、文化、科学、艺术,～,一切上层建筑都是跟社会的经济基础分不开的。Politics, culture, science and art, in short, all elements of the superstructure is inseparable from the economic base of a society.

【总装】zǒngzhuāng ❶ 把部件装配成总体的工序 process of putting all parts together; general assembly; final assembly ❷ 把部件装配

成总体 fit parts into a whole：～空间站 final assembly of a space station

捻(摠) zǒng〈书 *fml*.〉same as 总 zǒng

偬(傯) zǒng ☞［倥偬］kǒngzǒng on p.1106

zòng (ㄗㄨㄥˋ)

纵[1](縱) zòng ❶ 地理上南北向的(跟'横'相对，下 ②③ 同 as opposed to 'from east to west' or 'from west to east', same for ②③ below) (geographical direction) from north to south or from south to north：大运河北起北京，南至杭州，～贯河北、山东、江苏、浙江四省。The Grand Canal starts in Beijing in the north and ends in Hangzhou in the south, running through Hebei, Shandong, Jiangsu and Zhejiang provinces from north to south. ❷ 从前到后的 from the front to the back：～深 in depth; depth ❸ 跟物体的长的一边平行的 vertical; longitudinal; lengthwise：～剖面 vertical section; longitudinal section or profile ❹ 指军队编制上的纵队 column; file; military unit corresponding to an army

纵[2](縱) zòng ❶ 释放；放走 release; set free：欲擒故～ let loose the noose in order to catch; allow sb. some latitude at first in order to keep a tighter rein on him afterwards; give sb. line enough｜～虎归山 release the tiger and let it return to the mountains ❷ 放任；不约束 indulge; let loose; let oneself go：放～ indulge｜～情 to one's heart's content｜～欲 indulge in sensual pleasures｜不能～着孩子。Don't spoil the child. ❸ 纵身 jump up; jump into the air：花猫向前一～，就把老鼠扑住了。The spotted kitten leaped forward and caught the mouse.

纵[3](縱) zòng〈书 *fml*.〉纵然 even if; even though：～有千山万水，也挡不住英勇的勘探队员。Even though there are a thousand mountains and ten thousand rivers to conquer, they can't stop the dauntless prospectors.

纵[4](縱) zòng〈方 *dial*.〉有了皱纹 creased; crumpled：～金字(用有皱纹的金纸做成的字) creased golden characters (cut from creased, gold-plated paper)｜衣服压～了。The dress is crumpled.｜纸都～起来了。The paper got crumpled.

【纵步】zòngbù ❶ 放开脚步 stride：～向前走去 stride forward ❷ 向前跳跃的步子 jump; bound：一个～跳过壕沟 cross a trench in one big jump

【纵队】zòngduì ❶ 纵的队形 column; file：四路～ column of four lines ❷ 军队编制单位之一，我国解放战争时期，解放军曾编纵队，相当于军 military unit of the People's Liberation Army during the War of Liberation, equivalent to corps

【纵隔】zònggé 胸腔里左肺和右肺之间的脏器(如心脏、胸腺、食管等)和结缔组织的统称 mediastinum; organs (the heart, thymus and esophagus, etc.) and connective tissues between the left and right lungs

【纵横】zònghéng ❶ 竖和横；横一条竖一条的 in length and breadth; vertically and horizontally：～交错 criss-cross｜铁路～，像蜘蛛网一样。The railwayscriss-cross each other like a spider's web. ❷ 奔放自如 with great ease; freely：笔意～ write with great ease ❸ 奔驰无阻 sweep over; march over unhindered：红军长驱二万五千余里，～十一个省。The Red Army marched over more than 25,000 *li*, sweeping through eleven provinces.

【纵横捭阖】zònghéng bǎihé 指在政治、外交上运用手段进行联合或分化 manoeuvre among various states or political groupings (纵横 *zongheng*：用游说来联合 go about selling ideas among states for alliance; 捭阖 *baihe*：开合 opening and closing)

【纵虎归山】zòng hǔ guī shān〈比喻 *fig*.〉放走敌人，留下祸根 let the tiger return to the mountains—court calamity for the future; also 放虎归山 fàng hǔ guī shān

【纵火】zònghuǒ 放火 set on fire; commit arson：～犯 arsonist

【纵酒】zòngjiǔ 没有节制地饮酒 drink to excess

【纵览】zònglǎn 放开眼任意观看 look far and wide; scan：～四周 look all round｜～群书 read extensively

【纵令】[1] zònglìng〈连词 *conj*.〉即使 even if; even though：～有天大困难，也吓不倒我们。Even if there are insurmountable difficulties, we'll not be scared.

【纵令】[2] zònglìng 放任不加管束；听凭 give free rein to; indulge; connive：不得～坏人逃脱。Don't allow evil-doers to escape.

【纵目】zòngmù 尽着目力(远望) look as far as one's eyes can see：～四望 look far into the distance in all directions

【纵情】zòngqíng 尽情 to one's heart's content; as much as one likes：～欢乐 indulge in unbridled joy｜～歌唱 sing to one's heart's content; sing heartily

【纵然】zòngrán 即使 even if; even though：今天～有雨，也不会很大。Even if it rains today, it can't be heavy.

【纵容】zòngróng 对错误行为不加制止，任其发展 connive; wink at：不要～孩子的不良行为。Don't connive at your child's misdemeanours.

【纵身】zòngshēn 全身猛力向前或向上(跳) jump; leap：～上马 leap onto a horse｜～跳过

壕沟 jump across a trench

【纵深】zòngshēn 地域纵的方向的深度(多用于军事上 oft. used in military affairs) depth:突破前沿,向~推进 break through the forward line and push in deep

【纵使】zòngshǐ 即使 even if; even though:~你再聪明,不努力也难以成事。Even if you are clever, you can achieve nothing without working hard.

【纵谈】zòngtán 无拘束地谈 talk freely:~天下事 talk freely about the world affairs

【纵向】zòngxiàng ❶ 非平行的;上下方向的 vertical; longitudinal; lengthwise:~比较 vertical comparison|~联系 vertical link or contact ❷ 指南北方向 from north to south:京广铁路是~的,陇海铁路是横向的。The Beijing-Guangzhou Railway lies longitudinally while the Lanzhou-Lianyungang Railway runs laterally from west to east.

【纵欲】zòngyù 放纵肉欲,不加节制 give way to one's carnal desires; indulge in sensual pleasures

疭(瘲) zòng ☞ [瘛疭](chìzòng) on p. 266

粽(糉) zòng 粽子 pyramid-shaped dumpling made of glutinous rice wrapped in bamboo or reed leaves (eaten during the Dragon Boat Festival):肉~ glutinous rice dumpling stuffed with meat|豆沙~ glutinous rice dumpling stuffed with sweetened red bean paste

【粽子】zòng·zi 一种食品,用竹叶或苇叶等把糯米包住,扎成三角锥体或其他形状,煮熟后食用。我国民间端午节有吃粽子的习俗。pyramid-shaped dumpling made of glutinous rice wrapped in bamboo or reed leaves. It is a traditional folk custom to eat such dumplings during the Dragon Boat Festival.

猔 zòng 〈方 *dial.*〉公猪 boar

zōu (ㄗㄡ)

邹(鄒) Zōu ❶ 周朝国名,在今山东邹县一带 Zou, name of a principality in the Zhou Dynasty in and around present-day Zouxian, Shandong Province ❷ 姓 a surname

驺(騶) zōu ❶〈古代 *arch.*〉给贵族掌管车马的人 groom; person whose work is tending, feeding and currying horses for aristocrats ❷ (Zōu)姓 a surname

诹 zōu 〈书 *fml.*〉商量;咨询 consult; seek advice from:~吉(商订吉日) pick an auspicious day (for a marriage, etc.)

陬 zōu 〈书 *fml.*〉角落;山脚 corner; foot of a hill

缏 zōu 〈书 *fml.*〉黑里带红的颜色 dark red

鄹(❶郰) Zōu ❶ 春秋时鲁国地名,在今山东曲阜东南 Zou, name of a place in the state of Lu during the Spring and Autumn Period, in what is today's southeast Qufu, Shandong Province ❷〈书 *fml.*〉same as 邹 zōu ①

鲰 zōu 〈书 *fml.*〉❶ 小鱼 small fish; fry; fingerling ❷ 形容小 tiny; small

zǒu (ㄗㄡˇ)

走 zǒu ❶ 人或鸟兽的脚交互向前移动 walk; go; person, bird or animal moves feet forward alternately:行~ walk|~路 hit the road; walk|孩子会~了。The baby can walk now.|马不~了。The horse has stopped. ❷ 跑 run; move:奔~相告 run about spreading the news ❸ (车、船等)运行;移动;挪动 (of a vehicle, boat, etc.) move; drive; sail:钟不~了。The clock has stopped.|这条船一个钟头能~三十里。The ship can ply 30 *li* per hour.|你这步棋~坏了。You've made a bad move. ❹ 离开;去 leave; go away:车刚~。The bus (car, train, etc.) has just left.|我明天要~了。I'm leaving tomorrow.|请你~一趟吧。Please pay them a visit just once.|把土抬~ carry the earth away ❺ 指人死(婉辞 euph.) go; leave; die:她还这么年轻就~了。She died so young. ❻ (亲友之间)来往 (of ralatives and friends) visit; call on:~娘家 visit the bride's home|~亲戚 visit a relative|他们两家~得很近。The two families are in close touch. ❼ 通过;由 through; from:咱们~这个门出去吧。Let's go out through this door. ❽ 漏出;泄漏 leak; let out; escape:~气。The gas is leaking.|~风 disclose (a secret)|说~了嘴 make a slip of the tongue ❾ 改变或失去原样 depart from the original; lose the original shape, flavour, etc.:~样 depart from the original model|~调儿 out of tune|茶叶~味了。The tea has lost the original flavour.|你把原意讲~了。You failed to get across the original meaning.

【走板】zǒu//bǎn ❶ 指唱戏不合板眼 (of opera singing) be out of tune; be off the beat:黄腔~ go off the beat|唱得走了板 sing out of tune ❷ (~儿 zǒubǎnr)〈比喻 *fig.*〉说话离开主题或不恰当 digress from the subject; stray from the point:你的话~了。You have strayed from the point.|他说着说着就走了板儿。As he talked and talked, he forgot what he was talking about.

【走笔】zǒubǐ 〈书 *fml.*〉很快地写 write rapidly:~疾书 write rapidly (or swiftly)

【走避】zǒubì 为躲避而走开;逃避 flee; escape:

～他乡 go away and hide oneself in another place|～不及 fail to escape

【走边】zǒu//biān 武戏中表演夜间潜行、靠路边疾走的动作 (of actors playing military roles in traditional opera) walk with a light, cautious tread to suggest travel stealthily by the roadside at night

【走镖】zǒubiāo 指保镖的人押送货物 act as an armed escort for a convoy

【走道】zǒudào 街旁或室内外供人行走的道路 pavement; sidewalk; path; walk; footpath: 大楼的～窄。The corridors in the building are narrow. |留出一条～ leave a footpath

【走道儿】zǒu//dàor 走路 walk: 小孩儿刚会～。The baby has just learned to toddle. |她～一扭一扭的。She swings her hips all the time she walks.

【走电】zǒu//diàn 〈方 *dial*.〉跑电 leakage of electricity

【走调儿】zǒu//diàor 唱戏、唱歌、演奏乐器不合调子(of singing or playing musical instrument) out of tune: 他唱歌爱～。He often sings out of tune. *or* His singing often gets out of tune.

【走动】zǒudòng ❶ 行走而使身体活动 walk about; stretch one's legs: 坐的时间久了,应该～～。After sitting so long, we should go out for a stroll. ❷ 指亲戚朋友之间彼此来往 (of relatives and friends) visit each other: 两家常～,感情很好。The two families often visit each other. They are on very good terms.

【走读】zǒudú (学生)只在学校上课,不在学校住宿,叫走读(区别于'寄宿' as compared with 'attending a boarding school') attend a day school: ～生 day student; non-resident student

【走访】zǒufǎng 访问;拜访 interview; have an interview with: 记者～劳动模范。The reporter had an interview with a model worker.

【走风】zǒu//fēng 泄漏消息 let out a secret; leak out

【走钢丝】zǒu gāngsī ❶ 杂技的一种,演员在悬空的钢丝上来回走动,并表演各种动作 wire-walking; acrobatic show, in which an actor or actress walks to or fro and performs on a suspended steel wire ❷〈比喻 *fig*.〉做有风险的事情 do sth. risky

【走狗】zǒugǒu 本指猎狗,今比喻受人豢养而帮助作恶的人 hunting dog; (fig.)person who is paid to do evils; running dog; lackey; flunkey; stooge; servile follower

【走过场】zǒu guòchǎng ❶ 戏曲中角色出场后不停留,穿过舞台从另一侧下场,叫走过场 go through the stage in quick motions; actor or actress going from one end of the stage to the other without stopping ❷〈比喻 *fig*.〉敷衍了事 do sth. as a mere formality; do sth. perfunctorily or superficially

【走合】zǒuhé 磨(mó)合 (of a vehicle or machine) run in

【走红】zǒu//hóng ❶ 遇到好运气 have good luck; be in luck: 这几年他正～,步步高升。He is in good luck and has been promoted successively these years. also 走红运 zǒu//hóngyùn ❷ 指吃得开;受欢迎 in favour; in demand: 图书市场上音像制品开始～。The audio-visual products are now in good demand in the book market.

【走后门】zǒu hòumén (～儿 zǒu hòuménr)〈比喻 *fig*.〉用托情、行贿等不正当的手段,通过内部关系达到某种目的 get in by the back door; practise backdoorism; get sth. done through pull; secure advantages through influence; get sth. done through pull, bribery or other improper means

【走火】zǒu//huǒ ❶ 因不小心而使火器发火 (of firearms) discharge accidentally: 枪走了火。The rifle went off accidentally. ❷〈比喻 *fig*.〉说话说过了头 go too far in what one says; put sth. too strongly; overstate: 他说话好～。He often went far in speaking. ❸ 电线破损跑电引起燃烧 sparking; fire caused by the leakage of electricity due to to damged wire: 起火原因是电线～。The fire was caused by electric sparks from the wire. ❹ 失火 catch fire; be on fire: 仓房～了。The storehouse is on fire.

【走江湖】zǒu jiāng·hú 指四方奔走,靠武艺杂技或医卜星相谋生 wander from place to place and earn a living by juggling, fortune-telling, etc.; become a vagrant

【走廊】zǒuláng ❶ 屋檐下高出平地的走道,或房屋之间有顶的走道 corridor; passage; passageway; raised walkway under the eaves of a house; roofed walkway between two buildings ❷〈比喻 *fig*.〉连接两个较大地区的狭长地带 corridor; long, narrow strip of land linking two areas: 河西～ Hexi Corridor; Gansu Corridor; Corridor West of the Yellow River

【走漏】zǒulòu ❶ 泄漏(消息等) leak out; divulge: ～风声 divulge a secret; leak information ❷ 走私漏税 smuggling and tax evasion ❸ 大宗的东西部分失窃,叫有走漏 things stolen out of a bulk

【走露】zǒulòu same as 走漏 zǒulòu ①

【走路】zǒu//lù ❶ (人)在地上走 walk; go on foot: 孩子会～了。The baby has learned to walk. |走了两天的路,累坏了。We are completely exhausted after travelling on foot for two days. ❷ 指离开;走开 leave; go away: 不好好儿干,让他卷铺盖～。If he does not work properly, tell him to pack and go.

【走马】zǒumǎ 骑着马跑 gallop or trot along on horseback: 平原～ ride a horse across the plain|～看花 look at flowers while riding a horse; gain a shallow understanding from a fleeting glance

【走马灯】zǒumǎdēng 一种供玩赏的灯，用彩纸剪成各种人骑着马的形象(或别的形象)，贴在灯里特制的轮子上，轮子因蜡烛的火焰形成的空气对流而转动，纸剪的人物随着绕圈儿 running horse lantern; decorative lantern with a revolving circle of colourful paper-cut horses and other figures, which revolve as hot air ascends from the candle burning within it

【走马换将】zǒu mǎ huàn jiàng 指掉换将领，泛指掉换人员 change of command; reshuffle of personnel：领导班子～后，工作有了起色。Things are looking up as a result of a reshuffle of the leading group.

【走马看花】zǒu mǎ kàn huā 〈比喻 *fig*.〉粗略地观察事物 look at flowers while riding a horse; gain a shallow understanding from a fleeting glance; also 走马观花 zǒu mǎ guān huā

【走马上任】zǒu mǎ shàng rèn 指官吏就职 go to one's post; take up (or assume) office

【走南闯北】zǒu nán chuǎng běi 形容走的地方多，到过许多省份 journey north and south; travel widely

【走内线】zǒu nèixiàn 指通过对方的眷属或亲信，进行某种活动 take the inner line; use private influence to achieve one's end (e.g. seek sb.'s favour by approaching his confidants or family members); go through private channels

【走俏】zǒuqiào (商品)销路好 (of goods) sell well; be in great demand：近年金首饰～。Gold jewels have sold well in recent years.

【走禽】zǒuqín 鸟的一类，这类鸟翅膀短小，脚大而有力，只能在地面行走而不能飞行。如食火鸡和鸵鸟。cursores; cursorial birds; birds with small, short wings and big, strong legs, which can walk on the ground but cannot fly, as cassowary and ostrich

【走人】zǒurén (人)离开；走开 go away; leave：咱们～，不等他了。Let's go now and not wait for him any more.|他既不愿干，就叫他～。Tell him to pack up and quit if he is not willing to do it.

【走色】zǒu//shǎi 落色 lose colour; fade：这布一洗就～。The cloth loses colour when it is washed.

【走扇】zǒushàn 门扇或窗扇由于变形等原因而关不上或关不严 (of a door or window) won't shut properly (due to warping)

【走墒】zǒu//shāng 跑墒 evaporation of water in soil

【走神儿】zǒu//shénr 精神不集中，注意力分散 (of one's attention) wander; be absent-minded：开车可不能～。You must not be absent-minded when driving a car.|刚才走了神儿，没听见他说什么。I was absent-minded just now and did not hear what he was saying.

【走绳】zǒu//shéng 杂技的一种，演员在悬空的绳索上来回走动，并表演各种动作 rope-walk, a category of acrobatics, in which the performer moves to and fro on a rope suspended horizontally in the air while doing a variety of stunts; also 走索 zǒu//suǒ

【走失】zǒushī ❶(人或家畜)出去后迷了路，回不到原地，因而不知下落 (of humans or domestic animals) wander away; be lost; be missing：孩子在庙会上～了。The child got lost at the temple fair.|前天他家～了一只羊。A sheep of his has wandered away from the flock the other day. ❷改变或失去(原样) fail to keep; lose：译文～原意。The original meaning is lost in the translation.

【走时】zǒushí ❶钟表指针移动，指示时间 (of clocks or watches) tick; keep time：表～准确。The watch keeps good time. ❷〈方 *dial*.〉走运 have good luck; be in luck; also 走时运 zǒu shíyùn

【走势】zǒushì ❶趋势 trend; tendency：当前企业投资～看好。The trend of enterprise investment looks good. ❷走向 direction; alignment：勘察山谷的～ survey the run of a valley

【走兽】zǒushòu 泛指兽类 (in a broad sense) four-footed animals; quadrupeds; beasts：飞禽～ birds and beasts

【走水】zǒu//shuǐ ❶漏水 leak water：房顶～了。The roof is leaking. ❷流水 (of water) flow; run：渠道～通畅。Water runs well in the canal. ❸指失火(含避讳意 euph.) be on fire; catch fire：仓库～。The warehouse was on fire.

【走水】zǒu•shui 〈方 *dial*.〉帐子帘幕等上方装饰的短横幅 short streamer decorating the upper part of a curtain

【走私】zǒu//sī 违反海关法规，逃避海关检查，非法运输货物进出国境 smuggle; bring goods into or take out of a country secretly, under illegal conditions or without paying the required import and export duties：～毒品 smuggle drugs|～活动 smuggling activities

【走索】zǒu//suǒ same as 走绳 zǒu//shéng

【走题】zǒu//tí 做诗文或说话离开了主题 (of a speech, poem, etc.) digress from the subject; stray from the point：说话走了题 speak beside the point; wander from the subject

【走投无路】zǒu tóu wú lù 无路可走 have no way out;〈比喻 *fig*.〉处境极端困难，找不到出路 in an extremely difficult situation; in an impasse; come to a dead end

【走味儿】zǒu//wèir 失去原有的滋味、气味(多指食物、茶叶)(oft. of foods, tea, etc.) lose flavour

【走向】zǒuxiàng (岩层、矿层、山脉等)延伸的方

向（of rock stratum, mineral ore formation, mountains, etc.）run; trend; alignment：河流～ run of a river | 边界～ alignment of the boundary line | 一条南北～的道路 a road that runs from south to north

【走形】zǒu//xíng（～儿 zǒu//xíngr）失去原有的形状；变形 be out of shape：用潮湿木料做成的家具容易～。The furniture made of wet wood is liable to change shape. | 这件衣服洗了一次就走了形。This dress has gone out of shape after being washed once.

【走形式】zǒu xíngshì 指只图表面上应付，不讲实效 do sth. as a mere formality; go through the motions

【走穴】zǒuxué 指演员为了捞外快而私自外出演出（esp. of a performer）moonlight; make private performances in order to earn extra money

【走眼】zǒu//yǎn 看错 mistake for：拿着好货当次货，你可看～了。You've mistaken superior goods for inferior goods. | 买珠宝首饰，若是走了眼，可就吃大亏。If you make bad judgements when you buy jewels, you are in for great losses.

【走样】zǒu//yàng（～儿 zǒu//yàngr）失去原来的样子 lose shape; go out of form; be different from what is expected or intended：话三传两传就走了样儿。The words were completely different after they had made just a few rounds.

【走运】zǒu//yùn 所遇到的事情，恰巧符合自己的意愿；运气好 have good luck; be in luck：你真～，好事都让你赶上了。You are lucky enough to have all the good things coming your way.

【走账】zǒu//zhàng 把款项记在账簿上 enter a sum in the account book; charge a sum to account

【走卒】zǒuzú 差役 pawn; servant; 〈比喻 *fig.*〉受人豢养而帮助作恶的人 cat's paw; lackey; stooge

【走嘴】zǒu//zuǐ 说话不留神而泄漏机密或发生错误 make a slip of the tongue; let slip an inadvertent remark：她说着说着就走了嘴了。As she talked on and on, she blurted the secret out.

zòu（ㄗㄡˋ）

奏 zòu ❶ 演奏 play：独～ solo | 合～ ensemble | 伴～ accompany; to the accompaniment of an instrument | ～国歌 play the national anthem ❷ 发生；取得（功效等）achieve; produce; perform：～效 produce good effect | 大～奇功 perform a great merit ❸ 臣子对帝王陈述意见或说明事情 submit a memorial to an emperor：启～ present a memorial to the emperor（or the throne）| ～议 memorial to an emperor（or the throne）| ～本 present a memorial to an emperor（or the throne）

【奏捷】zòujié 取得胜利 win a battle; score a success：～归来 return in triumph | 频频～ win one victory after another

【奏凯】zòukǎi 得胜而奏凯歌，泛指胜利 sing a song of victory; win victory; be victorious; triumph

【奏鸣曲】zòumíngqǔ 乐曲形式之一，一般由三个或四个性质不同的乐章组成，用一件或两件乐器演奏 sonata; musical piece usu. composed of three or four different movements and played by one or two instruments

【奏疏】zòushū same as 奏章 zòuzhāng

【奏效】zòu//xiào 发生预期的效果；见效 prove effective; be successful; get the desired result：～显著 have notable efficacy | 吃了这药就能～。This medicine works if you take it.

【奏乐】zòu//yuè 演奏乐曲 play music; strike up a tune：乐队～。The band was playing music.

【奏章】zòuzhāng 臣子向帝王呈递的意见书 memorial to an emperor（or the throne）

【奏折】zòuzhé 写有奏章的折子 memorial to the throne（as written on paper folded in accordion form）：上～ present a memorial to an emperor（or the throne）

揍 zòu ❶ 打（人）beat; hit; strike：挨～ get a thrashing | ～他一顿。Beat him up. ❷〈方 *dial.*〉打碎 smash; break：小心别把玻璃～了。Be careful not to break the glass. | 把碗给～了。（He）broke a bowl.

zū（ㄗㄨ）

租 zū ❶ 租用 rent; hire; charter：～房 rent three rooms | ～了一辆汽车 rent a car ❷ 出租 rent out; let out; lease：这个书店开展～书业务。The bookstore offers leasing services. ❸ 出租所收取的金钱或实物 rent; money or kind received from sth. rented：房～ house rent | 地～ land rent | 减～减息 reduce rent and interest ❹〈旧指 *old*〉田赋 land tax：～税 land tax

【租户】zūhù 租用房屋或物品的人 tenant（of a building or part of it）; lessee; leaseholder; hirer（of a thing）

【租价】zūjià 出租的价格 rent; rental

【租界】zūjiè 帝国主义国家强迫半殖民地国家在通商都市内'租借'给他们做进一步侵略的据点的地区 concession; tract of land in a port city in a semi-colonial country supposedly on lease to, but actually seized by, an imperialist power which uses it as a stronghold for further aggression

【租借】zūjiè ❶ 租用 rent; hire; lease：～剧场开会 hire a theatre for a meeting ❷ 出租 rent out; let out; least:修车铺～自行车。The repair shop rent out bikes.

【租借地】zūjièdì 一国以租借名义在他国暂时取得使用、管理权的地区。租借地的所有权仍属于原来国家,出租国有权随时要求交还。leased territory; leasehold; tract of land leased by a country in another country for temporary use and management, with the leasing country retaining ownership of it and the right to ask for its return

【租金】zūjīn 租房屋或物品的钱 rent; rental

【租赁】zūlìn ❶ 租用 rent; lease; hire:～了两间平房 rent two rooms in a single-storeyed house ❷ 出租 lease:这家公司向外～建筑机械。The company leases building machinery.

【租钱】zū·qian same as 租金 zūjīn

【租用】zūyòng 以归还原物并付给一定代价为条件而使用别人的东西 rent; hire; take on lease; use sth. belonging to sb. else's on the condition that the goods will be returned with payment:～家具 rent furniture

【租约】zūyuē 确定租赁关系的契约 lease; a contract by which sth. is leased

【租子】zū·zi 地租 land rent; ground rent; rent:交～ pay rent|收～ collect rent

菹(葅) zū〈书 *fml*.〉❶ 多水草的沼泽地带 marshland ❷ 酸菜 pickled vegetables ❸ 切碎(菜、肉) cut or chop up (vegetables or meat) into very small pieces; mince; shred

zú (ㄗㄨˊ)

足[1] zú ❶ 脚;腿 foot; leg:～迹 footprint|～球 football|手舞～蹈 dance for joy|画蛇添～ draw a snake and put feet to it ❷ 器物下部形状像腿的支撑部分 leg (of certain utensils):鼎～ three legs of a tripod; confrontation between three rival powers

足[2] zú ❶ 充足;足够 enough; ample; sufficient:富～rich; abundant; wealthy|十～ fully|丰衣～食 amply clothed and well-fed|劲头很～ full of energy ❷ 够得上某种数量或程度 fully; as much as:这棵菜～有十几斤。The cabbage weighs more than 10 *jin*.|这些事有三小时～能做完。Three hours are enough to get these things done. ❸ 足以(多用于否定式 usu. in the negative) enough; sufficiently:不～为凭 cannot be taken as evidence|微不～道 insignificant; negligible

【足本】zúběn 指书籍没有残缺删削的本子 unabridged version (of a novel, etc.):大字～《三国演义》unabridged version of *Romance of the Three Kingdoms* in large print

【足赤】zúchì 足金 pure gold; solid gold:金无～,人无完人。There is no pure gold in the world, nor is there a perfect man.

【足够】zúgòu ❶ 达到应有的或能满足需要的程度 enough; ample; sufficient:～的燃料 sufficient fuel|～的认识 full knowledge; fully understand; know fully|已经有这么多了,～了。There is already so much. It's quite enough. ❷ 满足;知足 satisfied:有您这句话就～了。I'm quite satisfied with what you've said.

【足迹】zújì 脚印 footmark; footprint; track:祖国各个角落都有勘探队员的～。Our geological prospectors have left their footprints in every nook and cranny of our country.

【足见】zújiàn 完全可以看出 it serves to show; one can well perceive:这些难题通过集体研究都解决了,～走群众路线是非常必要的。All these difficult problems have been solved through collective discussion, which shows it is essential to take the mass line.

【足金】zújīn 成色十足的金子 pure gold; solid gold

【足球】zúqiú ❶ 球类运动项目之一,主要用脚踢球。球场长方形,较大,比赛时每队上场十一人,一人守门。除守门员外,其他队员不得用手或臂触球。把球射进对方球门算得分,得分多的获胜。football; soccer; ball game in which the players kick the ball with feet in a large rectangular field. A match involves two contesting teams each having eleven players, including a goalkeeper. Except for the goalkeeper, the players are not permitted to use their upper limbs to touch the ball. A goal is scored when the ball is netted. The team that scores more goals is the winner. ❷ 足球运动使用的球,用牛皮做壳,橡胶做胆,比篮球小 football; ball used in the football game, made of cattle skin for the outer covering and rubber for the inner bladder, smaller than the basketball

【足色】zúsè 金银的成色十足 (of gold or silver) of standard purity:～纹银 pure silver

【足岁】zúsuì 按十足月份和天数计算的年龄 actual age:这孩子已经七～了。The child has turned seven years old.

【足下】zúxià 对朋友的敬称(多用于书信 used mostly in letters) polite term of address between friends

【足以】zúyǐ 完全可以;够得上 enough; sufficiently:这些事实～说明问题。These facts are enough to illustrate the point.

【足银】zúyín 成色十足的银子 pure silver

【足月】zúyuè 指胎儿在母体中成长的月份已足 (of a foetus) born after the normal period of gestation; mature:孩子不～就生下来了。The baby was born prematurely. *or* The baby was born ahead of the normal period of gestation.

【足智多谋】zú zhì duō móu 智谋很多,形容善于料事和用计 wise and full of strategems; wise and resourceful

卒[1] zú ❶ 兵 soldier; private: 小～ pawn | 士～ rank and file | 马前～ pawn; cat's-paw ❷ 差役 servant: 走～ lackey; underling; stooge | 狱～ prison guard | 隶～ *yamen* runner

卒[2] zú ❶ 完毕;结束 finish; end: ～读 finish schooling | ～业 complete school education ❷ 到底;终于 finally; at last: ～底于成 finally achieve success ❸ 死 die: 病～ die of illness | 暴～ die a violent death | 生～年月 dates of birth and death

☞ cù on p. 330

【卒岁】zúsuì 〈书 *fml.*〉度过一年 get through the year: 聊以～ just to tide over the year

【卒业】zúyè 毕业 graduate; finish a course of study

崒(崪) zú 〈书 *fml.*〉险峻 precipitous; steep

族 zú ❶ 家族 clan: 宗～ patriarchal clan | 合～ all the members of a clan; the whole clan | 同～ of the same clan ❷ 古代的一种残酷刑法,杀死犯罪者的整个家族,甚至他母亲、妻子等的家族 death penalty in ancient times, imposed on an offender and his whole family, or even the families of his mother and wife ❸ 种族;民族 race; nationality: 汉～ Han people; Hans | 斯拉夫～ Slavdom ❹ 事物有某种共同属性的一大类 class or group of things with common features: 水～ aquatic animals | 语～family of languages | 芳香～化合物 aromatic compounds ◇打工～ wage earner | 上班～ commuter; working people

【族谱】zúpǔ 家族或宗族记载本族世系和重要人物事迹的书 family tree; genealogical tree; genealogy; genealogical chart showing the relationship of ancestors and descendants in a given family

【族权】zúquán 宗法制度下,族长对家族或宗族的支配权力,或家长对家庭成员的支配权力 clan authority; clan power; power of a patriarchal clan leader to control the clan or the power of a family head to control the family members under the patriarchal clan system

【族人】zúrén 同一家族或宗族的人 clansman; members of the same clan or family

【族长】zúzhǎng 宗法制度下家族或宗族的领头人,通常由族中辈分较高、年纪较长的有权势的人担任 patriarch; clan elder; head of a clan; leader of a family or a patriarchal clan under the patriarchal clan system, usu. an elder with an influential power

镞 zú 〈书 *fml.*〉箭头 arrowhead: 箭～ arrowhead

zǔ(ㄗㄨˇ)

诅 zǔ 〈书 *fml.*〉❶ 诅咒 curse; swear; wish sb. evil ❷ 盟誓;发誓 vow; swear; take an oath

【诅咒】zǔzhòu 原指祈祷鬼神加祸于所恨的人,今指咒骂 curse; swear; wish sb. evil; imprecate; abuse; revile

阻 zǔ 阻挡;阻碍 hinder; block; obstruct: ～止 stop; block | 拦～ block; stop; obstruct; hold back | 劝～ talk somebody out of doing something | 通行无～ smooth traffic; pass unobstructed; go through without any hindrance

【阻碍】zǔ'ài ❶ 使不能顺利通过或发展 hinder; block; impede: ～交通 block the traffic | 旧的生产关系～生产力的发展。The old relations of production hinder the development of the productive forces. ❷ 起阻碍作用的事物 obstacle; hindrance; impediment: 毫无～ without a hitch

【阻挡】zǔdǎng 阻止;拦住 stop; stem; resist; obstruct: 他一定要去就不要～了。If he insists on going, don't stop him any more. | 革命洪流不可～。The revolutionary torrent is irresistible.

【阻遏】zǔ'è same as 阻止 zǔzhǐ

【阻隔】zǔgé 两地之间不能相通或不易来往 separate; cut off: 山川～ be separated by mountains and rivers

【阻梗】zǔgěng 〈书 *fml.*〉阻塞 block; obstruct; clog: 交通～。The traffic is held up. *or* There's a traffic jam.

【阻击】zǔjī 以防御手段阻止敌人增援、逃跑或进攻 block; check; preventing enemy troops from reinforcements, fleeing or attaching by defensive means: ～战 blocking action

【阻截】zǔjié 阻挡;拦截 stop; obstruct; bar the way: ～南逃之敌 stop the enemy from fleeing south

【阻绝】zǔjué 受阻碍不能通过;阻隔 block; obstruct; clog: 交通～ traffic jam | 音信～ be cut off from the outside world

【阻抗】zǔkàng 电路中电阻、电感和电容对交流电流的阻碍作用的统称 impedance; total opposition offered by the resistor, inductor and capicitor of an electric circuit to the flow of an alternating current of a single frequency

【阻拦】zǔlán 阻止 stop; obstruct; bar the way; stymie: 他要去,谁也～不住。Since he wanted to go, no one could stop him.

【阻力】zǔlì ❶ 妨碍物体运动的作用力 resistance; drag: 空气～ air resistance | 水的～ water resistance ❷ 泛指阻碍事物发展或前进的外力 (in a broad sense) obstruction; resistance: 冲破各种～,克服一切困难 break through all kinds of obstructions and overcome all difficulties

【阻力臂】zǔlìbì 杠杆阻力点和支点间的距离 distance between the point of resistance and the fulcrum while applying a lever; 旧称 formerly called 重臂 zhòngbì

【阻力点】zǔlìdiǎn 杠杆中阻力的作用点 point of resistance at which a lever is applied at a weight；旧称 formerly called 重点 zhòngdiǎn

【阻难】zǔnàn 阻挠留难 thwart；obstruct；make things difficult for sb.；put obstacles in one's way：再三～ obstruct repeatedly｜无理～ obstruct one's way without reason

【阻挠】zǔnáo 阻止或暗中破坏使不能发展或成功 obstruct；thwart；stand in the way；put a spoke in one's wheel：从中～ obstruct；thwart；stand in the way；put a spoke in one's wheel｜～双方和谈 obstruct the peace talks between the two parties

【阻尼】zǔní 振动的物体或振荡电路，当能量逐渐减少时，振幅也相应减小的现象 damping；amplitude of oscillation of an oscillating object or circuit is reduced when the energy drops gradually

【阻塞】zǔsè ❶ 有障碍而不能通过 block；obstruct；clog：交通～。The traffic is held up. *or* There's a traffic jam. ❷ 使阻塞 hold up；obstruct：车辆～了道路。The vehicles held up the road. ◇～言路 muffle public opinion；block the channels for criticisms and suggestions

【阻止】zǔzhǐ 使不能前进；使停止行动 prevent；stop；hold back：别～他，让他去吧。Don't try to stop him. Let him go.

组 zǔ ❶ 组织 organize；form：改～ reorganize｜～字游戏 crossword puzzle｜十个人～成一个分队。Ten people form a squad. ❷ 由不多的人员组织成的单位 group；small unit consisting of a few people：小～ small group｜大～ large group｜～长 group leader｜～员 member of a group｜读报～ newspaper-reading group｜互助～ mutual aid group｜人事～ personnel group ❸〈量词 *classifier*〉用于事物的集体［used in a collective］：两～电池 two groups of batteries ❹ 合成一组的（文艺作品）(of literary works) suite；series：～诗 a suite of poems｜～画 a series of paintings｜～曲 a suite of music pieces｜～歌 a suite of songs

【组办】zǔbàn 组织筹办 organize：～音乐会 organize a concert

【组锉】zǔcuò 什锦锉 assorted files

【组分】zǔfèn 指混合物中的各个成分，如空气中的氧、氮、氢等都是空气的组分 component part；component. Elements of a mixture or compound, e. g. oxygen, nitrogen, hydrogen, etc. in the air, are all component parts of the air.

【组稿】zǔ//gǎo 书报刊物编者按照编辑计划向作者约定稿件（of newspaper, magazine and book editors) commission authors to write on given topics；solicit contributions

【组歌】zǔgē 由表现同一个主题的若干支歌曲组成的一组歌，如《长征组歌》suite of songs；a series of songs portraying the same theme, as 'The Suite of Long March'

【组阁】zǔ//gé ❶ 组织内阁 form (or set up, organize) a cabinet：受命～ be ordered to form a cabinet ❷ 泛指组织领导班子 (in a broad sense) form a leading group

【组合】zǔhé ❶ 组织成为整体 make up；compose；constitute：这本集子是由诗、散文和短篇小说三部分～而成的。This collection is made up of three parts：poems, essays and short stories. ❷ 组织起来的整体 association；combination：劳动～（工会的旧称）labour association (the old name for trade union)｜词组是词的～。A phrase is a group of words. ❸ 由 m 个不同的元素中取出 n 个并成一组，不论次序，其中每组所含成分至少有一个不同，所得到的结果叫做由 m 中取 n 个的组合。如由 a,b,c,d 中取 3 个的组合有 abc, abd, acd, bcd 四组。组合数用 C_m^n 来表示，公式是

$$C_m^n=\frac{m(m-1)(m-2)\cdots(m-n+1)}{1\times2\times3\times\cdots\times n}$$

combination；any of the various groupings, or subsets, of m elements out of n elements, into which a number, or set of units may be arranged without regard to order, and which contains at least one different element, and the result of which is called combinations of n elements out of m elements. For example, triple combinations of A, B, C and D are ABD, ABD, ACD and BCD. The combination is expressed by C_m^n, and its formula is

$$C_m^n=\frac{m(m-1)(m-2)\cdots(m-n+1)}{1\times2\times3\times\cdots\times n}.$$

【组画】zǔhuà 由表现同一主题的、形式统一的若干幅画组成的一组画。组画比连环画一般幅数少，画面较大，每幅画具有相对的独立性。group painting；series of paintings which portray the same theme in an identical form, have fewer pictures than a picture-story book and a large tableau, and are relatively independent of each other

【组建】zǔjiàn 组织并建立（机构、队伍等）put together (a group)；form：～剧团 put together a theatrical troupe｜～突击队 form a shock brigade

【组曲】zǔqǔ 由若干器乐曲组成的一组乐曲 suite；instrumental composition consisting of several music pieces

【组诗】zǔshī 由表现同一主题的若干首诗组成的一组诗 suite；poetic composition consisting of several poems under the same theme

【组团】zǔtuán 组成团体，特指组织剧团或代表团 form or organize an art troupe or delegation：～出国访问 form an art troupe for a foreign tour｜中央歌舞团重新～。The Central Song and Dance Ensemble has been reorganized.｜中国运动员～参加奥运会。A delegation of Chinese athletes was organized to take part in the Olympic Games.

【组织】zǔzhī ❶ 安排分散的人或事物使具有一定的系统性或整体性 organize; form; arrange separate persons or things into a systematic and organic whole: ～人力 organize human power | ～联欢晚会 organize an evening party | 这篇文章～得很好。This article is well organized. ❷ 系统;配合关系 system; coordination: ～严密 well organized | ～松散 loosely organized ❸ 纺织品经纬纱线的结构 (of fabrics) weave; warp-and-weft pattern: 平纹～ plain weave | 斜纹～ twill weave | 缎纹～ satin weave ❹ 机体中构成器官的单位,是由许多形态和功能相同的细胞按一定的方式结合而成的。人和高等动物体内有上皮组织、结缔组织、肌肉组织和神经组织。tissue; substance of an organic body or organ, consisting of cells and intercellular material in the same form and with the same function, as epithelial tissue, connective tissue, muscle tissue and nerve tissue ❺ 按照一定的宗旨和系统建立起来的集体 organization; organized system: 党团～ Party and Youth League organizations | 工会～ trade union organization | 向～汇报工作 report to the leadership of an organization on one's work

【组织生活】zǔzhī shēnghuó 党派、团体的成员每隔一段时间聚集在一起进行的交流思想、讨论问题等的活动 regular activities of a political party or other organization for exchange of ideas and discussions

【组织液】zǔzhīyè ❶ 促进血液和组织细胞进行物质交换的液体,存在于组织的空隙间,是由血浆经过毛细管管壁过滤进入组织空隙而形成的 tissue fluid; fluid that promotes the material exchange of the blood and tissue cells, exists in the spaces of the tissues and is formed when the blood plasma enters into the tissue spaces after being filtered through the walls of the capillaries ❷ 用动植物的某些组织制成的液体药剂,注射到人体内能治疗某些慢性病。如用胎盘制的组织液能治神经衰弱、胃溃疡等。medicinal liquid prepared from certain animal and plant tissues, which is injected into the human body to treat certain chronic diseases. For example, the tissue fluid made from placenta is used to treat neurasthenia, gastric ulcer, etc.

Z

【组装】zǔzhuāng 把零件组合起来,构成部件;把零件或部件组合起来,构成器械或装置 put together; assemble; put the separate parts together into units and put the units and parts into a machine: ～车间 assembly workshop | 进口原件,国内～ import parts for assembly at home | ～一台掘进机 assemble a tunnelling machine

俎 zǔ ❶〈古代 *arch.*〉祭祀时盛牛羊等祭品的器具 sacrificial vessel ❷〈古代 *arch.*〉割肉类用的砧板 chopping block used in slaughtering ❸ (Zǔ)姓 a surname

【俎上肉】zǔshàngròu〈书 *fml.*〉〈比喻 *fig.*〉任人欺压蹂躏的人或国家 meat on a chopping block; helpless victim; person or country subject to bullying, oppression and trampling by others

祖 zǔ ❶ 父母亲的上一辈 grandparents: ～父 grandfather | 伯～ grand uncle; grandfather's brother | 外～ grandfather; grandpa; maternal grandfather; mother's father ❷ 祖宗 ancestors: 曾～ great grandfather; grandfather's father | 高～ (paternal) great-great-grandfather; the earliest ancestor | 远～ remote ancestor ❸ 事业或派别的首创者 founder (of a craft, religious sect, etc.): 鼻～ founder; originator | ～师 founder of a school of learning, craft, etc.; founder of a religious sect ❹ (Zǔ)姓 a surname

【祖辈】zǔbèi 祖宗 ancestors; forefathers; ancestry; same as 祖先 zǔxiān ①

【祖本】zǔběn 书籍或碑帖最早的刻本或拓本 first edition (of a block-printed book); first rubbing (taken from a stone inscription)

【祖产】zǔchǎn 祖宗传下来的产业 property handed down from one's ancestors; ancestral estate

【祖传】zǔchuán 祖宗留传下来的 be handed down from one's ancestors: ～秘方 secret prescription handed down in the family from generation to generation | 三代～ handed down for three generations

【祖坟】zǔfén 祖宗的坟墓 ancestral grave

【祖父】zǔfù 父亲的父亲 (paternal) grandfather

【祖国】zǔguó 自己的国家 one's country; homeland; native land; motherland; fatherland

【祖籍】zǔjí 原籍 original family home; ancestral home; land of one's ancestors; native land

【祖居】zǔjū ❶ 祖辈居住过的房子或地方 ancestral home ❷ 世代居住 have one's ancestral home at; be a native of: ～南京 be a native of Nanjing

【祖率】zǔlǜ 南北朝时祖冲之算出圆周率的近似值在 3.1415926 和 3.1415927 之间,并提出圆周率的疏率为 22/7,密率为 355/113。为了纪念祖冲之,把他算出的近似值叫做祖率。approximate ratio of the circumference of a circle to its diameter as calculated by Zu Chongzhi (429-500) in the Southern and Northern Dynasties, i. e. between 3.1415926 and 3.1415927. He also said that the loose ratio is 22/7 and the close ratio is 355/113. In order to honour him, the approximate ratio he calculated is dubbed Zu's ratio.

【祖母】zǔmǔ 父亲的母亲 (paternal) grandmother

【祖上】zǔshàng 家族中较早的上辈 ancestors; forefathers; forebears:他～是从江西迁来的。His ancestor moved here from Jiangxi.

【祖师】zǔshī ❶ 学术或技术上创立派别的人 guru; founder of a school of learning, a craft, etc. ❷ 佛教、道教中创立宗派的人 founder of a sect of Buddhism or Taoism ❸ 会道门称本会门或本道门的创始人 originator of a superstitious sect or a secret society ❹〈旧时 *old*〉手工业者称本行业的创始者 originator of a trade or a profession ‖ also 祖师爷 zǔshīyé

【祖述】zǔshù〈书 *fml.*〉尊崇和效法前人的学说或行为 follow the example of former worthies

【祖先】zǔxiān ❶ 一个民族或家族的上代,特指年代比较久远的 ancestry; ancestors; forebears; forefathers ❷ 演化成现代各类生物的各种古代生物 ancient organisms from which present-day livings or beings are evolved:始祖鸟是鸟类的～。Archaeopteryx was the ancestor of the birds.

【祖业】zǔyè ❶ 祖产 property handed down from ancestors; ancestral estate ❷ 祖先创立的功业 ancestors' meritorious achievements

【祖茔】zǔyíng〈书 *fml.*〉祖坟 ancestral grave

【祖宗】zǔ·zong 一个家族的上辈,多指较早的。也泛指民族的祖先。forefathers (of a family and also of a nationality); (in a broad sense) ancestry; forebears

【祖祖辈辈】zǔzǔbèibèi 世世代代 for generations; from generation to generation:我家～都是农民。Our family have been farmers for generations. *or* I come from a long line of farmers.|勤劳俭朴是我国劳动人民～流传下来的美德。Industriousness and thrift are the virtues the Chinese working people have handed down through the ages.

zuān (ㄗㄨㄢ)

钻(鑽) zuān ❶ 用尖的物体在另一物体上转动,造成窟窿 drill; bore; use a pointed object to turn it on another object to make a hole:～孔 drill a hole|～个眼儿 drill a hole|～木取火 drill wood to make fire ❷ 穿过;进入 get into; go through; make one's way into:～山洞 pass through a mountain tunnel|～到水里 dive into water ❸ 钻研 study intensively; dig into:～书本 dig into books; bury oneself in books|边干边～,边学边用 dig into one's job while working, and put whatever one learns to use ❹ 指钻营 curry favour with sb. in authority for personal gain; secure personal gain
☞ zuàn on p. 2568

【钻空子】zuān kòng·zi 利用漏洞进行对自己有利的活动 avail oneself of loopholes (in a law, contract, etc.); exploit an advantage

【钻门子】zuān mén·zi 指巴结权贵 curry favour with the powerful and influential; jockey for favours; manoeuvre for advantage; fawn on

【钻谋】zuānmóu 钻营 use pull to get what one wants:～肥缺 curry favour with the authority for a lucrative position

【钻牛角尖】zuān niújiǎojiān〈比喻 *fig.*〉费力研究不值得研究的或无法解决的问题 split hairs; get into a dead end (or a blind alley); take pains to study an insignificant or insoluble problem; also 钻牛角 zuān niújiǎo or 钻牛犄角 zuān niújījiǎo

【钻探】zuāntàn 为了勘探矿床、地层构造、地下水位、土壤性质等,用器械向地下钻孔,取出土壤或岩心,作为分析研究的样品 (exploration) drilling; drill a hole through the ground to get some earth or rock as a sample for analysis to prospect for mineral resources, tectonics, subterranean water level and soil properties

【钻探机】zuāntànjī 钻井、钻探用的机器。包括动力设备和钻杆、钻头、岩心管、钢架等。一般有冲击式和旋转式两种。drilling machine; machine for drilling wells or prospecting, including the power equipment, drill rod, drill bit, coring pipe and derrick. Usu. there are two types: impact and rotary drill. also 钻机 zuànjī

【钻心】zuānxīn 指心里像被钻着那样难受 (of pain, itching, etc.) unbearable:痒得～ itch unbearably|疼得～ seized with sharp pains

【钻研】zuānyán 深入研究 study intensively; dig into:～理论 dig into theories|～业务 study professional knowledge intensively|刻苦～ study hard

【钻营】zuānyíng 设法巴结有权势的人以谋求私利 curry favour with sb. in authority for personal gain; secure personal gain:拍马～ fawn on and curry favour with sb.

躜 zuān 向上或向前冲 jump up; dash forward

zuǎn (ㄗㄨㄢˇ)

篹 zuǎn same as 纂 zuǎn ①
☞ zhuàn on p. 2523

缵 zuǎn〈书 *fml.*〉继承 inherit

纂(❷鬘) zuǎn ❶〈书 *fml.*〉编辑 compile; edit:～修 compile; edit|～辑 edit|编～ compile ❷〈方 *dial.*〉(～儿 zuǎnr) 妇女梳在头后边的发髻 woman's hair worn in a knot at the nape; bun

籑(饌) zuǎn same as 纂 zuǎn ①
☞ zhuàn on p. 2523

zuàn(ㄗㄨㄢˋ)

钻(鑽) zuàn ❶ 打眼儿用的工具,有手摇的、电动的、风动的多种 drill; auger; implement for drilling a hole, hand-operated, electrically operated or pneumatically operated ❷指钻石 diamond; jewel:～戒 diamond ring|十七～的手表 a 17-jewel watch ❸义同钻(zuān)①same as 钻 zuān ①in meaning
☞ zuān on p. 2567

【钻床】zuànchuáng 金属切削机床,用来加工工件上的圆孔。加工时工件固定在工作台上,钻头一面旋转,一面推进切削。drilling machine; drill; metal cutting tool for drilling round holes in work-pieces. A work piece is fixed at a working table and the drill cuts the hole while rotating.

【钻机】zuànjī 钻(zuān)探机 petroleum (drilling) rig; drilling machine

【钻戒】zuànjiè 镶着钻石的戒指 diamond ring

【钻石】zuànshí ❶ 经过琢磨的金刚石,是贵重的首饰 diamond; precious gem ❷ 用红、蓝宝石等做的精密仪器、仪表(如手表、航空仪表等)的轴承 jewel (used in a watch); bearings made of ruby or sapphire for precision instruments, as watch, aviation meters, etc.

【钻塔】zuàntǎ 井架用于钻井或钻探时叫做钻塔 derrick; boring tower

【钻台】zuàntái 安装钻探机的平台 drilling platform

【钻头】zuàntóu 钻、钻床、钻探机上用的刀具,金属切削上常用的是有螺旋槽的麻花钻头,地质勘探用的有硬质合金钻头、金刚石钻头等 bit (of a drill); cutter fitted on a drill or drilling machine. The bit used for metal cutting usu. have twisted grooves, and those used for geological prospecting are hard alloy bits or diamond bits.

赚 zuàn 〈方 *dial.*〉骗(人) kid; deceive; hoax:你～我白跑了一趟。You kidded me into going there for nothing.
☞ zhuàn on p. 2522

攥 zuàn 握 hold; grip; grasp:～紧拳头 clench one's fist|手里～着一把斧子 hold an axe in one's hand

zuī(ㄗㄨㄟ)

朘 zuī 〈方 *dial.*〉男子生殖器 man's sex organ
☞ juān on p. 1054

zuǐ(ㄗㄨㄟˇ)

咀 zuǐ '嘴'俗作咀 popular form for 嘴 zuǐ
☞ jǔ on p. 1047

觜 zuǐ same as 嘴 zuǐ
☞ zī on p. 2538

嘴 zuǐ ❶ 口的通称 general term for 口 kǒu:张～ open one's mouth|闭～ close one's mouth ❷(～儿 zuǐr)形状或作用像嘴的东西 anything shaped or functioning like a mouth:瓶～儿 mouth of a bottle|茶壶～儿 spout of a teapot|烟～儿 cigarette holder ❸ 指说话 speak; talk:别多～。Keep your mouth shut.

【嘴巴】zuǐ·ba ❶ 打嘴部附近的部位叫打嘴巴 slap one in the face:挨了一个～ get a slap in the face; also 嘴巴子 zuǐbà·zi ❷ same as 嘴 zuǐ ①:张开～。Open your mouth.

【嘴笨】zuǐ bèn 不善于说话 inarticulate; clumsy of speech:他～,有话说不出来。He is inarticulate, and doesn't know how to express himself.

【嘴唇】zuǐchún 唇的通称 general term for 唇 chún:上～ upper lip|下～ lower lip

【嘴刁】zuǐ diāo ❶ 指吃东西爱挑剔 be choosy about what one eats; be particular about food:她从小～,总是这不吃,那不吃的。She has always been picky and choosy about food since childhood. ❷〈方 *dial.*〉说话刁滑 cunning; tricky:这小鬼～,差点儿被她骗了。What a little trickster she is. (I) was almost taken in.

【嘴乖】zuǐ guāi 说话使人爱听(多指小孩儿 oft. of children) clever and pleasant when speaking to elders:这小姑娘～,挺逗人喜欢。What a dear little girl, talking so sweetly!

【嘴尖】zuǐ jiān ❶ 说话刻薄 sharp-tongued; cutting in speech:这人～,爱损人。He's sharp-tongued and always makes biting remarks. ❷ 指味觉灵敏,善于辨别味道 have a keen sense of taste:他～,喝一口就知道这是什么茶。He has a keen sense of taste and can tell the brand of the tea as soon as he drinks it. ❸ 嘴刁 be choosy about what one eats:这孩子～,不合口的一点也不吃。The child is very particular about food, and refuses to eat whatever is not to his taste.

【嘴角】zuǐjiǎo 上下唇两边相连的部分 corners of the mouth

【嘴紧】zuǐ jǐn 说话谨慎,不乱讲 tight-lipped; close-mouthed

【嘴快】zuǐ kuài 有话藏不住,马上说出来 have a loose tongue

【嘴脸】zuǐliǎn 面貌;表情或脸色(多含贬义 derog.) face; features; countenance:丑恶～ hideous face|他一直不给人家好～看。He never shows a kind look to others.

【嘴皮子】zuǐpí·zi 嘴唇(就能说会道而言)(of a glib talker) lips:耍～ talk glibly; be a slick talker|他那两片～可能说了。He has a ready tongue. *or* He can argue on any side of any question.

【嘴软】zuǐ ruǎn 说话不理直气壮 be unable to speak out what should be said after receiving small favours

【嘴松】zuǐ sōng 说话不谨慎,容易说出不应说的话 have a loose tongue

【嘴碎】zuǐ suì 说话啰唆 loquacious; garrulous:老太太~,遇事总爱唠叨。The old lady is loquacious and always babbling on something.

【嘴损】zuǐ sǔn〈方 *dial.*〉说话刻薄 sharp-tongued; sarcastic:~不饶人 be sharp-tongued and pick on someone

【嘴甜】zuǐ tián 说的话使人听着舒服 ingratiating in speech; smooth-tongued; honey-mouthed:孩子~,讨老人喜欢。The child is honey-mouthed and wins favour among old people.

【嘴头】zuǐtóu〈方 *dial.*〉(~儿 zuǐtóur)嘴(指说话时的) mouth (when speaking):~儿能说会道 have a glib tongue|我是打~儿上直到心眼儿里服了你了。You've convinced me completely. also 嘴头子 zuǐtóu·zi

【嘴稳】zuǐ wěn 说话谨慎,不说泄露秘密的话 able to keep a secret; discreet in speech

【嘴严】zuǐ yán 嘴紧;嘴稳 tight-lipped; close-mouthed

【嘴硬】zuǐ yìng 自知理亏而口头上不肯认错或服输 stubborn and reluctant to admit mistakes or defeats although one knows he is in the wrong:做错了事还要~。You know you're wrong, but still insist that you aren't.

【嘴直】zuǐ zhí 说话直爽 outspoken; plain-spoken:别怪我~,这事是你不对。Don't blame me for my frankness. You are wrong on this matter.

【嘴子】zuǐ·zi〈方 *dial.*〉same as 嘴 zuǐ ②:山~ mountain pass

zuì (ㄗㄨㄟˋ)

寂 zuì〈书 *fml.*〉same as 最 zuì

最 zuì ❶〈副词 *adv.*〉表示某种属性超过所有同类的人或事物[indicating that a certain attribute has surpassed all people or things of the same kind] most; least; best; to the highest or lowest degree:我国是世界上人口~多的国家。Ours is the most populous country in the world. ❷ 居首位的;没有能比得上的 in the first place; incomparable:中华之~ best of China|世界之~ best of the world

【最初】zuìchū 最早的时期;开始的时候 the earliest; at the beginning; first; initial; at first; originally:那里~还是不毛之地。Originally it was a barren land there.|我~认识他是在上中学的时候。I first knew him when we were in the middle school.

【最后】zuìhòu 在时间上或次序上在所有别的之后 final; last; ultimate:~胜利一定属于我们。Final victory is bound to be ours.|这是全书的~一章。This is the last chapter of the book.

【最后通牒】zuìhòu tōngdié 一国对另一国提出的必须接受其要求,否则将使用武力或采取其他强制措施的外交文书,这种文书限在一定时期内答复 ultimatum; diplomatic document which contains the final offer or demand, esp. by one of the parties engaged in negotiations, the rejection of which usu. leads to a break in relations and unilateral action, the use of force, etc. by the party issuing the ultimatum; also 哀的美敦书 āidìměidūnshū

【最惠国待遇】zuìhuìguó dàiyù 一国在贸易、航海等方面给予另一国的不低于任何第三国的优惠待遇 most-favoured-nation (MFN) treatment; MFN trading status; favoured treatment given by one country to another in trade, navigation, etc. which is not lower than any third country

【最近】zuìjìn 指说话前或后不久的日子 recently; lately; of late; soon; in the near future; in the next few days; in a couple of days:~我到上海去了一趟。I went to Shanghai recently.|这个戏~就要上演了。The play is about to be staged soon.

【最为】zuìwéi〈副词 *adv.*〉用在双音节的形容词前,表示某种属性超过所有同类的人或事物[used before disyllabic adjectives to indicate that a certain attribute surpasses all people or things of the same kind]:~重要 most important; extremely important|~可恶 most hideous; extremely detestable; abominable|用电话通知,~省事。It's much easier to inform by telephone.

【最终】zuìzhōng 最后;末了 final; ultimate:~目的 ultimate aim

晬 zuì〈书 *fml.*〉婴儿周岁 child's first birthday

罪(辠) zuì ❶ 作恶或犯法的行为 crime; guilt:有~ guilty|判~ declare guilty; convict|~大恶极 be guilty of the most heinous crimes ❷ 过失;过错 fault; blame:归~于人 blame sb. for a fault; shift the blame to others ❸ 苦难;痛苦 suffering; pain; hardship:受~ suffer hardships ❹ 把罪过归到某人身上;责备 put the blame on sb.:~己 blame oneself

【罪案】zuì'àn 犯罪的案情 details of a criminal case; case

【罪不容诛】zuì bù róng zhū 罪大恶极,处死都不能抵偿 even death cannot atone for the offence; be guilty of a crime for which even death is an insufficient punishment

【罪大恶极】zuì dà è jí 罪恶严重到极点 be guilty of the most heinous crimes

【罪恶】zuì'è 严重损害人民利益的行为 crime;

Z

evil：～滔天 be guilty of monstrous crimes

【罪犯】zuìfàn 有犯罪行为的人 criminal; offender; culprit

【罪过】zuì·guo ❶ 过失 fault; offence; sin：你这样训斥他，他有什么～？What sin has he committed to deserve all this reprimand from you? ❷〈谦辞 *hum.*〉表示不敢当 thanks, but this is really more than I deserve：为我的事让您老特地跑一趟，真是～。I'm really very sorry to have you come here especially for me.

【罪魁】zuìkuí 罪恶行为的首要分子 chief criminal; culprit; arch criminal：～祸首 chief culprit (or offender); arch criminal

【罪戾】zuìlì〈书 *fml.*〉罪过；罪恶 sin; crime

【罪名】zuìmíng 根据犯罪行为的性质和特征所规定的犯罪名称 charge; accusation; crime of which a person is accused

【罪孽】zuìniè 迷信的人认为应受到报应的罪恶 wrongdoing that brings retribution; sin：～深重 sinful; full of sin

【罪愆】zuìqiān〈书 *fml.*〉same as 罪过 zuì·guo ①

【罪人】zuìrén 有罪的人 guilty person; offender; sinner

【罪刑】zuìxíng 罪状和应判的刑罚 crime and punishment

【罪行】zuìxíng 犯罪的行为 crime; guilt; offence：～累累 countless crimes | 犯下严重～ commit a grave crime

【罪尤】zuìyóu〈书 *fml.*〉same as 罪过 zuì·guo ①

【罪有应得】zuì yǒu yīng dé 干了坏事或犯了罪得到应得的惩罚 deserve one's punishment; punishment fits the crime

【罪责】zuìzé ❶ 对罪行所负的责任 responsibility for an offence：～难逃 cannot escape the responsibility for the offence (or crime); cannot get away with it ❷〈书 *fml.*〉责罚 penal punishment：免于～ exempt from punishment

【罪证】zuìzhèng 犯罪的证据 evidence of a crime; proof of one's guilt：查明～ find out the evidence of a crime

【罪状】zuìzhuàng 犯罪的事实 facts about a crime; charges in an indictment：罗列～ list the facts about a crime

槜(檇) zuì [槜李](zuìlǐ) ❶ 李子的一个品种，果实皮鲜红，汁多，味甜 a variety of plum with bright red skinned, juicy, sweet fruits ❷ 这种植物的果实 fruit of the plant

蕞 zuì [蕞尔](zuì'ěr)〈书 *fml.*〉形容小(多指地区小 of a region) small; tiny：～小国 small country

醉 zuì ❶ 饮酒过量，神志不清 drunk; intoxicated; turn tipsy：～汉 drunk; drunkard; drunken person | 喝～了 be tipsy; be drunk | ～得不省人事 dead drunken; lose consciousness due to excessive drinking ❷ 沉迷；过分爱好 be drunk with; indulge in：～心 be preoccupied with; be immersed in | 陶～ drunk with joy ❸ 用酒泡制(食品) liquor-saturated; steeped in liquor：～枣 wine-soaked dates | ～蟹 liquor-saturated crab

【醉鬼】zuìguǐ 喝醉了酒的人，多指经常喝醉了酒的人(含厌恶意 implying disgust) drunkard; sot; inebriate; oft. referring to a person who oft. get drunk

【醉话】zuìhuà 喝醉酒时说的话 words uttered when a person becomes drunk

【醉人】zuìrén ❶ 酒容易使人喝醉 intoxicate; make drunk：这酒度数虽不高，可爱～。Though low in alcoholic content, the wine is liable to make one drunk. ❷ 使人陶醉 intoxicating; enchanting; fascinating：春意～ enchanting springtime | ～的音乐 intoxicating music

【醉生梦死】zuì shēng mèng sǐ 像喝醉了酒和在睡梦中那样糊里糊涂地活着 live as if drunk or dreaming; lead a befuddled life

【醉态】zuìtài 喝醉以后神志不清的样子 drunkenness; state of being drunk

【醉翁之意不在酒】zuì wēng zhī yì bù zài jiǔ 欧阳修《醉翁亭记》：'醉翁之意不在酒，在乎山水之间也。'后来用来表示本意不在此而在别的方面。*Story of Old Tippler's Pavilion* by Ouyang Xiu: 'The Old Tippler's delight resides not in wine but in the mountains and waters.' Now this line is used to indicate that someone has other things in mind or have ulterior motives.

【醉乡】zuìxiāng 喝醉以后昏昏沉沉、迷迷糊糊的境界 drunken stupor：沉入～ fall into a drunken stupor

【醉心】zuìxīn 对某一事物强烈爱好而一心专注 be bent on; be dead gone on sth.; be immersed in; be wrapped up in：他一向～于数学的研究。He is always bent on his mathematical research. *or* He is deeply engrossed in mathematical research.

【醉醺醺】zuìxūnxūn (～的 zuìxūnxūn·de) 形容人喝醉了酒的样子 buzzed; sottish; drunk; tipsy

【醉眼】zuìyǎn 醉后迷糊的眼睛 eyes showing the effects of drink：～乜斜 drunken with eyes half-closed | ～朦胧 drunken and bleary-eyed

【醉意】zuìyì 醉的感觉或神情 signs or feeling of getting drunk：他已经有三分～了。He is a bit tipsy.

zūn (ㄗㄨㄣ)

尊[1] zūn ❶ 地位或辈分高 senior; of a senior generation：～长 elders and betters | ～卑 order of seniority | ～亲 one's senior relatives

❷ 敬重；尊崇 respect; venerate; honour：～敬 respect; esteem; honour｜自～ self-respect｜～师爱徒 respect the master and cherish the apprentices ❸〈敬辞 *pol.*〉称跟对方有关的人或事物 your：～府 your residence｜～驾 you; your respected self｜～姓大名。May I know your name? ❹〈量词 *classifier*〉a)用于神佛塑像［used for Buddhist sculptures］：一～佛像 a statue of Buddha b)用于炮［used for artillery］：五十～大炮 fifty artillery pieces

尊² zūn same as 樽 zūn

【尊称】zūnchēng ❶ 尊敬地称呼 address sb. respectfully：～他为老师。They respectfully call him 'Teacher'. ❷ 对人尊敬的称呼 respectful form of address; honorific title：'您'是'你'的～。*Nin* 您 is an honorific form for *ni* 你, or 'you'.｜范老是同志们对他的～。'Venerable Fan' is the honorific term the comrades address him.

【尊崇】zūnchóng 尊敬推崇 worship; revere; venerate：他是一位受人～的学者。He is a revered scholar.

【尊贵】zūnguì 可尊敬；高贵 honourable; respectable; respected：～的客人 honoured guest

【尊敬】zūnjìng ❶ 重视而且恭敬地对待 respect; honour; esteem：～老师 respect a teacher｜受人～ be respected ❷ 可尊敬的 honourable; distinguished; respectable：～的总理阁下 Your Excellency Mr. Prime Minister

【尊亲】zūnqīn ❶ 辈分高的亲属 one's senior relatives; one's parents, grandparents and other relatives of the older generations ❷〈敬辞 *pol.*〉称对方的亲属 your relatives

【尊严】zūnyán ❶ 尊贵庄严 dignity; honour：～的讲台 platform of dignity ❷ 可尊敬的身份或地位 respectable status or position：民族的～ national dignity｜法律的～ sanctity of the law

【尊长】zūnzhǎng 地位或辈分比自己高的人 elders and betters：敬重～ respect the elders and betters

【尊重】zūnzhòng ❶ 尊敬；敬重 respect; value; esteem：～老人 respect for the old｜互相～ mutual respect; respect each other ❷ 重视并严肃对待 attach importance to and treat seriously：～历史 respect history｜～事实 cherish facts; face facts ❸ 庄重(指行为) serious; proper (behaviour)：放～些！Behave yourself!

遵 zūn 依照 abide by; obey; observe; follow：～照 obey; conform to; comply with; act in accordance with｜～循 follow; abide by; adhere to｜～守 observe; abide by; comply with｜～命 comply with your wish; obey your command

【遵从】zūncóng 遵照并服从 defer to; comply with; follow：～决议 comply with the resolution｜～上级的指示 in compliance with the directives of the leadership｜～老师的教导 follow the teacher's advice

【遵命】zūnmìng〈敬辞 *pol.*〉表示依照对方的嘱咐(办事) comply with your wish; obey your command：～照办 act in compliance with your instructions

【遵守】zūnshǒu 依照规定行动；不违背 observe; abide by; comply with：～时间 be on time; be punctual｜～交通规则 observe traffic regulations｜～劳动纪律 observe labour discipline

【遵行】zūnxíng 遵照实行或执行 act on; follow：即请批示，以便～。Please give your immediate instruction so that we can follow it.

【遵循】zūnxún 遵照 follow; abide by; adhere to：～原则 adhere to the principles｜无所～，碍难执行。With nothing to go by, we find it difficult to carry out the task.

【遵照】zūnzhào 依照 obey; conform to; comply with; act in accordance with：～执行 obey and implement｜～政策办事 act in accordance with the policies

樽(罇) zūn 古代的盛酒器具 *zun*, a kind of wine vessel used in ancient times

【樽俎】zūnzǔ〈古代 *arch.*〉盛酒食的器具。后来常用做宴席的代称 wine vessel used in ancient times; feast; banquet：折冲～ outmanoeuvre the enemy at the negotiating table; carry out diplomatic negotiations successfully

鳟 zūn 鳟鱼，背部淡青稍带褐色，侧线下部银白色，全身有黑点 brown trouts (*Salmo trutta Linnaeus*), usu. have black specks, a pale green and slightly brown back and a silver-white belly

zǔn (ㄗㄨㄣˇ)

撙 zǔn 节省 save：～节 save; retrench｜～下一些钱 save some money

【撙节】zǔnjié 节约；节省 retrench; practise economy：～开支 retrench; cut down expenses

zùn (ㄗㄨㄣˋ)

捘 zùn〈书 *fml.*〉用手指按 press with fingers

zuō (ㄗㄨㄛ)

作 zuō 作坊 workshop：石～ stone mason's workshop｜小器～ workshop for the making of small things

☞ zuò on p. 2574

【作坊】zuō·fang 手工业工场 workshop：造纸～

Z

paper mill

嘬 zuō 〈方 *dial*.〉吮吸 suck:小孩儿～奶。The baby is sucking its mother's breast.|～柿子 suck a persimmon

☞ chuài on p.297

【嘬瘪子】zuō biě·zi 〈方 *dial*.〉〈比喻 *fig*.〉受窘为难;碰壁 feel embarrassed; be nonplussed:我的外语不行,让我当翻译,非～不可。My foreign language is very poor. I'll feel embarrassed to be an interpreter.

zuó (ㄗㄨㄛˊ)

昨 zuó ❶ 昨天 yesterday:～夜 last night; yesterday evening ❷ 泛指过去 (in a broad sense) the past:觉今是而～非。I have to realize that I'm right now, but I was wrong in the past.

【昨儿】zuór 〈方 *dial*.〉昨天 yesterday; also 昨儿个 zuór·ge

【昨日】zuórì 昨天 yesterday

【昨天】zuótiān 今天的前一天 yesterday

捽 zuó 〈方 *dial*.〉揪 seize; grasp:小孩儿～住妈妈的衣服。The child held tightly to his mother's dress.|～着他胳膊就往外走。The man seized his arm and went out.

笮(筰) zuó 竹篾拧成的绳索 rope made of bamboo slips:～桥(竹索桥) bamboo rope bridge

☞ Zé on p.2399

琢 zuó ☞ below

☞ zhuó on p.2535

【琢磨】zuó·mo 思索;考虑 think over; turn over in one's mind; ponder:队长的话我～了很久。I pondered over what the team leader said for a long time.|你～～这里面还有什么问题。Please think over if there's still any problem in this.

☞ zhuómó on p.2535

zuǒ (ㄗㄨㄛˇ)

左 zuǒ ❶ 面向南时靠东的一边(跟'右'相对,下②⑥同 as opposed to 'the right', the same for ②⑥ below) the left side; the left; on the east side when one faces the south:～方 to the left; left side|～手 on the left|向～转 turn to the left ❷ 东 east:山～(太行山以东的地方,过去也专指山东省)(areas east of the Taihang Mountains; in the past, a special reference to Shandong Province) east of the mountain ❸ 偏;邪;不正常 queer; unorthodox; heretical:～脾气 eccentric or queer temperament|～道旁门 heretical sect; heterodox school; heresy; heterodoxy ❹ 错;不对头 wrong; incorrect:想～了 have misunderstood sth. or sb.|说～了 have said sth. incorrect ❺ 相反 different; contrary; opposite:意见相～ different ideas ❻ 进步的;革命的 progressive; revolutionary:～派 the Left|～翼作家 Leftist writer ❼ 〈书 *fml*.〉same as 佐 zuǒ ❽ (Zuǒ)姓 a surname

【左膀右臂】zuǒ bǎng yòu bì 〈比喻 *fig*.〉得力的助手 right-hand man; capable assistant

【左边】zuǒ·bian (～儿 zuǒ·bianr)靠左的一边 the left; the left (or left-hand) side

【左不过】zuǒ·buguò 〈方 *dial*.〉❶ 左右;反正 anyway; anyhow; in any event:不是你来,就是我去,～是这么一回事。Either you come or I go, but anyway, that's all that. ❷ 只不过 only; merely; just:这架机器～是上了点锈,不用修。There is only a little bit of rust on the machine. No repairs needed.

【左道旁门】zuǒ dào páng mén 指不正派的宗教派别,也借用在学术上 heretical sect; heterodox school; heresy; heterodoxy; also 旁门左道 páng mén zuǒ dào

【左顾右盼】zuǒ gù yòu pàn 向左右两边看 glance right and left; look around:他走得很慢,～,像在寻找什么。Walking very slowly and casting glances here and there, he seemed to be looking for something.

【左近】zuǒjìn 附近 close by; in the vicinity (or neighbourhood); nearby:房子～有一片草地。There is a meadow close by the house.

【左轮】zuǒlún 转轮手枪的一种,装子弹的轮能从左侧甩出来,所以叫左轮 revolver; handgun equipped with a revolving cylinder containing cartridges that can be released on the left side

【左面】zuǒmiàn 左边 the left (or left-hand) side; the left

【左派】zuǒpài 在阶级、政党、集团内,政治上倾向进步或革命的一派。也指属于这一派的人。the Left; the left wing; politically progressive and revolutionary faction of a class, political party or group; people belonging to the faction

【左撇子】zuǒpiě·zi 习惯于用左手做事(如使用筷子、刀、剪等器物)的人 left-handed person; left-hander; lefty (using chopsticks, knife, scissors, etc. with left hand)

【左迁】zuǒqiān 〈书 *fml*.〉指降职(古人以右为上 ancient people regarding 'right' superior to 'left') demote

【左倾】zuǒqīng ❶ 思想进步的;倾向革命的 left-leaning; progressive; inclined towards the revolution ❷ 分不清事物发展的不同阶段,在革命斗争中表现急躁盲动的(左字常带引号作'左')(左 zuǒ here always in quotes) left deviation, characterized by failure to distinguish the different stages of development of things and acting rashly and blindly in revolutionary struggles

【'左'倾机会主义】zuǒqīng jīhuì zhǔyì ☞ 机会

主义 jīhuì zhǔyì on p. 890

【左券】zuǒquàn 〈古代 *arch.*〉称契约为券，用竹做成，分左右两片，立约的各拿一片，左券常用做索偿的凭证。后来说有把握叫操左券。contract was called *quan* in ancient times. It was made of two bamboo slips, the left and the right, with each party keeping one of them, the left slip being oft. used as evidence for claiming compensation. When one is sure to win a competition, it is called 'having the left *quan* in hand!'

【左嗓子】zuǒsǎng·zi ❶ 指歌唱时声音高低不准 sing out of tune ❷ 左嗓子的人 person who sings out of tune

【左手】zuǒshǒu ❶ 左边的手 left hand ❷ same as 左首 zuǒshǒu

【左首】zuǒshǒu 左边（多指坐位 oft. referring to seats）left-hand side; the left：～坐着一位老太太。An old lady sat to the left; also 左手 zuǒshǒu

【左袒】zuǒtǎn 〈书 *fml.*〉汉高祖刘邦死后，吕后当权，培植吕姓的势力。吕后死，太尉周勃夺取吕氏的兵权，就在军中对众人说：'拥护吕氏的右袒（露出右臂），拥护刘氏的左袒。'军中都左袒（见于《史记·吕太后本纪》）。后来管偏护一方叫左袒。take sides with; be partial to. *Records of the Historian · Official Records of Queen Lü*: after Liu Bang, Emperor Gaozu of the Han Dynasty, died, his wife Queen Lü took power and cultivated her own influence. After the death of the queen, Defender-in-Chief Zhou Bo seized the military power and told those in the army: 'Those who support the Lü's have their right arms exposed, and those who support the Liu's have their left arms exposed.' All the army officers exposed their left arms. Hence the term, 左袒, meaning 'bias'.

【左性子】zuǒxìng·zi ❶ 性情执拗、怪僻 stubborn; pigheaded; wilful ❷ 性情执拗、怪僻的人 pigheaded person

【左翼】zuǒyì ❶ 作战时在正面部队左侧的部队 left wing; left flank; troops on the left of the front troops in a battle ❷ 政党或阶级、集团中在政治思想上倾向革命的一部分 left wing; Left; forces in a political party, class or group that are politically and ideologically inclined towards the revolution

【左右】zuǒyòu ❶ 左和右两方面 left and right sides：～为难 in a dilemma; in an awkward predicament | ～逢源 be have one's bread buttered on both sides; be smooth and slick in handling people or things | 主席台～的红旗迎风飘扬。Red flags are fluttering on both sides of the rostrum. ❷ 身边跟随的人 attendent; those in close attendance; retinue：吩咐～退下 order one's attendants to quit ❸ 支配；操纵 master; control; influence：～局势 have the situation in control | 他想～我，没那么容易！It's not so easy for him to control me. ❹ 用在数目字后面表示概数，跟'上下'相同［used after a numeral to indicate an approximate number, same as '上下 shàngxià'］about; or so：年纪在三十～ about thirty years old ❺ 〈方 *dial.*〉〈副词 *adv.*〉反正 anyway; anyhow; in any case：我～闲着没事，就陪你走一趟吧。Anyway I'm free now. Let me go with you.

【左…右…】zuǒ…yòu… 强调同类行为的反复 over and over again; repeatedly：～说～说 try again and again to talk sb. over | ～思～想 think over again and again | ～一趟～一趟地派人去请 send for sb. time and again

【左右逢源】zuǒ yòu féng yuán 〈比喻 *fig.*〉做事得心应手，怎样进行都很顺利。也比喻办事圆滑。be able to achieve success one way or another; have one's bread buttered on both sides; (fig.) be smooth and slick in handling things

【左右开弓】zuǒ yòu kāi gōng 〈比喻 *fig.*〉两手轮流做同一动作，或者左边一下右边一下做同一动作。也指同时做几项工作。shoot first with one hand, then with the other; use both hands alternately in quick succession; be ambidextrous

【左右手】zuǒyòushǒu 〈比喻 *fig.*〉得力的助手 right-hand man, capable assistant：儿子已长大成人，成了他的～。The son has grown up to be his right-hand man.

【左右袒】zuǒyòutǎn 偏袒某一方面 take sides with; be partial to：勿为～ refuse to take sides; remain neutral; ☞ 左袒 zuǒtǎn

【左证】zuǒzhèng same as 佐证 zuǒzhèng

【左支右绌】zuǒ zhī yòu chù 指力量不足，应付了这一方面，那一方面又有了问题 find it difficult to cope with the situation; be in straitened circumstances; have too many problems to cope with

佐 zuǒ ❶ 辅佐；辅助 assist：～理 assist somebody with a task | ～餐 be eaten together with rice or bread; go with rice or bread ❷ 辅佐别人的人 assistant：僚～ assistant in a government office in old times

【佐餐】zuǒcān 下饭 be eaten together with rice or bread; go with rice or bread：～佳肴 go well with rice or bread

【佐理】zuǒlǐ 〈书 *fml.*〉协助处理 assist sb. with a task：～军务 assist sb. in handling military affairs

【佐证】zuǒzhèng 证据 evidence; proof：伪造的单据就是他贪污的～。The faked documents are exact evidence of his corruption; also 左证 zuǒzhèng

撮 zuǒ（～儿 zuǒr）〈量词 *classifier*〉用于成丛的毛发（of hair）tuft：一～胡子 a tuft of moustache

☞ cuō on p. 338

【撮子】zuǒ·zi 撮 tuft (of hair):剪下一～头发 cut off a tuft of hair

zuò(ㄗㄨㄛˋ)

作 zuò ❶ 起 rise; grow; get up:振～ brace up; cheer up|日出而～ begin a day's work at sunrise|一鼓～气 press on without a letup; brace one's nerve in one vigorous effort|枪声大～。Heavy firing broke out. ❷ 从事某种活动 engage in certain activity:～孽 do evil; commit a sin|自～自受 reap what one sows; suffer the consequences of one's own doing ❸ 写作 write; compose:著～ writings; works|～曲 compose music|～书(写信) write a letter ❹ 作品 writings; work:佳～ excellent works|杰～ masterpiece|成功之～ successful work ❺ 装 pretend; affect:～态 pose; affect; strike an attitude|装模～样 act with affected manners; be pretentious; put on a show ❻ 当作;作为 regard as; take sb. or sth. for:过期～废 cancel after expiration; invalid after the expiry date|认贼～父 regard a thief as one's father ❼ 发作 feel; have:～呕 feel sick or nausea; feel like vomiting|～怪 make trouble

☞ zuō on p. 2571

【作案】zuò//àn 进行犯罪活动 commit a crime or an offence; take part in a criminal activity

【作罢】zuòbà 作为罢论;不进行 drop; relinquish; give up:既然双方都不同意,这件事就只好～了。Since neither side agrees, the matter has to be dropped.

【作保】zuò//bǎo 当保证人 be sb.'s guarantor; vouch for:请人～ ask a person to be one's guarantor

【作弊】zuò//bì 用欺骗的方式做违法乱纪或不合规定的事情 practise fraud; cheat; indulge in corrupt practices; do sth. unlawful or against rules by fraud:通同～ act fraudulently in collaboration with|考试～ cheat in an examination

【作壁上观】zuò bì shàng guān 人家交战,自己站在营垒上观看 watch a fight from the ramparts;〈比喻 *fig.*〉坐观成败,不给予帮助 sit by and watch; be an onlooker or bystander

【作别】zuòbié 〈书 *fml.*〉分别;分手 bid farewell; take one's leave:拱手～ bid farewell by cupping one hand in another before one's chest

【作成】zuòchéng 成全 help (sb. to achieve his or her aim):～他俩的亲事。(She) helped bringing the two of them together in marriage.

【作答】zuòdá 做出回答 answer; reply:听到问话,他没有马上～。Hearing the question, he didn't answer it at once.

【作对】zuò//duì ❶ 做对头;跟人为难 make things difficult for sb.; set oneself against; oppose:他成心跟我～。He deliberately set himself against me. ❷ 成为配偶 pair off in marriage; make a pair:成双～ in pairs

【作恶】zuò//è 做坏事 do evil:～多端 do all kinds of evil; be steeped in iniquity|乘机～ take a chance to do evil

【作伐】zuòfá 〈书 *fml.*〉做媒 act as matchmaker

【作法】zuò//fǎ 〈旧时 *old*〉指道士施行法术 (of a Taoist) exercise magic

【作法】zuòfǎ ❶ 作文的方法 technique of writing:文章～ technique of writing; art of composition ❷ 做法 way of doing things; course of action; practice

【作法自毙】zuò fǎ zì bì 自己立法反而使自己受害 make a law only to run afoul of it oneself; be hoist with one's own petard; get caught in one's own trap

【作废】zuò//fèi 因失效而废弃 become invalid:过期～ become invalid after the expiry date; cancel after expiry|～的票不能再用。An invalid ticket can't be used again.

【作风】zuòfēng ❶ (思想上、工作上和生活上)表现出来的态度、行为 style; style of work; way; attitude; behaviour; conduct (in ideology, work and life):反对官僚～ oppose bureaucratic style of work|～正派 be honest and upright in one's conduct; have moral integrity ❷ 风格 style:他的文章～朴实无华。He writes in an unaffected style.

【作梗】zuògěng 从中阻挠,使事情不能顺利进行 obstruct; hinder; create difficulties:从中～ make things difficult for sb.; create trouble

【作古】zuò//gǔ 〈书 *fml.*〉〈婉辞 *euph.*〉去世 die; pass away

【作怪】zuòguài 作祟 do mischief; make trouble:兴妖～ make trouble; conjure up demons to make trouble

【作家】zuòjiā 从事文学创作有成就的人 writer; author

【作假】zuò//jiǎ ❶ 制造假的,冒充真的;真的里头搀假的;好的里头搀坏的 counterfeit; falsify; make false for true; adulterate:弄虚～ adulterate; practise fraud ❷ 耍花招;装糊涂 cheat; play tricks:～骗人 play tricks to cheat people ❸ 故作客套,不爽直 behave affectedly:没吃饱就说没吃饱,别～! If you've not had enough, just say it. Don't pretend to be otherwise.

【作价】zuò//jià 在出让物品、赔偿物品损失或以物品偿还债务时估定物品的价格;规定价格 evaluate; fix a price for sth. on sale, compensation for damages or repayment of a debt in kind:合理～ reasonable pricing|～赔偿 reasonable compensation

【作奸犯科】zuò jiān fàn kē 为非作歹,触犯法令 violate the law and commit crimes; run afoul of law (奸 *jian*:坏事 evil;科 *ke*:法令 law)

【作茧自缚】zuò jiǎn zì fù 蚕叶丝作茧,把自己包在里面 spin a cocoon around oneself; get enmeshed in a web of one's own spinning; 〈比喻 *fig.*〉做了某事,结果反而使自己受困 do sth. to make it difficult for oneself

【作件】zuòjiàn 作为工作对象的零件,多指在机械加工过程中的零件 workpiece; work; mostly pieces processed in metal working; also 工件 gōngjiàn or 制件 zhìjiàn

【作践】zuò·jian (口语中多读 oft. pronounced 'zuó·jian' in spoken Chinese) 糟蹋 spoil; waste; violate; run sb. down: ~粮食 waste good grains; spoil food grains | 别~人。Don't run others down.

【作客】zuò//kè 〈书 *fml.*〉寄居在别处 sojourn: ~他乡 sojourn in an alien land

【作乐】zuòlè 取乐 make merry; enjoy oneself; have a good time: 寻欢~ seek pleasure and make merry | 苦中~ seek joy amidst hardships
☞ zuòyuè

【作脸】zuòliǎn 〈方 *dial.*〉争光;争气 win honour (or glory) for; try to make a good showing

【作料】zuò·liao (口语中多读 oft. pronounced 'zuó·liao' in spoken Chinese) (~儿 zuò·liaor) 烹调时用来增加滋味的油、盐、酱、醋和葱蒜、生姜、花椒、大料等 condiments; seasonings; dressings such as oil, salt, sauce, vinegar, onion, ginger, Chinese prickly ash, aniseed, etc.

【作乱】zuòluàn 发动叛乱 stage an armed rebellion: 犯上~ rebel against the authority; go against one's superiors and make trouble

【作美】zuòměi (天气等)成全人的好事(多用于否定 usu. used in the negative) (of weather, etc.) help; cooperate; make things easy for sb.: 我们去郊游的那天,天公不~,下了一阵雨,玩得不痛快。The weather didn't cooperate the day we went for an outing. It showered and damped our spirits.

【作难】zuònán 为难 feel embarrassed; feel awkward; find oneself in a predicament; make things difficult for sb.: 从中~ put a spoke in sb.'s wheel

【作难】zuònàn 〈书 *fml.*〉发动叛乱;起事 start a revolt; rise in revolt

【作孽】zuò//niè 造孽 do evil; commit a sin

【作弄】zuònòng (口语中多读 oft. pronounced 'zuōnòng' in spoken Chinese) 捉弄 tease; make a fool of; play a trick on; poke fun at

【作呕】zuò'ǒu ❶ 恶心,想呕吐 feel sick; feel like vomiting; be overcome by nausea ❷ 〈比喻 *fig.*〉对可憎的人或事非常讨厌 be utterly digusted by sb. or sth.: 令人~be nauseating

【作陪】zuòpéi 当陪客 help entertain a guest of honour; be invited along with the guest of honour

【作品】zuòpǐn 指文学艺术方面的成品 works (of literature and art): 绘画~ paintings | 诗词~ poems

【作色】zuòsè 脸上现出怒色 show signs of anger; get worked up: 愤然~ flush with indignation

【作势】zuòshì 做出某种姿态 assume a posture; attitudinize: 装腔~ be pretentious; strike a posture

【作数】zuò//shù 算数儿 count; be valid: 你说话~不~? Does what you said count?

【作死】zuòsǐ (口语中多读 oft. pronounced 'zuōsǐ' in spoken Chinese) 自寻死路 seek death; take the road to ruin; look for trouble: 酒后开快车,这不是~吗! Are you seeking death that you drive so fast after drinking?

【作速】zuòsù 赶快;赶紧 lose no time; hasten: ~处理 deal with the matter as soon as possible; settle the matter quickly | ~前往 lose no time in going to

【作祟】zuòsuì 迷信的人指鬼神跟人为难 (of ghosts, spirits, etc.) haunt; 〈比喻 *fig.*〉坏人或坏的思想意识捣乱,妨碍事情顺利进行 make mischief; cause trouble; exercise evil influence: 防止有人从中~ prevent sb. from making trouble

【作态】zuòtài 故意做出某种态度或表情 pose; affect; strike an attitude: 惺惺~ be affected | 忸怩~ affections; behave coyly

【作痛】zuòtòng 产生疼痛的感觉 have a pain; ache: 周身的筋骨隐隐~ feel a dull pain all over

【作威作福】zuò wēi zuò fú 原指统治者擅行赏罚,独揽威权,后来指妄自尊大,滥用权势abuse one's power tyrannically; ride roughshod over others; act like a tyrant; lord it over people

【作为】[1] zuòwéi ❶ 所作所为;行为 conduct; deed; action: 评论一个人,不但要根据他的谈吐,而且更需要根据他的~。Appraisal of a person should be based not only on what he says, but also on what he does. ❷ 做出成绩 accomplishment; achievement: 有所~ amount to sth.; do sth. useful ❸ 可以做的事 scope for one's abilities or talents: 大有~ plenty of scope for one's talents; be able to accomplish great things

【作为】[2] zuòwéi ❶ 当做 regard as; look on as; take as: ~罢论 regard sth. as abandoned; let a matter drop | ~无效 be declared null and void | 我把游泳~锻炼身体的方法。I take swimming as a physical exercise. ❷ 就人的某种身份或事物的某种性质来说 in the role and character of; as: ~一个学生,首先得把学

习搞好。As a student, you must first study well. |～一部词典,必须有明确的编写宗旨。To compile a dictionary, there must be a definite purpose.

【作伪】zuòwěi 制造假的,冒充真的(多指文物、著作等 oft. of cultural relics, works of art, etc.) fake; make an imitation; cheat

【作文】zuò//wén 写文章(多指学生练习写作 of students) write compositions:～比赛 composition contest

【作文】zuòwén 学生作为练习所写的文章 composition; article a student writes as practice: 写～ write a composition|他的～被评为优秀。His composition earned an excellent mark.

【作物】zuòwù 农作物的简称 abbr. for 农作物 nóngzuòwù:大田～ field crops|经济～ cash crops

【作息】zuòxī 工作和休息 work and rest:按时～ work and rest according to schedule|～制度 time schedule; timetable

【作兴】zuò·xīng〈方 *dial.*〉❶ 情理上许可(多用于否定 usu. in the negative) there's reason to; it's justifiable (or permissible) to:开口骂人,不～! It's impermissible to swear at people. ❷ 可能;也许 perhaps; possibly; maybe: 看这天气,～要下雨。It looks it's going to rain. ❸ 流行;盛行 prevail; prevalent; be in vogue; it's common practice:农村过春节,还～贴春联。It's still a common practice to have New Year couplets pasted up on the wall in the countryside during the Spring Festival.

【作业】zuòyè ❶ 教师给学生布置的功课;部队给士兵布置的训练性的军事活动;生产单位给工人或工作人员布置的生产活动 homework; assignment given by a teacher to his students; military drill assignment given by a commander to soldiers; production assignment given by a production unit to workers or staff:课外～ extracurricular work; homework|野外～ field assignment|～计划 work plan ❷ 从事这种军事活动或生产活动 military operation; production; task; work:高空～ work high above the ground|队伍开到野地上去～。The troops moved to the fields for operation.

【作揖】zuò//yī (口语中多读 oft. pronounced 'zuō//yī' in spoken Chinese)两手抱拳高拱,身子略弯,向人敬礼 make a slight bow with hands folded in front:打躬～ make a slight bow with hands folded in front|给老人家作了个揖 make a bow to an old man

【作艺】zuòyì〈旧时 *old*〉指艺人演出 (of artists) perform; put on a show:她从十一岁起就登台～。She started her stage life at the age of eleven.

【作俑】zuòyǒng〈书 *fml.*〉制造殉葬用的偶像 make idols to be buried with the dead;〈比喻 *fig.*〉倡导做不好的事 initiate an immoral and bad practice; create a bad precedent; ☞ 始作俑者 shǐ zuò yǒng zhě on p. 1750

【作用】zuòyòng ❶ 对事物产生影响 act on; affect:外界的事物～于我们的感觉器官,在我们的头脑中形成形象。External things act on our sense organs and give rise to impressions in our brains. ❷ 对事物产生某种影响的活动 action; function:同化～ assimilation|消化～ digestion|光合～ photosynthesis ❸ 对事物产生的影响;效果;效用 impact; result; effect:副～ side effect|起～ be effective|积极～ play a positive role ❹ 用意 purpose; intention; motive:他刚才说的那些话是有～的。He had an axe to grind, judging from what he said.

【作乐】zuòyuè ❶ 制定乐律 write music; compose music ❷ 奏乐 play music ☞ zuòlè

【作战】zuò//zhàn 打仗 fight; conduct operations; engage in a battle:～英勇 fight heroically

【作者】zuòzhě 文章或著作的写作者;艺术作品的创作者 writer; author; artist

【作准】zuòzhǔn ❶ 作数 count; be valid; be authentic ❷ 准许;承认 approve; recognize; acknowledge

坐 zuò ❶ 把臀部放在椅子、凳子或其他物体上,支持身体重量 sit; rest the weight of the body upon the buttocks and the back of the thighs, as on a chair, stool or other objects:请～。Sit down, please. *or* Please be seated. |咱们～下来谈。Let's sit down for a talk. |他～在河边钓鱼。He sat at the riverside fishing. ◇稳～江山 have the state power in one's control ❷ 乘;搭 take; travel by:～船 travel by boat|～火车 take a train ❸ (房屋)背对着某一方向 (of a building) have its back towards:这座大楼是～北朝南的。This building faces south. ❹ 把锅、壶等放在炉火上 put (a pan, pot, kettle, etc.) on a fire:～一壶水 put a kettle of water on the fire|火旺了,快把锅～上。The fire is ablaze. Put the pan on it quickly. ❺ (～儿 zuòr) same as 座 zuò ① ❻ 枪炮由于反作用而向后移动;建筑物由于基础不稳固而下沉(of rifles, guns, etc.) recoil; kick back; (of a building) sink; subside:步枪的～劲儿不小。The rifle kicks back powerfully. |这房子向后～了。This house is slanting backwards. ❼ 瓜果等植物结实 bear; fruit:～果 bear fruits|～瓜 bear melons or gourds ❽ 指定罪 be punished:连～ be punished for being related to or friendly with sb. who has committed an offence|反～ sentence the accuser to the punishment facing the person he falsely accused ❾ 形成(疾病) cause disease; develop into a disease:打那次受伤之后,就～

下了腰疼的病根儿。Since the injury was inflicted last time, I've come down with lumbago. ❿〈书 *fml*.〉因为 because; for the reason that:～此解职 be dismissed on account of this ⓫〈书 *fml*.〉〈副词 *adv*.〉表示无缘无故 for no reason; without reason:孤蓬自振,惊砂～飞。The solitary bitter fleabane fluttered by itself, and sand flew without being disturbed.

【坐班】zuò//bān 每天按规定时间上下班(多指坐办公室 usu. referring to sitting in one's office) keep office hours:～制 office hour system

【坐标】zuòbiāo 能够确定一个点在空间的位置的一个或一组数,叫做这个点的坐标。通常由这个点到垂直相交的若干条固定的直线的距离来表示。这些直线叫做坐标轴。坐标轴的数目在平面上为2,在空间里为3。coordinate; any of a set of numbers in a reference system that locates the position of a point; a number or a set of numbers that locates the position of a point in space is the coordinate. Usually, it is indicated by the distance between the point and the fixed straight lines that intersect each other at right angles. These straight lines are coordinate axes. The number of coordinate axes is two on a plane and three in space.

【坐禅】zuòchán〈佛教 *Budd*.〉指排除一切杂念,静坐修行 sits in meditation free from all distractions

【坐吃山空】zuò chī shān kōng 光是消费而不从事生产,即使有堆积如山的财物也会消耗完 sit eating away one's resources; eat one's way through one's property

【坐次】zuòcì 坐位的次序 order of seats; seating arrangements:～表 seating chart; also 座次 zuòcì

【坐待】zuòdài 坐等 sit back and wait:～胜利 sit and wait for victory

【坐等】zuòděng 坐着等待 sit back and wait:在他家～了半个多小时。I sat back and waited in his home for more than half an hour.

【坐地】zuòdì ❶ 固定在某个地方 stay at a fixed place:～户 family that has lived in the same place for generations|～行医 practise medicine at a fixed place ❷ 就地 on the spot:～加价 raise the price on the spot|货物～转手 resell goods right on the spot

【坐地分赃】zuò dì fēn zāng (匪首、窝主等)不亲自偷窃抢劫而分到赃物 (of a ringleader, criminal, receiver of stolen goods, etc.) take a share of the spoils without participating in the robbery

【坐垫】zuòdiàn (～儿 zuòdiànr)放在椅子、凳子上的垫子 cushion; pillow or soft pad put on a chair or stool

【坐蔸】zuòdōu 水稻在幼苗时期发生萎黄、生长迟缓的现象。多由水的温度低、肥料不足等引起。wilting or tardy growth of rice seedlings, usually caused by low temperatures of water or inadequate fertilizer

【坐而论道】zuò ér lùn dào 原指坐着议论政事,后泛指空谈大道理 sit back and pontificate; sit back and engage in empty talk

【坐骨】zuògǔ 人坐时支持上身重量的骨头,左右各一,跟耻骨和髂骨组成髋骨 ischium; bone on either side of the human body, on which the torso rests when sitting; lowermost of the three sections of the innominate bone, the other two being the sacrum and coccyx; (图见 ☞ figure for 骨骼 gǔgé on p. 693)

【坐骨神经】zuògǔ shénjīng 人体内最粗最长的神经,是脊髓神经分布到下肢的一支,主要作用是管下肢的弯曲运动 sciatic nerve; longest, thickest nerve in the human body, passing down from the spinal nerve to the lower limbs, its chief function to control the bending movements of the lower limbs

【坐观成败】zuò guān chéng bài 对于别人的成功或失败采取旁观态度 take an onlooker's attitude towards sb. else's success or failure; wait to see what will become of sb. else's endeavour; look on with folded arms; be a mere onlooker

【坐果】zuò//guǒ (果树)长出果实 bear fruit; fructify:果园的苹果树都已～。The apple trees in the garden have all begun to bear fruits.

【坐化】zuòhuà〈佛教 *Budd*.〉指和尚盘膝端坐死去 (of Buddhist monks) pass away (or die) in a sitting posture

【坐江山】zuò jiāngshān 指掌握国家政权 hold the state power

【坐井观天】zuò jǐng guān tiān〈比喻 *fig*.〉眼光狭小,看到的有限 look at the sky from the bottom of a well; have a very narrow view

【坐具】zuòjù 供人坐的用具,如椅子、凳子等 sitting tool, such as a chair, stool, bench, etc.; seat

【坐科】zuò//kē 在科班学戏 undergo professional training at an old-type opera school:他幼年～学艺,习青衣。He received professional training as in the female role at an old-type opera school in his childhood.

【坐困】zuòkùn 守在一个地方,找不到出路 be confined; be walled in; be shut up:～孤城 be confined within the walls of an isolated city

【坐蜡】zuò//là〈方 *dial*.〉陷入为难境地;遇到难以解决的困难 in trouble; be on the spot; be in the spot; be in a predicament:我不会的事硬让我干,这不是让人～吗? Doesn't it mean putting me in the spot, forcing me to do what I can't?

【坐牢】zuò//láo 关在监狱里 be in prison; be in jail; be imprisoned

【坐冷板凳】zuò lěngbǎndèng〈比喻 *fig*.〉因不

Z

受重视而担任清闲的职务。也比喻长期候差或久等接见。hold an unimportant job and be ignored; sit on a cold bench; hold an unimportant post and be neglected; (fig.) be kept waiting for an assignment or an audience with a VIP

【坐力】zuòlì 指枪弹、炮弹射出时的反冲力 recoil (of a gun); kick

【坐落】zuòluò 土地或建筑物位置(在某处) (of a building) be situated; be located: 我们的学校～在环境幽静的市郊。Our school is located in the outskirts with quiet surroundings.

【坐骑】zuòqí 供人骑的马,泛指供人骑的兽类 mount; horse or other animals for riding on

【坐鞦】zuòqiū ☞ 后鞦 hòuqiū on p. 811

【坐蓐】zuòrù 〈书 *fml.*〉坐月子 confinement in childbirth; lying in

【坐山观虎斗】 zuò shān guān hǔ dòu 〈比喻 *fig.*〉对双方的斗争采取旁观的态度,等到两败俱伤的时候,再从中取利 sit on top of a mountain to watch two tigers fight; watch in safety while others fight, then reap the spoils when both sides are exhausted

【坐商】zuòshāng 有固定营业地点的商人(区别于'行商' as compared with 'travelling merchant') tradesman; shopkeeper

【坐视】zuòshì 坐着看,指对该管的事故意不管或漠不关心 sit by and watch; sit tight and look on; sit by idly and remain indifferent

【坐胎】zuò//tāi 指怀孕 be pregnant; conceive

【坐探】zuòtàn 混入对方组织内部刺探情报的人 mole; person working inside an enemy organization to obtain secret information

【坐堂】zuò//táng ❶〈旧时 *old*〉指官吏在公堂上审理案件 (of a magistrate) sit in court to try a case ❷〈佛教 *Budd.*〉指在禅堂上坐禅 sit in meditation in the meditation room ❸ 营业员在店堂里营业;中药店聘请的医生在店堂里看病 serve at the counter in a shop; Chinese traditional doctor invited to see patients at a pharmacy: ～营业 keep (a shop) open for business | ～行医 (of a doctor) sit in a pharmacy to practise medicine

【坐天下】zuò tiānxià 指掌握国家政权 hold state power

【坐位】zuò•wèi ❶ 供人坐的地方(多用于公共场所 oft. in a public place) place to sit; seat: 票已经卖完,一个～也没有了。All tickets are sold out. There is no vacant seat. ❷ (～儿 zuò•wèir)指椅子、凳子等可以坐的东西 sth. to sit on; seat, such as chair, stool, bench, etc.: 搬个～儿来。Get me a seat. ‖ also 座位 zuò•wèi

【坐误】zuòwù 坐失(时机) let slip (an opportunity): 因循～ procrastinate until it is too late

【坐席】zuòxí ❶ 坐到筵席的坐位上,泛指参加宴会 take one's seat at a banquet table; attend a banquet ❷ 供坐的位子 seat

【坐享其成】zuò xiǎng qí chéng 自己不出力而享受别人劳动的成果 sit idle and enjoy the fruits of sb. else's work; reap where one has not sown

【坐像】zuòxiàng 用雕塑等方法制成的人物坐着的形象 statue of a person in a sitting posture

【坐药】zuòyào 〈中医 *Chin. med.*〉指栓剂 suppository

【坐夜】zuòyè 为了守岁、守灵等夜里坐着不睡 sit and stay up overnight on New Year's Eve or by the coffin to guard the spirit of the dead: ～等门 sit overnight to keep the door | ～守岁 stay up overnight on New Year's Eve

【坐以待毙】zuò yǐ dài bì 坐着等死或等待失败 sit still waiting for death or failure

【坐月子】zuò yuè•zi 指妇女生孩子和产后一个月里调养身体 confinement in childbirth; lying-in

【坐赃】zuòzāng ❶〈方 *dial.*〉栽赃 plant stolen or banned goods on sb. ❷〈书 *fml.*〉犯贪污罪 commit the crime of corruption

【坐镇】zuòzhèn (官长)亲自在某个地方镇守,也用于比喻 (of a commander) personally attend to garrison duty; assume personal command; also used in a figurative sense: 总经理亲临现场～。The General Manager came to the scene personally.

【坐支】zuòzhī 指某些企业单位经银行同意从自己业务收入的现金中直接支付的方式 (of an enterprise) use of business revenue to finance expenses; direct cash payment from its earnings with the permission of the bank

【坐庄】zuòzhuāng ❶ 商店派遣或特约的人常驻某地,采购货物、招揽生意 be a resident buyer of a business firm ❷ 打牌时继续做庄家 be the banker or dealer (in a gambling game)

阼 zuò 〈古代 *arch.*〉指东面的台阶,主人迎接宾客的地方 flight of steps on the eastern side of a hall where the host stands to welcome his guests

岞 zuò 岞山(Zuòshān),地名,在山东 Zuoshan, name of a place in Shandong Province

怍 zuò 〈书 *fml.*〉惭愧 ashamed: 惭～ ashamed | 愧～ ashamed

柞 zuò ☞ below
☞ zhà on p. 2405

【柞蚕】zuòcán 昆虫,比家蚕大,将变成蛹的幼虫全身长有褐色长毛,吃栎树的叶子,吐的丝是丝织品的重要原料 tussah (*Antheraea paphia*); Asiatic silkworm bigger than the mulberry silkworm that feeds on oak leaves, develops long, brown hair when it is about to become a pupa, and produces a kind of silk that is an important raw material for making silk fabrics

【柞树】zuòshù 栎的通称 general term for 栎 lì

【柞丝绸】zuòsīchóu 用柞蚕丝织成的平纹纺织

品,有光泽。适宜做夏季衣服。lustrous, tussah silk fabric with a plain weave, suitable for making summer dresses; pongee

胙 zuò〈古代 *arch.*〉祭祀时供的肉 sacrificial meat

祚 zuò〈书 *fml.*〉❶ 福 blessing:门衰～薄。The family is declining and its wealth depleting out. ❷ 君主的位置 throne:帝～imperial throne|践～ ascend the throne

唑 zuò 译音用字 character used for transliteration:咔～ carbazole|噻～ thiazole

座(❶坐) zuò ❶ (～儿 zuòr)坐位 seat; place:～次 seating order|满～ full house; packed to capacity|这个剧场有五千个～儿。The theatre seats 5,000. ❷ (～儿 zuòr)放在器物底下垫着的东西 stand; pedestal; base:茶碗～儿 coaster|石碑～儿 stone tablet base ❸ 星座 constellation:大熊～ Ursa Major|天琴～ Lyra ❹〈敬辞 *pol.*〉〈旧时 *old*〉称高级长官 term of address for a high-ranking officer:军～(称军长) army commander ❺〈量词 *classifier*〉多用于较大或固定的物体 [used mostly for large or fixed objects]:一～山 a mountain|一～水库 a reservoir|一～高楼 a tall building

【座舱】zuòcāng 指客机上载乘客的地方。也指战斗机的驾驶舱。passenger cabin (in an airliner); cockpit (of a fighter)

【座次】zuòcì same as 坐次 zuòcì

【座机】zuòjī 指专供某人乘坐的飞机 sb.'s private plane

【座儿】zuòr 影剧院、茶馆、商店、饭馆等指顾客;拉人力车、三轮车的指乘客 (of a cinema, teahouse, shop, restaurant, etc.) patron; (of a rickshaw, pedicab, etc.) passenger:上～ seat of honour|拉～ (of a taxi driver) solicit passengers

【座上客】zuòshàngkè 指在席上的受主人尊敬的客人,泛指受邀请的客人 guest of honour; honoured guest; invited guest

【座谈】zuòtán 不拘形式地讨论 have an informal discussion:～会 forum; symposium; informal discussion

【座位】zuò·wèi same as 坐位 zuò·wèi

【座无虚席】zuò wú xū xí 座位没有空着的,形容观众、听众或出席的人很多 be packed to capacity; there are no empty seats; full house

【座右铭】zuòyòumíng 写出来放在坐位旁边的格言。泛指激励、警戒自己的格言。motto; maxim; concisely expressed principle or rule of conduct

【座钟】zuòzhōng 摆在桌子上的时钟(区别于'挂钟' as compared with 'wall clock') desk clock

【座子】zuò·zi ❶ same as 座 zuò ②:钟～ clock stand ❷ 自行车、摩托车等上面供人坐的部分 saddle (of a bicycle, motorcycle, etc.)

做(作) zuò ❶ 制造 do; make; produce; manufacture:～衣服 make clothes|用这木头～张桌子 make a table using this piece of wood ❷ 写作 write; compose:～诗 write a poem|～文章 write an article ❸ 从事某种工作或活动 do; act; engage in:～工 do manual work; work|～事 do work|～买卖 do business; buy and sell ❹ 举行家庭的庆祝或纪念活动 hold a family or home celebration:～寿 hold a birthday party for an elder|～生日 celebrate sb.'s birthday ❺ 充当;担任 be; become:～母亲的 being a mother|～官 hold an official post; be an official|～教员 be a teacher; become a teacher|～保育员 be a nurse|今天开会由他～主席。He'll be the chairman at today's meeting. ❻ 用做 be used as:树皮可以～造纸的原料。Bark may be used as a raw material for making paper.|这篇文章可以～教材。This article may be used as teaching material. ❼ 结成(关系) form or contract a relationship:～亲 (of two families) become related by marriage|～对头 set oneself against sb.|～朋友 make friends with ❽ 假装出(某种模样) pretend; feign; make believe; do sth. for appearance's sake:～样子 make a show|～鬼脸 make faces|～痛苦状 grimace with pain

【做爱】zuò'ài 指人性交 make love

【做伴】zuò//bàn (～儿 zuò//bànr)当陪伴的人 keep one's company:母亲生病,需要有个人～。My mother is ill. She needs someone to keep her company.

【做东】zuò//dōng 当东道主 play the host; host sb.; act as host to sb.

【做法】zuòfǎ 处理事情或制作物品的方法 way of handling or making sth.; method of work; practice

【做工】zuò//gōng 从事体力劳动 do manual work; work:她在纺纱厂～。She works in a cotton mill.

【做工】zuògōng (～儿 zuògōngr) ❶ same as 做功 zuògōng ❷ 指制作的技术或质量 workmanship:这件衣服～很细。This dress is of excellent workmanship.

【做功】zuògōng 戏曲中演员的动作和表情 acting (in traditional opera); business; stage business:～戏 stage acting; also 做工 zuògōng

【做鬼】zuò//guǐ (～儿 zuò//guǐr)做骗人的勾当;捣鬼 play tricks; play an underhand game; get up to mischief:从中～ play tricks

【做活儿】zuò//huór 从事体力劳动 work; do manual labour:他们一块儿在地里～。They worked together in the fields.|孩子也能帮着做点活儿了。The child can also help with some work.

【做客】zuò//kè 访问别人,自己当客人 be a guest:到亲戚家～ be a guest at a relative's

【做礼拜】zuò lǐbài 基督教徒到礼拜堂聚会听讲道（of a Christian）go to church; be at church

【做买卖】zuò mǎi·mai 从事商业活动 do business; carry on trade:～的 businessman; trader; merchant | 到集上去～ do business at a fair

【做满月】zuò mǎnyuè 在婴儿满月时宴请亲友 host a dinner for relatives and friends when one's baby is one month old

【做媒】zuò//méi 当媒人；给人介绍婚姻 be a matchmaker (or go-between)

【做梦】zuò//mèng ❶ 睡眠中因大脑里的抑制过程不彻底，在意识中呈现种种幻象 have a dream; dream; a sequence of sensations, images, thoughts, etc. passing through a sleeping person's mind as a result of the incomplete inhibition of the cerebral cortex ❷〈比喻 *fig.*〉幻想 pipe dream; fancy: 白日～ daydream

【做派】zuò·pài 做功；戏曲中演员的动作、表演 acting; stage business; business

【做亲】zuò//qīn ❶ 结为姻亲（of two families）become related by marriage: 他们两家～，倒是门当户对。The two families have become related by marriage. They are well-matched in social status. ❷ 成亲；娶妻 get married; be united in marriage; take a wife

【做圈套】zuò quāntào 设计让人上当受骗 set a trap (to deceive sb.)

【做人】zuòrén ❶ 指待人接物 conduct oneself; behave: ～处世 conduct oneself in society | 她很会～。She knows how to conduct herself in society. ❷ 当个正派人 be an upright person: 痛改前非，重新～ sincerely mend one's ways and turn over a new leaf

【做人家】zuò rénjiā〈方 *dial.*〉俭省 thrifty; frugally: 他平时不乱花钱，很会～。He spends money carefully and is rather thrifty.

【做生活】zuò shēnghuó〈方 *dial.*〉从事体力劳动；做活儿 work; do manual labour

【做生日】zuò shēng·ri 庆祝生日 celebrate one's birthday

【做生意】zuò shēng·yi 做买卖 do business; carry on trade

【做声】zuòshēng（～儿 zuòshēngr）发出声音，指说话、咳嗽等 make a sound (as when speaking, coughing, etc.): 大家别～，注意听他讲。Keep quiet and listen to him!

【做事】zuò//shì ❶ 从事某种工作或处理某项事情 do work; do a deed; handle affairs: 他～一向认真负责。He is always earnest and conscientious in his work. ❷ 担任固定的职务；工作 work; hold a job: 你现在在哪儿～? Where do you work now?

【做手脚】zuò shǒujiǎo 背地里进行安排；暗中作弊 rig a situation; practise fraud; cheat

【做寿】zuò//shòu（为老年人）做生日 celebrate the birthday (usu. of elderly people); hold a birthday party for an elder

【做文章】zuò wénzhāng〈比喻 *fig.*〉抓住一件事发议论或在上面打主意 make an issue of it; make a fuss about sth. trivial

【做戏】zuò//xì ❶ 演戏 put on a play; act in a play ❷〈比喻 *fig.*〉故意做出虚假的姿态 play-act; pretend: 他这是在我面前～，不要相信。He is putting on a show of himself in front of me. Don't believe him.

【做学问】zuò xué·wen 钻研学问 engage in scholarship; do research

【做贼心虚】zuò zéi xīn xū 做了坏事怕人觉察出来而心里惶恐不安 have a guilty conscience like a thief; have sth. on one's conscience

【做针线】zuò zhēn·xian 做缝纫刺绣等活计 sew; do needlework

【做主】zuò//zhǔ 对某项事情负完全责任而做出决定 decide; take the responsibility for a decision: 当家～ be master of one's own destiny | 这事我做不了主。I have no say on this matter. *or* I am not in a position to decide.

【做作】zuò·zuo 故意做出某种表情、腔调等 affected; artificial: 他的表演太～了，一点也不自然。His acting is overdone. It is not at all natural.

酢 zuò〈书 *fml.*〉客人向主人敬酒 propose a toast to the host: 酬～ exchange of toasts

☞ cù on p. 330

Z

附

新词新义
New Words and New Senses

A

【艾滋病】àizībìng 获得性免疫缺陷综合征的通称，是一种传染病。病原体是人类免疫缺陷病毒，通过性接触或血液、母婴等途径传播，侵入人体后，使丧失对病原微生物的免疫能力。蔓延迅速，死亡率高。AIDS; acquired immune deficiency syndrome; infectious disease caused by the human immunodeficiency virus (HIV) which attacks the body's immune system, leaving it vulnerable to a variety of life threatening illnesses. AIDS is transmitted by infected blood (between intravenous drug users, and by blood transfusions) and sexual intercourse, and can also be passed on passively by pregnant HIV positive women to their fetuses. It spreads quickly and has a high mortality rate.

【安检】ānjiǎn 安全检查 security check: 旅客登机前要经过～。Passengers are requested to go through a security check before boarding the plane.

【安全套】ānquántào 避孕套。因使用避孕套有避孕和防止性病感染传播的作用，所以也叫安全套。condom; sheath; men's device of contraception that also functions as protection against venereal disease and the HIV

【按揭】ànjiē 一种购房或购物的贷款方式，以所购房屋或物品为抵押向银行贷款，然后分期偿还 mortgage; loan taken out from a bank to buy property or purchase goods, paid back in installments, on the basis that such property or goods are pledged to the bank until the loan is repaid

【案值】ànzhí 指案件涉及的物、款的价值 value of goods and money involved in a law case

【暗恋】ànliàn 暗中爱恋(多指男女之间 usu. between man and woman) love sb. in one's heart: 他对公司的一位女会计～已久。He has been secretly in love with a woman accountant at his company for a long time.

【暗物质】ànwùzhì 由天文观测推断存在于宇宙中的不发光物质。包括不发光天体，以及某些非重子中性粒子等。dark matter or substance, including non-luminous celestial bodies and certain non-baryon neutral particles, whose existence in the universe is inferred from astronomical observation

【暗箱操作】ànxiāng cāozuò 指利用职权暗地里做某事(多指不公正、不合法的) covert abuse of authority and trust; corrupt behaviour: 避免医院收费中的～。The abuse of power to impose fallacious charges in hospitals must be stopped. also 黑箱操作 hēixiāng cāozuò

【澳门币】àoménbì 澳门地方通行的货币，以圆为单位 Macao pataca, the basic monetary unit of which is the pataca

B

【吧台】bātái 酒吧里供应饮料等的柜台 bar; pub counter

【白色收入】báisè shōurù 指按规定获得的工资、津贴等劳动报酬，具有公开性(区别于'黑色收入、灰色收入' as compared with 'black income and grey income') white income; open, regular salary and allowances

【白色污染】báisè wūrǎn 指废弃塑料及其制品对环境造成的污染。塑料不易降解，影响环境的美观，所含成分有潜在危害。因塑料用做包装材料多为白色，所以叫白色污染。white pollution; environmental pollution caused by scrap non-biodegradable plastics that are an environmental eyesore and contain potentially hazardous elements. It is called 'white pollution' because plastic wrapping and packaging materials are generally white.

【白页】báiyè 电话号簿中登录党政机关、团体电话号码的部分，因用白色纸张印刷，所以叫白页（区别于‘黄页’ as compared with ‘yellow pages’）white pages; white pages in a telephone directory that list the telephone numbers of Party and government organs and people's organizations

【扳平】bānpíng 在体育比赛中扭转落后的局面，使成平局（of the losing team or competitor in a sports event）equalize the score; make the match a draw：终场前，甲队将比分～。Just before the match ended, Team A scored an equalizer.

【包养】bāoyǎng 为婚外异性（多为女性）提供房屋、金钱等并与之长期保持性关系 provide housing, money, etc. for an extramarital partner（usu. woman）and maintain a long-term sexual relationship with her：～情妇 provide for a kept woman

【包装】bāozhuāng ［补义 new sense］〈比喻 *fig.*〉对人或事物从形象上装扮、美化，使更具吸引力或商业价值 packaging; make sb. or sth. look beautiful and exciting to appeal to the public or enhance marketability：～歌星 package a pop star｜～体育比赛 presentation of a sports event

【保安】bǎo'ān ［补义 new sense］指保安员，在机关、企业、商店、宾馆等处做保安工作的人 security personnel employed by government organs, enterprises, stores, hotels, etc.：银行～ bank security staff

【保税区】bǎoshuìqū 一个国家或地区在其管辖范围内划出的特定区域，境外商人和商品可以自由进出，并在区内享受税收优惠政策 bonded zone; bonded area; designated area in a country or a region where international business people and commodities can come and go freely, within whose limits preferential tax policies apply

【崩盘】bēng//pán 指股票、期货等的市场由于行情大跌而彻底崩溃 stock market crash; collapse of a stock or futures market caused by a drastic drop in price

【蹦床】bèngchuáng ❶ 一种体育器械，外形像床，有弹性 trampoline; highly elastic sports apparatus resembling a bed ❷ 体育运动项目之一。运动员在蹦床上完成跳跃、翻腾、旋转等动作。sports event where competitors perform gymnastic springing, tumbling and spinning, etc. on the trampoline

【蹦极】bèngjí 一种体育运动，用一端固定的有弹性的绳索绑缚在踝部从高空跳下，身体在空中上下弹动 bungee jumping; bungy jumping; sport that entails jumping from a great height with one end of a long elastic rope attached to the jumper's ankles and the other firmly fixed. On jumping, the performer's body bounces up and down in mid air; also 蹦极跳 bèngjítiào

【逼抢】bīqiǎng 紧逼着争抢（多用于足球、篮球等球类比赛 usu. in ball games such as football and basketball）hassle：～凶狠 play physical and hassle for the ball

【比拼】bǐpīn 拼力比试 compete fiercely; go all out to win：双方将在半决赛中～，争夺决赛权。The two sides will compete fiercely in the semi-final to qualify for the final match.

【比萨饼】bǐsàbǐng 一种意大利式饼，饼上放蕃茄、奶酪、肉类等，用烤箱烘烤而成。因最早盛行于意大利城市比萨而得名。pizza; pie of Italian origin, consisting of a flat round base of dough baked with a topping of tomatoes, cheese, meat, etc., named after the Italian city of Pisa, where it first became popular

【比特】bǐtè 信息量单位，二进制数的一位所包含的信息量就是一比特。如二进制数 1010 包含的信息量为 4 比特。bit（blend of binary and digit）; basic unit of information, expressed by either of the digits 0 or 1 in binary notation, e.g. the binary number 1010 contains four bits of information

【笔记本电脑】bǐjìběn diànnǎo 便携式电子计算机的一种。因外形略像笔记本，所以叫笔记本电脑。notebook computer; laptop; portable computer in the shape of a notebook

【笔友】bǐyǒu 通过书信往来、诗文赠答结交的朋友 pen-friend; pen pal; friend whose acquaintance has been made and is maintained by correspondence or exchange of poems and compositions

【边境贸易】biānjìng màoyì 相邻国家的贸易组织或边境居民在国家接壤地区进行的贸易活动 frontier trade; border trade; trade activity in border areas between the trade organizations and residents of two neighbouring countries; 简称 abbr. 边贸 biānmào

【边贸】biānmào 边境贸易的简称 abbr. for 边境贸易 biānjìng màoyì

【编创】biānchuàng 编写创作 write; create：～人员 writer; designer｜～节目 compose a programme or an item on a programme in show business, etc.

【变频】biànpín 指改变交流电频率 frequency conversion：～机 frequency converter｜～空调 convertible frequency air-conditioner

【变现】biànxiàn 把非现金的资产和有价证券等换成现金 liquidate; liquidation; convert liquid assets and securities into cash

【标题新闻】biāotí xīnwén 以标题形式刊登在报纸上的新闻，内容简要，字号较大 headline news; title of news item in a newspaper, written in succinct language and printed in large type

【飙升】biāoshēng （价格、数量等）急速上升 (of price, quantity, etc.) soar; skyrocket; (of price, interest rate, etc.) hike：石油价格～。The price of petroleum soared. | 中档住宅的销量一路～。The sales volume of medium-quality housing has soared.

【冰毒】bīngdú 有机化合物，成分是去氧麻黄素。白色结晶，很像小冰块，对人的中枢神经和交感神经有强烈刺激作用，常用成瘾。因用做毒品，所以叫冰毒。ice; organic compound comprising methamphetamine, its crystalline form closely resembling that of ice. A highly addictive stimulant that works on the central and sympathetic nervous systems, it is used as narcotic drug.

【并购】bìnggòu 购并 merger and acquisition

【并轨】bìngguǐ 〈比喻 *fig.*〉将并行的体制、措施等合而为一 combine parallel systems, similar measures, etc., into one：两种教学体制实行～。The two educational systems have been unified.

【病毒】bìngdú ［补义 new sense］指计算机病毒 computer virus

【拨打】bōdǎ 打（电话）dial (a phone number); make a phone call：～国内长途 make a domestic long-distance call | ～投诉电话 dial the consumer complaints hotline

【播报】bōbào 通过广播、电视播送报道 air; broadcast sth. on radio or television; broadcast news on radio or television：～新闻 news broadcast

【博彩】bócǎi 指赌博、摸彩、抽奖一类活动 gambling in the form of a tombola, or lottery：～业 lottery industry

【博导】bódǎo 博士研究生导师的简称 abbr. for 博士研究生导师 bóshì yánjiūshēng dǎoshī (advisor for Ph. D candidates)

【博士后】bóshìhòu 获得博士学位后在高等院校或研究机构从事研究工作并继续深造的阶段。也指博士后研究人员。post-doctoral research; post-doctoral studies; period of research or further study at a higher-learning or research institute after getting a Ph. D; also referring to a person engaged in such research or studies

【补仓】bǔ//cāng 指投资者在持有一定数量的某种证券的基础上，又买入同一种证券 (of an investor) buy more of the same securities already held

【不可更新资源】bù kě gēngxīn zīyuán 经人类开发利用后，在相当长的时期内不可能再生的自然资源。如金属矿物、煤、石油等。unrenewable resources; natural resources that take more than a human lifetime to replenish after exploitation, such as metal ores, coal, and petroleum; also 非再生资源 fēizàishēng zīyuán

【不明飞行物】bù míng fēixíngwù 指天空中来历不明并未经证实的飞行物体。近几十年来屡有这类飞行物体出现的报道，据称形状有圆碟形、卵形、蘑菇形等。UFO; unidentified flying object. Over the past decades there have been frequent reported sightings of UFOs, describing them as disc, oval, or mushroom shaped. also 飞碟 fēidié

【不争】bùzhēng 不容置疑的 unassailable; unarguable; beyond doubt; undoubted：～的事实 unarguable facts

【不正当竞争】bùzhèngdàng jìngzhēng 经营者在经营活动中违反诚、信、公平等原则的竞争行为。如商业贿赂、侵犯商业秘密、虚假广告、倾销等。unfair competition; dishonest and unfair competitive tactics in business operations, such as bribery, fraudulently obtaining commercial information, false advertising, dumping, etc.

【布点】bù//diǎn 布设、安排有关基层单位、人员等 setup of organizations and arrangement of personnel, etc. at the grassroots level：住宅区商业～不够合理。The distribution of commercial outlets in residential areas has left something to be desired.

【布网】bù//wǎng 〈比喻 *fig.*〉公安部门为捕捉犯罪嫌疑人等在各处布置力量 spread a net; deploy police forces over a wide radius in order to apprehend a criminal suspect：～守候，捉拿绑匪 deploy police forces and monitor closely so as to apprehend a kidnapper

【布艺】bùyì 一种手工艺，用布料经过剪裁、缝缀、刺绣制成用品或饰物等 fabric art; handicraft in which a piece of cloth is fashioned into articles for use or ornamentation by cutting and sewing or embroidering：～沙发 cloth-upholstered sofa | ～装饰 fabric decoration

【布展】bùzhǎn 布置展览 arrange exhibits：精心～ take great pains to arrange exhibits | 油画展正在加紧～。The arrangement of exhibits for the oil painting exhibition is now under way.

【步道】bùdào 指人行道 pavement; sidewalk; footpath：加宽～ widen the pavement

C

【擦边球】cābiānqiú 打乒乓球时擦着球台边沿的球，后来把做在规定的界限边缘而不违反规定的事比喻为打擦边球 edge ball; touch ball; ball that hits the edge of the table in a table tennis match; (fig.) stretch the rules to their limit

【采认】cǎirèn 〈方 *dial.*〉承认 admit; acknowledge; recognize: ～学历 recognize sb.'s educational credentials

【采信】cǎixìn 相信(某种事实)并用来作为处置的依据 believe (a fact) and take it as grounds for dealing with sth. or sb.: 被告的陈述证据不足,法庭不予～。The accused's statement lacks verification and therefore provides insufficient grounds on which the court may proceed.

【彩券】cǎiquàn 彩票 lottery

【菜单】càidān [补义 new sense]选单的俗称 popular name for menu; bill of fare: 计算机屏幕上显示出操作～。The operating menu appeared on a computer screen. ◇本届服装节亮出精彩～。The fashion festival's spectacular programme of events is being unveiled.

【菜品】càipǐn 菜肴(多指饭馆、餐厅等供应的) dish (oft. referring to choice of dishes provided by a restaurant or in a dining hall): 这家餐厅新近推出几款新～。The restaurant has recently added several new dishes to its menu.

【参股】cān//gǔ 入股 become a shareholder; buy shares

【参拍】cānpāi ❶(物品)参加拍卖 (of goods) be auctioned; be put up for auction: 一批在海外收藏多年的书画作品近日回国～。A batch of calligraphic works and paintings that have been part of an overseas collection for many years are soon to be returned and put up for auction. ❷参加拍摄 (motion-picture making) join the shooting crew; play a part: 这部影片有多名影星～。Several film stars are to act in this film.

【参评】cānpíng 参加评比、评选或评定 submit sth. for public appraisal, competition, or selection: ～影片 film nominated for public appraisal | ～人员将统一进行外语考试。All the nominated candidates will take a foreign language test. | 住宅设计评比共有二十个方案～。Twenty designs have been nominated for competing for the housing design awards.

【餐饮】cānyǐn 指饭馆、酒馆的饮食买卖 food and drink: ～业 catering; catering trade | ～市场 catering market

【残障】cánzhàng 〈方 *dial.*〉残疾 handicap; deformity; physical disability: 重度～ seriously handicapped | 老师手把手教～孩子画画。The teacher helped the disabled children to paint by a hands-on approach.

【仓位】cāngwèi 指投资者所持的证券金额占其资金总量的比例 ratio of an investor's securities against the total volume of capital in his or her possession: 控制～ control the amount of securities in hand | ～过重 excessive security holdings; also 持仓量 chícāngliàng

【操控】cāokòng 操纵控制 operate and control; manipulate: 幕后～ pull strings behind the scenes; unobtrusively manipulate

【测评】cèpíng ❶检测评定 give an assessment after checking and measuring: 对职工进行技术～。A technological assessment of the staff will be conducted. ❷推测并评论 speculate and comment on sth.: 股市～ speculate and give comments on stock market situation

【层级】céngjí 层次;级别 level: 经过充分准备,双方进行了较高～的会谈。After ample preparations, the two parties held a conference at a higher level.

【查控】chákòng 侦查并控制 surveillance; investigate and control; monitor: 对嫌犯可能藏身的场所进行严密～。Put the suspects' possible hideouts under close surveillance.

【长线】chángxiàn [补义 new sense]经过较长的时间才能产生效益的(跟'短线'相对 as compared with 'short-term') (of investment) long-term; yielding economic returns in the long run: ～投资 long-term investment

【长项】chángxiàng 擅长的项目;擅长做的工作、事情等 forte; sth. at which one excels; one's strong point: 双杠是他的～。The parallel bars is his forte. | 每个人都有自己的～。Everyone has his strong points.

【长销】chángxiāo (商品)有市场潜力,在长时间内销路好 (of merchandise) have strong market potential; be likely to be in demand in the long run: ～产品 products popular for the long term

【常销】chángxiāo (商品)能经常不断地销售 (of merchandise) in constant demand: ～书 books in constant, popular demand

【厂价】chǎngjià 产品出厂时的价格 producer price; ex-factory price: 按～优惠销售 sell sth. at a preferential producer price

【超生】chāoshēng [补义 new sense]指超过计划生育指标生育 have more children than the family planning policy allows; have unplanned births: ～户 family that has more children than the family planning policy allows

【超市】chāoshì 超级市场的简称 abbr. for 超级市场 chāojí shìchǎng

【炒股】chǎo//gǔ 指从事股票交易 speculate in stocks and shares: 他炒了三年股。He has been dealing in stocks for three years.

【炒作】chǎozuò 为扩大人或事物的影响而通过媒体做反复的宣传 publicity hype; persistent media promotion publicizing a person or an event; hype：经过一番新闻～，这位歌星名气大振。The pop star became widely known after heavy promotional hype.

【车本】chēběn (～儿 chēběnr)机动车驾驶证的通称 general term for a driver's licence

【车程】chēchéng 车(一般指汽车)行驶的路程(用于表示道路的远近)(used to describe the distance of a journey, usu. of an automobile) distance covered in a certain amount of time：从广州到深圳，大约有三个多小时的～。It's a three-hour drive from Guangzhou to Shenzhen.

【车匪】chēfěi 在汽车、火车上进行抢劫等活动的匪徒 bandits that loot bus or train passengers

【撤资】chè//zī 撤销投资；撤出资金 withdraw investment; withdraw funds

【尘埃落定】chén'āi luò dìng 〈比喻 *fig.*〉事情有了结局或结果 when the dust has settled; come to an end：世界杯小组赛～。The qualifying matches for the World Cup are at an end.

【承保】chéngbǎo 承担保险 undertake or accept insurance; underwrite：～额 underwriting limit

【城市热岛效应】chéngshì rèdǎo xiàoyìng 指城市气温高于郊区的现象。造成这种现象的主要原因是城市工厂及车辆排热，人口密度大，建筑物多，地面干燥、水分蒸发少等。urban heat island effect; phenomenon in which the temperature in urban areas is higher than that in rural areas, owing to factory and vehicle emissions, denser population, excess construction, dry ground, and lack of evaporation; 简称 abbr. 热岛效应 rèdǎo xiàoyìng

【持仓】chícāng 指持有证券，不买也不卖，待机行事 wait for one's chance by refraining from selling and buying stocks

【赤潮】chìcháo 由于海洋富营养化，使某些浮游生物暴发性繁殖和高度密集所引起的海水变红的现象，多发生在近海海域。赤潮造成海水严重污染，鱼虾、贝类等大量死亡。red tide; reddening of seas, mainly coastal, caused by eutrophication-related explosive propagation and high density of marine plankton. Red tides cause severe contamination of sea water and the death of great numbers of marine life; also 红潮 hóngcháo

【冲顶】[1] chōngdǐng 足球比赛时运动员向前跃起用头顶球 (of a player) jump up to head the ball during a football match

【冲顶】[2] chōngdǐng 登山中临近顶峰时奋力攀登 (when mountaineering) scale the summit; make a particularly strenuous effort when the summit is in view

【充电】chōng//diàn [补义 new sense]〈比喻 *fig.*〉通过学习补充知识、提高技能等 supplement one's knowledge and improve one's skills by further study：为了适应形势的发展，每个人都需要通过不断～来提高自己的能力。To adapt to developing circumstances, everyone needs to improve their abilities through further study.

【重码】chóngmǎ ❶ 两个或两个以上的编码相同，造成重复，叫做重码 superimposed coding; two or more identical codes that are superimposed ❷ 两个或两个以上相同而重复的编码 two or more codes that are the same and are superimposed

【重组】chóngzǔ 重新组合 reorganize; reshuffle; regroup; realign：资产～ realignment of assets | 对小企业进行～改造 regroup small enterprises

【抽逃】chōutáo (为逃避债务、隐匿财产、抗拒纳税等)暗中抽走(资金) flight; surreptitiously withdraw one's capital to evade debts or taxes, conceal property, etc.

【臭氧洞】chòuyǎngdòng 指地球上空的臭氧层因臭氧大幅度减少而形成的空洞。人类向大气中排放的氟氯烷(氟利昂)等化合物进入臭氧层与臭氧发生化学反应，是使臭氧减少的重要因素。出现臭氧洞后，紫外线会过量地射到地表，危害人体健康，也会导致气候异常，影响生态平衡。ozone hole; hole in the ozone layer of the earth's stratosphere resulting from massive ozone depletion. A main cause for ozone depletion is the chemical reaction of ozone to such compounds as freon released into the atmosphere by humanity. Excessive ultraviolet radiation may reach the earth's surface through the ozone hole, affecting people's health, causing an abnormal climate, and upsetting the ecological balance.

【出警】chūjǐng 出动警察到案件或事故发生的地方 dispatch policemen to the scene of an crime or accident：巡警及时～，制止了一场械斗。The police were sent to the scene in time to prevent an armed gang fight.

【出镜】chū//jìng 指在电影或电视中露面 star in a film or a TV drama：青年演员频频～，演技提高很快。This young actor has starred in several films and his acting has rapidly improved.

【出局】chū//jú [补义 new sense] ❶ 泛指在体育比赛中因失利而不能继续参加后一阶段的比赛 (in a broad sense) be knocked out; be out; fail to qualify for the next round of matches：经过预赛，有三支球队被淘汰～。Three teams were knocked out after the preliminary matches. ❷〈比喻 *fig.*〉人或事物因不能适应形势或不能达到某种要求而无法在其领域继续存在下去 (of a person or a thing) be unable to survive in a certain field due to failure to adapt to the situation or meet the requirements：粗制滥造的产品必然被淘汰～。Slipshod products will inevitably be automatically eliminated.

【除权】chú//quán 股份公司因向股东送红股等，股份增加，每股股票的实际价值减少，需要从股票市场价格中除去减少的部分，叫做除权。ex rights. When a joint-stock company issues bonus stock to its shareholders, the number of shares increases, but the real value of each share decreases, and the difference is deducted from the stock market price, hence the term.

【除息】chú//xī 股份公司因向股东分配股息、红利，每股股票的实际价值减少，需要从股票市场价格中除去减少的部分，叫做除息 ex dividend. When a joint-stock company allocates dividends and bonuses to its shareholders, the real value of each share decreases, and the difference is deducted from the market price of the stock, hence the term.

【处方药】chǔfāngyào 必须凭执业医师处方才可调配、购买的药品，须在医师指导下服用 prescription drug; prescription medicine; medicine that is available by doctor's prescription only and taken under doctor's instructions

【处警】chǔjǐng （公安部门）处理紧急或危险情况（of public security department）deal with emergencies and dangerous situations：及时～。Policemen arrived in time to deal with the emergency.

【触摸屏】chùmōpíng 在显示器屏幕上加一层感应膜，用手指或其他笔形物轻触屏幕就可以使电子计算机执行操作，这种屏幕叫触摸屏 touch screen; screen on a monitor that is covered with induction film, which on being touched with a finger or other pen-like object sets the computer into operation

【穿帮】chuānbāng 〈方 *dial.*〉露出破绽；被揭穿 give the game away; let the cat out of the bag; be exposed; reveal one's true colours：弄虚作假迟早要～。Acts of deceit will sooner or later be revealed.

【传感器】chuángǎnqì 指利用一定规律把被检测量转换成便于处理的其他物理量的器件 sensor; transducer; device that converts an amount of input energy to be tested into another form of physical quantity according to certain laws to facilitate the testing

【串案】chuàn'àn 同一系统或单位的人串通一起所作的案 conspiracy; case of crime committed by a number of people of the same affiliation or profession in close collaboration

【创业资金】chuàngyè zījīn 风险资金 start-up funds; risk capital; venture capital

【创意】chuàngyì ❶ 有创造性的想法、构思等 creative concept; original thinking and concept：颇具～ most original in concept | 这个设计格调单一，毫无～可言。The style of this design is insipid and lacks originality. ❷ 提出有创造性的想法、构思等 create a new concept; break fresh ground; be original in thinking and concept：这项活动由工会～发起。This activity was initiated by the trade union.

【词频】cípín 一定范围的语言材料中词的使用频率 frequency of a word's use within a defined scope of language

【磁卡】cíkǎ 表面带有磁性物质可存储信息的卡片，存储的信息可通过电子计算机等读取或处理 magcard; magnetic card; card that has a magnetized strip or surface on which data can be recorded and read or processed by a computer

【磁盘】cípán 表面带有磁性物质的圆盘形存储载体，是电子计算机存储信息的设备，分为硬磁盘和软磁盘两种 disk; diskette; magnetic disk; circular device with a magnetic coating on which information is stored for computer use; of two types: hard and floppy disks

【磁盘驱动器】cípán qūdòngqì 电子计算机中磁盘存储器的一部分，用来驱动磁盘稳速旋转，并控制磁头在盘面磁层上按一定的记录格式和编码方式记录和读取信息。分为软盘驱动器和硬盘驱动器等。disk drive; part of the computer that turns the disk in a steady run and controls the magnetic head to record and read, according to certain recording and coding formats, the information stored in the magnetic coating of the disk. A computer contains disk drives for floppy and hard disks.

【磁悬浮列车】cíxuánfú-lièchē 利用电磁感应产生的磁斥力使车辆悬浮在轨道上方并以电机驱动前进的列车，列车在全封闭的U型导槽内行驶。行驶阻力小，速度快，能源消耗少，无噪声，无污染，安全性强。magnetically levitated train; magnetic suspension train; train that is suspended over the rails by magnetic repulsion produced by electromagnetic induction, and driven by an electric locomotive in a closed, U-shaped conduit ferrule. The magnetic suspension train travels faster than the conventional train as it meets far lower air resistance, saves energy, and is noiseless, pollution-free, and safe.

【次声武器】cìshēng wǔqì 发出次声波来杀伤人的武器。次声波能引起人体内脏的共振，使内脏发生位移和形变，功能损坏，甚至造成人死亡。infrasonic weapon; device that sends out lethal infrasonic sound waves to cause the internal organs of the human body to vibrate, displacing, distorting and rupturing them, and even resulting in death

【蹿红】cuānhóng 迅速走红 meteoric rise to stardom; become a star overnight; become instantly popular:她一夜之间～歌坛。She shot to fame in the singing circles overnight.

【蹿升】cuānshēng 疾速上升 climb sharply; soar; rise quickly:股市～。The stock market index rose sharply.

【存盘】cún//pán 把电子计算机中的信息存储到磁盘上 save information on a disk

【存续】cúnxù 存在并持续 exist and continue:夫妻在婚姻关系～期间所得财产归夫妻双方共有。All property acquired for the duration of a marriage is shared by the husband and wife.

【错失】cuòshī ❶ 错过;失去 let sth. good slip through; lose:～良机 squander a good opportunity ❷ 差错;过失 mistake; slip; fault:他工作认真负责,没有发生过～。He is very conscientious and never makes mistakes in his work.

【错位】cuò // wèi [补义 new sense]〈比喻 *fig.*〉失去正常的或应有的状态 dislocation; displacement:名和利使他的荣辱观发生了～。Fame and wealth have distorted his views on honour and disgrace.

D

【搭车】dā//chē 〈比喻 *fig.*〉借做某事的便利做另外的事,从而得利 take advantage of sth.; do sth. on a pretext amd with gain in mind:～涨价 chain-reaction price rise

【打车】dǎ//chē 租用出租汽车;乘坐出租汽车 hail a taxi; take a taxi:时间太紧了,咱们打个车去吧。There's not much time left. Let's hail a taxi.

【打非】dǎfēi 指打击制作、出售非法出版物和音像制品的行为 crack down on illegal publications and the unlawful manufacturing and sale of video and audio products:扫黄～ crack down on pornography

【打拐】dǎguǎi 指打击拐卖人口的犯罪活动 crack down on abduction and trafficking of human beings

【打黑】dǎhēi 指打击具有黑社会性质的犯罪团伙 crack down on organized crime gangs

【打假】dǎjiǎ 指打击制造、出售假冒伪劣商品的行为 crack down on the manufacturing and sale of fake and shoddy merchandise

【打卡】dǎ//kǎ 工作人员上下班时把考勤卡放在磁卡机上记录下到达和离开单位的时间叫打卡 punch the clock; record the time that one starts or finishes work by putting a card into a magnetic-card machine

【打拼】dǎpīn 〈方 *dial.*〉用力去干;拼搏 go all out; try one's utmost to do sth.:奋力～ do all one can | 为生活而～ try one's utmost to eke out a living

【打私】dǎsī 指打击走私、贩私活动 crack down on smuggling and sale of contraband

【打压】dǎyā 打击压制 combat and suppress:在对方无情的～下,他终于屈服了。He eventually succumbed to the ruthless pressure exerted by his rival.

【大本】dàběn 大学本科的简称 abbr. for 大学本科 dàxué běnkē

【大牌】dàpái ❶ 名气大、水平高、实力强的人(多指体育界、文艺界的)(usu. of people in sports and arts circles) bigwig; celebrity; personage; person of exceptional fame and ability ❷ 名气大、水平高、实力强的 having a high reputation and unusual ability:～球星 famous football or basketball star | ～歌星 famous pop singer | ～俱乐部 prestigious club

【大盘】dàpán 指证券市场交易的整体行情 overall situation in the securities market

【大片】dàpiàn 指投资大、制作成本高的电影片,多为题材重大、影响面广并由著名影星主演的 blockbuster film; big-budget film with a highly dramatic theme in which famous film stars act, and which is a huge success,:进口～ imported blockbuster film | 国产～ home-made big-budget film

【大气污染】dàqì wūrǎn 指大气中有害气体和悬浮颗粒物所造成的环境污染。核爆炸后散落的放射性物质、化学毒剂、工业废气、扬尘等都是污染大气的物质。air pollution; atmospheric pollution caused by hazardous gascs and suspended particles such as the scattered radioactive substances after a nuclear explosion, chemical toxins, industrial exhaust gases, drifting dust, etc.

【代培】dàipéi 学校等替出资单位培养(专业人员) student training course at a school or institute under the sponsorship of an organization:～生 student recruited or trained by an organization or work unit which pays relevant training expenses | 这所大学先后为企业～了二百多名学员。This university has trained more than 200 students for enterprises.

【代位继承】dàiwèi jìchéng 法定继承人先于被继承人死亡或丧失继承权时,由其晚辈直系血亲按照继承顺序继承 subrogation inheritance; instance when a legal heir to an estate dies or loses his right of inheritance, the next blood relative in line inherits

【带宽】dàikuān 频带的宽度。在通信中,指某一频带最高频率和最低频率的差(单位是赫兹);在电子计算机网络中,指数据传输能力的大小(单位是比特/秒) band width; numerical difference between the upper and lower frequencies of a frequency band in telecommunications (in units of hertz); data-transmitting capability in a computer network (in units of bits per second)

【待岗】dàigǎng (下岗人员)等待得到工作岗位 (of lay-off workers) wait for work opportunities; wait for a job; wait to be re-employed; be unemployed

【待聘】dàipìn 等待聘用 wait to be employed; wait for appointment or post; wait for work opportunities; wait for a job:~人员 unemployed people; people who have not signed a contract with any company|单位裁减编制后,有二十多名干部~。More than 20 clerks were laid off after their work unit was streamlined.

【担纲】dāngāng 指在艺术表演或体育比赛中担任主角或主力,泛指在工作中承担重任 play a leading role in an artistic performance or be the main player in a sports competition; (in a broad sense) play an important role in one's work; be the mainstay:这部影片由著名演员~。The leading roles in the film are played by famous actors.|设计方案由享有盛誉的建筑师~。Renowned architects have played a leading role in the design.

【单身贵族】dānshēn guìzú 指独身的成年人(多指比较年轻而且各方面条件比较优越的)(usu. of a relatively young and successful person) eligible bachelor; unmarried adult

【淡出】dànchū ❶影视片的画面由清晰明亮逐渐变得模糊暗淡,以至完全消失,是摄影方法造成的一种效果,表示剧情发展中一个段落的结束 fade-out; (in motion pictures or television) gradual disappearance of a scene, a cinematographic effect used to indicate the end of a scene or story ❷〈比喻 *fig.*〉逐渐退出(某一领域、范围) fade away; gradually retreat (from a field or circle):~演艺界 fade away from performing circles|~社会活动 fade out of social activity

【淡入】dànrù ❶影视片的画面由黑暗模糊逐渐变得清晰明亮,以至完全显露,是摄影方法造成的一种效果,表示剧情发展中一个段落的开始 fade-in; (in motion pictures or television) gradual appearance of a scene, a cinematographic effect used to indicate the beginning of a story ❷〈比喻 *fig.*〉逐渐进入(某一领域、范围)fade-in; gradually enter (a field or circle)

【淡市】dànshì 交易清淡的市场形势(跟'旺市'相对 as opposed to 'brisk market') slack market:中式快餐在~中显示了强大的生命力。Chinese-style fast food has emerged as a vital force in a slack market.

【当红】dānghóng (演员等)正走红 (performers) be in the height of one's popularity:~艺人 popular performer|~歌星 popular singing star

【档期】dàngqī 指影视片上演或播出所占的时间段 (of films or television programmes) slot; time or season to be shown:排定~ fix the slot of time to show or air a programme|延误~ miss a showing season because of delay|春节期间是贺岁片的最佳放映~。The Spring Festival is the best period for showing a New Year film.

【导播】dǎobō ❶组织和指导广播或电视节目的播出工作 organize and direct radio or television broadcasting:~任务 task of organizing and directing a broadcast|~节目 organize and direct programme broadcasts ❷担任导播工作的人 director of broadcasting

【倒计时】dàojìshí 从未来的某一时点往现在计算时间,用来表示距离某一期限还有多少时间(多含有时间越来越少,越来越紧迫的意思) count-down; counting off, in reverse order, of units of time on schedule (to show the urgency of an operation):~牌 count-down billboard|工程已进入~阶段。The project has entered the count-down stage.

【盗猎】dàoliè 非法捕猎 poaching; illegal hunting:禁止~国家保护动物。The hunting of animals under state protection is prohibited.

【盗印】dàoyìn 未经版权所有者同意而非法印制(出版物) (of publication) pirate; publish or reproduce without authorization:~畅销书 pirate a best-seller

【灯饰】dēngshì 用灯具做成的装饰;具有装饰作用的灯具 decorations comprising lamps; decorative lamps:绚丽的~美化了城市夜景。Bright and colourful lamps have beautified the night skyline of the city.

【灯箱】dēngxiāng 用玻璃等制成的、里面装有电灯的箱式标牌或广告设备 illuminated advertisement; box-shaped placard or advertisement made of glass incorporating electric or neon lights

【登陆】dēnglù [补义 new sense]〈比喻 *fig.*〉商品等打进某地市场 (of a commodity) enter the market of an area or region:这种新型空调已经在上海市场~。This new-style air-conditioner has landed on the Shanghai market.

【邓小平理论】Dèng Xiǎopíng Lǐlùn 马克思列

宁主义的基本原理同当代中国实践和时代特征相结合而形成的思想体系，是以邓小平为代表的中国共产党人在社会主义建设新时期对毛泽东思想的继承和发展，它阐明了建设有中国特色的社会主义的路线、方针、政策，是当代中国的马克思主义，是中国共产党集体智慧的结晶。Deng Xiaoping Theory; ideological system that combines the basic principles of Marxism-Leninism with the practice and zeitgeist of contemporary China. It is the inheritance and development of Mao Zedong Thought in the new era of socialist construction by the Chinese Communists represented by Deng Xiaoping. Expounding the line, principles, and policies for building socialism with Chinese characteristics, the Deng Xiaoping Theory is the Marxism of contemporary China, and a crystallization of the collective wisdom of the Chinese Communist Party.

【低谷】dīgǔ 〈比喻 *fig.*〉事物运行过程中低落或低迷的阶段 doldrums; low ebb; stage in which a matter is in decline, decreasing or weakening：用电～ power consumption hitting an all-time low | 经济开始走出～。The economy has begun to emerge from its low ebb.

【低龄】dīlíng 年龄较小的（就一般标准来说）(of age) juvenile; minor：～犯罪案件 case of juvenile delinquency | ～老人（指六十岁至七十岁的老人）junior old population (senior citizens aged between 60 and 70)

【低迷】dīmí 低落，多形容经济萧条，不景气 (oft. of an economic depression) sluggish; slumping：销售～ sluggish sales | ～的市场 recessed market

【底线】dǐxiàn ［补义 new sense］最低的标准、条件、限度 bottom line; minimum standard, conditions or limit：道德～ lowest permissible level of virtue | 谈判的～ bottom line for negotiations

【地板革】dìbǎngé 铺地面用的人造革，有各种图案花纹，坚固耐磨 plastic flooring; patterned artificial leather for flooring that stands tear and wear

【地板砖】dìbǎnzhuān 用来铺室内地面的地砖 tiles for indoor flooring

【地价】dìjià 指极低的价格 bottom price; minimum price：卖主要的是天价，买主给的是～。The seller asks an exorbitant price, while the buyer makes a rock-bottom offer.

【地量】dìliàng 指最低的数量 lowest amount：昨天成交量已减少至二十八亿元，接近年内～二十五亿元。Yesterday's turnover plummeted to 2.8 billion yuan, approaching the year's all-time low at 2.5 billion yuan.

【地球村】dìqiúcūn 随着科学技术的进步和交通、信息业的发展，地球上生活的人类感到彼此的距离大大缩短，地球似乎就像一个村庄那样联系紧密，所以把地球叫做地球村 global village; progress in science and technology and developments in communications and the information industry has had the effect of shortening the distance between various parts of the globe, inspiring the feeling that people worldwide are living in the same village, the global village

【地税】dìshuì 地方税的简称 abbr. for 地方税 dìfāngshuì

【地缘】dìyuán 由地理位置上的联系而形成的关系 geo-; relations formed through geographical links：～政治 geo-politics | ～文化 geo-culture

【地砖】dìzhuān 专门用来铺地的砖，多为方形，表面有色彩和图案，品种较多 floor tile; indoor tiles, generally square, in a good variety of patterns and colours

【第二课堂】dì èr kètáng ❶ 指有利于学生全面发展的有组织的课外活动 second classroom; organized extracurricular activities that are beneficial to the overall development of students：开辟～，让学生通过社会实践增长才干。Open a second classroom for students to enhance their abilities through social practice. ❷ 指职业教育或成人教育 vocational education; adult education

【第三状态】dì sān zhuàngtài 亚健康状态 third state; sub-healthy state; condition where there is no specific illness, but tiredness and depression are experienced

【第四宇宙速度】dì sì yǔzhòu sùdù 宇宙速度的一级，预计物体具有 110—120 公里/秒的速度时，就可以脱离银河系而进入其他星系，这个速度叫做第四宇宙速度 fourth cosmic velocity; galaxy exit velocity; grade in cosmic velocity to be reached when travelling at a speed of 110-120 km. per second, speed which makes it possible to leave the Milky Way and travel to other galaxies

【第一夫人】dì yī fū・rén 某些国家称国家最高领导人的妻子 First Lady; wife of the top leader of a country

【点击】diǎnjī 进行计算机操作时，移动鼠标，把鼠标指针指向要操作的地方并用手指敲击鼠标上的键 hit; click; when using a computer, move the cursor to a point and click the mouse

【点评】diǎnpíng ❶ 评点；评论 make comments on; discuss：佳作～ commentary on an excellent work | 最后专家进行了精彩的～。The expert finally gave a brilliant and illuminating commentary. ❷ 点评的话或文字 comment (spoken or written)：每篇文选的后面都附有～。At the end of every article there is a comment.

【电磁炮】diàncípào 利用电磁力发射炮弹的装置，主要由能源、加速器和开关三个部分组成。

炮弹射出的速度快，射程远，命中率高，安全性和隐蔽性好。electromagnetic artillery; electromagnetic-powered shell-launching device comprising three parts: the energy source, accelerator and switch. Shells thus launched are marked for their high speed, long range, accuracy, and a high degree of safety and concealment.

【电话卡】diànhuàkǎ 指打电话付费用的电话信用卡、磁卡、智能卡等 phone card; calling card; magnetic card or intelligence-capacity card used to dial and pay for telephone calls

【电离层暴】diànlícéngbào 电离层发生急剧而不规则变化的现象，是太阳表面耀斑异常活跃时发出大量带电粒子流扰动电离层引起的。发生时往往持续几小时到几天，影响短波通信正常进行，甚至造成通信中断。ionospheric storm; phenomenon of rapid and irregular changes caused to the ionosphere by the massive flow of charged particles released by abnormal solar flare activity on the sun's surface. An ionospheric storm may last several hours or days, and affects, sometimes to the extent of interrupting normal short-wave telecommunications.

【电子出版物】diànzǐ chūbǎnwù 需要通过电子计算机或其他电子设备阅读的以光盘、磁盘等为载体的出版物 electronic publication; publications carried on optical or magnetic disks, to be read on computers or other electronic devices

【电子函件】diànzǐ hánjiàn same as 电子邮件 diànzǐ yóujiàn

【电子货币】diànzǐ huòbì 银行发行的一种具有消费信用功能的电子磁卡，可以通过电子计算机网络系统转账结算、存取现款等 electronic currency; electronic magnetic card issued by banks that enables the consumer to transfer or settle accounts and deposit or withdraw cash through a computerized network

【电子商务】diànzǐ shāngwù 通过互联网构拟的空间和媒体，以数据的形式表达各种信息而进行的商务活动 electronic commerce; e-commerce; commercial activities transacted over the Internet, with information expressed in data form

【电子信箱】diànzǐ xìnxiāng 在互联网设置的电子邮政计算机系统中，用户拥有的一定的信息存储空间，叫做电子信箱。用户使用密码打开电子信箱，进行电子邮件的收发、编辑等各种操作。electronic mailbox; individualized information storage space in an electronic postal system on the Internet accessed with a password, on which operations such as receiving, dispatching, and editing can be conducted. also 电子邮箱 diànzǐ yóuxiāng

【电子眼】diànzǐyǎn 电视监控摄像器的俗称 electronic eye; popular name for television monitoring camera：重要交通路口都安装了～。Electronic eyes are installed at major traffic intersections.

【电子邮件】diànzǐ yóujiàn 指通过互联网传递的邮件，即用户之间通过互联网发出或收到的信息 electronic mail; e-mail; mails transmitted over the Internet; namely, information dispatched or received by users on the Internet. also 电子函件 diànzǐ hánjiàn

【电子邮箱】diànzǐ yóuxiāng same as 电子信箱 diànzǐ xìnxiāng

【跌幅】diēfú （物价等）下跌的幅度（of prices, etc.）margin of drop：昨日股市暴跌，～达8%。Yesterday saw a steep fall in share prices, with a drop of 8 per cent.

【跌停板】diētíngbǎn ☞ 涨停板 zhǎngtíngbǎn on p. 2641

【丁克家庭】dīngkè jiātíng 指夫妇都有收入并且不打算生育孩子的家庭 DINK（abbr. for 'double income, no kids'）; family of a married couple who both earn a lot of money but have no intention to have children

【盯防】dīngfáng 球类比赛中指紧跟着不放松地防守（in ball games）close-marking defence; man-for-man defence; method of defence entailing keeping close to（marking) an opponent：重点～对方的前锋 closely marking the forward of the opposing team

【顶风】dǐng//fēng ［补义 new sense］〈比喻 *fig.*〉公然违犯正在大力推行的法令、法规、政策等 go against the wind; brazenly flout a decree, law or policy that is being vigorously implemented：～违纪 violate discipline while discipline is being tightened up｜～作案 commit a crime during the height of a crackdown on crime

【顶级】dǐngjí 最高级别的；水平最高的 top-notch; first-class：～品牌 top-notch brand-name｜～餐厅 top-of-the-line restaurant｜～球员 top-notch ball players

【定岗】dìng//gǎng 确定工作岗位 fix job and responsibility：每个车间都要～到人。Jobs and responsibilities should be fixed for everyone in every workshop.

【动能武器】dòngnéng wǔqì 通过发射能够制导的高速弹头，以其整体或爆炸碎片击毁目标的武器。主要用来拦截弹道导弹和攻击军用卫星。动能武器的一些先进技术，也可用于某些常规武器。kinetic-energy weapon; weapon that launches high-speed guided warheads containing metal balls, mainly used to intercept ballistic missiles or attack military satellites. Some of the advanced technology for kinetic-energy weapons can also be applied to conventional weapons.

【动迁】dòngqiān 因原建筑物拆除或翻建而迁

移到别处 mobilize-evacuate; relocate; mobilization of residents into evacuation from dwellings to be demolished or reconstructed:～户 relocated household|这次拓宽马路,要～五百多户居民。In this street-widening project, more than 500 households will be relocated.

【动销】dòngxiāo 开始销售 begin to sell:刚过春节,空调就已～。Sales of air-conditioners began soon after the Spring Festival.

【动因】dòngyīn 动机;原因 motive; cause:创作～ creative motivation|贪欲是她作案的直接～。It was greed that motivated her to commit this crime.

【动作片】dòngzuòpiàn 以打斗场面为主的故事片 action film

【豆腐渣工程】dòu·fuzhā gōngchéng 〈比喻 *fig.*〉质量很差、极不坚固的建筑工程 bean-dregs project; construction project using poor quality materials

【豆奶】dòunǎi 以黄豆、牛奶为主要原料制成的饮品 soyamilk; drink made of soya beans and cow's milk

【督察警】dūchájǐng 对公安机关及人民警察现场执法、值勤等活动进行监督的警察 supervisory police; policeman that supervises public security organs and the police in law enforcement and performance of other duties

【毒案】dú'àn 涉及毒品犯罪的案件 criminal narcotics cases

【毒犯】dúfàn 制造、运输、贩卖毒品的罪犯 drug criminal; criminal that makes or traffics in narcotics:严厉打击～ crack down on drug criminals

【毒贩】dúfàn 贩卖毒品的人 drug trafficker

【毒资】dúzī 用来购买毒品的钱;贩毒所得的钱 drug-capital; money earned from drug trafficking or used to buy drugs:公安机关破获一起贩毒案,缴获～近五十万元。The public security organ has cracked a narcotics case and captured drug capital of nearly 500,000 yuan.

【读秒】dú//miǎo 围棋比赛中指某方用完自由支配的时间后,必须在很短时间(一般为一分钟,快棋多为30秒)内走一步棋,此时裁判员开始随时口报所用秒数,如超时则判负 countdown; compulsory time left for play; in a match of go, when a side has used up his or her time, moves must be made in a very short period of time (in general one minute, and for a faster game, 30 seconds). The referee then starts to count the seconds allowed, and the side exceeding the time limit is judged the loser:白方在～声的催促下出现了失误。Made nervous by the sound of seconds being counted off, the white counter side made a bad move. ◇高考一天天地临近,已进入最后的～阶段。The countdown to the college entrance examinations has begun.

【度假村】dùjiàcūn 一种供人们旅游度假居住的场所,多建在风景优美的地方 holiday resort; vacation village; place where vacationers go to spend their holidays, usu. in a scenic spot

【短线】duǎnxiàn [补义 new sense]经过较短的时间即可产生效益的(跟'长线'相对 as compared with 'long-term') short-term; (of investment) capable of producing quick results:～投资 short-term investment

【对手戏】duìshǒuxì 戏剧或影视片中两个演员相互配合表演的情节、内容 perform together; two actors that perform in a drama, film or TV play, portraying a couple or two characters that have frequent exchanges of dialogue:这两位影星在多部影片中演过～。These two stars have performed together in many films.

【蹲守】dūnshǒu 隐蔽在某处守候,多指公安人员隐蔽在暗处等待犯罪嫌疑人等出现以便抓捕 undercover; (of policemen) conceal their whereabouts and lie in wait to apprehend a criminal suspect:连夜～,抓获贩毒团伙。The police spent the night undercover, waiting to arrest the narcotics traffickers.

【多动症】duōdòngzhèng 一种儿童轻微脑功能失调的疾病,表现为注意力不能集中,异常好动,自我控制能力差,但没有明显的智力障碍。到青春期症状一般可自行缓解。hyperkinesis; hyperactivity disorder; disease of restlessness or excessive movement in children with a minimal brain dysfunction. Sufferers cannot focus their attention, are restless and lack self-control, but suffer no evident intellectual impediment, and in general the symptoms disappear at the onset of adolescence.

【多媒体】duōméitǐ 可用电子计算机处理的多种信息载体的统称,包括文本、声音、图形、动画、图像等 multi-media; carrier of many kinds of information that can be processed by electronic computer, including text, sound, graphics, animation, images, etc.

【多米诺骨牌】duōmǐnuò gǔpái 18世纪中叶出现在欧洲的一种用来游戏或赌博的长方形骨牌。把骨牌按一定距离竖立起来排成行,只要碰倒一张,后面的便会一张碰一张地相继倒下。后来把连锁反应称为多米诺骨牌效应或骨牌效应。domino; one of a set small, rectangular block of wood or plastic with different numbers of spots on, used in a game, sometimes to gamble, that first appeared in mid-18th century Europe. They can be laid flat, or set on end when, if evenly placed in erect rows, the first one knocked down, has a knock-on effect that makes all the others topple. This chain reaction has become known as the domino effect.

E

【额度】édù 规定的数额 quota; prescribed amount or proportion:贷款～ loan limit|融资～ financing limit

【厄尔尼诺现象】è'ěrnínuò xiànxiàng 位于赤道附近东太平洋的秘鲁洋流水温反常增高、鱼群大量死亡的现象。一般出现于圣诞节前后。每隔几年发生一次,海水表层增温范围扩大,持续时间长,对全球气候产生重大影响。El Niño phenomenon; phenomenon that occurs once every few years around Christmas in Peru in the eastern Pacific Ocean near the equator, when an abnormal rise in the temperature of ocean currents caused the death of large quantities of fish. With the affected ocean water surface expanding and the duration long lasting, the El Niño phenomenon exerts a major impact on the global climate.

【恩格尔系数】Ēngé'ěr xìshù 统计学中指家庭用于食品的支出与家庭消费总支出的比值。其数值越小说明生活越富裕,数值越大说明生活水平越低。因德国经济学家和统计学家恩格尔(Ernst Engel)最先提出而得名。Engel coefficient; (in statistics) ratio of expenses on food against the total a family spends on consumption. The smaller the figure, the wealthier the family, and vice versa; named after German economist and statistician Ernst Engel, who first devised it.

【二噁英】èr'èyīng 一类有毒的含氯有机化合物,有强烈的致畸和致癌作用。在垃圾焚烧、汽车尾气排放、纸浆漂白和金属热加工过程中都可能产生。进入人体的主要途径是饮食,尤其是受污染的肉类和乳制品。dioxin; toxic organic compound containing chlorine, which can cause malformation and cancer, produced by burning garbage, automobile exhaust emission, bleaching of paper pulp, and heat treatment of metals. It enters the human body mainly through food and drink, particularly contaminated meat and dairy products.

【二级市场】èr jí shìchǎng 指对已经售出的证券、商品房等再进行交易的市场 secondary market; market on which second-hand securities or commodity housing are traded

F

【罚单】fádān 罚款的通知单 ticket; notice for payment of fine:交通违规～ ticket; summons issued for a traffic or parking violation

【法定继承】fǎdìng jìchéng 按照法律规定的继承人范围、继承顺序、遗产分配原则继承死者遗产 inheritance through operation of the law; statutory succession; inheritance of the estate of the deceased according to legal stipulations in relation to the scope of inheritors, order of succession and principle of legacy distribution

【法人股】fǎréngǔ 企业法人或具有法人资格的单位、团体以其合法的资产向上市公司投资形成的股份 shares of a legal person; shares that constitute an enterprise, unit or organization as a legal person and its legitimate investment in a listed company

【反超】fǎnchāo 体育比赛中比分由落后转为领先叫反超 turn the tide; turning defeat into victory in a sports event:中国队在先失一球的情况下,频频发动攻势,以 2 比 1 将比分～。After losing one score, the Chinese team persistently attacked the opposing team's goal, finally turning the tide after tipping the score to 2∶1.

【反厄尔尼诺现象】fǎn'è'ěrnínuò xiànxiàng ☞ 拉尼娜现象 lānínà xiànxiàng on p.1708

【反讽】fǎnfěng 从反面讽刺;用反语进行讽刺 sarcastic retort:文章中充满了强烈的～意味。The article is strongly satirical.

【反腐倡廉】fǎn fǔ chàng lián 反对腐败,提倡廉洁 combat corruption and advocate an honest, aboveboard government

【反观】fǎnguān 反过来看;从相反的角度来观察 conversely; observed from an opposite angle:表面上看轰轰烈烈,～效果,却未必好。Superficially it appears spectacular, but conversely, it does not necessarily have a good effect.

【反季节】fǎnjìjié 不合当前季节的 out of season:～蔬菜 vegetables out of season|～销售 out of season sale; also 反季 fǎnjì

【反粒子】fǎnlìzǐ 正电子、反质子、反中子、反中微子、反介子、反超子等粒子的统称。反粒子与所对应的粒子在质量、自旋、平均寿命和磁矩大小上都相同;如果带电,两者所带电量相等而符号相反,磁矩和自旋的取向关系也相反。反粒子与所对应的粒子相遇就发生湮没而转变为别的粒子。anti-particle; any constituent particle of antimatter; general term for positive electron, anti-proton, anti-neutron, anti-neutrino, anti-mesotron, anti-hyperon, etc. An anti-particle and its corresponding particle are the same in quality, rotation, average life span and magnetic torque. When charged, the two have the same electrical charge in reverse directions, and this also applies to magnetic torque and rotation. When an anti-particle and its corresponding particle meet, they combine and become other particles.

【反倾销】fǎnqīngxiāo 国际贸易中,为保护本国利益,用高额征税的办法反对外国向本国倾销商品 anti-dumping; protect its interests in international trade, a country levies heavy taxes on the foreign goods being dumped

【反物质】fǎnwùzhì 物理学上指原子核由反质子和反中子组成的带负电荷的物质。反核子(反质子和反中子)组成反原子核,反原子核和正电子组成反原子,各种反原子组成各种反物质(phys.) anti-matter; form of matter in which the electrical charge or other property of each constituent particle is the reverse of that in the usual matter of the universe. The anti-nucleon (anti-proton and anti-neutron) forms an anti-atomic nucleus, the anti-atomic nucleus and positive electron form an anti-atom, and various kinds of anti-atoms form various anti-matter.

【返岗】fǎn//gǎng (下岗人员)返回原来的工作岗位 (of laid-off employees) return to original job:这家企业有四百多名下岗工人重新～。In this enterprise more than 400 laid-off workers have been reinstated in their original positions.

【返贫】fǎnpín 返回原来的贫困状态 slide back into poverty:确保脱贫户不再～。Families that have quitted poverty must have some guarantee that they will not be forced back into it.

【犯罪嫌疑人】fànzuì xiányírén 在法院判决之前,涉嫌有犯罪行为的人称为犯罪嫌疑人 criminal suspect; before the court makes its judgement, a person under suspicion of having committed a crime is referred to as a criminal suspect

【贩黄】fànhuáng 贩卖黄色书刊、录像带、光盘等 sell and distribute pornography in the form of magazines, books, videos, VCDs, etc.

【贩私】fànsī 贩卖走私物品 sell smuggled goods:严厉打击走私、～活动。Severely crack down on the smuggling and sale of smuggled goods.

【方程式赛车】fāngchéngshì sàichē 汽车比赛的一种。所用车的长、宽、重以及轮胎直径等数据都有严格规定,其复杂和精确程度就像数学方程式一样,因此得名。方程式赛车分为一、二、三级,其中一级速度最快。formula auto racing; a kind of car race that has strict stipulations as to the participating motor vehicles' length, width, weight, and tire diameter, the complexity and required accuracy of which resemble a formula, hence the name. Formula auto racing is divided into formulas one, two and three, formula one being the fastest.

【防火墙】fánghuǒqiáng [补义 new sense]指两个网络之间设立的安全设施,可以防止未经授权的访问,保护硬件和软件的安全 fire wall; safety facility between two networks to prevent unauthorized entry and ensure the safety of hardware and software

【防伪】fángwěi 防止伪造 counterfeit prevention:～标志 proof of authenticity

【防卫过当】fángwèi guòdàng 正当防卫明显超过必要限度造成重大损害的行为。我国刑法规定,防卫过当应负刑事责任,但应减轻或免除处罚。excessive defence; act in undue self-defence; act of self-defence that exceeds a reasonable limit and causes serious harm. According to Chinese criminal law, excessive defence is a criminal act, but punishment is generally either reduced or exempted.

【房车】fángchē ❶ 一种汽车,车厢大而长,像房子,配有家具,并设有厨房、浴室和卫生间,能提供基本生活条件。多用于长途旅行。caravan; tailer; large, long motor vehicle equipped with a kitchen and bathroom, that provides basic living conditions, mostly used on long journeys. ❷〈方 *dial.*〉指豪华的轿车 limousine

【房型】fángxíng 户型 layout of a house

【房展】fángzhǎn 房地产公司等单位举办的所售房屋模型、图片等的展览 housing exhibition; exhibition of models or pictures of houses for sale, held by real estate companics, etc.:看～ visit a housing exhibition

【仿生建筑】fǎngshēng jiànzhù 模仿某些生物的结构和形态而获得所期望的优良性能的建筑。如模仿蜂巢结构的墙壁,大大减轻了建筑物的自重;模仿蛋壳结构的屋顶,虽仅几厘米厚,却能承受风吹雨打和积雪的压力。Bionic architecture; architecture on the principle of imitating the structure and form of certain organisms so as to produce buildings with all the anticipated fine functions and qualities. For instance, a wall modelled on a honeycomb greatly reduces the weight of a building, and a roof imitating the structure of an eggshell, though only a few cm. thick, is capable of weathering heavy winds, rain and snow.

【仿真】fǎngzhēn ❶ 指利用模型模仿实际系统进行实验研究 emulate; experiment with a model that simulates the real thing ❷ 从外形上模仿逼真的 simulation; have or take on the external appearance: ～手枪 simulated pistol

【放射性污染】fàngshèxìng wūrǎn 指人类活动排放的放射性物质所造成的环境污染。各种放射性元素都是其污染物。radioactive pollution; radioactive contamination comprising various radioactive elements; environmental pollution caused by the discharge of radioactive matter in industrial processes

【放水】fàng//shuǐ 指体育比赛中串通作弊,一方故意输给另一方 disembogue; discharge water at the mouth of a river; (fig.) collusion in a sports competition, when one side intentionally loses to the other

【飞碟】fēidié 不明飞行物。因早期报道的不明飞行物形状像圆形碟子,所以叫飞碟 flying saucer; UFO (unidentified flying object). The appearance of the first UFO sighted was compared to a saucer, hence the name.

【非处方药】fēichǔfāngyào 不需凭执业医师处方就可自行购买并按照药品说明书使用的药品 over-the-counter medicine (OTC); nonprescription medicine; medicine that is purchasable and used according to indications on its container, rather than being obtainable on prescription by certified practitioners

【非礼】fēilǐ [补义 new sense]〈方 *dial.*〉指调戏、猥亵(妇女) indecent assault; take liberties with (a woman); behave indecently towards (a woman)

【非再生资源】fēizàishēng zīyuán 不可更新资源 unrenewable resource

【肥皂剧】féizàojù 某些国家称一种题材轻松的电视连续剧。因早期常在中间插播肥皂之类的生活用品广告而得名。soap opera; serialized television drama chiefly characterized by stock domestic situations imbued with melodrama and romance, called ‘soap opera’ because in its early days it was oft. interspersed with advertisements for soaps and other daily-use articles

【分保】fēnbǎo 再保险 re-insurance

【分税制】fēnshuìzhì 根据中央政府和地方政府的职能和事权范围,按税种、税源将全部税收划分为中央税、地方税和中央地方共享税的制度 system of tax division; system of dividing revenues from taxes between the central and local governments, where they are designated, according to type, source, function and administrative scope, into as well as taxes jointly shared by a locality and the central authorities

【粉领】fěnlǐng 某些国家和地区指从事秘书、打字等工作的职业妇女 pink-collar; professional women working as secretaries or typists; also 粉红领 fěnhónglǐng

【风景线】fēngjǐngxiàn 供游览的风景优美的狭长地带,多比喻某种景观、景象 scenic vista; narrow strip of area of beautiful scenery; (oft. fig.) a feast to the eyes; sight; scene: 街头秧歌表演已成为都市里的一道亮丽的～。Street *yanggo* performances are a feast to the eyes in the metropolis.

【风险资金】fēngxiǎn zījīn 投资者协助具有专门科技知识而缺乏资金的人创业、并承担失败风险的资金,特点是甘冒风险而追求较高的投资回报 risk capital; risk assets; venture capital; funds invested or available for investment, at considerable risk of loss, in potentially highly profitable enterprises; also 创业资金 chuàngyè zījīn

【封笔】fēngbǐ 指作家、画家、书法家等不再从事创作活动 seal off one's writing or painting brush; (of a writer, painter or calligrapher) quit creative activity once and for all: ～之作 the last piece of work; swan song|老画家由于健康原因已正式～。Due to poor health, the veteran painter has officially announced his retirement.

【封杀】fēngshā same as 封禁 fēngjìn ②: ～黄色刊物 prohibit pornography|一部优秀作品竟被～。An excellent piece of work has been unexpectedly banned.

【疯牛病】fēngniúbìng 牛的一种传染病,最早发现于英国。病牛的中枢神经系统受到侵害,出现狂躁不安,步态不稳,痉挛,心跳迟缓,极度消瘦等症状,直至死亡。对人有传染作用。BSE; bovine spongiform encephalopathy; mad cow disease; infectious brain disease of cows first found in Britain, that attacks the infected beast's central nervous system, with symptoms including hyperactivity, unsteady gait, fits, slow pulse rate, pathological emaciation, and eventual death. BSE can be transmitted to human beings through eating the meat of an infected cow.

【峰会】fēnghuì 高峰会议,一般指首脑会议 summit; summit meeting; meeting of heads of states

【峰位】fēngwèi 最高点的位置 peak; highest point; all-time high: 价格已经接近历史～。The price has approached a record high.

【峰值】fēngzhí 最高点的数值 peak value: 成交量达到八百亿元的～。Turnover has

reached a peak of 80 billion yuan.

【孵化器】fūhuàqì 〈比喻 *fig.*〉担负培育中小科技创新企业、加速高新技术成果转化以及对传统企业进行信息化改造任务的企业 incubator; enterprise whose task is to nurture innovative technological enterprises of medium and small sizes, accelerate commercialization of new and high-tech research results, and upgrade informatization in traditional enterprises

【服务器】fúwùqì 在网络环境或分布式处理环境中,为用户提供服务的计算机。可分为访问服务器、文件服务器、数据库服务器、通信服务器和应用服务器等。server; computer that provides service within a networking environment or distributive processing, including access server, file server, databank server, communications server and applications server

【氟利昂】fúlì'áng same as 氟氯烷 fúlǜwán

【氟氯烷】fúlǜwán 有机化合物的一类,含有氟和氯,常见的有 CCl_3F、CCl_2F_2,都是无色、无味、无毒的气体,容易液化。通常用作冷冻剂和分散剂,对大气臭氧层有破坏作用,国际上已规定控制并逐渐停止氟氯烷的生产和使用 chlorinated and fluorinated hydrocarbon; colourless, tasteless, non-toxic, and easily liquefied, organic compound containing fluorine and chlorine, with common varieties including CCl_3F and CCl_2F_2, generally used as refrigerants and solvents. According to an international convention, production and usage of freon are to be controlled and eventually banned because it is harmful to the ozone layer. also 氟利昂 fúlì'áng

【浮出水面】fú chū shuǐmiàn 从水下漂浮到水面上来 emerge through the water surface; 〈比喻 *fig.*〉事物显露出来 become evident: 被假象掩盖起来的矛盾逐渐～。The contradiction that had been hidden by a facade is gradually emerging.

【辅路】fǔlù 为缓解干道的运输压力而修建的较窄的辅助性道路,多位于干道的两旁并有隔离带与干道隔开 auxiliary lane; narrow roads used to alleviate traffic congestion, mainly flanking the main road and separated from it by a belt

【辅修】fǔxiū 大学生在学习本专业课程以外,利用课余时间学习第二专业的课程叫辅修 minor (compare major); selected subject that university students take in their spare time, in addition to their major subject

【负案】fù'àn 作案后被公安机关立案(多指尚未被抓获的) filed criminal case; criminal whose record is on file at the public security organ but who has not yet been arrested: 凶手～在逃。The murderer whose case is on police file is still at large.

【负增长】fùzēngzhǎng 指增长率为负数,即在规模、数量等方面有所减少或下降 negative growth; decrease; negative growth rate; reduction or drop in scale, amount, etc.

【复读】fùdú 中小学毕业生因未能考取高一级的学校而在原一级学校重新学习,以待来年再考 re-taking of a year or grade; (of a graduate of primary or middle school who fails to move on to the next stage) stay in the same grade for another year so as to be able to re-take the entrance examination the following year: ～生 re-take student | 高考～班 re-take class for college entrance examinations

【复岗】fù//gǎng (下岗人员)恢复原来的工作岗位 (laid-off employees) return to original job position: ～通知 notification to return to a job

【复合材料】fùhé cáiliào 两种或两种以上物理、化学性质不同的材料,按所设计的形式、比例、分布,由人工组合而成的材料。这种材料具有比单一材料更好的性能。compound material; artificial material formed by combining two or more materials of different physical or chemical properties in accordance with a specified form, proportion and distribution, which functions more efficiently than a single material

【复机】fù//jī 给通过寻呼机呼叫自己的人回电话 answer a pager's call; answer a call made to a pager: 刚呼过他,他还没有～。I called his pager a moment ago, but he has not yet answered.

【复牌】fùpái 指某种被停牌的证券恢复交易 resumption of a transaction; transaction of certain securities resumed after a period of suspension

【富营养化】fùyíngyǎnghuà 指湖泊、水库、河口、海湾等流动缓慢的水域里,生物营养物质(如氮、磷)不断积累,含量过多。富营养化使藻类等水生生物大量繁殖,水质污染,水体变色,鱼虾死亡。排放工业废水和生活污水是水体富营养化的重要原因。eutrophication; phenomenon occurring in a body of water, such as a lake, a reservoir, a river mouth or a sea bay, where water flows sluggishly, and where there is an excessive accumulation of dissolved nutrients (such as phosphates and nitrogen), which encourages the propagation of aquatic algae. These cloud the water surface, preventing other aquatic plant life from getting enough light. When the algae itself die and decompose, oxygen is removed from the water, making it difficult for other aquatic organisms to survive. The discharge of industrial liquid waste and daily-life sewage is a major cause of eutrophication.

G

【伽马刀】gāmǎdāo 利用伽马射线代替手术刀进行手术的医疗装置。以钴-60作为能源，将多束伽马射线聚焦在病灶并摧毁病灶。主要用来治疗脑血管畸形和颅内肿瘤等。gamma-knife; medical device used in surgical operations whereby a gamma ray performs the function of a scalpel. Taking cobalt-60 as its energy source, it concentrates gamma rays on the diseased area and eradicates it, mainly used to treat cerebrovascular malformations and intracranial tumours

【干租】gānzū 一种租赁方式，在租赁设备、交通工具等时，不配备操纵、维修人员（跟'湿租'相对 as compared with 'wet lease'） dry lease; lease of equipment or transport such as aircraft, exclusive of accompanying operators or maintenance workers

【干细胞】gànxìbāo 一切血细胞的原始细胞。主要分布于骨髓中，脾内也有少量存在，外形像小淋巴细胞。其中一部分可在一定激素的刺激下，向一定方向分裂、分化，形成红细胞、淋巴细胞等不同的血细胞 stem cell; cell from which all other blood cells arise, and which is found mainly in the bone marrow, and in a small quantity in the spleen. Some stem cells, stimulated by certain hormones, split and develop into various kinds of blood cells such as red cells and lymphocytes

【刚性】gāngxìng ❶坚强的性格；刚强的气质 fortitude; firmness; unyieldingness：一个男子汉应该有～。A man should be firm and strong. ❷坚硬不易变化的（跟'柔性'相对 as compared with 'flexible'） rigid; stiff：～物体 rigid object ❸不能改变或通融的（跟'柔性'相对 as compared with 'flexible'） inflexible, compulsory：～指标 inflexible target; compulsory quota

【高发】gāofā （疾病、事故等）发生频率高的（of disease, accident, etc.） frequent：胃癌～地区 district with a high incidence of stomach cancer｜交通事故～地段 stretch of road prone to traffic accidents

【高峰会议】gāofēng huìyì 指高级领导人的会议 summit; summit conference; conference attended by high government officials

【高架路】gāojiàlù 架在地面上空的道路，供机动车辆行驶 causeway; skyway; elevated road for motor vehicles

【高架桥】gāojiàqiáo 修建在地面或道路上空的形状像桥的路段，供机动车辆行驶，能够避免道路平面交叉，从而提高交通运输能力 flyover; bridge-like section of road built above ground or over a road to avoid intersecting with other roads, thus alleviating traffic congestion

【高企】gāoqǐ （价格、数值等）居高不下（of prices, numerical value, etc.） stay high; continue high：房价～。House prices remain high.

【高危】gāowēi 发生某种不良情况的危险性高的 be liable to; be susceptible to (sth. undesirable or threatening)：冠心病～人群 group of people at high risk of coronary heart disease

【高新技术】gāoxīn-jìshù 指处于当代科学技术前沿，具有知识密集型特点的新兴技术。如信息技术、生物工程技术、航天技术、纳米技术等。high and new technology; knowledge-intensive new technology that leads contemporary science and technology, such as information technology, bio-engineering technology, astronomic technology, nanometre technology, etc.

【搞定】gǎodìng 〈方 *dial.*〉把事情办妥；把问题解决 settle (a matter); solve (a problem)

【搞笑】gǎoxiào 〈方 *dial.*〉制造笑料，逗人发笑 provoke laughter; amuse：不要采取庸俗手法～。Don't use vulgarity as a way of raising a laugh.｜一味～的节目，效果不会好。A programme intended specifically to amuse often defeats the purpose.

【告破】gàopò 宣告破获 announce that sth. has been unearthed, or ferreted out; make known that a mystery or puzzle has been cracked：特大凶杀案～。It was announced that the major murder case had been cracked.

【告缺】gàoquē 指物品、货物等出现短缺（of goods, etc.） be short of; lack：药品～ shortage of medicine

【割肉】gēròu 〈比喻 *fig.*〉赔钱卖出（多用于证券交易 oft. of stock market dealing） sell sth. at a price lower than its original price：现在～，得赔30%。To sell the shares right now means a loss of 30 per cent.

【歌带】gēdài 录有歌曲的磁带 cassette tape of recorded songs

【歌厅】gētīng 演唱歌曲的营业性娱乐场所 karaoke hall; public place of entertainment where members of the public go to sing to the accompaniment of recorded music

【个股】gègǔ 指某一公司的股票 shares of an individual company：～行情 individual company share quotations

【个例】gèlì 个别的、特殊的事例 individual case; exceptional case:此类造假现象,绝非~。Forgery such as this is by no means an isolated case.

【个人数字助理】gèrén shùzì zhùlǐ 一种手持式电子设备,具有电子计算机的某些功能,可以用来管理个人信息(如通讯录、计划等),也可以上网浏览、收发电子邮件等。一般不配备键盘。personal digital assistant; hand-held electronic device that performs some of the functions of a computer but that has no keyboard, used to manage personal information (such as addresses, telephone numbers, social engagements, etc.), surf the Internet, send and receive e-mails, etc.; 俗称 commonly known as 掌上电脑 zhǎngshàng diànnǎo

【个人所得税】gèrén suǒdéshuì 国家对公民个人所得征收的税,征收范围主要包括工资、奖金、补贴收入以及个体工商户生产、经营所得的收入 personal income tax; tax imposed by the state on the personal incomes of its citizens, including salaries, and bonuses, and on the subsidies and incomes of individual industrial and commercial businesses earned through production and operation

【跟风】gēnfēng 指追随某种风气或潮流 go with the tide; be given to fads; be a faddist:~炒作 promotional hype|不要盲目~。Do not blindly follow the latest fad.

【工程院】gōngchéngyuàn 工程科学技术界最高荣誉性、咨询性学术机构,由全体院士组成,下设若干学部 academy of engineering; consultative academic organization of the highest reputation within engineering science and technology circles, that encompasses a number of academic committees

【工卡】gōngkǎ 工作时佩戴的表示身份的卡片式标志 employee's name badge; badge worn by an employee to show his or her position

【工薪阶层】gōngxīn jiēcéng 指有稳定的工作并以工资为主要经济来源的社会阶层 salariat; wage-earner; members of the social stratum that have stable, salaried jobs

【工薪族】gōngxīnzú 工薪阶层 salariat; salaried sector

【工业产权】gōngyè chǎnquán 对法律所确认的新技术和经济管理成果享有的权利,主要包括专利权、商标权。是知识产权的组成部分 industrial property right; right to a new technology or method of economic management recognized by law, which forms part of intellectual property, including patents and registered trade marks

【工作餐】gōngzuòcān 单位为上班职工提供的比较简单的饭菜,也指开会等公务活动时所吃的饭菜 working lunch; simple meal supplied to employees; meal provided during official business, such as meetings

【工作站】gōngzuòzhàn ❶为进行某项工作而设立的机构 working station; working centre; organization established for certain work:征兵~ drafting centre; draft centre|救灾~ disaster relief centre ❷计算机网络中作为分享网络资源的一个访问端点的计算机,性能高于微型计算机 workstation; computer that is more powerful than a microcomputer and that shares the resources of a computer network as a visiting terminal

【公示】gōngshì 公开宣示,让公众了解并征求意见 make known to the public and seek opinions:实行干部任前~制度 implement the system whereby the appointment of cadres is made public and opinions are sought before they take up office

【公信力】gōngxìnlì 使公众信任的力量 public credibility; ability to win public trust:提高政府部门的~ improve government departments' capacity to win public trust

【构架】gòujià [补义 new sense]建立(多用于抽象事物 usu. of abstract matters) establish:~新理论体系 establish a new theoretical system

【构拟】gòunǐ 构思设计 work out; design; conceive:~城市新蓝图 design a new blueprint for the city

【购并】gòubìng 用购买的方式兼并 acquire:这个企业集团最近~了两家公司。This enterprise group recently acquired two companies.

【股海】gǔhǎi 〈比喻 *fig.*〉变化不定并充满风险的股票市场 fluctuating stock market:~沉浮 rises and falls on the stock market

【股民】gǔmín 指从事股票交易的个人投资者 individual stock market investor

【股票价格指数】gǔpiào jiàgé zhǐshù 为反映股票市场总体价格的波动和走势而编制的股价统计指标。它是股市的重要参数,也是反映宏观经济发展趋势的重要指标之一。stock market index; index of stock prices that reflects the general fluctuations and trends on the stock market, and of macroeconomic development; 简称 abbr. 股指 gǔzhǐ

【股评】gǔpíng 对股市行情的分析和评论 analysis and comments on stock market quotations:晚间~ evening stock market analysis

【股权】gǔquán 股东对所投资的股份公司所享有的权益 stockholder's right; right of a stockholder within the limited liability company in which he or she has invested

【股灾】gǔzāi 指因股市行情大跌而造成的严重损失 stock exchange crash; serious damage caused by plummeting of stock prices

【股指】gǔzhǐ 股票价格指数的简称 abbr. for 股票价格指数 gǔpiào jiàgé zhǐshù

【骨龄】gǔlíng 骨骼年龄。用X射线透视手腕部，根据骨骼的钙化程度，可以推测少年儿童的年龄和发育情况。bone age; calcification of the wrist bone observed by X-ray, from which a child's age and growth can be inferred

【骨牌效应】gǔpái xiàoyìng ☞多米诺骨牌 duōmǐnuò gǔpái on p.2591

【固沙】gùshā 使流沙固定不再移动 stabilize sand dunes: ～造林 dune-fixating afforestation | ～植物 sand binder

【挂牌】guà//pái ［补义 new sense］❶挂出牌子，指某些单位正式成立或营业 officially start business by unveiling one's nameboard ❷指公司在股票市场上市（of a company) be listed on the stock market ❸体育主管部门公布要求转换所属职业体育组织的人员名单叫挂牌（of a sports club) announcement of a list of players available for trading

【拐点】guǎidiǎn 原指数学上改变曲线向上或向下方向的点，借指事物的发展趋势开始改变的地方 point of inflection; knee point; break point; mathematical term that refers to the point where a curve on a graph moves up or down, meaning the point where the development trend of sth. starts to change: 经济运行出现回升～。There is an upward inflection point in economic performance.

【关税壁垒】guānshuì bìlěi 指为阻止外国某些商品输入而采取的对其征收高额关税的措施 tariff wall; customs barrier; imposition of high duties on certain commodities from abroad to prevent or inhibit their importation

【观光农业】guānguāng nóngyè 旅游农业 tourism-oriented agriculture

【观照】guānzhào 原为美学术语，现也泛指仔细观察，审视（aesthetics) perception; (in a broad sense) scrutinize; study: ～传统文化 scrutinize traditional culture | ～现实，正视生活 study reality and face up to life

【管道】guǎndào ［补义 new sense］〈方 *dial*.〉same as 渠道 qúdào ②: 协商～中断。The consultation channel has been discontinued.

【管控】guǎnkòng 管理控制；管制 management and control: 严加～ strictly manage and control

【管涌】guǎnyǒng 堤坝渗水严重时，细沙随水带出，形成孔穴而集中涌水，叫做管涌。管涌会引起堤坝下陷，出现溃口，使洪水泛滥。piping; water erosion in a layer of subsoil under or through a dam, resulting in the formation of tunnels and cave-ins that eventually lead to its collapse

【冠名权】guànmíngquán 在某种事物前面加上自己名号的权利 right to name: 取得本次赛事的～ obtain the right to name the competition | 这家公司获得新建立交桥的～。This company won the right to name the newly built flyover.

【光笔】guāngbǐ 电子计算机的一种输入装置，与显示器配合使用。对光敏感，外形像钢笔，多用电缆与主机相连。可以在屏幕上进行绘图等操作。electronic pen; light pen; pen-shaped computer inputting device, light-sensitive, and usu. connected to the monitor by cable, used to write on an electronic whiteboard and to access programmes

【光标】guāngbiāo 在电子计算机显示器屏幕上用来指示当前操作位置的标志，是由若干光点组成的符号 cursor; indicator consisting of a number of light-spots on a visual display, marking the position of the current operation

【光电子技术】guāng-diànzǐ jìshù 由光子技术和电子技术结合而成的新技术，涉及光显示、光存储、激光等领域，是未来信息产业的核心技术 photoelectronic technology; new technology combining photonic and electronic technologies and involving optical display, optical storage, and lasers, being the core technology in the future information industry

【光碟】guāngdié same as 光盘 guāngpán

【光盘】guāngpán 用激光束记录和读取信息的圆盘形存储载体，分为可擦型、一写多读型和只读型三类 CD; compact disc; disc storing information that is recorded on it and read with a laser beam; divided into CD rewritable, CD recordable and CD read only; also 光碟 guāngdié

【光驱】guāngqū 光盘驱动器，能使光盘匀速转动，以便读出上面存储的信息 optical drive; device that revolves a CD at a uniform velocity so as to read the information stored on it

【光污染】guāngwūrǎn 指超量或杂乱的光辐射所造成的环境污染。多指眩光、电焊弧光等对人的视力和健康的不良影响。light pollution; environmental pollution caused by excessive amounts of or uncontrolled light rays; oft. refers to the harmful effect of dazzling light, and the arc lights produced by electric welding on human eyesight and health

【广域网】guǎngyùwǎng 指由若干局域网相互连接而成的网络。一般分布在方圆数十公里至数千公里的区域范围内。wide area network; network consisting of a number of area networks, usu. ranging between a few score to several thousand square km.

【硅谷】guīgǔ 美国加利福尼亚州北部圣克拉拉谷的电子工业中心，因生产电子工业基本材料硅片及地处谷地而得名。常用来借指高新技术工业园区。Silicon Valley; electronic industry centre located in the Santa Clara valley region in northern California, U.S.A., its name derives from its production of silicon chips, an essential material for the electronic industry, and its location in a valley; oft. a reference to a high-tech industrial zone

【柜员】guìyuán 柜台工作人员(多指金融机构的 usu. in financial organizations) counter clerk

【滚动】gǔndòng [补义 new sense] ❶逐步积累扩展;不断地周转 gradually accumulate and expand:～发展 develop at a progressive speed; snowball | 资金～capital turnover ❷一轮接一轮地连续不断进行 proceed one round after another:～播出 continual broadcasts

【滚梯】gǔntī 自动扶梯的通称(general term for) escalator

【国家公园】guójiā gōngyuán 国家为保护自然生态系统和自然景观的原始状态,为进行科学研究和科学普及,同时供公众参观旅游而划出的大面积场所 national park; large natural area set aside by the state in order to protect and preserve its natural ecological system and landscape for the sake of scientific research, popularization of science, and tourism

【国家税】guójiāshuì 中央税 state tax

【国企】guóqǐ 国有企业的简称 abbr. for 国有企业 guóyǒu qǐyè:～改革 reform of state-owned enterprises

【国有股】guóyǒugǔ 由政府或代表政府的机构投资购买的股份公司的股份。在我国,也指国有企业股份制改组中,以国有资产经评估后入股的股份。state-owned shares; shares bought by the government or by organizations on behalf of the government. In China, the term also refers to state-owned assets that become shares for their officially appraised value in a limited liability company converted from a state-owned enterprise.

【国有企业】guóyǒu qǐyè 指我国的社会主义全民所有制企业。是国家占有并控制全部或大部分财产的企业。原来由国家直接经营管理,称为国营企业。在经济体制改革中,所有权和经营权开始分离,国家原则上不参与直接经营,改称为国有企业。state-owned enterprise; enterprise under socialist public ownership in China, where the state owns and controls all or a major part of the property and assets. Such an enterprise was formerly under the direct management and control of the state, and called a state-run enterprise. Because ownership and management rights have been separated in economic restructuring, and the state no longer directly ran such enterprises, they are called state-owned enterprises. 简称 abbr. 国企 guǒqǐ

H

【含金量】hánjīnliàng ❶物体内所含黄金的数量 gold content; amount of gold contained in an object ❷〈比喻 *fig.*〉事物所包含的实际价值 real or intrinsic value of sth.:这篇论文的学术～相当高。This thesis is of high academic value.

【函售】hánshòu 用通信方式联系的销售 mail-order:～保健品 sell health products by mail-order

【航拍】hángpāi 利用航空器(如飞机、直升机、气球)对地面进行拍摄 aerial photography; photographs of the ground from an aircraft (e.g. airplane, helicopter or balloon):直升机在会场上空～。A helicopter is hovering over the meeting place, taking aerial photos.

【豪赌】háodǔ 以巨资为赌注进行赌博 play for high (or big) stakes:他在一场～中输了几十万元。He gambled away tens of thousands of dollars at a single sitting.

【豪宅】háozhái 豪华的住宅 luxury house

【荷兰豆】hélándòu 食荚豌豆的俗称,一年生或二年生草本植物,是豌豆的一个变种,嫩荚是常见蔬菜。原产欧洲。mangetout (*Pisum sativum* var. *macrocarpon*); snow pea; an annual or biennial herb with an edible pod, a variant of the common pea originating in Europe. The young pod of it is a common vegetable.

【核磁共振】hécí gòngzhèn 原子核在外加恒定磁场作用下产生能级分裂,对特定频率的电磁波发生共振吸收的现象。利用核磁共振可以测定有机物的结构,医疗上可以通过核磁共振成像技术进行脑部疾病、血管病、肿瘤等的检查和诊断。nuclear magnetic resonance; absorption of electromagnetic radiation of a specific frequency by an atomic nucleus that is placed in a stable magnetic field. Nuclear magnetic resonance imaging technology is used to identify and diagnose brain diseases, vascular diseases, and tumours.

【核糖核酸】hétáng hésuān 分子中含有核糖的一类核酸,存在于细胞以及某些病毒和噬菌体中。细胞内的核糖核酸,按其功能和性质的不同,可分为转移核糖核酸、信使核糖核酸和核糖体核糖核酸三种。RNA; ribonucleic acid; nucleic acid containing ribose found in cells, certain viruses and bacteriophages. RNA in cells, according to its functions and characteristics, can be divided into transfer ribonucleic acid, messenger ribonucleic acid and ribosomal ribonucleic acid

【核验】héyàn 审核检验 check; examine:购买时请～防伪标志。When making a purchase please check the authentication label.

【贺岁】hèsuì 贺年 celebrate the new year:～演出 New Year celebration performance

【黑车】hēichē 指没有牌照的或非法运营的汽车、三轮车等 unlicensed car, tricycle, etc., illegally used for business purposes

【黑金】hēijīn 〈方 *dial.*〉指官场上用于行贿等非法活动的钱 money used for bribery and other illegal activities within official circles

【黑客】hēikè ❶指精通电子计算机技术,善于从互联网中发现漏洞并提出改进措施的人 hacker; one skilled at computer programming and capable of pinpointing flaws in the Internet and suggesting improvements ❷ 指通过互联网非法侵入他人的电子计算机系统查看、更改、窃取保密数据或干扰计算机程序的人 hacker; one who illegally gains access to or enters sb. else's computer system through the Internet to read, change or steal secret data or interfere computer programmes

【黑色收入】hēisè shōurù 指通过贪污、受贿等非法手段取得的收入(区别于'白色收入、灰色收入' as opposed to 'while income' and 'grey income') black money; income from illegal activities such as embezzlement, bribes, etc.

【黑色幽默】hēisè yōumò 20世纪60年代在美国兴起的一个文学流派,对充满矛盾的荒谬的社会现实进行无奈、苦涩的冷嘲热讽。后也指这种无奈、苦涩的表现风格。black humour; literary genre that emerged in the 1960s in the United States, used to satirize, in helplessly bitter and astringent ways, a reality that is fraught with absurdity and paradox; helpless, bitter and astringent style of portrayal

【黑哨】hēishào 指球类比赛中故意做出的不公正的裁判行为 corrupt refereeing; intentionally unfair refereeing of a ball game

【黑箱】hēixiāng 通常指某种结构复杂的电子元件或电子仪器设备,能够对某个系统实行自动控制或自动记录。因使用中可作为一个独立的整体装配或拆卸,其内部工作特性不须透露,所以叫黑箱。black box; electronic device or piece of equipment with a complex structure, which automatically controls or records a system's operations and can be installed or uninstalled as an independent part without revealing its own operational features

【黑箱操作】hēixiāng cāozuò 暗箱操作 underhand operation

【红潮】hóngcháo 赤潮 red tide

【红筹股】hóngchóugǔ 指在中国境外注册,在香港上市的内地企业发行的股票 red chip stock; stock issued by a Chinese enterprise registered outside China and listed in Hong Kong

【红股】hónggǔ 股份公司向股东赠送的股票,是红利分配的一种形式 bonus share; bonus stock; share presented by a limited liability company to its shareholders as a form of distribution of dividend

【红马甲】hóngmǎjiǎ 指证券交易所内的证券交易员,因穿红色背心而得名 stock-broker's clerk that wears a red vest (or waistcoat) at a securities exchange

【红盘】hóngpán [补义 new sense]指证券交易市场电子显示屏上用红色数字表示的上涨的价格或指数(跟'绿盘'相对 as opposed to 'green listing') red listing; prices or indexes that have risen (shown in red on the electronic screen at a securities exchange market)

【后市】hòushì 指以后一段时间的证券等交易的行情 (of a securities or stock exchange) afternoon session; afternoon trading:～看涨 Prices are expected to rise in the afternoon session

【呼机】hūjī 寻呼机的简称 abbr. for 寻呼机 xúnhūjī

【呼台】hūtái 寻呼台的简称 abbr. for 寻呼台 xúnhūtái

【互动】hùdòng 互相作用;互相影响 interaction:良性～ beneficial interaction|形成～效应 produce an interactive effect

【互联网】hùliánwǎng 指由若干个电子计算机网络相互连接而成的网络 Internet; international computer network comprising a number of interconnected computer networks

【户型】hùxíng 房屋(多指单元房)内部格局的类型,如一室一厅、二室一厅、三室一厅等 type of layout of an apartment, such as one-bedroom, two-bedroom and three-bedroom apartments; also 房型 fángxíng

【护工】hùgōng 受雇担任住院病人生活护理工作的人员 nurse attendant; person hired to take care of in-patients' everyday needs

【花季】huājì 〈比喻 *fig.*〉人十五至十八岁青春期前后的年龄段 period between the ages 15 and 18; youthful time; bloom of youth:～少女 young maid; teenage girl; blooming girl | ～少年 youth; teenage boy

【花心】huāxīn ❶指爱情上不专一的感情(多指男性 oft. of men) two-timing; unfaithful; infidel:婚后不久,丈夫就起了～。Shortly after their wedding, the husband started seeing another woman. ❷指爱情上不专一 unfaithful:～丈夫 unfaithful husband

【画句号】huà jùhào 〈比喻 *fig.*〉事情做完或结束 finish; end; complete; put an end to

【画作】huàzuò 绘画作品 painting

【话费】huàfèi 电话的使用费 telephone bill:缴纳～ pay the telephone bill

【话机】huàjī same as 电话 diànhuà ①

【话网】huàwǎng 指电话的通信系统 telephone network; telephone communications system

【还迁】huánqiān 回迁 move back:旧房拆除后还要盖～房。After demolition, a new building will be constructed for residents to move back to.

【环境壁垒】huánjìng bìlěi 绿色壁垒 green barrier or rampart

【环境标志】huánjìng biāozhì 产品的一种证明性标志,表明产品在生产、使用和废弃处理过程中符合环保要求,对环境无害或危害极小,同时有利于资源的再生和回收利用。我国的环境标志图形由青山、绿水、太阳和十个环组成 environment-friendly mark, signifying that a product meets the requirements of environmental protection in its production, use and disposal, that it is harmless or almost harmless to the environment, and contributes towards regeneration and recycling of resources. The Chinese environment-friendly mark comprises images of mountains, clear waters, the sun and ten circles. It is also called 绿色标志 lǜsè biāozhì and 生态标志 shēngtài biāozhì

【环境要素】huánjìng yàosù 构成环境的基本单元,如自然环境要素有水、空气、生物、土壤、岩石以及阳光等。环境要素在形态、组成和性质上各不相同,彼此独立,通过物质转换和能量传递而相互联系,构成环境整体。environmental element; basic units of the environment, such as water, air, living beings, soil, rocks and sunlight, that differ in form, composition and characteristics and are independent of one another. They form the entire environment and are linked by material exchange and energy transmission.

【荒漠化】huāngmòhuà 指由于气候变异和人类活动等因素造成的干旱地区、半干旱地区和亚湿润干旱地区的土地退化 desertification; deterioration of land in arid, semi-arid and sub-humid dry areas owing to climatic changes, and human activity etc.; also 沙漠化 shāmòhuà

【黄毒】huángdú 指毒害人思想的淫秽的书刊、音像制品等 pornographic books, magazines, and audio and video products:扫除～ eradicate pornography

【黄页】huángyè 电话号簿中登录企事业单位(有时也包括住宅)电话号码的部分,因用黄色纸张印刷,所以叫黄页(区别于'白页' as compared with 'white pages') yellow pages; telephone directory for businesses and institutions (sometimes also residences), printed on yellow paper, hence the name

【灰色收入】huīsè shōurù 指职工获得的工资、津贴以外的经济收入,如稿酬、兼职收入、专利转让费等,有时也指一些透明度不高,不完全符合法规的收入(区别于'白色收入、黑色收入' as compared with 'white income' and 'black money') grey income; income from moonlighting; income other than one's salary and allowances, such as contribution fees, payment for part-time work, and for assignment of patent rights; sometimes refers to undeclared income

【回放】huífàng 已播放过的影视片、录像等的片段重新播放 replay; play clips of a movie, TV drama and video over again:精彩镜头～ reprise of some great scenes

【回馈】huíkuì 回赠;回报 repay; requite:～社会 repay debt to society | 以诚信～消费者。Repay the customers with honesty and reliability.

【汇市】huìshì ❶买卖外汇的市场 foreign exchange market ❷外汇的行市 foreign exchange quotations

【汇映】huìyìng 若干部有某种联系的影片在同一时期、同一地区集中上映 film festival; showing of a group of films related in some way, over a certain period of time and in the same area:法国电影～ French film festival

【会展经济】huìzhǎn jīngjì 指以承办各种会议、展览等并为之提供服务为主要内容的经济活动 exhibition economy; economic activities that involve organizing conventions, exhibitions, etc., and providing necessary services

【贿金】huìjīn same as 贿款 huìkuǎn

【贿款】huìkuǎn 行贿的钱 bribery money

【婚典】hūndiǎn 结婚典礼 wedding ceremony:传统～ traditional wedding

【婚介】hūnjiè 婚姻介绍 matchmaking:～机构 matchmaking service (or centre, agency); matrimonial agency

【婚庆】hūnqìng 结婚的庆祝仪式 wedding ceremony

【婚外情】hūnwàiqíng 指与配偶以外的人发生的恋情 extramarital affair; love affair with sb. other than one's spouse

J

【机顶盒】jīdǐnghé 数字视频解码接收器。通常放置在电视机的顶部,所以叫机顶盒。digital set-top box; device that decodes and receives digital video frequencies, usu. placed on top of a TV set

【积淀】jīdiàn ❶积累沉淀 accumulate:多年来～的艺术功底 artistic skills accumulated over the years ❷所积累沉淀下来的事物(多指文化、知识、经验等 usu. of culture, knowledge, experience, etc.) accumulation:历史的～ accumulation throughout history | 深厚的艺术～ deep artistic tradition

【基尼系数】Jīní xìshù 表示社会收入分配不平均程度的指标,系数数值在 0 与 1 之间,数值越大,分配的不平均程度越高。因由意大利统计学家基尼提出而得名。Gini Coefficient; index showing the degree of unevenness in the distribution of social incomes, ranging from 0 to 1. The higher the value, the higher the degree of unevenness. Named after its devisor, Corrado Gini, an Italian statistician.

【基因芯片】jīyīn xīnpiàn ☞ 生物芯片 shēngwù xīnpiàn on p. 2622

【基因组】jīyīnzǔ 指细胞和生物体的整套基因 genome; complete set of genes of a cell or an organism; also 染色体组 rǎnsètǐzǔ

【畸恋】jīliàn 不正常的恋情 abnormal love

【激光刀】jīguāngdāo 用激光代替手术刀进行手术的医疗装置。激光有单一方向性,能量密度高,可利用其热效应、光效应和电磁效应等切割身体组织。用激光刀进行手术,切口平滑,出血少,不易感染。常用的有二氧化碳激光刀、氩激光刀等。laser scalpel; medical device used in operations in place of a conventional scalpel. A laser beam does not diverge and maintains a high energy density and can be used to cut body tissue with its heat and luminous and electromagnetic effects. Surgery with a laser scalpel leaves a clean cut, causes minimal bleeding and carries a low risk of infection. The carbon dioxide laser and argon laser scalpels are most oft. used.

【激光电视】jīguāng diànshì 利用激光显示图像的电视系统,设备采用全数字化技术。彩色激光电视用红、绿、蓝三种颜色扫描,被调制的激光束投射在屏幕上,图像清晰逼真,色彩绚丽。laser television; television system using a laser for display and digital technology. A colour laser television scans in red, green and blue, and projects the modulated laser beam onto the screen, producing clear, distinct images in brilliant colour.

【激光武器】jīguāng wǔqì 利用激光束直接攻击并毁伤目标的武器。由激光器、精密瞄准跟踪系统、光束控制与发射系统组成。射击时快速、精确、灵活,不受电磁干扰。laser weapon; weapon that directly attacks and destroys its target with laser beams, comprising a laser, a precise aiming and tracking system, and a beam control and firing system. A laser weapon fires rapidly, accurately and flexibly, free from electromagnetic interruption.

【激活】jīhuó [补义 new sense]〈比喻 *fig.*〉刺激某事物使活跃起来 activate; stimulate:出台有力措施,～房地产市场。Introduce effective measures to stimulate the real estate market.

【极限运动】jíxiàn yùndòng 指某些带有冒险性与刺激性的体育运动。如攀岩、高山滑板、滑水、激流皮划艇、摩托艇、冲浪、蹦极等。elemental, thrilling sports that are oft. dangerous, such as rock-climbing, alpine skiing, water skiing, kayaking over rapids, speed-boating, surfing, bungee-jumping, etc.

【集藏】jícáng 收集保藏;收藏 collect:～品 collectables; collected object | 明清家具～ collection of furniture from the Ming and Qing dynasties

【集成电路卡】jíchéngdiànlùkǎ 智能卡 IC (integrated circuit) card

【集萃】jícuì 荟萃 fine collection:新闻～ cache of popular news dispatches

【挤提】jǐtí 〈方 *dial.*〉挤兑 squeeze; run on a bank:发生～风潮。A serious run on banks occurred.

【计划单列市】jìhuà dānliè shì 保持省辖市行政隶属关系,但在经济体制和管理权限上相当于省级,经济计划单列,直接向中央政府负责的城市 municipality with an independent budget; city enjoying provincial-level status in economic structure and management power, while remaining under the jurisdiction of the province where it is located, having the right of independent economic planning, and being directly responsible to the Central Government

【计算机断层扫描】jìsuànjī duàncéng sǎomiáo 计算机体层成像 computer tomography; computer laminography

【计算机体层成像】jìsuànjī tǐcéng chéngxiàng

用X射线透视人体，测定透视后的放射量，经过电子计算机处理，重建出人体器官断层图像，并做出诊断 computer tomography; computer laminography; restructuring of a tomogram of human organs, using a computer to process the levels of radiation of the human body that has been X-rayed, and making a diagnosis; also 计算机断层扫描 jìsuànjī duàncéng sǎomiáo

【计算机网络】jìsuànjī wǎngluò 用通信线路把若干台电子计算机互相连接起来，用来实现资源共享和信息交换的系统 computer network; system that connects a number of computers with telecommunication lines to enable the sharing of resources and exchange of information

【记忆合金】jìyì héjīn 形状记忆合金的简称 abbr. for 形状记忆合金 xíngzhuàng jìyì héjīn

【绩优股】jìyōugǔ 股市上指业绩优良，具有较高投资价值的股票 blue chip stock (or share); stock that has a high investment value because of its good record of performance on the stock market

【加密】jiāmì 给计算机、电话、存折等的有关信息编上密码，使不掌握密码的用户无法使用，达到保密的目的 encrypt; encode the relevant information on a computer, telephone or bankbook so as to prevent unauthorized access

【佳绩】jiājì 优秀的成绩；优良的业绩 outstanding achievement: 再创～ make another outstanding achievement

【家教】jiājiào ［补义 new sense］❶受聘到别人家中进行文化、艺术等教育（多指对孩子 usu. for children) tutoring; private instruction in culture, art, etc.: ～工作 private tutoring ❷ 受聘到别人家中进行文化、艺术等教育的人 tutor; private instructor: 请～ employ a tutor | 当～ work as a tutor

【家居】jiājū ［补义 new sense］家庭居室 home; residence; abode: 装点～ decorate one's home | ～陈设 home furnishings

【假球】jiǎqiú 球类比赛的双方在比赛中通同作弊，弄虚作假，叫打假球 rigged ball game or match; ball game where the two competing teams collude in cheating

【价差】jiàchā 价格之间的差距 price difference

【价位】jiàwèi 某一价格在市场行情中所处的位置 position of a price within the market: 低～ low price | ～合理 reasonable price

【价值观】jiàzhíguān 关于价值的一定信念、倾向、主张和态度的观点，起着行为取向、评价标准、评价原则和尺度的作用 values; views, beliefs, tendencies, opinions and attitudes that indicate behavioural tendencies, moral standards and principles

【驾龄】jiàlíng 驾驶汽车、飞机等的年数 number of years of experience or service as car driver, airplane pilot, etc.: 他是个老司机，已有二十年～了。He is a veteran driver, with a service record of 20 years.

【驾校】jiàxiào 汽车驾驶技术学校的简称 abbr. for 汽车驾驶技术学校 qìchē jiàshǐ jìshù xuéxiào

【驾照】jiàzhào 指驾驶证 driving licence

【假日经济】jiàrì jīngjì 利用假日集中消费带动餐饮业、旅游业和其他行业发展的经济活动 holiday economy; economic activities aimed at concentrated consumer patronage of the catering and tourist industries in holiday seasons

【监理】jiānlǐ ❶对工程项目等进行监督管理 supervise and manage an engineering project: 完善～制度 improve the system of supervision and management ❷做监理工作的人 supervisor

【监事】jiānshì 监事会的成员 supervisor; member of board of supervisors

【监事会】jiānshìhuì 对股份公司一般业务的执行情况进行监督的机构，其成员由股东大会选举产生 board of supervisors; organization that supervises a company's general business, whose members are elected at a shareholders' meeting

【检获】jiǎnhuò 通过检查而获得（赃物、违禁品等） root out; discover and seize (spoils, contraband goods, etc.): ～一批赌具 root out a quantity of gambling devices

【检控】jiǎnkòng ❶ 检举控告 prosecute: ～交通违章 charge sb. with traffic violation | ～不法商贩 prosecute illegal peddlers ❷检查并控制 investigation and control: 公安局对在逃犯罪嫌疑人部署～工作。Police are being deployed to investigate and capture the escaped suspect.

【减仓】jiǎn//cāng 指投资者减轻仓位（of investors) sell shares: 逢高～，注意风险。Sell shares when their price is high as a precaution against risk.

【减负】jiǎnfù 减轻过重的、不合理的负担 alleviate an excessive, unreasonable burden: 治理乱收费现象，给农民～ rectify arbitrary exaction of fees and alleviate the burden on farmers | 少留家庭作业是对学生～的主要措施。A major measure in alleviating the burden on students is to give them less homework.

【减亏】jiǎnkuī 减少亏损（多用于企业 usu. of enterprises) reduce losses: ～增盈 reduce losses and increase profits | 这家钢厂今年～三千万元。This year the steel plant has reduced losses by 30 million yuan.

【减灾】jiǎnzāi 采取措施，减少自然灾害造成的损失 take measures to reduce damage caused by natural disasters: 科技～ mitigate the effects of disasters by science and technology | ～贵在预防。Prevention is what counts in disaster mitigation.

【建仓】jiàn//cāng 指投资者买入股票、期货合约等 buy in; (of investors) buy stock shares, future contracts, etc.

【建构】jiàngòu 构建;建立(多用于抽象事物 usu. in an abstract sense) foster; cement: ～良好的人际关系 forster good personal relations | ～夏商周古史系统 chronicle the history of the Xia, Shang and Zhou dynasties

【键入】jiànrù 按动电子计算机键盘上的键输入(信息) key in; enter (information) by means of a keyboard: ～网址 key in an Internet address

【奖级】jiǎngjí 奖金或奖品的等级 grade of prizes (or awards): 大赛共设五个～。The competition offers five grades of award.

【奖项】jiǎngxiàng 指某一种奖划分的不同类别,也指某一项奖 prize; award: 大赛共设九类～。The competition has nine prizes. | 获得了最高～ win the highest prize

【叫价】jiào//jià 公开报出价格;开价 quoted price; offer; quote: ～竞买 competitive offer to buy

【教师节】Jiàoshī Jié 中国教师的节日。1985年1月21日第六届全国人民代表大会常务委员会第九次会议决定,9月10日为我国的教师节。Teacher's Day in China; on January 21, 1985, the Ninth Session of the Standing Committee of the Sixth National People's Congress designated September 10th as China's Teacher's Day

【接轨】jiē//guǐ [补义 new sense]〈比喻 *fig.*〉两种事物彼此衔接起来 link; hook up; couple up two matters: 与世界经济～ link up with world economy

【接柜】jiē//guì 在柜台接待(储户、顾客等) receive (depositors, customers, etc.) at the counter: ～员 desk clerk

【接警】jiē//jǐng (公安部门)接到报警 (of the police) receive a crime report: ～记录 record of crime reports received | 公安人员～后迅速赶赴现场。Having received the crime report, the police rushed to the scene.

【揭牌】jiē//pái 揭开蒙在机关、企业等名称牌子上的布,表示成立、开业等 (of organizations and enterprises) be founded; open: 公司在沪正式～。The company was officially founded in Shanghai. | 举行～仪式 hold an opening ceremony

【街区】jiēqū 由若干街道形成的一片区域 subdistrict; neighbourhood; area consisting of a few blocks: 他家所在的～离市中心较远。He lives far from the downtown area.

【节庆】jiéqìng 节日;庆祝日 festival; holiday: 举办～展销活动 hold sales exhibitions during festivals

【结构】jiégòu [补义 new sense]组织安排(文字、情节等) plot; arrange: 根据主线来～故事 formulate the plot of a story on the basis of its main thread

【解读】jiědú ❶ 阅读解释 read; interpret; decode: ～信息编码 read information codes | 传统的训诂学以～古籍为主要目的。The main purpose of the study of exegesis is to interpret ancient texts. ❷ 分析;研究 analyse; study: ～人生 study human life | ～史前文化 analyse pre-historic culture ❸ 理解;体会 understand; learn; realize: 持不同观点的人对这项政策会有不同的～。People of diverse views will interpret the policy differently.

【解构】jiěgòu 对某种事物的结构进行剖析 deconstruct; analyse the structure of a certain matter: ～作品 dissect a creative work | ～传统文化 deconstruct traditional culture

【解困】jiě//kùn 解决困难;从困境中解脱出来 resolve difficulties; get out of a difficult situation: ～房 housing built for the poor | 帮助国有企业～ deliver state-owned enterprises from financial doldrums

【解密】jiě//mì ❶ 解除对文件、档案等的保密规定,允许对外公布 declassify; remove official security classification from a document, archive, etc. ❷ 给经过加密的信息除去密码,使还原为加密前的状态,以便获取信息 decrypt; decode; decipher; convert enciphered information into its original form so as to be able to read it

【戒毒】jiè//dú 戒除毒瘾 come off drugs; drug detoxification: ～所 drug rehabilitation centre

【界面】jièmiàn [补义 new sense] 用户界面的简称 abbr. for 用户界面 yònghù jièmiàn

【金领】jīnlǐng 指掌握现代科技,能创造大量财富因而收入较高的高级科学技术人员,如软件设计工程师等 gold collar; senior technicians, such as software design engineers, who are masters of modern science and technology, create large wealth and therefore earn relatively high incomes: ～阶层 gold-collar stratum

【近亲繁殖】jìnqīn fánzhí 〈比喻 *fig.*〉在人员培养或使用中,亲属关系或师承关系近的人集中的现象 nepotism; phenomenon where the relatives and associates of a prominent operative in a company or organization are given preference of employment or training

【禁毒】jìndú 禁止吸食、贩卖和制造毒品 ban the production, sale and abuse of drugs: 开展～统一行动 implement a unified drugs ban

【禁赛】jìnsài 禁止参加体育比赛,是对违犯规则的运动队或运动员的一种处罚 suspend

from competition (as penalty to a sports team or its members for violating rules):因服用兴奋剂而被～两年 be suspended from competition for two years for using performance enhancing drugs

【经典】jīngdiǎn [补义 new sense](事物)具有典型性而影响较大的 classic; (of matters) typical and influential:～影片 classic movie

【经济技术开发区】jīngjì jìshù kāifāqū 我国为吸收外资、引进先进技术、开发新产业而在中心城市设立的特定区域,在区域内实行一系列优惠政策 economic and technological development zone; special zone set up in a central city of China where a series of favourable policies are implemented to attract foreign investment, introduce advanced technology, and develop new industries

【精准】jīngzhǔn 非常准确;精确 accurate; perfect:8号选手的远投～。The No. 8 player's long shot was accurate.

【精算】jīngsuàn ❶精确计算 accurate calculation:计划中的各项指标都是～后确定的。Every quota in the plan was fixed after minute and accurate calculation. ❷以数学、统计、会计、金融等学科为基础的交叉学科,用于商业保险和各种社会保障业务 actuarial evaluation; interdisciplinary practice and theory on statistics and probability based on mathematics, statistics, accounting and finance, applied to commercial insurance and various social security services:～师 actuary

【警匪片】jǐngfěipiàn 以表现警察与盗匪的斗争为主要内容的故事片 crime action movie; 'cops and robbers' action film

【警风】jǐngfēng 警察的作风 police mode of operation

【警花】jǐnghuā 对年轻女警察的称呼(含赞美意 complimentary term) young policewoman

【警龄】jǐnglíng 警察从事警务工作的年数 number of years a policeman has been in the service:他已有近十年～。He has worked as a policeman for ten years.

【警嫂】jǐngsǎo 对警察妻子的尊称 respectful term for a policeman's wife

【警示】jǐngshì 警告,启示 warning; caution:～后人 warning to younger generations|洪灾给了我们一个很大的～。The floods were a serious warning to us.

【警衔】jǐngxián 区别警察等级的称号,如警监、警督、警司、警员等。武装警察的警衔和军衔相同。police hierarchy; titles that distinguish the rank of police officers, i. e. senior police supervisor, police supervisor, police superintendent, police constable, etc. Armed police use the same hierarchy as the army.

【劲歌】jìnggē 节奏强烈有力的流行歌曲 pop song characterized by a strong beat

【劲升】jìngshēng 强有力地上升 soar; rise powerfully:股市行情～。Stock prices are soaring.

【劲舞】jìngwǔ 节奏强烈有力的现代舞蹈 modern dance characterized by a strong beat

【净菜】jìngcài 经过择洗等加工处理后出售的蔬菜 cleaned vegetable; vegetable sold after being washed and trimmed:～上市。Cleaned vegetables are available on the market.

【竞标】jìngbiāo (投标者)互相竞争以争取中标 (of bidders) compete in bidding:这个工程有好几家公司～。Many companies competed in bidding for the project.

【竞猜】jìngcāi 比赛谁先猜出答案或结果 guessing game or contest:～热线 guessing game hotline|灯谜～ contest to guess the answers to lantern riddles

【竞岗】jìnggǎng 通过竞争以得到工作岗位 compete for a post in the workplace

【竞价】jìngjià 竞相报价(以争取成交) compete in bidding at an auction:举牌～ hold up the card bearing a bidder's number|轮番～ bid in turns

【竞买】jìngmǎi 竞相报价,争取买到 compete to buy:房地产～ competitive buying of real estate|～失败 failure in competitive buying

【竞卖】jìngmài 竞相报价,争取卖出 compete to sell:～交易 competitive sale

【竞拍】jìngpāi ❶指拍卖 auction:～活动 auctioning activity ❷在拍卖中竞相报价以争取成交 make bids at an auction:～价格直线上升。The bids soared.

【竞聘】jìngpìn 通过竞争争取得到聘任 compete for a post:～执教 compete for a teaching post|推广干部～制 promote the system whereby functionaries compete for posts

【竞投】jìngtóu 以竞争的方式投标或参与拍卖 competitive bid; competitive bidding:无底价～ competitive bid with no bottomline

【纠风】jiūfēng 纠正行业不正之风 correct a wrong tendency; rectify malpractice in a certain trade or profession:抓好～工作。The work of rectifying malpractice in various trade and professions should be emphasized.

【局域网】júyùwǎng 把小区域范围内的若干电子计算机和数据通信设备直接连接而成的网络 local area network (LAN); network that directly connects a number of computers in a small area to digital telecommunications equipment

【焗油】júyóu 一种染发护发方法,一般是在头发上抹上染发剂或护发膏等,用特殊机具放出蒸汽加温,使油质渗入头发 hair dressing method where after applying colour or conditioner to the hair it is steam-heated to help the oil permeate the hair follicles

【举证】jǔzhèng 出示证据；提供证据 produce evidence; show evidence：原告、被告先后～，进行法庭辩论。After the plaintiff and defendant had produced their evidence, the court debate started.

【拒载】jùzài （出租汽车）拒绝载客（of a taxi driver）refuse to take a passenger：拦了三辆车，有两辆～。Of the three taxies he hailed, two refused to take the passenger.

【聚焦】jùjiāo ［补义 new sense］〈比喻 *fig.*〉视线、注意力等集中于某处 focus; concentrate：新闻报道～于一个共同的话题。The news reports focus on a common topic.

【军嫂】jūnsǎo 对军人妻子的尊称 respectful term for a service man's wife

【均线】jūnxiàn 在坐标图上显示的一段时间内指数、价位等的平均值所连成的线，如五日均线、十日均线等 average line; line formed by linking the points in a coordinate graph that represent the average values of an index or price during a certain period, such as five-day average line and ten-day average line

【均值】jūnzhí 几个数平均以后得出的值 mean value; value obtained by calculating the average

K

【开局】kāijú ［补义 new sense］❶泛指工作、活动等开始 start (or beginning) of work, activities, etc.：今年的工业生产一～就很顺利。This year's industrial production got off to a smooth start. ❷泛指工作、活动等的开始阶段 (in a broad sense) commencement stage of work, activities, etc.：今年的图书市场呈现出良好～。This year the book market got off to a promising start.

【看淡】kàndàn ❶ 行情、价格等将要出现不好的势头（of market, price, etc.）show a tendency towards decline：行情～ bear market | 销路～。The market shows a downward trend. ❷ 认为行情、价格等将要出现不好的势头 expect (market, price, etc.) to worsen：商界普遍～钟表市场。Commercial circles generally expect a falling market in clocks and watches.

【考级】kǎo//jí 某一专业或技能的定级或晋级考试 examination for determining or raising one's level in a certain field or specific skill：英语～ English level examination | 举办电子琴、手风琴的～活动 hold electric organ and accordion aptitude examinations

【考研】kǎo//yán 报考研究生 take postgraduate entrance examination

【科教兴国】kējiào xīngguó 通过发展科学和教育来振兴国家 revitalize the nation by developing science and education

【可持续发展】kěchíxù fāzhǎn 指自然、经济、社会协调统一的社会发展。发展过程中，在不牺牲后代人需求的情况下满足当代人的需求。sustainable development; social development coordinating and unifying nature, economy and society, in which the present demands are met without sacrificing those of later generations

【可更新资源】kěgēngxīn zīyuán 指通过天然作用或人工经营，在合理开发条件下，消耗速度和恢复速度达到平衡，能够为人类反复利用的各种自然资源，如土壤、水、动植物等 renewable resource; natural resource that humankind can use continuously by reaching a balance between the rate of consumption and replenishment through rational human development and natural effects; also 可再生资源 kězàishēng zīyuán

【可乐】kělè 美国生产的一种饮料，用可乐果树的子实为原料加工配制而成，含二氧化碳，不含酒精，味甜，呈棕色。也指其他类似的饮料。Cola; sweet, brown, carbonated soft drink containing an extract of the cola nut; also referring to similar drinks

【可圈可点】kě quān kě diǎn 文章精彩，值得加以圈点，形容表现好，值得肯定或赞扬（of writing or performance）good; laudable; commendable; admirable; praiseworthy：影片中男女主角的表演都～。The performances of the leading man and lady in the film are both commendable.

【可吸入颗粒物】kěxīrù kēlìwù 飘浮在空气中的可被人吸入呼吸器官的极微小颗粒 inhalable particulate matter; small particles suspended in the air that can be inhaled into the human respiratory organs

【可再生资源】kězàishēng zīyuán same as 可更新资源 kěgēngxīn zīyuán

【克隆】kèlóng ❶ 生物体通过体细胞进行无性繁殖，复制出遗传性状完全相同的生命物质或生命体 clone; process in which an organism regenerates asexually a group of genetically identical cells descended from a single common ancestor ❷〈比喻 *fig.*〉复制（强调跟原来的一模一样）（emphasizing the identity of the original）copy; duplicate

【空仓】kōng//cāng 指投资者将所持有的证券

等全部卖出，手中只有资金 (of investors) holding capital, having sold all securities

【空巢家庭】kōngcháo jiātíng 指子女长大成人离开后，只有老人单独生活的家庭 empty-nest household; household where an elderly couple lives alone after their children have grown up and left home

【空乘】kōngchéng ❶ 航空乘务，客机上为乘客服务的各种事务 services for passengers aboard a flight：～人员 airline attendants ❷指客机上的乘务员 airline steward (or stewardess); airline attendant：一名男～ an airline steward

【空港】kōnggǎng 航空港的简称 abbr. for 航空港 hángkōnggǎng

【空气污染指数】kōngqì wūrǎn zhǐshù 根据空气质量标准和各种污染物对人体健康和生态环境的影响来确定的污染物浓度的值，是评估空气质量的一种依据。计算方法为：将各种空气污染物的浓度分别除以国家标准，再乘以100，得到各种污染物指数，取其中最高的一项作为空气污染指数。我国目前计入空气污染指数的污染物项目有二氧化硫、一氧化碳、臭氧、二氧化氮、可吸入颗粒物等。air pollution index; extent of pollutant density determined on the basis of air-quality standards and the effects of various pollutants on human health and the ecological environment. The basis on which to appraise air quality, the air pollution index is computed by dividing the density of each air pollutant with the state standard and multiplying the quotient by 100, with the highest of the indices thus derived for all the pollutants serving as the air pollution index. In China, pollutants include sulphur dioxide, carbon monoxide, ozone, nitric dioxide, inhalable particulate matter, etc.

【空气质量】kōngqì zhìliàng 指空气的清洁程度。检测空气质量的项目主要有二氧化硫、一氧化碳、臭氧、二氧化氮、可吸入颗粒物等。我国现将空气质量分为五级 air quality; cleanness of air. The major factors denoting air quality are the amounts of sulphur dioxide, carbon monoxide, ozone, nitric dioxide, inhalable particulate matter, etc. In China, air quality is divided into five grades:

级别 Grade	空气污染指数 Air pollution index	空气质量 Air quality
一 Grade I	0～50	优 Excellent
二 Grade II	50～100	良 Good
三 Grade III	100～200	轻度污染 Lightly polluted
四 Grade IV	200～300	中度污染 Moderately polluted
五 Grade V	300 以上 Above 300	重度污染 Seriously polluted

【空天飞机】kōngtiān-fēijī 能在机场跑道上水平起飞和降落，既可在大气层内飞行，也可在大气层外飞行的飞机。动力装置在大气层内用吸气式发动机，在大气层外用火箭发动机。space plane; plane that takes off from and lands horizontally on an airport runway, capable of travelling both inside and outside the atmosphere layer. It is powered by an air-breathing engine when flying inside the atmosphere, and a rocket engine when flying outside it.

【空置】kōngzhì (房屋)没有人居住或使用 (of houses) empty; unoccupied：客房～率较高 relatively high rate of vacant rooms | 那栋楼已经～了一年。The building has been unoccupied for a year.

【控盘】kòngpán 操纵、控制股市行情 manipulate stock quotations

【垮塌】kuǎtā 倒塌；坍塌 collapse; give way; break down; yield; crumble：河堤～。The river embankment gave way. | 桥身突然～。The bridge collapsed suddenly.

【快递】kuàidì 特快专递的简称 abbr. for 特快专递 tèkuài zhuāndì

【宽带】kuāndài 模拟通信中指频率大大高于话音的带宽，数字通信中指传输速率超过2兆比特/秒的带宽 (in analogue communication) broadband; bandwidth of high magnetic frequency, higher than that of voice, (in digital communication) bandwidth with a transmission speed of over 2 megabit per second

【款型】kuǎnxíng (服装等的)款式 (of clothes, etc.) style; fashion; model; design：时髦的～ fashionable style; latest fashion

【框定】kuàngdìng 限定(在一定的范围内) pinpoint; delimit; isolate：公安人员经过反复分析～了作案人的范围。After repeated analysis, the police isolated the possible culprits.

【溃口】kuì//kǒu (堤坝)坍塌决口 (of a dike) crevasse; breach; break

【扩容】kuòróng ❶扩大通信设备的容量 expand the capacity of communication equipment：电信～工程 telecommunication capacity expansion project ❷泛指扩大规模、范围、数量等 (in a broad sense) expand (the scale and scope); increase (the number):去年股市～较快。Last year the stock market expanded relatively rapidly.

【扩招】kuòzhāo 扩大招收 expand admission; increase enrolment:今年我校又～了二百多名学生。Our school enrolled 200 more students this year than last.

L

【垃圾股】lājīgǔ 股市上指业绩差,没有投资价值的股票 junk bond; bond of a bad performance record on the stock market and of low investment value

【拉动】lādòng 采取措施使提高或发展 take measures to promote; spur:～经济增长 spur economic growth|～文化市场 activate the cultural market

【拉力赛】lālìsài 一种汽车或摩托车比赛,赛程较长,一般为连续性分站进行 rally; competition in which automobiles or motorcycles are driven over a long distance, usu. with stops

【拉尼娜现象】lānínà xiànxiàng 指赤道东太平洋水域大范围海水反常降温的现象。每隔几年发生一次,多出现在厄尔尼诺现象之后,持续时间长,对全球气候有重大影响。La Niña phenomenon; abnormal drop in temperature over large areas of seawater in the equatorial eastern Pacific Ocean that happens every few years, usu. in the wake of the El Niño phenomenon, and lasts for a long period to bring a major import to bear on the global climate. also 反厄尔尼诺现象 fǎn'è'ěrnínuò xiànxiàng[拉尼娜,西 Spanish: La Niña]

【蓝筹股】lánchóugǔ 指在某一行业内占有重要支配地位、业绩优良的大公司的股票。蓝筹是西方对赌博中使用的最高筹码的称呼。blue chip stock; stock of a large company that performs well and holds a dominant position in a specific industry. The blue chip is the term for the gambling chip of the highest value in Western casinos.

【蓝牙】lányá 一种近距离的无线传输应用技术,在10—100米范围内,把专用的半导体装入机器中,无需借助电线就可连接电子计算机、打印机、数字相机、电视机、微波炉等,并能同时进行数据和语音传输 blue tooth; short-range wireless transmission technology, which enables a device containing this special radio to connect to any computer, printer, digital camera, television, microwave oven, etc., within 10-100 metres, and simultaneously transmit data and voice

【揽储】lǎnchǔ 招揽储蓄存款 canvass deposit:制止高息～行为。Canvassing deposits at a high interest should be stopped. also 揽存 lǎncún

【老虎机】lǎohǔjī 一种赌博机器,内有电子计算机装置,参赌者将硬币投入机器,如获胜,机器会将储藏在内的硬币自动吐出,否则硬币便被机器吞掉 slot machine; gambling machine containing an electronic computer, which operates when the gambler inserts coins, sending out stored coins when the gambler wins, and retaining coins when he loses

【老年性痴呆】lǎoniánxìng chīdāi 由于老年性脑萎缩所导致的进行性智能缺损,初期不易被发现,病程进展缓慢,主要症状有个性改变,记忆力和判断力下降以致丧失等 senile dementia; progressive deterioration of the mental faculties caused by senile encephalanalosis, barely noticeable at its early stage, and which progresses slowly, its main symptoms being a change in personality, deterioration or loss of memory, and impaired judgement

【老总】lǎozǒng [补义 new sense]称担任总经理、总工程师、总编辑等职务的人 form of address for a general manager, chief engineer, editor-in-chief, etc.

【礼兵】lǐbīng 在隆重的庆典和迎宾、葬礼等活动中接受检阅或担任升旗、护卫灵柩等工作的士兵 honour guard; guard reviewed at a grand ceremony, responsible for raising flags at a welcoming ceremony, and escorting biers at a funeral:人民解放军～ honour guard of the People's Liberation Army

【礼仪小姐】lǐyí xiǎojiě 在宾馆、酒店或大型仪式、活动中从事礼节性服务工作的年轻女子 young lady giving etiquette-related assistance at a hotel or a grand ceremony

【理据】lǐjù 理由;根据 argument; reason:这篇论文观点明确,～充足。The thesis is clear in viewpoint and sufficient in reasoning.

【理念】lǐniàn ❶信念 belief; conviction:人生～ belief about life ❷思想;观念 idea; thought; concept:经营～ idea about operation|文化～ cultural concept

【理赔】lǐpéi 合同双方中的一方在对方要求赔偿时进行处理 settle claims; one party of a contract acceding to the claims of the other:保险公司按约～。The insurance company settles claims in accordance with contracts.

【利多】lìduō 指对市场行情有利,可能引起价格上涨的消息 favourable information for the market, which may lead to a rise in prices; also 利好 lìhǎo

【利空】lìkōng 指对市场行情不利,可能引起价格下跌的消息 unfavourable information for the market, which may lead to a fall in prices; also 利淡 lìdàn

【利息所得税】lìxī suǒdéshuì 国家对个人存款、有价证券等所得的利息征收的所得税 interest tax; tax the state imposes on the interest accrued on personal deposits, negotiable securities, etc.

【联动】liándòng 若干个相关联的事物,一个运动或变化时,其他的也跟着运动或变化 chain effect; chain reaction; situation where one of several related matters moves or changes and causes others to move or change in a similar way:这种空调降价可能产生～效应。The price reduction on this brand of air conditioner will produce a chain effect.

【联网】liánwǎng 若干单个的设备相互连接成网络;若干较小的网络相互连接成更大的网络 network; connect separate equipment to a network, and incorporate smaller networks into a larger one:～发电 networked electric power generating | 计算机～ computer networking

【链接】liànjiē 指在电子计算机程序的各模块之间传递参数和控制命令,并把它们组成一个可执行的整体的过程 interlinkage; process of transmitting parameters and controlling commands between modules in a computer programme and joining them into an executable whole

【亮点】liàngdiǎn 〈比喻 *fig.*〉有光彩而引人注目的人或事物 bright spot; person or event that occupies the limelight:在全国排球联赛上,几位再度出山的教练成为～。In the national volleyball league competition, it was the returned coaches that stole the limelight. | 作者亲笔签名的旧书是此次拍卖会的～。The old books with the author's autograph were the main focus of attention at the auction.

【亮丽】liànglì ❶ 明亮美丽 brilliant; splendid; bright and beautiful:色彩～ vibrant colour | ～的风景线 brilliant scenery ❷美好;优美 beautiful; graceful; brilliant:他的诗歌很有韵味,散文也写得～。He writes lyrical poems and brilliant prose.

【亮色】liàngsè 明亮的色彩,也用于比喻[used in a figurative sense] bright colour:两个小演员的出色表演为该剧增添了不少～。The excellent performance of the two child actors added colour to the drama.

【靓丽】liànglì 漂亮;美丽 pretty; beautiful:扮相～ prettily costumed and made up | ～的容颜 beautiful facial features

【料理】liàolǐ [补义 new sense]❶〈方 *dial.*〉菜肴 dish:日本～ Japanese dishes | 韩国～ South Korean dishes ❷烹调制作 cuisine; cooking:名厨～ famous chef's cuisine

【猎头】liètóu 指受企业等委托为其物色、挖掘高级人才 headhunting; looking for senior talents for enterprises:～公司 headhunting company | ～服务 headhunting service

【临终关怀】línzhōng guānhuái 对将要死亡的病人给予心理和生理上的关心照顾,使减轻痛苦,平静地度过人生的最后时间 hospice care; taking care of a dying patient physically and psychologically, so as to reduce his pain and help him live his last days peacefully

【零增长】língzēngzhǎng 指增长率为零,即在规模、数量等方面保持原状,没有变化 zero growth; status quo of an unchanging scale, number, etc.

【领军】lǐngjūn 率领军队,多比喻在某个行业或集体中起领头作用 command an army; (oft. fig.) lead; play a leading role in a trade or group:目前男子体操队实力平均,缺少～人物。At present all the members of the men's gymnastic team are at a similar level, and lack a leading light.

【另类】lìnglèi ❶ 另外的一类,指与众不同的、非常特殊的人或事物 people or things not of the mainstream; oddball; nonconformist:这样的女孩可以归入～。Such a girl can be regarded as a nonconformist. | 这部片子是当代电影中的～。This movie is totally different from typical contemporary movies. ❷ 与众不同;特殊 alien; different from the common run; unconventional; original; offbeat; out of the way:～服装 offbeat clothes | 她打扮得很～。She dresses in an offbeat way.

【留医】liúyī (病人)留在医院治疗;住院 (of patient) be hospitalized:由于病情严重,大夫坚持让病人～。As the patient was seriously ill, the doctor insisted on his being hospitalized.

【流标】liúbiāo 拍卖时,拍品因无人出价竞买而未成交 fail to be sold at auction because of no bids:一百多件拍卖物品全部成交,无一～。All of the 100 odd items were bid for and sold at the auction.

【隆胸】lóngxiōng 通过手术等使女性乳房丰满隆起 breast enhancement; enhancing the shape of a woman's breasts by way of surgery; also 隆乳 lóngrǔ

【楼花】lóuhuā 指预售的尚未竣工的楼房 building that is put up for sale before it is completed:出售～ sell unfinished buildings

【楼盘】lóupán 在建或出售的商品楼 commercial building being built or sold:开发新～ develop new commercial buildings | 推销～ market commercial buildings

【楼市】lóushì 楼房市场,也泛指房产市场(in a broad sense) real estate market

【漏诊】lòuzhěn 医生没有把病人的病症诊断出来 fail to pinpoint a disease in diagnosis:哮喘的发病原因很复杂,不少病人容易被误诊、~。The causes of asthma are complex, and doctors may misdiagnose or fail to diagnose many asthma sufferers.

【录入】lùrù 把文字等输入到电子计算机里 key; input; enter words, etc., into a computer:~员 keyboarder|平均每分钟~一百个汉字。On average 100 Chinese characters are keyed in per minute.

【路霸】lùbà 指非法在路上拦截过往车辆和行人强行收费的人或单位 person or unit illegally stopping passing vehicles and passengers and fraudulently charging tolls:严厉打击车匪~ crack down on illegal road tolls and highway and railroad banditry

【路向】lùxiàng 〈方 *dial.*〉道路延伸的方向,多用于比喻 direction of a road, usu. used in a figurative sense:青少年成长的~ direction of juvenile growth

【路演】lùyǎn 指股份公司为了与投资者沟通和交流而举行的股票发行推介会,是英语 road show 的意译 road show; promotion of stocks held by a limited liability company as a means to communicate with investors. 路演 is exactly the transliteration of road show.

【旅游农业】lǚyóu nóngyè 农事活动与旅游相结合的农业发展形式。利用农村的自然风光作为旅游资源,提供必要的生活设施,让游客从事农耕、收获、采摘、垂钓、饲养等活动,享受回归自然的乐趣。tourism-oriented agriculture; tourist agriculture; made of agricultural development that combines farming with tourism, using the natural landscape of rural areas as a tourist resource, providing appropriate accommodation, and enabling tourists to enjoy the pleasure of returning to nature by doing farm work such as tilling, harvesting, fruit picking, fishing, feeding domestic animals, etc.; also 观光农业 guānguāng nóngyè

【律动】lǜdòng ❶有规律的运动 rhythm; movement characterized by regular recurrence:脉搏的~ rhythm of the pulse|生命的~ rhythm of life ❷〈比喻 *fig.*〉有规律的发展、运行 rhythm; development or operation in a regular pattern:社会的~ rhythm of society|古城伴着现代化的~呈现出新的面貌。The old city is taking on a new look in sync with the pace of the modernization drive.

【绿菜花】lǜcàihuā 西蓝花的通称 general term for broccoli

【绿盘】lǜpán 指证券交易市场电子显示屏上用绿色数字显示的下跌的价格或指数(跟'红盘'相对 as opposed to 'red listing') green listing; prices or indexes that have fallen (shown in green on the electronic screen in a stock exchange market)

【绿色】lǜsè 指符合环保要求,无公害、无污染的 green; environment friendly:~食品 green food|~餐具 environment-friendly tableware

【绿色壁垒】lǜsè bìlěi 指为了保护本国或本地区环境和经济利益而附加的进出口贸易条件及限制措施,如提高进口产品质量标准或实行高额征税等 green barrier; extra conditions and limitations imposed on imports and exports to protect the environment and economic interests of a country or region, such as raising the quality standard of imported products or levying high tariffs; also 环境壁垒 huánjìng bìlěi

【绿色标志】lǜsè biāozhì 环境标志 environment label

【乱码】luànmǎ 电子计算机或通信系统中因出现某种错误而造成的内容、次序等混乱的编码或不能识别的字符 error codes; unintelligible or unidentifiable codes caused by an error in the computer or communications system

【裸机】luǒjī ❶指没有加入通信网的手机、寻呼机 bare cell phone; bare pager; cell phone or pager not connected to a communications network ❷指没有配置操作系统和其他软件的电子计算机 bare computer; computer without an operating system and other softwares

【落槌】luò//chuí ❶拍卖物品时,拍卖师最后用槌敲一下桌子表示成交 wind up a deal; (of the auctioneer) knock the table with the gavel as a sign that an auctioned item has been sold:~价 closing bid|那幅国画最终以一万元人民币~。The Chinese painting was auctioned off for 10,000 yuan RMB. ❷指拍卖会结束 wrap up; wind up:春季拍卖会已于昨日~。The spring auction wound up yesterday.

【落聘】luòpìn 在招聘或选聘中没有被聘用(of one's job application) be turned down:~人员 unsuccessful applicants|在人事改革中王副校长~了。Wang failed to retain his post as school vice-president during the personnel reform.

M

【埋单】máidān 〈方 *dial.*〉在饭馆用餐后结账付款，现也用于其他娱乐性消费。原为粤语，传入北方话地区后也说买单。pay the bill for a meal at a restaurant or for other entertainment. Originally Cantonese, the term was borrowed by northern areas and adapted to the variation 买单 mǎidān.

【买单】[1] mǎidān 金融市场作为买进凭证的单据 voucher of purchase; proof of purchase in a financial market

【买单】[2] mǎidān ☞埋单 máidān on p. 2611

【买点】mǎidiǎn ❶ 商品所具有的让消费者乐于购买的特点 buying point; distinctive features of a commodity that make a consumer happy to buy it ❷ 指买进证券、期货等的理想价位 buy point; ideal price for buying stocks or futures

【买方市场】mǎifāng shìchǎng 商品供大于求，买方处于有利地位并对价格起主导作用的现象（跟'卖方市场'相对 as opposed to the 'seller's market'）buyer's market. On a buyer's market, supply outstrips demand, thereby putting the buyer in a favourable position and giving him the final say on prices.

【卖场】màichǎng 〈方 *dial.*〉比较大的出售商品的场所 big marketplace for selling commodities：仓储式～ warehouse-type marketplace

【卖单】màidān 金融市场作为卖出凭证的单据 vouchers of sale at a financial market

【卖点】màidiǎn ❶ 商品能够吸引消费者并让消费者乐于购买的地方 selling point; salient feature of a commodity which attracts consumers and prompts them to buy it：经济、实用是目前商品房的最佳～。Economy and practicality are the biggest selling point of a commodity house. ❷ 指卖出证券、期货等的理想价位 sell point; ideal price for selling stocks or futures

【卖方市场】màifāng shìchǎng 商品供不应求，卖方处于有利地位并对价格起主导作用的现象（跟'买方市场'相对 as opposed to 'buyer's market'）seller's market. On a seller's market, supply falls behind demand, thereby landing the seller in a favourable position and giving him final say on the prices.

【满仓】mǎncāng 指投资者将所持有的资金全部买成证券等（of an investor）buy securities with all one's capital; turn all one's capital into securities

【漫游】mànyóu ［补义 new sense］移动电话或寻呼机的一种功能。通常指当用户离开自己注册登记的服务区域而到另一个服务区域后，移动电话或寻呼机系统仍能为其提供服务 roam; function of a mobile phone or a beeper enabling the subscriber to receive the same kind of servicces when he leaves his registered service area

【盲道】mángdào 在人行道上或其他场所为方便盲人行走而铺设的道路，用特制的砖块铺成，砖块上有凸出的条纹、圆点等 the blind's track; special track on the sidewalk for the blind, paved with bricks with special raised designs

【盲点】mángdiǎn ［补义 new sense］〈比喻 *fig.*〉没有被认识的或被忽略的地方 unrecognized or neglected spot; blind spot：当前儿童教育存在着一些～。There are some neglected spots in the current children's education.

【盲区】mángqū ［补义 new sense］〈比喻 *fig.*〉没有被认识的或被忽略的领域、方面 unrecognized or neglected areas or aspects：心理素质的培养成了一些学校教育的～。The cultivation of psychological qualities has become a neglected aspect of education in some schools

【盲杖】mángzhàng 盲人探路用的竿儿 blind man's stick; stick used by a blind man for pointing his way along a road

【猫步】māobù 指时装模特儿表演时走的台步，因为这种步子类似猫行走的样子，所以叫猫步 cat's walk; steps taken by a fashion model on a platform during a fashion show, which look like the walk of a cat

【帽子戏法】mào·zi xìfǎ （～儿 mào·zi xìfǎr）英国作家刘易斯·卡洛尔的童话《爱丽丝漫游奇境记》里，有一位做帽子的匠人能用帽子变出各种戏法。后来把在一场足球比赛中一名队员攻进对方球门三个球叫做上演帽子戏法。hat trick. In the fairy tale *Alice in Wonderland* by the English writer Lewis Carroll, a craftman making hats was capable of conjuring up many tricks out of a hat. The term today refers to three goals scored by the same player in a game of soccer.

【密码箱】mìmǎxiāng 一种装有密码锁的小型手提箱，用来放现金、票据、贵重物品或文件等 cipher suitcase; small suitcase with a cipher lock, in which money, bills, valuables or documents are kept

【面巾纸】miànjīnzhǐ 用来擦脸的纸巾 facial napkin; tissue

【面市】miànshì （产品）开始供应市场（of a

product) put on sale：一种新型移动电话即将～。A new mobile phone will soon be available on the market.

【灭失】mièshī 法律上指物品因自然灾害、被盗、遗失等原因不复存在(leg.) missing; any article that no long exists because of natural calamity, theft or otherwise

【民营经济】mínyíng jīngjì 国有经济以外的集体经济、合作经济、民间持股的股份经济、个体经济、私营经济等经济成分的统称 non-state sector; economic sectors other than the state economy, such as the collective economy, cooperative economy, joint-stock companies with private citizens holding stocks, individual economy, private economy, etc.

【名模】míngmó 著名的时装模特儿 famous fashion model：超级～ super fashion model

【摸排】mōpái 为侦破案件对一定范围内的人进行逐个摸底调查 sound out the people in a given scope one by one in order to break a criminal case

【模块】mókuài ❶ 在通信、计算机、数据处理控制系统的电路中，可以组合和更换的硬件单元 module; replaceable component part of a circuit in a communication network, computer or data processing control system ❷ 大型软件系统中的一个具有独立功能的部分 module; part of a large software system with an independent function

【磨合】móhé ［补义 new sense］〈比喻 *fig*〉在彼此接触的过程中逐渐相互适应、协调 break in; get to accommodate each other in the course of contacts among people：新组建的国家队还需要～。The newly formed national team needs breaking in.

【母亲河】mǔqīnhé 对与民族世代繁衍生息息息相关的河流的亲切称呼。如长江、黄河被称做中华民族的母亲河。mother river; term of endearment for a river closely related to the multiplication and reproduction of a nation. The Yangtze River and Yellow River are called the mother rivers of the Chinese nation.

【幕墙】mùqiáng 指多层建筑或高层建筑的装配式板材外墙。因远看墙体像舞台上的大幕，所以叫幕墙。curtain wall; external wall built of pre-fabricated panels of a multi-storied or tall building, as it looks like a curtain on the stage from a distance

N

【纳米】nàmǐ 长度单位，1纳米等于一百万分之一毫米 nanometre; unit of length that equals one billionth of a metre

【纳米材料】nàmǐ cáiliào 由直径1—50纳米的极小微粒所构成的固体材料，具有高强度、高韧性、高比热、高热膨胀率、高电导率等特性，有极强的电磁波吸收能力。可用来制高性能陶瓷和特种合金、红外吸收材料等 nanometre material; solid material consisting of particles 1-50 nanometres in diameter, which has high strength, resilience, specific heat, thermal expansion rate, conductivity, and the strong ability to absorb electromagnetic wave, and is used in making high performance ceramics and special alloys and infrared absorbents

【纳米技术】nàmǐ jìshù 在纳米尺度(0.1—100纳米)上研究电子、原子、分子运动规律和特性的技术。它使人类能够按照自己的意愿操纵单个原子或分子，实现对微观世界的有效控制，对一系列高新技术的产生和发展有着极为重要的影响。nanometre technology; technology dealing with the law and specific features of the motion of electronics, atoms and molecules by the standard of the nanometre (0.1-100 nanometres). Enabling man to manipulate an individual atom or molecule as he wishes and exercise effective control over the microcosmos, the nanometre technology has an extremely important impact on the emergence and development of new and high technologies.

【纳米科学】nàmǐ kēxué 在纳米尺度(0.1—100纳米)上研究物质的特征和相互作用，以及如何利用这些特征的科学。包括纳米生物学、纳米机械学、纳米材料学、原子/分子操纵和表征学、纳米制造学等。nanometre science; science dealing with the specific properties and interaction of matters and how to make use of these specific properties by the standard of the nanometre (0.1-100 nanometres), including nanometre biology, nanometre mechanics, nanometre material science, the science of atom/molecule manipulation and characterization, and the science of nanometre manufacturing

【纳税人】nàshuìrén 依法直接负有纳税义务的企业、单位和个人 taxpayer; enterprise, organization and individual legally bound to pay taxes; also 纳税主体 nàshuì zhǔtǐ and 纳税义务人 nàshuì yìwùrén

【脑死亡】nǎosǐwáng 指以大脑功能永久性丧失为死亡标准认定的死亡。严重昏迷，瞳孔放大、固定，脑干反应能力消失，脑波无起伏，呼吸停顿，就可认定为脑死亡。brain death; condition in which all vital functions of the brain are determined to have irreversibly ceased by such symptoms as: serious coma, dilation and fixation of the pupils of the eyes, loss of the ability of the brainstem to react, loss of brainwave, and cessation of breathing

【内存】nèicún 电子计算机内存储器的简称。也指内存储器的存储量。internal memory; storage or storage capacity as of a computer

【内功】nèigōng [补义 new sense]指人的内在的能力及修养 ability and self-cultivation; professional skill or ability: 驾御重大历史题材，编剧、导演首先要练好～。To handle a major historical subject, a playwright or director should, first of all, acquire his professional ability. ◇公司苦练～，重新赢得了市场。The company regained its market share by working hard to improve the professional skills of its employers.

【内敛】nèiliǎn ❶（性格、思想感情等）深沉，不外露（of one's character, thoughts, feelings, emotions, etc.）self-restraint; self-restrained; self-control; reserved; introvert: 班长一向少言寡语，性格～。The squad leader always keeps to himself, and is self-restrained by character. ❷（艺术风格）含蓄，耐人寻味（of an artistic style）implicit; intriguing: 她的诗像清清的流水，～而平静。Her poem is implicit and calm, like the flow of a clear and limpid stream.

【内退】nèituì 不到国家规定的退休年龄，在单位内部办理手续，享受退休人员待遇，叫内退 retire under legal age, but be entitled to all privileges as a normal retired person

【内需】nèixū 国内市场的需求（区别于'外需' as opposed to 'foreign market demand'）domestic market demand: 扩大～，拉动经济增长 increase the domestic demand in order to pull up economic growth

【内资】nèizī 国内的资本 domestic capital; domestic investment: ～企业 enterprise run with domestic investment

【逆价】nìjià （购销部门）销售商品时的价格低于收购时的价格（跟'顺价'相对 as opposed to 'favourable price'）（of purchasing and marketing departments）unfavourable price; adverse price; sales price of a commodity that is lower than its purchasing price

【牛市】niúshì 指价格持续上涨，成交额上升，交易活跃的证券市场行情（跟'熊市'相对 as opposed to 'bear market'）bull market; securities market at which prices and the volume of transactions keep rising, and business is brisk

【扭亏】niǔkuī 扭转亏损局面 wipe out deficits; make up for losses: ～为盈 turn a deficit into profit

【暖冬】nuǎndōng 大范围地区冬季三个月的平均气温比常年同期明显偏高，这样的冬季称为暖冬 warm winter; winter in which the average temperature in the three winter months is strikingly higher than in the same period of a normal year

O

【欧佩克】ōupèikè 石油输出国组织 OPEC; Organization of Petroleum Exporting Countries

【欧元】ōuyuán 欧洲经济和货币联盟确定的欧洲统一货币名称。奥地利、比利时、德国、希腊、法国、芬兰、爱尔兰、意大利、卢森堡、荷兰、葡萄牙、西班牙等 12 国为首批使用欧元的国家。欧元于 1999 年 1 月 1 日正式启用。2002 年 1 月 1 日现钞开始流通。Euro; euro; Eurodollar single European currency adopted by the European Economic and Mònetary Union. Austria, Belgium, Germany, Greece, France, Finland, Ireland, Italy, Luxembourg, the Netherlands, Portugal, and Spain are the first 12 European countries to use euro. The euro was officially launched on January 1, 1999 and went into cash circulation on January 1, 2002.

P

【拍价】pāijià 物品拍卖的价格 auction price

【拍品】pāipǐn 拍卖的物品 goods at auction: 古籍～中，宋、元刻本颇受关注。Of all the ancient books at the auction, the block-printed editions of books of the Song and Yuan dynasties have commanded the attention.

【拍戏】pāi//xì 指拍摄电影或电视剧 shoot a

film or a TV play

【排查】páichá 为侦破案件对一定范围内的人进行逐个审查 investigate people within a given scope one by one in order to break a case

【排行榜】páihángbǎng 公布出来的按某种统计结果排列顺序的名单 ranking list; published list of statistics arranged in sequence：流行歌曲～ list of best pop songs | 当代文学最新作品～ list of best-selling literary works

【排污】páiwū 排放废水、废气等污染物；排除污染物 discharge waste water, waste gas and other pollutants; dispose of the pollutants：提高汽车发动机的动力性能，降低～量 improve the performance of car engines to reduce the exhaust gas

【派对】pàiduì 指小型的聚会 party：生日～ birthday party

【派发】pàifā 分发；发放 distribute：街头常有人～商品广告。There are often people handing out advertisement leaflets in the streets.

【派送】pàisòng 分发赠送 distribute; give：这家餐厅节日期间将向客人～小礼品。This restaurant will hand out small presents to patrons during the holidays.

【攀高】pāngāo ❶ 攀升 climb up; rise：入夏以来，空调销量不断～。The sales of air conditioners have kept rising since the beginning of the summer. ❷ 跟在某方面高于自己的人攀比 try to compete with sb. who is better than oneself in a certain aspect; keep up with the Joneses：～心理 mentality of trying to keep up with sb. better than oneself ❸ 高攀 try to forge relations with people of higher social status：不敢～。I dare not aspire to this honour.

【攀升】pānshēng （数量等）向上升（of quantity, etc.）climb up; increase：市场行情一路～。The market quotations have kept climbing up. | 成交额逐年～。The volume of business rose year by year.

【攀岩】pānyán 一种体育运动，只使用少量器具，主要利用双手和双脚攀登岩石峭壁 rock climbing; sport in which the athlete climbs a rock or cliff mainly with his limbs, using only a few tools

【盘跌】pándiē （股价、期价等）缓慢小幅下跌（of stock price, future price, etc.）slow, small fall

【盘活】pánhuó 采取措施，使资产、资金等恢复活力，产生效益 adopt measures to revitalize the assets or capital funds to bring economic returns：～资金 revitalize the capital funds | ～了两家工厂 revitalized two factories

【盘面】pánmiàn 指某一时点或某一时段的股市、期市等的交易状况 market situation of stock, futures, etc. at a given point or during a given period of time

【盘升】pánshēng （股价、期价等）缓慢小幅上升（of stock price, future price, etc.）slow, small rise

【盘整】pánzhěng ❶（股价、期价等）在一定范围内小幅调整（of stock price, future price, etc.）slow, small adjustment in a given scope：大盘行情处于～格局之中。The whole market situation is being adjusted. ❷ 整顿；调整 rectify; consolidate; readjust; strengthen：音像制品市场的～已刻不容缓。It is extremely urgent to rectify the irregularities in the audio-video market.

【抛盘】pāopán 指卖出证券、期货等，也指一定时间内市场上卖出的证券、期货等 sell out stocks, futures, etc.; stocks, futures, etc. sold out at the market in a given period of time

【泡沫经济】pàomò jīngjì 指因投机交易极度活跃，金融证券、房地产等的市场价格脱离实际价值大幅上涨，造成表面繁荣的经济现象 bubble economy; foam economy; economic phenomenon in which the market prices of the financial securities, real estate, etc. rise abnormally due to the extremely brisk speculative business and create a false sense of prosperity

【陪读】péidú 陪伴他人读书，特指留学生在国外学习期间，其配偶前往陪伴 keep a person in company in his or her study; be a companion in one's study; especially when a person studies in another country, his or her spouse goes together to keep him or her company

【赔付】péifù 赔偿支付 pay as compensation：保险公司～金额二百万元。The insurance company paid two million yuan as compensation.

【配额】pèi'é 分配的数额 quota：进口物资实行～管理 exercise quota control over imported goods

【配股】pèigǔ 股份公司为进一步筹资，向股东按比例配售股票 rights issue; privilege given to a company's stockholders of buying shares in a new issue of stock, usually at a price below the current market price

【配送】pèisòng 一种营销方式，把某一类货物搭配好并负责运送 distribution; mode of marketing to distribute and deliver goods in packages：建立农副产品～中心 set up a farm and sideline products distribution centre | 加工、包装蔬菜，～到各大超市 process, package and deliver vegetables to the supermarkets

【批捕】pībǔ 批准逮捕 approve the arrest of：检察院已经～此案的犯罪嫌疑人。The procuratorate has approved the arrest of the criminal suspect in the case.

【批租】pīzū 批准租用(土地)approve the lease of (land):工业～用地呈上升势头。The trend for approved lease of land for industry is on the rise.

【皮草】pícǎo 〈方 *dial*.〉指裘皮及裘皮制品 furs and fur products:优质～ high-quality fur and fur products|～时装 fur fashions

【皮具】píjù 皮革制做的用品,如皮包、皮夹子、皮带等 leatherware, as briefcase, wallet, leather belt, etc.

【啤酒肚】píjiǔdù 指肥胖的人向前凸起的腹部,一般认为多饮啤酒容易形成这样的体形,所以叫啤酒肚 pot belly; big belly; protruding belly of a fat person. It is usu. believed that the excessive drinking of beer is apt to cause the bulging of the belly.

【飘尘】piāochén 颗粒较小、能够长时间在空中飘浮的灰尘,可以随气流飘到很远的地方,造成大范围污染 floating dust; small particles of dust suspended in the air, which may drift far away with the air current to cause pollution over a large area

【飘红】piāohóng 指股票等证券的价格普遍上涨。证券交易场所的电子显示屏上显示价格上涨时用红色,价格普遍上涨时显示屏上以红色为主,所以说飘红。general rise of prices of the stocks and other securities. When a price rises the figure on the electronic screen of a stock exchange is red. When most prices rise, the screen is displayed mainly in red.

【票房】piàofáng [补义 new sense]指票房价值 box office value; box office receipts:这部影片全市～已经突破一千万元。The box office value of this film has surpassed 10 million yuan in the whole city.

【贫化铀】pínhuàyóu 从金属铀中提炼出铀-235后的副产品,主要成分是铀-238,有低放射性 depleted uranium; by-product after uranium-235 is extracted from the metal uranium, consisting mainly of uranium-238 with low radioactivity; 简称 abbr. 贫铀 pínyóu

【贫铀】pínyóu 贫化铀的简称 abbr. for 贫化铀 pínhuàyóu

【贫铀弹】pínyóudàn 指以贫化铀为主要原料制成的炸弹、炮弹或枪弹,穿甲能力强,爆炸威力大。其中的放射性物质会长期污染环境,损害人的健康。depleted uranium bomb; bomb, shells or bullets made with depleted uranium as the main material, having a strong piercing ability and large explosive force, its radioactive discharge causing long-term environmental pollution and being a serious health hazard

【频密】pínmì (次数)多而密;频繁 frequent; too many (number of times):由于赛事过于～,运动员的体力普遍下降。As there were too many matches, the physical strength of the players has dropped as a whole.

【品读】pǐndú 仔细阅读、品味 read carefully; ponder on:有些老书多年后再来～,仍能读出新意。When you read some of the old books again after a few years, you can still get new inspirations from them.

【品牌】pǐnpái 产品的牌子,特指著名产品的牌子 brand of a product, esp. of a famous product:新～ new brand|～效应 brand effect

【平均期望寿命】píngjūn qīwàng shòumìng 人口学中反映人寿命长短的统计指标之一。指人活到某一年龄后还能继续生存的平均年数。出生时的平均期望寿命常简称为平均寿命。社会经济水平的提高,生活条件的改善,医疗卫生事业的发展,使死亡率降低,平均期望寿命增高。average life expectancy; one of the statistical indices for the life expectancy in demography; average expected number of years in man's life after reaching a given age. The average life expectancy at birth is also called 'average lifespan' for short. The rise of the social economic level, the improvement of the living conditions and the development of the medical service and public health lead to a drop in the mortality rate and a rise in the average life expectancy.

【平台】píngtái [补义 new sense]计算机的硬件系统和软件系统的组合。如将DOS操作系统装入计算机,就形成DOS平台。在平台上可以支持和开发各种应用软件。platform; combination of computer hardware and software system. If the DOS operating system is fitted in a computer, it forms a DOS platform. On the platform various application softwares can be developed.

【破解】pòjiě ❶ 揭破;解开 unravel; decode; unveil; unlock:～生命之谜 unravel the mystery of life ❷ 解决 resolve; solve:终于～了这道难题 solve the difficult problem in the end ❸ 分析解释 analyse and explain:经他这么一～,老人家明白了。The old man saw the light after he explained it. ❹ 迷信 指用法术破除(灾难)(superstition) avert (misfortune, calamity, etc.) by magic:～之术 magic for forestalling a calamity

Q

【期房】qīfáng 房产市场上指约定期限建成交付使用的房子（跟‘现房’相对 as opposed to ‘ready house’）forward house; house to be completed and delivered for use at an agreed date on the real estate market

【期价】qījià 期货的价格 futures price

【期市】qīshì ❶ 进行期货交易的市场 futures market ❷ 指期货的行情 futures prices

【期望值】qīwàngzhí 对人或事物所抱希望的程度 the running high or low of expectations

【歧见】qíjiàn 不一致的见解或意见 difference; divergent opinions; disagreement：消除～，增进共识 eliminate differences and promote common understanding

【祈盼】qípàn ❶ 恳切地盼望 look forward to; expect：～他早日康复 look forward to his early recovery ❷ 愿望；期望 wish; expectation：发展经济，过上幸福生活是山里人的～。It's the expectation of the people living in the mountains to develop the economy and live a happy life.

【企管】qǐguǎn 企业管理 enterprise management; business management：～知识 knowledge on enterprise management; management know-how

【企划】qǐhuà 策划；谋划 planning (for an enterprising project, etc.); plot：～人员 planning staff

【企业所得税】qǐyè suǒdéshuì 国家对生产、运输、贸易等企业按其所得情况所征收的税 enterprise income tax; tax levied on the income of an enterprise engaged in production, transport, trade, etc.

【启动】qǐdòng ［补义 new sense］❶（法令、规划、方案等）开始实施或进行（decree, plan, programme, etc.）come under way; come into effect; set in motion：扶贫工程已正式～。The aid-the-poor programme has officially begun. ❷ 开拓；发动 open up; initiate; rev up：～农村市场 open up the rural market|大力～消费需求 stimulate consumer demands in a big way

【起拍】qǐpāi 从某一价格开始拍卖 starting bid price：～价 starting price|从两千元～，连叫五次无人应拍。The bid started at 2,000 yuan, and no one responded after five calls.

【千分点】qiānfēndiǎn 统计学上称千分之一为一个千分点 one-tenth of a percentage point; per-millage point in statistics

【签单】qiān//dān 购物、用餐等消费后，不付现款，在单据上签署姓名，店方日后结账 sign a bill without paying cash after shopping and having a meal, leaving the accounts to be settled afterwards

【前台】qiántái ［补义 new sense］指酒店、旅馆、歌舞厅等负责接待、登记、结算工作的柜台 front desk; front counter in a restaurant, hotel, song and dance hall, etc. for reception, registration and accounts settlement

【前卫】qiánwèi ［补义 new sense］具有新异的特点而领先于潮流的 avant-garde; having originality and leading in a field：～作品 avant-garde work|～的服装 avant-garde clothes

【前瞻】qiánzhān ❶ 向前面看 look ahead：极目～ look as far as one's eyes can reach; stretch one's eyes over many a mile of terra incognita ❷ 展望；预测 forecast; predict：～性 foresightedness

【潜亏】qiánkuī 潜在的亏损 potential loss：下大力气解决企业的～问题 make big efforts to solve the problem of potential losses in an enterprise

【潜能】qiánnéng 潜在的能量或能力 potential energy or ability; latent energy：发挥～ give play to one's potential energy or ability|挖掘～ tap the potential energy

【潜质】qiánzhì 潜在的素质 potential quality; latent quality; (having the) makings of; promise：她是个很有表演天赋和～的歌手。She is a singer with the gift and promise for performance.

【强暴】qiángbào ［补义 new sense］特指强奸 sexual assault; rape：惨遭～ be brutally raped

【强势】qiángshì ❶ 变强的趋势 going strong; tendency to grow stronger：该股一段时间内仍将保持～。The stock will remain strong for a period of time. ❷ 强劲的势头 great momentum; high velocity：宣传要形成～。Publicity must be intensified and gain tremendous momentum. ❸ 势力或力量强大的 strong; powerful：～地位 powerful position; strong position

【抢断】qiǎngduàn（足球、篮球等比赛中）拦截并把球抢过来（in a football or basketball match）steal; intercept and control the ball：甲队～十分积极，占据了主动。Team A gained the upperhand by pulling off a succession of interceptions.

【抢滩】qiǎngtān ❶ 船只有沉没危险时，设法使船只搁浅在浅滩上，防止沉没 try to make a sinking ship run aground in order to avert its going under ❷ 军事上指抢占滩头阵地 (mil.) take hold of a beach position：我海军陆战队快速～登陆。Our marines took hold of the beach positions and landed quickly. ❸ 商业上指抢占市场 (com.) take and occupy a market by preempting one's rivals：各种品牌的空调～京城。Air conditioners of all brands are scrambling for the Beijing market.

【抢眼】qiǎngyǎn 引人注目；显眼 eye-catching：她的衣着打扮，在人群中格外～。In her dress she was rather eye-catching in the crowds.

【俏销】qiàoxiāo 畅销 sell well; good seller：各种披肩～沈阳。All kinds of capes and shawls sell well in Shenyang.

【切换】qiēhuàn 影片、电视片等从某一镜头或画面迅速转换到另一镜头或画面，也泛指转换 cut; make a sudden shift from one scene or frame to another in a film, TV, etc.; (in a broad sense) shift：这部影片采取同期录音，现场～镜头的方法摄制。This film was made through synchronization and on-the-spot cutting.｜股市在调整中完成热点的～。The stock market completed the shift of its hot spots in the course of its readjustment.

【切入】qiērù (从某个地方)深入进去 go deep into; penetrate：～点 penetration point｜写到这里，文章已～正题。By this paragraph, the article comes straight to the main theme.

【亲子鉴定】qīnzǐ jiàndìng 用测试双方 DNA (脱氧核糖核酸)或血型的方法，来确定两个人是否为亲生父子(女)或亲生母子(女)的关系 child identification; determination of the parent-child relationship between two people by testing their DNA or blood type

【轻轨铁路】qīngguǐ tiělù 城市公共交通所使用的铁路，列车由地铁车辆或改进的有轨电车组成，可以在地面下和地面上沿轻型轨道行驶 light railway; railway used for mass transit in a city, on which a train of subway coaches or improved trolleybuses moves along under or above the ground

【倾情】qīngqíng 倾注全部情感 pour one's feelings; devote heart and soul to：～之作 work of heart and soul｜歌手～演唱。The singer sang with all his emotions.

【清仓】qīng//cāng ❶ 清理仓库 make an inventory：～核资 make an inventory of the warehouses to check up the assets ❷ 指投资者将证券等全部卖出 (of an investor) sell out all one's securities

【清洁生产】qīngjié shēngchǎn 指从原料、能源、加工到产品制成，从产品使用到废弃处置的全过程，对资源、环境和人体健康都避免产生不良影响和危害的生产方式 clean production; environment-friendly production; process of production from raw material and energy consumption and processing to the finished products, and from the use of a product to its disposal, that does not produce any adverse effect on resources, the environment and human health

【清盘】qīng//pán ❶ 企业由于某种原因不再继续经营时，变卖资产以偿还债务、分配剩余财产等，叫清盘 liquidation; go into liquidation; close a business by selling assets, settling debts and distributing surplus assets ❷ 指房屋、货物、股票等全部卖出或抛出 close out; sell out all houses, goods, stocks, etc.

【情变】qíngbiàn 爱情的突然变化，多指恋人分手 love breakdown; abrupt breakdown of a love affair, usu. referring to the separation of lovers：在他周围，男男女女～、婚变的事情确实不少。There are indeed many breakdowns of love and marriage around him.

【情商】qíngshāng 心理学上指人的情绪品质和对社会的适应能力 (psychol.) EQ (emotion quotient); emotional quality and ability to adapt to society

【球市】qiúshì 指观众购票到球场观看比赛的情势 ball game market situation; situation in which fans buy tickets to watch a ball game：～火爆 hot sales of ball game tickets

【球星】qiúxīng 称著名的球类运动员 star player; famous ball player

【球员】qiúyuán 球类运动员 (ball) player

【区位】qūwèi 地区位置 geographical location：依托海岛的～优势，积极发展养殖业 positively develop aquaculture by taking advantage of the waters around an island

【趋同】qūtóng 趋于一致 monotonous regularity：重复建设，产业～，是众多产品供过于求的主要原因。Redundant construction and monotony regularity of industrial enterprises are main causes for the glut of many products.

【取向】qǔxiàng 选取的方向；趋向 tendency; orientation：价值～ orientation of value｜审美～ orientation of aesthetics

【全科医师】quánkē yīshī 指掌握医学各科知识的医师，他们主要在社区进行疾病的预防、诊断和治疗，必要时再转给相应的专科做进一步诊治 general practitioner; doctor with the general knowledge of all medical subjects, who is mainly responsible for the prevention, diagnosis and treatment of diseases in a community and, when necessary, for the transfer of patients to a medical specialist

【全球定位系统】quánqiú dìngwèi xìtǒng 通过导航卫星对地球上任何地点的用户进行定位并报时的系统。由导航卫星、地面台站和用户定位设备组成。用于军事，也用于其他领域。

global positioning system (GPS); system for pinpointing the position of subscribers and giving the correct time at any location on the globe through a navigational satellite. The GPS consists of a navigational satellite, ground station and subscriber's positioning equipment, used either for military or other purposes.

【全职】quánzhí 专门担任某种职务的(区别于'兼职' as opposed to 'part-time job') full-time job:～教师 full-time teacher

【缺失】quēshī ❶ 缺陷;缺点 fault; shortcoming; defect; flaw; drawback:公司的经营有很多～。There are many flaws in the company's management and operations. ❷ 缺少;失去 be short of; lack; lose; miss:体育比赛不能～公平公正的原则。The principle of fair play is indispensable in sports competitions.

【缺阵】quēzhèn 〈比喻 *fig.*〉运动员因故不能上场参加比赛 no-show; absence of players in a competition for one reason or another:多名主力～使球队实力大大降低。The absence of quite a few starters in the match dibilitated the team considerably.

R

【扰民】rǎomín 搅扰人民群众 disturb the residents:噪声～ noise disturbance|防止夜间施工～。Prevent night construction work from disturbing the residents in the neighbourhood.

【热岛效应】rèdǎo xiàoyìng 城市热岛效应的简称 abbr. for 城市热岛效应 chéngshì rèdǎo xiàoyìng

【热卖】rèmài (商品)受欢迎而卖得快;畅销 (of a commodity) sell like hot cakes; sell well:初夏的京城,空调正在～中。Air conditioners are selling briskly in the capital city in early summer.

【热污染】rèwūrǎn 通常指人类生活和生产活动排放废热等造成的环境污染 heat pollution; environmental pollution caused by waste heat discharged in everyday life and productive activities

【人机界面】rén-jī jièmiàn 用户界面 man-machine interface; user's interface

【人气】rénqì ❶ 人或事物受欢迎的程度 popularity of sb. or sth.:由于该影片获奖,扮演女主角的演员～急升。As the film won the award, the popularity of the leading actress soars. ❷〈方 *dial.*〉指人的品格 character; quality:这人好～。The man has a good character.|村里谁不知道他的～! Who in the village doesn't know his character!

【人蛇】rénshé 〈方 *dial.*〉指偷渡的人 illegal immigrant; one who pays highly to a snakehead for illegal passage into a foreign country

【人造土】rénzàotǔ 用某些废弃物与有机材料研磨混合而成的培养土,重量轻,没有污染,性能良好,可以完全取代自然土壤栽培植物 artificial soil; culture soil made from grinding and blending certain waste materials and organic materials. Light in weight, pollution-free and with a good property, this kind of soil can replace natural soil for plant culture.

【认养】rènyǎng ❶ 认领并抚养 adopt and bring up:从福利院～了一个女儿 adopt a girl from an orphanage ❷ 经有关部门确认而负责养护(花木、动物) assume the responsibility to raise flowers, trees, or animals with the approval of the departments concerned:今年本市开展了绿地～活动。Activities to take care of the green land was initiated in the city earlier this year.

【容错】róngcuò 指电子计算机系统在硬件发生故障或软件出现问题时,能自行采取补救措施,不会影响整个系统的工作及其效率 fault toleration; self-remedy in a computer system that does not affect the work and efficiency of the whole system when there is a fault in the hardware or a trouble in the software

【柔性】róuxìng ❶ 柔软而易变形的(跟'刚性'相对 as opposed to 'rigid' or 'rigidity') flexible; flexibility:～材料 flexible materials ❷ 可以改变或通融的(跟'刚性'相对 as opposed to 'rigid' or 'rigidity') flexible; can be accommodated; able to make changes:～处理 handle flexibly

【入网】rù//wǎng 指手机、寻呼机等加入某个通信网,也指电子计算机加入某个网络 (of mobile phone, beeper, etc.) link with a telecommunications network; (of a computer) link with the Internet

【入围】rù//wéi 经选拔进入某一范围 be included among those selected; qualify:中国象棋锦标赛八强产生,广东两名选手～。Two players from Guangdong were among the eight qualified for the quarter-finals at the Chinese Chess Championships.|经过评选,这部长篇小说～茅盾文学奖。This novel was selected and nominated for the Mao Dun Literature Award according to the decision of a selection panel.

【入住】rùzhù 住进去 move into：小区八月竣工，年底～。The residential quarter will be completed in August, and dwellers will be able to move in towards the end of the year. | 代表团抵京后，～北京饭店。The delegation moved into the Beijing Hotel after arriving in Beijing.

【软广告】ruǎnguǎnggào 指通过广播、影视节目、报刊等用间接的形式（如情节、对话、道具、新闻报道等）对某种商品所作的宣传（区别于'硬广告' as distinguished from 'hard advertisement'）soft advertisement; promotion of a certain commodity by using an indirect form (as scene, dialogue, stage property, news report, etc.) through radio broadcasts, films, TV programmes, newspapers, etc.)

【软环境】ruǎnhuánjìng 指物质条件以外的环境，如政策、法规、管理、服务、人员素质等方面的状况 soft environment; environments other than material conditions, as policies, laws and regulations, administration, services, qualities of personnel, etc.：提高办事效率，改善投资～。Increase the efficiency in getting things done and improve the soft environment for investment.

【软科学】ruǎnkēxué 运用自然科学和社会科学，研究决策和管理的综合性科学，如科学学、管理学等 soft science; comprehensive discipline of learning dealing with decision-making and administration through the use of natural science and social science, as science studies (scienology), science of administration, etc.

【软驱】ruǎnqū 软盘驱动器的简称 abbr. for 软盘驱动器 ruǎnpán qūdòngqì; ☞ 磁盘驱动器 cípán qūdòngqì on p. 2586

【软着陆】ruǎnzhuólù ［补义 new sense］〈比喻 *fig.*〉采取稳妥的措施使某些重大问题和缓地得到解决 soft landing; take safe and reliable measures to solve a major problem the soft way：扩大内需，实现经济的～。Increase the domestic market demand to achieve the soft landing of the economy.

【软资源】ruǎnzīyuán 指科学技术、信息等，它们在发展生产力中起着重要作用，又不同于矿产、水力等天然资源，所以叫软资源 soft resources; science, technology, information, etc., which play an important role in developing the productive forces, but are different from minerals, hydraulic power and other natural resources

【弱化】ruòhuà 变弱；使变弱 enfeeble; weaken; become weak; play down; downplay：由于老队员退役，球队后卫线优势在～。As the veteran players have retired, the defence line of the team has become weaker. | 作品有意～生活的阴暗面，力图为孩子们展现乐观的未来。The works intentionally played down the seamy side of life to show an optimistic future to the children.

【弱势】ruòshì ❶ 变弱的趋势 on a decline; become weak：股票市场渐显～。The stock market went on a decline. ❷ 力量弱小的 weak; underprivileged; disadvantaged：未成年人是社会的～群体，应该得到更多的保护。Minors are a disadvantaged group of society that calls for more protection.

S

【赛季】sàijì 某些体育项目每年或跨年度集中比赛的一段时间 season; a period of time during which matches are arranged one after another for a certain sports event：全国足球联赛本～已进行了五轮比赛。Five rounds of matches have been played in the current National Football League season.

【赛况】sàikuàng 比赛的情况 proceeding of a match：中央电视台将现场直播这场决赛的～。The CCTV will broadcast the final match live.

【赛制】sàizhì 关于比赛的规则和具体安排，如循环赛制，主客场赛制等 competition system; setup of a competition, as round-robin system, home-and-away system, etc.

【三个代表】sān gè dàibiǎo 指中国共产党要始终代表中国先进生产力的发展要求，代表中国先进文化的前进方向，代表中国最广大人民的根本利益。这一重要思想是以江泽民为代表的中国共产党人，根据国际国内形势的新变化，总结党的历史经验作出的科学论断，是对马克思主义建党学说的新发展。Three Represents, i.e. the Communist Party of China is required to always represent the demand for the development of advanced productive forces in China, the direction for the advance of the advanced Chinese culture, and the fundamental interests of the broadest masses of the Chinese people. This major concept is a scientific conclusion the Chinese Communists represented by Jiang Zemin have reached in the light of new changes in the international and domestic situations and by summing up the historical experience of the Party; it is also a new development in the Marxist theory on Party building.

【三围】sānwéi 指人的胸围、腰围和臀围 three measurements; measurement of chest, waist and seat, esp. of a woman

【三维动画】sānwéi dònghuà 利用电子计算机技术生成的、模拟三维空间中场景和实物的动画 three-dimensional cartoon; cartoon made by using the computer technology to imitate scenes and objects in three dimensions

【三资企业】sānzī qǐyè 我国境内的中外合资经营企业、中外合作经营企业、外商独资经营企业的合称 foreign-invested enterprises; three types of enterprises operated with foreign investment, namely, joint ventures with Chinese and foreign capital, Chinese-foreign cooperative enterprises, and wholly-owned foreign enterprises

【散户】sǎnhù 证券市场上指资金较少的个人投资者 small individual investors in the securities market

【色狼】sèláng 指贪色并凶恶地对女性进行性侵犯的坏人 sex maniac; wolf; lecher; man who is indulged in sex and violates a woman sexually and cruelly

【色魔】sèmó 指贪色并以暴力手段对女性进行性侵犯的坏人 satyr; man who is indulged in sex and uses violent force to assault a woman sexually

【杀毒】shā//dú 指用特别编制的程序清除存在于软件或存储载体中的电子计算机病毒 kill virus; use a special programme to get rid of viruses in the software or storage carrier of a computer

【沙尘暴】shāchénbào 挟带大量尘沙的风暴，发生时空气混浊，天色昏黄，水平能见度小于1,000米。春季在我国西北部和北部地区多有发生。sandstorm; storm carrying large quantities of sand and dust, which oft. occurs in northwest China and north China in spring. The air is foul and the sky darkish yellow, and visibility reduces to less than 1,000 metres when it occurs.

【沙雕】shādiāo 用沙土做堆积材料的造型艺术。也指这样的雕塑作品。sand sculpture; plastic art using sand and soil as materials; also its works

【沙化】shāhuà 土地因受侵蚀或水土流失等原因而退化 sandification; sandify; deterioration of the land caused by loss of water and soil erosion

【沙漠化】shāmòhuà ❶ 荒漠化 desertification ❷ 特指干旱、半干旱地区土地严重退化，地表出现流沙，有覆沙现象 worsening of land conditions in arid and semi-arid regions, characterized by shifting sand dunes and the covering up of earth's surface by sand

【沙滩排球】shātān páiqiú ❶ 球类运动项目之一，在沙滩场地上进行比赛，场地面积和比赛规则与排球基本相同。国际正式比赛有两人制、四人制和男女混合制，队员穿泳装，赤脚。beach volleyball; ball game played on the beach by two-player, four-player or mixed squads, dressed in swimming suits and bare-footed, similar to the volleyball game court size and rules ❷ 沙滩排球运动使用的球，用不吸水的柔软皮革制成，大小与排球相同，颜色为黄色或橙色 yellow or orange ball used in the game, made of soft leather that does not absorb water, and of the same size as the volleyball

【煽情】shānqíng ❶ 煽动人的感情或情绪 stir; rouse strong feelings or excitement in sb.: 导演很会营造氛围～。The director is very good at creating a stirring atmosphere. ❷ 能煽动人的感情或情绪 stirring; rousing: 这是一个浪漫、～的爱情故事。This is a romantic and stirring love story.

【善待】shàndài 友善地对待；好好对待 treat friendly; treat well: ～野生动物 treat wildlife well | ～生命 cherish life

【商海】shānghǎi 〈比喻 *fig.*〉充满竞争和风险的商业领域 business world; business area full of competition and risks: 在～中拼搏 fight a life-and-death struggle in the business world

【商机】shāngjī 商业经营的机遇 business opportunity: 把握～ seize a business opportunity | 西部开发带来了许多～。The government initiative to develop the western regions in a big way has brought about plenty of business opportunities.

【商厦】shāngshà 指多层的大型商场 large, multi-floor department store

【商业片】shāngyèpiàn 以营利为主要目的的影片 commercial film; film made mainly to make a profit

【商业银行】shāngyè yínháng 以经营工商业及个人存贷款为主要业务的综合性金融机构，利用吸收存款扩大资金规模，实行企业化经营 commercial bank; comprehensive financial organization that deals chiefly in industrial, commercial and individual savings and loans, uses the deposits to augment its funds and expand its financial operation, and carries out corporate-type management

【上班族】shàngbānzú 指在机关、企事业单位工作的人，因为这些人需按时上下班，所以叫上班族 commuter; office or factory worker; people working in government offices, companies and institutions as they have to go to work and leave offices at fixed times

【上浮】shàngfú （价格、利率、工资等）向上浮动 (price, interest rate, work pay, etc.) rise; increase: ～一级工资 raise sb.'s wage or salary by one grade | 物价指数～一个百分点

the price index rose by one percentage point

【上佳】shàngjiā 上好；非常好 optimal；best possible：竞技状态～ be in a very good competitive form｜推出～的营销策划 put forward an excellent marketing plan

【上镜】shàngjìng ❶ 出现在电影、电视中 appear in a film or TV：她还在电影学院学习期间就已经多次～。She appeared many times in films and TV plays when she was still a film academy student. ❷ 在电影、电视中的形象好 photogenic；have a good image in film or TV：这位节目主持人很～。This anchor has a good image on the TV screen.

【上市公司】shàngshì gōngsī 经有关部门核准，公开发行股票并在证券交易所上市交易的股份有限公司 listed company；joint stock company that issues stocks and is listed on the stock exchange market with the approval of the departments concerned

【上台阶】shàng//táijiē 〈比喻 *fig*.〉社会发展、工作、生产等达到一个新的高度 reach a new height in social development，work，production，etc.：粮食产量～。Grain production has reached a new height.｜本市经济又上了新台阶。The economy in this city has reachcd a new height.

【上网】shàng//wǎng 操作电子计算机进入互联网，在网络上进行信息检索、查询等（跟'下网'相对 as opposed to 'log off'）log on；log in；use a computer to connect with the Internet to read or retrieve information

【上扬】shàngyáng （数量、价格等）上升（of quantity，price，etc.）rise；climb up；increase；go up：收视率～ rising rating of a TV programme｜租金～。The rent rises.

【上载】shàngzǎi 把信息从某台电子计算机输入到互联网或其他电子计算机上（跟'下载'相对 as opposed to 'download'）upload；load or transfer information from one computer to another or the Internet

【蛇头】shétóu 〈方 *dial*.〉称组织偷渡并从中获取钱财的坏人 ringleader of organized illegal immigration

【社会保险】shèhuì bǎoxiǎn 国家以保险形式实行的社会保障制度，在劳动者或公民暂时或永久丧失劳动能力以及发生其他困难时，由国家、社会对他们给予物质保证 social insurance；social security system instituted by the government in the form of social insurance，by which the state or the public provides material guarantee in case a labourer or citizen loses his or her work ability temporarily or permanently or has other difficulties

【社情】shèqíng 社会情况 social conditions：了解～民意 get to known the social conditions and public opinions｜该地区～十分复杂。Conditions in that area are extremely complicated.

【涉案】shè'àn 牵涉到案件之中；案件所涉及的 involved in a case：这起经济案件～人员七人，～金额一千多万元。This financial case involves seven people and more than ten million yuan.

【申办】shēnbàn 申请举办 bid for：～奥运会 bid for the Olympic Games

【申购】shēngòu 申请购买 apply for the purchase of：～新股 apply for the purchase of new stocks｜～解困房 apply to buy a house built for those having housing problems

【审验】shěnyàn 审核查验；审查检验 inspect；examine，check：～驾驶证 check sb.'s driving licence｜～商店的注册资金和经营范围 examine and verify the registered capital and business line of a shop

【升班马】shēngbānmǎ 指在分级的体育比赛中由低一级升入高一级的运动队 team rising from a lower grade to a higher grade in a graded sports event

【生境】shēngjìng 指生物的个体、种群或群落生活地域的环境，包括必需的生存条件和其他对生物起作用的生态因素 environment for individuals，species，or communities organisms，including essential living conditions and other ecological factors that are vital to them

【生猛】shēngměng ［补义 new sense］指富有生气和活力 action-packed；full of vigour and life；(of seafood) fresh from the sea：～的武打动作 action-packed fighting movements

【生态标志】shēngtài biāozhì 环境标志 ecological label；environment label

【生态工程】shēngtài gōngchéng 运用生态学和系统工程原理建立的生产工艺体系。结构复杂、相对稳定的生态系统，能在有限空间养育最多的生物种类，各种有机物质和无机物质资源能被不同营养级的生物充分利用。ecological engineering；productive technological system established by using the principles of ecology and system engineering. A relatively stable eco-system with complicated structure can raise the greatest number of plants and animal species in a limited space and enable various organic and inorganic matters to be fully utilized by plants and animals of different trophic levels.

【生态环境】shēngtài huánjìng 生物和影响生物生存与发展的一切外界条件的总和。由许多生态因素综合而成，其中非生物因素有光、温度、水分、大气、土壤和无机盐类等，生物因素有植物、动物、微生物等。在自然界，生态因素相互联系，相互影响，共同对生物发生作用。eco-environment；ecological environment；sum total of organisms and all the external conditions that affect their survival and development. An eco-environment encompasses many ecological factors, including non-organic ones such as light, temperature, water, air, soil and inorganic salts, and organic ones such as plants, animals and microbes. In the nature, ecological factors are interrelated, affecting each other, and producing a joint effect on organisms.

【生态农业】shēngtài nóngyè 按照生态学原理,应用现代科学技术进行集约经营管理的农业,是一种新型综合农业生产体系 ecological agriculture; intensive farming using modern sciences and technology according to ecological principles; new type of multi-purpose farming system

【生物工程】shēngwù gōngchéng 借助生命物质参与改造自然现象的生物学技术。酶工程、基因工程、细胞工程等都属于生物工程。bioengineering; biological engineering; biological technology designed to involve life substances such as enzyme engineering, gene engineering and cell engineering in transformation of natural phenomena

【生物污染】shēngwù wūrǎn 寄生虫、细菌和病毒等有害生物对大气、水源、土壤、食物所造成的污染,主要由医院污水、肉类加工和食品加工产生的废水、污浊空气等引起 biological pollution; pollution of the air, water sources, soil and food caused by harmful organisms such as parasites, bacteria and viruses, mainly from the polluted water from hospitals and the waste water and foul air resulting from meat processing and food processing

【生物芯片】shēngwù xīnpiàn 用生物大分子为材料制造的分子电路系统,集成度高,能耗小,速度快,生物体系中的生物分子可以自我修复、自我复制。主要包括基因芯片、蛋白质芯片等。biological chip; molecular circuit system made from bio-macromolecules, of such major types as gene chip and protein chip, which is characterized by a high degree of integration, low energy consumption and fast speed. The bio-molecules in a biological system can repair and duplicate themselves.

【声讯】shēngxùn 由专设的电话提供的各类信息咨询业务 telephone information service: ～台 telephone information service; telephone information station | 求职者可拔打～电话查询有关事宜。Job seekers may dial the telephone information service for information.

【声讯台】shēngxùntái 从事有偿电话信息服务的机构 telephone information station; institution offering paid information services on the phone

【胜出】shèngchū (在比赛或竞争中)胜过对手 beat the rival; outplay an opponent (in a match or competition): 在大选中～ won a major election | 甲队在比赛中以3比0～。Team A won the game 3:0.

【胜机】shèngjī 取胜的机会 chance of winning; winning chance: 痛失～ lose the winning chance with regret | 把握～ seize the chance to win

【胜绩】shèngjì 在比赛中获胜的成绩 win; victory (in sports competition): 自开赛以来,该队尚无～。The team has had no wins yet since the season began.

【胜率】shènglǜ ❶ 获胜的概率 winning chance; winning probability: 乙队的～略高于甲队。Team B has a slightly better chance than Team A. ❷ 获胜的次数与参加比赛等的总次数的比率,如某选手参加比赛10场,获胜6场,胜率为60% winning rate; ratio between the number of wins to the number of appearances, e.g. a player appears in ten matches and wins six, then his winning rate is 60%

【失范】shīfàn 失去规范;违背规范 irregular; not obeying the usu. accepted legal or moral rules: 严重的市场～会危及整个经济秩序 serious non-standard market operations can jeopardize the whole economic order | 避免辞书用语～ avoid the use of non-standard words and terms in a dictionary

【失婚】shīhūn 指已经离婚或丧偶后未再婚 lose one's spouse to death or divorce and remain unmarried

【失序】shīxù 失去正常的秩序 lose order; go out of order: 一旦企业管理～,生产就会瘫痪。Once enterprise management runs out of order, production will be paralyzed.

【失业保险】shīyè bǎoxiǎn 社会保险的一种。保险机构在劳动者失业后发生经济困难时提供失业保险金等物质帮助。unemployment insurance, which is a kind of social insurance. An insurance company will provide unemployment insurance when a worker loses his job and has economic difficulties.

【湿租】shīzū 一种租赁方式,在租赁设备、交通工具等时,同时配备操纵、维修人员(跟'干租'相对 as opposed to 'dry lease') wet-lease; a kind of lease in which equipment or means of transportation are leased together with operating and maintenance personnel: 中国民航向国际市场～大型客机。Chinese airlines wet-lease large-capacity passenger planes to the international market.

【时间差】shíjiānchā ❶ 排球运动上指守方队员跳起拦网下落后攻方队员才攻球这两者之间短暂的时间差距,这种进攻方法叫打时间差 (in volleyball game) time difference; the difference between the time after a defending player jumps up to block and lands and the time an attacking player pounds an attacking smash. This offensive move is called attack with a time difference：北京队打了个～，赢得一分。The Beijing team won a point by attacking with a time difference. ❷ 泛指可以利用的两事之间的时间差距 time difference between two matters：商贩利用南北方水果成熟期不同的～牟利。Traders make use of the north-south difference in the fruit's ripening time to make profits.

【时蔬】shíshū 正当时令的蔬菜 seasonal vegetables

【实名】shímíng 真实的姓名 real name：存款～制 real-name savings deposit system

【实名制】shímíngzhì 办理存款等的一种制度。办理有关手续时必须出示有效的身份证明，并填写真实姓名。real-name savings deposit system; system for depositing savings in a bank, whereby the depositor is obliged to present his valid identity and fill his real name when he goes through the necessary formalities

【实时】shíshí 在某事发生、发展过程中的同一时间 live; real-time; time during which the occurrence of an event and the reporting or recording of it are simultaneous：进行～报道 report an event live｜～传递股市行情 transmit or convey real-time stock market prices

【实职】shízhí 非虚设的、有实际权力和责任的职务（跟'虚职'相对 as opposed to 'nominal position'）solid position; position with real power and responsibility

【士官】shìguān 我国志愿兵役制士兵称士官，一般从服役期满的义务兵中选取，必要时也从军外具有专业技能的公民中招收。士官的军衔分为三等六级。warrant officer; rank-and-file soldier in the Chinese army under the voluntary service system, who is usu. selected from among compulsory servicemen who have completed their term of service, and when necessary from among civilian citizens with professional knowledge and skills. Warrant officers are classified into three grades and six classes.

【示爱】shì'ài 表示爱慕之情 show one's love：向意中人～ show one's love to a person one is in love with｜壮族青年常常以山歌～。Young people of the Zhuang ethnic group often sing folk songs to express love to their sweethearts.

【世界贸易组织】Shìjiè Máoyì Zǔzhī 全球性的贸易组织。主要职责是规范、协调、促进世界范围内的贸易活动，消除关贸壁垒，降低关税，处理贸易纠纷等。1995年1月1日成立，总部设在日内瓦。其前身是关税和贸易总协定。WTO; World Trade Organization; global trade organization whose main duties and responsibilities are to standardize, coordinate and promote trade activities worldwide, eliminate tariff and trade barriers, reduce custom duties and handle trade disputes. Its predecessor was the General Agreement on Tariffs and Trade (GATT) set up on January 1, 1995 with headquarters in Geneva.

【市场机制】shìchǎng jīzhì 市场经济体系中各种要素之间的有机联系和相互作用及其对资源配置的调节功能。是价值规律调节商品生产和流通的主要形式。在社会主义市场经济中，市场机制在国家宏观调控下对资源配置起基础性作用。market mechanism; organic connection and interaction among various elements in a market economy and their function in regulating the allocation of resources. The market mechanism is a main form of using the law of value to regulate commodity production and circulation. In a socialist market economy, the market mechanism plays a basic role in the allocation of resources under the state's macroeconomic control.

【市道】shìdào 市场价格的状况；行市 market prices：～转暖。The market prices are turning for the better. ｜～低迷。The market prices are running low.

【市话】shìhuà 市区电话 inner-city telephone service

【市况】shìkuàng 市场的交易状况 situation with market transactions; business situation：鲜花～日益看好。The fresh flower trade is getting brisker day after day.

【市值】shìzhí 按照现时的市场行情计算的价值 market value; value calculated on the basis of current market prices：这所老房子～至少数百万元。The market value of this old house amounts to at least several million yuan.｜他拥有的个人股份～有七十多万元。The market value of his personal shares is at least more than 700,000 yuan.

【试播】shìbō ❶ 新建立的广播电台或电视台进行试验性播放，以检验设备的性能是否合乎要求 trial broadcasting of a new radio or television station to check if the performance of the equipment is up to the requirements ❷ 节目正式播放前为听取意见先在一定范围内播放 test showing of a programme to a limited number of people to collect their comments for improvement before the programme is officially released to the public

【试岗】shìgǎng 在某个工作岗位先试着工作一段时间，以考察是否适合这一岗位 work on probation; testing of a person's on the job ability for a period of time to see if he fits the job

【试管婴儿】shìguǎn yīng'ér 指体外受精成功后，受精卵在试管中培育一段时间再移入妇女子宫内发育诞生的婴儿 test-tube baby; after successful external insemination, the zygote is bred in the tube for a period of time before it is transplanted into the womb of a woman for the development of the baby

【试镜】shìjìng 在影片、电视片正式拍摄前，先让演员拍摄一些镜头，以确定该演员是否适合所扮演的角色 screen test; filmed audition to determine a person's suitability as a movie actor or for a particular role：首次～即被选中 be selected in the first screen test

【视点】shìdiǎn 观察或分析事物的着眼点 point of departure for observation or analysis：作者的～比较独特，文章很有新意。The writer has an original point of departure for observation and the article is full of new ideas.

【视界】shìjiè 视野；眼界 field of vision; view：船刚转弯，几点灯火进入～。A few lights came into view just as the boat turned round.｜参观了科技新成果展览，～大开。The exhibition of new scientific and technological achievements was a great eye-opener for us visitors.

【视盘】shìpán 视频光盘的简称 abbr. for 视频光盘 shìpín guāngpán

【视盘机】shìpánjī 一种放像设备，用激光光束将光盘上存储的数字视频和伴音信息读出并转换为视频信号和音频信号。根据记录密度和格式的不同，可分为 VCD 和 DVD 等。disc player; device which uses a laser beam to read the digital information on a disc and convert it into signals. According to the recording density and format, the players fall into VCD and DVD types.

【视频光盘】shìpín guāngpán 一种只读型光盘，可以存储图像信息。制作时，把记录的视频信号加以转换处理，刻录在光盘上。通过视盘机播放，再现动态的图像和声音。VCD; video compact disc; read-only disc which stores image information. The recorded signals are converted and recorded on the disc. When it is played on a disc player, the images in motion are shown with accompanying sound; 简称 abbr. 视盘 shìpán

【手包】shǒubāo （～儿 shǒubāor）手提的较小的包儿，多用皮革制成 handbag; small leather bag

【手袋】shǒudài 〈方 *dial.*〉手包（多指女用的 usu. for women's use) handbag

【手机】shǒujī 手持式移动电话机的简称 abbr. for 手持式移动电话机 shǒuchíshì yídòng diànhuàjī (cellphone; mobile phone)

【手链】shǒuliàn 戴在手腕子上的链形装饰品，多用金、银、玉石等制成 bracelet; ornamental band or chain worn about the wrist, mostly made of gold, silver, jade, etc.

【首播】shǒubō （广播电台、电视台）第一次播放 (of radio or TV station) premiere; broadcast a programme for the first time：这个节目每周二 19∶40～，周六 21∶50 重播。This programme is released at 19∶40 every Tuesday and rerun at 21∶50 on Saturday.

【首发】shǒufā ❶ 第一次发行 release; publish for the first time：大百科全书的～式在北京举行。A ceremony to release the Encyclopedia was held in Beijing. ❷ 第一次发车 dispatch the first bus：这路公共汽车每天早晨五点半～。The first bus for this route leaves at 5∶30 every morning. ❸ 第一次发放 first distribution：新式军服～仪式 ceremony marking the release of the new army uniform ❹ 球类比赛中首先出场 start (a ball game)：～阵容 start list; start line-up

【受众】shòuzhòng 新闻媒体的传播对象和各种文化、艺术作品的接受者，包括读者、听众和观众等 readership and audience, including readers, listeners, viewers, etc.：电视～ TV audience｜就文化产品而言，关键是心中要有～。So far as cultural products are concerned, the crucial point is to bear the readers in mind.

【疏离】shūlí 疏远隔离 be estranged and kept apart：关系～ be estranged and keep apart｜一个作家任何时候都不应～社会。A writer should not alienate himself from society at any time.

【蔬果】shūguǒ 蔬菜和水果的合称 vegetables and fruits：～专用清洗剂 vegetable and fruit wash

【鼠标器】shǔbiāoqì 电子计算机的一种输入设备。基本功能是将手的移动转换成计算机屏幕上光标的移动，用手指点击上面的键，可以对计算机进行操作，主要用于选单项目的选择以及计算机绘图。因外形略像老鼠，所以叫鼠标器。mouse; small hand-held device roughly in the shape of a mouse to be moved about on a flat surface in such a way as to move the cursor to the desired position on a computer screen. By clicking a button on the mouse, a signal is sent to the computer to select an item from the manu or draw a diagram. 简称 abbr. 鼠标 shǔbiāo

【数秒】shǔmiǎo 在爆破作业起爆前或人造卫星、宇宙飞船发射前的最后时刻倒着数出所剩的秒数，如 5、4、3、2、1，数完最后一秒起爆或发射。有时也用于其他活动。countdown; count down the seconds until a blasting operation or the launching of a man-made satellite or spaceship takes place, e.g., the blasting or launching starts right after the commander has counted from five, four... to one. The countdown is also used in other activities sometimes.

【数据库】shùjùkù 存放在电子计算机存储器中，按照一定格式编成的相互关联的各种数据的集合，供用户迅速有效地进行数据处理 database; conglomeration of data stored in the hard disc of a computer, organized according to a certain format in such a way that the data can be processed rapidly and efficiently

【数码相机】shùmǎ xiàngjī 数字相机 digital camera

【数字电视】shùzì diànshì 通过编码把图像、伴音的模拟信号转换成数字信号传输的电视。可减少畸变和干扰，提高电视画面的清晰程度。digital TV; television that converts analogue signals into digital signals by encoding the images and accompanying sounds. Digital television can reduce distortion and interference and increase the clarity of the screen display.

【数字化】shùzìhuà 指在某个领域的各个方面或某种产品的各个环节都采用数字信息处理技术 digitalize; use of digital information processing technology in all aspects of a certain field or in all links of a certain product

【数字相机】shùzì xiàngjī 能够将拍摄对象的影像变成数字信息的相机。拍摄的影像能输入电子计算机保存和修改加工，通过数字打印机可获得彩色照片。digital camera; camera capable of converting a photographed image into digital information. The photographed image can be programmed into a computer for storing and processing, and colour pictures can be obtained by using a colour printer; also 数码相机 shùmǎ xiàngjī

【刷卡】shuā//kǎ 把磁卡放在磁卡机上，使磁头阅读、识别磁卡中的信息，以确认持卡人的身份或增减磁卡中的储存金额。因有的磁卡需在磁卡机上移动，类似刷的动作，所以叫刷卡。swipe a magnetic card on a magnetic card reading machine so that the magnetic head can read and recognize the information in the card in order to identify the card holder or increase or decrease the amount of money deposited in the card

【双轨制】shuāngguǐzhì 指两种不同体制并行的制度 double-track system; two-tiered system：某些物资实行国家定价和市场调节的～。Some goods were tagged with dual prices — a state-fixed price, and a price to be regulated by the market.

【双休日】shuāngxiūrì 实行每周五天工作制时，每周连续的两个休息日叫双休日（一般为星期六、星期日）(usu. Saturday and Sunday) two-day weekend of the five-workday system

【双赢】shuāngyíng 双方都能得益 win-win situation; both sides benefit：本着平等互利的精神，谈判取得～的结果。The talks ended with both parties winning in the spirit of equality and mutual benefit.

【水华】shuǐhuá 淡水水域中一些藻类和其他浮游生物大量繁殖和过度密集而引起的水体污染现象，会造成水质恶化，鱼类死亡 water bloom; algal bloom; water pollution caused by massive reproduction and dense population of blooming algae and other plankton, resulting in the worsening of water quality and death of fishes; also 藻花 zǎohuā

【水体】shuǐtǐ 水的集合体。包括江、河、湖、海、冰川、积雪、水库、池塘等，也包括地下水和大气中的水汽。waters; body of waters, including rivers, lakes, seas, glaciers, accumulated snow, reservoirs, ponds, etc. as well as groundwater and vapours in the atmosphere

【水体污染】shuǐtǐ wūrǎn 工业废水、生活污水和其他废弃物进入江河湖海等，超过水体自净能力所造成的污染 pollution of waters; pollution caused to the water by the discharge of more industrial waste water, domestic sewage and other wastes than a river, lake or sea can clean by itself

【顺价】shùnjià （购销部门）销售商品时的价格高于收购时的价格（跟'逆价'相对 as opposed to 'unfavourable price'）favourable price; (of a purchasing and marketing department) sell a commodity at a price higher than its purchasing price：实行粮食～销售 sell grain at favourable prices; put grain up for sale at favourable prices

【硕导】shuòdǎo 硕士研究生导师的简称 abbr. for 硕士研究生导师 shuòshì yánjiūshēng dǎoshī (adviser for MA candidates)

【司职】sīzhí 担任某种职务；担负某种职责 take up a position or responsibility：他在这场比赛中～前锋。He played forward in this game.

【私密】sīmì ❶ 属于个人而比较隐私的 private and personal：卧室的设计讲究～性。The design of the bedroom is private and personal. ❷ 个人的秘密；隐私 privacy：窥探他人的～ nose into sb.'s privacy

【私企】sīqǐ 私营企业的简称 abbr. for 私营企业 sīyíng qǐyè

【私营企业】sīyíng qǐyè 私人投资经营的企业，包括独资企业、合伙企业、有限责任公司等。企业资产属私人所有，存在雇佣关系。私营企业是我国社会主义市场经济的重要组成部分。private enterprise; enterprise operated with private investment, including wholly owned enterprises, partnerships, and limited liability companies. In a private company the assets are privately owned and there is an employee-employer relationship. Private enterprises are an important component part of the socialist market economy in China. 简称 abbr. 私企 sīqǐ

【死机】sǐ//jī 电子计算机运行中因程序错误或其他原因而不正常地停止运行，此时屏幕图像静止不动，无法继续操作 (of a computer) crash; computer stops working due to a programme error or other factors and the image on its screen becomes still

【诉求】sùqiú ❶ 陈诉和请求 recount and request：他耐心地倾听老人的～。He listened to the old man's account and request with patience. ❷ 追求；要求 pursuit; demand; request：廉政成为广大群众对领导干部的一致～。Honest and clean government is what the broad masses unanimously require of their leaders.

【素质教育】sùzhì jiàoyù 以提高人的综合素质为根本宗旨的教育。要求对学生实施德、智、体、美、劳的全面教育，着重培养学生的创新精神和实践的能力。quality-oriented education; education with the fundamental aim of improving students' overall qualities, requiring schools to provide students with all-round development of moral, intellectual, physical, aesthetic and manual education, with stress on the training of their innovative spirit and practical ability

【速递】sùdì 特快专递 express delivery：邮政～ express mail delivery

【塑钢】sùgāng 一种用于制作门窗等的材料，用聚氯乙烯、树脂等原料，添加适当助剂、改性剂挤压成型，框架是中空的，里面嵌装槽形钢材 plastic and steel frame; material for making door and window frames, whereby polyvinyl chloride and resin added with assistants and modifiers, are extrusion-molded into hollow frames, which are filled with channel-section steel as reenforcement

【随机】suíjī ❶ 跟着情况的变化，掌握时机 act according to circumstances：密切关注经济的发展，～调整农业政策。Pay close attention to economic development and adjust the agricultural policy according to circumstances. ❷ 不设任何条件，随意地 random：～采样 random sampling | 记者在大街上～采访了几位市民。The reporter had random interviews with some citizens in streets.

【索偿】suǒcháng 索取赔偿 claim damages：根据保险合同向保险公司～ claim damages from an insurance company according to an insurance contract

【锁定】suǒdìng ❶ 使固定不动 keep to：只要有足球赛，他就会～电视频道。Whenever there is a football match, he keeps to the TV sports channel. | 按动照相机的快门，将这个美好的瞬间～。He clicked his camera button to record this wonderful moment. ❷ 最终确定 finally decide：终场前甲队前锋又攻进一球，把比分～在2比0上。Another goal by Team A's forward at the buzz sealed the match score at 2：0. | 根据目击者提供的情况，警方很快将凶犯的身份～。According to information provided by witnesses, the police quickly identified the murder suspect. ❸ 紧紧跟定 follow closely：这种电子侦测系统能同时搜索并～数百个来犯的目标。This electronic scouting system can search for and locate the whereabouts of several hundred intruding objects simultaneously.

T

【胎死腹中】tāi sǐ fù zhōng 〈比喻 *fig*.〉计划、方案等尚未实施就遭到失败或被取消 death in the womb; (of a plan, operation, etc.) fail or be cancelled before it gets started

【台海】Táihǎi 台湾海峡的简称 abbr. for 台湾海峡 Táiwān Hǎixiá (Taiwan Straits)

【抬升】táishēng [补义 new sense]泛指抬高；上升 lift：将左臂向上～ lift the left arm | 房地产的价格在逐步～。The real estate prices are rising step by step.

【跆拳道】táiquándào 体育运动项目之一，起源于朝鲜半岛，两人徒手赤足搏击，以脚踢、踹为主，手击打为辅，以击中对方身体的有效部位的次数多少判定胜负 tae kwon do; sport which originated on the Korean Peninsula, in which two contestants fight each other with bare limbs with kicking supplemented by punching, and the winner is decided on the basis of the number of hits scored on the valid parts of the body of the opponent

【太阳风暴】tàiyáng fēngbào 指太阳在黑子活动高峰阶段产生的剧烈爆发活动。爆发时释放大量带电粒子所形成的高速粒子流，严重影响地球的空间环境，破坏臭氧层，干扰无线通信，对人体健康也有一定的危害。solar storm; violent explosion of the sun at the peak time of sunspot activities. During the explosion, the sun releases massive flow of high-speed charged particles, gravely affecting the space environment of the earth, undermining the ozone layer, interfering in radio communications and causing certain harm to the human health.

【弹升】tánshēng (价格等)反弹;回升 bounce back; rebound; rise again:股价大跌后又小幅～。Stock prices rose slightly again after they had dropped sharply.

【坦陈】tǎnchén 坦率地陈述 state frankly:与会代表～自己的观点。The delegates stated their views frankly.

【坦承】tǎnchéng 坦白地承认 admit candidly:不少家长～在教育子女的问题上存在困惑。Many parents admitted frankly that they had felt uncertain on the question of educating their children.

【坦言】tǎnyán ❶ 坦率地说 be straightforward about; say frankly:他～自己对音乐懂得不多。He said frankly that he had little knowledge of music. ❷ 坦率的话 straightforward remarks:～相告 give candid advice to sb.

【碳三植物】tàn-sān zhíwù 植物进行光合作用时,固定二氧化碳形成的第一个产物是三碳糖,这类植物叫做碳三植物,如小麦、水稻等。碳三植物光吸收效率高,光合效率低,因而产量较低。C_3 plant. When a plant undergoes photosynthesis and the first product formed by the fixed carbon dioxide is a tricarbon sugar, such a plant is called C_3 plant, as wheat, rice, etc. C_3 plants have a high efficiency of light absorption, but a low efficiency of photosynthesis, and therefore their output is low.

【碳四植物】tàn-sì zhíwù 植物进行光合作用时,固定二氧化碳形成的第一产物是四碳糖,这类植物叫做碳四植物,如玉米、高粱等。碳四植物光吸收效率低,光合效率高,因而产量较高。C_4 plant. When a plant undergoes photosynthesis and the first product formed by the fixed carbon dioxide is a four-carbon sugar, such a plant is called C_4 plant, as maize, sorghum, etc. C_4 plants have a low efficiency of light absorption, but a high efficiency of photosynthesis, and therefore their output is high.

【碳纤维】tànxiānwéi 含碳量高于90%的无机高分子纤维。耐高温,耐腐蚀,抗疲劳,强度高,纤维密度低,可加工成织物等。有碳纤维加入的复合材料是制造飞机、火箭和化工厂耐腐蚀设备等的优良材料。carbon fibre; inorganic high polymer fibre containing 90% of carbon, resistant to high temperature, erosion and fatigue and with high strength and low density. It can be processed into fabric. Composite material with carbon fibre is a fine material for making airplanes, rockets and erosion-resistant equipment for chemical works.

【陶艺】táoyì 制作陶器的技艺,也指陶制的艺术品 craft of making ceramics; ceramics

【套牢】tàoláo 预期证券价格将上涨而买入,结果价格不涨反跌,投资者不甘心在低价位卖出,被动等待价格回升,致使资金在较长时间内被占用,这种情况叫套牢 in the court; buy securities when prices are expected to rise, but the prices do not rise as expected but fall. The investor is unwilling to sell them at low prices and has to wait passively for the prices to rise again. As a result, the funds are held up for a long time.

【特别行政区】tèbié xíngzhèngqū 按照一国两制的基本国策设置的具有特殊法律地位和高度自治权的地方行政区域,如香港特别行政区、澳门特别行政区 special administrative zone; administrative region with a special legal status and a high degree of autonomy, set up in accordance with the fundamental state policy of 'one country, two systems', as the Hong Kong Special Administrative Region and the Macao Special Administrative Region; 简称 abbr. 特区 tèqū

【特惠】tèhuì 特别优惠 specially preferential:～价格 specially preferential prices | 商厦～酬宾。The shopping centre sells goods at specially preferential prices.

【特警】tèjǐng 经过特殊训练,配有特殊装备,执行特殊任务的武装警察。主要任务是打击劫持、暗杀等暴力犯罪活动。special police force; armed police with special training and equipped with special arms to carry out special missions, mainly to strike at crimes of violence such as kidnapping, assassination, etc.

【特快专递】tèkuài zhuāndì 专门递送时间性特别强的邮件的快速寄递业务 express mail service (EMS); 简称 abbr. 快递 kuàidì; also 速递 sùdì

【特困】tèkùn 特别困难(多指经济、住房等)(oft. referring to economic and housing status) destitute; penurious; down and out:～户 destitute family; family in utter poverty | ～生 student with serious financial difficulties; student from a down-and-out family

【特卖】tèmài 以特别优惠的价格卖 special sales; sell at specially preferential prices:商场举办家电～活动。There is a special sale for household electric appliances in the shopping centre. | 女式大衣五折～。Ladies' overcoats sell at a 50% discount.

【特勤】tèqín ❶ 特殊勤务,如重大活动中的安全保卫、交通指挥等 special duty, such as security and traffic control on special occasions:出～ be on special duty ❷ 指执行特殊勤务的人 person on a special mission

【特区】tèqū [补义 new sense] 特别行政区的简称 abbr. for 特别行政区 tèbié xíngzhèngqū:香港～ Hong Kong SAR | 澳门

～Macao SAR

【特首】tèshǒu 称香港、澳门特别行政区行政长官 Chief Executive of Hong Kong or Macao SAR

【特许经营】tèxǔ jīngyíng 一种企业经营方式。拥有先进经营管理经验和名牌产品、特色服务或专利等优异条件的企业，用契约形式特许其他独立的企业使用自己的商标、店名和经营模式进行经营，并收取使用费。franchise; right to market a product under its trademark or provide a service in its name oft. exclusively for a specified area, as granted by a manufacturer or company with advanced management experience and famous brand products, excellent service or patent in the form of a contract and for a fee

【梯次】tīcì ❶ 依照一定次序分级或分批地 by echelon or by group; in order of age, size, etc.:按年轻化的标准～配备干部 fill leadership posts with functionaries in order and according to the requirement that the lower the position is the younger the functionary should become | 这个服装厂～推出了衬衫、西服、女装等产品。The garment factory developed shirts, Western suits, ladies' dresses and other products in order. ❷ 依照一定次序分成的级或批 by grades and in groups:这个厂的产品结构～合理。The grading of the product mix in this factory is reasonable.

【梯度】tīdù ❶ 坡度 slope; gradient ❷ 单位时间或单位距离内某种现象(如温度、气压、密度、速度等)变化的程度 gradient; change of temperature, atmospheric pressure, density, speed, etc. in a certain time or within a certain distance ❸ 依照一定次序分层次地 in order:我国经济发展由东向西～推进。The economic development in China has proceeded in good order from east to west. ❹ 依照一定次序分出的层次 classification by level:考试命题要讲究题型有变化，难易有～。When setting questions for exams see to it that the questions are varied in type and gradient in degree of difficulty.

【提存】tícún 债务人因债权人的原因无法对债权人履行义务时，依法将应偿还的物品(一般为动产)交由法院或有关机关保存，从而解除债务债权关系 deposit; when a debtor is unable to fulfil his obligation because of his creditor, he shall hand over the articles (usu. movables) he is bound to hand back to the court or a government organ for safekeeping according to law, thereby putting an end to the debtor-creditor relationship

【提速】tí//sù 提高速度 increase the speed:铁路列车全面～。Train speed has been raised on all the railways.

【提现】tíxiàn 提取现金 draw cash money:本行办理贷款、结算、～等业务。This bank offers loan, settlement, cash drawing and other services.

【题库】tíkù 大量习题或考题的汇编 examination question bank:高中数学～ senior middle school mathematics examination question bank | 从规定的～中提取试题 retrieve examination questions from an officially mandated examination question bank

【体测】tǐcè 对身体运动能力进行测试 testing of physical strength

【体能】tǐnéng 身体的运动能力，包括耐力和在单位时间内运动的速度等 physical strength, including stamina and speed of movement per time unit:～测试 physical strength test | 加强～训练 intensify physical strength training

【天价】tiānjià 指极高的价格 prohibitive price; exorbitant price:这种房子的价格是每平方米六万元，堪称～。This kind of house sells for a whopping 60,000 yuan per square metre. It's outrageous indeed!

【天量】tiānliàng 指极大的数量 staggering amount; monstrous quantity:商厦在国庆期间创下销售～。The shopping mall reported a staggering sales volume during the National Day holiday.

【填权】tiánquán 某只股票在除权、除息后交易价格高于除权、除息价格叫填权 trading price of a stock after ex rights and ex dividends is higher than the ex rights and ex dividends price

【调适】tiáoshì 调整使适应 modulate; adjust to adapt; fine-tune:～家庭成员关系 adjust and adapt the relationship in a family | 学会自我心理～ learn how to adjust one's own psychology

【调制解调器】tiáozhì-jiětiáoqì 电子计算机通信中模拟信号与数字信号的转换设备，由调制器和解调器组成。调制器把发送的数字信号转换为模拟信号，解调器把接收到的模拟信号还原为数字信号。modem; device that it consists of a modulator and a demodulator to convert data to a form that can be transmitted, as by telephone, to data-processing equipment where a similar device reconvert it. The modulator converts digital signals into analogue signals for transmission and the demodulator reconverts the received analogue signals into digital signals.

【跳舞毯】tiàowǔtǎn 一种娱乐用品，是一个带电子感应接口能够与家用电子计算机或电视机相连接的脚垫，人站在脚垫上随着音乐跳舞，同时按照屏幕上不断移动的箭头指示变换脚踩的点 dancing mat; foot mat with electronic inductions connected with a personal computer or TV set, on which a person dances to the accompaniment of music with the directional arrows changing on the screen to show changes in foot steps

【贴权】tiēquán 某只股票在除权、除息后交易价格低于除权、除息价格叫贴权 trading price of a stock after ex rights and ex dividends is lower than the ex rights and ex dividends price

【铁人三项】tiěrén sānxiàng 综合性体育比赛项目之一。由依次进行的天然水域游泳、公路自行车、公路长跑三个项目组成,要求运动员连续完成。由于这项运动需要运动员具有坚强的意志和充沛的体力,所以叫铁人三项。iron man triathlon; sporting event combining three separate events to be finished continuously: swimming in a natural water, road cycling and road running. As the sport requires an athlete to have strong will power and enormous physical stamina, it is thus called iron man triathlon.

【停牌】tíng//pái 指某只股票暂停交易 suspension of a stock for sale

【通关】tōngguān ❶ ☞ 打通关 dǎ tōngguān on p. 351 ❷ 通过海关 clear the customs:~口 customs clearance post | 进出境车辆的~速度提高了。It is a lot faster now for inbound and outbound vehicles to clear the customs.

【通货紧缩】tōnghuò jǐnsuō ❶ 国家纸币的发行量小于流通中所需要的货币量,引起物价下跌的现象。通货紧缩会造成国民经济增长乏力和衰退,失业率上升,人民生活水平下降。deflation; lessening of the amount of money in circulation, resulting in a sharp and sudden rise in its value and a fall in price. Deflation may hold back economic growth and cause economic recession. ❷ 缩减流通中的纸币数量,提高货币的购买力,以抑制通货膨胀 reduce the amount of money in circulation to raise its purchasing power so as to check inflation ‖ 简称 abbr. 通缩 tōngsuō

【通缩】tōngsuō 通货紧缩的简称 abbr. for 通货紧缩 tōnghuò jǐnsuō

【通胀】tōngzhàng 通货膨胀的简称 abbr. for 通货膨胀 tōnghuò péngzhàng:~率 inflation rate | 抑制~ check inflation

【统合】tǒnghé 统一,综合 uniform; overall:~开发旅游资源 exploit the tourist resources in an overall way

【投拍】tóupāi 投入拍摄 start shooting:这部电视剧日前已在京~。Shooting of the TV play has been started in Beijing.

【投向】tóuxiàng (资金等)投放的方向 orientation for (funds, etc.):优化贷款~ optimize the loan orientation

【投注】tóuzhù (精神、力量等)集中;倾注 (energy, strength, etc.) concentrate; devote:把全副精力~到扶贫工程中 concentrate oneself on an aid-the-poor programme | 大家的目光都~在厂长身上。All eyes are fixed on the factory director.

【投注】tóu//zhù 投放于博彩的钱 money poured into lottery:本期彩票~总额为八千余万元。The total sum of this lottery is more than 80 million yuan.

【投资基金】tóuzī jījīn 一种通过集合投资方式筹资的基金。由管理人或托管人进行证券、外汇等方面的运作,以使投资者获取收益,同时也共同承担其中的风险。investment fund; fund raised by pooling investments and operated by a manager or trustee in securities and foreign exchange trading to make profit for the investors with risks shared by all the investors

【透明度】tòumíngdù 〈比喻 *fig.*〉事情的公开程度 transparency; honest way of doing things that allow other people to know exactly what is being done:增加评奖工作的~。Increase the transparency in which award winners are prospective appraised and chosen.

【透析】tòuxī [补义 new sense] 透彻地分析 penetrating analysis:一周国际形势~ penetrating analysis of the international affairs in the week | 这部书从艺术鉴赏的角度~了诗歌创作的方法。This book made a deep analysis of the methods for composing poems and songs from the angle of artistic appreciation.

【凸显】tūxiǎn 清楚地显出 show clearly; set off; stand out:草地上~出一座花坛。A flower bed stands out clearly on the lawn. | 市场规范化的问题日益~出来。The problem of market standardization is manifesting itself clearly day after day.

【凸现】tūxiàn 清楚地显现 figure prominently; come into focus; appear clearly:在一排排的校舍中~出图书馆的高楼。The tall building that houses the library figures prominently in the rows of school buildings. | 经济的高速发展,使不少历史遗留问题~出来。A host of problems left behind by history came into sharp focus in the fast development of the economy.

【突审】tūshěn 突击审讯 interrogate sb. by surprise:对犯罪嫌疑人进行~ bring a suspect under a sudden trial

【突显】tūxiǎn 突出地显出 protrude conspicuously; distinct:手臂上~出一条条青筋。Blue veins protruded conspicuously from the arm. | 产品的包装也~出民族特色。The packing of the product is also imbued with a distinct national flavour.

【突现】tūxiàn ❶ 突然出现 catch the eye suddenly:转过山脚,一片美丽的景色~在眼前。

A beautiful landscape catches the eye behind the hill. ❷ 突出地显现 conspicuously reveal：语言和行为都～了他的个性。His words and deeds reveal his personal character conspicuously.

【土壤污染】tǔrǎng wūrǎn 工业废水、生活污水、农药、化肥和大气沉降物等进入土壤并逐渐积累所造成的污染。土壤污染使土质恶化，有毒物质通过食物链危害人畜健康。soil pollution; pollution caused by the gradual accumulation of industrial waste water, domestic sewage, insecticides, chemical fertilizers and deposits from the atmosphere that enter the soil. Soil pollution worsens soil quality, and the poisonous substances harm the health of the humans and animals through the food chain.

【团队精神】tuánduì jīngshén 指团结协作的集体主义精神 team spirit; collective spirit of unity and cooperation

【推介】tuījiè 推荐介绍 recommend：～新书 recommend a new book

【推展】[1] tuīzhǎn 推进；发展 promote; develop; push forward; advance：沉积的泥沙填满了海湾，促使海岸向前～。Deposits silted up the bay, forcing the seashore to push forward. *or* The bay was silted up with sediments, pushing the coastline forward.｜两国关系持续～。The relations between the two countries have continued to advance.

【推展】[2] tuīzhǎn 推介展销 recommend and exhibit for sale：商厦举办羊绒精品～活动。The shopping centre held exhibition activities to promote the sales of quality cashmere products.

【退耕】tuìgēng 为保护自然环境而对已经开垦耕种的农田不再耕种 reforest cultivated land; stop cultivating reclaimed land in order to protect natural surroundings：～还林 revert cultivated land to forests

【退税】tuìshuì 为鼓励投资和出口，税收部门根据税法退还原纳税人一定比率的税款，如再投资退税、出口退税等 tax rebate; refund part of import duties in accordance with the tax law after taxed commodities are exported, for the purpose of encouraging investment and exports

【托老所】tuōlǎosuǒ 专门照料老年人的处所 nursing house; home for the old; home to take care of the old

【脱岗】tuō//gǎng ❶ 在工作时间内擅自离开所在的岗位 leave one's job without authorization during work time：一些夜间值班人员存在～现象。Some people on night duty tend to leave their jobs without authorization. ❷ 暂时脱离工作岗位 be away from one's post temporarily：对不合格的人员进行～培训 provide off-the-job training to unqualified personnel

【脱困】tuō//kùn 摆脱困境 get out of a difficult position：经过整改，该厂两年就实现了～目标。After rectification and consolidation, the factory met its goal to overcome its difficulties in two years.

【脱氧核糖核酸】tuōyǎng-hétáng hésuān 分子中含有脱氧核糖的一类核酸，存在于细胞核、线粒体、叶绿素、某些细胞的细胞质以及某些病毒和噬菌体中，是储藏、复制和传递遗传信息的主要物质基础 deoxyribonucleic acid (DNA); nucleic acid containing deoxyribose in its molecules, found in nucleus, mitochondrion, chlorophyll, the cytoplasm of certain cells, and some viruses and bacteriophage. DNA is a major material base for storing, reproducing and transmitting hereditary information.

W

【外访】wàifǎng 出国访问 visit a foreign country：～活动 activities during a visit to a foreign country

【外卖】wàimài ❶ 餐饮业指销售供顾客带离店铺的食品(一般指自己店铺现做的 usu. prepared by a restaurant or a food shop) takeout; prepared food sold as by a restaurant to be eaten away from the premises：～烤鸭 takeout roast duck｜增加～业务 add the takeout service ❷ 外卖的食品 food for takeout：送～ deliver takeouts｜吃～ eat takeout

【外向型经济】wàixiàngxíng jīngjì 指面向国际市场，具有较强的引进外资能力和较大的进出口贸易额的经济类型 export-oriented economy; business oriented for the international market, which has a large capacity for foreign investment and a large import and export volume

【外需】wàixū 国外市场的需求，在我国也包括向香港、澳门、台湾地区出口的需求(区别于'内需' as distinguished from 'domestic market demand') international market demand, which in China also includes the demand for export to Hong Kong, Macao and Taiwan

【外援】wàiyuán [补义 new sense]指运动队从国外引进的运动员 players bought in from abroad：北京足球队添了三名～。The Beijing football team has added three foreign players.

【完败】wánbài 球类、棋类比赛中指一直处于明显劣势而输给对手 crushing defeat; lose due to apparently inferior strength in ball or chess games：甲队0比3～于乙队。Team A lost 0∶3 to Team B.

【完胜】wánshèng 球类、棋类比赛中指一直占据较大优势而战胜对手 win a complete victory; win a resounding victory in a ball or chess game：主队3比0～客队。The host team won a resounding victory 3∶0 over the visitors.

【婉拒】wǎnjù 以委婉的方式拒绝 decline politely：～谢礼 politely decline a gift in token of one's gratitude

【万维网】Wànwéiwǎng 电子计算机网络的一种信息服务系统，建立在超文本的基础上，方便用户在因特网上搜索和浏览各种信息 World Wide Web (WWW); web; computer web information service system established on the basis of hypertext, for the convenience of readers retrieving and reading information on the Internet

【网吧】wǎngbā 备有电子计算机可供上网并且兼售饮料等的营业性场所 cybercafe; Internet bar; business centre with computers for customers to log on the Internet and selling soft drinks; also called 电脑咖啡屋 diànnǎo kāfēiwū (computer cafe) or 公共电脑屋 gōnggòng diànnǎowū (public computer room) in some regions

【网虫】wǎngchóng 网迷〈含诙谐意 *humor.*〉 Internet buff; web enthusiast; Internet geek

【网络电话】wǎngluò diànhuà 指通过互联网接通的电话。它采用分组交换方式，使许多用户能共享网络资源，通话费用较低。Internet telephone service; Internet protocol (IP) telephone, whose packet-switching operation enables many subscribers to share the web resources at a low rate

【网络计算机】wǎngluò jìsuànjī 适于在网络环境中使用的简易型电子计算机。采用支持互联网标准的技术，应用软件从网络上实时下载，用户无需自己进行维护。network computer; simple computer that is used in the Internet, employs technology in support of Internet standards, downloads application software from the net, and frees users from maintenance chores

【网络经济】wǎngluò jīngjì 以互联网技术和信息技术的运用为主要特征的经济 cyber-economy; economy characterized by the use of Internet technology and information technology

【网迷】wǎngmí 指对电子计算机上网十分入迷的人 net enthusiast

【网民】wǎngmín 指电子计算机互联网的用户 netizen

【网页】wǎngyè 可以在互联网上进行信息查询的信息页 web page; information page on the Internet

【网友】wǎngyǒu 在电子计算机互联网上交往的朋友。也用于网民之间的互称。netizen; net friends; friend made through the Internet; term of address for netizens

【网站】wǎngzhàn 某个企业、组织或个人在互联网上的虚拟站点，一般由一主页和许多网页构成 website set up by an enterprise, organization or individual on the Internet, usu. consisting of a home page and many web pages

【网址】wǎngzhǐ 某一网站在互联网上的地址 website address on the Internet

【旺市】wàngshì ❶ 交易旺盛的市场形势（跟'淡市'相对 as opposed to 'dull market'） brisk market：营造节日～ build a brisk market during the holidays ❷ 市场交易兴旺 brisk market business：春节期间几家商场都是～一时。The shopping centres all had good business during the Spring Festival.

【旺势】wàngshì 旺盛的势头 hot sale; good sale：保健食品近年呈现出销售～。Health food has sold well in recent years.

【微波炉】wēibōlú 一种利用微波加热的炊具。由磁控管、波导、搅拌器、炉腔、电源和控制系统等组成。工作时微波从各个角度进入炉腔，使放在里面的食物的分子振荡、摩擦而产生热量，食物的内部和外部一起受热。microwave oven; cooking device using electricity-generated microwave rather than heat, consisting of magnetron, waveguide, mixer, chamber, power source and control system. When it works, microwave enters the chamber from all angles so that the molecules of the food inside it vibrate and rub each other to generate heat, enabling the food to be heated within and without.

【违规】wéi//guī 违反有关的规定或规程 violate regulations or rules：～现象 violations of the regulations and rules｜～操作 operate against the rules

【违纪】wéi//jì 违反纪律 breach the discipline：～行为 acts of violating the discipline｜查处～人员 investigate and deal with those violating the discipline

【违宪】wéixiàn 违反宪法的规定 violate the Constitution

【维和】wéihé 维持和平 peacekeeping：～部队 peacekeeping force｜～行动 peacekeeping action

【维权】wéiquán 维护合法权益 safeguard legitimate rights and interests：提高消费者的～意识 heighten the consumers' consciousness of safeguarding their legitimate rights and interests

【尾巴工程】wěi·ba gōngchéng 指有小部分长期完不成因而不能竣工的工程 project with a small part remaining unfinished for a long time

【尾款】wěikuǎn 结算账目时没有结清的数目较小的款项 small balance; arrears; odd: 所欠～五天内还清。Pay the small balance owed in five days.

【尾气】wěiqì 机动车辆或其他设备在工作过程中所排出的废气 tail exhaust; exhaust; used gas discharged by motor vehicles or other equipment in the course of their working: 汽车～ car exhaust

【委培】wěipéi 委托外单位培养 entrust sb. else to train one's own personnel: ～生 student trainees entrusted on an institution other than their own | 企业与高校合作，～专业人才。Through cooperation, the enterprises entrust universities and collegues to train professionals.

【卫视】wèishì 卫星电视的简称 abbr. for 卫星电视 wèixīng diànshì

【卫星电视】wèixīng diànshì 利用通信卫星传送和转播电视节目的电视系统。电视节目从某个地面站发往通信卫星，再转发到其他地面站，地面站收到信号后传送到当地电视台转播。卫星电视传送电视节目质量好，覆盖面积大，总投资成本低。satellite TV; TV programme transmitted through a satellite; television system using communication satellites to transmit and relay television programmes. A TV programme is transmitted from an earth station to a communication satellite which relays it to the other earth stations, which in turn transmit the signals they have received to local TV stations for relay broadcast. Satellite TV ensures good quality of the programmes and covers a large area and costs less. 简称 abbr. 卫视 wèishì

【未成年人】wèichéngniánrén 法律上指未达到成年年龄的人。在我国指 18 周岁以下的人。(leg.)person under legal age, in China referring to those under 18 years of age; minor

【温室效应】wēnshì xiàoyìng ❶ 农业上指不经人工加温的温室内气温高于室外的效应(agric.) greenhouse effect; effect of the temperature in an unheated greenhouse being higher than outside ❷ 指大气保温效应，即大气中二氧化碳、甲烷等气体含量增加，使地表和大气下层温度增高。这种效应曾被误认为与温室保温的机制相同，所以叫温室效应。gradual warming of earth's surface and atmosphere said to be caused by increased carbon dioxide, methane and other gases in the air

【文化衫】wénhuàshān 印有文字或图案的针织短袖衫，在一定程度上能反映出某些文化心态 T-shirt with printed words or designs, which reflect certain cultural mentality to a certain degree

【文秘】wénmì 文书和秘书的合称 clerk and secretary: ～工作 job for a clerk or secretary

【文胸】wénxiōng 乳罩 bra; brassiere

【文员】wényuán 在企业、事业单位的办公室中从事文字工作的职员 clerical worker; office worker handling clerical work in an enterprise or institution

【乌龙球】wūlóngqiú 足球比赛中指球员不慎踢进或顶进己方球门的球 own goal; goal scored by a team's own player by mistake

【污染源】wūrǎnyuán 造成环境污染的东西；产生污染物的根源 source of pollution; sth. that causes environmental pollution; root cause of pollution: 加快治理～，使湖水还清 accelerate the control of sources of pollution to make the lake clear and clean again

【无绳电话】wú shéng diànhuà 电话机的一种，分为主机和副机两部分，主机与电话线相接，副机和主机之间没有电话线相连。打电话时，副机可以离开主机一段距离移动通话。cordless phone; telephone consisting of a main set and an auxiliary set. The main set is linked with a telephone line while the auxiliary set is not linked. When a phone call is made, the auxiliary set can be used at some distance from the main set.

【物业】wùyè 产业，多指房地产(如公寓、办公楼等) real estate (as apartment building, office building, etc.); property: ～管理 property management

X

【夕阳】xīyáng [补义 new sense]〈比喻 *fig.*〉传统的、因缺乏竞争力而日渐衰落、没有发展前途的 sunset; traditional, declining and uncompetitive: ～产业 sunset industry; declining traditional industry

【西蓝花】xīlánhuā 青花菜的俗称。二年生草本植物，是甘蓝的一个变种。叶子大，主茎顶端形成肥大的花球，绿色或紫绿色，表面的小花蕾不密集在一起，侧枝的顶端各生小花球。原产意大利，是常见蔬菜。broccoli (*Brassica ol-*

eracea var. *italica*); popularly called 青花菜 qīnghuācài; biennial herbal plant and a variety of cabbage, with large leaves and loose green or purplish-green mass of fleshy flower stalks that form the head, a common vegetable originating in Italy; 通称 generally called 绿菜花 lǜcàihuā

【吸储】xīchǔ (银行、信用社等)吸收存款(of bank, credit union, etc.) absorb deposits; attract savings depositors: 增加储蓄种类,扩大～渠道。Increase the variety of savings deposits to open more channels to attract depositors.

【吸纳】xīnà ❶ 吸入 take in; inhale: ～新鲜空气 inhale fresh air ❷ 吸收;接纳 accept; admit: ～存款 accept savings deposits | ～下岗职工就业 give jobs to layoffs ❸ 接受;采纳 accept; adopt: ～先进技术 adopt advanced technology | ～合理化建议 accept rationalization proposals

【希望工程】Xīwàng Gōngchéng 通过社会集资和捐赠,救助贫困地区失学儿童的一种措施和活动。1989年10月由中国青少年发展基金会发起。Project Hope, project initiated by the China Youth and Children's Development Fund in October 1989 to enlist popular support to help school dropouts in underdeveloped regions return to school

【息影】xīyǐng [补义 new sense]指影视演员由于某种原因,不再拍戏(of film or TV actors) stop appearing in films for certain reason; retire

【惜败】xībài 体育比赛中实力与对方相当或强于对方的一方以相差很小的比分败给对方(含惋惜意 showing sympathy) lose unfortunately by a small margin: 整场比赛我方占有优势,但最后却以一分之差～。Our side had the advantage over the whole match, but we lost unfortunately by one point in the end.

【洗盘】xǐ//pán 股市庄家在拉高股价的过程中,有意让股价上下震荡,让先前买进股票的投资者卖出股票,这种操作手法叫洗盘 wash sale. While the leading investor is pulling up the stock price at the stock market, he intentionally makes the stock price to fluctuate, forcing other investors who have bought shares of the stock previously to sell them.

【戏歌】xìgē 把戏曲唱腔和通俗歌曲结合起来的一种艺术形式 artistic form combining opera singing with pop song

【戏说】xìshuō 附会历史题材,虚构一些有趣或引人发笑的情节进行创作或讲述 dramatization of history; create or tell a dramatic story about a historical subject: ～三国 dramatic fiction on the Three Kingdoms | 孩子们围坐着听老人～乾隆皇帝的故事。The children sat around the old man and listened to his dramatic tales about Emperor Qianlong.

【下挫】xiàcuò (价格、销量、汇率等)下降;下跌(of price, sales, exchange rate, etc.) fall; drop: 股市连续～。The stock market prices have kept falling. | 这个月电视机销售量～15%。Sales of TV sets have dropped by 15% this month.

【下浮】xiàfú (价格、利率、工资等)向下浮动(of price, interest rate, wage, etc.) fall; drop: 办公用房租金～。The rent of the office space fell. | 利率～一个百分点。The interest rate dropped by one percentage point.

【下岗】xià//gǎng [补义 new sense]职工因企业破产、裁减人员等原因失去工作岗位 be laid off; (of workers) lose job because one's factory has gone bankrupt or cut down on the payroll: ～待业 be laid off and wait for job

【下课】xià//kè [补义 new sense]指辞职或被撤换 resign; be fired: 几个队的主教练先后～。The head coaches of several teams resigned or were fired.

【下网】xià//wǎng 在互联网上结束信息的检索、查询等,操作电子计算机退出互联网(跟'上网'相对 as opposed to 'log on') log off; stop retrieving information from the Internet and operate the computer to disconnect it

【下载】xiàzài 把信息从互联网或其他电子计算机上输入到某台电子计算机上(跟'上载'相对 as opposed to 'upload') download; transfer information to one's own computer from the Internet or another computer

【嫌犯】xiánfàn 指犯罪嫌疑人 criminal suspect

【显示器】xiǎnshìqì 电子计算机的一种输出设备,能够显示文字、图像等 monitor; television screen that displays text and images and serves as a computer terminal

【险种】xiǎnzhǒng 保险公司所设的投保种类,如财产保险、人身保险等 insurance category, as property insurance, life insurance, etc.

【现代五项】xiàndài wǔxiàng 综合性体育比赛项目之一。由依次进行的越野障碍赛马、击剑、射击、游泳和越野赛跑五个项目组成。比赛每天进行一项,连续五天赛完,以各单项积分总和计算成绩。modern pentathlon; five-event sport consisting of cross-country horseback riding, fencing, shooting, swimming and cross-country running. Each event takes a day, the whole contest is required to finish in five days, and the results are calculated on the basis of the total score of each participant.

【现房】xiànfáng 房产市场上指已经建成、可以入住的房子(跟'期房'相对 as opposed to

'forward house') ready house; house already completed for an owner to move in on the real estate market

【现汇】xiànhuì 在国际贸易和外汇买卖中可以当时交付的外汇(主要指外国货币 chiefly of foreign currencies) spot exchange; exchange that can be paid out or delivered immediately; ready exchange

【限养】xiànyǎng (对某些动物)限制喂养 restricted raising (of certain animals):市有关部门最近制定出～犬的规定。The department concerned of the municipal government has recently issued regulations to restrict the raising of dogs.

【线报】xiànbào 〈方 *dial.*〉线人向警察、侦探提供的情报 tip; clue; information from an informer to the police or detective

【线人】xiànrén 〈方 *dial.*〉为警察、侦探充当暗探,提供侦查对象活动情报的人 inner connection; informer; plant; mole; spy; person who acts as an informer for the police or a detective and supplies information on a suspect

【乡镇企业】xiāngzhèn qǐyè 我国乡镇村集体经济组织、农村村民兴办的集体所有制企业、合作企业和个体企业的统称 rural enterprise; cottage industry; collective economic organization in Chinese rural areas; collective enterprise, cooperative enterprise or self-employed enterprise set up in rural areas

【消费税】xiāofèishuì 国家对烟、酒、化妆品、小轿车等消费品按销售额征收的税 consumer tax; excise; tax levied on consumer goods such as tobacco, wine, cosmetics, cars, etc.

【消费信贷】xiāofèi xìndài 金融机构向消费者个人发放的用于购买消费品的贷款 consumption credit; loan issued by a financial institution to an individual consumer for buying consumer goods

【销势】xiāoshì (商品)销售的势头 (of a commodity) sales trend:近来国产家用电器～看好。The sales trend of home-made household electrical appliances is looking up lately.

【小儿科】xiǎo'érkē ❶〈比喻 *fig.*〉价值小、水平低,不值得重视的事物 insignificant thing; thing of little value:零售日用小商品对商家来说不过是～罢了。Retail sale of small commodities of daily use means a mere pittance to a big business. ❷〈比喻 *fig.*〉极容易做的事情 a piece of cake; easy picking:写这种小文章,对大作家来说简直是～。Writing a small piece like this is simply an easy picking to a famous writer. ❸ 形容小气,被人看不上 stingy; miserly:送二十元礼金,也太～了。It's too stingy to give a gift of twenty yuan.

【小饭桌】xiǎofànzhuō 指街道或个体户为吃午饭有困难的中小学生开办的小型食堂 small canteen opened by a community service or self-employed business to provide lunches to primary and middle school students whose parents are too busy or too far away to prepare lunch for them

【小时工】xiǎoshígōng 指按小时计酬的临时工,多从事家庭服务工作 casual worker paid on an hourly basis, mostly hired to do household chores; also 钟点工 zhōngdiǎngōng

【协查】xiéchá 协助侦查或调查 assist in investigation:请临近地区公安部门～此案 ask the public security departments in nearby areas to assist in the investigation of the case

【邪教】xiéjiào 指打着宗教旗号蛊惑人心、危害社会的非法组织 cult; illegal organization that corrupt people's minds and jeopardize society under the banner of religion

【写字间】xiězìjiān 〈方 *dial.*〉❶ 办公室 office room ❷ 书房 study

【写字楼】xiězìlóu 〈方 *dial.*〉办公楼,多指配备现代化设施的商用办公楼 office building; chiefly commercial office building equipped with modern facilities

【心路】xīnlù [补义 new sense]指心理变化的过程 process of psychological changes:她经历了一段从失落到重新找回自我价值的～历程。She experienced a process of psychological changes from feeling lost to regaining her self-worth.

【心脏死亡】xīnzàng sǐwáng 指以心脏停止跳动为死亡标准认定的死亡 heart death; death judged with the cease of heartbeats as the standard

【心智】xīnzhì ❶ 思考能力;智慧 ability to think; wisdom; intelligence:启迪～ sharpen one's intellect ❷ 心理;性情 psychology; mentality; mood:～健康 health psychology | 陶冶～ cultivate one's intelligence

【芯片】xīnpiàn 指包含有许多条门电路的集成电路。体积小,耗电少,成本低,速度快,广泛应用在电子计算机、通信设备、机器人或家用电器设备等方面。chip; integrated circuit consisting of many gate circuits. Small in body, low in power consumption and cost, and fast in speed, it is widely used in computers, telecommunications equipment, robots and household electric appliances.

【新宠】xīnchǒng 新受宠爱的人或物 new favourite; new favourite person or thing:这种品牌的葡萄酒成为餐桌上的～。Wine of this brand has become a new favourite on the dining table.

【新低】xīndī 数量、水平等下降出现的新的低点

new low; new low point reached in quantity or level：黄金价格近来创历史～。The gold price has recorded an all-time low recently.

【新高】xīngāo 数量、水平等上升出现的新的高点 new high; new high point reached in quantity or level：股市指数连创～。The stock market index has chalked up new highs in a row.｜机场飞行保障再创历史～。The airport's safety record has hit another all-time high.

【新锐】xīnruì ❶ 新奇锐利 new and sharp; nascent：～武器 new and sharp weapon｜～的言论 new and cutting remarks ❷ 新出现而有锐气的（人）trendsetter; man with drive：～诗人 trendsetting new poet｜～导演 new director in his/her right ❸ 指新出现而有锐气的年轻人 rising, young star：棋坛～ rising young chess star

【信息产业】xìnxī chǎnyè 从事信息生产、流通和应用的产业。通常包括计算机产业、软件业、通信业以及信息服务业等。information industry; industry for information production, circulation and application, usu. including the computer, software, telecommunications and information service industries

【信息高速公路】xìnxī gāosù gōnglù 指能够高速运行的通信网络，可以迅速地传送文字、图像、声音等信息 information superhighway; telecommunications network capable of high-speed operation, which can transmit text, picture, sound and other information rapidly

【信息科学】xìnxī kēxué 研究信息的产生、获取、存储、传输、处理和使用的科学 information science; science dealing with the occurrence, collection, storage, transmission, processing, and retrieval of information

【信用卡】xìnyòngkǎ 由商业银行发行，专供消费者购买商品和支付费用的信用凭证。上面有持卡人姓名、签字和号码等信息。持卡人可在指定的银行、商店等处凭卡签字支取现金、购买商品等，有的可以透支小额现金。credit card; card issued by a commercial bank as a credit certificate to pay for ones purchases. The card bears the name of the holder, his signature and number and enables him to draw money from designated banks or buy commodities in designated shops on the strength of the card and signature. Some cards permit the holder to overdraw a small amount of money.

【信众】xìnzhòng 信仰某种宗教的人 believer in a certain religion

【形状记忆合金】xíngzhuàng jìyì héjīn 具有形状记忆功能的合金，能够在某一温度下经塑性变形而改变形状，在另一温度下又自动变回原来的形状 shape memory alloy; alloy with the function of shape memory, which can change its shape through plastic deformation under a certain temperature and automatically return to its original shape under another temperature；简称 abbr. 记忆合金 jìyì héjīn

【性贿赂】xìnghuìlù 以满足有权势的人的性欲为手段变相进行的贿赂 sex bribery; sexual bribery; bribe an influential person by gratifying his sexual desire

【性骚扰】xìngsāorǎo 指用轻佻、下流的语言或举动对异性进行骚扰（多指男性对女性）（mostly man to woman） sex harassment; harass a person of the opposing sex with frivolous, base words or behaviour

【凶嫌】xiōngxián 凶杀案的犯罪嫌疑人 murder suspect

【胸卡】xiōngkǎ 戴在胸前表示身份的卡片式标志，上面一般写有姓名、职务，有的还带有本人照片 chest placard; small card with name and position, pinned on one's chest showing identity and post, sometimes carrying a photo

【熊市】xióngshì 指价格持续下跌，成交额下降，交易呆滞的证券市场行情（跟'牛市'相对 as opposed to 'bull market'） bear market; stock market situation in which prices keep going down, business becomes dull and transaction volume drops

【休市】xiūshì 交易市场因节假日等原因暂停交易 close the market for holiday or other reasons：春节期间股市～一周。The market shall be closed for a week during the Spring Festival.

【休渔】xiūyú 为保护渔业资源在一定时期和范围禁止捕鱼 closed for fishing within a certain period of time and the limits of an area to protect the fish resources：南海海域实行伏季～制度。A system of prohibiting fishing in the hot months is enforced for the territorial waters of the South China Sea.

【虚拟现实】xūnǐ xiànshí 一种电子计算机技术。以视觉、听觉等数据库为基础，利用计算机生成高度逼真的虚拟环境，通过多种传感设备使人产生身临其境的感觉，并可实现人与该环境的交互作用 virtual reality; computer-generated simulation of three-dimensional images of an environment or sequence of events on the basis of a visual and audio database that someone using special electronic sensor equipment may view, as on a video screen, and interact with in a seemingly physical way

【虚职】xūzhí 有名义而没有实际权力和责任的职务（跟'实职'相对 as opposed to 'real position'） nominal position; position with name only and no real power and responsibility

【选单】xuǎndān 在电子计算机屏幕或图形输入板上，为使用者提供的用来选择项目的表。一般分为命令选单和操作选单。option sheet; menu; list, displayed as on a computer video screen or on a graphic input board, of the various functions available on a command menu and an operation menu for selection by the user; 俗称 popularly called 菜单 càidān

【眩光】xuànguāng 刺眼的、可引起视觉功能下降的光 dazzling light; light that dazzles the human eyes and may lead to a decline in eyesight

【雪藏】xuěcáng ❶〈方 *dial.*〉冷藏；冰镇 refrigerate; freeze; keep in a refrigerator:～汽水 cold soda water ❷〈比喻 *fig.*〉搁置不用 shelve; pigeon-hole; lay aside:这几篇批评文章遭到～。These critical articles were pigeon-holed. ❸〈比喻 *fig.*〉有意掩藏或保留 conceal or keep intentionally:球队把主力～起来，关键比赛才派上场。The team has reserved its top players and will not field them unless a crucial match comes along.

【雪雕】xuědiāo 用雪堆积、雕塑成形象的艺术。也指用雪堆积、雕塑成的作品 snow sculpture; art of piling snow and modelling it into figures; works of snow sculpture

【巡演】xúnyǎn 巡回演出 touring performances; performing tour:剧团这次南下～，受到各地观众的热烈欢迎。The troupe made a performing tour in the south and was warmly received by local audiences.

【巡展】xúnzhǎn 巡回展览 touring exhibition; exhibition tour:博物馆的珍藏文物将陆续到各地～。The treasured relics kept in the museum will be exhibited on a tour around the country.

【寻呼机】xúnhūjī 无线寻呼系统中的用户接收机。通常由超外差接收机、解码器、控制部分和显示部分组成。寻呼机收到信号后发出音响或产生振动，并显示有关信息 beeper (BP); electronic device consisting of superheterodyne receiver, decoding matrix, controller, and display, used to send or receive electronic signals, or beep a small portable receiver to contact people for messages; 简称 abbr. 呼机 hūjī

【寻呼台】xúnhūtái 无线寻呼系统中的单向无线电发射台 beeper station; one-way wireless transmitter for a beeping system; 简称 abbr. 呼台 hūtái

Y

【压产】yāchǎn 减少生产，降低产量 cut/curtail production:限期～，减少库存 cut production to reduce the stock in a limited period

【压锭】yā//dìng 减少纱锭的数目，限制纱厂的生产规模 reduce the number of spinning spindles to curtail production in a cotton mill:棉纺厂～减员后，效益显著提高。After reducing the number of spinning spindles and the employment, the cotton mill has conspicuously raised its economic returns.

【雅飞士】yǎfēishì 指西方国家中不求上进、境遇不佳的一类年轻人。他们一般穿短裤和T恤衫，戴棒球帽，主张乐天知命，安于现状。yuffie; any of those young, unambitious people who usually wear shorts, T-shirts and baseball caps and who are content with their lot

【雅皮士】yǎpíshì 指西方国家中年轻能干有上进心的一类人。他们一般受过高等教育，具有较高的知识水平和技能，工作勤奋，追求物质享受。yuppie; anyone who is young and capable and has the drive to excel, and who is usu. college educated, upscale in knowledge and skill, hard-working, and materialistic

【亚健康】yàjiànkāng 指身体虽然没有患病，却出现生理功能减退、代谢水平低下的状态。主要表现是疲劳、胸闷、头疼、失眠、健忘、腰背酸痛、情绪不安、做事效率低下等。因处于健康与疾病之间的状态，所以也叫第三状态。sub-health; state in which a person is not ill, but his physiological functions have declined and his metabolic level is low. Sub-health is characterized chiefly by fatigue, oppressed feeling in the chest, headache, insomnia, amnesia, back sore, restlessness and low work efficiency. As sub-health is a condition between healthiness and illness, it is thus also called the third state.

【严打】yándǎ ❶ 严厉打击 strike severely; deal a telling blow to:～行业违法行为。Deal a crushing blow to violations of law in various professions and trades. ❷ 严厉打击刑事犯罪活动的简称 abbr. for 严厉打击刑事犯罪活动 yánlì dǎjī xíngshì fànzuì huódòng:深入开展～斗争。Deepen the campaign to deal crushing blows to criminal activities.

【研发】yánfā 研制开发 research and develop:～新药 develop new drugs | 血液代用品～成功。A blood substitute has been successfully developed.

【研判】yánpàn 研究判断；研究评判 study and

judge; discuss and decide：～案情 discuss and judge a case｜～市场趋势 survey and discuss the market trend

【演艺】yǎnyì ❶ 戏剧、歌舞、杂技等表演艺术 performing art, such as the drama, singing, dancing, and acrobatics：～界 performing art circles｜～人员 performing artists ❷ 表演的技艺 performing skill; performance：他的精湛～受到人们赞赏。His superb performing skill was highly appreciated.

【演绎】yǎnyì ［补义 new sense］❶ 铺陈；发挥 narrate in detail; describe in length; elaborate; develop：～出感人的故事 relate a stirring story ❷ 阐发；展现 develop; elaborate：～时尚潮流 expound on the fashion trend｜～不同的风格 develop different styles

【验资】yànzī 查验资金或资产 check and verify capital funds or assets：～机构 capital examining institution｜～报告 asset examination report

【央行】yānghán 中央银行的简称 abbr. for 中央银行 zhōngyāng yínháng

【扬尘】yángchén ❶ 扬起灰尘 raise dust to the air：拆迁工地要落实防止～措施。When demolishing old houses, measures must be taken to prevent raising dust to the air. ❷ 扬起的灰尘 flying dust：控制～污染 control the pollution of flying dust

【扬升】yángshēng （价格等）往上升；上涨（of price, etc.）rise; increase：油价大幅～。The oil price has gone up greatly.｜这种邮票在交易市场上～至八十元。The price of this stamp has gone up to 80 yuan on the market.

【阳伞效应】yángsǎn xiàoyìng 由于大气中微粒的散射和云层的反射，到达地面的太阳辐射减弱，这种效应好像是在地面上撑起巨大的遮阳伞，所以叫阳伞效应。火山爆发、沙尘暴等造成的大气总悬浮颗粒物增多及云量增多，都会加强阳伞效应，使地面气温降低。umbrella effect; because of the scattering of particles in the atmosphere and the reflection of the clouds, the radiation of the sun becomes weaker when it reaches the ground. This is called the umbrella effect as it is evocative of a giant umbrella held up over the earth's surface. Increases in the amount suspended particles in the atmosphere by volcano eruption and sandstorm, and the thickening of clouds in the sky, may help exacerbate the umbrella effect and reduce the ground temperature.

【阳线】yángxiàn 证券市场上指收盘价高于开盘价的K线 positive line; K line at the securities market if the closing price is higher than the opening price

【氧吧】yǎngbā 备有输氧装置专供人吸取氧气的营业性场所 oxygen bar; commercial bar with oxygen therapy equipment for people to take oxygen

【摇头丸】yáotóuwán 有机化合物，成分是二亚甲基双氧苯丙胺，是冰毒的衍生物，有强烈的兴奋作用，是一种毒品。服用后使人出现幻觉，狂热舞蹈，产生暴力倾向等。过量服用会急性中毒甚至死亡。Ecstasy; MDMA（cmethylenedioxy methamphetamine）; organic chemical compound that is a derivative of methamphetamine hydrochloride with a deadly euphoric effect and is used as a narcotic. After taking it, man begins his hallucination and dances wildly and tends to commit violence. Excessive taking of it may lead to acute poisoning and even death.

【业内】yènèi 某种行业或业务范围以内 in the business; within the scope of a trade, business or profession：～人士 insider; people in a business circle or profession｜这家老店在～有很大影响。This old shop has a great influence in its field.

【业外】yèwài 某种行业或业务范围以外 beyond the scope of certain trade, business or profession：～人士 outsider; person who does not belong to a business circle or profession

【业态】yètài 业务经营的形式、状态 form or state of business operation：京城零售业在～上已形成新的格局。The retail service in the capital city has formed a new business pattern.

【业者】yèzhě 从事某种行业的人 practitioner of a certain business

【一国两制】yī guó liǎng zhì 指一个国家，两种制度。是中国共产党于1978年十一届三中全会后提出的完成国家统一的基本国策，在大陆实行社会主义制度，在香港、澳门设立特别行政区，实行资本主义制度。这项政策也适用于台湾。'one country, two systems' policy, China's fundamental state policy set forth by the Communist Party of China after the Third Plenary Session of the 11th Central Party Committee in 1978 for national unification. This policy calls for maintaining the socialist system on the mainland and establishing special administrative regions in Hong Kong and Macao that retain the capitalist system. This policy also applies to Taiwan.

【一级市场】yī jí shìchǎng 指证券、商品房等首次发行、发售的市场 primary market; market where stocks are issued or houses put up for sale for the first time

【一米线】yīmǐxiàn 银行、机场等距营业窗口或柜台前一米远的地面上划出的横线，正在办理存取款、验证等业务的人站在窗口、柜台前，其他等待办理的人站在线外 one-metre line; horizontal line drawn on the flour which is one metre from a business window or counter in a bank, airport etc. so that those who are drawing or depositing money in the bank or have their passports examined in the airport stand in front of the windows or counter while the others stand in waiting behind the line

【一头雾水】yī tóu wù shuǐ 形容摸不着头脑，糊里糊涂 be unable to make head or tail of sth.; be muddle-headed

【移动电话】yídòng diànhuà 不固定在一处，可以变换地点使用的电话，如手机、对讲机、车载电话等 mobile telephone; telephone not fixed at one location, but used at different locations, such as cell phone, intercom, vehicle-carried telephone, etc.

【移动通信】yídòng tōngxìn 不固定在一处，可以变换地点进行通信的通信方式 mobile telecommunication; mode of telecommunications that is not fixed at one location, but allows for changes in locations

【遗撒】yísǎ 丢弃，散落 litter and leak：防止垃圾清运中～渗漏。Prevent littering and leakage when clearing and transporting garbage.

【遗赠】yízèng 遗嘱中指明立遗嘱人于其死后把自己的财产赠给国家、集体或法定继承人以外的人 make a will to donate (sb.'s property to the state, an institution, or sb. other than the legal heir) upon one's death; bequeath

【遗嘱继承】yízhǔ jìchéng 按照被继承人生前所立的合法有效的遗嘱而继承遗产 inherit by will; inherit (sb.'s property or belongings) by a legal, valid will upon sb.'s death

【疑犯】yífàn 指犯罪嫌疑人 criminal suspect

【疑凶】yíxiōng 有行凶嫌疑的人 murderer suspect

【义工】yìgōng ❶ 自愿参加的无报酬的公益性工作 voluntary work without pay：学生们在居委会干部指导下从事～。The students do voluntary work under the guidance of neighbourhood committee leaders. ❷ 从事义工的人 volunteer：退休后他到福利院当起了～。After he retired, he became a volunteer in a nursing home for the old.

【义拍】yìpāi 为正义或公益事业筹款而拍卖物品，拍卖的物品往往是捐献的 charitable auction; fund-raising auction; auction goods (which are oft. donated) to raise funds for justice or public welfare

【义赛】yìsài 为正义或公益事业筹款而举行体育比赛 sports competition held for charity; sports competition held to raise funds for justice or public welfare

【艺员】yìyuán 〈方 *dial.*〉演员 actor or actress

【溢价】yìjià 指高于有价证券等的面值或高于平价的价格 premium; price that is above the face value of securities or parity

【因特网】Yīntèwǎng 目前全球最大的一个电子计算机互联网，是由美国的 ARPA 网发展演变而来的 Internet; largest global computer network that has grown from the ARPA in the United States

【因应】yīnyìng ❶ 适应（变动的情况）；顺应 keep up with (changing circumstances); conform to; comply with：～变局 keep up with the changing situation | ～市场的需求 keep up with the market demand ❷ 采取措施应付 take measures to cope with：～挑战 take steps to cope with the challenge | 针对形势的变化而妥善～ take proper measures to comply with the changing situation

【阴线】yīnxiàn 证券市场上指开盘价高于收盘价的 K 线 negative line; K line on the securities market if the opening price is higher than the closing price

【银团贷款】yíntuán dàikuǎn 指多家银行共同出资、共同承担风险的信贷经营形式 bank consortium loan; form of credit operation with several banks contributing funds and jointly bearing the risk

【引介】yǐnjiè 引进并介绍 import and introduce：～外国作品 import and introduce foreign works

【引资】yǐnzī 引进资金 attract investment; absorb capital：招商～ solicit investment from outside | ～一千万元发展蔬菜生产 solicit 10 million yuan for the development of vegetable production

【饮品】yǐnpǐn 饮料 drink

【隐身技术】yǐnshēn jìshù same as 隐形技术 yǐnxíng jìshù

【隐形技术】yǐnxíng jìshù 采取各种措施，减弱雷达反射波、红外线辐射及噪声等，以使飞机、导弹、舰船等不易被探测设备发现的综合技术 stealth technology; multifunctional technology of taking various measures to reduce the radar reflection wave, infrared radiation and noise so as to prevent military aircraft, missiles, naval vessels, etc. from being detected by enemy radar; also 隐身技术 yǐnshēn jìshù

【营销】yíngxiāo 经营销售 marketing：～观念 marketing notion | ～人员 marketing personnel

【赢面】yíngmiàn 竞赛中战胜对手的概率（多用于预测 oft. when making a prediction) winning rate; chance or probability of defeating the opponent in a competition：这场对抗赛主队的～要大些。The host team has a bigger chance in this contest.

【应拍】yìng//pāi 拍卖物品时，拍卖师报出起价后，竞买人对该价格表示接受，叫应拍 answer the bid, whereby when sth. is put up for auction, the auctioneer quotes the starting price and the competitive bidder accepts the price:一万元的起价叫出后,竞买人纷纷举牌～。After the starting price of 10,000 yuan is quoted, the bidders raised their plates one after another to bid.

【硬广告】yìngguǎnggào 指直接介绍商品、服务内容等的传统形式的广告,通过报刊刊登、设置广告牌、电台和电视台播出等进行宣传(区别于'软广告' as distinguished from 'soft ad') hard advertisement; traditional form of advertisement which directly introduces and promotes a commodity or service through newspapers, billboards, radio and TV broadcasts

【硬环境】yìnghuánjìng 指交通、通信、水电设施等物质环境 hard environment, including transportation, telecommunications, water and power supply, etc.:在抓好开发区～建设的同时,也要努力改善软环境。While stress is being laid on the construction of the hard environment in the development zone, something has got to be done to improve the soft environments.

【硬驱】yìngqū 硬盘驱动器的简称 abbr. for 硬盘驱动器 yìngpán qūdòngqì; ☞ 磁盘驱动器 cípán qūdòngqì on p. 2586

【硬着陆】yìngzhuólù [补义 new sense]〈比喻 *fig.*〉采取过急、过猛的措施较生硬地解决某些重大问题 hard landing; taking hasty, excessive and rigid measures to solve certain major problems

【拥堵】yōngdǔ 由于车辆多、秩序乱或道路狭窄等造成车辆拥挤、道路堵塞;拥塞 traffic congestion; traffic jam caused by heavy traffic, disorder or narrow road:采取措施缓解市区交通～状况。Take measures to relieve traffic congestion in the urban areas.

【泳装】yǒngzhuāng 游泳时所穿的专用服装,多指女性穿的,有文胸式、背心式、比基尼式等 bathing suit; swimsuit; suit worn for swimming, esp. lady's, such as brassiere suit, vest suit and bikini

【用户界面】yònghù jièmiàn 电子计算机系统中实现用户与计算机信息交换的软件、硬件部分。软件部分包括用户与计算机信息交换的约定、操作命令等处理软件,硬件部分包括输入装置和输出装置。目前常用的是图形用户界面,它采用多窗口系统,显示直接形象,操作简便。user interface; man-machine interface; software and hardware in a computer system for the exchange of information between the user and the computer. Software includes a contract for information exchange between the user and the machine, operation commands, while hardware includes the input device and output device. The common interface used nowadays is the easy-to-use graphical user interface, which adopts a multiple window system to display direct images. also 人机界面 rénjī jièmiàn; 简称 abbr. 界面 jièmiàn

【邮品】yóupǐn 邮政部门发行的邮票、小型张、明信片等的统称 philatelist's items; collective term for stamps, enlarged stamps, post cards, etc.

【有机农业】yǒujī nóngyè 一种农业生产体系,施用有机肥料,不使用化肥和植物激素,采用生物技术防治作物病虫害,不洒农药,用洁净水灌溉。利于保护土壤资源,实现农业生态系统的良性循环。organic agriculture; agricultural production system whereby organic fertilizers are applied instead of chemical fertilizers and plant hormones, biotechnology is used instead of insecticides to prevent plant diseases, and clean water is used for irrigation — all for the purpose of protecting the soil resources and achieving a virtuous cycle of the agricultural ecological system

【有机食品】yǒujī shípǐn 指来自有机农业生产体系,在生产、加工、贮存、运输过程中无污染,并经有关部门认证的优质安全保健食品 organic food; high-quality, safe health foods produced by organic agricultural production system, free from pollution in the course of production, processing, storing and transportation, and recognized by the department concerned

【与时俱进】yǔ shí jù jìn 随着时间的推移而不断发展、前进 keep pace with the times; keep on developing and advancing with the passing of time:马克思主义具有～的理论品格。Marxism possesses the theoretical character of keeping pace with the times.

【语音信箱】yǔyīn xìnxiāng 一种新型的电话通信服务业务。利用电信网和计算机处理系统存储、传递语音信息。用户向电信部门申请并办理手续取得自己的语音信箱号码和密码。别人可以拨通这个号码留言,本人拨通这个号码并输入密码能够听取留言。voicemail, a new type of telephone service; electronic system that uses telephones and a computer to store and deliver recorded voice messages. A subscriber may apply to the telecommunications department and go through the formalities for his voice mail box number and cipher. A caller may dial this number to leave a message and the subscriber may dial the number and submit the cipher to retrieve the message.

【域名】yùmíng 企业或机构在互联网上注册的名称,是互联网上企业或机构间相互联络的网络地址 domain name; name registered by an enterprise or institution on the Internet for correspondence on the Internet

【预警机】yùjǐngjī 飞机的一种,装有远程雷达,用来搜索和监视空中或海上目标，指挥、引导己方飞机执行作战任务。机身上装有带罩的雷达天线，舱内还装有敌我识别、数据处理、通信、导航等电子设备，易于探测和监控低空或超低空目标，续航力强。early-warning aircraft; plane equipped with remote radar to search for and keep under surveillance targets in the air or on the sea, and to direct and guide fellow aircraft to carry out a combat mission. With its fuselage fitted with a covered radar antenna and its cabin equipped with electronic devices for aircraft identification, data processing, communication and navigation, an early-warning aircraft is capable of detecting and supervising and controlling a target at low and minimum altitudes, and it is highly enduring as well.

【园区】yuánqū 指集中发展某种事业的地区 industrial park; area for concentrated development of a certain undertaking：高科技～ high-tech park

【原创】yuánchuàng 最早创作；首创 originate; initiate; pioneer created：～精神 pioneering spirit|～歌曲 original song

【远程教育】yuǎnchéng jiàoyù 指利用通信手段开展的异地教育。现代远程教育是以现代化网络技术为依托，利用数字多媒体通信网，特别是计算机网络开展交互式教学的教育方式。distance learning; teaching and learning at different locations conducted through communication. Modern distance learning, backed by the modern network technology, uses digital multi-media communication networks, esp. the computer network, to conduct interactive teaching.

【跃升】yuèshēng 跳跃式地上升，指在名次、地位、价位等方面越过前面的次第迅速上升（of ranking, position, prices, etc.）jump; rise by leaps：去年联赛的第十名今年～至第三名。The team which ranked 10th in the league last year has jumped to the third place.

【跃增】yuèzēng 跳跃式地增长；大幅度地增长 grow by leaps; grow by a big margin：年利润由三千万元～到八千万元。The annual profit jumped from 30 million yuan to 80 million yuan.

Z

【匝道】zādào 立交桥和高架路上下两条道路相连接的路段，也指高速公路与邻近的辅路相连接的路段 ring road; section of a road connecting a cloverleaf; also a section linking an expressway with a byroad

【灾变】zāibiàn 灾难和变故；灾害 natural calamity; disaster：提高应付各种～的能力 raise the capability of coping with all kinds of natural adversities

【在读】zàidú 正在学校或科研机关学习 studying in a school or research institute：～硕士研究生 student pursuing a MA degree

【在岗】zàigǎng 在工作岗位上 at one's post; employed; on job：～人员 employed people

【在线】zàixiàn ❶ 科学技术上指在某种系统的控制过程中（science and technology）controlled by a certain system ❷ 电子计算机系统上指在互联网上（of a computer）on-line; on the Internet

【再保险】zàibǎoxiǎn 保险人把所承担的保险业务的部分或全部分给其他保险人承保，以分散风险和责任的一种保险形式 reinsurance; insure again, esp. under a contract by which one insurer transfers all or part of the risk to another insurer; also 分保 fēnbǎo

【再生水】zàishēngshuǐ 中水 recycled water

【藻花】zǎohuā 水华 water bloom

【造势】zàoshì 制造声势 build up the momentum：利用广告为新产品～ use advertisements to promote a new product

【造血】zàoxuè〈比喻 *fig.*〉部门、单位、组织等从内部挖掘潜力，增强自身实力 internal functions; tap the internal potentials of a department, organization, etc. to increase its own strength：增收节支，强化企业的～机能 increase the revenue and reduce the expenses to strengthen an enterprise

【噪声污染】zàoshēng wūrǎn 干扰人们休息、学习和工作的声音所造成的污染，多由机械振动或流体运动引起。安静环境中，约30分贝的声音就是噪声，超过50分贝，会影响睡眠和休息，90分贝以上，会损伤人的听觉，影响工作效率，严重的可致耳聋或诱发其他疾病。noise pollution; pollution caused by noises that disturb people's rest, study and work, mostly arising from mechanical vibration or the flow of a liquid. In a quiet environment, a sound of about 30 decibels is regarded as a noise. A noise exceeding 50 decibels affects sleep and rest. A noise exceeding 90 decibels hurts people's sense of hearing and affects work efficiency, or even causes deafness or other diseases.

【择业】zéyè 选择职业 job selection：自主～ choose a job at one's own decision

【增值税】zēngzhíshuì 国家对商品生产、销售等各个环节新增的价值所征收的税 value-added

tax (VAT); tax levied on the value newly added on various links in the production and sale of a commodity

【扎啤】zhāpí 一种鲜啤酒，常用特制的大酒杯盛装 fresh beer held in a jar [扎 *zha*: jar; 啤 *pi*: beer]

【摘牌】zhāi//pái ❶ 指终止某种证券在股票市场的交易资格 cancel a security for trading on the stock market ❷ 职业体育组织吸收挂牌的其他体育组织人员叫摘牌 draft; (of a sports franchise) draft an athlete from another organization

【窄带】zhǎidài 数字通信中指传输速率低于 64 千比特/秒的带宽 narrow band; band with its width allowing a transmission speed of less than 64 kilobits per second in digital telecommunications

【斩仓】zhǎncāng 指以低于买入价的价格卖出所持有的证券 sell out all one's securities at a price lower than that when they are bought

【斩获】zhǎnhuò 原指战争中斩首与俘获，现指竞赛中在奖牌、进球等方面的收获(orig.) cut off enemies' heads and take those alive captive in a war; win medals or score a goal: 下半场比赛，双方俱无～。Both sides scored no goal in the second half of the match.

【展区】zhǎnqū 博物馆、展销会等按内容、地区等分设的区域 display zone set up in a museum or sales exhibition according to content or geographical division: 电脑～ computer zone | 北京～ Beijing zone

【展位】zhǎnwèi 陈列展品的地方 berth; display space: 科技馆有二百个～。The Science and Technology Hall has 200 display berths.

【展演】zhǎnyǎn 以展览为目的而演出(文艺节目等) (of art programme, etc.) festival; exhibition performance: 华东地区优秀剧目～ East China theatrical exhibition show

【展业】zhǎnyè 开展业务，特指保险公司的业务人员开展保险业务 promote business, esp. insurance business: 广泛运用直销、营销、代办三种～手段 make wide use of the three channels of direct sale, marketing and agency service to promote business

【展映】zhǎnyìng 以展览为目的而放映(影视片) (of movies and television plays) festival; exhibition show: 新片～ new film festival

【彰显】zhāngxiǎn ❶ 明显；显著 conspicuous; outstanding; well known: 名声～ well-reputed ❷ 鲜明地显示 show to advantage; bring out conspicuously: 英雄们的壮举，～了中国人民威武不屈的崇高品格。The death-defying exploits of the heroes serve to bring out the Chinese people's noble unyielding character to best advantage.

【涨停板】zhǎngtíngbǎn 证券交易机构为维护证券市场的稳定，采取措施对单只股票价格或整个股市指数的涨跌进行限制，使股价或股指只能在一定幅度内波动。对涨幅进行的限制叫涨停板，对跌幅进行的限制叫跌停板。ceiling. In order to maintain stability on a securities market, a securities trading institution adopts measures to restrict the rise or fall of the prices of individual stocks or the stock market index so that the stock prices or the stock market index fluctuate within bounds. The restriction to the rise is called 'ceiling' and the restriction to the fall is called 'floor'.

【掌控】zhǎngkòng 掌握控制 hold; control: 公司的人事任免权～在总经理手中。The power to appointments and dismissals in the company is in the hand of the general manager.

【掌上电脑】zhǎngshàng diànnǎo popular name for 个人数字助理 gèrén shùzì zhùlǐ

【招商】zhāoshāng 用广告、展览等方式吸引商家(投资、经营) attract investment or business through advertising, exhibition, etc.: ～引资 invite business and attract investment from the outside world

【朝阳】zhāoyáng [补义 new sense]〈比喻 *fig.*〉新兴的、有发展前途的 sunrise; rising; nascent; promising: ～产业 sunrise industries; rising industries

【找赎】zhǎoshú 〈方 *dial.*〉找零钱 small change: 自备零钞，恕不～。Get your small change ready. No change here, thanks.

【侦结】zhēnjié 侦查终结 conclusion of an investigation: 这一特大经济案件经检察院～后向法院提起诉讼。This extraordinary economic case has been submitted to the court for legal proceedings after the procuratorate concluded its investigation.

【征管】zhēngguǎn 征收管理(税款、公粮等) collect and manage (taxes, public grain, etc.): 加强税收～工作。Tighten up taxation and the management of tax revenues.

【整固】zhěnggù 调整巩固 readjust and consolidate: 大盘进入～阶段。The overall business of the securities market is now readjusted and consolidated. | 人民币汇率继续在高位～。The RMB exchange rate continues to be readjusted and consolidated at a high level.

【整合】zhěnghé 通过整顿、协调重新组合 reorganize through readjustment and coordination: 冰箱市场完成了从无序到有序的～ The refrigerator market has gone through the process of readjustment from disorder to order. | 该校通过～课程，明显地提高了教学效果。The school has obviously improved its teaching efficiency after readjusting its curriculum.

【正版】zhèngbǎn 出版单位正式出版的版本(区别于'盗版' as distinguished from 'pirated copy') legal copy; official edition: ～书 official edition book | ～光盘 legal copy of CD

【正当防卫】zhèngdàng fángwèi 为使公共利益、本人或他人的人身、财产等免受正在面对的不法侵害而采取制止侵害的行为。正当防卫对不法侵害人造成损害的一般可以免除法律责任。self-defence; legal defence; justifiable defence; legitimate defence; action taken to prevent public interests, or one's body or property, or those of sb. else from being infringed on

【证照】zhèngzhào 证件;执照 certificate; permit; licence: 取缔无～的非法经营活动 outlaw unlicensed, unlawful business activities

【知识产权】zhī·shi chǎnquán 人们对其通过脑力劳动创造出来的智力成果所享有的权利。包括工业产权和著作权 intellectual property right; right to own and use the intellectual achievement of one's mental work, including industrial property right and copyright

【知识经济】zhī·shi jīngjì 一种以现代科技知识为基础、以信息产业为核心的经济类型 intellectual economy; economy based on modern scientific and technological knowledge with the information industry at the core

【执业】zhíyè (律师、医生、会计和某些中介服务机构的人员等)进行业务活动 (of a lawyer, doctor, accountant, etc.) practise one's profession: ～律师 certified lawyer | 取得～资格的房地产估价师 certified real estate assessor

【直销】zhíxiāo 生产者不经过中间环节,直接把商品卖给消费者 direct sale; (of a producer) sell a commodity directly to consumers without intermediate links

【直选】zhíxuǎn 直接选举的简称 abbr. for 直接选举 zhíjiē xuǎnjǔ

【值守】zhíshǒu 值班看守 be on duty and on guard: 无人～公用电话 unguarded public telephone | 保安人员在厂区巡察～。Security guards were patrolling the factory.

【职高】zhígāo 职业高中的简称 abbr. for 职业高中 zhíyè gāozhōng

【职级】zhíjí 职务的等级 rank: 晋升～ be promoted to a higher rank or position

【职业高中】zhíyè gāozhōng 进行某种职业技能教育的高级中学,如旅游职业高中、烹饪职业高中等 senior middle technical school, such as senior middle tourist school, senior middle cooking school; 简称 abbr. 职高 zhígāo

【纸巾】zhǐjīn 一种像手绢那样大小用来擦脸、手等的质地柔软的纸片 tissue paper; napkin

【指称】zhǐchēng ❶ 指出;声称 point out; profess; claim: 该公司在诉状中～对方违约。In its plaint the company accused the other party of breaking the contract. ❷ 指示并称呼 call: 江西人用'老表'来相互～。People in Jiangxi call each other *lao biao*.

【指证】zhǐzhèng 指认并证明 identify and testify: 现场目击者出庭～凶犯。Eye witnesses appeared in court to identify and testify against the murder suspect.

【制衡】zhìhéng 相互制约,使不偏移 check and balance; check each other to balance: 董事会和经理分权～。The board of directors and the manager have a division of power in a check and balance relationship.

【智能材料】zhìnéng cáiliào 一种新型材料,由传感器或敏感元件等与传统材料结合而成。这种材料可以自我发现故障,自我修复,并根据实际情况做出优化反应,发挥控制功能。intelligent material; new type of material made by combining sensor or sensitive elements with traditional materials, and capable of detecting and repairing breakdowns or failures by itself and making optimum response in the light of the actual situation so as to perform its control function

【智能卡】zhìnéngkǎ 把智能化集成电路芯片嵌在塑料基片中封装而成的卡,外形跟磁卡相像,能够写入数据和存储数据,可以有条件地供外部读取 smart card; plastic card with memory provided by an integrated circuit embedded in it, looking like a magnetic card and capable of receiving and storing data for people to read and retrieve; also 集成电路卡 jíchéng diànlùkǎ

【智能武器】zhìnéng wǔqì 具有人工智能的武器,通常由信息采集与处理系统、知识库系统、辅助决策系统和任务执行系统等组成。能够自行完成侦察、搜索、瞄准、攻击目标和收集、整理、分析、综合情报等军事任务。intelligent weapon; weapon usu. consisting of an information collecting and processing system, a knowledge bank system, a supplementary decision-making system and a mission-performing system, capable of fulfulling on its own military duties as reconnaissance, search, sighting and attacking targets, and collecting, classifying, analysing and summerizing information

【中考】zhōngkǎo 高中和高中程度专科学校招收新生的考试 senior middle school or senior middle technical school entrance examination

【中水】zhōngshuǐ 经过处理的生活污水、工业废水、雨水等,水质介于清洁水和污水之间。可以用来灌溉田地、冲洗厕所、回补地下水等。recycled water; water recovered by treating domestic sewage, industrial waste water, rain water, etc., the quality of which is between clean water and sewage, and which is used to irrigate farmland, clean toilets and refill ground water. also 再生水 zàishēngshuǐ

【中文信息处理】zhōngwén xìnxī chǔlǐ 用电子计算机对中国语言文字(特指汉语言文字)的各种信息(如字、词、短语、句、篇章等)进行识别、转换、压缩、检索、分析、理解和生成等处理的技术 Chinese information processing; processing technology using computers to recognize, convert, condense, retrieve, analyse, comprehend and generate all kinds of information in the written Chinese language

【中央商务区】zhōngyāng shāngwùqū 大城市中地理位置优越,汇集商贸、金融、证券、保险等机构,以互联网为纽带,集中进行商务活动的地区 central business district (CBD); district that is centrally located in a large city and embraces trade, financial, securities, insurance and other institutions linked by the Internet for concentrated business activities

【中央税】zhōngyāngshuì 按照税法规定由中央税务部门征收管理,或由地方征收后划归中央所有的税种 central tax; tax collected by the central taxation department or collected and turned over to the central government by a local tax department; also 国家税 guójiāshuì

【中央银行】zhōngyāng yínháng 一国居主导地位的金融中心机构,是国家干预和调控国民经济的重要工具,负责制定并执行国家货币信用政策,独占货币发行权,实行金融监管等。我国的中央银行为中国人民银行。central bank; leading financial institution of a country, which is an important state apparatus to intervene in and control the national economy and responsible for making and implementing state monetary and credit policies, monopolizing the right to issue a currency and exercising supervision over financial affairs. The central bank in China is the People's Bank of China. 简称 abbr. 央行 yānghánq

【钟点工】zhōngdiǎngōng 小时工 hour worker

【重头】zhòngtóu ❶ 重要的部分 important part: 词典是工具书的～。Dictionaries are the foremost of all reference books. ❷ 意义或作用大的;重要的 significant; important: ～文章 important article|～项目 major project; major item

【重头戏】zhòngtóuxì [补义 new sense]〈比喻 *fig.*〉重要的任务或活动 important task; major activity: 营销是企业的～。Marketing is an important activity of an enterprise. | 探讨社区精神文明建设是这次研讨会的～。How to promote community culture and ethics is the major topic for this symposium.

【主板市场】zhǔbǎn shìchǎng 在一国的证券市场体系中居于主导地位的证券交易市场 stock exchange market that plays a leading role in a nation's securities market system

【主创】zhǔchuàng 在文学、艺术作品的创作过程中担负主要工作的 chief writer of a work of literature or art: 该剧～人员赴京进行艺术交流。The main writers of the play went to Beijing to swap experience in creative writing.

【主打】zhǔdǎ (文艺作品、商品等)在吸引受众、顾客,打开市场上起主要作用的 (of literary and artistic works, commodities, etc.) that plays the leading role in attracting readership, audience and customers or in taking a market share: ～歌 top song | 短篇小说是这个刊物的～栏目。Short stories are the mainstay column of this magazine. | 本商场以时装为～商品。This shopping centre features the latest fashion as its major commodities.

【主页】zhǔyè 可以在互联网上进行信息查询的起始信息页 homepage

【主因】zhǔyīn 主要的原因 main cause: 骄傲自满是他学习成绩下滑的～。Self-conceitedness is the main cause for the downslide in his studies.

【助残】zhùcán 帮助残疾人 aid the disabled: 开展大规模～活动 launch a large-scale campaign to aid the disabled

【助力】zhùlì ❶ 帮助 help; assist: 他对于促进双方的协作～不少。He is of much help to promoting cooperation between the two sides. ❷ 帮助的力量 help: 别人的鼓励是一种～,别人的批评也是一种～。Someone else's encouragement is a help, and so is his criticism.

【助力车】zhùlìchē 装有小型发动机的自行车,因可以借助机械动力代替脚蹬骑行,所以叫助力车 bicycle fitted with a small motor, using mechanical power to replace pedalling

【专卖店】zhuānmàidiàn 专门出售某一种类或某一品牌商品的商店 franchised shop; shop exclusively selling a certain category or brand of commodities

【转岗】zhuǎn//gǎng 转换工作岗位 be transferred to a new job: 一些伐木工～为护林工了。Some lumberjacks have been turned into forest conservation workers.

【转基因】zhuǎnjīyīn 运用科学手段从某种生物中提取所需要的基因,将其转入另一种生物中,使与另一种生物的基因进行重组,从而产生特定的具有优良遗传性状的物质。利用转基因技术可以改变动植物性状,培育新品种。也可以利用其他生物体培育出人类所需要的生物制品,用于医药、食品等方面。transgenic; use scientific means to extract the needed gene from a certain plant or animal and transfer it to another plant or animal for the reorganization of its genes, so as to produce a particular matter with fine hereditary characteristics. The transgenic technology can change the properties of a plant or animal and develop new breeds, and, by using certain organisms, help develop biological products needed by humans for the making of pharmaceuticals and foodstuffs.

【转型】zhuǎnxíng ❶ 社会经济结构、文化形态、价值观念等发生转变 in transition; transformation of a socioeconomic structure, cultural pattern, or values:我国正处在由计划经济向市场经济的～期。Our country is in transition from central planning to a market economy. ❷ 转换产品的型号或构造 change the design or structure of a product:这种产品正酝酿～。A new design for the product is in the offing.

【转制】zhuǎnzhì 转换体制 reshape; change a system or setup:后勤部门将在年底前完成～。The logistics departments will have been reshaped by the end of the year.

【庄家】zhuāng·jia ［补义 new sense］资金雄厚、买卖股票数量巨大并能影响股市行情走势的投资者 investor who has abundant capital, buy and sell huge amounts of shares and can affect the stock market trend

【追偿】zhuīcháng ❶ 事后给予赔偿 make compensation afterwards:以后再设法～ try to make up for it afterwards ❷ 追逼着使偿还 recover:向债务人～债款 recover a debt from its debtor

【追捧】zhuīpěng 追逐捧场 pursue and admire:这位歌坛新星受到不少青少年的～。The new star singer has quite a following among young people and children.

【追星族】zhuīxīngzú 对影星、歌星、球星等极度崇拜迷恋的一类人(多为青少年)(mostly young people and children) fan; movie star fan; pop music star fan; football star fan; groupie

【资费】zīfèi 指电信、邮政等方面的费用 telecommunications service charges; postage:调整电话～ readjust the telephone charges

【资信】zīxìn 指企业或个人的经济技术实力、履约守信水平等 credit; credentials and trustworthiness; economic and technical strength and trustworthiness of an enterprise or individual:～评估 credit assessment

【资讯】zīxùn 〈方 *dial.*〉信息 information

【资质】zīzhì ［补义 new sense］指企业所具备的从事工程设计、施工等业务活动的资格和能力 credentials and ability of a designing and engineering enterprise:建筑企业～年检 annual check for the credentials and ability of building enterprises|～证书 accreditation certificate

【自动扶梯】zìdòng fútī 电梯的一类,是链式输送机的特种形式,斜向上升或下降运行,外形像楼梯,由许多活动的台阶组成,两侧有扶手,人站在台阶上能自动升降。escalator; chain-like electric stairway with handrails on both sides, consisting of treads linked in an endless belt moving upstairs or downstairs; 通称 popularly called 滚梯 gǔntī

【自动柜员机】zìdòng guìyuánjī 自助式银行业务办理设备,由磁卡识别、控制和机电点钞等部分组成。信用卡的持有人可在无人值守的情况下自己进行简单的存款、取款或查询等操作。automated teller machine (ATM); automatic bank service equipment consisting of devices to authenticate magnetic cards and control and count the bank notes to be drawn or deposited. A card holder may deposit and draw money or retrieve information from the machine by himself. also 自动取款机 zìdòng qǔkuǎnjī

【自动取款机】zìdòng qǔkuǎnjī same as 自动柜员机 zìdòng guìyuánjī

【自净作用】zìjìng-zuòyòng 大气、土壤或水体等受到污染后能够自然净化的作用,通过物理、化学、生物等自然作用而使污染物总量减少,浓度降低,逐渐恢复到未污染的状态 self-purification; self-purification of polluted atmosphere, soil or water through physical, chemical and biological reactions to cut down the total quantity and density of the pollutants, and gradually restore itself to the unpolluted state

【自然保护区】zìrán bǎohùqū 国家为保护特殊的自然环境、自然资源、生态系统而划定的区域。保护对象还包括有特殊意义的文化遗迹等。nature reserve; natural preservation zone; zone designated by the government for the protection of a special natural environment, natural resources and the ecological system. A nature reserve also protects cultural relics and ruins of special cultural and historical interest.

【综艺】zōngyì 综合文艺 comprehensive arts:大型～联欢节目 programme for a full-length variety show; large comprehensive arts and entertainment programme

【总悬浮颗粒物】zǒng xuánfú kēlìwù 指悬浮在大气中不易沉降的所有的颗粒物,包括各种固体微粒、液体微粒等,直径通常在0.1—100微米之间 aggregate of suspended particles; all the particles suspended in the atmosphere, solid, liquid, and otherwise, usu. with a diameter of 0.1—100 microns

【走低】zǒudī (价格等)往下降(of price, etc.) fall; drop; go down:物价持续～。Prices have kept going down.|欧元汇率一度～。The exchange rate of the euro fell for a time.

【走高】zǒugāo (价格等)往上升(of price, etc.) rise; go up:消费需求增加,拉动物价～。The increased consumer demand pulled the prices up.

【走强】zǒuqiáng ❶(价格等)趋于上升(of price, etc.) go strong; on the rise:大盘指数～。The wholesale index is on the rise. ❷趋于旺盛 tend to flourish:技术人才的需求量～。The demand for technical personnel is increasing.

【走软】zǒuruǎn ❶(价格等)趋于下降(of price, etc.) tend to fall; become weak:油价开始～。The oil prices began to weaken. ❷趋于低迷 tend to slump:销售势头～。Sales showed a tendency to slump.

【走台】zǒu//tái 演员、时装模特儿等正式演出前在舞台上走动练习,熟悉位置 rehearse; walk-through; actors, actresses, fashion models, etc. walk on the stage before a public performance

【族群】zúqún 原指由共同语言、宗教、信仰、习俗、世系、种族、历史和地域等方面的因素构成的社会文化群体,现泛指具有某些共同特点的一群人 social and cultural group of people bound together by a common language, religion, belief, customs, pedigree, race, history, geography and other factors; group of people with certain common features:高血压患者是发生脑中风的危险～。Sufferers of hypertension are a dangerous group of people susceptible to cerebral stroke.

【罪错】zuìcuò 罪行和过错 crime and malfeasance

【作秀】zuò//xiù 〈方 *dial.*〉❶表演;演出 perform; show:歌星们依次上台～。The singing stars went onstage one after another to make a show. ❷指为了销售、竞选等而进行展览、宣传等活动 hold exhibition and promotion activities for sales, election, etc.:想方设法～促销 try every way to promote sales [秀 *xiu*: show]

【坐诊】zuòzhěn 医生在药店等固定地点给人看病 sit-in doctor; physician sitting in a pharmacy or other fixed places to see patients:本店聘请名医～。This shop has invited famous physicians to sit in and provide medical consultation.

西文字母开头的词语*

Acronyms and Words Beginning with Greek or Latin Letters

【α粒子】α lìzǐ ☞ 阿尔法粒子 ā'ěrfǎ lìzǐ on p. 1

【α射线】α shèxiàn ☞ 阿尔法射线 ā'ěrfǎ shèxiàn on p. 1

【β粒子】β lìzǐ ☞ 贝塔粒子 bèitǎ lìzǐ on p. 81

【β射线】β shèxiàn ☞ 贝塔射线 bèitǎ shèxiàn on p. 81

【γ刀】γ dāo ☞ 伽马刀 gāmǎdāo on p. 2596

【γ射线】γ shèxiàn ☞ 伽马射线 gāmǎ shèxiàn on p. 618

【A股】A gǔ 指人民币普通股票。由我国境内的公司发行，供境内（不含港、澳、台）投资者以人民币认购和交易 A-share; ordinary share issued in China by a domestic company, in denominations of, and payable in, Renminbi, and bought and sold by domestic investors (those of Hong Kong, Macao and Taiwan not included)

【AA制】AA zhì 指聚餐会账时各人平摊出钱或各人算各人账的做法 go Dutch; share expenses equally when dining out in numbers, or where people each pay for their own meal

【AB角】AB jué 指在AB制中担任同一角色的两个演员 two actors playing the same role in a theatrical work

【AB制】AB zhì 剧团排演某剧时，其中的同一主要角色由两个演员担任，演出时如A角不能上场则由B角上场，这种安排叫做AB制 AB system, in which two actors, respectively Actor A and Actor B, play the same role when a troupe rehearses a play. In the absence of Actor A, Actor B (also known as the understudy) takes his place.

【ABC】A、B、C是拉丁字母中的前三个。用来指一般常识或浅显的道理（有时也用做书名 sometimes used in book titles) basic knowledge; rudiments, of a subject: 连音乐的～也不懂，还作什么曲？How can you compose when you don't even know the ABC of music? |《股市交易～》*Stock Market ABC*

【ABS】制动防抱死装置 anti-lock braking system

【ADSL】非对称数字用户线路 asymmetrical digital subscriber line

【AIDS】获得性免疫缺陷综合征，即艾滋病 acquired immune deficiency syndrome

【AM】调幅 amplitude modulation

【APC】复方阿司匹林。由阿司匹林、非那西丁和咖啡因制成的一种解热镇痛药 aspirin, phenacetin and caffeine; compound aspirin; heat-relieving and pain-killing medicine consisting of aspirin, phenacetin and caffeine

【APEC】亚太经济合作组织 Asia Pacific Economic Cooperation

【API】空气污染指数 air pollution index

【ATM机】ATM jī 自动柜员机 automated teller machine

【B超】B chāo ❶ B型超声诊断的简称 ultrasonic diagnosis B: 做～ have an ultrasonic B check ❷ B型超声诊断仪的简称，利用超声脉冲回波幅度调制荧光屏辉度分布而显示人体断面像并从中获得临床诊断信息的装置 ultrasonograph B; apparatus for producing sectional body images by using the reflection of ultrasonic waves that produces different shades of brightness on a screen. From the images, information can be obtained for making clinic diagnoses

---

* 这里收录的常见西文字母开头的词语，有的是借词，有的是外语缩略语。在汉语中西文字母是按西文的音读的，这里就不用汉语拼音标注读音，词目中的汉字部分仍用汉语拼音标注读音。The words and expressions on this list are frequently encountered in contemporary Chinese, and all of them begin with Greek or Latin letters. Some are loanwords, and the others are abbreviations of foreign words. No *pinyin* transliterations are given to these letters because they have retained their original pronunciations even though they have already become part and parcel of the Chinese language. The Chinese characters in these entries are, like those on the preceding pages, transcribed into *pinyin*.

【B股】B gǔ　指人民币特种股票。以人民币标明面值，供投资者以美圆（沪市）或港币（深市）认购和交易。B-share; special share with a par value in RMB but subscribed and traded in US dollars in the Shanghai stock market, or in Hong Kong dollars in the Shenzhen stock market

【B淋巴细胞】B línbā xìbāo　一种免疫细胞，起源于骨髓，禽类在腔上囊发育成熟，人和哺乳动物在骨髓中发育成熟，再分布到周围淋巴器官和血液中去，占血液中淋巴细胞的15%—30%。能够产生循环抗体。bone marrow lymphocyte; a kind of immunocyte growing from the bone marrow, maturing in the bursa of the nasal cavity of poultry and in the bone marrow of human beings and mammals, and distributed to the surrounding lymph organs and blood, making up 15-30 per cent of the lymph cells in blood. Bone marrow lymphocytes can produce circulatory antibodies. 简称 abbr. B细胞 B xìbāo [B: bone marrow]

【B细胞】B xìbāo　B淋巴细胞的简称 abbr. for B淋巴细胞

【BBS】❶ 电子公告牌系统 bulletin board system ❷ 电子公告牌服务 bulletin board service

【BP机】BP jī　无线寻呼机 wireless beeper; pager

【CAD】　计算机辅助设计 computer-aided design

【CBD】　中央商务区 central business district

【CD】　激光唱盘 compact disc

【CDMA】　码分多址 code division multiple access

【CD-R】　可录光盘 compact disc-recordable

【CD-ROM】　只读光盘 compact disc-read only memory

【CD-RW】　可擦写光盘 compact disc-rewritable

【CEO】　首席执行官 chief executive officer

【CFO】　首席财务官 chief finance officer

【CGO】　首席沟通官 chief government officer

【CI】　❶ 企业标识 corporate identity ❷ 企业形象 corporate image

【C^3I系统】　指军队自动化指挥系统 military automatic commanding system [C^3I: command 指挥, control 控制, communication 通信 and intelligence 情报]

【CIMS】　计算机集成制造系统 computer integrated manufacturing system

【CIO】　首席信息官 chief information officer

【CIP】　在版编目；预编目录。在图书出版前，由图书馆编目部门根据出版商提供的校样先行编目，编目后将著录内容及标准格式交出版机构，将它印于图书的版权页上。cataloguing in publication. Before the publishing of a book, a library cataloguing department will make a catalogue of the book according to the proof sheet provided by the publisher and deliver the CIP, which indicates the content and standard format of the book, to the publishing house to be printed on the copyright page of the book.

【C^4ISR】　指军队自动化指挥系统。由C^3I系统发展而来。military automatic commanding system, developed from C^3I [C^4ISR: command 指挥, control 控制, communication 通信, computer 计算机, intelligence 情报, surveillance 监视 and reconnaissance 侦察]

【COO】　首席运营官 chief operating officer

【CPA】　注册会计师 certified public accountant

【CPU】　中央处理器 central processing unit; part of a computer that controls what it does

【CT】　❶ 计算机体层成像 computerized tomography; computer-controlled scanning technique that displays details of a cross-section, esp. through the body: 做～ make a CT check ❷ 计算机体层成像仪 computerized tomograph

【CTO】　首席技术官 chief technology officer

【DIY】　自己动手做 do it yourself

【DNA】　脱氧核糖核酸 deoxyribonucleic acid

【DNA芯片】DNA xīnpiàn　基因芯片 DNA chip

【DOS】　磁盘操作系统 disc operating system

【DSL】　数字用户线路 digital subscriber line

【DVD】　数字激光视盘 digital video disc

【e化】e huà　电子化 electronic [e: the first letter of 'electronic']

【ED】　男子生殖器勃起功能障碍 erectile dysfunction

【EDI】　电子数据交换 electronic data interchange

【E-mail】　电子邮件 electronic mail [E: the first letter of 'electronic']

【EMS】　邮政特快专递 express mail service

【EQ】　情商 emotional quotient

【FA】　工厂自动化 factory automation

【FAX】　❶ 传真件 faxed message or document; copy produced or messaged by facsimile transmission ❷ 用传真机传送 transmit a message through a fax machine ❸ 传真系统 facsimile system [fax: abbr. for facsimile]

【FM】　调频 frequency modulation

【GDP】　国内生产总值 gross domestic product

【GIS】　地理信息系统 geographical information system

【GMDSS】 全球海上遇险与安全系统 global maritime distress and safety system

【GNP】 国民生产总值 gross national product

【GPS】 全球定位系统 global positioning system

【GRE】 美国等国家研究生入学资格考试 graduate record examination in USA and other countries

【GSM】 全球移动通信系统 global system for mobile communications

【H股】H gǔ 指在我国境内（不含港、澳、台）注册，在香港上市的股票，以人民币标明面值，供港、澳、台及境外投资者以港币认购和交易 H-share; share registered in China (not including Hong Kong, Macao and Taiwan) and listed in the stock market of Hong Kong, with RMB par value, for investors from Hong Kong, Macao and Taiwan and overseas to subscribe and trade [H: Hong Kong（香港）的第一个字母 initial letter of 'Hong Kong']

【HA】 家庭自动化 home automation

【HDTV】 高清晰度电视 high definition television

【hi-fi】 高保真度 high-fidelity

【HIV】 人类免疫缺陷病毒；艾滋病病毒 human immunodeficiency virus

【HSK】 汉语水平考试 Chinese Standard Test [abbr. for the *pinyin* spelling for 汉语水平考试 Hànyǔ Shuǐpíng Kǎoshì]

【IC卡】IC kǎ 集成电路卡 IC card [IC: integrated circuit]

【ICP】 因特网信息提供商 Internet content provider

【ICQ】 网络寻呼机 device for network paging; network pager [partial tone for 'I seek you']

【ICU】 重病监护病房 intensive-care unit

【IDC】 互联网数据中心 internet data centre

【internet】 互联网 internet

【Internet】 因特网 Internet

【IOC】 国际奥林匹克委员会 International Olympic Committee

【IP地址】IP dìzhǐ 网际协议地址。因特网使用IP地址作为主机的标识。Internet protocol address; IP address, used on the Internet as identification for a host computer [IP: Internet protocol]

【IP电话】IP diànhuà 网络电话 IP telephone [IP: Internet protocol]

【IP卡】IP kǎ IP电话卡 IP telephone card [IP: Internet protocol]

【IQ】 智商 intelligence quotient

【ISDN】 综合业务数字网 integrated services digital network

【ISO】 国际标准化组织。从希腊语 isos（相同的）得名。international standard organization. ISO is derived from the Greek word 'isos', meaning 'identical'.

【ISP】 因特网服务提供商 Internet services provider

【IT】 信息技术 information technology

【ITS】 智能交通系统 intelligent transportation system

【KTV】 指配有卡拉OK和电视设备的包间 hotel or club room equipped with a karaoke unit and a television set that a patron can rent [K: karaoke; TV: television]

【LD】 激光视盘 laser disc

【MBA】 工商管理硕士 Master of Business Administration; master's degree in business management

【MD】 迷你光盘 mini disc

【MP3】 一种常用的数字音频压缩格式 MPEG 1 audio layer 3; method of reducing the size of a computer file that contains sound, so that it can be transmitted quickly by e-mail or the Internet

【MPA】 公共管理硕士 Master of Public Administration; master's degree in public administration

【MTV】 音乐电视，一种用电视画面配合歌曲演唱的艺术形式 music television

【NC】 网络计算机 network computer

【NMD】 国家导弹防御系统 National Missile Defense

【OA】 办公自动化 office automation

【OCR】 光学字符识别 optical character recognition

【OEM】 原始设备制造商 original equipment manufacturer

【OPEC】 石油输出国组织 Organization of Petroleum Exporting Countries

【PC】 个人电子计算机 personal computer

【PC机】PC jī 个人电子计算机 personal computer

【PDA】个人数字助理 personal digital assistant

【pH值】pH zhí 氢离子浓度指数 pH value; hydrogen ion concentration exponent [pH, French: potentiel hydrogène]

【POS机】POS jī ❶ 销售点终端机，供银行卡持卡人刷卡消费使用 POS terminal; terminal computer at a point of sale where bankcards may be used to pay ❷ 商场电子收款机 cash register in a store [POS: point of sale]

【PPA】 苯丙醇胺，即N-去甲麻黄碱。某些感冒药和减肥药中的一种成分，可以刺激鼻腔、喉头的毛细血管收缩，减轻鼻塞症状，也有促使中枢神经兴奋等作用。服用该药有可能引起血压升高、心脏不适、颅内出血、痉挛甚至中风。含有这种成分的感冒药已被我国医药部门通告停用。phenylpropanolamine; ingredient in certain flu medicines and weight-losing drugs, which stimulates the contraction of capillary vessels in the nasal cavity and larynx so as to alleviate symptoms of congestion and activate the central nerves. PPA may cause high blood pressure, intracranial haemorrhage, convulsions and haemorrhagic strokes. PPA-containing flu medicines are banned in China by the medical authorities.

【PT】 特别转让 particular transfer

【QC】 质量管理 quality control

【RAM】 随机存取存储器 random-access memory

【RMB】 人民币 Renminbi; Chinese currency [abbr. for the *pinyin* spelling for 'renminbi']

【ROM】 只读存储器 read-only memory

【SBS】 大楼综合征 sick building syndrome

【SCI】 科学引文索引 science citation index

【SIM卡】SIM kǎ 用户身份识别卡。移动通信数字手机中的一种IC卡，该卡存储有用户的电话号码和详细的服务资料。SIM card; IC card used in a digital mobile phone that stores the phone number of the subscriber and detailed service data [SIM: subscriber identification module]

【SOHO】 小型家居办公室 small office home office

【SOS】 国际上曾通用的紧急呼救信号，也用于一般的求救或求助 Save Our Souls; radio signal once used universally to appeal for help esp. by a ship or boat; urgent request for help from sb. in trouble

【SOS儿童村】SOS értóngcūn 一种专门收养孤儿的慈善机构。SOS children's village; charity organization that specializes in fostering and bringing up orphaned children [SOS: save our souls]

【ST】 特别处理 special treatment

【STD】 性传播疾病 sexually transmitted disease

【T淋巴细胞】T línbā xìbāo 一种免疫细胞，起源于骨髓，在胸腺中发育成熟，再分布到周围淋巴器官和血液中去，占血液中淋巴细胞的50%—70%。可分化为辅助细胞、杀伤细胞和抑制细胞。thymus lymphocyte; a kind of immunocyte growing from the bone marrow, maturing in the thymus and distributed to surrounding lymph organs and blood, making up 50-70 percent of the lymph cells in blood. Thymus lymphocytes are divided into helper cells, killer cells and inhibitory cells. 简称 abbr. T细胞 T xìbāo [T: the first letter of the Latin word *thymus*]

【T细胞】T xìbāo T淋巴细胞的简称 abbr. for T淋巴细胞 T línbā xìbāo

【T型台】T xíng tái 呈T形的表演台，多用于时装表演 catwalk; narrow T-shaped platform or gangway often used in fashion shows

【T恤衫】T xù shān 一种短袖套头上衣，因略呈T形而得名。恤，英语shirt的粤语音译。T-shirt; short-sleeved casual top in the form of T. *Xu* is the transliteration of the English word 'shirt' in Cantonese. also T恤 T xù

【Tel】 电话（号码） telephone (number) [Tel: telephone]

【TMD】 战区导弹防御系统 theatre missile defence

【TV】 电视 television

【UFO】 不明飞行物 unidentified flying object

【VCD】 激光视盘 video compact disc

【VDR】 光盘录像机 video disc recorder

【VIP】 要人；贵宾 very important person

【VOD】 视频点播 video on demand

【WAP】 无线应用协议 wireless application protocol

【WC】 盥洗室；厕所 water closet

【WTO】 世界贸易组织 World Trade Organization

【WWW】 万维网 World Wide Web

【X刀】X dāo 一种用于放射治疗的设备，采用三维立体定位，X射线能够准确地按照肿瘤的生长形状照射，使肿瘤组织和正常组织之间形成整齐的边缘，像用手术刀切除的一样 X-ray knife; radiotherapy device that locates and gives a clear three-dimensional image of a tumor, enabling X-rays to accurately trace the shape of the tumor and irradiate it, leaving a neat edge around it and separating it from healthy tissues, like what a scalpel does

【X光】X guāng X射线 X-ray

【X射线】X shèxiàn ☞ 爱克斯射线 àikèsī shèxiàn on p.6

附　录
Appendices

我国历代纪元表
Chronology of Chinese History

1. 本表从‘五帝’开始，到1949年中华人民共和国成立为止。This chronology runs from the period of the ‘Five August Emperors’ up to the founding of the People's Republic of China in 1949.

2. ‘五帝’以后，西周共和元年（公元前841年）以前，参考2000年公布的《夏商周年表》作了调整。The period from the end of the ‘Five August Emperors’ to the 1st year of the Gonghe reign of the Western Zhou Dynasty (841 B.C.) has been adjusted according to the Chronology of the Xia, Shang, and Zhou dynasties published in 2000.

3. 较小的王朝如‘十六国’、‘十国’、‘西夏’等不列表。Small regimes are not listed, such as the Sixteen States Periods, the Ten States Periods, and the Western Xia Dynasty.

4. 各个时代或王朝，详列帝王名号（‘帝号’或‘庙号’，以习惯上常用者为据），年号，元年的干支和公元纪年，以资对照。（年号后用括号附列使用年数，年中改元时在干支后用数字注出改元的月份。）The rulers of every period or dynasty are listed, including their temple titles or posthumous titles whichever is the better known, reign titles, the name of the 1st year of a reign according to the traditional Chinese calendar, and the corresponding year according to the Gregorian calendar. (The number in parentheses on the right of the reign title is the number of years the reign lasted. If a reign title was changed in the middle of a year, the month in which it was changed is given after the name of the year in traditional Chinese calendar.)

干支次序表
Heavenly Stems and Earthly Branches

(Translator's Note: The 10 Heavenly Stems are: 甲 *jia*, 乙 *yi*, 丙 *bing*, 丁 *ding*, 戊 *wu*, 己 *ji*, 庚 *geng*, 辛 *xin*, 壬 *ren*, and 癸 *gui*. The 12 Earthly Branches are: 子 *zi*, 丑 *chou*, 寅 *yin*, 卯 *mao*, 辰 *chen*, 巳 *si*, 午 *wu*, 未 *wei*, 申 *shen*, 酉 *you*, 戌 *xu*, and 亥 *hai*. Traditional Chinese calendar calculated the passage of years, months, days and hours by combining one Heavenly Stem and one Earthly Branch to form 60 unique pair in a complete cycle. In the lunar calendar in use today, only years and days are marked by such cyclic pairings. In this chronology, they indicate years.)

1. 甲子 *jia-zi*	2. 乙丑 *yi-chou*	3. 丙寅 *bing-yin*	4. 丁卯 *ding-mao*
5. 戊辰 *wu-chen*	6. 己巳 *ji-si*	7. 庚午 *geng-wu*	8. 辛未 *xin-wei*
9. 壬申 *ren-shen*	10. 癸酉 *gui-you*	11. 甲戌 *jia-xu*	12. 乙亥 *yi-hai*
13. 丙子 *bing-zi*	14. 丁丑 *ding-chou*	15. 戊寅 *wu-yin*	16. 己卯 *ji-mao*
17. 庚辰 *geng-chen*	18. 辛巳 *xin-si*	19. 壬午 *ren-wu*	20. 癸未 *gui-wei*
21. 甲申 *jia-shen*	22. 乙酉 *yi-you*	23. 丙戌 *bing-xu*	24. 丁亥 *ding-hai*
25. 戊子 *wu-zi*	26. 己丑 *ji-chou*	27. 庚寅 *geng-yin*	28. 辛卯 *xin-mao*
29. 壬辰 *ren-chen*	30. 癸巳 *gui-si*	31. 甲午 *jia wu*	32. 乙未 *yi-wei*
33. 丙申 *bing-shen*	34. 丁酉 *ding-you*	35. 戊戌 *wu-xu*	36. 己亥 *ji-hai*
37. 庚子 *geng-zi*	38. 辛丑 *xin-chou*	39. 壬寅 *ren-yin*	40. 癸卯 *gui-mao*
41. 甲辰 *jia-chen*	42. 乙巳 *yi-si*	43. 丙午 *bing-wu*	44. 丁未 *ding-wei*
45. 戊申 *wu-shen*	46. 己酉 *ji-you*	47. 庚戌 *geng-xu*	48. 辛亥 *xin-hai*
49. 壬子 *ren-zi*	50. 癸丑 *gui-chou*	51. 甲寅 *jia-yin*	52. 乙卯 *yi-mao*
53. 丙辰 *bing-chen*	54. 丁巳 *ding-si*	55. 戊午 *wu-wu*	56. 己未 *ji-wei*
57. 庚申 *geng-shen*	58. 辛酉 *xin-you*	59. 壬戌 *ren-xu*	60. 癸亥 *gui-hai*

五帝 Five August Emperors

(约前 30 世纪初—前 21 世纪初)
(c. 30th century B. C. — c. 21st century B. C.)

黄帝 Yellow Emperor			
颛顼 [zhuānxū] Emperor Zhuanxu			
帝喾 [kù] Emperor Ku			
尧 [yáo] Emperor Yao			
舜 [shùn] Emperor Shun			

夏 Xia Dynasty

(前 2070 —前 1600) (2070 B. C. —1600 B. C.)

禹 [yǔ] King Yu			
启 King Qi			
太康 King Taikang			
仲康 King Zhongkang			
相 King Xiang			
少康 King Shaokang			
予 King Yu			
槐 King Huai			
芒 King Mang			
泄 King Xie			
不降 King Bujiang			
扃 [jiōng] King Jiong			
廑 [jǐn] King Jin			
孔甲 King Kongjia			
皋 [gāo] King Gao			
发 King Fa			
癸 [guǐ] (桀 [jié]) King Gui (also King Jie)			

商　Shang Dynasty
（前 1600 —前 1046）（1600 B. C. —1046 B. C.）

商前期（前 1600 —前 1300）Early Shang Dynasty（1600 B. C. —1300 B. C.）

汤 King Tang			
太丁 King Taiding			
外丙 King Waibing			
中壬 King Zhongren			
太甲 King Taijia			
沃丁 King Woding			
太庚 King Taigeng			
小甲 King Xiaojia			
雍己 King Yongji			
太戊 King Taiwu			
中丁 King Zhongding			
外壬 King Wairen			
河亶[dǎn]甲 King Hedan Jia			
祖乙 King Zuyi			
祖辛 King Zuxin			
沃甲 King Wojia			
祖丁 King Zuding			
南庚 King Nangeng			
阳甲 King Yangjia			
盘庚（迁殷前）King Pangeng (before the Shang capital was moved to Yin)			

商后期（前 1300 —前 1046 ）Later Shang Dynasty（1300 B. C. —1046 B. C.）

盘庚（迁殷后）* King Pangeng (after the Shang capital was moved to Yin)			
小辛 King Xiaoxin	(50)		前 1300
小乙 King Xiaoyi			
武丁 King Wuding	(59)		前 1250
祖庚 King Zugeng			
祖甲 King Zujia			
廪辛 King Linxin	(44)		前 1191

康丁 King Kangding			
武乙 King Wuyi	(35)	甲寅 *jia-yin*	前 1147
文丁 King Wending	(11)	己丑 *ji-chou*	前 1112
帝乙 King Diyi	(26)	庚子 *geng-zi*	前 1101
帝辛(纣) King Dixin (or King Zhou)	(30)	丙寅 *bing-yin*	前 1075

*盘庚迁都于殷后，商也称殷。Shang was also called Yin, after King Pangeng moved the Shang capital to Yin.

周 Zhou Dynasty

(前 1046 —前 256) (1046 B.C. —256 B.C.)

西周 (前 1046—前 771) Western Zhou Dynasty (1046 B.C. —771 B.C.)

武王 King Wu (姬[jī]发 Ji Fa)	(4)	乙未 *yi-wei*	前 1046
成王 King Cheng (～诵 Ji Song)	(22)	己亥 *ji-hai*	前 1042
康王 King Kang (～钊[zhāo] Ji Zhao)	(25)	辛酉 *xin-you*	前 1020
昭王 King Zhao (～瑕[xiá] Ji Xia)	(19)	丙戌 *bing-xu*	前 995
穆王 King Mu (～满 Ji Man)	(55)共王当年改元 King Gong changed the reign title in the same year	乙巳 *yi-si*	前 976
共[gōng]王 King Gong (～繄[yī]扈 Ji Yihu)	(23)	己亥 *ji-hai*	前 922
懿[yì]王 King Yi (～囏[jiān] Ji Jian)	(8)	壬戌 *ren-xu*	前 899
孝王 King Xiao (～辟方 Ji Pifang)	(6)	庚午 *geng-wu*	前 891
夷王 King Yi (～燮[xiè] Ji Xie)	(8)	丙子 *bing-zi*	前 885
厉王 King Li (～胡 Ji Hu)	(37)共和当年改元 In the beginning of the Gonghe reign the reign title was changed.	甲申 *jia-shen*	前 877
共和 Gonghe reign	(14)	庚申 *geng-shen*	前 841
宣王 King Xuan (～静 Ji Jing)	(46)	甲戌 *jia-xu*	前 827
幽王 King You (～宫湦[shēng] Ji Gongsheng)	(11)	庚申 *geng-shen*	前 781

东周（前 770 —前 256）Eastern Zhou Dynasty（770 B. C. —256 B. C.）

平王 King Ping （姬宜臼 Ji Yijiu）	(51)	辛未 *xin-wei*	前 770
桓王 King Huan （～林 Ji Lin）	(23)	壬戌 *ren-xu*	前 719
庄王 King Zhuang （～佗［tuó］Ji Tuo）	(15)	乙酉 *yi-you*	前 696
釐［xī］王 King Xi （～胡齐 Ji Huqi）	(5)	庚子 *geng-zi*	前 681
惠王 King Hui （～阆［làng］Ji Lang）	(25)	乙巳 *yi-si*	前 676
襄［xiāng］王 King Xiang （～郑 Ji Zheng）	(33)	庚午 *geng-wu*	前 651
顷王 King Qing （～壬臣 Ji Renchen）	(6)	癸卯 *gui-mao*	前 618
匡王 King Kuang （～班 Ji Ban）	(6)	己酉 *ji-you*	前 612
定王 King Ding （～瑜［yú］Ji Yu）	(21)	乙卯 *yi-mao*	前 606
简王 King Jian （～夷 Ji Yi）	(14)	丙子 *bing-zi*	前 585
灵王 King Ling （～泄心 Ji Xiexin）	(27)	庚寅 *geng-yin*	前 571
景王 King Jing （～贵 Ji Gui）	(25)	丁巳 *ding-si*	前 544
悼王 King Dao （～猛 Ji Meng）	(1)	辛巳 *xin-si*	前 520
敬王 King Jing （～匄［gài］Ji Gai）	(44)	壬午 *ren-wu*	前 519
元王 King Yuan （～仁 Ji Ren）	(7)	丙寅 *bing-yin*	前 475
贞定王 King Zhending （～介 Ji Jie）	(28)	癸酉 *gui-you*	前 468
哀王 King Ai （～去疾 Ji Quji）	(1)	庚子 *geng-zi*	前 441
思王 King Si （～叔 Ji Shu）	(1)	庚子 *geng-zi*	前 441
考王 King Kao （～嵬［wéi］Ji Wei）	(15)	辛丑 *xin-chou*	前 440
威烈王 King Weilie （～午 Ji Wu）	(24)	丙辰 *bing-chen*	前 425
安王 King An （～骄 Ji Jiao）	(26)	庚辰 *geng-chen*	前 401
烈王 King Lie （～喜 Ji Xi）	(7)	丙午 *bing-wu*	前 375

显王 King Xian (～扁 Ji Bian)	(48)	癸丑 *gui-chou*	前 368
慎靓[jìng]王 King Shenjing (～定 Ji Ding)	(6)	辛丑 *xin-chou*	前 320
赧[nǎn]王 King Nan (～延 Ji Yan)	(59)	丁未 *ding-wei*	前 314

秦 Qin Dynasty

[秦帝国(前 221 —前 206) Qin Empire (221 B.C. —206 B.C.)]

周赧王 59 年乙巳(前 256),秦灭周。自次年(秦昭襄王 52 年丙午,前 255)起至秦王政 25 年己卯(前 222),史家以秦王纪年。秦王政 26 年庚辰(前 221)完成统一,称始皇帝。In 256 B.C., or the 59th year of the reign of King Nan, the Eastern Zhou was overthrown by the State of Qin. Historians chronicle the events taking place during the period from 255 B.C., or the 52nd year of the reign of King Zhaoxiang of Qin, to 222 B.C., or the 25th year of the reign of King Ying Zheng of Qin, along the lineage of the kings of Qin. Ying Zheng accomplished the unification of China in 221 B.C. or the 26th year of his reign, and proclaimed himself the First Emperor.

昭襄王 King Zhaoxiang (嬴则,又名稷 Ying Ze, also named Ji)	(56)	乙卯 *yi-mao*	前 306
孝文王 King Xiaowen (～柱 Ying Zhu)	(1)	辛亥 *xin-hai*	前 250
庄襄王 King Zhuangxiang (～子楚 Ying Zichu)	(3)	壬子 *ren-zi*	前 249
始皇帝 First Emperor (～政 Ying Zheng)	(37)	乙卯 *yi-mao*	前 246
二世皇帝 Second Emperor (～胡亥 Ying Huhai)	(3)	壬辰 *ren-chen*	前 209

汉 Han Dynasty

(前 206 —公元 220) (206 B.C. —A.D. 220)

西汉 (前 206 —公元 25) Western Han Dynasty (206 B.C. —A.D. 25)

包括王莽(公元 9—23)和更始帝(23—25)。Wang Mang (9-23) and Emperor Gengshi (23-25) included. (Translator's Note: Starting with the First Emperor of the Qin Dynasty, Chinese monarchs are all called emperors.

高帝 Emperor Gao (刘邦 Liu Bang)	(12)	乙未 *yi-wei*	前 206
惠帝 Emperor Hui (～盈 Liu Ying)	(7)	丁未 *ding-wei*	前 194

高后 Empress Gao (吕雉 Lü Zhi)	(8)	甲寅 *jia-yin*	前 187
文帝 Emperor Wen (刘恒 Liu Heng	(16)	壬戌 *ren-xu*	前 179
	(后元 Houyuan)(7)	戊寅 *wu-yin*	前 163
景帝 Emperor Jing (～启 Liu Qi)	(7)	乙酉 *yi-you*	前 156
	(中元 Zhongyuan)(6)	壬辰 *ren-chen*	前 149
	(后元 Houyuan)(3)	戊戌 *wu-xu*	前 143
武帝 Emperor Wu (～彻 Liu Che)	建元 Jianyuan(6)	辛丑 *xin-chou*	前 140
	元光 Yuanguang(6)	丁未 *ding-wei*	前 134
	元朔 Yuanshuo(6)	癸丑 *gui-chou*	前 128
	元狩 Yuanshou(6)	己未 *ji-wei*	前 122
	元鼎 Yuanding(6)	乙丑 *yi-chou*	前 116
	元封 Yuanfeng(6)	辛未 *xin-wei*	前 110
	太初 Taichu(4)	丁丑 *ding-chou*	前 104
	天汉 Tianhan(4)	辛巳 *xin-si*	前 100
	太始 Taishi(4)	乙酉 *yi-you*	前 96
	征和 Zhenghe(4)	己丑 *ji-chou*	前 92
	后元 Houyuan(2)	癸巳 *gui-si*	前 88
昭帝 Emperor Zhao (～弗陵 Liu Fuling)	始元 Shiyuan(7)	乙未 *yi-wei*	前 86
	元凤 Yuanfeng(6)	辛丑[八] *xin-chou*[8]	前 80
	元平 Yuanping(1)	丁未 *ding-wei*	前 74
宣帝 Emperor Xuan (～询 Liu Xun)	本始 Benshi(4)	戊申 *wu-shen*	前 73
	地节 Dijie(4)	壬子 *ren-zi*	前 69
	元康 Yuankang(5)	丙辰 *bing-chen*	前 65
	神爵 Shenjue(4)	庚申[三] *geng-shen*[3]	前 61
	五凤 Wufeng(4)	甲子 *jia-zi*	前 57
	甘露 Ganlu(4)	戊辰 *wu-chen*	前 53
	黄龙 Huanglong(1)	壬申 *ren-shen*	前 49
元帝 Emperor Yuan (～奭] [shì] Liu Shi)	初元 Chuyuan(5)	癸酉 *gui-you*	前 48
	永光 Yongguang(5)	戊寅 *wu-yin*	前 43
	建昭 Jianzhao(5)	癸未 *gui-wei*	前 38
	竟宁 Jingning(1)	戊子 *wu-zi*	前 33
成帝 Emperor Cheng (～骜 [ào] Liu Ao)	建始 Jianshi(4)	己丑 *ji-chou*	前 32

	河平 Heping(4)	癸巳三 gui-si3	前 28
	阳朔 Yangshuo(4)	丁酉 ding-you	前 24
	鸿嘉 Hongjia(4)	辛丑 xin-chou	前 20
	永始 Yongshi(4)	乙巳 yi-si	前 16
	元延 Yuanyan(4)	己酉 ji-you	前 12
	绥和 Suihe(2)	癸丑 gui-chou	前 8
哀帝 Emperor Ai (刘欣 Liu Xin)	建平 Jianping(4)	乙卯 yi-mao	前 6
	元寿 Yuanshou(2)	己未 ji-wei	前 2
平帝 Emperor Ping (～衎[kàn] Liu Kan)	元始 Yuanshi(5)	辛酉 xin-you	公元 1
孺子婴 Ruzi Ying (王莽摄政 with Wang Mang as regent)	居摄 Jushe(3)	丙寅 bing-yin	6
	初始 Chushi(1)	戊辰十一 wu-chen11	8
[新 Xin (New) Dynasty] 王莽 Wang Mang	始建国 Shijianguo(5)	己巳 ji-si	9
	天凤 Tianfeng(6)	甲戌 jia-xu	14
	地皇 Dihuang(4)	庚辰 geng-chen	20
更始帝 Emperor Gengshi (刘玄 Liu Xuan)	更始 Gengshi(3)	癸未二 gui-wei2	23

译者按:孺子婴即刘婴,孺子为其号。元始 5 年被王莽立为太子,时年两岁。Translator's Note: Ruzi Ying is the literary name of Liu Ying, who was two years old when Wang Mang installed him as the crown prince in the 5th year of the Yuanshi reign.

东汉 **Eastern Han Dynasty (25—220)**

光武帝 Emperor Guangwu (刘秀 Liu Xiu)	建武 Jianwu(32)	乙酉六 yi-you6	25
	建武中元 Jianwu Zhongyuan(2)	丙辰四 bing-chen4	56
明帝 Emperor Ming (～庄 Liu Zhuang)	永平 Yongping(18)	戊午 wu-wu	58
章帝 Emperor Zhang (～炟[dá] Liu Da)	建初 Jianchu(9)	丙子 bing-zi	76
	元和 Yuanhe(4)	甲申八 jia-shen8	84
	章和 Zhanghe(2)	丁亥七 ding-hai7	87
和帝 Emperor He (～肇[zhào] Liu Zhao)	永元 Yongyuan(17)	己丑 ji-chou	89
	元兴 Yuanxing(1)	乙巳四 yi-si4	105
殇[shāng]帝 Emperor Shang (～隆 Liu Long)	延平 Yanping(1)	丙午 bing-wu	106
安帝 Emperor An (～祜[hù] Liu Hu)	永初 Yongchu(7)	丁未 ding-wei	107
	元初 Yuanchu(7)	甲寅 jia-yin	114

	永宁 Yongning(2)	庚申四 geng-shen4	120
	建光 Jianguang(2)	辛酉七 xin-you7	121
	延光 Yanguang(4)	壬戌三 ren-xu3	122
顺帝 Emperor Shun (～保 Liu Bao)	永建 Yongjian(7)	丙寅 bing-yin	126
	阳嘉 Yangjia(4)	壬申三 ren-shen3	132
	永和 Yonghe(6)	丙子 bing-zi	136
	汉安 Han'an(3)	壬午 ren-wu	142
	建康 Jiankang(1)	甲申四 jia-shen4	144
冲帝 Emperor Chong (～炳 [bǐng] Liu Bing)	永憙 [xī]Yongxi (嘉 Jia)(1)	乙酉 yi-you	145
质帝 Emperor Zhi (～缵 [zuǎn] Liu Zuan)	本初 Benchu(1)	丙戌 bing-xu	146
桓帝 Emperor Huan (～志 Liu Zhi)	建和 Jianhe(3)	丁亥 ding-hai	147
	和平 Heping(1)	庚寅 geng-yin	150
	元嘉 Yuanjia(3)	辛卯 xin-mao	151
	永兴 Yongxing(2)	癸巳五 gui-si5	153
	永寿 Yongshou(4)	乙未 yi-wei	155
	延熹 [xī]Yanxi(10)	戊戌六 wu-xu6	158
	永康 Yongkang(1)	丁未六 ding-wei6	167
灵帝 Emperor Ling (～宏 Liu Hong)	建宁 Jianning(5)	戊申 wu-shen	168
	熹 [xī]平 Xiping(7)	壬子五 ren-zi5	172
	光和 Guanghe(7)	戊午三 wu-wu3	178
	中平 Zhongping(6)	甲子十二 jia-zi12	184
献帝 Emperor Xian (～协 Liu Xie)	初平 Chuping(4)	庚午 geng-wu	190
	兴平 Xingping(2)	甲戌 jia-xu	194
	建安 Jian'an(25)	丙子 bing-zi	196
	延康 Yankang(1)	庚子三 geng-zi3	220

三国 Three Kingdoms (220—280)

魏 Kingdom of Wei (220—265)

文帝 Emperor Wen (曹丕 [pī] Cao Pi)	黄初 Huangchu(7)	庚子十 geng-zi10	220

明帝 Emperor Ming(～叡[ruì] Cao Rui)	太和 Taihe(7)	丁未 *ding-wei*	227
	青龙 Qinglong(5)	癸丑二 *gui-chou*₂	233
	景初 Jingchu(3)	丁巳三 *ding-si*₃	237
齐王 King Qi(～芳 Cao Fang)	正始 Zhengshi(10)	庚申 *geng-shen*	240
	嘉平 Jiaping(6)	己巳四 *ji-si*₄	249
高贵乡公 Township Duke Gaogui(～髦[máo] Cao Mao)	正元 Zhengyuan(3)	甲戌十 *jia-xu*₁₀	254
	甘露 Ganlu(5)	丙子六 *bing-zi*₆	256
元帝 Emperor Yuan(～奂[huàn] Cao Huan)(陈留王 also called King Chenliu)	景元 Jingyuan(5)	庚辰六 *geng-chen*₆	260
	咸熙 Xianxi(2)	甲申五 *jia-shen*₅	264

蜀汉 Kingdom of Shuhan (221—263)

昭烈帝 Emperor Zhaolie(刘备 Liu Bei)	章武 Zhangwu(3)	辛丑四 *xin-chou*₄	221
后主 Later Master(～禅[shàn] Liu Shan)	建兴 Jianxing(15)	癸卯五 *gui-mao*₅	223
	延熙 Yanxi(20)	戊午 *wu-wu*	238
	景耀 Jingyao(6)	戊寅 *wu-yin*	258
	炎兴 Yanxing(1)	癸未八 *gui-wei*₈	263

吴 Kingdom of Wu (222—280)

大帝 Great Emperor(孙权 Sun Quan)	黄武 Huangwu(8)	壬寅十 *ren-yin*₁₀	222
	黄龙 Huanglong(3)	己酉四 *ji-you*₄	229
	嘉禾 Jiahe(7)	壬子 *ren-zi*	232
	赤乌 Chiwu(14)	戊午九 *wu-wu*₉	238
	太元 Taiyuan(2)	辛未五 *xin-wei*₅	251
	神凤 Shenfeng(1)	壬申二 *ren-shen*₂	252
会稽王 King Guiji(～亮 Sun Liang)	建兴 Jianxing(2)	壬申四 *ren-shen*₄	252
	五凤 Wufeng(3)	甲戌 *jia-xu*	254
	太平 Taiping(3)	丙子十 *bing-zi*₁₀	256
景帝 Emperor Jing(～休 Sun Xiu)	永安 Yong'an(7)	戊寅十 *wu-yin*₁₀	258
乌程侯 Marquis Wucheng(～皓[hào] Sun Hao)	元兴 Yuanxing(2)	甲申七 *jia-shen*₇	264
	甘露 Ganlu(2)	乙酉四 *yi-you*₄	265

	宝鼎 Baoding(4)	丙戌八 *bing-xu*8	266
	建衡 Jianheng(3)	己丑十 *ji-chou*10	269
	凤凰 Fenghuang(3)	壬辰 *ren-chen*	272
	天册 Tiance(2)	乙未 *yi-wei*	275
	天玺 Tianxi(1)	丙申七 *bing-shen*7	276
	天纪 Tianji(4)	丁酉 *ding-you*	277

晋 Jin Dynasty (265—420)

西晋 Western Jin Dynasty (265—317)

武帝 Emperor Wu(司马炎 Sima Yan)	泰始 Taishi(10)	乙酉十二 *yi-you*12	265
	咸宁 Xianning(6)	乙未 *yi-wei*	275
	太康 Taikang(10)	庚子四 *geng-zi*4	280
	太熙 Taixi(1)	庚戌 *geng-xu*	290
惠帝 Emperor Hui (～衷 Sima Zhong)	永熙 Yongxi(1)	庚戌四 *geng-xu*4	290
	永平 Yongping(1)	辛亥 *xin-hai*	291
	元康 Yuankang(9)	辛亥三 *xin-hai*3	291
	永康 Yongkang(2)	庚申 *geng-shen*	300
	永宁 Yongning(2)	辛酉四 *xin-you*4	301
	太安 Tai'an(2)	壬戌十二 *ren-xu*12	302
	永安 Yong'an(1)	甲子 *jia-zi*	304
	建武 Jianwu(1)	甲子七 *jia-zi*7	304
	永安 Yong'an(1)	甲子十一 *jia-zi*11	304
	永兴 Yongxing(3)	甲子十二 *jia-zi*12	304
	光熙 Guangxi(1)	丙寅六 *bing-yin*6	306
怀帝 Emperor Huai (～炽 [chì] Sima Chi)	永嘉 Yongjia(7)	丁卯 *ding-mao*	307
愍[mǐn]帝 Emperor Min (～邺 [yè] Sima Ye)	建兴 Jianxing(5)	癸酉四 *gui-you*4	313

东晋 Eastern Jin Dynasty (317—420)

元帝 Emperor Yuan (司马睿 [ruì] Sima Rui)	建武 Jianwu(2)	丁丑三 *ding-chou*3	317
	大兴 Daxing(4)	戊寅三 *wu-yin*3	318
	永昌 Yongchang(2)	壬午 *ren-wu*	322
明帝 Emperor Ming (～绍 Sima Shao)	永昌 Yongchang	壬午闰十一 *ren-wu*leap11	322

	太宁 Taining(4)	癸未$_{三}$ *gui-wei*$_{3}$	323
成帝 Emperor Cheng (～衍 [yǎn] Sima Yan)	太宁 Taining	乙酉$_{闰八}$ *yi-you*$_{leap8}$	325
	咸和 Xianhe(9)	丙戌$_{二}$ *bing-xu*$_{2}$	326
	咸康 Xiankang(8)	乙未 *yi-wei*	335
康帝 Emperor Kang (～岳 Sima Yue)	建元 Jianyuan(2)	癸卯 *gui-mao*	343
穆帝 Emperor Mu (～聃 [dān] Sima Dan)	永和 Yonghe(12)	乙巳 *yi-si*	345
	升平 Shengping(5)	丁巳 *ding-si*	357
哀帝 Emperor Ai (～丕 [pī] Sima Pi)	隆和 Longhe(2)	壬戌 *ren-xu*	362
	兴宁 Xingning(3)	癸亥$_{二}$ *gui-hai*$_{2}$	363
海西公 Duke Haixi (～奕 [yì] Sima Yi)	太和 Taihe(6)	丙寅 *bing-yin*	366
简文帝 Emperor Jianwen (～昱 [yù] Sima Yu)	咸安 Xian'an(2)	辛未$_{十一}$ *xin-wei*$_{11}$	371
孝武帝 Emperor Xiaowu (～曜 [yào] Sima Yao)	宁康 Ningkang(3)	癸酉 *gui-you*	373
	太元 Taiyuan(21)	丙子 *bing-zi*	376
安帝 Emperor An (～德宗 Sima Dezong)	隆安 Long'an (5)	丁酉 *ding-you*	397
	元兴 Yuanxing(3)	壬寅 *ren-yin*	402
	义熙 Yixi(14)	乙巳 *yi-si*	405
恭帝 Emperor Gong (～德文 Sima Dewen)	元熙 Yuanxi(2)	己未 *ji-wei*	419

南北朝
Southern and Northern Dynasties (420—589)

南朝 Southern Dynasties　宋 Song Dynasty (420—479)

武帝 Emperor Wu (刘裕 Liu Yu)	永初 Yongchu(3)	庚申$_{六}$ *geng-shen*$_{6}$	420
少帝 Emperor Shao (～义符 Liu Yifu)	景平 Jingping(2)	癸亥 *gui-hai*	423
文帝 Emperor Wen (～义隆 Liu Yilong)	元嘉 Yuanjia(30)	甲子$_{八}$ *jia-zi*$_{8}$	424
孝武帝 Emperor Xiaowu (～骏 [jùn] Liu Jun)	孝建 Xiaojian(3)	甲午 *jia-wu*	454
	大明 Daming(8)	丁酉 *ding-you*	457
前废帝 Former Dethroned Emperor (～子业 Liu Ziye)	永光 Yongguang(1)	乙巳 *yi-si*	465
	景和 Jinghe(1)	乙巳$_{八}$ *yi-si*$_{8}$	465

明帝 Emperor Ming (～彧[yù] Liu Yu)	泰始 Taishi(7)	乙巳十二 yi-si 12	465
	泰豫 Taiyu(1)	壬子 ren-zi	472
后废帝 Later Dethroned Emperor (～昱[yù] Liu Yu)(苍梧王 also called King Cangwu)	元徽 Yuanhui(5)	癸丑 gui-chou	473
顺帝 Emperor Shun (～準 Liu Zhun)	昇明 Shengming(3)	丁巳七 ding-si 7	477

齐 Qi Dynasty (479—502)

高帝 Emperor Gao (萧道成 Xiao Daocheng)	建元 Jianyuan(4)	己未四 ji-wei 4	479
武帝 Emperor Wu (～赜[zé] Xiao Ze)	永明 Yongming(11)	癸亥 gui-hai	483
鬱林王 King Yulin (～昭业 Xiao Zhaoye)	隆昌 Longchang(1)	甲戌 jia-xu	494
海陵王 King Hailing (～昭文 Xiao Zhaowen)	延兴 Yanxing(1)	甲戌七 jia-xu 7	494
明帝 King Ming (～鸾 Xiao Luan)	建武 Jianwu(5)	甲戌十 jia-xu 10	494
	永泰 Yongtai(1)	戊寅四 wu-yin 4	498
东昏侯 Marquis Donghun (～宝卷 Xiao Baojuan)	永元 Yongyuan(3)	己卯 ji-mao	499
和帝 Emperor He (～宝融 Xiao Baorong)	中兴 Zhongxing(2)	辛巳三 xin-si 3	501

梁 Liang Dynasty (502—557)

武帝 Emperor Wu (萧衍[yǎn] Xiao Yan)	天监 Tianjian(18)	壬午四 ren-wu 4	502
	普通 Putong(8)	庚子 geng-zi	520
	大通 Datong(3)	丁未三 ding-wei 3	527
	中大通 Mid-Datong(6)	己酉十 ji-you 10	529
	大同 Datong(12)	乙卯 yi-mao	535
	中大同 Mid-Datong(2)	丙寅四 bing-yin 4	546
	太清 Taiqing(3)*	丁卯四 ding-mao 4	547
简文帝 Emperor Jianwen (～纲 Xiao Gang)	大宝 Dabao(2)**	庚午 geng-wu	550
元帝 Emperor Yuan (～绎[yì] Xiao Yi)	承圣 Chengsheng(4)	壬申十一 ren-shen 11	552
敬帝 Emperor Jing (～方智 Xiao Fangzhi)	绍泰 Shaotai(2)	乙亥十 yi-hai 10	555

	太平 Taiping(2)	丙子九 *bing-zi*$_9$	556

* 有的地区用至 6 年。The reign title lasted for six years in some regions.
** 有的地区用至 3 年。The reign title lasted for three years in some regions.

陈 Chen Dynasty (557—589)

武帝 Emperor Wu（陈霸先 Chen Baxian）	永定 Yongding(3)	丁丑十 *ding-chou*$_{10}$	557
文帝 Emperor Wen（～蒨［qiàn］Chen Qian）	天嘉 Tianjia(7)	庚辰 *geng-chen*	560
	天康 Tiankang(1)	丙戌二 *bing-xu*$_2$	566
废帝 Dethroned Emperor（～伯宗 Chen Bozong）（临海王 also called King Linhai）	光大 Guangda(2)	丁亥 *ding-hai*	567
宣帝 Emperor Xuan（～顼［xū］Chen Xu）	太建 Taijian(14)	己丑 *ji-chou*	569
后主 Later Master（～叔宝）Chen Shubao	至德 Zhide (4)	癸卯 *gui-mao*	583
	祯明 Zhenming (3)	丁未 *ding-mo*	587

北朝 Northern Dynasties

北魏 Northern Wei Dynasty［拓跋氏，后改元氏 founded by the Tuoba family, which later changed its family name to Yuan］(386—534)

北魏建国于丙戌（386 年）正月，初称代国，至同年四月始改国号为魏，439 年灭北凉，统一北方。The Northern Wei Dynasty was known as the State of Dai when it was established in the first month of the year *bing-xu* (386). The dynasty was renamed Wei in the 4th month of the same year. In 439 the Wei Dynasty unified northern China after it overthrew the Northern Liang State.

道武帝 Emperor Daowu（拓跋珪［guī］Tuoba Gui）	登国 Dengguo(11)	丙戌 *bing-xu*	386
	皇始 Huangshi(3)	丙申七 *bing-shen*$_7$	396
	天兴 Tianxing(7)	戊戌十二 *wu-xu*$_{12}$	398
	天赐 Tianci(6)	甲辰十 *jia-chen*$_{10}$	404
明元帝 Emperor Mingyuan（～嗣［sì］Tuoba Si）	永兴 Yongxing(5)	己酉十 *ji-you*$_{10}$	409
	神瑞 Shenrui(3)	甲寅 *jia-yin*	414
	泰常 Taichang(8)	丙辰四 *bing-chen*$_4$	416
太武帝 Emperor Taiwu（～焘［tāo］Tuoba Tao）	始光 Shiguang(5)	甲子 *jia-zi*	424
	神䴥［jiā］Shenjia(4)	戊辰二 *wu-chen*$_2$	428
	延和 Yanhe(3)	壬申 *ren-shen*	432
	太延 Taiyan(6)	乙亥 *yi-hai*	435
	太平真君 Taiping Zhenjun(12)	庚辰六 *geng-chen*$_6$	440

	正平 Zhengping(2)	辛卯$_{\text{六}}$ *xin-mao*$_6$	451
南安王 King Nan'an (拓跋余 Tuoba Yu)	永(承)平 Yong (Cheng) Ping(1)	壬辰$_{\text{三}}$ *ren-chen*$_3$	452
文成帝 Emperor Wencheng (～濬[jùn] Tuoba Jun)	兴安 Xing'an(3)	壬辰$_{\text{十}}$ *ren-chen*$_{10}$	452
	兴光 Xingguang(2)	甲午$_{\text{七}}$ *jia-wu*$_7$	454
	太安 Tai'an(5)	乙未$_{\text{六}}$ *yi-wei*$_6$	455
	和平 Heping (6)	庚子 *geng-zi*	460
献文帝 Emperor Xianwen (～弘 Tuoba Hong)	天安 Tian'an(2)	丙午 *bing-wu*	466
	皇兴 Huangxing(5)	丁未$_{\text{八}}$ *ding-wei*$_8$	467
孝文帝 Emperor Xiaowen (元宏 Yuan Hong)	延兴 Yanxing(6)	辛亥$_{\text{八}}$ *xin-hai*$_8$	471
	承明 Chengming(1)	丙辰$_{\text{六}}$ *bing-chen*$_6$	476
	太和 Taihe(23)	丁巳 *ding-si*	477
宣武帝 Emperor Xuanwu (～恪[kè] Yuan Ke)	景明 Jingming(4)	庚辰 *geng-chen*	500
	正始 Zhengshi(5)	甲申 *jia-shen*	504
	永平 Yongping(5)	戊子$_{\text{八}}$ *wu-zi*$_8$	508
	延昌 Yanchang(4)	壬辰$_{\text{四}}$ *ren-chen*$_4$	512
孝明帝 Emperor Xiaoming (～诩[xǔ] Yuan Xu)	熙平 Xiping(3)	丙申 *bing-shen*	516
	神龟 Shengui(3)	戊戌$_{\text{二}}$ *wu-xu*$_2$	518
	正光 Zhengguang(6)	庚子$_{\text{七}}$ *geng-zi*$_7$	520
	孝昌 Xiaochang(3)	乙巳$_{\text{六}}$ *yi-si*$_6$	525
	武泰 Wutai(1)	戊申 *wu-shen*	528
孝庄帝 Emperor Xiaozhuang (～子攸[yōu] Yuan Ziyou)	建义 Jianyi(1)	戊申$_{\text{四}}$ *wu-shen*$_4$	528
	永安 Yong'an(3)	戊申$_{\text{九}}$ *wu-shen*$_9$	528
长广王 King Changguang (～晔[yè] Yuan Ye)	建明 Jianming(2)	庚戌$_{\text{十}}$ *geng-xu*$_{10}$	530
节闵[mǐn]帝 Emperor Jiemin (～恭 Yuan Gong)	普泰 Putai(2)	辛亥$_{\text{二}}$ *xin-hai*$_2$	531
安定王 King Anding (～朗 Yuan Lang)	中兴 Zhongxing(2)	辛亥$_{\text{十}}$ *xin-hai*$_{10}$	531
孝武帝 Emperor Xiaowu (～脩 Yuan Xiu)	太昌 Taichang(1)	壬子$_{\text{四}}$ *ren-zi*$_4$	532
	永兴 Yongxing(1)	壬子$_{\text{十二}}$ *ren-zi*$_{12}$	532
	永熙 Yongxi(3)	壬子$_{\text{十二}}$ *ren-zi*$_{12}$	532

东魏 Eastern Wei Dynasty (534—550)

孝静帝 Emperor Xiaojing (元善见 Yuan Shanjian)	天平 Tianping(4)	甲寅$_{十}$ *jia-yin*$_{10}$	534
	元象 Yuanxiang(2)	戊午 *wu-wu*	538
	兴和 Xinghe(4)	己未$_{十一}$ *ji-wei*$_{11}$	539
	武定 Wuding(8)	癸亥 *gui-hai*	543

北齐 Northern Qi Dynasty (550—577)

文宣帝 Emperor Wenxuan (高洋 Gao Yang)	天保 Tianbao(10)	庚午$_{五}$ *geng-wu*$_{5}$	550
废帝 Dethroned Emperor (～殷 Gao Yin)	乾明 Qianming(1)	庚辰 *geng-chen*	560
孝昭帝 Emperor Xiaozhao (～演 Gao Yan)	皇建 Huangjian(2)	庚辰$_{八}$ *geng-chen*$_{8}$	560
武成帝 Emperor Wucheng (～湛 Gao Zhan)	太宁 Taining(2)	辛巳$_{十一}$ *xin-si*$_{11}$	561
	河清 Heqing(4)	壬午$_{四}$ *ren-wu*$_{4}$	562
后主 Later Emperor (～纬 Gao Wei)	天统 Tiantong(5)	乙酉$_{四}$ *yi-you*$_{4}$	565
	武平 Wuping(7)	庚寅 *geng-yin*	570
	隆化 Longhua(1)	丙申$_{十二}$ *bing-shen*$_{12}$	576
幼主 Young Emperor (～恒 Gao Heng)	承光 Chengguang(1)	丁酉 *ding-you*	577

西魏 Western Wei Dynasty (535—556)

文帝 Emperor Wen (元宝炬 Yuan Baoju)	大统 Datong(17)	乙卯 *yi-mao*	535
废帝 Dethroned Emperor (～钦 Yuan Qin)	—(3)	壬申 *ren-shen*	552
恭帝 Emperor Gong (～廓 Yuan Kuo)	—(3)	甲戌$_{一}$ *jia-xu*$_{1}$	554

北周 Northern Zhou Dynasty (557—581)

孝闵[mǐn]帝 Emperor Xiaomin (宇文觉 Yuwen Jue)	—(1)	丁丑 *ding-chou*	557
明帝 Emperor Ming (～毓[yù] Yuwen Yu)	—(3)	丁丑$_{九}$ *ding-chou*$_{9}$	557
	武成 Wucheng(2)	己卯$_{八}$ *ji-mao*$_{8}$	559
武帝 Emperor Wu (～邕[yōng] Yuwen Yong)	保定 Baoding(5)	辛巳 *xin-si*	561
	天和 Tianhe(7)	丙戌 *bing-xu*	566

	建德 Jiande(7)	壬辰$_{三}$ *ren-chen*$_3$	572
	宣政 Xuanzheng(1)	戊戌$_{三}$ *wu-xu*$_3$	578
宣帝 Emperor Xuan (～赟[yūn] Yuwen Yun)	大成 Dacheng(1)	己亥 *ji-hai*	579
静帝 Emperor Jing (～阐[chǎn] Yuwen Chan)	大象 Daxiang(3)	己亥$_{二}$ *ji-hai*$_2$	579
	大定 Dading(1)	辛丑$_{一}$ *xin-chou*$_1$	581

隋 Sui Dynasty (581—618)

隋建国于 581 年，589 年灭陈，完成统一。The Sui Dynasty was established in 581 and reunited China in 589 after it overthrew the Chen Dynasty.

文帝 Emperor Wen (杨坚 Yang Jian)	开皇 Kaihuang(20)	辛丑$_{二}$ *xin-chou*$_2$	581
	仁寿 Renshou(4)	辛酉 *xin-you*	601
炀[yáng]帝 Emperor Yang (～广 Yang Guang)	大业 Daye(14)	乙丑 *yi-chou*	605
恭帝 Emperor Gong (～侑[yòu] Yang You)	义宁 Yining(2)	丁丑$_{十一}$ *ding-chou*$_{11}$	617

唐 Tang Dynasty (618—907)

高祖 Emperor Gaozu (李渊 Li Yuan)	武德 Wude(9)	戊寅$_{五}$ *wu-yin*$_5$	618
太宗 Emperor Taizong (～世民 Li Shimin)	贞观 Zhenguan(23)	丁亥 *ding-hai*	627
高宗 Emperor Gaozong (～治 Li Zhi)	永徽 Yonghui(6)	庚戌 *geng-xu*	650
	显庆 Xianqing(6)	丙辰 *bing-chen*	656
	龙朔 Longshuo(3)	辛酉$_{三}$ *xin-you*$_3$ *	661
	麟德 Linde(2)	甲子 *jia-zi*	664
	乾封 Qianfeng(3)	丙寅 *bing-yin*	666
	总章 Zongzhang(3)	戊辰$_{三}$ *wu-chen*$_3$	668
	咸亨 Xianheng(5)	庚午$_{三}$ *geng-wu*$_3$	670
	上元 Shangyuan(3)	甲戌$_{八}$ *jia-xu*$_8$	674
	仪凤 Yifeng(4)	丙子$_{十一}$ *bing-zi*$_{11}$	676
	调露 Tiaolu(2)	己卯$_{六}$ *ji-mao*$_6$	679

	永隆 Yonglong(2)	庚辰$_{八}$ *geng-chen*$_{8}$	680
	开耀 Kaiyao(2)	辛巳$_{九}$ *xin-si*$_{9}$	681
	永淳 Yongchun(2)	壬午$_{二}$ *ren-wu*$_{2}$	682
	弘道 Hongdao(1)	癸未$_{十二}$ *gui-wei*$_{12}$	683
中宗 Emperor Zhongzong (～显又名哲 Li Xian, also named Li Zhe)	嗣圣 Sisheng(1)	甲申 *jia-shen*	684
睿[ruì]宗 Emperor Ruizong (～旦 Li Dan)	文明 Wenming(1)	甲申$_{二}$ *jia-shen*$_{2}$	684
武后 Empress Wu (武曌[zhào] Wu Zhao)	光宅 Guangzhai(1)	甲申$_{九}$ *jia-shen*$_{9}$	684
	垂拱 Chuigong(4)	乙酉 *yi-you*	685
	永昌 Yongchang(1)	己丑 *ji-chou*	689
	载初 Zaichu** (1)	庚寅$_{正}$ *geng-yin*$_{1}$	690
武后称帝，改国号为周。Empress Wu ascended the throne and changed the name of the dynasty to Zhou.	天授 Tianshou(3)	庚寅$_{九}$ *geng-yin*$_{9}$	690
	如意 Ruyi (1)	壬辰$_{四}$ *ren-chen*$_{4}$	692
	长寿 Changshou(3)	壬辰$_{九}$ *ren-chen*$_{9}$	692
	延载 Yanzai(1)	甲午$_{五}$ *jia-wu*$_{5}$	694
	证圣 Zhengsheng(1)	乙未 *yi-wei*	695
	天册万岁 Tiance Wansui(2)	乙未$_{九}$ *yi-wei*$_{9}$	695
	万岁登封 Wansui Dengfeng(1)	丙申$_{腊}$ *bing-shen*$_{12}$	696
	万岁通天 Wansui Tongtian(2)	丙申$_{三}$ *bing-shen*$_{3}$	696
	神功 Shengong(1)	丁酉$_{九}$ *ding-you*$_{9}$	697
	圣历 Shengli(3)	戊戌 *wu-xu*	698
	久视 Jiushi(1)	庚子$_{五}$ *geng-zi*$_{5}$	700
	大足 Dazu(1)	辛丑 *xin-chou*	701
	长安 Chang'an(4)	辛丑$_{十}$ *xin-chou*$_{10}$	701
中宗（李显又名哲），复唐国号。Emperor Zhongzong (Li Xian, also named Li Zhe) changed the name of the dynasty back to Tang.	神龙 Shenlong (3)	乙巳 *yi-si*	705
	景龙 Jinglong(4)	丁未$_{九}$ *ding-wei*$_{9}$	707
睿[ruì]宗 Emperor Ruizong(～旦 Li Dan)	景云 Jingyun(2)	庚戌$_{七}$ *geng-xu*$_{7}$	710
	太极 Taiji (1)	壬子 *ren-zi*	712
	延和 Yanhe(1)	壬子$_{五}$ *ren-zi*$_{5}$	712
玄宗 Emperor Xuanzong (～隆基 Li Longji)	先天 Xiantian(2)	壬子$_{八}$ *ren-zi*$_{8}$	712
	开元 Kaiyuan(29)	癸丑$_{十二}$ *gui-chou*$_{12}$	713
	天宝 Tianbao(15)	壬午 *ren-wu*	742

肃宗 Emperor Suzong (～亨 Li Heng)	至德 Zhide(3)	丙申七 *bing-shen*$_7$	756
	乾元 Qianyuan(3)	戊戌二 *wu-xu*$_2$	758
	上元 Shangyuan(2)	庚子闰四 *geng-zi*$_{leap\ 4}$	760
	—(1) ***	辛丑九 *xin-chou*$_9$	761
代宗 Emperor Daizong (～豫 Li Yu)	宝应 Baoying(2)	壬寅四 *ren-yin*$_4$	762
	广德 Guangde(2)	癸卯七 *gui-mao*$_7$	763
	永泰 Yongtai(2)	乙巳 *yi-si*	765
	大历 Dali(14)	丙午十一 *bing-wu*$_{11}$	766
德宗 Emperor Dezong (～适 [kuò] Li Kuo)	建中 Jianzhong(4)	庚申 *geng-shen*	780
	兴元 Xingyuan(1)	甲子 *jia-zi*	784
	贞元 Zhenyuan(21)	乙丑 *yi-chou*	785
顺宗 Emperor Shunzong (～诵 Li Song)	永贞 Yongzhen(1)	乙酉八 *yi-you*$_8$	805
宪宗 Emperor Xianzong (～纯 Li Chun)	元和 Yuanhe(15)	丙戌 *bing-xu*	806
穆宗 Emperor Muzong (～恒 Li Heng)	长庆 Changqing(4)	辛丑 *xin-chou*	821
敬宗 Emperor Jingzong (～湛 Li Zhan)	宝历 Baoli(3)	乙巳 *yi-si*	825
文宗 Emperor Wenzong (～昂 Li Ang)	宝历 Baoli	丙午十二 *bing-wu*$_{12}$	826
	大(太)和 Da/Taihe (9)	丁未二 *ding-wei*$_2$	827
	开成 Kaicheng(5)	丙辰 *bing-chen*	836
武宗 Emperor Wuzong (～炎 Li Yan)	会昌 Huichang (6)	辛酉 *xin-you*	841
宣宗 Emperor Xuanzong (～忱 [chén] Li Chen)	大中 Dazhong(14)	丁卯 *ding-mao*	847
懿 [yì] 宗 Emperor Yizong (～漼 [cuǐ] Li Cui)	大中 Dazhong	己卯八 *ji-mao*$_8$	859
	咸通 Xiantong(15)	庚辰十一 *geng-chen*$_{11}$	860
僖 [xī] 宗 Emperor Xizong (～儇 [xuān] Li Xuan)	咸通 Xiantong	癸巳七 *gui-si*$_7$	873
	乾符 Qianfu(6)	甲午十一 *jia-wu*$_{11}$	874
	广明 Guangming(2)	庚子 *geng-zi*	880
	中和 Zhonghe(5)	辛丑七 *xin-chou*$_7$	881
	光启 Guangqi(4)	乙巳三 *yi-si*$_3$	885

昭宗 Emperor Zhaozong (~晔[yè] Li Ye)	文德 Wende(1)	戊申二 wu-shen2	888
	龙纪 Longji(1)	己酉 ji-you	889
	大顺 Dashun(2)	庚戌 geng-xu	890
	景福 Jingfu(2)	壬子 ren-zi	892
	乾宁 Qianning(5)	甲寅 jia-yin	894
	光化 Guanghua(4)	戊午八 wu-wu8	898
	天复 Tianfu(4)	辛酉四 xin-you4	901
	天祐 Tianyou(4)	甲子闰四 jia-zi leap 4	904
哀帝 Emperor Ai (~柷[chù] Li Chu)	天祐 Tianyou****	甲子八 jia-zi8	904

* 辛酉三月丙申朔改元,一作辛酉二月乙未晦改元。The reign title was changed on the 1st day of the 3rd month of the year *xin-you*, but another theory dates it to the last day of the 2nd month of that year.

** 始用周正,改永昌元年十一月为载初元年正月,以十二月为腊月,夏正月为一月。久视元年十月复用夏正,以正月为十一月,腊月为十二月,一月为正月。本表在这段期间内干支后面所注的改元月份都是周历,各年号的使用年数也是按照周历的计算方法。During this year Empress Wu adopted the Zhou calendar, according to which she instituted the 11th lunar month of the 1st year of the Yongchang reign (which used the Xia calendar) as the 1st month of the 1st year of her Zaichu reign, the 12th lunar month as the last month of the year, and the 1st lunar month of the Xia calendar as the 1st month of the year. In the 10th month of the 1st year of the Jiushi reign, she restored the Xia calendar, altering the 1st month of the Zhou calendar as the 11th month, and the last month of the Zhou calendar as the 12th month. In this table, the month in which a reign title was changed during this period, as indicated behind the year rendered in Heavenly Stems and Earthly Branches pairings, is calculated according to the Zhou calendar, so are the years a reign lasted. (Translator's Note: In ancient times the traditional Chinese calendar fell into three categories: the Xia calendar, which regards the 1st lunar month as the beginning of the year and is the same as the lunar calendar; the Shang calendar, with the 12th lunar month as the beginning of the year; and the Zhou calendar, with the 11th lunar month as the beginning of the year.)

*** 此年九月以后去年号,但称元年。The reign title was abolished in the 9th month of this year, which was incorporated as the 1st year of the Baoying reign.

**** 哀帝即位未改元。Emperor Ai did not change the reign title when he ascended the throne.

五代 Five Dynasties (907—960)

后梁 Later Liang Dynasty (907—923)

太祖 Emperor Taizu (朱晃,又名温、全忠 Zhu Huang, also named Wen or Quanzhong)	开平 Kaiping(5)	丁卯四 ding-mao4	907
	乾化 Qianhua(5)	辛未五 xin-wei5	911
末帝 Last Emperor (~瑱[zhèn] Zhu Zhen)	乾化 Qianhua	癸酉二 gui-you2	913
	贞明 Zhenming(7)	乙亥十一 yi-hai11	915
	龙德 Longde(3)	辛巳五 xin-si5	921

后唐 Later Tang Dynasty (923—936)

庄宗 Emperor Zhuangzong (李存勖 [xù] Li Cunxu)	同光 Tongguang(4)	癸未$_{四}$ *gui-wei*$_4$	923
明宗 Emperor Mingzong (~[dǎn] Li Dan)	天成 Tiancheng(5)	丙戌$_{四}$ *bing-xu*$_4$	926
	长兴 Changxing(4)	庚寅$_{二}$ *geng-yin*$_2$	930
闵[mǐn]帝 Emperor Min (~从厚 Li Conghou)	应顺 Yingshun(1)	甲午 *jia-wu*	934
末帝 Last Emperor (~从珂 [kē] Li Congke)	清泰 Qingtai(3)	甲午$_{四}$ *jia-wu*$_4$	934

后晋 Later Jin Dynasty (936—947)

高祖 Emperor Gaozu (石敬瑭 [táng] Shi Jingtang)	天福 Tianfu(9)	丙申$_{十一}$ *bing-shen*$_{11}$	936
出帝 Emperor Chu (~重贵 Shi Chonggui)	天福 Tianfu*	壬寅$_{六}$ *ren-yin*$_6$	942
	开运 Kaiyun(4)	甲辰$_{七}$ *jia-chen*$_7$	944

* 出帝即位未改元. Emperor Chu did not change the reign title when he ascended the throne.

后汉 Later Han Dynasty (947—950)

高祖 Emperor Gaozu (刘暠 gǎo],本名知远 Liu Gao, originally named Li Zhiyuan)	天福 Tianfu*	丁未$_{二}$ *ding-wei*$_2$	947
	乾祐 Qianyou(3)	戊申 *wu-shen*	948
隐帝 Emperor Yin (~承祐 Liu Chengyou)	乾祐 Qianyou**	戊申$_{二}$ *wu-shen*$_2$	948

* 后汉高祖即位,仍用后晋高祖年号,称天福十二年。Emperor Gaozu of the Later Han Dynasty adopted the same reign title of Emperor Gaozu of the Later Jin Dynasty, naming the 1st year of his own reign the 12th year of Tianfu.

** 隐帝即位未改元。Emperor Yin did not change the reign title when he ascended the throne.

后周 Later Zhou Dynasty (951—960)

太祖 Emperor Taizu (郭威 Guo Wei)	广顺 Guangshun(3)	辛亥 *xin-hai*	951
	显德 Xiande(7)	甲寅$_{一}$ *jia-yin*$_1$	954
世宗 Emperor Shizong (柴荣 Chai Rong)	显德 Xiande*	甲寅$_{一}$ *jia-yin*$_1$	954
恭帝 Emperor Gong (~宗训 Chai Zongxun)	显德 Xiande	己未$_{六}$ *ji-wei*$_6$	959

* 世宗、恭帝都未改元。Both Emperor Shizong and Emperor Gong retained the reign title of their respective predecessors.

宋 Song Dynasty (960—1279)

北宋 Northern Song Dynasty (960—1127)

太祖 Emperor Taizu (赵匡胤 [yìn] Zhao Kuangyin)	建隆 Jianlong(4)	庚申 *geng-shen*	960
	乾德 Qiande(6)	癸亥$_{十一}$ *gui-hai*$_{11}$	963
	开宝 Kaibao(9)	戊辰$_{十一}$ *wu-chen*$_{11}$	968
太宗 Emperor Taizong (～炅 [jiǒng],本名匡义,又名光义 Zhao Jiong, originally named Zhao Kuangyi, also named Zhao Guangyi)	太平兴国 Taiping Xingguo(9)	丙子$_{十二}$ *bing-zi*$_{12}$	976
	雍熙 Yongxi(4)	甲申$_{十一}$ *jia-shen*$_{11}$	984
	端拱 Duangong(2)	戊子 *wu-zi*	988
	淳化 Chunhua(5)	庚寅 *geng-yin*	990
	至道 Zhidao(3)	乙未 *yi-wei*	995
真宗 Emperor Zhenzong (～恒 Zhao Heng)	咸平 Xianping(6)	戊戌 *wu-xu*	998
	景德 Jingde(4)	甲辰 *jia-chen*	1004
	大中祥符 Dazhong Xiangfu(9)	戊申 *wu-shen*	1008
	天禧 [xǐ] Tianxi(5)	丁巳 *ding-si*	1017
	乾兴 Qianxing(1)	壬戌 *ren-xu*	1022
仁宗 Emperor Renzong (～祯 Zhao Zhen)	天圣 Tiansheng(10)	癸亥 *gui-hai*	1023
	明道 Mingdao(2)	壬申$_{十一}$ *ren-shen*$_{11}$	1032
	景祐 Jingyou(5)	甲戌 *jia-xu*	1034
	宝元 Baoyuan(3)	戊寅$_{十一}$ *wu-yin*$_{11}$	1038
	康定 Kangding(2)	庚辰$_{二}$ *geng-chen*$_{2}$	1040
	庆历 Qingli(8)	辛巳$_{十一}$ *xin-si*$_{11}$	1041
	皇祐 Huangyou(6)	己丑 *ji-chou*	1049
	至和 Zhihe(3)	甲午$_{三}$ *jia-wu*$_{3}$	1054
	嘉祐 Jiayou(8)	丙申$_{九}$ *bing-shen*$_{9}$	1056
英宗 Emperor Yingzong (～曙 Zhao Shu)	治平 Zhiping(4)	甲辰 *jia-chen*	1064
神宗 Emperor Shenzong (～顼 [xū] Zhao Xu)	熙宁 Xining(10)	戊申 *wu-shen*	1068
	元丰 Yuanfeng(8)	戊午 *wu-wu*	1078
哲宗 Emperor Zhezong (～煦 [xù] Zhao Xu)	元祐 Yuanyou(9)	丙寅 *bing-yin*	1086
	绍圣 Shaosheng(5)	甲戌$_{四}$ *jia-xu*$_{4}$	1094
	元符 Yuanfu(3)	戊寅$_{六}$ *wu-yin*$_{6}$	1098

徽宗 Emperor Huizong(～佶[jí] Zhao Ji)	建中靖国 Jianzhong Jingguo (1)	辛巳 *xin-si*	1101
	崇宁 Chongning(5)	壬午 *ren-wu*	1102
	大观 Daguan(4)	丁亥 *ding-hai*	1107
	政和 Zhenghe(8)	辛卯 *xin-mao*	1111
	重和 Chonghe(2)	戊戌十一 *wu-xu*₁₁	1118
	宣和 Xuanhe(7)	己亥二 *ji-hai*₂	1119
钦宗 Emperor Qinzong(～桓[huán] Zhao Huan)	靖康 Jingkang(2)	丙午 *bing-wu*	1126

南宋 Southern Song Dynasty (1127—1279)

高宗 Emperor Gaozong(赵构 Zhao Gou)	建炎 Jianyan(4)	丁未五 *ding-wei*₅	1127
	绍兴 Shaoxing(32)	辛亥 *xin-hai*	1131
孝宗 Emperor Xiaozong (～昚[shèn] Zhao Shen)	隆兴 Longxing(2)	癸未 *gui-wei*	1163
	乾道 Qiandao(9)	乙酉 *yi-you*	1165
	淳熙 Chunxi(16)	甲午 *jia-wu*	1174
光宗 Emperor Guangzong (～惇[dūn] Zhao Dun)	绍熙 Shaoxi(5)	庚戌 *geng-xu*	1190
宁宗 Emperor Ningzong (～扩 Zhao Kuo)	庆元 Qingyuan(6)	乙卯 *yi-mao*	1195
	嘉泰 Jiatai(4)	辛酉 *xin-you*	1201
	开禧 Kaixi(3)	乙丑 *yi-chou*	1205
	嘉定 Jiading(17)	戊辰 *wu-chen*	1208
理宗 Emperor Lizong (～昀[yùn] Zhao Yun)	宝庆 Baoqing(3)	乙酉 *yi-you*	1225
	绍定 Shaoding(6)	戊子 *wu-zi*	1228
	端平 Duanping(3)	甲午 *jia-wu*	1234
	嘉熙 Jiaxi(4)	丁酉 *ding-you*	1237
	淳祐 Chunyou(12)	辛丑 *xin-chou*	1241
	宝祐 Baoyou(6)	癸丑 *gui-chou*	1253
	开庆 Kaiqing(1)	己未 *ji-wei*	1259
	景定 Jingding(5)	庚申 *geng-shen*	1260
度宗 Emperor Duzong (赵禥[qí] Zhao Qi)	咸淳 Xianchun(10)	乙丑 *yi-chou*	1265
恭帝 Emperor Gong(～㬎[xiǎn] Zhao Xian)	德祐 Deyou(2)	乙亥 *yi-hai*	1275
端宗 Emperor Duanzong (～昰[shì] Zhao Shi)	景炎 Jingyan(3)	丙子五 *bing-zi*₅	1276

帝昺 Emperor Bing (～昺 [bǐng] Zhao Bing)	祥兴 Xiangxing(2)	戊寅五 wu-yin₅	1278

辽 Liao Dynasty

[耶律氏 Yelü Family] (907—1125)

辽建国于907年,国号契丹,916年始建年号,938年(一说947年)改国号为辽,983年复称契丹,1066年仍称辽。The Liao Dynasty was known as the Qidan (or Khitan) Kingdom when it was first established in 907. The dynasty began to use a reign title in 916, and renamed itself Liao in 938 (or 947 according to another theory), but it resumed the name of Qidan in 983, before changing it back to Liao in 1066.

太祖 Emperor Taizu (耶律阿保机 Yelü Abaoji, or Yelü A-pao-chi)	— (10)	丁卯 ding-mao	907
	神册 Shence(7)	丙子十二 bing-zi₁₂	916
	天赞 Tianzan(5)	壬午二 ren-wu₂	922
	天显 Tianxian(13)	丙戌二 bing-xu₂	926
太宗 Emperor Taizong (～德光 Yelü Deguang)	天显 Tianxian*	丁亥十一 ding-hai₁₁	927
	会同 Huitong(10)	戊戌十一 wu-xu₁₁	938
	大同 Datong(1)	丁未二 ding-wei₂	947
世宗 Emperor Shizong (～阮 [ruǎn] Yelü Ruan)	天禄 Tianlu(5)	丁未九 ding-wei₉	947
穆宗 Emperor Muzong (～璟[jǐng] Yelü Jing)	应历 Yingli(19)	辛亥九 xin-hai₉	951
景宗 Emperor Jingzong (～贤 Yelü Xian)	保宁 Baoning(11)	己巳二 ji-si₂	969
	乾亨 Qianheng(5)	己卯十一 ji-mao₁₁	979
圣宗 Emperor Shengzong (～隆绪 Yelü Longxu)	乾亨 Qianheng	壬午九 ren-wu₉	982
	统和 Tonghe(30)	癸未六 gui-wei₆	983
	开泰 Kaitai(10)	壬子十一 ren-zi₁₁	1012
	太平 Taiping(11)	辛酉十一 xin-you₁₁	1021
兴宗 Emperor Xingzong (～宗真 Yelü Zongzhen)	景福 Jingfu(2)	辛未六 xin-wei₆	1031
	重熙 Chongxi(24)	壬申十一 ren-shen₁₁	1032
道宗 Emperor Daozong (～洪基 Yelü Hongji)	清宁 Qingning(10)	乙未八 yi-wei₈	1055
	咸雍 Xianyong(10)	乙巳 yi-si	1065
	大(太)康 Dakang/Taikang(10)	乙卯 yi-mao	1075
	大安 Da'an(10)	乙丑 yi-chou	1085

	寿昌(隆) Shouchang/Shoulong(7)	乙亥 *yi-hai*	1095
天祚[zuò]帝 Emperor Tianzuo (～延禧[xī] Yelü Yanxi)	乾统 Qiantong(10)	辛巳$_{二}$ *xin-si*$_2$	1101
	天庆 Tianqing(10)	辛卯 *xin-mao*	1111
	保大 Baoda(5)	辛丑 *xin-chou*	1121

* 太宗即位未改元。Emperor Taizong did not change the reign title when he ascended the throne.

金 Jin Dynasty

[完颜氏 Wanyan Family] (1115—1234)

太祖 Emperor Taizu (完颜旻[mín], 本名阿骨打 Wanyan Min, originally named Wanyan Akutta)	收国 Shouguo(2)	乙未 *yi-wei*	1115
	天辅 Tianfu(7)	丁酉 *ding-you*	1117
太宗 Emperor Taizong (～晟[shèng] Wanyan Sheng)	天会 Tianhui(15)	癸卯$_{九}$ *gui-mao*$_9$	1123
熙宗 Emperor Xizong (～亶[dǎn] Wanyan Dan)	天会 Tianhui*	乙卯$_{一}$ *yi-mao*$_1$	1135
	天眷 Tianjuan(3)	戊午 *wu-wu*	1138
	皇统 Huangtong(9)	辛酉 *xin-you*	1141
海陵王 King Hailing (～亮 Wanyan Liang)	天德 Tiande(5)	己巳$_{十二}$ *ji-si*$_{12}$	1149
	贞元 Zhenyuan(4)	癸酉$_{三}$ *gui you*$_3$	1153
	正隆 Zhenglong(6)	丙子$_{二}$ *bing-zi*$_2$	1156
世宗 Emperor Shizong (完颜雍 Wanyan Yong)	大定 Dading(29)	辛巳$_{十}$ *xin-si*$_{10}$	1161
章宗 Emperor Zhang (～璟[jǐng] Wanyan Jing)	明昌 Mingchang(7)	庚戌 *geng-xu*	1190
	承安 Cheng'an(5)	丙辰$_{十一}$ *bing-chen*$_{11}$	1196
	泰和 Taihe(8)	辛酉 *xin-you*	1201
卫绍王 King Weishao (～永济 Wanyan Yongji)	大安 Da'an(3)	己巳 *ji-si*	1209
	崇庆 Chongqing(2)	壬申 *ren-shen*	1212
	至宁 Zhining(1)	癸酉$_{五}$ *gui-you*$_5$	1213
宣宗 Emperor Xuanzong (～珣[xún] Wanyan Xun)	贞祐 Zhenyou(5)	癸酉$_{九}$ *gui-you*$_9$	1213
	兴定 Xingding(6)	丁丑$_{九}$ *ding-chou*$_9$	1217
	元光 Yuanguang(2)	壬午$_{八}$ *ren-wu*$_8$	1222
哀宗 Emperor Ai (～守绪 Wanyan Shouxu)	正大 Zhengda(9)	甲申 *jia-shen*	1224

	开兴 Kaixing(1)	壬辰— *ren-chen*₁	1232
	天兴 Tianxing(3)	壬辰四 *ren-chen*₄	1232

*熙帝即位未改元。Emperor Xi did not change the reign title when he ascended the throne.

元 Yuan Dynasty

[孛儿只斤氏 Borzigin Family] (1206—1368)

蒙古孛儿只斤铁木真于1206年建国。1271年忽必烈定国号为元,1279年灭南宋。Borzigin Temuzin, a Mongol general, founded a kingdom in 1206. Kublai Khan renamed the kingdom Yuan in 1271, and overthrew the Southern Song Dynasty in 1279.

太祖 Emperor Taizu (孛儿只斤铁木真 Borzigin Temuzin)(成吉思汗 Genghis Khan)	— (22)	丙寅 *bing-yin*	1206
拖雷 Toloi (监国 regent)	— (1)	戊子 *wu-zi*	1228
太宗 Emperor Taizong (~窝阔台 Borzigin Ugedei)	— (13)	己丑 *ji-chou*	1229
乃马真后 Empress Naimazin (称制 claiming the throne)	— (5)	壬寅 *ren-yin*	1242
定宗 Emperor Dingzong (~贵由 Borzigin Guyug)	— (3)	丙午七 *bing-wu*₇	1246
海迷失后 Empress Haimig (称制 claiming the throne)	— (3)	己酉三 *ji-you*₃	1249
宪宗 Empress Xianzong (~蒙哥 Borzigin Monghe)	— (9)	辛亥六 *xin-hai*₆	1251
世祖 Emperor Shizu (~忽必烈 Borzigin Kublai)	中统 Zhongtong(5)	庚申五 *geng-shen*₅	1260
	至元 Zhiyuan(31)	甲子八 *jia-zi*₈	1264
成宗 Emperor Chengzong (~铁穆耳 Borzigin Temur)	元贞 Yuanzhen(3)	乙未 *yi-wei*	1295
	大德 Dade(11)	丁酉二 *ding-you*₂	1297
武宗 Emperor Wuzong (~海山 Borzigin Haisan)	至大 Zhida(4)	戊申 *wu-shen*	1308
仁宗 Emperor Renzong (~爱育黎拔力八达 Borzigin Ayurbalbad)	皇庆 Huangqing(2)	壬子 *ren-zi*	1312
	延祐 Yanyou(7)	甲寅 *jia-yin*	1314
英宗 Emperor Yingzong (~硕[shuò]德八剌 Borzigin Sidibala)	至治 Zhizhi(3)	辛酉 *xin-you*	1321
泰定帝 Emperor Taiding (~也孙铁木儿 Borzigin Yisuntemur)	泰定 Taiding(5)	甲子 *jia-zi*	1324
	致和 Zhihe(1)	戊辰二 *wu-chen*₂	1328

天顺帝 Emperor Tianshun (～阿速吉八 Borzigin Asazibao)	天顺 Tianshun(1)	戊辰九 *wu-chen*₉	1328
文宗 Emperor Wenzong (～图贴睦尔 Borzigin Tubtemur)	天历 Tianli(3)	戊辰九 *wu-chen*₉	1328
明宗 Emperor Mingzong (～和世㻋[là] Borzigin Husle) *		己巳 *ji-si*	1329
	至顺 Zhishun(4)	庚午五 *geng-wu*₅	1330
宁宗 Emperor Ningzong (～懿[yì]璘[lín]质班 Borzigin Irincinbala)	至顺 Zhishun	壬申十 *ren-shen*₁₀	1332
顺帝 Emperor Shun (～妥懽帖睦尔 Borzigin Togugantemur)	至顺 Zhishun	癸酉六 *gui-you*₆	1333
	元统 Yuantong(3)	癸酉十 *gui-you*₁₀	1333
	(后 Later) 至元 Zhiyuan(6)	乙亥十一 *yi-hai*₁₁	1335
	至正 Zhizheng(28)	辛巳 *xin-si*	1341

*明宗于己巳(1329)正月即位,以文宗为皇太子。八月明宗暴死,文宗复位。Emperor Mingzong ascended the throne in the 1st month of the year *ji-si* (1329) and made Wenzong the crown prince. Emperor Mingzong died a sudden death in the 8th month of that year, upon which Wenzong resumed the throne.

明 Ming Dynasty (1368—1644)

太祖 Emperor Taizu (朱元璋 Zhu Yuanzhang)	洪武 Hongwu(31)	戊申 *wu-shen*	1368
惠帝 Emperor Hui (～允炆[wén] Zhu Yunwen)	建文 Jianwen(4) *	己卯 *ji-mao*	1399
成祖 Emperor Chengzu (～棣[dì] Zhu Di)	永乐 Yongle(22)	癸未 *gui-wei*	1403
仁宗 Emperor Renzong (～高炽[chì] Zhu Gaochi)	洪熙 Hongxi(1)	乙巳 *yi-si*	1425
宣宗 Emperor Xuanzong (～瞻[zhān]基 Zhu Zhanji)	宣德 Xuande(10)	丙午 *bing-wu*	1426
英宗 Emperor Yingzong (～祁镇 Zhu Qizhen)	正统 Zhengtong(14)	丙辰 *bing-chen*	1436
代宗 Emperor Daizong (～祁钰[yù] Zhu Qiyu) (景帝 also called Emperor Jing)	景泰 Jingtai(8)	庚午 *geng-wu*	1450
英宗 Emperor Yingzong (～祁镇 Zhu Qizhen)	天顺 Tianshun(8)	V 丁丑一 *ding-chou*₁	1457
宪宗 Emperor Xianzong (～见深 Zhu Jianshen)	成化 Chenghua(23)	乙酉 *yi-you*	1465
孝宗 Emperor Xiaozong (～祐樘[chēng] Zhu Youcheng)	弘治 Hongzhi(18)	戊申 *wu-shen*	1488

武宗 Emperor Wuzong (～厚照 Zhu Houzhao)	正德 Zhengde(16)	丙寅 *bing-yin*	1506
世宗 Emperor Shizong (～厚熜 [cōng] Zhu Houcong)	嘉靖 Jiajing(45)	壬午 *ren-wu*	1522
穆宗 Emperor Muzong (～载垕 [hòu] Zhu Zaihou)	隆庆 Longqing(6)	丁卯 *ding-mao*	1567
神宗 Emperor Shenzong (～翊 [yì] 钧 Zhu Yijun)	万历 Wanli(48)	癸酉 *gui-you*	1573
光宗 Emperor Guangzong (～常洛 Zhu Changluo)	泰昌 Taichang(1)	庚申八 *geng-shen*8	1620
熹[xī]宗 Emperor Xizong (～由校 Zhu Youjiao)	天启 Tianqi(7)	辛酉 *xin-you*	1621
思宗 Emperor Sizong (～由检 Zhu Youjian)	崇祯 Chongzhen(17)	戊辰 *wu-chen*	1628

* 建文 4 年时成祖废除建文年号，改为洪武 35 年。In the 4th year of the Jianwen reign, Emperor Chengzu abolished the reign title of Jianwen and restored the reign title of Hongwu, counting that year as the 35th year of the Hongwu reign.

清 Qing Dynasty

[爱新觉罗氏 Aisin-Gioro Family] (1616—1911)

清建国于 1616 年，初称后金，1636 年始改国号为清，1644 年入关。The Qing Dynasty was known as Later Jin when it was first established in 1616, and the name Qing was not adopted until 1636. The Qing army fought its way across Shanhai Pass in 1644, thereby extending its rule south of the Great Wall.

太祖 Emperor Taizu (爱新觉罗努尔哈赤 Aisin-Gioro Nurhachi)	天命 Tianming(11)	丙辰 *bing-chen*	1616
太宗 Emperor Taizong (～皇太极 Aisin-Gioro Huangtaiji)	天聪 Tiancong(10)	丁卯 *ding-mao*	1627
	崇德 Chongde(8)	丙子四 *bing-zi*4	1636
世祖 Emperor Shizu (～福临 Aisin-Gioro Fulin)	顺治 Shunzhi(18)	甲申 *jia-shen*	1644
圣祖 Emperor Shengzu (～玄烨 [yè] Aisin-Gioro Xuanye)	康熙 Kangxi(61)	壬寅 *ren-yin*	1662
世宗 Emperor Shizong (～胤[yìn]禛[zhēn] Aisin-Gioro Yinzhen)	雍正 Yongzheng(13)	癸卯 *gui-mao*	1723
高宗 Emperor Gaozong (～弘历 Aisin-Gioro Hongli)	乾隆 Qianlong(60)	丙辰 *bing-chen*	1736
仁宗 Emperor Renzong (～颙[yóng]琰 [yǎn] Aisin-Gioro Yongyan)	嘉庆 Jiaqing(25)	丙辰 *bing-chen*	1796
宣宗 Emperor Xuanzong (～旻[mín]宁 Aisin-Gioro Minning)	道光 Daoguang(30)	辛巳 *xin-si*	1821

文宗 Emperor Wenzong (～奕[yì]詝[zhǔ] Aisin-Gioro Yizhu)	咸丰 Xianfeng(11)	辛亥 *xin-hai*	1851
穆宗 Emperor Muzong (～载淳 Aisin-Gioro Zaichun)	同治 Tongzhi(13)	壬戌 *ren-xu*	1862
德宗 Emperor Dezong (～载湉[tián] Aisin-Gioro Zaitian)	光绪 Guangxu(34)	乙亥 *yi-hai*	1875
～溥[pǔ]仪 Aisin-Gioro Puyi	宣统 Xuantong(3)	乙酉 *yi-you*	1909

中华民国 Republic of China (1912—1949)

中华民国 Republic of China(38)	壬子 *ren-zi*	1912

中华人民共和国 1949 年 10 月 1 日成立

Founding of the People's Republic of China on October 1, 1949

计量单位表
Tables of Weights and Measures

I 中华人民共和国法定计量单位
Legal Units of Weights and Measures of the People's Republic of China

中华人民共和国的法定计量单位（以下简称法定单位）包括 The legal units of weights and measures of the People's Republic of China (hereafter simplified as legal units) include:

(1) 国际单位制的基本单位（见表 1）;
Basic units in the international unit system (☞ Table 1);

(2) 国际单位制中具有专门名称的导出单位（见表 2）;
Derived units with special names in the international unit system (☞ Table 2);

(3) 国家选定的非国际单位制单位（见表 3）;
Non-international units stipulated by the State (☞ Table 3);

(4) 由以上单位构成的组合形式的单位;
Compound units formed by the above-mentioned units;

(5) 由词头和以上单位所构成的十进倍数和分数单位（词头见表 4）。
Decimal multiple and fraction units formed by prefixes and the above-mentioned units (☞ Table 4).

法定单位的定义、使用方法等，由国家计量局（其职权现由国家质量监督检验检疫总局执行）另行规定。The definitions and usage of the legal units are stipulated separately by the State Metrology Administration (whose authorities are being executed by the State Administration of Quality Supervision, Inspection and Quarantine).

表 Table 1
国际单位制的基本单位
Basic Units in the International Unit System

量的名称 Name of Quantity	单位名称 Name of Unit	单位符号 Symbol of Unit
长度 length	米 metre	m
质量 mass	千克（公斤）kilogramme	kg
时间 time	秒 second	s
电流 electric current	安［培］ampere	A
热力学温度 thermodynamic temperature	开［尔文］kelvin	K
物质的量 amount of a substance	摩［尔］mole	mol
发光强度 luminous intensity	坎［德拉］candela	cd

表 Table 2
国际单位制中具有专门名称的导出单位
Derived Units with Special Names in the International Unit System

量的名称 Name of Quantity	单位名称 Name of Unit	单位符号 Symbol of Unit	其他表示式例 Other Form
平面角 plane angle	弧度 radian	rad	1
立体角 solid angle	球面度 steradian	sr	1
频率 frequency	赫[兹] hertz	Hz	s^{-1}
力;重力 force	牛[顿] newton	N	$kg\cdot m/s^2$
压力,压强;应力 pressure; stress; intensity	帕[斯卡] pascal	Pa	N/m^2
能量;功;热 energy; work; heat	焦[耳] joule	J	N·m
功率;辐射通量 power; radiant flux	瓦[特] watt	W	J/s
电荷量 electric charge	库[仑] coulomb	C	A·s
电位;电压;电动势 potential; voltage; electromotive force	伏[特] volt	V	W/A
电容 capacitance	法[拉] farad	F	C/V
电阻 electrical resistance	欧[姆] ohm	Ω	V/A
电导 conductance	西[门子] siemens	S	A/V
磁通量 magnetic flux	韦[伯] weber	Wb	V·s
磁通量密度,磁感应强度 magnetic flux density; magnefic induction intensity	特[斯拉] tesla	T	Wb/m^2
电感 inductance	亨[利] henry	H	Wb/A
摄氏温度 Celsius temperature	摄氏度 degree Celsius	℃	
光通量 luminous flux	流[明] lumen	lm	cd·sr
光照度 illuminance	勒[克斯] lux	lx	lm/m^2
放射性活度 activity (referring to a radionuclide)	贝可[勒尔] becqucrel	Bq	s^{-1}
吸收剂量 absorbed dose	戈[瑞] gray	Gy	J/kg
剂量当量 dose equivalent	希[沃特] sievert	Sv	J/kg

表 Table 3
国家选定的非国际单位制单位
Non-international Units Stipulated by the State

量的名称 Name of Quantity	单位名称 Name of Unit	单位符号 Symbol of Unit	换算关系和说明 Conversion and Explanation
时间 time	分 minute [小]时 hour 天（日）day	min h d	1min=60s 1h=60min=3600s 1d=24h=86400s
平面角 plane angle	[角]秒 second [角]分 minute 度 degree	(″) (′) (°)	1″=(π/648000)rad(π 为圆周率 pi，ratio of the circumference of a circle to its diameter) 1′=60″=(π/10800)rad 1°=60′=(π/180)rad
旋转速度 speed of rotation	转每分 rotation per minute	r/min	$1r/min=(1/60)s^{-1}$
长度 length	海里 nautical mile	n mile	1n mile=1852m(只用于航程 only used in navigation)
速度 speed; velocity	节 knot	kn	1km = 1n mile/h = (1852/3600)m/s(只用于航行 only used in navigation)
质量 mass	吨 ton 原子质量单位 atomic mass unit	t u	$1t=10^3 kg$ $1u\approx1.6605402\times10^{-27} kg$
体积 cubic measure	升 litre	L,(l)	$1L=1dm^3=10^{-3} m^3$
能 energy	电子伏 electron volt	eV	$1eV\approx1.60217733\times10^{-19} J$
级差 logarithmic	分贝 decibel	dB	用于对数量 used for logarithm
线密度 count	特[克斯] tex	tex	1tex=1g/km
土地面积 acreage of land	公顷 hectare	hm^2,(ha)	$1hm^2=10^4 m^2=0.1km^2$

表 Table 4
用于构成十进倍数和分数单位的词头
Prefixes Forming Units of Decimal Multiples and Fractions

所表示的因数 Submultiple	词头名称 Name of Prefix	词头符号 Symbol of Prefix
10^{24}	尧[它] yotta	Y
10^{21}	泽[它] zetta	Z
10^{18}	艾[可萨] exa	E

10^{15}	拍［它］peta	P
10^{12}	太［拉］tera	T
10^{9}	吉［咖］giga	G
10^{6}	兆 mega	M
10^{3}	千 kilo	k
10^{2}	百 hecto	h
10^{1}	十 deka	da
10^{-1}	分 deci	d
10^{-2}	厘 centi	c
10^{-3}	毫 milli	m
10^{-6}	微 micro	μ
10^{-9}	纳［诺］nano	n
10^{-12}	皮［可］pico	p
10^{-15}	飞［母托］femto	f
10^{-18}	阿［托］atto	a
10^{-21}	仄［普托］zepto	z
10^{-24}	幺［科托］yocto	y

注 Notes：

1. 周、月、年（年的符号为 a），为一般常用时间单位。Week, month and year (with 'a' serving as the symbol for year) are commonly used time units.

2. [ ]内的字，是在不致混淆的情况下，可以省略的字。The characters in brackets can be omitted on condition that they do not cause confusion.

3. ( )内的字为前者的同义语。The characters in parentheses are synonyms for the preceding characters.

4. 角度单位度分秒的符号不处于数字后时，用括弧。When the symbols of angle units — degree, minute and second — do not follow a number, they are put into parentheses.

5. 升的符号中，小写字母 l 为备用符号。ha 为公顷的国际符号。The small letter 'l' is an alternate symbol for litre; 'ha' is the international symbol for hectare.

6. r 为'转'的符号。The symbol of 'rotation' is 'r'.

7. 人民生活和贸易中，质量习惯称为重量。In trade and everyday life, 'mass' is habitually called 'weight'.

8. 公里为千米的俗称，符号为 km。Gōnglǐ is the popular name for kilometre, its symbol being 'km'.

9. 10^4 称为万，10^8 称为亿，10^{12} 称为万亿，这类数词的使用不受词头名称的影响，但不应与词头混淆。In Chinese, 10^4 is called 万 wàn, 10^8 亿 yì and 10^{12} 万亿 wànyì. Their use is free from prefixes, but shall not be confused with the use of prefixes.

II 法定计量单位与常见非法定计量单位的对照和换算表
Legal and Non-legal Units of Weights and Measures with Conversion Table

	法定计量单位 Legal Unit		常见非法定计量单位 Common Non-legal Unit		换算关系 Conversion Table
	名称 Name	符号 Symbol	名称 Name	符号 Symbol	
长度 length	千米（公里）kilometre	km		KM	1 千米（公里 km）＝2 市里 *li* ＝0.6214 英里 mi
	米 metre	m	公尺 metre	M	1 米 ＝1 公尺 M ＝3 市尺 *chi* ＝3.2808 英尺 ft ＝1.0936 码 yd
	分米 decimetre	dm	公寸 decimetre		1 分米 dm＝1 公寸 dm＝0.1 米 m＝3 市寸 *cun*
	厘米 centimetre	cm	公分 centimetre		1 厘米 cm＝1 公分 cm＝0.01 米 m＝3 市分 *fen*＝0.3937 英寸 in
	毫米 millimetre	mm	公厘 millimetre	m/m, MM	1 毫米 mm＝1 公厘 MM
			公丝 decimillimetre		1 公丝 dmm＝0.1 毫米 mm
	微米 micron	μm	公微 micron	μ, mμ, μM	1 微米 μm ＝1 公微 mμ
			丝米 decimillimetre	dmm	1 丝米 dmm ＝0.1 毫米 mm
			忽米 centimillimetre	cmm	1 忽米 cmm＝0.01 毫米 mm
	纳米 nanometre	nm	毫微米 bicron	mμm	1 纳米 nm＝1 毫微米 mμm
			市里 *li*		1 市里 *li*＝150 市丈 *zhang*＝0.5 公里 km
			市引 *yin*		1 市引 *yin*＝10 市丈 *zhang*
			市丈 *zhang*		1 市丈 *zhang*＝10 市尺 *chi*＝3.3333 米 m
			市尺 *chi*		1 市尺 *chi*＝10 市寸 *cun*＝0.3333 米 m＝1.0936 英尺 ft
			市寸 *cun*		1 市寸 *cun* ＝10 市分 *fen*＝3.3333厘米 cm＝1.3123 英寸 in
			市分 *fen*		1 市分 *fen* ＝10 市厘 *li*
			市厘 *li*		1 市厘 *li*＝10 市毫 *hao*

	法定计量单位 Legal Unit		常见非法定计量单位 Common Non-legal Unit		换算关系 Conversion Table
	名称 Name	符号 Symbol	名称 Name	符号 Symbol	
长度 length			英里 mile	mi	1 英里 mi＝1760 码 yd＝5280 英尺 ft＝1.609344 公里 km
			码 yard	yd	1 码 yd＝3 英尺 ft＝0.9144 米 m
			英尺 foot	ft	1 英尺 ft＝12 英寸 in＝0.3048 米 m＝0.9144 市尺 *chi*
			英寸 inch	in	1 英寸 in＝2.54 厘米 cm
	飞米 femtometre	fm	费密 femtometre	fermi	1 飞米 fm＝1 费密 fm ＝10^{-15}米 m
			埃 angstrom	Å	1 埃 Å ＝10^{-10}米 m
面积 area	平方千米（平方公里）square kilometre	km^2		KM^2	1 平方千米（平方公里）km^2＝100 公顷 hm^2＝0.3861 平方英里 $mile^2$
			公亩 are	a	1 公亩 a＝100 平方米 m^2＝0.15 市亩 *mu*＝0.0247 英亩 acre
	平方米 square metre	m^2	平米，方 square metre		1 平方米 m^2＝1 平米 m^2＝9 平方市尺 square *chi*＝10.7639 平方英尺 ft^2＝1.1960 平方码 yd^2
	平方分米 square decimetre	dm^2			1 平方分米 dm^2＝0.01 平方米 m^2
	平方厘米 square centimetre	cm^2			1 平方厘米 cm^2＝0.0001 平方米 m^2
			市顷 *qing*		1 市顷 *qing*＝100 市亩 *mu*＝6.6667 公顷 hm^2
			市亩 *mu*		1 市亩 *mu*＝10 市分 *fen*＝60 平方市丈 square *zhang*＝6.6667 公亩 a＝0.0667 公顷 hm^2＝0.1644 英亩 acre
			市分 *fen*		1 市分 *fen*＝6 平方市丈 square *zhang*
			平方市里 square *li*		1 平方市里 square *li*＝22500 平方市丈 square *zhang*＝0.25 平方公里 km^2＝0.0965 平方英里 ft^2
			平方市丈 square *zhang*		1 平方市丈 square *zhang*＝100 平方市尺 square *chi*
			平方市尺 square *chi*		1 平方市尺 square *chi*＝100 平方市寸 square *cun*＝0.1111 平方米 m^2＝1.1960 平方英尺 ft^2

	法定计量单位 Legal Unit		常见非法定计量单位 Common Non-legal Unit		换算关系 Conversion Table
	名称 Name	符号 Symbol	名称 Name	符号 Symbol	
面积 area			平方英里 square mile	$mile^2$	1 平方英里 $mile^2$ = 640 英亩 acres = 2.58998811 平方公里 km^2
			英亩 acre		1 英亩 acre = 4840 平方码 yd^2 = 40.4686 公亩 a = 6.0720 市亩 *mu*
			平方码 square yard	yd^2	1 平方码 yd^2 = 9 平方英尺 ft^2 = 0.8361 平方米 m^2
			平方英尺 square foot	ft^2	1 平方英尺 ft^2 = 144 平方英寸 in^2 = 0.09290304 平方米 m^2
			平方英寸 square inch	in^2	1 平方英寸 in^2 = 6.4516 平方厘米 cm^2
			靶恩 barn	b	1 靶恩 b = 10^{-28} 平方米 m^2
体积 cubic measure	立方米 cubic metre	m^3	方，公方 cubic metre		1 立方米 m^3 = 1 方 m^3 = 35.3147 立方英尺 ft^3 = 1.3080 立方码 yd^3
	立方分米 cubic decimetre	dm^3			1 立方分米 dm^3 = 0.001 立方米 m^3
	立方厘米 cubic centimetre	cm^3			1 立方厘米 cm^3 = 0.000001 立方米 m^3
			立方市丈 cubic *zhang*		1 立方市丈 cubic *zhang* = 1000 立方市尺 cubic *chi*
			立方市尺 cubic *chi*		1 立方市尺 cubic *chi* = 1000 立方市寸 cubic *cun* = 0.0370 立方米 m^3 = 1.3078 立方英尺 ft^3
			立方码 cubic yard	yd^3	1 立方码 yd^3 = 27 立方英尺 ft^3 = 0.7646 立方米 m^3
			立方英尺 cubic foot	ft^3	1 立方英尺 ft^3 = 1728 立方英寸 in^3 = 0.028317 立方米 m^3
			立方英寸 cubic inch	in^3	1 立方英寸 in^3 = 16.3871 立方厘米 cm^3
容积 capacity	升 litre	L(l)	公升、立升 litre		1 升 L = 1 公升 litre = 1 立升 litre = 1 市升 *sheng*
	分升 decilitre	dL, dl			1 分升 dL = 0.1 升 L = 1 市合 *he*
	厘升 centilitre	cL, cl			1 厘升 cL = 0.01 升 L
	毫升 millilitre	mL, ml	西西 cubic centimetre	c. c., cc	1 毫升 mL = 1 西西 cc = 0.001 升 L

	法定计量单位 Legal Unit		常见非法定计量单位 Common Non-legal Unit		换算关系 Conversion Table
	名称 Name	符号 Symbol	名称 Name	符号 Symbol	
容积 capacity			市石 *shi*		1 市石 *shi*＝10 市斗 *dou*＝100 升 L
			市斗 *dou*		1 市斗 *dou*＝10 市升 *sheng*＝10 升 L
			市升 *sheng*		1 市升 *sheng*＝10 市合 *he*＝1 升 L
			市合 *he*		1 市合 *he*＝10 市勺 *shao*＝1 分升 dL
			市勺 *shao*		1 市勺 *shao*＝10 市撮 *cuo*＝1 厘升 cL
			市撮 *cuo*		1 市撮 *cuo*＝1 毫升 mL
			* 蒲式耳（英 UK) bushel		1 蒲式耳（英 UK) bushel＝4 配克（英 UK) pk
			* 配克（英 UK) peck	pk	1 配克（英 UK) pk＝2 加仑（英 UK) gal＝9.0922 升 L
			* * 加仑（英 UK) gallon	UKgal	1 加仑（英 UK) gal＝4 夸脱（英 UK) qt＝4.54609 升 L
			夸脱（英 UK) quart	UKqt	1 夸脱（英 UK) qt＝2 品脱（英 UK) pt＝1.1365 升 L
			品脱（英 UK) pint	UKpt	1 品脱（英 UK) pt＝4 及耳（英 UK) gi＝5.6826 分升 dL
			及耳（英 UK) gill	UKgi	1 及耳（英 UK) gi＝1.4207 分升 dL
			英液盎司 UK fluid ounce	UKfloz	1 英液盎司 UKfloz＝2.8413 厘升 cL
			英液打兰 UK fluid dram	UKfldr	1 英液打兰 UKfldr＝3.5516 毫升 mL
质量 mass	吨 ton	t	公吨 tonne; metric ton	T	1 吨 t＝1 公吨 T＝1000 千克 kg＝0.9842 英吨 UKton＝1.1023美吨 USton
			公担 quintal	q	1 公担 q＝100 千克 kg＝2 市担 piculs
	千克（公斤）kilogramme	kg		KG, kgs	1 千克 kg＝2 市斤 *jin* ＝2.2046 磅 lb(常衡 avoirdupois)
	克 gramme	g	公分 metric gramme	gm, gr	1 克 g＝1 公分 gm ＝0.001 千克 kg＝15.4324 格令 gr

	法定计量单位 Legal Unit		常见非法定计量单位 Common Non-legal Unit		换算关系 Conversion Table
	名称 Name	符号 Symbol	名称 Name	符号 Symbol	
质量 mass	分克 decigramme	dg			1 分克 dg=0.0001 千克 kg=2 市厘 *li*
	厘克 centigramme	cg			1 厘克 cg=0.00001 千克 kg
	毫克 milligramme	mg			1 毫克 mg =0.000001 千克 kg
			公两 metric *liang*		1 公两 metric *liang* =100 克 g
			公钱 metric *qian*		1 公钱 metric *qian*=10 克 g
			市担 picul		1 市担 picul=100 市斤 *jin*
			市斤 *jin*		1 市斤 *jin*=10 市两 *liang*=0.5千克 kg=1.1023 磅 lb(常衡 avoirdupois)
			市两 *liang*		1 市两 *liang* =10 市钱 *qian*=50 克 g=1.7637 盎司 oz(常衡 avoirdupois)
			市钱 *qian*		1 市钱 *qian*=10 市分 *fen*=5 克 g
			市分 *fen*		1 市分 *fen*=10 市厘 *li*
			市厘 *li*		1 市厘 *li*=10 市毫 *hao*
			市毫 *hao*		1 市毫 *hao*=10 市丝 *si*
			英吨（长吨）long ton	UKton	1 英吨（长吨）UKton=2240 磅 lb=1016.047 千克 kg
			美吨（短吨）short ton	sh ton, USton	1 美吨（短吨）USton=2000 磅 lb=907.185 千克 kg
			磅 pound	lb	1 磅 lb=16 盎司 oz=0.4536 千克 kg
			盎司 ounce	oz	1 盎司 oz = 16 打兰 dr = 28.3495克 g
			打兰 dram	dr	1 打兰 dr=27.34375 格令 gr=1.7718 克 g
			格令 grain	gr	1 格令 gr = 1/7000 磅 lb = 64.79891毫克 mg
时间 time	年 year	a		y, yr	1y=1yr=1 年 year
	天（日）day	d			
	［小］时 hour	h		hr	1hr=1 小时 hour

	法定计量单位 Legal Unit		常见非法定计量单位 Common Non-legal Unit		换算关系 Conversion Table
	名称 Name	符号 Symbol	名称 Name	符号 Symbol	
时间 time	分 minute	min		(′)	1′=1 分 min
	秒 second	s		S, sec, (″)	1″=1S=1sec=1 秒 s
频率 frequency	赫兹 hertz	Hz	周 cycle	C	1 赫兹 Hz=1 周 C
	兆赫 megahertz	MHz	兆周 megacycle	MC	1 兆赫 MHz=1 兆周 MC
	千赫 kilohertz	kHz	千周 kilocycle	KC, kc	1 千赫 kHz=1 千周 KC
温度 temperature	开［尔文］Kelvin	K	开氏度 Kelvin temperature	°K	1 开 K=1 开氏度°K
			绝对度 absolute temperature	°K	=1 绝对度°K =1 摄氏度℃
	摄氏度 Celsius degree	℃	度 degree	deg	1deg=1 开 K－1 摄氏度℃
			华氏度 Fahrenheit degree	°F	1 华氏度°F =1 列氏度°R =5/9 开 K
			列氏度 Reaumur degree	°R	
力、重力 force	牛［顿］newton	N	千克，公斤 kilogramme	kg	
			千克力，公斤力 kilogramme force	kgf	1 千克力 kgf=9.80665 牛 N
			达因 dyne	dyn	1 达因 dyn=10^{-5} 牛 N
压力、压强、应力 pressure; intensity; stress	帕［斯卡］pascal	Pa	巴 bar	bar, b	1 巴 b=10^5 帕 Pa
			毫巴 millibar	mbar	1 毫巴 mbar=10^2 帕 Pa
			托 Torr	Torr	1 托 Torr=133.322 帕 Pa
			标准大气压 standard atmosphere	atm	1 标准大气压 atm=101.325 千帕 kilopascal
			工程大气压 technical atmosphere	at	1 工程大气压 at=98.0665 千帕 kilopascal
			毫米汞柱 millimetre Hg	mmHg	1 毫米汞柱子 mmHg－133.322 帕 Pa
线密度 count	特［克斯］tex	tex	旦［尼尔］denier	den, denier	1 旦 den=0.111111 特 tex

	法定计量单位 Legal Unit		常见非法定计量单位 Common Non-legal Unit		换算关系 Conversion Table
	名称 Name	符号 Symbol	名称 Name	符号 Symbol	
功、能、热 work; energy; heat	焦［耳］joule	J	尔格 erg	erg	1 尔格 erg $=10^{-7}$焦 J
功率 power	瓦［特］watt	W	［米制 metric system］马力 horsepower		1 马力 horsepower =735.499 瓦 W
磁感应强度 magnetic induction intensity(磁通密度 magnetic flux density)	特［斯拉］tesla	T	高斯 gauss	Gs	1 高斯 Gs $=10^{-4}$特 T
磁场强度 intensity of magnetic field	安［培］每米 ampere/metre	A/m	奥斯特 oersted; 楞次 lenz	Oe	1 奥斯特 Oe=1000/4π 安/米 A/m 1 楞次 lenz=1 安/米 A/m
物质的量 molecular weight of a substance	摩［尔］mole	mol	克原子，克分子，克当量，克式量 gram atom; gram molecule; gram equivalent; gram molecular weight		与基本单元粒子形式有关 related to the forms of basic cell particles
发光强度 luminous intensity	坎［德拉］candela	cd	烛光，支光，支 candlepower		1 烛光 candlepower≈1 坎 cd
光照度 illuminance	勒［克斯］lux	lx	辐透 phot	ph	1 辐透 ph $=10^4$ 勒 lx
光亮度 brightness	坎［德拉］每平方米 candela/square metre	cd/m²	熙提 stilb	sb	1 熙提 sb$=10^4$ 坎/米² cd/m²
放射性活度 activity (referred to a radionuclide)	贝可［勒尔］becquerel	Bq	居里 curie	Ci	1 居里 Ci$=3.7\times10^{10}$贝可 Bq
吸收剂量 absorbed dose	戈［瑞］gray	Gy	拉德 rad	rad rd	1 拉德 rd $=10^{-2}$戈 Gy
剂量当量 dose equivalent	希［沃特］sievert	Sv	雷姆 rem	rem	1 雷姆 rem $=10^{-2}$希 Sv
照射量 quantity of irradiation	库［仑］每千克 coulomb/kilogramme	C/kg	伦琴 roentgen	R	1 伦琴 R$=2.58\times10^{-4}$库/千克 C/kg

* 蒲式耳、配克只用于固体。Bushel and peck are only used for solids.

** 英制 1 加仑＝4.54609 升（用于液体和干散颗粒）。One British gallon equals 4.54609 litres (used for liquids and dry and loose grains).

美制 1 加仑$=2.31\times10^2$ 立方英寸＝3.785411784 升（只用于液体）。One American gallon equals 2.31×10^2 cubic inches or 3.785411784 litres (only used for liquids).

汉字偏旁名称表
Names of Radicals of Chinese Characters

1. 本表列举一部分汉字偏旁的名称，以便教学。This table lists some of the radicals of Chinese characters for the convenience of teaching and learning.

2. 本表收录的汉字偏旁，大多是现在不能单独成字、不易称呼或者称呼很不一致的。能单独成字、易于称呼的，如山、马、日、月、石、鸟、虫等，不收录。Most of the radicals this table includes are not characters by themselves, or difficult to name, or have confusing names. The radicals that are Chinese characters by themselves and easily pronounced, such as 山 shān, 马 mǎ, 日 rì, 月 yuè, 石 shí, 鸟 niǎo, 虫 chóng, etc., have not been listed here.

3. 有的偏旁有几种不同的叫法，本表只取较为通行的名称。Some radicals have different names, but this table only offers the most commonly used ones.

偏旁 Radical	名称 Name	例字 Examples
冫	两点水儿(liǎngdiǎnshuǐr)	次、冷、准
冖	秃宝盖儿(tūbǎogàir)	写、军、冠
讠	言字旁儿(yánzìpángr)	计、论、识
厂	偏厂儿(piānchǎngr)	厅、历、厚
匚	三匡栏儿(sānkuānglánr); 三匡儿(sānkuāngr)	区、匠、匣
刂	立刀旁儿(lìdāopángr); 立刀儿(lìdāor)	列、别、剑
冂(⺆)	同字匡儿(tóngzìkuāngr)	冈、网、周
亻	单人旁儿(dānrénpángr); 单立人儿(dānlìrénr)	仁、位、你
勹	包字头儿(bāozìtóur)	匀、勾、旬
厶	私字儿(sīzìr)	允、去、矣
廴	建之旁儿(jiànzhīpángr)	廷、延、建
卩	单耳旁儿(dān'ěrpángr); 单耳刀儿(dān'ěrdāor)	卫、印、却
阝	双耳旁儿(shuāng'ěrpángr); 双耳刀儿(shuāng'ěrdāor) 左耳刀儿(zuǒ'ěrdāor)(在左) 右耳刀儿(yòu'ěrdāor)(在右)	防、阻、院 邦、那、郊
氵	三点水儿(sāndiǎnshuǐr)	江、汪、活
丬(爿)	将字旁儿(jiàngzìpángr)	壮、状、将
忄	竖心旁儿(shùxīnpángr); 竖心儿(shùxīr)	怀、快、性
宀	宝盖儿(bǎogàir)	宇、定、宾
广	广字旁儿(guǎngzìpángr)	庄、店、席
辶	走之儿(zǒuzhīr)	过、还、送

偏旁 Radical	名称 Name	例字 Examples
土	提土旁儿(títǔpángr); 剔土旁儿(tītǔpángr)	地、场、城
艹	草字头儿(cǎozìtóur); 草头儿(cǎotóur)	艾、花、英
廾	弄字底儿(nòngzìdǐr)	开、弁、异
尢	尤字旁儿(yóuzìpángr)	尤、龙、尥
扌	提手旁儿(tíshǒupángr); 剔手旁儿(tīshǒupángr)	扛、担、摘
匚	方匡儿(fāngkuāngr)	因、国、图
彳	双人旁儿(shuāngrénpángr); 双立人儿(shuānglìrénr)	行、征、徒
彡	三撇儿(sānpiěr)	形、参、须
夂	折文儿(zhéwénr)	冬、处、夏
犭	反犬旁儿(fǎnquǎnpángr); 犬犹儿(quǎnyóur)	狂、独、狠
饣	食字旁儿(shízìpángr)	饮、饲、饰
子	子字旁儿(zǐzìpángr)	孔、孙、孩
纟	绞丝旁儿(jiǎosīpángr); 乱绞丝儿(luànjiǎosīr)	红、约、纯
巛	三拐儿(sānguǎir)	甾、邕、巢
灬	四点儿(sìdiǎnr)	杰、点、热
火	火字旁儿(huǒzìpángr)	灯、灿、烛
礻	示字旁儿(shìzìpángr); 示补儿(shìbǔr)	礼、社、祖
王	王字旁儿(wángzìpángr); 斜玉旁儿(xiéyùpángr)	玩、珍、班
木	木字旁儿(mùzìpángr)	朴、杜、栋
牜	牛字旁儿(niúzìpángr); 剔牛儿(tīniúr)	牡、物、牲
攵	反文旁儿(fǎnwénpángr); 反文儿(fǎnwénr)	收、政、教
疒	病字旁儿(bìngzìpángr) 病旁儿(bìngpángr)	症、疼、痕
衤	衣字旁儿(yīzìpángr); 衣补儿(yībǔr)	初、袖、被
𡗗	春字头儿(chūnzìtóur)	奉、奏、秦
罒	四字头儿(sìzìtóur)	罗、罢、罪
皿	皿字底儿(mǐnzìdǐr); 皿墩儿(mǐndūnr)	盂、益、盔
钅	金字旁儿(jīnzìpángr)	钢、钦、铃

偏旁 Radical	名称 Name	例字 Examples
禾	禾木旁儿(hémùpángr)	和、秋、种
癶	登字头儿(dēngzìtóur)	癸、登、凳
龹	卷字头儿(juànzìtóur)	券、拳、眷
米	米字旁儿(mǐzìpángr)	粉、料、粮
虍	虎字头儿(hǔzìtóur)	虏、虑、虚
⺮	竹字头儿(zhúzìtóur)	笑、笔、笛
⻊	足字旁儿(zúzìpángr)	跃、距、蹄

汉语拼音方案
Phonetic System of the Chinese Language

（1957 年 11 月 1 日国务院全体会议第 60 次会议通过 Endorsed at the 60th meeting of the Plenary Session of the State Council on November 1, 1957）

（1958 年 2 月 11 日第一届全国人民代表大会第五次会议批准 Approved at the 5th Session of the 1st National People's Congress on February 11, 1958）

I 字母表 The Alphabet

字母 Alphabet / 名称 Name						
Aa	Bb	Cc	Dd	Ee	Ff	Gg
ㄚ	ㄅㄝ	ㄘㄝ	ㄉㄝ	ㄜ	ㄝㄈ	ㄍㄝ
Hh	Ii	Jj	Kk	Ll	Mm	Nn
ㄏㄚ	ㄧ	ㄐㄧㄝ	ㄎㄝ	ㄝㄌ	ㄝㄇ	ㄋㄝ
Oo	Pp	Qq	Rr	Ss	Tt	Uu
ㄛ	ㄆㄝ	ㄑㄧㄡ	ㄚㄦ	ㄝㄙ	ㄊㄝ	ㄨ
Vv	Ww	Xx	Yy	Zz		
ㄪㄝ	ㄨㄚ	ㄒㄧ	ㄧㄚ	ㄗㄝ		

v 只用来拼写外来语、少数民族语言和方言。The letter v is only used in loan words, ethnic minority languages and dialects.

字母的手写体依照拉丁字母的一般书写习惯。The letters are written in the same way as the Latin alphabets.

II 声母表 The Consonants

b	p	m	f	d	t	n	l
ㄅ玻	ㄆ坡	ㄇ摸	ㄈ佛	ㄉ得	ㄊ特	ㄋ讷	ㄌ勒
g	k	h		j	q	x	
ㄍ哥	ㄎ科	ㄏ喝		ㄐ基	ㄑ欺	ㄒ希	
zh	ch	sh	r	z	c	s	
ㄓ知	ㄔ蚩	ㄕ诗	ㄖ日	ㄗ资	ㄘ雌	ㄙ思	

在给汉字注音的时候，为了使拼式简短，zh ch sh 可以省作 ẑ ĉ ŝ。When phonetic notations are given to Chinese characters, zh, ch and sh can be abbreviated as ẑ, ĉ and ŝ to simplify the spelling.

III 韵母表 The Vowels

	i 丨 衣	u ㄨ 乌	ü ㄩ 迂
a ㄚ 啊	ia 丨ㄚ 呀	ua ㄨㄚ 蛙	
o ㄛ 喔		uo ㄨㄛ 窝	
e ㄜ 鹅	ie 丨ㄝ 耶		üe ㄩㄝ 约
ai ㄞ 哀		uai ㄨㄞ 歪	
ei ㄟ 欸		uei ㄨㄟ 威	
ao ㄠ 熬	iao 丨ㄠ 腰		
ou ㄡ 欧	iou 丨ㄡ 忧		
an ㄢ 安	ian 丨ㄢ 烟	uan ㄨㄢ 弯	üan ㄩㄢ 冤
en ㄣ 恩	in 丨ㄣ 因	uen ㄨㄣ 温	ün ㄩㄣ 晕
ang ㄤ 昂	iang 丨ㄤ 央	uang ㄨㄤ 汪	
eng ㄥ 亨的韵母	ing 丨ㄥ 英	ueng ㄨㄥ 翁	
ong (ㄨㄥ) 轰的韵母	iong ㄩㄥ 雍		

(1) "知、蚩、诗、日、资、雌、思"等七个音节的韵母用 i,即:知、蚩、诗、日、资、雌、思等字拼作 zhi,chi,shi,ri,zi,ci,si。The vowel i is used in the seven syllables of 知,蚩,诗,日,资,雌 and 思, and thus they are spelled respectively as zhi, chi, shi, ri, zi, ci and si.

(2) 韵母儿写成 er,用做韵尾的时候写成 r。例如:"儿童"拼作 ertong,"花儿"拼作 huar。The vowel 儿 is written as er, but as r when used as a tail vowel, i. e. 儿童 ertong and 花儿 huar.

(3) 韵母ㄝ单用的时候写成 ê。The vowel ㄝ is written as ê when used independently.

(4) i 行的韵母,前面没有声母的时候,写成 yi(衣),ya(呀),ye(耶),yao(腰),you(忧),yan(烟),yin(因),yang(央),ying(英),yong(雍)。The vowels in the i row are written as yi(衣),ya(呀),ye(耶),yao(腰),you(忧),yan(烟),yin(因),yang(央),ying(英) and yong(雍) if no consonants precede them.

u 行的韵母，前面没有声母的时候，写成 wu(乌)，wa(蛙)，wo(窝)，wai(歪)，wei(威)，wan(弯)，wen(温)，wang(汪)，weng(翁)。The vowels in the u row are written as wu(乌)，wa(蛙)，wo(窝)，wai(歪)，wei(威)，wan(弯)，wen(温)，wang(汪) and weng(翁) if no consonants precede them.

ü 行的韵母，前面没有声母的时候，写成 yu(迂)，yue(约)，yuan(冤)，yun(晕)；ü 上两点省略。The vowels in the ü row are written as yu(迂)，yue(约)，yuan(冤) and yun(晕) if no consonants precede them, and the two dots of ü are omitted.

ü 行的韵母跟声母 j，q，x 拼的时候，写成 ju(居)，qu(区)，xu(虚)，ü 上两点也省略；但是跟声母 n，l 拼写的时候，仍然写成 nü(女)，lü(吕)。When the vowels in the ü row are used together with the consonants of j, q and x, they are written as ju (居)，qu(区) and xu(虚) with the two dots of ü being omitted; when they are used together with the consonants of n and l, the two dots of ü are retained as in nü(女) and lü(吕).

(5) iou，uei，uen 前面加声母的时候，写成 iu，ui，un，例如 niu(牛)，gui(归)，lun(论)。When iou, uei and uen are preceded by consonants, they are written as iu, ui and un, such as in niu(牛)，gui(归) and lun(论).

(6) 在给汉字注音的时候，为了使拼式简短，ng 可以省作 ŋ。When phonetic notations are added to Chinese characters, ng may be abbreviated as ŋ to simplify the spelling.

IV 声调符号 The Symbols of Tones

阴平 high and level tone	阳平 rising tone	上声 falling-rising tone	去声 falling tone
ˉ	ˊ	ˇ	ˋ

声调符号标在音节的主要母音上，轻声不标。例如：The symbol of each tone is marked on the main vowel of a syllable, but it is omitted when the pronunciation is light. For example:

妈 mā	麻 má	马 mǎ	骂 mà	吗 ma
(阴平 high and level tone)	(阳平 rising tone)	(上声 falling-rising tone)	(去声 falling tone)	(轻声 light pronunciation)

V 隔音符号 The Syllable-dividing Mark

a，o，e 开头的音节连接在其他音节后面的时候，如果音节的界限发生混淆，用隔音符号（'）隔开，例如：pi'ao(皮袄)。When a syllable beginning with a，o，e follows another syllable, and the boundary of the two syllables are confusing, the syllable-dividing mark (') is used to separate them, i.e. pi'ao(皮袄).

元 素 周

The Periodic Table of Ch

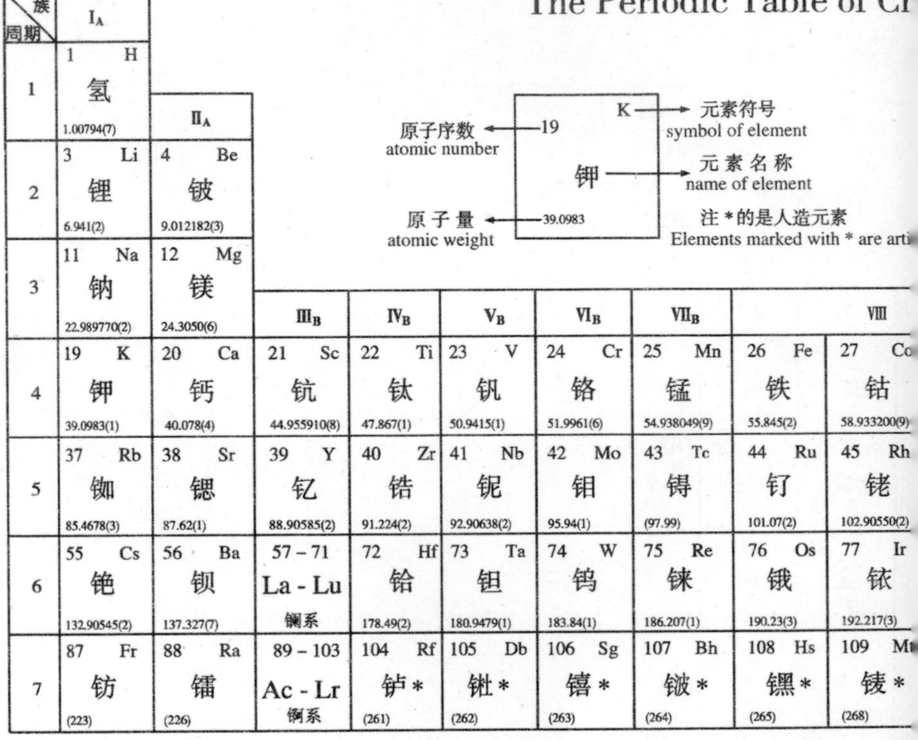

族 / 周期	I_A	II_A	III_B	IV_B	V_B	VI_B	VII_B	VIII	
1	1 H 氢 1.00794(7)								
2	3 Li 锂 6.941(2)	4 Be 铍 9.012182(3)							
3	11 Na 钠 22.989770(2)	12 Mg 镁 24.3050(6)							
4	19 K 钾 39.0983(1)	20 Ca 钙 40.078(4)	21 Sc 钪 44.955910(8)	22 Ti 钛 47.867(1)	23 V 钒 50.9415(1)	24 Cr 铬 51.9961(6)	25 Mn 锰 54.938049(9)	26 Fe 铁 55.845(2)	27 Co 钴 58.933200(9)
5	37 Rb 铷 85.4678(3)	38 Sr 锶 87.62(1)	39 Y 钇 88.90585(2)	40 Zr 锆 91.224(2)	41 Nb 铌 92.90638(2)	42 Mo 钼 95.94(1)	43 Tc 锝 (97.99)	44 Ru 钌 101.07(2)	45 Rh 铑 102.90550(2)
6	55 Cs 铯 132.90545(2)	56 Ba 钡 137.327(7)	57 – 71 La - Lu 镧系	72 Hf 铪 178.49(2)	73 Ta 钽 180.9479(1)	74 W 钨 183.84(1)	75 Re 铼 186.207(1)	76 Os 锇 190.23(3)	77 Ir 铱 192.217(3)
7	87 Fr 钫 (223)	88 Ra 镭 (226)	89 – 103 Ac - Lr 锕系	104 Rf 𬬻 * (261)	105 Db 𬭊 * (262)	106 Sg 𬭳 * (263)	107 Bh 𬭛 * (264)	108 Hs 𬭶 * (265)	109 Mt 鿏 * (268)

原子序数 atomic number	元素符号 symbol of element	元素名称 name of element	原子量 atomic weight
19	K	钾	39.0983

注 * 的是人造元素
Elements marked with * are arti

镧系	57 La 镧 138.9055(2)	58 Ce 铈 140.116(1)	59 Pr 镨 140.90765(2)	60 Nd 钕 144.24(3)	61 Pm 钷 * (147)	62 Sm 钐 150.36(3)	63 Eu 铕 151.964(1)
锕系	89 Ac 锕 (227)	90 Th 钍 232.0381(1)	91 Pa 镤 231.03588(2)	92 U 铀 238.02891(3)	93 Np 镎 (237)	94 Pu 钚 (239.244)	95 Am 镅 * (243)

注 Notes:

1. 原子量录自1999年国际原子量表，以$^{12}C=12$为基准。原子量的末位数的准 international table of atomic weights published in 1999, with $^{12}C=12$ as the cri brackets.
2. 括弧内数据是天然放射性元素较重要的同位素的质量数或人造元素半衰期 relatively important isotopes of natural radioactive elements or the mass numb
3. 105–109号元素中文名称分别读作dù(𬭊)、xǐ(𬭳)、bō(𬭛)、hēi(𬭶)、r hēi, and mài.